MOTOR
AUTO REPAIR MANUAL

42nd Edition

First Printing

Editor
Louis C. Forier, SAE

Managing Editor
Larry Solnik, SAE

Associate Editors
Michael Kromida, SAE · Dan Irizarry, SAE · Warren Schildknecht, SAE

Editorial Assistants
Katherine Keen · Ted Kolaya · William Lilieholm

Published by

MOTOR

1790 Broadway, New York, N. Y. 10019

The Automotive Business Magazine

Books Published by MOTOR

The nature of the automobile we know today makes it economically impractical to cover all phases of servicing in one book. A brief descriptive list of all titles is provided below for your convenience.

Auto Repair Manual–*Early Model Edition*

Mechanical specifications and service procedures for 1967-73 American built cars plus Volkswagen. Special sections on Engine Service, Wiper Motor Service, Alternators, Carburetors, Starting Motors and Switches, Transmissions, Tune Up, Emission Controls, Brakes, Headlamps, etc.

Imported Car Repair Manual

For the "Imported Car" owner who is totally involved with his car and is interested in Do-It-Yourself car repairs: the maintenance of peak performance . . . and in saving money.
Includes specifications and service procedures for 27 popular imported cars and pickups. Over 1150 pages and 2,600 plus illustrations and diagrams.

Truck Repair Manual

Service and repair is surprisingly easy with this new edition that covers 2,800 Truck Models, 1966 through 1979. Over 1,300 pages of step-by-step instructions, 2,000 cutaway pictures, 3,000 service and repair facts, specs and adjustments. Covers all popular makes of trucks. Manual also includes specs for gasoline and diesel engines used in off-highway equipment and farm tractors.

Auto Engines & Electrical Systems

Ideal basic book for car buffs, students, engineers, mechanics. Over 800 pages, 1,400 pictures and diagrams explain the workings of engines, fuel and electrical systems. Special chapters on the Diesel, Rotary and Turbine engines.

Automobile Trouble Shooter

This new hardback edition is a must for the glove compartment or tool box of every do-it-yourself car enthusiast. A handy guide to finding out what's wrong, it pinpoints over 2,000 causes of car trouble.

INDEX

This Edition Covers Mechanical Specifications and Service Procedures on 1974-79 Models

*For your convenience in locating this section, a black bar has been positioned beneath all odd page numbers.

American Motors

INDEX OF SERVICE OPERATIONS

SERIAL NUMBER LOCATION: 1974-79: Plate is attached to top of instrument panel, on driver's side.

ENGINE IDENTIFICATION

4-121 (1977-79): The engine code is located on a machined flange at the left rear of the cylinder block adjacent to the oil dipstick. The letter "G" denotes the 4-121 engine.

6-232 & 6-258 (1974-79): The engine code is located on a pad between number two and three cylinders. The letter "A" denotes the 258 engine with one barrel carburetor. The letter "C" denotes the 258 engine with two barrel carburetor. The letter "E" denotes the 232 engine.

V8-304, 360, & 401 (1974-79): The engine code is located on a tag attached to the right bank rocker cover. The letter "H" denotes the 304 engine. The letter "N" denotes the 360 engine with 2 barrel carburetor while the letter "P" denotes the 360 engine with 4 barrel carburetor. The letter "Z" denotes the 401 engine.

GRILLE IDENTIFICATION

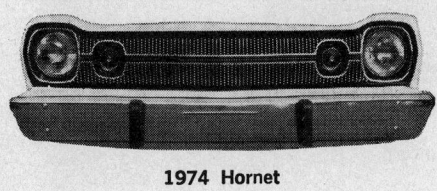
1974 Hornet

1974 Javelin

1974 Ambassador

1974 AMX

1974 Matador 4 Door

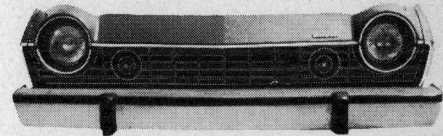
1974-75 Matador 2 Door

1974-75 Gremlin

1974-75 Gremlin X

1975 Matador 4 Door

1975-77 Hornet

1975-77 Pacer

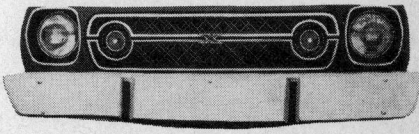
1976 Gremlin

1976-78 Matador 2 Door

1976-78 Matador 4 Door

1977 AMX

GRILLE IDENTIFICATION—Continued

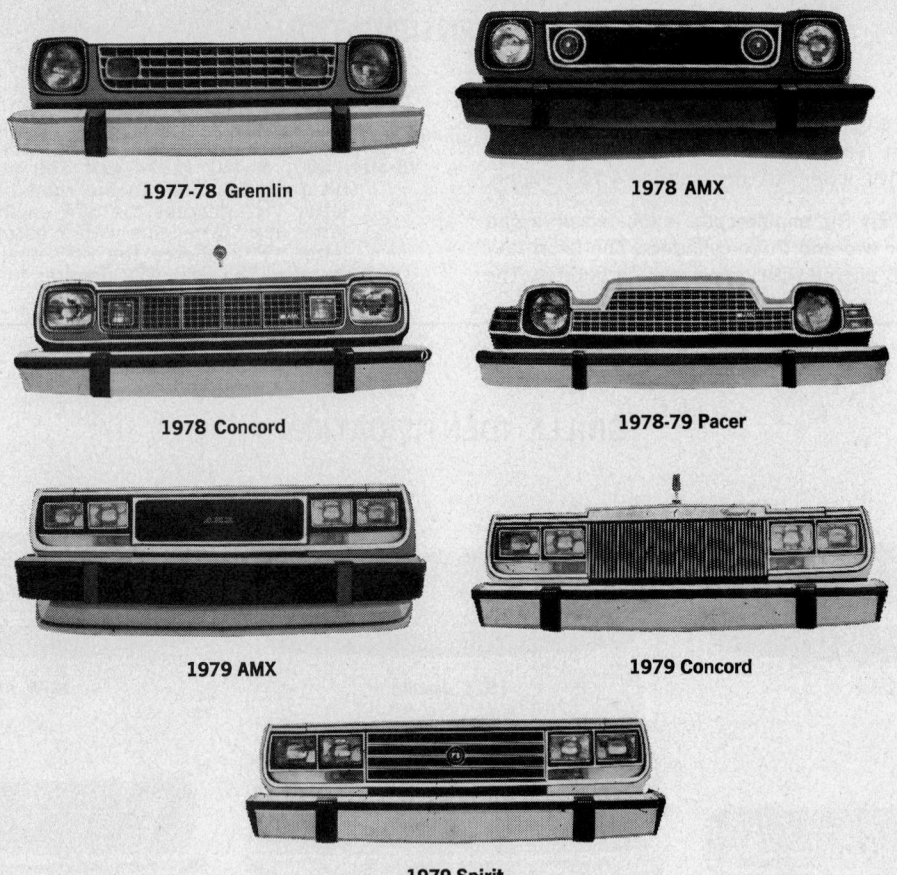

1977-78 Gremlin

1978 AMX

1978 Concord

1978-79 Pacer

1979 AMX

1979 Concord

1979 Spirit

GENERAL ENGINE SPECIFICATIONS

Year	Engine	Car-buretor	Bore and Stroke	Piston Dis-place-ment, Cubic Inches	Com-pres-sion Ratio	Maximum Brake H.P. @ R.P.M.	Maximum Torque Lbs. Ft. @ R.P.M.	Normal Oil Pressure Pounds
1974	100 Horsepower②..............6-232	1 Barrel	3.75 x 3.50	232	8.0	100 @ 3600	185 @ 1800	75
	110 Horsepower②..............6-258	1 Barrel	3.75 x 3.90	258	8.0	110 @ 3500	195 @ 2000	75
	150 Horsepower②............V8-304	2 Barrel	3.75 x 3.44	304	8.4	150 @ 4200	245 @ 2500	75
	175 Horsepower②............V8-360	2 Barrel	4.08 x 3.44	360	8.5	175 @ 4000	285 @ 2400	75
	195 Horsepower②............V8-360	4 Barrel	4.08 x 3.44	360	8.5	195 @ 4400	295 @ 2900	75
	220 Horsepower②③..........V8-360	4 Barrel	4.08 x 3.44	360	8.5	220 @ 4400	315 @ 3100	75
	255 Horsepower②............V8-401	4 Barrel	4.165 x 3.68	401	8.5	235 @ 4600	335 @ 3200	75
1975	90 Horsepower②..............6-232	1 Barrel	3.75 x 3.50	232	8.0	90 @ 3050	163 @ 2200	37–75
	95 Horsepower②..............6-258	1 Barrel	3.75 x 3.90	258	8.0	95 @ 3050	179 @ 2100	37–75
	120 Horsepower②............V8-304	2 Barrel	3.75 x 3.44	304	8.4	120 @ 3200	220 @ 2000	37–75
	140 Horsepower②............V8-360	2 Barrel	4.08 x 3.44	360	8.25	140 @ 3300	251 @ 1600	37–75
	180 Horsepower②............V8-360	4 Barrel	4.08 x 3.44	360	8.25	180 @ 3600	280 @ 2800	37–75
	Horsepower②........V8-401①	4 Barrel	4.165 x 3.68	401	8.25	—	—	37–75
1976	90 Horsepower②..............6-232	1 Barrel	3.75 x 3.50	232	8.0	90 @ 3050	170 @ 2000	37–75
	95 Horsepower②............6-258④	1 Barrel	3.75 x 3.90	258	8.0	95 @ 3050	180 @ 2100	37–75
	95 Horsepower②............6-258⑤	1 Barrel	3.75 x 3.90	258	8.0	95 @ 3050	180 @ 2000	37–75
	120 Horsepower②..............6-258	2 Barrel	3.75 x 3.90	258	8.0	120 @ 3400	200 @ 2000	37–75
	120 Horsepower②..........V8-304④	2 Barrel	3.75 x 3.44	304	8.4	120 @ 3200	220 @ 2200	37–75
	120 Horsepower②..........V8-304⑤	2 Barrel	3.75 x 3.44	304	8.4	120 @ 3200	220 @ 2000	37–75
	140 Horsepower②............V8-360	2 Barrel	4.08 x 3.44	360	8.25	140 @ 3200	260 @ 1600	37–75
	180 Horsepower②............V8-360	4 Barrel	4.08 x 3.44	360	8.25	180 @ 3600	280 @ 2800	37–75
	Horsepower②........V8-401①	4 Barrel	4.165 x 3.68	401	8.25	—	—	37–75
1977	80 Horsepower②..............4-121	2 Barrel	3.41 x 3.32	121	8.1	80 @ 5000	105 @ 2800	28½
	90 Horsepower②..............6-232	1 Barrel	3.75 x 3.50	232	8.0	90 @ 3050	163 @ 2200	37–75
	95 Horsepower②..............6-258	1 Barrel	3.75 x 3.90	258	8.0	95 @ 3050	179 @ 2100	37–75
	120 Horsepower②..............6-258	2 Barrel	3.75 x 3.90	258	8.0	120 @ 3600	200 @ 2000	37–75
	120 Horsepower②............V8-304	2 Barrel	3.75 x 3.44	304	8.4	120 @ 3200	220 @ 2000	37–75
	140 Horsepower②............V8-360	2 Barrel	4.08 x 3.44	360	8.25	140 @ 3300	251 @ 1600	37–75
1978	80 Horsepower②..............4-121	2 Barrel	3.41 x 3.32	121	8.2	80 @ 5000	105 @ 2800	28.5
	90 Horsepower②..............6-232	1 Barrel	3.75 x 3.50	232	8.0	90 @ 3400	168 @ 1600	37–75
	100 Horsepower②..............6-258	1 Barrel	3.75 x 3.90	258	8.0	100 @ 3400	200 @ 1600	37–75
	120 Horsepower②..............6-258	2 Barrel	3.75 x 3.90	258	8.0	120 @ 3600	201 @ 1800	37–75
	130 Horsepower②............V8-304	2 Barrel	3.75 x 3.44	304	8.4	130 @ 3200	238 @ 2000	37–75
	140 Horsepower②............V8-360	2 Barrel	4.08 x 3.44	360	8.25	140 @ 3350	278 @ 2000	37–75
1979	Horsepower②..............4-121	2 Barrel	3.41 x 3.32	121	8.1		105 @ 2800	
	Horsepower②..............6-232	1 Barrel	3.75 x 3.50	232	8.0		168 @ 2200	
	Horsepower②..............6-258	2 Barrel	3.75 x 3.90	258	8.3		210 @ 1800	
	Horsepower②............V8-304	2 Barrel	3.75 x 3.44	304	8.4		220 @ 2400	

①—Police
②—Ratings are net (as installed in the vehicle).
③—With dual exhausts.
④—Except Matador.
⑤—Matador.

TUNE UP SPECIFICATIONS

The following specifications are published from the latest information available. This data should be used only in the absence of a decal affixed in the engine compartment.

★When using a timing light, disconnect vacuum hose or tube at distributor and plug opening in hose or tube so idle speed will not be affected.

●When checking compression, lowest cylinder must be within 80 percent of highest.

▲Before removing wires from distributor cap, determine location of the No. 1 wire in cap, as distributor position may have been altered from that shown at the end of this chart.

Year	Spark Plug		Distributor		Ignition Timing★			Carb. Adjustments					
	Type	Gap Inch	Point Gap Inch	Dwell Angle Deg.	Firing Order Fig. ▲	Timing BTDC ①	Mark Fig.	Hot Idle Speed		Air Fuel Ratio		Idle CO%	
								Std. Trans.	Auto. Trans.②	Std. Trans.	Auto. Trans.	Std. Trans.	Auto. Trans.
1974													
6-232 L/EGR	N12Y	.035	.016	31–34	A	5°	D	700	600D	—	—	⑨	⑨
6-232 W/EGR	N12Y	.035	.016	31–34	A	5°	D	600	550D	—	—	⑨	⑨
6-232 Calif.	N12Y	.035	.016	31–34	A	5°	D	600	700D	—	—	⑨	⑨
6-258 L/EGR	N12Y	.035	.016	31–34	A	3°	D	550	700D	—	—	⑨	⑨
6-258 W/EGR	N12Y	.035	.016	31–34	A	3°	D	550	600D	—	—	⑨	⑨
6-258 Calif.	N12Y	.035	.016	31–34	A	3°	D	600	700D	—	—	⑨	⑨
V8-304	N12Y	.035	.016	29–31	B	⑩	C	750	700D	—	—	0.5-1.0	0.5-1.0
V8-360	N12Y	.035	.016	29–31	B	5°	C	750	700D	—	—	0.5-1.0	0.5-1.0
V8-401	N12Y	.035	.016	29–31	B	5°	C	750	700D	—	—	0.5-1.0	0.5-1.0
1975													
6-232	N12Y	.035	—	—	A	5°	E	600	⑥	—	—	—	⑪
6-258	N12Y	.035	—	—	A	3°③	E	600④	⑥	—	—	—	⑪
V8-304	N12Y	.035	—	—	B	5°	C	750	700D	—	—	—	—
V8-360	N12Y	.035	—	—	B	5°	C	—	700D	—	—	—	—
1976													
6-232	N12Y	.035	—	—	A	8°	E	850	⑥	—	—	⑧⑫	⑧⑪
6-258⑬	N12Y	.035	—	—	A	⑭	E	850	⑥	—	—	⑧⑫	⑧⑪
6-258⑮	N12Y	.035	—	—	A	⑭	E	600	700	—	—	⑧⑫	⑧⑪
V8-304	N12Y	.035	—	—	B	⑯	C	750	700D	—	—	—	—
V8-360	N12Y	.035	—	—	B	⑱	C	—	700D	—	—	—	—
V8-401⑰	N12Y	.035	—	—	B	⑱	C	—	700D	—	—	—	—
1977													
4-121	N8L	.035	.018	44–50	F	㉕	G	900	800D	—	—	—	—
6-232	N12Y	.035	—	—	A	⑲	E	⑳	⑥	—	—	1.0⑧	1.0⑧
6-258 Std. Tr.⑬	N12Y	.035	—	—	A	㉑	E	600	—	—	—	1.0⑧	—
6-258 Auto. Tr.⑬	N12Y	.035	—	—	A	㉒	E	—	⑥	—	—	—	1.0⑧
6-258⑮	N12Y	.035	—	—	A	⑭	E	600	㉓	—	—	1.0⑧	1.0⑧
V8-304	RN12Y	.035	—	—	B	⑱	C	—	⑦	—	—	—	—
V8-360	RN12Y	.035	—	—	B	⑱	C	—	㉔	—	—	—	—
1978													
4-121	N8L	.035	.018	44–50	F	㉖	G	900	800D	—	—	—	—
6-232	N13L	.035	—	—	H	㉖	E	600	550D	—	—	1.0⑧	1.0⑧
6-258⑬	N13	.035	—	—	H	⑭	E	850	700D	—	—	1.0⑧	1.0⑧
6-258⑮	N13L⑧	.035	—	—	H	⑭	E	600	600D	—	—	1.0⑧	1.0⑧
V8-304	N12Y	.035	—	—	I	⑱	C	—	㉔	—	—	—	—
V8-360	N12Y	.035	—	—	I	10°	C	—	㉟	—	—	—	—

Continued

TUNE UP SPECIFICATIONS—Continued

The following specifications are published from the latest information available. This data should be used only in the absence of a decal affixed in the engine compartment.

★When using a timing light, disconnect vacuum hose or tube at distributor and plug opening in hose or tube so idle speed will not be affected.

●When checking compression, lowest cylinder must be within 80 percent of highest.

▲Before removing wires from distributor cap, determine location of the No. 1 wire in cap, as distributor position may have been altered from that shown at the end of this chart.

Year	Spark Plug		Distributor		Ignition Timing★			Carb. Adjustments					
	Type	Gap Inch	Point Gap Inch	Dwell Angle Deg.	Firing Order Fig. ▲	Timing BTDC ①	Mark Fig.	Hot Idle Speed		Air Fuel Ratio		Idle CO%	
								Std. Trans.	Auto. Trans.②	Std. Trans.	Auto. Trans.	Std. Trans.	Auto. Trans.
1979													
4-121	N8L	.035	.018	44–50	F	㉖	G	900	800D	—	—	—	—
6-232	N13L	.035	—	—	H	㉖	E	600	550D	—	—	—	—
6-258㉝	N13L	.035	—	—	H	㊱	E	700	600D	—	—	—	—
6-258㉞	N13L	.035	—	—	H	8°	E	—	700D	—	—	—	—
V8-304	N12Y	.035	—	—	I	㊲	C	800	600D	—	—	—	—

① —BTDC: Before top dead center.
② —D: Drive. N: Neutral.
③ —Except distributor No. 3227331; distributor No. 3227331, Man. trans., 6° BTDC; auto. trans., 8° BTDC.
④ —Set Matador sta. wag. with distributor No. 3227331 at 850 RPM.
⑤ —Except Calif. models and vehicles with catalyic converter.
⑥ —Exc. Calif., 550D; Calif., 700D.
⑦ —Except Calif., early 1977 600D RPM; late 1977 700D RPM; Calif. all 700D RPM.
⑧ —On models equipped with auto. trans. & 2.53 axle ratio use N12Y.
⑨ —W/Air Guard 0.5-1.0%. W/O Air Guard 1.0-1.5%.
⑩ —Exc. Calif. auto. trans., 5° BTDC; Calif. auto. trans., 2½° BTDC.
⑪ —Exc. Calif. W/Air Guard, 0.8% maximum; Less Air Guard, 1.0% maximum.

⑫ —With Air Guard–0.5%, with Air Guard disconnected on 1 bar. carb. models; less Air Guard–1.0%.
⑬ —1 barrel carb.
⑭ —Man. trans., 6° BTDC; auto. trans., 8° BTDC.
⑮ —2 barrel carb.
⑯ —Auto. trans. except Calif., 10° BTDC; man. trans. & Calif. auto. trans., 5° BTDC.
⑰ —Police.
⑱ —Except Calif., 10° BTDC; Calif., 5° BTDC.
⑲ —Man. trans. except Calif. & high altitude, 8° BTDC; auto. trans., Calif. man. trans. & high altitude, 10° BTDC.
⑳ —Except Calif., 600 RPM; Calif., 850 RPM.
㉑ —Except high altitude, 6° BTDC; high altitude, 10° BTDC.
㉒ —Matador except Calif., 6° BTDC; Gremlin, Hornet & all Calif., models, 8° BTDC; high altitude all, 10° BTDC.
㉓ —Except Calif., 600D RPM; Calif., 700D RPM

㉔ —Except Calif. & high altitude, 600D RPM; Calif. & high altitude, 700D RPM.
㉕ —Exc. Calif. auto. trans., 12° BTDC; Calif. auto. trans., 8° BTDC.
㉖ —Manual trans., 8° BTDC; auto. trans., 10° BTDC.
㉗ —California & altitude.
㉘ —Calif., 6° BTDC; altitude, 10° BTDC.
㉙ —Calif., 850 RPM; altitude, 600 RPM.
㉚ —Calif., 8° BTDC; altitude, 10° BTDC.
㉛ —Calif., 700D RPM; altitude, 550D RPM.
㉜ —Except California & altitude.
㉝ —Exc. Calif.
㉞ —Calif.
㉟ —Exc. Calif. & altitude, 600D RPM; Calif., 650D RPM; altitude, 700D RPM.
㊱ —Manual trans., 4° BTDC; Auto. trans., 8° BTDC.
㊲ —Manual trans., 5° BTDC; Auto. trans., 8° BTDC.

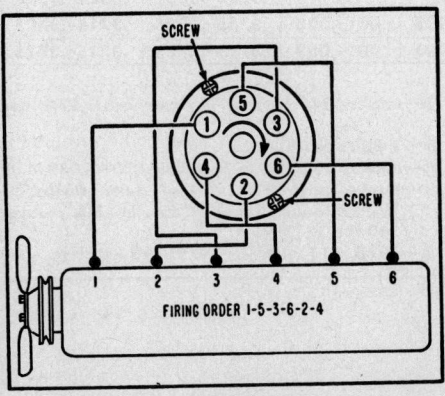

Fig. A

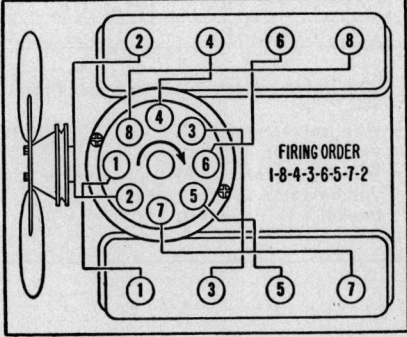

Fig. B

Fig. C

Continued

TUNE UP NOTES—Continued

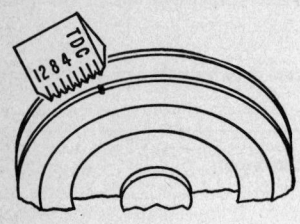

Fig. D

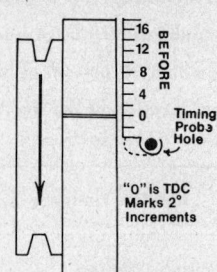

Fig. E

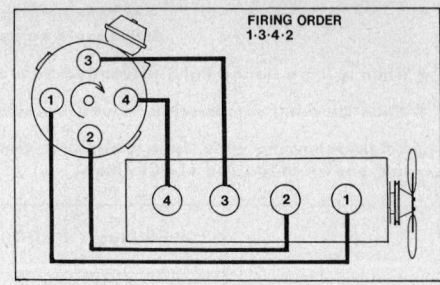

Fig. F

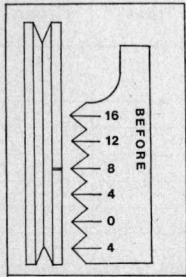

Fig. G

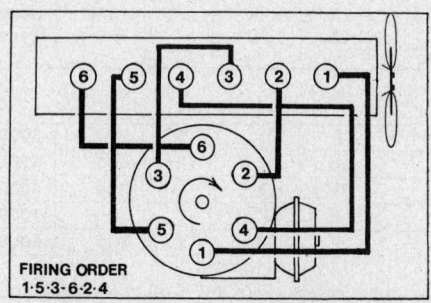

Fig. H

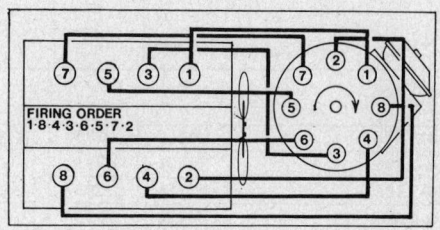

Fig. I

VALVE SPECIFICATIONS

Year	Model	Valve Lash		Valve Angles		Valve Spring Installed Height	Valve Spring Pressure Lbs. @ In.	Stem Clearance		Stem Diameter	
		Int.	Exh.	Seat	Face			Intake	Exhaust	Intake	Exhaust
1974	6-232, 258	Hydraulic③		⑦	②	⑧	⑨	.001–.003	.001–.003	.3715–.3725	.3715–.3725
	V8-304, 360, 401	Hydraulic③		⑦	②	⑧	⑩	.001–.003	.001–.003	.3715–.3725	.3715–.3725
1975	6-232, 258	Hydraulic③		⑦	③	1¹³⁄₁₆	195 @ 1⁷⁄₁₆	.001–.003	.001–.003	.3715–.3725	.3715–.3725
	V8-304, 360④	Hydraulic③		⑦	②	1¹³⁄₁₆	213 @ 1²³⁄₆₄	.001–.003	.001–.003	.3715–.3725	.3715–.3725
	V8-360, 401⑥	Hydraulic③		⑦	②	⑪	⑫	.001–.003	.001–.003	.3715–.3725	.3715–.3725
1976	6-232, 258⑬	Hydraulic③		⑦	②	1¹³⁄₁₆	195 @ 1⁷⁄₁₆	.001–.003	.001–.003	.3715–.3725	.3715–.3725
	V8-304, 360, 401	Hydraulic③		⑦	②	1¹³⁄₁₆	213 @ 1²³⁄₆₄	.001–.003	.001–.003	.3715–.3725	.3715–.3725
1977	6-232, 258⑬	Hydraulic③		⑦	②	1²⁵⁄₃₂	195 @ 1¹³⁄₃₂	.001–.003	.001–.003	.3715–.3725	.3715–.3725
	6-258⑤	Hydraulic③		⑦	②	1²⁵⁄₃₂	205 @ 1²⁵⁄₆₄	.001–.003	.001–.003	.3715–.3725	.3715–.3725
	V8-304, 360	Hydraulic③		⑦	②	1¹³⁄₁₆	213 @ 1²³⁄₆₄	.001–.003	.001–.003	.3715–.3725	.3715–.3725
1977–79	4-121	⑭		45	45	①	⑮	.031	.039	.3526–.3531	.3522–.3528
1978–79	6-232, 258	Hydraulic③		⑦	②	1²⁵⁄₃₂	195 @ 1¹³⁄₃₂	.001–.003	.001–.003	.3715–.3725	.3715–.3725
	V8-304, 360	Hydraulic③		⑦	③	1²⁵⁄₃₂	⑯	.001–.003	.001–.003	.3715–.3725	.3715–.3725

①—Inner 1½"; outer 1⁴⁵⁄₆₄".
②—Intake 29°, exhaust 44°.
③—No adjustment.
④—Except police and taxi.
⑤—2 Barrel carburetor.
⑥—Police and taxi.
⑦—Intake 30°, exhaust 44½°.

⑧—With valve rotator, 1⅝"; less valve rotator, 1¹³⁄₁₆".
⑨—With valve rotator, 218 lbs. @ 1³⁄₁₆"; less valve rotator, 195 lbs. @ 1⁷⁄₁₆".
⑩—With valve rotator, 213 lbs. @ 1³⁄₁₆"; less valve rotator, 213 lbs. @ 1²³⁄₆₄".
⑪—Intake: 1¹³⁄₁₆"; exhaust: 1⅝".

⑫—Intake: 270 lbs. @ 1⅜"; exhaust: 270 lbs. @ 1³⁄₁₆".
⑬—1 Barrel carburetor.
⑭—Intake, .006–.009 in. H; exhaust, .016–.019 in. H.
⑮—Intake, inner 39 lbs. @ 1³⁄₃₂"; outer 166 lbs. @ 1⁵⁄₁₆". Exhaust, inner 37 lbs. @ 1⁷⁄₆₄"; outer 160 lbs. @ 1²¹⁄₆₄".
⑯—1978, 211 @ 1²³⁄₆₄; 1979, 195 @ 1¹³⁄₃₂.

DISTRIBUTOR SPECIFICATIONS

★If unit is checked on vehicle, double the RPM and degrees to get crankshaft figures.

Breaker arm spring tension 17–21.

Distributor Part No.①	Centrifugal Advance Degrees @ RPM of Distributor					Vacuum Advance		Distributor Retard	
	Advance Starts	Intermediate Advance			Full Advance	Inches of Vacuum to Start Plunger	Max. Adv. Dist. Deg. @ Vacuum	In. of Mercury Start Retard	Max. Retard Dist. Deg. @ Vacuum
1974									
1110528	0–2 @ 600	3–5.5 @ 800	6–8.5 @ 1000	6.5–9 @ 1500	15 @ 2200	5–7	9 @ 13	—	—
1110529	0–2 @ 500	4.5–7 @ 800	7–9 @ 1000	7–9.5 @ 1500	14 @ 2300	5–7	9 @ 13	—	—
1112112	0–2 @ 500	4.5–6.5 @ 800	7.5–9.5 @ 1000	9¾–11¾ @ 1500	14 @ 2200	5–7	8¼ @ 12¾	—	—
1112179	0–2 @ 500	4.5–6.5 @ 750	8–10 @ 1000	12.5–13.5 @ 1600	17 @ 2200	5–7	8¼ @ 12¾	—	—
1112214	0–2.5 @ 500	6.5–8.5 @ 700	—	11–13 @ 1500	17 @ 2200	4–6	8¼ @ 13	—	—
1112215	0–1.5 @ 400	4–6¾ @ 600	6.5–8.5 @ 1000	10–12 @ 1600	16 @ 2200	4–6	8¼ @ 13	—	—
1975									
3224746	0–1½ @ 400	5–7 @ 750	6½–8½ @ 1000	—	9¼–14 @ 1500	—	16¾ @ 1000	—	—
3224965	0–1 @ 400	4½–6 @ 750	8–10 @ 1000	—	11–13 @ 1500	—	18 @ 1000	—	—
3224966	0–2½ @ 450	6¼–8¾ @ 750	8¼–10¼ @ 1000	—	11–13 @ 1500	—	18¼ @ 1000	—	—
3224968	0–½ @ 500	2–4¾ @ 750	6–8½ @ 1000	—	6½–9 @ 1500	5–7	9 @ 13.1	—	—
3224969	0–2 @ 500	3½–6 @ 750	7–9 @ 1000	—	7–9½ @ 1500	5–7	9 @ 13.1	—	—
1976									
3227331	0–.4 @ 500	2–4 @ 750	4–6 @ 1000	4.65–6.65 @ 1500	5¼–7¼ @ 2200	5–7	9 @ 12.6	—	—
1976-77									
3228263	0–2.8 @ 500	2.8–4.85 @ 750	4.2–6.25 @ 1000	7.05–9.05 @ 1500	11–13 @ 2200	4–6	8½ @ 12.7	—	—
3228264	0–2.4 @ 500	3.4–6.4 @ 750	6.3–8.3 @ 1000	9.3–11.3 @ 1500	13½–15½ @ 2200	5–7	8½ @ 12.5	—	—
3228265	0–2.7 @ 500	2.4–4.4 @ 750	3.3–5.3 @ 1000	5.1–7.1 @ 1500	7½–9½ @ 2200	4–6	8½ @ 12.7	—	—
3228266	0–3¾ @ 500	4.4–6.4 @ 750	5.4–7.4 @ 1000	7.3–9.3 @ 1500	10–12 @ 2200	4–6	8½ @ 12.7	—	—
3229719	0–1.8 @ 500	1–3 @ 750	4–6 @ 1000	6–8 @ 1500	9–11 @ 2200	5–7	9 @ 13	—	—
1977-78									
3250163	0 @ 550	4 @ 800	8 @ 1000	11 @ 1500	17 @ 2200	2–4	9 @ 9.5	—	—
3230443	–¾ @ 400	4.5 @ 800	6.5 @ 1200	9.5 @ 1800	13 @ 2200	5.5–6.5	9¼ @ 12½	—	—
3231340	–¾ @ 400	5.5 @ 800	8.5 @ 1200	12 @ 1800	15.5 @ 2200	6.5–8.5	9⅛ @ 12	—	—
3231341	–¾ @ 400	3.5 @ 800	5 @ 1200	7 @ 1800	9.5 @ 2200	5.5–6.5	9¼ @ 12½	—	—
3231915	–1 @ 400	3 @ 800	5.5 @ 1200	7.5 @ 1800	10.5 @ 2200	3.5–5.5	13¼ @ 11½	—	—
3232434	–¾ @ 400	2¾ @ 800	5¼ @ 1200	7 @ 1600	10.5 @ 2200	6.5–8.5	9½ @ 13	—	—
3233173	–⅝ @ 400	4 @ 800	6¼ @ 1200	9.5 @ 1800	13 @ 2200	4–6	13⅛ @ 11¼	—	—
3233174	–¾ @ 400	3.5 @ 800	4¾ @ 1200	6⅞ @ 1800	9.5 @ 2200	4–6	13⅛ @ 11	—	—
1979									
3231915	–1 @ 400	3 @ 800	5.5 @ 1200	7.5 @ 1800	10.5 @ 2200	3.5–5.5	13¼ @ 11.5	—	—
3232434	–¾ @ 400	2¾ @ 800	5¼ @ 1200	7 @ 1600	10.5 @ 2200	6.5–8.5	9.5 @ 13	—	—
3233959	–1 @ 400	2 @ 800	5¼ @ 1200	10 @ 1800	14.5 @ 2200	1.5–3	17¼ @ 12	—	—
3234693	–¾ @ 400	3¾ @ 800	6.5 @ 1200	9 @ 1600	14.5 @ 2200	2–3.5	12¾ @ 12	—	—
3250163	0 @ 550	4 @ 800	8 @ 1000	11 @ 1500	17 @ 2200	2–4	9 @ 9.5	—	—
3250497	0 @ 500	2 @ 700	4 @ 900	7 @ 1400	10¾ @ 1800	2–4	17 @ 13	—	—

①—Stamped on distributor housing plate.

PISTONS, PINS, RINGS, CRANKSHAFT & BEARINGS

Year	Model	Piston Clearance Top of Skirt	Ring End Gap①		Wrist-pin Diameter	Rod Bearings		Main Bearings		Thrust on Bear. No.	Shaft End Play
			Comp.	Oil		Shaft Diameter	Bearing Clearance	Shaft Diameter	Bearing Clearance		
1974	6-232, 250	.0009–.0017	.010	.010	.9304	2.0934–2.0955	.001–.003	2.4986–2.5001	.001–.003	3	.0015–.0065
	V8-304	.0010–.0018	.010	.010	.9308	2.0934–2.0955	.001–.003	②	.001–.003	3	.003–.008
	V8-360	.0012–.0020	.010	.015	.9308	2.0934–2.0955	.001–.003	②	.001–.003	3	.003–.008
	V8-401	.0010–.0018	.010	.015	1.0009	2.2464–2.2485	.001–.003	②	.001–.003	3	.003–.008
1975	6-232, 258	.0009–.0017	.010	.010	.9306	2.0934–2.0955	.001–.003	2.4986–2.5001	.001–.003	3	.0015–.0065
	V8-304	.0010–.0018	.010	.010	.9311	2.0934–2.0955	.001–.003	②	.001–.003	3	.003–.008
	V8-360	④	.010	.015	.9311	2.0934–2.0955	.001–.003	②	.001–.003	3	.003–.008
	V8-401	⑤	.010	.015	.9311	2.2464–2.2485	.001–.003	②	.001–.003	3	.003–.008
1976	6-232, 258	.0009–.0017	.010	.010	.9307	2.0934–2.0955	.001–.003	2.4986–2.5001	.001–.003	3	.0015–.0065
	V8-304	.0010–.0018	.010	.010	.9311	2.0934–2.0955	.001–.003	②	.001–.003	3	.003–.008
	V8-360	④	.010	.015	.9311	2.0934–2.0955	.001–.003	②	.001–.003	3	.003–.008
	V8-401	⑤	.010	.015	1.0011	2.2464–2.2485	.001–.003	②	.001–.003	3	.003–.008
1977	4-121	.0009–.0015	.010	.010	.945	1.888–1.889	.0008–.0028	2.1581–2.1587	.0008–.0031	3	.0039–.0075
	6-232, 258	.0009–.0017	.010	.010	.9307	2.0934–2.0955	.001–.0025	2.4986–2.5001	.001–.003	3	.0015–.0065
	V8-304	.0010–.0018	.010	.010	.9311	2.0934–2.0955	.001–.003	②	⑥	3	.003–.008
	V8-360	.0012–.0020	.010	.015	.9311	2.0934–2.0955	.001–.003	②	⑥	3	.003–.008
1978–79	4-121	.0007–.0017	.010	.010	.9448	1.8882–1.8888	.0007–.0024	2.1581–2.1587	.00098–.00311	3	.0039–.0075
	6-232, 258	.0009–.0017	.010	.010	.9307	2.0934–2.0955	.0010–.0025	2.4986–2.5001	.0010–.0030	3	.0015–.0065
	V8-304	.0010–.0018	.010	.010	.9311	2.0934–2.0955	.0010–.0030	②	⑥	3	.003–.008
	V8-360	.0012–.0020	.010	.015	.9311	2.0934–2.0955	.0010–.0030	②	⑥	3	.003–.008

①—Fit rings in tapered bores for clearance listed in tightest portion of ring travel.
②—Rear main 2.7464–2.7479″, others 2.7474–2.7489″.
③—Rear main .002–.003″, others .001–.002″.

④—Except police, .0012–.002″. Police, .0016–0024″.
⑤—Except police, .001–.0018″. Police, .0014–.0022″.
⑥—Rear main, .002″ to .004″; all others, .001″ to .003″.

REAR AXLE SPECIFICATIONS

Year	Model	Carrier Type ②	Ring Gear & Pinion Backlash		Pinion Bearing Preload			Differential Bearing Preload		
			Method	Adjustment	Method	New Bearings Inch-Lbs.	Used Bearings Inch-Lbs.	Method	New Bearings Inch-Lbs.	Used Bearings Inch-Lbs.
1974–78	7⁹⁄₁₆″ Dr. Gr.	Integral	Shims	.005–.009	Sleeve	15–25①	15–25①	Shims	.008	.008
	8⁷⁄₈″ Dr. Gr.	Integral	Shims	.005–.009	Sleeve	17–28①	17–28①	Shims	.008	.008

①—Adjust at drive pinion flange nut with inch-pound torque wrench.　②—Axle shaft end play .006″.

ENGINE TIGHTENING SPECIFICATIONS*

★Torque specifications are for clean and lightly lubricated threads only. Dry or dirty threads produce increased friction which prevents accurate measurement of tightness.

Year	Engine Model	Spark Plugs Ft. Lbs.	Cylinder Head Bolts Ft. Lbs.	Intake Manifold Ft. Lbs.	Exhaust Manifold Ft. Lbs.	Rocker Arm Shaft Bracket Ft. Lbs.	Rocker Arm Cover Ft. Lbs.	Connecting Rod Cap Bolts Ft. Lbs.	Main Bearing Cap Bolts Ft. Lbs.	Flywheel to Crankshaft Ft. Lbs.	Vibration Damper or Pulley Ft. Lbs.
1977–79	4-121	22	⑥	18	18	—	①②	41	⑦	65	∠
1974	6-232, 258	25–30	105	23	23	21	50①	28	80	105	55
1975–76	6-232, 258	28	105	23	23	19③	50①	④	80	105	55
1977–79	6-232, 258	28	105	23	23	19③	50①	33	80	105	80⑤
1974–75	V8-304, 360	28	110	43	25	19③	50①	28	100	105	55
1976	V8-304, 360	28	110	43	25	19③	50①	33	100	105	80
1977–79	V8-304, 360	28	110	43	⑧	19③	50①	33	100	105	90⑤
1974–75	V8-401	28	110	43	25	19③	50①	38	100	105	55
1976	V8-401	28	110	43	25	19③	50①	39	100	105	80

①—Inch pounds.
②—1977-78 50 in.-lb.; 1979, 35 in.-lb.
③—Rocker arm cap screw.
④—Except Pacer 28, Pacer 33.
⑤—Lubricate bolt threads lightly before assembly.
⑥—Cold, 65 ft. lbs.; warm, 73 ft. lbs.
⑦—Hex head, 58 ft. lbs.; rear main bearing socket head cap screw, 47 ft. lbs.
⑧—1977-78, 25 ft. lbs.; 1979, ⅜ inch bolts, 25 ft. lbs., ⁵⁄₁₆ inch bolts, 15 ft. lbs.

WHEEL ALIGNMENT SPECIFICATIONS

Year	Model	Caster Angle, Degrees		Camber Angle, Degrees				Toe-In. Inch	Toe-Out on Turns, Deg.①	
		Limits	Desired	Limits		Desired			Outer Wheel	Inner Wheel
				Left	Right	Left	Right			
1974	Hornet, Gremlin	−½ to +½	Zero	+⅛ to +⅝	0 to +½	+⅜	+⅛	¹⁄₁₆–³⁄₁₆	22	25
	Others	+½ to +1½	+1	+⅛ to +⅝	0 to +½	+⅜	+⅛	¹⁄₁₆–³⁄₁₆	22	25
1975–77	Hornet, Gremlin	−½ to +½	Zero	+⅛ to +⅝	0 to +½	+⅜	+⅛	¹⁄₁₆–³⁄₁₆	②	38
	Others	+½ to +1½	+1	+⅛ to +⅝	0 to +½	+⅜	+⅛	¹⁄₁₆–³⁄₁₆	②	③
1978	Pacer	+½ to +1½	+1	+⅛ to +⅝	0 to +½	+⅜	+¼	¹⁄₁₆–³⁄₁₆	②	35
	Except Pacer	0 to +2	+1	+⅛ to +⅝	0 to +½	+⅜	+¼	¹⁄₁₆–³⁄₁₆	②	38

①—Incorrect toe-out when other adjustments are correct, indicates bent steering arms.
②—Wheels at full turn.
③—Matador 38°; Pacer 35°.

ALTERNATOR SPECIFICATIONS

| Year | Alternator | | | | | | | Regulator | | | |
| | Make | Model | Ground Polarity | Rated Output | | Field Current | | Model | Regulator Test @ 120°F. | | |
				Amperes	Volts	Amperes ①	Volts		Ampere Load	Altern. R.P.M.	Volts
1974–75	Motorola	—	Negative	37	—	1.8–2.5	—	8RH2003②	10	2000	13.1–14.3
	Motorola	—	Negative	51	—	1.8–2.5	—	8RH2003②	10	2000	13.1–14.3
	Motorola	—	Negative	62	—	1.8–2.5	—	8RH2003②	10	2000	13.1–14.3
1975–77	Delco	—	Negative	37	—	4.0–4.5	—	1116387④	10③	3000③	14.0–14.3③
	Delco	—	Negative	55	—	4.0–4.5	—	1116387④	10③	3000③	14.0–14.3③
	Delco	—	Negative	63	—	4.0–4.5	—	1116387④	10③	3000③	14.0–14.3③
1976–78	Motorcraft	—	Negative	40	—	2.5–3.0	—	—	—	—	13.4–14.2
	Motorcraft	—	Negative	60	—	2.5–3.0	—	—	—	—	13.4–14.2
1978–79	Delco	—	Negative	37	—	4.0–5.0	—	1116387④	—	—	13.4–14.4
	Delco	—	Negative	55	—	4.0–5.0	—	1116387④	—	—	13.4–14.4
	Delco	—	Negative	63	—	4.0–5.0	—	1116387④	—	—	13.4–14.4
1979	Bosch	—	Negative	45	—	3.5–5.0	—	④⑤	—	—	13.4–14.4
	Bosch	—	Negative	55	—	3.5–5.0	—	④⑤	—	—	13.4–14.4

①—Excessive current drawn indicates shorted field winding. No current draw indicates an open winding.
②—Regulator is a sealed assembly, requiring no adjustments.
③—At 80° F.
④—Integral regulator.
⑤—B 192052 193 EE 14v3.

STARTING MOTOR SPECIFICATIONS

| Year | Engine Model | Rotation ① | Brush Spring Tension, Ounces | No Load Test | | | Torque Test | | |
				Amperes	Volts	R.P.M.	Amperes	Volts	Torque, Ft. Lbs.
1974–77	All	C	40	65	12	9250	600	3.4	13
1978–79	4-121	—	—	69	12	6709–10843	—	—	—
	6-232, 258	—	—	67	12	7380–9356	—	—	—
	V8-304	—	—	67	12	7380–9356	—	—	—
	V8-360	—	—	77	12	8900–9600	—	—	—

①—As viewed from drive end. C—Clockwise.

BRAKE SPECIFICATIONS

| Year | Model | Brake Drum Inside Diameter | Wheel Cylinder Bore Diameter | | | Master Cylinder Bore Diameter | | |
			Disc Brake	Front Drum Brake	Rear Drum Brake	Disc Brakes	Drum Brakes	Power Brakes
1974	Gremlin 6-Cyl.	9	2¾	1⅛	13/16	1⅛①	1	1
	Gremlin V8	10	2¾	1³⁄₁₆	⅞	1⅛①	1	1
	Hornet, Javelin 6-Cyl.	9	2¾	1⅛	⅞	1	1	1
	Hornet, Javelin V8	10	2¾	1³⁄₁₆	⅞	1	1	1
	Matador, Ambassador	10	2¾	1³⁄₃₂	15/16	1⅛①	1	1
	Station Wagons	10	2¾	1³⁄₃₂	15/16	1⅛①	1	1

Continued

BRAKE SPECIFICATIONS—Continued

Year	Model	Brake Drum Inside Diameter	Wheel Cylinder Bore Diameter			Master Cylinder Bore Diameter		
			Disc Brake	Front Drum Brake	Rear Drum Brake	Disc Brakes	Drum Brakes	Power Brakes
1975–76	Pacer	[6]	3.1	1 3/32	7/8	1 [1]	1	1
	Gremlin [3]	9	3.1	1 1/8	7/8	1 [1]	1	1
	Hornet [3]	9	3.1	1 1/8	13/16	1 [1]	1	1
	Gremlin, Hornet [4]	10	3.1	1 3/16	7/8	1 [1]	1	1
	Matador	10	3.1	—	[5]	1 1/16	—	1 1/8
1977	Pacer	10	2.6	—	13/16	1	—	1
	Gremlin, Hornet	10	2.6	—	13/16	1	—	1
	Matador	10	3.1	—	[5]	1	—	1 1/8
1978	Pacer	10	2.6	—	13/16	15/16	—	15/16
	Gremlin [2]	9	2.6	—	15/16	15/16	—	15/16
	Concord & Gremlin [7]	10	2.6	—	13/16 [8]	15/16	—	15/16
	Matador	10	3.1	—	[5]	1 1/8	—	1 1/8
1979	Pacer	10	2.6	—		15/16	—	15/16
	Spirit [2]	9	2.6	—		15/16	—	15/16
	Concord & Spirit [7]	10	2.6	—		15/16	—	15/16

[1]—Non power disc brakes 1 1/16".
[2]—Models equipped w/4 cyl. engine.
[3]—1975 & Early 1976 6 cyl. models.
[4]—1975–76 V8 models & 1976 mid-year 6 cyl. models.
[5]—Exc. sta. wag., 7/8"; sta. wag. 15/16".
[6]—Front drums, 10"; rear drums, 9".
[7]—Models equipped w/6 cyl. or V8 engines.
[8]—Exc. AMX models w/V8; AMX models w/V8, 7/8".

COOLING SYSTEM & CAPACITY DATA

Year	Model or Engine	Cooling Capacity, Qts.			Radiator Cap Relief Pressure, Lbs.		Thermo. Opening Temp. [1]	Fuel Tank Gals.	Engine Oil Refill Qts. [2]	Transmission Oil			Rear Axle Oils Pint
		No Heater	With Heater	With A/C	With A/C	No. A/C				3 Speed Pints	4 Speed Pints	Auto. Trans. Qts. [10]	
1974	6-232, 258	10	11	11 1/2	14	14	205	[16]	4	2 1/2 [3]	—	8 1/2	[7]
	6-232, 258 Mat. 2 Dr. Coupe	10	11	13 1/2 [17]	14	14	205	[16]	4	2 1/2	—	8 1/2	[7]
	V8-304 Hornet, Gremlin	15	16	16	14	14	195	[16]	4	2 1/2 [3]	—	8 1/2	[7]
	V8-304 Mat., Amb.	15 1/2	16 1/2	16 1/2	14	14	195	[16]	4	2 1/2	—	8 1/2	[7]
	V8-304, Mat. 2 Dr. Coupe	17 1/2	18 1/2 [17]	18 1/2 [17]	14	14	195	[16]	4	2 1/2	—	8 1/2	[7]
	V8-304 Javelin	—	15	15 1/2	14	14	195	[16]	4	2 1/2	—	8 1/2	[7]
	V8-360 Hornet	14	15	15	14	14	195	[16]	4	—	—	9 1/2	[7]
	V8-360, 401 Matador	14 1/2	15 1/2	15 1/2 [17]	14	14	195	[16]	4	—	—	9 1/2	[7]
	V8-360, 401 Mat. 2 Dr. Coupe	16 1/2	17 1/2 [17]	17 1/2 [17]	14	14	195	[16]	4	—	—	9 1/2	[7]
	V8-360, 401 Javelin	14	15	15	14	14	195	[16]	4	—	2 1/2	9 1/2	[7]
	V8-360, 401 Ambassador	14 1/2	15 1/2	15 1/2	14	14	195	[16]	4	—	—	9 1/2	[7]
1975	6-232, 258	—	[18]	[6]	15	15	195	[9]	4	3 1/2 [19]	—	8 1/2	[7]
	Gremlin, Hornet V8-304	—	16	16	15	15	195	[9]	4	3 1/2	—	8 1/2	[7]
	Matador [20] V8-304	—	16 1/2	16 1/2	15	15	195	[9]	4	3 1/2	—	8 1/2	[7]
	Matador [21] V8-304	—	18 1/2 [17]	18 1/2 [17]	15	15	195	24 1/2	4	3 1/2	—	8 1/2	[7]
	Matador [20] V8-360	—	15 1/2	15 1/2	15	15	195	[9]	4	3 1/2	—	9 1/2	[7]
	Matador [21] V8-360	—	17 1/2 [17]	17 1/2 [17]	15	15	195	24 1/2	4	3 1/2	—	9 1/2	[7]

Continued

COOLING SYSTEM & CAPACITY DATA—Continued

Year	Model or Engine	Cooling Capacity, Qts.			Radiator Cap Relief Pressure, Lbs.		Thermo. Opening Temp. ①	Fuel Tank Gals.	Engine Oil Refill Qts. ②	Transmission Oil			Rear Axle Oils Pint
		No Heater	With Heater	With A/C	With A/C	No. A/C				3 Speed Pints	4 Speed Pints	Auto. Trans. Qts. ⑩	
1976	6-232, 258	—	㉒	㉓	15	15	195	㉔	4	⑮	—	8½	⑦
	V8-304 Gremlin, Hornet	—	16	16	15	15	195	㉔	4	3½	—	9½	4
	V8-304 Matador⑳	—	16½⑰	16½⑰	15	15	195	㉔	4	3½	—	9½	4
	V8-304 Matador㉑	—	18½	18½	15	15	195	24½	4	3½	—	9½	4
	V8-360 Matador⑳	—	15½⑰	15½⑰	15	15	195	㉔	4	—	—	9½	4
	V8-360 Matador㉑	—	17½	17½	15	15	195	24½	4	—	—	9½	4
1977	4-121 Gremlin	—	6½	6½	14	14	189	15	4	—	2.4	7.1	3
	6-232, 258 Gremlin	—	11	14	15	15	195	21	4	3½	3½	8½	3
	6-232, 258 Hornet	—	11	11½	15	15	195	22	4	3½	3½	8½	3
	6-232, 258 Matador	—	⑪	⑪	15	15	195	⑫	4	—	—	8½	4
	6-232, 258 Pacer	—	14	14	15	15	195	22	4	3½	3½	8½	3
	V8-304 Hornet	—	16	16	15	15	195	22	4	3½	3½	8½	4
	V8-304 Matador	—	⑭	⑭	15	15	195	⑫	4	—	—	8½	4
	V8-360 Matador	—	⑭	⑭	15	15	195	⑫	4	—	—	9½	4
1978	4-121 Gremlin	—	6½	6½	14	14	190	④	3½⑤	—	2.4	7.1	3
	6-232, 258 Gremlin	—	11	14	14	14	195	⑬	4	3	3.3	8.5	3
	6-232, 258 Concord & AMX	—	11	14	14	14	195	⑬	4	3	3.3	8.5	3
	6-232, 258 Matador	—	⑪	⑪	14	14	195	㉕	4	—	—	8.5	4
	6-232, 258 Pacer	—	14	14	14	14	195	20	4	3	3.3	8.5	3
	V8-304 Concord & AMX	—	18	18	14	14	195	22	4	3	—	8.5	4
	V8-304 Pacer	—	18	18	14	14	195	20	4	—	—	8.5	4
	V8-360 Matador	—	㉖	㉖	14	14	195	㉕	4	—	—	8.2	4

①—With permanent type anti-freeze.
②—Add one quart with filter change.
③—Late 6-232, 3½ pts.
④—With man. trans., 13 gals.; with auto. trans., 15 gals.
⑤—Add ½ qt. with filter change.
⑦—7⁹⁄₁₆″ axle, 3 pints. 8⅞″ axle, 4 pints.
⑧—Matador 2 dr. coupe 13½ qts., all others 11½ qts.
⑨—Gremlin, 21 gals.; Hornet, early 17 gals.; late 22 gals.; Matador exc. wagon, 24½ gals.; wagon, 21 gals.; Pacer, 22 gals.
⑩—Approximate. Make final check with dipstick.
⑪—Coupe, 13½ qts.; sedan & wagon 11½ qts.
⑫—Except wagon, 24½ gals.; wagon, 21 gals.
⑬—Gremlin, 21 gals.; Concord, 22 gals.
⑭—Sedan & wagon: V8-304 16½ qts. V8-360 15½ qts. Add 2 quarts with coolant recovery system; Coupe models: V8-304 18½ qts., V8-360 17½ qts.
⑮—Except Pacer, Matador & overdrive, 2½ pt.; Pacer & Matador, 3½ pts.; all models with overdrive, 4 pts.
⑯—Hornet & Javelin, 16; Gremlin, 21; Matador Sedan & 2 Dr. Coupe, 24¾; Ambassador Sedan, 24¾; Mat. & Amb. Wagons, 21.
⑰—Add two quarts with coolant recovery system.
⑱—Exc. Pacer, 11 qts.; Pacer, 10½ qts.
⑲—With overdrive exc. Pacer, add 1 pt.; Pacer with overdrive, add ½ pt.
⑳—Sedan & wagon.
㉑—2 dr. coupe.
㉒—Exc. Pacer, 11 qts.; Pacer, 14 qts.
㉓—Exc. Pacer & Matador 2 dr. coupe, 11½ qts.; Pacer, 14 qts.; Matador 2 dr. coupe, 13½ qts.
㉔—Gremlin, 21 gals.; Hornet, 22 gals.; Matador exc. wagon, 24½ gals.; Wagon, 21 gals.; Pacer, 22 gals.
㉕—Except Sta. wag., 25 gals.; sta. wag., 21 gals.
㉖—Coupe 17½ qts.; Sedan & Sta. Wag., 15½ qts.⑰

Electrical Section

DISTRIBUTOR, REPLACE

1. Disconnect distributor primary wiring.
2. Remove distributor cap and rotor. Mark position of rotor arm on distributor housing so distributor can be installed in same position.
3. Remove vacuum line from distributor.
4. Remove distributor hold-down clamp.
5. Note relative position of distributor in block, then work it out of the engine.

Installation

1. Turn rotor about 1/8 of a turn counterclockwise past the mark previously placed on the distributor housing.
2. Push the distributor down into the block with the housing in the normal "installed" position. It may be necessary to move the rotor slightly to start gear into mesh with camshaft gear, but rotor should line up with mark when distributor is down in place.
3. Tighten distributor clamp screw snugly and connect vacuum line, primary wiring, and install cap.

Note

If the engine was disturbed while the distributor was removed from the engine, first crank the engine to bring No. 1 piston up on its compression stroke and continue cranking until the timing mark is adjacent to the timing indicator. Then rotate the distributor cam until the rotor is in position to fire No. 1 cylinder. Install the distributor as outlined above and set the ignition timing as directed elsewhere in this manual.

STARTER, REPLACE

To remove starter, disconnect cable from battery. Disconnect cable and solenoid lead wire from solenoid switch. Remove starter attaching bolts and take off starter.

IGNITION LOCK

1974-79

1. Remove turn signal switch as described further on.
2. Place key lock in "Lock" position and using a small flat blade screwdriver to depress the lock cylinder retaining tab, remove the lock cylinder, Fig. 1.

Fig. 1   Lock cylinder removal

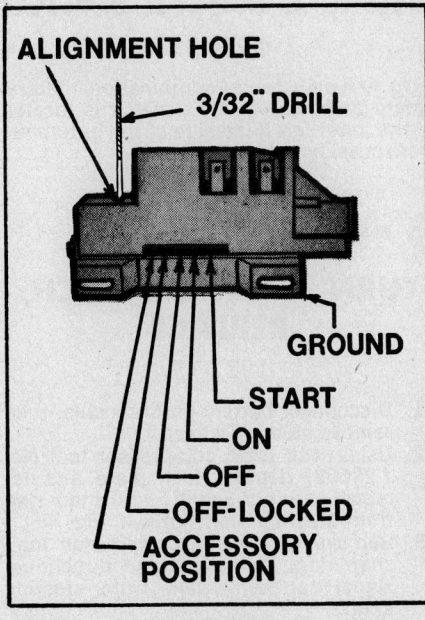

Fig. 2   Ignition switch alignment. 1974-79 (typical)

IGNITION SWITCH, REPLACE

1974-79

NOTE: On Pacer models, it may be necessary to remove steering tube cover and A/C duct to gain access to ignition switch. On Concord, Gremlin, Hornet and Spirit models, remove package tray, if equipped.

The ignition switch on all models is mounted on the lower section of the steering column and is connected to the lock by a remote control rod. To remove switch, place key in Off-Lock position and remove switch mounting screws. Disconnect switch from remote control rod, remove wire harness and remove switch.

To install switch on 1974-79 models equipped with standard steering column, move slider to extreme left position (left side of switch pointing inward toward steering column), Fig. 2. Place actuator rod in slider hole and install switch on column. Tighten retaining screws.

To install switch on 1974-79 models equipped with tilt steering column, move slider to extreme right position (right side of switch pointing downward from steering wheel). Place actuator rod in slider hole and install switch on column without tightening screws. Remove lash from actuator rod by pushing downward lightly on switch and tighten retaining screws.

LIGHT SWITCH, REPLACE

1976-79 Concord, Gremlin, Hornet & Spirit

1. Disconnect battery ground cable.
2. Remove package tray, if equipped, and disconnect speedometer cable.
3. Remove instrument cluster bezel attaching screws and tilt bezel away from instrument panel.
4. With switch in full "On" position, press release button on switch and remove shaft and knob assembly.
5. Remove switch mounting sleeve nut.
6. Disconnect electrical connectors from switch and remove switch from vehicle.

1975-79 Pacer

1. Disconnect battery ground cable.
2. Remove switch overlay attaching screws and pull overlay assembly rearward.
3. With switch in full "On" position, press release button on switch and remove shaft and knob assembly.
4. Remove switch mounting sleeve nut.
5. Disconnect electrical connectors from switch and remove switch from vehicle.

1974 Ambassador & 1974-78 Matador

1. Disconnect battery ground cable.
2. Remove instrument cluster bezel.
3. Remove screws attaching light switch and wiper-washer bracket to instrument panel.
4. With switch in full "On" position,

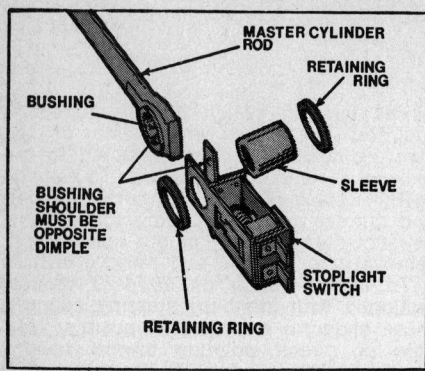

Fig. 3 Stoplight switch. 1974-79 (typical)

press release button on switch and remove shaft and knob assembly.
5. Remove switch mounting sleeve nut.
6. Disconnect electrical connectors from switch and remove switch from vehicle.

1974 Javelin

1. Remove knob from toggle switch by depressing a small spring steel retaining tab up toward the handle.
2. Remove seven screws from steering column lower cover and remove cover.
3. Remove wire connections, two retaining screws and remove switch.

1974-75 Gremlin & Hornet

1. Disconnect a battery cable.
2. With switch in full "On" position, press button on side or top of switch to release shaft and knob assembly.
3. Remove switch mounting sleeve nut.
4. Disconnect wire harness connector.
5. Reverse procedure to install. Position switch so that shaft is lined up properly before tightening.

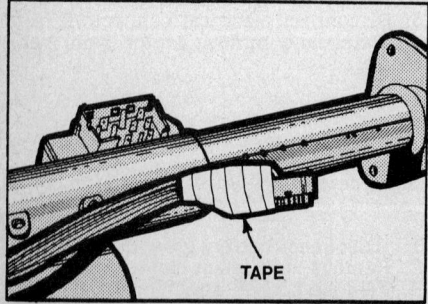

Fig. 5 Taping turn signal connector and wires

STOP LIGHT SWITCH, REPLACE
1974-79

1. On Concord, Gremlin, Hornet and Spirit models, remove package tray, if equipped.
2. On Pacer models, remove steering column tube cover and intermediate duct under instrument panel, if equipped with A/C.
3. On all models, disconnect wire connector from switch.
4. Remove brake pedal pivot bolt, nylon retaining rings, sleeve and remove switch.
5. When installing switch, be sure dimple on switch is opposite the bushing collar, Fig. 3.

NOTE: On 1977-79 models, there are two bolt holes on the brake pedal. On models equipped with power brakes, install bolt in lower hole. On models less power brakes, install bolt in upper hole.

NEUTRAL SAFETY SWITCH
1974-79

A non-adjustable combination neutral safety and back-up light switch is located at the lower left hand side of the automatic transmission case.

TURN SIGNAL SWITCH, REPLACE
1977-79

1. Disconnect battery ground cable, then remove steering wheel.
2. Using lock plate compressor tool No. J-23653, depress lock plate and remove and pry round wire snap ring from steering shaft groove, Fig. 4.
3. Remove lock plate compressor tool, snap ring, lock plate and directional signal canceling cam from steering shaft.
4. Place directional signal lever in the right turn position, then remove lever and directional signal switch mounting screws, Fig. 6.
5. Depress hazard warning switch and remove button by turning in counter clockwise direction.
6. Remove directional signal switch wiring harness connector from mounting bracket on right side of lower column.
7. On Concord, Gremlin, Hornet, Pacer & Spirit models, remove steering tube cover.
8. On Matador models, remove lower finish panel.
9. Remove steering column lower bracket bolts, then loosen steering column bracket nuts.
10. Fold connector over harness and wrap with tape to avoid snagging, Fig. 5.

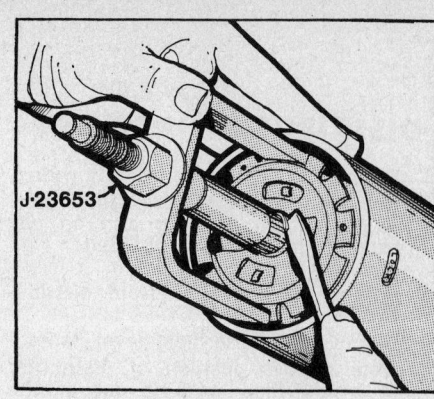

Fig. 4 Compressing lock plate and removing retaining ring

Raise column and pull harness out of column.

NOTE: On models with tilt column, raise column and remove plastic wiring harness protector.

11. On Concord and Hornet models, with column shift automatic transmission, use stiff wire, such as a paper clip, to depress lock tab which retains shift quadrant light wire to wiring harness connector. The shift quadrant light wire is the grey wire connected to terminal D on wiring harness connector.

1974-76

1. Disconnect negative battery cable.
2. Remove steering wheel.
3. Loosen anti-theft cover retaining screws and lift cover from column. *It is not necessary to remove these screws completely as they are held on the cover by plastic retainers.*
4. Using a suitable tool, depress lock plate and pry out snap ring from steering shaft groove, Fig. 4.
5. Remove tool, lock plate, cancelling cam, upper bearing preload spring and thrust washer.

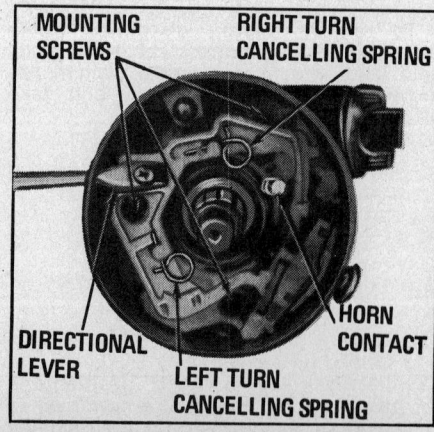

Fig. 6 Turn signal switch. 1974-79

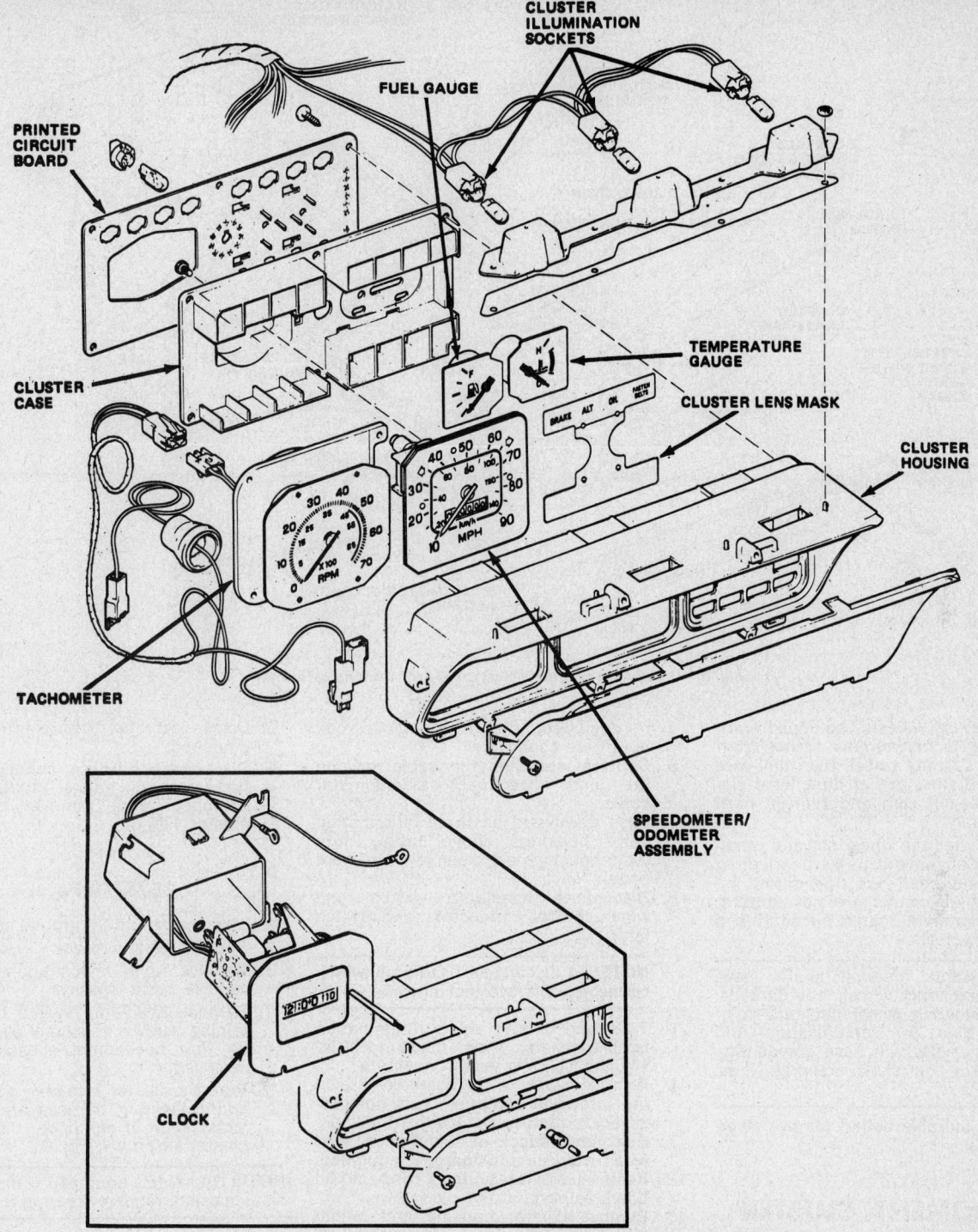

Fig. 7 Instrument cluster (typical). 1978-79 Concord, Gremlin & Spirit

6. Place directional signal lever in right turn position and remove lever.
7. Depress hazard warning light switch and remove the button by turning in a counterclockwise direction.
8. Remove directional signal wire harness from mounting bracket on lower column. Wrap upper part of connector with tape to prevent snagging the wire during removal, Fig. 5. On Shift Command, column shift, use a stiff wire to depress lock tab which retains the shift quadrant light wire in connector block.
9. Remove directional signal switch screws and remove switch, Fig. 6.

HORN SOUNDER & STEERING WHEEL

1. Disconnect battery ground cable.
2. On steering wheels with horn buttons, remove button by first lifting button upward, and then pulling button out.

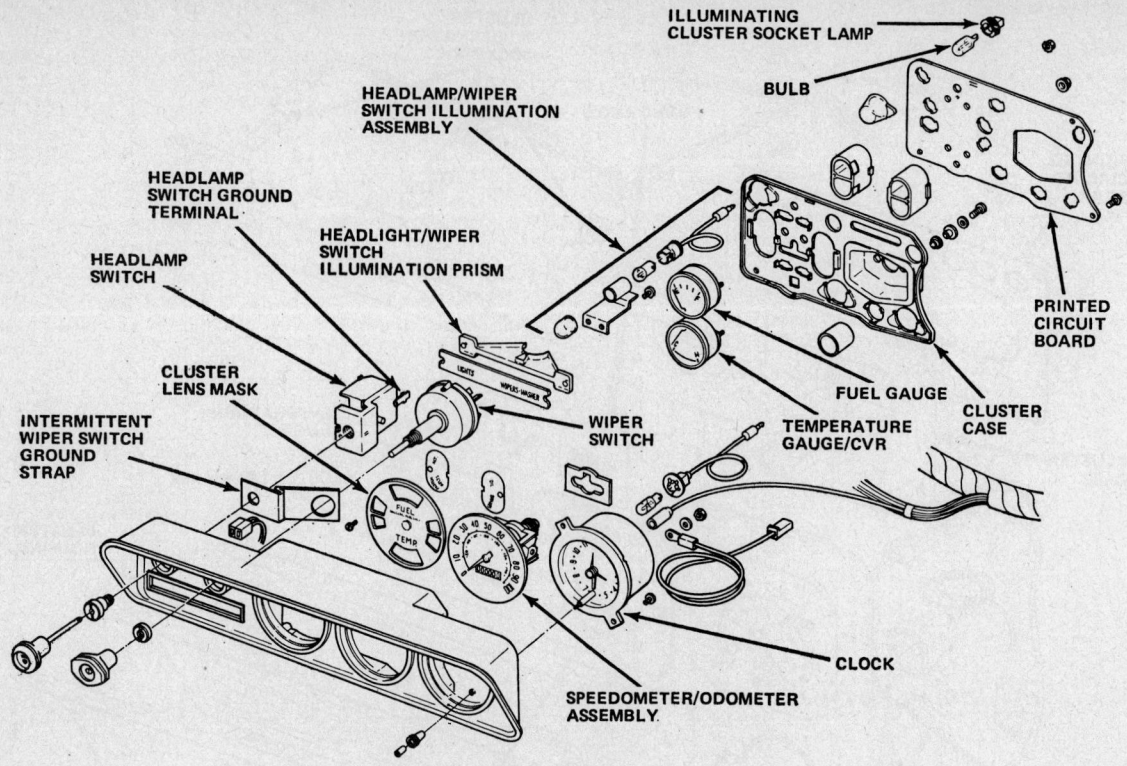

ILLUMINATING CLUSTER SOCKET LAMP

BULB

HEADLAMP/WIPER SWITCH ILLUMINATION ASSEMBLY

HEADLAMP SWITCH GROUND TERMINAL

HEADLIGHT/WIPER SWITCH ILLUMINATION PRISM

HEADLAMP SWITCH

PRINTED CIRCUIT BOARD

CLUSTER LENS MASK

INTERMITTENT WIPER SWITCH GROUND STRAP

WIPER SWITCH

FUEL GAUGE

CLUSTER CASE

TEMPERATURE GAUGE/CVR

CLOCK

SPEEDOMETER/ODOMETER ASSEMBLY

Fig. 8 Instrument cluster (typical). 1974-77 Gremlin & Hornet

On steering wheels equipped with horn ring or bar, remove screws from back of steering wheel, then pull wire plastic retainer out of directional signal canceling cam and remove horn ring or bar.

3. Remove steering wheel nut and washer. Note alignment marks on steering wheel and shaft for use during installation. If marks are not present, paint alignment marks on shaft and steering wheel.

NOTE: Some steering shafts have metric steering wheel nut threads. Metric steering wheel nuts are color coded blue for identification and steering shafts will have an identifying groove on shaft steering wheel splines.

4. Using a suitable puller, remove steering wheel.

INSTRUMENT CLUSTER

1978-79 Concord, Gremlin & Spirit

1. Disconnect battery ground cable.
2. On 1979 Concord and Spirit models, remove lower steering column cover. On models equipped with column shift automatic transmission, remove gear selector dial actuator cable from steering column shift shroud.
3. On all models, remove instrument cluster bezel attaching screws across top of bezel, above radio and behind glove box door.
4. Tip top of bezel outward and disengage tabs along bottom edge of bezel.

5. If equipped, disconnect glove box lamp wire connector.
6. Depress speedometer cable locking tab and disconnect speedometer cable.
7. Push downward on three illumination lamp housings above bezel, until lamp housings are clear of instrument panel.
8. Disconnect headlamp switch and wiper control connectors and switch lamp.

NOTE: To disconnect headlamp switch connector, lift two locking tabs.

9. Twist and remove cluster illumination lamp sockets, then disconnect instrument cluster wire connectors.
10. Remove clock or tachometer attaching screws, if equipped. It is not necessary to remove clock adjusting knob.
11. Disconnect clock or tachometer feed wires from circuit board, if equipped.
12. Remove cluster housing and circuit board to bezel attaching screws.
13. Remove cluster housing and circuit board assembly from bezel, Fig. 7. If equipped with clock or tachometer, position aside as necessary.

1976-77 Gremlin & Hornet

1. Disconnect battery ground cable.
2. Remove package tray if equipped to gain access speedometer cable.
3. Remove speedometer cable.
4. Remove top and side screws from instrument panel and tilt panel forward to gain access to headlamp and wiper control switch harness connectors.

5. Disconnect fiber-optic ashtray lamp if equipped.
6. Disconnect harness connectors and fuel economy gauge vacuum line if equipped and remove instrument cluster, Fig. 8.

1975-79 Pacer

1. Disconnect battery ground cable.
2. Remove cluster bezel.
3. Remove radio knobs and nuts, then remove radio overlay.
4. Remove headlamp switch overlay retaining screws, then pull overlay back so that speedometer cable can be removed.
5. Remove cluster retaining screws, disconnect wiring harness and gear selector cable if equipped, then remove cluster assembly, Fig. 9.

NOTE: On models equipped with automatic transmission, remove steering tube cover.

1974-78 Matador & Ambassador

1. Disconnect battery ground cable.
2. Remove radio knobs, attaching nuts and bezel retaining screws.
3. Remove right hand remote control mirror control from instrument panel, if equipped.
4. Tilt bezel forward and disconnect wiring.
5. Remove bezel, then remove clock or economy fuel gauge (if used) attaching screws, pull assembly away from

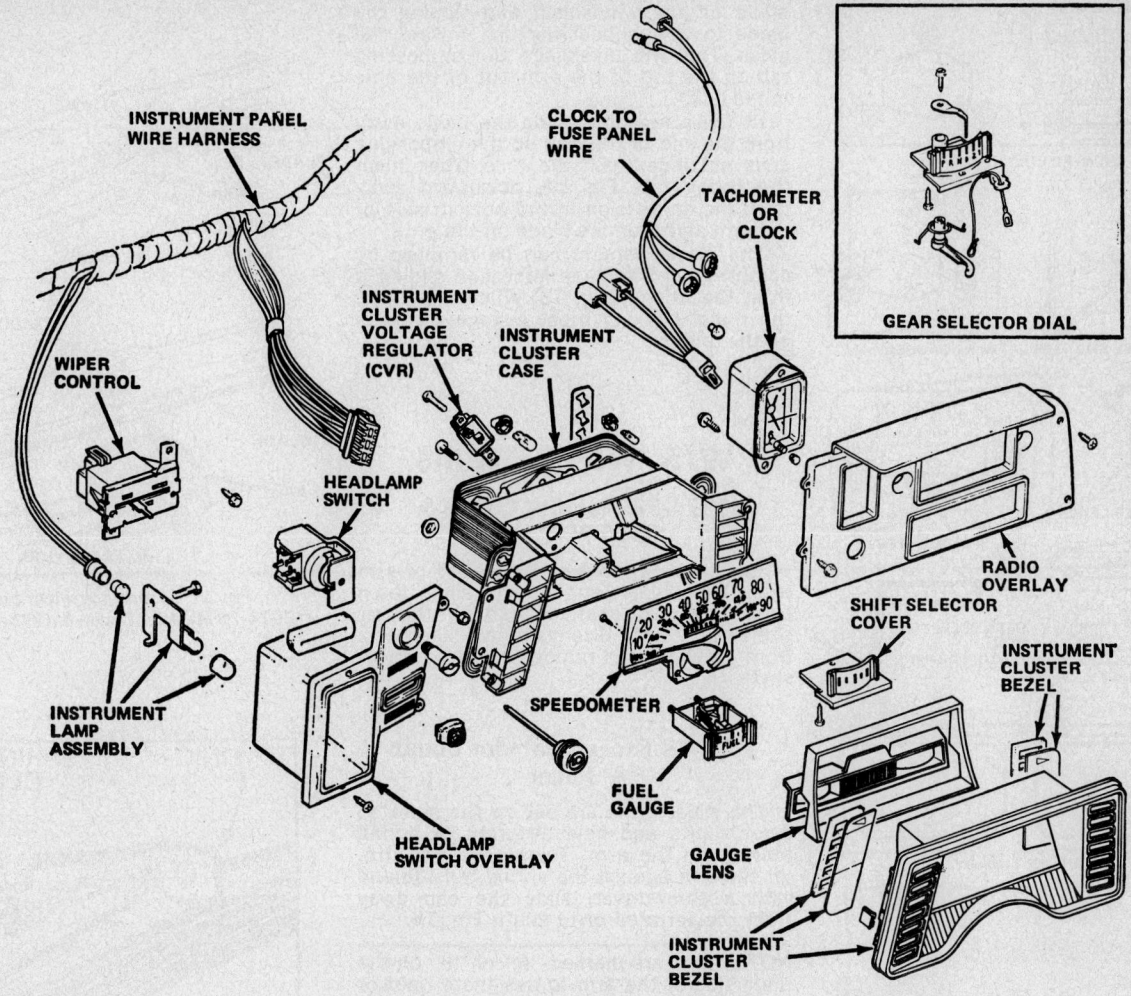

Fig. 9   Instrument cluster (typical). 1975-79 Pacer

cluster and disconnect bulbs and electrical leads. If equipped with fuel economy gauge, disconnect vacuum line and remove assembly.

6. Using clock opening, disconnect speedometer cable from instrument cluster, and disconnect gear selector dial cable from steering column.

7. Remove cluster mounting screws, disconnect any remaining electrical connections and remove cluster, Fig. 10.

1974-75 Hornet & Gremlin

1. Disconnect battery ground cable.
2. Remove package tray, if so equipped, to gain access to wiper control and speedo cable.
3. Remove wiper control knob and spanner nut. To remove control knob, rotate knob until slot in neck of knob is visible. Insert a small diameter tool

in slot and apply pressure toward knob to release pressure on spring metal clip. Remove knob.

4. Remove speedometer cable.
5. Remove four top and two side screws from instrument panel and tilt panel forward slightly to gain access to light switch and connectors.
6. Remove headlight switch knob, retaining nut and switch.
7. Cover steering column with a cloth to prevent scratches and disconnect harness connectors and remove cluster, Fig. 8.

1974 Javelin

1. Disconnect battery.
2. Cover painted surface of column with a cloth.
3. Remove the top, side and lower screws around bezel.
4. If equipped with radio, remove control knobs and retaining nuts.

5. Remove knobs from four instrument panel switches.
6. If equipped with A/C, release the speedometer cable hold-down clip on wheelhouse panel to allow movement of cable.
7. Move bezel and cluster out of opening far enough to reach in and disconnect speedometer cable, wire harness plug and wire connections.
8. The cluster can be removed from bezel by removing eight screws and the clock set knob.

W/S WIPER BLADES

1974-78 Matador Coupe & 1975-79 Pacer

Insert an appropriate tool into spring release opening of blade saddle, depress spring clip and pull blade from arm, Fig. 11. To install, push blade saddle onto pin so spring engages pin.

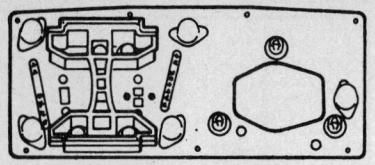

PRINTED CIRCUIT BOARD
FUEL AND TEMPERATURE GAUGES
INDICATOR BULB LENS
SPEEDOMETER
MASK
GEAR SELECTOR
DIAL
(AUTO. TRANS)
CLUSTER HOUSING
LENS

Fig. 10 Instrument cluster (typical). 1974 Ambassador & 1974-78 Matador

1974-79 Exc. Matador Coupe & Pacer

The wiper blade assembly can be removed from the wiper arm by lifting the blade off the windshield and tipping the blade to arm connecting link toward the glass. This will disengage the embossing tab on the top of the arm out of the hole in the link.

At the same time, slide the blade away from the end of the arm so the embossing does not index with the hole. Then push the spring tab, Fig. 12, downward away from the depression in the bottom side of the arm and slide the blade off the arm.

The blade element can be removed by compressing the blade latch and sliding it from the bridge, Fig. 13. When installing, the metal backing must engage the tabs on the bridge.

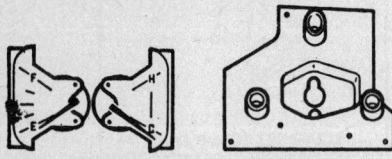

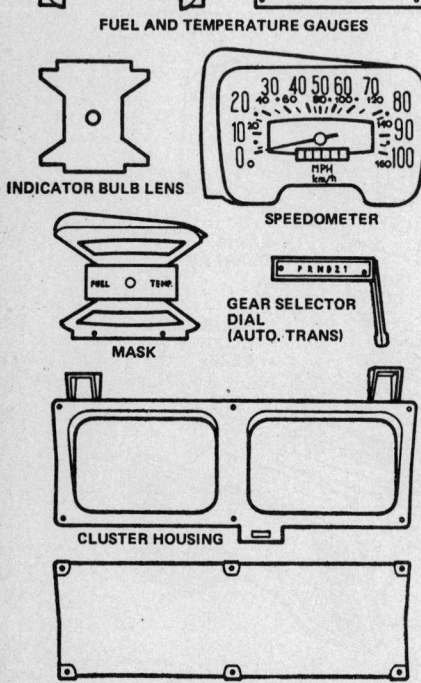

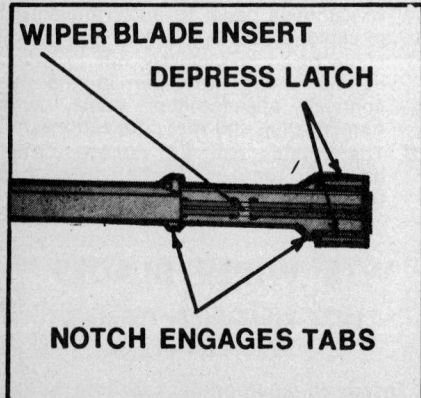

WIPER BLADE INSERT
DEPRESS LATCH
NOTCH ENGAGES TABS

Fig. 13 Removing blade element. 1974-79 Exc. Matador Coupe & Pacer

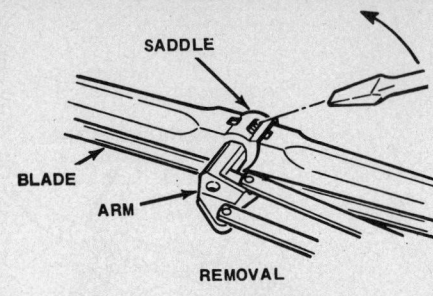

SADDLE
BLADE
ARM
REMOVAL
SADDLE
BLADE
PIN
ARM
INSTALLATION

Fig. 11 Removing wiper blade. 1974-78 Matador Coupe & 1975-79 Pacer

W/S WIPER ARMS

1974-78 Matador Coupe & 1975-79 Pacer

To remove arm, raise blade end of arm from windshield and move slide latch away from pivot shaft, Fig. 14. On the left side wiper arm, disengage auxillary arm from pivot pin and remove arm from pivot shaft.

1974-79 Except Matador Coupe & Pacer

The wiper arms are set on the serrated pivot shafts and held securely by spring tension on the arm. To remove the arm, lift the arm against the spring tension and with a screwdriver, slide the cap away from the serrated pivot shaft, Fig. 15.

NOTE: Arms are marked "R" or "L" on the underside of the arm to designate right or left arm.

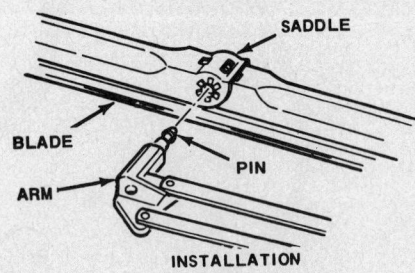

TIP LINK
SPRING
CLIP

Fig. 12 Removing wiper blade. 1974-79 Exc. Matador Coupe & Pacer

W/S WIPER MOTOR, REPLACE

1975-79 Pacer

1. Disconnect linkage drive arm from motor crankpin.
2. Remove vacuum canister and mounting bracket assembly, if necessary.
3. On models equipped with air conditioning, remove two nuts from left side of heater housing and one nut from the right side of the housing.
4. On models not equipped with air conditioning, remove two nuts and one screw from left side of heater housing and one nut from the right side of the housing.
5. On all models, remove screw from heater housing support.
6. Pull heater housing forward.

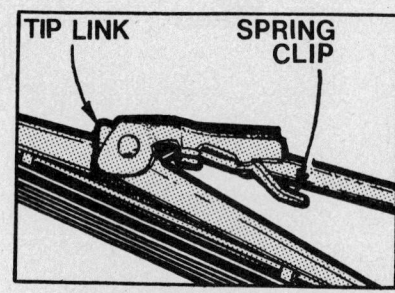

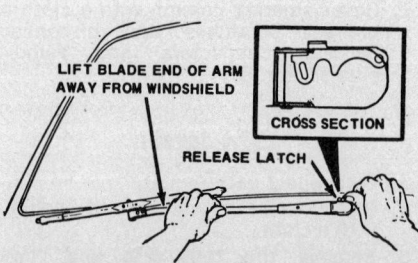

LIFT BLADE END OF ARM
AWAY FROM WINDSHIELD
CROSS SECTION
RELEASE LATCH

Fig. 14 Removing wiper arm. 1974-78 Matador Coupe & Pacer

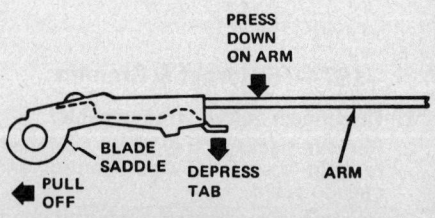

PRESS
DOWN
ON ARM
BLADE
SADDLE
DEPRESS
TAB
ARM
PULL
OFF

Fig. 15 Removing wiper arm. 1974-78 except Matador Coupe & Pacer

7. Remove screws from wiper motor mounting plate and disconnect wiring harness.
8. Remove attaching screws and wiper motor.

NOTE: Ensure output arm is in parked position before installing wiper motor.

1975-79 Pacer Liftgate Wiper

1. Remove wiper arm and blade.
2. Remove liftgate trim pad.
3. Disconnect wiring harness and ground wire.
4. Remove nut and pad securing wiper motor shaft to liftgate.
5. Remove screws securing wiper motor bracket, then separate bracket from motor.

1974-78 Matador Coupe

1. Remove wiper arms and cowl screen.
2. Remove retaining clip from linkage drive arm and disconnect electrical connectors from motor.
3. Remove wiper motor retaining screws and wiper motor.

NOTE: If output arm contacts dash panel, preventing wiper motor removal, hand turn output arm so arm clears dash opening.

4. Before installing motor, be sure output arm is in park position.

1974-79 Exc. Matador Coupe & Pacer

1. Remove wiper arms and blades.
2. Remove four screws holding motor to dash.
3. Separate harness connector at the motor.
4. Pull motor and linkage out of opening to expose the drive link to crank stud retaining clip. Raise up the lock tab of the clip with a flat bladed screwdriver and slide clip off stud.

W/S WIPER TRANSMISSION, REPLACE

1975-79 Pacer

1. Remove wiper arms and blades.
2. Remove pivot shaft bodies to cowl screws using tool J-25359 for 1975-76 models or tool No. J-25359-02 for 1977-79 models.
3. Disconnect linkage from motor output arm, then remove pivot shaft body assembly.

1974-78 Matador Coupe

1. Remove wiper arm and blade assemblies, then remove cowl screen.

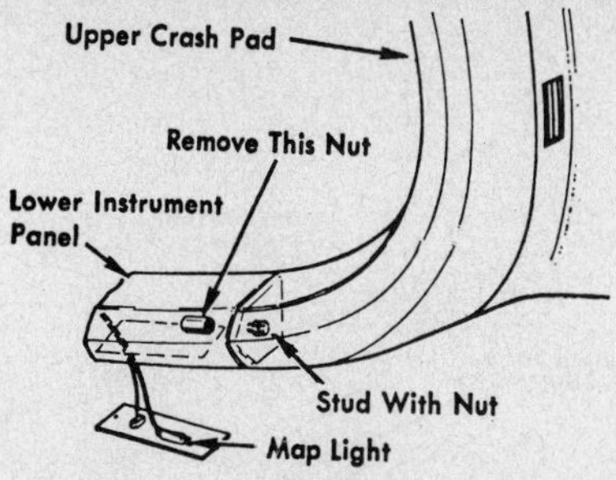

Fig. 16 Location of hidden stud nut. 1974 Javelin

2. Remove screws attaching right and left pivot bodies to cowl using tool No. J-24628-2 for 1974 models, tool No. J-25359 for 1975-76 models or tool No. J-25359-02 for 1977-78 models.
3. Disconnect linkage drive arm from motor output arm crankpin by removing retaining clip.
4. Remove pivot shaft body assembly through cowl opening.

1974-78 Ambassador & Matador Exc. Matador Coupe

1. Remove wiper arms and blades.
2. Remove cowl air intake cover.
3. Disconnect link-to-motor retainer and link from wiper arm through cowl top opening.
4. Remove screws holding each pivot shaft body to cowl top.
5. Remove both pivot body and link assemblies through cowl top opening.

1974 Javelin, 1974-79 Concord, Hornet, Gremlin & Spirit

1. Remove wiper arms and blades.
2. Remove pivot shaft-to-cowl top nuts.
3. Remove wiper motor.
4. Slide pivot shaft body and link assembly to the left to clear right pivot shaft opening and move assembly to the right side of car to remove as a unit.

NOTE

When installing pivot shafts to cowl top, flat side of pivot shaft indexes flat side of hole in cowl top when pivot shaft is in up position.

W/S WIPER CONTROL, REPLACE

1978-79 Pacer

1. Using a small screwdriver, remove knob from switch by releasing tension on clip.
2. Remove bezel from instrument cluster by pulling toward rear of vehicle.
3. Remove four screws attaching headlamp switch overlay, then pull toward rear of vehicle to gain access to rear of w/s wiper switch.
4. Remove connector from rear of switch.
5. Remove two screws attaching switch to instrument panel, then remove switch.

1975-77 Pacer

1. Remove instrument cluster bezel, then the four screws from headlamp overlay.
2. Remove control knob, using a small screw driver to release spring tension on clip.
3. Remove wire connector, then the two screws attaching switch to instrument panel.

1974-79 All Exc. Javelin & Pacer

1. Locate small notch at base of knob and insert a small screwdriver and apply pressure to release spring and pull knob from shaft.
2. Remove slotted trim nut from front of switch.
3. Push switch through instrument panel then disconnect wiring harness and remove switch.

1974 Javelin

1. Remove control knob.
2. Access can be gained to switch screws by removing steering column cover.

RADIO

NOTE: When installing radio, be sure to adjust antenna trimmer for peak performance.

1975-79 Pacer

1. Remove radio knobs, nuts and bezels, then the radio overlay.
2. Loosen radio attaching screws and lift radio from mounting bracket.
3. Disconnect antenna lead and wire connectors and remove radio.

1974 Ambassador & 1974-78 Matador

1. Remove radio knobs, retaining nuts and instrument cluster bezel.
2. Loosen upper radio retaining screw and lift radio disengaging bracket from screw, and pull radio slightly forward.
3. Disconnect antenna lead, electrical wiring and remove radio.

1974 Javelin

To remove the radio, the entire crash pad will have to be removed.

1. Disconnect battery ground cable.
2. Remove the six attaching screws that lie next to lower edge of windshield.
3. Remove radio knobs and retaining nuts.
4. Open right door and remove two panel attaching screws at door pillar area.
5. Remove the five attaching screws in the upper flange of the cluster bezel. Remove moulding attaching screws and assist handle at lower right finish panel.

NOTE: Remove map light to gain access to hidden stud nut which retains crash pad to lower instrument panel, Fig. 16.

6. Remove entire panel top cover to expose radio and speaker.
7. Disconnect and remove speaker. Slide radio back and lift up to disconnect speaker and bulb wires.
8. Remove radio input wire from fuse panel. Tie a heavy string to wire before removing radio to assist in dressing wire back through wiring and duct assemblies.
9. Remove radio.

1974-79 Concord, Gremlin, Hornet & Spirit

1. Disconnect battery ground cable.
2. Remove package tray, if equipped.
3. Disconnect fiber-optic ash tray lamp from instrument cluster, if equipped.
4. Remove ash tray and bracket.
5. Remove radio knobs and shaft nuts.
6. Remove bezel retaining screws and bezel.
7. On 1977-79 models equipped with A/C, remove instrument panel center housing and attaching screws and center housing.
8. Disconnect antenna, speaker and power lead.
9. Remove radio.

HEATER CORE, REMOVAL

1975-79 Pacer, Fig. 17

1. Drain approximately 2 qts. from cooling system.
2. Remove heater hoses and install plugs in hoses and core openings.
3. Position vacuum hoses away from core housing.

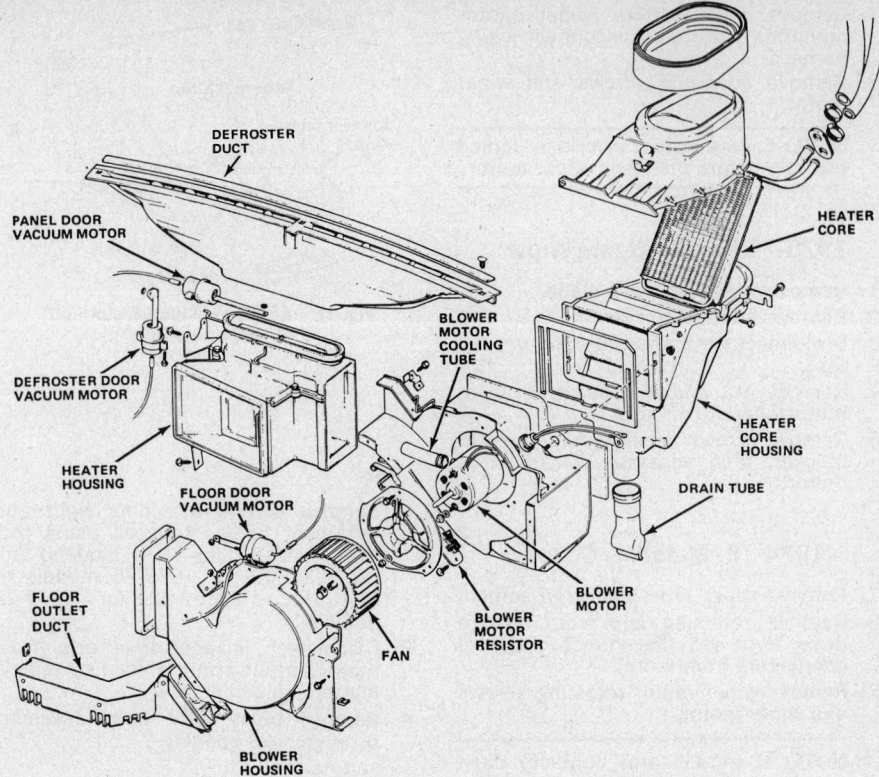

Fig. 17   Heater and blower housing assembly. 1975-79 Pacer (Typical)

4. On models with A/C, disconnect outside air door vacuum hose from vacuum motor.
5. Remove core housing cover screws, disconnect overcenter spring and remove cover.
6. Remove screws attaching core to housing and remove core.

1974 Ambassador & 1974-78 Matador, Fig. 18

Less Air Conditioning

1. Disconnect battery ground cable.
2. Drain about 2 quarts of coolant then disconnect heater hoses and plug ends of hoses and core openings, Fig. 18.
3. Remove lower instrument finish panel and glove box.
4. Disconnect control cables and vacuum motor hoses.
5. On 1975-78 models, remove right side windshield reveal moulding to gain access to upper right housing attaching screw.
6. On all models, remove retaining screws and remove heater core housing assembly.
7. Remove heater core from housing.
8. Reverse procedure to install.

With Air Conditioning

1. Disconnect battery ground cable and drain cooling system.

2. Disconnect heater hoses from core and plug core tubes, Fig. 18.
3. Remove glove box and door.
4. Remove blend-air door cable from core housing and remove fuse panel.
5. Remove lower instrument finish panel.
6. Remove right windshield pillar and corner finish mouldings.
7. Remove vacuum motor hoses.
8. Remove screw attaching instrument panel to right "A" pillar.
9. Pull out right side of instrument panel and remove heater core housing assembly.
10. Remove heater core from housing.
11. Reverse procedure to install.

1974 Javelin

1. Drain 2 qts. of water from cooling system and disconnect hoses from core tubes in engine compartment. Install corks in hoses and core tubes.
2. Disconnect blower motor wires.
3. Remove ground wire from dash panel ground stud and remove ground stud nut and washer.
4. Remove instrument panel top cover, right side mouldings, assist handle, lower right finish panel and right hand panel support brace.
5. Disconnect air vent cable at heater housing.
6. Remove heater housing attaching screws in front compartment.

7. After removal of housing assembly the heater core can be removed.

1974-79 Concord, Hornet, Gremlin & Spirit

1. Drain about 2 qts. from cooling system.
2. Disconnect heater hoses and plug heater core tubes.
3. Remove blower motor and fan.
4. Remove housing attaching nut(s) from inside engine compartment.
5. Remove package tray if so equipped.
6. Disconnect wire connector at resistor.
7. On models with A/C, remove instrument panel bezel, outlet and duct.
8. Disconnect control cables from damper levers.
9. Remove right side windshield pillar moulding and the instrument panel upper attaching screws and right side cap screw at the door hinge post.
10. Remove right side kick panel and heater housing attaching screws.
11. Pull the right side of the instrument panel slightly rearward and remove the housing.
12. Remove cover and screws attaching heater core to housing, then remove heater core from housing.

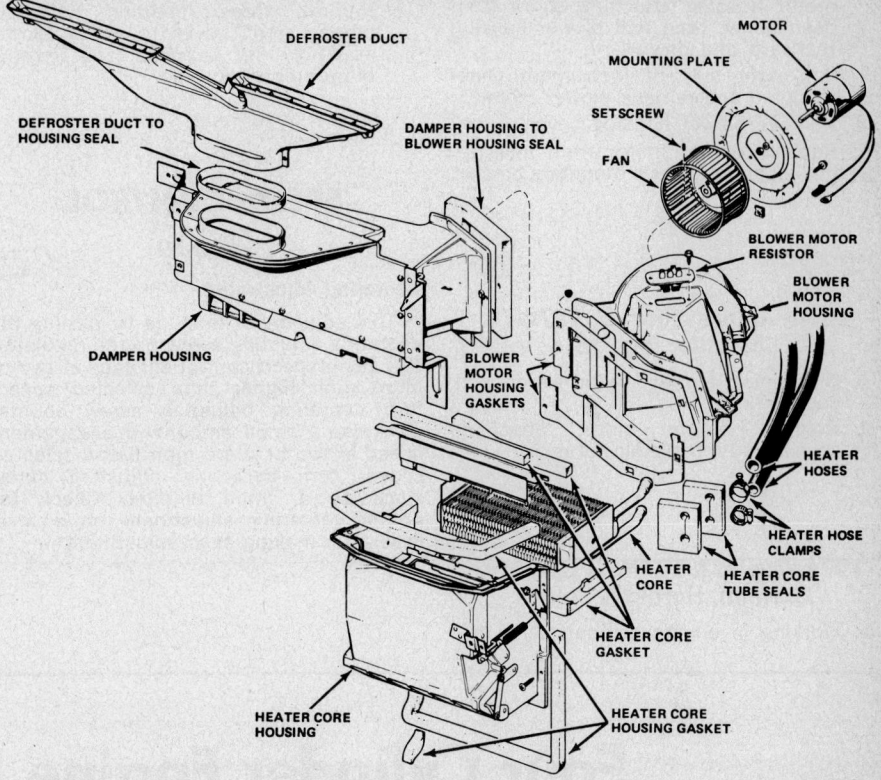

Fig. 18   Heater and blower housing assembly. 1974 Ambassador & 1974-78 Matador (Typical)

BLOWER MOTOR, REMOVE

1975-79 Pacer

Less Air Conditioning

1. Disconnect battery ground cable.
2. Remove right side windshield molding, then the instrument panel crash pad.
3. Remove right scuff plate and cowl panel.
4. Remove lower instrument panel to pillar attaching screws, then pull instrument panel rearward and reinstall attaching screws, allowing panel to rest on screws.
5. Remove heater core housing attaching nuts and screw, position vacuum lines aside, disconnect air door, then pull housing forward and position on upper control arm.
6. Remove blower motor attaching screws, disconnect relay ground wire and resistor wiring.
7. Remove blower motor brace.
8. Loosen heater housing to instrument panel attaching nuts.
9. Pull blower motor housing rearward and downward, disconnect vacuum hoses from motors and remove blower housing.
10. Remove housing cover, disconnect wire and remove blower to housing attaching screws.
11. Remove blower from housing, then separate fan and mounting bracket from motor.

With Air Conditioning

1. Disconnect battery ground cable.
2. Remove right scuff plate and cowl panel.
3. Remove radio overlay, then the instrument panel crash pad.
4. Remove instrument panel to right pillar attaching screws, then the upper to lower instrument panel attaching screws, located above glove box.
5. Disconnect air door cable from heater core housing and remove housing to floor pan brace screw.
6. Disconnect wires from blower motor resistor and vacuum lines from vacuum motors.
7. Remove heater core housing attaching nuts and screw, position vacuum lines aside, then pull housing forward

8. Remove floor duct.
9. Disconnect wires from blower motor relay and remove blower motor housing attaching screw from firewall.
10. Loosen evaporator housing to dash

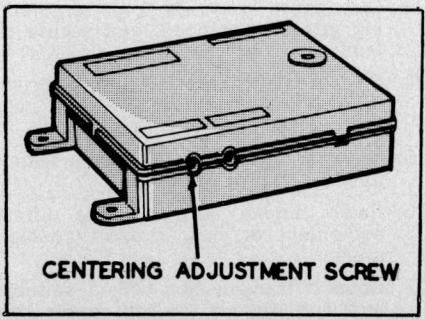

Fig. 19   Centering adjusting screw location. 1978-79

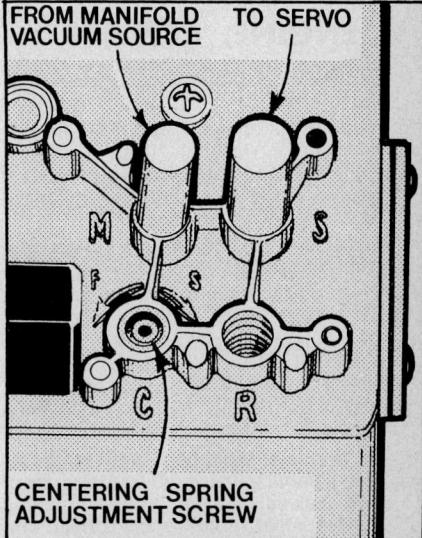

Fig. 20   Centering spring adjustment. 1974-77

panel attaching nuts, remove blower motor housing attaching screw from dash panel, then pull blower housing rearward and downward.

11. Pull right side of instrument panel rearward and remove blower motor.

12. Remove blower housing cover.

13. Remove blower motor from housing, the separate fan and mounting bracket from motor.

1974 Ambassador & 1974-78 Matador, Fig. 18

1. Disconnect blower motor wiring and cooling hose.

2. Remove blower motor attaching screws and remove blower motor.

1974 Javelin & 1974-79 Concord, Gremlin, Hornet & Spirit

1. Working in engine compartment, dis-connect blower motor wire.

2. Remove three retaining nuts for blower scroll cover to which blower assembly is attached and remove blower motor and fan.

SPEED CONTROL

1978-79

Centering Adjustment

This adjustment is made by turning the centering adjusting screw on the regulator, Fig. 19. If speed control engages at two or more mph higher than selected speed, turn centering adjusting screw counter clockwise a small amount. If engagement speed is two or more mph below selected speed, turn centering adjusting screw clockwise a small amount. Check for proper centering adjustment on a level road after making each adjustment.

1974-77

Chain Linkage, Adjust

Chain linkage should never be taut. To adjust, start engine and set carburetor at hot idle with anti-stall plunger backed off so as not to affect idle speed and discon-nect idle stop solenoid. Hook chain to ac-celerator linkage, pull taut, then loosen one ball at a time until a slight chain de-flection is obtained without moving car-buretor throttle or servo. After chain has been adjusted, bend servo hook tabs to-gether and chain must be free in hook.

NOTE: Whenever adjusting chain linkage, be sure chain does not hold carburetor throttle open.

Centering Springs, Adjust

If speed control system holds speed three or more mph higher than selected speed, turn centering spring adjusting screw (C) toward (S) $1/32$" or less, Fig. 20.

If speed control system holds speed three or more mph below selected speed, turn centering spring adjusting screw (C) toward (F) $1/32$" or less. *Do not move ad-justment screw (R).*

Four Cylinder Engine Section

ENGINE MOUNTS, REPLACE

1. Remove nut from cushion upper stud, Fig. 1.

2. If replacing right side cushion, remove TAC flexible hose.

3. Raise engine until engine bracket clears cushion stud.

4. Remove nut from lower cushion and the cushion.

5. Reverse procedure to install.

ENGINE, REPLACE

1. Scribe hood hinge locations and re-move hood.

2. Remove air cleaner and TAC flexible hose.

3. Drain coolant and disconnect battery ground cable from battery and alter-nator mounting bracket.

4. Remove fuel line, vapor return and canister lines.

5. Disconnect engine wiring at dash panel connectors.

6. Disconnect throttle cable and, if equipped with automatic transmis-sion, the throttle valve linkage.

7. Disconnect upper radiator hose from radiator.

8. On models equipped with A/C, re-move service valve covers and front seat valves. Loosen nuts attaching service valve to compressor head and allow compressor charge to bleed off. Remove service valves and cap com-pressor ports and service valves.

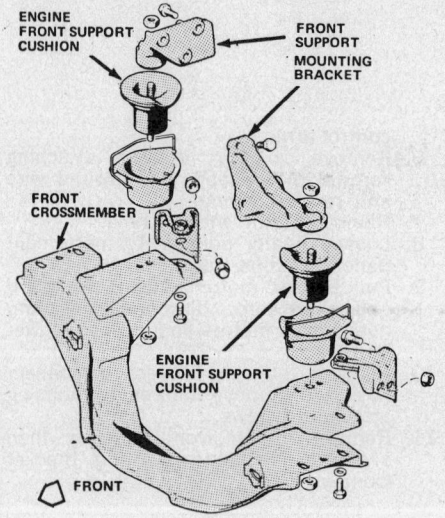

Fig. 1   Engine mounts. 4-121

9. Raise vehicle and remove starter.

10. Remove exhaust pipe support bracket and the bellhousing shield.

11. On automatic transmission vehicles, remove torque converter to flywheel nuts.

12. On all models, disconnect exhaust pipe from manifold.

13. Disconnect back-up light switch wire from switch and clips.

14. Disconnect the lower radiator hose and heater hose from radiator.

15. On automatic transmission vehicles, disconnect transmission oil cooler lines at flexible hose.

16. On all models, disconnect wiring har-ness from alternator.

17. Remove all bellhousing bolts except the top center.

18. Lower vehicle.

19. Remove screw securing cold air in-duction manifold to radiator.

20. Remove radiator attaching screws and move radiator approximately one inch toward the left side. Rotate radi-ator and remove with shroud at-tached.

21. Remove tie from upper heater hose, then disconnect hose from heater and secure to engine.

22. Pull back-up light harness upward and secure to engine.

23. Disconnect hoses from power steer-ing gear, if equipped, and secure to engine.

24. On automatic transmission vehicles, remove transmission filler tube sup-port screws.

25. On all models, remove engine mount cushion nuts on both sides.

26. Raise engine with suitable lifting equipment to clear support cushion studs.

27. Support transmission with a suitable jack and remove the top center bolt from bellhousing.

28. Remove engine from vehicle.

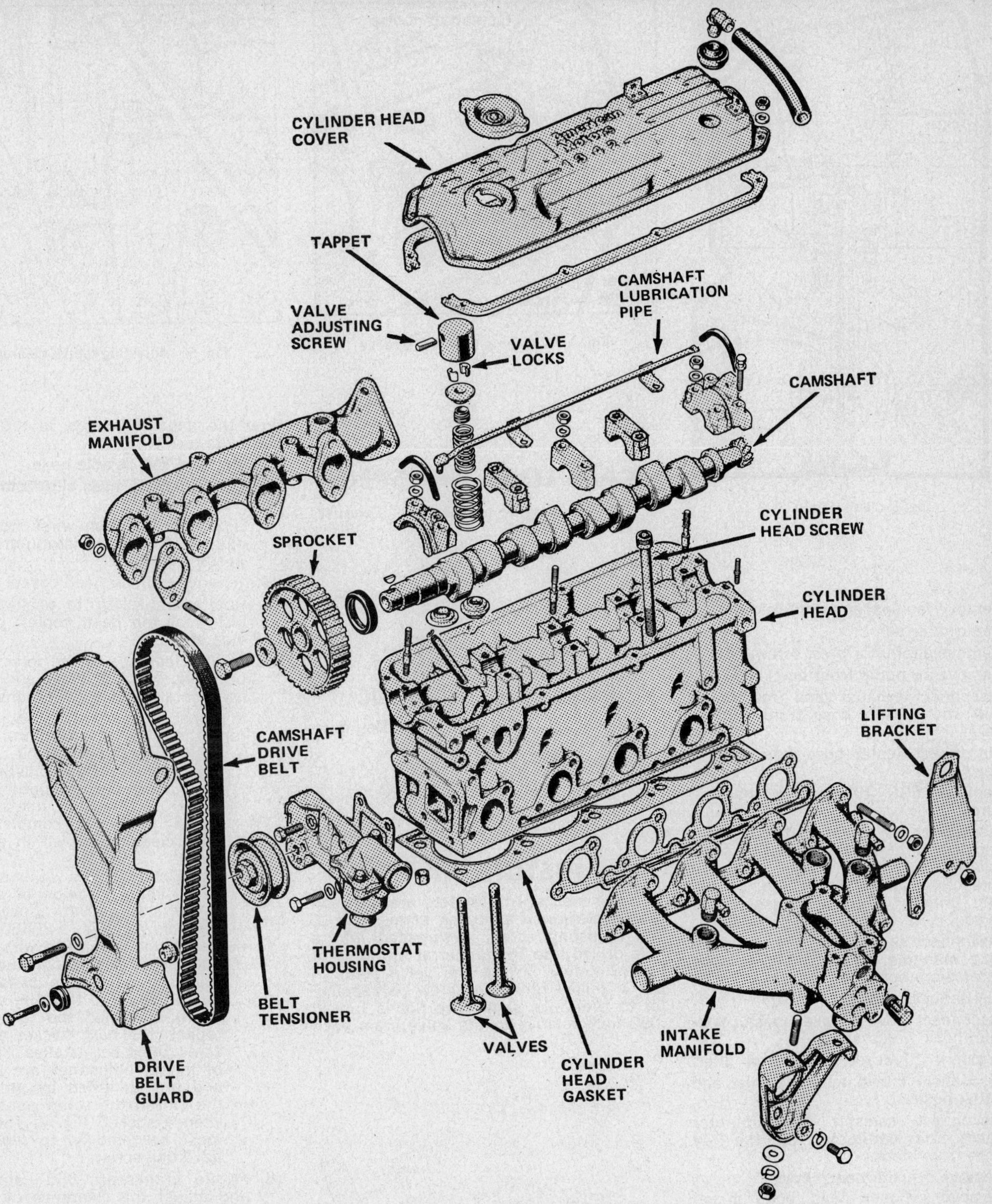

CYLINDER HEAD COVER

TAPPET

VALVE ADJUSTING SCREW

VALVE LOCKS

CAMSHAFT LUBRICATION PIPE

CAMSHAFT

EXHAUST MANIFOLD

SPROCKET

CYLINDER HEAD SCREW

CYLINDER HEAD

CAMSHAFT DRIVE BELT

BELT TENSIONER

THERMOSTAT HOUSING

DRIVE BELT GUARD

VALVES

CYLINDER HEAD GASKET

INTAKE MANIFOLD

LIFTING BRACKET

Cylinder head assembly

CYLINDER HEAD, REPLACE

1. Disconnect battery ground cable and drain coolant.
2. Remove air cleaner, TAC vacuum motor and valve assembly, and flexible hoses.

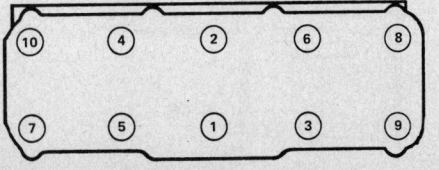

Fig. 2 Cylinder head tightening sequence

3. Disconnect upper radiator hose from radiator.
4. Remove bypass hose from bottom of thermostat housing.
5. Remove accessory drive belts.
6. Remove camshaft drive belt guard and the camshaft drive belt.

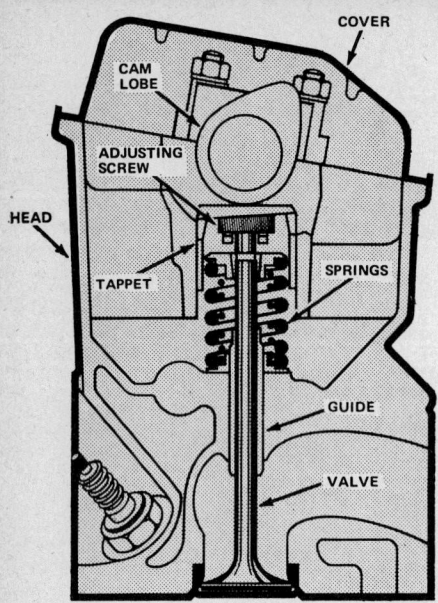

Fig. 3   Valve train

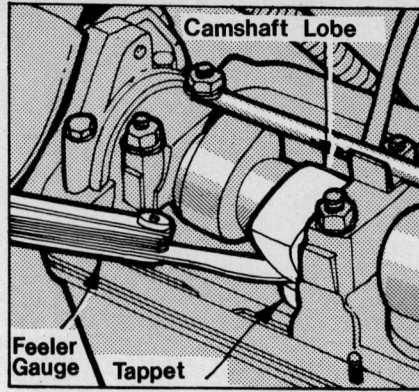

Fig. 4   Checking tappet clearance

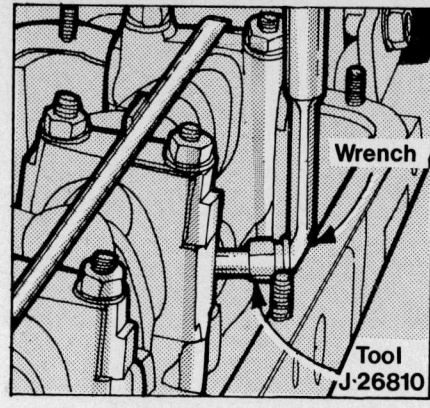

Fig. 5   Adjusting tappet clearance

7. Remove fan spacer and pulley.
8. Remove air pump.
9. Remove alternator pivot screw.
10. Remove air pump front bracket.
11. Disconnect exhaust pipe from manifold and the air hose from diverter valve.
12. Disconnect heater hose from rear of head.
13. Remove EGR tube to bellhousing screw.
14. Disconnect the following wiring connectors: temperature sender, oil pressure sender, electric choke, throttle solenoid, PCV valve solenoid, distributor primary and ignition secondary to coil.
15. Disconnect fuel line at bottom of intake manifold bracket, then remove screw from bottom of bracket.
16. Disconnect accelerator cable.
17. Disconnect power brake booster vacuum hose, if equipped.
18. Disconnect fuel return line from filter.
19. Disconnect intake manifold inlet and outlet hoses.
20. Disconnect canister to carburetor hoses from carburetor and the PCV hose from block.
21. Remove cylinder head cover.
22. Remove cylinder head bolts in reverse order of tightening sequence, Fig. 2.
23. Remove cylinder head from engine.
24. Reverse procedure to install. Torque cylinder head bolts in sequence, Fig. 2.

CAM LOBE LIFT SPEC.

Year	Engine	Intake	Exhaust
1977-79	4-121	.400	.380

VALVE TIMING

Intake Opens Before TDC

Year	Engine	Degrees
1977-79	4-121	41.8

ADJUSTING TAPPETS

These mechanical tappets are provided with a clearance adjusting screw, Fig. 3. The adjusting screw is threaded into a hole drilled into the tappet at an angle of approximately 86° to the valve stem. A flat is milled onto the screw perpendicular to the valve stem. The flat is moved .002 inch relative to the valve stem each

Fig. 6   Checking tappet adjusting screw position

time the adjusting screw is rotated one complete turn.

1. Remove TAC flexible hose.
2. Disconnect harness clip from cylinder head cover.
3. Disconnect ignition wires from spark plugs and remove distributor cap and position aside.
4. Remove cylinder head cover.
5. Rotate crankshaft to position No. 1 piston at top dead center, compression stroke.
6. Check clearance of the following tappets, Fig. 4: No. 1 intake and exhaust, No. 2 intake and No. 3 exhaust.
7. If tappet adjustment is required, perform the following procedure:
   a. With adjusting screw bit, J-26810, and wrench rotate adjusting screw one complete turn until it clicks, Fig. 5. Continue to rotate the adjusting screw in complete turns until clearance is within specifications.
   b. When clearance is within specifications, check position of adjusting screw in tappet with tappet adjusting screw gauge, J-26860, Fig. 6. The gauge is marked with a band. The outside edge of the tappet must be within the band. If the gauge indicated that the adjusting screw is turned too far into the tappet, the next thicker adjusting screw must be installed. Five sizes of tappet adjustings are available and are identified by grooves on the end of the screw opposite the wrench socket, Fig. 7. The tappet must be removed to replace the adjusting screw.
8. Rotate crankshaft 360° and check and adjust the clearance of the following tappets: No. 2 exhaust, No. 3 intake and No. 4 intake and exhaust. Perform step 7 if tappet adjustment is required.

TAPPETS, REPLACE

1. Remove camshaft as outlined under "Camshaft, Replace" procedure.
2. Remove tappets from bores by lifting upward.
3. Lubricate new tappets with AMC En-

VALVE ARRANGEMENT

Front to Rear

4-121 . . . . I-E-I-E-I-E-I-E

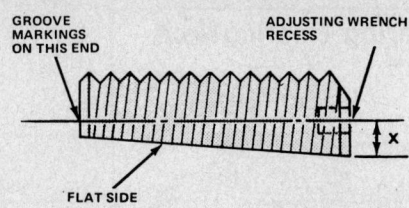

Fig. 7   Tappet adjusting screw markings

GROOVE MARKING	DIMENSION X-mm
NONE	3.00
I	3.45
II	3.57
III	3.69
IIII	3.81

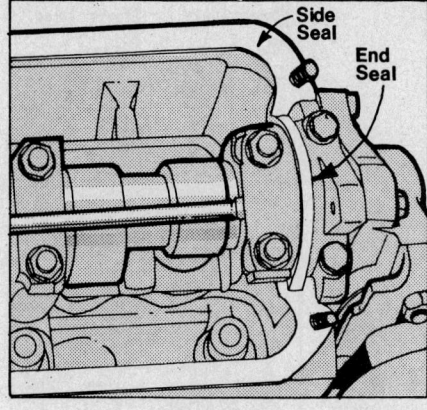

Fig. 8   Cylinder head cover gasket installation

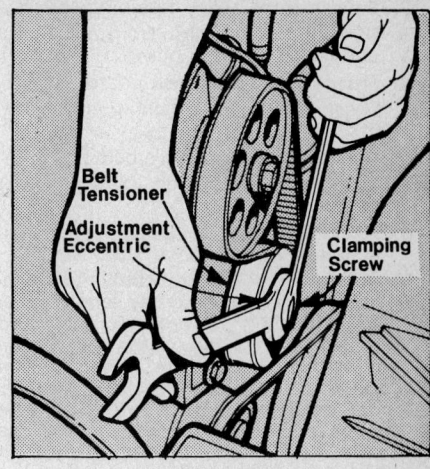

Fig. 10   Camshaft drive belt tensioner

gine Oil Supplement or suitable equivalent.

4. Install new tappets in bores.
5. Install camshaft.
6. Adjust tappet clearance.
7. Pour the remaining AMC Engine Oil Supplement or equivalent over the valve train.

NOTE: The engine oil supplement should remain in the engine for at least 1000 miles.

CYLINDER HEAD COVER, REPLACE

1. Remove TAC flexible hose.
2. Remove PCV valve hose from cylinder head cover.
3. Disconnect ignition wires from spark plugs, then the harness clip from the cover.
4. Remove cylinder head cover nuts and washers.
5. Clean gasket material from cylinder head and cover.
6. Install end pieces of replacement gasket in grooves of bearing caps at both ends of head, Fig. 8. Ensure the end pieces fit into the side seal slots. Also, apply silicone gasket material to all joints.

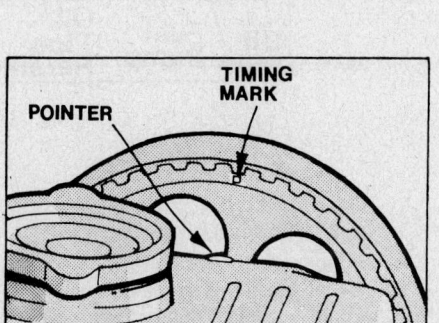

Fig. 9   Camshaft sprocket timing mark

7. Install side pieces of gasket over cylinder head studs.
8. Install cylinder head cover, reinforcement strips, washers and nuts. Torque nuts to specifications.
9. Install PCV valve hose into cylinder

head cover.
10. Connect ignition wires to spark plugs, then the harness clip to cover.
11. Install TAC flexible hose.

CAMSHAFT DRIVE BELT, REPLACE

1. Rotate engine to position crankshaft timing mark at "0". The camshaft sprocket timing mark should be aligned with the pointer on the cylinder head cover, Fig. 9.

NOTE: If camshaft timing mark is 180° out of position, rotate the crankshaft 360°. The camshaft mark should then align with the pointer.

Fig. 11   Replacing camshaft sprocket

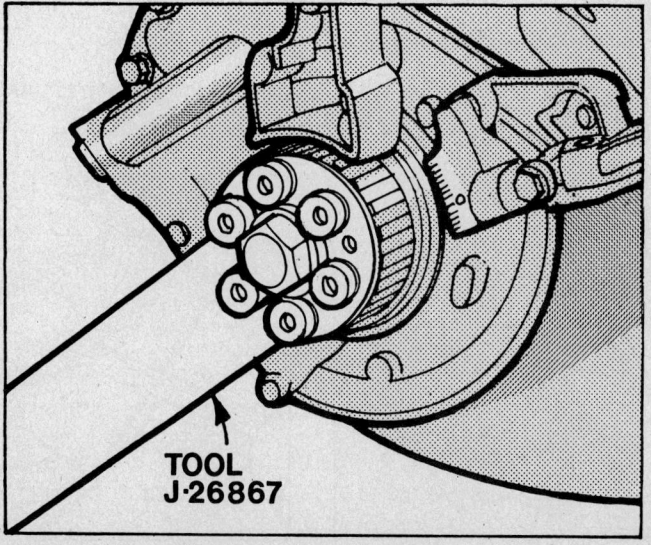

Fig. 12   Replacing crankshaft sprocket

2. Loosen front pulley retaining screws.
3. Remove drive belts from alternator and power steering pump.
4. Remove cam drive belt guard.
5. Loosen tensioner retaining screw, Fig. 10.
6. Remove camshaft drive belt.
7. Install new drive belt on crankshaft sprocket.
8. Position belt in tensioner pulley and install belt on camshaft sprocket.
9. Rotate tensioner adjusting nut counter-clockwise to increase tension, Fig. 10. The belt is properly tensioned when the drive side of the belt can be twisted 90° with the fingers. When checking belt tension, apply force to the crankshaft with a wrench in the counter-clockwise direction. This is done to position the belt slackness on the side of the belt being checked.
10. Maintain pressure to the tensioner pulley nut and torque the retaining screw to 29 ft. lbs. Recheck belt tension.
11. Install cam belt drive guard.
12. Install and tension alternator and power steering pump drive belts.

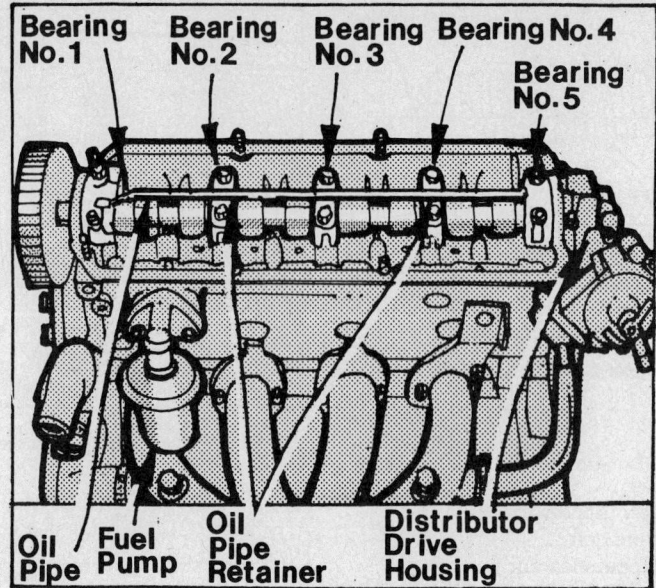

Fig. 13 Camshaft & bearings

CAMSHAFT DRIVE SPROCKETS, REPLACE

Upper

1. Remove cam drive belt as outlined previously.
2. Remove sprocket retaining bolt. Use a suitable tool wrapped in a shop cloth to prevent the sprocket from turning, Fig. 11.
3. Remove sprocket, key and washer.
4. Reverse procedure to install. Torque sprocket retaining bolt to 58 ft. lbs.

Lower

1. Raise vehicle and support on jack stands.
2. Loosen crankshaft pulley screws.
3. Remove accessory drive belts.

4. Remove crankshaft pulley.
5. Remove cam drive belt guard.
6. Loosen tensioner retaining screw.
7. Attach crankshaft holding tool, J-26867, Fig. 12, to crankshaft sprocket with the six pulley attaching screws. Remove crankshaft sprocket retaining bolt and the sprocket.
8. Remove tool from sprocket and attach to new sprocket, if replacing sprocket.
9. Install sprocket.

NOTE: The hole in the sprocket must index with the crankshaft locating pin.

10. Install and torque crankshaft sprocket retaining bolt to 181 ft. lbs.

11. Remove tool from sprocket and install crankshaft pulley.
12. Rotate crankshaft to position crankshaft timing mark at "0".
13. Rotate camshaft sprocket to align timing mark with pointer on cylinder head cover.
14. Install and tension camshaft drive belt.
15. Remove crankshaft pulley.
16. Install cam drive belt guard.
17. Install crankshaft pulley and torque attaching bolts to 15 ft. lbs.
18. Install accessory drive belts.

CAMSHAFT, REPLACE

Removal

1. Remove TAC flexible hose.

Fig. 14 Distributor drive housing installation

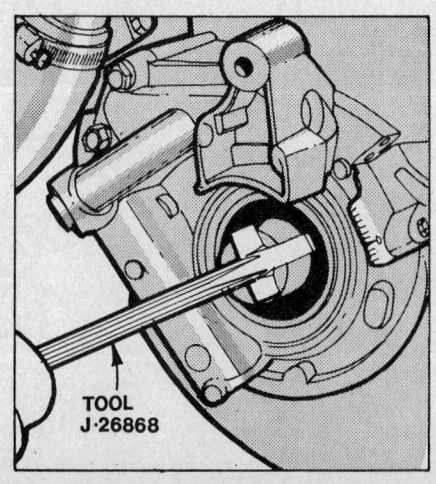

Fig. 15 Front oil seal removal

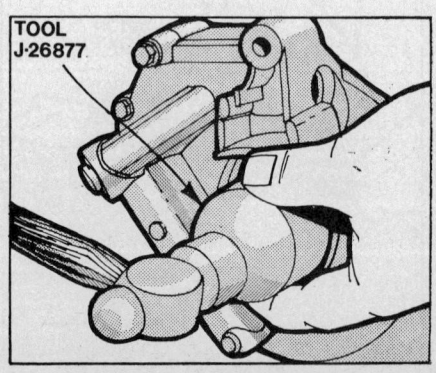

Fig. 16 Front oil seal installation

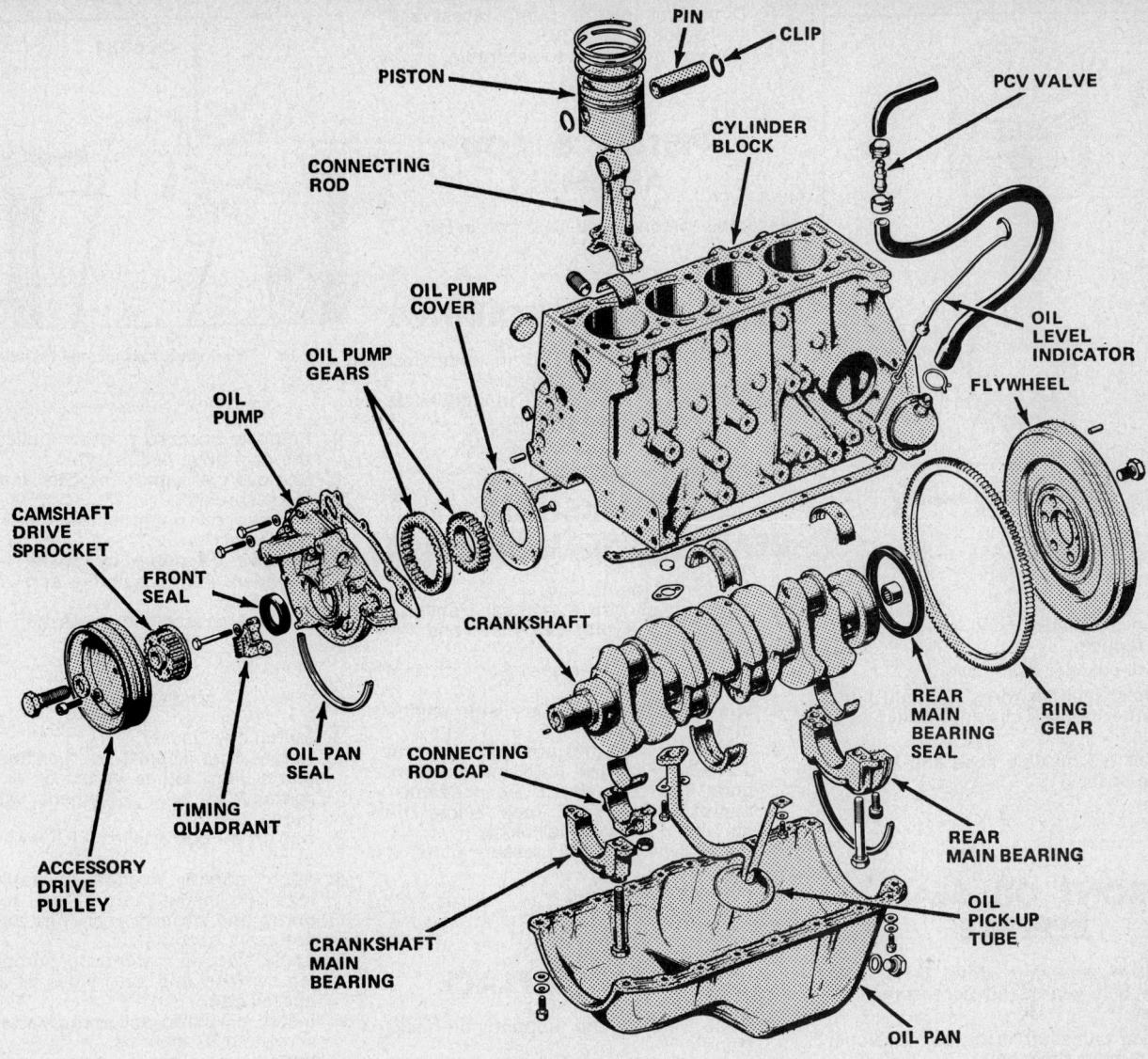

PISTON

CONNECTING ROD

OIL PUMP COVER

OIL PUMP GEARS

OIL PUMP

CAMSHAFT DRIVE SPROCKET

FRONT SEAL

ACCESSORY DRIVE PULLEY

TIMING QUADRANT

OIL PAN SEAL

CONNECTING ROD CAP

CRANKSHAFT MAIN BEARING

CRANKSHAFT

PIN

CLIP

CYLINDER BLOCK

PCV VALVE

OIL LEVEL INDICATOR

FLYWHEEL

REAR MAIN BEARING SEAL

RING GEAR

REAR MAIN BEARING

OIL PICK-UP TUBE

OIL PAN

Cylinder block assembly

2. Disconnect ignition wires from spark plugs, then the clip from cylinder head cover.
3. Remove distributor cap with wire attached.
4. Remove accessory drive belts.
5. Remove cam drive belt guard.
6. Loosen tensioner attaching bolt and remove camshaft drive belt.
7. Remove camshaft sprocket.
8. Disconnect the distributor primary wire and the vacuum advance hose.
9. Remove distributor housing and distributor assembly.
10. Disconnect PCV valve hose from cylinder head cover and remove the cylinder head cover.
11. Remove two 10mm screws from the No. 5 bearing cap, Fig. 13.
12. Remove nuts from bearing cap Nos. 1, 2, 3, 4 and 5.
13. Remove oil pipe, Fig. 13.

14. Remove bearing caps and the camshaft.
15. Remove distributor drive gear from camshaft with a suitable puller and install on replacement camshaft, if replacing camshaft.

Installation

1. Install camshaft.
2. Lubricate and install bearing caps.
3. Install oil pipe.
4. Install and torque nuts on cap Nos. 2 and 4 to 13 ft. lbs.
5. Install and torque nuts on cap Nos. 3 and 5 to 13 ft. lbs.
6. Install and torque the 10mm screws on cap No. 5 to 7 ft. lbs.
7. Install replacement seal on camshaft.
8. Install and torque nuts on cap No. 1 to 13 ft. lbs.

9. Install camshaft sprocket.
10. Install cylinder head cover seals and gaskets.
11. Install cylinder head cover and install nuts finger tight.
12. Align camshaft timing mark with pointer on cylinder head cover.
13. Install distributor housing, Fig. 14, with distributor rotor pointing to the No. 1 cylinder firing position. Install distributor cap.
14. Connect distributor primary wire and the vacuum advance hose.
15. Rotate crankshaft to position crankshaft timing mark at "0".
16. Install and tension camshaft drive belt.
17. Install cam drive belt guard.
18. Install pulley, spacer and fan.
19. Install and tension accessory drive belts.

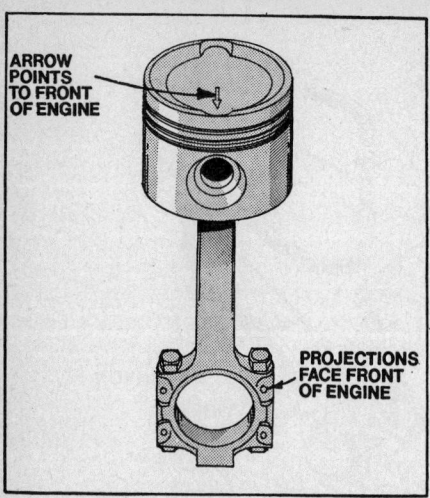

Fig. 17   Piston & rod assembly

20. Remove cylinder head cover and adjust tappets.
21. Install cylinder head cover.
22. Connect ignition wires to spark plugs and the harness clip to cylinder head cover.
23. Install TAC flexible hose and the PCV valve hose.

FRONT OIL SEAL, REPLACE

1. Remove accessory drive belts, cam drive belt guard and accessory drive pulley.
2. Loosen camshaft drive belt tensioner and remove drive belt.
3. Remove crankshaft sprocket.
4. Remove front oil seal from oil pump recess with tool J-26868, Fig. 15.
5. Lubricate seal inner lip with engine oil. Do not apply sealant to outer edge of seal.

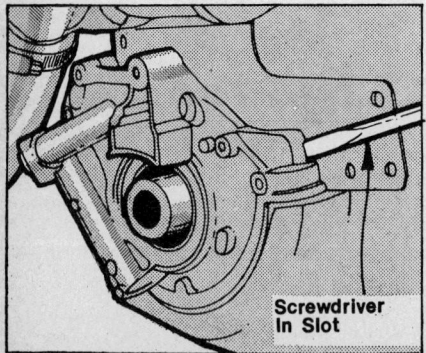

Fig. 19   Oil pump removal

6. Drive seal into oil pump recess with tool J-26877, Fig. 16.
7. Reverse procedure to assemble.

PISTON & ROD ASSEMBLY

Assemble piston to rod as shown in Fig. 17.

MAIN & ROD BEARINGS

Main bearings are available in undersizes of .25mm, .50mm and .75mm.
Rod bearings are available in undersizes of .25mm, .50mm and .75mm.

CRANKSHAFT REAR OIL SEAL, REPLACE

1. Remove transmission.
2. If equipped with a manual transmission, remove pressure plate and flywheel.
3. On all models, remove seal with tool J-26868.
4. Lubricate new seal lips with engine oil.
5. Drive new seal into position with tool J-26834, Fig. 18, until bottomed in bore. The seal should be positioned approximately 1/32 inch below the surface of the cylinder block.
6. Install flywheel and pressure plate, if removed.
7. Install transmission.

OIL PAN, REPLACE

1. Raise vehicle and support on jackstands.
2. Drain oil pan.
3. Install suitable engine lifting equipment.
4. Remove engine bracket to cushion nuts.
5. Loosen strut and bracket screws.
6. Raise engine approximately two inches.
7. Remove crossmember to sill attachments.
8. Remove steering gear idler bracket.
9. Pry crossmember loose and insert wooden blocks between crossmember and sill on both sides.
10. Remove oil pan attaching bolts and the oil pan.
11. Reverse procedure to install. Torque oil pan attaching bolts to 70 inch lbs. for side bolts and 90 inch lbs. for end bolts.

OIL PUMP, REPLACE

Removal

1. Remove fan shroud.
2. Raise and support vehicle on jackstands.
3. Remove accessory drive belts.

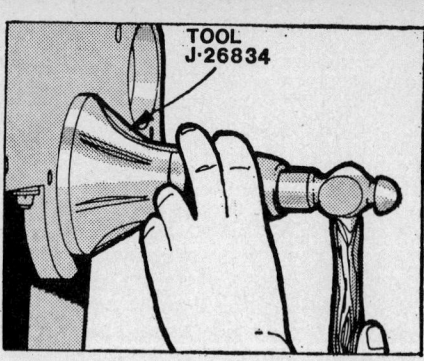

Fig. 18   Crankshaft rear oil seal installation

4. Remove accessory drive pulley and the cam drive belt guard.
5. Remove crankshaft sprocket and camshaft sprocket.
6. Remove oil pump screws and front oil pan screws.
7. Remove oil pump by prying in slot provided with a suitable screwdriver, Fig. 19.
8. Remove gasket and crankshaft seal.

Installation

1. Install new gasket.
2. Rotate crankshaft to position; oil pump lugs either vertically or horizontally to ease alignment with oil pump.
3. Cut off oil pan gasket flush with front of block.
4. Apply marking material to crankshaft lugs and install pump. Then, remove pump and observe markings and orient gears accordingly.
5. Apply silicone material to pump sealing surface and the edges of pump and oil pan.
6. Install oil pump and torque attaching screws to 87 inch lbs.
7. Install crankshaft and camshaft sprockets and the camshaft drive belt.
8. Install cam drive belt guard and accessory drive pulley.
9. Install accessory drive belts.
10. Install fan shroud.
11. Lower vehicle.

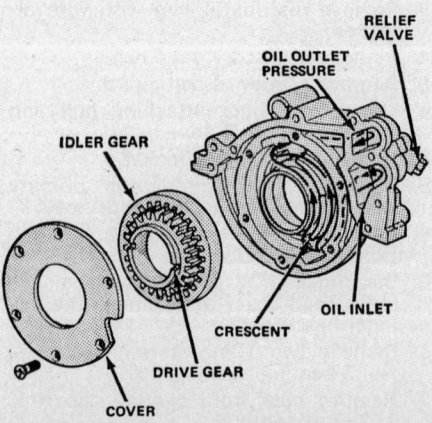

Fig. 20   Oil pump

Relief Valve Replacement

1. Remove relief valve from pump, Fig. 20.
2. Remove spring and piston from pump, if not removed with valve body.
3. Install spring and piston into valve body.
4. Install valve body into pump and torque to 35 ft. lbs.

BELT TENSION DATA

	New Lbs.	Used Lbs.
1977-79		
Air Pump	40-60	40-60
A/C, Fan & Alternator	125-155	90-115
Power Steering	125-155	90-115

WATER PUMP, REPLACE

1. Drain coolant.
2. Rotate crankshaft to place No. 1 piston at TDC, compression stroke.
3. Remove power steering drive belt, if equipped.
4. Loosen the alternator and air pump.
5. Remove fan, spacer and pulley.
6. Remove cam drive belt guard.
7. Remove air pump bracket.
8. Remove camshaft drive belt idler pulley.
9. Remove all hoses from water pump except the thermostat hose.
10. Remove water pump attaching screws and the water pump, pulling the pump from thermostat hose.
11. Reverse procedure to install.

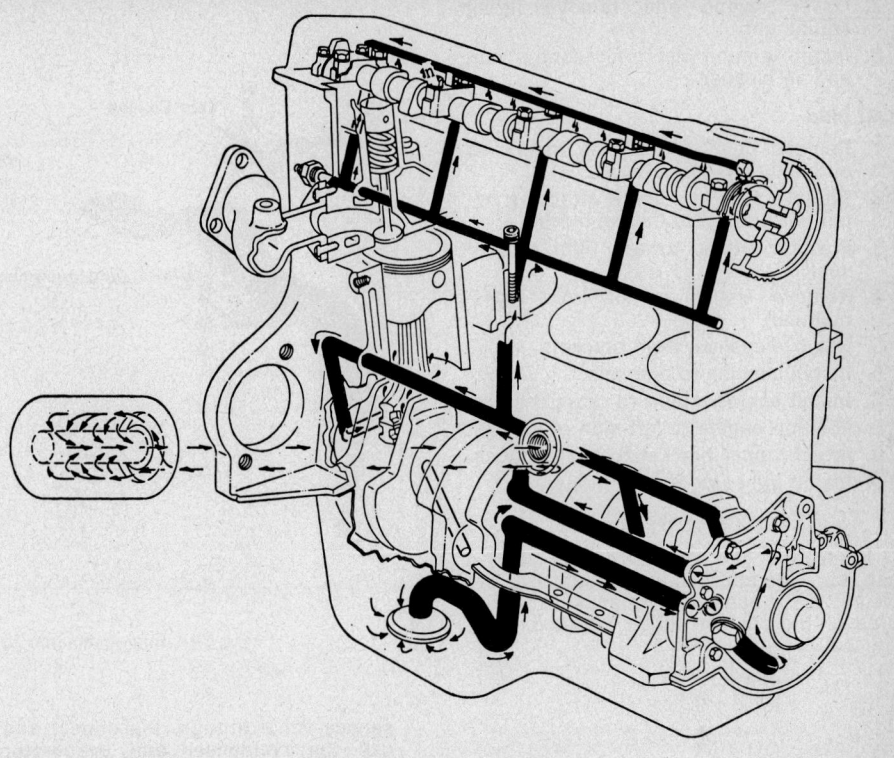

Engine oiling system. 4-121

FUEL PUMP PRESSURE

Year	Engine	Pressure Lbs.
1977-79	4-121	4-6

FUEL PUMP, REPLACE

1. Disconnect fuel lines from pump.
2. Remove pump retaining screws.
3. Remove pump, spacer and gaskets.
4. Reverse procedure to install.

NOTE: Ensure the pushrod is properly positioned against the pump actuating lever. If positioned improperly, the pump may be damaged when the screws are tightened.

Six Cylinder & V8 Engine Section

ENGINE MARKINGS

A letter code is used to denote size of the bore, main bearings and rod bearings. On V8 engines, this code is stamped on the engine code tag. On six cylinder engines, this code is located on a boss above the oil filter. This letter code is as follows:

Letter "B"
  Cyl. bore .010" oversize

Letter "M"
  Main bearings .010" undersize

Letter "P"
  Rod bearings .010" undersize

Letter "C"
  Camshaft block bore .010" oversize

Letters "PM"
  Main and rod bearings .010" undersize

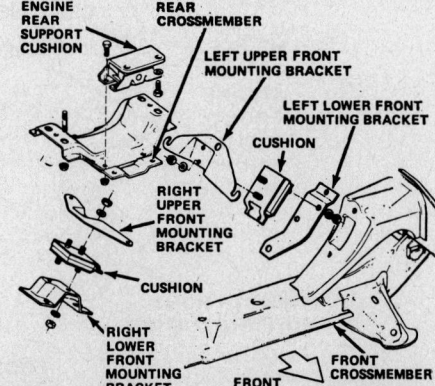

Fig. 1 Engine mounts. 1978-79 Pacer V8-304

ENGINE MOUNTS

1978-79 Pacer V8-304

NOTE: The right side mount must be removed before removing the left side mount.

Right Side

1. Remove air cleaner and ignition electronic control unit.
2. Attach suitable engine lifting equipment to engine and raise engine slightly.
3. Remove engine mount, Fig. 1.
4. Remove cushion from brackets.
5. Install cushion to brackets.
6. Install engine mount to engine and crossmember.

7. Lower engine and remove lifting equipment.
8. Install ignition electronic control unit and air cleaner.

Left Side

1. Remove right side engine mount as outlined previously, Fig. 1.
2. Remove nuts and screw attaching upper left bracket to engine block.
3. Position engine toward right side of vehicle.
4. Remove engine mount from crossmember.
5. Remove cushion from brackets.
6. Install cushion to brackets.
7. Install engine mount to crossmember.
8. Position engine to left side of vehicle.
9. Attach upper bracket to engine block.
10. Install right side engine mount.

Exc. Pacer w/V8-304

Removal or replacement of any cushion can be accomplished by supporting the weight of the engine or transmission at the area of the cushion to be replaced, Figs. 1A, 2 & 3.

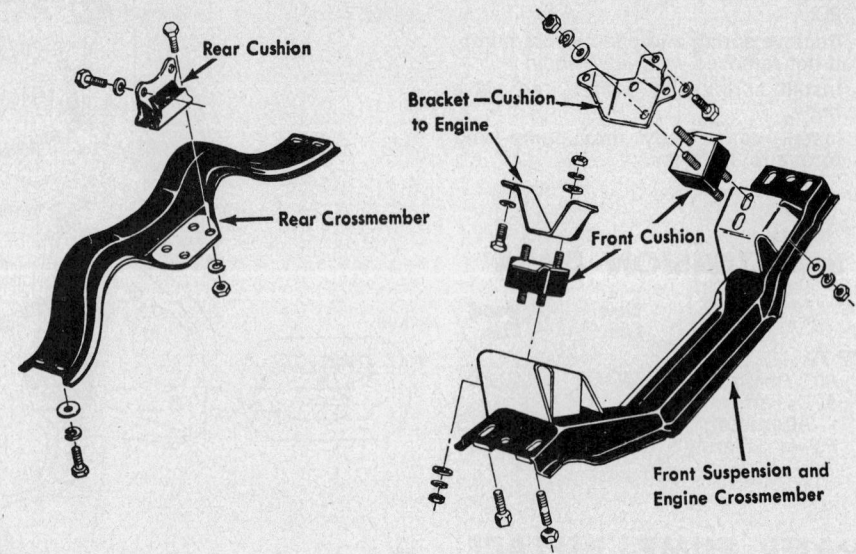

Fig. 1A   Engine mounts. 1974-79 V8 except Pacer (typical)

ENGINE REPLACE

1978-79 Pacer V8-304

NOTE: The engine and transmission is removed as an assembly.

1. Scribe hood hinge locations and remove hood. If equipped, disconnect underhood lamp wire.
2. Drain cooling system.
3. Remove grille, air cleaner and battery.
4. Disconnect transmission oil cooler lines from radiator, then remove the shroud and radiator assembly.
5. Remove fan attaching nuts and the fan.
6. If equipped with air conditioning, turn service valves clockwise to front seated position. Bleed refrigerant from compressor by slowly loosening the service valve fittings. Disconnect and cap the condenser and evaporator lines from compressor. Cap compressor service valve outlets. Disconnect receiver outlet at the coupling. Remove condenser and receiver assembly.
7. On all models, disconnect vacuum hoses, cable and heater hoses from heater housing.
8. Remove heater housing.
9. Disconnect the wiring at the following locations: alternator, oil pressure sending unit, ignition coil, A/C compressor, temperature sending unit, distributor, solenoid vacuum valve, TCS solenoid control switch and throttle solenoid.

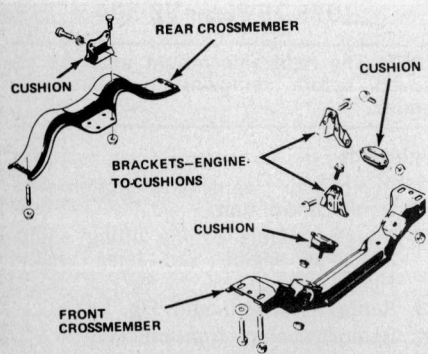

Fig. 2   Engine mounts. 1974-79 6 cyl. except Pacer (typical)

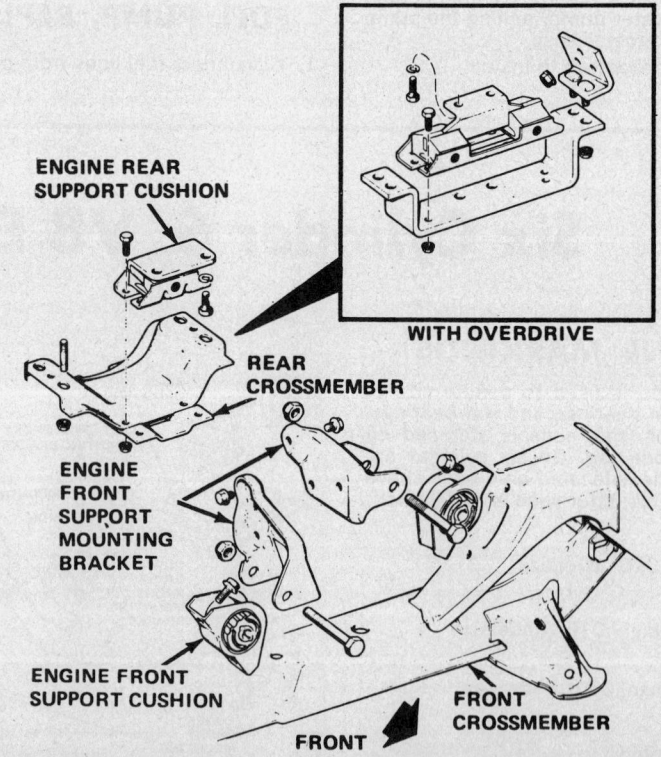

Fig. 3   Engine mounts. 1975-79 6 cyl. Pacer

10. Disconnect the hoses or lines at the following locations: fuel pump, power brake booster, fuel filter return, carburetor vapor vents, intake manifold heater vacuum hose and power steering pump.
11. Disconnect throttle cable and bracket.
12. Attach suitable engine lifting equipment to engine.
13. Raise vehicle and drain oil pan.
14. Disconnect neutral safety switch harness, starter motor wiring and speedometer cable.
15. Remove propeller shaft from vehicle.
16. Disconnect throttle valve and shift linkage.
17. Disconnect oil cooler lines from transmission.
18. Disconnect exhaust pipes from exhaust manifolds.
19. Loosen engine rear support crossmember to body retaining nuts. Do not remove the nuts.
20. Disconnect transmission linkage at shift lever.
21. On left side of engine, disconnect engine mount from engine block.
22. On right side of engine, disconnect engine mount from crossmember.
23. Disconnect steering shaft flexible coupling and position aside.
24. Support transmission with a suitable jack and remove the engine rear support crossmember to body nuts loosened previously.
25. Raise engine and transmission assembly from vehicle. Remove oil cooler lines when engine is moved forward.
26. Reverse procedure to install.

1977-79 V8 Concord, Gremlin, Hornet, Matador & Spirit

The engine is removed without the transmission.

1. Mark hood hinge locations, disconnect underhood lamp, if equipped, and remove hood.
2. Drain cooling system.
3. Disconnect transmission oil cooler lines, if equipped.
4. Disconnect radiator hoses from radiator.
5. Remove fan shroud screws, then the radiator and shroud.
6. Remove fan and spacer.
7. Remove air cleaner and disconnect purge hose at canister, TAC vacuum hose at manifold and TAC heat tube.
8. Install a $5/_{16}$ X $1/_2$ inch capscrew through the fan pulley, into the water pump flange.
9. Disconnect alternator wiring.
10. Disconnect neutral safety switch harness at cowl and the TCS harness at solenoid control switch and solenoid vacuum valve. Open clip on intake manifold and position harness on cowl.
11. Disconnect heater hoses from heater core and intake manifold.
12. Disconnect heater and A/C system vacuum hose from intake manifold.
13. Disconnect throttle cable and remove from bracket, then position aside.
14. Remove power brake vacuum check valve from power brake unit.
15. Disconnect temperature sender wire

and throttle stop solenoid wire from connector near ignition coil.
16. Disconnect TCS solenoid control switch and the transmission cooler lines, if equipped.
17. Disconnect distributor leads, primary leads at coil and ground wire from coil bracket.
18. Remove fuel return hose from fuel filter.
19. Remove vapor canister and bracket.
20. Disconnect flexible fuel line from steel fuel line and plug lines.
21. If equipped with air conditioning:
   a. Remove service valve covers and front-seat valves.
   b. Loosen nuts attaching service valves to compressor head.
   c. Bleed compressor refrigerant charge.
   d. Remove service valves and cap compressor ports and service valves.
   e. Disconnect clutch feed wire.
22. If equipped with power steering, disconnect hoses from steering gear, drain reservoir and cap hose fittings and gear ports.
23. On all models, raise and support vehicle on jackstands.
24. Remove starter.
25. Remove exhaust flange nuts, seals and heat valve.
26. Remove converter housing spacer cover.
27. Remove lower throttle valve bellcrank and inner manual linkage support. Disconnect throttle valve rod at lower end of bellcrank.
28. Remove converter attaching screws.
29. Remove exhaust support screws at transmission extension housing bracket, then lower the exhaust system.
30. Remove front motor mount to block attaching bolts.
31. Remove the four upper converter housing screws and loosen the lower screws.
32. Remove throttle cable housing retainer bracket.
33. Install suitable engine lifting equipment.
34. Slightly raise engine and support transmission with a suitable jack.
35. Remove the remaining converter housing screws.
36. Remove engine from vehicle.

1977-79 Six Cyl. Concord, Hornet, Matador & Spirit

The engine is removed without the transmission.

1. Drain cooling system.
2. Mark hood hinge locations, disconnect underhood lamp, if equipped, and remove hood.
3. Disconnect battery cables and on Gremlin and Hornet, remove battery.
4. Disconnect alternator wiring and the ignition coil, distributor and oil pressure sender leads.
5. Remove TCS switch bracket from cylinder block, if equipped.
6. Disconnect flexible fuel line from fuel pump and plug line and pump port.
7. Disconnect engine ground strap.
8. Remove the right front engine support cushion to bracket screw.

9. If equipped with air conditioning:
   a. Remove service valve covers and front-seat valves.
   b. Loosen service valve to compressor attaching nuts.
   c. Bleed compressor refrigerant charge.
   d. Remove service valves and cap compressor ports and service valves.
   e. Disconnect clutch feed wire.
10. Remove starter.
11. Remove air cleaner and disconnect purge hose from canister and TAC vacuum hose from manifold, if equipped.
12. Disconnect throttle stop solenoid lead, if equipped.
13. Disconnect fuel return hose from fuel filter and the carburetor bowl vent hose from canister.
14. Disconnect throttle cable and remove from bracket. Disconnect throttle valve rod at carburetor and the bellcrank.
15. Disconnect heater and air conditioning system vacuum hose from intake manifold.
16. Disconnect temperature sender wire and TCS vacuum solenoid wiring harness.
17. Disconnect radiator hoses from radiator and the heater hoses from engine.
18. Disconnect transmission oil cooler lines from radiator, if equipped.
19. Remove fan shroud attaching screws, then the radiator and shroud.
20. Remove fan and spacer. Install a $5/_{16}$ X $1/_2$ inch capscrew through fan pulley, into water pump flange.
21. Remove power brake vacuum check valve from power brake unit, if equipped.
22. If equipped with power steering, disconnect hoses from gear and drain reservoir. Cap gear ports and hoses.
23. Remove transmission filler tube bracket screw, if equipped.
24. Raise and support vehicle on jackstands.
25. If equipped with automatic transmission:
   a. Remove converter housing spacer cover.
   b. Remove converter attaching screws.
   c. Remove exhaust pipe support from converter housing. This also supports the inner end of the transmission linkage.
26. If equipped with manual transmission:
   a. Remove clutch housing cover and clutch bellcrank inner support screws.
   b. Disconnect springs and remove bellcrank.
   c. Remove outer bellcrank to strut rod bracket retainer.
   d. Disconnect back-up lamp switch wiring harness under hood at dash panel to gain access to clutch housing screw.
27. On all models, remove engine mount cushion to bracket screws.
28. Disconnect exhaust pipe from manifold.
29. Remove upper converter or clutch housing screws and loosen the bottom screws.
30. Raise vehicle and support on jackstands.
31. Remove air conditioning compressor

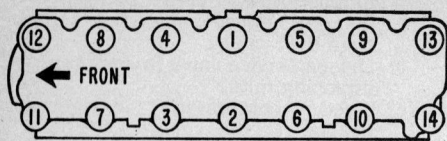

Fig. 4 Cylinder head tightening sequence 6-232, 258 engines. The No. 11 bolt must be sealed to prevent coolant leakage.

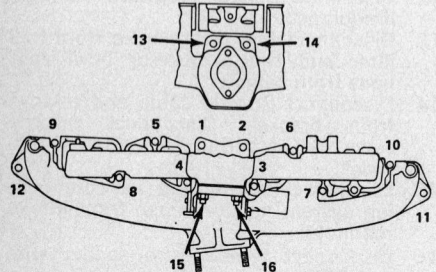

Fig. 5 Manifold tightening sequence. 1974-76 6-232, 258

drive belt idler pulley and the compressor mounting bracket, if equipped.

32. Install suitable engine lifting equipment and slightly raise engine. Support transmission with a suitable jack.
33. Remove remaining converter or clutch housing screws.
34. Remove engine from vehicle.

1975-79 Six Cyl Pacer

The engine and transmission are removed as an assembly.

1. Mark hood hinge locations, disconnect underhood lamp, if equipped, and remove hood.
2. Drain cooling system and oil pan.
3. Disconnect heater and radiator hoses from engine.
4. Park W/S wipers at center of windshield to provide clearance for valve cover removal.
5. Remove battery.
6. Disconnect and cap transmission oil cooler lines, if equipped.
7. Remove fan shroud and radiator.
8. If equipped with air conditioning:
   a. Remove service valve covers and front-seat the valves.
   b. Bleed refrigerant charge from compressor by loosening service valve fittings.
   c. Disconnect and cap condenser and evaporator lines from compressor. Cap the service valves.
   d. Disconnect receiver outlet at coupling.
   e. Remove condenser and receiver assembly.
9. Remove air cleaner assembly.

10. Disconnect wiring at the following components, if equipped: starter, ignition coil, distributor, alternator, A/C compressor, temperature sensing unit, oil pressure sending unit, solenoid vacuum valve, TCS solenoid control switch, throttle stop solenoid and brake warning lamp switch.
11. Disconnect the following lines, if equipped: fuel pump suction, power brake vacuum supply from manifold, fuel filter return, heater and A/C system vacuum supply from manifold, carburetor pressure vent and power steering.
12. Remove carburetor and cover intake manifold opening.
13. Remove valve cover and vibration damper.
14. Disconnect accelerator cable at control cable bracket.
15. Raise and support vehicle with jackstands.
16. Disconnect exhaust pipe at manifold.
17. Disconnect transmission linkage and, if equipped, clutch linkage.
18. Disconnect speedometer cable from transmission.
19. Remove propeller shaft and cap transmission output shaft.
20. Support transmission with a suitable jack and remove rear crossmember.
21. Install suitable engine lifting equipment and support engine weight.
22. Remove engine mount bracket to front support cushion attaching bolts, then
23. the front support cushions.
24. Lower jack from transmission.
25. Raise vehicle with a suitable positioned under front crossmember until bottom of front bumper is approximately three feet from floor, then support vehicle at that height with jackstands.
26. Remove oil filter and starter.
27. Raise front of engine and partially remove assembly by pulling upward until rear of cylinder head clears cowl.
28. Lower the vehicle and remove engine-transmission assembly.

1974-76 Except Pacer

The engine and transmission is removed as an assembly as follows:

1. Remove battery.
2. Remove hood. Mark hinges for alignment at installation.
3. Remove fender braces, if equipped.
4. Remove air cleaner.
5. Drain cooling system, crankcase and transmission.
6. Remove radiator upper air baffle, if equipped.
7. Disconnect radiator and heater hoses and remove radiator and fan.
8. Remove power steering pump and position aside, do not disconnect hoses.
9. If equipped with A/C, discharge refrigerant system. Disconnect refrigerant lines from compressor and the receiver outlet at disconnect coupling. Then, remove condenser and receiver assembly.
10. On all models, disconnect all electrical connections and lines and hoses

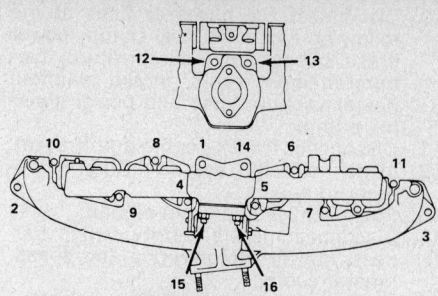

Fig. 6 Manifold tightening sequence. 1977-79 6-232 & 258

THREADS MUST BE SEALED TO PREVENT COOLANT LEAKAGE

Fig. 7 Cylinder head tightening sequence on V8-304, 360 & 401. The No. 7 bolt indicated (second from front on left bank only) must be sealed to prevent coolant leakage.

from engine.

11. Disconnect accelerator, clutch and transmission linkage.
12. Disconnect exhaust pipes from manifolds and the speedometer cable from transmission.
13. Support engine with suitable lifting equipment, then disconnect engine front support cushions and ground strap from engine brackets.
14. Remove rear crossmember.
15. Remove engine and transmission by pulling forward and upward. Support propeller shaft when disengaging transmission output shaft from slip joint.

CYLINDER HEAD

Tighten cylinder head bolts a little at a time in three steps in the sequence shown in the illustrations. Final tightening should be to the torque specifications listed in the *Engine Tightening* table.

6-232 & 258

NOTE: On Pacer models, park windshield wiper blades at center of windshield to aid in removal cylinder head.

1. Drain cooling system and disconnect hoses at thermostat housing.
2. Remove air cleaner and disconnect fuel line and vacuum advance line.
3. Remove valve cover and gasket.

Fig. 8 Rocker arms, push rod and pivot assembly. Late 1974 & 1975-79 6-232, 258 and all 1974-79 V8s

4. On early 1974 models, remove rocker arm and shaft assemblies and push rods. On late 1974 and 1975-79 models, remove rocker arms and bridged pivot assemblies. Alternately loosen each cap screw one turn at a time to prevent damage to bridge.

NOTE: Label push rods, rocker arms and bridge pivots so they can be installed in the same position.

5. Disconnect power steering pump and air pump and position pumps and brackets aside. Do not disconnect hoses from pumps.
6. Remove intake and exhaust manifold assembly from cylinder head.
7. On models equipped with A/C, remove A/C drive belt idler bracket from cylinder head. Loosen alternator drive belt, then remove alternator bracket to cylinder head mounting bolt. Remove bolts from compressor mounting bracket and position compressor aside.
8. Disconnect ignition wires and remove spark plugs.
9. Disconnect temperature sending unit wire and battery ground cable.
10. Remove ignition coil and bracket assembly.
11. Remove cylinder head bolts, cylinder head and gasket.
12. Reverse procedure to install. Torque cylinder head bolts in sequence shown in Fig. 4 and torque manifold bolts in sequence shown in Figs. 5 and 6.

V8-304, 360 & 401

1. Drain cooling system and cylinder block.
2. Remove valve cover and gasket.
3. Remove rocket arm, bridged pivot assemblies and push rods. Alternately loosen cap screws one turn at a time to prevent damage to bridge pivots.

NOTE: Label push rods, rocker arms and bridged pivot assemblies so they can be installed in the same position.

4. Disconnect ignition wires and remove spark plugs.

5. Remove intake and exhaust manifolds, then loosen all drive belts.
6. If right hand cylinder head is to be removed, remove battery ground cable from cylinder head. Detach alternator support brace from cylinder head. On models equipped with A/C, remove compressor mounting bracket from cylinder head.
7. If left hand cylinder head is to be removed, detach air pump and power steering pump mounting bracket, if equipped, from cylinder head.
8. Remove cylinder head bolts, cylinder head and gasket.
9. Reverse procedure to install. Torque cylinder head bolts in sequence shown in Fig. 7.

VALVE ARRANGEMENT
Front to Rear

All V8s . . . . E-I-I-E-E-I-I-E
6-232, 258 . . . . E-I-I-E-I-E-E-I-E-I-I-E

VALVE LIFT SPECS.

Year	Engine	Intake	Exhaust
Early 1974	Six	.381	.381
Late 1974[2] & 1975-76	Six	.372	.372
1977-79	6-232 & 258 1 Bbl. Carb.	.375	.375
1977-79	6-258 2 Bbl. Carb.	.400	.400
1974	V8-304, 360	.425[1]	.425[1]
1975-79	V8-304, 360	.430	.430
1974	V8-401	.457[1]	.457[1]
1975-76	V8-401	.464	.464

[1]Hi-Perf. cam, .477.
[2]Beginning with engine build date code 704 (A or E) 04.

VALVE TIMING
Intake Opens Before TDC

Year	Engine	Degrees
Early 1974	Six	12½
Late 1974[1] & 1975-79	Six[2]	12.12
1975-79	Six[3]	14.58
1974-79	V8-304, 360	14¾
1974-76	V8-401	12.12

[1]Beginning with engine build date code 704 (A or E) 04.
[2]1 barrel carb.
[3]2 barrel carb.

ROCKER ARMS
V8-304, 360, 401

All 1974-79 V8 engines have the intake and exhaust rocker arms pivoting on a bridged pivot assembly which is secured to the cylinder head by two cap screws, Fig. 8. When installing cap screws, turn each screw one turn at a time to avoid breaking the bridge. Torque cap screws to 19 ft. lbs.

LUBRICATION SUPPLY TO PUSH ROD

Fig. 9 Hydraulic lifter identification. V8-304, 360, 401 engines

The push rods are hollow, serving as oil galleries for lubricating each individual rocker arm assembly. Prior to installing, the push rods should be cleaned thoroughly, inspected for wear and deposits which may restrict the flow of oil to the rocker arm assembly.

The push rods also serve as guides to maintain correct rocker arm to valve stem relationship; therefore, a contact pattern on the push rods where they contact the cylinder head is normal.

Lubrication to each rocker arm is supplied by the corresponding hydraulic valve lifter. A metering system located in each valve lifter consists of a stepped lower surface on the push rod cap that contacts a flat plate, causing a restriction, Fig. 9. The restriction meters the amount of oil flow through the push rod cap, hollow push rod, and upper valve train components. A loss of lubrication to the rocker arm could be caused by a restricted or plugged push rod or a defective hydraulic valve lifter.

CAUTION: Correct installation of push rods in these engines is critical and more than normal care must be taken upon installation. When placing the push rods through the guide hole in the cylinder head, it is important that the push rod end is inserted in the plunger cap socket. It is possible that the push rod may seat itself on the edge of the plunger cap which will restrict valve lifter rotation and lubrication to rocker arms.

It is recommended that, just prior to installation of the cylinder head covers, the engine be operated and the supply of lubrication to each rocker arm be visually inspected. If inspection reveals that an individual rocker arm is not being supplied with lubrication, the push rod and/or valve lifter must be inspected to determine the cause.

6-232, 258 Engines

On early 1974 engines, the pressure

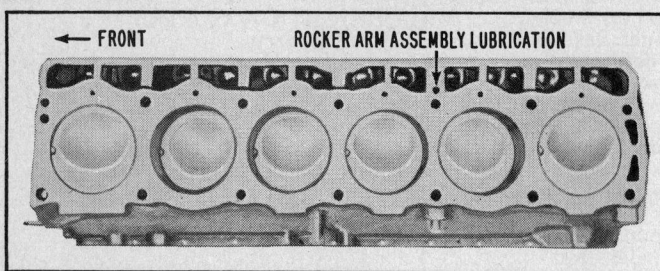

Fig. 10   Rocker arm lubrication gallery. Early 1974 6-232, 258 engines

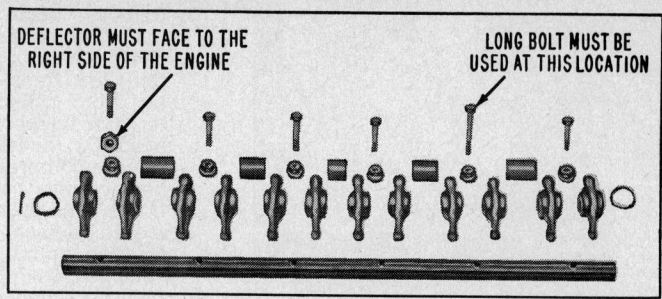

Fig. 11   Rocker arm assembly. Early 1974 6-232, 258 engines

supply for each rocker arm is obtained from No. 3 camshaft bearing location where the camshaft meters the flow of oil from the main lubricating gallery through a groove in the camshaft bearing surface to a gallery extending upwards to the cylinder head gasket surface, Fig. 10. On late 1974 and 1975-79 232, 258, oil is supplied through the valve lifters and hollow push rods. On early 1974 232 and 258, install the rocker arm shaft with oil holes facing down toward the cylinder head, Fig. 11. The late 1974 and 1975-79 232, 258 engines have the intake and exhaust rocker arms pivoting on a bridged pivot assembly which is secured to the cylinder head by two cap screws, Fig. 8.

NOTE: The new rocker arms used on late 1974 engines (beginning with build date code 704 (A or E) 04, have been redesigned with the oil hole on the push rod end relocated, pointing away from the valve assemblies allowing for improved oil control, Fig. 12. Also, these rocker arms are not interchangeable with earlier types, since the camshaft and rocker arm ratio has been modified.

6-232 & 258 Valve Train

The exhaust valve train on certain engines, has been modified to incorporate valve rotators to improve valve durability. The engines involved are those equipped with EGR systems less Air Guard.

NOTE: When replacing rocker arms on these engines, use only the cast type rocker arms, as they are designed to accommodate the valve rotators.

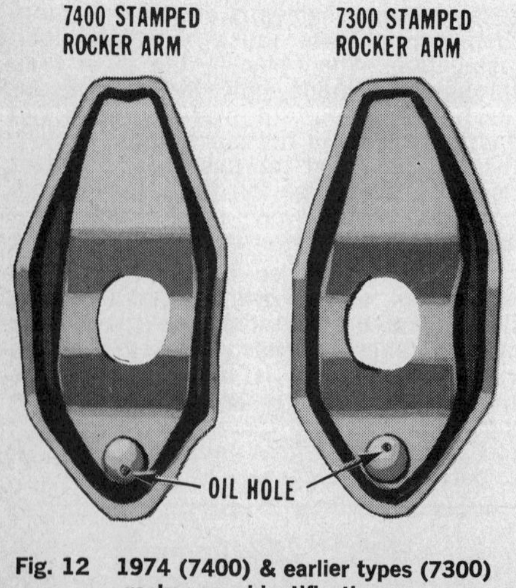

VALVE GUIDES

Excessive valve stem-to-guide clearance will cause lack of power, rough idling and noisy valves, and may cause valve breakage. Insufficient clearance will result in noisy and sticky functioning of valves and disturb engine smoothness of operation.

Valve stem-to-guide clearances are listed in the *Engine Valve Specifications* table. By using a micrometer and a suitable telescope hole gauge, check the diameter of the valve stem in three places (top, center and bottom). Insert telescope hole gauge in valve guide bore, measuring at the center. Subtract the highest reading of valve stem diameter from valve guide bore center diameter to obtain valve-to-guide clearance. If clearance is not within specified limits, use the next oversize valve and ream bore to fit. Valves with oversize stems are available in .003", .015" and .030".

HYDRAULIC LIFTERS

Valve lifters may be removed from their bores after removing the cylinder head. Adjustable pliers with taped jaws may be used to remove lifters that are stuck due to varnish, carbon, etc. Fig. 13 illustrates the type of lifter used.

TIMING CHAIN COVER
6-232, 258

1. Remove drive belts, fan and pulley.
2. Remove vibration damper.
3. Remove oil pan-to-timing chain cover screws and cover-to-block screws.
4. Raise the cover and pull the oil pan

front seal up enough to pull the retaining nibs from the holes in the cover.
5. Remove timing chain cover gasket from block. Cut off seal tab flush with front face of cylinder block. Clean gasket surfaces.
6. Remove oil seal.
7. Place gasket in position on cylinder block. Install new oil pan front seal, cut off protruding tab of seal to match portion of the original seal.
8. Insert suitable aligning tool in cover seal bore and on crankshaft. Install cover-to-oil pan screws and tighten lightly. Install cover screws and tighten.
9. Retighten all screws and install new cover seal.

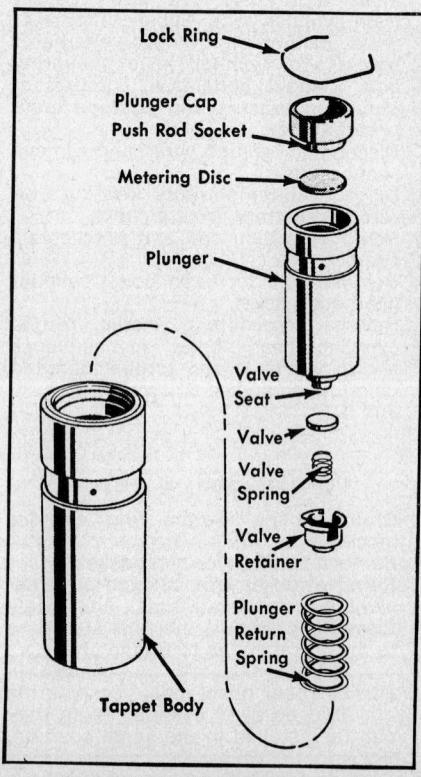

Fig. 13   Hydraulic valve lifter

Fig. 12   1974 (7400) & earlier types (7300) rocker arm identification

V8-304, 360, 401

The timing chain cover is a die casting incorporating an oil seal at the vibration damper hub, Fig. 14. On 1974-77 models, the crankshaft front seal is installed from the back side of the cover, therefore, it is necessary to remove the cover when replacement of the seal is required. On 1978-79 models, the oil seal may be installed from either side of the timing case cover, therefore it is not necessary to remove the cover to replace the oil seal. To remove cover, proceed as follows:

1. Drain cooling system completely.
2. Remove radiator hoses and bypass hose from cover.
3. Remove distributor, fuel pump, drive belts, fan and hub assembly, alternator, air pump and vibration damper, using a suitable puller.

NOTE: It is not necessary to disconnect power steering or discharge air conditioning system (if equipped). Remove units from their mounting brackets and place them aside.

4. Remove two front oil pan bolts and the eight hex head bolts retaining the cover to the cylinder block.

NOTE: Timing chain cover bolts are of various lengths. Note location of bolts during disassembly so they can be installed in original position.

5. Pull cover forward until free from locating dowel pins.
6. Remove used seal and clean seal bore and gasket surface of cover.
7. Apply sealing compound to outer surface of seal and a film of Lubriplate or equivalent to seal lips. Drive seal into cover bore until seal contacts outer flange of cover.

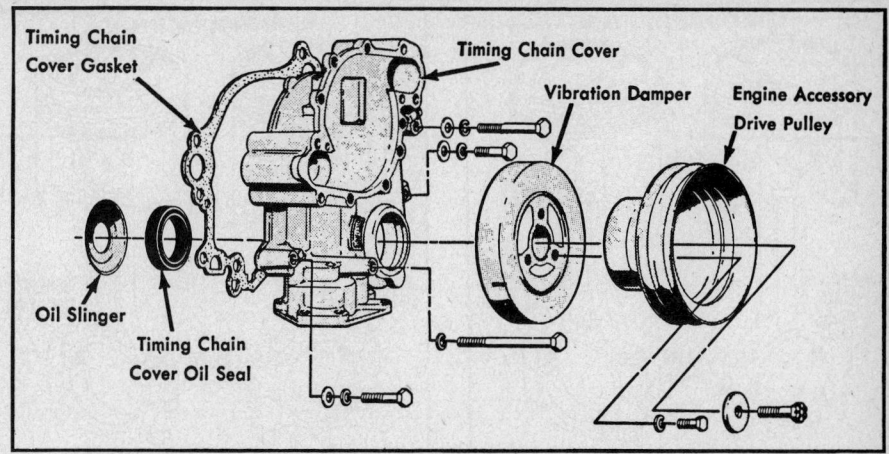

Fig. 14   Timing chain cover assembly. V8-304, 360, 401 engines

Installation of Cover

1. Prior to installation of cover, remove lower dowel pin from cylinder block.
2. Using a sharp knife or razor blade, cut oil pan gasket flush with cylinder block on both sides of oil pan.
3. Cut corresponding pieces of gasket from the replacement oil pan gasket set. Cement gasket to cover. Install replacement Neoprene oil pan seal into cover and align cork gasket tabs to the pan seal.
4. Apply a strip of sealing compound to both the cut-off oil pan gaskets at the oil pan to cylinder block location.
5. Place cover in position, install oil pan bolts in cover, tighten evenly and slowly until cover aligns with upper dowel. Then install lower dowel through cover. Drive dowel in corresponding hole in cylinder block.
6. Install cover attaching bolts and torque to 20-30 ft-lbs.

TIMING CHAIN

When installing a timing chain, see that the timing marks on the sprockets are in line as shown in Figs. 15, 16 and 17.

NOTE: All V8-360 and 401 heavy duty engines (Fleet) built after April 22, 1974 use a new double row roller type timing chain to improve timing chain durability. This new timing chain is available as a service replacement item and should be installed when timing chain failures occur to eliminate recurrence of the problem. Installation of the new timing chain requires the use of a new heavy duty camshaft sprocket and crankshaft sprocket.

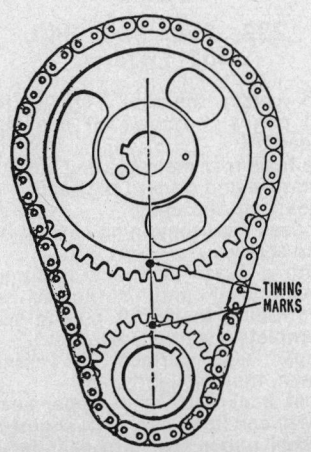

Fig. 15   Valve timing. V8 engines

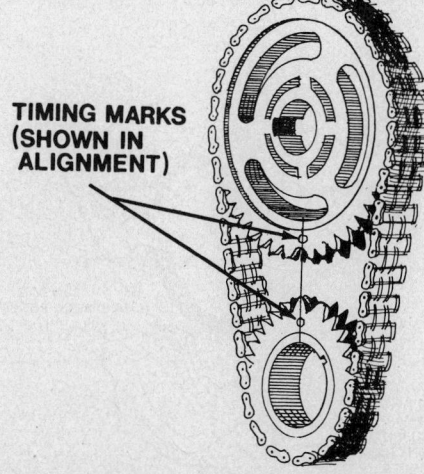

TIMING MARKS (SHOWN IN ALIGNMENT)

Fig. 16   Valve timing. V8-360 & 401 with double row roller timing chain

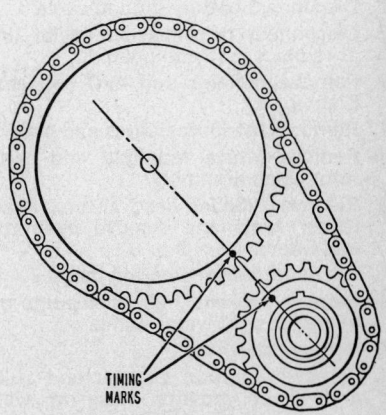

Fig. 17   Valve timing. 6-232, 258 engines

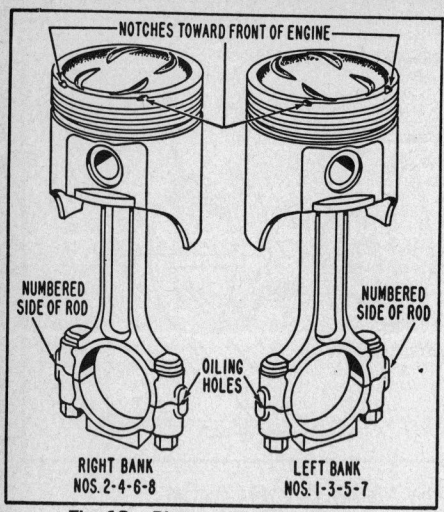

Fig. 18 Piston and rod assembly. V8-304, 360

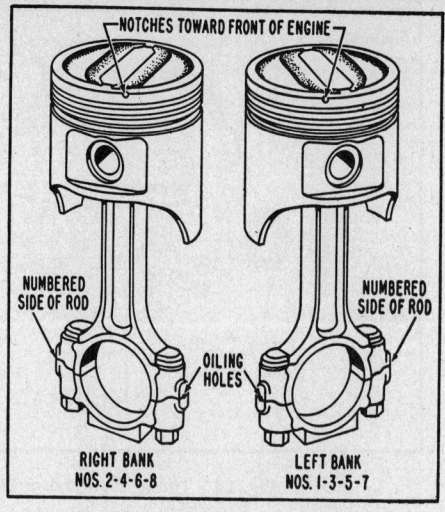

Fig. 19 Piston and rod assembly. V8-401

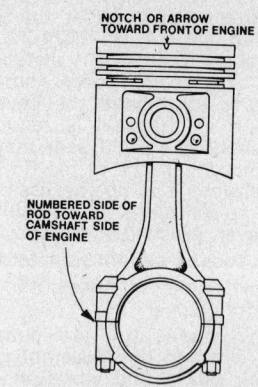

Fig. 20 Piston and rod assembly. 6-232, 258 engines

CAMSHAFT
6-232, 258

1. Remove distributor and ignition wires.
2. Remove cylinder head and valve lifters.
3. Remove radiator and, if so equipped, air conditioning condenser.
4. Remove timing chain cover.
5. Rotate crankshaft until timing marks on sprockets are aligned, Fig. 17.
6. Remove sprockets and chain.
7. On all models except Pacer, remove front bumper or grille as required to remove camshaft.
8. On Pacer models, remove hood and raise engine sufficiently to permit camshaft removal.

NOTE: Mark hinge locations on hood panel for alignment during installation.

9. Remove camshaft.

V8-304, 360, 401

1. Disconnect battery ground cable.
2. Disconnect transmission cooler lines at radiator if so equipped.
3. Remove radiator and A/C condenser if equipped.
4. Remove distributor, wires and coil.
5. Remove intake manifold and carburetor as an assembly.
6. Remove cylinder head covers, loosen rocker arms and remove push rods and lifters.
7. Dismount power steering pump.
8. Remove fan and hub, fuel pump and heater hose at water pump.
9. Remove alternator.
10. Remove vibration damper and pulley and lower radiator hose at water pump.
11. Remove timing chain cover, distributor-oil pump drive gear, fuel pump

eccentric, sprockets and chain.

NOTE: Remove camshaft sprocket, crankshaft bracket and timing chain as an assembly.

12. Remove hood latch support bracket upper retaining screws and move bracket as required to allow removal of camshaft.

PISTONS & RODS, ASSEMBLE
V8 Engines

Assemble piston to connecting rod as shown in Figs. 18 and 19.

6 Cyl. Engines

Pistons are marked with a depression

notch or arrow on the top perimeter, Fig. 20. When installed in the engine this notch or arrow must be toward the front of the engine. Always assemble rods and caps with the cylinder numbers facing the camshaft side of engine.

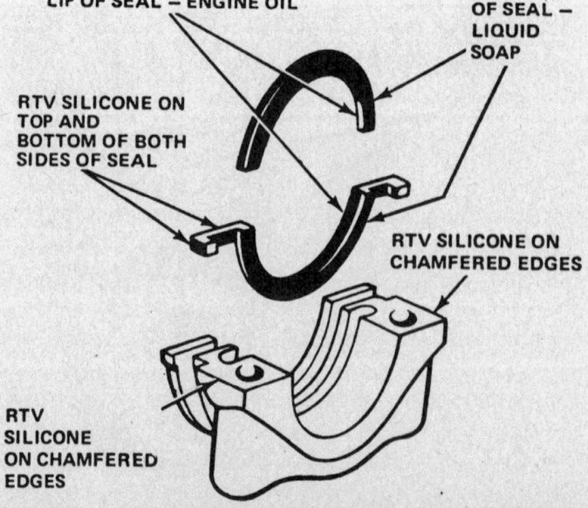

PISTONS, PINS & RINGS

Pistons are furnished in standard sizes and oversizes of .002, .005. .010 and .020".

Piston pins are furnished in oversizes of .003 and .005".

Piston rings are available in .020" oversizes.

MAIN & ROD BEARINGS

Both main and rod bearings are supplied in undersizes of .001, .002, .010 and .012".

CRANKSHAFT REAR OIL SEAL
232, 258, 304, 360, 401 Engines

1. To replace the seal, Fig. 21, remove oil pan and scrape oil pan surfaces clean.
2. Remove rear main bearing cap.
3. Remove and discard old seals.
4. Clean cap throughly.
5. Loosen all remaining main bearing cap screws.
6. With a brass drift and hammer, tap upper seal until sufficient seal is protruding to permit pulling seal out completely with pliers.
7. Wipe seal surface of crankshaft clean, then oil lightly.
8. Coat back surface of upper seal with soap, and lip of seal with engine oil.
9. Install upper seal into cylinder block. *Lip of seal must face to front of engine.*

Fig. 21 Rear main bearing sealing. 232, 258 304, 360, 401 engines

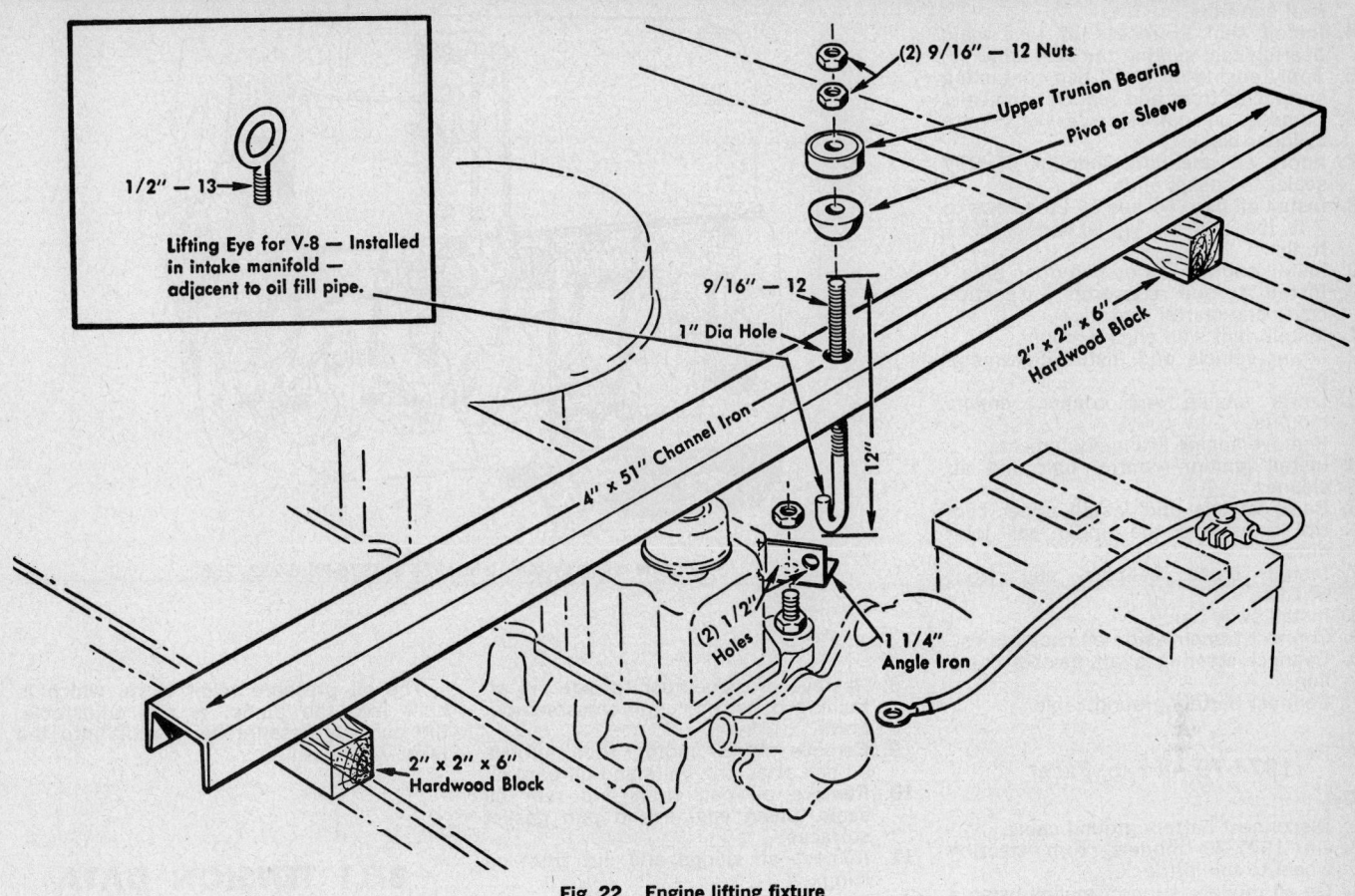

1/2" — 13

Lifting Eye for V-8 — Installed in intake manifold — adjacent to oil fill pipe.

(2) 9/16" — 12 Nuts

Upper Trunion Bearing

Pivot or Sleeve

9/16" — 12

1" Dia Hole

2" x 2" x 6" Hardwood Block

4" x 51" Channel Iron

12"

(2) 1/2" Holes

1 1/4" Angle Iron

2" x 2" x 6" Hardwood Block

Fig. 22 Engine lifting fixture

10. Coat cap and cylinder block mating surface portion of seal with RTV Silicone or equivalent, being careful not to apply sealer on lip of seal.
11. Coat back surface of lower seal with soap, and lip of seal with No. 40 engine oil. Place into cap, seating seal firmly into seal recess in cap.
12. Place RTV Silicone or equivalent on both chamfered edges of rear main bearing cap.
13. Install main bearings and install cap. Tighten all caps to correct torque as listed in the *Engine Tightening Specifications* table.
14. Cement oil pan gasket to cylinder block with tongue of gasket at each end coated with RTV Silicone or equivalent before installing into rear main bearing cap at joint of tongue and oil pan front neoprene seal.
15. Coat oil pan rear seal with soap. Place into recess of rear main bearing cap, making certain seal is firmly and evenly seated.
16. Install oil pan and tighten drain plug securely.

OIL PAN
1975-79 Pacer 6 Cyl.

1. Drain oil, then install engine holding

fixture.
2. Disconnect steering shaft flexible coupling and position out of way.
3. Raise vehicle and support on side sills.
4. Remove front engine mount through bolts.
5. Disconnect brake lines from front wheel cylinders, then disconnect upper ball joints from spindles.

NOTE: Ensure shock absorber is securely attached.

6. Remove upper control arm and position aside.
7. Support front crossmember with jack, then remove nuts from rear mounts and swing crossmember forward.
8. Remove starter.
9. Remove oil pan and front and rear oil pan seals.

1978-79 Pacer V8-304
Removal

1. Disconnect battery ground cable.
2. Remove air cleaner and ignition control unit.
3. Attach suitable engine lifting equipment to engine and lift engine.
4. Raise and support vehicle.
5. Remove front wheels.
6. Remove brake calipers and suspend

caliper with a wire.
7. Remove upper ball joint nuts, then the upper control arms.
8. Disconnect steering shaft flexible coupling and position aside.
9. On left side of engine, disconnect engine mount from engine block.
10. On right side of engine, remove engine mount.
11. Disconnect transmission oil cooler lines.
12. Remove sway bar.
13. Lower vehicle and support crossmember with a suitable jack.
14. Remove nuts from rear crossmember insulators and lower the crossmember.
15. Raise and support vehicle.
16. Drain oil pan and remove starter motor.
17. Remove torque converter inspection cover, then the oil pan.
18. Remove gaskets and seals.
19. Clean gasket surface of oil pan and cylinder block.
20. Clean oil pan sump.

Installation

1. Install oil pan front seal to timing case cover.
2. Apply an adequate amount of RTV sealer to end tabs.
3. Apply an adequate amount of RTV sealer to gasket contacting surface of

seal end tabs.

4. Install seal in recess of rear main bearing cap, seating the seal fully.
5. Apply engine oil to oil pan contacting surface of front and real oil pan seals.
6. Cement oil pan side gaskets onto cylinder block.
7. Apply an adequate amount of RTV sealer to gasket ends.
8. Install oil pan. Torque ¼-20 screws to 7 ft. lbs. and the ⁵⁄₁₆-18 screws to 11 ft. lbs.
9. Install and tighten oil pan drain plug.
10. Install torque converter inspection cover and starter motor.
11. Install right side engine mount.
12. Lower vehicle and install crossmember.
13. Lower engine and connect engine mounts.
14. Remove engine lifting equipment.
15. Install ignition control unit and air cleaner.
16. Raise vehicle and install upper control arms and the upper ball joint nuts.
17. Install brake calipers and front wheels.
18. Install sway bar.
19. Connect transmission oil cooler lines.
20. Connect steering shaft flexible coupling.
21. Connect battery ground cable.

1974-79 All Exc. Pacer

6 Cyl.

1. Disconnect battery ground cable.
2. On 1977-79 models, turn steering wheel to full left lock.
3. On all models, support engine using a suitable holding fixture.
4. Raise vehicle and support on side sills.
5. Disconnect steering idler arm at side sill.
6. Disconnect engine front support cushions at engine brackets.
7. Loosen sway bar link nuts to end of threads, if equipped.
8. Remove front crossmember to side sill attaching bolts, then pull crossmember down.
9. Remove engine right support bracket from engine.
10. On 1977-79 models, loosen strut rods at lower control arms; do not remove screws.
11. On 1977-79 models, remove starter motor.
12. On all models, drain crankcase, then remove oil pan attaching bolts and oil pan.
13. Clean gasket surfaces of oil pan and engine block. Remove all sludge and dirt from oil pan sump.

V8-304, 360 & 401

1. Disconnect battery ground cable.
2. Support engine using a suitable holding fixture.
3. Raise vehicle and support on side sills.
4. Drain engine oil, then disconnect steering idler arm and sway bar brackets at side sills.
5. Disconnect strut rods at lower control arms.
6. Disconnect engine to body ground cable.
7. Disconnect engine support cushions at crossmember.

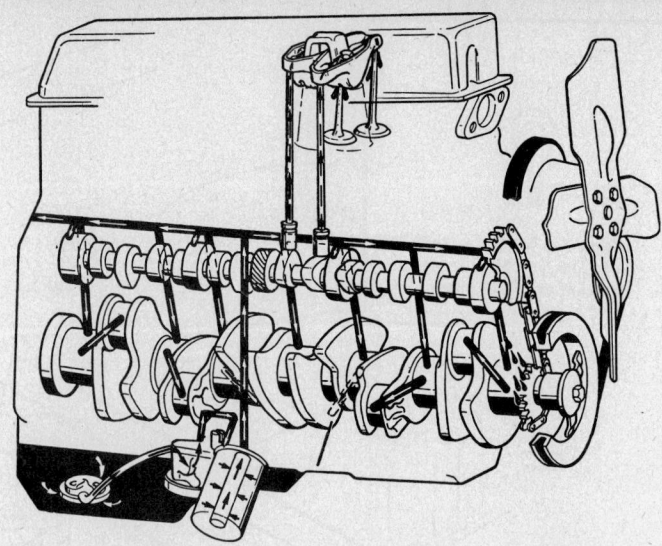

Engine oiling system, late 1974 & 1975-78 6-232, 258

8. Remove crossmember to side sill attaching bolts, then pull crossmember down.
9. Remove starter motor, then remove oil pan attaching bolts and oil pan.
10. Remove oil pan front and rear oil seals. Clean engine and pan gasket surfaces.
11. Remove all sludge and dirt from oil sump.

OIL PUMP

6-232, 258 & V8s

NOTE: When servicing oil pump on 6 cylinder engines if inlet tube is moved out of position a new inlet tube and screen assembly must be installed.

The oil pump on six cylinder models is located in the oil pan thus necessitating removal of the pan to gain access to the pump. The pump on V8 engines is an integral part of the timing case cover and it can be serviced after removal of the oil filter adapter body.

Oil pump removal or replacement will not affect distributor timing as the distributor drive gear remains in mesh with the camshaft gear.

Upon disassembly of the oil pump, place a straightedge across gears and pump body and check clearance between straightedge and pump body which should be .002-.006 inch for 1974-76 engines, .004-.008 inch for 1977 engines, and 1978-79 6 cyl. engines and .004-.0065 inch for 1978-79 V8 engines. Clearance between gears and pump housing should be .0005-.0025 for 1974-79 V8 engines and all 6 cylinder engines.

NOTE: The pump cover should be installed with the pump out of the engine and pump checked for freedom of operation before installation.

The oil pressure relief valve, which is built into the pump, is not adjustable, the correct pressure being built into the relief valve spring.

BELT TENSION DATA

	New Lbs.	Used Lbs.
1974—		
Air Condition	125-155	105-130
Air Pump—		
Exc. 6 cyl. With A/C	125-155	90-115
6 cyl. With A/C (¼ inch belt)	40-50	35-40
Fan and Alternator—		
Exc. V8 With A/C	125-155	90-115
V8 With A/C	125-155	105-130
Power Steering—		
Exc. V8 With A/C	125-145	90-110
V8 with A/C	125-145	105-120
1975—		
Air Condition	125-155	105-130
Air Pump—		
Exc. 6 cyl. With A/C	125-155	90-115
6 cyl. With A/C (⅜ inch belt)	65-75	60-70
Fan and Power Steering	125-155	90-115
1976-79—		
Air Condition	125-155	90-115
Air Pump—		
Except 6 cyl. With P.S.	125-155	90-115
6 cyl. with P.S. (⅜ inch belt)	65-75	60-70
Fan and Power Steering	125-155	90-115

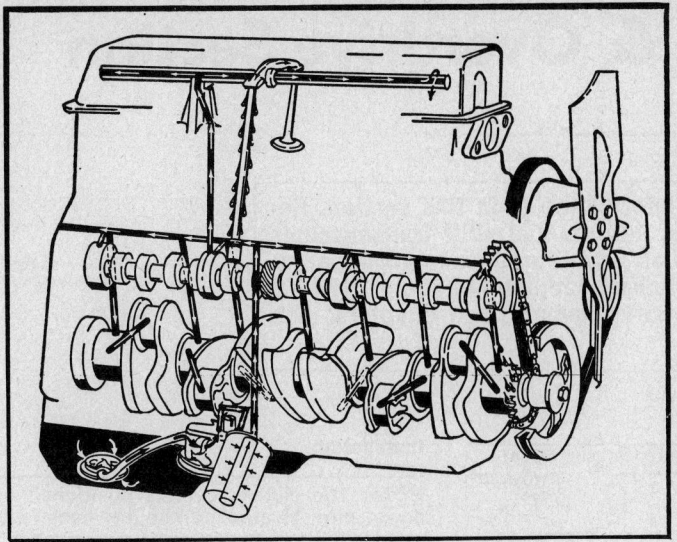

Engine oiling system. Early 1974 6-232, 258 engines

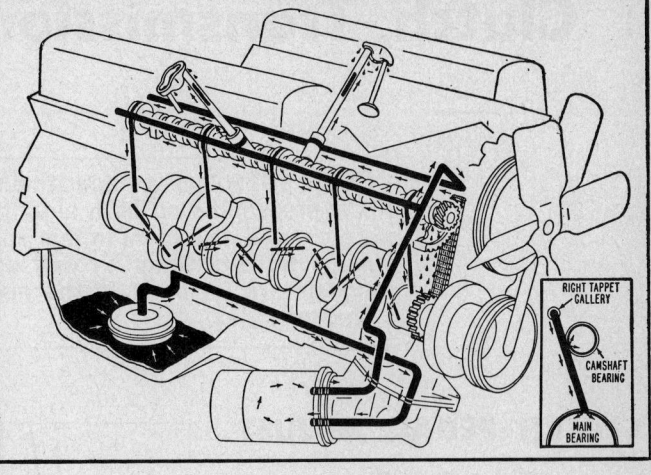

Engine oiling system. V8-304, 360, 401 engines

WATER PUMP

1. Disconnect battery ground cable.
2. Drain cooling system and disconnect radiator and heater hoses from pump.
3. Remove drive belts.
4. On V8 models, remove power steering pump, air pump and mounting bracket assembly from engine and position aside. Do not disconnect hoses.
5. On V8 models, remove A/C compressor and bracket as an assembly and position aside, if equipped. Do not discharge system.

NOTE: On some models it will be necessary to remove alternator front bracket and place alternator aside, without disconnecting wires.

6. Remove fan shroud attaching bolts, then remove fan, hub and shroud.
7. Remove water pump and gasket.

FUEL PUMP PRESSURE

Year	Engine	Pressure lbs.
1974-79	Six cyl.	4-5
1974-79	V8	5-6½

FUEL PUMP, REPLACE

1. Remove all gasket material from the pump and block gasket surfaces. Apply sealer to both sides of new gasket.

2. Position gasket on pump flange and hold pump in position against its mounting surface. Make sure rocker arm is riding on camshaft eccentric.
3. Press pump tight against its mounting. Install retaining screws and tighten them alternately.
4. Connect fuel lines. Then operate engine and check for leaks.

SERVICE NOTE: Before installing the pump, it is good practice to crank the engine so that the nose of the camshaft eccentric is out of the way of the fuel pump rocker arm when the pump is installed. In this way there will be the least amount of tension on the rocker arm, thereby easing the installation of the pump.

Clutch, Transmission & Overdrive Section

NOTE: 1979 Linkage adjustment information is in this section. Repair procedures on both automatic and manual shift transmissions are covered elsewhere in this manual. Procedures for removing automatic transmissions as well as linkage adjustments on 1974-78 models are included in the automatic transmission chapters. See Chapter Index.

CLUTCH PEDAL, ADJUST

Pedal Free Play

4-121

1. Raise vehicle and remove screw attaching throwout lever boot to clutch housing, then the boot.
2. Loosen clutch cable locknut at transmission side of clutch housing, Fig. 1, View A.
3. Pull cable housing toward front of vehicle until throwout lever free play is eliminated, then rotate the adjuster nut toward rear of vehicle until adjuster nut face tabs contact housing boss, Fig. 1, View B.
4. Release cable housing and rotate adjuster nut until adjuster nut tabs engage clutch housing slots.
5. Torque clutch cable locknut to 25 ft. lbs.
6. Install throwout lever boot and attaching screw.
7. Lower vehicle.

Exc. 4-121

In order to provide sufficient free movement of the clutch release bearing when the clutch is engaged and pedal fully released, free pedal play should be $7/8''$ to $1\frac{1}{8}''$ with desired free play of $1\frac{1}{8}''$ for 1974-79.

Adjustment for free pedal play is made by varying the length of the beam or link to the release lever rod. Lengthening this rod reduces pedal travel; shortening it increases pedal play, Fig. 2.

CLUTCH, REPLACE

4-121

Removal

1. Remove gearshift lever bezel and slide outer and inner boots toward top of lever.
2. Fold carpet and straighten all gearshift lever lock tabs bent downward.
3. Remove gearshift lever locknut and the gearshift lever.
4. Raise and support vehicle, then remove propeller shaft.
5. Disconnect speedometer cable and adapter from transmission.
6. Disconnect back-up lamp switch wires and disengage wire harness from clips on transmission top cover.
7. Remove starter motor.
8. Loosen clutch cable locknut and back off adjuster nut to slacken cable.

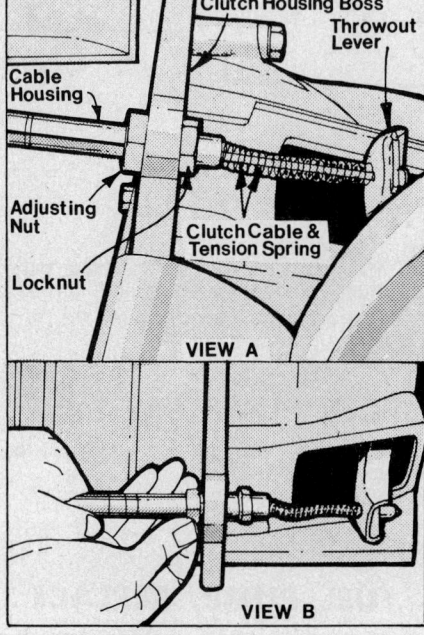

Fig. 1   Clutch adjustment. 4-121

Slide cable toward clutch housing until cushion and cable ball can be disengaged from throwout lever, Fig. 3.

9. Remove inspection cover at front of clutch housing.
10. Remove bolts attaching catalytic converter support bracket to transmission rear support bracket.
11. Support engine with a suitable jack.
12. Remove nuts and bolts attaching transmission support cushion to rear crossmember.
13. Remove rear crossmember.
14. Support transmission with a suitable jack and remove clutch housing to engine bolts.
15. Remove clutch housing and transmission.
16. Mark clutch cover and flywheel alignment.
17. Remove clutch cover bolts, then the cover and driven plate.

NOTE: Loosen the clutch cover bolts evenly and alternately to prevent cover distortion.

Installation

NOTE: The clutch cover is positioned on dowel pins located on the flywheel face.

When installing the driven plate and cover, the cover must be indexed with the alignment marks and be properly engaged with the dowel pins.

1. Position clutch driven plate and cover, then install the attaching bolts finger tight.
2. Align clutch driven plate with tool J-5824-01 or equivalent.
3. Torque clutch cover bolts to 23 ft. lbs. and remove alignment tool.
4. Install transmission and clutch housing assembly and torque attaching bolts to 54 ft. lbs.
5. Install rear crossmember, then the support cushion to crossmember attaching bolts and torque to 25 ft. lbs. Torque rear crossmember stud nuts to 35 ft. lbs.
6. Connect clutch cable to throwout lever and adjust as outlined previously.
7. Connect speedometer cable and adapter to transmission.
8. Connect back-up lamp switch wires and engage harness in retaining clips at top of transmission cover.
9. Install clutch housing inspection cover.
10. Install catalytic converter support bracket bolts, then the starter.
11. Install propeller shaft.
12. Lower vehicle.
13. Install gearshift lever. Ensure shift rail insert is facing downward and that offset side of lever fork is facing right side of extension housing before lever installation. Bend at least three lock tabs down to retain lever.
14. Install inner and outer lever boots, then the bezel.

Exc. 4-121

Removal

1. Remove transmission as described further on.
2. Remove starter, clutch housing, throwout lever, bearing and sleeve assembly.

NOTE: Mark clutch cover, pressure plate and flywheel to insure correct alignment during installation.

3. Remove clutch cover and pressure plate assembly.

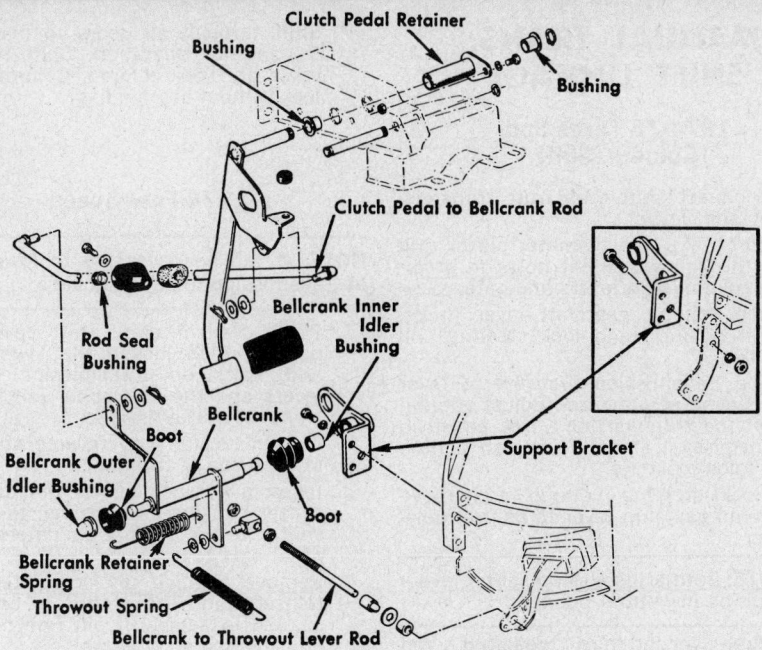

Fig. 2 Typical clutch linkage exc. 4-121

NOTE: When removing clutch cover and pressure plate assembly from flywheel, loosen screws evenly until spring tension is released, as cover could be warped by improper removal, resulting in clutch chatter when reassembled.

4. Remove pilot bushing lubricating wick and soak in engine oil.

NOTE: Unless special clutch rebuilding equipment is available, it is recommended that the clutch assembly be exchanged for a rebuilt unit should the clutch require rebuilding. The driven disc, however, may be replaced without special equipment. If clutch rebuilding equipment is available, follow the equipment manufacturer's instructions.

Installation

1. Inspect clutch release lever height and correct as necessary. If used, lubricate pilot bushing wick with engine oil.
2. Install clutch disc and cover on flywheel and loosely install bolts. Using clutch aligning tool or transmission clutch shaft, align clutch disc.
3. Tighten cover retaining bolts several turns at a time to prevent cover distortion, then torque bolts to 28 ft. lbs. on 1974-79 6 cylinder models and 1977 V8 models; 38 ft. lbs. on 1974-76 V8 models.
4. Install throwout lever, bearing and sleeve assembly, clutch housing and starter.

MANUAL TRANS., REPLACE

4-121

1977-79

Refer to Clutch, Replace 4-121 for manual transmission removal and installation procedures.

1977-78

Except 4-121

1. Remove knob, bezel, boot and gear shift lever.
2. Open hood and raise vehicle.
3. Mark rear universal joint and pro-

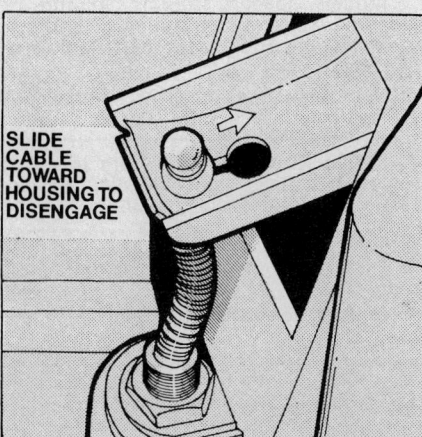

SLIDE CABLE TOWARD HOUSING TO DISENGAGE

Fig. 3 Clutch cable removal. 4-121

peller shaft to ensure proper alignment at time of installation, then remove propeller shaft.

4. Disconnect speedometer cable and backup lamp switch and TCS switch wires, if equipped.
5. If equipped with four speed transmission, release back-up lamp switch wires from clip on transmission top cover.
6. Install support stand under clutch housing to support engine when crossmember and transmission are removed.
7. On Pacer models, disconnect ground strap at support cushion bolt.
8. On all models, remove rear crossmember to frame side sill attaching nuts.
9. Remove catalytic converter support bracket, if equipped.
10. On Concord, Gremlin, Hornet and Spirit models, remove rear support cushion to crossmember attaching bolts and remove crossmember.

NOTE: On Pacer models, crossmember is removed with transmission.

11. On all models remove two lower transmission to clutch housing attaching bolts and install guide pins.
12. Remove two upper transmission to clutch housing attaching bolts and remove transmission.

NOTE: Care must be taken not to damage clutch shaft, pilot bushing or clutch disc.

1974-76

NOTE: On overdrive equipped vehicles, depress clutch then engage and disengage overdrive to relieve overrunning clutch and pinion carrier torque loading.

CAUTION: It is necessary to open the hood to avoid damage to the hood and air cleaner whenever the rear crossmember is removed.

NOTE: On cars equipped with floor shift, remove bezel, boot and shift selector lever.

1. Raise the vehicle.
2. Mark rear universal joint yoke and bearing prior to removal to insure proper alignment at time of installation.
3. Disconnect propeller shaft from rear axle.
4. Slide front universal joint yoke from transmission.
5. Unfasten and lower exhaust pipes on V8 models.
6. Support the engine and detach rear support cushion from transmission.

NOTE: On overdrive equipped vehicles, disconnect front cable from parking brake equalizer, remove adjuster and hooks from floor pan and lower parking brake equalizer to provide working clearance.

7. Remove bolts securing rear crossmember to side sills and remove rear crossmember.

8. Disconnect speedo cable, back up light switch wires and any other wiring.
9. Disconnect column shift rods and reverse lock up rod.
10. Lower engine until clearance is obtained to permit transmission removal.

NOTE: Care must be taken not to damage clutch shaft, pilot bushing or clutch disc.

OVERDRIVE REPLACE
1975-76

NOTE: In order to ease removal, operate vehicle, then engage and disengage overdrive with clutch pedal depressed. This procedure will relieve torque loading on overrunning clutch and pinion carrier.

1. On floorshift vehicles, remove gearshift lever bezel, boot, insulator, retaining bolts, crossover spring, and gearshift lever.
2. Raise and support vehicle on hoist.
3. On catalytic converter equipped vehicles, disconnect converter from exhaust pipes, and lower converter, muffler and tailpipes to obtain clearance.
4. Disconnect solenoid valve wires and disconnect speedometer cable from governor speed switch, then remove speedometer clamp, governor speed switch, speedometer support, adaptor and driven gear from speedometer bore.
5. Mark rear universal joint and pinion yoke for correct alignment at installation and remove propeller shaft.
6. On floorshift vehicles, disconnect shift rods at transmission shifter levers and slide rods forward out of gearshift lever retainer bushings, then remove retainer to transmission adapter bolts and remove retainer.
7. Place a support under clutch housing, then remove rear support cushion to transmission adaptor bolts and remove support cushion and crossmember.
8. Remove the eight locknuts and washers from overdrive main case-to-transmission adaptor studs and remove overdrive. Discard old adaptor gasket.
9. When installing overdrive, use a long screwdriver to align overrunning clutch splines with transmission output shaft splines, then align pump strap with drive cam and install overdrive. Torque locknuts to 18 ft. lbs.

NOTE: Make certain that transmission output shaft splines are aligned with splines in overrunning clutch hub. Do not force engagement when installing.

MANUAL TRANS. SHIFT LINKAGE

1974-76 Three Spd. Column Shift

1. Disconnect shift rods from transmission shift levers.
2. Insert a 3/16 inch diameter pin or drill bit through alignment holes in steering column shift levers and gate.
3. Place column gearshift lever in reverse position and lock steering column.
4. Place transmission first-reverse lever in reverse position and adjust column shift rod trunnion for a free pin fit in transmission shifter lever and tighten trunnion locknuts.
5. Unlock steering column and move column gearshift lever to neutral position.

NOTE: Both transmission shifter levers must be in neutral position.

6. Adjust second-third gearshift rod trunnion to obtain a free aligning fit in column levers. Tighten shift rod trunnion locknuts.
7. Remove aligning pin and shift through all gears to check for freedom of operation. Shift into reverse and lock column. Column must lock without any binding.

1974-79 Three Spd. Floor Shift

1. Place transmission shift levers in neutral and loosen second-third transmission lever retaining nut and adjustment bolt.
2. Place first-reverse shift rod in neutral position, then align second-third shift rod so shift notch is exactly aligned with first-reverse shift rod notch. Tighten adjustment bolt and nut.
3. Actuate shifter lever to assure a smooth crossover between first and second speed and for proper engagement in all gears.
4. If equipped with tilt steering column on 1974-75 models, or a steering column lock which is actuated by transmission shift linkage on 1976-79 models, loosen steering column reverse lockup rod trunnion locknuts to allow free movement of trunnion on rod.
5. Shift transmission into reverse and lock steering column.

NOTE: It may be necessary to rotate lower column shifter lever upward until it is in locked position.

6. Tighten lower trunnion locknut until it contacts trunnion, then tighten upper locknut while holding trunnion centered in column lever.

7. Shift through all gears to check for freedom of operation. Shift into reverse and lock column. Column must lock without any binding.

1974 Four Speed

NOTE: It will be necessary to lower rear of transmission to adjust linkage.

1. Place transmission shift levers in neutral, then loosen the lower nuts and bolts on transmission shifter levers and the two upper jamnuts at center of shifter levers.
2. Loosen locknuts on reverse shift rod at each end of trunnion.
3. Insert a 1/4 inch pin or drill bit into shifter housing and through the three shifter levers. Be sure pin enters notch at far side of housing.
4. Remove aligning pin completely and reinsert pin. The shifter is correctly aligned in neutral if pin freely enters housing and shift levers.
5. Tighten lower bolts and nuts at transmission forward shifter levers, then torque upper jamnuts to 10 ft. lbs. Making sure transmission reverse lever is in neutral position (trunnion must be loose on shift rod) tighten trunnion nuts. Use care to avoid binding trunnion in reverse lever.
6. Remove pin, then raise transmission, install crossmember and exhaust pipes.
7. If vehicle is equipped with tilt steering column, loosen steering column reverse lockup rod trunnion locknuts to allow free movement of trunnion on rod.
8. Shift transmission into reverse and lock steering column.

NOTE: It may be necessary to rotate lower column shifter lever upward until it is in locked position.

9. Tighten lower trunnion locknut until it contacts trunnion, then tighten upper locknut while holding trunnion centered in column lever.
10. Shift through all gears to check for freedom of operation. Shift into reverse and lock column. Column must lock without any binding.

1979 AUTO. TRANS.
LINKAGE ADJUST

Linkage adjustments for the 1979 models are the same as for 1978 models and can be found elsewhere in this manual.

Rear Axle, Propeller Shaft & Brakes

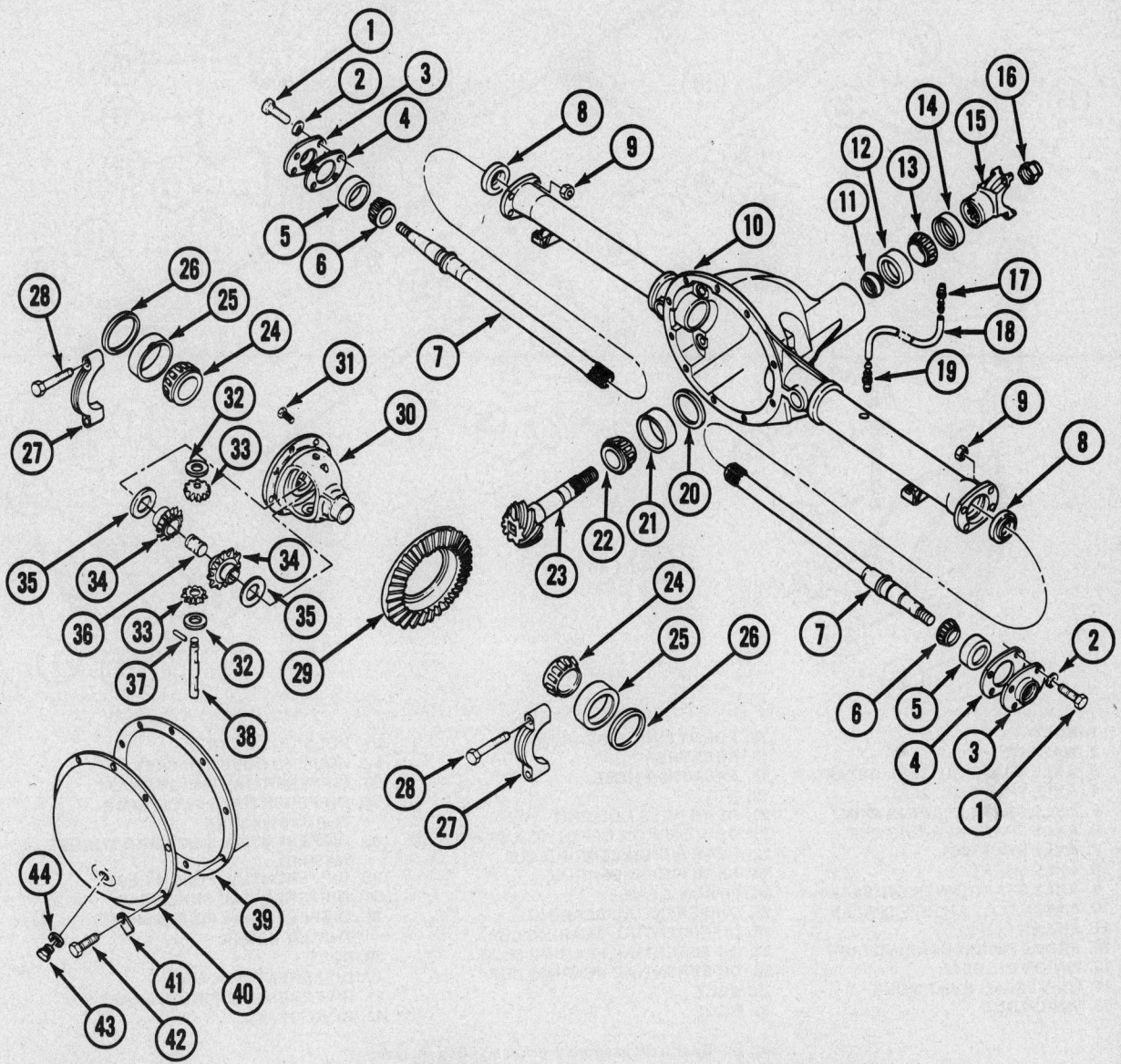

1. BOLT
2. WASHER
3. AXLE SHAFT OIL SEAL AND RETAINER ASSEMBLY
4. AXLE SHAFT BEARING SHIM
5. AXLE SHAFT BEARING CUP
6. AXLE SHAFT BEARING
7. AXLE SHAFT
8. AXLE SHAFT INNER OIL SEAL
9. NUT
10. AXLE HOUSING
11. COLLAPSIBLE SPACER
12. PINION BEARING CUP-FRONT
13. PINION BEARING-FRONT
14. PINION OIL SEAL
15. UNIVERSAL JOINT YOKE
16. PINION NUT
17. BREATHER
18. BREATHER HOSE
19. BREATHER
20. PINION DEPTH ADJUSTING SHIM
21. PINION REAR BEARING CUP
22. PINION BEARING-REAR
23. PINION GEAR
24. DIFFERENTIAL BEARING
25. DIFFERENTIAL BEARING CUP
26. DIFFERENTIAL BEARING SHIM
27. DIFFERENTIAL BEARING CAP
28. DIFFERENTIAL BEARING CAP BOLT
29. RING GEAR
30. DIFFERENTIAL CASE
31. RING GEAR BOLT
32. DIFFERENTIAL PINION WASHER
33. DIFFERENTIAL PINION
34. DIFFERENTIAL SIDE GEAR
35. DIFFERENTIAL SIDE GEAR THRUST WASHER
36. DIFFERENTIAL PINION SHAFT THRUST BLOCK
37. DIFFERENTIAL PINION SHAFT PIN
38. DIFFERENTIAL PINION SHAFT
39. AXLE HOUSING COVER GASKET
40. AXLE HOUSING COVER
41. AXLE IDENTIFICATION TAG
42. BOLT
43. AXLE HOUSING COVER FILL PLUG
44. WASHER

Fig. 1   Rear axle assembly (typical). 7-9/16 in. axle

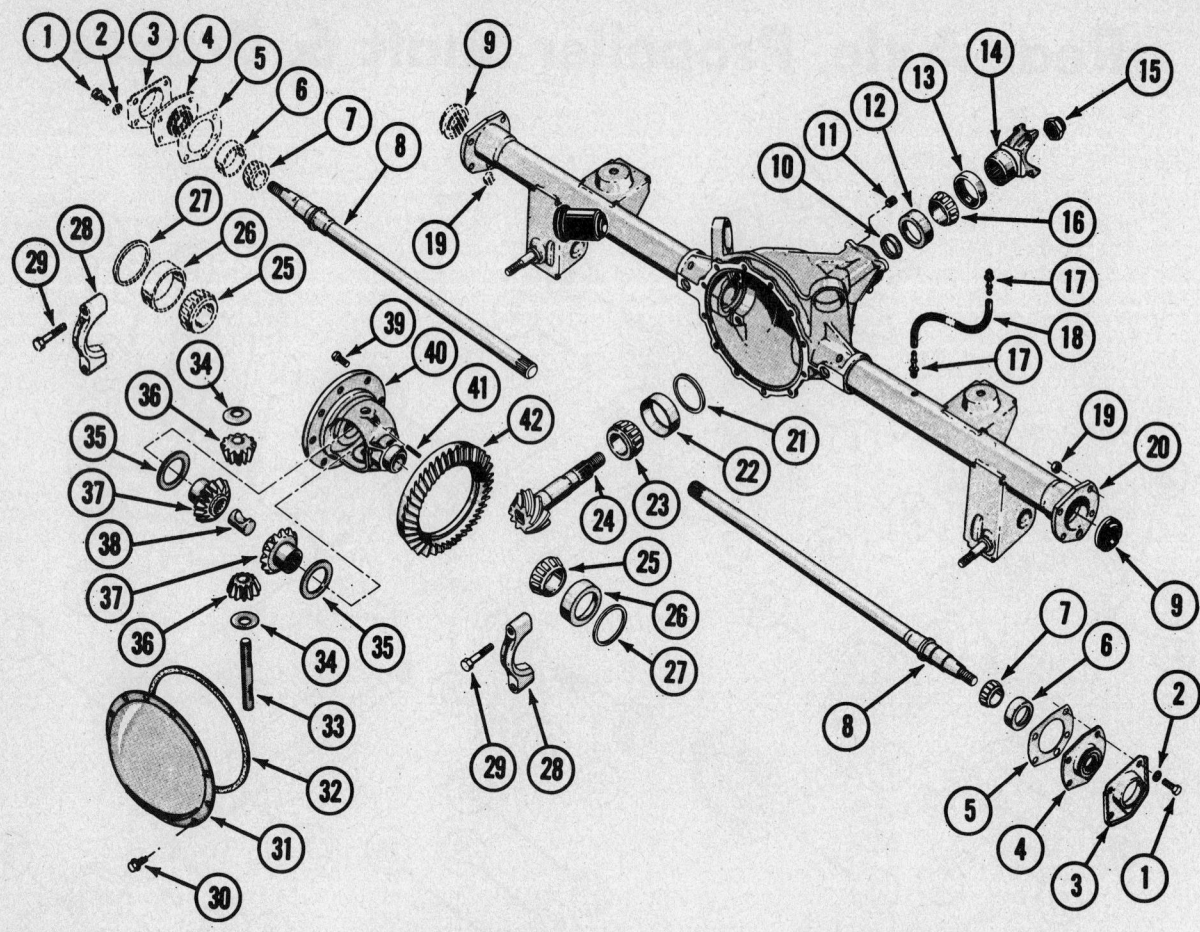

1. BOLT
2. WASHER
3. AXLE SHAFT OIL SEAL RETAINER
4. AXLE SHAFT OIL SEAL
5. AXLE SHAFT BEARING SHIM
6. AXLE SHAFT BEARING CUP
7. AXLE BEARING
8. AXLE SHAFT
9. AXLE SHAFT INNER OIL SEAL
10. PINION COLLAPSIBLE SPACER
11. FILLER PLUG
12. FRONT PINION BEARING CUP
13. PINION OIL SEAL
14. UNIVERSAL JOINT YOKE
15. PINION NUT

16. FRONT PINION BEARING
17. BREATHER
18. BREATHER HOSE
19. NUT
20. REAR AXLE HOUSING
21. DRIVE PINION DEPTH ADJUSTING SHIM
22. REAR PINION BEARING CUP
23. REAR PINION BEARING
24. PINION GEAR
25. DIFFERENTIAL BEARING
26. DIFFERENTIAL BEARING CUP
27. DIFFERENTIAL BEARING SHIM
28. DIFFERENTIAL BEARING CUP
29. BOLT
30. BOLT

31. HOUSING COVER
32. HOUSING COVER GASKET
33. DIFFERENTIAL PINION SHAFT
34. DIFFERENTIAL PINION GEAR THRUST WASHER
35. DIFFERENTIAL SIDE GEAR THRUST WASHER
36. DIFFERENTIAL PINION GEAR
37. DIFFERENTIAL SIDE GEAR
38. DIFFERENTIAL PINION SHAFT THRUST BLOCK
39. BOLT
40. DIFFERENTIAL CASE
41. DIFFERENTIAL PINION SHAFT PIN
42. RING GEAR

Fig. 2   Rear axle assembly (typical). 8⅞ in. axle

REAR AXLES

Figs. 1 and 2 illustrate the rear axle assembly used on these cars. When necessary to overhaul the unit, refer to the *Rear Axle Specifications* table in this chapter.

DESCRIPTION

In these rear axles, Figs. 1 and 2, the drive pinion is mounted in two tapered roller bearings. These bearings are pre-loaded by a washer behind the front bearing. The pinion is positioned by shims located in front of the rear bearing. The differential is supported in the carrier by two tapered roller side bearings. These bearings are preloaded by shims located between the bearings and carrier housing. The differential assembly is positioned for proper ring gear and pinion backlash by varying the position of these shims. The differential case houses two side gears in mesh with two pinions mounted on a pinion shaft which is held in place by a lock pin. The side gears and pinions are backed by thrust washers.

It is not necessary to remove the rear axle assembly. However, the underbody should be washed to prevent particles of road dirt from contaminating the parts.

REAR AXLE & PROP. SHAFT, REPLACE

1977-79

1. Remove cotter pins and remove axle shaft nuts.
2. Raise vehicle and position support

stands under rear frame side sills.

3. Remove wheels and brake drum retaining screws.
4. Remove brake drums, then disconnect brake lines at wheel cylinders.
5. Remove axle hub using tool No. J-1644-02, then remove support plates, oil seals, retainers and end play shims.

NOTE: Axle shaft end play shims are installed at left side of axle only.

6. Using a suitable puller, remove axle shafts.
7. Remove axle housing cover and drain lubricant, then reinstall cover.
8. Disconnect parking brake cables at equalizer.
9. Mark universal joint and rear axle yokes for reassembly, then disconnect propeller at rear yoke.
10. On Matador models, remove stabilizer bar, if equipped.
11. Disconnect brake hose at body floor pan bracket.
12. Disconnect vent tube from axle tube.
13. Support axle assembly using a suitable jack.
14. On Hornet, Gremlin and Pacer models:
   a. Disconnect shock absorbers at spring plates.
   b. Remove rear spring U-bolts and spring plates.
   c. Rotate axle until it clears springs, then lower axle assembly and remove from vehicle.
15. On Matador models:
   a. Disconnect shock absorbers from lower control arms. If equipped with air shocks, release all air pressure by opening valves before disconnecting.
   b. Lower jack and disconnect upper control arms from axle housing brackets.
   c. Pull left side axle tube downward and remove coil spring, then pull right side axle tube downward and remove coil spring.
   d. Disconnect lower control arms from axle tube brackets, then lower axle assembly and remove from vehicle.

1974-76 Hornet, Javelin, Gremlin & 1975-76 Pacer

1. Remove axle shaft nuts prior to raising the car weight from the wheels.
2. Remove the axle housing cover to drain the lubricant.
3. Raise and support the rear of the body.
4. Remove the rear wheels and rear wheel hubs and drums.
5. Disconnect rear parking brake cables at equalizer.
6. Remove the brake support plates.

NOTE: Retain the shims located between the left support plate and axle tube for use on reassembly.

7. Remove the axle shafts from the axle.
8. Mark the universal joint yoke and bearing before separating to insure same alignment at time of assembly.

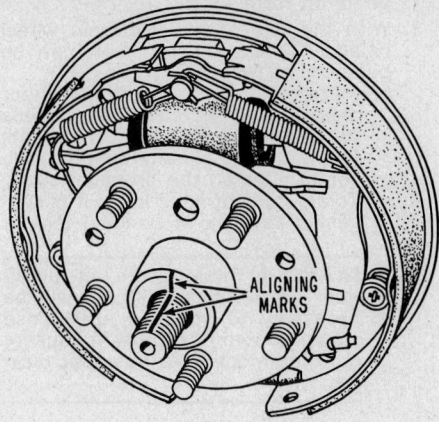

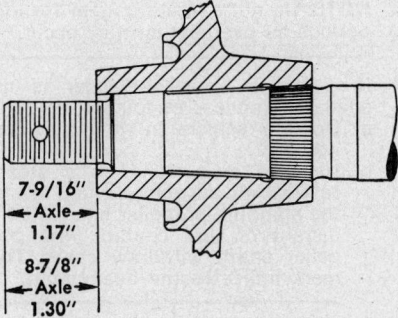

Fig. 3   Installing hub on axle shaft

Disconnect the propeller shaft at the rear universal joint.
9. Disconnect the rear shocks at the axle.
10. Disconnect the brake line at the body floor pan bracket.
11. Remove the rear spring U bolts and the axle may now be removed.

1974-76 Ambassador & Matador

1. Remove axle shaft nuts prior to raising the car weight from the wheels.
2. Raise and support the rear of the car.
3. Remove the axle housing cover and drain the lubricant.
4. Mark the rear universal joint and bearing and disconnect the propeller shaft at the rear universal joint.
5. Disconnect the parking brake cable at the equalizer.

NOTE: The left cable is routed to upper long end of equalizer. Disconnect the brake lines at the support plates.

6. Remove the wheels, hubs, drums, support plates, seals, axle shafts and bearings.
7. Support the axle assembly and dis-

connect the shocks at the axle tubes.
8. Lower axle assembly until it is supported by the control arms.
9. Pull one axle tube down and remove the spring. Pull the other axle tube and remove the other spring.
10. Support the axle assembly and disconnect the upper control arms at the axle housing.
11. Disconnect the lower control arms at the axle tubes and the axle may now be removed.

AXLE SHAFTS

The hub and drum are separate units, and the hub and axle shaft are serrated to mate and fit together on the taper. Both are punched marked to insure correct assembly, Fig. 3. The axle shaft and bearing may be removed as follows:

1. Remove rear wheel, drum and hub, then disconnect parking brake cable at equalizer.
2. Disconnect brake tube from wheel cylinder and remove brake support plate assembly, oil seal and axle shims from axle shaft.

NOTE: Axle shaft end play shims are located on the left side only.

3. Using suitable puller, pull axle shaft and bearing from axle tube, then remove and discard inner oil seal.

NOTE: The bearing cone must be pressed off the shaft, using an arbor press.

CAUTION: On models equipped with Twin Grip differential, do not rotate differential unless both axle shafts are in place.

When installing hub onto axle, install two well lubricated thrust washers and axle shaft nut. Tighten axle shaft nut until hub is installed to the dimensions shown in Fig. 3. Remove axle shaft nut and one thrust washer. Reinstall axle shaft nut and tighten to 250 ft. lbs. If cotter pin hole is not aligned, tighten the nut to the next castellation and install cotter pin.

NOTE

Do not use an original hub on a replacement axle shaft; use a new hub. A new hub may be installed on an original axle shaft providing the serrations on the shaft are not worn or damaged. Be certain that the hub and axle shaft are punch marked to insure proper alignment on installation. A replacement hub, which is not serrated, can be installed and serrations will be cut in the hub when installed on the shaft due to the difference in hardness of the shaft and the hub.

Assembly

Replace the parts in the reverse order of their removal. If the old parts are replaced and the shims have not been disturbed, the axle shaft end play should be correct when the parts are assembled. However, if a new shaft, bearing, differential carrier or housing has been installed, it will be necessary to check the end play.

The end play can be checked when all parts have been replaced except the wheel and hub. To make this check, rap each axle shaft after the nuts are tight to be sure the bearing cups are seated. Then place a dial indicator so that its stem contacts the end of the shaft and work the shaft in and out to determine the amount of existing end play. If an adjustment is necessary, remove the outer oil seal and brake support and add or remove shims as required. When making this adjustment, add or subtract shims on left side of axle only.

NOTE

The application of a bead of sealing material such as "Pliobond" or "Permatex" to the outer diameter of axle tube flange and the brake support contact area is recommended. The sealing material will be used in addition to the gasket for improved sealing.

PROPELLER SHAFT VIBRATION

1. Raise and support the rear of the car at the axle and remove rear wheels.
2. Remove all undercoating and accumulated dirt from shaft.
3. With the use of an electronic wheel balancer, the propeller shaft can be balanced as follows:
   a. Place electronic pick up unit under axle housing as close as possible to pinion yoke. Use crayon or chalk to mark four equally spaced horizontal lines on the propeller shaft. To aid in identifying lines, it is suggested they be of unequal length.

   NOTE: On models with an aluminum extension housing, it will be necessary to install a steel hose clamp on rear of extension housing to accommodate the magnetic pick-up.

   b. Operate the car in gear at the speed of greatest vibration. Locate the heavy spot.

   NOTE: Do not operate in gear for long periods as overheating may occur.

4. If electronic wheel balancer is not available, proceed as follows:
   a. Operate vehicle in gear at about 40 mph.
   b. Using a jack stand as a steady rest, slowly advance a chalk toward the spinning propeller shaft. At the instant of first contact with propeller shaft, withdraw chalk. This mark indicates the heavy spot.

   NOTE: Do not operate in gear for long periods as overheating may occur.

5. Place two worm type hose clamps on propeller shaft with heads of clamps located 180° from heavy spot noted previously. Slide clamps as far to rear as possible.
6. Again operate car in gear and if vibration still exists move both clamp heads an equal distance in opposite directions toward the heavy spot until vibration is at a minimum.
7. Replace rear wheels and road test car.

BRAKE ADJUSTMENTS

These brakes, Fig. 4, have self-adjusting mechanisms that assure correct lining-to-drum clearances at all times. The automatic adjusters operate only when the brakes are applied as the car is moving rearward.

Although the brakes are self-adjusting, an initial adjustment is necessary after the brake shoes have been relined or replaced, or when the length of the star wheel adjusting screw has been changed during some other service operation.

Frequent usage of an automatic transmission forward range to halt reverse vehicle motion may prevent the automatic adjusters from functioning, thereby inducing low pedal heights. Should low pedal heights be encountered on these models, it is recommended that numerous forward and reverse stops be made until satisfactory pedal height is obtained.

NOTE

If a low pedal condition cannot be corrected by making numerous stops (provided the hydraulic system is free of air) it indicates that the self-adjusting mechanism is not functioning. Therefore, it will be necessary to remove the brake drum, clean, free up and lubricate the adjusting mechanisms. Then adjust the brakes as follows, being sure the parking brake is fully released.

Adjustment

1. Remove access slot cover from brake support plate.

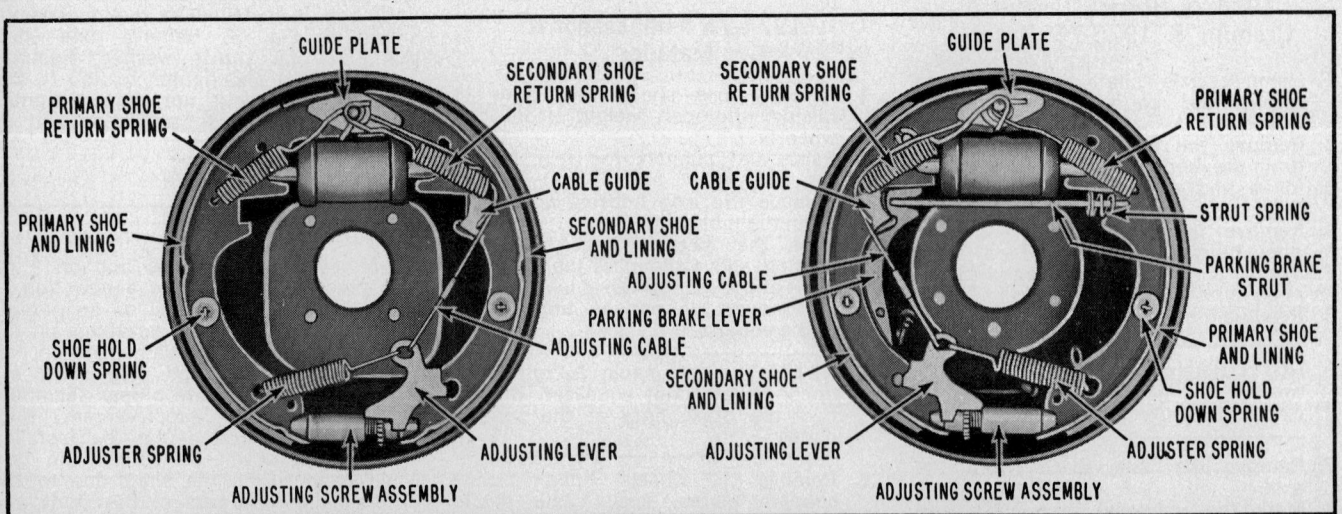

Fig. 4 Bendix Duo-Servo Brake (typical). Left view is a left front brake. Right view is a right rear brake

2. Using brake adjusting tool or screwdriver, rotate adjuster screw until wheel is locked.
3. Back off adjuster screw one complete turn.

NOTE: To back off adjuster screw, insert a piece of $\frac{1}{8}$ inch rod past adjuster screw and force adjusting lever off adjuster screw.

---

4. Install rubber access slot cover.
5. Following the initial adjustment and final assembly, check the brake pedal height to insure brake operation. Then drive the car forward and reverse, making 10 to 15 brake applications prior to road testing. This action balances the adjustment of the four brake units and raises the brake pedal.

PARKING BRAKE, ADJUST

1975-79 Pacer

1. Make sure service brakes are properly adjusted.
2. Apply and release parking brake several times.
3. Place parking lever in first notch from fully released position and place transmission in neutral.
4. Raise and support vehicle at rear axle using jack stands.
5. Loosen locknut and tighten cable adjuster until there is a heavy brake drag at rear wheels.
6. Loosen adjuster until heavy drag is just eliminated and tighten locknut.

1974-79 Exc. Pacer

With Adjustment Gauge J-23462

1. Make sure service brakes are properly adjusted.
2. Apply and release parking brake several times.
3. Raise and support vehicle at rear axle using jack stands.
4. Place parking brake in first notch from fully released position.
5. Place an inch lb. torque wrench on Parking Brake Cable Adjustment Gauge J-23462 and place gauge on from parking brake cable, centered between cable housing ferrule and cable equalizer.
6. Apply 50 inch lbs. of torque and note indicator reading. If reading is not within the green band, adjust parking brake at equalizer until satisfactory reading is obtained.
7. Release parking brake and check for brake drag. If brake drag is evident, inspect actuating cables and equalizer for freedom of movement and proper operation. Inspect cable condition, especially at areas where cable passes near exhaust components. Correct as necessary and readjust parking brake cable.

Without Adjustment Gauge J-23462

1. With service brakes properly adjusted, set parking brake pedal on the first notch from fully released position.

2. Tighten parking brake cable at equalizer to a point where the rear wheels are locked in forward rotation.
3. Release pedal and check for rear wheel drag—wheels should rotate freely.

BRAKE MASTER CYLINDER, REPLACE

1. Disconnect brake lines from master cylinder. Cap lines and master cylinder ports.
2. On models with manual brakes, disconnect master cylinder push rod at brake pedal.
3. On all models, remove nuts or bolts attaching master cylinder to dash panel or brake booster and remove master cylinder. On Matador and Pacer models, remove mounting bracket and boot retainer plate.
4. Install in the reverse order of removal and bleed the brake system.

POWER BRAKE UNIT

1. Disconnect booster push rod from brake pedal.
2. Remove vacuum hose from check valve.
3. Remove nuts and washers securing master cylinder to booster unit, then separate master cylinder from booster unit.

NOTE: Do not disconnect brake lines from master cylinder.

---

4. Remove booster unit to firewall attaching nuts and remove booster unit.

Rear Suspension

SHOCK ABSORBER, REPLACE

1. With the rear axle supported properly, disconnect lower end of shock absorber from stud on mounting bracket.
2. Remove upper mounting bracket from underbody.
3. Reverse procedure to install.

LEAF SPRINGS, REPLACE

1. Support rear axle, removing tension from springs.
2. Disconnect lower end of shock absorber from stud on mounting bracket.
3. Remove "U" bolts securing spring plate and spring to axle tube.
4. Disassemble rear shackle and remove eye bolt from spring forward mounting bracket.

NOTE: On Pacer, remove nuts attach-

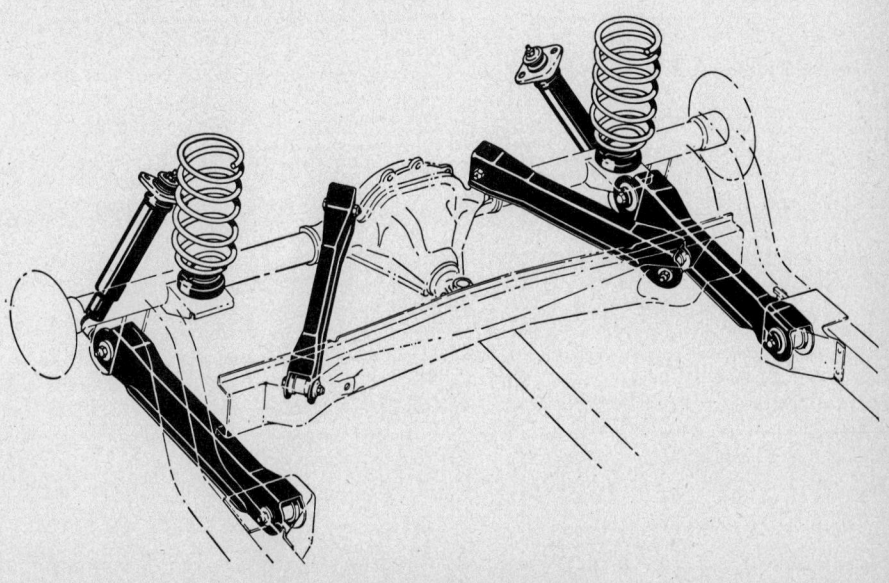

Fig. 1 Coil spring suspension (typical)

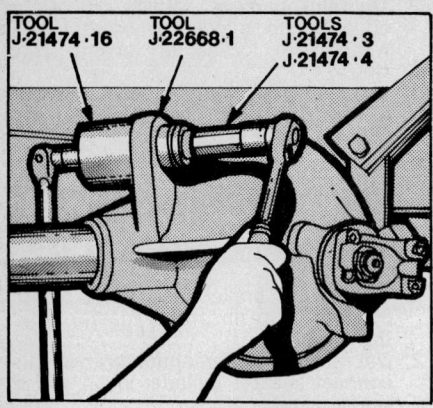

Fig. 2   Upper control arm rear bushing removal

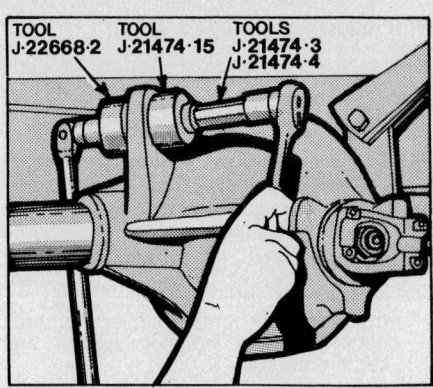

Fig. 3   Upper control arm rear bushing installation

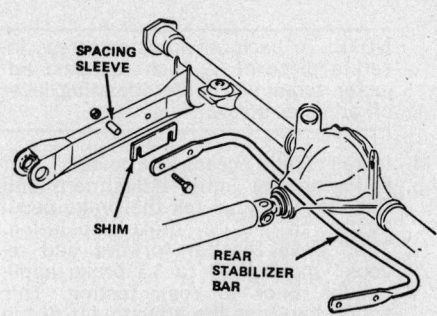

Fig. 4   Rear stabilizer bar. 1974-78 Ambassador & Matador

ing rear hanger bracket to mounting studs on side sill and remove spring.

5. Reverse procedure to install. Replace bushings as necessary.

COIL SPRINGS, REPLACE

1. Support vehicle at frame and support rear axle with a suitable jack.
2. Disconnect shock absorbers from lower mountings.
3. On 1975-79 models disconnect upper control arm at axle housing.
4. On all models, lower axle assembly until spring can be removed, Fig. 1.
5. Reverse procedure to install.

CONTROL ARMS & BUSHINGS, REPLACE

NOTE: Replace control arms one at a time to prevent axle assembly misalignment, making installation difficult.

Upper Control Arms

1. Support vehicle at frame.
2. Remove control arm bolts from frame crossmember and axle tube bracket.
3. To replace axle tube bracket bushings, refer to Figs. 2 & 3.
4. Reverse procedure to install.

Lower Control Arms

1. Support vehicle at rear axle.
2. Remove stabilizer bar, if equipped.
3. Remove control arm mount bolts from frame and axle tube brackets.

4. Reverse procedure to install

NOTE: Lower control arm bushings are not serviceable.

STABILIZER BAR, REPLACE
1974-78 Ambassador & Matador

1. Raise and support rear of vehicle.
2. Remove bolts attaching stabilizer bar to lower control arms, then remove stabilizer bar, shims (if used) and spacing sleeves, Fig. 4.
3. Install spacing sleeves in lower control arms.
4. Position stabilizer bar on lower control arms, then install attaching bolts and nuts. Hand tighten bolts and nuts only.
5. Install shims, if used, then torque stabilizer bar attaching bolts to 75 ft. lbs.

Front End and Steering Section

1975-79 Pacer

These models have an independent front coil spring front suspension system using unequal length upper and lower control arms, Figs. 1 and 1A. The coil springs are mounted between the lower control arms and the front crossmember with the lower arm functioning as the loaded member.

1974-79 Exc. Pacer

The front suspension, Figs. 2 & 3 is an independent linked type, with the coil springs located between seats in the wheel house panels and seats attached to the upper control arms.

Direct acting telescoping shock absorbers are located inside the coil springs.

Each upper control arm assembly has two rubber bushings attached to the wheel house panel and a ball joint attached to the steering knuckle.

Each lower control arm has a rubber bushing attached to the front crossmember and a ball joint attached to the steering knuckle.

The lower control arm strut rods are attached to the lower control arms and body side sill brackets.

LUBRICATION

Lubrication is required every 25,000 miles on 1974 models and 30,000 on 1975-79 models.

Under severe driving conditions, such as dusty or extreme wet conditions, earlier lubrication is recommended. Under these conditions the suspension system should be inspected every 12,000 miles or one year whichever occurs first, and lubricated as required.

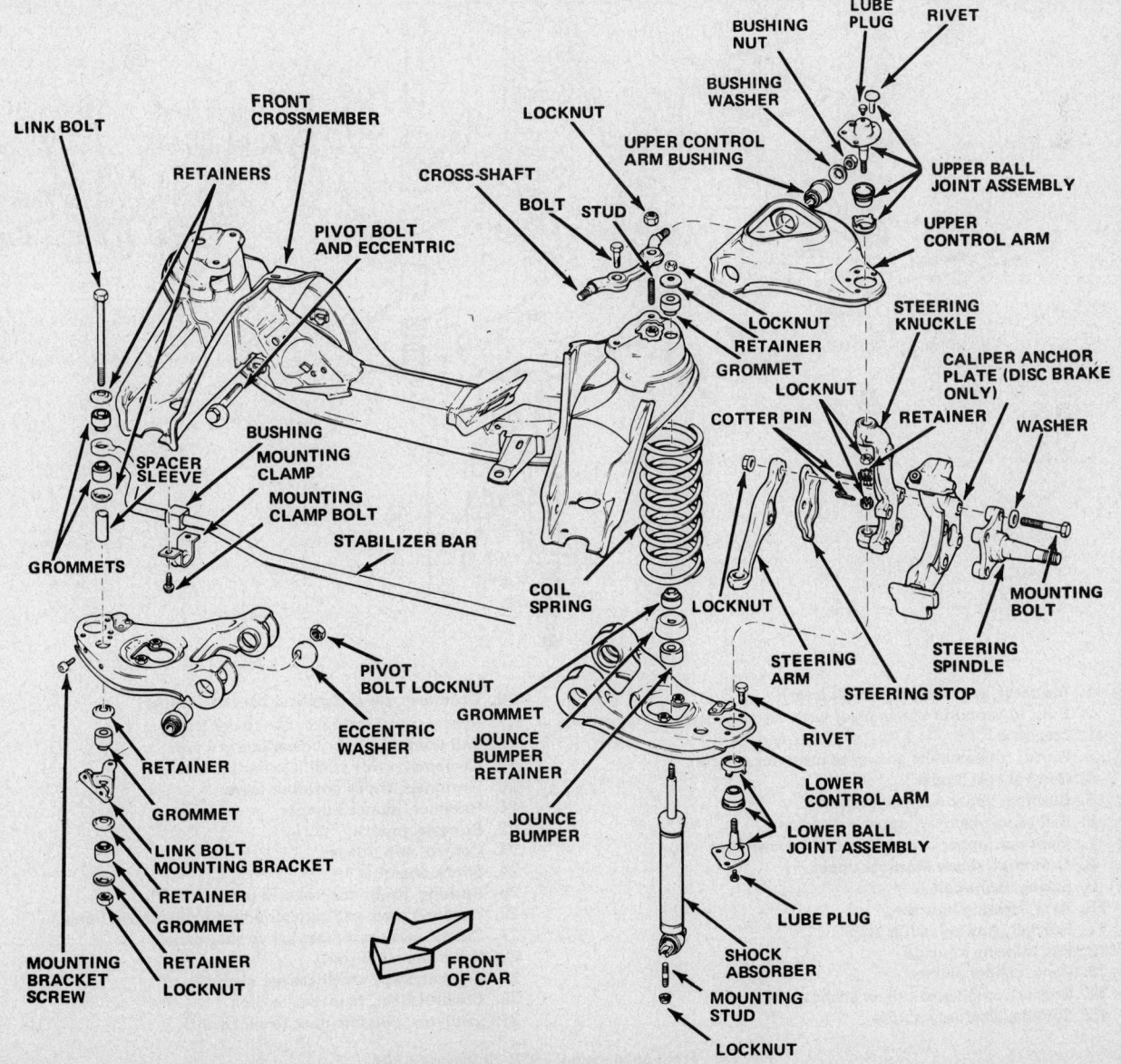

Fig. 1   Front suspension. 1975-79 Pacer 6 cyl.

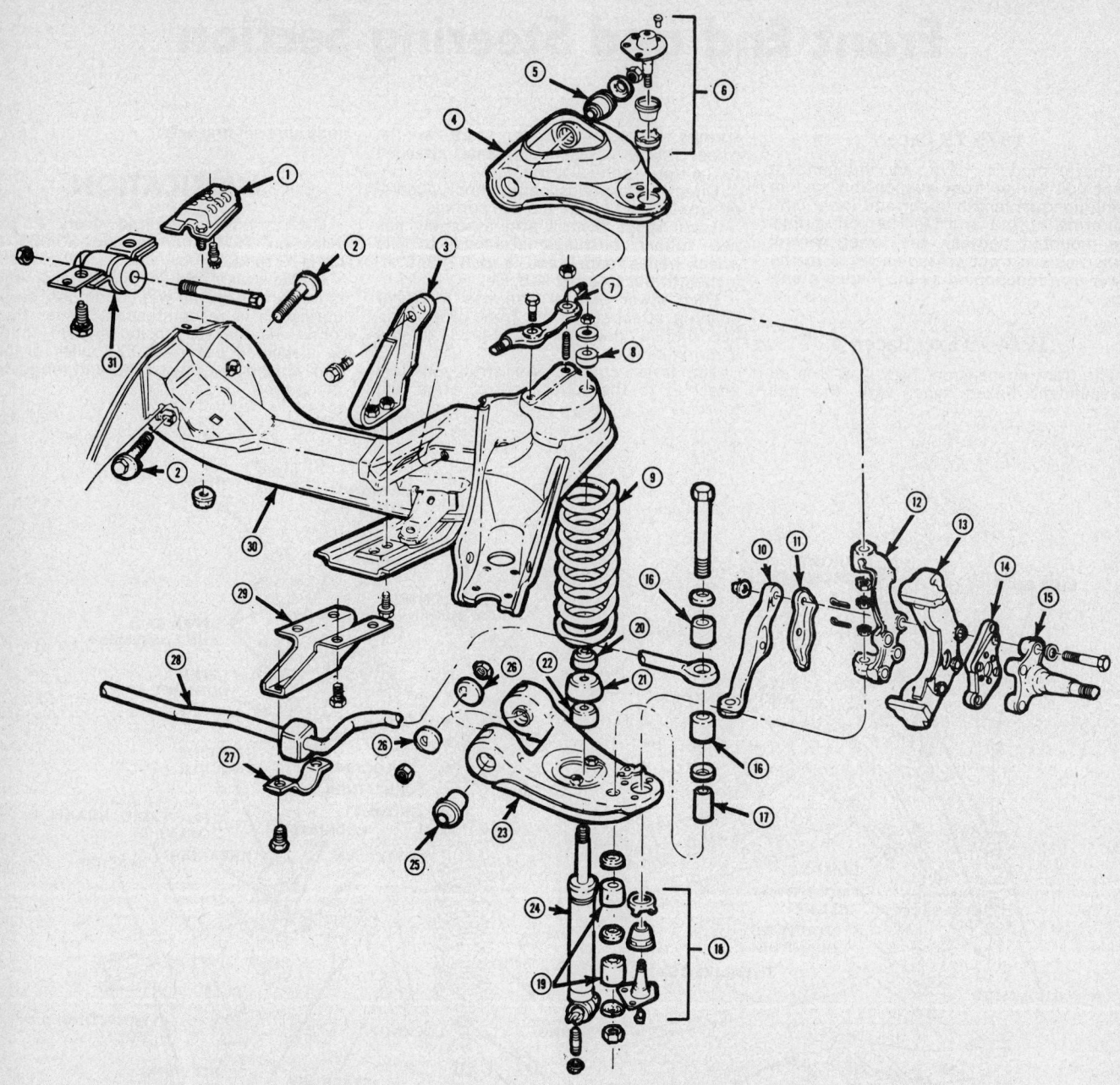

1. Insulator, crossmember to sill (rear)
2. Bolt, lower control arm pivot with caster and camber adjusting eccentric
3. Brace, crossmember to engine insulator support
4. Control arm, upper
5. Bushing, upper control arm pivot
6. Ball joint assembly, upper control arm
7. Pivot bar, upper control arm to crossmember
8. Grommet, shock absorber upper
9. Spring, front coil
10. Arm, steering knuckle
11. Bracket, turning radius stop
12. Pin, steering knuckle
13. Plate, caliper anchor
14. Bracket, spindle to caliper anchor adapter
15. Spindle, steering knuckle

16. Grommet, sway stabilizer bar bolt (upper)
17. Spacer, sway stabilizer bar to control arm
18. Ball joint assembly, lower control arm .
19. Grommet, sway stabilizer bar bolt (lower)
20. Grommet, shock absorber lower
21. Retainer, jounce bumper
22. Bumper, jounce
23. Control arm, lower
24. Shock absorber
25. Bushing, lower control arm pivot
26. Washer, caster and camber adjusting eccentric (inner)
27. Clamp, sway stabilizer bar to sill bracket
28. Bar, sway stabilizer
29. Bracket, sway stabilizer bar clamp to sill
30. Crossmember, front suspension
31. Insulator, crossmember to sill (front)

Fig. 1A   Front suspension. 1978-79 Pacer V8-304

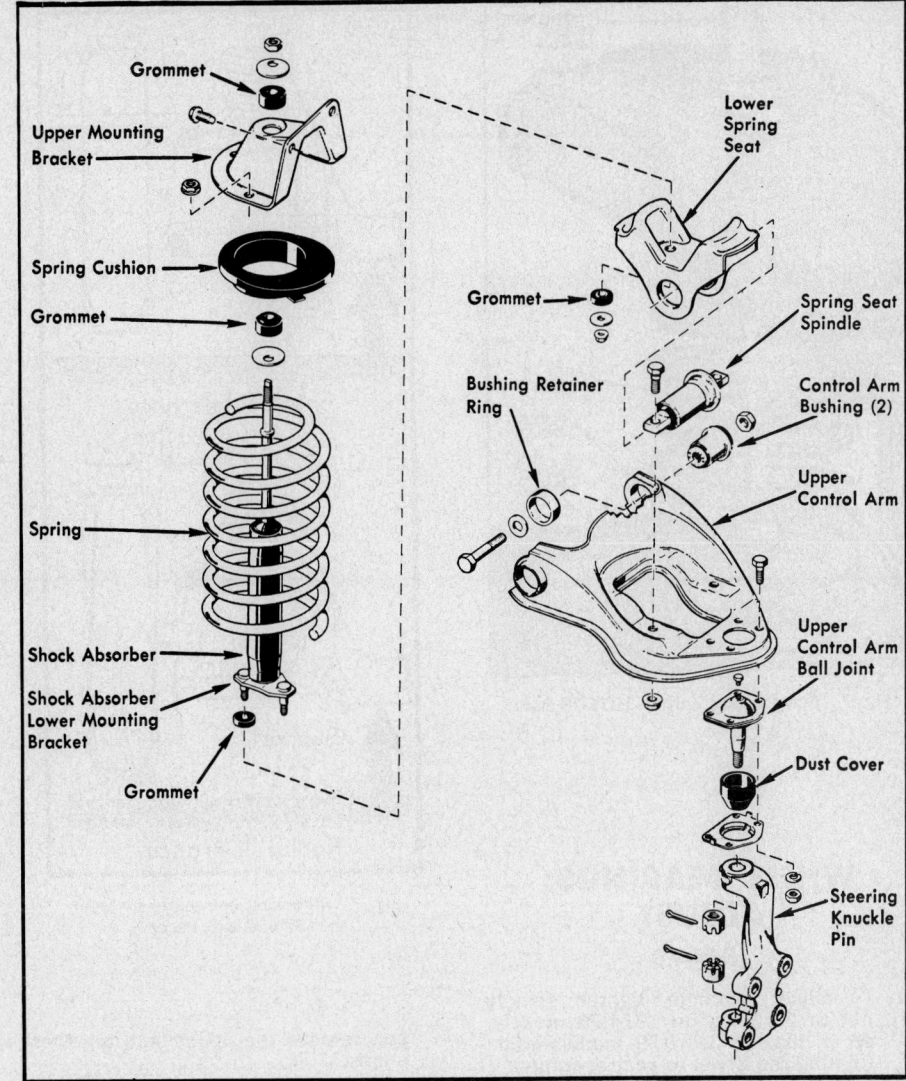

Fig. 2 Front suspension upper control arm components. 1974-79 except Pacer

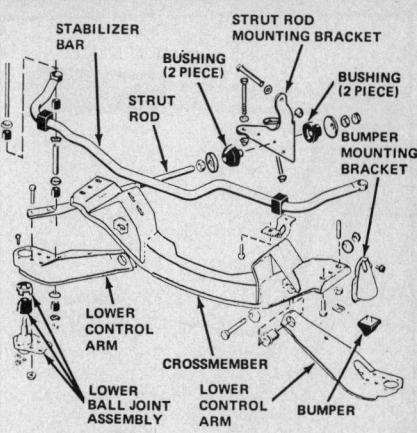

Fig. 3 Front suspension lower control arm components. 1974-79 except Pacer

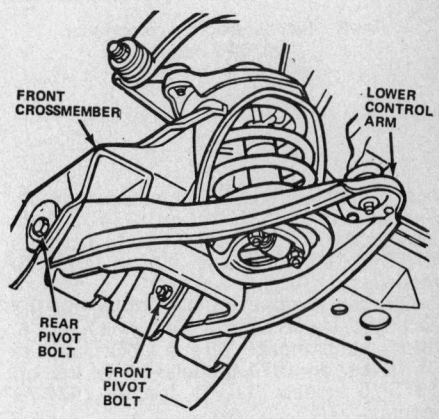

Fig. 4 Caster and camber adjustment. 1975-79 Pacer

WHEEL ALIGNMENT

1975-79 Pacer

Caster is adjusted by rotating the rear pivot bolt eccentric, Fig. 4. After adjustment, torque locknut to 95 ft. lbs. on 1975-76 and 110 ft. lbs. on 1977-79 models.

Camber is adjusted by rotating both front and rear lower control arm pivot bolt eccentrics, Fig. 4. After adjustment, torque locknut to 95 ft. lbs. on 1975-76 and 110 ft. lbs. on 1977-79 models.

1974-79 Exc. Pacer

Caster is obtained by moving the two adjusting nuts on the threaded strut rod, Fig. 5. One nut is on each side of the mounting bracket. Therefore, moving the nuts on the rod will move the lower control arm to front or rear for desired

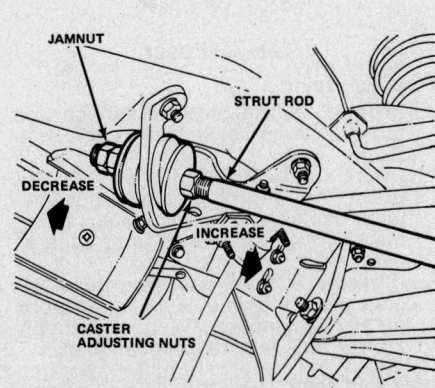

Fig. 5 Caster adjustment. 1974-79 except Pacer

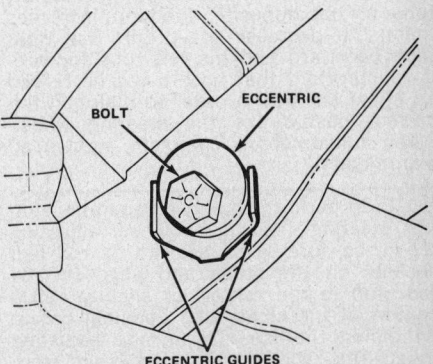

Fig. 6 Camber adjustment. 1974-79 except Pacer

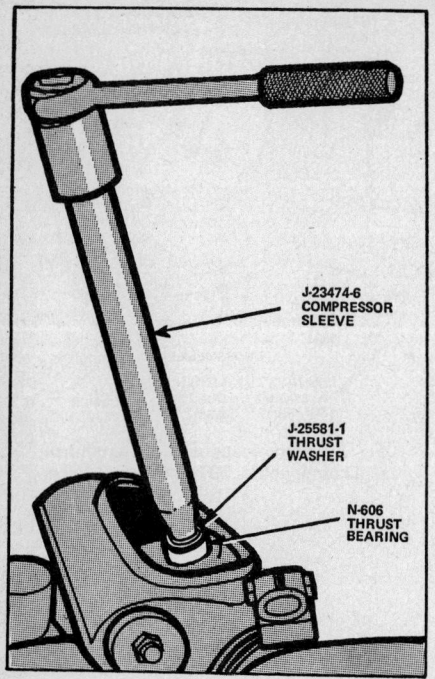

Fig. 8   Installing Spring compressor.
1975-79 Pacer

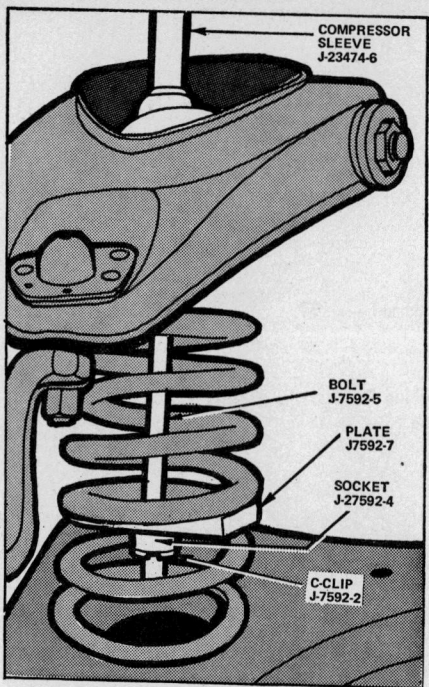

Fig. 9   Compressing spring. 1975-79 Pacer

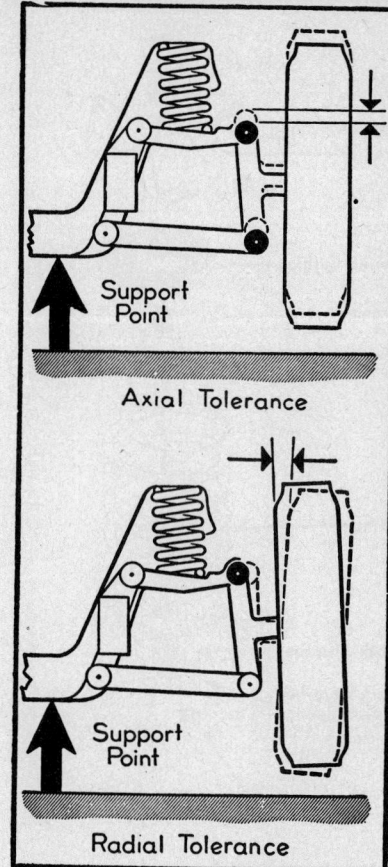

Fig. 7   Checking ball joints for wear.
1974-79 exc. Pacer

caster angle. After adjustment, torque adjusting nuts to 65 ft. lbs. on 1974-79 models. On 1974-76 models, torque locknuts to 55 ft. lbs. or 75 ft. lbs. on 1977-79 models.

Camber is obtained by turning on the eccentric lower control arm bolt, Fig. 6. After adjustment, torque lock nut to 95 ft.-lbs. on 1974 models, 85 ft. lbs. on 1975-76 models, 110 ft. lbs. on 1977-79 models.

TOE-IN, ADJUST

To adjust toe-in, loosen the clamps at both ends of the adjustable tubes on each tie rod. Turn the tubes an equal amount until the toe-in is correct. Turning the right tube in the direction the wheels revolve when the car is going forward increases the toe-in and turning the left tube in the opposite direction increases toe-in. To decrease toe-in turn the right tube backward and the left tube forward. It is important that both tubes be turned an equal amount in order to maintain the correct position of the steering wheel. When adjustment is complete, tighten all clamp bolts.

NOTE: In performing service operations on the steering linkage or when adjusting toe-in, be sure to square the tie rod ball sockets on the studs and align the tie rod stud in the center, or slightly above center, of the cross tube opening, before tightening the steering linkage adjusting tube. This will prevent the stud from contacting the side of the cross tube opening, which would otherwise result in noise problems or damage.

WHEEL BEARINGS, ADJUST

1974-79

1. To adjust bearings, tighten spindle nut to 22 ft-lbs on 1974-76 models, 25 ft. lbs. on 1977-79 models while rotating the wheel to seat bearings.
2. Then loosen spindle nut 1/3 turn and with wheel rotating, retorque spindle nut to 2-10 inch pound on 1974, and 6 inch pounds on 1975-79.
3. Place the nut retainer on spindle nut with the slots of the retainer aligned with the cotter pin hole on the spindle.
4. Install cotter pin and dust cap.

WHEEL BEARINGS, REPLACE

(Disc Brakes)

1. Remove two thirds of the total fluid capacity of the master cylinder reservoir to prevent fluid overflow when the caliper pistons are pushed back on their bores.
2. Raise car and remove front wheels.
3. Disconnect hydraulic tube from mounting bracket. Do not disconnect any hydraulic fitting.
4. Holding the lower edge of the caliper, remove the lower bolt. Any shims that fall out at this point should be labeled to insure that they be replaced in their original position.
5. Holding the upper edge of the cali-

per, remove the upper bolt, tag these shims.
6. Hang caliper from upper suspension to prevent strain being placed on brake hose.
7. Remove spindle nut and hub and disc assembly. Grease retainer and inner bearing can now be removed.

CHECKING BALL JOINTS FOR WEAR

1975-79 Pacer

Lower Ball Joint

1. Position vehicle on level surface and remove lower ball joint lubrication plug.
2. Insert a 2 to 3 in. piece of stiff wire or thin rod into plug hole until it contacts ball stud, then accurately scribe mark on wire or rod at outer edge of plug hole.
3. If distance from ball stud to outer edge of plug hole is 7/16 in. or more on 1975-77 models, 3/8 in. or more on 1978-79 models, replace ball joint.

Upper Ball Joint

1. Position suitable jack under lower control arm and raise vehicle until wheel is off floor.

2. Move top of tire toward and away from center of vehicle, if any looseness or play is present, replace ball joint.
3. Using a suitable tool, move upper control arm up and down. If looseness or play is present, replace ball joint.

1974-79 Except Pacer

Before checking ball joints for wear, make sure the front wheel bearings are properly adjusted and that the control arms are tight.

Referring to Fig. 7, raise wheel with a jack placed under the frame as shown. Then test by moving the wheel up and down to check axial play, and rocking it at the top and bottom to measure radial play.

The upper ball joint should be replaced if total travel when rocking wheel and tire exceeds .160".

The lower ball joint is spring loaded and should be replaced if there is any noticeable lateral shake.

BALL JOINTS, REPLACE

1975-79 Pacer

Upper Ball Joint

1. Raise vehicle and remove wheel and tire assembly.
2. Using a suitable jack, raise lower control arm approximately 1 in.
3. Remove cotter pin and retaining nut from upper ball joint stud.
4. Install tool J-9656 onto ball joint stud.
5. Lower jack supporting control arm slightly, then strike tool with hammer to loosen ball stud in steering knuckle.
6. Chisel heads from rivets attaching ball joint to upper control arm, then drive rivets out using a punch.
7. Remove tool from ball stud, then remove ball joint assembly.
8. Position ball joint on upper control arm and install nuts and bolts.

NOTE: Install bolts from bottom with nuts on top. Torque nuts to 25 ft. lbs.

9. Reverse procedure to assemble. Torque ball joint stud nut to 75 ft. lbs.

Lower Ball Joint

1. Raise vehicle and remove wheel and tire assembly.
2. Remove brake drum or caliper and rotor assembly.

NOTE: When removing caliper do not damage brake tubing or hose. Secure caliper to frame with wire.

3. Remove steering arm to steering knuckle attaching bolts and position steering arm aside.
4. Disconnect stabilizer bar link bolt at lower control arm, if equipped.
5. Support lower control arm with a suitable jack and remove cotter pin and nut from lower ball joint stud.
6. Install tool No. J-9656 on ball stud and remove jack.
7. Strike tool with hammer to loosen ball stud in steering knuckle.
8. Support lower control arm with jack and remove tool.

9. Disengage ball stud from steering knuckle and position components aside.

NOTE: Use wire to suspend components from upper control arm.

10. Chisel heads from rivets attaching ball joint to lower control arm, then drive rivets out using a punch and remove ball joint.
11. Position ball joint on lower control arm and install nuts and bolts.

NOTE: Install bolts from top with nuts on bottom. Torque bolts to 25 ft. lbs.

12. Reverse procedure to assemble. Torque lower ball joint stud nut to 75 ft. lbs., steering arm to knuckle bolts to 80 ft. lbs. on 1975-76 or 55 ft. lbs. on 1977-79, and the stabilizer bar link bolt to 8 ft. lbs. on 1975-76 or 7 ft. lbs. on 1977-79.

1974-79 Except Pacer

Upper Ball Joint

1. Position a 2x4x5 in. block of wood on side sill under upper control arm.
2. Raise vehicle and support at frame side sills.
3. Remove wheel and brake drum or caliper and rotor assembly.

NOTE: When removing caliper do not damage brake tubing or hose. Secure caliper to frame with wire.

4. Remove cotter pin and retaining nut from upper ball joint stud.
5. Install tool No. J-9656 on ball stud, then using a hammer strike tool to loosen ball stud in steering knuckle.
6. Support lower control arm with a suitable jack.
7. Chisel heads from rivets attaching ball joint to upper control arm, then drive rivets out using a punch.
8. Remove tool from ball stud and ball joint from steering knuckle.
9. Position ball joint on control arm and install nuts and bolts. Torque bolts to 25 ft. lbs.
10. Reverse procedure to assemble. Torque ball joint stud nut to 40 ft. lbs. on 1974-76 models or 75 ft. lbs. on 1977-79.

Lower Ball Joint

1. Position a 2x4x5 in. block of wood on side sill under upper control arm.
2. Raise vehicle and support at frame side sills.
3. Remove wheel and brake drum or caliper and rotor assembly.

NOTE: When removing caliper do not damage brake tubes or hoses. Secure caliper to frame with wire.

4. Disconnect strut rod from lower control arm and steering arm from steering knuckle.
5. Remove lower ball joint stud cotter pin and retaining nut.
6. Install tool No. 9656 on ball stud, then strike tool with hammer to loosen ball stud in steering knuckle.
7. Support lower control arm with a suitable jack.

8. Chisel heads from rivets attaching ball joint to lower control arm, then drive rivets out using a punch.
9. Remove tool from ball stud and ball joint from steering knuckle and lower control arm.
10. Position ball joint on lower control arm and install attaching bolts loosely.
11. Connect strut to lower control arm and torque bolts to 75 ft. lbs. on 1974-79 models.
12. Torque ball joint to lower control arm attaching bolts to 25 ft. lbs.
13. Lubricate steering stop, then install ball stud on steering knuckle. Torque stud nut to 40 ft. lbs. on 1974-76 and 75 ft. lbs. on 1977-79 models. Install cotter pin.
14. Install wheel and brake drum or caliper and rotor and lower vehicle.

SHOCK ABSORBER, REPLACE

Pacer

1. Disconnect shock absorber at upper mounting.
2. Raise and support vehicle.
3. Disconnect shock absorber at lower mounting.
4. Remove shock absorber.
5. Reverse procedure to install.

Exc. Pacer

After disconnecting shock absorber from wheelhouse panel at top and lower spring seat at the bottom, withdraw shock absorber out of top of wheelhouse.

SPRING, REPLACE

1975-79 Pacer

1. Remove shock absorber, then the stabilizer bar link bolt at lower control arm, if equipped.
2. On models with drum brakes, remove wheel, tire and drum. On disc brake models, remove wheel, tire, caliper and rotor.
3. Remove steering arm to knuckle attaching bolts and position arm aside.
4. Compress spring, Figs. 8 and 9.
5. Remove cotter pin and nut from lower ball joint, then using tool J-9656 and a hammer, disengage stud from steering knuckle and position knuckle aside.

NOTE: Use wire to support steering knuckle otherwise brake hoses may be damaged.

6. Position lower control arm aside and relieve spring tension. When all tension is relieved, remove tool and spring.

1974-79 Exc. Pacer

1. Remove shock absorber.
2. Install spring compressor (J-23474) through upper spring seat opening, Fig. 10. Place tool lower attaching screws through shock absorber mounting holes in the lower spring seat. Install tool lower retainer.

3. Remove lower spring seat pivot retaining nuts.
4. Tighten compressor until spring is compressed approximately 1".
5. Raise and support front of car under frame allowing control arms to fall free of lower spring seat. Remove wheel.
6. Pull lower spring seat away from car. Loosen compressor and allow lower spring seat to come out.
7. When all spring tension is released, remove tool lower retainer spring seat and spring.

STEERING GEAR, REPLACE

1976-79 Pacer

NOTE: Some 1976 and all 1977-79 models use a new design front crossmember. The new crossmember has a larger steering gear mounting plate and utilizes a reinforcement brace between mounting plate and left side engine support bracket.

Use the following procedure when replacing steering gear on vehicles utilizing this new design crossmember.

1. Unlock steering column, then raise and support front vehicle.
2. Remove reinforcement brace to crossmember and left engine support bracket attaching bolts, then remove brace.
3. On models with power steering, position a drain pan under steering gear housing and disconnect power steering hoses at gear.

NOTE: Cap hoses and connections to prevent entry of dirt.

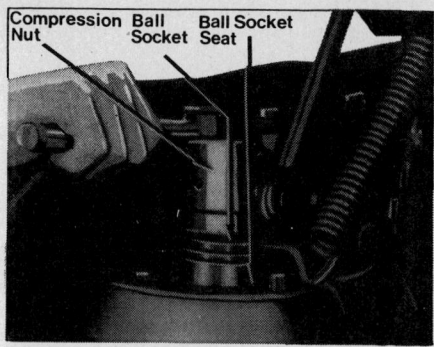

Fig. 10   Installation of spring compressor. 1974-79 exc. Pacer

4. Remove flexible coupling pinch bolt, then disconnect coupling from steering pinion shaft.
5. Turn wheels in direction of tie rod to be disconnected, then using a floor jack, raise lower control arm at least 2 in. Remove cotter pin and retaining nut from tie rod end and using tool J-3295, disconnect tie rod from steering arm.
6. Remove bolts attaching steering gear mounting clamp to right side of crossmember.
7. Remove steering gear housing to crossmember attaching nuts, then using a blunt punch, remove bolts, washers, sleeves and grommets from gear housing.
8. Rotate bottom of gear housing toward front of front of vehicle until pinion shaft is parallel with skid plate, then slide gear toward right side of vehicle until housing and tube clear mounting plate.

1975-76 Pacer

1. Unlock steering column and raise vehicle.
2. Remove flexible coupling to intermediate shaft flange attaching nuts.
3. Turn wheels to stop in direction of tie rod being disconnected, then using a floor jack, raise lower control arm at least 2 inches. Remove cotter pin and retaining nut from tie rod end and using tool J-3295, disconnect tie rod end from steering arm.
4. On models with power steering, disconnect and cap hoses.
5. Remove steering gear attaching bolts and the gear.

1974-79 Except Pacer

Manual Steering
1. Remove flexible coupling bolts.
2. Remove pitman arm, using a suitable puller.
3. Remove mounting screws and lower steering gear from vehicle.

Power Steering
1. Disconnect pressure and return hoses from gear. Raise hoses above pump level to keep oil from draining out of pump.
2. Remove flexible coupling bolt nuts, noting the different nut sizes to insure correct assembly.
3. Remove pitman arm with a suitable puller.
4. Remove gear attaching bolts.
5. Slide lower shaft free of coupling flange, then remove gear.
6. Reverse procedure to install.

BUICK
EXC. SKYHAWK

INDEX OF SERVICE OPERATIONS

GRILLE IDENTIFICATION

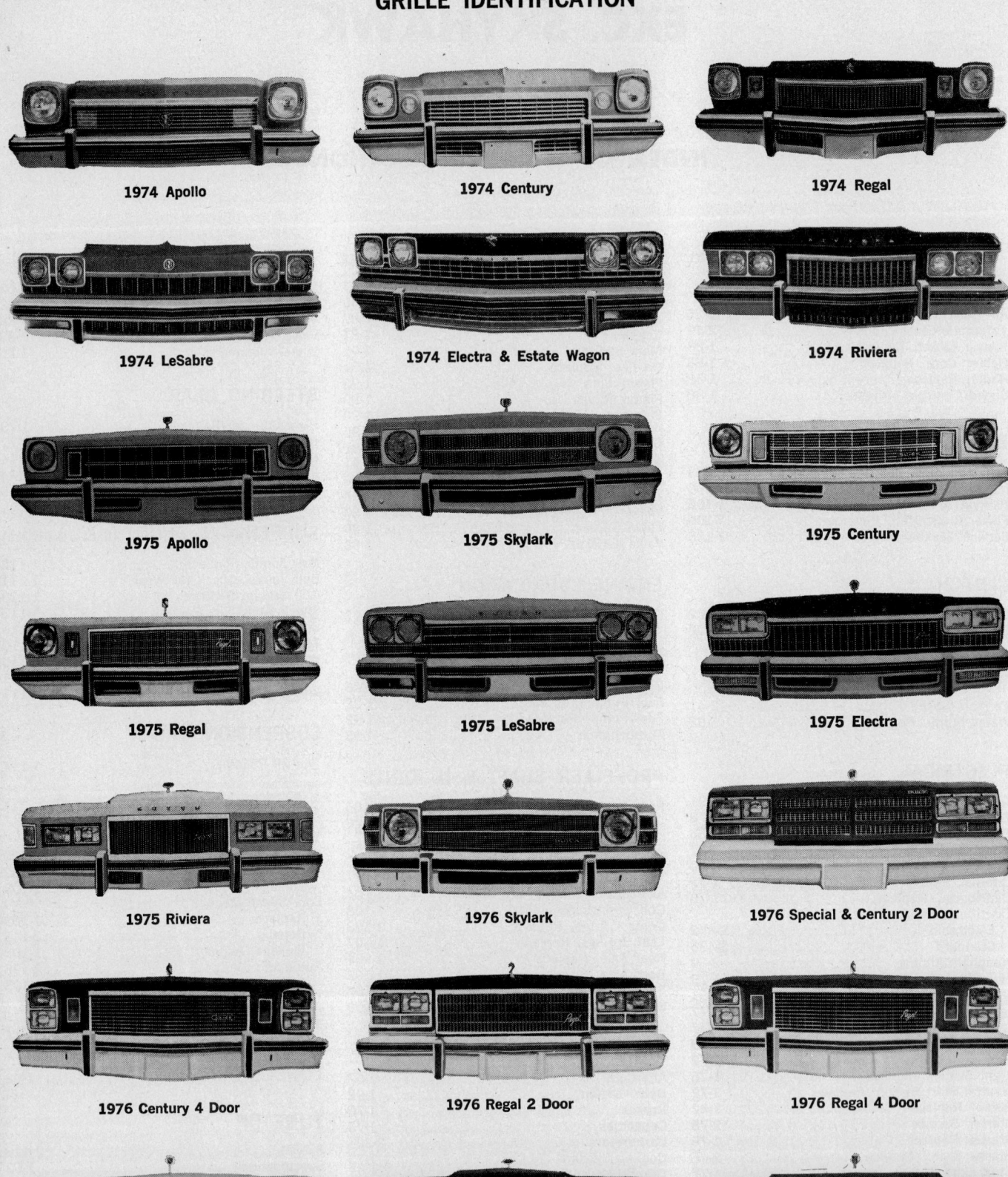

1974 Apollo

1974 Century

1974 Regal

1974 LeSabre

1974 Electra & Estate Wagon

1974 Riviera

1975 Apollo

1975 Skylark

1975 Century

1975 Regal

1975 LeSabre

1975 Electra

1975 Riviera

1976 Skylark

1976 Special & Century 2 Door

1976 Century 4 Door

1976 Regal 2 Door

1976 Regal 4 Door

1976 Electra

1976 Riviera

1977 Skylark

GRILLE IDENTIFICATION—Continued

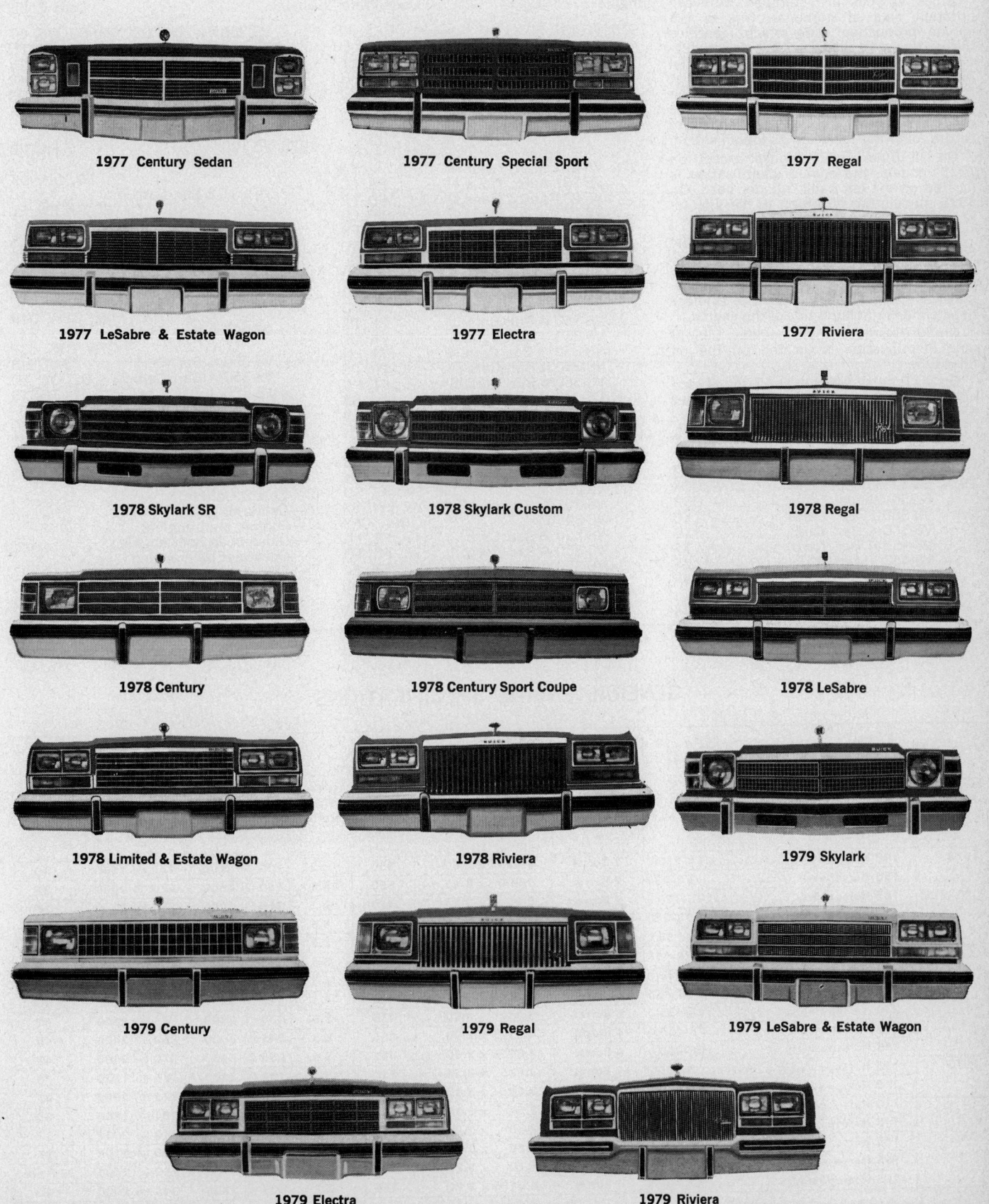

1977 Century Sedan

1977 Century Special Sport

1977 Regal

1977 LeSabre & Estate Wagon

1977 Electra

1977 Riviera

1978 Skylark SR

1978 Skylark Custom

1978 Regal

1978 Century

1978 Century Sport Coupe

1978 LeSabre

1978 Limited & Estate Wagon

1978 Riviera

1979 Skylark

1979 Century

1979 Regal

1979 LeSabre & Estate Wagon

1979 Electra

1979 Riviera

ENGINE IDENTIFICATION

Buick engines are stamped with two different sets of numbers. One is the engine production code which identifies the engine and its approximate production date. The other is the engine serial number which is the same number that is found on the vehicle identification plate. To identify an engine, look for the production code prefix letters, then refer to the following table for its identification.

On all Buick built engines except on 1975 models, the engine identification is located on the left bank cylinder head. On 1975 models the fifth digit in the VIN denotes the engine used.

On Chevrolet built 6-250 engines, the code is stamped on the cylinder block next to the distributor. On Chevrolet built V8 engines, the code is stamped on the engine case pad located below the cylinder head on the right hand side of the engine.

On all Oldsmobile built engines, the engine identification is located on the oil filler tube.

On all Pontiac built engines, the engine identification is located on the right front of the cylinder block.

Engine	Code Prefix
1974 6-250 Auto. Trans.[5]	CCW, CCX
6-250 Manual Trans.[5]	CCR
V8-350 2 Bar. Carb.	XC
V8-350 4 Bar. Carb.	XB
V8-455 4 Bar. Carb.	XF
V8-455 (Stage 1)	XS
V8-455 (Riviera G.S.)	XA

Engine	Code Prefix
1975 V6-231	C
6-250[5]	D
V8-260[4]	F
V8-350 2 Bar. Carb.	H
V8-350 4 Bar. Carb.	J
V8-400[3]	S
V8-455	T
1976 V6-231 Man. Trans.[1]	FA
V6-231 Auto. Trans.[1]	FB, FC
V6-231 Auto. Trans.[1]	FD, FE
V6-231 Auto. Trans.[2]	FF, FG
V6-231 Auto. Trans.[1]	FP, FR
V8-260 Man. Trans.[1][4]	QA, QD
V8-260 Auto. Trans.[1][4]	QB, QC
V8-260 Auto. Trans.[2][4]	TE, TJ
V8-350 2 Bar. Carb.[1]	PA, PB
V8-350 2 Bar. Carb.[1]	PC, PD
V8-350 4 Bar. Carb.[1]	PE, PF
V8-350 4 Bar. Carb.[2]	PK, PL
V8-350 4 Bar. Carb.[2]	PM, PN
V8-350 4 Bar. Carb.[2]	PR, PS
V8-350 4 Bar. Carb.[1]	PT, PU
V8-455 Auto. Trans.[1]	SA
V8-455 Auto. Trans.[2]	SB
1977 V6-231	RA, RB
V6-231	SG, SI, SJ, SK, SL
V6-231	SM, SN, ST, SU
V8-301[3]	YF, YJ, YW, YX
V8-305[5]	CPA, CPY
V8-350 2 Bar. Carb.	FA, FB, FK
V8-350 4 Bar. Carb.	FC, FD, FG
V8-350 4 Bar. Carb.	FH, FL
V8-350[4]	QK, QL

Engine	Code Prefix
V8-350[4]	QP, QQ, Q2, Q3, Q6, Q7
V8-350[4]	Q8, Q9, TK, TL, TN
V8-350[4]	TO, TQ, TX, TY
V8-350[5]	CKM, CKR
V8-403[4]	UA, UB, U2, U3
V8-403[4]	VA, VB, VJ, VK
1978 V6-196	PA, PB
V6-231 2 Bar. Carb.[6]	EA, EG, OH, OK
V6-231 2 Bar. Carb.[6]	EG, EI, EJ, EK, EL
V6-231 2 Bar. Carb.[7]	EO, OL
V6-231 4 Bar. Carb.[7]	EP, ER, ES
V8-301[3]	XA, XC
V8-305 2 Bar. Carb.[5]	CEK, CPZ, CRU, CRX
V8-305 2 Bar. Carb.[5]	CRY, CRZ, CTM, CTR
V8-305 2 Bar. Carb.[5]	CTW, CTX, C3P
V8-350 4 Bar. Carb.	MA, MB
V8-350 4 Bar. Carb.[4]	Q2, Q3, TO
V8-350 4 Bar. Carb.[4]	TP, TQ, TS
V8-350 4 Bar. Carb.	CHM, CKM, CMC
V8-403[4]	UA, UB, U2
V8-403[4]	U3, VA, VB

[1]—Except California
[2]—California
[3]—Pontiac built engine.
[4]—Oldsmobile built engine.
[5]—Chevrolet built engine.
[6]—Except turbocharged engine.
[7]—Turbocharged engine.

GENERAL ENGINE SPECIFICATIONS

Year	Engine	Carburetor	Bore and Stroke	Piston Displacement, Cubic Inches	Compression Ratio	Maximum Brake H.P. @ R.P.M.	Maximum Torque Lbs. Ft. @ R.P.M.	Normal Oil Pressure Pounds
1974	100 Horsepower[2]............6-250[1]	1 Barrel	3.875 x 3.53	250	8.25	100 @ 3600	175 @ 1600	40
	150 Horsepower[2]............V8-350	2 Barrel	3.800 x 3.85	350	8.5	150 @ 3600	270 @ 2000	37
	165 Horsepower[2]............V8-350[3]	2 Barrel	3.800 x 3.85	350	8.5	165 @ 3800	285 @ 2000	37
	175 Horsepower[2]............V8-350	4 Barrel	3.800 x 3.85	350	8.5	175 @ 3800	260 @ 2000	37
	195 Horsepower[2]............V8-350[3]	4 Barrel	3.800 x 3.85	350	8.5	195 @ 4000	280 @ 2000	37
	175 Horsepower[2]............V8-455	2 Barrel	4.3125 x 3.90	455	8.5	175 @ 3400	355 @ 2000	40
	190 Horsepower[2]............V8-455[3]	2 Barrel	4.3125 x 3.90	455	8.5	190 @ 3600	370 @ 2000	40
	210 Horsepower[2]............V8-455	4 Barrel	4.3125 x 3.90	455	8.5	210 @ 3600	335 @ 2200	40
	230 Horsepower[2]............V8-455[3]	4 Barrel	4.3125 x 3.90	455	8.5	230 @ 3800	355 @ 2200	40
	245 Horsepower[2]............V8-455[4]	4 Barrel	4.3125 x 3.90	455	8.5	245 @ 4000	360 @ 2400	40
	255 Horsepower[2]............V8-455[4]	4 Barrel	4.3125 x 3.90	455	8.5	255 @ 4400	370 @ 2800	40
1975	105 Horsepower[2]............6-250[1]	1 Barrel	3.875 x 3.53	250	8.25	105 @ 3800	185 @ 1200	40
	110 Horsepower[2]............V6-231	2 Barrel	3.80 x 3.40	231	8.0	110 @ 4000	175 @ 2000	37
	110 Horsepower[2]............V8-260[5]	2 Barrel	3.50 x 3.385	260	8.0	110 @ 3400	205 @ 1600	35
	145 Horsepower[2]............V8-350	2 Barrel	3.80 x 3.85	350	8.0	145 @ 3200	270 @ 2000	37
	165 Horsepower[2]............V8-350	4 Barrel	3.80 x 3.85	350	8.0	165 @ 3800	260 @ 2200	37
	190 Horsepower[2]............V8-400[6]	4 Barrel	4.12 x 3.75	400	7.6	190 @ 3400	350 @ 2400	55–60
	205 Horsepower[2]............V8-455	4 Barrel	4.3125 x 3.90	455	7.9	205 @ 3800	345 @ 2000	40

Continued

GENERAL ENGINE SPECIFICATIONS—Continued

Year	Engine	Carburetor	Bore and Stroke	Piston Displacement, Cubic Inches	Compression Ratio	Maximum Brake H.P. @ R.P.M.	Maximum Torque Lbs. Ft. @ R.P.M.	Normal Oil Pressure Pounds
1976	110 Horsepower② V6-231	2 Barrel	3.80 x 3.40	231	8.0	110 @ 4000	175 @ 2000	37
	110 Horsepower② V8-260⑤	2 Barrel	3.50 x 3.385	260	8.5	110 @ 3400	210 @ 1600	—
	145 Horsepower② V8-350⑦	2 Barrel	3.80 x 3.85	350	8.0	145 @ 3200	270 @ 2000	37
	160 Horsepower② V8-350⑧	4 Barrel	3.80 x 3.85	350	8.0	160 @ 3800	260 @ 2200	37
	165 Horsepower② V8-350	4 Barrel	3.80 x 3.85	350	8.0	165 @ 3800	260 @ 2200	37
	Horsepower② V8-455	4 Barrel	4.3125 x 3.90	455	7.9	—	—	40
1977	105 Horsepower② V6-231	2 Barrel	3.80 x 3.40	231	8.0	105 @ 3200	185 @ 2000	37
	135 Horsepower② V8-301⑥	2 Barrel	4.00 x 3.00	301	8.2	135 @ 4000	250 @ 1600	38–42
	145 Horsepower② V8-305①	2 Barrel	3.736 x 3.48	305	8.5	145 @ 3800	245 @ 2400	32–40
	140 Horsepower② V8-350	2 Barrel	3.80 x 3.85	350	8.1	140 @ 3200	280 @ 1400	37
	155 Horsepower② V8-350	4 Barrel	3.80 x 3.85	350	8.0	155 @ 3400	275 @ 1800	37
	170 Horsepower② V8-350	4 Barrel	3.80 x 3.85	350	8.0	170 @ 3800	275 @ 2400	37
	170 Horsepower② V8-350①	4 Barrel	4.00 x 3.48	350	8.5	170 @ 3800	270 @ 2400	32–40
	170 Horsepower② V8-350⑤	4 Barrel	4.057 x 3.385	350	8.5	170 @ 3800	275 @ 2400	30–45
	185 Horsepower② V8-403⑤	4 Barrel	4.351 x 3.385	403	8.5	185 @ 3600	315 @ 2400	30–45
1978	90 Horsepower② V6-196	2 Barrel	3.50 x 3.40	196	8.0	90 @ 3600	165 @ 2000	37
	105 Horsepower② V6-231	2 Barrel	3.80 x 3.40	231	8.0	105 @ 3400	185 @ 2000	37
	150 Horsepower② V6-231⑨	2 Barrel	3.80 x 3.40	231	8.0	150 @ 3200	245 @ 2400	37
	165 Horsepower② V6-231⑨	4 Barrel	3.80 x 3.40	231	8.0	165 @ 4000	265 @ 2800	37
	135 Horsepower② V8-301①	2 Barrel	4.00 x 3.00	301	8.2	135 @ 4000	245 @ 2000	35–40
	145 Horsepower② V8-305①	2 Barrel	3.736 x 3.48	305	8.5	145 @ 3800	245 @ 2400	32–40
	155 Horsepower② V8-350	4 Barrel	3.80 x 3.85	350	8.0	155 @ 3400	275 @ 1800	37
	170 Horsepower② V8-350⑤	4 Barrel	4.057 x 3.385	350	8.0	170 @ 3800	275 @ 2000	30–45
	170 Horsepower② V8-350①	4 Barrel	4.00 x 3.48	350	8.5	170 @ 3800	270 @ 2400	32–40
	185 Horsepower② V8-403⑤	4 Barrel	4.351 x 3.385	403	8.0	185 @ 3600	320 @ 2200	30–45
1979	105 Horsepower② V6-196	2 Barrel	3.50 x 3.40	196	8.0	105 @ 3800	160 @ 2000	37
	115 Horsepower② V6-231	2 Barrel	3.80 x 3.40	231	8.0	115 @ 3800	190 @ 2000	37
	170 Horsepower② V6-231⑨	4 Barrel	3.80 x 3.40	231	8.0			37
	175 Horsepower② V8-231③⑨	4 Barrel	3.80 x 3.40	231	8.0			37
	185 Horsepower② V6-231⑨⑩	4 Barrel	3.80 x 3.40	231	8.0			37
	140 Horsepower② V8-301⑥	2 Barrel	4.00 x 3.00	301	8.2	140 @ 3600	235 @ 2000	35–40
	150 Horsepower② V8-301⑥	4 Barrel	4.00 x 3.00	301	8.2	150 @ 4000	240 @ 2000	35–40
	Horsepower② V8-305①	2 Barrel	3.736 x 3.48	305	8.5			32–40
	160 Horsepower② V8-305①	4 Barrel	3.736 x 3.48	305	8.5	160 @ 4000	235 @ 2400	32–40
	155 Horsepower② V8-350	4 Barrel	3.80 x 3.85	350	8.0	155 @ 3400	280 @ 1800	34
	160 Horsepower② V8-350①	4 Barrel	4.00 x 3.48	350	8.5	160 @ 3800	260 @ 2400	32–40
	170 Horsepower② V8-350	4 Barrel	4.057 x 3.385	350	8.0	170 @ 3800	275 @ 2000	30–45
	185 Horsepower② V8-403⑤	4 Barrel	4.351 x 3.385	403	8.0	185 @ 3600	320 @ 2000	30–45

①—See Chevrolet chapter for service procedures on this engine.
②—Net Rating—As installed in vehicle.
③—Dual exhaust.
④—Stage 1.
⑤—See Oldsmobile chapter for service procedures on this engine.
⑥—See Pontiac chapter for service procedure on this engine.
⑦—Except California.
⑧—California.
⑨—Turbocharged engine.
⑩—Riviera.

TUNE UP SPECIFICATIONS

The following specifications are published from the latest information available. This data should be used only in the absence of a decal affixed in the engine compartment.

★When using a timing light, disconnect vacuum hose or tube at distributor and plug opening in tube or hose so idle speed will not be affected.

●When checking compression, lowest cylinder must be within 80 percent of highest.

▲Before removing wires from distributor cap, determine location of the No. 1 wire in cap, as distributor position may have been altered from that shown at the end of this chart.

| Year | Spark Plug | | Distributor | | Ignition Timing★ | | | Carb. Adjustments | | | | | |
| | Type | Gap Inch | Point Gap Inch | Dwell Angle Deg. | Firing Order Fig. ▲ | Timing BTDC ① | Mark Fig. | Hot Idle Speed ② | | Air Fuel Ratio | | Idle CO % | |
								Std. Trans.	Auto. Trans.	Std. Trans.	Auto. Trans.	Std. Trans.	Auto. Trans.
1974													
6-250⑧	R46T	.035	.019	31–34	A	③	D	950	600	—	—	—	—
V8-350	R45TS	.040	.016	29–31	④	4°	F	—	650	—	—	—	—
V8-455	R45TS	.040	.016	29–31	④	⑤	F	—	650	—	—	—	—
1975													
6-250⑧	R46TX	.060	—	—	I	10°	D	800	⑥	—	—	—	—
V6-231	R44SX	.060	—	—	J	12°	K	800	700	—	—	—	—
V8-260⑫	R46SX	.080	—	—	L	16°⑭	M	—	650	—	—	—	—
V8-350	R45TSX	.060	—	—	H	12°	F	—	600	—	—	—	—
V8-400 4 B. Carb.⑬	R45TSX	.060	—	—	N	16°	C	—	650	—	—	—	—
V8-455	R45TSX	.060	—	—	H	12°	F	—	600	—	—	—	—
1976													
V6-231	R44SX	.060	—	—	J	12°	㉖	800	600	—	—	—	—
V8-260⑫	R46SX	.080	—	—	L	⑨	M	—	650⑩	—	—	—	—
V8-350	R45TSX	.060	—	—	H	12°	F	—	600	—	—	—	—
V8-455	R45TSX	.060	—	—	H	12°	F	—	600	—	—	—	—
1977													
V6-231	R46TS	.040	—	—	O	12°	P㉗	500/800㉒	600	—	—	—	—
V6-231	R46TSX	.060	—	—	Q	15°	R㉗	—	600/670	—	—	—	—
V8-301⑬	R46TSX	.060	—	—	N	12°	G	—	550/650	—	—	—	—
V8-305⑧	R45TS	.045	—	—	E	8°	D	—	500/650	—	—	—	—
V8-350⑰	R46TS	.040	—	—	H	12°	P㉗	—	㉓	—	—	—	—
V8-350⑧⑱	R45TS	.045	—	—	E	8°	D	—	500/650㉑	—	—	—	—
V8-350⑫⑳	R46SZ	.060	—	—	L	㉔⑭	M	—	550/650㉑	—	—	—	—
V8-403⑫	R46SZ	.060	—	—	L	㉕⑭	M	—	550/650㉑	—	—	—	—
1978													
V6-196	R46TSX	.060	—	—	Q	15°	R㉗	600/800	600	—	—	—	—
V6-231⑦	R46TSX	.060	—	—	Q	15°	R㉗	600/800	600/670	—	—	—	—
V6-231⑪	R44TSX	.060	—	—	Q	15°	R㉗	—	650	—	—	—	—
V8-301⑬	R46TSX	.060	—	—	N	12°	G	—	550/650	—	—	—	—
V8-305⑧㉘	R45TS	.045	—	—	E	㉚	D	—	㉛	—	—	—	—
V8-305⑧㉙	R45TS	.045	—	—	E	4°	D	—	500/600	—	—	—	—
V8-350⑰	R46TSX	.060	—	—	H	15°	R㉗	—	550	—	—	—	—
V8-350⑧⑱	R45TS	.045	—	—	E	8°	D	—	㉜	—	—	—	—
V8-350⑫⑳	R46SZ	.060	—	—	L	20°⑭	M	—	㉝	—	—	—	—
V8-403⑫	R46SZ	.060	—	—	L	20°⑭	M	—	㉞	—	—	—	—

Continued

TUNE UP SPECIFICATIONS—Continued

The following specifications are published from the latest information available. This data should be used only in the absence of a decal affixed in the engine compartment.

★When using a timing light, disconnect vacuum hose or tube at distributor and plug opening in tube or hose so idle speed will not be affected.

●When checking compression, lowest cylinder must be within 80 percent of highest.

▲Before removing wires from distributor cap, determine location of the No. 1 wire in cap, as distributor position may have been altered from that shown at the end of this chart.

Year	Spark Plug		Distributor		Ignition Timing ★			Carb. Adjustments					
	Type	Gap Inch	Point Gap Inch	Dwell Angle Deg.	Firing Order Fig. ▲	Timing BTDC ①	Mark Fig.	Hot Idle Speed ②		Air Fuel Ratio		Idle CO %	
								Std. Trans.	Auto. Trans.	Std. Trans.	Auto. Trans.	Std. Trans.	Auto. Trans.
1979													
V6-196			—						—	—	—	—	—
V6-231			—						—	—	—	—	—
V6-231			—						—	—	—	—	—
V6-231			—						—	—	—	—	—
V6-231			—						—	—	—	—	—
V8-301			—						—	—	—	—	—
V8-301			—						—	—	—	—	—
V8-305			—						—	—	—	—	—
V8-305			—						—	—	—	—	—
V8-350			—						—	—	—	—	—
V8-350			—						—	—	—	—	—
V8-350			—						—	—	—	—	—
V8-403			—	—					—	—	—	—	—

① —BTDC: Before top dead center.
② —Idle speed on manual trans. equipped vehicles is adjusted in Neutral and on auto. trans. equipped vehicle adjusted in Drive unless otherwise specified. Where two idle speeds are listed, the higher speed is with the A/C solenoid energized.
③ —Manual trans., 8° BTDC; auto. trans., 6° BTDC.
④ —Exc. H.E.I., Fig. B; H. E. I., Fig. H.
⑤ —Exc. intermediate model Stage 1 eng., 4° BTDC; intermediate model Stage 1 eng., 10° BTDC.
⑥ —Except California, 550D with A/C on & compressor clutch wires disconnected; California, 600D.
⑦ —Exc. Turbocharged engine.
⑧ —See Chevrolet chapter for service procedures on this engine.
⑨ —Except California, 18° BTDC; California, 14° BTDC. At 1100 RPM.
⑩ —California models with A/C on & compressor clutch wires disconnected.

⑪ —Turbocharged engine.
⑫ —See Oldsmobile chapter for service procedures on this engine.
⑬ —See Pontiac chapter for service procedures on this engine.
⑭ —At 1100 RPM.
⑮ —Manual trans.
⑯ —Auto. trans.
⑰ —Distributor at front of engine.
⑱ —Distributor at rear of engine, clockwise rotor rotation.
⑲ —Exc. Calif. auto. trans., 8° BTDC; Calif. auto. trans. 6° BTDC.
⑳ —Distributor at rear of engine, counter-clockwise rotor rotation.
㉑ —High altitude, 600/650.
㉒ —California, 600/800.
㉓ —2 barrel carb., 600; 4 barrel carb., 550.
㉔ —Exc. Calif., 20° BTDC; Calif.—exc. Sta. Wag., 18° BTDC; Sta. Wag., 20° BTDC.
㉕ —Exc. Hi. Alt. & Calif., 24° BTDC; Hi. Alt. & Calif., 20° BTDC.

㉖ —These engines use two different harmonic balancers. The harmonic balancer on late engines has two timing marks. The mark measuring 1/16 inch is used when setting timing with a hand held light. The mark measuring 1/8 inch is used when setting timing with magnetic timing equipment.
㉗ —The harmonic balancer on these engines has two timing marks. The mark measuring 1/16 inch is used when setting timing with a hand held timing light. The mark measuring 1/8 inch is used when setting timing with magnetic timing equipment.
㉘ —Two barrel carburetor.
㉙ —Four barrel carburetor.
㉚ —Exc. Calif. & high altitude, 4° BTDC; Calif., 6° BTDC; high altitude, 8° BTDC.
㉛ —Exc. Calif. & high altitude, 600/500; Calif., 650/500; high altitude, 700/600.
㉜ —Calif., 600/500; high altitude, 650/600.
㉝ —Calif., 650/550; high altitude, 700/600.
㉞ —Exc. high altitude, 650/550; high altitude, 700/600.

Continued

TUNE UP NOTES—Continued

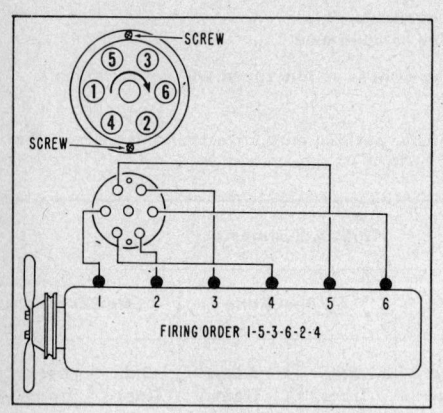

Fig. A

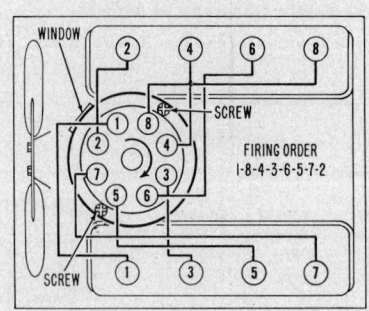

Fig. B

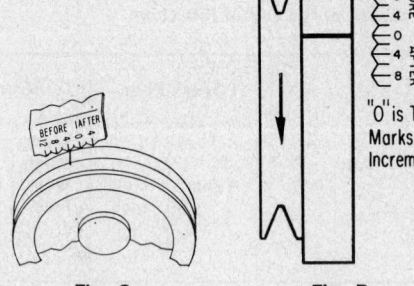

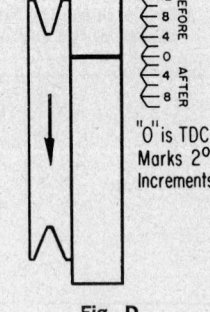

Fig. C

Fig. D

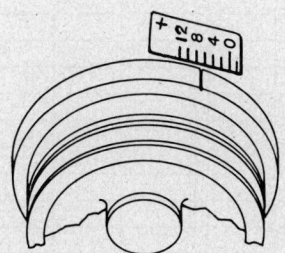

Fig. E

Fig. F

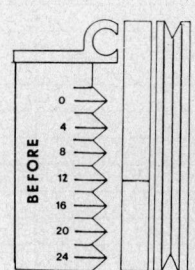

Fig. G

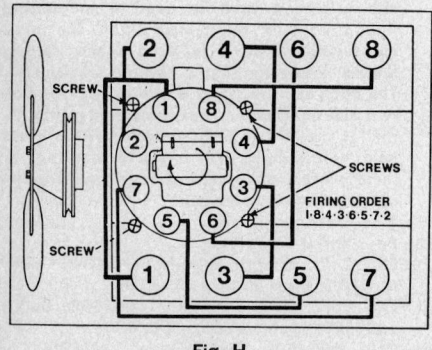

Fig. H

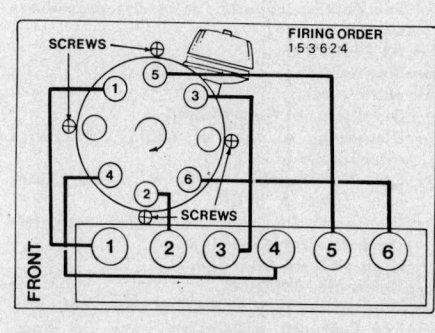

Fig. I

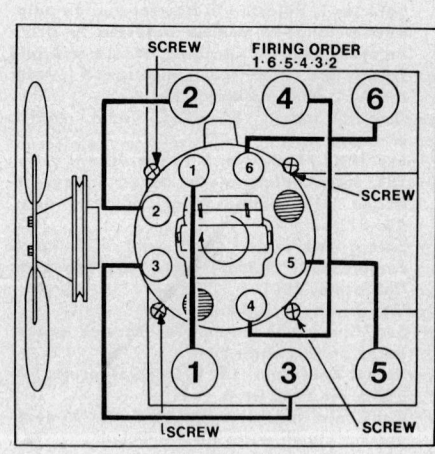

Fig. J

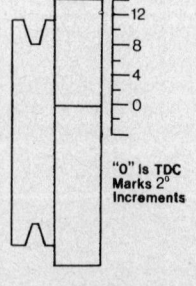

Fig. K

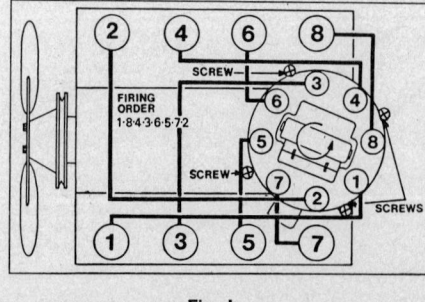

Fig. L

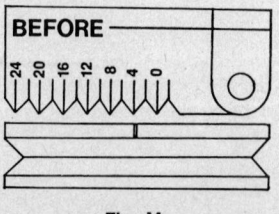

Fig. M

Continued

TUNE UP NOTES—Continued

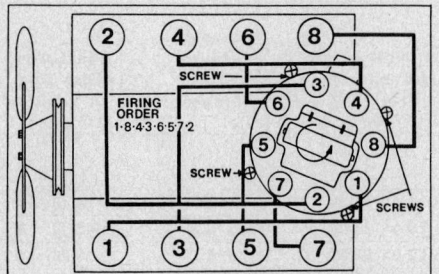

Fig. N

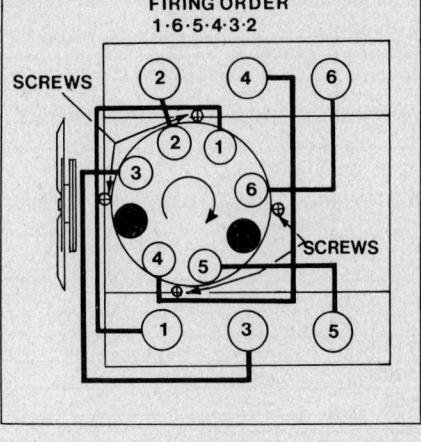

Fig. O

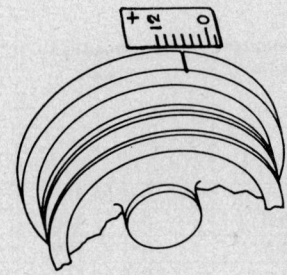

Fig. P

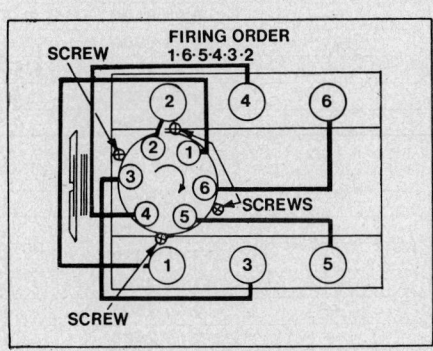

Fig. Q

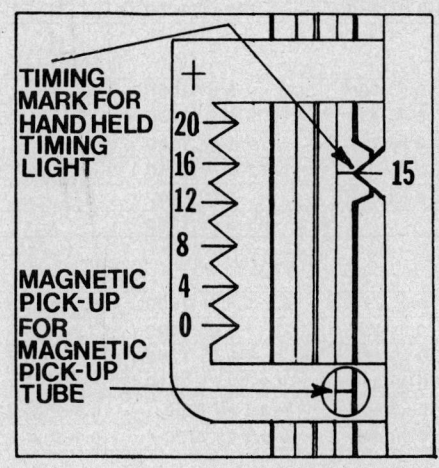

Fig. R

REAR AXLE SPECIFICATIONS

Year	Model	Carrier Type	Ring Gear & Pinion Backlash		Pinion Bearing Preload			Differential Bearing Preload		
			Method	Adjustment	Method	Adjustment New Bearings Inch-Lbs.	Adjustment Used Bearings Inch-Lbs.	Method	Adjustment New Bearings Inch-Lbs.	Adjustment Used Bearings Inch-Lbs.
1974	All Exc. Apollo	Integral	Shims	.006–.008	Spacer	20–25①	10–15①	Shims	35–40②	20–25②
1974	Apollo	Integral	Shims	.006–.008	Spacer	20–25①	10–15①	Shims	30–40②	20–25②
1975	All	Integral	Shims	.006–.008	Spacer	20–25①	10–15①	Shims	30–40②	20–25②
1976-78	All	Integral	Shims	.006–.008	Spacer	20–25①	10–15①	Shims	35–40②	20–25②

①—Measured with torque wrench at pinion flange nut.

②—Total preload measured with torque wrench at pinion flange nut with new seal installed.

DISTRIBUTOR SPECIFICATIONS

★Note: If unit is checked on the vehicle, double the RPM and degrees to get crankshaft figures.

Breaker arm spring tension—19–23.

Distributor Part No.①	Centrifugal Advance Degrees @ RPM of Distributor					Vacuum Advance	
	Advance Starts	Intermediate Advance			Full Advance	Inches of Vacuum to Start Plunger	Max. Adv. Dist. Deg. @ Vacuum
1974							
1110499	0–1 @ 550	7 @ 1150	—	—	10½ @ 2050	6	11 @ 14
1112520②	0–1 @ 450	7–9 @ 1200	—	—	10 @ 1500	6.5–8.5	9.5 @ 13
1112521②	0–1 @ 400	4½–6½ @ 900	—	—	12 @ 2300	6–8	9 @ 16
1112541	0–1 @ 450	5½–7½ @ 900	—	—	12 @ 1800	6–8	9 @ 16
1112542	0–1 @ 450	7–9 @ 1050	—	—	14 @ 2050	6.5–8.5	9.5 @ 13
1112802②	0–1 @ 450	5½–7½ @ 900	—	—	12 @ 1800	6–8	9 @ 16
1112803②	0–1 @ 450	7–9 @ 1050	—	—	14 @ 2050	6.5–8.5	9.5 @ 13
1975							
V6-231②	0 @ 500	5 @ 1000	—	—	8 @ 2050	5–7	9 @ 10
6-250②	0 @ 550	3½ @ 1150	—	—	8 @ 2100	4	③
V8-260②	0 @ 325	9½ @ 1200	—	—	14 @ 2200	4	12 @ 15
V8-350②	—	2–4 @ 1050	—	—	7 @ 2250	6½–8½	8 @ 11½
V8-400②	0 @ 600	2 @ 700	—	—	8 @ 2200	6–8	12½ @ 13½
V8-455②	—	4½–6 @ 1500	—	—	9 @ 2200	4–6	10 @ 11
1976							
V6-231②	0 @ 770	6.2–8.4 @ 1500	6.7–9 @ 1590	—	9 @ 2500	5.3	12¾ @ 12.8
V8-260④	0 @ 325	9½ @ 1200	—	—	14 @ 2200	4.5	15 @ 11
V8-260②⑤	0 @ 455	8½ @ 1190	—	—	13 @ 2230	6	10 @ 14¾
V8-350②	0 @ 872	8.9–11 @ 2215	—	—	11 @ 2500	6.9	11¾ @ 14.3
V8-455②④	0 @ 660	4–6.1 @ 1750	6.9–9 @ 1200	—	9 @ 2500	4½	12¾ @ 14.1
V8-455②⑤	0 @ 660	4–6.1 @ 1750	6.9–9 @ 2200	—	9 @ 2500	4½	9¾ @ 12
1977							
1103275②	0 @ 725	—	—	—	10 @ 2200	5½–7½	12 @ 14
1110677②	0 @ 766	8.9–11 @ 1800	—	—	7.95–11 @ 2500	6	12.7 @ 20
1110686②	0 @ 888	3.15–5.45 @ 1300	8.8–11 @ 1800	—	8.7–11 @ 2500	6	4.7 @ 20
1110694②	0 @ 764	8.9–11 @ 1800	—	—	7.95–11 @ 2500	3.5	15.5 @ 20
1978							
1103281②	—	4½–5½ @ 950	—	—	—	3–5	4½ @ 13
1103282②	—	4½–5½ @ 950	—	—	—	3–6	5 @ 12
1103285②	—	5–6 @ 1050	—	—	—	3–5	2½ @ 9
1103314②	—	4¾–5¾ @ 850	—	—	—	3–5	5 @ 12
1103322②	—	6¾–7¾ @ 1000	—	—	—	4–6	6 @ 14
1103323②	—	4¼–5¼ @ 1000	—	—	—	4–5	4 @ 12
1103324②	—	5¼–6¼ @ 900	—	—	—	4–6	6 @ 14
1103325②	—	3¼–3¾ @ 900	—	—	—	4–5	4 @ 12
1103342②	0 @ 950	3¾–4¾ @ 1100	—	—	8½ @ 2200	5–7	6 @ 13
1103346②	—	4¼–5¼ @ 1000	—	—	—	4–6	6 @ 14
1103347②	—	3¼–3¾ @ 900	—	—	—	4–6	6 @ 14
1103353②	—	5½–6 @ 1125	—	—	—	3–6	5 @ 12
1110695②	0 @ 840	3–4½ @ 900	—	—	7½ @ 1800	3–6	6 @ 13
1110723②	—	2–3 @ 1000	—	—	—	4–6	2 @ 7
1110728②	—	3½–4½ @ 800	—	—	—	1–5	5 @ 8
1110730②	0 @ 445	4¾–5¾ @ 1000	—	—	11½ @ 2000	4–6	6 @ 10

Continued

DISTRIBUTOR SPECIFICATIONS—Continued

★Note: If unit is checked on the vehicle, double the RPM and degrees to get crankshaft figures.

Breaker arm spring tension—19–23.

Distributor Part No.①	Centrifugal Advance Degrees @ RPM of Distributor					Vacuum Advance	
	Advance Starts	Intermediate Advance			Full Advance	Inches of Vacuum to Start Plunger	Max. Adv. Dist. Deg. @ Vacuum
1978—Continued							
1110731②	0 @ 840	3¼–4¼ @ 900	—	—	7½ @ 1800	4–6	4 @ 9
1110732②	0 @ 840	3¼–4¼ @ 900	—	—	7½ @ 1800	7–9	3½ @ 13
1110735②	—	4¾–5¾ @ 1000	—	—	—	2–4	5 @ 13
1110739②	—	3¼–4¼ @ 900	—	—	—	2–4	5 @ 13
1979							
1103266②	0 @ 500	—	—	—	10½ @ 2000	5	8 @ 11
1103342②	0 @ 950	—	—	—	8½ @ 2200	6½	12 @ 14
1110765②	0 @ 458	1½–3½ @ 600	—	—	8½ @ 2250	2½–3½	10½ @ 12
1110766②	0 @ 840	—	—	—	7½ @ 1800	3	12 @ 36.7
1110769②	0 @ 500	2½ @ 800	3 @ 1200	—	7½ @ 1800	4	12 @ 11
1110770②	0 @ 810	—	—	—	7½ @ 1800	3	10 @ 9
1110774②	0 @ 458	1½–3½ @ 600	—	—	6 @ 2250	2½–3½	10½ @ 12
1110775②	0 @ 500	—	—	—	7½ @ 1800	3	10 @ 9

①—Stamped on distributor housing plate.
②—High Energy Ignition.
③—Exc. Calif., 9 @ 12; Calif., 9 @ 15.
④—Except California.
⑤—California.

ALTERNATOR & REGULATOR SPECIFICATIONS

Year	Alternator					Regulator							
	Model	Rated Hot Output Amps.	Field Current 12 Volts @ 80 F.	Cold Output @ 14 Volts		Model	Field Relay			Voltage Regulator			
				2000 R.P.M. Amps.	5000 R.P.M. Amps.		Air Gap In.	Point Gap In.	Closing Voltage	Air Gap In.	Point Gap In.	Voltage @ 125° F.	
1974	1100497	37	4.0–4.5	13③	37	Integral	—	—	—	—	—	13.5–14.5	
	1100925	63	4.0–4.5	36③	58	Integral	—	—	—	—	—	13.5–14.5	
	1100926	42	4.0–4.5	15③	37	Integral	—	—	—	—	—	13.5–14.5	
	1100946	55	4.0–4.5	—	50	Integral	—	—	—	—	—	13.5–14.5	
	1100947	37	4.0–4.5	12③	32	Integral	—	—	—	—	—	13.5–14.5	
	1100948	61	4.0–4.5	24③	55	Integral	—	—	—	—	—	13.5–14.5	
	1101018	80	4.0–4.5	—	74	Integral	—	—	—	—	—	13.5–14.5	
1975	1101016	80	4.4–4.9	—	80④	Integral	—	—	—	—	—	—	
	1101024	80	4.4–4.9	—	80④	Integral	—	—	—	—	—	—	
	1101031	80	4.4–4.9	—	80④	Integral	—	—	—	—	—	—	
	1102388	37	4.0–4.5	—	37④	Integral	—	—	—	—	—	13.6–14.2	
	1102389	42	4.0–4.5	—	42④	Integral	—	—	—	—	—	13.6–14.2	
	1102390	55	4.0–4.5	—	55④	Integral	—	—	—	—	—	13.6–14.2	
	1102391	61	4.0–4.5	—	61④	Integral	—	—	—	—	—	13.6–14.2	

Continued

ALTERNATOR & REGULATOR SPECIFICATIONS—Continued

| Year | Alternator | | | | | Regulator | | | | | | |
| | Model | Rated Hot Output Amps. | Field Current 12 Volts @ 80 F. | Cold Output @ 14 Volts | | Model | Field Relay | | | Voltage Regulator | | |
				2000 R.P.M. Amps.	5000 R.P.M. Amps.		Air Gap In.	Point Gap In.	Closing Voltage	Air Gap In.	Point Gap In.	Voltage @ 125° F.
1975	1102392	63	4.0–4.5	—	63④	Integral	—	—	—	—	—	—
	1102394	37	4.0–4.5	—	37④	Integral	—	—	—	—	—	13.6–14.2
	1102399	37	4.0–4.5	—	37④	Integral	—	—	—	—	—	—
	1102400	42	4.0–4.5	—	42④	Integral	—	—	—	—	—	—
	1102457	55	4.0–4.5	—	55④	Integral	—	—	—	—	—	—
	1102460	61	4.0–4.5	—	61④	Integral	—	—	—	—	—	—
	1102461	63	4.0–4.5	—	63④	Integral	—	—	—	—	—	—
	1102467	63	4.0–4.5	—	63④	Integral	—	—	—	—	—	—
	1102478	55	4.0–4.5	—	55④	Integral	—	—	—	—	—	—
	1102483	37	4.0–4.5	—	37④	Integral	—	—	—	—	—	—
	1102488	55	4.0–4.5	—	55④	Integral	—	—	—	—	—	—
	1102491	37	4.0–4.5	—	37④	Integral	—	—	—	—	—	—
	1102494	55	4.0–4.5	—	55④	Integral	—	—	—	—	—	—
	1102495	55	4.0–4.5	—	55④	Integral	—	—	—	—	—	13.6–14.2
	1102497	37	4.0–4.5	—	37④	Integral	—	—	—	—	—	—
	1102861	42	4.0–4.5	—	42④	Integral	—	—	—	—	—	—
1976	1101024	80	4.4–4.9	—	80④	Integral	—	—	—	—	—	13.5–14.5①
	1102388	37	4.0–4.5	—	37④	Integral	—	—	—	—	—	13.5–14.5①
	1102389	42	4.0–4.5	—	42④	Integral	—	—	—	—	—	13.5–14.5①
	1102390	55	4.0–4.5	—	55④	Integral	—	—	—	—	—	13.5–14.5①
	1102391	61	4.0–4.5	—	61④	Integral	—	—	—	—	—	13.5–14.5①
	1102392	63	4.0–4.5	—	63④	Integral	—	—	—	—	—	13.5–14.5①
	1102394	37	4.0–4.5	—	37④	Integral	—	—	—	—	—	13.5–14.5①
	1102495	55	4.0–4.5	—	55④	Integral	—	—	—	—	—	13.5–14.5①
	1102840	55	4.0–4.5	—	55④	Integral	—	—	—	—	—	13.5–14.5①
1977	1101016	80	4.0–4.5	—	80④	Integral	—	—	—	—	—	13.6–14.2
	1101024	80	4.0–4.5	—	80④	Integral	—	—	—	—	—	13.6–14.2
	1102389	42	4.0–4.5	—	42④	Integral	—	—	—	—	—	13.6–14.2
	1102391	61	4.0–4.5	—	61④	Integral	—	—	—	—	—	13.6–14.2
	1102392	63	4.0–4.5	—	63④	Integral	—	—	—	—	—	13.6–14.2
	1102394	37	4.0–4.5	—	37④	Integral	—	—	—	—	—	13.6–14.2
	1102478	55	4.0–4.5	—	55④	Integral	—	—	—	—	—	13.6–14.2
	1102479	61	4.0–4.5	—	55④	Integral	—	—	—	—	—	13.6–14.2
	1102485	42	4.0–4.5	—	42④	Integral	—	—	—	—	—	13.6–14.2
	1102486	61	4.0–4.5	—	61④	Integral	—	—	—	—	—	13.6–14.2
	1102491	37	4.0–4.5	—	37④	Integral	—	—	—	—	—	13.6–14.2
	1102492	37	4.0–4.5	—	37④	Integral	—	—	—	—	—	13.6–14.2
	1102495	55	4.0–4.5	—	55④	Integral	—	—	—	—	—	13.6–14.2
	1102841	42	4.0–4.5	—	42④	Integral	—	—	—	—	—	13.6–14.2
	1102842	63	4.0–4.5	—	63④	Integral	—	—	—	—	—	13.6–14.2
	1102854	63	4.0–4.5	—	63④	Integral	—	—	—	—	—	13.6–14.2
	1102881	37	4.0–4.5	—	37④	Integral	—	—	—	—	—	13.6–14.2
	1102882	37	4.0–4.5	—	37④	Integral	—	—	—	—	—	13.6–14.2
	1102902	61	4.0–4.5	—	61④	Integral	—	—	—	—	—	13.6–14.2
	1102905	55	4.0–4.5	—	55④	Integral	—	—	—	—	—	13.6–14.2
	1102906	61	4.0–4.5	—	61④	Integral	—	—	—	—	—	13.6–14.2
	1102913	61	4.0–4.5	—	61④	Integral	—	—	—	—	—	13.6–14.2
1978	1101016	80	4.0–5.0	—	—	Integral	—	—	—	—	—	13.6–14.2
	1101024	80	4.0–5.0	—	—	Integral	—	—	—	—	—	13.6–14.2
	1102389	42	4.0–5.0	—	—	Integral	—	—	—	—	—	13.6–14.2
	1102391	61	4.0–5.0	—	—	Integral	—	—	—	—	—	13.6–14.2
	1102392	63	4.0–5.0	—	—	Integral	—	—	—	—	—	13.6–14.2

Continued

ALTERNATOR & REGULATOR SPECIFICATIONS—Continued

| Year | | Alternator | | | | | Regulator | | | | | | |
| | | | | Cold Output @ 14 Volts | | | | Field Relay | | | Voltage Regulator | | |
	Model	Rated Hot Output Amps.	Field Current 12 Volts @ 80 F.	2000 R.P.M. Amps.	5000 R.P.M. Amps.	Model	Air Gap In.	Point Gap In.	Closing Voltage	Air Gap In.	Point Gap In.	Voltage @ 125° F.
1978	1102394	37	4.0–5.0	—	33	Integral	—	—	—	—	—	13.6–14.2
	1102479	55	4.0–5.0	—	51	Integral	—	—	—	—	—	13.6–14.2
	1102485	42	4.0–5.0	—	—	Integral	—	—	—	—	—	13.6–14.2
	1102486	61	4.0–5.0	—	57	Integral	—	—	—	—	—	13.6–14.2
	1102495	55	4.0–5.0	—	—	Integral	—	—	—	—	—	13.6–14.2
	1102841	42	4.0–5.0	—	—	Integral	—	—	—	—	—	13.6–14.2
	1102842	63	4.0–5.0	—	—	Integral	—	—	—	—	—	13.6–14.2
	1102854	63	4.0–5.0	—	60	Integral	—	—	—	—	—	13.6–14.2
	1102901	61	4.0–5.0	—	—	Integral	—	—	—	—	—	13.6–14.2
	1102904	63	4.0–5.0	—	—	Integral	—	—	—	—	—	13.6–14.2
	1102906	61	4.0–5.0	—	—	Integral	—	—	—	—	—	13.6–14.2
	1102913	61	4.0–5.0	—	—	Integral	—	—	—	—	—	13.6–14.2
	1103033	42	4.0–5.0	—	—	Integral	—	—	—	—	—	13.6–14.2
1979	1101024	80	—	—	—	Integral	—	—	—	—	—	—
	1101043	80	—	—	—	Integral	—	—	—	—	—	—
	1102389	42	—	—	—	Integral	—	—	—	—	—	13.9–14.5
	1102392	63	—	—	—	Integral	—	—	—	—	—	13.9–14.5
	1102394	37	—	—	—	Integral	—	—	—	—	—	13.9–14.5
	1102479	55	—	—	—	Integral	—	—	—	—	—	13.9–14.5
	1102495	55	—	—	—	Integral	—	—	—	—	—	13.9–14.5
	1102841	42	—	—	—	Integral	—	—	—	—	—	13.9–14.5
	1102860	63	—	—	—	Integral	—	—	—	—	—	13.9–14.5
	1102904	63	—	—	—	Integral	—	—	—	—	—	—
	1103033	42	—	—	—	Integral	—	—	—	—	—	13.9–14.5
	1103055	42	—	—	—	Integral	—	—	—	—	—	—
	1103056	63	—	—	—	Integral	—	—	—	—	—	—
	1103058	63	—	—	—	Integral	—	—	—	—	—	13.9–14.5

①—At 2000 engine R.P.M.
②—At 1500 engine R.P.M.
③—At 600 engine R.P.M.
④—At 5500 R.P.M. & 80°F.

ENGINE TIGHTENING SPECIFICATIONS*

★Torque specifications are for clean and lightly lubricated threads only. Dry or dirty threads produce increased friction which prevents accurate measurement of tightness.

Year	Engine	Spark Plugs Ft. Lbs. ②	Cylinder Head Bolts Ft. Lbs.	Intake Manifold Ft. Lbs.	Exhaust Manifold Ft. Lbs.	Rocker Arm Shaft Bracket Ft. Lbs.	Rocker Arm Cover Ft. Lbs.	Connecting Rod Cap Bolts Ft. Lbs.	Main Bearing Cap Bolts Ft. Lbs.	Flywheel to Crankshaft Ft. Lbs.	Vibration Damper or Pulley Ft. Lbs.
1974	6-250	15	95	35	30	—	4	35	65	60	①
	V8-350	15	80	45	28	30	4	40	115	60	140 min.
	V8-455	15	100	45	28	30	4	45	115	60	200 min.
1975	6-250	15	95	35	30	—	4	35	65	60	60
	V6-231	15	75	45	25	30	5	40	115	55	150 min.
	V8-260	15	85	40	25	—	7	42	③	60	255
	V8-350	15	95	45	28	30	4	40	115	60	150
	V8-400	15	95	40	30	—	8	45	④	95	160
	V8-455	15	100	45	28	30	4	45	115	60	200

Continued

ENGINE TIGHTENING SPECIFICATIONS—Continued

Year	Engine	Spark Plugs Ft. Lbs. [2]	Cylinder Head Bolts Ft. Lbs.	Intake Manifold Ft. Lbs.	Exhaust Manifold Ft. Lbs.	Rocker Arm Shaft Bracket Ft. Lbs.	Rocker Arm Cover Ft. Lbs.	Connecting Rod Cap Bolts Ft. Lbs.	Main Bearing Cap Bolts Ft. Lbs.	Flywheel to Crankshaft Ft. Lbs.	Vibration Damper or Pulley Ft. Lbs.
1976	V6-231	20	80	45	25	30	4	40	115	60	175
	V8-260	25	85	40	25	25	7	42	[3]	60	255
	V8-350	20	80	45	25	30	4	40	115	60	175
	V8-455	20	100	45	25	30	4	45	115	60	225
1977-78	V6-196, 231	[12]	80	45	25	30	4	40	100	60	[13]
	V8-301	15	90	40	35	—	7	35	[5]	95	160
	V8-305	15	65	30	20	—	3¾	45	70	60	60
	V8-350 [6]	[12]	80	45	25	30	4	40	100	60	[13]
	V8-350 [7]	15	65	30	20 [8]	—	3¾	45	70 [9]	60	60
	V8-350 [10]	25	130	40	25	—	—	42	[3]	[11]	260
	V8-403	25	130	40	25	—	—	42	[3]	[11]	260

①—Pressed on.
②—Dry threads.
③—Nos. 1, 2, 3, 4—80 ft. lbs., No. 5—120 ft. lbs.
④—Rear main, 120 ft. lbs.; all others, 100 ft. lbs.
⑤—Rear main, 100 ft. lbs.; all others, 60 ft. lbs.
⑥—Distributor at front of engine.
⑦—Distributor at rear of engine, clockwise rotor rotation.

⑧—1977 only; Inside bolts; 30 ft. lbs.
⑨—Outer bolts on engines with 4 bolt caps, 65 ft. lbs.
⑩—Distributor at rear of engine, counter-clockwise rotor rotation.
⑪—Auto. trans. 60 ft. lbs.; man. trans., 90 ft. lbs.
⑫—1977; 20 ft. lbs. & 1978; 15 ft. lbs.
⑬—1977; 175 ft. lbs. & 1978; 225 ft. lbs.

BRAKE SPECIFICATIONS

Year	Model	Brake Drum Inside Diameter	Wheel Cylinder Bore Diameter			Master Cylinder Bore Diameter		
			Front Disc Brake	Front Drum Brake	Rear Drum Brake	With Disc Brakes	With Drum Brakes	With Power Brakes
1974	Apollo	9.50	2¹⁵⁄₁₆	1⅛	⅞	1⅛	1.00	①
	Century, Luxus, Regal	9.495–9.505	2¹⁵⁄₁₆	—	⅞	1⅛	—	1⅛
	Century Wagon	10.997–11.007	2¹⁵⁄₁₆	—	¹⁵⁄₁₆	1⅛	—	1⅛
	LeSabre, Centurion, Electra, Riviera	10.997–11.007	2¹⁵⁄₁₆	—	¹⁵⁄₁₆	1⅛	—	1⅛
	Estate Wagon	11.997–12.007	2¹⁵⁄₁₆	—	1	1⅛	—	1⅛
1975	Apollo, Skylark	9.495–9.505	2¹⁵⁄₁₆	—	⅞	1⅛	—	1⅛
	Century, Regal, Custom	9.495–9.505	2¹⁵⁄₁₆	—	⅞	1⅛	—	1⅛
	Century Wagon	10.997–11.007	2¹⁵⁄₁₆	—	¹⁵⁄₁₆	1⅛	—	1⅛
	LeSabre	10.997–11.007	2¹⁵⁄₁₆	—	¹⁵⁄₁₆	1⅛	—	1⅛
	Electra, Riviera	10.997–11.007	2¹⁵⁄₁₆	—	¹⁵⁄₁₆	1⅛	—	1⅛
	Estate Wagon	11.997–12.007	2¹⁵⁄₁₆	—	1	1⅛	—	1⅛
1976	Skylark	9.495–9.505	2¹⁵⁄₁₆	—	⅞	1⅛	—	1⅛
	Century, Regal	10.997–11.007	2¹⁵⁄₁₆	—	¹⁵⁄₁₆	1⅛	—	1⅛
	Century Wagon	10.997–11.007	2¹⁵⁄₁₆	—	¹⁵⁄₁₆	1⅛	—	1⅛
	LeSabre	10.997–11.007	2¹⁵⁄₁₆	—	1	1⅛	—	1⅛
	Electra, Riviera	10.997–11.007	2¹⁵⁄₁₆	—	1	1⅛	—	1⅛
	Estate Wagon	11.997–12.007	2¹⁵⁄₁₆	—	1	1⅛	—	1⅛
1977-78	Century, Regal	10.997–11.007	2¹⁵⁄₁₆	—	¹⁵⁄₁₆	1⅛	—	1⅛
	Electra, Riviera, Estate Wagon	10.997–11.007	2¹⁵⁄₁₆	—	¹⁵⁄₁₆	1⅛	—	1⅛
	LeSabre	9.5	2¹⁵⁄₁₆	—	⅞	1⅛	—	1⅛
	Skylark	9.5	2¹⁵⁄₁₆	—	¹⁵⁄₁₆	1⅛	—	1⅛
1979	Skylark	9.5	2¹⁵⁄₁₆	—	¹⁵⁄₁₆	1⅛	—	1⅛
	Century, Regal	9.45	2⁷⁄₁₆	—	¾	⅞	—	¹⁵⁄₁₆
	LeSabre	9.5	2¹⁵⁄₁₆	—	⅞	1⅛	—	1⅛
	Electra, Estate Wagon	11	2¹⁵⁄₁₆	—	¹⁵⁄₁₆	1⅛	—	1⅛
	Riviera	9.45	2½	—	¾	.945	—	.945

①—Drum brakes 1″, disc brakes 1⅛″.

PISTONS, PINS, RINGS, CRANKSHAFT & BEARINGS

Year	Engine	Piston Clearance	Ring End Gap①		Wrist-pin Diameter	Rod Bearings		Main Bearings			
			Comp.	Oil		Shaft Diameter	Bearing Clearance	Shaft Diameter	Bearing Clearance	Thrust on Bear. No.	Shaft End Play
1974	6-250②	.0005–.0015	.010	.015	.927	1.999–2.000	.0007–.0027	2.3004	.0003–.0029	7	.002–.006
	V8-350	.0008–.0020	.010	.015	.9393	2.000	.0002–.0023	③	.0004–.0015	3	.003–.009
	V8-455	.0010–.0016	.013	.015	.9993	2.249–2.250	.0002–.0023	3.250	.0007–.0018	3	.003–.009
1975	6-250②	.0005–.0015	.010	.015	.927	1.999–2.000	.0007–.0027	2.3004	.0003–.0029	7	.002–.006
	V6-231	.0008–.0020	.010	.015	.9393	1.9991–2.000	.0005–.0026	2.4995	.0004–.0015	2	.004–.008
	V8-260④	.001–.002	.010	.015	.9805	2.1238–2.1248	.0004–.0033	⑤	.0005–.0021⑥	3	.004–.008
	V8-350	.0008–.0014	.010	.015	.9393	1.9991–2.000	.0005–.0026	2.9995	.0004–.0015	3	.003–.009
	V8-400⑦	.003–.005	⑧	.035	.9802	2.25	.0005–.0025	3.00	.0002–.0017	4	.003–.009
	V8-455	.0007–.0013	.013	.015	.9991	2.487–2.495	.0005–.0026	3.250	.0007–.0018	3	.003–.009
1976	V6-231	.0008–.0020	.010	.015	.9393	1.9991–2.000	.0005–.0026	2.4995	.0004–.0015	2	.004–.008
	V8-260④	.001–.002	.010	.015	.9805	2.1238–2.1248	.0004–.0033	⑤	.0005–.0021⑥	3	.004–.008
	V8-350	.0008–.0020	.010	.015	.9393	1.9991–2.000	.0005–.0026	3.000	.0004–.0015	3	.003–.009
	V8-455	.0007–.0013	.013	.015	.9993	2.2487–2.2495	.0005–.0026	3.250	.0007–.0018	3	.003–.009
1977	V6-196, 231	.0008–.0020	.010	.015	.9393	1.9991–2.000	.0005–.0026	2.4995	.0004–.0015	2	.004–.008
	V8-301⑦	.0025–.0033	.010	.035	.927	2.25	.0005–.0025	3.00	.0004–.0020	4	.003–.009
	V8-305②	.0007–.0017	.010	.015	.9272	2.099–2.100	0013–.0035	⑪	⑫	3	.002–.006
	V8-350⑨	.0008–.0020	.010	.015	.9393	1.9991–2.000	.0005–.0026	3.00	.0004–.0015	3	.003–.009
	V8-350②⑩	.0007–.0017	⑭	.015	.9272	2.099–2.100	.0013–.0035	⑪	⑫	3	.002–.006
	V8-350④⑬	.001–.002	.010	.015	.9805	2.1238–2.1248	.0005–.0026	⑤	.0005–.0021⑥	3	—
	V8-403④	.001–.002	.010	.015	.9805	2.1238–2.1248	.0005–.0026	⑤	.0005–.0021⑥	3	—
1978	V6-196, 231	.0008–.0020	.010	.015	.9393	2.2487–2.2495	.0005–.0026	2.4995	.0003–.0018	2	.004–.008
	V8-301⑦	.0025–.0033	.010	.035	.927	2.25	.0005–.0025	3.00	.0004–.0020	4	.006–.022
	V8-305②	.0007–.0017	.010	.015	.9272	2.099–2.100	.0013–.0035	⑪	⑫	3	.002–.006
	V8-350⑨	.0008–.0020	.010	.015	.9393	1.991–2.000	.0005–.0026	3.00	.0004–.0015	3	.003–.009
	V8-350②⑩	.001–.002	.010	.015	.9272	2.099–2.100	.0013–.0035	⑪	⑫	3	.002–.006
	V8-350④⑬	.001–.002	.010	.015	.9805	2.1238–2.1248	.0004–.0033	⑤	.0005–.0021⑥	3	.0035–.0135
	V8-403④	.001–.002	.010	.015	.9805	2.1238–2.1248	.0004–.0033	⑤	.0005–.0021⑥	3	.0035–.0135
1979	V6-196, 231	.0008–.0020	.013	.015	.9393	2.2487–2.2495	.0005–.0026	2.4995	.0004–.0018	2	.003–.009
	V8-301⑦	.0025–.0033	.015	.015	.940	2.25	.0005–.0026	3.00	.0002–.0020	4	.0035–.0085
	V8-305②	.0017–.0042	⑭	.010	.9272	2.099–2.100	.0013–.0035	⑪	⑫	3	.002–.007
	V8-350⑨	.0008–.0020	.013	.015	.9393	1.9991–2.000	.0005–.0026	2.9995	.0004–.0015	3	.002–.006
	V8-350②⑩	.0007–.0017	⑭	.015	.9272	2.099–2.100	.0013–.0035	⑪	⑫	3	.002–.007
	V8-350④⑬	.0007–.0017	010	.015	.9805	2.1238–2.1248	—	2.50	—	3	—
	V8-403④	.0007–.0017	.010	.015	.9805	2.1238–2.1248	—	2.50	—	3	—

①—Fit rings in tapered bores for clearance given in tightest portion of ring travel. Clearances specified are minimum gaps.
②—See Chevrolet Chapter for service procedures on this engine.
③—1973, 2.9995 inch; 1974, 3.00 inch.
④—See Oldsmobile Chapter for service procedures on this engine.
⑤—No. 1: 2.4988–2.4998 inch; Nos. 2, 3, 4, 5: 2.4985–2.4995 inch.
⑥—Rear, .0015–.0031 inch.
⑦—See Pontiac Chapter for service procedures on this engine.

⑧—No. 1, .019; No. 2, .015.
⑨—Distributor at front of engine.
⑩—Distributor at rear of engine, clockwise rotation.
⑪—No. 1: 2.4484–2.4493 inch; Nos. 2, 3, 4: 2.4481–2.4490 inch; No. 5: 2.4479–2.4488 inch.
⑫—No. 1: .0008–.0020 inch; Nos. 2, 3, 4: .0011–.0023 inch; No. 5: .0017–.0032 inch.
⑬—Distributor at rear of engine, counter-clockwise rotation.
⑭—No. 1, .010; No. 2, .013.

VALVE SPECIFICATIONS

Year	Model	Valve Lash		Valve Angles		Valve Spring Installed Height ③	Valve Spring Pressure Lbs. @ In.	Stem Clearance		Stem Diameter	
		Int.	Exh.	Seat	Face			Intake	Exhaust	Intake	Exhaust
1974	6-250④	1 Turn⑤		46	45	1.66	186 @ 1.27	.001–.0027	.001–.0027	.3410–.3417	.3410–.3417
	V8-350	Hydraulic⑥		45	45	1.72	180 @ 1.34	.0015–.0035	.0015–.0032①	.3720–.3730	.3723–.3730②
	V8-455	Hydraulic⑥		45	45	1.89	177 @ 1.45	.0015–.0035	.0015–.0032①	.3720–.3730	.3723–.3730②
1975	6-250④	1 Turn⑤		46	45	1.66	186 @ 1.27	.001–.0027	.001–.0027	.3410–.3417	.3410–.3417
	V6-231	Hydraulic⑥		45	45	1.727	168 @ 1.327	.0015–.0032	.0015–.0032	.3405–.3412	.3405–.3412
	V8-260⑦	Hydraulic⑥		⑧	⑨	1.67	187 @ 1.27	.001–.0027	.0015–.0032	.3425–.3432	.3420–.3427
	V8-350	Hydraulic⑥		45	45	1.727	⑬	.0015–.0035	.0015–.0032	.3720–.3730	.3723–.3730
	V8-400⑩	Hydraulic⑥		⑪	⑫	—	—	.0016–.0033	.0021–.0038	.3412–.3419	.3407–.3414
	V8-455	Hydraulic⑥		45	45	1.89	177 @ 1.45	.0015–.0035	.0015–.0032	.3720–.3730	.3723–.3730
1976	V6-231	Hydraulic⑥		45	45	1.727	168 @ 1.327	.0015–.0032	.0015–.0032	.3405–.3412	.3405–.3412
	V8-260⑦	Hydraulic⑥		⑧	⑨	1.67	187 @ 1.27	.001–.0027	.0015–.0032	.3425–.3432	.3420–.3427
	V8-350	Hydraulic⑥		45	45	1.727	177 @ 1.45	.0015–.0035	.0015–.0032	.3720–.3730	.3723–.3730
	V8-455	Hydraulic⑥		45	45	1.89	177 @ 1.45	.0015–.0035	.0015–.0032	.3720–.3730	.3723–.3730
1977–78	V6-196, 231	Hydraulic⑥		45	45	1.727	168 @ 1.327	.0015–.0032	.0015–.0032	.3405–.3412	.3405–.3412
	V8-301⑩	Hydraulic⑥		46	45	1.69	170 @ 1.26	.0017–.0020	.0017–.0020	.3400	.3400
	V8-305④	¾ Turn⑤		46	45	⑲	⑳	.0010–.0037	.0010–.0037	.3410–.3417	.3410–.3417
	V8-350⑯	Hydraulic⑥		45	45	1.727	⑬	.0015–.0035	.0015–.0032	.3720–.3730	.3723–.3730
	V8-350④⑰	¾ Turn⑤		46	45	⑲	⑳	.0010–.0037	.0010–.0037	.3410–.3417	.3410–.3417
	V8-350⑦⑱	Hydraulic⑥		⑧	⑨	1.67	187 @ 1.27	.0010–.0027	.0015–.0032	.3425–.3432	.3420–.3427
	V8-403⑦	Hydraulic⑥		⑧	⑨	1.67	187 @ 1.27	.0010–.0027	.0015–.0032	.3425–.3432	.3420–.3427
1979	V6-196, 231	Hydraulic⑥		45	45	1.727	182 @ 1.34	.0015–.0035	.0015–.0032	.3402–.3412	.3405–.3412
	V8-301⑩	Hydraulic⑥		46	45	1.66	166 @ 1.296	.0010–.0027	.0010–.0027	.3418–.3425	.3418–.3425
	V8-305④	—		46	45	⑲	㉑	.0010–.0027	.0010–.0027	.3410–.3417	.3410–.3417
	V8-350⑯	Hydraulic⑥		45	45	1.727	175 @ 1.34	.0015–.0035	.0015–.0032	.3720–.3730	.3723–.3730
	V8-350④⑰	—		46	45	⑲	㉒	.0010–.0027	.0010–.0027	.3410–.3417	.3410–.3417
	V8-350⑦⑱	Hydraulic⑥		⑧	⑨	1.67	187 @ 1.27	.0010–.0027	.0015–.0032	.3425–.3432	.3420–.3427
	V8-403⑦	Hydraulic⑥		⑧	⑨	1.67	187 @ 1.27	.0010–.0027	.0015–.0032	.3425–.3432	.3420–.3427

①—Plus or minus .001". Guide tapers top to bottom with larger dimension at bottom.
②—Plus or minus .0005". Guide tapers top to bottom with larger dimension at top.
③—Outer spring.
④—See Chevrolet chapter for service procedures on this engine.
⑤—Turn rocker arm stud nut until all lash is eliminated, then tighten nut the additional turn listed.
⑥—No adjustment.
⑦—See Oldsmobile Chapter for service procedures on this engine.
⑧—Intake, 45°; exhaust 31°.
⑨—Intake 44°; exhaust, 30°.
⑩—See Pontiac Chapter for service procedure on this engine.

⑪—Intake, 30°; exhaust, 45°.
⑫—Intake, 29°; exhaust 44°.
⑬—Intake, 180 @ 1.34; exhaust, 177 @ 1.45.
⑭—Intake, 164 @ 1.34; exhaust, 182 @ 134.
⑮—Intake, 180 @ 1.34; exhaust, 175 @ 1.34.
⑯—Distributor at front of engine.
⑰—Distributor at rear of engine, clockwise rotation.
⑱—Distributor at rear of engine, counter-clockwise rotation.
⑲—Intake, 1.70 inch; exhaust, 1.61 inch.
⑳—Intake, 200 @ 1.25; exhaust 200 @ 1.16.
㉑—Intake, 180 @ 1.25; exhaust 190 @ 1.16.
㉒—Intake, 184 @ 1.25; exhaust, 190 @ 1.16.

STARTING MOTOR SPECIFICATIONS

Year	Model	Starter Number	Brush Spring Tension Oz①	Free Speed Test			Resistance Test③	
				Amps.	Volts	R.P.M.	Amps. ①	Volts
1974	6-250	1108365	35	50–80②	9	5500–10500	—	—
	V8-350	1108506	35	55–80②	9	3500–6000	—	—
	V8-455	1108507	35	45–80②	9	4000–6500	—	—
1975	6-250	1108366	35	50–80	9	5500–10500	—	—
	V6-231	1108763	35	55–80	9	3500–6000	—	—
	V8-260	230232	35	55–80	9	3500–6000	—	—
	V8-350	1108763	35	55–80	9	3500–6000	—	—
	V8-400	—	35	65–95	9	7500–10500	—	—
	V8-455	1108763	35	45–80	9	4000–6500	—	—
1976	V6-231	1108770	35	50–80	9	5500–10500	—	—
	V8-260	1109026	35	55–80	9	3500–6000	—	—
	V8-350	1108762	35	55–80	9	3500–6000	—	—
	V8-455	1108763	35	45–80	9	4000–6500	—	—
1977	V6-231	1108797	—	55–80	9	5500–10000	—	—
	V8-301	1108758	—	55–80	9	3500–6000	—	—
	V8-305 Auto. Trans.	1109056	—	50–80②	9	5500–10500	—	—
	V8-305 Man. Trans.	1108799	—	50–80②	9	5500–10500	—	—
	V8-350④	1108762	35	55–80	9	3500–6000	—	—
	V8-350⑤	1109052	—	65–95②	9	7500–10500	—	—
	V8-350⑥	1108765	—	55–80	9	3500–6000	—	—
	V8-403	1108794	—	65–95	9	7500–10000	—	—
1978–79	V6-196, 231	1109061	—	60–85	9	6800–10300	—	—
	V8-301	1109523	—	45–70	9	7000–11900	—	—
	V8-305 2 Bbl. Carb.	1109064	—	60–85	9	6800–10300	—	—
	V8-305 4 Bbl. Carb.	1109524	—	45–70	9	7000–11900	—	—
	V8-350④	1109061	—	60–85	9	6800–10300	—	—
	V8-350⑤⑦	1109065	—	65–95	9	7500–10500	—	—
	V8-350⑥	1109072	—	65–95	9	7500–10500	—	—
	V8-403	1109072	—	65–95	9	7500–10500	—	—
1979	V8-350⑤⑧	1109524	—	45–70	9	7000–11900	—	—
	V8-350⑤⑨	1109065	—	65–95	9	7500–10500	—	—

①—Minimum.
②—Includes solenoid.
③—Check capacity of motor by using a 500 ampere meter and a carbon pile rheostat to control voltage. Apply volts listed across motor with armature locked. Current should be as listed.
④—Distributor at front of engine.
⑤—Distributor at rear of engine, clockwise rotation.
⑥—Distributor at rear of engine, counter-clockwise rotation.
⑦—1978 only.
⑧—Exc. Skylark.
⑨—Skylark.

COOLING SYSTEM & CAPACITY DATA

Year	Model or Engine	Cooling Capacity, Qts.			Radiator Cap Relief Pressure, Lbs.		Thermo. Opening Temp.	Fuel Tank Gals.	Engine Oil Refill Qts. ①	Transmission Oil			Rear Axle Oil Pints
		No Heater	With Heater	With A/C	With A/C	No A/C				3 Speed Pints	4 Speed Pints	Auto. Trans. Qts. ⑬	
1974	6-250	—	14.0	14.0	15	15	195	21	4	3½	—	⑮	③
	V8-350 Apollo	—	16.5	17.0	15	15	190	21	4	3½	—	⑮	③
	V8-350⑪	—	17.3	④	15	15	190	22	4	—	—	⑮	②
	V8-350⑩	—	17.3	17.2	15	15	190	26	4	—	—	⑮	②
	V8-455⑪	—	19.4	19.9	15	15	190	22	4	—	—	⑯	②
	V8-455⑥	—	19.6	19.8⑤	15	15	190	26③	4	—	—	⑯	②

Continued

COOLING SYSTEM & CAPACITY DATA—Continued

Year	Model or Engine	Cooling Capacity, Qts.			Radiator Cap Relief Pressure, Lbs.		Thermo. Opening Temp.	Fuel Tank Gals.	Engine Oil Refill Qts. [1]	Transmission Oil			Rear Axle Oil Pints
		No Heater	With Heater	With A/C	With A/C	No A/C				3 Speed Pints	4 Speed Pints	Auto. Trans. Qts. [13]	
1975	6-250	—	16.3	16.4	15	15	190	21	4	3½	—	[15]	4.25
	V6-231[7]	—	16.5	16.6	15	15	190	21	4	3½	—	[15]	4.25
	V6-231[11]	—	15.3	15.3	15	15	190	22	4	3½	—	[15]	4.25
	V8-260[7]	—	22.4	22.9	—	—	195	21	4	3½	—	[13]	4.25
	V8-350[7]	—	17.9	18.6	15	15	190	21	4	—	—	[15]	4.25
	V8-350[11]	—	16.9	17.2	15	15	190	22	4	3½	—	[15]	[20]
	V8-350[10]	—	16.9	17.2	15	15	190	26	4	—	—	[15]	4.25
	V8-400	—	23.6[8]	[9]	15	15	190	26[3]	4	—	—	—	[20]
	V8-455	—	19.6	20[5]	15	15	190	26[3]	4	—	—	[16]	[20]
1976	V6-231[7]	—	16.6	16.7	15	15	195	21	4	3½	—	[15]	4.25
	V6-231[10]	—	15.5	15.4	15	15	195	26[3]	4	—	—	[15]	4¼
	V6-231[11]	—	15.5	15.4	15	15	195	22	4	3½	—	[15]	4.25
	V8-260[7]	—	22.4	22.9	15	15	195	21	4	3½	—	[15]	4.25
	V8-350[7]	—	17.9	18.5	15	15	195	21	4	—	—	[15]	4.25
	V8-350[11]	—	16.9	17.2[12]	15	15	195	22	4	—	—	[15]	4.25
	V8-350[10]	—	16.9	17.2[12]	15	15	195	26[3]	4	—	—	[15]	4.25
	V8-350[4]	—	16.9	17.2[12]	15	15	195	26	4	—	—	[15]	5½
	V8-455	—	19.7	20[21]	15	15	195	26[3]	4	—	—	[16]	5.5
1977	V6-231[7]	—	12.7	12.8	15	15	[17]	21	4	3½	—	[15]	3.5
	V6-231[11]	—	12.8	12.7	15	15	[17]	22	4	3½	—	[15]	4¼
	V6-231[10]	—	12.7	12.7	15	15	[17]	21	4	—	—	[15]	4¼
	V8-301[7]	—	18.6	19.2	15	15	195	21	4	—	—	[15]	3.5
	V8-301[10]	—	18.2[22]	18.1[22]	15	15	195	21	4	—	—	[15]	4¼
	V8-305[7]	—	17	18	15	15	195	21	4	—	—	[15]	3.5
	V8-350[11][23]	—	14.3[24]	14.9[24]	15	15	195	22	4	—	—	[15]	4¼
	V8-350[6][10][23]	—	14.2[25]	14.1[25]	15	15	195	[26]	4	—	—	[15]	[27]
	V8-350[7][18][28]	—	15.6	15.6	15	15	195	21	4	—	—	[15]	3.5
	V8-350[11][18][28]	—	15.3[29]	15.9[29]	15	15	195	22	4	—	—	[15]	4¼
	V8-350[6][10][28]	—	14.6[30]	14.5[30]	15	15	195	[26]	4	—	—	[15]	[27]
	V8-350[7][28]	—	17	18	15	15	195	21	4	—	—	[15]	3.5
	V8-350[11][28]	—	14.8	15.4	15	15	195	22	4	—	—	[15]	4¼
	V8-403[11]	—	16.4[31]	17[31]	15	15	195	22	4	—	—	[15]	4¼
	V8-403[6][10]	—	15.7[32]	15.6[32]	15	15	195	[26]	4	—	—	[15]	[27]
1978	V6-196	—	13.1	13.2	15	15	195	17.5	4	3½	—	[15]	4¼
	V6-231[7]	—	13.6	13.7	15	15	195	21	4	3½	—	[15]	4¼
	V6-231[11]	—	13.1	13.2	15	15	195	17.5	4	—	3½	[15]	4¼
	V6-231[10]	—	12.9	12.9	15	15	195	21	4	—	—	[15]	4¼
	V8-301	—	20.9[5]	20.9[5]	15	15	195	21	4	—	—	[15]	4¼
	V8-305[7]	—	15.9[33]	16.3[33]	15	15	195	21	4	3½	—	[15]	4¼
	V8-305[11]	—	19.2[34]	18.9[34]	15	15	195	17.5	4	—	—	[15]	4¼
	V8-305[10]	—	16.6	16.7	15	15	195	21	4	—	—	[15]	4¼
	V8-350[7]	—	16.1	16.9	15	15	195	21	4	—	—	[15]	4¼
	V8-350[11]	—	19.2[34]	18.9[34]	15	15	195	17.5	4	—	—	[15]	4¼
	V8-350[6][10][23]	—	14.1[35]	14.1[35]	15	15	195	[19]	4	—	—	[15]	4¼
	V8-350[6][10][18]	—	14.6[30]	14.5[30]	15	15	195	[19]	4	—	—	[15]	4¼
	V8-350[6][10][28]	—	16.6[36]	16.7[36]	15	15	195	[19]	4	—	—	[15]	4¼
	V8-403	—	15.7	16.6	15	15	195	[19]	4	—	—	—	4¼
1979	V6-196, 231[11]	—	13.5	13.5	15	15	195	18.1	4	3.12	3.12	[15]	3.5
	V6-231[10]	—	13.4	13.4	15	15	195	25.3	4	—	—	[15]	4.25
	V6-231[7]	—	13.8	14	15	15	195	21	4	3.12	—	[15]	4.25
	V6-231[37][10]	—	13.7	13.7	15	15	195	25.3	4	—	—	[15]	4.25
	V6-231[37][11]	—	13.4	13.4	15	15	195	18.1	4	—	—	[15]	3.5
	V6-231[37]	—	14.1	14.1	15	15	195	20	4	—	—	[16]	4.25
	V8-301[11]	—	17.6	17.9	15	15	195	18.1	4	—	—	[15]	3.5
	V8-301[10]	—	21	21[5]	15	15	195	25.3	4	—	—	[15]	4.25

Continued

COOLING SYSTEM & CAPACITY DATA—Continued

Year	Model or Engine	Cooling Capacity, Qts.			Radiator Cap Relief Pressure, Lbs.		Thermo. Opening Temp.	Fuel Tank Gals.	Engine Oil Refill Qts. ①	Transmission Oil			Rear Axle Oil Pint
		No Heater	With Heater	With A/C	With A/C	No A/C				3 Speed Pints	4 Speed Pints	Auto. Trans. Qts. ⑬	
1979	V8-305⑦	—	15.9	16.2㉜	15	15	195	21	4	—	—	⑮	4.25
	V8-305⑪	—	15.7	15.6㉔	15	15	195	18.1	4	—	—	⑮	3.5
	V8-350⑦	—	16.1	16.7	15	15	195	21	4	—	—	⑮	4.25
	V8-350⑪	—	15.7	16.4㊳	15	15	195	18.1	4	—	—	⑮	3.5
	V8-350⑩⑥㊴	—	14.6	14.5㉖	15	15	195	㊷	4	—	—	㊶	4.25
	V8-350⑩⑥㊵	—	14.6	14.5㉚	15	15	195	㊷	4	—	—	㊶	4.25
	V8-403	—	15.7	16.6	15	15	195	22.5	4	—	—	⑯	4.25

①—Add one quart with filter change.
②—8½ inch axle, 4¼ pts.; 8⅞ inch axle, 5¼ pts.; 9⅜ inch axle, 5½ pts.
③—Estate Wagon 22 gallons.
④—With 20 inch fan shroud, 17.6 qts.; with 22 inch fan shroud, 17.2 qts.
⑤—With heavy duty cooling system 21.6 qts.
⑥—Estate Wagon, Electra & Riviera.
⑦—Apollo & Skylark.
⑧—With heavy duty cooling system, 25.6 qts.
⑨—Exc. wagon & heavy duty, 24.4 qts;. wagon & heavy duty, 26.1 qts.
⑩—LeSabre.
⑪—Intermediates
⑫—With heavy duty cooling system, 18.7 qts.
⑬—Approximate. Make final check with dipstick.
⑭—Electra.
⑮—Total 10 qts.; pan only 3 qts.
⑯—Total 11½ qts. Oil pan only 3½ qts.
⑰—Exc. Calif., 195°; Calif., 180°.
⑱—Oil filler tube located on engine front cover.
⑲—LeSabre, 21; Estate Wagon, 22.5; Electra, Riviera, 25.3.
⑳—Exc. wagon, 4¼ pts.; wagon, 5.4 pts.
㉑—With heavy duty cooling system, 21.5 qts.
㉒—With heavy duty cooling system, 19.1 qts.
㉓—Distributor at front of engine.
㉔—With heavy duty cooling system, 16.4 qts.
㉕—With heavy duty cooling system, 15 qts.
㉖—LeSabre, 21 gal.; Electra & Riviera, 24.5 gal.; Estate wagon, 22 gal.
㉘—Distributor at rear of engine.
㉙—With heavy duty cooling system, 17.4 qts.
㉚—With heavy duty cooling system, 15.4 qts.
㉛—With heavy duty cooling system, 18.5 qts.
㉜—With heavy duty cooling system, 16.6 qts.
㉝—With heavy duty cooling system, 16.9 qts.
㉞—With heavy duty cooling system, 19.6 qts.
㉟—With heavy duty cooling system, 14.9 qts.
㊱—With heavy duty cooling system, 18.0 qts.
㊲—4 Barrel Carb.
㊳—With heavy duty cooling system, 17.9 qts.
㊴—Buick built engine.
㊵—Oldsmobile built engine.
㊶—LeSabre total 10 qts.; oil pan only 3 qts.; others total 11½ qts., oil pan 3½ qts.
㊷—Estate wagon, 22.5 gals.; Electra & LeSabre, 25.3 gal.; Riviera, 20 gal.

WHEEL ALIGNMENT SPECIFICATIONS

Year	Model	Caster Angle, Degrees		Camber Angle, Degrees				Toe-In. Inch	Toe-Out on Turns, Deg.	
		Limits	Desired	Limits		Desired			Outer Wheel	Inner Wheel
				Left	Right	Left	Right			
1974	Apollo	0 to +1	+½	−¼ to +¾	−¼ to +¾	+¼	+¼	⅛–¼	—	20
	Intermediates	−½ to +½	0	+½ to +1½	0 to +1	+1	+½	0–⅛	③	20
	Others	+½ to +1½	+1	+½ to +1½	0 to +1	+1	+½	0–⅛	18½	20
1975	Apollo, Skylark①	−½ to −1½	−1	+¼ to +1¼	+¼ to +1¼	+¾	+¾	0–⅛	18½	—
	Apollo, Skylark②	+½ to +1½	+1	+¼ to +1¼	+¼ to +1¼	+¾	+¾	0–⅛		—
	Century	+1½ to +2½	+2	+½ to +1½	0 to +1	+1	+½	0–⅛	③	20
	Others	+½ to +2½	+1½	+½ to +1½	0 to +1	+1	+½	0–⅛	18½	20
1976	Skylark①	−½ to −1½	−1	+¼ to +1¼	+¼ to +1¼	+¾	+¾	0–⅛	—	—
	Skylark②	+½ to +1½	+1	+¼ to +1¼	+¼ to +1¼	+¾	+¾	0–⅛	—	—
	Century, Regal	+1½ to +2½	+2	+½ to +1½	0 to +1	+1	+½	0–⅛	③	20
	Others	+1 to +2	+1½	+½ to +1½	0 to +1	+1	+½	0–⅛	18½	20
1977	Skylark①	−½ to −1½	−1	+¼ to +1¼	+¼ to +1¼	+¾	+¾	0–⅛	—	—
	Skylark②	+½ to +1½	+1	+¼ to +1¼	+¼ to +1¼	+¾	+¾	0–⅛	—	—
	Century, Regal④	+½ to +1½	+1	+½ to +1½	0 to +1	+1	+½	0–⅛	—	—
	Century, Regal⑤	+1½ to +2½	+2	+½ to +1½	0 to +1	+1	+½	0–⅛	—	—
	Others	+2½ to +3½	+3	+¼ to +1¼	+¼ to +1¼	+¾	+¾	1/16–3/16	—	—
1978	Skylark①	−.5 to −1.5	−1	+.3 to +1.3	+.3 to +1.3	+.8	+.8	0–⅛	—	—
	Skylark②	+.5 to +1.5	+1	+.3 to +1.3	+.3 to +1.3	+.8	+.8	0–⅛	—	—
	Century, Regal①	+.5 to +1.5	+1	0 to +1	0 to +1	+.5	+.5	0–⅛	—	—
	Century, Regal②	+2.5 to +3.5	+3	0 to +1	0 to +1	+.5	+.5	0–⅛	—	—
	Others	+2.5 to +3.5	+3	+.3 to +1.3	+.3 to +1.3	+.8	+.8	0–⅛	—	—

Continued

WHEEL ALIGNMENT SPECIFICATIONS—Continued

Year	Model	Caster Angle, Degrees		Camber Angle, Degrees				Toe-In. Inch	Toe-Out on Turns, Deg.	
				Limits		Desired				
		Limits	Desired	Left	Right	Left	Right		Outer Wheel	Inner Wheel
1979	Skylark①	−.5 to −1.5	−1	+.3 to +1.3	+.3 to +1.3	+.8	+.8	0–⅛	—	—
	Skylark②	+.5 to +1.5	+1	+.3 to +1.3	+.3 to +1.3	+.8	+.8	0–⅛	—	—
	Century, Regal	+2.5 to +3.5	+3	0 to +1	0 to +1	+.5	+.5	0–⅛	—	—
	Riviera	+2 to +3	+2.5	−.5 to +.5	−.5 to +.5	0	0	⑥	—	—
	Others	+2.5 to +3.5	+3	+.3 to +1.3	+.3 to +1.3	+.8	+.8	0–⅛	—	—

①—Manual steering.   ②—Power steering.
③—Manual steering & all Sta. Wag.—right turn, 19³⁄₁₆°; left turn, 18¹³⁄₁₆°:
power steering Exc. Sta. Wag.—right turn, 19°; left turn, 18¹¹⁄₁₆°.
④—Equipped with bias belted tires.
⑤—Equipped with radial tires.
⑥—¹⁄₁₆″ toe-in to ¹⁄₁₆″ toe-out.

Electrical Section

DISTRIBUTOR, REPLACE

Except H.E.I. System

1. Disconnect primary wire from ignition coil and hose from vacuum advance unit, then remove distributor cap.
2. Place a straight edge against distributor housing and water pump housing and make a chalk mark on rotor, distributor housing and water pump housing to ensure proper installation of distributor.
3. Remove distributor clamp bolt and clamp and lift out distributor.
4. Before installing distributor, install a new O-ring on distributor housing.
5. With chalk mark on rotor approximately 15-20 degrees counterclockwise from mark on distributor housing, install distributor with chalk marks on distributor housing and water pump housing aligned.

NOTE: It may be necessary to lift distributor and turn rotor slightly to align gears and oil pump drive shaft.

6. Install clamp and clamp bolt finger tight, then reconnect primary wire to coil and install distributor cap.
7. Check point dwell and timing and adjust as necessary.
8. Tighten distributor clamp bolt and reconnect vacuum hose.

With H.E.I. System

1. Disconnect battery ground cable.

2. Disconnect feed and module connectors from distributor cap.
3. Disconnect hose from vacuum advance unit and remove distributor cap.
4. Using chalk, make alignment marks on rotor and module and distributor housing and engine to ensure proper installation of distributor.
5. Remove clamp bolt and clamp.
6. Lift distributor out and note relative position of rotor and module alignment marks, then make a second mark on the rotor to align with mark on module.
7. Before installing distributor, install a new O-ring on distributor housing.
8. With the second mark on rotor aligned with mark on module, install distributor with mark on distributor housing aligned with mark on engine.

NOTE: It may be necessary to lift distributor slightly to align gears and oil pump drive shaft.

9. Install clamp and clamp bolt finger tight, then install distributor cap and reconnect feed and module connectors to distributor cap.
10. Check engine timing and adjust as necessary, then tighten clamp bolt and connect vacuum hose.

STARTER, REPLACE

To remove the starter, disconnect battery cable from battery. Disconnect cable and solenoid lead wire from solenoid switch. Remove flywheel inspection cover. Remove starter attaching bolts and remove starter.

LIGHT SWITCH, REPLACE

1974-79

CAUTION: On vehicles equipped with an Air Cushion Restraint System, turn ignition switch to "Lock," disconnect battery ground cable and tape end, thereby deactivating system.

1. Disconnect battery ground cable.
2. On 1975-79 intermediate models equipped with A/C, remove left hand duct.
3. On 1974-78 full size models, remove left hand trim panel.
4. On all models except 1978-79 Century and Regal, pull switch knob to full "On" position, depress latch button on rear of switch and pull knob and rod from switch. On 1978-79 Century and Regal, depress retainer tab behind switch knob and remove knob from stem. On all models, remove switch escutcheon or retaining nut, if used.
5. Pull switch down, disconnect electrical connector and remove switch.

NOTE: On 1975-76 Full Size Models, remove switch from mounting bracket.

6. Reverse procedure to install.

COLUMN-MOUNTED DIMMER SWITCH

1977-79 Full Size & 1978-79 Century & Regal

1. Disconnect battery ground cable.
2. Remove instrument panel lower trim and on models with A/C, remove A/C duct extension at column.
3. Disconnect shift indicator from column and remove toe-plate cover screws.
4. Remove two nuts from instrument panel support bracket studs and lower sterring column, resting steering wheel on front seat.
5. Remove dimmer switch retaining screw(s) and the switch. Tape actuator rod to column and separate switch from rod.
6. Reverse procedure to install. To adjust switch, depress dimmer switch slightly and install a $3/32$ inch twist drill to lock the switch to the body. Force switch upward to remove lash between switch and pivot. Torque switch retaining screw(s) to 35 inch lbs. and remove tape from actuator rod. Remove twist drill and check for proper operation.

1975-77 Intermediates

1. Remove switch cover.
2. Remove three switch to column attaching screws.
3. Disconnect switch lead at lower end of column and attach a wire to lead end of harness for ease of installation.
4. Hold switch and pull harness from column.
5. Reverse procedure to install.

IGNITION LOCK

1979

1. Remove steering wheel as described under Horn Sounder and Steering Wheel.
2. Remove turn signal switch as described under Turn Signal Switch, Replace, then remove buzzer switch.
3. Place ignition switch in Run position, then remove lock cylinder retaining screw and lock cylinder.
4. To install, rotate lock cylinder to stop while holding housing, Fig. 1. Align cylinder key with keyway in housing, then push lock cylinder assembly into housing until fully seated.
5. Install lock cylinder retaining screw. Torque screw to 40 in. lbs. for standard columns. On adjustable columns, torque retaining screw to 22 in. lbs.
6. Install buzzer switch, turn signal switch and steering wheel.

1974-78

1. Follow procedure to remove turn signal switch as described further on.
2. Place lock cylinder in "run" position.
3. Place a thin tool (small screw-driver or knife blade) into the slot next to the switch mounting screw boss (right hand slot) and depress spring latch at bottom of slot which releases lock Fig. 2. Remove lock.
4. To install lock, hold lock cylinder sleeve and rotate knob clockwise against stop, then insert cylinder with key on cylinder sleeve aligned with keyway in housing. Push in to abutment of cylinder and sector, then rotate knob counterclockwise, maintaining a light inward push on cylinder until drive section of cylinder mates with drive shaft.

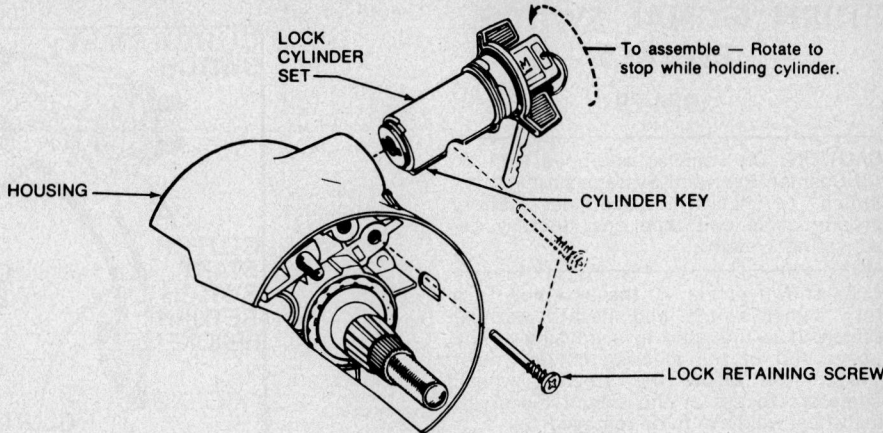

Fig. 1   Lock cylinder removal. 1979 models

LOCK CYLINDER SET

HOUSING

To assemble — Rotate to stop while holding cylinder.

CYLINDER KEY

LOCK RETAINING SCREW

IGNITION SWITCH, REPLACE

1974-79

CAUTION: On vehicles equipped with an Air Cushion Restraint System, turn ignition switch to "Lock" position, disconnect battery ground cable and tape end, thereby deactivating system.

The ignition switch is located on the top of the steering column under the instrument panel. To replace it the steering column must be lowered as follows:

1. Disconnect shift indicator link.
2. Remove nuts securing bracket to dash panel and carefully lower column.
3. Disconnect electrical connector from switch. Ensure switch is in "Accessory" position on 1977-79 models or "Off-Unlock" position on 1974-76 models.
4. Remove two screws securing switch and remove switch.
5. On 1974-76 models, the switch and lock are placed in the "Off-Unlock" position. On 1977-79 models, position switch and lock in the "Accessory" position.
6. Fit actuator rod into switch and assemble to column.
7. Complete assembly in reverse of removal procedure.

Fig. 2   Ignition lock removal. 1974-78

STOP LIGHT SWITCH, REPLACE

1974-79

The stop lights are controlled by a mechanical switch mounted on the brake pedal bracket. This spring loaded switch makes contact whenever the brake pedal is applied. When the brake pedal is released it depresses the switch to open the contacts and turn brake lights off.

CLUTCH START SWITCH

1974-78

A clutch start switch is installed on all manual transmission cars. The switch is mounted on the clutch pedal bracket and it prevents the car from being started until the clutch pedal is depressed, Fig. 3.

TURN SIGNAL SWITCH, REPLACE

1974-79

CAUTION: On vehicles equipped with an Air Cushion Restraint System, turn ignition switch to "Lock," disconnect battery ground cable and tape end, thereby de-activating system.

As shown in Fig. 4, the assembly is a turn signal switch and hazard warning switch. It is mounted in a housing at the upper end of the steering column mast jacket, just below the steering wheel. Therefore to get at the switch the steering wheel will have to be removed.

Also, on models equipped with tilt steering columns, it is necessary to lower the column assembly from instrument panel.

1. Disconnect battery ground cable.
2. Remove steering wheel and lock plate cover. On tilt columns, remove tilt lever.
3. With a suitable compressor, compress lock plate and spring, then remove snap ring from shaft, Fig. 5.

NOTE: On 1976-79 models, remove lock plate cover with a suitable screwdriver.

4. Remove lock plate, cancelling cam, preload spring and thrust washer.

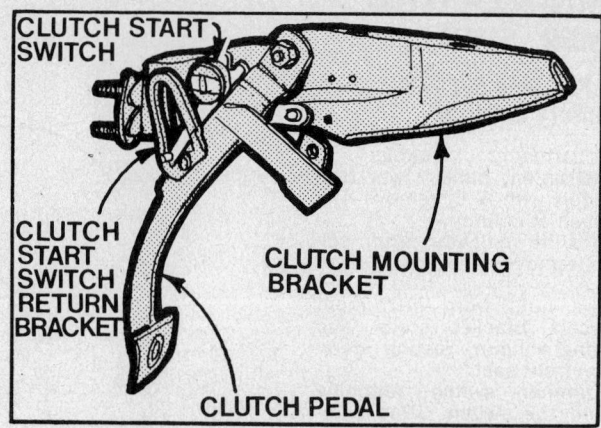

Fig. 3   Clutch start switch in start position. 1974-79

5. Remove turn signal lever and hazard warning switch knob.
6. Disconnect switch wiring connector and wrap a piece of tape around connector upper end and wiring harness, preventing snagging when removing switch, Fig. 6.
7. Remove three switch retaining screws and switch.
8. Reverse procedure to install.

NEUTRAL START & BACK-UP LIGHT SWITCH

1977-79 Full Size & 1978-79 Century, Regal

Actuation of the ignition switch is prevented by a mechanical lockout system, Figs. 7 and 8, which prevents the lock cylinder from rotating when the selector lever is out of Park or Neutral. When the selector lever is in Park or Neutral, the slots in the bowl plate and the finger on the actuator rod align allowing the finger to pass through the bowl plate in turn actuating the ignition switch, Fig. 9. If the selector lever is in any position other than Park or Neutral, the finger contacts the bowl plate when the lock cylinder is rotated, thereby preventing full travel of the lock cylinder.

NOTE: A back-up light switch is used and is similar to the combination neutral start—back-up lamp used on other models. Refer to the "Switch, Adjust" procedure for adjustment of this switch.

Exc. 1977-79 Full Size & 1978-79 Century, Regal

NOTE: To check operation of switch after adjustments are made as outlined below, proceed as follows:

1. With shift lever in Park starter should operate.
2. With shift lever in Reverse back-up lights should light but starter should not operate.
3. With shift lever in Neutral starter should operate but back-up lights should be out.
4. With shift lever in Drive, starter should not operate and back-up lights should be out.

Switch, Adjust

1. Place shift lever in Neutral.
2. Attempt to insert a 3/32" or a No. 42

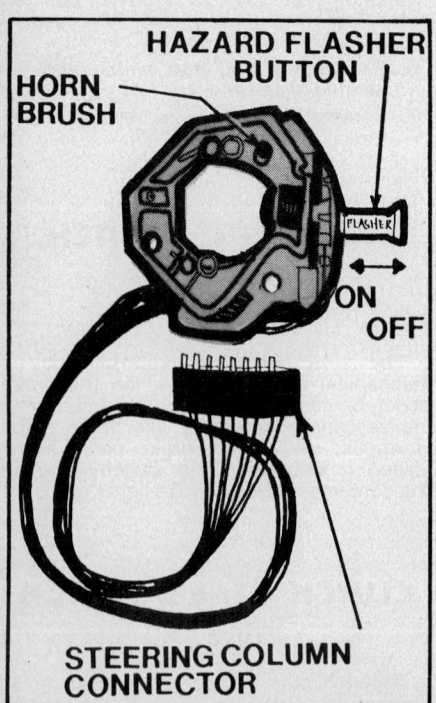

Fig. 4   Turn signal and hazard warning flasher switch assembly. 1974-79

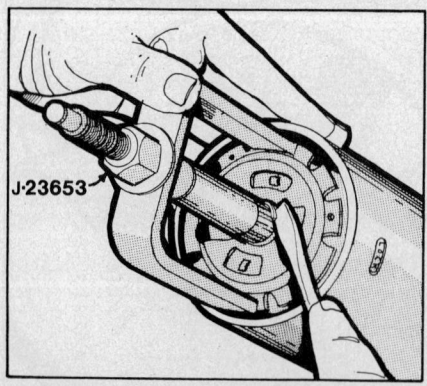

Fig. 5   Compressing lock plate & removing snap ring

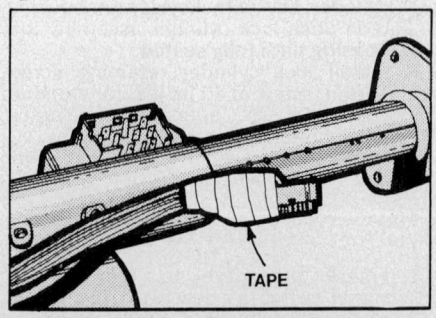

Fig. 6   Taping turn signal connector & wiring

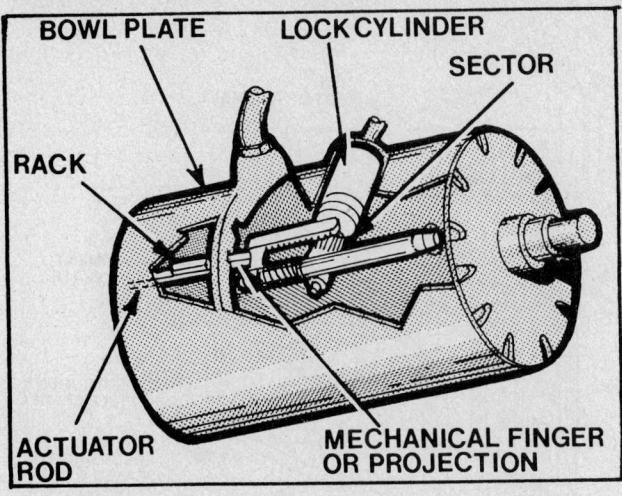

Fig. 7   Mechanical neutral start system with standard
column. 1977-78 Full Size & 1978-79 Century, Regal

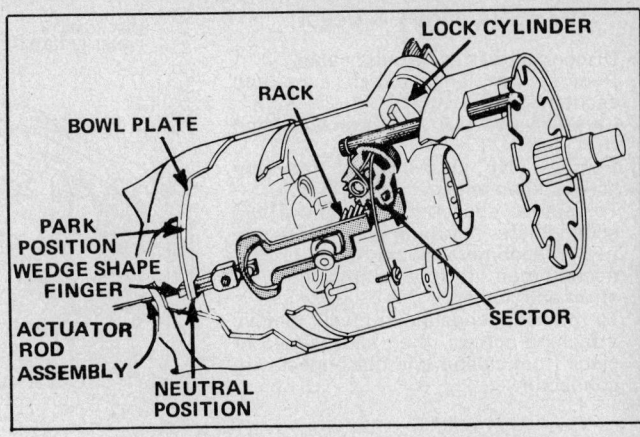

Fig. 8   Mechanical neutral start system with tilt
column. 1977-79 Full Size & 1978-79 Century, Regal

drill through gauging hole in switch body into inner hole in sliding part of switch, Fig. 10.

3. If drill does not enter inner hole, loosen two switch mounting screws and slide switch body as required to allow drill to enter inner hole. Tighten screws and remove drill.

HORN SOUNDER & STEERING WHEEL
1974-79

CAUTION: On vehicles equipped with an Air Cushion Restraint System, turn ignition switch to "Lock," disconnect battery ground cable and tape end, thereby de-activating system. Also, on these vehicles,

it is necessary to remove the drivers cushion module before removing steering wheel. With tool J-24628-2, remove the module to steering wheel screws, lift module and disconnect horn wire. Then, with tool J-24628-3, disconnect module wire connector from slip ring.

1. Remove horn cap or actuator bar.
2. Remove steering wheel nut retainer, if used.
3. On all models, back off nut until flush with top of steering shaft.
4. Use a suitable puller to remove wheel.

INSTRUMENT CLUSTER

CAUTION: On vehicles equipped with an

Air Cushion Restraint System, turn ignition switch to "Lock," disconnect battery ground cable and tape end, thereby de-activating system.

1979 Riviera

1. Disconnect battery ground cable.
2. Remove left hand trim cover, Fig. 11.
3. Remove headlamp and windshield wiper switches.
4. Disconnect headlamp and windshield wiper switch wire connectors from cluster carrier.
5. Disconnect speedometer cable, and wire connectors from cluster carrier.
6. Remove cluster carrier to instrument panel attaching screws, then remove cluster carrier.

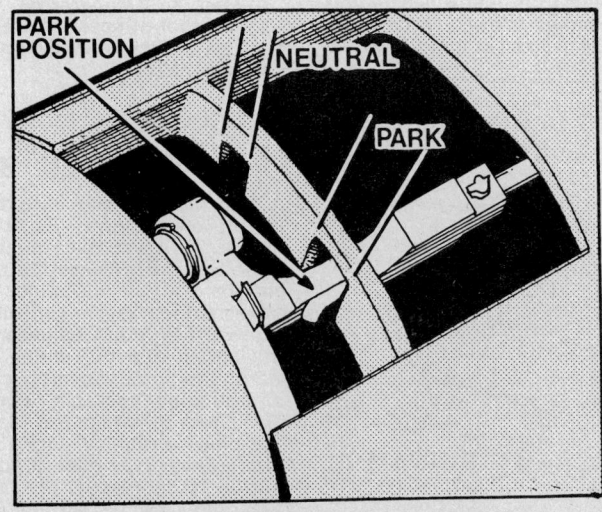

Fig. 9   Mechanical neutral start system
in Park position. 1977-79 Full Size & 1978-79 Century, Regal

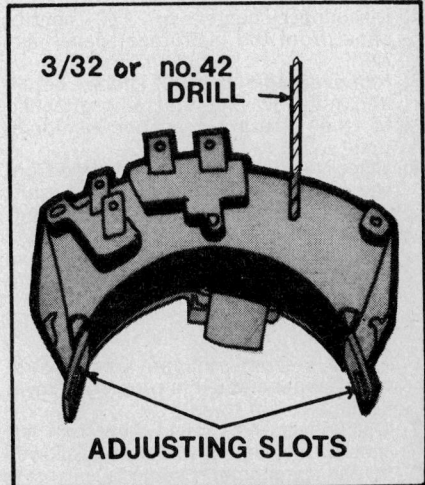

Fig. 10   Adjusting neutral
safety switch. Exc. 1977-79 Full Size &
1978-79 Century, Regal

1978-79 Century & Regal

1. Disconnect battery ground cable.
2. Remove headlamp switch knob and escutcheon.
3. Carefully pry out and remove clutch trim plate.
4. Remove five cluster lens attaching screws, then remove cluster lens.
5. To remove speedometer, remove two speedometer retaining screws. Disconnect speedometer cable and wire connector, then lift speedometer from instrument cluster.
6. To replace fuel gauge or clock, remove attaching screws, then slide gauge or clock from cluster and disconnect wire connector.

1977-79 Full Size Except 1979 Riviera

1. Disconnect battery ground cable.
2. Remove glove box door and glove box.
3. Remove trim plates and the steering column opening filler.
4. Disconnect electrical and vacuum connectors from gauges or controls.
5. Remove wiring harness from instrument panel carrier clips.
6. Remove instrument panel carrier attaching nuts and screws, then the carrier from vehicle.
7. Reverse procedure to install.

1975-76 Full Size

1. Disconnect battery ground cable.
2. Remove instrument cluster bezel and lens.
3. Remove screws securing speedometer head assembly and pull assembly from housing.
4. Remove screws securing fuel gauge assembly and pull assembly from housing.
5. Reverse procedure to install.

1974-79 Apollo & Skylark

1. Disconnect battery ground cable.
2. Disconnect heater or A/C control panel from the instrument panel carrier.
3. Remove radio control knobs, bezels and nuts, leaving the radio attached to the instrument panel reinforcement.
4. Disconnect instrument panel pad from the carrier and disconnect the shift quadrant indicator cable at the shift bowl. On automatic transmission equipped vehicles remove the two nuts securing the steering column to instrument panel.
5. Remove toe plate cover and disconnect from cowl.
6. Lower steering column from instrument panel and use a protective cover (such as shop towel).
7. Disconnect the ground wire from left side of instrument panel pad followed by the speedometer cable.
8. With carrier and cluster assembly tilted rearward, disconnect printed circuit and cluster ground connectors.
9. Rest assembly on top of column and

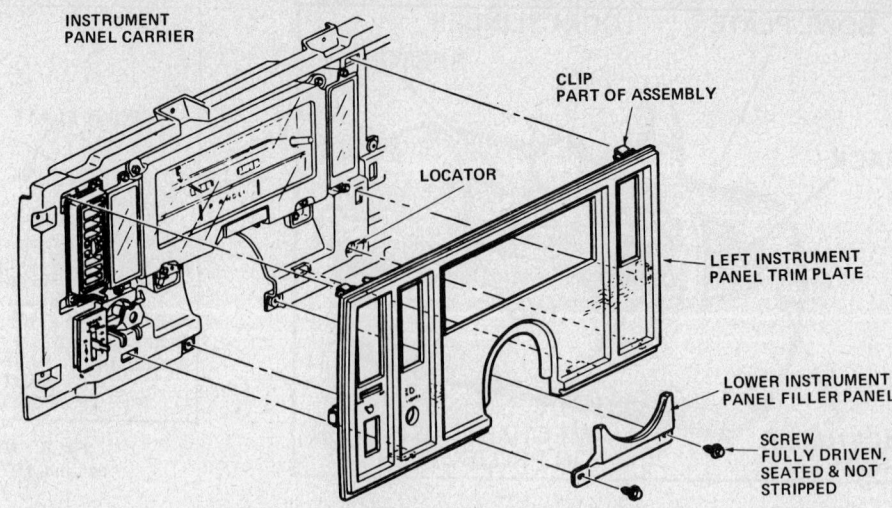

INSTRUMENT PANEL CARRIER

CLIP PART OF ASSEMBLY

LOCATOR

LEFT INSTRUMENT PANEL TRIM PLATE

LOWER INSTRUMENT PANEL FILLER PANEL

SCREW FULLY DRIVEN, SEATED & NOT STRIPPED

Fig. 11   Instrument cluster trim cover. 1979 Riviera

disconnect cluster from carrier assembly.
10. Reverse procedure to install.

1974-77 Century & Regal

Speedometer Cluster

1. Disconnect battery ground cable.
2. Place transmission selector lever in "L" position and disconnect shift indicator cable from steering column.
3. Pry trim plate from instrument panel.
4. Remove speedometer retaining screws, Fig. 12, disconnect speedometer cable and wiring connector, then remove speedometer.
5. Reverse procedure to install.

Fuel Gauge & Telltale Assembly

1. Disconnect battery ground cable.
2. Pry trim plate from instrument panel.
3. Remove retaining screws, Fig. 12, disconnect wiring connectors, then remove assembly.

NOTE: If equipped with temperature

and oil pressure gauges and one gauge of the assembly is defective, all three gauges must be replaced since the cluster is serviced as an assembly.

4. Reverse procedure to install.

1974 Full Size

1. Disconnect battery ground cable.
2. *Speedometer* removal is accomplished as follows: Remove lower instrument panel filler panel. Disconnect shift pointer cable with shift lever in L1. Remove speedo face glass by removing two screws on top of glass and remove speedometer by removing three screws on speedo face.
3. *Fuel & Temperature Gauges:* After removal of speedometer these gauges can be removed by removing attaching screws.

W/S WIPER BLADES

Two methods are used to retain wiper blades to wiper arms, Fig. 13. One method uses a press type release tab. When the release tab is depressed the blade assembly can be slid off the wiper arm pin. The other method uses a coil spring retainer. A screw driver must be inserted on top of the spring and the spring pushed downward. The blade assembly can then be slid off the wiper arm pin. Two methods are also used to retain the blade element in the blade assembly, Fig. 13. One method uses a press type release button. When the button is depressed, the two piece blade assembly can be slid off the blade element. The other method uses a spring type retainer clip in the end of the blade

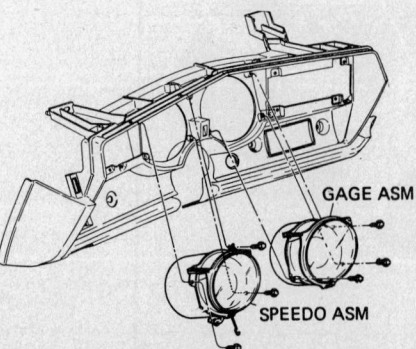

GAGE ASM

SPEEDO ASM

Fig. 12   Speedometer & telltale assembly. 1974-77 Century & Regal

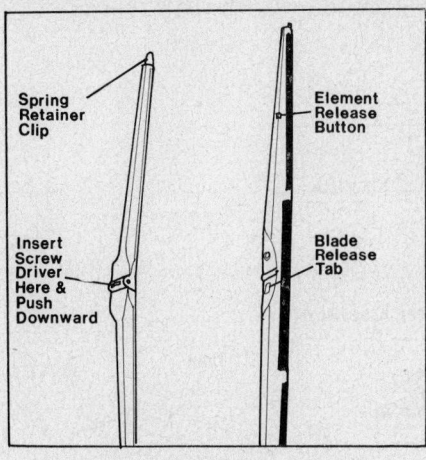

Fig. 13   Wiper blade assembly

element. When the retainer clip is squeezed together, the blade element can be slid out of the blade assembly.

NOTE: To be sure of correct installation, the element release button, or the spring element retaining clip should be at the end of the wiper blade assembly nearest the wiper transmission.

W/S WIPER ARMS

With Rectangular Motor

1. Wiper motor must be in park position.

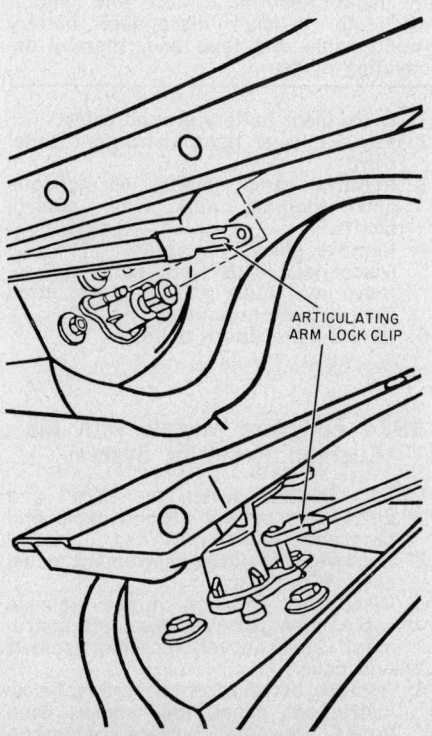

Fig. 15   Articulating arm lock clips

2. Use suitable tool to minimize the possibility of windshield or paint finish damage during arm removal, Fig. 14.
3. Remove arm by prying up with tool to disengage arm from serrated transmission shaft.
4. To install arm to transmission rotate the required distance and direction so that blades rest in proper position.

With Round Motor

1. Wiper motor must be in park position.
2. Raise hood to gain access to wiper arm.
3. On 1974-77 Intermediate Models: lift arm off transmission shaft. On left arm, slide articulating arm lock clip, Fig. 15, away from transmission pivot pin and lift arm off pin. On 1978-79 Intermediate Models: lift wiper arm and slide latch clip out from under arm, Fig. 17. On Full Size Models: lift wiper arm and slide latch clip, Figs. 16 and 17, out from under wiper arm.
4. Release wiper arm and lift arm assembly off transmission shaft.

W/S WIPER MOTOR, REPLACE
1974-79

1. Disconnect battery and remove cowl screen.
2. Loosen nuts on wiper drivelink to motor cranking arm and slip drivelink off cranking arm.
3. Disconnect washer hoses and electrical connections.
4. Unfasten motor and remove.

NOTE: On models with round motor, the motor must be in "Park" position when assembling crank arm to transmission drive link.

W/S WIPER TRANSMISSION
1974-79

1. Disconnect battery ground cable and

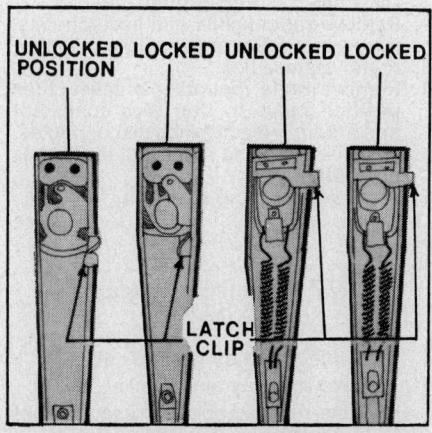

Fig. 16   Wiper arm latch clips. 1974-76 Full Size

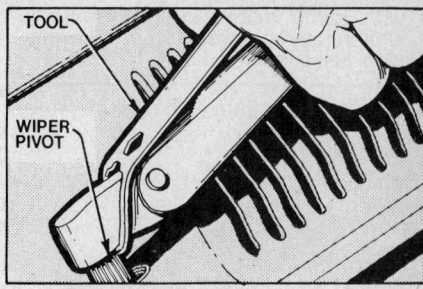

Fig. 14   Wiper arm removal. Models with rectangular motor

remove cowl vent screen or grille.
2. Disconnect wiper motor electrical connector.
3. Remove wiper arm and blade assemblies.

NOTE: 1974-76 full size models equipped with round motor, remove wiper arm and blade from transmission being removed.

4. Loosen transmission drive link to motor crankarm attaching nuts, then disconnect drive link from crankarm.

NOTE: 1974-76 full size models equipped with round motor, if left hand transmission is being removed, it is not necessary to disconnect the right hand transmission drive link.

5. Remove right and left transmission to body retaining screws and guide transmission and linkage through cowl opening.

NOTE: On full size models equipped

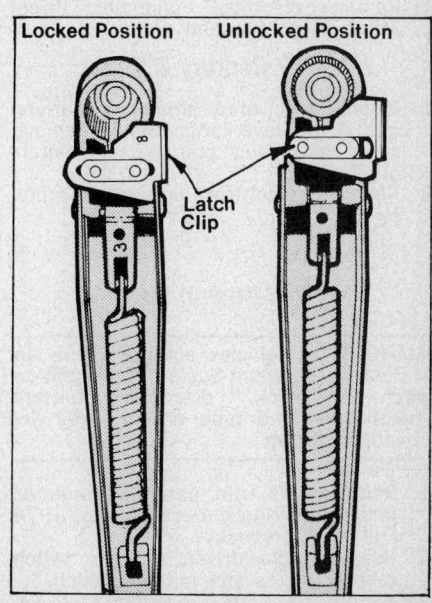

Fig. 17   Wiper arm latch clips. 1977-79 Full Size & 1978-79 Intermediates

with round motor, remove transmission retaining screws from transmission being removed.

6. Reverse procedure to install.

W/S WIPER SWITCH, REPLACE

1979 Riviera

1. Disconnect battery ground cable.
2. Remove left hand trim cover, Fig. 11.
3. Remove two switch to cluster attaching screws.
4. Pull switch rearward and remove.

1978-79 Century & Regal

1. Remove headlamp switch knob and escutcheon.
2. Remove trim plate.
3. Remove two switch attaching screws, then disconnect wire connector and remove switch.
4. Reverse procedure to install.

1977-79 Full Size Except 1979 Riviera

1. Remove left trim plate.
2. Remove switch attaching screws.
3. Disconnect electrical connector from switch and remove switch from vehicle.
4. Reverse procedure to install.

1974-79 Apollo & Skylark

1. Remove electrical connector, three attaching screws and switch.

1974-77 Century & Regal

1. Insert blade of a small screwdriver into slots above knobs, bend retaining clips down and pull top of switch outward.
2. Remove electrical connector from switch.

1974-76 Full Size

CAUTION: On vehicles equipped with an Air Cushion Restraint System, turn ignition switch to "Lock," disconnect battery ground cable and tape end, thereby deactivating system.

1. Remove left trim panel as outlined under the "Instrument Cluster, 1974 Full Size" procedure.
2. Using a screwdriver, depress switch retaining clips and remove switch.
3. Disconnect seelite cable and electrical connector.
4. Reverse procedure to install.

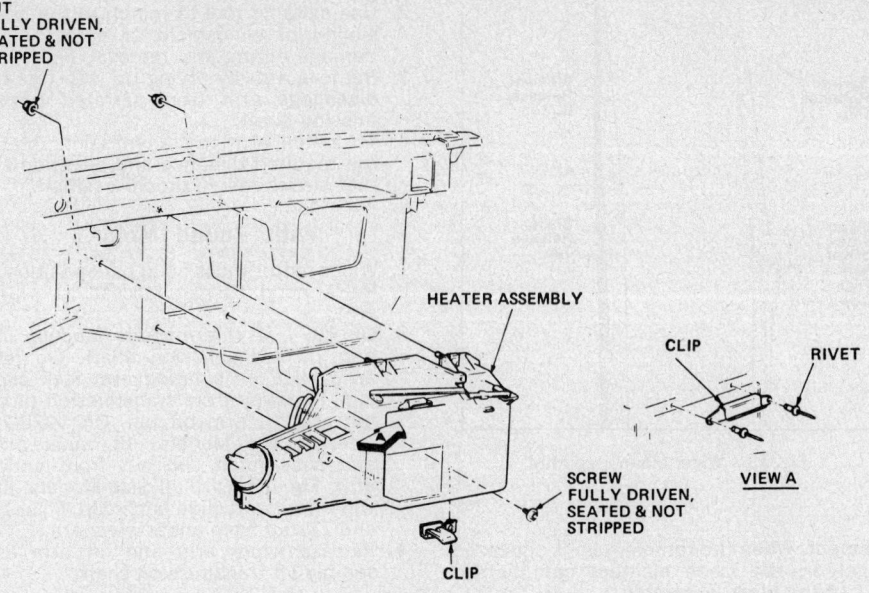

Fig. 18   Heater core. 1979 Riviera

RADIO, REPLACE

NOTE: When installing radio, be sure to adjust antenna trimmer for peak performance.

1979 Riviera

1. Disconnect battery ground cable.
2. Remove center trim cover, then remove screw attaching instrument panel wiring harness to radio bracket.
3. Remove screw attaching radio bracket to tie bar.
4. Remove four screws attaching radio mounting plate to instrument panel.
5. Disconnect radio wire connector and antenna lead.
6. Pull radio and mounting plate rearward and remove radio.

1978-79 Century & Regal

1. Disconnect battery ground cable.
2. Remove radio knobs and escutcheons, then remove center trim plate.
3. Remove glove box.
4. Remove radio mounting bracket, then position radio so that wire connector and antenna lead can be disconnected.
5. Remove radio and mounting bracket as an assembly.
6. Reverse procedure to install.

1977-79 Full Size Except 1979 Riviera

1. Disconnect battery ground cable.
2. Remove ash tray and bracket.
3. Remove radio knobs and escutcheons from shafts.
4. Remove lower left-hand air duct.
5. Remove retaining nuts from radio control shafts.
6. Disconnect electrical connections from radio.
7. Remove rear radio attaching nut, then the radio from vehicle.
8. Reverse procedure to install.

1975-76 Full Size Models

CAUTION: On vehicles equipped with an Air Cushion Restraint System, turn ignition switch to "Lock," disconnect battery ground cable and tape end, thereby deactivating system.

1. Disconnect battery ground cable.
2. Pry out lower right instrument panel trim.
3. Remove radio knobs, escutcheons and retaining nuts from control shafts.
4. Remove plastic trim plate.
5. Disconnect leads from radio and remove rear radio attaching nut, then pull radio from panel.
6. Reverse procedure to install.

1974 Full Size Models with Air Cushion Restraint System

1. Turn ignition switch to "Lock" and disconnect battery ground cable and tape end.
2. Remove both lower instrument panel cover trim plates.
3. Disconnect parking brake release cable, then remove lower left instrument panel cover retaining screws and cover.
4. Remove two horizontal screws below instrument panel, four screws from upper horizontal surface of instrument panel, two outer screws from glove box door hinge and screw from

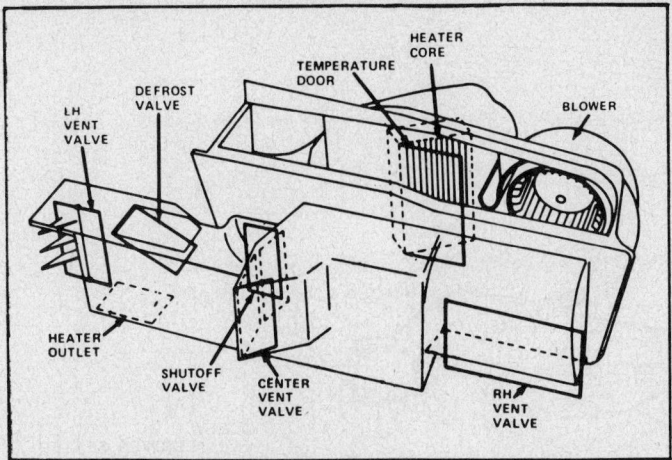

Fig. 19 Heater core & blower motor. 1977-79 Full Size Except 1979 Riviera without air conditioning

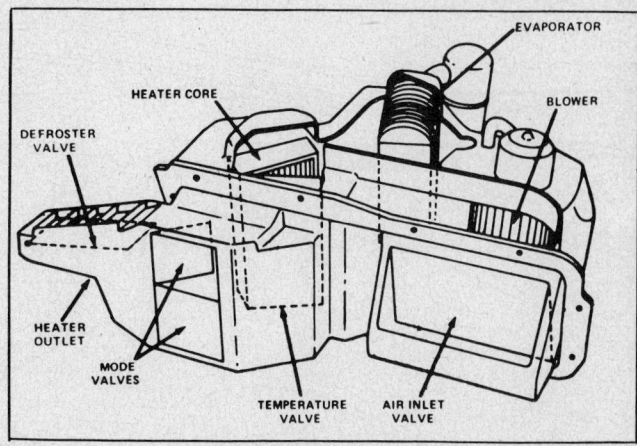

Fig. 20 Heater core & blower motor. 1977-79 Full Size Except 1979 Riviera with air conditioning

instrument panel cover right side.

5. Disconnect leads from radio.
6. Release four clips behind instrument panel by grasping tongue of right hand side clip, squeezing and pulling forward.
7. Remove radio knobs, escutcheons and instrument panel trim plate.
8. Remove retaining nuts from control shafts and power antenna relay retaining screws.
9. Loosen left radio support nut, re move right radio support nut and lower radio from instrument panel.
10. Reverse procedure to install.

1974-79 Apollo & Skylark

1. Remove radio knobs, bezels, nuts and side brace screw.
2. Disconnect antenna and leads.
3. Remove radio from under dash.
4. Reverse procedure to install.

1974-77 Century & Regal

1. Remove radio knobs and escutcheons. If equipped with center air duct assembly control, remove screws.
2. Disconnect antenna and leads.
3. Remove radio support nut.
4. Remove attaching nuts and slide radio to front of car and downward.
5. Reverse procedure to install.

1974 Full Size Models less Air Cushion Restraint System

1. Remove knobs and escutcheons. If equipped with trip-set and speed alert, unscrew the cone shaped knobs.
2. Remove right trim panel.
3. Remove retaining nuts from shafts.
4. Remove ash tray and separate connectors and antenna lead in from radio.

HEATER CORE REMOVAL

1979 Riviera

1. Disconnect battery ground cable and drain cooling system.
2. Disconnect heater hoses from heater core and install plugs in heater core outlets.
3. Remove instrument panel sound absorbers, then lower steering column.
4. Remove instrument cluster as described under Instrument Cluster, Replace.
5. Remove radio front speakers.
6. Remove screws attaching manifold to heater case.
7. Remove upper and lower instrument panel attaching screws.
8. Disconnect parking brake release cable.
9. Disconnect instrument panel wiring harness from dash wiring harness.
10. Disconnect right hand remote control mirror cable from instrument panel pad.
11. Disconnect speedometer cable and temperate control cable at heater case.
12. Disconnect radio, A/C wiring and vacuum lines, and all wiring necessary to remove instrument panel assembly. If equipped with pulse wiper, remove wiper switch, unlock wire connector from cluster carrier and separate pulse wiper jumper harness from wiper switch wire connector.
13. Remove instrument panel and harness assembly.

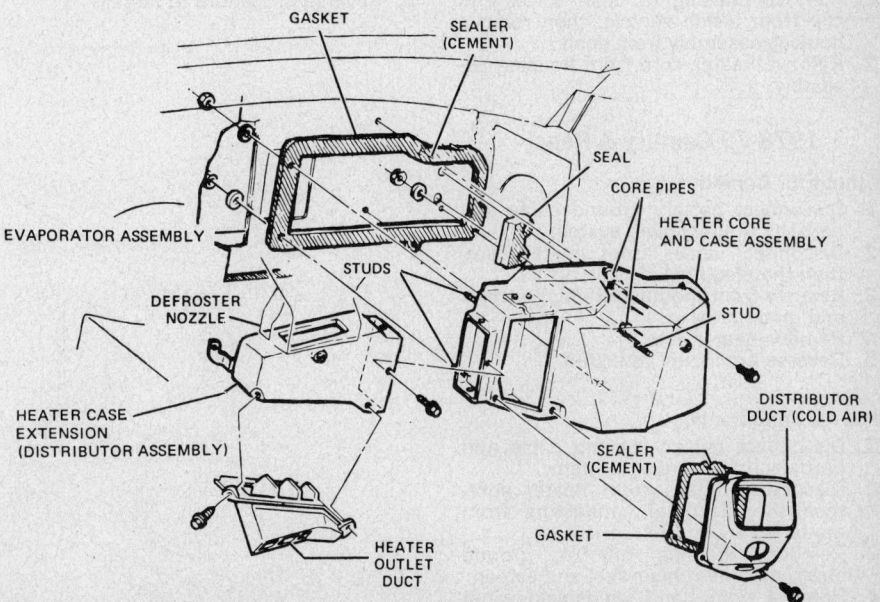

Fig. 21 Heater core. 1974-79 Apollo & Skylark (Typical)

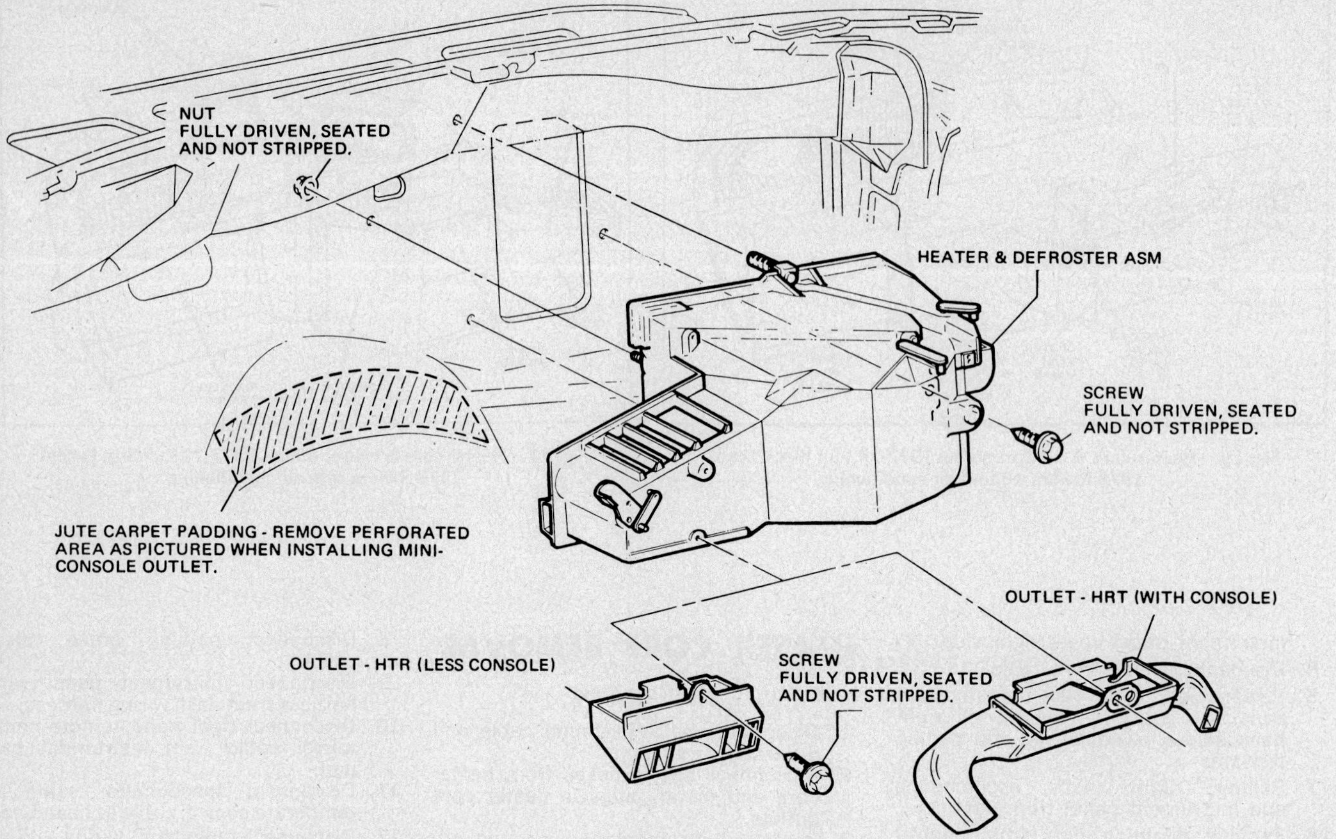

NUT
FULLY DRIVEN, SEATED
AND NOT STRIPPED.

HEATER & DEFROSTER ASM

SCREW
FULLY DRIVEN, SEATED
AND NOT STRIPPED.

JUTE CARPET PADDING - REMOVE PERFORATED
AREA AS PICTURED WHEN INSTALLING MINI-
CONSOLE OUTLET.

OUTLET - HRT (WITH CONSOLE)

OUTLET - HTR (LESS CONSOLE)

SCREW
FULLY DRIVEN, SEATED
AND NOT STRIPPED.

Fig. 22   Heater core. 1974-77 intermediate models exc. Apollo & Skylark (Typical)

14. Remove defroster ducts, then remove blower motor resistor.
15. Remove A/C-heater housing to dash panel nuts, Fig. 18.
16. Remove housing to dash screw and clip from inside vehicle, then remove housing assembly from dash.
17. Remove heater core from housing assembly.

1978-79 Century & Regal

Without Air Conditioning

1. Disconnect battery ground cable and partially drain cooling system.
2. Disconnect hoses from heater core, then the electrical connectors.
3. Remove front module retaining screws and module cover.
4. Remove heater core.
5. Reverse procedure to install.

With Air Conditioning

1. Disconnect battery ground cable and partially drain cooling system.
2. Disconnect hoses from heater core, then the electrical connectors from module.
3. Remove retaining bracket, ground strap, module rubber seal and screen.
4. Remove right hand windshield wiper arm.
5. Remove retaining screws from diag-

nostic connector, hi-blower relay and thermostatic switch.
6. Remove module top cover, then heater core.
7. Reverse procedure to install.

1977-79 Full Size Except
1979 Riviera
Without Air Conditioning

1. Disconnect battery ground cable and

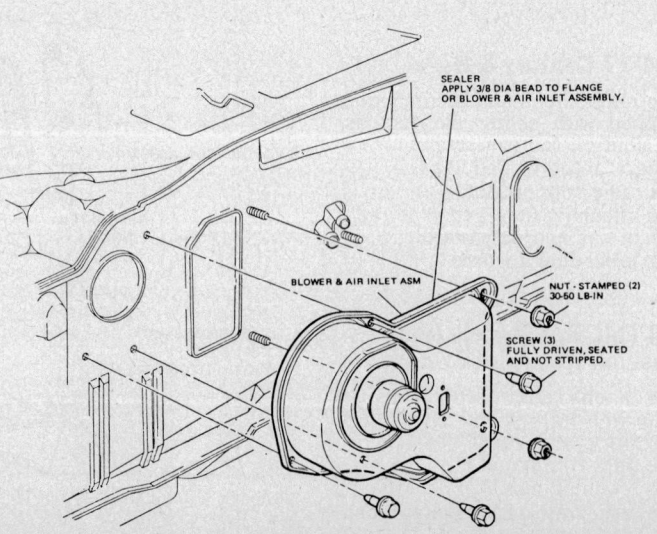

SEALER
APPLY 3/8 DIA BEAD TO FLANGE
OR BLOWER & AIR INLET ASSEMBLY.

BLOWER & AIR INLET ASM

NUT - STAMPED (2)
30-50 LB-IN

SCREW (3)
FULLY DRIVEN, SEATED
AND NOT STRIPPED.

Fig. 24   Blower motor. Intermediate Exc. 1978-79 Century & Regal (Typical)

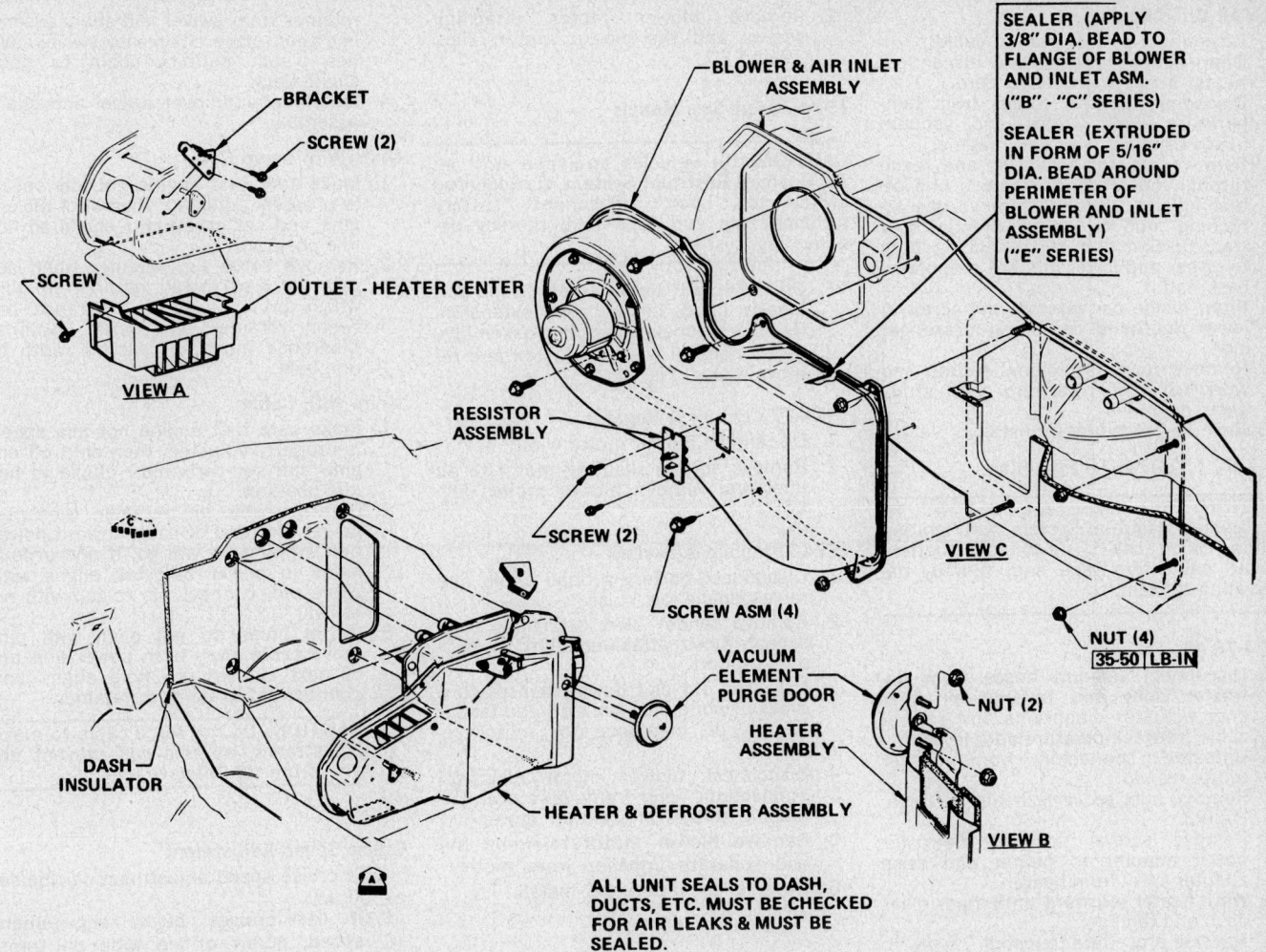

SEALER (APPLY 3/8" DIA. BEAD TO FLANGE OF BLOWER AND INLET ASM. ("B" - "C" SERIES)

SEALER (EXTRUDED IN FORM OF 5/16" DIA. BEAD AROUND PERIMETER OF BLOWER AND INLET ASSEMBLY) ("E" SERIES)

BLOWER & AIR INLET ASSEMBLY

BRACKET

SCREW (2)

SCREW

OUTLET - HEATER CENTER

VIEW A

RESISTOR ASSEMBLY

SCREW (2)

SCREW ASM (4)

VIEW C

NUT (4) 35-50 LB-IN

VACUUM ELEMENT PURGE DOOR

HEATER ASSEMBLY

NUT (2)

VIEW B

DASH INSULATOR

HEATER & DEFROSTER ASSEMBLY

ALL UNIT SEALS TO DASH, DUCTS, ETC. MUST BE CHECKED FOR AIR LEAKS & MUST BE SEALED.

Fig. 23 Heater core & blower motor. 1974-76 full size models (Typical)

drain radiator.
2. Disconnect heater hoses from module, then the electrical connections from module front case.
3. Remove module front case attaching screws, then the heater core, Fig. 19.
4. Reverse procedure to install.

With Air Conditioning

1. Disconnect battery ground cable and drain radiator.
2. Disconnect heater hoses from module.
3. Remove diagnostic connector and thermostatic switch from module.
4. Remove weather seal from top of module cover, then the cowl screen and windshield washer nozzle.
5. Remove module cover attaching screws.
6. Remove heater core retaining clip and the heater core from vehicle, Fig. 20.
7. Reverse procedure to install.

1974-79 Apollo & Skylark

Without Air Conditioning

1. Disconnect battery ground cable and drain radiator.
2. Disconnect heater hoses from core

and plug hoses and core openings to prevent coolant spillage.
3. Remove core case retaining nuts from engine side of dash, Fig. 21.
4. Remove glove compartment and door.
5. Using a 1/4 inch twist drill, drill out lower right hand heater case stud from inside vehicle.
6. Pull heater core and case assembly from dash.
7. Disconnect heater cables and blower motor resistor connector from case, then remove heater core and case assembly from vehicle.
8. Remove core tube seal and retaining strips, then heater core from case.
9. Reverse procedure to install.

With Air Conditioning

1. Disconnect battery ground cable and drain radiator.
2. Disconnect upper heater hose and plug hose and core openings. Remove accessible heater core and case attaching nuts.
3. Remove right front fender skirt bolts, lower skirt and disconnect lower heater hose from core tube. Plug hose and core openings.
4. Remove lower right hand heater core

and case attaching nuts, Fig. 21.
5. Remove glove compartment and door.
6. Remove right hand kick panel recirculation vacuum diaphragm.
7. Remove heater outlet from bottom of heater case, then cold air distributor duct.
8. Remove heater case extension screws, then separate extension from heater case.
9. Disconnect heater cables and electrical connectors from heater case, then remove heater core and case assembly. Separate core from case.
10. Reverse procedure to install.

1974-77 Century & Regal

Without Air Conditioning

1. Disconnect battery ground cable.
2. Drain cooling system and disconnect heater hoses from heater core.
3. Disconnect control cables from door levers.
4. Remove four nuts securing heater to dash, Fig. 22.
5. Remove screw securing defroster outlet to heater.
6. Work heater assembly rearward until studs clear dash.
7. Reverse procedure to install.

With Air Conditioning

1. Disconnect battery ground cable.
2. Drain cooling system and disconnect heater hoses from heater core.
3. Disconnect control cables from temperature door guides and vacuum hoses from actuator diaphragms.
4. Remove resistor assembly and reach through opening and remove one attaching nut to dash. Remove one attaching nut to dash directly over transmission and two attaching nuts to upper and lower inboard evaporator case half.
5. From inside car remove one screw in lower righthand corner on passenger side.
6. Remove lower attaching outlets and work assembly rearward until studs clear dash.
7. Reverse procedure to install.

1974-76 Full Size

CAUTION: On vehicles equipped with an Air Cushion Restraint System, turn ignition switch to "Lock," disconnect battery ground cable and tape end, thereby deactivating system.

1974-76 All

1. Disconnect vacuum hoses from defroster door and outside air inlet door actuator diaphrams and control cable from temperature door lever.
2. Unfasten connector from blower motor resistor.
3. Remove nuts securing heater to dash, Fig. 23.
4. Remove screws securing defroster outlet adapter to heater and raise adapter away from heater.
5. Work heater rearward until studs clear dash and remove.
6. Reverse procedure to install.

BLOWER MOTOR REMOVE

1979 Riviera

1. Disconnect battery ground cable.
2. Remove right fender skirt to provide clearance for blower motor removal.
3. Disconnect wire connector and cooling hose.
4. Remove blower motor attaching screws and blower motor.

1978-79 Century & Regal & 1977-79 Full Size Except Riviera

1. Disconnect blower motor wiring.

2. Remove blower motor attaching screws and the blower motor, Figs. 19 and 20.

1974-76 Full Size Models

CAUTION: On vehicles equipped with an Air Cushion Restraint System, turn ignition switch to "Lock", disconnect battery ground cable and tape end, thereby deactivating system.

1. On 1974-76 Riviera, support hood and loosen hood hinge from extension. Remove extension and plate assembly.
2. Disconnect all wires, unfasten and remove motor. Fig. 23.

1974-77 Century & Regal

1. Disconnect blower motor wire.
2. Remove screws securing motor to air inlet and remove blower motor, Fig. 24.

1974-79 Apollo & Skylark

1. Disconnect battery ground cable and raise vehicle on hoist.
2. Remove fender skirt attaching bolts except those attaching skirt to radiator support.
3. Pull skirt out and down, then place a block of wood between skirt and fender to provide clearance for motor removal.
4. Disconnect blower motor electrical connections and remove motor attaching screws and blower motor.
5. Remove blower motor retaining nut and separate impeller from motor.
6. Reverse procedure to install.

SPEED CONTROL

Power Unit, Adjust

Units With Bead Chain

1. Make sure that engine hot idle speed is properly adjusted, then shut off engine and set carburetor choke to hot idle position.
2. Check slack in chain by disconnecting swivel from ball stud and holding chain taut at ball stud. Center of swivel should extend $1/8$ inch beyond center of ball stud.
3. To adjust bead chain slack, remove

retainer from swivel and chain assembly, then place chain into swivel cavities which permits chain to have slight slack.
4. Install retainer over swivel and chain assembly.

Units With Servo Rod

1. Make sure that engine hot idle speed is properly adjusted, then shut off engine and set carburetor choke to hot idle position.
2. Remove servo rod retainer, then adjust rod and install retainer in hole which provides some clearance between retainer and servo bushing. Clearance must not exceed width of one hole.

Units With Cable

1. Make sure that engine hot idle speed is properly adjusted, then shut off engine and set carburetor choke to hot idle position.
2. Remove cable pin retainer, then pull power unit end of cable toward power unit as far as it will go. If one of four holes in power unit tab aligns with cable pin, connect pin to tab with retainer.
3. If tab holes do not align with pin, move cable away from power unit until next closest tab hole aligns and connect pin to tab with retainer.

CAUTION: Do not force cable to make adjustment, as this will prevent engine from returning to idle.

Cruise Speed Adjustment

The cruise speed adjustment can be set as follows:

1. If car cruises below engagement speed, screw orifice tube on transducer outward.
2. If car cruises above engagement speed, screw orifice tube inward.

NOTE: Each $1/4$ turn of the orifice tube will change cruise speed about one mile per hour. Snug up lock nut after each adjustment.

Brake Release Switch Adjustment

Fully depress brake pedal, then push switch and valve forward to contact bracket or arm. Pull pedal rearward with approximately 15 to 20 pounds of force to adjust switch and valve properly.

Engine Section

NOTE: For service see Chevrolet Chapter for 6-250, V8-305 and 1977-79 V8-350 with the distributor located at the rear of engine, clockwise distributor rotor rotation; Oldsmobile Chapter for V8-260, 1977-79 V8-350 with distributor located at the rear of engine, counter clockwise distibutor rotor rotation, V8-403 and the Pontiac Chapter for V8-301 and V8-400.

ENGINE MOUNTS, REPLACE

1. Raise car and provide frame support at front of car.
2. Support weight of engine at forward edge of pan.
3. Remove mount to engine block bolts. Raise engine slightly and remove mount to mount bracket bolt and nut, Figs. 1, 2 and 3. Remove mount.
4. Reverse above procedure to install.

ENGINE, REPLACE

1. Remove hood and drain radiator.
2. Remove fan shroud, radiator and air cleaner.
3. If equipped with A/C, disconnect compressor brackets and position out of way.
4. Remove power steering from bracket and position out of way.
5. Disconnect all hoses, linkages and electrical connections from engine.
6. Disconnect exhaust pipes and remove converter cover.
7. Remove flywheel to converter or pressure plate bolts, engine to transmission bolts and motor mount bolts.
8. Support transmission and remove engine.

CYLINDER HEADS

Some cylinder head gaskets are coated

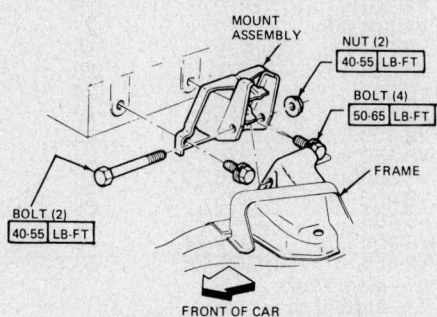

Fig. 1   Engine mounts. V6-196 & 231

with a special lacquer to provide a good seal once the parts have warmed up. Do not use any additional sealer on such gaskets. If the gasket does not have this lacquer coating, apply suitable sealer to both sides.

1. Drain coolant and disconnect battery.
2. Remove intake manifold.
3. When removing right cylinder head, remove Delcotron and/or A/C compressor with mounting bracket and move out of the way. *Do not disconnect hoses from A/C compressor.*
4. When removing left cylinder head, remove oil dipstick, power steering pump and move out of the way with hoses attached.
5. Disconnect exhaust manifold from head to be removed.
6. Remove rocker arm shaft and lift out push rods.
7. On 1974-78 Apollo & Skylark models

equipped with V6-231 and V8-350 engines, to replace left cylinder head, disconnect power brake unit hose at rear of cylinder head. Remove left front engine mount bolt and loosen right front engine mount bolt. Raise engine until exhaust manifold clears steering gear.

8. Remove cylinder head.
9. Reverse procedure to install and tighten bolts gradually and evenly in the sequence shown in Figs. 4 and 5.

NOTE: When installing intake manifold, refer to Figs. 6 and 7 for bolt tightening sequence.

ROCKER ARMS

V6-196, 231, V8-350 & 455

A nylon retainer is used to retain the rocker arm. Break them below their heads with a chisel, Fig. 8, or pry out with channel locks. Production rocker arms can be installed in any sequence since the arms are identical.

Replacement rocker arms for all engines are identified with a stamping, right (R) and left (L), Fig. 9 and must be installed as shown in Fig. 10.

VALVE ARRANGEMENT

Front to Rear

V6-196, 231 . . . . E-I-I-E-I-E
V8-350, 455 . . . . E-I-I-E-E-I-I-E

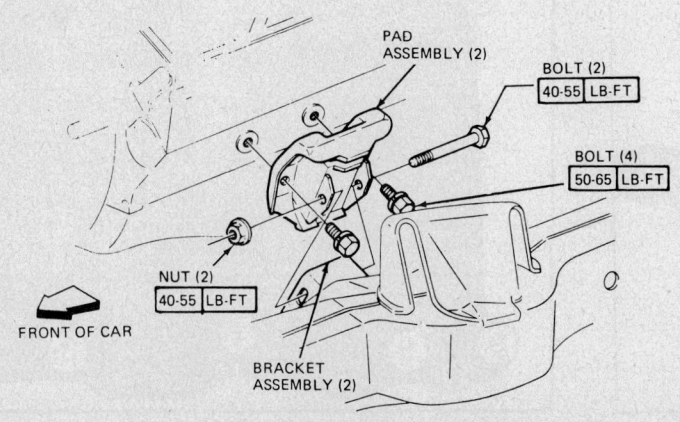

Fig. 2   Engine mounts. V8-350

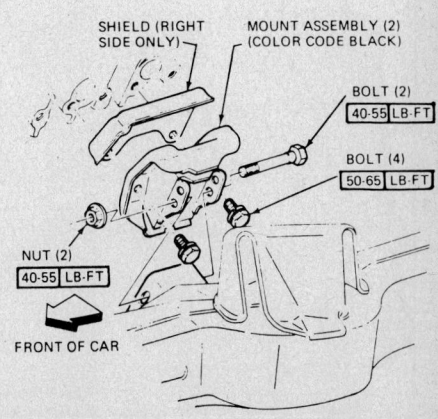

Fig. 3   Engine mounts. V8-455

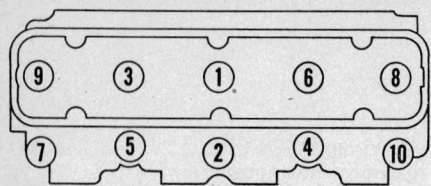

Fig. 4 Cylinder head tightening sequence. V8-350, 455

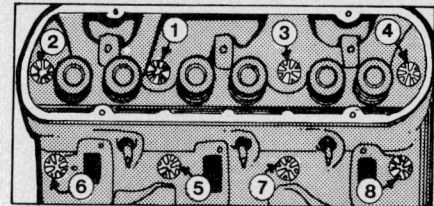

Fig. 5 Cylinder head tightening sequence. V6-196, 231

VALVE TIMING

Intake Opens Before TDC

Engine	Year	Degrees
6-250	1974-75	16
V6-196	1978	18
V6-196	1979	16
V6-231	1975-78	17
V6-231	1979	16
V8-260	1975-76	14
V8-301①	1977	31
V8-301②	1977-78	27
V8-301⑥	1979	16
V8-301①⑦	1979	27
V8-301②⑦	1979	16
V8-305	1977-79	28
V8-350	1973-74	24
V8-350	1975	19
V8-350③	1976-79	13.5
V8-350④	1976-79	28
V8-350⑤	1976-79	16
V8-400	1975	23
V8-403	1977-79	16
V8-455	1973-74	14
V8-455	1975-76	10

①—Man. trans.
②—Auto. trans.
③—Distributor located at front of engine.
④—Distributor located at rear of engine, clockwise distributor rotor rotation. Refer to Chevrolet chapter for engine service procedures.
⑤—Distributor located at rear of engine, counter clockwise distributor rotor rotation. Refer to Oldsmobile chapter for engine service procedures.
⑥—2 Bar. Carb.
⑦—4 Bar. Carb.

VALVE LIFT SPECS.

Engine	Year	Intake	Exhaust
6-250	1974	.3880	.3880
6-250	1975	.3880	.4051
V6-196	1978	.3230	.3660
V6-196	1979	.3410	.3660
V6-231	1975	.4011	.3768
V6-231	1976	.3768	.3768
V6-231	1977-78	.3830	.3660
V6-231⑧	1979	.3570	.3660
V6-231⑨	1979	.3410	—
V8-260	1975-76	.3950	.4000
V8-301③	1977	.3770	.3770
V8-301④	1977-79	.3640	.3640
V8-305	1977-79	.3727	.4100
V8-350	1974-75	.3818	.3984
V8-350	1976	.3873	.4930
V8-350⑤	1977-79	.3230	.3390
V8-350⑥	1977-79	.3900	.4100
V8-350⑦	1977-79	.4000	.4000
V8-400	1975	.4030	.4060
V8-403	1977-79	.4000	.4000
V8-455	1974	.3873	.4550
V8-455①	1975	.3873	.4450
V8-455②	1975	.3873	.4030
V8-455	1976	.3873	.4930

①—LeSabre.
②—Exc. LeSabre.
③—Man. trans.
④—Auto. trans.
⑤—Distributor located at front of engine.
⑥—Distributor located at rear of engine, clockwise distributor rotor rotation.
⑦—Distributor located at rear of engine, counter distributor rotor clockwise rotation
⑧—Exc. turbo charged engine.
⑨—Turbo charged engine.

VALVE GUIDES

The valve guides are an integral part of the cylinder head and cannot be replaced.

If valve stem clearance is excessive, the valve guide must be reamed and an oversize valve installed. On 1974-78 engines, valves are available in the oversizes of .010 inch for V8-350, 455 and .006 inch for V6-196, 231. On 1979 engines, valves are available in the oversize of .010 inch.

HYDRAULIC VALVE LIFTERS

Failure of an hydraulic valve lifter, Fig. 11, is generally caused by an inadequate oil supply or dirt. An air leak at the intake side of the oil pump or too much oil in the engine will cause air bubbles in the oil supply to the lifters, causing them to collapse. This is a probable cause of trouble if several lifters fail to function, but air in the oil is an unlikely cause of failure of a single unit.

The valve lifters may be lifted out of their bores after removing the rocker arms, push rods and intake manifold. Adjustable pliers with taped jaws may be used to remove lifters that are stuck due to varnish, carbon, etc. Fig. 11 illustrates the type of lifter used.

NOTE: 1974-75 in production .010" oversize lifters are being used for oversize lifter bores. The lifter bore will be marked with an "O" and the lifter will have two grooves in the lifter body. When replacing lifters, check bores for oversize markings.

TIMING CHAIN COVER
V6-196, 231 & V8-350, 455

1. Drain cooling system and remove

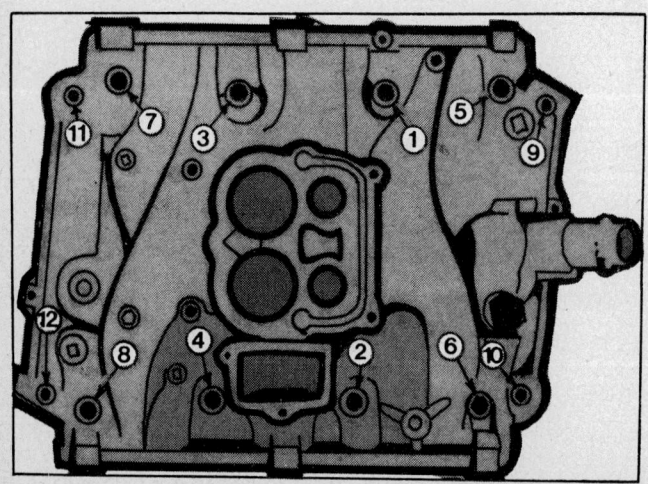

Fig. 6 Intake manifold tightening sequence. V8-350, 455

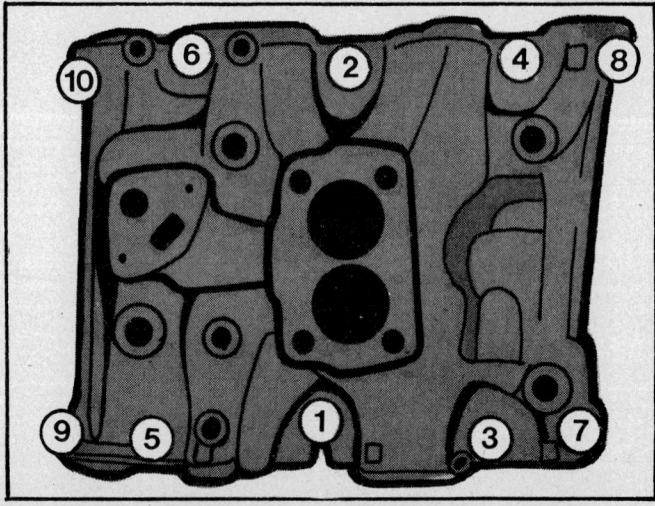

Fig. 7 Intake manifold tightening sequence. V6-196, 231

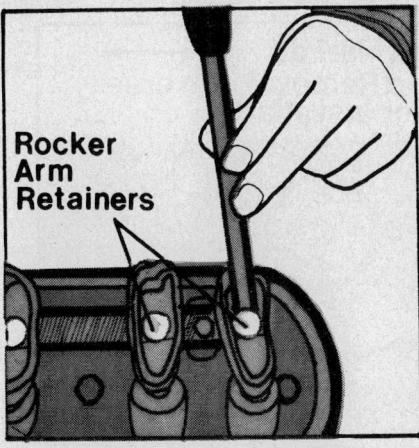

Fig. 8 Removing nylon retainer.
V6-196, 231 & V8-350, 455

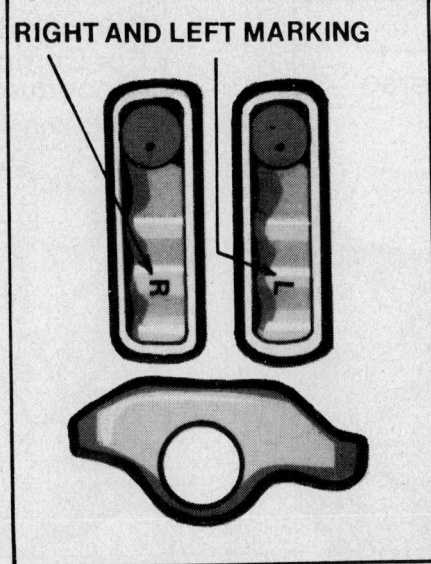

Fig. 9 Service rocker arms identification.
V6-196, 231 & V8-350, 455

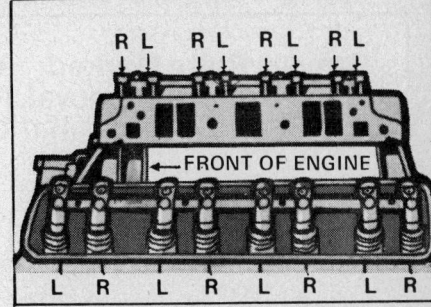

Fig. 10. Service rocker arms installation.
V6-196, 231 & V8-350, 455

radiator.

2. Remove fan, pulleys and belts.
3. Remove crankshaft pulley and reinforcement.
4. If equipped with power steering, remove any pump bracket bolts attached to timing chain cover and loosen and remove any other bolts necessary that will allow pump and brackets to be moved out of the way.
5. Remove fuel pump.
6. Remove Delcotron and brackets.
7. Remove distributor cap and pull spark plug wire retainers off brackets on rocker arm cover. Swing distributor cap with wires attached out of the way. Disconnect distributor primary lead.
8. Remove distributor. *If chain and sprockets are not to be disturbed, note position of distributor rotor for installation in the same position.*
9. Loosen and slide clamp on thermostat by-pass hose rearward.
10. Remove bolts attaching chain cover to block.
11. On V6-196, 231 and V8-350 engines, remove two oil pan-to-chain cover bolts and remove cover.
12. On V8-455 engines, remove four oil

pan-to-chain cover bolts.
Do not remove the five bolts attaching water pump to chain cover.
Remove cover, using care to avoid damaging oil pan gasket.
13. Reverse procedure to install, noting data shown in Figs. 12, 13 and 14.

IMPORTANT

Remove the oil pump cover and pack the space around the oil pump gears completely full of vaseline. There must be no air space left inside the pump. Reinstall the cover using a new gasket. This step is very important as the oil pump may lose its prime whenever the pump, pump cover or timing chain cover is disturbed. If the pump is not packed it may not begin to pump oil as soon as the engine is started.

TIMING CHAIN

V6-196, 231 & V8-350, 455

1. With the timing case cover removed as outlined above, temporarily install the vibration damper bolt and washer in end of crankshaft.
2. Turn crankshaft so sprockets are positioned as shown in Fig. 15. Use a sharp rap on a wrench handle to start the vibration damper bolt out without disturbing the position of the sprockets.
3. On V8-455 and 1977-79 V6 engines, remove the oil pan.
4. Remove oil slinger.
5. On V6-196, 231 and V8-350 remove camshaft distributor drive gear and fuel pump eccentric. On V8-455, remove sprocket bolts.
6. Use two large screwdrivers to alternately pry the camshaft sprocket

then the crankshaft sprocket forward until the camshaft sprocket is free. Then remove camshaft sprocket and chain, and crankshaft sprocket off crankshaft.
7. To install, assemble chain on sprockets and slide sprockets on their respective shafts with the "O" marks on the sprockets lined up as shown.
8. Complete the installation in the reverse order of removal.

CAMSHAFT

NOTE: If engine is in the car, the radiator, grille and A/C components will have to be removed. If engine is out of car, proceed as follows:

1. To remove camshaft, remove intake manifold, rocker arm shaft assemblies, push rods and valve lifters.
2. Remove timing chain and sprockets.
3. Slide camshaft out of engine, using care not to mar the bearing surfaces.

Fig. 12 Timing chain cover installation.
1975-79 V6-196 & 231

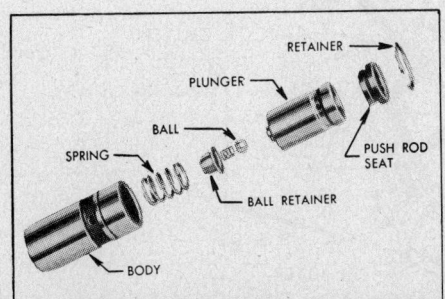

Fig. 11 Hydraulic valve lifter parts

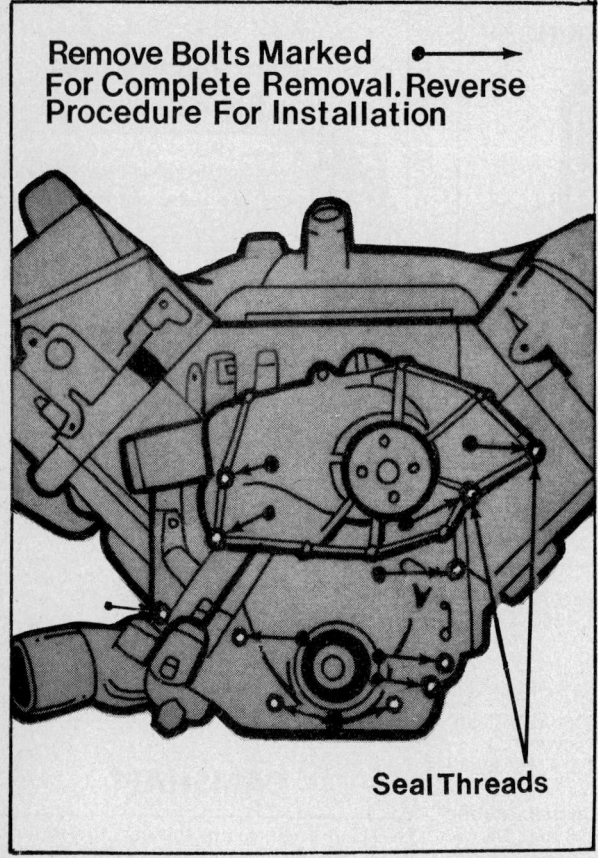

Remove Bolts Marked ● ⟶
For Complete Removal. Reverse
Procedure For Installation

Seal Threads

Fig. 13   Timing chain cover installation. 1974-76 V8-455

Remove Bolts Marked ○ ⟶
For Complete Removal. Reverse
Procedure For Installation

Seal
Threads

Fuel Pump Must Be Removed

Fig. 14   Timing chain cover installation. V8-350

PISTONS, PINS & RINGS

Pistons are available in standard sizes and oversizes of .005, .010 and .030 inch.

Rings are furnished in standard sizes and oversizes of .010 and .030 inch.

Piston pins are supplied in standard sizes only.

PISTONS & RODS, ASSEMBLE

Rods and pistons should be assembled and installed as shown in Figs. 16 through 18.

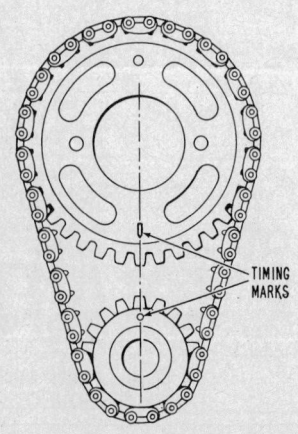

TIMING
MARKS

Fig. 15   Valve timing marks.
V6-196, 231 & V8-350, 455

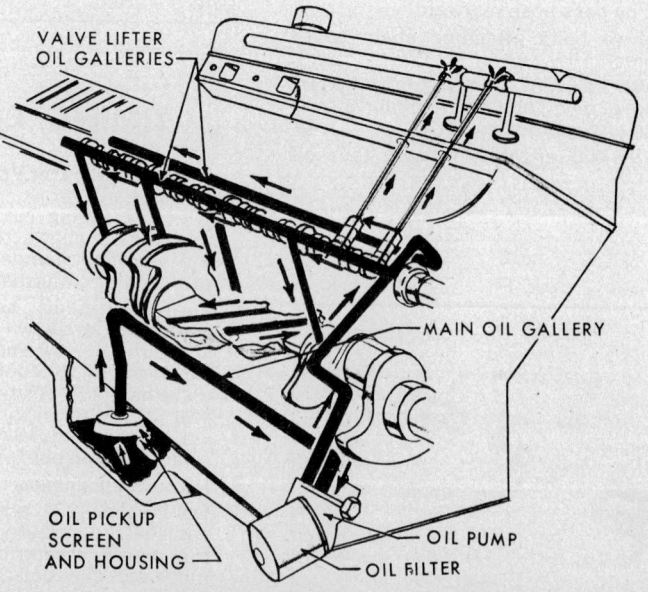

VALVE LIFTER
OIL GALLERIES

MAIN OIL GALLERY

OIL PICKUP
SCREEN
AND HOUSING

OIL PUMP

OIL FILTER

Engine lubrication system. V8-350, 455

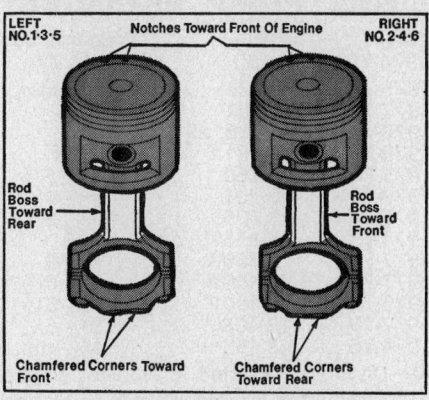

Fig. 16 Piston and rod assembly. V6-196, 231

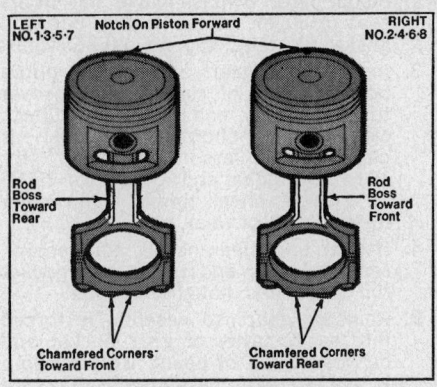

Fig. 17 Piston and rod assembly. 1974-79 V8-350

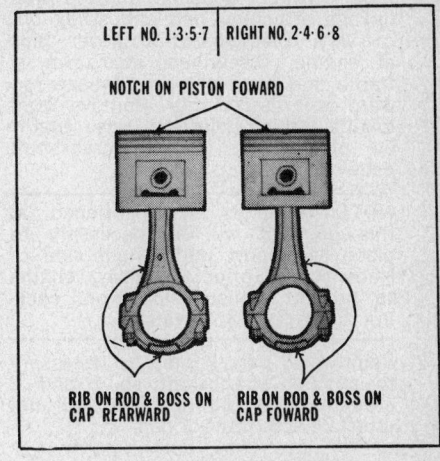

Fig. 18 Piston and rod assembly. 1974-76 V8-455

MAIN & ROD BEARINGS

Main bearings are available in standard sizes and undersizes of .001, .002, and .010 inch.

Rod bearings are furnished in standard sizes and undersizes of .001, .002 and .010", Fig. 19.

CRANKSHAFT OIL SEAL REPAIR

Since the braided fabric seal used on these engines can be replaced only when the crankshaft is removed, the following repair procedure is recommended.
1. Remove oil pan and bearing cap.

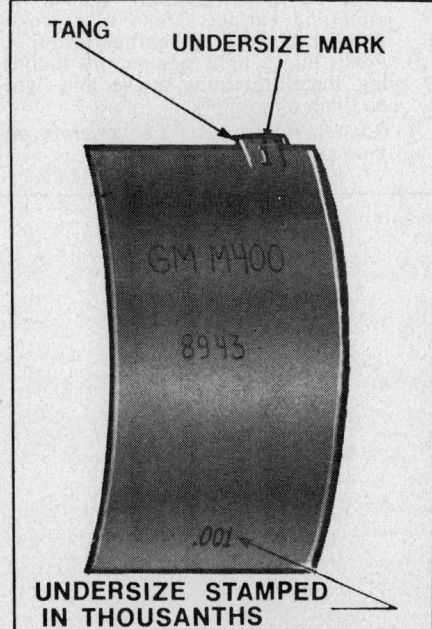

Fig. 19 Location of undersize mark on main and rod bearing shell

2. Drive end of old seal gently into groove, using a suitable tool, until packed tight. This may vary between $\frac{1}{4}$ and $\frac{3}{4}$ inch depending on amount of pack required.
3. Repeat previous step for other end of seal.
4. Measure and note amount that seal was driven up on one side. Using the old seal removed from bearing cap, cut a length of seal the amount previously noted plus $\frac{1}{16}$ inch.
5. Repeat previous step for other side of seal.
6. Pack cut lengths of seal into appropriate side of seal groove. A guide tool, J-21526-1, and packing tool, J-21526-2, may be used since these tools have been machined to provide a built-in stop.
7. Install new seal in bearing cap.

OIL PAN

1975-79 V6-196, 231

1. Support vehicle on hoist and drain oil.
2. Remove flywheel cover and exhaust crossover pipe.

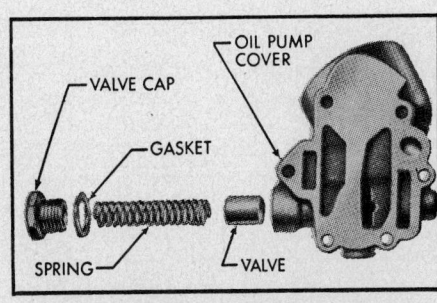

Fig. 20 Oil pump cover and by-pass valve. V6-196, 231 & V8-350, 455

3. Remove oil pan bolts and allow pan to drop.

NOTE: To remove oil pan, front wheels must be turned to the left, also the crankshaft may have to be turned to provide clearance.

4. Reverse procedure to install.

1974-79 V8-350, 455

NOTE: On 1974-78 models except Apollo and Skylark, it is no longer necessary to disconnect the idler arm. Otherwise, proceed as follows:

1. Disconnect battery and drain oil.
2. Remove fan shroud to radiator tie bar screws.
3. Remove air cleaner and disconnect linkage to throttle.
4. Raise and support car on stands.
5. With manual transmission, loosen clutch equalizer bracket to frame bolts. Disconnect crossover pipe at engine.
6. With automatic transmission, remove

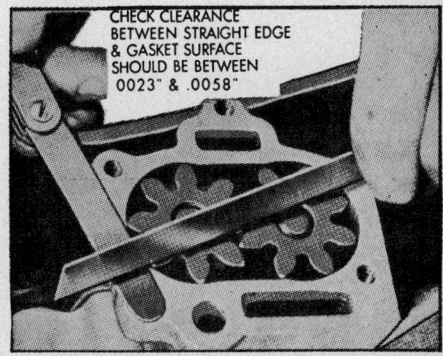

Fig. 21 Checking oil pump gear and clearance. V6-196, 231 & V8-350, 455

lower flywheel housing. Remove shift linkage attaching bolt and swing out of way. Disconnect crossover pipe at engine. Disconnect idler arm at frame and push steering linkage forward to crossmember. Remove front engine mount bolts and raise engine by placing jack under crankshaft pulley mounting.

NOTE: If car is air conditioned, at this point it will be necessary to place a support under right side of transmission prior to raising engine to prevent transmission from cocking to the right when raised.

7. Remove oil pan. It may be necessary to position crankshaft so 1 and 2 crankpin and counterweight will not interfere with front of pan.

OIL PUMP
V6-196, 231 & V8-350, 455

1. To remove pump, take off oil filter.
2. Disconnect wire from oil pressure indicator switch in filter by-pass valve cap (if so equipped).
3. Remove screws attaching oil pump cover to timing chain cover. Remove cover and slide out pump gears. Replace any parts not serviceable.
4. Remove oil pressure relief valve cap, spring and valve, Fig. 20. Remove oil filter by-pass valve cap, spring and valve. Replace any parts of valve not serviceable.
5. Check relief valve in its bore in cover. Valve should have no more clearance than an easy slip fit. If any perceptible side shake can be felt, the valve and/or cover should be replaced.
6. The filter by-pass valve should be flat and free of nicks and scratches.

Assembly & Installation

1. Lubricate and install pressure relief valve and spring in bore of pump cover. Install cap and gasket. Torque cap to 30-35 ft-lbs.

2. Install filter by-pass valve flat in its seat in cover. Install spring, cap and gasket. Torque cap to 30-35 ft-lbs.
3. Install pump gears and shaft in pump body section of timing chain cover to check gear end clearance. Check clearance as shown in Fig. 21. If clearance is less than .0018" for 1974-76 models and .0020" for 1977-79 models, check timing chain cover for evidence of wear.
4. If gear end clearance is satisfactory, remove gears and pack gear pocket *full* of vaseline, not chassis lube.
5. Reinstall gears so vaseline is forced into every cavity of gear pocket and between teeth of gears. *Unless pump is packed with vaseline, it may not prime itself when engine is started.*
6. Install cover and tighten screws alternately and evenly. Final tightening is 10-15 ft-lbs. torque. Install filter on nipple.

BELT TENSION DATA

	New lbs.	Used lbs.
1977-79—		
Alternator	130	75
Air Condition	155	90
A.I.R. Pump	70	60
Power Steering	155	90
1976—		
Alternator	130	65
Air Condition	155	90
A.I.R. Pump	70	60
Power Steering	155	90
1975—		
Alternator	125	80
Air Condition	150	100
A.I.R. Pump	70	65
Power Steering	150	90
1974—		
Alternator	80	80
Air Condition	90	90
A.I.R. Pump	65-80	65-80
Power Steering	100	100

WATER PUMP, REPLACE

Drain cooling system, being sure to drain into a clean container if antifreeze solution is to be saved. Remove the fan belt and disconnect all hoses from water pump. Remove water pump.

FUEL PUMP PRESSURE

Year	Engine	Pressure, Lbs.
1974-75	6-250	$3\frac{1}{2}$-$4\frac{1}{2}$
1975-76	V6-231	3 min.
1977	V6-231	3
1978-79	V6-196, 231 [4]	3
1978-79	V6-231 [5]	5
1975-76	V8-260	$5\frac{1}{2}$-$6\frac{1}{2}$
1977-79	V8-301	7-$8\frac{1}{2}$
1977-79	V8-305	$7\frac{1}{2}$-9
1974-79	V8-350 [1]	3
1977-79	V8-350 [2]	$7\frac{1}{2}$-9
1977-79	V8-350 [3]	$5\frac{1}{2}$-$6\frac{1}{2}$
1975	V8-400	$5\frac{1}{2}$-$6\frac{1}{2}$
1977-79	V8-403	$5\frac{1}{2}$-$6\frac{1}{2}$
1974-76	V8-455	$4\frac{1}{2}$ min.

[1]—Distributor located at front of engine.

[2]—Distributor located at rear of engine, clockwise distributor rotor rotation.

[3]—Distributor located at rear of engine, counter clockwise distributor rotor rotation.

[4]—Except turbocharged engine.

[5]—Turbocharged engine.

FUEL PUMP, REPLACE

NOTE: Before installing the pump, it is good practice to crank the engine so that the nose of the camshaft eccentric is out of the way of the fuel pump rocker arm when the pump is installed. In this way there will be the least amount of tension on the rocker arm, thereby easing the installation of the pump.

1. Remove all gasket material from the pump and block gasket surfaces. Apply sealer to both sides of new gasket.
2. Position gasket on pump flange and hold pump in position against its mounting surface. Make sure rocker arm is riding on camshaft eccentric.
3. Press pump tight against its mounting. Install retaining screws and tighten them alternately.
4. Connect fuel lines. Then operate engine and check for leaks.

Turbocharger Section

DESCRIPTION

The turbocharger, Fig. 1, is used to increase engine power on a demand basis, therefore allowing a smaller, more economical engine to be used. The turbocharged V6-231 is available with either two or four barrel carburetion.

As engine load increases and the throttle opens, more air-fuel mixture flows into the combustion chambers. As the increased flow is burned, a larger volume of high energy exhaust gasses enters the engine exhaust system and is directed through the turbocharger turbine housing, Fig. 2. Some of the exhaust gas energy is used to increase the speed of the turbine wheel which is connected to the compressor wheel. The increased speed of the compressor wheel compresses the air-fuel mixture from the carburetor and delivers the compressed air-fuel mixture to the intake manifold, Fig. 2. The high pressure in the intake manifold allows a denser charge to enter the combustion chambers, in turn developing more engine power during the combustion cycle.

The intake manifold pressure (Boost) is controlled to a maximum value by an exhaust gas bypass valve (Wastegate). The wastegate allows a portion of the exhaust gas to bypass the turbine wheel, thereby not increasing turbine speed. The wastegate is operated by a spring loaded diaphragm device sensing the pressure differential across the compressor. When intake manifold pressure reaches a set value above ambient pressure, the wastegate begins to bypass the exhaust gas.

An Electronic Spark Control System, Fig. 3, is used to retard ignition timing up to 20° to minimize detonation. The 1978 two barrel application uses a turbocharger vacuum bleed valve (TVBV) and the 1978 four barrel application uses a power enrichment control valve (PECV). These valves assist in proper vacuum control during boost. On 1979 applications, the power enrichment vacuum regulator (PEVR) is used to control vacuum flow to the carburetor power piston.

DIAGNOSIS & TESTING

Prior to performing any diagnostic or testing procedure check all vacuum hoses and wiring for proper routing and connections, carburetor linkage for freedom of movement, wastegate linkage for damage or any problems which may occur in a non-turbocharged engine.

Wastegate-Boost Pressure Test

1. Inspect actuator linkage for damage.
2. Check tubing from compressor housing to actuator assembly and the return tubing from the actuator to the PCV tee.
3. Tee the hand operated vacuum/pressure pump J-23738 into the tubing from the compressor housing to the actuator. At approximately 8 psi (16 inch Hg.) on 1978 engines, 9 psi. on 1979 engines, the lever should begin to move and actuate the wastegate. If not, replace actuator assembly and calibrate assembly to open at 8 psi (16 inch Hg.) on 1978 engines, 9 psi. on 1979 engines. Use J-23738 or perform "Road Test" as outlined below to measure boost pressure.

Road Test

1. Tee the compound gauge J-28474 into the tubing between compressor housing and actuator assembly with a sufficient length of hose to place the gauge in the passenger compartment.
2. With conditions and speed limits permitting, perform a zero to 40-50 mph wide open throttle acceleration and maintain top speed for two to three seconds. Boost pressures should reach 7-8 psi on 1978 two barrel engines or 8-9 psi for 1978 four barrel engines. On 1979 engines, boost pressure should reach 8-10 psi. If not, replace actuator assembly and, using tool J-23738, calibrate to open at 8 psi.

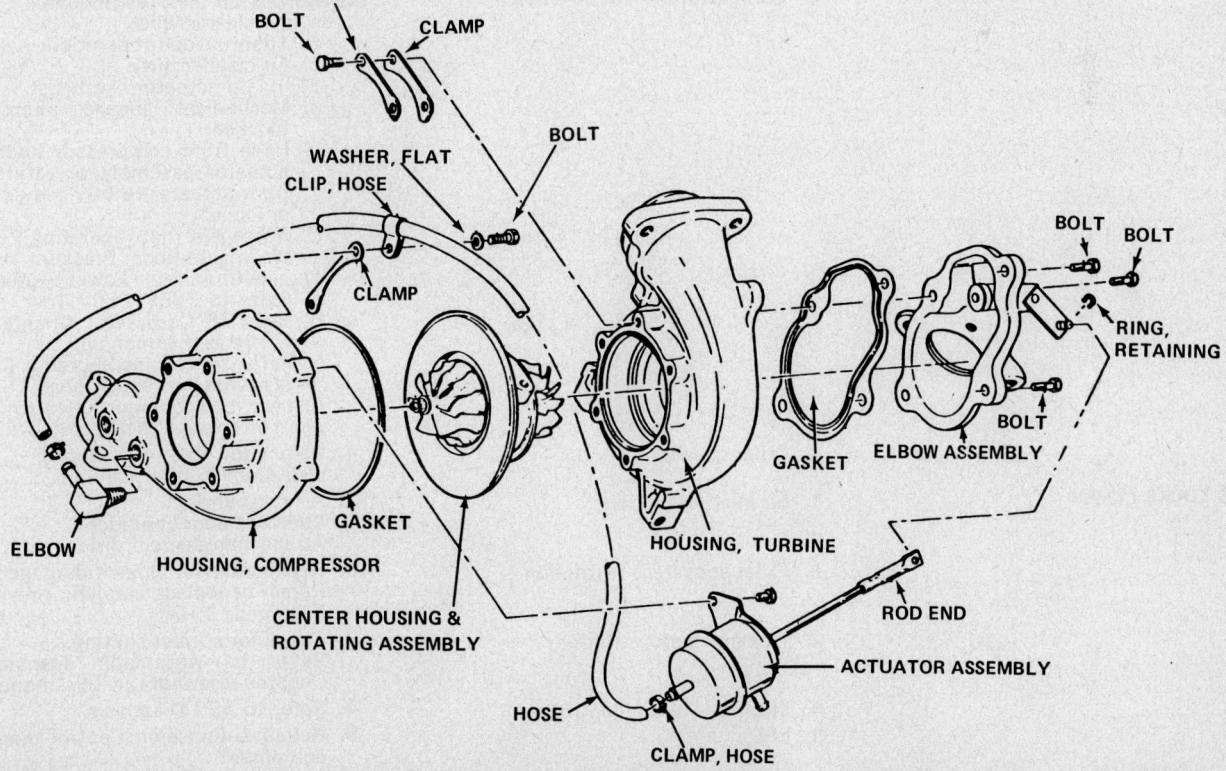

Fig. 1 Turbocharger assembly

1979 Power Enrichment Vacuum Regulator (PEVR) Test

1. Inspect PEVR and attaching hoses for deterioration, cracking or other damage and replace as necessary.
2. Tee one hose of manometer J-23951 between yellow stripped input hose and input port. Connect other hose directly to PEVR output port.
3. Start engine and operate at idle speed. There should be no more than 14" H_2O difference between manometer readings. If difference is greater than 14" H_2O, replace PEVR.
4. Remove PEVR from intake manifold and install a plug in intake manifold PEVR bore. Connect input and output hoses to PEVR.
5. Tee gauge J-28474 into output hose of PEVR.
6. Start engine and operate at idle speed. The gauge reading from the output port should be 7-9" Hg.
7. Apply 3 psi. to manifold signal port of PEVR. Vacuum reading from output port should be 1.4-2.6" Hg. If difficulty is encountered in measuring level of vacuum, apply 5 psi. to manifold sig-

nal port of PEVR. There should be no vacuum output from PEVR.
8. If PEVER does not perform as described above, replace PEVR.

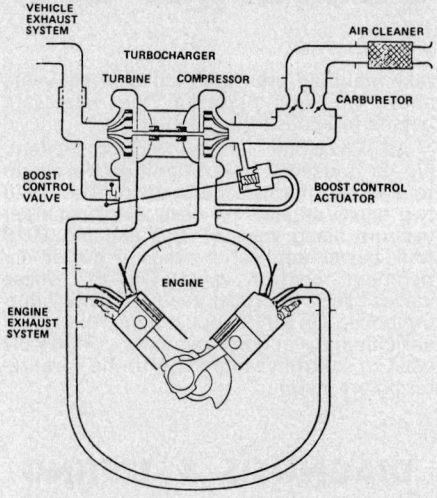

Fig. 2   Turbocharged V6 engine schematic

1978 Tubocharger Vacuum Bleed Valve (TVBV) Test

1. Inspect valve and attaching hoses deterioration, cracking or other damage and replace, if required.
2. Disconnect and plug the vacuum hose to the remote power enrichment port on the carburetor. Tee one hose from J-23951 manometer into the distributor vacuum hose between the carburetor and the TVBV. Tee the other hose into the hose between the TVBV and the distributor. Start and idle engine. There should be no more than a 14 inch H_2O difference on the manometer scale.
3. Repeat step 2 with the manometer teed into the vacuum hose from the Thermac sensor to the TVBV and the vacuum hose from the TVBV to the hot air door actuator.

NOTE: If the engine is at normal operating temperature, the hot air door may not have an applied vacuum signal. If so, connect manifold vacuum to port and recheck.

4. Plug the EGR hose at the EGR valve

ENGINE DIAGNOSIS CHART

Condition	Possible Cause	Correction
Engine Detonation	1. Electronic Spark Control.	1. Refer to ESC Diagnosis.
	2. EGR	2. Requires Emission Control diagnostic equipment.
	3. Carburetor or Turbocharger.	3. Correct air inlet restrictions. a. Air cleaner duct. b. Thermac door operation. c. Air cleaner dirty. Eliminate actuator overboost. a. Mechanical linkage jammed or blocked. b. Hose from compressor housing to actuator assembly or return hose from actuator to PCV tee damaged or loose. c. Wastegate not operating-Refer to Wastegate-Boost Pressure Test. Service Carburetor Power System. a. Refer to TVBV/PECV Test. b. Refer to Carburetor Chapter elsewhere in this manual. c. Refer to Trouble-Shooting Chapter elsewhere in this manual. Inspect turbocharger-Refer to Turbocharger Internal Inspection.
	4. Other causes.	4. Refer to Trouble-Shooting Chapter elsewhere in this manual.
Engine Lacks Power	1. Air inlet restriction	1. Air cleaner duct. Thermac door operation. Air cleaner element dirty.
	2. Exhaust system restriction.	2. Repair exhaust pipes if damaged. Repair or replace catalytic converter if damaged.
	3. Transmission.	3. Check for correct shifting. Refer to Automatic Transmission Chapter elsewhere in this manual.
	4. Electronic spark control.	4. Refer to ESC Diagnosis.
	5. EFE	5. Requires Emission Control diagnostic equipment.
	6. EGR	6. Requires Emission Control diagnostic equipment.

ENGINE DIAGNOSIS CHART—Continued

Condition	Possible Cause	Correction
	7. Carburetion	7. Refer to Carburetor Chapter elsewhere in this manual. Refer to Trouble-Shooting Chapter elsewhere in this manual.
	8. Turbocharger	8. Check for exhaust leaks or restrictions. Refer to TVBV/PECV test procedure. Inspect for collapsed or kinked plenum coolant hoses. Check wastegate operation. a. Refer to Wastegate-boost pressure test. b. Remove exhaust pipe from elbow assembly. Using a mirror, observe movement of wastegate while manually operating actuator linkage. Replace elbow assembly if valve does not open or close. Refer to Turbocharger Internal Inspection.
	9. Other causes.	9. Refer to Trouble-Shooting Chapter elsewhere in this manual.
Engine Surges	1. Electronic Spark Control.	1. Refer to ESC diagnosis.
	2. Carburetion.	2. Refer to TVBV/PECV Test Procedure. Refer to Carburetor Chapter elsewhere in this manual. Refer to Trouble-Shooting Chapter elsewhere in this manual.
	3. EGR	3. Requires Emission Control diagnostic equipment.
	4. Turbocharger.	4. Inspect turbocharger for loose bolts on compressor side of assembly, tighten.
	5. Other causes.	5. Refer to Trouble-Shooting Chapter elsewhere in this manual.
Excessive Oil Consumption Or Blue Exhaust Smoke	1. External turbocharger oil leaks.	1. Inspect turbocharger oil inlet for proper connection. Inspect turbocharger oil drain hose for leaks or restriction.
	2. PCV	2. Requires Emission Control diagnostic equipment.
	3. Other causes.	3. Refer to Trouble-Shooting Chapter elsewhere in this manual.
	4. Turbocharger.	4. Refer to Turbocharger Internal Inspection.
Black Exhaust Smoke	1. Carburetion.	1. Refer to TVBV/PECV Test. Refer to Carburetor Chapter elsewhere in this manual.
	2. Other causes.	2. Refer to Trouble-Shooting Chapter elsewhere in this manual.
Excessive Engine Noise	1. EFE	1. Requires Emission Control diagnostic equipment.
	2. Exhaust System.	2. Inspect for incorrect or loose mountings.
	3. AIR System.	3. Requires Emission Control diagnostic equipment.
	4. Other causes.	4. Refer to Trouble-Shooting Chapter elsewhere in this manual.
	5. Turbocharger.	5. Check for exhaust leaks. Inspect for restriction of turbocharger oil supply. Refer to Turbocharger Internal Inspection.

and install one hose from the manometer into the hose from the carburetor EGR signal port to the TVBV. Install the other manometer hose into the hose from the TVBV to the EGR-EFE switch. Start the engine and open the throttle slightly. There should be no more than a 14 inch H_2O difference on the manometer scale.

5. Disconnect all hoses from the TVBV. Connect one side of the manometer to the center vent port and vent the other side of the manometer to the atmosphere. Start and idle engine. There should be no vacuum signal at the port.

6. If conditions in steps 2, 3, 4 and 5 are not met, replace the TVBV and install all hoses.

7. If the TVBV tests normally but is still suspect, remove the TVBV from intake manifold. Plug the intake manifold and connect all hoses to the TVBV. Using J-23738, apply at least 6 inch Hg (3 psi) to the manifold signal port of the TVBV. Start and idle engine. Attach one side of the manometer to the output port of each pair of ports described in steps 2, 3 and four, in turn, and vent the other side of the manometer to the atmosphere. If the manometer indicates any pressure difference, replace the TVBV.

1978 Power Enrichment Control Valve (PECV) Test

1. Inspect the valve and attaching hoses for deterioration, cracking and other damage. Replace, if necessary.

2. Tee one side of manometer J-23951 into the input port and the other side into the output port of the PECV. Start and idle engine. There should be no more than a 12 inch H_2O difference on the manometer scale.

3. Disconnect all hoses from the PECV and plug the vacuum source hose. Connect one side of the manometer to the vent port and vent the other side to the atmosphere. Start and idle engine. The manometer should not indicate any pressure differential.

4. If conditions in steps 2 and 3 are not met, replace the PECV.

5. If the PECV tests normally but is still suspect, remove the PECV from intake manifold. Plug the intake manifold and connect hoses to the PECV. Tee one side of the manometer into the output port and vent the other side to the atmosphere. Apply at least 6 inch Hg (3 psi) to the manifold signal port of the PECV. Start and idle engine. If manometer indicates any pressure differential, replace the PECV.

Electronic Spark Control (ESC) System Diagnosis

Engine Detonation Or Poor Performance

1. Check all vacuum hoses and wires for proper connections and routing.

2. With ignition switch "On", check for voltage between light blue wire to black wire across ESC relay. If no voltage reading is obtained, replace ESC relay.

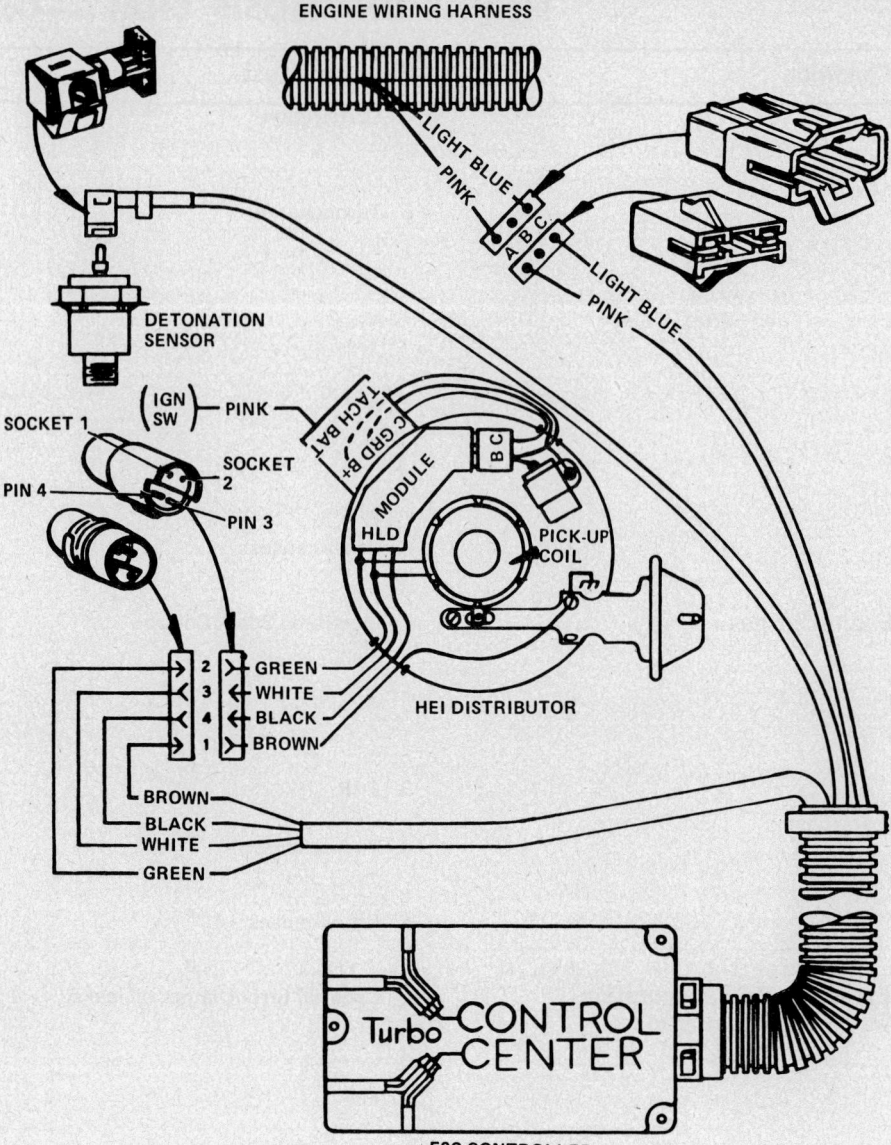

Fig. 3 Electronic spark control (ESC) system

3. If voltage reading is obtained in step 2, check initial ignition timing and correct, if necessary.

4. With engine at normal operating temperature, install a tachometer and timing meter, if available, to engine. Place air conditioner in "Off" position and the fast idle cam on high step. Run engine above 1800 RPM. Using a steel rod, tap intake manifold near detonation sensor with light to medium taps and observe tachometer or timing metering. Engine RPM should drop 300-500 RPM and timing should retard 18-22 degrees. Engine should return to original RPM and timing within 20 seconds after tapping stops.

5. If conditions are not met in step 4, check connection between ESC controller and detonation sensor, Fig. 3. Check detonation sensor for proper installation. Connect an ohmmeter

between detonation sensor and the ground, Fig. 3. If resistance is not 175-375 ohms, replace detonation sensor. If these checks and correction do not correct the problem, replace the ESC controller.

6. If conditions in step 4 are met, disconnect the four wire connector from ESC controller to distributor, Fig. 3. Using a jumper wire, connect socket No. 2 to pin No. 4 on the distributor side of the harness connector, Fig. 3. Test H.E.I. distributor as outlined in the "Tune-Up Chapter, Electronic Ignition Systems" section. After distributor repair, remove jumper wire and connect ESC controller.

Engine Cranks But Does Not Start

1. Check all vacuum hoses and wires for proper connections and routing.

2. Check for spark at spark plug.

3. If spark is present at spark plug, re-

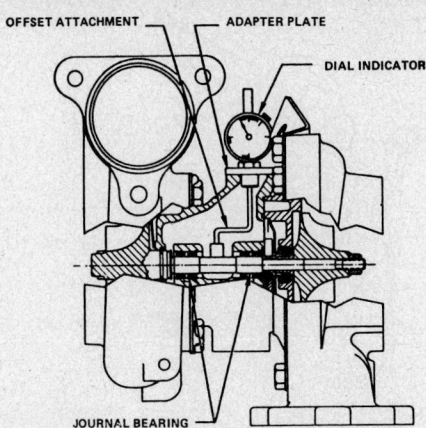

Fig. 4 Journal bearing clearance check

fer to the "Trouble-Shooting Chapter" and the "Tune-Up Chapter, Electronic Ignition Systems Section".

4. If spark is not present at spark plug, check ESC relay voltage between light blue wire and black wire while cranking. If voltage is present, replace ESC relay.
5. If no voltage was present in step 4, check voltage between the distributor "BAT" terminal and the ground with ignition "On". If voltage is under 7 volts, check for open circuit between distributor "BAT" terminal and ignition switch.
6. If voltage in step 5 is 7 volts or over, check voltage at "A" terminal, pink wire, on engine harness side of two wire connector from ESC controller to engine wiring harness, Fig. 3. If voltage is under 7 volts, check for open circuit between "A" terminal and the ignition switch.
7. If voltage in step 6 was 7 volts or over, disconnect four wire connector from ESC controller to distributor, Fig. 3. Connect a jumper wire between socket No. 2 and pin No. 4 on distributor side of harness connector, Fig. 3. Check for spark at spark plug while cranking engine. If spark is present at spark plug, replace ESC controller.
8. If spark is not present at spark plug in step 7, leave the jumper wire connected and test the H.E.I. distributor as outlined in the "Tune-Up Chapter, Electronic Ignition Section". After distributor repair, remove the jumper wire and connect the ESC controller.

TURBOCHARGER INTERNAL INSPECTION

1. Remove the turbocharger assembly but do not separate the center housing rotating assembly from the turbine housing.
2. Manually operate the wastegate linkage and using a small mirror, observe wastegate movement in the elbow assembly. Replace the elbow assembly if the wastegate fails to open or close.
3. Check for loose backplate to center housing rotating assembly bolts and

tighten, if necessary.
4. Spin the compressor wheel. If rotating assembly binds or drags, replace the center housing rotating assembly.
5. Inspect center rotating housing assembly for sludge in the oil drain area. Clean, if minor, or replace center housing rotating assembly if excessively sludged or coked.
6. Inspect compressor oil seal for damage or leakage on the compressor wheel side of the backplate. Replace center housing rotating assembly if oil seal damage or leakage is present.
7. If compressor wheel is damaged or severely coked, replace center housing rotating assembly.
8. If center housing rotating assembly is being replaced, pre-lubricate with engine oil.
9. Inspect compressor housing and turbine housing. If either housing is gouged, nicked or distorted, replace if necessary.
10. Remove turbine housing from center housing rotating assembly and check the journal bearing radial clearance and thrust bearing axial clearance as follows:
    a. Journal bearing radial clearance
    (1) Attach a rack and pinion type dial indicator (Starrett model 656-517 or equivalent with a two inch long, 3/4 to 1 inch offset extension rod) to the center housing so the indicator plunger extends through the oil output port and contacts the turbine wheel assembly shaft, Fig. 4. If required, a dial indicator mounting adapter can be utilized, Fig. 4.
    (2) Manually apply pressure equally and at the same time to both the compressor wheel and turbine wheel as required to move the turbine wheel as-

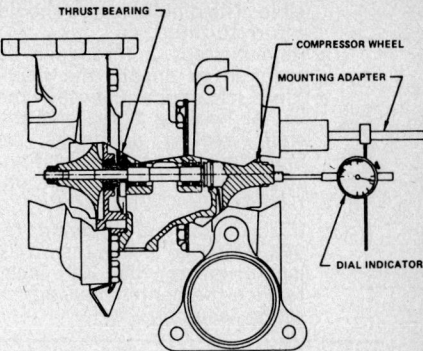

Fig. 5 Thrust bearing clearance check

sembly shaft away from the dial indicator as far as possible.
    (3) Zero the dial indicator.
    (4) Manually apply pressure equally and at the same time to both the compressor and turbine wheels as required to move the turbine wheel assembly shaft toward the dial indicator plunger as far as possible. Note maximum reading on dial indicator.

NOTE: To ensure that the dial indicator reading is the maximum obtainable, roll the wheels slightly in both directions while applying pressure.

    (5) Manually apply pressure equally and at the same time to both the compressor and turbine wheels as required to move the turbine wheel assembly shaft away from the dial indicator as far as pos-

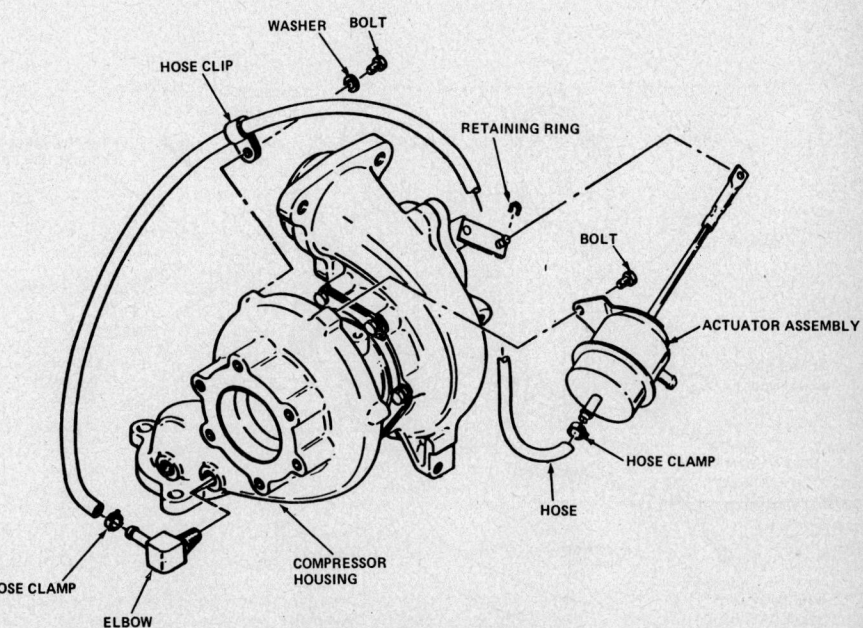

Fig. 6 Wastegate actuator assembly

sible. The dial indicator should return to zero.

(6) Repeat steps 2 through 5 as required to ensure the maximum clearance between the center housing bores and the shaft bearing diameters, as indicated by the maximum shaft travel, has been obtained.

(7) If the maximum bearing radial clearance is less than .003 inch or greater than .006 inch, replace the center housing rotating assembly.

NOTE: Continued operation of a turbocharger having excessive bearing radial clearance will result in severe damage to the compressor and turbine wheels and the housings.

b. Thrust bearing axial clearance.
(1) Mount a dial indicator (Starrett model 25-141 or equivalent) at the turbine end of the turbocharger so the dial indicator plunger contacts the end of the turbine wheel assembly, Fig. 5.

(2) Manually move the compressor wheel and turbine wheel assembly in each direction shown on the indicator dial.

(3) Repeat step 2 to ensure the maximum clearance between the thrust bearing components, as indicated by the maximum turbine wheel assembly travel, has been obtained.

(4) If the maximum thrust bearing axial clearance is less than .001 inch or greater than .003 inch, replace the center housing rotating assembly.

NOTE: Continued operation of a turbocharger having excessive thrust bearing axial clearance will result in severe damage to the compressor and turbine wheels and the housings.

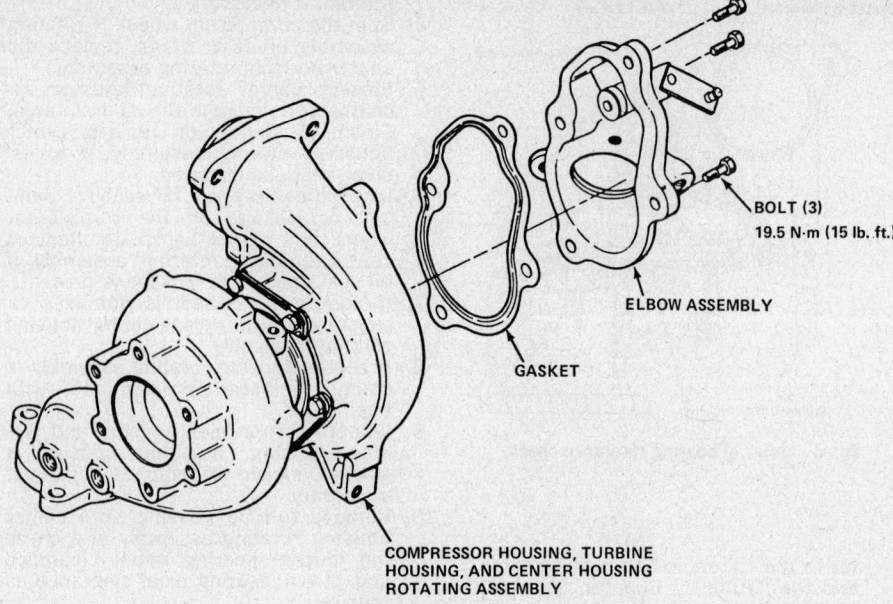

Fig. 7 Elbow assembly

SERVICE

Before performing turbocharger service, note the following general cautions:
1. Clean area around turbocharger assembly with a non-caustic solution before service. Cover openings of engine assembly connections to prevent entry of foreign material.
2. When removing the assembly, do not bend, nick or in any way damage the compressor or turbine wheel blades. Any damage may result in rotating assembly imbalance, failure of the center housing rotating assembly, and failure of the compressor and/or turbine housings.
3. Before disconnecting center housing rotating assembly from either compressor housing or turbine housing, scribe location of components for assembly in original position.

Wastegate Actuator Assembly, Replace

1. Disconnect two vacuum hoses from actuator.
2. Remove clip from wastegate linkage to actuator rod, Fig. 6.
3. Remove two bolts attaching actuator and the actuator.
4. Reverse procedure to install.

Elbow Assembly, Replace

1. Raise vehicle.
2. Loosen exhaust pipe at catalytic converter.
3. Lower the vehicle.
4. Disconnect turbocharger exhaust outlet pipe from elbow, Fig. 7.
5. Disconnect actuator rod from wastegate linkage.
6. Remove elbow from turbine housing.
7. Reverse procedure to install.

Turbine Housing & Elbow Assembly, Center Housing Rotating Assembly

1. Disconnect turbocharger exhaust outlet pipe from elbow.
2. Raise vehicle.

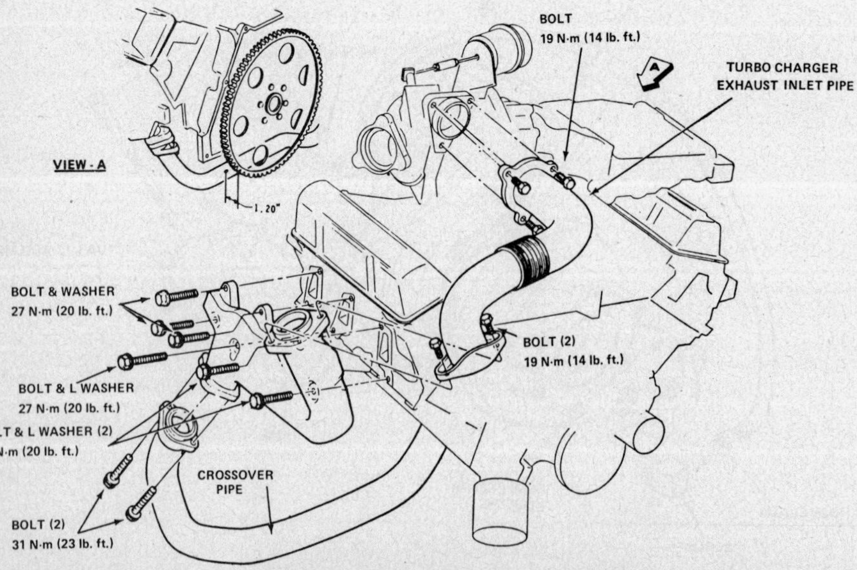

Fig. 8 Turbocharger exhaust inlet pipe

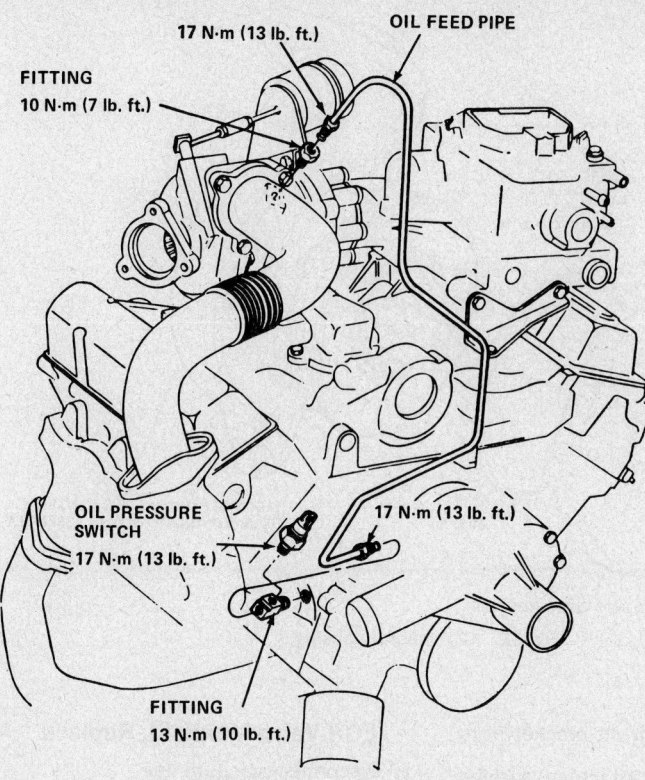

Fig. 9 Turbocharger oil feed pipe (typical)

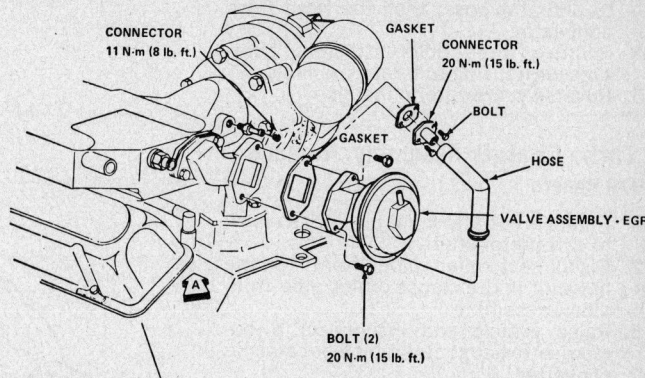

Fig. 10 EGR valve & turbocharger oil drain. Except 1979 Riviera

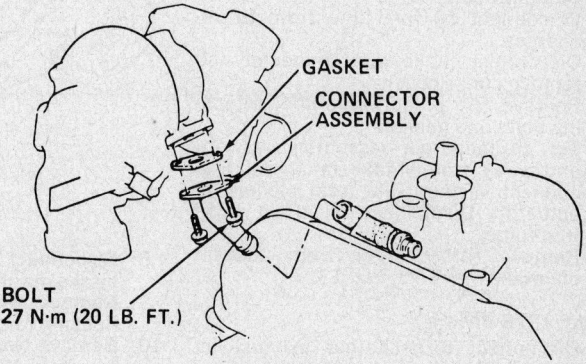

Fig. 10A Oil drain collector. 1979 Riviera

3. Disconnect catalytic converter from exhaust pipe and move pipe aside.
4. Lower vehicle.
5. Disconnect turbocharger exhaust inlet pipe from turbine housing, Fig. 8.
6. Disconnect turbocharger exhaust inlet pipe from right exhaust manifold, Fig. 8.
7. Disconnect turbine housing from bracket.
8. Disconnect turbocharger oil feed pipe, Fig. 9, and oil drain hose, Figs. 10 and 10A from center housing rotating assembly.
9. Disconnect actuator rod from wastegate linkage.
10. Remove six bolts and three clamps attaching center housing rotating assembly backplate to compressor housing.
11. Remove six bolts, three lockplates and three clamps attaching turbine housing to center housing rotating assembly, Fig. 11.
12. Reverse procedure to install.

Compressor Housing

1. Remove turbine housing and elbow assembly/center housing rotating assembly as outlined previously, however do not separate the turbine housing from the center housing rotating assembly.
2. Remove six bolts attaching compressor housing to the plenum, Figs. 12 and 13.
3. Remove clamp attaching compressor

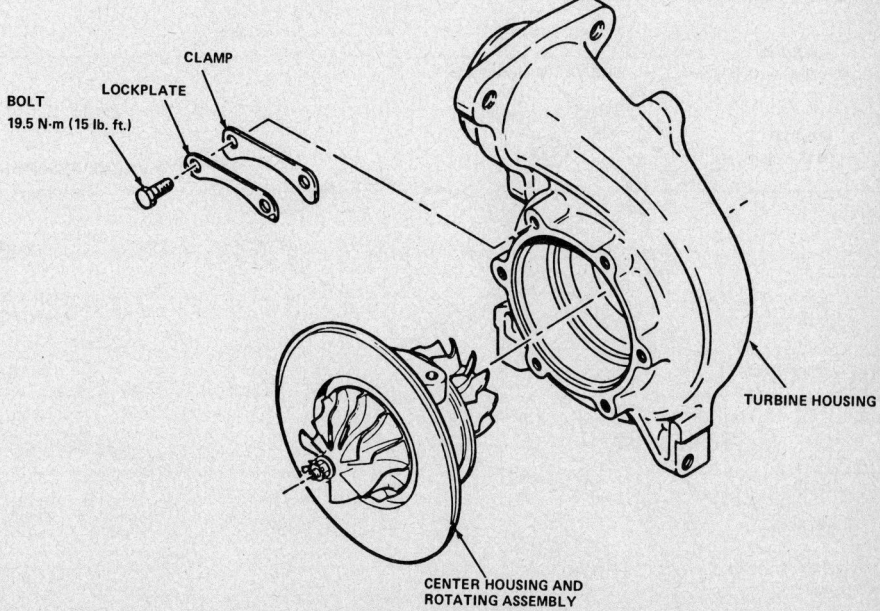

Fig. 11 Center housing rotating assembly

to actuator hose, then the hose from connector.
4. Remove three bolts attaching compressor housing to intake manifold.
5. Reverse procedure to install.

Turbo Charger Assembly, Replace

1979 Riviera

1. Remove nut attaching air intake elbow to carburetor stud.
2. Disconnect inlet pipe from turbine housing and exhaust outlet pipe from elbow assembly.
3. Raise vehicle and disconnect turbocharger exhaust outlet pipe at catalytic converter.
4. Lower vehicle and two bolts attaching turbocharger adjustment bracket to turbocharger support bracket on right cylinder head.
5. Disconnect oil feed line from turbocharger.
6. Disconnect choke wire connector and remove choke cover.
7. Remove five plenum chamber attaching bolts and gasket.
8. Tip turbocharger assembly upward and away from intake manifold. Disconnect vacuum line from plenum at actuator. Disconnect oil drain hose from pipe.
9. Remove turbocharger from adapter on intake manifold, Fig. 13.

Except 1979 Riviera

1. Disconnect turbocharger exhaust inlet and outlet pipes at turbocharger.
2. Disconnect oil feed pipe from center housing rotating assembly.
3. Remove nut attaching air intake elbow to carburetor and remove elbow.
4. Disconnect accelerator, cruise control and detent linkages at carburetor, then remove linkage bracket from plenum.
5. Remove two bolts attaching plenum to side bracket.
6. Disconnect fuel line and necessary vacuum hoses.
7. Disconnect coolant hoses and power brake vacuum hose from plenum.

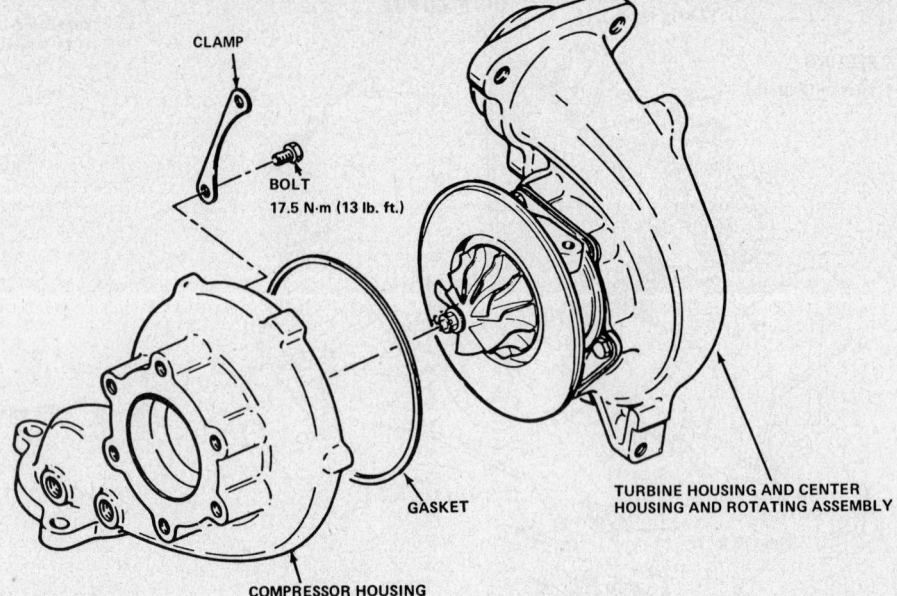

Fig. 12   Compressor housing

CLAMP

BOLT
17.5 N·m (13 lb. ft.)

TURBINE HOUSING AND CENTER HOUSING AND ROTATING ASSEMBLY

GASKET

COMPRESSOR HOUSING

8. Disconnect plenum front bracket from intake manifold.
9. Remove two bolts attaching turbine housing to bracket on intake manifold.
10. Remove two bolts attaching EGR valve manifold to plenum, then remove AIR bypass hose from pipe.
11. Remove three bolts attaching compressor housing to intake manifold.
12. Remove turbocharger and actuator with carburetor and plenum assembly attached from engine.
13. Remove six bolts attaching turbocharger and actuator assembly to plenum assembly and carburetor Fig. 13A.
14. Drain oil from center housing rotating assembly.

EGR Valve Manifold, Replace

1. Disconnect vacuum line.
2. Remove two bolts attaching EGR valve.
3. Remove bolts attaching EGR manifold, Figs. 14 and 14A.
4. Reverse procedure to install.

ESC Detonation Sensor, Replace

1. Disconnect wire connector from sensor. Do not pull on wire.
2. Remove the sensor with a deep socket, Fig. 15.
3. Reverse procedure to install. Torque ESC detonation sensor to 14 ft. lbs.

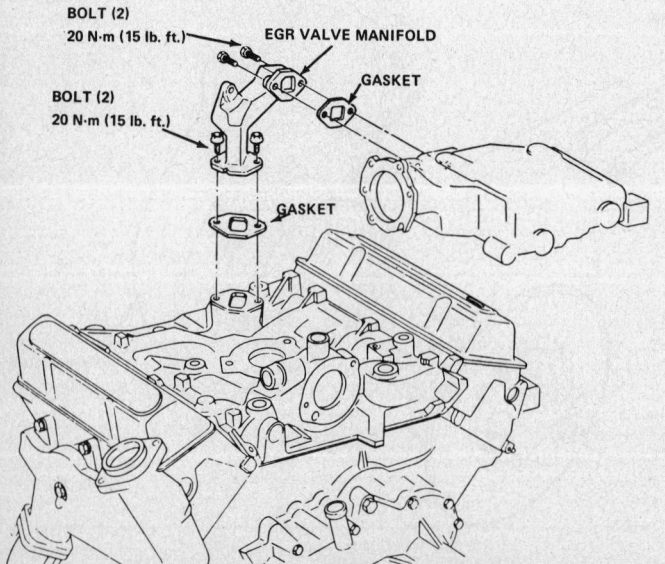

BOLT (2)
20 N·m (15 lb. ft.)
EGR VALVE MANIFOLD
BOLT (2)
20 N·m (15 lb. ft.)
GASKET
GASKET

Fig. 14   EGR valve manifold. Except 1979 Riviera

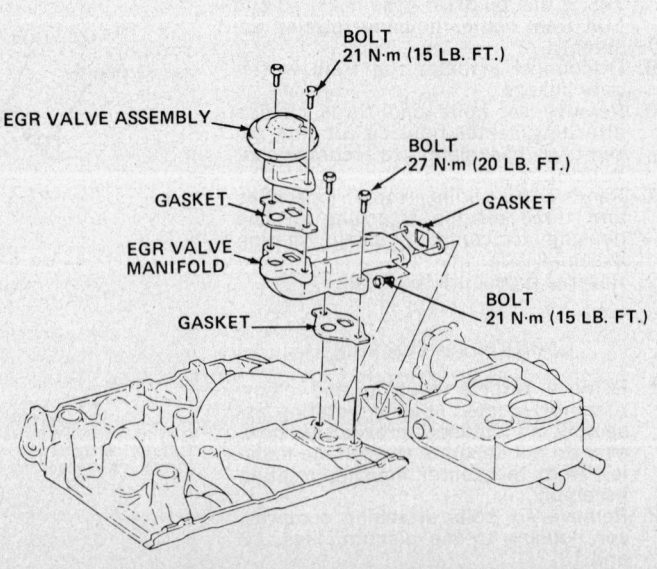

BOLT
21 N·m (15 LB. FT.)
EGR VALVE ASSEMBLY
BOLT
27 N·m (20 LB. FT.)
GASKET
GASKET
EGR VALVE MANIFOLD
GASKET
BOLT
21 N·m (15 LB. FT.)

Fig. 14A   EGR manifold. 1979 Riviera

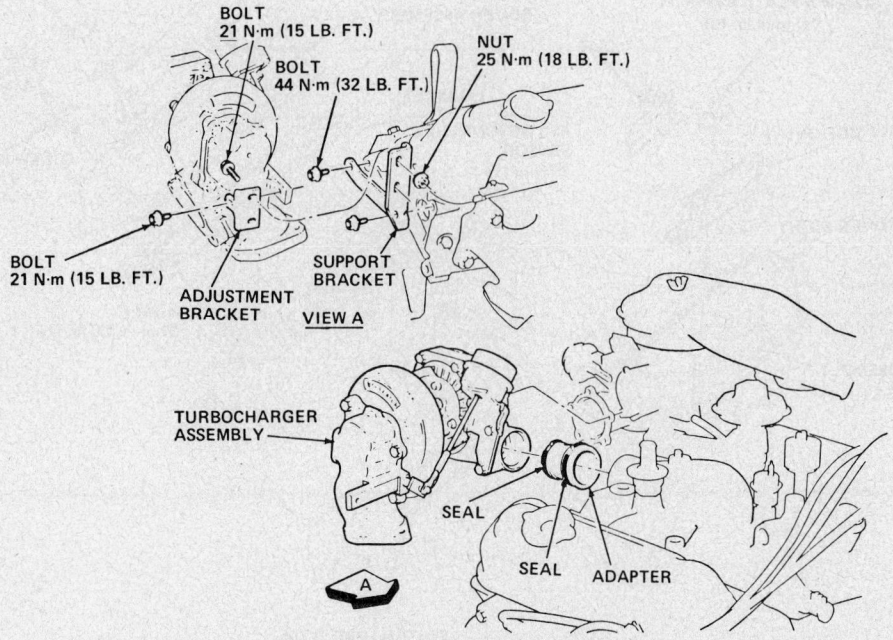

BOLT
21 N·m (15 LB. FT.)

BOLT
44 N·m (32 LB. FT.)

NUT
25 N·m (18 LB. FT.)

BOLT
21 N·m (15 LB. FT.)

ADJUSTMENT
BRACKET

SUPPORT
BRACKET

VIEW A

TURBOCHARGER
ASSEMBLY

SEAL

SEAL   ADAPTER

A

Fig. 13   Turbocharger assembly. 1979 Riviera

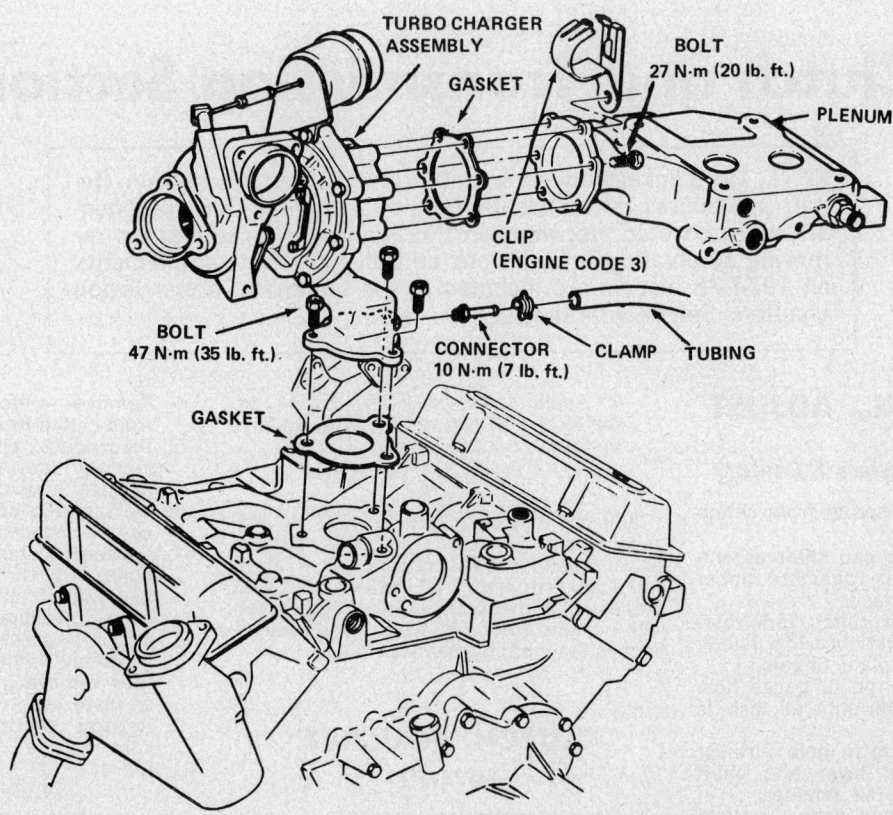

TURBO CHARGER
ASSEMBLY

GASKET

BOLT
27 N·m (20 lb. ft.)

PLENUM

CLIP
(ENGINE CODE 3)

BOLT
47 N·m (35 lb. ft.)

CONNECTOR
10 N·m (7 lb. ft.)

CLAMP   TUBING

GASKET

Fig. 13A   Plenum & turbocharger assembly. Except 1979 Riviera

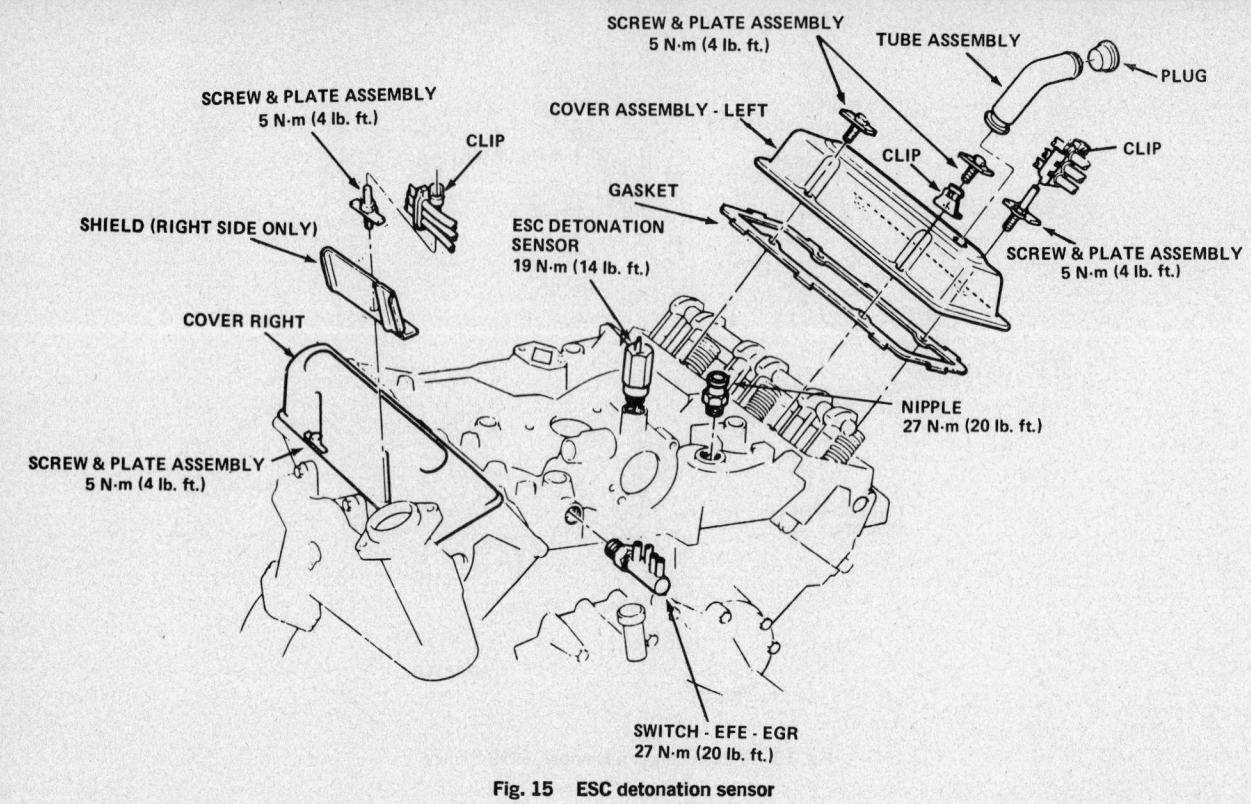

SCREW & PLATE ASSEMBLY
5 N·m (4 lb. ft.)

TUBE ASSEMBLY

PLUG

SCREW & PLATE ASSEMBLY
5 N·m (4 lb. ft.)

CLIP

COVER ASSEMBLY - LEFT

CLIP

CLIP

SHIELD (RIGHT SIDE ONLY)

GASKET

SCREW & PLATE ASSEMBLY
5 N·m (4 lb. ft.)

ESC DETONATION
SENSOR
19 N·m (14 lb. ft.)

COVER RIGHT

NIPPLE
27 N·m (20 lb. ft.)

SCREW & PLATE ASSEMBLY
5 N·m (4 lb. ft.)

SWITCH - EFE - EGR
27 N·m (20 lb. ft.)

Fig. 15   ESC detonation sensor

Clutch and Transmission Section

NOTE: 1979 linkage adjustment information is in this section. Repair procedures on both automatic and manual shift transmissions are covered elsewhere in this manual. Procedures for removing automatic transmissions as well as linkage adjustments on 1974-78 models are included in the automatic transmission chapters. See Chapter Index.

CLUTCH PEDAL, ADJUST

1975-79 Apollo, Skylark & Century

1. Disconnect return spring from clutch fork.
2. Rotate clutch lever and shaft assembly until pedal is against rubber bumper on dash brace.
3. Push outer end of clutch fork rearward until throwout bearing lightly contacts pressure plate fingers.
4. Install lower push rod in gauge hole and increase length until all lash is removed.
5. Install swivel or rod in hole furthest from centerline of lever and shaft assembly, then install retainer.
6. Tighten lock nut and spacer against swivel and connect clutch fork return spring.
7. Check clutch pedal free travel. Free play should be $^{55}/_{64}$ to $1^{29}/_{64}$ for 1975-

77 Apollo and Skylark, $^{45}/_{64}$ to $1^{5}/_{16}$ in. for 1975-79 Century and $1^{45}/_{64}$ to $2^{5}/_{16}$ in. for 1978-79 Skylark.

1974

Adjust linkage to provide $^5/_8$" to $^7/_8$" pedal free play. On LeSabre units, remove swivel retainer, disconnect swivel from equalizer arm and twin swivel to obtain proper adjustment. On other units, loosen lock nut and turn rod. When proper clearance is reached, tighten lock nut.

CLUTCH, REPLACE

1974-79

1. Remove transmission.
2. Remove pedal return spring from clutch fork and *disconnect rod assembly from clutch fork.*
3. Remove flywheel housing.

4. Remove clutch throw-out bearing from clutch fork.
5. Disconnect clutch fork from ball stud by moving it toward center of flywheel housing.
6. Mark clutch cover and flywheel so it can be installed in the same position.
7. Loosen clutch cover to flywheel bolts one turn at a time to avoid bending of clutch cover flange until spring pressure is released.
8. Support pressure plate and cover assembly while removing last bolts, then remove pressure plate and driven plate
9. Reverse procedure to install being sure to line up marks made in removal.

3 SPEED TRANS. REPLACE

All 1974-79

1. Disconnect speedometer cable from

driven gear fitting.

2. Disconnect shift control rods from shifter levers at transmission.
3. Remove propeller shaft.
4. Support rear of engine and remove transmission crossmember.
5. Remove two top transmission attaching bolts and insert guide pins in these holes.
6. Remove two lower bolts and slide transmission straight back and out of vehicle.
7. Reverse procedure to install.

3 SPEED TRANS. SHIFT LINKAGE

1974-79

Column Shift

1. Place column selector lever in Reverse detent, making sure the steering column selector plate engages lower most column lever (1st-reverse).
2. Loosen 1st-reverse adjusting clamp.
3. Shift transmission lever into reverse and tighten the 1st-reverse clamp.
4. Shift transmission levers into neutral and loosen 2nd-3rd clamp.

5. Install ³/₁₆″ diameter rod through 2nd-3rd lever selector plate and the 1st-reverse lever and alignment plate.
6. Tighten 2nd-3rd shift rod clamp.

Floor Shift

1. Place transmission levers in Neutral.
2. Loosen shift rod adjusting clamp bolts on shifter assembly.
3. Insert ¼″ drill rod through shift assembly and shift levers.
4. Tighten clamp bolts.

4 SPEED TRANS. REPLACE

1978-79 Century & Regal

1. Disconnect speedometer cable and remove driven gear.
2. Disconnect shift control rods from transmission.
3. Remove propeller shaft.
4. Support rear of engine and remove transmission support.
5. Remove two top transmission-to-flywheel housing bolts and insert guide pins.
6. Remove two lower bolts.
7. Slide transmission back and out.
8. Reverse procedure to install.

4 SPEED TRANS. SHIFT LINKAGE

1978-79 Century & Regal

Floor Shift

1. Place transmission in neutral.
2. Adjust all three shift rods so a ¼″ drill rod can be installed through shifter assembly and shift levers.
3. Tighten swivel nuts.

1979 AUTO. TRANS. LINKAGE ADJUST

NOTE: For service procedures on 1979 Riviera Turbo Hyra-Matic 325 refer to main index in front of book.

Except 1979 Riviera

This adjustment is the same as that described for previous models and is found elsewhere in this manual.

Rear Axle, Propeller Shaft & Brakes

REAR AXLES

Figs. 1 and 1A and illustrate the type rear axle assemblies used on Buicks. When necessary to overhaul any of these units, refer to the *Rear Axle Specifications* table in this chapter.

1974-79 All

In this rear axle, Figs. 1 and 1A the drive pinion is mounted in two tapered roller bearings which are preloaded by two selected spacers at assembly. The pinion is positioned by shims located between a shoulder on the drive pinion and the rear bearing. The front bearing is held in place by a large nut.

The differential is supported in the carrier by two tapered roller side bearings. These are preloaded by inserting shims between the bearings and the pedestals. The differential assembly is positioned for proper ring gear and pinion backlash by varying these shims. The ring gear is bolted to the case. The case houses two side gears in mesh with two pinions mounted on a pinion axle which

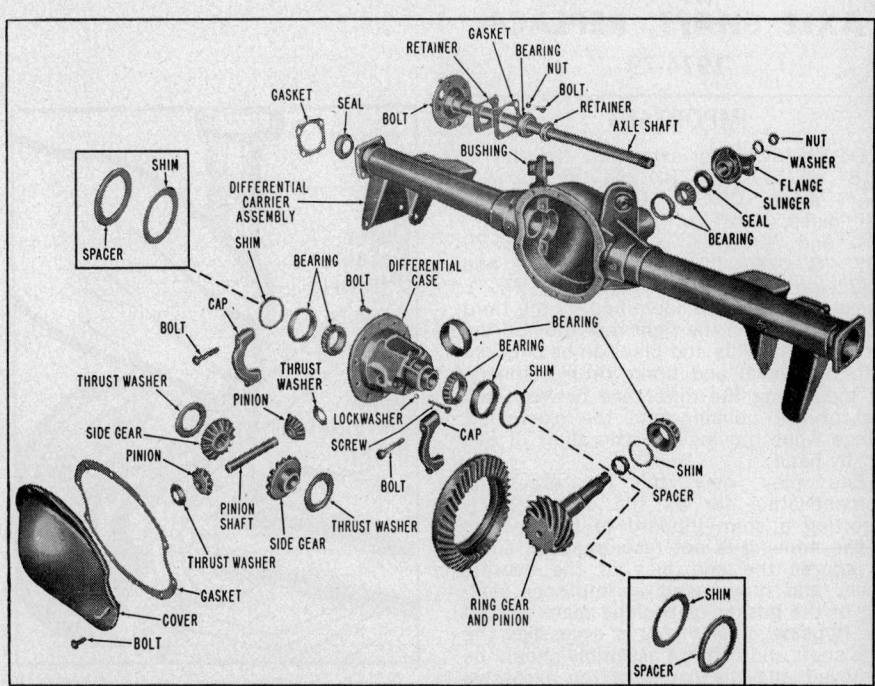

Fig. 1   Rear axle assembly (Typical). 1974-79 type "B & O" (Except 7½")

is anchored in the case by a spring pin. The pinions and side gears are backed by thrust washers.

REAR AXLE ASSEMBLY, REPLACE
1974-79

It is not necessary to remove the rear axle assembly for any normal repairs but if the housing must be replaced the assembly may be removed as follows:
1. Raise vehicle and support using jack stands under both frame side rails.
2. Mark rear universal joint and flange for proper reassembly and disconnect rear joint.
3. Push propeller shaft as far forward as possible and wire up out of way.
4. Disconnect parking brake cables and rear brake hose. Cover brake hose opening to prevent entrance of dirt.
5. Support axle with jack and disconnect shock absorbers at lower ends.
   On 1974-76 Estate Wagons, disconnect exhaust system right side by removing exhaust hanger screw at rear frame crossmember. On Apollo, Skylark and 1974-76 Estate Wagons, remove leaf spring as outlined under "Leaf Spring, Replace" procedure in the Rear Suspension section.
6. Disconnect upper control arms at axle housing.
7. Disconnect lower control arms and remove axle assembly.

AXLE SHAFT, REPLACE
1974-79

IMPORTANT

Design allows for axle shaft end play of .018" on 1974-77 "B" and "O" (except 7½") axles, .002 to .020" on 1978-79 "B" axles, .022" on 1974-77 "C", "G", "K", and "O" (7½"), .025" on 1978-79 "C", "G", "K", "O" and "P" (7½") and .032" on 1974-79 "P" (except 7½"). These axles may be identified by the third letter located on the right rear tube on the forward side. This end play can be checked with the wheel and brake drum removed by measuring the difference between the end of the housing and the axle shaft flange while moving the axle shaft in and out by hand.

End play over this is excessive. Compensating for all the end play by inserting a shim inboard of the bearing in the housing is not recommended since it ignores the end play of the bearing itself, and may result in improper seating of the gasket or backing plate against the housing. If end play is excessive, the axle shaft and bearing assembly should be removed and the cause of the excessive end play determined and corrected.

Fig. 1A Rear axle assembly (Typical). 1974-79 type "C, G, K, O (7½") & P"

Removing Axle Shaft
1974-79 C, G, K, O (7½") & P Axles
1. Remove wheels and brake drums.
2. Remove bolts and differential cover

and allow lubricant to drain.
3. Remove pinion shaft lock bolt and pinion shaft then push axle shafts inward, remove C-lock and axle shaft.

1974-79 B & O (Except 7½") Axles
1. Remove wheels and brake drums.
2. Remove retainer plate nuts. Pull retainers clear of bolts and reinstall two opposite nuts to hold brake backing plate in place.
3. Pull axle shaft assembly using a puller.

Replacing Axle Shaft Bearings & Seals
1974-79 C, G, K, O (7½") & P Axles

To remove axle shaft bearing & seal on all 1973 models and 1974-76 full size, use tool J-23689 or tool J-22813-01 on 1974-76 intermediate models and all 1977-78 models. To install bearing & seal, use tool J-23690 on all models.

1974-79 B & O (Except 7½")
1. Place axle shaft in a vise so that the retainer ring rests on vise jaws. Use a chisel and a hammer to crack the ring, Fig. 2.
2. Press bearing off shaft and remove seal. Inspect seal running surface for bad spots and replace if necessary.

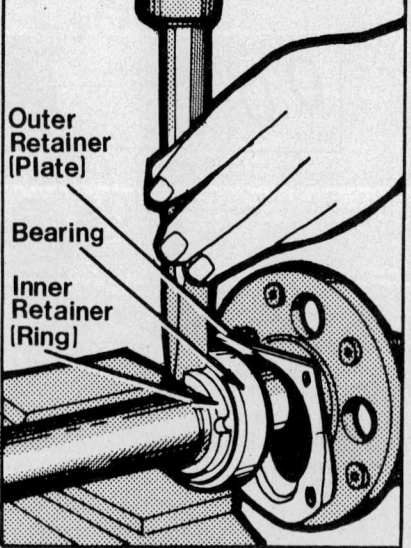

Fig. 2 Removing axle shaft bearing retainer

NOTE: Before installing seal, apply

grease between seal lips to avoid damaging the seal.

3. Press bearing against shoulder on shaft and retainer ring against bearing using Installer tool J-21022 for intermediate models and J-8609 for full size models.

Axle Shaft, Install

1. Apply a coat of wheel bearing grease in wheel bearing and seal recess.
2. For C, G, K, O (7½") and P axles:
   a. Install axle shaft through seal and bearing and through side gear as far in as possible.

   NOTE: Do not let shaft drag across seal lip and apply grease between seal lips.

   b. Install C-lock and move axle shaft outward to bottom C-lock in recess of side gear.
   c. Install pinion shaft and torque lock bolt to 15 ft. lbs.
   d. Install gasket and cover and torque bolts to 30 ft. lbs. After 20 minutes, retorque bolts to 30 ft. lbs.
   e. Install correct type and amount of lubricant.
3. For B and O (except 7½"), insert axle shaft through housing and install retaining nuts. Torque retaining nuts to 55 ft. lbs. on 1974-77 full size models, 35 ft. lbs. on 1978-79 full size models and all Century and Regal models.
4. Install drum and wheel.

PROPELLER SHAFT

NOTE

When service is required, the propeller shaft must be removed from the car as a complete assembly. While handling it out of the car, the assembly must be supported on a straight line as nearly as possible to avoid jamming or bending any of the parts.

The propeller shaft used on 1975-76 vehicles equipped with V6-231 engines and 1978-79 Riviera and Electra are constructed of concentric steel tubes with rubber elements between them, Fig. 3.

1974-79

NOTE: Two attachment methods are used to secure the propeller shaft to the pinion flange or end yoke, a pair of bolted straps or a set of bolted flanges.

1. Scribe alignment marks between propeller shaft and pinion flange or end yoke to aid reassembly.
2. Remove strap or flange bolts at rear of propeller shaft. Tape bearing cups to prevent loss of needle bearings.
3. Slide shaft assembly rearward, dis-

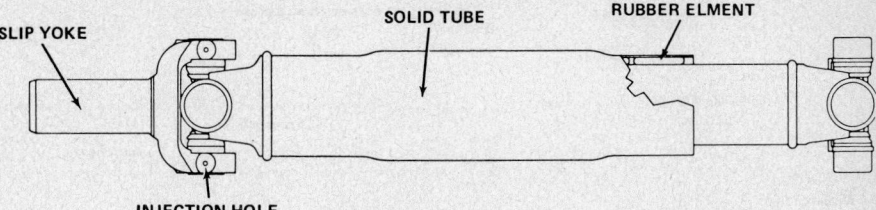

Fig. 3   Propeller shaft used with 1975-76 V6-231 engines & 1978 Riviera & Electra

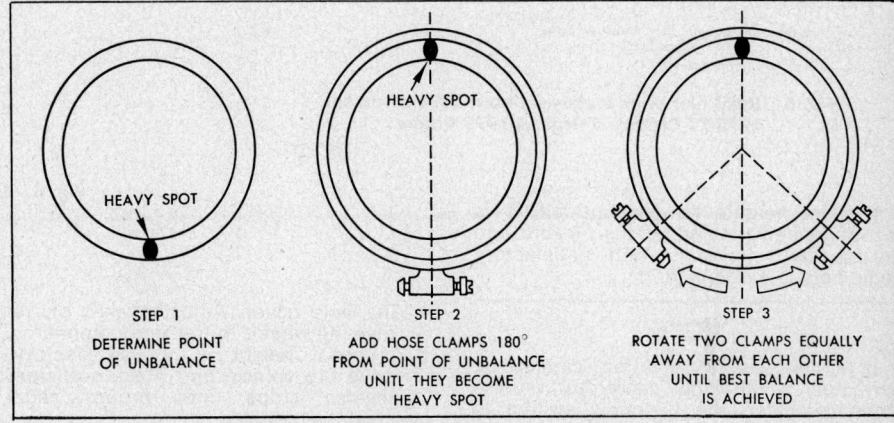

Fig. 4   Positioning hose clamps to balance shaft.

engaging front yoke from transmission output shaft splines and lower from vehicle.
4. Reverse procedure to install.

NOTE: Apply grease (Grade EP 1) to internal splines of front yokes having a .060 inch vent hole (automatic transmission models). Apply engine oil to same area of front yokes without vent holes (manual transmission models).

PROPELLER SHAFT BALANCE

A wheel balancer of the type equipped with a strobe light can be used to facilitate balancing of the driveshaft. The pick-up unit should be placed directly under the nose of the rear axle carrier and as far forward as possible.
1. Place car on twin post lift so rear of car is supported on the rear axle housing and rear wheels are free to rotate.
2. Remove both rear wheels and tire assemblies and reinstall wheel lug nuts with flat side next to drum.
3. Mark and number driveshaft at four points 90° apart at rear of shaft just forward of balance weights.
4. Place strobe light pick-up under nose of differential.
5. With car running in gear at car speed where unbalance is at its peak, allow driveline to stabilize by holding at

constant speed. Point strobe light at spinning shaft and note position of one of the reference marks.
6. Shut off engine and position shaft so reference mark will be in position noted when car was running.

CAUTION: Do not run car on hoist for extended periods due to danger of overheating transmission or engine.

7. When strobe light flashed, the heaviest point of the shaft was down. To balance shaft it will be necessary to apply weight 180° away. Screw type hose clamps can be used as weights as shown in Fig. 4.

BRAKE ADJUSTMENTS

1974-79 Self-Adjusting Drum Brakes

These brakes, Figs. 5, 6 and 7 have self-adjusting shoe mechanisms that assure correct lining-to-drum clearances at all times. The automatic adjusters operate only when the brakes are applied as the car is moving rearward.

Although the brakes are self-adjusting, an initial adjustment is necessary after the brake shoes have been relined or replaced, or when the length of the adjusting screw has been changed during some other service operation.

Frequent usage of an automatic transmission forward range to halt reverse vehicle motion may prevent the automatic adjusters from functioning, thereby inducing low pedal heights. Should

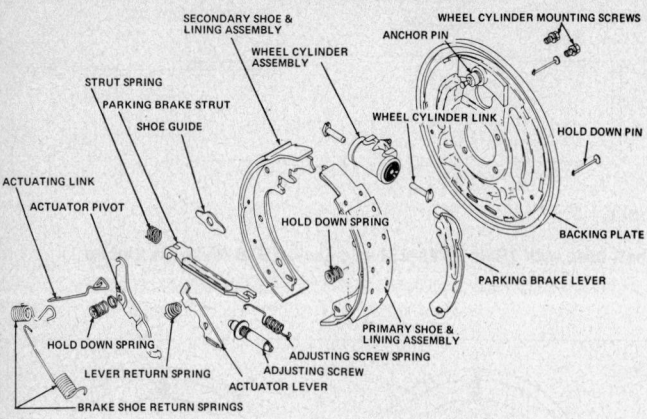

Fig. 5 Right rear drum brake assembly. 1974-79 except 1978-79 Century & Regal & 1979 Riviera

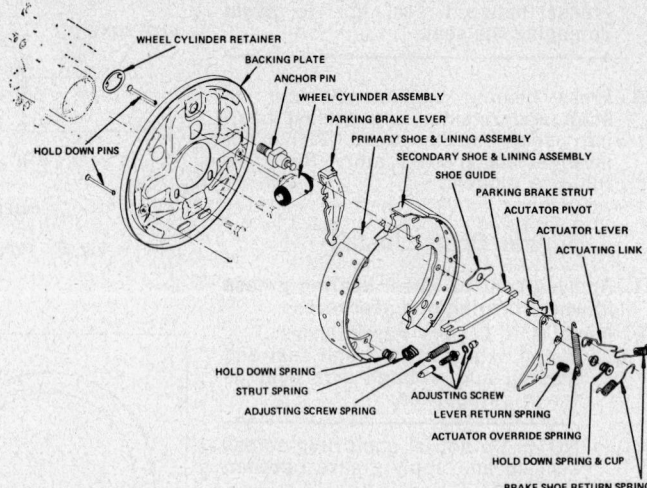

Fig. 6 Left rear drum brake assembly. 1978-79 Century & Regal

low pedal heights be encountered, it is recommended that numerous forward and reverse stops be made until satisfactory pedal height is obtained.

NOTE

If a low pedal condition cannot be corrected by making numerous reverse stops (provided the hydraulic system is free of air) it indicates that the self-adjusting mechanism is not functioning. Therefore, it will be necessary to remove the brake drum, clean, free up and lubricate the adjusting mechanism. Then adjust the brakes as follows, being sure the parking brake is fully released.

Adjustment

1. Remove adjusting hole cover from backing plate. Turn brake adjusting screw to expand shoes until wheel can just be turned by hand.
2. Using suitable tool to hold actuator away from adjuster, Fig. 8, back off adjuster 30 notches. If shoes still drag, back off one or two additional notches.

NOTE: Brakes should be free of drag when adjuster has been backed off approximately 12 notches. Heavy drag at this point indicates tight parking brake cables.

3. Install adjusting hole cover and check parking brake adjustment.

CAUTION

If finger movement will not turn the screw, free it up. If this is not done, the actuator will not turn the screw during subsequent vehicle operation. Lubricate the screw with oil and coat with wheel bearing grease. Any other adjustment procedure may cause damage to the adjusting screw with consequent self-adjuster problems.

4. Install wheel and drum, and adjust-

ing hole cover. Adjust brakes on remaining wheels in the same manner.
5. If pedal height is not satisfactory, drive the vehicle and make sufficient reverse stops until proper pedal height is obtained.

PARKING BRAKE, ADJUST

1977-79 W/Rear Disc Brakes

1. Lubricate parking brake cables at equalizer and underbody rub points. Check all cables for freedom of operation.
2. Fully release parking brake and raise vehicle.
3. Hold cable stud from turning and tighten equalizer nut until cable slack is removed and levers are against stops on caliper housing. If levers are off stops, loosen cable until levers return to stop.
4. Operate parking brake several times to check adjustment. When properly adjusted, the parking brake pedal should move 4-5 inches when a force of about 125 pounds is applied.

1974-79 W/Rear Drum Brakes

Need for parking brake adjustment is indicated if the service brake operates with good pedal reserve but the parking brake pedal can be depressed a minimum of 7 ratchet clicks but not more than 13 ratchet clicks on 1974 models and a minimum of 9 ratchet clicks but not more than 16 on 1976-79 models, under heavy foot pressure. After making sure that the service brakes are properly adjusted, adjust the parking brake as follows:
1. Depress parking brake exactly three ratchet clicks on 1974-77 models except Apollo and Skylark and 1974-76 Estate Wagon, two ratchet clicks on Apollo and Skylark and all 1978-79 models and 6 ratchet clicks on 1974-76 Estate Wagon.

2. Loosen jam nut, and tighten adjusting nut until rear wheels can just be turned rearward using both hands but are locked when forward motion is attempted.
3. Tighten jam nut and release parking brake. Rear wheels should turn freely in either direction with no brake drag.

MASTER CYLINDER, REPLACE

1974-79

1. Disconnect brake pipes from master cylinder and tape end of pipes to prevent entrance of dirt.
2. On manual brakes, disconnect brake pedal from master cylinder push rod.
3. Remove two nuts holding master cylinder to dash or power cylinder and remove master cylinder from car.

POWER BRAKE UNIT

1974-79

1. Remove two nuts attaching master cylinder to brake unit, then position master cylinder away from brake unit with brake lines attached.

NOTE: Use care not to bend or kink brake lines.

2. Disconnect vacuum hose from check valve. Plug vacuum hose to prevent dirt from entering.
3. Remove four nuts holding power unit to dash.
4. Remove retainer and washer from brake pedal pin and disengage push rod eye or clevis.
5. Remove power unit from car.

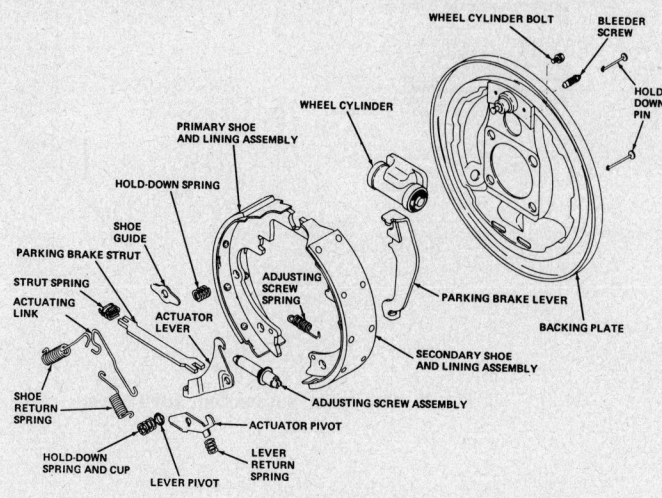

Fig. 7   Left rear drum brake assembly. 1979 Riviera

Fig. 8   Adjusting drum brakes. 1974-79

Rear Suspension

SHOCK ABSORBER, REPLACE

1. With the rear axle supported properly, disconnect shock absorber from lower mounting bracket. On models equipped with automatic level control, disconnect air hose from shock absorber.
2. Disconnect shock absorber upper end from underbody attachment.
3. Reverse procedure to install.

LEAF SPRINGS & BUSHINGS, REPLACE
1974-79 Apollo & Skylark

1. Support vehicle at frame and rear axle, relieving tension from spring.
2. Disconnect shock absorber from lower mounting.
3. Loosen spring front mount bolt.
4. Remove spring front mounting bracket attaching screws, lower axle and remove bracket.
5. Disconnect parking brake cable from spring plate bracket.
6. Remove "U" bolts and spring plate.
7. Support spring, remove front mount bolt and disassemble rear shackle.
8. Replace rear shackle and spring eye bushings as necessary, Figs. 1 and 2.
9. Reverse procedure to install.

1974-76 Estate Wagon

1. Support vehicle at frame and support rear axle, removing tension from springs.
2. Disconnect shock absorbers from lower mounting bracket and the exhaust system right side from hanger and support system, Fig. 3.
3. Remove "U" bolts and lower spring plates.
4. Disconnect spring at front and rear attachments.
5. Reverse procedure to install.

LEAF SPRING SERVICE
1974-79 Apollo & Skylark

NOTE: The spring leaves are not serviced

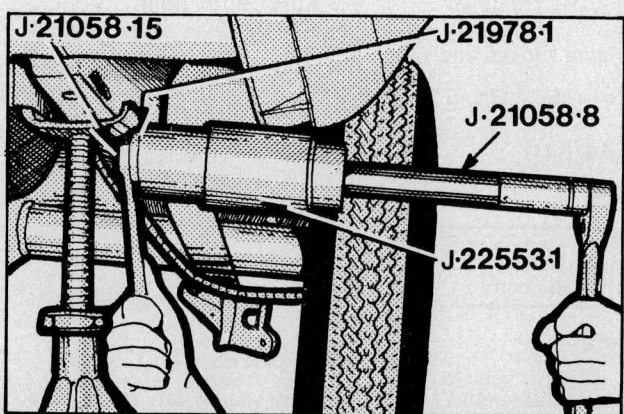

Fig. 1   Leaf spring bushings removal. 1974-78 Apollo & Skylark

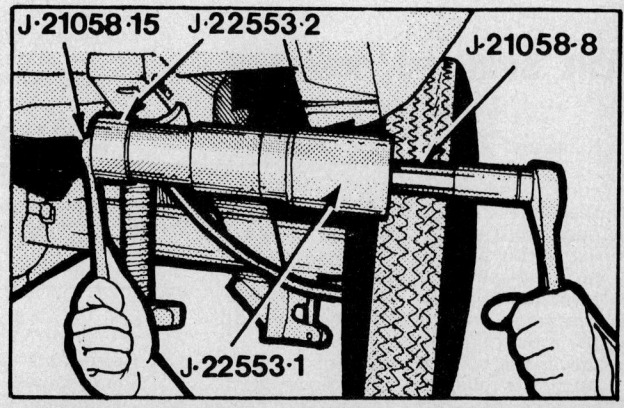

Fig. 2   Leaf spring bushings installation. 1974-78 Apollo & Skylark

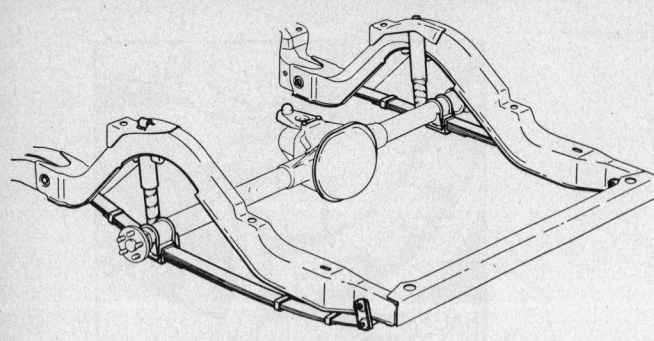

Fig. 3 Leaf spring suspension (typical)

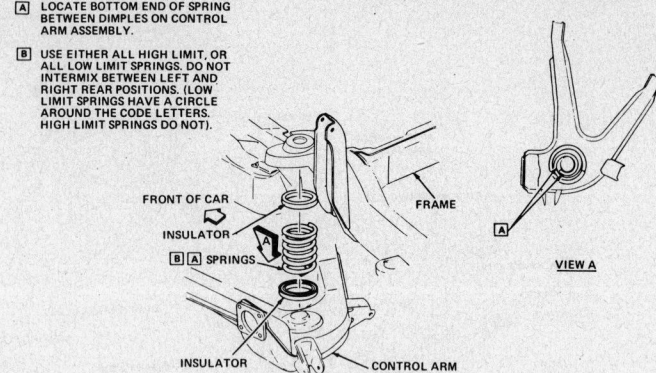

A LOCATE BOTTOM END OF SPRING BETWEEN DIMPLES ON CONTROL ARM ASSEMBLY.

B USE EITHER ALL HIGH LIMIT, OR ALL LOW LIMIT SPRINGS. DO NOT INTERMIX BETWEEN LEFT AND RIGHT REAR POSITIONS. (LOW LIMIT SPRINGS HAVE A CIRCLE AROUND THE CODE LETTERS. HIGH LIMIT SPRINGS DO NOT.)

Fig. 4 Coil spring suspension. 1979 Riviera

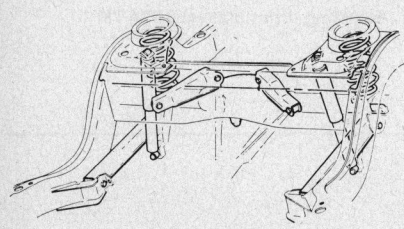

Fig. 5 Coil spring suspension. Except 1979 Riviera

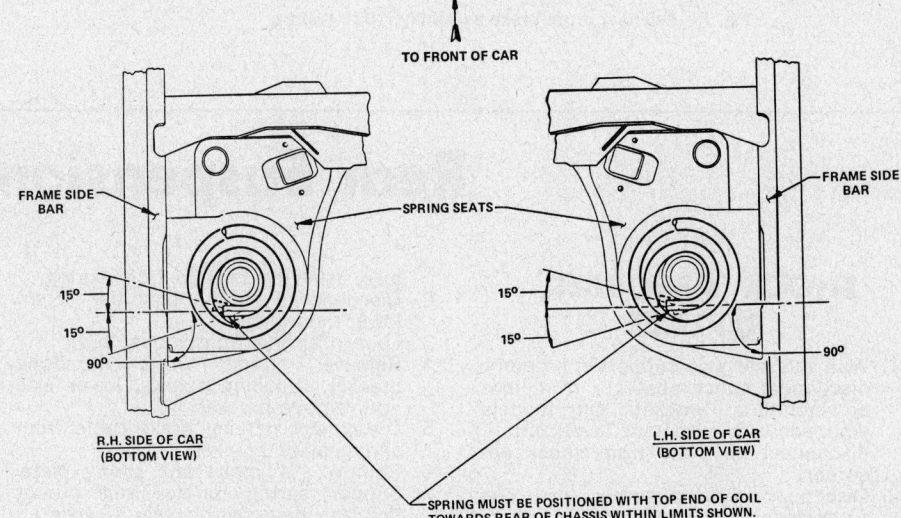

Fig. 6 Coil spring suspension. Except 1979 Riviera

separately, however, the spring leaf inserts may be replaced.

1. Clamp spring in a vise and remove spring clips.
2. File peened end of center bolt to permit nut removal, remove nut and open vise slowly, allowing spring to expand.
3. Replace spring leaf inserts as necessary.
4. Use a drift to align center bolt holes, compress spring in vise and install new center bolt and nut. Peen end of bolt to retain nut.
5. Align springs and bend spring clips into position.

NOTE: Overtightening of spring clips will cause spring binding.

COIL SPRINGS, REPLACE
1979 Riviera

1. Raise and support rear of vehicle.
2. Using a suitable jack support lower control arm.
3. Disconnect automatic level control air hose from shock absorber. If removing spring from left hand side of vehicle, disconnect level control link from control arm.
4. Disconnect shock absorber from upper mounting.
5. Lower the control arm until all spring tension is relieved, then remove spring.
6. Reverse procedure to install. Locate spring as shown in Fig. 4.

Except 1979 Riviera

1. Support vehicle at frame and support rear axle with a suitable jack.
2. Disconnect shock absorbers from lower mounting bracket, Fig. 5, and the brake lines from wheel cylinders.
3. Disconnect upper control arms at differential.
4. Lower jack fully extending springs and remove springs.
5. Reverse procedure to install, Fig. 6.

CONTROL ARMS, REPLACE

NOTE: Remove and replace one control arm at a time as axle assembly may slip sideways, making installation difficult.

1979 Riviera

1. Raise and support rear of vehicle, then remove wheel and tire assembly.
2. Disconnect brake line at bracket on control arm.

3. Remove brake caliper, then mark wheel stud and corresponding place on rotor for installation and remove rotor.
4. If removing left hand control arm, disconnect automatic level control link from control arm.
5. Using a suitable jack, support control arm.
6. Disconnect air hose from shock absorber, then detach shock absorber from upper and lower mountings.
7. Lower control arm until all spring tension is relieved, them remove spring and insulators.
8. Remove two bolts attaching control arm to frame and remove control arm, Fig. 7.

Except 1979 Riviera

Upper Control Arms

1. Support vehicle at frame and rear axle.
2. Remove control arm mount bolts from

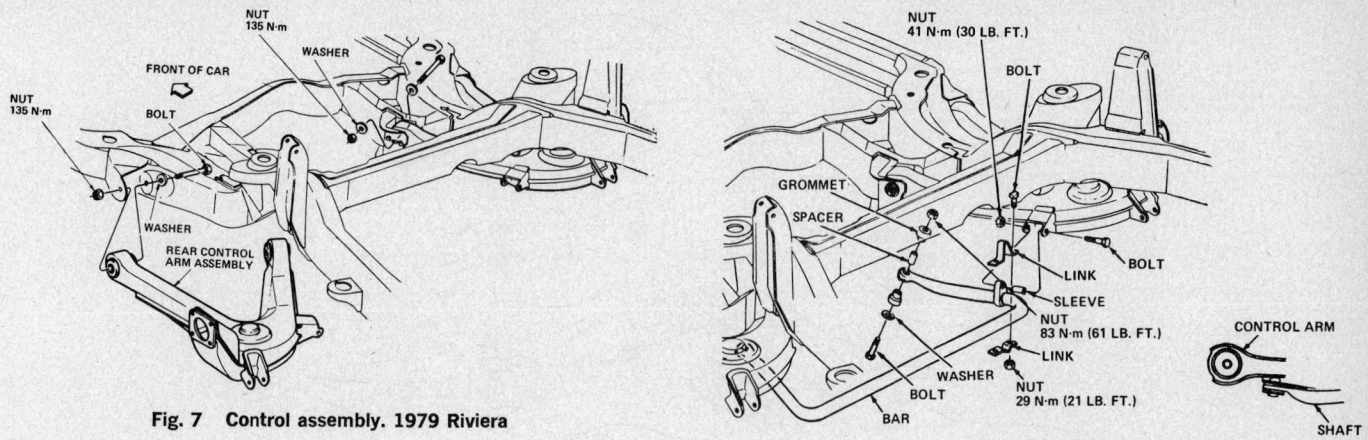

Fig. 7   Control assembly. 1979 Riviera

Fig. 8   Rear Stabilizer installation. 1979 Riviera

frame and axle housing attachments, Fig. 5.
3. Reverse procedure to install.

NOTE: Control arm bolts must be tightened with vehicle at curb height.

Lower Control Arm

Lower control arms may be removed and replaced using the "Upper Control Arms" procedure. However, it may be necessary to reposition the jack farther forward under carrier to aid in removing rear mount bolt. Also, a brass drift may be needed to remove mount bolts.

STABILIZER BAR, REPLACE

1974-79 Apollo & Skylark

1. Support vehicle at rear axle.
2. Disconnect stabilizer bar from spring plate brackets, Fig. 9.
3. Disconnect stabilizer bar from body brackets.
4. Reverse procedure to install. Tighten attaching bolts with vehicle at curb height.

1979 Riviera

1. Raise and support rear of vehicle, Fig. 8.
2. Remove bolts attaching front of stabilizer bar to control arms.
3. Remove inside nut and bolt from each side of stabilizer bar link, then loosen nut and bolt on outside of link.
4. Rotate bottom parts of link to one side and slide stabilizer bar out of bushings.

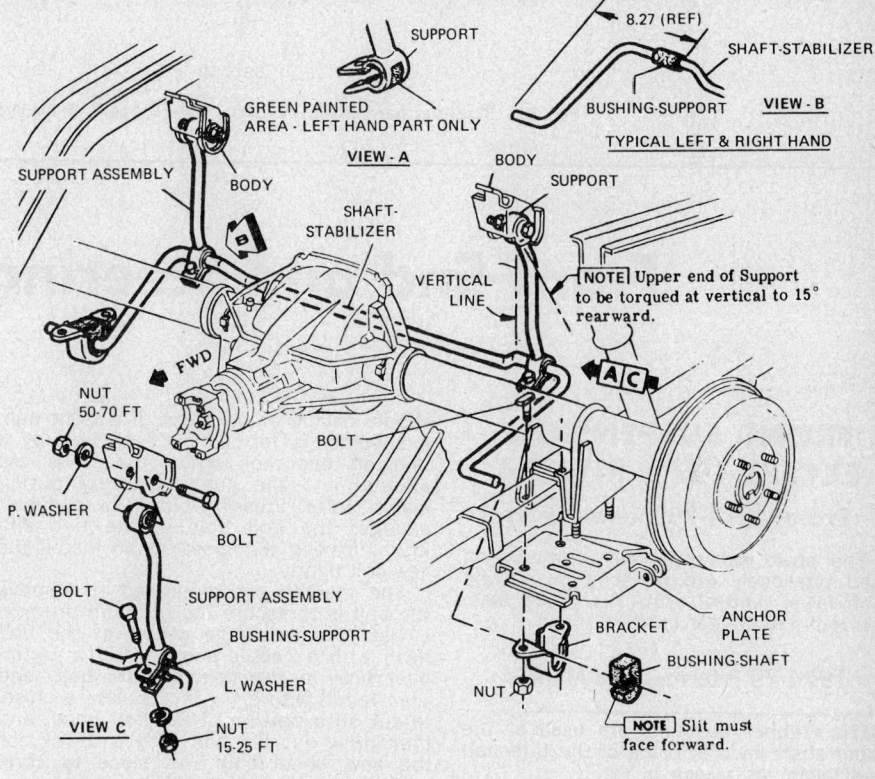

**Fig. 9   Stabilizer bar installation.
1974-79 Apollo & Skylark**

Except 1974-79 Apollo & Skylark & 1979 Riviera

1. Support vehicle at rear axle.

2. Remove stabilizer bar attaching bolts from brackets on lower control arms, Fig. 10.
3. Reverse procedure to install.

Continued

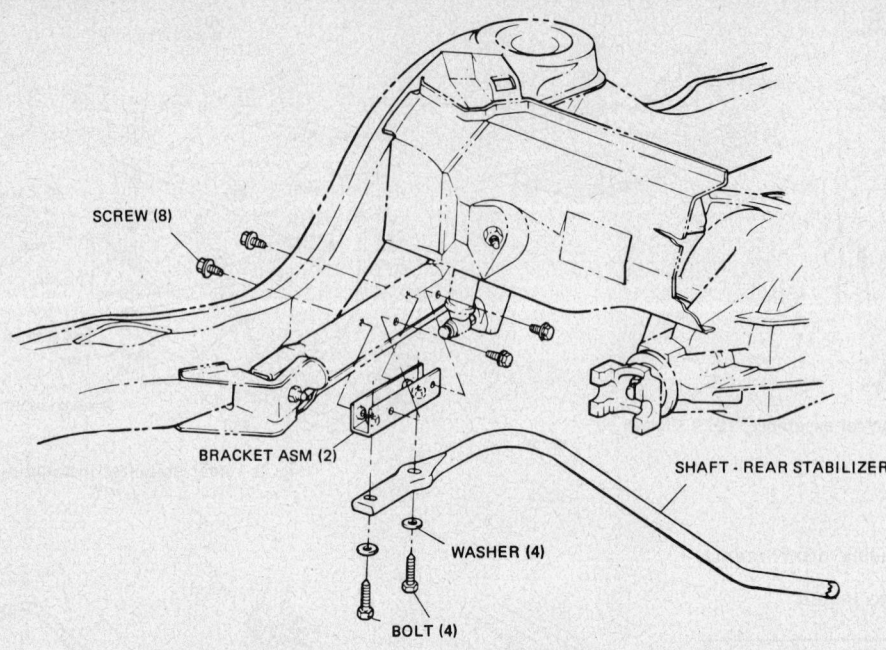

SCREW (8)

BRACKET ASM (2)

WASHER (4)

BOLT (4)

SHAFT - REAR STABILIZER

Fig. 10   Stabilizer bar installation exc. 1974-79 Apollo & Skylark & 1979 Riviera

Front End and Steering Section

FRONT SUSPENSION EXCEPT 1979 RIVIERA

Except 1974-79 Intermediates

The strut rod and lower control arm used previously are replaced by a wide span lower control arm. The brake reaction rod is no longer used.

1974-79 Intermediate Models

NOTE: Rubber bushings are used at the upper shaft ends in place of the threaded steel bushings shown in Fig. 1.

A ball joint is riveted to the outer end of the upper arm and is spring loaded to insure proper alignment of the ball in the socket.

The inner end of the lower control arm has pressed-in bushings. Two bolts, passing through the bushings, attach the arm to the frame. The lower ball joint is a press fit in the arm and attaches to the steering knuckle with a castellated nut that is retained with a cotter pin.

Rubber seals are provided on upper and lower shafts and at ball socket assemblies to exclude dirt and moisture from bearing surfaces. Grease fittings are provided at all bearing locations.

SERVICE BULLETIN

Wheel Bolt Replaced: Wheel bolts should not be pressed out of a front hub. A shoulder is formed on each bolt by a swaging operation when the bolts are pressed into the hub and drum during manufacture. Pressing out a swaged bolt enlarges the bolt hole in the hub and drum, making it impossible to install the new bolt tightly.

The method recommended to remove the bolt is to secure the hub and drum in a vise, and mark the center of the bolt head with a center punch. Drill a 1/8 in. pilot hole in the head of the bolt, and then redrill with a 9/16 in. bit. Use a chisel to cut off a portion of the bolt head, and then drive out the bolt with a drift. Press the new wheel bolt into place to complete the job.

Wheel Alignment
1974-79

Caster and camber are adjusted by shimming at the upper control arm shaft attaching points.

Adding shims at the front locations will change caster toward negative with practically no change in camber. Adding shims at the rear locations will change caster toward positive and camber toward negative. Adding equal shims at both front and rear locations will not change caster but will change camber toward negative.

To adjust, loosen both front and rear bolts to free shims for removal or addition. The maximum dimension for one shim pack is .750 inch. After installing or removing shims, torque shaft nuts to 70 ft. lbs. on 1974-76 models except Apollo and Skylark, 50 ft. lbs. on 1974-76 Apollo and Skylark, 75 ft. lbs. on all 1977 models and 1978-79 models except Century and Regal and 46 ft. lbs. for 1978-79 Century and Regal.

Toe-In, Adjust
1974-79

IMPORTANT

Vehicle must be at curb weight and running height; bounce front end and allow it to settle at running height. Steering gear and front wheel bearings must be properly adjusted with no looseness at tie rod ends. The car should be moved forward one complete revolution of the wheels before the toe-in check and adjustment is started and the car should never be moved backward while making the check and adjustment.

With front wheels in the straight ahead position, toe-in is adjusted by turning the tie rod adjusting sleeves as required. Left and right adjusting sleeves must be turned exactly the same amount but in opposite directions in order to maintain front wheels in straight ahead position when steering wheel is in straight ahead position.

IMPORTANT

The steering knuckle and steering arm "rock" or tilt as front wheel rises and falls. Therefore, it is vitally important to position the bottom face of the tie rod end parallel with the machined surface at the outer end of the steering arm when tie rod length is adjusted. Severe damage and possible failure can result unless this precaution is taken. The tie rod sleeve clamps must be straight down to 45° forward to provide clearance.

Wheel Bearings, Adjust

1974-79

1. Hand spin wheel in a forward direction and while wheel is spinning, snug up spindle nut to 12 ft. lbs. to fully seat bearings.
2. Back off nut 1/4 to 1/2 turn.
3. Snug up spindle nut by hand. Do not install cotter pin if hole in spindle lines up with a slot in spindle nut.
4. Loosen spindle nut 1/12 to 1/6 turn then insert cotter pin.
5. With bearings properly adjusted, the end play must be .001 to .005 inch.

Wheel Bearings, Replace

Disc Brakes

1. Raise car and remove front wheels.
2. Remove brake tube support bracket bolt. Do not disconnect hydraulic tube or hose.
3. Remove caliper to mounting bracket bolts. Hang caliper from upper suspension.

NOTE: Do not place strain on brake line.

4. Remove spindle nut and hub and disc assembly. Inner wheel bearing and grease retainer can now be removed.

Checking Ball Joints For Wear

If loose ball joints are suspected, first be sure front wheel bearings are properly adjusted and that control arms are tight. Then check ball joints as follows:

Upper Ball Joint 1976-79

1. Raise front of vehicle with jacks placed between coil spring pockets and ball joint of lower control arm.

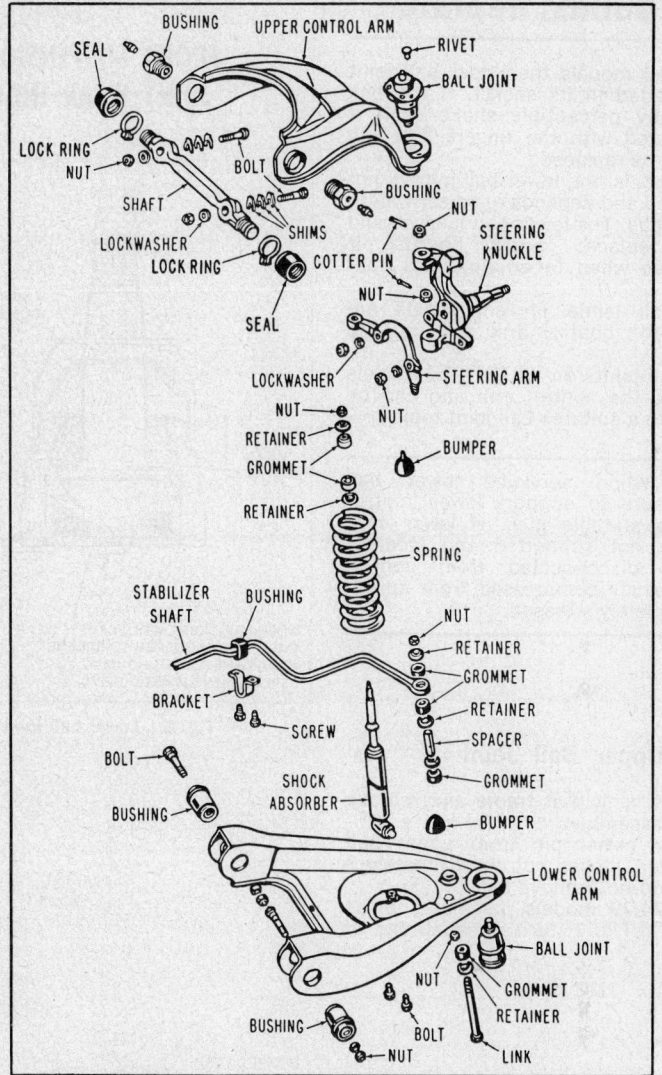

Fig. 1   Front suspension. 1974-79 intermediate models (Typical)

2. Shake top of wheel in and out. Observe steering knuckle for any movement relative to the control arm.
3. Replace ball joint if looseness is indicated.

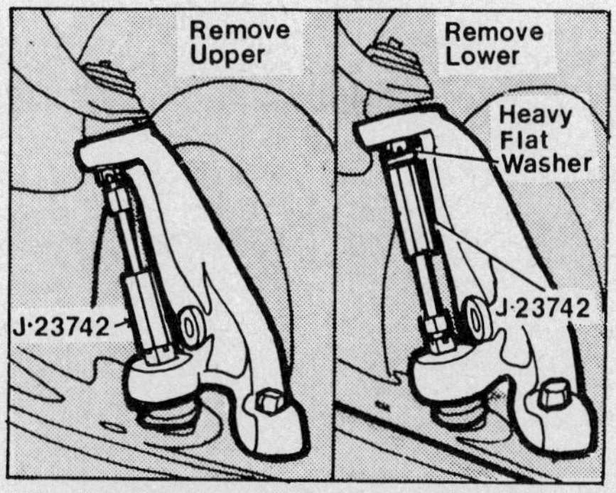

Fig. 3   Removing ball joint stud from steering knuckle. Except 1979 Riviera

Upper Ball Joint 1974-75

Using a regular ball joint nut and a second nut as a lock nut, turn joint in its socket with a torque wrench. If no torque is required and ball joint is properly lubricated, replace ball joint.

Lower Ball Joint Except 1974 Apollo

A wear indicator is built into the ball joint. Remove dirt deposits around service plug and observe position of nipple. Refer to Fig. 2 for wear tolerance.

Lower Ball Joint 1974 Apollo

1. Raise and support vehicle weight under lower control arm, then measure distance from grease fitting to end of threaded stud.
2. Raise tire, steering knuckle and brake assembly by levering under tire and re-measure distance between fitting and stud.
3. If difference is greater than 1/16 in., replace ball joint.

Ball Joints, Replace

NOTE: On all models the upper ball joint is spring-loaded in its socket. If the ball stud has any perceptible shake or if it can be twisted with the fingers, the ball joint should be replaced.

On all models, the lower ball joint is not spring-loaded and depends upon car weight to load the ball. The lower ball joint should never be replaced merely because it "feels" loose when in an unloaded condition.

Upper ball joints on all models are riveted to the control arm and can be replaced.

Lower ball joints on all 1974-79 models pressed into the control arm and can be replaced with a suitable ball joint tool.

CAUTION: When servicing lower ball joints, be sure to support lower control arm with a suitable jack. If lower control arm is not supported and steering knuckle is disconnected from control arm, the heavily compressed front spring will be completely released.

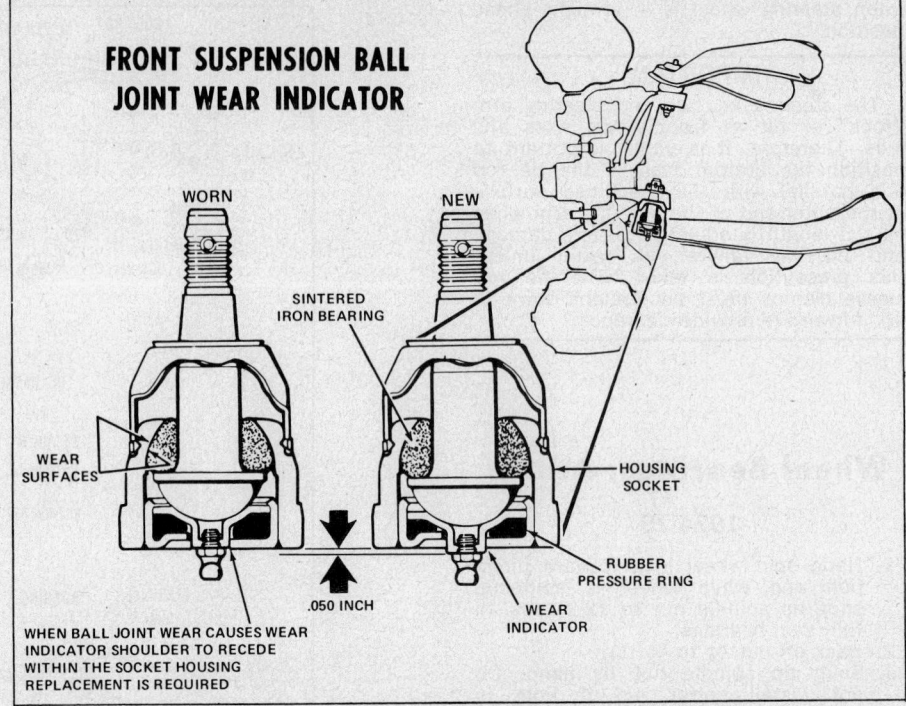

Fig. 2   Lower ball joint check. All models except 1974 Apollo & 1979 Riviera

Upper Ball Joint

1. Support vehicle at frame and remove wheel assembly.
2. Remove cotter pin from upper ball joint stud, loosen nut approximately 2 turns, do not remove nut.
3. On 1974-79 models, position tool as shown in Fig. 3, turn threaded end of

tool until stud disengages knuckle.
4. Position jack under lower control arm at spring seat, raise jack until compression is relieved from upper control arm bumper.
5. Remove stud nut, life control arm from steering knuckle and place a block of wood between control arm and frame.
6. On all models,
   a. Center punch rivet head as close to center as possible.
   b. Using a ⅛ inch twist drill, drill through center of rivet approximately ½ rivet length deep.
   c. Enlarge hole using a ⁷⁄₃₂ inch drill.

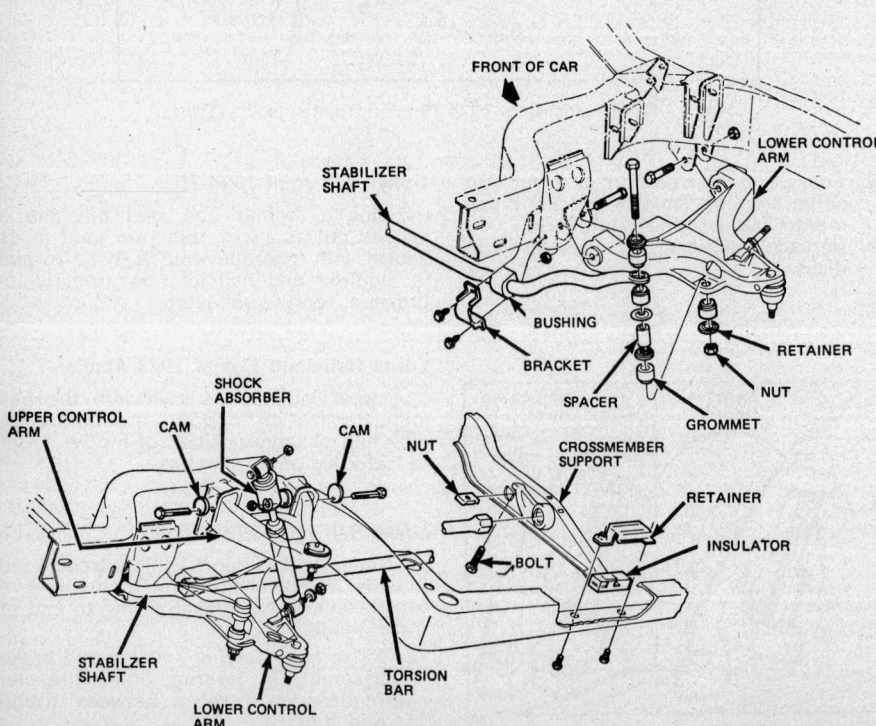

Fig. 4   Front suspension. 1979 Riviera

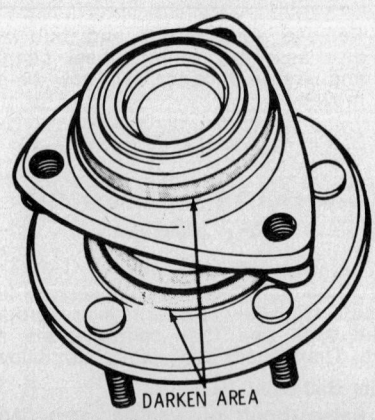

Fig. 5   Sealed wheel bearing assembly. 1979 Riviera

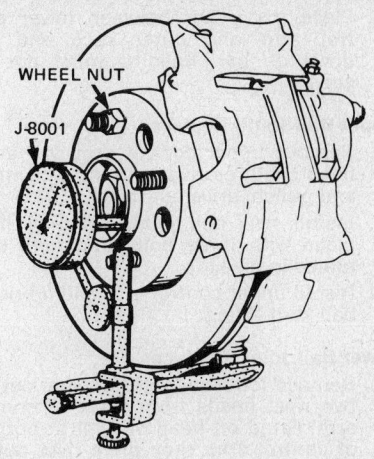

Fig. 6 Checking wheel bearing assembly for looseness. 1979 Riviera

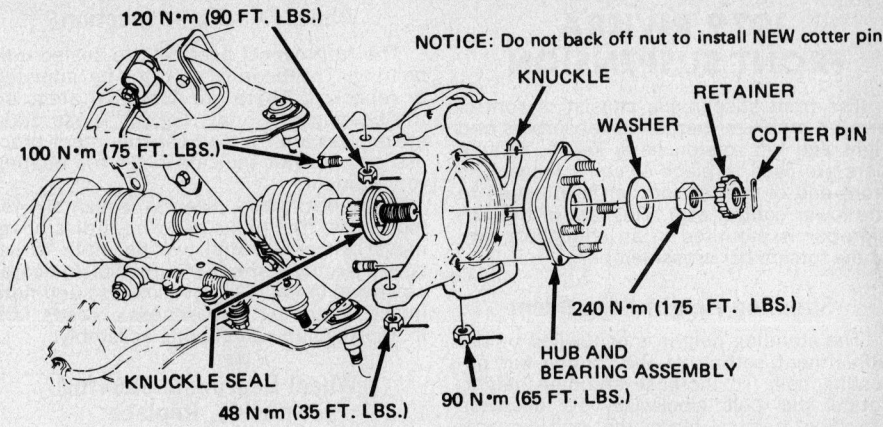

NOTICE: Do not back off nut to install NEW cotter pin

120 N·m (90 FT. LBS.)

100 N·m (75 FT. LBS.)

KNUCKLE

RETAINER

WASHER

COTTER PIN

KNUCKLE SEAL

48 N·m (35 FT. LBS.)

90 N·m (65 FT. LBS.)

240 N·m (175 FT. LBS.)

HUB AND BEARING ASSEMBLY

Fig. 7 Bearing & steering knuckle assembly. 1979 Riviera

d. Using a chisel, remove rivet heads, then drive rivets out using a suitable punch.

7. Position ball joint on upper control arm. Install bolts through bottom of control arm with nuts on top, torque to 8 ft. lbs.

8. On all models, position ball joint stud so cotter pin hole is facing forward and remove wooden block from between control arm and frame.

9. Place wheels in straight ahead position, raise jack under lower control until ball joint stud can be installed in steering knuckle.

10. Install castellated nut on ball joint stud. Torque nut to 50 ft. lbs. on 1974 Apollo and 1977 all models, 60 ft. lbs. on 1974 models except Apollo, 1975-76 all models and 1978-79 Apollo and Skylark, 61 ft. lbs. on 1978-79 Century, Regal and full size models.

NOTE: If cotter pin holes do not align, do not loosen nut, however, tighten until cotter pin can be installed.

11. Install wheel assembly and lower vehicle.

Lower Ball Joint

1. Support vehicle under frame side rails.

NOTE: Position jack under lower control at outboard end, raise jack until it is ½ inch below control arm.

2. Remove cotter pin, loosen ball joint stud nut approximately 2 turns, do not remove nut.

3. On 1974-79 models position tool as shown in Fig. 4, turn threaded end of tool until ball joint stud is disengaged from steering knuckle.

4. Position jack under lower control arm at spring seat and raise jack until compression is removed from upper

control arm bumper.

5. Remove lower ball joint stud nut and position steering knuckle aside.

6. Using tool No. J-9519-10, remove ball joint from lower control arm.

7. Position ball joint on control arm with bleed vent on rubber boot facing inward.

8. Install tools J-9519-17 and J-9519-10 and turn threaded end of tool until ball joint is fully seated in lower control arm.

9. Position new ball joint stud so cotter pin hole is facing forward.

10. Place wheels in the straight ahead position and install ball joint stud on steering knuckle.

11. Install stud nut and cotter pin. Torque nut to 80 ft. lbs. on 1974-76 Apollo and Skylark models, 90 ft. lbs. on 1974-76 models except Apollo and Skylark, 70 ft. lbs. on all 1977 models and 85 ft. lbs. on 1978-79 all models.

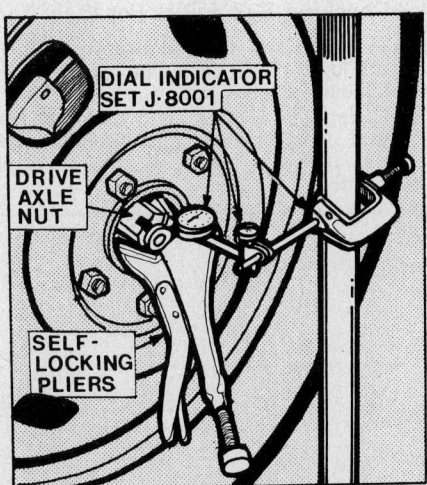

Fig. 8 Checking ball joints for wear. 1979 Riviera

NOTE: If cotter pin holes do not align do not loosen stud nut, tighten nut until cotter pin can be installed.

12. Install wheel assembly.

Shock Absorber, Replace

Unfasten shock absorber top and bottom and remove it through the spring seat. Check shock absorber for obvious physical damage or oil leakage. Push and pull shock absorber in an upright position. If smooth hydraulic resistance is not present in both directions, replace shock absorber.

Spring, Replace

1. Raise car and support with jack stands under frame. Remove wheel with hub and drum.

2. Disconnect stabilizer link from lower control arm and remove shock absorber.

3. Support lower control arm with a suitable floor jack to take up tension of front spring. Disconnect lower control arm ball joint stud from steering knuckle.

CAUTION: Be sure lower control arm is properly supported before disconnecting ball stud.

4. Lower floor jack under spring until spring is fully extended and remove spring.

5. Complete the installation in the reverse order of removal.

1979 RIVIERA FRONT SUSPENSION

The front suspension consist of control arms, a stabilizer bar, shock absorbers and right and left torsion bars, Fig. 4. Torsion bars are used in place of coil spirngs. The front end of the torsion bar is attached to the lower control arm. The rear of the torsion bar is mounted in an adjustable arm at the torsion bar crossmember.

Standing Height Adjustment

The standing height is controlled by the adjustment setting of the torsion bar adjusting bolt. To increase standing height, rotate the bolt clockwise. To decrease standing height rotate the bolt counter clockwise.

Wheel Alignment

Caster

Record camber reading, then hold front cam bolt and loosen nut. Turn front cam bolt to obtain $\frac{1}{4}$ of the desired caster change. At front cam bolt a positive camber change produces a positive caster change and a negative camber change produces a negative caster change. Hold cam bolt in position and tighten nut. Loosen rear cam bolt nut and rotate cam bolt to return camber to setting recorded previously. When adjustment has been completed hold rear cam bolt and torque nut to 80 ft. lbs.

Camber

While holding cam bolt in position, loosen cam bolt nut. Rotate cam bolt to obtain a change in camber equal to $\frac{1}{2}$ the needed correction. Hold cam bolt in position and tighten cam bolt nut. To obtain the remaining $\frac{1}{2}$ of needed correction apply the above procedure to other cam bolt.

Toe-In, Adjust

Toe-in is adjusted by turning the tie rod adjusting tubes at outer ends of each tie rod after loosening clamp bolts. Reading should only be taken when front wheels are in the straight ahead position and steering gear is on its high spot.
1. Loosen clamp bolts at each end of tie rod adjusting sleeve.
2. Turn tie rod adjusting sleeve to obtain the proper toe-in adjustment.
3. After completing adjustment, check to ensure that the number of threads at each end of sleeve are equal and ensure that tie rod end housings and clamps are properly positioned. Torque clamp bolt to 15 ft. lbs.

Wheel Bearing Inspection

The front wheel bearing is a sealed unit bearing. The bearing can not be adjusted or repacked. There are darkened areas on the bearing assembly, Fig. 5. These darkened areas are from a heat treatment process and do not indicate need for bearing replacement.

To check wheel bearing assembly for looseness, free brake pads from disc or remove calipers. Install two lug nuts to secure disc to bearing. Mount dial indicator as shown in Fig. 6, then rock disc and note indicator reading. If looseness exceeds .005 in. replace hub and bearing assembly.

Wheel Bearing & Steering Knuckle, Replace

1. Raise and support vehicle under lower control arms.
2. Remove drive axle nut and washer, then remove wheel and tire assembly, Fig. 7.
3. Remove brake hose clip from ball joint and replace nut, then remove brake caliper off disc, and using a length of wire support caliper on suspension.

NOTE: Do not allow caliper to hang from brake hose as this could cause damage and premature failure of hose.

4. Mark hub and disc assembly for alignment during assembly and remove disc, then strike steering knuckle in area of upper ball joint until upper ball joint is loose.

CAUTION: Use extreme care to prevent striking and damaging brake hose or ball joint seal.

5. Place a short length of rubber hose over lower control arm torsion bar connector to avoid damage to inboard tri-pot joint seal when hub and knuckle are removed.
6. Using appropriate puller, disconnect tie rod end, upper and lower ball joints and remove steering knuckle and hub assembly.

Checking Ball Joints For Wear

1. Raise car and position jack stands under lower control arms as near as possible to each ball joint.
2. Clamp vise grips on end of drive axle and position a dial indicator so that dial indicator ball rests on vise grip, Fig. 8.

3. Place a pry bar between lower control arm and outer race and pry down on bar. Reading must not exceed $\frac{1}{8}$".

Upper Ball Joint, Replace

1. Remove upper control arm and grind head off three rivets. Using a hammer and punch, drive out rivets.
2. Install new ball joint, securing it in place with three bolts and nuts contained in the kit.
3. Install upper control arm and lubricate ball joint fitting.

Lower Ball Joint, Replace

1. Remove lower control arm and cut off two rivet heads from sides of control arm. Grind off head of rivet at bottom of control arm, then drive rivet out of arm.
2. Install service ball joint, securing it to control arm with bolts and nuts contained in kit.

MANUAL STEERING GEAR, REPLACE

1974-79 All Models

1. Remove two nuts or pinch bolt securing lower coupling to steering shaft flange.
2. Use a suitable puller to remove pitman arm.
3. Unfasten gear (3 bolts) from frame and remove from car.

POWER STEERING, GEAR REPLACE

1974-79

1. Disconnect pressure and return line hoses at steering gear and elevate ends of hoses higher than pump to prevent oil from draining out of pump.
2. Remove pinch bolt securing coupling to steering gear.
3. Jack up car and remove pitman shaft nut, then use a suitable puller to remove pitman arm.
4. On full size models, remove sheet metal baffle that covers frame-to-gear attaching bolts, if equipped.
5. Loosen the three frame-to-steering gear bolts and remove steering gear.

CADILLAC

INDEX OF SERVICE OPERATIONS

VEHICLE IDENTIFICATION NUMBER LOCATION: On 1974-79 models it is located on rear upper portion of cylinder block, behind intake manifold and on left side of transmission.

ENGINE UNIT NUMBER LOCATION: On 1974-79 except V8-350 at rear of cylinder block. 1976-79 V8-350 at front left hand side of cylinder block below cylinder head.

GRILLE IDENTIFICATION

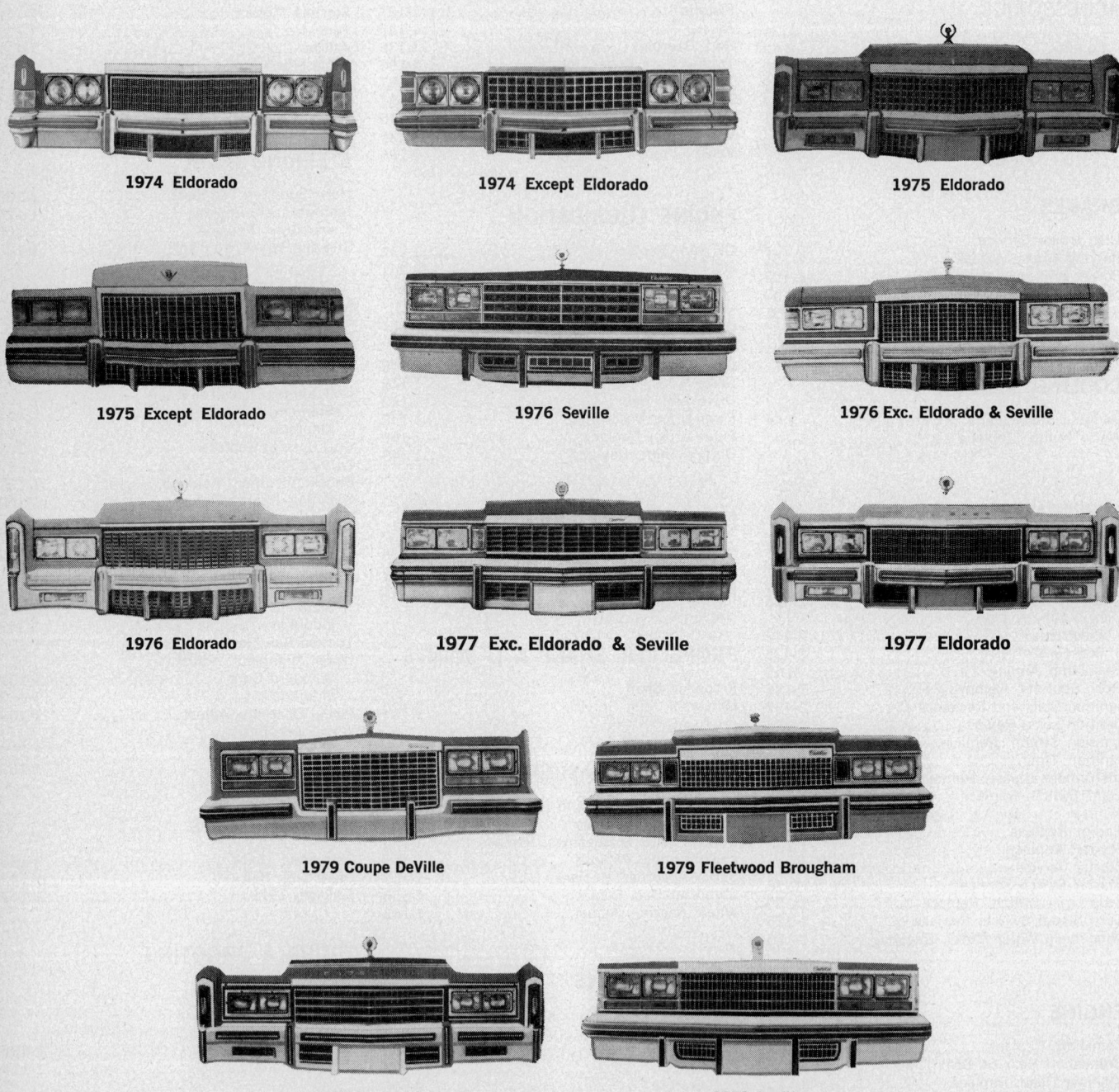

1974 Eldorado   1974 Except Eldorado   1975 Eldorado

1975 Except Eldorado   1976 Seville   1976 Exc. Eldorado & Seville

1976 Eldorado   1977 Exc. Eldorado & Seville   1977 Eldorado

1979 Coupe DeVille   1979 Fleetwood Brougham

1979 Eldorado   1979 Seville

GENERAL ENGINE SPECIFICATIONS

Year	Engine	Carburetor	Bore and Stroke	Piston Displacement, Cubic Inches	Compression Ratio	Maximum Brake H.P. @ R.P.M.	Maximum Torque Lbs. Ft. @ R.P.M.	Normal Oil Pressure Pounds
1974	205 Horsepower① V8-472	4 Barrel	4.300 x 4.060	472	8.25	205 @ 3600	365 @ 2000	35 Min.
	210 Horsepower① V8-500	4 Barrel	4.300 x 4.304	500	8.25	210 @ 3600	380 @ 2000	35 Min.
1975-76	190 Horsepower① V8-500	4 Barrel	4.300 x 4.304	500	8.5	190 @ 3600	360 @ 2000	35 Min.
1976	180 Horsepower① V8-350	Fuel Inj.	4.057 x 3.385	350	8.5	180 @ 4400	275 @ 2000	30–35
	215 Horsepower① V8-500	Fuel Inj.	4.300 x 4.304	500	8.5	215 @ 3600	400 @ 2000	35 Min.
1977	180 Horsepower① V8-350	Fuel Inj.	4.057 x 3.385	350	8.5	180 @ 4400	275 @ 2000	30–45
	180 Horsepower① V8-425	4 Barrel	4.082 x 4.060	425	8.2	180 @ 4000	320 @ 2000	35 Min.
	195 Horsepower① V8-425	Fuel Inj.	4.082 x 4.060	425	8.2	195 @ 3800	320 @ 2400	35 Min.
1978	120 Horsepower① V8-350②	Fuel Inj.	4.057 x 3.385	350	22.5	120 @ 3600	220 @ 1600	30–45
	170 Horsepower① V8-350	Fuel Inj.	4.057 x 3.385	350	8.0	170 @ 4280	270 @ 2000	30–45
	180 Horsepower① V8-425	4 Barrel	4.082 x 4.060	425	8.2	180 @ 4000	320 @ 2000	35 Min.
	180 Horsepower① V8-425	Fuel Inj.	4.082 x 4.060	425	8.2	180 @ 4000	320 @ 2000	35 Min.
1979	170 Horsepower① V8-350	Fuel Inj.	4.057 x 3.385	350	8.0	170 @ 4200	270 @ 2000	30–45
	180 Horsepower① V8-425	4 Barrel	4.082 x 4.060	425	8.2	180 @ 4000	320 @ 2000	40–48
	195 Horsepower① V8-425	Fuel Inj.	4.082 x 4.060	425	8.2	195 @ 3800	320 @ 2400	40–48

①—Net rating—as installed in the vehicle.　②—Diesel engine. See Oldsmobile Chapter for service.

TUNE UP SPECIFICATIONS

The following specifications are published from the latest information available. This data should be used only in the absence of a decal affixed in the engine compartment.

★When using a timing light, disconnect vacuum hose or tube at distributor and plug opening in hose or tube so idle speed will not be affected.

●When checking compression, lowest cylinder must be within 80 percent of highest.

▲Before removing wires from distributor cap, determine location of No. 1 wire in cap, as distributor position may have been altered from that shown at the end of this chart.

Year	Spark Plug Type	Spark Plug Gap Inch	Distributor Point Gap Inch	Distributor Dwell Angle Deg.	Firing Order Fig. ▲	Timing BTDC ①	Mark Fig.	Hot Idle Speed Std. Trans.	Hot Idle Speed Auto. Trans. ②	Air Fuel Ratio Std. Trans.	Air Fuel Ratio Auto. Trans.	Idle "CO" % Std. Trans.	Idle "CO" % Auto. Trans.
1974	R45NS	.035	③	30	⑥	10°	D	—	600D④	—	—	—	.4
1975–76 V8-500⑥	R45NSX	.060	—	—	E	6°	F	—	600D⑪	—	—	—	—
V8-500⑦	R45NSX	.060	—	—	E	12°	F	—	600D⑪	—	—	—	—
1976 V8-350	R47SX	.060	—	—	B	⑧	A	—	600D⑪	—	—	—	—
1977 V8-350	R47SX	.060	—	—	B	⑧	A	—	650D⑪	—	—	—	—
V8-425⑥	R45NSX	.060	—	—	E	18°⑩	F	—	600D⑪	—	—	—	—
V8-425⑦	R45NSX	.060	—	—	E	18°⑩	F	—	650D⑪	—	—	—	—
1978 V8-350	R47SX	.060	—	—	B	⑨	A	—	600D⑪	—	—	—	—
V8-350⑯	—	—	—	—	—	⑰	—	—	650D	—	—	—	—
V8-425⑥⑫	R45NSX	.060	—	—	E	⑬	F	—	600D⑪	—	—	—	—
V8-425⑥⑭	R45NSX	.060	—	—	E	⑮	F	—	600D⑪	—	—	—	—
V8-425⑦	R45NSX	.060	—	—	E	18°⑩	F	—	600D⑪	—	—	—	—
1979 V8-350	R47SX	.060	—	—	B	10°	A	—	600D	—	—	—	—
V8-350⑯	—	—	—	—	—	⑰	—	—	650D	—	—	—	—
V8-425⑥	R45NSX	.060	—	—	E	23°⑱	F	—	600N⑪	—	—	—	—
V8-425⑦	R45NSX	.060	—	—	E	18°⑩	F	—	650D	—	—	—	—

Continued

TUNE UP NOTES

①—BTDC: Before top dead center.
②—D: Drive. N: Neutral.
③—Turn adjusting screw in (clockwise) until engine begins to misfire; then back screw out ½ turn.
④—When making adjustments, air conditioner must be turned off (if equipped). Also, hose must be disconnected at parking brake vacuum release cylinder. The hot idle compensator must be closed; this can be done by pressing finger or eraser end of pencil on compensator.

⑤—Exc. H.E.I., Fig. C; H.E.I., Fig. E.
⑥—Exc. Electronic Fuel Injection models.
⑦—Electronic Fuel Injection models.
⑧—Except Calif. 10° BTDC; Calif. 6° BTDC.
⑨—Except Calif. 10° BTDC; Calif. 8° BTDC before Eng. #180291 and 6° BTDC after.
⑩—At 1400 Rpm.
⑪—When making adjustments, A/C must be turned off. Disconnect parking brake hose at vacuum release cylinder and plug hose. If equipped, disconnect air leveling compressor hose at air cleaner and plug hose.

⑫—Except Eldorado.
⑬—Except high altitude, 21° BTDC at 1600 Rpm; high altitude, 23° BTDC at 1600 Rpm.
⑭—Eldorado.
⑮—Except Calif. & high altitude, 21° BTDC at 1600 Rpm; Calif., 18° BTDC at 1600 Rpm; high altitude, 23° BTDC at 1600 Rpm.
⑯—Diesel engine.
⑰—Refer to Oldsmobile chapter for service on this engine.
⑱—At 1600 RPM.

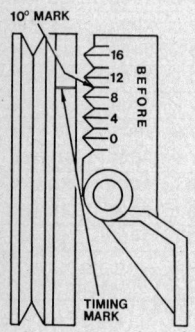

Fig. A

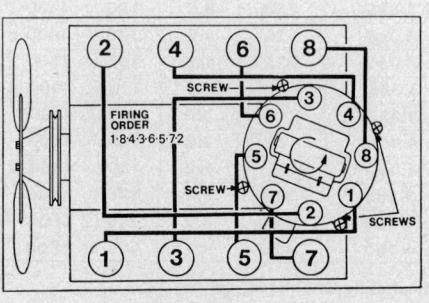

Fig. B

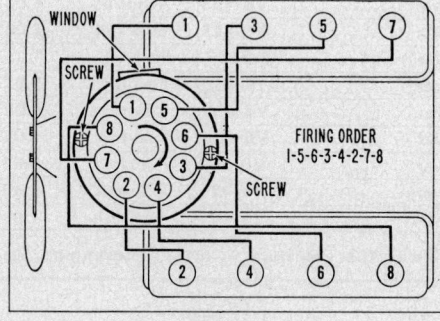

Fig. C

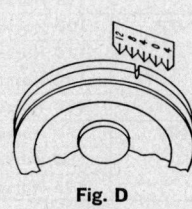

Fig. D

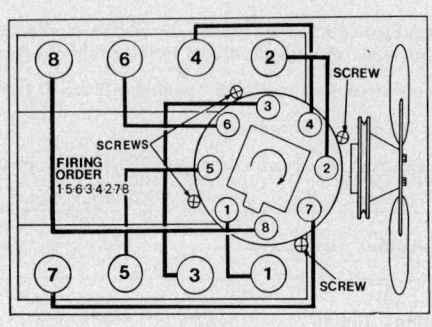

Fig. E

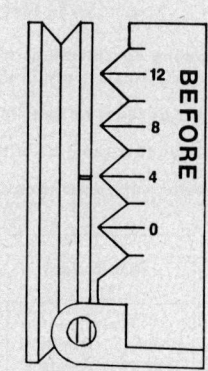

Fig. F

VALVE SPECIFICATIONS

Year	Model	Valve Lash	Valve Angles		Valve Spring Installed Height	Valve Spring Pressure Lbs. @ In.	Stem Clearance		Stem Diameter	
			Seat	Face			Intake	Exhaust	Intake	Exhaust
1974-76	V8-472, 500	Hydraulic①	45	44	1⁶¹⁄₆₄	160 @ 1½	.0010–.0027	.0010–.0027	.3413–.3420	.3413–.3420
1976-79	V8-350	Hydraulic①	②	③	1⁴³⁄₆₄	187 @ 1⁵⁄₃₂	.0010–.0027	.0015–.0032	.3425–.3432	.3420–.3427
1977-79	V8-425	Hydraulic①	45	44	1⁶¹⁄₆₄	160 @ 1³¹⁄₆₄	.0010–.0027	.0010–.0027	.3413–.3420	.3413–.3420
1978-79	V8-350④	Hydraulic①	②	③	1.670	151 @ 1.30	.0010–.0027	.0015–.0032	.3425–.3432	.3420–.3427

①—No adjustment.
②—Intake 45°; exhaust 31°.
③—Intake 44°; exhaust 30°.
④—Diesel engine. See Oldsmobile chapter for service.

DISTRIBUTOR SPECIFICATIONS

★**Note: If unit is checked on the vehicle, double the RPM and degrees to get crankshaft figures.**

Breaker arm spring tension—19-23.

Distributor Part No.①	Centrifugal Advance Degrees @ RPM of Distributor				Full Advance	Vacuum Advance	
	Advance Starts	Intermediate Advance				Inches of Vacuum to Start Plunger	Max. Adv. Dist. Deg. @ Vacuum
1103202②	0 @ 300	0 to −4 @ 500	2–6 @ 650	—	10 @ 1400	5½	9½–10½ @ 14
1103217②④	0 @ 200	0 to −¼ @ 300	3½–6 @ 600	7½–9½ @ 2000	9½ @ 3000	4	14½ @ 16
1103219②④	0 @ 200	0 to −¼ @ 300	3½–6 @ 600	7½–9½ @ 2000	9½ @ 3000	4	14½ @ 16
1103221②④	0 @ 200	0 to −⅜ @ 400	5–8 @ 725	20–22 @ 2500	22 @ 3000	7	12½ @ 18
1103222②③	0 @ 200	0 to −½ @ 350	5–8 @ 725	20–22 @ 2500	22 @ 3000	9⑤	9¾ @ 19⑥
1103277②③	0 @ 200	0 to −¼ @ 300	1–3 @ 600	6–8 @ 2500	8 @ 3000	3½	10½ @ 13
1103297②③	0 @ 200	0 to −¼ @ 300	¾–3 @ 600	6–8 @ 2500	8 @ 3000	3½	10½ @ 13
1103298②③	0 @ 200	0 to −¼ @ 300	1–3 @ 600	5⅞–8 @ 2500	8 @ 3000	4¼	5½ @ 9¾
1103300②③	0 @ 200	0 to −¼ @ 300	2½–6 @ 575	7½–9½ @ 2000	9½ @ 3000	7½	5½ @ 12
1103307②	0 @ 200	−½ to +1⅗ @ 450	4⅕–7³⁄₁₀ @ 700	11½–13⅘ @ 1450	22 @ 2500	9½	9½ @ 20⁷⁄₁₀
1103331②	0 @ 200	½–3½ @ 450	5½–8 @ 700	7½–9½ @ 1450	9½ @ 2500	3½	14½ @ 20⁷⁄₁₀
1103332②	0 @ 200	½–3½ @ 450	5½–8 @ 700	7½–9½ @ 1450	9½ @ 2500	3½	10½ @ 20⁷⁄₁₀
1103334②	0 @ 200	½–3½ @ 450	4⅕–6³⁄₁₀ @ 700	6–8 @ 1450	9½ @ 2500	4⅖	14½ @ 20⁷⁄₁₀
1103335②	0 @ 200	−½ to +1⅗ @ 450	1⅕–3³⁄₁₀ @ 700	3–5³⁄₁₀ @ 1450	8 @ 2500	3½	10½ @ 20⁷⁄₁₀
1103345②	0 @ 200	½–3½ @ 450	5½–8 @ 700	7½–9½ @ 1450	9½ @ 2500	3½	8½ @ 20⁷⁄₁₀
1103348②	0 @ 200	−½ to +1⅗ @ 450	4⅕–7³⁄₁₀ @ 700	11½–13⅘ @ 1450	22 @ 2500	5⅗	12½ @ 20⁷⁄₁₀
1103349②	0 @ 200	−½ to +1⅗ @ 450	4⅕–7⅘ @ 700	11½–13⅘ @ 1450	22 @ 2500	5⅗	14½ @ 20⁷⁄₁₀
1103352②	0 @ 200	½–3½ @ 450	5½–8 @ 700	7½–9½ @ 1450	9½ @ 2500	5⅗	5½ @ 20⁷⁄₁₀
1103389	0 @ 350	—	7 @ 700	—	8½ @ 1450	4	14 @ 15
1103392	0 @ 350	—	7 @ 700	—	8½ @ 1450	6	10 @ 13.5
1103393	0 @ 450	—	7 @ 750	—	21 @ 2500	5	12 @ 12
1103394	0 @ 450	—	7 @ 750	—	21 @ 2500	5	14 @ 15.5
1103395	0 @ 350	—	7 @ 700	—	8½ @ 1450	8	5 @ 12
1111262	0–2¼ @ 400	3¼–7¼ @ 800	4¾–8½ @ 1000	6¼–10 @ 1200	16 @ 2000	10–12	13¼–15¼ @ 11¼
1112065	0–1 @ 400	3–5 @ 800	4¾–6¾ @ 1000	6–8 @ 1200	13 @ 2000	8–10	11.30–12.60 @ 13
1112108	0–1 @ 400	3–5 @ 800	4¾–6¾ @ 1000	6–8 @ 1200	13 @ 2000	8–10	11.30–12.60 @ 13
1112219	0 @ 400	—	4½–6½ @ 950	—	13 @ 2000	5–7	12 @ 13
1112835	0 @ 400	5 @ 600	—	—	10 @ 2500	5	16 @ 11.5
1112836	0 @ 400	5 @ 600	—	—	10 @ 2500	7	16 @ 13.5
1112837	0 @ 400	4 @ 600	—	—	9 @ 2500	5	16 @ 11.5
1112838	0 @ 400	4 @ 600	—	—	9 @ 2500	7	16 @ 13.5
1112839	0 @ 400	5 @ 600	—	—	10 @ 2500	5	16 @ 11.5
1112840	0 @ 400	5 @ 600	—	—	10 @ 2500	7	16 @ 13.5
1112841	0 @ 400	4 @ 600	—	—	9 @ 2500	5	16 @ 11.5
1112842	0 @ 400	4 @ 600	—	—	9 @ 2500	7	16 @ 13.5
1112845	1 @ 500	—	—	—	12 @ 2000	5	16 @ 11.5
1112855	1 @ 500	—	—	—	12 @ 2000	5	16 @ 11.5
1112892②③	−¼–0 @ 330	−½ to 2½ @ 450	2½–5 @ 600	5–7 @ 1400	10 @ 3000	5.5	9.5–10.5 @ 14
1112954②④	−¼–0 @ 330	−½ to 2½ @ 450	2½–5 @ 600	5–7 @ 1400	10 @ 3000	4.5	13.5–14.5 @ 16
1112897②	0 @ 200	−½ to +2½ @ 450	2½–5 @ 600	5–7 @ 1400	10 @ 2500	5½	9½–10½ @ 13½
1112924②	0 @ 200	−1 to +1¾ @ 450	1½–3 @ 800	4–6 @ 1700	8 @ 2500	5	13½–14½ @ 16
1112931②	0 @ 200	½ to 1¾ @ 450	6¼–8½ @ 800	13½–15¾ @ 1700	22 @ 2500	5	13½–14½ @ 18
1112932②	0 @ 200	½ to 1¾ @ 450	6¼–8½ @ 800	13½–15¾ @ 1700	22 @ 2500	5	8½–9½ @ 18
1112954②	−¼–0 @ 330	−½ to +2½ @ 450	2½–5 @ 600	5–7 @ 1400	10 @ 3000	4½	13½–14½ @ 16

①—Stamped on distributor housing plate.
②—High energy ignition.
③—California.
④—Exc. California.
⑤—Vacuum retard, 1½ inch Hg.
⑥—Vacuum retard, 4¾° @ 11 inch Hg.

PISTONS, PINS, RINGS, CRANKSHAFT & BEARINGS

Year	Model	Fitting Pistons		Ring End Gap①		Wrist-pin Diameter	Rod Bearings		Main Bearings			
		Shim To Use	Pounds Pull On Scale	Comp.	Oil		Shaft Diameter	Bearing Clearance	Shaft Diameter	Bearing/Clearance	Thrust on Bear. No.	Shaft End Play
1974–75	All	②	②	.013	.015	.9995	2.500	.0005–.0028	3.250	.0001–.0026	3	.002–.012
1976	V8-350	③	—	.010	.015	.9805	2.1238–2.1248	.0004–.0033	④	⑤	3	.004–.008
	V8-500	②	②	.013	.015	.9997	2.500	.0005–.0028	3.250	.0001–.0026	3	.002–.012
1977–79	V8-350	—	—	.010	.015	.9805	2.1238–2.1248	.0005–.0026	④	⑤	3	.004–.008
	V8-425	②	②	.013	.015	.9997	2.500	.005–.0028	3.250	.0001–.0026	3	.002–.012
1978–79	V8-350⑥	—	—	.015	.015	1.0951	2.1238–2.1248	.0005–.0026	2.9998	⑤	3	.0035–.0135

①—Fit rings in tapered bores for clearance given in tightest portion of ring travel.
②—See text under "Pistons".
③—Piston clearance .001–.002.
④—Exc. No. 1, 2.4985–2.4995; No. 1, 2.4988–2.4998.
⑤—Exc. No. 5, .0005–.0021; No. 5 .0015–.0031.
⑥—Diesel engine. See Oldsmobile Chapter for service.

ENGINE TIGHTENING SPECIFICATIONS*

★Torque specifications are for clean and lightly lubricated threads only. Dry or dirty threads produce increased friction which prevents accurate measurement of tightness.

Year	Spark Plugs Ft. Lbs.	Cylinder Head Bolts Ft. Lbs.	Intake Manifold Ft. Lbs.	Exhaust Manifold Ft. Lbs.	Rocker Arm Shaft Bracket Ft. Lbs.	Rocker Arm Cover Ft. Lbs.	Connecting Rod Cap Bolts Ft. Lbs.	Main Bearing Cap Bolts Ft. Lbs.	Flex Plate to Crankshaft Ft. Lbs.	Vibration Damper or Pulley Ft. Lbs.
1974–75	25	115	30	35	—	24①	40	90	75	17
1976–79 V8-350	25	85③	40	25⑧	—	7	42	②	60	310
1978–79 V8-350⑤	—	130	40⑥	25	25⑦	—	42	120	60	200–310
1976 V8-500	25	115	30	35	—	30①	40	90	75	17
1977–79 V8-425	25	95	30	④	—	30	40	90	75	17

①—Inch pounds. Retorque after engine has been run.
②—Exc. No. 5, 80 ft. lbs.; No. 5, 120 ft. lbs.
③—1977–78, 130 ft. lbs.
④—Long screws, 35 ft. lbs. Short screw, 12 ft. lbs.
⑤—Diesel. See Oldsmobile Chapter for service.
⑥—Clean and dip entire bolt in engine oil before tightening.
⑦—Rocker arm pivot bolt to head.
⑧—1979 with lock tabs, 30 ft. lbs.

ALTERNATOR & REGULATOR SPECIFICATIONS

Year		Alternator					Regulator						
				Output @ 14 Volts			Field Relay			Voltage Regulator		
	Model	Rated Hot Output Amps.	Field Current 12 Volts @ 80° F.	2000 R.P.M. Amps.	5000 R.P.M. Amps.	Model	Air Gap In.	Point Gap In.	Closing Voltage	Air Gap In.	Point Gap In.	Voltage @ 125 F.
1974	1100558	42	2.2–2.6	—	—	1119515	.015	.030	2.3–3.7	.060	.014	13.8–14.8
	1100940	42	4.0–4.5	—	—		—	—	—	—	—	—
	1100557	63	2.8–3.2	—	—	1119519	—	—	—	—	—	13.8–14.8
	1100937	63	4.0–4.5	—	—		—	—	—	—	—	—
	1101015	80	4.0–4.5	—	—		—	—	—	—	—	—
1975–76	—	63	4.0–4.5	—	—	Integral	—	—	—	—	—	—
	—	80	4.0–4.5	—	—	Integral	—	—	—	—	—	—
	—	145	4.0–4.5	—	—	Integral	—	—	—	—	—	—
1977–79	1101023	80	4.0–4.5	—	—	Integral	—	—	—	—	—	—
	1101033	80	4.0–4.5	—	—	Integral	—	—	—	—	—	—
	1102380	63	4.0–4.5	—	—	Integral	—	—	—	—	—	—

WHEEL ALIGNMENT SPECIFICATIONS

Year	Model	Caster Angle, Degrees		Camber Angle, Degrees				Toe-In. Inch	Toe-Out on Turns, Deg.	
		Limits	Desired	Limits		Desired			Outer Wheel	Inner Wheel
				Left	Right	Left	Right			
1974	Eldorado	−½ to +½	Zero	−⅜ to +⅜	−⅝ to +⅛	Zero	−¼	0 to 1/16	—	—
	Series 75	−½ to +½	Zero	−⅜ to +⅜	−⅝ to +⅛	Zero	−¼	1/16 to 3/16	—	—
	Others	−½ to −1½	−1	−⅜ to +⅜	−⅝ to +⅛	Zero	−¼	1/16 to 3/16	—	—
1975–76	Eldorado	−½ to +½	Zero	−⅜ to +⅜	−⅝ to +⅛	Zero	−¼	0 to 1/16	—	—
	Series 75	−½ to −1½	−1	−⅜ to +⅜	−⅝ to +⅛	Zero	−¼	1/16 to 3/16	—	—
	Others Exc. Seville	−½ to +1½	Zero	−⅜ to +⅜	−⅝ to +⅛	Zero	−¼	1/16 to 3/16	—	—
1976	Seville	+1½ to +2½	+2	+⅛ to ⅞	−⅛ to +⅝	+½	+¼	0 to ⅛	—	—
1977–78	Eldorado	−½ to +½	Zero	−⅜ to +⅜	−⅜ to +⅜	Zero	Zero	−1/16 to +1/16	—	—
	Seville	+1½ to +2½	+2	−⅜ to +⅜	−⅜ to +⅜	Zero	Zero	0 to +⅛	—	—
	Others	+2½ to +3½	+3	+⅛ to +⅞	+⅛ to +⅞	+½	+½	−1/16 to +3/16	—	—
1979	Eldorado	+ 2 to +3	+2.5	−½ to +½	−½ to +½	+½	+½	−1/16 to +1/16	—	—
	Seville	+1½ to +2½	+2	−⅜ to +⅜	−⅜ to +⅜	Zero	Zero	0 to +⅛	—	—
	Others	+2½ to +3½	+3	+⅛ to +⅞	+⅛ to +⅞	+½	+½	−1/16 to +3/16	—	—

STARTING MOTOR SPECIFICATIONS

Year	Model	Starter Number	Brush Spring Tension Oz①	Free Speed Test			Resistance Test③	
				Amps.	Volts	R.P.M.	Amps.	Volts
1974	Std. Cars	1108521	35	65–95②	—	7000–10500	—	—
	Eldorado	1108522	35	70–99②	10.6	7800–12000	435–535③	3.0
1975–76	All	—	35	65–95②	9	7000–10500	—	—
1977–78	Exc. Eldorado & Seville	1109038	35	65–95②	9	7000–10500	—	—
	Eldorado	1109039	35	65–95②	9	7000–10500	—	—
	Seville	1108765	35	65–95②	9	7000–10500	—	—
1979	Exc. Eldorado & Seville	1109062	—	—	—	—	—	—
		1109063	—	—	—	—	—	—
	Eldorado & Seville	1109072	—	—	—	—	—	—
		1998205	—	—	—	—	—	—

①—Minimum.　②—Includes solenoid.
③—Check capacity of motor by using a 500-ampere meter and a carbon pile rheostat to control voltage. Apply volts listed across motor with armature locked. Current should be as listed.

COOLING SYSTEM & CAPACITY DATA

Year	Model or Engine	Cooling Capacity, Qts.			Radiator Cap Relief Pressure, Lbs.		Thermo. Opening Temp. ①	Fuel Tank Gals.	Engine Oil Refill Qts. ③	Transmission Oil			Rear Axle Oil Pints
		No Heater	With Heater	With A/C	With A/C	No. A/C				3 Speed Pints	4 Speed Pints	Auto. Trans. Qts. ⑦	
1974	Eldorado	—	21.3	23.8	15	15	180	27	5	—	—	⑨	4⑧
	Series 75	—	—	26.8	15	—	180	27	4	—	—	⑤	5
	Others	—	21.3	23.8	15	15	180	27	4	—	—	⑤	5
1975	Eldorado	—	23	23	15	15	180	27½	5	—	—	⑥	4⑧
	Series 75	—	25.8	25.8	15	15	180	27½	4	—	—	⑤	5
	Others	—	23	23	15	15	180	27½	4	—	—	⑤	5
1976	Eldorado	—	23	23	15	15	180	27½	5	—	—	②	4④⑧
	Series 75	—	25.8	25.8	15	15	180	27½	4	—	—	⑤	4④
	Seville	—	18.9	18.9	15	15	180	21	4	—	—	⑤	4¼
	Others	—	23	23	15	15	180	27½	4	—	—	⑤	4④
1977–78	Eldorado	—	—	25.8	15	15	195	27½	5	—	—	⑥	4
	Fleetwood	—	—	20.8	15	15	195	24	4	—	—	⑤	4¼
	Seville	—	—	17.2	15	15	202	21	4	—	—	⑤⑪	4¼
	Others	—	—	20.8	15	15	195	24	4	—	—	⑤	4¼
1979	Eldorado	—	—	17.2⑭	15	15	178	20.3	4	—	—	⑩	3⅔
	Seville	—	—	17.2⑭	15	15	178	21	⑬	—	—	⑫	4¼
	Others	—	—	20	15	15	195	25	⑬	—	—	⑫	4¼

①—For permanent anti-freeze.
②—Oil pan 5¾ qts. Total capacity 13½ qts.
③—Add one quart with filter change.
④—Exc. 3.15:1 ratio axle; 3.15:1 ratio axle, 5 pts.
⑤—Oil pan 4 qts. Total capacity 12½ qts.
⑥—Oil pan 5 qts. Total capacity 13 qts.
⑦—Approximate. Make final check with dipstick.
⑧—Front drive axle.
⑨—Oil pan 6 qts. Total capacity 13½ qts.
⑩—Oil pan 5 qts. Total capacity 12 qts.
⑪—Diesel oil pan 3 qts. Total capacity 9 qts.
⑫—Exc. Diesel oil pan 4½ qts. Total capacity 12½ qts.; Diesel oil pan 3 qts. Total capacity 9 qts.
⑬—Exc. Diesel, 4 qts.; Diesel, 6 qts.
⑭—Diesel engine, 20 qts.

BRAKE SPECIFICATIONS

Year	Model	Brake Drum Inside Diameter	Wheel Cylinder Bore Diameter			Master Cylinder Bore Diameter		
			Disc Brake	Front Drum Brake	Rear Drum Brake	Disc Brakes	Drum Brakes	Power Brakes
1974–75	Eldorado	11	$2^{15}\!/_{16}$	—	$^{15}\!/_{16}$	$1\frac{1}{8}$	—	$1\frac{1}{8}$
	Others	12	$2^{15}\!/_{16}$	—	$^{15}\!/_{16}$	$1\frac{1}{8}$	—	$1\frac{1}{8}$
1976	Seville	11	$2^{15}\!/_{16}$	—	$^{15}\!/_{16}$	$1\frac{1}{8}$	—	$1\frac{1}{8}$
	Eldorado	—	$2^{15}\!/_{16}$	—	$2\frac{1}{2}$①	$1\frac{1}{8}$	—	$1\frac{1}{8}$
	Others	12	$2^{15}\!/_{16}$	—	$^{15}\!/_{16}$②	$1\frac{1}{8}$	—	$1\frac{1}{8}$
1977–78	Brougham	—	$2^{15}\!/_{16}$	—	$2\frac{1}{2}$①	$1\frac{1}{8}$	—	$1\frac{1}{8}$
	Deville	11	$2^{15}\!/_{16}$	—	1	$1\frac{1}{8}$	—	$1\frac{1}{8}$
	Eldorado	—	$2^{15}\!/_{16}$	—	$2\frac{1}{2}$①	$1\frac{1}{8}$	—	$1\frac{1}{8}$
	Fleetwood	12	$2^{15}\!/_{16}$	—	$^{15}\!/_{16}$	$1\frac{1}{8}$	—	$1\frac{1}{8}$
	Seville	—	$2^{15}\!/_{16}$	—	$2\frac{1}{2}$①	$1\frac{1}{8}$	—	$1\frac{1}{8}$
1979	Deville	11	$2^{5}\!/_{16}$	—	1	$1\frac{1}{8}$	—	$1\frac{1}{8}$
	Eldorado	—	$2\frac{1}{2}$	—	$2\frac{1}{8}$①	1	—	1
	Others	—	$2^{5}\!/_{16}$	—	$2\frac{1}{2}$①	$1\frac{1}{8}$	—	$1\frac{1}{8}$

①—Rear disc brake.   ②—Commercial Chassis 1″.

Electrical Section

DISTRIBUTOR, REPLACE

1. Remove distributor cap.
2. On vehicles without H.E.I. system, disconnect primary wire from coil. On vehicles equipped with H.E.I. system, disconnect harness connector from side of distributor cap.
3. On vehicles equipped with electronic fuel injection disconnect speed sensor connector at distributor trigger.
4. Disconnect vacuum advance pipe or hose from distributor.
5. Crank engine until rotor is pointing to No. 1 spark plug wire position on cap.
6. Remove distributor hold-down nut and clamp.
7. Lift distributor from engine.
8. Note that the rotor will turn slightly as the drive gear becomes disengaged from the camshaft gear. Therefore, when installing the distributor, the rotor should be turned slightly counter-clockwise from No. 1 spark plug position to insure proper engagement of gears. When properly installed, rotor should point directly to No. 1 spark plug position.

STARTER, REPLACE

1979

1. Disconnect battery ground cable, then raise and support front of vehicle.
2. Remove spring clip securing battery positive cable to solenoid housing.

3. Disconnect battery cable and wiring from solenoid.
4. Remove three starter motor attaching blots and remove starter motor.

1974-78

1. Disconnect battery ground cable at battery.
2. On Eldorado, disconnect starter harness at connector at right rear of engine.
3. Raise front end of car.
4. On all except Eldorado models, disconnect battery lead at starter solenoid and disconnect neutral switch wire and coil feed wire at starter solenoid terminals.
5. On all except 1974 Eldorado and H.E.I. equipped vehicles, disconnect interlock relay wire and solenoid wire at starter solenoid terminals.
6. On Eldorado, remove spring clip securing wire to solenoid housing.
7. On Seville, remove crossover pipe.
8. Remove screw and nut securing support bracket to starter and crankcase.
9. Unfasten starter motor from crankcase and remove starter by pulling it forward, then toward RH front wheel and up over steering linkage toward rear of car.

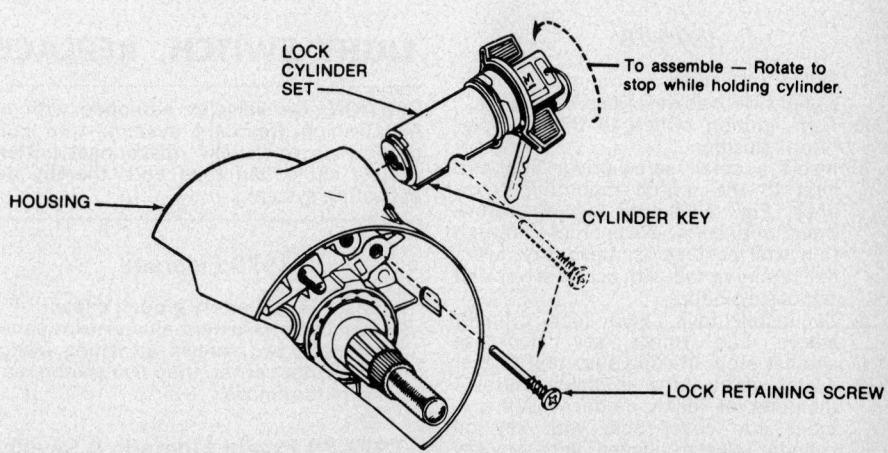

Fig. 1   Ignition lock removal. 1979 models

Fig. 2   Lock cylinder removal, 1974-78 models

IGNITION LOCK

CAUTION: On vehicles equipped with an Air Cushion Restraint system, turn ignition switch to "Lock," disconnect battery ground cable and tape end, thereby deactivating system.

1979

1. Remove steering wheel as described under Horn Sounder and Steering Wheel.
2. Remove turn signal switch as described under Turn Signal Switch, Replace, then remove buzzer switch.
3. Place ignition switch in Run position, then remove lock cylinder retaining screw and lock cylinder.
4. To install, rotate lock cylinder to stop while holding housing, Fig. 1. Align cylinder key with keyway in housing, then push lock cylinder assembly into housing until fully seated.
5. Install lock cylinder retaining screw. Torque screw to 40 in. lbs. for standard columns. On adjustable columns, torque retaining screw to 22 in. lbs.
6. Install buzzer switch, turn signal switch and steering wheel.

1974-78

1. Follow procedure to remove the turn signal switch as described further on.
2. Turn ignition switch to the "On" or "Run" position.
3. Insert a small screw-driver into slot next to the switch mounting screw boss, Fig. 2. Gently tap on screwdriver until screw-driver breaks through thin wall casting. Depress lock cylinder retaining tab with screw-driver and remove cylinder.
4. To install lock, hold lock cylinder sleeve and rotate key clockwise against stop. Making sure that buzzer switch drive tang is below outside diameter of lock cylinder, insert cylinder into cover bore with key on cylinder sleeve aligned with keyway in housing until cylinder touches lock sector shaft.

NOTE: Insert a $1/16$ inch drill shank between lock cylinder knob and column housing to avoid assembling lock cylinder too far into steering column.

5. While maintaining a light inward force, rotate lock cylinder counterclockwise until drive section of cylinder mates with sector drive shaft. Push in until snap ring on lock snaps into groove in housing.
6. Check for freedom of operation of lock cylinder.

IGNITION SWITCH, REPLACE

CAUTION: On vehicles equipped with an Air Cushion Restraint system, turn ignition switch to "Lock," disconnect battery ground cable and tape end, thereby deactivating system.

1974-79

1. Disconnect battery cable and position ignition key in "Lock".
2. Remove steering column lower cover.
3. Loosen two upper column support nuts and allow column to drop as far as possible without removing the nuts.

NOTE: Do not remove nuts as column may bend under its own weight.

4. Disconnect switch connector and remove switch, Fig. 3.
5. When reassembling, make sure the ignition key is in the "Lock" position. Assemble switch on actuator rod. Hold rod stationary and move switch towards bottom of column then back off one detent on standard steering column models. On models with tilt column, move switch toward upper end of column and back off one detent.

LIGHT SWITCH, REPLACE

CAUTION: On vehicles equipped with an Air Cushion Restraint system, turn ignition switch to "Lock," disconnect battery ground cable and tape end, thereby deactivating system.

1979 Eldorado

1. Disconnect battery ground cable.
2. Remove instrument cluster trim panel.
3. Remove two screws attaching switch to cluster carrier, then pull switch rearward to remove.

1977-79 Except Eldorado & Seville

1. Disconnect battery ground cable.

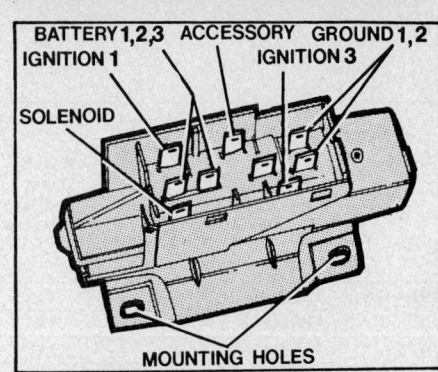

Fig. 3   Ignition switch. 1974-79

2. Remove left hand instrument panel insert.
3. Remove three screws attaching light switch to instrument panel.
4. On vehicles equipped with Cruise Control and Twilight Sentinel, remove two screws retaining Cruise Control switch to instrument panel.
5. Slide Cruise Control switch forward to remove headlamp switch.
6. Disconnect electrical connector from headlamp switch, then if used, disconnect Guidematic connector from under instrument panel.
7. Remove switch.
8. Reverse procedure to install.

1976-79 Seville

1. Disconnect battery ground cable.
2. Remove lower left instrument panel assembly.
3. Pull knob to "ON" position, depress button on bottom of switch and remove knob and shaft assembly.
4. Remove headlamp case to lower instrument panel attaching screws.
5. Remove sleeve attaching headlamp switch to case.
6. On vehicles without Guide-Matic and Twilight Sentinel remove sleeve retaining escutcheon, washer and lens to backplate.
7. On vehicles equipped with Guide-Matic and Twilight Sentinel, remove Guide-Matic knob, wave washer and Twilight Sentinel lever by pulling outward. Remove lens, then spanner nut and potentiometer from backplate.
8. Reverse procedure to install.

1974-76 Exc. Seville & 1977-79 Eldorado

1. Disconnect battery ground cable.
2. Remove steering column lower cover.
3. Disconnect headlamp electrical connector and lower bulb.
4. Pull knob to "ON" position, depress spring loaded button and remove knob and shaft, escutcheon and washer.
5. Remove case to instrument support screw.
6. Lower switch assembly, disconnect upper bulb and remove switch.
7. Reverse procedure to install.

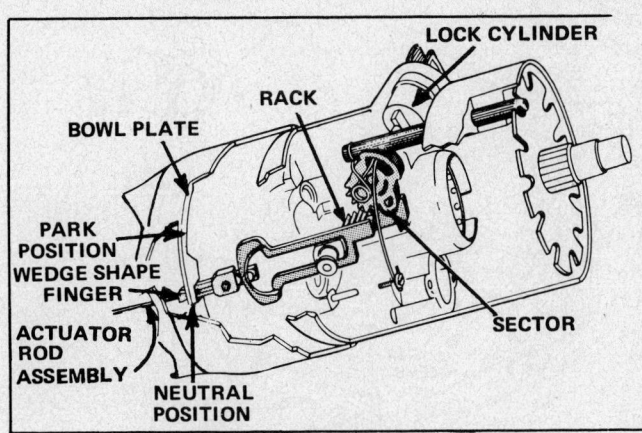

Fig. 4 Mechanical neutral switch system with Tilt-Telescope column. 1974-79

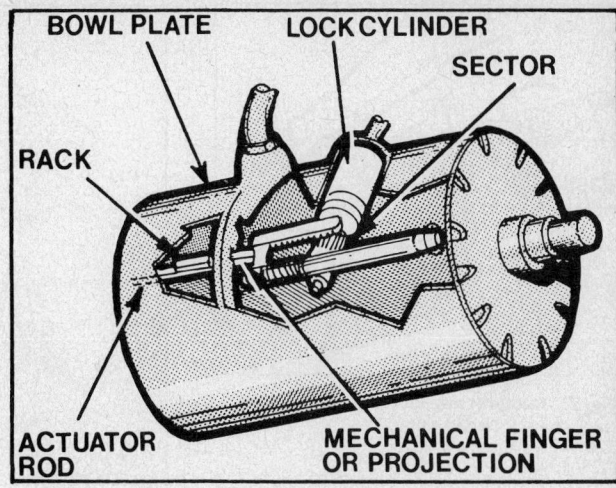

Fig. 5 Mechanical neutral start system with standard column. 1974-79 models

STOP LIGHT SWITCH

1974-79

The stoplight is retained to the brake pedal bracket. To adjust, pull the brake pedal fully up to its stop. This action automatically adjusts the switch.

NEUTRAL START SWITCH

1974-79 Models

Actuation of the ignition switch is prevented by a mechanical lockout system, Figs. 4 and 5, which prevents the lock cylinder from rotating when the selector lever is out of Park or Neutral. When the selector lever is in Park or Neutral, the slots in the bowl plate and the finger on the actuator rod align allowing the finger to pass through the bowl plate in turn actuating the ignition switch, Fig. 6. If the selector lever is in any position other than Park or Neutral, the finger contacts the bowl plate when the lock cylinder is rotated, thereby preventing full travel of the lock cylinder.

NOTE: On all models incorporating an electric neutral start switch, this switch plus the back-up light switch and parking brake vacuum release valve are combined into one unit. This unit is mounted on the steering column under the instrument panel.

TURN SIGNAL SWITCH, REPLACE

CAUTION: On vehicles equipped with an Air Cushion Restraint system, turn ignition switch to "Lock", disconnect battery

ground cable and tape end, thereby deactivating system.

1974-79

Standard column

1. Disconnect battery cable and remove steering wheel.
2. Remove lock plate cover screws and cover.
3. With a suitable compressor, compress lock plate and spring and remove snap ring from shaft, Fig. 7.
4. Remove lock plate, cancelling cam, preload spring and thrust washer.
5. Remove steering column lower cover and the signal lever.
6. On car equipped with cruise control proceed as follows:
   a. Disconnect cruise control wire from harness.
   b. Remove harness protector from cruise control.
   c. Wrap wire around turn signal lever until lever is disconnected. Do not remove wire from column.
7. On all models remove bolts at upper support.
8. Remove four screws securing upper mounting bracket to column and remove bracket.
9. Disconnect turn signal harness and remove wires from plastic protector. Wrap a piece of tape around connector and harness to facilitate removal, Fig. 8.
10. Remove screw securing turn signal switch to column and pull switch out.

Tilt & Telescope Wheel

1. Disconnect battery cable.
2. Remove steering wheel and slide rub-

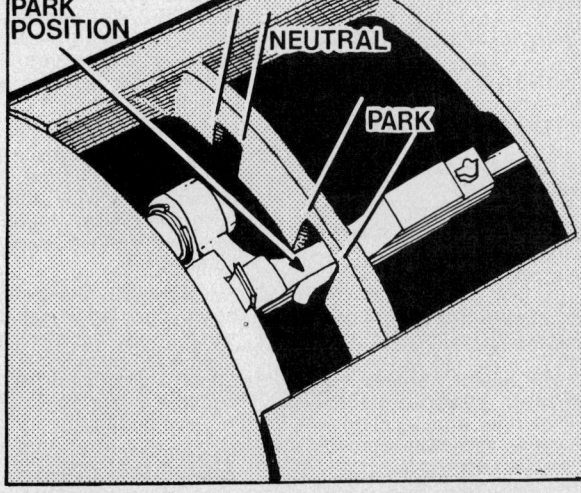

Fig. 6 Mechanical neutral start system in Park position

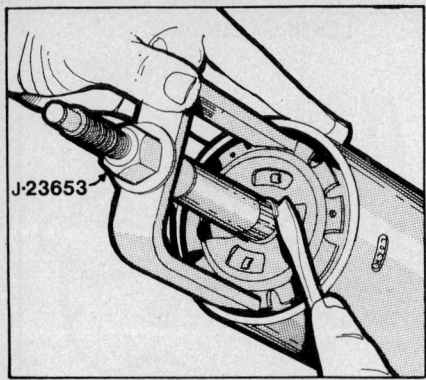

Fig. 7 Compressing lock plate & removing snap ring

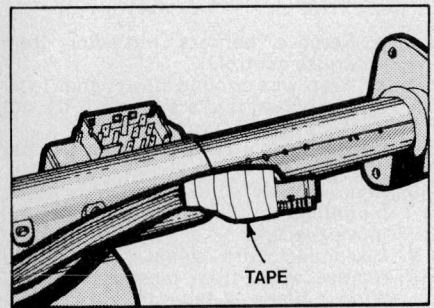

Fig. 8 Taping turn signal connector & wiring

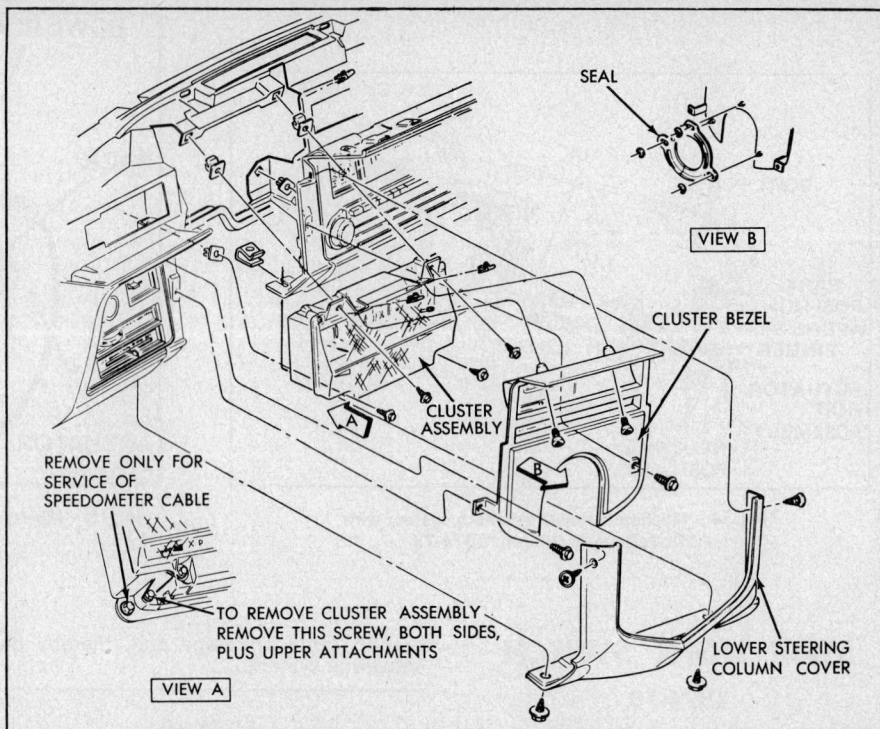

REMOVE ONLY FOR SERVICE OF SPEEDOMETER CABLE

TO REMOVE CLUSTER ASSEMBLY REMOVE THIS SCREW, BOTH SIDES, PLUS UPPER ATTACHMENTS

VIEW A

SEAL

VIEW B

CLUSTER BEZEL

CLUSTER ASSEMBLY

LOWER STEERING COLUMN COVER

Fig. 9 Instrument cluster. 1976-79 Seville

ber sleeve from steering shaft.

3. Remove plastic retainer from C-ring.
4. With a suitable compressor, thread bolt into steering shaft lock hole.
5. Compress preload spring and remove C-ring, Fig. 7.
6. Remove compressor and remove lock plate, horn contact carrier and preload spring.
7. Remove steering lower cover and the signal lever.
8. On cars equipped with cruise control proceed as follows:
   a. Disconnect cruise control wire from harness.
   b. Remove harness protector from cruise control.
   c. Wrap wire around turn signal lever until lever is disconnected. Do not remove wire from column.
9. On all models remove bolts at upper support.
10. Remove four screws securing upper mounting bracket to column and remove bracket.
11. Disconnect turn signal harness and remove wires from plastic protector. Wrap a piece of tape around connector and harness to facilitate removal, Fig. 8.
12. Remove screw securing turn signal switch to column and pull switch out.

HORN SOUNDER & STEERING WHEEL

1974-79

CAUTION: On vehicles equipped with an Air Cushion Restraint system, turn ignition switch to "Lock," disconnect battery ground cable and tape end, thereby deactivating system.

1. Disconnect battery ground cable.
2. On vehicles equipped with Air Cushion Restraint System, remove the driver module attaching screws using tool J-24628-2. On vehicles not equipped with Air Cushion Restraint System, remove three screws from back of spokes and lift pad assembly from wheel.
3. On tilt and telescope wheels remove three screws securing lever and knob assembly to flange and screw assembly. Unscrew flange and screw assembly from steering shaft and remove. Remove lever and knob assembly.
4. On standard wheels, scribe an alignment mark on wheel hub in line with slash mark on steering shaft to be used upon installation.
5. Loosen steering shaft nut, apply a suitable puller to loosen wheel; then remove puller, nut and wheel.
6. Remove three screws securing three contact wires to wheel.
7. Reverse procedure to install.

INSTRUMENT CLUSTER

CAUTION: On vehicles equipped with an Air Cushion Restraint system, turn ignition switch to "Lock," disconnect battery ground cable and tape end, thereby deactivating system.

1979 Eldorado

1. Disconnect battery ground cable.
2. Remove instrument cluster trim panel.
3. Remove headlamp and windshield wiper switches.
4. Unlock headlamp, windshield wiper and cruise control wire connectors from cluster carrier.
5. Disconnect speedometer cable and instrument cluster wiring.
6. Remove instrument cluster attaching screws and remove cluster assembly.

1976-79 Seville

1. Disconnect battery ground cable.
2. Remove steering column lower cover, 4 screws attaching cluster bezel to instrument panel, then press bezel downward, rotate top outward and carefully remove bezel.
3. Position shift lever in "Park" and remove screw attaching indicator cable to steering column.
4. Remove two screws securing top of cluster to instrument panel support and two screws securing speedometer cable retainer to cluster, Fig. 9.

NOTE: Do not remove speedometer

cable retainer.

5. Pull cluster outward to disengage speedometer cable, then rotate cluster downward and disconnect wire connector. Remove cluster.

1974-79 Except 1976-79 Seville & 1979 Eldorado

1. Disconnect battery ground cable.
2. Remove cluster bezel, then with shift lever in "Park" remove screw securing shift indicator cable to steering column.
3. Remove four screws securing cluster to instrument horizontal support, Figs. 10 and 11.

NOTE: Do not remove the 2 outboard screws which retain speedometer cable mounting.

4. On 1977-78 except Eldorado models, remove screw located directly above steering column, retaining cluster to speedometer mounting plate.
5. Disengage speedometer cable at neck by pulling cluster straight out and depressing retaining spring.

NOTE: To remove cluster, place shift lever in low range and on cars with tilt wheel, place wheel in lowest position.

6. Rotate cluster downward, disconnect printed circuit connector and remove cluster.

RADIO, REPLACE

NOTE: When installing radio, be sure to adjust antenna trimmer for peak performance.

1979 Eldorado

1. Disconnect battery ground cable.
2. Remove instrument panel center trim panel.
3. Remove screws attaching instrument panel wiring harness to radio bracket and screw attaching radio bracket to tie bar. Position tone generator aside, if equipped.
4. Remove screws attaching radio mounting plate to instrument panel.
5. Disconnect antenna lead and radio wire connector.
6. Pull radio and mounting plate assembly rearward to remove.

1977-79 Except Eldorado & Seville

1. Remove center instrument panel insert.
2. Remove the four screws retaining radio to lower instrument panel.
3. Disconnect electrical connectors and antenna leads(s) and remove radio.

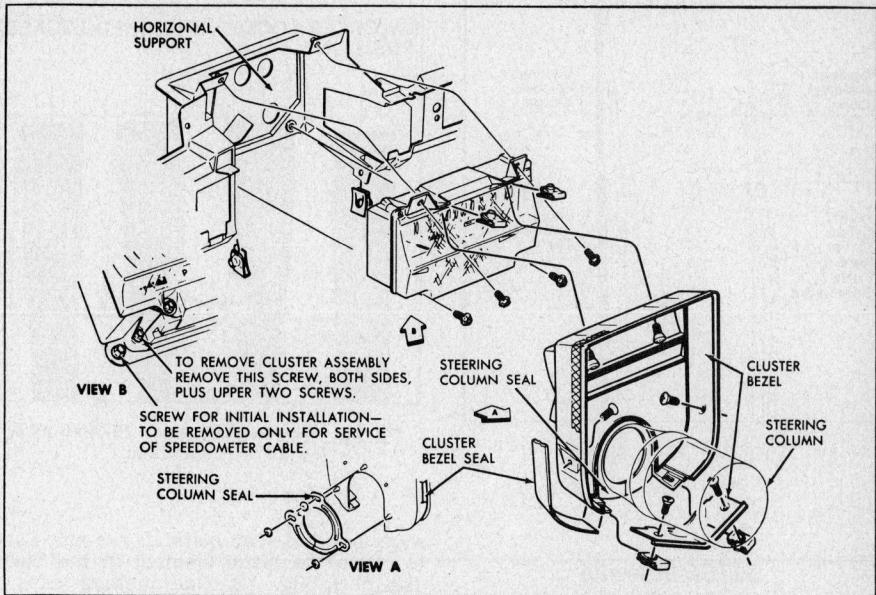

Fig. 10   Instrument panel cluster. 1974-76 Except Seville & 1977-79 Eldorado

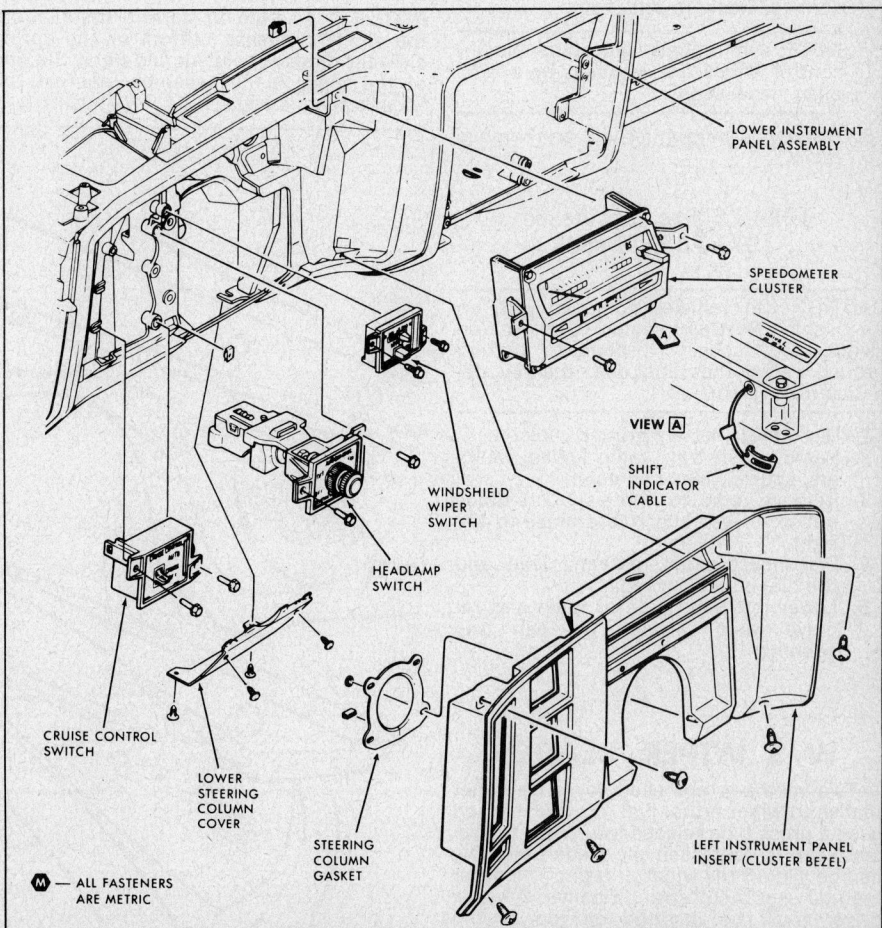

Fig. 11   Instrument cluster. 1977-79 Except Eldorado & Seville

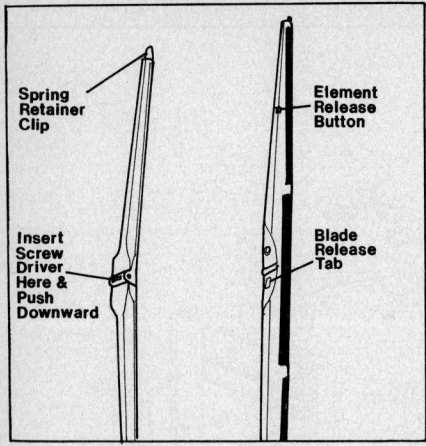

Fig. 12   Wiper Blades

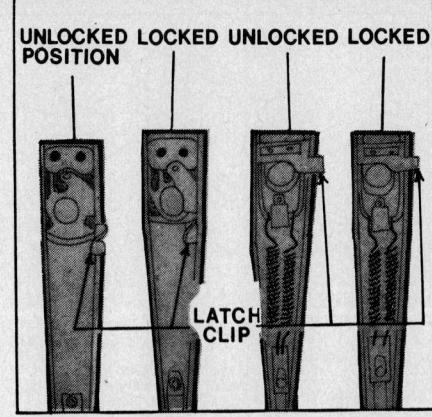

Fig. 13   Wiper arm removal. 1974-76 all & 1977-79 Eldorado

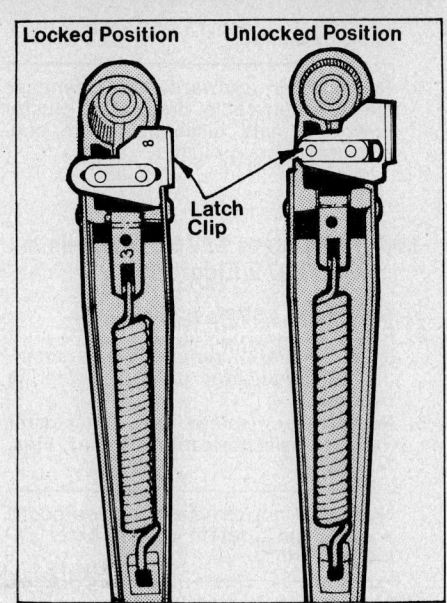

Fig. 14   Wiper arm removal. 1976 Seville & 1977-79 Except Eldorado

1976-79 Seville

1. Remove E.F.I. Electronic Control Unit as described in "Electronic Fuel Injection Section".
2. Remove screw attaching A/C outlet to heater case.
3. Disconnect antenna lead, then remove nut securing radio to rear mounting bracket.
4. Remove control knobs, anti-rattle springs, washers and nuts.

NOTE: On models with tape player, control knobs are retained by a $\frac{5}{64}$" allen head screw.

5. Disconnect wiring harness and remove radio.

1974-76 Exc. Seville & 1977-78 Eldorado

CAUTION: On vehicles equipped with an Air Cushion Restraint system, turn ignition switch to "Lock," disconnect battery ground cable and tape end, thereby deactivating system.

1. Disconnect battery ground cable.
2. Remove ash tray, radio knobs, washers, control rings and nuts.
3. Remove radio to lower support brace nut from rear and rotate brace to the right.
4. Disconnect wires, antenna lead and the dial bulb from radio.
5. Lower left hand side of radio and remove radio through the ash tray opening.

W/S WIPER BLADES

Two methods are used to retain wiper blades to wiper arms, Fig. 12. One method uses a press type release tab. When the release tab is depressed the blade assembly can be slid off the wiper arm pin. The other method uses a coil spring retainer. A screw driver must be inserted on top of the spring and the spring pushed downward. The blade assembly can then slide off the wiper arm pin. Two methods are also used to retain the blade element in the blade assembly, Fig. 12. One method uses a press type release button. When the button is depressed, the two piece blade assembly can be slid off the blade element. The other method uses a spring type retainer clip in the end of the blade element. When the retainer clip is squeezed together, the blade element can be slid out of the blade assembly.

NOTE: To be sure of correct installation, the element release button, or the spring element retaining clip should be at the end of the wiper blade assembly nearest the wiper transmission.

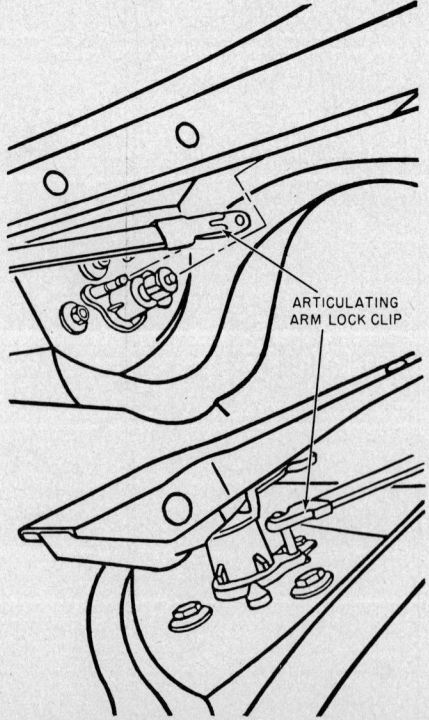

Fig. 15   Articulating arm lock clip.

W/S WIPER ARMS

1974-79

1. Raise hood to gain access to wiper arms. On Seville models, remove front cowl panel and screen.
2. Lift wiper arm and slide latch clip, Figs. 13 and 14, out from under wiper arm.
3. Release wiper arm and lift wiper arm assembly off transmission shaft.
4. On 1977-79 Eldorado and 1974-76 models except Seville, at left arm, slide articulating arm lock clip away from transmission pivot pin, Fig. 15, and lift arm off pin.
5. On 1977-79 Eldorado and 1974-76 models except Seville, to install left wiper arm assembly, position the articulating arm over the transmission pivot pin and slide the lock clip toward the pivot pin until it locks in place on the pin. Install the left wiper arm assembly to the transmission shaft aligning the keyway to the shaft.
6. On 1977-79 Eldorado and 1974-76 models except Seville, align keyway in right wiper arm assembly to transmission shaft and install arm assembly to shaft.
7. On 1977-79 models except Eldorado and Seville, align slot in arm and blade assembly to keyway in transmission spindle and position wiper arm on shaft. Lift blade assembly and slide latch clip into place.

NOTE: W/s wiper blade assembly release button or clip must face toward base of arm assembly for proper matching of blade to glass contour.

8. On Seville, position wiper arm assembly on transmission spindle, then lift blade and slide latch clip into place.

9. On all models, release wiper arms and check wiper pattern and park position.

W/S WIPER MOTOR

1974-79

1. Raise hood and remove cowl screen. On Seville it is necessary to first remove cowl panel.
2. Reach through opening and loosen transmission drive link to crank arm nuts.
3. Remove transmission drive link from motor crank arm.
4. Disconnect wiring and washer hoses.
5. Remove motor attaching screws.
6. Remove motor while guiding crank-arm through hole.

NOTE: Ensure wiper motor is in "Park" position before assembling crank arm to transmission drive link.

W/S WIPER TRANSMISSION

1974-79

1. Raise hood and remove cowl vent screen. On Seville it is first necessary to remove cowl panel.
2. On 1976 Seville and 1977-79 models except Eldorado, remove left and right wiper arm and blade assemblies. On 1977-79 Eldorado and 1974-76 models except Seville, remove wiper arm and blade from transmission to be removed.
3. Loosen attaching nuts securing transmission drive link to motor crank arm.

NOTE: On 1977-79 Eldorado and 1974-76 models except Seville, if only left side is to be removed, it will not be necessary to loosen nuts securing right drive link to motor crank arm.

4. Disconnect transmission drive link from crank arm.
5. Remove attaching screws securing transmission to body.
6. Remove transmission and linkage assembly through plenum chamber opening.

W/S WIPER SWITCH

1979 Eldorado

1. Disconnect battery ground cable.
2. Remove instrument cluster trim panel.
3. Remove two screws attaching switch to cluster carrier, then pull switch rearward to remove.

Except 1979 Eldorado

1. Disconnect battery ground cable.
2. Remove left hand climate control outlet grille.

3. Remove screw securing switch to instrument panel.
4. Pull control switch and electrical connector out and disconnect from panel.

HEATER CORE REMOVAL

CAUTION: On vehicles equipped with an Air Cushion Restraint system, turn ignition switch to "Lock," disconnect battery ground cable and tape end, thereby deactivating system.

After draining radiator and disconnecting heater hoses and battery ground cable proceed as follows:

1979 Eldorado

1. Plug heater core outlets to prevent spillage when removing heater core.
2. Remove instrument panel sound absorbers, then lower steering column.

3. Remove instrument cluster trim panel and instrument cluster as described under Instrument Cluster, Replace.
4. Remove radio front speakers.
5. Remove screws attaching manifold to heater case.
6. Remove instrument panel upper and lower attaching screws, then disconnect parkbrake release cable.
7. Disconnect instrument panel wiring harness from dash wiring assembly.
8. Disconnect right hand remote control mirror cable from instrument panel pad.
9. Disconnect speedometer cable from clip and temperature control cable from heater case.
10. Disconnect radio and A/C wiring, vacuum lines and all necessary wiring to remove instrument panel. If equipped with pulse wipers, remove wiper switch, and then disconnect wire connector from instrument cluster carrier

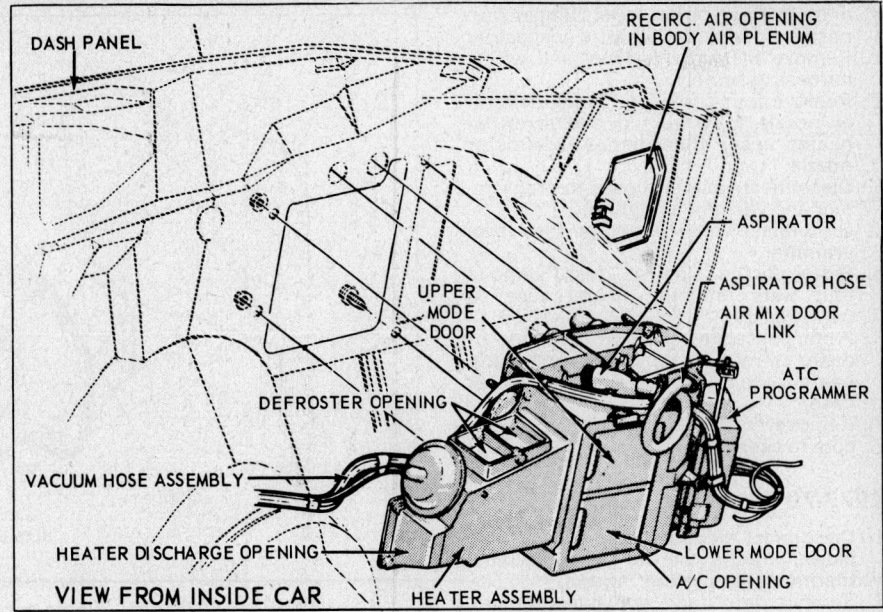

Fig. 16   Heater core. 1974-76 (Typical Except Seville)

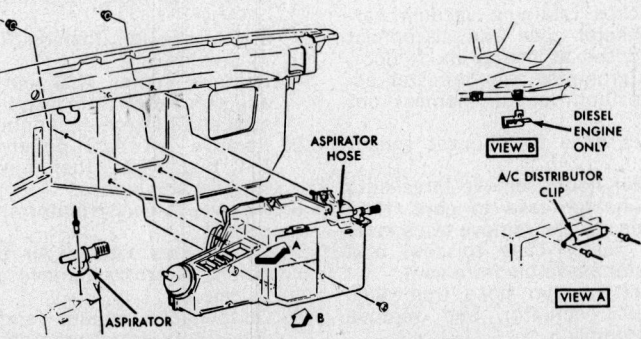

Fig. 17   Heater core. 1979 Eldorado

1-129

and separate pulse wiper jumper harness from wiper switch wire connector.

11. Remove instrument panel and wiring harness assembly.
12. Remove four screws retaining defroster nozzle to cowl and one screw at heater case, then remove defroster nozzle.
13. Disconnect vacuum hoses to programmer and vacuum actuators.
14. Disconnect wire connector from programmer.
15. From engine side of dash, remove four nuts retaining heater case to cowl, Fig. 17.
16. From passenger compartment side of dash, remove one screw retaining heater case to cowl, and remove heater case.
17. Remove four screws securing heater core to case and remove heater core.

1977-79 Except Eldorado & Seville

1. Disconnect electrical connectors from blower motor, blower resistors and thermostatic cycling switch.
2. Remove right hand windshield washer nozzle and remove right hand air inlet screen from plenum and cover plate at center of plenum opening.
3. Remove screws retaining thermostatic cycling switch and position switch aside.
4. Remove the 16 fasteners retaining cover and remove cover.
5. Remove one screw and retainer holding heater core to frame at top.
6. Place temperature door in the max. heat position and reach through temperature housing and push lower forward corner of heater core away from housing, then rotate core parallel to housing. This will cause core to snap out of lower clamp. Remove heater core from temperature housing.
7. Reverse procedure to install.

1976-79 Seville

1. Remove right hand wheel housing.
2. Plug heater core tubes to prevent spilling coolant into vehicle when core is removed.
3. Remove instrument panel right hand insert and applique.
4. Remove fuel injection control unit.
5. Remove radio, glove box door and glove box.
6. Remove A/C programmer.
7. Remove right hand lower instrument panel.
8. Remove screws retaining A/C distributor to heater case and remove distributor.
9. Remove clips retaining vacuum harness to heater case and disconnect vacuum hoses at heater mode door, bulkhead grommet and defroster actuator. Position vacuum harness out of way.
10. Disconnect hose from in-car sensor aspirator.
11. From under hood, remove three nuts retaining heater case to cowl, then from inside vehicle, remove two screws retaining heater case to cowl and move heater assembly from cowl.
12. Disconnect vacuum hose from A/C mode door actuator and remove heater assembly.

CAUTION: Heater core pipes are very

long. Use care when removing heater assembly.

13. Remove rubber seal from around heater core pipes, then remove screw and clip from beneath seal.
14. Remove screws from opposite side of core and remove core.
15. Reverse procedure to install.

1977-78 Eldorado & 1974-76 All Except Seville

1. Plug heater core tubes to prevent spilling coolant into vehicle when core is removed.
2. Remove instrument panel pad.

CAUTION: If the following step is performed, be sure to disable the Air Cushion Restraint System as described previously, to prevent accidental deployment of the system.

3. If equipped with Air Cushion Restraint System, proceed as follows:
   a. Remove knee restraint.
   b. Remove right hand lower trim cover.
   c. Remove Air Cushion Restraint assembly.
4. Remove center A/C outlet support and connector from position between cowl and horizontal support.
5. Remove left A/C outlet hose from A/C distributor, then remove center support and braces.
6. Remove A/C distributor and defroster nozzle.
7. On vehicles without Air Cushion Restraint System, remove glove compartment.
8. Disconnect vacuum and electrical connectors from programmer.
9. Disconnect vacuum hoses from recirc. door actuator, defroster door actu-

ator, mode door actuators and position hoses out of way.
10. Disconnect aspirator hose from in-car sensor.
11. Remove three nuts and one screw retaining heater case to cowl at engine side of cowl.
12. Remove heater case from under instrument panel.
13. Remove seal from around core tubes and remove screw and clip from beneath seal.
14. Remove two screws and clip from opposite side of core and remove core from case.
15. Reverse procedure to install.

BLOWER MOTOR REPLACE

CAUTION: On vehicles equipped with an Air Cushion Restraint system, turn ignition switch to "Lock," disconnect battery ground cable and tape end, thereby deactivating system.

1979 Eldorado

1. Disconnect battery ground cable.
2. Remove fender skirt from right hand side of vehicle.
3. Disconnect wire connector and cooling hose.
4. Remove five blower motor attaching screws and remove blower motor.

Except 1979 Eldorado

1. Disconnect battery ground cable.
2. Remove cooling hose from nipple and blower.

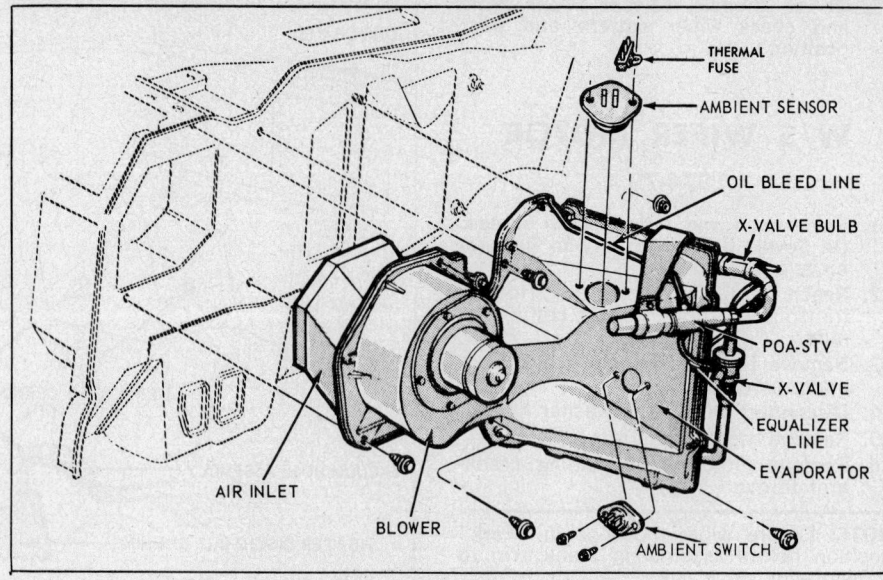

Fig. 18   Blower motor. 1974-79 (Typical)

THERMAL FUSE
AMBIENT SENSOR
OIL BLEED LINE
X-VALVE BULB
POA-STV
X-VALVE
EQUALIZER LINE
EVAPORATOR
AMBIENT SWITCH
BLOWER
AIR INLET

3. Disconnect electrical connector at lead to motor.
4. Unfasten and remove motor, Fig. 18.

SPEED CONTROL

Bead Chain Adjustment

On 1977-79 Eldorado and 1974-76 models except Seville, install the bead chain with second ball on the inboard slot of the throttle plate clip. This will provide the proper adjustment.

On 1976-79 Seville models, install bead chain to throttle plate clip, and adjust chain in clip to provide a minimum of sag without holding the throttle open. Inboard to outboard slot on the clip will provide a ½ ball adjustment.

On 1977-79 models except Eldorado and Seville, a control cable is used in place of the bead chain. With cable installed in throttle bracket and throttle lever, pull power unit end of cable as far as it will go. If one of four holes in power unit tab is aligned with cable pin, connect pin to tab with retainer. If tab does not align, move cable away from tab until the next closest hole in tab aligns with cable pin and connect pin to tab with retainer.

Brake Release Switch Adjustment, 1974

1. Turn ignition switch and Cruise Control on and connect a test light between one terminal of brake release switch and ground. Select terminal where light goes out when pedal is depressed.
2. Adjust switch so test light goes out when pedal is depressed $1/4$-$5/8$ inch on 1974 models.

NOTE: The release switch must disengage the system before the dump valve, otherwise a hissing sound will be heard in the vehicle when the brakes are applied.

Brake Release Switch Adjustment, 1975-79

With brake pedal depressed, push cruise control/stoplight switch fully into retainer and pull brake pedal fully back to rest position. Switch will back out of retainer and adjust automatically.

Vacuum Dump Valve Adjustment

With brake pedal depressed, push vacuum valve switch all the way into the retaining clip. Pull the brake pedal to the stop to automatically adjust the valve.

Engine Section

See Oldsmobile Chapter for Service Procedure on V8-350 Diesel Engine

ENGINE MOUNTS

1977-79 Exc. Eldorado & Seville

1. Open hood.
2. Remove two screws on each side securing radiator cover to strut support rods. Loosen one screw on each side and position support rods aside.
3. Remove two screws securing upper radiator shroud to radiator cover and one screw securing upper radiator hose bracket to shroud. Drill out the nine rivets securing upper shroud to lower shroud and remove the upper shroud.
4. Raise and support vehicle.
5. Remove through bolt from mount being replaced, Fig. 1.
6. Loosen the through bolt on the mount on the opposite side.
7. Using a suitable jack under the oil pan, raise engine until the bracket is free from the engine mount. Remove three flanged locking nuts and bolts, then the engine mount.
8. Reverse procedure to install.

1976-78 Seville

1. Remove fan shroud, then the wheel housing struts from both sides.
2. Raise vehicle, then remove crossover pipe and engine mount through bolts.
3. Support vehicle, raise engine until support can be removed from engine block.
4. Working through opening between lower control arm and frame, remove bolts attaching engine mount to frame and the mount, Fig. 1A.

1974-76 Except Eldorado & Seville

1. Open hood and remove radiator cover.

2. Raise and support vehicle on hoist.
3. Remove two through bolts from mount to be replaced, Fig. 2A.
4. If left hand (driver side) mount is being replaced, remove nut and washer from both mounts.
5. If right hand (passenger side) mount is being replaced, remove nut and washer from left hand mount and loosen right hand nut until no threads are visible on stud.
6. Support car with stands at each front frame horn.
7. Apply pressure (hoist, jack, etc.) to oil pan. Apply pressure over entire bottom with no concentration of pressure due to bumps or knobs on lift.

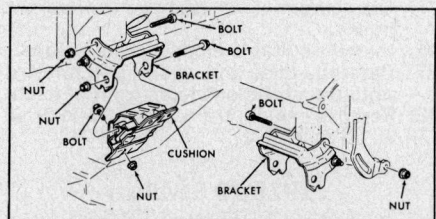

Fig. 1   Front engine mounts 1977-79 Exc. Eldorado & Seville

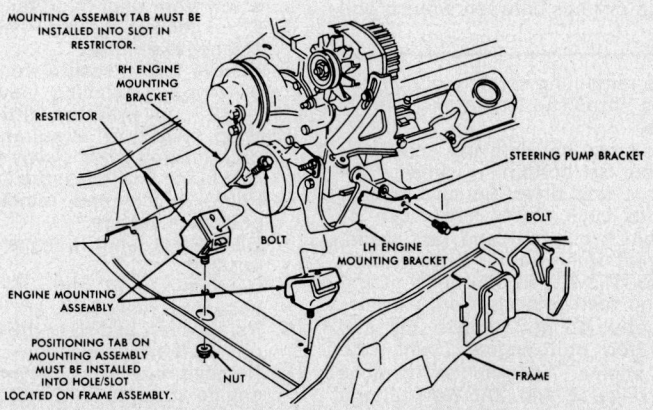

Fig. 2   Front engine mounts. 1979 Eldorado

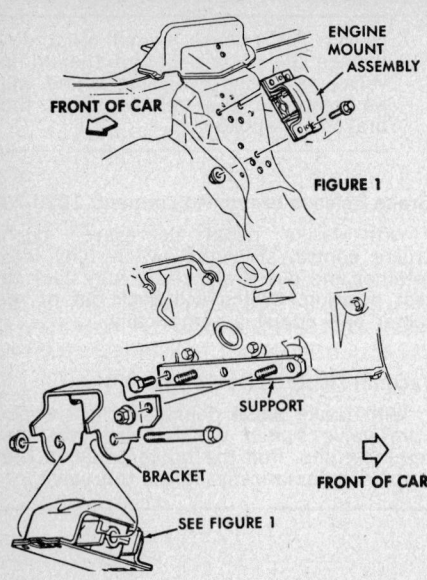

Fig. 1A Front Engine mounts. 1976-79 Seville

8. Raise engine until mount may be removed.

CAUTION: Amount engine may be raised is limited due to clearance between fan and shroud. Use caution when raising engine to avoid damage to these components.

1974-79 Eldorado

Left Front Mount

1. Remove radiator cover and disconnect battery ground cable.
2. Raise car and remove nut and washer from mount stud.
3. Remove capscrew securing transmission cooler lines to final drive bracket.
4. Remove screw securing top of steering gear flex coupling shroud to frame.
5. Remove nut from large through bolt securing top of engine mount and top of final drive bracket to engine.
6. Remove nut from lower engine mount through bolt.

NOTE: Attach box end wrench to nut, then use pry bar between wrench and engine.

7. Remove remaining screw securing flex coupling shroud to frame and remove shroud.
8. Remove cross bar bolt, nut and washers securing bottom of final drive bracket to final drive. Remove bracket by tipping back and to left of car.
9. Using block of wood and jack stand, lift engine from frame at crankshaft pulley to relieve load on engine mount bolts and remove bolts from mount.
10. Loosen, but do not remove, nut and washer from right engine mount stud.
11. Raise engine enough to remove mount, Figs. 2 and 2A. Work mount down and forward between fuel pump and frame.

Right Front Mount

1. Remove radiator cover.
2. Remove nut and washer securing left engine mount to frame.
3. Raise car and remove nut and washer securing right mount to frame.
4. Reach between right mount and oil pump to attach open end wrench to nut on lower bolt securing mount to engine. Holding this wrench in place, remove lower mounting bolt from rear, using ratchet, U-joint socket and 18" extension.
5. Work end wrench up between oil pump and crankshaft pulley and position wrench in a straight vertical position to engage nut on upper mounting bolt. Holding wrench in place, use same tools as in Step 4 to remove upper mounting bolt.

NOTE: If nut is impossible to engage, an alternative is to first perform the following Step, then use a 5" extension and a 9/16" crowfoot adapter and engage tool on nut by slipping between oil pump and A.I.R. pump.

6. Place jackstand under crankshaft pulley and, using wood block to avoid damage to pulley, either raise engine or lower chassis to remove mount.

CAUTION: When separating engine and chassis, observe relative position of frame rail and right drive axle tri-pot housing. Interference between these parts requires removal of right drive axle before mount can be removed. Furthermore, if tri-pot housing does clear the frame, vertical movement is limited by presence of fuel lines. Do not allow tri-pot housing to contact fuel lines.

7. Work mount free and pull rearward over tri-pot housing to remove, Figs. 2 and 2A.

ENGINE, REPLACE

1979 Eldorado

1. Mark hood hinge location on hood, then remove hood.
2. Disconnect battery cables and remove battery from vehicle.
3. Remove battery ground cable ground screw from right hand fender.
4. Drain cooling system, then remove air cleaner assembly.
5. Relieve fuel pressure from E.F.I. lines by loosely installing valve depressor J-5420 on pressure fitting. Position shop towels or a suitable container under fitting, then slowly tighten valve depressor until pressure is relieved.
6. Raise vehicle and remove crossover pipe from vehicle.
7. Disconnect shift linkage from transmission.
8. Remove clamp and disconnect fuel hose from fuel pipe.
9. Remove left and right drive axle to output shaft attaching screws.
10. Remove nuts from left and right hand engine mounts and nut and washer from left and right hand transmission mounts.

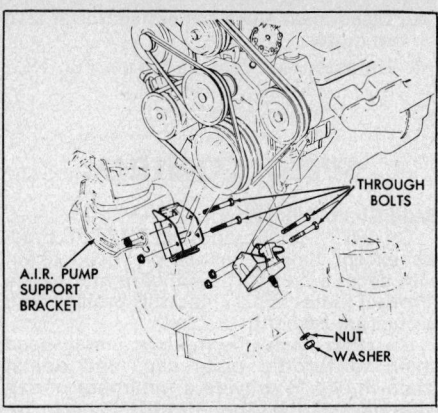

Fig. 2A Front engine mounts. 1974-76 Exc. Seville & 1977-78 Eldorado

11. Remove two fan shroud lower attaching screws and disconnect lower radiator hose from radiator, then lower vehicle.
12. Disconnect upper radiator hose and transmission cooler lines from radiator, then remove radiator upper cover and slide radiator out of vehicle.
13. Remove clutch fan and radiator shroud.
14. Disconnect power steering hoses at steering gear and cap hoses and fittings.
15. Remove clamp and disconnect fuel return hose from pressure regulator fuel return pipe.
16. Disconnect M.A.P. hose at throttle body, then pull hose out of tie straps and position aside.
17. If equipped with cruise control, disconnect vacuum hose from power unit, then pull hose out of tie strap and position on top of cowl.
18. Disconnect canister hose, vacuum supply hose and throttle cable from throttle body and position out of way.
19. Disconnect heater hoses at water valve and water pump.
20. Disconnect power brake unit vacuum hose.
21. Disconnect speedometer cable from transmission.
22. Disconnect engine wiring harness from bulkhead connector, E.S.S. connector from distributor, heater wire from water valve, wiring from wiper motor and washer bottle and ground strap from cowl.
23. Remove coolant reservoir and disconnect wiring from A/C compressor clutch.
24. Remove A/C compressor and A.I.R. pump drive belts.
25. Remove compressor to mounting bracket attaching bolts and position compressor on right hand fender skirt. Use care not to damage refrigerant hoses.
26. Install a suitable engine lifting fixture.
27. Carefully raise engine and pull forward until transmission clears front of dash.
28. Remove engine, transmission and drive as an assembly.

1976-79 Seville

1. Disconnect battery ground cable.
2. Drain cooling system and remove air cleaner.
3. Remove hood and wheel housing

struts from both sides.

NOTE: Scribe outline of hinge on underside of hood before removing to aid alignment at installation.

4. Remove fan shroud and disconnect power brake vacuum hose at steel line.
5. Disconnect wiring harness left side branch at fuel injectors, coolant sensor, oil pressure switch, HEI feed, heater turn-on switch, speed sensor and generator. Position harness aside.
6. Remove heater hose at rear of intake manifold.
7. Remove radiator hoses.
8. Remove fan and clutch assembly.
9. Remove distributor cap and secondary wiring.
10. Disconnect wiring harness right side branch at fuel injectors, throttle switch, EGR solenoid, fast idle valve, air temperature sensor, A/C compressor, MAP sensor, economy lite hose and two compressor ground wires.
11. Disconnect throttle linkage and position aside, remove vapor canister hose from throttle body.
12. Remove fuel inlet line from fuel rail.

NOTE: Use backup wrench on fuel rail to prevent damage to fitting. Ensure fuel pressure is relieved before loosening fittings.

13. Disconnect power steering hoses at steering gear and cap hoses and connections.
14. Disconnect fuel return line from pressure regulator outlet.
15. Remove compressor from engine and position aside.

NOTE: Do not disconnect refrigerant hoses from compressor.

16. Raise vehicle and remove exhaust pipe from right bank manifold.
17. Remove torque converter cover, then remove starter.
18. Remove clip securing transmission oil cooler lines to oil pan.
19. Remove bolts securing flex plate to converter.
20. Remove engine mount through bolts, then the crossover pipe.
21. Remove engine to transmission attaching bolts.
22. Remove screws attaching heater water valve to evaporator and position valve aside.
23. Support transmission, then raise engine off mounts and reposition transmission mount. Raise engine, then pull forward to disengage transmission and remove engine.

1974-78 Eldorado

1. Disconnect battery ground cable.
2. Scribe hood hinge locations and remove hood.
3. Drain cooling system.
4. Remove air cleaner, inlet duct, vacuum hoses and hot air ducts.
5. Disconnect upper radiator hose from thermostat housing and remove at cradle.
6. Remove radiator cover.
7. Remove fan assembly.

8. Disconnect alternator wiring, right bank spark plug wires and heater turn-on switch wiring and position harness aside.
9. Disconnect water control valve hose at rear of cylinder block.
10. Disconnect starter motor wiring harness at multiple connector.
11. Remove power steering pump and position aside with hoses attached.
12. Remove all drive belts.
13. Remove A/C compressor mounts and position aside with refrigerant hoses attached.
14. Disconnect throttle and Cruise Control linkage from carburetor or throttle body and bracket, then position cables aside.
15. Disconnect wiring on left branch of engine harness and position harness aside.
16. On vehicles equipped with Electronic Fuel Injection, disconnect manifold harness and position aside.
17. On all models, disconnect vacuum lines from carburetor or throttle body and position aside.
18. Remove left exhaust manifold flange nuts.
19. Remove transmission cooler line bracket screw, then the filler pipe nut from exhaust manifold.
20. Remove upper screw securing steering gear flex coupling shroud to frame.
21. Raise and support vehicle.
22. Remove remaining screw securing steering gear flex coupling shroud to frame.
23. Remove bolt and nut securing final drive bracket to engine mount.
24. Disconnect fuel pump fuel lines and plug lines and pump ports.
25. Remove lower radiator hose.
26. Remove right exhaust manifold flange nuts.
27. Remove starter motor and position aside with wiring attached.
28. Remove flywheel inspection cover.
29. Remove converter to flywheel retaining screws.
30. Remove the two lower transmission to engine screws.
31. Remove right output shaft screws.
32. Remove two output shaft bracket to cylinder block screws and one screw securing bracket to final drive.
33. Loosen right shock absorber mounting nut and position shock absorber outboard.
34. Move drive axle rearward as far as possible and remove output shaft.
35. Lower vehicle.
36. Remove four screws securing transmission to engine, two screws at the top and two screws at the left side.
37. Attach suitable engine lifting equipment to engine.
38. Support transmission with a suitable jack.
39. Remove engine from vehicle.
40. Reverse procedure to install.

1974-79 Except Eldorado & Seville

1. Disconnect battery ground cable.
2. Drain cooling system.
3. Remove self-tapping screw and washer securing each wheelhouse strut to radiator cover and position struts aside.

4. On 1974-75 models, remove six screws and washers securing radiator cover to cradle and one screw securing upper radiator hose to cover, then the radiator cover.
5. On 1976-79 models, remove two screws securing top radiator shroud to cradle and one screw securing upper radiator hose to shroud. Drill out nine rivets securing upper shroud to lower shroud. Remove two screws securing radiator cover to cradle and the cover.
6. On all models, scribe hood hinge locations. and remove hood.
7. Remove air cleaner and inlet duct.
8. Disconnect upper radiator hose from thermostat housing.
9. Disconnect wiring at the following locations: coolant temperature sender, ignition coil or H.E.I. distributor, downshift switch, engine metal temperature switch, anti-dieseling solenoid, oil pressure switch, heater turn-on switch and A/C compressor.
10. On vehicles equipped with Electronic Fuel Injection, disconnect EFI wiring harness and position aside.
11. On all models, bend back clips on rocker cover and position harness aside.
12. Disconnect brake hose from brake pipe.
13. Remove Cruise Control servo and disconnect bead chain at carburetor.
14. Disconnect throttle linkage from carburetor and position aside.
15. Disconnect vapor canister hose.
16. Disconnect power steering pump and position aside with hoses attached.
17. Remove fan and spacer.
18. Remove right side spark plug wires and position aside.
19. Remove A/C compressor and position aside with refrigerant line attached.
20. Disconnect alternator wiring and bend back clips securing harness to right valve cover and position harness aside.
21. Disconnect PCV vacuum line and the automatic level control vacuum line, if equipped.
22. Disconnect modulator line from carburetor.
23. Remove hot water valve hose from rear of right cylinder head.
24. Remove two nuts securing each cowl to wheelhouse tie strut to wheelhousing. Loosen nuts securing each strut to cowl and swing the struts outboard.
25. Remove two top screws securing engine to transmission.
26. Raise and support vehicle.
27. Remove nut and washer securing each engine mount to frame.
28. Remove starter motor.
29. Remove flywheel inspection cover.
30. Remove screws securing converter to flywheel.
31. Support the exhaust system and disconnect exhaust pipes from exhaust manifolds.
32. Disconnect fuel line and vapor return line from fuel pump.
33. Support transmission with a suitable jack. Remove remaining engine to transmission bolts.
34. Attach suitable engine lifting equipment to engine.
35. Remove engine from vehicle.
36. Reverse procedure to install.

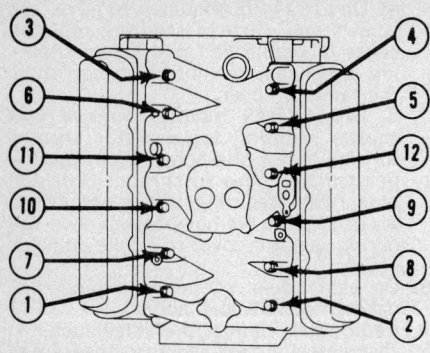

Fig. 3   Intake manifold tightening sequence. V8-350

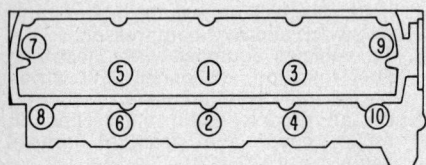

Fig. 4   Cylinder head tightening sequence. V8-350

INTAKE MANIFOLD, REPLACE

With E.F.I.

V8-350

1. Disconnect battery ground cable and drain cooling system.
2. Remove air cleaner and crankcase filter.
3. Disconnect throttle and Cruise Control linkage from throttle body. Remove cable from bracket and position aside.
4. Disconnect coolant temperature tell-tale switch, H.E.I. lead wire, speed sensor connector and injector valve wiring.
5. Disconnect EGR solenoid leads, throttle position switch, fast idle valve, air temperature sensor connector and MAP sensor hose.
6. Disconnect the two ground wires from A/C compressor bracket.
7. Disconnect the two vacuum hoses from throttle body to TVS switch.
8. Disconnect vacuum hoses and power brake pipe from rear of throttle body.
9. Disconnect fuel line from fuel rail.
10. Remove PCV valve from rocker cover.
11. Disconnect spark plug leads and position aside.
12. Disconnect upper radiator hose, bypass hose and the heater hose, located at the rear of the manifold.
13. Remove A/C compressor and position aside with refrigerant hoses attached.
14. Remove fuel return hose from pressure regulator.
15. On 1978-79 models, remove oil pressure switch and oil fill tube.
16. Remove intake manifold bolts and the intake manifold.
17. Reverse procedure to install. Torque intake manifold bolts in sequence, Fig. 3, to 40 ft. lbs.

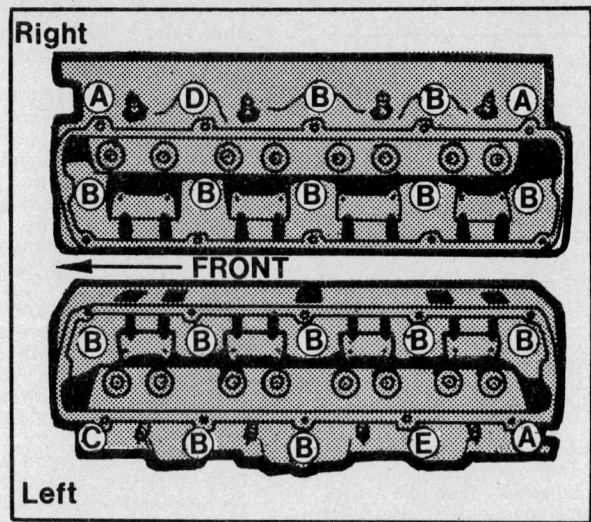

Bolt Location	Length
A (Bolt)	2.96 (Short)
B (Bolt)	4.16 (Long)
C (Bolt/Stud Head)	2.96 (Short)
D (Bolt/Stud Head)	4.16 (Long)
E (Bolt-Special)*	4.16 (Long)*

* This special bolt has an extra thick hex head which is drilled and tapped to accept the temperature switch.

Fig. 4A   Location and length of cylinder head bolts. V8-350

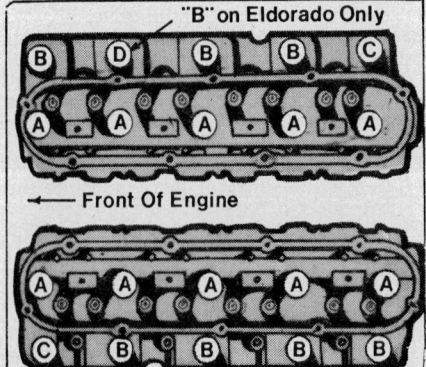

Bolt Location	Length
A (Bolt)	4.36'' (Medium)
B (Bolt)	4.77'' (Long)
C (Bolt)	3.02'' (Short)
D (Bolt/stud)	4.77'' (Long)

Fig. 5   Location and length of cylinder head screws. V8-425, 472, 500

V8-425, 472 & 500

1. Disconnect battery ground cable and remove air cleaner and crankcase filter.
2. Disconnect throttle cable and cruise control linkage, if equipped, from throttle body. Remove cable from bracket and position aside.
3. Working on engine left side, disconnect coolant temperature tell-tale switch wire, HEI lead wire, speed sensor connector, downshift switch and injector wires. Disconnect harness from fuel rail brackets and position aside.
4. Disconnect two vacuum hoses from throttle body to TVS switch.
5. Disconnect vacuum hoses and power brake pipe from throttle body.

NOTE: Use a back-up wrench when removing power brake pipe to prevent damage to fitting.

6. Disconnect fuel line from fuel rail.

NOTE: Use a back-up wrench on fuel rail to prevent damage to fitting.

7. Working on engine right side, disconnect injector wires, EGR solenoid leads, air temperature sensor connector and MAP sensor hose. Dis-

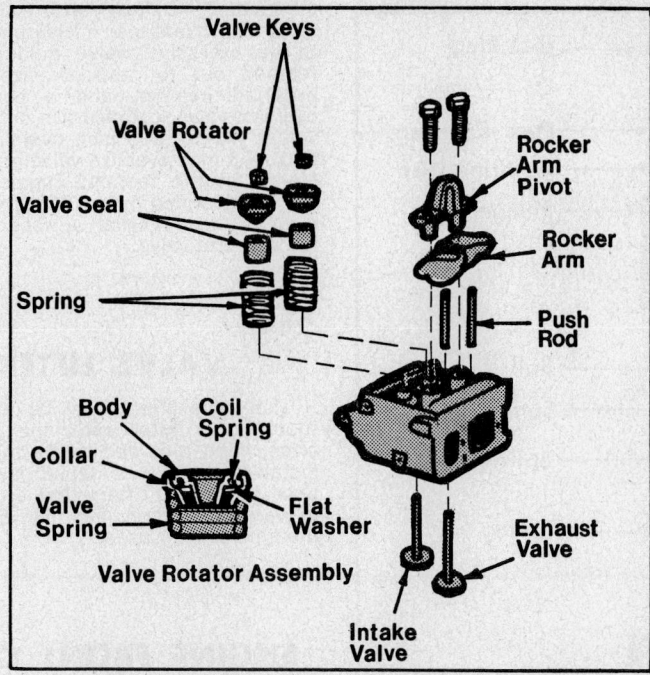

Fig. 6 Rocker arm components disassembled. V8-350

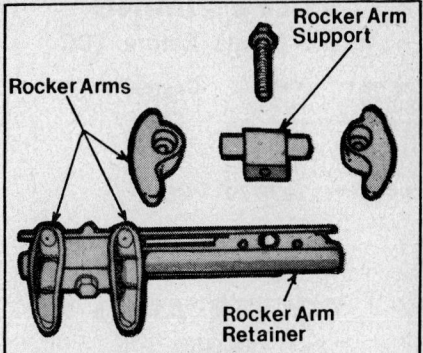

Fig. 7 Rocker arm components disassembled. V8-425, 472, 500

connect harness from fuel rail brackets and position aside.
8. Remove PCV valve from rocker cover and position aside.
9. Remove spark plug leads and distributor cap.
10. Remove front fuel rail.
11. Position A/C compressor aside, do not disconnect refrigerant lines.
12. Remove fuel return hose from pressure regulator.
13. Remove manifold bolts and lift manifold from engine. Do not pry or lift manifold by the fuel rails or the mounting brackets.
14. Reverse procedure to install. Torque manifold bolts to 30 ft. lbs.

Less E.F.I.

1. Disconnect battery ground cable and remove air cleaner.
2. Disconnect throttle linkage and Cruise Control linkage, if equipped.
3. Disconnect coil wires at H.E.I. connector, then remove distributor cap. On 1976-79 models, disconnect right hand spark plug wires at spark plugs and place aside.
4. Disconnect wire connectors from temperature sender, down shift switch and anti-dieseling solenoid.
5. Remove coil, anti-dieseling solenoid and solenoid bracket.
6. Disconnect vacuum lines from carburetor, remove Cruise Control servo top mounting bolt and position brake hose aside, if equipped.
7. Disconnect wiring connector from A/C compressor, if equipped.
8. Disconnect fuel line at carburetor and remove vacuum lines from intake manifold.

9. Loosen power steering mounting bolts and pivot pump toward engine. Remove A/C compressor drive belt, then the screws attaching compressor rear mounting to engine and the screws attaching compressor mounting flange to front mounting bracket. Position compressor aside.
10. Remove PCV valve from rocker cover.
11. Remove manifold to cylinder head bolts, intake manifold, manifold shield and gaskets.

CYLINDER HEAD, REPLACE

V8-350

1. Drain cooling system and remove intake manifold as described under "Intake Manifold Replace".
2. Remove exhaust manifolds.
3. Remove rocker cover, rocker arm bolts, pivots, rocker arms and push rods.

NOTE: Note location of rocker arms and pivots to ensure installation in original position.

4. Remove cylinder head bolts and the cylinder head.
5. When installing cylinder head it is important that cylinder head bolts are installed in the correct position, refer to Fig. 3. Torque bolts to 60 ft. lbs. in sequence, then retorque to 85 ft. lbs., Fig. 4. Torque intake manifold bolts in sequence shown in Fig. 3.

V8-425, 472, 500

1. Remove intake manifold.
2. Drain coolant from radiator.

3. Disconnect ground strap at rear of cylinder heads from cowl where used.
4. Disconnect wiring connector for high engine temperature warning system from sending unit at rear of left cylinder head.
5. Remove alternator if working on right cylinder head, or partially remove power steering pump if working on left cylinder head.
6. Remove A.I.R. manifold from both cylinder heads if equipped.
7. Disconnect wiring harness from cylinder head and position out of the way.
8. Remove exhaust manifold from cylinder head.
9. Remove rocker arm cover.
10. Remove rocker arm assemblies and lift out push rods.
11. Remove cylinder head bolts, remove head.
12. After carefully removing all gasket material from mating surfaces of head and block, position new gasket over dowels and install cylinder head in reverse order of removal, being sure to install the bolts as indicated in Fig. 5.

NOTE: When installing cylinder head bolts no torque sequence is required, start at center and work from side to side outwards and towards the ends.

VALVE ARRANGEMENT

Front to Rear

V8-425, 472, 500-
Left . . . . E-I-E-I-E-I-E-I
Right . . . . I-E-I-E-I-E-I-E
V8-350 . . . . I-E-I-E-E-I-E-I

VALVE LIFT SPECS.

Engine	Year	Intake	Exhaust
V8-472	1974	.457	.473
V8-500	1974-76	.475	.473
V8-350	1976-79	.400	.400
V8-425	1977-79	.457	.473

VALVE TIMING
Intake Opens Before TDC

Engine	Year	Degrees
V8-472	1974	21
V8-500	1974-76	21
V8-350	1976-79	16
V8-425	1977	11
V8-425	1978-79	21

ROCKER ARMS
V8-350

1. Remove rocker cover, rocker arm bolts, pivot and rocker arms.

   NOTE: Remove each set as a unit.

2. Position rocker arms on cylinder head, apply lubricant 1050169 or equivalent to wear points on pivot, then install pivot.

3. Install rocker arm bolts, tighten alternately, torque to 25 ft. lbs., Fig. 6.

V8-425, 472, 500

When disassembling the rocker arm assembly, be sure to keep the supports and rocker arms in order so they can be installed in the exact same position.

Install rocker arms on supports and place supports in retainers as shown in Fig. 7. Be sure that the "EX" on support is positioned toward the exhaust valve and "IN" toward the intake valve.

Place capscrews through the reinforcements, supports and retainers and position assemblies on cylinder head. Make sure that push rods are properly seated in the lifter seats and in the rocker arms. Lubricate rocker arm bearing surfaces before assembling in order to prevent wear. Torque rocker arm support bolts to 70 ft. lbs.

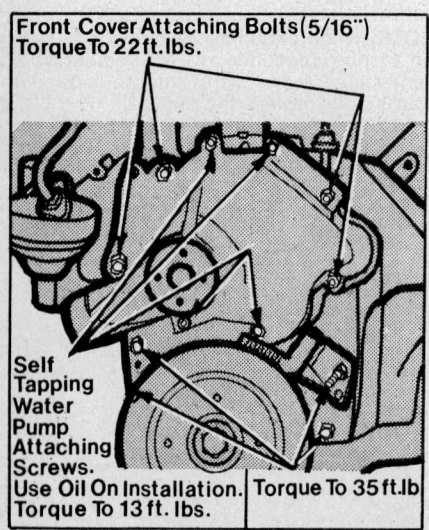

Front Cover Attaching Bolts (5/16")
Torque To 22 ft. lbs.

Self Tapping Water Pump Attaching Screws. Use Oil On Installation. Torque To 13 ft. lbs.

Torque To 35 ft. lb.

Fig. 9   Engine front cover attaching screws. V8-350

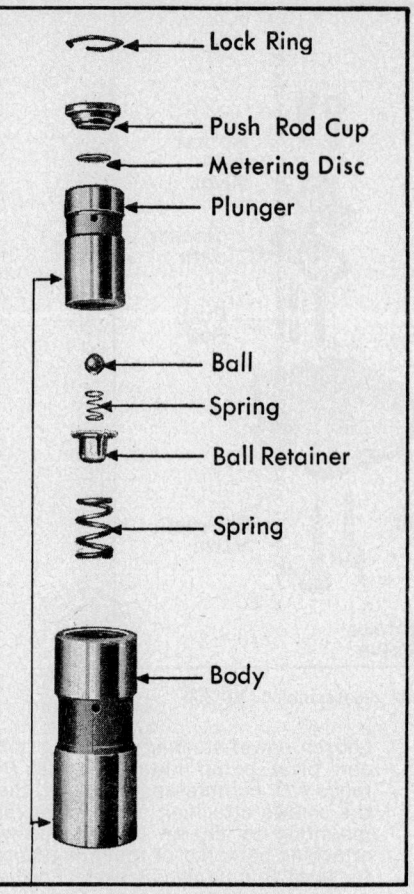

- Lock Ring
- Push Rod Cup
- Metering Disc
- Plunger
- Ball
- Spring
- Ball Retainer
- Spring
- Body

Fig. 8   Hydraulic valve lifter

VALVE GUIDES
V8-350

Valve stem to guide clearance should be .001-.003 inch. Service valves are available in standard (.343 inch) and .003, .005, .010, .013 inch oversizes. If stem to guide clearance is excessive, ream valve guide bore to the next oversize using appropriate reamer. Install proper oversize valve and valve seal. Valve seals can be identified as follows,

Intake
   Std.-.005 O.S. . . . . Gray Colored
   .010-.013 O.S. . Orange Colored
Exhaust
   Std.-.005 O.S. . . . Ivory Colored
   .010-.013 O.S. . . . Blue Colored

On occasion an engine will be manufactured with an oversize valve and valve guide bore. A number stamped on the inboard side of the head will indicate which valve and valve guide bore are oversize. The number 10 would indicate that a .010 inch oversize valve is installed in the adjacent valve guide bore.

V8-425, 472, 500

Check valve stem to valve guide clearance, clearance should be no more than .005 inch. Service valves are available in

standard (.343 inch) and .003, .006 and .013 inch oversizes. If clearance is found to be excessive, valve guide should be reamed out to next oversize using appropriate reamer, and a corresponding oversize valve installed. On some engines, valves with a .003 inch oversize diameter and .003 inch oversize valve guides are installed at the factory. Engines so fitted will be identified by a "3" stamped on the cylinder head gasket surface inline with the oversize valve.

VALVE LIFTERS

The valve lifters may be lifted out of their bores after removing the rocker arms, push rods and intake manifold. Adjustable pliers with taped jaws may be used to remove lifters that are stuck due to varnish, carbon, etc. Fig. 8 illustrates the type of lifter used.

ENGINE FRONT COVER
V8-350

1. Drain cooling system, disconnect radiator hoses, heater hose and bypass hose.

2. Remove radiator upper support and radiator.

3. Remove belts, fan, fan pully, crankshaft pully and harmonic balancer.

4. Remove oil pan, front cover attaching bolts, front cover and water pump.

5. Reverse procedure to install, refer to Fig. 9.

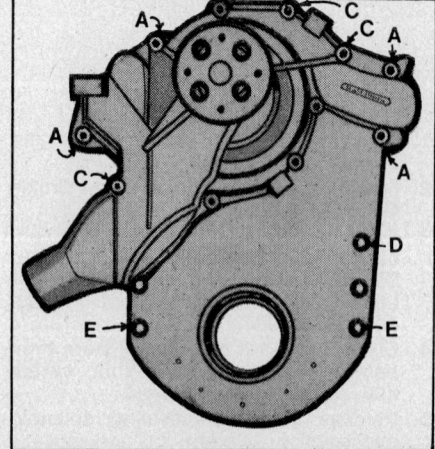

Key	(No.)	Size	Torque
A	(4)	3/8-16 x 1-3/8	25 Foot-Pounds
C	(3)	5/16-18 x 1-1/4	15 Foot-Pounds
D	(1)	5/16-18 x 5/8	15 Foot-Pounds
E	(2)	3/8-16 x 5/8	25 Foot-Pounds

Fig. 10   Engine front cover attaching screws. V8-425, 472, 500

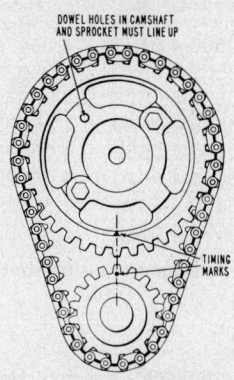

Fig. 11 Timing gear locating marks. V8-425, 472, 500

V8-425, 472, 500

1. On 1974-75 Eldorado models, remove engine from vehicle.
2. Remove harmonic balancer.
3. Loosen starter sufficiently to gain access to oil pan screws and lower front of oil pan until it clears front studs.
4. Drain radiator and remove lower hose from water pump.
5. Remove the 10 screws securing front cover to the cylinder block and remove cover with water pump as an assembly.
6. Reverse removal procedure, to install, referring to Fig. 10.

FRONT COVER OIL SEAL

V8-350

1. Remove drive belts, crankshaft pulley and harmonic balancer.
2. Using tool J-1859-03 or a suitable puller, remove front cover oil seal.

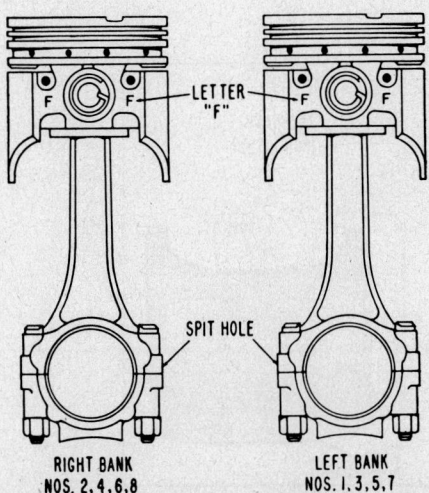

RIGHT BANK NOS. 2, 4, 6, 8
LEFT BANK NOS. 1, 3, 5, 7

Fig. 12 Piston and rod assembly. V8-350

3. Apply sealer to outside diameter of seal.
4. Position seal on front cover, then using tools No. J-25264 and J-21150, drive seal into place.
5. Install harmonic balancer and crankshaft pulley, install and adjust drive belts.

V8-425, 472, 500

1. Remove vibration damper.
2. With a thin blade screw driver or similar tool, pry out front cover oil seal.
3. Lubricate new seal and fill cavity with wheel bearing grease. Position seal on end of crankshaft with garter spring side toward engine.
4. Using a suitable installer drive seal into cover until it bottoms against cover.

TIMING CHAIN

1. Remove engine front cover as outlined above.
2. Remove two capscrews and washers that hold sprocket to camshaft.
3. Remove camshaft sprocket with chain.
4. Remove crankshaft sprocket, if necessary.
5. To install, reverse removal procedure, being sure to line up the timing marks as shown in Figs. 11 and 11A.

CAMSHAFT

V8-350

1. Disconnect battery, then remove air cleaner.
2. Drain cooling system and remove radiator, four bolts attaching A/C condenser to radiator and position condenser aside.
3. Remove crankshaft pulley and balancer, then the front cover.
4. Remove A/C compressor from engine and position aside.

NOTE: Do not disconnect refrigerant hoses from compressor.

5. Remove intake manifold as described under "Intake Manifold Replace".
6. Remove rocker covers, rocker arms, push rods and lifters.

NOTE: Note position of rocker arms, pivots, push rods and lifters to ensure installation in original position.

7. Remove camshaft.

V8-425, 472, 500

1. Remove engine front cover.
2. Remove distributor and oil pump.
3. Remove oil slinger from crankshaft.
4. Remove fuel pump and fuel pump eccentric.

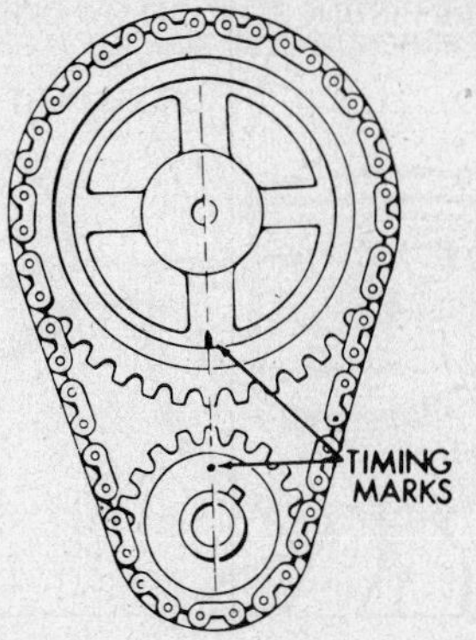

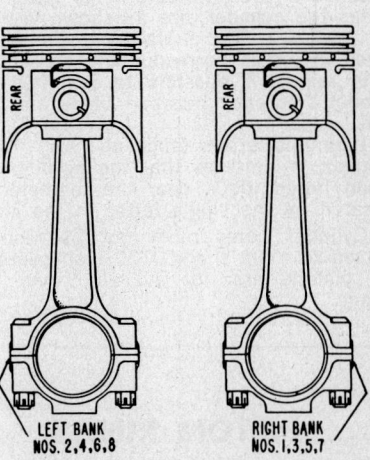

Fig. 11A Timing gear locating marks. V8-350

5. Unfasten and remove camshaft sprocket with chain attached.
6. Remove valve lifters as previously outlined.
7. Remove radiator.
8. Carefully slide camshaft forward until it is out of engine.

PISTONS & RODS ASSEMBLE

On all engines, assemble and install the piston and rod assemblies as shown in Figs. 12 & 13.

PISTONS

V8-350

Measure pistons for size, Fig. 14. Measure cylinder bore, piston to cylinder bore clearance should be .00075-.00175 inch. Measure piston for taper, the largest reading must be at the bottom of the skirt. Allowable taper is .000-.0001 inch.

LEFT BANK NOS. 2, 4, 6, 8
RIGHT BANK NOS. 1, 3, 5, 7

Fig. 13 Piston and rod assembly. V8-425, 472, 500

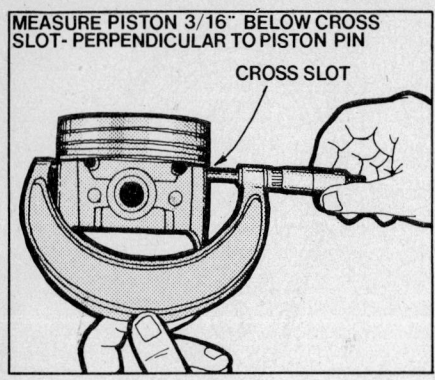

Fig. 14   Measuring piston diameter

Cylinder and piston sizes are indicated by a letter stamped on the cylinder gasket surface of the block. The letters that denote cylinder and piston sizes are listed in Fig. 15.

V8-425, 472, 500

The V8-472 and 500 engines both have identical bore sizes (4.300 inch), therefore it is important that the correct piston be installed for the engine being worked on. Refer to Fig. 16 for correct piston identification.

Pistons should be measured for size as shown in Fig. 14. Cylinders should be measured 1⅛" from the top, crosswise to the cylinder block. The clearance should be .0006-.0010" for V8-472 and 500 engines and .0006-.0014 for V8-425 engines in this position at room temperature (70°F). Subtract .0001" from measurement for every 6° above 70°.

On V8-472 and 500 engines, an identification letter is stamped on the valve lifter compartment cover next to lower inside edge of cylinder head, on V8-425 engine an identification letter is stamped on the cylinder head face of cylinder block located directly below cylinder bore. The letters are in groups of two for adjacent cylinders (such as "A" "B") midway between the two cylinders. This letter denotes the cylinder size as shown in Figs. 17 and 18. The table indicates piston sizes to match corresponding bore sizes. This makes it possible to maintain the proper clearance between block and piston.

If double letters (such as "AA" "BB") appear, it indicates that the cylinder has been bored .010" over the diameter indicated by the single letter in the chart.

Cylinder bores must not be reconditioned to more than .0100 inch oversize, as pistons are not available over this range.

PISTON RINGS

Replacement rings are available from Cadillac in standard size and .010"oversize.

PISTON PINS

V8-350

Piston pin to piston clearance should be .0003-.0005 inch. If clearance is more than .0005 inch, a new piston pin should be installed. Piston pin to connecting rod is a press fit and clearance should be .0008-.0018 inch tight fit.

V8-425, 472, 500

Piston pins are a matched fit with the piston and are not available separately. Piston pins are pressed in the connecting rods and will not become loose enough to cause a knock or tapping until after very high mileages. In such cases a new piston and pin assembly should be installed.

MAIN & ROD BEARINGS

V8-350

Main bearing clearance should not exceed .0035 inch. If clearance is more than .0035 inch replace both bearing shells. Main bearings are available in undersizes, Fig. 19.

Rod bearing clearance should not exceed .0035 inch. If clearance is more than .0035 inch replace both bearing shells and recheck clearance.

V8-425, 472, 500

Main and rod bearings are supplied by Cadillac in standard sizes only.

CRANKSHAFT OIL SEAL

V8-350

To replace upper rear main bearing seal, the crankshaft must be removed. After

Letter	Cylinder Size (Diameter in inches)	Piston Size (Diameter in inches)
A	4.0560-4.0565	4.05475-4.05525
B	4.0565-4.0570	4.05525-4.05575
C	4.0570-4.0575	4.05575-4.05625
D	4.0575-4.0580	4.05625-4.05675
J	4.0660-4.0665	4.06475-4.06525
K	4.0665-4.0670	4.06525-4.06575
L	4.0670-4.0675	4.06575-4.06625
M	4.0675-4.0680	4.06625-4.06675

Fig. 15   Cylinder and piston sizes. V8-350

removing crankshaft use tool No. J-25285 to install seal, Fig. 20.

Lower rear main bearing seal can be installed with crankshaft in place and engine in vehicle. Remove oil pan, than the rear main bearing cap. Remove bearing and seal from cap. Position new seal in groove in bearing cap. Using tool J-25285, hammer seal into groove. Rotate tool slightly, then cut seal ends flush with bearing cap surface. Pack seal end fibers away from edges, using a screw driver. Install bearing in cap, then install cap, lubricate bolt threads and torque to 120 ft. lbs. Install oil pan and lower flywheel cover.

V8-425, 472, 500

Rear main bearing installation tool can be made from shim stock or a metal banding strap using dimensions in Fig. 21. The two seal halves are identical and can be used in either the lower or upper location. However, both seal halves are pre-lubricated with a film of wax for break-in. Do not remove or damage this film.

To install the lower half of the seal into the bearing cap, slide either end of seal into position at one end of bearing cap and place tool on seal land at other end of bearing. Make sure seal is positioned over bearing ridge and lip of seal is facing forward (car position).

Hold thumb over end of seal that is flush with split line to prevent it from slipping upward, and push seal into seated position by applying pressure to the other end. Make sure seal is pressed

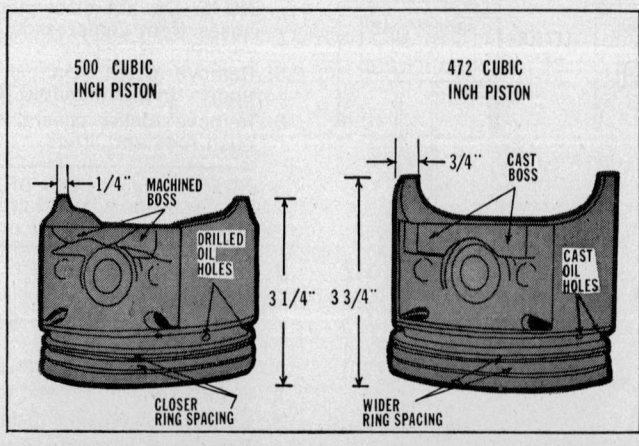

Fig. 16   Piston identification. 1974 V8-472 and 1974-76 V8-500

Cylinder and piston sizes (as indicated by letters stamped on the cylinder head gasket surface). The letters are in groups of two for adjacent cylinders (such as "H" and "B") midway between the two cylinders. The letters denote the cylinder piston sizes as shown below).

Letter	Cylinder Size (Diameter in Inches)	Piston Size (Diameter in Inches)
A	4.3000 - 4.3002	4.2992 - 4.2994
B	4.3002 - 4.3004	4.2994 - 4.2996
C	4.3004 - 4.3006	4.2996 - 4.2998
D	4.3006 - 4.3008	4.2998 - 4.3000
E	4.3008 - 4.3010	4.3000 - 4.3002
H	4.3010 - 4.3012	4.3002 - 4.3004
J	4.3012 - 4.3014	4.3004 - 4.3006
K	4.3014 - 4.3016	4.3006 - 4.3008
L	4.3016 - 4.3018	4.3008 - 4.3010
M	4.3018 - 4.3020	4.3010 - 4.3012
AA	4.3100 - 4.3102	4.3092 - 4.3094
BB	4.3102 - 4.3104	4.3094 - 4.3096
CC	4.3104 - 4.3106	4.3096 - 4.3098
DD	4.3106 - 4.3108	4.3098 - 4.3100
EE	4.3108 - 4.3110	4.3100 - 4.3102
HH	4.3110 - 4.3112	4.3102 - 4.3104
JJ	4.3112 - 4.3114	4.3104 - 4.3106
KK	4.3114 - 4.3116	4.3106 - 4.3108
LL	4.3116 - 4.3118	4.3108 - 4.3110
MM	4.3118 - 4.3120	4.3110 - 4.3112

Fig. 17 Cylinder & piston sizes. V8-425 V8-472, 500

down firmly and is flush on each side to avoid possibility of a leak at seal split line. Avoid pressing on lip as damage to sealing edge could result.

To install upper half of seal in cylinder block (with crankshaft in car), position "shoehorn" tool on land of block, Fig. 22. Start seal into groove in block with lip facing forward and rotate seal into position. Do not press on lip or sealing edge may be damaged. Both ends of seal must be flush at seal split line to avoid leaks. If necessary, Lubriplate or its equivalent may be used to facilitate installation of both upper and lower seal halves. Do not use silicone or a leak may result.

OIL PAN, REPLACE

1977-79 Except Eldorado & Seville

1. Disconnect battery ground cable.
2. Remove two screws on each side securing radiator cover to strut rods, support rods and loosen two screws at strut. Position support rods aside.
3. Remove two screws securing upper radiator shroud to radiator and one screw securing upper radiator hose clamp to shroud.
4. Drill out the six rivets securing the upper shroud to the lower shroud and remove shroud.
5. Loosen drive belts and remove crankshaft pulleys.
6. Raise vehicle and drain oil pan.
7. Remove exhaust "Y" pipe at exhaust manifold and converter.
8. Remove through bolts from engine mounts.
9. Remove starter motor.
10. Remove transmission lower cover.
11. Using a suitable jack, raise engine to gain clearance for oil pan removal
12. Remove nuts and screws securing oil pan to cylinder block.
13. Reverse procedure to install

1976-79 V8-350 Seville

1. Remove wheel housing struts from both fenders.
2. Remove fan shroud.
3. Remove front motor mount through bolts, disconnect crossover pipe at manifold.
4. Remove starter, then remove converter cover.
5. Remove oil pan attaching bolts, raise engine until pan can be removed.

1974-76 Except Eldorado & Seville

NOTE: For easier removal of the oil pan past the stabilizer bar, first remove the two front dowel studs from the block by running a jam nut on each stud to lock the pan nut on the stud. Working over the front frame crossmember, use a socket to remove the stud with the two nuts attached.

1. Disconnect battery ground cable.

Letter	Cylinder Size (Diameter in Inches)	Piston Size (Diameter in Inches)
A	4.0820-4.0824	4.0810-4.0814
B	4.0824-4.0828	4.0814-4.0818
C	4.0828-4.0832	4.0818-4.0822
D	4.0832-4.0836	4.0822-4.0826
E	4.0836-4.0840	4.0826-4.0830
AA	4.0920-4.0924	4.0910-4.0914
BB	4.0924-4.0928	4.0914-4.0918
CC	4.0928-4.0932	4.0918-4.0922
DD	4.0932-4.0936	4.0922-4.0926
EE	4.0936-4.0940	4.0926-4.0930

Fig. 18 Cylinder & piston sizes. V8-425

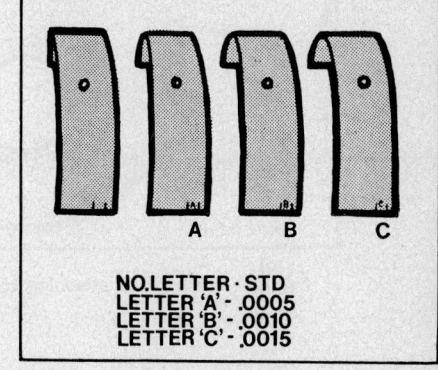

NO.LETTER · STD
LETTER 'A' - .0005
LETTER 'B' - .0010
LETTER 'C' - .0015

Fig. 19 Main bearing identification. V8-350

2. Drain engine oil.
3. Remove "Y" exhaust pipe at exhaust manifold.
4. Remove starter.
5. Unfasten and lower idler arm support.
6. Disconnect pitman arm at center link and lower steering linkage.
7. Remove transmission lower cover.
8. Unfasten and lower oil pan.

NOTE: To align the oil pan at the rear and prevent damage from the flywheel teeth during installation, first locate the oil pan on the crankcase with two screws at mid-point. Then install two

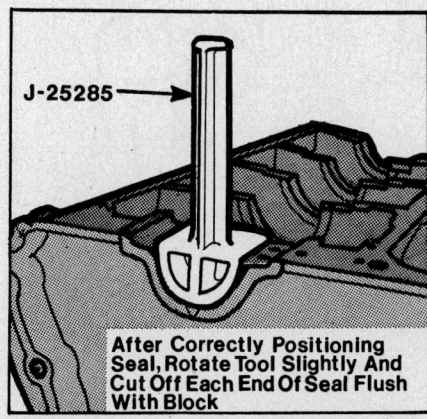

J-25285

After Correctly Positioning Seal, Rotate Tool Slightly And Cut Off Each End Of Seal Flush With Block

Fig. 20 Rear main bearing oil seal installation. V8-350

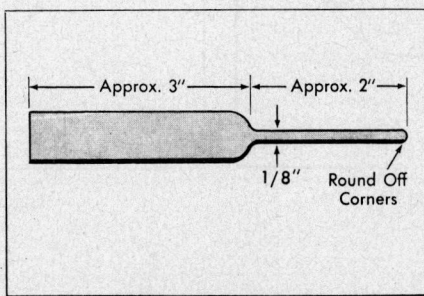

Approx. 3"   Approx. 2"
1/8"   Round Off Corners

Fig. 21 Main bearing oil seal tool. V8-425, 472, 500

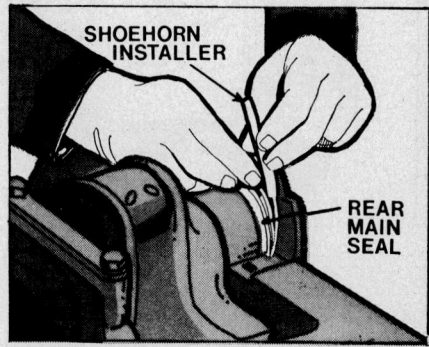

SHOEHORN INSTALLER

REAR MAIN SEAL

Fig. 22 Installing rear main bearing oil seal. V8-425, 472, 500

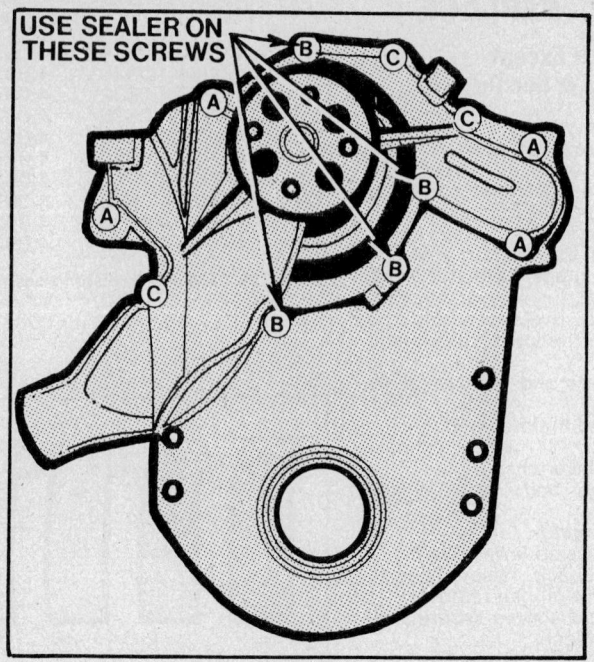

Fig. 23 Water pump attaching screws. V8-425, 472, 500

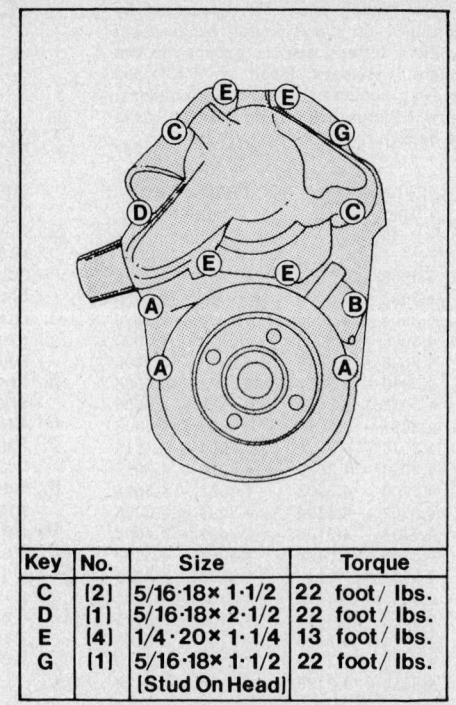

Key	No.	Size	Torque
C	[2]	5/16-18× 1-1/2	22 foot/lbs.
D	[1]	5/16-18× 2-1/2	22 foot/lbs.
E	[4]	1/4-20× 1-1/4	13 foot/lbs.
G	[1]	5/16-18× 1-1/2 (Stud On Head)	22 foot/lbs.

Fig. 24 Water pump attaching screws. V8-350

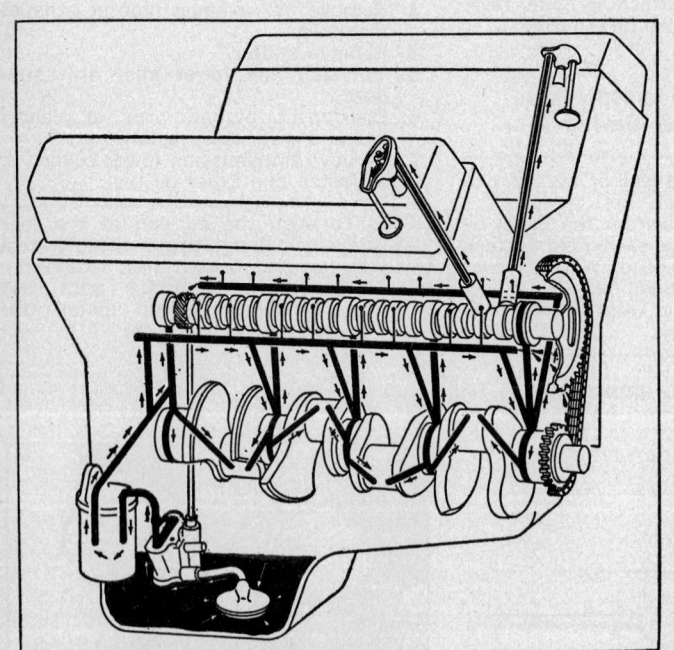

Engine oiling system. V8-350

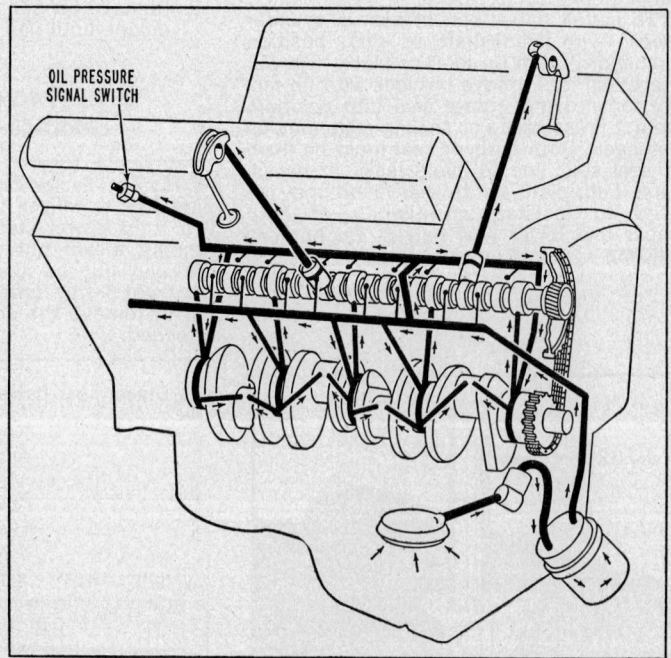

Engine oiling system. V8-425, 472, 500

screws at the rear while checking gasket alignment.

1974-79 Eldorado

To remove the oil pan it is necessary to remove the engine as described previously.

OIL PUMP
V8-350

1. Remove oil pan, then remove pump to rear main bearing attaching screws, remove pump.

V8-425, 472, 500

1. Raise car and remove oil filter.
2. Remove five screws securing pump to engine. *The screw nearest the pressure regulator should be removed last, allowing the pump to come down with screw.*
3. Remove pump drive shaft.
4. Reverse procedure to install, being sure to pack the pump with petrolatum.

BELT TENSION DATA

	New Lbs.	Used Lbs.
1974-76 Exc. Seville—		
Air Conditioning	170	120
A.I.R. Pump	170	120
Generator—		
Exc. 145 Amp.	100	70
145 Amp.	170	120
Power Steering	170	120
1976 Seville		
Air Conditioning	125	90
A.I.R. Pump	125	90
Generator	125	90
Power Steering	125	90
1977-79—		
All	110-140	60-120

WATER PUMP, REPLACE
1974-78

1. Disconnect battery ground cable.
2. Drain radiator and remove fan shroud.
3. Remove fan assembly. *On A/C cars, be sure to keep the fan clutch in the "on car" position when removed to prevent leakage of silicone fluid into clutch mechanism.*
4. Remove all drive belts.
5. Pull pump pulley off shaft.
6. Disconnect water inlet from pump.
7. On Seville models, remove A/C Compressor front bracket, A.I.R. pump bracket and support rod and power steering pump adjusting bracket.
8. Unfasten and remove pump from front cover.
9. Reverse procedure to install, being sure to install bolts as shown in Figs. 23 and 24.

FUEL PUMP PRESSURE

Year	Engine	Pressure, Lbs.
1974-79	All Exc. E.F.I.	5¼-6½

FUEL PUMP, REPLACE
1975-79 With Fuel Injection
Chassis-Mounted Fuel Pump

NOTE: The chassis-mounted fuel pump is located under the vehicle, forward of the left rear wheel on all models except Eldorado. On 1975-78 Eldorado models, the pump is mounted forward of the right rear wheel. On 1979 Eldorado models, the pump is mounted in front of the left rear suspension arm.

1979 Eldorado

1. Disconnect battery ground cable, then raise and support vehicle.
2. Release clamp and disconnect inlet hose from rear of pump.

3. Remove two screws attaching pump bracket to frame.
4. Disconnect wire connector from pump.
5. Release clamp and disconnect outlet hose at front of pump.
6. Tilt fuel pump and remove from vehicle.
7. Reverse procedure to install. Torque pump to frame attaching screws to 135 inch lbs. and hose clamps to 9 inch lbs.

Except 1979 Eldorado

1. Remove fuel inlet and outlet hoses.
2. Pull back rubber boot and remove nuts from electrical terminals, then the electrical leads.
3. Remove fuel pump to mounting bracket screws, then the fuel pump assembly.
4. Reverse procedure to install. Torque fuel pump mounting screws to 25 inch lbs. Connect 14 dark green wire to the positive terminal and the 14 black wire to the negative terminal.

In-Tank Fuel Pump

1. Remove fuel tank.
2. Remove fuel gauge tank unit locknuts and the fuel pump feed wires to tank unit.
3. Using tool J-24187, disengage lock ring from fuel tank. Remove tool and lift gauge-pump unit from tank.
4. Reverse procedure to install.

1974-79 Less Fuel Injection

1. Raise car and disconnect fuel line at pump and plug line.
2. Disconnect fuel pipe to fuel filter at pump.
3. Remove mounting screw on upper pump flange.
4. Remove nut from mounting stud at lower pump flange.
5. Tipping pump upward, pull pump straight out from engine and remove.
6. Reverse procedure to install.

Automatic Transmission

1979 AUTO. TRANS. LINKAGE ADJUSTMENTS
1979 Eldorado

Service and adjustment procedures for the Turbo Hydra-Matic 325 are located elsewhere in this manual, refer to Main Index.

1979 Except Eldorado

Linkage adjustment procedures for 1979 models are the same as those for 1974-78 models as outlined elsewhere in this manual.

NOTE: 1979 linkage adjustment information is in this section. Repair procedures on both automatic and manual shift transmissions are covered elsewhere in this manual. Procedures for removing automatic transmissions as well as linkage adjustments on 1974-78 models are included in the automatic transmission chapters. See Chapter Index.

Eldorado Drive Link Belt

For service procedure on the 1979 Eldorado, refer to Main Index

1974-78
LINK BELT OR SPROCKETS

Removal

After removal of transmission as described elsewhere in this manual, proceed as follows:

1. Remove sprocket housing cover attaching bolts and cover.
2. Remove sprocket bearing retaining snap rings from retaining grooves in support housing located under drive and driven sprockets, Fig. 1.

NOTE: Do not remove the snap rings from beneath the sprockets, leave them in a loose position between the sprockets and the bearing assemblies.

3. Remove drive and driven sprockets, link belt, bearings and shafts simultaneously by alternately pulling upwards and driven support housing, Fig. 2.

NOTE: If sprockets and link belt are difficult to remove, place a small piece of masonite, or similar material between the sprocket and a short pry bar. Alternately pry upward under each sprocket. Do not pry on links or aluminum case, Fig. 3.

4. Remove link belt from drive and driven sprockets.

Installation

1. Place link belt around the drive and driven sprockets so that the links engage the teeth of the sprockets, colored guide link which has etched numerals facing link cover.

Fig. 1   Removing or installing retaining rings

Fig. 2   Removing or installing sprockets and link assembly

Fig. 3   Removing tight sprockets

2. Simultaneously place link belt, drive and driven sprockets into support housing, Fig. 1.
3. Using a plastic mallet, gently seat the sprocket bearing assemblies into the support housings.

4. Install sprocket assembly to support housing snap rings, Fig. 2.
5. Install new case to cover and plate assembly sprocket housing gasket.

NOTE: Important: One sprocket cover housing attaching bolt is ¼ inch longer. This bolt must be installed in the tapped hole located directly over the cooler fittings on the transmission case.

6. Install sprocket housing cover and plate assembly and eighteen attaching bolts. Torque bolts to 8 ft. lbs.

Rear Axle, Propeller Shaft & Brakes

For 1979 Eldorado rear axle & drive axle service procedures refer to Main Index

REAR AXLE

1974-78 Eldorado

On these axles the rear wheel spindles are a press fit and bolted to the rear axle, Figs. 1 and 1A. As shown, tapered roller bearings and are used in the rear wheels. These bearings do not require regularly scheduled repacking. When major brake service work is to be performed, however, it is recommended that the bearings be cleaned and repacked.

Wheel Bearing Adjustment

Adjustment of the rear wheel bearings should be made while revolving the wheel at least three times the speed of the nut rotation when taking torque readings.

1. Check to make sure that hub is completely seated on wheel spindle.
2. While rotating wheel, tighten spindle nut to 30 ft-lbs. Make certain all parts are properly seated and that threads are free.
3. Back nut off ½ turn, then retighten nut to 2 ft. lbs. and install cotter pin.
4. If cotter pin cannot be installed in either of the two holes in the spindle, with the nut at 2 ft. lbs., back nut off until cotter pin can be installed.
5. The rear hub must be rotated at least

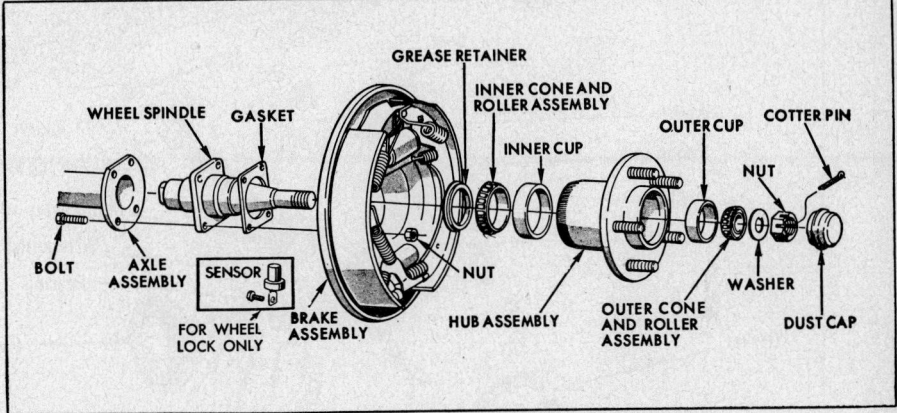

Fig. 1   Rear wheel spindle disassembled. 1974-75 Eldorado (typical)

three revolutions during tightening of spindle nut. The final adjustment to be 2 ft. lbs. to provide .004″ bearing end play.
6. Peen end of cotter pin snug against side of nut. If it can be moved with a finger, vibration may cause it to wear and break.

Wheel Spindle, Replace

1. Raise and support rear of vehicle.
2. Remove tire and wheel assembly.
3. Remove rear brake drum or caliper and disc assembly.
4. Remove dust cap, cotter pin, spindle nut, washer and outer cone and roller bearing assembly.
5. Carefully pull hub off spindle.
6. On vehicles with rear drum brakes:
   a. If equipped with Track Master, loosen sensor mounting screw, and pull sensor downward, part way out of installed position. This will avoid possible damage to sensor when hub is reinstalled.
   b. Disconnect brake line from brake cylinder, then remove backing plate retaining nuts and position backing plate out of the way.

CAUTION: Do not allow backing plate to hang unsupported, as parking brake cable or sensor wiring harness can be damaged.

7. On vehicles with rear disc brakes, remove the four nuts retaining spindle to axle housing.
8. Install one axle housing to spindle nut just far enough to engage threads, then using a slide hammer puller, pull spindle from axle housing.
9. Remove the remaining nut and bolt and remove spindle.

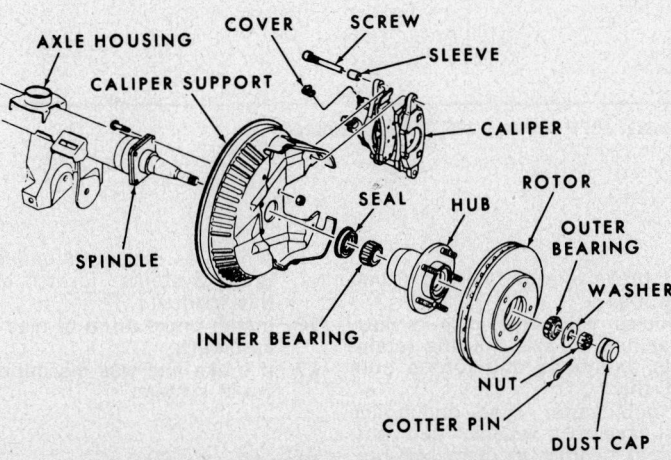

Fig. 1A   Rear wheel spindle disassembled. 1976-78 Eldorado

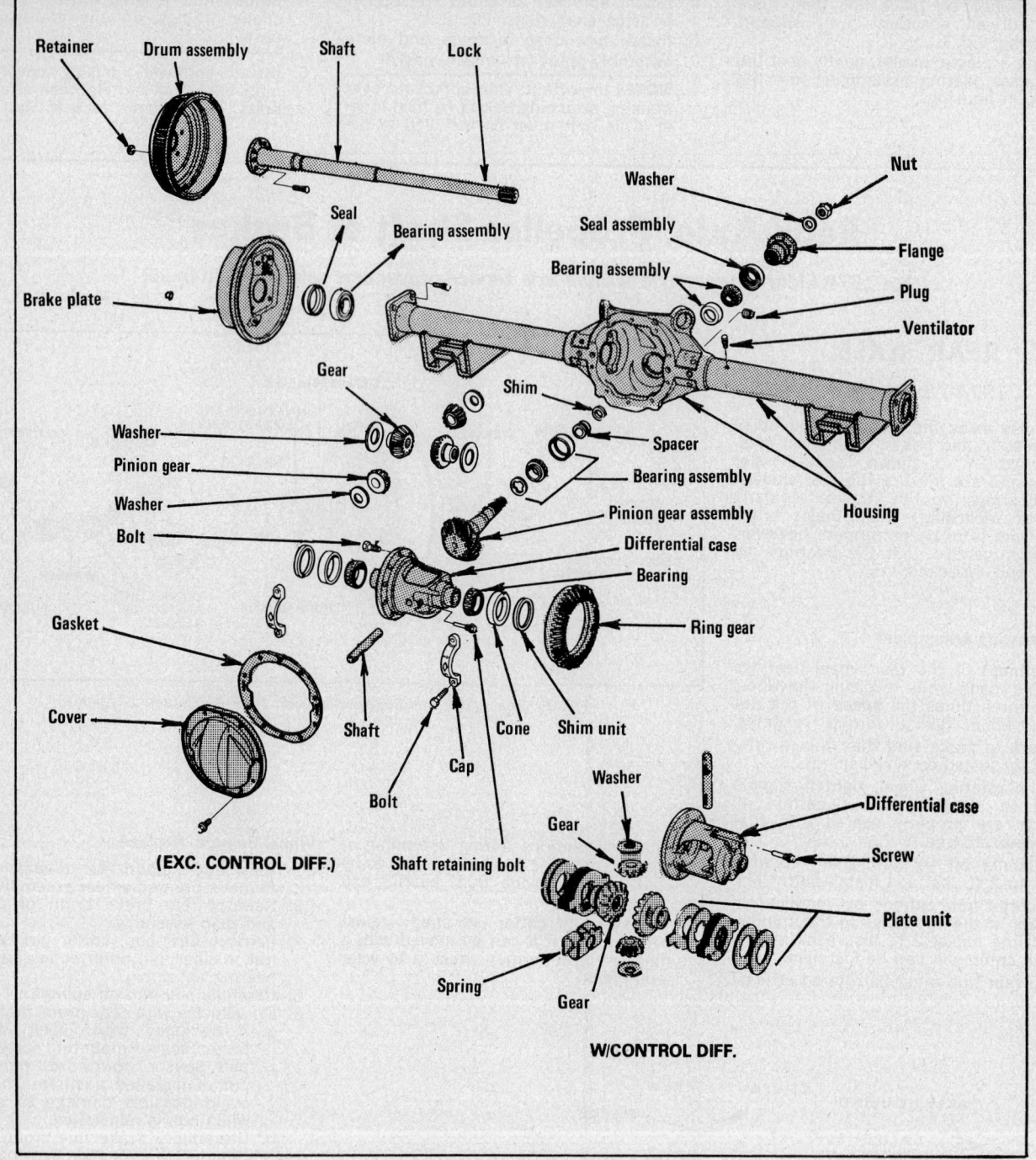

Fig. 2   Rear axle assembly. 1976 Seville & 1977-79 Exc. Eldorado

NOTE: If spindle threads were damaged during removal, use a ¾"-20 thread chaser to repair threads.

10. To install, use a slide hammer puller and drive spindle into axle until spindle is fully seated.
11. Install a new gasket on wheel spindle.
12. On vehicles with rear drum brakes, reinstall backing plate and torque retaining nuts to 40 ft. lbs., then re-connect brake line and torque fitting to 14 ft. lbs.
13. On vehicles with rear disc brakes, install spindle to axle housing retaining nuts and bolts and torque nuts to 40 ft. lbs.
14. Install hub, outer cone and roller bearing assembly, washer and nut. Adjust rear bearing as described previously.
15. On vehicles with Track Master, adjust sensor as described under "Anti-Skid Brake Systems" located elsewhere in this manual.
16. Install brake drum or disc and caliper assembly.
17. If brake line was disconnected, bleed brake system.

Rear Axle, Replace

1. Raise and support vehicle with jack

stands placed underneath frame side rails.

2. On 1974 models, remove stabilizer bar.
3. Using a suitable jack, support weight of axle by raising it about ⅜ inch.
4. Remove brake drums or disc and caliper assembly.
5. Remove hubs.
6. If equipped with Track Master, disconnect wiring connectors from sensor harness and brake pipe and position harness out of the way.
7. On vehicles with rear drum brakes, disconnect brake lines at wheel cylinders and remove the four brake backing plate nuts.

CAUTION: Do not allow backing plate to hang unsupported, as parking brake cable can be damaged.

8. Disconnect rubber brake hose and plug hose to minimize fluid leakage.
9. Disconnect overtravel link from bracket and deflate shock absorbers.
10. On vehicles with rear drum brakes, remove screw retaining rear brake pipe distributor to axle and disconnect brake pipes from the four retaining clips.
11. Disconnect shock absorbers at lower mounts, then raise axle to relieve tension on upper control arms and remove bolt and nut retaining each upper control arm to axle brackets.

CAUTION: Stand clear of axle assembly before performing next step, as springs can snap from their seats, resulting in personal injury or damage.

12. Carefully lower axle assembly until spring tension is relieved, then remove springs.
13. Remove bolt and nut retaining each lower control arm to axle brackets.

NOTE: It may be necessary to rotate axle slightly to remove bolts.

14. Remove rubber bumpers from top of axle housing, then lower axle assembly and remove from vehicle.
15. Reverse procedure to install.
16. Torque upper control arm bolts at frame end to 145 ft. lbs. and at axle end to 110 ft. lbs. Torque lower control arm bolts to 145 ft. lbs. Torque shock absorber lower mounting nuts to 50 ft. lbs. Torque spindle or brake backing retaining nuts to 40 ft. lbs.
17. On vehicles with Track Master, adjust sensor as described under "Anti-Skid Brake Systems" located elsewhere in this manual.

1976 Seville & 1977-79 Exc. Eldorado

In this axle, Fig. 2, the rear axle housing and differential carrier are cast into an integral assembly. The drive pinion assembly is mounted in two opposed tapered roller bearings. The pinion bearings are preloaded by a spacer behind the front bearing. The pinion is positioned by a washer between the head of the pinion and the rear bearing.

The differential is supported in the carrier by two tapered roller side bearings. These bearings are preloaded by spacers

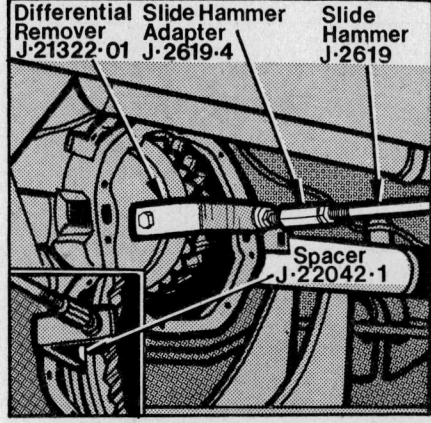

Fig. 3   Removing differential. 1976 Seville & 1977-79 Exc. Eldorado

located between the bearings and carrier housing. The differential assembly is positioned for proper ring gear and pinion backlash by varying these spacers. The differential case houses two side gears in mesh with two pinions mounted on a pinion shaft which is held in place by a lock pin. The side gears and pinions are backed by thrust washers.

Rear Axle, Replace 1977-79 Exc. Eldorado & Seville

1. Raise vehicle and support rear axle and frame.
2. Disconnect overtravel lever from link, if equipped.
3. Remove shock absorbers from lower mount.
4. Place jack under front differential to relieve tension on lower control arm.
5. Remove upper and lower control arms as outlined under "Control Arms and Bushings, Replace" procedure in Rear Suspension Section.
6. Remove propeller shaft and support with wire.
7. Remove brake hose at differential housing and plug.

CAUTION: If axle is allowed to wind up as it is lowered, springs may snap from their seats and could cause injury or damage. Use extreme caution to prevent wind-up condition.

8. Lower axle shaft and remove springs from vehicle.

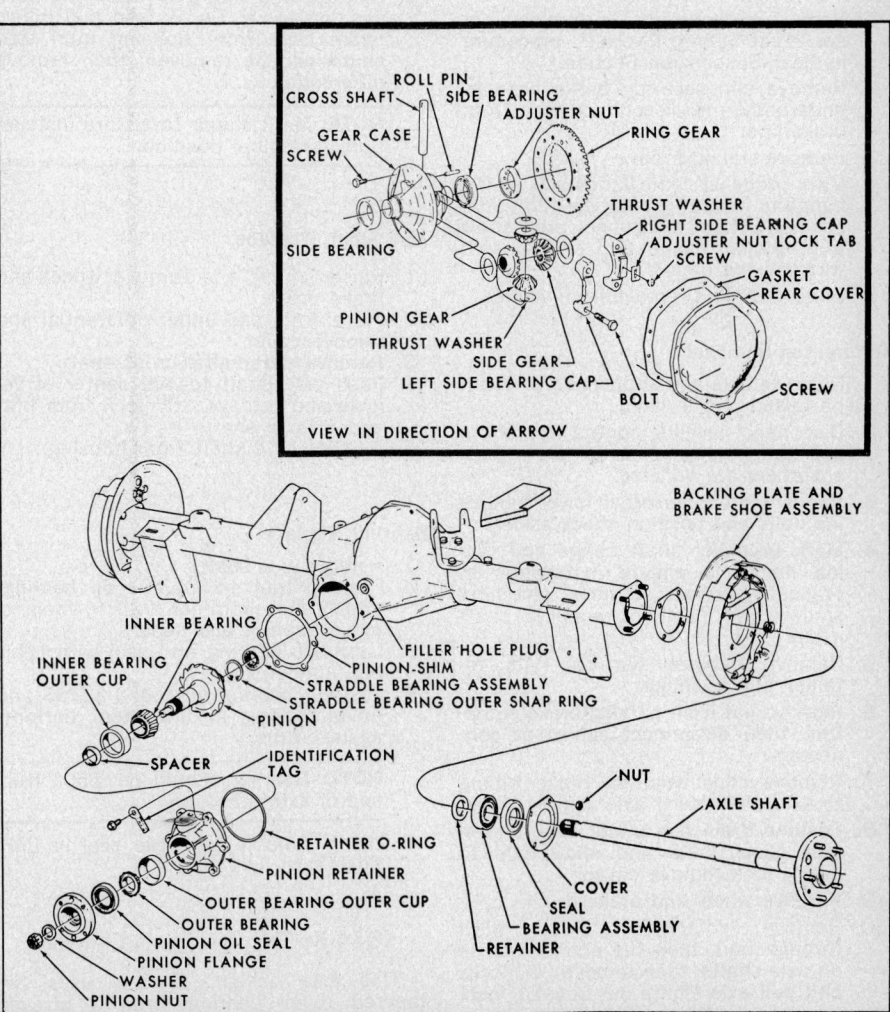

Fig. 4   Rear axle assembly. 1974-76 exc. Seville & Eldorado

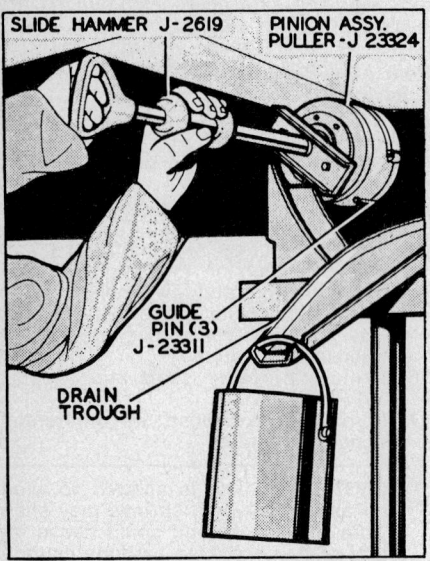

Fig. 5   Removing pinion assembly.
1974-76 standard cars exc. Seville

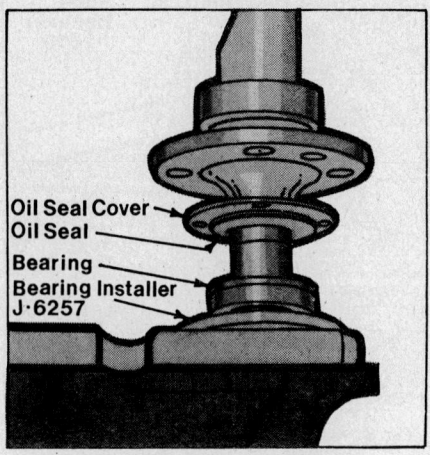

Fig. 6   Installing wheel bearing.
1974-76 standard cars exc. Seville

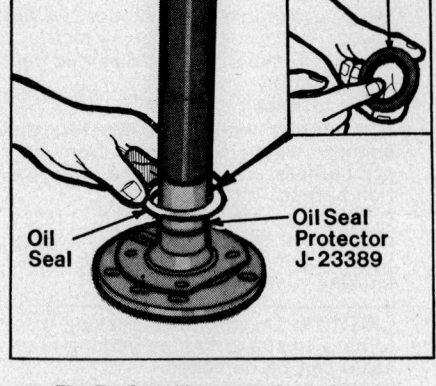

Fig. 7   Installing rear wheel oil seal.
1974-76 exc. Seville & Eldorado

Rear Axle, Replace 1976-79 Seville

1. Remove rear springs as outlined under "Leaf Spring, Replace" procedure in Rear Suspension Section.
2. Remove clip securing brake hose to underbody and disconnect hose from brake line.
3. Remove stabilizer bar.
4. Mark propeller shaft flange and pinion flange to insure installation in original position. Then, disconnect prop shaft from pinion flange and secure with wire to underbody.
5. Lower axle and remove from vehicle.

Differential Removal

1. Raise vehicle and support so axle can be raised and lowered.
2. Disconnect leveling control lever from link and hold lever down until shock absorbers are deflated.
3. Remove shock absorber lower mounting bolts and position shock aside.
4. Mark propeller shaft flange and pinion flange to ensure installation in original position. Remove attaching screws and position propeller shaft aside.
5. Remove stabilizer bar link nuts, retainer and bushings.
6. Remove nut from parking brake equalizer, then disconnect cables at connectors.
7. Remove clips securing brake tubing to axle, then lower axle slightly.
8. Position drain pan under axle, loosen rear cover bolts and allow axle to drain, then remove cover.
9. Remove wheel and brake drum.
10. Remove differential cross shaft through bolt, then the shaft. Push in on axle shafts, then remove "C" locks and pull axle shafts out about 1 inch.
11. Install cross shaft and bolt, then remove side bearing cap and bearing.

NOTE: Mark bearing caps to ensure installation in original position.

12. Remove one ring gear attaching bolt, position tools, Fig. 3, and pull differential case from housing until side shims can be removed, then remove differential.

NOTE: Mark shims to ensure installation in original position.

Axle Shaft, Replace

1. Raise vehicle and remove wheel and brake drum.
2. Place drain pan under differential and remove cover.
3. Remove differential cross shaft.
4. Push axle shaft toward center of vehicle and remove "C" lock from butt end of axle shaft.
5. Remove axle shaft from housing.

Bearing Replace

1. Remove axle shaft.
2. Position tool J-22813-01 on bearing, attach slide hammer J-2619, then remove bearing and seal.
3. Lubricate bearing and seal with bearing lubricant.
4. Position bearing on tool J-23765 and drive bearing in until tool bottoms against tube.

NOTE: Bearing should be .550" from end of axle tube.

5. Using suitable tool, tap seal in until flush with axle tube.

1974-76 Exc. Seville & Eldorado

This axle design, Fig. 4, uses two tapered roller bearings and a straight roller straddle bearing to support the pinion and provide rigidity. Adjustment of the pinion is done by the use of shims at the pinion retainer to differential carrier connection. Pinion-ring gear backlash adjustment of .005-.010" is accomplished through the use of a shim located to the left of the left side bearing. The differential preload is adjusted by means of an adjuster nut that is retained under the right side bearing cap which in addition to the shim provides the correct backlash.

The rear wheel bearing is called a "unit bearing". It is a tapered roller bearing that is completely assembled as a unit.

Differential Removal

1. Raise car on a hoist.
2. Remove wheel shields, rotors, wheels and brake drums.
3. Remove four nuts that secure retainer and backing to rear axle housing.
4. Attach a suitable tool to axle shaft and remove axle shafts.
5. Install two nuts on backing plate mounting studs to prevent plates from falling and damaging brake lines.
6. Remove two attaching screws and lockwashers that secure differential carrier nose bumper arm.
7. Support propeller shaft with a chain and disconnect shaft at axle flange.
8. Place a drain pan under differential and remove axle housing cover.
9. Remove five pinion retainer to carrier screws and loosen remaining screw.

CAUTION: Do not remove remaining screw.

10. Install guide pins, Fig. 5.
11. Position drain pan under pinion retainer and attach puller.
12. Using slide hammer, unseat pinion from carrier, removing remaining screw and slide pinion assembly over guide pins and out of carrier.
13. Remove adjuster lock tab, bearing caps, adjuster nut and remove carrier case.

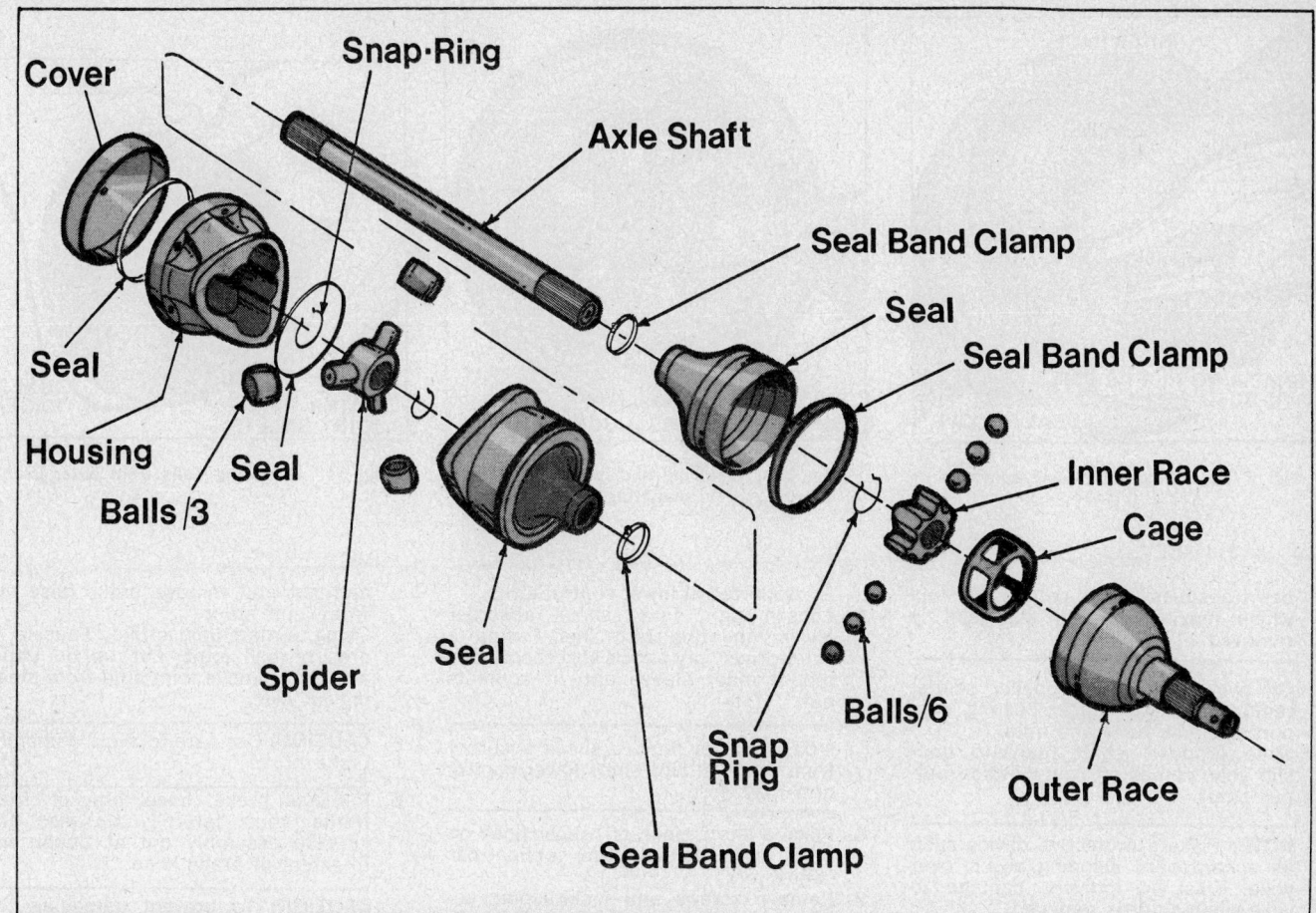

Fig. 8 Eldorado drive axle, exploded

Axle Shaft, Replace

1. Raise car and remove wheel and brake drum.
2. Remove axle retaining nuts and lockwashers.
3. Attach slide type puller and remove axle shaft.

NOTE: When removing axle shaft, the bearing may separate leaving the outer race in the housing. This is normal and does not indicate failure. If the bearing is to be replaced, make sure the old bearing outer race is removed from the housing.

Removing Bearings

1. Remove axle shaft.
2. Using a cold chisel and hammer, split bearing retainer next to bearing, being careful not to damage bearing or shaft.

NOTE: Bearing retainer must be completely split. Drive chisel into retainer until it separates and remove retainer.

3. Stand axle upright on flanged end and using two screwdrivers pry seal away from bearing.
4. Position shaft in a press and press shaft out of bearing.
5. To reassemble, install bearing cover on shaft with raised side of cover against shaft flange, Fig. 6.
6. Install seal protector on shaft with small end of protector toward splined end of shaft, Fig. 7.
7. Lubricate lip of seal and install by pressing down over protector. Seal is properly installed when the lip of the seal clears the large end of the protector.
8. Position bearing on shaft with narrow ring of bearing facing flanged end of shaft.
9. Press bearing on shaft until bearing bottoms against shoulder on shaft.
10. Position retainer on shaft with chamfer on retainer next to bearing.
11. Press retainer on shaft until retainer bottoms against bearing.

PROPELLER SHAFT

IMPORTANT

If drive line shudder, roughness, vibra-tion or rumble is experienced, it may be due to misalignment of the propeller shaft assembly. To make this check, however, a special Propeller Shaft Alignment Gauge Set. No. J-8905 must be used. Inasmuch as this equipment is not likely to be found in general repair shops, it is recommended that a Cadillac dealer having this equipment do the work.

1. Raise vehicle on hoist with transmission in neutral.

NOTE: Mark propeller shaft relationship to axle pinion flange to maintain balance.

2. Remove propeller shaft flange retaining bolts.

CAUTION: Do not allow propeller shaft to be supported by front or center universal joint, as damage to universal joint may result. Rear of propeller shaft must be supported to underbody of vehicle.

3. Pull propeller shaft forward to clear pinion flange and support rear end of shaft.

NOTE: Place a suitable container un-

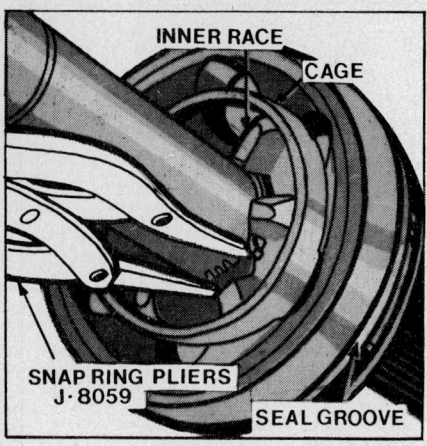

Fig. 9   Removing outer joint from axle

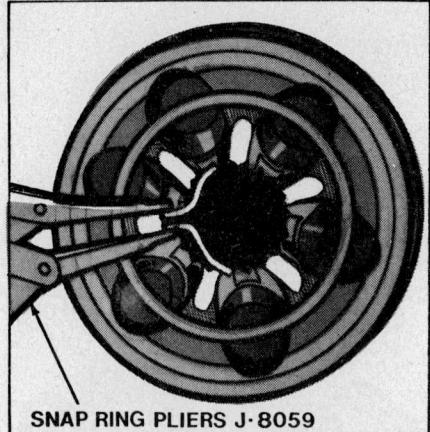

Fig. 10   Removing and installing inner snap ring

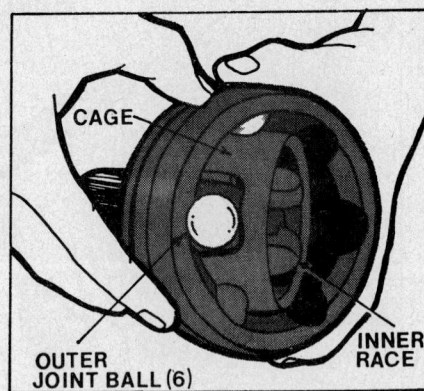

Fig. 11   Removing balls from outer joint

der transmission, to catch any fluid which may leak when slip joint is removed.

4. On two piece type propeller shafts, remove the two center bearing support to frame bolts and nuts.
5. Slide propeller shaft rearward until slip yoke comes off transmission output shaft.

NOTE: Place a protective device such as a cardboard shipping cover, over yoke. This will prevent damage to yoke when shaft is removed.

6. Remove shaft and install a spare yoke into transmission extension housing to prevent loss of oil.
7. Reverse procedure to install. Torque flange attaching bolts to 70 ft. lbs.
8. Check transmission oil.

ELDORADO DRIVE AXLES

General Description

Each drive axle, Fig. 8, consists of an axle shaft, with a ball type constant velocity joint at the outboard end and a tri-pot type at the inboard end. The torsional damper on the right hand shaft is not serviceable and must be replaced as a unit.

The inboard joint is not only flexible to operate at various angles, but can also move in and out as required by suspension movement.

Right Drive Axle

1974-78
1. Disconnect battery ground cable and remove wheel and the wheel disc.

NOTE: If drive axle is to be removed, remove cotter pin and loosen but do not remove spindle nut.

2. Raise vehicle so front vehicle weight

is supported at lower control arms.
3. Loosen right front shock absorber lower mounting nut, then, using a screwdriver, pry shock absorber at the mount inner sleeve until it contacts nut.

NOTE: Do not remove shock absorber from lower mount since lower control arm may drop.

4. Place a short piece of rubber hose on both lower control arm torsion bar connectors.
5. Remove screws and lockwashers securing right drive axle to output shaft.
6. Position inboard end of axle rearward toward starter to provide access to output shaft.
7. Remove output shaft support strut to final drive housing screw, then the two screws securing right output shaft support to the engine.
8. Slide output shaft outboard to disengage splines, then move inboard end of the assembly forward and downward until clear of vehicle.
9. Using a block of wood and a hammer, strike end of drive axle to unseat axle at hub.

NOTE: Loosen spindle nut just enough to allow axle to unseat.

10. Rotate axle inboard and forward, guiding axle over front cross-member and from under vehicle.

Left Drive Axle

1974-78
1. Raise and support vehicle with jack stands underneath frame side rails.
2. Remove wheel and tire and drive axle spindle nut.
3. Remove the six drive axle to output shaft screws and lockwashers.

NOTE: Discard the six screws and lockwashers. Use new ones during reassembly.

4. Loosen shock absorber upper bolt, then remove the ball joint cotter pin

and nut and remove brake hose clip from joint stud.
5. Using a hammer, strike, knuckle in area of ball joint. Lift up on upper arm and remove joint stud from steering knuckle.

CAUTION: Use care to avoid damaging brake hose.

6. Remove brake hose bracket from frame, then carefully tip disc and knuckle assembly out at upper end to extent of brake hose.

CAUTION: To prevent damaging the brake hose, wire the assembly to upper control arm so that brake hose does not support weight of knuckle assembly.

7. Rotate inner end of drive axle toward front of vehicle, then guide drive axle out of knuckle and remove drive axle.
8. Remove output shaft retaining bolt.

NOTE: To prevent output shaft from rotating, install two screws in output shaft flange.

9. Remove output shaft by pulling straight out.

CAUTION: Use care when removing output shaft to avoid damaging oil seal.

Outer Constant Velocity Joint

1. Remove inner and outer seal clamps by cutting with a chisel and slide seal down axle shaft to gain access to joint.
2. Wipe excess grease from joint and spread snap ring and slide joint off spline, Fig. 9.
3. Remove inner race snap ring, Fig. 10.
4. Hold constant velocity joint in one hand then tilt cage and inner race so that one ball can be removed, Fig. 11. Continue until all balls have been

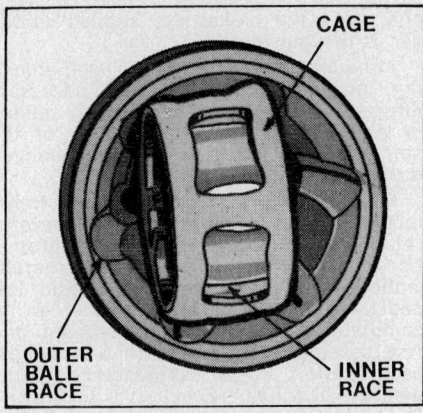

Fig. 12   Removing cage and inner race

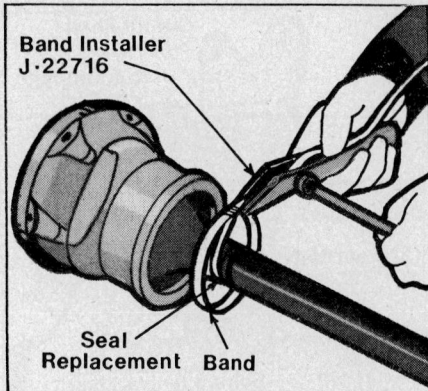

Fig. 14   Installing new seal clamp

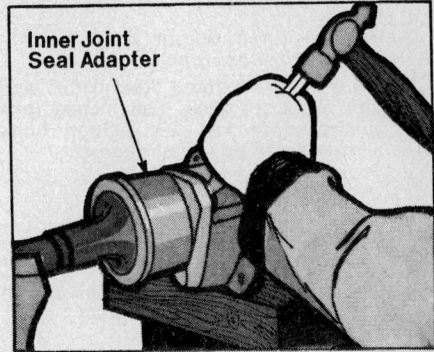

Fig. 15   Removing seal adapter

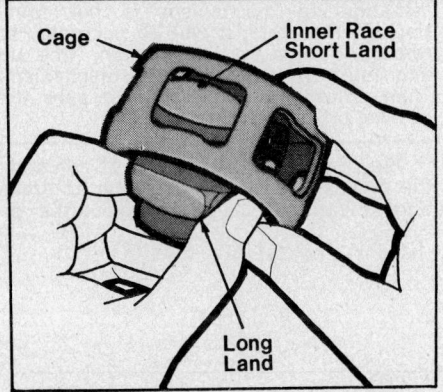

Fig. 13   Removing inner race from cage

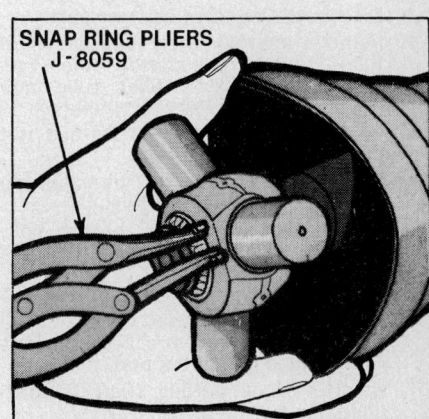

Fig. 16   Removing spider snap ring

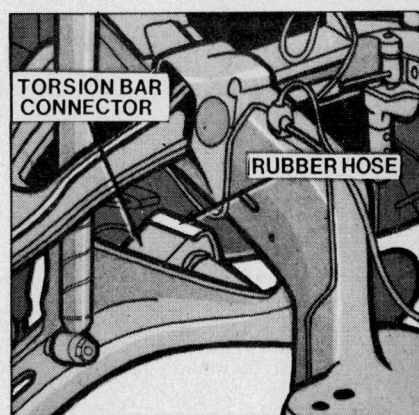

Fig. 17   Installing seal adapter on joint housing

removed.

NOTE: It may be necessary to tap the outer cage to rotate it.

5. Turn cage 90° with slot in cage aligned with short land on outer race and lift cage out of race, Fig. 12.
6. Turn short land of inner race 90° in line with hole in cage. Lift land on inner race up through hole in cage, then turn up and out to separate, Fig. 13.
7. Reverse procedure to install, using new seal clamps, Fig. 14. Cut off excess strap.

Inner Constant Velocity Joint

1. Remove small seal clamp bank by cutting it with a chisel.
2. Remove large end of seal from joint housing by prying up crimped edge on seal adapter. Drive seal adapter and seal off of joint housing with hammer and chisel, Fig. 15.

NOTE: Use care when removing seal adapter not to damage it or the seal.

3. Slide seal and adapter down axle shaft until joint is exposed.

NOTE: Do not allow spider leg balls to fall off by accident as adapter is moved.

4. Remove spider leg balls.
5. Remove spider outer snap ring, Fig. 16.
6. Tap spider assembly from shaft.
7. Reverse procedure to install, being sure to stake seal adapter to joint housing, Fig. 17.

Right Hand Output Shaft

1. Disconnect negative battery cable.
2. Raise car and install a short length of rubber hose on lower control arm torsion bar connector, Fig. 18.
3. Remove six drive axle-to-output shaft bolts and lock washers.
4. Remove output shaft support mounting bolts.

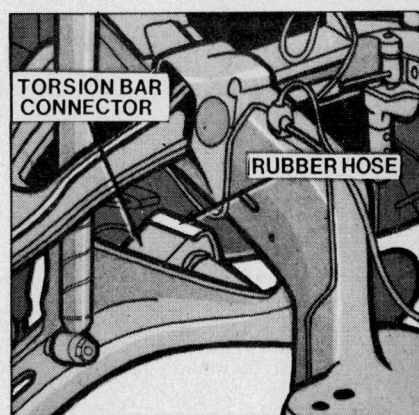

Fig. 18   Rubber hose location

5. Rotate inboard end of drive axle rearward.
6. Pull output shaft out until it clears final drive then lower splined end and remove from car.

Right Hand Output Shaft Bearing, Replace

1. Remove output shaft as described

above.

2. Remove three output shaft bearing retainer-to-support bolts.
3. Using two fabricated steel plates and four ⅜ x 24 bolts five inches long illustrated in Fig. 19, tighten bolts alternately to press out bearing.

Left Hand Output Shaft

1. Remove left drive axle.
2. Remove output shaft retaining bolt and pull shaft out of final drive.

Final Drive, Replace

The final drive unit is not serviced but is replaced as a unit.

1. Disconnect negative battery cable.
2. Remove approximately one gallon of fluid from transmission then remove transmission filler tube and plug tube hole.
3. Remove bolts "A" and "B" and nut "H", Fig. 20.
4. Remove bolt securing transmission oil cooler lines to final drive.
5. Remove nut from large through bolt, final drive support bracket to final drive.
6. Disconnect left front engine mount support bracket from engine. And final drive support bracket from left front engine mount support.
7. Remove right output shaft as outlined above.
8. Remove six left output shaft-to-drive axle bolts and lock washers.
9. Loosen final drive cover screws and drain fluid, then remove cover.
10. Compress left hand inner constant velocity joint and secure drive axle to frame with a piece of wire to provide clearance.
11. Disconnect left tie strut from crossmember and loosen strut to side rail bolt. Then rotate strut outboard until clear of final drive.
12. Remove final drive support bracket.
13. Remove remaining final drive-to-transmission bolts and nut "G".
14. Disengage final drive splines from transmission.

NOTE: To avoid damage to seals, final drive unit should be supported by a suitable jack and proper alignment must be maintained throughout removal.

15. Remove final drive unit from underside of car by sliding unit toward front of car, permitting ring gear to rotate up over steering linkage and work unit free from car.
16. Reverse procedure to install, being very careful to maintain proper final drive-to-transmission alignment to prevent seal damage.

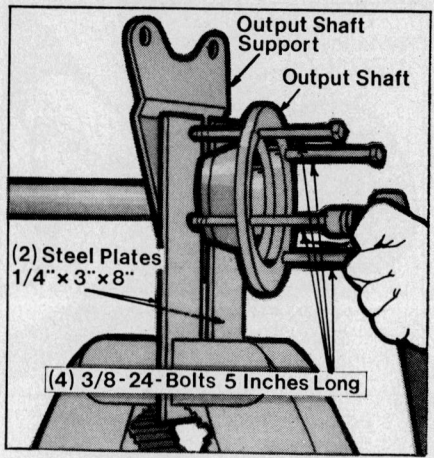

Fig. 19 Removing right hand output shaft support and bearing

DRUM BRAKE ADJUSTMENTS

Self-Adjusting Brakes

These brakes, Fig. 21, have self-adjusting shoe mechanisms that assure correct lining-to-drum clearances at all times. The automatic adjusters operate only when the brakes are applied as the car is moving rearward.

Although the brakes are self-adjusting, an initial adjustment is necessary after the brake shoes have been relined or replaced, or when the length of the star wheel adjuster has been changed during some other service operation.

Frequent usage of an automatic transmission forward range to halt reverse vehicle motion may prevent the automatic adjusters from functioning, thereby inducing low pedal heights. Should low pedal heights be encountered, it is recommended that numerous forward and reverse stops be made with a moderate pedal effort until satisfactory pedal height is obtained.

NOTE

If a low pedal height condition cannot be corrected by making numerous reverse stops (provided the hydraulic system is free of air) it indicates that the self-adjusting mechanism is not functioning. Therefore, it will be necessary to remove the brake drum, clean, free up and lubricate the adjusting mechanism. Then adjust the brakes, being sure the parking brake is fully released.

The recommended method of adjusting the brakes is by using the Drum-to-Brake Shoe Clearance Gauge to check the di-

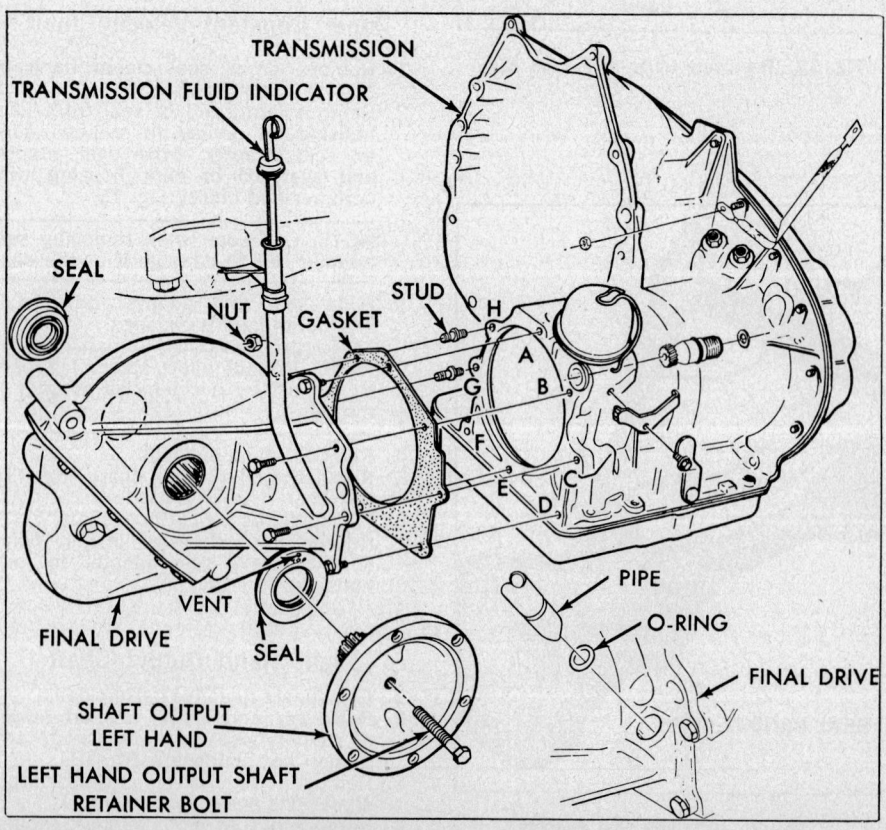

Fig. 20 Final drive attachment

ameter of the brake drum inner surface, Fig. 22, Turn the tool to the opposite side and fit over the brake shoes by turning the star wheel until the gauge just slides over the linings, Fig. 23. Rotate the gauge around the brake shoe lining surface to assure proper clearance.

PARKING BRAKE, ADJUST

1976-79 W/Rear Disc Brakes

1. Lubricate parking brake cables at equalizer and underbody rub points. Check all cables for freedom of operation.
2. Fully release parking brake and raise vehicle.
3. Hold cable stud from turning and tighten equalizer nut until cable slack is removed and levers are against stops on caliper housing. If levers are off stops, loosen cable until levers return to stop.
4. Operate parking brake several times to check adjustment. When properly adjusted, the parking brake pedal should move 4 to 5" on 1976 Eldorado, 5¼ to 6¾" on 1977-79 models except Seville and 1978-79 Eldorado, 6¼ to 7¼" on 1977-79 Seville, 4 to 5½" on 1978-79 Eldorado when a force of about 125 pounds is applied.

1974-79 W/Rear Drum Brakes

1. With service brakes properly adjusted, lubricate parking brake linkage at equalizer and cable stud with heat-resistant lubricant, and check for free movement of cables.
2. Depress parking brake pedal about 1" on 1974-75 models and 1976 Seville and 1½" on 1976-79 models except Seville from full released position.
3. Raise rear wheels off floor.

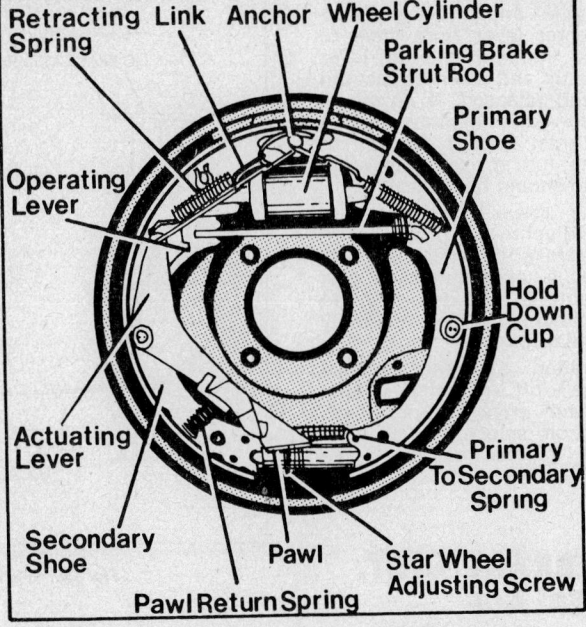

Fig. 21   Rear drum brake. Except 1976-78 Eldorado

4. Hold brake cable and stud from turning and tighten equalizer nut until a slight drag is felt on either wheel (going forward). After each turn of equalizer nut, check to see if either wheel begins to drag.
5. Release parking brake. No brake drag should be felt at either rear wheel. Operate several times to check adjustment.

VACUUM RELEASE PARKING BRAKE

1974-79

The foot-operated parking brake is mounted on the cowl to the left of the steering column. It incorporates a vacuum release, Fig. 24, operated by a vacuum diaphragm that is connected to the parking brake mechanism. When the transmission selector is moved into any Drive position, a vacuum valve in the neutral safety switch opens, allowing diaphragm to be actuated by engine vacuum.

The diaphragm is connected by a link to a release mechanism on the parking brake. Vacuum acting on the diaphragm unlocks the parking brake pedal, permitting it to return to the release position by spring action. Any abnormal leaks in the vacuum release system will prevent proper brake release. A manual release is provided and may be used if the automatic release is inoperative or if manual release is desired at any time.

NOTE: Under some conditions, aided by cold weather, the parking brake vacuum release valve (integral with the back-up light switch on steering column) may not release the parking brake automatically. Although when the brake is applied, the "Brake" indicator light will go on, brake can be released manually. If this condition is present the back-up light switch must be replaced.

Testing Vacuum Release

1. If the mechanism is inoperative, first check for damaged or kinked vacuum hoses and for loose hose connections at the diaphragm, vacuum release valve at neutral safety switch, and at engine manifold connection.
2. Check adjustment of neutral safety switch and operation of vacuum release valve.

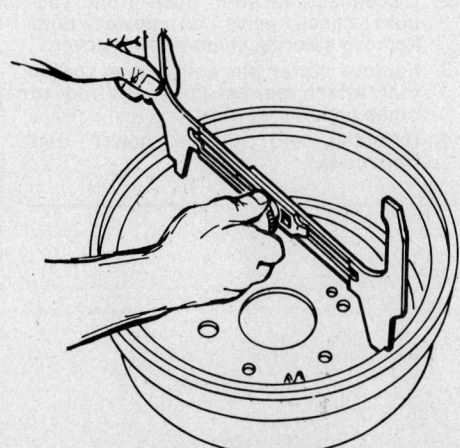

Fig. 22   Measuring brake drum inner diameter

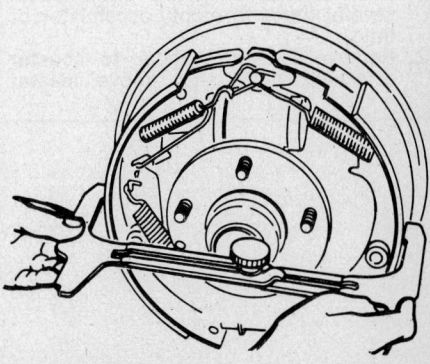

Fig. 23   Checking brake shoe lining clearance

3. Check diaphragm piston travel by running engine and moving transmission selector lever from drive to neutral. The manual release lever should move up and down as vacuum is applied and released. If no movement is observed, or if movement is slow (more than 1 or 2 seconds to complete the full stroke) diaphragm is leaking and should be replaced.

4. Check brake release with vacuum applied. If diaphragm piston completes full stroke but does not release brake, a malfunction of the pedal assembly is indicated, and the complete parking brake assembly should be replaced.

5. Check operation of parking brake with engine off. Parking brake should remain engaged regardless of transmission selector lever position. If not, replace parking brake assembly.

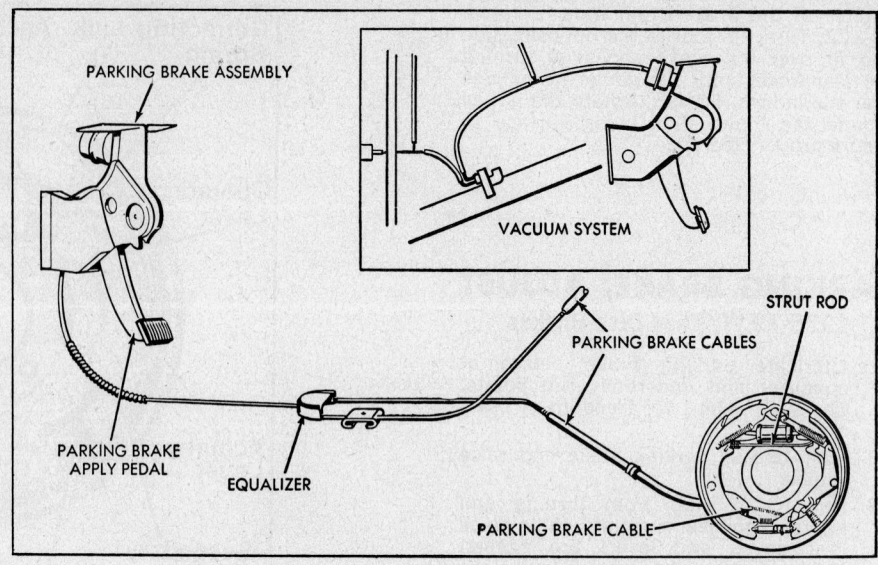

Fig. 24   Parking brake linkage. 1974-79 drum brake (typical)

POWER BRAKE UNIT, REPLACE

Service Bulletin

A sign of brake fluid dampness below the master cylinder at the power brake unit or on wheel cylinders at the bottom of the boot, does not necessarily indicate that these cylinders are leaking.

A small amount of fluid leakage at these areas can occur due to the creeping action of a very light film of fluid on the cylinder bores around the seals. This action provides proper seal lubrication. In addition, normal brake heat will produce a slight escape of lubricant from the impregnated, porous-metal wheel cylinder pistons.

Normal dampness at the master cylinder or wheel cylinders is not easily distinguishable from a definite leak. Therefore, this condition must be checked carefully.

If there is sufficient dampness to form a "teardrop" of fluid at the bottom of the master cylinder or on the bottom of the wheel cylinders at the boot area, the rate of fluid seepage is too high and the cause should be determined and corrected.

Hydro-Boost

1976-79

1. With engine off pump brake pedal several times to empty accumulator of fluid.
2. Remove master cylinder to booster attaching nuts, then move master

cylinder away from booster with brakes lines attached.
3. Remove three hydraulic lines from booster, cap all ports and lines to prevent entry of dirt and loss of fluid.
4. Remove retainer and washer securing booster pedal rod to brake pedal arm.
5. Remove four booster to firewall attaching nuts.
6. Loosen booster from firewall and move booster pedal rod inboard until it disconnects from brake arm.
7. Remove spring washer from brake pedal arm and remove booster.

Vacuum Booster

1979 Eldorado

1. Disconnect engine wiring harness clips from brake unit.
2. Remove two nuts retaining master cylinder to brake unit, and position master cylinder away from brake unit.

NOTE: Do not disconnect brake lines from master cylinder. Use care not to bend or kink lines.

3. Remove check valve from brake unit.
4. Remove four nuts attaching brake unit to cowl and pedal support bracket.
5. Disconnect brake unit push rod from brake pedal, then remove brake unit from vehicle.

1976-79 Seville

1. Disconnect and cap brake lines, remove wiring harness from combination valve.
2. Remove master cylinder to brake booster attaching nuts, then the master cylinder and combination valve.
3. Disconnect vacuum line from check valve.
4. Remove clip and washer from push rod pin at brake pedal, however, do not remove push rod.
5. Remove twilight sentinel amplifier attaching screws and wiring harness and lower unit, if equipped.
6. Remove brake booster to cowl attaching nuts, slide booster out and disconnect push rod from brake pedal pin.

1974-79 Exc. Seville & 1979 Eldorado

1. Disconnect hydraulic lines from master cylinder on power unit. Cap line fittings to prevent dirt entering system.
2. Disconnect vacuum hose from vacuum check valve on power unit. Remove steering column lower cover.
3. Remove cotter pin and spring spacer that attach power unit push rod to brake pedal relay lever.
4. Unfasten and remove power unit from cowl.

Rear Suspension

SHOCK ABSORBER, REPLACE
1974-79

1. If equipped with Automatic Level Control, disconnect air lines from shock absorber fittings.
2. With the rear axle supported properly disconnect shock absorber at upper and lower mountings.

NOTE: Use care not to damage brake hoses or lines when removing shock asborber.

3. Reverse procedure to install.

COIL SPRINGS, REPLACE
1979 Eldorado

1. Raise and support rear of vehicle, then remove wheel and tire assembly.
2. Remove stabilizer bar as described under Stabilizer Bar, Replace.
3. Using a suitable jack support lower control arm.
4. Disconnect automatic level air line at shock absorber. If removing left hand spring from vehicle, disconnect automatic level control link from ball pivot

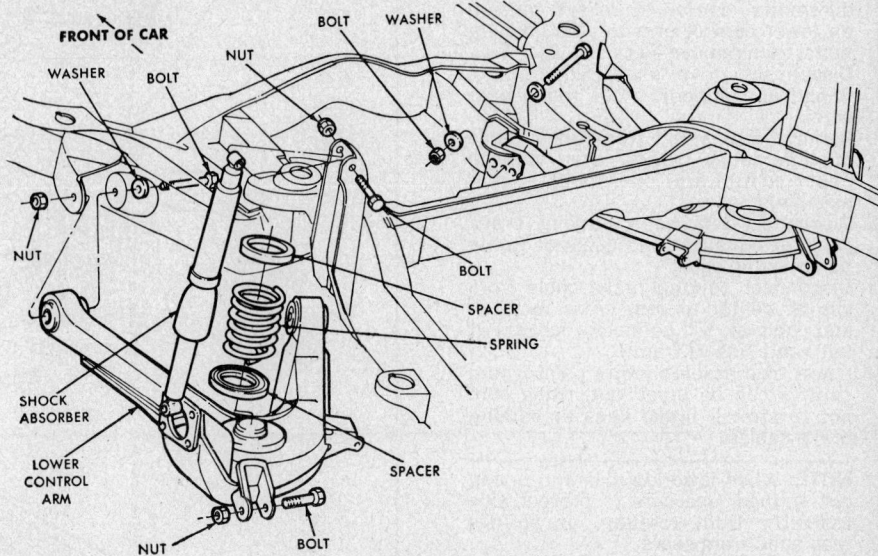

Fig. 1   1979 Eldorado rear suspension

at control arm.
5. Disconnect shock absorber from upper and lower mountings and remove shock absorber.
6. Carefully lower control arm until spring

tension is relieved, then remove spring and insulator, Fig. 1.
7. Reverse procedure to install. Locate bottom end of spring between dimples on lower control arm assembly.

1977-79 Except Eldorado

1. Support vehicle at frame and support rear axle using a suitable jack.
2. Remove shock absorbers.
3. If equipped with Automatic Level Control, remove bolts attaching stabilizer bar to lower control arms and remove stabilizer bar.
4. Remove bolt attaching brake line

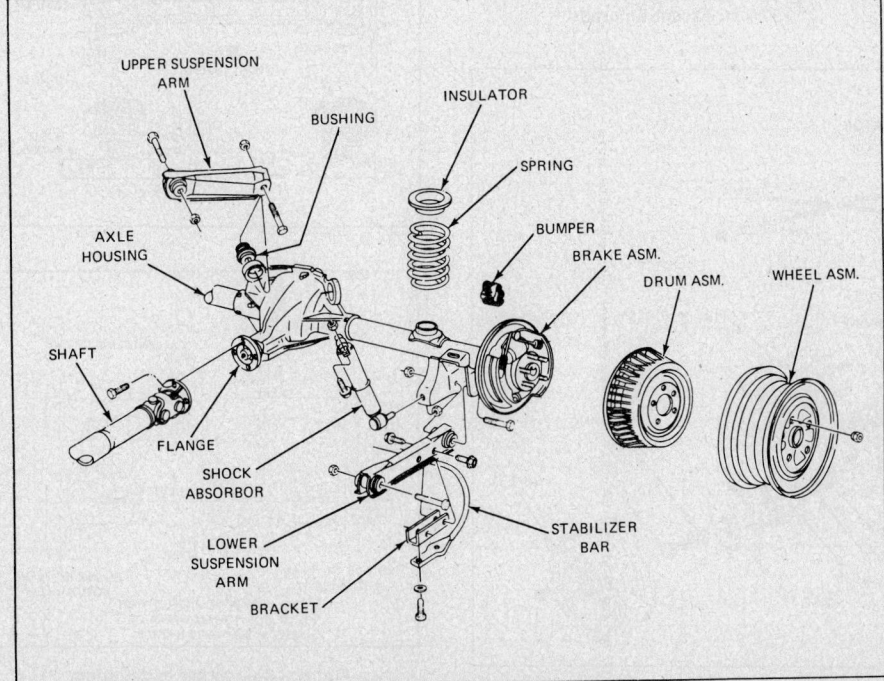

Fig. 2   1977-79 rear suspension (typical). Except Eldorado

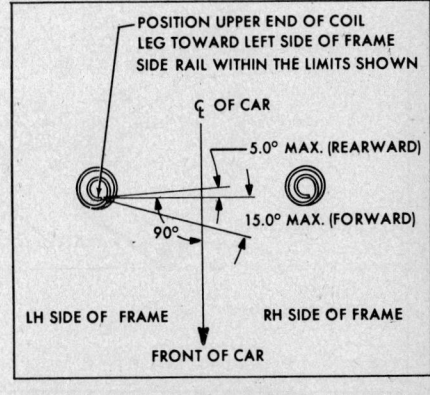

Fig. 2A   Coil spring installation. 1977-79 Except Eldorado

junction block to rear axle housing, then disconnect brake lines from clips on rear axle housing.

5. If equipped with Automatic Level Control, disconnect link from leveling valve arm.

6. Position a jack stand under nose of differential carrier to relieve tension on lower control arm to axle housing bolts, Fig. 2, then remove bolts.

7. Disconnect drive shaft from pinion flange and support from frame with wire.

8. Remove jack stand from under nose of differential carrier, then remove upper control arm pivot bolts at rear axle housing.

9. Disconnect left hand parking brake cable at equalizer and cable at frame by removing clip.

10. Disconnect parking brake cable from clip at center of rear cross member and cable at "C" connector located at left hand side of frame.

11. Lower axle assembly to a point where springs can be pryed out, using care not to stretch brake lines or parking brake cables.

NOTE: When lowering axle and prying out springs, use care to prevent axle assembly from rotating, as springs may snap from seats.

12. Reverse procedure to install. Note spring positions, Fig. 2A.

1974-76 All & 1977-78 Eldorado

1. Support vehicle at frame and support rear axle with a suitable jack.

2. If equipped with Automatic Level Control, disconnect overtravel lever link and place lever in center position.

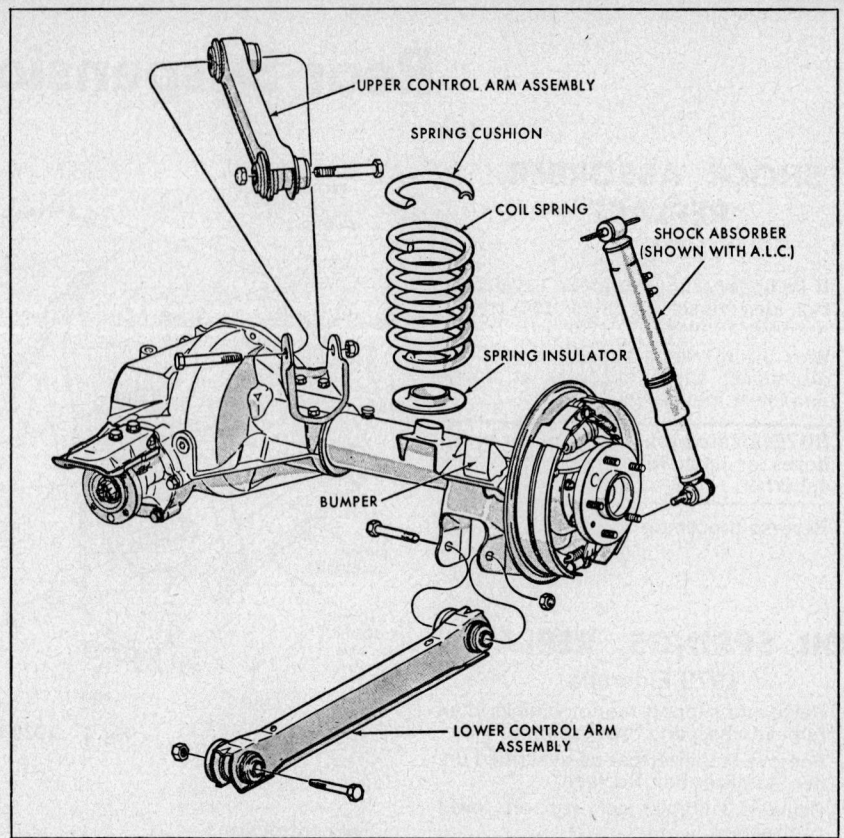

Fig. 3   1974-76 rear suspension (typical). Except Eldorado

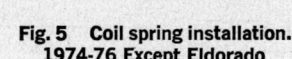

Fig. 5   Coil spring installation. 1974-76 Except Eldorado

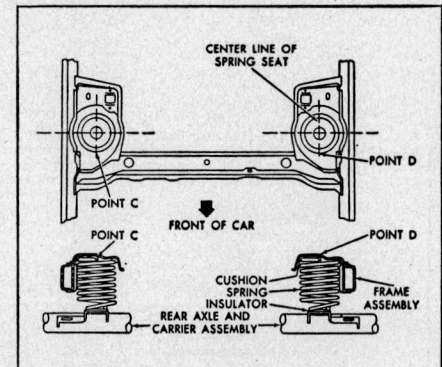

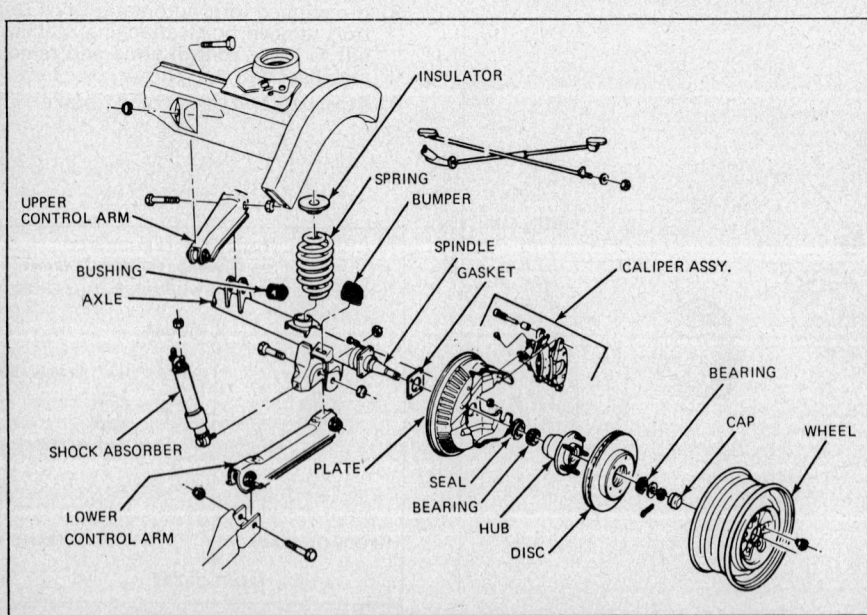

Fig. 4   1974-78 Eldorado rear suspension (typical)

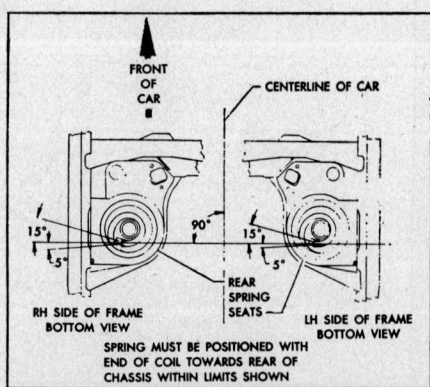

Fig. 6   Coil spring installation. 1974-78 Eldorado

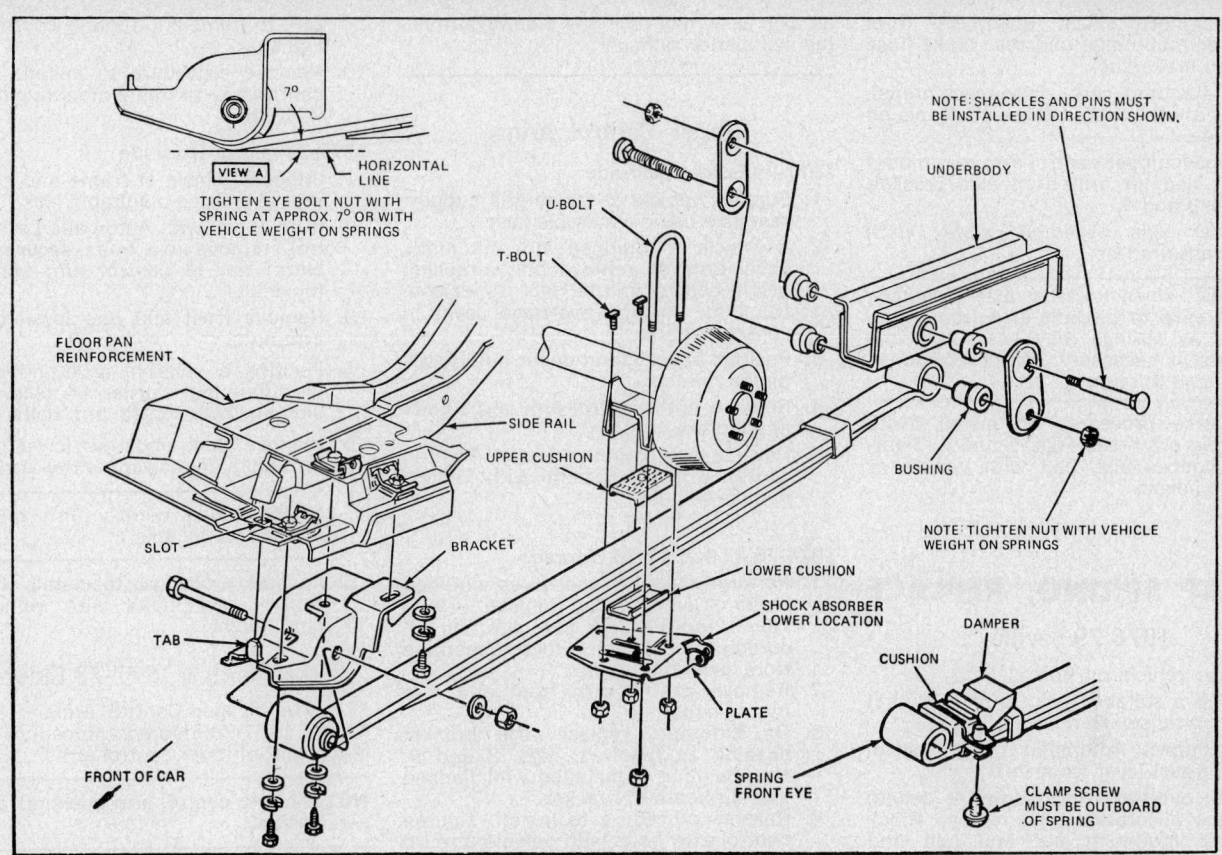

Fig. 7   Rear suspension. 1976-79 Seville

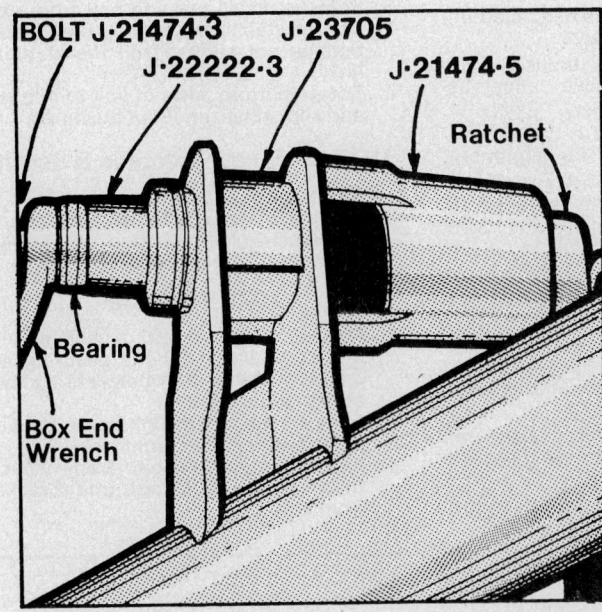

Fig. 8   Upper control arm axle bracket bushing removal, 1974-78 Eldorado

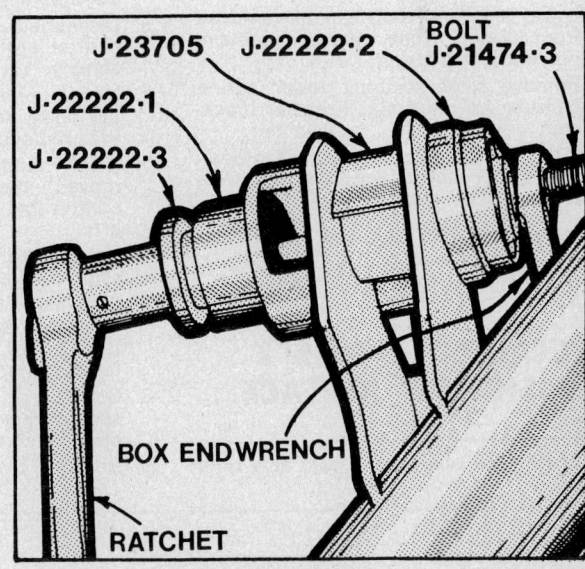

Fig. 9   Upper control arm axle bracket bushing installation, 1974-78 Eldorado

3. Disconnect shock absorbers from lower mountings and rear brake hose from brake line.
4. On standard cars, disconnect propeller shaft from differential pinion flange.
5. Remove upper control arm rear mount bolt and lift arm from axle bracket, Figs. 3 and 4.
6. Lower axle assembly slowly until springs are free.

NOTE: When lowering axle assembly, use care to prevent axle from rotating, as springs may snap from the seats. If necessary, compress springs by hand to remove.

7. Reverse procedure to install. Note spring positions, Figs. 5 and 6. Tighten control arm bolt with vehicle at curb height.

LEAF SPRING, REPLACE

1976-79 Seville

1. Raise vehicle on hoist.
2. Using a suitable jack, raise axle until spring tension is relieved, Fig. 7.
3. Disconnect Automatic Level Control overtravel lever from link.
4. Push overtravel lever down to deflate shock absorbers, then remove shock lower mounting nut and bolt and position shock absorber aside.
5. Back off parking brake adjustment at equalizer and remove cable clip from spring front retaining bracket and cable clamps from bottom of spring.
6. Loosen spring front eye to retaining bracket bolt.
7. Remove spring front bracket to underbody attaching screws.
8. Lower axle until bolt can be removed from spring front eye and remove bracket from spring.
9. Remove nuts securing lower spring plate to axle and stabilizer bar brackets.
10. Remove upper and lower spring pads and spring plate, support spring, then remove both nuts from rear shackle.
11. Separate spring and shackle and remove spring.

CONTROL ARMS & BUSHINGS, REPLACE

NOTE: Replace one control arm at a time

as axle assembly may slip sideways, making installation difficult.

Upper Control Arms

1977-79 Except Eldorado

1. Support vehicle at frame and support rear axle using a suitable jack.
2. If vehicle is equipped with Automatic Level Control, remove bolt attaching height control link to right upper control arm. Position overtravel lever in center position.
3. Position a jack stand under differential pinion retainer.
4. Remove both control arm pivot bolts and control arm.
5. Reverse procedure to install. Tighten control arm pivot bolts with vehicle at curb height.

1974-76 All & 1977-78 Eldorado

1. Perform steps 1 and 2 as outlined under "Coil Springs, Replace" 1974-76 All and 1977-78 Eldorado. On Eldorado disconnect shock absorbers from lower mountings.
2. Remove control arm front and rear mount bolts.
3. On Eldorado, replace axle bracket bushing as required, Figs. 8 and 9. New bushing is installed with flanged side outboard of bracket.
4. Reverse procedure to install. Tighten control arm bolts with vehicle at curb height.

Lower Control Arms

1979 Eldorado

1. Raise and support rear of vehicle, then remove wheel and tire assembly.
2. Remove stabilizer bar as described under Stabilizer Bar, Replace.
3. Disconnect brake line bracket from control arm, then remove caliper assembly.
4. Mark a wheel stud and a corresponding point on the rotor for alignment, then remove rotor.
5. If left hand control arm is to be removed, disconnect automatic level control link from ball pivot on control arm.
6. Using a suitable jack support control arm.
7. Disconnect air line from shock absorber, then disconnect shock absorber from upper and lower mountings and remove shock absorber.
8. Carefully lower the control arm until spring tension is relieved, then remove spring and insulator.
9. Remove two bolts mounting control

arm to frame and remove control arm, Fig. 1.
10. Reverse procedure to install. Torque control arm to frame mounting bolts to 75 ft. lbs.

1977-79 Except Eldorado

1. Support vehicle at frame and support rear axle using a suitable jack.
2. If equipped with Automatic Level Control, remove two bolts securing stabilizer bar to control arm being removed.
3. Remove front and rear lower control arm nuts.
4. Position a suitable jack under front of differential carrier to relieve tension on lower control arm bolts.
5. Remove front and rear lower control arm bolts and lower control arm.

NOTE: Lower control arm bushings are not serviceable.

6. Reverse procedure to install. Tighten control arm bolts with vehicle at curb height.

1974-76 All & 1977-78 Eldorado

Follow "Upper Control Arms" 1974-76 All and 1977-78 Eldorado procedure for replacement of lower control arms.

NOTE: Lower control arm bushings are not serviceable.

STABILIZER BAR, REPLACE

1979 Eldorado

1. Raise and support rear of vehicle.
2. Remove nuts and bolts securing front of stabilizer bar to control arms.
3. Remove inside nut and bolt from each side of stabilizer bar link, then loosen outside nut and bolt on the stabilizer link.
4. Rotate bottom parts of link to one side and slip stabilizer out of bushings.

1977-79 Except Eldorado & Seville

1. Raise and support rear of vehicle.
2. Remove bolts securing stabilizer bar to lower control arms, then remove stabilizer bar from vehicle.

1976-79 Seville

1. Raise and support rear of vehicle.
2. Remove nuts and bolts securing stabilizer bushings and brackets to lower spring plates.
3. Remove nuts from link bolts, then remove washers and grommets.
4. Remove stabilizer bar from vehicle, then remove bushings and brackets from bar.

Front End and Steering Section

FRONT SUSPENSION EXC. ELDORADO

1976 Seville & 1977-79 All

The front suspension consist of two upper and lower control arm assemblies, steel coil springs, shock absorbers, stabilizer bar, two integral steering arms, and knuckles, Fig. 1.

Ball joints are used at outer ends of upper and lower control arms. The upper ball joints is riveted to the upper control arm. The lower ball joint is pressed into the lower control arm.

A stabilizer bar is mounted in rubber bushings to the front frame side rails and is attached to the lower control arms by means of steel links.

1974-76 Exc. Seville

The front suspension system consists of two upper and lower control arm assemblies, steel coil springs, shock absorbers, front diagonal tie struts, and a stabilizer bar. Rubber bushings are used at all frame attaching points. Fig. 2.

Ball joints are used at the outer ends of the upper and lower control arms. The upper ball joint is pressed into the upper control arm and tack-welded to the arm at two points. It connects the upper control arm to the steering knuckle through a camber adjustment eccentric. The lower ball joint, a tension type joint, is pressed into the lower control arm. It connects the lower control arm to the steering knuckle.

The steering knuckle is a combination steering knuckle, brake caliper support and steering arm.

The upper control arms pivot at their inner ends on two flanged rubber bushings, one at each end of the one-piece control arm shaft which is bolted to the top surface of the spring tower on the front frame crossmember. The lower control arms pivot on a single rubber bushing that is bolted to the front suspension frame crossmember.

Diagonal tie struts are used to control the fore and aft movement of the wheels. The struts are bolted to the outer ends of the lower control arms and extend through the frame crossmember. Rubber bushings and a steel spacer are used at the frame mount.

Lubrication

On 1974 models, the ball joints are packed with lubricant and sealed at assembly and should not require further lubrication throughout their service life under normal driving conditions. The only maintenance they normally require is an inspection of the seals for physical damage each time the engine oil is changed.

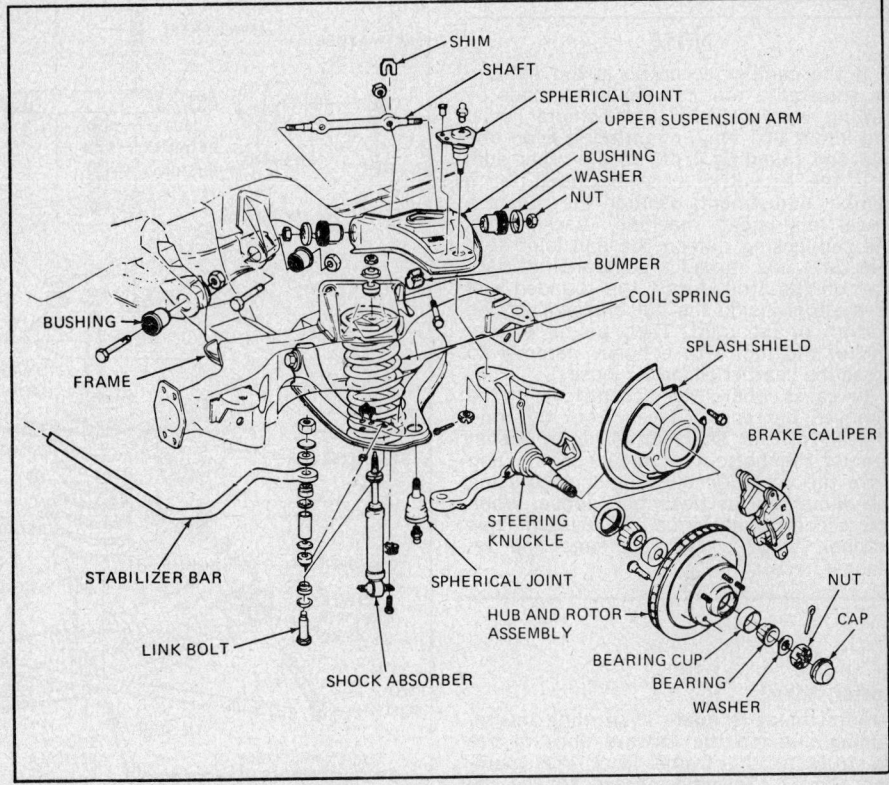

Fig. 1 Front suspension disassembled. 1976 Seville & 1977-79 All

Service plugs are provided in the ball joint covers so that the joints may be packed in the event a seal should become damaged and require replacement. Both the seals and plugs are serviceable.

On 1975-79 models, lubrication fittings are provided in ball joint covers. Lubrication is required every 6 months or 7500 miles.

Wheel Alignment
1976 Seville & 1977-79 All

Caster and camber are adjusted by adding or removing shims from between the upper control arm and frame bracket, Fig. 3. Caster is adjusted by transfering shims from front to rear and rear to front. Transfering shims from front bolt to rear bolt will increase positive caster, from rear bolt to front bolt will increase negative caster.

Camber is adjusted by adding or removing an equal number of shims from the front and rear bolts. To increase positive camber remove an equal amount of shims from front and rear bolts, to increase negative camber add an equal amount of shims to front and rear bolts.

After adjusting caster and camber torque nut to 70-80 ft-lbs. Tighten bolt with the least amount of shims first. After adjusting caster and camber toe-in must be ad-

justed.

NOTE: The differance in thickness between front and rear shim packs should not exceed .40 inch. If difference is greater than .40 inch check arms, frame and related parts for damage.

1974 Exc. Seville

Camber, Adjust

Adjustment is made at the camber eccentric located in the steering knuckle upper support, Fig. 4. The upper ball joint stud fits through the camber eccentric and knuckle support. Turning the eccentric repositions the upper ball joint stud.

To adjust camber, loosen locknut on ball joint stud one turn and strike steering knuckle in area of ball joint stud to free eccentric from steering knuckle, Fig. 5.

CAUTION: Use extreme care to prevent striking and damaging brake hose or ball joint seal.

Using adjustable wrench shown in Fig. 6, turn eccentric as required to obtain the camber specifications listed in the Wheel Alignment chart. The final position of the stud should be in the rear portion of the camber eccentric in order to keep steering angle correct. After proper adjustment has been established, torque stud nut to 60 ft. lbs.

NOTE

If the camber eccentric is too tight to be adjusted a tool can easily be made by cutting a piece of $7/16$" diameter steel rod about 20" long, chamfering it on one end and rounding it off on the other end.

If the eccentric must be freed for a camber adjustment, position the car on a wheel alignment machine, backing off the self-locking nut on the ball joint stud one turn, and thread a standard nut half-way on the stud. Insert the rounded end of the tool inside the nut and against the bottom of the stud. Then pound on the end of the tool with a heavy hammer to break the camber eccentric loose.

In cases where the eccentric is to be removed but comes loose from the stud instead of the knuckle, place a washer against the bottom of the eccentric and drive the eccentric out from below, using the same tool as described above. When the eccentric must be removed in this manner, inspect it for damage and replace if necessary.

Caster, Adjust

Adjustment is made by turning the retaining nuts on the forward ends of the tie-struts at the frame front crossmember, Fig. 7. To gain access to the retaining nuts, it is necessary to remove the splash shield.

Proper caster adjustment is obtained by shortening or lengthening the struts between the lower suspension arms and the frame front crossmember. To provide more negative caster, lengthen the struts by loosening the front bushing retaining nuts and tightening the rear bushing retaining nuts. One turn of the nuts results in approximately $1/2°$ change in caster.

To provide more positive caster, shorten the struts by loosening the rear bushing retaining nuts and tightening the front bushing retaining nuts.

After proper adjustment has been made, tighten front retaining nuts to 50 ft. lbs. on 1974-76 models, being sure to hold the rear nut with a wrench so as not to disturb the adjustment.

Toe-In, Adjust

Toe-in is adjusted by turning the tie rod adjusters at the outer ends of each tie rod after loosening the clamp bolts. (Both right and left pivot ends have right-hand threads.) Be sure to turn both adjusters an equal amount so that the relation of the steering gear high spot to the straight ahead position of the front wheels will not be changed.

When adjustment has been completed according to the specification listed in the *Wheel Alignment* chart, tighten nuts on clamp bolts to 22 ft. lbs. torque.

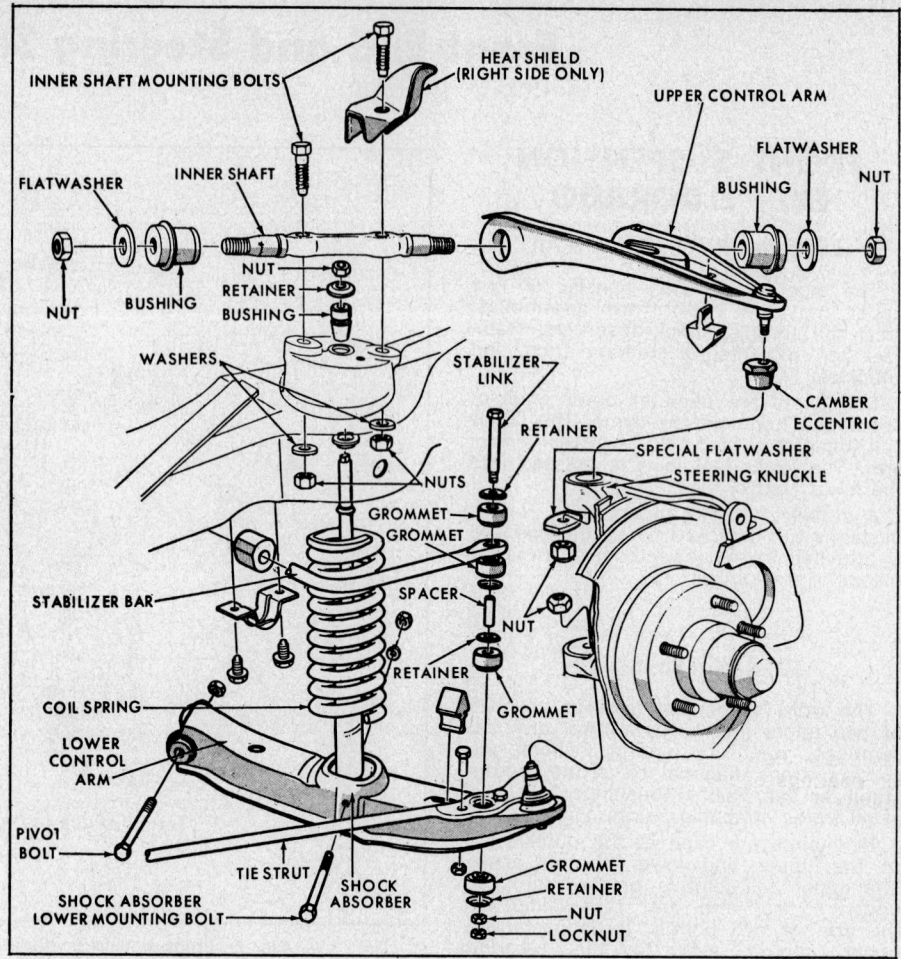

Fig. 2   Front suspension disassembled. 1974-76 Exc. Seville

NOTE

Make certain that both inner and outer tie rod ball pivots are centered in their respective housings prior to tightening the tie rod adjusting clamps.

If the tie rods are not properly positioned, a binding condition may occur, resulting in poor return of wheels to the straight ahead position.

Each tie rod should be checked after adjustment by grasping the center of the tie rod and rotating it fore and aft. The movement should be equal in both directions. If not, it indicates that the pivot studs are not properly positioned.

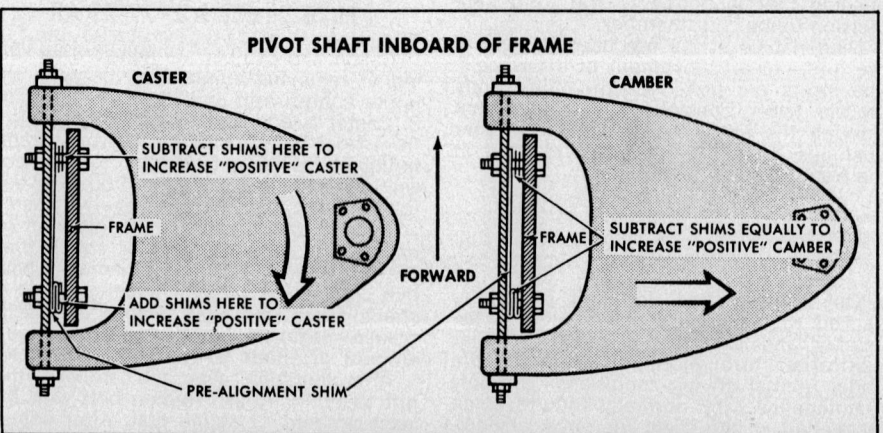

Fig. 3   Caster and camber adjustment. 1976 Seville & 1977-79 All

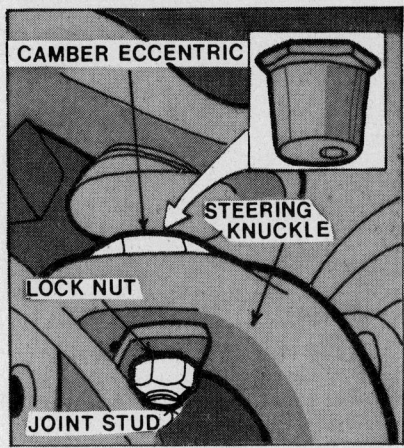

Fig. 4 Camber adjustment eccentric. 1974-76

Wheel Bearings, Adjust

Service Bulletin

Looseness at a front wheel does not necessarily indicate worn bearings or a loose spindle nut, since the tapered roller bearings used on front wheels of all standard Cadillacs should not be preloaded and normally can have up to .004" end play.

1. While rotating wheel and tire assembly, tighten spindle nut to 15 ft. lbs. for 1974-77 vehicles and 12 ft. lbs. for 1978-79 vehicles making certain that hub is fully seated on spindle.
2. Back off spindle nut until free, and on 1974-79 vehicles tighten nut finger tight.
3. Install new cotter pin. If pin cannot be installed, back off nut to next hole

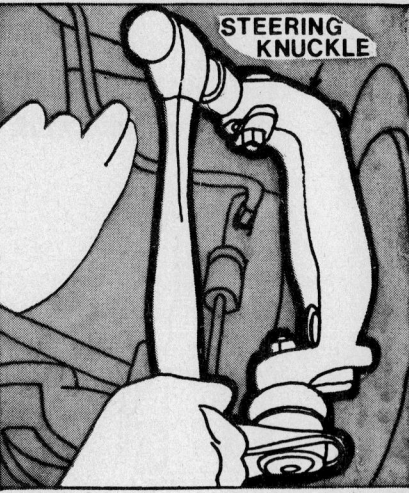

(left image: CROW FOOT ADAPTER J-23415)

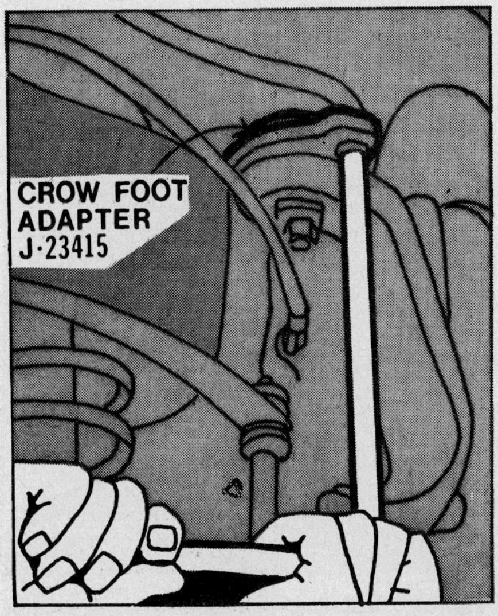

Fig. 6 Adjusting camber. 1974-76

and install pin.

NOTE: Cotter pin must be tight after installation, as vibration can break pin.

Wheel Bearings, Replace

1974-79

1. Remove caliper retaining bolts, then slide caliper off disc and using a length of wire, attach caliper to upper control arm.

   NOTE: Never allow caliper to hang from brake hose.

2. Remove dust cap, cotter pin, spindle nut, washer and outer bearing assembly.
3. Remove hub and disc assembly, being careful to avoid damage to spindle threads or grease seal.
4. Remove inner bearing grease seal and bearing assembly.

NOTE: Inner and outer bearing cups are press fit in hub and can be driven out from the opposite side using a brass drift. Tap alternately on opposite sides to prevent cocking cup and damaging hub.

Checking Ball Joints For Wear

Upper Ball Joint

1976 Seville & 1977-79 All

If ball joint has any noticeable lateral movement or can be twisted within its socket using finger pressure, the joint must be replaced.

1974-76 Exc. Seville

Using the regular ball joint stud nut and a second nut as a lock nut, turn joint in its socket with a torque wrench. If the torque is not within the limits of 2 to 4 ft-lbs, the joint should be replaced.

Lower Ball Joint

1974-79

A wear indicator is built in the ball joint. Remove dirt deposits around service plug and observe position of nipple. Refer to Fig. 8, for wear tolerance.

Upper Ball Joint, Replace

1976 Seville & 1977-79 All

1. Raise vehicle and remove wheel.
2. Remove cotter pin from upper ball joint stud.
3. Remove caliper and position aside.

NOTE: When removing caliper use care not to damage brake tubing or hose. Secure caliper to frame with wire.

Fig. 5 Loosening camber eccentric

4. Loosen stud nut, however, not more than one turn.
5. Using tool No. J-23742, free ball joint stud from steering knuckle, Fig. 9.

NOTE: The lower control arm must be supported so spring can not force arm down.

6. Remove upper ball joint stud nut, allow steering knuckle to swing out of way and place block of wood between frame and upper control arm.
7. To remove rivets securing ball joint to upper control arm, grind rivet heads off, then, using a punch, drive rivets out.

NOTE: Use care not to damage ball joint seat or upper control arm when removing rivets.

8. Position ball joint on upper control arm, install bolts through bottom of control arm, install and torque nuts to 25 ft. lbs.
9. Remove block of wood from between frame and upper control arm, position upper ball stud to steering

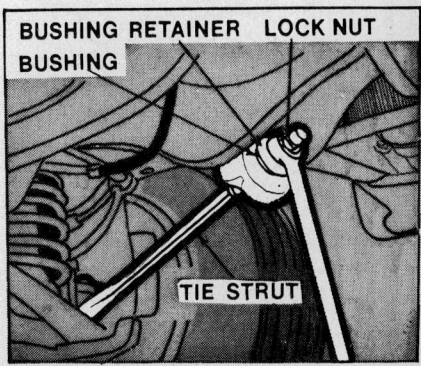

(BUSHING RETAINER LOCK NUT, BUSHING, TIE STRUT)

Fig. 7 Adjusting caster. 1974-76 Exc. Seville

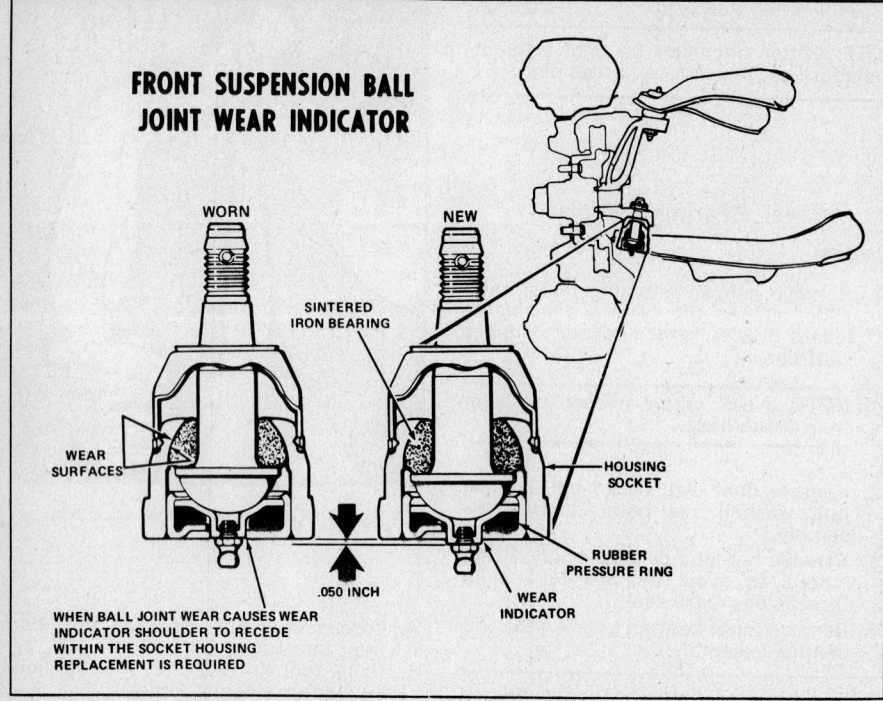

FRONT SUSPENSION BALL JOINT WEAR INDICATOR

WORN

NEW

SINTERED IRON BEARING

WEAR SURFACES

HOUSING SOCKET

.050 INCH

RUBBER PRESSURE RING

WEAR INDICATOR

WHEN BALL JOINT WEAR CAUSES WEAR INDICATOR SHOULDER TO RECEDE WITHIN THE SOCKET HOUSING REPLACEMENT IS REQUIRED

Fig. 8   Ball joint wear indicator. 1974-79 except Eldorado

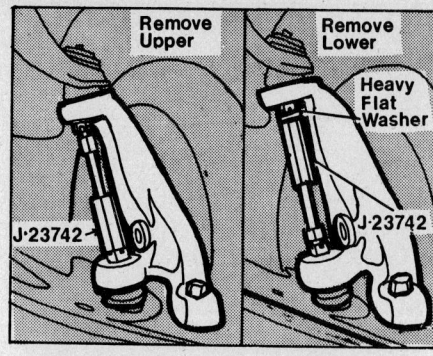

Fig. 9   Removing ball joint studs from steering knuckle. 1976 Seville & 1977-79 All

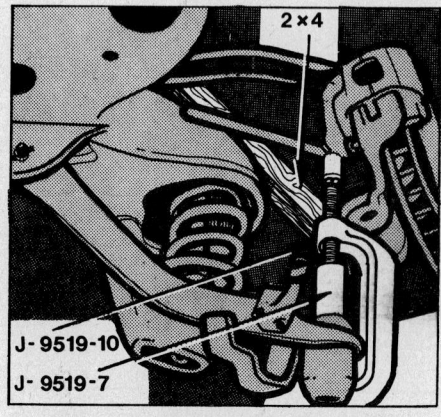

Fig. 10   Removing ball joint from lower control arm. 1976 Seville & 1977-79 All

knuckle, install and torque nut to 60 ft. lbs. Install cotter pin.

NOTE: If cotter pin hole is not aligned do not back nut off. Nut may be torqued to a maximum of 100 ft. lbs. (1/6 additional turn) to align cotter pin hole.

10. Install caliper, lubricate ball joint and install wheel.
11. Check wheel alignment.

1974-76 Exc. Seville

The upper ball joints are pressed into the upper control arm and tack-welded to the arm. Therefore, the upper ball joints are supplied only with the upper control arm.

Lower Ball Joint, Replace

1976 Seville & 1977-79 All

1. Raise vehicle and remove wheel.
2. Remove cotter pin from lower ball joint stud and loosen nut one turn.
3. Using tool No. J-23742, free ball joint stud from steering knuckle, Fig. 9.

NOTE: Lower control arm must be supported so spring can not force arm down.

4. Remove lower stud nut and pull upward and outward on bottom of brake disc to free ball joint stud from steering knuckle.
5. Lift upper control arm up with steering knuckle and hub attached and place a block of wood between frame and upper control arm.

NOTE: It maybe necessary to remove tie rod from steering knuckle.

6. Using tools J-9519-10 and J-9519-7, remove ball joint from lower control arm, Fig. 10.
7. Install ball joint in lower control arm using tools J-9519-9 and J-9519-10.

NOTE: Position bleed vent in ball joint rubber boot to face inward and the stud cotter pin hole to face forward.

8. Remove block of wood from between frame and upper control arm, then install lower ball joint stud in steering knuckle. Install and torque nut to 80 ft. lbs. and install cotter pin.

NOTE: If cotter pin hole is not aligned do not back nut off. Nut maybe torqued to a maximum of 125 ft. lbs. (1/6 additional turn) to align cotter pin holes.

9. Lubricate ball joint and install tie rod, if removed. Torque tie rod nut to 35 ft. lbs. and install cotter pin.
10. Install wheel and check wheel alignment.

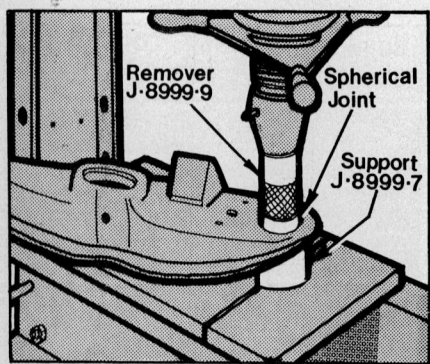

Fig. 11   Removing ball joint from lower control arm. 1974-76 Exc. Seville

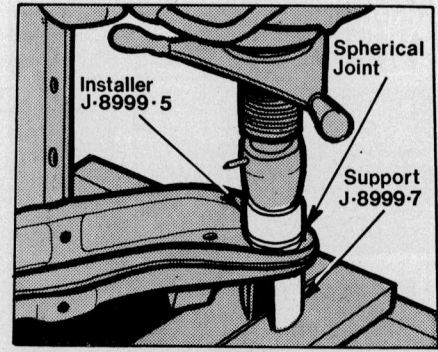

Fig. 12   Installing ball joint in lower control arm. 1974-76 Exc. Seville

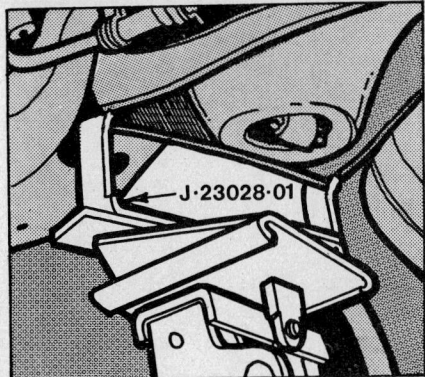

Fig. 13 Removing and installing front spring. 1976 Seville 1977-79 All

1974-76 Exc. Seville

1. Remove coil spring as outlined under "Coil Spring, Replace" procedure.
2. Remove pivot bolt and washer from lower control arm at frame mount, then remove lower control arm.
3. Remove band and seal from lower ball joint.
4. Using a suitable press and tools J-8999-9 and J-8999-7, Fig. 11, press lower ball joint from lower control arm.
5. Install new ball joint with tools J-8999-7 and J-8999-5, Fig. 12. Press ball joint into lower control arm until the ball joint flange bottoms on mounting hole flange.
6. Reverse procedure to install lower control arm.

Shock Absorber, Replace

The shock absorbers are removed through the bottom of the lower control arm after unfastening it at the top and bottom.

To install, place the retainer and rubber grommet on the upper stem and fully extend the shock absorber rod. Insert the shock absorber up into the coil spring and guide the stem through the tower in the crossmember. Then place the lower end in position on the lower control arm. On 1974-76 models except Seville, install bolt, washer and nut and torque nut to 55 ft. lbs. On all other models, install bolts and torque to 19 ft. lbs. On all models, install shock stud retaining nut and tighten to end of threads on stud (about 1⅛ inch).

Tie-Strut & Bushings
1974-76 Exc. Seville

Raise car and disconnect stabilizer link from lower arm on side from which tie-strut is to be removed. Remove strut and bushings and replace as follows:

1. Replace rear locknut on threaded end of tie-strut and run nut about ¾" from end of thread.
2. Install rear bushing retainer on tie-strut with concave side against nut.
3. Insert metal spacer part way through conical shaped bushing

from small end and install on tie-strut with small end toward front of car.
4. With strut held in horizontal position install threaded end through frame front cross member.
5. Position opposite end of strut on lower arm with pointed end inward, and install attaching bolts and nuts loosely.
6. Install front bushing on end of strut, cupped side toward frame, and slide bushing against cross member.
7. Install front bushing retainer on strut with concave side against bushing.
8. Start new locknut on threaded end of strut and connect stabilizer link to lower arm.
9. Lower car and with car weight on all four wheels, position front bushing on metal spacer and torque locknut on front end of strut to 50 ft. lbs.
10. Tighten tie-strut to lower arm nuts and bolts to 55 ft. lbs.

Coil Spring, Replace

1976 Seville & 1977-79 All

1. Raise vehicle on hoist, remove shock absorber lower mounting bolts and push shock through control arm up into spring.
2. Support vehicle so control arms hang free and disconnect stabilizer bar from lower control arm.
3. Secure tool No. J-23028-01 to a suit-

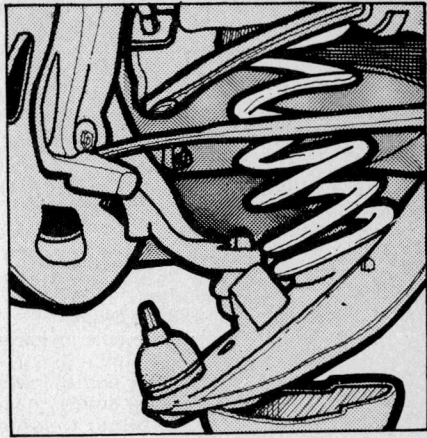

Fig. 14 Coil spring installation. 1974-76 Exc. Seville

able jack, position tool so lower control arm is supported by inner bushings, Fig. 13.
4. Raise jack to relieve spring tension from lower control arm pivot and install a safety chain around spring and through lower control arm.
5. Remove bolt from rear of lower control arm, then remove other bolt and slowly lower control arm until all spring tension is relieved.
6. Remove safety chain, spring and spring insulator.
7. Reverse procedure to install.

NOTE: When installing spring, bottom coil must cover all or part of one inspection hole on the lower control

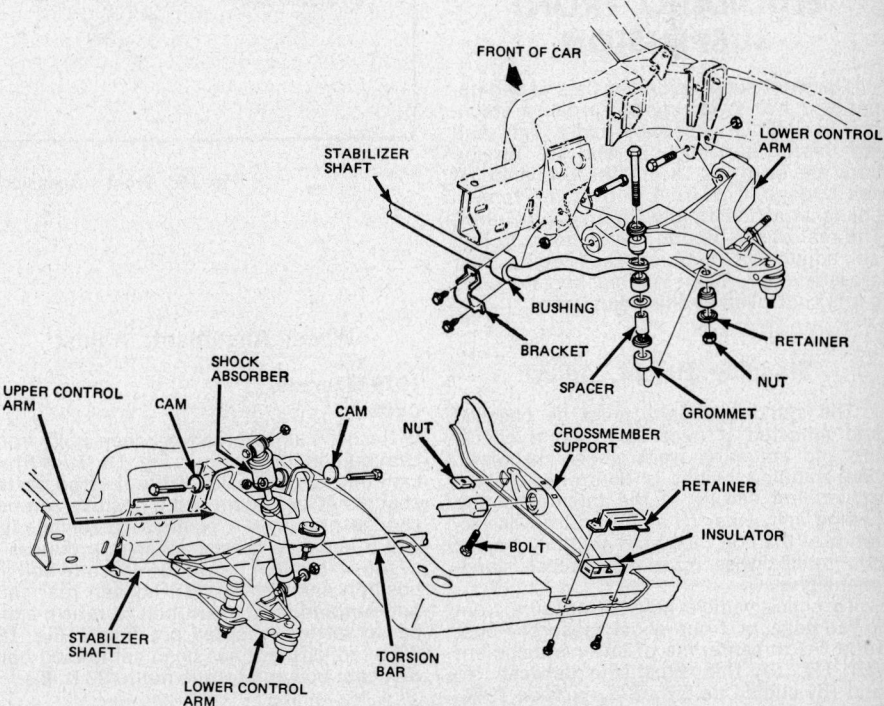

Fig. 15 Front suspension disassembled. 1979 Eldorado

arm, the other inspection hole must be fully or partially uncovered.

1974-76 Exc. Seville

1. Disconnect shock absorber at upper end.
2. Raise front of car and place jack stands under frame side rails.
3. Disconnect stabilizer link from side from which spring is to be removed.
4. Disconnect tie strut at lower arm.
5. Remove shock absorber.
6. Remove wheel and brake drum.
7. Remove nut from pivot bolt in lower control arm at frame mount.
8. Position jack under outer end of lower control arm and install a safety chain around spring and through lower control arm.
9. Remove stud nut from lower ball joint, install a standard nut on stud and tighten nut to within two threads of steering knuckle.
10. Using a suitable hammer, strike steering knuckle to free from ball joint stud.

NOTE: It maybe necessary to raise opposite rear wheel of vehicle to further compress spring when freeing ball joint stud from steering knuckle.

11. Raise jack to relieve spring tension from ball joint stud nut, remove nut and slowly lower jack until all spring tension is relieved, then remove safety chain and spring, Fig. 14.
12. Reverse procedure to install.

ELDORADO FRONT SUSPENSION

The front suspension consists of two upper and two lower control arms, a stabilizer bar, shock absorbers and a right and left torsion bar, Figs. 15 and 16. Torsion bars are used instead of the conventional coil springs. The front end of the torsion bar is attached to the lower control arm. The rear of the torsion bar is mounted into an adjustable arm in the torsion bar crossmember. The standing height of the car is controlled by this adjustment.

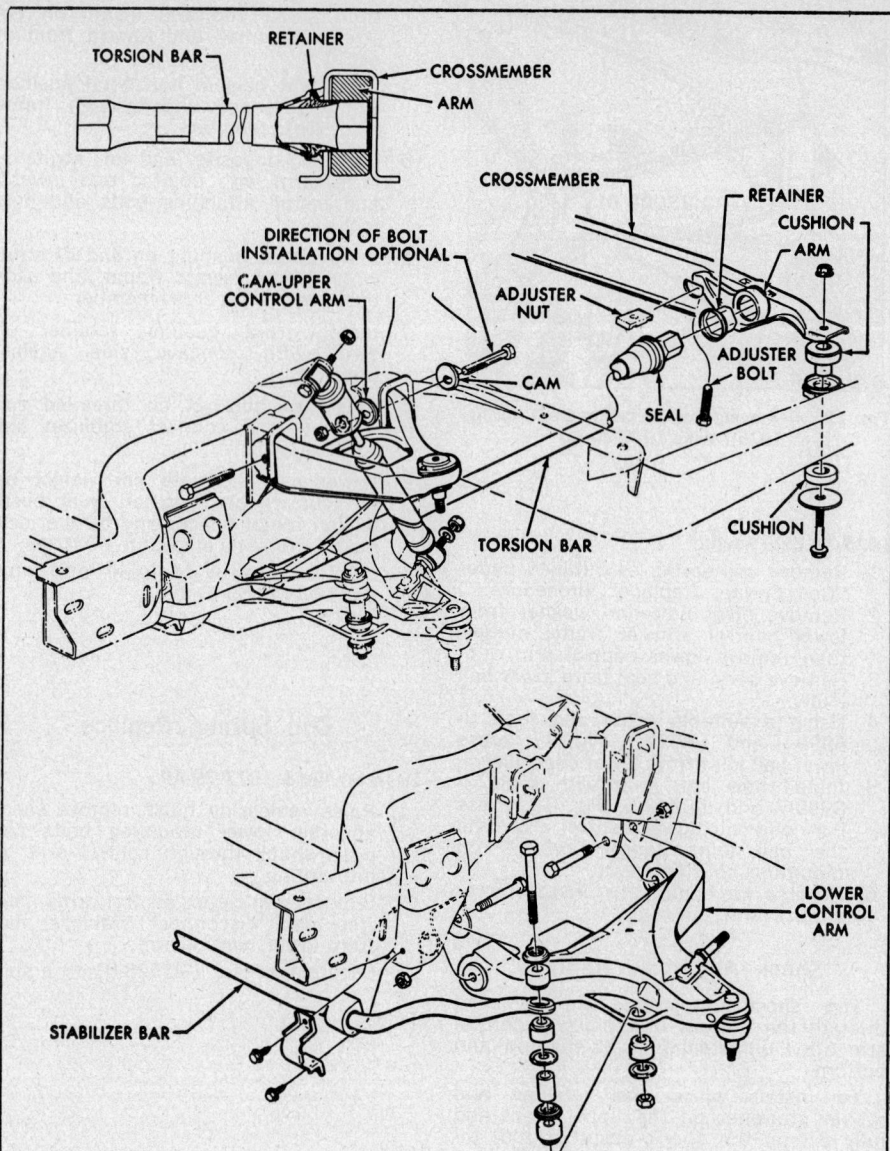

Fig. 16   Front suspension disassembled. 1974-78 Eldorado

Standing Height, Adjust

The standing height must be checked and adjusted if necessary before checking and adjusting front wheel alignment. The standing height is controlled by the adjustment setting of the torsion bar adjusting bolt, Figs. 15 and 16. Clockwise rotation of the bolt increases standing height; counterclockwise rotation decrease standing height.

To check vehicle height, measure from lower edge of front shock absorber dust tube (A) to centerline of lower attachment (B), Fig. 17, this dimension between (A) and (B) should be $8\frac{3}{16}$-$8\frac{7}{16}$ inch on 1974-78 vehicles and $10\frac{5}{8}$-$11\frac{3}{8}$" on 1979 vehicles.

Wheel Alignment, Adjust

1979 Eldorado
Caster

Record camber reading, then hold front cam bolt and loosen nut, Fig. 18. Turn front cam bolt to obtain $\frac{1}{4}$ of the desired caster change. At front cam bolt a positive camber change produces a positive caster change and a negative camber change produces a negative caster change. Hold cam bolt in position and tighten nut. Loosen rear cam bolt nut and rotate cam bolt to return camber to setting recorded previously, Fig. 18. When adjustment has been completed hold rear cam bolt and torque nut to 80 ft. lbs.

Camber

While holding cam bolt in position,

loosen cam bolt nut, Fig. 18. Rotate cam bolt to obtain a change in camber equal to $\frac{1}{2}$ the needed correction. Hold cam bolt in position and tighten cam bolt nut. To obtain the remaining $\frac{1}{2}$ of needed correction apply the above procedure to the other cam bolt.

1974-78 Eldorado

Caster and camber can be adjusted from under hood or under car. If under hood method is used, adjustments must be rechecked due to the change in weight distribution. After checking vehicle standing height adjust caster and camber as follows:

1. Loosen front and rear adjusting cam nuts, Fig. 18.
2. Rotate front cam to correct for $\frac{1}{2}$ of

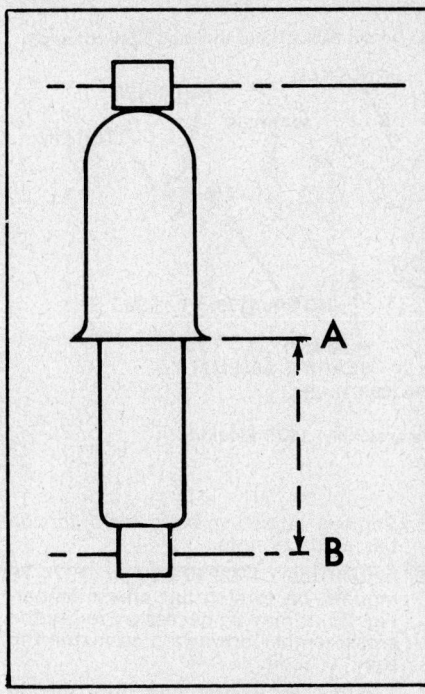

Fig. 17 Checking standing height. 1974-79 Eldorado

reading will change caster reading about 2°. To correct for excessive negative caster rotate front cam bolt to increase positive camber. To correct for excessive positive caster rotate front cam bolt to increase negative camber.

---

7. Set camber to specifications by rotating rear cam bolt.
8. Torque front and rear cam nuts to 95 ft. lbs.

NOTE: When tightening cam nuts ensure cam bolt does not move, any movement of cam bolt will effect wheel alignment.

Toe-In, Adjust

Toe-in is adjusted by turning the tie rod adjusting tubes at outer ends of each tie rod after loosening clamp bolts. Readings should be taken only when front wheels are straight ahead and steering gear is on its high spot.

1979 Eldorado

1. Loosen clamp bolts at each end of tie rod adjusting sleeve.
2. Turn tie rod adjusting sleeve to obtain the proper toe-in adjustment.
3. After completing adjustment, check to ensure that the number of threads at each end of sleeve are equal and tie rod end housings and clamps are properly positioned. Torque clamp bolt to 15 ft. lbs.

1974-78 Eldorado

1. Center steering wheel, raise car and check wheel run-out.
2. Loosen tie rod adjuster nuts and adjust tie rods to obtain the specified toe-in.
3. Tighten tie rod adjuster nuts to 20-22 ft-lbs.
4. Position adjuster clamps so that opening of clamps are facing up. Interference with front suspension components could occur while turning if clamps are facing down.

---

incorrect camber reading.

3. Rotate rear cam to bring camber reading to 0°.
4. Tighten front and rear cam nuts, then check caster.

NOTE: If caster is within specifications, procede to step 7.

---

5. If caster is to be adjusted, loosen front and rear cam nuts.
6. Rotate front cam bolt so that camber will change ¼ of desired caster change.

NOTE: A change of 1° in camber

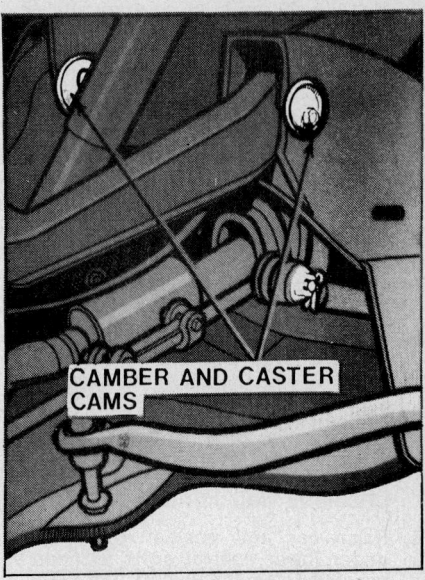

Fig. 18 Caster-camber cam locations. 1974-79 Eldorado

Wheel Bearing & Steering Knuckle, Replace

1974-79 Eldorado

1. Raise and support vehicle under lower control arms.
2. Remove drive axle nut and washer and remove wheel and tire assembly.
3. Remove brake hose clip from ball joint and replace nut, then remove brake caliper off disc, and using a length of wire support caliper on suspension.

NOTE: Do not allow caliper to hang from brake hose as this could cause damage and premature failure of hose.

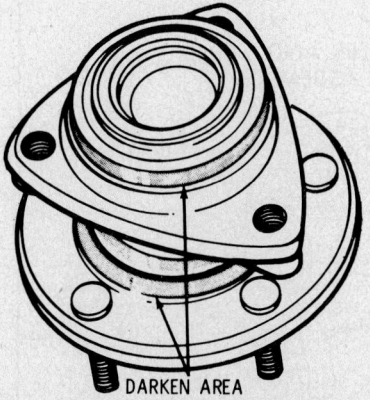

Fig. 19 Sealed wheel bearing assembly. 1979 Eldorado

Wheel Bearing Inspection

1979 Eldorado

The front wheel bearing is a sealed unit bearing. The bearing can not be adjusted or repacked. There are darkened areas on the bearing assembly. These darkened areas are from a heat treatment process and do not indicate need for bearing replacement, Fig. 19.

To check wheel bearing assembly for looseness, free brake pads from disc or remove calipers. Install two lug nuts to secure disc to bearing. Mount dial indicator as shown in Fig. 20, then rock disc and note indicator reading. If looseness exceeds .005 in. replace hub and bearing assembly.

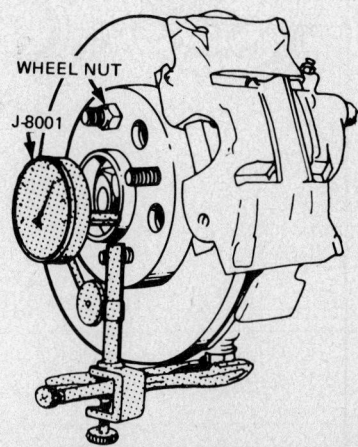

Fig. 20 Checking wheel bearing for looseness. 1979 Eldorado

4. Mark hub and disc assembly for alignment during assembly and remove disc, then strike steering knuckle in area of upper ball joint until upper ball joint is loose.

CAUTION: Use extreme care to prevent striking and damaging brake hose or ball joint seal.

5. Place a short length of rubber hose over lower control arm torsion bar connector to avoid damage to inboard tri-pot joint seal when hub and knuckle are removed.

6. Using appropriate puller, disconnect tie rod end, upper and lower ball joints and remove steering knuckle and hub assembly, Figs. 21 and 22.

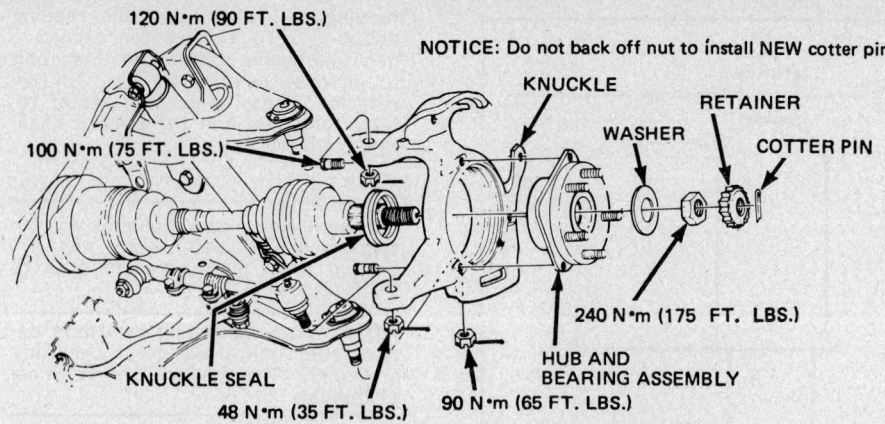

Fig. 21   Bearing & steering knuckle assembly. 1979 Eldorado

Checking Ball Joints For Wear

1. Raise car and position jack stands under lower control arms as near as possible to each ball joint.

2. Clamp vise grips on end of drive axle and position a dial indicator so that dial indicator ball rests on vise grip, Fig. 23.

3. Place a pry bar between lower control arm and outer race and pry down on bar. Reading must not exceed 1/8".

Upper Ball Joint, Replace

1. Remove upper control arm and grind head off three rivets. Using a hammer and punch, drive out rivets.

2. Install new ball joint, securing it in place with three bolts and nuts contained in the kit.

3. Install upper control arm and lubricate ball joint fitting until grease escapes between seal and steering knuckle, Fig. 24.

Lower Ball Joint, Replace

1. Remove lower control arm and cut off two rivet heads from sides of control arm. Grind off head of rivet at bottom of control arm, then drive rivet out of arm.

2. Install service ball joint, securing it to control arm with bolts and nuts contained in kit.

Torsion Bar, Replace

1974-78 Eldorado

Removal

1. Support vehicle so front suspension hangs at full rebound position.

2. Remove adjusting bolts from torsion bar adjuster nuts.

3. Install tool J-22517-01 on 1974-78 models, on torsion bar crossmember, Fig. 25. It may be necessary to pry the crossmember downward to install the tool "U"-bolt.

4. Tighten tool center bolt until torsion bar adjusting arm is raised enough to permit removal of adjuster nut, then remove nut.

5. Loosen tool center bolt until clear of adjusting arm.

6. Repeat steps 3 through 5 on other end of crossmember.

7. Remove parking brake cable from guide at right side of vehicle.

8. Remove torsion bar crossmember bolts, nuts, shim and retainer from both ends of crossmember. Move crossmember as far as possible to-

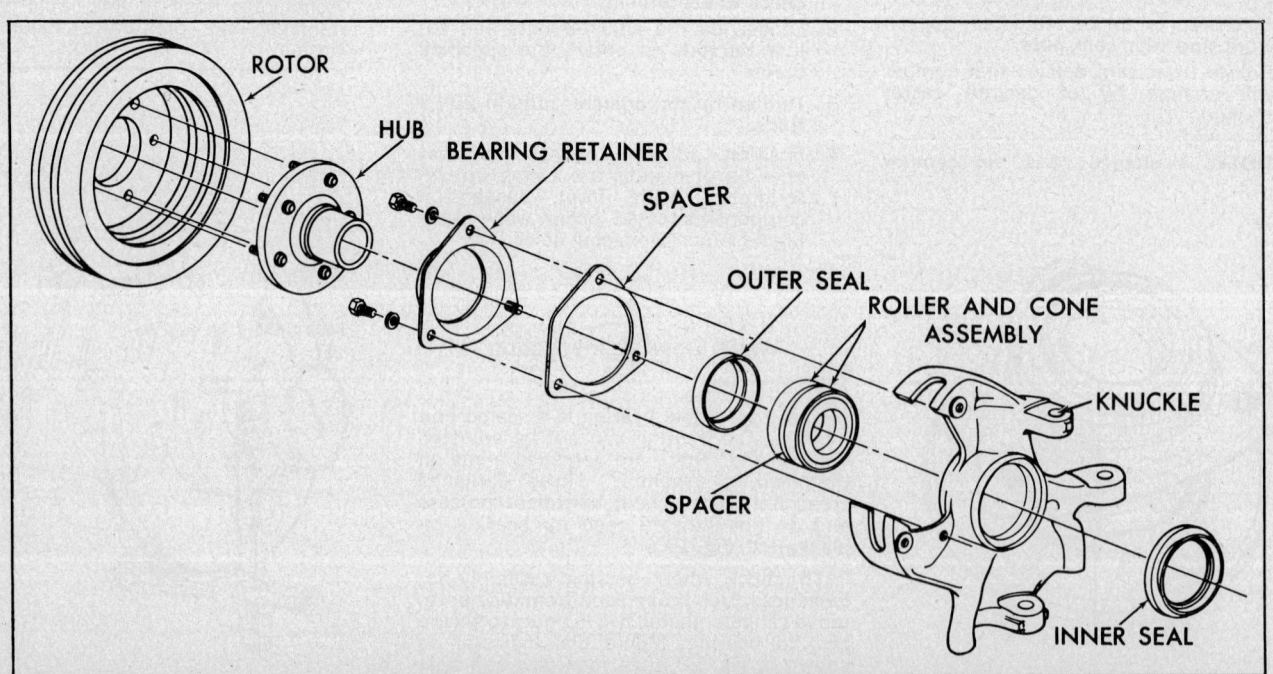

Fig. 22   Wheel bearing and steering knuckle assembly. 1974-78 Eldorado

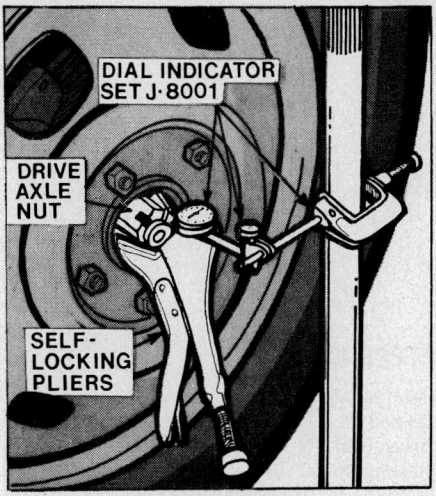

Fig. 23 Checking ball joints for wear.
1974-79 Eldorado

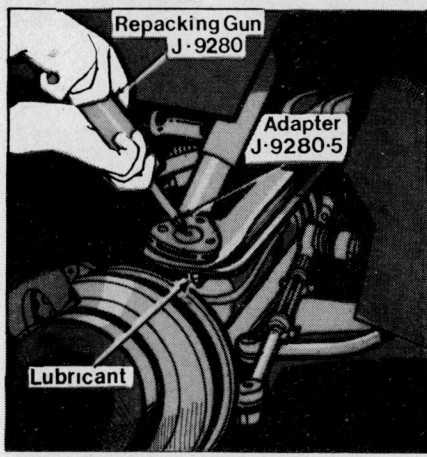

Fig. 24 Repacking upper ball
joint. 1977-78 Eldorado

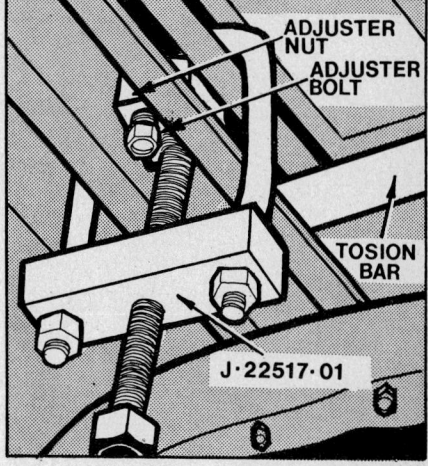

Fig. 25 Torsion bar removal tool installation
1974-78 Eldorado

ward the side opposite torsion bar being removed. One end of cross-member should be clear of frame.

9. Lower end of crossmember and drive rearward until torsion bar is free from crossmember.

NOTE: Use caution not to damage parking brake cable when lowering crossmember. It may be necessary to loosen parking brake cable at equalizer to provide additional slack.

10. Remove torsion bar from lower control arm connector.

NOTE: It is possible to remove both torsion bars at one time, however, installation is easier with one torsion mounted at all times.

Inspection

1. Check torsion bar for nicks, scratches or dents. If any of these conditions exist the torsion bar must be replaced.

Installation

1. Lubricate approximately three inches of each end of torsion bar with suitable lubricant, P/N 9985092 or equivalent.
2. Install torsion bar into lower control arm connector.

NOTE: Torsion bars are stamped with letters "R" for right hand and "L" for left hand. The stamped end of torsion bar is installed in lower control chamber.

3. Position torsion bar adjusting arm in crossmember, hold arm in place and slide torsion bar rearward until seated in adjusting arm.

NOTE: The tape on torsion bar, located near lower control arm connector, should be fully visable but within $1/4$ inch of connector.

4. Position crossmember on frame and install shim between crossmember and frame on each side. Install retainer over crossmember insulator.
5. Ensure torsion bar adjusting arms are properly positioned and install and torque crossmember nuts and bolts to 120 inch lbs.
6. Install parking brake cable through guide on vehicle right side and adjust cable if loosened.
7. Install tool J-22517 or J-22517-01 and tighten tool center bolt until torsion bar adjusting arm is raised enough to install adjustor nut and install nut. Remove tool.
8. Lubricate threads on new torsion bar adjusting bolts and install bolts into adjuster nuts.
9. Check vehicle standing height and wheel alignment. Adjust if necessary.

POWER STEERING, REPLACE

1974-79 Except Eldorado

1. Place container under gear to catch dripping fluid, then disconnect pressure and return lines from gear. Plug all openings to prevent loss of fluid and entrance of dirt into system.
2. Disconnect stone shield (if used) from return pipe, then remove pinch bolt or bolts and washers and disconnect flex coupling from gear.
3. Raise and support vehicle.
4. Remove pitman arm nut and lock-washer, then using a suitable puller, separate pitman arm from pitman shaft.

NOTE: Residual torque on nut after driving, may vary from 10-200 ft. lbs.

5. Remove steering gear to frame retaining bolts and remove steering gear.
6. Reverse procedure to install.

1974-79 Eldorado

1. Place container under gear to catch dripping fluid, then disconnect pressure and return lines from gear. Plug all openings to prevent loss of fluid and entrance of dirt into system.
2. Raise and support vehicle.
3. Remove cotter pin and nut from pitman arm, then using a suitable puller, separate pitman arm from intermediate shaft.
4. If used, remove plastic retainers securing flexible coupling shield to frame side rail and remove shield.
5. Remove nuts and washers from flexible coupling.
6. Remove steering gear to frame bolts, then remove steering gear by moving forward and downward.
7. Remove pitman shaft nut, then using a suitable puller, separate pitman arm from shaft.
8. Reverse procedure to install.

CHECKER MOTORS

INDEX OF SERVICE OPERATIONS

SERIAL NUMBER LOCATION: Plate on left front door pillar, cowl left side above master cylinder or top of left side instrument panel

ENGINE NUMBER LOCATION

SIX CYL.: Pad at front righthand side of cylinder block at rear of distributor

V8 ENGINES: Pad at front righthand side of cylinder block

ENGINE IDENTIFICATION CODE

Engines are identified in the following table by the code letter or letters immediately following the engine serial number.

CODE	TRANS.	ENGINE	CODE	TRANS.	ENGINE	CODE	TRANS.	ENGINE
1974			**1976**			7WD............................V8-350⑤		
4SB............⑨............6-250			6SB.......................................6-250			7WF............................V8-350④		
4SC............⑨............6-250⑤			6SC....................................6-250⑤			**1978**		
4WD............⑨............V8-350			6WD.................................V8-350			8SB.................................6-250⑥⑦		
4WF............⑨............V8-350④			6WF..............................V8-350④			8SC.................................6-250⑤		
1975			**1977**			8SJ.................................6-250⑥⑧		
5SB............⑨............6-250			7SB.......................................6-250			8MK..............................V8-305⑥		
5SC............⑨............6-250⑤			7MK..............................V8-305			8WD..............................V8-350⑤		
5WD............⑨............V8-350								

①—Std. trans.
②—Auto. trans.

③—High performance.
④—Aerobus.
⑤—California.

⑥—Except Calif.
⑦—Less A/C.
⑧—With A/C.

GENERAL ENGINE SPECIFICATIONS

Note: See Chevrolet chapter for engine service procedures.

Year	Engine	Carburetor	Bore and Stroke	Piston Displacement, Cubic Inches	Compression Ratio	Maximum Brake H.P. @ R.P.M.	Maximum Torque Lbs. Ft. @ R.P.M.	Normal Oil Pressure Pounds
1974	100 Horsepower①..............6-250	1 Barrel	3.875 x 3.53	250	8.25	100 @ 3600	175 @ 1800	40
	145 Horsepower①............V8-350	2 Barrel	4.000 x 3.48	350	8.5	145 @ 3800	250 @ 2200	40
	160 Horsepower①............V8-350	4 Barrel	4.000 x 3.48	350	8.5	160 @ 3800	250 @ 2400	40
1975	105 Horsepower①..............6-250	1 Barrel	3.875 x 3.53	250	8.25	105 @ 3800	185 @ 1200	40
	145 Horsepower①............V8-350	2 Barrel	4.000 x 3.48	350	8.5	145 @ 3800	250 @ 2200	40
1976	105 Horsepower①..............6-250	1 Barrel	3.875 x 3.53	250	8.25	105 @ 3800	185 @ 1200	40
	145 Horsepower①............V8-350	2 Barrel	4.000 x 3.48	350	8.5	145 @ 3800	250 @ 2200	40
	Horsepower①..........V8-350②	4 Barrel	4.000 x 3.48	350	8.5	—	—	32–40
1977	110 Horsepower①..............6-250	1 Barrel	3.875 x 3.53	250	8.25	110 @ 3800	195 @ 1600	36–41
	145 Horsepower①............V8-305	2 Barrel	3.736 x 3.48	305	8.5	145 @ 3800	245 @ 2400	32–40
	170 Horsepower①............V8-350	4 Barrel	4.000 x 3.48	350	8.5	170 @ 3800	270 @ 2400	32–40
	Horsepower①..........V8-350②	4 Barrel	4.000 x 3.48	350	8.5	—	—	32–40
1978	90 Horsepower①..............6-250	1 Barrel	3.875 x 3.53	250	8.1	90 @ 3600	180 @ 1600	36–41
	110 Horsepower①..............6-250	1 Barrel	3.875 x 3.53	250	8.1	110 @ 3800	195 @ 1600	36–41
	145 Horsepower①............V8-305	2 Barrel	3.736 x 3.48	305	8.4	145 @ 3800	245 @ 2400	45
	170 Horsepower①............V8-350	4 Barrel	4.000 x 3.48	350	8.2	170 @ 3800	270 @ 2400	32–40

①—Ratings are net—As installed in vehicle.   ②—Aerobus

TUNE UP SPECIFICATIONS

The following specifications are published from the latest information available. This data should be used only in the absence of a decal affixed in the engine compartment.

★When using a timing light, disconnect vacuum hose or tube at distributor and plug opening in hose or tube so idle speed will not be affected.

●When checking compression, lowest cylinder must be within 80 percent of highest.

▲Before removing wires from distributor cap, determine location of the No. 1 wire in cap, as distributor position may have been altered from that shown at the end of this chart.

| Year | Spark Plug | | Distributor | | Ignition Timing ★ | | | Carb. Adjustments | | | | | |
| | Type | Gap Inch | Point Gap Inch | Dwell Angle Deg. | Firing Order Fig. ▲ | Timing BTDC ① | Mark Fig. | Hot Idle Speed | | Air Fuel Ratio | | Idle "CO" % | |
								Std. Trans.	Auto. Trans.②	Std. Trans.	Auto. Trans.	Std. Trans.	Auto. Trans.
1974													
6-250	R46T	.035	⑤	31–34	A	6°	D	—	600D	—	—	—	—
V8-350	R44T	.035	⑤	29–31	B	8°	D	—	600D	—	—	—	—
1975													
6-250	R46TX	.060	—	—	E	10°	D	—	550D⑦	—	—	—	—
V8-350	R44TX	.060	—	—	C	6°	D	—	600D	—	—	—	—
1976													
6-250	R46TS	.035	—	—	E	10°	D	—	550D⑦	—	—	—	—
V8-350⑧	R45TS	.045	—	—	C	6°	D	—	600D	—	—	—	—
V8-350⑨	R44TX	.060	—	—	C	2°	D	—	700N	—	—	—	—
1977													
6-250	R46TS	.035	—	—	E	⑩	D	—	550D③	—	—	—	—
V8-305	R45TS	.045	—	—	C	8°	D	—	500D④	—	—	—	—
V8-350⑧	R45TS	.045	—	—	C	8°	D	—	500D④	—	—	—	—
V8-350⑥⑧	R45TS	.045	—	—	C	8°	D	—	600D④	—	—	—	—
V8-350⑨	R45TS	.045	—	—	C	—	D	—	—	—	—	—	—
1978													
6-250⑪	R46TS	.035	—	—	E	⑫	D	—	⑬	—	—	—	—
6-250⑭	R46TS	.035	—	—	E	6°	D	—	600D	—	—	—	—
V8-305⑪	R45TS	.045	—	—	C	4°	D	—	500D	—	—	—	—
V8-350⑭	R45TS	.045	—	—	C	8°	D	—	500D	—	—	—	—

① —BTDC: Before top dead center.
② —D: Drive. N: Neutral.
③ —With A/C & High Altitude, 600D RPM.
④ —On models with A/C, 650D RPM with A/C solenoid energized.
⑤ —New points, .019″, used, .016″. On V8's,

turn adjusting screw in (clockwise) until engine misfires, then back off ½ turn.
⑥ —High Altitude.
⑦ —Calif. 600D RPM.
⑧ —Marathon & Taxicab.
⑨ —Aerobus.

⑩ —Except high altitude, 8° BTDC; high altitude 10° BTDC.
⑪ —Exc. Calif.
⑫ —Less A/C, 10° BTDC; with A/C, 8° BTDC.
⑬ —Less A/C, 550D RPM; with A/C, 600D RPM.
⑭ —California.

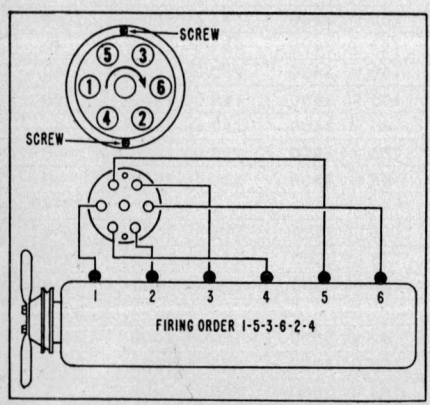

Fig. A

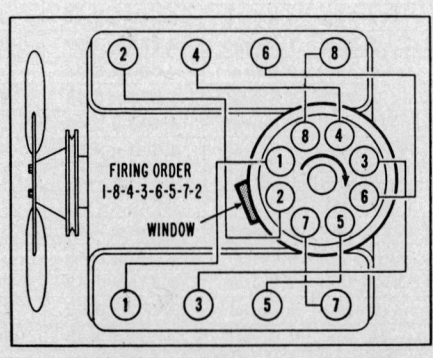

Fig. B

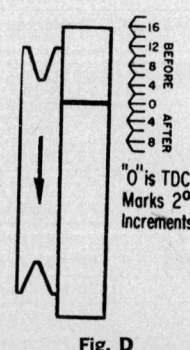

Fig. D

Continued

TUNE UP SPECIFICATIONS—Continued

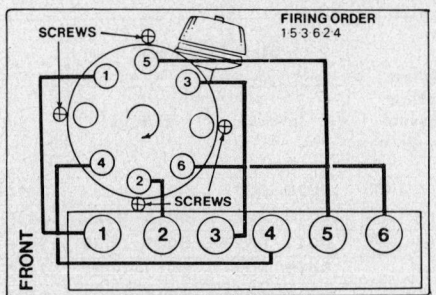

Fig. E

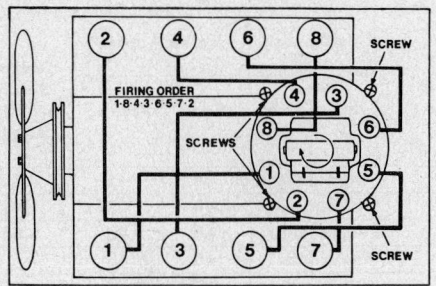

Fig. C

DISTRIBUTOR SPECIFICATIONS

★Note: If unit is checked on vehicle, double the RPM and degrees to get crankshaft figures.

Distributor Part No.①	Advance Starts	Centrifugal Advance Degrees @ RPM of Distributor			Vacuum Advance	
		Intermediate Advance		Full Advance	Inches of Vacuum to Start Plunger	Max. Adv. Dist. Deg. @ Vacuum
1974						
1110499	0 @ 550	—	—	11½ @ 2100	6	11 @ 14
1112093	0 @ 550	5½ @ 1200	—	9 @ 2100	6	7½ @ 13½
1112844	0 @ 500	—	—	9 @ 2100	4	7 @ 7
1975						
1110650②	0 @ 550	3½ @ 1150	—	8 @ 2100	4	7½ @ 12
1975-76						
1112863②	0 @ 800	3 @ 1100	—	7 @ 1900	4	9 @ 12
1112880②	0 @ 600	6 @ 1000	—	11 @ 2100	4	9 @ 12
1976						
1112884②	0 @ 575	8½ @ 1450	—	11 @ 2100	8	5 @ 13
1977						
1103239②	0 @ 600	6½ @ 1000	—	10 @ 2100	4	7½ @ 10
1103246②	0 @ 600	6 @ 1000	—	11 @ 2100	4	9 @ 12
1103248③	0 @ 600	6 @ 1000	—	11 @ 2100	4	9 @ 12
1110678③	0 @ 500	3½ @ 800	—	10 @ 2100	4	12 @ 15
1978						
6-250②③④	0 @ 500	3½ @ 800	—	10 @ 2100	4	12 @ 15
6-250②⑤	0 @ 500	3½ @ 800	—	10 @ 2100	4	9 @ 13
6-250②⑥	0 @ 500	3½ @ 800	—	10 @ 2100	4	7½ @ 12
V8-305②③	0 @ 500	5 @ 850	—	10 @ 1900	4	10 @ 10
V8-350②⑥	0 @ 600	6 @ 1000	—	11 @ 2100	4	10 @ 10

①—Stamped on distributor housing cover.
②—High Energy Ignition.
③—Except Calif.
④—Less A/C.
⑤—With A/C.
⑥—California.

VALVE SPECIFICATIONS

Year	Engine Model	Valve Lash		Valve Angles		Valve Spring Installed Height	Valve Spring Pressure Lbs. @ In.	Stem Clearance		Stem Diameter	
		Int.	Exh.	Seat	Face			Intake	Exhaust	Intake	Exhaust
1974–75	6-250	Hydraulic①		46	45	1.66	186 @ 1.27	.0010–.0027	.0015–.0032	.3410–.3417	.3410–.3417
1976–77	6-250	Hydraulic②		46	45	1²¹⁄₃₂	175 @ 1.26	.0010–.0027	.0015–.0032	.3410–.3417	.3410–.3417
1978	6-250	Hydraulic①		46	45	1.66	175 @ 1.26	.0010–.0027	.0015–.0032	.3410–.3417	.3410–.3417
1977	8-305	Hydraulic②		46	45	③	④	.0010–.0027	.0010–.0027	.3410–.3417	.3410–.3417
1978	V8-305	Hydraulic①		46	45	③	④	.0010–.0027	.0010–.0027	.3410–.3417	.3410–.3417
1974–75	8-350	Hydraulic①		46	45	1.66	189 @ 1.20	.0010–.0027	.0012–.0029	.3410–.3417	.3410–.3417
1976–77	8-350	Hydraulic②		46	45	③	④	.0010–.0027	.0010–.0027	.3410–.3417	.3410–.3417
1978	V8-350	Hydraulic①		46	45	③	④	.0010–.0027	.0010–.0027	.3410–.3417	.3410–.3417

①—1 turn down from zero lash.
②—¾ turn down from zero lash.

③—Intake, 1.70; exhaust, 1.61.
④—Intake, 200 @ 1.25; exhaust, 200 @ 1.16.

PISTONS, PINS, RINGS, CRANKSHAFT & BEARINGS

Year	Engine Model	Piston Clearance	Ring End Gap①		Wrist-pin Diameter	Rod Bearings		Main Bearings			
			Comp.	Oil		Shaft Diameter	Bearing Clearance	Shaft Diameter	Bearing Clearance	Thrust on Bear. No.	Shaft End Play
1974–75	6-250	.0015–.0025	.010	.015	.9272	1.9928–2.000	.0007–.0027	2.2983–2.2993	.0003–.0029	7	.002–.006
1976–77	6-250	.0010–.0020	.010	.015	.9272	1.9928–2.000	.0007–.0027	2.2983–2.2993	.0003–.0029	7	.002–.006
1978	6-250	.0010–.0020	.010	.015	.9272	1.9928–2.000	.0010–.0026	2.2979–2.2994	⑤	7	.002–.006
1977	8-305	.0007–.0017	.010	.015	.9272	2.099–2.100	.0013–.0035	④	③	5	.002–.006
1978	V8-305	.0007–.0017	.010	.015	.9272	2.0986–2.0998	.0013–.0035	④	③	5	.002–.006
1974–77	8-350	.0007–.0017	②	.015	.9272	2.099–2.100	.0013–.0035	④	③	5	.002–.006
1978	V8-350	.0007–.0017	.010	.015	.9272	2.0986–2.0998	.0013–.0035	④	③	5	.002–.006

①—Fit rings in tapered bores to the clearance listed in tightest portion of ring travel. Clearance specified are mimimum gaps.
②—Top ring, .010; lower ring, .013.

③—No. 1: .0008–.0020; No. 2, 3, 4: .0011–.0023; No. 5: .0017–.0033.
④—No. 1: 2.4484–2.4493; No. 2, 3, 4: 2.4481–2.4490; No. 5: 2.4475–2.4488.
⑤—Except No. 7, .0010–.0024; No. 7, .0016–.0035.

ALTERNATOR SPECIFICATIONS

Year	Alternator							Regulator②			
	Make	Model	Ground Polarity	Rated Output		Field Current		Model	Regulator Test @ 120°F		
				Amperes	Volts	Amperes①	Volts		Ampere Load	Altern. R.P.M.	Volts
1974	Motorola	8AL-2002	Negative	55	15	1.8–2.4	12.6	8RD2009	10	2000	13.4–13.9
1975	Delco-Remy	1100542	Negative	63	—	4.0–4.5	12	Integral	—	—	—
	Delco-Remy	1102854	Negative	63	—	4.0–4.5	12	Integral	—	—	—
1976–77	Delco-Remy	1102854	Negative	63	—	4.0–4.5	12	Integral	—	—	13.8–14.8
	Delco-Remy	1102860	Negative	63	—	4.0–4.5	12	Integral	—	—	13.8–14.8
1978	Delco-Remy	—	Negative	62	—	4.0–4.5	12	Integral	—	—	—

①—Excessive current drain indicates shorted field windings.
②—Regulator is a sealed assembly, requiring no adjustments.

ENGINE TIGHTENING SPECIFICATIONS*

★Torque specifications are for clean and lightly lubricated threads only. Dry or dirty threads produce increased friction which prevents accurate measurement of tightness.

Year	Engine Model	Spark Plugs Ft. Lbs.	Cylinder Head Bolts Ft. Lbs.	Intake Manifold Ft. Lbs.	Exhaust Manifold Ft. Lbs.	Rocker Arm Stud Ft. Lbs.	Rocker Arm Cover Ft. Lbs.	Connecting Rod Cap Bolts Ft. Lbs.	Main Bearing Cap Bolts Ft. Lbs.	Flywheel to Crankshaft Ft. Lbs.	Vibration Damper or Pulley Ft. Lbs.
1974	6-250	15	95	②	②	—	45③	35	65	60	60
1975	6-250	15	95	—	20④	—	45③	35	65	60	60
1976-78	6-250	15	95⑤	—	30	—	45③	35	65	60	60
1974	8-350	15	65	30	20④	50	45③	45	75①	60	60
1975	8-350	15	65	30	20④	50	45③	45	70①	60	60
1976-78	8-305, 350	15	65	30	20④	50	45③	45	70①	60	60

①—Outer bolts on engines with 4 bolt caps, 65 ft. lbs.
②—End clamp bolts 20 ft. lbs.; center bolts, 30 ft. lbs.
③—Inch lbs.
④—Inside bolts, 30 ft. lbs.
⑤—Left hand front head bolt, 85 ft. lb.

STARTING MOTOR SPECIFICATIONS

Year	Engine	Starter Number	Brush Spring Tension Oz.①	Free Speed Test Amps.③	Volts	R.P.M.①	Resistance Test③ Amps.	Volts
1974	V8-350	1108361	35	65-100	10.6	3600-5100	300-360	3.5
1974	6-250	1108480	35	50-80	9	5500-10500	—	—
1974	V8-350	1108430	35	65-95	9	7500-10500	—	—
1975-76	6-250	1108778	—	50-80②	9	5500-10500	—	—
	V8-350	1108776	—	65-95②	9	7500-10500	—	—
1977	6-250	1108778	—	50-80②	9	5500-10500	—	—
	V8-305	1109052	—	65-95②	9	7500-10500	—	—
	V8-350	1109052	—	65-95②	9	7500-10500	—	—
1978	6-250	—	—	60-85②	9	6800-10300	—	—
	V8-305	—	—	65-95②	9	7500-10500	—	—
	V8-350	—	—	65-95②	9	7500-10500	—	—

①—Minimum.
②—Includes solenoid.
③—Check capacity of motor by using a 500 ampere meter and a carbon pile rheostat to control voltage. Apply the volts listed across motor with armature locked. Current should be as listed.

WHEEL ALIGNMENT SPECIFICATIONS

Year	Model	Caster Angle, Degrees Limits	Desired	Camber Angle, Degrees Limits Left	Right	Desired Left	Right	Toe-In Inch	Toe-Out on Turns, Deg.① Outer Wheel	Inner Wheel
1974	Aerobus	+2	+2	+1 to +2	+1 to +2	+1½	+1½	⅛ to 3/16	—	—
1974-77	Exc. Aerobus	+2	+2	0 to +1	0 to +1	+½	+½	1/16 to ⅛	—	—
1978	All	+1 to +2	+1½	+½ to +1½	+½ to +1½	+1	+1	1/16-⅛	—	—

①—Incorrect toe-out when other adjustments are correct, indicates bent steering arms.

REAR AXLE SPECIFICATIONS

Year	Model	Carrier Type	Ring Gear & Pinion Backlash		Pinion Bearing Preload			Differential Bearing Preload		
			Method	Adjustment	Method	New Bearings Inch-Lbs.	Used Bearings Inch-Lbs.	Method	New Bearings Inch-Lbs.	Used Bearings Inch-Lbs.
1974-77	44	Integral	Shims	.005-.010	Shims	20-40①	10-20①	Shims	.015	.015
1974-77	62	Integral	Shims	.005-.009	Shims	20-40①	10-20①	Shims	.015	.015
1978	44	Integral	Shims	.005-.009	Shims	20-40①	—	Shims	—	—

①—Use inch-pound torque wrench on pinion shaft nut.

COOLING SYSTEM & CAPACITY DATA

Year	Model or Engine	Cooling Capacity, Qts.			Radiator Cap Relief Pressure, Lbs.		Thermo. Opening Temp. ①	Fuel Tank Gals.	Engine Oil Refill Qts. ②	Transmission Oil			Rear Axle Oil Pints
		No Heater	With Heater	With A/C	With A/C	No A/C				3 Speed Pints	4 Speed Pints	Auto. Trans. Qts.③	
1974-77	6-250	—	12	12	15	15	195	21½	4	—	—	9	3
1974-77	V8-350④	—	17	17	15	15	195	21½	4	—	—	9	3
1974-77	V8-350⑤	—	21	21	15	15	195	21½	4	—	—	9	6
1978	6-250	11	12⑥				195		4	—	—		
	V8-305	16	17⑦				195		4	—	—		
	V8-350	16	17⑦				195		4	—	—		

①—For permanent type anti-freeze.
②—Add one quart with filter change.
⑧—Approximate. Make final check with dipstick.

④—Marathon & Taxicab.
⑤—Aerobus.

⑥—If equipped w/dash & floor mounted heater 13 qts.
⑦—If equipped w/dash & floor mounted heater 18 qts.

BRAKE SPECIFICATIONS

Year	Model	Brake Drum Inside Diameter	Wheel Cylinder Bore Diameter			Master Cylinder Bore Diameter		
			Disc Brake	Front Drum Brake	Rear Drum Brake	Disc Brakes	Drum Brakes	Power Brakes
1974-77	All Exc. Aerobus	11	2¹⁵⁄₁₆	—	¹⁵⁄₁₆	1⅛	—	1
	Aerobus	11	—	1⅛	1	1	—	1
1978	All	11	—	—	¹⁵⁄₁₆	1⅛	—	1⅛

Electrical Section

DISTRIBUTOR

Refer to the Chevrolet chapter for removal and installation procedures.

STARTER, REPLACE

Refer to the Chevrolet chapter for replacement procedure.

IGNITION LOCK

Refer to the Chevrolet chapter for replacement procedure.

IGNITION SWITCH, REPLACE

Refer to the Chevrolet chapter for replacement procedure.

LIGHT SWITCH, REPLACE

1974-78 All

1. Disconnect battery ground cable.
2. Pull switch knob to "ON" position, reach under instrument panel and depress shaft retainer, then pull knob and shaft from switch.
3. Remove ferrule nut and switch from instrument panel and disconnect wiring.
4. Reverse procedure to install.

STOP LIGHT SWITCH, REPLACE

1974-78 All

1. Disconnect electrical connector from switch on brake pedal support.
2. Remove retaining nut, if so equipped, then remove switch from bracket.
3. Install and adjust new switch so stop lights are actuated when brake pedal is depressed ⅜ inch from fully released position.

NEUTRAL SAFETY SWITCH, REPLACE

Refer to the Chevrolet chapter, "1974-78 Column Shift".

TURN SIGNAL SWITCH, REPLACE

Refer to the Chevrolet chapter, "1974-78" replacement procedures.

HORN SOUNDER & STEERING WHEEL

Refer to the Chevrolet chapter, "1974-78 Standard Wheel" procedures.

INSTRUMENT CLUSTER

1974-78 All

1. Disconnect battery ground cable.
2. Remove instrument cluster retaining screws.
3. Pull cluster forward, disconnect wiring and remove instrument cluster.
4. Reverse procedure to install.

W/S WIPER BLADES

Two methods are used to retain wiper blades to wiper arms, Fig. 1. One method uses a press type release tab. When the release tab is depressed the blade assembly can be slid off the wiper arm pin. The other method uses a coil spring retainer. A screwdriver must be inserted on top of the spring and the spring pushed downward. The blade assembly can then be slid off the wiper arm pin. Two methods are also used to retain the blade element in the blade assembly, Fig. 1. One method uses a press type release button. When the button is depressed the two piece blade assembly can be slid off the blade element. The other method uses a spring type retainer clip in the end of the blade element. When the retainer clip is squeezed together, the blade element can be slid out of the blade assembly.

NOTE: To be sure of correct installation, the element release button, or the spring element retaining clip should be at the end of the wiper blade assembly nearest the wiper transmission.

W/S WIPER ARMS

1. Wiper motor must be in park position.
2. Use suitable tool to minimize the possibility of windshield or paint finish damage during arm removal.
3. Remove arm by prying up with tool to disengage arm from serrated transmission shaft.
4. To install arm to transmission shaft rotate the required distance and direction so that the blades rest in proper position.

W/S WIPER MOTOR

1. Remove nut and lock washer through center hole of pivot arm drive disc and separate drive disc from motor.
2. Remove bolts securing motor to cowl, lower transmission and disconnect motor electrical connector.
3. Remove motor from vehicle.

W/S WIPER TRANSMISSION

1. Perform step 1 as outlined under "W/S Wiper Motor".
2. Remove retaining clip from stud and disconnect right hand arm from transmission.
3. Remove wiper arm assemblies, outside linkage nut and transmission and linkage from under dash.

RADIO, REPLACE

1. Remove inner and outer knobs and right hand shaft insert.
2. Remove mounting nuts, escutcheon inserts and escutcheon.
3. Disconnect antenna, speaker and power feed leads.
4. Remove mounting nut from bracket and remove radio.

BLOWER MOTOR, REMOVAL

1. Disconnect wiring from motor.
2. Remove blower to heater housing screws and remove blower motor.

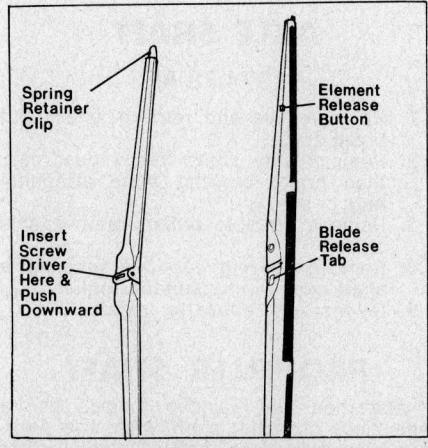

Spring Retainer Clip

Element Release Button

Insert Screw Driver Here & Push Downward

Blade Release Tab

Fig. 1   Wiper blades

HEATER CORE, REMOVAL

1. Disconnect resistor wires and remove heater core cover.
2. Disconnect heater hoses from core and plug hoses and core openings.
3. Slide heater core from housing.

Engine Section

Refer to Chevrolet Chapter for Engine Service Procedures.

Transmission Section

TURBO-HYDRAMATIC 400, REPLACE

1974-78

1. Disconnect battery negative cable and raise vehicle.
2. Remove filler tube and drain transmission.
3. Support engine and remove converter underpan.
4. Remove converter to flywheel bolts.
5. Disconnect speedometer cable, kickdown switch wiring and shift linkage.
6. Disconnect vacuum modulator line and remove vacuum modulator.
7. Disconnect oil cooler lines.
8. Reinstall vacuum modulator with retaining bolt finger tight.
9. Disconnect parking brake cable from frame lever and on all models except Aerobus, remove parking brake lever bracket.
10. Remove propeller shaft.
11. Place a jack under transmission and remove rear engine support.
12. Lower engine and transmission slightly and remove engine to transmission bolts. Move transmission rearward and install a suitable converter holding tool. Lower transmission and remove from vehicle.
13. Reverse procedure to install.

IN-CAR ADJUSTMENTS

NOTE: Refer to the Automatic Transmission section, Turbo-Hydramatic 400 chapter, for other adjustments and minor service.

Manual Linkage, Adjust

Refer to Turbo-Hydramatic 400 chapter, "Chevrolet Column Shift" 1974-78 manual linkage adjustment.

Kickdown Switch, Adjust

Adjust switch, located under accelerator pedal, so plunger is depressed when carburetor throttle is in the wide open position.

Rear Axle, Propeller Shaft & Brakes

REAR AXLE, REPLACE

1. Support vehicle at frame and rear axle, relieving tension from springs and remove rear wheels.
2. Disconnect parking brake cable at equalizer and brake line at axle tube connector.
3. Disconnect shock absorbers from lower mountings.
4. Place an alignment mark between rear propeller shaft yoke, universal joint and pinion flange yoke for alignment during assembly. Disconnect propeller shaft from pinion flange.
5. Remove axle shafts and brake support plates.
6. Remove leaf spring "U" bolts and spring plates.
7. Remove axle assembly from vehicle.
8. Reverse procedure to install.

AXLE SHAFT

1974-78 All

1. Raise vehicle and remove wheel and brake drum.
2. Remove axle shaft flange dust cap, then brake backing plate attaching nuts or screws.
3. Using a suitable puller, remove axle shaft.
4. Remove bearing cup and inner axle shaft seal with a suitable puller.
5. Reverse procedure to install.

PROPELLER SHAFT

Marathon and Taxicab models use a one piece propeller shaft while the Aerobus has a two piece shaft. Universal joints must be lubricated every 2500 miles with a suitable lithium soap base grease. When lubricating these joints, lubricant must flow from all four bearing seals.

BRAKE ADJUSTMENTS

Refer to the Chevrolet chapter for brake adjustments on the Marathon and Taxicab models.

Refer to the Chrysler chapter for brake adjustments on Aerobus models.

PARKING BRAKE, ADJUST

1978

1. Raise vehicle and apply parking brake two notches from the fully released position.

2. Tighten adjusting at rear cable equalizer while rotating rear wheels forward until brake drag is evident.
3. Release parking brake and check to ensure that no drag is present at rear wheels.

1974-77

Depress parking brake pedal approximately ½ inch, then remove slack from cable at clevis. Check cable adjustment to ensure against brake drag.

MASTER CYLINDER, REPLACE

Disconnect hydraulic lines from master cylinder. Remove bolts securing master cylinder to mounting.

POWER BRAKE UNIT

Refer to the Chevrolet chapter for replacement procedures.

Rear Suspension Section

SHOCK ABSORBER, REPLACE

1. With rear axle properly supported, remove nuts securing shock absorber to spring plate bracket, Fig. 1.
2. Remove nuts securing shock absorber to upper mounting bracket.
3. Reverse procedure to install.

LEAF SPRING, REPLACE

1. Support vehicle at frame and rear axle, removing tension from spring.
2. Disconnect shock absorber from spring plate mounting bracket.
3. Remove "U" bolt nuts, spring plate and "U" bolts.
4. Disassemble rear shackle.
5. Remove nuts securing spring front mounting bracket to the frame, pull spring assembly rearward and remove from vehicle. Remove spring front mounting bracket from spring.
6. Reverse procedure to install.

HELPER SPRING, REPLACE

1. Perform steps 1 to 3 as outlined under "Leaf Spring, Replace" procedure.
2. Remove rubber bumper "U" bolt nuts, plate, "U" bolt and rubber bumper, Fig. 2.
3. Reverse procedure to install.

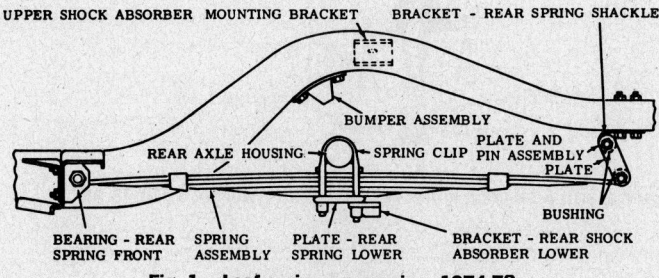

Fig. 1   Leaf spring suspension. 1974-78

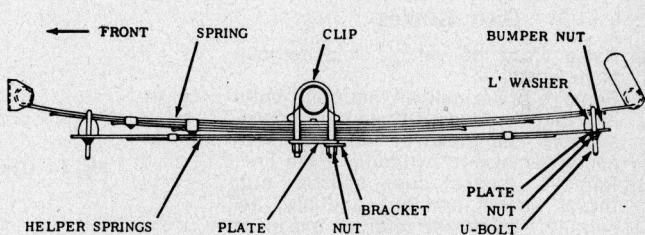

Fig. 2   Helper spring installation. 1974-78

Front End and Steering Section

FRONT SUSPENSION

All front suspension systems incorporate independent coil springs riding on the lower control arms. Ball joints connect the upper and lower control arms to the steering knuckles, Figs. 1 and 2.

LUBRICATION

Lubrication is recommended at 2,500 mile intervals with a suitable lithium base grease. When lubricating the ball joints, the joint must be unloaded.

WHEEL ALIGNMENT

Caster and camber adjustments are made by means of shims between the upper control arm shaft and the frame. Shims may be added, subtracted or transferred to change the readings as follows:

Caster, Adjust

Transfer shims from front to rear or rear to front. The transfer of one shim (.06 inch) from rear to front will increase positive caster by ½°. In any case, the total thickness of the shim pack should not exceed .562 inch.

Camber, Adjust

Add or subtract shims at both bolts (front and rear). Adding one shim (.06 inch) at front and rear bolts will increase positive camber by ¼°.

TOE-IN, ADJUST

Toe-in can be adjusted by loosening the

clamp bolts at each end of the tie rods and turning each tie rod to increase or decrease its length as necessary until proper toe-in is obtained with the steering gear on the high point for straight ahead driving and the steering wheel centered.

WHEEL BEARINGS, ADJUST

1978

1. While rotating hub and rotor, torque spindle nut to 10 to 16 ft. lbs. to seat bearings, then loosen spindle nut.
2. Retorque spindle nut to 2 ft. lbs.
3. Install retainer nut. Align one pair of slots with the cotter pin hole in the spindle.
4. Back nut off one slot, then install cotter pin.

1974-77

1. While rotating wheel, snug-up spindle nut.
2. Back nut off, then snug-up nut by hand.
3. Loosen nut to nearest cotter pin hole and insert cotter pin.
4. When bearings are properly adjusted, there should be .001-.005 inch end play present.

WHEEL BEARINGS, REPLACE

Disc Brakes

1. Raise front of vehicle and remove front wheels.
2. Remove brake caliper mounting bolts and caliper. Once caliper is removed, support caliper away from disc to avoid damage to hydraulic brake line.
3. Remove grease cup, spindle nut, thrust washer and hub and disc assembly. The grease retainer and inner wheel bearing can now be removed.

CHECKING BALL JOINTS FOR WEAR

Upper Ball Joint

The upper ball joint is checked for wear by measuring the amount of torque required to rotate the ball stud in the assembly. To make this type of check, it is necessary to remove the stud from the steering knuckle.

Install a nut on the ball stud and using a torque wrench, turn the stud. Acceptable torque for an upper ball joint is 28-40 inch lbs. If torque readings are excessively low or high, replace the ball joint.

Lower Ball Joint

1978

Raise vehicle and support lower control

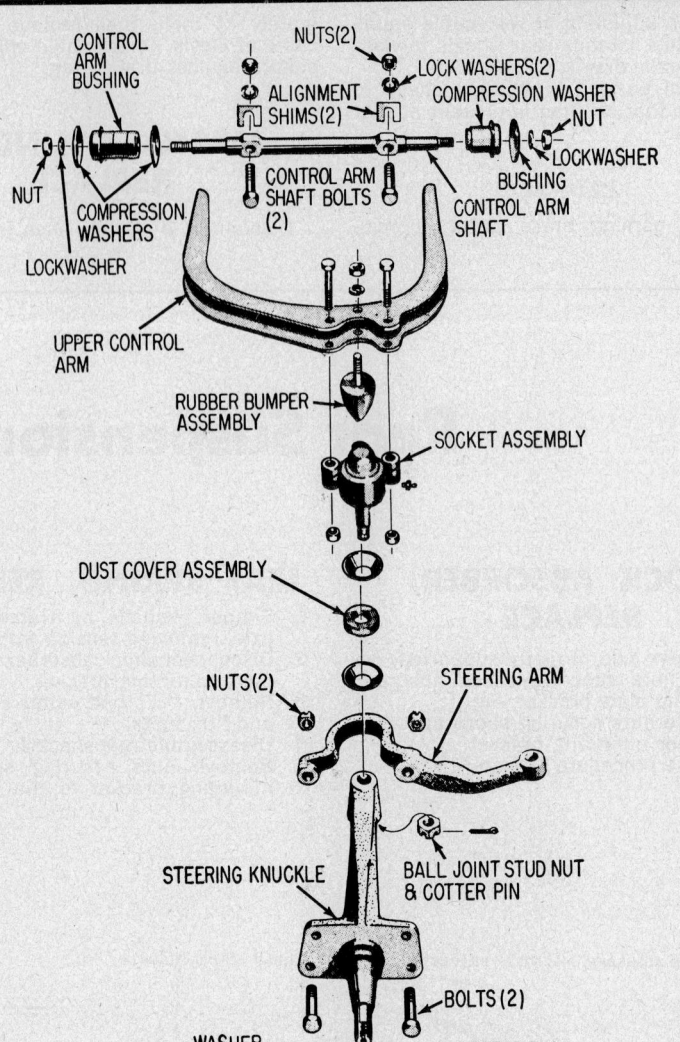

Fig. 1   Upper control arm & steering knuckles installation (typical). 1974-78 All

arm. Grasp wheel and move in an upward and downward motion. If vertical play at lower ball joint socket exceeds .065 in., replace ball joint.

1974-77

The lower ball joint is checked for wear by measuring the amount of "pull" required to move the ball stud in the assembly. This check is made with the stud removed from the steering knuckle.

With a spring scale attached to the stud cotter pin hole, pull the spring scale until the stud moves and note the reading. The specified "pull" for an acceptable lower ball joint is 8 lbs. If reading is lower than specified, replace the ball joint.

UPPER BALL JOINT, REPLACE

1. Support vehicle at lower control

and remove wheel.
2. Remove cotter pin from ball stud and loosen stud nut.
3. Lightly tap ball stud to loosen stud and remove stud nut.
4. Remove bolts securing ball joint to control arm.
5. Install new ball joint and torque bolts to 20-30 ft. lbs.
6. Assemble ball joint to steering knuckle and torque stud nut to 75-95 foot pounds and install cotter pin.

LOWER BALL JOINT, REPLACE

1978

1. Raise and support front of vehicle, then remove wheel and tire assembly. Position a suitable jack under lower control arm and compress coil spring.

2. Disconnect tie rod end from steering arm.
3. Remove cotter pin from lower ball joint stud, then loosen stud nut two turns.

NOTE: Install a safety chain around lower control arm and spring.

4. Lightly tap ball joint bracket to loosen stud, then remove nut.

NOTE: Ensure spring is sufficiently compressed before removing stud nut.

5. Remove bolts attaching steering arm to steering knuckle, then remove steering arm.
6. Position steering arm in a vise and drive out ball joint.
7. Press ball joint into steering arm.
8. Reverse procedure to install. Torque steering arm to steering knuckle bolts to 90-103 ft. lbs., tie rod end to steering arm nut to 40-45 ft. lbs. and ball joint stud nut to 80-90 ft. lbs.

1974-77

1. Support vehicle at lower control arm and remove wheel.
2. If equipped with disc brakes, remove caliper assembly.
3. Perform steps 2, 3 and 4 as outlined in above procedure.
4. Install new ball joint and torque bolts to 20-30 ft. lbs.
5. Raise control arm with jack until ball stud contacts spindle, install and torque stud nut to 100 ft. lbs.

SHOCK ABSORBER, REPLACE

1. Support vehicle at lower control arm.
2. Remove shock absorber upper mounting nuts.
3. Remove shock absorber mounting plate to lower control arm bolts. After shock absorber is removed, disconnect mounting plate from shock absorber.
4. Reverse procedure to install.

COIL SPRING, REPLACE

1978

1. Raise and support front of vehicle.
2. Remove shock absorber as described under Shock Absorber, Replace.
3. Disconnect outer tie rod socket from steering arm.
4. Remove wheel and tire assembly, then position a suitable jack under lower control arm and compress coil spring.
5. Disconnect stablizer bar at lower control arm.
6. Remove cotter pin from lower ball joint stud, then loosen stud nut two turns.

NOTE: Install a safety chain around lower control arm and frame side rail.

7. Lightly tap ball joint bracket to loosen stud, then remove stud from nut.

NOTE: Ensure spring is sufficently compressed before removing stud nut.

8. Disconnect safety chain, then carefully and slowly lower the control arm

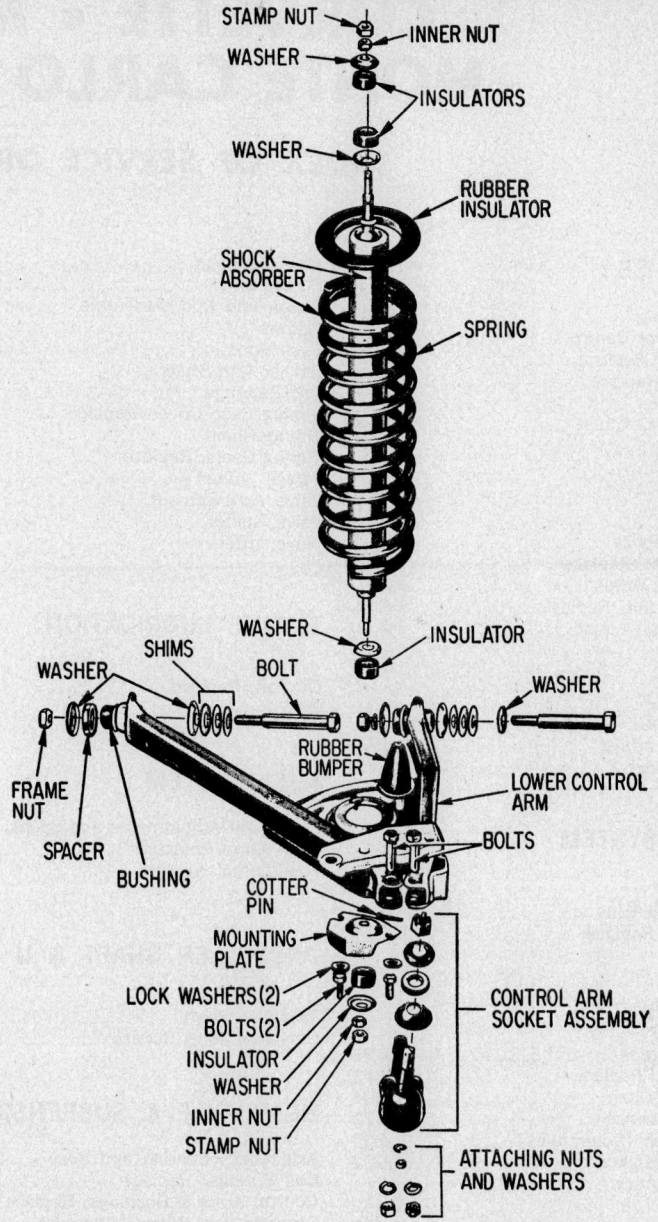

Fig. 2 Lower control arm, coil spring & shock absorber installation (typical). 1974-78 All

until all spring tension is relieved and remove spring and insulator.

1974-77

1. Support vehicle at frame and lower control arm with a suitable jack.
2. Disconnect stabilizer bar from lower control arm and loosen lower ball joint stud nut two turns. Lightly tap steering knuckle to loosen ball stud, then remove stud nut.
3. Lower jack slowly until tension is relieved from spring and remove spring and insulator.

NOTE: Install a safety chain through coil spring and lower control arm to prevent injury or damage if spring slips from mounting.

STEERING GEAR, REPLACE

1. Disconnect pressure and return hoses from gear housing. Cap hoses and gear housing outlets.
2. Raise and support front of vehicle.
3. Remove nuts and washers from steering coupling.
4. Remove nut and washer retaining pitman arm to pitman shaft.
5. Mark relation of pitman arm to pitman shaft, then using a suitable puller, remove arm from shaft.
6. Remove three steering gear housing attaching bolts, then remove gear assembly from vehicle.

CAMARO · CHEVELLE · CHEVROLET
CORVETTE · MALIBU
MONTE CARLO · NOVA

INDEX OF SERVICE OPERATIONS

SERIAL NUMBER LOCATION: Plate on left front door pillar or top of left side instrument panel

ENGINE NUMBER LOCATION

4 & 6 CYL.: Pad at front righthand side of cylinder block at rear of distributor	**V8 ENGINES:** Pad at front righthand side of cylinder block

ENGINE IDENTIFICATION CODE

Engines are identified in the following table by the code letter or letters immediately following the engine serial number.

CAMARO

CODE			CODE			CODE		
CCD	6-250	1977	CRC	8-350	1975	C3Y	6-250	1978
CCF	6-250	1977	CMF	8-350	1975	CTH	8-305	1978
CCR	6-250 with M/T	1974	CMH	8-350	1975	CTJ	8-305	1978
CCW	6-250 with T/H, E.E.C.	1974	CRX	8-350	1975	CTK	8-305	1978
CCW	6-250	1977	CHW	8-350	1975	C3N	8-305	1978
CCX	6-250 with T/H	1974	CHS	8-350	1975	CHF	8-350	1978
CJL	6-250	1975	CHT	8-350	1975	CHJ	8-350	1978
CJM	6-250	1975	CPA	8-305	1977	CHL	8-350	1978
CJR	6-250	1975	CPC	8-305	1977	CHR	8-350	1978
CJT	6-250	1975	CPY	8-305	1977	CHS	8-350	1978
CJU	6-250	1975	CCC	6-250	1976	CHT	8-305	1978
CJF	6-250	1975	CCD	6-250	1976	CHU	8-350	1978
CJY	6-250	1975	CCF	6-250	1976	C3T	8-350	1978
CJZ	6-250	1975	CHT	8-350	1976	DKA	6-250	1979
CKH	6-250	1977	CHU	8-350	1976	DKB	6-250	1979
CKM	8-350	1977	CML	8-350	1976	DKD	6-250	1979
CKR	8-350	1977	CPA	8-305	1976	DNF	8-305	1979
CKS	8-350	1977	CPB	8-305	1976	DNH	8-305	1979
CMA	8-350 with T/H	1974	CPJ	8-305	1976	DNK	8-305	1979
CMC	8-350 with M/T	1974	C2K	8-305	1977	DRC	8-350	1979
CKB	8-350 with M/T, 185 H.P.	1974	C2L	8-305	1977	DRD	8-350	1979
CKH	8-350 with 4 BC, M/T	1974	C8Y	6-250	1977	DRF	8-350	1979
CKH	8-350 with M/T, E.E.C., 185 H.P.	1974	9M	8-350	1976	DRH	8-350	1979
CLJ	8-350 with M/T, 245 H.P.	1974	9W	8-305	1976	DRL	8-350	1979
CKU	8-350 with T/H, 185 H.P.	1974	CCC	6-250	1977	DRY	8-350	1979
CKD	8-350 with 4BC, T/H	1974	CCH	6-250	1978	DTM	8-305	1979
CKD	8-350 with T/H, E.E.C., 185 H.P.	1974	CCJ	6-250	1978	DTR	8-305	1979
CLK	8-350 with 4BC, T/H	1974	CCK	6-250	1978	C8B	8-305	1979
CMU	8-350	1975				C8C	8-350	1979

CHEVROLET

CODE			CODE			CODE		
CCC	6-250	1977	CTC	8-400 with 4BC, E.E.C., 180 H.P.	1974	CXA	8-454	1974
CCF	6-250	1977	CTD	8-400 with 4BC, 180 H.P.	1974	CXX	8-454	1975
CCR	6-250	1977	CTK	8-400 with 4BC, E.E.C., 180 H.P., police	1974	CXY	8-454	1975
CCS	6-250	1977	CTJ	8-400 with 4BC, 180 H.P., police	1974	CHS	8-350	1976
CKA	8-350	1977	CTA	8-400 with 150 H.P.	1974	CMJ	8-350	1976
CKB	8-350	1977	CTB	8-400 with 150 H.P., police	1974	CMM	8-350	1976
CKC	8-350	1977	CPM	8-305	1977	CSF	8-400	1976
CLL	8-350	1977	CPR	8-305	1977	CTL	8-400	1976
CMK	8-350 with 4BC, E.E.C., taxi & police	1974	CTL	8-400	1975	CXX	8-454	1976
CMA	8-350 with E.E.C., taxi & police	1974	CTM	8-400	1975	CCA	6-250	1977
CMD	8-350 with taxi & police	1974	CTU	8-400	1975	CJA	6-250	1977
CMH	8-350 with 4BC, E.E.C., police	1974	CTW	8-400	1975	CJB	6-250	1977
CMJ	8-350 with 4BC, police	1974	CTY	8-400	1975	CJF	6-250	1977
CMJ	8-350	1975	CTZ	8-400	1975	CCH	6-250	1978
CMM	8-350	1977	CUB	8-350	1977	CCK	6-250	1978
CKD	8-350 with 4BC, E.E.C.	1974	CUC	8-350	1977	CCL	6-250	1978
CRU	8-350	1975	CUD	8-350	1977	CCM	6-250	1978
CRW	8-350	1975	CWU	8-454 with police	1974	CEJ	8-305	1978
CRY	8-350	1975	CWW	8-454 with E.E.C., police	1974	CEK	8-305	1978
CSA	8-400	1975	CWY	8-454 with E.E.C.	1974	CTL	8-305	1978
						CHF	8-350	1978

Continued

ENGINE IDENTIFICATION CODE—Continued

CHEVROLET—Continued

CODE			CODE			CODE		
CHH	8-350	1978	DKB	6-250	1979	DRJ	8-350	1979
CHJ	8-350	1978	DKC	6-250	1979	DRK	8-350	1979
CHK	8-350	1978	DKD	6-250	1979	DRL	8-350	1979
CHL	8-350	1978	DKF	6-250	1979	DRY	8-350	1979
CHM	8-350	1978	DNL	8-305	1979	DRZ	8-350	1979
CNT	8-350	1978	DNM	8-305	1979	DTC	8-305	1979
DCA	6-250	1979	DNR	8-305	1979	DTD	8-305	1979
DCB	6-250	1979	DRA	8-350	1979	DUB	8-350	1979
DCC	6-250	1979	DRB	8-350	1979	DUC	8-350	1979
DCD	6-250	1979	DRH	8-350	1979	DUD	8-350	1979

CHEVELLE, MALIBU & MONTE CARLO

CODE			CODE			CODE		
CCC	6-250	1977	CRX	8-350	1975	CMD	8-350	1978
CCD	6-250	1977	CSM	8-400	1975	NJ	V6-231	1979
CCF	6-250	1977	CTL	8-400	1975	RA	V6-231	1979
CCR	6-250 with M/T	1974	CTU	8-400	1975	RB	V6-231	1979
CCW	6-250 with T/H, E.E.C.	1974	CTX	8-400	1975	RJ	V6-231	1979
CCX	6-250 with T/H	1974	CXW	8-454	1975	RM	V6-231	1979
CCK	6-250	1974	CCC	6-250	1976	DHA	V6-200	1979
CJL	6-250	1975	CCD	6-250	1976	DHB	V6-200	1979
CLM	6-250	1975	CCF	6-250	1976	DHC	V6-200	1979
CJR	6-250	1975	CPB	8-305	1976	DMA	8-267	1979
CJT	6-250	1975	CMH	8-350	1976	DMB	8-267	1979
CJU	6-250	1975	CMJ	8-350	1976	DMC	8-267	1979
CJF	6-250	1975	CMM	8-350	1976	DMD	8-267	1979
CJZ	6-250	1975	CSB	8-400	1976	DMF	8-267	1979
CKH	8-350	1977	CSF	8-400	1976	DMH	8-267	1979
CKJ	8-350	1977	CSX	8-400	1976	DNS	8-305	1979
CKK	8-350	1977	9R	8-350	1976	DNT	8-305	1979
CKM	8-350	1977	9W	8-305	1976	DNU	8-305	1979
CKR	8-350	1977	EA	6-231	1978	DNW	8-305	1979
CMC	8-350 with M/T	1974	OH	6-231	1978	DNX	8-305	1979
CMA	8-350 with T/H	1974	OK	6-231	1978	DNY	8-305	1979
CKH	8-350 with 4BC, M/T	1974	CWA	6-250	1978	DRX	8-350	1979
CKD	8-350 with 4BC, T/H	1974	CWB	6-250	1978	DTA	8-305	1979
CMF	8-350	1975	CWC	6-250	1978	DTB	8-305	1979
CMH	8-350	1975	CWD	6-250	1978	DTF	8-305	1979
CMJ	8-350	1975	CER	8-305	1978	DTH	8-305	1979
CMU	8-350	1975	CPZ	8-305	1978	DTJ	8-305	1979
CTC	8-400 with T/H, E.E.C., 180 H.P.	1974	CRU	8-305	1978	DTS	8-305	1979
CTA	8-400 with T/H, 150 H.P.	1974	CRW	8-305	1978	DTU	8-305	1979
CPY	8-305	1977	CRX	8-305	1978	DTW	8-305	1979
CWA	8-454 with M/T	1974	CRY	8-305	1978	DTX	8-305	1979
CWX	8-454 with T/H	1974	CRZ	8-305	1978	DUF	8-350	1979
CWD	8-454 with T/H, E.E.C.	1974	CMA	8-350	1978	DUH	8-350	1979
CRT	8-350	1975	CMB	8-350	1978	DUJ	8-350	1979
CRU	8-350	1975	CMC	8-350	1978			

CHEVY NOVA

CODE			CODE			CODE		
CCR	6-250 with M/T	1974	CCT	6-250	1975	CGD	8-262	1975
CCW	6-250 with T/H, E.E.C.	1974	CCT	6-250	1977	CGF	8-262	1975
CCX	6-250 with T/H	1974	CCU	6-250	1977	CGH	8-262	1975
CCK	6-250	1974	CCU	6-250	1975	CHW	8-350	1975
CCD	6-250	1977	CCW	6-250	1975	CJF	6-250	1975
CCF	6-250	1977	CCW	6-250	1977	CJL	6-250	1975
CCS	6-250	1975	CGC	8-262	1975	CJM	6-250	1975

Continued

ENGINE IDENTIFICATION CODE—Continued

CHEVY NOVA—Continued

CODE			CODE			CODE		
CJR	6-250	1975	CCC	6-250	1976	CCJ	6-250	1978
CJS	6-250	1975	CCD	6-250	1976	C2D	6-250	1978
CJT	6-250	1975	CCF	6-250	1976	CTH	8-305	1978
CJU	6-250	1975	CHT	8-350	1976	CTJ	8-305	1978
CJW	6-250	1975	CHU	8-350	1976	CTK	8-305	1978
CJX	6-250	1975	CML	8-350	1976	C2K	8-305	1978
CJZ	6-250	1975	CPA	8-305	1976	CHJ	8-350	1978
CKH	8-350	1977	CPB	8-305	1976	CHL	8-350	1978
CMC	8-350 with M/T	1974	CPJ	8-305	1976	NG	V6-231	1979
CMA	8-350 with T/H	1974	C2D	6-250	1977	NL	V6-231	1979
CKB	8-350 with M/T, 185 H.P.	1974	C2K	8-305	1977	NO	V6-231	1979
CKH	8-350 with 4BC, M/T	1974	C2L	8-305	1977	RF	V6-231	1979
CKH	8-350 with M/T, E.E.C., 185 H.P.	1974	C8Y	6-250	1977	RX	V6-231	1979
CKM	8-350	1977	9M	8-350	1976	RY	V6-231	1979
CKR	8-350	1977	9W	8-305	1976	SL	V6-231	1979
CKS	8-350	1977	CRX	8-350	1975	SR	V6-231	1979
CKU	8-350 with T/H, 185 H.P.	1974	CZF	8-262	1975	DKA	6-250	1979
CKD	8-350 with 4 BC, T/H, E.E.C.	1974	CZH	8-262	1975	DKB	6-250	1979
CMF	8-350	1975	CZJ	8-262	1975	DKD	6-250	1979
CMH	8-350	1975	CZK	8-262	1975	DNF	8-305	1979
CMU	8-350	1975	CZL	8-262	1975	DNJ	8-305	1979
CPA	8-305	1977	CZM	8-262	1975	DNK	8-305	1979
CPC	8-305	1977	CZY	8-262	1975	DRJ	8-350	1979
CPY	8-305	1977	CZZ	8-262	1975	DRY	8-350	1979
CRC	8-350	1975	CCH	6-250	1978	DTM	8-305	1979
CCB	6-250	1976	CCK	6-250	1978	C8B	8-305	1979

CORVETTE

CODE			CODE			CODE		
CHA	8-350	1975	CLB	8-350	1977	CKD	8-350	1977
CHB	8-350	1975	CLC	8-350	1977	CHW	8-350	1978
CHC	8-350	1975	CLD	8-350	1977	CLM	8-350	1978
CHR	8-350	1975	CLF	8-350	1977	CLR	8-350	1978
CHU	8-350	1975	CLH	8-350	1977	CLS	8-350	1978
CHZ	8-350	1975	CWM	8-454 with M/T	1974	CMR	8-350	1978
CKZ	8-350 with M/T	1974	CWR	8-454 with T/H	1974	CMS	8-350	1978
CLB	8-350 with M/T, E.E.C.	1974	CWS	8-454 with T/H, E.E.C.	1974	ZAA	8-350	1979
CLR	8-350 with M/T, 245 H.P.	1974	CLS	8-350	1976	ZAB	8-350	1979
CLA	8-350 with T/H	1974	CHC	8-350	1976	ZAC	8-350	1979
CLC	8-350 with T/H, E.E.C.	1974	CKC	8-350	1976	ZAD	8-350	1979
CLD	8-350 with T/H, 245 H.P.	1974	CKW	8-350	1976	ZBA	8-350	1979
CKZ	8-350	1977	CKX	8-350	1976	ZBB	8-350	1979
CLA	8-350	1977	CHD	8-350	1977			

NOTES

AIR: Air injection reactor
4BC: Four barrel carburetor

E.E.C.: Exhaust emission control.
HDC: Heavy duty clutch
M/T: Manual transmission

P/G: Powerglide
T/H: Turbo Hydramatic

GRILLE IDENTIFICATION—Continued

1974 Corvette

1974 Camaro

1974 Chevelle Laguna

1974 Chevelle Malibu

1974 Chevy Nova

1974 Monte Carlo

1974 Bel Air & Impala

1974 Caprice & Estate Wagon

1975 Camaro

1975 Chevelle

1975 Nova

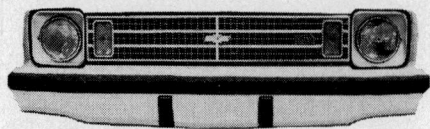

1975 Nova Custom

1975 Monte Carlo

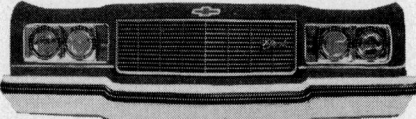

1975 Bel Air & Impala

1975 Caprice & Estate Wagon

1975-78 Corvette

1975 Laguna S-3

1976 Malibu Classic

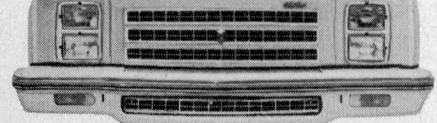

1976 Monte Carlo

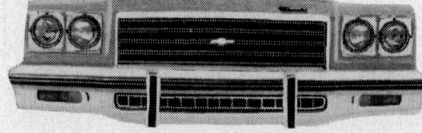

1976 Impala

1976 Caprice & Estate Wagon

1976-77 Nova

1977 Nova Concours

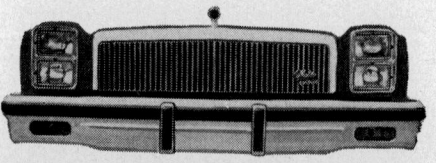

1977 Malibu Classic

GRILLE IDENTIFICATION—Continued

1977 Monte Carlo

1977 Impala

1977 Caprice & Estate Wagon

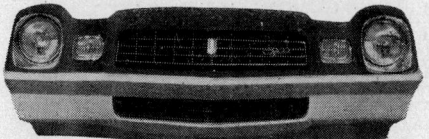

1978 Camaro LT

1978 Camaro Z28

1978 Caprice & Estate Wagon

1978 Chevy Nova

1978 Impala

1978 Malibu

1978 Malibu Classic

1978-79 Monte Carlo

1979 Malibu

1979 Chevy Nova

1979 Caprice

1979 Corvette

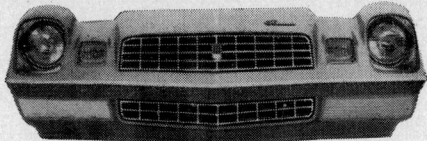

1979 Camaro

1979 Camaro Z28

GENERAL ENGINE SPECIFICATIONS

Year	Engine	Car-buretor	Bore and Stroke	Piston Dis-place-ment, Cubic Inches	Com-pres-sion Ratio	Maximum Brake H.P. @ R.P.M.	Maximum Torque Lbs. Ft. @ R.P.M.	Normal Oil Pressure Pounds
1974	100 Horsepower① 6-250	1 Barrel	3.875 x 3.53	250	8.25	100 @ 3600	175 @ 1800	40
	145 Horsepower① V8-350	2 Barrel	4.00 x 3.48	350	8.50	145 @ 3600	250 @ 2200	40
	160 Horsepower① V8-350	4 Barrel	4.00 x 3.48	350	8.50	160 @ 3800	250 @ 2400	40
	185 Horsepower① V8-350	4 Barrel	4.00 x 3.48	350	8.50	185 @ 4000	270 @ 2600	40
	195 Horsepower① V8-350	4 Barrel	4.00 x 3.48	350	8.50	195 @ 4400	275 @ 2800	40
	245 Horsepower① V8-350	4 Barrel	4.00 x 3.48	350	9.0	245 @ 5200	280 @ 4000	40
	250 Horsepower① V8-350	4 Barrel	4.00 x 3.48	350	9.0	250 @ 5200	285 @ 4000	40
	150 Horsepower① V8-400	2 Barrel	4.125 x 3.75	400	8.50	150 @ 3200	295 @ 2000	40
	180 Horsepower① V8-400	4 Barrel	4.125 x 3.75	400	8.50	180 @ 3800	290 @ 2400	40
	235 Horsepower① V8-454	4 Barrel	4.250 x 4.00	454	8.50	235 @ 4000	360 @ 2800	45
	270 Horsepower① V8-454	4 Barrel	4.250 x 4.00	454	8.50	270 @ 4400	380 @ 2800	45
1975	105 Horsepower① 6-250	1 Barrel	3.875 x 3.53	250	8.25	105 @ 3800	185 @ 1200	36–41
	110 Horsepower① V8-262	2 Barrel	3.671 x 3.10	262	8.5	110 @ 3600	200 @ 2000	32–40
	145 Horsepower① V8-350	2 Barrel	4.00 x 3.48	350	8.5	145 @ 3800	250 @ 2200	32–40
	155 Horsepower① V8-350	4 Barrel	4.00 x 3.48	350	8.5	155 @ 3800	250 @ 2400	32–40
	165 Horsepower① V8-350	4 Barrel	4.00 x 3.48	350	8.5	165 @ 3800	255 @ 2400	32–40
	205 Horsepower① V8-350	4 Barrel	4.00 x 3.48	350	9.0	205 @ 4800	255 @ 3600	32–40
	175 Horsepower① V8-400	4 Barrel	4.125 x 3.75	400	8.5	175 @ 3600	305 @ 2000	42–46
	215 Horsepower① V8-454	4 Barrel	4.251 x 4.00	454	8.15	215 @ 4000	350 @ 2400	42–46
1976	105 Horsepower① 6-250	1 Barrel	3.875 x 3.53	250	8.25	105 @ 3800	185 @ 1200	36–41
	140 Horsepower① V8-305	2 Barrel	3.736 x 3.48	305	8.5	140 @ 3800	245 @ 2000	32–40
	145 Horsepower① V8-350	2 Barrel	4.00 x 3.48	350	8.5	145 @ 3800	250 @ 2200	32–40
	165 Horsepower① V8-350	4 Barrel	4.00 x 3.48	350	8.5	165 @ 3800	260 @ 2400	32–40
	185 Horsepower① V8-350	4 Barrel	4.00 x 3.48	350	8.5	185 @ 4000	275 @ 2400	32–40
	195 Horsepower① V8-350	4 Barrel	4.00 x 3.48	350	8.5	195 @ 4400	275 @ 2800	32–40
	210 Horsepower① V8-350	4 Barrel	4.00 x 3.48	350	9.0	210 @ 5200	255 @ 3600	32–40
	270 Horsepower① V8-350	4 Barrel	4.00 x 3.48	350	8.5	270 @ 4400	380 @ 2800	32–40
	175 Horsepower① V8-400	4 Barrel	4.125 x 3.75	400	8.5	175 @ 3600	305 @ 2000	32–40
	235 Horsepower① V8-454	4 Barrel	4.251 x 4.00	454	8.5	235 @ 4000	360 @ 2800	42–46
1977	110 Horsepower① 6-250	1 Barrel	3.875 x 3.53	250	8.25	110 @ 3800	195 @ 1600	36–41
	145 Horsepower① V8-305	2 Barrel	3.736 x 3.48	305	8.5	145 @ 3800	245 @ 2400	32–40
	170 Horsepower① V8-350	4 Barrel	4.00 x 3.48	350	8.5	170 @ 3800	270 @ 2400	32–40
	180 Horsepower① V8-350	4 Barrel	4.00 x 3.48	350	8.5	180 @ 4000	270 @ 2400	32–40
	210 Horsepower① V8-350	4 Barrel	4.00 x 3.48	350	9.0	210 @ 5200	255 @ 3600	32–40
1978	95 Horsepower① V6-200	2 Barrel	3.50 x 3.48	200	8.2	95 @ 3800	160 @ 2000	34–39
	103 Horsepower①② V6-231	2 Barrel	3.80 x 3.40	231	8.0	103 @ 3800	180 @ 2000	37
	90 Horsepower① 6-250	1 Barrel	3.875 x 3.53	250	8.2	90 @ 3600	180 @ 1600	36–41
	110 Horsepower① 6-250	1 Barrel	3.875 x 3.53	250	8.2	110 @ 3800	195 @ 1600	36–41
	135 Horsepower① V8-305	2 Barrel	3.736 x 3.48	305	8.5	135 @ 3800	240 @ 2000	45
	145 Horsepower① V8-305	2 Barrel	3.736 x 3.48	305	8.5	145 @ 3800	245 @ 2000	45
	160 Horsepower① V8-350	4 Barrel	4.00 x 3.48	350	8.2	160 @ 3800	260 @ 2400	32–40
	170 Horsepower① V8-350	4 Barrel	4.00 x 3.48	350	8.2	170 @ 3800	270 @ 2400	32–40
	175 Horsepower① V8-350	4 Barrel	4.00 x 3.48	350	8.2	175 @ 3800	265 @ 2400	32–40
	185 Horsepower① V8-350	4 Barrel	4.00 x 3.48	350	8.2	185 @ 4000	280 @ 2400	32–40
1979	95 Horsepower① V6-200	2 Barrel	3.50 x 3.48	200	8.2	95 @ 3800	160 @ 2000	45
	Horsepower①② V6-231	2 Barrel	3.80 x 3.40	231	8.0	—	—	37
	Horsepower① 6-250	1 Barrel	3.876 x 3.53	250	8.1	—	—	40
	Horsepower① 6-250	1 Barrel	3.876 x 3.53	250	8.0	—	—	40
	Horsepower① V8-267	2 Barrel	3.50 x 3.48	267	8.2	—	—	45
	155 Horsepower① V8-305	2 Barrel	3.736 x 3.48	305	8.4	155 @ 4000	225 @ 2400	45
	160 Horsepower① V8-305	4 Barrel	3.736 x 3.48	305	8.4	160 @ 4000	235 @ 2400	45
	160 Horsepower① V8-350	4 Barrel	4.00 x 3.48	350	8.2	160 @ 3800	260 @ 2400	45
	170 Horsepower① V8-350	4 Barrel	4.00 x 3.48	350	8.2	170 @ 3800	270 @ 2400	45
	Horsepower① V8-350	4 Barrel	4.00 x 3.48	350	8.2	—	—	45
	Horsepower① V8-350	4 Barrel	4.00 x 3.48	350	8.9	—	—	45

①—Ratings are net—As installed in the vehicle.   ②—For service on this engine, see Buick chapter.

TUNE UP SPECIFICATIONS

The following specifications are published from the latest information available. This data should be used only in the absence of a decal affixed in the engine compartment.

★When using a timing light, disconnect vacuum hose or tube at distributor and plug opening in hose or tube so idle speed will not be affected.

●When checking compression, lowest cylinder must be within 80 percent of highest.

▲Before removing wires from distributor cap, determine location of the No. 1 wire in cap, as distributor position may have been altered from that shown at the end of this chart.

| Year | Spark Plug | | Distributor | | Ignition Timing ★ | | | Carb. Adjustments | | | | | |
| | Type | Gap Inch | Point Gap Inch | Dwell Angle Deg. | Firing Order Fig. ▲ | Timing BTDC ① | Mark Fig. | Hot Idle Speed ② | | Air Fuel Ratio | | Idle "CO" % | |
								Std. Trans.	Auto. Trans.	Std. Trans.	Auto. Trans.	Std. Trans.	Auto. Trans.
CAMARO													
1974													
6-250⑱	R46T	.035	④	31–34	D	8°	B	850	—	—	—	.3	.3
6-250⑲	R46T	.035	④	31–34	D	6°	B	—	600D	—	—	.3	.3
8-350, 145 H.P.⑱	R44T	.035	④	29–31	E	TDC	B	900	—	—	—	.5	.5
8-350, 145 H.P.⑲	R44T	.035	④	29–31	E	8°	B	—	600D	—	—	.5	.5
8-350, 160 H.P.⑱	R44T	.035	④	29–31	E	4°	B	900	—	—	—	.5	.5
8-350, 160 H.P.⑲	R44T	.035	④	29–31	E	8°	B	—	600D	—	—	.5	.5
8-350, 185 H.P.⑱	R44T	.035	④	29–31	E	8°⑥	B	900	—	—	—	.5	.5
8-350, 185 H.P.⑲	R44T	.035	④	29–31	E	8°	B	—	600D	—	—	.5	.5
8-350, 245 H.P.	R44T	.035	④	29–31	⑫	8°	B	900	700D	—	—	.5	.5
1975													
6-250	R46TX	.060	—	—	H	8°	B	850	600D	—	—	—	—
6-250⑦	R46TX	.060	—	—	H	10°	B	850	550D⑨	—	—	—	—
8-350 2 Bbl. Carb.	R44TX	.060	—	—	I	6°	B	800	600D	—	—	—	—
8-350⑱	R44TX	.060	—	—	I	6°⑥	B	800	—	—	—	—	—
8-350⑲	R44TX	.060	—	—	I	8°⑧	B	—	600D	—	—	—	—
1976													
6-250	R46TS	.035	—	—	H	6°	B	850	550D⑨	—	—	—	—
8-305⑱	R45TS	.045	—	—	I	6°	B	800	—	—	—	—	—
8-305⑲	R45TS	.045	—	—	I	8°⑬	B	—	600D	—	—	—	—
8-350 2 Bbl. Carb.	R45TS	.045	—	—	I	6°	B	—	600D	—	—	—	—
8-350 4 Bbl. Carb.	R45TS	.045	—	—	I	8°⑧	B	800	600D	—	—	—	—
1977													
6-250⑱	R46TS	.035	—	—	H	6°	B	③	—	—	—	—	—
6-250⑲	R46TS	.035	—	—	H	8°⑧	B	—	600	—	—	—	—
8-305	R45TS	.045	—	—	I	8°⑧	B	700	500/650	—	—	—	—
8-350⑱	R45TS	.045	—	—	I	8°	B	700	—	—	—	—	—
8-350⑲	R45TS	.045	—	—	I	8°	B	—	500/650	—	—	—	—
1978													
6-250⑱	R46TS	.035	—	—	H	6°	B	800	—	—	—	—	—
6-250⑲	R46TS	.035	—	—	H	10°⑧	B	—	550D⑨	—	—	—	—
8-305㉓	R45TS	.045	—	—	I	4°	B	600	500	—	—	—	—
8-305㉑	R45TS	.045	—	—	I	6°	B	—	500	—	—	—	—
8-350㉓	R45TS	.045	—	—	I	6°	B	700	500	—	—	—	—
8-350㉑	R45TS	.045	—	—	I	8°	B	—	500	—	—	—	—

Continued

TUNE UP SPECIFICATIONS—Continued

The following specifications are published from the latest information available. This data should be used only in the absence of a decal affixed in the engine compartment.

★When using a timing light, disconnect vacuum hose or tube at distributor and plug opening in hose or tube so idle speed will not be affected.

●When checking compression, lowest cylinder must be within 80 percent of highest.

▲Before removing wires from distributor cap, determine location of the No. 1 wire in cap, as distributor position may have been altered from that shown at the end of this chart.

| Year | Spark Plug | | Distributor | | Ignition Timing★ | | | Carb. Adjustments | | | | | |
| | Type | Gap Inch | Point Gap Inch | Dwell Angle Deg. | Firing Order Fig. ▲ | Timing BTDC ① | Mark Fig. | Hot Idle Speed ② | | Air Fuel Ratio | | Idle "CO" % | |
								Std. Trans.	Auto. Trans.	Std. Trans.	Auto. Trans.	Std. Trans.	Auto. Trans.
CAMARO—Continued													
1979													
6-250	R46TS	.035	—	—	H	㉘	B	—	—	—	—	—	—
V8-305	R45TS	.045	—	—	I	4°	B	—	—	—	—	—	—
V8-350	R45TS	.045	—	—	I	6°⑮	B	—	—	—	—	—	—
CHEVELLE, MALIBU & MONTE CARLO													
1974													
6-250⑱	R46T	.035	④	31–34	D	8°	B	850	—	—	—	.3	.3
6-250⑲	R46T	.035	④	31–34	D	6°	B	—	600D	—	—	.3	.3
8-350, 145 H.P.⑱	R44T	.035	④	29–31	E	TDC	B	900	—	—	—	.5	.5
8-350, 145 H.P.⑲	R44T	.035	④	29–31	E	8°	B	—	600D	—	—	.5	.5
8-350, 160 H.P.⑱	R44T	.035	④	29–31	E	4°	B	900	—	—	—	.5	.5
8-350, 160 H.P.⑲	R44T	.035	④	29–31	E	8°	B	—	600D	—	—	.5	.5
8-350, 185 H.P.⑱	R44T	.035	④	29–31	E	8°⑥	B	900	—	—	—	.5	.5
8-350, 185 H.P.⑲	R44T	.035	④	29–31	E	8°	B	—	600D	—	—	.5	.5
8-400	R44T	.035	④	29–31	E	8°	B	—	600D	—	—	.5	.5
8-454	R44T	.035	④	29–31	E	10°	B	800	600D	—	—	.5	.5
1975													
6-250	R46TX	.060	—	—	H	8°	B	850	600D	—	—	—	—
6-250⑦	R46TX	.060	—	—	H	10°	B	850	550D⑨	—	—	—	—
8-350 2 BBl. Carb.	R44TX	.060	—	—	I	6°	B	800	600D	—	—	—	—
8-350⑱	R44TX	.060	—	—	I	6°⑥	B	800	—	—	—	—	—
8-350⑲	R44TX	.060	—	—	I	8°⑧	B	—	600D	—	—	—	—
8-400	R44TX	.060	—	—	I	8°	B	—	600D	—	—	—	—
8-454	R44TX	.060	—	—	I	16°	B	—	600D	—	—	—	—
1976													
6-250	R46TS	.035	—	—	H	6°	B	850	550D⑨	—	—	—	—
8-305⑱	R45TS	.045	—	—	I	6°	B	800	—	—	—	—	—
8-305⑲	R45TS	.045	—	—	I	8°⑬	B	—	600D	—	—	—	—
8-350 2 Bbl. Carb.	R45TS	.045	—	—	I	6°	B	—	600	—	—	—	—
8-350 4 Bbl. Carb.	R45TS	.045	—	—	I	8°⑧	B	800	600D	—	—	—	—
8-400	R45TS	.045	—	—	I	8°	B	—	600D	—	—	—	—
1977													
6-250⑱	R46TS	.035	—	—	H	6°	B	③	—	—	—	—	—
6-250⑲	R46TS	.035	—	—	H	8°⑧	B	—	600⑤	—	—	—	—
8-305⑱	R45TS	.045	—	—	I	8°	B	700	—	—	—	—	—
8-350	R45TS	.045	—	—	I	8°	B	—	⑪	—	—	—	—

Continued

TUNE UP SPECIFICATIONS—Continued

The following specifications are published from the latest information available. This data should be used only in the absence of a decal affixed in the engine compartment.

★When using a timing light, disconnect vacuum hose or tube at distributor and plug opening in hose or tube so idle speed will not be affected.

●When checking compression, lowest cylinder must be within 80 percent of highest.

▲Before removing wires from distributor cap, determine location of the No. 1 wire in cap, as distributor position may have been altered from that shown at the end of this chart.

| Year | Spark Plug | | Distributor | | Ignition Timing★ | | | Carb. Adjustments | | | | | |
| | Type | Gap Inch | Point Gap Inch | Dwell Angle Deg. | Firing Order Fig. ▲ | Timing BTDC ① | Mark Fig. | Hot Idle Speed ② | | Air Fuel Ratio | | Idle "CO" % | |
								Std. Trans.	Auto. Trans.	Std. Trans.	Auto. Trans.	Std. Trans.	Auto. Trans.
CHEVELLE, MALIBU & MONTE CARLO—Continued													
1978													
6-200	R45TS	.045	—	—	F	8°	G	700	600	—	—	—	—
6-231 ㉔	R46TSX	.060	—	—	J	15°	K	—	600	—	—	—	—
8-305 ⑳	R45TS	.045	—	—	I	4°	B	600	500	—	—	—	—
8-305 ㉑	R45TS	.045	—	—	I	6°	B	—	500	—	—	—	—
8-305 ㉒	R45TS	.045	—	—	I	8°	B	—	600	—	—	—	—
8-350 ⑳	R45TS	.045	—	—	I	6°	B	700	500	—	—	—	—
8-350 ㉑㉒	R45TS	.045	—	—	I	8°	B	—	500	—	—	—	—
1979													
V6-200 ⑱	R45TS	.045	—	—	F	8°	G	—	—	—	—	—	—
V6-200 ⑲	R45TS	.045	—	—	F	14°	G	—	—	—	—	—	—
V6-231 ㉔	R46TSX	.060	—	—	J	15°	K	—	—	—	—	—	—
V8-267 ⑱	R45TS	.045	—	—	I	4°	B	—	—	—	—	—	—
V8-267 ⑲	R45TS	.045	—	—	I	10°	B	—	—	—	—	—	—
V8-305	R43TS	.045	—	—	I	4°	B	—	—	—	—	—	—
V8-350	R43TS	.045	—	—	I	8°	B	—	—	—	—	—	—
CHEVY NOVA													
1974													
6-250 ⑱	R46T	.035	④	31–34	D	8°	B	850	—	—	—	.3	.3
6-250 ⑲	R46T	.035	④	31–34	D	6°	B	—	600D	—	—	.3	.3
8-350, 145 H.P. ⑱	R44T	.035	④	29–31	E	TDC	B	900	—	—	—	.5	.5
8-350, 145 H.P. ⑲	R44T	.035	④	29–31	E	8°	B	—	600D	—	—	.5	.5
8-350, 160 H.P. ⑱	R44T	.035	④	29–31	E	4°	B	900	—	—	—	.5	.5
8-350, 160 H.P. ⑲	R44T	.035	④	29–31	E	8°	B	—	600D	—	—	.5	.5
8-350, 185 H.P. ⑱	R44T	.035	④	29–31	E	8°⑥	B	900	—	—	—	.5	.5
8-350, 185 H.P. ⑲	R44T	.035	④	29–31	E	8°	B	—	600D	—	—	.5	.5
1975													
6-250	R46TX	.060	—	—	H	8°	B	850	600D	—	—	—	—
6-250 ⑦	R46TX	.060	—	—	H	10°	B	850	550D⑨	—	—	—	—
8-262	R44TX	.060	—	—	I	8°	A	800	600D	—	—	—	—
8-350 2 BBl. Carb.	R44TX	.060	—	—	I	6°	B	800	600D	—	—	—	—
8-350 ⑱	R44TX	.060	—	—	I	6°⑥	B	800	—	—	—	—	—
8-350 ⑲	R44TX	.060	—	—	I	8°⑧	B	—	600D	—	—	—	—
1976													
6-250	R46TS	.035	—	—	H	6°⑩	B	850	550D⑨	—	—	—	—
8-305 ⑱	R45TS	.045	—	—	I	6°	B	800	—	—	—	—	—
8-305 ⑲	R45TS	.045	—	—	I	8°⑬	B	—	600D	—	—	—	—
8-350 2 Bbl. Carb.	R45TS	.045	—	—	I	6°	B	—	600D	—	—	—	—
8-350 4 Bbl. Carb.	R45TS	.045	—	—	I	8°⑧	B	800	600D	—	—	—	—

Continued

TUNE UP SPECIFICATIONS—Continued

The following specifications are published from the latest information available. This data should be used only in the absence of a decal affixed in the engine compartment.

★When using a timing light, disconnect vacuum hose or tube at distributor and plug opening in hose or tube so idle speed will not be affected.

●When checking compression, lowest cylinder must be within 80 percent of highest.

▲Before removing wires from distributor cap, determine location of the No. 1 wire in cap, as distributor position may have been altered from that shown at the end of this chart.

Year	Spark Plug Type	Gap Inch	Distributor Point Gap Inch	Dwell Angle Deg.	Ignition Timing ★ Firing Order Fig. ▲	Timing BTDC ①	Mark Fig.	Hot Idle Speed ② Std. Trans.	Auto. Trans.	Air Fuel Ratio Std. Trans.	Auto. Trans.	Idle "CO" % Std. Trans.	Auto. Trans.
CHEVY NOVA—Continued													
1977													
6-250[18]	R46TS	.035	—	—	H	6°	B	[8]	—	—	—	—	—
6-250[19]	R46TS	.035	—	—	H	8°[8]	B	—	600[5]	—	—	—	—
8-305[18]	R45TS	.045	—	—	I	8°	B	700	—	—	—	—	—
8-305[19]	R45TS	.045	—	—	I	8°[8]	B	—	500/650	—	—	—	—
8-350	R45TS	.045	—	—	I	8°	B	700	[11]	—	—	—	—
1978													
6-250[26]	R46TS	.035	—	—	H	6°	B	800	—	—	—	—	—
6-250[19][23]	R46TS	.035	—	—	H	10°[26]	B	—	600D	—	—	—	—
8-305[23]	R45TS	.045	—	—	I	4°	B	600	500D	—	—	—	—
8-305[21]	R45TS	.045	—	—	I	6°	B	—	500D	—	—	—	—
V8-350	R45TS	.045	—	—	I	8°	B	—	650D[9]	—	—	—	—
1979													
6-250	R46TS	.035	—	—	H	[28]	B	—	—	—	—	—	—
V8-305	R45TS	.045	—	—	I	4°	B	—	—	—	—	—	—
V8-350	R45TS	.045	—	—	I	8°	B	—	—	—	—	—	—
CHEVROLET													
1974													
8-350, 145 H.P.	R44T	.035	④	29–31	E	8°	B	—	600D	—	—	.5	.5
8-350, 160 H.P.	R44T	.035	④	29–31	E	8°	B	—	600D	—	—	.5	.5
8-400	R44T	.035	④	29–31	E	8°	B	—	600D	—	—	.5	.5
8-454	R44T	.035	④	29–31	[12]	10°	B	—	600D	—	—	.5	.5
1975													
8-350 2 BBl. Carb.	R44TX	.060	—	—	I	6°	B	—	600D	—	—	—	—
8-350	R44TX	.060	—	—	I	8°[8]	B	—	600D	—	—	—	—
8-400	R44TX	.060	—	—	I	8°	B	—	600D	—	—	—	—
8-454	R44TX	.060	—	—	I	16°	B	—	600D	—	—	—	—
1976													
8-350 2 Bbl. Carb.	R45TS	.045	—	—	I	6°	B	—	600D	—	—	—	—
8-350 4 Bbl. Carb.	R45TS	.045	—	—	I	8°[8]	B	—	600D	—	—	—	—
8-400	R45TS	.045	—	—	I	8°	B	—	600D	—	—	—	—
8-454	R45TSX	.060	—	—	I	12°	B	—	550D	—	—	—	—

Continued

TUNE UP SPECIFICATIONS—Continued

The following specifications are published from the latest information available. This data should be used only in the absence of a decal affixed in the engine compartment.

★When using a timing light, disconnect vacuum hose or tube at distributor and plug opening in hose or tube so idle speed will not be affected.

●When checking compression, lowest cylinder must be within 80 percent of highest.

▲Before removing wires from distributor cap, determine location of the No. 1 wire in cap, as distributor position may have been altered from that shown at the end of this chart.

| Year | Spark Plug | | Distributor | | Ignition Timing★ | | | Carb. Adjustments | | | | | |
| | Type | Gap Inch | Point Gap Inch | Dwell Angle Deg. | Firing Order Fig. ▲ | Timing BTDC ① | Mark Fig. | Hot Idle Speed ② | | Air Fuel Ratio | | Idle "CO" % | |
								Std. Trans.	Auto. Trans.	Std. Trans.	Auto. Trans.	Std. Trans.	Auto. Trans.
CHEVROLET—Continued													
1977													
6-250	R46TS	.035	—	—	H	8°⑧	B	—	600⑤	—	—	—	—
8-305	R45TS	.045	—	—	I	8°⑧	B	—	500/650	—	—	—	—
8-350	R45TS	.045	—	—	I	8°	B	—	⑪	—	—	—	—
1978													
6-250㉓	R46TS	.035	—	—	H	10°㉖	B	—	500D	—	—	—	—
6-250㉑	R46TS	.035	—	—	H	6°	B	—	600D	—	—	—	—
8-305㉓	R45TS	.045	—	—	I	4°	B	—	500D	—	—	—	—
8-305㉑	R45TS	.045	—	—	I	6°	B	—	500D	—	—	—	—
8-350㉓	R45TS	.045	—	—	I	6°	B	—	500D	—	—	—	—
8-350㉑	R45TS	.045	—	—	I	8°	B	—	500D	—	—	—	—
1979													
6-250	R46TS	.035	—	—	H	⑧㉙	B	—	—	—	—	—	—
8-305	R45TS	.045	—	—	I	4°	B	—	—	—	—	—	—
8-350	R45TS	.045	—	—	I	⑮㉚	B	—	—	—	—	—	—
CORVETTE													
1974													
8-350, 195 H.P.⑱	R44T	.035	④	29-31	C	8°⑥	B	900	—	—	—	.5	.5
8-350, 195 H.P.⑲	R44T	.035	④	29-31	C	8°	B	—	600D	—	—	.5	.5
8-350, 250 H.P.	R44T	.035	④	29-31	C	8°	B	900	700D	—	—	.5	.5
8-454	R44T	.035	④	29-31	E	10°	B	800	600D	—	—	.5	.5
1975													
8-350⑱	R44TX	.060	—	—	I	6°⑥	B	800	—	—	—	—	—
8-350⑲	R44TX	.060	—	—	I	6°	B	—	600D	—	—	—	—
1976													
8-350	R45TS	.045	—	—	I	8°⑧	B	1000	700D	—	—	—	—
8-350⑭	R45TS	.045	—	—	I	12°	B	1000	700D	—	—	—	—
1977													
8-350	R45TS	.045	—	—	I	8°	B	700	⑪	—	—	—	—
8-350⑭	R45TS	.045	—	—	I	12°	B	800	700/800	—	—	—	—
1978													
V8-350⑯	R45TS	.045	—	—	I	6°⑯	B	700	500㉗	—	—	—	—
V8-350⑰	R45TS	.045	—	—	I	12°	B	900	700	—	—	—	—

Continued

TUNE UP SPECIFICATIONS—Continued

The following specifications are published from the latest information available. This data should be used only in the absence of a decal affixed in the engine compartment.

★When using a timing light, disconnect vacuum hose or tube at distributor and plug opening in hose or tube so idle speed will not be affected.

●When checking compression, lowest cylinder must be within 80 percent of highest.

▲Before removing wires from distributor cap, determine location of the No. 1 wire in cap, as distributor position may have been altered from that shown at the end of this chart.

| Year | Spark Plug | | Distributor | | Ignition Timing ★ | | | Carb. Adjustments | | | | | |
| | Type | Gap Inch | Point Gap Inch | Dwell Angle Deg. | Firing Order Fig. ▲ | Timing BTDC ① | Mark Fig. | Hot Idle Speed ② | | Air Fuel Ratio | | Idle "CO" % | |
								Std. Trans.	Auto. Trans.	Std. Trans.	Auto. Trans.	Std. Trans.	Auto. Trans.
CORVETTE—Continued													
1979													
8-350	R45TS	.045	—	—	I	6°③①	B	—	—	—	—	—	—
8-350	R45TS	.045	—	—	I	12°	B	—	—	—	—	—	—

① —BTDC: Before top dead center.
② —Idle speed on manual trans. equipped vehicles is adjusted in Neutral and on auto. trans. equipped vehicles is adjusted in Drive unless otherwise specified. Where two speeds are listed, the higher speed is with A/C solenoid energized.
③ —Less A/C, 750 R.P.M.; with A/C, 800 R.P.M.
④ —New points, .019", used .016". On V8s, turn adjusting screw in (clockwise) until engine misfires; then back off ½ turn.
⑤ —California, 550 R.P.M.
⑥ —For California set at 4° BTDC.
⑦ —With integral intake manifold and all California models.

⑧ —For California set at 6° BTDC.
⑨ —For California 600 R.P.M.
⑩ —With Distributor 1110662 set at 8° BTDC.
⑪ —Exc. high altitude, 500/650; high altitude 600/650.
⑫ —Exc. H.E.I., Fig. E; H.E.I., Fig. I.
⑬ —For California set at TDC.
⑭ —210 H.P.
⑮ —For California, 8° BTDC.
⑯ —Exc. high performance.
⑰ —High performance.
⑱ —With standard transmission.
⑲ —With automatic transmission.
⑳ —Exc. Calif. & high altitude.
㉑ —Calif.

㉒ —High altitude.
㉓ —Exc. Calif.
㉔ —For service on this engine, see Buick chapter.
㉕ —With A/C, 8° BTDC.
㉖ —With manual trans. exc. Calif.: with auto trans. Calif. only.
㉗ —For high altitude, 600 R.P.M.
㉘ —With manual trans., 8° BTDC; auto. trans. Exc. Calif., 10° BTDC; Calif., 6° BTDC.
㉙ —Exc. Calif., 10° BTDC.
㉚ —Exc. Calif., 6° BTDC.
㉛ —For Calif. & high altitude, 8° BTDC.

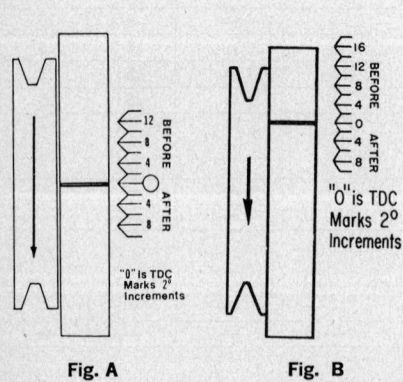

Fig. A

Fig. B

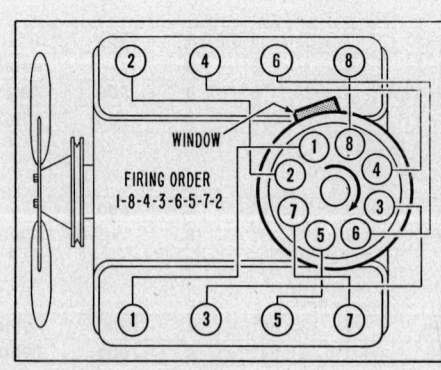

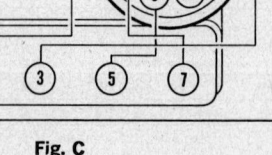

Fig. C

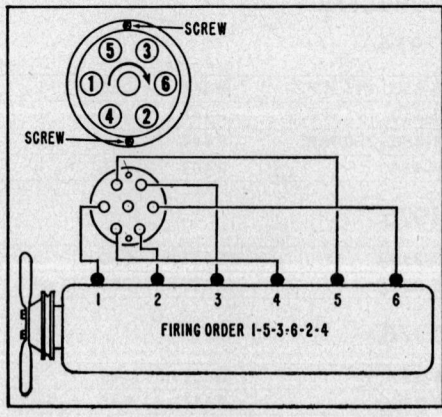

Fig. D

Continued

TUNE UP NOTES—Continued

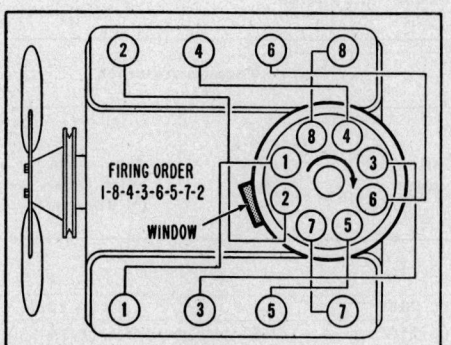

Fig. E

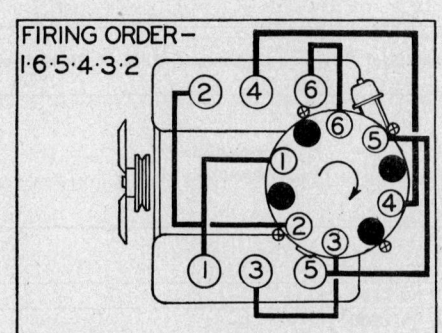

Fig. F

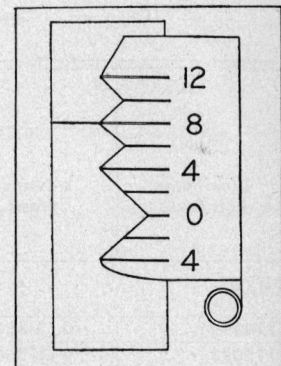

Fig. G

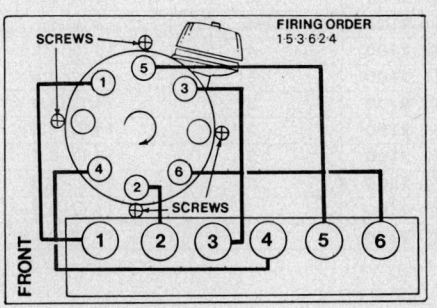

Fig. H

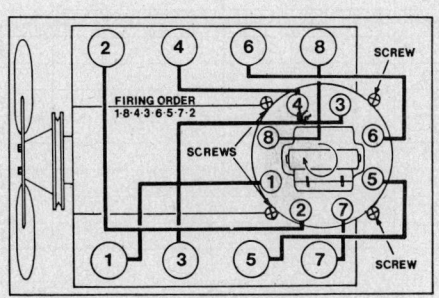

Fig. I

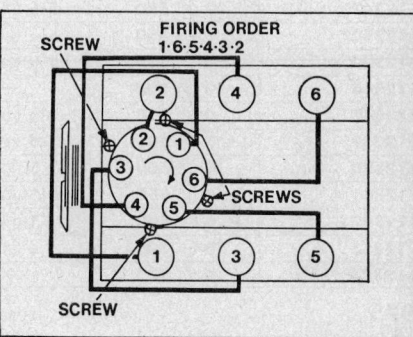

Fig. J

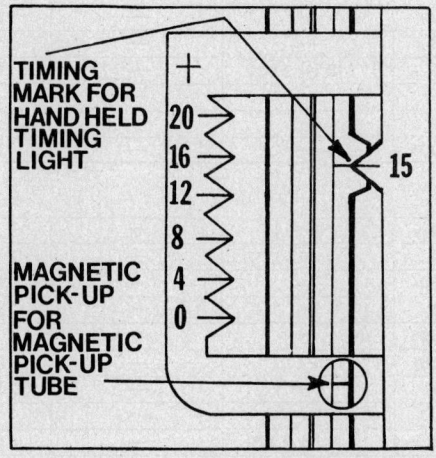

Fig. K

DISTRIBUTOR SPECIFICATIONS

★Note: If unit is checked on vehicle, double the RPM and degrees to get crankshaft figures.

| Distributor Part No.① | Centrifugal Advance Degrees @ RPM of Distributor | | | | | Vacuum Advance | |
	Advance Starts	Intermediate Advance			Full Advance	Inches of Vacuum to Start Plunger	Max. Adv. Dist. Deg. @ Vacuum
1974							
1110499②	0 @ 550	7 @ 1150	—	—	12 @ 2050	7	12 @ 15.5
1112093②	0 @ 550	5½ @ 1200	—	—	9 @ 2100	6	7½ @ 14
1112113③	0 @ 550	5½ @ 1200	—	—	9 @ 2100	6	10 @ 15.7
1112114③	0 @ 550	5½ @ 1200	—	—	9 @ 2100	6	10 @ 15.7
1112168	0 @ 500	—	—	—	10 @ 1100	4	7 @ 8.5
1112247②	0 @ 550	5½ @ 1200	—	—	9 @ 2100	6	7½ @ 14
1112250③	0 @ 550	5½ @ 1200	—	—	9 @ 2100	10	5 @ 15.5
1112504③	0 @ 550	5½ @ 1200	—	—	9 @ 2100	8	8 @ 16
1112846	0 @ 500	—	—	—	10 @ 2100	4	15 @ 10.5
1112847	0 @ 550	5½ @ 1200	—	—	9 @ 2100	6	14 @ 8.5
1112849	0 @ 500	5 @ 900	7½ @ 1200	—	11 @ 2100	3	14 @ 8.5
1112850	0 @ 500	5 @ 900	7½ @ 1200	—	11 @ 2100	3	14 @ 8.5
1112851	0 @ 550	5½ @ 1200	—	—	9 @ 2100	3	14 @ 8.5
1112852	0 @ 600	1 @ 730	6 @ 1100	—	10 @ 2500	3	14 @ 8.5
1112853	0 @ 500	6 @ 1100	—	—	10 @ 2500	3	14 @ 8.5
1112854	0 @ 500	—	—	—	10 @ 2100	4	15 @ 10.5
1975							
1110650	0 @ 550	3½ @ 1150	—	—	8 @ 2100	4	9 @ 12
1110652	0 @ 550	7 @ 1150	—	—	12 @ 2050	7	12 @ 15
1112863	0 @ 550	3½ @ 1150	—	—	8 @ 2100	4	9 @ 12
1112880	0 @ 600	6 @ 1000	—	—	11 @ 2100	4	9 @ 12
1112882	0 @ 500	4 @ 800	—	—	7½ @ 1400	8	7½ @ 15.5
1112883	0 @ 550	6 @ 800	8 @ 1200	—	11 @ 2300	4	7½ @ 10
1112886	0 @ 650	—	—	—	6 @ 2100	4	9 @ 7
1112888	0 @ 550	6 @ 800	—	—	8 @ 2100	4	9 @ 12
1112933	0 @ 600	4½ @ 1000	—	—	11 @ 2000	3	8 @ 8
1976							
1103200	0 @ 600	6½ @ 800	—	—	8 @ 1000	4	5 @ 8
1103203	0 @ 500	4 @ 800	—	—	7½ @ 1400	6	7½ @ 12
1110662	0 @ 550	7 @ 1150	—	—	12 @ 2050	4	9 @ 12
1110666	0 @ 500	3½ @ 800	—	—	10 @ 2100	4	12 @ 15
1112863	0 @ 550	3½ @ 1150	—	—	8 @ 2100	4	9 @ 12
1112880	0 @ 600	6 @ 1000	—	—	11 @ 2100	4	9 @ 12
1112882	0 @ 500	4 @ 800	—	—	7½ @ 1400	8	7½ @ 15.5
1112886	0 @ 650	—	—	—	6 @ 2100	4	9 @ 7
1112888	0 @ 550	6 @ 800	8 @ 1200	—	11 @ 2300	4	9 @ 12
1112905	0 @ 600	6 @ 1000	—	—	11 @ 2100	6	7½ @ 12
1112977	0 @ 500	5 @ 850	—	—	10 @ 1900	4	9 @ 12
1112999	0 @ 500	5 @ 850	—	—	10 @ 1900	4	5 @ 8
1977							
1103239	—	—	—	—	—	—	—
1103244	—	—	—	—	—	—	—
1103246	—	—	—	—	—	—	—
1103248	—	—	—	—	—	—	—
1103256	—	—	—	—	—	—	—
1110678	0 @ 500	3½ @ 800	—	—	10 @ 2050	4	12 @ 15
1110681	0 @ 500	3½ @ 800	—	—	10 @ 2100	4	7½ @ 12

Continued

DISTRIBUTOR SPECIFICATIONS—Continued

★Note: If unit is checked on vehicle, double the RPM and degrees to get crankshaft figures.

Distributor Part No.①	Centrifugal Advance Degrees @ RPM of Distributor				Vacuum Advance	
	Advance Starts	Intermediate Advance		Full Advance	Inches of Vacuum to Start Plunger	Max. Adv. Dist. Deg. @ Vacuum
1978						
1103281	0 @ 500	5 @ 850	—	10 @ 1900	—	—
1103282	0 @ 500	5 @ 850	—	10 @ 1900	4	10 @ 10
1103285	0 @ 600	6 @ 1000	—	11 @ 2200	4	5 @ 8
1103286	0 @ 550	6 @ 800	8 @ 1200	11 @ 2300	—	—
1103291	0 @ 600	6½ @ 800	—	8 @ 1000	—	—
1103337	0 @ 550	6 @ 800	—	8 @ 1200	4	12 @ 10
1103353	0 @ 550	6 @ 800	—	8 @ 1200	4	10 @ 10
1110695	0-3 @ 1000	—	—	6-9 @ 1800	7	12 @ 13
1110696	0 @ 500	5 @ 850	—	10 @ 1900	3	8 @ 6½
1110697	0 @ 500	5 @ 850	—	10 @ 1900	3	8 @ 6½
1110715	0 @ 500	3½ @ 800	—	10 @ 2100	4	12 @ 15
1110716	0 @ 500	3½ @ 800	—	10 @ 2100	4	7½ @ 12
1110718	0 @ 500	3½ @ 800	—	10 @ 2100	4	9 @ 12
1110731	0-2 @ 1000	—	—	6-9 @ 1800	4	8 @ 9
1979						
1103281	0 @ 500	5 @ 850	—	10 @ 1900	—	—
1103282	0 @ 500	5 @ 850	—	10 @ 1900	4	10 @ 10
1103285	0 @ 600	6 @ 1000	—	11 @ 2200	4	5 @ 8
1103291	0 @ 600	6½ @ 800	—	8 @ 1000	—	—
1103337	0 @ 550	6 @ 800	—	8 @ 1200	4	12 @ 10
1103353	0 @ 550	6 @ 800	—	8 @ 1200	4	10 @ 10
1103370	0 @ 700	2 @ 850	—	7 @ 1900	3	15 @ 9½
1103371	0 @ 500	5 @ 850	—	10 @ 1900	3	15 @ 9½
1110695	0-3 @ 1000	—	—	6-9 @ 1800	7	12 @ 13
1110716	0 @ 500	3½ @ 800	—	10 @ 2100	4	7½ @ 12
1110731	0-2 @ 1000	—	—	6-9 @ 1800	4	8 @ 9
1110737	0 @ 500	5 @ 850	—	10 @ 1900	3	15 @ 9½
1110748	0 @ 500	3½ @ 800	—	10 @ 2100	4	10 @ 10
1110756	0 @ 700	2 @ 850	—	7 @ 1900	3	15 @ 9½

①—Stamped on distributor housing cover.　②—Breaker arm spring tension—19-23.　③—Breaker arm spring tension—28-32.

REAR AXLE SPECIFICATIONS

Year	Model	Carrier Type	Ring Gear & Pinion Backlash		Pinion Bearing Preload			Differential Bearing Preload		
			Method	Adjustment	Method	New Bearings Inch-Lbs.	Used Bearings Inch-Lbs.	Method	New Bearings Inch-Lbs.	Used Bearings Inch-Lbs.
1974-79	Corvette	Integral	Shims	.005-.008	Spacer	20-25①	5-10①	Shims	.010	.010
1974-79	Exc. Corvette	Integral	Shims	.005-.008	Spacer	15-30①	5-10①	Shims	.010	.010

①—Use inch-pound torque wrench on pinion shaft nut.

VALVE SPECIFICATIONS

★Adjust hydraulic lifters by tightening rocker arm stud nut just to the point where all lash is eliminated.   Then turn nut the additional turns listed.   See Valves Adjust text for details.

Year	Engine Model	Valve Lash★		Valve Angles		Valve Spring Installed Height	Valve Spring Pressure Lbs. @ In.	Stem Clearance		Stem Diameter	
		Int.	Exh.	Seat	Face			Intake	Exhaust	Intake	Exhaust
1974	6-250	1 Turn⑤		46	45	1.66	186 @ 1.27	.001–.0027	.0015–.0032	.3410–.3417	.3410–.3417
	8-350, 145, 160 H.P.	1 Turn⑤		46	45	②	③	.001–.0027	.0012–.0029	.3410–.3417	.3410–.3417
	8-350, 185, 245 H.P.	1 Turn⑤		46	45	②	③	.001–.0027	.0012–.0029	.3410–.3417	.3410–.3417
	8-350, 250 H.P.	1 Turn⑤		46	45	1.70	200 @ 1.25	.001–.0027	.0012–.0029	.3410–.3417	.3410–.3417
	8-400	1 Turn⑤		46	45	1.70	200 @ 1.25	.001–.0027	.0012–.0027	.3410–.3417	.3410–.3417
	8-454	1 Turn⑤		46	45	1.88	300 @ 1.38	.001–.0027	.0012–.0027	.3715–.3722	.3715–.3722
1975	6-250	1 Turn⑤		46	45	1.66	186 @ 1.27	.001–.0027	.0015–.0032	.3410–.3417	.3410–.3417
	8-262	1 Turn⑤		46	45	②	①	.001–.0027	.001–.0027	.3410–.3417	.3410–.3417
	8-350	1 Turn⑤		46	45	②	①	.001–.0027	.0012–.0029	.3410–.3417	.3410–.3417
	8-400	1 Turn⑤		46	45	②	①	.001–.0027	.0012–.0027	.3410–.3417	.3410–.3417
	8-454	1 Turn⑤		46	45	1.88	300 @ 1.38	.001–.0027	.0012–.0027	.3715–.3722	.3713–.3720
1976	6-250	$\frac{3}{4}$ Turn⑤		46	45	1.66	175 @ 1.26	.0010–.0027	.0015–.0032	.3410–.3417	.3410–.3417
	8-305	$\frac{3}{4}$ Turn⑤		46	45	②	①	.0010–.0027	.0010–.0027	.3410–.3417	.3410–.3417
	8-350	$\frac{3}{4}$ Turn⑤		46	45	②	①	.0010–.0027	.0010–.0027	.3410–.3417	.3410–.3417
	8-400	$\frac{3}{4}$ Turn⑤		46	45	②	①	.0010–.0027	.0010–.0027	.3410–.3417	.3410–.3417
	8-454	$\frac{3}{4}$ Turn⑤		46	45	1.88	300 @ 1.38	.0010–.0027	.0010–.0027	.3715–.3722	.3713–.3720
1977	6-250	$\frac{3}{4}$ Turn⑤		46	45	$1\frac{21}{32}$	175 @ 1.26	.0010–.0027	.0010–.0027	.3410–.3417	.3410–.3417
	8-305	$\frac{3}{4}$ Turn⑤		46	45	②	①	.0010–.0027	.0010–.0027	.3410–.3417	.3410–.3417
	8-350④	$\frac{3}{4}$ Turn⑤		46	45	②	①	.0010–.0027	.0010–.0027	.3410–.3417	.3410–.3417
	8-350⑥	$\frac{3}{4}$ Turn⑤		46	45	1.70	200 @ 1.25	.0010–.0027	.0010–.0027	.3410–.3417	.3410–.3417
1978	V6-200	1 Turn⑤		46	45	$1\frac{23}{32}$	200 @ 1.25	.0010–.0027	.0010–.0027	.3410–.3417	.3410–.3417
	V6-231	Hydraulic⑭		45	45	1.727	⑪	.0015–.0032	.0015–.0032	.3402–.3412	.3405–.3412
	6-250	1 Turn⑤		46	45	$1\frac{21}{32}$	175 @ 1.26	.0010–.0027	.0010–.0027	.3410–.3417	.3410–.3417
	V8-305	1 Turn⑤		46	45	$1\frac{23}{32}$	200 @ 1.25	.0010–.0027	.0010–.0027	.3410–.3417	.3410–.3417
	V8-350⑦	1 Turn⑤		46	45	$1\frac{23}{32}$	200 @ 1.25	.0010–.0027	.0010–.0027	.3410–.3417	.3410–.3417
	V8-350⑧	1 Turn⑤		46	45	⑨	⑩	.0010–.0027	.0010–.0027	.3410–.3417	.3410–.3417
1979	V6-200	1 Turn⑤		46	45	$1\frac{45}{64}$	⑫	.0010–.0027	.0010–.0027	.3410–.3417	.3410–.3417
	V6-231	Hydraulic⑭		45	45	$1\frac{23}{32}$	182 @ $1\frac{11}{32}$	.0015–.0032	.0015–.0032	.3402–.3412	.3405–.3412
	6-250	1 Turn⑤		46	45	$1\frac{21}{32}$	175 @ $1\frac{17}{64}$	.0010–.0027	.0010–.0027	.3410–.3417	.3410–.3417
	V8-267	1 Turn⑤		46	45	$1\frac{45}{64}$	⑫	.0010–.0027	.0010–.0027	.3410–.3417	.3410–.3417
	V8-305	1 Turn⑤		46	45	$1\frac{45}{64}$	⑫	.0010–.0027	.0010–.0027	.3410–.3417	.3410–.3417
	V8-350⑦	1 Turn⑤		46	45	$1\frac{45}{64}$	190 @ $1\frac{5}{32}$	.0010–.0027	.0010–.0027	.3410–.3417	.3410–.3417
	V8-350⑧④	1 Turn⑤		46	45	$1\frac{45}{64}$	⑬	.0010–.0027	.0010–.0027	.3410–.3417	.3410–.3417
	V8-350⑧⑥	1 Turn⑤		46	45	$1\frac{45}{64}$	200 @ 1¼	.0010–.0027	.0010–.0027	.3410–.3417	.3410–.3417

①—Intake 200 @ 1.25; exhaust 200 @ 1.16.
②—Intake 1.70; exhaust 1.61.
③—Intake 200 @ 1.25; exhaust 189 @ 1.20.
④—Except Corvette High Performance.
⑤—Turn rocker arm stud nut until all lash is eliminated, then tighten nut the additional turn listed.
⑥—Corvette High Performance.
⑦—Except Corvette.
⑧—Corvette.
⑨—Intake, $1\frac{23}{32}$. Exhaust, $1\frac{19}{32}$.
⑩—Intake, 200 @ 1.25. Exhaust, 200 @ 1.16.
⑪—Intake, 164 @ 1.34. Exhaust, 182 @ 1.34.
⑫—Intake, 180 @ 1¼; Exhaust, 190 @ $1\frac{5}{32}$.
⑬—Intake, 184 @ 1¼; Exhaust, 190 @ $1\frac{5}{32}$.
⑭—No adjustment.

PISTONS, PINS, RINGS, CRANKSHAFT & BEARINGS

Year	Engine Model	Piston Clearance	Ring End Gap① Comp.	Ring End Gap① Oil	Wristpin Diameter	Rod Bearings Shaft Diameter	Rod Bearings Bearing Clearance	Main Bearings Shaft Diameter	Main Bearings Bearing Clearance	Thrust on Bear. No.	Shaft End Play
1978	V6-200	.0007–.0017	.010	.015	.9272	2.0986–2.0998	.0013–.0035	③	④	4	.002–.006
1979	V6-200	.0005–.0015	.010	.010	.9272	2.099–2.100	.0010–.0025	⑯	⑰	4	.002–.007
1978	V6-231	.0008–.0020	.010	.015	.9392	1.9991–2.000	.0005–.0026	2.4995	.0004–.0015	2	.004–.008
1979	V6-231	.0008–.0020	.013	.015	.9392	2.2487–2.2495	.0005–.0026	2.4995	.0004–.0017	2	.003–.009
1974–75	6-250	.0005–.0015	.010	.015	.9272	1.9928–2.000	.0007–.0027	2.2983–2.2993	.0003–.0029	7	.002–.006
1976–77	6-250	.0010–.0020	.010	.015	.9272	1.9928–2.000	.0007–.0027	2.2983–2.2993	.0003–.0029	7	.002–.006
1978	6-250	.0010–.0020	.010	.015	.9272	1.9928–2.000	.0010–.0026	2.2979–2.2994	⑩	7	.002–.006
1979	6-250	.0005–.0015⑲	.010	.015	.9272	1.999–2.000	.0007–.0027	2.2999	.0003–.0029	7	.002–.006
1975	8-262	.0007–.0013	②	.015	.9272	2.098–2.099	.0013–.0035	③	④	5	.002–.007
1976	8-305	.0007–.0017	.010	.015	.9272	2.099–2.100	.0014–.0035	③	⑤	5	.002–.006
1977–78	8-305	.0007–.0017	.010	.015	.9272	2.099–2.100	.0013–.0035	③	④	5	.002–.006
1979	8-305	.0017–.0042⑱	.010	.010	.9272	2.099–2.100	.0013–.0035	③	④	5	.002–.007
1974–75	8-350⑫	.0007–.0013	②	.015	.9272	2.099–2.100	.0013–.0035	③	④	5	.002–.006
	8-350⑬	.0036–.0042	②	.015	.9272	2.099–2.100	.0013–.0035	③	⑤	5	.002–.006
1976	8-350	.0007–.0017	②	.015	.9272	2.099–2.100	.0013–.0035	③	⑤	5	.002–.006
1976	8-350	.0007–.0017	⑭	.015	.9272	2.099–2.100	.0013–.0035	③	⑤	5	.002–.006
	8-350⑮	.0046–.0056	.010	.015	.9272	2.099–2.100	.0013–.0035	③	⑤	5	.002–.006
1977–79	8-350⑥	.0007–.0017	②	.015	.9272	2.099–2.100	.0013–.0035	③	④	5	.002–.006
	8-350⑦	.0046–.0056	.010	.015	.9272	2.099–2.100	.0013–.0035	③	④	5	.002–.006
1974–75	8-400	.0014–.0020	.010	.015	.9272	2.099–2.100	.0013–.0035	⑪	④	5	.002–.006
1976	8-400	.0014–.0024	.010	.015	.9272	2.099–2.100	.0013–.0035	⑪	④	5	.002–.006
1974–76	8-454	.0018–.0028	.010	.015	.9897	2.199–2.200	.0009–.0025	⑧	⑨	5	.006–.010

①—Fit rings tapered bores to the clearance listed in tightest portion of ring travel. Clearances specified are minimum gaps.

②—1977 & 79, top ring; .010. Lower ring; .013. 1978, .010 for both rings.

③—No. 1: 2.4484–2.4493; No. 2, 3 & 4: 2.4481–2.4490; No. 5: 2.4479–2.4488.

④—No. 1: .0008–.0020; No. 2, 3, 4: .0011–.0023; No. 5: .0017–.0033.

⑤—Manual/Trans.; No. 1, 2, 3 & 4: .0013–.0025; No. 5: .0023–.0033. Auto/Trans.; No. 1: .0019–.0032; No. 2 3 & 4; .0013–.0025; No. 5: .0023–.0033.

⑥—Except Corvette High Performance engine.

⑦—Corvette High Performance engine.

⑧—No. 1:27485–2.7494; No. 2, 3 & 4: 2.7481–2.7490; No. 5: 2.7478–2.7488.

⑨—No. 1, 2, 3, 4: .0013–.0025; No. 5: .0024–.0040.

⑩—Nos. 1–6; .0010–.0024. Nos. 7; .0016–0035.

⑪—No. 1, 2, 3 & 4: 2.6484–2.6493; No. 5: 2.6479–2.6488.

⑫—Exc. 245; 250 H.P.

⑬—245, 250 H.P.

⑭—Exc. 145 H.P., top ring .010, bottom ring .013; 145 H.P. top & bottom ring .010.

⑮—210 H.P.

⑯—No. 1, 2.4489; No. 2 & 3, 2.4486; No. 4, 2.4484.

⑰—No. 1, 2 & 3, .0020–.0035; No. 4 .0005–.0015.

⑱—Measured 1.56 in. from top of piston.

⑲—Measured 1.66 in. from top of piston.

BRAKE SPECIFICATIONS

Year	Model	Brake Drum Inside Diameter	Wheel Cylinder Bore Diameter: Disc Brake	Wheel Cylinder Bore Diameter: Front Drum Brake	Wheel Cylinder Bore Diameter: Rear Drum Brake	Master Cylinder Bore Diameter: Disc Brakes	Master Cylinder Bore Diameter: Drum Brakes	Master Cylinder Bore Diameter: Power Brakes
1974	Camaro	$9\frac{1}{2}$	$2\frac{15}{16}$	—	$\frac{7}{8}$	1	—	$1\frac{1}{8}$
	Chevelle & Monte Carlo	$9\frac{1}{2}$⑥	$2\frac{15}{16}$	—	$\frac{7}{8}$①	1	1	$1\frac{1}{8}$
	Nova	$9\frac{1}{2}$	$2\frac{15}{16}$	$1\frac{1}{8}$	$\frac{7}{8}$	1	1	$1\frac{1}{8}$
	Chevrolet	11⑦	$2\frac{15}{16}$	—	$\frac{15}{16}$⑤	$1\frac{1}{8}$	—	$1\frac{1}{8}$
	Corvette	—	③	—	—	1	—	$1\frac{1}{8}$
1975	Camaro	$9\frac{1}{2}$	$2\frac{15}{16}$	—	$\frac{7}{8}$	1	—	$1\frac{1}{8}$
	Chevelle & Monte Carlo	$9\frac{1}{2}$⑥	$2\frac{15}{16}$	—	$\frac{7}{8}$①	1	—	$1\frac{1}{8}$
	Nova	$9\frac{1}{2}$	$2\frac{15}{16}$	—	$\frac{7}{8}$	1	—	$1\frac{1}{8}$
	Chevrolet	11⑦	$2\frac{15}{16}$	—	$\frac{15}{16}$⑤	$1\frac{1}{8}$	—	$1\frac{1}{8}$
	Corvette	—	③	—	—	1	—	$1\frac{1}{8}$

Continued

BRAKE SPECIFICATIONS—Continued

Year	Model	Brake Drum Inside Diameter	Wheel Cylinder Bore Diameter			Master Cylinder Bore Diameter		
			Disc Brake	Front Drum Brake	Rear Drum Brake	Disc Brakes	Drum Brakes	Power Brakes
1976	Camaro	9½	2¹⁵⁄₁₆	—	¹⁵⁄₁₆	1.00	—	1⅛
	Chevelle & Monte Carlo	11	2¹⁵⁄₁₆	—	1②	¹⁵⁄₁₆④	—	1⅛
	Nova	9½	2¹⁵⁄₁₆	—	¹⁵⁄₁₆	1	—	1⅛
	Chevrolet	11⑦	—	—	1	1⅛	—	1⅛
	Corvette	—	③	—	—	1	—	1⅛
1977	Camaro	9½	2¹⁵⁄₁₆	—	¹⁵⁄₁₆	¹⁵⁄₁₆	—	1⅛
	Chevelle & Monte Carlo	11	2¹⁵⁄₁₆	—	¹⁵⁄₁₆	¹⁵⁄₁₆	—	1⅛
	Nova	9½	2¹⁵⁄₁₆	—	¹⁵⁄₁₆	¹⁵⁄₁₆	—	1⅛
	Chevrolet	9½⑥	2¹⁵⁄₁₆	—	⅞①	1⅛①	—	1⅛
	Corvette	—	③	—	—	1⅛	—	1⅛
1978	Camaro	9½	2¹⁵⁄₁₆	—	¹⁵⁄₁₆	¹⁵⁄₁₆	—	1⅛
	Malibu	9½	2½	—	¾	—	—	1⅛
	Monte Carlo	9½	2½	—	¾	—	—	1⅛
	Nova	9½	2¹⁵⁄₁₆	—	¹⁵⁄₁₆	¹⁵⁄₁₆	—	1⅛
	Chevrolet	9½⑥	2¹⁵⁄₁₆	—	⅞①	1⅛	—	1⅛
	Corvette	—	③	—	—	1⅛	—	1⅛
1979	Camaro	9½	2¹⁵⁄₁₆	—	¹⁵⁄₁₆	1.00	—	1⅛
	Malibu	9½	2½	—	¾	⑧	—	⑧
	Monte Carlo	9½	2½	—	¾	⑧	—	⑧
	Nova	9½	2¹⁵⁄₁₆	—	¹⁵⁄₁₆	1.00	—	1⅛
	Chevrolet	9½⑥	2¹⁵⁄₁₆	—	⅞①	1⅛	—	1⅛
	Corvette	—	③	—	—	1⅛	—	1⅛

①—Sta. Wagon ¹⁵⁄₁₆".
②—Power brakes ¹⁵⁄₁₆".
③—Front 1⅞; Rear 1⅜.
④—Malibu Classic and all V-8; 1⅛".
⑤—1974–75 Sta. Wag., 1".
⑥—Sta. Wagon 11".
⑦—Sta. Wagon, 12".
⑧—Exc. V6 Less A/C, ¹⁵⁄₁₆"; V6 Less A/C, ⅞".

ENGINE TIGHTENING SPECIFICATIONS*

★Torque specifications are for clean and lightly lubricated threads only. Dry or dirty threads produce increased friction which prevents accurate measurement of tightness.

Year	Engine Model	Spark Plugs Ft. Lbs.	Cylinder Head Bolts Ft. Lbs.	Intake Manifold Ft. Lbs.	Exhaust Manifold Ft. Lbs.	Rocker Arm Stud Ft. Lbs.	Rocker Arm Cover Ft. Lbs.	Connecting Rod Cap Bolts Ft. Lbs.	Main Bearing Cap Bolts Ft. Lbs.	Flywheel to Crankshaft Ft. Lbs.	Vibration Damper or Pulley Ft. Lbs.
1978	V6-200	15	65	30	20	—	45③	45	70	60	60
1978	V6-231	20	80	45	25	30⑨	4	40	100	60	175
1974	6-250	15	95	②	②	—	45③	35	65	60	60
1975	6-250	15	95	⑥	30⑦	—	45③	35	65	60	60
1976–78	6-250	15	95⑧	⑥	30	—	80③	35	65	60	60
1975	8-262	15	65	30	20	—	45③	45	70	60	60
1976–78	8-305	15	65	30	20	50	45③	45	70	60	60
1974	8-350	15	65	30	20①	50	45③	45	75⑤	60	60
1975–78	8-350	15	65	30	20①	50	45③	45	70⑤	60	60
1974	8-400④	25	65	30	20	—	55③	45	75	60	60
1975–76	8-400	15	65	30	20	50	45③	45	70⑤	60	60
1974–76	8-454	15	80	30	20	50	50③	50	110	65	85

①—Inside bolts 30 ft. lbs.
②—End clamp bolts 20, center bolts 30.
③—Inch lbs.
④—Exc. 330 H.P.
⑤—Outer bolts on engines with 4 bolt caps 65 ft. lbs.
⑥—Integral Intake Manifold.
⑦—Outer bolts 20 ft. lb.
⑧—Left hand front head bolt 85 ft. lbs.
⑨—Rocker arm shaft to cylinder head bolts.

STARTING MOTOR SPECIFICATIONS

Year	Model	Starter Number	Brush Spring Tension Oz.①	Free Speed Test			Resistance Test③	
				Amps.	Volts	R.P.M.①	Amps.	Volts
1974	6-250	1108365	35	50–80②	9	5500–10500	—	—
	8-307	1108367	35	50–80②	9	5500–10500	—	—
	④	1108418	35	65–95②	9	7500–10500	—	—
	④	1108430	35	65–95②	9	7500–10500	—	—
	8-454	1108429	35	65–95②	9	7500–10500	—	—
	8-454	1108400	35	65–95②	9	7500–10500	—	—
1975	6-250	1108365	—	50–80②	9	5500–10500	—	—
	6-250	1108774	—	50–80②	9	5500–10500	—	—
	V8-262	1108512	—	55–80②	9	3500–6000	—	—
	V8-262	1108790	—	55–80②	9	3500–6000	—	—
	8-350, 400, 454	1108430	—	65–95②	9	7500–10500	—	—
	8-350, 400, 454	1108776	—	65–95②	9	7500–10500	—	—
	8-350, 454	1108418	—	65–95②	9	7500–10500	—	—
	8-350, 454	1108775	—	65–95②	9	7500–10500	—	—
1976	6-250	1108774	—	50–80②	9	5500–10500	—	—
	8-305	1108798	—	50–80②	9	5500–10500	—	—
	8-305	1108799	—	50–80②	9	5500–10500	—	—
	8-350, 400, 454	1108776	—	65–95②	9	7500–10500	—	—
	8-350, 454	1108775	—	65–95②	9	7500–10500	—	—
1977–78	6-250	1108774	—	50–80②	9	5500–10500	—	—
	V8-305⑥	1109056	—	50–80②	9	5500–10500	—	—
	V8-305⑦	1108799	—	50–80②	9	5500–10500	—	—
	V8-350⑦	1109059	—	65–95②	9	7500–10500	—	—
	V8-350⑥	1109052	—	65–95②	9	7500–10500	—	—
1978	V6-200	1109524	—	—	—	—	—	—
	V6-231	1108797	—	—	—	—	—	—
1979	V6-200	1109524	—	—	—	—	—	—
	V6-231	1109065	—	—	—	—	—	—
	6-250	1109061	—	—	—	—	—	—
	V8-267	1109524	—	—	—	—	—	—
	V8-305⑧	1109067	—	—	—	—	—	—
	V8-305⑨⑥	1109064	—	—	—	—	—	—
	V8-305⑨⑦	1109074	—	—	—	—	—	—
	V8-305, 350⑧⑩	1109524	—	—	—	—	—	—
	V8-350⑥	1109065	—	—	—	—	—	—
	V8-350⑪⑦	1109067	—	—	—	—	—	—
	V8-350⑫⑦	1109068	—	—	—	—	—	—

①—Minimum.
②—Includes solenoid.
③—Check capacity of motor by using a 500 ampere meter and a carbon pile rheostat to control voltage. Apply the volts listed across motor with armature locked. Current should be as listed.
④—Used on V8-350, 400, 402, and 454 engines.

⑥—With auto. trans.
⑦—With manual trans.
⑧—4 Barrel.
⑨—2 Barrel.
⑩—Malibu & Malibu Classic.
⑪—Corvette.
⑫—Exc. Corvette, Malibu & Malibu Classic.

ALTERNATOR & REGULATOR SPECIFICATIONS

| Year | Alternator | | | | | Regulator | | | | | | |
| | Model | Rated Hot Output Amps. | Field Current 12 Volts @ 80° F. | Output @ 14 Volts | | Model | Field Relay | | | Voltage Regulator | | |
				2000 R.P.M. Amps.	5000 R.P.M. Amps.		Air Gap In.	Point Gap In.	Closing Voltage	Air Gap In.	Point Gap In.	Voltage @ 125° F.
1974–75	1100497	37	③	—	①	Integral	—	—	—	—	—	13.8–14.8
	1100934	37	4–4.5	—	32	Integral	—	—	—	—	—	13.8–14.8
	1100950	42	4–4.5	—	38	Integral	—	—	—	—	—	13.8–14.8
	1100544	61	4–4.5	—	55	Integral	—	—	—	—	—	—
	1100573	42	4–4.5	—	37	Integral	—	—	—	—	—	—
	1100597	61	4–4.5	—	55	Integral	—	—	—	—	—	—
	1102353	42	4–4.5	—	37	Integral	—	—	—	—	—	—
	1100560	55	4–4.5	—	50	Integral	—	—	—	—	—	—
	1100575	55	4–4.5	—	50	Integral	—	—	—	—	—	—
	1102347	61	4–4.5	—	55	Integral	—	—	—	—	—	—
1975	1102397	37	4–4.5	—	33	Integral	—	—	—	—	—	—
	1102483	37	4–4.5	—	33	Integral	—	—	—	—	—	—
	1102493	42	4–4.5	—	38	Integral	—	—	—	—	—	—
1976	1102394	37	4–4.5	—	33	Integral	—	—	—	—	—	—
	1102474	61	4–4.5	—	57	Integral	—	—	—	—	—	—
	1102478	55	4–4.5	—	51	Integral	—	—	—	—	—	—
	1102479	55	4–4.5	—	51	Integral	—	—	—	—	—	—
	1102480	61	4–4.5	—	57	Integral	—	—	—	—	—	—
	1102484	42	4–4.5	—	38	Integral	—	—	—	—	—	—
	1102486	61	4–4.5	—	57	Integral	—	—	—	—	—	—
	1102491	37	4–4.5	—	33	Integral	—	—	—	—	—	—
1977–78	1102394	37	4–4.5	—	33	Integral	—	—	—	—	—	—
	1102474	61	4–4.5	—	57	Integral	—	—	—	—	—	—
	1102478	55	4–4.5	—	51	Integral	—	—	—	—	—	—
	1102479	55	4–4.5	—	51	Integral	—	—	—	—	—	—
	1102480	61	4–4.5	—	57	Integral	—	—	—	—	—	—
	1102484	42	4–4.5	—	38	Integral	—	—	—	—	—	—
	1102486	61	4–4.5	—	57	Integral	—	—	—	—	—	—
	1102491	37	4–4.5	—	33	Integral	—	—	—	—	—	—
1979	1102394	37	4–4.5	—	33	Integral	—	—	—	—	—	—
	1102484	42	—	—	—	Integral	—	—	—	—	—	—
	1102491	37	4–4.5	—	33	Integral	—	—	—	—	—	—
	1102881	37	—	—	—	Integral	—	—	—	—	—	—
	1103033	42	—	—	—	Integral	—	—	—	—	—	—
	1103036	37	—	—	—	Integral	—	—	—	—	—	—

①—1974, 36 @ 7000 RPM; 1975, 33 @ 5000 RPM.   ②—At 7000 RPM.   ③—1974–75: 4–4.5.

WHEEL ALIGNMENT SPECIFICATIONS

Year	Model	Caster Angle, Degrees		Camber Angle, Degrees				Toe-In. Inch	Toe-Out on Turns, Deg.①	
		Limits	Desired	Limits		Desired			Outer Wheel	Inner Wheel
				Left	Right	Left	Right			

CAMARO

Year	Model	Limits	Desired	Left	Right	Left	Right	Toe-In	Outer	Inner
1974	Z-28	−½ to −1½	−1	+¼ to +1¼	+¼ to +1¼	+¾	+¾	⅛ to ¼	—	—
	Others	−½ to +½	Zero	+½ to +1½	+½ to +1½	+1	+1	⅛ to ¼	—	—
1975	All	−½ to ½	Zero	+½ to +1½	+½ to +1½	+1	+1	0 to ⅛	—	—
1976–77	All	+½ to +1½	+1	+½ to +1½	+½ to +1½	+1	+1	0 to ⅛	—	—
1978-79	All	+½ to +1½	+1	+½ to +1½	+½ to +1½	+1	+1	⑧	—	—

CHEVELLE, MALIBU & MONTE CARLO

Year	Model	Limits	Desired	Left	Right	Left	Right	Toe-In	Outer	Inner
1974	Chevelle③	−½ to −1½	−1	+½ to +1½	0 to +1	+1	+½	0 to ⅛	—	—
	Chevelle④	−½ to +½	Zero	+½ to +1½	0 to +1	+1	+½	0 to ⅛	—	—
	Monte Carlo	+4½ to +5½	+5	+½ to +1½	0 to +1	+1	+½	0 to ⅛	—	—
1975–76	Chevelle③	+½ to +1½	+1	+½ to +1½	0 to +1	+1	+½	0 to ⅛	—	—
	Chevelle④	+1½ to +2½	+2	+½ to +1½	0 to +1	+1	+½	0 to ⅛	—	—
	Monte Carlo	+4½ to +5½	+5	+½ to +1½	0 to +1	+1	+½	0 to ⅛	—	—
1977	Chevelle③	+½ to +1½	+1	+½ to +1½	0 to +1	+1	+½	0 to ⅛	—	—
	Chevelle④	②	⑦	+½ to +1½	0 to +1	+1	+½	0 to ⅛	—	—
	Monte Carlo	+4½ to +5½	+5	+½ to +1½	0 to +1	+1	+½	0 to ⅛	—	—
1978-79	All③	+½ to +1½	+1	0 to +1	0 to +1	+½	+½	1/16 to 3/16	—	—
	All④	+2½ to +3½	+3	0 to +1	0 to +1	+½	+½	1/16 to 3/16	—	—

CHEVY NOVA

Year	Model	Limits	Desired	Left	Right	Left	Right	Toe-In	Outer	Inner
1974	All	0 to +1	+½	−¼ to +¾	−¼ to +¾	+¼	+¼	⅛ to ¼	—	—
1975–76	All③	−½ to −1½	−1	+¼ to +1¼	+¼ to +1¼	+¾	+¾	0 to ⅛	—	—
	All④	+½ to +1½	+1	+¼ to +1¼	+¼ to +1¼	+¾	+¾	0 to ⅛	—	—
1977	All③	−1½ to −½	−1	+.3 to +1.3	+.3 to +1.3	+.8	+.8	0 to ⅛	—	—
	All④	+½ to +1½	+1	+.3 to +1.3	+.3 to +1.3	+.8	+.8	0 to ⅛	—	—
1978-79	All③	−1½ to −½	−1	+.3 to +1.3	+.3 to +1.3	+.8	+.8	⑨	—	—
	All④	+½ to +1½	+1	+.3 to +1.3	+.3 to +1.3	+.8	+.8	⑨	—	—

CHEVROLET

Year	Model	Limits	Desired	Left	Right	Left	Right	Toe-In	Outer	Inner
1974	All	+½ to +1½	+1	+½ to +1½	0 to +1	+1	+½	0 to ⅛	—	—
1975	All	+1 to +2	+1½	+½ to +1½	0 to +1	+1	+½	0 to ⅛	—	—
1976	All	⑤	⑥	+½ to +1½	0 to +1	+1	+½	0 to ⅛	—	—
1977	All	+2½ to +3½	+3	+.3 to +1.3	+.3 to +1.3	+.8	+.8	+1/16 to ⅛	—	—
1978-79	All	+2½ to +3½	+3	+.3 to +1.3	+.3 to +1.3	+.8	+.8	⑨	—	—

CORVETTE

Year	Model	Limits	Desired	Left	Right	Left	Right	Toe-In	Outer	Inner
1974	Manual Steer.	+½ to +1½	+1	+¼ to +1¼	+¼ to +1¼	+¾	+¾	3/16 to 5/16	—	20
	Power Steer.	+1¾ to +2¾	+2¼	+¼ to +1¼	+¼ to +1¼	+¾	+¾	3/16 to 5/16	—	20
	Rear Whl. Align.	—	—	−⅝ to −1⅛	−⅝ to −1⅛	−⅞	−⅞	1/32 to 3/32	—	—
1975	Manual Steer.	+½ to +1½	+1	+¼ to +1¼	+¼ to +1¼	+¾	+¾	3/16 to 5/16	—	—
	Power Steer.	+1¾ to +2¾	+2¼	+¼ to +1¼	+¼ to +1¼	+¾	+¾	3/16 to 5/16	—	—
	Rear Whl. Align.	—	—	−1 to 0	−1 to 0	−½	−½	0 to 3/16	—	—
1976	Manual Steer.	+½ to +1½	+1	+¼ to +1¼	+¼ to +1¼	+¾	+¾	3/16 to 5/16	—	—
	Power Steer.	+1¾ to +2¾	+2¼	+¼ to +1¼	+¼ to +1¼	+¾	+¾	3/16 to 5/16	—	—
	Rear Whl. Align.	—	—	−1⅛ to −⅝	−1⅛ to −⅝	−⅞	−⅞	1/32 to 3/32	—	—
1977–79	Front Whl. Align.	+2 to +2.5	+2¼	+¼ to +1¼	+¼ to +1¼	+¾	+¾	3/16 to 5/16	—	—
	Rear Whl. Align.	—	—	+⅝ to +1⅛	+⅝ to +1⅛	+⅞	+⅞	−1/32 to +1/32	—	—

①—Incorrect toe-out, when other adjustments are correct, indicates bent steering arms.
②—Equipped with radial tires, +1½° to +2½°; equipped with bias belted tires, +½° to 1½°.
③—Manual steering.
④—Power steering.
⑤—Equipped with radial tires, +1° to +2°; equipped with bias belted tires, +½° to +1½°.
⑥—Equipped with radial tires, +1½°; equipped with bias belted tires, +1°.
⑦—Equipped with radial tires, +2°; equipped with bias belted tires, +1°.
⑧—1978, 1/16″ to 3/16″; 1979, 1/16″ to 5/32″.
⑨—1978, 1/16 to 3/16 inch, 1979, 10° degree to 20° degree.

COOLING SYSTEM & CAPACITY DATA

Year	Model or Engine	Cooling Capacity, Qts.			Radiator Cap Relief Pressure, Lbs.		Thermo. Opening Temp. ①	Fuel Tank Gals.	Engine Oil Refill Qts. ②	Transmission Oil			Rear Axle Oil Pints
		No Heater	With Heater	With A/C	With A/C	No A/C				3 Speed Pints	4 Speed Pints	Auto. Trans. Qts. ⑬	
CAMARO													
1974	6-250	14	14	—	15	15	195	21	4	3	—	⑦	4¼
	8-350, 145 H.P.	18	18	—	15	15	195	21	4	3	3	⑦	4¼
	8-350, 160 H.P.	18	18	—	15	15	195	21	4	3	3	⑦	4¼
	8-350, 185 H.P.	18	18	—	15	15	195	21	4	3	3	⑦	4¼
	8-350, 245 H.P.	18	18	—	15	15	180	21	4	3	3	⑦	4¼
1975	6-250	—	12½	12½	15	15	195	21	4	3	—	4⑥	4¼
	8-350	—	15½	16½	15	15	195	21	4	3	3	4⑥	4¼
	8-350, Z28	—	15½	16½	15	15	180	21	4	—	3	4⑥	4¼
1976	6-250	—	15	16	15	15	195	21	4	3	—	⑥	4¼
	8-305	—	17½	18½	15	15	195	21	4	3	—	⑥	4¼
	8-350	—	17½	18½	15	15	195	21	4	—	3	⑥	4¼
1977	6-250	—	14.6	14.7	15	15	195	21	4	3	—	⑥	4¼
	8-305	—	17.2	17.9	15	15	195	21	4	3	—	⑥	4¼
	8-350	—	17.3	18.0	15	15	195	21	4	—	3	⑥	4¼
1978	6-250	—	15	16	15	15	195	21	4	3	—	⑲	4¼
	8-305	—	17.5	18.5	15	15	195	21	4	—	3	⑲	4¼
	8-350	—	17.5	18.5	15	15	195	21	4	—	3	⑲	4¼
1979	6-250	—	—	—	15	15	195	21	4	3	—	㉔	4¼
	8-305	—	—	—	15	15	195	21	4	—	3.4	㉔	4¼
	8-350	—	—	—	15	15	195	21	4	—	㉓	㉔	4¼
CHEVELLE, MALIBU & MONTE CARLO													
1974	6-250	—	14	14	15	15	195	22	4	3	—	⑦	④
	8-350, 145 H.P.	—	18	18③	15	15	195	22	4	3	—	⑦	④
	8-350, 160 H.P.	—	18	18③	15	15	195	22	4	3	—	⑦	④
	8-400, 150 H.P.	—	18	18③	15	15	195	22	4	—	—	⑦	④
	8-400, 180 H.P.	—	18	18③	15	15	195	22	4	—	—	⑦	④
	8-454, 235 H.P.	—	24	18⑤	15	15	195	22	4	—	3	⑦	④
1975	6-250	—	12½	12½	15	15	195	22	4	3	—	4⑥	④
	8-350	—	16	17	15	15	195	22	4	3	—	4⑥	④
	8-400	—	16	17	15	15	195	22	4	—	—	4⑥	④
	8-454	—	23	24	15	15	195	22	4	—	—	4½⑥	④
1976	6-250	—	15	17	15	15	195	22	4	3	—	⑥	4¼
	8-305	—	17½	18½	15	15	195	22	4	—	—	⑥	4¼
	8-350	—	17½	18½	15	15	195	22	4	—	—	⑥	4¼
	8-400	—	17½	18½	15	15	195	22	4	—	—	⑥	4¼
1977	6-250	—	15	17	15	15	195	22	4	3	—	⑥	4
	8-305	—	17½	18½	15	15	195	22	4	—	—	⑥	4
	8-350	—	17½	18½	15	15	195	22	4	—	—	⑥	4
1978	6-200	—	15	17	15	15	195	17.5	4	3	3	⑲	3¼
	6-231	—	15	17	15	15	195	17.5	4	3	3	⑲	3¼
	8-305	—	18	20	15	15	195	17.5	4	—	3	⑲	3¼
	8-350	—	18	20	15	15	195	17.5	4	—	—	⑲	3¼
1979	6-200	—	—	—	15	15	195	18.1	4	3	—	㉔	3¼
	6-231	—	—	—	15	15	195	18.1	4	—	—	㉔	3¼
	8-267	—	—	—	15	15	195	18.1	4	—	3.4	㉔	3¼
	8-305	—	—	—	15	15	195	18.1	4	—	3.4	㉔	3¼
	8-350	—	—	—	15	15	195	18.2	4	—	—	㉔	3¼

Continued

COOLING SYSTEM & CAPACITY DATA—Continued

Year	Model or Engine	Cooling Capacity, Qts.			Radiator Cap Relief Pressure, Lbs.		Thermo. Opening Temp. ①	Fuel Tank Gals.	Engine Oil Refill Qts. ②	Transmission Oil			Rear Axle Oil Pints
		No Heater	With Heater	With A/C	With A/C	No A/C				3 Speed Pints	4 Speed Pints	Auto. Trans. Qts. ⑬	
CHEVY NOVA													
1974	6-250	—	12½	12½	15	15	195	21	4	3	—	⑦	4¼
	8-350, 145 H.P.	—	15½	16½	15	15	195	21	4	3	—	⑦	4¼
	8-350, 160 H.P.	—	15½	16½	15	15	195	21	4	3	—	⑦	4¼
	8-350, 185 H.P.	—	15½	16½	15	15	195	21	4	—	3	⑦	4¼
1975	6-250	—	12½	12½	15	15	195	21	4	3	—	4⑥	4¼
	8-262	—	—	—	15	15	195	21	4	3	—	4⑥	4¼
	8-350	—	15½	16½	15	15	195	21	4	3	—	4⑥	4¼
1976	6-250	—	14	15	15	15	195	21	4	3	—	⑥	4¼
	8-305	—	17	18	15	15	195	21	4	3	—	⑥	4¼
	8-350	—	17	18	15	15	195	21	4	3	3	⑥	4¼
1977	6-250	—	14	15	15	15	195	21	4	3	—	㉑	⑩
	8-305	—	17	18	15	15	195	21	4	3	—	㉑	⑩
	8-350	—	17	18	15	15	195	21	4	—	3	㉑	⑩
1978-79	6-250	—	14	15	15	15	195	21	4	3	—	⑲	⑩
	8-305	—	16	17	15	15	195	21	4	—	3	⑲	⑩
	8-350	—	16	17	15	15	195	21	4	—	—	⑲	⑩
CHEVROLET													
1974	8-350, 145 H.P.	—	16	17	15	15	195	26㉑	4	—	—	⑦	④
	8-350, 160 H.P.	—	16	17	15	15	195	26㉑	4	—	—	⑦	④
	8-400, 150 H.P.	—	16½	17½	15	15	195	26㉑	4	—	—	⑦	④
	8-400, 180 H.P.	—	16½	17½	15	15	195	26㉑	4	—	—	⑦	④
	8-454, 235 H.P.	—	23	24	15	15	195	26㉑	4	—	—	⑦	④
1975	8-350	—	16	17	15	15	195	26㉑	4	—	—	4⑥	④
	8-400	—	16½	17½	15	15	195	26㉑	4	—	—	4½⑥	④
	8-454	—	23	24	15	15	195	26㉑	4	—	—	4½⑥	④
1976	8-350	—	18	18	15	15	195	26㉑	4	—	—	⑥	④
	8-400	—	18	18	15	15	195	26㉑	4	—	—	⑥	④
	8-454	—	23	25	15	15	195	26㉑	4	—	—	⑥	④
1977	6-250	—	15	16	15	15	195	21㉑	4	—	—	4⑧	⑩
	8-305	—	18	20	15	15	195	21㉑	4	—	—	4⑧	⑩
	8-350	—	18	20	15	15	195	21㉑	4	—	—	4⑧	⑩
1978-79	6-250	—	14	15	15	15	195	21㉑	4	—	—	⑲	⑩
	8-305	—	16½	18½	15	15	195	21㉑	4	—	—	⑲	⑩
	8-350	—	16½	18½	15	15	195	21㉑	4	—	—	⑲	⑩
CORVETTE													
1974	8-350, 195 H.P.	17	19	—	15	15	195	18	4	—	3	⑦	4
	8-350, 250 H.P.	17	19	—	15	15	180	18	4	—	3	⑦	4
	8-454, 270 H.P.	24	24	—	15	15	195	18	4	—	3	⑦	4
1975	8-350	—	18	18	15	15	180	18	4	—	3	4⑥	4
1976	8-350	—	21	21	15	15	195⑫	17	4	—	3	11	4
1977	8-350	—	21	21	15	15	195	17	4	—	3	㉒	3¾
1978	8-350	—	21	21	15	15	195	23.7	4	—	3	10	3¾
1979	8-350	—	—	—	15	15	195	24	4	—	㉓	㉔	3¾

①—For permanent type anti-freeze.
②—Add one quart with filter change.
③—Monte Carlo 20 qts.
④—4¼ for 8⅛″ and 8½″ ring gears and 4.9 for 8⅞″ ring gear.
⑤—Monte Carlo 26 qts.
⑥—Turbo Hydramatic 200, 250 & 350 total capacity 10 qts., T.H. 400 total capacity 11 qts.
⑦—Turbo Hydramatic 250 & 350 refill 2½ qts., T.H. 400 refill 3¾ qts.
⑧—Refill capacity.
⑩—3¼ pts. for 7½″ ring gear; 4 pts. for 8½″ and 8¾″ ring gears.
⑪—Refill capacity. With High Performance engine, 4½ qts.
⑫—Optional 350 engine: 180°.
⑬—Standard trans.
⑭—Auto. trans.
⑮—Approximate. Make final check with dipstick.
⑲—Turbo Hydramatic 200 oil pan only, 3 qts. Total capacity, 4.5 qts.; CBC 350, oil pan only. 3 qts. Total capacity 10 qts.
⑳—Wagons 22 gallons.
㉑—Refill capacities: THM 200—8¼ qts., THM 350—6¾ qts.
㉒—THM 350, 10 qts.; THM 400, 11 qts.
㉓—Exc. close ratio trans., 3.4 pts.; Close ratio trans., 2¾ pts.
㉔—Oil pan only, 4 qts. Total capacity, 10 qts.

Electrical Section

DISTRIBUTOR
Removal

1. Disconnect distributor primary wire from coil terminal.

   NOTE: On H.E.I. systems, disconnect feed and module connectors from distributor cap.

2. Remove distributor cap and rotor. *Mark position of rotor arm on distributor housing so distributor can be installed in same position.*
3. Remove vacuum line and distributor hold down clamp. On Corvette, units, remove tachometer drive cable.
4. Note relative position of distributor in block, then work it out of the engine.

Installation

1. Turn rotor about ⅛ of a turn counterclockwise past the mark previously placed on the distributor housing.
2. Push the distributor down into the block with the housing in the normal "installed" position. *It may be necessary to move the rotor slightly to start gear into mesh with camshaft gear, but rotor should line up with mark when distributor is down in place.*

NOTE: Because the lower end of the distributor shaft drives the oil pump, use extra care when installing the distributor to be sure it is completely seated and engaged in oil pump.

NOTE

If the engine was disturbed while the distributor was removed from the engine, first crank the engine to bring No. 1 piston up on its compression stroke and continue cranking until the timing mark is aligned to the timing indicator. Then rotate the distributor cam until the rotor

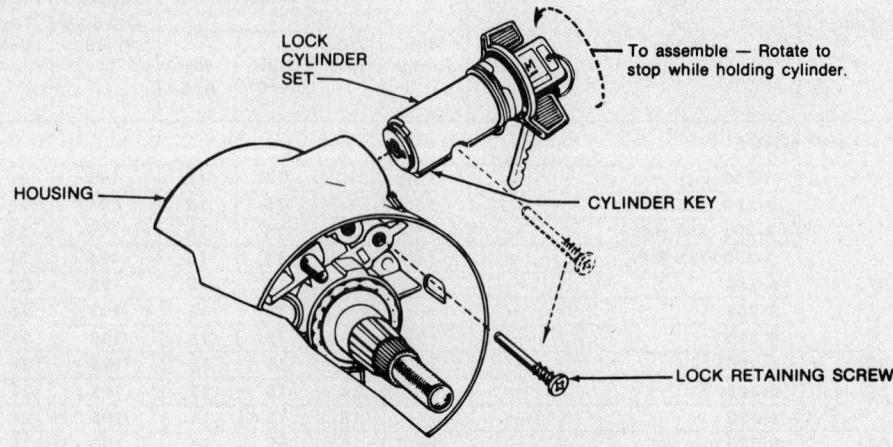

Fig. 1   Ignition lock. 1979 models

is in position to fire No. 1 cylinder. Install the distributor.

3. Tighten distributor clamp screw snugly and connect vacuum line, primary wire to coil, and install cap.
4. Set ignition timing.

NOTE: When using a timing light to adjust ignition timing, the connection should be made at the No. 1 spark plug. Forcing foreign objects through the boot at the No. 1 terminal of the distributor cap will damage the boot and could cause engine misfiring.

STARTER, REPLACE
1974-79 All Models

1. Disconnect ground cable at battery.
2. Raise vehicle to working height.
3. Disconnect all wires at solenoid.

   NOTE: Reinstall terminal nuts as each wire is disconnected as thread size is different but may be mixed and stripped.

4. Loosen starter front bracket (nut on V8 and bolt on Sixes) then remove two mounting bolts.

NOTE: On V8 engines using solenoid heat shield, remove front bracket upper bolt and detach bracket from starter.

5. Remove front bracket bolt or nut and rotate bracket clear of work area. Then lower starter from vehicle by lowering front end first (hold starter against bell housing and sort of roll end-over end).
6. Reverse removal procedure to install and torque mount bolts to 25-35 ft. lbs. On 1974-79 Corvette, apply a suitable sealing compound around starter where it enters engine splash shield.

IGNITION LOCK
1979

1. Remove steering wheel as described under Horn Sounder and Steering Wheel.
2. Remove turn signal switch as described under Turn Signal Switch, Replace, then remove buzzer switch.
3. Place ignition switch in Run position, then remove lock cylinder retaining screw and lock cylinder.
4. To install, rotate lock cylinder to stop while holding housing, Fig. 1. Align cylinder key with keyway in housing, then push lock cylinder assembly into housing until fully seated.
5. Install lock cylinder retaining screw. Torque screw to 40 in. lbs. for standard columns. On adjustable columns, torque retaining screw to 22 in. lbs.
6. Install buzzer switch, turn signal switch and steering wheel.

1974-78

1. Follow the procedure to remove the turn signal switch as described further on.

Fig. 2   Ignition lock removal

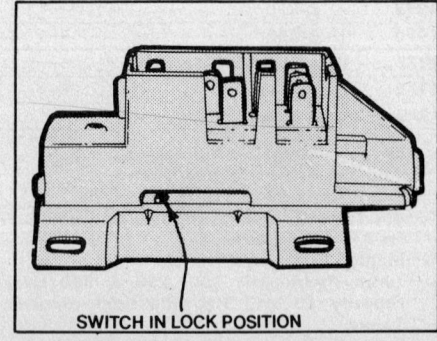

SWITCH IN LOCK POSITION

Fig. 3   Ignition switch replacement. 1974-79

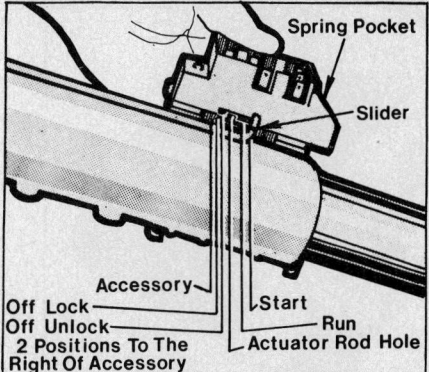

Fig. 4   Ignition switch assembly. 1977-79 models

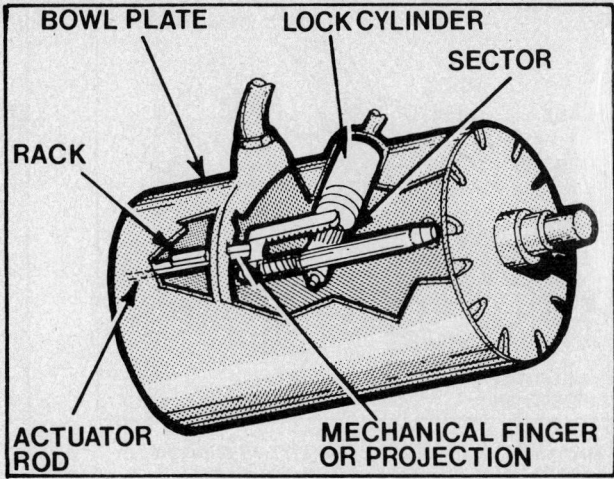

Fig. 5   Mechanical neutral start system. 1977-79 Chevrolet & 1978-79 Malibu & Monte Carlo with standard column

2. The lock cylinder should be removed in the "RUN" position only.

NOTE: On all models except Corvette, do not remove buzzer switch since damage to the lock cylinder will result.

3. Place a thin tool (small screwdriver or knife blade) into the slot, Fig. 2, next to the switch mounting screw boss (right hand slot) and depress spring latch at bottom of slot which releases lock. Remove lock.

IGNITION SWITCH, REPLACE

1974-79

The ignition switch is mounted on top of the mast jacket inside the brake pedal support and is actuated by a rod and rack assembly.

1. Disconnect battery cable.
2. Disconnect and lower steering column.

NOTE: It may be necessary, on some models, to remove the upper column mounting bracket if it hinders servicing of switch.

CAUTION: Use extreme care when lowering steering column to prevent damage to column assembly. Only lower steering column a sufficient distance to perform ignition switch service.

3. On all except 1977-79 models, the switch should be in the "Lock" position before removal, Fig. 3. If the lock cylinder was removed, pull actuator rod upward to the stop, then downward one detent. Remove ignition switch retaining screws and the switch.
4. On 1977-79 models, the switch should be in the "Off" unlocked position before removal, Fig. 4. If the lock cylinder was removed, pull actuator rod to the full downward position. Remove ignition switch retaining screws and the ignition switch.
5. Reverse procedure install. Ensure ignition switch is in "Lock" position on all except 1977-79 models. On 1977-

79 models, place gear shift lever in neutral position and install ignition switch in "Off" unlocked position, Fig. 4.

LIGHT SWITCH, REPLACE

1978-79 Malibu & Monte Carlo

1. Disconnect battery ground cable.
2. Remove instrument panel bezel.
3. Pull switch knob to "On" position.
4. Remove three screws attaching windshield wiper/light switch mounting plate to cluster and pull assembly rearward.
5. Depress shaft retainer button on switch and pull knob and shaft assembly from switch.
6. Remove ferrule nut and switch assembly from mounting plate.
7. Reverse procedure to install.

1978-79 Corvette

1. Disconnect battery ground cable.
2. Remove left air distribution duct.
3. Remove instrument cluster to instrument panel attaching screws and pull cluster rearward.
4. Disconnect speedometer cable and electrical connectors and remove cluster.
5. Remove two instrument panel to left door pillar attaching screws and pull left side of instrument panel slightly rearward.
6. Depress light switch shaft retainer button and pull out knob and shaft assembly from switch. Remove the switch retaining bezel.
7. Disconnect vacuum hoses from switch and the electrical connector.
8. Remove light switch from vehicle.
9. Reverse procedure to install.

1977-79 Chevrolet

1. Disconnect battery ground cable.
2. Pull switch knob to "On" position and reach up under instrument panel and depress switch shaft retainer, then

pull knob and shaft assembly from switch.
3. Remove windshield wiper switch.
4. Remove light switch ferrule nut and remove switch from panel.
5. Disconnect electrical connector from switch and remove switch from vehicle.
6. Reverse procedure to install.

1974-77 Chevelle & Monte Carlo

1. Disconnect battery ground cable.
2. Remove instrument panel pad.
3. Remove left radio speaker to one side.
4. Pull headlamp control knob to "ON" position and while standing outside vehicle on left side, reach in and behind instrument panel and depress switch shaft retainer and pull knob and shaft assembly out.
5. Remove ferrule nut and switch from panel.

1974-77 Corvette

1. Disconnect battery cable.
2. Remove screws securing mast jacket trim covers and remove covers.
3. Remove left side console forward trim panel.
4. Lower steering column.
5. Remove screws securing left instrument panel to door opening, top of dash and left side of center instrument panel.
6. Pull cluster down and tip forward for access.
7. Depress switch shaft retainer and remove the knob and shaft assembly. Remove switch retaining bezel.
8. Disconnect vacuum hoses from switch, tagging them for assembly. Pry the connector from the switch and remove the switch.

1974-79 Camaro

1. Disconnect battery ground cable.
2. Remove steering column lower cover.

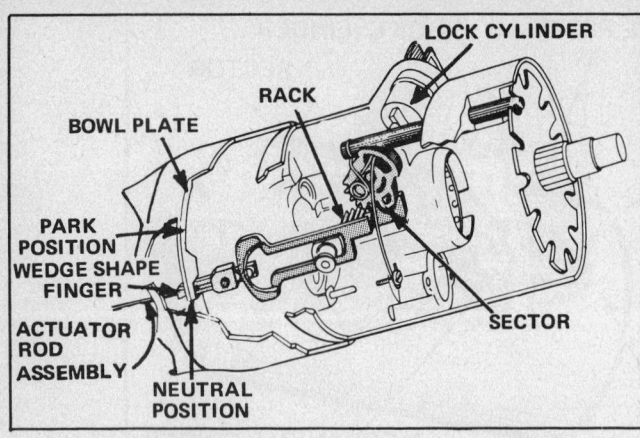

Fig. 6 Mechanical neutral start system. 1977-79 Chevrolet & 1978-79 Malibu & Monte Carlo with tilt column

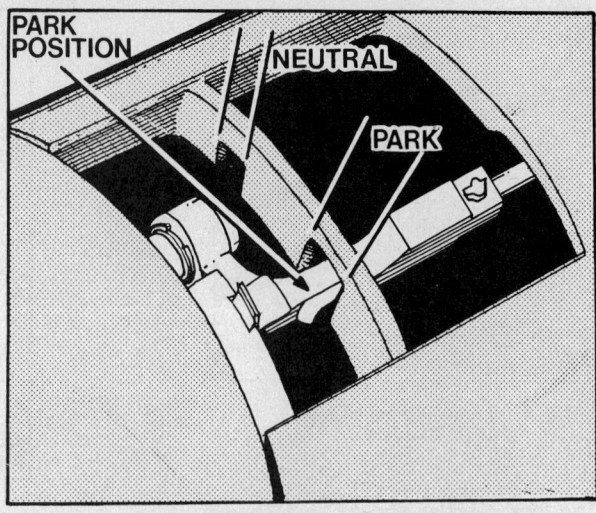

Fig. 7 Mechanical neutral start system in Park position. 1977-79 Chevrolet & 1978-79 Malibu & Monte Carlo

3. Reach up under cluster and depress lighting switch shaft retainer while pulling gently on shaft.
4. Remove nut securing switch to carrier.
5. Remove cluster carrier screws and tilt right side of cluster out.
6. Unplug connector and remove switch.

1974-76 Chevrolet & 1974-79 Nova

1. Disconnect battery ground cable.
2. Pull switch knob to "ON" position.
3. Reach up under instrument panel and depress switch shaft retainer, then remove knob and shaft assembly.
4. Remove ferrule nut and switch from panel.
5. Disconnect multi-contact connector from light switch.
6. Reverse procedure to install.

STOP LIGHT SWITCH, REPLACE

1974-79 Except Corvette

1. Disconnect wiring connector at switch.
2. Remove retaining nut, if so equipped, and unscrew switch from bracket.
3. To install: Depress brake pedal and push new switch into clip until shoulder bottoms out.
4. Plug connector onto switch and check operation. Electrical contact should be made when pedal is depressed ⅜" to ⅝" from fully released position.

1974-79 Corvette

1. Disconnect wiring connector at switch.
2. Remove retaining nut and unscrew switch from bracket.
3. Upon installation, check for proper operation. Electrical contact should be made when pedal is depressed ¼" to ⅝". Switch bracket has a slotted screw hole for adjustment.

CLUTCH START SWITCH

1974-79 Corvette

1. Unplug connector from switch.
2. Remove retainer from pins or link on clutch pedal arm.
3. Remove retaining screw and switch.

1974-79 Except Corvette

1. Unplug connector from switch.
2. Compress switch actuating shaft retainer and remove shaft with switch attached from switch bracket.

NEUTRAL SAFETY SWITCH, REPLACE

1977-79 Chevrolet & 1978-79 Malibu & Monte Carlo

Actuation of the ignition switch is prevented by a mechanical lockout system,

J-23653

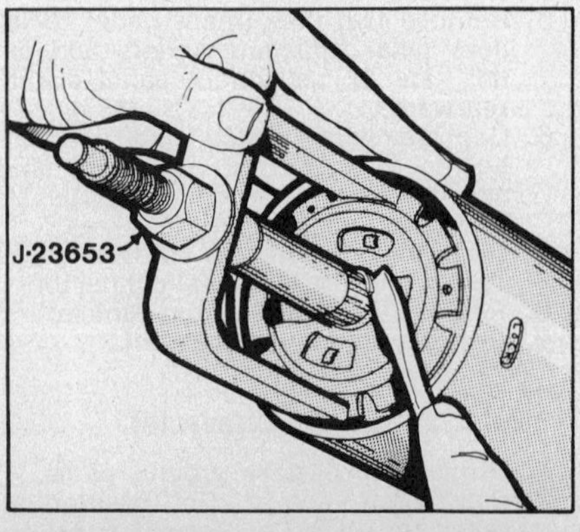

Fig. 8 Removing lock plate retaining ring

Figs. 5 and 6, which prevents the lock cylinder from rotating when the selector lever is out of Park or Neutral. When the selector lever is in Park or Neutral, the slots in the bowl plate and the finger on the actuator rod align allowing the finger to pass through the bowl plate in turn actuating the ignition switch, Fig. 7. If the selector lever is in any position other than Park or Neutral, the finger contacts the bowl plate when the lock cylinder is rotated, thereby preventing full travel of the lock cylinder.

1974-79 All Except 1977-79 Chevrolet & 1978-79 Malibu & Monte Carlo

Column Shift & 1974-79 Floor Shift Exc. Corvette

1. Disconnect wiring connector at switch terminals.
2. Unfasten and remove switch from mast jacket.
3. To install: position shift lever against PARK gate by rotating lower lever counterclockwise as viewed from drivers seat.
4. Assemble switch to column by inserting actuating tang in shifter tube slot.
5. Tighten screws, connect wiring connector and move selector lever out of PARK to shear pin which is part of new switch.

1974-79 Corvette

1. Disconnect shift control lever arm from transmission control rod.
2. Remove shift control knob.
3. Remove trim plate.
4. Remove control assembly from seal and disconnect switch wiring.
5. Remove switch from control assembly.
6. To install, position gearshift in Drive position, align hole in contact

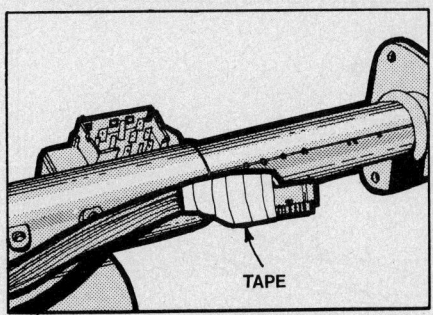

Fig. 9   Taping turn signal connector and wires. 1974-79

support with hole in switch and insert a pin (3/32") to hold support in place.

7. Place contact support drive slot over drive tang and tighten switch mounting screws.
8. Connect wiring harness to switch wiring.
9. Install trim plate control knob and connect shift lever arm to transmission control rod.

TURN SIGNAL SWITCH, REPLACE

1974-79

1. Disconnect battery cable, then remove steering wheel and column to instrument panel trim cover.
2. Remove cover from shaft. *The cover retaining screws need not be completely removed from the cover.*
3. Using a suitable tool, compress lock plate (horn contact carrier on tilt models) and remove snap ring ("C" ring on tilt models), Fig. 8.

NOTE: On 1976-79 models, remove lock plate cover with a suitable screwdriver. On 1976-79 Corvette models with tilt-telescopic column, place a 5/16 in. nut under each leg of puller.

4. Remove lock plate, cancelling cam, upper bearing preload spring, thrust washer and signal lever.
5. Push hazard warning knob in and unscrew knob.
6. Pull connector from bracket and wrap upper part of connector with tape to prevent snagging the wires during removal. On Tilt models, position shifter housing in "Low" position. Remove harness cover.
7. Remove retaining screws and remove switch, Figs. 9 and 10.

COLUMN-MOUNTED DIMMER SWITCH

1977-79 Chevrolet & 1978-79 Corvette, Malibu & Monte Carlo

1. Disconnect battery ground cable.

---

2. Remove instrument panel lower trim and on models with A/C, remove A/C duct extension at column.
3. Disconnect shift indicator from column and remove toe-plate cover screws.
4. Remove two nuts from instrument panel support bracket studs and lower steering column, resting steering wheel on front seat.
5. Remove dimmer switch retaining screws and the switch. Tape actuator rod to column and separate switch from rod.

NOTE: On 1978 models, two dimmer switch retaining screws are used.

6. Reverse procedure to install. To adjust switch, depress dimmer switch slightly and install a 3/32 inch twist drill to lock the switch to the body. Force switch upward to remove lash between switch and pivot. Torque switch retaining screw to 35 inch lbs. and remove tape from actuator rod. Remove twist drill and check for proper operation.

HORN SOUNDER & STEERING WHEEL

1974-79 Cushioned Rim Wheel

1. Disconnect battery ground cable.
2. Pry off horn button cap.
3. Remove three spacer screws, spacer, plate and belleville spring.
4. Remove steering wheel nut and washer and, using a suitable puller, remove steering wheel.

NOTE: On 1975-79 models, remove snap ring before steering wheel nut.

1974-79 Standard Wheel

1. Disconnect battery ground cable.

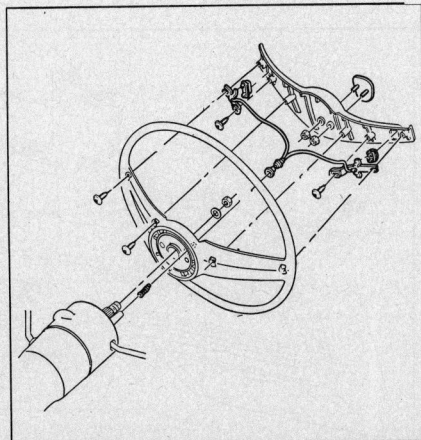

Fig. 11   Steering wheel and horn attachments. 1974-79 standard wheel

---

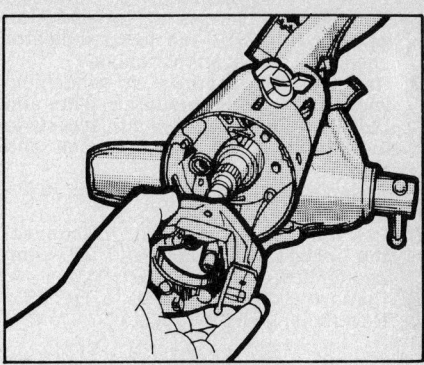

Fig. 10   Removing turn signal switch. 1974-79

2. Remove attaching screws on underside of the steering wheel, Fig. 11.
3. Lift steering wheel shroud and pull horn wires from cancelling cam tower.
4. Remove steering wheel nut and washer, and use a suitable puller to remove steering wheel.

NOTE: On 1975-79 models, remove snap ring before steering wheel nut.

1974-79 Corvette

1. Disconnect steering column harness at wiring connector. Disconnect battery ground cable.
2. Pry off horn button cap.
3. Remove three screws securing horn contact to spacer and hub.
4. On telescoping wheels, remove shim, if used, then the screw securing the center star screw and the star screw and lever.

NOTE: If wheel only is to be replaced, perform Step 5. If turn signal cancelling cam is to be replaced, omit Step 5 and proceed with Steps 6 and 7.

5. Remove wheel from hub (6 screws).
6. Remove nut and washer from shaft and use a suitable puller to remove wheel and hub.

NOTE: On 1975-78 models, remove snap ring before steering wheel nut.

7. Slide cancelling cam and spring off shaft.

INSTRUMENT CLUSTER

1978-79 Malibu Standard Cluster

1. Disconnect battery ground cable.
2. Remove clock set stem knob, if equipped.
3. Remove instrument bezel retaining screws, Fig. 12.
4. Pull bezel from panel slightly and disconnect rear defogger switch, if equipped.
5. Remove bezel, Fig. 12.

6. Remove two screws at transmission selector indicator and lower indicator assembly to disconnect cable.
7. Remove three screws at windshield wiper/light switch mounting plate and pull assembly rearward for access to lower left cluster attaching bolt and nut.
8. Remove nuts attaching cluster to instrument panel.
9. Pull cluster rearward and disconnect the speedometer cable and all wiring and cables.
10. Remove cluster from vehicle, Fig. 13.
11. Reverse procedure to install.

1978-79 Malibu Optional Cluster & Monte Carlo

1. Disconnect battery ground cable.
2. Remove radio knobs and clock set stem knob.
3. Remove instrument bezel retaining screws, Fig. 12.
4. Pull bezel rearward slightly and disconnect the rear defogger switch and remote control mirror control, if equipped.
5. Remove bezel, Fig. 12.
6. Remove speedometer retaining screws, pull speedometer from cluster slightly, disconnect speedometer cable and remove speedometer.
7. Remove fuel gauge or tachometer retaining screws, disconnect electrical connectors and remove fuel gauge or tachometer.
8. Remove clock or voltmeter retaining screws, disconnect electrical connectors and remove clock or voltmeter.
9. Disconnect transmission shift indicator cable from steering column.
10. Disconnect all wiring connectors and remove cluster case, Fig. 13.
11. Reverse procedure to install.

1977-79 Chevrolet

1. Disconnect battery ground cable.
2. Remove four steering column lower cover screws and the cover.
3. If equipped with automatic transmission, disconnect shift indicator cable from steering column.
4. Remove two steering column to instrument panel screws and lower steering column.

CAUTION: Use extreme care when lowering steering to prevent damage to column assembly.

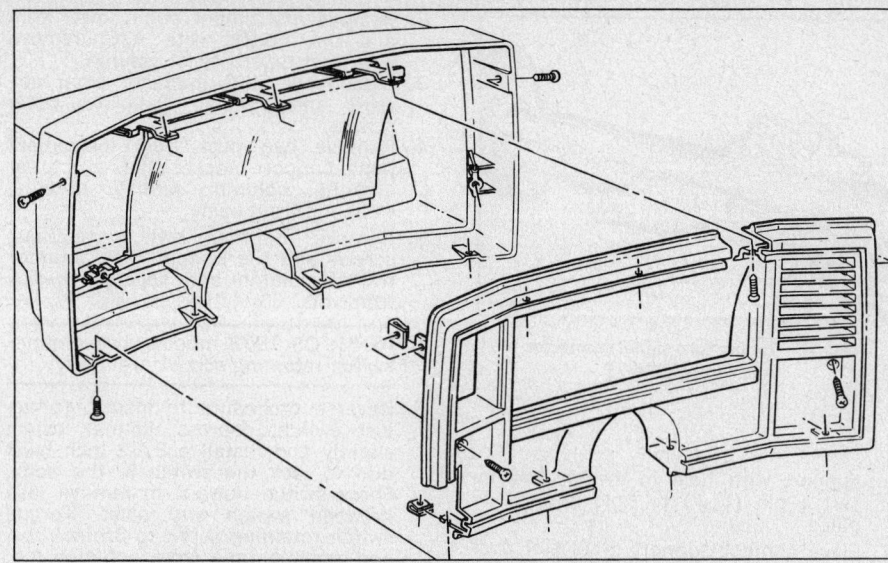

Fig. 12 Instrument cluster bezel removal (Typical). 1978-79 Malibu & Monte Carlo

5. Remove six screws and the three snap-in fasteners from perimeter of instrument cluster lens, Fig. 14.
6. Remove two screws from upper surface of grey sheet metal trim plate.
7. Remove two stud nuts from lower corner of cluster.
8. Disconnect speedometer cable and pull cluster from instrument panel.
9. Disconnect electrical connectors from cluster and remove from vehicle.

1974-77 Chevelle & Monte Carlo

1. Disconnect battery ground cable.
2. Remove radio knobs and clock stem set knob, if equipped.
3. Remove instrument bezel retaining screws, Figs. 15 and 16.
4. Pull bezel out to disconnect tail gate release or rear defogger switch, if equipped.
5. Remove instrument bezel.

1974-76 Chevrolet

1. Disconnect battery ground cable.
2. Remove cigar lighter knob and hidden screw in shroud where knob was.
3. Pull on headlamp switch shaft then remove hidden screw above middle of shaft.
4. Remove two screws at bottom corners of shroud and lift off shroud, Fig. 17.
5. To service instruments, remove clock stem set knob.
6. Remove lens retaining strip secured by three screws at top of lens. Be careful not to mar lens.
7. Lift off lens carefully—guide pins are on bottom of lens.
8. Gently lift up on bottom of filter housing and rotate housing up and rearward, toward technician on front seat. Top of housing should clear top of instrument carrier. Use

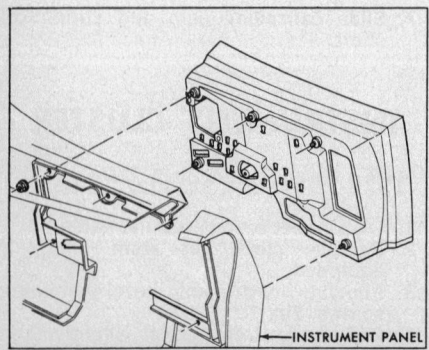

Fig. 13 Instrument cluster removal (Typical). 1978-79 Malibu & Monte Carlo

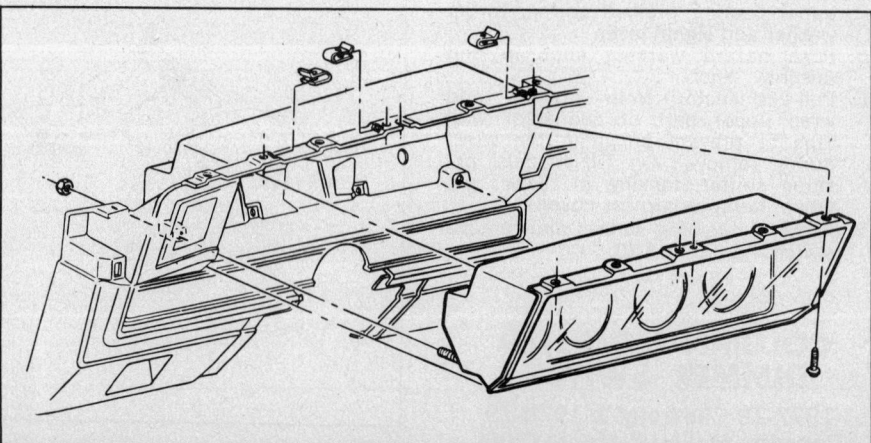

Fig. 14 Instrument cluster. 1977-79 Chevrolet

care around PRNDL housing and lift filter assembly off. Speedometer, fuel gauge and clock can now be removed.

1974-79 Camaro

1. Disconnect battery ground cable.
2. Remove 6 screws securing trim cover beneath steering column. Two of these screws are located above the ash tray.
3. Remove headlamp switch retaining nut.
4. From behind panel, disconnect cigar lighter and unscrew retainer. Note grounding ring.
5. From under lower edge of cluster, remove screw on either side of column, Fig. 18.
6. Remove 4 screws visible on front of carrier.
7. Remove screw retaining ground wire for wiper switch. Screw is fastened under top left corner of switch.
8. Carefully tilt carrier out of access to the connectors on headlamp and wiper switches.
9. Remove lens screws then cluster screws.
10. Disconnect shift indicator from steering column.
11. Disconnect speedometer cable and tilt cluster forward and remove remaining connectors.
12. Lift cluster out.

1974-79 Nova

1. Disconnect battery ground cable.
2. Lower steering column and apply protective covering to mast jacket to protect paint.
3. Remove three screws above front of heater control securing it to instrument cluster, Fig. 19.
4. Remove radio control knobs, washers, bezel nuts and front support at lower edge of cluster. This will allow radio to remain in panel.
5. Remove screws at top, bottom and sides of cluster securing it to panel.
6. Tilt console forward and reach behind to disconnect speedometer cable and all other connections and lift instrument panel out of carrier after removing screws.

1974-79 Corvette

Left Hand Side 1978-79
1. Disconnect battery ground cable.
2. Remove left air distribution duct.
3. Remove lens to bezel attaching screws and the lens.
4. Remove cluster to instrument panel attaching screws.
5. Pull cluster rearward slightly, then disconnect speedometer cable and electrical connectors.
6. Remove cluster from vehicle.
7. Reverse procedure to install.

Left Hand Side 1974-77
1. Disconnect battery ground cable.

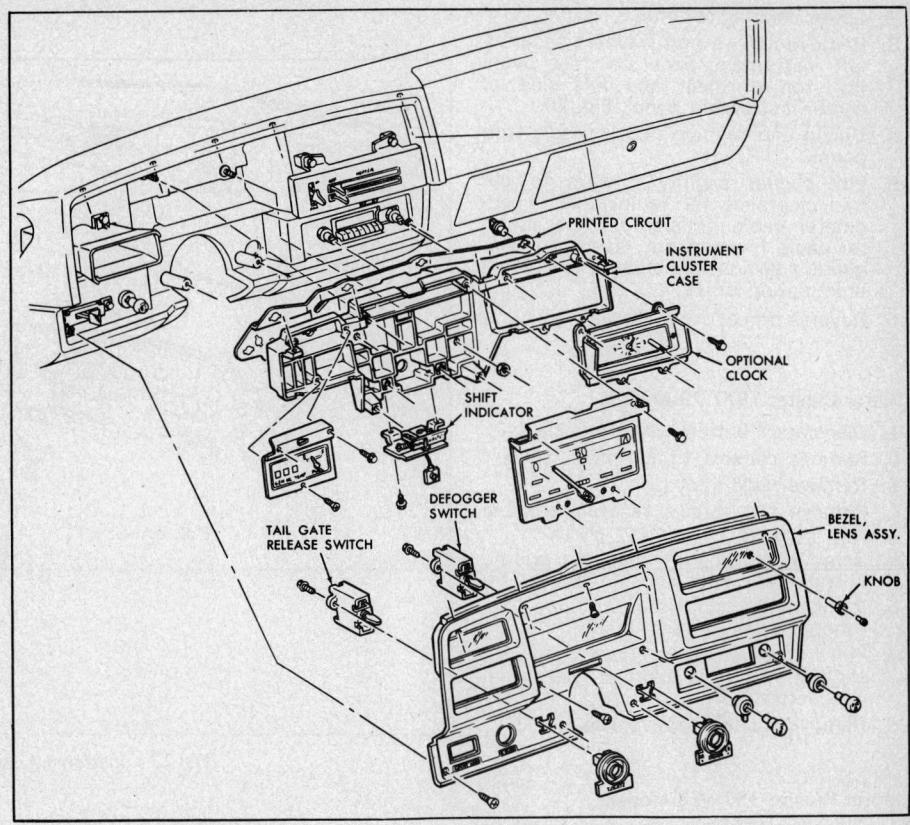

Fig. 15   Instrument cluster. 1974-77 Chevelle with standard cluster

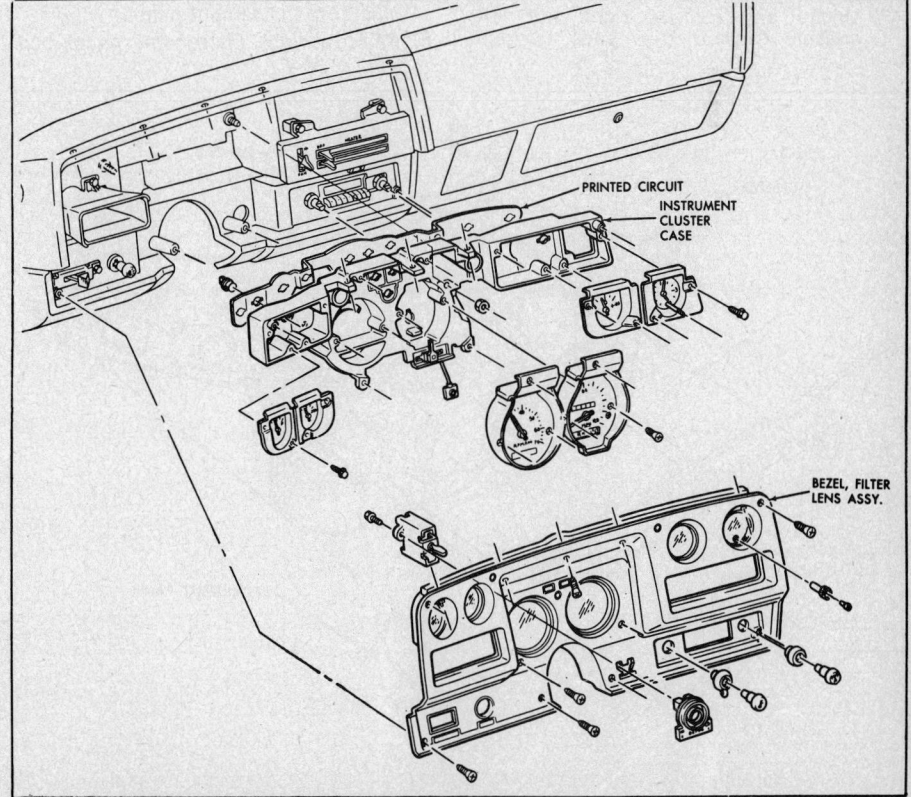

Fig. 16   Instrument cluster. 1974-77 Chevelle with optional cluster & Monte Carlo

2. Lower steering column.

3. Remove screws and washers securing left instrument panel to door opening, top of dash and left side of center instrument panel, Fig. 20.

4. Unclip and remove floor console trim panel.

5. Pull cluster slightly forward to obtain clearance for removal of speedometer cable housing nut, tachometer cable housing nut, headlamp and ignition switch connectors and panel illuminating lamps.

6. Reverse procedure to install.

Center Cluster 1977-79 Models

1. Disconnect battery ground cable.

2. Remove console tunnel side panels.

3. Remove radio knobs.

4. Remove two screws securing console trim plate to instrument cluster.

5. Remove rear window defogger switch, if equipped, from console trim plate.

6. Remove five screws from upper perimeter of instrument cluster.

7. Pull instrument cluster outward slightly and disconnect electrical connectors.

8. Remove cluster from vehicle.

Center Cluster 1974-76 Models

1. Disconnect battery ground cable at battery.

2. Remove wiper switch trim plate screws and tip plate forward for access to switch connector. Lift trim plate out from cluster, Fig. 20.

3. Unclip and remove right and left console forward trim pads to gain

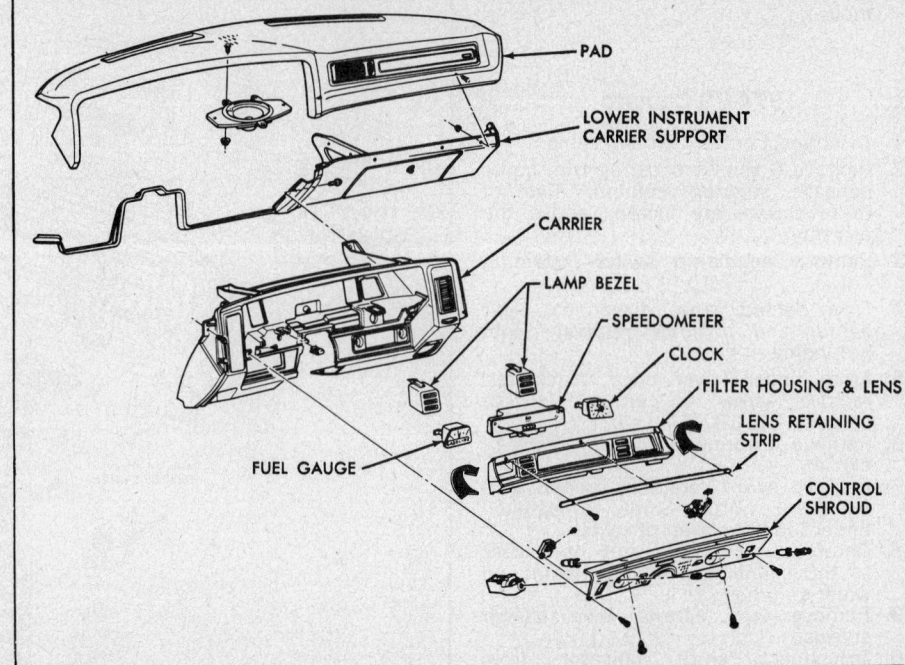

Fig. 17   Instrument cluster. 1974-76 Chevrolet

access to studs at lower edge of cluster.

4. Remove nuts from studs at lower edge of cluster, Fig. 21.

5. Remove remaining screws retaining cluster to instrument panel.

6. Remove right instrument panel pad.

7. Remove radio knobs, bezel retaining nuts and one radio support bolt (from behind cluster).

8. Slide radio back towards firewall and pull cluster forward. Reach behind cluster, disconnect oil pressure line, wiring harness and bulbs.

CAUTION: The center cluster trim plate is designed to collapse under impact, Consequently, do not try to deflect the cluster plate forward to gain access to back of gauges.

9. Lift cluster assembly up and forward to remove.

10. Reverse procedure to install cluster.

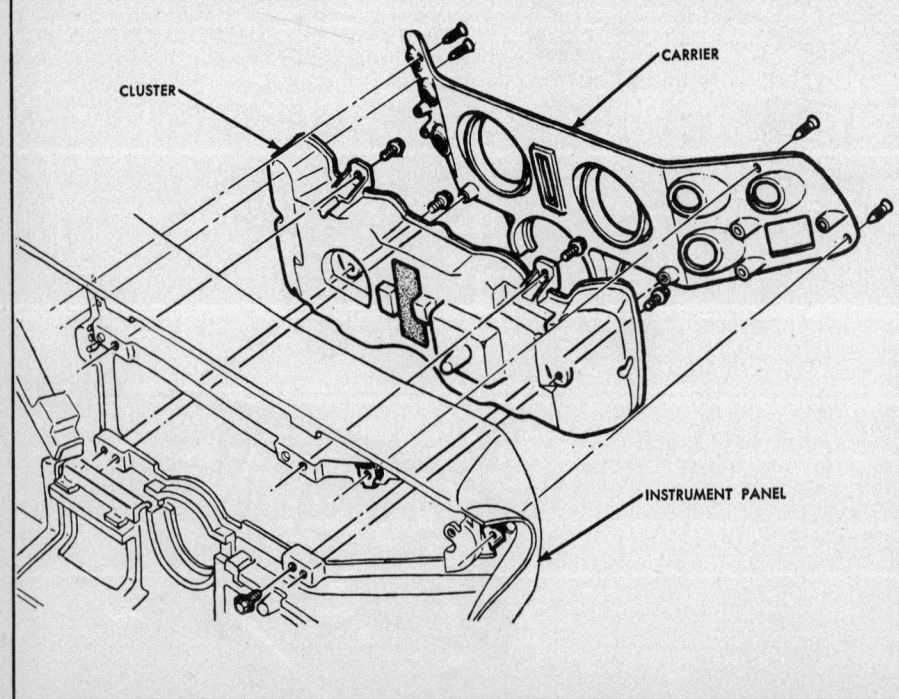

Fig. 18   Instrument cluster. 1974-79 Camaro

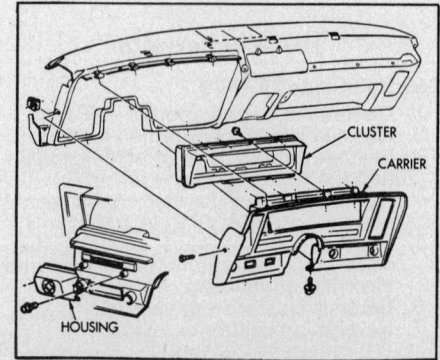

Fig. 19   Instrument cluster (Typical). 1974-79 Chevy Nova

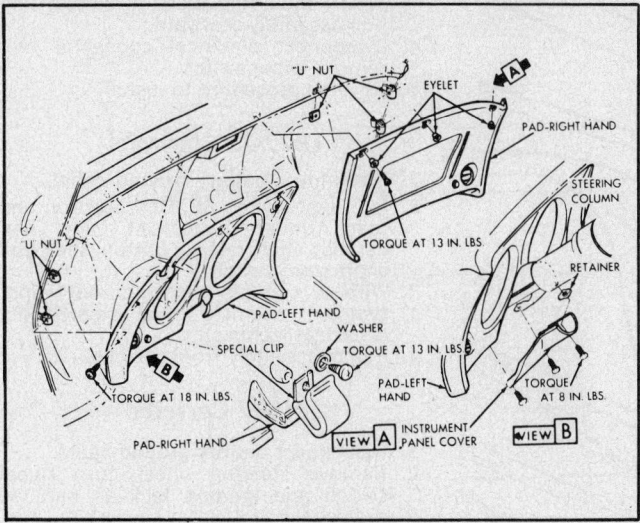

Fig. 20   Instrument panel. 1974-77 Corvette

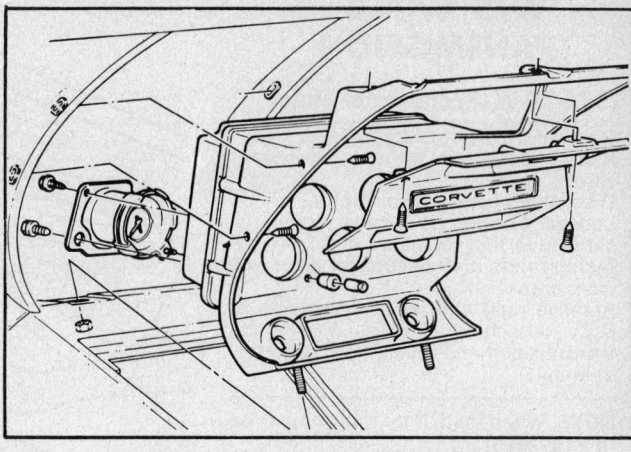

Fig. 21   Instrument cluster. 1974-76 Corvette

W/S WIPER BLADES

Two methods are used to retain wiper blades to wiper arms, Fig. 22. One method uses a press type release tab. When the release tab is depressed the blade assembly can be slid off the wiper arm pin. The other method uses a coil spring retainer. A screwdriver must be inserted on top of the spring and the spring pushed downward. The blade assembly can then be slid off the wiper arm pin. Two methods are also used to retain the blade element in the blade assembly, Fig. 22. One method uses a press type release button. When the button is depressed the two piece blade assembly can be slid off the blade element. The other method uses a spring type retainer clip in the end of the blade element. When the retainer clip is squeezed together, the blade element can be slid out of the blade assembly.

NOTE: To be sure of correct installation, the element release button, or the spring element retaining clip should be at the end of the wiper blade assembly nearest the wiper transmission.

W/S WIPER ARMS

Models with Rectangular Motor

1. Wiper motor must be in park position.
2. Use suitable tool to minimize the possibility of windshield or paint finish damage during arm removal.
3. Remove arm by prying up with tool to disengage arm from serrated transmission shaft, Fig. 23.
4. To install arm to transmission shaft rotate the required distance and direction so that the blades rest in proper position.

Models with Round Motor

1. Wiper motor must be in park position.
2. Raise hood to gain access to wiper arms.
3. *Corvette only:* Remove the rubber plug from the front of the wiper door actuator then insert a screwdriver, pushing the internal piston rearward to actuate the wiper door open.
4. *On 1974-77 Intermediate Models:* Lift arm off transmission shaft. On left arm, slide articulating arm lock clip, Fig. 24, away from transmission pivot pin and lift arm off pin. *On Full Size and 1978-79 Intermediate Models:* Lift arm and slide latch clip, Figs. 25 and 26 out from under wiper arm.
5. Release the wiper arm and lift assembly off transmission shaft.

W/S WIPER MOTOR

1974-79 Except Corvette

1. Raise hood and remove cowl screen or grille.
2. Disconnect wiring and washer hoses.
3. Reaching through cowl opening, loosen transmission drive link attaching nuts to motor crankarm.
4. Disconnect drive link from motor crankarm.
5. Remove motor attaching screws.
6. Remove motor while guiding crankarm through hole.

1974-79 Corvette

1. Make sure wiper motor is in park position.
2. Disconnect washer hoses and electrical connectors from assembly.
3. Remove the air intake screen.
4. Remove the nut which retains the crank arm to the motor.
5. Remove the ignition shield and distributor cap to gain access to the motor retaining screws or nuts.

NOTE: *Remove left bank spark plug wires from the cap and mark both cap and wires for aid in reinstallation.*

6. Remove three motor retaining screws or nuts and remove motor.

CAUTION: Wiper motor must be in the park position prior to installation on the cowl. Do not install a motor that was dropped or hung by the drive link.

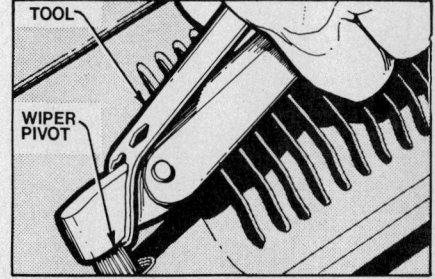

**Fig. 23   Wiper arm removal.
Models with rectangular motor**

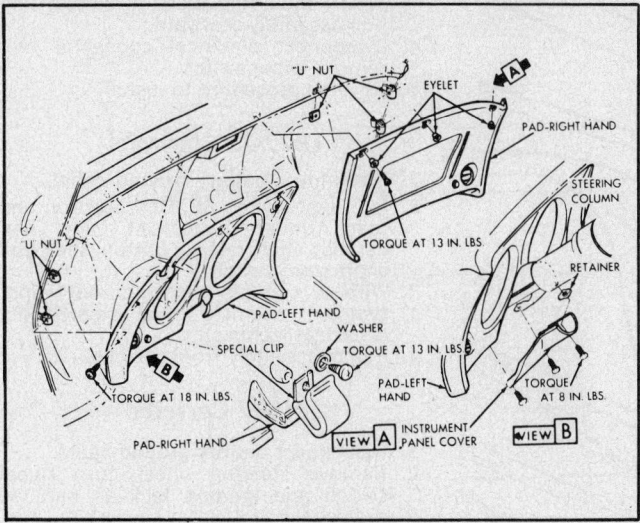

Spring Retainer Clip

Element Release Button

Insert Screw Driver Here & Push Downward

Blade Release Tab

Fig. 22   Wiper blades

W/S WIPER TRANSMISSION

1974-79 W/Rectangular Motor

1. Remove wiper arms and blades.
2. Raise hood and remove cowl vent screen or grille.
3. Disconnect wiring from motor.
4. Loosen, but do not remove, transmission drive link to motor crankarm attaching nuts and disconnect drive link from crankarm.
5. Remove right and left transmission to body attaching screws and guide transmission and linkage through cowl opening.

NOTE: When installing, motor must be in Park position.

1974-79 W/Round Motor

1. Raise hood and remove cowl vent screen.
2. On Chevelle, Monte Carlo, Camaro and 1977-79 Chevrolet models, remove right and left wiper arm and blades.
3. On 1974-76 Chevrolet models, remove arm and blade only from transmission to be removed.
4. Loosen, do not remove, attaching nuts securing drive link to motor crankarm.
5. Disconnect transmission drive link from motor crankarm.
6. On Chevelle, Monte Carlo, Camaro and 1977-79 Chevrolet models, remove right and left transmission to body screws.
7. On 1974-76 Chevrolet models, remove attaching screws securing only the transmission to be removed.
8. Remove transmission and linkage through cowl opening.

NOTE: When installing, motor must be in Park position.

1974-79 Corvette

1. Make sure motor is in PARK position.

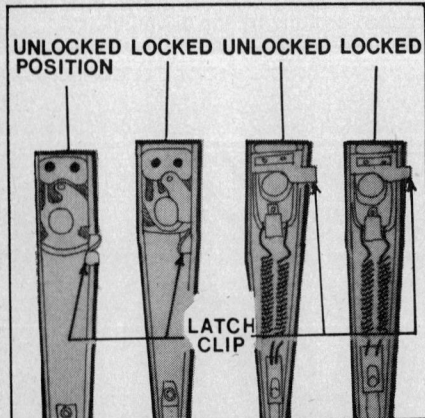

Fig. 25 Wiper arm latch clips. 1974-76 Chevrolet Full Size

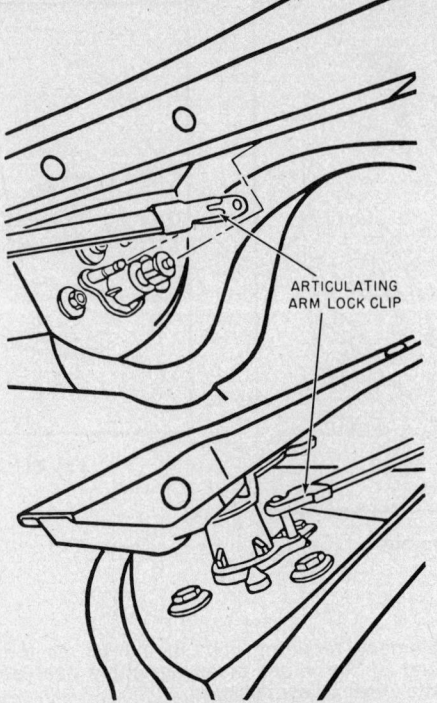

Fig. 24 Wiper articulating arm lock clip. 1974-77 Intermediate Models

2. Disconnect battery ground cable.
3. Open hood and remove chamber screen.
4. Loosen nuts retaining ball sockets to crankarm and detach drive rod from crankarm.
5. Remove transmission nuts, then lift rod assemblies from chamber.
6. Remove transmission linkage from chamber.

W/S WIPER SWITCH

1978-79 Corvette

1. Disconnect battery ground cable.
2. Remove left air distribution duct.
3. Remove instrument cluster attaching screws and pull cluster rearward.
4. Disconnect speedometer cable and all electrical connectors, then remove cluster.
5. Remove two instrument panel to left door pillar attaching screws and pull left side of instrument panel rearward for access.
6. Remove wiper switch to mounting plate screws, disconnect electrical connector and remove switch.
7. Reverse procedure to install.

1978-79 Malibu & Monte Carlo

1. Disconnect battery ground cable.
2. Remove instrument panel bezel.
3. Remove three screws securing wiper switch mounting plate to cluster and pull assembly rearward.
4. Disconnect electrical connector and remove wiper switch.
5. Reverse procedure to install.

1977-79 Chevrolet

1. Disconnect battery ground cable.
2. Pull light switch to "On" position and reach under instrument panel and depress shaft release button, then pull shaft from switch.
3. With a suitable tool, pry out wiper switch assembly and disconnect electrical connector.
4. Remove switch from vehicle.

1977 Corvette

1. Disconnect battery ground cable.
2. Remove steering wheel, turn signal switch and ignition lock as outlined previously.
3. Remove tilt release lever.
4. Remove three turn signal housing attaching screws, then remove housing while guiding the w/s wiper switch wire connector up through column shroud.
5. Turn housing over, then remove $7/16$ in. pivot bolt and lift switch from housing.

1974-79 Nova

1. Disconnect battery ground cable.
2. Disconnect wire connector from rear of wiper switch.
3. Remove three attaching screws from rear of switch.
4. Lift switch out from rear of instrument panel.

1974-76 Chevrolet

1. Disconnect battery ground cable.

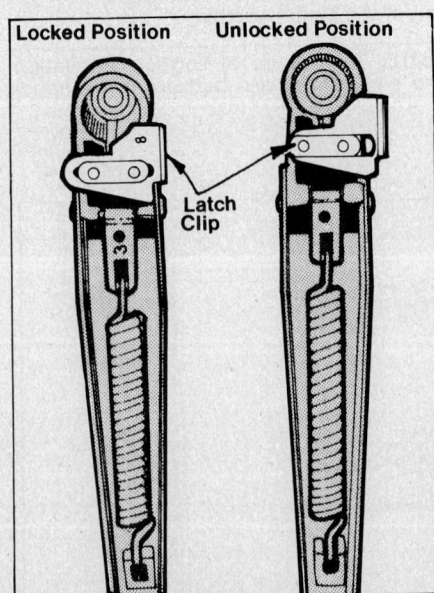

Fig. 26 Wiper arm latch clips. 1977-79 Chevrolet Full Size & 1978-79 Malibu & Monte Carlo

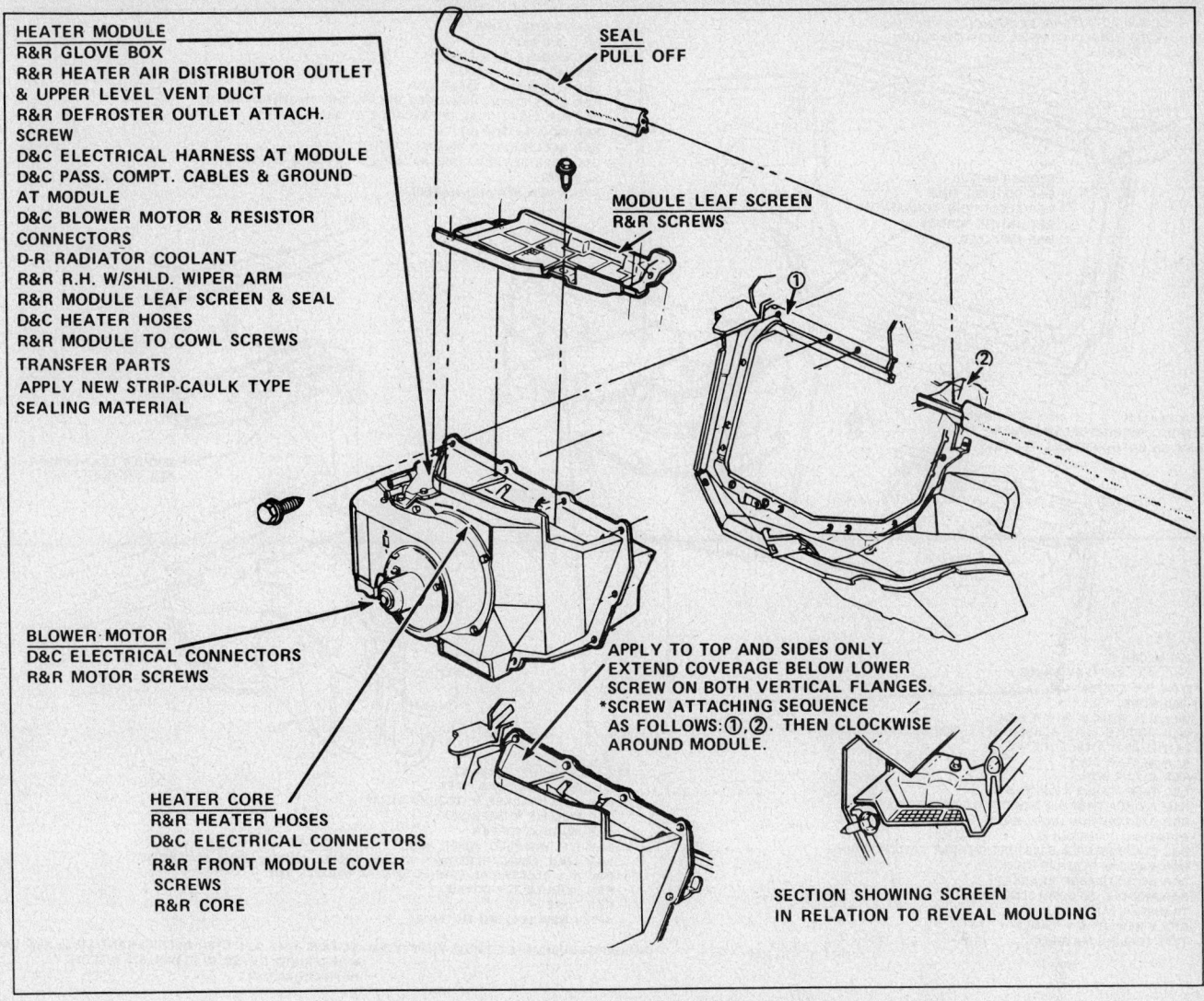

HEATER MODULE
R&R GLOVE BOX
R&R HEATER AIR DISTRIBUTOR OUTLET
& UPPER LEVEL VENT DUCT
R&R DEFROSTER OUTLET ATTACH.
SCREW
D&C ELECTRICAL HARNESS AT MODULE
D&C PASS. COMPT. CABLES & GROUND
AT MODULE
D&C BLOWER MOTOR & RESISTOR
CONNECTORS
D-R RADIATOR COOLANT
R&R R.H. W/SHLD. WIPER ARM
R&R MODULE LEAF SCREEN & SEAL
D&C HEATER HOSES
R&R MODULE TO COWL SCREWS
TRANSFER PARTS
APPLY NEW STRIP-CAULK TYPE
SEALING MATERIAL

SEAL
PULL OFF

MODULE LEAF SCREEN
R&R SCREWS

BLOWER MOTOR
D&C ELECTRICAL CONNECTORS
R&R MOTOR SCREWS

HEATER CORE
R&R HEATER HOSES
D&C ELECTRICAL CONNECTORS
R&R FRONT MODULE COVER
SCREWS
R&R CORE

APPLY TO TOP AND SIDES ONLY
EXTEND COVERAGE BELOW LOWER
SCREW ON BOTH VERTICAL FLANGES.
*SCREW ATTACHING SEQUENCE
AS FOLLOWS: ①,②. THEN CLOCKWISE
AROUND MODULE.

SECTION SHOWING SCREEN
IN RELATION TO REVEAL MOULDING

Fig. 27   Blower motor & heater core. 1978-79 Malibu & Monte Carlo Less A/C

2. Remove screws securing control shroud on instrument panel. (One screw is hidden above headlight switch shaft and one is hidden above cigarette lighter knob.)
3. Lift off shroud and remove remaining screws.
4. Unplug wiper switch and remove.

1974-77 Chevelle & Monte Carlo

1. Disconnect battery ground cable.
2. Remove instrument cluster.
3. Pull electric connector off rear of wiper switch.
4. Remove screws from front of switch and lift switch out front of panel.

1974-79 Camero

1. Disconnect battery ground cable.
2. Remove trim plate and A/C outlet

from below steering column if so equipped.
3. Remove light switch.
4. Remove 6 screws securing instrument carrier. Two of these are behind the cluster on either side of steering column.

NOTE: Cigar lighter grounding ring may have to be removed with lighter housing to gain access to left side of carrier.

5. Disconnect wiper switch wiring.
6. Tilting carrier forward, reach behind and remove 3 switch retaining screws and lift out switch.

1974-76 Corvette

1. Disconnect battery ground cable.
2. Remove screws from upper part of center console marked "Corvette".
3. Disconnect and remove switch and plate.

4. Carefully pry knob from switch then remove switch from plate.
5. To install, insert a small rod in the switch arm before pushing the knob on the arm outside of the trim plate then reverse the above procedure.

RADIO, REPLACE

NOTE: When installing radio, be sure to adjust antenna trimmer for peak performance.

NOTE: When installing, be sure to connect speaker before applying power to radio.

1978-79 Malibu & Monte Carlo

1. Disconnect battery ground cable.
2. Remove control knobs from control shafts.
3. Remove trim plate attaching screws and trim plate.
4. Disconnect antenna lead and wire connector from radio.

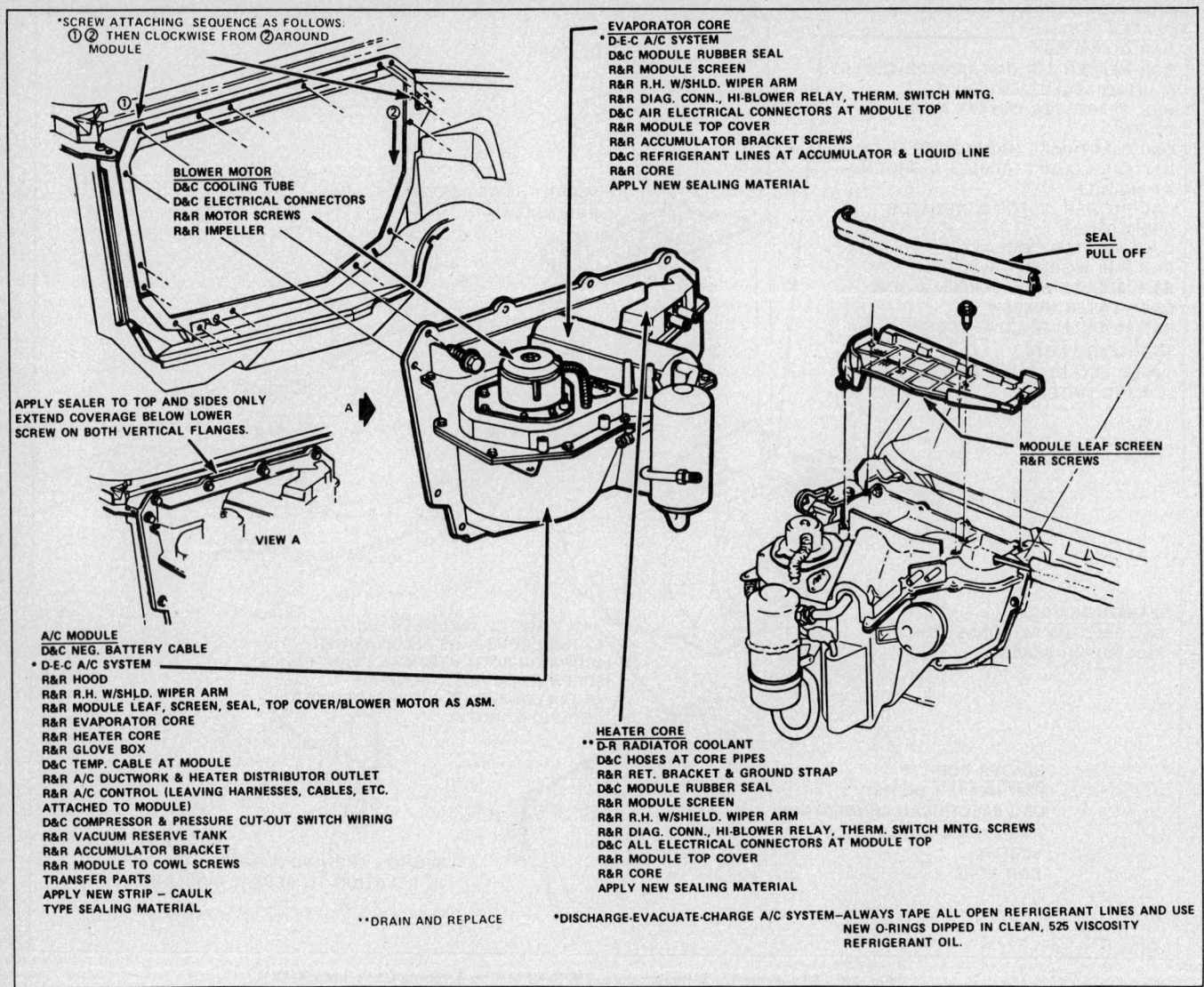

Fig. 28   Blower motor & heater core. 1978-79 Malibu & Monte Carlo with A/C

Within the figure:

*SCREW ATTACHING SEQUENCE AS FOLLOWS:
①② THEN CLOCKWISE FROM ②AROUND MODULE

BLOWER MOTOR
D&C COOLING TUBE
D&C ELECTRICAL CONNECTORS
R&R MOTOR SCREWS
R&R IMPELLER

EVAPORATOR CORE
*D-E-C A/C SYSTEM
D&C MODULE RUBBER SEAL
R&R MODULE SCREEN
R&R R.H. W/SHLD. WIPER ARM
R&R DIAG. CONN., HI-BLOWER RELAY, THERM. SWITCH MNTG.
D&C AIR ELECTRICAL CONNECTORS AT MODULE TOP
R&R MODULE TOP COVER
R&R ACCUMULATOR BRACKET SCREWS
D&C REFRIGERANT LINES AT ACCUMULATOR & LIQUID LINE
R&R CORE
APPLY NEW SEALING MATERIAL

SEAL
PULL OFF

APPLY SEALER TO TOP AND SIDES ONLY
EXTEND COVERAGE BELOW LOWER
SCREW ON BOTH VERTICAL FLANGES.

VIEW A

MODULE LEAF SCREEN
R&R SCREWS

A/C MODULE
D&C NEG. BATTERY CABLE
*D-E-C A/C SYSTEM
R&R HOOD
R&R R.H. W/SHLD. WIPER ARM
R&R MODULE LEAF, SCREEN, SEAL, TOP COVER/BLOWER MOTOR AS ASM.
R&R EVAPORATOR CORE
R&R HEATER CORE
R&R GLOVE BOX
D&C TEMP. CABLE AT MODULE
R&R A/C DUCTWORK & HEATER DISTRIBUTOR OUTLET
R&R A/C CONTROL (LEAVING HARNESSES, CABLES, ETC. ATTACHED TO MODULE)
D&C COMPRESSOR & PRESSURE CUT-OUT SWITCH WIRING
R&R VACUUM RESERVE TANK
R&R ACCUMULATOR BRACKET
R&R MODULE TO COWL SCREWS
TRANSFER PARTS
APPLY NEW STRIP – CAULK
TYPE SEALING MATERIAL

HEATER CORE
**D-R RADIATOR COOLANT
D&C HOSES AT CORE PIPES
R&R RET. BRACKET & GROUND STRAP
D&C MODULE RUBBER SEAL
R&R MODULE SCREEN
R&R R.H. W/SHIELD. WIPER ARM
R&R DIAG. CONN., HI-BLOWER RELAY, THERM. SWITCH MNTG. SCREWS
D&C ALL ELECTRICAL CONNECTORS AT MODULE TOP
R&R MODULE TOP COVER
R&R CORE
APPLY NEW SEALING MATERIAL

**DRAIN AND REPLACE

*DISCHARGE-EVACUATE-CHARGE A/C SYSTEM—ALWAYS TAPE ALL OPEN REFRIGERANT LINES AND USE NEW O-RINGS DIPPED IN CLEAN, 525 VISCOSITY REFRIGERANT OIL.

---

5. Remove stud nut at right side of bracket attachment.
6. Remove control shaft nuts and washers.
7. Remove instrument panel bracket screws and bracket.
8. Remove radio through opening in instrument panel.

1977-79 Chevrolet

1. Disconnect battery ground cable.
2. Remove control knobs from control shafts.
3. Remove three radio trim plate attaching screws.
4. Remove two screws and bottom nut attaching radio bracket to instrument panel.
5. Disconnect antenna lead and wire connector from radio.
6. Remove radio with mounting bracket attached from instrument panel.
7. Remove bracket from radio.

1977-79 Corvette

1. Disconnect battery ground cable.
2. Remove control knobs from control shafts.
3. Remove instrument cluster as described under Instrument Cluster, Replace.
4. Remove screw attaching radio mounting bracket to reinforcement on floor pan.
5. Pull radio outward and disconnect antenna lead and wire connector from rear of radio.
6. Remove mounting bracket from radio.

1974-76 Chevrolet

1. Disconnect battery ground cable.
2. On A/C equipped vehicles, it may be necessary to remove the lap cooler duct.
3. Turn radio knobs until slot in base in knob is visible. Depress the metal retainer and remove knobs and bezels.

4. Remove control shaft nuts and washers.
5. Remove right hand bracket to instrument panel bolt and the stud nut on left side of radio.
6. Push radio forward and then lower it far enough to gain access to electrical connections.
7. Disconnect antenna, speaker and power feed and remove radio.

1974-77 Chevelle & Monte Carlo

1. Disconnect battery ground cable.
2. On A/C vehicles, remove left lap cooler duct.
3. Pull off radio knobs and bezels.
4. Remove control shaft nuts and washers.
5. Disconnect antenna, speaker and power wires.
6. Remove radio to support bracket stud nut.
7. Push radio forward until shafts clear

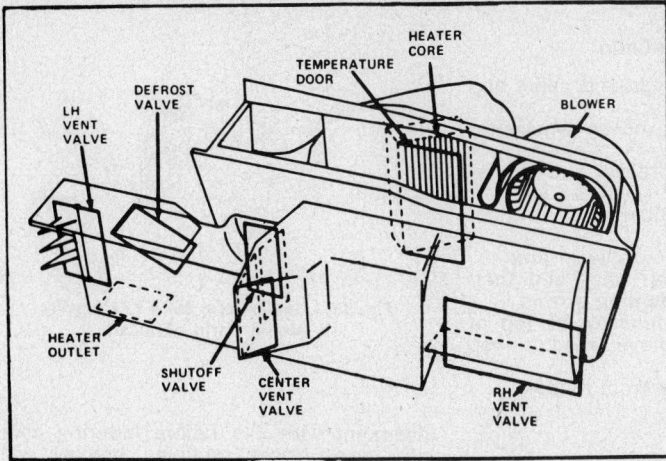

Fig. 29 Blower motor & heater core. 1977-79 Chevrolet less A/C

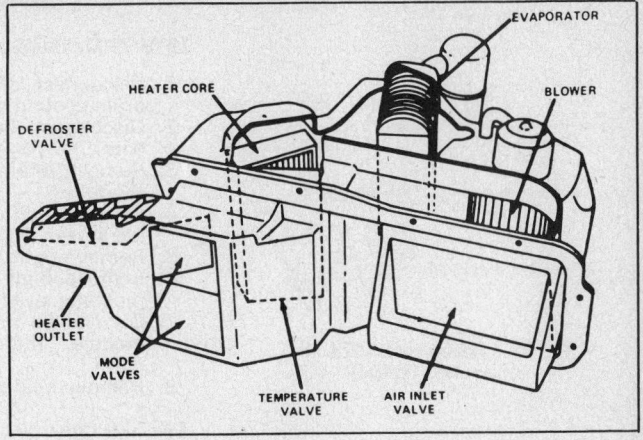

Fig. 30 Blower motor & heater core. 1977-79 Chevrolet with A/C

instrument panel and then lower from car.

1974-79 Camaro & Nova

1. Disconnect battery ground cable.
2. Pull off radio control knobs and bezels.
3. Remove control shaft nuts and washers.
4. Remove screws or nuts from radio brackets.
5. Push radio forward until shafts clear instrument panel and lower unit enough to remove electrical connections.
6. Disconnect antenna, speaker and power leads and remove radio.

1974-76 Corvette

1. Disconnect battery ground cable.
2. Remove right instrument panel pad.
3. Disconnect speaker connectors.
4. Remove wiper switch trim plate screws and tip plate for access to switch connector. Remove switch connector and trim plate from cluster.
5. Unclip and remove right and left console forward trim pads. Remove forward most screw on right and left side of console.
6. Insert a flexible drive socket between console and metal horseshoe brace and remove nuts from two studs on lower edge of console cluster.
7. Remove remaining screws retaining cluster to instrument panel.
8. From rear of console, disconnect electric connector, brace and antenna.
9. Remove knobs and bezel retaining nuts.
10. Pull top of console rearward and separate radio from console and remove it from right side opening.

CAUTION: The center instrument cluster trim plate is designed to collapse under impact. DO NOT try to deflect the cluster plate forward to gain more access to remove radio. Also use care so as not to damage the plastic oil pressure line when pulling console forward.

BLOWER MOTOR REMOVAL

1977-79 Chevrolet & 1974-79 Chevelle & Monte Carlo

1. Disconnect battery ground cable.
2. Disconnect blower motor lead wire. On models with A/C, disconnect cooling tube.
3. Remove blower motor to case attaching screws, then remove blower motor, Figs. 27 through 31.

1974-79 Corvette

1. Disconnect battery ground cable.
2. Remove radiator supply tank, if so equipped.
3. Disconnect blower motor wires.
4. Remove blower motor to case mounting screws and remove motor, Fig. 31.

1974-76 Chevrolet, 1974-79 Camaro & Nova

1. Disconnect battery ground cable.
2. Disconnect blower lead and remove all hoses and wires connected to fender skirt then raise vehicle.

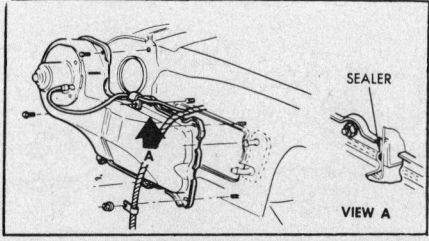

Fig. 31 Blower motor (Typical). Except 1977-79 Chevrolet & 1978-79 Chevelle & Monte Carlo

3. On all except Nova, remove all fender skirt retaining bolts except those retaining skirt to radiator support. On Nova, remove the eight rearmost fender skirt to fender retaining screws.
4. Pull out and down on fender skirt and wedge a 2x4 inch block of wood between skirt and fender to allow room for blower motor removal.
5. Remove blower to case retaining screws and remove blower assembly. Gently pry flange, since sealer will act as an adhesive, Fig. 31.

NOTE: On Nova, remove blower retaining nut and separate wheel and motor before removing through fender and skirt.

6. Reverse procedure to install.

HEATER CORE REMOVAL

L/Air Cond.

1978-79 Malibu & Monte Carlo

1. Disconnect battery ground cable and drain cooling system.
2. Disconnect heater hoses from heater core. Plug core outlets to prevent coolant spillage.
3. Disconnect wire connectors, then remove front module cover attaching screws and cover.
4. Remove heater core from module, Fig. 27.

1977-79 Chevrolet

1. Disconnect battery ground cable and drain cooling system.
2. Disconnect heater hoses from heater core. Plug core outlets to prevent coolant spillage.
3. Remove attaching screws from around perimeter of heater core cover on engine side of dash panel.
4. Pull heater core cover from dash panel mounting.
5. Remove heater core from module assembly, Fig. 29.

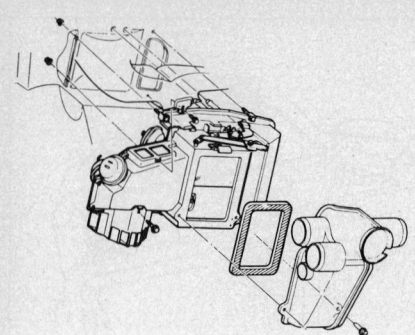

Fig. 32 Heater core. 1974-76 Chevrolet (Typical)

1974-79 Exc. 1977-79 Chevrolet & 1978-79 Malibu & Monte Carlo

1. Disconnect battery ground cable.
2. Drain radiator, disconnect heater hoses at core and plug openings to prevent spillage of water.
3. Remove nuts from air distributor duct studs on engine side of firewall, Figs. 32 through 36.
4. On 1974-76 Chevrolet and 1974-77 Chevelle and Monte Carlo, remove distributor duct retaining screw.
5. On Nova, remove glove box and door and drill out lower right hand distributor stud with a 1/4" drill.
6. On Camaro, remove glove box, radio, and defroster duct to distributor duct screw.
7. On Corvette, remove right instrument panel pad, right hand dash braces, center dash console duct and floor outlet duct, radio and center dash console.
8. On all models, pull distributor duct from firewall being careful not to bend cable.
9. On Camaro, disconnect cable and resistor wires and remove distributor and core.
10. On all other models, remove core assembly from duct.

W/Air Cond.

1978-79 Malibu & Monte Carlo

1. Disconnect battery ground cable and drain cooling system.
2. Disconnect heater hoses at heater core.
3. Remove retaining bracket and ground strap.
4. Remove module rubber seal and module screen, Fig. 28.
5. Remove right hand w/s wiper arm.
6. Remove high blower relay and thermostatic switch mounting screws.
7. Disconnect wire connector at top of module, then remove module top cover.
8. Remove heater core from module.

1977-79 Chevrolet

1. Disconnect battery ground cable and drain cooling system.
2. Disconnect heater hoses at heater core. Cap core outlets to prevent coolant spillage.
3. Remove diagnosis connector to upper case attaching screws.
4. Disconnect wire connectors from blower motor, resistor, blower relay and thermostatic switch.
5. Remove wiring harness retainer from blower case shroud.
6. Remove module screen to cowl attaching screws and remove screen.
7. Remove upper case to lower case attaching screws.

NOTE: Two screws are located inside air intake area at case separation point.

8. Disconnect wire connector from thermostatic switch, then remove screws attaching switch to evaporator case. Carefully remove insulation and loosen two clamps enough to pull formed end of switch capillary tube from under clamps attaching tube to evaporator inlet pipe for installation.
9. Remove evaporator inlet pipe support bracket to case attaching screws and remove bracket.
10. Remove heater-evaporator core case cover, using care not to damage sealer.
11. Remove heater core to case attaching screws at top of heater core, then remove heater core, Fig. 30.

NOTE: The heater core is held in position at bottom by a spring clip. Pull up firmly on heater core to disengage from clip. When installing, position core base in

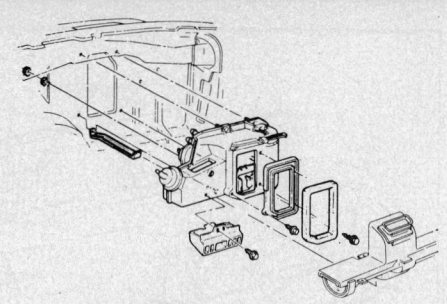

Fig. 33 Heater core. 1974-77 Chevelle & Monte Carlo (Typical)

alignment with clip before lowering core into case. Upper retaining bracket will line up with hole at top of core when core is properly seated.

Chevrolet 1974-76 Comfortron & 1974-76 4 Seasons

1. Disconnect battery ground cable and compressor clutch connector.
2. Drain radiator and disconnect heater hoses from core. Plug hoses and core openings.
3. On all 1974-76 systems, disconnect vacuum hose from vacuum check valve and push hose grommet through firewall.
4. Remove accessible screws and stud nuts from heater and air selector duct from dash side of firewall, Fig. 32.
5. On all 1974-76 systems, remove two screws and three stud nuts, accessible from engine side of dash.
6. On all 1974-76 systems, the last screw is accessible by removing the screws securing the fender skirt and holding skirt away from rear of wheelwell.
7. Remove lap cooler assembly, glove box door and glove box.
8. Remove floor outlet duct and instrument panel pad. On 1974-76 Comfortron, disconnect aspirator and in-car sensor connector.
9. Remove distributor duct hoses and

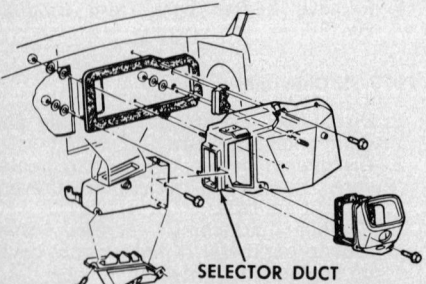

Fig. 34 Heater core. 1974-79 Chevy Nova (Typical)

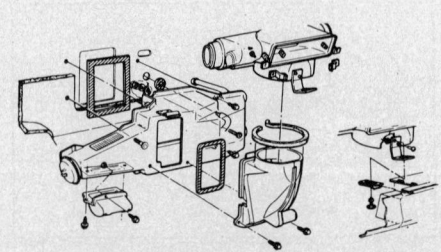

Fig. 35 Heater core. 1974-79 Camaro (Typical)

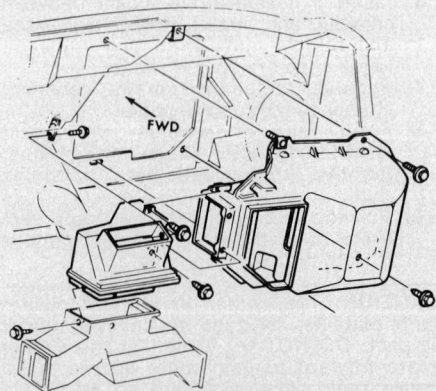

Fig. 36 Heater core. 1974-78 Corvette (Typical)

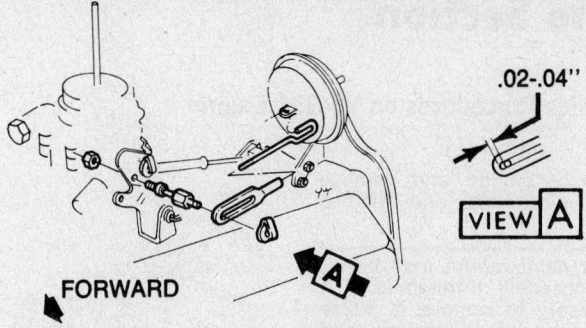

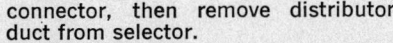

FORWARD

Fig. 37 Servo unit rod adjustment

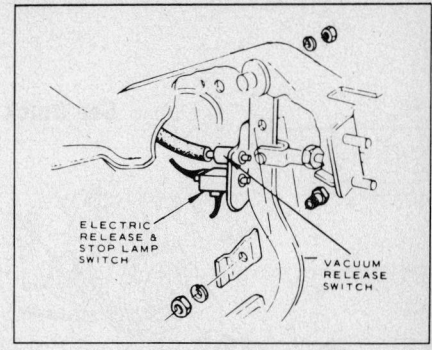

ELECTRIC RELEASE & STOP LAMP SWITCH

VACUUM RELEASE SWITCH

Fig. 38 Release switches and brackets (Typical). 1974-78

connector, then remove distributor duct from selector.

10. Remove defroster duct screw and move duct to gain access to selector and heater core. On 1974-76 Comfortron, disconnect in-line vacuum connector and line from outside air diaphragm, then disconnect electrical and vacuum connections from programmer.

11. Disconnect cables and vacuum lines from selector, then remove heater core and selector. Separate heater core from selector by removing clamp screws.

Chevelle & Monte Carlo, 1974-77

1. Disconnect battery ground cable and drain radiator.

2. Disconnect heater hoses from core and plug hoses and core openings.

3. Remove distributor case stud nuts projecting through firewall, Fig. 33. On 1974-77, remove resistor assembly and the last stud nut through its opening.

4. Remove glove box door and glove box.

5. On all models, remove right hand lap cooler and kick pad cover.

6. On all models, disconnect center duct hoses and remove center duct to selector duct screws, then remove center duct.

7. Remove floor distributor duct.

8. On 1974-77, remove lower right hand distributor duct to dash panel screw.

9. On all models, remove air selector retaining screws, then lower selector assembly. Disconnect all wiring, vacuum lines and cables.

10. On all models, remove core and housing from selector assembly, then core from housing.

Nova, 1974-79

1. Disconnect battery ground cable and drain radiator.

2. Disconnect heater hoses and plug hoses and core openings to prevent coolant spillage.

3. Remove accessible stud nut from air selector duct, Fig. 34.

4. Remove right hand fender skirt to fender and skirt reinforcing screws. Lower skirt to wheel and remove remaining stud nut.

5. Remove glove box door, glove box and right hand kick pad recirculating air valve.

6. Remove center and floor ducts. Remove screws securing selector duct halves together, then separate.

7. Remove selector duct right half to firewall screws and remove duct.

8. Disconnect all wiring and cables. Scribe location of temperature camming plate on selector duct and remove plate and core.

Camaro, 1974-79

1. Disconnect battery ground cable. Drain radiator and disconnect heater hoses from core. Plug openings to prevent spillage of coolant.

2. Remove nuts from engine side distributor duct, Fig. 36.

3. Remove right hand dash pad and center instrument cluster. Remove dash braces.

4. Disconnect right dash outlet duct from center duct. Remove screws attaching center duct to selector duct and remove center duct.

5. Remove screws attaching selector duct to firewall and pull selector rearward and to the right. Disconnect cables and wiring.

6. Remove selector duct from car. Remove temperature door camming plate from duct and remove core and housing.

Corvette, 1974-79

1. Disconnect battery ground cable.

2. Drain radiator and disconnect heater hoses from core. Plug openings to prevent spillage of coolant.

3. Remove nuts from distributor studs on engine side of firewall, Fig. 35.

4. Remove glove box and radio.

5. Remove defroster duct to distributor duct screw. With radio removed, the defroster duct can be pulled rearward to gain clearance for distributor duct removal.

6. Carefully pull distributor from firewall and disconnect wiring and cables. Remove duct and core from vehicle.

SPEED CONTROLS
1974-79 Cruise Master

Servo Unit Adjustment

Adjust the bead chain cable or rod so that it is as tight as possible without holding the throttle open when the carburetor is set as its lowest idle throttle position. The cable is adjusted by turning the hex portion of servo. The bead chain or cable is adjusted so there is 1/16 inch of lost motion in servo cable. The rod is adjusted by turning link onto rod. With rod hooked through tab, on power unit, turn link onto rod until dimension in Fig. 37 is obtained, then install link and retainer. This adjustment should be made with ignition off and fast idle cam in off position with throttle completely closed.

When connecting the bead chain or cable (engine stopped) manually set the fast idle cam at its lowest step and connect the chain so that it does not hold the idle screw off the cam. If the chain needs to be cut, cut it three beads beyond the bead that pulls the linkage.

Regulator Unit Adjustment

To remove any difference between engagement and cruising speed, one adjustment is possible. However, no adjustment should be made until the following items have been checked or serviced.

1. Bead chain or cable properly adjusted.

2. All hoses in good condition, properly attached, not leaking, pinched or cracked.

3. Regulator air filter cleaned and properly oiled.

4. Electric and vacuum switches properly adjusted.

Engagement - Cruising Speed Zeroing

If the cruising speed is lower than the engagement speed, loosen the orifice tube locknut and turn the tube outward; if higher turn the tube inward. Each 1/4 turn will alter the engagement-cruising speed difference one mph. Tighten locknut after adjustment and check the system operation at 50 mph.

Brake Release Switch

The electric brake switch is actuated when the brake pedal is depressed .38-.64 inch, Fig. 38. The vacuum release switch is actuated when brake pedal is moved 5/16 inch on all units.

Engine Section

See Buick Chapter for Service Procedures on V6-231 Engine

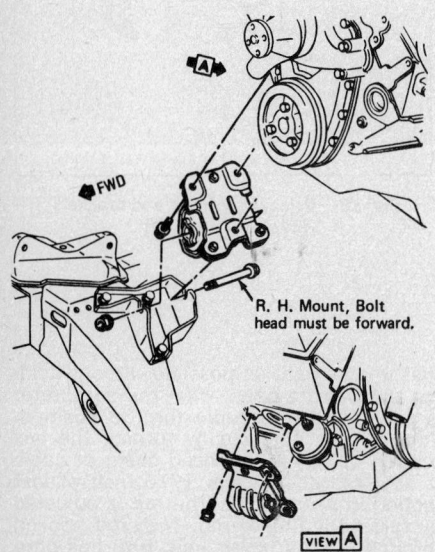

Fig. 1 Engine mounts (Typical). V6-200

NOTE
Throughout the engine section there will be references to Small V8s and Mark IV V8s. These can be distinguished as follows:

Small V8s: V8-262, 267, 305, 307, 350 and V8-400.

Mark IV V8s: V8-454.

ENGINE MOUNTS, REPLACE

1978-79 V6-200

1. Remove mount retaining bolt from below frame mounting bracket, Fig. 1.

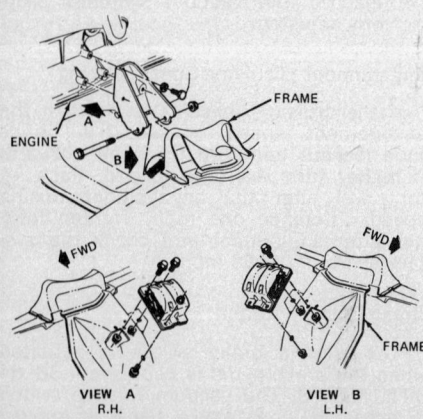

Fig. 3 Engine mounts (Typical). 1974-76 Camaro & 1977-79 Nova 6-250

2. Raise front of engine and remove mount to engine bolts and remove mount.

NOTE: Right hand mount may be removed by loosening through bolt. It is not necessary to remove it. Raise engine only enough to provide sufficient clearance for mount removal. Check for interference between rear of engine and cowl panel.

1974-79 6-250

1. Remove nut, washer and engine mount through-bolt.
2. Raise engine to release weight from mount.
3. Remove bracket-to-mount bolt, then remove mount.
4. Install new mount on bracket.
5. Lower engine, install through-bolt and tighten all mount bolts, Figs. 2, 3 and 4.

1974-79 All V-8

NOTE: On some V8 engines, the mount on the right side of the engine cannot be removed without first removing the fuel pump.

1. Remove nut, washer and engine mount through-bolt.
2. Raise engine to release weight from mount.
3. Remove mount from engine.
4. Install new mount on engine.
5. Lower engine, install through-bolt and tighten all mount bolts, Figs. 5 and 6.

ENGINE, REPLACE

NOTE: V8 engines are equipped with two strap type lifting rings, one at the right front the other at the left rear of the engine. Use of these rings eliminates the need to remove the rocker arm covers to install lifting adapters.

1977-79 Exc. Corvette

1. Disconnect battery ground cable.
2. Scribe hood hinge locations and remove hood.
3. Remove air cleaner.
4. Drain cooling system.
5. Disconnect radiator and heater hoses, then remove radiator and shroud.
6. Disconnect wiring at following locations: starter solenoid, alternator, temperature switch, oil pressure switch and ignition coil.
7. Disconnect accelerator linkage, fuel line from tank to pump, hoses from vapor storage canister and vacuum line to power brake unit at manifold.

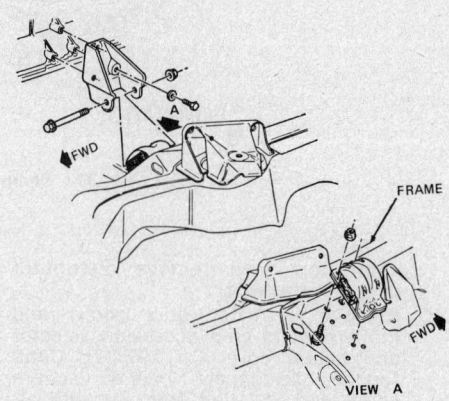

Fig. 2 Engine mounts (Typical). Chevelle, Chevrolet Malibu & Monte Carlo 6-250

8. Remove power steering pump and position aside with hoses attached.
9. Raise and support vehicle.
10. Drain oil pan.
11. Disconnect exhaust pipe at manifold and catalytic converter bracket from rear transmission mount.
12. Remove starter.
13. Remove flywheel splash shield or converter housing cover.
14. On models equipped with automatic transmission, remove converter to flywheel attaching bolts.
15. On all models, remove engine mount through bolts.
16. Remove bell housing bolts.
17. Lower vehicle.
18. Support transmission with a suitable jack.
19. Attach suitable engine lifting equipment to engine and raise engine slightly.
20. Remove engine mount to engine brackets.
21. Remove engine assembly from vehicle.
22. Reverse procedure to install.

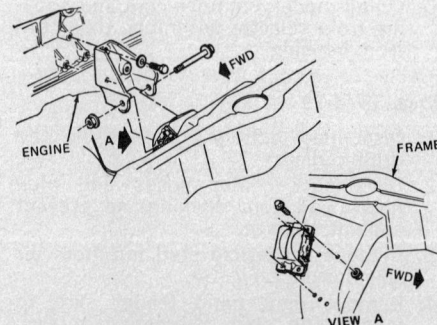

Fig. 4 Engine mounts (Typical). 1974-76 Nova & 1977-79 Camaro 6-250

automatic transmission, remove propeller shaft.

12. On all vehicles except Corvette with automatic transmission, disconnect shift linkage, speedometer cable, transmission oil cooler lines and TCS switch wiring from transmission.
13. On vehicles equipped with manual transmission, disconnect clutch linkage at cross-shaft, then remove cross-shaft engine or frame bracket.
14. Lower vehicle.
15. Attach suitable engine lifting equipment to engine and raise engine slightly.
16. On all vehicles except Corvette equipped with an automatic transmission, remove rear mount to crossmember bolts.
17. On Corvette equipped with automatic transmission, remove converter to flywheel attaching bolts.
18. On all models, remove engine or engine-transmission assembly from vehicle.
19. Reverse procedure to install.

CYLINDER HEAD

1977-79 V6-200 & All V-8

1. Drain cooling system and engine block.
2. Remove intake and exhaust manifolds.
3. Remove alternator lower mounting bolt and position alternator aside.
4. If equipped with A/C, remove compressor and forward mounting bracket and position aside.
5. Remove rocker arm cover, rocker arms and push rods.

NOTE: Keep rocker arm, rocker arm balls and push rods in order so they can be installed in the same position.

6. Remove cylinder head bolts and cylinder head.
7. Reverse procedure to install. Tighten cylinder head and intake manifold bolts in sequence shown in Figs. 7 and 8 and 10 through 13.

1974-77 6-250

Less Integral Intake Manifold

1. Drain cooling system and remove air cleaner.
2. Disconnect choke rod, accelerator pedal rod at bellcrank on manifold, and fuel and vacuum lines at carburetor.
3. Disconnect exhaust pipe at manifold flange, then unfasten and remove manifolds and carburetor as an assembly.
4. Remove fuel and vacuum line retaining clip from water outlet and disconnect wire harness from temperature sending unit and coil, leaving harness clear of clips on rocker arm cover.
5. Disconnect radiator hose at water outlet housing and battery ground strap at cylinder head.
6. Remove spark plugs and coil.
7. Remove rocker arm cover. Back off rocker arm nuts, pivot rocker arms to clear push rods and lift out push rods.

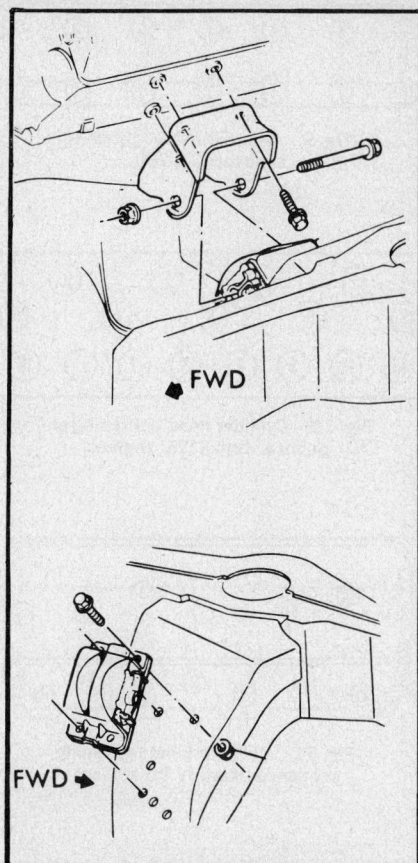

Fig. 5 Engine mounts. 1974-79 V8 Except Corvette (typical)

1974-76 All & 1977-79 Corvette

NOTE: On all vehicles except Corvette equipped with an automatic transmission, the engine and transmission is removed as an assembly. On Corvette equipped with an automatic transmission, the engine is removed separately without the transmission. Support transmission and torque converter properly to prevent damage.

1. Disconnect battery ground cable.
2. Scribe hood hinge locations and remove hood.
3. Remove air cleaner and drain cooling system.
4. On all models except Corvette with automatic transmission, disconnect radiator hoses and transmission oil cooler lines from radiator, then remove radiator and shroud.
5. On all models, remove fan and pulley.
6. Disconnect wiring at following locations: vacuum advance solenoid, idle stop solenoid, starter solenoid, alternator, temperature switch, oil pressure switch, and ignition coil.
7. Disconnect accelerator linkage, exhaust pipes from manifold, fuel line from tank to pump and vacuum line to power brake unit at manifold.
8. Raise and support vehicle.
9. Raise and support vehicle.
10. Drain oil pan.
11. On all vehicle except Corvette with

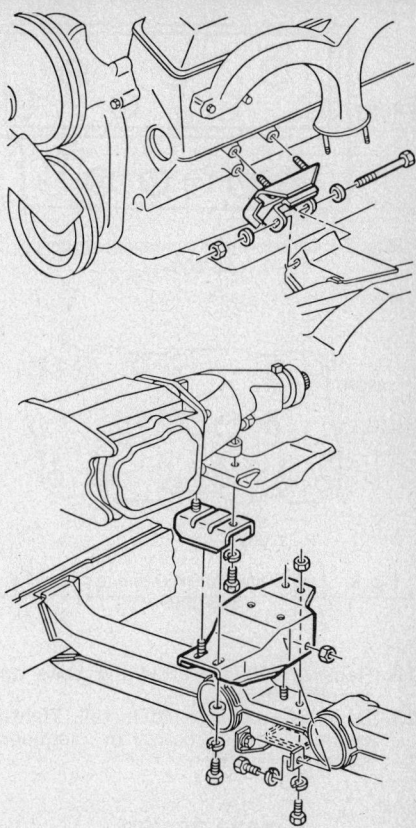

Fig. 6 Engine mounts. 1974-79 Corvette (typical)

8. Unfasten and remove cylinder head.
9. Reverse procedure to install and tighten head bolts in the sequence shown in Fig. 6.

With Integral Intake Manifold

1. Disconnect battery ground cable and remove air cleaner.
2. Remove power steering pump and A.I.R. pump brackets, if equipped.
3. Raise vehicle and disconnect exhaust pipe at manifold and converter bracket at transmission mount. If equipped with manifold converter, disconnect exhaust pipe from converter and remove converter.
4. Lower vehicle and remove rear heat shield and accelerator cable bracket.
5. Remove exhaust manifold attaching bolts and exhaust manifold.
7. Remove rocker arm covers, rocker arms and push rods.

NOTE: Keep rocker arms, rocker arm balls and push rod in order so they can be installed in the same position.

8. Drain cooling system and engine block.
9. Remove fuel and vacuum line from retaining clip at water outlet, then disconnect wires at temperature sending unit.
10. Disconnect air injection hose at check valve, if equipped.
11. Disconnect radiator hose at water outlet housing and battery ground cable at cylinder head.

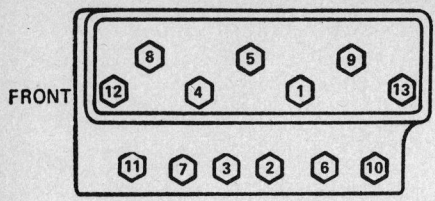

Fig. 7 Cylinder head tightening sequence. V6-200

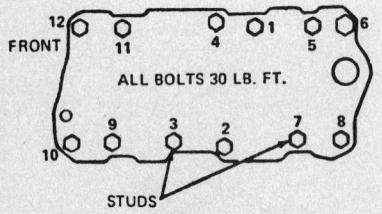

Fig. 8 Intake manifold tightening sequence. V6-200

12. Remove cylinder attaching bolts and cylinder head.
13. Reverse procedure to install. Tighten cylinder head bolts in sequence shown in Fig. 9.

1974-76 V8s

1. Remove intake and exhaust manifolds.
2. Remove rocker arm covers.
3. Back off rocker arm nuts, pivot rocker arms to clear push rods and remove push rods.
4. Unfasten and remove cylinder heads.
5. Reverse procedure to install and tighten intake manifold and head bolts in the sequence shown in Figs. 10 to 13.

VALVES, ADJUST
Hydraulic Lifters

NOTE: *After the engine has been thoroughly warmed up the valves may be adjusted with the engine shut off as follows: With engine in position to fire No. 1 cylinder the following valves may be adjusted: V6-200, Exhaust 1-5-6, intake 1-2-3. 6-250, Exhaust 1-3-5, intake 1-2-4. V8's, Exhaust 1-3-4-8, intake 1-2-5-7. Then crank the engine one more complete revolution which will bring No. 4 cylinder on V6-200 engine and No. 6 cylinder on 6-250 and V8 engines, to the firing position at which time the following valves may be adjusted: V6-200, Exhaust 2-3-4, intake 4-5-6. 6-250, Exhaust 2-4-6, intake 3-5-6. V8's, Exhaust 2-5-6-7, intake 3-4-6-8.*

The following procedure, performed with the engine running should be done only in case readjustment is required.

1. After engine has been warmed up to operating temperature, remove valve cover and install a new valve cover gasket.

2. With engine running at idle speed, back off valve rocker arm nut until rocker arm starts to clatter.
3. Turn rocker arm nut down slowly until the clatter just stops. This is the zero lash position.
4. Turn nut down ¼ additional turn and pause 10 seconds until engine runs smoothly. Repeat additional ¼ turns, pausing 10 seconds each time, until nut has been turned down the number of turns listed in the *Valve Specifications Chart* from the zero lash position.

NOTE
This preload adjustment must be done slowly to allow the lifter to adjust itself to prevent the possibility of interference between the intake valve head and top of piston, which might result in internal damage and/or bent push rods. Noisy lifters should be replaced.

VALVE ARRANGEMENT
Front to Rear

6-250 . . . . E-I-I-E-I-I-E-I-I-E
Small V8 . . . . E-I-I-E-E-I-I-E
Mark IV V8 . . . . I-E-I-E-I-E-I-E

ROCKER ARM STUDS

Rocker arm studs that have damaged threads may be replaced with standard studs. If studs are loose in the head, oversize studs (.003" or .013") may be installed after reaming the holes with a proper size reamer.
1. Remove the old stud by placing a suitable spacer, Fig. 14, over stud. Install nut and flat washer and remove stud by turning nut.
2. Ream hole for oversize stud.

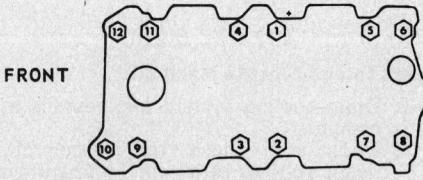

Fig. 12 Intake manifold tightening sequence. Small V8 engines

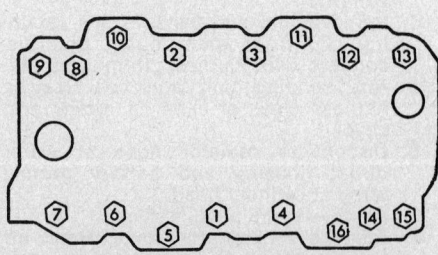

Fig. 13 Intake manifold tightening sequence. Mark IV V8 engines

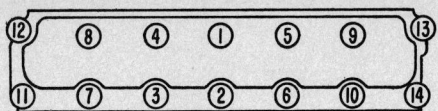

Fig. 9 Cylinder head tightening sequence. 6-250

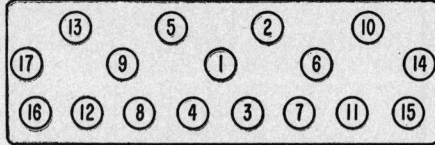

Fig. 10 Cylinder head tightening sequence. Small V8 engines

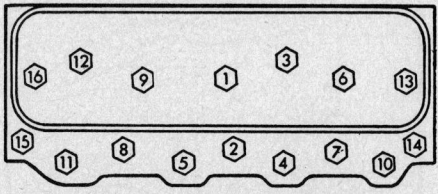

Fig. 11 Cylinder head tightening sequence. Mark IV V8 engines

3. Coat press-fit area of stud with rear axle lube. Then install new stud, Fig. 15. If tool shown is used, it should bottom on the head.

VALVE LIFT SPECS

Engine	Year	Intake	Exhaust
V6-200	1978–79	.373	.410
V6-231	1978	.383	.366
	1979	.357	.366
6-250	1974	.388	.388
	1974①	.388	.4051
	1975-79	.388	.4051
8-262	1975	.3727	.3900
8-267	1979	.373	.410
8-305	1976-79	.3727	.4100
8-350	1974-79③	.3900	.4100
	1974-79③	.4500	.4600
8-400	1974-76	.390	.410
8-454	1974-75	.440	.440
	1976	.3983	.4300

①—California vehicles.
②—Exc. L82 & Z28
③—L82 & Z28
④—Buick engine. Refer to Buick chapter for service procedures.

VALVE TIMING
Intake Opens Before TDC
All Except Corvette

Engine	Year	Degrees
V6-200	1978–79	34
V6-231①	1978	17
	1979	16

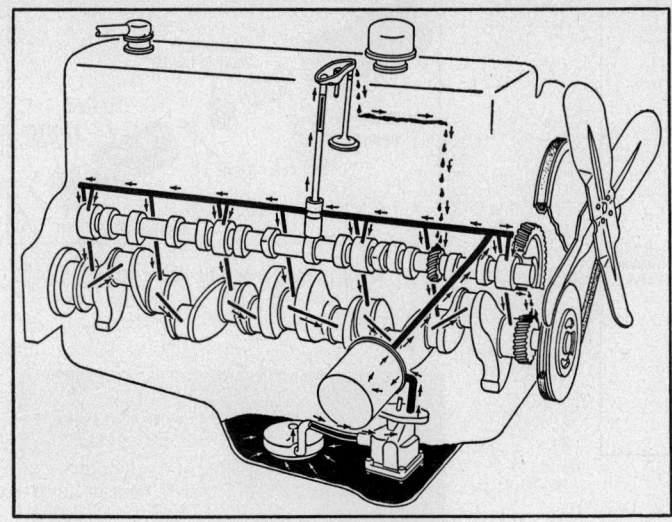

Engine oiling system. 6-250

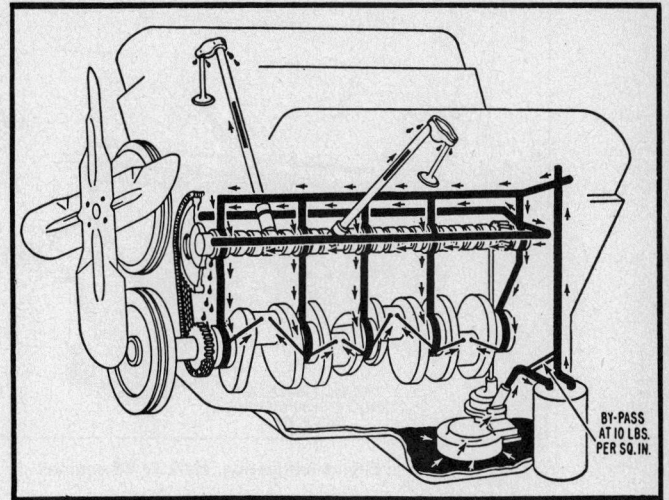

Engine oiling system. Small V8 engines

BY-PASS
AT 10 LBS.
PER SQ. IN.

6-250	1974-79	16
8-262	1975	26
8-267	1979	28
8-305	1976-79	28
8-350	1974-79 Exc. Z28	28
	1974-75 Z28	52
	1974 Calif.	44
8-400	1974-76	28
	1974 Calif.	44
8-454	1974-75	55
	1976	42

①—Buick engine. Refer to Buick chapter for service procedures.

Corvette

8-350	1974-79 Exc. L82	28
	1974-79 L82	52
8-454	1974	55

PUSH RODS

On engines that use push rods with a hardened insert at one end, the hardened end is identified by a color stripe and should always be installed toward the rocker arm during assembly.

Service Bulletin

On 6-250 engines with air conditioning, it is not necessary to remove the distributor wires, etc. to replace the valve push rod cover and/or gasket.
1. Remove coil and bracket from block.
2. Remove distributor hold-down clamp.
3. Lift distributor up for clearance (do not disengage from cam gear), then remove push rod cover.
4. Use new gasket and reverse procedure to install.

VALVE GUIDES

On all engines valves operate in guide holes bored in the head. If clearance becomes excessive, use the next oversize valve and ream the bore to fit. Valves with oversize stems are available in .003, .015 and .030".

HYDRAULIC LIFTERS

Valve lifters may be lifted from their bores after removing rocker arms and push rods. Adjustable pliers with taped jaws may be used to remove lifters that are stuck due to varnish, carbon, etc. Fig. 16 illustrates the type of lifter used.

TIMING CASE COVER

NOTE: On all engines the cover oil seal

may be replaced without taking off the timing gear cover. After removing the vibration damper, pry out the old seal with a screwdriver. Install the new seal with the lip or open end toward inside of cover and drive it into position.

1973-77 6-250

1. To remove cover, remove radiator.
2. Remove vibration damper.
3. Remove the two oil pan to front cover attaching screws.
4. Remove front cover to cylinder block attaching screws.
5. Pull cover slightly forward, then, using a sharp knife, cut oil pan front seal flush with cylinder block at both sides of cover.
6. Remove cover and attached portion of oil pan front seal.
7. Pry oil seal out of cover with a large screwdriver. Install new seal with open side of seal inside of cover and drive or press seal into place.

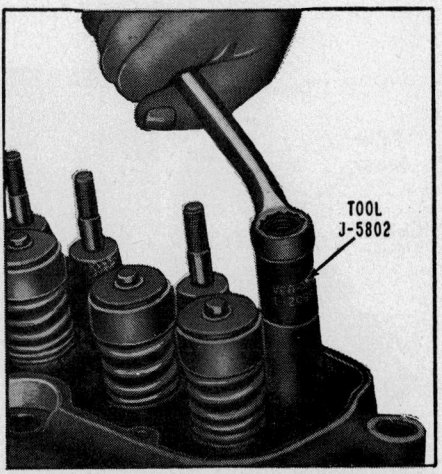

Fig. 14   Removing valve rocker arm stud.

TOOL
J-5802

Fig. 15   Installing valve rocker arm stud.

TOOL
J-6880

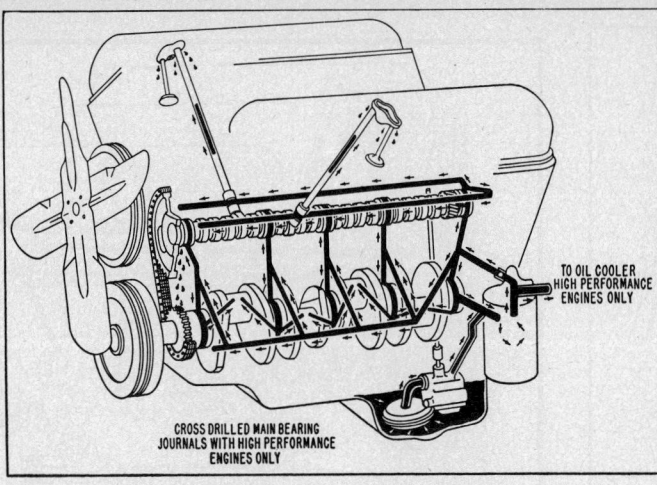

Engine lubrication. Mark IV V8 engines

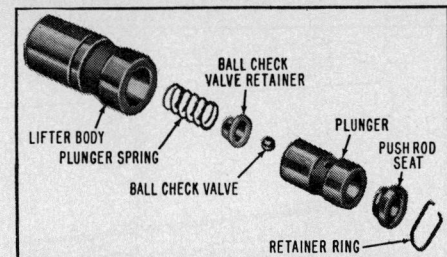

Fig. 16 Hydraulic valve lifter

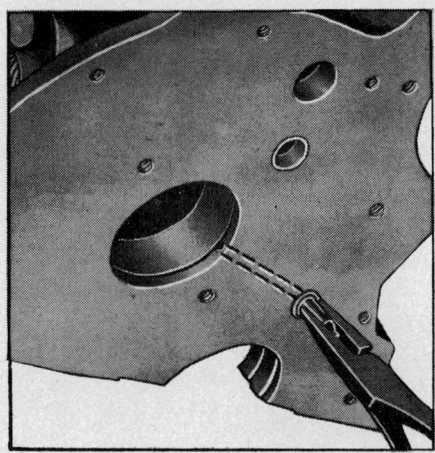

Fig. 17 Timing gear oil nozzle removal. 6-250

8. If oil nozzle is to be replaced, re-move it with pliers as shown in Fig. 17. Drive new nozzle in place, using a suitable light plastic or rubber hammer.

9. Clean gasket surfaces.

10. Cut tabs from new oil pan front seal, then install seal on cover, pressing tips into cover holes.

11. Install a suitable centering tool over end of crankshaft.

12. Coat gasket with light grease and stick it in position on cover.

13. Apply a 1/8 inch bead of RTV sealer at joint of oil pan and cover.

14. Install cover over centering tool, Fig. 18, and install cover screws, tighten-ing them to 6 to 8 ft. lbs. *It is im-portant that the centering tool be used to align the cover so the vibration damper installation will not damage the seal and position seal evenly around damper hub surface.*

V6 & V8 Engines

NOTE: The timing chain cover has been redesigned on 1974-79 small V8 engines to facilitate removal. The inner flange seal retainer has been shortened enough to clear the oil pan lip, making oil pan re-moval unnecessary.

Remove vibration damper, heater hose from water pump, and water pump from cylinder block. Unfasten and remove cover and gaskets.

Pry old seal out of cover from the front with a large screwdriver. Install the new seal so the open end of the seal is to-ward the inside of the cover and drive it into position with a suitable driver, be-ing sure to support cover at sealing area.

1. Make certain that the mating faces of cover and block are clean and flat.

2. Make certain oil slinger is in place against crankshaft sprocket.

3. Coat oil seal with light grease and, using a new cover gasket, install cov-er and gasket over dowel pins in cylinder block.

4. Install and torque cover screws to 80 inch lbs.

5. Install oil pan, harmonic balancer and water pump.

6. Start engine and check for leaks.

Fig. 18 Installing timing case cover. 6-250

Fig. 19 Removing camshaft gear from camshaft. 6-250

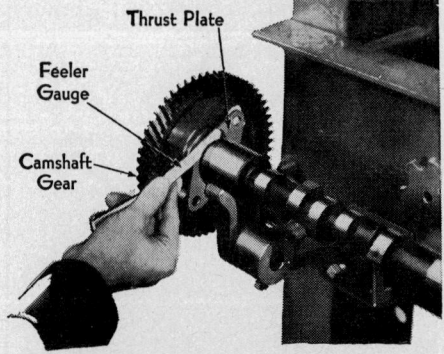

Fig. 20 Checking camshaft end play which should be .001 to .005''. 6-250

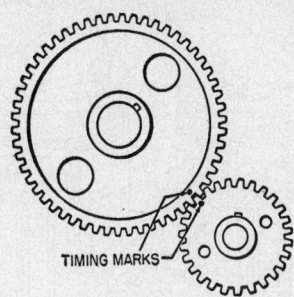

Fig. 21   Timing gear locating marks. 6-250 engines

Fig. 22   Checking timing gear backlash with dial indicator. Lash should be .004 to .006". 6-250 engines

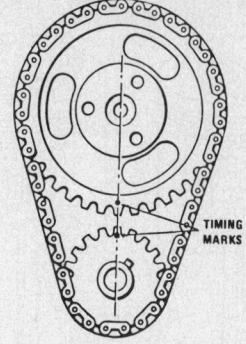

Fig. 23   Timing gear locating marks. V6 & V8 engines

TIMING GEARS

6-250

When necessary to install a new camshaft gear, the camshaft will have to be removed as the gear is a pressed fit on the shaft. The camshaft is held in position by a thrust plate which is fastened to the crankcase by two capscrews which are accessible through two holes in the gear web.

Use an arbor press to remove the gear and when doing so, a suitable sleeve, Fig. 19, should be employed to support the gear properly on its steel hub.

Before installing a new gear, assemble a new thrust plate on the shaft and press the gear on just far enough so that the thrust plate has practically no clearance, yet is free to turn. The correct clearance is from .001" to .005", Fig. 20.

The crankshaft gear can be removed by utilizing the two tapped holes in conjunction with a gear puller.

When the timing gears are installed, be sure the punch-marks on both gears are in mesh, Fig. 21. Backlash between the gears should be from .004" to .006", Fig. 22. Check the run-out of the gears,

and if the camshaft gear run-out exceeds .004" or the crank gear run-out is in excess of .003", remove the gear (or gears) and examine for burrs, dirt or some other fault which may cause the run-out. If these conditions are not the cause, replace the gear (or gears).

TIMING CHAIN

V6 & V8 Engines

1. Remove timing chain cover as outlined previously.
2. Remove crankshaft oil slinger.
3. Crank engine until timing marks on sprockets are in alignment, Fig. 23.
4. Remove three camshaft-to-sprocket bolts.
5. Remove camshaft sprocket and timing chain together. Sprocket is a light press fit on camshaft for approximately 1/8". If sprocket does not come off easily, a light blow with a plastic hammer on the lower edge of the sprocket should dislodge it.
6. If crankshaft sprocket is to be replaced, remove it with a suitable gear puller. Install new sprocket, aligning key and keyway.
7. Install chain on camshaft sprocket. Hold sprocket verticle with chain hanging below and shift around to align the timing marks on sprockets.
8. Align dowel in camshaft with dowel hole in sprocket and install sprocket on camshaft. *Do not attempt to drive sprocket on camshaft as welch plug at rear of engine can be dislodged.*
9. Draw sprocket onto camshaft, using the three mounting bolts. Tighten to 20 lb. ft. torque.
10. Lubricate timing chain and install cover.

CAMSHAFT

6-250 Engines

It is recommended that the engine be removed from the vehicle for camshaft

removal. Remove valve train components, engine front cover, fuel pump and distributor. Remove camshaft thrust plate screws and pull camshaft from cylinder block.

V8 Engines

1. Remove valve lifters and engine front cover.
2. On 1974-79 models except 1974-76 Nova, remove grille.
3. On 1974-76 Nova, remove front engine mount through bolts, then the right front engine mount and lower engine on frame. Remove the two center and one lower bolts attaching the hood catch support to the grille and radiator support.
4. On all models, remove fuel pump and the push rod.
5. Remove timing chain as outlined previously.
6. Install two 5/16"-18x4 bolts in camshaft bolt holes, then remove camshaft.

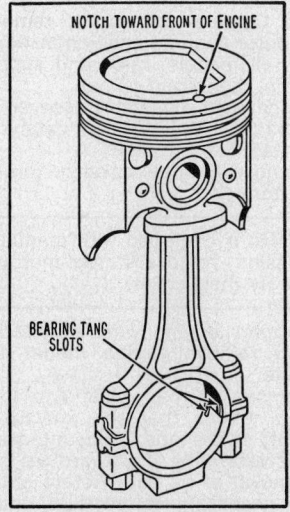

Fig. 23A   Piston and rod assembly. 6-250 engine

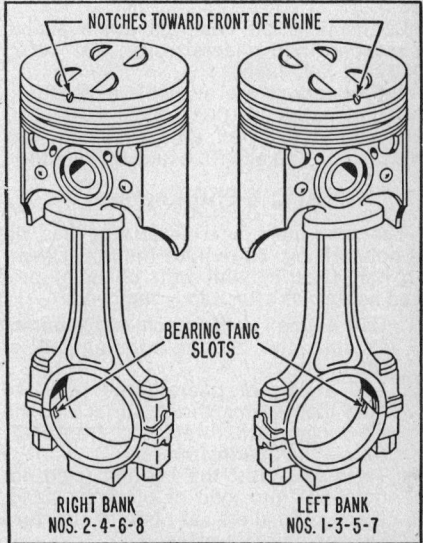

Fig. 23B   V8-350

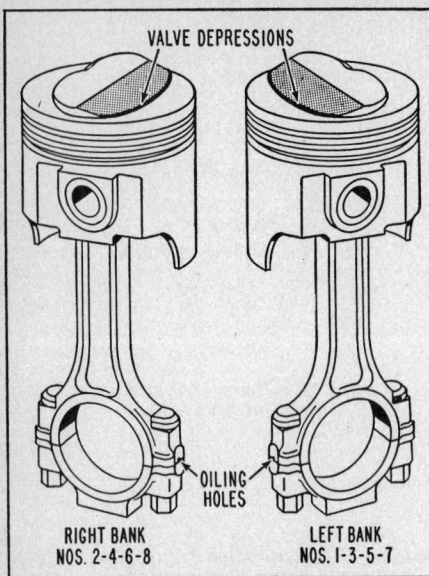

Fig. 23C   V8-350 Z-28
High performance

PISTONS & RODS, ASSEMBLE

1974-79

Assemble pistons to connecting rods as shown in Figs. 23A to 25.

PISTONS, PINS & RINGS

Pistons are available in standard and oversizes of .001 and .030 inch on all except V6-200 and .030 inch on V6-200.

Piston rings are available in standard and oversizes of .030 inch.

MAIN & ROD BEARINGS

Connecting rod bearings are available in standard and undersizes of .001, .002, .010 and .020 inch.

Main bearings are available in standard and undersizes of .001, .002, .009, .010 and .020 inch on all except V8-454, and .001, .002, .010 and .020 inch on V8-454.

NOTE: 6-250 Engines

The rear main bearing journal has no oil hole drilling. To remove the upper bearing half (bearing half with oil hole) proceed as follows after cap is removed:

1. Use a small drift punch and hammer to start the bearing rotating out of the block.
2. Use a pair of pliers (tape jaws) to hold the bearing thrust surface to the oil slinger and rotate the crankshaft to pull the bearing out.
3. To install, start the bearing (side not notched) into side of block by hand, then use pliers as before to turn bearing half into place.
4. The last ¼" movement may be done by holding just the slinger with the

pliers or tap in place with a drift punch.

CRANKSHAFT REAR OIL SEAL

NOTE: These engines are equipped with helix type rear seal. A seal starting tool, Fig. 26, must be used to prevent the upper seal half from coming into contact with the sharp edge of the block.

1974-79

When necessary to correct an oil leak due to a defective seal, always replace the upper and lower seal halves as a unit, Fig. 27. *When installing either half, lubricate the lip portion only with engine oil, keeping oil off the parting line surface as this is treated with glue.* Always clean crankshaft surface berore installing a new seal.

1. To replace the lower seal, remove seal from groove in bearing cap, using a small screwdriver to pry it out.
2. Insert new seal and roll it in place with finger and thumb.
3. To replace the upper seal (with engine in car) use a small hammer and tap a brass pin punch on one end of the seal until it protrudes far enough to be removed with pliers.
4. Position tip of tool, Fig. 26, between crankshaft and seal seat in cylinder block.
5. Position seal between crankshaft and tip of tool with seal bead contacting tip of tool. Ensure oil seal lip is facing toward front of engine.
6. Roll seal around crankshaft, using tool as a "Shoehorn" to protect seal bead from sharp corner of seal seat surface in cylinder block.

NOTE: Tool must remain in position until seal is properly seated with both ends flush with block.

7. Remove tool, using care not to dis-

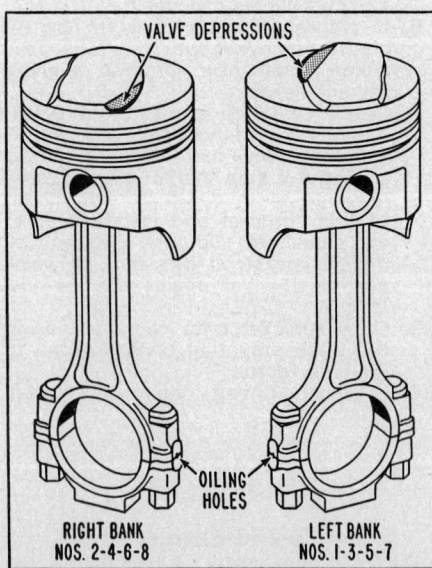

Fig. 25   V8-400 High performance

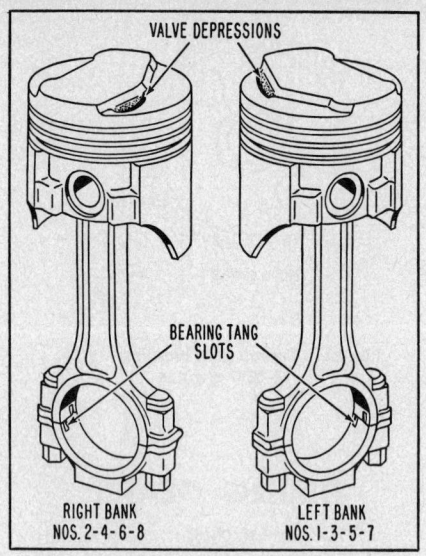

Fig. 24   V8-454 engines

lodge seal.
8. Install new seal into bearing cap with tool as outlined previously.
9. Install bearing cap with sealant applied to the cap to case interface. Do not apply sealant to seal ends. Torque rear main bearing cap bolts to specifications as listed in the "Engine Tightening Specification Chart".

OIL PAN

1977-79 V8 Exc. Corvette

1. Disconnect battery ground cable.
2. Remove air cleaner and snorkle.
3. Remove upper half of fan shroud.

NOTE: On Camaro and Nova equipped with heavy duty cooling system, remove fan shroud since it is of one piece construction.

4. On Malibu and Monte Carlo, remove engine oil dipstick and tube.
5. On Chevrolet, remove vacuum reservoir, if equipped.
6. On Camaro and Nova, remove distributor cap and position aside.
7. On all models, raise and support vehicle, then drain oil pan.
8. Disconnect exhaust crossover pipe at exhaust manifold and catalytic converter.
9. Remove flywheel cover or torque converter cover.

NOTE: If equipped with manual transmission, remove starter motor before the flywheel cover.

10. Support engine with a suitable jack and remove engine mount through bolts.
11. Remove oil pan bolts and lower oil pan. Check that the forward crankshaft throw and/or counterweight is not extending downward as to block removal of oil pan. Rotate crankshaft as necessary to position crankshaft to permit pan removal.
12. Raise engine and install engine mount through bolts.

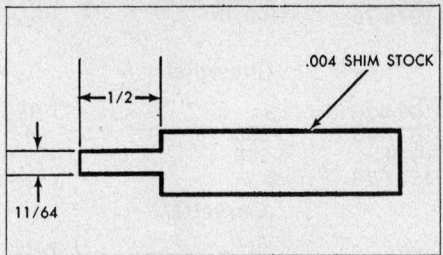

Fig. 26 Fabricated seal starting tool for helix type seal

13. Remove oil pan.
14. Reverse procedure to install. Torque oil pan bolts to 80 inch lbs.

1977-79 6-250

1. Disconnect battery ground cable.
2. Raise vehicle on hoist, then drain engine oil.
3. Remove starter, then remove flywheel housing cover, or torque converter housing cover.
4. Remove engine mount through bolts, then raise engine, reinstall through bolts to engine mounts and lower the engine.
5. Remove oil pan bolts and oil pan.
6. Reverse procedure to install.

1974-76 6-250

1. Disconnect battery positive cable.
2. Remove radiator upper mounting panel or side mount bolts.
3. Place a piece of heavy cardboard between fan and radiator.
4. Disconnect fuel suction line at fuel pump.
5. Raise vehicle on a hoist and drain engine oil.
6. Disconnect and remove starter and flywheel underpan or converter housing underpan and splash shield.
7. On Nova, disconnect steering rod at idler lever and position linkage to one side for pan clearance.
8. Rotate crankshaft until timing mark on damper is at 6 o'clock.
9. Remove bolts attaching brake line to front crossmember and move brake line away from crossmember.
10. Remove through bolts from engine front mounts.
11. Remove oil pan bolts.
12. On Chevrolet models, raise engine slowly until motor mount through bolts can be removed, remove bolts, then continue to raise engine about 3".
13. On Nova, remove left engine mount and frame bracket. Remove oil pan by lowering slightly and then rolling it into opening created by removal of left engine mount. Tilt front of pan upward and remove by pulling pan down and to rear.
14. On Camaro, raise engine enough to insert 2" x 4" block of wood under engine mounts. Then lower engine onto blocks and lower and remove pan.

1978-79 V6-200 & 1977 V8 Exc. Corvette

1. Disconnect battery ground cable.
2. Remove oil dipstick and tube.
3. Remove exhaust crossover pipe.
4. If equipped with automatic transmission, remove converter housing cover.
5. Remove starter bolt and inboard brace, then swing starter aside.
6. Remove oil pan retaining bolts and oil pan.
7. Reverse procedure to install.

1974-76 V8 Except Corvette

NOTE: On Chevelle equipped with V8-454 and manual transmission, it is necessary to remove the starter and the flywheel shield. Also, remove rear transmission mount to crossmember nut and raise rear of transmission.

1. Disconnect battery ground cable.
2. Remove distributor cap and fan shroud retaining bolts.
3. On Mark IV engines, place a piece of heavy cardboard between fan and radiator.
4. Raise vehicle on hoist and drain oil.
5. Disconnect exhaust or crossover pipes.
6. If equipped with automatic transmission, remove converter underpan and splash shield.
7. On 1974 Nova, disconnect steering idler lever at frame and swing linkage down for pan clearance.
8. Rotate crankshaft until timing mark on damper is at 6 o'clock.
9. On all except V8-350 and Mark IV engines with automatic transmission, disconnect starter brace at starter. Remove inboard starter bolt and loosen outboard starter bolt. Swing starter outward to gain clearance.
10. Remove both through bolts from engine front mounts.
11. Using suitable equipment, raise engine until wood blocks of 2" on

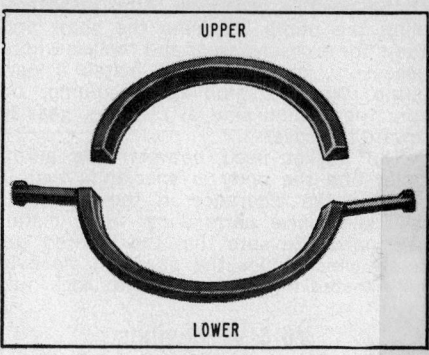

Fig. 27 Crankshaft and rear oil seal (typical)

Chevrolet and Nova and 3" on Chevelle and Monte Carlo can be inserted under engine mounts. Lower engine onto blocks.
12. Remove oil pan bolts and lower oil pan.

1974-78 Corvette

1. Disconnect battery ground cable.
2. Raise and support vehicle, then drain oil pan.
3. Remove engine oil dipstick and tube.
4. Disconnect idler arm and lower steering linkage.
5. Remove flywheel splash shield.
6. Disconnect exhaust pipe from exhaust manifold and catalytic converter.
7. Remove oil pan bolts and oil pan.
8. Reverse procedure to install. Torque oil pan bolts to 80 inch lbs.

OIL PUMP

6-250

The pumps used in these engines are

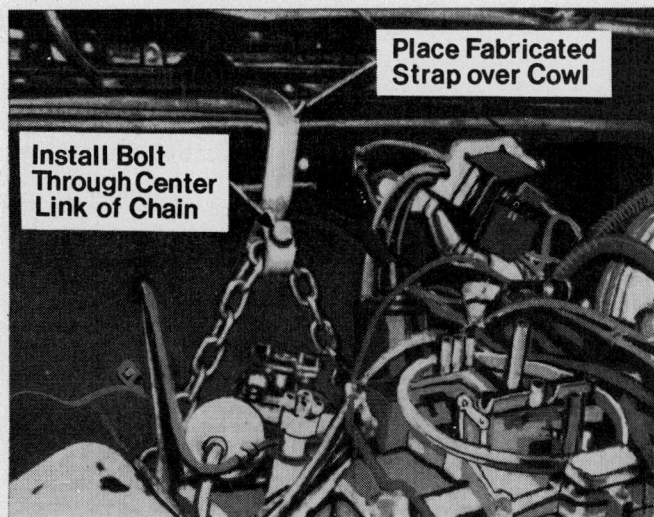

Fig. 28 Install strap over crowl

of the positive gear type. After disassembling the pump, examine the shaft and gears for excessive wear and replace where necessary, or better still, install a new pump. When assembling the pump, be sure the ground side of the idler gear is toward the cover.

The gasket used between the pump cover and the body is special in that it controls the clearance in the pump. If the relief valve parts show wear, install new parts. Be sure that the tapered set screw which holds the pump in place is fully seated and locked with its lock nut.

V6 & V8 Engines

After removing the oil pan, unfasten pump from rear main bearing cap. Disconnect pump shaft from extension by removing clip from collar. Remove pump cover and take out idler gear, drive gear and shaft.

Should any of the following conditions be found it is advisable to replace the pump assembly.

1. Inspect pump body for cracks or wear.
2. Inspect gears for wear or damage.
3. Check shaft for looseness in housing.
4. Check inside of cover for wear that would permit oil to leak past the ends of gear.
5. Check oil pick-up screen for damage to screen, by-pass valve or body.
6. Check for oil in air chamber.

BELT TENSION DATA

	New Lbs.	Used Lbs.
1974-79		
Air Condition	135-145	95
Air Pump		
Fan and Power Steering	120-130	75

WATER PUMP, REPLACE
All Models

1. Drain radiator and break loose fan pulley bolts.
2. Disconnect heater hose at water pump.
3. Loosen Delcotron and remove fan belt, then unfasten and remove pump. On 6-250 engines, pull pump straight out of block first to prevent damage to impeller.
4. Reverse procedure to install.

FUEL PUMP PRESSURE

Year	Engine	Pressure Lbs.
	Camaro	
1974-76	6-250	3½-4½
1977-78	6-250	4-5
1979	6-250	4½-6
1976	V8-305	7-8½
1977-79	V8-305	7½-9
1974-76	V8-350	7-8½
1977-79	V8-350	7½-9
	Chevelle, Malibu & Monte Carlo	
1978-79	V6-200	4½-6
1978-79	V6-231 ①	4.2-5.7
1974-76	6-250	3½-4½
1977	6-250	4-5
1979	V8-267	7½-9
1974-76	V-8-350, 400, 454	7-8½
1976	V8-305	7-8½
1977-79	V8-305, 350	7½-9

①—Buick engine. Refer to Buick chapter for service procedures.

	Chevy Nova	
1974-76	6-250	3½-4½
1977-78	6-250	4-5
1979	6-260	4½-6
1975	V8-262	7-8½
1976	V8-305	7-8½

1977-79	V8-305, 350	7½-9
1974-76	V8-350	7-8½
	Chevrolet	
1974-76	V8	7-8½
1977-78	6-250	4-5
1979	6-250	4½-6
1977-79	V8	7½-9
	Corvette	
1974-76	All	7-8½
1977-79	All	7½-9

FUEL PUMP, REPLACE
1974-79

1. Disconnect fuel lines at pump.
2. Unfasten and remove pump.
3. If push rod is to be removed on 454 engines, remove pipe plug, then remove push rod. On 262, 267, 305, 350 and V8-400, remove fuel pump adapter and gasket then remove push rod.
4. Reverse procedure to install. On V8 engines, a pair of mechanical fingers may be used to hold fuel pump push rod up while installing pump.

Service Bulletin

On Mark IV engines the access hole for removal of the fuel pump push rod is located below the fuel pump mounting bolts. This access hole, which permits removal of the push rod after the pump has been removed, has a threaded plug with a square recessed hole. The plug may be removed by using a hand-made tool. A ⁵⁄₁₆" square end for inserting and turning the plug for removal is required. A piece of bar stock, approximately 1½" long is suggested.

Clutch and Transmission Section

NOTE: 1979 linkage adjustment information is in this section. Repair procedures on both automatic and manual shift transmissions are covered elsewhere in this manual. Procedures for removing automatic transmissions as well as linkage adjustments on 1974-78 models are included in the automatic transmission chapters. See Chapter Index.

CLUTCH PEDAL, ADJUST

1974-79 Except Corvette

1. Disconnect return spring at clutch fork.
2. Rotate clutch lever and shaft assembly until pedal is against rubber bumper on dash brace.
3. Push outer end of clutch fork rearward until throwout bearing lightly contacts pressure plate fingers.
4. Install push rod in gauge hole and increase length until all lash is removed, Fig. 1.

NOTE: On 1974-77 Chevelle, it may be necessary to move rubber bumper rearward to obtain additional clutch pedal travel.

5. Remove swivel or rod from gauge hole and insert into lower hole on lever. Install retainer and tighten lock nut being careful not to change rod length.
6. Reinstall return spring and check pedal free travel:
1975-78 Malibu & Monte Carlo, ⁴³⁄₆₄" to 1¹⁷⁄₆₄".
1975-79 Camaro & Nova, ⁵⁵⁄₆₄" to 1²⁹⁄₆₄".
1975-77 Chevelle & Monte Carlo, ⁴⁵⁄₆₄" to 1⁵⁄₁₆".

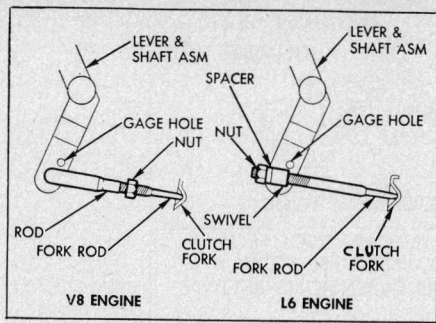

Fig. 1 Clutch pedal adjust. Except Corvette

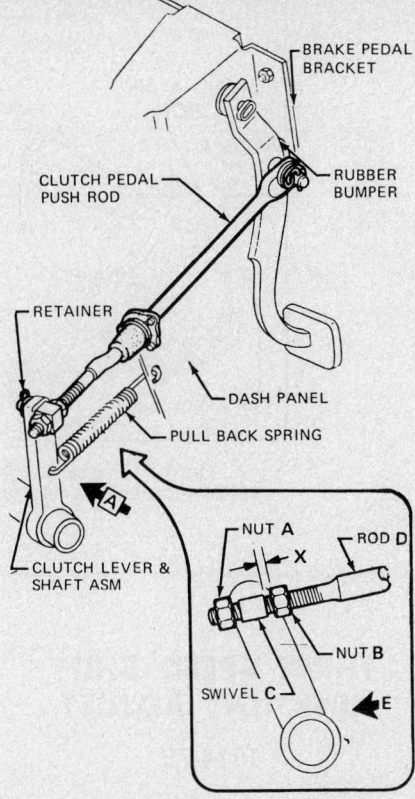

Fig. 2 Clutch pedal adjust. 1978-79 Corvette

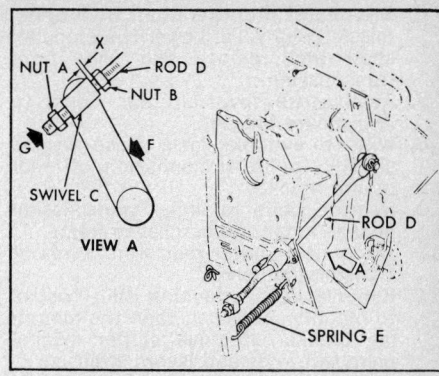

Fig. 3 Clutch pedal adjust. 1974-78 Corvette

1974 Camaro, 1" to 1⅜".
  Chevelle, ¾" to 1⁵⁄₁₆".
  Nova, ¾" to 1⅜".

1978-79 Corvette

1. Rotate clutch lever and shaft assembly until clutch pedal is firmly against rubber bumper on dash brace.
2. Install swivel "C", Fig. 2, in hole in clutch lever and shaft assembly.
3. Install retainer.
4. With nuts "A" and "B", Fig. 2, loose on rod "D", apply approximately 5 lbs. load in direction of arrow "E" until bearing lightly contacts belleville spring fingers.
5. Tighten lock nut "B", Fig. 2, toward swivel "C" until dimension "X" is .37-.43 inch.
6. Tighten nut "A", Fig. 2, to lock swivel "C" against nut "B".
7. Clutch pedal free play should be 1-1½ inch.

1975-77 Corvette

1. Disconnect return spring between toe pan brace and cross shaft lever, Fig. 3.
2. Rotate clutch lever and shaft assembly until pedal is against dash brace rubber bumper.
3. Install swivel (C) into clutch lever hole and install retainer.
4. Loosen nuts (A) and (B), then apply a 5 pound load in direction of arrow (F) until bearing lightly contacts plate fingers.
5. Rotate nut (B) toward swivel until dimension "X" is approximately ⅜ to ⁷⁄₁₆ inch, then tighten nut (A) to lock swivel against nut (B).
6. Reinstall return spring and adjust clutch pedal free travel which should be 1 to 1½ inch.

1974 Corvette

1. Referring to Fig. 3, disconnect spring (E) between toe pan brace and cross shaft lever.
2. With pedal against stop, loosen jam nuts sufficiently to allow adjusting rod to move against clutch fork until release bearing contacts pressure plate fingers lightly.
3. Rotate upper nut (B) against swivel and back off 4½ turns. Tighten lower nut (A) to lock swivel against nut (B).
4. Install return spring (E) and check pedal free travel. It should be 1" to 1½".

CLUTCH, REPLACE

Clutch Disc Installation

On all 6-cylinder engines the clutch disc is installed with the damper springs to the flywheel side. On V8's install clutch disc with damper springs and grease slinger to transmission side.

1974-79

1. Support engine and remove transmission as outlined further on.
2. Disconnect clutch fork push rod and spring.
3. Remove flywheel housing.
4. Slide clutch fork from ball stud and remove fork from dust boot.

NOTE: Look for "X" mark on flywheel and on clutch cover. If "X" mark is not evident, prick punch marks on flywheel and clutch cover for indexing purposes during installation.

5. Loosen clutch-to-flywheel attaching bolts evenly one turn at a time until spring pressure is released. Then remove bolts and clutch assembly.
6. Reverse procedure to install.

THREE SPEED TRANSMISSION, REPLACE

NOTE: On 1975-79 models, it may be necessary to remove the catalytic converter and its support bracket to facilitate transmission removal.

1974-79 Exc. Corvette

1. Disconnect battery ground cable.
2. Remove shift lever knob and, on four speed models, the spring and "T" handle.
3. Raise and support vehicle.
4. Disconnect speedometer cable and TCS wiring at transmission.
5. Remove propeller shaft.
6. Remove transmission mount to crossmember bolts and the crossmember to frame bolts.
7. Remove shift lever attaching bolts and shift levers from transmission. Disconnect back drive rod at bell housing crank on floor shift models.
8. On floor shift models, remove bolts attaching shift control assembly to support on transmission. Carefully pull unit downward until shift lever clears rubber boot and remove assembly from vehicle.
9. On all models, remove transmission to clutch housing upper retaining bolts and install guide pins in holes and remove the lower retaining bolts.
10. Slide transmission rearward until clutch drive gear clears the clutch assembly and remove transmission from vehicle.
11. Reverse procedure to install.

1974-79 Corvette

1. Disconnect battery ground cable.
2. Remove shifter ball spring and "T" handle.
3. Remove console trim plate.
4. Raise and support vehicle.
5. Remove right and left exhaust pipes from vehicle.

6. Disconnect propeller shaft from transmission slip yoke. Lower the propeller shaft and remove slip yoke from transmission.
7. Remove transmission rear mount to rear mount bracket.
8. With a suitable jack, raise engine slightly to lift transmission off rear mount bracket.
9. Remove bolts retaining transmission linkage mounting bracket to frame.
10. Disconnect shifter rods from levers at transmission cover.
11. Remove bolts attaching shift control to mounting bracket, then the mounting bracket. Remove shifter mechanism with rods and levers attached.
12. Remove shift levers from transmission and disconnect the speedometer cable and TCS switch wiring.
13. Remove transmission mount bracket to crossmember bolts, then the mount bracket. Remove bolts retaining rear mount cushion and exhaust pipe yoke.
14. Remove transmission to clutch housing bolts and the lower left extension bolt.
15. Pull transmission rearward until clear of clutch housing, rotating transmission clockwise while pulling rearward. To allow clearance for transmission removal, slowly lower rear of engine until tachometer drive cable at distributor clears horizontal ledge across front of dash.
16. Remove transmission from vehicle.
17. Reverse procedure to install.

FOUR SPEED TRANSMISSION, REPLACE

1974-79

The procedure for removing this transmission is similar to that described for the "1974-79" 3-speed unit.

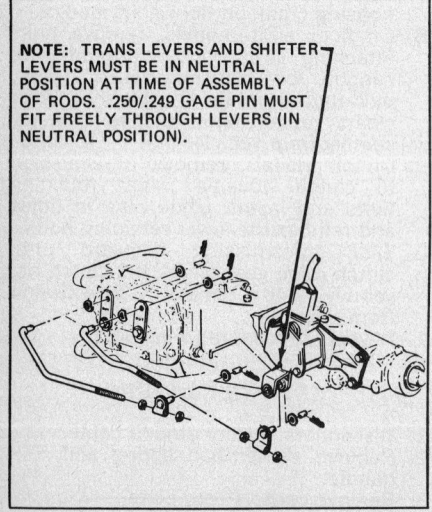

NOTE: TRANS LEVERS AND SHIFTER LEVERS MUST BE IN NEUTRAL POSITION AT TIME OF ASSEMBLY OF RODS. .250/.249 GAGE PIN MUST FIT FREELY THROUGH LEVERS (IN NEUTRAL POSITION).

Fig. 5 3 Speed floor shift linkage adjustment. 1978-79 Malibu & Monte Carlo (typical)

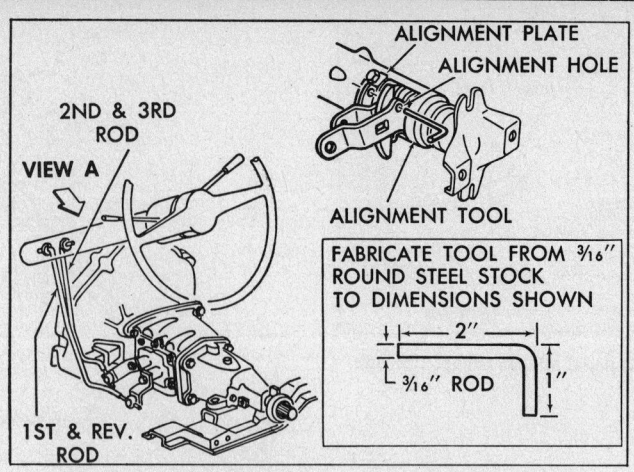

Fig. 4 Three-speed column shift linkage adjustment. 1974-79 Chevrolet, Chevy Nova, Chevelle and Camaro (typical)

THREE SPEED SHIFT LINKAGE, ADJUST

1974-79

Column Shift

1. Place shift lever in "Reverse" position and ignition switch in "Lock".
2. Raise vehicle on a hoist.
3. Loosen shift control rod swivel lock nuts. Pull down slightly on 1/R rod attached to column lever to remove any slack and then tighten clevis lock nut at transmission lever, Fig. 4.
4. Unlock ignition switch and shift column lever to "Neutral". Position column lower levers in "Neutral", align gauge holes in levers and insert gauge pin.
5. Support rod and swivel to prevent movement and tighten 2/3 shift control rod lock nut.
6. Remove alignment tool from column lower levers and check operation. Then place column lever in "Reverse" and check interlock control.

Floor Shift, 1974-79

1. Place ignition switch in "Off" position and raise vehicle.
2. Loosen lock nuts at shift rod swivels, Figs. 5 and 6. The rods should pass freely through the swivels.
3. Place transmission shift levers in neutral position.
4. Move shift control lever into the neutral detent position, align control assembly levers and insert locating pin into lever alignment slot.
5. Tighten lock nuts at shift rod swivels and remove locating pin.
6. Place transmission control lever in reverse position and the ignition switch in "Lock" position. Loosen lock nut at backdrive control rod swivel, then pull rod downward slightly to remove slack in the column mechanism, then tighten the lock nut.
7. Check interlock control. The ignition switch should move freely to and from the "Lock" position.
8. Check transmission shift operation and if satisfactory, lower vehicle.

FOUR SPEED SHIFT LINKAGE, ADJUST

1974-79

Exc. Corvette

The procedure, Figs. 7 and 8, is the same as that for Three Speed transmissions described previously.

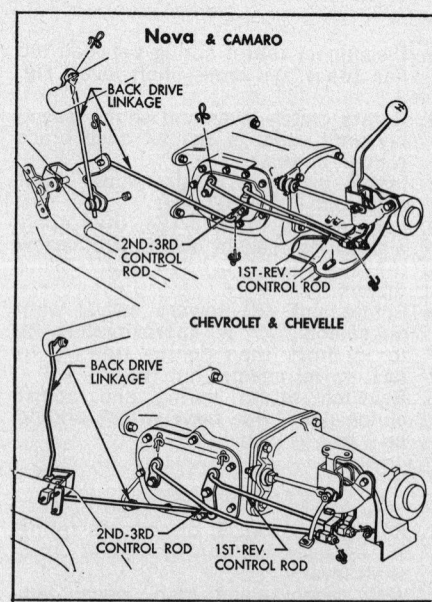

Fig. 6 3-Speed floor shift linkage. 1974-79 except Corvette & 1978-79 Malibu & Monte Carlo (typical)

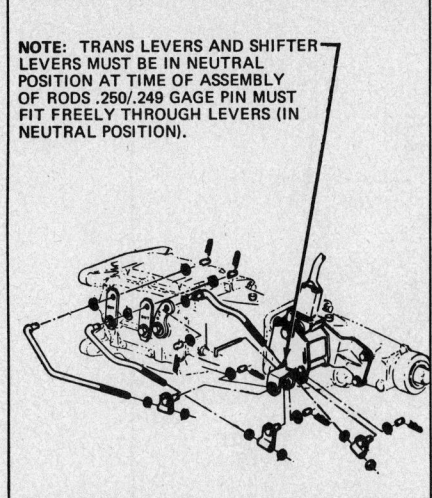

NOTE: TRANS LEVERS AND SHIFTER LEVERS MUST BE IN NEUTRAL POSITION AT TIME OF ASSEMBLY OF RODS .250/.249 GAGE PIN MUST FIT FREELY THROUGH LEVERS (IN NEUTRAL POSITION).

Fig. 8 4 Speed shift linkage adjustment.
1978-79 Malibu & Monte Carlo

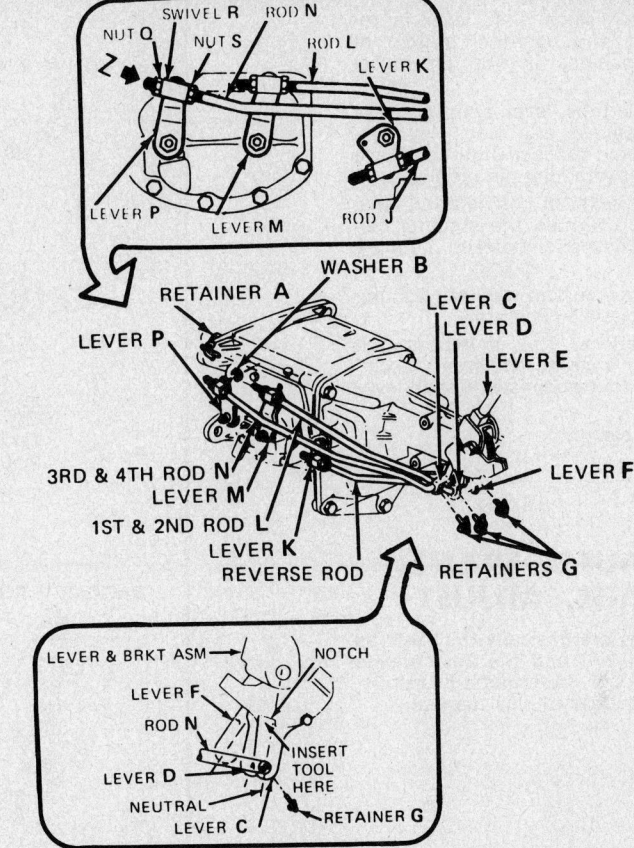

Fig. 9 4 Speed shift linkage adjustment. 1978-79 Corvette

1978-79 Corvette

1. Place levers (K), (M) and (P) in neutral position, Fig. 9. To obtain neutral position, move levers counter-clockwise to forward detent, then clockwise one detent.
2. Move lever (E) to neutral position. Align levers (C), (D) and (F) with notch in lever and bracket assembly, then insert a suitable tool to secure levers in neutral position.
3. Attach rod (N) to lever (C) with retainer (G).
4. Loosely assembly nuts (Q) and (S) and swivel (R) on rod (N).
5. Insert swivel (R) into lever (P), attach washer (B) and secure retaining (A). Apply a load on lever (P) in direction of arrow (Z). Tighten nut (S) against swivel, then nut (Q) against swivel.
6. Repeat steps 3, 4 and 5 for rod (J) and levers (F) and (K).
7. Repeat steps 3, 4 and 5 for rod (L) and levers (D) and (M).
8. Remove alignment tool from levers. The centerlines of shift levers must be aligned to provide free crossover motion.
9. Check for proper operation. Be sure all cables have adequate clearance around control rods.

1974-77 Corvette

1. Place ignition switch in "Lock" position and raise vehicle.
2. Loosen swivel and clevis lock nuts from both shift rods, Fig. 10. The rods should pass freely through the swivels. Disconnect backdrive cable from column lock tube lever.
3. Place shift control lever in neutral position and insert a locking pin, .644 inch diameter, in notch of lever and bracket assembly.
4. Place transmission levers in neutral position.
5. Hold reverse rod and lever rearward against locating pin, tighten rear lock nut against swivel and tighten the

front lock nut.
6. Hold 1st.-2nd. rod against locating pin and adjust clevis so clevis pin passes freely through clevis and lever. Tighten lock nut against clevis and install washer and lock pin.
7. Hold 3rd.-4th. rod and lever rearward

against locating pin and adjust swivel so swivel pin freely passes through lever. Tighten forward nut against lever, then the rear nut. Remove locating pin.
8. Check for proper operation.
9. Loosen two nuts at steering column

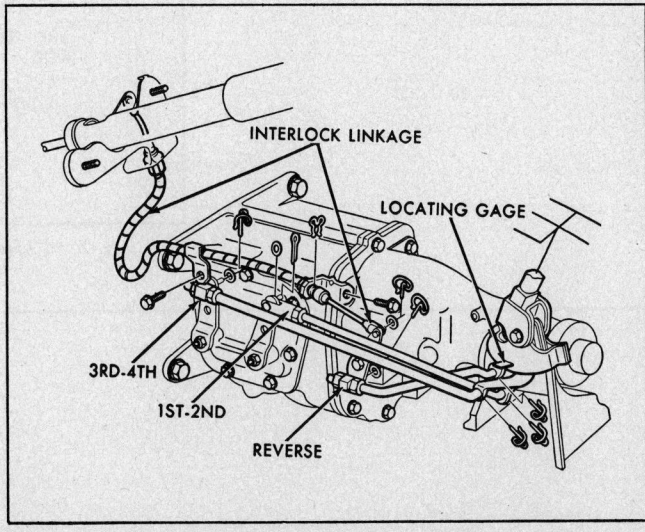

Fig. 10 4 Speed linkage. 1974-77 Corvette (typical)

to dash panel bracket.

10. Place transmission shift lever in reverse and the ignition switch in "Lock" position, if not previously done.

11. Rotate lock tube lever counter-clockwise to remove any free play. Reposition cable bracket until cable eye passes over retaining pin on lever.

12. Hold the bracket in position and have an assistant tighten the steering column to dash panel bracket retaining nuts.

13. Install cotter pin and washer retaining backdrive cable to lever pin.

14. Check interlock. The ignition switch must move freely to and from "Lock" position with transmission shift lever in reverse.

15. Lower vehicle.

1979 AUTO. TRANS. LINKAGE, ADJUST

1979 linkages are basically the same as those used in 1978 and the adjustments are covered in the "Automatic Transmission section" in rear of this manual.

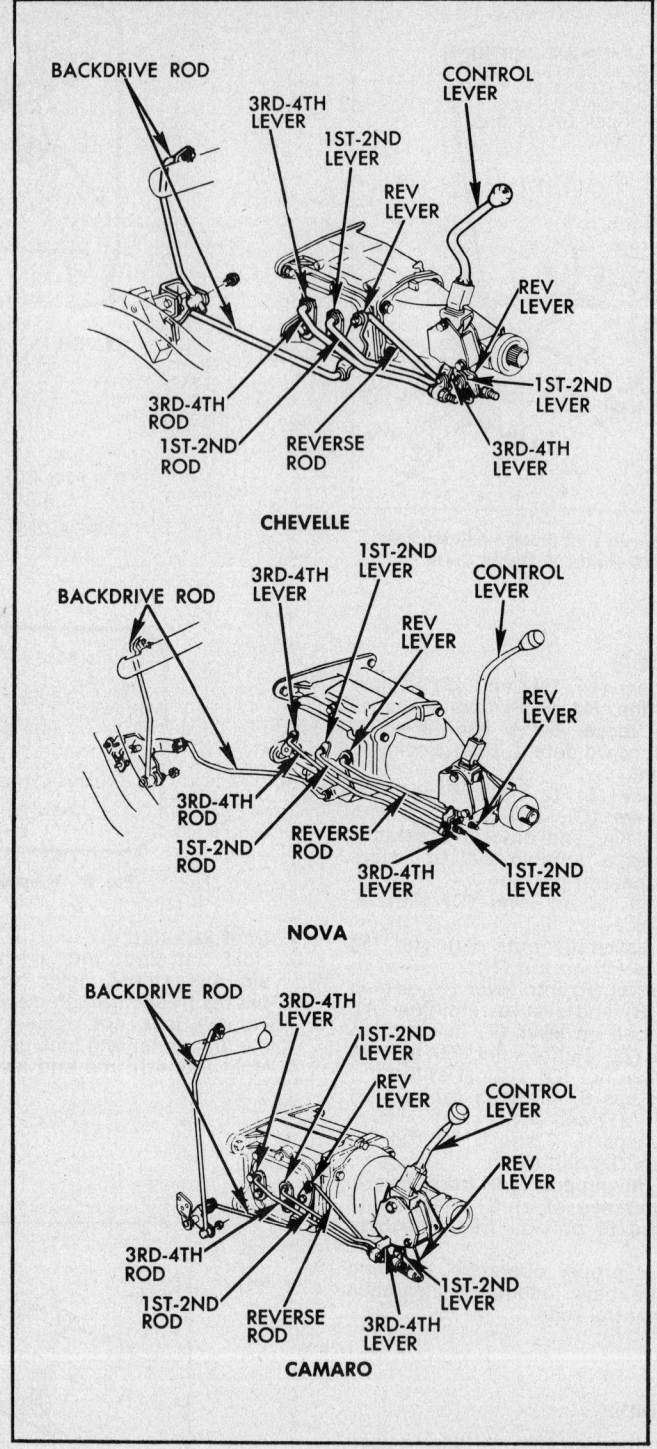

Fig. 7   4 Speed linkage. 1974-78 except Corvette (typical)

Rear Axle, Propeller Shaft & Brakes

REAR AXLE

Figs. 1 and 2 illustrate the rear axle assemblies used. When necessary to overhaul any of these units, refer to the *Rear Axle Specifications* table in this chapter.

1974-79 Corvette

NOTE: 1974-79 models are equipped with Positraction differentials.

In this axle, the drive pinion is mounted in two tapered roller bearings that are preloaded by a spacer. The pinion is positioned by a shim located between the head of the drive pinion and the rear pinion bearing. The front bearing is held in place by a large washer and a locking pinion nut.

The differential is supported in the carrier by two tapered roller side bearings.

The differential side bearings are preloaded by shims between the bearings and carrier housing, Fig. 2. The differential assembly is positioned for proper ring gear and pinion backlash by varying the position and thickness of these shims.

The ring gear is bolted to the case. The case houses two side gears in mesh with two pinions mounted on a pinion shaft which is held in place by a lock screw. The side gears are backed by thrust washers.

The differential side gears drive two splined yokes which are retained by snap rings located on the yoke splined end. The yokes are supported on caged needle bearings pressed into the carrier, adjacent to the differential bearings. A lip seal, pressed into the carrier outboard of the bearing, prevents oil leakage and dirt entry.

Remove & Replace

It is not necessary to remove the rear axle assembly for any normal repairs. The axle shafts and carrier assembly can easily be removed from the vehicle, leaving the rear axle housing in place.
1. Raise and support vehicle.
2. Remove exhaust system components located behind front crossmember for clearance.
3. Disconnect driveshaft at carrier yokes.
4. Remove carrier front mounting bracket bolt.
5. Remove propeller shaft.
6. Disconnect strut rod bracket from carrier and lower bracket with strut rods attached.
7. Loosen the four spring to carrier bolts.
8. Remove eight carrier cover bolts, allowing lubricant to drain from carrier.
9. Position drive yokes in a position to facilitate carrier removal.
10. Remove carrier from vehicle.
11. Reverse procedure to install.

1974-79 Camaro, Chevrolet, Chevelle, Nova, Malibu & Monte Carlo

In these rear axles, Fig. 1, the rear axle housing and differential carrier are

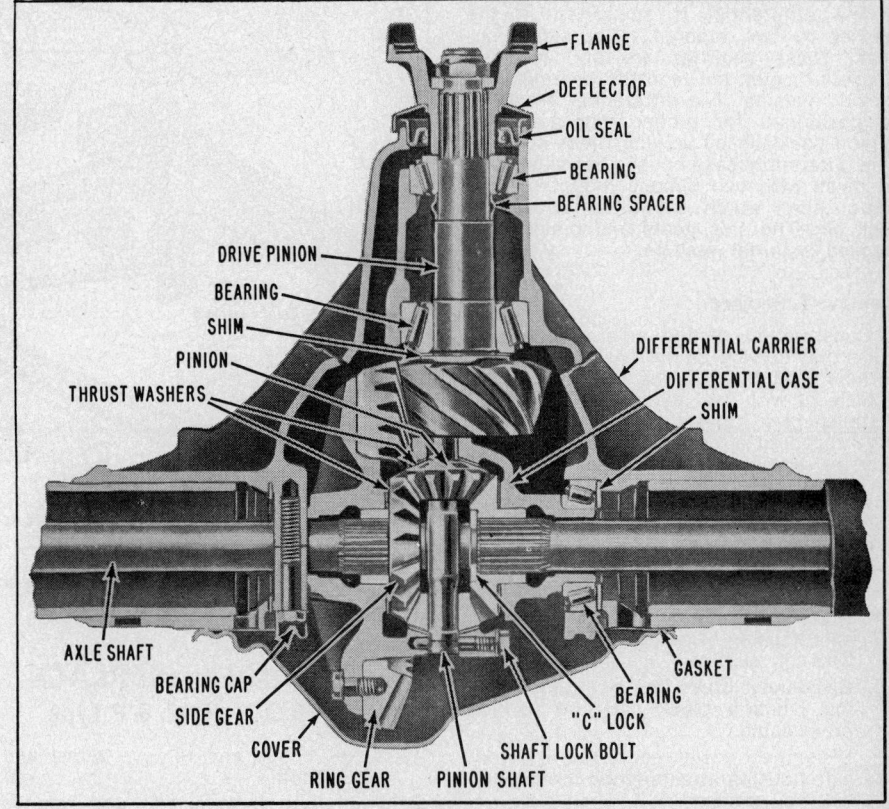

Fig. 1   Rear axle. 1974-79 Camaro, Chevrolet, Chevelle, Malibu, Monte Carlo and Nova. "C" Type

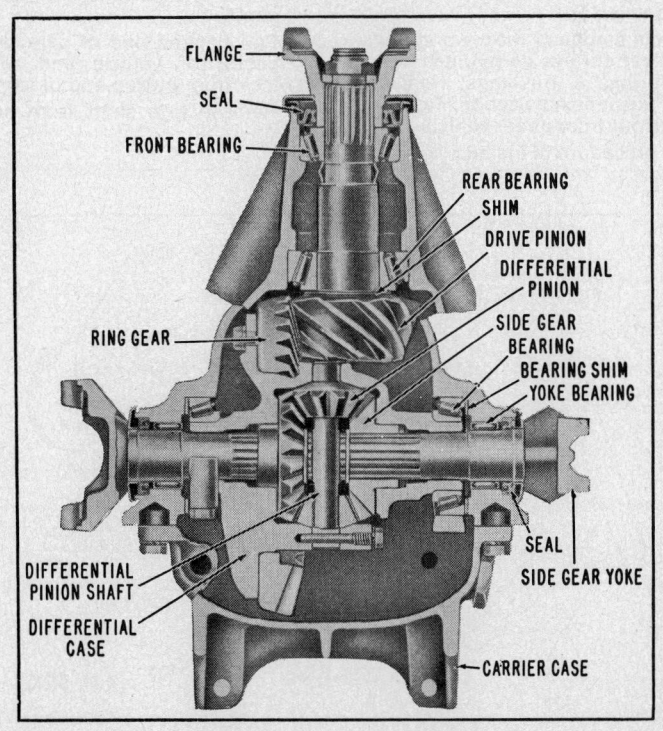

Fig. 2   Rear axle. 1974-79 Corvette

cast into an integral assembly. The drive pinion assembly is mounted in two opposed tapered roller bearings. The pinion bearings are preloaded by a spacer behind the front bearing. The pinion is positioned by a washer between the head of the pinion and the rear bearing.

The differential is supported in the carrier by two tapered roller side bearings. These bearings are preloaded by spacers located between the bearings and carrier housing. The differential assembly is positioned for proper ring gear and pinion backlash by varying these spacers. The differential case houses two side gears in mesh with two pinions mounted on a pinion shaft which is held in place by a lock pin. The side gears and pinions are backed by thrust washers.

Remove & Replace

Construction of the axle assembly is such that service operations may be performed with the housing installed in the vehicle or with the housing removed and installed in a holding fixture. The following procedure is necessary only when the housing requires replacement.

1. Raise and support vehicle, then support rear axle with a suitable jack.
2. Disconnect shock absorbers from lower mountings.
3. Remove propeller shaft.
4. Disconnect upper control arms from axle housing attachments, if equipped with coil springs.
5. Disconnect brake line from axle housing junction block and the parking brake cable.
6. Disconnect lower control arms from axle housing attachments, if equipped with coil springs.
7. On models equipped with coil springs, lower axle slowly until springs can be moved. Roll axle assembly out from under vehicle.
8. On models equipped with leaf springs, remove leaf springs as outlined under "Leaf Springs & Bushings, Replace" in Rear Suspension Section. Roll axle assembly out from under vehicle.
9. Reverse procedure to install.

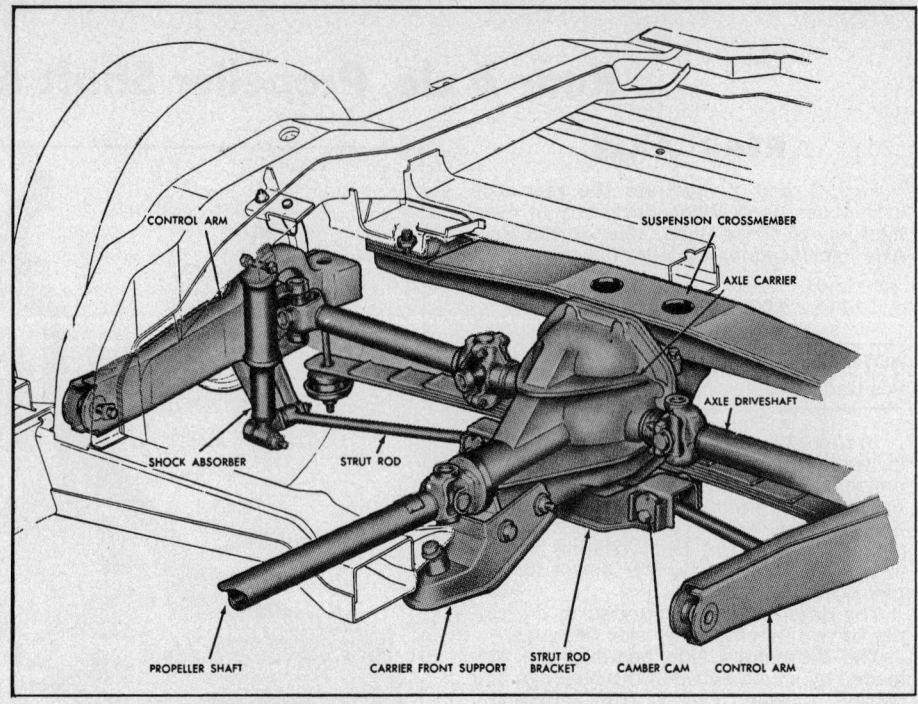

Fig. 3   Rear suspension. 1974-79 Corvette

AXLE SHAFT, REPLACE
1974-79 C, G, K, M, & P Type

1. Raise vehicle and remove wheel and brake drum.
2. Drain lube from carrier and remove cover.
3. Remove differential pinion shaft lock screw and remove differential pinion shaft.
4. Pull flanged end of axle shaft toward center of vehicle and remove "C" lock from button end of shaft.
5. Remove axle shaft from housing, be-

ing careful not to damage seal.
6. Reverse foregoing procedure to install the axle shaft.

1974-79 "B" & "O" Type

1. Raise vehicle and remove wheel and brake drum.
2. Remove bolts attaching axle shaft retainer plate to backing plate.
3. Using a slide hammer/puller, the axle shaft can now be removed.

NOTE: You may find the wheel bearing will come out in pieces as you remove the shaft. The inner race with bearing and one retainer plate will come out with the shaft. The outer race and inner retainer plate will remain in the axle housing. These

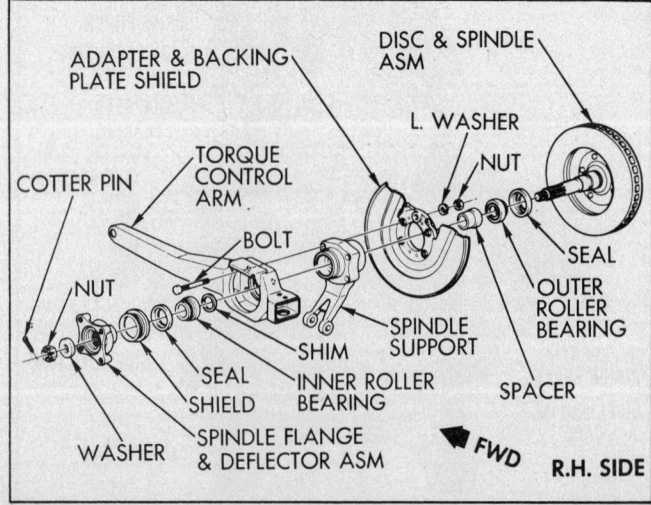

Fig. 4   Corvette rear wheel spindle

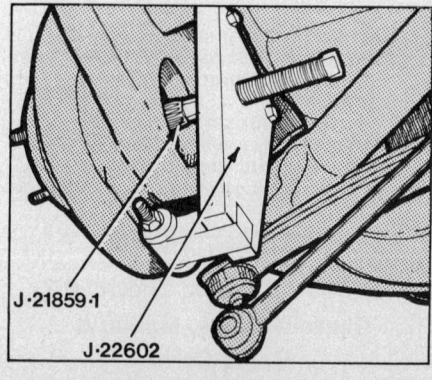

Fig. 4A   Corvette rear wheel spindle removal

pieces can easily be removed. Even though the bearing is not in one piece it is no indication that the bearing has failed.

Corvette 1974-79

1. Raise and support vehicle.
2. Disconnect inboard driveshaft trunnion from side gear yoke.
3. Bend bolt lock tabs downward.
4. Remove bolts securing shaft flange to spindle drive flange.
5. Scribe a mark on the camber adjusting cam and mounting bracket for alignment during assembly.
6. Loosen camber adjusting nut and rotate cam so the high point of the cam faces inboard. This pushes the control arm outboard providing spindle-drive-shaft clearance.
7. Remove driveshaft by withdrawing outboard end first.
8. Reverse procedure to install.

CORVETTE REAR SPINDLE

1. Referring to Fig. 4, raise vehicle and remove wheel and tire.
2. Apply parking brake to prevent spindle from turning and remove cotter pin and nut from spindle.
3. Release parking brake and remove drive spindle flange from splined end of spindle.
4. Remove brake caliper and disc.
5. Using the puller, Fig. 4A, remove spindle.

NOTE: When using puller tool J-22602, ensure puller plate is positioned vertically in the torque control arm before applying pressure to the puller screw.

6. When spindle is removed, the outer bearing will remain on the spindle. The inner bearing, tubular spacer, end play shim and both outer races will remain in the spindle support.

PROPELLER SHAFT
1974-79

These models use a one-piece propeller shaft.

BRAKE ADJUSTMENTS
1974-79 Self-Adjusting Brakes

These brakes, Figs. 5 and 5A have self-adjusting shoe mechanisms that assure correct lining-to-drum clearances at all times. The automatic adjusters operate only when the brakes are applied as the car is moving rearward or when the car comes to an uphill stop.

Although the brakes are self-adjusting, an initial adjustment is necessary after

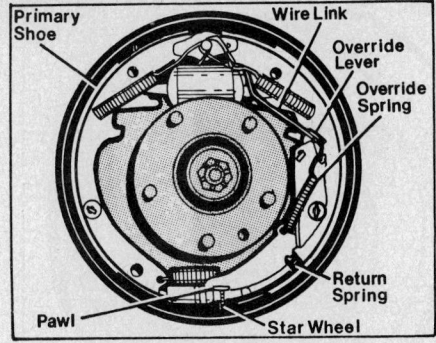

Fig. 5 Left front brake. 1974-75

the brake shoes have been relined or replaced, or when the length of the adjusting screw has been changed during some other service operation.

Frequent usage of an automatic transmission forward range to halt reverse vehicle motion may prevent to automatic adjusters from functioning, thereby inducing low pedal heights. Should low pedal heights be encountered, it is recommended that numerous forward and reverse stops be made until satisfactory pedal height is obtained.

NOTE

If a low pedal condition cannot be corrected by making numerous reverse stops (provided the hydraulic system is free of air) it indicates that the self-adjusting mechanism is not functioning. Therefore it will be necessary to remove the brake drum, clean, free up and lubricate the ad-

justing mechanism. Then adjust the brakes, being sure the parking brake is fully released.

Adjustment

A lanced "knock out" area, Fig. 6, is provided in the web of the brake drum for servicing purposes in the event retracting of the brake shoes is required in order to remove the drum.

1. With brake drum off, disengage the actuator from the star wheel and rotate the star wheel by spinning or turning with a screwdriver.
2. Using the brake drum as an adjustment fixture, turn the star wheel until the drum slides over the brake shoes with a slide drag.
3. Turn the star wheel 1¼ turns to retract the brake shoes. This will allow sufficient lining-to-drum clearance so final adjustment may be made.
4. Install drum and wheel.

NOTE: If lanced area in brake drum was knocked out, be sure all metal has been removed from brake compartment. Install new hole cover in drum to prevent contamination of brakes. Make certain that drums are installed in the same position as when removed with the drum locating tang in line with the locating hole in the wheel hub, Fig. 7.

5. Make final adjustment by driving and stopping in forward and reverse until satisfactory pedal height is obtained.

NOTE: The recommended method of ad-

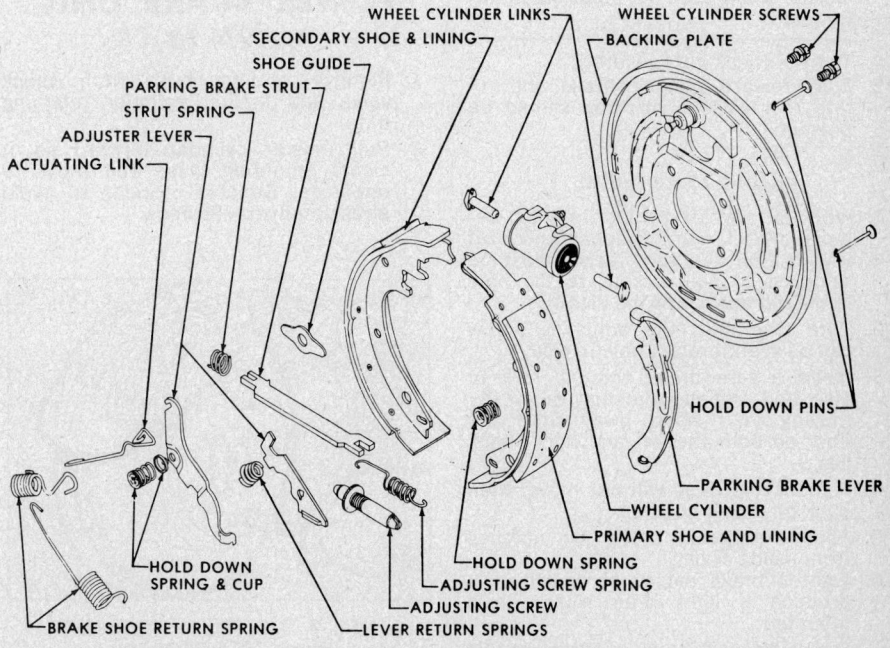

Fig. 5A Rear drum brake (Typical)

Fig. 6   Brake drum access hole

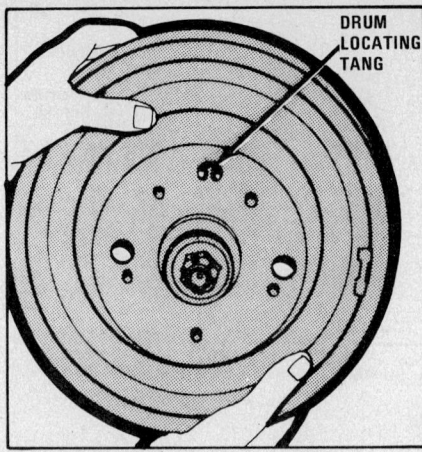

Fig. 7   Aligning drum tang with wheel hub. 1974-79

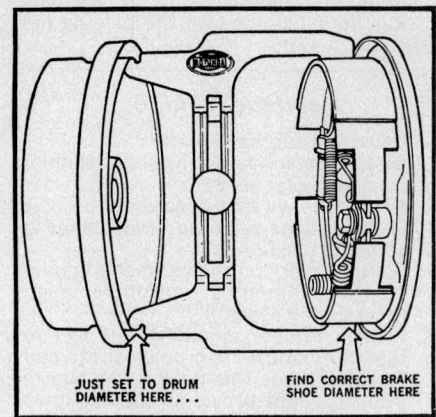

Fig. 8   Use of Drum-to-Brake Shoe Clearance Gauge (J-21177)

justing the brakes is by using the Drum-to-Brake Shoe Clearance Guage shown in Fig. 8 to check the diameter of the brake drum inner surface. Turn the tool to the opposite side and fit over the brake shoes by turning the star wheel until the gauge just slides over the linings. Rotate the gauge around the brake shoe lining surface to assure proper clearance.

PARKING BRAKE, ADJUST

1974-79 Except Corvette

1. Jack up both rear wheels.
2. Apply parking brake two notches from fully released position.
3. Loosen equalizer forward check nut and tighten rear nut until a light to moderate drag is felt when rear wheels are rotated rearward.

NOTE: The rear wheels should be locked when forward rotation is attempted.

4. Tighten check nuts securely.
5. Fully release parking brake and rotate rear wheels; no drag should be present.

1974-79 Corvette

1. With car on lift or jack stands, remove wheel. (On optional knock-off wheels, the adapter bracket must be removed to gain access to the hole in the hat section of the disc.)
2. Turn disc until the adjusting screw can be seen through hole in disc.
3. Insert a screwdriver through hole in disc and tighen adjusting screw by moving your hand away from the floor on both the left and right sides, Fig. 9.
4. Tighten until disc will not move, then back off 6 to 8 notches.
5. Apply emergency brake two notches from inside of car.
6. Tighten brake cables at equalizer to produce a light drag with wheels mounted.
7. Fully released parking brake handle

and rotate rear wheels. No drag should be evident with handle released.

MASTER CYLINDER, REPLACE

1974-78

1. Disconnect brake pipes from master cylinder. Plug lines and master cylinder ports to prevent entry of foreign material.
2. Disconnect brake pedal from master cylinder push rod, if equipped with manual brakes.
3. Remove master cylinder attaching nuts and the master cylinder.
4. Reverse procedure to install.

POWER BRAKE UNIT

1974-79

1. Remove vacuum hose from check valve and master cylinder retaining nuts.
2. Pull master cylinder forward so it clears mounting studs and move to one side. Support cylinder to avoid stress on hydraulic lines.

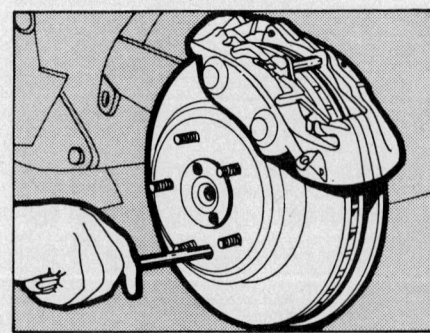

Fig. 9   Adjusting parking brake shoes. 1974-79 Corvette

3. Remove power unit to dash nuts. On 1974-77 Chevelle and Monte Carlo, remove brake line clip from power unit. On some Nova models, it may be necessary to apply road oil or tar remover to stud nuts to loosen sealer.
4. Remove brake pedal push rod retainer and disconnect push rod from pin.

NOTE: On 1974-77 Chevelle and Monte Carlo, push brake pedal to floor. This pushes power unit away from dash, providing clearance to remove push rod.

5. Remove power unit from vehicle.

1974-79 CORVETTE REAR WHEEL ALIGNMENT

Rear wheel camber and toe-out should be inspected and corrected if rear tires show unusual wear.

Camber, Adjust

Wheel camber is obtained by adjusting the eccentric cam and bolt assembly located at the inboard mounting of the strut rod (see Fig. 2). Place rear wheels on alignment machine and determine camber angle.

To adjust, loosen camber bolt nut and rotate cam and bolt assembly until the camber angle is within specifications listed in the front of this chapter.

Toe-Out, Adjust

Rear wheel toe-out is adjusted by inserting slotted shims of varying thickness inside the frame side member on both sides of the torque control arm pivot bushing. Shims are available in thicknesses of $1/64''$, $1/32''$, $1/8''$ and $1/4''$.

To adjust, loosen torque arm pivot bolts until shims are free enough to remove. Position torque arm assembly to obtain toe-out of $1/32''$ to $3/32''$ per wheel. Shim gap toward vehicle centerline between end of control arm bushing and frame side inner wall.

Rear Suspension

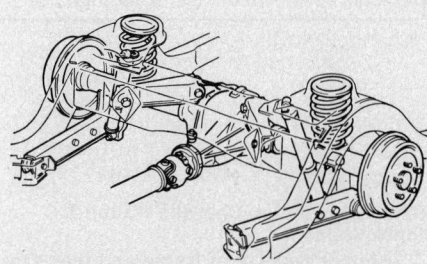

Fig. 1   Rear suspension. 1974-79 Chevrolet, Chevelle, Malibu & Monte Carlo (typical)

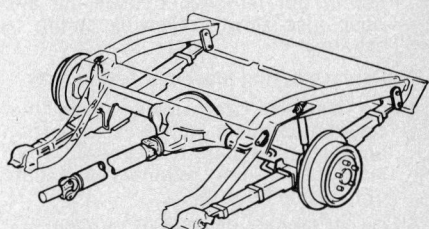

Fig. 2   Rear suspension. 1974-79 Camaro, Nova & 1974-76 125″ Wheelbase station wagon (typical)

SHOCK ABSORBER, REPLACE

1974-79 All

1. If equipped with Superlift shock absorbers, disconnect air lines from shock absorber fittings.
2. With rear axle properly supported, disconnect shock absorber from upper and lower mountings, Figs. 1, 2 and 3.
3. Reverse procedure to install.

COIL SPRINGS, REPLACE

1974-79 Chevrolet, Chevelle, Malibu & Monte Carlo

1. Support vehicle at frame and rear axle.
2. Disconnect shock absorbers at lower mountings.
3. Disconnect upper control arms from axle housing.
4. If necessary on 1974-77 models, disconnect brake line at junction block on axle housing. On 1978-79 models, remove brake hose support bolt and support without disconnecting the brake lines.
5. Lower axle until it reaches end of its travel and using a suitable tool, pry lower pigtail over retainer on axle bracket. Remove spring and insulator.
6. Reverse procedure to install. Springs must be installed with an insulator between upper seat and spring and positioned properly, Fig. 4.

LEAF SPRINGS & BUSHINGS, REPLACE

1974-76 125″ Wheelbase Wagon

1. Support vehicle at frame and rear axle, removing tension from spring.
2. Disconnect shock absorber from lower mounting.
3. Remove rear shackle upper bolt and spring front mount bolt.

4. Support spring, remove "U" bolts, spring plate and spring. Remove rear shackle from spring.
5. Replace shackle and spring eye bushings as necessary. To replace spring eye bushing, use a press and a suitably sized piece of pipe, tubing or similar tool as a ram, press out bushing. Press in new bushing with a suitable tool pressing on outer steel shell of bushing. Bushing is correctly installed when it protrudes equally on both sides of eye.
6. Reverse procedure to install.

1974-79 Camaro & Nova

1. Perform steps 1 and 2 as outlined in above procedure.
2. Loosen spring front mount bolt.
3. Remove spring front mounting bracket attaching screws, lower axle and remove bracket.
4. Disconnect parking brake cable from spring plate bracket.
5. Remove spring plate by removing axle bracket nuts on single leaf models and the "U" bolts on multi-leaf models.
6. Support spring, remove front mount bolt and disassemble rear shackle.
7. Replace rear shackle and spring eye bushings as necessary, Figs. 5 and 6.
8. Reverse procedure to install.

1974-79 Corvette

1. Support vehicle at frame and remove rear wheels.
2. Install a "C" clamp approximately 9 inches from end of spring.
3. Place a suitable jack under spring, Fig. 7, and place a wooden block between "C" clamp and jack pad.
4. Raise jack until load is off spring link, then remove cotter pin, link nut and spring cushion. Lower jack, removing tension from spring.
5. Repeat steps 2, 3 and 4 on opposite side of spring.
6. Remove bolts from spring center clamp plate, then remove clamp plate.
7. Remove spring from vehicle, Fig. 8.
8. Reverse procedure to install.

LEAF SPRING SERVICE

NOTE: The spring leaves are not serviced separately, however, the spring leaf in-

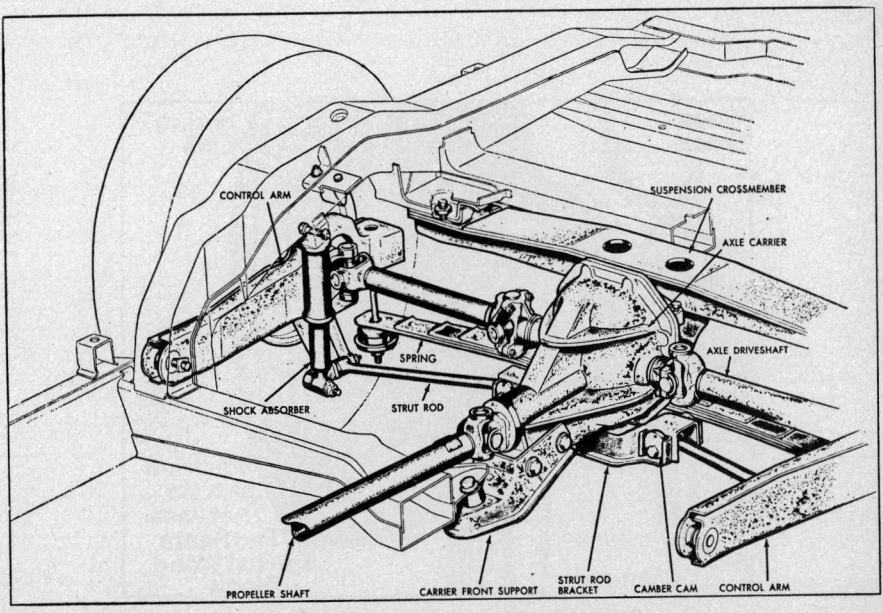

Fig. 3   Rear suspension. 1974-79 Corvette

serts may be replaced.

1. Clamp spring in a vise and remove spring clips.

2. File peened end of center bolt to permit nut removal, remove nut and open vise slowly, allowing spring to expand.

3. Replace spring leaves or leaf inserts.

4. On Corvette, to replace main leaf cushion retainers, chisel flared portion until retainer can be removed from leaf. Install new retainers and flare over with a hammer.

5. On all models use a drift to align center bolt holes, compress spring in vise and install new center bolt and nut. Peen end of bolt to retain nut.

6. Align springs and bend spring clips into position.

NOTE: Overtightening of spring clips will cause spring binding.

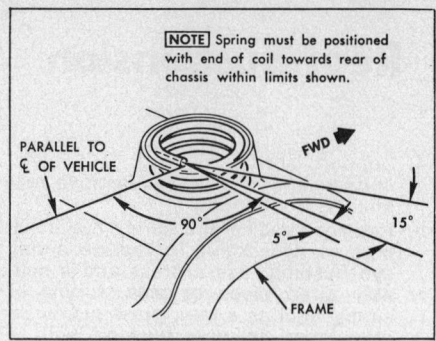

Fig. 4   Coil spring installation. 1974-79 all models

CONTROL ARMS & BUSHINGS, REPLACE

NOTE: On Chevelle, Monte Carlo & 119″

wheelbase station wagons, if both upper or lower control arms are to be removed at the same time, remove coil springs as outlined previously.

NOTE: When replacing bushings, use suitable tools as shown in Figs. 9 through 13.

Upper Control Arms

1974-79 Chevrolet, Chevelle Malibu & Monte Carlo

1. Support vehicle at frame and rear axle with a suitable jack.

2. Remove control arm front and rear mounting bolts.

3. Replace bushings as necessary.

4. Reverse procedure to install. Control arm bolts must be tightened with vehicle at curb height.

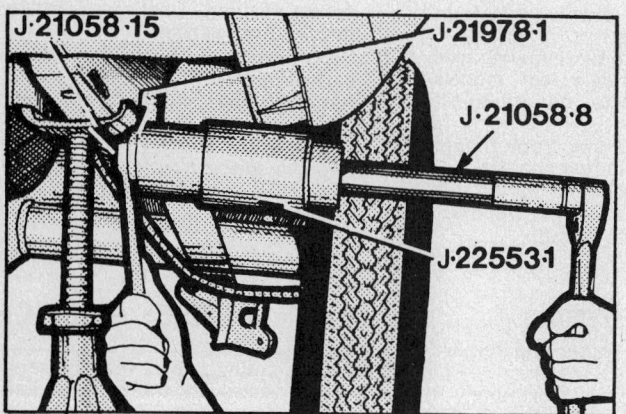

Fig. 5   Leaf spring bushings removal. 1974-79 Camaro. Nova & 1974-76 125″ Wheelbase station wagon

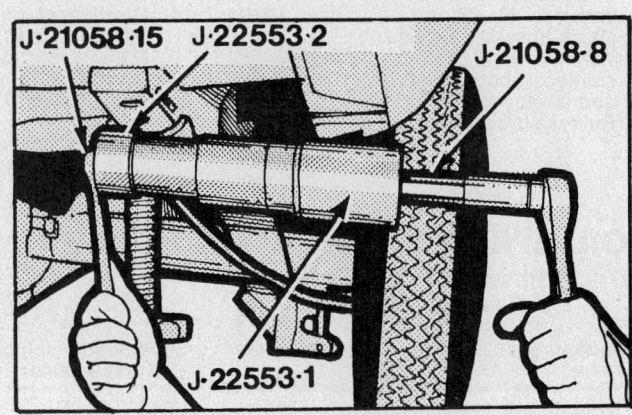

Fig. 6   Leaf spring bushing installation. 1974-79 Camaro, Nova & 1974-76 125″ Wheelbase station wagon

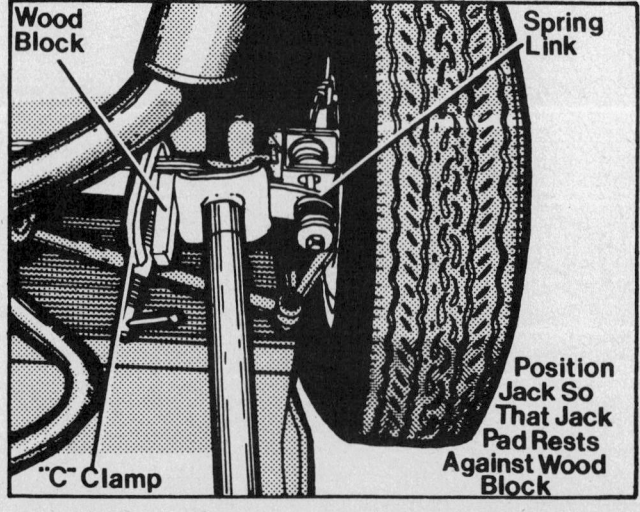

Fig. 7   Supporting leaf spring. 1974-79 Corvette

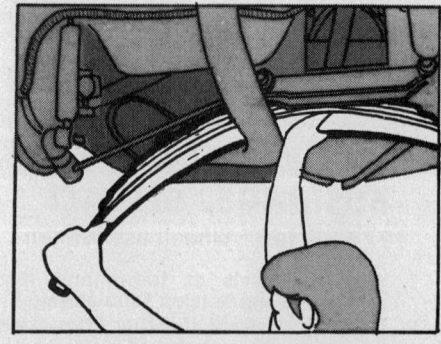

Fig. 8   Removing leaf spring. 1974-79 Corvette

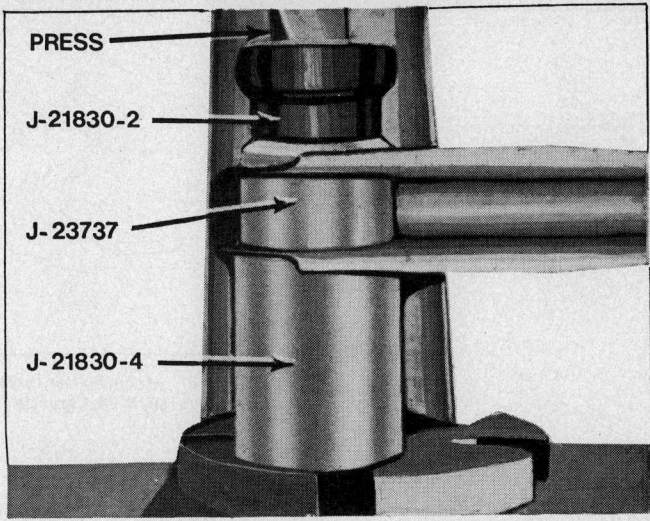

Fig. 9 Control arms front all & lower control arm
rear bushing removal. 1974-79 Chevrolet

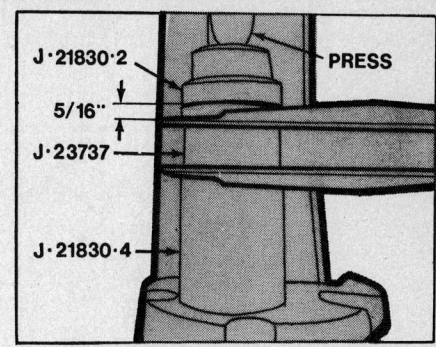

Fig. 10 Control arms front all & lower
control arm rear bushings installation.
1974-79 Chevrolet

Lower Control Arms

**1974-79 Chevrolet, Chevelle Malibu &
Monte Carlo**

Follow "Upper Control Arms" 1974-79
procedure for replacement of lower control
arms.

NOTE: When replacing bushings, use suitable tools as shown in Figs. 9, 10 and 11.

STABILIZER BAR, REPLACE

1974-79 Chevrolet, Chevelle, Malibu & Monte Carlo

1. Support vehicle at rear axle.
2. Remove bolts securing stabilizer bar to lower control arms, Fig. 14.
3. Reverse procedure to install. Use spacer shims, if needed, placed equally on each side of stabilizer bar. Tighten attaching bolts with vehicle at curb height.

1974-79 Camaro & Nova

1. Support vehicle at rear axle.
2. Disconnect stabilizer bar from spring plate brackets, Fig. 15.
3. Disconnect stabilizer bar from body brackets.
4. Reverse procedure to install. Tighten attaching bolts with vehicle at curb height.

1974-79 Corvette

1. Disconnect stabilizer bar from torque control arms and remove stabilizer bar frame brackets, Fig. 16.
2. Replace bushings as necessary, Fig. 16.
3. Reverse procedure to install.

STRUT ROD, REPLACE

1974-79 Corvette

1. Support vehicle at frame.

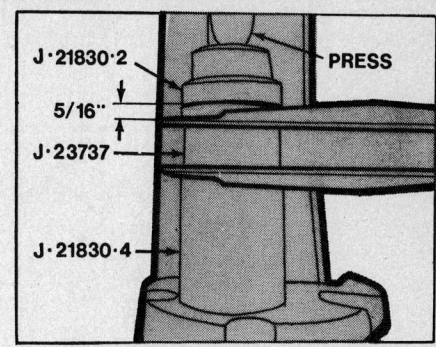

Fig. 11 Upper control arm front & all
lower control arm bushing. 1974-79
Chevelle, Malibu & Monte Carlo removal.
Also upper control arm rear bushing removal.
1974-79 Chevrolet

Fig. 12 Upper control arm rear bushing
removal. 1974-79 Chevelle & Monte Carlo

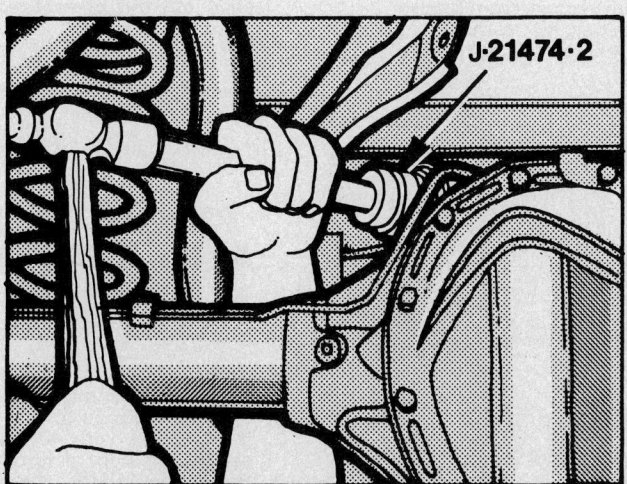

Fig. 13 Upper control arm rear bushing installation.
1974-79 Chevelle & Monte Carlo

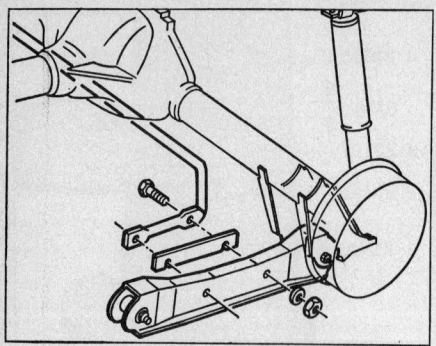

**Fig. 14   Stabilizer bar installation.
1974-79 Chevrolet, Chevelle, Malibu &
Monte Carlo (Typical)**

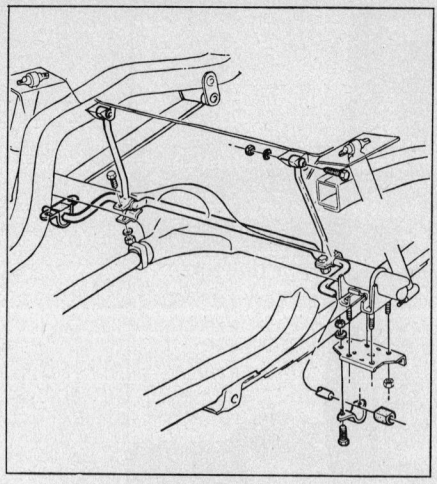

**Fig. 15   Stabilizer bar installation.
1974-79 Camaro & Nova (Typical)**

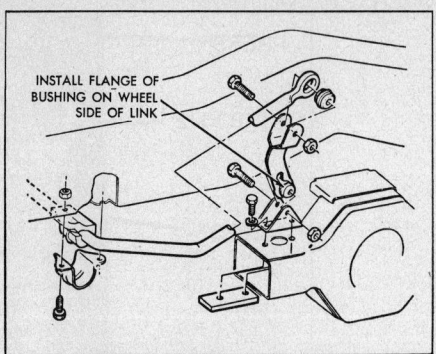

**Fig. 16   Stabilizer bar installation.
1974-79 Corvette**

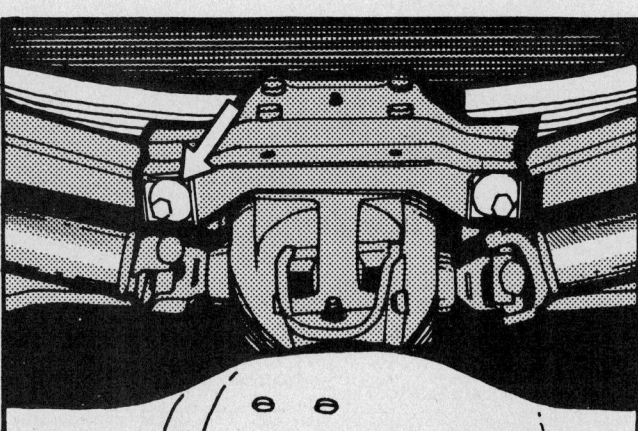

Fig. 17   Indexing camber cam & bracket. 1974-79 Corvette

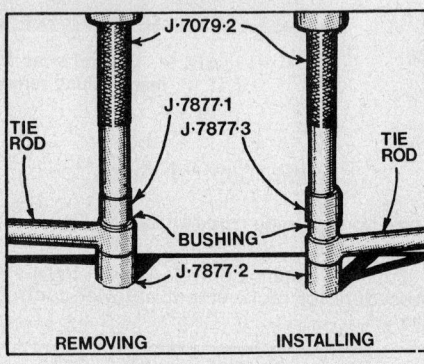

**Fig. 18   Strut rod bushing. 1974-79
Corvette replacement**

2. Disconnect shock frame from lower mounting.
3. Remove cotter pin and nut from strut rod shaft. Pull shaft toward front of vehicle and remove from bracket.
4. Mark position of camber adjusting cam to ensure proper installation,

Fig. 17 and loosen camber bolt nut.
5. Remove bolts securing strut rod bracket to carrier.
6. Remove camber bolt and nut, pull strut rod out of bracket and remove bushing caps.
7. Replace bushings as necessary, Fig. 18.
8. Reverse procedure to install.

spindle flange by removing attaching bolts.

NOTE: It may be necessary to force torque arm outboard providing clearance to lower axle drive shaft.

6. Disconnect brake line from caliper and from torque arm. Disconnect parking brake cable.
7. Remove torque arm forward mounting bolt and toe-in shims, Fig. 19, and pull torque arm out of frame attachment.
8. Replace bushings if necessary as described under "Torque Control Arm Bushing Service."
9. Reverse procedure to install.

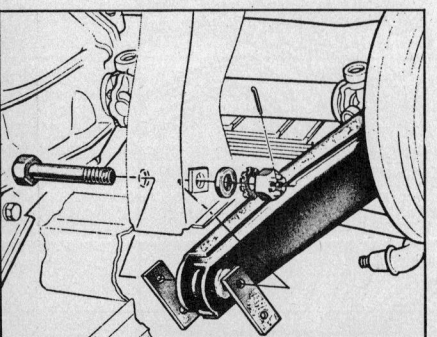

Fig. 19   Torque control arm insallaion 1974-79 Corvette

TORQUE CONTROL ARMS & BUSHINGS, REPLACE
1974-79 Corvette

1. Perform steps 1 thru 4 as outlined under "Leaf Spring Replace" 1973-78 Corvette procedure.
2. If equipped with a stabilizer shaft, disconnect shaft at torque arms.
3. Disconnect shock absorber at lower mounting.
4. Disconnect and lower strut rod shaft.
5. Disconnect axle drive shaft from

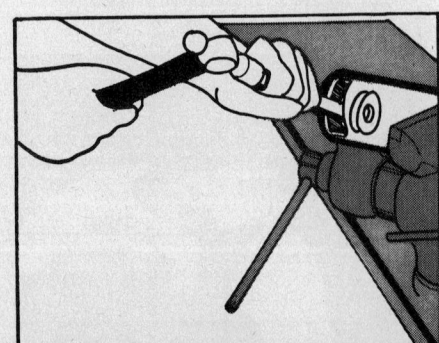

Fig. 20   Torque control arm bushing removal. 1974-79 Corvette

Fig. 21 Torque control arm bushing installation. 1974-79 Corvette

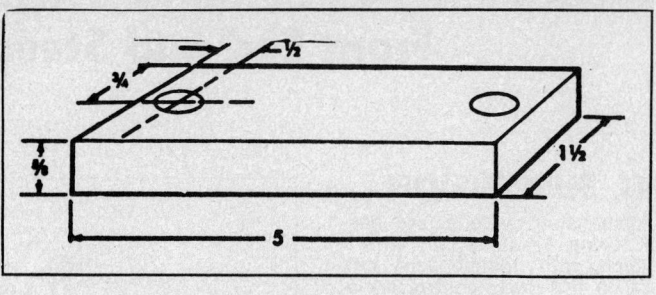

Fig. 22 Flaring tool back-up plate dimension

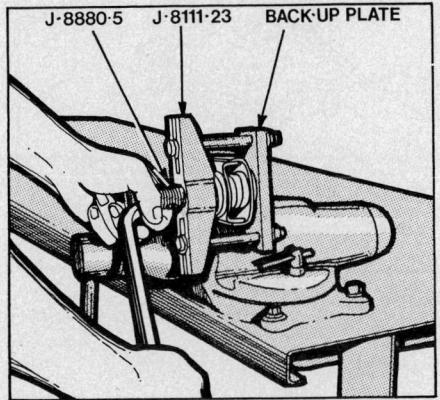

Fig. 23 Flaring torque control arm bushing retainer 1974-79 Corvette

Torque Control Arm Bushing Service

1. Using an 11/16 inch twist drill, drill out flared end of bushing retainer, remove retainer plate and retainer from bushing.
2. Spread bushing with a chisel, Fig. 20, and tap bushing from arm.

NOTE: If bushing is rusted in torque arm, torque arm may spread during bushing removal. Install a "C" clamp torque arm, preventing torque arm spreading.

3. Oil steel portion of new bushing and press bushing into arm, Fig. 21.
4. Place retainer plate over flared portion of bushing retainer and insert retainer into bushing.
5. Make a flaring tool back-up plate, Fig. 22, with ½ inch bolt holes.
6. Place back-up plate on flared end of bushing retainer and assemble tool to plate, Fig. 23, with ½ x 5 inch bolts. Center threaded hole in tool # J-8111-23 over unflared end of bushing retainer. Also center chamfered retainer plate over retainer tube.
7. Lubricate end of tool # J-8880-5 and thread screw into tool, flaring retainer.

CROSSMEMBER & ISOLATION MOUNT, REPLACE

1974-79 Corvette

1. Remove leaf spring as outlined under "Leaf Spring Replace" 1974-78 Corvette procedure.
2. Remove differential carrier and cover as outlined in "Rear Axle, Propeller Shaft & Brakes" section 1974-78 Corvette procedure.

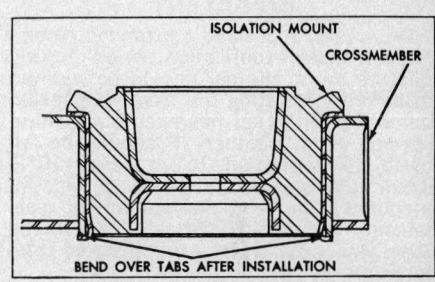

Fig. 24 Crossmember isolation mount replacement. 1974-79 Corvette

3. Support crossmember and remove bolts securing isolation mounts to frame and lower the crossmember.
4. To replace isolation mount, straighten isolation mount tabs and using a suitable ram, press on outer steel shell or inner steel insert, removing mount from crossmember. Install new mount into position, compress outer sleeve, press mount into crossmember and bend over locking tabs, Fig. 24.
5. Reverse procedure to install crossmember.

Front End and Steering Section

FRONT SUSPENSION

All front suspension systems are basically similar, being of the S.L.A. (short-long arm) type with independent coil springs riding on the lower control arms. Ball joints connect the upper and lower control arms to the steering knuckles, Fig. 1.

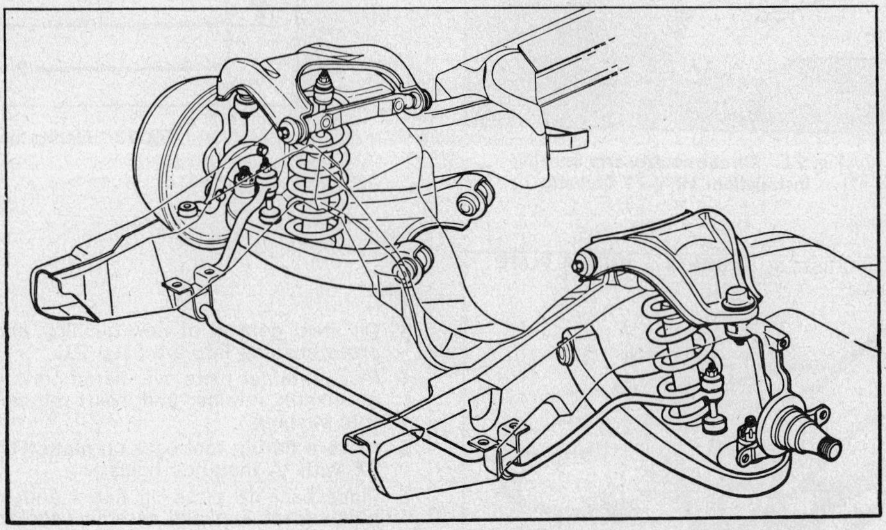

LUBRICATION

IMPORTANT

On models that have a extended recommended chassis lubrication period of 6000 miles or more, the car should be warmed up before lubricating the front suspension ball joints. If the car has been outdoors in extreme cold weather it should be allowed to warm up to at least 10°F. above zero before this job is started. Inadequate ball joint lubrication or seal damage can result should the job be done while the parts are at lower temperatures.

Fig. 1 Front suspension. (Typical)

WHEEL ALIGNMENT

NOTE: Before adjusting caster and camber angles after complaint of excessive tire wear or poor handling, the front bumper should be raised and quickly released to allow car to return to its normal height.

Caster and camber adjustments are made by means of shims between the upper control arm inner support shaft and the support bracket attached to the frame. Shims may be added, subtracted or transferred to change the readings as follows:

Caster, Adjust

Transfer shims from front to rear or rear to front. The transfer of one shim to the front bolt from the rear bolt will decrease positive caster. On shim ($1/32$") transferred from the rear bolt to the front bolt will change caster about $1/2$ degree.

Camber, Adjust

Change shims at both the front and rear of the shaft. Adding an equal number of shims at both front and rear of the support shaft will decrease positive camber. One shim ($1/32$") at each location will move camber approximately 1/5 degree on Camaro, Chevelle and Nova, on Chevrolet and Corvette the change will be about 1/6 degree.

TOE-IN, ADJUST

Toe-in can be adjusted by loosening

the clamp bolts at each end of each tie rod and turning each tie rod to increase or decrease its length as necessary until proper toe-in is secured and the steering gear is on the high point for straight-ahead driving.

WHEEL BEARINGS, ADJUST

1974-79

1. While rotating wheel forward, torque spindle nut to 12 ft. lbs.
2. Back off nut until "just loose" then hand tighten nut and back it off again until either hole in spindle lines up with hole in nut.

NOTE: Do not back off nut more than $1/2$ flat.

3. Install new cotter pin. With wheel bearing properly adjusted, there will be .001-.005 inch end play.

WHEEL BEARINGS, REPLACE

Disc Brakes

1. Raise car and remove front wheels.
2. Remove bolts holding brake caliper to its mounting and insert a fabricated block ($1^1/_{16}$ x $1^1/_{16}$ x 2 inches in length) between the brake pads as the caliper is being removed. Once

removed, the caliper can be wired or secured in some manner away from the disc.

3. Remove spindle nut and hub and disc assembly. Grease retainer and inner wheel bearing can now be removed.

CHECKING BALL JOINTS FOR WEAR

1974-79 All

Upper Ball Joint, 1976-79

1. Raise front of vehicle with jacks placed between the coil spring pocket and ball joint of lower control arm.
2. Shake top of wheel in and out. Observe steering knuckle for any movement relative to the control arm.
3. Replace upper ball joint if looseness is indicated.

Upper Ball Joint, 1974-75

The upper ball joint is checked for wear by checking the torque required to rotate the ball stud in the assembly. To make this type of check it will be necessary to remove the stud from the steering knuckle.

Install a nut on the ball stud and measure the torque required to turn the stud in the assembly with a torque wrench. Specified torque for a new ball joint is 3 to 10 ft-lbs. If torque readings are excessively high or low, replace the ball joint. If excessive wear is indicated in the upper ball joint, both upper and

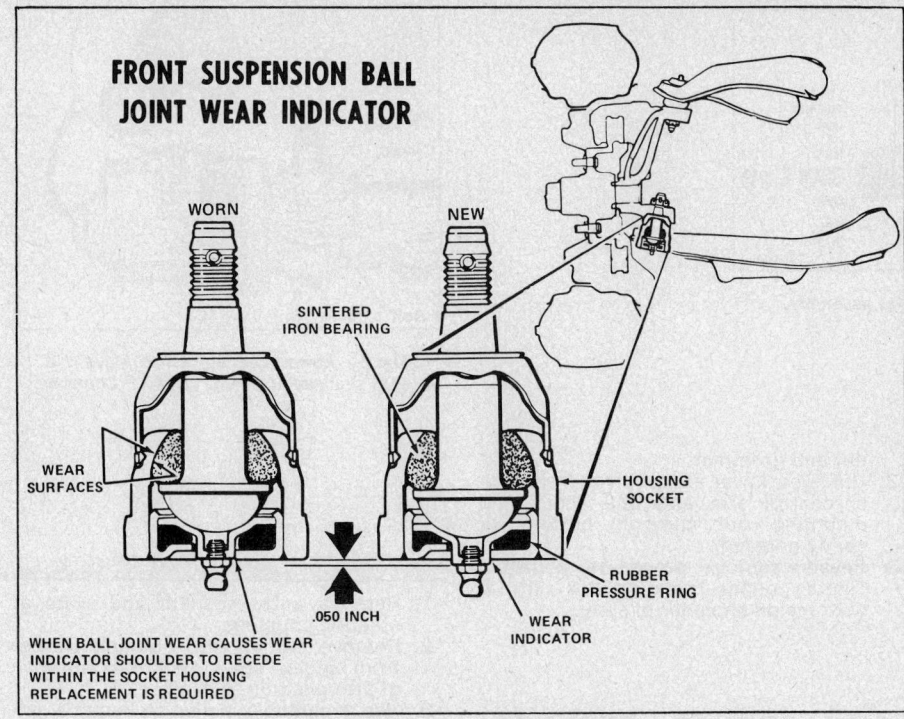

Fig. 2 Lower ball joint wear indicator.
1974 Exc. Corvette, Nova & 1975-78 Exc. Corvette

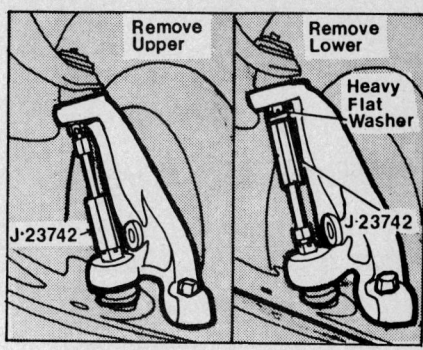

Fig. 3 Removing upper & lower ball joint stud from knuckle.

lower ball joints should be replaced.

Lower Ball Joint

Raise car and support lower control arm so spring is compressed in the same manner as if the wheels were on the ground and check axial (up and down) play at ball joint. If play exceeds $1/16''$, replace the joint.

Another indication of lower ball joint excessive wear is when difficulty is experienced when lubricating the joint. If the liner has worn to the point where the lubrication grooves in the liner have been worn away, then abnormal pressure is required to force lubricant through the joint. Should this condition be evident, replace both lower ball joints.

NOTE: 1974 except Corvette and Nova and 1975-79 models except Corvette have a wear indicator built into the lower ball joint, Fig. 2.

UPPER BALL JOINT, REPLACE

1974-79 All

1. Support weight of vehicle at outer end of lower control arm.
2. Remove wheel assembly.
3. Remove nut from upper ball joint stud.
4. Remove stud from knuckle, Fig. 3.
5. Cut off ball rivets with a chisel.
6. Enlarge ball stud attaching holes in control arm (if necessary) to accept the bolts included in the ball joint replacement kit.
7. Install and tighten new ball joint.
8. Reassemble ball joint to steering knuckle.

NOTE: On 1978-79 Malibu and Monte Carlo, the cotter pin must be installed from the rear, Fig. 3A.

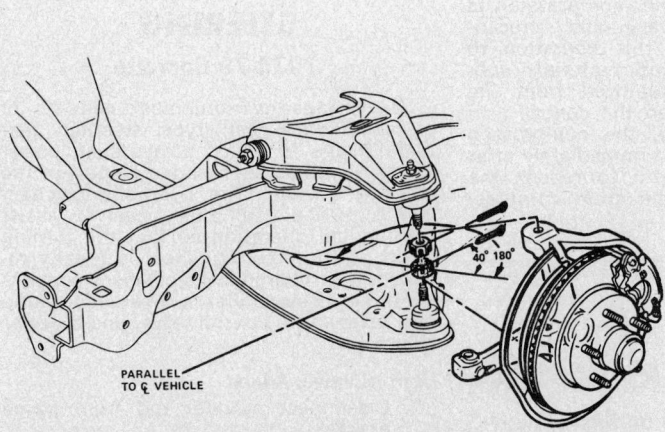

Fig. 3A Ball joint cotter pin installation.
1978-79 Malibu & Monte Carlo

Fig. 4 Supporting coil spring. 1974-79 All

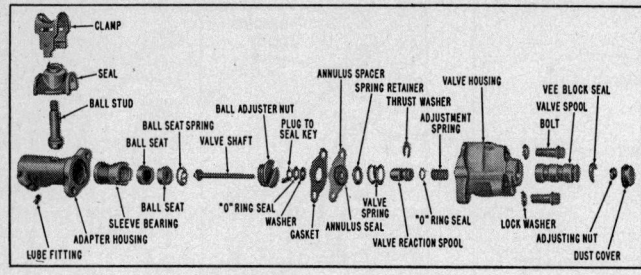

Fig. 5   Power steering control valve and adapter assembly. 1974-79 Corvette

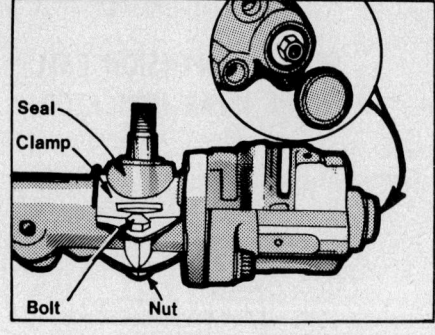

Fig. 6   Power steering control valve ball stud seal replacement. 1974-79 Corvette

LOWER BALL JOINT, REPLACE

1974-79 Exc. 1974-76 Corvette

1. Support vehicle at frame and lower control arm with suitable jacks.
2. Remove wheel and, if equipped with disc brakes, caliper assembly.
3. Loosen ball joint stud nut not more than one turn and, using a suitable tool, Fig. 3, press ball stud free of steering knuckle, then remove stud nut.
4. Lower the jack from under the control arm.
5. With a suitable tool, replace lower ball joint.
6. Reverse procedure to assemble.

NOTE: On 1978-79 Malibu and Monte Carlo, the cotter pin must be installed from the rear, Fig. 3A.

1974-76 Corvette

1. Support lower control arm at outer end on floor jack with hoist or jack pad clear of lower ball stud nut and seal.
2. If equipped with disc brakes, remove caliper assembly.
3. Remove upper and lower ball stud nuts, free ball studs from steering knuckle and wire knuckle and brake drum or disc assembly out of the way.
4. Being careful not to enlarge holes in control arm, cut off rivets.
5. Install new joint against underside of control arm and retain in place with special bolts supplied with replacement ball joint kit. Use only the alloy bolts supplied for this operation. The special thick headed bolt must be installed in the forward side of the control arm.
6. Tighten bolts and nut on ball stud and lubricate joint.

SHOCK ABSORBER, REPLACE

1974-79 All

1. Hold shock upper stem from turning with a suitable wrench and remove nut and grommet.
2. Unfasten lower shock pivot from lower control arm and pull shock and mounting out through bottom of spring housing.
3. Reverse removal procedure to install. Tighten upper retaining nut until it bottoms on shoulder of stem.

COIL SPRING, REPLACE

1974-79 All

1. Disconnect shock absorber from lower mounting, push shock absorber through hole in lower control arm and compress into spring.
2. Support vehicle by frame so control arms hang free.
3. Install a safety chain through spring and lower control arm.
4. Install tool J-23028 onto a suitable jack and position jack so control arm is supported by bushings seated in grooves of tool, Fig. 4.
5. Raise jack to relieve tension on control arm bolts and remove bolts.
6. Lower jack until tension is removed from spring, remove chain and spring from vehicle.

CAUTION

The spring force under compression is very great. Exercise every safety precaution when performing this operation to see that individuals and materials subject to damage are removed from the path of the spring when the control arm is being lowered. Also, the compressed spring should be relaxed immediately after lowering the control arm to reduce the time of exposure to the great compressive force.

STEERING GEAR, REPLACE

1974-78 All Models

NOTE: On models where shield is installed, remove shield from coupling.

1. Remove nuts, washers and bolts at steering coupling.
2. Remove pitman arm nut and washer from sector shaft and mark relation of arm position to shaft.
3. Use a suitable puller to remove pitman arm.
4. Unfasten gear from frame and remove assembly.
5. Reverse procedure to install.

INTEGRAL POWER STEERING

1974-79 Exc. Corvette

To remove gear assembly, disconnect pressure and return hoses from gear housing and cap both hoses and steering gear outlets to prevent foreign material from entering system, then follow procedure as outlined under *Steering Gear, Replace.*

LINKAGE TYPE POWER STEERING

1974-79 Corvette

Power steering equipment consists of a recirculating ball type steering gear and linkage to which a hydraulic power mechanism has been added as part of the steering linkage. The hydraulic mechanism furnishes additional power to *assist* the manual operation so that the turning effort at the steering wheel is greatly reduced. The hydraulic mechanism consists of three basic units: a hydraulic pump and reservoir, a control valve, and a power cylinder.

Control Valve, Adjust
1. Disconnect cylinder rod from frame bracket.
2. With car on a hoist, start the engine. One of the following two con-

ditions will exist:

a. If piston rod remains retracted, turn the adjusting nut clockwise until the rod begins to move out. Then turn the nut counterclockwise until the rod just begins to move in. Now turn the nut clockwise to exactly one half the rotation needed to change the direction of shaft movement.

b. If the rod extends upon starting the pump, move the nut counterclockwise until the rod begins to retract, then clockwise until the rod begins to move out again. Now turn the rod to exactly one half the rotation needed to change the direction of shaft movement.

Do not turn the nut back and forth more than is absolutely necessary to balance the valve.

---

3. Restart engine. Front wheels should not turn from center if valve has been properly balanced.

Power Cylinder Repairs

Removal

1. Disconnect two hydraulic lines at power cylinder.
2. Unfasten power cylinder rod from brace at frame.
3. Unfasten power cylinder from relay rod bracket.
4. Remove power cylinder from car.

Inspection

1. Inspect seals for leaks around cylinder rod and if leaks are present, replace seals as follows:
2. Use a hook tool to remove retaining ring. Remove wiper ring, back-up washer, back-up ring and seal. *Piston rod seal should not be removed unless there are signs of leakage along the piston shaft at shaft seal.*
3. Examine brass fitting hose connection seats for cracks or damage and replace if necessary.
4. For service other than seat or seal replacement, replace the power cylinder.

Installation

1. Install power cylinder on car by reversing removal procedure.
2. Reconnect two hoses, fill system with fluid and bleed system as outlined below.

Filling & Bleeding System

1. Fill reservoir to proper level with Automatic Transmission Fluid and let fluid remain undisturbed for about two minutes.
2. Raise front wheels off floor.
3. Run engine at idle for two minutes.
4. Increase engine speed to about 1500 rpm.
5. Turn wheels from one extreme to the other, lightly contacting stops.

6. Lower wheels to floor and turn wheels right and left.
7. Recheck for leaks.
8. Check oil level and refill as required. Pump pressure should be 870 lbs.

Control Valve Repairs

Removal, Fig. 5

1. Loosen relay rod-to-control valve clamp.
2. Disconnect hose connections at control valve.
3. Disconnect control valve from pitman arm.
4. Unscrew control valve from relay rod.
5. Remove control valve from car.

Ball Stud Seal, Replace

In servicing the control valve, refer to Fig. 5. To replace the ball stud seal, refer to Fig. 6 and proceed as follows:

1. Remove pitman arm with a suitable puller.
2. Remove clamp by removing nut, bolt and spacer. If crimped type clamp is used, straighten clamp end and pull clamp and seal off end of stud.
3. Install new seal and clamp over stud so lips on seal mate with clamp. (A nut and bolt attachment type clamp replaces the crimped type for service, Fig. 6).
4. Center the ball stud, seal and clamp in opening in adapter housing, then install spacer, bolt and nut.

CHEVROLET CHEVETTE

CAUTION

This vehicle contains many parts dimensioned in the metric system. Most fasteners are metric and many are very close in dimension to familiar customary measurements in the inch system. However, it is important to note that, during any vehicle maintenance procedures, replacement fasteners must have the same measurements as those removed, whether metric or customary. Mismatched or incorrect fastners can result in vehicle damage or malfunction or possible personal injury. Therefore, fasteners removed from the vehicle should be saved for re-use or care should be taken to select a replacement that matches the original.

INDEX OF SERVICE OPERATIONS

SERIAL NUMBER LOCATION

On top of instrument panel, left front.

ENGINE NUMBER LOCATION

On pad at right side of cylinder block, below No. 1 spark plug.

ENGINE IDENTIFICATION CODE

Engines are identified in the following table by the code letter or letters immediately following the engine serial number.

Year	Engine	Code	Year	Engine	Code	Year	Engine	Code
1976	4-85	CDD, CDS, CDT		4-97	CNR, CNS, CNT		4-97	ZTT, ZTU, ZTW
	4-85	CDU, CVA, CVB		4-97	CNU		4-97	ZTX
	4-97	CNA, CNB, CYC		4-97	CYC, CYD, CYF	1979	4-97	DBA, DBB, DBC
	4-97	CYD, CYJ, CYK		4-97	CYH, CYY, CYZ		4-97	DBD, DBF, DBH
	4-97	CYW, CYX	1978	4-97	CYA, CYB, CYJ		4-97	DBJ, DBK, DBL
1977	4-85	CDS, CVA, CVB		4-97	CYK, CYL, CYM		4-97	DBM, DBR, DBS
	4-97	CNA, CNB, CNC		4-97	CYR, CYS, CYT		4-97	DBT, DBU, DBW
	4-97	CND, CNF, CNH		4-97	CYU, CYW, CYX		4-97	DBX, DBY, DBZ
							4-97	DSA, DSB

GRILLE IDENTIFICATION

1976-77

1978

1979

GENERAL ENGINE SPECIFICATIONS

Year	Engine	Carburetor	Bore and Stroke	Piston Displacement, Cubic Inches	Compression Ratio	Maximum Brake H.P. @ R.P.M.	Maximum Torque Lbs. Ft. @ R.P.M.	Normal Oil Pressure Pounds
1976-77	52 Horsepower① .... 4-85 1400 c.c.	1 Barrel —	3.228 x 2.606 82.0 x 66.2 mm.	85 1.4 ltr.	8.5 —	52 @ 5300 —	67 @ 3400 97 Joules @ 3400	36-46 —
	60 Horsepower① .... 4-97 1600 c.c.	1 Barrel —	3.228 x 2.980 82.0 x 75.7 mm.	97.6 1.6 ltr.	8.5 —	60 @ 5300 —	77 @ 3200 104 Joules @ 3200	36-46 —
1978	63 Horsepower① .... 4-97 1600 c.c.	1 Barrel —	3.228 x 2.980 82.0 x 75.7 mm.	97.6 1.6 ltr.	8.5 —	63 @ 4800 —	82 @ 3200 —	34-42 —
	68 Horsepower① .... 4-97② 1600 c.c.	1 Barrel —	3.228 x 2.980 8.20 x 75.7 mm.	97.6 1.6 ltr.	8.5 —	68 @ 5000 —	84 @ 3200 —	34-42 —
1979	Horsepower① .... 4-97 1600 c.c.	2 Barrel —	3.228 x 2.980 82.0 x 75.7 mm.	97.6 1.6 ltr.	— —	— —	— —	55 —
	Horsepower① .... 4-97② 1600 c.c.	2 Barrel —	3.228 x 2.980 82.0 x 75.7 mm.	97.6 1.6 ltr.	— —	— —	— —	55 —

①—Ratings are net—as installed in vehicle.　②—High output engine.

TUNE UP SPECIFICATIONS

The following specifications are published from the latest information available. This data should be used only in the absence of a decal affixed in the engine compartment.

★When using a timing light, disconnect vacuum hose or tube at distributor and plug opening in hose or tube so idle speed will not be affected.

●When checking compression, lowest cylinder must be within 80 percent of highest.

▲Before removing wires from distributor cap, determine location of the No. 1 wire in cap, as distributor position may have been altered from that shown at the end of this chart.

Year	Spark Plug		Distributor		Ignition Timing ★			Carb. Adjustments					
	Type	Gap Inch	Point Gap Inch	Dwell Angle Deg.	Firing Order Fig. ▲	Timing BTDC ①	Mark Fig.	Hot Idle Speed		Air Fuel Ratio		Idle "CO" %	
								Std. Trans.	Auto. Trans. ②	Std. Trans.	Auto. Trans.	Std. Trans.	Auto. Trans.
1976													
4-85	R43TS	.035 (.889 mm.)	—	—	A	10°	B	④	⑤	—	—	—	—
4-97.6	R43TS	.035 (.889 mm.)	—	—	A	③	B	④	⑤	—	—	—	—
1977													
4-85	R43TS	.035 (.889 mm.)	—	—	A	12°	B	800	800D	—	—	—	—
4-97.6	R43TS	.035 (.889 mm.)	—	—	A	8°⑦	B	800	⑧	—	—	—	—
1978													
4-97.6	R43TS	.035 (.889 mm.)	—	—	A	8°⑦	B	800	⑧	—	—	—	—
1979													
4-97.6		.035 (.889 mm.)	—	—	A		B			—	—	—	—

①—BTDC—Before top dead center.
②—D-Drive.
③—Man. trans., 8° BTDC; auto. trans., 10° BTDC.
④—All with solenoid energized—exc. Calif., 800 RPM; Calif., 1000 RPM. With solenoid de-energized—600 RPM.
⑤—All with solenoid energized—except Calif.: less A/C 800D RPM, with A/C 950D RPM; Calif.: 850D RPM. With solenoid de-energized—except Calif.: less A/C 700D RPM, with A/C 800D RPM; Calif.: 600D RPM.

⑥—All with solenoid energized—except Calif.: less A/C 800D RPM, with A/C 950D RPM; Calif.: less A/C 850D RPM, with A/C 950D RPM. With solenoid de-energized—except Calif.: less A/C 700D RPM, with A/C 800D RPM; Calif.: less A/C 600D RPM, with A/C 850D RPM.
⑦—At 800 RPM.
⑧—With A/C, 950D RPM; less A/C, 800D. RPM

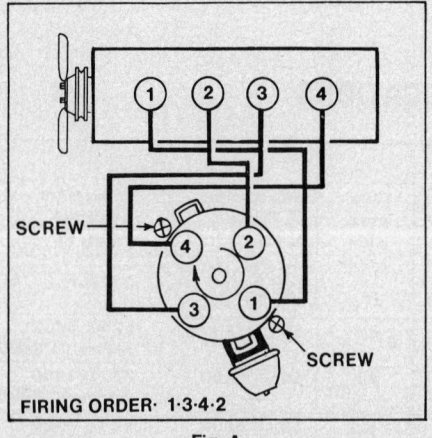

FIRING ORDER· 1·3·4·2

Fig. A

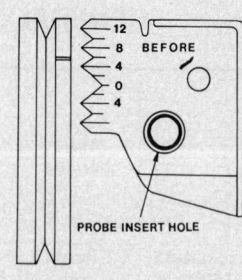

Fig. B

DISTRIBUTOR SPECIFICATIONS

★Note: If unit is checked on vehicle, double the RPM and degrees to get crankshaft figures.

Distributor Part No.①	Advance Starts	Intermediate Advance			Full Advance	Inches of Vacuum to Start Plunger	Max. Adv. Dist. Deg. @ Vacuum
1976							
1110654	0 @ 600	4 @ 1000	—	—	10 @ 2400	4② (14 kPa③)	7 @ 8② (27 kPa③)
1110655	0 @ 600	4 @ 1000	—	—	10 @ 2400	5② (17 kPa③)	6 @ 12② (41 kPa③)
1110657	0 @ 600	4 @ 1000	—	—	10 @ 2400	5② (17 kPa③)	12 @ 12② (41 kPa③)
1110658	0 @ 600	4 @ 1000	—	—	10 @ 2400	5② (17 kPa③)	13 @ 14.5② (49 kPa③)
1110659	0 @ 750	1 @ 800	—	—	8 @ 2400	4② (14 kPa③)	13 @ 12② (41 kPa③)
1977							
1110687	0 @ 600	4 @ 1200	—	—	12 @ 2400	4② (14 kPa③)	13 @ 12② (41 kPa③)
1110693	0 @ 600	4 @ 1200	—	—	12 @ 2400	4② (14 kPa③)	7 @ 8② (27 kPa③)
1110702	0 @ 600	4 @ 1200	—	—	12 @ 2400	4② (14 kPa③)	15 @ 12② (41 kPa③)
1110703	0 @ 600	4 @ 1200	—	—	12 @ 2850	4② (14 kPa③)	15 @ 12② (41 kPa③)
1978							
1110705	0 @ 600	4 @ 1000	—	—	10 @ 2400	4② (14 kPa③)	15 @ 12② (41 kPa③)
1110707	0 @ 600	4 @ 1000	—	—	10 @ 2400	4② (14 kPa③)	7 @ 8② (27 kPa③)
1110712	0 @ 600	4 @ 1000	—	—	10 @ 2400	4② (14 kPa③)	13 @ 12② (41 kPa③)
1110713④	0 @ 600	4 @ 1000	—	—	11 @ 2625	4② (14 kPa③)	15 @ 12② (41 kPa③)
1979							
1110740	0 @ 760	1½ @ 1100	—	—	8 @ 1625		
1110741							
1110742							
1110743							
1110744							
1110759							

①—Stamped on distributor housing. ②—Inches Hg. ③—kPa—kilopascals. ④—High output engine.

PISTONS, PINS, RINGS, CRANKSHAFT & BEARINGS

Year	Model	Piston Clearance Top of Skirt	Ring End Gap① Comp.	Oil	Wrist-pin Diameter	Rod Bearings Shaft Diameter	Bearing Clearance	Main Bearings Shaft Diameter	Bearing Clearance	Thrust on Bear. No.	Shaft End Play
1976	All	.0008–.0016 .020–.040 mm	.009 .229 mm	.015 .381 mm	.9052 22.992 mm	1.8093–1.8103 45.958–45.984 mm	.0014–.0031 .036–.078 mm	2.0078–2.0088 51.0–51.024 mm	.0009–.0026 .024–.066 mm	4	.004–.008 .100–.202 mm
1977–78	All	.0008–.0016 .020–.040 mm	.009 .229 mm	.015 .381 mm	.9052 22.992 mm	1.8093–1.8103 45.958–45.984 mm	.0014–.0031 .036–.078 mm	2.0078–2.0088 51.0–51.024 mm	②	4	.004–.008 .100–.202 mm

①—Fit ring in tapered bore for clearance listed in tightest portion of ring travel.
②—1977, No. 1, 2, 3 & 4, .0006–.0018 (.014–046 mm); No. 5, .0009–.0026 (.024–.066 mm) & 1978, All, .0009–.0026 (.024–.066 mm).

VALVE SPECIFICATIONS

Year	Model	Valve Lash		Valve Angles		Valve Spring Installed Height	Valve Spring Pressure Lbs. @ In.	Stem Clearance		Stem Diameter	
		Int.	Exh.	Seat	Face			Intake	Exhaust	Intake	Exhaust
1976–78	All	Hydraulic		46	45	1.26 32 mm.	173 @ .886 770N @ 22.5 mm.	.0006–.0017 .015–.045 mm.	.0014–.0025 .035–.065 mm.	.3138–.3144 7.970–7.986 mm.	.3130–.3136 7.950–7.965 mm.
1979	All	Hydraulic		46	45	1.26 32 mm.	173 @ .886 770N @ 22.5 mm.	.0018–.0021 .046–.053 mm.	.0026–.0029 .066–.074 mm.	.3138–.3144 7.970–7.986 mm.	.3130–.3136 7.950–7.965 mm

ENGINE TIGHTENING SPECIFICATIONS★

★Torque specifications are for clean and lightly lubricated threads only. Dry or dirty threads produce increased friction which prevents accurate measurement of tightness.

Year	Engine Model	Spark Plugs Ft. Lbs.	Camshaft Carrier Bolts Ft. Lbs.	Intake Manifold Ft. Lbs.	Exhaust Manifold Ft. Lbs.	Camshaft Sprocket Bolt Ft. Lbs.	Cam Cover In. Lbs.	Connecting Rod Cap Bolts Ft. Lbs.	Main Bearing Cap Bolts Ft. Lbs.	Flywheel to Crankshaft Ft. Lbs.	Vibration Damper or Pulley Ft. Lbs.
1976	All	15 20.3 N-m	75 102 N-m	16 22 N-m	①	75 102 N-m	14 1.6 N-m	37 50 N-m	46 63 N-m	46 63 N-m	75 102 N-m
1977–78	All	15 20.3 N-m	71 97 N-m	16 22 N-m	②	75 102 N-m	14 1.6 N-m	37 50 N-m	46 63 N-m	46 63 N-m	75 102 N-m

①—Center bolts, 16 ft. lbs. (22 Newton-meters); end legs, 22 ft. lbs. (30 Newton-meters).
②—1977, 22 ft. lbs. (30 Newton-meters) & 1978, Center bolts 15 ft. lbs. (20 Newton-meter); End legs, 22 ft. lbs. (30 Newton-meters).

REAR AXLE SPECIFICATIONS

Year	Model	Carrier Type	Ring Gear & Pinion Backlash		Pinion Bearing Preload			Differential Bearing Preload		
			Method	Adjustment	Method	New Bearings Inch-Lbs.	Used Bearings Inch-Lbs.	Method	New Bearings Inch-Lbs.	Used Bearings Inch-Lbs.
1976	All	Integral	Shims	—	Spacer	5–11 .5–1.2 N-m	3–6 .3–.6 N-m	Shims	—	—
1977–78	All	Integral	Shims	—	Spacer	15–25 1.7–2.82 N-m	5–10 0.56–1.3 N-m	Shims	—	—

WHEEL ALIGNMENT SPECIFICATIONS

Year	Model	Caster Angle, Degrees		Camber Angle, Degrees				Toe-In. Inch	Toe-Out on Turns, Deg.	
		Limits	Desired	Limits		Desired			Outer Wheel	Inner Wheel
				Left	Right	Left	Right			
1976	All	+4 to +5	+4½	−¼ to +¾	−¼ to +¾	+¼	+¼	¹⁄₆₄–⁷⁄₆₄ .5–2.5 mm	—	—
1977–78	All	+3½ to +5½	+4½	−.2 to +.6	−.2 to +.6	+.2	+.2	①	—	—
1979	All	+3½ to +5½	+4½	−.2 to +.6	−.2 to +.6	+.2	+.2	②	—	—

①—1977, .5 to 2.5 mm, 1978, 1.3 to 2.7 mm.
②—+.02° to +.10°.

ALTERNATOR & REGULATOR SPECIFICATIONS

| Year | Model | Alternator | | Output @ 14 Volts | | Regulator | Field Relay | | | Voltage Regulator | | |
		Rated Hot Output Amps.	Field Current 12 Volts @ 80° F.	2000 R.P.M. Amps.	5000 R.P.M. Amps.	Model	Air Gap In.	Point Gap In.	Closing Voltage	Air Gap In.	Point Gap In.	Voltage @ 125° F.
1976	1102845	32	4.0–4.5	—	31	Integral	—	—	—	—	—	13.8–14.8①
	1102846	55	4.0–4.5	—	51	Integral	—	—	—	—	—	
1977–79	1102845	32	4.0–4.5	—	31	Integral	—	—	—	—	—	13.8–14.8①

①—At 85° F.

STARTING MOTOR SPECIFICATIONS

| Year | Model | Starter Number | Brush Spring Tension Oz① | Free Speed Test | | | Resistance Test | |
				Amps.	Volts	R.P.M.①	Amps.	Volts
1976	All	1109411	—	50–75②	9	6500	—	—
1977	All	1109414	—	50–75②	9	6500	—	—
1978	All	1110941	—	—	—	—	—	—
1979	All	1109522						

①—Minimum. ②—Includes solenoid.

COOLING SYSTEM & CAPACITY DATA

| Year | Model or Engine | Cooling Capacity, Qts. | | | Radiator Cap Relief Pressure, Lbs. | | Thermo. Opening Temp. ① | Fuel Tank Gals. | Engine Oil Refill Qts. | Transmission Oil | | | Rear Axle Oils Pints |
		No Heater	With Heater	With A/C	With A/C	No. A/C				3 Speed Pints	4 Speed Pints	Auto. Trans. Qts. ②	
1976–78	All	—	8½ 8 ltr.	9 8.5 ltr.	15 —	15 —	190 —	13 49.2 ltr.	4 3.8 ltr.	— —	3 1.5 ltr.	4.5 4.2 ltr.	2 .9 ltr.

①—Use with permanent type anti-freeze. ②—Approximate. Make final check with dipstick.

BRAKE SPECIFICATIONS

Year	Model	Brake Drum Inside Diameter	Wheel Cylinder Bore Diameter			Master Cylinder Bore Diameter		
			Disc Brake	Front Drum Brake	Rear Drum Brake	Disc Brakes	Drum Brakes	Power Brakes
1976–79	All	7.88 200.15 mm	1⅞ 47.625 mm	—	¾ 19.05 mm	¾ 19.05 mm	—	¾ 19.05 mm

Electrical Section

ELECTRICAL DIAGNOSIS

This vehicle is equipped with either one or two "Master Electrical Connectors," Fig. 1. One connector is the "Engine Electrical Master Diagnostic Connector" and the other is the "Air Conditioning Electrical Master Diagnostic Connector." These connectors are used to diagnose electrical Malfunctions in the air conditioning, charging, cranking and ignition systems.

CAUTION: When performing any of the following tests, ensure transmission is in Neutral on manual transmission models or Park on automatic transmission models. Also, fully apply the parking brake.

ENGINE ELECTRICAL DIAGNOSTIC TESTS, FIG. 2

NOTE: The following tests are performed with a 14 gauge jumper wire and the ignition switch in the "Off" position.

Starter Does Not Crank Or Cranks Slowly

Test T-1

1. Connect jumper wire between terminal Nos. 1 and 8.
2. If malfunction remains there may be an open wire between terminal No. 8 and the starter solenoid "S" terminal, a faulty connection at the starter solenoid "S" terminal or a poor connection at battery or starter. If the wiring and connections are satisfactory, the starter solenoid may be defective.
3. If starter cranks in step 1, proceed to Test T-2.

Test T-2

1. Connect jumper wire between terminals Nos. 1 and 9.
2. If malfunction remains, the neutral starter switch may be defective or faulty neutral starter switch wiring.
3. If starter cranks in step 1, the ignition

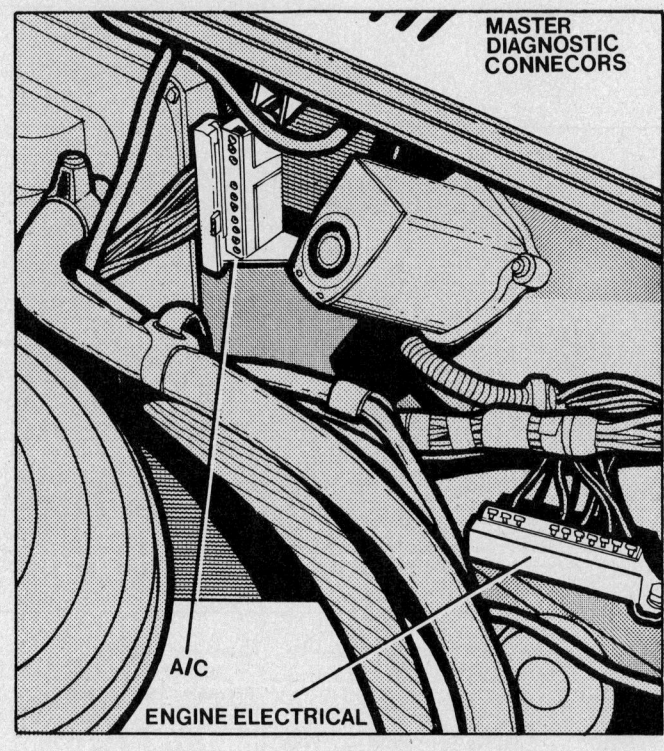

Fig. 1   Master electrical diagnostic connector locations

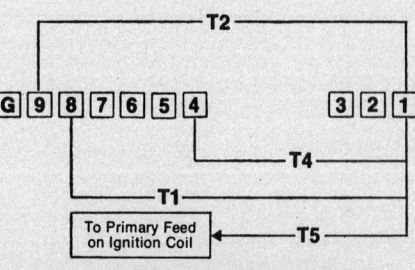

Fig. 2   Engine electrical diagnostic test connections

switch may be defective or improperly connected.

Engine Cranks But Will Not Start

Test T-3

1. Check for ignition output by removing a spark plug wire, insert an extension into the boot and crank engine while holding the spark plug wire with insulated pliers approximately ¼ inch (6mm) from engine block.
2. If spark is noted in step 1, the malfunction is not in ignition system (excluding the spark plugs).

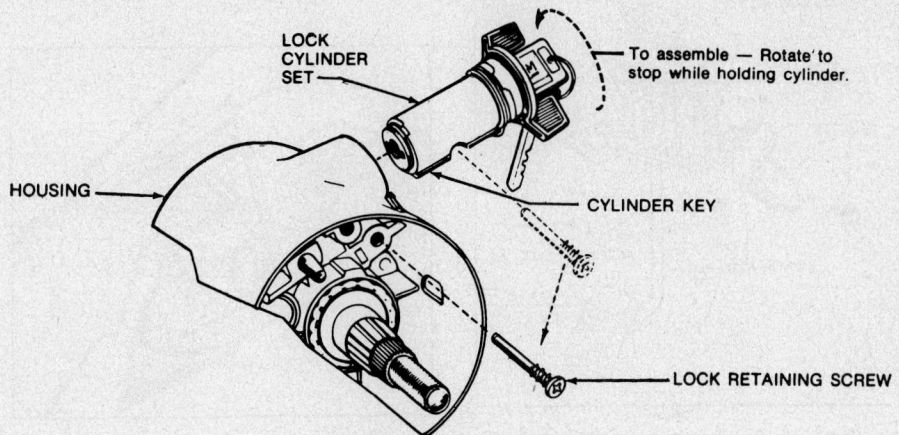

Fig. 3 Ignition lock removal & installation. 1979

Fig. 3A Ignition lock removal. 1976-78

3. If no spark occurs in step 1, proceed to Test T-4.

Test T-4

1. Connect jumper wire between terminals Nos. 1 and 4 and crank engine.
2. If engine starts, the ignition switch may be defective or not connected properly.
3. If engine does not start in step 1, proceed to Test T-5.

Test T-5

1. Connect jumper wire between terminal No. 1 and the ignition coil primary feed terminal and crank engine.
2. If engine starts, there is an open wire between test terminal No. 4 and the coil or a faulty coil connection.
3. If engine does not start, the H.E.I. system is malfunctioning.

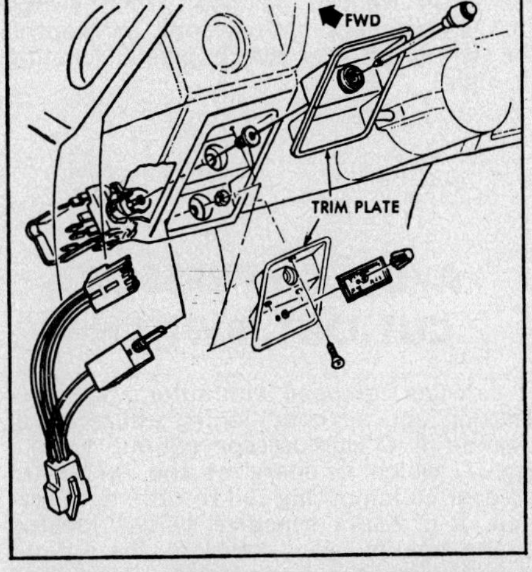

DISTRIBUTOR, REPLACE

1. On models equipped with A/C, disconnect wire connector from compressor, then remove through bolt, two adjusting bolts, and upper compressor mounting bracket.
2. Raise vehicle, then remove two retaining bolts and position lower compressor bracket outward for clearance.
3. On all models, remove air cleaner and distributor cap, position distributor cap out of way.
4. Remove ignition coil cover and mounting bracket bolts.
5. Disconnect distributor primary lead from coil terminal.
6. Remove fuel pump and push rod.

NOTE: Push rod must be installed in same direction as removed.

7. Scribe a mark on engine in line with rotor, noting approximate position of distributor housing in relation to engine.
8. Remove distributor hold down bolt and clamp and remove distributor.

NOTE: Avoid rotating engine while distributor is removed.

9. Reverse procedure to install.

STARTER, REPLACE

Less A/C

1. Disconnect battery ground cable and remove air cleaner.
2. Remove distributor cap and position aside.
3. Remove the fuel line from fuel pump and carburetor.
4. Disconnect electrical connectors from ignition coil, remove coil bracket retaining screws and the coil and bracket assembly.

5. Disconnect vacuum hose from vacuum advance unit and the electrical connector from the oil pressure sender, then remove the sender.
6. Disconnect electrical leads from starter and remove the brace screw from bottom of starter housing.
7. Remove starter retaining screws and the starter from vehicle.
8. Reverse procedure to install.

With A/C

1. Disconnect battery ground cable and remove air cleaner.
2. Remove starter upper retaining screw.
3. Remove steering column lever cover attaching screws.
4. Remove mast jacket lower bracket screw and the steering column upper mounting bracket.
5. Disconnect the four electrical connectors from steering column, then raise vehicle.
6. Disconnect steering column flexible coupling and position aside.

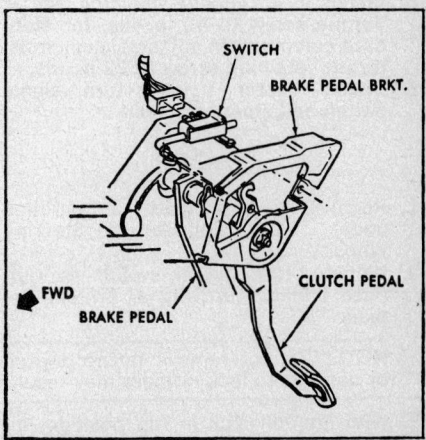

Fig. 5 Clutch start switch replacement

Fig. 4 Light switch replacement

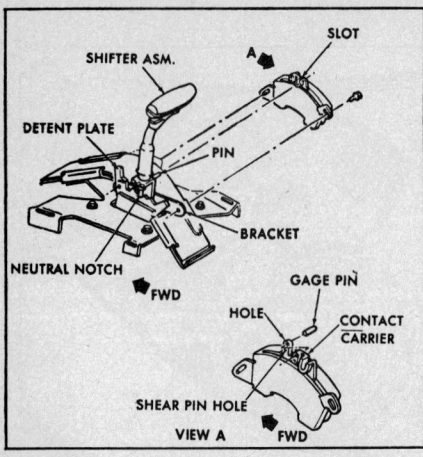

Fig. 6 Neutral start switch replacement

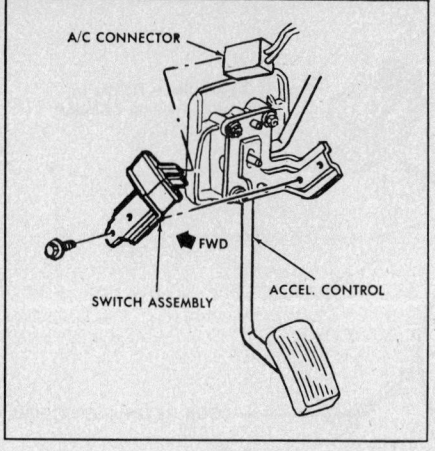

Fig. 7 A/C compressor cut-out switch

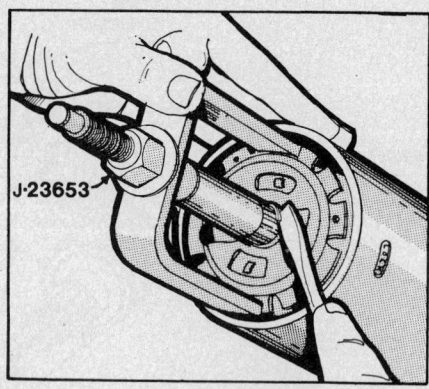

Fig. 9 Compressing lock plate and removing retaining ring

7. Disconnect electrical leads from starter and remove brace screw from bottom of starter.
8. Remove starter lower mounting screw.
9. With a suitable jack, raise engine approximately ½ inch to provide clearance for starter removal.
10. Lower starter and remove from vehicle.
11. Reverse procedure to install.

IGNITION LOCK, REPLACE

1979

1. Remove steering wheel as described under Horn Sounder and Steering Wheel.
2. Remove turn signal switch as described under Turn Signal Switch, Replace, then remove buzzer switch.
3. Place ignition switch in Run position, then remove lock cylinder retaining screw and lock cylinder.
4. To install, rotate lock cylinder to stop while holding housing, Fig. 3. Align cylinder key with keyway in housing, then push lock cylinder assembly into housing until fully seated.
5. Install lock cylinder retaining screw. Torque screw to 40 in. lbs. for standard columns. On adjustable columns, torque retaining screw to 22 in. lbs.
6. Install buzzer switch, turn signal switch and steering wheel.

1976-78

1. Remove steering wheel as outlined under "Horn Sounder & Steering Wheel".
2. Remove turn signal switch as outlined under "Turn Signal Switch, Replace".

NOTE: Do not remove buzzer switch or damage to lock cylinder may result.

3. With ignition lock in run position, insert a small screw driver or similar tool into turn signal housing slot,

Fig. 3. Keep tool to right side of housing slot and depress retainer at bottom of slot.
4. Remove lock cylinder from housing.

LIGHT SWITCH, REPLACE

1. Disconnect battery ground cable.
2. Pull headlamp switch knob to "ON" position, Fig. 4.
3. Reach under instrument panel and depress switch shaft retainer button while pulling on the switch control shaft knob.
4. With a large bladed screwdriver, remove the light switch ferrule nut from front of instrument panel.
5. Disconnect the multi-contact connector from side of switch and remove switch.
6. Reverse procedure to install.

STOP LIGHT SWITCH

1. Reach under right side of instrument panel at brake pedal support and release wiring harness connector at switch.
2. Pull switch from mounting bracket.
3. When installing switch, adjust by bringing brake pedal to normal position. Electrical contact should be made when pedal is depressed .53 inch (13.5 mm). To adjust, the switch may be rotated or pulled in the clip.

CLUTCH START SWITCH

NOTE: The clutch pedal must be fully depressed and the ignition switch in START position for the vehicle to start.

The clutch switch assembly mounts with two tangs to the clutch pedal brace switch pivot bracket and the clutch pedal arm, Fig. 5.

1. Under the instrument panel on the clutch pedal support remove the multi-contact connector from switch.
2. Compress switch assembly actuating shaft barb retainer and push out of clutch pedal.
3. Compress switch assembly pivot bracket barb and lift off switch.
4. When installing new switch, no adjustments are necessary as the switch is self aligning.

NEUTRAL SAFETY SWITCH, REPLACE

1. Remove floor console cover.
2. Disconnect electrical plugs on back-up contacts, seat belt warning contacts and neutral start contacts of switch assembly, Fig. 6.
3. Place shift lever in Neutral.
4. Remove two screws securing switch to lever assembly.
5. When installing switch, make sure it is in Neutral position. When switch is installed, shifting out of Neutral will shear the switch plastic locating pin.

A/C COMPRESSOR CUT-OUT SWITCH

Vehicles equipped with automatic transmission and air conditioning utilize a full throttle A/C compressor cut-out switch, Fig. 7, which de-energizes the A/C compressor clutch during full throttle acceleration. A pressure sensitive switch, located in the transmission, overrides the cut-out switch when the transmission is in third gear during full throttle acceleration.

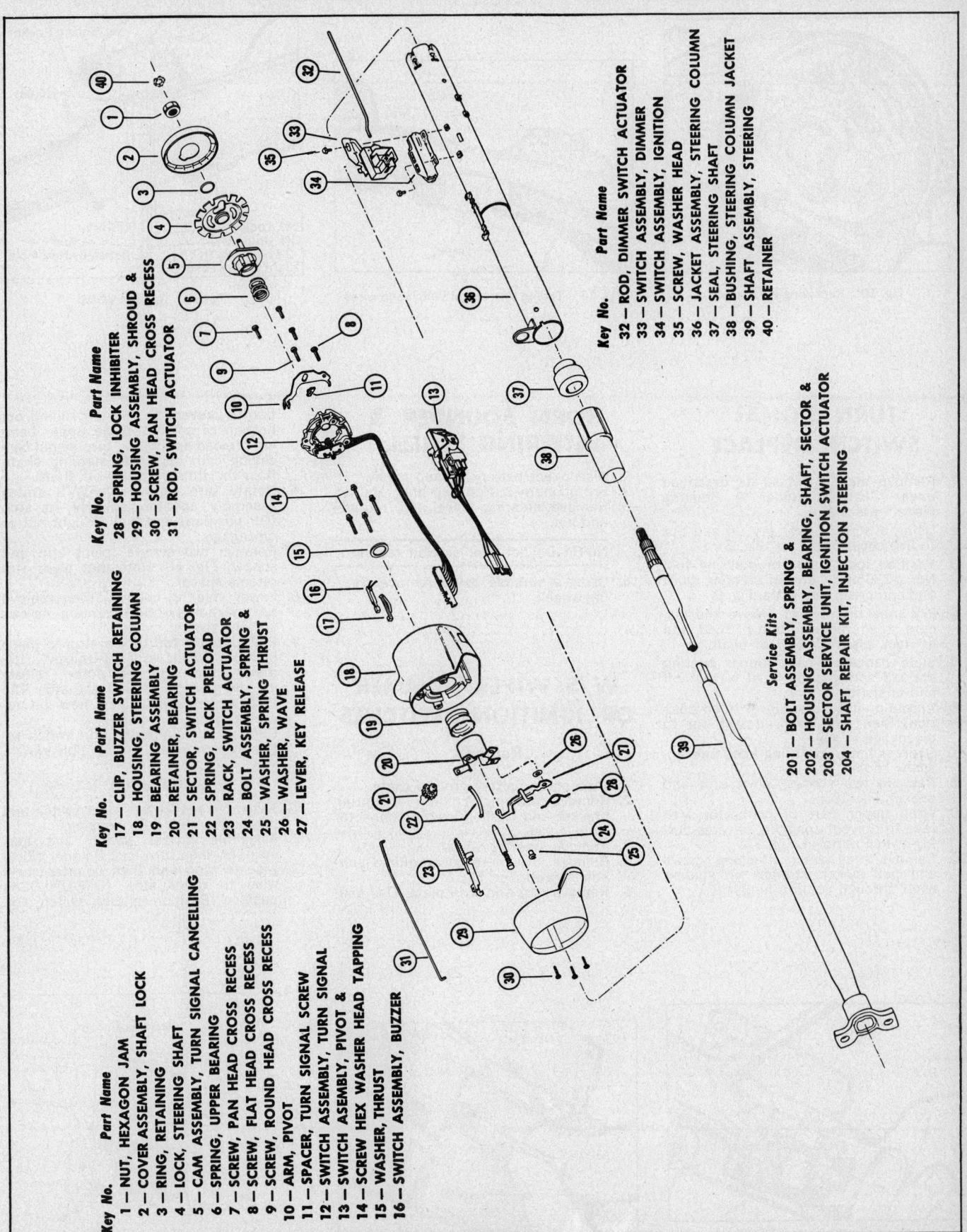

Key No.   Part Name

1 — NUT, HEXAGON JAM
2 — COVER ASSEMBLY, SHAFT LOCK
3 — RING, RETAINING
4 — LOCK, STEERING SHAFT
5 — CAM ASSEMBLY, TURN SIGNAL CANCELLING
6 — SPRING, UPPER BEARING
7 — SCREW, PAN HEAD CROSS RECESS
8 — SCREW, FLAT HEAD CROSS RECESS
9 — SCREW, ROUND HEAD CROSS RECESS
10 — ARM, PIVOT
11 — SPACER, TURN SIGNAL SCREW
12 — SWITCH ASSEMBLY, TURN SIGNAL
13 — SWITCH ASSEMBLY, PIVOT &
14 — SCREW HEX WASHER HEAD TAPPING
15 — WASHER, THRUST
16 — SWITCH ASSEMBLY, BUZZER

Key No.   Part Name

17 — CLIP, BUZZER SWITCH RETAINING
18 — HOUSING, STEERING COLUMN
19 — BEARING ASSEMBLY
20 — RETAINER, BEARING
21 — SECTOR, SWITCH ACTUATOR
22 — SPRING, RACK PRELOAD
23 — RACK, SWITCH ACTUATOR
24 — BOLT ASSEMBLY, SPRING &
25 — WASHER, SPRING THRUST
26 — WASHER, WAVE
27 — LEVER, KEY RELEASE

Key No.   Part Name

28 — SPRING, LOCK INHIBITER
29 — HOUSING ASSEMBLY, SHROUD &
30 — SCREW, PAN HEAD CROSS RECESS
31 — ROD, SWITCH ACTUATOR

Key No.   Part Name

32 — ROD, DIMMER SWITCH ACTUATOR
33 — SWITCH ASSEMBLY, DIMMER
34 — SWITCH ASSEMBLY, IGNITION
35 — SCREW, WASHER HEAD
36 — JACKET ASSEMBLY, STEERING COLUMN
37 — SEAL, STEERING SHAFT
38 — BUSHING, STEERING COLUMN JACKET
39 — SHAFT ASSEMBLY, STEERING
40 — RETAINER

Service Kits

201 — BOLT ASSEMBLY, SPRING &
202 — HOUSING ASSEMBLY, BEARING, SHAFT, SECTOR &
203 — SECTOR SERVICE UNIT, IGNITION SWITCH ACTUATOR
204 — SHAFT REPAIR KIT, INJECTION STEERING

Fig. 8   Chevette steering column, disassembled

Fig. 10   Removing pivot arm

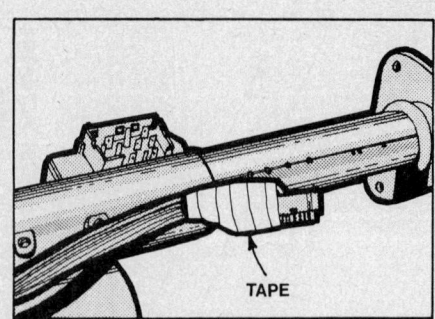

Fig. 11   Taping turn signal switch and wires

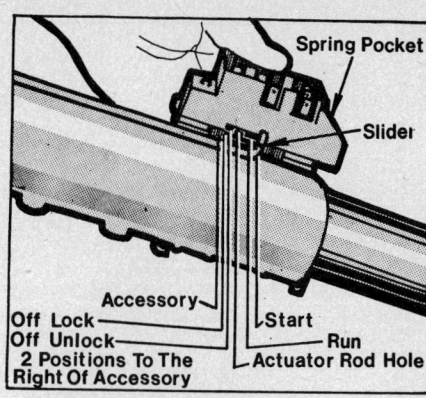

Fig. 12   Ignition switch

TURN SIGNAL SWITCH, REPLACE

1. Remove steering wheel as described under "Horn Sounder & Steering Wheel" procedure.
2. Using a screw driver pry up and out to free cover from lock, Fig. 8.
3. Position lock plate compressing tool No. J-23653 on end of steering shaft and compress lock plate, Fig. 9.
4. Pry snap ring out of groove and discard, then remove tool J-23653 and lift lock plate off end of shaft.
5. Slide canceling cam, upper bearing preload spring and thrust washer off end of shaft.
6. Rotate multi-function lever to off position, then pull lever straight out to disengage.
7. Depress hazard warning knob and unscrew knob.
8. Remove two screws, pivot arm and spacer, Fig. 10.
9. Wrap upper part of connector with tape to prevent snagging of wires during switch removal, Fig. 11.
10. Remove three switch attaching screws and pull switch straight up guiding wires through column housing.

HORN SOUNDER & STEERING WHEEL

1. Disconnect battery ground cable.
2. Pry off horn button cap and retainer.
3. Remove steering wheel nut retainer and nut.

NOTE: Do not over expand retainer.

4. Using a suitable puller remove steering wheel.

W/S WIPER, DIMMER OR IGNITION SWITCHES

Removal

1. Disconnect battery ground cable.
2. Remove steering column mounting bracket and unsnap switch connector from jacket.
3. Remove steering wheel.
4. Remove lock plate cover with a suitable screwdriver, Fig. 8.
5. Remove ring and lock plate. Use cau-

tion to prevent shaft from sliding out bottom of column. Slide upper bearing preload spring and turn signal cancelling cam off upper steering shaft, then the thrust washer off shaft.
6. Rotate turn signal lever-W/S switch assembly counter-clockwise to stop (Off position) and pull straight out to disengage.
7. Remove two screws, pivot arm and spacer, Fig. 10. Note that pivot arm retains spacer.
8. Lower steering column, then remove turn signal switch mounting screws and the switch.
9. Pull actuator rod to the stop to place ignition switch in "Off-Unlock". Remove upper attaching screw, releasing dimmer switch and actuator. The W/S wiper switch may now be removed, Figs. 12 and 13.
10. Remove remaining ignition switch retaining screw and the ignition switch.

Installation

1. Assemble windshield wiper switch and pivot assembly onto housing.
2. Assemble buzzer switch and lock cylinder, then turn lock cylinder clockwise to stop and then counter-clockwise to other stop (OFF-UNLOCK) position. Position ignition switch, Fig.

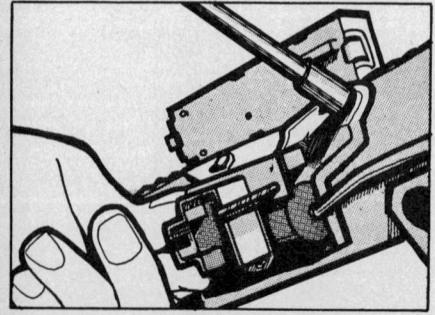

Fig. 13   Dimmer & ignition switch replacement

Fig. 14   Dimmer switch alignment

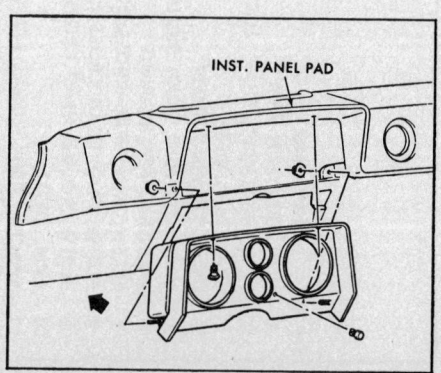

Fig. 15   Instrument cluster

12, then move slider to extreme left (ACC) and slide back two positions to the right to OFF-UNLOCK position. Install actuator rod into slider and install the bottom screw only, to retain the ignition switch. Do not move switch out of detent.

3. Install washer, spring and cancelling cam on steering shaft. Position cancelling cam lobes in relation to signal switch springs and assemble shaft lock and install new retaining ring, Fig. 8.
4. Install cover and snap ring, then install multi-function switch lever. Align lever pin with switch slot and push lever until it seats.
5. Install pinched end of dimmer switch actuator rod into dimmer switch, then install other end of rod into pivot switch. Install but do not tighten upper ignition switch screw. Depress dimmer switch and insert a 3/32 inch drill to lock switch body, Fig. 14.
6. Move dimmer switch up, removing lash between both switches and rod, then install and tighten upper ignition switch screw. Remove drill and check dimmer switch for proper operation.
7. Snap electrical connector into place and raise steering column, then install mounting nuts and torque to 22 ft. lbs. (30 Nm) and install steering wheel.

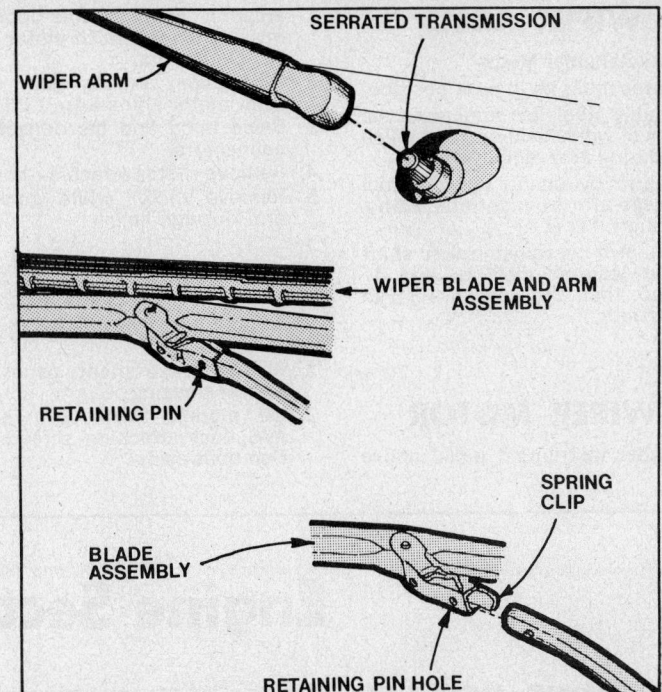

Fig. 16   Wiper blade clip location

INSTRUMENT CLUSTER

1. Disconnect battery ground cable.
2. Remove clock stem knob.
3. Remove cluster bezel and lens retaining screws, then the bezel and lens, Fig. 15.
4. Remove instrument cluster to instrument panel retaining nuts and pull cluster toward vehicle rear.
5. Disconnect all electrical connectors and speedometer cable from cluster, then remove cluster.
6. Reverse procedure to install.

RADIO, REPLACE

1. Disconnect battery ground cable.
2. Remove mounting stud nut from bottom of radio, and the control knobs from shafts.
3. Remove screws from center trim panel and pull panel and radio toward the rear of the vehicle.
4. Disconnect all electrical connectors from radio.
5. Remove radio retaining nuts from radio control shafts.
6. Remove radio from vehicle.
7. Reverse procedure to install.

HEATER CORE, REPLACE

1. Disconnect battery ground cable and drain cooling system.
2. Disconnect heater hoses from core and plug openings in core.

3. Remove heater core housing to dash panel attaching screws, then the housing.
4. Remove core from housing.

BLOWER MOTOR, REPLACE

1. Disconnect battery ground cable.
2. Disconnect blower lead wire.
3. Remove blower motor to case attaching screws then the blower and wheel as an assembly.

NOTE: Scribe mark on blower motor and case so motor is installed in original position.

Fig. 17   Removing wiper arm

4. Remove nut and separate motor from wheel.
5. Reverse procedure to install.

NOTE: At assembly position open end of blower wheel away from blower motor. Replace sealer at blower motor flange if necessary.

W/S WIPER BLADES

1. Remove the wiper blade from the arm by depressing the spring type blade clip, Fig. 16, away from the under side of the arm and slide the arm out of the blade clip.
2. To install wiper blade to wiper arm, slide tip end of arm into blade clip, until pin on tip end of arm engages hole in clip.
3. The blade element is retained in the blade assembly by a spring type retainer clip in the end of the blade element. When the retainer clip is squeezed together, the blade element can be slid out of the blade assembly.
4. When installing a blade element into a blade assembly, be certain to engage the metal insert in the element into all retaining tabs of the blade assembly.

NOTE: When properly installed, the spring type element retaining clip should be at the end of the wiper blade assembly nearest the wiper transmission.

W/S WIPER ARMS

Models with Rectangular Motor

1. Wiper motor must be in park position.
2. Use suitable tool to minimize the possibility of windshield or paint finish damage during arm removal.
3. Remove arm by prying up with tool to disengage arm from serrated transmission shaft, Fig. 17.
4. To install arm to transmission shaft rotate the required distance and direction so that the blades rest in proper position.

W/S WIPER MOTOR

1. Reach under instrument panel above steering column and loosen transmission drive link to motor crank arm attaching nuts.
2. Disengage transmission drive link from motor crank arm.
3. Raise hood and disconnect electrical connectors.
4. Remove motor attaching bolts.
5. Remove motor while guiding crank arm through hole.

W/S WIPER TRANSMISSION

1. Remove instrument panel pad and cluster housing.
2. On models with A/C, remove left A/C duct attaching screws and position duct aside.
3. On all models, remove left side air duct.
4. Remove speedometer cable shield and left side instrument brace.
5. From under instrument panel, loosen transmission drive link to motor crank arm attaching nuts and disengage drive link.
6. Remove wiper arms and blades, then remove transmission to dash panel attaching bolts.
7. Move transmission assembly to left, then while rotating assembly, work out through instrument panel access hole at right upper center of instrument panel.

NOTE: When installing, ensure motor is in park position.

Engine Section

ENGINE MOUNT, REPLACE

Front

1. Remove heater assembly and position on top of engine.
2. Remove radiator upper support.
3. Remove engine mount nuts and the restraint cable.
4. Raise vehicle, install engine lifting device and raise engine to relieve weight from mounts.
5. Remove mount to engine bracket, then using tool J-25510, remove mount.

Rear

1. Raise vehicle and remove crossmember to mount bolts.
2. Raise transmission at extension housing to relieve weight from mount.
3. Remove mount to transmission bolts and the mount.

ENGINE, REPLACE

1. Remove hood.
2. Disconnect battery cables and remove clips securing battery cable to right side frame rail.
3. Drain cooling system and disconnect radiator and heater hoses.
4. Disconnect engine wiring harness.
5. Remove radiator upper support, radiator and fan.
6. Remove air cleaner.
7. Disconnect fuel line at rubber hose located along left side frame rail.
8. Disconnect accelerator and automatic transmission throttle valve linkage, if equipped.
9. Remove A/C compressor from mounting bracket and position aside, if equipped.
10. Raise vehicle and disconnect exhaust pipe at manifold.
11. Remove flywheel dust cover.
12. On models with automatic transmission, remove converter to flywheel bolts.
13. Remove converter housing to engine bolts on automatic transmission models or flywheel housing to engine bolt on manual transmission models, then lower vehicle.
14. Support transmission using a suitable jack.
15. Remove safety straps from engine mounts, then remove engine mount bolts.
16. Install engine lifting device, raise engine slowly, pull engine forward to clear transmission and remove engine from vehicle.

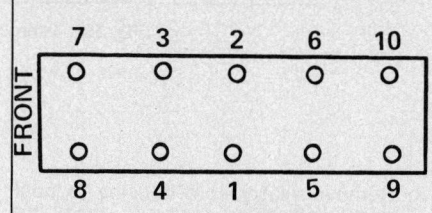

Fig. 1 Cylinder head tightening sequence

INTAKE MANIFOLD

1. Disconnect battery ground cable and drain cooling system.
2. Remove air cleaner and disconnect upper radiator hose and heater hoses from intake manifold.
3. Remove EGR valve.
4. Disconnect fuel line, electrical wiring, vacuum hoses and linkage from carburetor.
5. If equipped with A/C, perform the following.
   a. Remove radiator upper support, alternator and A/C drive belts.
   b. Remove fan, pulley and timing belt cover.
   c. Position A/C compressor aside.
   d. Raise vehicle and remove the lower A/C compressor bracket.
   e. Lower vehicle and remove the upper A/C compressor bracket.
6. On all models, remove ignition coil and position aside.
7. Remove intake manifold attaching bolts and the intake manifold.
8. Reverse procedure to install.

CYLINDER HEAD

1. Remove timing belt.
2. Drain cooling system, remove upper radiator hose and heater hose at intake manifold.
3. Remove air cleaner, then remove accelerator support bracket.
4. Disconnect spark plug wires.
5. Disconnect wiring harnesses at idle solenoid, choke, temperature sending switch and alternator.
6. Raise vehicle and disconnect exhaust pipe at manifold.
7. Lower vehicle and remove bolt retaining dipstick bracket to manifold.
8. Disconnect fuel line at carburetor.
9. Remove coil bracket bolts and position coil aside.
10. Remove camshaft cover, then remove camshaft cover to housing attaching studs.
11. Remove rocker arms, guides and lash adjusters.

NOTE: Rocker arms, guides and lash adjusters must be installed in original location during assembly.

12. Remove camshaft carrier from cylinder head.

> **NOTE:** It may be necessary to use a wedge to separate camshaft carrier from cylinder head.

13. Remove cylinder head and manifold as an assembly.
14. Reverse procedure to install, tighten cylinder bolts in the sequence as shown in Fig. 1.

HYDRAULIC VALVE LIFTERS

Failure of an hydraulic valve lifter is generally caused by an inadequate oil supply or dirt. An air leak at the intake side of the oil pump or too much oil in the engine will cause air bubbles in the oil supply to the lifters, causing them to collapse. This is a probable cause of trouble if several lifters fail to function, but air in the oil is an unlikely cause of failure of a single unit.

ROCKER ARMS

1. Remove camshaft cover.
2. Using tool J-25477, depress valve spring and remove rocker arm, guide and lash adjuster, Fig. 2.

NOTE: Rocker arms, guides and lash adjusters must be installed in the same location during assembly.

VALVE GUIDES

Valve guides are an integral part of the cylinder head. If stem to guide clearance is excessive, the guide should be reamed to the next oversize and the appropriate oversize valve installed. Valves are available in standard size and oversizes of .003 in. (.075mm), .006 in. (.150mm), and .012 in. (.300mm).

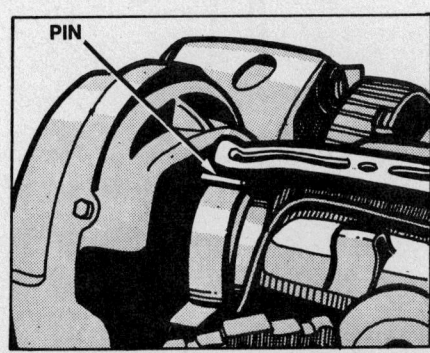

Fig. 3   Aligning camshaft sprocket

Fig. 2   Depressing valve spring

CAMSHAFT COVER

1. Raise hood to fully open position.
2. Disconnect battery ground cable.
3. Remove air cleaner, PCV valve, air cleaner snorkle and heat tube assembly.
4. Remove spark plug wires from retainer on camshaft cover.
5. Remove accelerator cable support and position aside.
6. Remove nut and gasket from stud and the camshaft cover.

CAMSHAFT SPROCKET

1. Remove drive belts, then the fan and pulley.
2. Remove engine front cover.
3. Loosen idler pulley and remove timing belt from camshaft sprocket.
4. Remove camshaft sprocket bolt and washer, remove camshaft sprocket.

CAMSHAFT, REMOVAL

1. Remove camshaft sprocket as described under "Camshaft Sprocket" procedure.
2. Remove rocker arms.
3. Remove heater assembly and position aside.
4. Remove camshaft carrier rear cover.
5. Remove camshaft thrust plate bolts, slide camshaft rearward and remove thrust plate.
6. Raise engine, then carefully slide camshaft from carrier.

CAM LOBE LIFT SPECS.

Year	Intake	Exhaust
All 1976	.232 (5.893mm)	.232 (5.893mm)
All 1977	.232 (5.893mm)	.232 (5.893mm)
All 1978	.2407 (6.1163mm)	.2407 (6.1163 mm)

VALVE TIMING

Intake Open Before TDC

Engine	Year	Degrees
All	1976	32
All	1977	29
Exc. Hi Output	1978-79	28
Hi Output	1978-79	31

ENGINE FRONT COVER

Upper Cover

1. Raise hood and disconnect battery ground cable.
2. Remove fan.
3. Remove upper cover retaining screw and the upper cover.

Lower Cover

1. Remove crankshaft pulley.
2. Remove upper front cover.
3. Remove lower cover attaching nut and the lower cover.

UPPER REAR TIMING BELT COVER, REMOVE

1. Remove engine front cover, timing belt and camshaft sprocket.
2. Remove three upper rear timing belt cover to camshaft carrier attaching screws.
3. Inspect camshaft seal and replace, if necessary.

TIMING BELT

1. Remove engine front upper and lower covers and crankshaft pulley.
2. Loosen idler pulley bolt and remove

Fig. 4   Timing belt idler arm and pulley

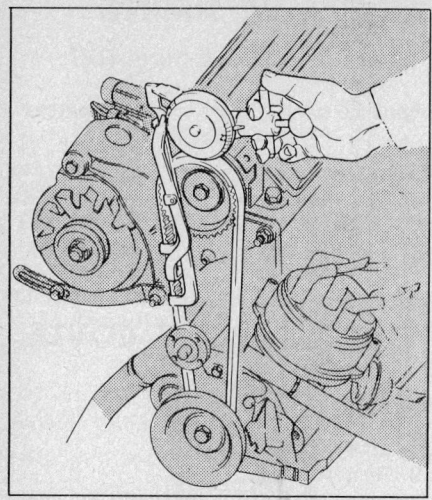

Fig. 5 Adjusting timing belt tension

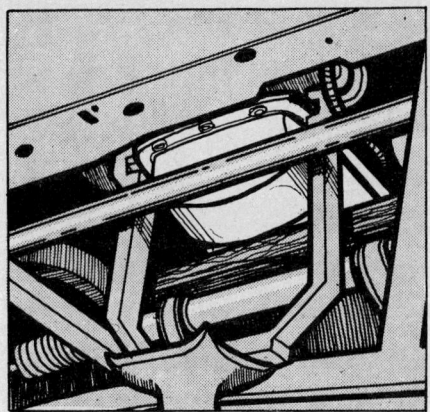

Fig. 6 Installing engine lifting device to facilitate oil pan removal

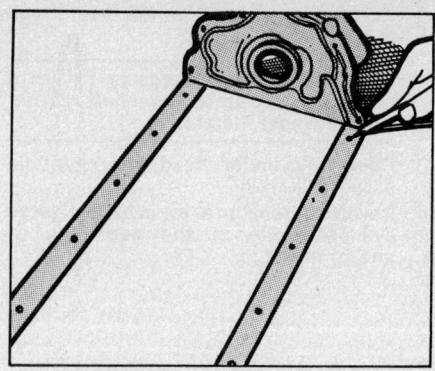

Fig. 7 Fabricating crankcase front cover to oil pan seal

timing belt from camshaft and crankshaft sprockets.

3. Position timing belt over crankshaft sprocket, then install crankshaft pulley.

4. Position crankshaft at TDC number 1 cylinder.

5. Align timing mark on camshaft sprocket with hole in upper rear cover, Fig. 3.

6. Install timing belt on crankshaft and camshaft sprockets, then adjust belt tension.

TIMING BELT TENSION, ADJUST

1. Remove fan, drive belt, pulley and upper cam belt cover.

2. Rotate crankshaft at least one revolution and position No. 1 piston at top dead center.

3. Install belt tension gauge, Tool J-26486, Fig. 5, on timing belt midway between the cam sprocket and idler pulley. Ensure the gauge center finger engages in a notch on the belt.

4. On 1976 engines, correct belt tension is 55 ft. lbs. and on 1977 engines, correct belt tension is 70 ft. lbs. To adjust, loosen idler pulley attaching bolt. Then, using a ¼ inch allen wrench, rotate the pulley counterclockwise on the attaching bolt until correct belt tension is obtained and torque attaching bolt to 13-18 ft. lbs. (18-24 N·m).

5. Remove gauge and install upper cam belt cover, pulley, drive belt and fan.

CRANKSHAFT SPROCKET

1. Remove engine front cover, crankshaft pulley and timing belt.

2. Remove crankshaft sprocket.

PISTON & ROD ASSEMBLE

Assemble pistons and rods as indicated in Fig. 9.

PISTONS, & RINGS

Pistons and rings are available in standard size, .001 and .030 in. (.750mm) oversize.

MAIN & ROD BEARINGS

Main bearings are available standard size and undersizes of .001 in. (.026mm), .002 in. (.050mm), .010 in. (.250mm) and .020 in. (.500mm).

Rod bearings are available in standard size and undersizes of .001 in. (.026mm), .010 in. (.250mm) and .020 in. (.500mm).

OIL PAN

1. Remove heater housing from dash and position on top of engine.

2. Remove motor mount nuts, then pull back motor mount restraint cables.

3. Remove radiator upper support, on models with A/C remove upper fan shroud.

4. Remove flywheel splash shield.

5. On models with manual transmission, remove rack and pinion to front crossmember attaching bolts and position aside.

6. On all models, loosen converter to exhaust pipe clamp bolts.

7. Remove oil pan bolts.

8. Install engine lifting device and raise engine until oil pan can be removed, Fig. 6.

Fig. 8 Installing crankcase front cover

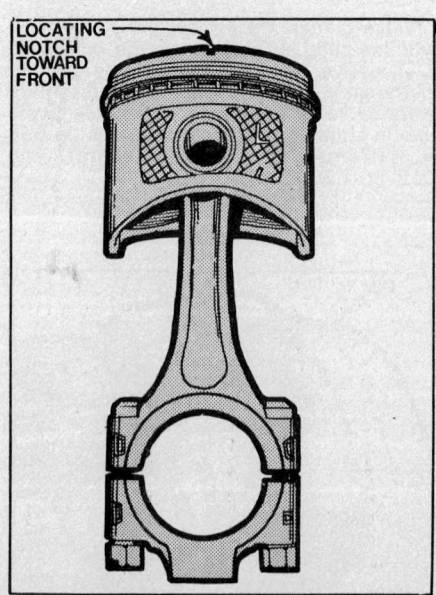

LOCATING NOTCH TOWARD FRONT

Fig. 9 Piston and rod assembly

OIL PUMP

1. Remove coil bracket attaching bolts and position coil aside.
2. Remove fuel pump and push rod.
3. Remove distributor.
4. Remove oil pan, then remove oil pump screen and pipe assembly and oil pump.

CRANKSHAFT REAR OIL SEAL

1. Remove engine and place on stand.
2. Remove oil pan and rear main bearing cap.
3. Clean bearing cap and case. Inspect crankshaft seal for damage.
4. Install seal in case, ensure seal is fully seated.
5. Coat bearing cap split line with sealer.
6. Install rear main bearing cap.
7. Install sealer in bearing cap vertical grooves, remove any excess sealer.
8. Install oil pan, then install engine in vehicle.

CRANKCASE FRONT COVER

1. Remove engine upper and lower front covers, crankshaft pulley, timing belt and crankshaft sprocket.
2. Remove three crankcase front cover to oil pan attaching bolts, then the crankcase cover to engine attaching bolts.
3. Remove crankcase front cover, cover gasket and front portion of oil pan gasket.

NOTE: To fabricate a replacement crankcase front cover to oil pan gasket, position crankcase cover over a new oil pan gasket as shown in Fig. 7. When installing gasket apply sealer to cut off portion of gasket.

---

4. Inspect crankshaft oil seal, replace if necessary.
5. Install crankcase front cover using tool J-26434, Fig. 8.

BELT TENSION DATA

	New Lbs.	Used Lbs.
1976-79—		
Air Condition	120-150	—
A.I.R. Pump	70-100	—
Generator	70-100	—
Timing Belt		
15 mm	55	—
19 mm	70	—

FUEL PUMP PRESSURE

Year	Engine	Pressure Lbs.
1976-79	All	5-6½

FUEL PUMP, REPLACE

1. Raise vehicle and remove ignition coil.
2. Remove A/C compressor rear bracket, if equipped.
3. Remove fuel pump attaching bolts and fuel pump.

WATER PUMP, REPLACE

1. Disconnect battery ground cable.
2. Remove drive belts, fan and pulley.
3. Remove engine front cover.
4. Drain cooling system and disconnect radiator hose and heater hose from water pump.
5. Loosen idler pulley bolt and remove belt from camshaft pulley.
6. Remove water pump attaching bolts and the water pump.

Clutch & Transmission Section

CLUTCH, ADJUST

Initial Ball Stud Adjustment

1. Place gage, J-23644 for 1976-77 models, J-28449 for 1978-79 models, with flat end against clutch housing front face and the hooked end is positioned in the bottom depression of the clutch fork, Fig. 1.
2. Turn ball inward until clutch release bearing contacts clutch spring.
3. Install and torque lock nut to 25 ft. lbs. (33 N·m).
4. Remove gage.

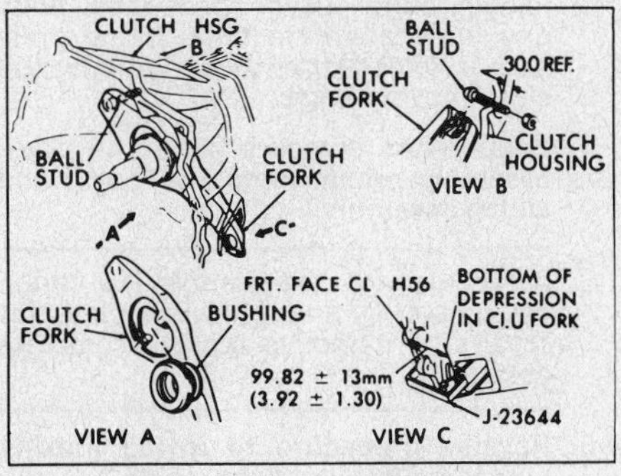

Clutch Cable Attachment & Adjustment

Late 1977 & 1978-79

1. Install clutch cable through hole in clutch fork and seat, then install return spring.
2. From engine compartment, pull cable until clutch pedal is firmly against pedal stop and hold in position, Fig. 2.
3. Install snap ring in first fully visible groove in cable from sleeve, then release cable.

Fig. 1 Ball stud adjustment

4. Clutch pedal lash should be .58 to 1.08 in. (15-27 mm), if not, adjust clutch pedal as described under Clutch Pedal Adjustment.

1976 & Early 1977

1. Install cable through clutch fork hole and pull until clutch pedal firmly contacts bumper. Hold cable in position.

2. Push clutch fork forward until throwout bearing contacts clutch spring fingers. Then, thread nut on cable until bottomed against spherical surface of clutch fork.
3. To adjust clutch pedal free play, follow either of the two methods outlined below Fig. 3.
4. Attach return spring.
5. Clutch pedal free travel should be .812 inch (20.6mm).

Method 1—Place a .171 inch (4.35 mm) shim stock against surface D of nut B. Thread locknut onto cable until it contacts shim stock. Remove shim stock and back off nut B until it contacts lock nut. Torque lock nut to 4 ft. lbs. (6 N·m).

Method 2—Rotate nut B 4.35 turns counter-clockwise. Thread lock nut on cable until it contacts nut B. Torque lock nut to 4 ft. lbs. (6 N·m).

Clutch Pedal Adjustment

Late 1977 & 1978-79

1. If clutch pedal lash is insufficient, re-

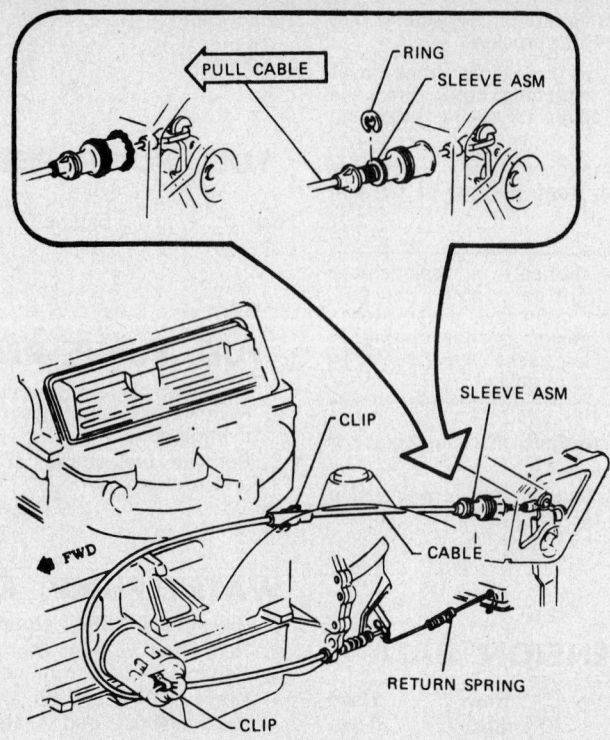

Fig. 2 Clutch cable adjustment. Late 1977 & 1978-79

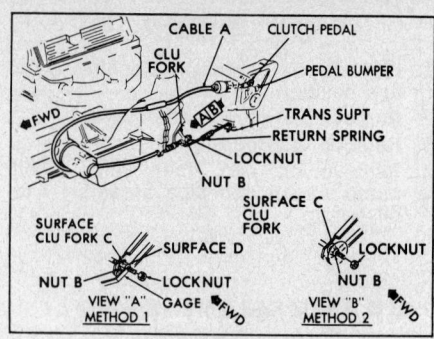

Fig. 3 Clutch cable adjustment.
1976 & early 1977

move snap ring from cable and allow cable to move into dash by one cable notch, then reinstall snap ring, Fig. 2.

2. If clutch pedal lash is excessive, remove snap ring from cable, and pull cable out of dash by one cable notch, then reinstall snap ring, Fig. 2.

3. Check to ensure clutch pedal lash is .58 to 1.08 in. (15-27 mm).

1976 & Early 1977

1. Loosen cable ball stud lock nut, located on the clutch housing right side.

2. Adjust ball stud to obtain .812 inch (20.6mm) clutch pedal free travel.

3. Torque lock nut to 25 ft. lbs. (33 N·m).

4. Check adjustment.

CLUTCH, REPLACE

1. Raise vehicle and remove transmission as outlined under "Manual Transmission, Replace" procedure.

2. Remove release bearing from the clutch fork and sleeve by sliding lever off ball stud and against spring force. If ball stud is to be replaced, remove cap, lock nut and stud from housing.

3. Make sure alignment marks on clutch assembly and flywheel are distinguishable.

4. Loosen clutch cover to flywheel bolts one turn at a time until spring pressure is released, to avoid bending the clutch cover flange.

5. Support the pressure plate and cover assembly while removing bolts and clutch assembly.

NOTE: Do not disassemble the clutch cover, spring and pressure plate for repairs. If defective replace complete assembly.

6. Reverse procedure to install making sure to index alignment marks.

CAUTION: Check position of engine in front mounts and realign as necessary.

MANUAL TRANSMISSION, REPLACE

1. Remove shifter assembly.

2. Raise vehicle and drain transmission lubricant.

3. Remove propeller shaft.

4. Disconnect speedometer cable and the back-up lamp switch.

5. Disconnect return spring and clutch cable from clutch fork.

6. Remove transmission to crossmember bolts.

7. Remove exhaust manifold nuts and the catalytic converter to transmission bracket bolts.

8. Remove crossmember to frame bolts, then the crossmember from vehicle.

9. Remove dust cover.

10. Remove clutch housing to engine retaining bolts, slide transmission rearward and remove from vehicle.

11. Reverse procedure to install.

1979 AUTO. TRANS. LINKAGE ADJUSTMENTS

Linkage adjustment procedures for 1979 models are the same as those for 1978 models as outlined elsewhere in this manual.

Rear Axle, Propeller Shaft & Brakes

REAR AXLE

Description

The rear axle, Fig. 1, is a semi-floating type consisting of a cast carrier and large bosses on each end into which two welded steel tubes are fitted. The carrier contains an overhung hypoid pinion and ring gear. The differential is a two pinion arrangement.

The overhung hypoid drive pinion, is supported by two preloaded tapered roller bearings. The pinion shaft is sealed by means of a molded, spring loaded, rubber seal. The seal is mounted on the pinion shaft flange which is splined and bolts to the hypoid pinion shaft.

The ring gear is bolted to a one piece differential case and is supported by two preloaded tapered roller bearings.

A rear axle extension housing is bolted to the axle housing and is attached to the underbody by a center bearing support. An extension shaft inside the housing is splined to the drive pinion at the rear end and to the companion flange at the forward end.

Removal

1. Raise vehicle on a hoist.
2. Place adjustable lifting device under axle.
3. Disconnect rear shock absorbers from axle and remove propeller shaft and extension housing, Fig. 2.
4. Remove both rear wheels.
5. Retract shoes and remove right and left brake drums, Fig. 3.
6. Disconnect brake lines from clips on axle tubes.
7. Disconnect track and stabilizer bars from axle tube.
8. Remove differential cover and drain lubricant.
9. Unscrew differential lock screw, remove pinion shaft and axle shaft "C" locks. Reinstall pinion shaft and tighten lock screw to retain differential gears.
10. Remove both axle shafts.
11. Remove brake backing plate retain-

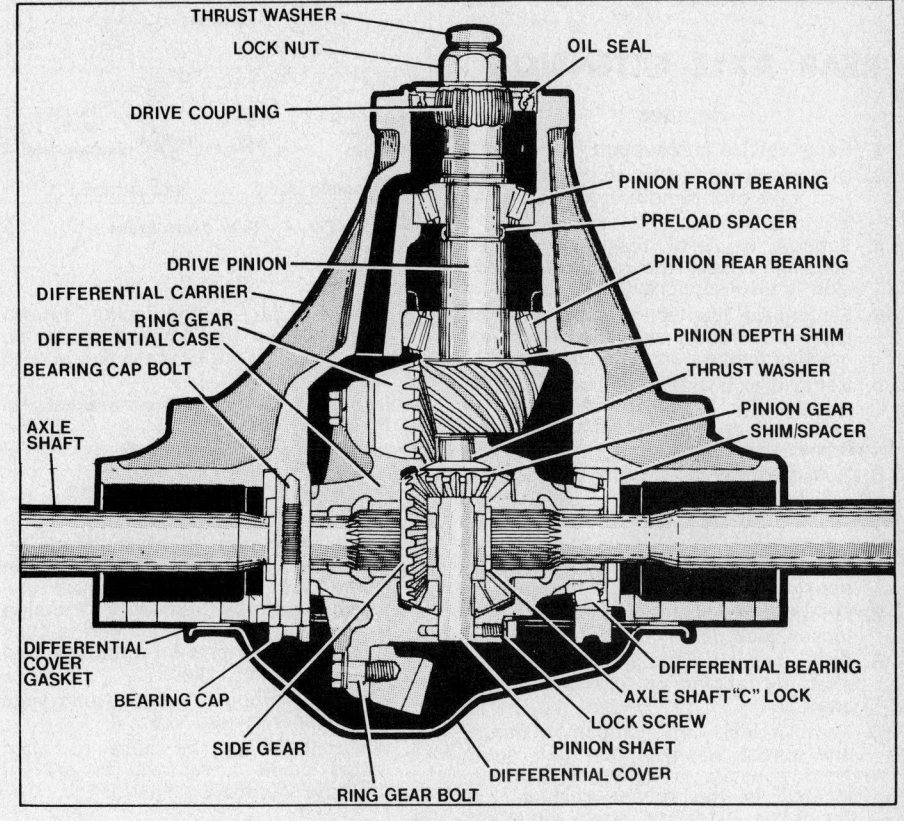

Fig. 1   Rear axle cross section

ing nuts and remove backing plates, with shoes and brake lines attached, and wire to frame.
12. Remove right and left lower control arm pivot bolts at axle.
13. Lower axle assembly slowly until coil spring tension is released, then remove axle.

AXLE SHAFT

1. Raise vehicle on a hoist and remove wheel and tire assembly and brake drum.
2. Drain lubricant from axle by removing carrier cover.
3. Unscrew pinion shaft lock screw and remove pinion shaft.
4. Push flanged end of exle shaft toward center of car and remove "C" lock from button end of shaft.
5. Remove axle shaft from housing being careful not to damage seal.

Oil Seal &/or Bearing Replacement

1. If replacing seal only, remove the seal by using the button end of axle shaft. Insert the button end of shaft behind the steel case of the seal and pry seal out of bore being careful not to damage housing.

2. If replacing bearings, insert tool J-25593 into bore so tool head grasps behind bearing. Slide washer against seal, or bearing, and turn nut against washer. Attach slide hammer J-2619 and remove bearing.

3. Lubricate bearing with rear axle lubricant, then install bearing into housing bore with tool J-25594 and slide hammer J-8092. Make sure tool contacts end of axle housing to insure proper bearing depth.

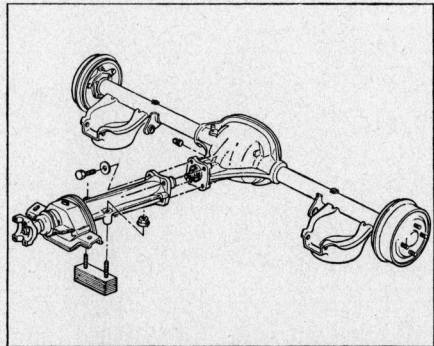

Fig. 2   Rear axle assembly

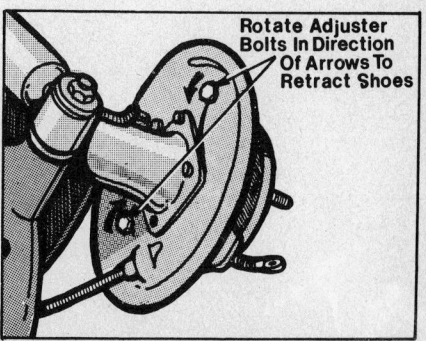

Fig. 3   Retracting brake shoes

4. Pack cavity between seal lips with a high melting point wheel bearing lubricant. Position seal on tool J-22922 and position seal in axle housing bore, tap seal in bore until flush with end of axle housing.

REAR AXLE EXTENSION

Replace

1. Raise vehicle and support rear axle.
2. Disconnect propeller shaft from the rear yoke and remove from transmission, Fig. 2.
3. Support front of rear axle carrier housing. Ensure the rear axle extension is also supported.
4. Disconnect center support bracket from underbody and the extension housing flange from axle housing.
5. Remove axle extension housing from vehicle. Pry extension housing from axle housing with a suitable screwdriver, if necessary.
6. Reverse procedure to install.

Service

1. Remove bolt securing extension housing to center support bracket.
2. Mount companion flange in a vise and loosen lock nut.
3. Drive splined companion flange off shaft by tapping on lock nut end of shaft.
4. Remove lock nut, companion flange and thrust washer, then pull shaft from housing. If centering bearing, located in the rubber cushion, remains on extension shaft, drive off shaft with a suitable drift.
5. Note position of bearing in rubber cushion and the cushion in center support. Then, using a suitable screwdriver, separate rubber cushion from center support bracket and remove bearing from cushion.
6. Clean, inspect and replace components, if necessary.
7. Install rubber cushion into center support bracket and place center support assembly over extension housing.
8. Press bearing onto extension shaft and insert shaft into housing through rubber cushion. Install thrust washer

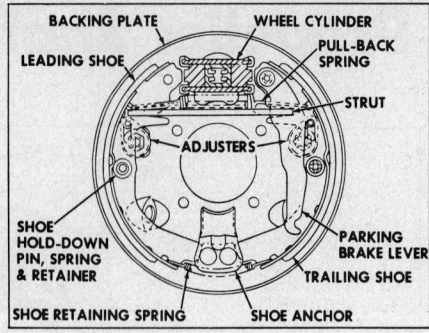

Fig. 4 Rear drum brake

with circular cavity facing toward bearing, then the companion flange, using the lock nut to press flange onto shaft splines.
9. Install bolts retaining bracket to housing.

PROPELLER SHAFT

1. Raise vehicle on a hoist. Mark relationship of shaft to companion flange and disconnect the rear universal joint by removing trunnion bearing "U" bolts. Tape bearing cups to trunnion to prevent dropping and loss of bearing rollers.
2. Withdraw propeller shaft front yoke from transmission.
3. When installing, be sure to align marks made in removal to prevent driveline vibration.

BRAKE ADJUSTMENTS

Disc brakes are used on front wheels and drum brakes are used on rear wheels. Rear brake adjustment is automatic. Adjustment takes place whenever brakes are applied. An adjuster is attached to each brake shoe by means of a pin, Fig. 4. This pin is smaller than the slot in the brake shoe. When brakes are applied and brake shoes move outward the automatic adjuster follows. When brakes are released the brake shoe moves inward until it contacts the automatic adjuster pin. The space between adjuster pin and slot in

brake shoe provides shoe to drum clearance.

NOTE: If manual adjustment or shoe retraction is necessary refer to Fig. 3.

PARKING BRAKE, ADJUST

1. Raise vehicle.
2. Apply parking brake one notch from fully released position.
3. Tighten equalizer adjusting nut until a light drag is felt when rear wheels are rotated in a forward direction.
4. Release parking brake and rotate rear wheels. No drag should be felt.

MASTER CYLINDER, REPLACE

1. Disconnect push rod from brake pedal and remove push rod boot.
2. Remove air cleaner.
3. Disconnect brake lines from master cylinder. Cap ends of lines to prevent entry of dirt.
4. Remove master cylinder to dash attaching nuts and the master cylinder.

POWER BRAKE UNIT, REPLACE

1. Remove air cleaner, then disconnect vacuum hose from check valve.
2. Remove master cylinder brace rod.
3. Remove remaining master cylinder to brake unit attaching nuts, then pull master forward until it clears brake unit mounting studs. Carefully move master cylinder aside with brake lines attached.

NOTE: Support master cylinder to avoid stress on brake lines. Move master cylinder only enough to provide clearance for brake unit removal.

4. Remove nuts attaching brake unit to dash panel.
5. Remove push rod to pedal retainer and slide push rod off pedal pin.
6. Remove power brake unit from vehicle.

Rear Suspension Section

DESCRIPTION

This suspension system, Fig. 1, incorporates two tubular lower control arms, a straight track rod, two shock absorbers, two coil springs and a stabilizer bar.

SHOCK ABSORBER, REPLACE

1. Raise vehicle and support rear axle with a suitable jack.
2. Disconnect shock absorber from upper and lower mounting.
3. Reverse procedure to install.

COIL SPRING, REPLACE

1. Raise vehicle and support rear axle with a suitable jack.
2. Disconnect both shock absorbers from lower brackets.

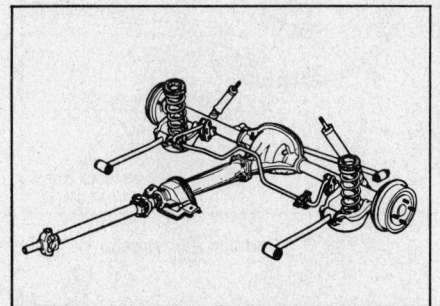

Fig. 1   Rear suspension

3. Disconnect rear axle extension bracket.

NOTE: Ensure axle is properly supported before disconnecting extension bracket.

4. Slowly lower axle until springs and insulators can be removed.

NOTE: When lower axle ensure that brake hoses do not stretch or become damaged.

5. Reverse procedure to install.

TRACK ROD, REPLACE

1. Raise vehicle and support rear axle with a suitable jack.
2. Disconnect stabilizer bar, if equipped, Fig. 2.
3. Remove control arm front and rear attaching bolts and control arm, Fig. 3.
4. Remove attaching bolts and track rod.
5. Reverse procedure to install.

NOTE: Vehicle must be at curb height when tightening pivot bolts.

LOWER CONTROL ARMS, REPLACE

1. Raise vehicle and support rear axle.
2. Disconnect stabilizer bar, if equipped, Fig. 2.
3. Disconnect the front and rear control arm attaching bolts and remove control arm from vehicle, Fig. 3.

NOTE: Replace one control arm at a time to prevent axle from rolling or slipping sideways.

4. Reverse procedure to install.

STABILIZER BAR, REPLACE

1. Raise vehicle and support rear axle.
2. Disconnect stablizer bar from underbody and axle tube connections, Fig. 2, then remove stabilizer bar from vehicle.
3. Reverse procedure to install.

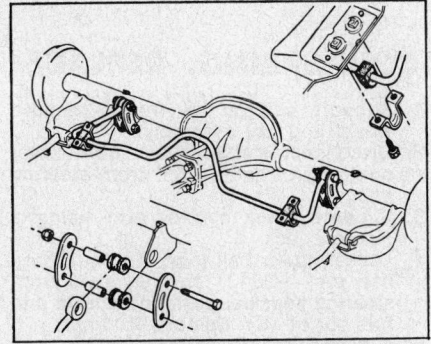

Fig. 2   Stabilizer bar installation

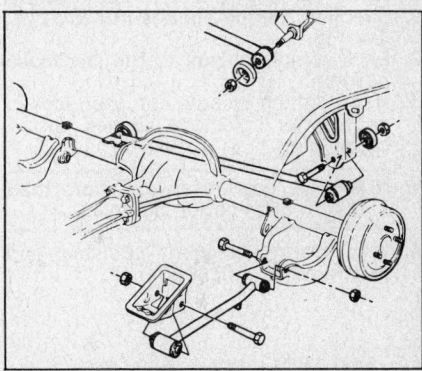

Fig. 3   Track rod and lower control arm

Front End & Steering Section

DESCRIPTION

This front suspension system, Fig. 1, uses long and short control arms with coil springs mounted between the lower control arms and front suspension crossmember.

WHEEL ALIGNMENT

Caster

Caster angle is adjusted by rearranging washers located at both ends of the upper

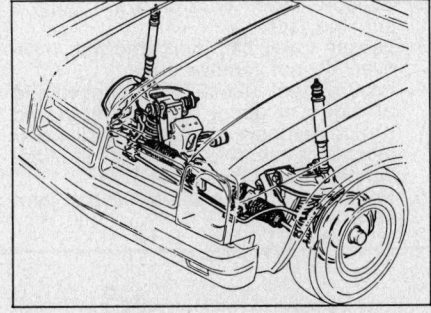

Fig. 1   Front suspension

control arm, Fig. 2. A kit consisting of two washers, one of 3 mm thickness and one of 9mm thickness, must be used when adjusting caster angle.

Camber

Camber is adjusted by removing the upper ball joint, rotating it $\frac{1}{2}$ turn and reinstalling it with flat of upper flange on inboard side of control arm, Fig. 3. This will increase positive camber by approximately 1°.

TOE-IN ADJUST

To adjust toe-in, loosen tie rod jam nuts

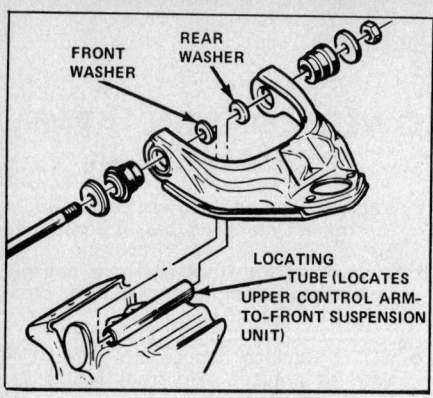

Fig. 2   Caster adjustment

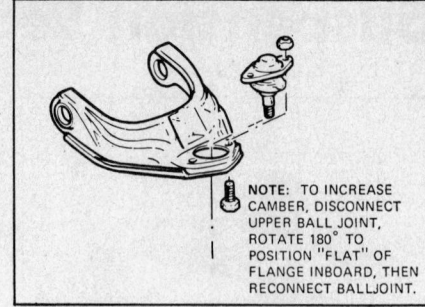

Fig. 3   Camber adjustment

NOTE: TO INCREASE CAMBER, DISCONNECT UPPER BALL JOINT, ROTATE 180° TO POSITION "FLAT" OF FLANGE INBOARD, THEN RECONNECT BALLJOINT.

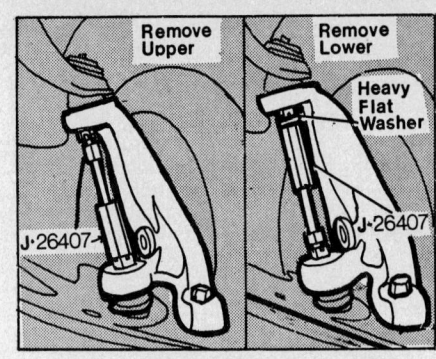

Fig. 4   Separating ball joint studs from steering knuckle

at tie rod ends and loosen clamp at rubber bellows. Turn each tie rod to increase or decrease its length until proper toe-in is obtained.

WHEEL BEARINGS, ADJUST

1. While rotating wheel in the forward direction, torque spindle nut to 12 ft. lbs, Fig. 2.
2. Back spindle nut off to the just loose position.
3. Hand tighten spindle nut, then loosen until cotter holes are aligned, install cotter pin.

NOTE: Do not loosen nut more than ½ flat to align cotter pin holes.

4. With bearings properly adjusted, end play must be .001-.005 inch.

WHEEL BEARINGS, REPLACE

1. Raise vehicle, remove wheel and tire assembly.
2. Remove two caliper mounting bracket to steering knuckle attaching bolts, remove caliper.
3. Remove hub dust cap, cotter pin, spindle nut, washer, outer wheel bearing and hub.
4. Pry out grease seal, then remove inner bearing from hub.

SHOCK ABSORBER, REPLACE

1. Hold upper stem of shock absorber, and remove nut, retainer and grommet.

2. Raise vehicle and remove lower shock absorber retaining bolts.
3. Lower shock absorber from vehicle.
4. Reverse procedure to install. Torque shock absorber lower retaining bolts to 35-50 ft. lbs. and the upper retaining nut to 60-120 in. lbs.

BALL JOINTS, REPLACE

Upper Ball Joint

1. Raise vehicle and remove wheel and tire assembly.
2. Support lower control arm using a suitable jack.
3. Loosen upper ball joint stud nut, however, do not remove nut.
4. Position tool J-26407 with cupped end over lower ball joint stud and turn threaded end of tool until upper ball joint stud is free of steering knuckle, Fig. 4.
5. Remove tool, then the upper stud nut.
6. Remove two nuts securing ball joint to upper control arm and the ball joint.

NOTE: Inspect tapered hole in steering knuckle. If out of round or damaged, the knuckle must be replaced.

7. Install ball joint on upper control arm and torque bolts to 29 ft. lbs.
8. Position upper ball joint stud on steering knuckle, then install and torque stud nut to 29-36 ft. lbs.
9. Install wheel and tire assembly and lower vehicle.

Lower Ball Joint

1. Raise vehicle and remove wheel and tire assembly.
2. Support lower control arm using a suitable jack.
3. Loosen lower ball joint stud nut, however, do not remove nut.
4. Position tool J-26407 with cupped end of tool over upper ball joint stud and turn threaded end of tool until lower ball joint stud is free of steering knuckle, Fig. 4.
5. Remove tool, then the lower ball joint stud nut.

6. Remove ball joint from lower control arm.

NOTE: Inspect tapered hole in steering knuckle, if out of round or damaged, the knuckle must be replaced.

7. Insert ball joint through lower control arm and into steering knuckle.
8. Install ball joint stud nut and torque to 41-54 ft. lbs.
9. Install wheel and tire assembly and lower vehicle.

COIL SPRING, REPLACE

1. Support vehicle by frame, remove wheel and tire assembly.
2. Disconnect stabilizer bar from lower control arm and tie rod from steering knuckle.
3. Support lower control arm using a suitable jack.
4. Loosen lower ball joint stud nut, then use tool J-26407 to free stud from steering knuckle, position knuckle and hub out of way. Remove stud nut.
5. Loosen lower control arm pivot bolts.
6. Install a safety chain around spring and through lower control arm.
7. Slowly lower control arm until spring is extended as far as possible, then use pry bar to carefully lift spring over lower control arm spring seat.

STEERING GEAR, REPLACE

1. Raise vehicle and remove bolts and shield.
2. Remove tie rod cotter pins and nuts from tie rod ends and separate tie rods from steering knuckles.
3. Remove flexible coupling pinch bolt.
4. Remove steering gear clamp bolts, then the steering gear assembly from vehicle.
5. Reverse procedure to install.

CHEV. MONZA • BUICK SKYHAWK OLDS STARFIRE • PONT. SUNBIRD

INDEX OF SERVICE OPERATIONS

SERIAL NUMBER LOCATION

On top of instrument panel, left front.

ENGINE NUMBER LOCATION

4-140 Cyl: On pad at right side of cylinder block, above starter.

4-151: On pad at right front side by distributor shaft hole. V6 & V8: Pad at front righthand side of cylinder block.

ENGINE IDENTIFICATION CODE

4-140 and Chevrolet V8 engines are identified by the code letters immediately following the engine number. 4-151 engines are identified by the code letters on the pad. V6-231 engines are identified by the code letters immediately preceding the engine number.

Monza

1975	4-140	CAM, CAR, CAS
	4-140	CAT, CBB, CBC
	V8-262 Std. Tr.	CZA, CZB, CZC
	V8-262 Std. Tr.	CZD, CZT, CZU
	V8-262 Auto. Tr.	CZE, CZG
	V8-262 Auto. Tr.	CGA, CGJ, CGK
	V8-350	CHY
	4-122	ZCA
1976	4-140	CAY, CAZ, CBK, CBL
	4-140	CBS, CBT, CBU, CBW
	4-140	CBX, CBY, CBZ
	V8-262	CGA, CGB, CGL, CZU, CZT
	4-140	CAA, CAB
1977	4-140	CAY, CAZ, CBK, CBL
	4-140	CBS, CBT, CBU, CBW
	4-140	CBX, CBY, CBZ
	V8-305	CPK, CPL, CPU, CPX
	V8-305	CRC, CRD
1978	4-151	WB, WD, WH
	4-151	XL, XN
	4-151	AC, AD
	4-151	ZA, ZB, ZC, ZD, ZF
	4-151	ZH, ZJ, ZK, ZL, ZN
	V6-196	PC, PD
	V6-231	OC, OD, OE, OF
	V8-305	CTA, CTB, CTC, CTD, CTF
1979	4-151	AB, AC, AD, AF, AM
	4-151	WD, WJ, XJ, XK
	4-151	ZA, ZB, ZP, ZR
	V6-196	FC, FD
	V6-231	NA, NB, NC, NF
	V8-305	DNA, DNB, DNC, DND
	V8-305	DTK, DTL

Skyhawk

1975	V6-231	AD
1976	V6-231 Std. Tr.①	FH
	V6-231 Std. Tr.②	FO
	V6-231 Auto. Tr.①	FI
	V6-231 Auto. Tr.②	FJ
1977	V6-231	SA, SB, SD
	V6-231	SO, SX, SY
1978	V6-231	OA, OB, OC
	V6-231	OD, OE, OF
	V6-231	OG

Starfire

1975	V6-231 Std. Tr.①	FP
	V6-231 Auto. Tr.①	FR
	V6-231 Auto. Tr.②	FS

1976	4-140 Std. Tr.①	BS
	4-140 Std. Tr.②	BK
	4-140 Auto. Tr.①	BT
	4-140 Auto. Tr.②	BL
1977	4-140 Std. Tr.①	CAY, CBS
	4-140 Std. Tr.②	CAZ, CBK
	4-140 Auto. Tr.①	CBT
	4-140 Auto. Tr.①	CBL
	4-140 Auto. Tr.①	CBS
	4-140 Auto. Tr.③	CBT
	V6-231 Std. Tr.①	SA
	V6-231 Std. Tr.②	SB
	V6-231 Auto. Tr.①	SD, SW
	V6-231 Auto. Tr.②	SE, SY
	V6-231 Auto. Tr.③	SF
	V6-231 Std. Tr.①	FH
	V6-231 Std. Tr.②	FO
	V6-231 Auto. Tr.①	FI
	V6-231 Auto. Tr.②	FJ
	V6-231	SQ, SR
	V8-305 Auto. Trans.①	CRL
	V8-305 Auto. Trans.②	CRM, CRS
	V8-305 Auto. Trans.③	CRT
	V8-305	CPX, CPY
1978	4-151 Auto. Trans.①	XL, XN
	4-151 Man. Trans.①	WD, WH
	4-151 Auto. Trans.②	ZK, ZJ
	4-151	WB, ZA, ZB
	V6-231 Man. Trans.①	OA
	V6-231 Auto. Trans.①	ED, OB
	V6-231 Man. Trans.②	OD
	V6-231 Auto. Trans.②	OE
	V6-231 Man. Trans.③	OF
	V6-231 Auto. Trans.③	OC
	V6-231	OH
	V8-305 Man. Trans.①	CTA
	V8-305 Auto. Trans.①	CTB
	V8-305 Auto. Trans.②	CTF
	V8-305 Auto. Trans.②	CTD
1979	4-151 Auto. Trans.①	XJ, XK
	4-151 Man. Trans.①	WJ, WM
	4-151 Auto. Trans.①	ZP, ZR
	4-151 Man. Trans.②	AF, AH
	V6-231 Auto. Trans.④	NB, NM
	V6-231 Auto. Trans.①	NH
	V6-231 Man. Trans.④	NA
	V6-231 Man. Trans.②	NC
	V6-231 Auto. Trans.③	NE
	V6-231 Auto. Trans.④	DTL
	V8-305 Man. Trans.④	DTK
	V8-305 Auto. Trans.④	DND

Sunbird

1976	4-140 Std. Tr.①	AY, BH, BS
	4-140 Std. Tr.①	BW, BX, BZ
	4-140 Std. Tr.②	AZ, BK, BY

1977	4-140 Auto. Tr.①	BJ, BT, BU
	4-140 Auto. Tr.②	BL
	V6-231 Std. Tr.①	FH
	V6-231 Std. Tr.②	FC, FO
	V6-231 Auto. Tr.①	FI
	V6-231 Auto. Tr.②	FJ
1977	4-140 Std. Tr.①	CAY, CBS, CBZ
	4-140 Std. Tr.②	CAZ, CBK, CBV
	4-140 Std. Tr.③	CBS, CBZ
	4-140 Auto. Tr.①③	CBT
	4-140	CAK, CBL, CBU
	4-140	CBW, CBX, CBY
	4-151 Std. Tr.①	WC, WD
	4-151 Auto. Tr.①	YL, YM
	4-151 Auto. Tr.②	ZH, ZJ
	4-151	ZD, ZF, ZN, ZP
	V6-231 Std. Tr.①	SA
	V6-231 Std. Tr.②	SB
	V6-231 Auto. Tr.①	SD
	V6-231 Auto. Tr.②	SY
	V6-231 Auto. Tr.③	SX
	V6-231	SO
1978	4-151 Man. Trans.①	WB, WD, WH
	4-151 Auto. Trans.①	XN, XL
	4-151 Auto. Trans.②	ZJ, ZK
	4-151	AC, AD
	4-151	ZA, ZB, ZC, ZD
	4-151	ZH, ZF, ZL, ZN
	V6-231 Auto. Trans.①	ED
	V6-231 Man. Trans.①	OA
	V6-231 Auto. Trans.②	EK, EL, EE, OE, EG
	V6-231 Man. Trans.②	OD
	V6-231 Auto. Trans.③	OC
	V6-231 Man. Trans.③	OF
	V6-231	OE, OB
1979	4-151 Man. Trans.①	WJ, WM
	4-151 Man. Trans.②	AF, AH
	4-151 Auto. Trans.①	XJ, XK
	4-151 Auto. Trans.②	ZP, ZR
	V6-231 Man. Trans.①	NA, NG, RA
	V6-231 Man. Trans.②	NC
	V6-231 Auto. Trans.④	NB, NJ, RB, RC, RX
	V6-231 Auto. Trans.②	NH, RG, RW, RY
	V6-231 Auto. Trans.③	NE
	V8-305 Man. Trans.④	DTK, DTM
	V8-305 Auto. Trans.④	DNJ, DTL
	V8-305 Auto. Trans.②	DND

①—Except California.
②—California.
③—High altitude.
④—Exc. High altitude & Calif.

GRILLE IDENTIFICATION

1975-76 Chevrolet Monza Hatchback & 1976-77 Towne Coupe with Sport Option

1975-76 Chevrolet Monza Towne Coupe Less Sport Option

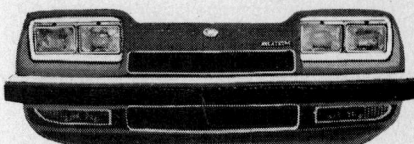

1975-76 Buick Skyhawk

1975-76 Oldsmobile Starfire

1976 Pontiac Sunbird

1977 Chevrolet Monza Towne Coupe Less Sport Option

1977-78 Buick Skyhawk

1977-78 Oldsmobile Starfire

1977 Pontiac Sunbird

1977 Pontiac Formula Sunbird

1978 Pontiac Sunbird

1978-79 Chevrolet Monza

1978 Chevrolet Monza 2+2

1979 Buick Skylark

1979 Oldsmobile Starfire

1979 Pontiac Sunbird Sport Safari

1979 Pontiac Sunbird Coupe & Hatchback

GENERAL ENGINE SPECIFICATIONS

Year	Engine	Carburetor	Bore and Stroke	Piston Displacement, Cubic Inches	Compression Ratio	Maximum Brake H.P. @ R.P.M.	Maximum Torque Lbs. Ft. @ R.P.M.	Normal Oil Pressure Pounds
1975	78 Horsepower①........4-140	1 Barrel	3.501 x 3.625	140	8.0	78 @ 4200	120 @ 2000	40
	80 Horsepower①②......4-140	2 Barrel	3.501 x 3.625	140	8.0	80 @ 4400	116 @ 2800	40
	87 Horsepower①.......4-140	2 Barrel	3.501 x 3.625	140	8.0	87 @ 4400	122 @ 2800	40
	110 Horsepower①.......V6-231	2 Barrel	3.80 x 3.40	231	8.0	110 @ 4000	175 @ 2000	37
	110 Horsepower①.......V8-262	2 Barrel	3.67 x 3.10	262	8.5	110 @ 3600	200 @ 2000	32-40
	125 Horsepower①.......V8-350	2 Barrel	4.00 x 3.48	350	8.5	125 @ 3600	235 @ 2000	32-40
1976	70 Horsepower①.......4-140	1 Barrel	3.501 x 3.625	140	8.0	70 @ 4400	107 @ 2400	40-45
	79 Horsepower①②......4-140	2 Barrel	3.501 x 3.625	140	8.0	79 @ 4400	109 @ 2800	40-45
	84 Horsepower①.......4-140	2 Barrel	3.501 x 3.625	140	8.0	84 @ 4400	109 @ 2800	40-45
	110 Horsepower①.......V6-231	2 Barrel	3.80 x 3.40	231	8.0	110 @ 4000	175 @ 2000	37
	110 Horsepower①.......V8-262	2 Barrel	3.671 x 3.100	262	8.5	110 @ 3600	195 @ 2000	32-40
	140 Horsepower①.......V8-305	2 Barrel	3.736 x 3.48	305	8.5	140 @ 3800	245 @ 2000	32-40
1977	84 Horsepower①.......4-140	2 Barrel	3.501 x 3.625	140	8.0	84 @ 4400	117 @ 2400	36-45
	87 Horsepower①.......4-151	2 Barrel	4.00 x 3.00	151	8.3	87 @ 4400	128 @ 2400	36-41
	105 Horsepower①.......V6-231	2 Barrel	3.80 x 3.40	231	8.0	105 @ 3200	185 @ 2000	37
	145 Horsepower①.......V8-305	2 Barrel	3.736 x 3.48	305	8.5	145 @ 3800	245 @ 2400	32-40
1978	85 Horsepower①.......4-151	2 Barrel	4.00 x 3.00	151	8.3	85 @ 4400	123 @ 2800	36-41
	86 Horsepower①.......V6-196	2 Barrel	3.50 x 3.40	196	8.0	86 @ 3600	160 @ 2000	37
	103 Horsepower①.......V6-231	2 Barrel	3.80 x 3.40	231	8.0	103 @ 3800	180 @ 2000	37
	135 Horsepower①.......V8-305	2 Barrel	3.736 x 3.48	305	8.5	135 @ 3800	240 @ 2000	32-40
	145 Horsepower①.......V8-305	2 Barrel	3.736 x 3.48	305	8.5	145 @ 3800	245 @ 2400	32-40
1979	90 Horsepower①........4-151	2 Barrel	4.00 x 3.00	151	8.3	90 @ 4400	128 @ 2400	36-41
	105 Horsepower①.......V6-196	2 Barrel	3.50 x 3.40	196	8.0	105 @ 3800	160 @ 2000	37
	115 Horsepower①.......V6-231	2 Barrel	3.80 x 3.40	231	8.0	115 @ 3800	190 @ 2000	37
	Horsepower①.......V8-305	2 Barrel	3.736 x 3.48	305	8.4	—	—	32-40

①—Ratings are net—As installed in vehicle.
②—California.

TUNE UP SPECIFICATIONS

The following specifications are published from the latest information available. This data should be used only in the absence of a decal affixed in the engine compartment.

★When using a timing light, disconnect vacuum hose or tube at distributor and plug opening in hose or tube so idle speed will not be affected.

●When checking compression, lowest cylinder must be within 80 percent of highest.

▲Before removing wires from distributor cap, determine location of No. 1 wire in cap, as distributor position may have been altered from tha shown at the end of this chart.

Year	Spark Plug		Distributor		Ignition Timing★			Carb. Adjustments					
	Type	Gap Inch	Point Gap Inch	Dwell Angle Deg.	Firing Order Fig. ▲	Timing BTDC ①	Mark Fig.	Hot Idle Speed ②		Air Fuel Ratio		Idle "CO" %	
								Std. Trans.	Auto. Trans.	Std. Trans.	Auto. Trans.	Std. Trans.	Auto. Trans.
1975													
4-140	R43TSX④	.060	—	—	A	③	B	700	750	—	—	.5	.5
V6-231	R44SX	.060	—	—	C	12°	D	800	650	—	—	—	—
V8-262	R44TX	.060	—	—	E	8°	F	800	600	—	—	—	—
V8-350	R44TX	.060	—	—	E	6°	G	800	600	—	—	—	—

Continued

TUNE UP SPECIFICATIONS—Continued

The following specifications are published from the latest information available. This data should be used only in the absence of a decal affixed in the engine compartment.

★When using a timing light, disconnect vacuum hose or tube at distributor and plug opening in tube or hose so idle speed will not be affected.

●When checking compression, lowest cylinder must be within 80 percent of highest.

▲Before removing wires from distributor cap, determine location of the No. 1 wire in cap, as distributor position may have been altered from that shown at the end of this chart.

Year	Spark Plug		Distributor		Ignition Timing★			Carb. Adjustments					
	Type	Gap Inch	Point Gap Inch	Dwell Angle Deg.	Firing Order Fig. ▲	Timing BTDC [1]	Mark Fig.	Hot Idle Speed [2]		Air Fuel Ratio		Idle "CO" %	
								Std. Trans.	Auto. Trans.	Std. Trans.	Auto. Trans.	Std. Trans.	Auto. Trans.
1976													
4-140 1 Bar. Carb.	R43TS	.035	—	—	A	[7]	B	[8]	750	—	—	—	—
4-140 2 Bar. Carb.[5]	R43TS	.035	—	—	A	[9]	B	700	750	—	—	—	—
4-140 2 Bar. Carb.[6]	R43TS	.035	—	—	A	[9]	B	[10]	750	—	—	—	—
V6-231	R44SX	.060	—	—	C	12°	D[25]	800	600	—	—	—	—
V8-262	R45TS	.045	—	—	E	8°	F	800	600	—	—	—	—
V8-305	R45TS	.045	—	—	E	[11]	G	—	600	—	—	—	—
1977													
4-140[12]	R43TS	.035	—	—	A	[13]	B	700/1250	650/850	—	—	—	—
4-140[6]	R43TS	.035	—	—	A	[17]	B	800/1250	650/850	—	—	—	—
4-140[15]	R43TS	.035	—	—	A	[13]	B	800/1250	700/850	—	—	—	—
4-151[5]	R44TSX	.060	—	—	H	14°	I	500/1200	650/850	—	—	—	—
4-151[6]	R44TSX	.060	—	—	H	12°	I	500/1000[20]	500/650[20]	—	—	—	—
V6-231[14]	R46TS	.040	—	—	J	12°	K[25]	800	600/670	—	—	—	—
V6-231[16]	R46TSX	.060	—	—	L	15°	M[25]	—	600/670	—	—	—	—
V8-305	R43TS	.035	—	—	E	[22]	G	700	500/650[23]	—	—	—	—
1978													
4-151	R44TSX	.060	—	—	H	[24]	I	1210/1000 [31]	850/650	—	—	—	—
V6-196	R46TSX	.060	—	—	L	15°	M[25]	800	600	—	—	—	—
V6-231	R46TSX	.060	—	—	L	15°	M[25]	800	600	—	—	—	—
V8-305	R45TS	.045	—	—	E	[18]	G	700	[19]	—	—	—	—
1979													
4-151	R43TSX	.060	—	—	H	[26]	I	[28][29]	[27][29]	—	—	—	—
V6-196	—	—	—	—	L	—	M[25]			—	—	—	—
V6-231	R46TSX	.060	—	—	L	15°	M[25]	600/800[20]	[29][30]	—	—	—	—
V8-305	R45TS	.045	—	—	E	4°	G	600	[29][21]	—	—	—	—

[1]—BTDC—Before Top Dead Center.

[2]—Idle speed on manual trans. equipped vehicles is adjusted in Neutral and on auto. trans. equipped vehicles is adjusted in Drive unless otherwise specified. Where two speeds are listed, the higher speed is with A/C solenoid energized.

[3]—Standard trans. 10°, Automatic trans. 12°.

[4]—If cold weather starting problems are encountered, use R43TS spark plug, gapped at .035 inch.

[5]—Exc. Calif.

[6]—California.

[7]—Man. trans., 10° BTDC; auto. trans., 8° BTDC.

[8]—Monza, 1200 RPM; Sunbird, 700 RPM.

[9]—Monza & Starfire man. trans., 10° BTDC; auto. trans. 12° BTDC. Sunbird man. trans., 8° BTDC; auto. trans., 10° BTDC.

[10]—Monza & Starfire; 1000 RPM; Sunbird, 700 RPM.

[11]—Except Calif., 8° BTDC; Calif., TDC.

[12]—Except high altitude & California engines.

[13]—Man. trans., TDC; auto. trans., 2° BTDC.

[14]—Exc. Even fire engine.

[15]—High altitude engine.

[16]—Even fire engine.

[17]—Man. trans., 2° ATDC; auto. trans. TDC.

[18]—Exc. Calif. & High Altitude, 4°; Calif. 6°; High Altitude, 8°.

[19]—Manual trans., 600 R.P.M.; Auto. trans. Exc. High altitude, 500 RPM & High altitude, 600 RPM.

[20]—Higher speed is with idle solenoid energized.

[21]—Exc. Calif., Less A/C 500, with A/C 550/600. Calif. 600/650.

[22]—Except Calif., 8° BTDC; Calif., 6° BTDC.

[23]—High altitude, 600/700.

[24]—Auto. Trans. 12°; Man. trans. 14°.

[25]—The harmonic balancer on these engines has two timing marks. The mark measuring 1/16 inch is used when setting timing with a hand held timing light. The mark measuring 1/8 inch is used when setting timing with magnetic timing equipment.

[26]—Exc. Calif., 12° BTDC; Calif. 14° BTDC.

[27]—Less A/C, 500/650 see note [20]; with A/C, 650/850.

[28]—Less A/C, 500/900 see note [20]; with A/C, 950/1200.

[29]—A/C "on", clutch wires disconnected.

[30]—Exc. Calif. & High altitude, Less A/C 550, with A/C 550/670; Calif. & High altitude, 600 Drive.

[31]—California models less A/C 500/1000 see [20].

Continued

TUNE UP NOTES—Continued

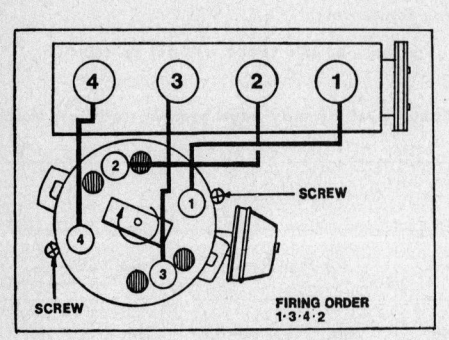

Fig. A

FIRING ORDER 1·3·4·2

SCREW

SCREW

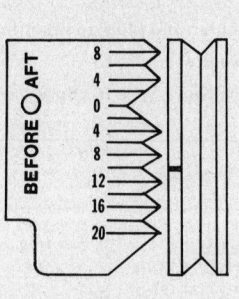

Fig. B

BEFORE ○ AFT

8 4 0 4 8 12 16 20

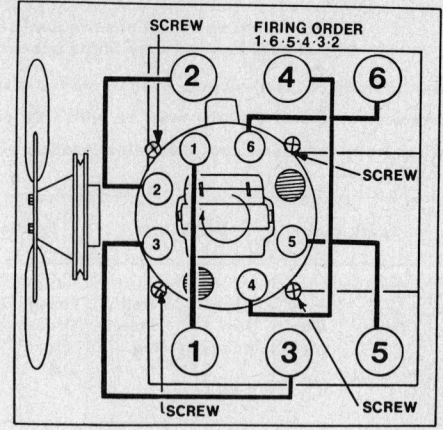

Fig. C

SCREW

FIRING ORDER 1·6·5·4·3·2

SCREW

SCREW

SCREW

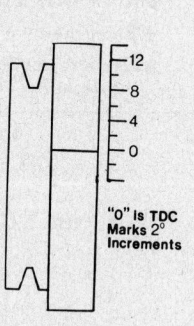

Fig. D

12 8 4 0

"0" Is TDC Marks 2° Increments

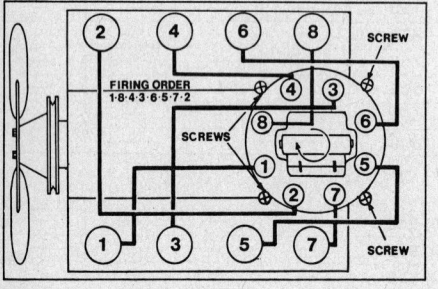

Fig. E

FIRING ORDER 1·8·4·3·6·5·7·2

SCREW

SCREWS

SCREW

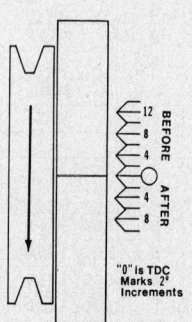

Fig. F

BEFORE AFTER

12 8 4 0 4 8

"0" Is TDC Marks 2° Increments

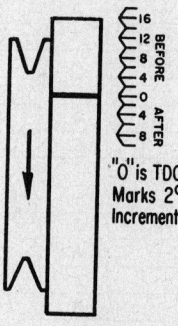

Fig. G

16 12 8 4 0 4 8

BEFORE AFTER

"0" is TDC Marks 2° Increments

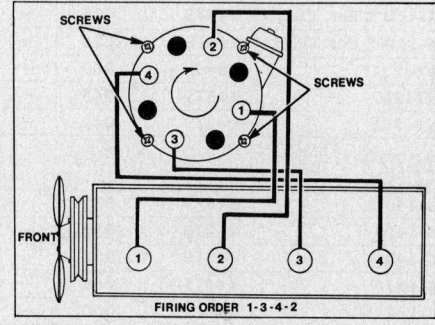

Fig. H

SCREWS

SCREWS

FRONT

FIRING ORDER 1·3·4·2

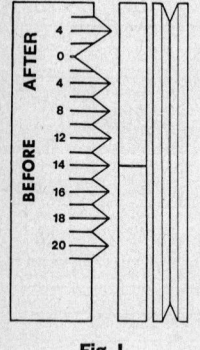

Fig. I

BEFORE AFTER

4 0 4 8 12 14 16 18 20

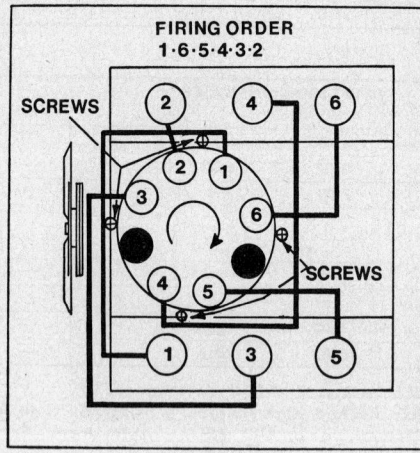

Fig. J

FIRING ORDER 1·6·5·4·3·2

SCREWS

SCREWS

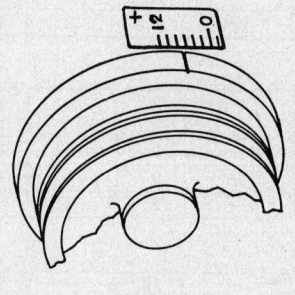

Fig. K

+ 12 0

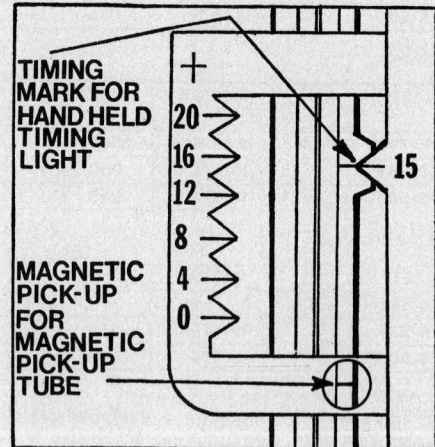

Fig. M

TIMING MARK FOR HAND HELD TIMING LIGHT

MAGNETIC PICK-UP FOR MAGNETIC PICK-UP TUBE

+ 20 16 12 8 4 0

15

Fig. L

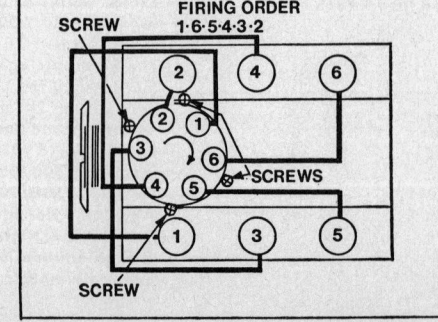

FIRING ORDER 1·6·5·4·3·2

SCREW

SCREWS

SCREW

DISTRIBUTOR SPECIFICATIONS

★If unit is checked on vehicle double the RPM and degrees to get crankshaft figures.

Distributor Part No.①	Centrifugal Advance Degrees @ RPM of Distributor				Vacuum Advance		Distributor Retard
	Advance Starts	Intermediate Advance		Full Advance	Inches if Vacuum To Start Plunger	Max. Adv. Dist. Deg. @ Vacuum	Max. Ret. Dist. Deg. @ Vacuum
1975							
1110650	0 @ 500	5 @ 1000	—	8 @ 2050	5-7	9 @ 10	—
1110651	0 @ 540	3 @ 1000	4½ @ 1750	8 @ 2050	5-7	9 @ 10	—
1112862	0 @ 810	2½ @ 1000	—	11 @ 2400	5	12 @ 12	—
1112880	0 @ 600	6 @ 1000	—	11 @ 2100	4	9 @ 12	—
1112933	0 @ 600	4½ @ 1000	—	11 @ 2000	3	8 @ 8	—
1976							
1103209	0 @ 600	4 @ 1000	—	11 @ 2000	4	5 @ 8	—
1119661	0 @ 525	3 @ 1000	—	8 @ 2050	6	9 @ 10	—
1110668	0 @ 638	—	—	8 @ 1600	6	12 @ 12	—
1112862	0 @ 810	2½ @ 1000	—	11 @ 2400	5	②	—
1112977	0 @ 500	5 @ 850	—	10 @ 1900	4	9 @ 12	—
1112983	0 @ 600	4½ @ 1000	—	11 @ 2000	4	7½ @ 10	—
1112999	0 @ 500	5 @ 850	—	10 @ 1900	4	5 @ 8	—
1977							
1103229	0 @ 600	3 @ 800	—	10 @ 2200	3½	10 @ 12	—
1103230	0 @ 600	3 @ 800	—	10 @ 2200	3½	10 @ 9	—
1103231	0 @ 600	—	—	10 @ 2200	3½	10 @ 12	—
1103239	—	—	—	—	—	—	—
1103244	—	—	—	—	—	—	—
1103252	—	—	—	—	—	—	—
1110538	0 @ 425	4 @ 600	—	8½ @ 1000	5	12 @ 10	—
1110539	0 @ 425	4 @ 600	—	8½ @ 1000	5	12 @ 10	—
1110677	0-2.2 @ 760	8.9-11 @ 1800	—	11 @ 2500	6	12¾ @ 20	—
1110686	0-2.15 @ 890	3.15-5.5 @ 1300	8.8-11 @ 1800	11 @ 2500	6	4¾ @ 20	—
1978							
1103281	0 @ 500	5 @ 850	—	10 @ 1900	4	9 @ 12	—
1103282	0 @ 500	5 @ 850	—	10 @ 1900	4	10 @ 10	—
1103312	0 @ 600	—	—	10 @ 2200	5	8 @ 11	—
1103328	0 @ 600	—	—	10 @ 2200	3½	10 @ 9③	—
1103329	0 @ 600	—	—	10 @ 2200	3½	10 @ 12	—
1103365	0 @ 600	—	—	10 @ 2200	5	8 @ 11	—
1110695	0-3 @ 1000	—	—	9 @ 1800	3-6	12 @ 13④	—
1110731	0-2 @ 1000	—	—	7½ @ 1800	4-6	8 @ 9	—
1110732	0-2 @ 1000	—	—	7½ @ 1800	4-6	7 @ 13	—
1979							
1103281	1 @ 575	5 @ 850	—	10 @ 1900	4	10 @ 13	—
1103285	1 @ 675	6 @ 1000	—	11 @ 2100	4	12 @ 7	—
1103365	0 @ 1000	—	—	10 @ 2350	5	11 @ 11½	—
1103379	1 @ 575	5 @ 850	—	10 @ 1900	2½	11 @ 8½	—
1110677	0 @ 638	—	—	10 @ 1800	5	12 @ 9½	—
1110695	0 @ 840	—	—	7½ @ 1800	4	12 @ 11	—
1110726	0 @ 600	5 @ 1200	—	9 @ 2000	3½	10½ @ 8	—
1110757	0 @ 600	5 @ 1200	—	9 @ 2000	3½	10½ @ 8	—
1110766	1 @ 875	—	—	7½ @ 1800	4	12½ @ 11½	—
1110767	1 @ 875	—	—	7½ @ 1800	3½	10½ @ 12½	—
1110768	1 @ 625	3 @ 1200	—	7½ @ 1800	3½	10½ @ 12½	—
1110770	1 @ 875	—	—	7½ @ 1800	3	10½ @ 9½	—

①—Located on distributor housing plate.   ③—Manual trans., 10° @ 12".   ④—High altitude, 8° @ 9".
②—Monza, 12 @ 12; Sunbird, 10 @ 14.

ALTERNATOR & REGULATOR SPECIFICATIONS

| Year | Model | Alternator | | Cold Output @ 14 Volts | | Model | Regulator | | | | | |
| | | Rated Hot Output Amps. | Field Current 12 Volts @ 80° F. | 2000 R.P.M. Amps. | 5000 R.P.M. Amps. | | Field Relay | | | Voltage Regulator | | |
							Air Gap In.	Point Gap In.	Closing Voltage	Air Gap In.	Point Gap In.	Voltage @ 125° F.
1975	1100545	32	4–4.5	—	31	Integral	—	—	—	—	—	13.5–14.5
	1100546	55	4–4.5	—	50	Integral	—	—	—	—	—	13.5–14.5
	1100559	32	4–4.5	—	31	Integral	—	—	—	—	—	13.5–14.5
	1100560	55	4–4.5	—	50	Integral	—	—	—	—	—	13.5–14.5
	1102394	37	4–4.5	—	37①	Integral	—	—	—	—	—	13.5–14.5
	1102483	37	4–4.5	—	37①	Integral	—	—	—	—	—	13.5–14.5
	1102494	55	4–4.5	—	55①	Integral	—	—	—	—	—	13.5–14.5
	1102495	55	4–4.5	—	55①	Integral	—	—	—	—	—	13.5–14.5
	1102500	55	4–4.5	—	50	Integral	—	—	—	—	—	13.5–14.5
	1102854	63	4–4.5	—	60	Integral	—	—	—	—	—	13.5–14.5
	1102856	37	4–4.5	—	33	Integral	—	—	—	—	—	13.5–14.5
	1102857	63	4–4.5	—	60	Integral	—	—	—	—	—	13.5–14.5
1976	1102840	55	4–4.5	—	51	Integral	—	—	—	—	—	—
	1102845	37	4–4.5	—	33	Integral	—	—	—	—	—	—
	1102846, 51	55	4–4.5	—	51	Integral	—	—	—	—	—	—
	1102854, 93	63	4–4.5	—	60	Integral	—	—	—	—	—	—
	1102891	55	4–4.5	—	51	Integral	—	—	—	—	—	—
	1102894	37	4–4.5	—	33	Integral	—	—	—	—	—	—
1976–78	1102394	37	4–4.5	—	33	Integral	—	—	—	—	—	13.8–14.8②
	1102479	55	4–4.5	—	51	Integral	—	—	—	—	—	13.6–14.2
	1102495	55	4–4.5	—	55①	Integral	—	—	—	—	—	13.6–14.2
	1102858	37	4–4.5	—	33	Integral	—	—	—	—	—	13.8–14.8②
1977	1102881	37	4–4.5	—	33	Integral	—	—	—	—	—	13.6–14.2
	1102854	63	4–4.5	—	60	Integral	—	—	—	—	—	—
1978	1102394	37	4–4.5	—	33	Integral	—	—	—	—	—	—
	1102478	55	4–4.5	—	51	Integral	—	—	—	—	—	13.6–14.2
	1102479	55	4–4.5	—	51	Integral	—	—	—	—	—	—
	1102495	55	—	—	—	Integral	—	—	—	—	—	—
	1102844	63	4–4.5	—	60	Integral	—	—	—	—	—	13.6–14.2
	1102851	55	4–4.5	—	51	Integral	—	—	—	—	—	—
	1102854	63	4–4.5	—	60	Integral	—	—	—	—	—	13.6–14.2
	1102858	37	4–4.5	—	33	Integral	—	—	—	—	—	—
	1102891	55	4–4.5	—	51	Integral	—	—	—	—	—	—
	1102893	63	4–4.5	—	60	Integral	—	—	—	—	—	—
	1102910	63	4–4.5	—	60	Integral	—	—	—	—	—	13.6–14.2
	1102911	55	4–4.5	—	51	Integral	—	—	—	—	—	13.6–14.2
	1102913	61	4–4.5	—	57	Integral	—	—	—	—	—	13.6–14.2

①—At 5500 RPM.   ②—At 85°F.

BRAKE SPECIFICATIONS

| Year | Model | Brake Drum Inside Diameter | Wheel Cylinder Bore Diameter | | | Master Cylinder Bore Diameter | | |
			Disc Brake	Front Drum Brake	Rear Drum Brake	Disc Brakes	Drum Brakes	Power Brakes
1975	All	9	1⅞	—	¾	¾	—	¾
1976–77	All	9½	2½	—	①	②	—	②
1978–79	All	③	2½	—	11⁄16	⅞	—	⅞

①—Exc. Sunbird, ¾"; Sunbird, 11⁄16".   ③—Exc. Monza, 9⅞"; Monza 9½".
②—Exc. Sunbird, & 1977 Monza, ¾"; Sunbird & 1977 Monza ⅞".

STARTING MOTOR SPECIFICATIONS

Year	Model	Starter Number	Brush Spring Tension Oz.[1]	Free Speed Test			Resistance Test	
				Amps.	Volts	R.P.M.[1]	Amps.	Volts
1975	4-140 Std. Trans.	1108771	35	50–75[2]	9	6500–10000	—	—
	4-140 Auto. Trans.	1108772	35	50–75[2]	9	6500–10000	—	—
	V6-231	1108770	35	50–80[2]	9	3500–6000	—	—
	V8-262	1108790	35	50–80[2]	9	3500–6000	—	—
	V8-350	1108775	35	65–95[2]	9	7500–10500	—	—
	V8-350	1108776	35	65–95[2]	9	7500–10500	—	—
1976	4-140 Std. Trans.	1108771	35	50–75[2]	9	6500–10000	—	—
	4-140 Auto. Trans.	1108772	35	50–75[2]	9	6500–10000	—	—
	V6-231	1108797	35	55–80[2]	9	5500–10500	—	—
	V8-262, 305	1108790	35	50–80[2]	9	3500–6000	—	—
1977	4-140 Std. Trans.	1108771	35	50–75[2]	9	6500–10000	—	—
	4-140 Auto. Trans.	1108772	35	50–75[2]	9	6500–10000	—	—
	4-151	1109412	—	—	—	—	—	—
	V6-231	1108797	35	50–80[2]	9	5500–10500	—	—
	V8-305	1108790	35	55–80[2]	9	3500–6000	—	—
1978–79	4-151	1109521	—	45–75[2]	9	6500–9700	—	—
	4-151	1108771	—	50–75	9	6500–10000	—	—
	4-151	1108772	—	50–75	9	6500–10000	—	—
	V6-196	1108797	—	55–80	9	5500–10500	—	—
	V6-231	1108797	—	55–80	9	5500–10500	—	—
	V6-231	1109061	—	60–85	9	6800–10300	—	—
	V8-305	1108415	—	35–75	9	6000–9000	—	—
	V8-305	1108790	—	55–80	9	3500–6000	—	—
	V8-305	1109064	—	60–85	9	6800–10300	—	—
	V8-305	1109524	—	45–70	9	7000–11900	—	—
1979	V8-305	1109062	—	65–95	9	7500–10500	—	—

[1]—Minimum. [2]—Includes solenoid.

VALVE SPECIFICATIONS

Year	Engine Model	Valve Lash		Valve Angles		Valve Spring Installed Height	Valve Spring Pressure Lbs. @ In.	Stem Clearance		Stem Diameter	
		Int.	Exh.	Seat	Face			Intake	Exhaust	Intake	Exhaust
1975	4-140	.015C	.030C	46	45	1.75	[1]	.0010–.0027	.0010–.0027	.3410–.3417	.3410–.3417
	V6-231	Hydraulic[4]		45	45	1.727	168 @ 1.327	.0015–.0032	.0015–.0032	.3405–.3412	.3405–.3412
	V8-262	1 Turn[7]		46	45	[2]		.0010–.0027	.0010–.0027	.3410–.3417	.3410–.3417
	V8-350	1 Turn[7]		46	45	1.70	200 @ 1.25	.0010–.0027	.0012–.0029	.3410–.3417	.3410–.3417
1976	4-140	Hydraulic[4]		46	45	1.746	190 @ 1.31	.0010–.0027	.0010–.0027	.3410–.3417	.3410–.3417
	V6-231	Hydraulic[4]		45	45	1.727	168 @ 1.327	.0015–.0032	.0015–.0032	.3405–.3412	.3405–.3412
	V8-262	¾ Turn[7]		46	45	[2]	[5]	.0010–.0027	.0010–.0027	.3410–.3417	.3410–.3417
	V8-305	¾ Turn[7]		46	45	[2]	[5]	.0010–.0027	.0010–.0027	.3410–.3417	.3410–.3417
1977	4-140	Hydraulic[4]		46	45	1.746	190 @ 1.31	.0010–.0027	.0010–.0027	.3410–.3417	.3410–.3417
	4-151	Hydraulic[4]		46	45	1.69	82 @ 1.66	.0017–.0030	.0017–.0030	.340	.340
	V6-231	Hydraulic[4]		45	45	1.727	168 @ 1.327	.0015–.0032	.0015–.0032	.3402–.3412	.3405–.3412
	V8-305	¾ Turn[7]		46	45	[2]	[5]	.0010–.0027	.0010–.0027	.3410–.3417	.3410–.3417
1978	4-151	Hydraulic[4]		46	45	1.69	176 @ 1.254	.0010–.0027	.0010–.0027	.340	.340
	V6-196	Hydraulic[4]		45	45	1.727	168 @ 1.327	.0015–.0035	.0015–.0032	.3402–.3412	.3405–.3412
	V6-231	Hydraulic[4]		45	45	1.727	168 @ 1.327	.0015–.0035	.0015–.0032	.3402–.3412	.3405–.3412
	V8-305	1 Turn[7]		46	45	[2]	[5]	.0010–.0027	.0010–.0027	.3410–.3417	.3410–.3417
1979	4-151	Hydraulic[4]		46	45	1.66	151 @ 1.254	.0010–.0027	.0010–.0027	.3425–.3418	.3418–.3425
	V6-196	Hydraulic[4]		45	45	1.727	168 @ 1.34	.0015–.0035	.0015–.0032	.3402–.3412	.3405–.3412
	V6-231	Hydraulic[4]		45	45	1.727	168 @ 1.34	.0015–.0035	.0015–.0032	.3402–.3412	.3405–.3412
	V8-305	1 Turn[7]		46	45	[2]	[6]	.0010–.0027	.0010–.0027	.3410–.3417	.3410–.3417

[1]—Intake 190 @ 1.31, Exhaust 186 @ 1.29.
[2]—Intake 1.70, Exhaust 1.61.
[3]—Intake 200 @ 1.25, Exhaust 189 @ 1.20.
[4]—No adjustment.
[5]—Intake 200 @ 1.25, Exhaust 200 @ 1.16.
[6]—Intake, 180 @ 1.25; exhaust 190 @ 1.16.
[7]—Turn rocker arm stud nut until all lash is eliminated, then tighten nut the additional turn listed.

PISTONS, PINS, RINGS, CRANKSHAFT & BEARINGS

Year	Engine Model	Piston Clearance	Ring End Gap①		Wrist-pin-Diameter	Rod Bearings		Main Bearings			
			Comp.	Oil		Shaft Diameter	Bearing Clearance	Shaft Diameter	Bearing Clearance	Thrust on Bear. No.	Shaft End Play
1975	4-140	.0018-.0028	②	.010	.9272	1.999-2.000	.0007-.0038	2.2983-2.2993	③	4	.002-.007
	V6-231	.0008-.0020	.010	.015	.9393	1.991-2.000	.0005-.0026	2.4995	.0004-.0015	2	.004-.008
	V8-262	.0007-.0013	④	.015	.9272	2.098-2.099	.0013-.0035	⑤	⑥	5	.002-.007
	V8-350	.0007-.0013	④	.015	.9272	2.098-2.099	.0013-.0035	⑤	⑦	5	.002-.007
1976	4-140	.0018-.0028	②	.010	.9272	1.999-2.000	.0007-.0038	2.2983-2.2993	③	4	.002-.007
	V6-231	.0008-.0020	.010	.015	.9393	1.9991-2.000	.0005-.0026	2.4995	.0004-.0015	2	.004-.008
	V8-262	.0008-.0018	.010	.015	.9272	2.099-2.100	.0013-.0035	⑤	⑥	5	.002-.007
	V8-305	.0007-.0017	.010	.015	.9272	2.099-2.100	.0013-.0035	⑤	⑥	5	.002-.007
1977	4-140	.0018-.0028	②	.010	.9272	1.999-2.000	.0007-.0027	2.3004	.0003-.0029	4	.002-.008
	4-151	.0025-.0033	.010	.010	.9272	1.999-2.000	.0006-.0026	2.2983-2.2993	.0003-.0022	5	.0015-.0085
	V6-231	.0008-.0020	.013	.015	.9393	1.9991-2.000	.0005-.0026	2.4995	.0004-.0015	2	.004-.008
	V8-305	.0007-.0027	.010	.015	.9272	2.099-2.100	.0013-.0035	2.4502	⑥	5	.002-.007
1978	4-151	.0025-.0033	.010	.010	.9400	2.000	.0005-.0026	2.2983-2.2993	.0002-.0022	5	.0015-.0085
	V6-196	.0008-.0020	.010	.015	.9393	2.2487-2.2495	.0005-.0026	2.4995	.0004-.0017	2	.0004-.0008
	V6-231	.0008-.0020	.010	.015	.9393	2.2487-2.2495	.0005-.0026	2.4995	.0003-.0017	2	.003-.009
	V8-305	.0007-.0027	.010	.015	.9272	2.099-2.100	.0013-.0035	⑥	⑥	5	.002-.006
1979	4-151	.0025-.0033	②	.015	.940	2.000	.0005-.0026	2.3000	.0005-.0022	5	.0035-.0085
	V6-196	.0008-.0020	.010	.010	.9393	2.2487-2.2495	.0005-.0026	2.4995	.0003-.0018	2	.003-.009
	V6-231	.0008-.0020	.013	.015	.9393	2.2487-2.2495	.0005-.0026	2.4995	.0003-.0018	2	.003-.009
	V8-305	.0007-.0017	.010	.015	.9272	2.086-2.098	.0013-.0035	⑤	⑥	5	.002-.006

①—Fit rings in tapered bore for clearance listed in tightest portion of ring travel.
②—#1—.015", #2—.009".
③—#1—.0003-.002, #2, 3, 4 & 5—.0003-.0027.
④—#1—.010", #2—.013".

⑤—#1—2.4484-2.4493, #2, 3 & 4—2.4481-2.4490, #5—2.4479-2.4488.
⑥—#1—.0008-.0020, #2, 3 & 4—.0011-.0023, #5—.0017-.0032.
⑦—#1,2,3,4—.0013-.0025, #5—.0023-.0033.

ENGINE TIGHTENING SPECIFICATIONS*

★Torque specifications are for clean and lightly lubricated threads only. Dry or dirty threads produce increased friction which prevents accurate measurement of tightness.

Year	Engine Model	Spark Plugs Ft. Lbs.	Cylinder Head Bolts Ft. Lbs.	Intake Manifold Ft. Lbs.	Exhaust Manifold Ft. Lbs.	Rocker Arm Stud Ft. Lbs.	Cam Cover Ft. Lbs. ①	Connecting Rod Cap Bolts Ft. Lbs.	Main Bearing Cap Bolts Ft. Lbs.	Flywheel to Crankshaft Ft. Lbs.	Vibration Damper or Pulley Ft. Lbs.
1975	4-140	15	60	30	30	—	35②	35	65	60	80
	V6-231	20	75	45	25	30③	5	40	115	55	150 min.
	V8-262,350	15	65	30	20④	—	45②	45	70	60	60
1976-77	4-140	20	60	30	30	—	80②	35	65	65	80
	V6-231	20	80	45	25	30③	4	40	⑥	60	175
	V8-262, 305, 350	15	65	30	20④	—	45②	45	70	60	60
1977	4-151	15	95	⑤	⑤	—	—	32	65	55	160
1978	4-151	15	95	⑤	⑤	20	85②	30	65	55	160
1978-79	V6-196	20	80	45	25	30③	4	40	100	60	225
	V6-231	20	80	45	25	30③	4	40	100	60	225
	V8-305	20	65	30	20④	—	⑦	45	80	60	60
1979	4-151	—	85	29	44	75	6	32	70	50	200

①—Rocker arm cover ft. lbs.
②—In. lbs.
③—Rocker arm shaft to cylinder head.
④—Inside bolts 30 ft. lbs.
⑤—Bolts, 40; Nuts, 30.
⑥—1976, 115 ft. lbs.; 1977, 100 ft. lbs.
⑦—1978, 45 in. lbs.; 1979, 50 in. lbs.

WHEEL ALIGNMENT SPECIFICATIONS

Year	Model	Caster Angle, Degrees		Camber Angle, Degrees					Toe-In. Inch	Toe-Out on Turns, Deg.①	
		Limits	Desired	Limits		Desired				Outer Wheel	Inner Wheel
				Left	Right	Left	Right				
1975–76	All	−¼ to −1¼	−¾	−¼ to +¾	−¼ to +¾	+¼	+¼	0 to ⅛	—	—
1977–79	All	−1¼ to −¼	−¾	−¼ to +¾	−¼ to +¾	+¼	+¼	0 to ⅛②	—	—

①—Incorrect toe out when other adjustments are correct indicates bent steering arms.   ②—Toe-out.

COOLING SYSTEM & CAPACITY DATA

Year	Model or Engine	Cooling Capacity, Qts.		Radiator Cap Relief Pressure, Lbs.		Thermo. Opening Temp.①	Fuel Tank Gals.	Engine Oil Refill Qts.②	Transmission Oil				Rear Axle Oil Pints
		With Heater	With A/C	With A/C	No A/C				3 Speed Pints	4 Speed Pints	5 Speed Pints	Auto. Trans. Qts.③	
1975	4-140	8	8	15	15	195	18½	3	24	24	—	④	2¼
	V6-231	13¼	13¾	15	15	190	18½	4	24	⑤	—	④	2¼
	V8-262, 350	18	18	15	15	195	18½	4	24	24	3½	④	2¼
1976	4-140	8½	8½	15	15	195	18½	3½	3	3	3	⑥	2¾
	V6-231	13½	14	15	15	195	18½	4	—	⑦	⑧	⑥	⑨
	V8-262	18½	18½	15	15	195	18½	4	—	3	3	④	2¾
1977	4-140	8	8	15	15	195	18½	3	—	2.4	3½	④	3.5
	4-151	12	12	15	15	195	18½	3	—	2.4	3½	④	3.5
	V6-231	⑪	⑪	15	15	195	18½	4	—	2.4	3½	④	⑩
	V8-305	18	18	15	15	195	18½	4	—	2.4	3½	④	2.8
1978–79	4-151	10.7	10.7	15	15	195	⑫	3	—	3	3½	④	3½⑬
	V6-196	12	12	15	15	195	⑫	4	—	3	3½	④	3½⑬
	V6-231	12	12	15	15	195	⑫	4	—	3	3½	④	3½⑬
	V8-305	16.6	18.0	15	15	195	⑫	4	—	3	3½	④	3½⑬

①—For permanent type anti freeze.
②—Add 1 qt. with filter change.
③—Approximate. Make final check with dip stick.
④—Refill 3 qts., total capacity 10 qts.
⑤—Exc. Skyhawk, 2½ pts.; Skyhawk, 3½ pts.
⑥—Exc. Sunbird, refill 3 qts., total capacity 10 qts.; Sunbird, refill 2½ pts.; total capacity 10½ qts.

⑦—Skyhawk, 3½ pts.; Starfire, 2½ pts.; Sunbird, 3 pts.
⑧—Exc. Sunbird, 3½ pts.; Sunbird, 3 pts.
⑨—Exc. Sunbird, 3½ pts.; Sunbird, 2¾ pts.
⑩—Skyhawk; 2.8. Sunbird; 3.5.
⑪—Exc. Sunbird, 12 qts.; Sunbird 13 qts.
⑫—Exc. Sunbird Station Wagon, Monza "S" Coupe & Station Wagon 18½; Sunbird

Station Wagon 16; Monza "S" Coupe & Station Wagon 15.
⑬—3¾ qts. on Skyhawk.

REAR AXLE SPECIFICATIONS

Year	Model	Carrier Type	Ring Gear & Pinion Backlash		Pinion Bearing Preload			Differential Bearing Preload		
			Method	Adjustment	Method	New Bearings Inch-Lbs.	Used Bearings Inch-Lbs.	Method	New Bearings Inch-Lbs.	Used Bearings Inch-Lbs.
1975–79	Monza	Integral	Shim	.005–.008	Spacer	10–25	8–12	Shim	—	—
	Skyhawk	Integral	Shim	.006–.008	Spacer	10–25	8–12	Shim	35–40	20–25
	Starfire	Integral	Shim	.005–.009	Spacer	10–25	8–12	Shim	—	—
	Sunbird	Integral	Shim	.006–.008	Spacer	10–25	8–12	Shim	35–40	20–25

Electrical Section

DISTRIBUTOR

Removal

1. Disconnect wiring connectors from distributor cap.
2. Remove distributor cap and position out of way, then disconnect vacuum advance hose.
3. Scribe a mark on engine in line with rotor, noting approximate position of distributor housing in relation to engine.
4. Remove hold-down nut and clamp and lift distributor from engine. Do not crank engine after distributor is removed, otherwise the distributor will have to be initially timed to the engine.
5. Install distributor in reverse order of removal, making certain to align scribe marks, then start engine and adjust timing.

STARTER, REPLACE

4-140, 151 & V8-262, 305, 350

1. Disconnect battery ground cable and disconnect all wires at solenoid ter-

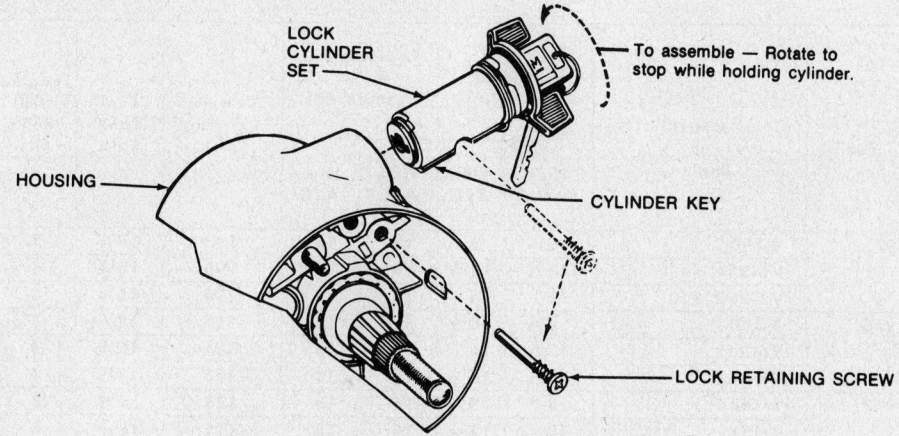

Fig. 1   Ignition lock removal. Late 1978 & 1979

minals.

NOTE: Reinstall the nuts on the terminals as each wire is removed, as thread size is different and if mixed, stripping of threads may occur.

2. Loosen starter front bracket and remove the two mounting bolts.
3. Remove from bracket bolt or nut and rotate brace clear of work area, then remove starter from vehicle by lowering front end of starter first.
4. Reverse procedure to install.

V6-196, 231

1. Disconnect battery ground cable.
2. On models with manual transmission, loosen engine crossmember attaching bolts.
3. On models with automatic transmission, remove crossover pipe and flywheel inspection cover.
4. On all models, remove starter attaching bolts, then lower starter and disconnect wiring.

NOTE: On models with manual transmission, it may be necessary to pull down on engine crossmember to gain clearance when removing starter as-

sembly.

5. Reverse procedure to install.

IGNITION SWITCH, REPLACE

Late 1978 & 1979

1. Remove steering wheel as described under Horn Sounder and Steering

Fig. 1A   Ignition lock removal 1975-77 & Early 1978

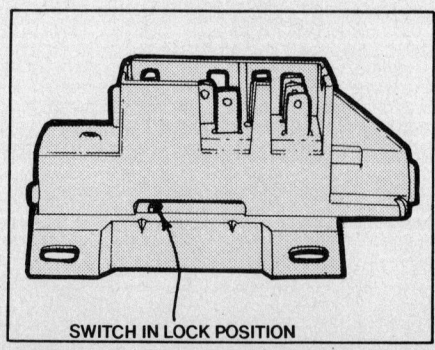

SWITCH IN LOCK POSITION

Fig. 2   Ignition switch assembly

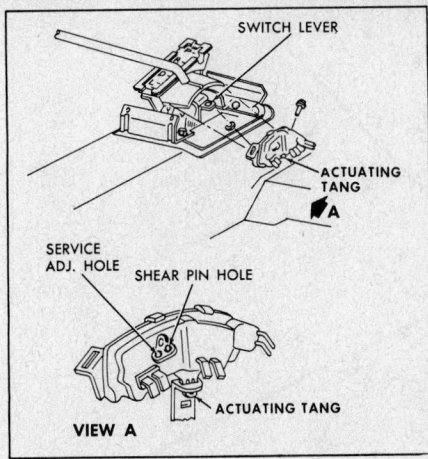

Fig. 3 Neutral safety switch installation. 1978-79 Coupe, S Coupe & Station Wagon

Wheel.

2. Remove turn signal switch as described under Turn Signal Switch, Replace, then remove buzzer switch.
3. Place ignition switch in Run position, then remove lock cylinder retaining screw and lock cylinder.
4. To install, rotate lock cylinder to stop while holding housing, Fig. 1. Align cylinder key with keyway in housing, then push lock cylinder assembly into housing until fully seated.
5. Install lock cylinder retaining screw. Torque screw to 40 in. lbs. for standard columns. On adjustable columns, torque retaining screw to 22 in. lbs.
6. Install buzzer switch, turn signal switch and steering wheel.

1975-77 & Early 1978

1. Remove steering wheel as described under "Horn Sounder & Steering Wheel" procedure.
2. On 1978-79 Coupe, S Coupe and station wagon models, remove turn signal switch as described under "Turn Signal Switch, Replace" procedure.
3. On all models except 1978-79 Coupe, S Coupe and station wagon, pull directional switch rearward far enough to slip it over end of shaft. Do not pull harness out of column.
4. With ignition switch in "Run" position, insert a small screwdriver or similar tool into turn signal housing slot, Fig. 1. Keeping tool to right side of slot, break housing flash loose and at same time depress spring latch at lower end of lock cylinder.
5. Remove lock cylinder from housing.

IGNITION LOCK, REPLACE

Exc. 1978-79 Coupe, S Coupe & Station Wagon

1. Disconnect battery ground cable.
2. Remove left A/C outlet duct.
3. Remove steering column to support retaining nuts and allow column to lower.
4. Disconnect connector from switch, then remove switch retaining screws and remove switch.
5. Reverse procedure to install with ignition switch in "lock" position, Fig. 2.

1978-79 Coupe, S Coupe & Station Wagon

The ignition switch is mounted on the top of the steering column jacket near the front of the dash. It is located inside the channel section of the brake pedal support and is completely inaccessible without first lowering the steering column.

1. Lower the steering column and be sure it is properly supported before proceeding.
2. The switch should be positioned in Lock position before removing, Fig. 2.
3. Unfasten and remove the switch, detaching it from the actuating rod.
4. When installing, make sure the lock and the switch are in the Lock position. Then install the activating rod into the switch and fasten the switch.

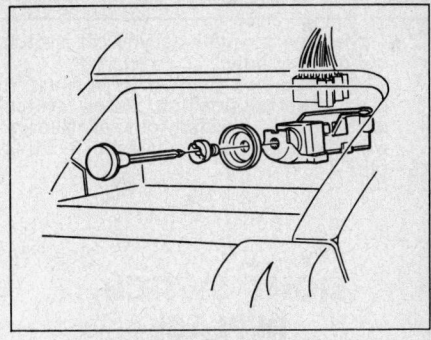

Fig. 4 Light switch replacement. 1978-79 Coupe, S Coupe & Station Wagon

NEUTRAL SAFETY SWITCH, REPLACE

Exc. 1978-79 Coupe, S Coupe & Station Wagon

1. Disconnect battery ground cable.
2. Remove console cover.
3. Disconnect connector from switch, then remove switch retaining screws and remove switch.
4. Reverse procedure to install and make certain that switch is correctly adjusted.

1978-79 Coupe, S Coupe & Station Wagon

1. Remove screws securing floor console, Fig. 3.
2. Disconnect electrical plugs on back-up contacts and neutral start contacts of switch assembly.
3. Place shift lever in Neutral.
4. Remove two screws securing shift indicator plate.
5. Remove two screws securing shift lever curved cover.
6. Remove two screws securing switch to lever assembly.

NOTE: Screws are hidden beneath lever

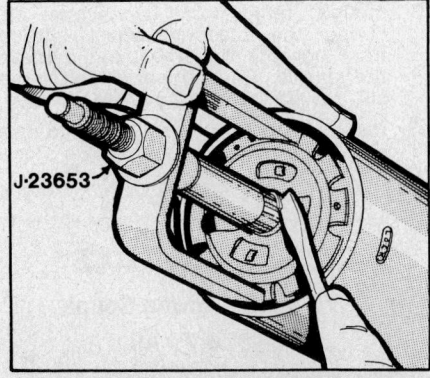

Fig. 5 Compressing lock plate and removing retaining ring

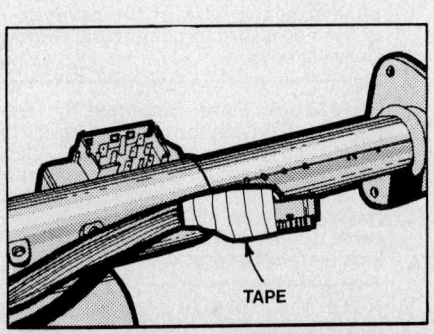

Fig. 6 Taping turn signal connector and wires

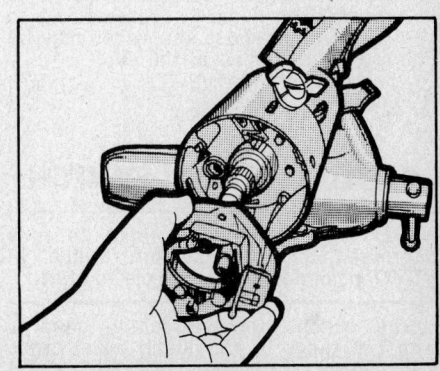

Fig. 7 Removing turn signal switch

cover.

7. Tilt switch to right as you lift switch out of lever hole.
8. When installing switch, make sure it is in Neutral position. When switch is installed, shifting out of Neutral will shear the switch plastic locating pin.

LIGHT SWITCH, REPLACE

Exc. 1978-79 Coupe, S Coupe & Station Wagon

1. Disconnect battery ground cable.
2. Remove left A/C duct if equipped.
3. Reaching under instrument panel, release and pull switch knob and shaft assembly out of switch.
4. Remove switch bezel retaining nut, then disconnect switch connector and remove switch.
5. Reverse procedure to install.

1978-79 Coupe, S Coupe & Station Wagon

1. Disconnect ground cable at battery.
2. Pull headlamp switch knob to "ON" position.
3. Reach under instrument panel and depress switch shaft retainer button while pulling on the switch control shaft knob.
4. With a large bladed screwdriver, remove the light switch ferrule nut from front of instrument panel, Fig. 4.
5. Disconnect the multi-contact connector from side of switch and remove switch.

STOP LIGHT SWITCH

1. Reach under right side of instrument panel at brake pedal support and disconnect wiring harness connector at switch.
2. Pull switch from mounting bracket.
3. When installing switch, adjust by bringing brake pedal to normal position. Electrical contact should be made when pedal is depressed $3/8$ to $5/8$ inch. To adjust, the switch may be rotated or pulled in the clip.

CLUTCH START SWITCH

NOTE: The clutch pedal must be fully depressed and the ignition switch in START position for the vehicle to start.

The clutch switch assembly mounts with two tangs to the clutch pedal brace switch pivot bracket and the clutch pedal arm.

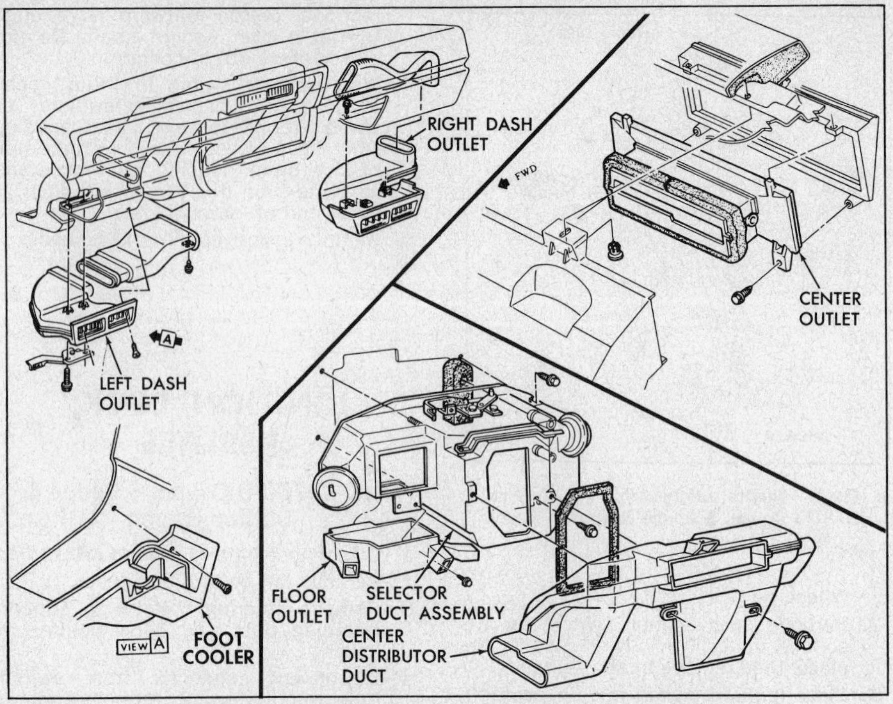

Fig. 8   Air distribution ducts and outlets on air conditioned models. 1978-79 Coupe, S Coupe & Station Wagon

1. Under the instrument panel on the clutch pedal support remove the multi-contact connector from switch.
2. Compress switch assembly actuating shaft barb retainer and push out of clutch pedal.
3. Compress switch assembly pivot bracket barb and lift off switch.
4. When installing new switch, no adjustments are necessary as the switch is self aligning.

TURN SIGNAL SWITCH, REPLACE

1. Remove steering wheel with suitable puller.
2. Remove three cover screws and lift cover off the shaft.

NOTE: These screws have plastic retainers on the back of the cover so it is not necessary to completely remove these screws.

3. Place Lock Plate Compressing Tool J 23653, Fig. 5, on end of steering shaft and compress the lock plate as far as possible using the shaft nut as shown. Pry the round wire snap ring out of the shaft groove and discard the ring. Remove tool and lift lock plate off end of shaft.

NOTE: On 1976-79 models, remove lock plate cover.

4. Slide the signal cancelling cam, upper bearing preload spring and thrust washer off the end of shaft.
5. Remove turn signal lever screw and remove the lever.
6. Push hazard warning knob in and unscrew the knob.
7. Wrap upper part of connector with tape, Fig. 6 to prevent snagging of wires during switch removal.
8. Remove three screws on switch and pull switch straight up through housing, Fig. 7.

HORN SOUNDER & STEERING WHEEL

1. Disconnect battery ground cable.
2. On regular production steering wheel models, remove the two screws securing the steering wheel shroud from beneath the wheel and remove the shroud. On optional wheels models, pry off horn button cap.
3. Remove steering wheel nut and use a suitable puller to remove the steering wheel.

RADIO, REPLACE

1975 Monza Towne Coupe & 1976-79 All

1. Disconnect battery ground cable.
2. Remove radio control knobs and

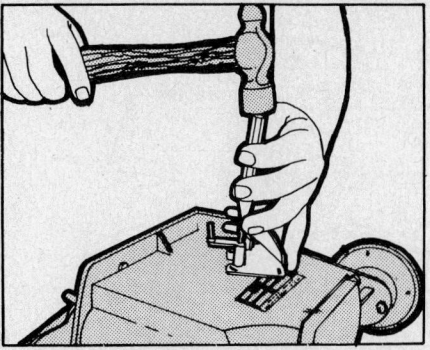

Fig. 9 Removing temperature door bell crank on air conditioned vehicles. 1978-79 Coupe, S Coupe and Station Wagon

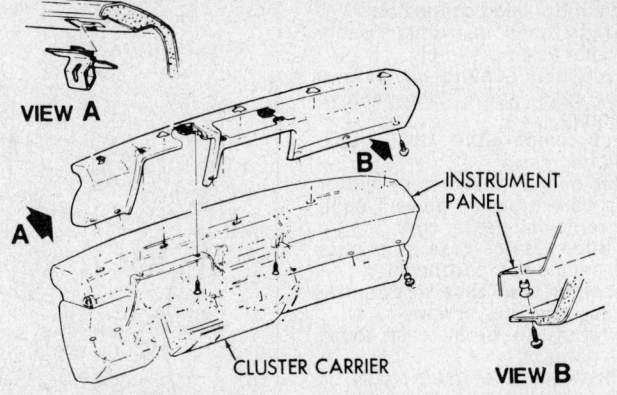

Fig. 10 Instrument panel pad. 1976-79 Except Coupe, S Coupe & Station Wagon

bezels, then the shaft nuts and washers.
3. Disconnect antenna lead from radio rear and remove screws securing radio to instrument panel reinforcement.
4. Lower radio from instrument panel and disconnect electrical connectors from radio.
5. Remove mounts from radio.
6. Reverse procedure to install.

1975 Exc. Monza Towne Coupe

1. Disconnect battery ground cable.
2. Remove clock stem knob, instrument panel bezel and glove box.
3. Remove instrument panel pad and radio knobs.

4. Remove the two lower screws from radio mounting bracket and remove the left lap cooler and duct, if equipped with A/C.
5. Remove two nuts from steering column mounting bracket, three screws from top of instrument panel and three bolts from instrument panel carrier reinforcement.

CAUTION: The two steering column mounting nuts are important attaching parts as they could affect the operation of the collapsible steering column. If replacement becomes necessary, they must be replaced with one of the same or equivalent part number. Also, the 15-25 ft. lb. torque must be adhered to.

6. Disconnect speedometer cable from instrument cluster, then pull complete instrument panel slightly forward and disconnect all electrical leads and antenna.
7. Remove radio from instrument panel.
8. Reverse procedure to install.

HEATER CORE REMOVAL

Exc. 1978-79 Coupe, S Coupe & Station Wagon

Less Air Conditioning

1. Disconnect battery ground cable and disconnect blower motor electrical lead.
2. Place a pan under vehicle, then disconnect heater hoses from core and secure hoses in a raised position.
3. Remove blower inlet to dash panel screws and nuts, then remove blower inlet and blower motor and wheel assembly.
4. Remove core retaining strap screws and remove core.
5. Reverse procedure to install making certain that blower inlet sealer is intact, replace as necessary.

1977-79 With Air Conditioning

NOTE: The heater core can be removed without purging the A/C refrigerant system or removing the evaporator case half of the assembly by using the following procedure.

1. Disconnect battery ground cable.
2. Remove floor outlet duct, then remove glove box and door as an assembly.
3. Remove left and right hand dash outlets using a suitable tool.
4. Remove instrument panel pad.
5. Disconnect vacuum hoses at valves on left end of heater and evaporator unit.
6. Remove insulation tray located below instrument cluster, then loosen console and slide console rearward.
7. Remove instrument panel to dash attaching screws. Place a protective covering over steering column, then lower instrument panel to steering column.

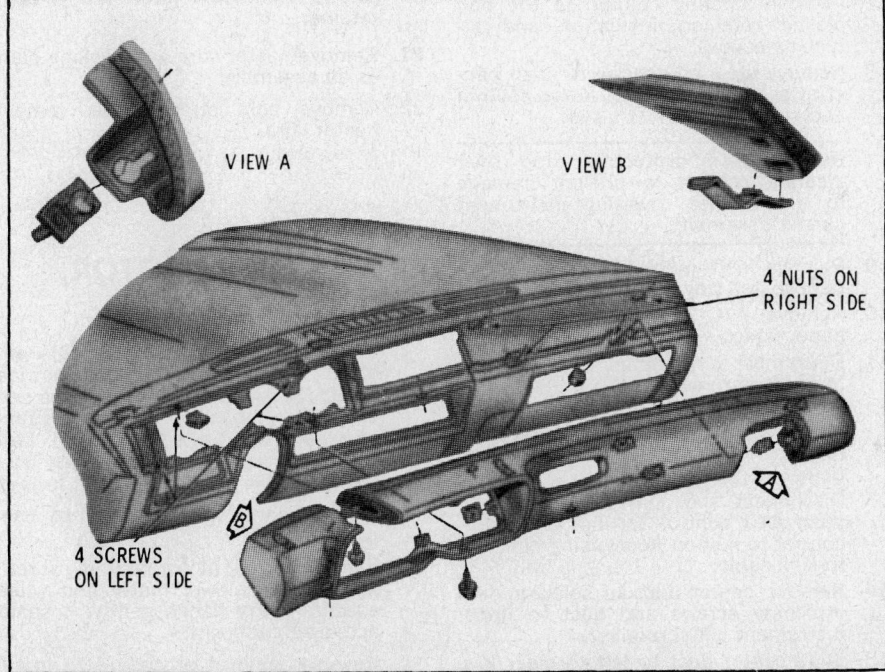

Fig. 10A Instrument panel pad (Typical). 1975 models

Disconnect speedometer cable, radio leads and control head connectors.

8. Remove right hand instrument panel and lap cooler as an assembly.
9. Remove modular duct to heater and evaporator case screw, then remove duct assembly.
10. Disconnect temperature door cable and wiring harness.
11. Disconnect heater hoses from heater core. Plug core tubes to prevent spillage when removing heater core.
12. Remove three heater case stud nuts located in engine compartment.
13. Remove heater core case to evaporator core case attaching screws.
14. Drive on studs to break case loose from dash panel.
15. Remove heater core case assembly.
16. Remove heater core to case attaching screws, then remove heater core.

1975-76 With Air Conditioning

1. Disconnect battery ground cable.
2. Remove glove box and right air duct.
3. Remove instrument panel bezel and pad.
4. Remove left air duct and feed duct.
5. Lower steering column and remove instrument panel.
6. Remove control assembly, radio, defroster duct and large distribution duct.
7. Purge system of refrigerent.
8. Disconnect heater hoses at core.
9. Clean VIR exterior surface and line connections, then disconnect compressor inlet line, oil bleed line and condenser outlet line from VIR assembly.

NOTE: Cap all line and VIR ports.

10. Loosen evaporator inlet and outlet lines and remove VIR mounting clamp, then slide VIR assembly from evaporator lines.
11. Remove heater—distributer case to cowl attaching nuts and remove case, then disconnect wiring harness and vacuum lines.
12. Separate heater case from distributor, then remove heater core from case.

1978-79 Coupe, S Coupe & Station Wagon

Less Air Conditioning

1. Disconnect battery ground cable.
2. Disconnect blower motor lead wire.
3. Place a pan under vehicle and disconnect heater hoses at core connections and secure ends of hoses in a raised position.
4. Remove the coil bracket to dash panel stud nut and move coil out of way.
5. Remove the blower inlet to dash panel screws and nuts and remove the blower inlet, blower motor and wheel as an assembly.
6. Remove the core retainer strap screws and remove the core.
7. When replacing core, be sure the blower inlet sealer is intact.

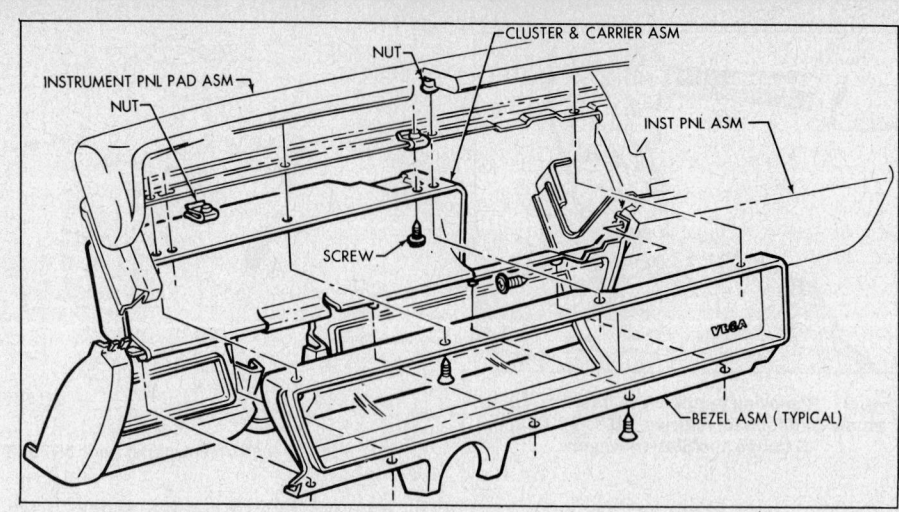

Fig. 11   Standard instrument panel cluster. 1978-79 Coupe, S Coupe & Station Wagon

With Air Conditioning

1. Disconnect battery ground cable.
2. Position a pan under heater core tubes, then disconnect heater hoses and secure in a raised position. Cap core tubes to prevent coolant spillage during removal.
3. From engine side of dash panel remove nuts from selector duct studs, Fig. 8.
4. Remove glove box and door as an assembly.
5. Remove right hand outlet to instrument panel attaching screws, then remove outlet and flexible hose.
6. Remove intermediate duct to left hand outlet.
7. Remove steering column to toe pan plastic retainer, insulation and attaching screws.
8. Remove steering column to dash panel attaching nuts, then lower column and support on driver's seat.

NOTE: Place protective tape over steering column to prevent damage to finish when lowering instrument cluster assembly.

9. Remove instrument panel bezel, then remove ash tray and retainer.
10. Remove A/C control to instrument panel attaching screws.
11. Disconnect wire connector and antenna lead from radio.
12. Remove instrument cluster to dash panel attaching screws and allow cluster assembly to rest on steering column.
13. Disconnect speedometer cable, then push A/C control forward and allow control to rest on floor, using care not to kink cable.
14. Remove center duct to selector duct attaching screws and duct to upper instrument panel retainer.
15. Slide center duct to left to clear lower instrument panel to cluster tab, then slide to right to remove.

16. Remove defroster duct to selector duct attaching screws.
17. Remove remaining selector duct to dash panel attaching screws, then pull duct rearward and disconnect all electrical leads and vacuum lines.
18. Disconnect temperature door cable and remove selector duct assembly.

NOTE: Ensure all electrical leads and vacuum lines are disconnected before removing duct assembly.

19. Pry off or punch out temperature door bell crank, then remove temperature door, Fig. 9.
20. Remove backing plate attaching screws and temperature door cable retainer.
21. Remove heater core and backing plate as an assembly.
22. Remove core straps, then remove heater core.

BLOWER MOTOR, REPLACE

1. Disconnect battery ground cable and disconnect blower motor electrical leads. On some models, it may be necessary to remove coolant recovery tank attaching screws and position tank aside. Do not disconnect hoses from tank.
2. Scribe blower motor flange to case position.
3. Remove blower motor retaining screws and remove blower motor and wheel assembly. Pry flange gently, if sealer acts as an adhesive.
4. Reverse removal procedure to install aligning scribe marks made during removal.

INSTRUMENT PANEL PAD

1978-79 Coupe, S Coupe & Station Wagon

1. Remove clock stem knob, then remove instrument cluster bezel, Figs. 11 and 12.
2. Remove one screw at lower left edge of pad and three screws located along lower right hand side of pad.
3. Sharply rap lower right edge of pad upward to disengage retaining clips at top right of pad, then remove pad assembly.

1976-79 Except Coupe, S Coupe & Station Wagon

1. Remove eleven screws from around edge of pad, Fig. 10.
2. On models equipped with A/C, disconnect left hand duct.
3. Pry upward on pad to disengage clips located rear of pad, then remove pad assembly

1975 Models

The instrument panel pad must be removed to service all gauges and instruments.
1. Remove glove box, then reaching through glove box opening, remove the nuts retaining the right side of pad, Fig. 10A.
2. Remove clock set knob and instrument panel bezel.
3. Remove two screws at top of cluster, then remove screws along lower edge of cover and remove instrument panel pad.
4. Reverse procedure to install.

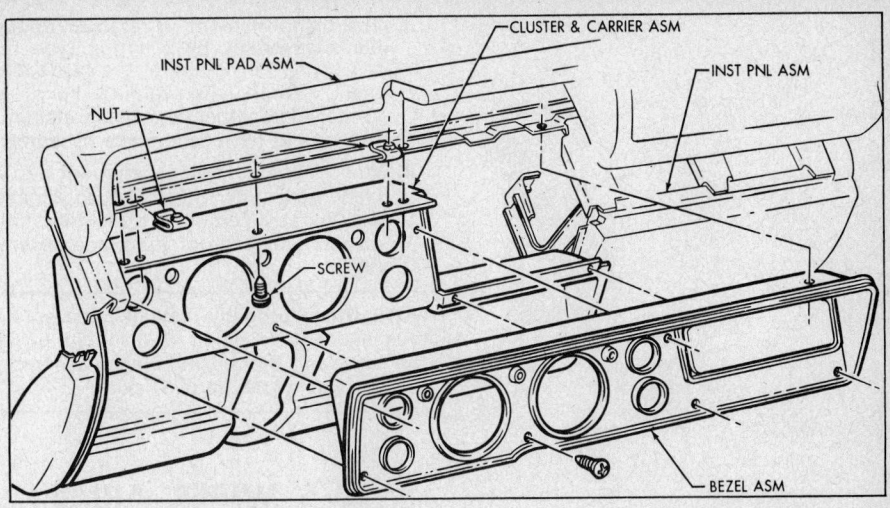

Fig. 12 Optional instrument panel cluster. 1978-79 Coupe, S Coupe & Station Wagon

INSTRUMENT CLUSTER

1978-79 Coupe, S Coupe & Station Wagon

Standard Cluster

The instrument cluster bezel is retained by nine screws, Fig. 11. After removal of bezel, remove cluster lens-light shield combination (2 screws at top of lens and 2 screws at bottom of light shield). The lens tips out at the top and then lifts off. Instruments are then easily removed.

GT Cluster

The cluster bezel is retained by six screws, Fig. 12. After removal of bezel, remove the lens light shield (6 screws). Then lift lens and light shield straight out. Instruments are then accessible for replacement.

1976-79 Coupe, S Coupe & Station Wagon

Standard Cluster

Remove four screws securing bezel and lens to instrument pane. Remove bezel and lens. Instruments are then accessible for replacement.

GT Cluster

Disconnect battery ground cable. Remove knob from clock stem, then remove six screws attaching cluster bezel to instrument panel. Remove six lens and light shield attaching screws, then remove lens and light shield. Instruments are then accessible for replacement.

1975 Models

After removing instrument panel pad as described under Instrument Panel Pad, remove cluster lens. Instruments are then accessible for removal.

W/S WIPER SWITCH

1975 Monza Towne Coupe & 1976-79 All Exc. Coupe, S Coupe & Station Wagon

1. Disconnect battery ground cable.
2. Remove screws securing light shield to wiper switch and position light shield aside.

NOTE: The light shield retaining screws also retains the upper portions of the wiper switch to the mounting bosses.

3. Remove lower switch mounting screw, lower switch from panel and disconnect electrical connector, then remove switch.
4. Reverse procedure to install.

1978-79 Coupe, S Coupe & Station Wagon

1. Beneath instrument panel, unplug the headlamp switch multi-connector for clearance to wiper switch screw.
2. Unplug connector on bottom of wiper switch.

3. Remove two mounting screws from switch and lower switch from instrument panel.

1975 Starfire

1. Disconnect battery ground cable and remove instrument panel pad as outlined under "Instrument Panel Pad" procedure.
2. Remove left A/C duct.
3. Remove two nuts securing steering column to upper bracket and lower steering column.
4. Remove screw securing upper column bracket to instrument cluster and pull cluster toward rear of vehicle.
5. Disconnect electrical connector and remove switch retaining screws, then the switch from vehicle.
6. Reverse procedure to install.

1975 Monza 2+2 & Skyhawk

1. Disconnect battery ground cable.
2. Remove left A/C duct if equipped, then disconnect headlight switch from instrument panel.
3. Disconnect electrical connectors from wiper switch and seat belt buzzer and remove wiper switch.
4. Reverse procedure to remove.

W/S WIPER BLADES

1. Remove the wiper blade from the arm by depressing the spring type blade clip, Fig. 13, away from the under side of the arm and slide the arm out of the blade clip.
2. To install wiper blade to wiper arm, slide tip end of arm into blade clip, until pin on tip end of arm engages hole in clip.

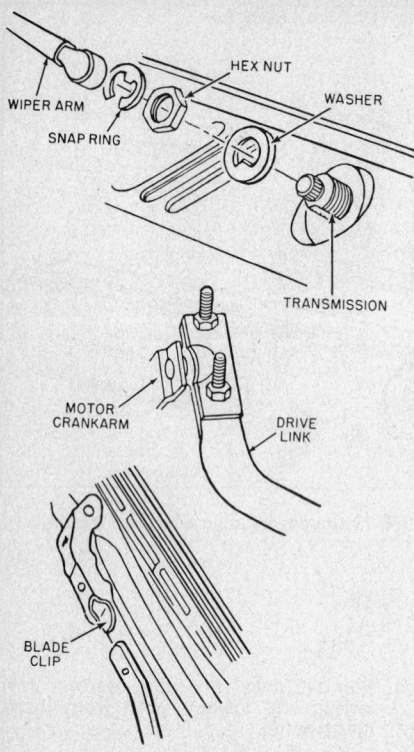

Fig. 13   Wiper blade clip location

3. The blade element is retained in the blade assembly by a spring type retainer clip in the end of the blade element. When the retainer clip is squeezed together, the blade element can be slid out of the blade assembly.

4. When installing a blade element into a blade assembly, be certain to engage the metal insert in the element into all retaining tabs of the blade assembly.

NOTE: When properly installed, the spring type element retaining clip should be at the end of the wiper blade assembly nearest the wiper transmission.

W/S WIPER ARMS

1. Wiper motor must be in park position.
2. Use suitable tool to minimize the possibility of windshield or paint finish damage during arm removal.
3. Remove arm by prying up with tool to disengage arm from serrated transmission shaft, Fig. 14.
4. To install arm to transmission shaft rotate the required distance and direction so that blades rest in proper parked position.

CAUTION: The parked position for the left

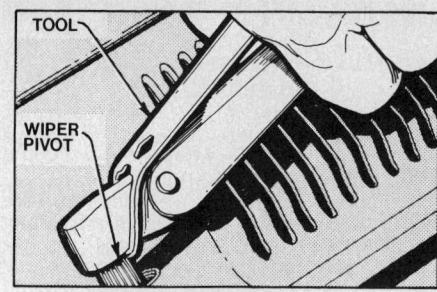

Fig. 14   Wiper arm removal

blade tip is approx. 2" above lower windshield reveal mounting and the right blade tip within 2" of the lower windshield reveal moulding.

W/S WIPER MOTOR

1. Raise hood, remove cowl screen.
2. Reaching through cowl opening, loosen the two transmission drive link attaching nuts to motor crankarm.
3. Remove transmission drive link from motor crankarm.
4. Disconnect wiring and unfasten motor and remove.

Engine Section

ENGINE MOUNTS, REPLACE

4-140

1. Raise vehicle on hoist and support front of engine to take weight off front mounts.
2. If only one mount is being replaced, remove the mount-to-engine bracket nut on the mount not being replaced.
3. Remove the stud nut and two bolts securing mount to housing support.
4. Remove the three stud nuts securing the bracket to the engine. On the right side remove the starter brace at starter and on air conditioned equipped vehicles, remove the compressor rear lower brace at the compressor.
5. Raise front of engine to provide maximum clearance without imposing stress on other engine components.
6. Reverse procedure to install.

4-151

1. Remove bracket to engine bolts and the chassis to engine mount attaching nut, Fig. 1.
2. Raise engine to release weight from mount.
3. Remove mount and separate from engine bracket.
4. Reverse procedure to install.

V6-196, 231

1. Raise car and provide frame support at front of car.
2. Support weight of engine at forward edge of pan.
3. Remove mount to engine block bolts. Raise engine slightly and remove mount to mount bracket bolt and nut. Remove mount.
4. Reverse above procedure to install and torque to specifications as shown on Fig. 1A.

V8-262, 305, 350

1. Remove lower mount bolts from frame bracket, Fig. 1B, and raise engine to relieve weight from mount.
2. Remove mount from engine.
3. Install new mount on engine, lower engine and install lower mount bolts to frame bracket.

ENGINE, REPLACE

4-140 & V8-262, 305, 350

1. Scribe relationship between hood

hinges and the hood, then remove hood from hinges.
2. Disconnect battery positive cable at battery and negative cable at engine block (except on air conditioned vehicles).
3. Drain cooling system and disconnect hoses at radiator. Disconnect heater hoses at water pump and at heater inlet (bottom hose).
4. Disconnect emission system hoses: PCV at cam cover; cannister vacuum hose at carburetor; PCV vacuum at inlet manifold and bowl vent at carburetor.
5. Remove radiator panel or shroud and remove radiator, fan and spacer.
6. Remove air cleaner, disconnecting vent tube at base of cleaner.
7. Disconnect electrical leads at: Delcotron, ignition coil, starter solenoid, oil pressure switch, engine temperature switch, transmission controlled spark switch at transmission, transmission controlled spark solenoid and engine ground strap at cowl.
8. Disconnect: Fuel line at rubber hose to rear of carburetor, transmission vacuum modulator and air conditioning vacuum line at inlet manifold, accelerator cable at manifold bellcrank.
9. On air conditioned cars, disconnect

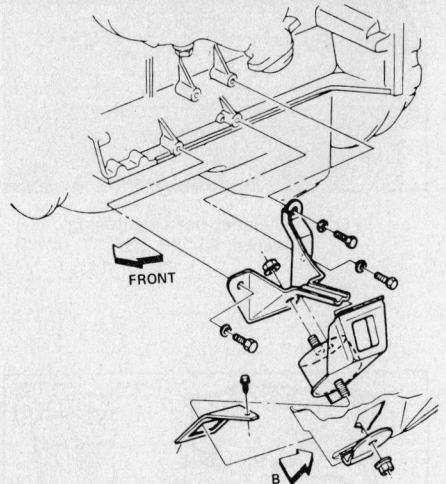

Fig. 1 Engine mounts. 4-151

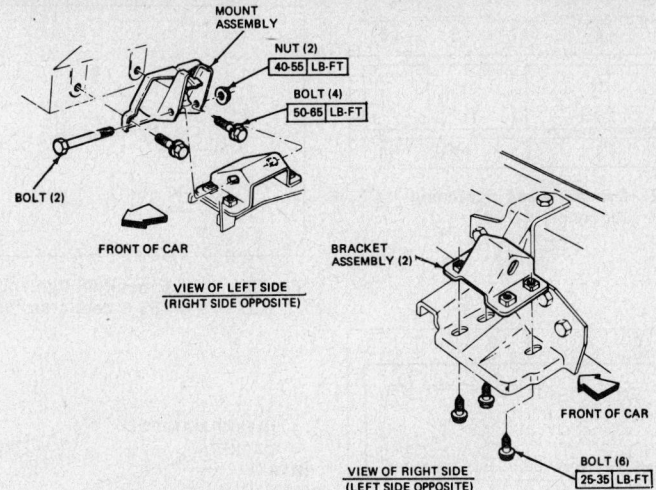

Fig. 1A Engine mounts. V6-196, 231

compressor at front support, rear support, rear lower bracket and remove drive belt from compressor.

10. Move compressor slightly forward and allow front of compressor to rest on frame forward brace, then secure rear of compressor to engine compartment so it is out of way.
11. Disconnect power steering pump, if equipped, and position it out of way.
12. Raise car on a hoist and disconnect exhaust pipe at manifold.
13. Remove engine flywheel dust cover or converter underpan.
14. On automatic transmission cars, remove converter-to-flywheel retaining bolts and nuts and install coverter safety strap.
15. Remove converter housing or flywheel housing-to-engine retaining bolts.
16. Loosen engine front mount retaining bolts at frame attachment and lower vehicle.
17. Install floor jack under transmission.
18. Install suitable engine lifting equipment and raise engine slightly to take weight from engine mounts and remove engine front mount retaining bolts.
19. Remove engine and pull forward to clear transmission while slowly lifting engine from car.

4-151

1. Disconnect battery cables and drain cooling system.
2. Scribe relationship between hood hinges and the hood, then remove hood from hinges.
3. Disconnect distributor, starter and alternator wiring, engine to body ground strap, oil pressure and engine temperature sender wires, and all external vacuum hoses.
4. Remove air cleaner.
5. Remove radiator shroud assembly and fan, then disconnect coolant hoses from engine.
6. Disconnect accelerator linkage.
7. If equipped with power steering or A/C, remove pump or compressor from mounting brackets and position

aside. Do not disconnect hoses or lines.
8. Disconnect fuel lines.
9. Raise vehicle and drain oil pan.
10. Disconnect exhaust pipe from manifold.
11. If equipped with automatic transmission, remove converter cover and the converter retaining bolts, then slide converter rearward.
12. If equipped with manual transmission, disconnect clutch linkage and remove clutch cross shaft.
13. On all models, remove four lower bell housing bolts.
14. Disconnect transmission filler tube support and the starter wiring harness.
15. Remove front engine mount bolts.
16. Lower vehicle and, using a suitable jack and block of wood, support transmission.
17. Install suitable engine lifting equipment and support engine.
18. Remove the two remaining bell housing bolts.
19. Raise transmission slightly.
20. Move engine forward to separate from transmission, tilt front of engine upward and remove from vehicle.

V6-196, 231

NOTE: On models with manual transmission, engine and transmission are removed as an assembly.

1. Scribe alignment marks at hood hinge and hinge bracket, then remove hood.
2. Disconnect battery ground cable, then drain cooling system.
3. Remove air cleaner.
4. On models equipped with A/C, disconnect compressor ground wire and wire connector, then remove compressor mounting bracket bolts and position compressor aside.
5. Remove drive belts, fan and pulley.
6. Disconnect radiator and heater hoses from engine and position out of way.
7. Remove fan shroud assembly.
8. Remove power steering pump bracket bolts and position pump aside, if equipped.
9. Disconnect fuel pump hoses and install plugs.
10. Disconnect battery ground cable from engine.
11. Disconnect vacuum hose from carburetor to manifold and vacuum hoses to vacuum modulator and power brake unit, if equipped.
12. Disconnect throttle cable from carburetor.

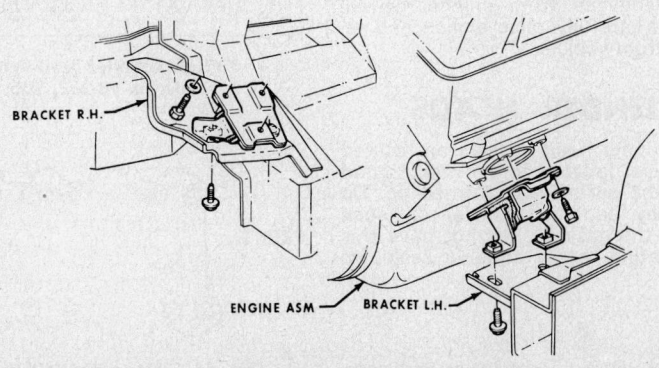

Fig. 1B Engine mounts, V8-262, 305, 350

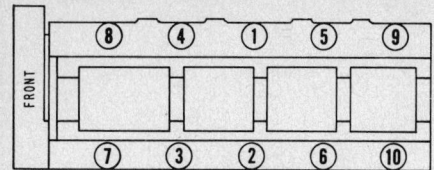

Fig. 2 Cylinder head tightening sequence. 4-140

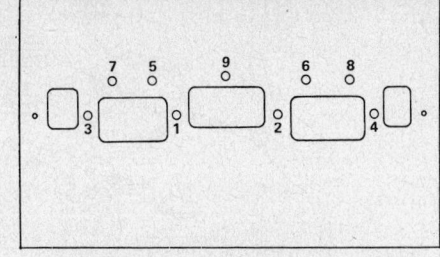

Fig. 2B Intake manifold tightening sequence. 1977-79 4-151 except cross flow engine

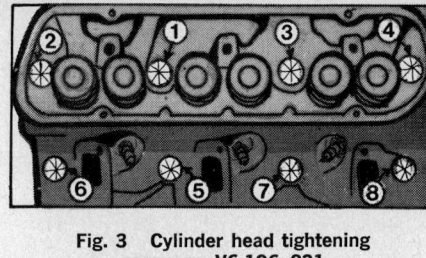

Fig. 3 Cylinder head tightening sequence. V6-196, 231

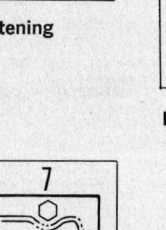

Fig. 2A Cylinder head tightening sequence. 4-151

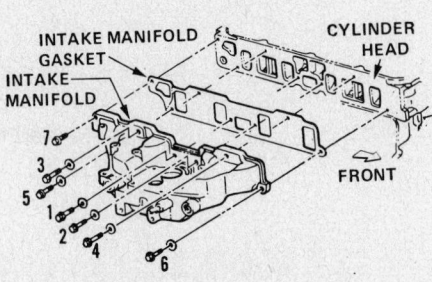

Fig. 2C Intake manifold tightening sequence. 1979 4-151 cross flow engine

Fig. 3A Intake manifold tightening sequence. V6-196, 231

13. Disconnect wire connectors from alternator, oil and coolant sending units.
14. Disconnect engine to body ground straps at engine.
15. Raise vehicle and disconnect starter cables and cable shields, if equipped.
16. Disconnect exhaust pipe from exhaust manifold.
17. Remove lower flywheel cover.
18. On models with automatic transmission, remove flywheel to converter attaching bolts. Mark converter and flywheel so they can be installed in the same position. Remove transmission to engine attaching bolts.
19. On models with manual transmission, disconnect driveshaft, shift linkage, clutch equalizer shaft and transmission.
20. Remove motor mount through bolts and cruise control bracket, if equipped, then lower vehicle.
21. On models with automatic transmission, support transmission.
22. Attach a suitable lifting device to engine and raise engine so that mounting through bolts can be removed. Ensure all wiring harness, vacuum lines and other components are clear before removing engine from vehicle.
23. On models with automatic transmission, raise engine clear of mounts and raise transmission support accordingly and alternately until transmission can be disengaged from engine. On all models carefully raise engine and remove from vehicle.

CYLINDER HEADS

Some cylinder head gaskets are coated with a special lacquer to provide a good seal once the parts have warmed up. Do not use any additional sealer on such gaskets. If the gasket does not have this lacquer coating, apply suitable sealer to both sides.

4-140

1. Remove engine front cover and camshaft cover as outlined further on.

2. Remove timing belt and camshaft sprocket.
3. Remove intake and exhaust manifolds.
4. Disconnect hose at thermostat housing.
5. Remove cylinder head bolts and with the aid of an assistant lift head and gasket from engine. Place head on two blocks of wood to prevent damage to valves.
6. Reverse procedure to install and tighten head bolts in sequence shown in Fig. 2.

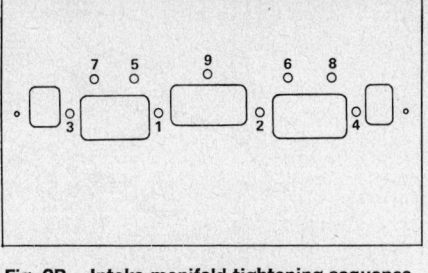

Fig. 4 Cylinder head tightening sequence. V8-262, 305, 350

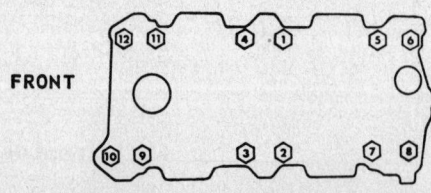

Fig. 4A Intake manifold tightening sequence. V8-262, 305, 350

4-151

1979 Cross Flow Engine

1. Drain cooling system and remove air cleaner.
2. Remove alternator, power steering pump and A/C compressor brackets from cylinder head and engine block.
3. Remove intake and exhaust manifolds.
4. Disconnect all electrical connectors from cylinder head.
5. Disconnect ignition wire from spark plugs, then remove spark plugs.
6. Disconnect fuel line at rear engine lifting bracket.
7. Remove rocker arm cover and back off rocker arm nuts. Pivot rocker arm and remove push rods.
8. Remove cylinder head attaching bolts, cylinder head and gasket.
9. Reverse procedure to install. Torque cylinder head bolt in sequence shown in Fig. 2A and intake manifold bolts in sequence shown, Fig. 2C.

1977-79 Except Cross Flow Engine

1. Disconnect battery ground cable.
2. Drain cooling system and remove air cleaner.
3. Disconnect accelerator cable from bellcrank at manifold, then the fuel and vacuum lines at carburetor.
4. Remove intake and exhaust manifolds.
5. Remove alternator to cylinder head bracket bolts.

NOTE: If equipped with power steering or A/C, remove right side front

Fig. 5 Removing nylon rocker arm retainer. V6-196, 231

Fig. 6 Removing rocker arm stud. V8-262, 305, 350

Fig. 7 Installing rocker arm stud. V8-262, 305, 350

bracket to facilitate cylinder head removal.

6. Disconnect wiring harness from temperature sender and remove from clips on rocker arm cover.
7. Disconnect coolant hoses at water outlet housing and the ground strap at cylinder head.
8. Remove spark plugs and rocker arm cover. Loosen rocker arm nuts, pivot rocker arms aside and remove push rods.
9. Remove cylinder head bolts and the cylinder head.
10. Reverse procedure to install. Torque cylinder head and intake manifold bolts in sequence shown in Figs. 2A and 2B.

V6-196, 231

1. Drain coolant and disconnect battery.
2. Remove intake manifold.
3. When removing right cylinder head, remove Delcotron and/or A/C compressor with mounting bracket and move out of the way. *Do not disconnect hoses from air compressor.*
4. When removing left cylinder head, remove oil dipstick, power steering pump and move out of the way with hoses attached.
5. Disconnect exhaust manifold from head to be removed.
6. Remove rocker arm shaft and lift out push rods.
7. Remove cylinder head.
8. Reverse procedure to install. Torque cylinder head and intake manifold bolts in sequence shown in Figs. 3 and 3A.

V8-262, 305, 350

1. Remove intake and exhaust manifolds.
2. Remove rocker arm covers.
3. Remove rocker arm nuts, rocker arm balls and rocker arms.

NOTE: Rocker arms, rocker arm balls and push rods must be installed in the original position.

4. Drain coolant from cylinder block, then remove cylinder head bolts and cylinder head.
5. Reverse procedure to install. Torque cylinder head and intake manifold bolts on sequence shown in Figs. 4 and 4A.

ROCKER ARMS

V6-196, 231

A nylon retainer is used to retain the rocker arms. Break them below their heads with a chisel, Fig. 5, or pry out with channel locks. Production rocker arms can

Fig. 8 Adjusting valve lash. 1975 4-140

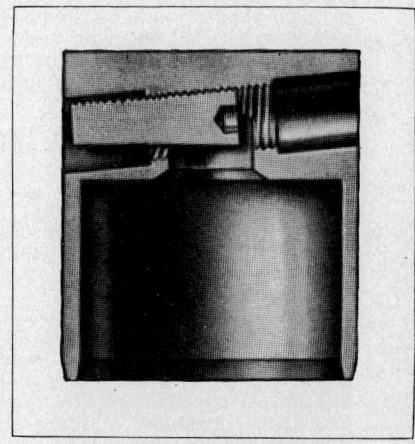

Fig. 9 Tappet and adjusting screw assembly. Screw is threaded in all areas except in valve stem contact surface. 1975 4-140

be installed in any sequence since the arms are identical, however, replacement arms are identified with a stamping right (R) and left (L).

ROCKER ARM STUDS

4-151

Rocker arm studs that are cracked or have damaged heads, can be removed from the cylinder head using a deep socket. Install and torque replacement rocker arm stud to 60 ft. lbs. on 1977-79 except cross flow engine and 75 ft. lbs. on 1979 cross flow engine.

V8-262, 305, 350

Rocker arm studs that have damaged threads may be replaced with standard studs. If studs are loose in the head, oversize studs (.003" or .013") may be installed after reaming the holes with a proper size reamer.
1. Remove old stud by placing a suitable spacer, Fig. 6 over stud. Install nut and flat washer and remove stud by turning nut.
2. Ream hole for oversize stud.
3. Coat press-fit area of stud with rear axle lube. Then install new stud, Fig. 7. If tool J-6880 shown is used, it should bottom on the head.

VALVES, ADJUST

4-140

NOTE: On 1976-77 engines, new type hydraulic valve lifters are used and no valve lash adjustment is required. These new type lifters are not interchangeable with the type previously used since the cylinder head has been re-designed to facilitate installation of the new type lifter.

1. To adjust valves, the tappet must be on the base circle of the cam lobe. Do this as follows:
   a. Rotate camshaft timing sprocket to align timing mark on sprocket with inverted "V" notch on timing belt upper cover. The following valves can be adjusted with cam in this position (number one firing).
   Number one cylinder—Intake and Exhaust
   Number two cylinder—Intake
   Number three cylinder—Exhaust
   b. Use a feeler gauge and measure clearance between tappet and cam lobe. Adjust clearance by turning adjusting screw in tappet, Fig. 8.

   NOTE: It is mandatory that the adjusting screw, Fig. 9, be turned one complete revolution to maintain proper stem-to-screw relationship. Each revolution of screw alters clearance by .003".

   c. Rotate camshaft timing sprocket 180 degrees so timing mark is at 12 o'clock position and in line with

notch on timing belt upper cover. The following valves can be adjusted with camshaft in this position (number four firing).
Number two cylinder—Exhaust
Number three cylinder—Intake
Number four cylinder—Intake and Exhaust

V8-262, 305, 350

NOTE: *After the engine has been thoroughly warmed up the valves may be adjusted with the engine shut off as follows: With engine in position to fire No. 1 cylinder the following valves may be adjusted: Exhaust 1-3-4-8, intake 1-2-5-7. Then crank the engine one more complete revolution which will bring No. 6 cylinder to the firing position at which time the following valves may be adjusted: Exhaust 2-5-6-7, intake 3-4-6-8.*

The following procedure, performed with the engine running should be done only in case readjustment is required.
1. After engine has been warmed up to operating temperature, remove valve cover and install a new valve cover gasket on cylinder head to prevent oil from running out.
2. With engine running at idle speed, back off valve rocker arm nut until rocker arm starts to clatter.
3. Turn rocker arm nut down slowly until the clatter just stops. This is the zero lash position.
4. Turn nut down ¼ additional turn and pause 10 seconds until engine runs smoothly. Repeat additional ¼ turns, pausing 10 seconds each time, until nut has been turned down the number of turns listed in the *Valve Specifications Chart* from the zero-lash position.

NOTE

This preload adjustment must be done slowly to allow the lifter to adjust itself to prevent the possibility of interference between the intake valve head and top of piston, which might result in internal damage and/or bent push rods. Noisy lifters should be replaced.

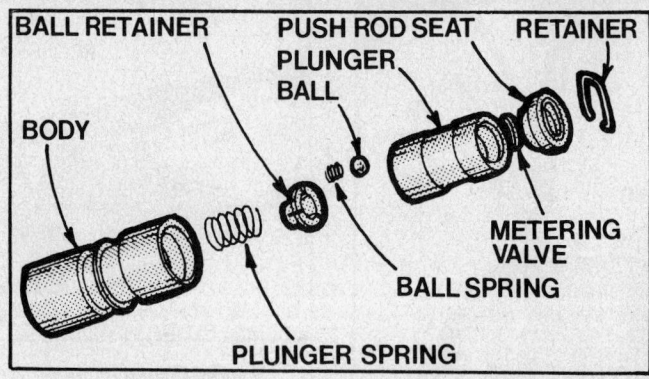

Fig. 10 Hydraulic valve lifter. 4-151, V6-196, 231 and V8-262, 305, 350

VALVE ARRANGEMENT

Front to Rear

4-140	I-E-I-E-I-E-I-E
4-151	E-I-I-E-E-I-I-E
V6-196, 231	E-I-E-I-I-E
V8-262, 305, 350	E-I-I-E-E-I-I-E

CAM LOBE LIFT SPECS.

	Year	Intake	Exhaust
4-140 1 bar. carb.			
	1975	.4199	.4302
4-140 2 bar. carb.			
	1975	.4369	.4150
4-140	1976-77	.4000	.4150

VALVE LIFT SPECS.

Engine	Year	Intake	Exhaust
4-151	1977-79	.406	.406
V6-196	1978	.323	.366
V6-231	1975	.4011	.3768
V6-231	1976	.3768	.3768
V6-231	1977-79	.3830	.3660
V8-262	1975-76	.3727	.3900
V8-305	1976-79	.3727	.4100
V8-350	1975	.3900	.4100

VALVE TIMING

Intake Opens Before TDC

Engine	Year	Degrees
4-140 1 bar. carb.	1975	22
4-140 2 bar. carb.	1975	28
4-140	1976-77	34
4-151	1977-79	33
V6-196	1978	18
V6-231	1975-79	17
V8-262	1975-76	26
V8-305	1976-79	28
V8-350	1975	28

VALVE GUIDES

Valve guides are an integral part of the

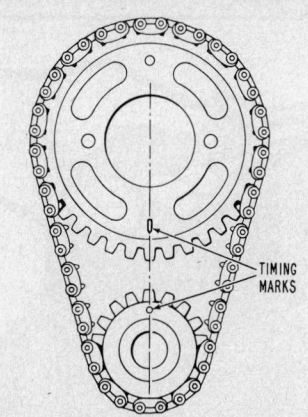

Fig. 11 Valve timing marks aligned for correct valve timing. V6-196, 231

ENGINE FRONT COVER

4-140

1. Raise hood to fully open position and install hood hold-open bolt.
2. Disconnect battery ground cable at battery.
3. Remove fan and spacer.
4. Loosen, but do not remove, the two cover lower screws. Cover is slotted to permit easy removal.
5. Remove the two cover upper retaining screws and remove cover.

4-151

1. Disconnect battery ground cable.
2. Remove torsional damper and the two oil pan to front cover screws, then front cover bolts.
3. Pull cover forward slightly and cut oil pan front seal flush with cylinder block at both side of cover.
4. Remove front cover.

V6-196, 231

1. Drain cooling system and remove radiator.
2. Remove fan, pulleys and belts.
3. Remove crankshaft pulley and reinforcement.
4. If equipped with power steering, remove any pump bracket bolts attached to timing chain cover and loosen and remove any other bolts necessary that will allow pump and brackets to be moved out of the way.
5. Remove fuel pump.
6. Remove Delcotron and brackets.
7. Remove distributor cap and pull spark plug wire retainers off brackets on rocker arm cover. Swing distributor cap with wires attached out of the way.
8. Remove distributor. *If chain and sprockets are not to be disturbed, note position of distributor rotor for installation in the same position.*
9. Loosen and slide clamp on thermostat by-pass hose rearward.
10. Remove bolts attaching chain cover to block.
11. Remove two oil pan-to-chain cover bolts and remove cover.
12. If seal replacement is required, drive seal from cover using a suitable punch.
13. Position packing around opening with

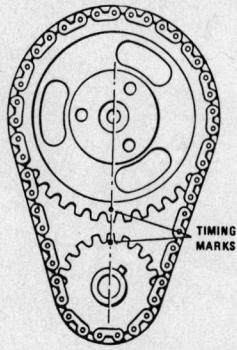

Fig. 12 Valve timing marks aligned for correct valve timing. V8-262, 305, 350

ends of packing facing upward. Drive shedder into position using a suitable punch and stake in three locations.
14. Rotate a hammer handle around packing until balancer hub can be inserted through opening.

V8-262, 305, 350

1. Drain cooling system.
2. Remove alternator and A.I.R. pump, if necessary.
3. Remove fan, fan shroud and radiator.
4. Remove crankshaft damper.
5. Remove front cover attaching bolts and front cover.
6. If seal replacement is required, pry seal from cover using a screw driver.
7. Position seal so open end faces toward inside of cover.
8. Drive seal into position using tool No. J-23042.

TIMING CHAIN

V6-196, 231 & V8-262, 305, 350

1. Remove timing chain cover.
2. Turn crankshaft so that sprockets are aligned as shown in Figs. 11 and 12.
3. Remove oil slinger.
4. On V6-196, 231, remove camshaft distributor drive gear and fuel pump eccentric, then using two large screwdrivers, alternately pry camshaft sprocket and crankshaft sprocket until camshaft is free. Remove camshaft sprocket and chain, then slide crankshaft sprocket off crankshaft.
5. On V8-262, 305, 350 remove three camshaft to sprocket bolts, then remove camshaft sprocket and timing chain together. Sprocket is a light press fit on camshaft, if sprocket does not come off easily, a light blow with a plastic hammer should dislodge it. If crankshaft sprocket is to be replaced, remove it with a suitable puller.
6. To install, assemble chain on sprockets with timing marks aligned as shown in Figs. 11 & 12.
7. Complete installation in reverse order of removal.

cylinder head and are not removable. If valve stem clearance is excessive, the valve stem should be reamed to the next oversize and the appropriate oversize valves installed. Valves are available in .003, .015 and .030 inch oversize for the 4-140 and V8-262, 305 and 350, .003 and .005 for the 4-151 and .010 and .006 inch for the V6-196, 231.

HYDRAULIC VALVE LIFTERS

4-151, V6-196, 231 & V8-262, 305, 350

Failure of an hydraulic valve lifter, is generally caused by an inadequate oil supply or dirt. An air leak at the intake side of the oil pump or too much oil in the engine will cause air bubbles in the oil supply to the lifters, causing them to collapse. This is a probable cause of trouble if several lifters fail to function, but air in the oil is an unlikely cause of failure of a single unit.

The valve lifters may be lifted out of their bores after removing the rocker arms, push rods and intake manifold. Adjustable pliers with taped jaws may be used to remove lifters that are stuck due to varnish, carbon, etc. Fig. 10 illustrates the type of lifter used.

CAMSHAFT COVER

4-140

1. Raise hood to fully open position and install bolt through the hood holdopen link.
2. Disconnect battery negative cable at battery.
3. Remove air cleaner wing nut. Disconnect ventilation tube at camshaft cover or at air cleaner; then remove air cleaner.
4. Remove PCV valve from grommet at front of cover.
5. Remove cover-to-cylinder head screws and withdraw cover from head.

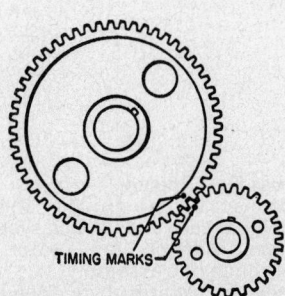

Fig. 12A Valve timing marks aligned for correct valve timing. 4-151

Fig. 13   Camshaft removal tool installed. 4-140

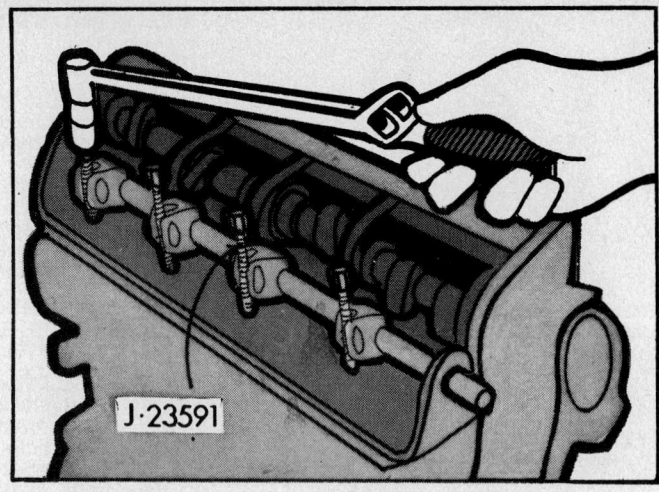

Fig. 14   Depressing valve tappets. 4-140

TIMING GEARS

4-151 Engine

When necessary to install a new camshaft gear, the camshaft will have to be removed as the gear is a pressed fit on the camshaft. The camshaft is held in place by a thrust plate which is retained to the engine by two capscrews which are accessible through the two holes in the gear web.

To remove gear, use an arbor press and a suitable sleeve to properly support gear on its steel hub.

Before installing gear, assemble thrust plate and gear spacer ring, then press gear onto shaft until it bottoms against spacer ring. The thrust plate end clearance should be .0015-.0050 inch. If clearance is less than .0015 inch, the spacer ring should be replaced. If clearance is greater than .0050 inch, the thrust plate should be replaced.

The crankshaft gear can be removed using a puller and two bolts in the tapped holes of the gear.

When installing timing gears, make sure that the marks on the gears are properly aligned, Fig. 12A.

CAMSHAFT, REMOVAL

4-140

1. Remove hood.
2. Remove camshaft timing sprocket.
3. Remove timing belt upper cover and cam retainer and seal assembly.
4. Remove camshaft cover.
5. Disconnect fuel line at carburetor and remove idle solenoid from bracket.
6. Remove carburetor choke coil, cover and rod assembly.
7. Remove distributor.
8. Raise vehicle on a hoist, disconnect engine front mounts at body attachment, raise front of engine and install wood blocks, about 1½" thick, between engine mounts and body. Lower vehicle.
9. Install camshaft removal tool as

shown in Fig. 13, to cylinder head as follows:
a. Position tool to cylinder head so attaching holes align with cam cover lower attaching holes.
b. Align tappet depressing levers on tool so each lever will depress both intake and exhaust valve for their respective cylinder. Lever should fit squarely in notches adjacent to valve tappets.
c. With tool aligned, make sure screws in bottom of tool are backed off so they do not make contact with bosses beneath tool.
d. Install hardened screws supplied with tool, to attach tool to head. Torque screws securely.
e. Turn screws in bottom of tool downward until they just seat against corresponding bosses on head.
f. Apply a heavy body lubricant to ball end of lever depressing screws and proceed to tighten screws to depress tappets, Fig. 14.

NOTE: Use a torque wrench to tighten screws the final few turns. About 10 ft. lbs. is required to depress tappets.

10. At this point the camshaft can be removed by sliding it forward from the head.

4-151

1979 Cross Flow Engine

1. Disconnect battery ground cable, then drain crankcase and cooling system.
2. Remove radiator, fan, water pump pulley and grille assembly.
3. Remove rocker arm cover, then loosen remove rocker arm stud nuts and pivot rocker arms so that push rod can be removed.

4. Remove push rod cover, then remove push rods and valve lifters.
5. Remove oil pump driveshaft and gear assembly.
6. Remove front pulley hub and timing gear cover, then remove spark plugs.
7. Remove two camshaft thrust plate screws through holes in camshaft gear.
8. Pull camshaft and gear assembly from block. Use care not to damage camshaft bearings.

1977-79 Except Cross Flow Engine

1. Disconnect battery ground cable.
2. Drain oil pan and cooling system.
3. Remove fan, water pump pulley, radiator and the grille.
4. Remove distributor, fuel pump and spark plugs.
5. Remove valve train components.
6. Remove engine front cover.
7. Remove two camshaft thrust plate screws.
8. Remove camshaft and gear assembly from engine. Use care not to damage camshaft bearing surfaces.

V6-196, 231 & V8-262, 305, 350

NOTE: If engine is in the car, the radiator, grille and A/C components will have to be removed. If engine is out of car, proceed as follows:

1. To remove camshaft, remove rocker arm assemblies, push rods and valve lifters.
2. Remove timing chain and sprockets.
3. On V8-262, 305, 350 engines install two 5/16" (18x4") bolts in camshaft bolt holes.
4. On all engines, slide camshaft out of engine using care not to damage the bearing surfaces.

TIMING BELT

4-140

1. Remove engine front cover as previously described.
2. Remove accessory drive pulley or damper.
3. Drain coolant and loosen water pump bolts to relieve tension on belt.
4. Remove timing belt lower cover, then remove belt from sprockets.

CAMSHAFT SPROCKET

4-140

After removal of timing belt, the camshaft sprocket can be removed as follows:

1. Align one hole in sprocket with bolt head behind sprocket, then using a socket on bolt head to prevent cam from turning, remove sprocket retaining bolt and withdraw sprocket from camshaft.
2. When installing, be sure timing marks are aligned as in Fig. 15.

NOTE: A simplified method is provided for checking camshaft and crankshaft alignment. Proper alignment is assured by making sure hole in left rear of the timing belt upper cover is in line with the corresponding hole in the camshaft sprocket. Check alignment by inserting a pencil or other similar tool through hole in cover. If alignment is correct, the tool will enter small hole in cam gear, Fig. 16.

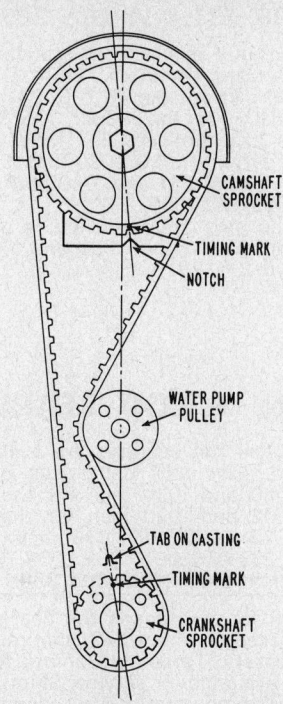

Fig. 15   Sprocket alignment marks. 4-140

CRANKSHAFT SPROCKET

4-140

1. Remove engine front cover, accessory drive pulley, timing belt and timing belt lower cover.

2. Install suitable puller to crankshaft sprocket and remove sprocket.

OIL PUMP (CRANKCASE FRONT COVER) SEAL

4-140

1. Remove engine front cover, accessory drive pulley, timing belt and timing belt lower cover and crankshaft sprocket.
2. Pry old seal from front cover being careful not to damage seal housing or seal lip contact surfaces.
3. Coat seal with light engine oil and apply an approved sealing compound to outside diameter of seal.
4. Position seal, closed end outward, onto crankshaft. Then install seal into bore using tool J-23624, Fig. 17.

PISTONS & RODS, ASSEMBLE

4-140

The "F" on the front of the piston must face the front of the engine when the piston and rod assembly is installed in its proper cylinder, Fig. 18.

4-151

Assemble piston to rod with the notch on piston facing toward front of engine and the raised notch side of rod at bearing end facing toward rear of engine, Fig. 18A.

Fig. 16   Checking sprocket alignment. 4-140

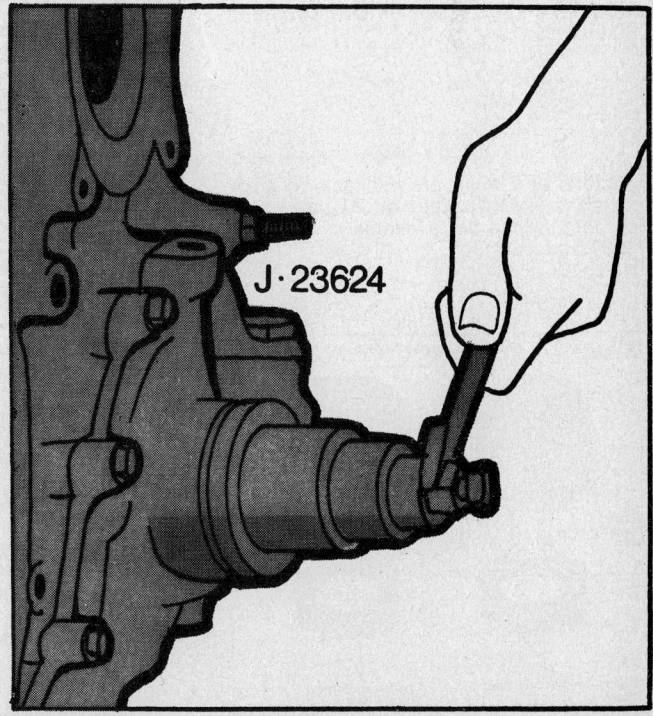

Fig. 17   Installing crankcase front oil seal. 4-140

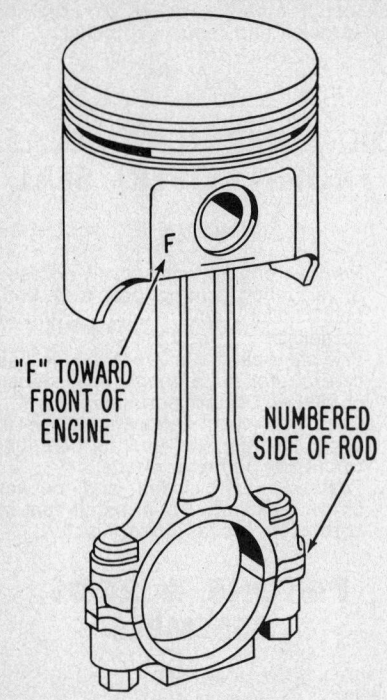

Fig. 18 Piston and rod assembly. 4-140

V6-196, 231 & V8-262, 305, 350

Rods and pistons should be assembled and installed as shown in Figs. 19 & 19A.

PISTONS, PINS & RINGS

4-140

Pistons and rings are available in standard sizes and oversizes of .010, .020 and .030 inch.

4-151

Pistons and rings are available in standard sizes and oversizes of .010 and .030 inch. Piston pins are available in oversizes of .001 and .003 inch.

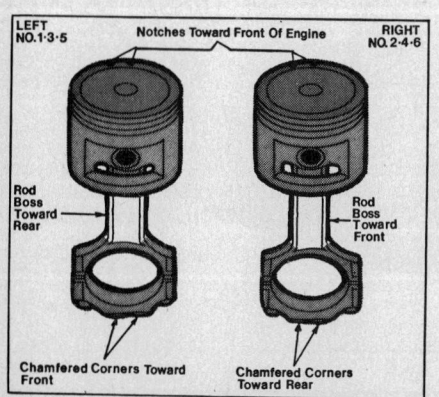

Fig. 19 Piston and rod assembly. V6-196, 231

V6-196, 231 & V8-262, 305, 350

Pistons are available in standard sizes and oversizes of .001, .005, .010, .020 and .030 inch for the V6-196, 231 & .001, .020 and .030 for the V8-262, 305, 350.
Rings are furnished in standard sizes and oversizes of .010, .020 and .030 inch for the V6-196, 231 and .020 and .030 for the V8-262, 305, 350.
Pistons pins are furnished in standard sizes and oversizes of .003 and .005 inch for the V6-196, 231.

MAIN & ROD BEARINGS

Main and rod bearings are available in standard sizes and undersizes of .001, .002, .020 and .030 inch for the 4-140, .001, .002 and .010 inch for the 4-151, .001, .002, .003 and .010 inch for the V6-196, 231 and .001, .002, .009, .010 and .020 inch for the V8-262, 305, 350.

NOTE: If for any reason the bearing caps are replaced on the 4-140, shimming may be necessary. Laminated shims for each cap are available for service. Shim requirements will be determined by bearing clearance.

OIL PAN

4-140

1. Raise vehicle on a hoist and drain engine oil.
2. Support front of engine so weight is off front mounts, and remove frame crossmember and both front crossmember braces.
3. Disconnect idler arm at frame side rail.

NOTE: On air conditioned vehicles, disconnect idler arm at relay rod.

4. Mark relationship of steering linkage pitman arm to steering gear pitman shaft and remove pitman arm.

NOTE: Do not rotate steering gear pitman shaft while arm is disconnected as this will change steering wheel alignment.

5. Remove flywheel cover or converter underpan.
6. Remove oil pan to cylinder case screws, tap pan lightly to break sealing bond and remove oil pan.
7. Remove pick up screen to baffle support bolts, then remove support from baffle.
8. Remove bolt securing oil pan drain back tube to baffle. Then rotate baffle 90 degrees towards left side of car and remove baffle from pick up screen, Fig. 20.

4-151

1. Disconnect battery ground cable.

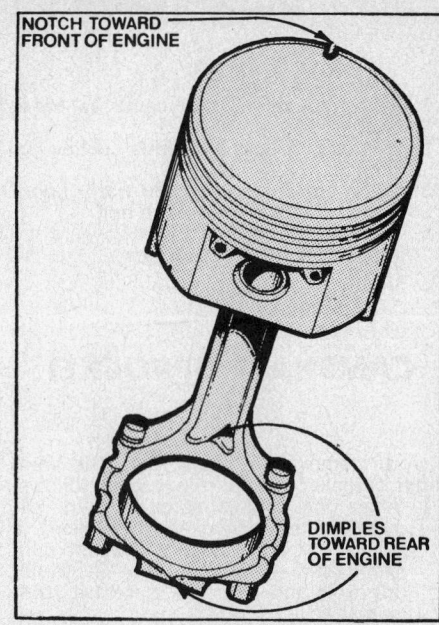

Fig. 18A Piston and rod assembly. 4-151
Engine oiling system (typical). V6-196, 231

2. Raise vehicle and drain oil pan.
3. Remove rear section of frame crossmember.
4. Disconnect exhaust pipe from manifold and loosen hanger bracket.
5. Remove starter and position aside.
6. Remove flywheel housing inspection cover.
7. Disconnect steering linkage at steering gear and idler arm support.
8. Remove oil pan bolts and the oil pan.

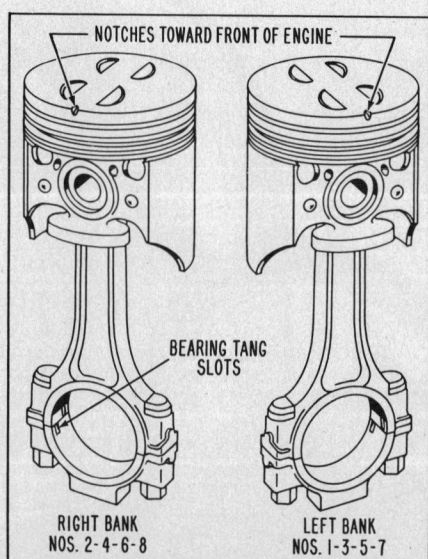

Fig. 19A Piston and rod assembly. V8-262, 305, 350

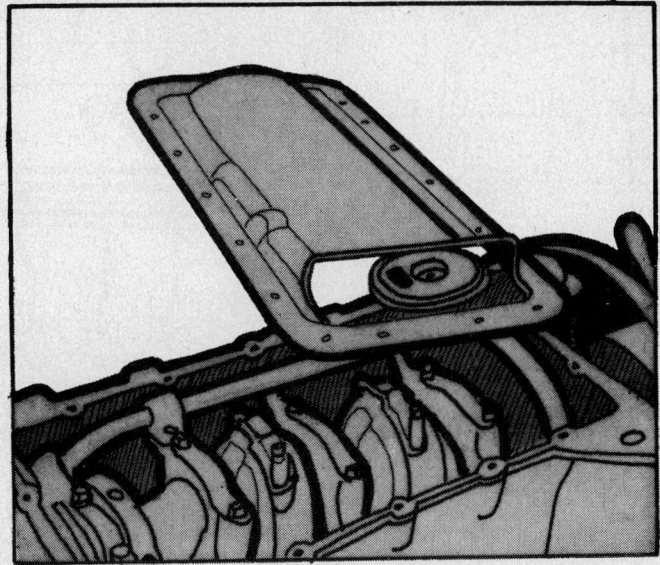

Fig. 20   Removing oil pan baffle. 4-140

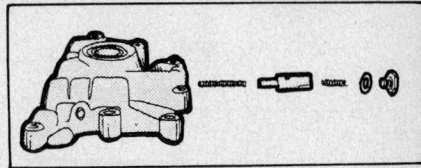

Fig. 21   Oil pump pressure regulator. 4-140

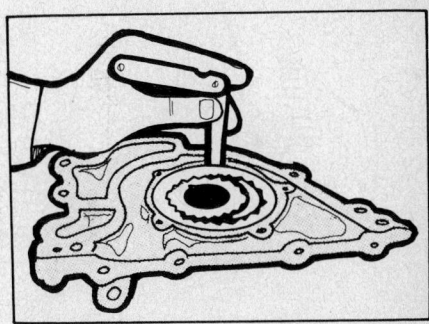

Fig. 22   Checking driven gear to housing clearance. 4-140

V6-196, 231

1. Support vehicle on hoist and drain oil.
2. Remove transmission dust cover and exhaust crossover pipe.
3. Remove oil pan bolts and allow pan to drop.
4. Reverse removal procedure to install.

V8-262, 305, 350

1. Disconnect battery ground cable.
2. Raise vehicle, drain oil pan and disconnect crossover pipe.
3. Remove underpan and splash shield from converter housing.
4. On 1975-76 models, support engine, then remove crossmember and braces.

NOTE: Scribe reference marks on each side of brace to ensure crossmember installation in original position.

5. On 1975-76 models, disconnect idler arm at frame side rail.
6. On all models, remove starter, then the oil pan.

OIL PUMP

4-140

1. Remove engine front cover, accessory drive pulley, timing belt, timing belt lower cover and crankshaft sprocket.
2. Raise vehicle on a hoist and remove oil pan and baffle.
3. Remove bolts and stud securing oil pump to cylinder case.

Inspection

1. Clean gasket surfaces, then wash parts in approved solvent and blow out all passages.
2. Check pressure regulator for free operation, Fig. 21.
3. Inspect pump gears for nicks, broken parts and other damage.
4. Check clearance between outside diameter, of driven gear and pump. Clearance should be .0038-.0068", Fig. 22.
5. Check clearance between outside diameter of drive gear and crescent. Clearance should be .0023-.0093", Fig. 23.
6. Check clearance between inside diameter of driven gear and pump crescent. Clearance should be .0068-.0148", Fig. 24.
7. Check gear end clearance. It should be .0009-.0023", Fig. 25.

NOTE: The pump gears and body are not serviced separately. If pump gears or body are worn, replacement of the entire oil pump is necessary.

4-151

1. Remove oil pan as outlined previously.
2. Remove two flange mounting bolts and nut from main bearing cap bolt, then the oil pump and screen assembly.

Should any of the following conditions be found, it is advisable to replace the pump assembly:
1. Inspect pump body for cracks or wear.
2. Inspect gears for wear or damage.
3. Check shaft for looseness in housing.
4. Check inside of cover for wear that would permit oil to leak past ends of gear.
5. Check oil pick-up screen for damage.
6. Check pressure regulator valve plunger for proper fit in body.

V6-196, 231

1. To remove pump, take off oil filter.
2. Disconnect wire from oil pressure indicator switch in filter by-pass valve cap (if so equipped).
3. Remove screws attaching oil pump cover to timing chain cover. Remove cover and slide out pump gears. Replace any parts not serviceable.
4. Remove oil pressure relief valve cap, spring and valve, Fig. 26. Remove oil filter by-pass valve cap, spring and valve. Replace any parts of valve not serviceable.
5. Check relief valve in its bore in cover. Valve should have no more clearance than an easy slip fit. If any perceptible side shake can be felt, the valve and/or cover should be replaced.
6. The filter by-pass valve should be flat and free of nicks and scratches.

Assembly & Installation

1. Lubricate and install pressure relief valve and spring in bore of pump cover. Install cap and gasket. Torque cap to 30-35 lbs.
2. Install filter by-pass valve flat in its seat in cover. Install spring, cap and gasket. Torque cap to 30-35 ft-lbs.
3. Install pump gears and shaft in pump body section of timing chain cover to check gear end clearance. Check clearance as shown in Fig. 27. If clearance is less than .0018" check timing chain cover for evidence of wear.
4. If gear end clearance is satisfactory, remove gears and pack gear pocket *full* of vaseline, not chassis lube.
5. Reinstall gears so vaseline is forced into every cavity of gear pocket and between teeth of gears. *Unless pump is packed with vaseline, it may not prime itself when engine is started.*
6. Install cover and tighten screws alternately and evenly. Final tightening is 10-15 ft-lbs. torque. Install filter on nipple.

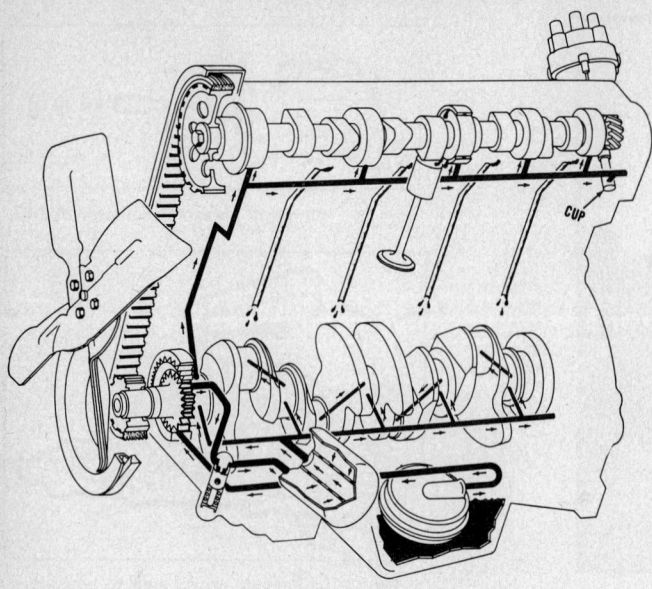

Engine oiling system. 4-140

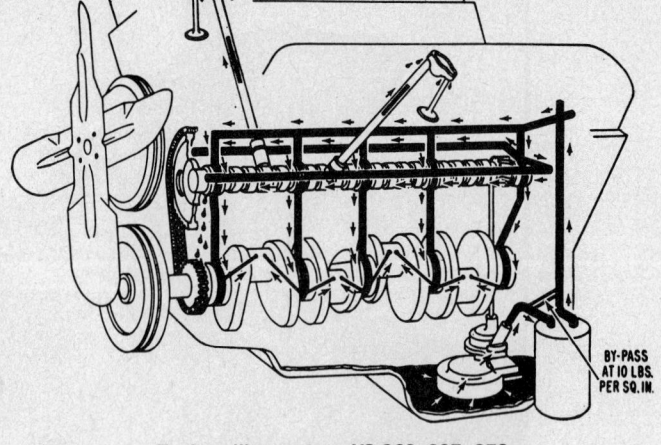

Engine oiling system. V8-262, 305, 350

BY-PASS
AT 10 LBS.
PER SQ. IN.

V8-262, 305, 350

After removing the oil pan, remove pump from rear main bearing cap. Disconnect pump shaft from extension by removing clip from collar. Remove pump cover and take out idler gear, drive gear and shaft.

Should any of the following conditions be found it is advisable to replace the pump assembly.

1. Inspect pump body for cracks or wear.
2. Inspect gears for wear or damage.
3. Check shaft for looseness in housing.
4. Check inside of cover for wear that would permit oil to leak past the ends of gear.
5. Check oil pick-up screen for damage to screen, by-pass valve or body.
6. Check for oil in air chamber.

CRANKSHAFT REAR OIL SEAL

When necessary to correct an oil leak

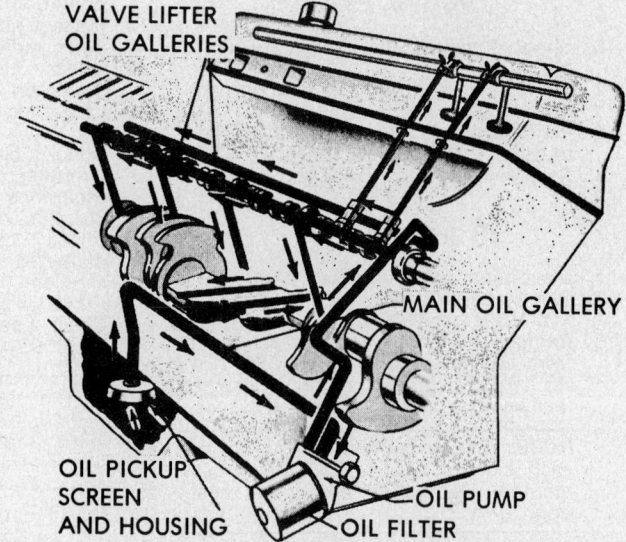

VALVE LIFTER
OIL GALLERIES

MAIN OIL GALLERY

OIL PICKUP
SCREEN
AND HOUSING

OIL PUMP
OIL FILTER

Engine oiling system (typical). V6-196, 231.

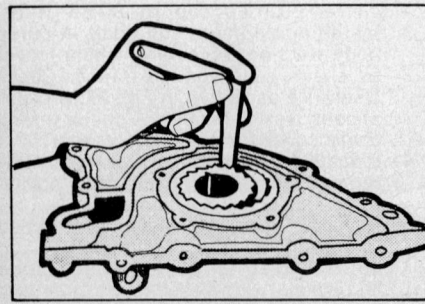

Fig. 23 Checking drive gear to crescent clearance. 4-140

Fig. 24 Checking driven gear to crescent clearance. 4-140

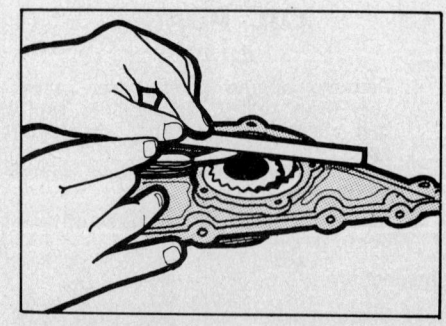

Fig. 25 Checking gear end clearance. 4-140

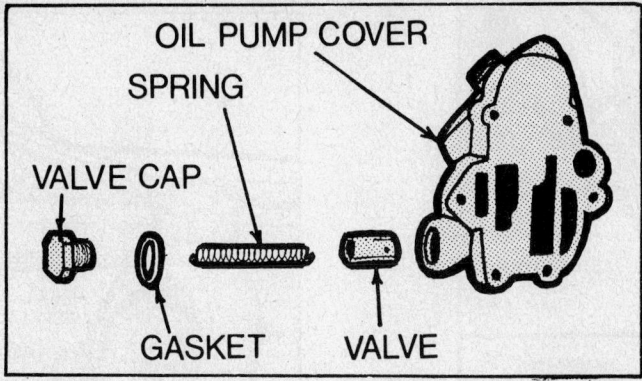

Fig. 26   Oil pump cover and pressure relief valve. V6-196, 231

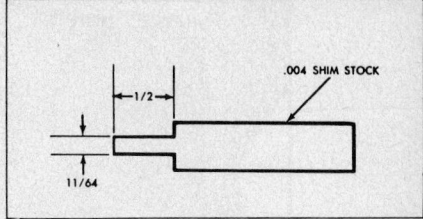

Fig. 28   Fabricated seal starting tool for helix type seal. V8-262, 305, 350

due to a defective seal, always replace the upper and lower halves as a unit. *When installing either half, lubricate the lip portion only with engine oil, keeping oil off the parting line surface as this is treated with glue.* Always clean crankshaft surface before installing a new seal. Be careful of seal retainer tang while inserting a new seal so that it doesn't cut the seal.

4-151

1979 Cross Flow Engine
The rear main bearing oil seal is a one piece unit and is replaced without removing the oil pan or crankshaft.
1. Remove transmission, flywheel housing and flywheel.
2. Using a suitable screwdriver, remove rear main bearing oil seal. Use care not to scratch crankshaft.
3. Lubricate inside and outside diameters of replacement seal with engine oil. In-

stall seal by hand onto rear crankshaft flange with helical lip side facing toward engine. Ensure seal is firmly and evenly seated.
4. Install flywheel, flywheel housing and transmission.

1977-79 Except Cross Flow Engine
The rear main bearing oil seal can be replaced without removing the crankshaft.
1. Remove oil pan and rear main bearing cap.
2. To replace the lower seal, remove seal from groove in bearing cap, using a small screwdriver to pry it out.
3. Insert new seal and roll it in place with finger and thumb.
4. To replace the upper seal (with engine in car) use a small hammer and tap a brass pin punch on one end of the seal until it protrudes far enough to be removed with pliers.
5. Insert the new seal, gradually push-

ing with a hammer handle until seal is rolled into place.
6. Install bearing cap with new seal and tighten bearing cap bolts.

V8-262, 305, 350

NOTE: V8-262, 305, 350 engines are equipped with helix type rear seal. A seal starting tool, Fig. 28, must be used to prevent the upper seal half from coming into contact with the sharp edge of the block. Place the tip of the tool into the seal channel and "shoehorn" the seal into the upper seal channel.

1. To replace the lower seal, remove seal from groove in bearing cap, using a small screwdriver to pry it out.
2. Insert new seal and roll it in place with finger and thumb.
3. To replace the upper seal (with engine in car) use a small hammer and tap a brass pin punch on one end of the seal until it protrudes far enough to be removed with pliers.
4. Position tip of tool, Fig. 28, between

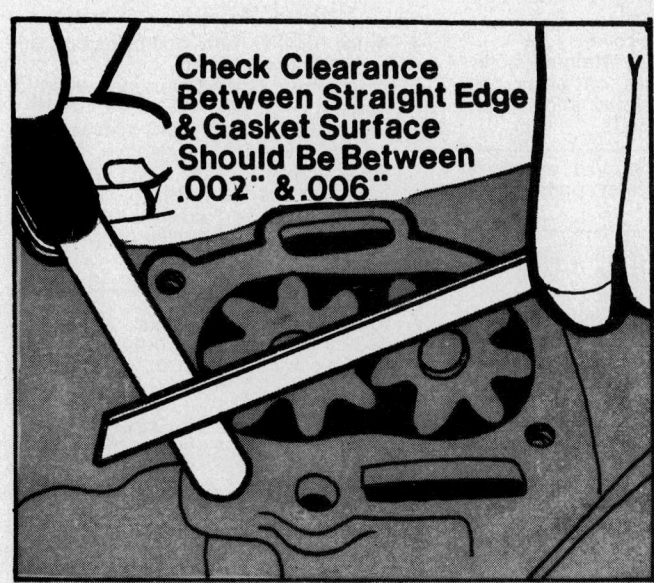

Fig. 27   Checking oil pump gear end clearance. V6-196, 231

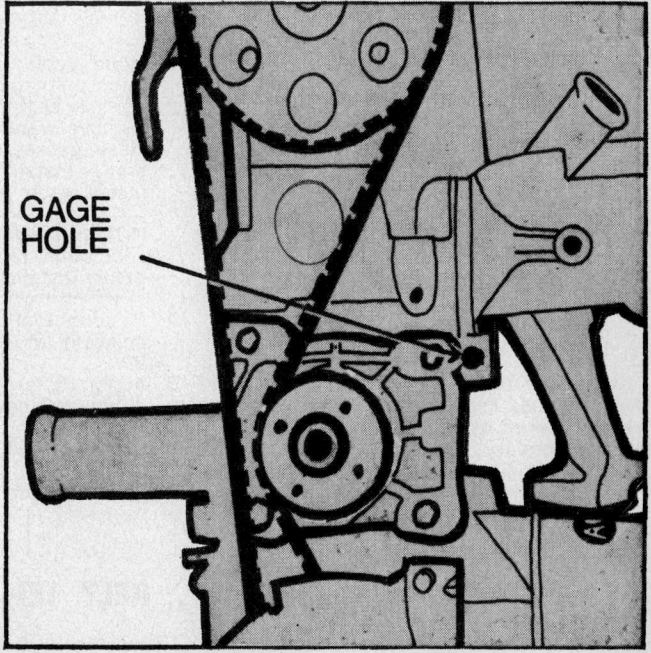

Fig. 29   Tensioning adaptor locating hole

J-23654

Fig. 30   Adjusting timing belt

Fig. 31   Removing fuel pump and gauge unit

crankshaft and seal seat in cylinder block.
5. Position seal between crankshaft and tip of tool with seal bead contacting tip of tool. Ensure oil seal lip is facing toward front of engine.
6. Roll seal around crankshaft, using tool as a "Shoehorn" to protect seal bead from sharp corner of seal seat surface in cylinder block.

NOTE: Tool must remain in position until seal is properly seated with both ends flush with block.

7. Remove tool, using care not to dislodge seal.
8. Install new seal into bearing cap with tool as outlined previously.
9. Install bearing cap with sealant applied to the cap to case interface. Do not apply sealant to seal ends. Torque rear main bearing cap bolts to specifications as listed in the "Engine Tightening Specification Chart".

CRANKSHAFT REAR OIL SEAL REPAIR

V6-196, 231

Since the braided fabric seal used on these engines can be replaced only when the crankshaft is removed, the following repair procedure is recommended.
1. Remove oil pan and bearing cap.
2. Drive end of old seal gently into groove, using a suitable tool, until packed tight. This may vary between 1/4 and 3/4 inch depending on amount of pack required.
3. Repeat previous step for other end of seal.
4. Measure and note amount that seal was driven up on one side. Using the old seal removed from bearing cap,

cut a length of seal the amount previously noted plus 1/16 inch.
5. Repeat previous step for other side of seal.
6. Pack cut lengths of seal into appropriate side of seal groove. A guide tool, J-21526-1, and packing tool, J-21526-2, may be used since these tools have been machined to provide a built-in stop.
7. Install new seal in bearing cap.

TIMING BELT TENSION, ADJUST

4-140

1. Drain coolant at engine block and remove fan and extension.
2. Remove engine front cover.
3. Remove water pump retaining bolts, clean gasket surfaces on block and pump. Install new gasket and loosely install water pump bolts.

NOTE: Apply an approved anti-seize compound to the water pump bolts before installation.

4. Position tool J-23564 in gauge hole adjacent to left side of pump, Fig. 29.
5. Apply 15 ft. lbs. of torque to water pump as shown in Fig. 30. Tighten water pump bolts while maintaining torque on side of pump.
6. Reinstall front cover, fan, extension and fill cooling system.

BELT TENSION DATA

	New lbs.	Used lbs.
Air Conditioning		
4-140, 151	110-140	75-80
V6-196, 231	135-165	100-105
V8-301	135-165	100-105
V8-305, 350	135-165	80
Air Pump		
4-140	120-130	75
4-151	110-140	70
V6-196, 231	60-80	50-55
V8-305, 350	120-150	55
Delcotron		
Exc. V8-305, 350	110-140	75-80
V8-305, 350	120-150	55
Power Steering		
4-140, 151	110-140	75-80
V6-196, 231	135-165	100-105
V8-301	135-165	100-105
V8-305, 350	120-150	55
Timing Belt		
4-140	100-140	

WATER PUMP, REPLACE

4-140

1. Raise hood to fully open position and install hold-open bolt.
2. Disconnect battery ground cable at battery.
3. Remove engine fan and spacer.
4. Loosen, but do not remove, the two cover lower screws. Cover is slotted to permit easy removal.
5. Remove the two cover upper retaining screws and remove cover.
6. Drain coolant and loosen water pump bolts to relieve tension in timing belt.
7. Remove radiator lower hose and heater hose at water pump.
8. Remove water pump bolts and water pump.

4-151, V6-196, 231 & V8-262, 305, 350

1. Drain cooling system and loosen fan pulley bolts.
2. On V8-262, 305, 350 engines, remove alternator and A.I.R. pump, if necessary.
3. On all engines, disconnect radiator and heater hoses from water pump.

4. Remove fan and pulley, then remove water pump.

FUEL PUMP PRESSURE

Year	Engine	Pressure lbs.
1975-76	4-140	3-4½
1977-78	4-151	3-4½
1979	4-151	6½-8
1978-79	V6-196	4¼-5¾
1975-78	V6-231	4-5
1979	V6-231	4.1-6½
1975-76	V8-262	7-8½
1976	V8-305	7-8½
1977-79	V8-305	7½-9
1975	V8-350	7½-9

FUEL PUMP, REPLACE
4-151

NOTE: Before installing the pump, it is good practice to crank the engine so that the nose of the camshaft eccentric is out of the way of the fuel pump rocker arm when the pump is installed. In this way there will be the least amount of tension on the rocker arm, thereby easing the installation of the pump.

1. Remove all gasket material from the pump and block gasket surfaces. Apply sealer to both sides of new gasket.
2. Position gasket on pump flange and hold pump in position against its mounting surface. Make sure rocker arm is riding on camshaft eccentric.
3. Press pump tight against its mounting. Install retaining screws and tighten them alternately.
4. Connect fuel lines. Then operate engine and check for leaks.

Except 4-151
Removal
1. Disconnect battery ground cable.
2. Disconnect meter and pump wires at rear wiring harness connector.
3. Raise vehicle on hoist and drain fuel tank.
4. Disconnect fuel line hose at gauge unit pick up line.
5. Disconnect tank vent lines to vapor separator.
6. Remove gauge ground wire screw at underbody floorpan.
7. Remove tank straps bolts and lower tank carefully.
8. Unscrew retaining ring using spanner wrench J-22554, Fig. 31, and remove pump-tank unit assembly.

Replacement
1. Remove flat wire conductor from plastic clip on fuel tube.
2. Squeeze clamp and pull pump straight back about ½ inch.
3. Remove two nuts and lockwashers and conductor wires from pump terminals.
4. Squeeze clamp and pull pump straight back to remove it from tank unit. Take care to prevent bending of circular support bracket.
5. Slide replacement pump through circular support bracket until it rests against rubber coupling. Make sure pump has rubber isolator and saran strainer attached.
6. Attach two conductor wires to pump terminals using lockwashers and nuts being certain flat conductor is attached to terminal located on side away from float arm.
7. Squeeze clamp and push pump into rubber coupling.
8. Replace flat wire conductor in plastic clip on fuel pick up tube.
9. Install unit into tank and replace fuel tank.

Clutch & Transmission Section

CLUTCH PEDAL, ADJUST
Ball Stud Adjustment
1. Before attaching clutch cable, place gauge J-23644 with flat end against face of clutch housing and locate hooked end of gauge at point of cable attachment to fork, Fig. 1.
2. Turn ball stud inward until clutch release bearing contacts clutch spring fingers.
3. Install lock nut and torque to 25 ft. lbs., use care not to change ball stud adjustment.
4. Install ball stud cap, then remove gauge by pulling outward at housing end.

Clutch Cable Adjustment
NOTE: Ball stud adjustment must be correct before adjusting clutch cable.

1. With return spring disconnected, place cable through hole in clutch fork, Figs. 2 and 3.
2. Pull cable until clutch pedal is firmly against clutch pedal stop.
3. Push clutch fork forward until release bearing contacts clutch spring fingers.
4. Tighten adjusting pin on cable until it contacts fork surface.
5. Rotate cable pin an additional ¼ turn clockwise and position pin into groove on fork.
6. Attach return spring, then cycle clutch pedal approximately 3 times. Lash at clutch pedal should be .65 to 1.15 in. for 1975 and 1978-79 Skyhawk, 1975-79 Monza and Sunbird, ⅝ to 1⅛ in. for 1976-77 Skyhawk and ¹¹⁄₁₆ to 1⅛ in. for 1975-79 Starfire.

CLUTCH REPLACE
1. Remove transmission.
2. Remove clutch fork cover then disconnect clutch return spring and control cable from clutch fork.
3. Remove flywheel housing lower cover and flywheel housing.
4. Remove release bearing from the clutch fork and sleeve by sliding lever off ball stud and against spring pres-

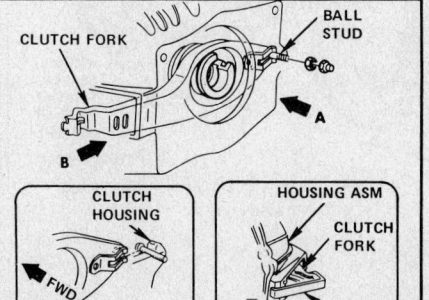

Fig. 1   Ball stud adjustment

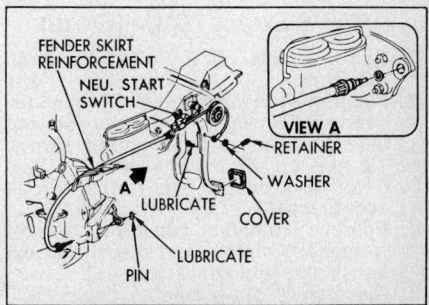

Fig. 2   Clutch cable adjustment. 1975 models

sure. If ball stud is to be replaced, remove cap, lock nut and stud from housing.

5. Make sure alignment marks on clutch assembly and flywheel are distinguishable.

6. Loosen clutch cover to flywheel bolts one turn at a time until spring pressure is released to avoid bending clutch cover flange, Fig. 4.

7. Support the pressure plate and cover assembly while removing bolts and clutch assembly.

NOTE: Do not disassemble the clutch cover, spring and pressure plate for repairs. If defective, replace complete assembly.

8. Reverse procedure to install making sure to index alignment marks.

9. After installing crossmember, loosely install retaining bolts, then the crossmember to transmission mount bolts. Tighten all bolts to specifications and remove the engine support.

CAUTION: Check position of engine in front mounts and realign as necessary.

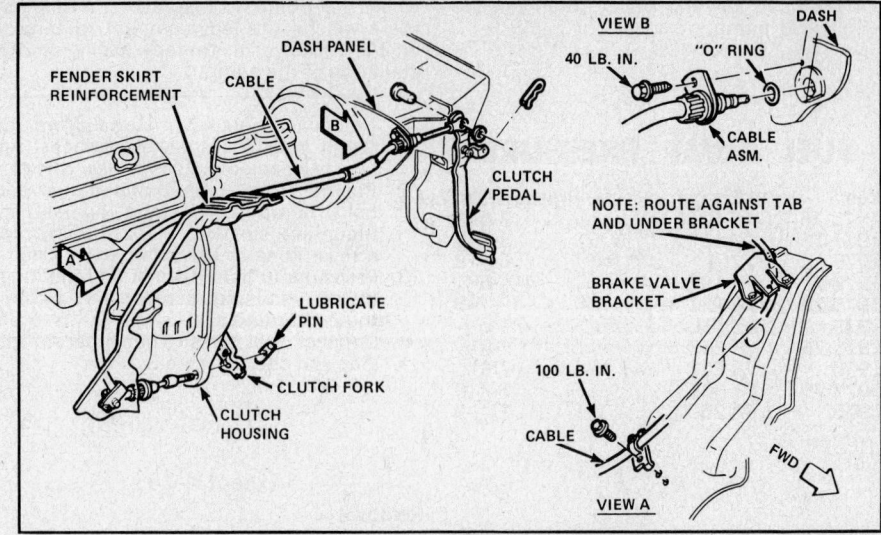

Fig. 3   Clutch cable adjustment. 1976-79 models

FOUR SPEED TRANSMISSION, REPLACE

1976 70MM (Brazil)

1. Push shift lever boot down and loosen lock nut, remove upper portion of shift lever.
2. Remove console, retainer and boot, then remove shift control from extension housing.
3. Raise vehicle and drain lubricant.
4. Remove torque arm, referring to the "Rear Suspension" section, then remove propeller shaft, and disconnect speedometer cable and back-up light from transmission.
5. Disconnect clutch return spring and cable from fork.
6. Remove transmission to crossmember bolts.
7. Remove converter bracket and damper, if equipped.
8. Remove crossmember to frame bolts, support transmission, then remove crossmember.
9. Remove clutch housing to engine attaching bolts, slide transmission and clutch housing rearward and remove from vehicle.

1975-79 Except 70MM (Brazil)

1. Raise vehicle on a hoist and drain lubricant.
2. Place shift lever in neutral, then disconnect transmission control rod and lever assemblies from shifter shafts. Tie rods up and out of way.
3. Remove propeller shaft and torque arm bracket.
4. Remove catalytic converter bracket from transmission and disconnect exhaust pipe and converter.
5. Disconnect speedometer cable, TCS switch and back-up lamp switch.
6. Remove crossmember to transmission

mount bolts.
7. Support engine with an appropriate jack stand and remove crossmember to frame bolts and remove crossmember.
8. Remove transmission to clutch housing upper retaining bolts and install guide pins in holes.
9. Remove lower bolts, then slide transmission rearward and remove from vehicle.

NOTE: Inspect throwout bearing support gasket located beneath lip of support. If necessary, replace gasket before installing transmission.

LINKAGE ADJUST

1975-79 4 Speed Except 70mm (Brazil)

1. Place ignition switch in off position.
2. Raise vehicle, then loosen lock nuts at swivels on shift rods, Fig. 5. Rods should pass freely through swivels.
3. Place transmission shift levers in neutral position.
4. Place shift control lever in neutral position, then align control levers and install gauge pin into levers and bracket.
5. Tighten 1st-2nd shift rod nut against swivel, then tighten 3rd-4th shift rod

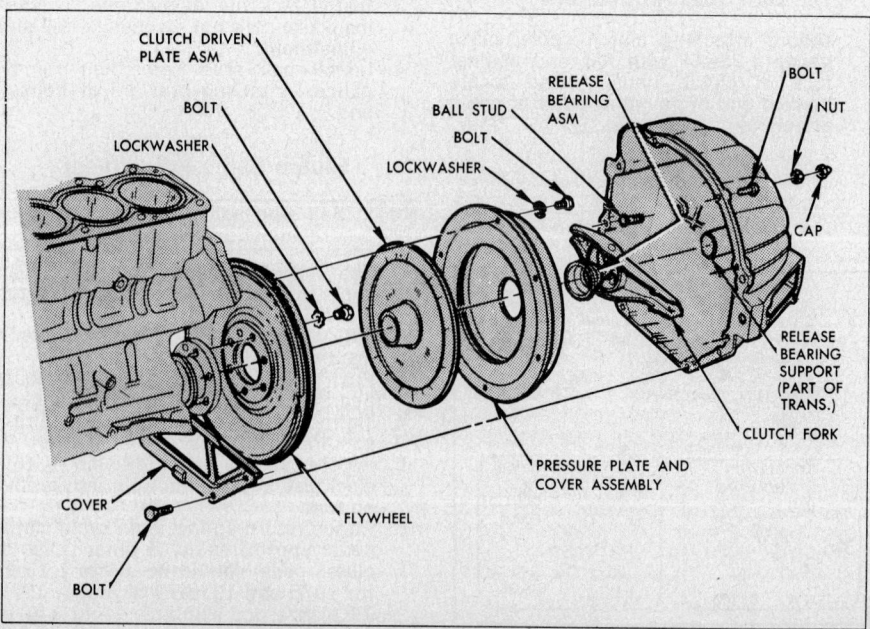

Fig. 4   Clutch & components (typical)

nut against swivel. Torque nuts to 120 in. lbs.

6. Torque reverse shift rod control nut to 120 in. lbs.

7. Remove gauge pin from shifter assembly and check linkage adjustment.

FIVE SPEED TRANS. REPLACE

1. Remove shifter assembly and raise vehicle.
2. Remove propeller shaft and torque arm bracket, then disconnect speedometer cable from transmission.
3. Remove crossmember to transmission bolts and the catalytic converter support bracket.
4. Support engine and remove crossmember.
5. Remove transmission to clutch housing upper retaining bolts and install guide pins.
6. Remove lower transmission to clutch housing bolts, slide transmission rearward and lower from vehicle.
7. Remove back-up lamp switch and fill plug, then drain transmission.

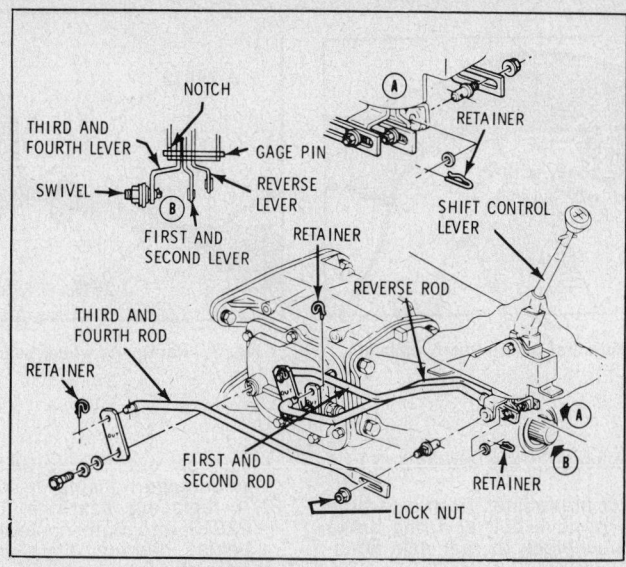

Fig. 5   Shift linkage adjustment. 1975-79 4 speed transmission except 70 mm (Brazil)

1979 AUTO. TRANS. LINKAGE, ADJUST

Linkage adjustments for these models are the same as the 1978 linkage adjustments found in the "Automatic Transmission" chapter, Turbo Hydra-matic 200 & 250, 350 sections.

Rear Axle, Propeller Shaft & Brakes

REAR AXLE

Description

The rear axle, Fig. 1, is a semi-floating type consisting of a cast carrier and large bosses on each end into which two welded steel tubes are fitted. The carrier contains an overhung hypoid pinion and ring gear. The differential is a two pinion arrangement.

The overhung hypoid drive pinion is supported by two preloaded tapered roller bearings. The pinion shaft is sealed by means of a molded, spring loaded, rubber seal. The seal is mounted on the pinion shaft flange which is splined and bolts to the hypoid pinion shaft.

The ring gear is bolted to a one piece differential case and is supported by two preloaded tapered roller bearings.

Removal

1. Support vehicle at frame and using a suitable jack support axle housing.

Fig. 1   Rear axle cross section →

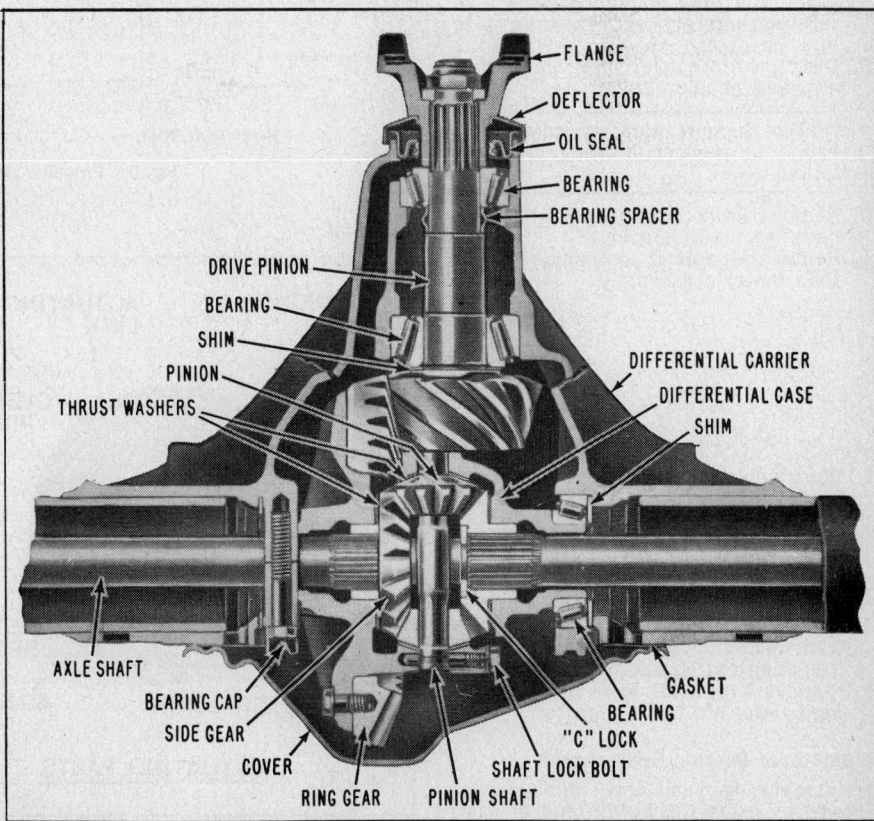

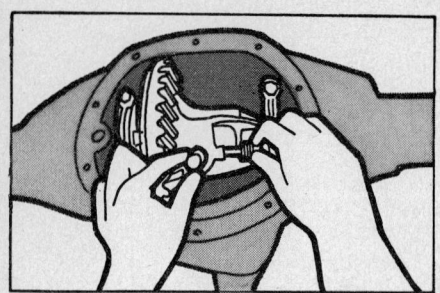

Fig. 2 Differential pinion shaft removal

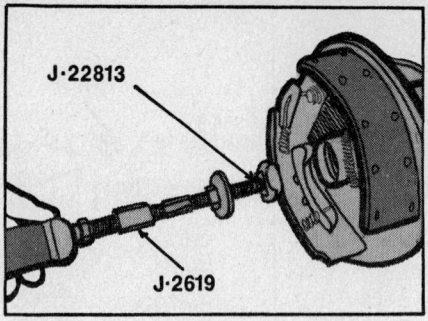

Fig. 3 Removing wheel bearing and seal

Fig. 4 Installing seal and wheel bearing

2. Remove wheels, brake drums and axle shafts.
3. Disconnect brake lines from axle tube clips and remove bolt securing brake line junction block to rear axle housing.

NOTE: Do not disconnect brake lines from wheel cylinders or junction block.

4. Remove brake backing plates and secure backing plates to frame.
5. Remove parking brake cable adjusting nuts at equalizer, pull center cable rearward and disconnect two rear cables from body connectors.
6. Disconnect rear brake hose at floor pan and cap ends of hose and line.
7. Disconnect shock absorber from rear axle.
8. Disconnect track rod, then slowly lower axle until all spring tension is relieved and pry springs from axle housing pads.
9. Disconnect propeller shaft and torque arm and position aside.

NOTE: Support axle at companion flange to prevent housing from rotating.

10. Remove lower control arm attaching bolts from axle housing.
11. Remove support at companion flange, then the axle assembly.

AXLE SHAFT

1. Raise vehicle on a hoist and remove wheel and tire assembly and brake drum.
2. Drain lubricant from axle by removing carrier cover.
3. Unscrew pinion shaft lock screw and remove pinion shaft, Fig. 2.
4. Push flanged end of axle shaft toward center of car and remove "C" lock from button end of shaft.
5. Remove axle shaft from housing being careful not to damage seal.

Oil Seal &/or Bearing Replacement

1. If replacing seal only, remove the seal by using the button end of axle shaft. Insert the button end of shaft behind the steel case of the seal and

pry seal out of bore being careful not to damage housing.
2. If replacing bearings, insert tool J-22813 into bore so tool head grasps behind bearing, Fig. 3. Slide washer against seal, or bearing, and turn nut against washer. Attach slide hammer J-2619 and remove bearing.
3. Pack cavity between seal lips with a high melting point wheel bearing lubricant. Position seal on tool J-21491 and position seal in axle housing bore, tap seal in bore just below end of housing, Fig. 4.

PROPELLER SHAFT

The propeller shaft used is made up of concentric steel tubes with rubber elements between, Fig. 5.

Propeller Shaft, Replace

1. Raise vehicle on a hoist.
2. Disconnect torque arm at rear axle, then referring to the "Rear Suspension" section, loosen attaching bolt at

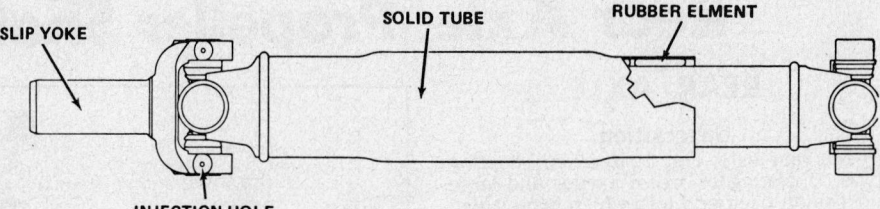

Fig. 5 Propeller shaft cross section (typical)

SLIP YOKE SOLID TUBE RUBBER ELMENT INJECTION HOLE

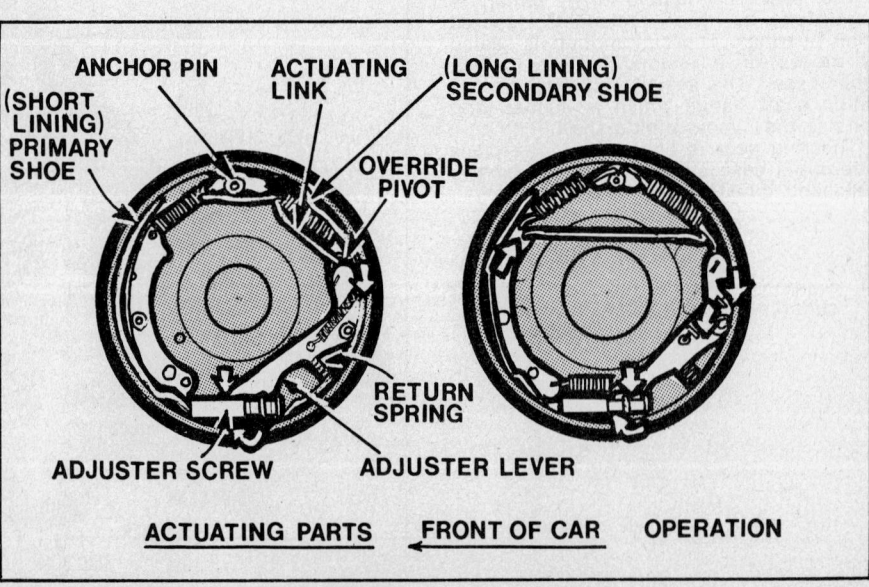

ANCHOR PIN ACTUATING LINK (LONG LINING) SECONDARY SHOE (SHORT LINING) PRIMARY SHOE OVERRIDE PIVOT RETURN SPRING ADJUSTER SCREW ADJUSTER LEVER

ACTUATING PARTS ← FRONT OF CAR OPERATION

Fig. 6 Self-adjusting brakes. 1976-79

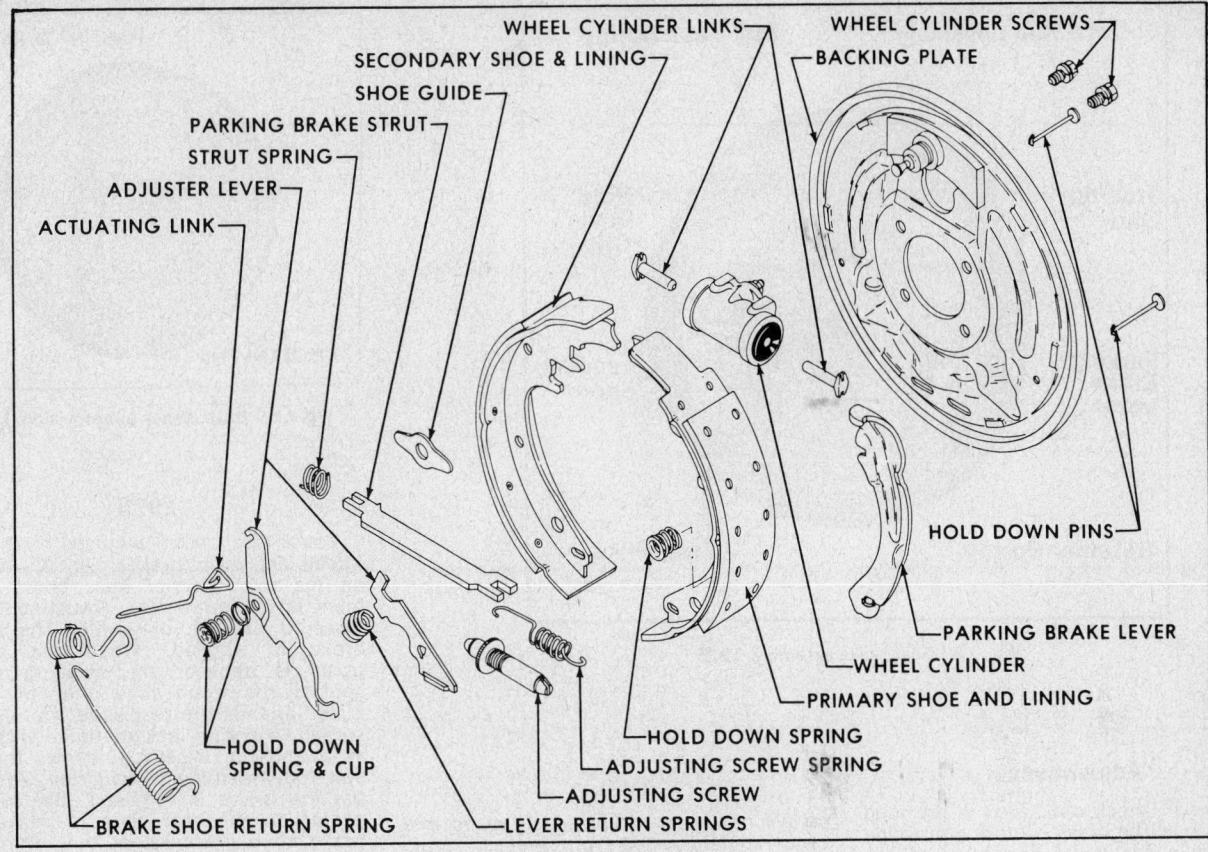

Fig. 7 Rear brake disassembled. 1976-79

transmission and swing torque arm away from shaft. Mark relationship of shaft to companion flange and disconnect the rear universal joint by removing trunnion bearing "U" bolts. Tape bearing cups to trunnion to prevent dropping and loss of bearing rollers.

3. Withdraw propeller shaft front yoke from transmission.
4. When installing, be sure to align marks made in removal to prevent driveline vibration.

rected by making numerous reverse stops (provided the hydraulic system is free of air) it indicates that the self-adjusting mechanism is not functioning. Therefore it will be necessary to remove the brake drum, clean, free up and lubricate the adjusting mechanism. Then adjust the brakes, being sure the parking brake is fully released.

BRAKE ADJUSTMENTS
1976-79

These rear wheel brakes, Figs. 6 and 7, have self-adjusting shoe mechanisms that assure correct lining-to-drum clearances at all times. The automatic adjusters operate only when the brakes are applied as the car is moving rearward.

Although the brakes are self-adjusting, an initial adjustment is necessary after the brake shoes have been relined or replaced, or when the length of the adjusting screw has been changed during some other service operation.

Frequent usage of an automatic transmission forward range to halt reverse vehicle motion may prevent to automatic adjusters from functioning, thereby inducing low pedal heights. Should low pedal heights be encountered, it is recommended that numerous forward and reverse stops be made until satisfactory pedal height is obtained.

NOTE
If a low pedal condition cannot be cor-

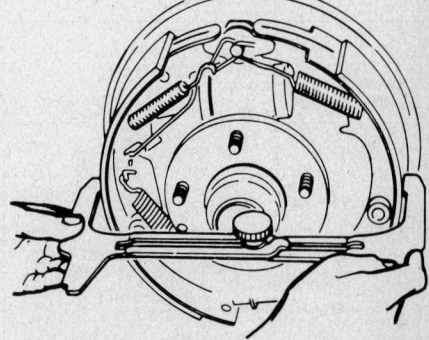

Fig. 9 Checking brake shoe lining clearance. 1976-79

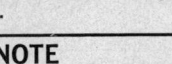

Fig. 8 Measuring brake drum inner diameter. 1976-79

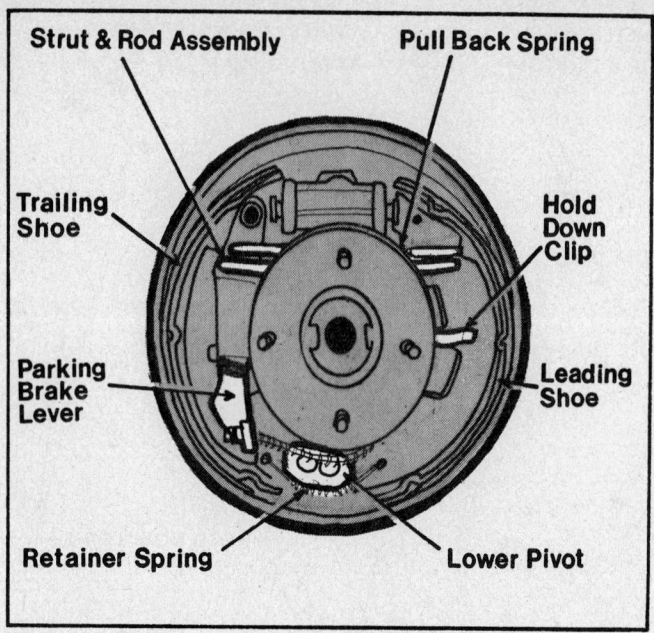

Fig. 10   Rear brake assembly. 1975

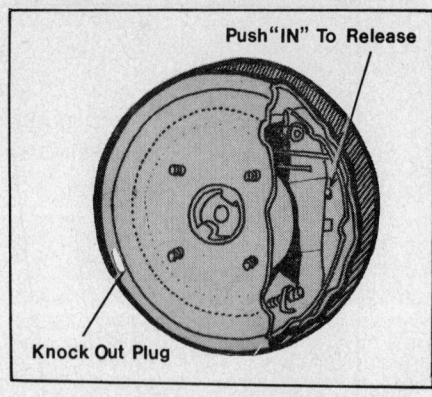

Fig. 11   Drum knock out provision. 1975

1975

Power disc brakes are used on the front wheels and drum brakes, Fig. 10, are used on the rear wheels. Rear brake adjustment is not automatic. Adjustment takes place, if needed, only when the parking brake is applied. When the parking brake is applied, the strut is pushed against the front shoe and the rod is pulled against the rear shoe. As the shoes spread, a spring lock mounted within the strut and rod assembly, allows the strut and rod assembly to lengthen. When the parking brake is released, the rod connected to the rear shoe is relaxed and brake shoe pressure on the drum is released providing running clearance. Clearance is obtained by the difference in the diameter of the rod and the diameter of the hole in the rear shoe.

NOTE: If the brake drum cannot be removed, it will be necessary to release the brake adjuster. To gain access to the adjuster, knock out the lanced area in web of brake drum, Fig. 11, using a chisel or similar tool. Release the rod from the trailing shoe by pushing in on the rod until it is clear of the shoe. The pull back spring will then pull the shoes toward each other and the drum may be removed.

CAUTION: After knocking out the lanced area, be sure to remove the piece of metal from inside the drum.

Adjustment

A lanced "knock out" area is provided in the web of the brake drum for servicing purposes in the event retracting of the brake shoes is required in order to remove the drum.

1. With brake drum off, disengage the actuator from the star wheel and rotate the star wheel by spinning or turning with a screwdriver.
2. Using the brake drum as an adjustment fixture, turn the star wheel until the drum slides over the brake shoes with a slide drag.
3. Turn the star wheel 1¼ turns to retract the brake shoes. This will allow sufficient lining-to-drum clearance so final adjustment may be made.
4. Install drum and wheel.

NOTE: If lanced area in brake drum was knocked out, be sure all metal has been removed from brake compartment.

Install new hole cover in drum to prevent contamination of brakes. Make certain that drums are installed in the same position as when removed with the drum locating tang in line with the locating hole in the wheel hub.

5. Make final adjustment by driving and stopping in forward and reverse until satisfactory pedal height is obtained.

NOTE: The recommended method of adjusting the brakes is by using the Drum-to-Brake Shoe Clearance Gauge to check the diameter of the brake drum inner surface, Fig. 8, Turn the tool to the opposite side and fit over the brake shoes by turning the star wheel until the gauge just slides over the linings, Fig. 9. Rotate the gauge around the brake shoe lining surface to assure proper clearance.

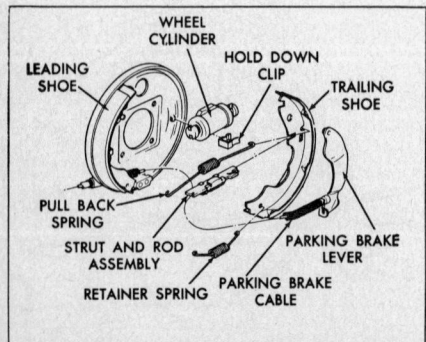

Fig. 12   Rear brake disassembled. 1975

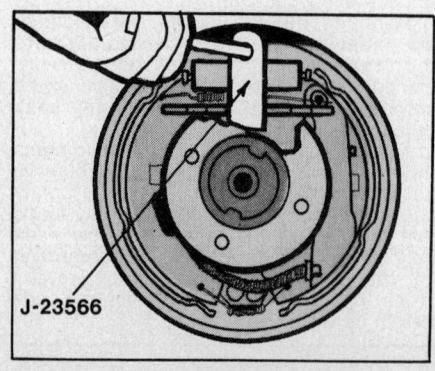

Fig. 13   Releasing adjuster on vehicle. 1975

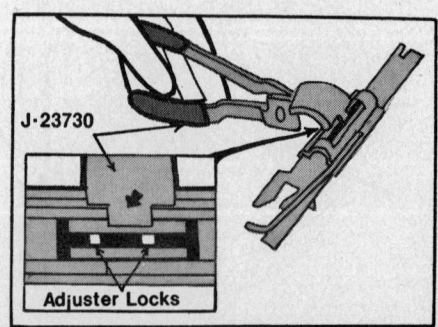

Fig. 14   Releasing adjuster locks. 1975

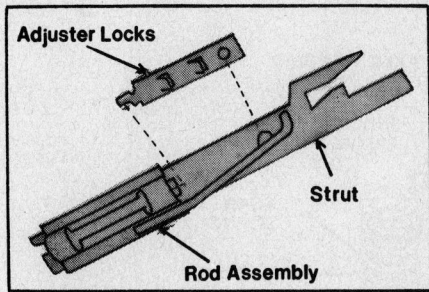

Fig. 15   Adjuster lock positioning. 1975

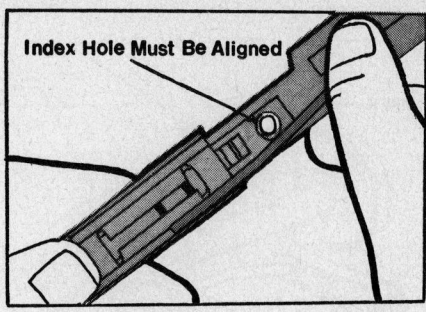

Fig. 16   Installing rod assembly. 1975

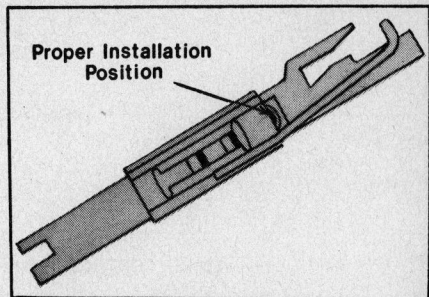

Fig. 17   Properly positioned adjuster rod assembly. 1975

When installing new brake shoes, Fig. 12, the adjuster assembly must be released and repositioned. To release adjuster on vehicle, position tool J-23566 as shown in Fig. 13. The tool releases the adjuster assembly by unseating the clips from the rod assembly. Both clips must be unseated at the same time.

To release adjuster off vehicle, position tool J-23730 so that tang of tool rests on flat portion of locks (between lock tangs) Fig. 14, then press down on adjuster locks. Work rod assembly free of adjuster locks, then when both adjuster tangs are clear of rod assembly, slide rod off lever. Subassemble rod assembly to strut making certain that index hole is lined up and seated Fig. 15, then slide rod assembly over adjuster locks, Fig. 16, until both locks are positioned as shown in Fig. 17. Note that adjuster lock index is about ½ covered by rod assembly.

PARKING BRAKE, ADJUST

1. Raise vehicle and remove propeller shaft.
2. Apply parking brake one notch from fully released position and raise hoist.
3. Loosen equalizer check nut and tighten the adjusting nut until a slight drag is felt when rear wheels are rotated.

NOTE: It may be necessary to remove drive shaft to gain access to parking brake equalizer.

4. Tighten check nut securely.
5. Release parking brake and rotate rear wheels. No drag should be present.

MASTER CYLINDER, REPLACE

1. Disconnect cylinder push rod from brake pedal.
2. Disconnect brake lines from two outlets on cylinder and cover ends of lines to prevent entry of dirt.
3. Unfasten and remove cylinder from brake booster.

POWER BRAKE UNIT
1975-79

1. Remove the vacuum hose from check valve and then remove the master cylinder retaining nuts.
2. Remove the bolt securing the brake pipe distributor and switch assembly to fender skirt.
3. Pull master cylinder forward until it just clears mounting studs and move aside. Support cylinder to avoid stress on hydraulic lines.
4. Remove power unit to dash nuts.
5. Remove brake pedal pushrod retainer and disconnect push rod from pin.
6. Remove power unit from vehicle.

Rear Suspension

DESCRIPTION

This rear suspension system does not use upper control arms, instead, it uses a torque arm mounted rigidly to the differential housing at the rear and to the transmission through a rubber bushing at the front. This torque arm prevents axle housing rotation caused by starting and stopping. Along with the torque arm a track rod is used to connect the axle housing to the body to control side sway and a rear stabilizer shaft is used for improved handling, Figs. 1 and 1A.

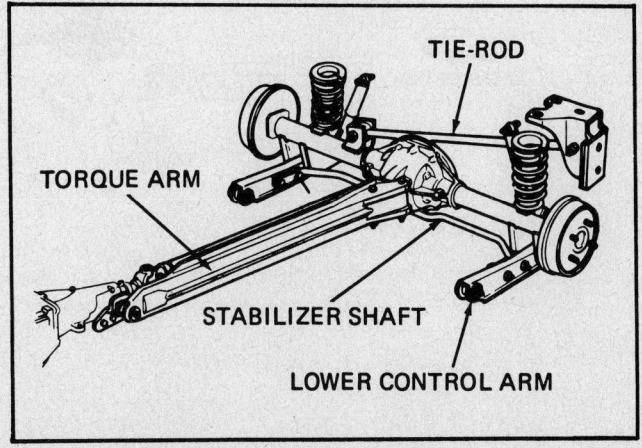

Fig. 1A   Rear suspension. 1976-79

SHOCK ABSORBER, REPLACE

1. With the rear axle supported properly

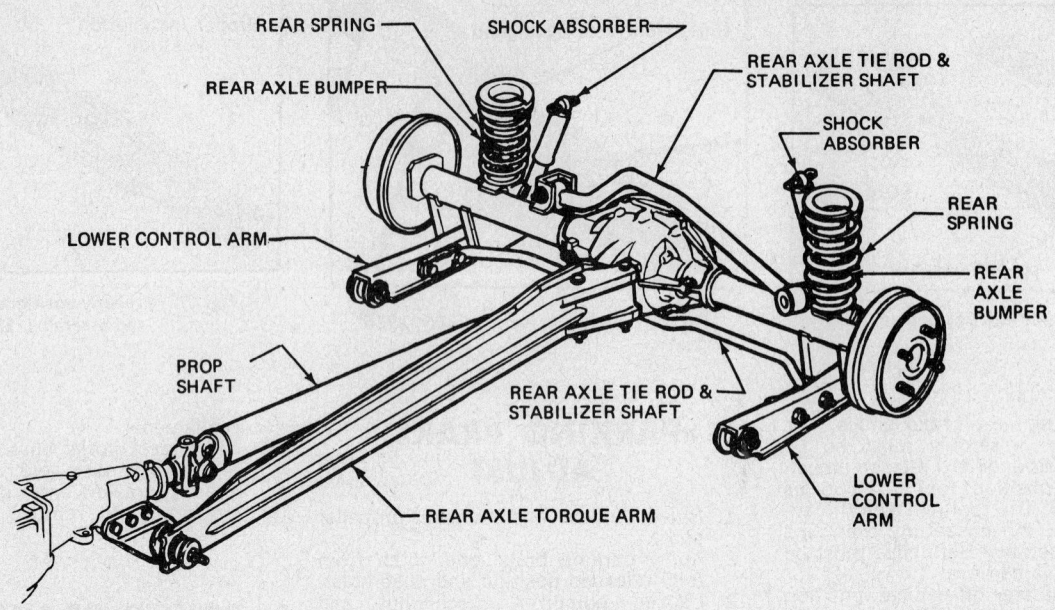

Fig. 1   Rear suspension. 1975

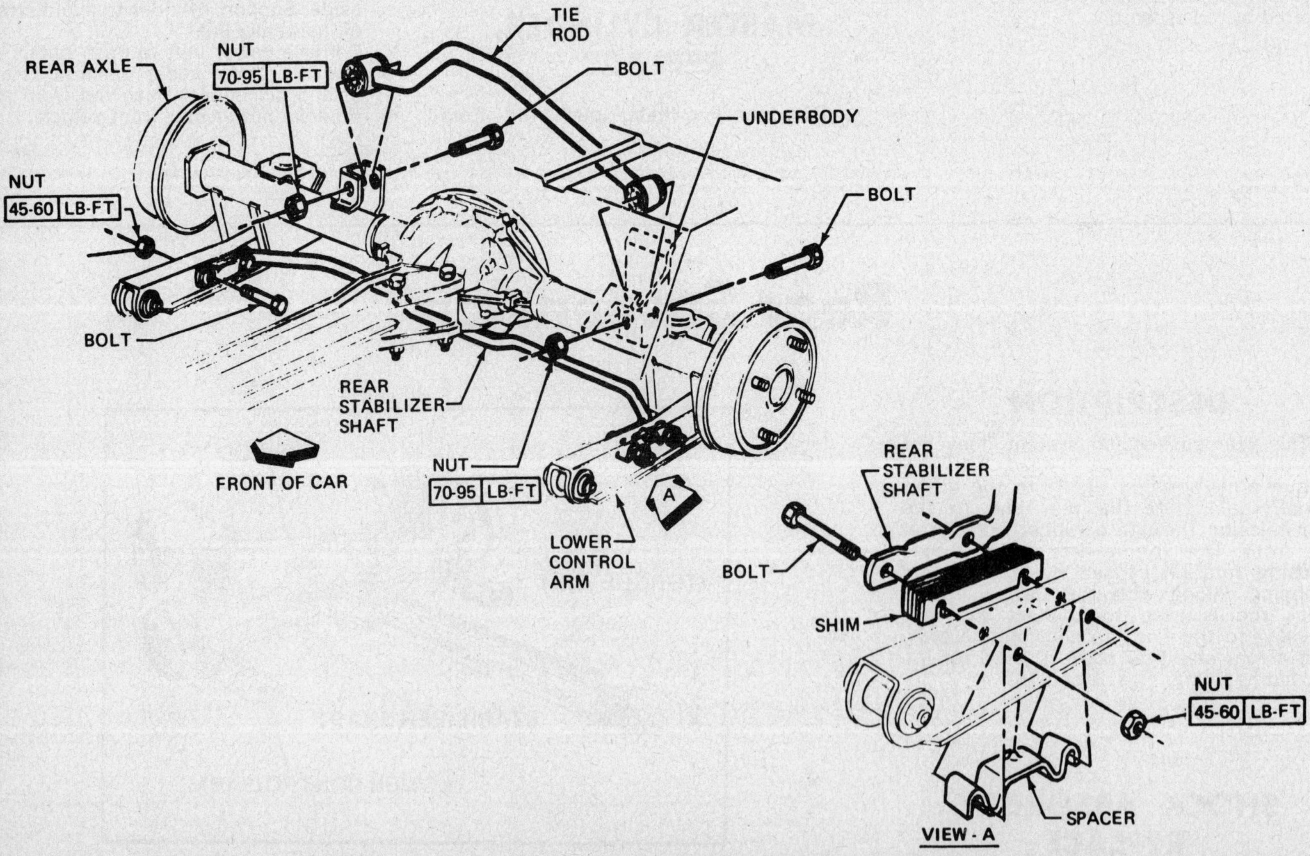

Fig. 2   1975 track rod and 1975-79 stabilizer bar removal

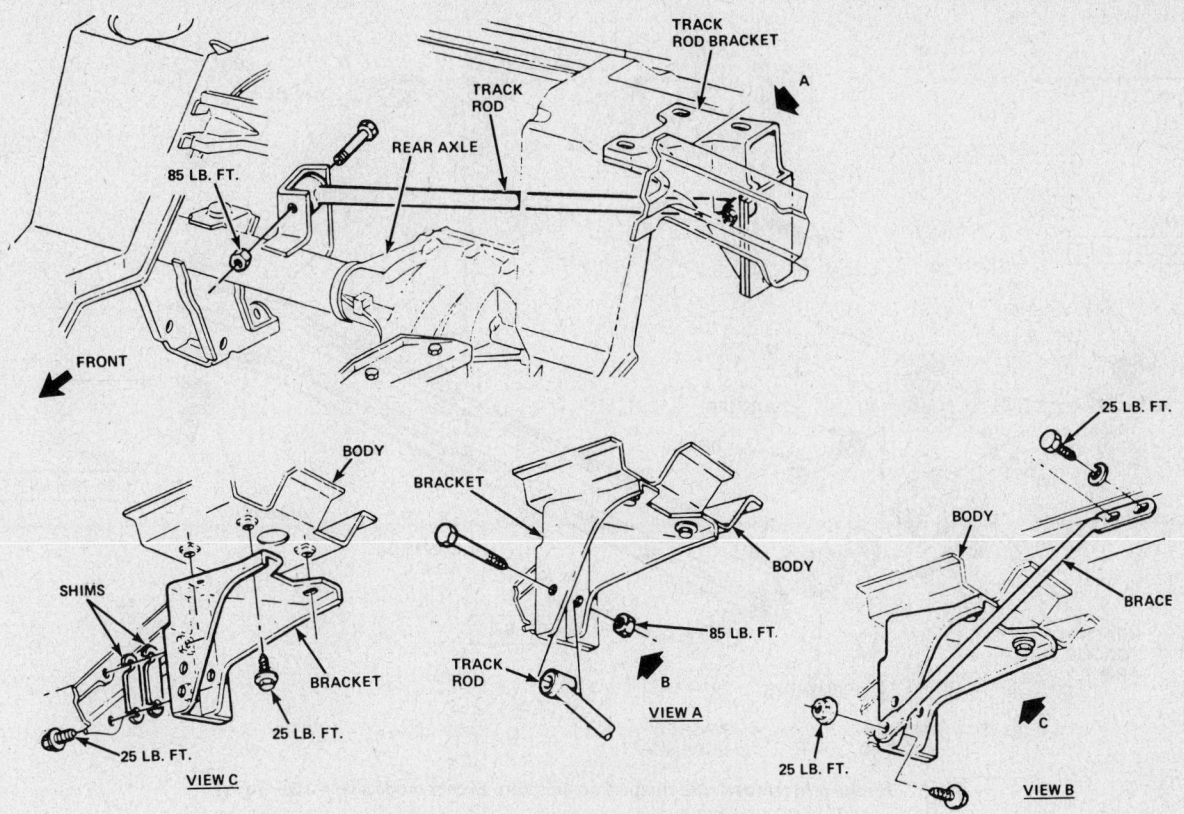

Fig. 3   Track rod removal. 1976-78

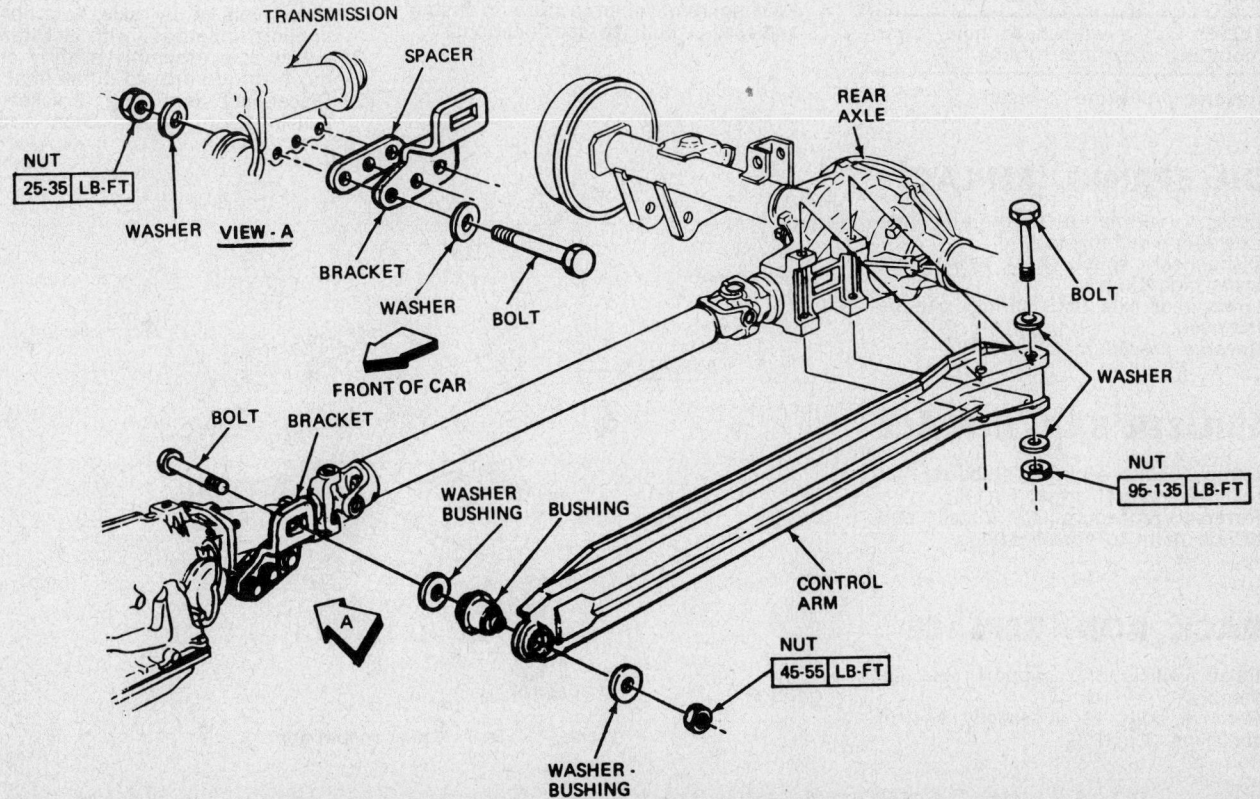

Fig. 4   Torque arm removal. Manual transmission. Except models w/4-151 engine

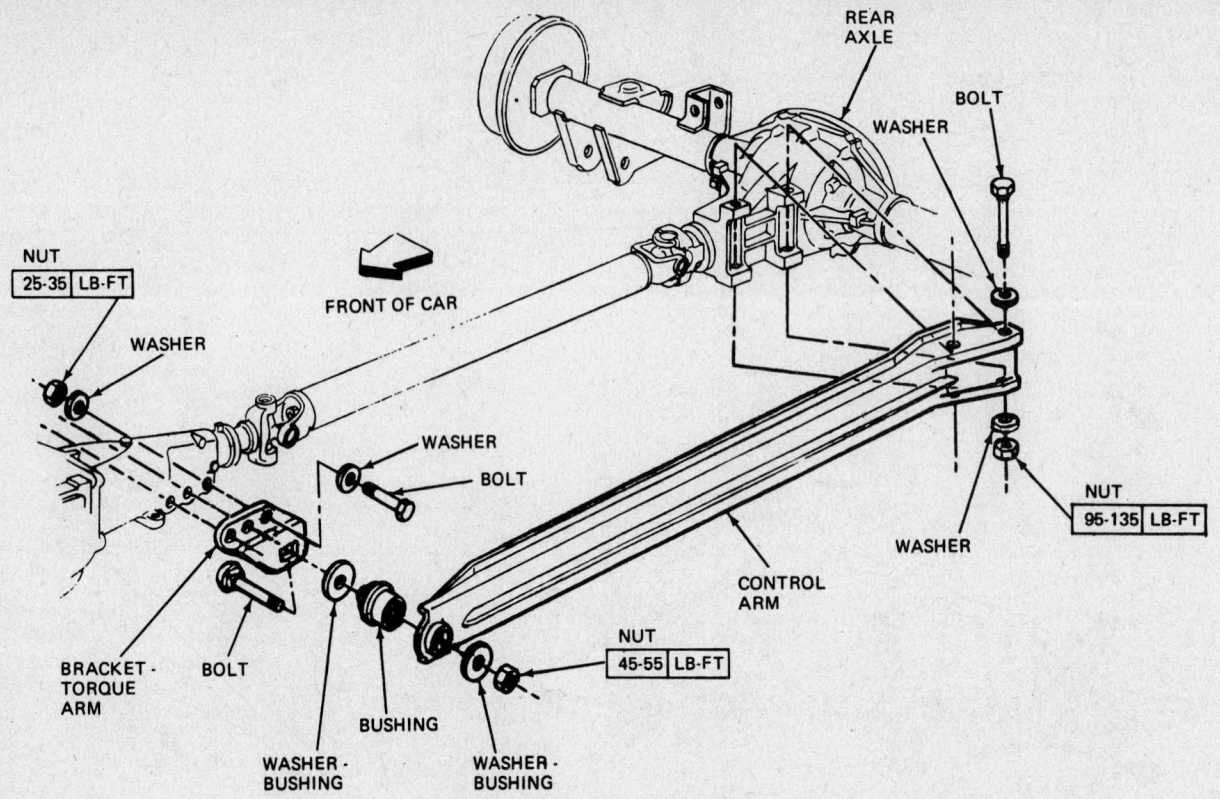

Fig. 5   Torque arm removal. Automatic transmission. Except models w/4-151 engine

disconnect shock absorber from upper and lower mounting, Fig. 1.

NOTE: Use a wrench to hold lower mounting stud from turning.

2. Reverse procedure to install.

COIL SPRING, REPLACE

1. Support vehicle at frame and rear axle with a suitable jack.
2. Disconnect shock absorbers from lower mountings.
3. Lower rear axle until springs can be removed.
4. Reverse procedure to install.

STABILIZER BAR, REPLACE

1. Remove bolts securing stabilizer bar to lower control arms, Fig. 2.
2. Reverse procedure to install and torque bolts to specifications.

TRACK ROD, REPLACE

1. Raise vehicle and support axle assembly.
2. Remove bolts at underbody end of rod, Figs. 2 and 3.

3. Remove bolts at axle bracket and remove track rod.
4. Reverse removal procedure to install and torque bolts to specifications.

TORQUE ARM, REPLACE

1. Raise vehicle by axle assembly and support underbody with jackstands.
2. Lower axle assembly slightly and remove torque arm to differential bolts.
3. Disconnect mounting bracket from transmission and then remove

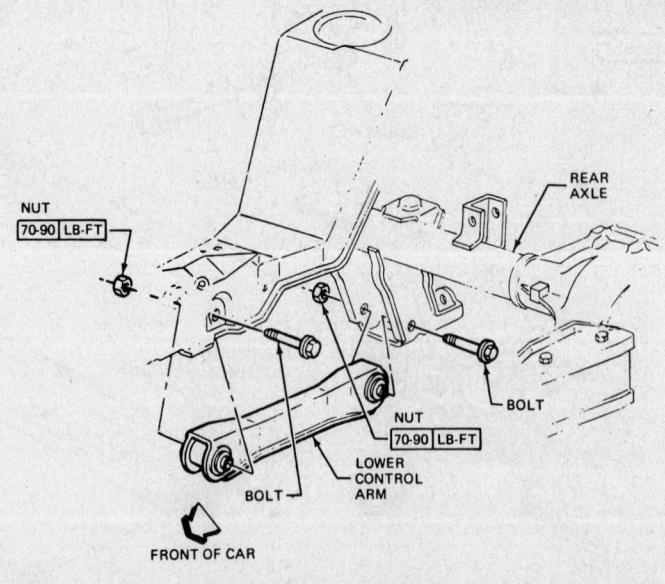

Fig. 7   Lower control arm

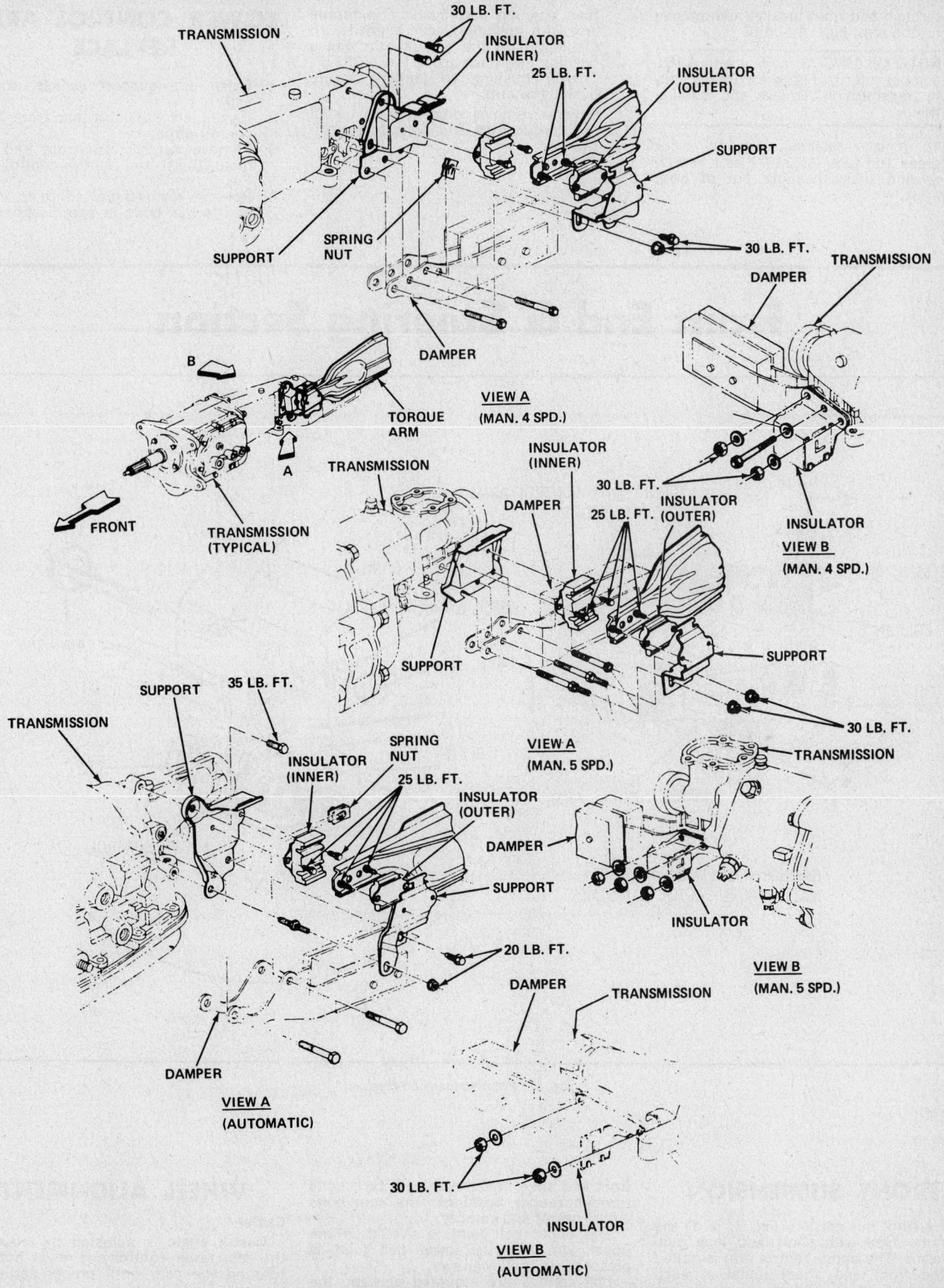

Fig. 6 Torque arm removal. 1977-79 models w/4-151 engine

through bolt from bracket and remove torque arm, Figs. 4 and 5.

NOTE: On 1977-78 models with 4-151 engine, refer to Fig. 6 for torque arm to transmission removal and installation.

4. To replace bushing, use an arbor press and tool J-25317-2 as a receiver and press bushing out of arm,

then position new bushing in torque arm with bushing sleeve aligned with the length of the torque arm. Press bushing into place using tool J-25317-1 over bushing to properly locate bushing in arm.

5. Reverse removal procedure to install and torque nuts and bolts to specifications.

LOWER CONTROL ARM, REPLACE

1. Raise and support vehicle at rear axle.
2. Disconnect stabilizer bar from lower control arms.
3. Remove control arm front and rear mount bolts and remove control arm, Fig. 7.
4. Reverse removal procedure to install and torque bolts to specifications.

Front End & Steering Section

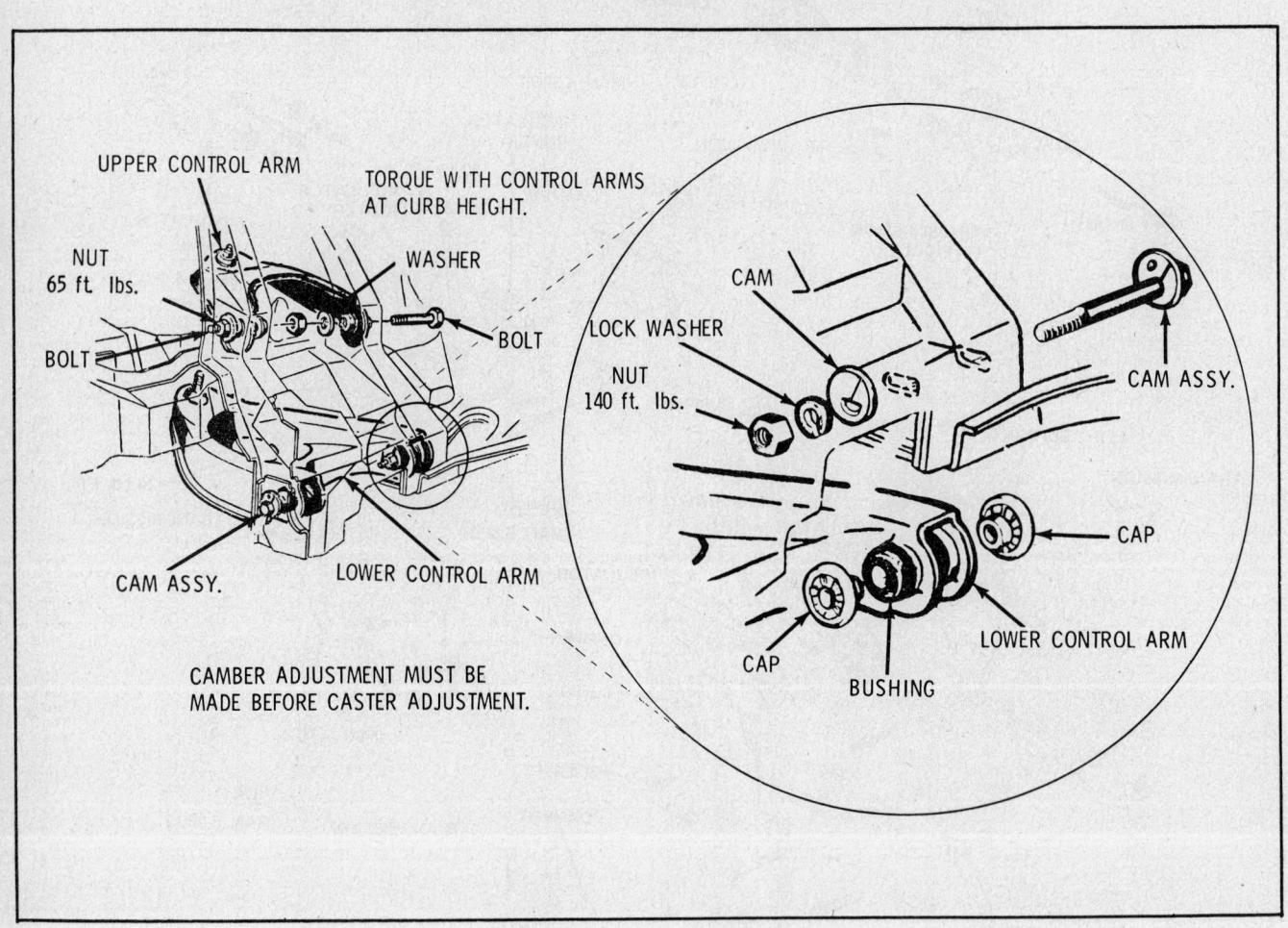

Fig. 1 Front suspension (typical)

FRONT SUSPENSION

The front suspension, Fig. 1, is of the A frame type with short and long control arms. The upper control arm is bolted to the front end sheet metal at each inner pivot point. Rubber bushings are used for mounting.

The lower control arms attach to the

front end sheet metal with cam type bolts through rubber bushings. The cam bolts adjust caster and camber.

The upper ball joint is riveted in the upper arm and the lower ball joint is pressed into the lower arm.

Coil springs are mounted between the lower control arms and the shock absorber tower.

WHEEL ALIGNMENT

Caster

Caster angle is adjusted by loosening the rear lower control arm pivot nut and rotating the cam until proper setting is reached, Fig. 2.

NOTE: This eccentric cam action will tend

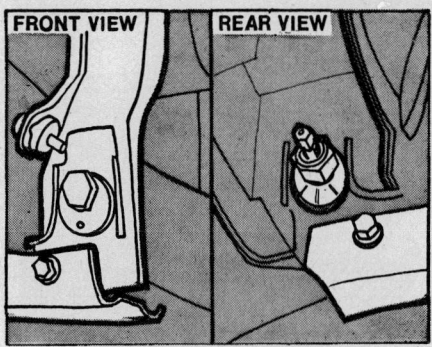

Fig. 2 Caster and camber adjustment

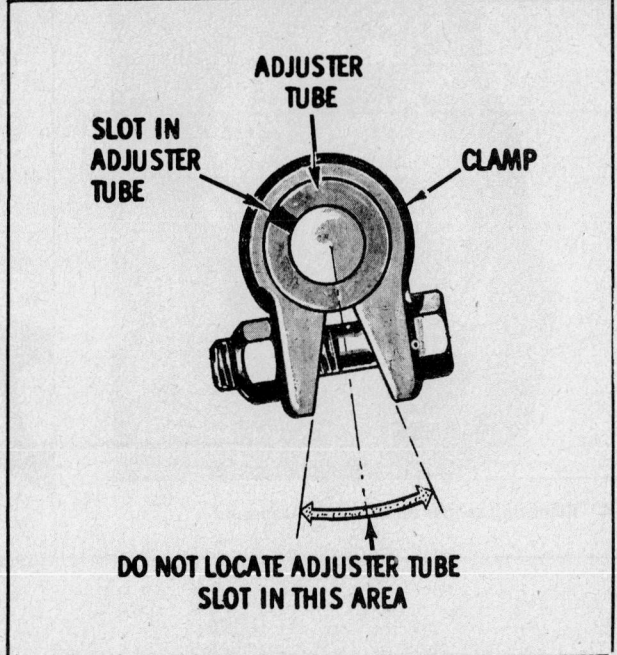

DO NOT LOCATE ADJUSTER TUBE SLOT IN THIS AREA

Fig. 3 Adjuster sleeve and clamp location

to move the lower control arm fore or aft thereby varying the caster. Hold the cam bolt while tightening the nut.

Camber

Camber angle is adjusted by loosening the front lower control arm pivot nut and rotating the cam until setting is reached, Fig. 2.

NOTE: This eccentric cam action will move the lower arm in or out thereby varying the setting. Hold the cam bolt head while tightening the nut.

TOE-IN, ADJUST

1. Loosen clamp bolt nut at each end of each tie rod and rotate the sleeve until proper toe-in is reached.
2. Position tie rod ball stud assembly straight on a center line through their attaching points.
3. Position clamp as shown in Fig. 3 and tighten clamp nuts.

WHEEL BEARINGS, ADJUST

1975-79 Monza, 1976-79 Sunbird, 1977-79 Skyhawk & 1978-79 Starfire

1. While rotating wheel, tighten spindle nut to 12 ft. lbs.
2. Backoff adjusting nut to the just loose position, then retighten nut hand tight.
3. Loosen until either hole in spindle is aligned with slot in nut, then install cotter pin.
4. Spin wheel to check that it rolls freely and then lock the cotter pin.

NOTE: Wheel bearings should have zero preload and the allowable end play is .001-.005 inch.

1975-76 Skyhawk

1. While rotating wheel, snug up spindle nut to fully seat bearing.
2. Back off nut 1/4-1/2 turn to the just loose position.
3. Tighten spindle nut finger tight, then back off nut a minimum of 1/12 turn or a maximum of 1/6 turn to align cotter pin hole. Insert cotter pin.
4. With bearings properly adjusted, end play should be .001-.005 inch.

1975-77 Starfire

1. While rotating wheel, torque spindle nut to 30 ft. lbs.
2. Back off nut 1/2 turn.
3. Tighten spindle nut finger tight and insert cotter pin. If cotter pin cannot be installed, back off nut not more than 1/24 turn to align slot and pin hole.
4. With bearings properly adjusted, end play should be .001-.008 inch.

WHEEL BEARINGS, REPLACE

1. Raise vehicle on a hoist and remove the wheel and tire assembly.
2. Remove the brake caliper from the disc by removing the mounting pins and stamped nuts, Figs. 4 & 5.
3. Remove hub grease cap, cotter pin, spindle nut and washer and remove hub and bearings.

4. Remove inner bearing by prying out the grease seal.

CHECKING BALL JOINTS FOR WEAR

Upper Ball Joint

The upper ball joint is checked for wear by checking the torque required to rotate the ball joint stud in the assembly. This is done after first dislodging the ball joint from the steering knuckle.
1. Install the stud nut to the ball stud in the seat.
2. Check the torque required to turn the ball stud.

NOTE: Specified torque for a new joint is 2 to 4 ft. lbs. rotating torque. If readings are excessively high or low, replace the joint.

Lower Ball Joint

The lower ball joints incorporate wear indicators for visual inspection, Fig. 5.

UPPER BALL JOINT, REPLACE

1. Raise vehicle on a hoist and remove wheel and tire assembly.
2. Support lower control arm with a floor jack.
3. Remove upper ball stud nut and re-

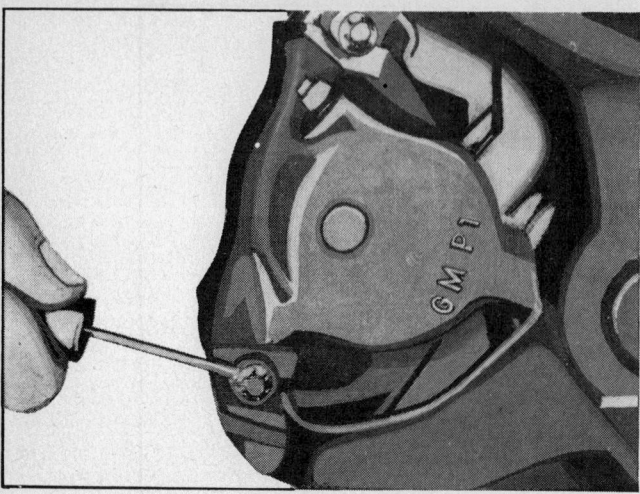

Fig. 4   Removing caliper retaining stamped nuts

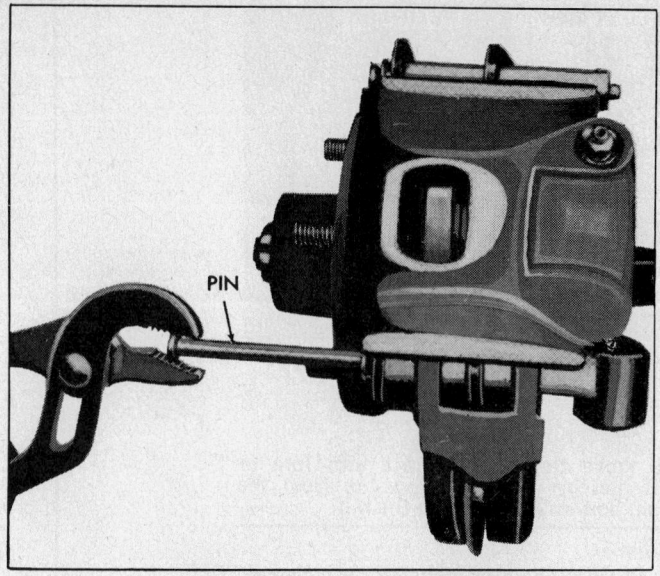

Fig. 5   Removing caliper mounting pins

move ball stud from knuckle, Fig. 7.
4. Remove control arm pivot bolts and remove control arm.
5. Grind off rivets securing ball joint to arm.
6. Install new ball joint using bolts and nuts supplied in kit.

LOWER BALL JOINT, REPLACE

1. Place vehicle on hoist and support lower control arm at outer end on a jack.
2. Free lower ball stud from knuckle, Fig. 7.

3. Using tool shown in Fig. 8, press ball joint out of control arm.
4. Position new ball joint so that grease bleed vent in rubber boot is facing inboard.
5. Install tool shown in Fig. 9 and press new joint into arm.
6. Install lube fitting in joint and install stud into steering knuckle.

SHOCK ABSORBER, REPLACE

1. Hold shock absorber stem and re-

move the nut, upper retainer and rubber grommet, Fig. 10.
2. Raise vehicle on a hoist.
3. Remove bolts from lower end of shock absorber and lower the shock from the vehicle.

COIL SPRING, REPLACE

Exc. Starfire

1. With shock absorber removed and stabilizer bar removed, raise the vehicle and place jackstands under front braces.
2. Remove the wheel and tire assembly.
3. Place a floor jack under the lower arm and support the arm. Use a block of wood between the control arm and the jack, Fig. 11.
4. Remove the lower ball stud from the knuckle.

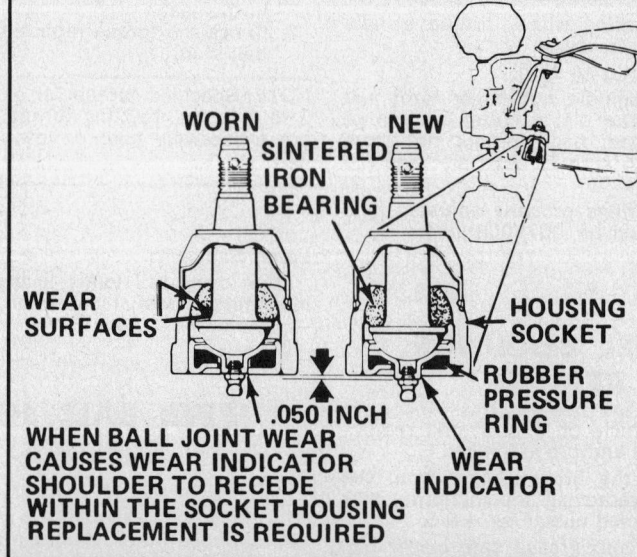

Fig. 6   Lower ball joint wear indicator

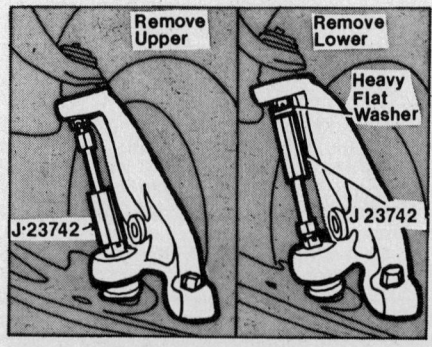

Fig. 7   Removing upper and lower ball joint from steering knuckle

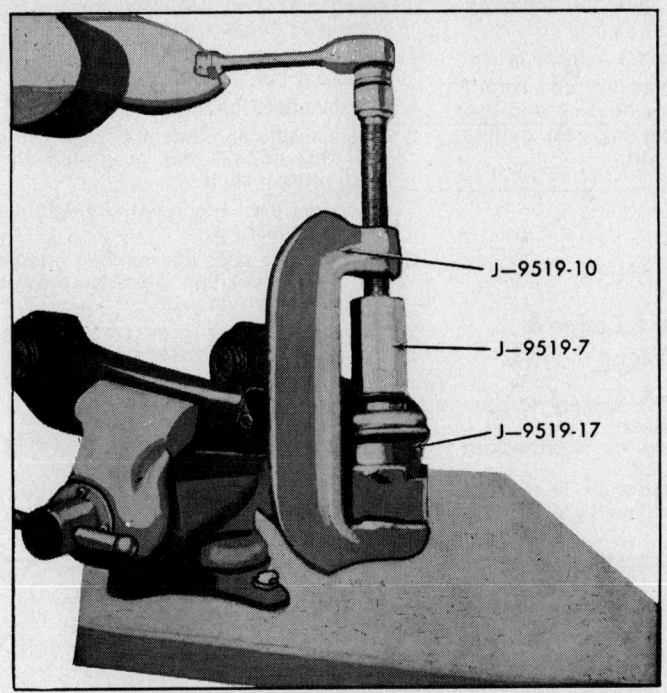

Fig. 8   Removing lower ball joint

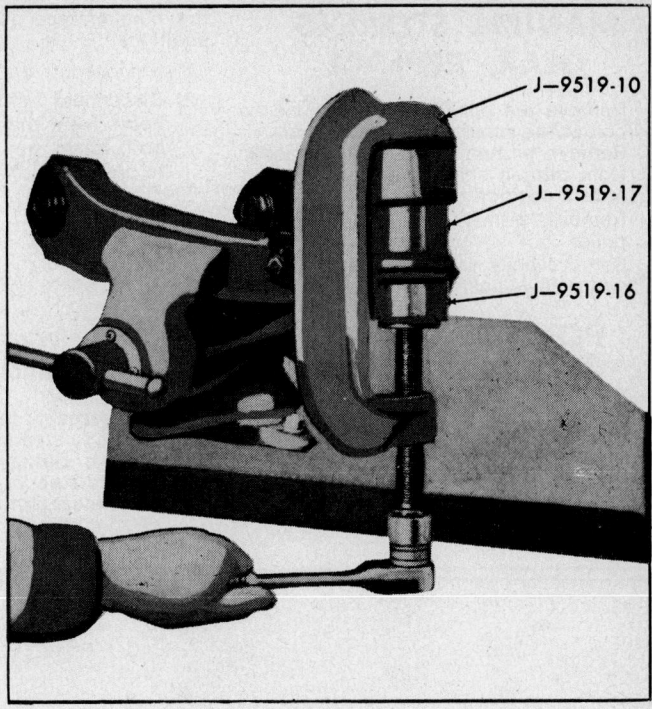

Fig. 9   Installing lower ball joint

5. Remove the tie rod end from the knuckle.
6. Lower the control arm by slowly lowering the jack until the spring can be removed.

Starfire

1. Place transmission in Neutral.
2. Disconnect shock absorber from upper mounting.
3. Raise vehicle, support at frame and remove wheel.
4. Remove stabilizer link nut, grommets, washers and bolt.
5. Remove shock absorber.
6. Install lower plate BT-7522, Fig. 12, with pivot ball seat facing downward

into spring coils. Rotate plate to fully seat it in lower control arm spring seat.
7. Install upper plate BT-7522, Fig. 12, with pivot ball seat facing upward into spring coils. Insert ball nut BT-7408-4 through spring coils and onto upper plate.
8. Install rod BT-7408-5 through shock absorber opening in lower control arm and through the lower and upper plates. Depress lock pin on shaft and thread shaft into upper ball nut BT-7408-4. Ensure lock pin is fully extended above ball nut upper surface.
9. With ball nut tang engaged in upper plate slot, rotate upper plate until it

contacts upper spring seat.
10. Install lower pivot ball, thrust bearing and nut on rod, then rotate nut until coil spring is compressed to be free in the seat.
11. Mark location of lower control arm pivot bolt cams and remove the pivot bolts. Move control arm forward and remove coil spring.
12. Reverse procedure to install.

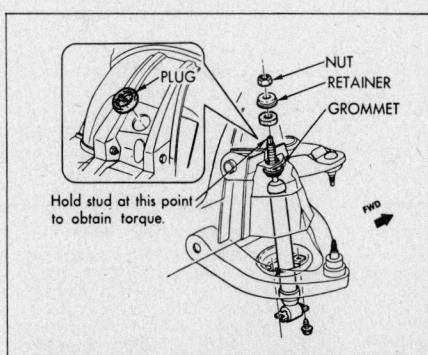

Fig. 10   Front shock absorber mountings

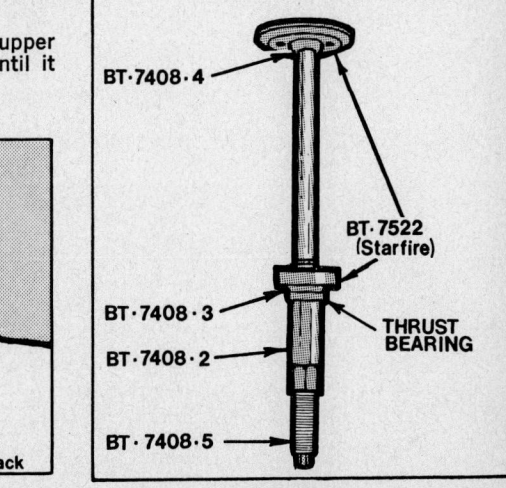

Fig. 11   Removing front coil spring. Exc. Starfire

Fig. 12   Coil spring replacement tool. Starfire

MANUAL STEERING GEAR, REPLACE

1. Remove the pot joint coupling clamp bolt at the steering gear wormshaft.
2. Remove pitman arm nut and washer from pitman shaft and mark relation of arm position to shaft.
3. Remove pitman arm with suitable puller.
4. Remove bolts securing gear to frame and remove gear assembly.

POWER STEERING GEAR, REPLACE

Exc. 1978-79 Coupe, S Coupe & Station Wagon

Replacement procedures for removing the gear assembly are the same as for the manual type gear with the following additions:

1. Remove left front crossmember brace.
2. Disconnect both pressure and return hoses from the gear housing and cap both hoses and steering gear outlets to prevent entry of dirt.

1978-79 Coupe, S Coupe & Station Wagon

1. If necessary, remove battery to gain access to steering gear.
2. Remove clamp securing intermediate shaft to steering shaft.
3. Disconnect both hydraulic lines from steering gear and allow to drain. Position lines out of way to provide clearance for gear removal.
4. Raise vehicle and remove clamps at stabilizer bar.
5. Remove left front crossmember.
6. Remove pitman shaft nut, then using tool No. J-6632, remove pitman arm from pitman shaft.
7. Remove three steering mounting bolts and lock washers.
8. Lift steering gear and remove pitman arm, then position gear to provide clearance for removal.
9. Remove steering gear and intermediate shaft as an assembly, the steering gear spacer is also removed.
10. Remove plastic shield.
11. Remove pot joint clamp and separate steering gear from pot joint.
12. Remove pot joint from intermediate shaft.

CHEVROLET VEGA · PONTIAC ASTRE

INDEX OF SERVICE OPERATIONS

SERIAL NUMBER LOCATION

On top of instrument panel, left front.

ENGINE NUMBER LOCATION

4-140, On pad at right side of cylinder block below No. 3 spark plug at cylinder head parting line.
4-151, On distributor mounting pad.

ENGINE IDENTIFICATION CODE

Engines are identified in the following table by the code letter or letters immediately following the engine serial number.

Code			Code			Code		
CAB with T.H. 350, W/E.E.C.	....	1974	CAZ 4-140	....	1976	CBK 4-140	....	1977
CAA with M/T, W/E.E.C.	......	1974	CBK 4-140	....	1976	CBL 4-140	....	1977
CAH with T.H. 350, W/E.E.C.	...	1974	CBL 4-140	....	1976	CBS 4-140	....	1977
CAJ with M/T, W/E.E.C.	....	1974	CBS 4-140	....	1976	CBT 4-140	....	1977
CAC with T.H. 350, W/E.E.C.	...	1974	CBT 4-140	....	1976	CBU 4-140	....	1977
CAD with M/T, W/E.E.C.	......	1974	CBU 4-140	....	1976	CBV 4-140	....	1977
CAK with T.H. 350, W/E.E.C.	...	1974	CBW 4-140	....	1976	CBW 4-140	....	1977
CAL with M/T, W/E.E.C.	......	1974	CBX 4-140	....	1976	CBX 4-140	....	1977
CAM 4-140	....	1975	CBY 4-140	....	1976	CBY 4-140	....	1977
CAR 4-140	....	1975	CBZ 4-140	....	1976	CBZ 4-140	....	1977
CAS 4-140	....	1975	ZCB 4-122	....	1976	WC 4-151	....	1977
CAT 4-140	....	1975	CAA 4-140	....	1977	WD 4-151	....	1977
CBB 4-140	....	1975	CAB 4-140	....	1977	YL 4-151	....	1977
CBC 4-140	....	1975	CAC 4-140	....	1977	YM 4-151	....	1977
ZCA 4-122	....	1975	CAY 4-140	....	1977	ZH 4-151	....	1977
CAY 4-140	....	1976	CAZ 4-140	....	1977	ZJ 4-151	....	1977

M/T: Manual transmission
P/G: Powerglide
T/D: Torque drive

T/H: Turbo Hydramatic
L/E.E.C.: Less Exhaust Emission Control

W/E.E.C.: With Exhaust Emission Control

GRILLE IDENTIFICATION

1974

1975 Vega

1975 Astre

1976 Astre

1976 Vega

1977 Astre

1977 Vega

GENERAL ENGINE SPECIFICATIONS

Year	Engine	Car-buretor	Bore and Stroke	Piston Dis-place-ment, Cubic Inches	Com-pres-sion Ratio	Maximum Brake H.P. @ R.P.M.	Maximum Torque Lbs. Ft. @ R.P.M.	Normal Oil Pressure Pounds
1974	75 Horsepower①..............4-140	1 Barrel	3.500 x 3.625	140	8.00	75 @ 4400	115 @ 2400	40
	85 Horsepower①..............4-140	2 Barrel	3.500 x 3.625	140	8.00	85 @ 4400	122 @ 2400	40
1975	78 Horsepower①..............4-140	1 Barrel	3.500 x 3.625	140	8.00	78 @ 4200	120 @ 2000	40
	87 Horsepower①..............4-140	2 Barrel	3.500 x 3.625	140	8.00	87 @ 4400	122 @ 2800	40
	110 Horsepower①..............4-122	②	3.500 x 3.160	122	8.50	110 @ 5600	107 @ 4800	40
1976	70 Horsepower①..............4-140	1 Barrel	3.500 x 3.625	140	8.00	70 @ 4400	107 @ 2400	27–41
	79 Horsepower①③..............4-140	2 Barrel	3.500 x 3.625	140	8.00	79 @ 4400	109 @ 2800	27–41
	84 Horsepower①..............4-140	2 Barrel	3.500 x 3.625	140	8.00	84 @ 4400	113 @ 3200	27–41
	110 Horsepower①..............4-122	②	3.500 x 3.160	122	8.00	110 @ 5600	107 @ 4800	27–41
1977	84 Horsepower①..............4-140	2 Barrel	3.500 x 3.625	140	8.00	84 @ 4400	117 @ 2400	36–45
	87 Horsepower①..............4-151	2 Barrel	4.00 x 3.00	151	8.25	88 @ 4400	128 @ 2400	36–41

①—Ratings Net—as installed in the vehicle. ②—Fuel Injection. ③—California.

DISTRIBUTOR SPECIFICATIONS

★If unit is checked on vehicle double the RPM and degrees to get crankshaft figures.

Distributor Part No.①	Centrifugal Advance Degrees @ RPM of Distributor			Vacuum Advance		Distributor Retard
	Advance Starts	Intermediate Advance	Full Advance	Inches of Vacuum To Start Plunger	Max. Adv. Dist. Deg. @ Vacuum	Max. Ret. Dist. Deg. @ Vacuum
1974						
1110496	0 @ 800	1 @ 875	6 @ 1600	—	11 @ 2400	7½	12 @ 15	—
1975-76						
1110649②	0 @ 1000	—	—	—	8½ @ 1800	—	—	8 @ 8
1112862②	0 @ 810③	2½ @ 1000	—	—	11 @ 2400	5	12 @ 12④	—
1977						
1103229②	0 @ 600	3 @ 800	—	—	10 @ 2200	3½	10 @ 12	—
1103230②	0 @ 600	3 @ 800	—	—	10 @ 2200	3½	10 @ 9	—
1103231②	0 @ 600	—	—	—	10 @ 2200	3½	10 @ 12	—
1103263②	0 @ 600	—	—	—	10 @ 2200	3½	10 @ 9	—
1103303②	0 @ 600	—	—	—	10 @ 2200	9	10 @ 16	—
1110538②	0 @ 425	4 @ 600	—	—	8½ @ 1000	5	12 @ 10	—
1110539②	0 @ 425	4 @ 600	—	—	8½ @ 1000	5	12 @ 10	—

①—Located on distributor housing plate. ③—Exc. 1976 Astre; 1976 Astre, 0 @ 450. ④—Exc. 1976 Astre; 1976 Astre, 10 @ 14.
②—High Energy Ignition.

TUNE UP SPECIFICATIONS

The following specifications are published from the latest information available. This data should be used only in the absence of a decal affixed in the engine compartment.

★When using a timing light, disconnect vacuum hose or tube at distributor and plug opening in hose or tube so idle speed will not be affected.

●When checking compression, lowest cylinder must be within 80 percent of highest.

▲Before removing wires from distributor cap, determine location of the No. 1 wire in cap, as distributor position may have been altered from that shown at the end of this chart.

| Year | Spark Plug | | Distributor | | Ignition Timing★ | | | Carb. Adjustments | | | | | |
| | Type | Gap Inch | Point Gap Inch | Dwell Angle Deg. | Firing Order Fig. ▲ | Timing BTDC ① | Mark Fig. | Hot Idle Speed ② | | Air Fuel Ratio | | Idle "CO" % | |
								Std. Trans.	Auto. Trans.	Std. Trans.	Auto. Trans.	Std. Trans.	Auto. Trans.
1974													
75 Horsepower	R42TS	.035	③	31–34	A	⑪	B	700/1000⑤	550/750⑤	—	—	.5	.5
85 Horsepower	R42TS	.035	③	31–34	A	⑪	B	700/1200⑤	500/750⑤	—	—	.5	.5
1975													
78 Horsepower	R43TSX	.060	—	—	C	⑬	D	700/1200⑤	550/750⑤	—	—	—	—
87 Horsepower	R43TSX⑭	.060	—	—	C	⑪	D	⑦	600/750⑤	—	—	—	—
Cosworth Vega	R43LTSX	.060	—	—	E	12°⑮	F	600	—	—	—	—	—
1976													
1 Bar. Carb.⑩	R43TS	.035	—	—	C	⑬	D	750/1200⑤	550/750⑤	—	—	—	—
2 Bar. Carb.⑩	R43TS	.035	—	—	C	⑰	D	700/1200⑤	600/750⑤	—	—	—	—
2 Bar. Carb.⑫	R43TS	.035	—	—	C	⑰	D	700/1000⑤	600/750⑤	—	—	—	—
Cosworth Vega	R43LTS	.035	—	—	E	12°⑮	F	600	—	—	—	—	—
1977													
4-140⑱	R43TS	.035	—	—	C	⑲	D	700/1250	650/850	—	—	—	—
4-140⑫	R43TS	.035	—	—	C	⑳	D	800/1250	650/850	—	—	—	—
4-140④	R43TS	.035	—	—	C	⑲	D	800/1250	700/850	—	—	—	—
4-151⑩	R44TSX	.060	—	—	G	⑧	H	500/1000⑤	500/650⑤	—	—	—	—
4-151⑥	R44TSX	.060	—	—	G	⑧	H	500/1200	650/850	—	—	—	—

① —BTDC—Before top dead center.
② —Idle speed on manual trans. equipped vehicles is adjusted in Neutral and on auto. trans. equipped vehicles is adjusted in Drive unless otherwise specified. Where two speeds are listed, the higher speed is with A/C solenoid energized.
③ —New points .019", used .016".
④ —High altitude.
⑤ —Higher speed is with idle solenoid energized.
⑥ —With air conditioning.
⑦ —Exc. Calif., 700; Calif., 700/1200⑤.
⑧ —Except Calif., 14° BTDC; Calif., 12° BTDC.
⑩ —Exc. California.

⑪ —Synchromesh trans. 10° BTDC; automatic trans. 12° BTDC.
⑫ —California.
⑬ —Synchromesh trans. 8° BTDC, automatic trans. 10° BTDC.
⑭ —If cold weather starting problems are encountered, use R43TS spark plug, gapped at .035 inch.
⑮ —At 1600 RPM.
⑯ —Less air conditioning.
⑰ —Astre man. trans., 8° BTDC; auto. trans., 10° BTDC. Vega man. trans., 10° BTDC; auto. trans., 12° BTDC.
⑱ —Except California & high altitude.
⑲ —Man. trans., TDC; auto. trans., 2° BTDC.
⑳ —Man. trans., 2° ATDC; auto. trans., TDC.

Continued

TUNE UP NOTES—Continued

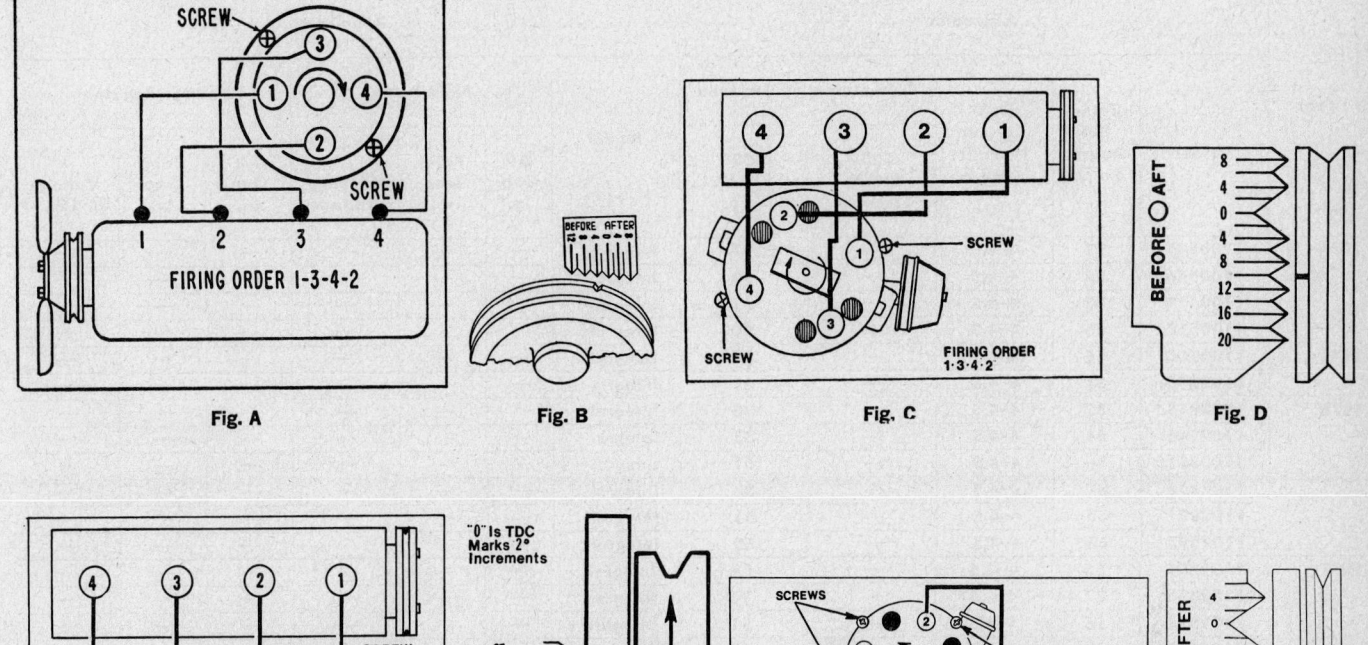

Fig. A   Fig. B   Fig. C   Fig. D

Fig. E   Fig. F   Fig. G   Fig. H

STARTING MOTOR SPECIFICATIONS

Year	Model	Starter Number	Brush Spring Tension Oz.①	Free Speed Test			Resistance Test	
				Amps.	Volts	R.P.M.	Amps.	Volts
1974	Std. Trans.	1108195	—	50–75②	9	6500–10000	—	—
	Auto. Trans.	1108196	—	50–75②	9	6500–10000	—	—
1975–76	4-140 Std. Trans.	1108771	—	50–75②	9	6500–10000	—	—
	4-140 Auto. Trans.	1108772	—	50–75②	9	6500–10000	—	—
	4-122 Cosworth Vega	1108773	—	50–75②	9	6500–10000	—	—
1977	4-140 Std. Trans.	1108771	—	50–75②	9	6500–10000	—	—
	4-140 Auto. Trans.	1108772	—	50–75②	9	6500–10000	—	—
	4-151	1109412	—	50–75②	9	6500–10500	—	—

①—Minimum.
②—Includes solenoid.

ALTERNATOR & REGULATOR SPECIFICATIONS

Year	Model	Rated Hot Output Amps.	Field Current 12 Volts @ 80 F.	Cold Output @ 14 Volts		Model	Field Relay			Voltage Regulator		
				2000 R.P.M. Amps.	5000 R.P.M. Amps.		Air Gap In.	Point Gap In.	Closing Voltage	Air Gap In.	Point Gap In.	Voltage @ 125° F.
1974–75	1100545	32	4–4.5	—	31	Integral	—	—	—	—	—	—
	1100546	55	4–4.5	—	50	Integral	—	—	—	—	—	—
	1100559	32	4–4.5	—	31	Integral	—	—	—	—	—	—
	1100560	55	4–4.5	—	50	Integral	—	—	—	—	—	—
1975	1102500	55	4–4.5	—	50	Integral	—	—	—	—	—	—
	1102856	37	4–4.5	—	33	Integral	—	—	—	—	—	—
1976	1102845	37	4–4.5	—	33	Integral	—	—	—	—	—	—
	1102846	55	4–4.5	—	51	Integral	—	—	—	—	—	—
	1102851	55	4–4.5	—	51	Integral	—	—	—	—	—	—
	1102858	37	4–4.5	—	33	Integral	—	—	—	—	—	—
	1102891	55	4–4.5	—	51	Integral	—	—	—	—	—	—
	1102893	63	4–4.5	—	60	Integral	—	—	—	—	—	—
1977	1102851	55	4–4.5	—	51	Integral	—	—	—	—	—	—
	1102858	37	4–4.5	—	33	Integral	—	—	—	—	—	—
	1102891	55	4–4.5	—	51	Integral	—	—	—	—	—	—
	1102893	63	4–4.5	—	60	Integral	—	—	—	—	—	—

VALVE SPECIFICATIONS

Year	Engine Model	Valve Lash		Valve Angles		Valve Spring Installed Height	Valve Spring Pressure Lbs. @ In.	Stem Clearance		Stem Diameter	
		Int.	Exh.	Seat	Face			Intake	Exhaust	Intake	Exhaust
1974	All	.015C	.030C	46	45	1.746	190 @ 1.31	.001–.0027	.001–.0027	.3410–.3417	.3410–.3417
1975	4-140 1 BBl.	.015C	.030C	46	45	1.75	186 @ 1.29	.001–.0027	.001–.0027	.3410–.3417	.3410–.3417
	4-140 2 BBl.	.015C	.030C	46	45	1.75	190 @ 1.31	.001–.0027	.001–.0027	.3410–.3417	.3410–.3417
1975–76	4-122	.014C	.014C	46	45	1.30	110 @ .92	.001–.0027	.001–.0027	.2788–.2795	.2788–.2795
1976–77	4-140	Hydraulic①		46	45	1.75	190 @ 1.31	.001–.0027	.001–.0027	.3410–.3417	.3410–.3417
1977	4-151	Hydraulic①		46	45	1.69	82 @ 1.66	.001–.0027	②	.3400	.3400

①—No adjustment.
②—Top, .0010–.0027″; bottom, .0020–0037″.

ENGINE TIGHTENING SPECIFICATIONS★

★Torque specifications are for clean and lightly lubricated threads only. Dry or dirty threads produce increased friction which prevents accurate measurement of tightness.

Year	Engine Model	Spark Plugs Ft. Lbs.	Cylinder Head Bolts Ft. Lbs.	Intake Manifold Ft. Lbs.	Exhaust Manifold Ft. Lbs.	Rocker Arm Stud Ft. Lbs.	Cam Cover Ft. Lbs.	Connecting Rod Cap Bolts Ft. Lbs.	Main Bearing Cap Bolts Ft. Lbs.	Flywheel to Crankshaft Ft. Lbs.	Vibration Damper or Pulley Ft. Lbs.
1974–77	4-140	15	60	30	30	—	35①	35	65	60	80
1975–77	4-122	15	60	20	15	—	65①	40–45	65	60	15
1977	4-151	15	95	②	②	60	③	30	65	55	160

①—Inch pounds.
②—Intake to exhaust manifold, 40 ft. lbs. Manifold to cylinder head nut, 30 ft. lbs. Manifold to cylinder head bolt, 40 ft. lbs.
③—Rocker arm cover, 85 inch lbs.

PISTONS, PINS, RINGS, CRANKSHAFT & BEARINGS

Year	Engine Model	Piston Clearance	Ring End Gap①		Wrist-pin Diameter	Rod Bearings		Main Bearings			
			Comp.	Oil		Shaft Diameter	Bearing Clearance	Shaft Diameter	Bearing Clearance	Thrust on Bear. No.	Shaft End Play
1974-75	4-140	.0018-.0028	④	.010	.9272	1.999-2.000	.0007-.0038	2.2983-2.2993	③	4	.002-.007
1975	4-122	.002-.003	④	.010	.9272	1.999-2.000	.0007-.0027	2.2983-2.2993	.0003-.0019	4	.002-.007
1976	4-140	.0018-.0028	④	.010	.9272	1.999-2.000	.0007-.0027	2.2983-2.2993	.0003-.0029	4	.002-.008
	4-122	.002-.003	④	.010	.9272	1.999-2.000	.0007-.0027	⑤	②	4	.002-.008
1977	4-140	.0018-.0028	④	.010	.9272	1.999-2.000	.0007-.0027	2.2983-2.2993	.0003-.0029	4	.002-.008
	4-151	.0025-.0033	.010	.010	.9400	2.000	.0005-.0026	2.2983-2.2993	.0002-.0022	5	.0015-.0085

①—Fit rings in tapered bores for clearance listed in tightest portion of ring travel.
②—No. 1,2,3,5: .0008-.0034; No. 4: .0002-.0029.
③—#1 .0003-.002; others .0003-.0027.
④—Top ring .015; lower ring .009.
⑤—No. 1,2,3,5: 2.3011; No. 4: 2.3006.

WHEEL ALIGNMENT SPECIFICATIONS

Year	Model	Caster Angle, Degrees		Camber Angle, Degrees				Toe-In. Inch	Toe-Out on Turns, Deg.①	
		Limits	Desired	Limits		Desired			Outer Wheel	Inner Wheel
				Left	Right	Left	Right			
1974	All	−¼ to −1¼	−¾	−¼ to +¾	−¼ to +¾	+¼	+¼	3/16 to 5/16	—	—
1975-76	All	−¼ to −1¼	−¾	−¼ to +¾	−¼ to +¾	+¼	+¼	②	—	—
1977	All	−.3 to −1.3	−.8	−.3 to +.7	−.3 to +.7	+.2	+.2	②	—	—

①—Incorrect toe-out when other adjustments are correct, indicates bent steering arms.
②—0 to ⅛ inch toe-out.
③—0 to .12 degree toe-out.

BRAKE SPECIFICATIONS

Year	Model	Brake Drum Inside Diameter	Wheel Cylinder Bore Diameter			Master Cylinder Bore Diameter		
			Disc Brake	Front Drum Brake	Rear Drum Brake	Disc Brakes	Drum Brakes	Power Brakes
1974-75	All	9	1⅞	—	¾	¾	—	¾
1976-77	All	9½	1⅞	—	11/16	¾	—	¾

COOLING SYSTEM & CAPACITY DATA

Year	Model or Engine	Cooling Capacity, Qts.		Radiator Cap Relief Pressure, Lbs.		Thermo. Opening Temp. ①	Fuel Tank Gals.	Engine Oil Refill Qts. ②	Transmission Oil				Rear Axle Oil Pints
		With Heater	With A/C	With A/C	No A/C				3 Speed Pints	4 Speed Pints	5 Speed Pints	Auto. Trans. Qts. ⑥	
1974	4-140	7.6	8.0	15	15	195	16	3	3	3	—	⑤	2.8
1975	4-140	7	7	15	15	195	16	3	2.4	2.4	—	⑤	2¼
1975–76	4-122	6.8	6.8	15	15	195	16	3½	—	3	—	—	2¼
1976	4-140⑦	7	7½	15	15	195	16	3½⑧	2.4	2.4	3.5	⑤	2¼
	4-140③	8	8	15	15	195	16	3½⑧	3	3	3	⑤	2¾
1977	4-140⑦	8.8	8.8	15	15	195	16	3½⑧	—	2.4	3.5	④	2.8
	4-140③	8	8	15	15	195	16	3½⑧	—	3	3	④	2¾
	4-151	11.2	11.2	15	15	195	16	3	—	2.4	3.5	④	2¾

①—For permanent type anti-freeze.
②—Add 1 quart with filter change.
③—Vega.
④—Turbo Hydra-Matic 200, refill 3 qts., total capacity 9.6 qts. Turbo Hydra-Matic 250, refill 2½ qts., total capacity 10 qts.
⑤—Refill 2½ qts. Total capacity 10 qts.
⑥—Approximate; make final check with dipstick.
⑦—Astre.
⑧—Add ½ quart with filter change.

REAR AXLE SPECIFICATIONS

Year	Model	Carrier Type	Ring Gear & Pinion Backlash		Pinion Bearing Preload			Differential Bearing Preload		
			Method	Adjustment	Method	New Bearings Inch-Lbs.	Used Bearings Inch-Lbs.	Method	New Bearings Inch-Lbs.	Used Bearings Inch-Lbs.
1974–77	All	Integral	Shims	.005–.008	Spacer	10–25	8–12	Shims	—	—

Electrical Section

DISTRIBUTOR

Removal

1. Release distributor cap hold-down screws and remove cap.
2. Disconnect distributor primary lead from coil terminal.

NOTE: On H.E.I. systems, disconnect feed and module connectors from distributor cap.

3. Scribe an alignment mark on the distributor and engine in line with the rotor.
4. Remove distributor hold-down bolt and clamp, then remove distributor.

CAUTION: Avoid rotating engine while distributor is removed.

Installation

1. Turn rotor about ⅛ turn in a clockwise direction past the mark previously made to locate rotor.

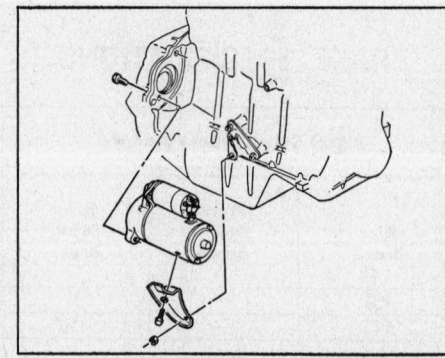

Fig. 1   Starter motor installation

2. Push distributor down into position in cylinder head with distributor housing in a normal installed position.

NOTE: It may be necessary to move rotor slightly to start gear into mesh with camshaft gear, but rotor should line up with the mark when distributor is down in place.

NOTE

If the engine was disturbed while the distributor was removed, it will be necessary to crank the engine to bring No. 1 cylinder piston up on the compression stroke. Continue cranking until timing mark is adjacent to pointer. Then rotate the distributor cam until rotor is in position to fire No. 1. Install distributor in this position.

3. Tighten distributor clamp bolt and connect vacuum line, primary wire and install the cap.
4. Set ignition timing.

NOTE: When using a timing light to ad-

Fig. 2   Ignition lock removal

IGNITION LOCK, REPLACE

1. Remove the turn signal switch as described further on.
2. The lock cylinder should be removed in the "Run" position only. Removal in any other position will damage the buzzer switch.
3. Insert a small screw driver or similar tool into the turn signal housing slot, Fig. 2. Keeping the tool to the right side of the slot, break the housing flash loose, and at the same time depress the spring latch at the lower end of the lock cylinder. With the latch depressed, the lock cylinder can be removed from the housing.

IGNITION SWITCH, REPLACE

The ignition switch is mounted on the top of the steering column jacket near the front of the dash. It is located inside the channel section of the brake pedal support and is completely inaccessible without first lowering the steering column.

1. Lower the steering column and be sure it is properly supported before proceeding.
2. The switch should be positioned in Lock position before removing, Fig. 3.
3. Unfasten and remove the switch, detaching it from the actuating rod.
4. When installing, make sure the lock and the switch are in the Lock position. Then install the activating rod into the switch and fasten the switch.

LIGHT SWITCH, REPLACE

1. Disconnect ground cable at battery.
2. Pull headlamp switch knob to "ON" position.
3. Reach under instrument panel and depress switch shaft retainer button while pulling on the switch control shaft knob.
4. With a large bladed screwdriver, remove the light switch ferrule nut

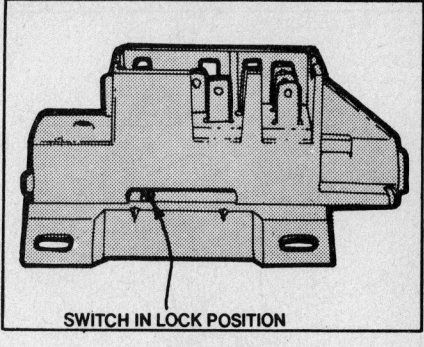

SWITCH IN LOCK POSITION

Fig. 3   Ignition switch assembly

from front of instrument panel, Fig. 4.
5. Disconnect the multi-contact connector from side of switch and remove switch.

STOP LIGHT SWITCH

1. Reach under right side of instrument panel at brake pedal support and release wiring harness connector at switch.
2. Pull switch from mounting bracket.
3. When installing switch, adjust by bringing brake pedal to normal position. Electrical contact should be made when pedal is depressed as shown in Fig. 5. To adjust, the switch may be rotated or pulled in the clip.

CLUTCH START SWITCH

NOTE: The clutch pedal must be fully depressed and the ignition switch in START position for the vehicle to start.

The clutch switch assembly mounts with two tangs to the clutch pedal brace switch pivot bracket and the clutch pedal arm, Fig. 6.
1. Under the instrument panel on the clutch pedal support remove the multi-contact connector from switch.

just ignition timing, the connection should be made at the No. 1 spark plug. Forcing foreign objects through the boot at the No. 1 terminal of the distributor cap will damage the boot and could cause engine misfiring.

STARTER, REPLACE

NOTE: The following procedure may vary slightly depending on model and series of vehicle.

1. Disconnect battery ground cable at battery.
2. Disconnect all wires at solenoid terminals.

NOTE: Reinstall the nuts on the terminals as each wire is removed as thread size is different and if mixed, stripping of threads may occur.

3. Loosen starter front bracket then remove two mount bolts, Fig. 1.
4. Remove front bracket bolt and rotate bracket clear of work area then lower starter from vehicle by lowering front end first.
5. Reverse procedure to install.

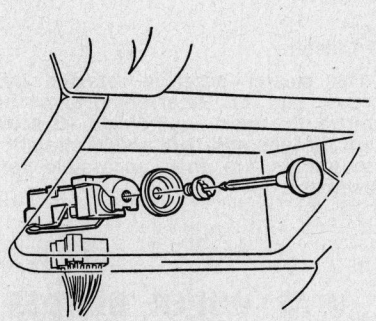

Fig. 4   Light switch replacement

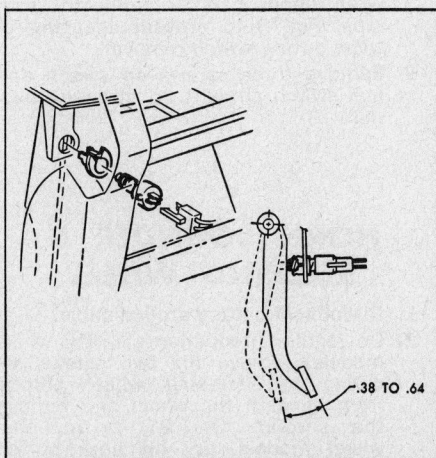

.38 TO .64

Fig. 5   Stop light switch replacement

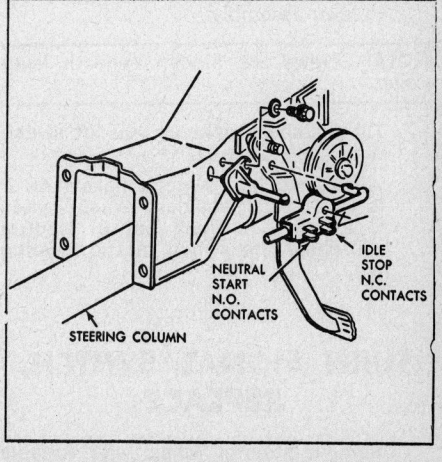

NEUTRAL START N.O. CONTACTS

IDLE STOP N.C. CONTACTS

STEERING COLUMN

Fig. 6   Clutch operated neutral start switch

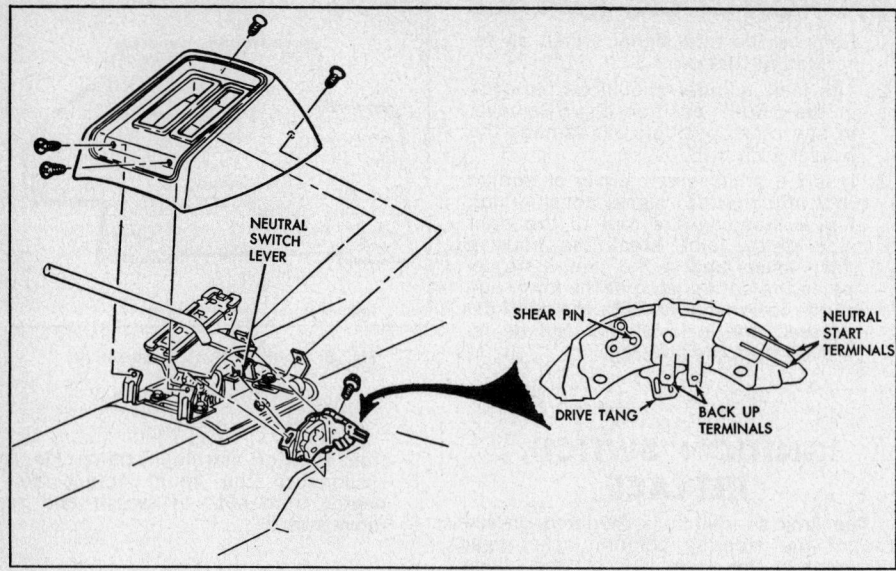

Fig. 7   Neutral safety switch installation (Typical)

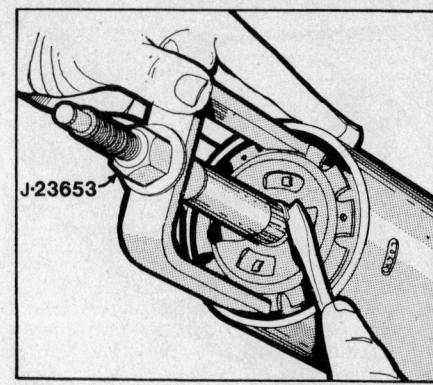

Fig. 8   Removing lock plate retaining ring

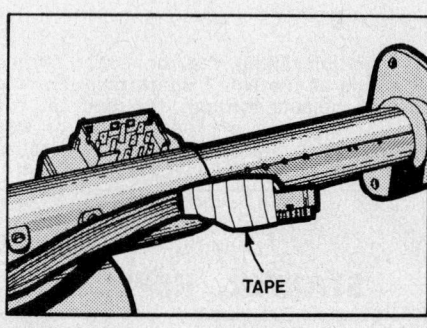

Fig. 9   Taping turn signal connector and wires

2. Compress switch assembly actuating shaft barb retainer and push out of clutch pedal.
3. Compress switch assembly pivot bracket barb and lift off switch.
4. When installing new switch, no adjustments are necessary as the switch is self aligning.

NEUTRAL SAFETY SWITCH, REPLACE

1. Remove screws securing floor console, Fig. 7.
2. Disconnect electrical plugs on back-up contacts and neutral start contacts of switch assembly.
3. Place shift lever in Neutral.
4. Remove two screws securing shift indicator plate.
5. Remove two screws securing shift lever curved cover.
6. Remove two screws securing switch to lever assembly.

NOTE: Screws are hidden beneath lever cover.

7. Tilt switch to right as you lift switch out of lever hole.
8. When installing switch, make sure it is in Neutral position. When switch is installed, shifting out of Neutral will shear the switch plastic locating pin.

TURN SIGNAL SWITCH, REPLACE

1. Remove steering wheel with suitable puller.

2. On 1974-75 models remove three cover screws and lift cover off the shaft. NOTE: These screws have plastic retainers on the back of the cover so it is not necessary to completely remove these screws.
3. On 1976-77 models, place screw driver blade into cover slot, pry up and out to free cover from lock plate.
4. On all models, place Lock Plate Compressing Tool J-23653, Fig. 8, on end of steering shaft and compress the lock plate as far as possible using the shaft nut as shown. Pry the round wire snap ring out of the shaft groove and discard the ring. Remove tool and lift lock plate off end of shaft.
5. Slide the signal cancelling cam, upper bearing preload spring and thrust washer off the end of shaft.
6. Remove turn signal lever screw and remove the lever.
7. Push hazard warning knob in and unscrew the knob.
8. Wrap upper part of connector with tape, Fig. 9 to prevent snagging of wires during switch removal.
9. Remove three screws on switch and pull switch straight up through housing.

HORN SOUNDER & STEERING WHEEL

1. Disconnect battery ground cable.
2. On regular production steering wheel models, remove the two screws securing the steering wheel shroud from beneath the wheel and remove the shroud. On GT or optional wheel models, pry off horn button cap.
3. Remove steering wheel nut and use

a suitable puller to remove the steering wheel.

NOTE: On 1975-77 models, remove snap ring before steering wheel nut.

INSTRUMENT CLUSTER

Standard Cluster

The instrument cluster bezel is retained by nine screws, Fig. 10. After removal of bezel, remove cluster lens-light shield combination (2 screws at top of lens and 2 screws at bottom of light shield). The lens tips out at the top and then lifts off. Instruments are then easily removed.

GT Cluster

The cluster bezel is retained by six screws, Fig. 11. After removal of bezel, remove the lens light shield (6 screws). Then lift lens and light shield straight out. Instruments are then accessible for replacement.

W/S WIPER BLADES

1. Remove the wiper blade from the arm by depressing the spring type blade

clip, Fig. 12, away from the under side of the arm and slide the arm out of the blade clip.

2. To install wiper blade to wiper arm, slide tip end of arm into blade clip, until pin on tip end of arm engages hole in clip.

3. The blade element is retained in the blade assembly by a spring type retainer clip in the end of the blade element. When the retainer clip is squeezed together, the blade element can be slid out of the blade assembly.

4. When installing a blade element into a blade assembly, be certain to engage the metal insert of the element into all retaining tabs of the blade assembly.

NOTE: When properly installed, the spring type element retaining clip should be at the end of the wiper blade assembly nearest the wiper transmission.

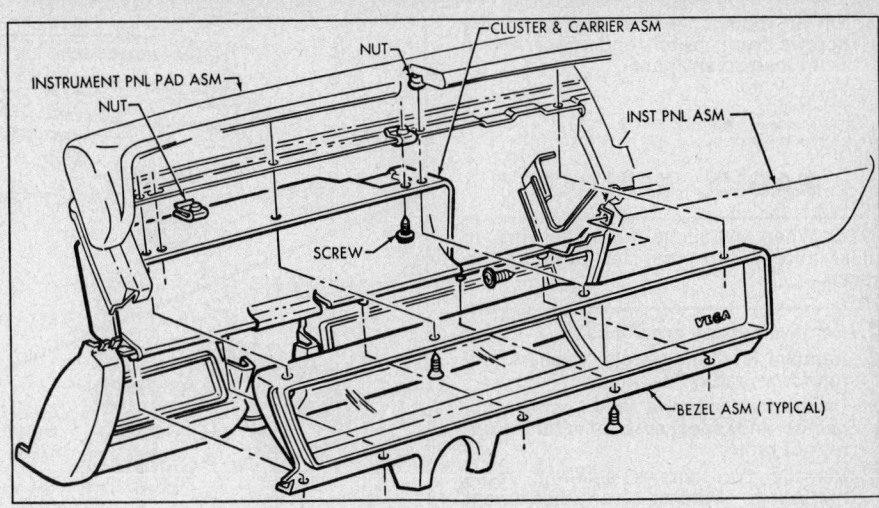

Fig. 10   Instrument panel. Standard cluster

W/S WIPER ARMS

1. Wiper motor must be in park position.

2. Use suitable tool to minimize the possibility of windshield or paint finish damage during arm removal.

3. Remove arm by prying up with tool to disengage arm from serrated transmission shaft, Fig. 13.

4. To install arm to transmission shaft rotate the required distance and direction so that blades rest in proper

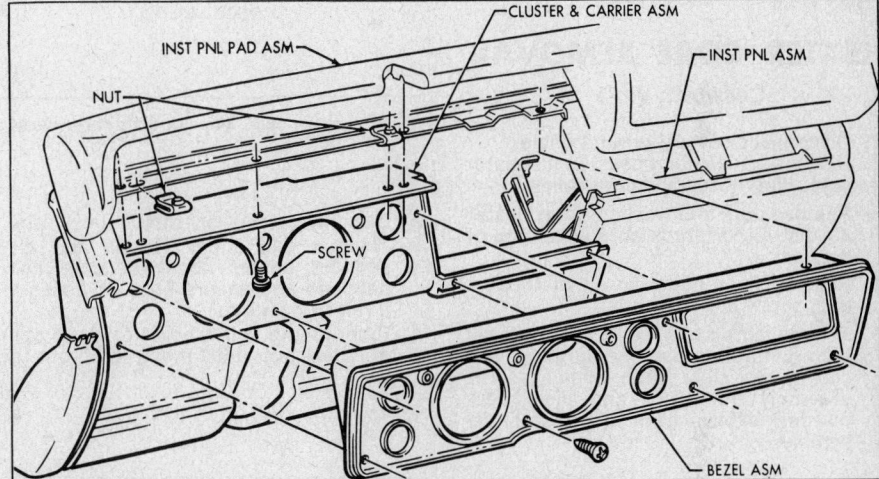

Fig. 11   Instrument panel. GT cluster

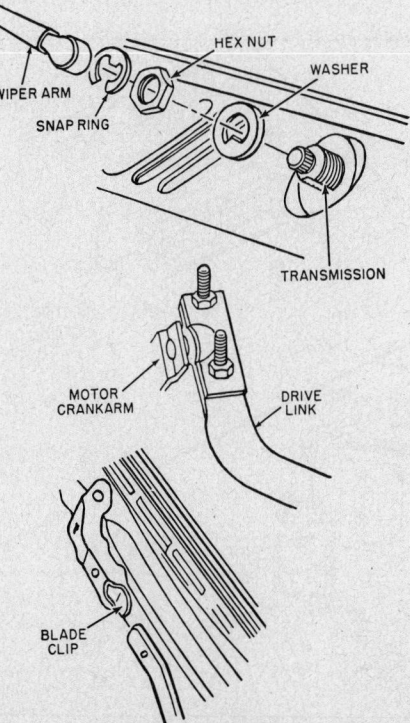

Fig. 12   Wiper blade clip

parked position.

CAUTION: The parked position for the left blade tip is approx. 2″ above lower windshield reveal moulding and the right blade tip within 2″ of the lower windshield reveal moulding.

W/S WIPER MOTOR

1. Raise hood.

2. Reaching through cowl opening, loosen the two transmission drive link attaching nuts to motor crankarm.

3. Remove transmission drive link from motor crankarm.

4. Disconnect wiring and unfasten motor and remove.

W/S WIPER SWITCH

1. Beneath instrument panel, unplug the headlamp switch multi-connector for clearance to wiper switch screw.

2. Unplug connector on bottom of wiper switch.

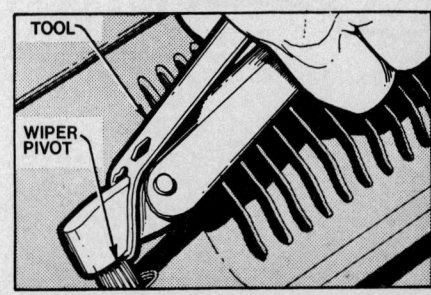

Fig. 13   Wiper arm removal

3. On all models, remove two mounting screws from switch and lower switch from instrument panel.

RADIO, REPLACE

NOTE: When installing radio, be sure to adjust antenna trimmer for peak performance.

1. Remove battery ground cable.
2. Remove knobs, controls, washers and nuts from radio bushings.
3. Disconnect antenna lead, power connector and speaker connectors from rear of radio.
4. Remove two screws securing radio mounting bracket to instrument panel lower reinforcement and lift out radio.

HEATER CORE REMOVAL
Cosworth Vega

1. Disconnect battery ground cable.
2. Disconnect heater hoses from heater core. Plug hoses and core tubes.
3. Remove nuts and washers from heater air distributor studs on engine side of dash.
4. Remove floor outlet to air distributor duct screw and the outlet.
5. Remove air distributor to dash screws, then pull duct assembly rearward until core tubes clear dash openings. Tilt assembly downward and disconnect bowden cables from distributor assembly.
6. Disconnect resistor wiring harness and remove air distributor assembly from vehicle.
7. Remove core retaining strap screw and the heater core.

All Exc. Cosworth Vega

Without Air Conditioning

1. Disconnect battery ground cable.

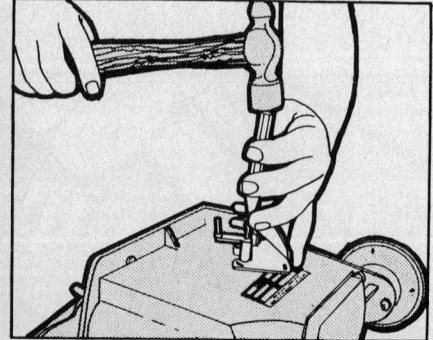

Fig. 15 Removing temperature door bell crank on air conditioned vehicles

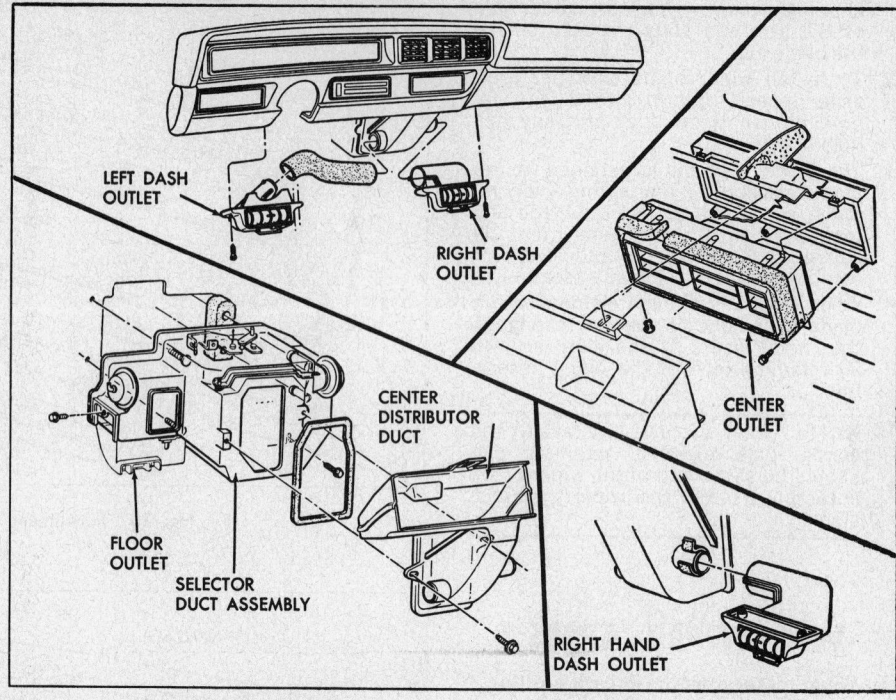

Fig. 14 Air distributor ducts and outlets on air conditioned models.

2. Disconnect blower motor lead wire.
3. Place a pan under vehicle and disconnect heater hoses at core connections and secure ends of hoses in a raised position.
4. Remove the coil bracket to dash panel stud nut and move coil out of way.
5. Remove the blower inlet to dash panel screws and nuts and remove the blower inlet, blower motor and wheel as an assembly.
6. Remove the core retainer strap screws and remove the core.
7. When replacing core, be sure the blower inlet sealer is intact.

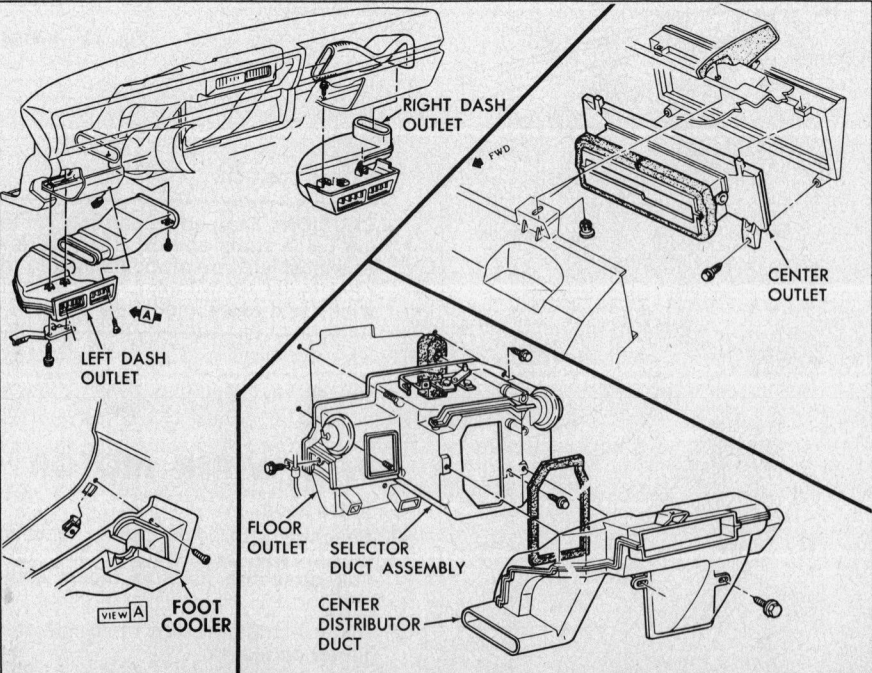

Fig. 16 Air distribution ducts and outlets on air conditioned models. 1974-76

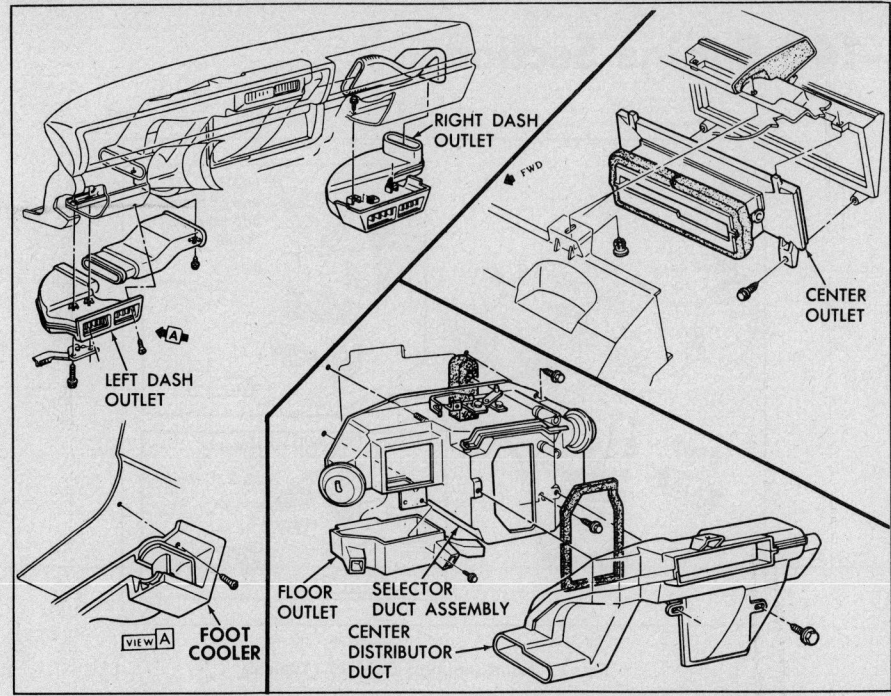

Fig. 17 Air distribution ducts and outlets on air conditioned models. 1977

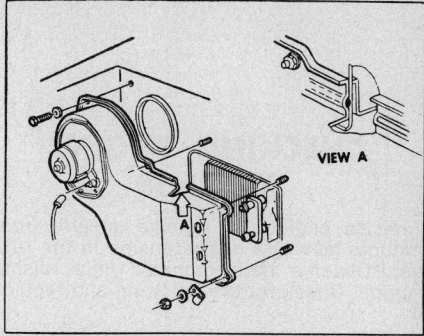

Fig. 18 Blower motor (Typical)

19. Pry off or punch out temperature door bell crank, then remove temperature door, Fig. 15.
20. Remove backing plate attaching screws and temperature door cable retainer.
21. Remove heater core and backing plate as an assembly.
22. Remove core straps, then remove heater core.

With Air Conditioning
1974-77 Models

1. Disconnect battery ground cable.
2. Position a pan under heater core tubes, then disconnect heater hoses and secure in a raised position. Cap core tubes to prevent coolant spillage during removal.
3. From engine side of dash panel remove nuts from selector duct studs, Figs. 16 and 17.
4. Remove glove box and door as an assembly.
5. Remove right hand outlet to instrument panel attaching screws, then remove outlet and flexible hose.
6. Remove intermediate duct to left hand outlet.
7. Remove steering column to toe pan plastic retainer, insulation and attaching screws.
8. Remove steering column to dash panel attaching nuts, then lower column and support on driver's seat.

NOTE: Place protective tape over steering column to prevent damage to finish when lowering instrument cluster assembly.

9. Remove instrument panel bezel, then remove ash tray and retainer.
10. Remove A/C control to instrument panel attaching screws.
11. Disconnect wire connector and antenna lead from radio.
12. Remove instrument cluster to dash panel attaching screws and allow cluster assembly to rest on steering column.
13. Disconnect speedometer cable, then push A/C control forward and allow control to rest on floor, using care not kink cable.
14. Remove center duct to selector duct attaching screws and duct to upper instrument panel retainer.
15. Slide center duct to left to clear lower instrument panel to cluster tab, then slide to right to remove.
16. Remove defroster duct to selector duct attaching screws.
17. Remove remaining selector duct to dash panel attaching screws, then pull duct rearward and disconnect all electrical leads and vacuum lines.
18. Disconnect temperature door cable and remove selector duct assembly.

NOTE: Ensure all electrical leads and vacuum lines are disconnected before removing duct assembly.

BLOWER MOTOR, REPLACE

1. Disconnect the battery ground cable.
2. On Cosworth Vega, loosen air cleaner seal to intake manifold clamp, then remove air cleaner bracket screws and rotate filter assembly upward.
3. On all models, disconnect blower motor lead wire.
4. Scribe the blower motor flange to case position.
5. Remove the blower to case attaching screws and remove the blower wheel and motor assembly, Fig. 18. Pry the flange gently if the sealer acts as an adhesive.
6. Remove the blower motor wheel retaining nut and separate the motor and wheel.
7. To install, reverse steps 1 thru 6, lining up the scribe marks on the motor flange which were made at removal.

NOTE: Assemble the blower wheel to the motor with the open end of the blower away from the motor. Replace sealer at the motor flange if necessary.

4-140 Engine Section

CHECKING ENGINE MOUNTS

Raise engine to remove weight from mounts leaving a slight tension in the rubber. Observe both mounts while raising engine. Check for the following and replace if:

a. Hard rubber surface is covered with heat check cracks.
b. Rubber separated from metal plate of mount.
c. Rubber split through center.

If there is relative movement between a metal plate of the mount and its attaching points lower the engine on the mounts and tighten the screws or nuts attaching the mounts to the engine, frame, or bracket.

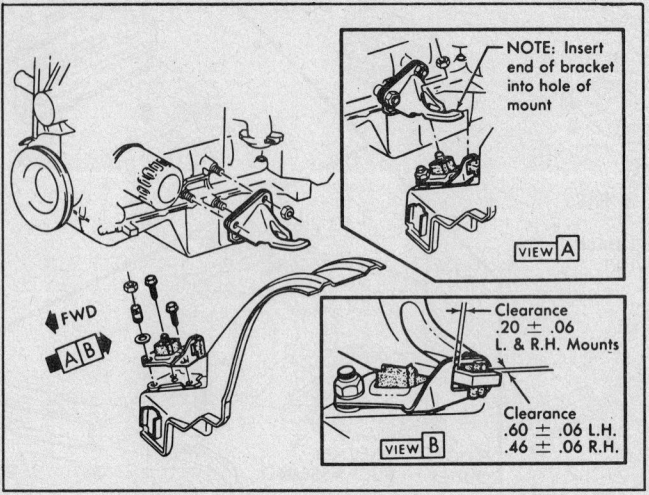

Fig. 1   Front mounts. 1974-77 (Typical)

ENGINE MOUNTS, REPLACE

1974-77 Front

1. Raise vehicle on hoist and support front of engine to take weight off front mounts.
2. If only one mount is being replaced, remove the mount-to-engine bracket nut on the mount not being replaced, Fig. 1.
3. Remove the stud nut and two bolts securing mount to housing support.
4. Remove the three stud nuts securing the bracket to the engine. On the right side remove the starter brace at starter and on air conditioned equipped vehicles, remove the compressor rear lower brace at the compressor.
5. Raise front of engine to provide maximum clearance without imposing stress on other engine components.

6. Remove mount and bracket as a unit and separate by removing stud nut.

1974-77 Rear

CAUTION: The rear mount serves to locate the power train fore and aft and side to side; therefore mark relationship of rear mount to transmission support cross member to ensure proper alignment when new mount is installed.

1. Remove crossmember-to-mount bolts, Figs. 2 and 3.
2. Raise transmission at extension housing to release weight from mount.
3. Remove mount-to-transmission bolts, then remove mount.

ENGINE, REPLACE

1. Remove hood.
2. Disconnect battery positive cable at battery and negative cable at engine block (except on air conditioned vehicles).
3. Drain cooling system and disconnect hoses at radiator. Disconnect heater hoses at water pump and at heater inlet (bottom hose).
4. Disconnect emission system hoses: PCV at cam cover; cannister vacuum hose at carburetor; PCV vacuum at inlet manifold and bowl vent at carburetor.
5. Remove radiator panel or shroud and remove radiator, fan and spacer.
6. Remove air cleaner, disconnecting vent tube at base of cleaner.

7. Disconnect electrical leads at: Delcotron, ignition coil, starter solenoid, oil pressure switch, engine temperature switch, transmission controlled spark switch at transmission, transmission controlled spark solenoid and engine ground strap at cowl.
8. Disconnect: Automatic transmission throttle valve linkage at manifold mounted bellcrank, fuel line at rubber hose to rear of carburetor, transmission vacuum modulator and air conditioning vacuum line at inlet manifold, accelerator cable at manifold bellcrank.

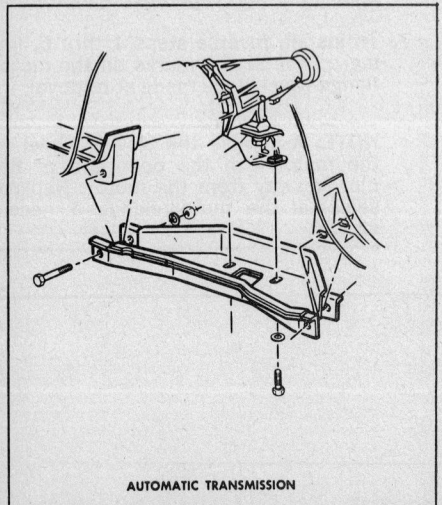

AUTOMATIC TRANSMISSION

Fig. 2   Rear mount. Automatic trans

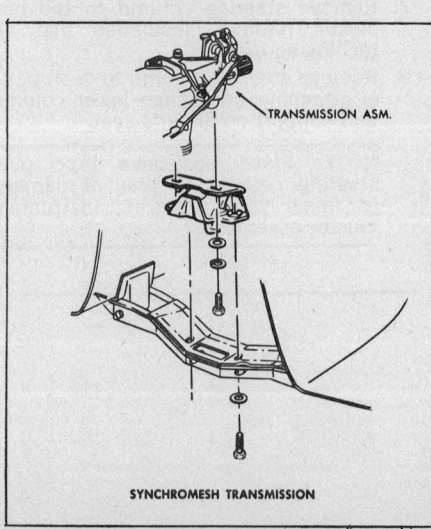

SYNCHROMESH TRANSMISSION

Fig. 3   Rear mount. Synchromesh trans

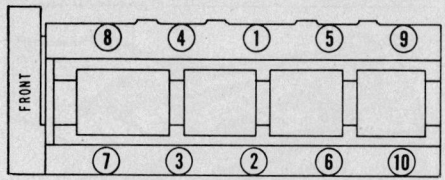

Fig. 4 Cylinder head tightening sequence

9. On air conditioned cars, disconnect compressor at front support, rear support, rear lower bracket and remove drive belt from compressor.
10. Move compressor slightly forward and allow front of compressor to rest on frame forward brace, then secure rear of compressor to engine compartment so it is out of way.
11. Disconnect power steering pump, if equipped, and position it out of way.
12. Raise car on a hoist and disconnect exhaust pipe at manifold.
13. Remove engine flywheel dust cover or converter underpan.
14. On automatic transmission cars, remove converter-to-flywheel retaining bolts and nuts and install coverter safety strap.
15. Remove converter housing or flywheel housing-to-engine retaining bolts.
16. Loosen engine front mount retaining bolts at frame attachment and lower vehicle.
17. Install floor jack under transmission.
18. Install suitable engine lifting equipment and raise engine slightly to take weight from engine mounts and remove engine front mount retaining bolts.
19. Remove engine and pull forward to clear transmission while slowly lifting engine from car.

VALVES, ADJUST

1976-77

These engines use new hydraulic valve lifters which require no lash adjustment. Also, these lifters are not interchangeable with the previous type valve lifters since the cylinder head has been re-designed to facilitate the use of the new type lifters.

1974-75

1. To adjust valves, the tappet must be on the base circle of the cam lobe.

   Do this as follows:
   a. Rotate camshaft timing sprocket to align timing mark on sprocket with inverted "V" notch on timing belt upper cover. The following valves can be adjusted with cam in this position (number one firing).
      Number one cylinder—Intake and Exhaust
      Number two cylinder—Intake
      Number three cylinder—Exhaust
   b. Use a feeler gauge and measure clearance between tappet and cam lobe. Adjust clearance by turning adjusting screw in tappet, Fig. 5.

   NOTE: It is mandatory that the adjusting screw, Fig. 6, be turned one complete revolution to maintain proper stem-to-screw relationship. Each revolution of screw alters clearance by .003".

   c. Rotate camshaft timing sprocket 180 degrees so timing mark is at 12 o'clock position and in line with notch on timing belt upper cover.

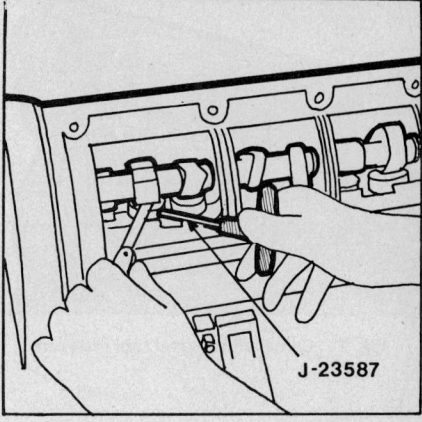

Fig. 5 Adjusting valve lash. 1974-75

The following valves can be adjusted with camshaft in this position (number four firing).
Number two cylinder—Exhaust
Number three cylinder—Intake
Number four cylinder—Intake and Exhaust

VALVE ARRANGEMENT
Front to Rear

4-140 . . . . I-E-I-E-I-E-I-E

CAMSHAFT COVER

1. Raise hood to fully open position and support with the hood hold-open link, Fig. 7.
2. Disconnect battery negative cable at battery.
3. Remove air cleaner wing nut. Disconnect ventilation tube at camshaft cover or at air cleaner; then remove air cleaner.
4. Remove PCV valve from grommet at front of cover.
5. Remove cover-to-cylinder head screws and withdraw cover from head.

CAMSHAFT, REMOVAL

1. Remove hood.
2. Remove camshaft timing sprocket.
3. Remove timing belt upper cover and cam retainer and seal assembly.
4. Remove camshaft cover.
5. Disconnect fuel line at carburetor and remove idle solenoid from bracket.
6. Remove carburetor choke coil, cover and rod assembly.
7. Remove distributor.
8. Raise vehicle on a hoist, disconnect engine front mounts at body attachment, raise front of engine and in-

CYLINDER HEAD, REPLACE

1. Remove engine front cover and camshaft cover as outlined further on.
2. Remove timing belt and camshaft sprocket.
3. Remove intake and exhaust manifolds.
4. Disconnect hose at thermostat housing.
5. Remove cylinder head bolts and with the aid of an assistant lift head and gasket from engine. Place head on two blocks of wood to prevent damage to valves.
6. Reverse procedure to install and tighten head bolts in sequence shown in Fig. 4.

NOTE: Cylinder head bolts are of different lengths. Install the longer bolts adjacent to intake manifold.

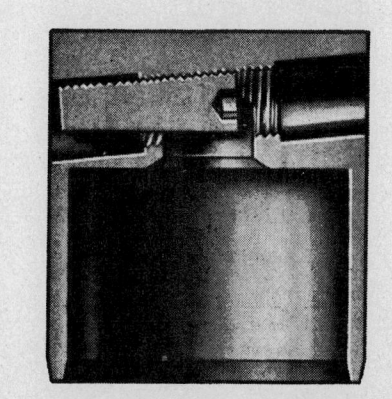

Fig. 6 Tappet and adjusting screw assembly. Screw is threaded in all areas except in valve stem contact surface. 1974-75

Fig. 7   Camshaft removal tool installed

downward until they just seat against corresponding bosses on head.

f. Apply a heavy body lubricant to ball end of lever depressing screws and proceed to tighten screws to depress tappets, Fig. 8.

NOTE: Use a torque wrench to tighten screws the final few turns. About 10 ft. lbs. is required to depress tappets.

10. At this point the camshaft can be removed by sliding it forward from the head.

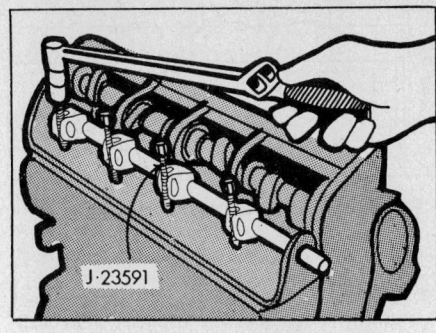

Fig. 8   Depressing valve tappets

stall wood blocks, about 1½″ thick, between engine mounts and body. Lower vehicle.

9. Install camshaft removal tool as shown in Fig. 7, to cylinder head as follows:

a. Position tool to cylinder head so attaching holes align with cam cover lower attaching holes.

b. Align tappet depressing levers on tool so each lever will depress both intake and exhaust valve for their respective cylinder. Lever should fit squarely in notches adjacent to valve tappets.

c. With tool aligned, make sure screws in bottom of tool are backed off so they do not make contact with bosses beneath tool.

d. Install hardened screws supplied with tool, to attach tool to head. Torque screws securely.

e. Turn screws in bottom of tool

CAMSHAFT BEARINGS

After removal of the camshaft as described previously, the bearings can be removed without removing the camshaft end plug.

NOTE: Install bearings from rear to front. Align oil holes in the rear three bearings with oil holes in bearing bore. Position oil holes in the first two bearings at 11 O'clock with oil groove in front bearing facing forward.

CAM LOBE LIFT SPECS.

		Intake	Exhaust
75 H.P.	1974	.4199	.4302
85 H.P.	1974	.4367	.4379

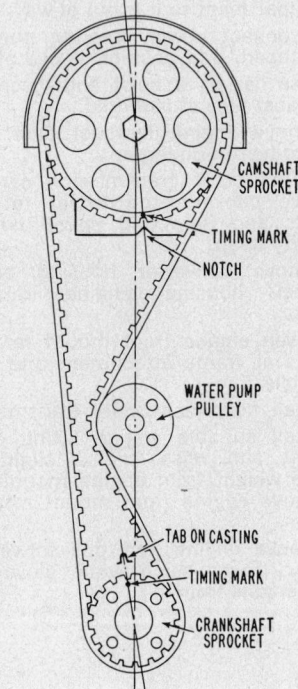

Fig. 10   Sprocket alignment marks

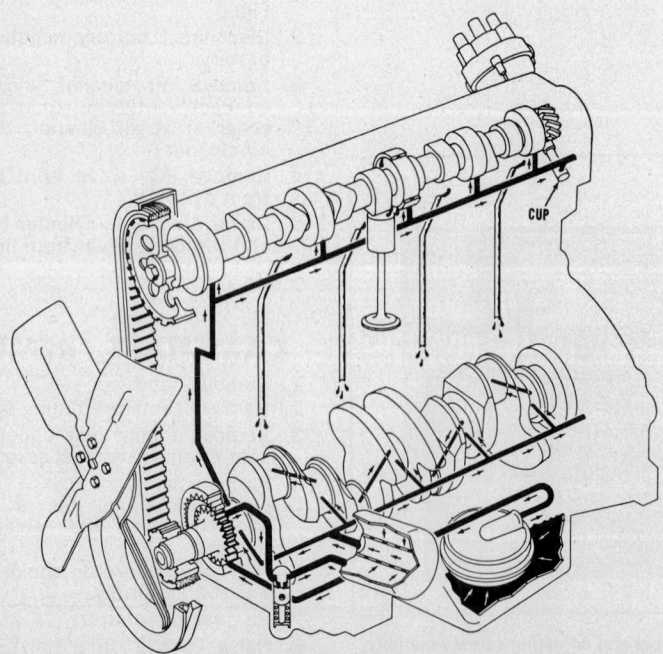

Fig. 9   Engine lubrication system

Fig. 11   Checking sprocket alignment. 1974-77

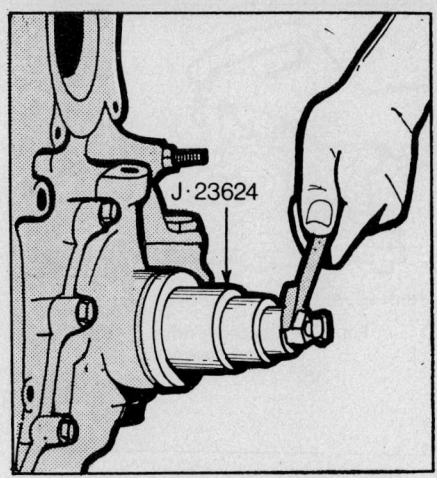

Fig. 12 Installing crankshaft front seal

78 H.P.	1975	.4199	.4302
87 H.P.	1975	.4369	.4379
All	1976-77	.4000	.4150

1 —Except California vehicles.
2 —California vehicles.

VALVE TIMING
Intake Open Before TDC

85 H.P.	1974	28
75 H.P.	1974	22
78 H.P.	1975	22
87 H.P.	1975	28
All	1976-77	34

1 —Except California vehicles.
2 —California vehicles.

VALVE GUIDES

On all engines, valves operate in guide holes bored in the cylinder head. If clearance becomes excessive, use the next oversize valve and ream the bore to fit. Valves with oversize stems are available in .003, .015 and 030".

ENGINE FRONT COVER

1. Raise hood to fully open position and install hood hold-open bolt.
2. Disconnect battery ground cable at battery.
3. Remove fan and spacer.
4. Loosen, but do not remove, the two cover lower screws. Cover is slotted to permit easy removal.
5. Remove the two cover upper retaining screws and remove cover.

TIMING BELT & WATER PUMP

1. Remove engine front cover as previously described.
2. Remove accessory drive pulley or damper.
3. Drain coolant and loosen water pump bolts to relieve tension on belt.
4. Remove timing belt lower cover, then remove belt from sprockets.
5. Remove water pump bolts and lift off pump after removing hoses.

CAMSHAFT SPROCKET

After removal of timing belt, the camshaft sprocket can be removed as follows:
1. Align one hole in sprocket with bolt head behind sprocket, then using a socket on bolt head to prevent cam from turning, remove sprocket retaining bolt and withdraw sprocket from camshaft.
2. When installing, be sure timing marks are aligned as in Fig. 10.

NOTE: A simplified method is provided for checking camshaft and crankshaft alignment. Proper alignment is assured by making sure hole in left rear of the timing belt upper cover is in line with the corresponding hole in the camshaft sprocket with engine at TDC compression stroke. Check alignment by inserting a pencil or other similar tool through the hole in cover. If alignment is correct, tool will also enter small hole in cam gear, Fig. 11.

CRANKSHAFT SPROCKET

1. Remove engine front cover, accessory drive pulley, timing belt and timing belt lower cover.
2. Install suitable puller to crankshaft sprocket and remove sprocket.

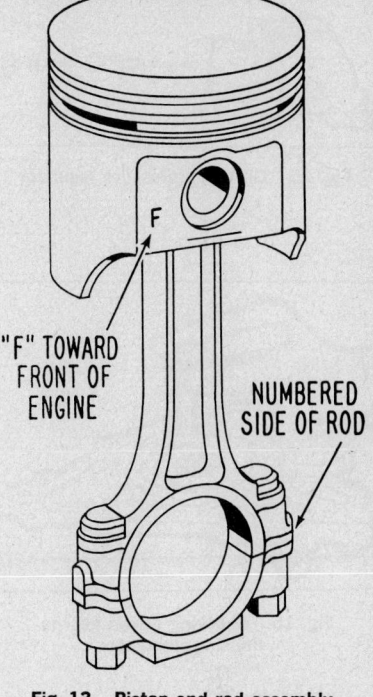

"F" TOWARD FRONT OF ENGINE

NUMBERED SIDE OF ROD

Fig. 13 Piston and rod assembly

OIL PUMP (CRANKCASE FRONT COVER) SEAL

1. Remove engine front cover, accessory drive pulley, timing belt and timing belt lower cover and crankshaft sprocket.
2. Pry old seal from front cover being careful not to damage seal housing or seal lip contact surfaces.
3. Coat seal with light engine oil and apply an approved sealing compound to outside diameter of seal.
4. Position seal, closed end outward, onto crankshaft. Then install seal into bore using tool J-23624, Fig. 12.

PISTONS & RODS, ASSEMBLE

The "F" on the front of the piston must face the front of the engine when the piston and road assembly is installed in its proper cylinder, Fig. 13.

Piston Oversizes

Oversize pistons are available in oversizes of .010 and .020 inch.

Fig. 14 Removing oil pan baffle

MAIN & ROD BEARINGS
Undersizes

Bearings are available in .001, .002,

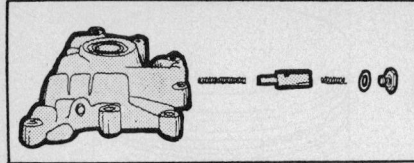

Fig. 15   Oil pump pressure regulator

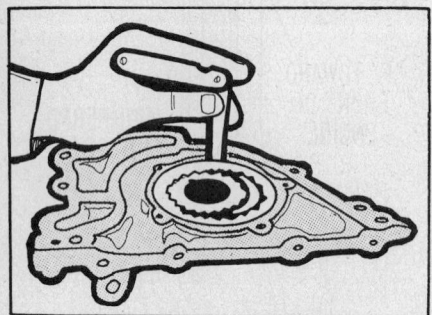

Fig. 16   Checking driven gear-to-housing clearance

.010 and .020" undersizes.

NOTE: If for any reason main bearing caps are replaced, shimming may be necessary. Laminated shims for each cap are available for service. Shim requirements will be determined by bearing clearance.

OIL PAN

1. Raise vehicle on a hoist and drain engine oil.
2. Support front of engine so weight is off front mounts, and remove frame crossmember and both front crossmember braces.
3. Disconnect idler arm at frame side rail.

NOTE: On air conditioned vehicles, disconnect idler arm at relay rod.

4. Mark relationship of steering linkage pitman arm to steering gear pitman shaft and remove pitman arm.

NOTE: Do not rotate steering gear pitman shaft while arm is disconnected as this will change steering wheel alignment.

5. Remove flywheel cover or converter underpan.
6. Remove oil pan to cylinder case screws, tap pan lightly to break sealing bond and remove oil pan.
7. Remove pick up screen to baffle support bolts, then remove support from baffle.
8. Remove bolt securing oil pan drain back tube to baffle. Then rotate baffle 90 degrees towards left side of car and remove baffle from pick up screen, Fig. 14.

OIL PUMP (CRANKCASE FRONT COVER)

1. Remove engine front cover, accessory drive pulley, timing belt, timing belt lower cover and crankshaft sprocket.
2. Raise vehicle on a hoist and remove oil pan and baffle.
3. Remove bolts and stud securing oil pump to cylinder case.

Inspection

1. Clean gasket surfaces, then wash parts in approved solvent and blow out all passages.
2. Check pressure regulator for free operation, Fig. 15.
3. Inspect pump gears for nicks, broken parts and other damage.
4. Check clearance between outside diameter of driven gear and pump. Clearance should be .0038-.0068", Fig. 16.
5. Check clearance between outside diameter of drive gear and crescent. Clearance should be .0023-.0093", Fig. 17.
6. Check clearance between inside diameter of driven gear and pump crescent. Clearance should be .0068-.0148", Fig. 18.
7. Check gear end clearance. It should be .0009-.0023", Fig. 19.

NOTE: The pump gears and body are not serviced separately. If pump gears or body are worn, replacement of the entire is necessary.

BELT TENSION DATA

1974-77—	New Lbs.	Used Lbs.
Air Condition	135-145	95
A.I.R. Pump	120-130	75
Generator	120-130	75
Power Steering	120 130	75
Timing Belt	100-140	—

WATER PUMP, REPLACE

1. Raise hood to fully open position and install hold-open bolt.

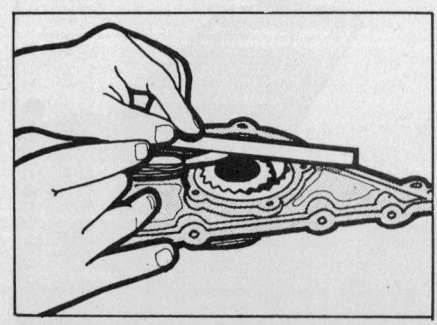

Fig. 19   Checking gear end clearance

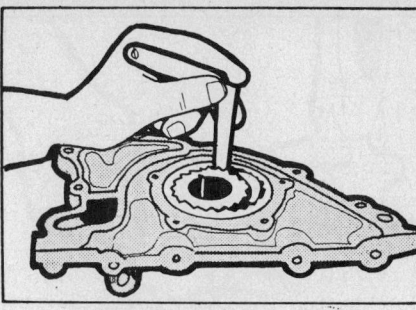

Fig. 17   Checking drive gear-to-crescent clearance

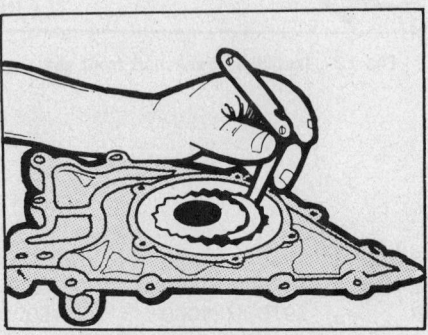

Fig. 18   Checking driven gear-to-crescent clearance

2. Disconnect battery ground cable at battery.
3. Remove engine fan and spacer.
4. Loosen, but do not remove, the two cover lower screws. Cover is slotted to permit easy removal.
5. Remove the two cover upper retaining screws and remove cover.
6. Drain coolant and loosen water pump bolts to relieve tension in timing belt.
7. Remove radiator lower hose and heater hose at water pump.
8. Unfasten and remove water pump.

TIMING BELT TENSION, ADJUST

1. Drain coolant at engine block and remove fan and extension.
2. Remove engine front cover.
3. Remove water pump retaining bolts, clean gasket surfaces on block and pump. Install new gasket and loosely install water pump bolts.

NOTE: Apply an approved anti-seize compound to the water pump bolts before installation.

4. Position tool J-23564 in gauge hole adjacent to left side of pump, **Fig. 20.**
5. Apply 15 ft. lbs. of torque to water pump as shown in Fig. 21. Tighten water pump bolts while maintaining

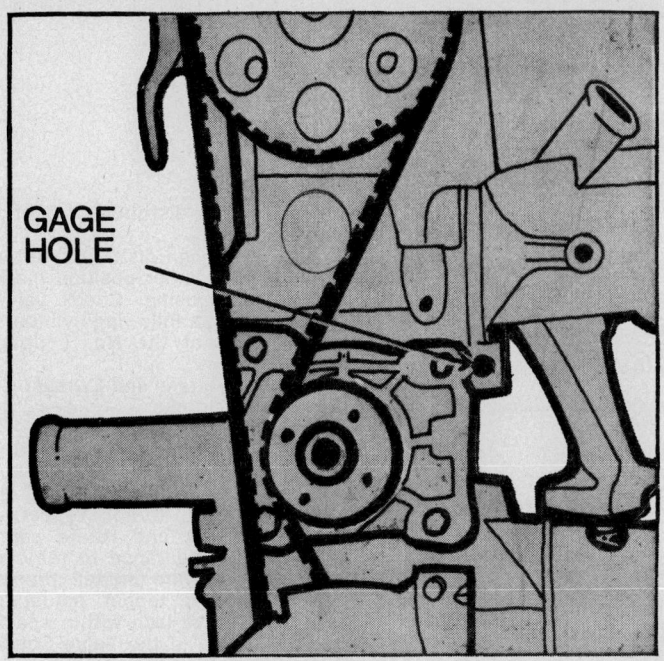

GAGE HOLE

Fig. 20   Tensioning adapter locating hole

Fig. 21   Adjusting timing belt

J-23654

torque on side of pump.

6. Reinstall front cover, fan, extension and fill cooling system.

FUEL PUMP PRESSURE

Year	Engine	Pressure, Lbs.
1974-77	All	3-4½

FUEL PUMP, REPLACE

Removal

1. Disconnect battery ground cable.
2. Disconnect meter and pump wires at rear wiring harness connector.
3. Raise vehicle on hoist and drain fuel tank.
4. Disconnect fuel line hose at gauge unit pick up line.
5. Disconnect tank vent lines to vapor separator.
6. Remove gauge ground wire screw at underbody floorpan.
7. Remove tank straps bolts and lower tank carefully.

Fig. 22   Removing fuel pump and gauge unit

8. Unscrew retaining ring using spanner wrench J-24187, Fig. 22, and remove pump-tank unit assembly.

Replacement

1. Remove flat wire conductor from plastic clip on fuel tube.
2. Squeeze clamp and pull pump straight back about ½ inch.
3. Remove two nuts and lockwashers and conductor wires from pump terminals.
4. Squeeze clamp and pull pump straight back to remove it from tank unit. Take care to prevent bending of circular support bracket.
5. Slide replacement pump through circular support bracket until it rests against rubber coupling. Make sure pump has rubber isolator and saran strainer attached.
6. Attach two conductor wires to pump terminals using lockwashers and nuts being certain flat conductor is attached to terminal located on side away from float arm.
7. Squeeze clamp and push pump into rubber coupling.
8. Replace flat wire conductor in plastic clip on fuel pick up tube.
9. Install unit into tank and replace fuel tank.

4-151 Engine Section

Refer to the "Monza, Skyhawk, Starfire & Sunbird" chapter for service procedures on this engine.

Cosworth Engine Section

ENGINE, REPLACE

1. Remove hood.
2. Disconnect battery positive cable from battery and the ground cable from engine block.
3. Drain cooling system and disconnect hoses from radiator and water pump.
4. Remove fan and spacer, then the radiator shroud and radiator.
5. Disconnect electrical leads from oil pressure switch and water temperature switch, then disconnect wiring harness from block and position aside.
6. Disconnect EFI coolant temperature sensor lead and position aside.
7. Disconnect air cleaner bellows from throttle body and remove air cleaner to fender skirt attaching bolts, then the air cleaner from vehicle.
8. Disconnect accelerator cable from throttle body and position aside.
9. Remove intake manifold to support bolts from underside of manifold, then the manifold attaching bolts and nuts. Position intake manifold with electrical leads and hoses attached, on fender skirt.
10. Disconnect electrical leads from starter solenoid, starter and alternator.
11. Disconnect fuel lines, PCV hose and the electrical leads from distributor.
12. Raise vehicle and disconnect exhaust pipe from manifold.
13. Remove flywheel housing to engine attaching bolts and loosen engine front mount retaining bolts at frame, then lower vehicle.
14. Support transmission with a suitable jack.
15. Install suitable engine lifting equipment and raise engine slightly to relieve weight from engine mounts. Remove engine front mount retaining bolts.
16. Pull engine forward to clear transmission and raise engine slowly. Also, turn engine sideways (engine front toward vehicle left side) to obtain maximum clearance. Remove engine from vehicle.
17. Reverse procedure to install.

CYLINDER HEAD

1. Remove engine front cover and camshaft carrier cover.
2. Remove timing belt and sprockets, then timing belt upper cover and camshaft carrier.
3. Remove intake manifold and position manifold with electrical leads and hoses attached on fender skirt.
4. Disconnect exhaust pipe from header.
5. Remove exhaust header and cylinder head.
6. Reverse procedure to install. Torque cylinder head bolts in sequence, Fig. 1, to 60 ft. lbs.

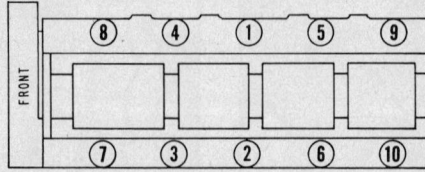

Fig. 1   Cylinder head tightening sequence

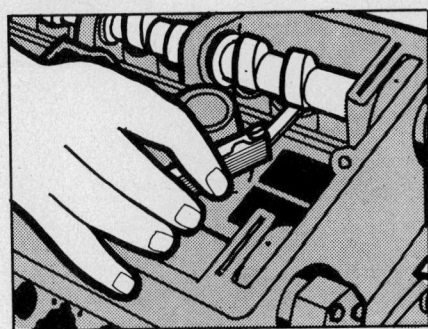

Fig. 2   Checking valve lash

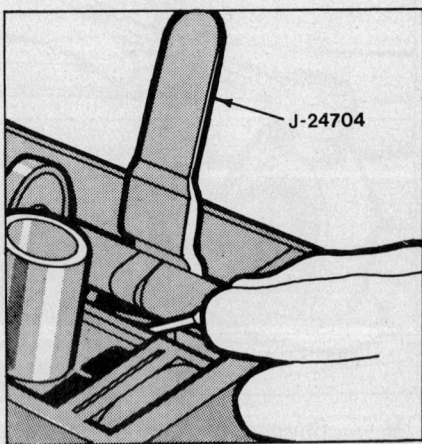

Fig. 3   Adjusting valve lash

VALVES, ADJUST

1. Remove camshaft carrier cover and gasket.
2. Mark distributor housing, with chalk, at plug wire locations Nos. 1 and 4. Then, disconnect plug wires at spark plugs and all other wiring from distri-

butor cap. Remove distributor cap and plug wire assembly.
3. Crank engine to align distributor rotor with the No. 1 cylinder position mark on distributor housing. Check valve lash, Fig. 2, on the following cylinders with the engine at the No. 1 firing position:
No. 1 cylinder—Intake and Exhaust
No. 2 cylinder—Intake
No. 3 cylinder—Exhaust
4. To adjust valve lash, crank engine until camshaft lobe fully depresses tappet of valve being adjusted. Install tool J-24704, Fig. 3, to hold tappet in depressed position and rotate camshaft to provide clearance to remove tappet adjusting shim. Install proper selective thickness tappet adjusting shim to bring valve lash within specifications as listed in the Valve Specifications Chart found in the front of this chapter. Rotate camshaft to fully depress tappet and remove tool J-24704.
5. Crank engine to align distributor rotor with the No. 4 cylinder position mark on distributor housing. Check valve lash on the following cylinders with the engine at the No. 4 firing position:
No. 2 cylinder—Exhaust
No. 3 cylinder—Intake
No. 4 cylinder—Intake and Exhaust
Adjust valve lash as outlined previously.
6. Install distributor cap and spark plug wire assembly, then the camshaft carrier cover gasket and cover.

VALVE ARRANGEMENT

Right side: all intake
Left side: all exhaust

CAMSHAFT CARRIER COVER

1. Raise hood and install hold-open link.
2. Disconnect battery ground cable.
3. Disconnect PCV hose from cover right side.
4. Remove spark plug leads from spark plugs and position aside.
5. Remove screws securing pulse air pipe brackets to cover, then the four hoses from pulse air manifold to pulse air pipe check valves.
6. Remove cover attaching screws, then the cover and gasket.
7. Reverse procedure to install.

CAMSHAFT CARRIER

1. Remove engine front cover, timing belts and camshaft sprockets.
2. Remove timing belt upper cover.
3. Remove camshaft carrier cover as

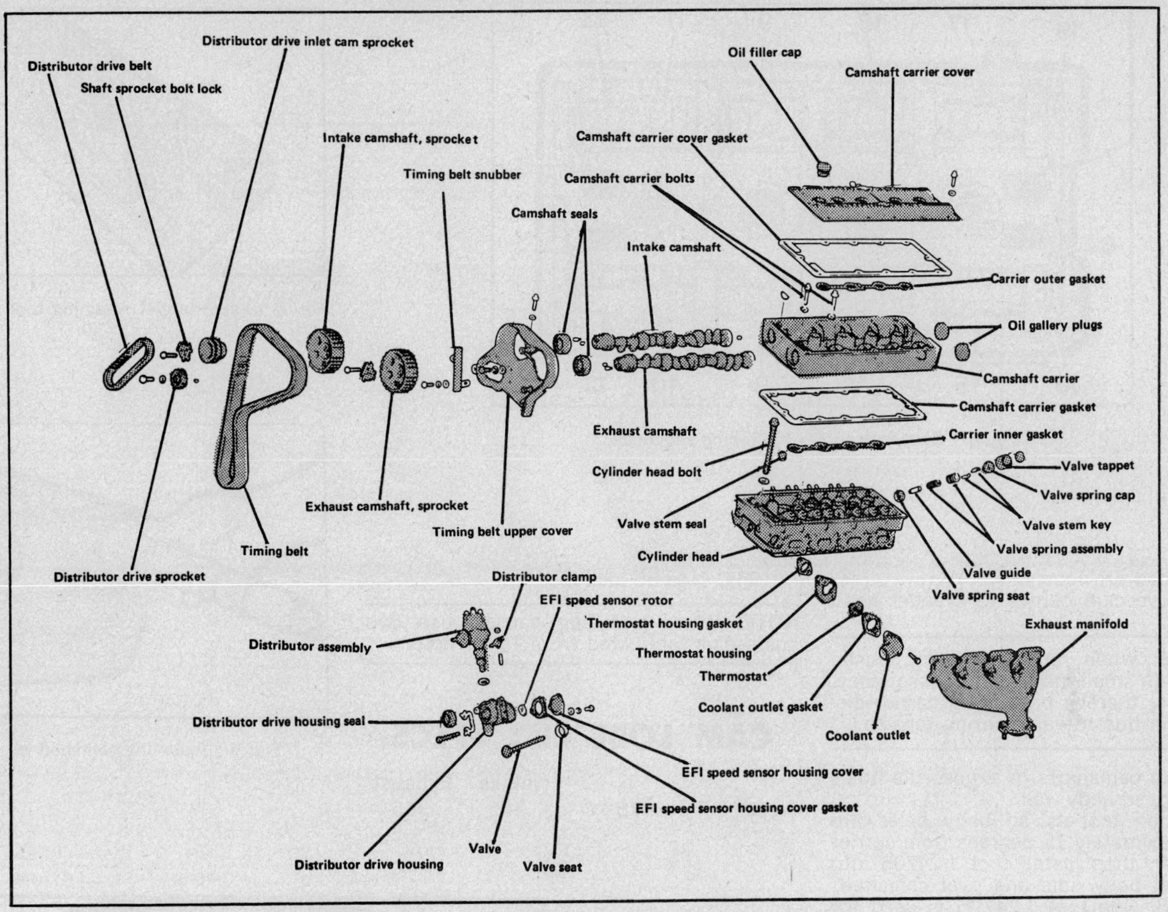

Distributor drive belt

Shaft sprocket bolt lock

Distributor drive inlet cam sprocket

Intake camshaft, sprocket

Timing belt snubber

Camshaft seals

Intake camshaft

Oil filler cap

Camshaft carrier cover

Camshaft carrier cover gasket

Camshaft carrier bolts

Carrier outer gasket

Oil gallery plugs

Camshaft carrier

Camshaft carrier gasket

Carrier inner gasket

Valve tappet

Valve spring cap

Valve stem key

Valve spring assembly

Valve guide

Valve spring seat

Exhaust camshaft

Cylinder head bolt

Valve stem seal

Cylinder head

Exhaust manifold

Exhaust camshaft, sprocket

Timing belt upper cover

Timing belt

Distributor drive sprocket

Distributor assembly

Distributor clamp

EFI speed sensor rotor

Thermostat housing gasket

Thermostat housing

Thermostat

Coolant outlet gasket

Coolant outlet

Distributor drive housing seal

EFI speed sensor housing cover

EFI speed sensor housing cover gasket

Distributor drive housing

Valve

Valve seat

Exploded view of Cosworth engine cylinder head assembly

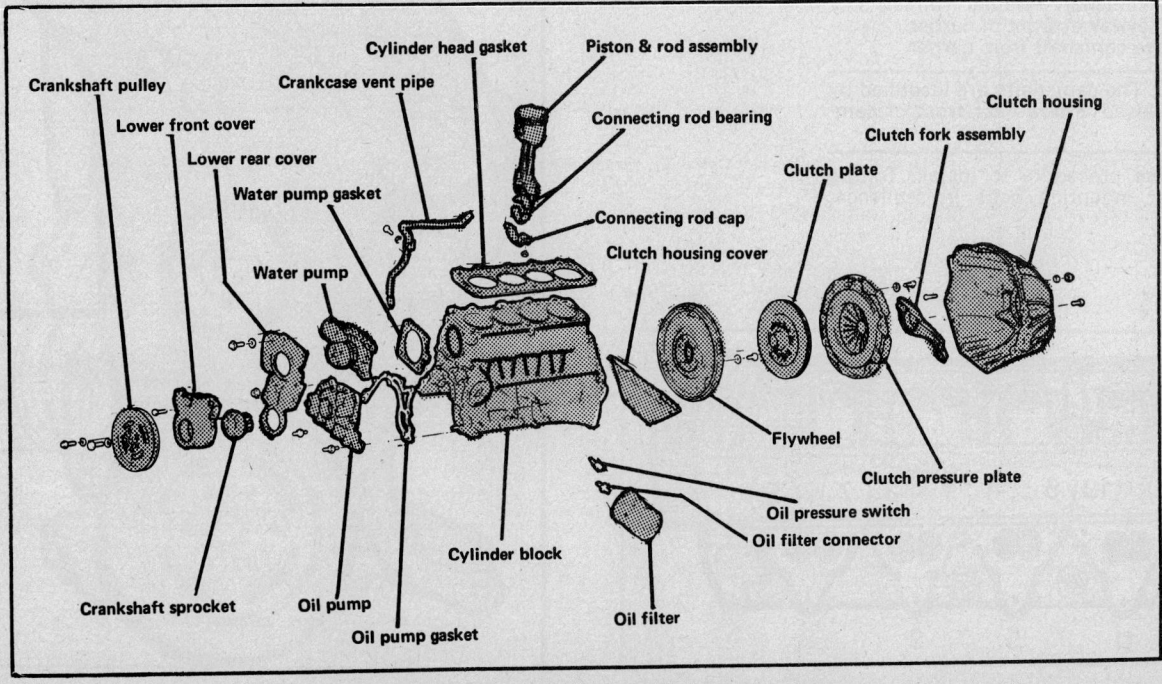

Crankshaft pulley

Lower front cover

Lower rear cover

Water pump gasket

Water pump

Cylinder head gasket

Crankcase vent pipe

Piston & rod assembly

Connecting rod bearing

Connecting rod cap

Clutch housing cover

Clutch plate

Clutch fork assembly

Clutch housing

Flywheel

Clutch pressure plate

Oil pressure switch

Oil filter connector

Cylinder block

Crankshaft sprocket

Oil pump

Oil pump gasket

Oil filter

Exploded view of Cosworth engine cylinder block assembly

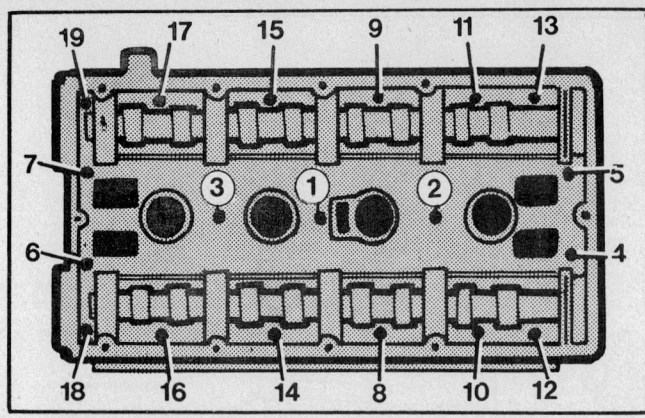

Fig. 4   Camshaft carrier tightening sequence

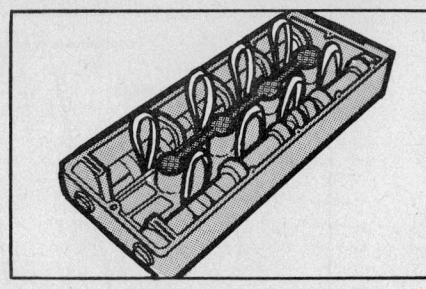

Fig. 5   Valve tappet retaining tool installation

Fig. 6   Installing camshaft oil seals

outlined previously.

4. Remove cam carrier to cylinder head bolts.

   NOTE: When removing bolts, loosen bolts in small increments in sequence, Fig. 4, thereby preventing carrier distortion due to valve spring tension.

5. Rotate camshafts to expose the holes in tapped body wall.
6. Position tappets so body holes are approximately 15 degrees from carrier center, then install tool J-24705 into tappet body hole and over camshaft, Fig. 5. One tool J-24705 is used for each pair of tappets.
7. Lift cam carrier from cylinder head.
8. Remove tools J-24705 from tappets and identify each tappet and adjusting shim to facilitate re-installation in original position.
9. Pry camshaft seal from carrier and remove camshaft retainer (thrust) key from keyway at front of carrier.
10. Remove camshaft from carrier.

    NOTE: The camshafts are identified by cast raised letters near front of camshaft.

11. Reverse procedure to install. Torque carrier mounting bolts in sequence,

Fig. 4, to 65 inch lbs.

NOTE: When installing carrier, use two guide pins fabricated from ¼-20 bolts.

CAM LOBE LIFT SPECS.

		Intake	Exhaust
4-122	1975-76	.355	.355

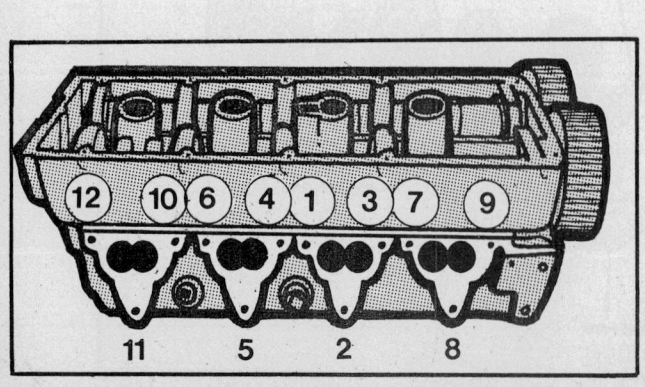

Fig. 7   Intake manifold tightening sequence

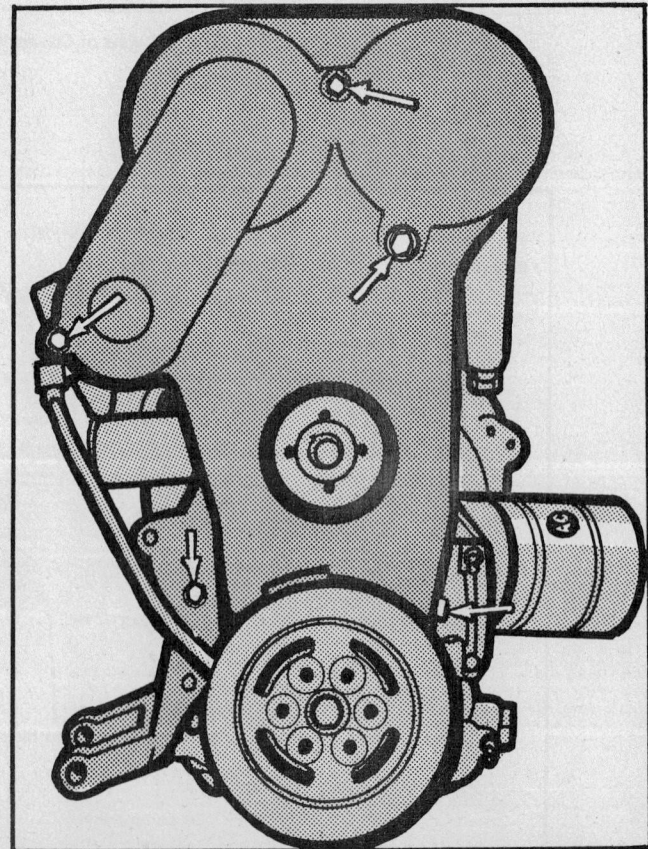

Fig. 8   Engine front cover

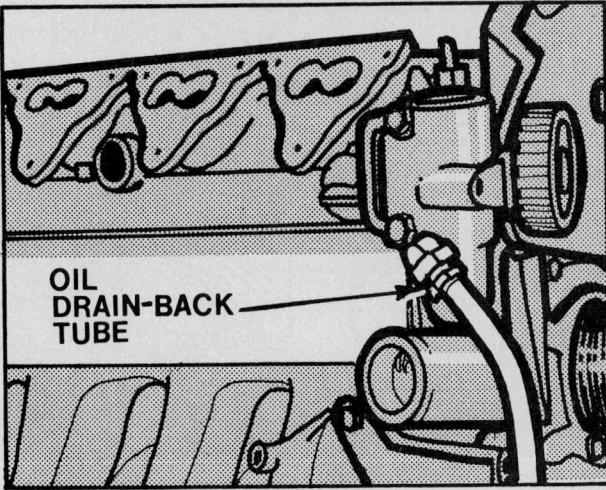

OIL DRAIN-BACK TUBE

Fig. 9   Distributor drive housing oil drain-back tube

J-24777

Fig. 10   Installing distributor drive housing seal

VALVE TIMING

Intake Open Before TDC

4-122   1975-76. 38

VALVE GUIDES

Valves with oversize stems are available in .003 inch oversize for replacement. Ream valve guide bores for oversize valves with tool J-24703.

CAMSHAFT OIL SEAL

1. Remove engine front cover and timing belts as outlined previously.
2. Remove sprocket from cam.
3. Pry seal from cam carrier, using caution not to damage carrier surfaces.
4. Coat outside diameter of new seal with a suitable sealant, then using tool J-24777, Fig. 6, install seal into cam carrier.

INTAKE MANIFOLD, REPLACE

NOTE: When replacing the intake manifold gasket only, it is not necessary to remove the fuel rail and throttle body from the manifold.

1. Raise hood and install hold-open link.
2. Disconnect battery ground cable.
3. Disconnect harness at air temperature sensor, throttle body air enrichment valve, distributor and fuel injectors.
4. Disconnect air cleaner bellows and MAP sensor lines from throttle body.
5. Disconnect fuel lines from fuel rail.
6. Remove bolts securing intake manifold to engine brace.
7. Disconnect accelerator cable from throttle body and position aside.

8. Disconnect PCV hose and position aside, then remove fuel rail and throttle body from intake manifold.
9. Remove manifold retaining nuts and bolts, then the intake manifold.
10. Clean gasket surfaces on cylinder head and intake manifold, then place new gasket over manifold studs on head.
11. Place intake manifold on cylinder head and apply a suitable anti-seize compound to manifold studs and mounting bolts. Install and torque manifold mounting nuts and bolts to 20 ft. lbs., Fig. 7.
12. Loosen lower nuts on intake manifold brace, ensuring brace is free to move. Then, attach brace to underside of manifold and torque bolts to 20 ft. lbs. Tighten lower nuts on manifold brace.
13. Install throttle body and connect accelerator cable.
14. Install fuel rail and fuel injectors, then connect harness to fuel injectors, air temperature sensor, throttle body air enrichment valve and the distributor.
15. Connect fuel inlet and return lines to fuel rail, then install air cleaner bellows on throttle body.
16. Connect MAP sensor lines to throttle body and install PCV hose in camshaft cover.
17. Connect battery ground cable, start engine and check for proper operation.

ENGINE FRONT COVER

1. Raise hood and install hold-open link. Disconnect battery ground cable.
2. Remove fan and spacer.
3. Remove the two lower cover screws and the three, cover attaching bolts, Fig. 8. Lift upward on cover right side and pull forward to clear accessory drive belt and water pump hub. Push

downward on cover left side, disengaging cover from support and lift cover from engine.
4. Reverse procedure to install.

DISTRIBUTOR DRIVE HOUSING

1. Remove engine front cover and distributor drive belt.
2. Remove distributor drive housing oil drain-back tube from carrier, Fig. 9.
3. Disconnect speed sensor terminal from housing rear.
4. Bend bolt lock tabs from bolt head and remove housing to head bolts.
5. Install new housing seal with tool J-24777, Fig. 10.
6. Reverse procedure to install.

TIMING BELT

1. Remove engine front cover.
2. Align timing marks, Fig. 11.
3. Drain cooling system and loosen water pump mounting bolts, thereby relieving timing belt tension.
4. Pry distributor drive belt from drive sprocket with a suitable tool.
5. Remove timing belt lower cover, then the timing belt from camshaft and crankshaft sprockets.
6. If engine was rotated with timing belt off, position No. 1 piston at TDC compression stroke and align all timing marks, Fig. 11.

NOTE: The camshaft sprockets may be aligned by using a straight edge or

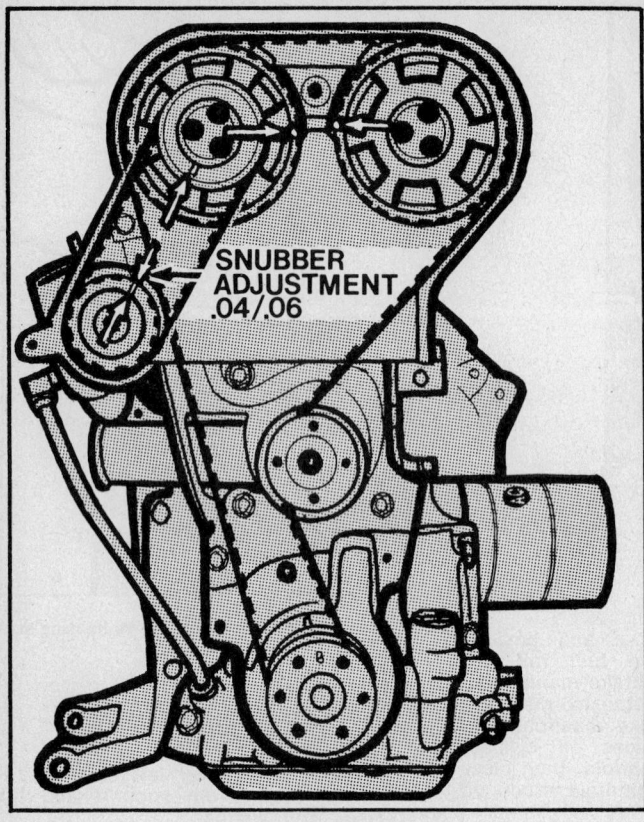

Fig. 11   Camshaft sprocket alignment

Fig. 12   Timing belt lower rear cover

by aligning the small hole in the sprocket tooth space with the "V" notch of the upper sheet metal cover.

7. Slide water pump to extreme left hand position and install timing belt over crankshaft sprocket and water pump pulley. Stretch belt tight and mesh belt with camshaft sprockets, starting with the inlet sprocket.
8. Using tool J-23654, slide water pump to the right and torque two pump attaching bolts to 15 ft. lbs.
9. Rotate engine clockwise two or three revolutions, then rotate engine counter-clockwise approximately 10 degrees to place the long slack side of the belt in tension.
10. Loosen the water pump attaching bolts and apply 15 ft. lbs. of torque to tool J-23654. Then, while holding tool J-23654 at specified torque, torque water pump attaching bolts to 15 ft. lbs.
11. Rotate engine clockwise to position No. 1 piston on TDC, compression stroke, and check timing mark alignment.
12. Install engine front cover.

TIMING BELT LOWER REAR COVER

1. Remove engine front cover and timing belt.
2. Remove alternator bracket to block bolt that passes through the rear cover.
3. Remove nut from oil pump mounting stud.
4. Remove water pump bolts, Fig. 12, and hold water pump in position. Then, remove rear cover and re-install two water pump bolts.
5. Reverse procedure to install.

PISTONS

Oversize pistons are available in .020 inch oversize.

MAIN BEARINGS

Bearings are available in undersizes of .001, .002, .010 and .020 inch.

FUEL PUMP PRESSURE

1975-76 In-tank Unit .... 7-8½ PSI
Chassis-mounted Unit   39 PSI

FUEL PUMPS, REPLACE

In-tank Unit
1. Remove fuel tank as outlined under "Fuel Tank, Replace" procedure.
2. Unscrew retaining ring using spanner wrench J-22554 and remove pump-tank unit assembly.
3. Remove flat wire conductor from plastic clip on fuel tube.
4. Squeeze clamp and pull pump straight back about ½ inch.
5. Remove two nuts and lockwashers and conductor wires from pump terminals.
6. Squeeze clamp and pull pump straight back to remove it from tank unit. Take care to prevent bending of circular support bracket.
7. Slide replacement pump through circular support bracket until it rests against rubber coupling. Make sure pump has rubber isolator and saran strainer attached.
8. Attach two conductor wires to pump terminals using lockwashers and nuts being certain flat conductor is attached to terminal located on side away from float arm.
9. Squeeze clamp and push pump into rubber coupling.
10. Replace flat wire conductor in plastic clip on fuel pick up tube.
11. Install unit into tank.

Cosworth Vega Chassis-Mounted Unit
1. Disconnect battery ground cable and raise vehicle.
2. Disconnect fuel lines from pump.
3. Remove two shield screws and the cable strap securing electrical harness to pump assembly.
4. Disconnect electrical connectors from pump and remove pump.
5. Reverse procedure to install.

Clutch & Transmission Section

CLUTCH PEDAL, ADJUST

Initial adjustment after clutch and/or cable replacement is made at two points, at the ball stud and the lower end of the cable.

1. Ball stud adjustment is made before attaching the cable as follows: using gauge J-23644, place it so flat end is against the front face of the clutch housing and the hooked end is located at the point of cable attachment on the fork, Fig. 1.
2. Turn ball stud inward until clutch release bearing lightly contacts the clutch spring levers, then install the lock nut and tighten being careful not to change the adjustment. Remove the gauge by pulling outward at the housing end.
3. To adjust the cable, place it through the hole in the fork and pull it until the clutch pedal is firmly against the rubber bumper.
4. Push the clutch fork forward until the throwout bearing lightly contacts the clutch spring levers, then screw the lock pin on the cable until it bottoms out on the fork. Turn it ¼ additional clockwise revolution, set pin into groove in the fork and attach return spring. This procedure will produce .90″ lash at the pedal. Adjustment for normal clutch wear is accomplished by loosening the lock nut and by turning the clutch fork ball stud counterclockwise until .90″ of free play is obtained at the pedal.

CLUTCH REPLACE

1. Remove transmission.

Fig. 1 Clutch adjusting gauge in place

2. Remove clutch fork cover then disconnect clutch return spring and control cable from clutch fork.
3. Remove flywheel housing lower cover and flywheel housing, Fig. 2.
4. Remove release bearing from the clutch fork and sleeve by sliding lever off ball stud and against spring force. If ball stud is to be replaced, remove cap, lock nut and stud from housing.
5. Make sure alignment marks on clutch assembly and flywheel are distinguishable.
6. Loosen clutch cover to flywheel bolts one turn at a time until spring pressure is released, to avoid bending the clutch cover flange.
7. Support the pressure plate and cover assembly while removing bolts and clutch assembly.

NOTE: Do not disassemble the clutch cover, spring and pressure plate for repairs. If defective replace complete assembly.

8. Reverse procedure to install making sure to index alignment marks.
9. After installing crossmember, loosely install retaining bolts, then the crossmember to transmission mount bolts. Tighten all retaining bolts to specifications and remove the engine support.

CAUTION: Check position of engine in front mounts and realign as necessary.

LINKAGE ADJUST

1974-77 3 & 4 Speed Exc. 70mm (Brazil)

1. Place ignition switch in "Off" position.
2. Raise vehicle and loosen shift rod nuts at swivels.
3. Position shift levers in neutral.
4. Place shift control in neutral position, align control levers and install gauge pin into levers and brackets.
5. On 3 speed models, tighten 1st-Rev. shift rod nut against swivel, then tighten 2-3 shift rod nut against swivel, torque nuts to 120 in. lbs.
6. On 4 speed models, tighten 1-2 shift rod nut against swivel, then tighten 3-4 shift rod nut against swivel, torque nuts to 120 in. lbs.
7. On 4 speed models, torque reverse shift rod nut to 120 in. lbs.
8. On all models, remove gauge pin and check linkage for operation.

TRANSMISSION, REPLACE

3 & 4 Speed Exc. 70mm (Brazil)

1. Raise vehicle on a hoist and drain lubricant.
2. On 1976-77 models, remove torque arm, referring to the "Rear Suspension" section. On all models, remove the propeller shaft.
3. Disconnect speedo cable, TCS switch and back-up lamp switch.
4. Disconnect transmission control rod and lever assemblies from shifter shafts. Tie rods up out of way.
5. Remove crossmember to transmission mount bolts.
6. Support engine with an appropriate jack stand and remove crossmember to frame bolts and remove crossmember.
7. Remove transmission to clutch housing upper retaining bolts and install guide pins in holes.
8. Remove lower bolts, then slide transmission rearward and remove from vehicle.

NOTE: Inspect throwout bearing support gasket located beneath lip of support. If necessary, replace gasket before installing transmission.

4 Speed 70mm (Brazil)

1. Push shift lever boot down and loosen

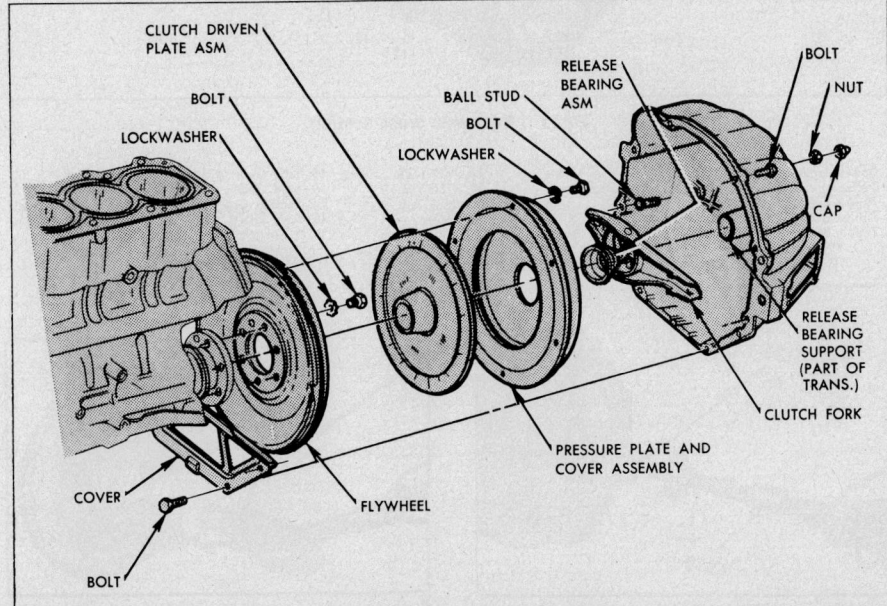

Fig. 2 1974-77 Clutch & housing

lock nut, remove upper portion of shift lever.
2. Remove console, retainer and boot, then remove shift control from extension housing.
3. Raise vehicle and drain lubricant.
4. Remove torque arm, referring to the "Rear Suspension" section.
5. Remove propeller shaft, then disconnect speedometer cable and back-up light switch.
6. Disconnect clutch return spring and cable at fork.
7. Remove transmission to crossmember bolts.

8. Remove converter bracket and damper, if equipped.
9. Remove crossmember to frame bolts, support transmission, then remove crossmember.
10. Remove clutch housing to engine attaching bolts, slide transmission and clutch housing rearward and remove from vehicle.

5 Speed Unit
1. Remove boot retainer, then slide boot up on control lever.
2. Remove foam insulator, then remove four control lever attaching bolts and

control lever.
3. Raise vehicle and remove propeller shaft.
4. Remove damper assembly, converter bracket and torque arm bracket.
5. Disconnect speedometer cable and back-up light switch wire connector.
6. Support transmission using a suitable jack.
7. Remove transmission support, then remove transmission to clutch housing attaching bolts and slide exhaust bracket forward.
8. Slide transmission rearward and remove from vehicle.

Rear Axle, Propeller Shaft & Brakes

REAR AXLE
Description

The rear axle, Fig. 1, is a semi-floating type consisting of a cast carrier and large bosses on each end into which two welded steel tubes are fitted. The carrier contains an overhung hypoid pinion and ring gear. The differential is a two pinion arrangement.

The overhung hypoid drive pinion is supported by two preloaded tapered roller bearings. The pinion shaft is sealed by means of a molded, spring loaded, rubber seal. The seal is mounted on the pinion shaft flange which is splined and bolts to the hypoid pinion shaft.

The ring gear is bolted to a one piece differential case and is supported by two preloaded tapered roller bearings.

Removal

1976-77
1. Support vehicle at frame and using a suitable jack support axle housing.
2. Remove wheels, brake drums and axle shafts.
3. Disconnect brake lines from axle tube clips and remove bolt securing brake line junction block to rear axle housing.

NOTE: Do not disconnect brake lines from wheel cylinders or junction block.

4. Remove brake backing plates and secure backing plates to frame.
5. Remove parking brake cable adjusting nuts at equalizer, pull center cable rearward and disconnect two rear cables from body connectors.

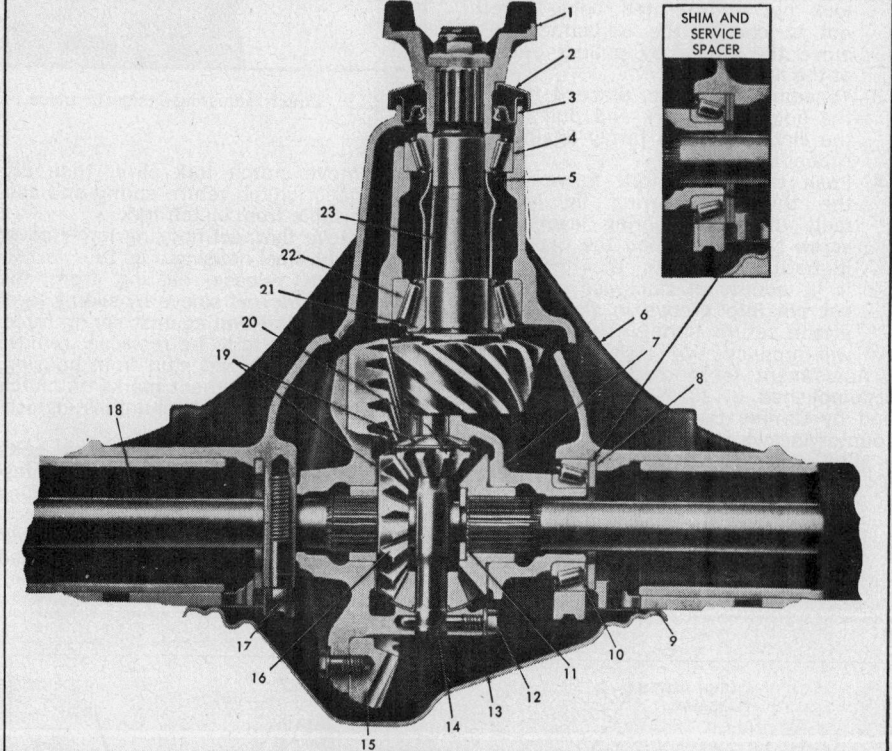

Fig. 1   Rear axle cross section

1. Companion Flange	6. Differential Carrier	11. "C" Lock	15. Ring Gear	20. Differential Pinion
2. Deflector	7. Differential Case	12. Pinion Shaft Lock Bolt	16. Side Gear	21. Shim
3. Pinion Oil Seal	8. Shim	13. Cover	17. Bearing Cap	22. Pinion Rear Bearing
4. Pinion Front Bearing	9. Gasket	14. Pinion Shaft	18. Axle Shaft	23. Drive Pinion
5. Pinion Bearing Spacer	10. Differential Bearing		19. Thrust Washer	

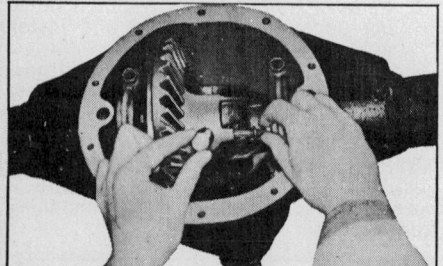

Fig. 2   Differential pinion shaft removal

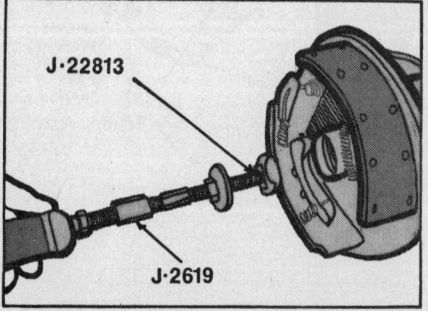

Fig. 3   Removing wheel bearing and seal

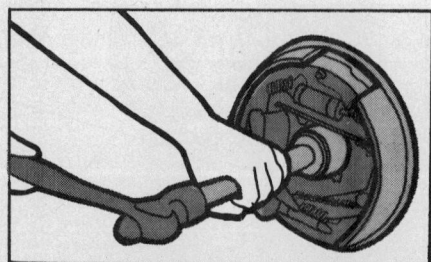

Fig. 4   Installation seal and wheel bearing

6. Disconnect rear brake hose at floor pan and cap ends of hose and line.
7. Disconnect shock absorber from rear axle.
8. Disconnect track rod, then slowly lower axle until all spring tension is relieved and pry springs from axle housing pads.
9. Disconnect propeller shaft and torque arm and position aside.

NOTE: Support axle at companion flange to prevent housing from rotating.

10. Remove lower control arm attaching bolts from axle housing.
11. Remove support at companion flange, then the axle assembly.

1974-75

1. Raise vehicle on a hoist.
2. Place adjustable lifting device under axle.
3. Disconnect rear shock absorbers from axle and remove propeller shaft.
4. Disconnect upper control arm from axle and remove both rear wheels.
5. Remove right and left brake drums.
6. Disconnect brake lines from clips on axle tubes.
7. Remove differential cover and drain lubricant.
8. Unscrew differential lock screw, remove pinion shaft and axle shaft "C" locks. Reinstall pinion shaft and tighten lock screw to retain differential gears, Fig. 2.
9. Remove both axle shafts.
10. Remove brake backing plate retaining nuts and remove backing plates, with shoes and brake lines attached, and wire to frame.
11. Remove right and left lower control arm pivot bolts at axle.
12. Lower axle assembly slowly until coil spring tension is released, then remove axle.

AXLE SHAFT

1. Raise vehicle on a hoist and remove wheel and tire assembly and brake drum.
2. Drain lubricant from axle by removing carrier cover.
3. Unscrew pinion shaft lock screw and remove pinion shaft, Fig. 2.
4. Push flanged end of axle shaft toward center of car and remove "C" lock from button end of shaft.
5. Remove axle shaft from housing being careful not to damage seal.

Oil Seal &/or Bearing Replacement

1. If replacing seal only, remove the seal by using the button end of axle shaft. Insert the button end of shaft behind the steel case of the seal and pry seal out of bore being careful not to damage housing.
2. If replacing bearings, insert tool J-22813 into bore so tool head grasps behind bearing, Fig. 3. Slide washer against seal, or bearing, and turn nut against washer. Attach slide hammer J-2619 and remove bearing.
3. Pack cavity between seal lips with a high melting point wheel bearing lubricant. Position seal on tool J-21491 and position seal in axle

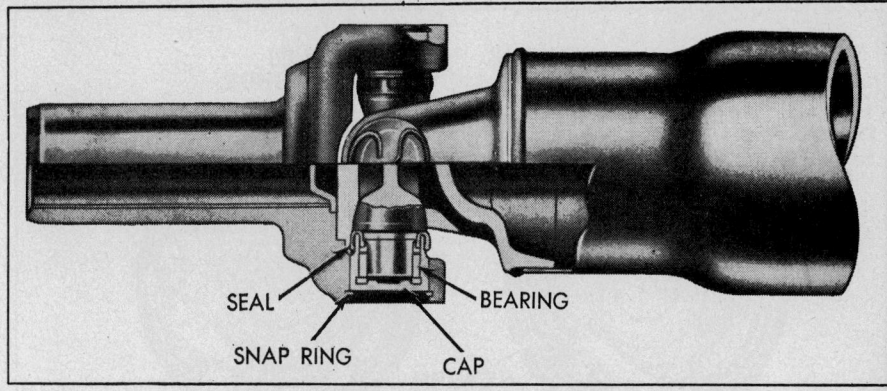

SEAL — BEARING
SNAP RING — CAP

Fig. 5 Propeller shaft cross section

housing bore, tap seal in bore just below end of housing, Fig. 4.

PROPELLER SHAFT

1. Raise vehicle on a hoist.
2. On 1976-77 models, remove torque arm bolts at rear axle, then referring to the "Rear Suspension" section, loosen attaching bolt at transmission and swing arm away.
3. On all models mark relationship of shaft to companion flange and disconnect the rear universal joint by removing trunnion bearing "U" bolts. Tape bearing cups to trunnion to prevent dropping and loss of bearing rollers.
4. Withdraw propeller shaft front yoke from transmission.
5. When installing, be sure to align marks made in removal to prevent driveline vibration.

BRAKE ADJUSTMENTS

1976-77

These brakes, Fig. 6A, have self-adjusting shoe mechanisms that assure correct lining-to-drum clearances at all times. The automatic adjusters operate only when the brakes are applied as the car is moving rearward.

Although the brakes are self-adjusting, an initial adjustment is necessary after the brake shoes have been relined or replaced, or when the length of the adjusting screw has been changed during some other service operation.

Frequent usage of an automatic transmission forward range to halt reverse vehicle motion may prevent to automatic adjusters from functioning, thereby inducing low pedal heights. Should low pedal heights be encountered, it is recommended that numerous forward and reverse stops be made until satisfactory pedal height is obtained.

NOTE

If a low pedal condition cannot be corrected by making numerous reverse stops (provided the hydraulic system is free of air) it indicates that the self-adjusting mechanism is not functioning. Therefore

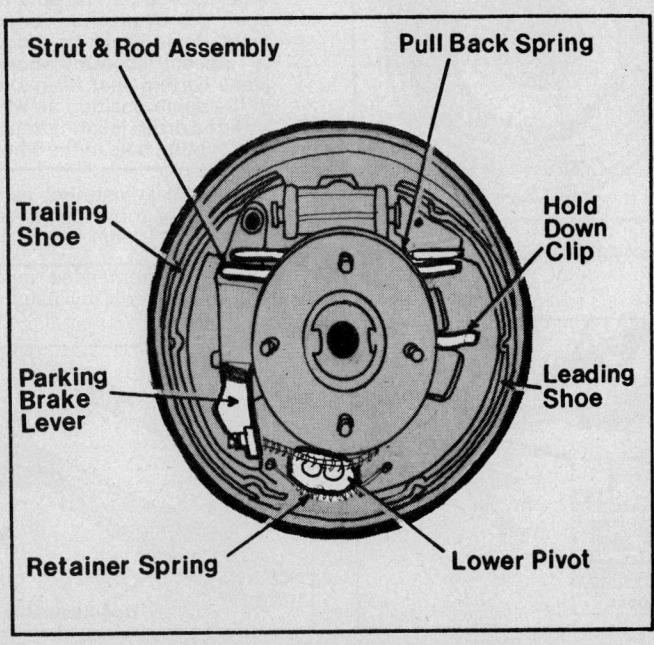

Strut & Rod Assembly   Pull Back Spring
Trailing Shoe   Hold Down Clip
Parking Brake Lever   Leading Shoe
Retainer Spring   Lower Pivot

Fig. 6 Rear brake assembly. 1974-75

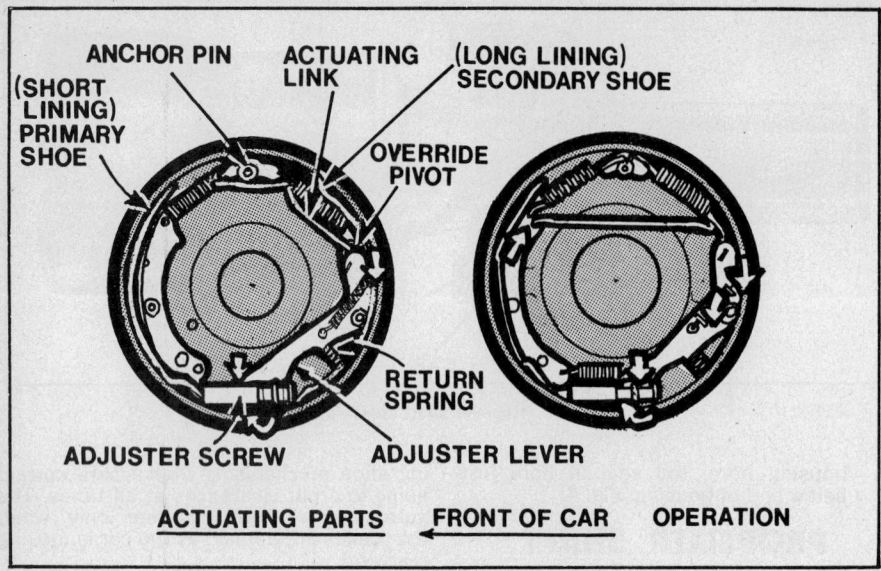

Fig. 6A   Self-adjusting brakes. 1976-77

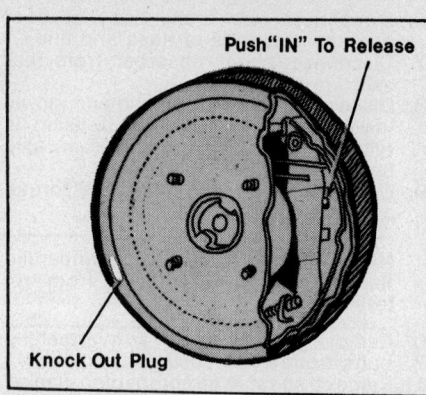

Fig. 7   Drum knock out provision. 1974-75

it will be necessary to remove the brake drum, clean, free up and lubricate the adjusting mechanism. Then adjust the brakes, being sure the parking brake is fully released.

Adjustment

A lanced "knock out" area is provided in the web of the brake drum for servicing

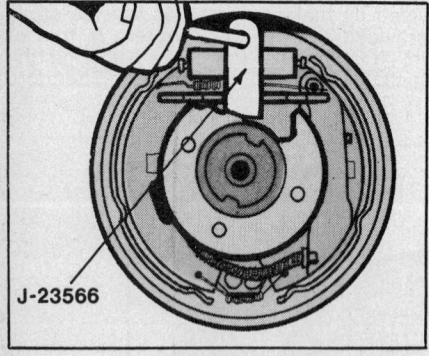

Fig. 8   Releasing adjuster on car. 1974-75

purposes in the event retracting of the brake shoes is required in order to remove the drum.

1. With brake drum off, disengage the actuator from the star wheel and rotate the star wheel by spinning or turning with a screwdriver.
2. Using the brake drum as an adjustment fixture, turn the star wheel until the drum slides over the brake shoes with a slide drag.
3. Turn the star wheel 1¼ turns to retract the brake shoes. This will allow sufficient lining-to-drum clearance so final adjustment may be made.
4. Install drum and wheel.

NOTE: If lanced area in brake drum was knocked out, be sure all metal has been removed from brake compartment. Install new hole cover in drum to prevent contamination of brakes. Make certain that drums are installed in the same position as when removed with the drum locating tang in line with the locating hole in the wheel hub.

5. Make final adjustment by driving and stopping in forward and reverse until satisfactory pedal height is obtained.

NOTE: The recommended method of adjusting the brakes is by using a Drum-to-

Brake Shoe Clearance Guage to check the diameter of the brake drum inner surface. Turn the tool to the opposite side and fit over the brake shoes by turning the star wheel until the gauge just slides over the linings. Rotate the gauge around the brake shoe lining surface to assure proper clearance.

1974-75

Drum brakes, Fig. 6, are used on the rear wheels. Rear brake adjustment is not automatic. Adjustment takes place, if needed, only when the parking brake is applied. When the parking brake is applied, the strut is pushed against the front shoe and the rod is pulled against the rear shoe. As the shoes spread, a spring lock mounted within the strut and rod assembly, allows the strut and rod assembly

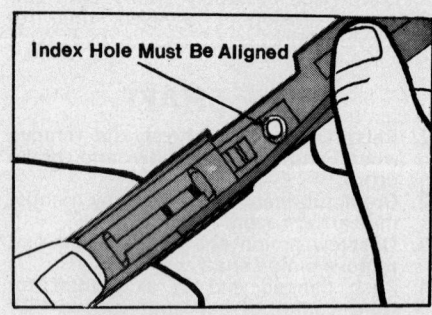

Fig. 11   Installing rod assembly. 1974-75

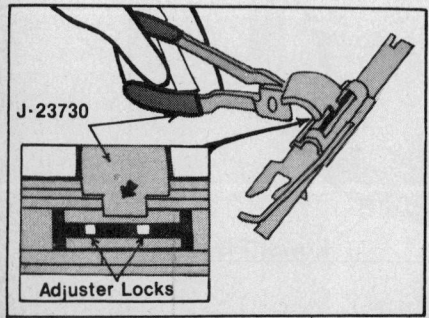

Fig. 9   Releasing adjuster off car. 1974-75

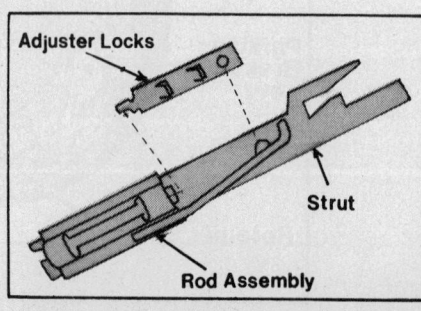

Fig. 10   Adjuster lock positioning. 1974-75

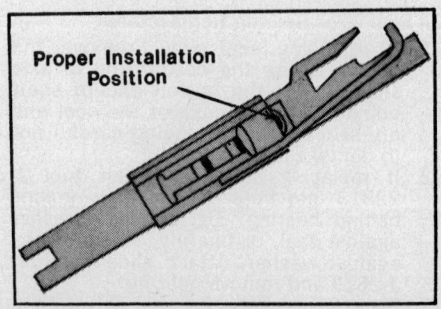

Fig. 12   Adjuster position for new shoes. 1974-75

to lengthen. When the parking brake is released, the rod connected to the rear shoe is relaxed and brake shoe pressure on the drum is released providing running clearance. Clearance is obtained by the difference in the diameter of the rod and the diameter of the hole in the rear shoe.

NOTE: If the brake drum cannot be removed, it will be necessary to release the brake adjuster. To gain access to the adjuster, knock out the lanced area in web of brake drum, Fig. 7, using a chisel or similar tool. Release the rod from the trailing shoe by pushing in on the rod until it is clear of the shoe. The pull back spring will then pull the shoes toward each other and the drum may be removed.

CAUTION: After knocking out the lanced area, be sure to remove the piece of metal from inside the drum.

Installation

When installing new brake shoes the adjuster assembly must be released and repositioned. To release adjuster on vehicle, position tool J-23566, Fig. 8. The tool releases the adjuster assembly by unseating the clips from the rod assembly. Both clips must be unseated at the same time.

To release adjuster off vehicle, position tool J-23730 so that tang of tool rests on flat portion of locks (between lock tangs) Fig. 9, then press down on adjuster locks. Work rod assembly free of adjuster locks, then when both adjuster tangs are clear of rod assembly, slide rod off lever. Sub-assemble rod assembly to strut making certain that index hole is lined up and seated, Fig. 10, then slide rod assembly over adjuster locks, Fig. 11, until both locks are positioned as shown in Fig. 12. Note that adjuster lock index is about $\frac{1}{2}$ covered by rod assembly.

PARKING BRAKE, ADJUST

1. Raise vehicle and on 1975 Cosworth Vega and all 1976-77 models, remove propeller shaft.
2. Apply parking brake one notch from fully released position and raise hoist.
3. Loosen equalizer check nut and tighten the adjusting nut until a slight drag is felt when rear wheels are rotated.
4. Tighten check nut securely.
5. Release parking brake and rotate rear wheels. No drag should be present.

MASTER CYLINDER, REPLACE

1. Disconnect cylinder push rod from brake pedal.
2. Disconnect brake lines from two outlets on cylinder and cover ends of lines to prevent entry of dirt.
3. Unfasten and remove cylinder from dash.

POWER BRAKE UNIT

1975-77

1. Remove the vacuum hose from check valve and then remove the master cylinder retaining nuts.
2. Remove the bolt securing the brake pipe distributor and switch assembly to fender skirt.
3. Pull master cylinder forward until it just clears mounting studs and move aside. Support cylinder to avoid stress on hydraulic lines.
4. Remove power unit to dash nuts.
5. Remove brake pedal pushrod retainer and disconnect push rod from pin.
6. Remove power unit from vehicle.

Rear Suspension

DESCRIPTION

1975 Cosworth Vega & All 1976-77 Models

This rear suspension system does not use upper control arms, instead, it uses a torque arm mounted rigidly to the differential housing at the rear and to the transmission through a rubber bushing or insulator at the front. This torque arm prevents axle housing rotation caused by starting and stopping. Along with the torque arm a track rod is used to connect the axle housing to the body to control side sway and a rear stabilizer shaft is used for improved handling, Fig. 1.

1974-75 Exc. Cosworth Vega

The rear suspension system on these models use two upper and two lower control arms mounted between the axle tube

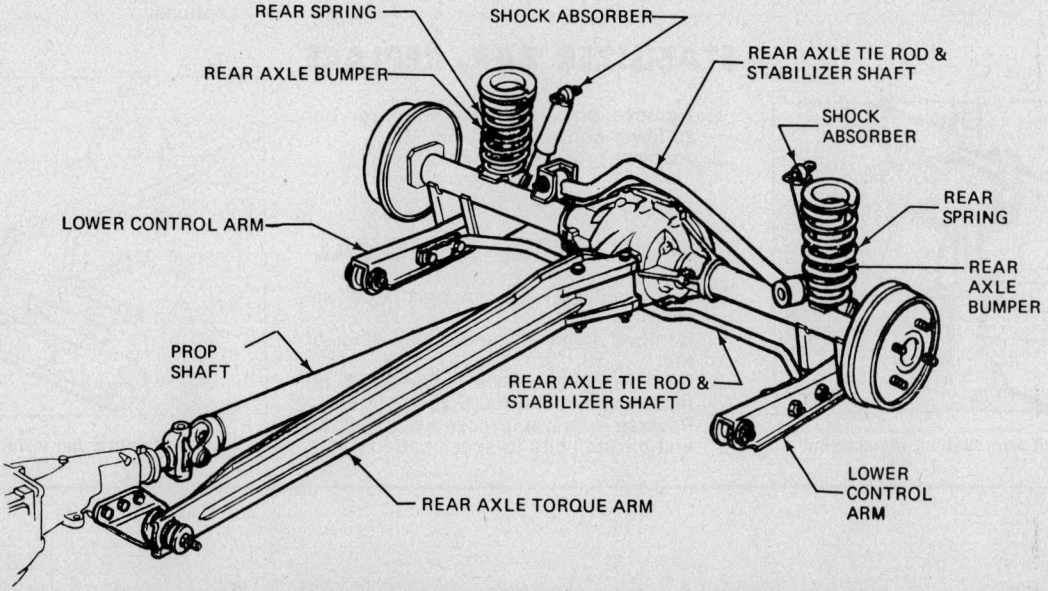

Fig. 1   Rear suspension. 1975 Cosworth Vega & all 1976-77 models (Typical)

and frame, Fig. 2. The upper control arms are shorter than the lower arm, thereby allowing the axle tube assembly to "Rock" or tilt forward on compression. The upper control arms control drive forces, side sway and pinion nose angle. The lower control arms maintain fore and aft relationship of the axle assembly to the chassis.

SHOCK ABSORBER, REPLACE

1. With the rear axle supported properly disconnect shock absorber from upper and lower mounting, Figs. 1 and 2.

   NOTE: Use a wrench to hold lower mounting stud from turning.

2. Reverse procedure to install.

COIL SPRING, REPLACE

1. Support vehicle at frame and rear axle with a suitable jack.
2. Disconnect shock absorbers from lower mountings.
3. Lower rear axle until springs can be removed.

   NOTE: Do not stretch or damage brake hoses.

4. Reverse procedure to install.

CONTROL ARMS & BUSHINGS, REPLACE

NOTE: Replace control arms one at a time to prevent axle misalignment, making installation difficult.

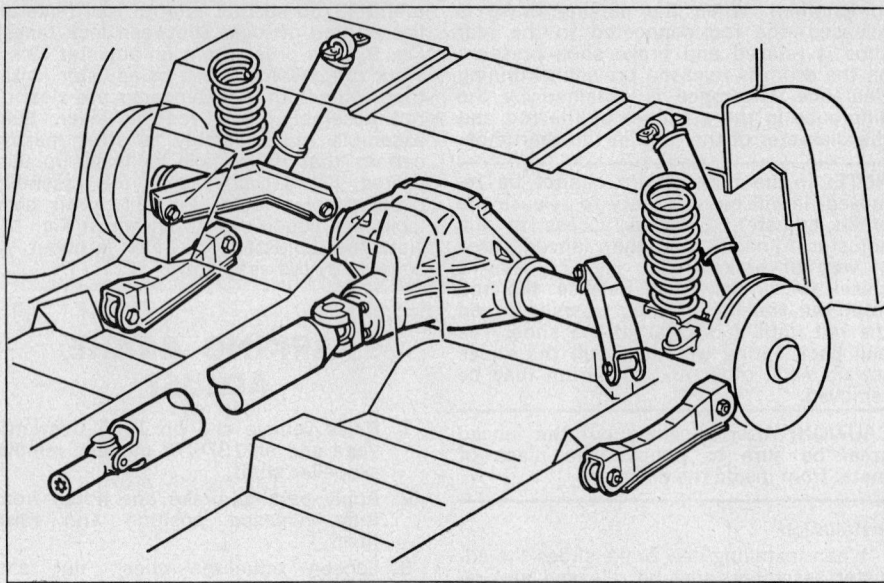

Fig. 2   Rear Suspension. 1974-75

Upper Control Arms, 1974-75

1. Support vehicle at rear axle.
2. Remove control arm front and rear mount bolts.
3. Replace bushings as necessary, Fig. 3.
4. Reverse procedure to install. Control arm bolts must be tightened with vehicle at curb height.

Lower Control Arms, 1974-77

1. Support vehicle at rear axle.
2. Disconnect stabilizer bar, if used, from lower arms.
3. Remove control arm front and rear mount bolts.
4. Replace bushings as necessary, Fig. 3.
5. Reverse procedure to install. Control arm bolts must be tightened with vehicle at curb height.

STABILIZER BAR, REPLACE

1. Remove bolts securing stabilizer bar to lower control arms, Fig. 4.
2. Reverse procedure to install.

TRACK ROD, REMOVAL

1. Raise vehicle and support axle assembly.
2. Remove bolts at underbody end of rod.
3. Remove bolts at axle bracket and remove track rod, Figs. 5 and 6.
4. Reverse removal procedure to install and torque bolts to specifications.

TORQUE ARM, REPLACE

1. Raise vehicle by axle assembly and support underbody with jackstands.
2. Disconnect mounting bracket from transmission, then remove through bolt and separate bracket from torque arm.
3. Remove bolts attaching torque arm to rear axle housing, then remove torque arm, Figs. 7, 8 and 9.
4. To replace bushing, use an arbor press and tool J-25317-2 as a receiver and press bushing out of arm, then position new bushing in torque arm with bushing sleeve aligned with the length of the torque arm. Press bushing into place using tool J-25317-1 over bushing to properly locate bushing in arm.
5. Reverse removal procedure to install and torque nuts and bolts to specifications.

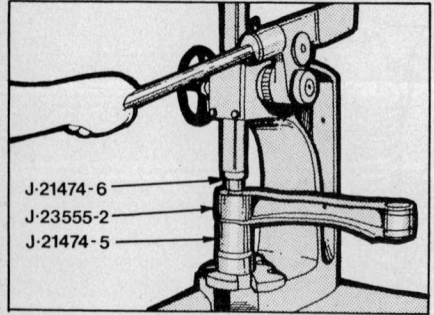

Fig. 3   Control arm bushing replacement

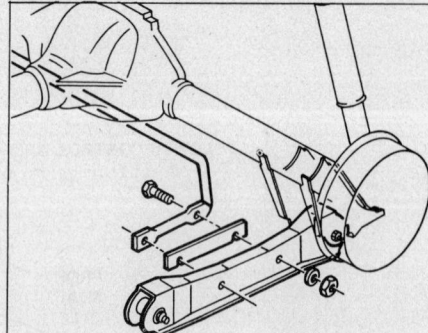

Fig. 4   Stabilizer bar installation. 1974-77

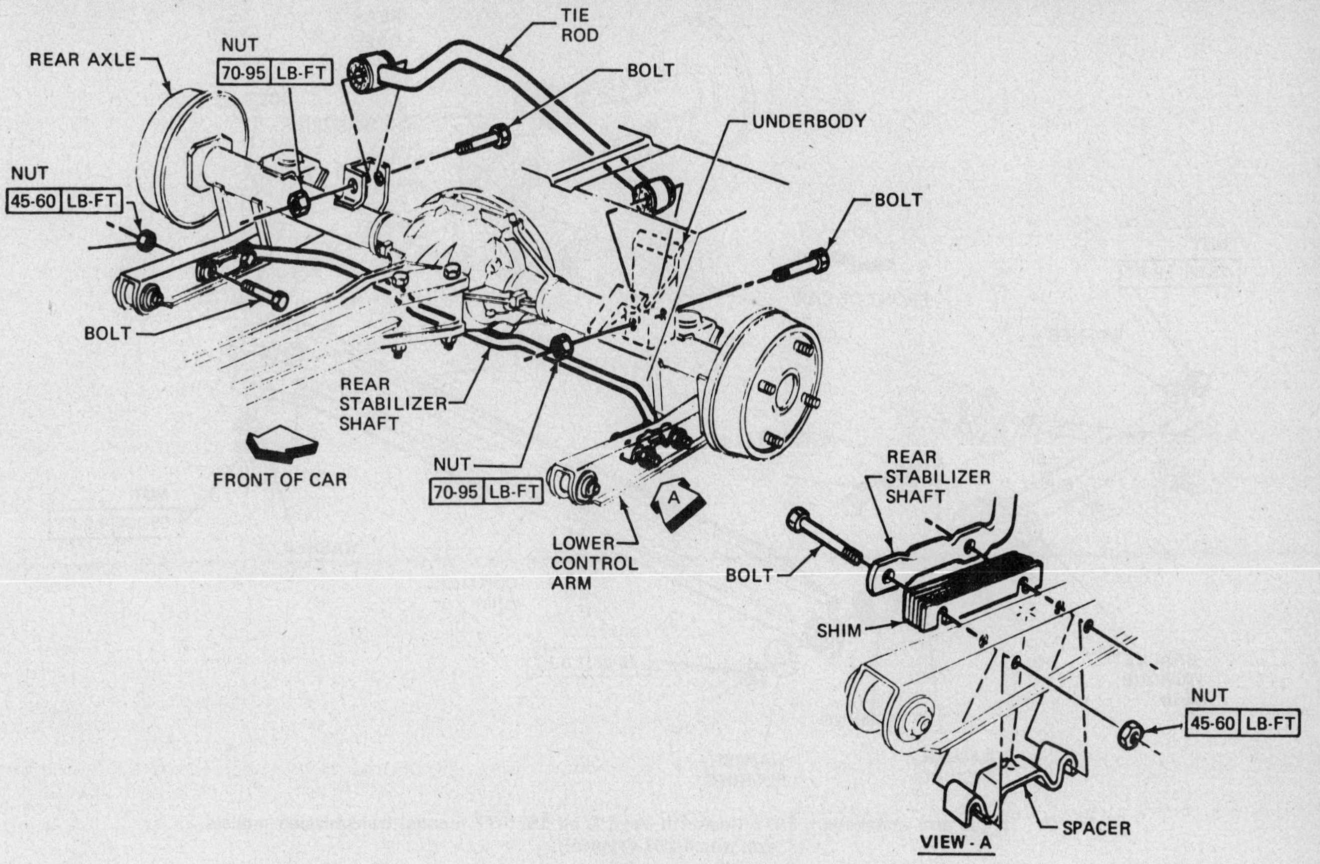

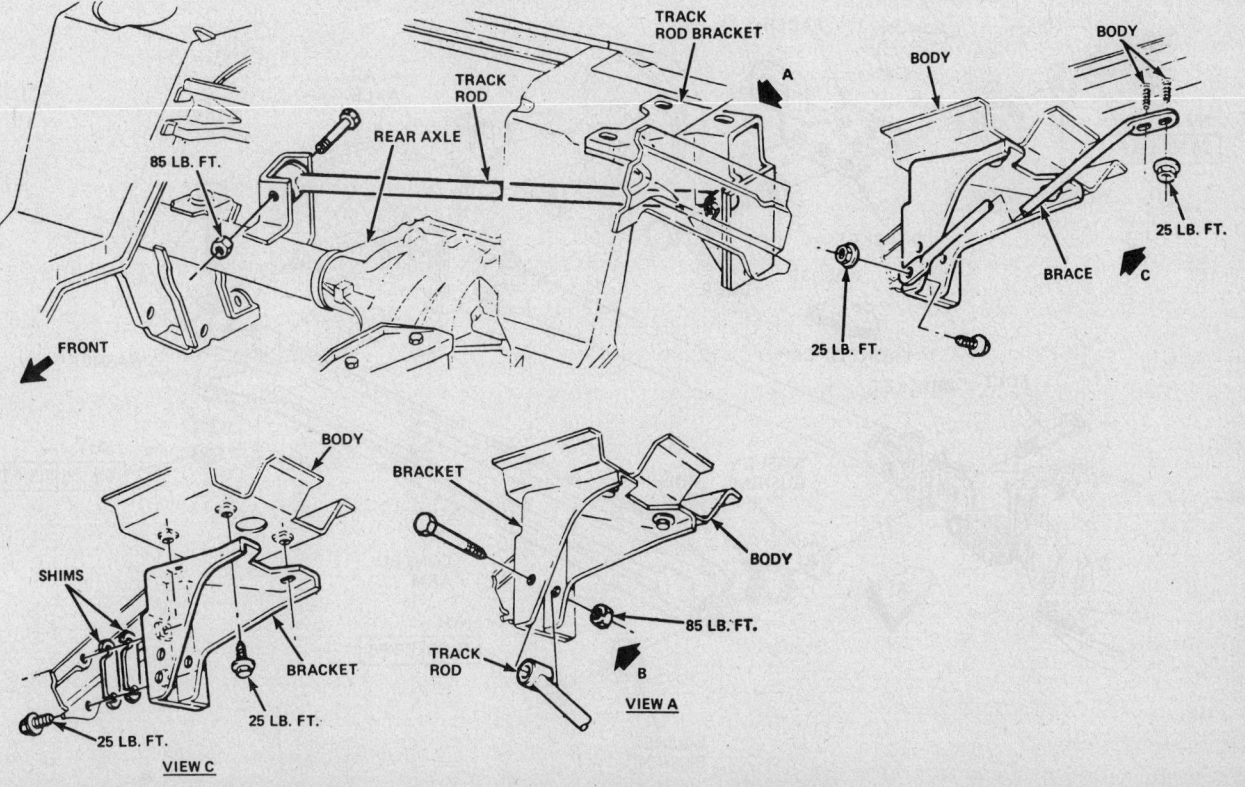

**Fig. 5 Track rod & stabilizer bar installation. 1975 Cosworth Vega & all 1976 models
Stabilizer bar installation. 1977 models**

Fig. 6 Track rod installation. 1977 models

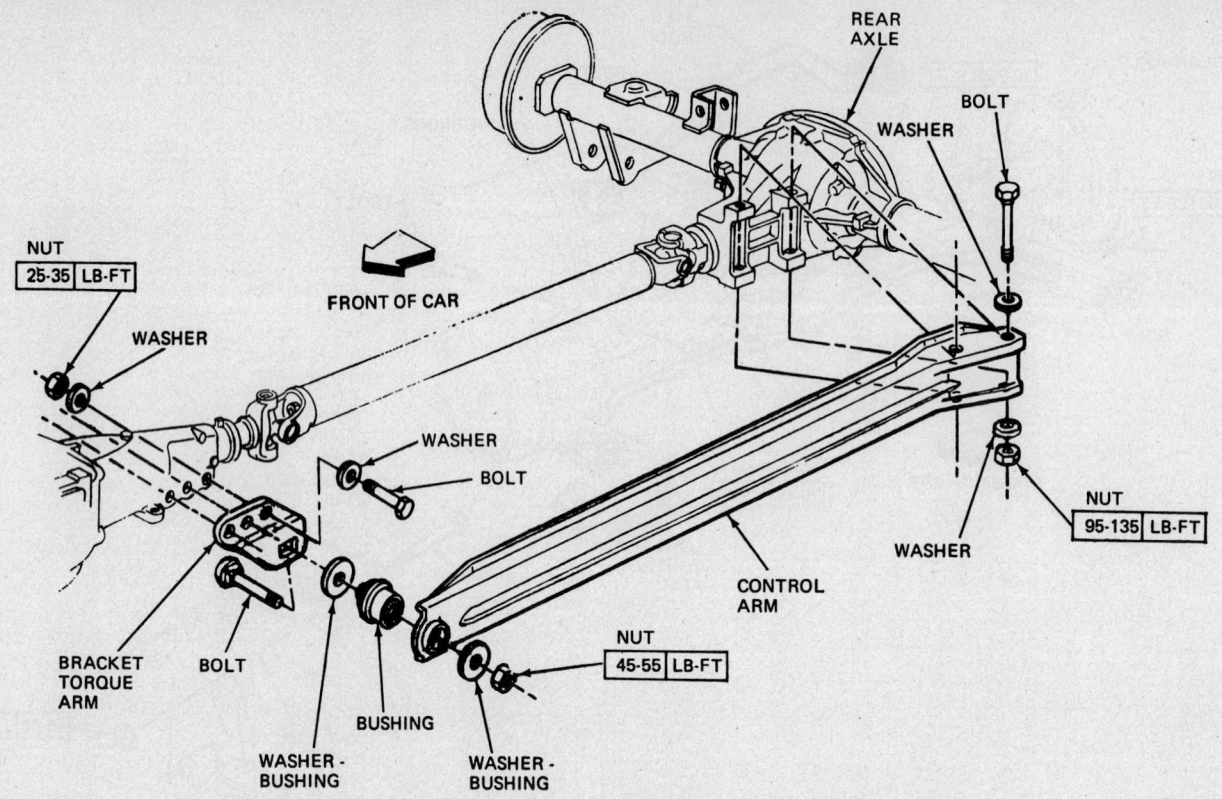

Fig. 7 Torque arm installation. 1975 Cosworth Vega & all 1976-77 manual transmission models exc. with 4-151 (Typical)

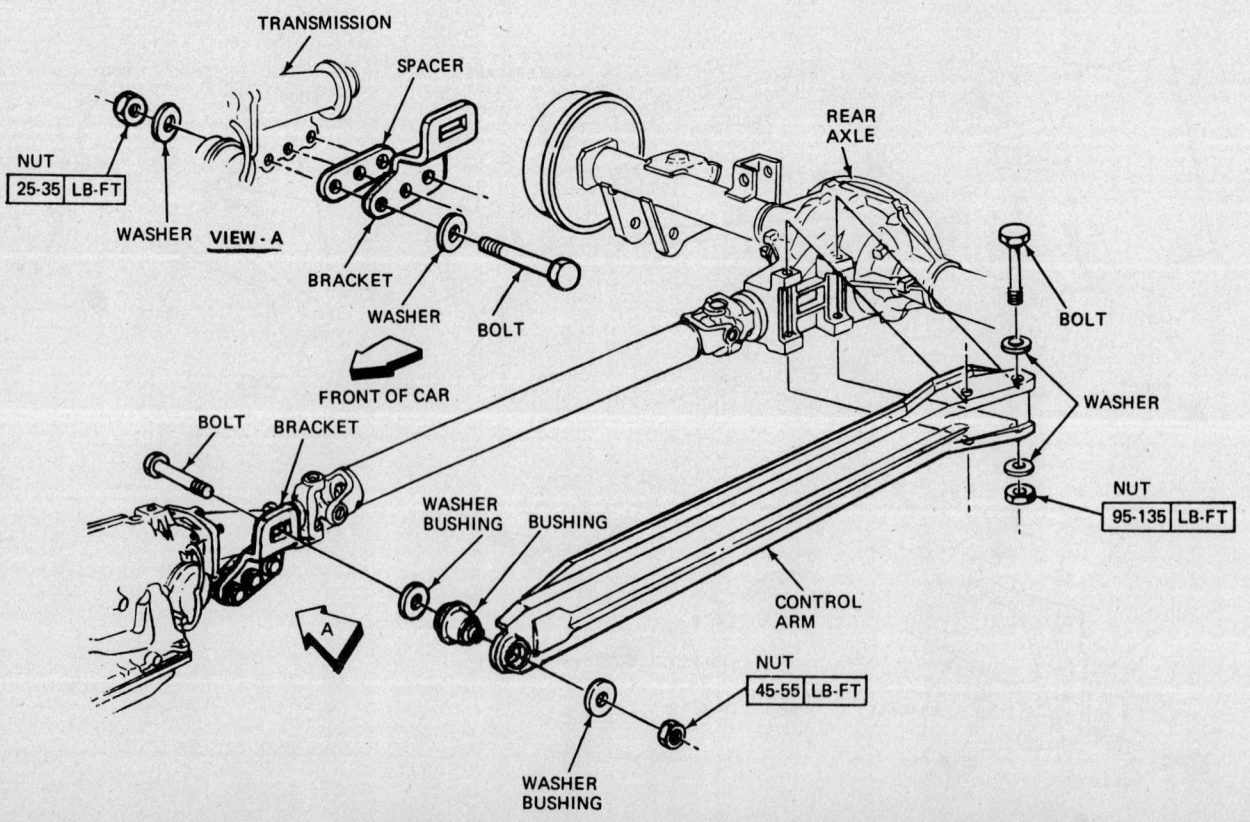

Fig. 8 Torque arm installation. All 1976-77 automatic transmission models exc. with 4-151 (Typical)

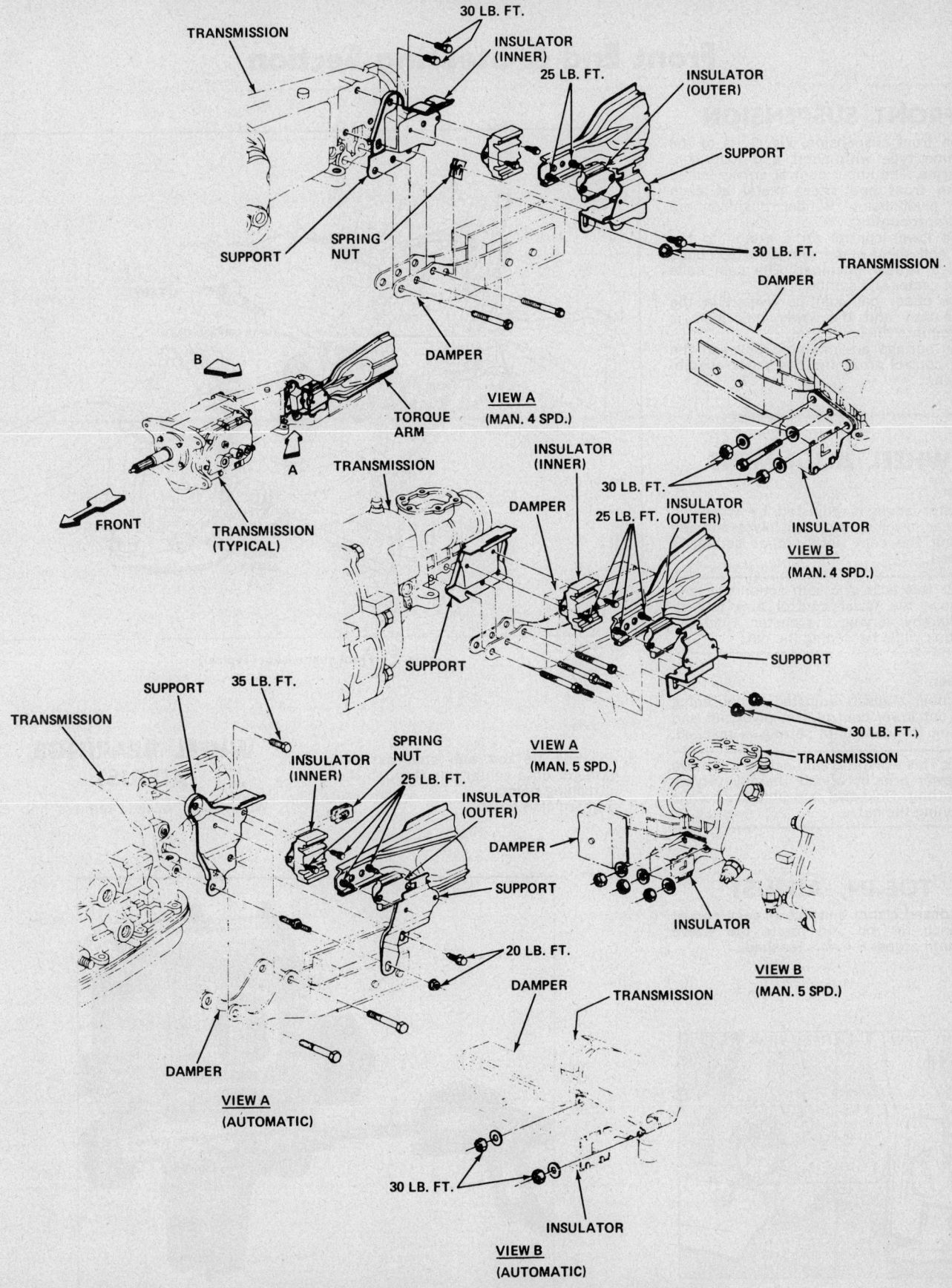

Fig. 9   Torque arm installation. 1977 models equipped with 4-151 (Typical)

Front End & Steering Section

FRONT SUSPENSION

The front suspension, Fig. 1, is of the A frame type with short and long control arms. The upper control arm is bolted to the front end sheet metal at each inner pivot point. Rubber bushings are used for mounting.

The lower control arms attach to the front end sheet metal with cam type bolts through rubber bushings. The cam bolts adjust caster and camber.

The upper ball joint is riveted in the upper arm and the lower ball joint is pressed into the lower arm.

Coil springs are mounted between the lower control arms and the shock absorber tower.

WHEEL ALIGNMENT

Caster

Caster angle is adjusted by loosening the rear lower control arm pivot nut and rotating the cam until proper setting is reached.

NOTE: This eccentric cam action will tend to move the lower control arm fore or aft thereby varying the caster. Hold the cam bolt while tightening the nut.

Camber

Camber angle is adjusted by loosening the front lower control arm pivot nut and rotating the cam until setting is reached.

NOTE: This eccentric cam action will move the lower arm in or out thereby varying the setting. Hold the cam bolt head while tightening the nut.

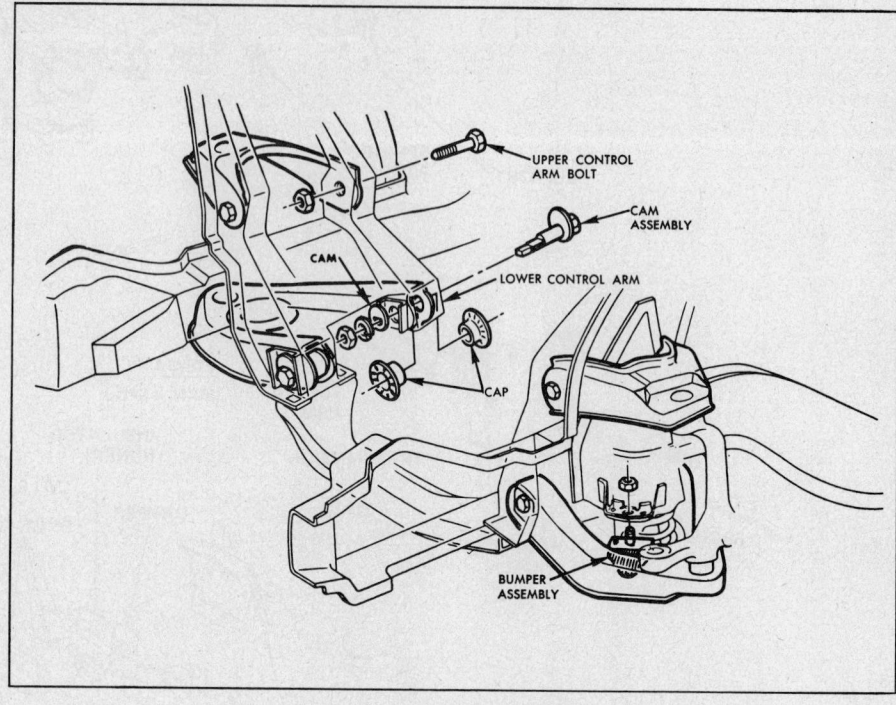

Fig. 1   Front suspension (Typical)

2. Position tie rod ball stud assembly straight on a center line through their attaching points.
3. Tighten clamp nuts.

WHEEL BEARINGS, ADJUST

1. With wheel raised, remove hub cap,

TOE-IN, ADJUST

1. Loosen clamp bolt nut at each end of each tie rod and rotate the sleeve until proper toe-in is reached.

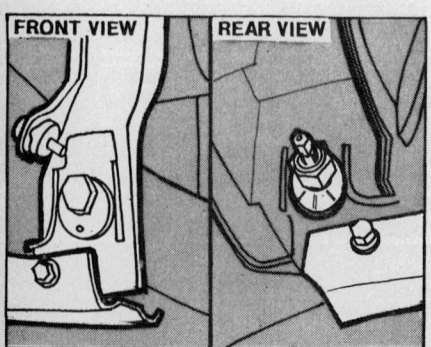

Fig. 2   Caster and camber adjustment

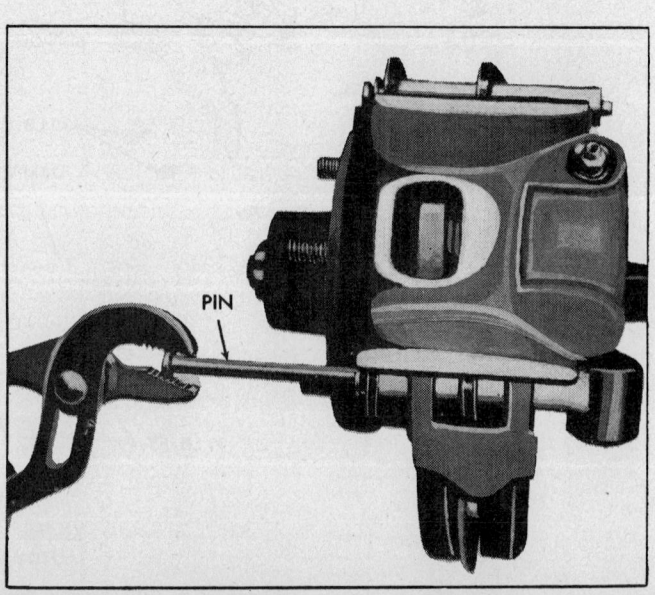

Fig. 3   Removing caliper mounting pins

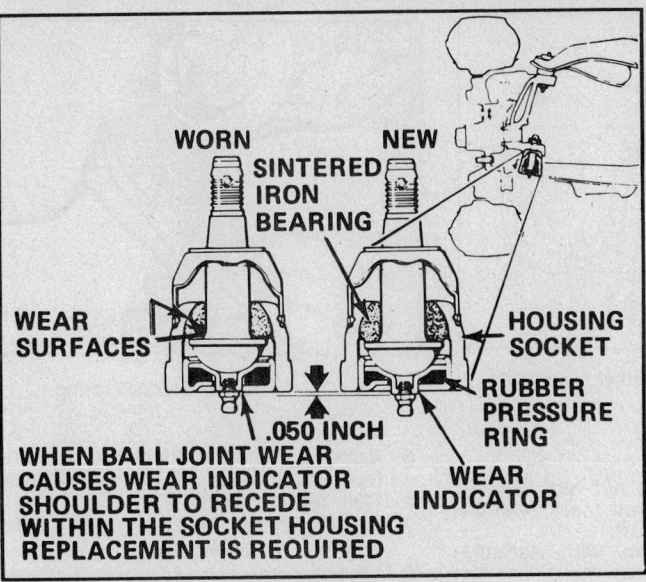

Fig. 4   Lower ball joint wear indicator

dust cap and cotter pin from end of spindle.
2. While rotating wheel, tighten spindle nut to 12 ft. lbs.
3. Backoff adjusting nut to the just loose position, then retighten nut hand tight.
4. Loosen until either hole in spindle is aligned with slot in nut, then install cotter pin.
5. Spin wheel to check that it rolls freely and then lock the cotter pin.

NOTE: Wheel bearings should have zero preload and the allowable end play is .001-.005 inch for 1974-77 models.

WHEEL BEARINGS, REPLACE

1. Raise vehicle on a hoist and remove the wheel and tire assembly.

2. Remove the brake caliper from the disc by removing the mounting pins and stamped nuts, Fig. 3.
3. Remove hub grease cap, cotter pin, spindle nut and washer and remove hub and bearings.
4. Remove inner bearing by prying out the grease seal.

CHECKING BALL JOINTS FOR WEAR

Upper Ball Joint

The upper ball joint is checked for wear by checking the torque required to rotate the ball joint stud in the assembly. This is done after first dislodging the ball joint from the steering knuckle.
1. Install the stud nut to the ball stud. in the seat.
2. Check the torque required to turn the ball stud.

NOTE: Specified rotating torque for a new joint is 1 to 4 ft. lbs. If readings are excessively high or low replace joint.

Lower Ball Joint

NOTE: All 1975-77 vehicles use lower ball joints incorporating wear indicators, Fig. 4.

The lower ball joint is checked for wear by checking to be sure torque is present. After dislodging ball joint from steering knuckle perform the following:
1. Install the stud nut to the ball stud.
2. Check the torque required to turn the ball stud in the seat.

NOTE: Some torque is required, if zero torque is observed, sufficient wear has taken place for replacement of the ball joint.

UPPER BALL JOINT, REPLACE

1. Raise vehicle on a hoist and remove wheel and tire assembly.
2. Support lower control arm with a floor jack.
3. Remove upper ball stud nut and remove ball stud from knuckle, Fig. 4A.
4. Remove control arm pivot bolts and remove control arm.
5. Grind off rivets securing ball joint to arm.
6. Install new ball joint using bolts and nuts supplied in kit.

LOWER BALL JOINT, REPLACE

1. Place vehicle on hoist and support lower control arm at outer end on a jack.
2. Free lower ball stud from knuckle, Fig. 4A.
3. Using tool shown in Fig. 5, press ball joint out of control arm.
4. Position new ball joint so that grease bleed vent in rubber boot is facing inboard.
5. Install tool shown in Fig. 6 and press new joint into arm.
6. Install lube fitting in joint and install stud into steering knuckle.

SHOCK ABSORBER, REPLACE

1. Hold shock absorber stem and remove the nut, upper retainer and rubber grommet, Fig. 7.
2. Raise vehicle on a hoist.
3. Remove bolts from lower end of shock absorber and lower the shock from the vehicle.

Fig. 4A   Removing upper & lower ball joint stud from knuckle. 1974-77

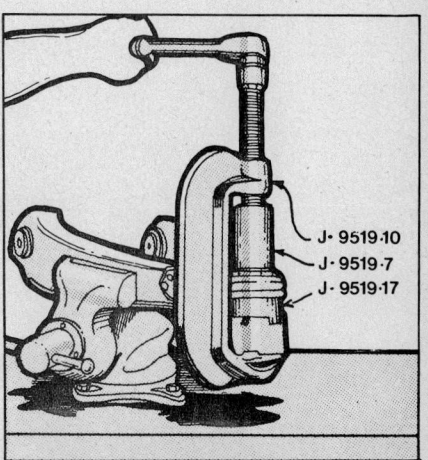

Fig. 5   Removing lower ball joint

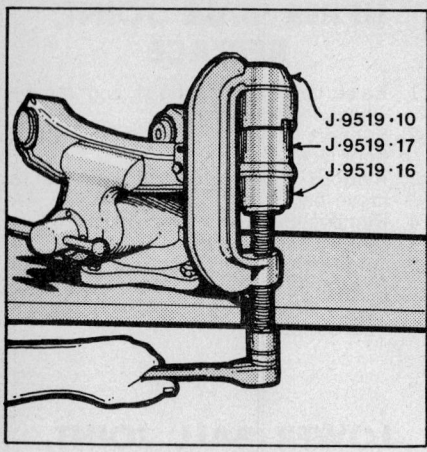

Fig. 6   Installing lower ball joint

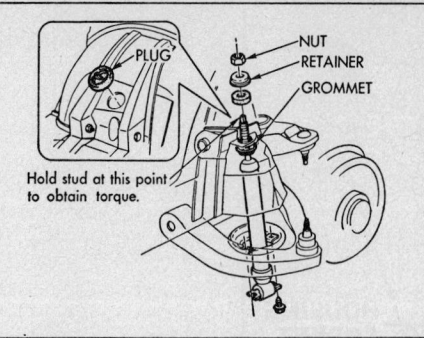

Fig. 7   Front shock absorber mountings

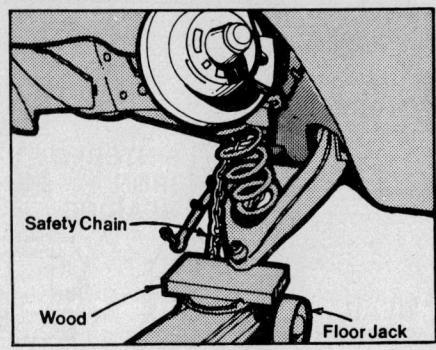

Fig. 8   Removing front coil spring

COIL SPRING, REPLACE

1. With shock absorber removed and stabilizer bar removed, raise the vehicle and place jackstands under front braces.
2. Remove the wheel and tire assembly.
3. Place a floor jack under the lower arm and support the arm. Use a block of wood between the control arm and the jack, Fig. 8.
4. Remove the lower ball stud from the knuckle.
5. Remove the tie rod end from the knuckle.
6. Lower the control arm by slowly lowering the jack until the spring can be removed.

STEERING GEAR, REPLACE

1. Remove the pot joint coupling clamp bolt at the steering gear wormshaft.

2. Remove "K" brace.
3. Remove pitman arm nut and washer from pitman shaft and mark relation of arm position to shaft.
4. Remove pitman arm with suitable puller.
5. Remove bolts securing gear to frame and remove gear assembly.

INTEGRAL POWER STEERING

1976-77 Models

1. Remove battery from vehicle to provide access to steering gear.
2. Remove clamp securing intermediate shaft to steering shaft.
3. Disconnect both hydraulic lines from steering gear and allow to drain. Position lines out of way to provide clearance for gear removal.
4. Raise vehicle and remove clamps at stabilizer bar.
5. Remove left front crossmember.

6. Remove pitman shaft nut, then using tool No. J-6632, remove pitman arm from pitman shaft.
7. Remove three steering mounting bolts and lock washers.
8. Lift steering gear and remove pitman arm, then position gear to provide clearance for removal.
9. Remove steering gear and intermediate shaft as an assembly, the steering gear spacer is also removed.
10. Remove plastic shield.
11. Remove pot joint clamp and separate steering gear from pot joint.
12. Remove pot joint from intermediate shaft.

1974-75 Models

Replacement procedures for removing the gear assembly are the same as for the manual type gear with the following additions:
1. Disconnect both pressure and return hoses from the gear housing and cap both hoses and steering gear outlets to prevent entry of dirt.

CHRYSLER · DODGE
IMPERIAL · PLYMOUTH

INDEX OF SERVICE OPERATIONS

VEHICLE NUMBER LOCATION

1974-79: ON PLATE ATTACHED TO DASH PAD AND VISIBLE THROUGH WINDSHIELD.

ENGINE NUMBER LOCATION

1974-79 Six: Right front of block below cylinder head.

1974-78 318, 360: Left front of block below cylinder head.

1974-79 V8-400, 1974-75 V8-440: Upper right front of cylinder block.

1976-79 V8-440: Top of block left bank next to front tappet rail.

ENGINE IDENTIFICATION CODE

1974-79 engines are identified by the cubic inch displacement found within the engine number stamped on the pad.

CHRYSLER GRILLE IDENTIFICATION

1974 Newport

1974 New Yorker & Town & Country

1975 Cordoba

1975-76 Newport

1975 New Yorker & Town & Country
1976 Newport Custom & Town & Country
1977 Newport & Town & Country
1978 Newport

1976 Cordoba

1976-77 New Yorker

1977 Cordoba

1977-78 LeBaron
1978 Town & Country

1978 Cordoba

1978 New Yorker

1979 Cordoba

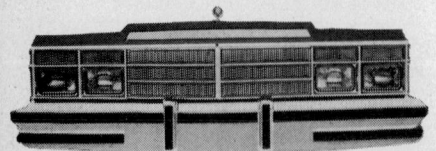

1979 LeBaron & Town & Country

1979 Newport

1979 New Yorker

DODGE GRILLE IDENTIFICATION

1974 Dart

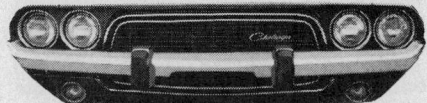

1974 Challenger

1974 Charger

1974 Charger SE

1974 Coronet

1974 Monaco

1975-76 Dart

**1975 Coronet
1976 Charger**

**1975 Coronet Brougham & Crestwood
1976 Coronet**

1975 Charger S.E.

1975 Monaco

**1975 Royal Monaco
1976 Monaco
1977 Royal Monaco**

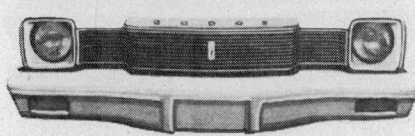

1976-77 Aspen

1976 Charger SE

1976 Charger Daytona

1977 Aspen R/T

1977-78 Monaco

1977 Charger Daytona

1977-78 Charger SE

1977-78 Diplomat

1978-79 Aspen

DODGE GRILLE IDENTIFICATION—Continued

1978-79 Magnum

1979 Diplomat

1979 St. Regis

IMPERIAL GRILLE IDENTIFICATION

1974

1975

PLYMOUTH GRILLE IDENTIFICATION

1974 Valiant & Duster

1974 Barracuda

1974 Satellite 2-Door, Sebring & Road Runner

1974 Satellite 4-Door

1974 Fury

1975-76 Valiant & Duster

1975 Road Runner

1975-76 Fury & Custom

1975-76 Fury Sport

1975 Gran Fury

1975 Gran Fury Custom

**1975 Gran Fury Sport & Brougham
1976 Gran Fury**

PLYMOUTH GRILLE IDENTIFICATION—Continued

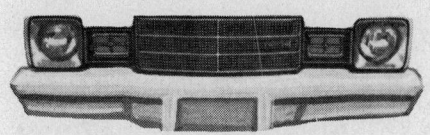
1976-77 Volaré & Road Runner

1977-78 Fury

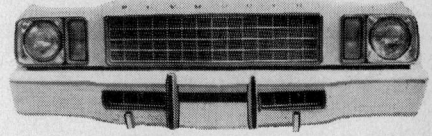
1977 Gran Fury

1978 Volaré & Road Runner

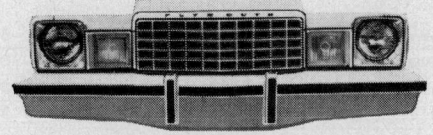
1979 Volaré & Road Runner

GENERAL ENGINE SPECIFICATIONS

Year	Engine	Carburetor	Bore and Stroke	Piston Displacement, Cubic Inches	Compression Ratio	Maximum Brake H.P. @ R.P.M.	Maximum Torque Lbs. Ft. @ R.P.M.	Normal Oil Pressure Pounds
CHRYSLER AND IMPERIAL								
1974	185 Horsepower①............V8-400	2 Barrel	4.34 x 3.38	400	8.2	185 @ 4000	315 @ 2400	45–65
	200 Horsepower①..........V8-400④	4 Barrel	4.34 x 3.38	400	8.2	200 @ 4400	310 @ 2400	45–65
	205 Horsepower①..........V8-400③	4 Barrel	4.34 x 3.38	400	8.2	205 @ 4400	310 @ 2400	45–65
	220 Horsepower①..........V8-440④	4 Barrel	4.32 x 3.75	440	8.2	220 @ 4000	345 @ 3200	45–65
	230 Horsepower①..........V8-440③	4 Barrel	4.32 x 3.75	440	8.2	230 @ 4000	350 @ 3200	45–65
1975	135 Horsepower①..........V8-318④	2 Barrel	3.91 x 3.31	318	8.5	135 @ 3600	245 @ 1600	30–80
	150 Horsepower①..........V8-318③	2 Barrel	3.91 x 3.31	318	8.5	150 @ 4000	255 @ 1600	30–80
	180 Horsepower①..........V8-360③	2 Barrel	4.00 x 3.58	360	8.4	180 @ 4000	290 @ 2400	30–80
	190 Horsepower①..........V8-360④	4 Barrel	4.00 x 3.58	360	8.4	190 @ 4000	270 @ 3200	30–80
	165 Horsepower①..........V8-400④	2 Barrel	4.34 x 3.38	400	8.2	165 @ 4000	295 @ 3200	30–80
	175 Horsepower①..........V8-400③	2 Barrel	4.34 x 3.38	400	8.2	175 @ 4000	300 @ 2400	30–80
	185 Horsepower①..........V8-400④	4 Barrel	4.34 x 3.38	400	8.2	185 @ 4000	285 @ 3200	30–80
	190 Horsepower①..........V8-400③	4 Barrel	4.34 x 3.38	400	8.2	190 @ 4000	290 @ 3200	30–80
	195 Horsepower①..........V8-400④	4 Barrel	4.34 x 3.38	400	8.2	195 @ 4000	285 @ 3200	30–80
	235 Horsepower①②.........V8-400③	4 Barrel	4.34 x 3.38	400	8.2	235 @ 4000	320 @ 3200	30–80
	215 Horsepower①..........V8-440	4 Barrel	4.32 x 3.75	440	8.2	215 @ 4000	330 @ 3200	30–80
1976	140 Horsepower①..........V8-318④	2 Barrel	3.91 x 3.31	318	8.6	140 @ 3600	250 @ 2000	30–80
	150 Horsepower①..........V8-318③	2 Barrel	3.91 x 3.31	318	8.6	150 @ 4000	255 @ 1600	30–80
	170 Horsepower①..........V8-360③	2 Barrel	4.00 x 3.58	360	8.4	170 @ 4000	280 @ 2400	30–80
	175 Horsepower①..........V8-360④	4 Barrel	4.00 x 3.58	360	8.4	175 @ 4000	270 @ 1600	30–80
	175 Horsepower①..........V8-400③	2 Barrel	4.34 x 3.38	400	8.2	175 @ 4000	300 @ 2400	30–80
	185 Horsepower①..........V8-400④	4 Barrel	4.34 x 3.38	400	8.2	185 @ 3600	285 @ 3200	30–80
	210 Horsepower①..........V8-400③	4 Barrel	4.34 x 3.38	400	8.2	210 @ 4000	305 @ 3200	30–80
	240 Horsepower①②.........V8-400③	4 Barrel	4.34 x 3.38	400	8.2	240 @ 4400	325 @ 3200	30–80
	200 Horsepower①..........V8-440④	4 Barrel	4.32 x 3.75	440	8.2	200 @ 3600	310 @ 2400	30–80
	205 Horsepower①..........V8-440③	4 Barrel	4.32 x 3.75	440	8.2	205 @ 3600	320 @ 2000	30–80
1977	135 Horsepower①..........V8-318④	2 Barrel	3.91 x 3.31	318	8.6	135 @ 3600	235 @ 1600	30–80
	145 Horsepower①..........V8-318	2 Barrel	3.91 x 3.31	318	8.6	145 @ 3600	245 @ 1600	30–80
	155 Horsepower①..........V8-360③	2 Barrel	4.00 x 3.58	360	8.4	155 @ 3600	275 @ 2000	30–80
	170 Horsepower①..........V8-360④	4 Barrel	4.00 x 3.58	360	8.4	170 @ 4000	270 @ 1600	30–80
	190 Horsepower①..........V8-400	4 Barrel	4.34 x 3.38	400	8.2	190 @ 3600	305 @ 3200	30–80
	185 Horsepower①..........V8-440⑥	4 Barrel	4.32 x 3.75	440	8.2	185 @ 3600	310 @ 2400	30–80
	195 Horsepower①..........V8-440③	4 Barrel	4.32 x 3.75	440	8.2	195 @ 3600	320 @ 2000	30–80

Continued

GENERAL ENGINE SPECIFICATIONS—Continued

Year	Engine	Carburetor	Bore and Stroke	Piston Displacement, Cubic Inches	Compression Ratio	Maximum Brake H.P. @ R.P.M.	Maximum Torque Lbs. Ft. @ R.P.M.	Normal Oil Pressure Pounds
CHRYSLER—Continued								
1978	100 Horsepower①.............6-225	1 Barrel	3.40 x 4.12	225	8.4	100 @ 3600	170 @ 1600	30–70
	110 Horsepower①.............6-225	2 Barrel	3.40 x 4.12	225	8.4	110 @ 3600	180 @ 2000	30–70
	140 Horsepower①.........V8-318③⑦	2 Barrel	3.91 x 3.31	318	8.5	140 @ 4000	245 @ 1600	30–80
	145 Horsepower①..........V8-318⑧	2 Barrel	3.91 x 3.31	318	8.5	145 @ 4000	245 @ 1600	30–80
	155 Horsepower①.........V8-318⑥⑦	4 Barrel	3.91 x 3.31	318	8.5	155 @ 4000	245 @ 1600	30–80
	155 Horsepower①..........V8-360③	2 Barrel	4.00 x 3.58	360	8.4	155 @ 3600	270 @ 2400	30–80
	170 Horsepower①..........V8-360⑥	4 Barrel	4.00 x 3.58	360	8.4	170 @ 4000	270 @ 1600	30–80
	190 Horsepower①............V8-400	4 Barrel	4.34 x 3.38	400	8.2	190 @ 3600	305 @ 3200	30–80
	185 Horsepower①..........V8-440⑥	4 Barrel	4.32 x 3.75	440	8.2	185 @ 3600	310 @ 2400	30–80
	195 Horsepower①. V8-440③	4 Barrel	4.32 x 3.75	440	8.2	195 @ 3600	320 @ 2000	30–80
1979	100 Horsepower①.............6-225	1 Barrel	3.40 x 4.12	225	8.4	100 @ 3600	165 @ 1600	—
	110 Horsepower①.............6-225	2 Barrel	3.40 x 4.12	225	8.4	110 @ 2000	180 @ 2000	—
	135 Horsepower①..........V8-318③	2 Barrel	3.91 x 3.31	318	8.5	135 @ 4000	250 @ 1600	—
	155 Horsepower①..........V8-318④	4 Barrel	3.91 x 3.31	318	8.5	155 @ 4000	245 @ 1600	—
	150 Horsepower①..........V8-360③	2 Barrel	4.00 x 3.58	360	8.4	150 @ 3600	265 @ 2400	—
	170 Horsepower①..........V8-360④	4 Barrel	4.00 x 3.58	360	8.4	170 @ 4000	270 @ 1600	—
	195 Horsepower①............V8-360	4 Barrel	4.00 x 3.58	360	8.0	195 @ 4000	280 @ 2400	—
DODGE								
1974	95 Horsepower①.............6-198	1 Barrel	3.40 x 3.64	198	8.4	95 @ 4000	145 @ 2000	45–65
	105 Horsepower①.............6-225	1 Barrel	3.40 x 4.12	225	8.4	105 @ 3600	180 @ 1600	45–65
	150 Horsepower①...........V8-318	2 Barrel	3.91 x 3.31	318	8.6	150 @ 4000	255 @ 2200	45–65
	180 Horsepower①..........V8-360③	2 Barrel	4.00 x 3.58	360	8.4	180 @ 4000	290 @ 2400	45–65
	200 Horsepower①.........V8-360④	4 Barrel	4.00 x 3.58	360	8.4	200 @ 4000	290 @ 3200	45–65
	245 Horsepower①②..........V8-360③	4 Barrel	4.00 x 3.58	360	8.4	245 @ 4800	320 @ 3600	45–65
	185 Horsepower①..........V8-400③	2 Barrel	4.34 x 3.38	400	8.2	185 @ 4000	315 @ 2400	45–65
	200 Horsepower①..........V8-400④	4 Barrel	4.34 x 3.38	400	8.2	200 @ 4400	310 @ 2400	45–65
	205 Horsepower①..........V8-400③	4 Barrel	4.34 x 3.38	400	8.2	205 @ 4400	310 @ 2400	45–65
	250 Horsepower①②..........V8-400④	4 Barrel	4.34 x 3.38	400	8.2	250 @ 4800	330 @ 3400	45–65
	230 Horsepower①..........V8-440③	4 Barrel	4.32 x 3.75	440	8.2	230 @ 4000	350 @ 3200	45–65
	220 Horsepower①..........V8-440④	4 Barrel	4.32 x 3.75	440	8.2	220 @ 4000	345 @ 3200	45–65
	275 Horsepower①②..........V8-440	4 Barrel	4.32 x 3.75	440	8.2	275 @ 4400	375 @ 3200	45–65
1975	90 Horsepower①.............6-225④	1 Barrel	3.40 x 3.64	225	8.4	90 @ 3600	165 @ 1600	30–70
	95 Horsepower①.............6-225③	1 Barrel	3.40 x 3.64	225	8.4	95 @ 3600	170 @ 1600	30–70
	135 Horsepower①..........V8-318④	2 Barrel	3.91 x 3.31	318	8.5	135 @ 3600	245 @ 1600	30–80
	140 Horsepower①..........V8-318④	2 Barrel	3.91 x 3.31	318	8.5	140 @ 3600	255 @ 1600	30–80
	145 Horsepower①..........V8-318③	2 Barrel	3.91 x 3.31	318	8.5	145 @ 4000	255 @ 1600	30–80
	150 Horsepower①..........V8-318③	2 Barrel	3.91 x 3.31	318	8.5	150 @ 4000	255 @ 1600	30–80
	180 Horsepower①..........V8-360③	2 Barrel	4.00 x 3.58	360	8.4	180 @ 4000	290; @ 2400	30–80
	190 Horsepower①..........V8-360④	4 Barrel	4.00 x 3.58	360	8.4	190 @ 4000	270 @ 3200	30–80
	230 Horsepower①②..........V8-360③	4 Barrel	4.00 x 3.58	360	8.4	230 @ 4200	320 @ 3200	30–80
	165 Horsepower①..........V8-400③	2 Barrel	4.34 x 3.38	400	8.2	165 @ 4000	295 @ 3200	30–80
	175 Horsepower①..........V8-400③	2 Barrel	4.34 x 3.38	400	8.2	175 @ 4000	300 @ 2400	30–80
	185 Horsepower①..........V8-400④	4 Barrel	4.34 x 3.38	400	8.2	185 @ 4000	285 @ 3200	30–80
	190 Horsepower①..........V8-400③	4 Barrel	4.34 x 3.38	400	8.2	190 @ 4000	290 @ 3200	30–80
	195 Horsepower①..........V8-400④	4 Barrel	4.34 x 3.38	400	8.2	195 @ 4000	285 @ 3200	30–80

Continued

GENERAL ENGINE SPECIFICATIONS—Continued

Year	Engine	Car-buretor	Bore and Stroke	Piston Dis-place-ment, Cubic Inches	Com-pres-sion Ratio	Maximum Brake H.P. @ R.P.M.	Maximum Torque Lbs. Ft. @ R.P.M.	Normal Oil Pressure Pounds
DODGE—Continued								
1975	235 Horsepower①②..........V8-400③	4 Barrel	4.34 x 3.38	400	8.2	235 @ 4200	320 @ 3200	30–80
	240 Horsepower①②..........V8-400③	4 Barrel	4.34 x 3.38	400	8.2	240 @ 4400	325 @ 3200	30–80
	215 Horsepower①..........V8-440③	4 Barrel	4.32 x 3.75	440	8.2	215 @ 4000	330 @ 3200	30–80
	250 Horsepower①..........V8-440④	4 Barrel	4.32 x 3.75	440	8.2	250 @ 4000	350 @ 3200	30–80
	260 Horsepower①②..........V8-440③	4 Barrel	4.32 x 3.75	440	8.2	260 @ 4400	355 @ 3200	30–80
1976	90 Horsepower①..........6-225④	1 Barrel	3.40 x 4.12	225	8.4	90 @ 3600	165 @ 1600	30–70
	100 Horsepower①..........6-225③	1 Barrel	3.40 x 4.12	225	8.4	100 @ 3600	170 @ 1600	30–70
	140 Horsepower①..........V8-318④	2 Barrel	3.91 x 3.31	318	8.6	140 @ 3600	250 @ 2000	30–80
	150 Horsepower①..........V8-318③	2 Barrel	3.91 x 3.31	318	8.6	150 @ 4000	255 @ 1600	30–80
	170 Horsepower①..........V8-360③	2 Barrel	4.00 x 3.58	360	8.4	170 @ 4000	280 @ 2400	30–80
	175 Horsepower①..........V8-360④	4 Barrel	4.00 x 3.58	360	8.4	175 @ 4000	270 @ 1600	30–80
	220 Horsepower①..........V8-360③	4 Barrel	4.00 x 3.58	360	8.4	220 @ 4400	280 @ 3200	30–80
	175 Horsepower①..........V8-400③	2 Barrel	4.34 x 3.38	400	8.2	175 @ 4000	300 @ 2400	30–80
	185 Horsepower①..........V8-400④	4 Barrel	4.34 x 3.38	400	8.2	185 @ 3600	285 @ 3200	30–80
	210 Horsepower①..........V8-400③	4 Barrel	4.34 x 3.38	400	8.2	210 @ 4000	305 @ 3200	30–80
	240 Horsepower①②..........V8-400③	4 Barrel	4.34 x 3.38	400	8.2	240 @ 4400	325 @ 3200	30–80
	200 Horsepower①..........V8-440④	4 Barrel	4.32 x 3.75	440	8.2	200 @ 3600	310 @ 2400	30–80
	205 Horsepower①..........V8-440③	4 Barrel	4.32 x 3.75	440	8.2	205 @ 3600	320 @ 2000	30–80
	250 Horsepower①②..........V8-440④	4 Barrel	4.32 x 3.75	440	8.2	250 @ 4000	350 @ 3200	30–80
	255 Horsepower①②..........V8-440③	4 Barrel	4.32 x 3.75	440	8.2	255 @ 4400	355 @ 3200	30–80
1977	90 Horsepower①..........6-225④	1 Barrel	3.40 x 4.12	225	8.4	90 @ 3600	170 @ 1600	30–70
	100 Horsepower①..........6-225③	1 Barrel	3.40 x 4.12	225	8.4	100 @ 3600	170 @ 1600	30–70
	110 Horsepower①..........6-225	2 Barrel	3.40 x 4.12	225	8.4	110 @ 3600	180 @ 2000	30–70
	135 Horsepower①..........V8-318④	2 Barrel	3.91 x 3.31	318	8.6	135 @ 3600	235 @ 1600	30–80
	145 Horsepower①..........V8-318	2 Barrel	3.91 x 3.31	318	8.6	145 @ 4000	245 @ 1600	30–80
	155 Horsepower①..........V8-360③	2 Barrel	4.00 x 3.58	360	8.4	155 @ 3600	275 @ 2000	30–80
	170 Horsepower①..........V8-360④	4 Barrel	4.00 x 3.58	360	8.4	170 @ 4000	270 @ 1600	30–80
	175 Horsepower①..........V8-360③	4 Barrel	4.00 x 3.58	360	8.0	175 @ 4000	275 @ 2000	30–80
	190 Horsepower①..........V8-400	4 Barrel	4.34 x 3.38	400	8.2	190 @ 3600	305 @ 3200	30–80
	185 Horsepower①..........V8-440⑥	4 Barrel	4.32 x 3.75	440	8.2	185 @ 3600	310 @ 2400	30–80
	195 Horsepower①..........V8-440	4 Barrel	4.32 x 3.75	440	8.2	195 @ 3600	320 @ 2000	30–80
	230 Horsepower①..........V8-440④⑤	4 Barrel	4.32 x 3.75	440	7.8	230 @ 4000	330 @ 3200	30–80
	245 Horsepower①..........V8-440③⑤	4 Barrel	4.32 x 3.75	440	7.8	245 @ 4000	350 @ 3200	30–80
1978	90 Horsepower①..........6-225⑬	1 Barrel	3.40 x 4.12	225	8.4	90 @ 3600	160 @ 1600	30–70
	100 Horsepower①..........6-225③	1 Barrel	3.40 x 4.12	225	8.4	100 @ 3600	170 @ 1600	30–70
	110 Horsepower①..........6-225	2 Barrel	3.40 x 4.12	225	8.4	110 @ 3600	180 @ 2000	30–70
	140 Horsepower①..........V8-318	2 Barrel	3.91 x 3.31	318	8.5	140 @ 4000	245 @ 1600	30–80
	155 Horsepower①..........V8-318④	4 Barrel	3.91 x 3.31	318	8.5	155 @ 4000	245 @ 1600	30–80
	155 Horsepower①..........V8-360	2 Barrel	4.00 x 3.58	360	8.4	115 @ 3600	270 @ 2400	30–80
	155 Horsepower①..........V8-360③⑨	2 Barrel	4.00 x 3.58	360	8.0	115 @ 3600	270 @ 2400	30–80
	155 Horsepower①..........V8-360③⑩	2 Barrel	4.00 x 3.58	360	8.4	115 @ 3600	270 @ 2400	30–80
	160 Horsepower①..........V8-360⑥	4 Barrel	4.00 x 3.58	360	8.0	160 @ 3600	265 @ 1600	30–80
	170 Horsepower①..........V8-360④	4 Barrel	4.00 x 3.58	360	8.4	170 @ 3600	270 @ 1600	30–80
	170 Horsepower①..........V8-360③⑬	4 Barrel	4.00 x 3.58	360	8.4	170 @ 4000	270 @ 2400	30–80
	175 Horsepower①..........V8-360	4 Barrel	4.00 x 3.58	360	8.0	175 @ 4000	260 @ 2400	30–80
	190 Horsepower①..........V8-400	4 Barrel	4.34 x 3.38	400	8.2	190 @ 3600	305 @ 3200	30–80
1979	90 Horsepower①..........6-225④	1 Barrel	3.40 x 4.12	225	8.4	90 @ 3600	170 @ 1600	—
	100 Horsepower①..........6-225③	1 Barrel	3.40 x 4.12	225	8.4	100 @ 3600	160 @ 1600	—
	110 Horsepower①..........6-255③	2 Barrel	3.40 x 4.12	225	8.4	110 @ 3600	180 @ 2000	—
	135 Horsepower①..........V8-318③	2 Barrel	3.91 x 3.31	318	8.5	135 @ 4000	250 @ 1600	—
	155 Horsepower①..........V8-318④	4 Barrel	3.91 x 3.31	318	8.5	155 @ 4000	245 @ 1600	—
	150 Horsepower①..........V8-360③	2 Barrel	4.00 x 3.58	360	8.4	150 @ 3600	265 @ 2400	—
	170 Horsepower①..........V8-360④	4 Barrel	4.00 x 3.58	360	8.4	170 @ 4000	270 @ 1600	—
	190 Horsepower①..........V8-360④	4 Barrel	4.00 x 3.58	360	8.0	190 @ 3600	275 @ 1600	—
	195 Horsepower①..........V8-360③	4 Barrel	4.00 x 3.58	360	8.0	195 @ 4000	280 @ 2400	—

GENERAL ENGINE SPECIFICATIONS—Continued

Year	Engine	Carburetor	Bore and Stroke	Piston Displacement, Cubic Inches	Compression Ratio	Maximum Brake H.P. @ R.P.M.	Maximum Torque H.P. @ R.P.M.	Normal Oil Pressure Pounds
PLYMOUTH								
1974	95 Horsepower①..............6-198	1 Barrel	3.40 x 3.64	198	8.4	95 @ 4000	145 @ 2000	45–65
	105 Horsepower①..............6-225	1 Barrel	3.40 x 4.12	225	8.4	105 @ 3600	180 @ 1600	45–65
	150 Horsepower①..............V8-318	2 Barrel	3.91 x 3.31	318	8.6	150 @ 4000	255 @ 2200	45–65
	170 Horsepower①②..........V8-318	2 Barrel	3.91 x 3.31	318	8.6	170 @ 4000	265 @ 2600	45–65
	180 Horsepower①..............V8-360	2 Barrel	4.00 x 3.58	360	8.4	180 @ 4000	290 @ 2400	45–65
	200 Horsepower①..............V8-360④	4 Barrel	4.00 x 3.58	360	8.4	200 @ 4000	290 @ 3200	45–65
	245 Horsepower①②..........V8-360③	4 Barrel	4.00 x 3.58	360	8.4	245 @ 4800	320 @ 3600	45–65
	185 Horsepower①..............V8-400	2 Barrel	4.34 x 3.38	400	8.2	185 @ 4000	315 @ 2400	45–65
	205 Horsepower①..............V8-400	4 Barrel	4.34 x 3.38	400	8.2	205 @ 4400	310 @ 2400	45–65
	250 Horsepower①②..........V8-400	4 Barrel	4.34 x 3.38	400	8.2	250 @ 4800	330 @ 3400	45–65
	230 Horsepower①..............V8-440③	4 Barrel	4.32 x 3.75	440	8.2	230 @ 4000	350 @ 3200	45–65
	220 Horsepower①..............V8-440④	4 Barrel	4.32 x 3.75	440	8.2	220 @ 4000	345 @ 3200	45–65
	275 Horsepower①②..........V8-440	4 Barrel	4.32 x 3.75	440	8.2	275 @ 4400	375 @ 3200	45–65
1975	90 Horsepower①..............6-225④	1 Barrel	3.40 x 4.12	225	8.4	90 @ 3600	165 @ 1600	30–70
	95 Horsepower①..............6-225③	1 Barrel	3.40 x 4.12	225	8.4	95 @ 3600	170 @ 1600	30–70
	135 Horsepower①..........V8-318④	2 Barrel	3.91 x 3.31	318	8.5	135 @ 3600	245 @ 1600	30–80
	140 Horsepower①..........V8-318④	2 Barrel	3.91 x 3.31	318	8.5	140 @ 3600	255 @ 1600	30–80
	145 Horsepower①..........V8-318③	2 Barrel	3.91 x 3.31	318	8.5	145 @ 4000	255 @ 1600	30–80
	150 Horsepower①..........V8-318③	2 Barrel	3.91 x 3.31	318	8.5	150 @ 4000	255 @ 1600	30–80
	180 Horsepower①..........V8-360③	2 Barrel	4.00 x 3.58	360	8.4	180 @ 4000	290 @ 2400	30–80
	190 Horsepower①..........V8-360④	4 Barrel	4.00 x 3.58	360	8.4	190 @ 4000	270 @ 3200	30–80
	230 Horsepower①②..........V8-360③	4 Barrel	4.00 x 3.58	360	8.4	230 @ 4400	300 @ 3600	30–80
	165 Horsepower①..........V8-400③	2 Barrel	4.34 x 3.38	400	8.2	165 @ 4000	295 @ 3200	30–80
	175 Horsepower①..........V8-400③	2 Barrel	4.34 x 3.38	400	8.2	175 @ 4000	300 @ 2400	30–80
	185 Horsepower①..........V8-400④	4 Barrel	4.34 x 3.38	400	8.2	185 @ 4000	285 @ 3200	30–80
	190 Horsepower①..........V8-400③	4 Barrel	4.34 x 3.38	400	8.2	190 @ 4000	290 @ 3200	30–80
	195 Horsepower①..........V8-400④	4 Barrel	4.34 x 3.38	400	8.2	195 @ 4000	285 @ 3200	30–80
	235 Horsepower①②..........V8-400③	4 Barrel	4.34 x 3.38	400	8.2	235 @ 4200	320 @ 3200	30–80
	240 Horsepower①②..........V8-400③	4 Barrel	4.34 x 3.38	400	8.2	250 @ 4400	325 @ 3200	30–80
	215 Horsepower①..............V8-440	4 Barrel	4.32 x 3.75	440	8.2	215 @ 4000	330 @ 3200	30–90
	250 Horsepower①②..........V8-440④	4 Barrel	4.32 x 3.75	440	8.2	250 @ 4000	350 @ 3200	30–80
	260 Horsepower①②..........V8-440③	4 Barrel	4.32 x 3.75	440	8.2	260 @ 4400	355 @ 3200	30–80
1976	90 Horsepower①..............6-225④	1 Barrel	3.40 x 4.12	225	8.4	90 @ 3600	165 @ 1600	30–70
	100 Horsepower①..............6-225③	1 Barrel	3.40 x 4.12	225	8.4	100 @ 3600	170 @ 1600	30–70
	140 Horsepower①..........V8-318④	2 Barrel	3.91 x 3.31	318	8.6	140 @ 3600	250 @ 2000	30–80
	150 Horsepower①..........V8-318③	2 Barrel	3.91 x 3.31	318	8.6	150 @ 4000	255 @ 1600	30–80
	170 Horsepower①..........V8-360③	2 Barrel	4.00 x 3.58	360	8.4	170 @ 4000	280 @ 2400	30–80
	175 Horsepower①..........V8-360④	4 Barrel	4.00 x 3.58	360	8.4	175 @ 4000	270 @ 1600	30–80
	220 Horsepower①②..........V8-360③	4 Barrel	4.00 x 3.58	360	8.4	220 @ 4400	280 @ 3200	30–80
	175 Horsepower①..........V8-400③	2 Barrel	4.34 x 3.38	400	8.2	175 @ 4000	300 @ 2400	30–80
	185 Horsepower①..........V8-400④	4 Barrel	4.34 x 3.38	400	8.2	185 @ 3600	285 @ 3200	30–80
	210 Horsepower①..........V8-400④	4 Barrel	4.34 x 3.38	400	8.2	210 @ 4000	305 @ 3200	30–80
	240 Horsepower①②..........V8-400③	4 Barrel	4.34 x 3.38	400	8.2	240 @ 4400	325 @ 3200	30–80
	200 Horsepower①..........V8-440④	4 Barrel	4.32 x 3.75	440	8.2	200 @ 3600	310 @ 2400	30–80
	205 Horsepower①..........V8-440③	4 Barrel	4.32 x 3.75	440	8.2	205 @ 3600	320 @ 2000	30–80
	250 Horsepower①②..........V8-440④	4 Barrel	4.32 x 3.75	440	8.2	250 @ 4000	350 @ 3200	30–80
	255 Horsepower①②..........V8-440③	4 Barrel	4.32 x 3.75	440	8.2	255 @ 4400	355 @ 3200	30–80
1977	90 Horsepower①..............6-225④	1 Barrel	3.40 x 4.12	225	8.4	90 @ 3600	170 @ 1600	30–70
	100 Horsepower①..............6-225③	1 Barrel	3.40 x 4.12	225	8.4	100 @ 3600	170 @ 1600	30–70
	110 Horsepower①..............6-225	2 Barrel	3.40 x 4.12	225	8.4	110 @ 3600	180 @ 2000	30–70

Continued

GENERAL ENGINE SPECIFICATIONS—Continued

Year	Engine	Carburetor	Bore and Stroke	Piston Displacement, Cubic Inches	Compression Ratio	Maximum Brake H.P. @ R.P.M.	Maximum Torque H.P. @ R.P.M.	Normal Oil Pressure Pounds
PLYMOUTH—Continued								
1977	135 Horsepower①..........V8-318④	2 Barrel	3.91 x 3.31	318	8.6	135 @ 3600	235 @ 1600	30-80
	145 Horsepower①..........V8-318③	2 Barrel	3.91 x 3.31	318	8.6	145 @ 4000	245 @ 1600	30-80
	155 Horsepower①............V8-360	2 Barrel	4.00 x 3.58	360	8.4	155 @ 3600	275 @ 2000	30-80
	170 Horsepower①............V8-360	4 Barrel	4.00 x 3.58	360	8.4	170 @ 4000	270 @ 1600	30-80
	175 Horsepower①..........V8-360⑤	4 Barrel	4.00 x 3.58	360	8.0	175 @ 4000	275 @ 2000	30-80
	190 Horsepower①............V8-400	4 Barrel	4.34 x 3.38	400	8.2	190 @ 3600	305 @ 3200	30-80
	185 Horsepower①..........V8-440⑥	4 Barrel	4.32 x 3.75	440	8.2	185 @ 3600	310 @ 2400	30-80
	195 Horsepower①............V8-440	4 Barrel	4.32 x 3.75	440	8.2	195 @ 3600	320 @ 2000	30-80
	230 Horsepower①........V8-440④⑤	4 Barrel	4.32 x 3.75	440	7.8	230 @ 4000	330 @ 3200	30-80
	245 Horsepower①........V8-440③⑤	4 Barrel	4.32 x 3.75	440	7.8	245 @ 4000	350 @ 3200	30-80
1978	90 Horsepower①............6-225⑬	1 Barrel	3.40 x 4.12	225	8.4	90 @ 3600	160 @ 1600	30-70
	100 Horsepower①.............6-225	1 Barrel	3.40 x 4.12	225	8.4	100 @ 3600	170 @ 1600	30-70
	110 Horsepower①.............6-225	2 Barrel	3.40 x 4.12	225	8.4	110 @ 3600	180 @ 2000	30-70
	140 Horsepower①........V8-318③⑪	2 Barrel	3.91 x 3.31	318	8.5	140 @ 4000	245 @ 1600	30-80
	145 Horsepower①........V8-318⑫	2 Barrel	3.91 x 3.31	318	8.5	145 @ 4000	245 @ 1600	30-80
	155 Horsepower①..........V8-318⑥	4 Barrel	3.91 x 3.31	318	8.5	155 @ 4000	245 @ 1600	30-80
	155 Horsepower①............V8-360	2 Barrel	4.00 x 3.58	360	8.4	155 @ 3600	270 @ 2400	30-80
	175 Horsepower①............V8-360	4 Barrel	4.00 x 3.58	360	8.4	175 @ 4000	260 @ 2400	30-80
	190 Horsepower①............V8-400	4 Barrel	4.34 x 3.38	400	8.2	190 @ 3600	305 @ 3200	30-80
1979	100 Horsepower①.............6-225	1 Barrel	3.40 x 4.12	225	8.4	100 @ 3600	165 @ 1600	—
	110 Horsepower①...........6-225③	2 Barrel	3.40 x 4.12	225	8.4	110 @ 3600	180 @ 2000	—
	135 Horsepower①..........V8-318③	2 Barrel	3.91 x 3.31	318	8.5	135 @ 4000	250 @ 1600	—
	155 Horsepower①..........V8-318④	4 Barrel	3.91 x 3.31	318	8.5	155 @ 4000	245 @ 1600	—
	195 Horsepower①............V8-360	4 Barrel	4.00 x 3.58	360	8.0	195 @ 4000	280 @ 2400	—

①—Ratings are NET—as installed in the vehicle.
②—With dual exhausts.
③—Exc. California.
④—California.
⑤—High Performance.
⑥—California and high altitude.
⑦—LeBaron.
⑧—Cordoba.
⑨—Exc. Aspen coupe & sedan.
⑩—Aspen coupe & sedan.
⑪—Fury.
⑫—Volaré.
⑬—High Altitude.

TUNE UP SPECIFICATIONS

The following specifications are published from the latest information available. This data should be used only in the absence of a decal affixed in the engine compartment.

★ When using a timing light, disconnect vacuum hose or tube at distributor and plug opening in hose or tube so idle speed will not be affected.

● When checking compression, lowest cylinder must be within 80 percent of highest.

▲ Before removing wires from distributor cap, determine location of the No. 1 wire in cap, as distributor position may have been altered from that shown at the end of this chart.

Year	Spark Plug		Distributor		Ignition Timing★			Carb. Adjustments					
	Type [7]	Gap Inch	Point Gap Inch	Dwell Angle Deg.	Firing Order Fig. ▲	Timing BTDC [1]	Mark Fig.	Hot Idle Speed		Air Fuel Ratio		Idle CO % [8]	
								Std. Trans.	Auto. Trans. [2]	Std. Trans.	Auto. Trans.	Std. Trans.	Auto. Trans.
CHRYSLER & IMPERIAL													
1974													
V8-400 [21]	J13Y	.035	—	—	J	[9]	F	—	750	—	14.3	—	—
V8-400 [4] [24]	J13Y	.035	—	—	J	5°	F	—	750	—	14.3	—	—
V8-400 [4] [25]	J13Y	.035	—	—	J	5°	F	—	750	—	14.1	—	—
V8-440 [24]	J11Y	.035	—	—	J	10°	F	—	750	—	14.3	—	—
V8-440 [25]	J11Y	.035	—	—	J	5°	F	—	750	—	14.1	—	—
1975													
V8-318 [5]	N13Y	.035	—	—	H	[14]	B	—	750N	—	—	.3 [19]	[33]
V8-318 [8]	N13Y	.035	—	—	H	2° [15]	B	—	900N	—	—	—	.5 [20]
V8-360	N12Y	.035	—	—	H	6°	B	—	750N	—	—	—	[33]
V8-400 [21]	J13Y	.035	—	—	J	10°	F	—	750N	—	—	.3 [19]	
V8-400 [4]	J13Y	.035	—	—	J	8°	F	—	750N	—	—	—	[32]
V8-400 [22]	RJ87P	.035	—	—	J	6°	F	—	850N	—	—	.5 [20]	
V8-440	RJ87P	.040	—	—	J	6°	D	—	750N	—	—	—	[34]
1976													
V8-318 [5]	RN12Y	.035	—	—	H	[36]	B	—	750	—	—	—	[37]
V8-318 [8]	RN12Y	.035	—	—	H	2° [15]	B	—	900	—	—	—	.5 [20]
V8-360 [21]	RN12Y	.035	—	—	H	6°	B	—	700	—	—	—	.3 [19]
V8-360 [4]	RN12Y	.035	—	—	H	6°	B	—	750	—	—	—	2.0 [19]
V8-400 [21]	RJ13Y	.035	—	—	J	10°	F	—	700	—	—	—	.3 [19]
V8-400 [4] [24]	[38]	.035	—	—	J	6°	F	—	850	—	—	—	.5 [20]
V8-400 [4] [25]	RJ13Y	.035	—	—	J	8°	F	—	750	—	—	—	.5 [19]
V8-440	RJ13Y	.035	—	—	J	8°	D	—	750	—	—	—	.3 [19]
1977													
V8-318	RN12Y	.035	—	—	H	[46]	B	[47]	[47]	—	—	.5 [19] [25]	—
V8-360 [21]	RN12Y	.035	—	—	H	10°	B	—	700	—	—	—	—
V8-360 [4] [48]	RN12Y	.035	—	—	H	6°	B	—	750	—	—	—	.5 [19] [25]
V8-360 [4] [49]	RJ13Y	.035	—	—	H	10°	B	—	750	—	—	—	—
V8-400 [49]	RJ13Y	.035	—	—	J	10°	F	—	750	—	—	—	—
V8-440 [48]	RJ13Y	.035	—	—	J	8°	D	—	750	—	—	—	1.0 [19] [25]
V8-440 [49]	RJ13Y	.035	—	—	J	[50]	D	—	750	—	—	—	.3 [19] [25]
1978													
6-225 [42]	RBL16Y	.035	—	—	G	[50]	K	750	750	—	—	—	—
6-225 [21]	RBL16Y	.035	—	—	G	12°	K	750	750	—	—	—	—
V8-318 [21]	RN12Y	.035	—	—	H	16°	L	700	750	—	—	—	—
V8-318 [4] [25]	RN12Y	.035	—	—	H	10°	L	—	750	—	—	—	—
V8-360 [21]	RN12Y	.035	—	—	H	20°	L	—	750	—	—	—	—
V8-360 [4] [48]	RN12Y	.035	—	—	H	[6]	L	—	750	—	—	—	—
V8-360 [4] [49]	RN12Y	.035	—	—	H	16°	L	—	750	—	—	—	—
V8-400	[17]	.035	—	—	J	[26]	M	—	750	—	—	—	—
V8-440	[17]	.035	—	—	J	[27]	L	—	750	—	—	—	—

Continued

TUNE UP SPECIFICATIONS—Continued

The following specifications are published from the latest information available. This data should be used only in the absence of a decal affixed in the engine compartment.

★When using a timing light, disconnect vacuum hose or tube at distributor and plug opening in hose or tube so idle speed will not be affected.

●When checking compression, lowest cylinder must be within 80 percent of highest.

▲Before removing wires from distributor cap, determine location of the No. 1 wire in cap, as distributor position may have been altered from that shown at the end of this chart.

Year	Spark Plug Type ⑦	Spark Plug Gap Inch	Distributor Point Gap Inch	Distributor Dwell Angle Deg.	Ignition Timing Firing Order Fig. ▲	Ignition Timing BTDC ①	Ignition Timing Mark Fig.	Hot Idle Speed Std. Trans.	Hot Idle Speed Auto. Trans. ②	Air Fuel Ratio Std. Trans.	Air Fuel Ratio Auto. Trans.	Idle "CO" % ③ Std. Trans.	Idle "CO" % ③ Auto. Trans.
CHRYSLER & IMPERIAL—Continued													
1979													
6-225 ⑫	4091678	.035	—	—	G	�							

TUNE UP SPECIFICATIONS—Continued

The following specifications are published from the latest information available. This data should be used only in the absence of a decal affixed in the engine compartment.

★When using a timing light, disconnect vacuum hose or tube at distributor and plug opening in hose or tube so idle speed will not be affected.

●When checking compression, lowest cylinder must be within 80 percent of highest.

▲Before removing wires from distributor cap, determine location of the No. 1 wire in cap, as distributor position may have been altered from that shown at the end of this chart.

Year	Spark Plug Type (7)	Spark Plug Gap Inch	Distributor Point Gap Inch	Distributor Dwell Angle Deg.	Firing Order Fig. ▲	Timing BTDC (1)	Mark Fig.	Hot Idle Speed Std. Trans.	Hot Idle Speed Auto. Trans. (2)	Air Fuel Ratio Std. Trans.	Air Fuel Ratio Auto. Trans.	Idle "CO" % (3) Std. Trans.	Idle "CO" % (3) Auto. Trans.
DODGE—Continued													
1977													
6-225 (42)(43)	RBL15Y	.035	—	—	G	(50)	A	(44)	(44)	—	—	.3 (19)(25)	.3 (19)(25)
6-225 (42)(45)	RBL15Y	.035	—	—	G	(29)	A	(24)	(44)	—	—	.3 (19)(25)	.3 (19)(25)
6-225 (21)	RBL15Y	.035	—	—	G	(30)	A	750 (29)	750 (29)	—	—	.5 (19)(25)	.3 (19)(25)
V8-318	RN12Y	.035	—	—	H	(46)	B	(47)	(47)	—	—	.5 (19)(25)	—
V8-360 (21)	RN12Y	.035	—	—	H	10°	B	—	700	—	—	—	—
V8-360 (4)(48)	RN12Y	.035	—	—	H	6°	B	—	750	—	—	—	.5 (19)(25)
V8-360 (4)(49)	RJ13Y	.035	—	—	H	10°	B	—	750	—	—	—	—
V8-400 (49)	RJ13Y	.035	—	—	J	10°	F	—	750	—	—	—	—
V8-440 (48)	RJ13Y	.035	—	—	J	8°	D	—	750	—	—	—	1.0 (19)(25)
V8-440 (49)	RJ13Y	.035	—	—	J	(50)	D	—	750	—	—	—	.3 (19)(25)
V8-440 (22)(49)	RJ11Y	.035	—	—	J	8°	D	—	750	—	—	—	1.0 (19)(25)
1978													
6-225 (42)	RBL16Y	.035	—	—	G	(50)	K	(44)	(44)	—	—	—	—
6-225 (21)	RBL16Y	.035	—	—	G	12°	K	750	750	—	—	—	—
V8-318 (21)	RN12Y	.035	—	—	H	16°	L	700	750	—	—	—	—
V8-318 (4)(25)	RN12Y	.035	—	—	H	10°	L	—	750	—	—	—	—
V8-360 (21)	RN12Y	.035	—	—	H	20°	L	—	750	—	—	—	—
V8-360 (4)(48)	RN12Y	.035	—	—	H	(6)	L	—	750	—	—	—	—
V8-360 (4)(49)	RN12Y	.035	—	—	H	16°	L	—	750	—	—	—	—
V8-400	(17)	.035	—	—	J	(26)	M	—	750	—	—	—	—
V8-440	(17)	.035	—	—	J	(28)	L	—	750	—	—	—	—
1979													
6-225 (42)	4091678	.035	—	—	G	(51)	K	(52)	(52)	—	—	—	—
6-225 (21)	4091678	.035	—	—	G	12°	K	—	725	—	—	—	—
V8-318 (21)	3874490	.035	—	—	H	16°	L	—	730	—	—	—	—
V8-318 (4)	3874490	.035	—	—	H	16°	L	—	750	—	—	—	—
V8-360 (21)	3874490	.035	—	—	H	12°	L	—	750	—	—	—	—
V8-360 (4)	3874490	.035	—	—	H	16°	L	—	750	—	—	—	—
PLYMOUTH													
1974													
6-198	N14Y	.035	—	—	G	2½°	C	800	750	14.3 to 1	14.3 to 1	—	—
6-225	N14Y	.035	—	—	G	TDC	C	800	750	14.3 to 1	14.3 to 1	—	—
V8-318	N13Y	.035	—	—	H	TDC	E	750	750	14.3 to 1	14.3 to 1	—	—
V8-360	N12Y	.035	—	—	H	5° (11)	E	850	850	14.3 to 1	14.3 to 1	—	—
V8-400 Auto. Trans. (21)	J13Y	.035	—	—	J	(9)	F	—	750	—	14.3 to 1	—	—
V8-400 Auto. Trans. (4)	J13Y	.035	—	—	J	5°	F	—	750	—	14.3 to 1	—	—
V8-400 Std. Trans. (22)	J11Y	.035	—	—	J	5°	F	900	—	14.3 to 1	—	—	—
V8-400 Auto. Trans. (18)	J11Y	.035	—	—	J	5° (13)	F	—	850	—	14.3 to 1	—	—
V8-440	J11Y	.035	—	—	J	(35)	F	—	850	—	14.3 to 1	—	—

Continued

TUNE UP SPECIFICATIONS—Continued

The following specifications are published from the latest information available. This data should be used only in the absence of a decal affixed in the engine compartment.

★ When using a timing light, disconnet vacuum hose or tube at distribtor and plug opening in hose or tube so idle speed will not be affected.

● When checking compression, lowest cylinder must be within 80 percent of highest.

▲ Before removing wires from distributor cap, determine location of the No. 1 wire in cap, as distributor position may have been altered from that shown at the end of this chart.

Year	Spark Plug Type [7]	Gap Inch	Distributor Point Gap Inch	Dwell Angle Deg.	Firing Order Fig. ▲	Timing BTDC [1]	Mark Fig.	Hot Idle Speed Std. Trans.	Hot Idle Speed Auto. Trans. [2]	Air Fuel Ratio Std. Trans.	Air Fuel Ratio Auto. Trans.	Idle "CO" % [3] Std. Trans.	Idle "CO" % [3] Auto. Trans.
PLYMOUTH—Continued													
1975													
6-225	BL13Y	.035	—	—	G	TDC	A	800	750N	—	—	.3[19]	[34]
V8-318[5]	N13Y	.035	—	—	H	[14]	B	750	750N	—	—	.3[19]	[33]
V8-318	N13Y	.035	—	—	H	2°[15]	B	—	900N	—	—	—	.5[20]
V8-360	N12Y	.035	—	—	H	6°	B	—	750N	—	—	—	[33]
V8-360[22]	N12Y	.035	—	—	H	2°	B	—	850N	—	—	—	.5[20]
V8-400[21]	J13Y	.035	—	—	J	10°	F	—	750N	—	—	—	.3[19]
V8-400[4]	J13Y	.035	—	—	J	8°	F	—	750N	—	—	—	[32]
V8-400[22]	RJ87P	.035	—	—	J	6°	F	—	850N	—	—	—	5[20]
V8-440	RJ87P	.040	—	—	J	6°	D	—	750N	—	—	—	[34]
V8-440[22]	J11Y	.035	—	—	J	10°	D	—	750N	—	—	—	[33]
1976													
6-225 Std. Tr.[23]	RBL13Y	.035	—	—	G	[39]	A	750[30]	—	—	—	[37]	—
6-225 Auto. Tr.[23]	RBL13Y	.035	—	—	G	2°	A	—	750	—	—	—	[37]
6-225[41]	RBL13Y	.035	—	—	G	12°	A	750[30]	750	—	—	—	—
V8-318[5]	RN12Y	.035	—	—	H	[36]	B	750	750	—	—	.3[19]	[37]
V8-318[8]	RN12Y	.035	—	—	H	2°[15]	B	—	900	—	—	—	.5[20]
V8-360[21]	RN12Y	.035	—	—	H	6°	B	—	700	—	—	—	.3[19]
V8-360[4]	RN12Y	.035	—	—	H	6°	B	—	750	—	—	—	2.0[19]
V8-360[22]	RN12Y	.035	—	—	H	2°	B	—	850	—	—	—	.5[20]
V8-400[21]	RJ13Y	.035	—	—	J	10°	F	—	700	—	—	—	.3[19]
V8-400[4][24]	[38]	.035	—	—	J	6°	F	—	850	—	—	—	.5[20]
V8-400[4][25]	RJ13Y	.035	—	—	J	8°	F	—	750	—	—	—	.5[19]
V8-440	RJ13Y	.035	—	—	J	8°	D	—	750	—	—	—	.3[19]
V8-440[22]	RJ11Y	.035	—	—	J	[40]	D	—	750	—	—	—	[32]
1977													
6-225[42][43]	RBL15Y	.035	—	—	G	[50]	A	[44]	[44]	—	—	.3[19][25]	.3[19][25]
6-225[42][45]	RBL15Y	.035	—	—	G	[29]	A	[44]	[44]	—	—	.3[19][25]	.3[19][25]
6-225[21]	RBL15Y	.035	—	—	G	[30]	A	750[29]	750[29]	—	—	.5[19][25]	.5[19][25]
V8-318	RN12Y	.035	—	—	H	[46]	B	[47]	[47]	—	—	.5[19][25]	—
V8-360[21]	RN12Y	.035	—	—	H	10°	B	—	700	—	—	—	—
V8-360[4][45]	RN12Y	.035	—	—	H	6°	B	—	750	—	—	—	.5[19][25]
V8-360[4][46]	RJ13Y	.035	—	—	H	10°	B	—	750	—	—	—	—
V8-400[49]	RJ13Y	.035	—	—	J	10°	F	—	750	—	—	—	—
V8-440[48]	RJ13Y	.035	—	—	J	8°	D	—	750	—	—	—	1.0[19][25]
V8-440[49]	RJ13Y	.035	—	—	J	[50]	D	—	750	—	—	—	.3[19][26]
V8-440[22][49]	RJ11Y	.035	—	—	J	8°	D	—	750	—	—	—	1.0[19][25]

Continued

TUNE UP SPECIFICATIONS—Continued

The following specifications are published from the latest information available. This data should be used only in the absence of a decal affixed in the engine compartment.

★ When using a timing light, disconnect vacuum hose or tube at distributor and plug opening in tube or hose so idle speed will not be affected.

● When checking compression, lowest cylinder must be within 80 percent of highest.

▲ Before removing wires from distributor cap, determide location of the No. 1 wire in cap, as distributor position may have been altered from that shown at the end of this chart.

| Year | Spark Plug | | Distributor | | Ignition Timing★ | | | Carb. Adjustments | | | | | |
| | Type (7) | Gap Inch | Point Gap Inch | Dwell Angle Deg. | Firing Order Fig. ▲ | Timing BTDC (1) | Mark Fig. | Hot Idle Speed | | Air Fuel Ratio | | Idle "CO" % (3) | |
								Std. Trans.	Auto. Trans.(2)	Std. Trans.	Auto. Trans.	Std. Trans.	Auto. Trans.
PLYMOUTH—Continued													
1978													
6-225 (42)	RBL16Y	.035	—	—	G	(50)	K	(44)	(44)	—	—	—	—
6-225 (21)	RBL16Y	.035	—	—	G	12°	K	750	750	—	—	—	—
V8-318 (21)	RN12Y	.035	—	—	H	16°	L	700	750	—	—	—	—
V8-318 (4)(26)	RN12Y	.035	—	—	H	10°	L	—	750	—	—	—	—
V8-360 (21)	RN12Y	.035	—	—	H	20°	L	—	750	—	—	—	—
V8-360 (4)(48)	RN12Y	.035	—	—	H	(6)	L	—	750	—	—	—	—
V8-360 (4)(49)	RN12Y	.035	—	—	H	16°	L	—	750	—	—	—	—
V8-400	(17)	.035	—	—	J	(26)	M	—	750	—	—	—	—
V8-440	(17)	.035	—	—	J	(28)	L	—	750	—	—	—	—
1979													
6-225 (42)	4091678	.035	—	—	G	(51)	K	(52)	(52)	—	—	—	—
6-225 (21)	4091678	.035	—	—	G	12°	K	—	725	—	—	—	—
V8-318 (21)	3874490	.035	—	—	H	16°	L	—	730	—	—	—	—
V8-318 (4)	3874490	.035	—	—	H	16°	L	—	750	—	—	—	—
V8-360 (21)	3874490	.035	—	—	H	12°	L	—	750	—	—	—	—
V8-360 (4)	3874490	.035	—	—	H	16°	L	—	750	—	—	—	—

①—BTDC: Before top dead center.

②—D: Drive. N: Neutral.

③—Before adjusting idle "CO", disconnect air pump outlet hose and plug tube leading to exhaust manifold, if equipped.

④—Four barrel carburetor.

⑤—With catalytic converter.

⑥—Dist. No. 3874115, 6° BTDC. Dist. No. 3874858, 8° BTDC.

⑦—Champion.

⑧—With air pump.

⑨—Early production—Exc. sta. wag., 7½° BTDC; sta. wag., 5° BTDC. Late production—Exc. sta. wag., 10° BTDC; sta. wag., 7½° BTDC.

⑩—Dist. No. 3656780, TDC. Dist. No. 3755336, 7½°. Dist. No. 3755337 & 3755365, 5°.

⑪—Calif. V8-360 Hi Perf. Manual Trans. 2½° BTDC.

⑫—Auto. trans.

⑬—Exc. Calif. auto. trans. & Police; Calif. auto. trans. & Police, 2½°.

⑭—Except Calif., 2° BTDC; Calif.: Early production, TDC, Late production, 2° ATDC.

⑮—ATDC: after top dead center.

⑯—High performance & Police.

⑰—Exc. high performance engine, OJ13Y; high performance engine, OJ11Y.

⑱—Exc. Calif. late production; Calif. late production, TDC.

⑲—Measured ahead of catalytic converter.

⑳—Measured in tailpipe.

㉑—Two barrel carburetor.

㉒—High performance engine.

㉓—Except "Dodge Lite" and "Feather Duster".

㉔—Exc. California.

㉕—California only.

㉖—Engine code E-64, 4500 lbs. vehicle curb weight, 24° BTDC; all others, 20° BTDC.

㉗—Calif. & high altitude, 8° BTDC; Exc. Calif. & high altitude—Chrysler, 12° BTDC, Cordoba, 16° BTDC.

㉘—Exc. Calif., 16° BTDC; Calif., 8° BTDC.

㉙—Exc. high altitude & Calif.—manual trans., 6° BTDC; auto trans., 2° BTDC; high altitude & Calif., 8° BTDC.

㉚—Exc. Calif., 12° BTDC; Calif. 4° BTDC.

㉛—Std. trans.

㉜—Exc. Calif., .3 (see note 19); Calif., .5 (see note 19).

㉝—Except Calif. .3 (see note 19), Calif. .5 (see note 20).

㉞—Except Calif. .3 (see note 19), Calif. 1.5 (see note 20).

㉟—Exc. Calif., 10° BTDC; Calif., 5° BTDC.

㊱—Exc. Calif., 2° BTDC; Calif., TDC.

㊲—Exc. Calif., .3 (see note 19); Calif., 1.0 (see note19).

㊳—Exc. high performance engine, RJ13Y; high performance engine, RJ87P.

㊴—Exc. Calif., 6° BTDC; Calif., 4° BTDC.

㊵—Exc. Calif., 10° BTDC; Calif., 8° BTDC.

㊶—"Dodge Lite" and "Feather Duster".

㊷—Aspen & Volaré.

㊸—Except high altitude & Calif., 700 RPM; high altitude & Calif., 750 RPM.

㊹—Fury & Monaco.

㊺—Except high altitude & Calif. engines, 8° BTDC; high altitude & Calif., TDC.

㊻—Except high altitude & Calif., 700; High Altitude & Calif., 850.

㊼—Except Electronic Lean Burn engines.

㊽—Electronic Lean Burn engines.

㊾—Except high altitude & Calif., 12° BTDC; high altitude & Calif. 8° BTDC.

㊿—Except California, 12° BTDC; California, 8° BTDC.

52—Except Calif., 675 RPM; Calif., 750 RPM.

Continued

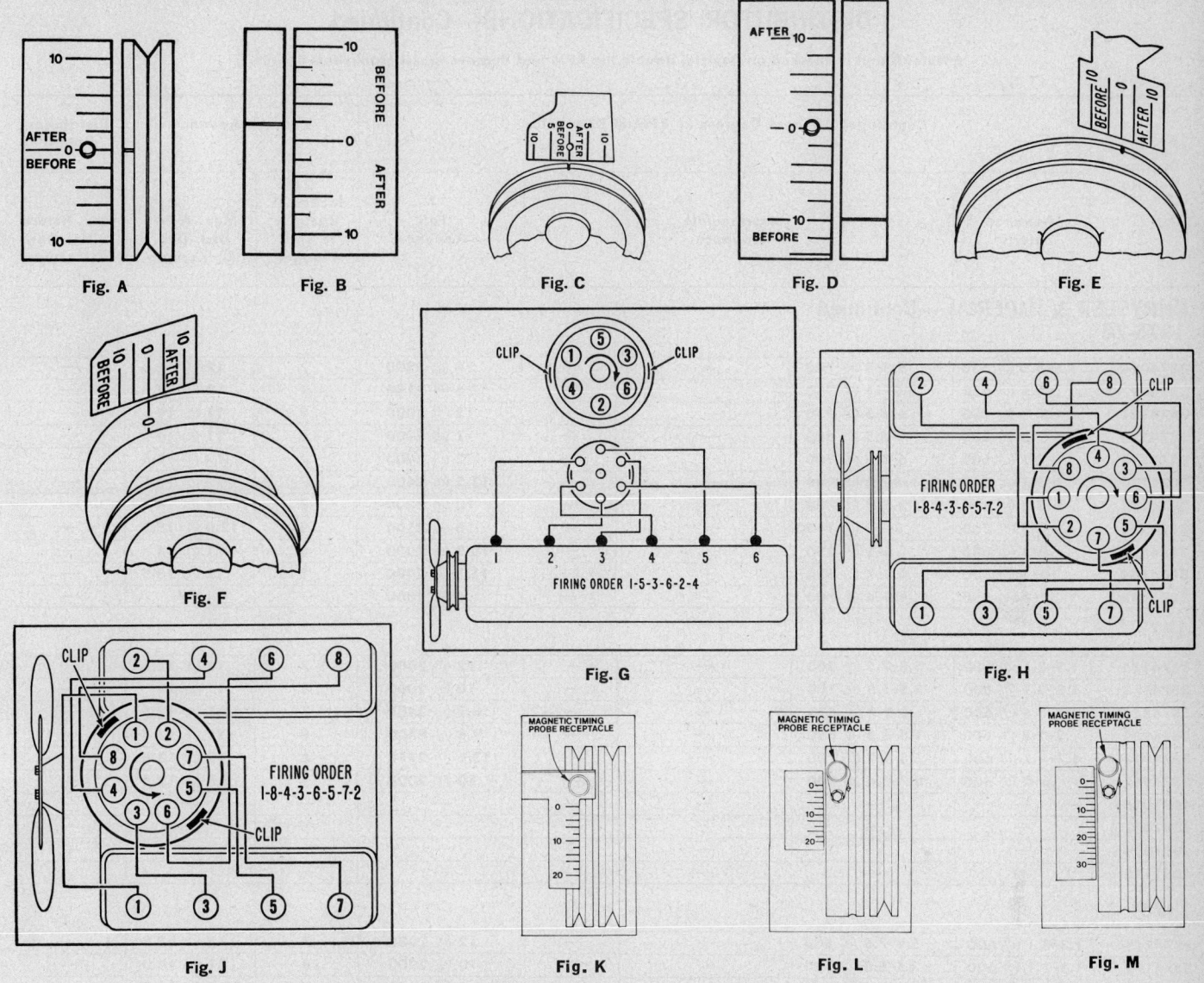

Fig. A

Fig. B

Fig. C

Fig. D

Fig. E

Fig. F

Fig. G

Fig. H

Fig. J

Fig. K

Fig. L

Fig. M

DISTRIBUTOR SPECIFICATIONS

★Note: If unit is checked on vehicle, double the RPM and degrees to get crankshaft figures.

Breaker arm spring tension—17–20.

Distributor Part No.①	Centrifugal Advance Degrees @ RPM of Distributor					Vacuum Advance		Distributor Retard
	Advance Starts	Intermediate Advance			Full Advance	Inches of Vacuum to Start Plunger	Max. Adv. Dist. Deg. @ Vacuum	Max. Retard Dist. Deg. @ Vacuum
CHRYSLER & IMPERIAL **1974**								
3755518	0.5–3.5 @ 650	5.5–8 @ 900	—	—	12 @ 2000	8	10 @ 14	—
3755522	0.5–3 @ 650	4–6.5 @ 900	—	—	10 @ 2000	8	10 @ 14	—
3755681	1–4.5 @ 650	8.5–11 @ 950	—	—	16 @ 2150	8	10 @ 14	—

Continued

DISTRIBUTOR SPECIFICATIONS—Continued

★Note: If unit is checked on vehicle, double the RPM and degrees to get crankshaft figures.

Distributor Part No.①	Centrifugal Advance Degrees @ RPM of Distributor					Vacuum Advance		Distributor Retard
	Advance Starts	Intermediate Advance			Full Advance	Inches of Vacuum to Start Plunger	Max. Adv. Dist. Deg. @ Vacuum	Max. Retard Dist. Deg. @ Vacuum
CHRYSLER & IMPERIAL—Continued								
1975-76								
3874090	1.5–5.5 @ 550	5.5–8 @ 700	—	—	14 @ 2200	7	12 @ 12.5	—
3874097	1–4.5 @ 650	8.5–11 @ 950	—	—	16 @ 2150	7	12 @ 12.5	—
3874101	.5–3 @ 600	6–8.5 @ 950	—	—	12 @ 2000	8	11 @ 14	—
3874110	1–3.5 @ 600	6–8.5 @ 900	—	—	12 @ 2000	8	11 @ 14	—
3874115	1–3.5 @ 600	6–8.5 @ 900	—	—	12 @ 2000	7	12 @ 12.5	—
3874119	1–3.5 @ 600	8–10 @ 900	—	—	11.5 @ 2400	7	12 @ 12.5	—
3874173	1–3.5 @ 600	3.5–6 @ 750	—	—	10 @ 2000	8	11 @ 14	—
3874298	.5–3.5 @ 700	7–10 @ 1100	—	—	16 @ 2100	9	12.5 @ 15.5	—
3874596	.5–4 @ 600	6–9 @ 850	—	—	10.9 @ 2000	8	11 @ 14	—
3874754	0–4 @ 500	4.5–7 @ 650	—	—	13.5 @ 2400	8	12 @ 13.5	—
3874848②	.5–3 @ 550	1.5–4 @ 700	—	—	9 @ 2300	—	—	—
1977								
3874115	1.3–3.1 @ 600	5.8–7.5 @ 800	—	—	12 @ 2000	7	12 @ 12.5	—
3874173	1.3–3.1 @ 600	3.5–5.5 @ 700	—	—	10 @ 2000	8	11 @ 14	—
3874858	1.4–3.4 @ 600	6–8 @ 800	—	—	8.5 @ 2400	7	12.5 @ 12.5	—
3874909	.2–2.2 @ 600	1.5–3.5 @ 650	—	—	9.6 @ 2300	8	12 @ 13.5	—
3874913	1.7–4.1 @ 600	4.8–7 @ 700	—	—	13.6 @ 2350	8	12 @ 13.5	—
3874917	.6–2 @ 500	3.7–5.4 @ 700	—	—	10 @ 2000	7	12.5 @ 12.5	—
4091015②	—	—	—	—	—	—	—	—
4091017②	—	—	—	—	—	—	—	—
4091019②	—	—	—	—	—	—	—	—
4091140②	—	—	—	—	—	—	—	—
1978								
3874115	1.3–3.1 @ 600	5.8–7.5 @ 800	—	—	12 @ 2000	7	12 @ 12.5	—
3874173	1.3–3.1 @ 600	3.5–5.5 @ 700	—	—	10 @ 2000	8	11 @ 14.0	—
3874858	1.4–3.4 @ 600	6–8 @ 800	—	—	8.5 @ 2400	7	12.5 @ 12.5	—
3874876	.2–2.2 @ 600	1.5–3.5 @ 650	—	—	5.7 @ 2500	7	9.8 @ 11.5	—
3874929	1.4–3.4 @ 600	5.6–7.6 @ 800	—	—	11.7 @ 2300	7	9.8 @ 11.5	—
4091101	1–1.2 @ 600	1.7–3.7 @ 800	—	—	5.8–7.8 @ 2060	9	9.5 @ 12.5	—
4091140②	—	—	—	—	—	—	—	—
4091709②	—	—	—	—	—	—	—	—
4091711②	—	—	—	—	—	—	—	—
1979								
3874876	.2–2.2 @ 600	1.5–3.5 @ 650	—	—	3.7–5.7 @ 2500	7	9.8 @ 11.5	—
4091101	1.0–1.2 @ 600	1.7–3.7 @ 800	—	—	5.8–7.8 @ 2060	9	9.5 @ 12.5	—
4091140②	—	—	—	—	—	—	—	—

①—Stamped on distributor housing. ②—Electronic Lean Burn distributor cannot be checked on vehicle.

DISTRIBUTOR SPECIFICATIONS—Continued

★Note: If unit is checked on vehicle, double the RPM and degrees to get crankshaft figures.

Breaker arm spring tension—17-20.

Distributor Part No.①	Centrifugal Advance Degrees @ RPM of Distributor				Vacuum Advance		Distributor Retard
	Advance Starts	Intermediate Advance		Full Advance	Inches of Vacuum to Start Plunger	Max. Adv. Dist. Deg. @ Vacuum	Max. Retard Dist. Deg. @ Vacuum
DODGE & PLYMOUTH							
1974							
3755037	1–4 @ 550	9–11.5 @ 900	—	—	14 @ 2000	9	8.5 @ 15.5	—
3755042	1–4 @ 550	9–11.5 @ 900	—	—	14 @ 2000	7	8.5 @ 11.5	—
3755467	0.5–3.5 @ 550	7–9.5 @ 950	—	—	14 @ 2000	9	8.5 @ 15.5	—
3755470	0.5–3.5 @ 550	7–9.5 @ 950	—	—	14 @ 2000	7	8.5 @ 11.5	—
3755475	0.5–4 @ 550	8–11.5 @ 800	—	—	14 @ 2000	7	11 @ 12.5	—
3755486	1–5 @ 600	8–10 @ 850	—	—	14 @ 2000	8	11 @ 13.5	—
3755503	0.5–4 @ 650	8–10.5 @ 850	—	—	16 @ 2200	8	10 @ 14	—
3755508	1–4.5 @ 650	8–10.5 @ 950	—	—	14 @ 2000	8	10¼ @ 16	—
3755512	0.5–3.5 @ 650	5.5–8 @ 900	—	—	12 @ 2000	8	10 @ 14	—
3755518	0.5–3.5 @ 650	5.5–8 @ 900	—	—	12 @ 2000	8	10 @ 14	—
3755522	0.5–3 @ 650	4–6.5 @ 900	—	—	10 @ 2000	8	10 @ 14	—
3755681	1–4.5 @ 650	8.5–11 @ 950	—	—	16 @ 2150	8	10 @ 14	—
3755686	0.5–4 @ 550	8–10.5 @ 850	—	—	16 @ 2200	8	10¼ @ 16	—
3656763	1.5–5.5 @ 550	6–8.5 @ 700	—	—	16 @ 2100	9	11 @ 15.5	—
3656859	0.5–4 @ 550	8–10.5 @ 800	—	—	14 @ 2000	7	8.5 @ 11.5	—
1975-76							
3874082	1–4.5 @ 600	8–10.5 @ 900	—	—	14 @ 2200	7	10 @ 11.5	—
3874090	1.5–5.5 @ 550	5.5–8 @ 700	—	—	14 @ 2200	7	12 @ 12.5	—
3874097	1–4.5 @ 650	8.5–11 @ 950	—	—	16 @ 2150	7	12 @ 12.5	—
3874101	.5–3 @ 600	6–8.5 @ 950	—	—	12 @ 2000	8	11 @ 14	—
3874110	1–3.5 @ 600	6–8.5 @ 900	—	—	12 @ 2000	8	11 @ 14	—
3874115	1–3.5 @ 600	6–8.5 @ 900	—	—	12 @ 2000	7	12 @ 12.5	—
3874173	1–3.5 @ 600	3.5–6 @ 750	—	—	10 @ 2000	8	11 @ 14	—
3874298	.5–3.5 @ 700	7–10 @ 1100	—	—	16 @ 2100	9	12.5 @ 15.5	—
1976							
3874596	.5–4.0 @ 600	6–9 @ 850	—	—	10.9 @ 2000	8	11 @ 14	—
3874598	1–4.5 @ 600	6.5–8.5 @ 800	—	—	11.5 @ 2300	7	10 @ 11.5	—
3874714	1–4.5 @ 450	4–6.5 @ 650	—	—	9 @ 2500	7	10 @ 11.5	—
3874754	0–4 @ 500	4.5–7 @ 650	—	—	13.5 @ 2400	8	12 @ 13.5	—
3874795	1.5–3.5 @ 650	—	—	—	5.5 @ 2300	7	12 @ 8.5	—
3874796	1.5–3.5 @ 650	—	—	—	5.5 @ 2300	7	12 @ 8.5	—
3874848②	.5–3 @ 550	1.5–4 @ 700	—	—	9 @ 2300	—		—
1977							
3874115	1.3–3.1 @ 600	5.8–7.5 @ 800	—	—	12 @ 2000	7	12 @ 12.5	—
3874173	1.3–3.1 @ 600	3.5–5.5 @ 700	—	—	10 @ 2000	8	11 @ 14	—
3874714	.3–2.4 @ 500	4.2–6.2 @ 650	—	—	8.9 @ 2500	7	9.8 @ 11.5	—
3874858	1.4–3.4 @ 600	6–8 @ 800	—	—	8.5 @ 2400	7	12.5 @ 12.5	—
3874876	.2–2.2 @ 600	1.5–3.5 @ 650	—	—	5.7 @ 2500	7	9.8 @ 11.5	—
3874909	.2–2.2 @ 600	1.5–3.5 @ 650	—	—	9.6 @ 2300	8	12 @ 13.5	—
3874913	1.7–4.1 @ 600	4.8–7.0 @ 700	—	—	13.6 @ 2350	8	12 @ 13.5	—
3874917	.6–2 @ 500	3.7–5.4 @ 700	—	—	10 @ 2000	7	12.5 @ 12.5	—
3874929	1.4–3.4 @ 600	5.6–7.6 @ 800	—	—	11.7 @ 2300	7	9.8 @ 11.5	—

Continued

DISTRIBUTOR SPECIFICATIONS—Continued

—Note: If unit is checked on vehicle, double the RPM and degrees to get crankshaft figures.

Breaker arm spring tension—17-20.

Distributor Part No.①	Centrifugal Advance Degrees @ RPM of Distributor				Vacuum Advance		Distributor Retard
	Advance Starts	Intermediate Advance		Full Advance	Inches of Vacuum to Start Plunger	Max. Adv. Dist. Deg. @ Vacuum	Max. Retard Dist. Deg. @ Vacuum
DODGE & PLYMOUTH—Continued							
1977							
4091015②	—	—	—	—	—	—	—
4091017②	—	—	—	—	—	—	—
4091019①	—	—	—	—	—	—	—
4091039	.2–2.2 @ 600	1.5–3.5 @ 650	—	—	5.7 @ 2500	7	9.8 @ 11.5	—
4091101	1.0–1.2 @ 600	1.7–3.7 @ 800	—	—	7.8 @ 2060	9	9.5 @ 12.5	—
4091140②	—	—	—	—	—	—	—
1978							
3874115	1.3–3.1 @ 600	5.8–7.5 @ 800	—	—	12 @ 2000	7	12 @ 12.5	—
3874173	1.3–3.1 @ 600	3.5–5.5 @ 700	—	—	10 @ 2000	8	11 @ 14.0	—
3874858	1.4–3.4 @ 600	6–8 @ 800	—	—	8.5 @ 2400	7	12.5 @ 12.5	—
3874876	.2–2.2 @ 600	1.5–3.5 @ 650	—	—	5.7 @ 2500	7	9.8 @ 11.5	—
4091101	1–1.2 @ 600	1.7–3.7 @ 800	—	—	5.8–7.8 @ 2060	9	9.5 @ 12.5	—
4091140②	—	—	—	—	—	—	—
4091709②	—	—	—	—	—	—	—
4091711②	—	—	—	—	—	—	—
1979							
3874876	.2–2.2 @ 600	1.5–3.5 @ 650	—	—	3.7–5.7 @ 2500	7	9.8 @ 11.5	—
4091101	1–1.2 @ 600	1.7–3.7 @ 800	—	—	5.8–7.8 @ 2060	9	9.5 @ 12.5	—
4091140①	—	—	—	—	—	—	—

①—Stamped on distributor housing.

②—Electronic Lean Burn system distributor, cannot be checked on vehicle.

VALVE SPECIFICATIONS

Year	Model	Valve Lash Int.	Valve Lash Exh.	Valve Angles Seat	Valve Angles Face	Valve Spring Installed Height	Valve Spring Pressure Lbs. @ In.	Stem Clearance Intake	Stem Clearance Exhaust	Stem Diameter Intake	Stem Diameter Exhaust
CHRYSLER & IMPERIAL											
1974	8-400, 440	Hydraulic①		45	45	1.86	200 @ 1.42	.001-.003	.002-.004	.372-.373	.371-.372
1975-76	V8-318	Hydraulic①		45	②	1 11/16	177 @ 1 5/16	.001-.003	.002-.004	.372-.373	.371-.372
	V8-360	Hydraulic①		45	②	1 11/16	⑧	.001-.003	.002-.004	.372-.373	.371-.372
	V8-400, 440	Hydraulic①		45	45	1 55/64	200 @ 1 7/16	.0011-.0028	④	.3723-.373	⑥
	V8-400, 440③	Hydraulic①		45	45	1 55/64	246 @ 1 23/64	.0016-.0033	⑤	.3718-.3725	⑦
1977	V8-318	Hydraulic①		45	②	1 11/16	177 @ 1 5/16	.001-.003	.002-.004	.372-.373	.371-.372
	V8-360	Hydraulic①		45	②	1 21/32	193 @ 1 1/4	.001-.003	.002-.004	.372-.373	.371-.372
	V8-400, 440	Hydraulic①		45	45	1 55/64	200 @ 1 7/16	.0011-.0028	④	.3723-.3730	⑥
1978	6-225	.010H	.020H	45	②	1 21/32	144 @ 1 5/16	.001-.003	.002-.004	.372-.373	.371-.372
	V8-318	Hydraulic①		45	②	1 21/32	177 @ 1 5/16	.001-.003	.002-.004	.372-.373	.371-.372
	V8-360	Hydraulic①		45	②	1 21/32	177 @ 1 5/16	.001-.003	.002-.004	.372-.373	.371-.372
	V8-360③	Hydraulic①		45	②	1 21/32	193 @ 1 1/4	.0015-.0035	.0025-.0045	.3715-.3725	.3705-.3715
	V8-400, 440	Hydraulic①		45	45	1 55/64	200 @ 1 7/16	.0011-.0028	④	.3723-.3730	⑥
	V8-400, 440③	Hydraulic①		45	45	1 55/64	246 @ 1 23/64	.0016-.0033	⑤	.3718-.3725	⑦
1979	6-225	.010H	.020H	45	②	1 21/32	144 @ 1.31	.001-.003	.002-.004	.372-.373	.371-.372
	V8-318	Hydraulic		45	45	1 21/32	177 @ 1.31	.001-.003	.002-.004	.372-.373	.371-.372
	V8-360	Hydraulic		45	45	1 21/32	177 @ 1.31	.001-.003	.002-.004	.372-.373	.371-.372
	V8-360③	Hydraulic		45	45	1 21/32	193 @ 1.25	.002-.004	.0025-.0045	.3175-.3725	.3705-.3715
DODGE & PLYMOUTH											
1974	6-198, 225	.010H	.020H	45	②	1.65	147 @ 1 5/16	.001-.003	.002-.004	.372-.373	.371-.372
	8-318	Hydraulic①		45	②	1.65	177 @ 1 5/16	.001-.003	.002-.004	.372-.373	.371-.372
	8-360, 2 Bar. Carb.	Hydraulic①		45	②	1.65	177 @ 1 5/16	.001-.003	.002-.004	.372-.373	.371-.372
	8-360, 4 Bar. Carb.	Hydraulic①		45	②	1.65	238 @ 1 5/16	.001-.003	.002-.004	.372-.373	.371-.372
	8-400, 440	Hydraulic①		45	45	1.86	200 @ 1 7/16	.001-.003	.002-.004	.372-.373	.371-.372
	8-400, 440 Hi Perf.	Hydraulic①		45	45	1.86	246 @ 1 23/64	.001-.003	.002-.004	.372-.373	.371-.372
1975-76	6-225⑮	.010H	.020H	45	45	1 11/16	144 @ 1 5/16	.001-.003	.002-.004	.372-.373	.371-.372
	V8-318	Hydraulic①		45	②	1 11/16	177 @ 1 5/16	.001-.003	.002-.004	.372-.373	.371-.372
	V8-360	Hydraulic①		45	②	1 11/16	⑧	.001-.003	.002-.004	.372-.373	.371-.372
	V8-360③⑨	Hydraulic①		45	②	1 21/32	238 @ 1 5/16	⑩	⑪	⑫	⑬
	V8-360③⑭	Hydraulic①		45	②	1 21/32	193 @ 1 1/4	⑩	⑪	⑫	⑬
	V8-400, 440	Hydraulic①		45	45	1 55/64	200 @ 1 7/16	.0011-.0028	④	.3723-.373	⑥
	V8-400, 440③	Hydraulic①		45	45	1 55/64	246 @ 1 23/64	.0016-.0033	⑤	.3718-.3725	⑦
1977	6-225	.010H	.020H	45	②	1 11/16	144 @ 1 5/16	.001-.003	.002-.004	.372-.373	.371-.372
	V8-318	Hydraulic①		45	②	1 11/16	177 @ 1 5/16	.001-.003	.002-.004	.372-.373	.371-.372
	V8-360	Hydraulic①		45	②	1 21/32	193 @ 1 1/4	.001-.003	.002-.004	.372-.373	.371-.372
	V8-360③	Hydraulic①		45	②	1 21/32	193 @ 1 1/4	.0015-.0035	.0025-.0045	.3715-.3725	.3705-.3715
	V8-400, 440	Hydraulic①		45	45	1 55/64	200 @ 1 7/16	.0011-.0028	④	.3723-.373	⑥
	V8-400, 440③	Hydraulic①		45	45	1 55/64	246 @ 1 23/64	.0016-.0033	⑤	.3718-.3725	⑦
1978	6-225	.010H	.020H	45	②	1 21/32	144 @ 1 5/16	.001-.003	.002-.004	.372-.373	.371-.372
	V8-318	Hydraulic①		45	②	1 21/32	177 @ 1 5/16	.001-.003	.002-.004	.372-.373	.371-.372
	V8-360	Hydraulic①		45	②	1 21/32	177 @ 1 5/16	.001-.003	.002-.004	.372-.373	.371-.372
	V8-360③	Hydraulic①		45	②	1 21/32	193 @ 1 1/4	.0015-.0035	.0025-.0045	.3715-.3725	.3705-.3715
	V8-400, 440	Hydraulic①		45	45	1 55/64	200 @ 1 7/16	.0011-.0028	④	.3723-.3730	⑥
	V8-400, 440③	Hydraulic①		45	45	1 55/64	246 @ 1 23/64	.0016-.0033	⑤	.3718-.3725	⑦
1979	6-225	.010H	.020H	45	②	1 21/32	144 @ 1.31	.001-.003	.002-.004	.372-.373	.371-.372
	V8-318	Hydraulic		45	45	1 21/32	177 @ 1.31	.001-.003	.002-.004	.372-.373	.371-.372
	V8-360	Hydraulic		45	45	1 21/32	177 @ 1.31	.001-.003	.002-.004	.372-.373	.371-.372
	V8-360③	Hydraulic		45	45		193 @ 1.25	.002-.004	.0025-.0045	.3175-.3725	.3705-.3715

①—No adjustment.
②—Intake 45°, exhaust 43°.
③—High Performance.
④—Hot end .0021-.0038, Cold end .0011-.0028.
⑤—Hot end .0026-.0043, Cold end .0016-.0033.
⑥—Hot end .3713-.372, Cold end .3723-.373.
⑦—Hot end .3708-.3715, Cold end .3718-.3725.
⑧—1975, 208 @ 1 5/16; 1976, 177 @ 1 5/16.
⑨—Except California.
⑩—1975: .001-.003; 1976: .0015-.0035.
⑪—1975: .002-.004; 1976: .0025-.0045.
⑫—1975: .372-.373; 1976: .3715-.3725.
⑬—1975: .371-.372; 1976: .3705-.3715.
⑭—California.
⑮—Some Aspen & Volaré models w/6-225 2 bar. carb. will be equipped W/hydraulic lifters which cannot be adjusted.

PISTONS, PINS, RINGS, CRANKSHAFT & BEARINGS

Year	Model	Piston Clearance Top of Skirt	Ring End Gap①		Wrist-pin Diam-eter	Rod Bearings		Main Bearings			
			Comp.	Oil		Shaft Diameter	Bearing Clearance	Shaft Diameter	Bearing Clearance	Thrust on Bear. No.	Shaft End Play
CHRYSLER & IMPERIAL											
1974	8-400	.0003–.0013	.013	.015	1.0935	2.374–2.375	②	2.6245–2.6255	.0005–.0025	3	.002–.007
	8-440	.0003–.0013	.013	.015	1.0935	2.374–2.375	.001–.0025	2.7495–2.7505	.0005–.0025	3	.002–.007
1975–76	V8-318	.0005–.0015	.010	.015	.9842	2.124–2.125	.0005–.0025	2.4995–2.5005	.0005–.0020	3	.002–.010
	V8-360	.0005–.0015	.010	.015	.9842	2.124–2.125	.0005–.0025	2.8095–2.8105	.0005–.0020	3	.002–.010
	V8-400	.0003–.0013	.013	.015	1.0936	2.375–2.376	③	2.6245–2.6255	.0005–.0020	3	.002–.007
	V8-440	.0003–.0013	.013	.015	1.0936	2.375–2.376	.0005–.0030	2.7495–2.7505	.0005–.0020	3	.002–.007
1977	V8-318	.0005–.0015	.010	.015	.9842	2.124–2.125	.0005–.0025	2.4995–2.5005	.0005–.0020	3	.002–.009
	V8-360	.0005–.0015	.010	.015	.9842	2.124–2.125	.0005–.0025	2.4995–2.5005	.0005–.0020	3	.002–.009
	V8-400	.0003–.0013	.013	.015	1.0936	2.375–2.376	.0005–.0025	2.6245–2.6255	.0005–.0020	3	.002–.009
	V8-440	.0003–.0013	.013	.015	1.0936	2.375–2.376	.0005–.0025	2.7495–2.7505	.0005–.0020	3	.002–.009
1978	6-225	.0005–.0015	.010	.015	.9008	2.1865–2.1875	.0005–.0025	2.7495–2.7505	.0005–.0020	3	.002–.009
	V8-318	.0005–.0015	.010	.015	.9842	2.1240–2.1250	.0005–.0025	2.4995–2.5005	.0005–.0020	3	.002–.009
	V8-360	⑥	.010	.015	.9842	2.1240–2.1250	.0005–.0025	2.8095–2.8105	.0005–.0020	3	.002–.009
	V8-400	.0003–.0013	.013	.015	1.0936	2.375–2.376	⑦	2.6245–2.6255	.0005–.0020	3	.002–.009
	V8-440	.0003–.0013	.013	.015	1.0936	2.375–2.376	⑦	2.7495–2.7505	.0005–.0020	3	.002–.009
1979	6-225	.0005–.0015	.010	.015	.9008	2.187	.0005–.0025	2.7495–2.7505	.0005–.002	3	.002–.009
	V8-318	.0005–.0015	.015	.015	.9842	2.125	.0005–.0025	2.4995–2.5005	.0005–.002	3	.002–.009
	V8-360	⑥	.015	.015	.9842	2.125	.0005–.0025	2.8095–2.8105	.0005–.002	3	.002–.009
DODGE & PLYMOUTH											
1974	6-198, 225	.0005–.0015	.010	.015	.9008	2.1865–2.1875	.0005–.0025	2.7495–2.7505	.0005–.0025	3	.002–.010
	8-318	.0005–.0015	.010	.015	.9842	2.124–2.125	.0005–.0025	2.4995–2.5005	.0005–.0025	3	.002–.010
	8-340	.0005–.0015	.010	.015	.9842	2.124–2.125	.0005–.0030	2.4995–2.5005	.0005–.0025	3	.002–.010
	8-360	.0005–.0015	.010	.015	.9842	2.124–2.125	.0005–.0025	2.8095–2.8105	.0005–.0025	3	.002–.010
	8-400	.0003–.0013	.013	.015	1.0936	2.374–2.375	②	2.6245–2.6255	.0005–.0025	3	.002–.010
	8-440	.0003–.0013	.013	.015	1.0936	2.374–2.375	.001–.0025	2.7495–2.7505	.0005–.0025	3	.002–.010
1975–76	6-225	.0005–.0015	.010	.015	.9008	2.1865–2.1875	④	2.7495–2.7505	.0005–.002	3	.002–.007
	V8-318	.0005–.0015	.010	.015	.9842	2.124–2.125	.0005–.0025	2.4995–2.5005	.0005–.002	3	.002–.010
	V8-360	.0005–.0015	.010	.015	.9842	2.124–2.125	.0005–.0025	2.8095–2.8105	.0005–.002	3	.002–.010
	V8-400	.0003–.0013	.013	.015	1.0936	2.375–2.376	③	2.6245–2.6255	.0005–.002	3	.002–.010
	V8-440	.0003–.0013	.013	.015	1.0936	2.375–2.376	.0005–.0030	2.7495–2.7505	.0005–.002	3	.002–.010
1977	6-225	.0005–.0015	.010	.015	.9008	2.1865–2.1875	.0005–.0025	2.7495–2.7505	.0005–.0020	3	.002–.009
	V8-318	.0005–.0015	.010	.015	.9842	2.124–2.125	.0005–.0025	2.4995–2.5005	.0005–.0020	3	.002–.009
	V8-360	.0005–.0015	.010	.015	.9842	2.125–2.125	.0005–.0025	2.4995–2.5005	.0005–.0020	3	.002–.009
	V8-400	.0003–.0013	.013	.015	1.0936	2.375–2.376	.0005–.0025	2.6245–2.6255	.0005–.0020	3	.002–.009
	V8-440	.0003–.0013	.013	.015	1.0936	2.375–2.376	.0005–.0025	2.7495–2.7505	.0005–.0020	3	.002–.009
1978	6-225	.0005–.0015	.010	.015	.9008	2.1865–2.1875	.0005–.0025	2.7495–2.7505	.0005–.0020	3	.002–.009
	V8-318	.0005–.0015	.010	.015	.9842	2.1240–2.1250	.0005–.0025	2.4995–2.5005	.0005–.0020	3	.002–.009
	V8-360	⑥	.010	.015	.9842	2.1240–2.1250	.0005–.0025	2.8095–2.8105	.0005–.0020	3	.002–.009
	V8-400	.0003–.0013	.013	.015	1.0936	2.375–2.376	⑦	2.6245–2.6255	.0005–.0020	3	.002–.009
	V8-440	.0003–.0013	.013	.015	1.0936	2.375–2.376	⑦	2.7495–2.7505	.0005–.0020	3	.002–.009
1979	6-225	.0005–.0015	.010	.015	.9008	2.187	.0005–.0025	2.7495–2.7505	.0005–.002	3	.002–.009
	V8-318	.0005–.0015	.015	.015	.9842	2.125	.0005–.0025	2.4995–2.5005	.0005–.002	3	.002–.009
	V8-360	⑥	.015	.015	.9842	2.125	.0005–.0025	2.8095–2.8105	.0005–.002	3	.002–.009

①—Fit rings in tapered bores for clearance listed in tightest portion of ring travel.
②—W/2 bbl. carb., .0005–.0020"; W/4 bbl. carb., .001–.0025".
③—1975: 2 bbl. carb., .0002–.0022, 4 bbl. carb., .0004–.0029; 1976: 2 bbl. carb., .0005–.0025, 4 bbl. carb., .0005–.0030.
④—1975: .0005–.0020; 1976; .0005–.0025.
⑤—With 2 bbl. carb., .0005–.0025; 4 bbl. carb., .0005–.0030.
⑥—Exc. High perf. engine, .0005"–.0015"; High perf. engine, .001"–.002".
⑦—Exc. High perf. engine, .0005"–.0025"; High perf. engine, .0005"–.0030".

ALTERNATOR & REGULATOR SPECIFICATIONS

Year	Unit Number	Ground Polarity	Field Coil Draw Amperes	Current Output			Operating Voltage			Voltage Regulator Point Gap	Regulator Armature Air Gap
				Engine R.P.M.	Amperes	Volts	Engine R.P.M.	Volts	Voltage @ 120° ①		
1974	Black Tag	Negative	2.5–3.7②	1250	65③	15	1250	15	13.8–14.4⑩	—	—
	Yellow Tag	Negative	2.5–3.7②	1250	36⑪	15	1250	15	13.8–14.4⑩	—	—
	Red Tag	Negative	2.5–3.7②	1250	40⑪	15	1250	15	13.8–14.4⑩	—	—
	Green Tag	Negative	2.5–3.7②	1250	47⑪	15	1250	15	13.8–14.4⑩	—	—
	Blue or Natural Tag	Negative	2.5–3.7②	1250	57⑪	15	1250	15	13.8–14.4⑩	—	—
1975	Yellow Tag④	Negative	2.5–3.7②	1250	36⑪	15	1250	15	13.9–14.6⑩	—	—
	Red Tag	Negative	2.5–3.7②	1250	40⑪	15	1250	15	13.9–14.6⑩	—	—
	Green Tag	Negative	2.5–3.7②	1250	47⑪	15	1250	15	13.9–14.6⑩	—	—
	Blue Tag	Negative	2.5–3.7②	1250	57⑪	15	1250	15	13.9–14.6⑩	—	—
	Natural Tag	Negative	2.5–3.7②	1250	57⑪	15	1250	15	13.9–14.6⑩	—	—
	Black Tag	Negative	2.5–3.7②	1250	62⑪	15	1250	15	13.9–14.6⑩	—	—
	Yellow Tag⑤	Negative	4.75–6②	900	72⑪	13	900	13	13.9–14.6⑩	—	—
1976–79	Bronze Tag	Negative	4.5–6.5②	1250	40⑪	15	1250	15	13.9–14.6⑩	—	—
	Natural Tag	Negative	4.5–6.5②	1250	47⑪	15	1250	15	13.9–14.6⑩	—	—
	Yellow Tag⑫	Negative	4.5–6.5②	1250	57⑪	15	1250	15	13.9–14.6⑩	—	—
	Brown Tag	Negative	4.5–6.5②	1250	62⑪	15	1250	15	13.9–14.6⑩	—	—
	Yellow Tag⑤	Negative	4.75–6.0②	900	72⑪	13	900	13	13.9–14.6⑩	—	—
1978-79	Violet Tag	Negative	4.5–6.5②	1250	40⑪	15	1250	15	13.9–14.6⑩	—	—

①—For each 10 degree rise in temperature subtract .04 volt. Temperature is checked with thermometer two inches from installed voltage regulator cover.
②—Current draw at 12 volts while turning rotor shaft by hand.
③—Plus or minus three amperes. If output is low, stator or rectifier is shorted.
④—34 amp rating.
⑤—100 amp rating.
⑥—Standard with 6-cyl. engines.
⑦—Standard with V8 engines.
⑧—Heavy duty and/or air conditioning.
⑨—Special equipment.
⑩—At 80 degrees F.
⑪—Minimum output.
⑫—60 amp rating.

STARTING MOTOR SPECIFICATIONS

Year	Part No.	Rotation ①	Brush Spring Tension, Ounces	No Load Test			Torque Test		
				Amperes	Volts	R.P.M.	Amperes	Volts	Torque, Ft. Lbs.
1974	3656575	Clockwise	32–36	90	11	3700–4200	475–550	4	—
1975–79	3755250	Clockwise	32–36	90	11	5700	475–550	4	—
	3755900	Clockwise	32–36	90	11	3700	475–550	4	—

①—Viewed from drive end.

ENGINE TIGHTENING SPECIFICATIONS★

★Torque specifications are for clean and lightly lubricated threads only. Dry or dirty threads produce increased friction which prevents accurate measurement of tightness.

Year	Engine	Spark Plugs Ft. Lbs.	Cylinder Head Bolts Ft. Lbs.	Intake Manifold Ft. Lbs.	Exhaust Manifold Ft. Lbs.	Rocker Arm Shaft Bracket Ft. Lbs.	Rocker Arm Cover Ft. Lbs.	Connecting Rod Cap Bolts Ft. Lbs.	Main Bearing Cap Bolts Ft. Lbs.	Flywheel to Crank-shaft Ft. Lbs.	Vibration Damper or Pulley Ft. Lbs.
1974	6-198, 225	30	70	240①	10	25	40①	45	85	55	②
1974	8-318, 360	30	95	35	20	200①	40①	45	85	55	100
1974	8-400, 440	30	70	40	30	25	40①	45	85	55	135
1975–76	6-225	10	70	240①	120①	25	40①	45	85	55	②
	V8-318, 360	30	95	40	20	200①	40①	45	85	55	100
	V8-400, 440	30	70	45	30	25	40①	45	85	55	135
1977	6-225	10	70	240①	120①	24	40①	45	85	55	②
	V8-318, 360	30	95	45	20	200①	40①	45	85	55	100
	V8-400, 440	30	70	45	40	24	40①	45	85	55	135
1978	6-225	10	70	④	120①	24	40①	45	85	55	②
	V8-318, 360	30	105	45	③	200①	40①	45	85	55	100
	V8-400, 440	30	70	45	30	25	40①	45	85	55	135
1979	6-225	10	70	④	120①	24	40①	45	85	55	②
	V8-318, 360	30	105	45	③	200①	40①	48	85	55	100

①—Inch pounds.
②—Press fit.
③—Screw, 20 ft. lbs.; Nut, 15 ft. lbs.
④—Intake to exhaust manifold studs 240 in. lbs., Intake to exhaust manifold bolts 200 in. lbs.

WHEEL ALIGNMENT SPECIFICATIONS

NOTE: See that riding height is correct before checking wheel alignment.

Year	Model	Caster Angle, Degrees		Camber Angle, Degrees				Toe-In. Inch	Toe-Out on Turns, Deg.	
		Limits	Desired	Limits		Desired			Outer Wheel	Inner Wheel
				Left	Right	Left	Right			
CHRYSLER & IMPERIAL										
1974-76	All	+¼ to +1¼	+¾	+¼ to +¾	0 to +½	+½	+¼	⅛–3/16	17.5	20
1977–79	Chrysler	−½ to +2	+¾	0 to +1	−¼ to +¾	+½	+¼	⅛	18.3	20
	Cordoba	−½ to +2	+¾	0 to +1	−¼ to +¾	+½	+¼	⅛	18	20
	LeBaron	+1½ to +3¾	+2½	0 to +1	−¼ to +¾	+½	+¼	⅛	18	20

①—Exc. Cordoba, 18.3°; Cordoba, 18°.

Year	Model	Caster Limits	Caster Desired	Camber Limits Left	Camber Limits Right	Camber Desired Left	Camber Desired Right	Toe-In. Inch	Outer Wheel	Inner Wheel
DODGE										
1974	Man. Steer.	−1 to 0	−½	+¼ to +¾	0 to +½	+½	+¼	⅛ to 3/16	②	20
	Power Steer.	+¼ to +1¼	+¾	+¼ to +¾	0 to +½	+½	+¼	⅛ to 3/16	②	20
1975	Man. Steer.	−1 to 0	−½	+¼ to +¾	0 to +½	+½	+¼	⅛–3/16	③	20
	Power Steer.	+¼ to +1¼	+¾	+¼ to +¾	0 to +½	+½	+¼	⅛–3/16	③	20
1976	Man. Steer.④	−1 to 0	−½	+¼ to +¾	0 to +½	+½	+¼	⅛–3/16	③	20
	Power Steer.④	+¼ to +1¼	+¾	+¼ to +¾	0 to +½	+½	+¼	⅛–3/16	③	20
	Aspen	+2 to +3	+2½	+¼ to +¾	0 to +½	+½	+¼	⅛–3/16	18.0	20
1977	Man. Steer.④	−1¾ to +¾	−½	0 to +1	−¼ to +¾	+½	+¼	1/16–¼	①	20
	Power Steer.④	−½ to +2	+¾	0 to +1	−¼ to +¾	+½	+¼	1/16–¼	①	20
	Aspen	+1½ to +3¾	+2½	0 to +1	−¼ to +¾	+½	+½	1/16–¼	18.0	20
	Diplomat	+1½ to +3¾	+2½	0 to +1	−¼ to +¾	+½	+¼	⅛	18.0	20

Continued

WHEEL ALIGNMENT SPECIFICATIONS—Continued

NOTE: See that riding height is correct before checking wheel alignment.

Year	Model	Caster Angle, Degrees		Camber Angle, Degrees				Toe-In. Inch	Toe-Out on Turns, Deg.	
		Limits	Desired	Limits		Desired			Outer Wheel	Inner Wheel
				Left	Right	Left	Right			

DODGE—Continued

Year	Model	Limits	Desired	Left	Right	Left	Right	Toe-In. Inch	Outer Wheel	Inner Wheel
1978-79	Man. Steer.④	−1¾ to +¾	−½	0 to +1	−¼ to +¾	+½	+¼	⅛	18.0	20
	Power. Steer.④	−½ to +2	+¾	0 to +1	−¼ to +¾	+½	+¼	⅛	18.0	20
	Aspen	+1½ to 3¾	+2½	0 to +1	−¼ to +¾	+½	+¼	⅛	18.0	20
	Diplomat	+1½ to 3¾	+2½	0 to +1	−¼ to +¾	+½	+¼	⅛	18.0	20

①—Charger SE & Monaco, 18°; Royal Monaco, 18.3°.
②—Dart 18.5°, Challenger 18.4°, Charger & Coronet 18°, Monaco 18.3°.
③—Dart, 18.5°; Charger SE & Coronet, 18° Monaco, 18.3°.
④—Except Aspen & Diplomat.

PLYMOUTH

Year	Model	Limits	Desired	Left	Right	Left	Right	Toe-In. Inch	Outer Wheel	Inner Wheel
1974	Man. Steer.	−1 to 0	−½	+¼ to +¾	0 to +½	+½	+¼	⅛-³⁄₁₆	②	20
	Power Steer.	+¼ to +1¼	+¾	+¼ to +¾	0 to +½	+½	+¼	⅛-³⁄₁₆	②	20
1975	Man. Steer.	−1 to 0	−½	+¼ to +¾	0 to +½	+½	+¼	⅛-³⁄₁₆	③	20
	Power Steer.	+¼ to +1¼	+¾	+¼ to +¾	0 to +½	+½	+¼	⅛-³⁄₁₆	③	20
1976	Man. Steer.④	−1 to 0	−½	+¼ to +¾	0 to +½	+½	+¼	⅛-³⁄₁₆	③	20
	Power Steer.④	+¼ to +1¼	+¾	+¼ to +¾	0 to +½	+½	+¼	⅛-³⁄₁₆	③	20
	Volaré	+2 to +3	+2½	+¼ to +¾	0 to +½	+½	+¼	⅛-³⁄₁₆	18.0	20
1977	Man. Steer.④	−1¾ to +¾	−½	0 to +1	−¼ to +¾	+½	+¼	¹⁄₁₆-¼	①	20
	Power Steer.④	−½ to +2	+¾	0 to +1	−¼ to +¾	+½	+¼	¹⁄₁₆-¼	①	20
	Volaré	+1½ to +3¾	+2½	0 to +1	−¼ to +¾	+½	+½	¹⁄₁₆-¼	18.0	20
1978	Man. Steer.④	−1¾ to +¾	−½	0 to +1	−¼ to +¾	+½	+¼	⅛	18.0	20
	Power. Steer.④	−½ to +2	+¾	0 to +1	−¼ to +¾	+½	+¼	⅛	18.0	20
	Volaré	+1½ to 3¾	+2½	0 to +1	−¼ to +¾	+½	+¼	⅛	18.0	20
1979	Volaré	+1½ to +3¾	+2½	0 to +1	−¼ to +¾	+½	+¼	⅛		

①—Barracuda & Valiant, 17.5°; 1973 Satellite, 18.5°; Fury, 18.8°.
②—Valiant 18.5°, Barracuda 18.4°, Satellite 18°, Fury 18.3°
③—Valiant, 18.5°; Fury, 18°; Gran Fury, 18.3°.
④—Except Volaré.
⑤—Fury, 18°; Gran Fury, 18.3°.

BRAKE SPECIFICATIONS

Year	Model	Brake Drum Inside Diameter	Wheel Cylinder Bore Diameter			Master Cylinder Bore Diameter		
			Disc Brake	Front Drum Brake	Rear Drum Brake	Disc Brakes	Drum Brakes	Power Brakes
CHRYSLER & IMPERIAL								
1974	Chrysler	11	3.10	—	15/16	1 1/32	—	1 1/32
	Imperial	—	(5)	—	—	1 1/16	—	1 1/16
1975	Cordoba	10	2¾	—	15/16	1.03	—	1.03
	Chrysler	11	3.1	—	15/16	1.03	—	1.03
	Imperial	—	(5)	—	—	1.06	—	1.06
1976	Cordoba	10	2¾	—	15/16	1.03	—	1.03
	Chrysler	11	3.1	—	15/16	1.03	—	1.03
1977	Chrysler	11	3.1	—	15/16	1.03	—	1.03
	Cordoba	11	2¾	—	15/16	1.03	—	1.03
	LeBaron	10	2.755	—	15/16	1.031	—	1.031
1978	Chrysler	11	3.102	—	15/16	1.031	—	1.031
	Cordoba	(6)	2.755	—	15/16	1.031	—	1.031
	LeBaron	10	2.755	—	15/16	1.031	—	1.031
1979	Chrysler	(6)	2.75	—	15/16	1.03	—	1.03
	Cordoba	(6)	2.75	—	15/16	1.03	—	1.03
	LeBaron	10	2.75	—	15/16	1.03	—	1.03
DODGE								
1974	Dart, 6 cyl.	(3)	—	1⅛	13/16	—	1 1/32	1 1/32
	Dart, V8	10	2.60	—	15/16	1 1/32	—	15/16
	Challenger	10	2.75	—	15/16	1	—	1 1/32
	Charger, Coronet Exc. Sta. Wag.	10	2.75	—	15/16	1	—	1 1/32
	Coronet Sta. Wag.	11	2.75	—	15/16	1	—	1 1/32
	Monaco, Polara	11	3.10	—	15/16	1 1/32	—	1 1/32
1975	Dart 6 cyl.	(3)	—	1⅛	13/16	—	1.03	—
	Dart V8	10	2.6	—	15/16	1.03	—	15/16
	Coronet, Charger SE	10①	2.75	—	15/16	1	—	1.03
	Monaco	11	3.1	—	15/16	1.03	—	1.03
1976	Aspen	10②	2¾	—	15/16	1.03	—	1.03
	Dart 6 cyl.	(3)	—	15/16	13/16	—	1.03	—
	Dart V8	10	2¾	—	15/16	1.03	—	.937
	Coronet, Charger	10①	2¾	—	15/16	1.03	—	1.03
	Monaco	11	3.1	—	15/16	1.03	—	1.03
1977	Aspen	10①	2¾	—	15/16	1.03	—	1.03
	Charger	11	2¾	—	15/16	1.03	—	1.03
	Monaco	11	2¾	—	15/16	1.03	—	1.03
	Royal Monaco	11	3.1	—	15/16	1.03	—	1.03
	Diplomat	10	2.755	—	15/16	1.031	—	1.031
1978	Aspen	(7)	2.755	—	15/16	1.031	—	1.031
	Charger	(6)	2.755	—	15/16	1.031	—	1.031
	Diplomat	10	2.755	—	15/16	1.031	—	1.031
	Monaco	(6)(7)	2.755	—	15/16	1.031	—	1.031
1979	Aspen	(7)	2.75	—	15/16	1.03	—	1.03
	Diplomat	10	2.75	—	15/16	1.03	—	1.03
	Magnum XE	(6)	2.75	—	15/16	1.03	—	1.03
	St. Regis	(6)	2.75	—	15/16	1.03	—	1.03

BRAKE SPECIFICATIONS—Continued

Year	Model	Brake Drum Inside Diameter	Wheel Cylinder Bore Diameter			Master Cylinder Bore Diameter		
			Disc Brake	Front Drum Brake	Rear Drum Brake	Disc Brakes	Drum Brakes	Power Brakes
PLYMOUTH								
1973	Valiant, 6 cyl. (Early)	9	—	1 1/16	13/16	—	15/16	15/16
	Valiant, 6 cyl. (Late)	10	—	1 3/16	13/16	—	1 1/32	1 1/32
	Valiant, V8	10	2.599	1 1/16	15/16	1 1/32	1 1/32	1 1/32
	Barracuda	10	2.750	—	15/16	1 1/32	1 1/32	1 1/32
	Satellite	10④	2.750	—	15/16	1 1/32	1 1/32	1 1/32
	Fury	11	2.750	—	15/16	1 1/32	1 1/32	1 1/32
1974	Valiant, 6 cyl.	③	—	1 1/8	13/16	—	1 1/32	1 1/32
	Valiant, V8	10	2.60	—	15/16	1 1/32	—	15/16
	Barracuda	10	2.75	—	15/16	1	—	1 1/32
	Satellite Exc. Sta. Wag.	10	2.75	—	15/16	1	—	1 1/32
	Satellite Sta. Wag.	11	2.75	—	15/16	1	—	1 1/32
	Fury	11	3.10	—	15/16	1 1/32	—	1 1/32
1975	Valiant 6 cyl.	③	—	1 1/8	13/16	—	1.03	—
	Valiant V8	10	2.6	—	15/16	1.03	—	15/16
	Fury	10①	2.75	—	15/16	1	—	1.03
	Gran Fury	11	3.1	—	15/16	1.03	—	1.03
1976	Volaré	10②	2 3/4	—	15/16	1.03	—	1.03
	Valiant 6 cyl.	③	—	15/16	13/16	—	1.03	1.03
	Valiant V8	10	2 3/4	—	15/16	1.03	—	.937
	Fury	10①	2 3/4	—	15/16	1.03	—	1.03
	Gran Fury	11	3.1	—	15/16	1.03	—	1.03
1977	Volaré	10①	2 3/4	—	15/16	1.03	—	1.03
	Fury	11	2 3/4	—	15/16	1.03	—	1.03
	Gran Fury	11	3.1	—	15/16	1.03	—	1.03
1978	Fury	⑥⑦	2.755	—	15/16	1.031	—	1.031
	Volaré	⑦	2.755	—	15/16	1.031	—	1.031
1979	Volaré	⑦	2.75	—	15/16	1.03	—	1.03

①—Wagon 11".
②—Wagon, early 1976 models 11"; late 1976 models 10".
③—Front 10", rear 9".
④—Heavy duty 11".
⑤—Front, 3.1; Rear, 2.6.
⑥—Exc. 9 1/4" axle, 10"; 9 1/4" axle, 11".
⑦—Exc. taxi & police, 10"; taxi & police 11".

COOLING SYSTEM & CAPACITY DATA

Year	Model or Engine	Cooling Capacity, Qts.			Radiator Cap Relief Pressure, Lbs.		Thermo. Opening Temp. ①	Fuel Tank Gals.	Engine Oil Refill Qts. ②	Transmission Oil			Rear Axle Oil Pints
		No Heater	With Heater	With A/C	With A/C	No A/C				3 Speed Pints	4 Speed Pints	Auto. Trans. Qts. ⑫	
CHRYSLER													
1974	8-400, 440	—	16 1/2	16 1/2	16	16	195	25⑰	4	—	—	9 1/2	4.5
1975	V8-318	—	16	18	16	16	195	25 1/2	4	—	—	8 1/2⑥	4 1/2
	V8-360	—	16	16	16	16	195	⑤	4	—	—	9 1/2	4 1/2
	V8-400	—	16 1/2	16 1/2	16	16	195	㉑	4	—	—	9 1/2	4 1/2
	V8-440	—	16	16	16	16	195	26 1/2⑰	4㉚	—	—	9 1/2	4 1/2
1976	V8-318	—	16	18	16	16	195	⑤	4	—	—	9 1/2	4 1/2
	V8-360	—	16	16	16	16	195	⑤	4㉚	—	—	㉝	4 1/2
	V8-400	—	16 1/2	16 1/2	16	16	195	⑤	4㉚	—	—	㉝	4 1/2
	V8-440	—	16	16	16	16	195	⑤	4㉚	—	—	㉝	4 1/2
1977	V8-318	—	16 1/2	18	16	16	195	⑤	4	—	—	8 1/2	4 1/2
	V8-360	—	16	16	16	16	195	⑤	4	—	—	8 1/2③	4 1/2
	V8-400	—	16 1/2	16 1/2	16	16	195	⑤	4	—	—	8 1/4	4 1/2
	V8-440	—	16	16	16	16	195	⑤	4	—	—	8 1/4	4 1/2

Continued

COOLING SYSTEM & CAPACITY DATA—Continued

Year	Model or Engine	Cooling Capacity, Qts.			Radiator Cap Relief Pressure, Lbs.		Thermo. Opening Temp. ①	Fuel Tank Gals.	Engine Oil Refill Qts. ②	Transmission Oil			Rear Axle Oil Pints
		No Heater	With Heater	With A/C	With A/C	No A/C				3 Speed Pints	4 Speed Pints	Auto. Trans. Qts. ⑫	
CHRYSLER—Continued													
1978	6-225	—	12	14	16	16	195	19½	4	—	—	8½	2
	V8-318	—	16	17½	16	16	195	⑯	4	—	—	8½	4½
	V8-360	—	16	16	16	16	195	⑮	4	—	—	8¼	4½
	V8-400	—	16½	16½	16	16	195	⑮	4	—	—	8¼	4½
	V8-440	—	16½	16½	16	16	195	⑮	4	—	—	8¼	4½
1979	6-225	—	11.5	㊳	16	16	195	㊱	4	—	—	8½	㊲
	V8-318	—	15	㊴	16	16	195	㊱	4	—	—	8½	㊲
	V8-360	—	㊵	㊵	16	16	195	㊱	4	—	—	8½	
IMPERIAL													
1974	All	—	17	17	16	16	195	25	4	—	—	9½	4.5
1975	All	—	16	16	16	16	195	26½	4	—	—	9½	4½
DODGE													
1974	Dart 6 cyl.	—	13	14	16	16	195	16	4	6½	—	8¼	2
	Dart 8-318	—	16	17½	16	16	195	16	4	4¾	7	8¼	4½
	Dart 8-360	—	16	16	16	16	195	16	4	4¾	7	8	4½
	Challenger 8-318	—	16	17½	16	16	195	18	4	4¾	—	8¼	4½
	Challenger 8-360	—	16	16	16	16	195	18	4	4¾	7½	8	4½
	Coro., Charger 6-225	—	13	15	16	16	195	19½㉘	4	4¾	—	8¼	4½
	Coro., Charger 8-318	—	16	18	16	16	195	19½㉘	4	4¾	7½	8¼	4½
	Coro., Charger 8-360	—	16½	16½	16	16	195	19½㉘	4	—	7½	8	4½
	Coro., Charger 8-400	—	16½	16½	16	16	195	19½㉘	4	—	7½	9½㉙	4½
	Coro., Charger 8-440	—	16	16	16	16	195	19½㉘	4	—	—	8	4½
	Monaco 8-360	—	16	16	16	16	195	25㉗	4	—	—	8	4½
	Monaco 8-400	—	16½	16½	16	16	195	25㉗	4	—	—	9½	4½
	Monaco 8-440	—	16	16	16	16	195	25㉗	4	—	—	9½	4½
1975	Dart 6-225	—	13	14	16	16	195	16	4	3½	—	8½	2.1
	Dart 8-318	—	16	17½	16	16	195	16	4	4¾	7	8½⑥	4½
	Dart 8-360	—	16	16	16	16	195	16	4	4¾	—	8¼	4½
	Coronet 6-225	—	13	—	16	16	195	25½	4	4¾	—	8½	4½
	Coro., Charger 8-318	—	16½	18	16	16	195	25½⑪	4	4¾	—	8½⑥	4½
	Coro., Charger 8-360	—	16	16	16	16	195	25½⑪	4	—	—	9½	4½
	Coro., Charger 8-400	—	16	16	16	16	195	25½⑪	4	—	—	9½	4½
	Coronet 8-440	—	16	16	16	16	195	25½⑪	4㉚	—	—	8¼	4½
	Monaco 8-318	—	17½	17½	16	16	195	26½㉗	4	—	—	8½⑥	4½
	Monaco 8-360	—	16	16	16	16	195	26½㉗	4	—	—	9½	4½
	Monaco 8-400	—	16½	16½	16	16	195	26½㉗	4	—	—	9½	4½
	Monaco 8-440	—	16	16	16	16	195	26½㉗	4㉚	—	—	9½	4½
1976	Aspen, Dart 6-225	—	13	14	16	16	195	㉛	4	㉜	7	8½	4
	Aspen, Dart 8-318	—	16	17	16	16	195	㉛	4	4¾	7	8½	4
	Aspen 8-360	—	16	16	16	16	195	㉛	4	4¾	7	8½	4
	Charger, Coronet 6-225	—	13	14½	16	16	195	25½⑪	4	4¾	—	8½	4½
	Charger, Coronet 8-318	—	16½	18	16	16	195	25½⑪	4	4¾	—	8½	4½
	Charger, Coronet 8-360	—	16	16	16	16	195	25½⑪	4	4¾	—	8½	4½
	Charger, Coronet 8-400	—	16½	16½	16	16	195	25½⑪	4	4¾	—	㉝	4½
	Coronet 8-440	—	16	16	16	16	195	25½⑪	4	4¾	—	㉝	4½
	Monaco 8-318	—	17½	17½	16	16	195	26½㉗	4	—	—	9½	4½
	Monaco 8-360	—	16	16	16	16	195	26½㉗	4	—	—	9½	4½
	Monaco 8-400	—	16½㉞	16½㉞	16	16	195	26½㉗	4㉚	—	—	㉝	4½
	Monaco 8-440	—	16㉞	16㉞	16	16	195	26½㉗	4㉚	—	—	㉝	4½

Continued

COOLING SYSTEM & CAPACITY DATA—Continued

Year	Model or Engine	Cooling Capacity, Qts.			Radiator Cap Relief Pressure, Lbs.		Thermo. Opening Temp. ①	Fuel Tank Gals.	Engine Oil Refill Qts. ②	Transmission Oil			Rear Axle Oil Pints
		No Heater	With Heater	With A/C	With A/C	No A/C				3 Speed Pints	4 Speed Pints	Auto. Trans. Qts. ⑫	
DODGE—Continued													
1977	Aspen 6-225	—	12	14	16	16	195	18⑦	4	4¾	7	8½	2
	Aspen 8-318	—	16	17½	16	16	195	20	4	4¾	7	8½	4½
	Aspen 8-360	—	16	17½	16	16	195	20	4	—	—	8½	4½
	Charger 8-318	—	16½	18	16	16	195	25½	4	—	—	8½	4½
	Charger 8-360	—	16	16	16	16	195	25½	4	—	—	8½③	4½
	Charger 8-400	—	16½	16½	16	16	195	25½	4	—	—	8¼	4½
	Monaco 6-225	—	13	14½	16	16	195	25½⑦	4	4¾	—	8½	4½
	Monaco 8-318	—	16½	18	16	16	195	25½⑦	4	4¾	—	8½	4½
	Monaco 8-360	—	16	16	16	16	195	25½⑦	4	—	—	8½③	4½
	Monaco 8-400	—	16½	16½	16	16	195	25½⑦	4	—	—	8¼	4½
	Monaco 8-440	—	16	16	16	16	195	20½	4	—	—	8½	4½
	Royal Monaco 8-318	—	17½	17½	16	16	195	20½	4	—	—	8½③	4½
	Royal Monaco 8-360	—	16	16	16	16	195	26½㉗	4	—	—	8½③	4½
	Royal Monaco 8-400	—	16½	16½	16	16	195	26½㉗	4	—	—	8½③	4½
	Royal Monaco 8-440	—	16	16	16	16	195	20½	4	—	—	8½③	4½
1978	Diplomat	—	16	17½	16	16	195	19½	4	—	—	8½	4½
	Aspen 6-225	—	12	14	16	16	195	⑭	4	4¾	7	8½	2
	Aspen V8-318	—	16	17½	16	16	195	⑭	4	4¾	7	8½	2
	Aspen V8-360	—	16	16	16	16	195	⑭	4	4¾	7	8½	4½
	Charger V8-318	—	16½	18	16	16	195	25½	4	—	—	8½	4½
	Charger V8-360	—	16	16	16	16	195	25½	4	—	—	8¼	4½
	Charger V8-400	—	16½	16½	16	16	195	25½	4	—	—	8¼	4½
	Diplomat 6-225	—	12	14	16	16	195	19½	4	—	7	8½	2
	Diplomat V8-318	—	16	17½	16	16	195	19½	4	—	7	8½	2
	Diplomat V8-360	—	16	16	16	16	195	19½	4	—	7	8½	4½
	Monaco 6-225	—	13	14½	16	16	195	20½	4	4¾	—	8½	4½
	Monaco V8-318	—	16½	18	16	16	195	25½⑦	4	4¾	—	8½	4½
	Monaco V8-360	—	16	16	16	16	195	25½⑦	4	4¾	—	8½	4½
	Monaco V8-400	—	16½	16½	16	16	195	25½⑦	4	4¾	—	8¼	4½
1979	Aspen 6-225	—	11.5	12.5	16	16	195	⑭	4	4.8	7	8.5	2
	Aspen V8-318	—	15	16.5	16	16	195	19.5	4	—	—	8.5	2
	Aspen V8-360	—	15	15	16	16	195	19.5	4	—	—	8.5	4.5
	Diplomat 6-225	—	11.5	12.5	16	16	195	19.5	4	—	7	8.5	2
	Diplomat V8-318	—	15	16.5	16	16	195	19.5	4	—	—	8.5	2
	Diplomat V8-360	—	15	15	16	16	195	19.5	4	—	—	8.5	4.5
	Magnum XE V8-318	—	15	17.5	16	16	195	21	4	—	—	8.5	4.5
	Magnum XE V8-360	—	16	16	16	16	195	21	4	—	—	8.5	4.5
	St. Regis 6-225	—	11.5	14.5	16	16	195	21	4	—	—	8.5	4.5
	St. Regis V8-318	—	15	17.5	16	16	195	21	4	—	—	8.5	4.5
	St. Regis V8-360	—	16	16	16	16	195	21	4	—	—	8.5	4.5
PLYMOUTH													
1974	Satellite 6-225	12	13	13	16	16	185	21	4	6½	—	8½	4½
	Satellite 8-318	15	16	18	16	16	185	21	4	4¾	7.5	8½	4½
	Satellite 8-340	14	15	16	16	16	185	21	4	4¾	7.5	8	4½
	Satellite 8-400	15	16	17	16	16	185	21	4	4¾	7.5	8	4½
	Satellite 8-440	16	17	17	16	16	185	21	4	—	—	9½	4½
	Fury 8-318	15	16	19	16	16	185	23	4	—	—	8½	4½
	Fury 8-360	15	16	16	16	16	185	23	4	—	—	8	4½
	Fury 8-400	15㉒	16㉓	17㉖	16	16	185	23	4	—	—	8⑱	4½
	Fury 8-440	15㉒	16㉓	17㉖	16	16	185	23	4	—	—	9½	4½

Continued

COOLING SYSTEM & CAPACITY DATA—Continued

Year	Model or Engine	Cooling Capacity, Qts.			Radiator Cap Relief Pressure, Lbs.		Thermo. Opening Temp. ①	Fuel Tank Gals.	Engine Oil Refill Qts. ②	Transmission Oil			Rear Axle Oil Pints
		No Heater	With Heater	With A/C	With A/C	No A/C				3 Speed Pints	4 Speed Pints	Auto. Trans. Qts. ⑫	
PLYMOUTH—Continued													
1975	Fury 6-225	—	13	—	16	16	195	25½	4	4¾	—	8½	4½
	Fury 8-318	—	16½	18	16	16	195	25½⑪	4	4¾	—	⑧	4½
	Fury 8-360	—	16	16	16	16	195	25½⑪	4	—	—	9½	4½
	Fury 8-400	—	16½	16½	16	16	195	25½⑪	4	—	—	9½	4½
	Fury 8-440	—	16	16	16	16	195	25½⑪	4㉚	—	—	8¼	4½
	Gran Fury 8-318	—	17½	17½	16	16	195	26½㉗	4	—	—	⑥	4½
	Gran Fury 8-360	—	16	16	16	16	195	26½㉗	4	—	—	9½	4½
	Gran Fury 8-400	—	16½	16½	16	16	195	26½㉗	4	—	—	9½	4½
	Gran Fury 8-440	—	16	16	16	16	195	26½㉗	4㉚	—	—	9½	4½
1976	Fury 6-225	—	13	14½	16	16	195	25½⑪	4	4¾	—	8½	4½
	Fury 8-318	—	16½	18	16	16	195	25½⑪	4	4¾	—	8½	4½
	Fury 8-360	—	16	16	16	16	195	25½⑪	4	4¾	—	8½	4½
	Fury 8-400	—	16½	16½	16	16	195	25½⑪	4	4¾	—	㉝	4½
	Fury 8-440	—	16	16	16	16	195	25½⑪	4	4¾	—	㉝	4½
	Gran Fury 8-318	—	17½	17½	16	16	195	19½㉗	4	—	—	9½	4½
	Gran Fury 8-360	—	16	16	16	16	195	26½㉗	4	—	—	9½	4½
	Gran Fury 8-400	—	16½�34	16½�34	16	16	195	26½㉗	4	—	—	㉝	4½
	Gran Fury 8-440	—	16�34	16�34	16	16	195	26½㉗	4	—	—	㉝	4½
1977	Fury 6-225	—	13	14½	16	16	195	25½⑦	4	4¾	—	8½	4½
	Fury 8-318	—	16½	18	16	16	195	25½⑦	4	4¾	—	8½	4½
	Fury 8-360	—	16	16	16	16	195	25½⑦	4	—	—	8½	4½
	Fury 8-400	—	16½	16½	16	16	195	25½⑦	4	—	—	8¼	4½
	Fury 8-440	—	16	16	16	16	195	20½	4	—	—	8½	4½
	Gran Fury 8-318	—	17½	17½	16	16	195	20½	4	—	—	8½③	4½
	Gran Fury 8-360	—	16	16	16	16	195	26½㉗	4	—	—	8½③	4½
	Gran Fury 8-400	—	16½	16½	16	16	195	26½㉗	4	—	—	8½③	4½
	Gran Fury 8-440	—	16	16	16	16	195	26½㉗	4	—	—	8½③	4½
1978	Fury 6-225	—	13	14½	16	16	195	25½⑦	4	4¾	—	8½	4½
	Fury V8-318	—	16½	18	16	16	195	25½⑦	4	4¾	—	8½	4½
	Fury V8-360	—	16	16	16	16	195	25½⑦	4	4¾	—	8½	4½
	Fury V8-400	—	16½	16½	16	16	195	25½⑦	4	4¾	—	8¼	4½
VALIANT, BARRACUDA & VOLARÉ													
1974	Valiant 6-198	—	13	14	16	16	195	16	4	6½	—	8¼	2
	Valiant 6-225	—	13	14	16	16	195	16	4	6½	—	8¼	2
	Valiant 8-318	—	16	17½	16	16	195	16	4	4¾	7	8¼	4½
	Valiant 8-360	—	16	16	16	16	195	16	4	4¾	7	8	4½
	Barracuda 8-318	—	16	17½	16	16	195	16½	4	4¾	—	8¼	4½
	Barracuda 8-360	—	16	16	16	16	195	16½	4	4¾	7½	8	4½
1975	Valiant 6-225	—	13	14	16	16	195	16	4	3½	—	8½	2.1
	Valiant V8-318	—	16	17½	16	16	195	16	4	4¾	7	8½⑥	4½
	Valiant V8-360	—	16	16	16	16	195	16	4	—	—	8¼	4½
1976	Valiant, Volaré 6-225	—	13	14	16	16	195	㉟	4	㉜	7	8½	2
	Valiant, Volaré V8-318	—	16	17	16	16	195	㉟	4	4¾	7	8½	4½
	Valiant, Volaré V8-360	—	16	16	16	16	195	㉟	4	4¾	7	8½	4½
1977	Volaré 6-225	—	12	14	16	16	195	18⑦	4	4¾	7	8½	2
	Volaré 8-318	—	16	17½	16	16	195	20	4	4¾	7	8½	4½
	Volaré 8-360	—	16	17½	16	16	195	20	4	—	—	8½	4½

Continued

COOLING SYSTEM & CAPACITY DATA—Continued

Year	Model or Engine	Cooling Capacity, Qts.			Radiator Cap Relief Pressure, Lbs.		Thermo. Opening Temp. ①	Fuel Tank Gals.	Engine Oil Refill Qts. ②	Transmission Oil			Rear Axle Oil Pints
		No Heater	With Heater	With A/C	With A/C	No A/C				3 Speed Pints	4 Speed Pints	Auto. Trans. Qts. ⑫	

VALIANT, BARRACUDA & VOLARÉ—Continued

Year	Model	No Heater	With Heater	With A/C	With A/C	No A/C	Thermo	Fuel	Engine	3 Speed	4 Speed	Auto	Rear Axle
1978	Volaré 6-225	—	12	14	16	16	195	⑭	4	4¾	7	8½	2
	Volaré V8-318	—	16	17½	16	16	195	⑭	4	4¾	7	8½	2
	Volaré V8-360	—	16	16	16	16	195	⑭	4	4¾	7	8½	4½
1979	Volaré 6-255	—	11.5	12.5	16	16	195	⑭	4	4.8	7	8.5	2
	Volaré V8-318	—	15	16.5	16	16	195	19.5	4	—	—	8.5	2
	Volaré V8-360	—	15	15	16	16	195	19.5	4	—	—	8.5	4.5

①—With permanent type anti-freeze.
②—Add one qt. with filter change.
③—With A-727 transmission (heavy duty), 8¼ qts.
④—With 7¼" ring gear, 2 pts.; 8¼" ring gear, 4½ pts.
⑤—Cordoba 25½ gals., Chrysler 26½, Wagon 24 gals.
⑥—With 727 transmission (heavy duty), 9½ qts.
⑦—Station wagons, 20 gals.
⑧—With 727 transmission (heavy duty), 9½ qts.; Roadrunner models 8¼ qts.
⑪—Wagon 20 gals., Sedan Models with dual exhaust 20½ gals.

⑫—Approximate. Make final check with dipstick.
⑭—6 cyl. exc. Station Wag. 18 gal.; 8 cyl. & Wag., 19.5 gals.
⑮—LeBaron, 19½; Cordoba, 25½; Chrysler, 26½.
⑱—With 2 bar. carb. 9½ qts.
㉑—Chrysler exc. wagon, 26½ gals.; wagon, 24 gals.; Cordoba exc. dual exhaust, 25½ gals.; dual exhaust 20.5 gals.
㉒—16 quarts with 4 Bar. Carb. or Hi-Perf.
㉓—17 quarts with 4 Bar. Carb. or Hi-Perf.
㉔—8 quarts with 4 Bar. Carb. or Hi-Perf.
㉖—18 quarts with 4 Bar. Carb. or Hi-Perf.
㉗—Wagons 24 gals.

㉘—Wagons 21 gals.
㉙—Hi Perf. 8 qts.
㉚—High performance engine 5 qts.
㉛—Aspen, 18 gals.; Dart, 16 gals.
㉜—Exc. floorshift, 3.6 pts.; floor shift, 4¾ pts.
㉝—Exc. High Perf., 9½ qts.; High Perf., 8¼ qts.
㉞—Add 1 qt. with maximum cooling or trailer towing package.
㉟—Volaré, 18 gal.; Valiant, 16 gals.
㊱—Exc. Le Baron, 21 qts.; Le Baron, 19.5 qts.
㊲—Exc. Le Baron, 4½ pts.; Le Baron, 7¼" ring gear, 2 pts.; 8¼", 9¼" ring gear, 4½ pts.
㊳—Exc. Le Baron, 14.5 qts.; Le Baron 12.5 qts.
㊴—Exc. Le Baron, 17.5 qts.; Le Baron, 16.5 qts.
㊵—Exc. Le Baron, 16.0 qts.; Le Baron, 15.0 qts.

REAR AXLE SPECIFICATIONS

Year	Model	Carrier Type	Ring Gear & Pinion Backlash		Pinion Bearing Preload			Differential Bearing Preload		
			Method	Adjustment	Method	New Bearings Inch-Lbs.	Used Bearings Inch-Lbs.	Method	New Bearings Inch-Lbs.	Used Bearings Inch-Lbs.
1974	8¾"	Integral	②	.006–.008	①	20–30	—	②	③	③
1974–79	8¼" ⑤	Integral	②	.006–.008	①	20–35④	10–25④	②	③	③
1974–79	9¼" ⑤	Integral	②	.006–.008	①	20–35④	10–25④	②	③	③
1974–79	7¼"	Integral	②	.004–.006	①	15–25	—	②	③	③

①—Collapsible spacer.
②—Threaded adjusters.
③—Preload is correct when ring gear and pinion backlash is properly adjusted.

④—Adjust by turning pinion shaft nut with an inch-pound torque wrench and seal removed.
⑤—"C" lock type.

Electrical Section

DISTRIBUTOR, REPLACE

Removal

1. Disconnect vacuum line at distributor.
2. Disconnect distributor pickup lead at wiring harness connector, then remove distributor cap.
3. Rotate crankshaft to bring No. 1 piston to top of compression stroke and mark on crankshaft pulley in line with "O" mark on timing chain cover.
4. Mark position of rotor on distributor body and engine block surface so that distributor can be installed in the same position.
5. Remove distributor screw and clamp and lift distributor from engine.

Installation

1. If engine was disturbed while distributor was removed from engine, rotate crankshaft to bring No. 1 piston up on its compression stroke, and position mark on inner edge of crankshaft pulley in line with the "O" (TDC) mark on timing chain cover.
2. With distributor gasket in position, hold distributor over mounting pad.
3. Turn rotor to a position just ahead of the No. 1 distributor cap terminal.
4. Install distributor, engaging distributor gear with drive gear on camshaft. With distributor fully seated on engine, rotor should be under No. 1 cap terminal and on conventional systems, breaker points just opening.
5. Install hold-down bolt.
6. Adjust timing with timing light.

SERVICE BULLETIN

FUSIBLE LINK REPAIR: Alternator equipped 1974-79 cars have charging circuits protected by a fuse-type wire. This fusible link is installed on the starter relay battery terminal.

If the charging circuit becomes overloaded, the inner fuse wire of this link burns out and the insulation heats up and breaks apart. This cuts off the battery from the charging system.

In the event one of these cars has none of its electrical parts functioning, check for a burned out fusible link. After locating and correcting the short, a new fusible link should be installed. Do not allow the insulation to contact any other wiring.

In situations like this, never use an uninsulated wire as a jumper if a fusible link replacement is not available. This can cause a fire in the electrical system.

STARTER, REPLACE

1. To remove starter, disconnect ground

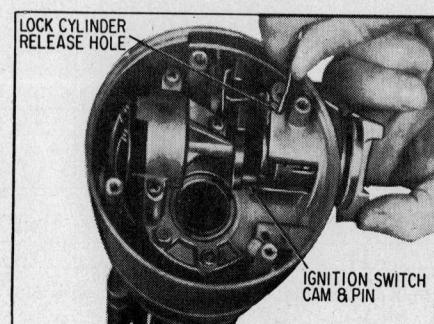

Fig. 1 Lock cylinder removal. 1974-78

cable at battery.
2. Remove cable at starter.
3. Disconnect wires at solenoid.
4. Remove one stud nut and one bolt attaching starter motor to flywheel housing.
5. Slide transmission oil cooler bracket off stud (if so equipped).
6. Remove starter motor and removeable seal.
7. Reverse above procedure to install.

NOTE: When tightening attaching bolt and nut be sure to hold starter away from engine to insure proper alignment.

CLUTCH SWITCH
1974-79

A clutch switch is used which necessitates depressing the clutch pedal before the engine can be started.

IGNITION SWITCH & LOCK, REPLACE

1975-78

1. Disconnect battery ground cable and remove turn signal switch as outlined elsewhere in this chapter.
2. Remove ignition key lamp assembly retaining screw and the assembly.
3. Remove snap ring from upper end of steering shaft.
4. Remove bearing housing to lock housing retaining screws, then the bearing housing from shaft.
5. Remove bearing lower snap ring from shaft.
6. Pry sleeve from steering shaft lock plate hub, then, using a suitable punch, drive lock plate groove pin

from lock plate.

NOTE: Drive pin from end without grooves.

7. Remove lock plate from shaft, then the shaft through lower end of column.
8. Remove shift indicator pointer screw, if equipped.
9. Remove buzzer switch retaining screw and the switch.
10. Remove lock lever guide plate retaining screws and the guide plate.
11. Place lock cylinder in the "Lock" position and remove key. With a suitable tool, depress spring loaded lock retainer and pull lock cylinder from housing bore, Fig. 1.
12. Remove ignition switch retaining screws and the ignition switch.

1974 All

1. Disconnect battery ground cable.
2. Remove steering column cover and remove two screws attaching wiring cover from column.
3. Disconnect wiring connectors at column.
4. Remove horn ring ornament, horn ring or rim blow switch pad and ornament if so equipped.
5. Disconnect horn wires at steering wheel hub.
6. Remove horn ring.
7. Remove steering wheel with suitable puller.
8. Remove screw attaching turn signal lever and remove lever.

NOTE: On Tilt & Tel columns, lever screws out.

9. Attach a string or fine wire to signal switch wiring before removing switch from column. When switch is removed leave wire in column jacket tube as an aid in replacement.
10. Remove screws attaching signal switch and upper bearing retainer screws and remove retainer and signal switch and flasher switch.
11. Remove screw and lift out ignition key lamp assembly.
12. Remove snap ring from upper end of steering shaft.
13. Remove three bearing housing attaching screws.
14. With tool C-3044 attached to threaded holes for signal switch retaining screws, pull bearing and housing from steering shaft.
15. Remove lower snap ring from steering shaft.
16. Remove lock plate pin retaining ring from lock plate hub.
17. Use tool C-4113 and press steering shaft lock plate pin out of shaft and

plate and remove lock plate.

NOTE: Do not use hammer as damage to column may result.

18. Remove lock lever guide plate screws and plate.
19. Depress key cylinder retainer toward the cylinder to disengage it from slot in housing bore, then withdraw key cylinder from lock housing, Fig. 1.
20. Remove ignition switch retaining screws and the ignition switch.

IGNITION SWITCH, ADJUST

1979 Except Cordoba & Magnum

1. Place transmission in Park and ignition lock in the lock position.
2. If switch was not removed from column, loosen two mounting bolts and insert a lock pin into hole on switch marked lock. If switch was removed from column, pin switch in the lock position, then place switch into rod and rotate 90 degrees over mounting holes. Loosely install mounting bolts. Replacement switches are supplied with locking pins.
3. Apply light upward pressure to align rod and switch and hold switch in this position while tightening retaining bolts. Remove locking pin.
4. Remove lock pin from switch.

COLUMN MOUNTED DIMMER SWITCH, ADJUST

1979 Newport, New Yorker & St. Regis

1. Loosen two switch mounting screws, then depress switch plunger slightly and insert locking pin.
2. Apply light upward pressure to remove free play between switch and rod.
3. While holding switch with slight upward pressure tighten the two mounting screws.
4. Remove locking pin and check switch for proper operation.

LIGHT SWITCH, REPLACE

1979 Newport, New Yorker & St. Regis

1. Depress switch stem release button and pull knob and stem from switch.
2. Using a small screwdriver, snap out switch trim bezel, then remove mounting nut.
3. Pull switch from cluster and disconnect wire connector.

1976-79 Aspen, Volaré & 1977-79 Diplomat & LeBaron

1. Remove cluster bezel.
2. Remove switch mounting plate attaching screws and pull switch and plate assembly outward.

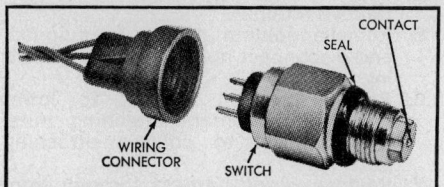

Fig. 2   Neutral safety switch

3. Depress headlight switch stem, then depress release button and pull knob and stem from switch.
4. Remove switch mounting nut, then disconnect electrical connector and remove switch.

1975-76 Coronet, 1975-78 Fury, 1975-79 Charger, Cordoba, 1977-78 Monaco & 1978-79 Magnum

1. Disconnect battery ground cable and fusible link.
2. Remove instrument cluster upper bezel and escutcheon mounting screw.
3. Remove switch mounting plate to cluster housing screws, pull switch from housing and disconnect electrical connector.
4. Depress release button on rear of switch and pull knob and stem from switch.
5. Remove switch escutcheon and mounting nut.
6. Reverse procedure to install.

1974-75 Imperial & 1974-78 Chrysler Newport & New Yorker

1. Remove headlight switch lens.
2. Remove headlight switch to mounting plate retaining nut.
3. Remove switch.

1974 Fury, 1974-76 Monaco, 1975-77 Gran Fury & 1977 Royal Monaco

1. Remove instrument cluster bezel.
2. Remove windshield wiper switch mounting screws and headlight switch mounting screws.
3. Pull switch outwards and disconnect electrical leads, then pull switch to the "ON" position and depress release button on side of switch. Remove knob and stem from switch.
4. Remove escutcheon and mounting plate retaining nut and remove switch.

1974-76 Dart & Valiant

1. Depress release button on rear of switch and remove knob and stem.
2. Remove spanner nut and drop switch below panel and disconnect wiring from switch.

1974 Coronet & Charger

1. Reaching under instrument panel, disconnect wiring to switch.
2. Remove switch mounting screws and remove switch.

1974 Satellite

1. Reaching under instrument panel, disconnect switch wiring.
2. Unfasten and remove switch.

1974 Barracuda, Challenger

1. Disconnect battery ground cable.
2. Remove lamp panel retaining screws and carefully slide panel out and lay it on top of instrument panel.
3. Remove bezel retaining screws and slide assembly out and disconnect wiring harness.
4. Remove switch mounting screws and remove switch.

STOP LIGHT SWITCH REPLACE

1974-79

The switch and mounting bracket assembly are attached to the brake pedal bracket.

To remove the switch, disconnect wires from switch and remove switch from its mounting. Install the new switch and connect the wires.

NEUTRAL SAFETY & BACK-UP SWITCH

1974-79

1. Unscrew switch from transmission case, allowing fluid to drain into a container, Fig. 2.
2. Move shift lever to "Park" and then to "Neutral" positions and inspect to see that lever operating is centered in switch opening in case.
3. Screw switch into transmission case and torque to 24 ft-lbs.
4. Add fluid to proper level.
5. Check to see that switch operates only in "Park" and "Neutral".

HORN SOUNDER & STEERING WHEEL

1974-79

1. Disconnect ground cable at battery.
2. Remove horn ring ornament by turning counterclockwise or remove rim blow switch pad and ornament if so equipped.
3. Disconnect wires at horn switch.
4. Remove three screws attaching horn

ring and switch to steering wheel, then remove horn ring and switch.

5. Remove wheel nut and use a suitable puller to remove steering wheel.

CAUTION: Do not bump or hammer on steering shaft to remove wheel as damage to shaft may result. See *Steering Gear, Replace* for other precautions.

TURN SIGNAL SWITCH

1976-79

1. Disconnect battery ground cable and remove steering wheel.
2. Remove steering column cover. On Charger, Cordoba, Coronet, Fury, Magnum and 1977-78 Monaco, it is necessary to remove the lower instrument panel bezel.
3. On models with Tilt and Telescope columns and Aspen, Diplomat, LeBaron and Volaré models with Tilt columns:
   a. On all models except Charger, Cordoba, Coronet, Fury, Magnum and 1977-78 Monaco, remove gearshift indicator.
   b. On all models, remove steering column to lower panel reinforcement nuts.
   c. Remove mounting bracket attaching bolts and the mounting bracket from steering column.
   d. Remove wiring trough screws and the wiring trough.
4. On all models except models with Tilt and Telescope columns and Aspen, Diplomat, LeBaron and Volaré with Tilt columns, unsnap retainer clips attaching wiring trough to steering column and remove wiring trough.
5. Position shift lever at the full clockwise position except on Tilt columns. On Tilt columns, position shift lever at the mid-point.
6. Disconnect turn signal switch wiring harness connector.
7. Remove turn signal lever attaching screw and the lever.

NOTE: On models equipped with speed control, it is not necessary to remove lever but allow lever to hang.

8. Remove hazard warning switch and upper bearing retainer mounting screws.
9. Carefully pull switch from column, guiding wires through column opening.

1974-75

1. Disconnect battery ground cable.
2. Remove steering wheel as previously outlined.
3. Remove turn signal lever mounting nut and lever.

NOTE: On vehicles equipped with speed control, do not remove lever, but let lever hang.

4. Remove the switch and upper bearing retainer attaching screws, then

remove retainer.

5. Remove column cover, if equipped, and disconnect horn wire from mounting nut.
6. Remove column bracket to lower panel reinforcement attaching nuts, then bracket to column attaching nuts.
7. Remove wiring harness through from steering column and the tape securing wiring harness to column, then disconnect wiring harness connector.
8. Pull switch outward from column, guiding wires and connector through column opening.

INSTRUMENT CLUSTER REMOVAL

1979 Newport, New Yorker & St. Regis

1. Disconnect battery ground cable.
2. Remove upper cluster bezel attaching screws, then pull cluster bezel outward and upward away from steering column.
3. Reach up behind instrument panel and depress release button on headlamp switch and remove switch knob and shaft assembly.
4. Using needle nose pliers, remove eight plastic pins retaining cluster masks to cluster housing, then remove cluster masks. Cluster masks separate to ease removal from around steering column.
5. With the cluster masks removed, individual gauges can be removed and replaced as necessary.
6. Reverse procedure to install. Cluster masks must be interlocked before installing on cluster housing.

1977-79 Diplomat & LeBaron

1. Disconnect battery ground cable.
2. Remove lower panel assembly.
3. Remove left lower reinforcement by removing two screws located at left end.
4. Remove gear shift indicator.
5. Remove steering column toe plate mounting bolts and upper steering column mounting nuts, then lower steering column.
6. Disconnect speedometer cable.
7. Remove two mounting screws and detach fuse block from mid reinforcement.
8. Remove one screw attaching radio to mid reinforcement.
9. Remove four upper and four lower cluster mounting screws, Fig. 3.
10. Pull cluster out from instrument panel and disconnect wire connectors, control cables and vacuum harness, then remove cluster assembly.
11. Reverse procedure to install.

1976-79 Aspen & Volaré

1. Remove steering column cover and instrument panel end cap.
2. Remove lower left reinforcement and remove gearshift indicator.
3. Remove steering column toe plate

bolts, then remove the two upper mounting nuts and lower steering column.

4. Remove left side cowl mouldings, then disconnect speedometer cable.
5. Remove two mounting screws, then detach fuse block from mid reinforcement.
6. Remove 1 screw attaching radio to mid-reinforcement, 4 screws at bottom of cluster and 3 screws at top of cluster, Fig. 4.
7. Pull cluster from panel, then disconnect all electrical connectors, control cables and vacuum hoses and remove cluster.

1975-76 Coronet, 1975-78 Fury, 1975-79 Charger, Cordoba, 1977-78 Monaco & 1978-79 Magnum

1. Disconnect battery ground cable.
2. Remove trim pad, radio and heater or A/C controls, Fig. 5.
3. Remove cluster housing reinforcement bracket.
4. Disconnect speedo cable, all electrical connectors and three wiring through clips from cluster.
5. Remove upper cluster bezel and instrument panel end cap.
6. Remove steering column to support bracket nuts.
7. Remove cluster housing to instrument panel retaining screws, then remove cluster.
8. Reverse procedure to install.

1975-76 Monaco, 1975-77 Gran Fury & 1977 Royal Monaco

Refer to the "1974 Fury & Monaco" procedure for instrument cluster removal.

1974-75 Imperial, 1974-78 Chrysler Newport & New Yorker

1. Disconnect battery ground cable.
2. Remove instrument panel upper cover, then working through top of panel, disconnect speedometer cable and printed circuit multiple connector.
3. Remove instrument cluster bezel, Fig. 6.
4. On Chrysler, remove gear selector and warning lamp bezel.
5. On all models disconnect instrument cluster lens and cluster housing from carrier.
6. Pull cluster out and disconnect two illumination and warning light modules.
7. Disconnect remaining electrical leads and remove cluster assembly.

1974 Fury & Monaco

1. Place selector lever in low position and remove ash tray and cigarette lighter.
2. Center the windshield wiper switch,

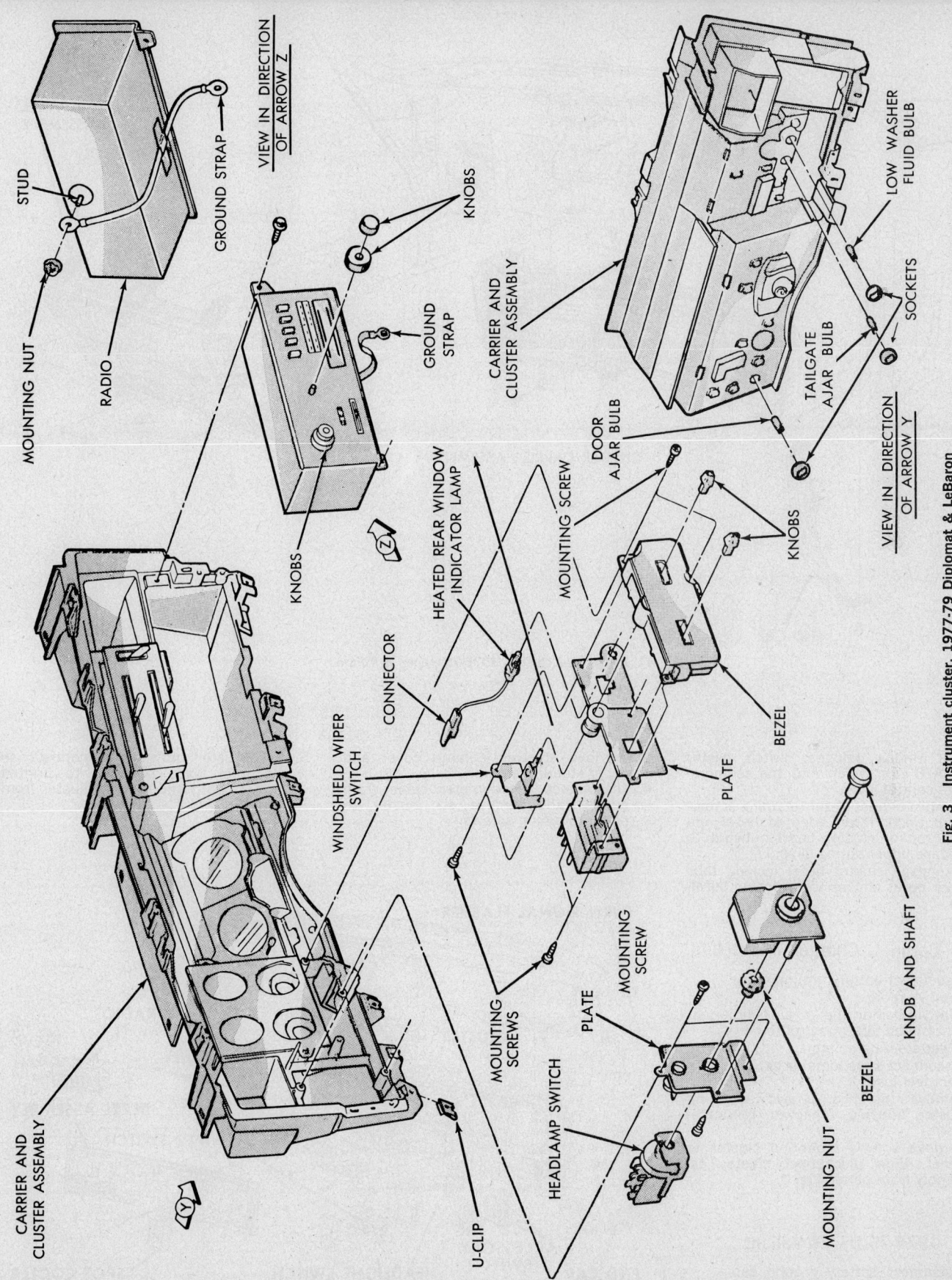

STUD

MOUNTING NUT

RADIO

GROUND STRAP

VIEW IN DIRECTION OF ARROW Z

KNOBS

GROUND STRAP

KNOBS

CARRIER AND CLUSTER ASSEMBLY

LOW WASHER FLUID BULB

SOCKETS

TAILGATE AJAR BULB

VIEW IN DIRECTION OF ARROW Y

DOOR AJAR BULB

MOUNTING SCREW

KNOBS

HEATED REAR WINDOW INDICATOR LAMP

CONNECTOR

BEZEL

WINDSHIELD WIPER SWITCH

PLATE

MOUNTING SCREWS

MOUNTING SCREW

PLATE

KNOB AND SHAFT

U-CLIP

PLATE

HEADLAMP SWITCH

MOUNTING NUT

BEZEL

CARRIER AND CLUSTER ASSEMBLY

Fig. 3 Instrument cluster, 1977-79 Diplomat & LeBaron

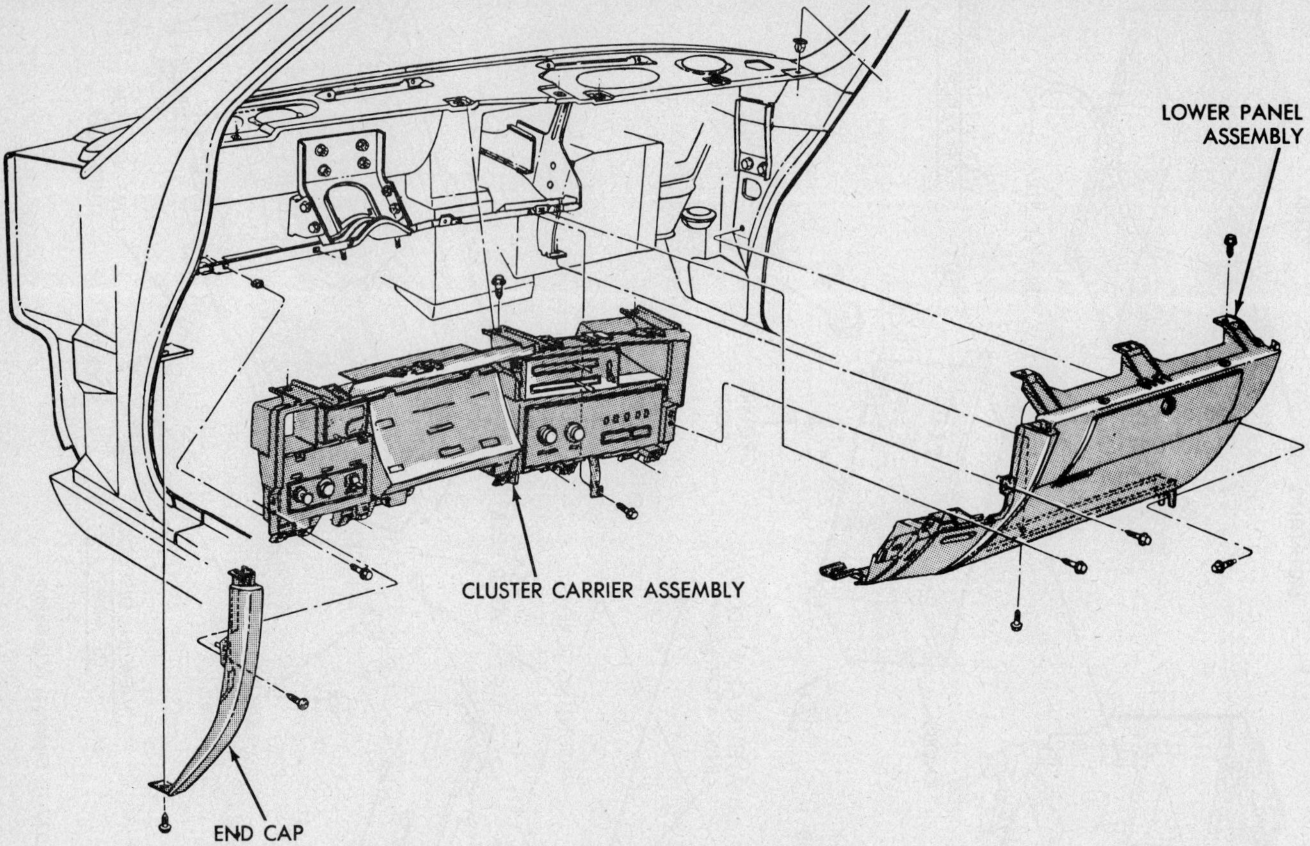

LOWER PANEL ASSEMBLY

CLUSTER CARRIER ASSEMBLY

END CAP

Fig. 4   Instrument cluster. 1976-79 Aspen & Volaré

rear window defogger switch, heater or A/C fan switch and the temperature control lever.
3. Remove cluster bezel retaining screws from under lower edge of bezel and pull top of cluster bezel outward to release upper spring clips, Fig. 7.
4. Disengage cluster bezel locking tabs from bezel and remove cluster bezel.

1974 Coronet, Charger & Satellite

1. Disconnect battery ground cable.
2. Remove radio.
3. Remove heater and/or air conditioner control and allow control to hang.
4. Lower steering column.
5. Disconnect speedometer cable and all electrical leads.
6. Remove the two screws attaching cluster housing to lower reinforcement.
7. Remove screws mounting cluster to panel, then disconnect cluster assembly from panel, Fig. 8.

1974-76 Dart & Valiant

1. Disconnect battery ground cable.
2. Tape steering column to prevent damage to finish and remove center A/C duct (if equipped).

3. Remove steering column cover and lower steering column.
4. Disconnect speedometer cable from cluster and remove six cluster to panel retaining screws.

5. Pull cluster outward, disconnect all electrical leads attached to printed circuit board and remove cluster from panel.

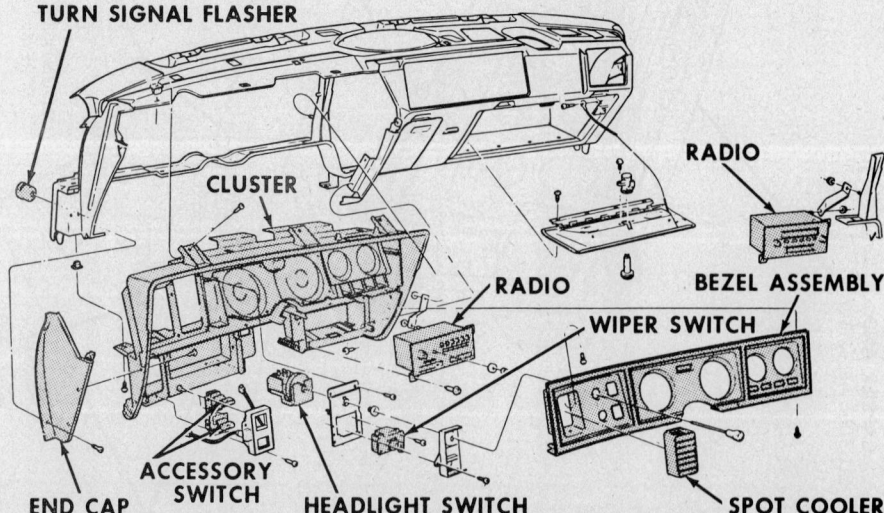

TURN SIGNAL FLASHER

RADIO

CLUSTER

RADIO

BEZEL ASSEMBLY

WIPER SWITCH

ACCESSORY SWITCH

END CAP

HEADLIGHT SWITCH

SPOT COOLER

Fig. 5   Instrument cluster. 1975-76 Coronet, 1975-78 Fury, 1975-79 Charger, Cordoba, 1977-78 Monaco & 1978 Magnum

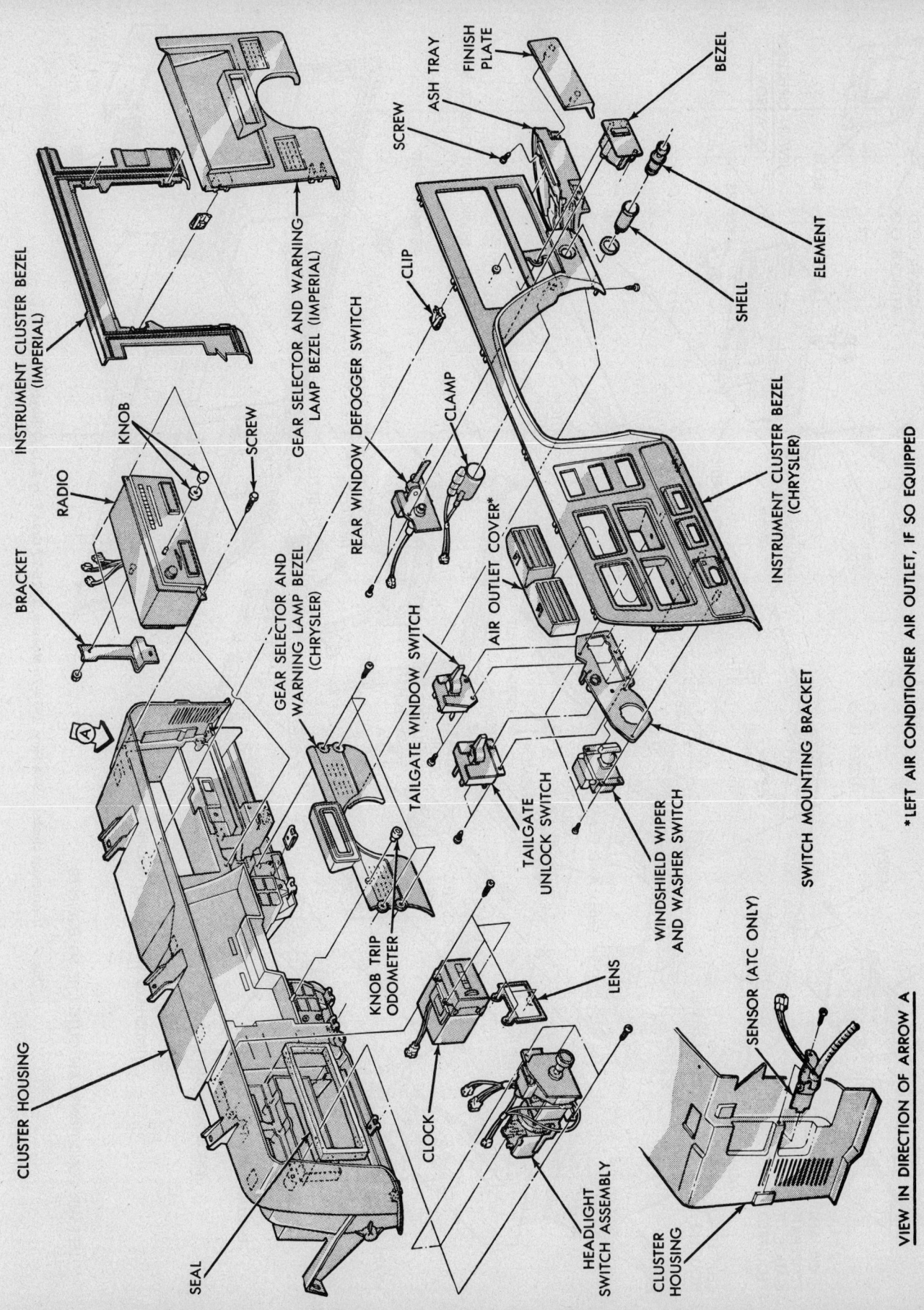

INSTRUMENT CLUSTER BEZEL (IMPERIAL)

ASH TRAY

FINISH PLATE

SCREW

BEZEL

ELEMENT

SHELL

KNOB

RADIO

GEAR SELECTOR AND WARNING LAMP BEZEL (IMPERIAL)

REAR WINDOW DEFOGGER SWITCH

CLIP

BRACKET

SCREW

CLAMP

AIR OUTLET COVER*

INSTRUMENT CLUSTER BEZEL (CHRYSLER)

GEAR SELECTOR AND WARNING LAMP BEZEL (CHRYSLER)

TAILGATE WINDOW SWITCH

TAILGATE UNLOCK SWITCH

WINDSHIELD WIPER AND WASHER SWITCH

SWITCH MOUNTING BRACKET

KNOB TRIP ODOMETER

CLUSTER HOUSING

LENS

CLOCK

SENSOR (ATC ONLY)

HEADLIGHT SWITCH ASSEMBLY

CLUSTER HOUSING

SEAL

VIEW IN DIRECTION OF ARROW A

*LEFT AIR CONDITIONER AIR OUTLET, IF SO EQUIPPED

Fig. 6   Instrument cluster. 1974-75 Imperial & 1974-78 Chrysler Newport & New Yorker

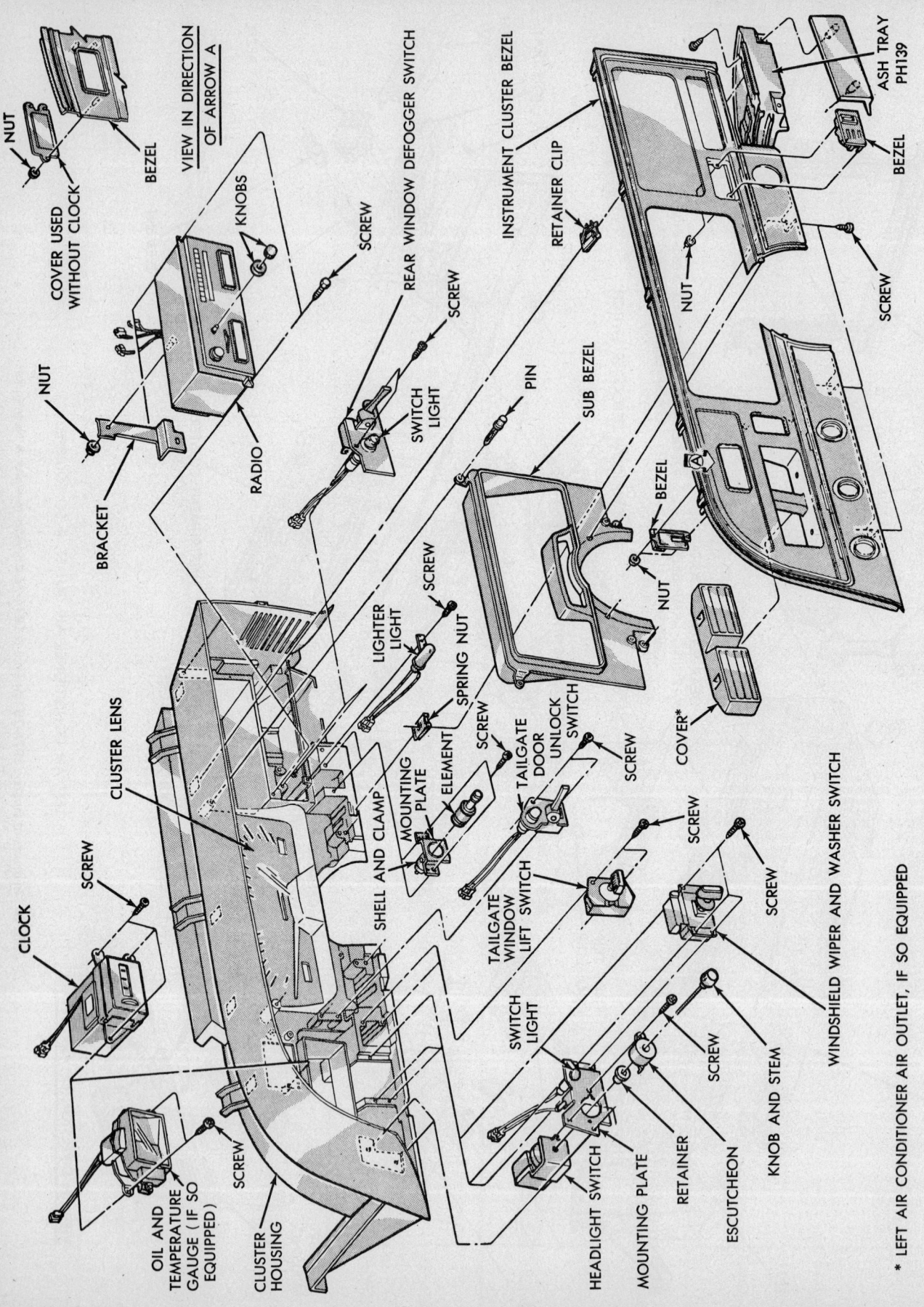

NUT

BEZEL

COVER USED WITHOUT CLOCK

VIEW IN DIRECTION OF ARROW A

KNOBS

SCREW

REAR WINDOW DEFOGGER SWITCH

INSTRUMENT CLUSTER BEZEL

RETAINER CLIP

ASH TRAY PH139

BEZEL

NUT

SCREW

NUT

SCREW

SWITCH LIGHT

PIN

SUB BEZEL

BEZEL

NUT

RADIO

BRACKET

SCREW

COVER*

LIGHTER LIGHT

SPRING NUT

SCREW

ELEMENT

TAILGATE DOOR UNLOCK SWITCH

SCREW

SCREW

CLUSTER LENS

MOUNTING PLATE

SHELL AND CLAMP

TAILGATE WINDOW LIFT SWITCH

SCREW

WINDSHIELD WIPER AND WASHER SWITCH

CLOCK

SCREW

SWITCH LIGHT

SCREW

HEADLIGHT SWITCH

MOUNTING PLATE

RETAINER

ESCUTCHEON

SCREW

KNOB AND STEM

OIL AND TEMPERATURE GAUGE (IF SO EQUIPPED)

CLUSTER HOUSING

SCREW

* LEFT AIR CONDITIONER AIR OUTLET, IF SO EQUIPPED

Fig. 7 Instrument cluster, 1974 Fury, 1974-76 Monaco, 1975-77 Gran Fury & 1977 Royal Monaco

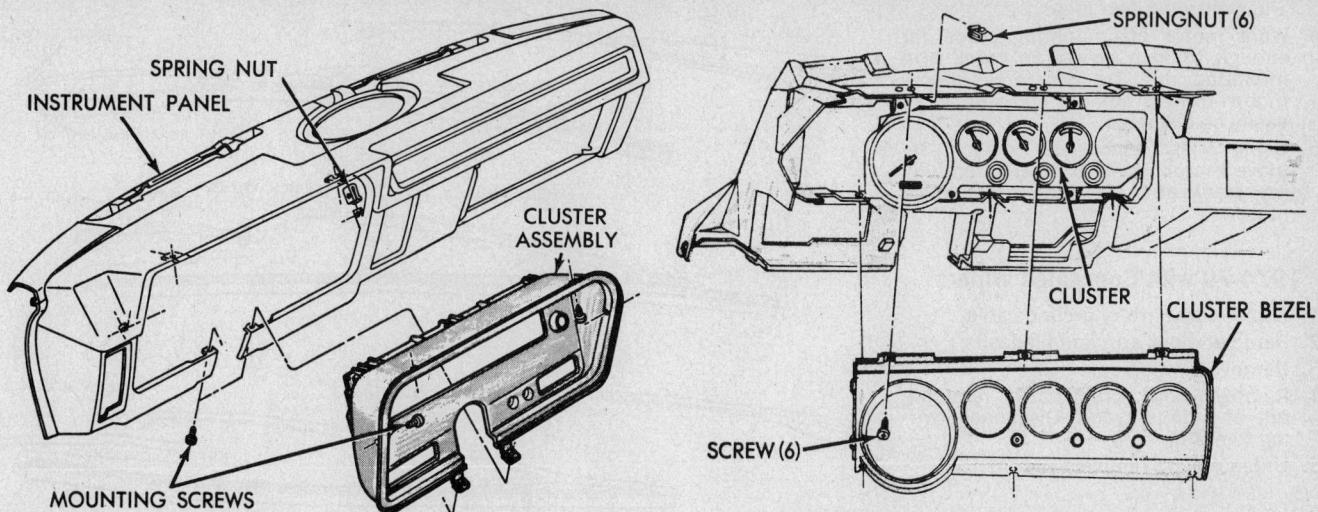

Fig. 8   Instrument cluster. 1974 Charger, Coronet & Satellite

Fig. 9   Instrument cluster. 1974 Barracuda & Challenger with standard cluster

1974 Barracuda, Challenger

1. Disconnect battery ground cable.
2. Remove lamp panel mounting screws and carefully slide panel out and lay it on top of instrument panel. It is not necessary to disconnect wiring.
3. Remove switch bezel mounting screws and allow bezel to hang loose.
4. Remove steering column plate and disconnect column clamps and allow column to rest on seat.
5. Disconnect speedometer cable.
6. Remove six cluster bezel mounting screws, angle bezel out to clear clock button. Reach behind bezel and disconnect stereo control wiring, if so equipped.
7. On Rallye cluster, remove clock and odometer reset knobs.
8. Remove four cluster-to-panel mounting screws, disconnect wiring harnesses and remove cluster, Figs. 9 and 10.

W/S WIPER BLADES

1. Turn wiper switch "ON", move blades to a convenient position by turning the ignition switch "ON" and "OFF".
2. Lift wiper arm and blade off glass.
3. Depress release lever on center bridge and remove blade from arm, Fig. 11.
4. Remove wiper blade element from wiper blade, Fig. 11.
5. Pull rubber wiping element from the end bridge.
6. When replacing rubber element use caution to insure that all four bridge claws are engaged and properly positioned on filler assembly.
7. Check each release point for positive locking when installing blade and blade assembly.

W/S WIPER ARMS

CAUTION: The use of a screwdriver or other prying tool to remove an arm may distort it in a manner that will cause the arm to come off the pivot shaft in the future, regardless of how carefully it is re-installed. *Do not* under any circumstances push or bend the spring clip in the base of the arm in an attempt to release the arm. This clip is self-releasing.

1974-79

1. Place wiper motor in park position.
2. On Barracuda and Challenger models, position tool on wiper arm assembly, Fig. 12, and remove wiper arm assembly.
3. On all other models, lift arm to permit

the latch, Fig. 13, to be pulled out and remove the arm from the pivot using a rocking motion.

W/S WIPER MOTOR REPLACE

1974-76 with Non-Concealed Wipers

1. Disconnect battery ground cable.
2. Disconnect wiper motor harness.
3. Remove three motor mounting nuts. On vehicles without A/C it is easier to remove crank arm nut and crank arm from under instrument panel first

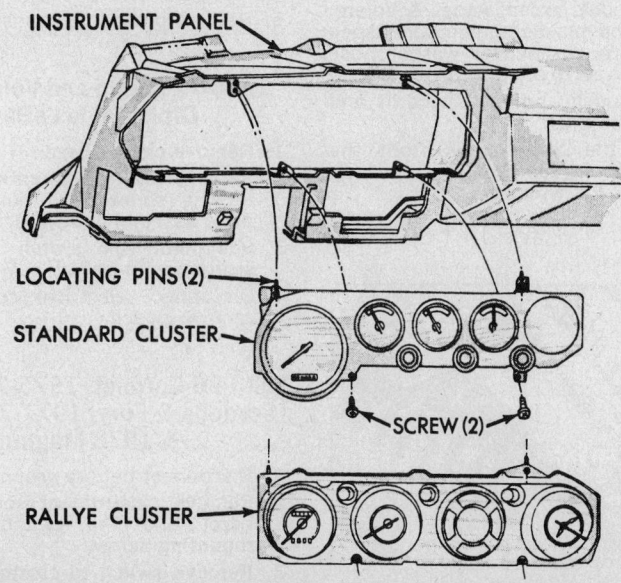

Fig. 10   Instrument cluster. 1974 Barracuda & Challenger with Rallye cluster

4. Work motor off mounting studs far enough to gain access to crank arm mounting nut. Do not force or pry motor from studs as drive link can easily be distorted.

5. Using a ½″ open end wrench, remove motor crank arm nut. Carefully pry crank arm off shaft and remove motor.

1974-79 with Concealed Wipers

1. Disconnect battery ground cable.
2. Remove wiper arm and blades.
3. Remove cowl screen.
4. Remove drive crank arm retaining nut and drive crank. Disconnect wiring to motor.
5. Unfasten and remove wiper motor.

W/S WIPER TRANSMISSION

1974-76 with Non-Concealed Wipers

1. Disconnect the battery ground cable.
2. For non A/C equipped models, remove the drive crank from the motor by removing the attaching nut (above the accelerator pedal) with a ⅜″ wrench. For A/C equipped vehicles, remove the wiper motor nuts and/or bolts with ½″ wrench.
3. Move wiper motor forward and to the right to gain access to the drive attaching nut. Loosen nut with a ⅜″ wrench and remove the drive crank from the motor.
4. Remove the drive link and crank assembly from the left pivot by prying the link bushing from the pivot pin.

1974-79 with Concealed Wipers

1. Disconnect the battery ground cable.
2. On all models except Aspen & Volaré, remove top plastic screen. On Aspen and Volaré, disconnect washer hose to gain access to drive crank.
3. On all models, remove the arm and blade assemblies.
4. Remove the drive crank from the wiper motor by removing the attaching nut with a ⅜″ wrench.

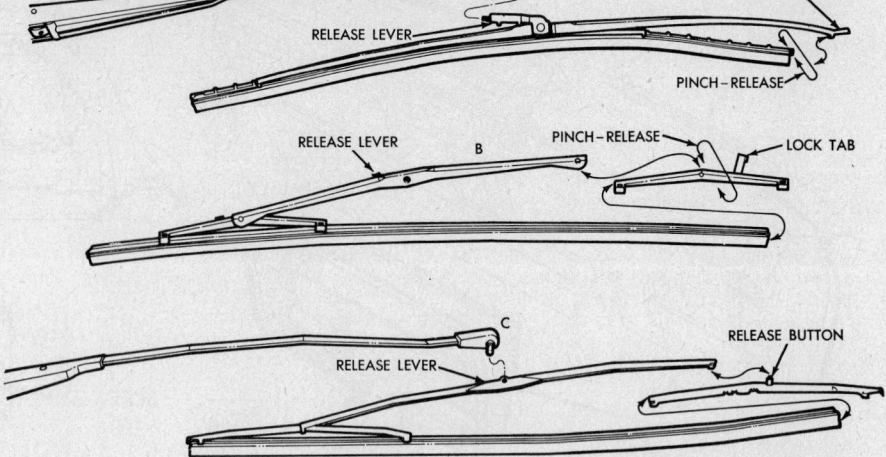

Fig. 11 Windshield wiper blade & element removal

5. On all models except Aspen, Diplomat, LeBaron and Volaré, remove six pivot mounting screws. On Aspen, Diplomat, LeBaron and Volaré models, remove pivot mounting nut and washer. On Diplomat and LeBaron models, also remove pivot mounting plate.

W/S WIPER SWITCH

1978 Aspen, Diplomat, LeBaron & Volaré

1. Disconnect battery ground cable.
2. Remove instrument cluster bezel.
3. Remove switch module assembly attaching screws, then pull assembly out and let hang in order to gain access to switch.
4. Remove switch knob from stem, then remove switch mounting screws.
5. Disconnect switch wire connector and remove switch.
6. Reverse procedure to install.

1976-77 Aspen and Volaré, 1977 Diplomat & LeBaron

1. Remove cluster bezel.
2. Remove switch mounting plate attaching screws and pull switch and plate assembly outward.
3. Pull knob off switch and remove switch retaining nut
4. Disconnect electrical connector and remove switch.

1975-76 Coronet, 1975-78 Charger, Cordoba & Fury, 1977-78 Monaco & 1978 Magnum

1. Disconnect battery ground cable.
2. Remove instrument cluster upper bezel and the switch escutcheon mounting screw.
3. Remove switch to cluster housing retaining screws and pull headlamp switch to the "On" position.

4. Slide escutcheon on shaft toward rear of vehicle and rotate upward, thereby gaining clearance for switch removal.
5. Pull switch from cluster housing, disconnect electrical connector and remove switch.
6. Reverse procedure to install.

1975 Imperial, 1975-76 Monaco, 1975-77 Gran Fury, 1977-78 Chrysler Newport & New Yorker & 1977 Royal Monaco

1. Disconnect battery ground cable.
2. Remove instrument cluster bezel.
3. Remove switch mounting screws.
4. Disconnect electrical connector and remove switch from bezel.

1974 Chrysler, Fury, Imperial, Monaco

1. Remove instrument cluster bezel.
2. Remove switch mounting screws.
3. Disconnect electric leads and remove switch from bezel.

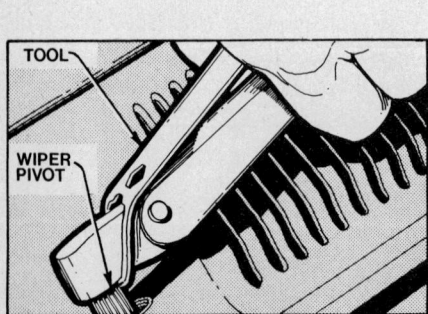

Fig. 12 Wiper arm removal. Barracuda & Challenger

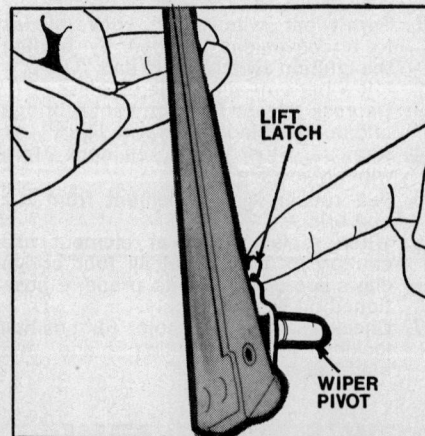

Fig. 13 Wiper arm removal. Except Barracuda & Challenger

1974 Charger, Coronet, & Satellite

1. Remove wiper switch knob.
2. Remove wiper switch bezel nut.
3. Remove wiper switch from instrument cluster and disconnect electrical leads.

1974 Barracuda, Challenger

1. Disconnect battery ground cable.
2. Remove lamp panel retaining screws and carefully slide panel out and lay it on top of instrument panel.
3. Remove bezel retaining screws and slide assembly out and disconnect wiring harness.
4. Pull control knob from shaft. Remove mounting nut and remove switch from bezel.

1974-76 Dart & Valiant

1. Remove air conditioning duct (if so equipped).
2. Pull knob from switch.
3. Remove spanner nut.
4. Remove wiring harness from clip. Disconnect wiring and remove switch.

RADIO, REPLACE

NOTE: When installing radio, be sure to adjust antenna trimmer for peak performance.

1979 Newport, New Yorker & St. Regis

1. Remove center bezel, then remove radio to panel attaching screws.
2. Pull radio from instrument panel, then disconnect antenna and electrical leads.

1976-79 Aspen, Volaré & 1977-79 Diplomat & LeBaron

1. Disconnect battery ground cable.
2. Remove instrument cluster bezel, then the radio mounting screws.
3. Pull radio from panel and disconnect all wiring, then remove radio from vehicle.
4. Reverse procedure to install.

1975-76 Coronet, 1975-78 Fury, 1975-79 Charger, Cordoba, 1977-78 Monaco & 1978 Magnum

1. Disconnect battery ground cable.
2. Remove lower cluster bezel.
3. Remove radio knobs and mounting screws.
4. Remove radio rear support bracket mounting nut.
5. Disconnect electrical leads from radio and pull radio from cluster housing.
6. Reverse procedure to install.

1975 Imperial, 1975-76 Monaco, 1975-77 Gran Fury, 1975-78 Chrysler Newport & New Yorker & 1977 Royal Monaco

Refer to the "1974 Fury, Monaco, Chrysler & Imperial" procedure for radio replacement.

1974 Barracuda & Challenger

1. Disconnect battery ground cable.
2. Remove radio retaining screws and disconnect antenna lead.
3. Remove radio support bracket nut and move radio forward and down.
4. Disconnect electrical and speaker leads and remove radio.

1974 Charger, Coronet, & Satellite

1. Disconnect battery ground cable.
2. Remove ash tray and right radio retaining screw which is accessible through lower left corner of ash tray housing.
3. Loosen radio support bracket nut and remove radio knobs and mounting nuts.
4. Disconnect antenna and electrical leads and remove radio.

1974-76 Valiant & Dart

1. Disconnect battery ground cable.
2. If equipped with A/C, remove outlet duct assembly, ash tray and ash tray housing mounting screws.
3. Remove radio knobs, mounting nuts and radio support bracket screw.
4. Lift radio, relocate ash tray housing for additional clearance and disconnect antenna lead.
5. Move radio forward and down, disconnect electrical and speaker leads and remove radio.

1974 Fury, Monaco, Chrysler & Imperial

1. Disconnect battery ground cable.
2. Remove bezel. On Fury and Monaco, also remove sub bezel.
3. Remove lamp assembly from radio (monaural only).
4. Remove radio to panel retaining screws and instrument panel upper cover.
5. Working through top of panel, disconnect antenna lead and remove radio mounting bracket nut.
6. On monaural radio, disconnect speaker lead from speaker. On stereo radio, disconnect speaker lead from radio.
7. Pull radio out from panel and disconnect electrical lead.

HEATER CORE REMOVAL

Before attempting to remove a heater core, disconnect the battery ground cable, drain the radiator and remove inlet and outlet hoses from heater assembly in engine compartment.

1976-79 Aspen, Volaré & 1977-79 Diplomat & LeBaron

Less Air Conditioning

1. Disconnect battery ground cable and drain cooling system.
2. Disconnect and plug heater hoses from dash panel.
3. Remove heater core tube dash panel seals and retainer.
4. Remove instrument cluster bezel assembly, upper cover, steering column cover, right intermediate side cowl trim panel and the lower instrument panel.
5. Remove instrument panel center to lower reinforcement.
6. Remove right vent control cable from unit.
7. Disconnect temperature and mode door control cables from unit, then the blower motor resistor block wiring.
8. Remove heater assembly mounting nuts in engine compartment.
9. Remove heater support to plenum bracket and pull heater unit from dash panel.
10. Separate heater housing by removing retainer clips.
11. Remove heater core tube support clamp and side heater core from housing.
12. Reverse procedure to install.

With Air Conditioning

1. Disconnect battery ground cable and drain cooling system.
2. Discharge refrigerant system.
3. Remove air cleaner, then disconnect heater hoses from heater core. Install plugs in heater core tubes to prevent coolant from spilling when removing unit.
4. Remove "H" valve, then cap refrigerant lines to prevent dirt and moisture from entering.
5. Remove instrument cluster bezel assembly.
6. Remove instrument panel upper cover, steering column cover and right intermediate side cowl trim panel.
7. Remove lower instrument panel.
8. Remove instrument center to lower reinforcement.
9. Remove floor console, if equipped.
10. Remove right center air distribution duct.
11. Disconnect locking tab on defroster distribution duct.
12. Disconnect temperature control cable from evaporator housing.
13. Disconnect blower motor resistor block wire connector.
14. Disconnect vacuum lines from water valve and vacuum source tee.
15. Remove wiring from evaporator housing and vacuum lines from inlet air housing, then disconnect vacuum harness coupling.
16. Remove drain tube from engine compartment.
17. Remove nuts from evaporator housing mounting studs on engine side of dash panel.

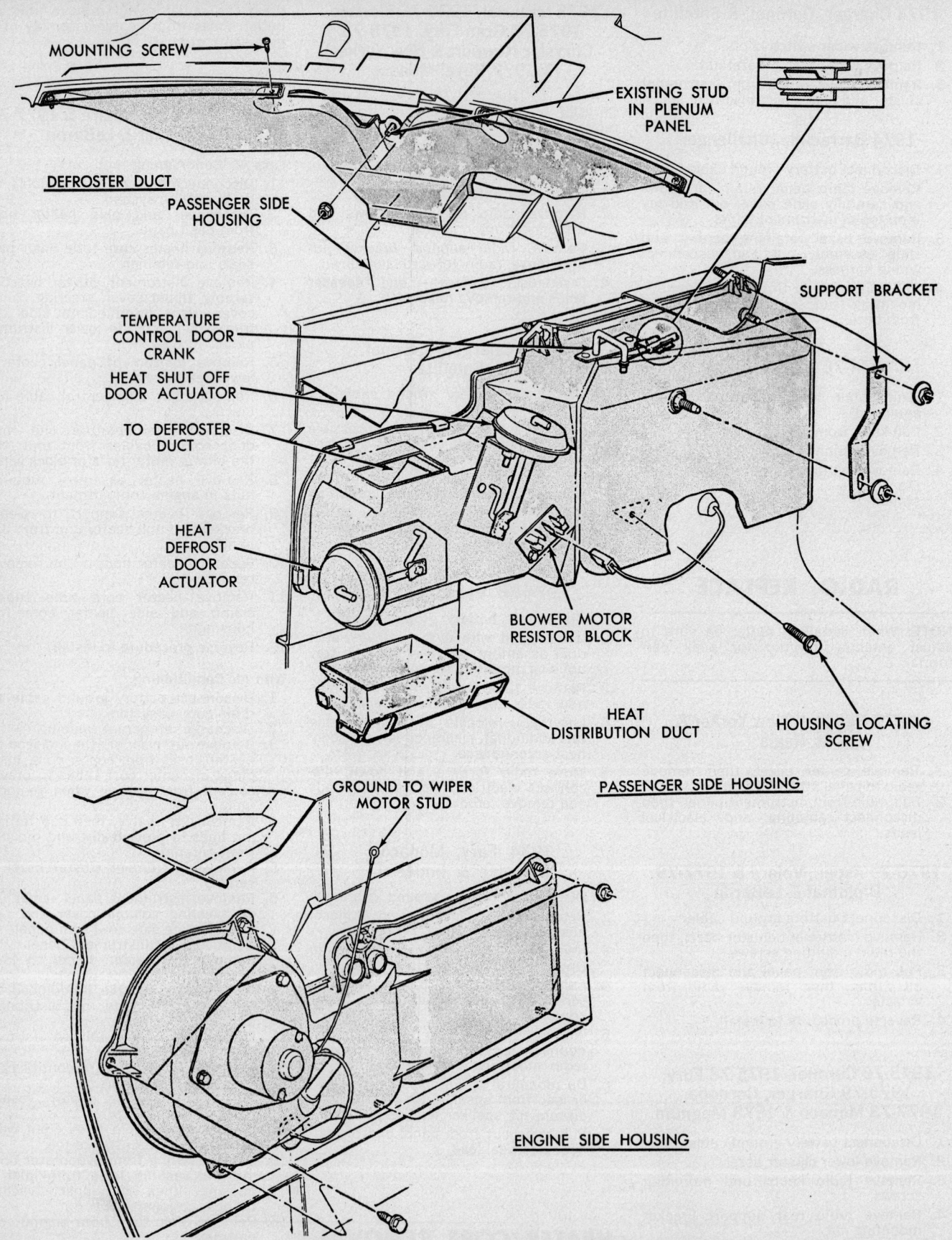

MOUNTING SCREW

EXISTING STUD
IN PLENUM
PANEL

DEFROSTER DUCT

PASSENGER SIDE
HOUSING

SUPPORT BRACKET

TEMPERATURE
CONTROL DOOR
CRANK

HEAT SHUT OFF
DOOR ACTUATOR

TO DEFROSTER
DUCT

HEAT
DEFROST
DOOR
ACTUATOR

BLOWER MOTOR
RESISTOR BLOCK

HEAT
DISTRIBUTION DUCT

HOUSING LOCATING
SCREW

PASSENGER SIDE HOUSING

GROUND TO WIPER
MOTOR STUD

ENGINE SIDE HOUSING

Fig. 14 Heater core & blower motor. 1974-79 less air conditioning (Typical)

18. Remove hanger strap from plenum stud above evaporator housing, then tilt evaporator housing back to clear dash panel and remove housing from vehicle.
19. Remove blend air door lever from shaft.
20. Remove top cover screws and the cover.
21. Remove heater core from housing.

1975-76 Coronet, 1975-78 Fury, 1975-79 Charger, Cordoba, 1977-78 Monaco & 1978-79 Magnum

Less Air Conditioning

1. Disconnect fusible link and drain coolant.
2. Disconnect heater hoses from core tubes and plug tubes to prevent coolant from spilling into interior of vehicle.
3. Remove nuts from around blower motor and one from center of dash panel, then remove lower instrument panel bezel, glove box and door.
4. Disconnect antenna lead from radio, then remove screw from housing to plenum support rod on right side of housing above outside air opening.
5. Disconnect air door control cables and wire from blower motor resistor.
6. Tip heater assembly down and out from under instrument panel.
7. Remove screws retaining front cover to heater assembly, then cut rubber seal in two places where front cover separates cover from housing.
8. Remove core tube retaining screw located behind housing and between core tubes.
9. Remove sponge rubber gaskets from core tubes and remove heater core from housing.

With Air Conditioning

1. Disconnect fusible link and drain coolant.
2. Disconnect heater hoses from core tubes and plug tubes to prevent coolant from spilling into interior of vehicle.
3. Discharge A/C refrigerant and disconnect line from H-valve and cover tubing sealing plate. Remove expansion valve from evaporator and cover evaporator sealing plate and both sealing surfaces of expansion valve.
4. Disconnect blower motor wires and remove blower motor cooling tube.
5. Remove glove box, ash tray and housing bezel, right lap cooler, right side cowl panel and air distribution duct.
6. Remove A/C mode door vacuum actuator from bracket and shift actuator forward on top of unit.
7. Disconnect connector from seat belt interlock control module and disconnect wires from blower motor resistor.
8. Disconnect antenna lead from radio

and remove radio.
9. Remove housing retaining nuts through engine compartment, then remove rubber drain tube.
10. Remove support bracket from rear of unit to plenum.
11. Pull unit back so that tubes clear dash panel, then rotate so that right end of unit comes out first from under the instrument panel.
12. Carefully remove plenum air seal, then disconnect vacuum hose from inlet air door actuator.
13. On 1975-76 models, remove 14 clamps and four screws and separate housings. On 1977-79 models, remove 18 clamps holding front and rear covers separate housings.
14. On all models, carefully lift left half of housing seal from rear cover. Do not remove entire seal as the lower portion is a water seal.
15. Remove two retaining screws from mounting plate and one from between heater core tubes and lift heater core from housing.

1974 Fury; 1974-75 Imperial; 1974-76 Monaco; 1975-77 Gran Fury, 1974-78 Chrysler Newport & New Yorker; 1977 Royal Monaco

Less Air Conditioning

1. Disconnect battery and drain radiator.
2. Disconnect heater hoses and plug hose fittings on heater core.
3. Move front seat rearward and remove instrument panel lower cover. Unplug antenna lead from radio and disconnect upper level vent vacuum line.
4. Disconnect the upper level vent from heater housing and the mounting bracket from dash, then swing duct back.
5. Disconnect electrical connectors from blower motor resistor and control cable from clip and crank.
6. Disconnect support bracket and swing bracket out of way.
7. From engine compartment, remove five retaining nuts from studs.
8. Roll or tip housing out from under instrument panel and disconnect control cable from clip and the blend air door crank.
9. Remove core tube locating screw from between core tubes, remove housing retaining nuts, separate housing and remove core.

With Air Conditioning

1. Discharge refrigerant system.
2. Disconnect fusible link, drain cooling system, remove air cleaner and disconnect heater hoses at heater core. Install plugs in heater core tube to prevent coolant spillage when removing heater core.
3. Remove "H" valve, then cap refriger-

ant lines to prevent entry of dirt and moisture.
4. Move front seat rearward to provide room to remove unit.
5. Remove lap cooler and instrument panel lower cover.
6. Remove A/C distribution duct.
7. Disconnect antenna lead from radio and wires and vacuum lines from unit.
8. Remove drain tube. On models with ATC, disconnect wire connectors and vacuum connector from servo, amplifier and master and compressor switches. Disconnect aspirator tube.
9. On all models, remove temperature control cable from clip on unit.
10. Remove retaining nut from support bracket.
11. From engine side of dash panel, remove retaining nuts from studs.
12. Tilt housing and remove from under instrument panel.
13. Remove mode door and blend air door levers.
14. Remove attaching screws and lift off top cover.
15. Remove four heater core retaining screws and three screws from core tube seal, then lift heater core from housing.

1974-76 Dart & Valiant

Less Air Conditioning

1. Remove heater hoses to dash panel seal and retainer plate.
2. Remove heater motor seal retainer plate and seal from dash panel.
3. Disconnect control cables from heater.
4. Remove heater motor resistor wire from resistor.
5. Remove defroster tubes from heater.
6. Disconnect heater housing support rod from outside air duct.
7. Remove heater assembly.

With Air Conditioning

1. Remove battery, drain radiator and disconnect heater from unit.
2. Remove core tube seal nut, bracket and seal.
3. Remove A/C duct, ash tray and housing and radio.
4. Remove heat-defrost vacuum actuator pot; let hang by rod.
5. To remove heat distribution duct, remove three screws on front cover, two on each end and work housing out of lip and remove to left side.
6. Remove left defroster duct. Remove right defroster duct and let it hang from top.
7. To remove the rear distribution housing, reach through radio opening and remove three screws top and bottom and one at left end.
8. With housing off, core will be settling loose. Separate seal and lift out.

1974 Barracuda, Challenger, Coronet & Satellite

Less Air Conditioning

1. Remove three mounting nuts from

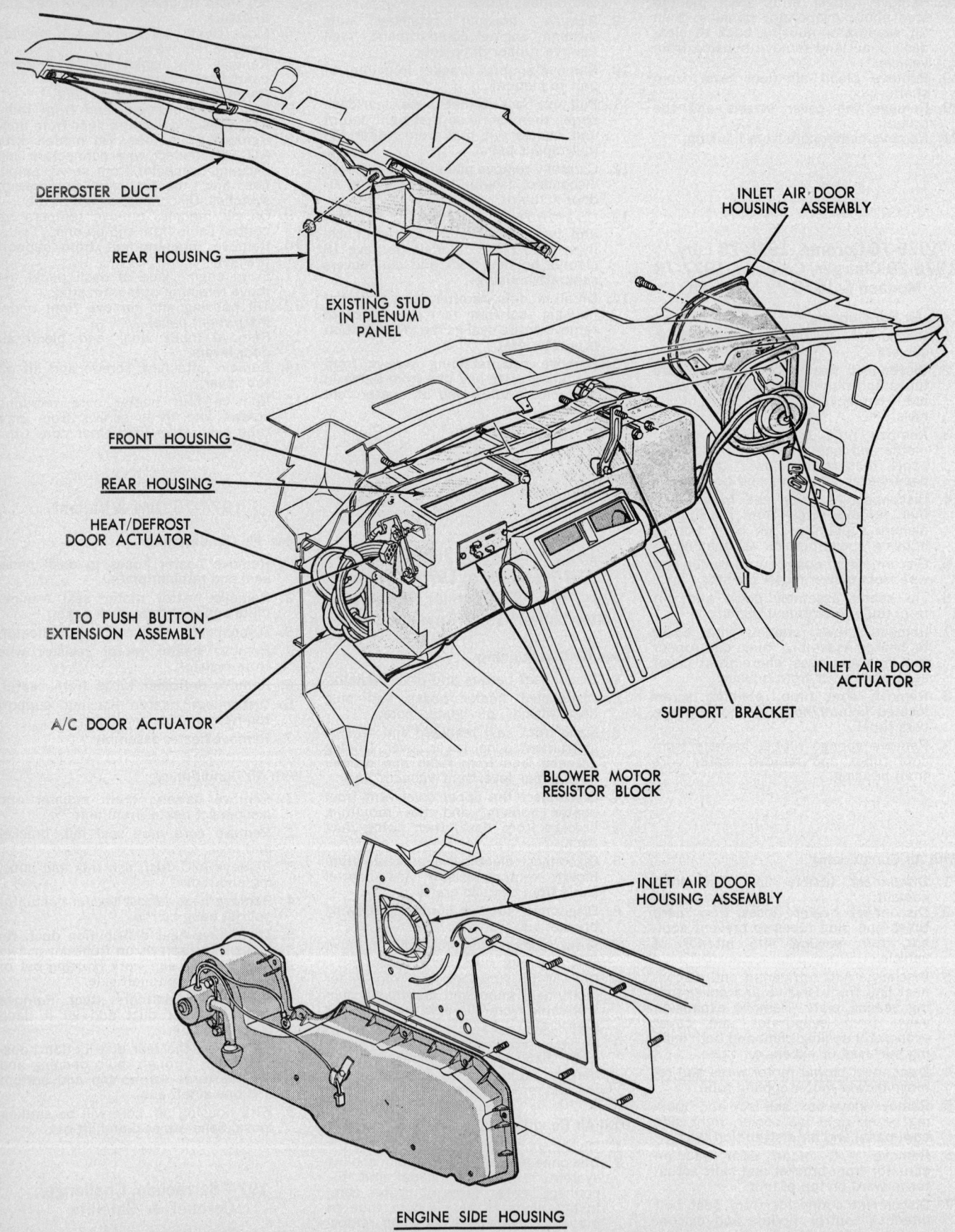

DEFROSTER DUCT

REAR HOUSING

EXISTING STUD
IN PLENUM
PANEL

INLET AIR DOOR
HOUSING ASSEMBLY

FRONT HOUSING

REAR HOUSING

HEAT/DEFROST
DOOR ACTUATOR

TO PUSH BUTTON
EXTENSION ASSEMBLY

A/C DOOR ACTUATOR

INLET AIR DOOR
ACTUATOR

SUPPORT BRACKET

BLOWER MOTOR
RESISTOR BLOCK

INLET AIR DOOR
HOUSING ASSEMBLY

ENGINE SIDE HOUSING

Fig. 15   Heater core & blower motor. 1974-79 with air conditioning (Typical)

studs around blower motor and remove flange and air seal.

2. Unplug antenna from radio and place to one side.
3. Remove screw from housing to plenum support rod on right side of housing above fresh air opening.
4. Disconnect three air door cables.
5. Disconnect wires from blower resistor.
6. Tip unit down and out from under panel.

With Air Conditioning

1. Remove air cleaner and slowly discharge refrigerant from system.
2. Disconnect refrigerant lines at dash panel. Leave expansion valve attached to line. Cap all lines.
3. Disconnect blower motor wires and remove motor cooling tube and motor.
4. Remove glove box and appearance shield from lower edge of dash panel.
5. Remove left spot cooler duct and air distribution duct.
6. Disconnect wires from blower resistor and antenna wire from radio.
7. Remove radio.
8. Disconnect vacuum harness from back of control switch.
9. Remove water valve cable from bracket on left end of housing.
10. Remove nuts from housing mounting studs in engine compartment.
11. Remove rubber drain tube.
12. Remove support bracket from housing plenum panel.
13. Carefully remove plenum air seal.
14. Disconnect vacuum hose from inlet air door actuator and by-pass door actuator.
15. Remove air seal from heater and evaporator core tubes.
16. Remove 18 screws holding front and rear covers together and one screw from between core tubes. Separate housings.
17. Remove 3 screws from evaporator core access plate, remove plate, this provides access to two evaporator core mounting screws.
18. Remove four screws holding evaporator core to front cover and remove core. Carefully lift left half of housing seal from rear cover. Do not remove entire seal as bottom portion is a water seal.
19. Remove two core retaining screws from mounting plates and one from between core tubes in back of rear cover. Lift core out of housing.

BLOWER MOTOR REMOVE

1976-79 Aspen, Volaré & 1977-79 Diplomat & LeBaron

Less Air Conditioning

1. Remove heater assembly and heater core as outlined under "Heater Core, Replace" 1976-79 Aspen, Volaré & 1977-79 Diplomat & LeBaron.

2. Remove blower motor vent tube.
3. Remove blower motor mounting nuts and the blower motor.

With Air Conditioning

NOTE: All service to the blower motor is performed under the right side of the instrument panel.

1. Disconnect battery ground cable and the blower motor feed wire.
2. Remove blower motor mounting nuts from bottom of recirculation housing.
3. Separate upper and lower blower motor housing, then remove blower motor mounting plate screws.
4. Remove wire grommet, mounting plate and blower motor.

1975 Imperial, 1975-76 Monaco, 1975-77 Gran Fury, 1975-78 Chrysler Newport & New Yorker & 1977 Royal Monaco

Refer to the "1974 Chrysler, Imperial, Fury, Polara & Monaco" procedure for blower motor removal.

1974 Barracuda, Challenger & Satellite; 1974-76 Coronet; 1974-79 Charger; 1975-78 Fury; 1975-79 Cordoba; 1977-78 Monaco; 1978-79 Magnum

Less Air Conditioning

The heater assembly must be removed to service the blower motor. See procedure for *Heater Core Removal* to remove assembly, then proceed to *Remove Blower Motor* as follows:

1. Disconnect blower motor lead from resistor block. Disconnect the ground wire from the mounting plate.
2. Remove six screws and retaining clips holding blower motor mounting plate to housing. Separate the blower motor and mounting plate from the housing, Fig. 14.
3. Remove the blower wheel from the motor shaft.
4. Remove the two retaining nuts and separate the motor from the mounting plate. Remove the motor.

With Air Conditioning

NOTE: All service to the blower motor is made from the engine compartment side.

1. Disconnect the feed wire at the connector and the ground wire. Remove the air tube.
2. Remove three screws located on the outer surface of the mounting plate.
3. Remove the mounting plate and blower motor as an assembly, Fig. 15.

1974 Chrysler, Imperial, Fury, Polara & Monaco

The blower motor is mounted to the engine side housing under the right front fender between the inner fender shield and the fender, Figs. 14 and 15. The inner fender shield must be removed to service the blower motor.

1974-76 Dart & Valiant

Less Air Conditioning

The heater assembly must be removed to service the blower motor. See procedure for *Heater Core Removal* to remove assembly, then proceed to *Remove Blower Motor* as follows:

1. Disconnect lead wire from the blower motor to the heater assembly.
2. Remove motor cooler tube.
3. Remove heater backplate assembly from heater.
4. Remove fan from motor shaft. Remove blower motor from backplate, Fig. 14.

With Air Conditioning

NOTE: All service to the blower motor is made from the engine compartment side.

1. Disconnect the feed wire at the connector and the ground wire. Remove the air tube.
2. Remove three screws located on the outer surface of the mounting plate.
3. Remove the mounting plate and blower motor as an assembly, Fig. 15.

SPEED CONTROLS
1974-79 Speed Control

Servo Adjustments

There are two adjustment set screws in the servo housing, Figs. 16 and 17. The adjustment of these set screws have been factory set and under normal conditions there should be no need for altering the factory setting during the life of the vehicle.

Need for adjustment can be determined only after accurate diagnosis of the system operation. If adjustment is found to be necessary, perform the appropriate adjustment outlined below; if screw is loose stake side of servo housing adjacent to screw to insure a snug fit.

Lock-in Screw Adjustment, Fig. 16

Lock-in accuracy will be affected by poor engine performance (need for tune-up), loaded gross weight of car (trailering), improper slack in control cable. After the foregoing items have been considered and the speed sags or drops more than 2 to 3 mph when the speed control is activated, the lock-in adjusting screw should be turned counter-clockwise approximately 1/4 turn per one mph correction required.

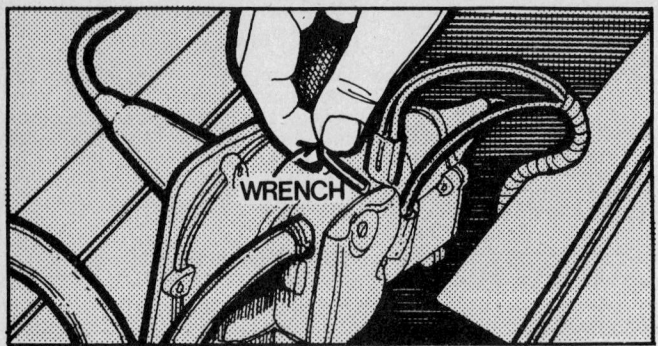

Fig. 16 Speed Control lock-in screw adjustment. 1974-79

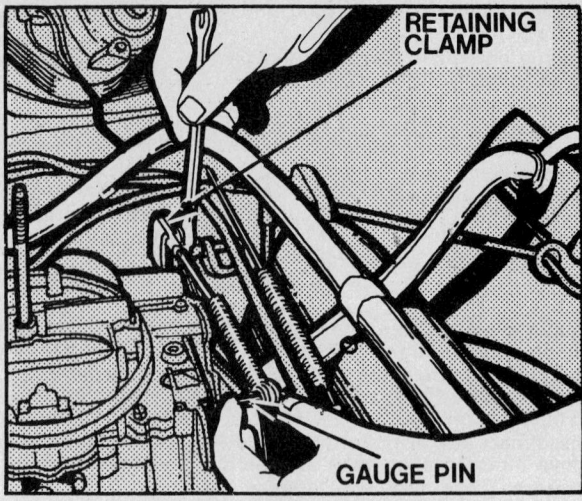

Fig. 17 Speed Control servo cable throttle adjustment. 1974-79

If a speed increase of more than 2 to 3 mph occurs, the lock-in adjusting screw should be turned clockwise ¼ turn per one mph correction required.

CAUTION: This adjustment must not exceed two turns in either direction or damage to the unit may occur.

Throttle Cable Adjustment, Fig. 17

Optimum servo performance is obtained with a given amount of free play in the throttle control cable. To obtain proper free play, insert a ¹⁄₁₆″ diameter pin between forward end of slot in cable end of carburetor linkage pin (hair pin clip removed from linkage pin). With choke in full open position and carburetor at curb idle, pull cable back toward dash panel without moving carburetor linkage until all free play is removed. Tighten cable clamp bolt to 45 inch-pounds, remove ¹⁄₁₆″ pin and install hair pin clip.

Brake Switch Adjustment, 1974-79

1. Loosen switch bracket.
2. Insert proper spacer gauge between brake push rod and switch with pedal in free position. The spacer must be .120 in. for full size models and Dart and Valiant models with manual brakes, .170 in. Dart and Valiant models with power brakes and .140 in. for intermediates except Dart and Valiant.
3. Push switch bracket assembly toward brake push rod until plunger is fully depressed and switch contacts spacer.
4. Tighten bracket bolt to 75 in-lbs. and remove spacer.

Engine Section

ENGINE MOUNTS REPLACE

1. Disconnect throttle linkage at transmission and at carburetor.
2. Raise hood and position fan to clear radiator hose and radiator top tank.
3. Remove torque nuts from insulator studs.
4. Raise engine just enough to remove front engine mount.
5. Reverse above to install.

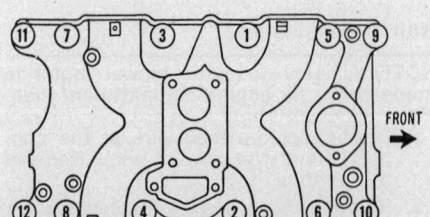

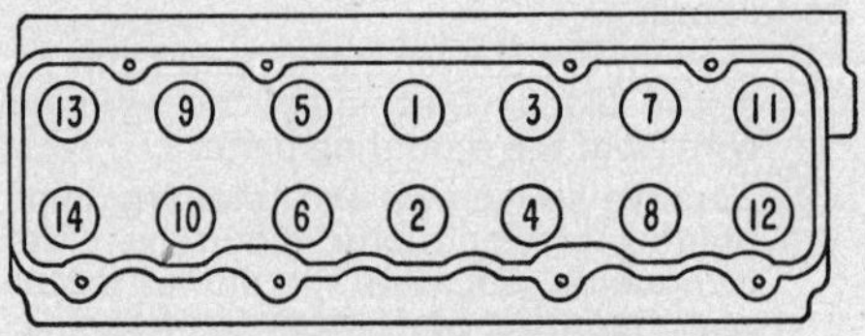

Fig. 1 Cylinder head tightening sequence. 6-198, 225

ENGINE, REPLACE
All V8 Engines

1. Scribe a line on hinge brackets on hood to assure proper adjustments when installing. Then remove hood.
2. Remove battery, drain cooling system, remove all hoses, fan shroud, disconnect oil cooler lines and remove radiator.
3. On models with A/C, remove compressor from mounting bracket and position on right fender.

NOTE: Do not tilt compressor when removed from mounting bracket. Before installing compressor turn pulley several revolutions by hand to ensure all oil is back in compressor oil sump.

4. On all models, remove distributor cap, vacuum lines and wiring.
5. Remove carburetor, linkage, starter wires and oil pressure wire.
6. Disconnect power steering hoses, if equipped.
7. Remove starter, alternator, charcoal canister and horns.
8. Disconnect exhaust pipe at manifold.
9. On vehicles with automatic transmission:
   a. Mark converter and drive plate to aid in installation.
   b. Remove torque converter drive plate bolts.
   c. Install a C-clamp on bottom front

Fig. 2 Intake manifold tightening sequence. V8-318, 360

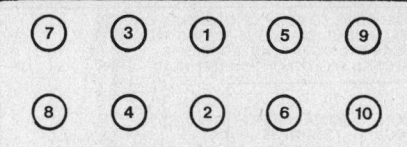

Fig. 3 Cylinder head tightening sequence. V8-318, 360

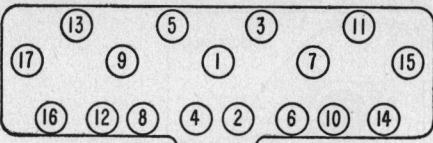

Fig. 4 Cylinder head tightening sequence. V8-400, 440

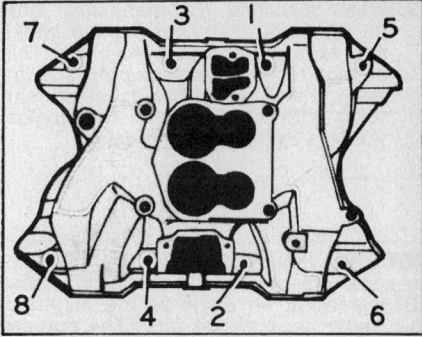

Fig. 4A Intake manifold tightening sequence. V8-400 & 440

of torque converter, to assure that converter remains properly positioned in transmission housing.

   d. Remove converter housing to engine bolts.

   e. Support transmission in its normal position to assure ease of installation.

10. On vehicles with manual transmission, remove transmission.
11. Attach engine lifting fixture.
12. Remove engine front mounting bolts, then raise and work engine out of chassis.
13. Reverse procedure to install.

6-198, 225

1. Scribe hood hinge outlines on hood and remove hood.
2. Drain cooling system and remove battery and carburetor air cleaner.
3. Disconnect transmission cooler lines at radiator (if equipped).
4. Remove radiator and hoses.
5. On models with A/C, remove compressor from mounting bracket and position on right fender.

NOTE: Do not tilt compressor when removed from mounting bracket. Before installing compressor turn pulley several revolutions by hand to ensure all oil is back in compressor sump.

6. On all models, remove closed ventilation system and evaporative control system from cylinder head cover.
7. Disconnect fuel lines, vacuum lines, carburetor linkage and wiring to engine.
8. Disconnect power steering hoses, if equipped.
9. Remove starter, alternator and horns.
10. Disconnect exhaust pipe at manifold.
11. Remove converter cover plate.
12. On manual transmission equipped vehicles disconnect propeller shaft, tie out of the way and disconnect wires and linkage at transmission.
13. On manual transmission equipped vehicles attach engine support fixture, remove engine rear crossmember and remove transmission.
14. On automatic transmission equipped vehicles disconnect torque converter drive plate from engine. Mark converter and drive plate to aid in installation. Support transmission in its normal position in relation to the vehicle, to insure ease of installation.
15. Attach lifting fixture to cylinder head and attach chain hoist.
16. Remove engine support and front en-

gine mounting bolts and lift engine from chassis.

CYLINDER HEAD

Some cylinder head gaskets are coated with a special lacquer to provide a good seal once the parts have warmed up. Do not use any additional sealer on such gaskets. If the gasket does not have this lacquer coating, apply suitable sealer to both sides.

6-198, 225

1. Drain cooling system.
2. Remove carburetor air cleaner and fuel line.
3. Disconnect accelerator linkage.
4. Remove vacuum control tube at carburetor and distributor.
5. Disconnect spark plug wires, heater hose and clamp holding by-pass hose.
6. Disconnect heat indicator sending unit wire.

NOTE: On models equipped with air pump, disconnect diverter valve vacuum line from intake manifold and remove air tubes from cylinder head.

7. Disconnect exhaust pipe at manifold.
8. On 1974-77 models, remove intake and exhaust manifold and carburetor as a unit.
9. On all models, remove closed vent system and rocker arm cover.
10. Remove rocker shaft assembly and push rods.

NOTE: During disassembly note location of push rods so they can be installed in the same position.

11. On 1974-77 models, remove cylinder head bolts and lift off cylinder head. On 1978-79 models, remove cylinder head bolts, then remove cylinder head and intake and exhaust manifolds as an assembly.
12. Install the head in the reverse order of removal, and tighten the bolts in the sequence shown in Fig. 1.

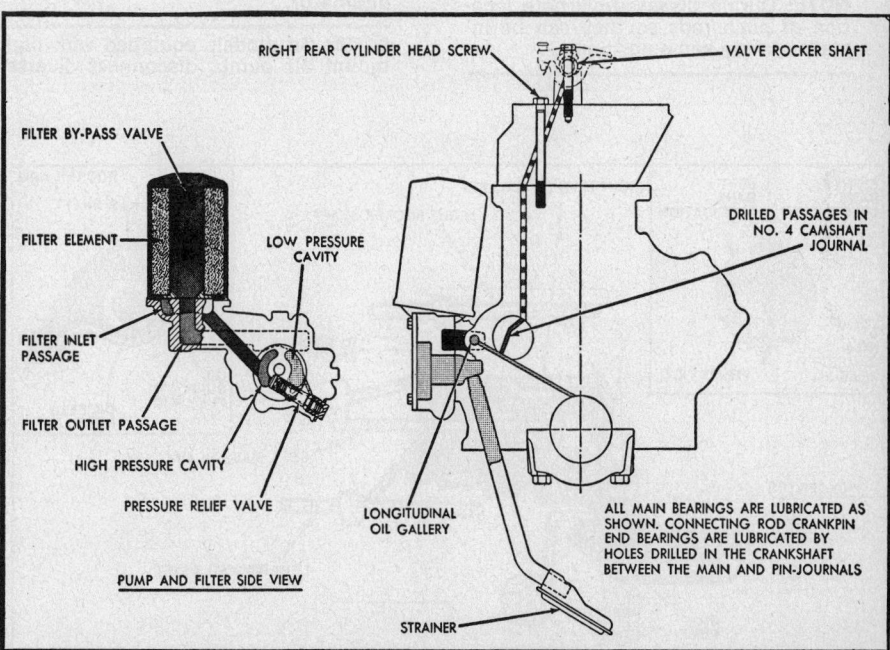

Engine oiling system. 6-198, 225

13. *When installing the manifolds, loosen the three bolts holding the intake and exhaust manifolds together. This is required to maintain proper alignment.* Install intake and exhaust manifolds with cup side of the conical washers against the manifolds.

V8-318, 360

NOTE: The intake manifold attaching bolts on some engines are tilted upward about 30 degrees at an angle to the manifold-to-cylinder head gasket face. The purpose of this design is to provide more effective sealing at the cylinder block end gaskets. If the intake manifold is removed the installation should be such that the bolt tightening is done evenly and in the sequence shown in Fig. 2.

With gaskets in place start all bolts, leaving them loose. Run bolts 1 through 4 down so the heads just touch manifold. Then tighten these four bolts to 25 foot-pounds torque. After checking to see that gaskets are properly seated at all surfaces, tighten remaining bolts to 25 foot-pounds. Finally tighten all bolts in the sequence shown to 35 foot-pounds.

1. Drain cooling system and disconnect battery ground cable.
2. Remove alternator, carburetor air cleaner and fuel line. Disconnect accelerator linkage.
3. Remove vacuum advance hose and distributor cap and wires.
4. Disconnect coil wires, heat indicator wire, heater and by-pass hoses.
5. Remove closed ventilation system and rocker arm covers.
6. Remove intake manifold, coil and carburetor as an assembly.
7. Remove exhaust manifolds.
8. Remove rocker arm and shaft assemblies. Remove push rods.

NOTE: During disassembly note location of push rods so they can be installed in the same position.

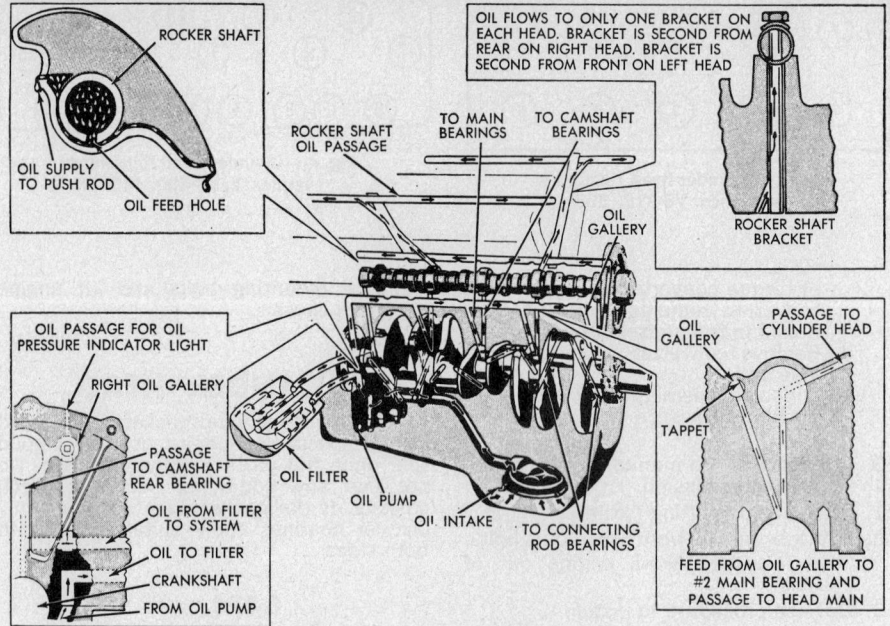

Engine oiling system, V8-318, 360

9. Remove head bolts and lift off cylinder heads.
10. Reverse procedure to install heads and tighten bolts in sequence shown in Fig. 3.

V8-400, 440

1. Drain cooling system, remove air cleaner, fuel line from pump and carburetor, distributor vacuum tube and alternator.

NOTE: On models equipped with high mount air pump, disconnect diverter valve vacuum line from intake manifold and air pump line from exhaust manifolds.

2. Disconnect throttle linkage at carburetor, distributor cap, coil wires, heat indicator sending unit wire and heater hoses at engine.
3. Remove spark plugs and cables, and closed vent system.
4. Remove intake manifold, carburetor and coil as an assembly.
5. Remove exhaust manifolds.
6. Remove cylinder head covers and spark plug cable support brackets.
7. Remove rocker shaft assemblies. *Do not remove bolts from end brackets.*
8. Remove push rods and valve lifter chamber cover.

NOTE: During disassembly note location of push rods so they can be installed in the same position.

9. Remove attaching bolts and lift off heads.
10. Reverse the foregoing procedure to install the heads. Tighten bolts in the sequence shown in Fig. 4. Tighten intake manifold bolts in sequence shown in Fig. 4A.

VALVES, ADJUST

6-198, 225

NOTE: Some 1978 Aspen and Volare models with 6-225 2 bar. carb. engines will be equipped with hydraulic lifters which can not be adjusted.

Before the final valve lash adjustment

Engine oiling system. V8-400, 440 engines

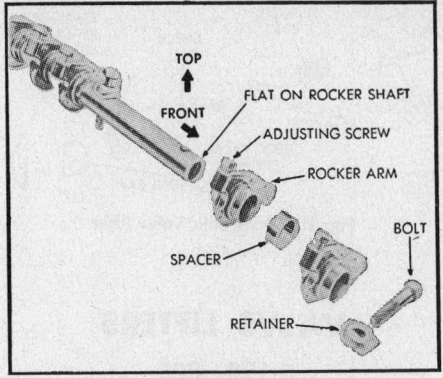

Fig. 5 Rocker arm and shaft assembly. 6-198, 225

VALVE LIFT SPECS.

Engine	Year	Intake	Exhaust
6-198	1974	.406	.414
6-225	1974-79	.406	.414
8-318	1974-77	.373	.399
	1978-79	.373	.400
8-360	1974	.410	.412
	1974②	.429	.444
	1975-76③		
		.410	.410
	1975-76④	.429	.444
	1977-79	.410	.410
8-400	1974①	.434	.430
	1974②	.450	.464
	1975-77④	.434	.464
	1975-77③	.434	.430
	1978 All	.434	.430
	1974-77③	.434	.430
	1974④	.450	.464
	1975-76④	.434	.464
	1977-78④	.449	.464

① —2 bar. carb. ② —4 bar. carb.

③ —Exc. Hi. Perf.

④ —Hi. Perf.

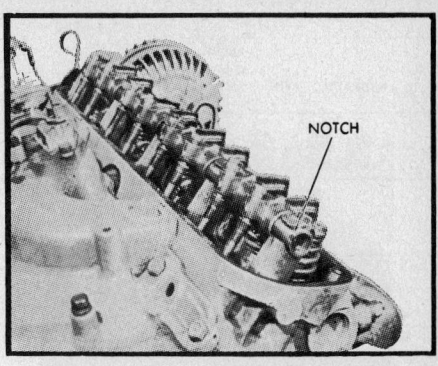

Fig. 6 Notches at end of both rocker arm shafts must face toward center of engine. V8-318, 360

VALVE TIMING SPECS.

Intake Opens Before TDC

Engine	Year	Degrees
6-198	1974	16
6-225	1974-79	16
8-318	1974-79	10
8-360	1974	16
	1974 4 B. C.	20
	1975-76 Exc. Hi. Perf.	18
	1975-76 Hi Perf.	22
	1977-79	18
8-400	1974 2 bar. carb.	18
	1974 4 bar. carb.	21
	1975-76 All	18
	1977 All	20
	1978 All	18
8-440	1974-76 Exc. Hi. Perf.	18
	1974-76 Hi. Perf.	21
	1977 All	20
	1978 Exc. Hi Perf	18
	1978 Hi Perf	21

is made, operate the engine for 5 minutes at a fast idle to stabilize engine temperatures.

Before starting the adjustment procedure, make two chalk marks on the vibration damper. Space the marks approximately 120° apart (⅓ of circumference) so that with the timing mark the damper is divided into three equal parts. Adjust the valves for No. 1 cylinder. Repeat the procedure for the remaining valves, turning the crankshaft ⅓ turn in the direction of normal rotation while adjusting the valves in the firing order sequence of 153624.

VALVE ARRANGEMENT

Front to Rear

8-318:
Right Bank . . . . I-E-I-E-I-E-I-E
Left Bank . . . . E-I-E-I-E-I-E-I
8-360 . . . . E-I-I-E-E-I-I-E
8-400, 440 . . . . E-I-I-E-E-I-I-E
6-198, 225 . . . . E-I-E-I-E-I-I-E-I-E-I-E

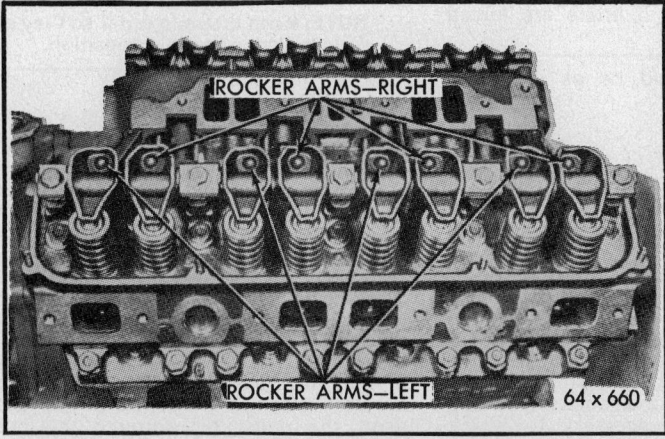

Fig. 7 Rocker arm and shaft assembly installed. 8-318, 360, 400, 440

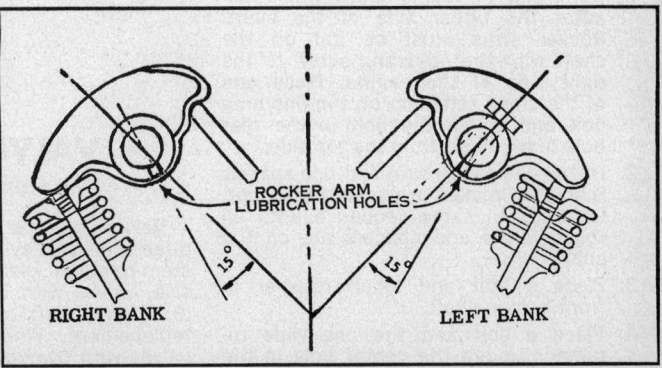

Fig. 8 Rocker arm shaft installation. V8-400, 440

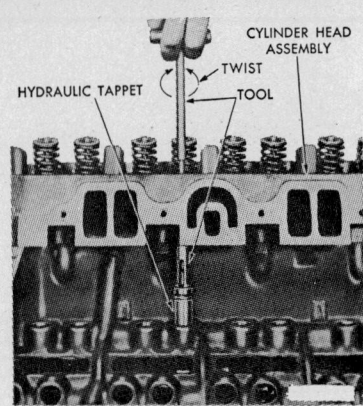

Fig. 9   Removing valve lifter

ROCKER ARMS

6-198, 225

1. Remove closed ventilation and evaporation control systems.
2. Remove rocker arm cover.
3. Remove rocker shaft bolts and retainers.
4. Lift off rocker arms and shaft.

Inspection

Clean all parts with a suitable solvent. Be sure the inside of the shaft is clean and the oil holes are open. The drilled oil hole in the bore of the rocker arm must be open to the trough and valve end of the arms. The trough also feeds oil to the adjusting screw and push rod.

The shaft should be free from excessive wear in arm contact areas. The shaft should be smooth in retainer contact areas. The adjusting screws in the rocker arms should have a uniform round end. The drag torque should be smooth and uniform. The retainers should be smooth and undamaged in the shaft contact area.

Assemble and Install

1. Referring to Fig. 5, note flat on forward end of rocker shaft which denotes the upper side of the shaft. Rocker arms must be put on the shaft with the adjusting screw to the right side of the engine. Place one of the small retainers on the one long bolt and install the bolt in the rear hole in the shaft from the top side.
2. Install one rocker arm and one spacer; then two rocker arms and a spacer. Continue in same sequence until all rocker arms and spacers are on the shaft.
3. Place a bolt and small retainer in front hole in shaft.
4. Place a bolt and the one *wide* retainer through the center hole in the shaft with six rocker arms on each side of center.

5. Install remaining bolts and retainers.
6. Locate the assembly on the cylinder head and position rocker arm adjusting screws in push rods.
7. Tighten bolts finger tight, bringing retainers in contact with the shaft *between rocker arms*.
8. Tighten bolts to specified torque.
9. After running engine to normal operating temperature, adjust valve lash to specifications.
10. Complete the job by installing the remaining parts removed.

V8-318, 360

To provide correct lubrication for the rocker arms on these engines, the rocker shafts have a small notch machined at one end, Fig. 6, and these notches must always face inward toward the center of the engine when installed. In other words, the notched end must be toward the rear of the engine on the right bank, and to the front of the engine on the left bank.

Rocker arms must be correctly positioned on the shaft prior to installation on cylinder head, Fig. 7.

It is also important when installing the rocker shaft assembly on the cylinder head to position the short retainers at each end and in the center, and to place long retainers in the two remaining positions.

V8-400, 440

1. Install rocker shafts so that the $\frac{3}{16}''$ diameter rocker arm lubrication holes point downward into rocker arm, and so that the 15 degree angle of these holes point outward toward valve end of rocker arm, Fig. 8. The 15 degree angle is determined from the center line of the bolt holes through the shaft which are used to attach the shaft assembly to the cylinder head.
2. On all engines, install rocker arms and shaft assembly, making sure to install long stamped steel retainers in No. 2 and 4 positions.

NOTE: Use extreme care in tightening the bolts so that valve lifters have time to bleed down to their operating length. Bulged lifter bodies, bent push rods and permanent noisy operation may result if lifters are forced down too rapidly.

3. Installation should be as shown in Fig. 7.

VALVE GUIDES
Non-Removable Type

Valves operate in guide holes bored directly in the cylinder head. When valve stem-to-guide clearance becomes excessive, valves with oversize stems of .005" .015" and .030" are available for service replacement. When necessary to install valves with oversize stems the valve bores should be reamed to provide the proper operating clearance.

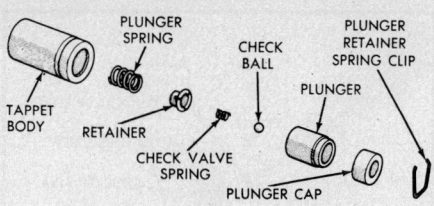

Fig. 10   Hydraulic valve lifter

VALVE LIFTERS

6-198, 225

NOTE: Some 1978 Aspen and Volaré models equipped with 6-225 2 bar. carb. will be equipped with hydraulic lifters. The lifters can be replaced after removing the cylinder head.

After taking off rocker arm and shaft assembly, lift out push rods. The valve lifters may then be removed with a suitably long magnet rod. If the lifters cannot be removed with the magnet rod, a special tool (C-4129) may be used, Fig. 9. Insert the tool through the push rod opening in the cylinder head and into lifter. Turn the handle to expand the tool in the lifter, then with a twisting motion remove the lifter from its bore.

HYDRAULIC LIFTERS

Lifter, Replace
1978-79 V8-318, 360

1. Drain cooling system and remove air cleaner.
2. Remove valve covers, rocker shaft assemblies and push rods.

NOTE: Keep push rods in order so they can be installed in the same position.

3. Remove upper radiator hose, heater hose and bypass hose from intake manifold.
4. Remove distributor and intake manifold assembly, then remove lifters.

NOTE: Keep lifters in order so they can be installed in the same position.

1974-77 V8-318, 360 & 1974-78 V8-400, 440

Chrysler Tool is available for this operation. To remove the lifter, insert the tool in the lifter body. (This portion of the tool can be used to remove lifters without a varnish build-up around the bottom of the body.) Lift the lifter out of the bore, Fig. 10. If they are struck proceed as follows:

Slide the puller portion of the tool through the cylinder head push rod holes and seat it firmly in the top of the lifter. Insert the puller pin through the body and tool shaft in the holes provided, Fig. 9. Grasp the tool handle and pull the lifter out of the bore as shown.

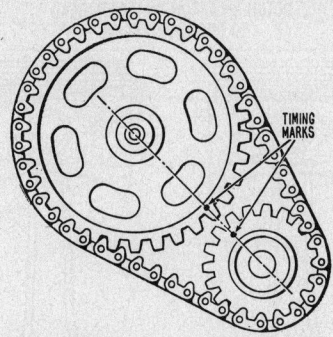

Fig. 11   Valve timing marks aligned for correct valve timing. All Sixes

TIMING CHAIN COVER

6-198, 225

1. To remove cover, drain cooling system and remove radiator and fan.
2. Remove vibration damper with a puller.
3. Loosen oil pan bolts to allow clearance and remove chain case cover.
4. Reverse above procedure to install cover.

V8-400, 440

1. Drain cooling system.
2. Remove radiator, fan and belt.
3. Remove power steering pump and alternator attaching bolts and position pump and alternator aside.
4. If equipped with A/C, position compressor aside.
5. Remove water pump and housing as an assembly.
6. Remove crankshaft bolt and pulley from vibration damper and remove damper with a puller.
7. Remove key from crankshaft.
8. Remove chain case cover and gasket, *Use extreme caution to avoid damaging the oil pan gasket; if damaged it will be necessary to remove the oil pan in order to install a new pan gasket.*

V8-318, 360

1. Remove radiator, fan and belt.
2. Remove water pump and housing as a unit.
3. Remove power steering pump, if necessary.
4. Remove crankshaft pulley.
5. Remove key from crankshaft.
6. Remove fuel pump.
7. Loosen oil pan bolts and remove front bolt at each side.
8. Remove chain case cover and gasket, *using extreme caution to avoid damaging oil pan gasket otherwise oil pan will have to be removed. It is normal to find particles of neoprene collected between crankshaft seal retainer and oil slinger.*

TIMING CHAIN

6-198, 225

1. After removing chain case cover as outlined above, take off camshaft sprocket attaching bolt.
2. Remove chain with camshaft sprocket.
3. Clean all parts and dry with compressed air.
4. Inspect timing chain for broken or damaged links. Inspect sprockets for cracks and chipped, worn or damaged teeth.

Installation

1. Turn crankshaft so sprocket timing mark is toward and directly in line with centerline of camshaft.
2. Temporarily install camshaft sprocket. Rotate camshaft to position sprocket timing mark toward and directly in line with centerline of crankshaft; then remove camshaft sprocket.
3. Place chain on crankshaft sprocket and position camshaft sprocket in chain so sprocket can be installed with timing marks aligned without moving camshaft, Fig. 11.
4. Install parts removed in reverse order of removal.

V8 Engines

To install chain and sprockets, lay both the camshaft and crankshaft sprockets on the bench. Position the sprockets so that the timing marks are next to each other. Place the chain on both sprockets, then push the gears apart as far as the chain will permit. Use a straightedge to form a line through the exact centers of both gears. The timing marks must be on this line, Fig. 12.

Slide the chain with both sprockets on the camshaft and crankshaft at the same time; then recheck the alignment.

NOTE: On V8-400 & 440 engines, use tool No. C-3509 to prevent camshaft from contacting welch plug in rear of engine block. Remove distributor and oil pump-distributor drive gear. Position tool against rear side of cam gear and attach tool with distributor retainer plate bolt.

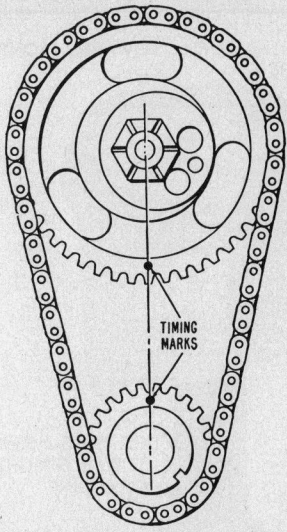

Fig. 12   Valve timing marks aligned for correct valve timing. All V8s

CAMSHAFT & BEARINGS

6-198, 225

The camshaft is supported by four precision type, steel backed, babbitt-lined bearings. Rearward thrust is taken by the rear face of the sprocket hub contacting the front of the engine block.

The camshaft, Fig. 13, can be removed after removing the grille, radiator and timing chain. To remove the camshaft bearings, the engine must be removed from the vehicle.

1. Remove valve lifters, oil pump, fuel pump and distributor.
2. Install a long bolt into front of camshaft to aid removal. Remove camshaft using care not to damage bearings.
3. Remove welch plug back of rear camshaft bearing.
4. Remove bearings with suitable puller equipment.
5. Install new bearings, being sure the oil holes in bearings line up with the corresponding oil holes in the crankcase.

NOTE: Install No. 1 camshaft bearing 3/32 in. inward from front face of cylinder block.

6. Apply sealer to welch plug and plug bore, then install plug at rear of camshaft.

V8 Engines

To remove the camshaft, remove all valve lifters, timing chain and sprockets. Remove distributor and oil pump-distributor drive gear. Remove fuel pump and see that push rod has moved away from eccentric drive cam. On V8-318 & 360 engine, remove thrust plate, 1974-79 engines incorporate a timing chain oil tab, before removing, note position of tab so it can be installed in the same manner. On all engines withdraw camshaft from engine, using care to see that camshaft lobes do

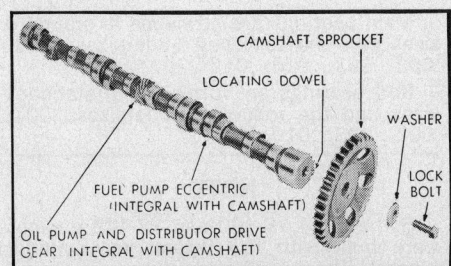

Fig. 13   Camshaft and related parts. 6-198, 225

CAMSHAFT SPROCKET
LOCATING DOWEL
WASHER
LOCK BOLT
FUEL PUMP ECCENTRIC (INTEGRAL WITH CAMSHAFT)
OIL PUMP AND DISTRIBUTOR DRIVE GEAR INTEGRAL WITH CAMSHAFT)

Fig. 14   Piston and rod assembly. 1974-77 6-198, 225, engines

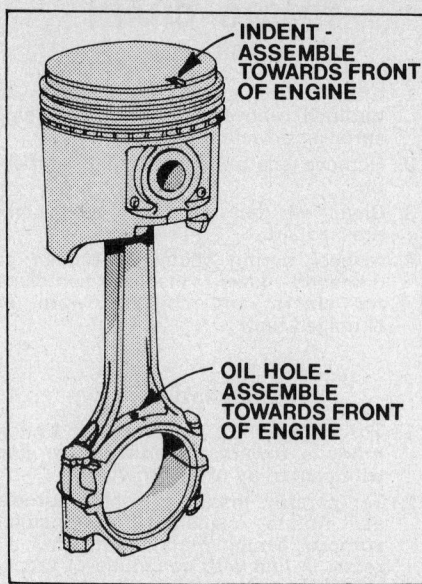

Fig. 15   Piston and rod assembly. 1978-79 6-225

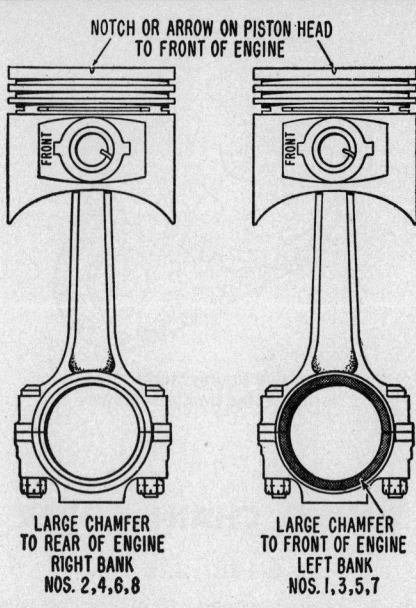

Fig. 16   Piston and rod assembly, V8 engines

not damage the camshaft bearings.

If camshaft bearings are to be replaced, it is recommended that the engine be removed from the chassis and the crankshaft taken out in order that any chips or foreign material may be removed from the oil passages.

NOTE: On V8-400 & 440 engines, install No. 1 camshaft bearing $1/32$ in. inward from front face of cylinder block.

Apply sealer to welch plug and plug bore, then install plug at rear of camshaft.

PISTON & ROD, ASSEMBLE

6-198, 225

Piston and rod assemblies must be installed as shown in Figs. 14 and 15.

V8 Engines

When installing piston and rod assemblies in the cylinders, the compression ring gaps should be diametrically opposite one another and not in line with the oil ring gap. The oil ring expander gap should be toward the outside of the "V" of the engine. The oil ring gap should be turned toward the inside of the engine "V".

Immerse the piston head and rings in clean engine oil and, with a suitable piston ring compressor, insert the piston and rod assembly into the bore. Tap the piston down into the bore, using the handle of a hammer.

Assemble the pistons to the rods as shown in Fig. 16.

PISTONS, PINS & RINGS

Pistons are available in standard sizes and the following oversizes: 1974-79 6 cylinder, .005, .020, .040, .060"; 1974 V8, .005, .020, .040"; 1975-79 V8, .020".

Pins are available in the following oversizes: V8-318 & 360, .003, .008". Not furnished on all other engines.

Rings are available in the following oversizes: std. to .009, .020-.029, .040-.049".

MAIN & ROD BEARINGS

Main bearings are furnished in standard sizes and the following undersizes: .001, .002, .003, .010, .012".

Rod bearings are furnished in standard sizes and the following undersizes: .001, .002, .003, .010, .012".

NOTE

Some 1974 V8-400 and V8-440 engines were built with low thrust wall cylinder blocks. These engines require a small thrust wall or flange (No. 3) crankshaft main bearing. The dimension "A" in Fig.

17, must be noted if the thrust bearing (No. 3) is to be replaced.

Engines using the small thrust wall (flange) bearing, Fig. 17, can be identified by the yellow "X" painted on the engine identification pad and also engine will be date coded 8-12 on the pad.

All other 1974 V8-400 and V8-440 engines require the large thrust wall bearing.

1974-76 V8-400 and 440 use either forged or cast crankshafts. These engines require that a matching torque converter, short block, damper and connecting rods be used.

If replacement of the crankshaft, torque converter, crankshaft damper or short engine is required, it is important that matching parts are used otherwise severe engine vibration will result, (Consult Chrysler Parts Dept.).

The cast crankshaft engine can be easily identified since it has the letter "E" stamped on the engine numbering pad following the built date.

Also, V8-440 engines built starting January 1975, will have external balance weights at the front damper and torque converter and a clock face will appear on the number 1 counterweight of the cast crankshaft.

6-225 engines built after June 1, 1976 may be equipped with either a cast or forged crankshaft. The following parts are not interchangeable between cast and forged crankshaft engines, crankshaft, crankshaft bearings, connecting rods and bearings and cylinder block. On models equipped with manual transmission, cast crankshaft engine vibration damper is not interchangeable with forged crankshaft engine and requires that a crankshaft screw and washer be used and torqued to 135 ft. lbs. On models equipped with automatic transmission, vibration damper and torque converter are interchangeable between cast and forged crankshaft engines.

CRANKSHAFT REAR OIL SEAL

SERVICE BULLETIN

V8 318 SEAL: When oil seal replacement is necessary on these engines, thoroughly clean the bearing cap and block to assure proper seating of the cap. Install a new rope seal in the conventional manner. Then apply an All Purpose cement (Mopar 1316241) on the joint face on the ends of the rope and ¼" to each side of the rubber side gaskets. Do not use sealer on the rope where it contacts the crankshaft or near the bearing shell.

OIL PAN

CAUTION: *Engine oil pan bolts on V8-440 engines are ¹³⁄₁₆" long with the exception of two bolts at the rear center of the oil pan. The two rear center bolts are ⁹⁄₁₆" long and thread into the aluminum seal retainer. Do not use longer bolts than ⁹⁄₁₆" at this location as they will bottom in the aluminum seal retainer and, if forced in may strip the threads and damage the seal retainer, causing an oil leak.*

1974-78 Six

1. Drain radiator, disconnect battery and radiator hoses and remove oil dipstick.
2. Remove shroud attaching screws, separate shroud from radiator and position rearward on engine.
3. Raise vehicle and drain oil pan.
4. Remove engine to transmission support bracket.
5. Disconnect exhaust pipe, then torque converter inspection shield.
6. Remove center link from steering arm and idler arm ball joints.
7. Support front of engine with a jack stand placed under the right front corner of oil pan.
8. Remove engine front mount bolts. Raise engine approx. 1½ to 2".
9. Remove oil pan attaching screws, rotate engine crankshaft to clear counterweights and remove oil pan.

V8-400, 440

1. Disconnect battery cable and drain crankcase.
2. Raise car on hoist and disconnect steering linkage from idler arm and pitman arm.
3. Remove outlet vent pipe and disconnect exhaust pipe branches from

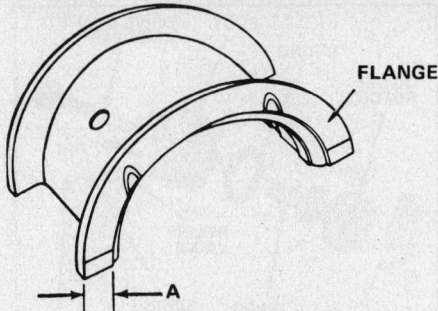

Fig. 17   Main bearing with small thrust wall flange (A)

manifolds.
4. Remove clamp attaching exhaust pipe to extension and remove exhaust pipe.
5. Remove converter dust shield.
6. Remove oil pan bolts and turn flywheel until counterweight and connecting rods at the front end of crankshaft are at their highest position to provide clearance, and lower the pan. Turn the pan to clear oil screen and suction pipe.
7. On some models, it may be necessary to release motor mounts and raise engine approximately 1½ to 2 inches.

V8-318, 360

1974-75 All

1. Disconnect battery ground cable.
2. Remove oil level dipstick.
3. Raise vehicle and drain oil.
4. Remove engine-to-torque converter left housing brace.
5. Remove steering and idler arm ball joints from steering center link.
6. Disconnect exhaust crossover pipe from exhaust manifolds and leave it hang without disconnecting it from muffler.
7. On some models it will be necessary to remove crossover pipe.
8. On 1974 Charger and Satellite, 1974-75 Coronet and 1975 Fury models with V8-360 high performance engine, remove motor mount bolts and raise engine about 2 inches.
9. Unfasten and remove oil pan.

1976 Coronet, 1976-78 Fury, 1976-79 Charger, Cordoba, 1977-78 Monaco & 1978-79 Magnum Except 4 Bar. Carb.

1. Disconnect battery ground cable and remove oil level dipstick.
2. Raise vehicle and drain crankcase, then remove engine to torque converter left housing strut.
3. Remove steering idler arm ball joints from center link.
4. Disconnect exhaust pipes from exhaust manifolds.
5. Remove oil pan attaching bolts.
6. Position a suitable jack under transmission remove rear engine mount to transmission extension attaching bolts.
7. Raise transmission until rear of oil pan

can be lowered to clear transmission.

1976 Monaco, 1976-77 Gran Fury, 1977 Royal Monaco, 1976-78 Newport, New Yorker, 1976-79 Aspen, Volaré & 1977-79 Diplomat & LeBaron Except 4 Bar. Carb.

1. Disconnect battery ground cable and remove engine oil level dipstick.
2. Raise vehicle and drain crankcase.
3. Remove exhaust crossover pipe, then disconnect and lower center link.
4. Remove starter and starter mounting stud.
5. Remove torque converter inspection cover.
6. Remove oil pan attaching bolts and oil pan.

1976-79 V8-360 4 Bar. Carb.

1. Disconnect battery ground cable and remove oil dipstick.
2. Remove fan shroud attaching bolts and place shroud over fan.
3. Raise vehicle and disconnect steering linkage center link.
4. Remove oil pan bolts.
5. Raise transmission slightly with a suitable jack and remove rear engine mount to transmission bolts.
6. Lower rear of oil pan until clear of transmission.
7. Lower transmission and loosely install the rear engine mount bolts.
8. Loosen front engine mounts from frame.
9. Raise engine with a suitable jack approximately one inch and remove oil pan.

OIL PUMP, REPLACE

Six Cylinder

1. Drain radiator and disconnect upper and lower hoses.
2. Remove fan shroud (if equipped).
3. Raise vehicle on a hoist, support front of engine with a jack stand place under right front corner of engine oil pan. *Do not support engine at crankshaft pulley or vibration damper.*
4. Remove front engine mounts.
5. Raise engine 1½ to 2 inches.
6. Remove oil filter, pump attaching bolts and remove pump assembly.

V8 Engines

On 318, 360 engines, remove oil pump from rear main bearing cap.

On V8-400 and 440 engines, unfasten oil pump from engine and remove pump and filter assembly from bottom of engine.

OIL PUMP REPAIRS

6-198, 225

To disassemble, remove the pump

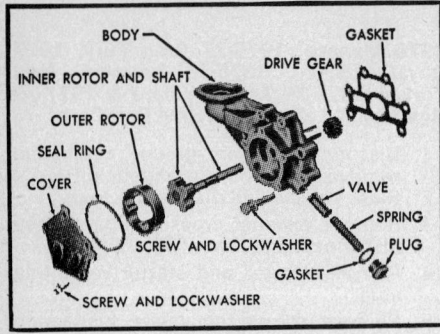

Fig. 18   Oil pump. 6-198, 6-225

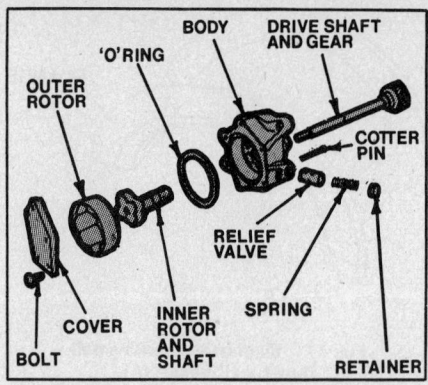

Fig. 19   Oil pump. V8-318 & 360

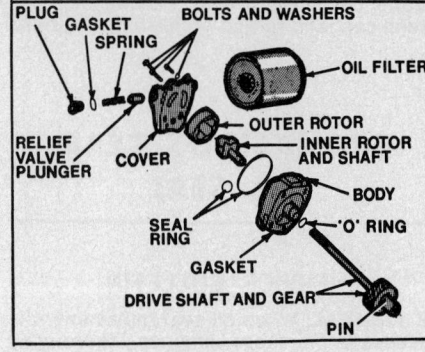

Fig. 20   Oil pump. V8-400 & 440

cover seal ring, Fig. 18. Press off the drive gear, supporting the gear to keep load off aluminum body. Remove rotor and shaft and lift out outer pump rotor. Remove oil pressure relief valve plug and lift out spring and plunger. Remove oil pressure sending unit.

Inspection

1. The rotor contact area and the bores for the shaft and valve in the pump body should be smooth, free from scratches, scoring or excessive wear.
2. The pump cover should be smooth, flat and free from scoring or ridges. Lay a straightedge across the cover. If a .0015″ feeler gauge can be inserted under the straightedge, the cover should be replaced.
3. All surfaces of the outer rotor should be smooth and uniform, free from ridges, scratches or uneven wear. Discard a rotor less than .649″ thick and/or less than 2.469″ in diameter.
4. The inner rotor and shaft assembly should be smooth, free from scoring and uneven wear. Discard rotors less than .649″ thick.
5. Place outer rotor in pump body and measure clearance between rotor and body. Discard pump body if clearance is more than .014″.
6. Install inner rotor and shaft in pump body. Shaft should turn freely but without side play. If clearance between rotor teeth is more than .010″, replace both rotors.
7. Measure rotor end clearance. If feeler gauge of more than .004″ can be inserted between straightedge and rotors, install a new pump body.
8. The oil pressure relief valve should be smooth, free from scratches or scoring, and should be a free fit in its bore.
9. Relief valve springs are painted either gray, red or brown to denote free lengths of 2.19, 2.29 and 2.39 inches. Rather than change the length, replace a spring with one of the same color.

Assemble and Install

1. With pump rotors in body, press drive gear on shaft, flush with end of shaft.

2. Install seal ring in groove in body and install cover. Tighten bolts to 10 ft. lbs. Test pump for free turning.
3. Install oil pressure relief valve spring. Use new washer (gasket) and tighten plug securely.
4. If pump shaft turns freely, remove pump cover and outer rotor before installation of pump on engine.
5. Install oil pressure sending unit and tighten to 60 inch lbs. (5 ft. lbs.)
6. Using a new gasket, install pump on engine and tighten bolts to 200 inch lbs. (16 ft. lbs.)
7. Install oil filter reservoir on pump. Install filter element and tighten cover nuts to 25 ft. lbs.
8. Connect oil pressure sending unit wire.
9. Complete the installation by reversing steps as given under Oil Pump, Replace.

V8 Engines

After removing the pump from the engine it should be disassembled, cleaned and inspected for wear, Figs. 19 and 20.

1. Remove the cotter pin holding the oil strainer to the oil suction pipe. Then remove the pipe from the pump body.
2. Remove the pump cover and discard the oil seal ring.
3. Remove pump rotor and shaft and lift out rotor body.
4. Remove oil pressure relief valve plug and lift out the spring and plunger.
5. Wash all parts in cleaning solvent and inspect carefully for damage or wear.
6. The mating face of the oil pump cover should be smooth. If it is scratched or grooved, the cover should be replaced with a new one.
7. Check for excessive cover-to-rotor wear by laying a straight edge across the cover surface. If a .0015″ feeler gauge can be inserted between cover and straight edge, the

cover should be discarded and a new one installed.

8. Slide rotor body and rotor into pump body and then place a straight edge across the face of the pump body between the bolt holes. If a feeler gauge of less than .003″ or more than .006″ can be inserted between the rotors and straight edge, install a new pump body.
9. Remove the pump rotor and shaft, leaving rotor body in pump cavity. Press rotor body to one side with the fingers and measure the clearance between rotor and pump bodies. If it is more than .014″, install a new pump body.
10. Check the clearance between the pump rotor and rotor body. If the measurement is more than .014″, install a new pump rotor and rotor body.
11. Check the oil pump relief valve plunger for scoring and free operation in its bore. If the plunger is scored, install a new one.

BELT TENSION DATA

	New[1]	Used[1]
1974-79 All	120	70

[1]—Belt tension in lbs.

WATER PUMP, REPLACE

CAUTION: When it becomes necessary to remove a fan clutch of the silicone type, the assembly must be supported in the vertical position to prevent leaks of silicone fluid from the clutch mechanism. This loss of fluid will render the fan clutch inoperative.

6-198, 225

1. Drain cooling system, then remove battery, upper and lower radiator hoses and fan shroud.
2. Remove all drive belts, then remove fan attaching bolts, fan, spacer and pulley.
3. Remove A/C compressor and air pump bracket to water pump attaching bolts, then position compressor and air pump aside. Keep compressor in upright position.

4. Disconnect by-pass and heater hoses from water pump.
5. Remove water pump attaching bolts and remove pump assembly.

V8-318, 360

1. Drain cooling system and disconnect battery ground cable.
2. Remove all drive belts, then remove radiator shroud and position over fan.
3. Remove fan assembly, pulley and fan shroud.
4. Remove alternator adjusting strap and mounting bolts and position alternator aside.
5. Remove A/C compressor with mounting brackets and position aside, if equipped. Keep compressor in upright position.
6. Remove power steering pump mounting bolts and position pump aside, if equipped.
7. Remove air pump and mounting brackets, if equipped. Disconnect air hose at pump fittings.
8. Disconnect by-pass and heater hoses at water pump.
9. Disconnect lower radiator hose from pump.
10. Remove remaining water pump attaching bolts and remove pump assembly.

V8-400, 440

1. Drain cooling system and disconnect battery ground cable.
2. Remove upper radiator hose and fan shroud. Position shroud back on engine.

3. Remove all drive belts, then remove fan attaching bolts, fan, spacer and pulley.
4. Remove water pump attaching bolts and remove pump assembly.

Service Bulletin

CORE HOLE PLUG SIZES: When replacing a cup-type core hole plug in an engine, the size of the hole in the cylinder head, water jacket or rear bearing bore for the camshaft should be checked. At these locations a $1/16$" oversize hole is sometimes bored in production and an oversize core plug installed.

Core plugs $1/16$" oversize are available for replacement should they be required at these locations.

FUEL PUMP PRESSURE

Year	Engine	Pressure(PSI)
1974-79	Six Cylinder	$3\frac{1}{2}$-5
1974-79	V8-318, 360	
1974-75	V8-400, 440 Except Below	$3\frac{1}{2}$-5
1975	V8-400-2	$6-7\frac{1}{2}$
1975	V8-400-4 [1]	$6-7\frac{1}{2}$
1975	V8-440 [2]	$4-5\frac{1}{2}$
1975	V8-440 [1]	$6-7\frac{1}{2}$
1976-78	V8-400, 440 [3]	5-7

1974-78	V8-440 High Performance	$6-7\frac{1}{2}$

[1]—California.
[2]—Except California.
[3]—Except High Performance.

FUEL PUMP, REPLACE

SERVICE NOTE: Before installing the pump, it is good practice to crank the engine so that the nose of the camshaft eccentric is out of the way of the fuel pump rocker arm when the pump is installed. In this way there will be the least amount of tension on the rocker arm, thereby easing the installation of the pump.

1. Remove all gasket material from the pump and block gasket surfaces. Apply sealer to both sides of new gasket.
2. Position gasket on pump flange and hold pump in position against its mounting surface. Make sure rocker arm is riding on camshaft eccentric.
3. Press pump tight against its mounting. Install retaining screws and tighten them alternately.
4. Connect fuel lines. Then operate engine and check for leaks.

Clutch and Transmission Section

NOTE: 1979 linkage adjustment information is in this section. Repair procedures on both automatic and manual shift transmissions are covered elsewhere in this manual. Procedures for removing automatic transmissions as well as linkage adjustments on 1974-78 models are included in the automatic transmission chapters. See Chapter Index.

CLUTCH PEDAL, ADJUST

1. Inspect condition of clutch pedal rubber stop, if stop is damaged install a new one.
2. Where necessary, disconnect interlock clutch rod at transmission end.
3. Adjust linkage by turning self-locking adjusting nut to provide $5/32$" free movement at outer end of fork. This movement will provide the prescribed one-inch free play at pedal.
4. Assemble interlock clutch rod (if used) to transmission pawl.

CLUTCH, REPLACE

Removal

1. Remove transmission and clutch housing pan.
2. Remove return spring from clutch

release fork and clutch housing or torque shaft lever.
3. Remove spring washer securing fork rod to torque shaft lever and remove rod from torque shaft and release fork.
4. On 1974-76 6 cylinder models, remove clip and plain washer securing interlock rod to torque shaft lever and remove spring washer, plain washer and rod.
5. Remove clutch release bearing assembly, release fork and boot from clutch housing.
6. Mark clutch cover and flywheel so that they may be assembled in their original position to maintain balance.
7. Loosen clutch cover retaining screws one or two turns at a time in succession until cover is loose and remove screws.
8. Remove clutch assembly and disc from clutch housing using care to

avoid contaminating the friction surfaces of the clutch disc.

Installation

1. Lubricate pilot bushing in crankshaft with Multi-Purpose Grease number 2932524 or equivalent.
2. Clean surfaces of flywheel and pressure plate, making certain no oil or grease remains on these parts.
3. Hold cover plate and disc in place and insert a special clutch aligning tool or a spare clutch shaft through the hub of the disc and into the crankshaft pilot bearing.
4. Bolt clutch cover loosely to flywheel, being sure marks previously made are lined up.
5. To avoid distortion of clutch cover, tighten cover bolts a few turns each in progression until all are tight. The final tightening should be 15-20 ft-

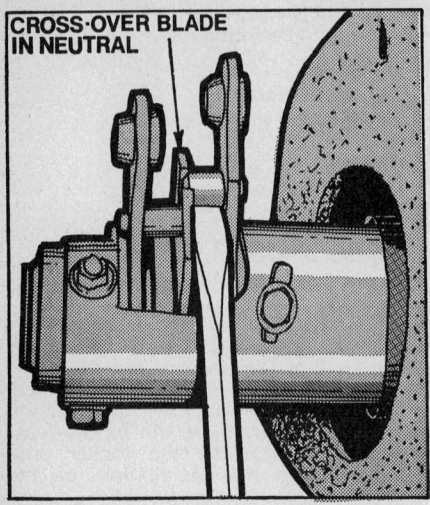

Fig. 1 Gearshift lever adjustment. 1974-79 three speed transmission

nents.
2. Drain fluid from transmission.
3. Disconnect propeller shaft at rear universal joint and carefully pull yoke out of extension housing. *Be careful not to scratch or nick ground surface on sliding spline yoke during removal and installation of shaft.*
4. Disconnect speedometer cable and stop light switch leads.
5. Disconnect left-hand exhaust pipe (dual exhaust) from manifold.
6. Disconnect parking cable where necessary.
7. Support rear of engine with a jack.
8. Raise engine slightly and disconnect extension housing from removable center crossmember.
9. Support transmission with a suitable jack and remove center crossmember.
10. Remove transmission-to-clutch housing bolts.
11. Slide transmission rearward and out of vehicle.
12. Reverse procedure to install.

SHIFT LINKAGE, ADJUST THREE SPEED TRANS.

Column Shift

1974
1. Loosen both shift rod swivels.
2. With transmission shift levers in neu-

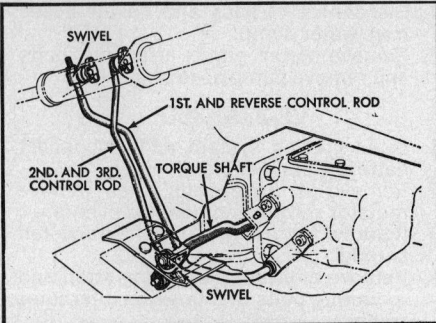

Fig. 2 Gearshift controls. 1974 Three Speed Transmission

tral (middle detent) move shift lever to align locating slots in bottom of steering column shift housing and bearing housing. Install suitable tool in slot to maintain alignment.
3. Place screwdriver or other suitable tool between crossover blade and 2nd-3rd lever at steering column so that both lever pins are engaged by crossover blade, Fig. 1.
4. Rotate 1st-reverse lever on transmission clockwise to reverse position, then adjust 1st-reverse rod swivel by loosening clamp bolt and sliding swivel along rod until it enters 1st-reverse

lbs. for 5/16″ bolts and 30 ft-lbs. for 3/8″ bolts.
6. Lubricate release bearing sleeve and fork fingers with Milti-Purpose Grease number 2932524 or equivalent and install release bearing, fork and dust boot.
7. Install transmission by guiding it into place with guide studs inserted in the two top holes of the housing.
8. Adjust clutch pedal free travel.

THREE SPEED TRANSMISSION, REPLACE

1. Disconnect shift rods from transmission levers.

NOTE: If shift rods are retained by plastic grommets, disconnect the shift levers from the transmission to avoid replacing the grommets.

2. Drain lubricant from transmission and disconnect propeller shaft.
3. Disconnect speedometer cable and back-up light switch connector.
4. If necessary, disconnect exhaust pipes from exhaust manifolds.
5. Raise engine slightly using a suitable support fixture or jack and disconnect extension housing from center crossmember.
6. Support transmission with a suitable jack and remove center crossmember.
7. Remove transmission to clutch housing retaining bolts, then slide transmission rearward until input shaft clears clutch disc and remove transmission.
8. Reverse procedure to install.

FOUR SPEED & OVERDRIVE TRANSMISSION, REPLACE

1. Remove console and shift compo-

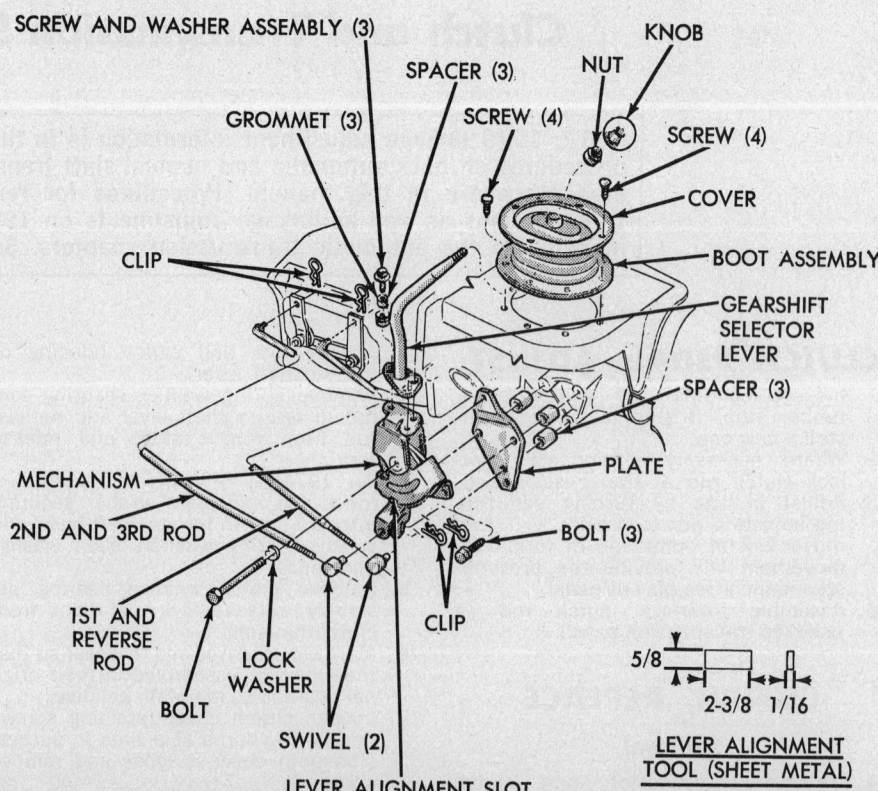

Fig. 3 Gearshift linkage adjustment. 1974-79 three speed floor shift transmission

lever at transmission, Fig. 2. Install washers and clip and torque swivel bolt to 125 inch lbs.

5. Adjust 2nd-3rd rod swivel by loosening clamp bolt and sliding swivel along rod until it enters 2nd-3rd lever, Fig. 2. Install washers and clip and torque swivel bolt to 125 inch lbs.

6. Remove tool from crossover blade at steering column and shift through all gears to check adjustment and crossover smoothness.

7. Check for proper operation of steering column lock in reverse and other gear positions. If properly adjusted, ignition should lock in reverse position only without having to force the shift lever.

1975-79

1. Loosen both shift rod swivels.

2. With transmission shift levers in neutral (middle detent), move shift lever to align locating slots in bottom of steering column shift housing and bearing housing. Install suitable tool in slot to maintain alignment.

3. Place screwdriver or other suitable tool between crossover blade and 2nd-3rd lever at steering column so that both lever pins are engaged by crossover blade, Fig. 1.

4. Torque both shift rod swivel bolts to 125 inch lbs.

5. Remove gearshift housing locating tool and remove tool from crossover blade at steering column.

6. Shift through all gears to check adjustment and crossover smoothness.

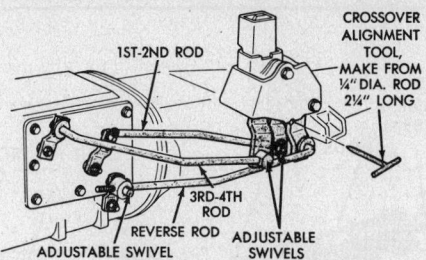

Fig. 4 Gearshift linkage adjustment. 1974-78 four speed transmission

Check for operation of steering column lock in reverse and other gear positions, If properly adjusted, ignition should lock in reverse position only without having to force the shift lever.

Floor Shift

1. Place shift lever in neutral position and disconnect shift rods from levers.

2. Fabricate alignment tool from $1/16$ in. thick sheet metal as shown in Fig. 3.

3. Insert alignment tool into slots in levers and frame to hold levers in neutral position, Fig. 3.

4. Place transmission levers in neutral position and adjust shift rod swivels so that rods will install freely into levers.

5. Secure rods with washers and clips, then remove alignment tool and check shifter operation.

SHIFT LINKAGE, ADJUST FOUR SPEED TRANS.

1974-79

1. Install floor shift lever aligning tool, Fig. 4, to hold levers in neutral position. Crossover alignment tool shown in Fig. 4, will have to be fabricated.

2. With all rods disconnected from transmission shift levers, place levers in neutral position.

3. Starting with 1-2 shift rod, rotate shift rods until ends of rods enter shift levers. It may be necessary to remove clip at shifter end to rotate rods.

4. Replace washers and clips, then remove aligning tool and check shifting action.

1979 AUTO. TRANS. LINKAGE, ADJUST

Column Shift

Linkage adjustment procedures are the same as 1978 models described in the Automatic Transmission section of this manual.

Rear Axle, Propeller Shaft & Brakes

NOTE: Figs. 1, 2, 4 and 5 illustrate the various rear axle assemblies used on these cars. When necessary to overhaul any of these units, refer to the *Rear Axle Specifications* table in this chapter.

INTEGRAL TYPE REAR AXLE

Two types of integral carrier axles are used. In both types, the drive pinion is mounted in two opposing tapered roller bearings which are preloaded by a spacer positioned between them.

In the unit shown in Fig. 1, the differential is supported by two tapered roller side bearings. These bearings are preloaded by spacers located between the bearings and carrier housing. The differential assembly is positioned for ring and pinion backlash by varying these spacers.

Axle shafts in this unit are held in place by retainers at the outer ends of the shafts. These retainers are bolted

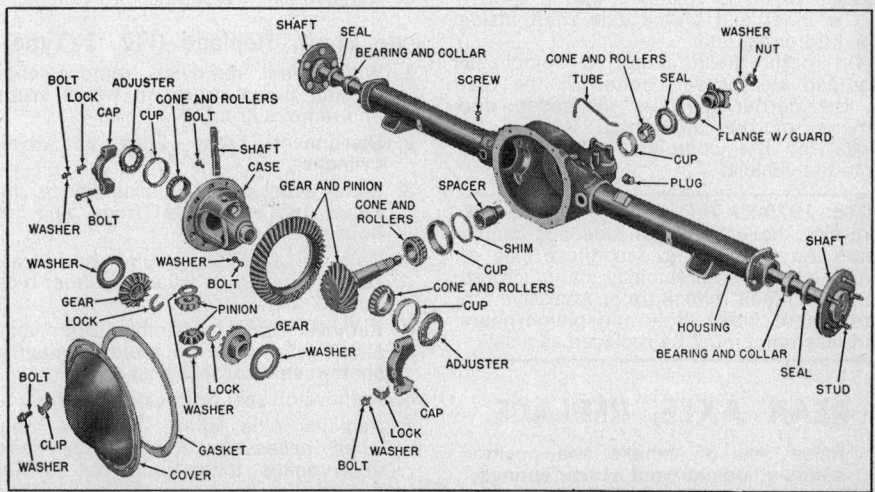

Fig. 2 Integral "C" washer type rear axle (typical). 1974-79

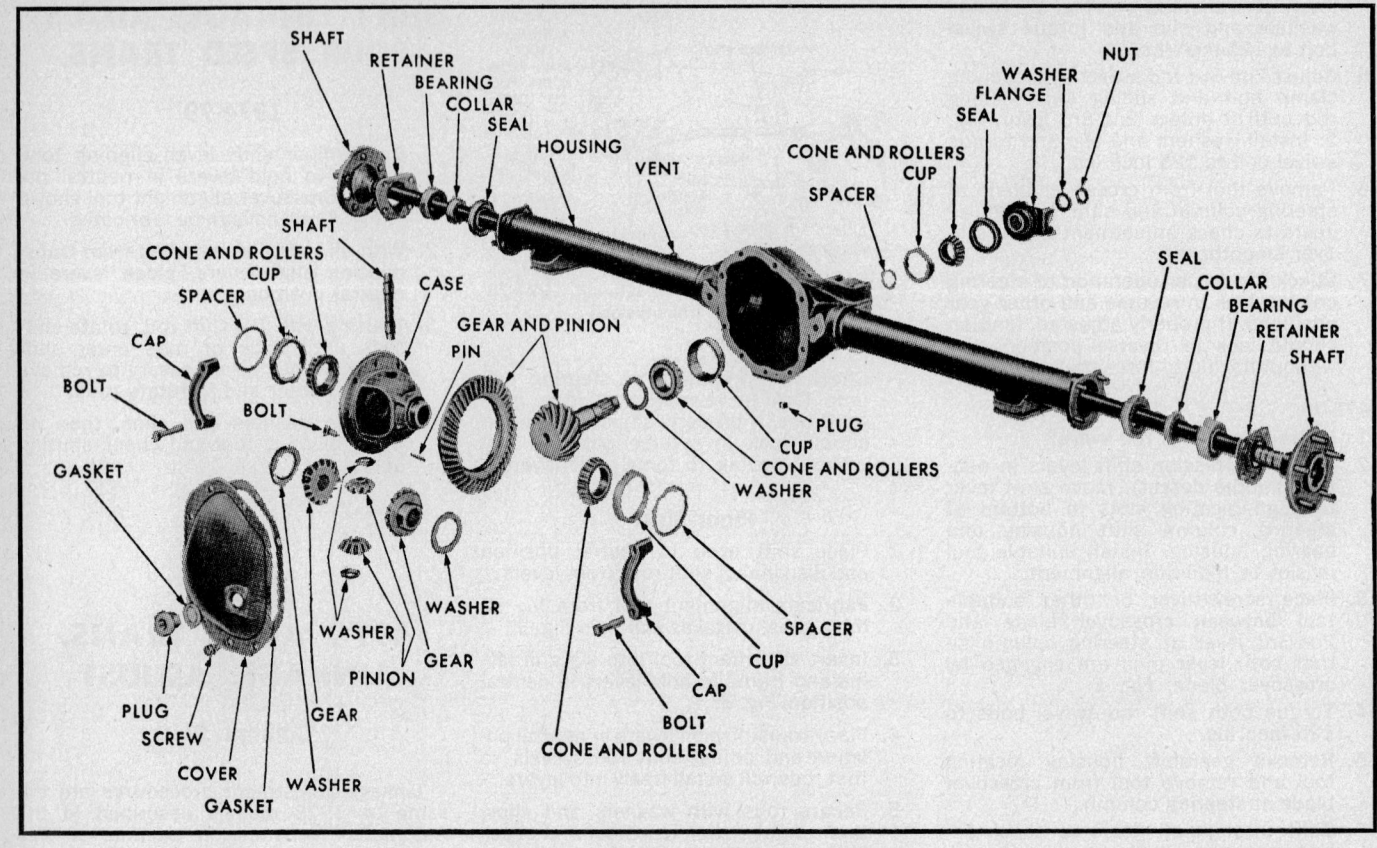

Fig. 1   Integral rear axle (typical). 1974-79

through the brake backing plates to the rear axle tubes.

In the unit shown in Fig. 2, the differential is also supported by two tapered roller bearings. A threaded differential bearing adjuster is located in each bearing pedestal cap to eliminate differential side play, adjust and maintain ring and pinion backlash and provide a means of obtaining differential bearing preload.

Axles are retained by means of a "C" washer which is installed into a groove in the inner end of the axle shaft inside the differential unit.

On both these units, a removable stamped steel cover, bolted to the rear of the carrier, permits inspection and service of the differential without removal of the complete axle assembly from the vehicle.

NOTE: 1975-79 7¼ and 8¼ in. axle differentials have balanced side and pinion gears. Any attempt to mix these side or pinion gears with previously manufactured ones will result in lock up or excessive differential backlash. Side and pinion gears on these units must be replaced as a set.

REAR AXLE, REPLACE

1. Raise rear of vehicle and position safety stands at front of rear springs.
2. Remove rear wheels, then disconnect brake lines at wheel cylinders. Cap brake line fittings to prevent loss of fluid.
3. Disconnect parking brake cables.
4. Mark drive shaft and pinion flanges for reassembly, then remove drive shaft.
5. Disconnect shock absorbers from spring plate studs, then loosen rear spring U-bolt nuts and remove U-bolts.
6. Remove axle assembly from vehicle.

Axle Shaft, Replace (Fig. 1 Type)

1. With wheel removed, remove clips holding brake drum on wheel studs and remove drum.
2. Disconnect brake lines at wheel cylinders.
3. Using access hole in axle flange, remove retainer nuts from end of housing.
4. Remove axle shaft and brake assembly, using a slide hammer-type puller.
5. Remove brake assembly from axle shaft with care to avoid damaging shaft in seal contact area.
6. Remove oil seal from axle housing.
7. *Remove axle shaft bearings only when necessary. Removal of bearings makes them unfit for further use.*
8. *Axle shaft end play is pre-set and*

not adjustable. End play is accomplished by the amount of end play built into the bearings. The two axle housing brake support plate gaskets on each side are used for sealing purposes only. Always replace the gaskets once they have been removed.
9. Press bearing and collar on shaft firmly against shoulders on shaft.
10. Install new oil seal in housing.
11. Install brake assembly on axle housing and carefully slide axle shaft through oil seal and into side gear splines.
12. Tap end of axle shaft lightly to position axle shaft bearing into bearing bore and attach retainer plate to housing.
13. Install brake drums and wheels.

Axle Shaft, Replace (Fig. 2 Type)

1. With wheel and brake drum removed, or caliper and rotor assembly removed, loosen differential housing cover and drain lubricant. Remove cover.
2. Turn differential case to make pinion shaft lock screw accessible and remove lock screw and shaft.
3. Push axle shaft inward toward center of car and remove "C" washer from groove in axle shaft, Fig. 3.
4. Remove axle shaft from housing, being careful not to damage the axle

bearing, which will remain in the housing.

5. The axle bearing and/or seal can now be removed if necessary.
6. Reverse procedure to install.

REMOVABLE CARRIER TYPE

In these rear axles, Figs. 4 and 5, the drive pinion is mounted in two tapered roller bearings. The bearings are preloaded by a spacer and shims behind the front bearing. The drive pinion is positioned by an adjusting washer between the head of the drive pinion and the rear pinion bearing. The front bearing is held in place by a large washer and nut.

The differential is supported in the carrier by two tapered roller side bearings. These bearings are preloaded by two threaded ring nuts between the bearings and the pedestals. The differential assembly is positioned for proper ring gear and pinion backlash by varying the adjustment of these ring nuts. The differential case houses two side gears in mesh with two pinions mounted on a pinion shaft which is held in place by a lock pin. The side gears and pinions are backed up by thrust washers. Side thrust of the wheels is transferred from one axle shaft to the other by means of a thrust block in the center of the differential case.

Carrier, Remove & Replace

It is not necessary to remove the rear axle assembly for any normal repairs. The axle shafts and carrier assembly can easily be moved from the vehicle, leaving the rear axle housing in place.

1. Remove axle shafts as outlined be-

Fig. 3   Location of "C" washer locks

low.
2. Disconnect rear universal joint and move propeller shaft out of the way. Support shaft to relieve strain on the front universal joint.
3. Remove lubricant from axle housing with a suction gun.
4. Remove attaching nuts and lift carrier assembly out of axle housing.
5. Reverse removal procedure to install.

Axle Shaft, Replace

1. With wheels removed, remove clips holding brake drum on axle shaft studs and remove brake drum.
2. Using access hole in axle shaft flange, remove retainer nuts. The right shaft with threaded adjuster in retainer plate will have a lock under one of the studs that should be removed at this time, Fig. 6.
3. Remove parking brake strut.
4. Attach axle shaft remover tool, Fig. 7, to axle shaft flange and remove

axle shaft. Remove brake assembly and foam gaskets.

5. Remove oil seal, Fig. 8.
6. Wipe axle shaft housing seal bore clean and install a new seal, Fig. 9.

Disassembly

To prevent the possibility of damaging axle shaft seal surface, slide a protective sleeve over seal surface next to bearing collar, Fig. 10.

1. Position axle shaft bearing collar on a heavy vise and, using a chisel, cut deep grooves into retaining collar at 90-degree intervals, as shown in Fig. 10. This will enlarge bore of collar and permit it to be driven off axle shaft.
2. Remove bearing roller retainer flange by cutting off lower edge with a chisel, Fig. 11.
3. Grind a section off flange of inner bearing cone, Fig. 12, and remove bearing rollers, Fig. 13.
4. Pull bearing roller retainer down as far as possible and cut with side cutters and remove, Fig. 14.
5. Remove roller bearing cup and protective sleeve from axle shaft.

CAUTION: Sleeve should not be used as a protector for the seal journal when pressing off bearing cone as it was not designed for this purpose.

6. To avoid scuffing seal journal when bearing cone is being removed, it should be protected by a single wrap of .002" shim stock held in place by a rubber band, Fig. 15.
7. Remove bearing cone with tool set shown in Fig. 7. Tighten bolts of

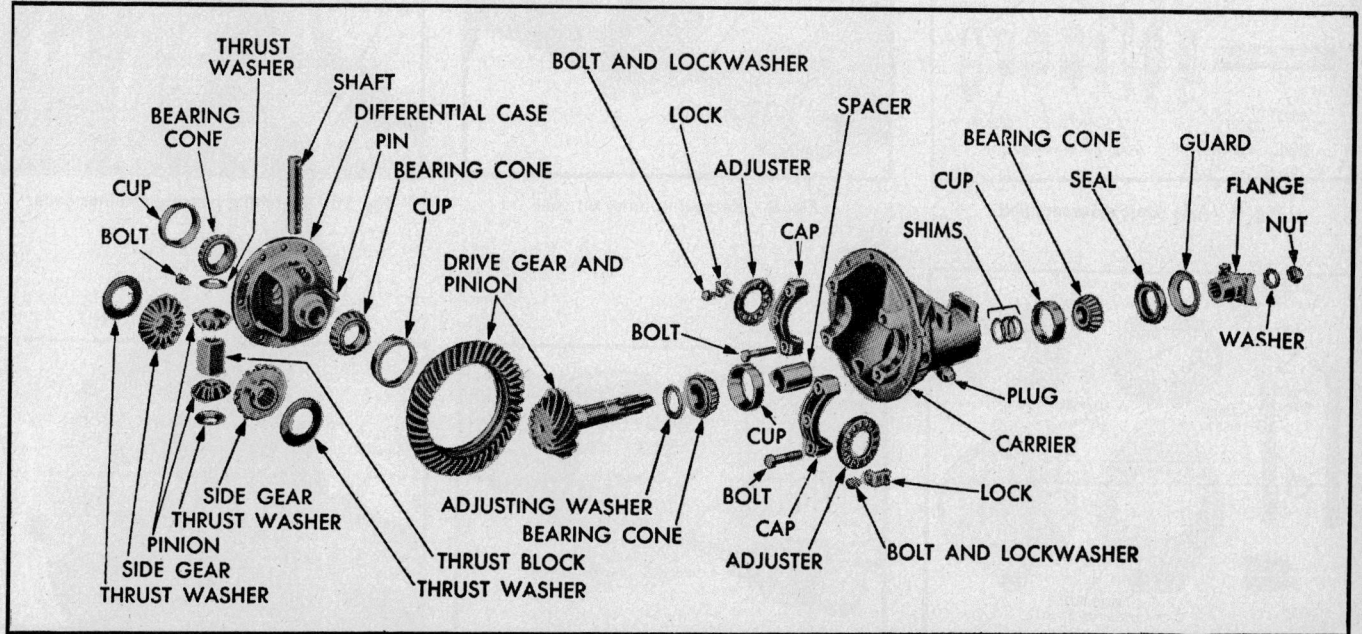

Fig. 4   Removable type rear axle assembly with large pinion

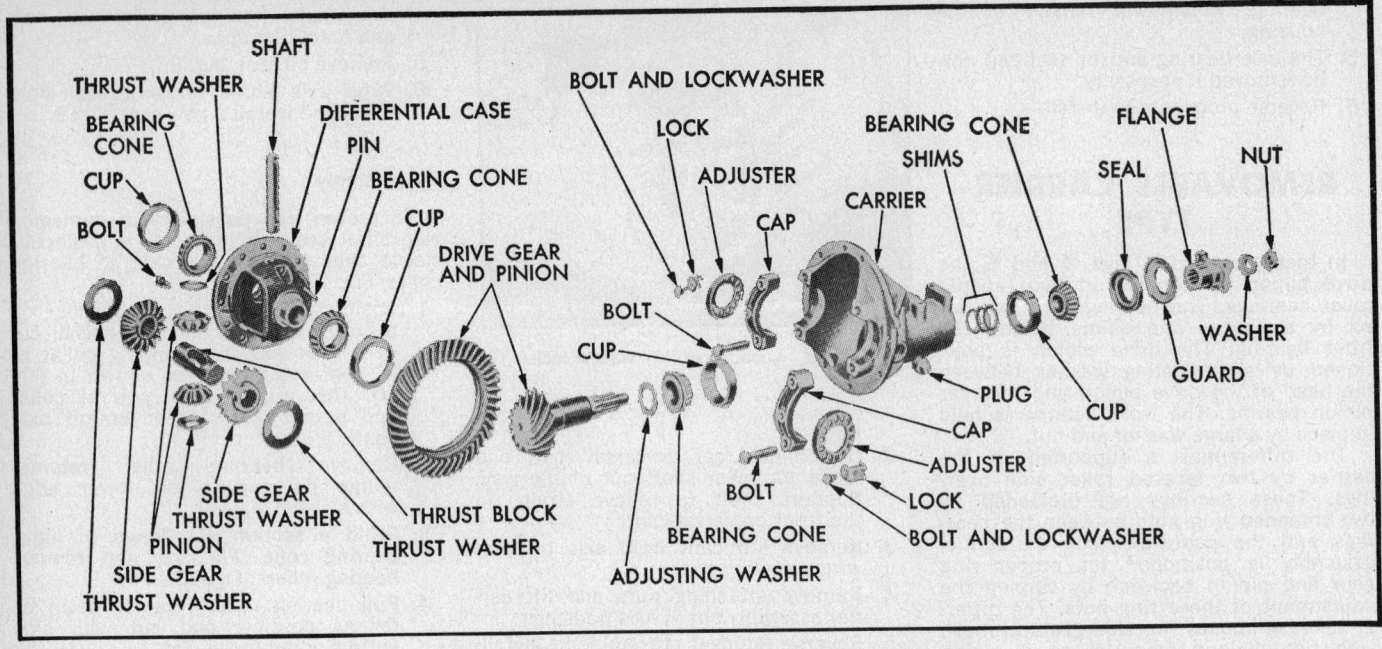

Fig. 5   Removable type rear axle assembly with small pinion

tool alternaterly until cone is removed, Fig. 16.

8. Remove seal in bearing retainer plate and replace with a new seal.

Assembly

1. Install retainer plate and seal on axle shaft.

2. Install new axle shaft bearing cup, cone and collar on shaft, using tool shown in Fig. 17. Tighten bolts of tool alternately until bearing and collar are seated properly.

3. Inspect axle shaft seal journal for scratches and polish with #600 crocus cloth if necessary.

4. Lubricate wheel bearings with approved grease.

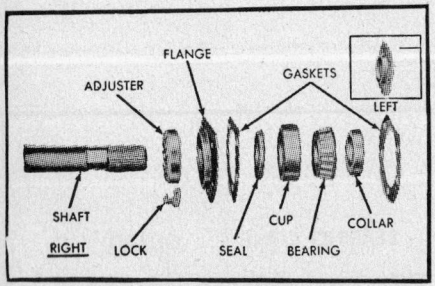

Fig. 6   Axle shaft disassembled

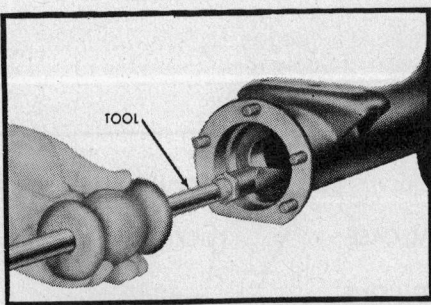

Fig. 8   Removing inner oil seal

Fig. 10   Notching bearing retainer collar

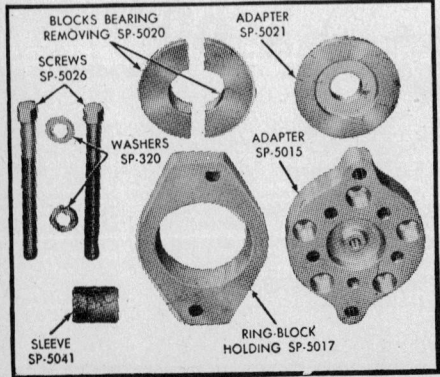

Fig. 7   Tool set for removing axle shaft

Fig. 9   Installing inner oil seal

Fig. 11   Removing roller retainer

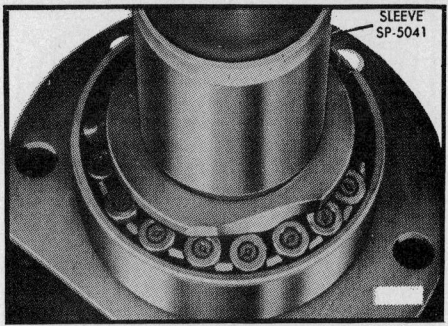

Fig. 12 Flange ground off inner bearing cone

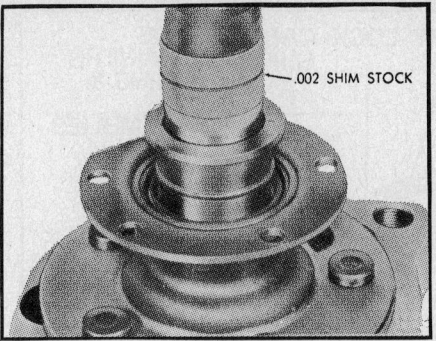

Fig. 15 Seal journal protection

Fig. 16 Removing bearing cone

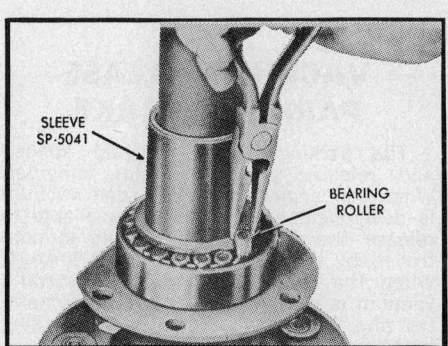

Fig. 13 Removing bearing rollers

Fig. 14 Cutting out bearing retainer

Installation

1. Clean axle shaft flange face and install new gasket followed by brake support plate on left side of axle housing.
2. Install foam gasket on studs of axle housing and slide shaft through oil seal and engage splines in differential side gear.
3. Tap end of axle shaft lightly with a plastic mallet to position axle shaft bearing in housing bearing bore. Position retainer plate over axle housing studs. Install retainer nuts and torque to 30-35 ft-lbs. Start by tightening bottom nut.

4. Repeat Step 1 on right side of axle housing.
5. Back off threaded adjuster on right axle shaft until inner face of adjuster is flush with inner face of retainer plate. Carefully slide axle shaft through oil seal and engage splines in differential side gears.
6. Repeat Step 3.

Axle Shaft End Play

When setting end play both rear wheels must be off the ground, otherwise a false end play setting will occur.

1. Using a dial indicator mounted as shown in Fig. 18, turn the adjuster clockwise until both wheel bearings are seated and there is zero end play in axle shafts. Back off adjuster counterclockwise four notches to establish an axle shaft end play of .013-.023".
2. Tap end of axle shaft lightly with a plastic mallet to seat right wheel bearing cup against adjuster, and rotate axle shaft several revolutions so that a true end play reading is indicated.
3. Remove one retainer plate nut and install adjuster lock. If tab on lock does not mate with notch in adjuster, turn adjuster slightly until it does. Install nut and torque to 30-35 ft-lbs.
4. Recheck axle shaft end play. If not within prescribed limits, repeat adjustment procedure.
5. Remove dial indicator and install brake drum, drum retaining clips and wheel.

PROPELLER SHAFT

1. Remove both rear universal joint roller and bushing assembly clamps from pinion yoke. Do not disturb retaining strap holding roller assemblies on cross.
2. Lower front of vehicle slightly to prevent loss of transmission oil and pull drive shaft out as an assembly.
3. To install, carefully slide yoke into splines on transmission output shaft.
4. Align rear of propeller shaft with pinion yoke and position roller and bush-

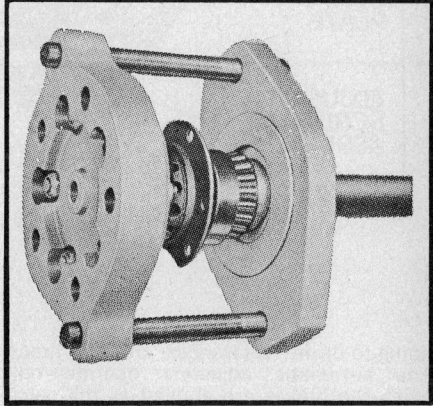

Fig. 17 Installing bearing and collar

Fig. 18 Measuring axle shaft end play

ing assemblies into seats of pinion yoke.
5. Install bushing clamps and tighten clamp bolts to 170 inch lbs.

BRAKE ADJUSTMENTS

1974-79 Self Adjusting Brakes

These brakes, Fig. 19, have self-adjusting shoe mechanisms that assure correct

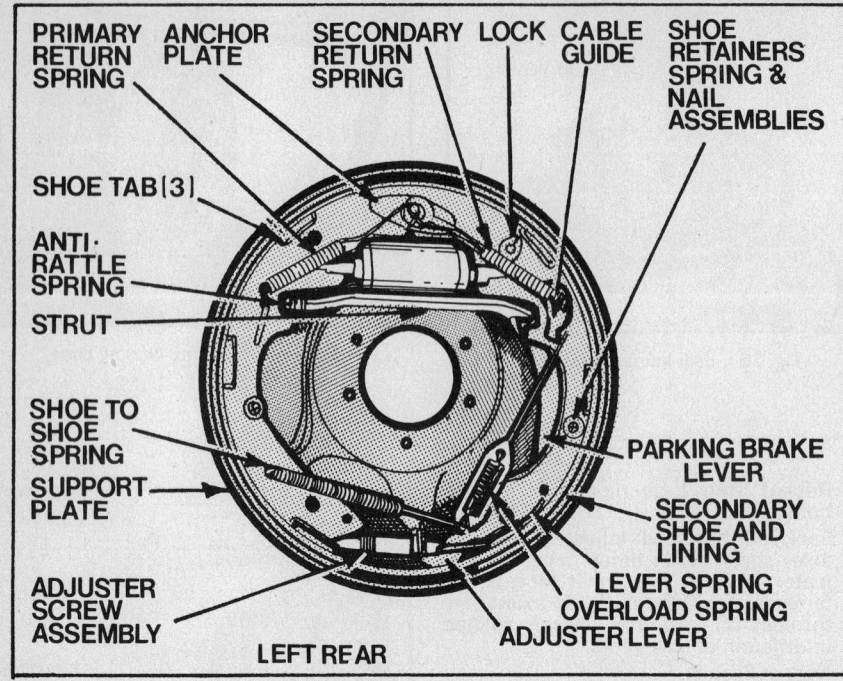

PRIMARY RETURN SPRING | ANCHOR PLATE | SECONDARY RETURN SPRING | LOCK | CABLE GUIDE | SHOE RETAINERS SPRING & NAIL ASSEMBLIES

SHOE TAB (3)

ANTI-RATTLE SPRING

STRUT

SHOE TO SHOE SPRING

SUPPORT PLATE

ADJUSTER SCREW ASSEMBLY

PARKING BRAKE LEVER

SECONDARY SHOE AND LINING

LEVER SPRING
OVERLOAD SPRING
ADJUSTER LEVER

LEFT REAR

Fig. 19   Left rear brake (10-11 inch). 1974-79

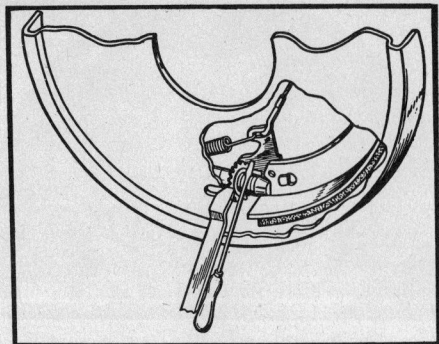

Fig. 20   Releasing brake lever with screwdriver while adjusting star wheel

lining-to-drum clearances at all times. The automatic adjusters operate only when the brakes are applied as the car is moving rearward.

Although the brakes are self-adjusting, an initial adjustment is necessary when the brake shoes have been relined or replaced, or when the length of the star wheel adjuster has been changed during some other service operation.

Frequent usage of an automatic transmission forward range to halt reverse vehicle motion may prevent the automatic adjusters from functioning, thereby inducing low pedal heights. Should low pedal heights be encountered, it is recommended that numerous forward and reverse stops be made until satisfactory pedal height is obtained.

Service Note

If a low pedal height condition cannot be corrected by making numerous reverse stops (provided the hydraulic system is free of air) it indicates that the self-adjusting mechanism is not functioning. Therefore, it will be necessary to remove the drum, clean, free up and lubricate the adjusting mechanism. Then adjust the brakes, being sure the parking brake is fully released.

Adjustment

1. Each backing plate has two adjusting hole covers; remove the rear cover and turn the adjusting screw upward with a screwdriver or other suitable tool to expand the shoes until a slight drag is felt when the drum is rotated.
2. While holding the adjusting lever out of engagement with the adjusting screw, Fig. 20; back off the adjusting screw until wheel rotates freely with no drag.
3. Install wheel and adjusting hole cover. Adjust brakes on remaining wheels in the same manner.
4. If pedal height is not satisfactory, drive the vehicle and make sufficient reverse stops until proper pedal height is obtained.

PARKING BRAKE, ADJUST

Exc. 1974-75 Imperial

1. Release parking brake lever and loosen cable adjusting nut to be sure cable is slack.
2. With rear wheel brakes properly adjusted, tighten cable adjusting nut until a slight drag is felt when the rear wheels are rotated. Then loosen the cable adjusting nut until both rear wheels can be rotated freely.
3. To complete the operation, back off an additional two turns of the cable adjusting nut.
4. Apply and release parking brake several times to be sure rear wheels are not dragging when cable is in released position.

1974-75 Imperial

Adjust parking brake by rotating adjuster wheel with tool C-4223, Fig. 21, until brakes seat against drums, then back off adjuster wheel 12 clicks to prevent brake drag.

VACUUM RELEASE PARKING BRAKE

The parking brake is pedal applied and released by a vacuum chamber. When the engine is started and vacuum is developed, energy is then available to release the parking brake. This is controlled by the transmission shift linkage. When the transmission is in "Neutral", vacuum is cut off from the release chamber and there is no action of the parking brake pedal.

When the transmission is shifted into a drive gear (forward or reverse), the vacuum control valve is opened, actuating the vacuum release chamber mounted on the parking brake assembly.

NOTE: *In the event of engine failure and no vacuum, the brake may be released by a manual release lever mounted on the left side of the parking brake pedal assembly. This assembly prevents the vehicle from being driven with the parking brake in the applied position.*

Testing Vacuum Release

1. If the mechanism is inoperative, first check for damaged or kinked vacuum hoses and for loose hose connections at the vacuum chamber, vacuum release valve at neutral safety switch, and at engine manifold connection.
2. Check adjustment of neutral safety switch and operation of vacuum release valve.
3. Check vacuum chamber piston travel by running engine and shifting transmission selector from drive to neutral. The manual release lever should move up and down as vacuum is applied and released. If no movement is observed or if movement is slow (more than 1 or 2 seconds to complete full stroke), the vacuum chamber is leaking and should be replaced.
4. Check brake release with vacuum applied. If vacuum chamber piston completes full stroke but does not release brake, a malfunction of the pedal assembly is indicated.

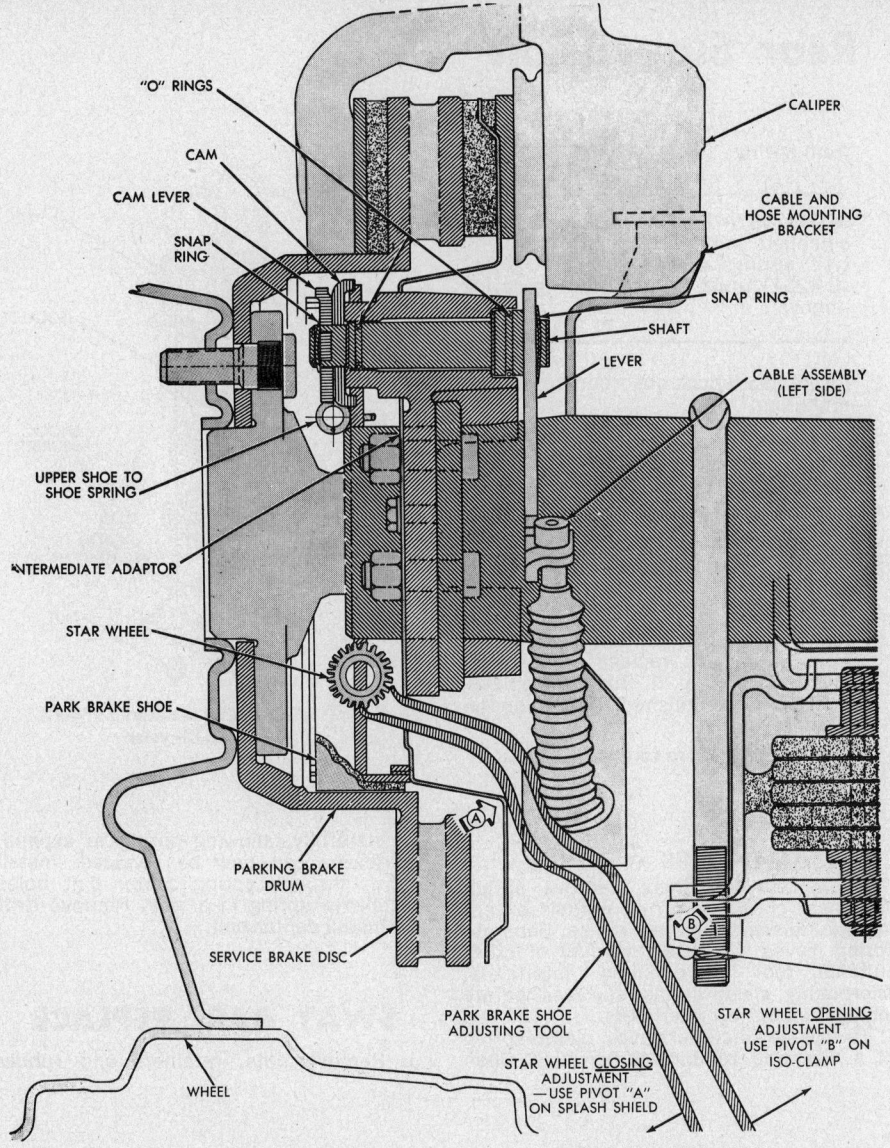

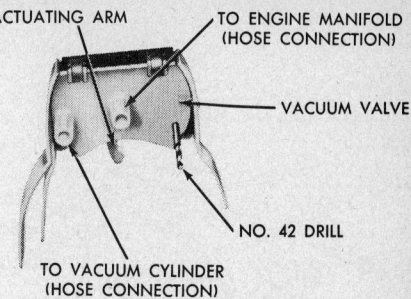

Fig. 22 Parking brake vacuum release valve. 1974-78 (typical)

Fig. 21 Rear wheel disc brake drum type parking brake shoe adjustment. 1974-75 Imperial

5. Check operation of parking brake with engine off. Parking brake should remain engaged regardless of transmission selector position.

Parking Brake Vacuum Valve, Replace

1. With engine off, place shift lever in drive, remove vacuum hoses and retaining screws and remove valve from steering column.
2. To install, move actuating arm on valve against spring to extreme position or until locating holes line up and install a #42 drill in hole, Fig. 22.
3. Place shift lever in park and install valve but do not tighten screws. Rotate valve clockwise until actuating arm contacts tab in steering column then tighten screws.
4. Remove drill and install vacuum hoses

making sure that hose from engine manifold is attached to center fitting on valve, Fig. 22.
5. Start engine and check that parking brake can be set in neutral and park and will release in reverse and drive positions.

BRAKE MASTER CYLINDER, REPLACE
Exc. 1978-79 With Aluminum Master Cylinder & Manual Brakes

1. Disconnect front and rear brake tubes from master cylinder (residual pressure valves will keep cylinder from draining).

NOTE: On 1975-79 models, residual valves are not used, therefore plugs should be installed in master cylinder

outlets after disconnecting tubes.
2. Remove nuts that attach master cylinder to cowl panel or power brake unit.
3. Disconnect pedal push rod (manual brakes) from brake pedal.
4. Slide master cylinder straight out from cowl panel and/or power brake unit.
5. Reverse procedure to install.

1978-79 With Aluminum Master Cylinder & Manual Brakes

1. Disconnect brake lines from master cylinder. Install plugs in outlets to prevent fluid leakage.
2. From under instrument panel, disconnect stop lamp switch mounting bracket and position aside.
3. Grasp brake pedal and pull backward to disengage push rod from master cylinder piston.

NOTE: This will require a pull of about 50 pounds. Also, the retention grommet will be destroyed.

4. Remove master cylinder to cowl retaining nuts and remove master cylinder by pulling straight out.

CAUTION: Make sure to remove all traces of old grommet from push rod groove and master cylinder piston.

5. Reverse procedure to install. Install new grommet on push rod, then lubricate grommet with water and align push rod with master cylinder piston. Using brake pedal, apply pressure to fully seat push rod into piston.

POWER BRAKE, REPLACE
1974-79

1. Remove master cylinder retaining nuts, then carefully slide out master cylinder from power brake and allow it to rest on fender shield.
2. Disconnect vacuum hose from power brake.
3. From under instrument panel, disconnect push rod from brake pedal. On linkage type power brake unit, also remove lower pivot retaining bolt.
4. Remove power brake retaining nuts and remove power brake unit.
5. Reverse procedure to install.

Rear Suspension

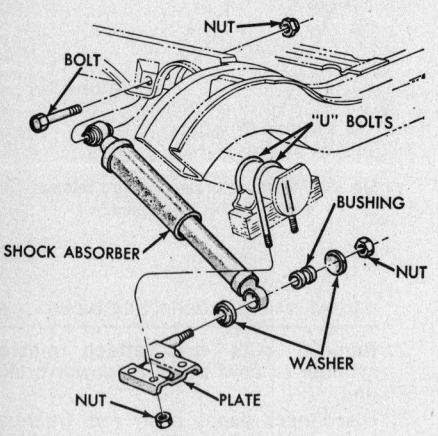

Fig. 1   Spring plate (typical)

SHOCK ABSORBER, REPLACE

To replace shock absorber, support rear axle properly and disconnect shock absorber at upper and lower mountings. On 1974 Barracuda and Challenger, the upper nut is accessible from trunk.

LEAF SPRINGS & BUSHINGS, REPLACE

1. Support rear axle, relieving tension

from spring.

NOTE: 1974-78 Full Size Models are equipped with preloaded "tension" type springs and a spring stretcher (C-4211) must be used during spring removal.

2. Disconnect shock absorber from lower mounting.
3. Remove "U" bolts and spring plate, Fig. 1, or lower spring seat isolator retainer and isolator, Figs. 2 and 3.
4. Remove spring front hanger to body mount bracket nuts, Fig. 4.
5. Remove rear shackle bolts, lower spring, thus pulling spring front hanger bolts out of holes.
6. Remove front hanger and rear shackle from spring. To replace pivot bushings, refer to Fig. 5. Bushing replacement is accomplished in one operation.
7. Reverse procedure to install.

Leaf Spring Service

To replace interliners, remove spring alignment clips and on all models except Imperial, discard alignment clips. Separate spring leaves with a screwdriver or other suitable tool and remove interliners. Thoroughly clean spring surfaces before installation of new interliners.

To replace zinc interleaves, clamp spring in a vise and remove center bolt. Open vise carefully, allowing spring to expand. Interleaves can now be serviced. Install a drift through spring center bolt holes and clamp spring in a vise. Remove drift and install center bolt.

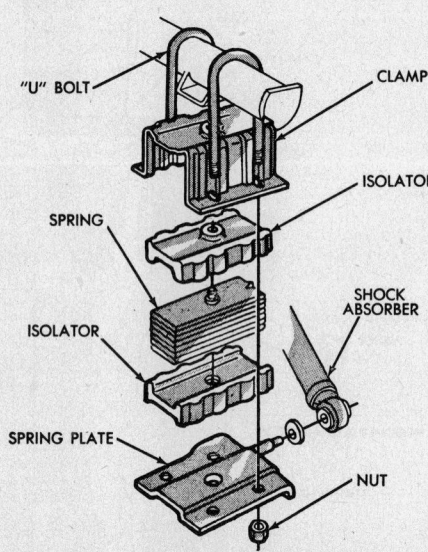

Fig. 2   Rear spring isolator. 1974-77 All & 1978 Chrysler

SWAY BAR, REPLACE

1. Remove nuts, retainers and rubber

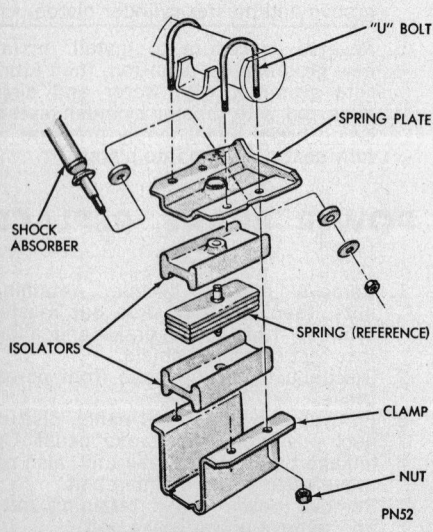

Fig. 3   Rear spring isolator. 1978 except Chrysler & 1979 All

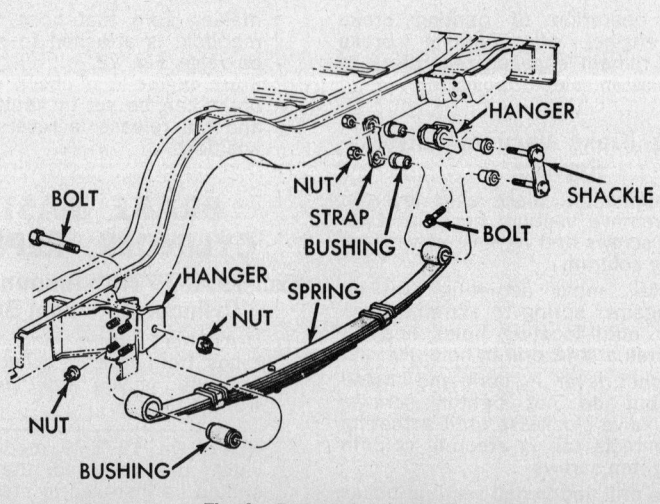

Fig. 4   Rear spring (typical)

insulators from sway bar upper links, Figs. 6 and 7.

2. Disconnect sway bar brackets from frame.

3. Remove link from support assembly and replace insulators.
Reverse procedure to install.

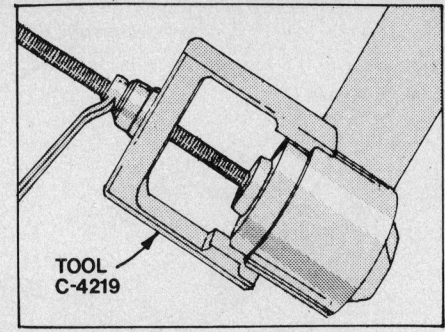

Fig. 5   Spring pivot bushing replacement

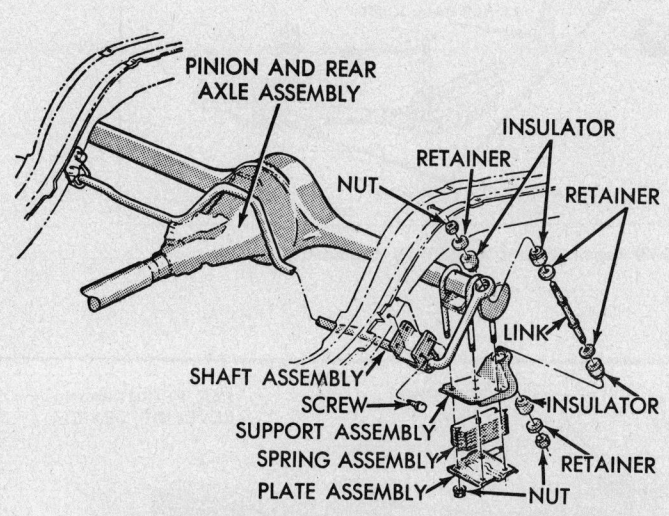

Fig. 6   Sway bar installation (typical). 1974 Barracuda, Challenger & 1979 Aspen, Diplomat, LeBaron & Volare

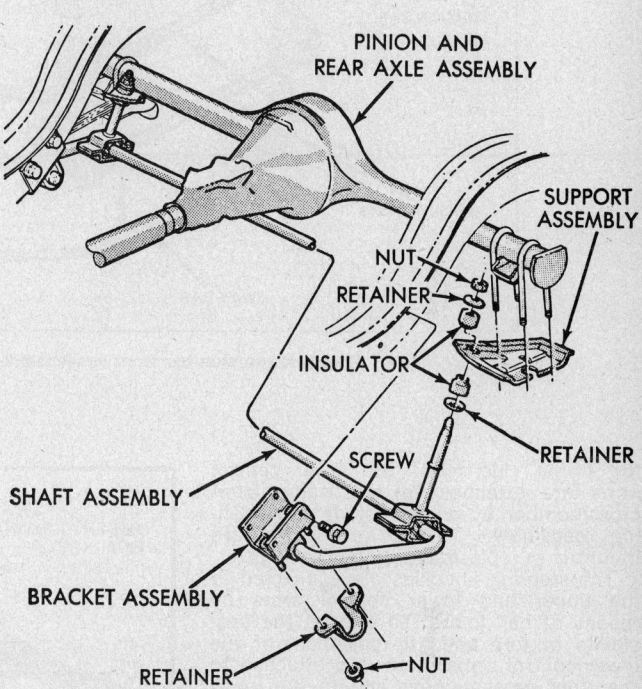

Fig. 7   Sway bar installation (typical). Except 1974 Barracuda, Challenger & 1979 Aspen, Diplomat, LeBaron & Volare

Front End and Steering Section

FRONT SUSPENSION

1976-79 Aspen, Volaré & 1977-79 Diplomat & LeBaron

This front suspension, Fig. 1, incorporates two transverse torsion bars which react on the outboard end of the lower control arms. The torsion bars are anchored in the front crossmember opposite the affected wheel. The torsion bars are mounted parallel to the front crossmember through a "Pivot Cushion Bushing", attached to the crossmember, and turns and extends rearward to the lower control arm. The torsion bar ends are provided with an isolated bushing, bolted to the lower control arm and sway bar, which acts as the lower control arm strut.

Riding height is controlled by the torsion bar adjusting bolts on the anchor end of the torsion bar. The right torsion bar is adjusted from the left side and the left torsion bar is adjusted from the right side.

The torsion bar assembly incorporates the "Pivot Cushion Bushing" and "Bushing to Lower Control Arm". The lower control arm inner ends are bolted to the crossmember and pivots through bushings.

Caster and camber settings are made by loosening the upper control arm pivot bar bolt nuts and adjusting as necessary.

All Exc. 1976-79 Aspen, Volaré & 1977-79 Diplomat & LeBaron

This suspension, Fig. 2, consists of two torsion bar springs (right and left), two sets of upper and lower control arms, four ball joints and two struts.

The front ends of the torsion bar springs engage the lower control arms at the inner pivot points. The rear end of the torsion bars engage adjustable anchor and cam assemblies that are supported by brackets welded to the frame side rails and a removable crossmember.

The upper control arms are mounted on removable brackets that are bolted to

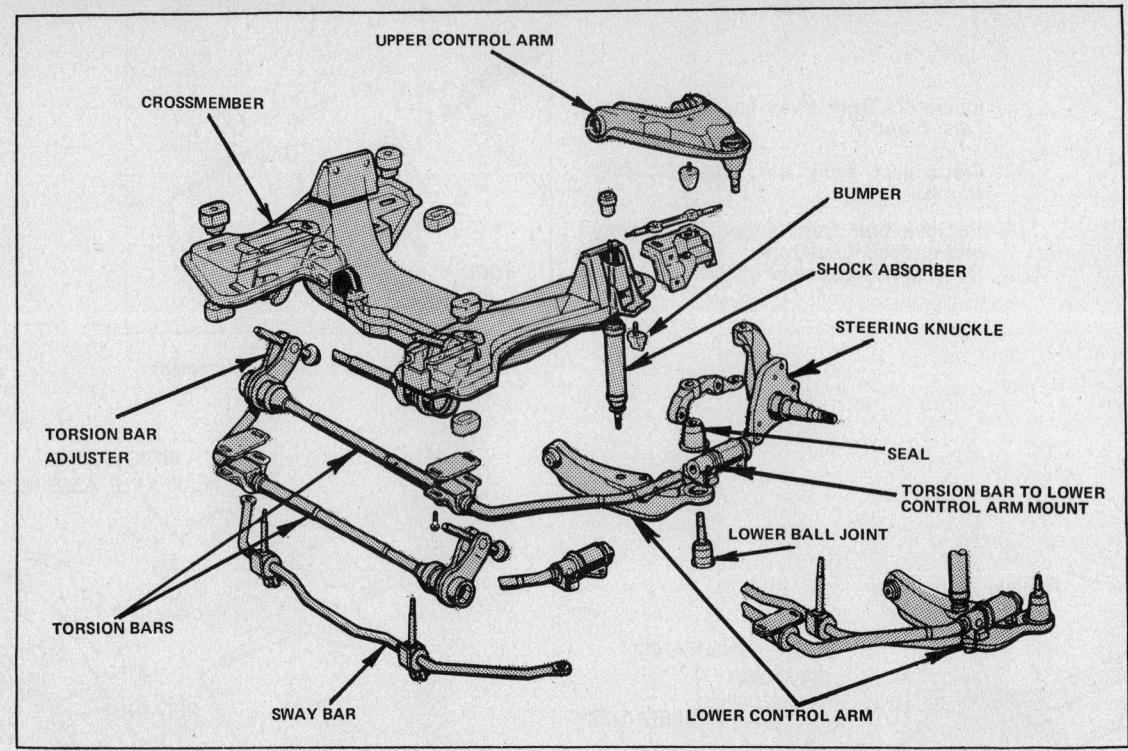

Fig. 1   Transverse torsion bar front suspension. 1976-79 Aspen, Volare, & 1977-79 Diplomat & LeBaron

the frame side rails. The lower control arms are attached to the frame front crossmember by a pivot shaft and bushing assembly. The pivot shafts are mounted in replaceable rubber bushings.

The steering knuckles are connected to the upper and lower control arms by means of ball joints. To prevent the possibility of fore and aft movement of the lower control arms, a strut is attached to the front crossmember and to the lower control arm.

1974 Fury; 1974-75 Imperial, 1974-76 Monaco 1974-78 Chrysler Exc. Cordoba; 1975-77 Gran Fury; 1977 Royal Monaco

This suspension has new lower control arms with pressed in ball joints and more serviceable struts. Caster and camber settings are made by loosening the upper control arm pivot bar bolt nuts and adjusting as necessary.

1974 Satellite; 1974-76 Coronet; 1974-79 Charger; 1975-78 Fury; 1975-79 Cordoba; 1977-78 Monaco; 1978-79 Magnum; 1979 Newport, New Yorker & St. Regis

This suspension has a rubber mounted crossmember, a torsion bar crossmember, more serviceable struts and a lower control arm with pressed in ball joints. Caster and camber settings are made by loosening the upper control arm pivot bar bolt nuts and adjusting as necessary.

LUBRICATION

All ball joints and torsion bars are effectively sealed against road splash by

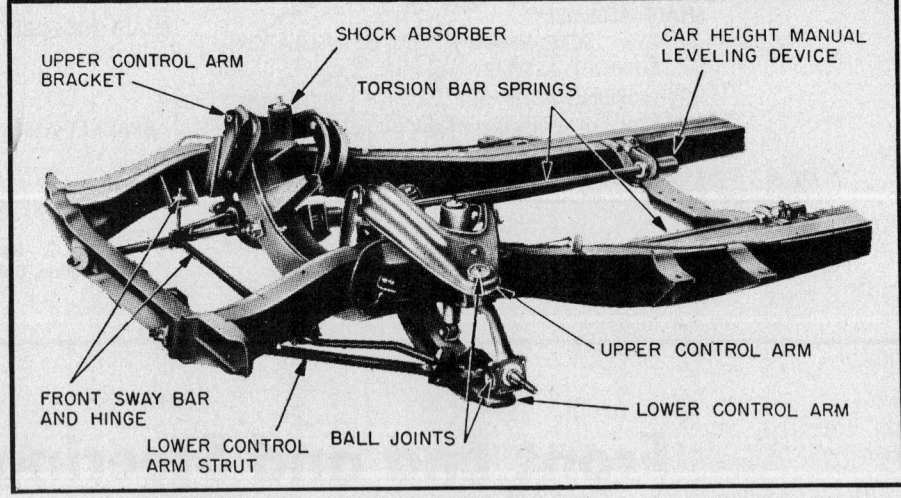

Fig. 2   Longitudinal torsion bar front suspension (typical). Exc. 1976-79 Aspen, Volare & 1977-79 Diplomat & LeBaron

tightly fitted balloon type flexible type seals. The ball joints are semi-permanently lubricated with special lubricant, and should not under normal conditions require lubrication before 30,000 miles.

All ball joints, tie rod end seals and protectors should be inspected at all oil change periods. Damaged seals must be replaced to prevent lubricant leakage or contamination and subsequent component failure.

WARNING

Do not use pressure type lubrication equipment as the pressure may damage the balloon type seals. Use a hand type lubrication gun filled only with the special lubricant specified for the job. Fill each unit slowly to avoid rupturing the seal.

Every 30,000 miles remove the plug from the ball joint and install a grease

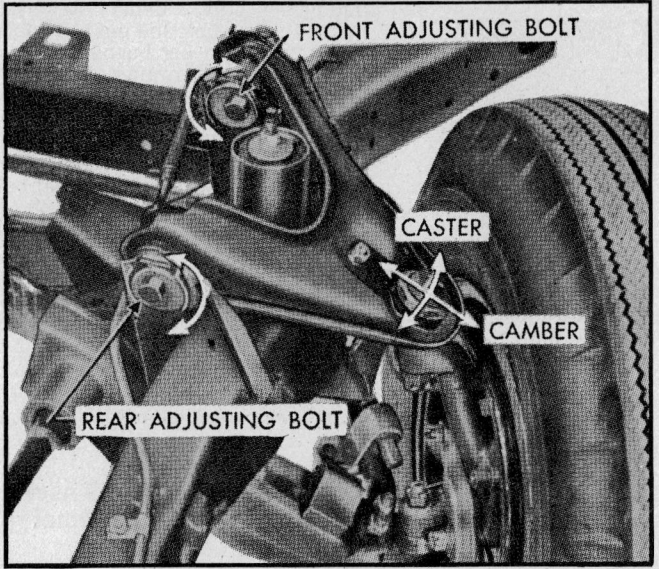

Fig. 3 Camber and caster adjusting bolts. 1974 Barracuda & Challenger & 1974-76 Dart & Valiant

Fig. 4 Checking lower ball joint for wear

fitting. Using a hand gun, pump the grease into the unit until the seal balloons—indicating fullness. Remove the grease fitting and reinstall the plug.

WHEEL ALIGNMENT

NOTE: Front suspension height must be checked and corrected as necessary before performing wheel alignment.

1. Remove all foreign material from exposed threads of cam adjusting bolt nuts or pivot bar adjusting bolt nuts.
2. Record initial camber and caster readings before loosening cam bolt nuts or pivot bar bolt nuts.
3. On vehicles using cam bolts, the camber and caster is adjusted by loosening the cam bolt nuts and turning the cam bolts as necessary until the desired setting is obtained Fig. 3. On vehicles using pivot bars, tool C-4576 is required to adjust caster and camber. When performing adjustments, the camber settings should be held as close as possible to the "desired" setting, and the caster setting should be held as nearly equal as possible on both wheels.

TOE-IN, ADJUST

1974-79

With the front wheels in straight ahead position, loosen the clamps at each end of both adjusting tubes. Adjust toe-in by turning the tie rod sleeve which will "center" the steering wheel spokes. If the steering wheel was centered, make the toe-in adjustment by turning both sleeves an equal amount. Position the clamps so they are on the bottom and tighten bolts to 15 ft. lbs.

WHEEL BEARINGS, ADJUST

1. Tighten adjusting nut to 20-25 ft. lbs. while rotating wheel.
2. Back off nut to completely release bearing preload, then finger tighten adjusting nut and install cotter pin.
3. The resulting adjustment should be .0001-.003 end play.

WHEEL BEARINGS, REPLACE

(Disc Brakes)

1. Raise car and remove front wheels.
2. Remove grease cap, cotter pin, lock nut and bearing adjusting nut.
3. Remove bolts that attach caliper to steering knuckle.
4. Slowly slide caliper up and away from disc and support caliper on steering knuckle arm.

NOTE: Do not allow caliper to hang by brake hose.

5. Remove thrust washer and outer bearing cone. Remove hub and disc

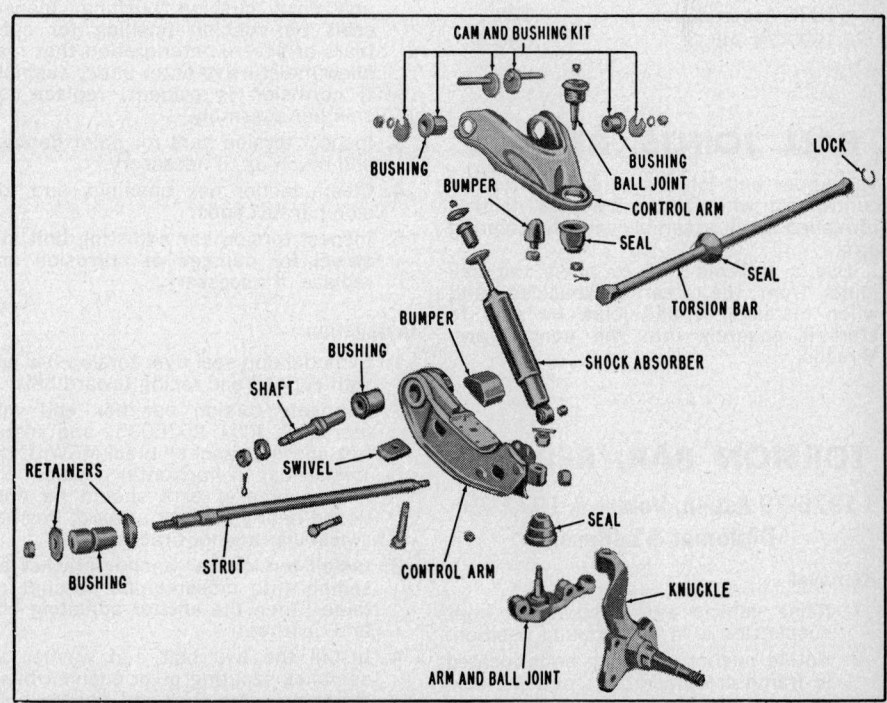

Fig. 5 Front suspension. 1974 Barracuda, Challenger & 1974-76 Dart & Valiant

assembly. Grease retainer and inner bearing can now be removed.

CHECKING BALL JOINTS FOR WEAR

NOTE: If loose ball joints are suspected, first make sure the front wheel bearings are properly adjusted and that the control arms are tight.

1. Raise front of vehicle and place jack stands underneath each lower control arm as far out as possible.

   NOTE: The upper control arms must not contact the rubber rebound bumpers.

2. With weight of vehicle on lower control arms, attach dial indicator onto lower control arm, Fig. 4.

3. Place dial indicator plunger tip against ball joint housing and zero dial indicator.

4. Using a pry bar under the center of the tire, raise and lower the tire and measure the axial travel of the ball joint housing with respect to the ball joint. If the axial travel is as specified or more than specified, the ball joint should be replaced. Refer to chart below.

   1974 Barracuda &
   1973-74 Barracuda &
     Challenger .... .070
   1974-76 Dart & Valiant ... .070
   1974 Satellite .... .020
   1974-75 Imperial .... .020
   1974-76 Charger & Coronet .020
   1974-76 Full Size .... .020
   1975-76 Cordoba & Fury .. .020
   1976 Aspen & Volaré ..... .020
   1977-79 All .... .030

BALL JOINTS, REPLACE

The upper ball joint is threaded into the control arm whereas the lower ball joint is furnished as an assembly with the steering arm.

Use a suitable tool to press the ball joints from the steering knuckles, and when installing a ball joint, be sure to start it squarely into the control arm threads.

TORSION BAR, REPLACE

1976-79 Aspen, Volaré & 1977-79 Diplomat & LeBaron

Removal

1. Raise vehicle and support so front suspension is in full rebound position.

2. Rotate anchor adjusting bolts located in frame crossmember, counter-clockwise to release load on both torsion bars. Then, remove anchor adjusting bolt from torsion bar to be removed.

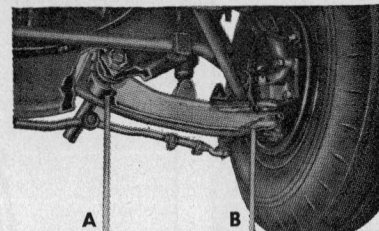

Fig. 6 Measuring front suspension height (typical)

3. Raise lower control arms until 2⅞ inch clearance is obtained between crossmember ledge at jounce bumper and the torsion bar end bushing and support lower arms at this height.

   NOTE: This procedure will align the sway bar and the lower control arm attaching points for disassembly and component realignment and attachment during assembly.

4. Remove sway bar to control arm attaching bolt and retainers, then the two bolts securing torsion bar end bushing to lower control arm.

5. Remove two bolts securing torsion bar pivot cushion bushing to crossmember, then the torsion bar and anchor assembly from crossmember.

6. Separate anchor from torsion bar.

Inspection

1. Inspect seal for damage and replace, if necessary.

2. Inspect bushing to lower control arm and pivot cushion bushing. Inspect seals on cushion bushing for cuts, tears or severe deterioration that may allow moisture to enter under cushion. If corrosion is evident, replace torsion bar assembly.

3. Inspect torsion bars for paint damage and touch up, if necessary.

4. Clean anchor hex openings and torsion bar hex ends.

5. Inspect torsion bar adjusting bolt and swivel for damage or corrosion and replace, if necessary.

Installation

1. Slide balloon seal over torsion bar end with cupped end facing toward hex.

2. Lubricate torsion bar hex end with lubricant, P/N 2525035, and install hex end into anchor bracket. With the torsion bar in horizontal position, the anchor bracket ears should be positioned nearly straight upward. Position swivel into anchor bracket ears.

3. Install torsion bar anchor bracket assembly into crossmember anchor retainer, then the anchor adjusting bolt and bearing.

4. Install the two bolt and washer assemblies securing pivot cushion bushing to crossmember and tighten bolts finger tight.

5. With lower control arms supported as

outlined in step 3 under "Removal", install the two bolt and nut assemblies securing torsion bar bushing to lower control arm and torque nuts to 50 ft. lbs. on 1976 models and 70 ft. lbs. on 1977-79 models.

6. Ensure anchor bracket is fully seated in crossmember, then torque pivot cushion retainer to crossmember bolts to 75 ft. lbs. on 1976 models and 85 ft. lbs. on 1977-79 models. Place balloon seal over anchor bracket.

7. Install new bolt through sway bar, retainer cushions and sleeve and attach to lower control arm end bushing, then torque bolt to 50 ft. lbs.

8. Rotate anchor adjusting bolt clockwise to load torsion bar.

9. Lower vehicle and adjust riding height.

1974-79 All Exc. 1976-79 Aspen, Volaré & 1977-78 Diplomat & LeBaron

The torsion bars are not interchangeable side for side. The bars are marked either right or left by an "R" or an "L" stamped on one end of the bar. The general procedure for replacing a torsion bar is as follows:

Removal

1. Remove upper control arm rebound bumper.

2. If vehicle is to be raised on a hoist, make sure it is lifted on the body only so suspension is in full rebound position (no load).

3. Release all load from torsion bar by turning anchor adjusting bolt counterclockwise.

4. Slide rear anchor balloon seal off of rear anchor and remove lock ring from anchor.

5. Remove torsion bar, by sliding bar out through rear of rear anchor. Use care not to damage balloon seal when it is removed from torsion bar.

   NOTE: On some models, it may be necessary to remove transmission torque shaft to provide clearance.

Inspection

1. Inspect balloon seal for damage and replace if necessary.

2. Inspect torsion bar for scores or nicks. Dress down all scratches and nicks to remove sharp edges, then paint repaired areas with a rust preventive.

3. Remove all foreign material from hex openings in anchors and from hex ends of torsion bars.

4. Inspect adjusting bolt and swivel and replace if there is any sign of corrosion or other damage. Lubricate for easy operation.

Installation

1. Insert torsion bar through rear anchor.

2. Slide balloon seal over torsion bar with cupped end toward rear of bar.

3. Coat both ends of torsion bar with a long mileage lubricant.

GRILLE IDENTIFICATION

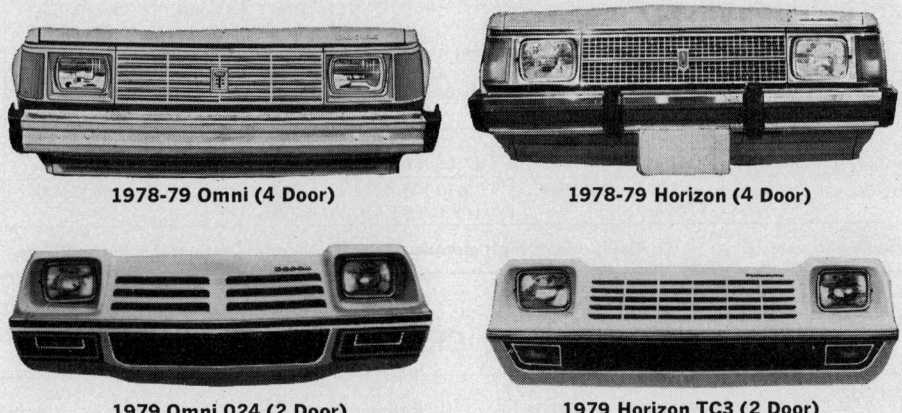

1978-79 Omni (4 Door)   1978-79 Horizon (4 Door)

1979 Omni 024 (2 Door)   1979 Horizon TC3 (2 Door)

TUNE UP SPECIFICATIONS

The following specifications are published from the latest information available. This
data should be used only in the absence of a decal affixed in the engine compartment.

▲Before removing wires from distributor cap, determine location of the No. 1 wire in cap, as distributor position may have been altered from that
shown at the end of this chart.

Year	Spark Plug		Distributor		Ignition Timing			Carb. Adjustments					
	Type	Gap Inch	Point Gap Inch	Dwell Angle Deg.	Firing Order Fig. ▲	Timing BTDC	Mark Fig.	Hot Idle Speed		Air Fuel Ratio		Idle "CO" %	
								Std. Trans.	Auto. Trans.	Std. Trans.	Auto. Trans.	Std. Trans.	Auto. Trans.
1978-79													
4-105 Man. trans.	RN-12Y	34-45	—	—	A	15°	B	900	—	—	—	—	—
4-105 Auto. trans.	RN-12Y	34-45	—	—	A	15°	C	—	900	—	—	—	—

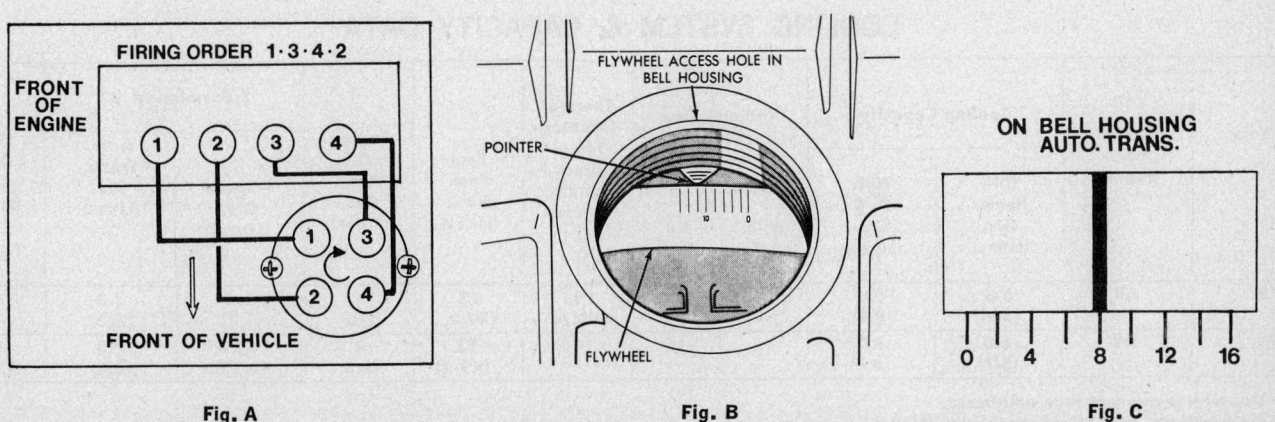

FRONT OF ENGINE   FIRING ORDER 1·3·4·2

1   2   3   4

1   3

2   4

FRONT OF VEHICLE

Fig. A

FLYWHEEL ACCESS HOLE IN BELL HOUSING

POINTER

10   0

FLYWHEEL

Fig. B

ON BELL HOUSING AUTO. TRANS.

0   4   8   12   16

Fig. C

GENERAL ENGINE SPECIFICATIONS

Year	Engine	Carburetor	Bore and Stroke Inch (Millimeters)	Piston Displacement, Cubic Inches	Compression Ratio	Maximum Brake H.P. @ R.P.M.	Maximum Torque Ft. Lbs. (Nm) @ R.P.M.	Normal Oil Pressure Pounds @ 2000 RPM
1978-79	50 Horsepower①② 4-105 1700cc	2 Barrel	3.13×3.40 (79.5×86.4)	105 1.7 ltr.	8.2	50@5600 —	115@3200 85@3200 Nm	70④
	55 Horsepower①③ 4-105 1700cc	2 Barrel	3.13×3.40 (79.5×86.4)	105 1.7 ltr.	8.2	55@5600 —	120@3200 90@3200 Nm	70④

①—Ratings are net—as installed in vehicle.　②—California & high altitude.　③—Except California & high altitude.　④—At 2000 R.P.M.

PISTONS, PINS, RINGS, CRANKSHAFT & BEARINGS

Year	Engine Model	Piston Clearance Top of Skirt Inch (Millimeter)	Ring End Gap① Comp. Inch (Millimeter)	Ring End Gap① Oil Inch (Millimeter)	Wrist-pin Diameter Inch (Millimeter)	Rod Bearings Shaft Diameter Inch (Millimeter)	Rod Bearings Bearing Clearance Inch (Millimeter)	Main Bearings Shaft Diameter Inch (Millimeter)	Main Bearings Bearing Clearance Inch (Millimeter)	Thrust on Bear. No.	Shaft End Play Inch (Millimeter)
1978-79	4-105 1700 cc	.0004–.0015 (.011–.039 mm)	.012 (.3 mm)	.012 (.3 mm)	.866 (21.997–22.001 mm)	1.81 (46 mm)	.0004–.0025 (.010–.064 mm)	2.12 (54 mm)	.0008–.003 (.020–.080 mm)	3	.003–.015 (.075–.38 mm)

①—Minimum.

ENGINE TIGHTENING SPECIFICATIONS★

★Torque specifications are for clean and lightly lubricated threads only. Dry or dirty threads produce increased friction which prevents accurate measurement of tightness.

Year	Engine Model	Spark Plugs Ft. Lbs.	Cylinder Head Bolts Ft. Lbs.	Intake Manifold Inch Lbs.	Exhaust Manifold Inch Lbs.	Camshaft Cover Inch Lbs.	Connecting Rod Cap Bolts Ft. Lbs.	Main Bearing Cap Bolts Ft. Lbs.	Flywheel to Crankshaft Ft. Lbs.	Crankshaft Pulley Ft. Lbs.
1978-79	4-105 (1700 cc)	20	60①	200②	150	48	35	47	52	58

①—Turn torque wrench an additional 90 degrees after the specified torque has been achieved.　②—Intake to exhaust manifold inboard nut, 150 inch lbs. Intake to exhaust manifold outboard nut, 200 inch lbs.

COOLING SYSTEM & CAPACITY DATA

Year	Model or Engine	Cooling Capacity With Heater Qts. (Litres)	Cooling Capacity With A/C Qts. (Litres)	Radiator Cap Relief Pressure, Lbs. With A/C	Radiator Cap Relief Pressure, Lbs. No A/C	Thermo. Opening Temp. Degrees F. (Centigrade)①	Fuel Tank Gals. (Litres)	Engine Oil Refill Qts. (Litres)	Transmission Oil 4 Speed Qts. (Litres)	Transmission Oil Auto. Trans. Qts. (Litres)②	Final Drive Qts. (Litres)
1978	All	6.5 (6.2)	6.5 (6.2)	16	16	195 (90.6)	13 (49.2)	4 (3.8)	1.4 (1.3)	7.3 (6.8)	③
1979	All	6.0 (5.7)	6.0 (5.7)	16	16	195	13 (49.2)	4 (3.8)	1.32 (1.25)	7.3 (6.8)	1.0 (.94)

①—Use with permanent type anti-freeze.　②—Approximate. Make final check with dipstick.　③—Horizon, 1 qt. (.94 Litre); Omni, 1.1 qts. (1.2 Litres).

VALVE SPECIFICATIONS

Year	Model	Valve Lash 95°F		Valve Angles		Valve Spring Installed Height Inch (Millimeters)	Valve Spring Pressure Lbs. @ In. (Kg. @ mm)	Stem Clearance		Stem Diameter	
		Int. in. (MM)	Exh. in. (MM)	Seat	Face			Intake Inch (Millimeters) ①	Exhaust Inch (Millimeters) ①	Intake Inch (Millimeters)	Exhaust Inch (Millimeters)
1978-79	4-105 (1700 cc)	.010 (.25)	.018 (.45)	45°	45° 33'	1.28 (32.6)	38.8 @ 1.28 (17.6 @ 32.6)	.020 (.5)	.027 (.7)	.313–.314 (7.955–7.970)	.312–.313 (7.935–7.950)

①—Refer to text.

ALTERNATOR & REGULATOR SPECIFICATIONS

Year	Alternator				Regulator						
	Part Number	Rated Hot Output Amps.	Field Current 12 Volts @ 80° F.	Output @ 15 Volts 1250 R.P.M.	Part Number	Field Relay			Voltage Regulator		
						Air Gap In.	Point Gap In.	Closing Voltage	Air Gap In.	Point Gap In.	Voltage @ 80° F.
1978-79	Yellow	60	5	57	4091050	—	—	—	—	—	13.9–14.6
	Brown	65	5	62	—	—	—	—	—	—	13.9–14.6

STARTING MOTOR SPECIFICATIONS

Year	Model	Starter Number	Brush Spring Tension Oz.	Free Speed Test		
				Amps.	Volts	R.P.M.
1978-79	Bosch④	5206255	—	47①	11	6600②
	Bosch③	5206260	—	47①	11	6600②
	Nippondenso④	5206265	—	47①	11	6600②
	Nippondenso③	5206270	—	47①	11	6600②

①—Maximum current draw. ②—Minimum speed. ③—Automatic Transmission. ④—Manual Transmission.

BRAKE SPECIFICATIONS

Year	Model	Brake Drum Inside Diameter Inch (Millimeter)	Wheel Cylinder Bore Diameter		Master Cylinder Bore Diameter
			Disc Brake Inch (Millimeter)	Rear Drum Brake Inch (Millimeter)	Inch (Millimeter)
1978-79	All	7⅞ (200)	1.89 (48)	⅝ (15.94)	.877 (22.27)

WHEEL ALIGNMENT SPECIFICATIONS

Year	Model	Camber Angle, Degrees				Toe Front out to in	Inches (Degrees) Rear out to in
		Front Wheel Camber		Rear Wheel Camber			
		Limits	Desired	Limits	Desired		
1978	All	− ¼ to + ¾	+ 5/16	− 1½ to − ½	− 1	5/32 to ⅛ (.3 to .1)	5/32 to 11/32 (.3 to .7)
1979	All	− .2° to + .8	+ .3	—	—	(.3 to .1)	—

Electrical Section

DISTRIBUTOR, REPLACE

Removal

1. Disconnect distributor pickup lead wire at harness connector.
2. Remove distributor cap.
3. Rotate engine until distributor rotor faces toward cylinder block then scribe a mark on the block to indicate rotor position.
4. Remove distributor hold down screw.
5. Remove distributor from engine.

NOTE: Do not crank engine while distributor is removed.

Installation

1. Position distributor in engine.
2. Engage distributor drive gear with camshaft drive gear so the distributor rotor will align with the scribe mark on cylinder block.
3. If the engine was cranked while the distributor was removed, proceed as follows:
   a. Rotate crankshaft until No. 1 piston is at top dead center, compression stroke. The pointer on clutch housing should align with the "0" mark on the flywheel.
   b. Rotate distributor rotor to a position ahead of the No. 1 distributor cap terminal.
   c. Install distributor into engine, engaging distributor drive gear with camshaft drive gear. The rotor should be properly positioned under the distributor cap No. 1 terminal.
4. Install distributor cap.

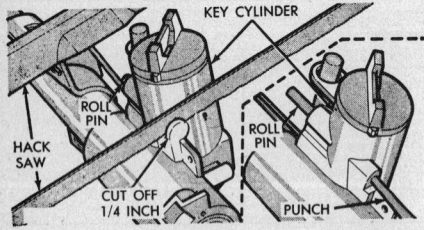

Fig. 1   Key cylinder roll pin removal

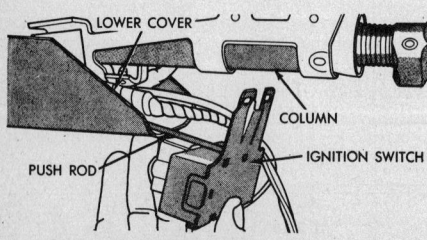

Fig. 2   Ignition switch replacement

5. Install distributor hold down screw finger tight.
6. Connect distributor pickup lead wire.
7. Adjust ignition timing. Refer to the "Tune Up Specifications" found in the front of this chapter.

STARTER, REPLACE

1. Disconnect battery ground cable.
2. Disconnect starter cable at starter.
3. Disconnect solenoid lead wire from solenoid.
4. Remove starter attaching bolts and the starter.
5. Reverse procedure to install.

IGNITION LOCK, REPLACE

1. Remove steering wheel, column covers and turn signal switch.
2. With a hack saw blade, cut the upper 1/4 inch from the retainer pin boss, Fig. 1.
3. Using a suitable drift, drive roll pin from housing and remove lock cylinder, Fig. 1.
4. Insert new cylinder into housing, ensuring that it engages the lug on ignition switch driver.
5. Install roll pin.
6. Check for proper operation.

IGNITION SWITCH, REPLACE

1. Disconnect battery ground cable.
2. Remove connect from ignition switch.
3. Place ignition lock in "Lock" position and remove key.
4. Remove the two ignition switch mounting screws and permit the switch and push rod to drop below the column jacket, Fig. 2.
5. Rotate the switch 90° for removal of switch from push rod.
6. Position ignition switch in "Lock" position, the second detent from the top of the switch.
7. Place switch at right angle to column and insert push rod.
8. Align switch on bracket and loosely install screws.
9. With a light rearward load on the switch, tighten attaching screws.

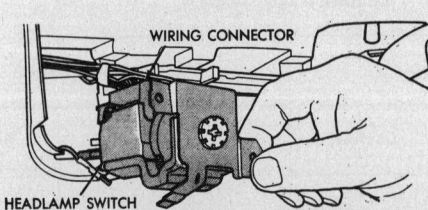

Fig. 3   Light switch replacement

10. Connect ignition switch wiring connector and battery ground cable.
11. Check for proper operation.

LIGHT SWITCH, REPLACE

1. Disconnect battery ground cable.
2. Reach under instrument panel and depress light switch knob release button, then pull light switch knob and shaft from switch.
3. Remove four bezel attaching screws and the bezel.
4. Remove switch attaching screws and disconnect electrical connector from switch, Fig. 3.
5. Remove switch from panel.
6. Reverse procedure to install.

TURN SIGNAL SWITCH, REPLACE

Removal

1. Disconnect battery ground cable.
2. Remove horn button, three screws and the horn switch.
3. Remove steering wheel nut and the steering wheel with a suitable puller.
4. Remove four screws from the lower steering column cover and the cover.
5. Remove screw securing washer-wiper switch and position switch aside.
6. Disconnect turn signal and hazard warning wiring connector, disengage wiring harness from support bracket and remove vinyl tape securing key in buzzer wires to turn signal harness.
7. Remove three turn signal switch retainer screws, Fig. 4.
8. Remove turn signal and hazard warning switch while guiding wiring harness out from column.

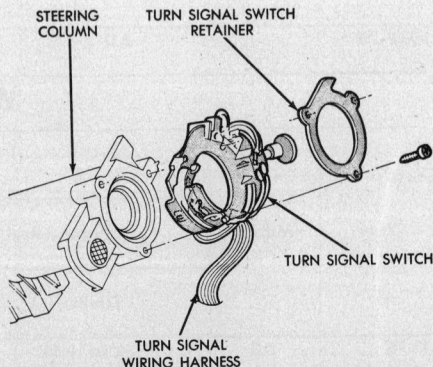

Fig. 4   Turn signal switch replacement

Installation

1. Guide wiring harness downward through column until the switch is properly seated.
2. Install switch retainer and the three screws.
3. Snap plastic harness retainer into support bracket, connect harness connector and tape key in buzzer wires to harness.
4. Install washer-wiper switch and retaining screw.
5. Install lower steering column cover.
6. Install steering wheel, horn switch and horn button.
7. Connect battery ground cable.

INSTRUMENT CLUSTER, REPLACE

1. Disconnect battery ground cable.
2. Remove two mask-lens assembly lower attaching spring pins by pulling rearward with suitable pliers.
3. Pull mask-lens rearward, lower slightly and remove from cluster.
4. Disconnect speedometer cable.
5. Remove two speedometer attaching screws and the speedometer.
6. Disengage two wiring harness connectors.
7. Remove two cluster attaching screws, Fig. 5.
8. Remove cluster upper attaching spring pins and pull cluster from panel.
9. Disconnect clock wiring, if equipped.
10. Remove cluster from vehicle.
11. Reverse procedure to install.

WIPER SWITCH, REPLACE

1. Disconnect battery ground cable.
2. Disconnect wiper switch and turn signal switch wiring harness connectors.
3. Remove lower column cover.
4. Remove horn button.
5. Place ignition lock in "Off" position and turn steering wheel so the access hole in hub area is at 9 o'clock position.
6. With a suitable screwdriver, loosen turn signal lever screw through access hole, Fig. 6.
7. Disengage dimmer push rod from wiper switch.
8. Unsnap wiring clip and remove wiper switch.
9. Reverse procedure to install.

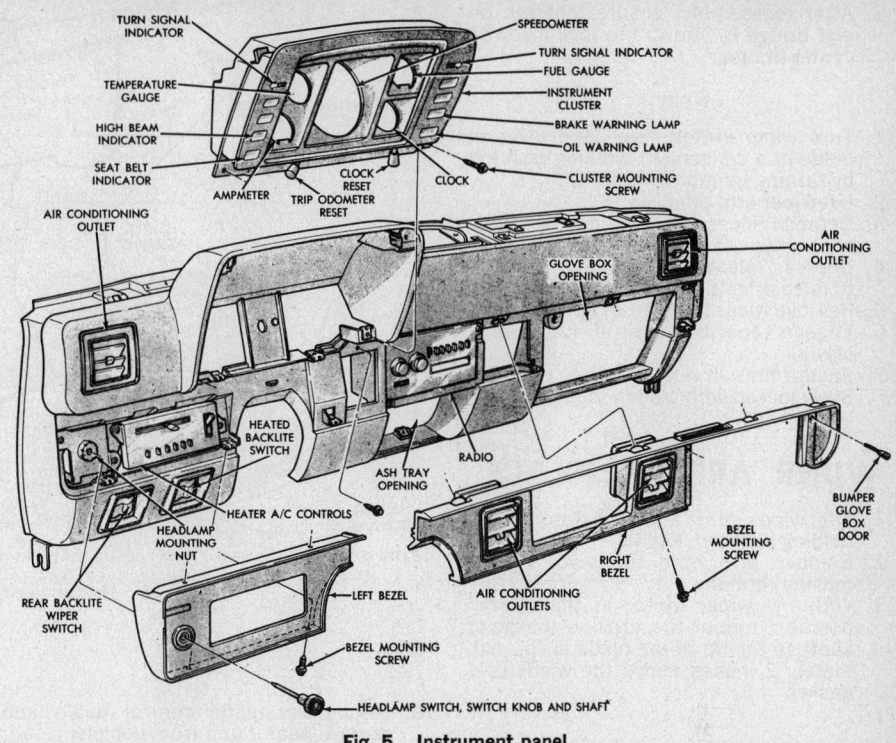

Fig. 5   Instrument panel

WINDSHIELD WIPER MOTOR, REPLACE

Front

1. Remove wiper arm assemblies.
2. Remove the nuts from the left and right pivots.
3. Remove wiper motor plastic cover.
4. Disconnect wiper motor wiring harness.
5. Remove three bolts from wiper motor mounting bracket.
6. Disengage the pivots from cowl top mounting positions.
7. Remove wiper motor, cranks, pivots and drive link assembly from cowl plenum chamber.
8. Remove wiper motor from drive crank linkage.
9. Reverse procedure to install.

Rear

1. Remove wiper motor plastic cover.
2. Remove arm and blade assembly.
3. Remove pivot shaft chromed nut and ring from pivot shaft.
4. Remove two wiper motor mounting screws.
5. Disconnect wiper motor wiring harness from motor pigtail wire.
6. Remove wiper motor from vehicle.
7. Reverse procedure to install.

WIPER BLADES, REPLACE

Front

1. Turn wiper switch "On" and position blades to a convenient working position by turning the ignition switch "Off".
2. Lift wiper arm off glass.
3. Depress release lever on center bridge and remove blade from arm, Fig. 7.
4. Lift tab and pinch end bridge to release from center bridge. Slide end bridge from wiper blade assembly and wiper blade from opposite end bridge.

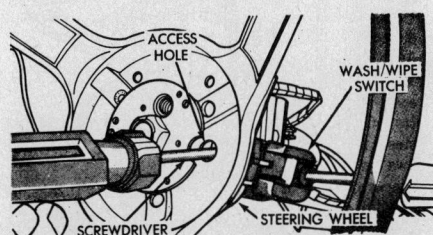

Fig. 6   Loosening turn signal lever screw

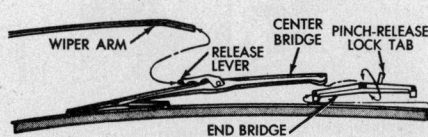

Fig. 7   W/S wiper blade replacement. Front

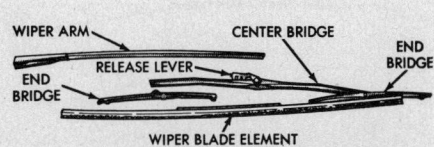

Fig. 8   W/S wiper blade replacement. Rear

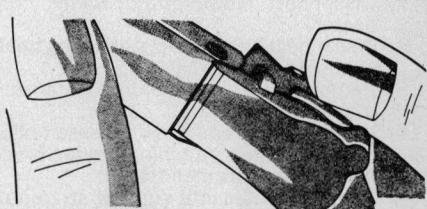

Fig. 9   Wiper arm removal

5. After reassembly, ensure that tab on end bridge is "Down" to lock blade to center bridge.

Rear

1. Turn wiper switch "On" and position blade at a convenient working position by turning ignition switch "Off".
2. Lift wiper arm off glass.
3. Depress release lever on center bridge and remove center bridge, Fig. 8.
4. Depress release button on end bridge to release from center bridge.
5. Remove wiper blade from end bridge.
6. Engage wiper blade on all four bridge claws.
7. Ensure that all release points are positively locked with blade assembly.

WIPER ARMS, REPLACE

1. Lift wiper arm and pull latch from holding position, Fig. 9.
2. Remove arm from the pivot with a rocking motion.
3. With the wiper motor in the "Park" position, mount the arm on the pivot shaft so the tip of the blade is approximately 2 inches above the windshield gasket.

RADIO, REPLACE

1. Disconnect battery ground cable.
2. Remove seven bezel attaching screws and open the glove box.
3. Remove bezel, guiding the right end around glove box.
4. Remove radio mounting screws.
5. Pull radio from panel and disconnect wiring, ground strap and antenna lead from radio.
6. Remove radio from vehicle.
7. Reverse procedure to install.

HEATER CORE, REPLACE

Less A/C

1. Disconnect battery ground cable and drain cooling system.
2. Remove center outside air floor vent housing.
3. Remove ash tray.
4. Remove two screws retaining defroster duct adapter to heater unit.

NOTE: The left hand screw is accessible through the ash tray housing access hole.

5. Remove the adapter and push the flexible connector upward and position aside.
6. Disconnect temperature control cable.
7. Disconnect blower motor wiring connector.
8. Disconnect heater hoses and plug heater core tube openings.
9. Remove two nuts retaining heater unit to dash panel, Fig. 10.
10. Remove glove box and door assembly.
11. Remove screw attaching heater brace bracket to instrument panel.
12. Remove heater unit support strap nut. Disconnect strap from plenum stud and lower heater unit from panel.

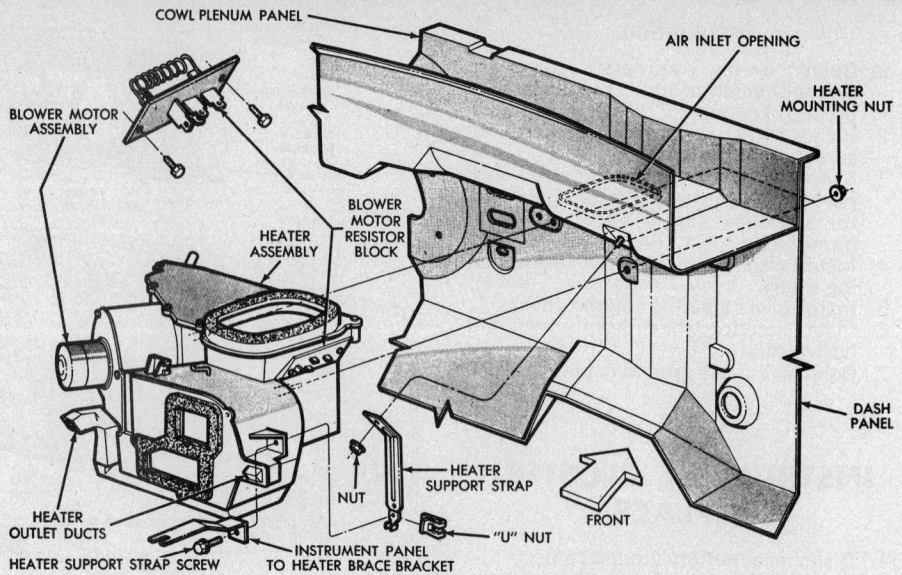

Fig. 10 Heater assembly. Less air conditioning

13. Disconnect mode control cable and remove heater unit from vehicle.
14. Remove left heater outlet duct.
15. Remove four screws from blower motor mounting plate, then the blower motor from heater unit.
16. Remove defroster duct adapter.
17. Remove outside air and defroster door cover.
18. Remove screw from center of defroster door, then the door, screw and screw retaining plate.
19. Remove defroster door control rod from heater unit.
20. Remove heater core cover.
21. Slide heater core from heater unit.
22. Reverse procedure to install.

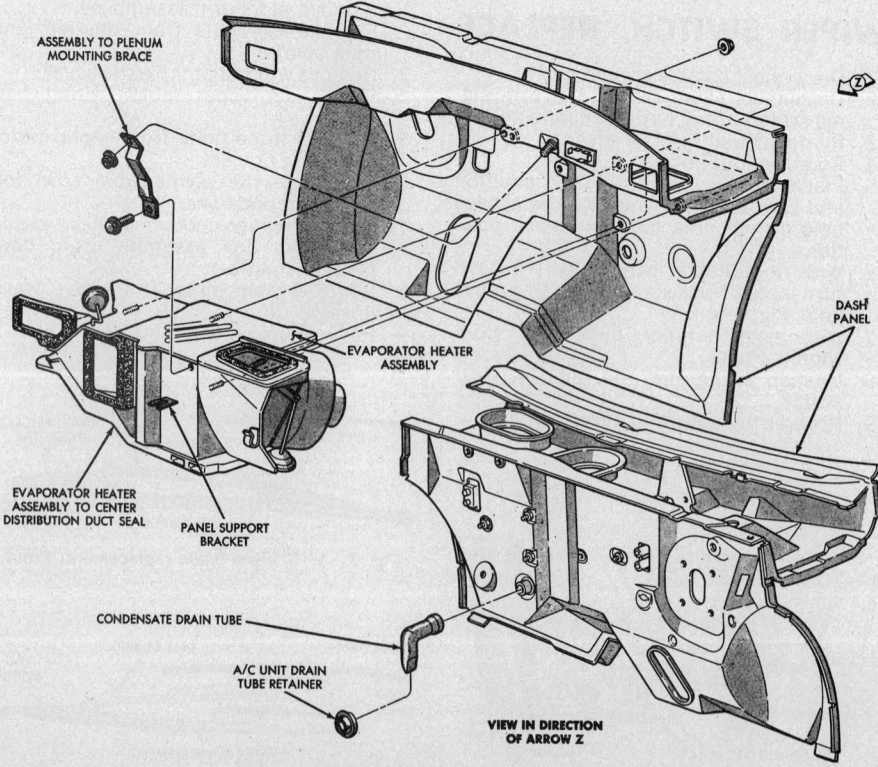

Fig. 11 Heater assembly. With air conditioning

Fig. 12 Blower motor replacement. Less air conditioning

With A/C

1. Disconnect ground cable, drain radiator and discharge refrigerant system.
2. Disconnect temperature door cable from evaporator heater assembly.
3. Remove glove box.
4. Disconnect vacuum harness from control panel and the blower motor feed wire and anti-diesel relay wires.
5. Remove right hand bezel.
6. Remove central air duct cover from central air distribution duct.
7. Remove three screws retaining central air distribution duct, then the duct.
8. Remove defroster duct adapter.
9. Remove "H" valve and disconnect heater hoses. Plug heater core tube openings.
10. Remove condensate drain tube from evaporator heater unit.
11. Disconnect vacuum lines at intake manifold and water valve.
12. Remove evaporator heater unit to dash panel retaining nuts, Fig. 11.
13. Remove panel support bracket.
14. Remove right side cowl lower bracket.
15. Remove instrument panel pivot bracket screw from right side.

16. Remove screws securing lower instrument panel at steering column.
17. Pull back carpet from under evaporator heater assembly as far as possible.
18. Remove nut from A/C to plenum mounting brace and blower motor ground cable.
19. Support unit and remove brace from stud.
20. Lift evaporator heater unit and pull rearward to clear dash panel and liner. Also, the lower instrument panel will have to be pulled rearward to provide adequate clearance for unit removal. Slowly lower the evaporator heater unit, slide rearward and remove from vehicle.
21. Remove 1/4-20 nut from mode door actuator arm on top cover and two retaining clips from front edge of cover.
22. Remove mode door actuator attaching screws and the actuator.
23. Remove fifteen screws securing cover to evaporator heater assembly and the cover.
24. Remove mode door from unit.
25. Remove screw from heater core tube retaining bracket, then the heater core from evaporator heater assembly.
26. Reverse procedure to install.

BLOWER MOTOR, REPLACE

Less A/C

1. Disconnect battery ground cable.
2. Disconnect blower motor wiring connector.
3. Remove left heater outlet duct.
4. Remove four screws retaining blower

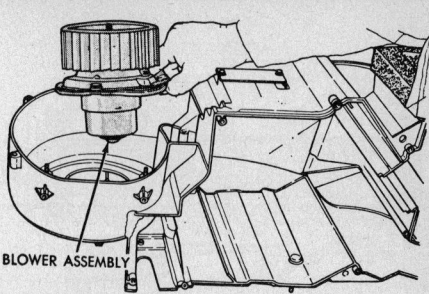

Fig. 13 Blower motor replacement. With air conditioning

motor mounting plate to heater unit.
5. Remove blower motor assembly, Fig. 12.
6. Reverse procedure to install.

With A/C

1. Disconnect battery ground cable.
2. Remove three screws securing glove box to instrument panel and the glove box.
3. Disconnect blower motor feed and ground wires. Remove wires from retaining clip on recirculating housing.
4. Disconnect blower motor vent tube from A/C unit.
5. Loosen recirculation door actuator from bracket and remove actuator from housing. Do not disconnect vacuum lines.
6. Remove seven screws securing recirculating housing to A/C unit, then the housing.
7. Remove three blower motor mounting flange nuts and the blower motor, Fig. 13.
8. Reverse procedure to install.

Engine Section

ENGINE MOUNTS

Refer to Figs. 1 and 2 when replacing the engine mounts.

ENGINE, REPLACE

1. Disconnect battery ground cable and drain cooling system.
2. Scribe hood hinge locations and remove hood.
3. Remove radiator hoses and transmission oil cooler lines, if equipped, then the radiator and shroud assembly.
4. Remove air cleaner.
5. Remove A/C compressor mounting bolts and position compressor aside, if equipped.
6. Disconnect all wiring, hoses, lines and cables from engine.
7. Remove air diverter valve and lines from air pump.
8. Remove alternator belt and alternator.
9. Disconnect clutch and speedometer cables.
10. Raise and support vehicle.

Fig. 1 Engine mount. Right side

TIGHTENING TORQUE	
Ⓐ	54.2 N.M (40 FT. LB.)
Ⓑ	28.2 N.M (250 IN. LB.)
Ⓒ	95.0 N.M (70 FT. LB.)
Ⓓ	14.7 N.M (130 IN. LB.)

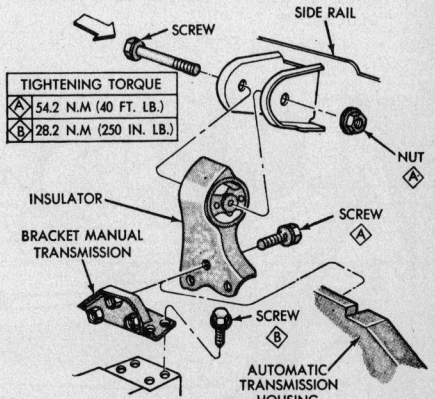

TIGHTENING TORQUE	
Ⓐ	54.2 N.M (40 FT. LB.)
Ⓑ	28.2 N.M (250 IN. LB.)

Fig. 2 Engine mount. Left side

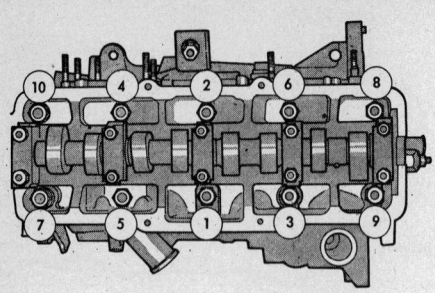

Fig. 3 Cylinder head tightening sequence

11. Disconnect drive shafts from transmission and secure aside with wire.
12. Disconnect exhaust pipe from manifold.
13. Remove air pump hoses and lines, then the air pump belt and the air pump.
14. Disconnect transmission linkage.
15. Lower vehicle.
16. Attach suitable engine lifting equipment to engine.
17. Raise engine slightly and remove front engine mount bolt.
18. Remove right and left engine mount bolts.
19. Remove engine and transmission assembly from vehicle.
20. Reverse procedure to install.

CYLINDER HEAD, REPLACE

1. Drain cooling system and perform Steps 1 through 18 as outlined under "Timing Belt, Replace" procedure.
2. Remove intake and exhaust manifolds from cylinder head.
3. Disconnect all wiring, hoses and cables attached to cylinder head.
4. Remove cam cover bolts and the cam cover.
5. Loosen cylinder head attaching bolts in reverse sequence found in Fig. 3.
6. Remove cylinder head from engine, Fig. 4.
7. Reverse procedure to install. Insert bolts No. 8 and 10 first, to center the cylinder head on engine block. Torque bolts to specifications in sequence, Fig. 3. To properly tension the timing belt, perform Steps 19 through 23 as outlined under "Timing Belt, Replace" procedure.

CAMSHAFT BEARING CAPS

5 N•m (48 IN. LB.)

COVER GASKET REPLACE IF DAMAGED

ALWAYS REPLACE

19 N•m (168 IN. LB.)

CAMSHAFT

VALVE ADJUSTING DISC

CAM FOLLOWER BEFORE INSTALLING CHECK FOR WEAR AND CHECK CAMSHAFT END PLAY

VALVE SPRINGS

VALVE SPRING SEAT, LOWER

VALVE STEM SEAL

VALVE GUIDE

CYLINDER HEAD BOLT

OIL SEAL

CYLINDER HEAD

CYLINDER HEAD GASKET

VALVES

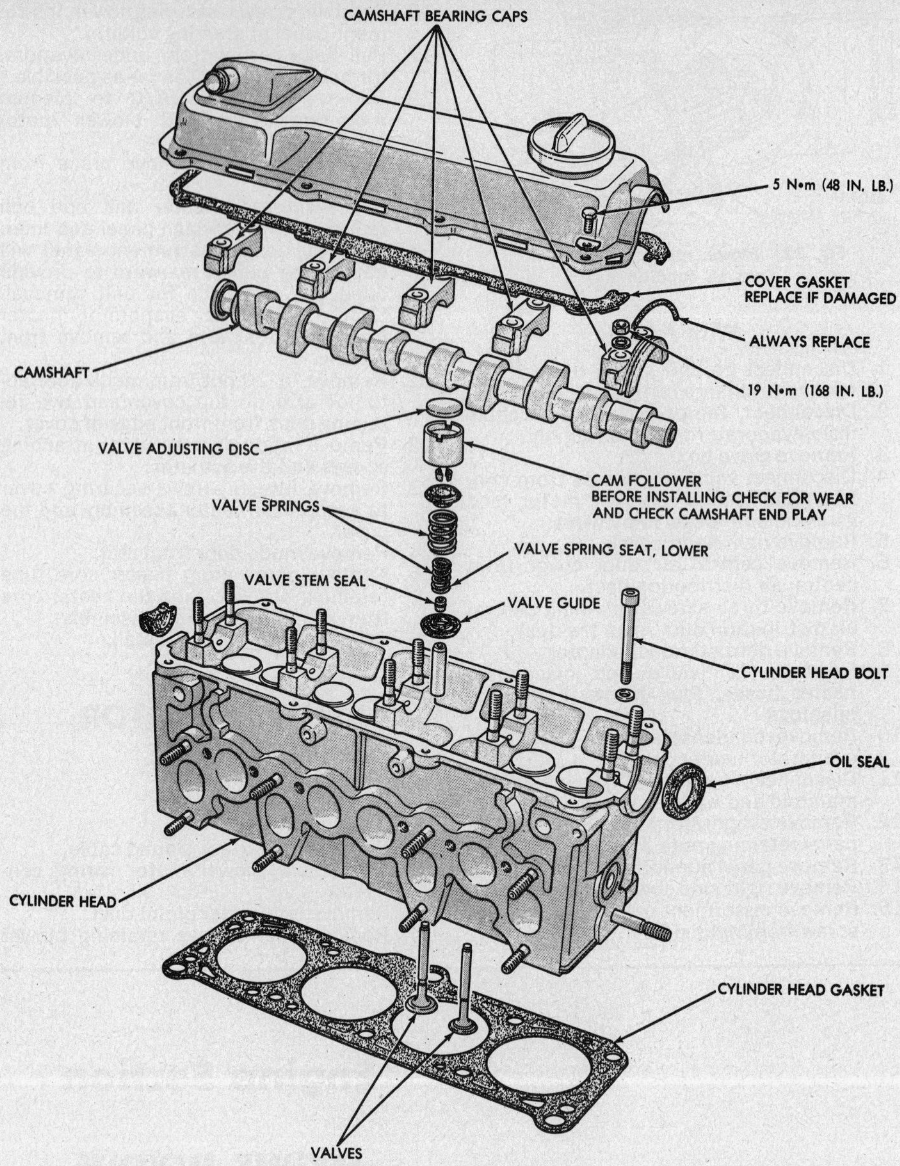

Fig. 4 Cylinder head assembly

VALVE ARRANGEMENT

Front to Rear

4-105 . . . . E-I-E-I-I-E-I-E

VALVE LIFT SPECS.

Engine	Year	Intake	Exhaust
4-105	1978-79	.406	.406

VALVE TIMING

Engine	Year	Degrees
4-105	1978	23
	1979	14

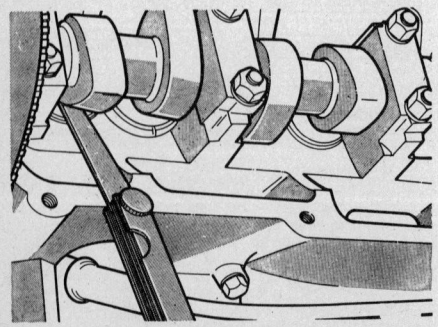

Fig. 5 Checking valve clearance

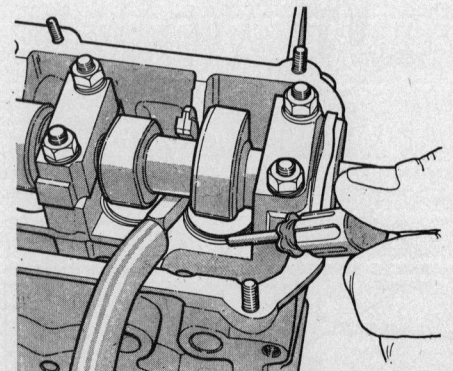

Fig. 6 Valve adjusting disc replacement

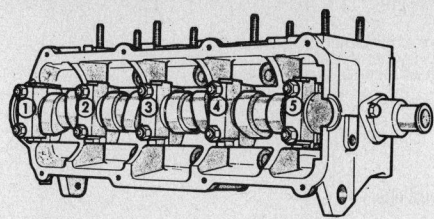

Fig. 7 Camshaft bearing cap identification

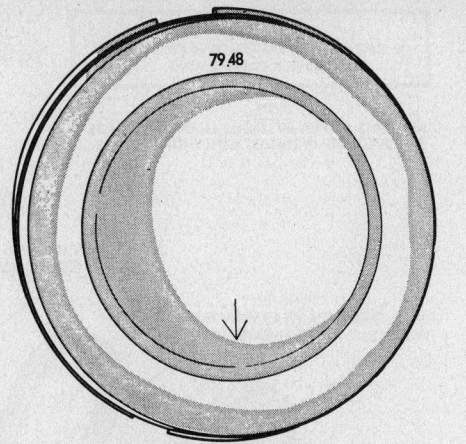

Fig. 8 Piston markings

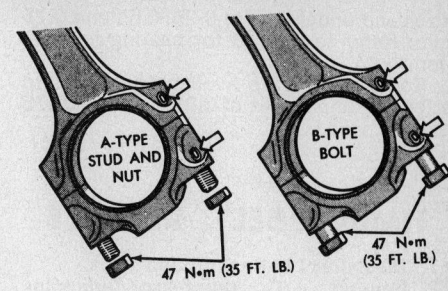

Fig. 9 Connecting rod assemblies

VALVES, ADJUST

1. Using a feeler gauge, check valve clearance, Fig. 5. The cylinder head should be moderately warm, coolant temperature 95° F. Check clearances on all valves following the firing order, 1-3-4-2.
2. If valve clearance is greater than specified, remove valve adjusting disc and insert a thicker disc to obtain proper clearance.
3. If valve clearance is less than specified, remove valve adjusting disc and insert a thinner disc to obtain proper clearance.
4. To replace valve adjusting disc, depress cam follower with tool L-4417 or equivalent and remove with a narrow screwdriver, Fig. 6, and a magnet. Install new disc and recheck clearance.
5. Valve adjusting discs are available in thicknesses of 3.00 mm to 4.25 mm in increments of .05 mm.

VALVE GUIDES

The valve guides may be removed by pressing out from the combustion chamber side. Coat the new valve guide with oil and press into cold cylinder head until the shoulder is seated. The replacement valve guides have a shoulder. Do not exert a pressure greater than one ton after the valve guide shoulder is seated since the shoulder may break. Ream valve guide to .315-.316 inch.

CAMSHAFT, REPLACE

1. Remove timing belt as outlined under "Timing Belt, Replace".
2. Remove camshaft sprocket.
3. Remove bearing caps 5, 1 and 3, Fig. 7.
4. Diagonally loosen and remove bearing caps 2 and 4, Fig. 7.
5. Remove camshaft from cylinder head.
6. Lubricate bearing shells, journals and contact faces of bearing caps.
7. Install caps in proper order, observing off center bearing position.
8. Reverse Steps 1 through 5 to complete installation.

PISTON & ROD ASSEMBLY

When installing the piston and connecting rod assembly the arrow on top of the piston must face toward the front of engine, Fig. 8, and the forged mark on the connecting rod must face toward the intermediate shaft, Fig. 9.

NOTE: There are two types of connecting rod assemblies. One uses a stud and nut to retain the bearing cap and the other uses a bolt to retain the bearing cap, Fig. 9.

PISTONS, RINGS & PINS

Pistons are available in standard sizes and oversizes of 0.25, 0.50 and 1.0 mm.
Rings are available in standard sizes and oversizes of 0.25, 0.50 and 1.0 mm.

MAIN & ROD BEARINGS

Main bearings are available in standard

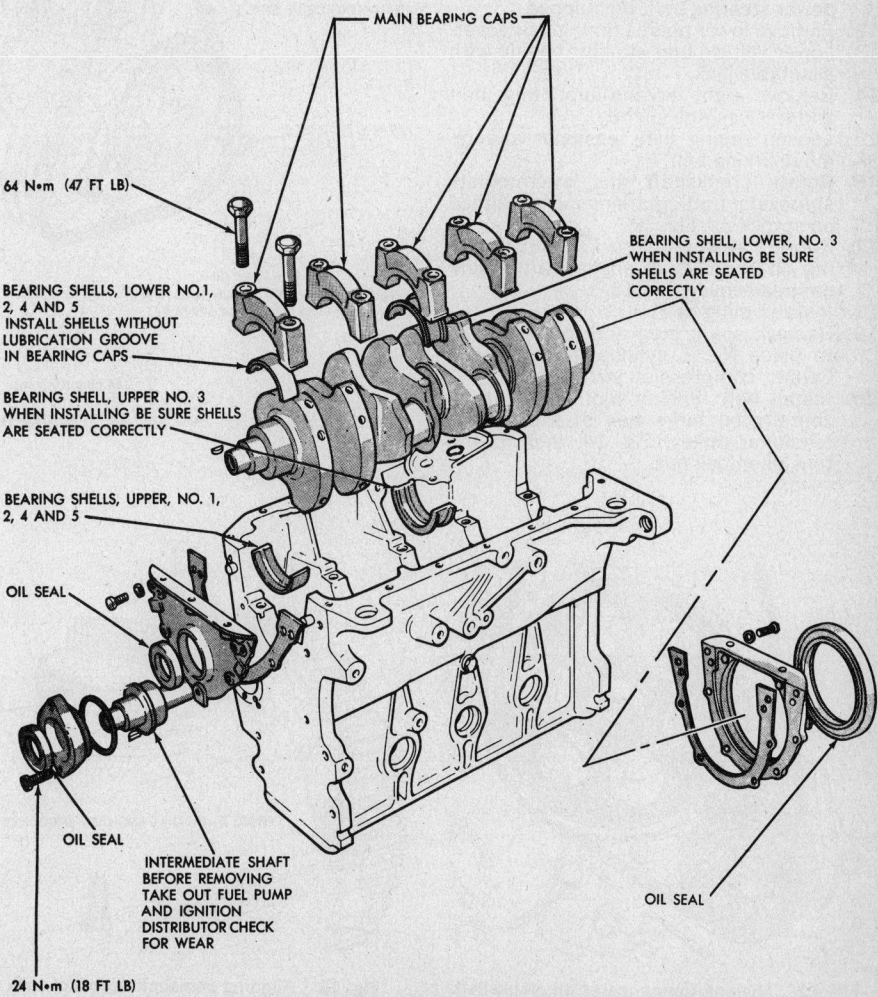

Fig. 10 Crankshaft assembly

sizes and undersizes of 0.25, 0.50 and 0.75 mm. Refer to Fig. 10 for bearing installation.

Rod bearings are available in standard sizes and undersizes of 0.25, 0.50 and 0.75 mm.

TIMING BELT, REPLACE

1. Disconnect battery ground cable.
2. Remove A/C compressor adjusting strap screws and the drive belt, if equipped. Remove screws from compressor mount and stabilizer brackets, then position compressor aside. Remove compressor bracket from alternator and the compressor mount bracket.
3. Loosen alternator adjusting strap and remove drive belt.
4. Remove alternator mount bolts and position alternator aside.
5. Remove alternator and compressor mounting bracket from retainer bracket.
6. Loosen power steering pump drive belt, if equipped.
7. Raise and support vehicle.
8. Remove inner fender shield.
9. Remove air compressor, water pump and air pump drive belts, if equipped.
10. Remove idler pulley assembly.
11. Remove crankshaft pulley, Fig. 11, and power steering belt, if equipped.
12. Remove lower plastic timing belt cover.
13. Lower vehicle and support engine with a suitable jack.
14. Remove right engine mounting bolt and raise engine slightly.
15. Loosen timing belt tensioner and remove timing belt.
16. Rotate crankshaft and intermediate sprockets until markings are aligned on sprockets, Fig. 12.
17. Rotate camshaft sprocket until marking on sprocket is aligned with cylinder head cover, Fig. 13.
18. Install timing belt.
19. Remove spark plug and rotate engine to place No. 1 cylinder at Top Dead Center, compression stroke.
20. Install belt tension tool L-4502 horizontally on large hex of timing belt tensioner pulley, Fig. 14, then loosen tensioner lock nut.

CAUTION
IF TIMING BELT WAS REMOVED OR REPLACED, RECHECK VALVE TIMING.

NOTE
ALL PARTS SHOWN IN THIS ILLUSTRATION CAN BE REMOVED AND INSTALLED WITH ENGINE IN CAR.

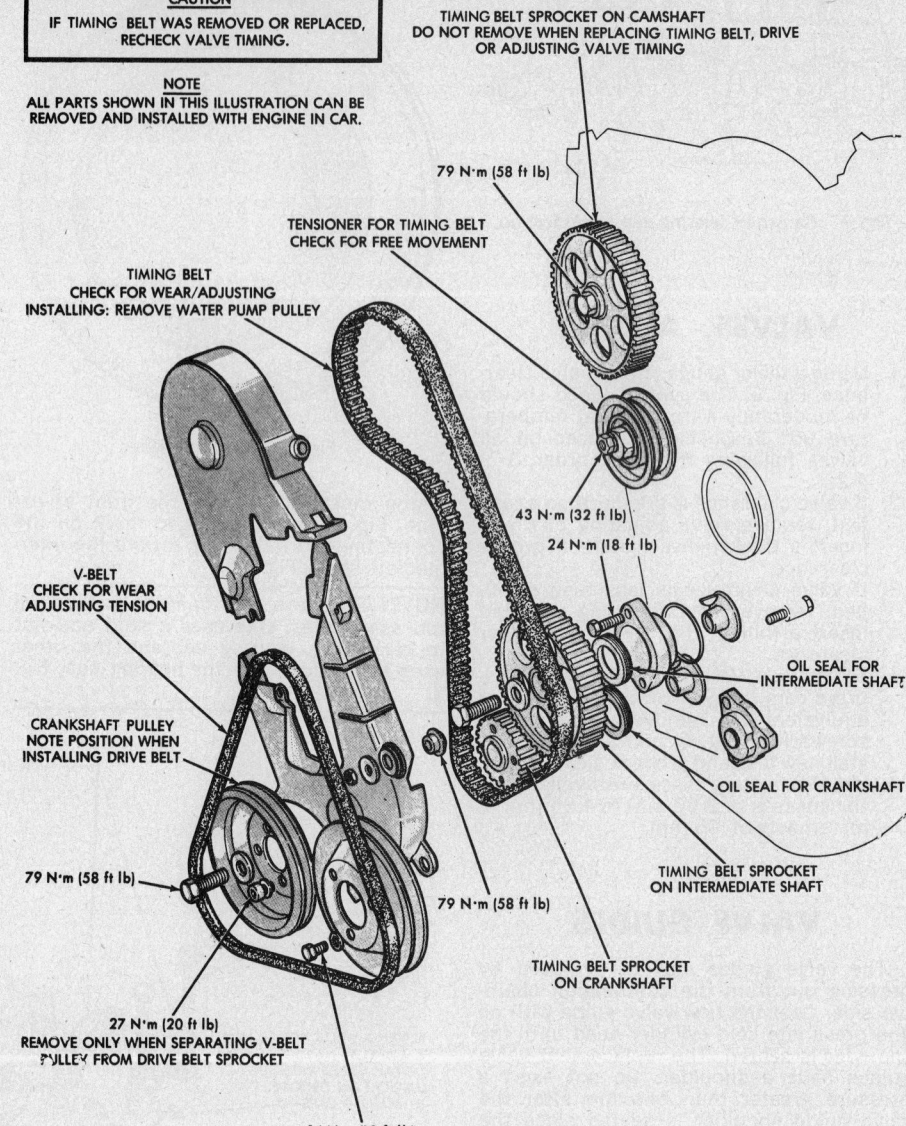

Fig. 11   Timing belt & sprockets installation

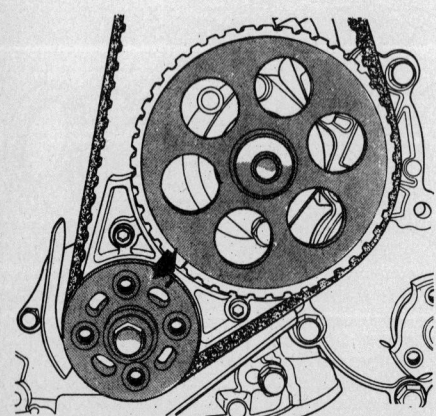

Fig. 12   Aligning timing marks on crankshaft & intermediate shaft sprockets

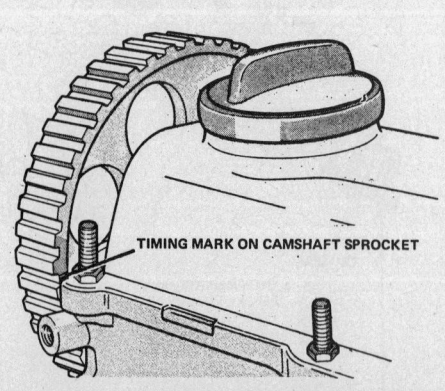

Fig. 13   Aligning camshaft sprocket with cylinder head cover

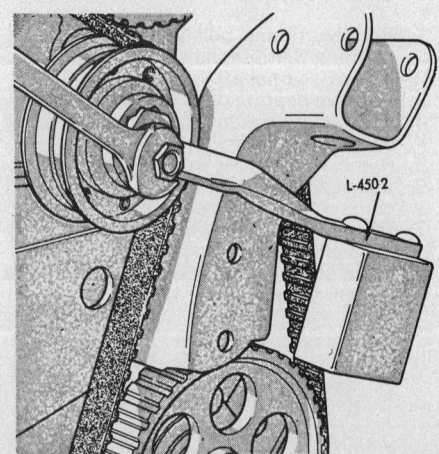

Fig. 14   Timing belt tensioner tool installation

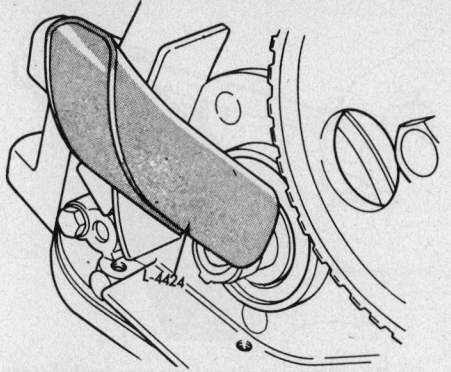

Fig. 15   Front engine oil seals removal

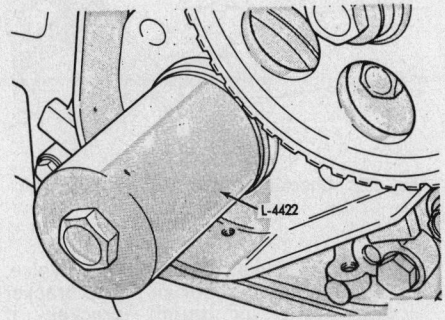

Fig. 16   Front engine oil seals installation

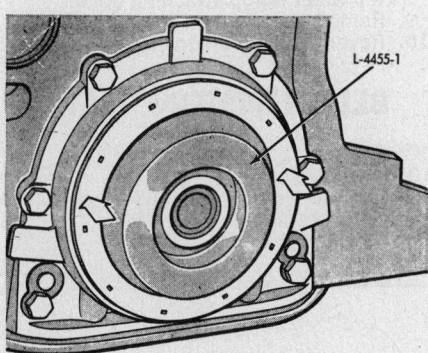

Fig. 17   Rear crankshaft oil seal installation

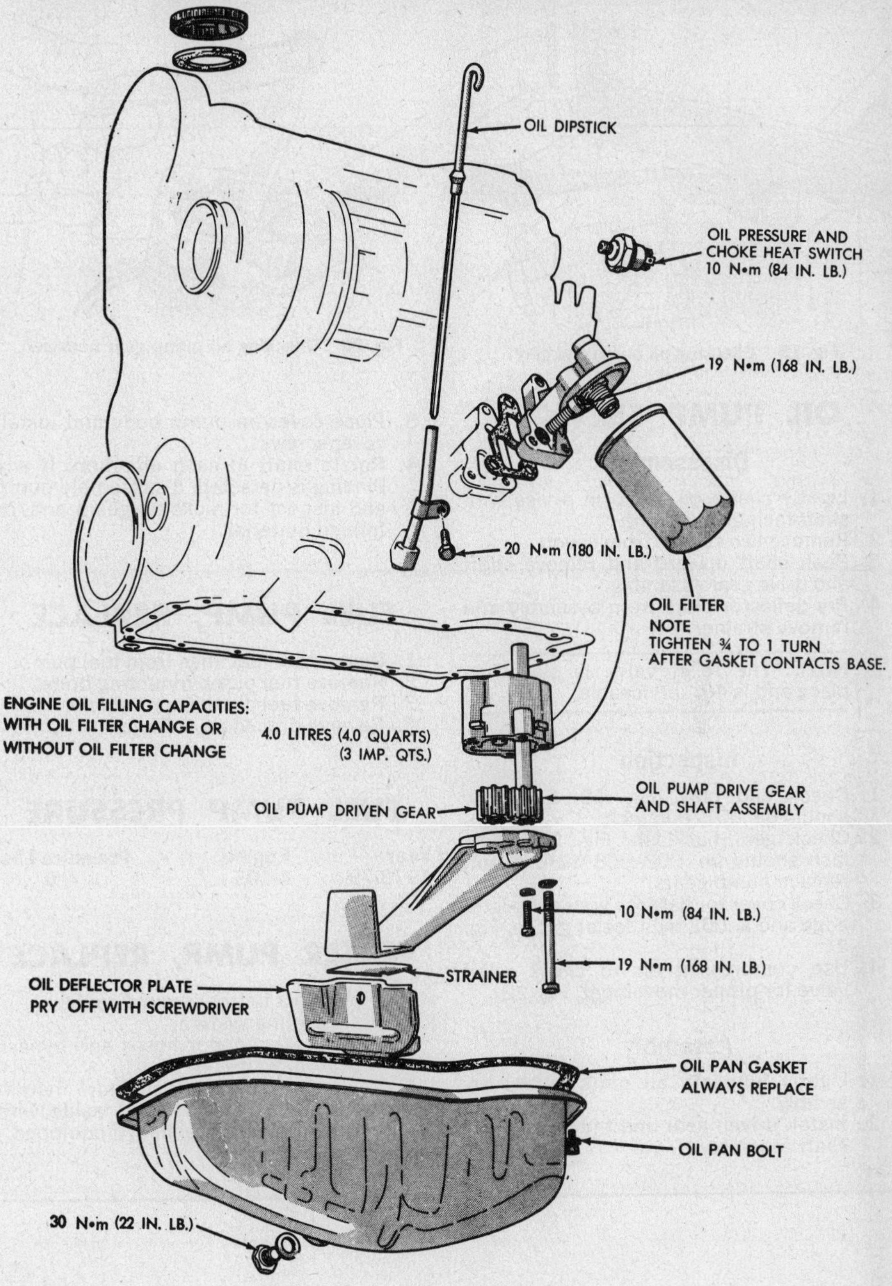

OIL DIPSTICK

OIL PRESSURE AND
CHOKE HEAT SWITCH
10 N•m (84 IN. LB.)

19 N•m (168 IN. LB.)

20 N•m (180 IN. LB.)

OIL FILTER
NOTE
TIGHTEN ¾ TO 1 TURN
AFTER GASKET CONTACTS BASE.

ENGINE OIL FILLING CAPACITIES:
WITH OIL FILTER CHANGE OR
WITHOUT OIL FILTER CHANGE

4.0 LITRES (4.0 QUARTS)
(3 IMP. QTS.)

OIL PUMP DRIVEN GEAR

OIL PUMP DRIVE GEAR
AND SHAFT ASSEMBLY

10 N•m (84 IN. LB.)

19 N•m (168 IN. LB.)

STRAINER

OIL DEFLECTOR PLATE
PRY OFF WITH SCREWDRIVER

OIL PAN GASKET
ALWAYS REPLACE

OIL PAN BOLT

30 N•m (22 IN. LB.)

Fig. 18   Engine lubrication system

21. Reset tension tool, if necessary, to be within 15 degrees of the horizontal.
22. Rotate engine clockwise two crankshaft revolutions, then tighten tensioner lock nut.
23. Remove tension tool and reverse Steps 1 through 14 to assemble.

FRONT ENGINE OIL SEAL SERVICE

Refer to Figs. 15 and 16 to replace the crankshaft, intermediate shaft or camshaft seal.

REAR CRANKSHAFT OIL SEAL SERVICE

1. Using a suitable screwdriver, pry oil seal out. Use caution not to nick or damage crankshaft flange seal surface.
2. Place tool L-4455-1 over crankshaft, Fig. 17.
3. Place replacement oil seal over tool and tap seal into position with a mallet.

OIL PUMP, REPLACE

Removal

1. Remove oil pan and gasket.
2. Remove oil pump mounting screws, then the oil pump from engine block, Fig. 18.

Installation

1. Install oil pump with shaft in bore until pump mounting face contacts engine block. It may be necessary to rotate pump body to engage pump shaft tongue in distributor shaft groove.
2. Install oil pump mounting screws.
3. Install oil pan gasket and oil pan.

Fig. 19   Checking oil pump end play

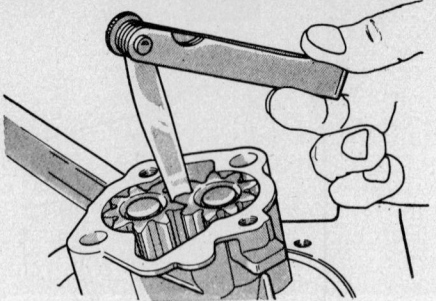

Fig. 20   Checking oil pump gear backlash

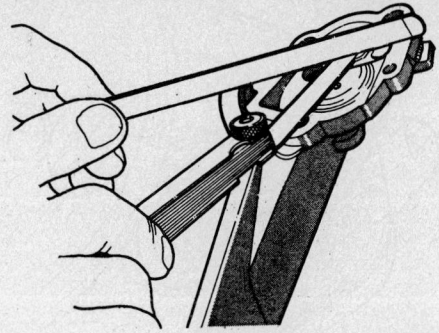

Fig. 21   Checking oil pump cover for flatness

OIL PUMP SERVICE

Disassembly

1. Lightly clamp oil pump in a vise with shaft facing downward.
2. Remove two screws from cover.
3. Push shaft upward and remove shaft and drive gear assembly.
4. Pry deflector plate from assembly and remove strainer.

NOTE: The relief valve is staked in place and is not serviceable.

Inspection

1. Check end play, Fig. 19. End play should be .001-.006 inch.
2. Check gear backlash, Fig. 20. Backlash should be .002-.008 inch. If not, replace pump gears.
3. Check cover for flatness with a straightedge and a .002 inch feeler gauge, Fig. 21.
4. Use compressed air to check relief valve for proper movement, Fig. 22.

Assembly

1. Lightly lubricate all parts before assembly.
2. Install driven gear and the drive gear/shaft assembly.

3. Place cover on pump body and install cover screws.
4. Rotate shaft in each direction. If any binding is detected, disassemble pump and inspect for nicks on gears and/or foreign material.

FUEL PUMP, REPLACE

1. Disconnect fuel lines from fuel pump.
2. Remove fuel pump mounting bolts.
3. Remove fuel pump from vehicle.
4. Reverse procedure to install.

FUEL PUMP PRESSURE

Year	Engine	Pressure Lbs.
1978-79	4-105	4-6

WATER PUMP, REPLACE

1. Disconnect battery ground cable.
2. Drain cooling system.
3. Disconnect radiator hoses and bypass hose from water pump.
4. Remove A/C compressor from mounting brackets and position aside with refrigerant lines attached, if equipped.
5. Remove alternator.

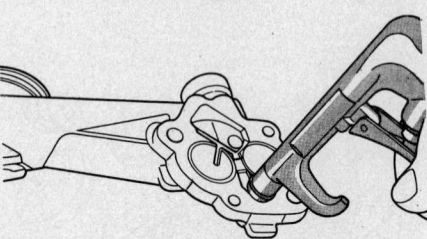

Fig. 22   Checking oil pump relief valve with compressed air

6. Disconnect diverter valve hose at valve, then remove the rear air pump bracket and front air pump bracket, if equipped.
7. Remove alternator bracket from water pump.
8. Remove timing belt cover bolt and two top water pump attaching bolts.
9. Remove water pump from vehicle.
10. Reverse procedure to install.

BELT TENSION DATA

		New	Used
1978-79	Air Cond.	55	40
	Air Pump	65	45
	Alternator	75	55
	Power Steer.	40	25

Clutch & Transaxle Section

CLUTCH, ADJUST

1. Pull upward on clutch cable at housing attachment, Fig. 1.
2. Rotate sleeve downward until sleeve snugly contacts grommet.
3. Rotate sleeve so end of sleeve seats into rectangular groove in grommet.
4. Check for proper operation.

CLUTCH, REPLACE

Removal

1. Remove transmission as outlined under "Manual Transaxle, Replace" procedure.
2. Gradually loosen and remove bolts attaching flywheel to pressure plate.
3. Remove flywheel and clutch disc, Fig. 2.
4. Remove retaining ring and release plate.
5. Mark position of pressure plate on crankshaft.
6. Gradually loosen and remove bolts attaching pressure plate to flywheel.
7. Remove spacer and pressure plate.

Installation

1. Thoroughly clean surfaces of flywheel and pressure plate with fine sandpaper or crocus cloth. Also, ensure that all oil or grease has been removed.
2. Align marks on pressure plate and crankshaft and install pressure plate and spacer on crankshaft. Install and torque attaching bolts to 55 ft. lbs. (74.5 Nm).
3. Install release plate and retaining ring.
4. Using tool L-4533 to center clutch disc,

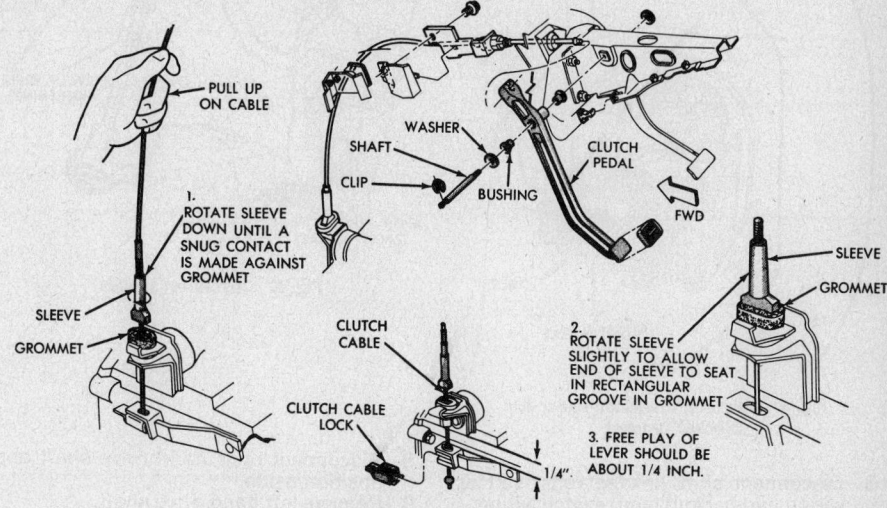

Fig. 1 Adjusting clutch free play

Fig. 3, install disc and flywheel onto pressure plate. Ensure the drilled mark on flywheel is at the top so the two dowels in the flywheel align the proper holes in the pressure plate.
5. Install and torque flywheel to pressure plate attaching bolts to 14.5 ft. lbs. (19.8 Nm).
6. Remove centering tool.
7. Install transaxle and adjust clutch.
8. Check for proper operation.

GEARSHIFT LINKAGE, ADJUST

1. Place shift lever in neutral at 3-4 position.

2. Loosen shift tube clamp.
3. Align tab on slider with hole in blocker bracket, Fig. 4.
4. Install a 1/2 inch spacer, Fig. 5, to set gearshift unit lock-out.

NOTE: If the blocket bracket has a 5/8 stamp imprint at the forward vertical face of the reinforcement strap, Fig. 6, it indicates that a 5/8 inch spacer must be used in place of the 1/2 inch spacer.

5. Tighten shift tube clamp and remove spacer.
6. Check for proper operation.

MANUAL TRANSAXLE, REPLACE

1. Remove engine timing access hole plug, then rotate engine to align drilled mark on flywheel with pointer on clutch housing.
2. Disconnect battery ground cable.

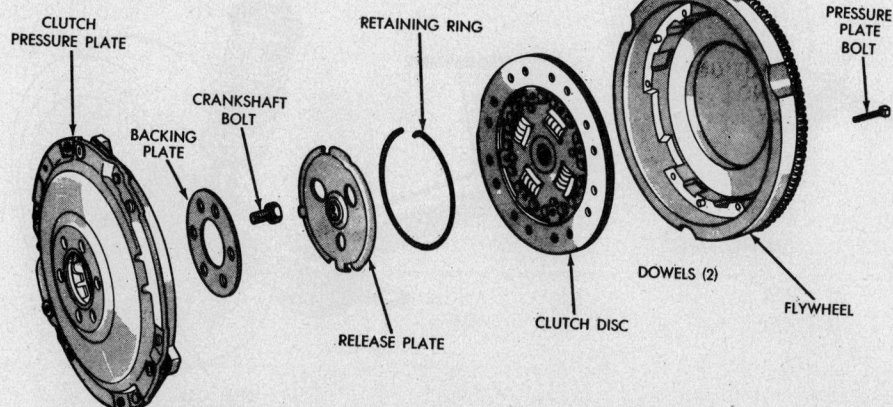

Fig. 2 Clutch assembly

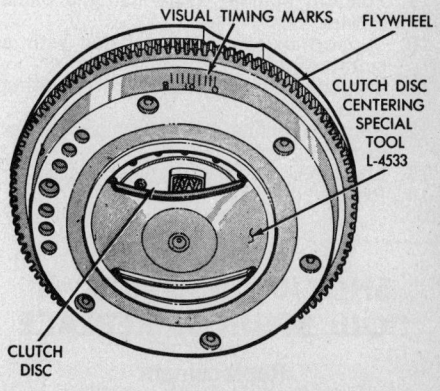

Fig. 3 Centering clutch disc

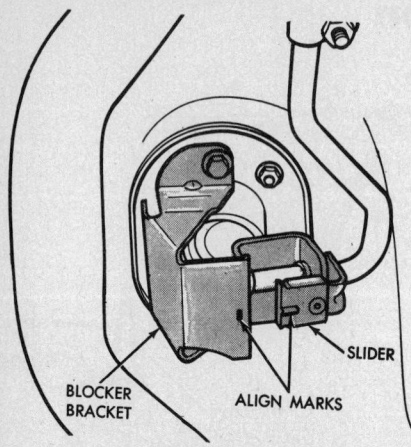

Fig. 4   Aligning marks on slider & blocker bracket

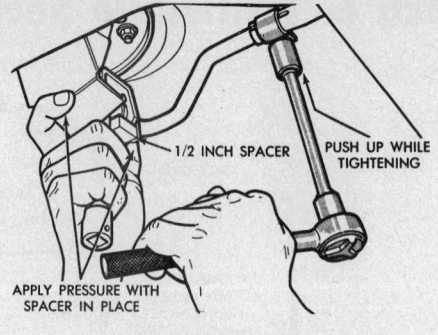

Fig. 5   Installing spacer

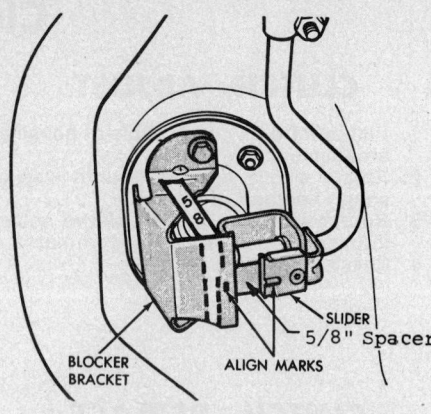

Fig. 6   Revised gearshift blocker bracket

3. Disconnect shift linkage rods, starter wiring and backup lamp switch wiring.
4. Remove starter and disconnect clutch cable.
5. Remove bolt attaching speedometer adapter to transaxle.
6. With speedometer cable housing connected, pull adapter and pinion from transaxle.
7. Raise and support vehicle. Also, support engine with suitable equipment.

8. Disconnect right hand drive shaft and position aside.
9. Remove left hand drive shaft.
10. Remove left splash shield.
11. Drain transaxle fluid.
12. Remove bolts from left engine mount.
13. Remove transaxle to engine attaching nuts and bolts.
14. Slide transaxle toward left side of vehicle until mainshaft clears clutch.
15. Lower and remove transaxle from vehicle.

16. Reverse procedure to install.

1979 AUTO. TRANSAXLE LINKAGE, ADJUST

Linkage adjustments for the 1979 models are the same as those for the 1978 models outlined elsewhere in this manual.

Rear Axle, Rear Suspension & Brakes Section

REAR AXLE, REPLACE

1. Raise and support vehicle.
2. Remove wheels.
3. Remove brake fittings and retaining clips securing flexible brake line.
4. Remove parking brake cable adjusting connection nut.
5. Release parking brake cables from bracket by slipping ball-end of cables through brake connectors.
6. Pull parking brake cable through bracket.
7. Remove brake drums.
8. Remove brake assembly and spindle retaining bolts.
9. Position spindle aside using a piece of wire.
10. Support axle and suspension with a suitable jack.
11. Remove shock absorber mounting bolts.
12. Remove trailing arm to hanger bracket mounting bolt.
13. Lower rear axle from vehicle, Fig. 1.
14. Reverse procedure to install.

ing protective cap, located inside vehicle at upper rear wheel well area.
2. Remove upper shock absorber mounting nut, isolator retainer and upper isolator, Fig. 1.

3. Raise and support vehicle.
4. Remove shock absorber lower mounting bolt.
5. Remove shock absorber and coil spring assembly from vehicle.

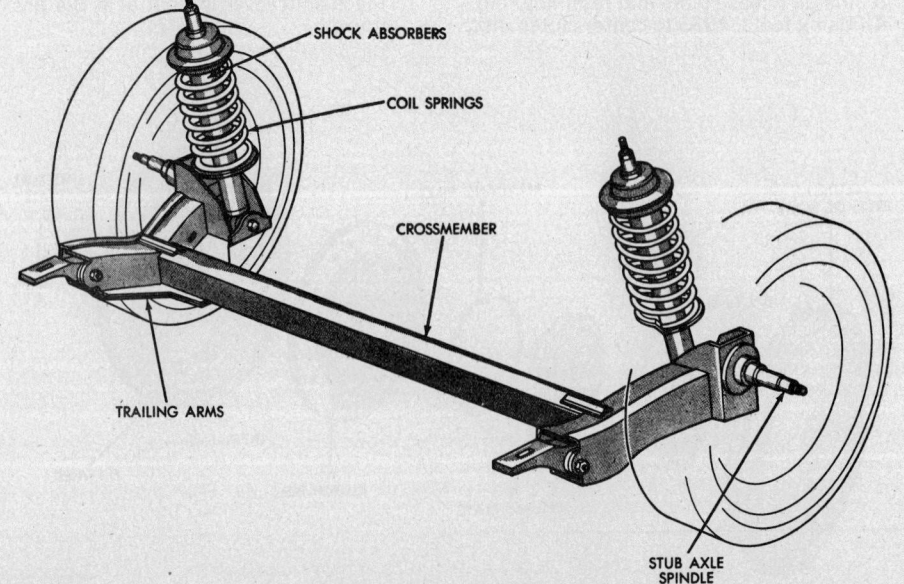

Fig. 1   Rear axle & suspension assembly

SHOCK ABSORBER & COIL SPRING, REPLACE

Replacement

1. Remove upper shock absorber mount-

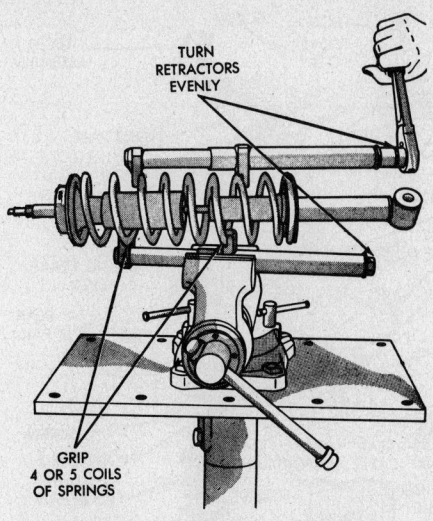

Fig. 2 Retracting coil spring

6. Reverse procedure to install.

Service

1. Install coil spring retractors, tool L-4514, on coil spring and support in a vise, Fig. 2. Grip 4 or 5 coils of the spring in the retractors. Also, do not extend retractors more than 9¼ inches.
2. Tighten retractors evenly until spring pressure is released from upper spring seat.
3. Hold flat end of push rod and loosen retaining nut.

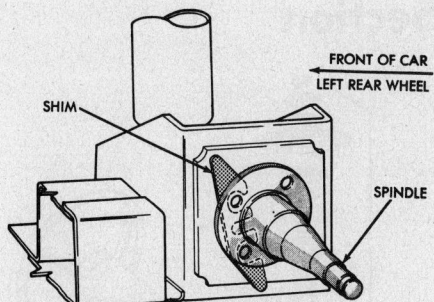

Fig. 4 Shim installation for toe-out

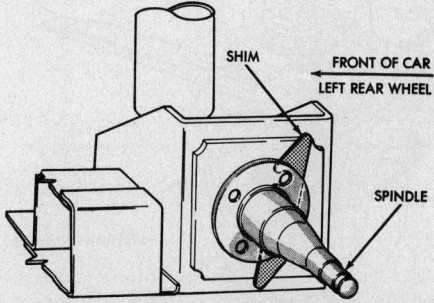

Fig. 5 Shim installation for toe-in

CAUTION: Ensure that spring is properly compressed before loosening retaining nut since personal injury may result.

4. Remove lower isolator, push rod sleeve and upper spring seat.
5. Remove shock absorber from coil spring.
6. Remove jounce bumper and dust shield from push rod, Fig. 3.
7. Remove lower spring seat. Fig. 3.
8. Reverse procedure to assemble.

REAR WHEEL BEARING, ADJUST

1. Torque adjusting nut to 270 inch lbs. (35 Nm) while rotating wheel.
2. Stop wheel and loosen adjusting nut.
3. Tighten adjusting nut finger tight. End play should be .004-.12 inch.
4. Install castle lock with slots aligned with cotter pin hole.
5. Install cotter pin and grease cap.

REAR WHEEL ALIGNMENT

Due to the design of the rear suspension and the incorporation of stub axles or wheel spindles, it is possible to adjust the camber and toe of the rear wheels on these vehicles. Adjustment is controlled by adding shims approximately .010 inch thick between the spindle mounting surface and spindle mounting plate. The amount of adjustment is approximately 0° 18' per shim. Refer to Figs. 4 through 7 for proper placement of the shims.

SERVICE BRAKES, ADUST

Since the rear brakes on these vehicles are not self-adjusting, periodic adjustment is required as follows:
1. Raise and support vehicle.
2. Remove adjusting hole covers from brake supports.
3. Release parking brake and back off cable adjustment to slacken cable.
4. Insert a narrow screwdriver into adjusting nut hole. Move screwdriver handle downward on left side or upward on right side until drag is felt when wheel is rotated, Fig. 8.
5. Back off nut so no drag is present when wheel is rotated.
6. Adjust parking brake.

PARKING BRAKE, ADJUST

1. Raise and support vehicle.
2. Release parking brake and back off adjustment to slacken cable.
3. Tighten cable adjusting nut until a slight drag is obtained while rotating wheels.
4. Loosen cable adjusting nut until the wheels rotate freely, Fig. 9, then an additional two turns.

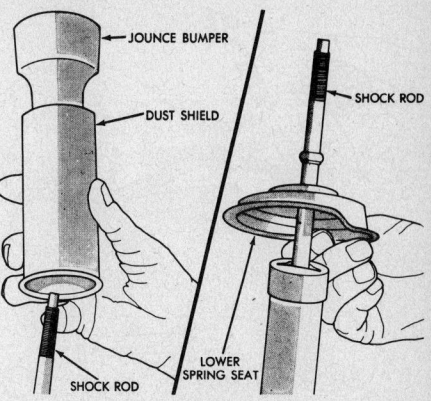

Fig. 3 Jounce bumper, dust shield & lower spring seat replacement

5. Apply and release parking brake to check for proper operation. The rear wheels should rotate without dragging.

MASTER CYLINDER, REPLACE

Manual Brakes

1. Disconnect and plug brake tubes from master cylinder. Cap master cylinder ports.
2. Disconnect stop lamp switch mounting bracket from beneath instrument panel.
3. Pull brake pedal rearward to disengage push rod from master cylinder.

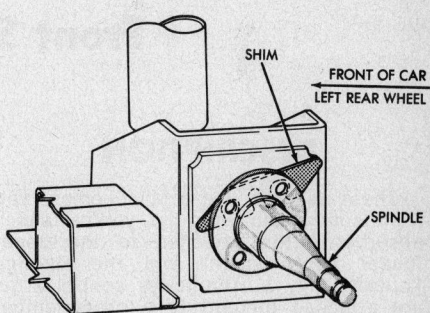

Fig. 6 Shim installation for positive camber

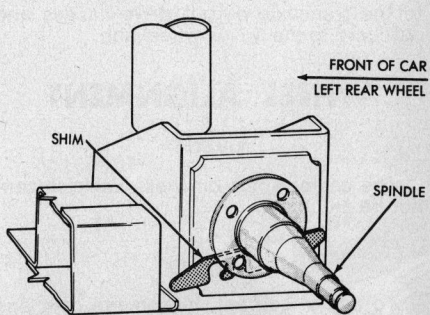

Fig. 7 Shim installation for negative camber

Fig. 8 Adjusting service brakes

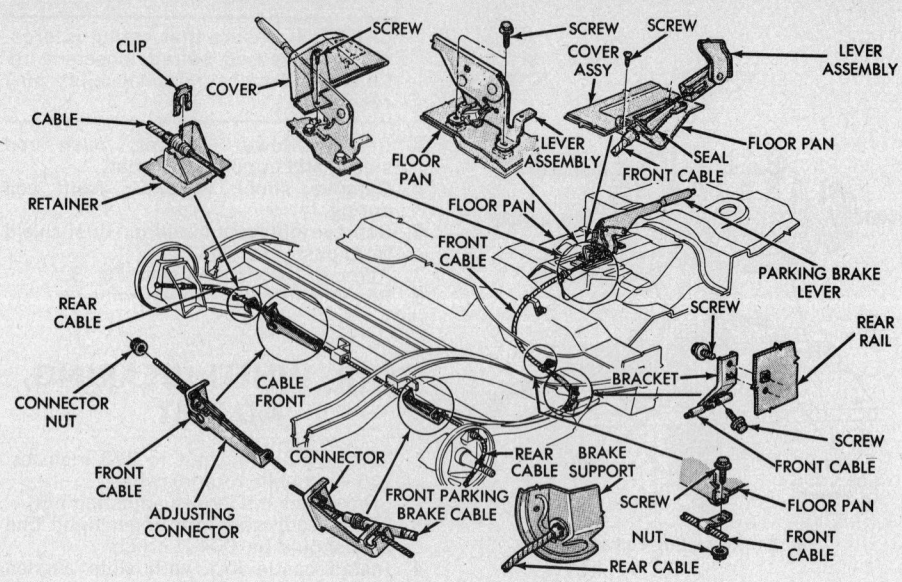

Fig. 9 Parking brake cable routing

NOTE: Pulling the brake pedal rearward will destroy the grommet. Install a new grommet when installing the push rod.

4. Remove master cylinder attaching nuts.
5. Remove master cylinder from vehicle.
6. Reverse procedure to install.

Power Brakes

1. Disconnect and plug brake tubes from master cylinder. Cap master cylinder ports.
2. Remove master cylinder attaching nuts.
3. Remove master cylinder from power brake unit.
4. Reverse procedure to install.

POWER BRAKE UNIT, REPLACE

1. Remove master cylinder attaching nuts, slide master cylinder from mounting studs and support on fender shield. Do not disconnect brake tubes from master cylinder.
2. Disconnect vacuum hose from power brake unit.

3. From beneath instrument panel, install a suitable screwdriver between the center tang on retainer clip and the brake pedal pin. Rotate the screwdriver so the retainer center tang will pass over brake pedal pin. Pull retainer clip from pin.
4. Remove power brake unit attaching nuts and the power brake unit from vehicle.
5. Reverse procedure to install.

Front Suspension & Steering Section

DESCRIPTION

These vehicles use a MacPherson type front suspension with the vertical shock absorber struts attached to the upper fender reinforcement and the steering knuckle, Fig. 1. The lower control arms are attached inboard to a crossmember and outboard to the steering knuckle through a ball joint to provide lower steering knuckle position. During steering maneuvers, the strut and steering knuckle rotate as an assembly.

The drive shafts are attached inboard to the transaxle output drive flanges and outboard to the driven wheel hub.

WHEEL ALIGNMENT

Caster

The caster angle on these vehicles cannot be adjusted.

Camber

To adjust camber, loosen the cam and through bolts, Fig. 2. Rotate the upper cam bolt to move the top of the wheel

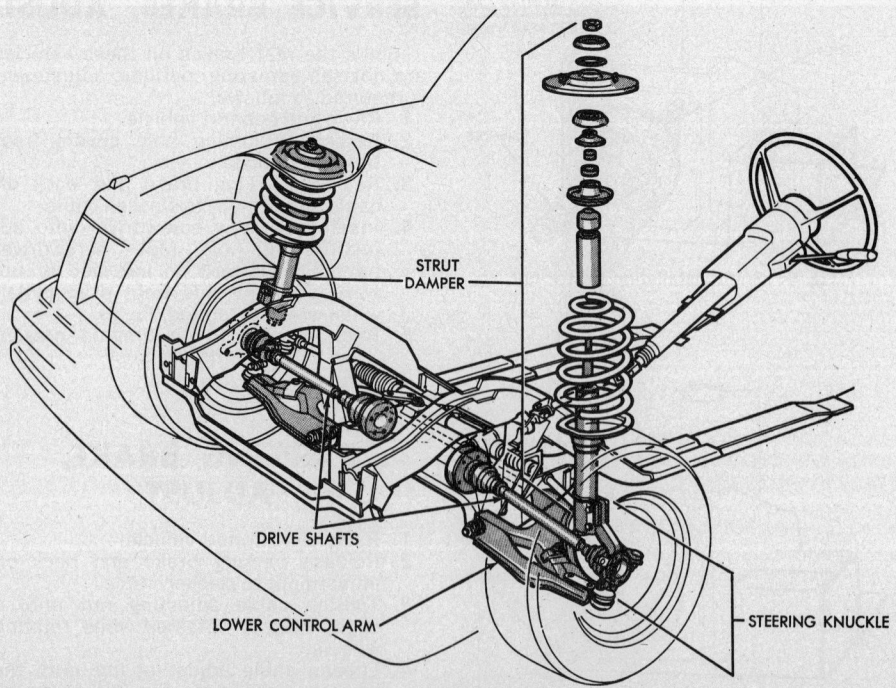

Fig. 1 Front suspension

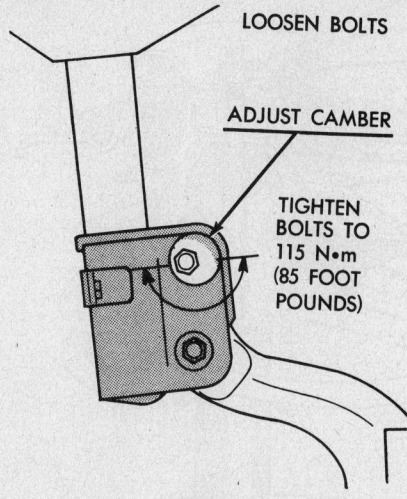

Fig. 2   Camber adjustment

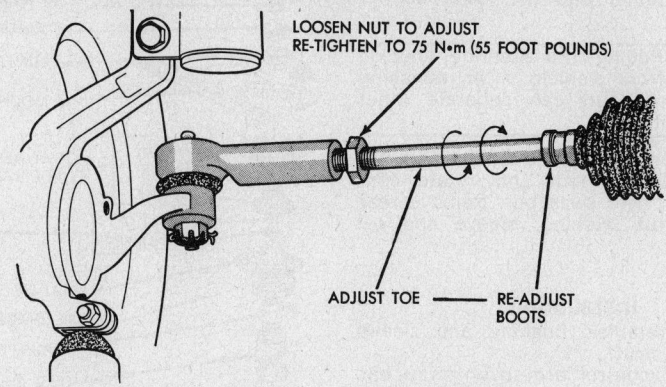

Fig. 3   Toe-in adjustment

in or out to achieve the specified camber angle. Torque cam bolts to 85 ft. lbs. (115 Nm).

Toe-In

To adjust toe-in, center the steering wheel and hold in position with a suitable tool. Loosen the tie rod lock nuts and rotate the rod, Fig. 3, to adjust toe-in to specifications. Use care not to twist the steering gear rubber boots. Torque the tie rod lock nuts to 55 ft. lbs. (75 Nm). Adjust position of steering gear rubber boots. Remove steering wheel holding tool.

STRUT DAMPER ASSEMBLY, REPLACE

1. Raise and support vehicle, then remove front wheels.
2. Mark position of camber adjusting cam, then remove the camber adjusting bolt and through bolt and the brake hose to damper bracket retaining screw, Fig. 4.
3. Remove strut damper to fender shield mounting nut and washer assemblies.
4. Remove strut damper from vehicle.
5. Reverse procedure to install.

COIL SPRING, REPLACE

1. Remove strut damper assembly as outlined previously.
2. Using a suitable tool, compress coil spring.
3. Remove strut rod nut while holding strut rod to prevent rotation.
4. Remove the mount assembly, Fig. 5.
5. Remove coil spring from strut damper.
6. Inspect mount assembly for deterioration of rubber isolator, retainers for cracks and distortion and bearings for binding.
7. Install the bumper dust shield assembly.
8. Install spring and seat, upper spring retainer, bearing and spacer, mount assembly and the rebound bumper, retainer and rod nut upper.

NOTE: Position the spring retainer alignment notch paralled to the damper lower attaching brackets.

9. Torque strut rod nut to 60 ft. lbs. (81 Nm). Do not release spring compressor before torquing nut.
10. Remove spring compressor.

BALL JOINTS

The lower control arm ball joints are premanently lubricated, operate with no free play and are riveted or bolted to the lower control arm.

If the ball joint is bolted to the lower control arm, it is required that the lower control arm assembly be replaced if the ball joint is defective.

If the ball joint is bolted to the lower control arm, the ball joint can be replaced without replacing the entire lower control arm. When installing the ball joint, torque attaching bolts to 60 ft. lbs. (81 Nm).

LOWER CONTROL ARM, REPLACE

Removal

1. Raise and support vehicle.
2. Remove the front inner pivot through bolt, the rear stub strut nut, retainer and bushing and the ball joint to steering knuckle clamp bolt, Fig. 6.
3. Separate the ball joint from the steering knuckle by prying between the ball

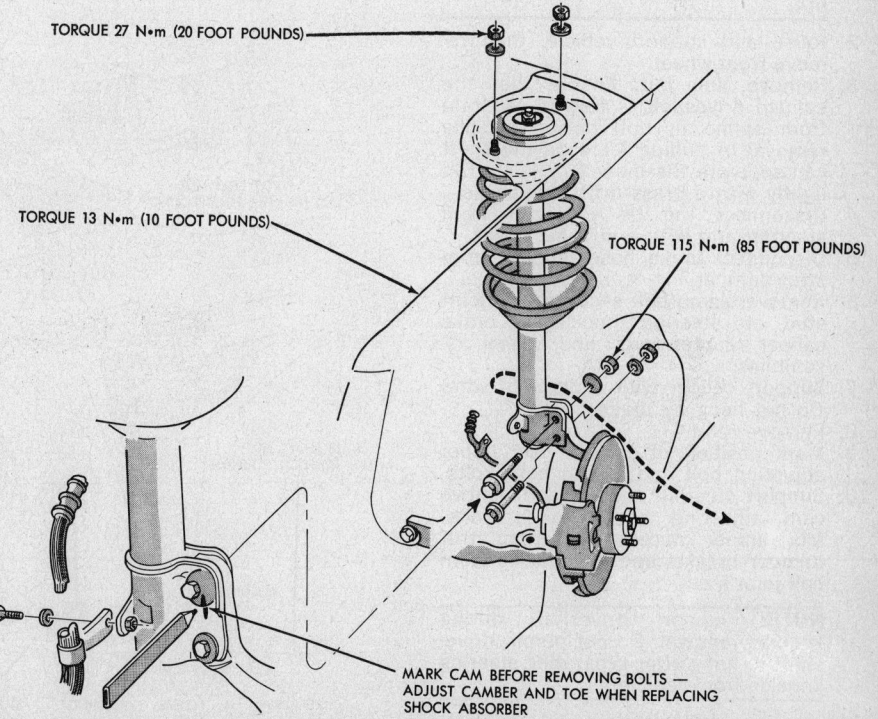

Fig. 4   Strut damper replacement

stud retainer and the lower control arm.

NOTE: Pulling the steering knuckle "Out" from vehicle after releasing from ball joint can separate inner C/V joint.

4. Remove sway bar to control arm nut and reinforcement and rotate control arm over sway bar. Remove rear stub strut bushing, sleeve and retainer.

Installation

1. Install retainer, bushing and sleeve on stub strut.
2. Position control arm over sway bar and install rear stub strut and front pivot into crossmember.
3. Install front pivot bolt and loosely assemble nut, Fig. 6.
4. Install stub strut bushing and retainer and loosely assemble nut.
5. Place sway bar bracket stud through control arm and install retainer and nut. Torque nut to 10 ft. lbs. (13 Nm).
6. Install ball joint stud into steering knuckle, then the clamp bolt. Torque bolt to 50 ft. lbs. (67 Nm).
7. Lower vehicle and with suspension support vehicle torque front pivot bolt to 105 ft. lbs. (142 Nm) and the stub strut nut to 70 ft. lbs. (94 Nm).

STEERING KNUCKLE, REPLACE
Removal

1. Loosen hub nut with brakes applied, Fig. 7.

NOTE: The nub and driveshaft are splined together through the knuckle (Bearing) and retained by the hub nut.

2. Raise and support vehicle, then remove front wheel.
3. Remove hub nut. Ensure that the splined driveshaft is free to separate from spline in hub during knuckle removal. A pulling force on the shaft can separate the inner C/V joint. Tap lightly with a brass drift, if required.
4. Disconnect the tie rod end from steering arm with a suitable puller.
5. Disconnect brake hose retainer from strut damper.
6. Remove clamp bolt securing ball joint stud into steering knuckle and brake caliper adapter screw and washer assemblies.
7. Support caliper with a piece of wire. Do not hang by brake hose.
8. Remove rotor.
9. Mark position of camber cam upper adjusting bolt and loosen both bolts.
10. Support steering knuckle and remove cam adjusting and through bolts. Move upper knuckle "Leg" from strut damper bracket and lift knuckle from ball joint stud.

NOTE: Support driveshaft during knuckle removal. Do not permit driveshaft to hang after separating steering knuckle from vehicle.

Installation

1. Place steering knuckle on lower ball

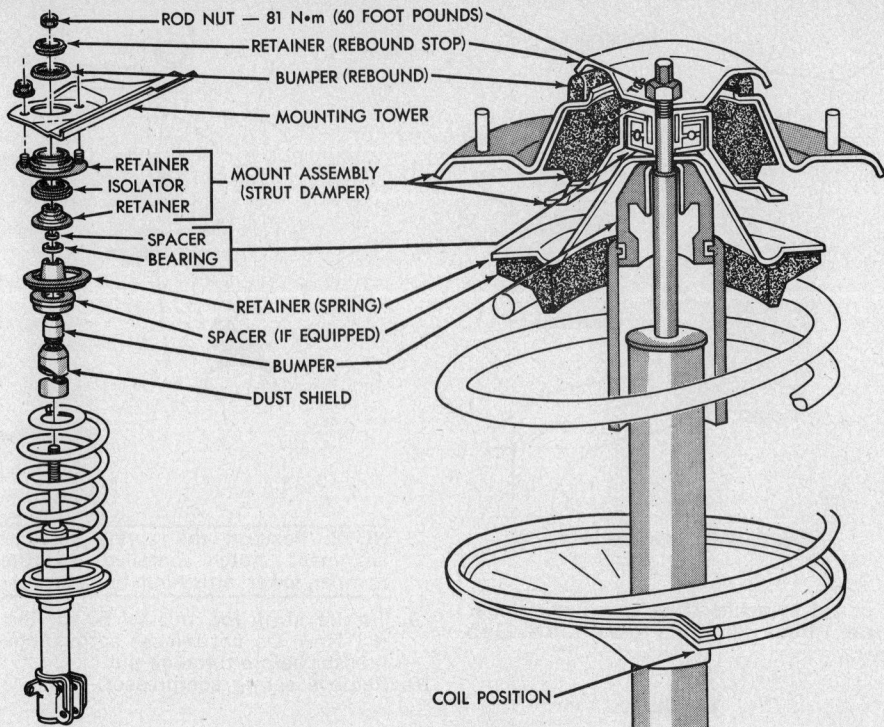

Fig. 5 Strut damper assembly

joint stud and the driveshaft through hub.

2. Position upper "Leg" of knuckle into strut damper bracket and install cam and through bolts. Place cam in original position and torque both bolts to 85 ft. lbs. (115 Nm).

3. Install and torque ball joint to steering knuckle clamp bolt to 50 ft. lbs. (68 Nm).

4. Install tie rod end into steering arm, torque nut to 25 ft. lbs. (33 Nm) and install cotter pin.

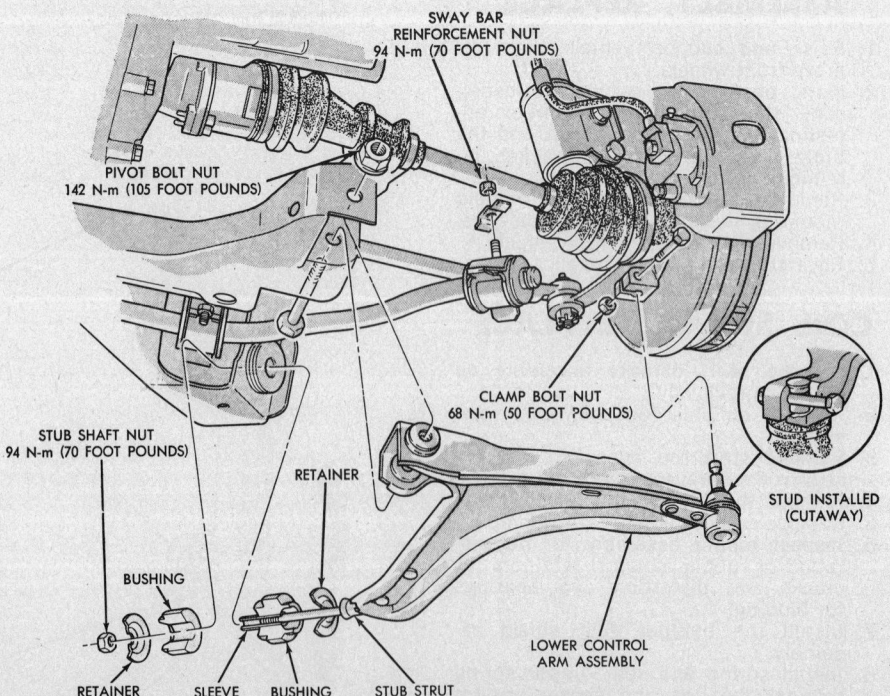

Fig. 6 Lower control arm assembly

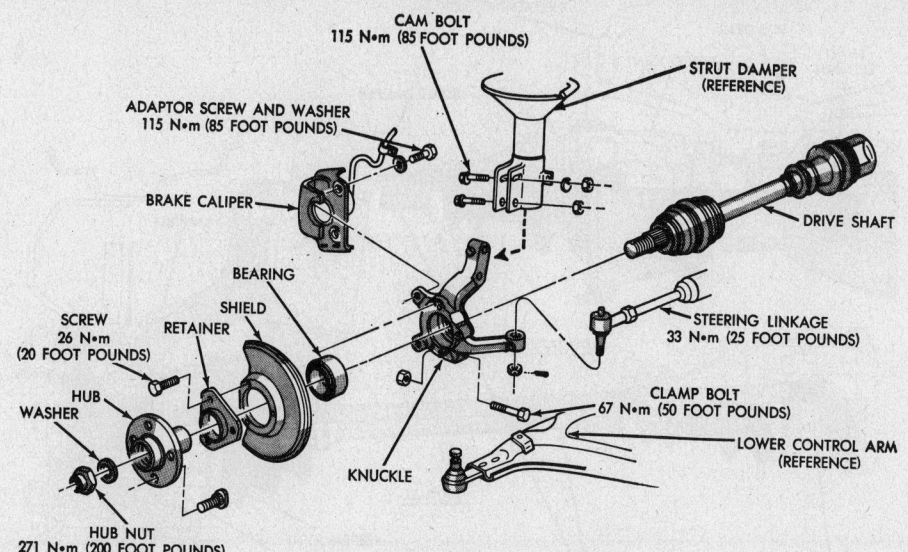

CAM BOLT
115 N•m (85 FOOT POUNDS)

STRUT DAMPER
(REFERENCE)

ADAPTOR SCREW AND WASHER
115 N•m (85 FOOT POUNDS)

BRAKE CALIPER

DRIVE SHAFT

BEARING

SHIELD

SCREW
26 N•m
(20 FOOT POUNDS)

RETAINER

STEERING LINKAGE
33 N•m (25 FOOT POUNDS)

HUB
WASHER

CLAMP BOLT
67 N•m (50 FOOT POUNDS)

LOWER CONTROL ARM
(REFERENCE)

KNUCKLE

HUB NUT
271 N•m (200 FOOT POUNDS)
AND STAKE

Fig. 7   Steering knuckle assembly

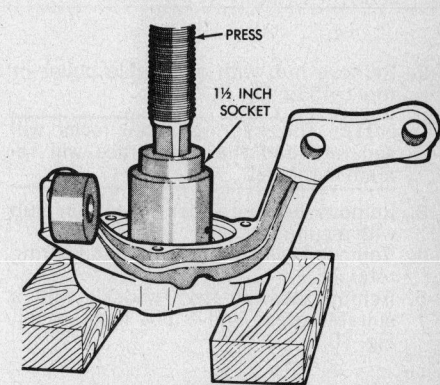

TOOL
L-4539

BACK OUT
RETAINER
SCREW TO HUB

THRUST
BUTTON

SHIELD

HUB

Fig. 9   Hub removal

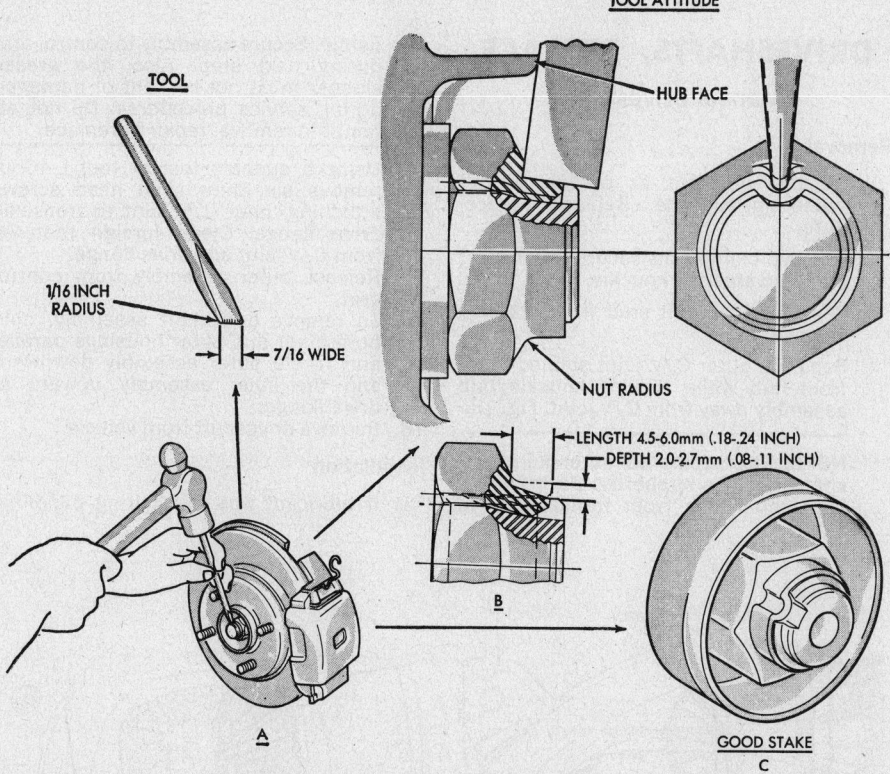

TOOL ATTITUDE

TOOL

HUB FACE

1/16 INCH
RADIUS

7/16 WIDE

NUT RADIUS

LENGTH 4.5-6.0mm (.18-.24 INCH)
DEPTH 2.0-2.7mm (.08-.11 INCH)

B

A

GOOD STAKE
C

Fig. 8   Staking hub nut

PRESS

1½ INCH
SOCKET

Fig. 10   Removing bearing from knuckle

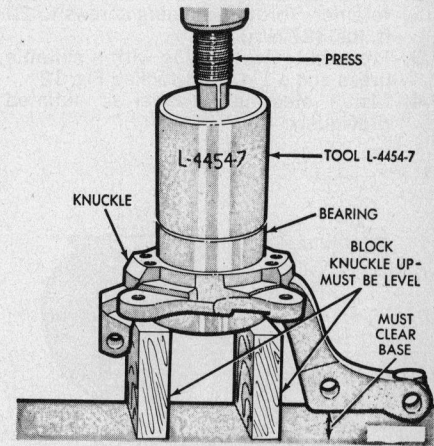

PRESS

L-4454-7

TOOL L-4454-7

KNUCKLE

BEARING

BLOCK
KNUCKLE UP—
MUST BE LEVEL

MUST
CLEAR
BASE

Fig. 11   Installing bearing into knuckle

5. Install rotor.
6. Install caliper over rotor and position adapter to steering knuckle. Install adapter to knuckle bolts and torque to 85 ft. lbs. (115 Nm).
7. Attach brake hose retainer to strut damper and torque screw to 10 ft. lbs. (13 Nm).

8. Install washer and new hub nut after cleaning chips from thread lock groove.

NOTE: The hub nuts are not to be reused.

9. With brakes applied, torque hub nut to 200 ft. lbs. (271 Nm).
10. Stake the hub nut as shown in Fig. 8.

HUB & BEARING, REPLACE

Removal

1. Remove steering knuckle as outlined previously.

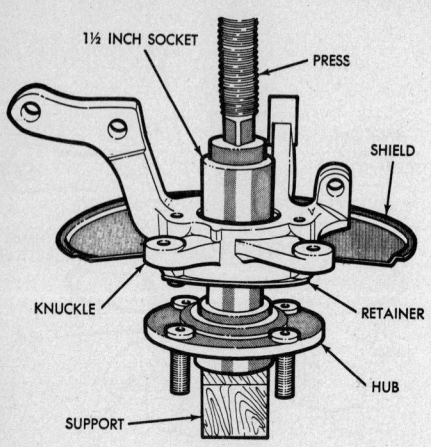

Fig. 12 Installing hub into knuckle

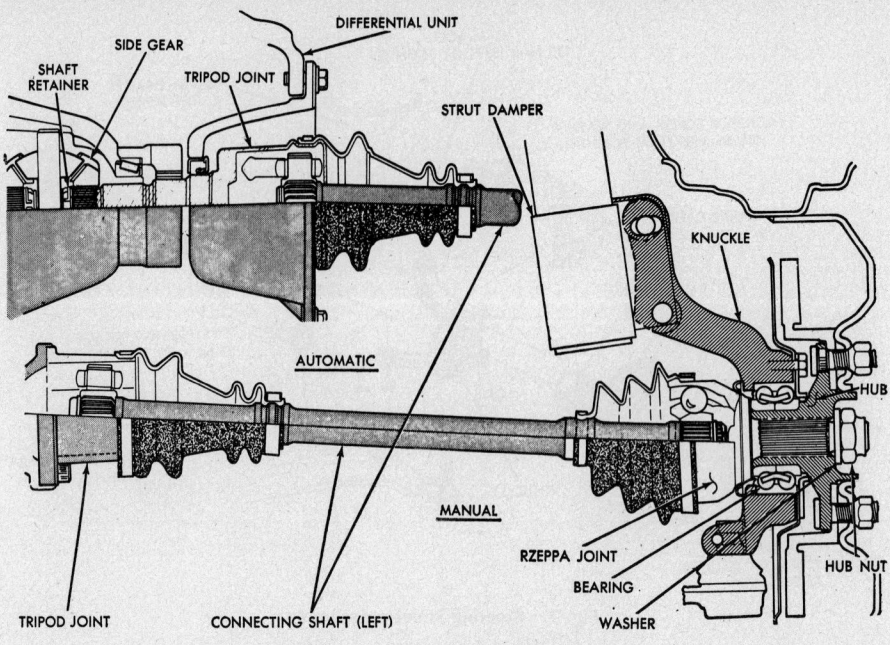

Fig. 13 Driveshaft assemblies

2. Remove hub with a suitable puller or tool L-4539, Fig. 9.

NOTE: The bearing inner races will separate and the outer race will remain in the hub.

3. Remove bearing inner race from hub with a suitable puller.
4. Remove brake dust shield and bearing retainer.
5. Remove bearing from knuckle with a suitable press and a 1½ inch socket, Fig. 10.

Installation

1. Press new bearing into knuckle with a suitable press and installer tool L-4454-7, Fig. 11.
2. Install brake dust shield and bearing retainer. Torque retaining screws to 20 ft. lbs. (27 Nm).
3. Press hub into bearing with a suitable press and a 1½ inch socket, Fig. 12.
4. Install steering knuckle as outlined previously.

DRIVESHAFTS, REPLACE

Manual Driveshaft

Removal

1. Remove hub nut as outlined under "Steering Knuckle, Replace" procedure.
2. Remove clamp bolt securing ball joint stud into steering knuckle.
3. Separate ball joint stud from steering knuckle.
4. Separate outer C/V joint splined shaft from hub while moving knuckle/hub assembly away from C/V joint, Fig. 13.

NOTE: The separated outer joint and shaft must be supported during inner joint separation from transaxle drive flange. Secure assembly to control arm during next step. Also, the grease slonger must not be bent or damaged during service procedures. Do not attempt to remove, repair or replace.

5. Using a suitable tool or tool L-4550, remove six 8mm allen head screws attaching inner C/V joint to transaxle drive flange. Clean foreign material from C/V joint and drive flange.
6. Release outer assembly from control arm.
7. To remove driveshaft assembly, hold both inner and outer housings parallel and rotate outer assembly downward and the inner assembly upward at drive flange.
8. Remove driveshaft from vehicle.

Installation

1. If lubricant was lost during handling,

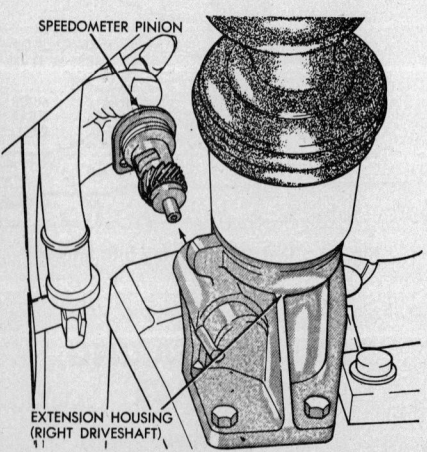

Fig. 14 Speedometer pinion replacement. Automatic units

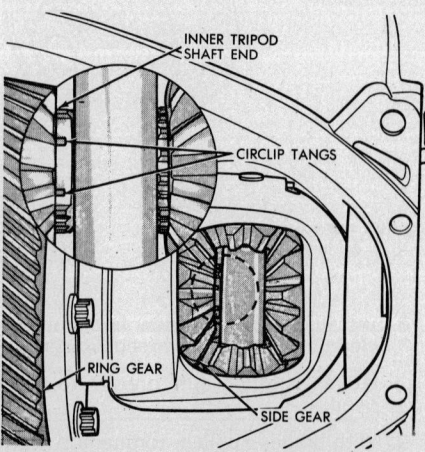

Fig. 15 Circlips exposed. Automatic units

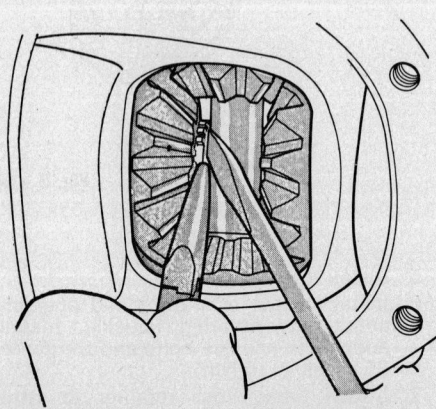

Fig. 16 Compressing circlips. Automatic units

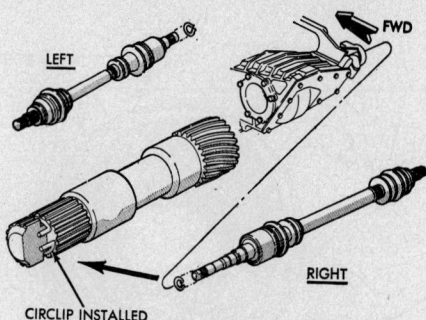

Fig. 17   Circlip installation. Automatic units

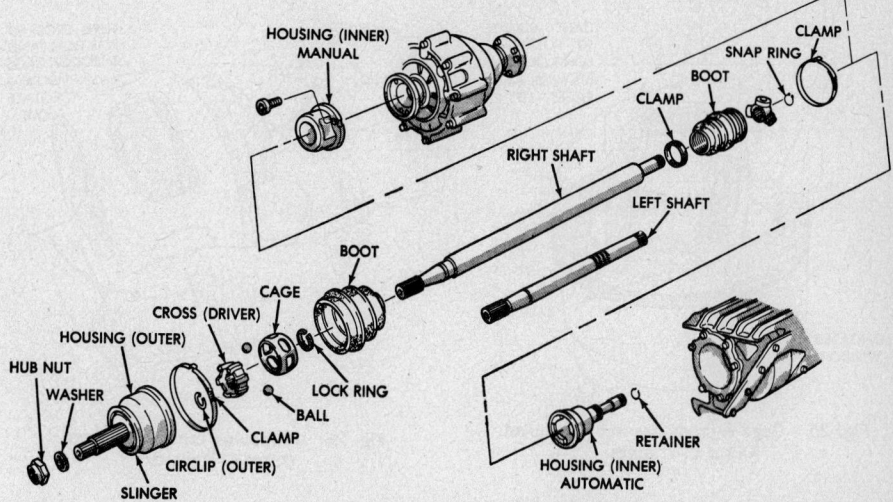

Fig. 18   Driveshaft components

fill C/V joint housing with lubricant, P/N 4131389 or equivalent.

2. Clean grease from joint housing, face, screw holes and transaxle drive flange prior to installation.

3. Support assembly vertically with inner housing upward.

NOTE: Do not move inner joint in or out during reassembly to drive flange since this movement can force the lubricant from the joint.

4. Position inner housing to drive flange and rotate assembly upward. Locate inner housing in drive flange. Support the outer end of driveshaft, Fig. 13. Do not permit assembly to hang.

5. Secure inner C/V joint to drive flange

with new allen head screws. Then, using tool L-4550 or equivalent, torque the six screws to 220 inch lbs. (25 Nm).

NOTE: Failure to properly torque screws may result in failure during vehicle operation.

6. Push knuckle/hub assembly out and

install splined outer C/V joint shaft into hub.

7. Install knuckle assembly on ball joint stud. Install and torque clamp bolt to 50 ft. lbs. (68 Nm).

8. Install and torque hub nut to 200 ft. lbs. (271 Nm). Stake hub nut as shown in Fig. 8.

9. If, after attaching driveshaft assembly in the vehicle the inboard boot appears

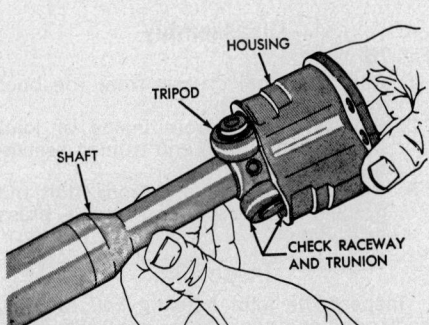

Fig. 19   Removing 3-ball tripod, housing & shaft assembly. Inner C/V joints

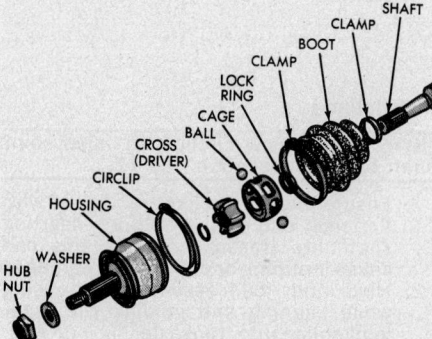

Fig. 21   Outer C/V joint disassembled

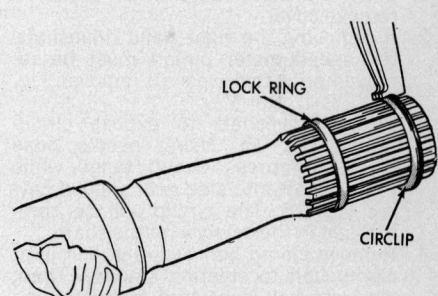

Fig. 23   Circlip removal. Outer C/V joints

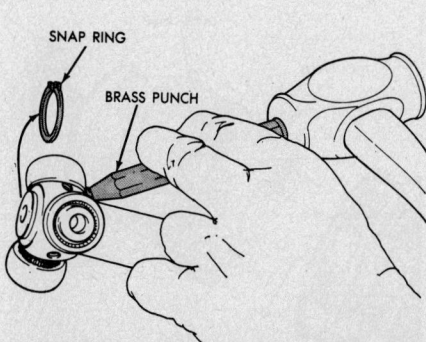

Fig. 20   Remove snap ring & tripod. Inner C/V joints

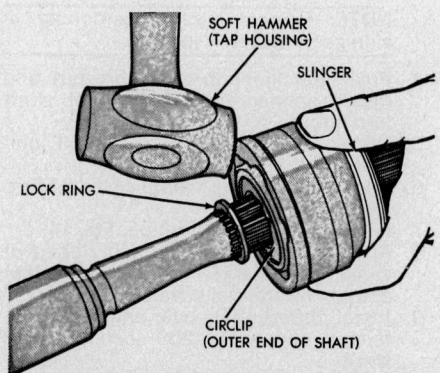

Fig. 22   Removing joint from shaft. Outer C/V joints

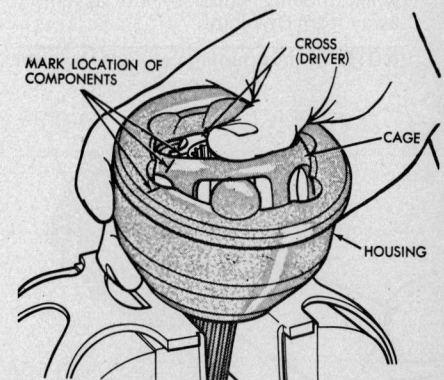

Fig. 24   Ball removal. Outer C/V joints

1-433

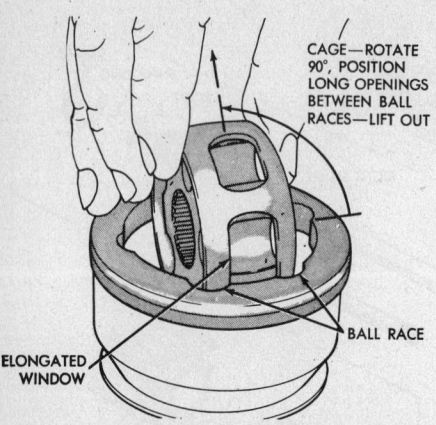

Fig. 25 Cage & cross assembly removal. Outer C/V joints

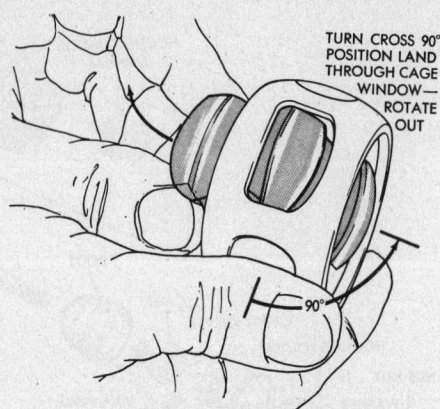

Fig. 26 Removing cross from cage. Outer C/V joints

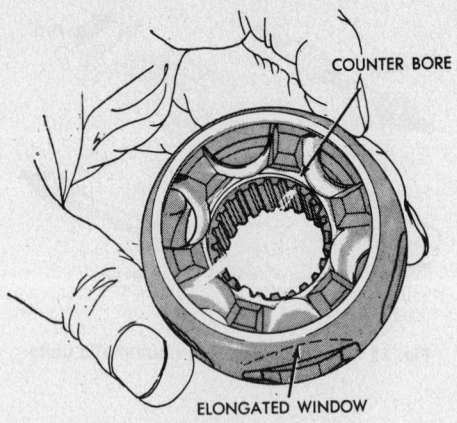

Fig. 27 Cage & cross assembly. Outer C/V joints

collapsed or deformed, vent the inner boot by inserting a round tipped, small diameter rod between the boot and shaft. As venting occurs, the boot will return to the normal shape.

Automatic Driveshafts

Removal

NOTE: The inboard C/V joints have stub shafts splined into the differential side gears and are retained with circlips. The circlip "Tangs" are located on a machined surface on the inner end of the stub shafts and are removed and installed with the shaft.

1. Drain transaxle differential unit and remove cover.
2. If removing the right hand driveshaft, the speedometer pinion must be removed prior to driveshaft removal, Fig. 14.
3. Rotate driveshaft to expose circlip tangs, Fig. 15. Using needle nose pliers, compress circlip tangs while prying shaft into side gear splined cavity, Fig. 16. The circlip will be compressed in the cavity with the shaft.
4. Remove clamp bolt securing ball joint clamp bolt to steering knuckle. Then, separate ball joint stud from steering knuckle. Do not damage ball joint or C/V joint boots.
5. Separate outer C/V joint splined shaft from hub by holding C/V housing while moving knuckle/hub assembly away from C/V joint.

NOTE: Do not damage slinger on outer

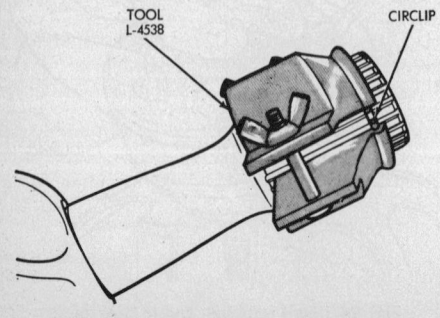

Fig. 28 Compressing circlip. Outer C/V joints

C/V joint. Do not attempt to remove, repair or replace.

6. Support assembly at C/V joint housings and remove by pulling outward on the inner C/V joint housing. Do not pull on the shaft.

NOTE: If removing left hand driveshaft assembly, the removal may be aided by inserting a screwdriver blade between the differential pinion shaft and carefully prying against the end face of stub.

7. Remove driveshaft assembly from vehicle.

Installation

NOTE: Install new circlips on inner joint shaft before installation, Fig. 17.

1. Ensure tang on circlips are aligned with flattened end of shaft before inserting shaft into transaxle. If not, this can cause jamming or component damage.
2. Hold inner joint assembly at housing while aligning and guiding the inner joint spline into transaxle.
3. While holding the inner joint housing, quickly thrust the shaft into the differential. This will complete the lock-up of the circlip on the axle side gear.

NOTE: Inspect circlip positioning in side gears to verify lock-up.

4. Push knuckle/hub assembly out and install splined outer C/V joint shaft into hub.
5. Install knuckle assembly on ball joint stud.
6. Install and torque clamp bolt to 50 ft. lbs. (68 Nm).
7. Install speedometer pinion, Fig. 14.
8. Apply a $\frac{1}{8}$ inch by $\frac{1}{8}$ inch ribbon of gasket material (RTV sealer) to gasket area of differential cover.
9. Install differential cover and torque retaining screws to 250 inch lbs. (28 Nm).
10. Fill differential to bottom of filler plug hole with Dexron automatic transmission fluid.
11. Install and torque hub nut to 200 ft.

lbs. (271 Nm). Stake nut as shown in Fig. 8.
12. If, after attaching driveshaft assembly in vehicle the inboard boot appears collapsed or deformed, vent the inner boot by inserting a round tipped, small diameter rod between the boot and shaft. As venting occurs, the boot will return to the normal shape.

INNER CONSTANT VELOCITY JOINT SERVICE

Disassembly

Fig. 18

1. Cut the metal clamps from the boot and discard boot.
2. Remove grease from inside of joint housing and 3-ball and trunion assembly, Fig. 19.
3. Remove retaining rings from shaft-end groove, then the tripod with a brass drift, Fig. 20.

Inspection

Inspect the joint housing ball raceway and tripod components for excessive wear. Replace if necessary.

Assembly

Fig. 18

1. To install new boot, slide small rubber

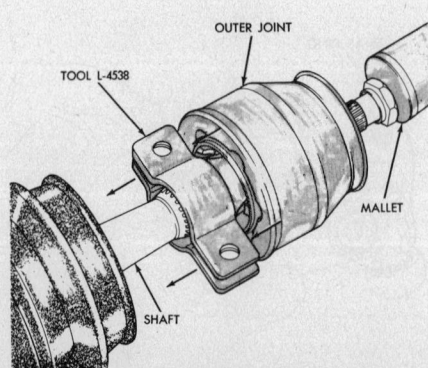

Fig. 29 Positioning joint into shaft splined. Outer C/V joints

clamp onto shaft, then the small end of boot over the shaft.

NOTE: On tubular shafts, position the boot lip face in line with the mark on the shaft outside diameter. On solid shafts, position the small boot end in the machined groove.

2. Clamp the small boot end by placing the rubber clamp over the boot groove.
3. Install the tripod on the shaft with the non-chamfered face of the tripod body facing the shaft retainer groove.
4. Install the retaining ring in the groove to lock the tripod assembly on the shaft.
5. Distribute two packets of grease in the boot. The packets of proper lubricant are provided in the boot joint kits.
6. On manual driveshafts, install the joint housing over the tripod and position the large end of boot in the groove on the housing. Two additional packets of grease are to be added after the boot is secured to the housing.
7. On automatic driveshafts, position housing over tripod and position boot over housing groove. One additional packet of grease is to be added after securing boot to housing.
8. On all driveshafts, install large metal clamp on boot, ensuring that the boot is properly located on the shaft and is not twisted.
9. Install the clamp tags in the slots and tighten clamp by hand.
10. Clamp bridge with tool C-4124 and squeeze to complete tightening the clamp. Do not cut through the clamp bridge and/or damage the boot.
11. On manual driveshafts, distribute two additional packets of grease in the joint housing. First push forward gently on the housing to provide space to accommodate volume of grease required.

OUTER CONSTANT VELOCITY JOINT SERVICE

Disassembly

Figs. 18 & 21

1. Cut boot clamps from boot and discard boot and clamps.
2. Clean grease from joint.
3. Support shaft in a soft jawed vise, support the outer joint and tap with a mallet to dislodge joint from internal circlip installed in a groove at the outer end of the shaft, Fig. 22. Do not remove slinger from housing.
4. Remove circlip from shaft groove and discard, Fig. 23.
5. Unless the shaft requires replacement, do not remove the heavy lock ring from the shaft, Fig. 23.
6. If the constant velocity joint was operating satisfactorily and the grease

does not appear contaminated, proceed to "Assembly" procedure, Step 7.
7. If the constant velocity joint is noisy or badly worn, replace entire unit. The repair kit will include boot, clamps, circlip and lubricant. Clean and inspect the joint outlined in the following steps.
8. Clean surplus grease and mark relative position of inner cross, cage and housing with a dab of paint.
9. Hold joint vertically in a soft jawed vise.
10. Press downward on one side of the inner race to tilt cage and remove ball from opposite side, Fig. 24. If joint is tight, use a hammer and a brass drift to tap inner race. Do not strike the cage. Repeat this step until all six balls are removed. A screwdriver may be used to pry the balls loose.
11. Tilt the cage assembly vertically and position the two opposing, enlongated cage windows in area between ball grooves. Remove cage and inner race assembly by pulling upward from the housing, Fig. 25.
12. Rotate inner cross 90 degrees to cage and align one of the race spherical lands with an enlongated cage window. Raise land into cage window and remove inner race by swinging outward, Fig. 26.

Inspection

1. Check housing ball races for excessive wear.
2. Check splined shaft and nut threads for damage.
3. Inspect the balls for pitting, cracks, scouring and wear. Dulling of the surface is normal.
4. Inspect cage for excessive wear on inner and outer spherical surfaces, heavy brinelling of cage, window cracks and chipping.
5. Inspect inner race (Cross) for excessive wear or scouring of ball races.
6. If any of the defects listed in Steps 1 through 5, are found, replace the C/V assembly as a unit.

NOTE: Polished areas in races (Cross and housing) and on cage spheres are normal and does not indicate a need for joint replacement unless they are suspected of causing noise and vibration.

Assembly

Figs. 18 & 21

1. Lightly lubricate all components before assembling joint.
2. Align parts according to paint markings.
3. Insert one inner race (Cross) lands into an elongated cage window and feed race into cage. Pivot cross 90 degrees to complete cage assembly.

4. Align opposite elongated cage windows with housing land and insert cage assembly into housing. Pivot cage 90 degrees to complete installation.

NOTE: When properly assembled, the curved side of the elongated cage windows and the inner cross counterbore should face outward from the joint, Fig. 27.

5. Apply lubricant to ball races between all sides of ball grooves.
6. Insert balls into raceway by tilting cage and inner race assembly. Ensure that locking ring is seated in the groove.
7. To install new boot, slide small metal clamp over lock ring and shaft.
8. Slide end of boot over lock ring and shaft, then position in machined groove.
9. Place small metal clamp over boot groove. Locate clamp tags in slots and hand tighten. Clamp bridge with tool C-4124 and squeeze to complete tightening.
10. Insert new circlip in shaft groove. Do not expand or twist circlip during assembly.
11. Position tool L-4538 on shaft splines with the tapered end outboard and compress circlip, Fig. 28. Ensure that sufficient spline area is left ahead of the tool to provide entry of outer joint onto shaft, Fig. 29.
12. Place outer joint on splined end, engage splines and rap with a mallet, allowing tool to slide along with the joint.
13. Remove too and check that circlip is properly seated by attempting to pull joint from shaft.
14. Place large end of boot over joint housing, ensuring that boot is not twisted.
15. Place large metal clamp over boot and locate clamp tags in slots, hand tightening the clamp.
16. Clamp bridge with tool L-4124 and squeeze to complete tightening. Do not cut through clamp bridge and/or damage boot.

RACK & PINION STEERING GEAR, REPLACE

1. Raise and support vehicle, then remove front wheels.
2. Remove tie rod ends with a suitable puller.
3. Remove splash shields and boot seal shields.
4. Drive out lower roll pin attaching pinion shaft to lower universal joint.
5. On power steering units, disconnect hoses from steering gear.
6. On all models, remove bolts attaching steering gear to front suspension crossmember. Loosen crossmember from vehicle frame.
7. Remove steering gear from left side of vehicle.
8. Reverse procedure to install.

FORD & MERCURY
Compact & Intermediate Models

NOTE: The 1974-79 Ford Mustang, Pinto, Mercury Bobcat and 1979 Capri are located elsewhere in this manual.

INDEX OF SERVICE OPERATIONS

ENGINE & SERIAL NUMBER LOCATION: Vehicle warranty plate on rear face of left front door.

ENGINE IDENTIFICATION: Engine code is last letter in serial number on vehicle warranty plate.

Year	Engine	Engine Code
1974	6-200	T
	6-250	L
	8-302	F
	8-351①	H
	8-351②	Q
	8-351③	R
	8-400	S
	8-460	A
	8-460④	C
1975–77	6-200	T
	6-250	L
	8-302	F

Year	Engine	Engine Code
	8-351	H
	8-400	S
	8-460	A
	8-460④	C
1978	8-400	S
1978–79	4-140	Y
	6-200	T
	6-250	L
	8-302	F
	8-351	H

①—Two barrel carburetor.
②—Four barrel carburetor.
③—High Performance.
④—Police Interceptor.

GRILLE IDENTIFICATION

1974 Comet

1974 Cougar

1974-76 Elite

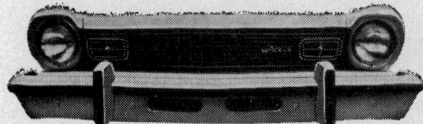
1974-75 Maverick

1974 Montego

1974 Torino

1974-75 Gran Torino

1975-77 Granada

1975 Comet

1975-76 Cougar

1975-76 Montego

1975-77 Monarch

GRILLE IDENTIFICATION—Continued

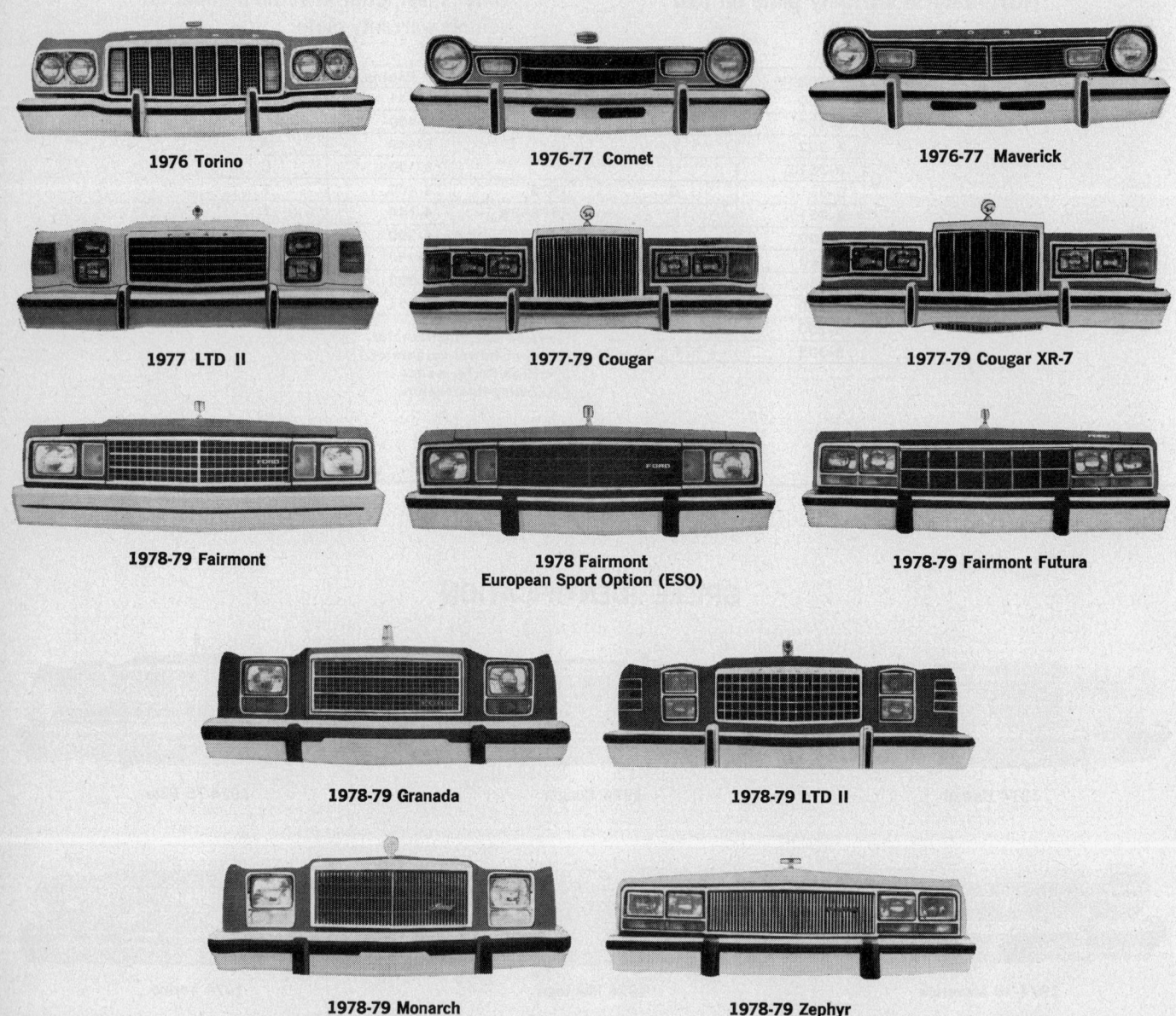

1976 Torino

1976-77 Comet

1976-77 Maverick

1977 LTD II

1977-79 Cougar

1977-79 Cougar XR-7

1978-79 Fairmont

1978 Fairmont
European Sport Option (ESO)

1978-79 Fairmont Futura

1978-79 Granada

1978-79 LTD II

1978-79 Monarch

1978-79 Zephyr

GENERAL ENGINE SPECIFICATIONS

Year	Engine	Car-buretor	Bore and Stroke	Piston Dis-place-ment, Cubic Inches	Com-pres-sion Ratio	Maximum Brake H.P. @ R.P.M.	Maximum Torque Lbs. Ft. @ R.P.M.	Normal Oil Pressure Pounds
1974	84 Horsepower②.............6-200	1 Barrel	3.68 x 3.13	200	8.0	84 @ 3800	150 @ 1800	30–50
	91 Horsepower②.............6-250	1 Barrel	3.68 x 3.91	250	8.0	91 @ 3200	190 @ 1600	40–60
	140 Horsepower②...........V8-302	2 Barrel	4.00 x 3.00	302	8.0	140 @ 3800	230 @ 2600	40–60
	162 Horsepower②...........V8-351	2 Barrel	4.00 x 3.50	351	8.0	162 @ 4000	275 @ 2200	40–65
	163 Horsepower②...........V8-351	2 Barrel	4.00 x 3.50	351	8.0	163 @ 4200	278 @ 2000	45–75
	255 Horsepower②...........V8-351	4 Barrel	4.00 x 3.50	351	8.0	255 @ 5600	290 @ 3400	45–75
	170 Horsepower②...........V8-400	2 Barrel	4.00 x 4.00	400	8.0	170 @ 3400	330 @ 2000	45–75
	195 Horsepower②...........V8-460	4 Barrel	4.36 x 3.85	460	8.0	195 @ 3800	335 @ 2600	35–65
	220 Horsepower②③........V8-460	4 Barrel	4.36 x 3.85	460	8.0	220 @ 4000	355 @ 2600	35–65
	260 Horsepower②...........V8-460	4 Barrel	4.36 x 3.85	460	8.0	260 @ 4400	355 @ 2700	35–65
1975	70 Horsepower②.............6-200	1 Barrel	3.68 x 3.13	200	8.3	—	—	30–50
	70 Horsepower②⑤...........6-250	1 Barrel	3.68 x 3.91	250	8.0	70 @ 2800	175 @ 1400	40–60
	72 Horsepower②④...........6-250	1 Barrel	3.68 x 3.91	250	8.0	72 @ 2900	180 @ 1400	40–60
	122 Horsepower②⑥.........V8-302	2 Barrel	4.00 x 3.00	302	8.0	122 @ 3800⑥	208 @ 1800⑦	40–60
	129 Horsepower②⑧.........V8-302	2 Barrel	4.00 x 3.00	302	8.0	129 @ 3800⑧	220 @ 1800⑨	40–60
	148 Horsepower②④㉒.......V8-351	2 Barrel	4.00 x 3.50	351	8.0	148 @ 3800	243 @ 2400	50–75
	150 Horsepower②④㉒.......V8-351	2 Barrel	4.00 x 3.50	351	8.0	150 @ 3800	244 @ 2800	50–75
	143 Horsepower②⑩㉑.......V8-351	2 Barrel	4.00 x 3.50	351	8.1	143 @ 3600⑩	255 @ 2200⑪	40–65
	154 Horsepower②⑩㉑.......V8-351	2 Barrel	4.00 x 3.50	351	8.1	154 @ 3800⑫	268 @ 2200	40–65
	144 Horsepower②⑤.........V8-400	2 Barrel	4.00 x 4.00	400	8.0	144 @ 3600	255 @ 2200	50–65
	158 Horsepower②④.........V8-400	2 Barrel	4.00 x 4.00	400	8.0	158 @ 4000	276 @ 2000	50–65
	216 Horsepower②④.........V8-460	4 Barrel	4.36 x 3.85	460	8.0	216 @ 4000	366 @ 2600	40–65
	217 Horsepower②⑤.........V8-460	4 Barrel	4.36 x 3.85	460	8.0	217 @ 4000	365 @ 2600	40–65
1976	78 Horsepower②④⑬.........6-200	1 Barrel	3.68 x 3.13	200	8.3	78 @ 3300	152 @ 1600	30–50
	81 Horsepower②④⑭.........6-200	1 Barrel	3.68 x 3.13	200	8.3	81 @ 3400	151 @ 1700	30–50
	76 Horsepower②⑬⑮.........6-250	1 Barrel	3.68 x 3.91	250	8.0	76 @ 3000	179 @ 1300	40–60
	78 Horsepower②⑬⑯.........6-250	1 Barrel	3.68 x 3.91	250	8.0	78 @ 3000	187 @ 1200	40–60
	78 Horsepower②⑬⑰.........6-250	1 Barrel	3.68 x 3.91	250	8.0	78 @ 3000	183 @ 1400	40–60
	81 Horsepower②⑬⑱.........6-250	1 Barrel	3.68 x 3.91	250	8.0	81 @ 3000	192 @ 1200	40–60
	87 Horsepower②⑭⑱.........6-250	1 Barrel	3.68 x 3.91	250	8.0	87 @ 3000	187 @ 1900	40–60
	90 Horsepower②⑭⑱.........6-250	1 Barrel	3.68 x 3.91	250	8.0	90 @ 3000	190 @ 2000	40–60
	130 Horsepower②⑬⑱.......V8-302	2 Barrel	4.00 x 3.00	302	8.0	130 @ 3600	238 @ 1600	40–60
	133 Horsepower②⑬⑯.......V8-302	2 Barrel	4.00 x 3.00	302	8.0	133 @ 3600	243 @ 1800	40–60
	134 Horsepower②⑭⑯.......V8-302	2 Barrel	4.00 x 3.00	302	8.0	134 @ 3600	242 @ 2000	40–60
	137 Horsepower②⑬⑲.......V8-302	2 Barrel	4.00 x 3.00	302	8.0	137 @ 3600	⑳	40–60
	138 Horsepower②⑭⑯.......V8-302	2 Barrel	4.00 x 3.00	302	8.0	138 @ 3600	245 @ 2000	40–60
	140 Horsepower②⑯㉑.......V8-351	2 Barrel	4.00 x 3.50	351	8.0	140 @ 3400	276 @ 1600	45–65
	143 Horsepower②⑯㉑.......V8-351	2 Barrel	4.00 x 3.50	351	8.0	143 @ 3200	285 @ 1600	46–65
	152 Horsepower②㉒.........V8-351	2 Barrel	4.00 x 3.50	351	8.0	152 @ 3800	274 @ 1600	45–75
	154 Horsepower②⑬㉓.......V8-351	2 Barrel	4.00 x 3.50	351	8.0	154 @ 3400	286 @ 1800	45–65
	180 Horsepower②...........V8-400	2 Barrel	4.00 x 4.00	400	8.0	180 @ 3800	336 @ 1800	45–75
	202 Horsepower②...........V8-460	4 Barrel	4.36 x 3.85	460	8.0	202 @ 3800	352 @ 1600	35–65
1977	96 Horsepower②④⑭.........6-200	1 Barrel	3.68 x 3.13	200	8.5	96 @ 4400	151 @ 2000	30–50
	97 Horsepower②④⑬.........6-200	1 Barrel	3.68 x 3.13	200	8.5	97 @ 4400	153 @ 2000	30–50
	86 Horsepower②⑤⑬.........6-250	1 Barrel	3.68 x 3.91	250	8.1	86 @ 3000	185 @ 1800	40–60
	98 Horsepower②④⑬.........6-250	1 Barrel	3.68 x 3.91	250	8.1	98 @ 3600	190 @ 1400	40–60
	98 Horsepower②④⑭.........6-250	1 Barrel	3.68 x 3.91	250	8.1	98 @ 3400	182 @ 1800	40–60
	122 Horsepower②⑤⑬.......V8-302	2 Barrel	4.00 x 3.00	302	8.1	122 @ 3400	222 @ 1400	40–65
	122 Horsepower②④㉔.......V8-302	2 Barrel	4.00 x 3.00	302	8.4	122 @ 3200	237 @ 1600	40–65
	130 Horsepower②⑬㉕.......V8-302	2 Barrel	4.00 x 3.00	302	8.4	130 @ 3400	243 @ 1800	40–65
	134 Horsepower②⑬⑯.......V8-302	2 Barrel	4.00 x 3.00	302	8.4	134 @ 3600	245 @ 1600	40–65
	137 Horsepower②⑬⑯.......V8-302	2 Barrel	4.00 x 3.00	302	8.4	137 @ 3600	245 @ 1600	40–65
	135 Horsepower②⑬⑯㉑.....V8-351	2 Barrel	4.00 x 3.50	351	8.3	135 @ 3200	275 @ 1600	40–65
	149 Horsepower②④⑬㉑㉖...V8-351	2 Barrel	4.00 x 3.50	351	8.3	149 @ 3200	291 @ 1600	40–65

Continued

GENERAL ENGINE SPECIFICATIONS—Continued

Year	Engine	Carburetor	Bore and Stroke	Piston Displacement, Cubic Inches	Compression Ratio	Maximum Brake H.P. @ R.P.M.	Maximum Torque Lbs. Ft. @ R.P.M.	Normal Oil Pressure Pounds
1977	161 Horsepower②④⑬㉒㉕.....V8-351	2 Barrel	4.00 x 3.50	351	8.0	161 @ 3600	285 @ 1800	50–75
	161 Horsepower②⑤⑬㉒㉕.....V8-351	2 Barrel	4.00 x 3.50	351	8.0	161 @ 3600	286 @ 1800	50–75
	173 Horsepower②④⑬㉕.......V8-400	2 Barrel	4.00 x 4.00	400	8.0	173 @ 3800	326 @ 1600	50–75
	168 Horsepower②⑤⑬㉕.......V8-400	2 Barrel	4.00 x 4.00	400	8.0	168 @ 3800	323 @ 1600	50–75
1978	88 Horsepower②.............4-140	2 Barrel	3.781 x 3.126	140	9.0	88 @ 4800	118 @ 2800	50
	85 Horsepower②.............6-200	1 Barrel	3.68 x 3.13	200	8.5	85 @ 3600	250 @ 1600	30–50
	97 Horsepower②.............6-250	1 Barrel	3.68 x 3.91	250	8.5	97 @ 3200	210 @ 1400	40–60
	133 Horsepower②⑤..........V8-302	2 Barrel	4.00 x 3.00	302	8.1	133 @ 3600	243 @ 1600	40–60
	134 Horsepower②④.........V8-302	2 Barrel	4.00 x 3.00	302	8.4	134 @ 3400	248 @ 1600	40–60
	139 Horsepower②④.........V8-302	2 Barrel	4.00 x 3.00	302	8.4	139 @ 3600	250 @ 1600	40–60
	144 Horsepower②㉑.........V8-351	2 Barrel	4.00 x 3.50	351	8.3	144 @ 3200	277 @ 1600	40–60
	152 Horsepower②㉒.........V8-351	2 Barrel	4.00 x 3.50	351	8 0	152 @ 3600	278 @ 1800	50–75
	166 Horsepower②..........V8-400	2 Barrel	4.00 x 4.00	400	8.0	166 @ 3800	319 @ 1800	50–75
1979	Horsepower②.............4-140	2 Barrel	3.781 x 3.126	140				
	Horsepower②.............6-200	1 Barrel	3.68 x 3.13	200				
	Horsepower②.............6-250	1 Barrel	3.68 x 3.91	250				
	Horsepower②...........V8-302	2 Barrel	4.00 x 3.00	302				
	Horsepower②㉑.........V8-351	2 Barrel	4.00 x 3.50	351				
	Horsepower②㉒.........V8-351	2 Barrel	4.00 x 3.50	351				

②—Ratings are NET—as installed in the vehicle.
③—Cougar XR-7 requires A/C in California.
④—Except California.
⑤—California.
⑥—Comet & Maverick, California vehicles rated at 115 H.P. @ 3600 RPM.
⑦—California vehicles rated at 203 @ 1400 RPM.
⑧—Granada & Monarch, California vehicles rated at 115 H.P. @ 3600 RPM.
⑨—California vehicles rated at 203 @ 1800 RPM.
⑩—Granada, Monarch, Torino & Elite, California vehicles rated at 153 H.P. @ 3400 RPM.
⑪—California vehicles rated at 270 @ 2400 RPM.
⑫—Cougar & Montego, not available in California.
⑬—With auto. trans.
⑭—With manual trans.
⑮—Calif. Granada and Monarch.
⑯—Exc. Calif. Granada and Monarch.
⑰—Calif. Comet and Maverick.
⑱—Exc. Calif. Comet and Maverick.
⑲—All Comet and Maverick.
⑳—Exc. Calif.; 246 @ 1800. Calif.; 247 @ 1800.
㉑—Windsor engine.
㉒—Modified engine.
㉓—Exc. Calif. Montego and Torino.
㉔—Granada and Monarch man. trans.
㉕—LTD II, Cougar, XR-7 (sedan).

TUNE UP SPECIFICATIONS

The following specifications are published from the latest information available. This data should be used only in the absence of a decal affixed in the engine compartment.

★When using a timing light, disconnect vacuum hose or tube at distributor and plug opening in hose or tube so idle speed will not be affected.

●When checking compression, lowest cylinder must be within 75% of the highest.

▲Before removing wires from distributor cap, determine location of the No. 1 wire in cap, as distributor position may have been altered from that shown at the end of this chart.

Year	Spark Plug Type	Gap Inch	Point Gap Inch	Dwell Angle Deg.	Firing Order Fig.▲	Timing BTDC①	Mark Fig.	Hot Idle Speed Std. Trans.	Hot Idle Speed Auto. Trans.②	Air Fuel Ratio Std. Trans.	Air Fuel Ratio Auto. Trans.	Idle "CO" % Std. Trans.	Idle "CO" % Auto. Trans.
1974													
6-200	BRF-82	.034	.025	33	D	6°	A	750	550D	—	—	—	—
6-200⑭	BRF-82	.034	—	—	D	6°	A	750	550D	—	—	—	—
6-250	BRF-82	.034	.025	33	D	6°	A	600	600D	—	—	—	—
6-250⑭	BRF-82	.034	—	—	D	6°	A	600	600D	—	—	—	—
V8-302	BRF-42	.034	.017	26–30	E	6°	B	850	575D	—	—	—	.5
V8-302⑭	BRF-42	.034	—	—	E	6°	B	850	575D	—	—	—	.5
V8-351⑦㉓	BRF-42	.034	.017	26–30	F	6°	B	—	600D	—	—	—	.4
V8-351⑦㉓⑭	BRF-42	.034	—	—	F	6°	B	—	600D	—	—	—	.4
V8-351⑦㉒	ARF-42	.044	.017	26–30	F	10°	B	—	650D	—	—	—	.5
V8-351⑦㉒⑭	ARF-42	.044	—	—	F	10°	B	—	650D	—	—	—	.5
V8-351⑧	ARF-42	.034	㉑	26–31	F	⑳	B	900	800D	—	—	—	—
V8-351⑧⑭	ARF-42	.034	—	—	F	⑳	B	900	800D	—	—	—	—
V8-400⑭	ARF-42	.044	—	—	F	⑩	B	—	625D	—	—	—	—
V8-460⑭	ARF-52	.054	—	—	E	⑱	B	—	650D	—	—	—	.25
1975													
6-200⑭	BRF-82	.044	—	—	D	6°	A	750	600D	—	—	—	—
6-250⑭	BRF-82	.044	—	—	G	6°	A	750	600D	—	—	—	—
V8-302⑭	ARF-42	.044	—	—	E	6°	B	900	650D	—	—	—	—
V8-351④⑭	ARF-42	.044	—	—	F	12°	B	—	650D	—	—	—	—
V8-351⑭㉓	ARF-42	.044	—	—	F	12°	B	—	650D	—	—	—	—
V8-400⑭	ARF-42	.044	—	—	F	12°	B	—	650D	—	—	—	—
V8-460⑭	ARF-52	.044	—	—	E	14°	B	—	650D	—	—	—	—
1976													
6-200⑭	BRF-82	.044	—	—	D	6°	A	800	650D	—	—	—	—
6-250⑭㉚	BRF-82	.044	—	—	G	㉙	A	850	600D	—	—	—	—
6-250⑭㉛	BRF-82	.044	—	—	G	㉜	A	850	600D	—	—	—	—
V8-302⑭⑯㉛㉝	ARF-42	.044	—	—	E	4°	B	—	700D	—	—	—	—
V8-302⑭㉚㉝	ARF-42	.044	—	—	E	㉙	B	750	650D	—	—	—	—
V8-302⑭⑰㉚	ARF-42	.044	—	—	E	⑱	B	750	650D	—	—	—	—
V8-302⑭⑯⑰㉛	ARF-42	.044	—	—	E	8°	B	—	700D	—	—	—	—
V8-351⑭㉓	ARF-42	.044	—	—	F	10°	B	—	650D	—	—	—	—
V8-351④⑭	ARF-42	.044	—	—	F	8°	B	—	650D	—	—	—	—
V8-400⑭㉚	ARF-42	.044	—	—	F	㉔	B	—	650D	—	—	—	—
V8-400⑭㉖㉛	ARF-42	.044	—	—	F	10°	B	—	625D	—	—	—	—
V8-400⑭㉖㉛	ARF-42	.044	—	—	F	12°	B	—	625D	—	—	—	—
V8-460⑭	ARF-52	.044	—	—	E	㉗㉘	B	—	650D	—	—	—	—

Continued

TUNE UP SPECIFICATIONS—Continued

The following specifications are published from the latest information available. This data should be used only in the absence of a decal affixed in the engine compartment.

★When using a timing light, disconnect vacuum hose or tube at distributor and plug opening in hose or tube so idle speed will not be affected.

●When checking compression, lowest cylinder must be within 75% of the highest.

▲Before removing wires from distributor cap, determine location of the No. 1 wire in cap, as distributor position may have been altered from that shown at the end of this chart.

| Year | Spark Plug | | Distributor | | Ignition Timing ★ | | | Carb. Adjustments | | | | | |
| | | | | | | | | Hot Idle Speed | | Air Fuel Ratio | | Idle "CO" % | |
	Type	Gap Inch	Point Gap Inch	Dwell Angle Deg.	Firing Order Fig. ▲	Timing BTDC ①	Mark Fig.	Std. Trans.	Auto. Trans. ②	Std. Trans.	Auto. Trans.	Std. Trans.	Auto. Trans.
1977													
6-200	BRF-82	.050	—	—	L	6°	M	800	—	—	—	—	—
6-250⑤⑰	BRF-82	.050	—	—	L	4°	A	850	—	—	—	—	—
6-250⑱㉚	BRF-82	.050	—	—	L	6°	A	—	⑥	—	—	—	—
6-250⑯㉛	BRF-82	.050	—	—	L	8°	A	—	600	—	—	—	—
6-250⑤㉝	BRF-82	.050	—	—	L	⑥	A	⑥	—	—	—	—	—
V8-302㉛	ARF-52-6	.060	—	—	J	12°	B	—	600	—	—	—	—
V8-302㉚	⑥	⑥	—	—	J	⑥	B	⑥	⑥	—	—	—	—
V8-351㉝	ARF-52	.050	—	—	K	4°	B	—	625	—	—	—	—
V8-351⑪㉓	ARF-52	.050	—	—	K	⑥	B	—	625	—	—	—	—
V8-351④	ARF-52	.050	—	—	K	⑥	B	—	650	—	—	—	—
V8-400㉛	ARF-52-6	.060	—	—	K	⑥	B	—	⑥	—	—	—	—
V8-400㉚	ARF-52	.050	—	—	K	⑥	B	—	⑥	—	—	—	—
1978													
4-140⑭㉚	AWSF-42	.034	—	—	H	6°	I	850	—	—	—	—	—
4-140⑭㉛	AWSF-42	.034	—	—	H	㊳	I	850	800D	—	—	—	—
6-200⑭㉛	BSF-82	.050	—	—	L	6°	M	600	650D	—	—	—	—
6-200⑭㉞	BSF-82	.050	—	—	L	12°	M	600	650D	—	—	—	—
6-200⑬⑭	BSF-82	.050	—	—	L	10°	M	700	650D	—	—	—	—
6-250⑭㉚	BSF-82	.050	—	—	L	6°	A	—	600/700D㊱	—	—	—	—
6-250⑭㉛	BSF-82	.050	—	—	L	㊴	A	800	600/700D㊱	—	—	—	—
V8-302⑭㉛	ARF-52-6	.060	—	—	J	12°	B	—	600D	—	—	—	—
V8-302⑭㉞	ARF-52	.050	—	—	J	14°	B	—	650/725D㊱	—	—	—	—
V8-302⑭㉚㉝	ARF-52	.050	—	—	J	㊵	B	800	600/675D㊱	—	—	—	—
V8-302⑪⑭	ARF-52	.050	—	—	J	14°	B	—	600D	—	—	—	—
V8-302⑫⑭	ARF-52	.050	—	—	J	6°	B	—	600/675D㊱	—	—	—	—
V8-351⑭㉓	ARF-52	.050	—	—	K	14°	B	—	600/650D㊱	—	—	—	—
V8-351④⑭㉛	ASF-52	.050	—	—	K	16°	B	—	600/650D㊱	—	—	—	—
V8-351④⑭㉞	ASF-52	.050	—	—	K	12°	B	—	650D	—	—	—	—
V8-351④⑭㉚㊶	ASF-52	.050	—	—	K	⑨	B	—	600/675D㊱	—	—	—	—
V8-351③④⑭㉚	ASF-52	.050	—	—	K	14°	B	—	600/650D㊱	—	—	—	—
V8-400⑭㉞	ASF-52	.050	—	—	K	8°	B	—	650D	—	—	—	—
V8-400⑭㉛	ASF-52	.050	—	—	K	14°	B	—	600/675D㊱	—	—	—	—
V8-400⑭㉚	ASF-52	.050	—	—	K	⑲	B	—	600/675D㊱	—	—	—	—

Continued

TUNE UP SPECIFICATIONS—Continued

The following specifications are published from the latest information available. This
data should be used only in the absence of a decal affixed in the engine compartment.

★When using a timing light, disconnect vacuum hose or tube at distributor and plug opening in hose or tube so idle speed will not be affected.

●When checking compression, lowest cylinder must be within 75% of the highest.

▲Before removing wires from distributor cap, determine location of the No. 1 wire in cap, as distributor position may have been altered from that shown at the end of this chart.

Year	Spark Plug		Distributor		Ignition Timing★			Carb. Adjustments					
	Type	Gap Inch	Point Gap Inch	Dwell Angle Deg.	Firing Order Fig. ▲	Timing BTDC ①	Mark Fig.	Hot Idle Speed		Air Fuel Ratio		Idle "CO" %	
								Std. Trans.	Auto. Trans.②	Std. Trans.	Auto. Trans.	Std. Trans.	Auto. Trans.
1979													
4-140⑭	AWSF-42	.034	—	—	H	20°	I	—	800D	—	—	—	—
6-200⑫⑭⑯	BSF-82	.050	—	—	L	10°	M	—	650D	—	—	—	—
6-200⑤⑫⑭	BSF-82	.050	—	—	L	8°	M	700/850㊱	—	—	—	—	—
6-250⑭⑲㉝㊲	BSF-82	.050	—	—	L	10°	A	—	600D	—	—	—	—
6-250⑤⑭㉝	BSF-82	.050	—	—	L	4°	A	800	—	—	—	—	—
V8-302⑭	ASF-52	.050	—	—	J	8°	B	—	600/675㊱	—	—	—	—
V8-351⑭㉓	ASF-42	.050	—	—	K	15°	B	—	600/650㊱	—	—	—	—
V8-351④⑭	ASF-45	.050	—	—	K	12°	B	—	600/650㊱	—	—	—	—

① —BTDC: Before top dead center.
② —D: Drive.
③ —Engineless air pump.
④ —Modified Engine.
⑤ —With manual trans.
⑥ —Must refer to engine decal due to running production changes.
⑦ —With two barrel carburetor.
⑧ —With four barrel carburetor.
⑨ —Early production models, 12° BTDC; mid production models, 9° BTDC; late production models, 14° BTDC.
⑩ —Cougar 12°, all others 6°.
⑪ —LTD II & Cougar.
⑫ —Fairmont & Zephyr.
⑬ —Exc. Calif. & high altitude.
⑭ —Breakerless distributor.

⑮ —Cougar 14°, all others 10°.
⑯ —With auto. trans.
⑰ —Comet and Maverick.
⑱ —With auto. trans.; 8°. With manual trans.; 4°.
⑲ —Early production models, 14° BTDC; late production models, 13° BTDC.
⑳ —Manual trans. 16° BTDC, Auto. trans. 18° BTDC.
㉑ —Manual trans. .020, Auto. trans. .017.
㉒ —Cleveland engine.
㉓ —Windsor engine.
㉔ —Cougar; 10°. Elite, Montego, Torino; 12°.
㉕ —Cougar.
㉖ —Elite, Torino and Montego.
㉗ —In drive with service and parking brake applied.
㉘ —California and Police Interceptor; 14°. All

others; 10°.
㉙ —With auto. trans.; 6°. With manual trans.; 4°.
㉚ —Except Calif.
㉛ —California.
㉜ —With auto. trans.; 8°. With manual trans.; 6°.
㉝ —Granada and Monarch.
㉞ —High altitude.
㉟ —LTD II.
㊱ —High RPM is for A/C, A/C on.
㊲ —Less A/C.
㊳ —Manual trans., 6° BTDC; Auto. trans., 20° BTDC.
㊴ —Manual trans., 4° BTDC; Auto. trans., 14° BTDC.
㊵ —Manual trans., 12° BTDC; Auto. trans., 2° BTDC.
㊶ —Engine with air pump.

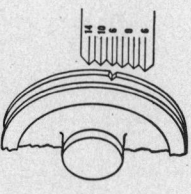

Fig. A

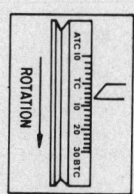

Fig. B

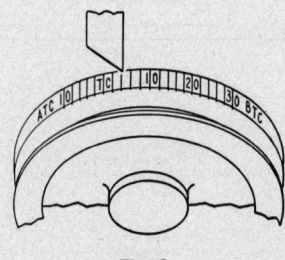

Fig. C

Continued

TUNE UP NOTES—Continued

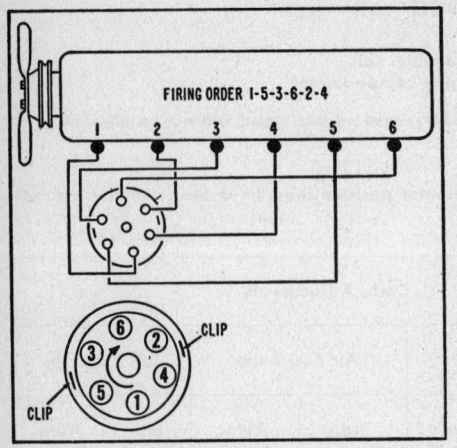

Fig. D

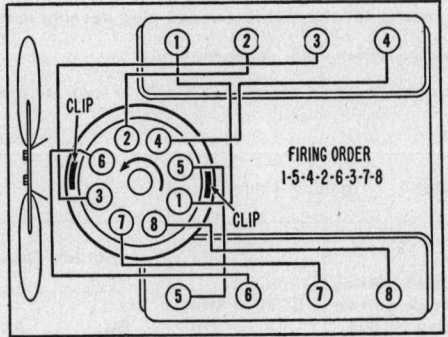

Fig. E

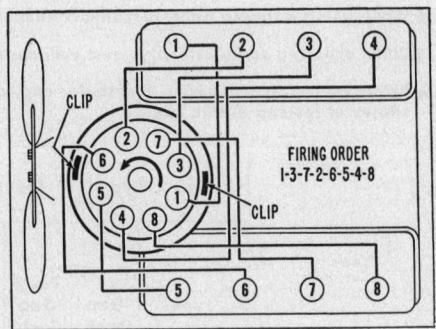

Fig. F

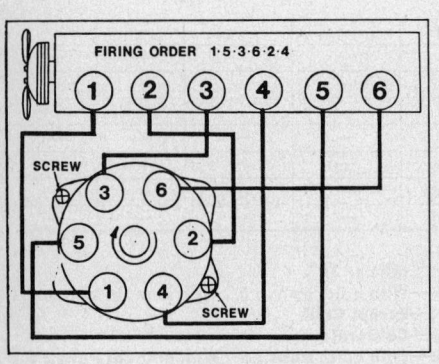

Fig. G

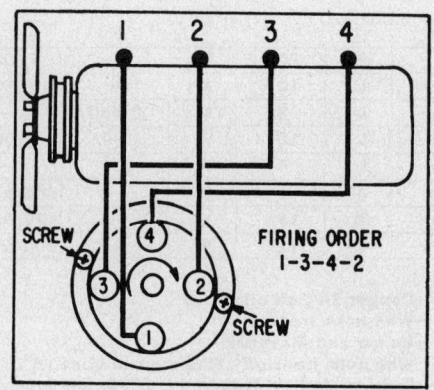

Fig. H

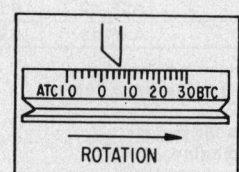

Fig. I

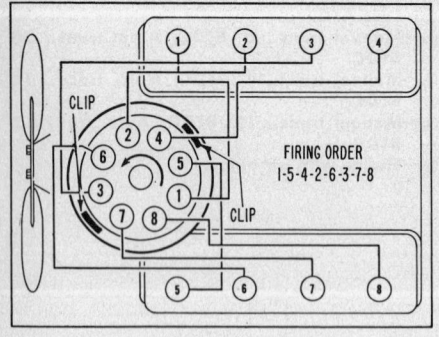

Fig. J

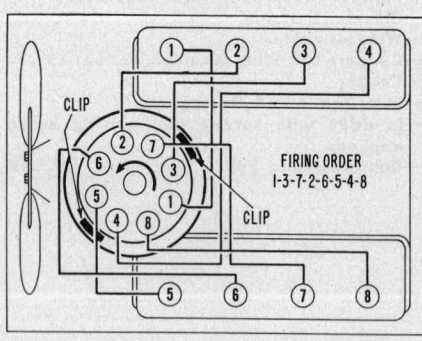

Fig. K

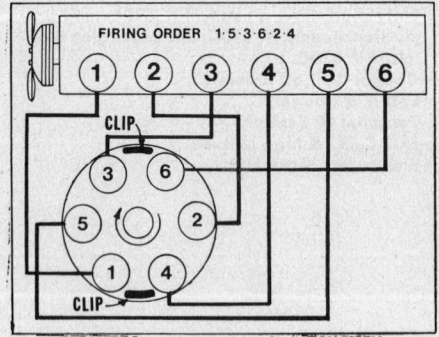

Fig. L

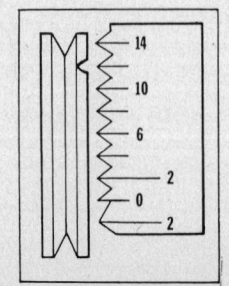

Fig. M

DISTRIBUTOR SPECIFICATIONS

★Note: If unit is checked on vehicle, double the RPM and degrees to get crankshaft figures.

Breaker arm spring tension—17–21.

Distributor Ident. No.①	Centrifugal Advance Degrees @ RPM of Distributor					Vacuum Advance		Distributor Retard
	Advance Starts	Intermediate Advance			Full Advance	Inches of Vacuum to Start Plunger	Max. Adv. Dist. Deg. @ Vacuum	Max. Retard Dist. Deg. @ Vacuum
1974								
D3AF-AA	0–1½ @ 500	4–6 @ 750	6–8¼ @ 1000	10–12½ @ 1500	16½ @ 2000	5	13¼ @ 20	—
D3BF-DA	0–1¼ @ 500	2½–4½ @ 750	5½–7½ @ 1000	8½–10½ @ 1500	12 @ 2000	5	11¼ @ 20	5–7 @ 20
D3DF-FA	0–1½ @ 500	1½–3½ @ 750	4½–6½ @ 1000	6½–9 @ 1500	9¼ @ 2000	5	9¼ @ 20	2–4 @ 20
D3DF-HA	0–1½ @ 500	3½–5½ @ 750	7½–9½ @ 1000	9½–11½ @ 1500	11¼ @ 2000	5	7¼ @ 20	—
D3DF-KA	0–1½ @ 500	4½–6½ @ 750	7½–9½ @ 1000	8½–11 @ 1500	11¼ @ 2000	5	7¼ @ 20	2–4 @ 20
D3OF-FA	0–1 @ 500	0–1½ @ 750	1–3 @ 1000	5½–8½ @ 1500	13 @ 2000	5	5¼ @ 20	5–7 @ 20
D3OF-GA	0–1 @ 500	0–1½ @ 750	1–3½ @ 1000	6½–8½ @ 1500	13½ @ 2000	5	5¼ @ 20	—
D3OF-HB	0–1½ @ 500	½–3 @ 750	2½–5 @ 1000	6½–9 @ 1500	13½ @ 2000	5	11¼ @ 20	—
D3OF-RA	0–1½ @ 500	3½–5½ @ 750	5½–7½ @ 1000	6½–8½ @ 1500	10 @ 2000	5	9¼ @ 20	2–4 @ 20
D3UF-EA	0–1¼ @ 500	2½–4½ @ 750	5½–7½ @ 1000	9–11 @ 1500	14½ @ 2000	5	9¼ @ 20	5–7 @ 20
D3ZF-GA	0–1 @ 500	0–2½ @ 750	2¼–4¼ @ 1000	5½–7½ @ 1500	11 @ 2000	5	12½ @ 20	—
D4AE-AA	0–½ @ 500	0–2 @ 750	2½–4½ @ 1000	5½–7½ @ 1500	11 @ 2000	5	12½ @ 20	—
D4AE-HA	0–1½ @ 500	5–7 @ 750	6–8 @ 1000	8–10½ @ 1500	12½ @ 2000	5	9½ @ 20	5–7 @ 20
D4DE-FA	0–1½ @ 500	4½–6½ @ 750	7½–9½ @ 1000	9–11 @ 1500	12½ @ 2000	5	7¼ @ 20	2–4 @ 20
D4DE-LA	0–1½ @ 500	4–6 @ 750	4½–6½ @ 1000	6–8 @ 1500	9½ @ 2000	5	9 @ 20	2–4 @ 20
D4DE-MA	0–½ @ 500	½–2½ @ 750	3½–5½ @ 1000	7½–9½ @ 1500	13½ @ 2000	5	11½ @ 20	—
D4DE-NA	0–1½ @ 500	3½–5½ @ 750	5½–7½ @ 1000	6½–8½ @ 1500	10 @ 2000	5	9¼ @ 20	2–4 @ 20
D4DE-RA	0–1½ @ 500	3½–5½ @ 750	5½–7½ @ 1000	6½–8½ @ 1500	10½ @ 2000	5	9¼ @ 20	2–4 @ 20
D4OE-CA	0–½ @ 500	0–1½ @ 750	2–4 @ 1000	5½–7½ @ 1500	10½ @ 2000	5	13½ @ 20	—
D4VE-CA	0–½ @ 500	0–½ @ 750	3–5 @ 1000	7–9 @ 1500	10½ @ 2000	5	11¼ @ 20	—
1975								
D3ZF-GA	0–2 @ 775	2–4 @ 975	5.4–7.7 @ 1500	—	10¾ @ 2500	6	13¼ @ 24	—
D4OE-EA	0–2 @ 520	4½–7½ @ 800	10–12½ @ 1500	—	17¾ @ 2000	4	13 @ 17	—
D4VE-CA	0–2 @ 825	4–6 @ 1025	7–9¼ @ 1500	8⅓–11¼ @ 2000	12½ @ 2500	4	11¾ @ 14.6	—
D5AE-BA	0–2½ @ 975	—	3¾–6¼ @ 1500	—	11¼ @ 2150	4	13¼ @ 13	—
D5AE-DA	0–2½ @ 975	—	3¾–6¼ @ 1500	—	11¼ @ 2150	4.3	15¼ @ 13	—
D5AE-EA	0–2½ @ 975	—	3¾–6¼ @ 1500	—	11¼ @ 2150	3	13¼ @ 11	—
D5DE-HA	0–2 @ 550	3½–5½ @ 1000	7–9¼ @ 1500	10½–13 @ 2000	16½ @ 2500	4½	13¼ @ 19	—
1976								
D4VE-CA	−¾ to +½ @ 500	−1¼ to +½ @ 700	—	—	5 @ 1000	5	11¼ @ 15	—
D5DE-AFA	−¾ to +1¼ @ 500	3–5¼ @ 700	—	—	6½ @ 1000	5	13¼ @ 15	—
D5DE-AGA	−1 to +½ @ 500	¼–2¼ @ 700	—	—	5½ @ 1000	5	15¼ @ 15	—
D5DE-DA	−1 to +½ @ 500	0–2 @ 700	—	—	11¼ @ 1000	5	5¼ @ 15	—
D5DE-FA	−1 to +½ @ 500	1¼–3¼ @ 700	—	—	5 @ 1000	5	5¼ @ 15	—
D5DE-SA	−1 to +1 @ 500	1¼–3¼ @ 700	—	—	5½ @ 1000	5	13¼ @ 15	—
D5VE-CA	−1 to +½ @ 500	½–2½ @ 700	—	—	6½ @ 1000	5	13¼ @ 15	—
D6AE-AA	¼–2¼ @ 500	4–6 @ 700	—	—	7½ @ 1000	5	15¼ @ 15	—
D6AE-BA	−¾ to +2¼ @ 500	3¾–6 @ 700	—	—	7¾ @ 1000	5	9½ @ 15	—
D6AE-CA	0–3¼ @ 500	4¼–6½ @ 700	—	—	7 @ 1000	5	15¼ @ 15	—
D6AE-DA	0–3¼ @ 500	6–8¾ @ 700	—	—	9¾ @ 1000	5	15¼ @ 15	—
D6BE-BA	0–3¼ @ 500	3¼–5¼ @ 700	—	—	7 @ 1000	5	15¼ @ 15	—
D6DE-AA	−1 to +½ @ 500	0–2 @ 700	—	—	7 @ 1000	5	11¼ @ 15	—

Continued

DISTRIBUTOR SPECIFICATIONS—Continued

★Note: If unit is checked on vehicle, double the RPM and degrees to get crankshaft figures.

Breaker arm spring tension—17–21.

Distributor Ident. No.①	Centrifugal Advance Degrees @ RPM of Distributor					Vacuum Advance		Distributor Retard
	Advance Starts	Intermediate Advance			Full Advance	Inches of Vacuum to Start Plunger	Max. Adv. Dist. Deg. @ Vacuum	Max. Retard Dist. Deg. @ Vacuum
D6DE-BA	−¾ to +1 @ 500	2¼–4½ @ 700	—	—	8½ @ 1000	5	11¼ @ 15	—
D6DE-CA	−¾ to +½ @ 500	3–5 @ 700	—	—	6½ @ 1000	5	13¼ @ 15	—
D6DE-EA	−1 to +½ @ 500	3–5¾ @ 700	—	—	9 @ 1000	5	13¼ @ 15	—
D6DE-GA	−1 to +½ @ 500	1¼–3¼ @ 700	—	—	4½ @ 1000	5	11¼ @ 15	—
D6DE-JA	1–4 @ 500	5–7¼ @ 700	—	—	9½ @ 1000	5	13¼ @ 15	—
D6DE-KA	−1 to +1 @ 500	1¼–3¼ @ 700	—	—	4¾ @ 1000	5	7¼ @ 15	—
D6OE-AA	−1 to +½ @ 500	½–2¼ @ 700	—	—	5 @ 1000	5	15¼ @ 15	—
D6VE-AA	0–2½ @ 500	4½–6½ @ 700	—	—	9 @ 1000	5	13½ @ 15	—
D6VE-BA	−1 to +2¾ @ 500	6–9½ @ 700	—	—	11¾ @ 1000	5	13¼ @ 15	—
D6VE-CA	−½ to +3 @ 500	6–9½ @ 700	—	—	10¼ @ 1000	5	13¼ @ 15	—
D6ZE-AA	−1 to +½ @ 500	−¼ to +1 @ 700	—	—	5¼ @ 1000	5	13¼ @ 15	—
1977								
D5DE-AFA	−¾ to +1¼ @ 500	3–5¼ @ 700	—	—	6½ @ 1000	5	13¼ @ 15	—
D6DE-JA	1–4 @ 500	5–7¼ @ 700	—	—	9½ @ 1000	5	13¼ @ 15	—
D6AE-AA	0–2 @ 500	4–6 @ 700	7¾–9½ @ 1500	—	14 @ 2500	3	19¾ @ 11½	—
D7AE-BA	0–1 @ 425	2¾–4¾ @ 625	—	—	13½ @ 2250	3.5	15¼ @ 12	—
D7AE-CA	0–1 @ 700	3½–6 @ 1600	—	—	10¾ @ 2500	3	15½ @ 11	—
D7AE-DA	0–1 @ 450	3¾–5¾ @ 675	—	—	14 @ 2500	3.2	15½ @ 14½	—
D7BE-CA	—	—	—	—	—	—	—	—
D7BE-DA	0–1 @ 500	1¾–3¾ @ 600	—	—	8½ @ 2500	3	11¼ @ 11	—
D7BE-EA	0–1 @ 550	4¾–6¾ @ 625	—	—	13¾ @ 2450	3	11¼ @ 13½	—
D7BE-FA	0–1 @ 500	1–3 @ 575	—	—	8¼ @ 2500	3.1	7¼ @ 6½	—
D7DE-CA	0–1 @ 450	4¾–6¾ @ 700	—	—	15½ @ 2500	3	15¼ @ 11	—
D7DE-DA	—	—	—	—	—	—	—	—
D7DE-FA	0–1 @ 425	2½–4½ @ 575	—	—	13¾ @ 2500	3	15¼ @ 13½	—
D7DE-GA	0–1 @ 525	2¼–4¼ @ 700	—	—	7¼ @ 2500	3	13¼ @ 13	—
D7OE-CA	0–1 @ 450	2¾–4¾ @ 575	—	—	16 @ 2500	3.5	15¼ @ 14½	—
D7ZE-BA	0–1 @ 425	6–8 @ 650	—	—	16 @ 2500	3.5	13¼ @ 15.2	—
1978								
D7AE-CA	0–1 @ 700	3½–6 @ 1600	—	—	10¾ @ 2500	3	15¼ @ 11	—
D7BE-CA	0–1 @ 550	5¾–8 @ 1100	—	—	14¾ @ 2500	3.5	9¼ @ 13	—
D7BE-GA	0–1 @ 500	1–2¾ @ 600	—	—	6½–8¾ @ 2500	3	7¼ @ 7	—
D7DE-CA	0–1 @ 450	4¾–6¾ @ 700	—	—	15½ @ 2500	3	15¼ @ 11	—
D7DE-DA	—	—	—	—	—	—	—	—
D8AE-GA	0–1 @ 450	3½–5½ @ 700	—	—	8¼ @ 2500	5.5	15¼ @ 16.5	—
D8BE-CA	0–1 @ 1000	—	—	—	4¾ @ 2500	3	11¼ @ 11.5	—
D8BE-DA	—	—	—	—	—	—	—	—
D8DE-EA	0–1 @ 450	3–5 @ 600	—	—	12¼ @ 2500	3	13.5 @ 14	—
D8BE-FA	0–1 @ 500	1½–3½ @ 1200	—	—	7–9½ @ 2500	3.5	11 @ 13.5	—
D8DE-CA	0–1 @ 475	1–3 @ 600	—	—	6½–9 @ 2500	2	13¼ @ 10.8	—
D8DE-DA	—	—	—	—	—	—	—	—

①—Basic Ident. No. 12127.

Continued

VALVE SPECIFICATIONS

Year	Engine	Valve Lash Int.	Valve Lash Exh.	Valve Angles Seat	Valve Angles Face	Valve Spring Installed Height	Valve Spring Pressure Lbs. @ In.	Stem Clearance Intake	Stem Clearance Exhaust	Stem Diameter, Standard Intake	Stem Diameter, Standard Exhaust
1974	6-200	.079-.129[4]		45	44	1 37/64	[16]	.0008-.0025	.0010-.0027	.3100-.3107	.3098-.3105
	6-250	.095-.195[4]		45	44	1 37/64	146 @ 1.18	.0008-.0025	.0010-.0027	.3100-.3107	.3098-.3105
	8-302	.090-.140[4]		45	44	[6]	[14]	.0010-.0027	.0015-.0032	.3416-.3423	.3411-.3418
	8-351[9][10]	.100-.150[4]		45	44	1 53/64	226 @ 1.39	.0010-.0027	.0015-.0032	.3416-.3423	.3411-.3418
	8-351[9][10]	.106-.156[4]		45	44	1 51/64	200 @ 1.34	.0010-.0027	.0015-.0032	.3416-.3423	.3411-.3418
	8-351[11]	.100-.150[4]		45	44	1 53/64	285 @ 1.32	.0010-.0027	.0015-.0032	.3416-.3423	.3411-.3418
	8-400	.100-.150[4]		45	44	1 53/64	226 @ 1.39	.0010-.0027	.0015-.0032	.3416-.3423	.3411-.3418
	8-460	.075-.125[4]		45	44	1 13/16	253 @ 1.33	.0010-.0027	.0010-.0027	.3416-.3423	.3416-.3423
1975	6-200	.079-.129[4]		45	44	1 37/64	[16]	.0008-.0025	.001-.0027	.3100-.3107	.3098-.3105
	6-250	.095-.145[4]		45	44	1 37/64	150 @ 1.18	.0008-.0025	.001-.0027	.3100-.3107	.3098-.3105
	8-302	.115-.130[4]		45	44	[13]	[14]	.001-.0027	.0015-.0032	.3416-.3423	.3411-.3418
	8-351[8]	.131-.181[4]		45	44	1 51/64	200 @ 1.34	.001-.0027	.0015-.0032	.3416-.3423	.3411-.3418
	8-351[5], 400	.125-.175[4]		45	44	1 53/64	226 @ 1.39	.001-.0027	.0015-.0032	.3416-.3423	.3411-.3418
	8-460	.100-.150[4]		45	44	1 13/16	253 @ 1.33	.001-.0027	.001-.0027	.3416-.3423	.3416-.3423
1976	6-200	.079-.129[4]		45	44	1 37/64	[16]	.0008-.0025	.0010-.0027	.3100-.3107	.3098-.3105
	6-250	.079-.129[4]		45	44	1 37/64	150 @ 1.18	.0008-.0025	.0010-.0027	.3100-.3107	.3098-.3105
	8-302	.115-.165[4]		45	44	[17]	[15]	.0010-.0027	.0015-.0032	.3416-.3423	.3411-.3418
	8-351[8]	.131-.181[4]		45	44	1 51/64	200 @ 1.34	.0010-.0027	.0015-.0032	.3416-.3423	.3411-.3418
	8-351[5], 400	.125-.175[4]		45	44	1 13/16	226 @ 1.39	.0010-.0027	.0015-.0032	.3416-.3423	.3411-.3418
	8-460	.100-.150[4]		45	44	1 13/16	229 @ 1.33	.0010-.0027	.0010-.0027	.3416-.3423	.3416-.3423
1977	6-200	.110-.160[4]		45	44	1 37/64	[18]	.0008-.0025	.0010-.0027	.3100-.3107	.3098-.3105
	6-250	.096-.184[4]		45	44	1 37/64	[19]	.0008-.0025	.0010-.0027	.3100-.3107	.3098-.3105
	8-302	.096-.168[4]		45	44	[17]	[15]	.0010-.0027	.0015-.0032	.3416-.3423	.3411-.3418
	8-351[8]	.096-.168[4]		45	44	[20]	[12]	.0010-.0027	.0015-.0032	.3416-.3423	.3411-.3418
	8-351[5], 400	.125-.175[4]		45	44	1 53/64	226 @ 1.39	.0010-.0027	.0015-.0032	.3416-.3423	.3411-.3418
1978	4-140	.0040-.0050[4]		45	44	1 9/16	189 @ 1.16	.0010-.0027	.0015-.0032	.3416-.3423	.3411-.3418
	6-200	.110-.160[4]		45	44	1 37/64	150 @ 1.22	.0008-.0025	.0010-.0027	.3100-.3107	.3098-.3105
	6-250	.096-.184[4]		45	44	1 37/64	150 @ 1.22	.0008-.0025	.0010-.0027	.3100-.3107	.3098-.3105
	V8-302[1]	.096-.168[4]		45	44	[7]	[16]	.0010-.0027	.0015-.0032	.3416-.3423	.3411-.3418
	V8-302[2]	[3][4]		45	44	[7]	[16]	.0010-.0027	.0015-.0032	.3416-.3423	.3411-.3418
	V8-351[1][8]	.096-.168[4]		45	44	[20]	[12]	.0010-.0027	.0015-.0032	.3416-.3423	.3411-.3418
	V8-351[2][8]	.142		45	44	[20]	[12]	.0010-.0027	.0015-.0032	.3416-.3423	.3411-.3418
	V8-351	.125-.175[4]		45	44	1 53/64	226 @ 1.39	.0010-.0027	.0015-.0032	.3416-.3423	.3411-.3418
	V8-400	.125-.175[4]		45	44	1 53/64	226 @ 1.39	.0010-.0027	.0015-.0032	.3416-.3423	.3411-.3418

①—Early 1978 engines.
②—Late 1978 engines.
③—Exc. Calif., .121; Calif., .142.
④—Clearance is obtained at valve stem tip with hydraulic lifter collapsed. If clearance is less than the minimum install an undersize push rod; if clearance is greater than the maximum install an oversize push rod.
⑤—Modified engine.
⑥—Intake 1 11/16, exhaust 1 9/16.
⑦—Intake, 1 51/64; Exhaust, 1 3/64.
⑧—Windsor engine.
⑨—Cleveland engine.
⑩—2 barrel carb.
⑪—4 barrel carb.
⑫—Intake, 200 @ 1.34; exhaust, 200 @ 1.20.
⑬—Intake, 1 53/64; Exhaust, 1 11/16.
⑭—Intake 200 @ 1.31, exhaust 200 @ 1.22.
⑮—Intake 200 @ 1.31, exhaust 200 @ 1.20.
⑯—Intake, 150 @ 1.18; exhaust, 150 @ 1.22.
⑰—Intake, 1 11/16; exhaust, 1 19/32.
⑱—Intake, 156 @ 1.20; exhaust, 148 @ 1.23.
⑲—Intake, 156 @ 1.20; exhaust, 154 @ 1.20.
⑳—Intake, 1 51/64; exhaust, 1 39/64.

STARTING MOTOR SPECIFICATIONS

Year	Engine Model	Ident. No.	Brush Spring Tension, Ounces	No Load Test			Torque Test		
				Amperes	Volts	R.P.M.	Amperes	Volts	Torque Lbs. Ft.
1974	6-200	D2ZF-BA, CA	80	90	12	—	670	5	15.5
	6-200	D2OF-AA, BA	80	90	12	—	670	5	15.5
	6-250, 8-302, 351	D2AF-CA	80	90	12	—	670	5	15.5
	8-302, 351	D4AF-AA, BA	80	90	12	—	670	5	15.5
	8-302, 351	D5TF-DA	80	80	12	—	670	5	15.5
	8-400	D2AF-AA	80	80	12	—	670	5	15.5
	8-460	D4OF-AA	80	90	12	—	—	—	—
1975	6-200	D2OF-BA	80	80	12	—	670	5	15.5
	6-200	D2ZF-CA	80	80	12	—	670	5	15.5
	6-250, 8-302, 351①	D5OF-BA	80	80	12	—	670	5	15.5
	8-351②	D2AF-JA	80	80	12	—	670	5	15.5
	8-400	D5AF-EA	80	80	12	—	670	5	15.5
	8-460	D5AF-AB	40	70	12	—	—	—	—
1976	6-200	D2ZF-BA	80	80	12	—	670	5	15.5
	6-250, 8-302, 351①	D5OF-AA	80	80	12	—	670	5	15.5
	8-351②, 400	D2AF-AA	80	80	12	—	670	5	15.5
	8-351②, 400	D5AF-EA	80	80	12	—	670	5	15.5
	8-460	D5AF-B	40	70	12	—	—	—	—
	8-460	D6AF-AA	40	70	12	—	—	—	—
1977	6-200	D6BF-AA, BA	80	80	12	—	670	5	15.5
	6-250, 8-302, 351①	D6OF-AA	80	80	12	—	670	5	15.5
	8-351①	D6DF-AA	80	80	12	—	670	5	15.5
	8-351②	D5AF-EA	80	80	12	—	670	5	15.5
	8-400	D6OF-AA	80	80	12	—	670	5	15.5
1978	4-140③	D8BF-AA	40	70	12	—	460	5	9
	4-140④	D8EF-AA	40	70	12	—	460	5	9
	6-200③	D8BF-AA	80	80	12	—	670	5	15.5
	6-200④	D8BF-CA	80	80	12	—	670	5	15.5
	6-250	D8OF-AA	80	80	12	—	670	5	15.5
	8-302	D8OF-AA	80	80	12	—	670	5	15.5
	8-351①	D8OF-AA	80	80	12	—	670	5	15.5
	8-351②	D8AF-AA	80	80	12	—	670	5	15.5
	8-400	D8AF-AA	80	80	12	—	670	5	15.5

①—Windsor engine.
②—Modified engine.
③—Manual trans.
④—Auto. trans.

PISTONS, PINS, RINGS, CRANKSHAFT & BEARINGS

Year	Engine	Piston Clearance	Ring End Gap①		Wrist-pin Diameter	Rod Bearings		Main Bearings			
			Comp.	Oil		Shaft Diameter	Bearing Clearance	Shaft Diameter	Bearing Clearance	Thrust on Bear. No.	Shaft End Play
1974	6-200	.0013–.0021	.008	.015	.9122	2.1232–2.1240	.0008–.0015	2.2482–2.2490	.0008–.0015	5	.004–.008
	6-250	.0013–.0021	.008	.015	.9122	2.1232–2.1240	.0008–.0015	2.3982–2.3990	.0008–.0015	5	.004–.008
	8-302	.0018–.0026	.010	.015	.9122	2.1228–2.1236	.0008–.0015	2.2482–2.2490	⑥	3	.004–.008
	8-351②	.0018–.0026	.010	.015	.9122	2.3103–2.3111	.0008–.0015	2.9994–3.0002	.0008–.0015	3	.004–.008
	8-351③	⑩	.010	.015	.9122	2.3103–2.3111	⑦	2.7484–2.7492	⑪	3	.004–.008
	8-400	.0014–.0022	.010	.015	.9752	2.3103–2.3111	.0008–.0015	2.9994–3.0002	.0009–.0015	3	.004–.008
	8-460	.0022–.0030	.010	.015	1.0401	2.4992–2.5000	.0008–.0015	2.9994–3.0002	⑨	3	.004–.008
	8-460⑤	.0034–.0042	.010	.015	1.0401	2.4992–2.5000	.0008–.0015	2.9994–3.0002	.0009–.0015	3	.004–.008

Continued

PISTONS, PINS, RINGS, CRANKSHAFT & BEARINGS—Continued

Year	Engine	Piston Clearance	Ring End Gap①		Wrist-pin Diameter	Rod Bearings		Main Bearings			Shaft End Play
			Comp.	Oil		Shaft Diameter	Bearing Clearance	Shaft Diameter	Bearing Clearahce	Thrust on Bear. No.	
1975	6-200	.0013-.0021	.008	.015	.9122	2.1232-2.1240	.0008-.0015	2.2482-2.2490	.0008-.0015	5	.004-.008
	6-250	.0013-.0021	.008	.015	.9122	2.1232-2.1240	.0008-.0015	2.3982-2.3990	.0008-.0015	5	.004-.008
	8-302	.0018-.0026	.010	.015	.9122	2.1228-2.1236	.0008-.0015	2.2482-2.2490	⑥	3	.004-.008
	8-351②	.0018-.0026	.010	.015	.9122	2.3103-2.3111	.0008-.0015	2.9994-3.0002	.0008-.0015	3	.004-.008
	8-351⑧	.0014-.0022	.010	.015	.9752	2.3103-2.3111	.0008-.0015	2.9994-3.0002	.0008-.0015	3	.004-.008
	8-400	.0014-.0022	.010	.015	.9752	2.3103-2.3111	.0008-.0015	2.9994-3.0002	.0008-.0015	3	.004-.008
	8-460	.0014-.0022	.010	.015	1.0401	2.4992-2.5000	.0008-.0015	2.9994-3.0002	⑩	3	.004-.008
	8-460⑤	.0022-.0030	.010	.015	1.0401	2.4992-2.5000	.0008-.0015	2.9994-3.0002	④	3	.004-.008
1976	6-200	.0013-.0021	.008	.015	.9122	2.1232-2.1240	.0008-.0015	2.2482-2.2490	.0008-.0015	5	.004-.008
	6-250	.0013-.0021	.008	.015	.9122	2.1232-2.1240	.0008-.0015	2.3982-2.3990	.0008-.0015	5	.004-.008
	8-302	.0018-.0026	.010	.015	.9122	2.1228-2.1236	.0008-.0015	2.2482-2.2490	.0008-.0015	3	.004-.008
	8-351②	.0018-.0026	.010	.015	.9122	2.3103-2.3111	.0008-.0015	2.9994-3.0002	.0008-.0015	3	.004-.008
	8-351⑧	.0022	.010	.015	.9752	2.3103-2.3111	.0008-.0015	2.9994-3.0002	.0008-.0015	3	.004-.008
	8-400	.0022	.010	.015	.9752	2.3103-2.3111	.0008-.0015	2.9994-3.0002	.0008-.0015	3	.004-.008
	8-460	.0014-.0022	.010	.015	1.0401	2.4992-2.5000	.0008-.0015	2.9994-3.0002	.0008-.0015	3	.004-.008
	8-460⑤	.0022-.0030	.010	.015	1.0401	2.4992-2.5000	.0008-.0015	2.9994-3.0002	④	3	.004-.008
1977	6-200	.0013-.0021	.008	.015	.9121	2.1232-2.1240	.0008-.0015	2.2482-2.2490	.0008-.0015	5	.004-.008
	6-250	.0013-.0021	.008	.015	.9121	2.1232-2.1240	.0008-.0015	2.3982-2.3990	.0008-.0015	5	.004-.008
	8-302	.0018-.0026	.010	.015	.9121	2.1228-2.1236	.0008-.0015	2.2482-2.2490	⑥	3	.004-.008
	8-351②	.0018-.0026	.010	.015	.9121	2.3103-2.3111	.0008-.0015	2.9994-3.0002	.0008-.0015	3	.004-.008
	8-351⑧	.0014-.0022	.010	.015	.9752	2.3103-2.3111	.0008-.0015	2.9994-3.0002	.0008-.0015	3	.004-.008
	8-400	.0014-.0022	.010	.015	.9752	2.3103-2.3111	.0008-.0015	2.9994-3.0002	.0008-.0015	3	.004-.008
1978	4-140	.0014-.0022	.010	.015	.9120	2.0464-2.0472	.0008-.0015	2.3986	.0008-.0015	3	.004-.008
	6-200	.0013-.0021	.008	.015	.9121	2.1232-2.1240	.0008-.0015	2.2486	.0008-.0015	5	.004-.008
	6-250	.0013-.0021	.008	.015	.9121	2.1232-2.1240	.0008-.0015	2.3986	.0008-.0015	5	.004-.008
	8-302	.0018-.0026	.010	.015	.9121	2.1228-2.1236	.0008-.0015	2.2486	⑥	3	.004-.008
	8-351M②	.0014-.0022	.010	.015	.9752	2.3103-2.3111	.0008-.0015	2.9998	.0008-.0015	3	.004-.008
	8-351W⑤	.0018-.0026	.010	.015	.9122	2.3103-2.3111	.0008-.0015	2.9998	.0008-.0015	3	.004-.008
	8-400	.0014-.0022	.010	.015	.9752	2.3103-2.3111	.0008-.0015	2.9998	.0008-.0015	3	.004-.008

①—Fit rings in tapered bores for clearance listed in tightest portion of ring travel.
②—Windsor engine.
③—Cleveland engine.
④—No. 1: .0004-.0015; No. 2, 3, 4, 5: .0008-.0015.
⑤—Police.
⑥—No. 1: .0001-.0015; No. 2, 3, 4, 5: .0005-.0015.
⑦—2 Barrel: .0008-.0015; 4 Barrel: .0011-.0015.
⑧—Modified engine.
⑨—No. 1: .0004-.0015; No. 2, 3, 4, 5: .0012-.0015.
⑩—No. 1: .0004-.0015; No. 2, 3, 4, 5: .0009-.0015.
⑪—2 Barrel: .0009-.0015; 4 Barrel: .0011-.0015.

ENGINE TIGHTENING SPECIFICATIONS*

★Torque specifications are for clean and lightly lubricated threads only. Dry or dirty threads produce increased friction which prevents accurate measurement of tightness.

Year	Engine	Spark Plugs Ft. Lbs.	Cylinder Head Bolts Ft. Lbs.	Intake Manifold Ft. Lbs.	Exhaust Manifold Ft. Lbs.	Rocker Arm Shaft Bracket Ft. Lbs.	Rocker Arm Cover Ft. Lbs.	Connecting Rod Cap Bolts Ft. Lbs.	Main Bearing Cap Bolts Ft. Lbs.	Flywheel to Crankshaft Ft. Lbs.	Vibration Damper or Pulley Ft. Lbs.
1974	6-200	15–20	70–75	—	13–18	30–35	3–5	19–24	60–70	75–85	85–100
	6-250	15–20	70–75	—	13–18	30–35	3–5	21–26	60–70	75–85	85–100
	8-302	15–20	65–72	19–27	12–16	17–23②	3–5	19–24	60–70	75–85	70–90
	8-351③	15–20	105–112	19–27	18–24	17–23②	3–5	40–45	95–105	75–85	100–130
	8-351④	10–15	95–105	⑤	12–22	18–25⑧	3–5	40–45	⑥	75–85	70–90
	8-400	10–15	95–105	⑤	12–16	18–25⑧	3–5	40–45	⑥	75–85	70–90
	8-460	10–15	130–140	22–32	28–33	18–25⑧	5–6	40–45	95–105	75–85	70–90
1975	6-200	15–25	70–75	—	13–18	30–35	3–5	21–26	60–70	75–85	85–100
	6-250	15–25	70–75	18–24	13–18	30–35	3–5	21–26	60–70	75–85	85–100
	8-302	7–15	65–72	23–25	18–24	17–23②	3–5	19–24	60–70	75–85	70–90
	8-351③	7–15	105–112	23–25	18–24	17–23②	3–5	40–45	95–105	75–85	70–90
	8-351①	7–15	95–105	⑦	18–24	18–25⑧	3–5	40–45	⑥	75–85	70–90
	8-400	7–15	95–105	⑦	18–24	18–25⑧	3–5	40–45	⑥	75–85	70–90
	8-460	7–15	130–140	25–30	28–33	18–25⑧	5–6	40–45	95–105	75–85	70–90
1976	6-200, 250	20–25	70–75	—	18–24	30–35	3–5	21–26	60–70	75–85	85–100
	8-302	7–15	65–72	23–25	18–24	17–23②	3–5	19–24	60–70	75–85	70–90
	8-351③	7–15	105–112	23–25	18–24	17–23②	3–5	40–45	95–105	75–85	70–90
	8-351①	7–15	95–105	⑨	18–24	18–25⑧	3–5	40–45	⑥	75–85	70–90
	8-400	7–15	95–105	⑨	18–24	18–25⑧	3–5	40–45	⑥	75–85	70–90
	8-460	7–15	130–140	22–32	28–33	18–25⑧	5–6	40–45	95–105	75–85	70–90
1977–78	4-140	5–10	80–90	14–21	16–23	—	4–7	30–36	80–90	54–64	100–120
	6-200, 250	10–15	70–75	—	18–24	30–35	3–5	21–26	60–70	75–85	85–100
	8-302	10–15	65–72	23–25	18–24	⑩	3–5	19–24	60–70	75–85	70–90
	8-351③	10–15	105–112	23–25	18–24	⑩	3–5	40–45	95–105	75–85	70–90
	8-351①	10–15	95–105	⑨	18–24	18–25⑧	3–5	40–45	95–105	75–85	70–90
	8-400	10–15	95–105	⑨	18–24	18–25⑧	3–5	40–45	95–105	75–85	70–90

①—Modified engine.
②—Rocker arm stud nut.
③—Windsor engine.
④—Cleveland engine.
⑤—5⁄16″ bolts, 21–25, 3⁄8″ bolts, 27–33, 1⁄4″ bolt, 6–9.
⑥—1⁄2″ bolts, 95–105, 3⁄8″ bolts, 35–45.
⑦—5⁄16″ bolts, 21–25, 3⁄8″ bolts, 27–33.
⑧—Fulcrum bolt to cylinder head.
⑨—5⁄16″ bolts, 19–25 ft. lbs.; 3⁄8″ bolts, 22–32 ft. lbs.
⑩—1977 & early 1978 rocker arm stud nut, 17–23 ft. lbs.; late 1978 fulcrum bolt to cylinder head, 18–25 ft. lbs.

ALTERNATOR & REGULATOR SPECIFICATIONS

Year	Ident. No. (10300)	Current Rating①		Field Current @ 75°F.		Voltage Regulator②				Field Relay	
		Amperes	Volts	Amperes	Volts	Model No. (10316)	Voltage @ 75°F.	Contact Gap	Armature Air Gap	Armature Air Gap	Closing Voltage @ 75°F.
1974	Purple③	38	15	2.9	12	D4AF-AA	13.5–15.3	④	④	④	2.5–4.0
	Orange③	42	15	2.9	12	D4AF-AA	13.5–15.3	④	④	④	2.5–4.0
	Red③	55	15	2.9	12	D4AF-AA	13.5–15.3	④	④	④	2.5–4.0
	Green③	61	15	2.9	12	D4AF-AA	13.5–15.3	④	④	④	2.5–4.0
	All	70	15	2.9	12	D4TF-AA	13.5–15.3	④	④	④	2.5–4.0
	All	90	15	2.9	12	D4TF-AA	13.5–15.3	④	④	④	2.5–4.0
1975–76	Orange③	40	15	2.9	12	D4AF-AA	13.5–15.3	④	④	④	2.5–4.0
	Green③	60	15	2.9	12	D4AF-AA	13.5–15.3	④	④	④	2.5–4.0
	All	70	15	2.9	12	D4TF-AA	13.5–15.3	④	④	④	2.5–4.0
	All	90	15	2.9	12	D4TF-AA	13.5–15.3	④	④	④	2.5–4.0

Continued

ALTERNATOR & REGULATOR SPECIFICATIONS—Continued

Year	Ident. No. (10300)	Current Rating[1] Amperes	Volts	Field Current @ 75°F. Amperes	Volts	Voltage Regulator[2] Model No. (10316)	Voltage @ 75°F.	Contact Gap	Armature Air Gap	Field Relay Armature Air Gap	Closing Voltage @ 75°F.
1977	Orange[3]	40	15	2.9	12	D4AF-AA	13.5–15.3	[4]	[4]	[4]	2.5–4.0
	Green[3]	60	15	2.9	12	D4AF-AA	13.5–15.3	[4]	[4]	[4]	2.5–4.0
	All	70	15	2.9	12	D4TF-AA	13.5–15.3	[4]	[4]	[4]	2.5–4.0
	All	90	15	2.9	12	D4TF-AA	13.5–15.3	[4]	[4]	[4]	2.5–4.0
1978	Orange[3]	40	15	2.9	12	D4AF-AA	13.5–14.3	[4]	[4]	[4]	—
	Green[3]	60	15	2.9	12	D4AF-AA	13.5–14.3	[4]	[4]	[4]	—
	Green[3][5]	60	15	4.0	12	D8BF-AA	13.8–14.6	[4]	[4]	[4]	—
	Black[3]	70	15	2.9	12	D4TF-AA	13.5–14.3	[4]	[4]	[4]	—
	Red[3]	90	15	2.9	12	D4TF-AA	13.5–14.3	[4]	[4]	[4]	—
	Red[3][6]	90	15	4.0	12	D8BF-AA[6]	13.8–14.6	[4]	[4]	[4]	—
1979	D8BF-BA	70				D8BF-AA[6]	13.8–14.6	[4]	[4]	[4]	—
	D8BF-CA	65				D8BF-AA[6]	13.8–14.6	[4]	[4]	[4]	—
	D8BF-DA	70				D8BF-AA[6]	13.8–14.6	[4]	[4]	[4]	—
	D8VF-BA	100				D8BF-AA[6]	13.8–14.6	[4]	[4]	[4]	—
	D8ZF-AA	40				D8BF-AA[6]	13.8–14.6	[4]	[4]	[4]	—
	D8ZF-BA	60				D8BF-AA[6]	13.8–14.6	[4]	[4]	[4]	—
	D8ZF-CA	60				D8BF-AA[6]	13.8–14.6	[4]	[4]	[4]	—
	D8ZF-EA	40				D8BF-AA[6]	13.8–14.6	[4]	[4]	[4]	—
	D8ZF-FA	70				D8BF-AA[6]	13.8–14.6	[4]	[4]	[4]	—
	D8ZF-HA	65				D8BF-AA[6]	13.8–14.6	[4]	[4]	[4]	—
	D9DF-AA	70				D8BF-AA[6]	13.8–14.6	[4]	[4]	[4]	—
	D9UF-GA	100				D8BF-AA[6]	13.8–14.6	[4]	[4]	[4]	—

[1]—Current rating stamped on housing.
[2]—Voltage regulation stamped on cover.
[3]—Stamp color.
[4]—Not adjustable.
[5]—Solid state alternator.
[6]—Electronic voltage regulator. These units are color coded black for systems w/warning indicator lamp & blue for systems w/ammeter.

WHEEL ALIGNMENT SPECIFICATIONS

Year	Model	Caster Angle, Degrees Limits	Desired	Camber Angle, Degrees Limits Left	Right	Desired Left	Right	Toe-In. Inch	Toe-Out on Turns, Deg Outer Wheel	Inner Wheel
1974	Maverick	−2½ to +1½	−½	−¾ to +1¼	−¾ to +1¼	+¼	+¼	3/16	18.16[4]	20
	Torino	+½ to +3½	+2	−3/8 to +1 5/8	−7/8 to +1 1/8	+½	+1/8	1/8	18.11	20
	Comet	−2½ to +1½	−½	−¾ to +1¼	−¾ to +1¼	+¼	+¼	3/16	18.16[4]	20
	Montego	+½ to +3½	+2	−3/8 to +1 5/8	−7/8 to +1 1/8	+5/8	+1/8	1/8	18.11	20
	Cougar	+½ to +3½	+2	−3/8 to +1 5/8	−7/8 to +1 1/8	+5/8	+1/8	1/8	18.84	20
1975–76	Comet	+¼ to −1¼	−½	−½ to +1	−½ to +1	+¼	+¼	1/8	18.36[1]	20
	Cougar	+3¼ to +4¾	+4	−¼ to +1¼	−½ to +1	+½	+¼	1/8	18.06	20
	Elite	+3¼ to +4¾	+4	−¼ to +1¼	−½ to +1	+½	+¼	1/8	18.06	20
	Granada	+¼ to −1¼	−½	−½ to +1	−½ to +1	+¼	+¼	1/8	18.43[2]	20
	Maverick	+¼ to −1¼	−½	−½ to +1	−½ to +1	+¼	+¼	1/8	18.36[1]	20
	Monarch	+¼ to −1¼	−½	−½ to +1	−½ to +1	+¼	+¼	1/8	18.43[2]	20
	Montego	+3¼ to +4¾	+4	−¼ to +1¼	−½ to +1	+½	+¼	1/8	18.06	20
	Torino	+3¼ to +4¾	+4	−¼ to +1¼	−½ to +1	+½	+¼	1/8	18.06	20

Continued

WHEEL ALIGNMENT SPECIFICATIONS—Continued

Year	Model	Caster Angle, Degrees		Camber Angle, Degrees					Toe-In. Inch	Toe-Out on Turns, Deg	
				Limits		Desired					
		Limits	Desired	Left	Right	Left	Right			Outer Wheel	Inner Wheel
1977	Comet	−1¼ to +¼	−½	−½ to +1	−½ to +1	+¼	+¼	⅛	18.36①	20
	Cougar	+3¼ to +4¾	+4	−¼ to +1¼	−½ to +1	+½	+¼	⅛	18.06	20
	Granada	−1¼ to +¼	−½	−½ to +1	−½ to +1	+¼	+¼	⅛	18.43②	20
	Maverick	−1¼ to +¼	−½	−½ to +1	−½ to +1	+¼	+¼	⅛	18.36①	20
	Monarch	−1¼ to +¼	−½	−½ to +1	−½ to +1	+¼	+¼	⅛	18.43②	20
	LTD II	+3¼ to +4¾	+4	−¼ to +1¼	−½ to +1	+½	+¼	⅛	18.06	20
1978	Cougar	+3¼ to +4¾	+4	−¼ to +1¼	−½ to +1	+½	+¼	⅛	18.06	20
	Fairmont	+⅛ to +1⅝	+⅞	−⅜ to +1⅛	−⅜ to +1⅛	+⅜	+⅜	5⁄16	19.74	20
	Granada	−1¼ to +¼	−½	−½ to +1	−½ to +1	+¼	+¼	¼	②③	20
	LTD II	+3¼ to +4¾	+4	−¼ to +1¼	−½ to +1	+½	+¼	⅛	18.06	20
	Monarch	−1¼ to +¼	−½	−½ to +1	−½ to +1	+¼	+¼	¼	②③	20
	Zephyr	+¼ to +1⅝	+⅞	−⅜ to +1⅛	−⅜ to +1⅛	+⅜	+⅜	5⁄16	19.74	20

①—Power steering 18.13°.
②—Power steering 18.20°.
③—Manual Steering 18.44°.
④—Manual Steering 18.39°.

COOLING SYSTEM & CAPACITY DATA

Year	Model or Engine	Cooling Capacity, Qts.			Radiator Cap Relief Pressure, Lbs.		Thermo. Opening Temp. ①	Fuel Tank Gals.	Engine Oil Refill Qts. ②	Transmission Oil			Rear Axle Oil Pints
		No Heater	With Heater	With A/C	With A/C	No A/C				3 Speed Pints	4 Speed Pints	Auto. Trans. Qts. ⑨	
1974	6-200③	8.0	9.0	9.0	12–16	12–16	191	15	4	3½	—	8	4
	6-250③	8.7	9½	9½	12–16	12–16	191	15	4	3½	—	9	4
	6-250⑩	—	11.9	—	12–16	12–16	191	26½	4	3½	—	9	4
	8-302③	12.4	13½	14¼	12–16	12–16	191	15	4	3½	—	9	4
	8-302⑩	14.2	15½	15½	12–16	12–16	191	④	4	3½	—	⑤	4
	8-351C⑩	14.8	16	16½	12–16	12–16	191	④	4	—	—	10¼	4
	Cougar 8-351C	14.9	16	16½	12–16	12–16	191	26½	4	—	—	⑭	5
	8-351 W⑩	15.3	16½	16½	12–16	12–16	191	④	4	—	—	⑭	4
	Cougar 8-351 W	15.3	16½	16½	12–16	12–16	191	26½	4	—	—	⑭	5
	8-351 "CJ"⑩	14.7	16½	16½	12–16	12–16	191	④	4	—	4	⑭	4
	Cougar 8-351 "CJ"	14.9	16½	16½	12–16	12–16	191	26½	4	—	—	⑭	5
	8-400⑩	16.7	17¾	18.3	12–16	12–16	191	④	4	—	—	⑭	5
	8-460⑩	18.4	19	19½	12–16	12–16	191	④	4	—	—	⑭	5
	Cougar 400	—	17½	18½	12–16	12–16	191	26½	4	—	—	⑭	5
	Cougar 460	—	19	19½	12–16	12–16	191	26½	6	—	—	⑭	5
1975	6-200③	8	9	9	11–17	11–17	191	19.2	4	3½	—	8¾	4
	6-250③	8	9.7	9.7	11–17	11–17	191	19.2	4	3½	—	8¾	4
	6-250⑱	—	10.5	10.7	13–19	13–19	191	19.2	4	3½	—	8¾	4
	8-302③	—	13.5	14.1	11–17	11–17	191	19.2	4	3½	—	8¾	4
	8-302⑱	—	14.4	14.6	13–19	13–19	191	19.2	4	3½	—	8¾	4
	8-351W⑱	—	15.7	16.7	13–19	13–19	191	19.2	4	3½	—	⑯	4
	8-351W⑮	—	15.9	16.2	13–19	13–19	191	④	4	—	—	⑯	5
	8-351M⑮	—	17.1	18	13–19	13–19	191	④	4	—	—	⑯	5
	8-400⑮	—	17.1	17.5	13–19	13–19	191	④	4	—	—	⑯	5
	8-460⑮	—	19.2	19.7	13–19	13–19	191	④	6	—	—	⑯	5

Continued

COOLING SYSTEM & CAPACITY DATA—Continued

Year	Model or Engine	Cooling Capacity, Qts.			Radiator Cap Relief Pressure, Lbs.		Thermo. Opening Temp. [1]	Fuel Tank Gals.	Engine Oil Refill Qts. [2]	Transmission Oil			Rear Axle Oil Pints
		No Heater	With Heater	With A/C	With A/C	No A/C				3 Speed Pints	4 Speed Pints	Auto. Trans. Qts. [9]	
1976	6-200[3]	8.2	9	9	11–17	11–17	191	19.2	4	3½	—	7.8	4
	6-200[18]	9.1	9.9	9.9	13–19	13–19	191	[6]	4	3½	—	8¾	[12]
	6-250[3]	8.9	9.7	9.7	11–17	11–17	191	19.2	4	3½	—	8.8	4
	6-250[18]	9.7	10.5	10.7	13–19	13–19	191	[6]	4	3½	—	8¾	[12]
	8-302[3]	12.7	13.5	14.1	11–17	11–17	191	19.2	4	3½	—	8.8	4
	8-302[18]	—	14.4	14.6	13–19	13–19	191	19.2	4	3½	—	8¾	[12]
	8-351W[18]	14.9	15.7	16.7	13–19	13–19	191	19.2	4	3½	—	10¼	[12]
	8-351W[15]	15.1	15.9	16.2	13–19	13–19	191	[4]	4	—	—	[21]	5
	8-351M	16.3	17.1	18	13–19	13–19	191	[4]	4	—	—	[21]	5
	8-400	16.3	17.1	17.5	13–19	13–19	191	[4]	4	—	—	12.2	5
	8-460	18.4	19.2	19.7	13–19	13–19	191	[4]	4	—	—	12.2	5
1977	6-200[3]	—	8.7	8.7	14–18	14–18	191	19.2	4	3.5	—	7¼	4½
	6-200[18]	—	9.9	9.9	14–18	14–18	191	19.2	4	—	4.5[17]		[4]
	6-250[3]	—	9.6	9.6	14–18	14–18	191	19.2	4	3.5	—	8¼	4
	6-250[18]	—	10.5	10.7	14–18	14–18	191	19.2	4	—	4.5[17]	8¼	[4]
	8-302[3]	—	13.5	14.1	14–18	14–18	191	19.2	4	3.5	—	10¼	4
	8-302[18]	—	14.4	14.6	14–18	14–18	191	19.2	4	—	4.5[17]	8¼	[4]
	8-302[11]	—	14.8	15.1	14–18	14–18	191	[20]	4	—	—	10½	5
	8-351[18]	—	15.7	16.7	14–18	14–18	191	19.2	4	—	4.5	10½	[7]
	8-351M[11]	—	[19]	[19]	12–16	12–16	191	[20]	4	—	—	[16]	5
	8-351W[11]	—	15.9	16.2	12–16	12–16	191	[20]	4	—	—	[16]	5
	8-400[11]	—	[21]	[21]	12–16	12–16	191	[20]	4	—	—	[16]	5
1978	4-140	7.9	8.7	9.1	12–15	12–15	191	16	4	—	2.8	8	3.5
	6-200	8.9	9.7	9.1	12–15	12–15	191	16	4	3.5	—	8	3.5
	6-250	9.7	10.5	10.7	14–18	14–18	191	18	4	—	4.5[17]	10	[7]
	8-302[8]	13.2	14.1	14.3	12–15	12–15	191	16	4	—	—	10	3.5
	8-302[18]	13.8	14.6	14.6	14–18	14–18	191	18	4	—	4.5[17]	10	[7]
	8-302[11]	—	14.3[13]	14.6[13]	14–18	14–18	191	22	4	—	—	10	5
	8-351M	—	17	17	14–18	14–18	191	22	4	—	—	11	5
	8-351W	14.7	15.4	15.7	14–18	14–18	191	22	4	—	—	11	5
	8-400	—	16.5	16.5	14–18	14–18	191	22	4	—	—	12.5	5

[1]—Use with permanent type anti-freeze.
[2]—Add 1 qt. with filter change.
[3]—Maverick and Comet.
[4]—Sta. Wagons 21 gals.; others 26½ gals.
[5]—C4 9 quarts, FMX 11 quarts.
[6]—Except fuel economy models—19.2 gals; fuel economy models—18.1.
[7]—With 8″ ring gear, 4.5 pts.; with 8.7″ ring gear, 4.0 pts.; with 9″ ring gear, 5.0 pts.
[8]—Fairmont & Zephyr.
[9]—Approximate. Make final check with dipstick.
[10]—Torino & Montego.
[11]—Cougar and LTD II.
[12]—Less 4 wheel disc brakes—5 pts.; with 4 wheel disc brakes—4 pts.
[13]—Police & Taxi, 15.1 qts.
[14]—C4, 10.25 qts.; FMX, 11 qts; C6, 12.5 qts.
[15]—Torino, Montego, Cougar & Elite.
[16]—C4 trans. 10.3 qts.; FMX trans. 11.0 qts.; C6 trans. 12.2 qts.
[17]—With overdrive.
[18]—Granada and Monarch.
[19]—A/C & non A/C, 17.1; police & taxi, 17.5.
[20]—Passenger cars, 26 gals.; station wagons, 21.2.
[21]—A/C & non A/C, 17.1 qts.; trailer tow class III and police, 17.5 qts.

FORD & MERCURY — Compact & Intermediate Models

BRAKE SPECIFICATIONS

Year	Model	Brake Drum Inside Diameter	Wheel Cylinder Bore Diameter			Master Cylinder Bore Diameter		
			Front Disc Brake	Front Drum Brake	Rear Brake	With Disc Brakes	With Drum Brakes	With Power Brakes
1974	Maverick & Comet	10.00	2.600	1.125	.875	.9375	.9375	—
	Montego & Torino	①	3.100	—	1.00	1.00	1.00	1.00
	Cougar	9.00	3.100	—	.875	1.00	.9375	.9375
1975	Maverick & Comet	10.00	2.600	1.125	.843	.9375	.9375	.9375
	Granada & Monarch	10.00	2.600	—	②	.9375	—	③
	Torino, Montego, Cougar, Elite	①	3.100	—	1.00	1.00	—	1.00
1976	Maverick & Comet	10.00	2.600	—	.9375	.9375	—	.9375
	Granada & Monarch	10.00	2.600	—	②	.9375	—	③
	Torino, Montego, Cougar, Elite	11.00	3.100	—	.938	1.00	—	1.00
1977	Maverick & Comet	10.00	2.600	—	.938	.938	—	.938
	Granada & Monarch	10.00	2.600	—	②	.938	—	③
	Cougar & LTD II	11.03	3.100	—	④	1.00	—	1.00
1978	Cougar & LTD II	11.03	3.100	—	1.00	1.00	—	1.00
	Fairmont & Zephyr	⑤	2.360	—	.813	.875	—	.875
	Granada & Monarch	10.00	2.600	—	②	.938	—	③

①—Exc. Sta. Wagons 10.00, Sta. Wagons 11.00.
②—Drum .938"; Disc 2.1".
③—Power rear drum .938"; Power rear disc 1.00".
④—Except Station Wagon—.938"; Station Wagon—1.00".
⑤—Exc. sta. wag. 9"; Sta. wag. 10".

REAR AXLE SPECIFICATIONS

Year	Model	Carrier Type	Ring Gear & Pinion Backlash Inch	Nominal Pinion Locating Shim, Inch	Pinion Bearing Preload				Differential Bearing Preload	Pinion Nut Torque Ft.-Lbs. ①
					New Bearings With Seal Inch-Lbs.	Used Bearings With Seal Inch-Lbs.	New Bearings Less Seal Inch-Lbs.	Used Bearings Less Seal Inch-Lbs.		
1974		Removable	.008–.012	.015③	17–27④	8–14	—	—	.008–.012⑥	⑤
1975–78		Integral	.008–.012	.030	17–27	8–14	—	—	.008–.012②	140
		Removable	.008–.012	.015③	17–27④	8–14	—	—	.008–.012⑥	⑤

①—If torque cannot be obtained, install new spacer.
②—Case spread with new bearings. With used bearings .006–.010".
③—With 8" ring gear .022".
④—Solid spacer 13–33 inch-lbs.
⑤—With collapsible spacer 170 ft. lbs., with solid spacer 200 ft. lbs.
⑥—Case spread with new bearings. With used bearings .005–.008".

Electrical Section

DISTRIBUTOR, REPLACE

1. On vehicles with conventional ignition systems, disconnect primary wire from ignition coil. On vehicles with breakerless ignition systems, disconnect distributor wiring from connector from main wiring harness.
2. Disconnect vacuum advance lines and remove distributor cap.
3. Scribe a mark on the distributor body indicating the position of the rotor, and scribe another mark on the body and engine block indicating position of distributor body in block. These marks can be used as guides when installing distributor in a correctly timed engine.
4. Remove hold down screw or screws and lift distributor out of block. *Do not crank engine while distributor is removed or the initial timing operation will have to be performed.*

Installation

If the crankshaft has not been disturbed, install the distributor, using the scribed marks previously made on the distributor body and engine block as guides.

If the crankshaft has been rotated while the distributor was removed from the engine, it will be necessary to retime the engine. Crank the engine to bring No. 1 piston on top dead center of its compression stroke. Align the timing mark on the crankshaft pulley with the timing pointer (see *Tune Up* chart). Install the distributor so that the rotor points to the No. 1 spark plug wire terminal in the distributor cap.

NOTE: If equipped with breakerless igni-

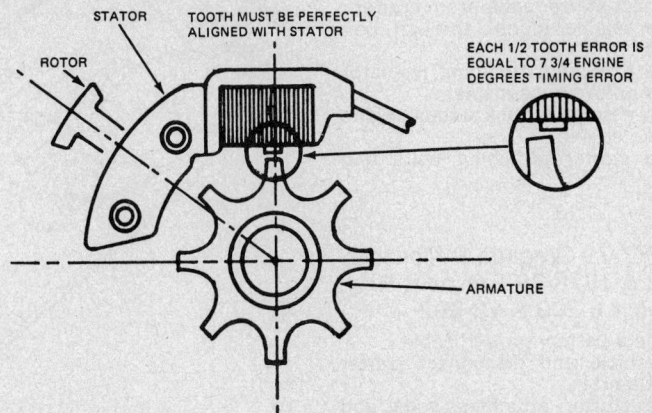

Fig. 1   Distributor stator & armature segment alignment. Breakerless distributors

tion system, the distributor must be installed with one of the armature segments aligned with the starter, Fig. 1, and the rotor at the number 1 firing position.

Make sure the oil pump intermediate shaft properly engages the distributor shaft. It may be necessary to crank the engine with the starter, after the distributor drive gear is properly engaged, in order to engage the oil pump intermediate shaft.

Check ignition timing and adjust to specifications.

NOTE: When using an inductive timing light on 1977-79 Dura Spark ignition systems, it is recommended that a split piece of vacuum hose be placed on the ignition wire where the inductive pick-up is placed.

STARTER, REPLACE

1978-79 Fairmont & Zephyr 6-200

1. Disconnect battery ground cable, then remove upper starter attaching bolt.
2. Remove exhaust heat shield, then disconnect starter cable from starter motor.
3. Raise vehicle and remove wishbone brace.
4. Remove two starter mounting bolts, then remove starter motor.

1978-79 Fairmont & Zephyr V8-302

1. Disconnect battery ground cable.
2. Raise vehicle and remove wishbone brace.
3. Remove starter motor attaching bolts and remove starter assembly.
4. Disconnect starter cable from starter motor.

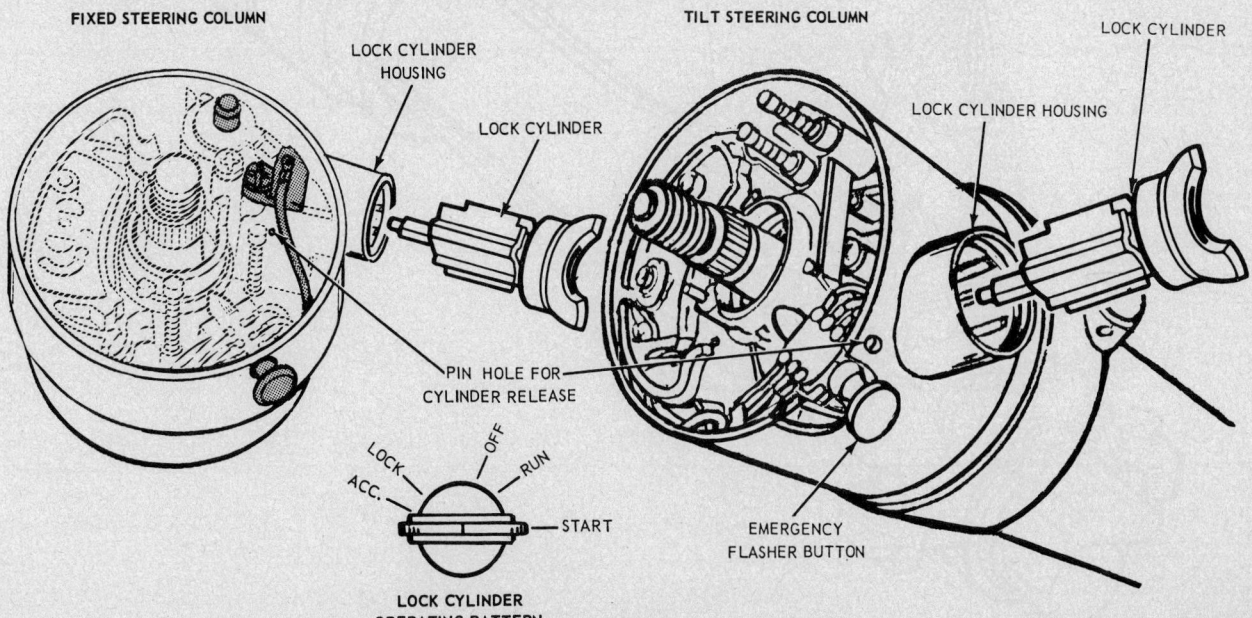

Fig. 2   Ignition lock

1977-79 Granada & Monarch V8-302

1. Disconnect battery ground cable.
2. Disconnect starter cable from starter.
3. Remove engine mount through bolt and nut.
4. Remove two bolts retaining insulator to block and remove insulator.
5. Position a suitable jack under engine and raise engine.
6. Remove starter attaching bolts and starter.

Except 1977-79 Granada & Monarch V8-302 & 1978-79 Fairmont & Zephyr 6-200 & V8-302

1. Disconnect battery ground cable.
2. Raise vehicle and disconnect starter cable at starter.
3. Remove starter attaching bolts and

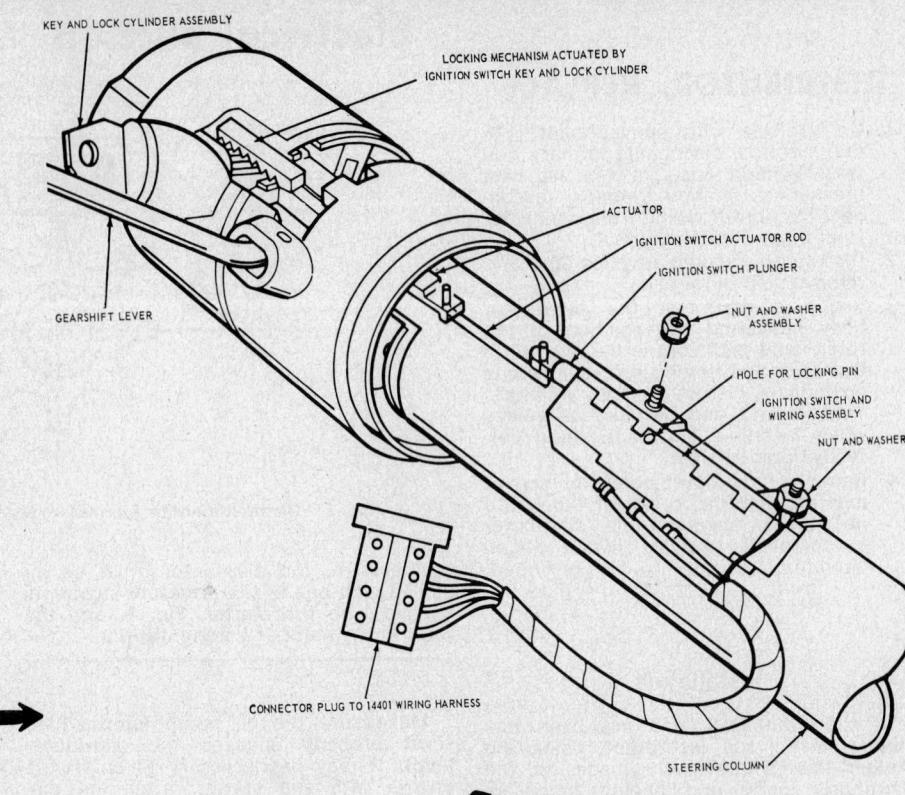

KEY AND LOCK CYLINDER ASSEMBLY

LOCKING MECHANISM ACTUATED BY IGNITION SWITCH KEY AND LOCK CYLINDER

ACTUATOR

IGNITION SWITCH ACTUATOR ROD

IGNITION SWITCH PLUNGER

NUT AND WASHER ASSEMBLY

HOLE FOR LOCKING PIN

IGNITION SWITCH AND WIRING ASSEMBLY

NUT AND WASHER

GEARSHIFT LEVER

CONNECTOR PLUG TO 14401 WIRING HARNESS

STEERING COLUMN

Fig. 3   Ignition switch installation 1974-77 Comet & Maverick ➡

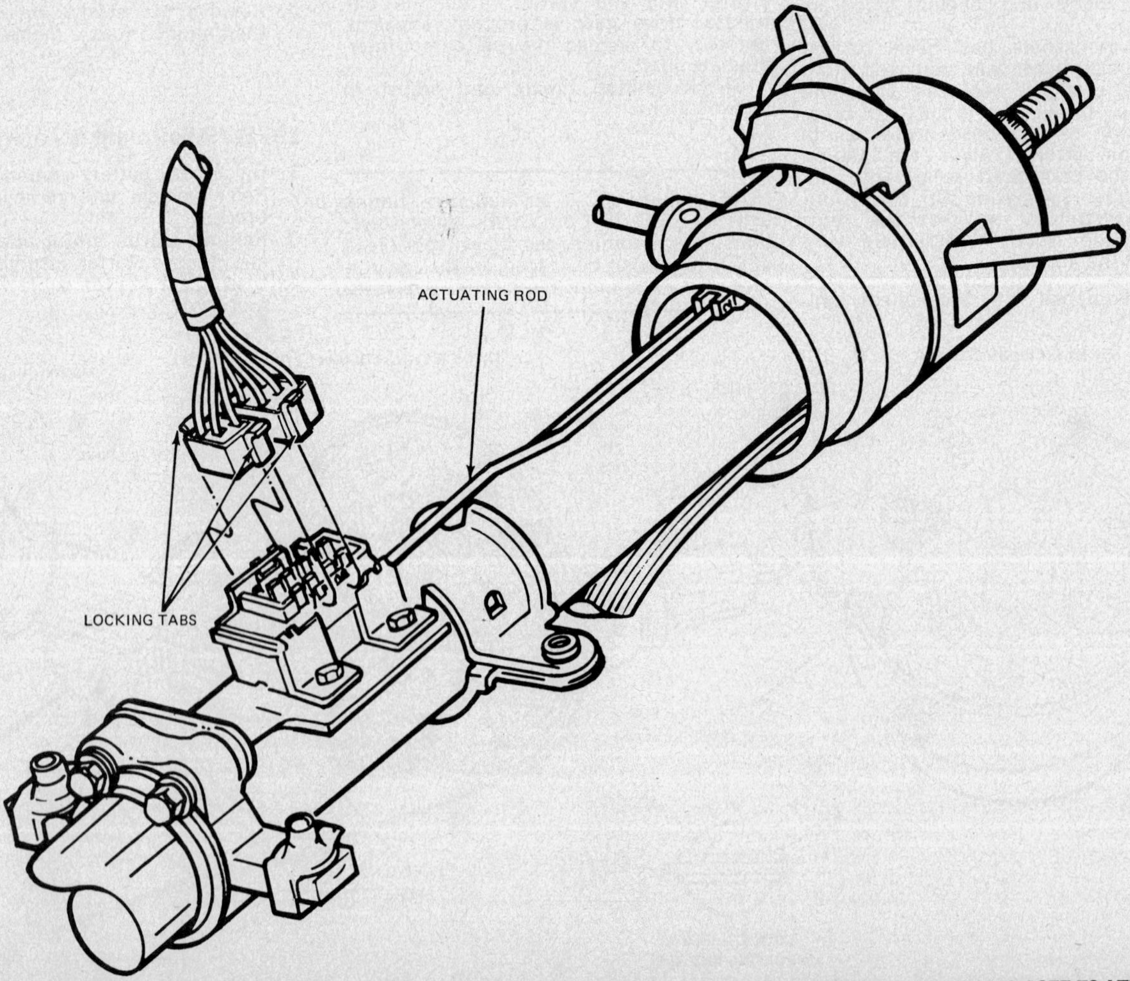

ACTUATING ROD

LOCKING TABS

Fig. 4   Ignition switch installation. 1974-76 Elite, Montego, Torino, 1974-79 Cougar, 1975-79 Granada, Monarch & 1977-79 LTD II

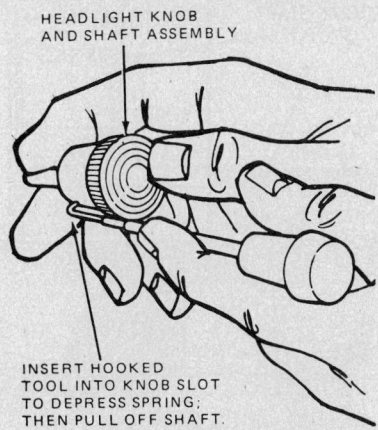

HEADLIGHT KNOB
AND SHAFT ASSEMBLY

INSERT HOOKED
TOOL INTO KNOB SLOT
TO DEPRESS SPRING;
THEN PULL OFF SHAFT.

Fig. 5 Light switch knob removal. Granada, LTD II & Monarch

starter.

NOTE: On engines equipped with a solenoid actuated starter, turn wheel to full right and remove the idler arm to frame bolts. On some models, it may be necessary to turn wheels aside to aid starter removal.

NOISY STARTER OR STARTER LOCKUP: If either of these situations occur, loosen the three mounting bolts enough to hand fit the starter properly into pilot plate. Then tighten starter mounting bolts, starting with top bolt. Starter should not be replaced until it has been proven noisy after proper alignment has been established by the above method.

IGNITION LOCK, REPLACE

1. Disconnect the battery ground cable.
2. *Units With Fixed Steering Columns:* Remove steering wheel and trim pad. Insert a wire pin into the hole inside the column halfway down the lock cylinder housing, Fig. 1. *Units with Tilt Steering Columns:* Insert wire pin in the hole located on the outside of the flange casting next to the emergency flasher button, Fig. 2.
3. Place the gear shift lever in *Park* (with automatic trans) or *Reverse* (with manual trans) position, and turn the lock cylinder with the ignition key to *Run* position.
4. Depress the wire pin while pulling up on the lock cylinder to remove. Remove the wire pin.
5. To install insert the lock cylinder into housing in the flange casting, and turn the key to *Off* position. Be certain that the cylinder is fully inserted before turning to the *Off* position. This action will extend the cylinder retaining pin into the cylinder housing.
6. Turn the key to check for correct operation in all positions.
7. Install the steering wheel and trim pad on fixed column units.
8. Connect the battery ground cable.

IGNITION SWITCH, REPLACE

1978-79 Fairmont & Zephyr

1. Disconnect battery ground cable, then remove steering column trim shroud by removing four screws.
2. Disconnect ignition switch wire connector.
3. Drill out bolts that attach switch to lock cylinder housing using a 1/8 in. drill. Remove the two bolts using an easy out.
4. Disengage ignition switch from actuator pin.
5. Adjust ignition switch by sliding carrier to lock position and inserting a 7/16 in. drill bit through switch housing and into carrier.
6. Rotate ignition key to lock position, then install ignition switch on actuator pin.
7. Install new switch to lock cylinder housing break away bolts and torque bolt until heads break away.
8. Remove drill bit from switch housing, then connect switch wire connector.
9. Connect battery ground cable and check switch for proper operation, then install steering column trim shroud.

Except 1978-79 Fairmont & Zephyr

1. On 1977-79 Cougar and LTD II, remove instrument cluster as described under Instrument Cluster, Replace.
2. On all models, remove steering column shroud and lower steering column from brake support bracket.
3. Disconnect battery cable.
4. Disconnect switch wiring and remove two switch retaining nuts. Disconnect switch from actuator and remove switch, Figs. 3 and 4.
5. Move shift lever to Park position on automatic transmissions and Reverse on standard transmission units. Place ignition key in Lock position and remove the key.

NOTE: New replacement switches

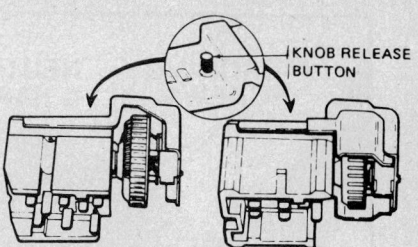

KNOB RELEASE BUTTON

Fig. 6 Light switches. Typical

are pinned in the Lock position by a plastic shipping pin inserted in a locking hole in the switch. For an existing switch, pull plunger out as far as it will go then back one detent to Lock position and insert a 3/32" drill in locking hole to retain switch in Lock position.

6. With locking pin in place, install switch on steering column, determine mid position of actuator lash and tighten retaining bolts.
7. Remove locking pin.

LIGHT SWITCH, REPLACE

1974-79 All

1. Disconnect battery ground cable.
2. On Granada, LTD II and Monarch models, to remove light switch knob, bend a discarded bowden cable into shape shown in Fig. 5. Insert hooked end of cable into knob slot to depress spring, then pull knob from shaft.
3. On all other models, remove control knob and shaft assembly, by placing knob in full on position, then pressing knob release button on switch and pulling out knob and shaft, Fig. 6. To gain access to the release button on Comet, Fairmont, Maverick and Zephyr models with air conditioning it will be necessary to first disconnect the left A/C duct.

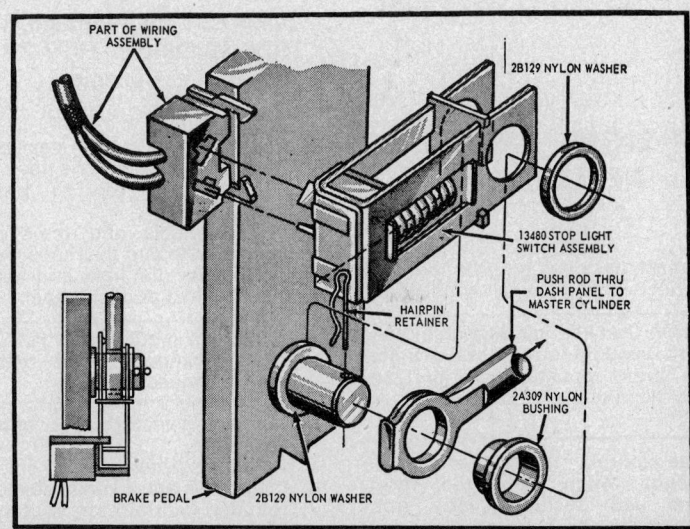

PART OF WIRING ASSEMBLY

2B129 NYLON WASHER

13480 STOP LIGHT SWITCH ASSEMBLY

PUSH ROD THRU DASH PANEL TO MASTER CYLINDER

HAIRPIN RETAINER

2A309 NYLON BUSHING

BRAKE PEDAL   2B129 NYLON WASHER

Fig. 7 Mechanical stop light switch.

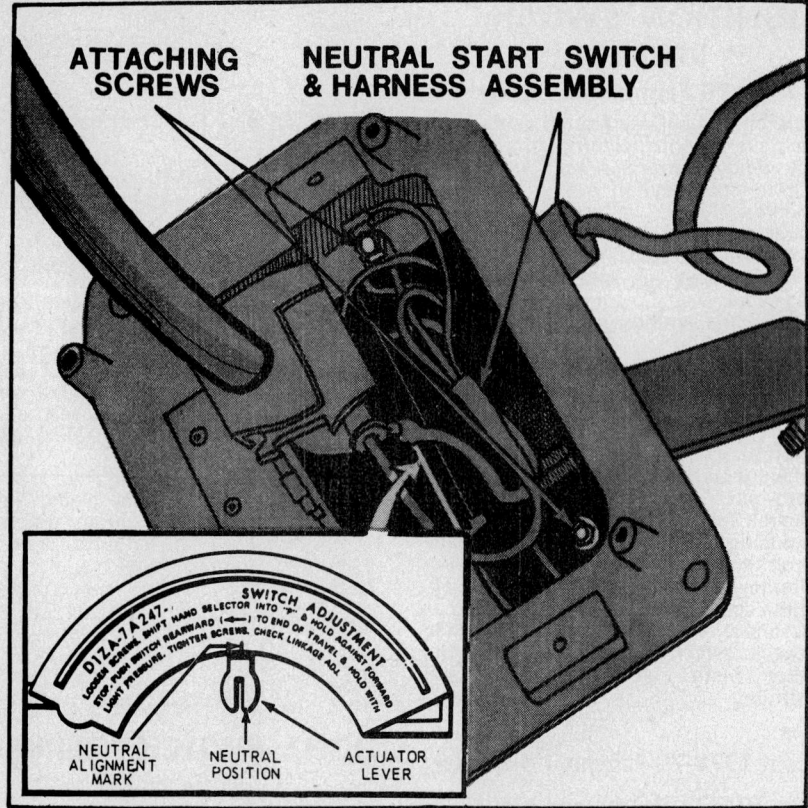

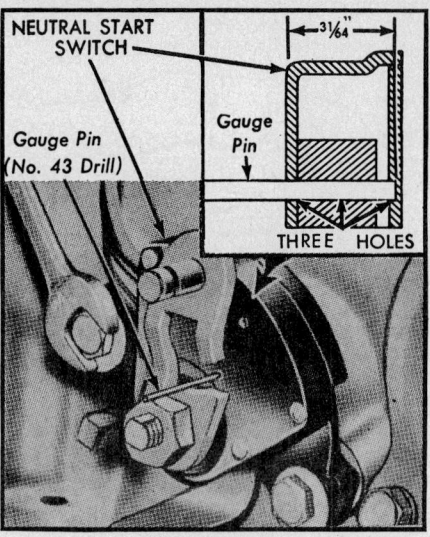

Fig. 9   Neutral safety switch. 1974-77 Maverick, Comet & 1975-79 Granada & Monarch

Fig. 8   Neutral safety switch. 1974-79 Cougar, 1974-76 Elite, Montego, Torino & 1977-79 LTD II with console

4. On all models, remove bezel nut. Disconnect multiple plug connector, vacuum hoses if vehicle is equipped with headlight doors and remove switch.
5. Reverse procedure to install. On Granada, LTD II and Monarch models, align triangular holes in knob and shaft, then press knob onto shaft until knob bottoms. On all other models, install knob and shaft by inserting shaft into the switch until a distinct click is heard. In some instances it may be necessary to rotate the shaft slightly until it engages the switch carrier.

STOP LIGHT SWITCH, REPLACE

1. Disconnect battery ground cable and disconnect wires at switch connector.

NOTE: On Granada and Monarch models with vacuum power brake units, loosen brake booster nut $1/4$ turn, thereby eliminating binding during removal.

2. Remove hairpin retainer and slide stop light switch, push rod, nylon washers and bushings away from brake pedal, and remove switch, Fig. 7.

3. Reverse procedure to install and on Granada and Monarch models, torque brake booster retaining nuts to 13-25 ft. lbs.

NEUTRAL SAFETY SWITCH, REPLACE

1974-76 Elite, Montego, Torino, 1974-79 Cougar, 1977-79 LTD II Console

Removal & Adjustment, Fig. 8
1. Place selector lever in neutral.
2. Raise vehicle and remove nut that secures shift rod to transmission manual lever.
3. Lower vehicle and remove selector level handle and dial housing.
4. Disconnect dial light and neutral start switch wires at dash panel.

NOTE: On models with FMX transmission, disconnect seat belt warning circuit connector.

5. Remove selector lever and housing assembly.
6. Remove pointer back up shield attaching screws and remove shield.
7. Remove neutral start switch to selector lever housing attaching screws.
8. Push neutral start switch harness plug

inward and remove switch and harness assembly.
9. Position switch and harness assembly on selector lever housing, then install but do not tighten attaching screws.

NOTE: Before installing switch and harness assembly, ensure selector lever is against neutral detent stop and actuator lever is properly aligned in neutral position.

10. Place selector lever in park position and hold against forward stop.
11. Move neutral start switch rearward to end of its travel, then while holding switch in rearward position tighten attaching screws.
12. Install pointer back up shield, then position selector lever and housing assembly on console and install attaching bolts.
13. Connect dial indicator, neutral start switch and seat belt warning circuit (if equipped) wire connectors.
14. Install dial housing and shift lever handle, then place selector lever in Drive position.
15. Raise vehicle and install shift rod on transmission manual lever.
16. Check shift linkage adjustment, then lower vehicle and check operation of neutral start switch.

1974-77 Comet, Maverick & 1975-79 Granada & Monarch

Transmission Mounted Switch, Fig. 9
1. Remove downshift linkage rod from transmission downshift lever.
2. Apply penetrating oil to downshift lever shaft and nut; then remove downshift outer lever.
3. Remove switch attaching bolts.
4. Disconnect multiple wire connector and remove switch from transmission.
5. Install new switch.
6. With transmission manual lever in neutral, rotate switch and install

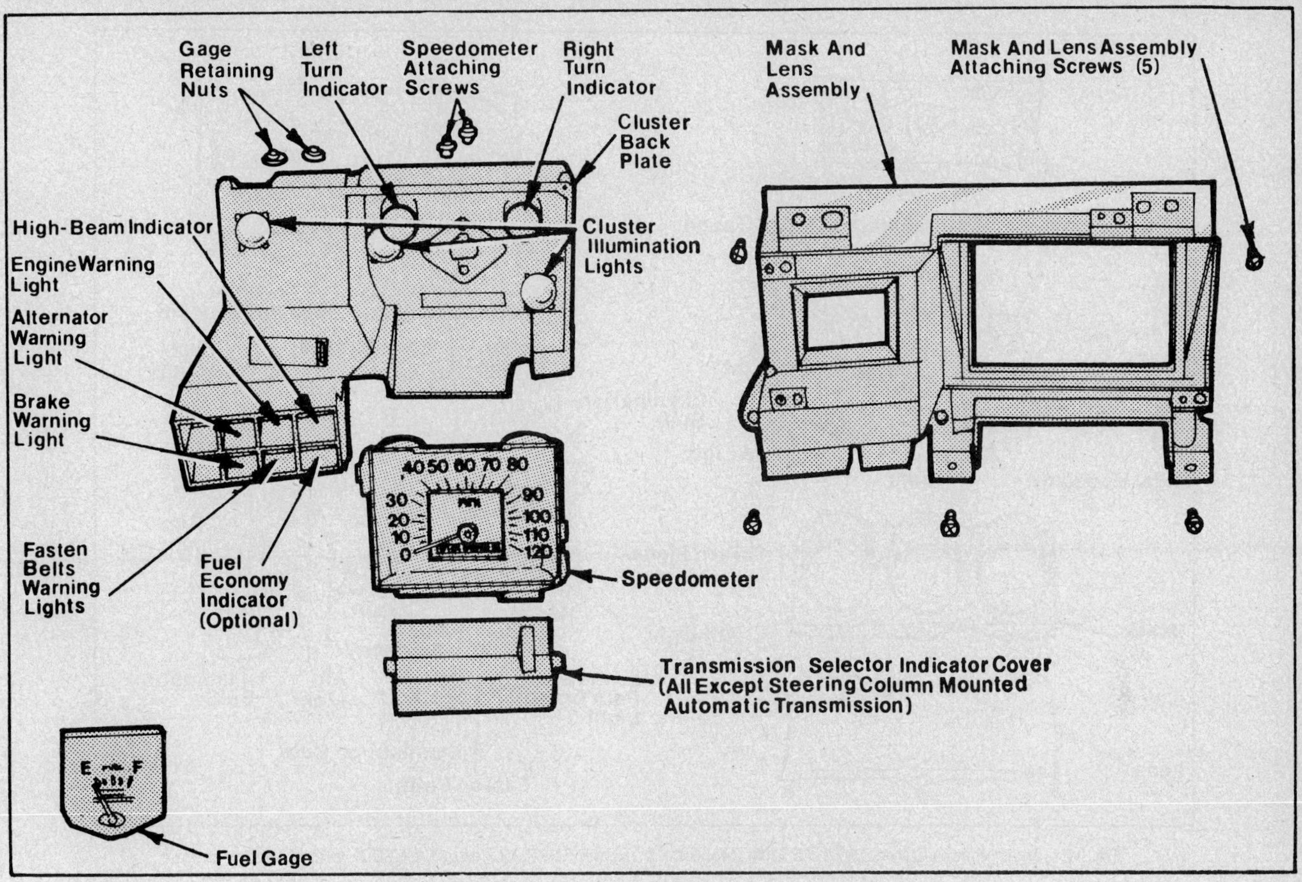

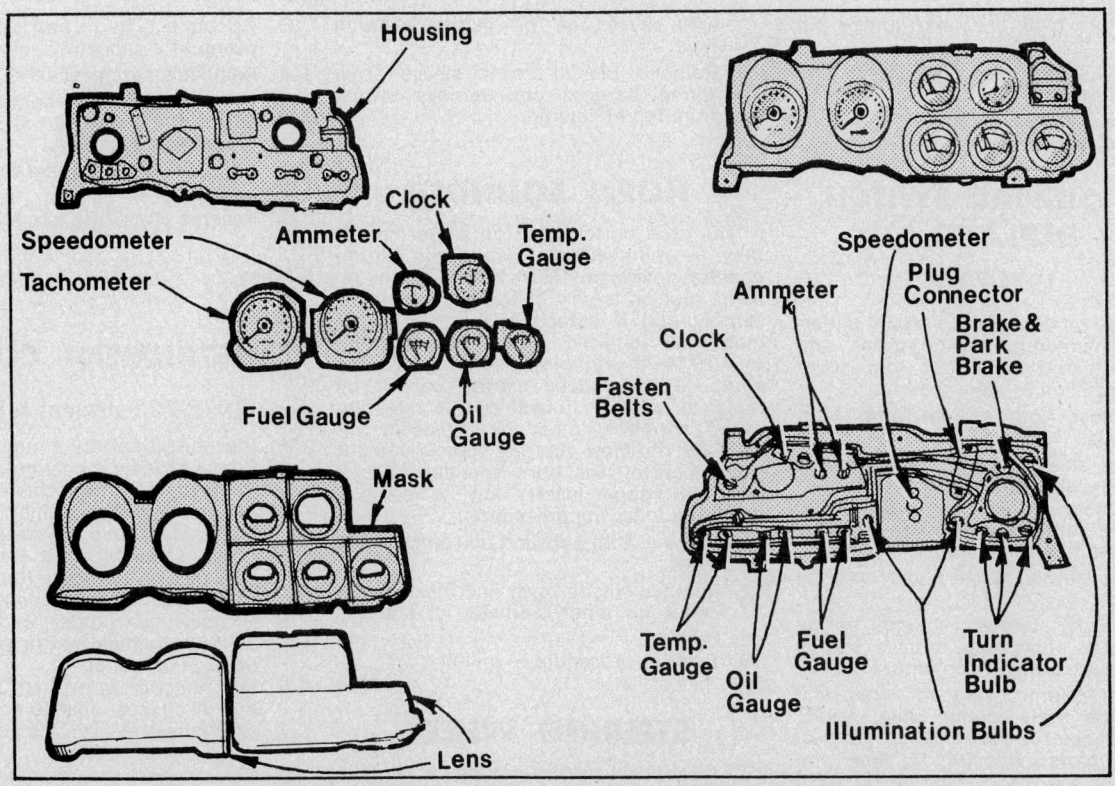

Gage Retaining Nuts
Left Turn Indicator
Speedometer Attaching Screws
Right Turn Indicator
Cluster Back Plate
Mask And Lens Assembly
Mask And Lens Assembly Attaching Screws (5)
High-Beam Indicator
Cluster Illumination Lights
Engine Warning Light
Alternator Warning Light
Brake Warning Light
Fasten Belts Warning Lights
Fuel Economy Indicator (Optional)
Speedometer
Transmission Selector Indicator Cover (All Except Steering Column Mounted Automatic Transmission)
Fuel Gage

Fig. 10   Instrument cluster. 1975-79 Granada & Monarch

Housing
Clock
Temp. Gauge
Speedometer
Ammeter
Tachometer
Fuel Gauge
Oil Gauge
Mask
Lens
Speedometer
Plug Connector
Ammeter
Clock
Brake & Park Brake
Fasten Belts
Temp. Gauge
Oil Gauge
Fuel Gauge
Turn Indicator Bulb
Illumination Bulbs

Fig. 11   Instrument cluster. 1974-76, Elite, Montego & Torino, 1974-79
Cougar & 1977-79 LTD II with performance cluster

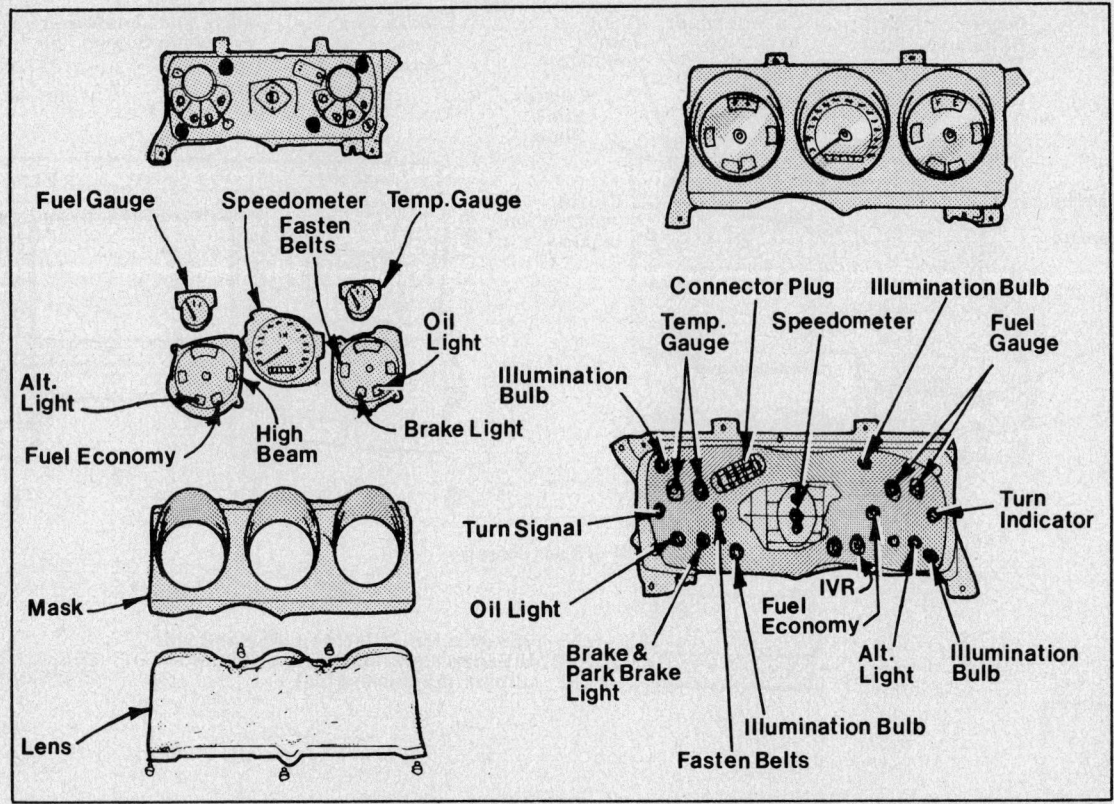

Fig. 12 Instrument cluster. 1974-76 Elite, Montego & Torino, 1977-79 Cougar & LTD II with standard cluster

gauge pin (#43 drill) into gauge pin holes.

7. Tighten switch attaching bolts and remove gauge pin.

8. Complete the installation in reverse order of removal.

TURN SIGNAL SWITCH, REPLACE

1974-79

1. Remove retaining screw from underside of steering wheel spokes and lift off pad horn switch/trim cover and medallion as an assembly.

2. Disconnect horn switch wires from terminals.

3. Remove steering wheel retaining nut and remove steering wheel with suitable puller.

4. Remove turn signal switch lever by unscrewing it from steering column.

5. Remove shroud from under steering column.

6. Disconnect steering column wiring connector plugs and remove screws that secure switch to column.

7. On tilt column, remove wires and terminals from column plug. *NOTE: Record color code and position of wires before removing. A hole provided in the flange casting on fixed columns makes it unnecessary to separate wires from plug as the plug*

with wires can be guided through hole.

8. Remove plastic cover sleeve from wiring harness and remove switch from top of column.

HORN SOUNDER

The horn button used on some models may be removed by twisting the button counter-clockwise. The horn switch on some models is part of the trim cover assembly and if defective, the trim cover must be replaced. The horn sounder on 1974-79 rim-blow steering wheels equipped with speed control cannot be replaced and if defective, the steering wheel assembly must be replaced. On 1974-79 rim-blow steering wheels without speed control, the horn sounder (plastic strip and copper insert) may be replaced using the following procedure:

1. Remove trim pad and disconnect lead wires.

2. Remove plastic cover and lift out horn insert on inner diameter of steering wheel.

3. Reverse procedure to install.

STEERING WHEEL

1. Disconnect battery ground cable.

2. Remove steering wheel trim pad, horn button or ring.

3. Disconnect horn and speed control wiring, if equipped.

4. Remove steering wheel nut.

5. Mark relationship between steering shaft and steering wheel hub for proper reinstallation.

6. Remove steering wheel with a suitable puller.

7. Reverse procedure to install.

INSTRUMENT CLUSTER

1978-79 Fairmont & Zephyr

1. Disconnect battery ground cable.

2. Remove steering column shroud.

3. Remove instrument cluster trim cover.

4. Remove screw retaining PRND21 control cable clamp to steering column. Then, disconnect the cable from pin on steering column. Remove plastic clamp from steering column.

5. Remove two upper and two lower screws retaining instrument cluster to instrument panel.

6. Pull cluster from instrument panel and disconnect speedometer cable.

7. Disconnect electrical connectors from instrument cluster.

8. Remove instrument cluster from vehicle.

9. Reverse procedure to install.

1975-79 Granada & Monarch

1. Disconnect battery ground cable.
2. Remove lower cluster cover from below steering column.
3. Remove steering column shroud.
4. On early 1975 models remove windshield wiper switch control knob.
5. On all models, remove headlamp switch knob and shaft assembly and bezel.
6. Remove four cluster finish panel attaching screws.
7. Using a right angle screwdriver, pry along edges of finish panel, thereby removing studs from retainers and remove finish panel.
8. Disconnect automatic transmission indicator cable and speedometer cable.
9. Remove four screws retaining cluster to instrument panel, then pull cluster out and disconnect feed plug from printed circuit, Fig. 10.
10. Disconnect wires from fuel gauge if equipped with low fuel warning light and remove cluster.

1974-76 Elite, Montego, Torino, 1974-79 Cougar XR7 & 1977-79 LTD II

1. Disconnect battery ground cable.
2. Remove upper and lower retaining screws from cluster trim cover and remove the cover, Figs. 11 and 12.
3. On 1977-79 models with standard cluster, remove clock or cover to cluster attaching screw and clock or cover to instrument panel retaining screw.
4. On all models, remove two upper and two lower screws retaining cluster to the panel.
5. Pull cluster away from panel and disconnect speedo cable.
6. Disconnect cluster feed plug from receptable in printed circuit.
7. If equipped, remove Park, Belts and Fuel Economy lights from receptacles.
8. On Elite, Montego and Torino performance cluster, disconnect clock and tachometer wire loom at connector.
9. On Cougar and Ltd II models, disconnect over-lay harness connector.
10. Remove cluster.

1974-77 Comet & Maverick

1. Disconnect battery ground cable.
2. From under instrument panel, disconnect speedometer cable.
3. Remove two retaining screws at the top of the cluster and swing it down from the panel, Fig. 13.
4. Disconnect electrical connections and remove cluster.

W/S WIPER BLADES

1978-79 Fairmont & Zephyr

Side Saddle Pin Type: Remove blade by pulling up on spring lock and pulling blade assembly from pin, Fig. 14. To replace rubber element, locate 7/16 in. long notch on the plastic backing strip. Place frame of wiper blade assembly on a firm surface with notched end of locking strip visible. Grasp frame portion of wiper blade assembly and push down until blade is slightly bowed, then grasp tip of backing strip firmly and pull up and twist counter clockwise at the same time, Fig. 15. The backing strip will snap out of the retaining tab at the end of the frame. Lift wiper blade assembly from surface and slide

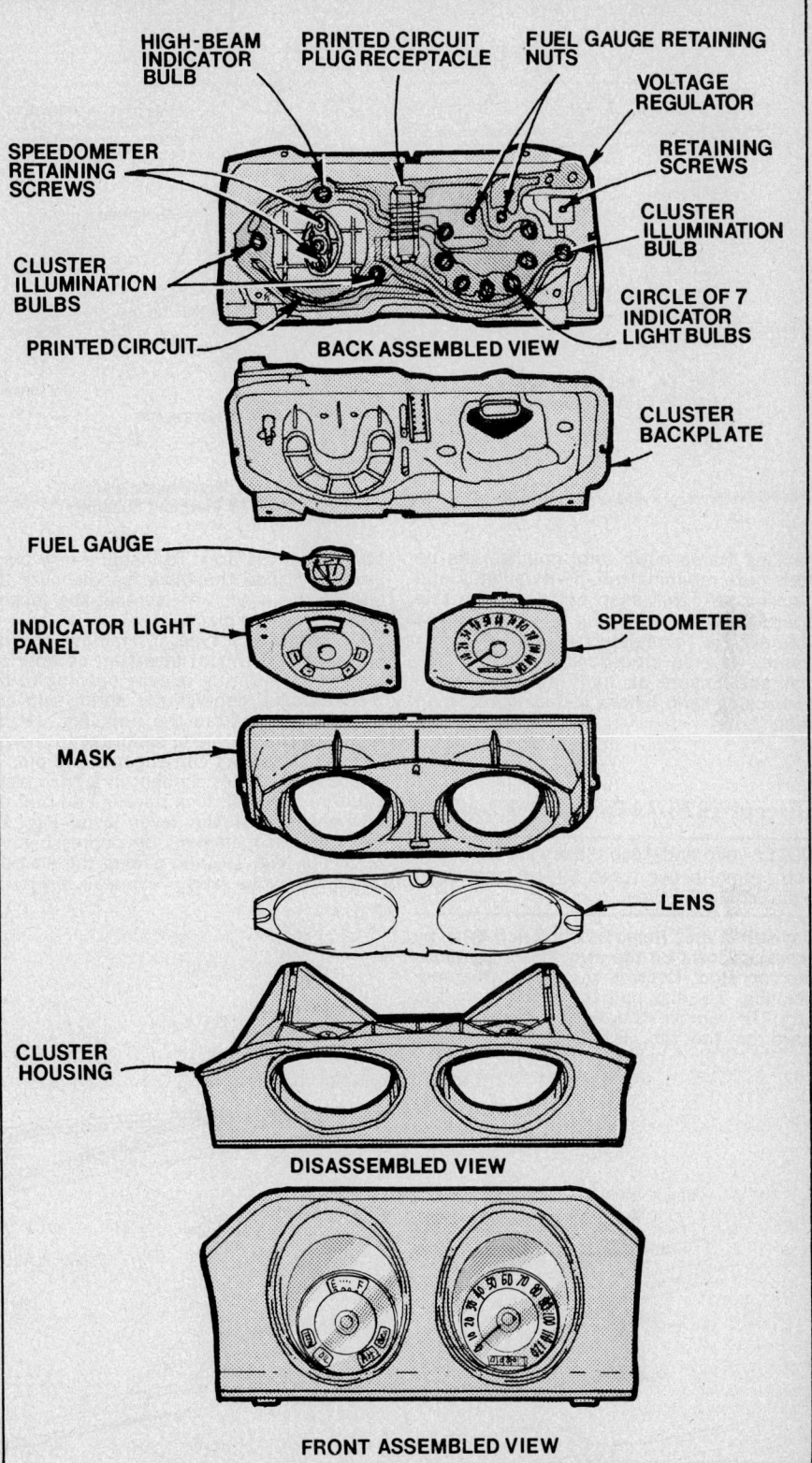

Fig. 13   Instrument cluster. 1974-77 Comet & Maverick

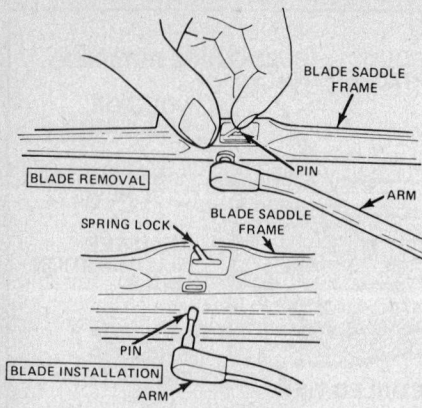

Fig. 14 Pin type blade.
1978-79 Fairmont & Zephyr

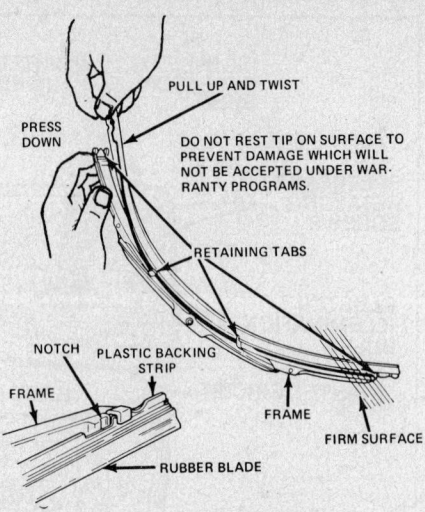

Fig. 15 Wiper blade element.
1978-79 Fairmont & Zephyr

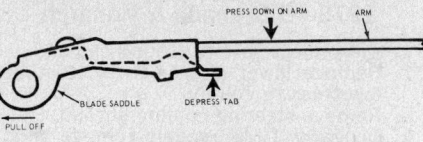

Fig. 16 Trico bayonet type blade.
Exc. Fairmont & Zephyr

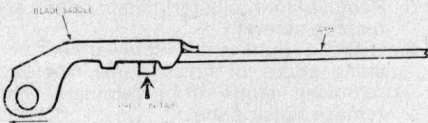

Fig. 17 Anco bayonet type blade.
Exc. Fairmont & Zephyr

backing frame down until notches line up with next retaining tab. Twist slightly and backing strip will snap out. Continue this operation with remaining tabs until blade element is completely detached from frame. Reverse procedure to install blade element. Ensure all four tabs are locked to backing strip before installing blade on wiper arm.

Except 1978-79 Fairmont & Zephyr

NOTE: Trico and Anco blades are used and both come in two types Bayonet type and Side Saddle Pin type.

Bayonet Type: Remove the Trico type by pressing down on the arm, this will unlock the top stud. Depress the tab on the saddle, Fig. 16, and pull the blade from the arm. To remove the *Anco* type press inward on the tab, Fig. 17, and pull the

blade from the arm. To install a new blade assembly slide the blade saddle over the end of the wiper arm so that the locking stud snaps into place.

Side Saddle Pin Type: To remove the pin type (Trico or Anco) insert an appropriate tool into the spring release opening of the blade saddle, depress the spring clip and pull the blade from the arm, Fig. 18. To install, push the blade saddle onto the pin so that the spring clip engages the pin. To replace the rubber element in a *Trico* blade squeeze the latch lock release and pull the element out of the lever jaws, Fig. 19. Remove *Anco* element by depressing the latch pin, Fig. 19, and sliding the element out of the yoke jaws. To install insert the

element through the yoke or lever jaws. Be sure the element is engaged at all points.

W/S WIPER ARMS

1974-77 Comet & Maverick

NOTE: These models do not have a pin and hole arrangement to hold the attaching clip in the released position.

To remove, swing the arm and blade assembly away from the windshield to release the spring loaded attaching clip in the arm from the pivot. Hold in this position and pull the arm off the pivot shaft using tool, Fig. 20. To install, hold the arm

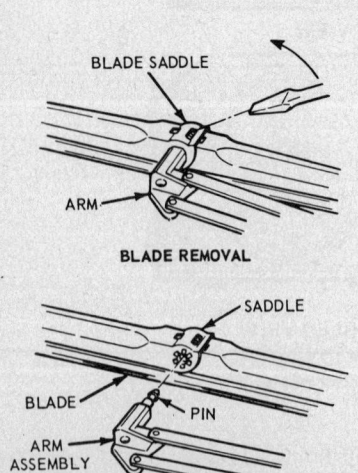

Fig. 18 Pin type blade.
Exc. Fairmont & Zephyr

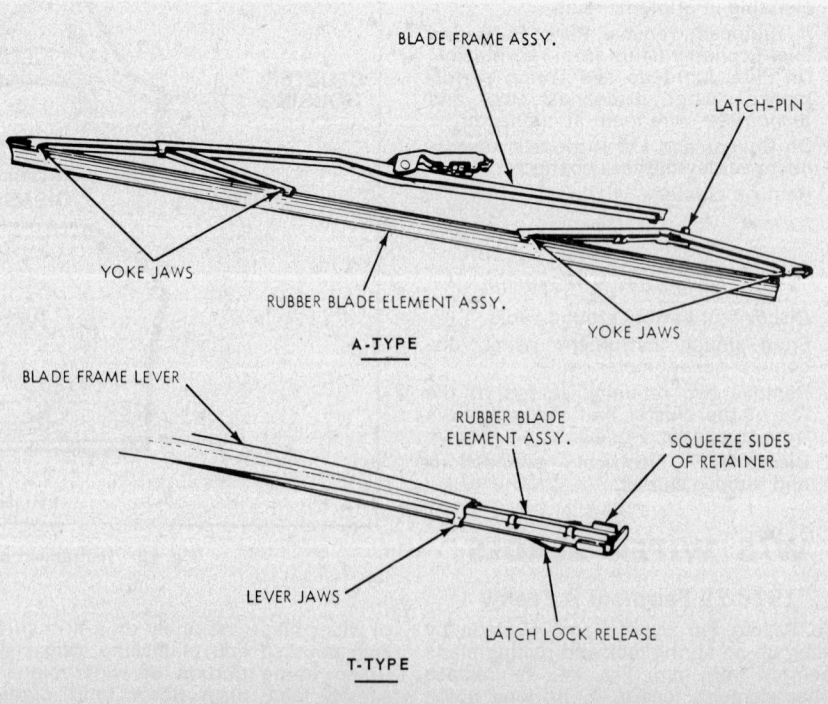

Fig. 19 Wiper blade element. Exc. Fairmont & Zephyr

and blade assembly in the swing out position and push the arm on to the pivot shaft. The arm will lock to the pivot when it is moved back against the windshield.

1974-79 Except Comet & Maverick

Raise the blade end of the arm off of the windshield and move the slide latch, Fig. 21, away from the pivot shaft. This action will unlock the wiper arm from the pivot shaft and hold the blade end of the arm off the glass at the same time. The wiper arm can now be pulled off of the pivot shaft without the aid of any tools.

W/S WIPER MOTOR

1978-79 Fairmont & Zephyr

1. Disconnect battery ground cable.
2. Remove left hand wiper arm from pivot shaft and place on cowl grille.
3. Remove cowl grille attaching screws, then raise left hand corner of cowl grille to gain access to linkage drive arm.
4. Disconnect linkage arm from motor output arm pin by removing retaining clip.
5. Disconnect wiper motor wire connector.
6. Remove wiper motor to cowl attaching bolts, then remove wiper motor.

1978-79 Granada & Monarch

1. Disconnect battery ground cable.
2. Remove instrument panel pad.
3. Remove speaker mounting bracket, then disconnect wire connector and remove speaker.
4. Remove defroster nozzle and air distribution duct.
5. Remove wiper motor to cowl attaching bolts, then remove wiper motor.

1975-77 Comet, Maverick, Granada & Monarch

1. Disconnect battery ground cable.
2. On 1975 models remove seat belt interlock module.
3. On all models, remove evaporator case center distribution duct assembly.
4. Working over top of brake support assembly, remove wiper motor pivot clip and disconnect linkage from motor arm.
5. Remove wiper motor attaching bolts and wiper motor.

NOTE: Some Granada and Monarch models may have an additional instrument panel brace which must be detached from the floor pan and swung to one side to provide access to wiper motor attaching bolts.

1974-76 Elite, Montego, Torino, 1974-79 Cougar & 1977-79 LTD II

1. Disconnect battery ground cable.
2. Remove wiper arm and blade assembly.
3. Remove left cowl screen, then remove retaining clip and disconnect drive arm from motor crankpin.
4. Disconnect wire connectors from

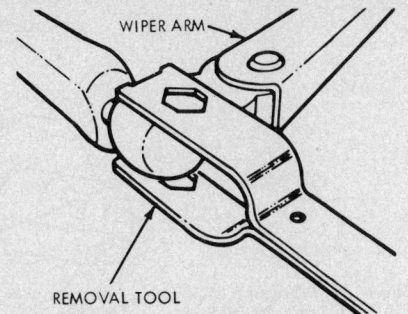

Fig. 20   Wiper arm removal. 1974-77 Comet & Maverick

motor, then remove attaching bolts and motor.

NOTE: If output arm catches on dash during removal, handturn arm clockwise so it will clear. Before installing ensure output arm is in park position.

1974 Comet & Maverick

1. Remove instrument cluster.
2. On air conditioned units, remove center connector and duct assembly.
3. Working through cluster opening, disconnect two pivot shaft links from motor drive arm by removing retaining clip.
4. Disconnect wiring and remove mounting bolts and remove motor through cluster opening.

W/S WIPER TRANSMISSION

1978-79 Fairmont & Zephyr

1. Disconnect battery ground cable.
2. Remove wiper arms and blade assemblies from pivot shafts, then remove cowl grille attaching screws.
3. If left pivot shaft assembly is to be removed, disconnect linkage drive arm from right drive arm by removing retaining clip.
4. If right pivot shaft assembly is to be removed, disconnect linkage drive arm from motor and left drive arm by removing retaining clips.
5. Remove pivot shaft retaining screws, then remove linkage and pivot shaft assemblies.

1974-76 Elite, Montego, Torino, 1974-79 Cougar & 1977-79 LTD II

1. Disconnect battery ground cable.
2. Remove wiper arm and blade assemblies.
3. Remove cowl screen. Screen snaps into cowl and the arm stop is integral with the screen.
4. Disconnect linkage drive arm from motor by removing retaining clip.
5. Remove pivot shaft retaining bolts and remove linkage and pivot shaft assemblies.

1974-77 Comet, Maverick & 1975-79 Granada & Monarch

Left Side:
1. Remove instrument cluster.

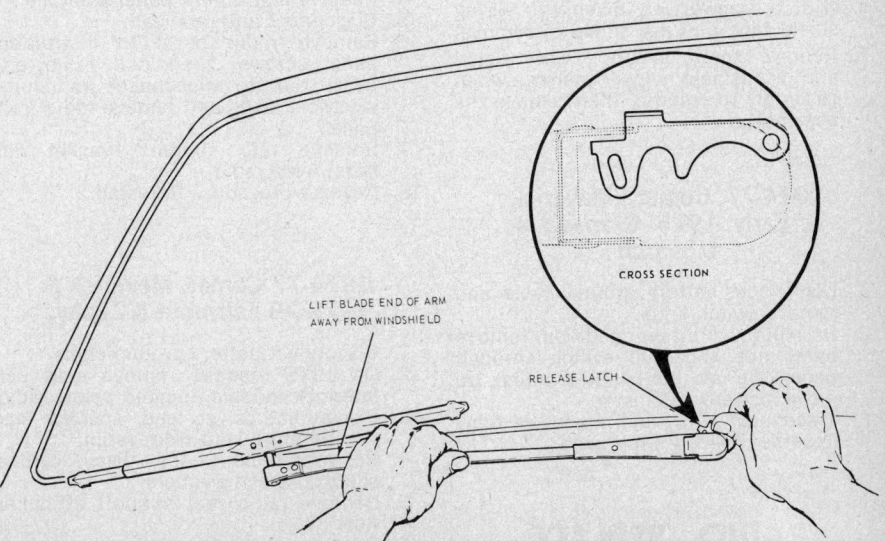

Fig. 21   Wiper arm. 1974-79 Except Comet & Maverick

2. Remove wiper arm and blade.
3. Working through cluster opening, disconnect both pivot shaft links from motor drive arm by removing retaining clip.
4. Remove three pivot shaft assembly retaining bolts and remove assembly through cluster opening.

Right Side:

1. Disconnect battery ground cable and remove wiper blade and arm.
2. On air conditioned units, remove right duct assembly.
3. From under the instrument panel, disconnect first left then right pivot shaft link from motor drive arm.
4. Reaching between utility shelf and instrument panel, remove pivot shaft retaining bolts and lower assembly out from under panel.

W/S WIPER SWITCH

1974-79 Except Comet, Granada, Maverick & Monarch

1. Disconnect battery ground cable.
2. Remove wiper switch knob, bezel nut and bezel. The wiper switch knob is removed in the same manner as the headlight switch knob, Fig. 5.
3. Pull out switch from under panel and disconnect plug connector from switch.

Late 1975 & 1976-79 Granada, Monarch & 1978-79 Fairmont & Zephyr Column Mounted Switch

1. Disconnect battery ground cable.
2. Disconnect turn signal and wiper/washer switch wire connector.
3. Remove lower instrument panel shield.
4. Remove two screws and separate steering column cover halves.
5. Pull wire cover from bottom on column and remove cover.
6. With a screwdriver, disengage wiring shield tang and pry shield to remove.
7. Remove screw securing turn signal and windshield wiper/washer switch assembly to column, then remove the assembly.

1974-77 Comet, Maverick & Early 1975 Granada & Monarch

1. Disconnect battery ground cable and remove switch knob.
2. On units without air condition, remove bezel nut and pull switch through panel. On air conditioned units, remove instrument cluster.
3. Disconnect wiring and remove switch.
4. Reverse procedure to install.

RADIO, REPLACE

NOTE: When installing radio, be sure to

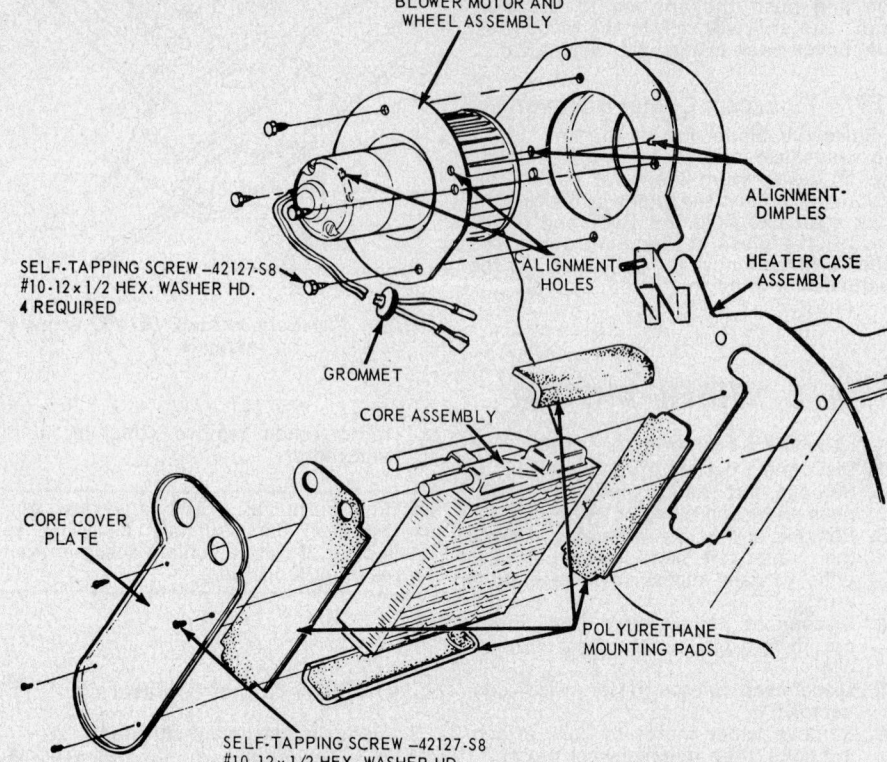

SELF-TAPPING SCREW –42127-S8
#10-12 x 1/2 HEX. WASHER HD.
4 REQUIRED

GROMMET

BLOWER MOTOR AND WHEEL ASSEMBLY

ALIGNMENT DIMPLES

HEATER CASE ASSEMBLY

ALIGNMENT HOLES

CORE ASSEMBLY

CORE COVER PLATE

POLYURETHANE MOUNTING PADS

SELF-TAPPING SCREW –42127-S8
#10-12 x 1/2 HEX. WASHER HD.
4 REQUIRED

Fig. 22 Heater core & blower motor less air conditioning. 1974-76 Elite, Montego & Torino; 1974-79 Cougar; 1975-79 Granada & Monarch; 1977-79 LTD II

adjust antenna trimmer for peak performance.

1975-79 Granada & Monarch

1. Disconnect battery ground cable.
2. Remove headlamp switch.
3. Remove knobs from heater and A/C control, windshield wiper switch and radio.
4. Remove instrument panel applique.
5. Disconnect antenna lead.
6. Remove radio bezel to instrument panel screws, then pull radio and bezel out to disconnect remaining electrical leads and remove radio from panel.
7. Remove rear support bracket and bezel from radio.
8. Reverse procedure to install.

1974-77 Comet, Maverick & 1978-79 Fairmont & Zephyr

1. Disconnect battery ground cable.
2. On 1975 models, remove seat belt interlock module, located below radio.
3. Disconnect power lead, speaker lead and antenna lead from radio.
4. Remove radio knobs, discs, control shaft nuts and washers.
5. Remove radio rear support attaching nut.
6. Remove radio from bezel and from rear support.
7. Reverse procedure to install.

1974-76 Elite, Montego, Torino, 1974-79 Cougar & 1977-79 LTD II

1. Disconnect battery ground cable.
2. Pull off radio control knobs.
3. Remove radio support to instrument panel attaching screw.
4. Remove bezel nuts from radio control shafts, then lower radio and disconnect speaker, power and antenna wire from radio.
5. Reverse procedure to install.

HEATER CORE REMOVAL

1978-79 Fairmont & Zephyr

Less Air Conditioning

1. Disconnect battery ground cable and drain cooling system.
2. Disconnect heater hoses from heater core and seal the core tubes.
3. Remove glove box liner.
4. Remove instrument panel to cowl brace retaining screws and brace.
5. Place temperature control lever in the warm position.
6. Remove heater core cover retaining screws and the cover.
7. From engine compartment, remove heater case assembly mounting stud nuts.

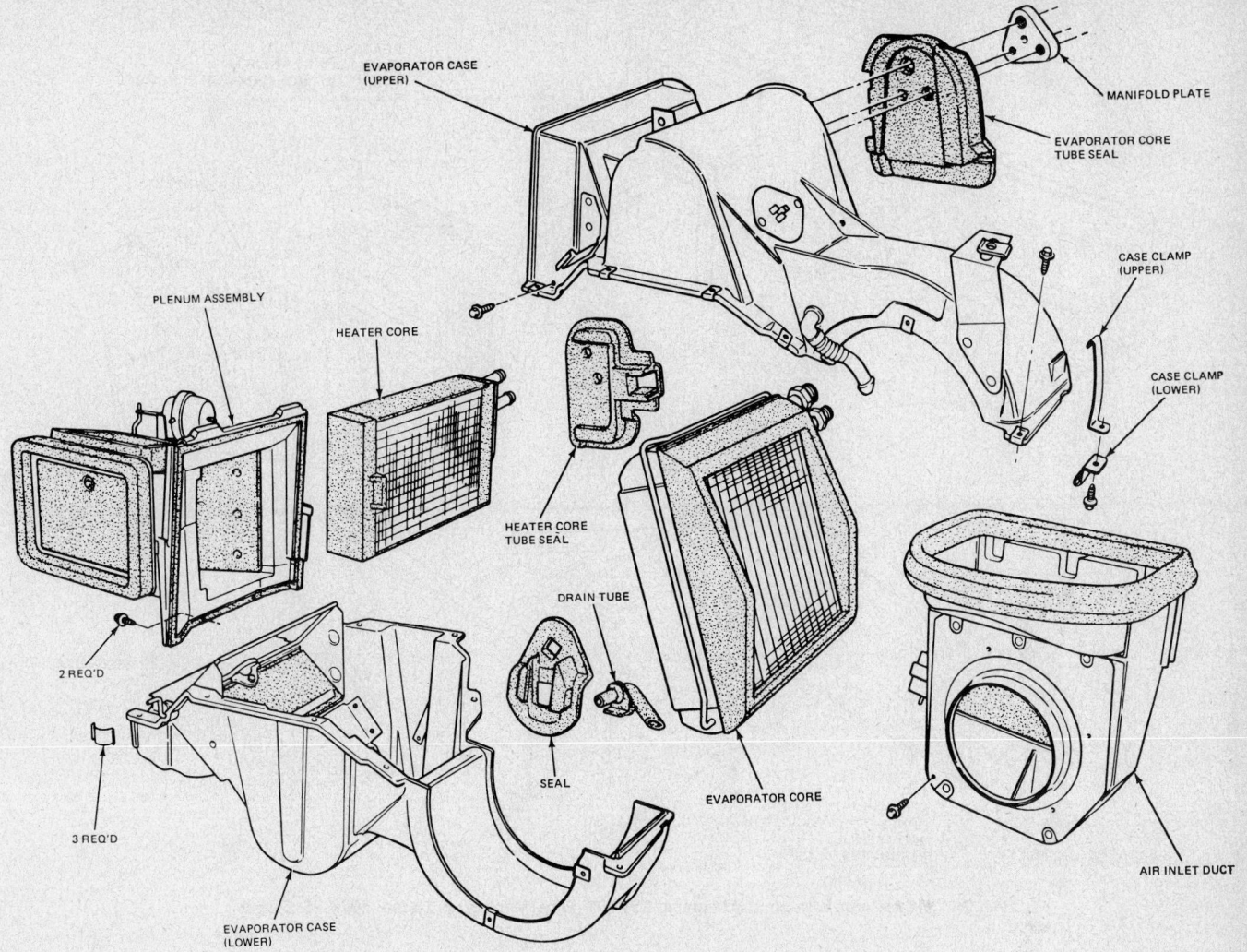

EVAPORATOR CASE (UPPER)

MANIFOLD PLATE

EVAPORATOR CORE TUBE SEAL

PLENUM ASSEMBLY

HEATER CORE

CASE CLAMP (UPPER)

CASE CLAMP (LOWER)

HEATER CORE TUBE SEAL

DRAIN TUBE

2 REQ'D

SEAL

EVAPORATOR CORE

3 REQ'D

AIR INLET DUCT

EVAPORATOR CASE (LOWER)

Fig. 23   Heater core. 1975-79 Granada & Monarch with air conditioning

8. Push heater core tubes and seal toward passenger compartment to loosen heater core from case assembly.
9. Remove heater core through glove box opening.
10. Reverse procedure to install.

With Air Conditioning

1. Disconnect battery ground cable.
2. Remove screws attaching instrument cluster trim panel to instrument panel pad.
3. Remove instrument panel pad to instrument panel screws at each defroster opening.
4. Remove instrument panel pad edge to instrument panel screws and pad.
5. Remove steering column lower cover to instrument panel screws then the cover.
6. Remove two nuts and bracket securing steering column to instrument panel and brake pedal support. Support steering column on front seat.
7. Remove instrument panel to brake pedal support screw at steering column opening.
8. Remove screw attaching lower brace to lower edge of instrument panel below radio.
9. Remove screw attaching the brace to lower edge of instrument panel.
10. Disconnect temperature control cable from blend door and evaporator case bracket.
11. Disconnect vacuum hose connectors from evaporator case.
12. Disconnect blower resistor wire connector from resistor on evaporator housing, then the blower motor feed wire at in-line connector.
13. Support instrument panel and, with an angle Phillips screwdriver, remove three screws attaching top of instrument panel to the cowl.
14. Remove screws attaching instrument panel to cowl side panels.
15. Move instrument panel rearward and disconnect speedometer cable and any wiring that will not permit the instrument panel to be positioned on the front seat.
16. Drain cooling system.
17. Disconnect heater hoses from heater core and seal core tubes.
18. From engine compartment, remove nuts retaining evaporator case to dash panel.
19. From passenger compartment, remove screws attaching evaporator case support bracket and air inlet duct support bracket to cowl top panel.
20. Remove one nut retaining bracket at left end of evaporator case to dash panel and one nut retaining bracket beneath the case to dash panel.
21. Pull evaporator case assembly from dash panel.
22. Remove screws attaching heater core access cover from evaporator case.
23. Remove heater core from evaporator case.
24. Reverse procedure to install.

1975-79 Granada & Monarch

Less Air Conditioning

1. Drain cooling system and disconnect heater hoses from heater core.
2. Remove glove box and the right and floor air distribution ducts.
3. Disconnect heater control cables and wiring harness from resistor assembly.

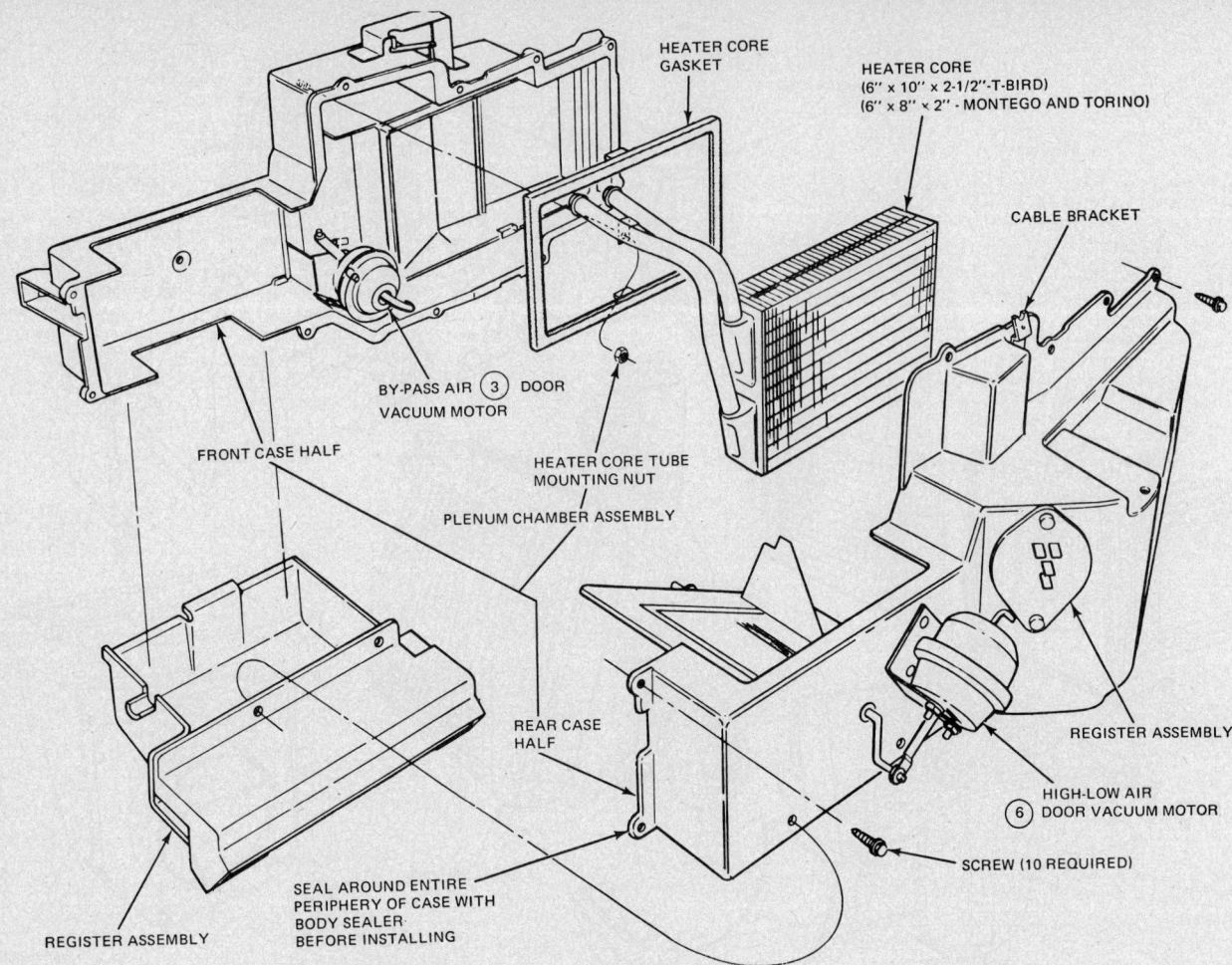

Fig. 24 Heater core with air conditioning. 1974-76 Elite, Montego & Torino; 1974-76 Cougar

Remove right vent cable bracket from instrument panel.

4. Remove vent duct to upper cowl mounting bolt.

5. Remove heater case to dash panel nuts, then the heater case and vent duct assembly.

6. Remove core cover and seal, then slide core from case, Fig. 22.

With Air Conditioning

1. Disconnect battery ground cable and drain coolant system, then disconnect heater hoses from core at engine side of dash panel.

NOTE: Easier access may be obtained by first disconnecting suction hose and moving it out of the way.

2. Remove heat distribution duct from instrument panel, seat belt interlock module and glove box liner, then loosen right door sill scuff plate and remove right cowl side from trim panel.

3. Loosen instrument panel to right cowl side bolt and remove instrument panel brace bolt at lower rail under glove box.

4. Remove tunnel to cowl brace, located to left of evaporator plenum assem-

bly, if equipped.

5. Remove defroster nozzle by removing instrument panel crash pad, removing radio speaker or panel cowl brace, removing four nozzle to cowl bracket screws and lifting defroster nozzle upward through crash panel, Fig. 23.

6. Disconnect vacuum hoses from A/C-Defrost and A/C-Heat door motors and remove vacuum harness to plenum clip screw, then remove the two A/C-Heat mounting nuts and swing door rearward on crankarm.

7. Remove two plenum to left mounting bracket screws and remove the two screws and three clips securing plenum to evaporator case.

8. Swing bottom of plenum away from evaporator case and disengage S-clip on forward flange of plenum, then raise plenum to clear tabs on top of evaporator case.

9. Move plenum to left as far as possible (about 4 inches), pulling rearward on instrument panel to gain clearance.

NOTE: Use extreme care when pulling back on instrument panel to avoid cracking plastic panel. Also, there is very little clearance between plenum and wiper motor assembly.

10. Using tab molded into rear heater core seal, pull heater core to left, then as rear surface of heater core clears evaporator case, pull core rearward and downward to clear instrument panel.

11. Reverse procedure to install, making certain that heater core tube to dash panel seal is in place between evaporator case and dash panel.

1974-76 Elite, Montego, Torino, 1974-79 Cougar & 1977-79 LTD II

Less Air Conditioning

1. Disconnect battery ground cable and drain cooling system.

2. Disconnect heater hoses from heater core and plug core openings.

3. Remove heater assembly to dash retaining nuts.

4. Disconnect control cables from door crank arms.

5. Disconnect electrical wiring from resistor and blower motor.

6. Remove glove box.

7. Remove right air duct control to instrument panel retaining nuts and

bolts and the screws securing the right air duct, then remove the duct.

8. Remove heater assembly from vehicle.
9. Remove heater core cover pad and slide heater core from case, Fig. 22.

With Air Conditioning: 1974-76 Elite, Montego, Torino & 1974-76 Cougar

1. Drain engine coolant and disconnect heater hoses from core.
2. Remove glove box.
3. Remove heater air outlet register from plenum assembly (2 snap clips).
4. Remove temperature control cable assembly mounting screw, and disconnect the end of the cable from the blend door crank arm (1 spring nut).
5. Remove the blue and red vacuum hoses from the high-low door vacuum motor; the yellow hose from the panel-defrost door motor, and the brown hose at the inline tee connector to the temperature by-pass door motor.
6. Disconnect wiring connector from resistor.
7. Remove ten screws from around flange of plenum case and remove rear case half of the plenum, Fig. 24.
8. Remove mounting nut from heater core tube support bracket.
9. Remove heater core.

NOTE: During installation of heater core, be sure to apply body sealer around the case flanges to provide a positive seal. Also make sure core mounting gasket is properly installed.

With Air Conditioning: 1977-79 Cougar & LTD II

1. Disconnect battery ground cable and drain cooling system.
2. Disconnect heater hoses from heater core and plug core openings.
3. Remove heater core cover plate retaining screws and the plate.
4. Press downward on heater core and tip toward front of vehicle to release the heater core seal from housing Fig. 25.
5. Lift heater core from case and remove from vehicle.

1974-77 Comet & Maverick

Less Air Conditioning

1. Disconnect battery ground cable and drain engine cooling system.
2. Disconnect blower motor ground wire from fender apron at engine side of dash.
3. Disconnect heater hoses at engine block.
4. Remove heater assembly to dash panel mounting nuts.
5. Remove glove compartment and on all models remove right cowl trim panel.
6. Remove cable retaining clips and the push nuts at door crank arms. Disconnect control cables from crank arms.
7. Remove defroster air duct from left side of heater assembly.
8. Disconnect motor lead from resistor assembly on bottom of heater.

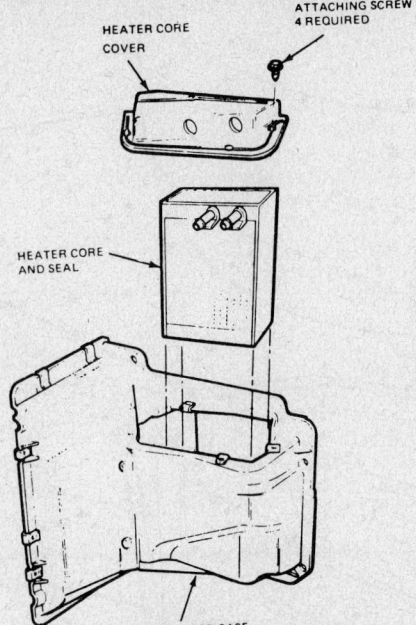

Fig. 25   Heater core with air conditioning. 1977-79 Cougar & LTD II

9. Remove heater case to instrument panel support bracket mounting screw.
10. Pull heater hoses through dash panel and disconnect hoses from heater core.
11. Separate halves of heater and remove core, Fig. 26.

With Air Conditioning: 1974 Comet & Maverick

1. Disconnect battery ground cable, remove air cleaner and drain cooling system.
2. Connect gauge set to compressor and discharge system.
3. Disconnect evaporator core tubes and tape ends to keep out foreign material and disconnect heater hoses from heater core tubes.
4. Remove A/C assembly-to-dash panel stud nuts.
5. Remove right cowl trim panel and remove glove compartment.
6. Disconnect right and left A/C air ducts.
7. Remove floor distribution duct from blower. Disconnect vacuum hoses from door motor and the vacuum harness multiple connector.
8. Disconnect temperature control cable from door crank arm on evaporator.
9. Remove screw that retains evaporator to cowl upper support and remove A/C rearward and away from dash panel.
10. Disconnect wire connectors from A/C thermostat switch on the evaporator housing and also the resistor on blower housing.
11. Disconnect blower motor ground wire from wiper mounting bracket and lower the blower and evaporator housing removing it from vehicle.
12. Separate halves of evaporator housing and remove water valve vacuum

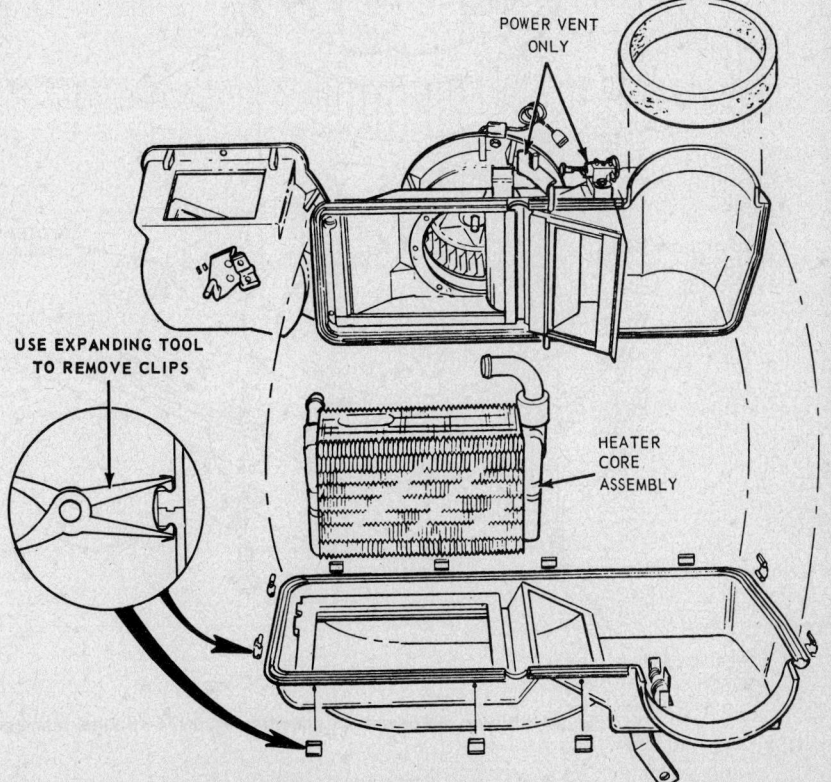

Fig. 26   Heater core less air conditioning. 1974-77 Comet & Maverick

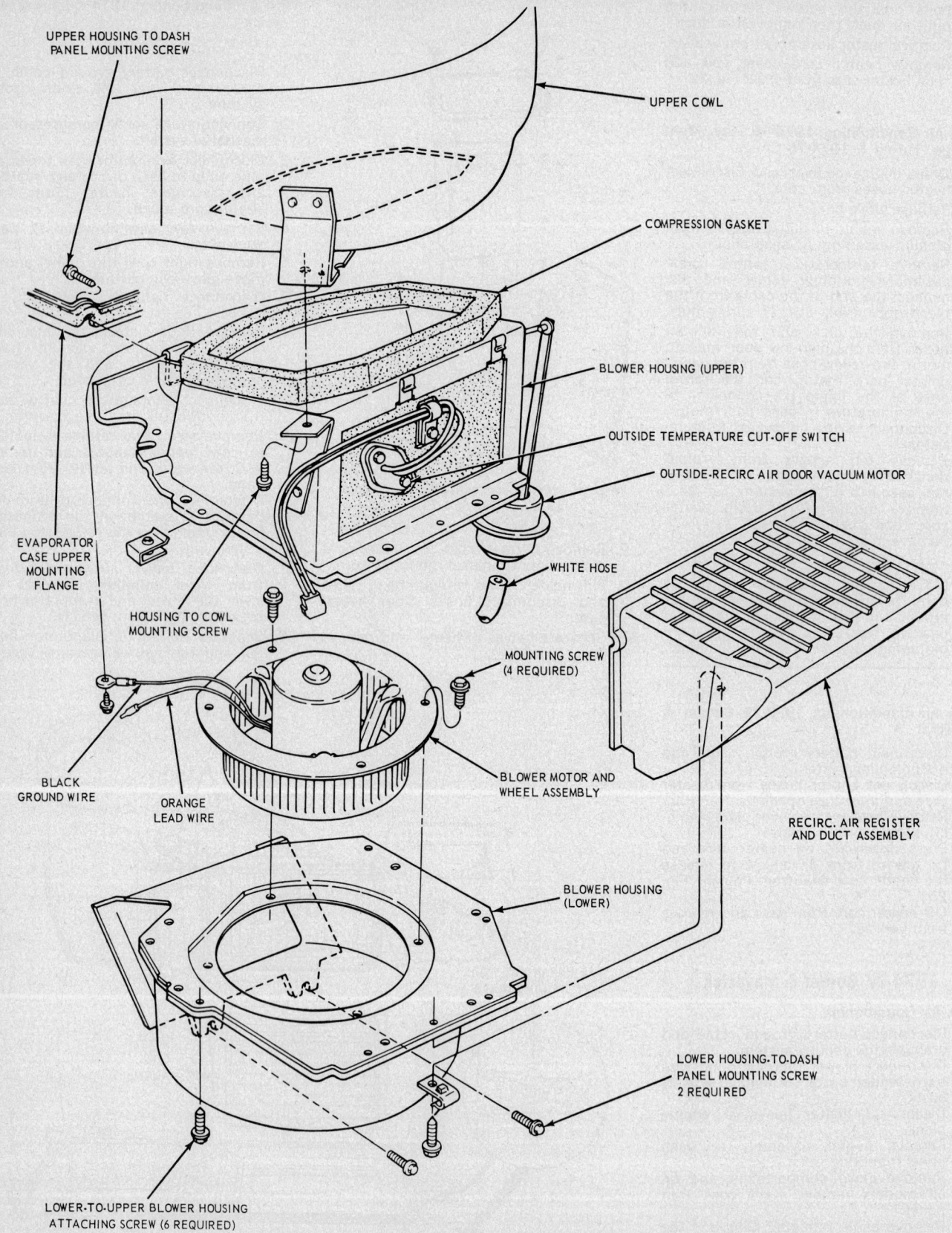

UPPER HOUSING TO DASH
PANEL MOUNTING SCREW

UPPER COWL

COMPRESSION GASKET

BLOWER HOUSING (UPPER)

OUTSIDE TEMPERATURE CUT-OFF SWITCH

OUTSIDE-RECIRC AIR DOOR VACUUM MOTOR

WHITE HOSE

EVAPORATOR
CASE UPPER
MOUNTING
FLANGE

HOUSING TO COWL
MOUNTING SCREW

MOUNTING SCREW
(4 REQUIRED)

BLACK
GROUND WIRE

ORANGE
LEAD WIRE

BLOWER MOTOR AND
WHEEL ASSEMBLY

RECIRC. AIR REGISTER
AND DUCT ASSEMBLY

BLOWER HOUSING
(LOWER)

LOWER HOUSING-TO-DASH
PANEL MOUNTING SCREW
2 REQUIRED

LOWER-TO-UPPER BLOWER HOUSING
ATTACHING SCREW (6 REQUIRED)

Fig. 27   Blower motor with air conditioning. 1974-76 Elite, Montego & Torino; 1974-76 Cougar

switch.

13. Remove temperature blend door shaft, frames and door from lower half of evaporator housing.
14. Lift heater core out of lower housing and remove pads from core.

With Air Conditioning: 1975-77 Comet & Maverick

1. Disconnect battery ground cable and remove air cleaner.
2. Drain cooling system, then discharge refrigerant from A/C system.
3. Disconnect evaporator core tubes from expansion valve and heater hose from heater core.

NOTE: Place tape over evaporator core tubes and expansion valve fittings. Install plugs in heater hoses and core outlets to prevent coolant spillage.

---

4. Remove three A/C assembly to dash panel attaching nuts.
5. Remove lower instrument extension.
6. On 1976-77 models remove radio.
7. On all models, disconnect right and left A/C register air duct assemblies from plenum chamber.
8. Remove floor distribution duct from blower housing.
9. On 1975 models, remove center register from instrument panel, then pull plenum chamber to disengage from blower housing.
10. On all models, disconnect vacuum lines from actuators and water valve.
11. Remove any tape or clips retaining vacuum switch and control cable from door crank arm.
    vacuum lines to unit, then disconnect wires from A/C thermostat and resistor.
12. On 1975 models, disconnect blower motor ground wire from windshield wiper motor mounting bracket.
13. On 1976-77 models, disconnect blower motor wire connector and vacuum source line at connector and remove blower motor.
14. On all models, remove evaporator housing to cowl upper support attaching screw, then move assembly rearward to clear mounting studs.
15. Pull drain tube from floor pan, then lower evaporator assembly and remove from vehicle.
16. Remove clips and seperate housing halves.
18. Remove water valve vacuum switch and blend air door shaft, door and door frame from lower half of housing.
19. Lift heater core out of lower housing.

BLOWER MOTOR, REPLACE
1978 Fairmont & Zephyr

Less Air Conditioning
1. Disconnect battery ground cable.
2. Remove screw securing right register duct mounting bracket to lower edge of instrument panel.
3. Remove screws securing ventilator control cable lever assembly to lower edge of instrument panel.
4. Remove glove box liner.

5. Remove plastic rivets securing grille to ventilator floor outlet, then the grille from the bottom of the ventilator assembly.
6. Remove right register duct and register assembly.
7. Remove screws securing ventilator assembly to blower housing portion of the heater case assembly.
8. Slide ventilator assembly toward the right, then downward to remove from under instrument panel.
9. Remove push nut from door crank arm.
10. Remove control cable housing retaining screw, then control cable assembly from ventilator assembly.
11. Disconnect blower lead wire from resistor assembly, push through hole in case.
12. Remove right side cowl trim panel and the ground terminal lug retaining screw.
13. Remove blower motor retaining screws and the blower motor.
14. Reverse procedure to install.

With Air Conditioning
1. Disconnect battery ground cable.
2. Remove glove box and disconnect vacuum hose from outside—recirc air door motor.
3. Remove instrument panel lower right to side attaching bolt.
4. Remove screw attaching support brace to top of air inlet duct.
5. Disconnect blower motor lead wire.
6. Remove nut securing blower motor housing lower bracket to evaporator case.
7. Remove side cowl trim panel and the blower ground wire screw.
8. Remove screw securing top of air inlet duct to evaporator case.
9. Move air inlet duct and blower housing assembly downward from evaporator case.
10. Remove blower motor mounting plate screws and the blower motor.
11. Reverse procedure to install.

1975-79 Granada & Monarch

Less Air Conditioning
Remove heater case as outlined in the "1975-79 Granada & Monarch" procedure under "Heater Core, Removal," then remove screws securing blower motor to case, Fig. 22.

With Air Conditioning
1. Disconnect battery ground cable.
2. Loosen right door sill scuff plate and remove right cowl side trim panel, then remove right lower instrument panel to cowl side bolt.
3. Remove cowl to loosen instrument panel brace bolt, then disconnect wiring harness connectors from blower motor and remove cooling tube from motor.
4. Remove the four blower motor attaching screws and remove blower motor from scroll by pulling on lower edge of instrument panel to gain clearance.

NOTE: Use extreme care when pulling back on instrument panel to avoid cracking plastic panel.

---

5. Reverse procedure to install.

1974-76 Elite, Montego, Torino, 1974-79 Cougar & 1977-79 LTD II

Less Air Conditioning
1. Follow the procedure to remove the heater core as described previously.
2. Remove the heater assembly from the vehicle, and place it on a bench.
3. Remove the four mounting screws and remove the blower motor, and wheel assembly from the blower, Fig. 22.
4. Reverse procedure to install.

With Air Conditioning: 1974-76 Elite, Montego, Torino & 1974-76 Cougar
1. Remove the glove box to gain access.
2. Remove the recirculation air register and duct assembly from the blower assembly.
3. Remove the two screws that attach the blower lower housing to the dash panel.
4. Disconnect the white hose from the outside-recirculation air door vacuum motor, and remove the vacuum motor from the blower lower housing (2 screws). Leave the motor actuator connected to the door crank arm.
5. Disconnect the blower motor lead wire (orange) from the harness connector, and disconnect the motor ground wire (black).
6. Remove six upper to lower blower housing flange screws.
7. Separate the blower lower housing and motor assembly from the upper housing and remove it from under the instrument pad.
8. Remove the blower motor and wheel assembly from the lower housing (4 screws), Fig. 27.
9. The upper flange of the recirculating duct is retained to the blower upper housing with two S-clips that remained on the housing during removal. Make sure that the duct is installed properly in the two clips during installation.

With Air Conditioning: 1977-79 Cougar & LTD II
1. Remove instrument panel pad, glove box and side cowl trim panel.
2. Remove instrument panel attachment on right side.
3. Remove one nut attaching blower motor housing to engine side of dash panel.
4. Remove one nut attaching blower motor to passenger compartment side of dash panel.
5. Remove one blower housing mounting bracket and cowl top inner screw.
6. Disconnect vacuum line from outside-recirculating air door vacuum motor.
7. Disconnect blower motor lead wire from connector and blower motor ground wire.
8. Remove blower housing assembly.
9. Remove blower motor and wheel as an assembly from blower housing.

1974-77 Comet & Maverick

Less Air Conditioning
1. Remove the heater core as described previously.
2. Disconnect the blower motor lead wire (orange) from the resistor.
3. Remove the four blower motor mounting plate nuts and remove the motor and wheel assembly from the heater assembly.

With Air Conditioning

The blower housing has to be removed to gain access to the blower motor.

1. On 1976-77 models, remove lower instrument panel extension.
2. On all models, remove radio.
3. On 1974 models, remove package shelf.
4. On 1974-75 models, disconnect right and left A/C register air duct assemblies from plenum chamber.
5. On all models, remove the floor air distribution duct from the bottom of the blower housing. Remove the blower housing mounting stud nut and lock plate.
6. Rotate the blower housing to unlock the slotted tabs on the blower housing from their lock pins on the evaporator housing. There are two tabs and two pins. Disconnect the red and yellow hoses at the vacuum motor on the blower housing. Disconnect the resistor and ground wires, and remove the blower housing.
7. On 1974-75 models, cut gaskets around A/C outlets at break line.
8. On all models, remove seven clips and separate blower motor housing halves.
9. Remove three blower motor mounting plate retaining nuts, and remove the motor and wheel assembly from the housing.
10. When installing be sure that the A/C Heat-Door is positioned properly before clipping the right and left housings together.

SPEED CONTROLS

Exc. 1979 Fairmont & Zephyr

Adjust bead chain to obtain .06-.25" actuator arm free travel when engine is at hot idle. The adjustment should be made to take as much slack as possible out of the chain without restricting the carburetor lever from returning to idle.

On vehicles with a solenoid anti-diesel valve, perform adjustment with ignition switch in the "ON" position.

Engine Section

NOTE: Refer to "FORD MUSTANG & PINTO • MERCURY BOBCAT & CAPRI" Section for service on the 2300 cc (4-140) engine.

ENGINE MOUNTS

Caution: Whenever self-locking mounting bolts and nuts are removed, they must be replaced with new self-locking bolts and nuts.

1974-79 Six

1. Remove the insulator to support bracket retaining nuts, Fig. 1.
2. Using a wood block placed under the oil pan, raise the engine enough to clear the insulator.
3. Remove the retaining screws and nuts from the insulator(s). Remove the insulator(s).
4. Reverse procedure to install.

1977-79 Fairmont & Zephyr V8-302

1. Remove fan shroud attaching screws.
2. Remove nuts attaching insulators to lower bracket, Fig. 2.
3. Raise engine slightly using a block of wood placed under the oil pan and a suitable jack.
4. Remove bolts attaching insulator to engine block.
5. Remove insulator assembly.
6. Reverse procedure to install.

1974-77 Comet, Maverick, 1975-79 Granada & Monarch V8-302, 351W

1. Using a block of wood and jack placed under oil pan, support engine.
2. Remove through bolt attaching motor mount to crossmember, Figs. 3 and 4.
3. Remove engine mount to engine attaching bolts.
4. Raise engine slightly and remove engine mount and heat shield (if used).
5. Reverse procedure to install.

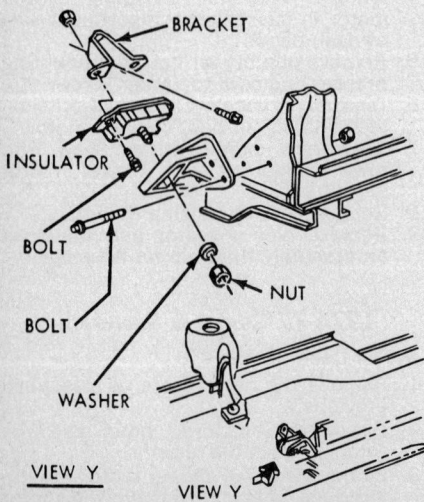

Fig. 1   Engine mounts. All 1974-79 Six (typical)

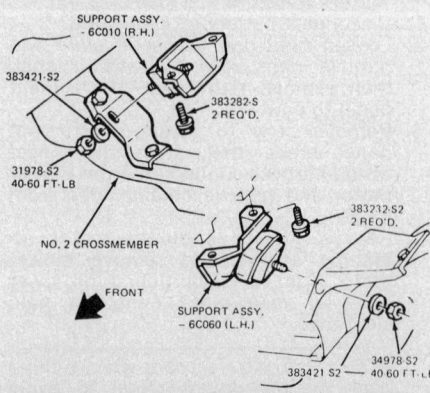

Fig. 2   Engine mounts. 1978-79 Fairmont & Zephyr V8-302

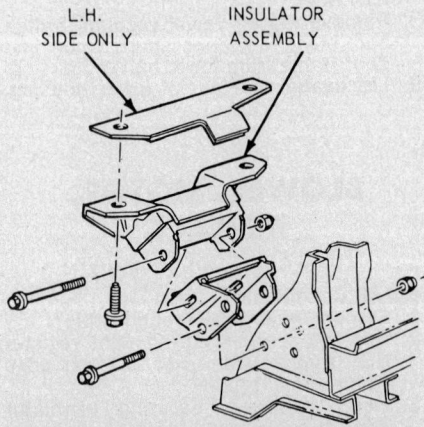

Fig. 3   Engine mounts. 1974-77 Comet & Maverick V8

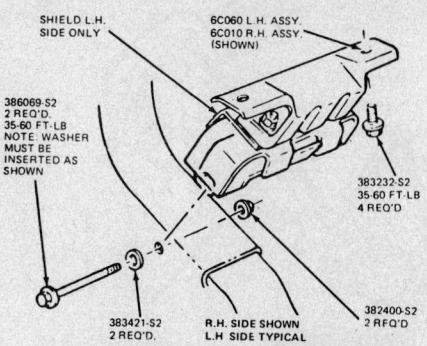

SHIELD L.H.
SIDE ONLY

6C060 L.H. ASSY.
6C010 R.H. ASSY.
(SHOWN)

386069-S2
2 REQ'D.
35-60 FT-LB
NOTE: WASHER
MUST BE
INSERTED AS
SHOWN

383232-S2
35-60 FT-LB
4 REQ'D

383421-S2
2 REQ'D.

R.H. SIDE SHOWN
L.H. SIDE TYPICAL

382400-S2
2 REQ'D

Fig. 4 Engine mounts. 1975-79 Granada & Monarch V8-302, 351W

1974-79 V8-302 & 351W Exc. Fairmont, Granada, Monarch & Zephyr

1. Remove fan shroud attaching screws.
2. Support engine using a block of wood placed under the oil pan and a suitable jack.
3. Remove nut and through bolt attaching insulator to frame crossmember, Fig. 5.
4. Raise engine slightly and remove insulator and heat shield, if equipped.
5. Reverse procedure to install.

1974 V8-351C, 1974-78 V8-400 & 1975-79 V8-351M

1. Remove fan shroud attaching bolts.
2. Remove through bolt and nut attaching insulator to insulator support bracket, Fig. 6.
3. Raise engine slightly using a block of wood placed under the oil pan and a suitable jack.
4. Remove insulator assembly to engine block attaching bolts and lock washers.
5. Remove insulator and heat shield, if equipped.
6. Reverse procedure to install.

1974-76 V8-460

1. Remove the fan shroud attaching screws and support the engine using a jack and block of wood under the oil pan.
2. Remove the through bolt and nut attaching the insulator to the frame crossmember.
3. Remove the insulator to upper bracket attaching nuts, Fig. 7.
4. Raise the engine enough to remove the insulator and heat shield if so equipped.
5. If necessary, the upper bracket can now be removed by removal of the three screws holding the bracket to the cylinder block.

ENGINE, REPLACE
Six Cylinder

1. Remove battery ground cable.
2. Remove hood assembly.
3. Drain cooling system and oil pan.
4. Disconnect crankcase ventilation hose and remove air cleaner.
5. Disconnect canister purge hose from P.C.V. valve.
6. Disconnect radiator and heater hoses and remove all drive belts.
7. If equipped with automatic transmission, disconnect transmission oil cool-

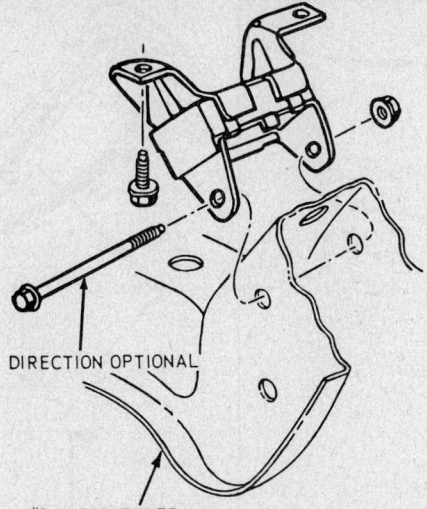

DIRECTION OPTIONAL

#2 CROSSMEMBER

Fig. 5 Engine mounts. 1974-79 V8-302, 351W exc. Comet, Fairmont, Granada, Maverick Monarch & Zephyr

er lines from radiator.
8. On all models, remove radiator, then the fan, spacer and pulley.
9. Disconnect alternator and starter wiring, then the accelerator cable from carburetor.
10. If equipped with Thermactor system, remove or disconnect components that may interfere with engine replacement.
11. If equipped with A/C, remove compressor from mounting bracket and position aside with refrigerant line attached.
12. On all models, disconnect and plug fuel pump inlet line.
13. Disconnect ignition coil wires, then the oil pressure and water temperature wiring from sending units.
14. Remove starter motor.
15. If equipped with manual transmission, disconnect clutch retracting spring, then the clutch equalizer shaft and arm bracket from underbody rail. Remove arm bracket and equalizer shaft.
16. On all models, raise vehicle and remove flywheel or converter housing upper attaching bolts.
17. Disconnect exhaust pipe from manifold. Loosen exhaust pipe clamp and slide off support bracket on engine.
18. Disconnect front engine mounts from underbody bracket.
19. Remove flywheel or converter housing cover.
20. If equipped with manual transmission, remove flywheel housing lower attaching bolts.
21. If equipped with automatic transmission, remove converter to flywheel bolts, then the converter housing lower attaching bolts.
22. On all models, lower vehicle and support transmission and flywheel or converter housing with a suitable jack.
23. Attach suitable lifting equipment to engine and remove engine from vehicle.
24. Reverse procedure to install.

V8-302 & 351W

1. Remove battery ground cable.
2. Remove hood.

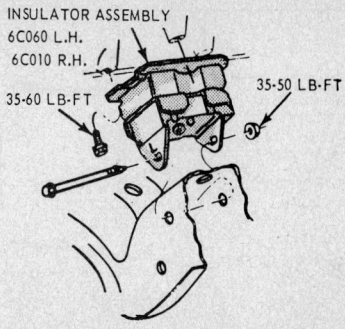

INSULATOR ASSEMBLY
6C060 L.H.
6C010 R.H.

35-60 LB-FT

35-50 LB-FT

Fig. 6 Engine mounts. 1974 V8-351C, 1974-79 V8-400 & 1975-79 V8-351M

3. Drain cooling system and oil pan.
4. Remove air cleaner and intake duct assembly.
5. Disconnect radiator and heater hoses, then remove all drive belts.
6. If equipped with automatic transmission, disconnect transmission oil cooler lines from radiator.
7. On all models, remove fan shroud attaching bolts, then the radiator, fan, spacer, pulley and shroud.
8. Remove alternator mounting bolts and position alternator aside with wiring attached.
9. Disconnect oil pressure and water temperature wiring from sending units, then the accelerator cable from carburetor.
10. Disconnect and plug fuel pump inlet line.
11. If equipped with automatic transmission, disconnect throttle valve vacuum line from intake manifold. Disconnect manual shift rod and the retracting spring at shift rod stud. Disconnect transmission filler tube bracket from engine block.
12. If equipped with Thermactor system, remove or disconnect components that may interfere with engine replacement.
13. If equipped with A/C, isolate and remove compressor.
14. If equipped with power steering, disconnect pump bracket from cylinder head and position assembly aside.
15. If equipped with power brakes, disconnect brake vacuum line from intake manifold.
16. On all models, remove flywheel or converter housing upper attaching bolts.
17. Disconnect ignition coil wiring.
18. Remove wiring harness from left side rocker arm cover and position aside. Disconnect ground strap from engine block.
19. Raise front of vehicle. Disconnect starter wiring, then remove starter motor.
20. Disconnect exhaust pipes from manifolds.
21. Disconnect engine mounts from brackets on frame.
22. If equipped with manual transmission, remove bolts attaching clutch equalizer bar to frame rail, then the equalizer from engine block. Remove remaining flywheel housing to engine bolts.
23. If equipped with automatic transmission, disconnect transmission oil cooler lines from retainer and remove converter housing inspection cover.

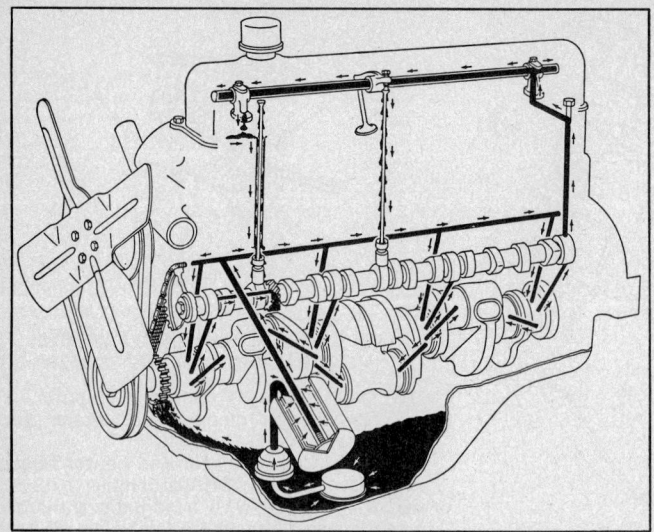

Engine oiling system for 6 cylinder engines

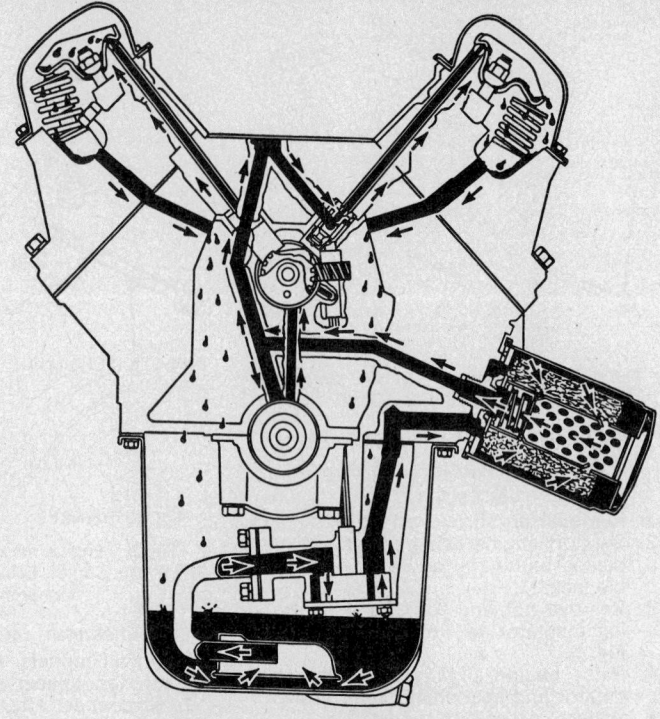

Engine oiling system. V8-302, 351, 400

Remove converter to flywheel bolts and secure converter in housing. Remove remaining converter housing to engine bolts.

24. On all models, lower vehicle and support transmission with a suitable jack.
25. Attach suitable engine lifting equipment to engine.
26. Lift engine slightly and pull forward to disengage from transmission, then remove engine from vehicle.
27. Reverse procedure to install.

V8-351C, 351M & 400

1. Remove battery ground cable.
2. Drain cooling system and oil pan.
3. Remove hood.
4. Remove air cleaner and air intake duct.
5. Disconnect radiator and heater hoses, then remove all drive belts.
6. If equipped with automatic transmission, disconnect transmission oil cooler lines from radiator.
7. On all models, remove fan shroud attaching bolts, then the radiator, fan, spacer, pulley and shroud.
8. Remove power steering pump brackets and position pump aside with lines attached.
9. If equipped with Thermactor system, remove or disconnect components that may interfere with engine replacement.
10. If equipped with A/C, isolate and remove compressor.
11. On all models, remove alternator bracket mounting bolts and position alternator aside with wiring attached. Disconnect alternator ground wire from engine block.
12. Remove wires from engine block and right hand cylinder head.
13. Disconnect and plug fuel pump inlet line.
14. Disconnect vacuum lines at rear of intake manifold. Disconnect vacuum control valve hoses and wiring, if equipped.
15. Disconnect accelerator cable or linkage from carburetor, then the transmission downshift linkage, if equipped.
16. Disconnect engine wiring harness

from ignition coil, water temperature sending unit and oil pressure sending unit. Remove wiring harness from hold down clips.
17. Raise and support vehicle.
18. Disconnect exhaust pipes from exhaust manifolds and remove the heat control valve, if equipped, or the manifold to pipe spacer.
19. Disconnect starter motor wiring and remove starter motor.
20. Remove engine front support through bolts and the starter motor cable clamp from right front engine support.
21. If equipped with automatic transmission, remove converter inspection cover, then the converter to flywheel bolts. Remove downshift rod, then the four lower converter housing to engine bolts and the adapter plate to converter housing bolt.
22. If equipped with manual transmission, disconnect clutch linkage from engine block and remove the four lower flywheel housing bolts.
23. On all models, lower the vehicle and remove the two upper converter housing or flywheel housing bolts.
24. Attach suitable engine lifting equipment to engine and support transmission with a suitable jack.
25. Raise engine slightly and pull forward to disengage from transmission, then remove engine from vehicle.
26. Reverse procedure to install.

V8-460

1. Remove battery ground cable.
2. Remove hood.
3. Drain cooling system and oil pan.
4. Remove air cleaner and intake duct assembly.
5. Disconnect radiator and heater hoses, then remove all drive belts.
6. Disconnect transmission oil cooler

lines from radiator.
7. Remove fan shroud attaching bolts, then the fan, pulley and shroud.
8. Remove radiator upper support and the radiator.
9. If equipped with A/C, discharge refrigerant system. Remove clamp bolt at A/C muffler support and position refrigerant lines aside. Remove compressor bracket mounting bolts. Remove power steering pump and position aside. Disconnect compressor clutch wire and remove compressor, mounting bracket and idler pulley.
10. On all models, disconnect and plug fuel pump inlet line.
11. Remove alternator mounting bracket bolts and position assembly aside with wiring connected.
12. Remove transmission filler tube attaching bolt from right hand rocker arm cover and position filler tube aside.
13. Disconnect all vacuum lines from rear of intake manifold.
14. Disconnect speed control cable from carburetor and bracket, if equipped, then the accelerator and transmission cables.
15. Disconnect the engine wiring harness at multi-connector on dash.
16. Raise and support vehicle.
17. Disconnect exhaust pipes from exhaust manifolds, then the starter motor wiring. Remove starter motor.
18. Remove converter housing access cover, then the converter to flywheel bolts.
19. Remove converter to engine lower rear cover plate attaching bolts.
20. Remove nuts securing front support insulator to crossmember.
21. Lower vehicle and support transmission with a suitable jack.
22. Remove converter housing to engine block upper attaching bolts.

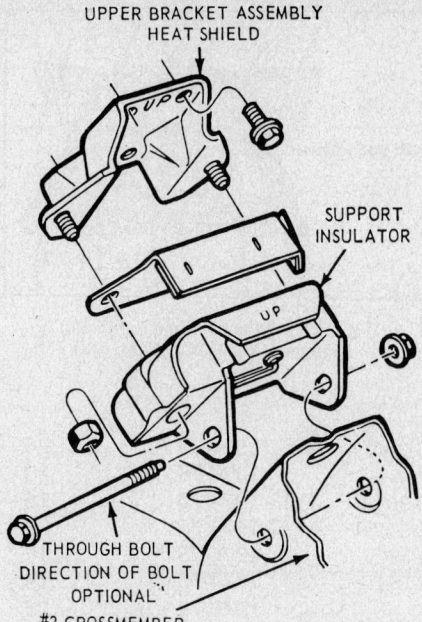

UPPER BRACKET ASSEMBLY HEAT SHIELD

SUPPORT INSULATOR

UP

THROUGH BOLT
DIRECTION OF BOLT OPTIONAL
#2 CROSSMEMBER

Fig. 7   Engine mounts. 1974-76 V8-460 Cougar, Montego & Torino

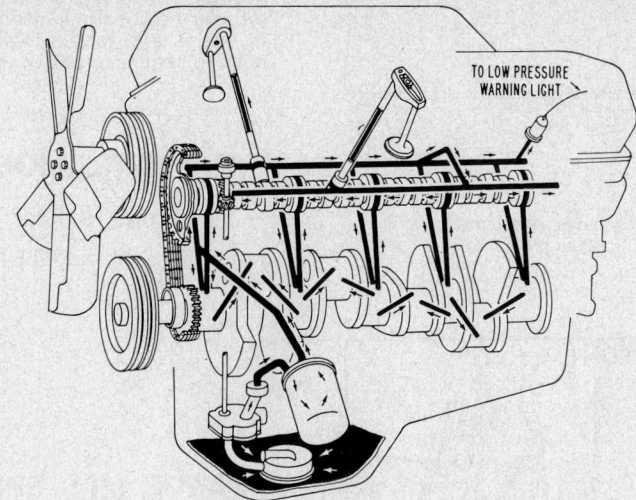

TO LOW PRESSURE WARNING LIGHT

Engine oiling system. V8-460

23. Disconnect ignition coil wiring and remove ignition coil and bracket assembly from intake manifold.
24. Attach suitable engine lifting equipment to engine.
25. Remove engine from vehicle.
26. Reverse procedure to install.

CYLINDER HEAD, REPLACE

Tighten cylinder head bolts a little at a time in three steps in the sequence shown in the illustrations. Final tightening should be to the torque specifications listed in the *Engine Tightening* table. After tightening the bolts to specifications, *they should not be disturbed.*

1974-79 Six-Cylinder

1. Drain cooling system and remove air cleaner.
2. Unfasten exhaust pipe from manifold and pull it down.
3. Disconnect accelerator cable and transmission downshift rod from carburetor.
4. Disconnect fuel inlet line at fuel filter hose, and distributor vacuum line at carburetor.

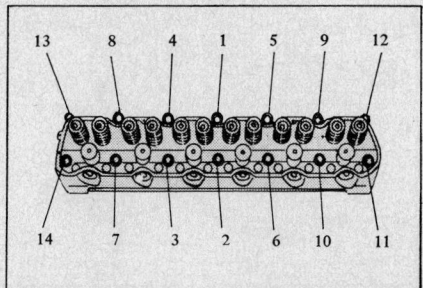

Fig. 8   Cylinder head tightening sequence. 1974-77 Six cylinder

5. Disconnect coolant lines at carburetor spacer. Remove radiator upper hose at outlet housing.
6. Disconnect distributor vacuum line at distributor. Disconnect carburetor fuel inlet line at fuel pump. Remove lines as an assembly.
7. Disconnect spark plug wires at plugs and temperature sending unit wire at sending unit.
8. Remove crankcase ventilation system. Remove hoses from Thermactor system as necessary for accessability.
9. Remove valve rocker arm cover.
10. Remove rocker arm shaft assembly.
11. Remove valve push rods.
12. Remove remaining cylinder head bolts and lift off head.
13. Reverse procedure to install and tighten head bolts in the sequence shown in Figs. 8 and 8A.

1974-79 V8-302, 351, 400

1. Remove intake manifold and carburetor as an assembly.
2. Disconnect battery ground cable at cylinder head.
3. If left head is being removed, remove A/C compressor (if equipped). Also remove and wire power steering pump out of the way. If equipped with Thermactor System, disconnect hose from air manifold on left cylinder head.
4. If right head is to be removed, remove alternator mounting bracket bolt and spacer, ground wire and air cleaner inlet duct.
5. If right head is to be removed on an engine with Thermactor System, remove air pump from bracket. Disconnect hose from air manifold.
6. Disconnect exhaust manifolds at exhaust pipes.
7. Remove rocker arm covers. If equipped with Thermactor System, remove check valve from air manifold.

8. Loosen rocker arm nuts or bolts so rocker arms can be rotated to one side. Remove push rods.
9. Remove head bolts and lift head off block.
10. Reverse procedure to install. Torque cylinder head bolts in sequence shown in Fig. 9, and torque intake manifold bolts in sequence shown in Figs. 10, 11 and 12.

1974-76 V8-460

1. Remove intake manifold and carburetor as an assembly and disconnect exhaust pipes from manifold.
2. Loosen A/C belt if equipped and remove alternator.
3. If equipped with A/C, isolate compressor at service valves and disconnect valves and hoses from compressor. Remove compressor attaching bolts and position unit out of way.
4. If not equipped with A/C, remove power steering retaining bolts and position unit out of way.
5. Remove valve covers, then remove rocker arm bolts, rocker arms, oil de-

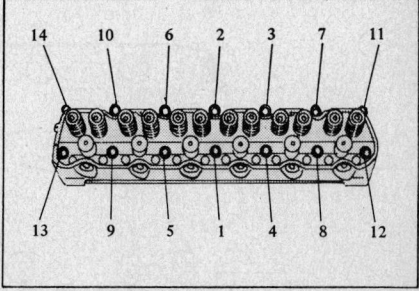

Fig. 8A   Cylinder head tightening sequence. 1978-79 six cylinder

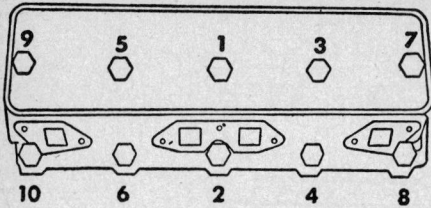

Fig. 9 Cylinder head tightening. V8 engines

7. Reverse procedure to install. Torque cylinder head bolts in sequence shown in Fig. 9, and torque intake manifold bolts in sequence shown in Fig. 13.

VALVE ARRANGEMENT

Front to Rear

Sixes	E-I-I-E-I-E-E-I-E-I-I-E
302 Right	I-E-I-E-I-E-I-E
302 Left	E-I-E-I-E-I-E-I
8-351, 400 Right	I-E-I-E-I-E-I-E
8-351, 400 Left	E-I-E-I-E-I-E-I
V8-460 Right	I-E-I-E-I-E-I-E
V8-460 Left	E-I-E-I-E-I-E-I

VALVE LIFT SPECS.

Engine	Year	Intake	Exhaust
6-200	1974	.382	.350
	1975-78	.372	.372
6-250	1974-75	.382	.350
	1976[1]	.385	.353
	1976[2]	.372	.372
	1977-78	.372	.372
V8-302	1974-75	.3707	.3823
	1976-77	.3823	.3884
	1978	.3823	.3980
V8-351W	1974-75	.418	.448
	1976-78	.4186	.4186
V8-351C	1974[3]	.407	.406
	1974[4]	.481	.490
V8-351M	1975-78	.4065	.4065
V8-400	1974	.427	.433
	1975-78	.428	.4325
V8-460	1974	.437	.480
	1975	.437	.4509
	1976	.437	.4809

[1]—Manual trans.
[2]—Auto. trans.
[3]—Two barrel carb.
[4]—Four barrel carb.

VALVE TIMING

Intake Opens Before TDC

Engine	Year	Degrees
6-200	1974-75	28
	1976-78	20

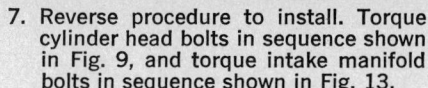

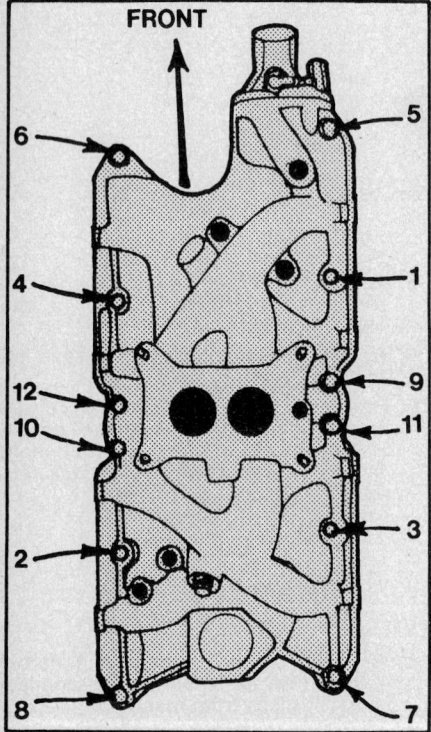

Fig. 10 Intake manifold tightening sequence. V8-302 & 1976-79 V8-351W

flectors, fulcrums and push rods.

NOTE: Remove all parts in sequence so that they are installed in their original positions.

6. Remove cylinder head bolts and cylinder head.

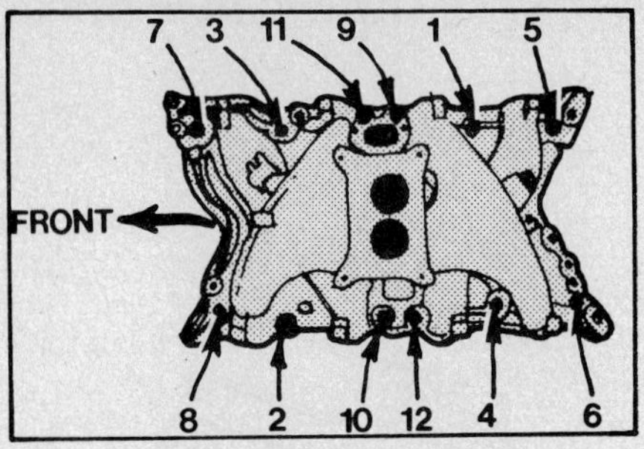

Fig. 12 Intake manifold tightening sequence. V8-351C, 351M, 400

Engine	Year	
6-250	1974-75	26
	1976-78	18
8-302[6]	1974-75	16
8-302[4]	1974-75	20
8-302	1976-78	16
8-351[5]	1974-75	15
	1976-78	23
8-351[3][1]	1974	19½
8-351[2]	1974	14
8-351[7]	1975-78	19.5
8-400	1974-78	17
8-460	1974-76	8
8-460[8]	1974-76	18

[1]—Cleveland engine.
[2]—Four bar. carb.
[3]—Two bar. carb.
[4]—Auto. trans.
[5]—Windsor engine.
[6]—Std. trans.
[7]—Modified.
[8]—Police Interceptor.

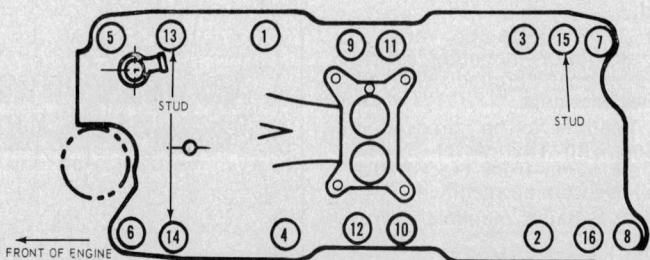

Fig. 11 Intake manifold tightening sequence. 1974-75 V8-351W

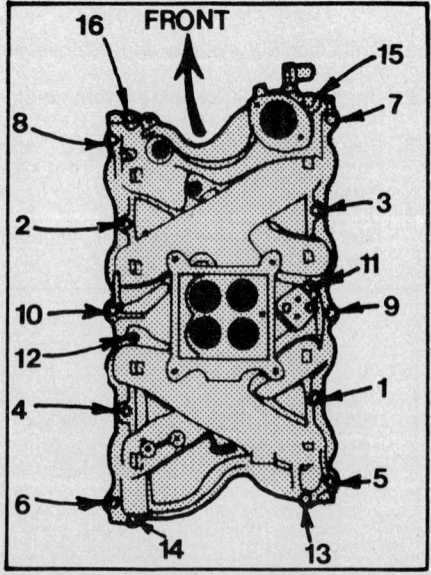

Fig. 13 Intake manifold tightening sequence. V8-460

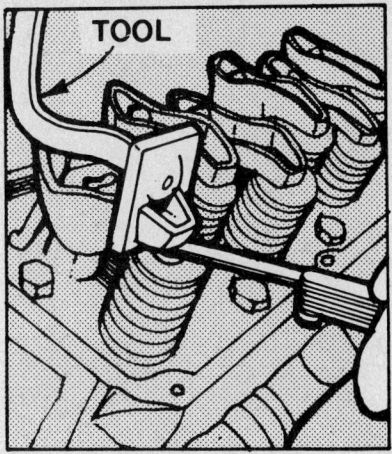

Fig. 14   Compressing lifter to check valve clearance. V8 engines (typical of 6 cylinder engines)

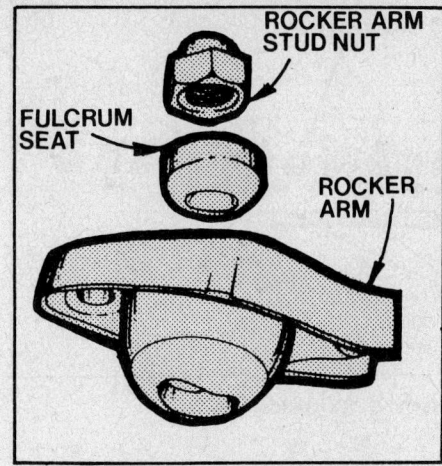

Fig. 15   Rocker arm assembly. 1974-77 & early 1978 V8-302, 351W

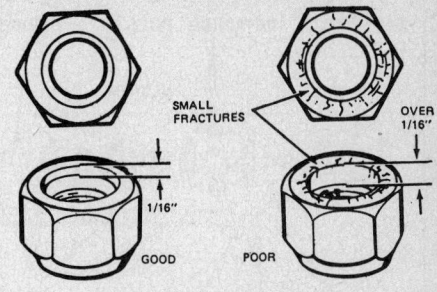

Fig. 16 Rocker arm stud nut. 1974-77 & early 1978 V8-302, 351W

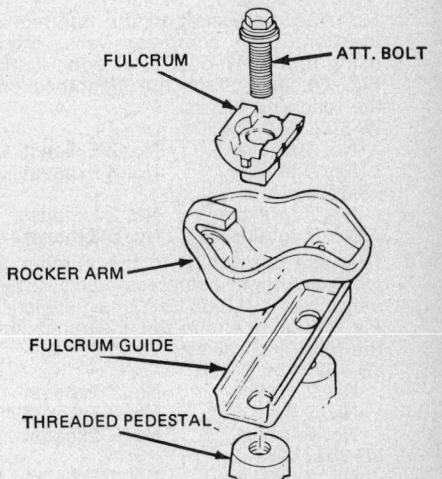

Fig. 17   Rocker arm assembly. Late 1978 & 1979 V8-302, 351W

VALVES, ADJUST

Six Cylinder

A .060 inch longer or a .060 inch shorter push rod is available to compensate for dimensional changes in the valve train. If clearance is less than the minimum, the .060 inch shorter push rod should be used. If clearance is more than the maximum, the .060 inch longer push rod should be used.

The procedure used to check the valve clearance is to rotate the crankshaft with an auxiliary starter switch until the No. 1 piston is near TDC at the end of the compression stroke, and then compress the valve lifter using tool 6513-K or equivalent, Fig. 14. At this point the following valves can be checked:

No. 1 Intake	No. 3 Exhaust
No. 1 Exhaust	No. 4 Intake
No. 2 Intake	No. 5 Exhaust

After the clearance of these valves have been checked, rotate the crankshaft until the No. 6 piston is on TDC at the end of its compression stroke (1 revolution of the crankshaft), and then compress the valve lifter using tool 6513-K or equivalent, Fig. 14, and check the following valves:

No. 2 Exhaust	No. 5 Intake
No. 3 Intake	No. 6 Intake
No. 4 Exhaust	No. 6 Exhaust

V8 Engines

For these engines, a .060″ longer or a .060″ shorter push rod is available to provide a means of compensating for dimensional changes in the valve train. and rocker arm. If the clearance is less than the minimum, the .060″ shorter push rod should be used. If clearance is more than the maximum the .060″ longer push rod should be used.

1974-77 and early 1978 V8-302 and 351W engines use a positive stop rocker arm stud and nut, Fig. 15. Before checking valve lash, check condition of stud nut, Fig. 16. Torque stud nut to 18-22 ft. lbs.

Late 1978 and 1979 V8-302 and 351W engines use a bolt and fulcrum attachment, Fig. 17.

To check valve clearance, proceed as follows:

1. Mark crankshaft pulley at three locations with number 1 location at TDC timing mark (end of compression stroke), number 2 location one half turn (180°) from TDC and number 3 location three quarter turn clockwise (270°) from TDC.

2. Turn the crankshaft to the number 1 location, then compress valve lifter using tool T71P-6513-A or equivalent, Fig. 14, and check the clearance on the following valves;

V8-302, 429 & 460

No. 1 Intake	No. 1 Exhaust
No. 7 Intake	No. 5 Exhaust
No. 8 Intake	No. 4 Exhaust

V8-351, 400

No. 1 Intake	No. 1 Exhaust
No. 4 Intake	No. 3 Exhaust
No. 8 Intake	No. 7 Exhaust

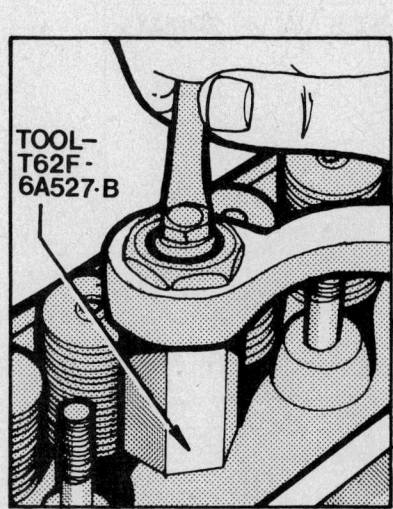

Fig. 18   Rocker arm stud removal. 1974-77 & early 1978 V8-302 & 351W

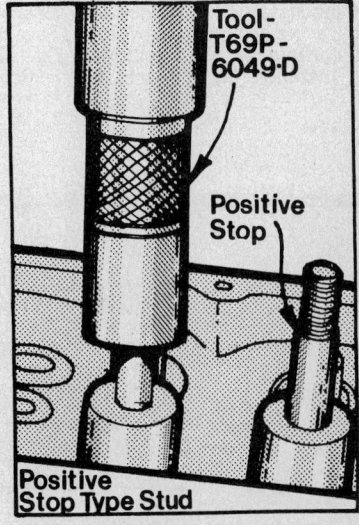

Fig. 19   Positive stop type rocker arm stud installation. 1974-77 & early 1978 V8-302 & 351W

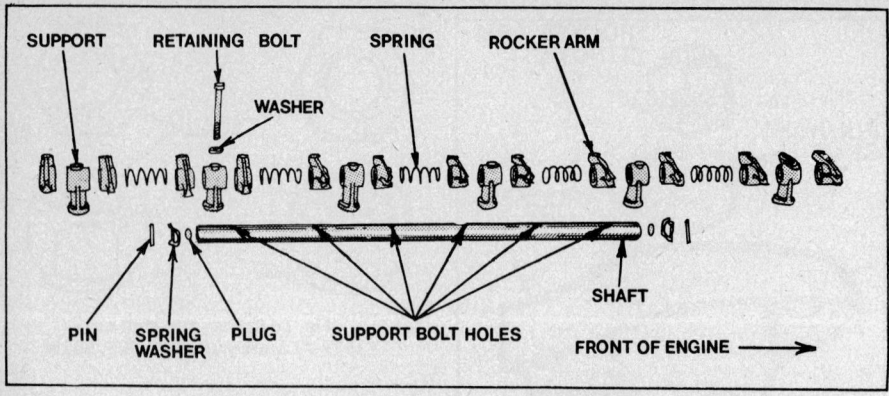

Fig. 20   Rocker arm shaft assembly. Six cylinder engines

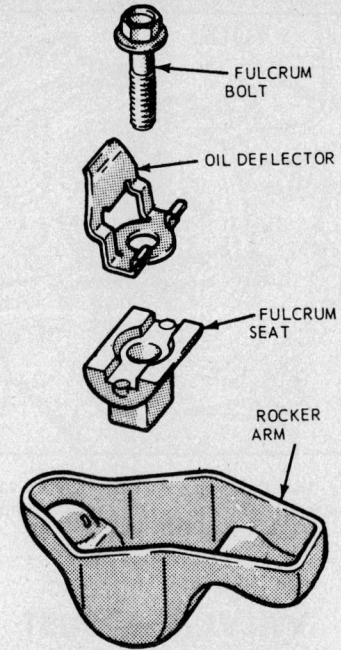

Fig. 21   Rocker arm assembly.
V8-351C, 351M, 400 & 460

3. Turn the crankshaft to the number 2 location, then compress valve lifter using tool T71P-6513-A or equivalent, Fig. 14, and check the clearance on the following valves:

V8-302, 429 & 460
No. 4 Intake   No. 2 Exhaust
No. 5 Intake   No. 6 Exhaust

V8-351, 400
No. 3 Intake   No. 2 Exhaust
No. 7 Intake   No. 6 Exhaust

4. Turn the crankshaft to the number 3 location, then compress valve lifter using tool T71P-6513-A or equivalent, Fig. 14, and check the clearance on the following valves:

V8-302, 429 & 460
No. 2 Intake   No. 3 Exhaust
No. 3 Intake   No. 7 Exhaust
No. 6 Intake   No. 8 Exhaust

V8-351, 400
No. 2 Intake   No. 4 Exhaust
No. 5 Intake   No. 5 Exhaust
No. 6 Intake   No. 8 Exhaust

adjust valve lash.

ROCKER ARM STUD
V8-302, 351W

If necessary to replace a rocker arm stud, a rocker arm stud kit is available and contains a stud remover, Fig. 18, a stud installer, Fig. 19, and two removers,

one .003" and the other .015".

Rocker arm studs that are broken or have damaged threads may be replaced with standard studs. Loose studs in the head may be replaced with .003" or .015" oversize studs which are available for service. *The standard studs have no identification marks, whereas the .003" oversize stud has a groove around the pilot end of the stud. The .015" oversize stud has a step produced by the increased diameter of the stud approximately 1⁵⁄₃₂" from the pilot end.*

When going from a standard size stud to a .015" oversize stud, always use a .003" reamer before finish reaming with a .015" reamer.

If a stud is broken off flush with the stud boss, use an easy-out to remove the broken stud, following the instructions of the tool manufacturer.

Installation

1. Position the piston of the cylinder being worked on at TDC compression stroke.

2. Locate stud properly with tool T69P-6049D, Fig. 16. Make sure tool

bottoms on the head.

3. Lubricate rocker arm components and place rocker arm and fulcrum on the stud.

4. Thread nut onto the stud until it contacts the shoulder, then tighten nut to 18-22 ft lbs.

VALVE GUIDES

Valve guides consist of holes bored in the cylinder head. For service the guide

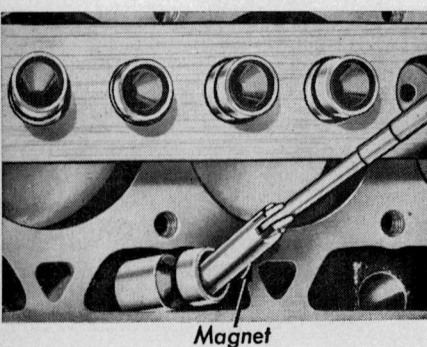

Magnet

Fig. 22   Removing valve lifter
with magnetic rod

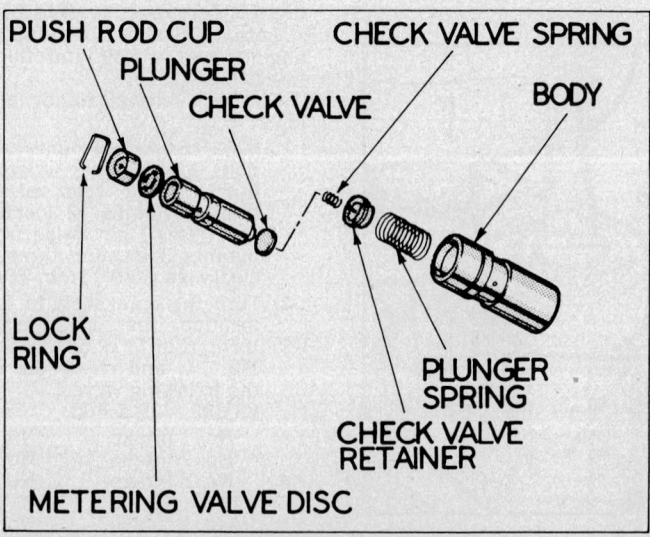

Fig. 23   Hydraulic valve lifter

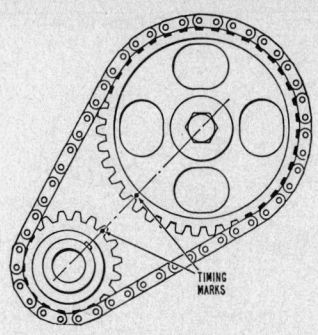

Fig. 24 Timing marks aligned for correct valve timing. Six cylinder engines

holes can be reamed oversize to accommodate valves with oversize stems of .003, .015 and .030".

ROCKER ARM SERVICE

6 Cylinder Engines

1. To disassemble, remove pin and spring washer from each end of rocker shaft, Fig. 20.
2. Slide rocker arms, springs and supports off the shaft, being sure to identify location of parts for reassembly.
3. If it is necessary to remove the plugs from the shaft ends, drill or pierce the plug on one end. Then use a steel rod to knock out the plug on the opposite end. Working from the open end, knock out the remaining plug.

Assemble

1. Lubricate all parts with engine oil. Apply Lubriplate to the rocker arm pads.
2. If plugs were removed from shaft ends, use a blunt tool or large diameter pin punch and install a plug (cup side out) in each end of shaft.
3. Install spring washer and pin on one end of shaft.
4. Install rocker arms, supports and springs in order shown in Fig. 20. *Be sure oil holes in shaft are facing downward.*
5. Complete the assembly by installing remaining spring washer and pin.

V8-351C, 351M, 400, 460 & Late 1978-79 V8-302, 351W

These engines use stamped steel rocker arms retained by a fulcrum seat, Figs. 17 and 21. The fulcrum seat bolts directly to the cylinder head and guides the rocker arm.

VALVE LIFTERS, REPLACE

6 Cylinder Engines

When necessary to replace valve lifters, remove cylinder head and related parts as outlined previously. Then, using a magnet rod, Fig. 22, remove and install one lifter at a time to be sure they are placed in their original bores.

When installing, apply Lubriplate to each lifter foot and coat the remainder of lifter with oil before installation.

V8 Engines

1. Remove intake manifold.
2. Remove rocker arm covers. On engines with stud-mounted rocker arms, loosen stud nuts and rotate rocker arms to one side. On other engines, remove rocker arms and shafts.
3. Remove push rods in sequence so they can be installed in their original bores.
4. Using a magnet rod, Fig. 22, remove the lifters and place them in a numbered rack so they can be installed in their original bores. *If the lifters are stuck in their bores by excessive varnish, etc., it may be necessary to use a plier-type tool to remove them. Rotate the lifter back and forth to loosen it from the gum or varnish.*
5. The internal parts of each lifter are matched sets. Do not intermix parts. Keep the assemblies intact until they are to be cleaned, Fig. 23.

TIMING CASE COVER

NOTE: To replace the seal in the timing gear cover, it is necessary to remove the cover as outlined below.

6 Cylinder Engines

Removal
1. Disconnect battery ground cable.
2. Drain cooling system and oil pan.
3. Disconnect radiator hoses from engine, then the transmission oil cooler lines from radiator, if equipped.
4. Remove radiator, then the drive belt, fan and pulley.
5. If equipped with A/C, remove condenser attaching bolts and position condenser forward with refrigerant lines attached. Remove compressor drive belt.
6. On all models, remove accessory drive pulley and the crankshaft damper with a suitable puller.
7. On 6-200 engines, remove front cover attaching screws from cover and oil pan. Pry cover from cylinder block slightly and cut oil pan gasket flush with front face of cylinder block.
8. On 6-250 engines, remove oil pan, then the front cover.
9. On all models, clean mating surfaces of cylinder block and front cover.

Installation
1. Apply oil resistant sealer to new front cover gasket and position gasket on front cover. Apply sealer to exposed area of gasket.
2. On 6-200 engines, apply sealer to gasket surface of oil pan. Cut and position the required portions of a new gasket on oil pan. Apply sealer to exposed areas of gasket, including the corners where contact is made with the front cover gasket.

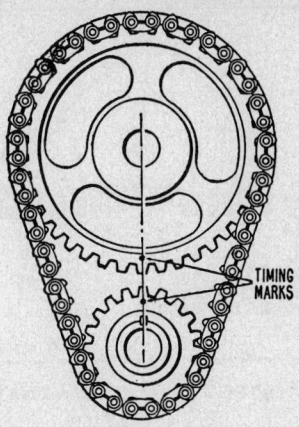

Fig. 25 Timing marks aligned for correct valve timing. V8 engines

3. On all models, install front cover.
4. Lubricate hub of crankshaft damper with Lubriplate or equivalent, then install damper. Torque attaching bolt to specifications.
5. On 6-250 engines, install oil pan.
6. On all models, install accessory drive pulley.
7. Reverse "Removal" steps 1 through 5 to complete installation.

V8 Engines

1. To remove cover, drain cooling system and crankcase. Remove air cleaner and disconnect battery ground cable.
2. Remove water hose as necessary.
3. Remove generator support bolt at water pump, and loosen generator mounting bolts.
4. Remove fan, spacer and pulley.
5. Remove power steering drive belt (if equipped). If air conditioned, remove compressor drive belt.
6. Remove crankshaft pulley and adapter.
7. Remove fuel pump and lay it to one side with flexible fuel line attached.
8. Remove oil level dipstick tube bracket and oil filler tube bracket.
9. Remove oil pan-to-front cover bolts.
10. Remove cover and water pump as an assembly.
11. Drive out cover seal with a pin punch. Clean out recess in cover.
12. Coat a new seal with grease and drive seal in until it is fully seated in recess. Check seal after installation to be sure spring is properly positioned in seal.
13. Reverse removal procedure to install cover.

TIMING CHAIN

After removing the cover as outlined above, remove the crankshaft front oil slinger. Crank the engine until the timing marks are aligned as shown in Figs. 24 and 25. Remove camshaft sprocket retaining bolt and washer. Slide both sprockets and chain forward and remove them as an assembly.

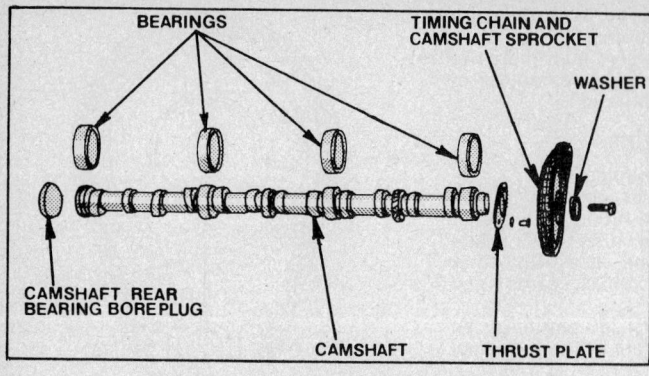

Fig. 26 Camshaft and related parts. Six cylinder engines

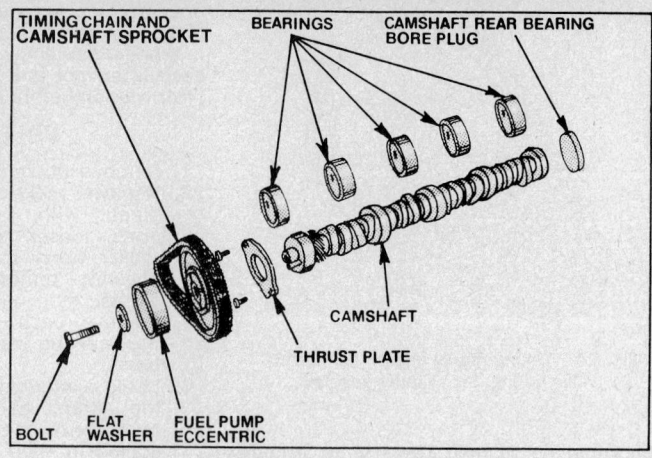

Fig. 27 Camshaft and related parts. V8 engines

Reverse the order of the foregoing procedure to install the chain and sprockets, being sure the timing marks are aligned.

CAMSHAFT, REPLACE

6 Cylinder Engine

1. Remove air cleaner, then drain cooling system and radiator.
2. Remove radiator and grille.
3. If equipped with air conditioning, remove condensor retaining bolts and position condensor aside.

NOTE: Do not disconnect refrigerant lines.

4. Disconnect accelerator spring, accellator cable and distributor vacuum line from carburetor.
5. Remove fuel line and distributor vacuum line.
6. Disconnect engine temperature sensor wire, then remove distributor,

fuel pump and oil filter.
7. Remove cylinder head and lifters.
8. Remove damper and oil level dipstick.
9. On vehicles with 6-250 engines, remove oil pan and oil pump.
10. Remove front cover, timing chain and sprockets.
11. Remove camshaft thrust plate, then the camshaft by pulling toward front of engine, Fig. 26.

CAUTION: Use care to avoid damaging camshaft bearings.

12. Reverse procedure to install.

V8 Engines

1. Drain cooling system and remove radiator.
2. If equipped with air conditioning:
   a. On 302, 351W, 429 and 460 engines, remove condensor retaining bolts and position condensor aside without disconnecting refrigerant lines.
   b. On 351C, 351M and 400 engines, purge refrigerant from system and remove condensor.
3. On vehicles equipped with 460 engines, remove grille.
4. Remove front cover, timing chain and sprockets.
5. Remove intake manifold.
6. Remove push rods and lifters.

NOTE: On 400 engines, make sure that number one cylinder is at top dead center position.

7. Remove thrust plate, then carefully remove camshaft by pulling toward front of engine, Fig. 27.

CAUTION: Use care to avoid damaging camshaft bearings.

8. Reverse procedure to install.

PISTON & ROD ASSEMBLY

When installed, piston and rod assembly should have the notch or arrow in piston head toward front of engine

with connecting rod numbers positioned as shown in Figs. 28 and 29.

PISTONS, PINS & RINGS

Pistons and rings are furnished in standard sizes and oversizes of .020, .030 and .040". On 6-200 engines, .060" oversizes are also available.
Oversize pins are not furnished.

SERVICE BULLETIN

PISTON & PIN REPLACEMENT: When servicing engines using press fit piston pins, the piston and pin must be replaced as an assembly if either does not meet specifications. These components are not serviced separately for the principle reason that excess clearances are usually caused by piston wear rather than pin wear. Elimination of excess clearance by using oversize pins may result in fracture of the connecting rod.

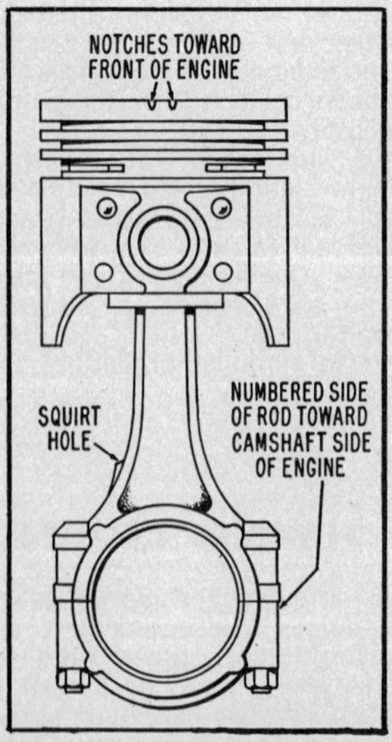

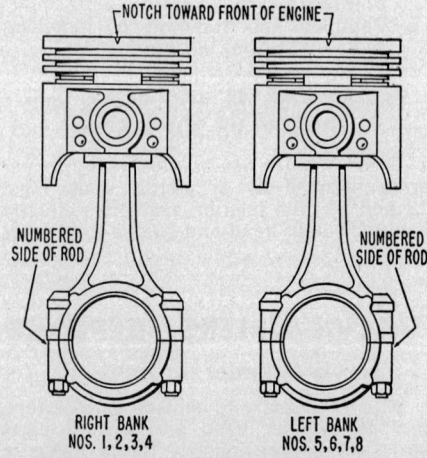

Fig. 28 Piston and rod assembly. Six cylinder engines

Fig. 29 Piston and rod assembly. V8s

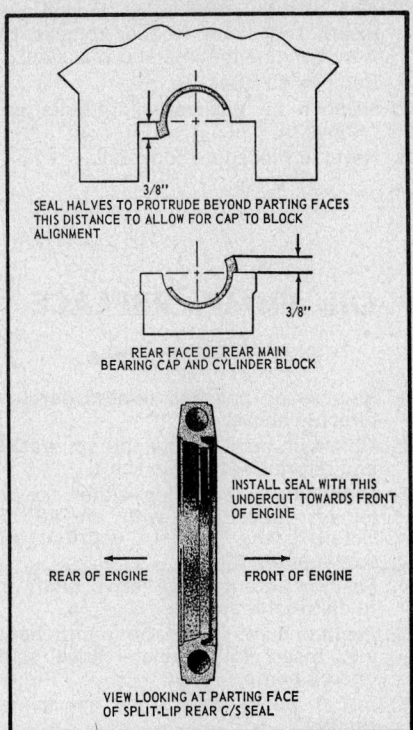

SEAL HALVES TO PROTRUDE BEYOND PARTING FACES THIS DISTANCE TO ALLOW FOR CAP TO BLOCK ALIGNMENT — 3/8"

3/8"

REAR FACE OF REAR MAIN BEARING CAP AND CYLINDER BLOCK

INSTALL SEAL WITH THIS UNDERCUT TOWARDS FRONT OF ENGINE

REAR OF ENGINE ← → FRONT OF ENGINE

VIEW LOOKING AT PARTING FACE OF SPLIT-LIP REAR C/S SEAL

Fig. 30   Split-lip crankshaft rear seal installation

CRANKSHAFT OIL SEAL

Split Lip Type

1. Remove oil pan.
2. Remove rear bearing cap.
3. Loosen remaining bearing caps, allowing crankshaft to drop down about 1/32".
4. Remove old seals from both cylinder block and rear main bearing cap. Use a brass rod to drift upper half of seal from cylinder block groove. Rotate crankshaft while drifting to facilitate removal.
5. Carefully clean seal groove in block with a brush and solvent. Also clean seal groove in bearing cap. Remove the oil seal retaining pin from the bearing cap if so equipped. *The pin is not used with the split-lip seal.*
6. Dip seal halves in clean engine oil.
7. Carefully install upper seal half in its groove with undercut side of seal toward front of engine, Fig. 30, by rotating it on shaft journal of crankshaft until approximately 3/8" protrudes below the parting surface. *Be sure no rubber has been shaved from outside diameter of seal by bottom edge of groove.*
8. Retighten main bearing caps and torque to specifications.
9. Install lower seal in main bearing cap with undercut side of seal toward front of engine, and allow seal to protrude about 3/8" above parting surface to mate with upper seal upon cap installation.
10. Apply suitable sealer to parting faces of cap and block. Install cap and torque to specifications.

NOTE: If difficulty is encountered in installing the upper half of the seal in

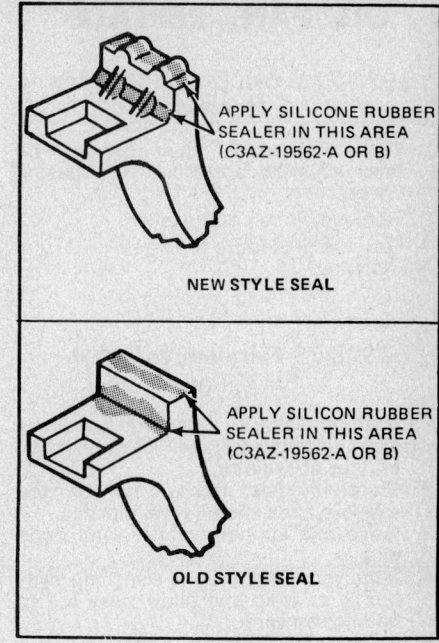

APPLY SILICONE RUBBER SEALER IN THIS AREA (C3AZ-19562-A OR B)

NEW STYLE SEAL

APPLY SILICON RUBBER SEALER IN THIS AREA (C3AZ-19562-A OR B)

OLD STYLE SEAL

Fig. 31   Crankshaft oil seals

position, lightly lap (sandpaper) the side of the seal opposite the lip side using a medium grit paper. After sanding, the seal must be washed in solvent, then dipped in clean engine oil prior to installation.

SERVICE BULLETIN

A new crankshaft rear oil seal has been released for service. This new seal may be received when ordering an oil pan gasket kit and is installed in the same manner as described above, Fig. 31.

MAIN & ROD BEARINGS

NOTE: Some High Output engines are equipped with an oil baffle tray connected to the main bearing caps. This baffle must be removed to service main and rod bearings.

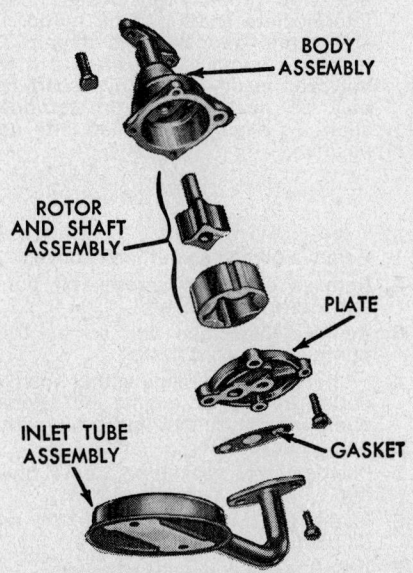

BODY ASSEMBLY

ROTOR AND SHAFT ASSEMBLY

PLATE

INLET TUBE ASSEMBLY

GASKET

Fig. 32   Oil pump assembly. Six cylinder engines

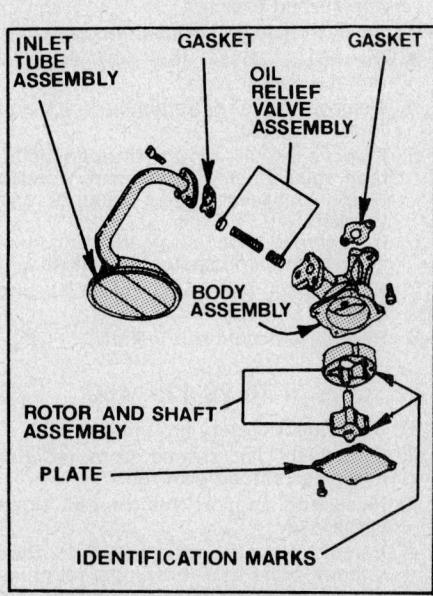

INLET TUBE ASSEMBLY

GASKET   GASKET

OIL RELIEF VALVE ASSEMBLY

BODY ASSEMBLY

ROTOR AND SHAFT ASSEMBLY

PLATE

IDENTIFICATION MARKS

Fig. 33   Oil pump assembly. V8-302, 351W

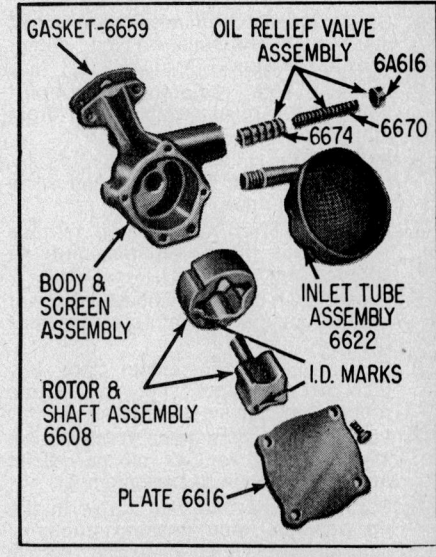

GASKET-6659

OIL RELIEF VALVE ASSEMBLY

6A616

6674   6670

BODY & SCREEN ASSEMBLY

INLET TUBE ASSEMBLY 6622

ROTOR & SHAFT ASSEMBLY 6608

I.D. MARKS

PLATE 6616

Fig. 34   Oil pump assembly. V8-351C, 351M & 400

OIL PAN, REPLACE

1974-77 6 Cyl. Except Granada & Monarch

1. Drain crankcase, then remove oil level dipstick and flywheel housing cover.
2. Remove oil pan and gasket.
3. Reverse procedure to install.

1978-79 Fairmont & Zephyr Six Cylinder

1. If equipped with automatic transmission, disconnect transmission oil cooler lines at radiator.
2. On all models, remove radiator top support, then the oil level dipstick.
3. Raise and support vehicle, and drain oil pan.
4. Remove nuts and bolts attaching sway bar to chassis and allow sway bar to hang downward.
5. Remove "K" brace.
6. Lower rack and pinion steering gear.
7. Remove starter motor.
8. Remove nuts attaching engine mounts to support brackets.
9. Loosen rear insulator to crossmember attaching bolts.
10. Slightly raise engine and place a 1¼ inch spacer between engine support insulator and chassis bracket.
11. Support and raise transmission slightly with a suitable jack.
12. Remove oil pan attaching bolts and lower oil pan to crossmember.
13. Position transmission oil cooler lines aside, if equipped, and remove oil pan from vehicle. It may be necessary to rotate crankshaft.
14. Reverse procedure to install.

1975-79 Granada & Monarch 6 Cyl.

1. On automatic transmission vehicles, disconnect transmission oil cooler lines at radiator.
2. Remove both radiator top support bolts, then raise vehicle and drain crankcase.
3. Remove the four bolts and nuts retaining sway bar to chassis and allow bar to hang down.
4. Remove starter motor, then remove both engine mount retaining nuts to support brackets.
5. Loosen but do not remove both rear mount insulator to crossmember bolts.
6. Raise front of engine and place 1¼ inch wooden blocks between engine mount and chassis bracket.
7. Lower engine and raise transmission slightly, then remove oil pan bolts and lower oil pan to crossmember.
8. Position crankshaft rear throw in the up position, then position transmission oil cooler lines aside and remove oil pan.
9. Reverse procedure to install.

1978-79 Fairmont & Zephyr V8-302

1. Remove fan shroud attaching bolts and position shroud over fan.
2. Raise and support vehicle, then drain oil pan.
3. Remove two bolts attaching steering gear to main crossmember and let steering gear rest on frame away from oil pan.
4. Remove engine mount attaching bolts.
5. Raise engine with a suitable jack and place wood blocks between engine mounts and frame.
6. Remove rear "K" braces.
7. Remove oil pan attaching bolts and lower oil pan to frame.
8. Remove oil pump attaching bolts and the inlet tube attaching nut, then lower pump into oil pan.
9. Remove oil pan, rotating crankshaft as necessary to provide clearance for oil pan.
10. Reverse procedure to install.

1974-77 Comet & Maverick & 1975-79 Granada & Monarch V8-302

1. Raise and support vehicle, then drain oil pan.
2. Remove stabilizer bar from chassis.
3. Remove engine front support through bolts, then the supports. If equipped, remove bolt and nut securing power steering lines to rear side of lower arm.
4. Remove idler arm bracket retaining bolts and pull linkage downward and aside.
5. Remove oil pan attaching bolts and the oil pan.
6. Reverse procedure to install.

Cougar, Elite, LTD II, Montego & Torino V8-302, 351 & 400

1. Remove oil level dipstick, then remove fan shroud retaining screws and position shroud over fan.
2. Raise vehicle and drain crankcase.
3. On 351C, 351M and 400 engines, remove starter.
4. Remove stabilizer retaining bolts and lower sway bar.
5. Remove engine mount through bolts, then raise engine and insert wooden blocks between engine mounts and brackets.
6. If equipped with automatic transmission, position oil cooler lines aside.
7. Remove oil pan retaining bolts and oil pan.
8. Reverse procedure to install.

1974-76 V8-429, 460

1. Disconnect battery ground cable.
2. Disconnect fan shroud from radiator and place shroud over fan.
3. Raise and support vehicle and drain crankcase.
4. Remove sway bar retaining bolts, then remove bolts and bushings retaining sway bar to lower control arms and move sway bar foward on struts.
5. Remove through bolt from each engine mount, then raise engine and insert 1-¼ inch wooden blocks between engine mounts and brackets.
6. Remove oil filter.
7. Remove oil pan retaining bolts and remove oil pan.
8. Reverse procedure to install.

OIL PUMP, REPLACE

6 Cylinder Engines

1. Remove oil pan and related parts as directed above.
2. Unfasten and remove pump, gasket and intermediate drive shaft.
3. Prime pump by filling either the inlet or outlet port with engine oil. Rotate pump shaft to distribute oil within pump body.
4. Position intermediate drive shaft into distributor socket.
5. Position new gasket on pump housing. Insert intermediate drive shaft into oil pump.
6. Install pump and shaft as an assembly.
7. Install oil pan.

V8-302, 351, 400

1. Remove oil pan as outlined above.
2. Remove pump inlet tube and screen.
3. Remove pump retaining bolts and remove pump, gasket and intermediate shaft.
4. To install, position intermediate drive shaft into distributor socket. With shaft seated in socket, stop on shaft should touch roof of crankcase. Remove shaft and position stop as necessary.
5. With new gasket on pump housing and stop properly positioned, insert intermediate shaft into oil pump. Install pump and shaft as a unit. Do not force pump into position if it will not seat readily. The drive shaft hex may be misaligned with distributor shaft. To align, rotate shaft into new position.

V8-460

1. Remove oil pan as outlined above.
2. Remove oil pump screws, oil pump and intermediate shaft.
3. Remove inlet tube and screen from pump and discard gasket.
4. Prime pump by filling either inlet or outlet port with engine oil. Rotate pump shaft to distribute oil within pump body.
5. Position new gasket on pump housing.
6. Insert intermediate drive shaft into oil pump.
7. Install pump and shaft as a unit.
8. Complete installation in reverse order of removal.

OIL PUMP, REPAIRS

V8-460

See Ford-Mercury Full Size Car chapter for an illustration and service procedure for the oil pump used on this engine.

V8-302, 351, 400 & All Sixes

Referring to Figs. 30, 31 and 32, disassemble pump. To remove the oil pressure relief valve, insert a self-threading sheet metal screw of the proper diameter into the oil pressure relief valve chamber cap and pull cap out of chamber. Remove spring and plunger.

The inner rotor and shaft and the outer race are serviced as an assembly. One part should not be replaced without replacing the other.

Install the pump cover and tighten to 6-9 ft. lbs. torque.

BELT TENSION DATA

	New	Used
1974-78 All ①	140	110
1974-78 ②	80	60

①—Exc. ¼″ Belts.
②—¼″ Belts.

WATER PUMP, REPLACE

Drain cooling system and disconnect radiator lower hose and heater hose at water pump. Remove drive belt, fan and pulley (also spacer on V8's). Unfasten and remove pump.

FUEL PUMP PRESSURE

Year	Engine	Pressure Lbs.
1974-75	Six cyl.	4-6
1976-78	Six cyl.	5-7
1974-75	V8-302, 351, 400	5-7
1974-75	V8-460	5.7-7.7
1976	V8-460	6.7-8.7
1976-78	V8-302, 351, 400	6-8

FUEL PUMP, REPLACE

1. Remove all gasket material from pump and block gasket surfaces. Apply sealer to both sides of new gasket.
2. Position gasket on pump flange and hold pump in position against its mounting surface. Make sure rocker arm is riding on camshaft eccentric.
3. Press pump tight against its mounting. Install retaining screws and tighten them alternately.
4. Connect fuel lines. Then operate engine and check for leaks.

NOTE: Before installing the pump, it is good practice to crank the engine so that the nose of the camshaft eccentric is out of the way of the fuel pump rocker arm when the pump is installed. In this way there will be the least amount of tension on the rocker arm, thereby easing installation of the pump.

Clutch and Transmission Section

NOTE: 1979 linkage adjustment information is in this section. Repair procedures on both automatic and manual shift transmissions are covered elsewhere in this manual. Procedures for removing automatic transmissions as well as linkage adjustments on 1974-78 models are included in the automatic transmission chapters. See Chapter Index.

CLUTCH PEDAL, ADJUST

1978-79 Fairmont & Zephyr

4-140
1. From under vehicle, remove release lever return spring and dust shield.
2. Loosen clutch cable lock nut and adjusting nut at release lever.
3. Move release lever forward until free play is eliminated and hold lever in this position for adjustment.
4. Insert a .30 in. spacer against release lever cable spacer, then tighten adjusting nut against spacer finger tight.
5. Tighten lock nut against adjusting nut, using care not to disturb adjustment. Torque lock nut to 5 to 8 ft. lbs. Cycle clutch pedal several times, then recheck free play. Free play at clutch pedal should be approximately 1½ in.
6. Install dust shield and return spring.

6-200
1. Pull clutch toward front of vehicle until adjusting nut can be rotated. Rotate adjusting away from rubber insulator approximately .30 in. Do not rotate nylon nut until it is free of rubber insulator. If necessary, to free adjusting nut from dash insulator it may be necessary to remove clutch pedal bumper stop from clutch pedal.

The clutch pedal bumper stop must be reinstalled before adjusting clutch pedal free play.
2. Release cable, then pull cable until free play at release lever is eliminated.
3. Rotate adjusting nut until it contacts rubber insulator, then index tabs into next notch. Free play at clutch pedal should be approximately 1½ in. Cycle clutch pedal several times and recheck free play.

Except 1978-79 Fairmont & Zephyr

1. Disconnect clutch return spring from release lever.
2. On 1974-76 models loosen lock nut, on 1977-79 models remove locking pin, then on all models loosen adjusting nut.
3. Move release lever rearward until release bearing lightly contacts clutch pressure plate release fingers.
4. Slide rod until it seats in release lever pocket.
5. Insert proper feeler gauge (see below) between adjusting nut and swivel sleeve, then tighten adjusting nut finger tight against feeler gauge.

1974-77 Comet & Maverick	.136″
1974 Except Comet & Maverick	.194″
1975-79 Granada & Monarch	.136″

6. On 1974-76 models, tighten lock nut against adjusting nut, then remove feeler gauge.

NOTE: When tightening lock nut, use care not to disturb adjustment.

7. On 1977-79 models, rotate rod slightly to align flat with pin hole in adjusting nut, then install locking pin and remove feeler gauge.
8. On all models, connect return spring to release lever.
9. Depress clutch pedal a minimum of five times, then recheck free play setting with the feeler gauge. Check free travel of pedal which should be ⅞ to 1⅛ inch.

CLUTCH, REPLACE

1978-79 Fairmont & Zephyr

4-140
1. Raise vehicle and remove release lever spring and dust shield.
2. Loosen clutch cable lock nut and adjusting nut, then disconnect clutch cable from release lever.
3. Remove retaining clip, then remove clutch cable from clutch housing.
4. Remove starter motor.
5. Remove bolts attaching engine rear plate to lower front portion of flywheel housing.

6. Remove transmission and flywheel housing as described under Transmission, Replace.

7. Remove clutch release lever from housing by pulling lever through opening in housing until retainer spring is disengaged from pivot.

8. Remove pressure plate cover attaching bolts.

   NOTE: Loosen bolts evenly to relieve spring tension without distorting cover. Mark cover and flywheel so that pressure plate can be installed in the same position.

9. Remove pressure plate and clutch disc from flywheel.

10. Reverse procedure to install. Adjust clutch pedal as described under Clutch Pedal, Adjust.

6-200

1. Raise vehicle, then remove transmission as described under Transmission, Replace.

2. Remove dust shield and loosen clutch cable adjusting nut, then disengage clutch cable from release lever.

3. Disengage clutch cable from flywheel housing.

4. Remove starter.

5. Remove bolts attaching engine rear plate to front lower portion of flywheel housing.

6. Remove bolts attaching housing to cylinder block.

7. Move housing back just far enough to clear pressure plate and remove housing.

8. Remove clutch release lever from housing by pulling lever through housing opening until retainer spring is disengaged from pivot.

9. Remove pressure plate cover attaching bolts.

   NOTE: Loosen bolts evenly to relieve spring tension without distorting cover. Mark cover and flywheel so that pressure plate can be installed in the same position.

10. Remove pressure plate and clutch disc from flywheel.

11. Reverse procedure to install. Adjust clutch pedal as described under Clutch Pedal, Adjust.

Except 1978-79 Fairmont & Zephyr

1. Remove transmission as described under Transmission, Replace.

2. Disconnect clutch release lever retaining spring.

3. Loosen clutch adjusting rod nuts and remove adjusting rod.

4. Remove starter motor.

5. Remove engine rear plate to lower flywheel housing attaching bolts.

6. Remove flywheel housing to engine attaching bolts and clutch equalizer bar pivot bracket, if equipped.

7. Move flywheel housing back just far enough to clear pressure plate and remove housing.

   NOTE: Use care not to disturb clutch linkage.

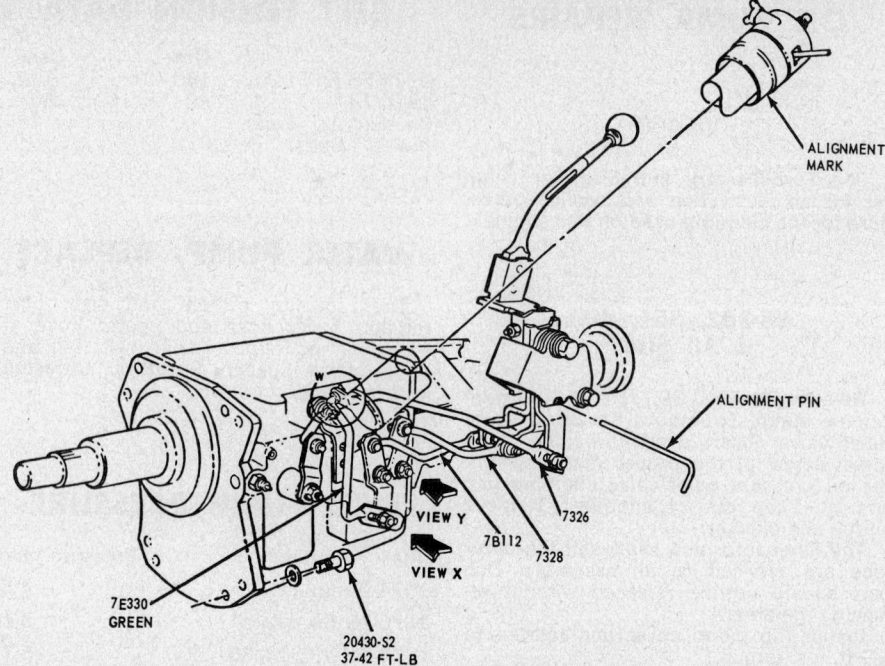

Fig. 1 Installing alignment pin in shift control

8. Pull clutch release lever through opening in housing until retainer spring is disengaged from pivot.

9. Remove pressure plate cover attaching bolts.

   NOTE: Loosen bolts evenly to relieve spring tension without distorting cover. Mark cover and flywheel so that pressure plate can be installed in the same position.

10. Remove pressure plate and clutch disc from flywheel.

11. Reverse removal procedure to install the clutch and adjust the pedal as outlined in Clutch Pedal, Adjust.

THREE SPEED TRANS. REPLACE

1974-79

1. Raise and support vehicle on a hoist or safety stands.

2. Disconnect electrical connectors from transmission.

3. Mark drive shaft so that it may be installed in the same position, then disconnect it from rear U joint and remove it from output shaft.

   NOTE: Plug extension housing to prevent loss of lubricant.

4. Disconnect speedometer cable and shift linkages from transmission.

5. Support transmission with suitable jack and remove engine rear support nuts. Remove the crossmember and rear support insulator.

6. Support engine and remove transmission.

   NOTE: Do not depress clutch pedal with transmission removed.

FOUR SPEED OVERDRIVE TRANSMISSION, REPLACE

1977-79 Granada & Monarch

1. Disconnect battery ground cable.

2. Remove shift lever boot bezel and the four shift lever boot to floor attaching screws. Lift boot upward.

3. Remove two bolts attaching shift lever to shift control, then the shift lever and boot.

4. From beneath vehicle, disconnect shift rods from shift control levers.

5. Disconnect back-up lamp switch electrical connector and remove switch from retainer by pulling and twisting the switch in both directions.

   NOTE: Do not use pliers or other tools since damage to the switch may result.

6. Remove shift control assembly to extension housing attaching bolts, then the shift control assembly.

7. Raise vehicle and remove propeller shaft.

8. Disconnect speedometer cable from extension housing.

9. Support engine with a suitable jack and remove extension housing to engine rear support attaching bolts.

10. Support transmission with a suitable jack and release weight from crossmember. Remove bolts attaching crossmember to frame side supports and the crossmember.
11. Remove transmission to flywheel housing bolts.
12. Move transmission rearward and lower from vehicle.
13. Reverse procedure to install. Adjust shift linkage as outlined under "Gearshift Linkage".

FOUR SPEED TRANS. REPLACE

1978-79 Fairmont & Zephyr

1. Remove coin tray, then remove four screws attaching boot to floor pan and pull boot up on shift lever. Remove three lever attaching screws, then remove shift lever and boot assembly.
2. From under hood, remove flywheel housing to engine block upper attaching bolts or nuts.
3. Raise and support vehicle.
4. Mark driveshaft so that it can be installed in the same position, then remove driveshaft and install a plug in transmission extension housing to prevent lubricant leakage.
5. Remove clutch release lever dust cover, then disconnect clutch cable from release lever.
6. Remove starter motor.
7. Remove speedometer cable attaching screw, then lift cable from extension housing.
8. Support rear of engine using a suitable jack, then remove bolts attaching crossmember to body.
9. Remove bolts attaching crossmember to extension housing and remove crossmember.
10. Lower engine as required to permit removal of bolts attaching flywheel housing to engine. Slide transmission rearward from engine and lower from vehicle.

NOTE: It may be necessary to slide mounting bracket forward from catalytic converter heat shield to provide clearance to move transmission rearward for removal.

11. Remove cover attaching bolts and drain lubricant.
12. Remove flywheel housing to transmission attaching bolts, then remove flywheel housing.

GEARSHIFT LINKAGE

NOTE: *If the transmission shifts hard or will not engage, the gearshift levers may need adjusting at the cross-over. Move the shift lever through all positions to see that the cross-over operation is smooth. If not, adjust as follows:*

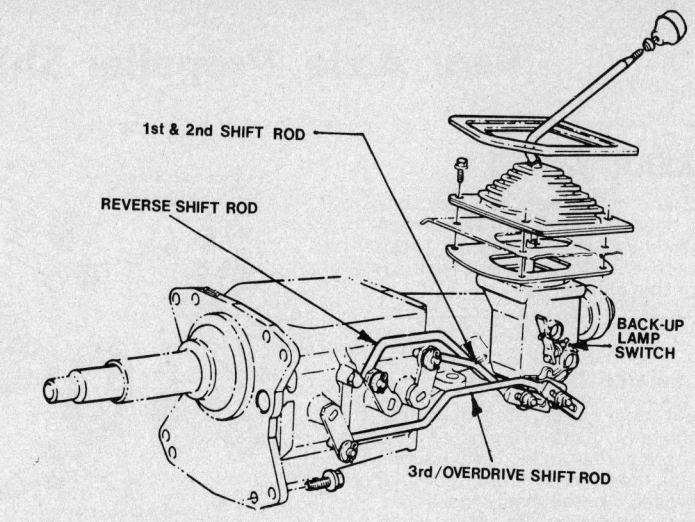

Fig. 2 Four speed overdrive gear shift linkage. 1977-79 Granada & Monarch

1974 Montego & Torino Column Shift

1. Working inside car, loosen clamp nut holding gearshift tube and shaft.
2. Loosen shift rod adjusting nuts at transmission.
3. Remove plastic covers over gearshift lever assembly and insert 1/4" rod.
4. Set gearshift lever in Neutral in the 2-3 plane and torque clamp nut inside car to 12-18 ft. lbs.
5. Set transmission levers in Neutral and insert 1/4" rod in locator holes in lower end of steering column.
6. Torque shift rod adjusting nuts using care to prevent motion between the rods and the studs on transmission levers.
7. Remove alignment pins and install covers.
8. Check operation to assure smooth crossover.

Except 1974 Montego & Torino

1. Place shift lever in neutral.
2. Loosen two gearshift rod adjustment nuts.
3. See that transmission shift levers are in neutral position.
4. Insert a 3/16" diameter rod through holes in both levers and both holes in lower casting. It may be necessary to align levers to insert tool.
5. Tighten shift rod adjustment nuts.
6. Remove alignment tool and check operation of shift levers.

1974-76 3 Speed Floor Shift

NOTE: 1974-76 floor shift linkages incorporate a transmission lock rod. This rod must be adjusted AFTER the shift linkage has been adjusted. With shift lever in Neutral and lock rod adjustment nut loose, align hole in steering column socket casting with alignment mark and insert a .180" dia. rod. The casting must not rotate with the rod in this position. Tighten lock rod adjustment nut.

1. Loosen three shift linkage adjusting nuts. Install a 1/4" diameter alignment pin through control bracket and levers, Fig. 1.
2. Tighten three linkage adjusting nuts and remove alignment pin.
3. Check gearshift lever for smooth crossover.

1978-79 3 Speed

1. Connect shift rods to transmission levers, Fig. 2.
2. Ensure transmission is in neutral.
3. Insert alignment pin through hole in boot and into shift control assembly alignment hole.
4. Install slotted ends of shift rods over flats of studs in shift control assembly, then install and torque lock nuts.
5. Remove alignment pin.

1977-79 4 Speed Overdrive

1. Attach shift rods to transmission levers.
2. Shift reverse lever (middle) clockwise to place transmission in reverse.
3. Insert alignment pin through hole in boot and into shift control assembly alignment hole.
4. Attach slotted ends of 1-2 and 3-overdrive shift rods over flats of studs on shift control assembly. Install lock nuts and torque to 10 to 20 ft. lbs.
5. Shift transmission to neutral and attach reverse lever. Torque lock nut to 10 to 20 ft. lbs.
6. Remove alignment pin.

1979 AUTO. TRANS. LINKAGE, ADJUST

NOTE: All 1979 vehicles, use the same procedure as previous models and can be found elsewhere in this book.

Rear Axle, Propeller Shaft & Brakes

REAR AXLES

Figs. 1, 2 and 4 illustrate the rear axle assemblies used on these cars. When necessary to overhaul either of these units, refer to the *Rear Axle Specifications* table in this chapter.

Service Bulletin

All Ford Built Rear Axles: Recent manufacturing changes have eliminated the need for marking rear axle drive pinions for individual variations from nominal shim thicknesses. In the past, these pinion markings, with the aid of a shim selection table, were used as a guide to select correct shim thicknesses when a gear set or carrier assembly replacement was performed.

With the elimination of pinion markings, use of the shim selection table is no longer possible and the methods outlined below must be used.

1. Measure the thickness of the original pinion depth shim removed from the axle. Use the same thickness upon installation of the replacement carrier or drive pinion. If any further shim change is necessary, it will be indicated in the tooth pattern check.
2. If the original shim is lost, substitute a nominal shim for the original and use the tooth pattern check to determine if further shim changes are required.

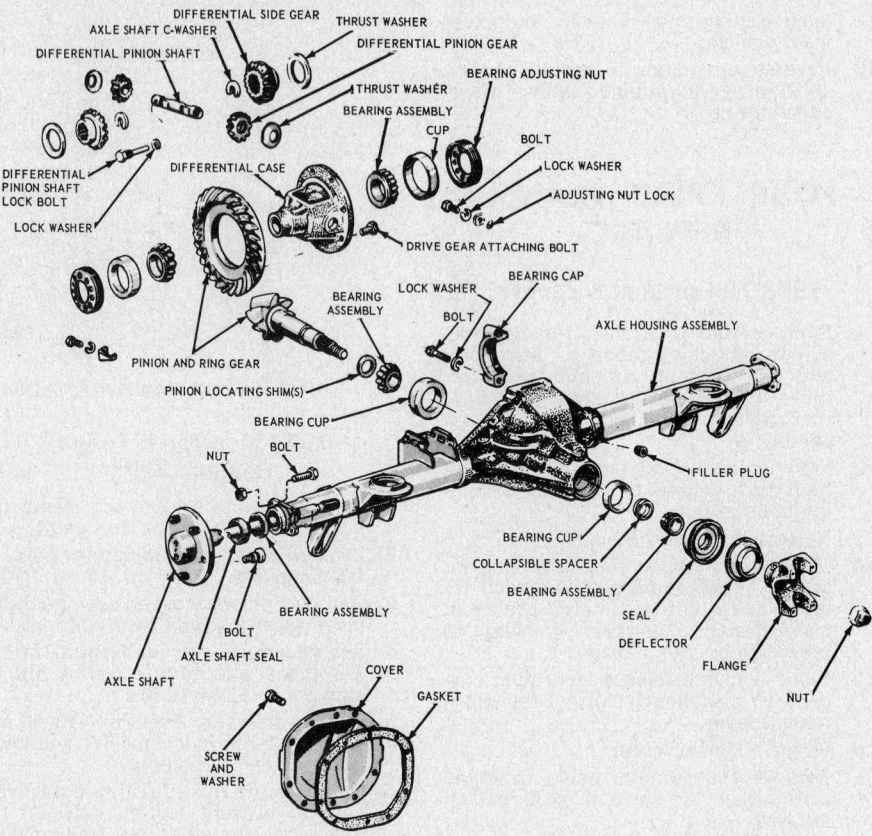

Fig. 1   Disassembled view of Ford WER integral carrier type rear axle assembly

Ford WER Integral Carrier, Fig. 1

The gear set consists of a ring gear and an overhung drive pinion which is supported by two opposed tapered roller bearings. The differential case is a one-piece design with openings allowing assembly of the internal parts and lubricant flow. The differential pinion shaft is retained with a threaded bolt (lock) assembled to the case.

The roller type wheel bearings have no inner race, and the rollers directly contact the bearing journals of the axle shafts. The axle shafts do not use an inner and outer bearing retainer. Rather, they are held in the axle by means of C-locks, Fig. 2. These C-locks also fit into a machined recess in the differential side gears within the differential case. There is no retainer bolt access hole in the axle shaft flange.

Ford WGX Integral Carrier, Fig. 3

The gear set consist of a ring gear and an overhung drive pinion which is supported by two opposed tappered roller bearings. Pinion bearing preload is maintained by a collapsible spacer on the pinion shaft and adjusted by the pinion nut. The differential case is a one piece design

with two openings to allow assembly of internal components and lubricant flow. The pinion shaft is retained with a threaded bolt assembled to the case. The differential case is mounted in the carrier between two opposed tapered roller bearings. The bearings are retained in the carrier by removal bearing caps. Differential bearing preload and ring gear backlash are adjusted by the use of shims located between the differential bearing cups and

Fig. 2   Axle shaft C-locks. Ford WER & WGX integral type axles

the carrier housing. Axle shafts are held in the housing by C-locks positioned in a slot on the axle shaft splined end, Fig. 2.

Removable Carrier Type

In these axles, Fig. 4, the drive pinion is straddle-mounted by two opposed tapered roller bearings which support the pinion shaft in front of the drive pinion gear, and a straight roller bearing that supports the pinion shaft at the rear of the pinion gear. The drive pinion is assembled in a pinion retainer that is bolted to the differential carrier. The tapered roller bearings are preloaded by a collapsible spacer between the bearings. The pinion is positioned by a shim or shims located between the drive pinion retainer and the differential carrier.

The differential is supported in the carrier by two tapered roller side bearings. These bearings are preloaded by two threaded ring nuts or sleeves between the bearings and the pedestals. The differential assembly is positioned for proper ring gear and pinion backlash by varying the adjustment of these ring nuts. The differential case houses two side gears in mesh with two pinions mounted on a pinion shaft which are held in place by a pin. The side gears and pinions are backed by thrust washers.

The axle shafts are of unequal length, the left shaft being shorter than the right. The axle shafts are mounted in sealed ball bearings which are pressed on the shafts.

Rear Axle, Replace

Leaf Spring Suspension

1. Raise vehicle and support at rear frame members.
2. Drain lubricant from axle.
3. Mark drive shaft and pinion flanges for reassembly, then disconnect drive shaft at rear axle U-joint and remove drive shaft from transmission extension housing. Install seal replacer tool in extension housing to prevent leakage.
4. Disconnect shock absorbers at lower mountings.
5. Rear wheels and brake drums, then disconnect brake lines at wheel cylinders.
6. Disconnect vent hose from vent tube, then remove vent tube from brake junction and axle housing.
7. Remove clips retaining brake lines to axle housing.
8. Support rear axle housing using a suitable jack, remove U-bolts and plates.
9. Lower rear axle and remove vehicle.
10. Reverse procedure to install.

Coil Spring Suspension

1. Raise rear of vehicle support at frame members and rear axle, then remove wheel and tire assembly.
2. Remove brake drums and disconnect brake lines at wheel cylinders.
3. Make marks on drive shaft yoke and pinion flange for reassembly, then disconnect drive shaft at rear U-joint and remove drive shaft from transmission extension housing. Install seal replacer tool in extension housing to prevent leakage.
4. Position a drain pan under differential carrier, then remove carrier attaching bolts and allow differential to drain.
5. Disconnect stabilizer bar, if equipped.
6. Disconnect shock absorbers from lower mountings.
7. Remove brake lines from retaining clips on rear axle housing, then remove brake line junction block retaining screw.
8. Position a suitable jack under axle housing to prevent housing from tilting when removing control arms.
9. Disconnect lower control arms from axle housing and position control arms downward.
10. Disconnect upper control arms from axle housing and position control arms upward.
11. Disconnect air vent line.
12. Lower axle slightly and remove coil springs and insulators.
13. Lower axle housing and remove from vehicle.

Axle Shaft, Replace

Removable Carrier Type

1. Remove wheel assembly.
2. Remove brake drum or rotor and caliper assembly.

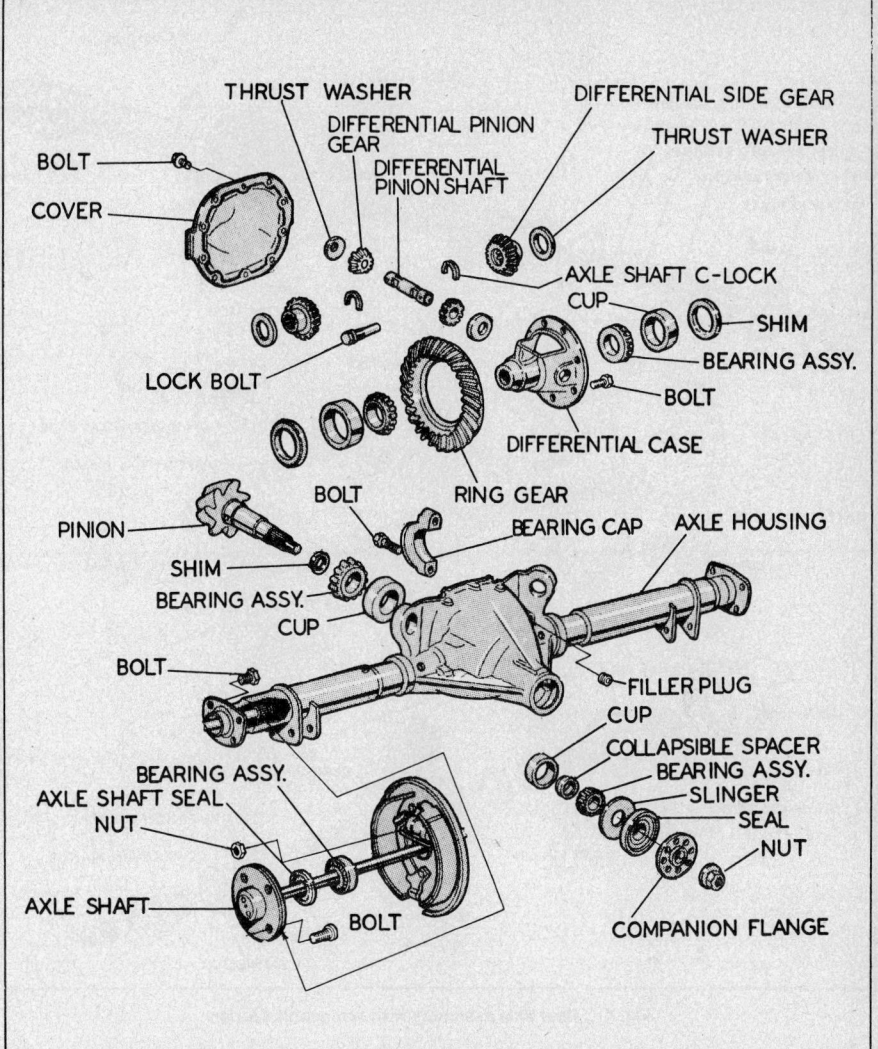

Fig. 3 Disassemble view of Ford WGX integral carrier type rear axle assembly

3. Working through hole provided in axle shaft flange, Fig. 5, remove nuts that secure wheel bearing retainer.
4. Pull axle shaft out of housing. If bearing is a tight fit in axle housing use a slide hammer-type puller, Fig. 6. Remove brake backing plate and secure to frame rail with wire.
5. If the axle shaft bearing is to be replaced, loosen the inner retainer by nicking it deeply with a chisel in several places, Fig. 7. The bearing will then slide off easily.
6. Press bearing from axle shaft.
7. Inspect machined surface of axle shaft and housing for rough spots that would affect sealing action of the oil seal. Carefully remove any burrs or rough spots.

8. Press new bearing on shaft until it seats firmly against shoulder on shaft.
9. Press inner bearing retainer on shaft until it seats firmly against bearing.
10. If oil seal is to be replaced, use a hook-type tool to pull it out of housing, Fig. 8. Wipe a small amount of oil resistant sealer on outer edge of seal before it is installed, Fig. 9.

Installation

1. Place a new gasket on each side of brake carrier plate and slide axle shaft into housing.
2. Start the splines into the differential side gear and push the shaft in until bearing bottoms in housing.

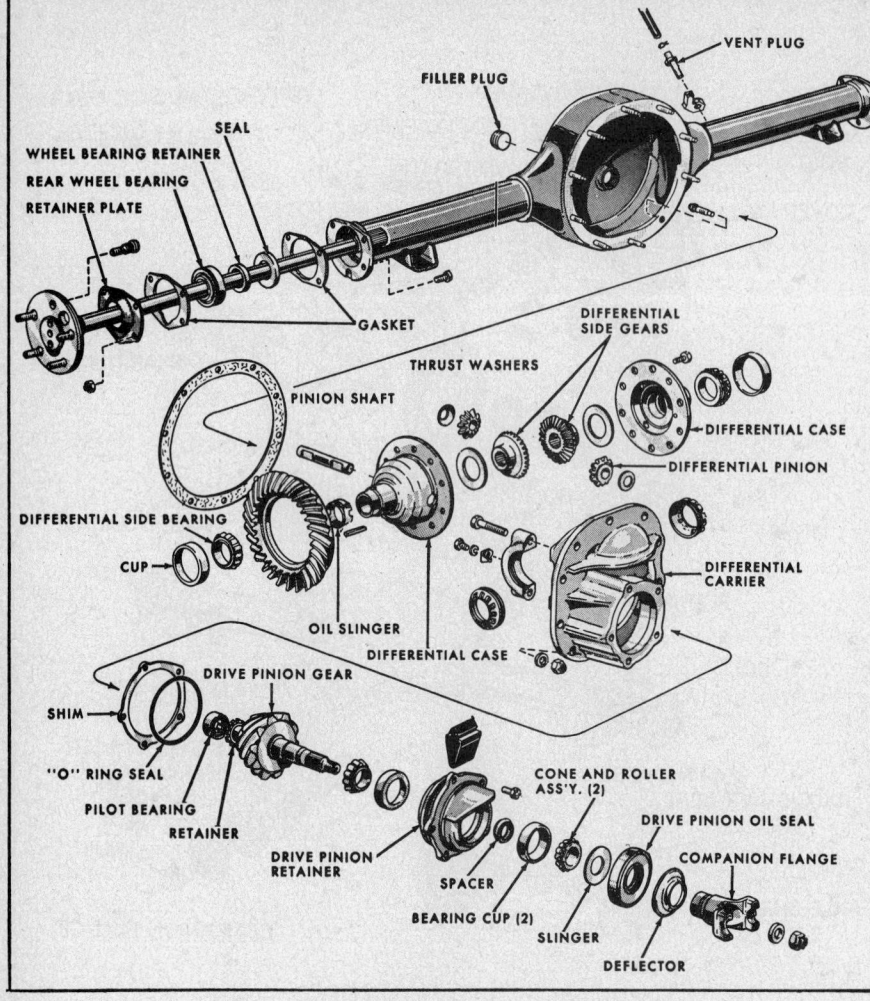

Fig. 4 Rear axle assembly with removable carrier

AXLE SHAFT FLANGE

Fig. 5 Removing nuts from wheel bearing retainer

sembly using a suitable slide hammer, Fig. 8, if necessary.

NOTE: Two of bearing are used. One requires a light press fit in the housing flange, while on the other a loose fit is acceptable. Therefore, if a loose fitting bearing is encountered, it does not indicate excessive wear or damage.

8. Lubricate bearing with rear axle lubricant and install bearing into housing bore using tool No. T78P-1225-A.
9. Install axle shaft seal into housing using tool No. T78P-1177-A, Fig. 9.
10. Reverse procedure to install axle shaft.

3. Install retainer. On 1974-77 Comet, Granada, Maverick, Monarch and all 1978 models, torque retaining nuts to 20 to 40 ft. lbs. On 1974-77 models except Comet, Granada, Maverick and Monarch, torque retaining nuts to 35 to 55 ft. lbs.
4. Install brake drum or caliper and rotor and wheel assembly.

Ford WER Integral Carrier Type

1. Raise car on hoist and remove wheels.
2. Drain differential lubricant.
3. Remove brake drums.
4. Remove differential housing cover.
5. Position safety stands under rear frame member and lower hoist to allow axle to lower as far as possible.
6. Working through differential case opening, remove pinion shaft lock bolt and pinion shaft.
7. Push axle shaft(s) inward toward center of axle housing and remove C-lock(s) from housing, Fig. 3.
8. Remove axle shaft, using extreme care to avoid contact of shaft seal lip with any portion of axle shaft except seal journal.
9. Use a hook-type puller to remove seal

and bearing, Fig. 8.

NOTE: Two types of bearings are used. One requires a light press fit in the housing flange, while on the other, a loose fit is acceptable. Therefore, if a loose fitting bearing is encountered, it does not indicate excessive wear or damage.

10. Reverse procedure to install, using suitable driving tools, Fig. 9, to install seal and bearing. New seals are pre-packed with lubricant and do not require oil soaking before installation.

Ford WGX Integral Carrier Type

1. Raise and support rear of vehicle.
2. Remove wheel and tire assembly and brake drum.
3. Remove rear axle housing cover and drain lubricant.
4. Remove differential pinion lock screw and differential pinion shaft.
5. Push axle shafts inward and remove C-locks.
6. Remove axle shaft from housing using care not to damage oil seal.
7. Remove bearing and seal as an as-

PROPELLER SHAFT

Remove & Replace

1. Disconnect rear U-joint from drive pinion flange.
2. Pull drive shaft toward rear of car until front U-joint yoke clears transmission extension housing and output shaft.
3. Install a suitable tool, such as a seal driver, in seal to prevent lube from leaking from transmission.
4. Before installing, check U-joints for freedom of movement. If a bind has resulted from misalignment after overhauling the U-joints, tap the ears of the drive shaft sharply to relieve the bind.
5. If rubber seal installed on end of transmission extension housing is damaged, install a new seal.
6. On a manual shift transmission, lubricate yoke spline with conventional transmission grease. On an automatic transmission, lubricate yoke spline with special spline grease. *This spline is sealed so that transmission fluid does not "wash" away spline lubricant.*
7. Install yoke on transmission output shaft.
8. Install U-bolts and nuts which attach U-joint to pinion flange. Tighten U-bolts evenly to prevent binding U-joint bearings.

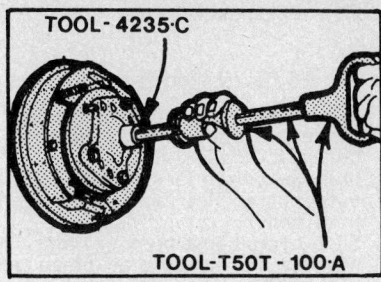

Fig. 6 Removing axle shaft with slide hammer-type puller

BRAKE ADJUSTMENTS

SERVICE BULLETIN

REVISED BRAKE ADJUSTMENT PROCEDURE: Some models use a new front and rear brake backing plate which omits the adjusting slot for manual brake adjustment. The backing plates have a partially stamped knock-out slot for use ONLY when the brake drums cannot be removed in a normal manner. The open slot is then covered with a rubber plug as used in the past to prevent contamination of the brakes.

When servicing a vehicle requiring a brake adjustment, the metal knock-out plugs should NOT be removed. Rather the drums should be removed and brakes inspected for a malfunction.

Although the brakes are self-adjusting, an initial adjustment will be necessary after a brake repair, such as relining or replacement. The initial adjustment can be obtained by the new procedure which follows:

1. Use the brake shoe adjustment gauge shown in Fig. 10 to obtain the drum inside diameter as shown. Tighten the adjusting knob on the gauge to hold this setting.
2. Place the opposite side of the gauge over the brake shoes and adjust the shoes by turning the adjuster screw until the gauge just slides over the linings. Rotate the gauge around the lining surface to assure proper lining diameter adjustment and clearance.

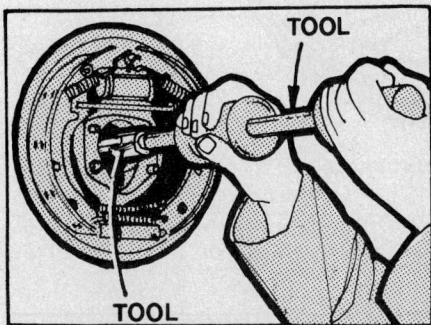

Fig. 8 Using hook-type tool to remove oil seal

3. Install brake drum and wheel. Final adjustment is accomplished by making several firm reverse stops, using the brake pedal.

Self-Adjusting Brakes

These brakes, Fig. 11 have self-adjusting shoe mechanisms that assure correct lining-to-drum clearances at all times. The automatic adjusters operate only when the brakes are applied as the car is moving rearward.

Although the brakes are self-adjusting, an initial adjustment in necessary after the brake shoes have been relined or replaced, or when the length of the star wheel adjuster has been changed during some other service operation.

Frequent usage of an automatic transmission forward range to halt reverse vehicle motion may prevent the automatic adjusters from functioning, thereby inducing low pedal heights. Should low pedal heights be encountered, it is recommended that numerous forward and reverse stops be made until satisfactory peda! height is obtained.

NOTE

If a low pedal condition cannot be corrected by making numerous reverse stops (provided the hydraulic system is free of air) it indicates that the self-adjusting mechanism is not functioning. Therefore, it will be necessary to remove the brake drum, clean, free up and lubricate the adjusting mechanism. Then adjust the brake, being sure the parking brake is fully released.

PARKING BRAKE, ADJUST

1974-79 All

Rear Drum Brakes

1. Make sure parking brake is released.
2. Place transmission in neutral and raise the vehicle.
3. Tighten the adjusting nut against the cable equalizer to cause rear brakes to drag.
4. Then loosen the adjusting nut until the rear wheels are fully released. There should be no drag.
5. Lower vehicle and check operation.

Rear Disc Brakes

1. Fully release parking brake, then place transmission in neutral and support vehicle at rear axle.
2. Tighten adjuster nut until levers on calipers just begin to move, then loosen adjuster nut until levers just return to stop position.
3. Apply and release parking brake. Check levers on caliper to determine if they are fully returned by attempting to pull lever rearward. If lever

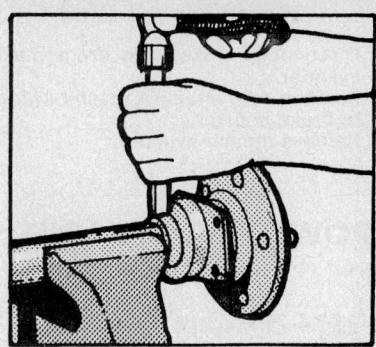

Fig. 7 Splitting bearing inner retainer for bearing removal

moves, the adjustment is too tight and must be readjusted.

MASTER CYLINDER, REPLACE

1974-78 Less Power Brakes

1. Working from inside vehicle below instrument panel, disconnect master cylinder push rod from brake pedal.
2. Disconnect stop light switch wires, remove hairpin retainer and slide stop light switch off brake pedal pin just far enough to clear end of pin. Then lift switch straight upward from pin.
3. Slide master cylinder push rod with nylon washers and bushings from brake pedal pin.
4. Remove brake tubes from outlet ports of master cylinder.
5. Remove lock nuts that secure master cylinder to dash panel and lift cylinder forward and upward from vehicle.
6. Reverse procedure to install.

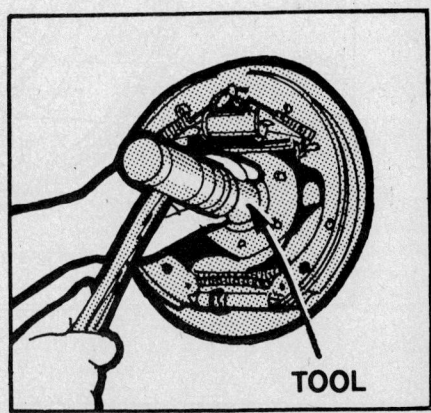

Fig. 9 Using special driver to install oil seal

1974-79 Power Brakes

1. Disconnect brake lines from master cylinder.
2. Remove nuts retaining master cylinder to brake booster.
3. Remove master cylinder.

POWER BRAKE UNIT, REPLACE

1974-78 Except Hydro-Boost

1. Working under instrument panel, disconnect stop light switch wires at connector.
2. Remove hairpin type retainer. Slide stop light switch off brake pedal pin just far enough for the switch outer hole to clear the pin, then lower switch away from pin.
3. Slide booster push rod link and nylon washers and bushing off brake pedal pin.
4. On 1978-79 Fairmont & Zephyr, remove air cleaner. On models with 4-140 engine, disconnect accelerator cable from carburetor, then remove screw that secures accelerator cable to shaft bracket and remove cable from bracket. Remove two screws that secure accelerator shaft bracket to manifold and rotate bracket toward engine.
5. On 1975-77 Comet and Maverick with 6-250 engine, remove air cleaner and disconnect accelerator cable from car-

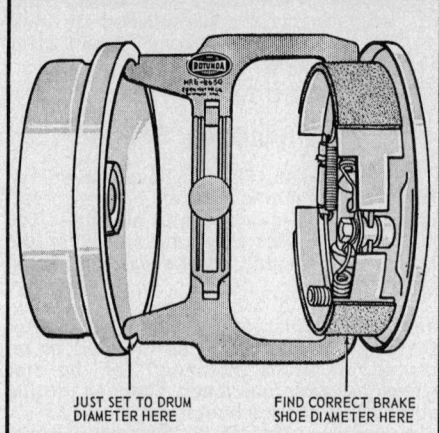

JUST SET TO DRUM DIAMETER HERE   FIND CORRECT BRAKE SHOE DIAMETER HERE

Fig. 10   Revised brake adjustment

buretor.

6. On all 1975-77 Comet and Maverick models, remove fender to cowl brace.
7. On 1975-76 Montego, Torino, Elite, 1975-79 Cougar and 1977-79 LTD II models equipped with speed control, remove left cowl screen, then remove servo mounting bracket attaching nuts and position servo cable.
8. On all models, disconnect brake line from master cylinder.
9. Disconnect vacuum hose from booster at check valve.
10. Unfasten and remove booster and bracket assembly from dash panel, sliding push rod link out from engine

side of dash panel.

1975-79 Hydro-Boost

1. Disconnect stoplight switch wires at connector and remove hairpin retainer, then slide stoplight switch off brake pedal pin far enough for switch outer hole to clear pin and remove pin from switch.
2. Slide hydro-boost push rod and nylon washers and bushing off brake pedal pin.
3. Remove master cylinder and position to one side without disturbing hydraulic lines.

NOTE: It is not necessary to disconnect brake lines, but care should be taken not to deform lines.

4. Disconnect pressure, steering gear and return lines from booster, then plug lines and ports in hydro-boost to prevent entry of dirt.
5. Remove hydro-boost retaining nuts, and remove assembly sliding push rod link from engine side of dash panel.
6. Reverse procedure to install. To purge system, disconnect coil wire so that engine will not start. Fill power steering pump reservoir, then while engaging starter, pump brake pedal. Do not cycle steering wheel until all residual air has been purged from the hydro boost unit. Check fluid level, then connect coil wire and start engine. Apply brakes with a pumping action and cycle steering wheel, then check system for leaks.

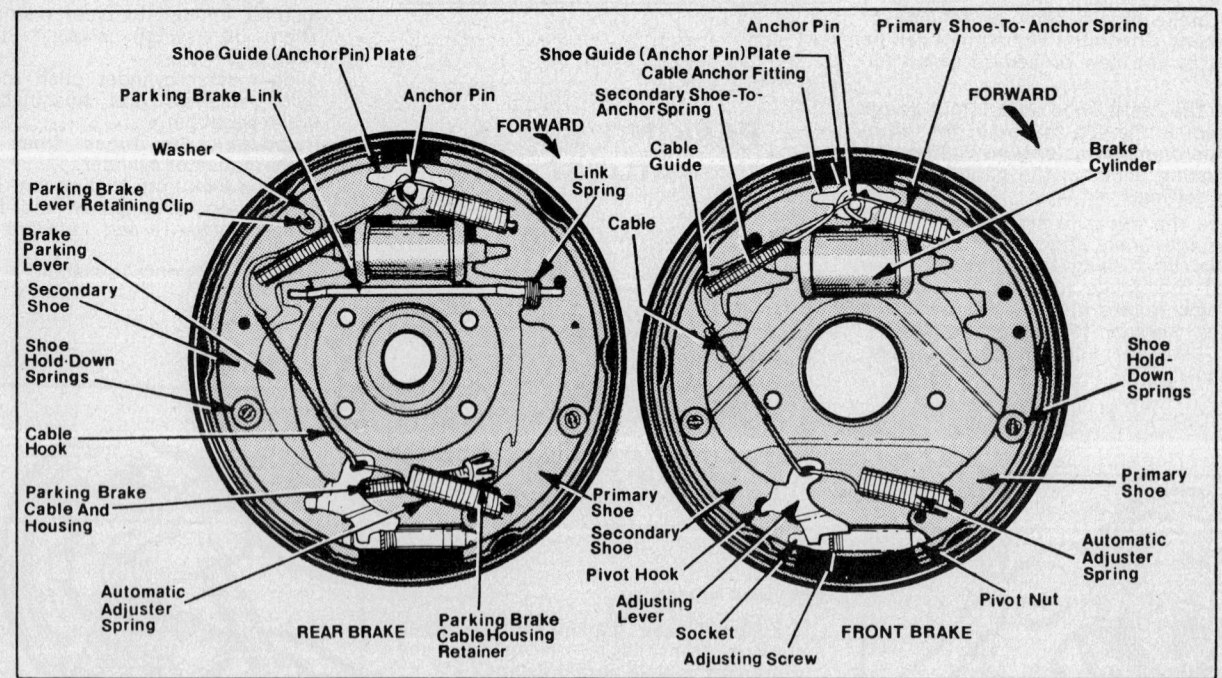

Fig. 11   Right front and rear drum brake mechanism

Rear Suspension

SHOCK ABSORBER, REPLACE

1978-79 Fairmont & Zephyr

1. On sedans, open trunk to gain access to upper shock absorber attachment. On station wagons, remove side panel trim covers.
2. On sedans, remove rubber cap from shock absorber stud.
3. On all models, remove shock absorber attaching nut, washer and insulator.
4. Raise vehicle and support rear axle.
5. Compress shock absorber to clear hole in upper shock absorber tower.
6. Remove nut and washer from shock absorber lower mounting stud, then remove shock absorber.

Except 1978-79 Fairmont & Zephyr

LEAF SPRINGS & BUSHINGS REPLACE

1974-77 Comet & Maverick & 1975-79 Granada & Monarch

1. Raise rear of vehicle and support at frame. Support axle with a suitable jack.
2. Disconnect shock absorbers from lower mountings.

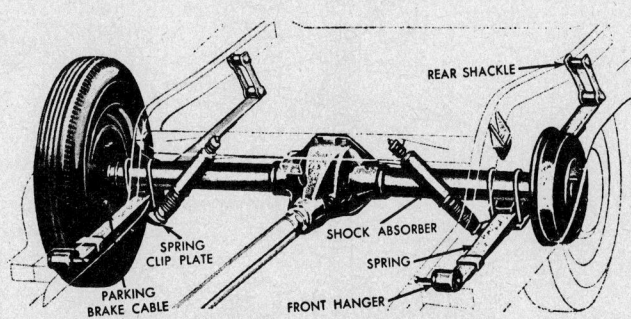

Fig. 1   Leaf spring suspension (typical)

3. Lower jack and remove spring plate "U" bolts and spring plate, Fig. 1.
4. Raise axle to remove weight from spring and disassemble rear shackle.
5. Remove spring front mount bolt.
6. Replace spring front eye bushings as necessary, Figs. 2 and 3.
7. Reverse procedure to install.

STABILIZER BAR, REPLACE

1978-79 Fairmont & Zephyr

1. Raise and support rear of vehicle.
2. Remove four bolts attaching stabilizer bar to lower control arms.
3. Remove stabilizer bar from vehicle.

1974-76 Elite, Montego, Torino, 1974-79 Cougar & 1977-79 LTD II

1. Remove bolts securing stabilizer bar to rear link assemblies on both sides, Fig. 4.
2. Remove nuts securing mounting bracket to lower mounting clamp and remove bar.
3. Reverse procedure to install.

COIL SPRING, REPLACE

1978-79 Fairmont & Zephyr

1. Remove stabilizer bar as described under Stabilizer Bar, Replace, if equipped.
2. Position a suitable jack under rear axle, then raise vehicle and support

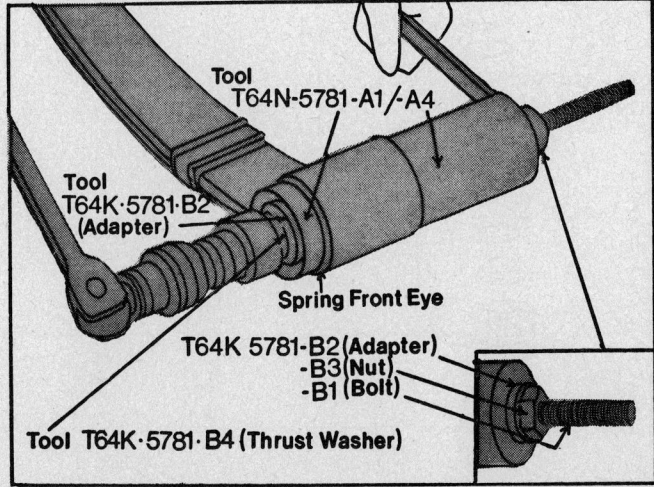

Fig. 2   Spring front bushing removal

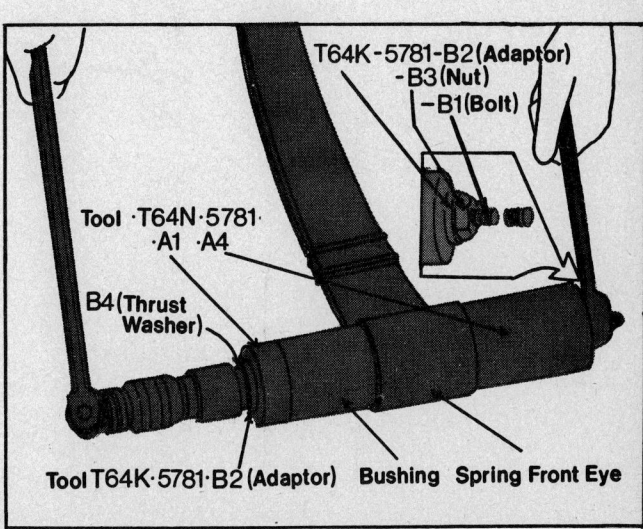

Fig. 3   Spring front bushing installation

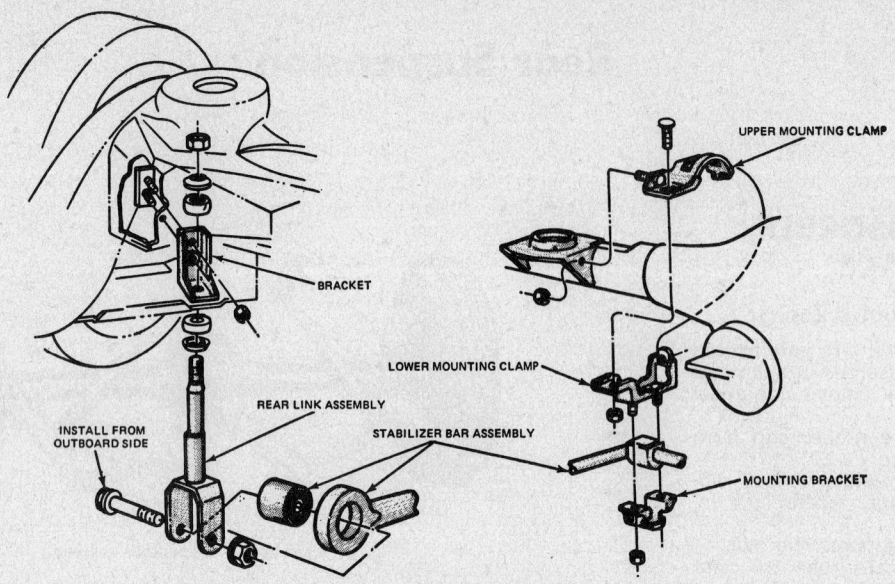

**Fig. 4   Stabilizer bar installation
1974-76 Elite, Montego, Torino,
1974-79 Cougar & 1977-79 LTD II**

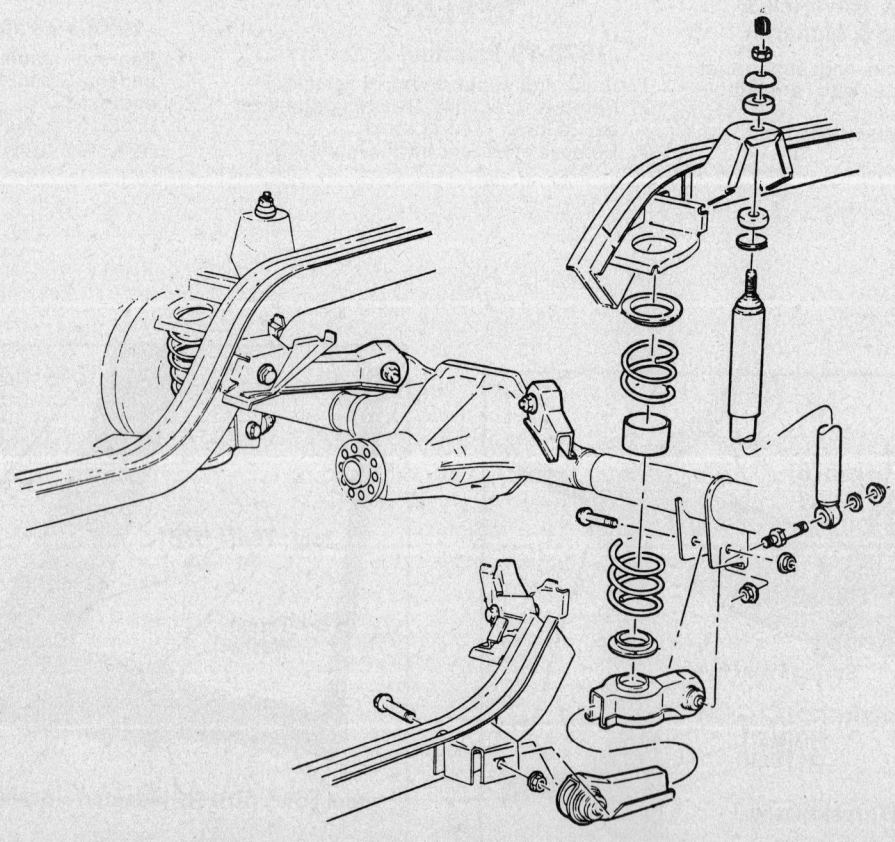

Fig. 5   Rear suspension. 1978-79 Fairmont & Zephyr

body at rear body crossmember.
3. Lower axle until shock absorbers are fully extended.

NOTE: Support axle with jack stands or a suitable jack.

4. Position a suitable jack under lower control arm pivot bolt and remove nut and bolt. Carefully and slowly lower the control arm until all spring tension is relieved.
5. Remove coil spring and insulators from vehicle, Fig. 5.

1974-76 Elite, Montego, Torino, 1974-79 Cougar & 1977-79 LTD II

1. Raise rear of vehicle and support at frame. Support axle with a suitable jack.
2. Disconnect shock absorbers from lower mountings.
3. Lower axle to remove springs.
4. Reverse procedure to install. Install an insulator between upper and lower seats and spring.

CONTROL ARMS, REPLACE

NOTE: Upper and lower control arms must be replaced in pairs.

1978-79 Fairmont & Zephyr

Upper Arm
1. Raise vehicle and support body at rear body crossmember.
2. Remove upper arm pivot bolt and nut, Fig. 5.
3. Remove front pivot bolt and nut, then remove upper arm from vehicle.

Lower Arm
1. Remove stabilizer bar as described under Stabilizer Bar, Replace, if equipped.
2. Position a suitable jack under rear axle, then raise vehicle and support body at rear body crossmember.
3. Lower axle until shock absorbers are

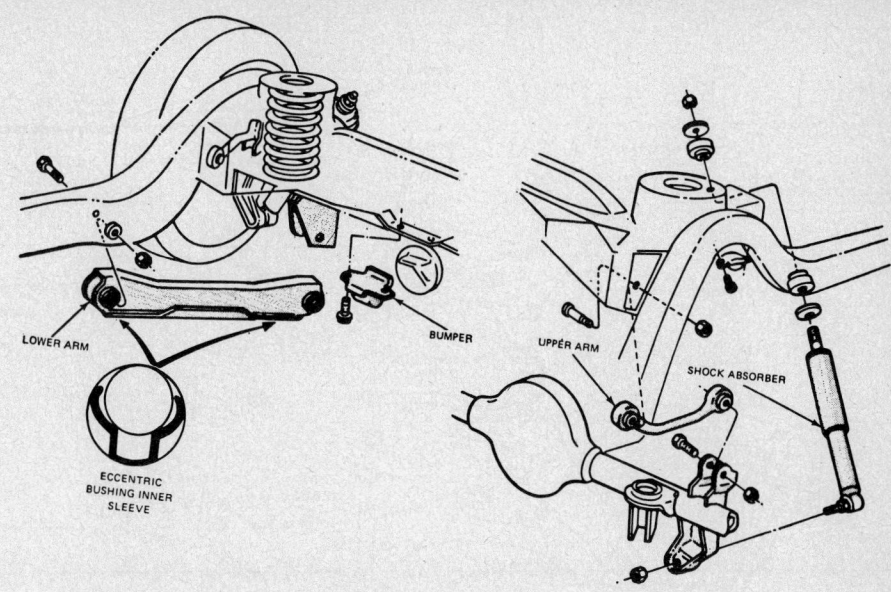

Fig. 6   Rear suspension, 1974-76 Elite, Montego & Torino, 1974-79 Cougar & 1977-79 LTD II

fully extended.

NOTE: Support axle with jack stands or a suitable jack.

4. Position a suitable jack under lower control arm rear pivot bolt and remove nut bolt, Fig. 5. Carefully and slowly lower the control arm until all spring tension is relieved, then remove coil spring and insulators.
5. Remove lower control arm front pivot bolt and nut, then remove lower control arm assembly.

1974-76 Elite, Montego, Torino, 1974-79 Cougar & 1977-79 LTD II

Upper Arm
1. Raise vehicle and support at frame side rails.
2. Lower axle and support axle under differential nose as well as under axle.
3. Remove nut and bolt attaching upper arm to axle housing, then disconnect arm from housing, Fig. 6.
4. Remove nut and bolt attaching upper arm to crossmember, then remove control arm from vehicle.

Lower Arm
1. Raise vehicle and support at frame side rails.
2. Lower axle until all spring tension is relieved.
3. Support axle under differential pinion nose as well as under axle.
4. Remove lower control arm pivot bolt and nut from axle bracket, then disconnect arm from bracket, Fig. 6.
5. Remove pivot bolt and nut from frame bracket, then remove lower control arm from vehicle.

Front End & Steering Section

FRONT SUSPENSION

1978-79 Fairmont & Zephyr

This suspension, Fig. 1, is a modified McPherson strut design, which uses shock struts and coil springs. The springs are mounted between the lower control arm and a spring pocket in the crossmember.

1974-76 Elite, Montego, Torino, 1974-79 Cougar & 1977-79 LTD II

The front suspension, Fig. 1A, has the coil spring mounted on the lower arm.

1974-77 Comet & Maverick & 1975-79 Granada & Monarch

Referring to Fig. 2, each front wheel rotates on a spindle. The upper and lower ends of the spindle are attached to ball joints that are mounted to an upper and lower control arm. The upper arm pivots on a bushing and shaft assembly that is bolted to the underbody. The lower arm pivots on a bolt that is located in an underbody bracket.

A coil spring seats between the upper arm and the top of the spring housing. A double-acting shock absorber is bolted to the arm and the top of the spring housing.

Struts, which are connected between the lower control arms and the underbody, prevent the arms from moving fore and aft.

LUBRICATION

These cars are equipped with an extended chassis lubrication feature which is made possible by a new type of special lubricant combined with special seals and bearing materials which extends the lubrication period to 36,000 miles, on 1974-76 models and 30,000 miles on 1977-79 models.

SERVICE BULLETIN

BALL JOINT LUBRICATION: The ball joint seals have been redesigned to provide improved sealing and longer life. The new seals can be damaged and sealing characteristics destroyed if excessive lubricant is used. Specifications call for the addition of only 10 grams (one level teaspoonful) of lubricant to the ball joint at the recommended intervals. The initial application of 10 grams of lubricant insures forcing grease into the bearing area

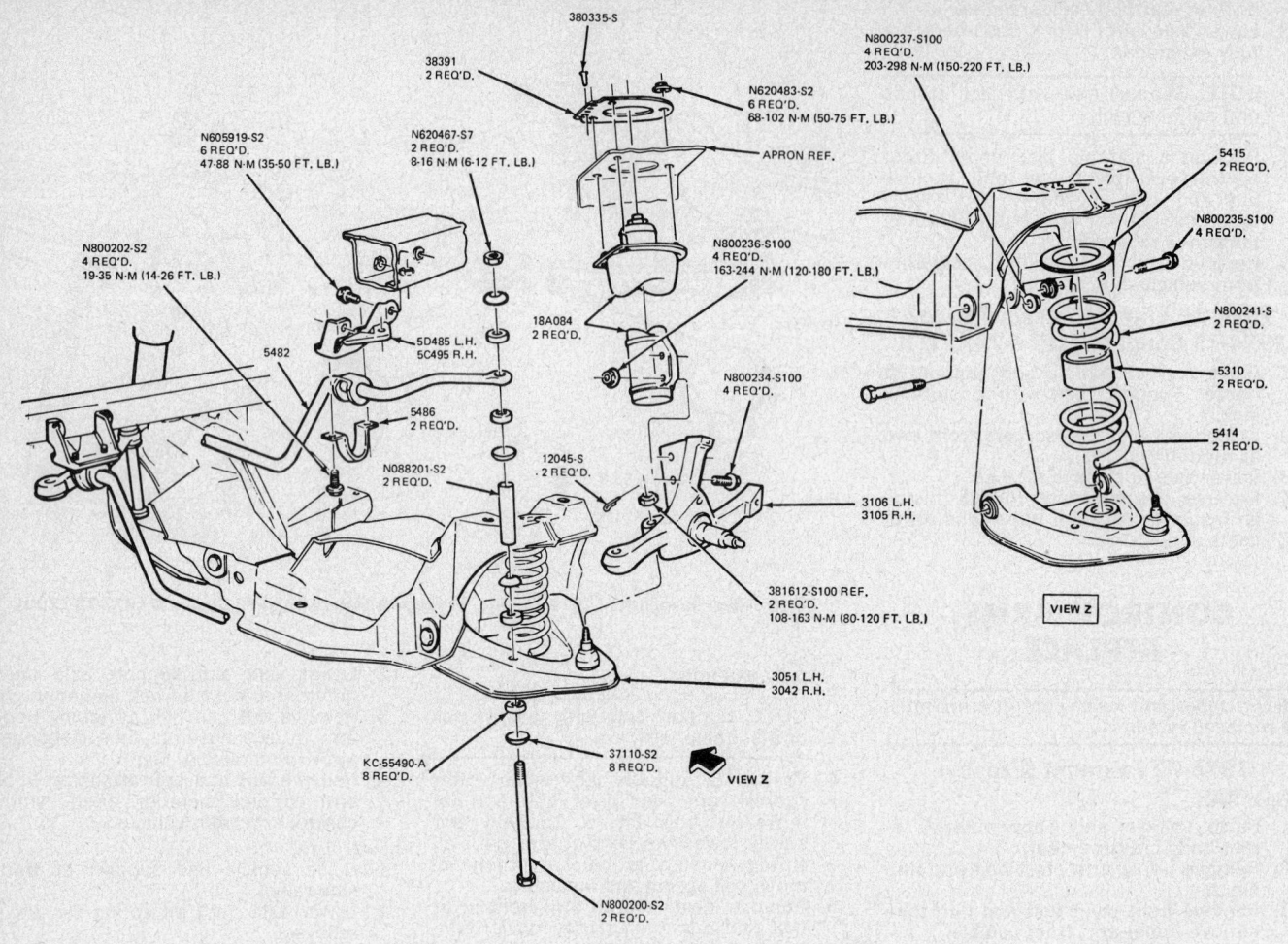

380335-S

38391
2 REQ'D.

N620483-S2
6 REQ'D.
68-102 N·M (50-75 FT. LB.)

N800237-S100
4 REQ'D.
203-298 N·M (150-220 FT. LB.)

N605919-S2
6 REQ'D.
47-88 N·M (35-50 FT. LB.)

N620467-S7
2 REQ'D.
8-16 N·M (6-12 FT. LB.)

APRON REF.

5415
2 REQ'D.

N800202-S2
4 REQ'D.
19-35 N·M (14-26 FT. LB.)

N800236-S100
4 REQ'D.
163-244 N·M (120-180 FT. LB.)

N800235-S100
4 REQ'D.

5D485 L.H.
5C495 R.H.

18A084
2 REQ'D.

N800241-S
2 REQ'D.

5482

5486
2 REQ'D.

N800234-S100
4 REQ'D.

5310
2 REQ'D.

N088201-S2
2 REQ'D.

12045-S
2 REQ'D.

3106 L.H.
3105 R.H.

5414
2 REQ'D.

381612-S100 REF.
2 REQ'D.
108-163 N·M (80-120 FT. LB.)

VIEW Z

3051 L.H.
3042 R.H.

KC-55490-A
8 REQ'D.

37110-S2
8 REQ'D.

VIEW Z

N800200-S2
2 REQ'D.

Fig. 1   Front suspension. 1978-79 Fairmont & Zephyr

and still allows for three subsequent lubrications of 10 grams each without ballooning the seals and resultant premature failure.

For the above reasons the ball joint seals on new vehicles might appear to be collapsed and give the mistaken impression that additional lubricant is required. This is not the case and under no circumstances should more than 10 grams of grease be added to the ball joint at the 30,000 or 36,000 mile intervals.

SERVICE BULLETIN
STEERING LINKAGE LUBRICATION:

The steering linkage should be greased at the recommended intervals. Normal breathing of the socket joints permits moisture condensation within the joint. Moisture inside the joint will cause no appreciable damage and the joint will function normally. However, if the moisture is concentrated in the bearing grease grooves and is frozen at the time of lubrication, grease cannot flow and pressure greasing may damage the joint.

Do not attempt to grease the steering linkage on these models if it has set in temperatures lower than 20 deg. above zero F. The car should be allowed to warm up in a heated garage for 30 minutes or until the joints accept lubrication.

IMPORTANT: A torch must not be used to heat joints because this quantity of heat will melt the nylon bearing within the joint.

WHEEL ALIGNMENT
1978-79 Fairmont & Zephyr

Caster & Camber

The caster and camber angles of this suspension are factory pre-set and cannot be adjusted in the field.

1974-77 Comet & Maverick & 1975-79 Granada & Monarch

As shown in Fig. 3, caster is controlled by the front suspension strut. To obtain positive caster, loosen the strut rear nut and tighten the strut front nut against the bushing. To obtain negative caster, loosen the strut front nut and tighten the strut rear nut against the bushing. Camber is controlled by the eccentric cam located at the lower arm attachment

to the side rail. To adjust camber, loosen the camber adjustment bolt nut at the rear of the body bracket. Spread the body bracket at the camber adjustment bolt area just enough to permit lateral travel of the arm when the adjustment bolt is turned. Rotate the bolt and eccentric clockwise from the high position to increase camber or counterclockwise to decrease it.

1974-76 Elite, Torino, Montego, 1974-79 Cougar & 1977-79 LTD II

Caster and camber can be adjusted by loosening the bolts that attach the upper suspension arm to the shaft at the frame side rail, and moving the arm assembly in or out in the elongated bolt holes, Fig. 4. Since any movement of the arm affects both caster and camber, both factors should be balanced against one another when making the adjustment.

Install the tool with the pins in the frame holes and the hooks over the upper arm inner shaft. Tighten the hook nuts snug before loosening the upper arm inner shaft attaching bolts, Fig. 4.

Caster, Adjust

1. Tighten the tool front hook nut or loosen the rear hook nut as required

to increase caster to the desired angle.
2. To decrease caster, tighten the rear hook nut or loosen the front hook nut as required.

NOTE: The caster angle can be checked without tightening the inner shaft retaining bolts.

3. Check the camber angle to be sure it did not change during the caster adjustment and adjust if necessary.
4. Tighten the upper arm inner shaft retaining bolts and remove tool.

Camber, Adjust

1. Install tool as previously outlined.
2. Loosen both inner shaft retaining bolts.
3. Tighten or loosen the hook nuts as necessary to increase or decrease camber.
4. Recheck caster angle.

TOE-IN, ADJUST

1978-79 Fairmont & Zephyr

1. Check to see that steering shaft and steering wheel marks are in alignment and in the top position.
2. Loosen clamp screw on the tie rod bellows and free the seal on the rod to prevent twisting of the bellows, Fig. 4A.
3. Place opened end wrench on flats of tie rod socket to prevent socket from turning, then loosen tie rod jam nuts.
4. Use suitable pliers to turn the tie rod inner end to correct the adjustment to specifications. Do not use pliers on tie rod threads. Turning to reduce number of threads showing will increase toe-in. Turning in the opposite direction will reduce toe-in.

Exc. Fairmont & Zephyr

Check the steering wheel spoke position when the front wheels are in the straight-ahead position. If the spokes are not in the normal position, they can be adjusted while toe-in is being adjusted.
1. Loosen clamp bolts on each tie rod end sleeve.
2. Adjust toe-in. If steering wheel spokes are in their normal position, lengthen or shorten both rods equally to obtain correct toe-in. If spokes are not in normal position, make necessary rod adjustments to obtain correct toe-in and steering wheel spoke alignment.

WHEEL BEARINGS, ADJUST

1. With wheel rotating, tighten adjusting nut to 17-25 ft. lbs.
2. Back off adjusting nut ½ turn and retighten nut to 10-15 inch lbs.
3. Place nut lock on nut so that castellations on lock are aligned with cotter

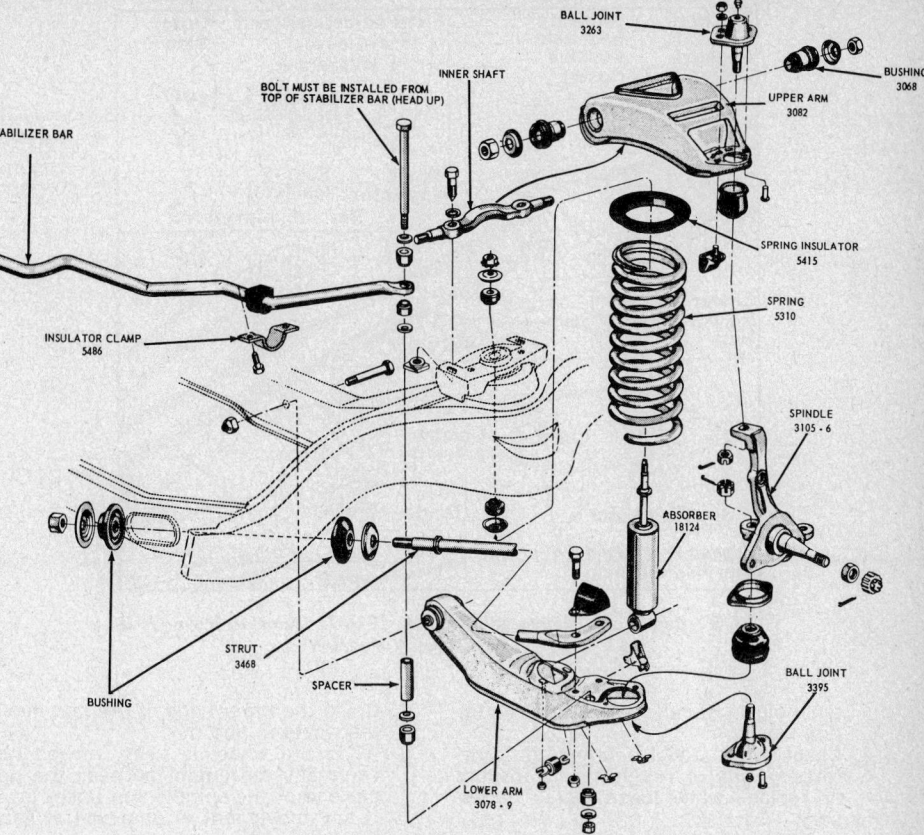

Fig. 1A   Front suspension (typical). 1974-76 Elite, Montego, Torino, 1974-79 Cougar & 1977-79 LTD II

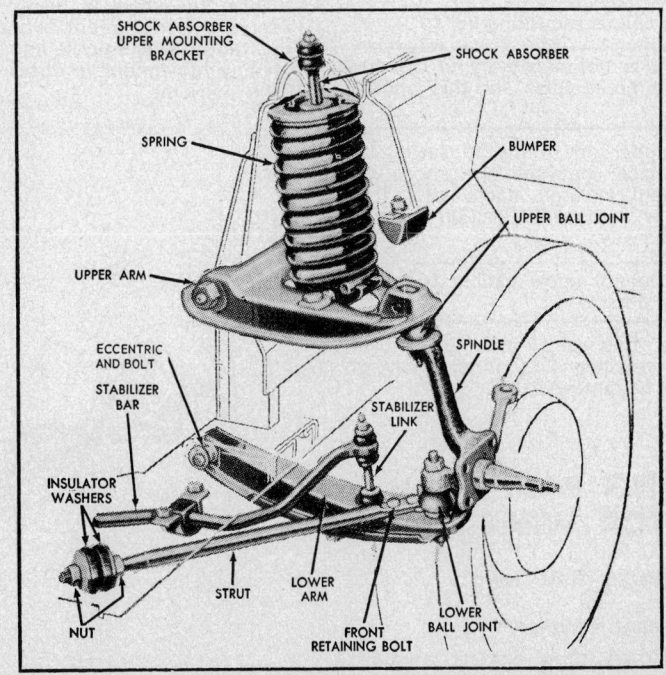

Fig. 2   Front suspension (typical). 1974-77 Comet & Maverick & 1975-79 Granada & Monarch

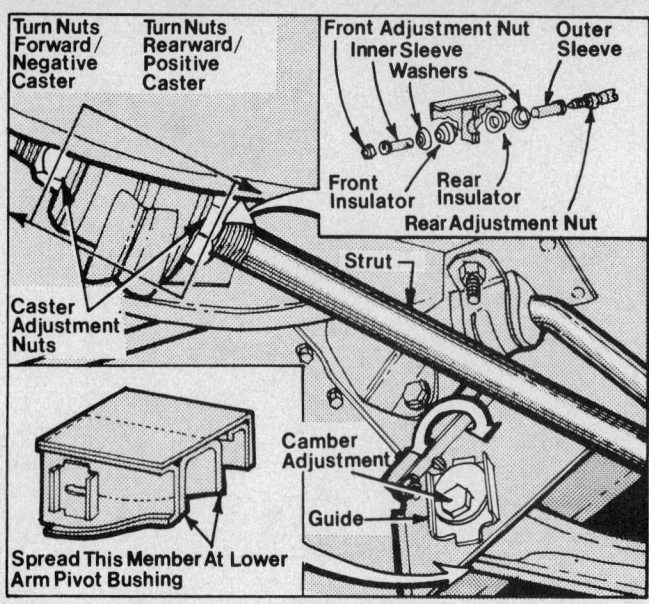

Fig. 3   Caster and camber adjustments. 1974-77 Comet & Maverick &
1975-79 Granada & Monarch

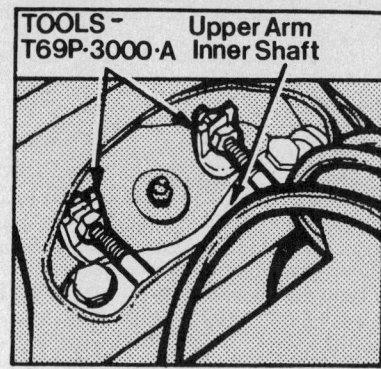

Fig. 4   Caster and Camber adjustment.
1974-76 Elite, Torino, Montego,
1974-79 Cougar & 1977-79 LTD II

pin hole in spindle and install cotter pin, Fig. 5.
4. Check front wheel rotation, if it rotates noisily or rough, clean, inspect or replace wheel bearings as necessary.

WHEEL BEARINGS, REPLACE

(Disc Brakes)

1. Raise car and remove front wheels.
2. Remove caliper mounting bolts.

NOTE: It is not necessary to disconnect the brake lines for this operation.

3. Slide caliper off of disc, inserting a clean spacer between the shoes to hold them in their bores after the caliper is removed. Position caliper out of the way.

NOTE: Do not allow caliper to hang by brake hose.

4. Remove hub and disc assembly. Grease retainer and inner bearing can now be removed.

CHECKING BALL JOINTS FOR WEAR

Upper Ball Joint

1975-79 Granada & Monarch

1. Raise car on frame contact hoist or by floor jacks placed beneath underbody until wheel falls to full down position.

2. Grasp the lower edge of tire and move the wheel in and out.
3. While the wheel is being moved observe any movement between the upper end of the spindle and upper arm. If any movement is observed replace the ball joint.

1974-76 Elite, Montego, Torino, 1974-79 Cougar & 1977-79 LTD II

1. Raise vehicle and place floor jacks beneath lower control arms.
2. Grasp the lower edge of tire and move the wheel in and out.
3. While the wheel is being moved observe any movement between the upper end of the spindle and upper arm. If any movement is observed replace the ball joint.

1974-77 Comet & Maverick

1. Raise car on frame contact hoist or by floor jacks placed beneath underbody until wheel falls to full down position as shown in Fig. 6. This will unload upper ball joint.
2. With front wheel bearings properly adjusted, attach a dial indicator to the upper control arm and position the indicator so that its plunger rests against the inner side of the wheel rim adjacent to the upper arm ball joint.
3. Grasp tire at top and bottom and slowly move it in and out, Fig. 6. Reading on dial will indicate the amount of radial play. If reading exceeds $\frac{1}{4}''$, replace the upper ball joint.

Lower Ball Joint

1978-79 Fairmont & Zephyr
1. Support vehicle in normal driving po-

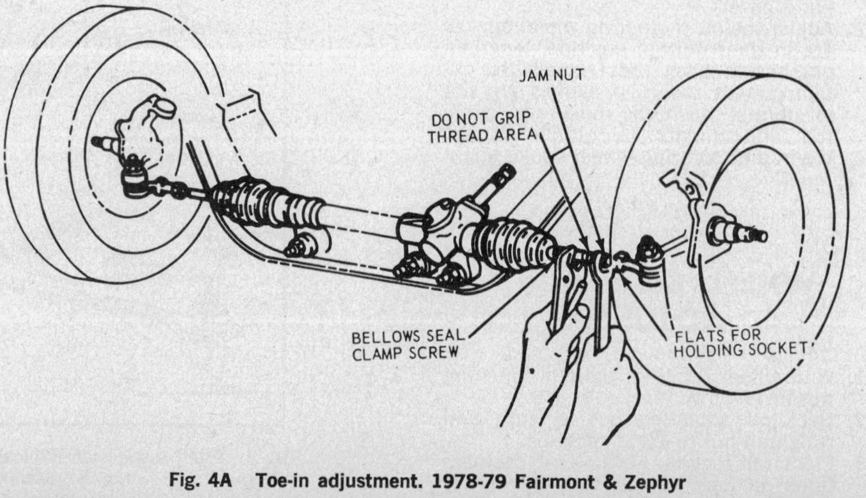

Fig. 4A   Toe-in adjustment. 1978-79 Fairmont & Zephyr

With Drum and Wheel Rotating, Torque the Adjusting Nut

Install Lock on Nut so that Castellations are Aligned with Cotter Pin Hole.

Back off Nut and Nut Lock one Castellation Install Cotter Pin.

Fig. 5 Front wheel bearing adjustment

sition with both ball joints loaded.

2. Clean area around grease fitting and checking surface.

NOTE: The checking surface is the round boss into which the grease fitting is installed.

3. The checking surface should project outside the cover, Fig. 7. If surface is inside cover replace lower arm assembly.

1974-76 Elite, Montego, Torino, 1974-79 Cougar & 1977-79 LTD II

1. Raise vehicle and place floor jacks under the lower control arms, Fig. 8.

2. Adjust wheel bearings and place a dial indicator to the lower arm and position the indicator so that the plunger rests against the inner side of the wheel rim adjacent to the lower ball joint.

3. Grasp tire at top and bottom and move it slowly in and out. Reading on dial will indicate the amount of radial play. If reading exceeds ¼ inch replace the ball joint.

1974-77 Comet & Maverick, 1975-79 Granada & Monarch

1. With car jacked up as directed above, grasp the lower edge of the tire and move it in and out.

2. As wheel is being moved in and out, observe lower end of spindle and lower arm.

3. Any movement between lower end of spindle and lower arm indicates ball joint wear and loss of preload. If such movement is observed, replace

lower arm and/or ball joint.

NOTE: During the foregoing check, the ball joints will be unloaded and may move. Therefore disregard any movement of the upper ball joint when checking the lower ball joint and any movement of the lower ball joint when checking the upper ball joint. Also, do not mistake loose wheel bearings for a worn ball joint.

BALL JOINT, REPLACE

NOTE: Ford Motor Company recommends that new ball joints should not be installed on used control arms and that the control arm be replaced if ball joint replacement is required. However, aftermarket ball joint repair kits which do not require control arm replacement, are available and can be installed using the following procedure.

1978-79 Fairmont & Zephyr

These ball joints are not serviceable. If they require replacement, the control arm and ball joint must be replaced as an assembly.

Exc. 1978-79 Fairmont & Zephyr

The ball joints are riveted to the upper and lower control arms. The upper ball joint can be replaced by removing the rivets and retaining the new ball joint to the upper control arm with bolts, nuts and washers furnished with the ball joint repair kit. When removing an upper ball joint, use a suitable pressing tool to loosen the ball joint from the spindle.

SHOCK STRUT, REPLACE

1978-79 Fairmont & Zephyr

1. Raise and support vehicle, then remove wheel and tire assembly.

2. Place a floor jack under lower con-

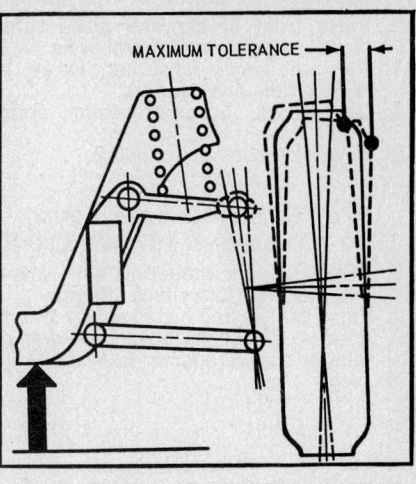

Fig. 6 Measuring upper ball joint for radial play. 1974-77 Comet & Maverick

trol arm and raise jack to compress spring.

3. Remove the lower and then the upper shock strut retaining bolts and nuts.

4. Compress and remove shock strut.

5. Reverse procedure to install. Torque the upper retaining nuts to 60-75 ft. lbs., and the lower bolts and nuts to 150-180 ft. lbs.

SHOCK ABSORBER, REPLACE

1974-77 Comet & Maverick & 1975-79 Granada & Monarch

1. Raise hood and remove upper mounting bracket-to-spring tower retain-

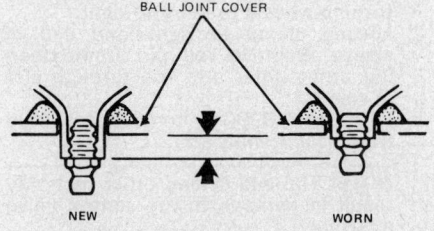

Fig. 7 Checking lower ball joint. 1978-79 Fairmont & Zephyr

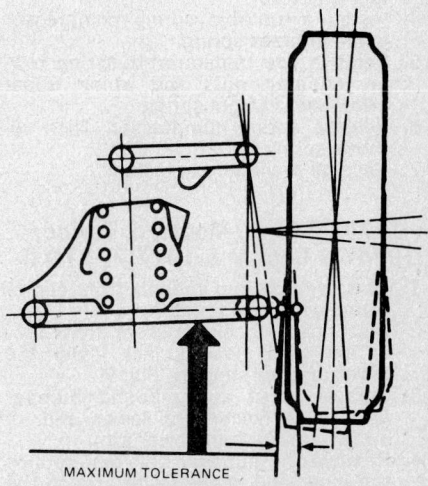

Fig. 8 Measuring lower ball joint for radial play. 1974-76 Elite, Montego, Torino, 1974-79 Cougar & 1977-79 LTD II

ing nuts.

2. Raise front of car and place safety stands under lower control arms.
3. Remove shock absorber lower retaining nuts and washers.
4. Lift shock absorber from spring tower.
5. Reverse procedure to install.

1974-76 Elite, Montego, Torino, 1974-79 Cougar & 1977-79 LTD II

1. Remove upper mounting nut, washer and bushing from shock absorber.
2. Raise vehicle and install safety stands.
3. Remove the shock absorber lower retaining screws and remove shock absorber.

COIL SPRING, REPLACE

1978-79 Fairmont & Zephyr

1. Raise vehicle and place stands under both sides at jack pads directly behind the control arms, then remove wheel and tire assembly.
2. Disconnect stabilizer link from control arm, then remove disc brake caliper and rotor assembly.
3. Place a jack stand under lower arm at bushing area supporting the arm under both bushings, then remove steering gear bolts and move steering gear aside.
4. Remove the control arm to crossmember bolts and nuts.
5. Lower the floor jack slowly to relieve spring tension and remove spring.
6. Reverse procedure to install. Torque control arm nuts to 200-220 ft. lbs. and stabilizer link nut to 9-12 ft. lbs.

1974-77 Comet & Maverick & 1975-79 Granada & Monarch

1. Remove shock absorber and upper mounting bracket as an assembly.
2. Raise car on hoist and install safety stands.
3. Remove wheel, hub and drum or caliper and rotor.
4. Install a suitable spring compressor and compress spring.
5. Remove two upper-arm-to-spring tower retaining nuts and swing upper arm outward from spring.
6. Release spring compressor. Then remove spring.
7. Reverse procedure to install.

1974-76 Elite, Montego, Torino, 1974-79 Cougar & 1977-79 LTD II

1. Raise vehicle and support front end of frame with jack stands.
2. Disconnect shock absorber from lower arm and place a jack under the lower arm for support, Fig. 9.
3. Remove strut and rebound bumper bolts and disconnect lower end of sway bar stud from lower arm.
4. Remove the nut and bolt that retains the inner end of the lower arm to the crossmember.
5. Carefully lower jack relieving spring pressure on the lower arm, then remove the spring.

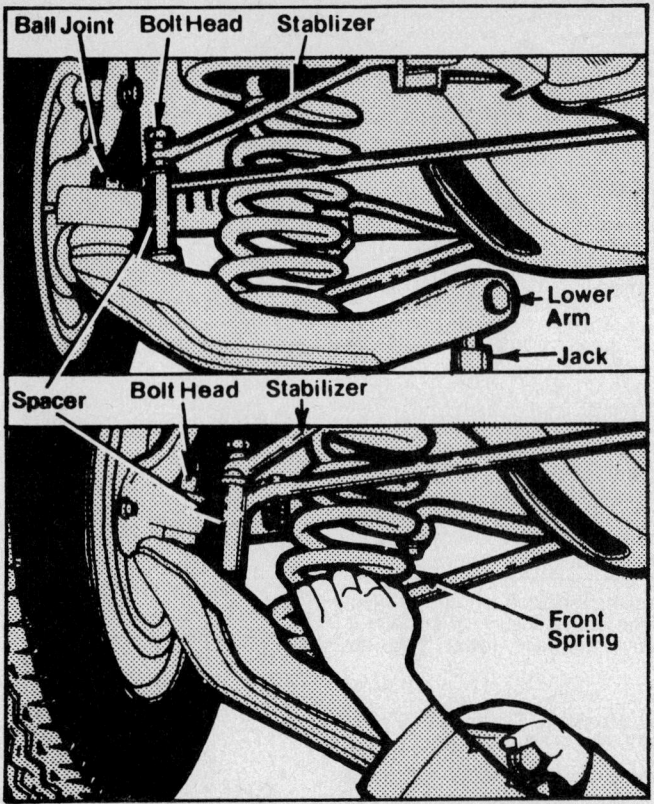

Fig. 9 Removing or installing front spring. 1974-76 Elite, Montego, Torino, 1974-79 Cougar & 1977-79 LTD II

STABILIZER BAR &/OR INSULATOR

1978-79 Fairmont & Zephyr

1. Raise vehicle and place jack stands under lower control arms.
2. Disconnect stabilizer bar from links, then remove stabilizer insulator retaining clamps and remove stabilizer.
3. To remove insulator, cut insulators and plastic sleeves from stabilizer bar. Before installing new insulators, coat the necessary parts of the stabilizer with grease, then install the insulators and sleeves.
4. Reverse procedure to install stabilizer bar. Install new stabilizer link bolts with heads facing down and torque to 9-12 ft. lbs. Using new bolts, install stabilizer insulator retaining clamps and torque to 20-26 ft. lbs.

POWER STEERING GEAR, REPLACE

Integral Power Steering Gear

1. Disconnect pressure and return lines from gear and plug openings to prevent entry of dirt.
2. Remove two bolts that secure flex coupling to gear and column.
3. Raise vehicle and remove pitman arm with suitable puller.
4. If vehicle is equipped with synchromesh transmission, remove clutch release lever retracting spring to provide clearance to remove gear.
5. Support gear and remove three gear attaching bolts.

MANUAL STEERING GEAR, REPLACE

1. Remove flex coupling bolts.
2. Remove pitman arm nut and remove arm from shaft using a puller.
3. With manual transmission it may be necessary to disconnect the clutch linkage and on V8 models it may be necessary to lower the exhaust system.
4. Unfasten and remove steering gear.

CONTROL VALVE, REPLACE

Non-Integral Power Steering

1. Disconnect fluid fittings at control valve and drain fluid from lines by turning wheels to left and right.
2. Loosen clamp at right-hand end of sleeve. Remove roll pin from steering arm-to-idler arm rod through slot in sleeve.
3. Using tool 3290-C, remove ball stud from sector shaft arm.

NOTE: The use of any other tool may result in damage to the control valve assembly.

4. Turn wheels fully to left and unthread control valve from idler arm rod.

FORD & MERCURY
Full Size Models

INDEX OF SERVICE OPERATIONS

ENGINE & SERIAL NUMBER LOCATION
Plate On Left Front Door Pillar

ENGINE IDENTIFICATION

★Serial number on Vehicle Warranty Plate

Engine code for 1974-79 is the last letter in the serial number.

Year	Engine	Engine Code★	Year	Engine	Engine Code★	Year	Engine	Engine Code★
1974	V8-351	H		V8-400	S		V8-400	S
	V8-400	S		V8-460	A		V8-460	A
	V8-460	A	1979	V8-302	F	1979	V8-302	F
1975-77	V8-351②	Q		V8-351①	H		V8-351	H
				V8-351②	Q			

①—Windsor engine.
②—Modified engine.

GRILLE IDENTIFICATION

1974 Ford Custom, Galaxie

1974 Ford "LTD"

1974 Mercury Monterey

1974 Mercury Marquis

1975-78 Ford "LTD" & Custom

1975-78 Ford "LTD" Landau

1975-78 Mercury

1979 Mercury Marquis

1979 LTD 2 Dr.

1979 Ford LTD Landau 4 Dr. & Country Squire

GENERAL ENGINE SPECIFICATIONS

Year	Engine	Carburetor	Bore and Stroke	Piston Displacement, Cubic Inches	Compression Ratio	Maximum Brake H.P. @ R.P.M.	Maximum Torque Lbs. Ft. @ R.P.M.	Normal Oil Pressure Pounds
FORD								
1974	162 Horsepower① V8-351	2 Barrel	4.00 x 3.50	351	8.0	162 @ 4000	275 @ 2200	45–75
	163 Horsepower① V8-351	2 Barrel	4.00 x 3.50	351	8.0	163 @ 4200	278 @ 2000	45–65
	170 Horsepower① V8-400	2 Barrel	4.00 x 4.00	400	8.0	170 @ 3400	330 @ 2000	45–75
	195 Horsepower① V8-460	4 Barrel	4.36 x 3.85	460	8.0	195 @ 3800	335 @ 2600	35–65
	275 Horsepower① V8-460	4 Barrel	4.36 x 3.85	460	8.8	275 @ 4400	395 @ 2800	35–65
1975	148 Horsepower① V8-351	2 Barrel	4.00 x 3.50	351	8.0	148 @ 3800	243 @ 2400	50–75
	150 Horsepower① V8-351	2 Barrel	4.00 x 3.50	351	8.0	150 @ 3800	244 @ 2800	50–75
	158 Horsepower① V8-400	2 Barrel	4.00 x 4.00	400	8.0	158 @ 3800	276 @ 2000	50–75
	144 Horsepower① V8-400	2 Barrel	4.00 x 4.00	400	8.0	144 @ 3600	255 @ 2200	50–75
	218 Horsepower① V8-460	4 Barrel	4.36 x 3.85	460	8.0	218 @ 4000	369 @ 2600	40–65
1976	152 Horsepower① V8-351	2 Barrel	4.00 x 3.50	351	8.0	152 @ 3800	274 @ 1600	50–75
	180 Horsepower① V8-400	2 Barrel	4.00 x 4.00	400	8.0	180 @ 3800	336 @ 1800	50–75
	202 Horsepower① V8-460	4 Barrel	4.36 x 3.85	460	8.0	202 @ 3800	352 @ 1600	40–65
1977	135 Horsepower V8-302	2 Barrel	4.00 x 3.00	302	8.4	—	—	40–65
	161 Horsepower①②④ V8-351	2 Barrel	4.00 x 3.50	351	8.0	161 @ 3600	285 @ 1800	50–75
	149 Horsepower①②⑤ V8-351	2 Barrel	4.00 x 3.50	351	8.3	149 @ 3200	291 @ 1600	40–65
	173 Horsepower①② V8-400	2 Barrel	4.00 x 4.00	400	8.0	173 @ 3800	326 @ 1600	50–75
	168 Horsepower①③ V8-400	2 Barrel	4.00 x 4.00	400	8.0	168 @ 3800	323 @ 1600	50–75
	197 Horsepower① V8-460	4 Barrel	4.36 x 3.85	460	8.0	197 @ 4000	353 @ 2000	35–65
1978	134 Horsepower① V8-302	2 Barrel	4.00 x 3.00	302	8.4	134 @ 3400	248 @ 1600	40–60
	145 Horsepower①④ V8-351	2 Barrel	4.00 x 3.50	351	8.3	145 @ 3400	273 @ 1800	50–75
	144 Horsepower①⑤ V8-351	2 Barrel	4.00 x 3.50	351	8.0	144 @ 3200	277 @ 1600	40–60
	160 Horsepower① V8-400	2 Barrel	4.00 x 4.00	400	8.0	160 @ 3800	314 @ 1800	50–75
	— Horsepower①⑥ V8-460	4 Barrel	4.36 x 3.85	460	8.0	—	—	35–65
	202 Horsepower①⑦ V8-460	4 Barrel	4.36 x 3.85	460	8.0	202 @ 4000	348 @ 2000	35–65
1979	— Horsepower① V8-302	2 Barrel	4.00 x 3.00	302	8.4	—	—	—
	— Horsepower① V8-351	2 Barrel	4.00 x 3.50	351	8.3	—	—	—
MERCURY								
1974	170 Horsepower① V8-400	2 Barrel	4.00 x 4.00	400	8.0	170 @ 3400	330 @ 2000	45–75
	195 Horsepower① V8-460	4 Barrel	4.36 x 3.85	460	8.0	195 @ 3800	335 @ 2600	35–65
	275 Horsepower① V8-460	4 Barrel	4.36 x 3.85	460	8.8	275 @ 4400	395 @ 2800	35–65
1975	148 Horsepower① V8-351	2 Barrel	4.00 x 3.50	351	8.0	148 @ 3800	243 @ 2400	50–75
	150 Horsepower① V8-351	2 Barrel	4.00 x 3.50	351	8.0	150 @ 3800	244 @ 2800	50–75
	144 Horsepower① V8-400	2 Barrel	4.00 x 4.00	400	8.0	144 @ 3600	255 @ 2200	50–75
	158 Horsepower① V8-400	2 Barrel	4.00 x 4.00	400	8.0	158 @ 3800	276 @ 2000	50–75
	218 Horsepower① V8-460	4 Barrel	4.36 x 3.85	460	8.0	218 @ 4000	369 @ 2600	40–65
1976	152 Horsepower① V8-351	2 Barrel	4.00 x 3.50	351	8.0	152 @ 3800	274 @ 1600	50–75
	180 Horsepower① V8-400	2 Barrel	4.00 x 4.00	400	8.0	180 @ 3800	336 @ 1800	50–75
	202 Horsepower① V8-460	4 Barrel	4.36 x 3.85	460	8.0	202 @ 3800	352 @ 1600	40–65
1977	173 Horsepower①② V8-400	2 Barrel	4.00 x 4.00	400	8.0	173 @ 3800	326 @ 1600	50–75
	168 Horsepower①③ V8-400	2 Barrel	4.00 x 4.00	400	8.0	168 @ 3800	323 @ 1600	50–75
	197 Horsepower① V8-460	4 Barrel	4.36 x 3.85	460	8.0	197 @ 4000	353 @ 2000	35–65
1978	145 Horsepower① V8-351	2 Barrel	4.00 x 3.50	351	8.0	145 @ 3400	273 @ 1800	50–75
	160 Horsepower① V8-400	2 Barrel	4.00 x 4.00	400	8.0	160 @ 3800	314 @ 1800	45–75
	— Horsepower①⑥ V8-460	4 Barrel	4.36 x 3.85	460	8.0	—	—	35–65
	202 Horsepower①⑦ V8-460	4 Barrel	4.36 x 3.85	460	8.0	202 @ 4000	348 @ 2000	35–65
1979	— Horsepower① V8-302	2 Barrel	4.00 x 3.00	302	8.4	—	—	—
	— Horsepower① V8-351	2 Barrel	4.00 x 3.50	351	8.3	—	—	—

① —Ratings are NET—as installed in the vehicle.
② —Exc. Calif.
③ —Calif. only.
④ —Modified engine.
⑤ —Windsor engine.
⑥ —Police Interceptor
⑦ —Exc. Police Interceptor

TUNE UP SPECIFICATIONS

The following specifications are published from the latest information available. This
data should be used only in the absence of a decal affixed in the engine compartment.

★When using a timing light, disconnect vacuum hose or tube at distributor and plug opening in tube or hose so idle speed will not be affected.

●When checking compression, lowest cylinder must be within 75% of the highest.

▲Before removing wires from distributor cap, determine location of the No. 1 wire in cap, as distributor position may have been altered from that shown at the end of this chart.

| Year | Spark Plug | | Distributor | | Ignition Timing★ | | | Carb. Adjustments | | | | | |
| | Type ⑤ | Gap Inch | Point Gap Inch | Dwell Angle Deg. | Firing Order Fig. ▲ | Timing BTDC ① | Mark Fig. | Hot Idle Speed | | Air Fuel Ratio | | Idle "CO" % | |
								Std. Trans.	Auto. Trans.②	Std. Trans.	Auto. Trans.	Std. Trans.	Auto. Trans.
1974													
V8-351⑪	BRF-42	.034	.017	26–30	A	6°	E	—	600	—	—	—	—
V8-351⑪④	BRF-42	.044	—	—	A	6°	E	—	600	—	—	—	—
V8-351⑫	ARF-42	.044	.017	26–30	A	14°	E	—	650	—	—	—	—
V8-351⑫④	ARF-42	③	—	—	A	14°	E	—	650	—	—	—	—
V8-400④	ARF-42	.044	—	—	A	12°	E	—	625	—	—	—	—
V8-460④	ARF-52	.054	—	—	B	⑬	E	—	⑭	—	—	—	.25
1975													
V8-351	ARF-42	.044	—	—	A	14°	E	—	700D	—	—	—	—
V8-400	ARF-42	.044	—	—	A	12°	E	—	625D	—	—	—	—
V8-460	ARF-52	.044	—	—	B	14°	E	—	650D	—	—	—	—
1976													
V8-351	ARF-42	.044	—	—	A	8°	E	—	650D	—	—	—	—
V8-400	ARF-42	.044	—	—	A	10°	E	—	⑩	—	—	—	—
V8-460	ARF-52	.044	—	—	B	10°	E	—	650D	—	—	—	—
1977													
V8-351	ARF-52	.050	—	—	F	⑧	E	—	⑧	—	—	—	—
V8-400⑥	ARF-52-6	.060	—	—	G	6°	E	—	600D	—	—	—	—
V8-400⑦	ARF-52	.050	—	—	G	⑧	E	—	⑧	—	—	—	—
V8-460⑮⑰	ARF-52	.050	—	—	G	⑧	E	—	⑧	—	—	—	—
V8-460⑯	ARF-52	.050	—	—	G	16°	E	—	700D	—	—	—	—
V8-460⑮⑱	ARF-52	.050	—	—	G	18°	E	—	600D	—	—	—	—
1978													
V8-302	ARF-52	.050	—	—	G	14°	E	—	650D	—	—	—	—
V8-351⑪	ARF-52	.050	—	—	F	14°	E	—	650D	—	—	—	—
V8-351⑲	ARF-52	.050	—	—	F	⑳⑧	E	—	600/675D㉑	—	—	—	—
V8-400⑥	ARF-52-6	.060	—	—	F	㉒⑧	E	—	㉓	—	—	—	—
V8-400⑦	ARF-52	.050	—	—	F	16°	E	—	650D	—	—	—	—
V8-460	ARF-52	.050	—	—	G	⑧⑨	E	—	580/650D㉑	—	—	—	—
1979													
V8-302	ASF-52	.050	—	—	G	6°	E	—	550/625㉑	—	—	—	—
V8-351	ASF-52	.050	—	—	F	—	E	—	550/640㉑	—	—	—	—

①—BTDC: Before top dead center.
②—D: Drive. N: Neutral.
③—Exc. Calif., .044; Calif., .054.
④—Breakerless distributor.
⑤—Autolite/Motorcraft.
⑥—Calif.
⑦—Exc. Calif.
⑧—Must refer to engine decal due to running production changes.
⑨—Early production models, 16° BTDC; Late production model, 10° BTDC.
⑩—Except Calif., 650D; Calif., 625D.
⑪—Windsor engine.
⑫—Cleveland engine.
⑬—Except Police Interceptor, 14° BTDC; Police Interceptor, 10° BTDC.
⑭—Except Police Interceptor, 650D; Police Interceptor, 700D.
⑮—Exc. Police Interceptor.
⑯—Police Interceptor.
⑰—Low altitude vehicles.
⑱—High altitude vehicles.
⑲—Modified engine.
⑳—Early production models, 9° BTDC; Late production models, 12° BTDC.
㉑—Higher RPM is for A/C, A/C on.
㉒—With A/C, 13° BTDC; Less A/C, 8° BTDC.
㉓—Less A/C, 650; With A/C A/C on, 650; A/C off, 575.

Continued

TUNE UP NOTES—Continued

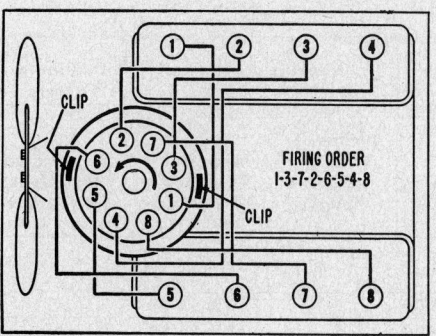

Fig. A

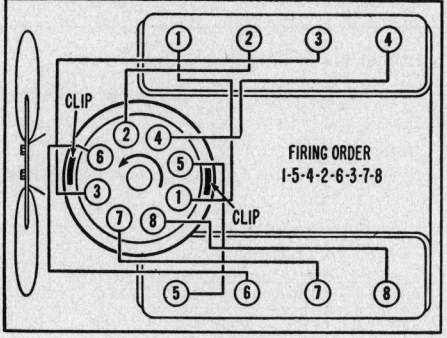

Fig. B

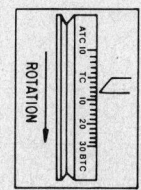

Fig. E

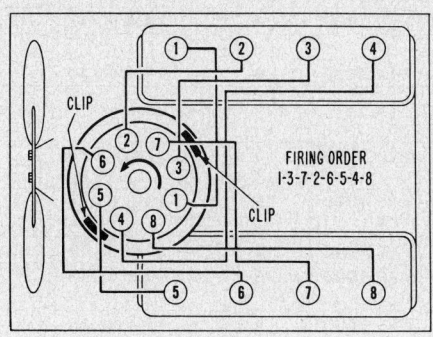

Fig. F

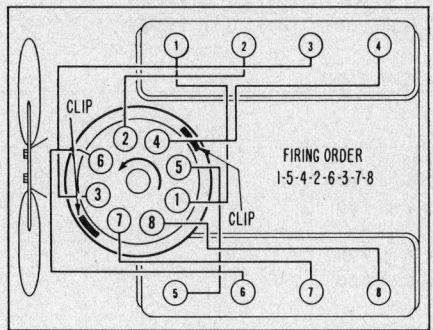

Fig. G

REAR AXLE SPECIFICATIONS

Year	Model	Carrier Type	Ring Gear & Pinion Backlash Inch	Nominal Pinion Locating Shim, Inch	Pinion Bearing Preload				Differential Bearing Preload	Pinion Nut Torque Ft.-Lbs.①
					New Bearings With Seal Inch-Lbs.	Used Bearings With Seal Inch-Lbs.	New Bearings Less Seal Inch-Lbs.	Used Bearings Less Seal Inch-Lbs.		
1974–78	—	Integral	.008–.012	.030	17–27	8–14	—	—	.008–.012⑥	140
	—	Removable	.008–.012	.015	17–27⑤	8–14	—	—	.008–.012③	②

①—If torque cannot be obtained, install new spacer.
②—Collapsible spacer 170 ft. lbs.; solid spacer 200 ft. lbs.
③—Case spread with new bearings; with used bearings .005–.008".
④—8-302 engine with two-barrel carburetor.
⑤—Solid spacer 13–33 inch-lbs.
⑥—Case spread with new bearing; with used bearings .006–.010".
⑦—Collapsible spacer 175 ft. lbs.; solid spacer 200 ft. lbs.

DISTRIBUTOR SPECIFICATIONS

★Note: If unit is checked on vehicle, double the RPM and degrees to get crankshaft figures.
Breaker arm spring tension—17–21.

Distributor Part No.①	Centrifugal Advance Degrees @ RPM of Distributor				Vacuum Advance		Distributor Retard
	Advance Starts	Intermediate Advance		Full Advance	Inches of Vacuum to Start Plunger	Max. Adv. Dist. Deg. @ Vacuum	Max. Retard Dist. Deg. @ Vacuum
1974							
D3AF-AA	0–1½ @ 500	4–6 @ 750	6–8¼ @ 1000	10–12½ @ 1500	15¼ @ 2000	5	13¼ @ 20	—
D3ZF-GA	0–1 @ 500	0–2½ @ 750	2¼–4¼ @ 1000	5½–7½ @ 1500	9½ @ 2000	5	12½ @ 20	—
D4OE-CA	0–½ @ 500	0–1½ @ 750	2–4 @ 1000	5½–7½ @ 1500	9¼ @ 2000	5	13½ @ 20	—
D4VE-CA	0–½ @ 500	0–½ @ 750	3–5 @ 1000	7–9 @ 1500	9½ @ 2000	5	11¼ @ 20	—
1975							
D4AE-AA	0–2 @ 520	4½–7½ @ 800	10–12½ @ 1500	—	15¼ @ 2000	4	12¾ @ 17	—
D4OE-EA	0–2 @ 520	4½–7½ @ 800	10–12½ @ 1500	—	15¼ @ 2000	4	12¾ @ 17	—
D4VE-CA	−1½–+½ @ 800	3–5 @ 1000	—	—	19 @ 2000	4	19¾ @ 14	—
1976							
D4VE-CA	−¾ to +½ @ 500	−1¼ to +½ @ 700	—	—	5 @ 1000	5	11¼ @ 15	—
D5VE-CA	−1 to +½ @ 500	½–2½ @ 700	—	—	6½ @ 1000	5	13¼ @ 15	—
D6AE-AA	¼–2¼ @ 500	4–6 @ 700	—	—	7½ @ 1000	5	15¼ @ 15	—
D6AE-BA	−¾ to +2¼ @ 500	3¾–6 @ 700	—	—	7¾ @ 1000	5	9½ @ 15	—
D6AE-CA	0–3¼ @ 500	4¼–6½ @ 700	—	—	7 @ 1000	5	15¼ @ 15	—
D6AE-DA	0–3¼ @ 500	6–8¾ @ 700	—	—	9¾ @ 1000	5	15¼ @ 15	—
D6VE-AA	0–2½ @ 500	4½–6½ @ 700	—	—	9 @ 1000	5	13½ @ 15	—
D6VE-BA	−1 to +2¾ @ 500	6–9½ @ 700	—	—	11¾ @ 1000	5	13¼ @ 15	—
D6VE-CA	−½ to +3 @ 500	6–9½ @ 700	—	—	10¼ @ 1000	5	13¼ @ 15	—
1977							
D6AE-AA	0–2 @ 500	4–6 @ 700	—	—	14 @ 2500	3	15¼ @ 11½	—
D6VE-CA	0–1 @ 450	7½–9½ @ 725	—	—	14 @ 2500	3½	13¼ @ 15	—
D7AE-BA	0–1 @ 425	2¾–4¾ @ 625	—	—	13½ @ 2250	3½	15¼ @ 12	—
D7AE-CA	0–1 @ 700	3½–6 @ 1600	—	—	10¾ @ 2500	3	15¼ @ 11	—
D7AE-DA	0–1 @ 450	3¾–5¾ @ 675	—	—	14 @ 2500	3.2	15¼ @ 14.5	—
D7DE-CA	0–1 @ 450	4¾–6¾ @ 700	—	—	15½ @ 2500	3	15¼ @ 11	—
D7OE-CA	0–1 @ 450	2¾–4¾ @ 575	—	—	16 @ 2500	3½	15¼ @ 14.5	—
1978							
D8AE-CA	0 @ 1100	3.5–6 @ 1600	—	—	9.5 @ 2500	3	17.5 @ 14	—
D8AE-GA	0 @ 450	3.5–5.5 @ 700	—	—	8.25 @ 2500	5.5	15.25 @ 16.5	—
1979							
D7AE-UA	0 @ 750	2 @ 700	—	—	7.5–10.5 @ 2500	1	13.5 @ 15	—
D8AE-BA	0 @ 450	4–6 @ 700	—	—	11.25–14 @ 2500	4	17.25 @ 14.5	—

①—Basic part No. 12127.

VALVE SPECIFICATIONS

Year	Engine Model	Valve Lash		Valve Angles		Valve Spring Installed Height	Valve Spring Pressure Lbs. @ In.	Stem Clearance		Stem Diameter	
		Int.	Exh.	Seat	Face			Intake	Exhaust	Intake	Exhaust
1974	8-351③	.106–.156④		45	44	1⁵¹⁄₆₄	75 @ 1.79	.0010–.0027	.0015–.0032	.3416–.3423	.3411–.3418
	8-351⑥	.100–.150④		45	44	1¹³⁄₁₆	80 @ 1.82	.0010–.0027	.0015–.0032	.3416–.3423	.3411–.3418
	8-400	.100–.150④		45	44	1¹³⁄₁₆	80 @ 1.82	.0010–.0027	.0015–.0032	.3416–.3423	.3411–.3418
	8-460	.075–.125④		45	44	1¹³⁄₁₆	80 @ 1.81	.0010–.0027	.0010–.0027	.3416–.3423	.3416–.3423
1975	8-351②	.125–.175④		45	44	1⁵³⁄₆₄	226 @ 1.39	.001–.0027	.0015–.0032	.3416–.3423	.3411–.3418
	8-400	.125–.175④		45	44	1⁵³⁄₆₄	226 @ 1.39	.001–.0027	.0015–.0032	.3416–.3423	.3411–.3418
	8-460	.100–.150④		45	44	1¹³⁄₁₆	253 @ 1.33	.001–.0027	.0010–.0027	.3416–.3423	.3416–.3423
1976	8-351②	.125–.175④		45	44	1⁵³⁄₆₄	226 @ 1.39	.0010–.0027	.0015–.0032	.3416–.3423	.3411–.3418
	8-400	.125–.175④		45	44	1⁵³⁄₆₄	226 @ 1.39	.0010–.0027	.0015–.0032	.3416–.3423	.3411–.3418
	8-460	.100–.150④		45	44	1¹³⁄₁₆	229 @ 1.33	.0010–.0027	.0010–.0027	.3416–.3423	.3416–.3423
1977	8-302	.096–.168④		45	44	⑦	⑨	.0010–.0027	.0015–.0032	.3416–.3423	.3411–.3418
	8-351③	.096–.168④		45	44	⑧	⑩	.0010–.0027	.0015–.0032	.3416–.3423	.3411–.3418
	8-351②	.125–.175④		45	44	1⁵³⁄₆₄	226 @ 1.39	.0010–.0027	.0015–.0032	.3416–.3423	.3411–.3418
	8-400	.125–.175④		45	44	1⁵³⁄₆₄	226 @ 1.39	.0010–.0027	.0015–.0032	.3416–.3423	.3411–.3418
	8-460	.100–.150④		45	44	1¹³⁄₁₆	229 @ 1.33⑪	.0010–.0027	.0010–.0027	.3416–.3423	.3416–.3423
1978	8-302	.071–.193④		45	44	⑦	⑨	.0010–.0027	.0015–.0037	.3416–.3423	.3411–.3418
	8-351②	.100–.200④		45	44	1¹³⁄₁₆	226 @ 1.39	.0010–.0027	.0015–.0037	.3416–.3423	.3411–.3418
	8-351③	.071–.193④		45	44	①	⑤	.0010–.0027	.0015–.0037	.3416–.3423	.3411–.3418
	8-400	.100–.200④		45	44	1¹³⁄₁₆	226 @ 1.39	.0010–.0027	.0015–.0037	.3416–.3423	.3411–.3418
	8-460	.075–.175④		45	44	1¹³⁄₁₆	229 @ 1.33	.0010–.0027	.0010–.0027	.3416–.3423	.3416–.3423

①—Intake, 1⁵¹⁄₆₄; exhaust, 1³⁹⁄₆₄.
②—Modified engine.
③—Windsor engine.
④—Clearance specified is obtainable at valve stem tip with lifter collapsed. See "Valves, Adjust" text.
⑤—Intake, 200 @ 1.34; exhaust, 200 @ 1.20.
⑥—Cleveland engine.
⑦—Intake, 1¹¹⁄₁₆; exhaust, 1³⁹⁄₆₄.
⑧—Intake, 1²⁵⁄₃₂; exhaust, 1³⁹⁄₆₄.
⑨—Intake, 200 @ 1.31; exhaust, 200 @ 1.20.
⑩—Intake, 200 @ 1.34; exhaust, 200 @ 1.20.
⑪—Police, 315 @ 1.32.

BRAKE SPECIFICATIONS

Year	Model	Brake Drum Inside Diameter	Wheel Cylinder Bore Diameter			Master Cylinder Bore Diameter		
			Front Disc Brake	Front Drum Brake	Rear Brake	With Disc Brakes	With Drum Brakes	With Power Brakes
1974	All	11.03	3.100	—	1.00	1.00	1.00	1.00
1975–78	All①	11.03	3.100	—	1.00	1.00	—	1.00
	All②	—	3.100	—	2.60	③	—	③
1979	All Passenger Cars	10.00	—	—	0.875	1.00	—	1.00
	All Wagons	11.03	—	—	0.9375	1.00	—	1.00

①—Except 4 wheel disc brakes with hydro boost.　　②—With 4 wheel disc brakes with hydro boost.
③—1975-77, 1.00; 1978, 1.25.

PISTONS, PINS, RINGS, CRANKSHAFT & BEARINGS

Year	Engine Model	Piston Clearance	Ring End Gap①		Wrist-pin Diameter	Rod Bearings		Main Bearings			
			Comp.	Oil		Shaft Diameter	Bearing Clearance	Shaft Diameter	Bearing Clearance	Thrust on Bear. No.	Shaft End Play
1974	8-351③	.0018–.0026	.010	.015	.9122	2.3103–2.3111	.0008–.0015	2.9994–3.0002	.0008–.0015	3	.004–.008
	8-351④	.0014–.0022	.010	.015	.9122	2.3103–2.3111	⑦	2.7484–2.7492	⑧	3	⑨
	8-400	.0014–.0022	.010	.015	.9752	2.3103–2.3111	.0008–.0015	2.9994–3.0002	.0009–.0015	3	⑨
	8-460	.0014–.0022	.010	.015	1.0401	2.4992–2.5000	.0008–.0015	2.9994–3.0002	⑥	3	.004–.008
	8-460⑩	.0034–.0042	.010	.015	1.0401	2.4992–2.5000	.0008–.0015	2.9994–3.0002	.0009–.0015	3	.004–.008
1975–76	8-351⑪	.0014–.0022	.010	.015	.9752	2.3103–2.3111	.0008–.0015	2.9994–3.0002	.0008–.0015	3	.004–.008
	8-400	.0014–.0022	.010	.015	.9752	2.3103–2.3111	.0008–.0015	2.9994–3.0002	.0008–.0015	3	.004–.008
	8-460	.0014–.0022	.010	.015	1.0401	2.4992–2.5000	.0008–.0015	2.9994–3.0002	⑫	3	.004–.008
	8-460⑩	.0022–.0030	.010	.015	1.0401	2.4992–2.5000	.0008–.0015	2.9994–3.0002	⑬	3	.004–.008
1977	8-302	.0018–.0026	.010	.015	.9122	2.1228–2.1236	.0008–.0015	2.2482–2.2490	⑭	3	.004–.008
	8-351③	.0018–.0026	.010	.015	.9122	2.3103–2.3111	.0008–.0015	2.9994–3.0002	.0008–.0015	3	.004–.008
	8-351⑪	.0014–.0022	.010	.015	.9752	2.3103–2.3111	.0008–.0015	2.9994–3.0002	.0008–.0015	3	.004–.008
	8-400	.0014–.0022	.010	.015	.9752	2.3103–2.3111	.0008–.0015	2.9994–3.0002	.0008–.0015	3	.004–.008
	8-460	.0014–.0022	.010	.015	1.0401	2.4992–2.5000	.0008–.0015	2.9994–3.0002	.0008–.0015	3	.004–.008
	8-460⑩	.0022–.0032	.010	.015	1.0401	2.4992–2.5000	.0008–.0015	2.9994–3.0002	.0008–.0015	3	.004–.008
1978	8-302	.0018–.0026	.010	.015	.9122	2.1228–2.1236	.0007–.0024	2.2482–2.2490	⑤	3	.004–.008
	8-351③	.0018–.0026	.010	.015	.9122	2.3103–2.3111	.0008–.0025	2.9994–3.0002	.0008–.0026	3	.004–.008
	8-351⑪	.0014–.0022	.010	.015	.9752	2.3103–2.3111	.0008–.0025	2.9994–3.0002	.0008–.0026	3	.004–.008
	8-400	.0014–.0022	.010	.015	.9752	2.3103–2.3111	.0008–.0025	2.9994–3.0002	.0008–.0026	3	.004–.008
	8-460	.0014–.0022	.010	.015	1.040	2.4992–2.5000	.0008–.0028	2.9994–3.0002	②	3	.004–.008

①—Fit rings in tapered bores for clearance listed in tightest portion of ring travel.
②—No. 1, .0001–.0015; all others, .0005–.0015.
③—Windsor engine.
④—Cleveland engine.
⑤—No. 1, .0001–.0020; all others, .0005–.0024.
⑥—No. 1: .0004–.0015; No. 2, 3, 4, 5: .0012–.0015.

⑦—2 Bbl.: .0008–.0015; 4 Bbl.: .0011–.0015.
⑧—1973–74: 2 Bbl.—.0009–.0015; 4 Bbl.: 1973—.0010–.0015; 1974—.0011–.0015.
⑨—1973: .004–.010; 1974: .004–.008.
⑩—Police.
⑪—Modified engine.

⑫—1975: No. 1—.0004–.0015; No. 2, 3, 4, 5—.0009–.0015; 1976: .0008–.0015.
⑬—No. 1: .0004–.0015; No. 2, 3, 4, 5: .0008–.0015.
⑭—No. 1: .0004–.0020; No. 2, 3, 4, 5: .0009–.0027.

WHEEL ALIGNMENT SPECIFICATIONS

Year	Model	Caster Angle, Degrees		Camber Angle, Degrees				Toe-In. Inch	Toe-Out on Turns, Deg.①	
		Limits	Desired	Limits		Desired			Outer Wheel	Inner Wheel
				Left	Right	Left	Right			
1974	All	0 to +4	+2	−½ to +1½	−¾ to +1¼	+½	+¼	³⁄₁₆	18¾	20
1975–78	All	+1¼ to +2¾	+2	−¼ to +1¼	−½ to +1	+½	+¼	³⁄₁₆	18.72	20
1979	All	+2¼ to +3¾	+3	−¼ to +¼	−¼ to +¼	+½	+½	³⁄₁₆	—	—

①—Incorrect toe-out, when other adjustments are correct, indicates bent steering arms.

ENGINE TIGHTENING SPECIFICATIONS*

★Torque specifications are for clean and lightly lubricated threads only. Dry or dirty threads produce increased friction which prevents accurate measurement of tightness.

Year	Engine Model	Spark Plugs Ft. Lbs.	Cylinder Head Bolts Ft. Lbs.	Intake Manifold Ft. Lbs.	Exhaust Manifold Ft. Lbs.	Rocker Arm Shaft Bracket Ft. Lbs.	Rocker Arm Cover Ft. Lbs.	Connecting Rod Cap Bolts Ft. Lbs.	Main Bearing Cap Bolts Ft. Lbs.	Flywheel to Crank-shaft Ft. Lbs.	Vibration Damper or Pulley Ft. Lbs.
1974	V8-351②	15-20	105-112	19-27	18-24	17-23①	3-5	40-45	95-105	75-85	100-130
	V8-351⑤	15-20	95-105	⑨	12-22	18-25⑦	3-5	40-45	⑧	75-85	70-90
	V8-400	15-20	95-105	⑨	12-16	18-25⑦	3-5	40-45	⑧	75-85	70-90
	V8-460	15-20	130-140	22-32	28-33	18-25⑦	5-6	40-45	95-105	75-85	70-90
1975-76	V8-351④	10-15	95-105	⑥	18-24	18-25⑦	3-5	40-45	95-105	75-85	70-90
	V8-400	10-15	95-105	⑥	18-24	18-25⑦	3-5	40-45	95-105	75-85	70-90
	V8-460	10-15	130-140	③	28-33	18-25⑦	5-6	40-45	95-105	75-85	70-90
1977-78	V8-302	10-15	65-72	23-25	18-24	17-23⑦	3-5	19-24	60-70	75-85	70-90
	V8-351②	10-15	105-112	23-25	18-24	17-23⑦	3-5	40-45	95-105	75-85	70-90
	V8-351④	10-15	95-105	⑥	18-24	18-25⑦	3-5	40-45	95-105	75-85	70-90
	V8-400	10-15	95-105	⑥	18-24	18-25⑦	3-5	40-45	95-105	75-85	70-90
	V8-460	10-15	130-140	22-32	28-33	18-25⑦	5-6	40-45	95-105	75-85	70-90

①—Rocker arm stud nut.
②—Windsor engine.
③—1975 except police: 25-30 ft. lbs.; 1975 police & 1976-77 all: 22-32 ft. lbs.
④—Modified engine.
⑤—Cleveland engine.

⑥—1973-76: 5/16″ bolts 21-25 ft. lbs., 3/8″ bolts 27-33 ft. lbs., 1/4″ bolts 6-9 ft. lbs.; 1977-78: 5/16″ bolts 19-25 ft. lbs., 3/8″ bolts 22-32 ft. lbs.
⑦—Fulcrum bolt to cylinder head.
⑧—1/2″ bolts 95-105 ft. lbs., 3/8″ bolts 35-45 ft. lbs.
⑨—5/16″ bolts 17-25 ft. lbs., 3/8″ bolts 22-32 ft. lbs., 1/4″ bolts 6-9 ft. lbs.

STARTING MOTOR SPECIFICATIONS

Year	Model	Ident. No.	Rotation	Brush Spring Tension Ounces	No Load Test			Torque Test		
					Amperes	Volts	R.P.M.	Amperes	Volts	Torque Ft. Lbs.
1974	8-351	D2AF-CA	C	80	80	12	—	670	5.0	15.5
	8-400	D4AF-AA	C	80	80	12	—	670	5.0	15.5
	8-460	D4OF-AA, BA	C	40	90	12	—	—	—	—
1975	8-351	D2AF-JA	C	80	80	12	—	670	5.0	15.5
	8-400	D5AF-EA	C	80	80	12	—	670	5.0	15.5
	8-460	D5AF-AB	C	40	70	12	—	—	—	—
1976	8-351	D5AF-FA	C	80	80	12	—	670	5.0	15.5
	8-400	D5AF-EA	C	80	80	12	—	670	5.0	15.5
	8-460	D6AF-AA	C	40	70	12	—	—	—	—
1977	8-351	D5AF-EA	C	80	80	12	—	670	—	15.5
	8-400	D5AF-EA	C	80	80	12	—	670	—	15.5
	8-460	D6AF-AA	C	40	70	12	—	—	—	—
1978	8-302	D8OF-AA	C	80	80	12	—	670	5.0	15.5
	8-351	D8AF-AA	C	80	80	12	—	670	5.0	15.5
	8-351	D8OF-AA	C	80	80	12	—	670	5.0	15.5
	8-400	D8AF-AA	C	80	80	12	—	670	5.0	15.5
	8-460	D8AF-BA	C	40	40	12	—	460	5.0	9.0
1979	8-302	D8BF-AA	—	—	—	—	—	—	—	—
	8-351	D8BF-AA	—	—	—	—	—	—	—	—

ALTERNATOR & REGULATOR SPECIFICATIONS

Year	Make or Model	Current Rating		Field Current @ 75°F.		Voltage Regulator				Field Relay	
		Amperes	Volts	Amperes	Volts	Part No. (10316)	Voltage @ 75°F.	Contact Gap	Armature Air Gap	Armature Air Gap	Closing Voltage @ 75°F.
1974	Purple①	38	15	2.9	12	D4TZ-A	—	—	—	—	—
	Orange①	42	15	2.9	12	D4TZ-A	—	—	—	—	—
	Red①	55	15	2.9	12	D4TZ-A	—	—	—	—	—
	Green①	61	15	2.9	12	D4TZ-A	—	—	—	—	—
	All	70	15	2.9	12	D4TZ-A	—	—	—	—	—
	All	90	15	2.9	12	D4TZ-A	—	—	—	—	—
1975–77	Orange①	40	15	2.9	12	D4AF-AA	13.5–15.3	—	—	—	2.5–4
	Green①	60	15	2.9	12	D4AF-AA	13.5–15.3	—	—	—	2.5–4
	All	70	15	2.9	12	D4TF-AA	13.5–15.3	—	—	—	2.5–4
	All	90	15	2.9	12	D4TF-AA	13.5–15.3	—	—	—	2.5–4
1978	D7AF-AA	40	15	2.9	12	—	13.5–15.3	—	—	—	—
	D7AF-CA	60	15	2.9	12	—	13.5–15.3	—	—	—	—
	D7TF-AA	65	15	2.9	12	—	13.5–15.3	—	—	—	—
	D7OF-CA	70	15	2.9	12	—	13.5–15.3	—	—	—	—
	D7OF-BA	90	15	2.9	12	—	13.5–15.3	—	—	—	—
1979	D9ZF-AA	60	—	—	—	—	13.8–14.6	—	—	—	—
	D9ZF-BA	65	—	—	—	—	13.8–14.6	—	—	—	—
	D9Z-CA	70	—	—	—	—	13.8–14.6	—	—	—	—

①—Identification tag.

COOLING SYSTEM & CAPACITY DATA

Year	Model or Engine	Cooling Capacity, Qts.			Radiator Cap Relief Pressure, Lbs.		Thermo. Opening Temp.	Fuel Tank Gals.	Engine Oil Refill Qts. ①	Transmission Oil			Rear Axle Oil Pints
		No Heater	With Heater	With A/C	With A/C	No A/C				3 Speed Pints	4 Speed Pints	Auto. Trans. Qts. ②	
FORD													
1974	8-351⑧	15.3	16½	17.2	12–16	12–16	191	22④	4	—	—	⑪	⑤
	8-351⑨	15.3	16½	16½	12–16	12–16	191	22④	4	—	—	⑭	⑤
	8-400	17	18	18½	12–16	12–16	191	22④	4	—	—	⑭	⑤
	8-460	18.4	19½	19½	12–16	12–16	191	22④	4	—	—	12½	⑥
1975	8-351	—	17.1	17.6	13–19	13–19	191	24.2④	4	—	—	⑬	⑤
	8-400	—	17.1	17.6	13–19	13–19	191	24.2④	4	—	—	⑬	⑤
	8-460	—	18.5	18.5⑮	13–19	13–19	191	24.2④	4⑫	—	—	⑬	⑤
1976	8-351	16.3	17.1	17.6	13–19	13–19	191	24.2④	4	—	—	⑬	⑤
	8-400	16.3	17.1	17.6	13–19	13–19	191	24.2④	4	—	—	⑬	⑤
	8-460	—	18.5	18.5⑮	13–19	13–19	191	24.2④	4⑫	—	—	12¼	⑤
1977	8-351	16.3	17.1	17.2	13–19	13–19	191	24.2④	4	—	—	⑬	⑤
	8-400	16.3	17.1	17.2	13–19	13–19	191	24.2④	4	—	—	⑬	⑤
	8-460	18.4	18.5	18.5	13–19	13–19	191	24.2④	4	—	—	⑬	⑤
	8-460	18.4	19.0	19.0	13–19	13–19	191	24.2④	6	—	—	⑬	⑤
1978	8-302	—	14.7	15.2	14–18	14–18	191	24.2⑭	4	—	—	10	⑥
	8-351⑨	—	15.9	16.3	14–18	14–18	191	24.2⑭	4	—	—	11	⑥
	8-351⑩	—	17.0	17.0	14–18	14–18	191	24.2⑭	4	—	—	11	⑥
	8-400	—	17.0	17.0	14–18	14–18	191	24.2⑭	4	—	—	11	⑥
	8-460③	18.9	19.7	19.7	14–18	14–18	191	24.2⑭	6	—	—	12½	⑥
	8-460⑦	17.8	18.6	18.6	14–18	14–18	191	24 2⑭	4	—	—	12½	⑥
1979	8-302	—	—	—	14–18	14–18	191	—	4	—	—	⑬	⑯
	8-351	—	—	—	14–18	14–18	191	—	4	—	—	⑬	⑯

COOLING SYSTEM & CAPACITY DATA—Continued

Year	Model or Engine	Cooling Capacity, Qts.			Radiator Cap Relief Pressure, Lbs.		Thermo. Opening Temp.	Fuel Tank Gals.	Engine Oil Refill Qts. ①	Transmission Oil			Rear Axle Oil Pints
		No Heater	With Heater	With A/C	With A/C	No A/C				3 Speed Pints	4 Speed Pints	Auto. Trans. Qts. ②	
MERCURY													
1974	8-351⑧	15.3	16½	17	12–16	12–16	191	22④	4	—	—	10½	⑤
	8-400	17	18	18½	12–16	12–16	191	22④	4	—	—	⑬	⑤
	8-460	18.4	19½	19½	12–16	12–16	191	22④	4	—	—	12½	⑤
1975	8-351	—	17.1	17.6	13–19	13–19	191	24.2④	4	—	—	⑬	⑤
	8-400	—	17.1	17.6	13–19	13–19	191	24.2④	4	—	—	⑬	⑤
	8-460	—	18.5	18.5⑮	13–19	13–19	191	24.2④	4⑫	—	—	⑬	⑤
1976	8-351	16.3	17.1	17.6	13–19	13–19	191	24.2④	4	—	—	⑬	⑤
	8-400	16.3	17.1	17.6	13–19	13–19	191	24.2④	4	—	—	⑬	⑤
	8-460	17.6	18.5	18.5⑮	13–19	13–19	191	24.2④	4⑫	—	—	12¼	⑤
1977	8-400	16.3	17.1	17.2	13–19	13–19	191	24.2⑥	4	—	—	⑬	⑤
	8-460	18.4	18.5	18.5	13–19	13–19	191	24.2④	4	—	—	⑬	⑤
	8-460	18.4	19.0	19.0	13–19	13–19	191	24.2④	6	—	—	⑬	⑤
1978	8-351	—	16.3	17.0	14–18	14–18	191	24.2⑭	4	—	—	⑬	⑯
	8-400	—	17.0	17.5	14–18	14–18	191	24.2⑭	4	—	—	11	⑯
	8-460③	18.9	19.7	19.7	14–18	14–18	191	24.2⑭	6	—	—	12½	⑯
	8-460⑦	17.8	18.6	18.6	14–18	14–18	191	24.2⑭	4	—	—	12½	⑯
1979	8-302	—	—	—	14–18	14–18	191	—	4	—	—	⑬	⑯
	8-351	—	—	—	14–18	14–18	191	—	4	—	—	⑬	⑯

①—Add one quart with filter change.
②—Approximate. Make final check with dipstick.
③—Police models.
④—Station Wagons 21 gals. Add 8 gals. with auxiliary tank.
⑤—WER axles 4, all others 5.
⑥—Exc. models with 460 engine, locking or optional axles, 4 pts.; Models with 460 engine, locking or optional axles, 5 pts.
⑦—Exc. police models.
⑧—Cleveland engine.
⑨—Windsor engine.
⑩—Modified engine.
⑪—C4 10½ qts., FMX 11 qts.
⑫—Police Models 6½ qts.
⑬—FMX 11 qts., C6 12¼ qts. C4, 10¼ qts.
⑭—Station wagons, 21 gals.
⑮—Medium duty 19 qts., Heavy duty and Police 20 qts.
⑯—7.5″ Ring gear 3¾ pints; 8.5″ Ring gear, 4¼ pints.

Electrical Section

DISTRIBUTOR, REPLACE
Removal

1. On vehicles with conventional ignition systems, disconnect primary wire from ignition coil. On vehicles with electronic ignition, disconnect harness connector from engine wiring.
2. Disconnect vacuum control line and remove distributor cap.
3. Scribe a mark on the distributor body indicating the position of the rotor, and scribe another mark on the body and engine block indicating position of distributor body in block. These marks can be used as guides when installing distributor in a correctly timed engine.
4. Remove hold down screw or screws and lift distributor out of block. *Do not crank engine while distributor is removed or the initial timing operation will have to be performed.*

Installation

If the crankshaft has not been disturbed, install the distributor, using the scribed marks previously made on the distributor body and engine block as guides.

If the crankshaft has been rotated while the distributor was removed from the engine, it will be necessary to retime the engine. Crank the engine to bring No. 1 piston on top dead center of its compression stroke. Align the timing mark on the vibration damper or pulley with the timing pointer (see *Tune Up* chart). On models with electronic ignition, install distributor so that armature tooth is aligned with stator and rotor is pointing to No. 1 spark plug wire, Fig. 1. On models with breaker type ignition, install the distributor so that the rotor points to the No. 1 spark plug wire terminal in the distributor cap.

NOTE: Make sure the oil pump intermediate shaft properly engages the distributor shaft. It may be necessary to crank the engine with the starter, after the distributor drive gear is properly engaged, in order to engage the oil pump intermediate shaft.

CAUTION: When checking ignition timing on 1977-79 models using an inductive pickup type timing light, a length of split vacuum hose should be installed around the plug wire.

STARTER, REPLACE

SERVICE BULLETIN

STARTER PROBLEMS: If the starter is noisy or if it locks up, before condemning the starter, loosen the three mounting bolts enough to hand fit the starter properly into the pilot plate. Then tighten the mounting bolts, starting with the top bolt.

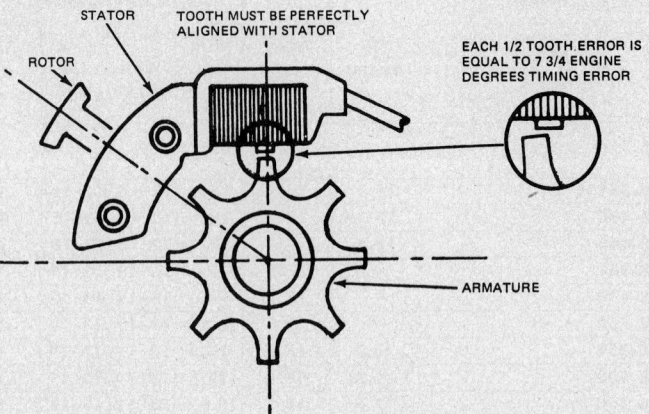

Fig. 1 Armature tooth and stator alignment. 1974-78 models with electronic ignition

1974-79 Ford & Mercury

1. Disconnect battery ground cable, then disconnect starter cable at starter terminal.
2. Remove mounting bolts and starter.

NOTE: On some models, it may be necessary to turn the wheels right or left to remove starter.

3. Reverse procedure to install and torque bolts to 15-20 ft. lbs.

IGNITION LOCK, REPLACE

1979

1. Disconnect battery ground cable.
2. Remove steering column trim shroud.
3. Disconnect key warning switch electrical connector.
4. Turn ignition lock to "On" position.
5. Using a ⅛" pin or punch located in the 4 o'clock hole and 1¼ inch from outer edge of lock cylinder housing, depress retaining pin while pulling the lock cylinder from housing.
6. Turn lock cylinder to "On" position and insert cylinder into housing. Ensure that the lock cylinder is fully seated and aligned into the interlocking washer before turning key to "Off" position. This will permit the retaining pin to extend into the lock cylinder housing hole.
7. Rotate key to check for proper mechanical operation.
8. Connect key warning switch electrical connector.
9. Connect battery ground cable.
10. Check for proper operation.

1974-78

1. Disconnect battery ground cable.

2. *Units with Fixed Steering Columns:* Remove steering wheel and trim pad. Insert a wire pin in the hole located inside the column halfway down the lock cylinder housing, Fig. 1. *Units with Tilt Steering Columns:* Insert wire pin in the hole located on the outside of the flange casting next to the emergency flasher button, Fig. 2.
3. Place the gear shift lever in PARK position, and turn the lock cylinder with the ignition key to RUN position.
4. Depress the wire pin while pulling up on the lock cylinder to remove. Remove the wire pin.
5. To install insert the lock cylinder into housing in the flange casting, and turn the key to OFF position. Be certain that the cylinder is fully inserted before turning to the OFF position. This action will extend the cylinder retaining pin into the cylinder housing.
6. Turn the key to check for correct operation in all positions.
7. Install the steering wheel and trim pad on fixed column units.
8. Connect the battery ground cable.

IGNITION SWITCH, REPLACE

1979

1. Disconnect battery ground cable.
2. Remove upper column shroud.
3. Disconnect ignition switch electrical connector.
4. With a ⅛ inch twist drill, drill out the switch retaining bolt heads. Then, remove the bolts with a "Easy Out" or equivalent.
5. Disengage ignition switch from actuator and remove from vehicle.

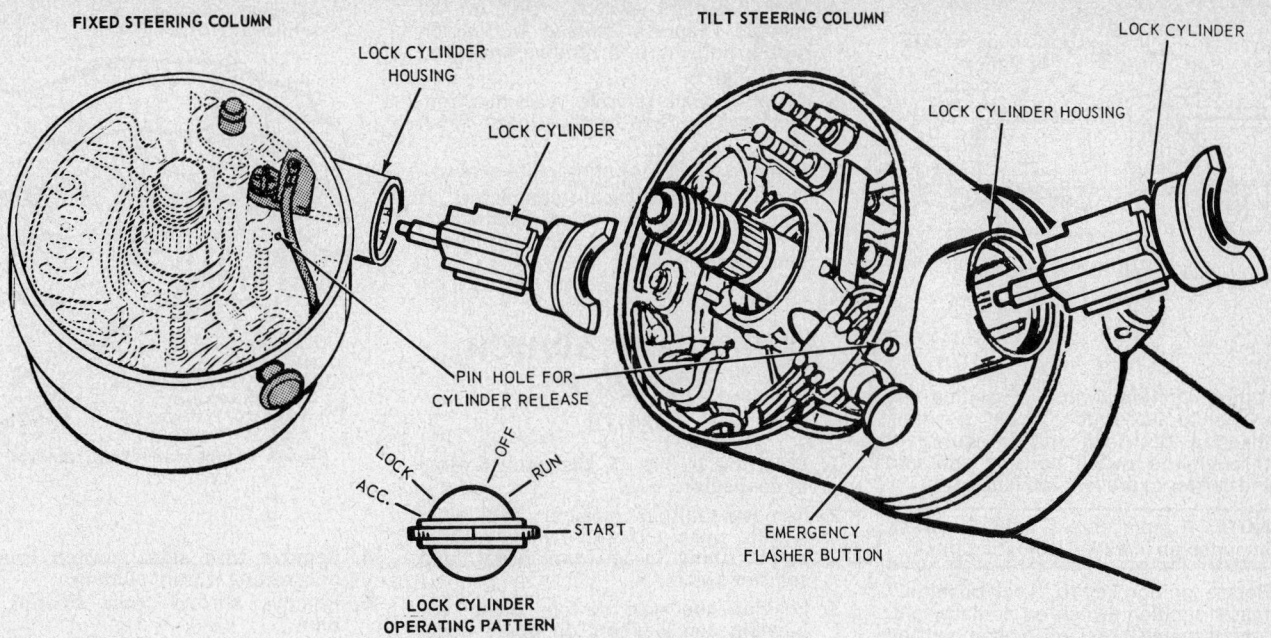

FIXED STEERING COLUMN

TILT STEERING COLUMN

LOCK CYLINDER HOUSING

LOCK CYLINDER

LOCK CYLINDER

LOCK CYLINDER HOUSING

LOCK CYLINDER

PIN HOLE FOR CYLINDER RELEASE

LOCK

OFF

RUN

ACC.

START

EMERGENCY FLASHER BUTTON

LOCK CYLINDER OPERATING PATTERN

Fig. 2   Ignition Lock. 1974-78

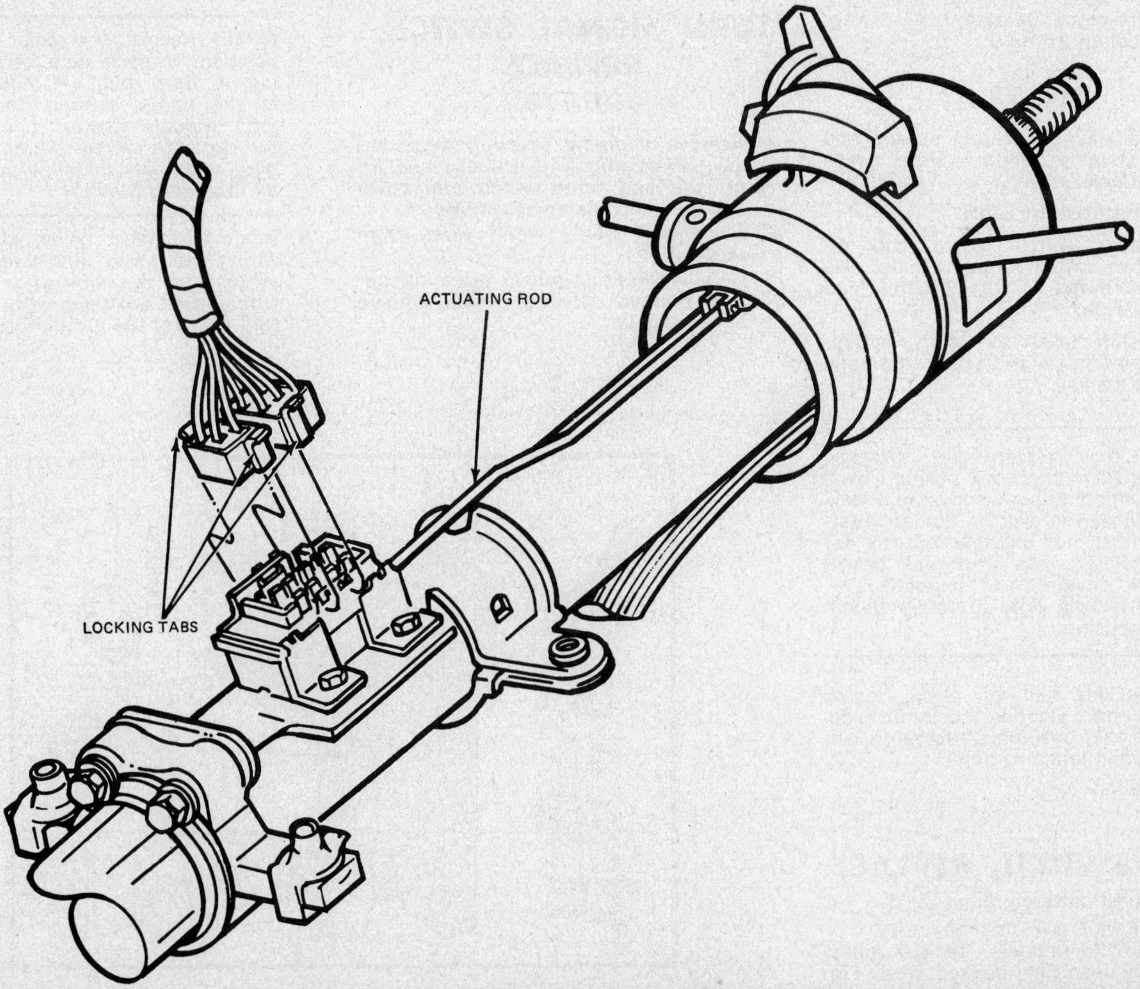

ACTUATING ROD

LOCKING TABS

Fig. 3   Ignition switch. 1974-78 All

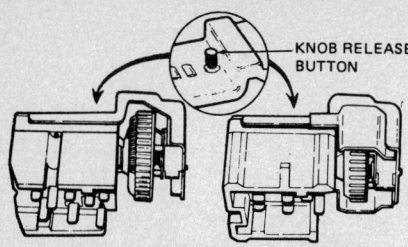

Fig. 4   Light switch. Ford and Mercury. Typical

6. Adjust ignition switch by sliding the carrier to the switch "Lock" position. Insert a .050 inch drill or equivalent through the switch housing and into the carrier to prevent movement.

NOTE: A replacement ignition switch includes an installed adjusting pin.

7. Rotate ignition key to "Lock position."
8. Install ignition switch on actuator pin.
9. Install switch break-off heat mounting bolts and tighten until the bolt heads shear.
10. Remove adjusting pin or drill.
11. Connect ignition switch electrical connector.
12. Connect battery ground cable and check for proper operation.
13. Install column shroud.

1974-78

1. Remove steering column shroud and lower steering column from brake support bracket.
2. Disconnect battery cable.
3. Disconnect switch wiring and remove two switch retaining nuts. Disconnect switch from actuator and remove switch, Fig. 3.
4. Move shift lever to Park position. Place ignition key in Lock position and remove the key.

NOTE: New replacement switches are pinned in the Lock position by a plastic shipping pin inserted in a locking hole in the switch. For an existing switch, pull plunger out as far as it will go then back one detent to Lock position and insert a $3/32''$ drill in locking hole to retain switch in Lock position.

5. With locking pin in place, install switch on steering column, determine mid position of actuator lash and tighten retaining bolts.
6. Remove locking pin.

LIGHT SWITCH, REPLACE

1. Disconnect battery ground cable.
2. Remove wiper switch knob.
3. On 1977-78 models, remove shaft knob by inserting hooked wire, Fig. 4A, into knob slot and depressing spring.

4. With headlight switch "On" on all models, depress release button on switch housing and remove knob and shaft, Fig. 4.
5. On all models remove bezel nut from light switch, then remove lower finish panel.
6. Remove three mounting plate screws.
7. Disconnect electrical connector. If equipped with concealed headlamps, disconnect vacuum hoses from switch and remove switch.

STOP LIGHT SWITCH, REPLACE
1974-78

1. Referring to Fig. 5, disconnect wires at connector.
2. Remove hairpin retainer and slide switch, push rod and nylon washers and bushing away from pedal, and remove switch.
3. Position the new switch, push rod, bushing and washers on brake pedal pin and secure with hairpin retainer.
4. Connect wires at connector and install wires in retaining clip.

TURN SIGNAL SWITCH, REPLACE
1974-78

1. Remove retaining screw from underside of steering wheel spoke and lift off the pad horn switch/trim cover and medallion as an assembly.
2. Disconnect horn switch wires from terminals.
3. Remove steering wheel retaining nut and remove steering wheel with a suitable puller.

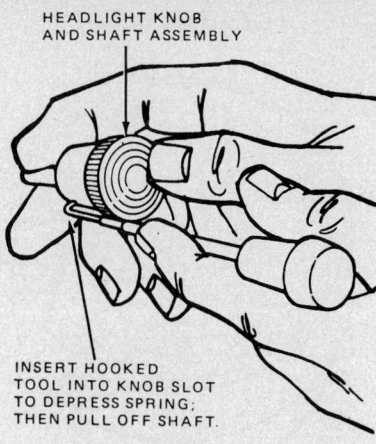

Fig. 4A   Light switch knob removal

4. Remove turn signal switch lever by unscrewing it from column.
5. Remove shroud from steering column.
6. Disconnect column wiring connector plug and remove screws that secure switch to column.
7. On tilt column models, remove wires and terminals from column wiring plug.

NOTE: Record the color code and position of each wire before removing it from plug. A hole provided in the flange casting on fixed column models makes it unnecessary to separate wires from plug. The plug with wires installed can be guided through the hole.

8. Remove plastic cover sleeve from wiring harness and remove the switch from top of column.
On vehicles equipped with speed control, transfer the ground brush located

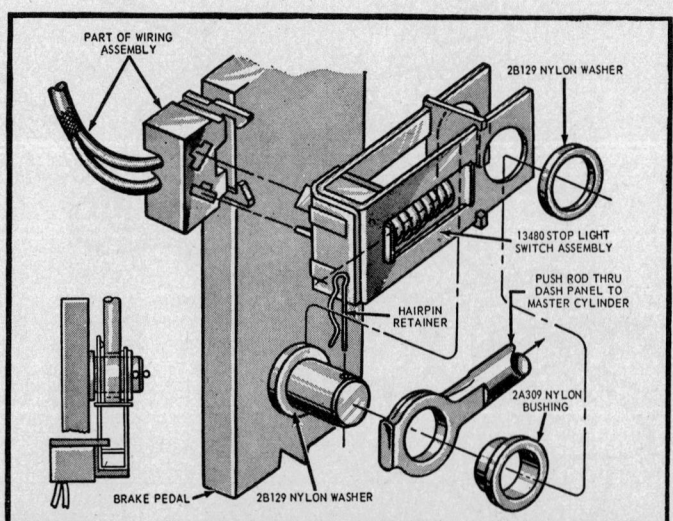

**Fig. 5   Mechanical stop light switch.
1974-78 Ford and Mercury**

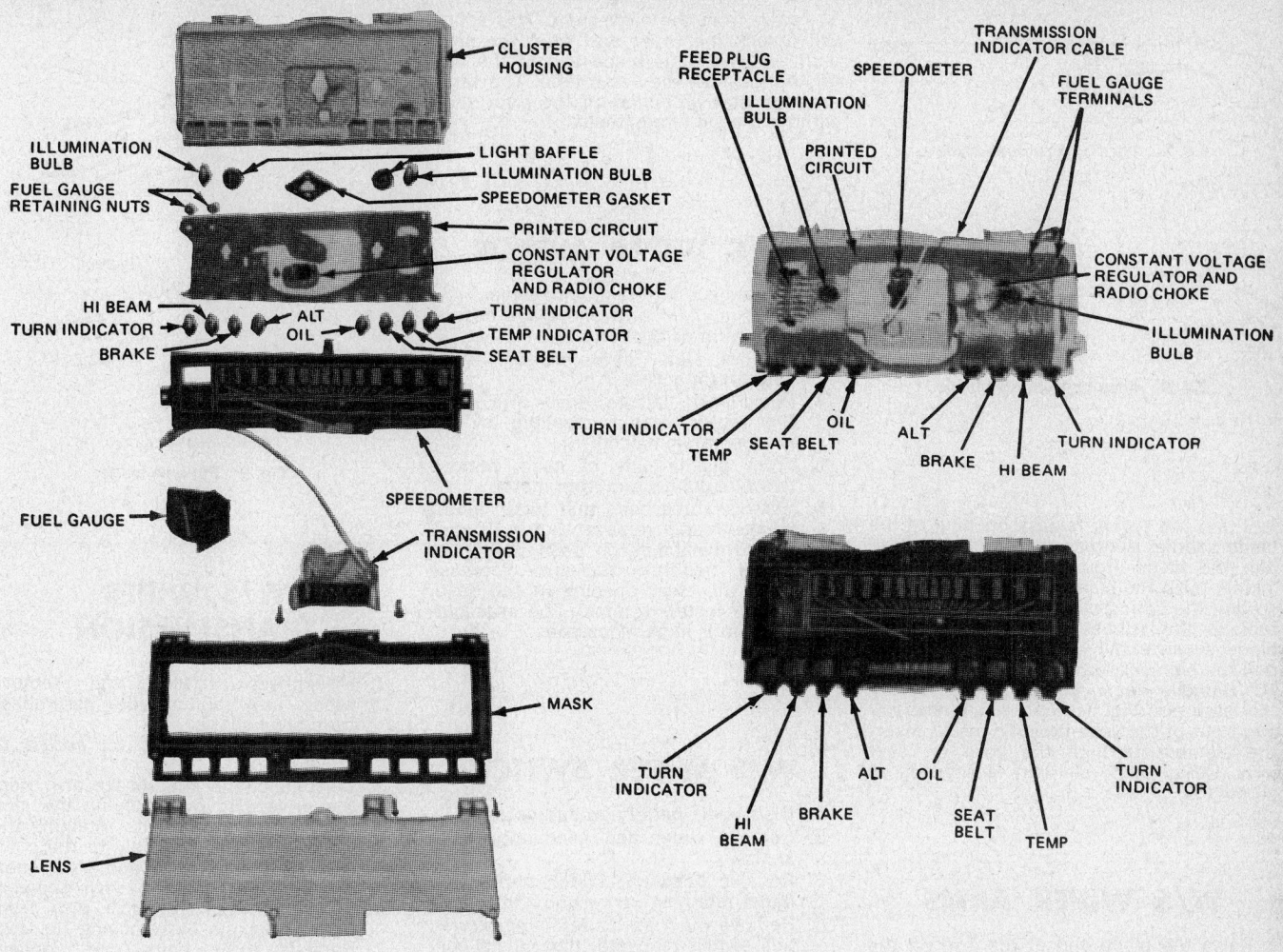

CLUSTER HOUSING

ILLUMINATION BULB

FUEL GAUGE RETAINING NUTS

LIGHT BAFFLE

ILLUMINATION BULB

SPEEDOMETER GASKET

PRINTED CIRCUIT

CONSTANT VOLTAGE REGULATOR AND RADIO CHOKE

HI BEAM

TURN INDICATOR

BRAKE

ALT

OIL

TURN INDICATOR

TEMP INDICATOR

SEAT BELT

FUEL GAUGE

SPEEDOMETER

TRANSMISSION INDICATOR

MASK

LENS

FEED PLUG RECEPTACLE

ILLUMINATION BULB

SPEEDOMETER

TRANSMISSION INDICATOR CABLE

FUEL GAUGE TERMINALS

PRINTED CIRCUIT

CONSTANT VOLTAGE REGULATOR AND RADIO CHOKE

ILLUMINATION BULB

TURN INDICATOR

TEMP

OIL

SEAT BELT

ALT

BRAKE

HI BEAM

TURN INDICATOR

TURN INDICATOR

HI BEAM

BRAKE

ALT

OIL

SEAT BELT

TEMP

TURN INDICATOR

Fig. 6.   Instrument cluster. 1974-78 Ford & Mercury

in the turn signal cancelling cam to the new switch assembly.

NEUTRAL SAFETY SWITCH

1974-78 Ford & Mercury

Column Shift

The neutral safety switch has been eliminated and is replaced by a series of steps designed into the steering column selector lever hub casting.

HORN SOUNDER, REPLACE

Rim-Blow Type

The rubber insert and copper strip assembly is not replaceable on vehicles with speed control. If a new insert assembly is required the entire steering wheel must be replaced.

1. Remove the pad from the steering

wheel (three screws).
2. Remove medallion from the pad.
3. After removing the steering wheel nut the wheel can be removed from the shaft with a wheel puller.

Except Rim-Blow Type

1. Disconnect battery ground cable.
2. Remove steering column pad (2 screws).
3. Push down and turn horn ring and remove ring and spring.
4. Reverse procedure to install.

INSTRUMENT CLUSTER

1. Disconnect the battery ground cable.
2. Remove two steering column cover screws and remove the cover.
3. Remove two instrument cluster trim cover attaching screws and remove cover, Fig. 6.
4. Reach behind the cluster and disconnect the cluster feed plug from its receptacle.

5. Disconnect the speedometer cable.
6. Remove steering column cover shroud, then remove the screw attaching the transmission indicator cable to the steering column.
7. Remove the four cluster attaching screws and remove the cluster assembly.

W/S WIPER BLADES

NOTE: Trico and Anco blades are used and both come in two types Bayonet type and Side Saddle Pin type.

Bayonet Type: To remove the *Trico* type press down on the arm to unlock the top stud. Depress the tab on the saddle, Fig. 7, and pull the blade from the arm. To remove the *Anco* type press inward on the tab, Fig. 8, and pull the blade from the arm. To install a new blade assembly slide the blade saddle over the end of the wiper arm so that the locking stud snaps into place.

Side Saddle Pin Type: To remove the pin type (Trico or Anco) insert an appropiate

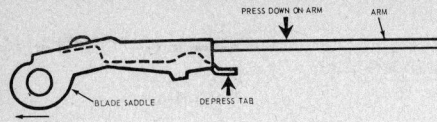

Fig. 7   Trico bayonet type blade

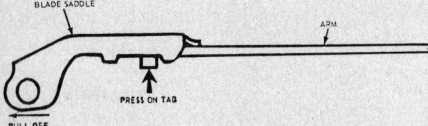

Fig. 8   Anco bayonet type blade

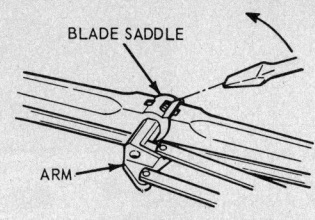

BLADE REMOVAL

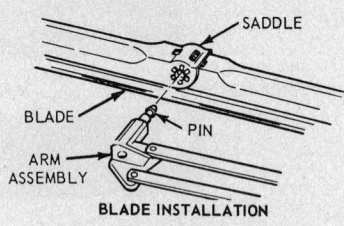

BLADE INSTALLATION

Fig. 9   Pin type blade

11, away from the pivot shaft. This action will unlock the wiper arm from the pivot shaft and hold the blade end of the arm off the glass at the same time. The wiper arm can now be pulled off the pivot shaft without the aid of any tools.

W/S WIPER MOTOR

1. Disconnect battery ground cable.
2. Remove wiper arm and blade assemblies from pivot shafts.
3. Remove left cowl screen (four screws) for access.
4. Disconnect linkage drive arm from the motor output crankpin by removing retaining clip.
5. From engine side of dash, remove two wire connectors from motor.
6. Remove three bolts that retain motor to dash and remove motor. If output arm catches on dash during removal, handturn the arm clockwise so it wil! clear opening in the dash. Before installing motor, be sure output arm is in park position.

W/S WIPER SWITCH

1. Disconnect battery ground cable.
2. Remove wiper and headlight switch knobs.
3. Remove headlight switch bezel, trim panel retaining screw and trim panel.
4. Remove wiper switch retaining screws, pull switch rearward, disconnect connector and remove switch.

tool into the spring release opening of the blade saddle, depress the spring clip and pull the blade from the arm, Fig. 9 to install, push the blade saddle on to the pin so that the spring clip engages the pin. To replace the rubber element in a *Trico* blade squeeze the latch lock release and pull the element out of the lever jaws, Fig. 10, Remove *Anco* element by depressing the latch pin, Fig. 10, and sliding the element out of the yoke jaws. To install insert the element through the yoke or lever jaws. Be sure the element is engaged at all points.

W/S WIPER ARMS

Raise the blade end of the arm off the windshield and move the slide latch, Fig.

W/S WIPER TRANSMISSION

1. Disconnect battery and remove wiper arm and blade assemblies from pivot shafts.
2. Remove cowl screens for access to linkage.
3. Disconnect the left linkage arm from the drive arm by removing the clip.
4. Remove the three bolts retaining the left pivot shaft assembly to the cowl.
5. Remove the left arm and pivot shaft assembly through the cowl opening.
6. Disconnect linkage drive arm from motor crankpin by removing the clip.
7. Remove three bolts that connect drive arm pivot shaft assembly to the cowl and remove the pivot shaft drive arm and right arm as an assembly.

RADIO, REPLACE

NOTE: When installing radio, be sure to adjust antenna trimmer for peak performance.

1. Disconnect battery ground cable.

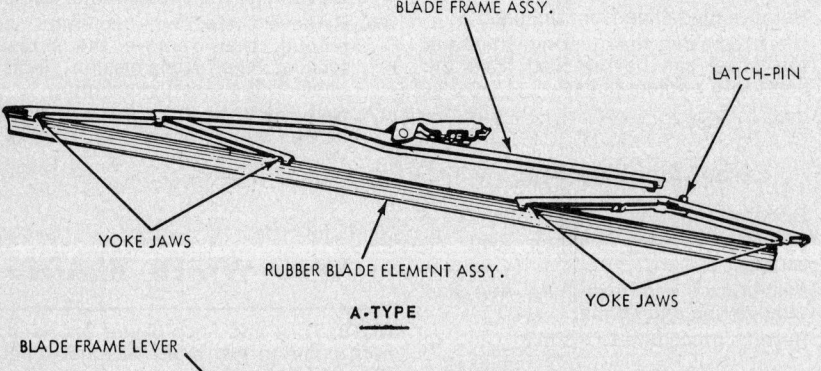

A-TYPE

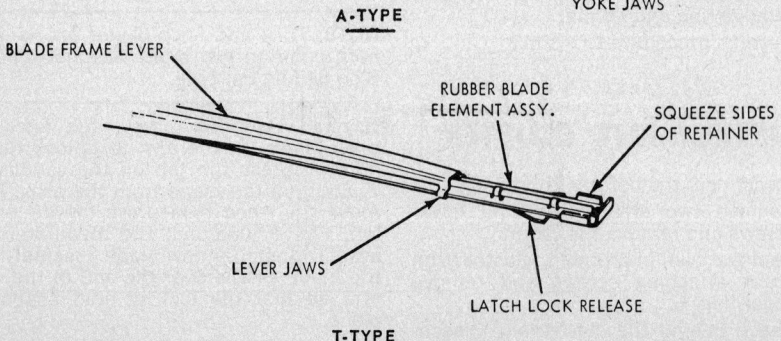

T-TYPE

Fig. 10   Wiper blade element

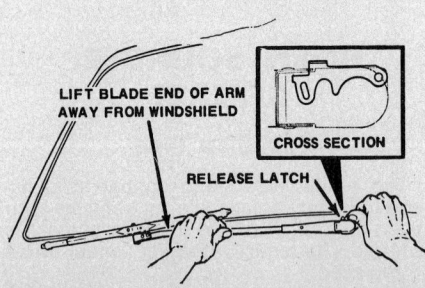

Fig. 11   Wiper arm. 1974-78 models

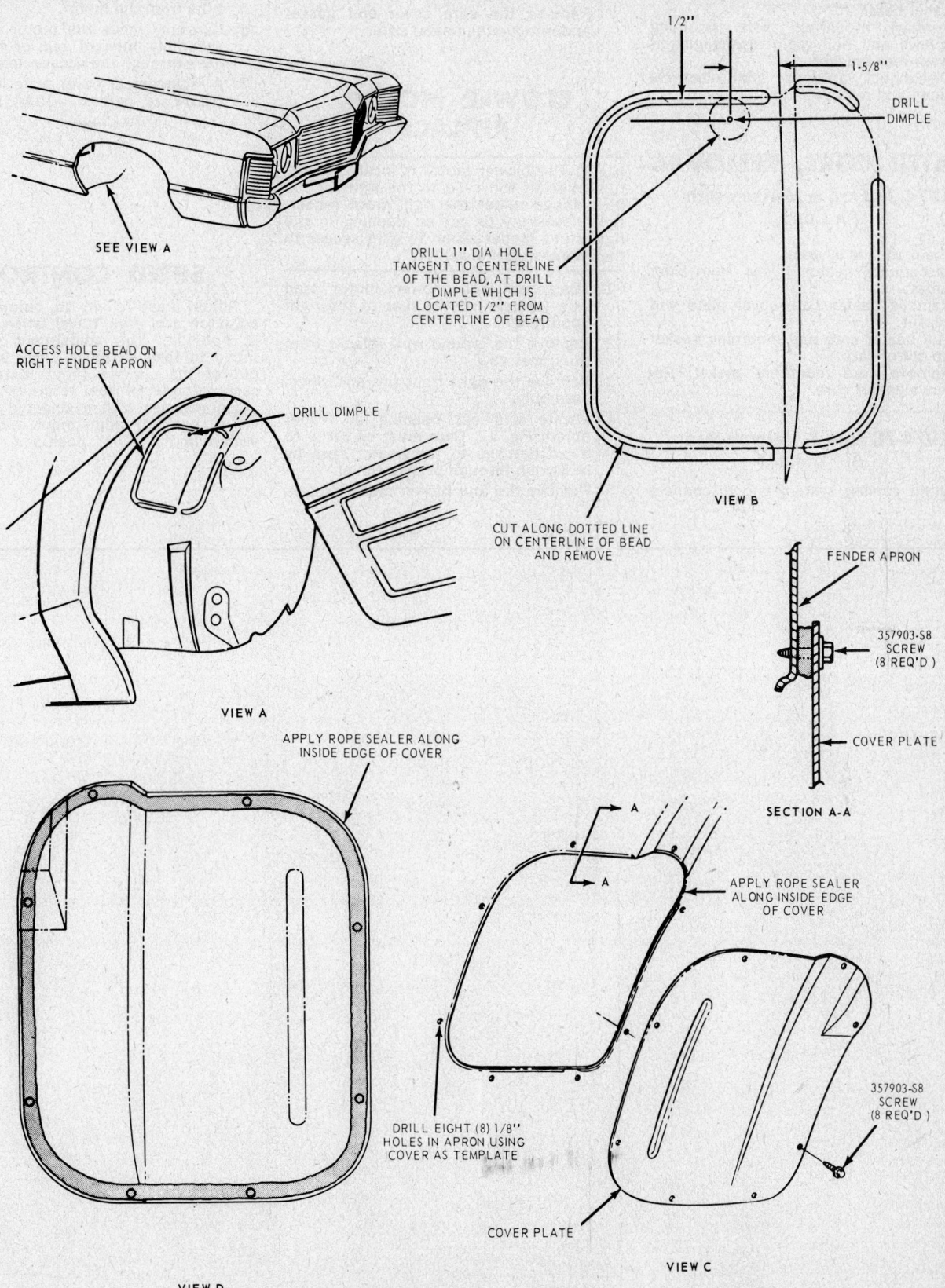

SEE VIEW A

1/2"

1-5/8"

DRILL DIMPLE

DRILL 1" DIA HOLE TANGENT TO CENTERLINE OF THE BEAD, AT DRILL DIMPLE WHICH IS LOCATED 1/2" FROM CENTERLINE OF BEAD

ACCESS HOLE BEAD ON RIGHT FENDER APRON

DRILL DIMPLE

VIEW B

CUT ALONG DOTTED LINE ON CENTERLINE OF BEAD AND REMOVE

FENDER APRON

357903-S8 SCREW (8 REQ'D)

COVER PLATE

SECTION A-A

VIEW A

APPLY ROPE SEALER ALONG INSIDE EDGE OF COVER

A

A

APPLY ROPE SEALER ALONG INSIDE EDGE OF COVER

DRILL EIGHT (8) 1/8" HOLES IN APRON USING COVER AS TEMPLATE

357903-S8 SCREW (8 REQ'D)

COVER PLATE

VIEW D

VIEW C

Fig. 12   Blower motor access. 1974-78 Ford & Mercury

2. Remove radio knobs and instrument panel bezel.
3. Remove mounting plate retaining screws and pull radio disengaging it from rear bracket.
4. Disconnect antenna and electrical wires and remove radio.

HEATER CORE, REMOVAL

1974-78 Ford & Mercury with Air Cond.

1. Drain cooling system.
2. Disconnect heater hoses from core tubes.
3. Remove heater core cover plate and gasket.
4. Pull heater core and mounting gasket up out of case.
5. Remove core mounting gasket. Remove heater core.

1974-78 Ford & Mercury less Air Cond.

1. Drain cooling system and disconnect heater hoses from the core.
2. Remove the core cover and gasket and remove the heater core.

BLOWER MOTOR, REPLACE

NOTE: The blower motor is located in the right side of the case to the right of the hood hinge under the right front fender. It is necessary to cut an opening in the right front fender apron to gain access to the blower motor assembly.

1. Disconnect the blower motor lead wire (orange) at the rear of the right hood hinge.
2. Remove the ground wire (black) from the upper cowl.
3. Remove the right front tire and wheel assembly.
4. Locate and cut opening in fender apron, Fig. 12. Care must be taken to avoid damage to the heater case by drill push-through or over-travel.
5. Remove the four blower motor mounting screws and disconnect the cooler tube from the motor.
6. Carefully move the motor and wheel assembly forward out of the heater case through the access hole.
7. A replacement cover plate is available from Ford, part no. #18A475.

SPEED CONTROLS

Adjust bead chain to obtain .06-.25" actuator arm free travel when engine is at hot idle. The adjustment should be made to take as much slack as possible out of the chain without restricting the carburetor lever from returning to idle.

On vehicles with a solenoid anti-diesel valve, perform adjustment with ignition switch in the "ON" position.

Engine Section

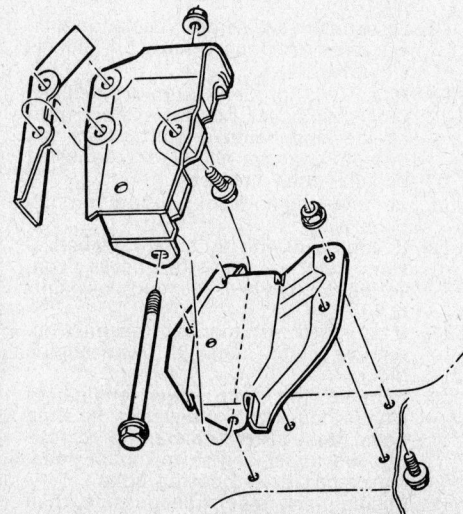

Fig. 1 Engine mount (typical). 1974-78 V8-302, 351W

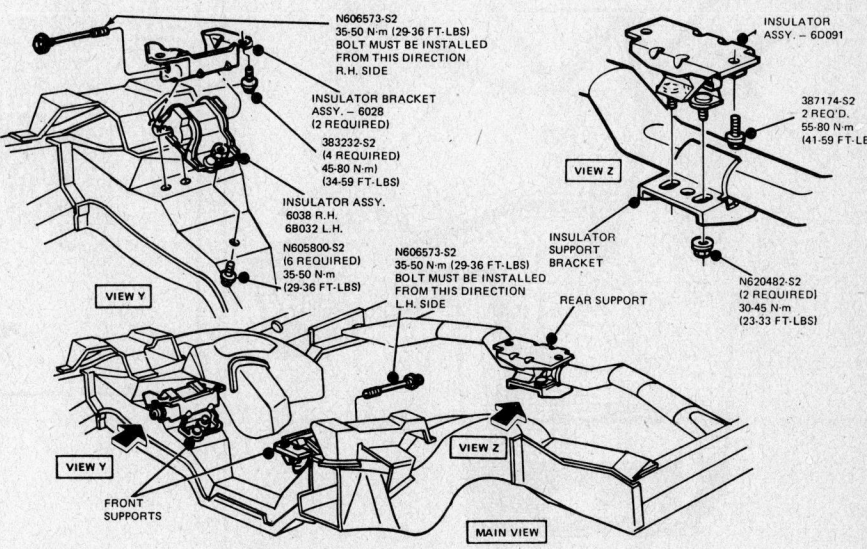

N606573-S2
35-50 N·m (29-36 FT·LBS)
BOLT MUST BE INSTALLED
FROM THIS DIRECTION
R.H. SIDE

INSULATOR BRACKET
ASSY. – 6028
(2 REQUIRED)

383232-S2)
(4 REQUIRED)
45-80 N·m
(34-59 FT-LBS)

INSULATOR ASSY.
6038 R.H.
6B032 L.H.

N605800-S2
(6 REQUIRED)
35-50 N·m
(29-36 FT·LBS)

N606573-S2
35-50 N·m (29-36 FT·LBS)
BOLT MUST BE INSTALLED
FROM THIS DIRECTION
L.H. SIDE

INSULATOR
ASSY. – 6D091

387174-S2
2 REQ'D.
55-80 N·m
(41-59 FT-LB)

VIEW Z

INSULATOR
SUPPORT
BRACKET

N620482-S2
(2 REQUIRED)
30-45 N·m
(23-33 FT-LBS)

REAR SUPPORT

VIEW Y

VIEW Y

VIEW Z

FRONT
SUPPORTS

MAIN VIEW

Fig. 1A Engine mounts. 1979 V8-302 & 351W

ENGINE MOUNTS

CAUTION: Whenever self-locking mounting bolts and nuts are removed, they must be replaced with new self-locking bolts and nuts.

1974-79 V8-302, 351W

1. Remove the nut and through bolt attaching the insulator to the support bracket, Figs. 1 and 1A.
2. Raise the engine slightly with a jack and a wood block placed under the oil pan.
3. Remove the engine insulator assembly to cylinder block attaching bolts.

Remove the engine insulator assembly and the heat shield, if so equipped.
4. Reverse procedure to install.

1974-78 V8-351C, 351M, 400

1. Remove the fan shroud attaching bolts. Remove the transmission oil cooler lines from the retaining bracket on the block.
2. Remove the through bolt and lock nut attaching the insulator support bracket, Fig. 3. Remove the bolt and nut on the opposite mount to prevent distortion of the insulator.
3. Raise the engine slightly with a jack and a wood block placed under the oil pan.
4. Remove the engine insulator assembly to cylinder block attaching bolts and lockwashers.
5. Remove the engine insulator assembly and heat shield, if equipped.
6. Reverse procedure to install.

1974-78 V8-460

1. Block rear wheels and set parking brake. Raise front of vehicle with floor jack and install safety stands.
2. Position jack under the front area of the oil pan. Place a wood block between the jack and oil pan. Raise the jack just enough to support the engine.
3. Remove the nut through bolt that attaches the front support insulator to the lower support bracket, Fig. 2.
4. Remove the bolts attaching the support insulator and heat shield to the cylinder block. Replace the insulator

on one side before proceding to the other insulator.
5. Reverse procedure to install.

ENGINE, REPLACE

NOTE: Because of engine compartment

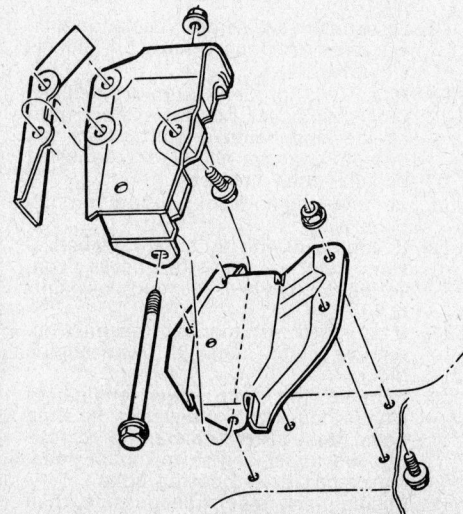

Fig. 2 Engine mount (typical). 1974-78 V8-460

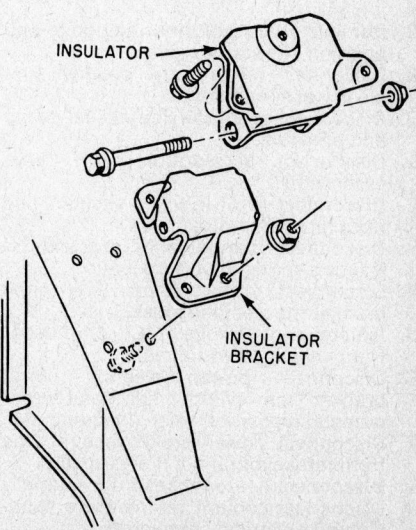

Fig. 3 Engine mount. 1974-78 V8-351C, 351M, 400

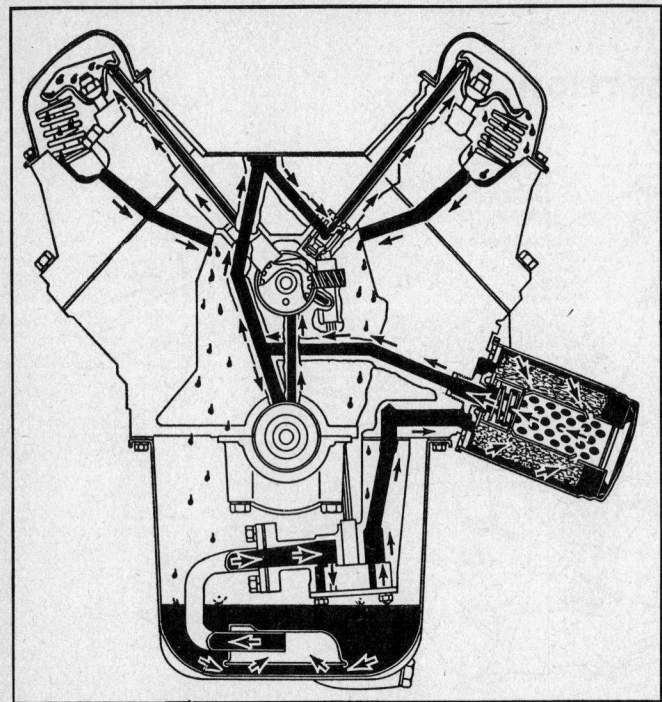

Engine oiling system. V8-302, 351, 400

Engine oiling system. V8-460

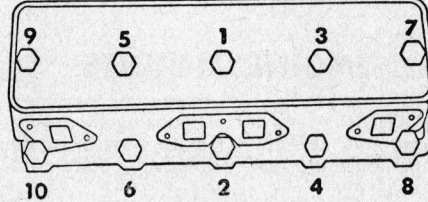

Fig. 4 Cylinder head tightening sequence. V8 engines

tolerances, the engine should not be removed and installed with the transmission attached.

1979

1. Disconnect battery and alternator ground cables.
2. Drain cooling system and oil pan.
3. Remove hood.
4. Remove air cleaner and intake duct assembly.
5. Disconnect radiator hoses from engine.
6. Disconnect transmission oil cooler lines from radiator.
7. Remove fan shroud attaching bolts, then the radiator, fan, spacer, pulley and shroud.
8. Remove alternator mounting bolts and position alternator aside.
9. Disconnect oil pressure sending unit electrical connector.
10. Disconnect fuel tank line at fuel pump and plug line.
11. Disconnect accelerator cable from carburetor.
12. Disconnect throttle valve vacuum line from intake manifold.
13. Disconnect manual shift rod and retracting spring at shift rod stud.
14. Disconnect transmission filler tube bracket from engine block.
15. Isolate and remove A/C compressor from vehicle, if equipped.
16. Disconnect power steering pump bracket from cylinder head and water pump and position aside, if equipped.
17. Disconnect power brake vacuum line from intake manifold, if equipped.
18. Disconnect heater hoses from engine.
19. Disconnect coolant temperature sending unit electrical connector.
20. Remove upper converter housing to engine attaching bolts.

21. Disconnect ignition coil and distributor wiring. Remove harness from left hand rocker arm cover and position aside. Disconnect ground strap from engine block.
22. Raise and support front of vehicle.
23. Disconnect starter motor wiring and remove starter motor.
24. Disconnect exhaust pipes from manifold.
25. Disconnect engine mounts from frame brackets.
26. Disconnect secondary air line to catalytic converter, if equipped.
27. Disconnect transmission oil cooler lines from retainer.
28. Remove converter housing inspection cover.
29. Disconnect converter from flywheel. Secure converter in housing.
30. Remove remaining converter housing to engine bolts.
31. Lower vehicle and attach suitable engine lifting equipment to engine.
32. Raise engine slight and pull forward to disengage from transmission.
33. Remove engine from vehicle.
34. Reverse procedure to install.

1974-78

1. Disconnect battery ground cable, drain cooling system and crankcase and remove hood and air cleaner assembly.
2. Disconnect or remove all Thermactor components that may interfere with engine removal.
3. Disconnect hoses and oil cooler lines from radiator, then remove radiator, fan shroud and fan.
4. Remove all drive belts.
5. Disconnect power steering pump and alternator and position units out of the way.

6. If equipped with air conditioning, isolate and remove compressor.
7. Disconnect all hoses, lines and wiring from engine. Make certain to remove ground wires from block and right cylinder head.
8. Disconnect fuel line from pump and plug line.
9. Disconnect accelerator cable or linkage, then disconnect downshift linkage (if used).
10. Raise and properly support vehicle, then disconnect exhaust system from engine and remove starter. On six cylinder engines, remove transmission oil filler tube bracket.
11. Remove engine front support through bolts.
12. If equipped with automatic transmission, remove converter cover, converter to flywheel bolts, and downshift rod.
13. If equipped with manual transmission, remove clutch linkage from engine block.
14. Remove the four lower engine to clutch housing or converter housing bolts, then lower vehicle and remove the two upper engine to clutch housing or converter housing bolts.
15. Position jack under transmission, then using a suitable hoist, carefully remove engine from vehicle.
16. Reverse procedure to install.

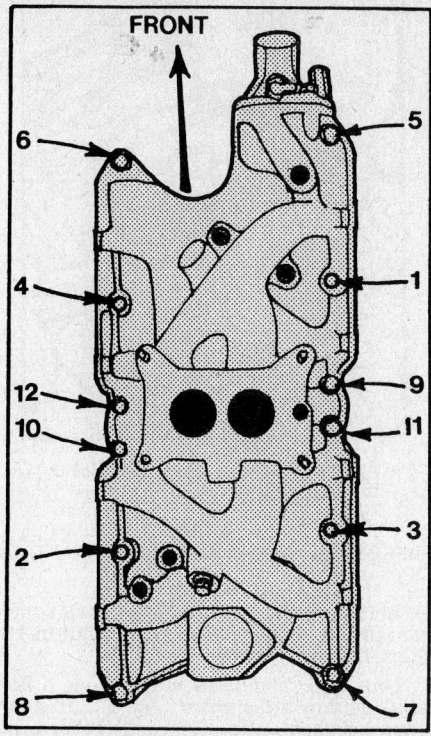

Fig. 5   Intake manifold tightening sequence. V8-302 & 1976-79 V8-351W

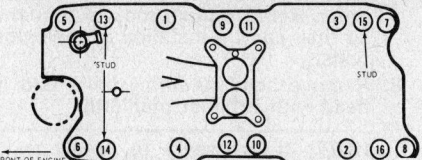

Fig. 6   Intake manifold tightening sequence. 1974-75 V8-351W

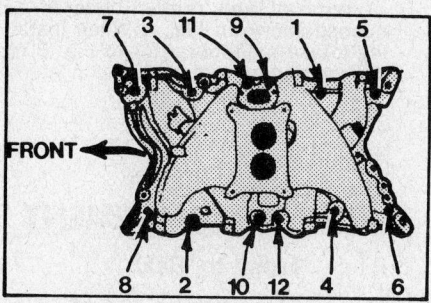

Fig. 7   Intake manifold tightening sequence. V8-351C, 351M, 400

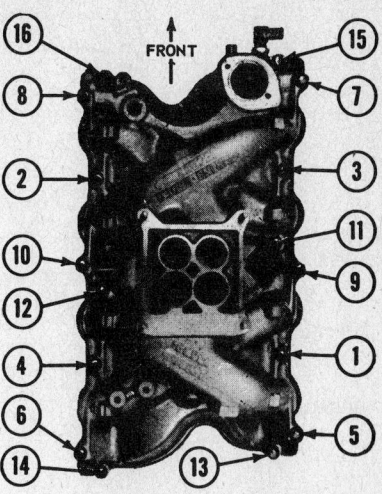

Fig. 8   Intake manifold tightening sequence. V8-429, 460

CYLINDER HEAD, REPLACE

Tighten cylinder head bolts a little at a time in three steps in the sequence shown in Fig. 4. Final tightening should be to the torque specifications listed in the *Engine Tightening* table. After bolts have been tightened to specifications, *they should not be disturbed.*

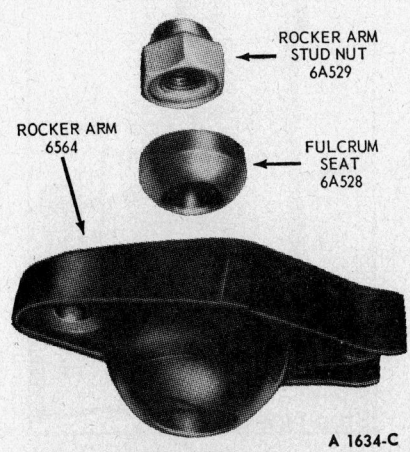

Fig. 9   Valve rocker arm parts. 1974-77 & early 1978 V8-302, 351W

1979 V8-302 & 351W

1. Disconnect battery ground cable.
2. Remove intake manifold and carburetor as an assembly.
3. Remove rocker arm cover.
4. If right cylinder head is being removed, isolate and remove A/C compressor, if equipped.
5. Remove EGR cooler, if equipped with V8-351W and EEC system.
6. If left cylinder head is being removed, and is equipped with power steering, disconnect power steering pump bracket from cylinder head and engine block and position assembly aside.
7. Remove ignition coil, alternator mounting bracket bolt and spacer.
8. Remove rocker arms and push rods.
9. Remove cylinder head bolts and the cylinder head.
10. Reverse procedure to install. Torque cylinder head bolts to specifications in sequence, Fig. 4. Torque intake manifold bolts to specifications in sequence, Fig. 5.

1974-78 V8-302, 351, 400

1. Remove intake manifold and carburetor as an assembly.
2. Disconnect battery ground cable at cylinder head.
3. Remove rocker arm cover.
4. On air conditioned cars, remove compressor.
5. On car with power steering, disconnect pump bracket from left cylinder head and remove drive belt. Wire power steering pump out of the way and in position that will prevent oil from draining out.

NOTE: If left cylinder head is being re-

moved on an engine equipped with Thermactor Exhaust Emission Control System, disconnect hose from air manifold on left head. If a right head is to be removed, remove air pump and bracket and disconnect hose on right head.

6. Remove generator or alternator.
7. Disconnect exhaust manifold at exhaust pipes.
8. Loosen rocker arm stud nuts or bolts so that rocker arms can be rotated to the side.
9. Remove push rods, keeping them in sequence so they may be returned to their original locations.
10. Unfasten and remove cylinder head.
11. Reverse removal procedure to install the head. Tighten cylinder head down in the sequence shown in Fig. 4. When installing intake manifold refer to Figs. 5, 6 and 7 for bolt tightening sequence.

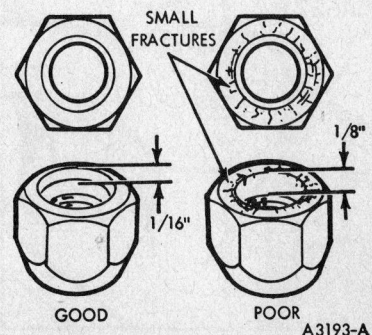

Fig. 10   Inspection of rocker arm stud nut. 1974-77 & early 1978 V8-302, 351W

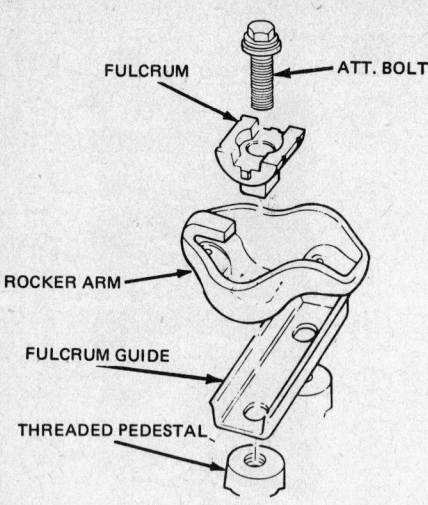

FULCRUM

ATT. BOLT

ROCKER ARM

FULCRUM GUIDE

THREADED PEDESTAL

Fig. 11   Rocker arm. Late 1979 & 1979 V8-302 & 351W

1974-78 V-8-460

1. Remove intake manifold and carburetor as an assembly.
2. Disconnect muffler inlet pipe at exhaust manifold.
3. Loosen air conditioner compressor belt if so equipped.
4. Loosen alternator retaining bolts and remove bolt retaining alternator bracket to right head.
5. If air conditioned, isolate compressor at service valves and hoses from compressor. Remove nuts retaining compressor bracket to water pump. Remove bolts retaining compressor to upper mounting bracket and lay compressor out of way. Remove compressor upper bracket from head.
6. If not air conditioned, remove bolts retaining power steering reservoir bracket to left head and position reservoir out of way.

7. Remove rocker arm covers and rocker arms. Remove push rods in sequence so they can be installed in their positions.
8. Remove head retaining bolts and lift head with exhaust manifold.

NOTE: If necessary to break gasket seal, pry at forward corners of cylinder heads against casting bosses provided on cylinder block. Avoid damaging machined surfaces on head and gasket.

9. Install cylinder heads in reverse order of removal and torque bolts in sequence shown in Fig. 4. When installing intake manifold refer to Fig. 8 for bolt tightening sequence.

VALVE ARRANGEMENT

Front to Rear

Right . . . . I-E-I-E-I-E-I-E
Left . . . . E-I-E-I-E-I-E-I

VALVE LIFT SPECS.

Engine	Year	Intake	Exhaust
8-302	1977-79	.382	.398
8-351	1974-75[1]	.418	.448
	1974[2]	.407	.407
	1975-78[3]	.406	.406
	1978-79[1]	.419	.419
8-400	1974-77	.427	.433
	1978	.428	.432
8-460	1974	.437	.480
	1975-78	.437	.481

[1]—Windsor engine.
[2]—Cleveland engine.
[3]—Modified engine.

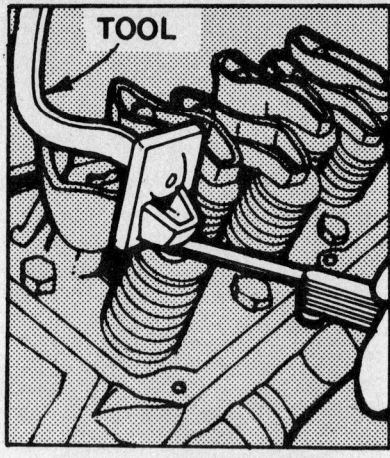

Fig. 12   Checking valve clearance on models with hydraulic lifters

9. Before checking valve lash, check condition of nut, Fig. 10. Torque stud nut to 18-22 ft. lbs.

Late 1978 and 1979 engines use a bolt and fulcrum attachment, Fig. 11. If clearance between valve stem and rocker arm, with lifter collapsed, as in Fig. 12, is not shown in *Valve Specifications* table a .060″ shorter or a .060″ longer push rod is available to compensate for dimensional changes in valve train. If clearance is less than specified, install an undersized push rod. If clearance is greater install an oversize push rod.

V8-351C, 351M, 400 & 460

For these engines a .060″ shorter push rod (color coded white) or a .060″ longer

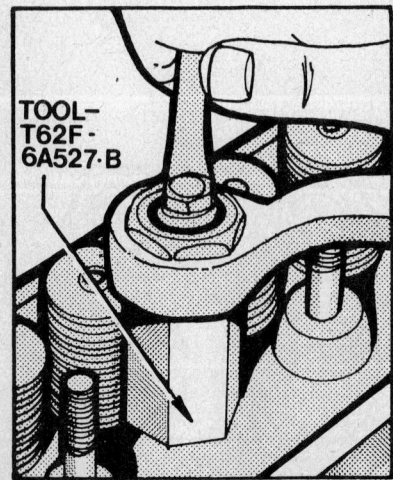

TOOL-T62F-6A527-B

Fig. 13   Rocker arm stud removal. 1974-77 & early 1978 V8-302, 351W

VALVE TIMING

Intake Opens Before TDC

Engine	Year	Degrees
8-302	1977	16
8-351	1974[1]	15
	1974[2]	19½
	1975-78[3]	19½
	1978[1]	23
8-400	1974-78	17
8-460	1974-78	8

[1]—Windsor engine.
[2]—Cleveland engine.
[3]—Modified engine.

VALVES, ADJUST

V8-302, 351W

1974-77 and early 1978 engines use a positive stop rocker arm stud and nut, Fig.

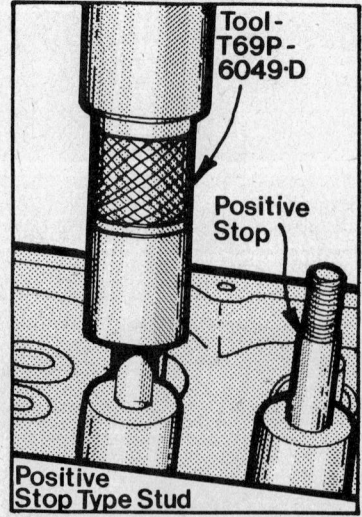

Tool-T69P-6049-D

Positive Stop

Positive Stop Type Stud

Fig. 14   Positive stop type rocker arm stud installation. 1974-77 & early 1978 V8-302, 351W

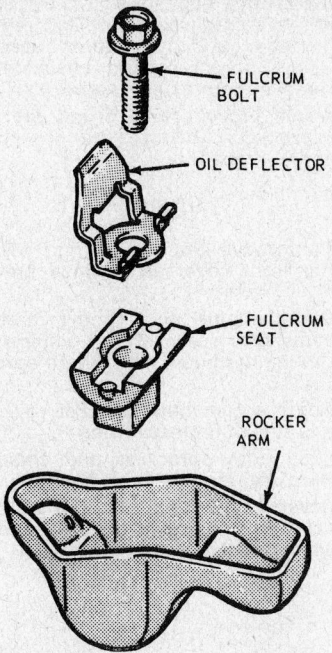

Fig. 15 Rocker arm and related parts. V8-351C, 351M, 400, 460

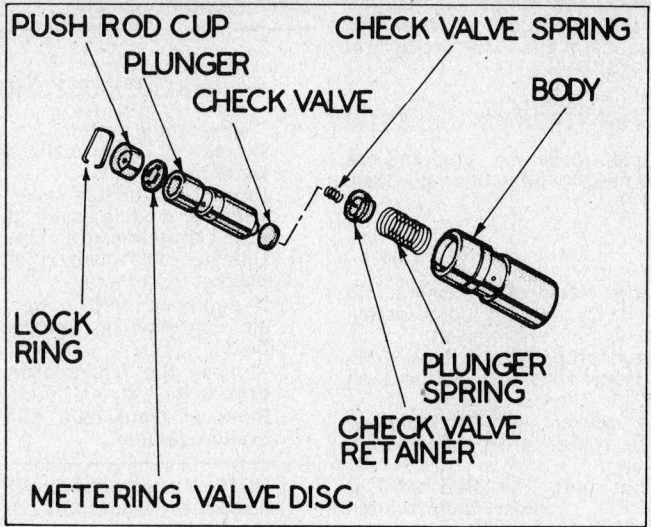

Fig. 16 Hydraulic valve lifter disassembled (typical)

push rod (color coded yellow) are available for service to provide a means of compensating for dimensional changes in the valve mechanism.

To check the clearance, bring the piston of the cylinder being checked on top dead center of the compression stroke. Then with hydraulic lifter collapsed, Fig. 9 check the clearance between valve stem and rocker arm. If the clearance is less than the minimum listed in the *Valve Specifications* table, the .060" shorter push rod should be used. If the clearance is more than the maximum specified, the .060" longer push rod should be used.

VALVE GUIDES

Valve guides in these engines are an integral part of the head and, therefore, cannot be removed. For service, guides can be reamed oversize to accommodate one of three service valves with oversize stems (.003", .015" and .030").

Check the valve stem clearance of each valve (after cleaning) in its respective valve guide. If the clearance exceeds the service limits of .0055", ream the valve guides to accommodate the next oversize diameter valve.

ROCKER ARM & STUD

1974-77 & Early 1978 V8-302 & 351W

If necessary to replace a rocker arm stud, a kit is available which contains a

stud remover, Fig. 13, a stud installer, Fig. 14, and two reamers, one .006" and the other .015". For .010" oversize studs, use reamer No. T66P-6A527-B.

Rocker arm studs that are broken or have damaged threads may be replaced with standard studs. Loose studs in the head may be replaced with .006", .010" or .015" oversize studs which are available for service.

When going from a standard size stud to a .010 or .015" oversize stud, always use a .006" reamer before finish reaming with a .010 or .015" reamer.

If a stud is broken off flush with the stud boss, use an easy-out to remove the broken stud, following the instructions of the tool manufacturer.

ROCKER ARMS

Late 1978 & 1979 V8-302, 351W

These engines use a bolt and fulcrum at-

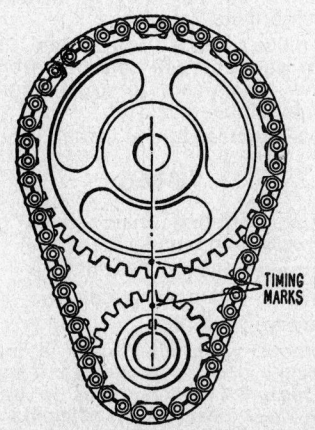

Fig. 17 Timing marks aligned for correct valve timing. V8s

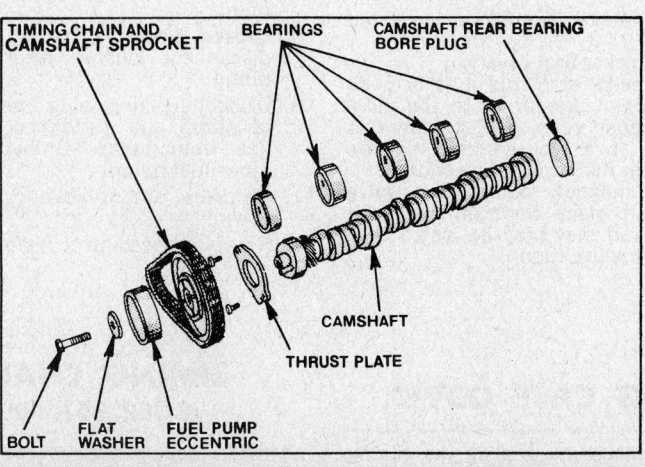

Fig. 18 Camshaft and related parts. All V8

tachment, Fig. 11. To remove, remove attaching bolt, then the fulcrum, rocker arm and fulcrum guide, if the other rocker arm is being removed.

1974-77 & Early 1978 V8-302, 351W

A positive stop rocker arm stud and nut eliminates the need for adjusting valve lash, Fig. 9.

Installation

1. Position the piston of the cylinder to be worked on at TDC compression stroke.
2. Locate stud properly with tool T69P-6049D. Make sure tool bottoms on the head.
3. Lubricate rocker arm components and place rocker arm and fulcrum on the stud.
4. Thread nut onto the stud until it contacts the shoulder then tighten nut to 18-22 ft-lbs.

V8-351C, 351M, 400, 460

The rocker arm is supported by a fulcrum bolt which fits through the fulcrum seat and threads into the cylinder head. To disassemble, remove the bolt, oil deflector, fulcrum seat and rocker arm, Fig. 15.

HYDRAULIC VALVE LIFTERS

The internal parts of each hydraulic valve lifter assembly are a matched set. If these are mixed, improper valve operation may result. Therefore, disassemble, inspect and test each assembly separately to prevent mixing the parts.

Fig. 16 illustrates the type of hydraulic lifter used. See the *Trouble Shooting Chapter* under the heading *Engine Noises* for causes of hydraulic valve lifter noise.

Hydraulic Lifters, Replace V8-302, 351, 400, 460

1. Remove intake manifold and related parts.
2. Remove rocker arm covers.
3. Loosen rocker arm stud nuts or bolts and rotate rocker arms to the side.
4. Lift out push rods, keeping them in sequence in a rack so they may be installed in their original location.
5. Using a magnet rod, remove valve lifters and place them in sequence in a rack so they may be installed in their original location.

TIMING CASE COVER

NOTE: To replace the seal in the timing gear cover, it is necessary to remove the cover as outlined below.

V8-302, 351, 400

1. Drain cooling system and oil pan.
2. Disconnect lower radiator hose from water pump.
3. Disconnect heater hose from water pump and slide water pump bypass hose clamp toward pump.
4. Unfasten and position alternator and bracket out of way.
5. If equipped with power steering or air conditioning, remove the drive belts.
6. Remove the fan, spacer, pulley and drive belt.
7. Remove crankshaft pulley and vibration damper.

NOTE: If equipped with EEC II system, disconnect crankshaft position sensor electrical connector.

8. Disconnect fuel pump outlet line from pump and remove pump retaining bolts and lay pump to one side with flex line attached.
9. Remove oil dipstick and the oil pan to front cover attaching bolts.
10. Unfasten and remove the front cover and water pump as an assembly.
11. Reverse procedure to install.

V8-460

1. Drain cooling system and crankcase.
2. Remove bolts attaching fan to water pump and remove screws attaching radiator shroud to radiator.
3. Remove fan assembly and radiator shroud.
4. Disconnect radiator hoses at engine and cooler lines at radiator and remove radiator upper support and radiator assembly.
5. Loosen alternator and air pump, then remove drive belt with water pump pulley.
6. If air conditioned, loosen idler pulley and remove compressor support.
7. Remove vibration damper from crankshaft.
8. Disconnect power steering lines at pump and unfasten and remove the pump.
9. Loosen bypass hose at pump and disconnect heater return tube at pump.
10. Disconnect and plug fuel inlet line at pump and disconnect fuel outlet line from pump. Unfasten and remove fuel pump.
11. Unfasten and remove cylinder front cover.
12. Reverse procedure to install.

TIMING CHAIN
V8-302, 351, 400

After removing the cover as outlined above, crank the engine until the timing marks are aligned as shown in Fig. 16. Remove crankshaft sprocket retaining bolt, washer and fuel pump eccentric. Slide both sprockets and chain forward and remove them as an assembly.

Reverse procedure to install the chain and sprockets, being sure the timing marks are aligned.

V8-460

1. To remove the chain, first take off the front cover as outlined previously.
2. Crank engine until timing marks on camshaft sprocket is adjacent to timing mark on crankshaft sprocket, Fig. 16.
3. Remove camshaft sprocket cap screw and fuel pump eccentric.
4. Slide both sprockets and chain forward and remove as an assembly.
5. Reverse procedure to install the chain, being sure to align the timing marks as shown.

CAMSHAFT, REPLACE
V8-302, 351, 400

NOTE: It may be necessary to remove or reposition radiator, A/C compressor and grille components to provide adequate clearance.

1. To remove camshaft, remove cylinder front cover and timing chain.
2. Remove distributor cap and spark plug wires, then remove distributor.
3. Disconnect automatic transmission oil cooler lines from radiator and remove radiator.
4. Remove intake manifold and carburetor as an assembly.
5. Remove rocker arm covers.
6. Loosen rocker arm stud nuts or bolts and rotate rocker arms to one side.
7. Remove push rods, keeping them in sequence in a rack so they may be installed in their original location.
8. Using a magnet, remove valve lifters and place them in a rack in sequence so they may be installed in their original location.
9. Remove camshaft thrust plate, Fig. 17 and carefully pull camshaft from engine, using care to avoid damaging camshaft bearings.
10. Reverse procedure to install.

V8-460

1. Remove timing chain cover, chain, sprockets and intake manifold.
2. Remove grille and distributor.
3. Remove rocker arm assembly.
4. Remove push rods.
5. Remove valve lifters with a magnet through push rod openings. *It may be necessary in some cases to transfer the lifter over to an adjoining push rod opening in order to remove it.*
6. Slide camshaft out of engine, Fig. 18.

CAMSHAFT BEARINGS

When necessary to replace camshaft bearings, the engine will have to be removed from the vehicle and the plug at the rear of the cylinder block will have to be removed in order to utilize the special camshaft bearing removing and installing tools required to do this job. It properly installed, camshaft bearings require no reaming—nor should this type bearing be reamed or altered in any manner in an attempt to fit bearings.

PISTON & ROD, ASSEMBLE

All V8's

Assemble the pistons to the rods as shown in Fig. 19.

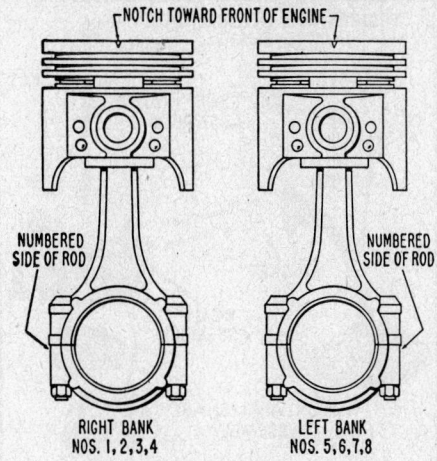

NOTCH TOWARD FRONT OF ENGINE

NUMBERED SIDE OF ROD

NUMBERED SIDE OF ROD

RIGHT BANK NOS. 1, 2, 3, 4

LEFT BANK NOS. 5, 6, 7, 8

Fig. 19   Piston and rod assembly. All V8 engines

PISTONS, PINS & RINGS

SERVICE BULLETIN

Piston and Pin Replacement: When servicing engines using press fit piston pins, the piston and pin must be replaced as an assembly if either does not meet specifications. These components are not serviced separately for the principle reason that excess clearances are usually caused by piston wear rather than pin wear. Elimination of excessive clearance by using oversize pins may result in fracture of the connecting rod.

Pistons and rings are available in standard sizes and oversizes of .003, .020, .030 and .040 inch.

Oversizes piston pins of .001 and .002" are available.

MAIN & ROD BEARINGS

Main and rod bearings are available in standard sizes and the following under-sizes:

V8-302, 351, 400, 429, 460: .001, .002, .010, .020, .030, .040".

CRANKSHAFT OIL SEAL

V8-302, 351, 400, 460

A rubber split-lip rear crankshaft oil seal is available for service. This seal can be installed without removal of the crankshaft and also eliminates the necessity of seal installation tools.

1. Remove oil pan.
2. Remove rear main bearing cap.
3. Loosen remaining bearing caps, allowing crankshaft to drop down about 1/32".
4. Remove old seals from both cylinder block and rear main bearing cap. Use a brass rod to drift upper half of seal from cylinder block groove. Rotate crankshaft while drifting to facilitate removal.
5. Carefully clean seal groove in block with a brush and solvent. Also clean seal groove in bearing cap. Remove the oil seal retaining pin from the bearing cap if so equipped. *The pin is not used with the split-lip seal.*
6. Dip seal halves in clean engine oil.
7. Carefully install upper seal half in its groove with undercut side of seal toward front of engine, Fig. 20, by rotating it on shaft journal of crankshaft until approximately 3/8" protrudes below the parting surface. *Be sure no rubber has been shaved from outside diameter of seal by bottom edge of groove.*
8. Retighten main bearing caps and torque to specifications.
9. Install lower seal in main bearing cap with undercut side of seal toward front of engine, and allow seal to protrude about 3/8" above parting surface to mate with upper seal upon cap installation.
10. Apply suitable sealer to parting faces of cap and block. Install cap and torque to specifications.

NOTE: If difficulty is encountered in installing the upper half of the seal in position, lightly lap (sandpaper) the side of the seal opposite the lip side using a medium grit paper. After sanding, the seal must be washed in solvent, then dipped in clean engine oil prior to installation.

SERVICE BULLETIN

A revised crankshaft rear oil seal has been released for service. This new seal may be received when ordering an oil pan gasket kit and is installed in the same manner as described previously, Fig. 21.

OIL PAN, REPLACE

1979 V8-302 & 351W

1. Disconnect battery ground cable and remove air cleaner assembly.
2. Disconnect accelerator cable and kickdown rod from carburetor.

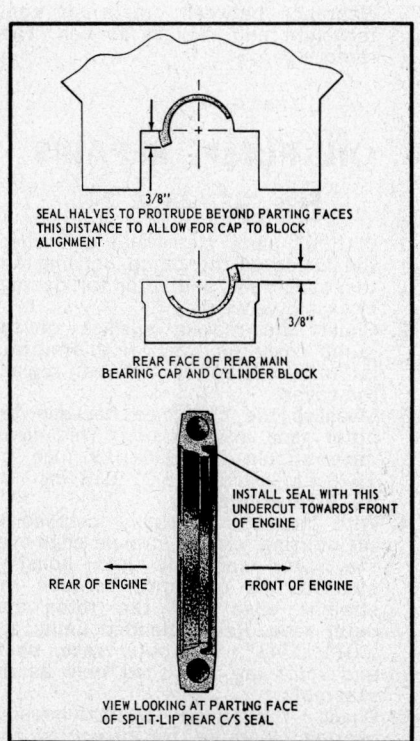

SEAL HALVES TO PROTRUDE BEYOND PARTING FACES THIS DISTANCE TO ALLOW FOR CAP TO BLOCK ALIGNMENT

3/8"

3/8"

REAR FACE OF REAR MAIN BEARING CAP AND CYLINDER BLOCK

INSTALL SEAL WITH THIS UNDERCUT TOWARDS FRONT OF ENGINE

REAR OF ENGINE

FRONT OF ENGINE

VIEW LOOKING AT PARTING FACE OF SPLIT-LIP REAR C/S SEAL

Fig. 20   Split-lip rear crankshaft seal installation on V8-302, 351, 400, 460

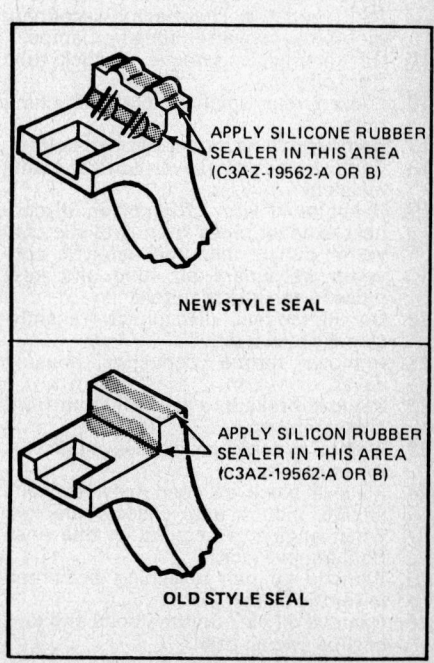

APPLY SILICONE RUBBER SEALER IN THIS AREA (C3AZ-19562-A OR B)

NEW STYLE SEAL

APPLY SILICON RUBBER SEALER IN THIS AREA (C3AZ-19562-A OR B)

OLD STYLE SEAL

Fig. 21   Crankshaft rear oil seals

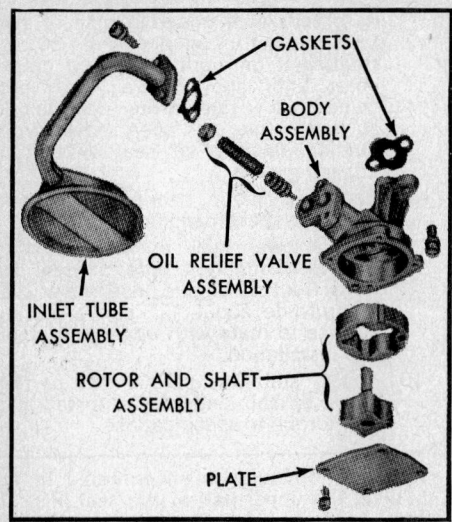

Fig. 22   Oil pump. V8-302, 351W

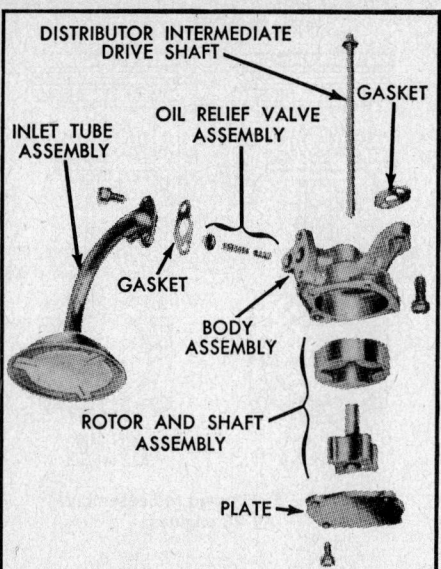

Fig. 23   Oil pump. V8-460

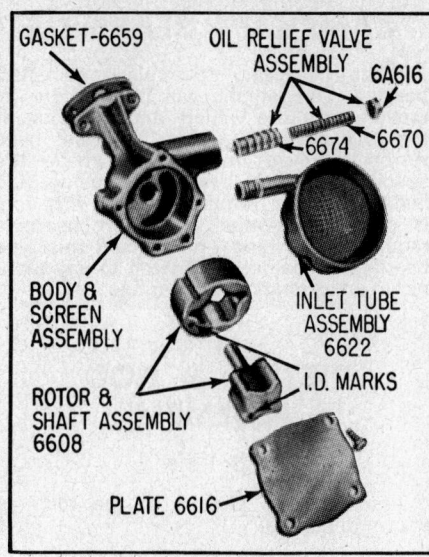

Fig. 24   Oil pump assembly. V8-351C, 351M and 400

3. Remove accelerator mounting bracket bolts and bracket.
4. Remove fan shroud attaching screws and position shroud over fan.
5. Disconnect wiper motor electrical connector and remove wiper motor.
6. Disconnect windshield washer hose.
7. Remove wiper motor mounting cover.
8. Remove oil level dipstick, then the dipstick tube retaining bolt from exhaust manifold.
9. If equipped with EGR cooler, remove Thermactor air dump tube retaining clamp, then the Thermactor crossover tube at rear of engine.
10. On all models, raise and support vehicle.
11. Drain oil pan.
12. Disconnect fuel tank fuel line at fuel pump and plug line.
13. Disconnect exhaust pipes from manifolds.
14. If equipped with EGR cooler, remove exhaust gas sensor from exhaust manifold, then the Thermactor secondary air tube to converter housing clamps.
15. On all models, remove dipstick tube from oil pan.
16. Loosen rear engine mount attaching nuts.
17. Remove engine mount through bolts.
18. Remove shift crossover bolts at transmission.
19. If equipped with EGR cooler, disconnect exhaust pipes from catalytic converter outlet, then the catalytic converter secondary air tube and inlet pipes to exhaust manifold.
20. On all models, disconnect transmission kickdown rod.
21. Remove torque converter housing cover.
22. Remove brake line retainer from front crossmember.
23. With a suitable jack, raise engine as far as possible.
24. Place a block of wood between each engine mount and chassis bracket. When engine is secured in this position, remove jack.
25. Remove oil pan attaching bolts and lower the oil pan.
26. Remove oil pick-up tube bolts and lower tube into oil pan.
27. Remove oil pan from vehicle.
28. Reverse procedure to install.

1974-78 V8-302, 351, 400

1. Drain oil pan and remove dip stick.
2. Remove fan shroud bolts and place shroud over fan.
3. On V8-351C, 351M, 400 engines, remove starter.
4. On all engines, remove engine front mount to chassis bolts, raise engine and install wood blocks between mounts and chassis, then lower engine onto the wood blocks.
5. On V8-302, 351W engines, disconnect stabilizer bar from lower control arms and position stabilizer bar and control arms to permit oil pan removal. Also, on all models with automatic transmission, position oil cooler lines aside for pan removal.
6. Remove oil pan bolts and oil pan.

Installation

1. Coat all gasket surfaces with a suitable sealer and install gaskets on engine.
2. On V8-351C, 351M, 400 engines, install pan seal on cylinder front cover and pan rear seal on rear main bearing cap.
3. On all engines, install oil pan.
4. On V8-302, 351W engines, connect stabilizer bar to lower control arms and torque bolts to 6-12 ft. lbs.
5. On all engines, raise engine, remove wood blocks, lower engine and install front mount to chassis bolts.
6. Install starter, if removed, fan shroud and dip stick.

V8-460

1. Drain oil pan, then remove starter.
2. Disconnect sway bar and pull forward on struts.
3. Remove fan shroud bolts, place shroud on fan and remove oil filter.

NOTE: *To allow clearance for removal of oil pan, remove the front engine mount nuts. Then position floor jack under front leading edge of oil pan (use wood block between pan and jack). Raise engine about 1¼" and insert a 1" block of wood between insulators and frame crossmember. Then remove floor jack.*

4. Remove oil pan screws and lower pan to crossmember.
5. Crank engine to obtain necessary clearance between crankshaft counterweight and rear of oil pan. Then remove pan.

OIL PUMP, REPAIRS

Figs. 22, 23 & 24

1. With all parts clean and dry, check the inside of the pump housing and the outer race and rotor for damage or excessive wear.
2. Check the mating surface of the pump cover for wear. If this surface is worn, scored or grooved, replace the cover.
3. Measure the clearance between the outer race and housing. This clearance should be .006-.013 inch on 1973 engines and .001-.013 inch on 1974-78 engines.
4. With the rotor assembly installed in the housing, place a straight edge over the rotor assembly and housing. Measure the clearance between the straight edge and the rotor and outer race. Recommended limits are .0011-.0041". *The outer race, shaft and rotor are furnished only as an assembly.*
5. Check the drive shaft-to-housing bearing clearance by measuring the O.D. of the shaft and the I.D. of the housing bearing. The recommended clearance limits are .0015-.0030".

6. Inspect the relief valve spring for a collapsed or worn condition.
7. Check the relief valve piston for scores and free operation in the bore. The specified piston clearance is .0015-.0030".

BELT TENSION DATA

	New Lbs.	Used Lbs.
1974-79 Exc. ¼"	140	110
¼" inch	65	50

WATER PUMP, REPLACE

V8-351C, 351M, 400, 429, 460

1. Drain cooling system, remove fan shroud, fan and all belts.
2. Disconnect alternator bracket and position bracket out of way.
3. Remove power steering pump, A/C compressor and position units out of way.

4. Remove A/C compressor bracket and disconnect hoses from water pump.
5. Remove water pump and remove separator plates from pump.

V8-302, 351W

1. Drain cooling system.
2. Remove power steering drive belt (if equipped). If air conditioned, remove compressor belt.
3. Disconnect radiator lower hose and heater hose at water pump.
4. Remove drive belt, fan, spacer or fan drive clutch and pulley.
5. Unfasten and remove water pump from cylinder front cover.

FUEL PUMP PRESSURE

Year	Engine	Pressure Lbs.
1974-75	V8 exc. 1974-75 460	5-7
1974	V8-460 Calif.	5.7-7.7
1974	V8-460 exc. Calif.	5-7
1976	V8-351, 400	6-8
	V8-460	6.7-8.7
1977	V8-351, 400	6-8
1978	V8-460	5.7-7.7
	V8-302	5.5-6.5
	V8-351W	4-6
	V8-351M, 400	6.5-7.5
	V8-460	7.2-8.2
1979	V8-302, 351W	6-8

FUEL PUMP, REPLACE

1. Remove all gasket material from the pump and block gasket surfaces. Apply sealer to both sides of new gasket.
2. Position gasket on pump flange and hold pump in position against its mounting surface. Make sure rocker arm is riding on camshaft eccentric.
3. Press pump tight against its mounting. Install retaining screws and tighten them alternately.
4. Connect fuel lines. Then operate engine and check for leaks.

NOTE: Before installing the pump, it is good practice to crank the engine so that the nose of the camshaft eccentric is out of the way of the fuel pump rocker arm when the pump is installed. In this way there will be the least amount of tension on the rocker arm, thereby easing the installation of the pump.

Transmission Section

NOTE: 1979 linkage adjustment information is in this section. Repair procedures on both automatic and manual shift transmissions are covered elsewhere in this manual. Procedures for removing automatic transmissions as well as linkage adjustments on 1974-78 models are included in the automatic transmission chapters. See Chapter Index.

1979 AUTO. TRANS. LINKAGE, ADJUST

Linkage adjustment procedures are the same as those described for 1978 models described in the "Automatic Transmissions" section of this manual.

Rear Axle, Propeller Shaft & Brakes

REAR AXLES

Figs. 1 and 3 illustrate the rear axle assemblies used on these cars. When necessary to overhaul either of these units, refer to the *Rear Axle Specifications* table in this chapter.

Integral Carrier Type

The gear set consists of a ring gear and an overhung drive pinion which is supported by two opposed tapered roller bearings, Fig. 1. The differential case is a one-piece design with openings allowing assembly of the internal parts and lubricant flow. The differential pinion shaft is retained with a threaded bolt (lock) assembled to the case.

The roller type wheel bearings have no inner race, and the rollers directly contact the bearing journals of the axle shafts. The axle shafts do not use an inner and outer bearing retainer. Rather, they are held in the axle by means of C-locks, Fig. 2. These C-locks also fit into a machined recess in the differential side gears within the differential case. There is no retainer bolt access hole in the axle shaft flange.

Rear Axle, Replace

1. Raise rear of vehicle and remove wheel and tire assembly.
2. Remove brake drums.
3. Mark drive shaft and pinion flange for reassembly, then disconnect drive shaft at pinion flange and remove drive shaft from transmission extension housing. Install seal replacer tool in extension housing to prevent leakage.
4. Disconnect vent hose from rear vent tube, then all the hydraulic brake lines from axle housing retaining clips and wheel cylinders.
5. Disconnect parking brake cable.
6. Position safety stands under rear frame members, then lower axle far enough to relieve spring tension.
7. Disconnect shock absorbers at lower mounting brackets.
8. Disconnect track bar from axle housing stud.
9. Remove nuts, washers and pivot bolts connecting lower suspension arms to axle housing, then disconnect both arms from housing.
10. Remove nuts, bolts, washers and two eccentric washers, then disconnect upper suspension arm from axle housing.
11. Lower rear axle and remove from vehicle.

Axle Shaft, Bearing & Seal

1. Raise car on hoist and remove wheels.
2. Drain differential lubricant.
3. Remove brake drums.
4. Remove differential housing cover.
5. Position safety stands under rear frame member and lower hoist to allow axle to lower as far as possible.
6. Working through differential case opening, remove pinion shaft lock bolt and pinion shaft.
7. Push axle shaft(s) inward toward center of axle housing and remove C-lock(s) from housing, Fig. 2.
8. Remove axle shaft, using extreme care to avoid contact of shaft seal lip with any portion of axle shaft except seal journal.
9. Use a hook-type puller to remove seal and bearing, Fig. 7.

NOTE: On 1975-79 models, two types of bearings are used, one requires a snug press fit in the axle housing flanges and the other has a ground race and a loose fit is acceptable, Fig. 7A. Therefore, when removing bearings, if a loose fit is encountered it does not indicate excessive wear or damage.

10. Reverse procedure to install, using suitable driving tools, Fig. 8, to install seal and bearing. New seals are pre-packed with lubricant and do not require oil soaking before installation.

Removable Carrier Type

In these axles, Fig. 3, the drive pinion is straddle-mounted by two opposed tapered roller bearings which support

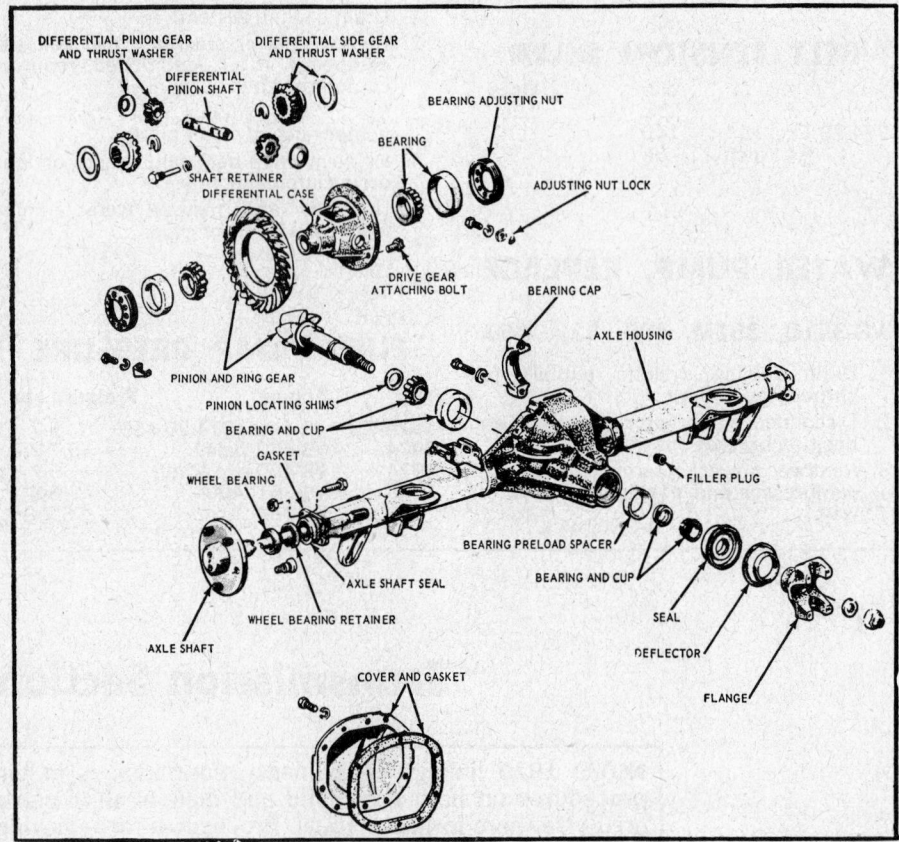

Fig. 1   Integral type rear axle assembly (typical)

Fig. 2   Axle shaft C-locks. 1974-79 Ford integral type axle

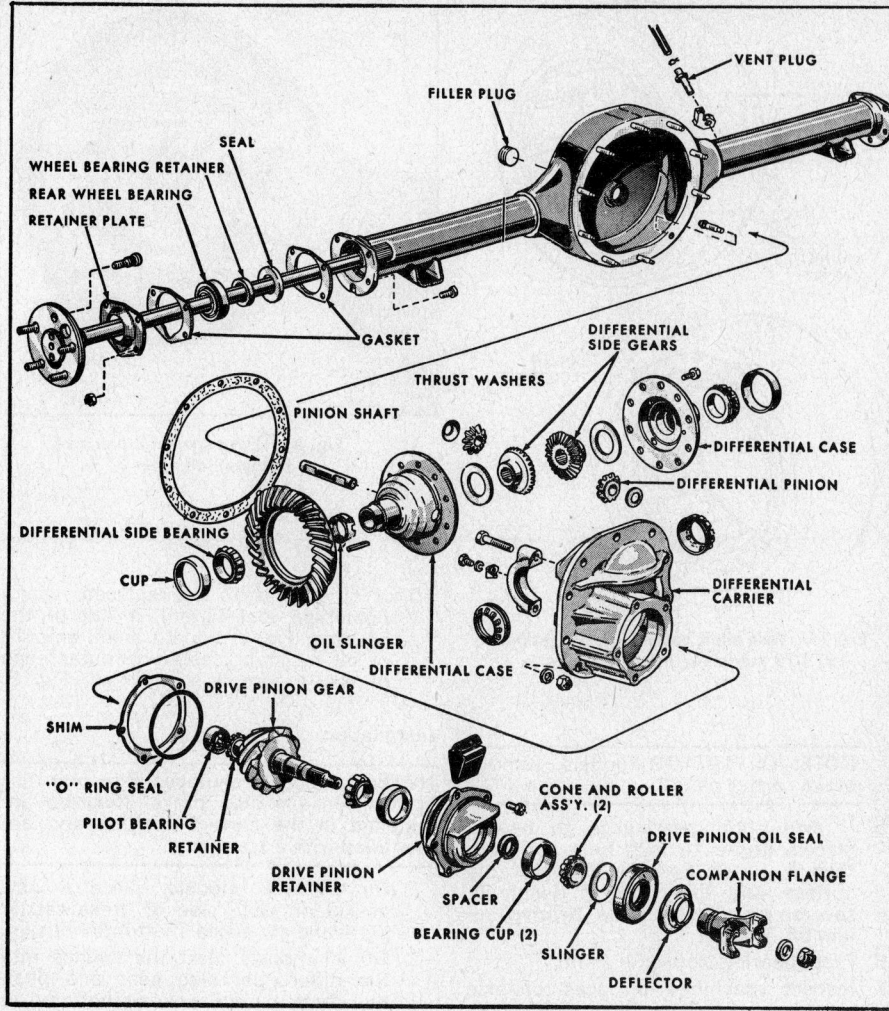

Fig. 3   Removable carrier type of rear axle assembly (typical)

Fig. 4   Removing nuts from rear bearing retainer

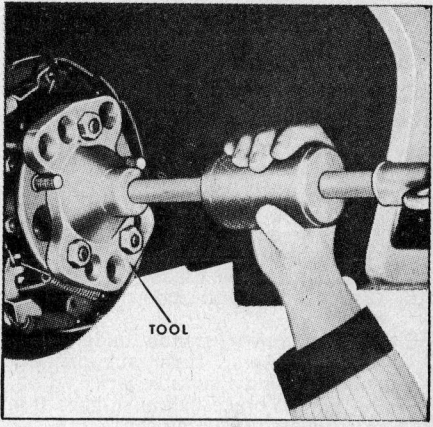

Fig. 5   Removing axle shaft with slide hammer-type puller

the pinion shaft in front of the drive pinion gear, and straight roller bearing that supports the pinion shaft at the rear of the pinion gear. The drive pinion is assembled in a pinion retainer that is bolted to the differential carrier. The tapered roller bearings are preloaded by a collapsible spacer between the bearings. The pinion is positioned by a shim or shims located between the drive pinion retainer and the differential carrier.

The differential is supported in the carrier by two tapered roller side bearings. These bearings are preloaded by two threaded ring nuts or sleeves between the bearings and pedestals. The differential assembly is positioned for proper ring gear and pinion backlash by varying the adjustment of these ring nuts. The differential case houses two side gears in mesh with two pinions mounted on a pinion shaft which is held in place by a pin. The side gears and pinions are backed by thrust washers. With high performance engines, an optional rear axle having a four-pinion differential is also used.

The axle shafts are of unequal length, the left shaft being shorter than the right.

The axle shafts are mounted on sealed ball bearings or tapered roller bearings which are pressed on the shafts.

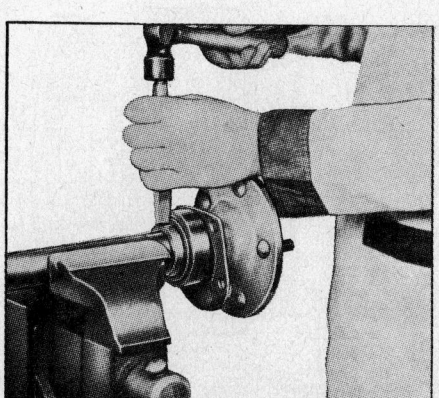

Fig. 6   Splitting bearing inner retainer for bearing removal

Service Bulletin

All Ford Built Rear Axles: Recent manufacturing changes have eliminated the need for marking rear axle drive pinions for individual variations from nominal shim thicknesses. In the past, these pinion markings, with the aid of a shim selection table, were used as a guide to select correct shim thicknesses when a gear set or carrier assembly replacement was performed.

With the elimination of pinion markings, use of the shim selection table is no longer possible and the methods outlined below must be used.

1. Measure the thickness of the original pinion depth shim removed from the axle. Use the same thickness upon installation of the replacement carrier or drive pinion. If any further shim change is necessary, it will be indicated in the tooth pattern check.

2. If the original shim is lost, substitute a nominal shim for the original and use the tooth pattern check to determine if further shim changes are required.

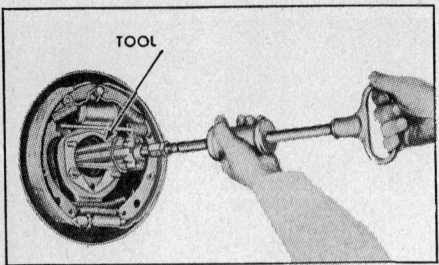

Fig. 7 Using hook-type tool to remove oil seal

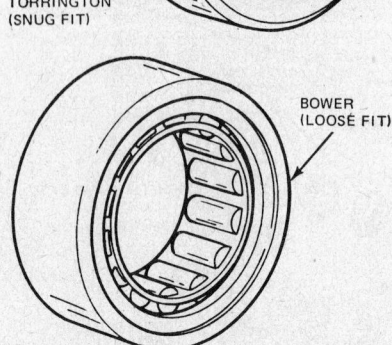

TORRINGTON (SNUG FIT)

BOWER (LOOSE FIT)

Fig. 7A Axle shaft bearing identification. 1975-79 models w/integral type axle

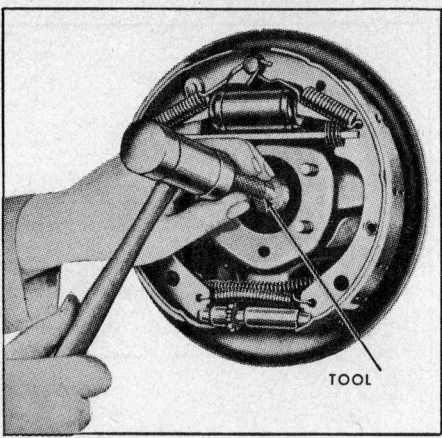

Fig. 8 Using special driver to install oil seal

Rear Axle, Replace

1. Raise rear of vehicle and remove wheel and tire assembly.
2. On models equipped with rear drum brakes, remove brake drums.
3. On models equipped with rear disc brakes, remove calipers from anchor plates, then remove two retaining nuts and slide rotors off axle shafts.

NOTE: Secure calipers to frame with wire.

4. Make marks on drive shaft yoke and pinion flange for reassembly, then disconnect drive shaft at rear axle U-joint and remove drive shaft from transmission extension housing. Install seal replacer tool in extension housing to prevent leakage.
5. Disconnect anti-skid sensor, if equipped.
6. Position safety stands under frame rear members, then support axle housing using a suitable jack.
7. Disconnect brake hydraulic lines from axle housing retaining clips.
8. Disconnect vent tube from rear housing.
9. Disconnect shock absorbers from lower mounting brackets.
10. Disconnect track bar from mounting stud on rear axle housing bracket.

NOTE: The axle housing mounting bracket has two holes, the track bar should be attached to the lower hole.

11. Lower rear axle housing until coil springs are released, then remove springs and insulators.
12. Disconnect suspension lower arms from axle housing, then disconnect suspension upper arms from housing.
13. Lower axle housing and remove from vehicle.

Axle Shaft, Bearing & Seal

1. Remove wheel assembly.
2. Remove brake drum or caliper.
3. Working through hole provided in axle shaft flange, Fig. 4, remove nuts that secure bearing retainer.
4. Pull axle shaft out of housing. If bearing is a tight fit in axle housing, use a slide hammer-type puller, Fig. 5. *Brake carrier plate must not be dislodged. Install one nut to hold plate in place after axle shaft is removed.*

NOTE: On 1974-78 models, remove brake carrier plate.

5. If axle shaft bearing is to be replaced, drill a $\frac{1}{4}$ inch hole not more than $\frac{5}{16}$ inch deep in retainer ring surface and then nick it deeply in several places and slide bearing retain off, Fig. 6.
6. Press bearing from axle shaft.
7. Inspect machined surfaces of axle shaft and housing for rough spots that would affect the sealing action of the oil seal. Carefully remove any burrs or rough spots.
8. Press new bearing on shaft until it seats firmly against shoulder on shaft.
9. Press inner bearing retainer on shaft until it seats firmly against bearing.

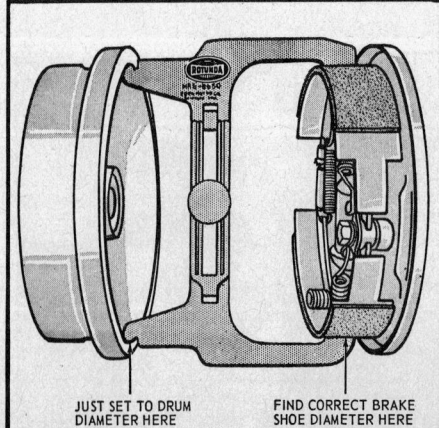

JUST SET TO DRUM DIAMETER HERE

FIND CORRECT BRAKE SHOE DIAMETER HERE

Fig. 9 Brake adjustment gauge

10. If oil seal is to be replaced, use a hook-type tool to pull it out of the housing, Fig. 7. Wipe a small amount of oil resistant sealer on outer edge of seal before it is installed, Fig. 8.

Installation

NOTE: On models equipped with rear disc brakes, ensure disc brake adapters are installed in the correct position and are identified with a stamping.

1. On 1974-78 models, place a new gasket on each side of brake carrier plate and slide axle shaft into housing.
2. On all models start the splines into the differential side gear and push the shaft in until bearing bottoms in housing.
3. Install retainer and tighten nuts to 20-40 ft. lbs.
4. Install brake drum and wheel.

PROPELLER SHAFT

Remove & Replace

1. Disconnect rear U-joint from drive pinion flange.
2. Pull drive shaft toward rear of car until front U-joint yoke clears transmission extension housing and output shaft.
3. Install a suitable tool, such as a seal driver, in seal to prevent lube from leaking from transmission.
4. Before installing, check U-joints for freedom of movement. If a bind has resulted from misalignment after overhauling the U-joints, tap the ears of the drive shaft sharply to relieve the bind.
5. If rubber seal installed on end of transmission extension housing is damaged, install a new seal.
6. Lubricate yoke spline with special spline lubricant. *This spline is sealed so that transmission fluid does not "wash" away spline lubricant.*

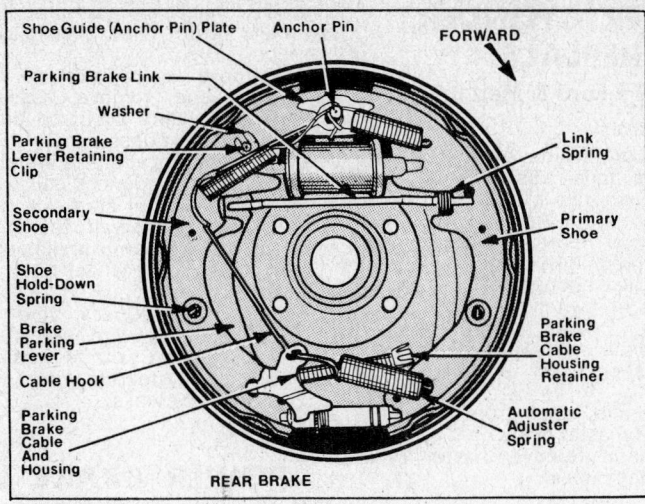

Fig. 10 Rear drum type brakes

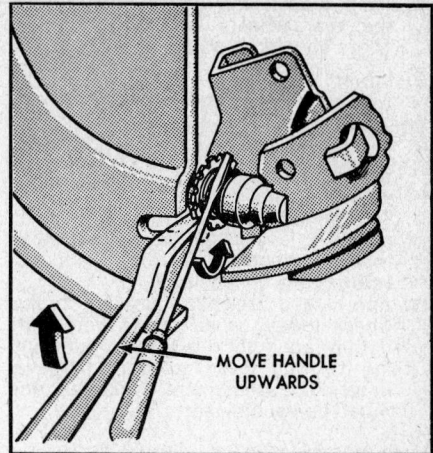

Fig. 11 Backing off brake adjustment by disengaging adjusting lever with screwdriver

7. Install yoke on transmission output shaft.
8. Install U-bolts and nuts which attach U-joint to pinion flange. Tighten U-bolts evenly to prevent binding U-joint bearings.

BRAKE ADJUSTMENTS

1. Use the brake shoe adjustment gauge shown in Fig. 9 to obtain the drum inside diameter as shown. Tighten the adjusting knob on the gauge to hold this setting.
2. Place the opposite side of the gauge over the brake shoes and adjust the shoes by turning the adjuster screw until the gauge just slides over the linings. Rotate the gauge around the lining surface to assure proper lining diameter adjustment and clearance.
3. Install brake drum and wheel. Final adjustment is accomplished by making several firm reverse stops, using the brake pedal.

Self-Adjusting Brakes

These brakes, Fig. 10, have self-adjusting shoe mechanisms that assure correct lining-to-drum clearances at all times. The automatic adjusters operate only when the brakes are applied as the car is moving rearward.

Although the brakes are self-adjusting, an initial adjustment is necessary after the brake shoes have been relined or replaced, or when the length of the star wheel adjuster has been changed during some other service operation.

Frequent usage of an automatic transmission forward range to halt reverse vehicle motion may prevent the automatic adjusters from functioning, thereby inducing low pedal heights. Should low pedal heights be encountered, it is recommended that numerous forward and reverse stops be performed with a firm pedal effort until satisfactory pedal height is obtained.

NOTE

If a low pedal height condition cannot be corrected by making numerous reverse stops (provided the hydraulic system is free of air), it indicates that the self-adjusting mechanism is not functioning. Therefore, it will be necessary to remove the brake drums, clean, free up and lubricate the adjusting mechanism. Then adjust the brakes, being sure the parking brake is fully released.

Initial Adjustment

1. Remove adjusting hole cover from brake backing plate and, from the backing plate side, turn the adjust-

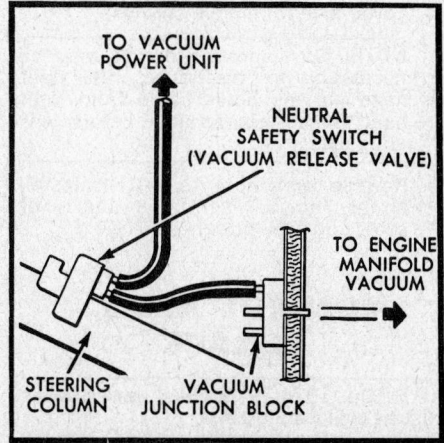

Fig. 12 Connections for automatic parking brake release. Typical

ing screw upward with a screwdriver or other suitable tool to expand the shoes until a slight drag is felt when the drums are rotated.
2. Remove the drum.
3. While holding the adjusting lever out of engagement with the adjusting screw, Fig. 11, back off the adjusting screw about one full turn with the fingers.

NOTE: *If finger movement will not turn the screw, free it up. If this is not done, the adjusting lever will not turn the screw during vehicle operation. Lubricate the screw with oil and coat with wheel bearing grease. Any other adjustment procedure may cause damage to the adjusting screw with consequent self-adjuster problems.*

4. Install wheel and drum, and adjusting hole cover. Adjust brakes on remaining wheels in the same manner.
5. If pedal height is not satisfactory, drive the vehicle and make sufficient reverse stops with a firm pedal effort until proper pedal height is obtained.

PARKING BRAKE, ADJUST

Check parking brake cables when brakes are fully released. If cables are loose, adjust as follows:

Ford & Mercury

1974-79 Rear Drum Brakes

1. Make sure parking brake is released.
2. Place transmission in neutral and raise the vehicle.
3. Tighten the adjusting nut against the cable equalizer to cause rear brakes to drag.

4. Then loosen the adjusting nut until the rear wheels are fully released. There should be no drag.

5. Lower vehicle and check operation.

1975-78 Rear Disc Brakes

1. Fully release parking brake, then place transmission in neutral and support vehicle at rear axle.

2. Tighten adjuster nut until levers on calipers just begin to move, then loosen adjuster nut until levers just return to stop position.

3. Apply and release parking brake. Check levers on caliper to determine if they are fully returned by attempting to pull lever rearward. If lever moves, the adjustment is too tight and must be readjusted.

VACUUM RELEASE PARKING BRAKE

The vacuum power unit will release the parking brakes automatically when the shift lever is moved into any drive position with the engine running. The brakes will not release automatically, however, when the shift lever is in neutral or park position with the engine running, or in any position with the engine off.

The power unit piston rod is attached to the release lever. Since the release lever pivots against the pawl, a slight movement of the release lever will disengage the pawl from the ratchet, allowing the brakes to release. The release lever pivots on a rivet pin in the pedal mount.

As shown in Fig. 12, hoses connect the power unit and the engine manifold to a vacuum release valve in the transmission neutral safety switch. Moving the transmission selector lever into any drive position with the engine running will open the release valve to connect engine manifold vacuum to one side of the actuating piston in the power unit. The pressure differential thus created will cause the piston and link to pull the release lever.

MASTER CYLINDER, REPLACE

1974-79 Ford & Mercury

Less Power Brakes

1. Working from inside of car beneath instrument panel, disconnect master cylinder push rod from brake pedal.

2. Disconnect stop light switch wires at connector. Remove hairpin retainer. Slide stop light switch off brake pedal pin just enough to clear end of pin, then lift switch straight upward from pin.

3. Slide master cylinder push rod, nylon washers and bushings from pedal pin.

4. Remove brake tubes from both outlet ports of master cylinder.

5. Unfasten and remove master cylinder from dash panel.

With Power Brakes

1. Disconnect brake lines from master cylinder.

2. Remove nuts retaining master cylinder to brake booster.

3. Remove master cylinder.

HYDRO-BOOST BRAKE BOOSTER, REPLACE

1975-78 Mercury & 1976-78 Ford

1. Working from inside of car under instrument panel, disconnect booster push rod link from brake pedal. To do this, proceed as follows:

2. Disconnect stop light switch wires at connector. Remove hairpin retainer. Slide switch off brake pedal pin just far enough for switch outer hole to clear pin. Then lift switch straight upward from pin. Slide master cylinder push rod and nylon washers and bushing off brake pedal pin.

3. Open hood and disconnect brake line at master cylinder outlet fitting.

4. Disconnect the pressure, steering gear and return lines, then plug lines and ports.

5. Remove Hydro-Boost to dash panel nuts and remove assembly from panel, sliding push rod link from engine side of dash panel.

6. Reverse procedure to install. To purge system, disconnect coil wire so that engine will not start. Fill power steering pump reservoir, then while engaging starter, pump brake pedal. Do not cycle steering wheel until all residual air has been purged from the hydro boost unit. Check fluid level, then connect coil wire and start engine. Apply brakes with a pumping action and cycle steering wheel, then check system for leaks.

POWER BRAKE UNIT, REPLACE

1974-79 Ford & Mercury

1. Working from inside of car under instrument panel, disconnect booster push rod link from brake pedal. To do this, proceed as follows:

2. Disconnect stop light switch wires at connector. Remove hairpin retainer. Slide switch off brake pedal pin just far enough for switch outer hole to clear pin. Then lift switch straight upward from pin. Slide master cylinder push rod and nylon washers and bushing off brake pedal pin.

3. Open hood and disconnect brake line at master cylinder outlet fitting.

4. Disconnect vacuum hose from booster unit. If equipped with automatic transmission disconnect transmission vacuum unit hose.

5. Remove four attaching nuts and remove booster and bracket from dash panel, slide push rod link out from engine side of dash panel. Remove four spacers.

6. Remove push rod link boot from dash panel.

7. Reverse procedure to install.

Rear Suspension

SHOCK ABSORBER, REPLACE

1. With the rear axle supported properly disconnect shock absorber at upper mounting and compress it to clear hole in spring seat.

2. Disconnect shock absorber from stud on axle bracket.

3. Reverse procedure to install!.

COIL SPRING, REPLACE

1. Raise rear of vehicle and support at frame. Support rear axle with a suitable jack.

2. Disconnect shock absorbers at lower mountings.

3. Disconnect brake line from rear brake hose and remove hose to bracket clip.

4. Lower axle to remove springs.

NOTE: On some models, it may be necessary to disconnect the right hand parking brake cable from right hand upper arm retainer before lowering axle.

5. Reverse procedure to install. Install an insulator between upper and lower seats and the spring.

CONTROL ARMS, REPLACE

NOTE: On 1974-79 models, lower arms must be replaced in pairs.

1. Raise rear of vehicle and support at frame. Support axle with a suitable jack.

2. On 1974-78 models, disconnect track bar from frame mounting bracket.

3. On 1979 models, remove stabilizer bar.

4. Lower axle and install a second jack under differential pinion nose.

5. Disconnect control arm from axle bracket. On upper arms, disconnect arm from crossmember and on lower arms, disconnect arm from frame attachment bracket.

6. Reverse procedure to install.

TRACK BAR, REPLACE

1974-78

1. Remove cover from track bar axle attachment and disconnect track bar from mounting stud, Fig. 1.

2. Disconnect track bar from frame side rail.

3. Reverse procedure to install.

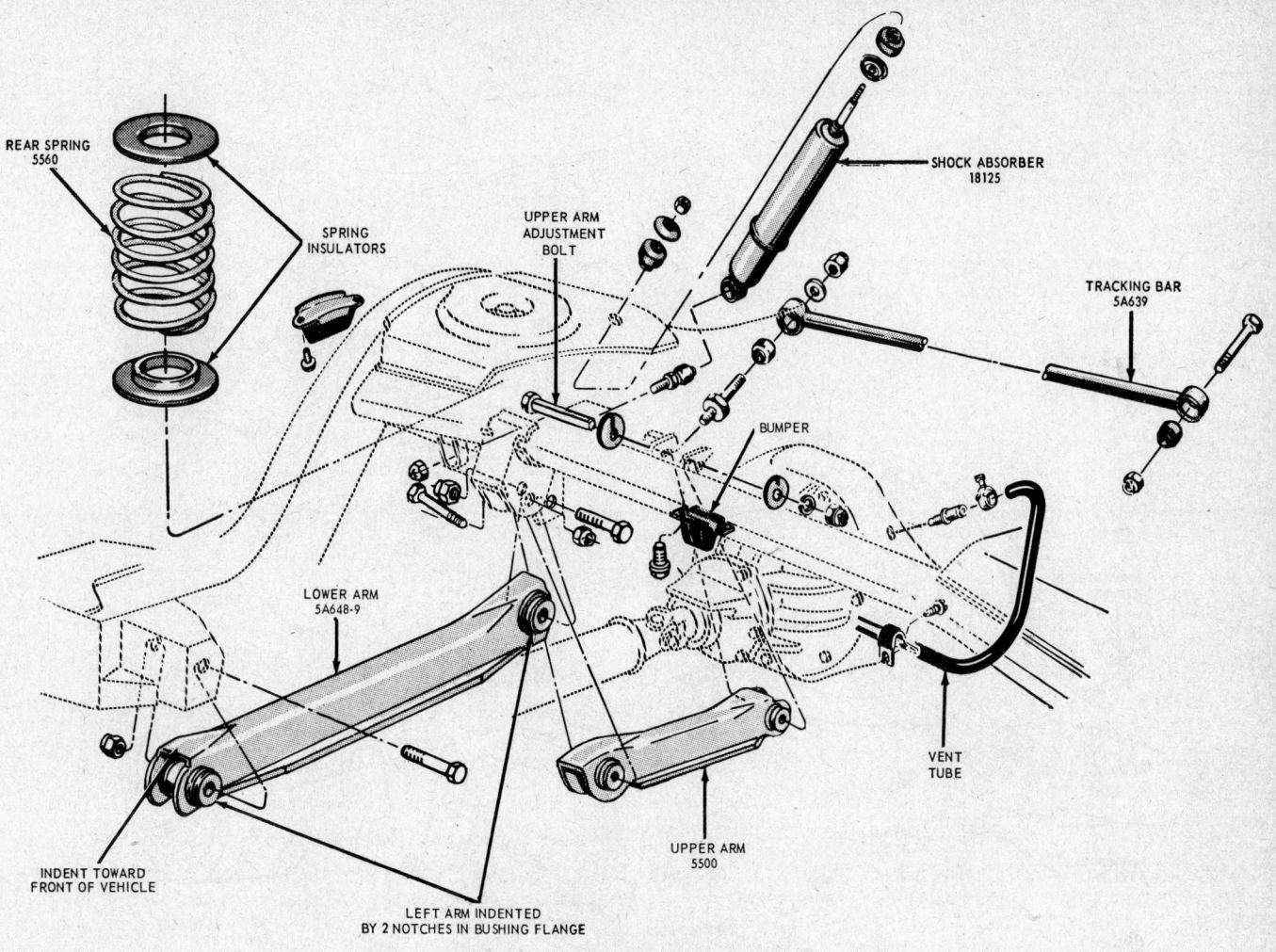

REAR SPRING 5560

SPRING INSULATORS

UPPER ARM ADJUSTMENT BOLT

SHOCK ABSORBER 18125

TRACKING BAR 5A639

BUMPER

LOWER ARM 5A648-9

VENT TUBE

INDENT TOWARD FRONT OF VEHICLE

UPPER ARM 5500

LEFT ARM INDENTED BY 2 NOTCHES IN BUSHING FLANGE

Fig. 1 Rear suspension (typical). 1974-78

STABILIZER BAR, REPLACE
1979

1. Raise and support vehicle at frame side rails.

2. Support rear axle with a suitable jack and position axle so the shock absorbers are fully extended.

3. Remove bolts, nuts and spacers attaching stabilizer bar to lower arms, Fig. 2.
4. Remove stabilizer bar from vehicle.

Continued

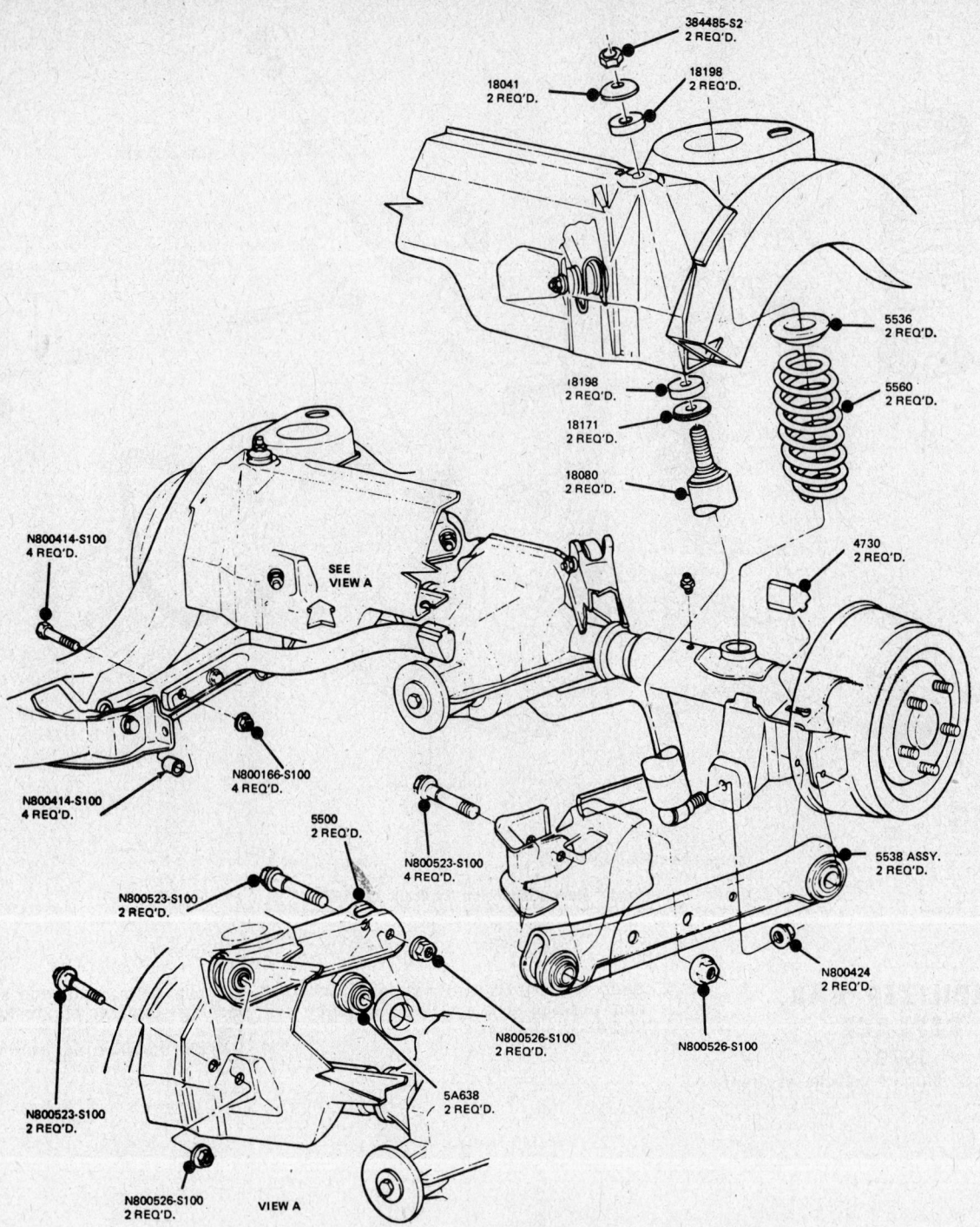

384485-S2
2 REQ'D.

18041
2 REQ'D.

18198
2 REQ'D.

5536
2 REQ'D.

18198
2 REQ'D.

5560
2 REQ'D.

18171
2 REQ'D.

18080
2 REQ'D.

4730
2 REQ'D.

N800414-S100
4 REQ'D.

SEE
VIEW A

N800414-S100
4 REQ'D.

N800166-S100
4 REQ'D.

5538 ASSY.
2 REQ'D.

5500
2 REQ'D.

N800523-S100
4 REQ'D.

N800523-S100
2 REQ'D.

N800526-S100
2 REQ'D.

N800424
2 REQ'D.

N800526-S100

5A638
2 REQ'D.

N800523-S100
2 REQ'D.

N800526-S100
2 REQ'D.

VIEW A

Fig. 2   Rear suspension. 1979

Front End and Steering Section

FRONT SUSPENSION

1979

Referring to Fig. 1, note that the lower control arms pivot on two bolts and bushings attached to the crossmember. Previous models used only one bolt and bushing to attach the lower control arm to the suspension crossmember.

1974-78

Referring to Fig. 2, note that the lower control arm pivots on a bolt in the front crossmember. The struts, which are connected between the lower control arms and frame crossmember, prevent the control arms from moving forward and backward.

LUBRICATION

1974-78

Ball joints are prelubricated with a special lubricant. The lubricating interval is 36,000 miles on 1974-75 models and 30,000 miles on 1976-78 models. At these intervals, remove the plugs, apply the special lubricant, remove the fittings and replace the plugs.

SERVICE BULLETIN

Some uninformed service people recommend that conventional grease fittings be installed and that the car be lubricated every 1000 miles. This is completely unnecessary and, in fact, may cause damage to the special seals used in the lubrication points.

The use of conventional lubricants not only can do damage to the special seals but is incompatible with the special lubricant. Moreover, after the special sealing plugs have been replaced by conventional grease fittings, dirt and water can enter and cause excessive wear, rendering the units unfit for further service.

SERVICE BULLETIN, 1974-78

BALL JOINT LUBE: The ball joint seals on these models have been redesigned to provide improved sealing and longer life. The new seals can be damaged and the sealing characteristics destroyed if excessive lubricant is used. Specifications call for the addition of only 10 grams (level teaspoon) of lubricant to the ball joints at 36,000 mile intervals on 1974-75 models and 30,000 mile intervals on 1976-78 models. The initial application of 10 grams of lubricant insures forcing grease into the bearing area and still allows for three subsequent lubrications of 10 grams each without ballooning the seals and resultant premature failure.

For the above reasons the ball joint

seals on new cars might appear to be collapsed and give the mistaken impression that additional lubricant is required. This is not the case and under no circumstances should more than 10 grams of lubricant be added to the ball joints at the 36,000 mile intervals.

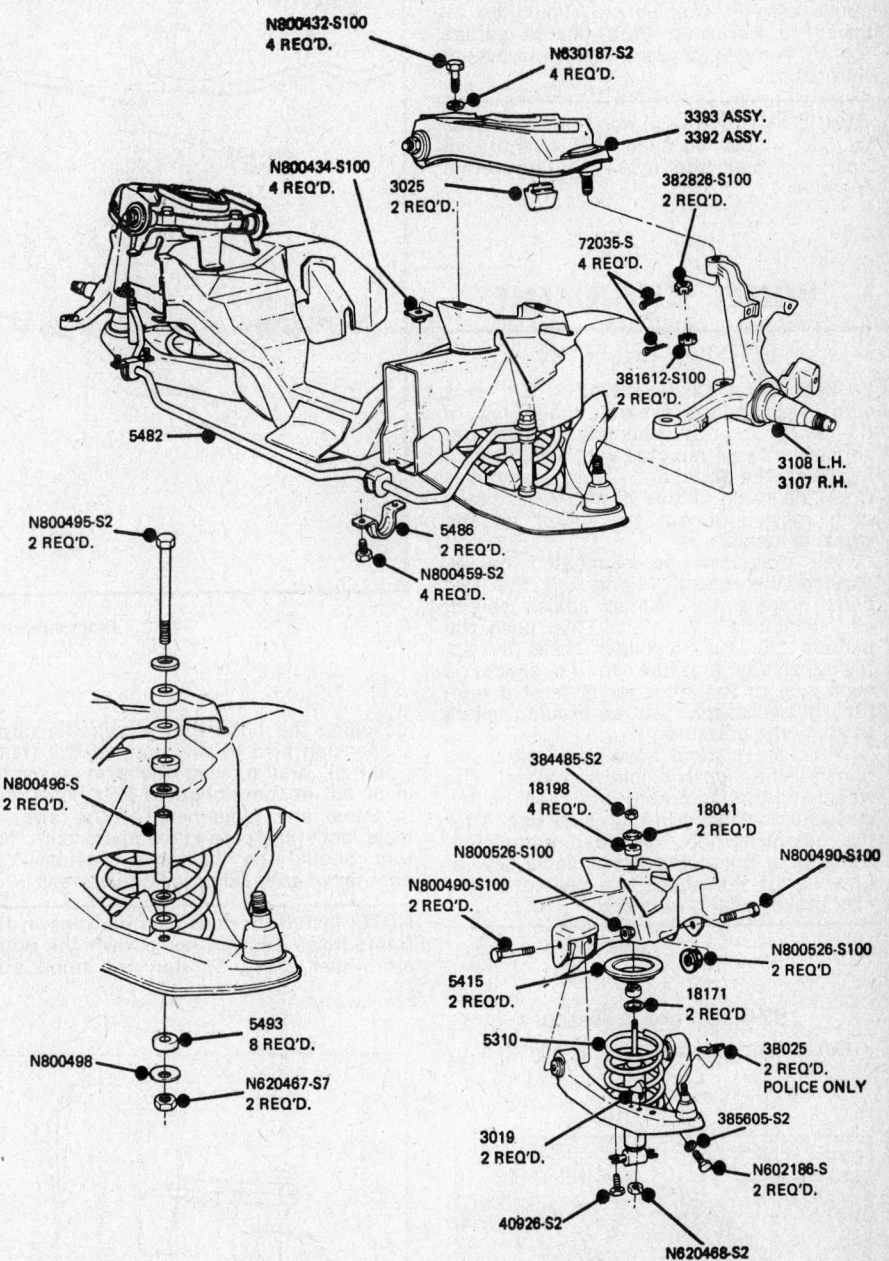

Fig. 1   Front suspension. 1979 Ford & Mercury

SERVICE BULLETIN

1974-78 STEERING LINKAGE LUBE: The steering linkage on these models should be lubricated at intervals of 36,000 miles on 1974-75 models and 30,000 miles on 1976-78 models. Normal breathing of socket joints permits moisture condensation within the joint. Moisture inside the joint assembly will cause no appreciable damage and the joint will function normally. However, if the moisture is concentrated in the bearing grease grooves and is frozen at the time of attempted lubrication, grease cannot flow and pressure greasing may damage the joint.

Do not attempt to lubricate the steering linkage on these vehicles if it has set in temperatures lower than 20 deg. above zero F. The vehicle should be allowed to warm up in a heated garage for 30 minutes or until the joints accept lubrication.

IMPORTANT: A torch must not be used to heat joints because this quantity of heat will melt the nylon bearing within the joint.

WHEEL ALIGNMENT

SERVICE BULLETIN

WHEEL BALANCING DIFFERS: On cars with disc brakes, dynamic balancing of the wheel-and-tire assembly on the car should not be attempted without first pulling back the shoe and lining assemblies from the rotor. If this is not done, brake drag may burn out the motor on the wheel spinner.

The drag can be eliminated by removing the wheel, taking out the two bolts holding the caliper splash shield, and detaching the shield. Then push the pistons into their cylinder bores by applying steady pressure on the shoes on each side of the rotor for at least a minute. If necessary, use waterpump pliers to apply the pressure.

After the pistons have been retracted, reinstall the splash shield and wheel. The wheel-and-tire assembly can then be dynamically balanced in the usual way. After the balancing job has been completed, be sure to pump the brake pedal several times until the shoes are seated and a firm brake pedal is obtained.

1974-79 Ford & Mercury

Caster and camber can be adjusted by

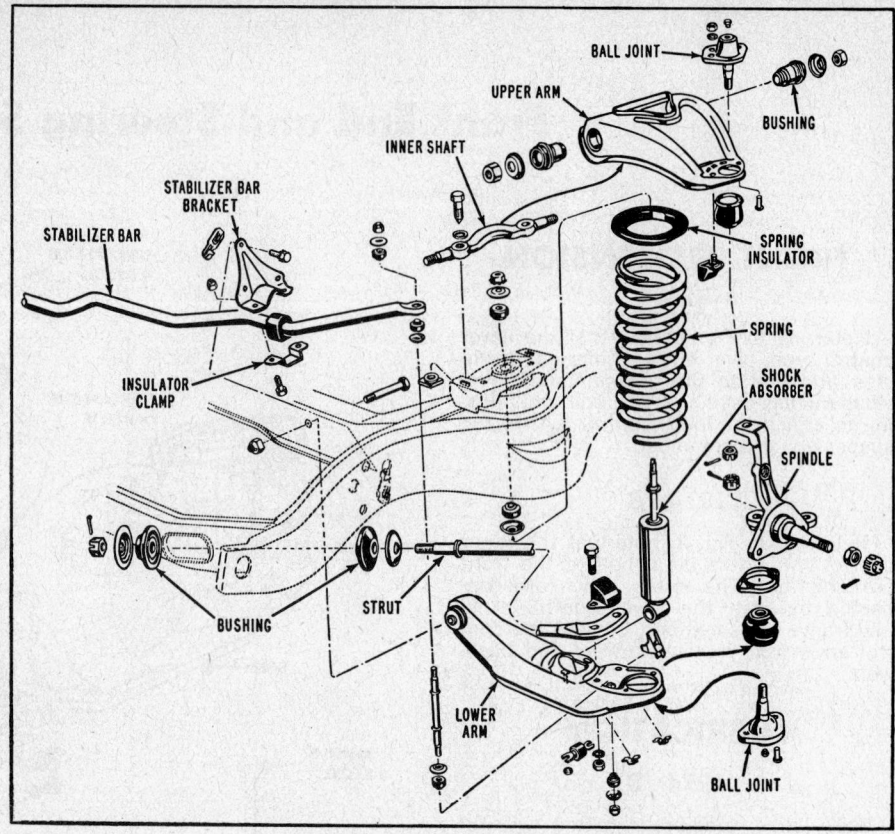

Fig. 2   Front suspension. 1974-78 Ford & Mercury

loosening the bolts that attach the upper suspension arm to the shaft at the frame side rail, and moving the arm assembly in or out in the elongated bolt holes, Fig. 3. Since any movement of the arm affects both caster and camber, both factors should be balanced against one another when making the adjustment.

NOTE: Install the tool with the pins in the frame holes and the hooks over the upper arm inner shaft. Tighten the hook nuts

snug before loosening the upper arm inner shaft attaching bolts.

Caster, Adjust

1. Tighten the tool front hook nut or loosen the rear hook nut as required to increase caster to the desired angle.
2. To decrease caster, tighten the rear hook nut or loosen the front hook nut as required.

NOTE: The caster angle can be

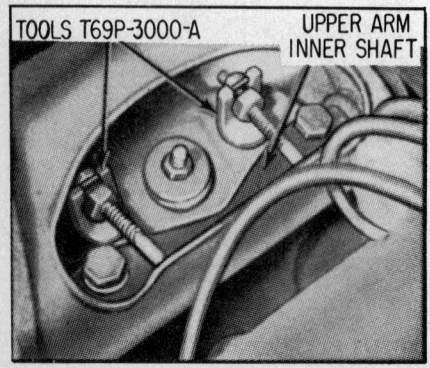

Fig. 3   Adjusting caster and camber. 1974-79 Ford and Mercury

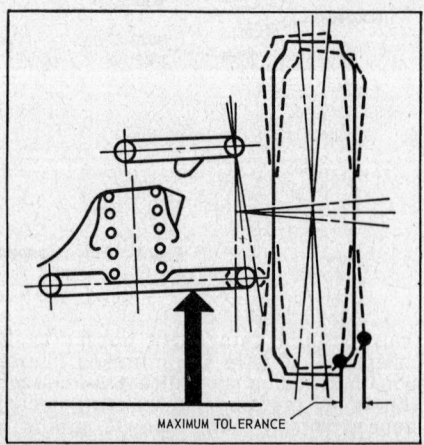

Fig. 4   Measuring lower ball joint radial play, which should not exceed ¼"

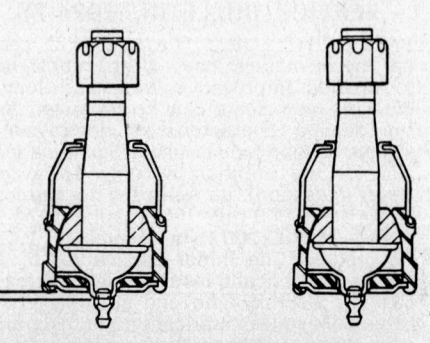

Fig. 5   Lower ball joint wear indicator. 1979 Ford & Mercury

checked without tightening the inner shaft retaining bolts.

3. Check the camber angle to be sure it did not change during the caster adjustment and adjust if necessary.
4. Tighten the upper arm inner shaft retaining bolts and remove tool.

Camber, Adjust

1. Loosen both inner shaft retaining bolts.
2. Tighten or loosen the hook nuts as necessary to increase or decrease camber.
3. Recheck caster and readjust if necessary.

TOE-IN, ADJUST

Position the front wheels in their straight-ahead position. Then turn both tie rod adjusting sleeves an equal amount until the desired toe-in setting is obtained.

WHEEL BEARINGS, ADJUST

1. With wheel rotating, tighten adjusting nut to 17-25 ft. lbs.
2. Back off adjusting nut ½ turn and retighten nut to 10-15 inch lbs.
3. Place nut lock on nut so that castellations on lock are aligned with cotter pin hole in spindle and install cotter pin.
4. Check front wheel rotation, if it rotates noisily or roughly, clean, inspect or replace wheel bearings as necessary.

WHEEL BEARINGS, REPLACE

(Disc Brakes)

1. Raise car and remove front wheels.
2. Remove caliper mounting bolts.

   NOTE: It is not necessary to disconnect the brake lines for this operation.

3. Slide caliper off of disc, inserting a spacer between the shoes to hold them in their bores after the caliper is removed. Position caliper assembly out of the way.

   NOTE: Do not allow caliper to hang by brake hose.

4. Remove hub and disc assembly. Grease retainer and inner bearing can now be removed.

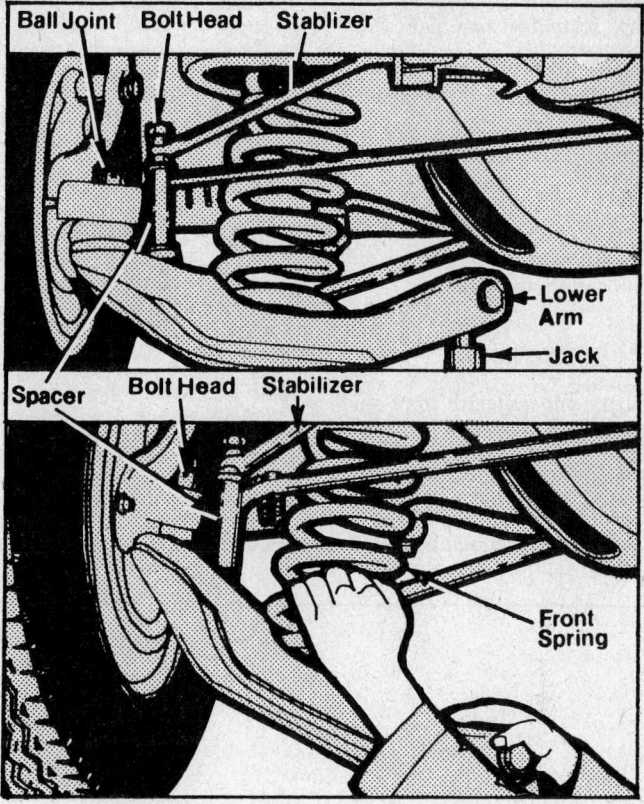

Fig. 6   Replacing coil spring. 1974-78

CHECKING BALL JOINTS FOR WEAR

Upper Ball Joint

1. Raise car on floor jacks placed beneath lower control arms.
2. Grasp lower edge of tire and move wheel in and out.
3. As wheel is being moved in and out, observe upper end of spindle and upper arm.
4. Any movement between upper end of spindle and upper arm indicates ball joint wear and loss of preload. If any such movement is observed, replace upper ball joint.

   NOTE: During the foregoing check, the lower ball joint will be unloaded and may move. Disregard all such movement of the lower ball joint. Also, do not mistake loose wheel bearings for a worn ball joint.

Lower Ball Joint

1. Raise car on jacks placed under lower control arms as shown in Fig. 4. This will unload ball joints.
2. Adjust wheel bearings.
3. Attach a dial indicator to lower control arm and position so that its plunger rests against the inner side of the wheel rim adjacent to the lower ball joint.
4. Grasp tire at top and bottom and slowly move it in and out as shown in Fig. 4.
5. If reading on dial indicator exceeds ¼", replace lower ball joint.

NOTE: 1979 models are equipped with lower ball joint wear indicators, Fig. 5. To check ball joint for wear, support vehicle in normal driving position with both ball joints loaded. Observe the checking surface of the ball joint. If the checking surface is inside the cover, Fig. 5, replace the ball joint.

SHOCK ABSORBER, REPLACE

To remove a shock absorber, unfasten it at the top and bottom and lower it through the opening in the lower control arm.

COIL SPRING, REPLACE
1979

1. Raise and support vehicle.

2. Remove wheel.
3. Disconnect stabilizer bar link from lower control arm.
4. Remove shock absorber.
5. Remove steering center link from pitman arm.
6. Compress coil spring with a suitable spring compressor, tool D-78P-5310-A or equivalent.
7. Remove two lower control arm pivot bolts and disengage arm from crossmember.
8. Remove spring from vehicle.
9. Reverse procedure to install.

1974-78

1. Raise vehicle and support front end of frame with jack stands.
2. Disconnect shock absorber from lower arm, collapse shock absorber into the spring and place a jack under the lower arm for support, Fig. 6.
3. Remove strut and rebound bumper bolts and disconnect lower end of sway bar stud from lower arm.
4. Remove the nut and bolt retaining the inner end of the lower arm to the crossmember.
5. Carefully lower jack to relieve spring pressure on lower arm, then remove the spring.

BALL JOINTS, REPLACE

NOTE: Ford Motor Company recommends that new ball joints should not be installed on used control arms and that the control arm be replaced if ball joint replacement is required. However, aftermarket ball joint repair kits which do not require control arm replacement, are available and can be installed using the following procedure.

The ball joints are riveted to the upper and lower control arms. The ball joints can be replaced on the car by removing the rivets and retaining the new ball joint to the control arm with the attaching bolts, nuts and washers furnished with the ball joint kit.

When removing a ball joint, use a suitable pressing tool to force the ball joint out of the spindle.

POWER STEERING GEAR
1974-79 Ford & Mercury

1. Remove stone shield, if equipped.
2. Disconnect pressure and return lines from steering gear. Plug lines and ports in gear to prevent entry of dirt.
3. Remove two bolts that secure flex coupling to steering gear and to column.
4. Raise car and remove sector shaft nut.
5. Use a puller to remove pitman arm.
6. Support steering gear, then remove attaching bolts.
7. Work steering gear free of flex coupling and remove it from car.
8. Reverse procedure to install.

INDEX OF SERVICE OPERATIONS

ENGINE & SERIAL NUMBER LOCATION: Vehicle warranty plate on rear face of left front door.

ENGINE IDENTIFICATION: Engine code is last letter in serial number on vehicle warranty plate.

Year	Engine	Engine Code
1974	4-122②	X
1974-79	4-140③⑤	Y
1979	4-140③⑥	W
1974-79	V6-171④	Z
1975-79	V8-302	F

①—1600 cc engine. ④—2800 cc engine.
②—2000 cc engine. ⑤—Non-turbocharged.
③—2300 cc engine. ⑥—Turbocharged.

GRILLE IDENTIFICATION

1973 Pinto

1974 Mustang II

1975 Mustang II
1976 Mustang II
Base Model

1976 Mustang II Stallion, Mach 1

1975-78 Mercury Bobcat

1976 Pinto

1977-78 Mustang II

1977 Mustang II Cobra

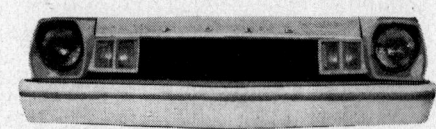

1977 Pinto

1977 Pinto Wagon
With Cruising Option

1978 Mustang II Cobra

1978 Pinto

1979 Bobcat

1979 Capri

1979 Mustang

1979 Pinto

GENERAL ENGINE SPECIFICATIONS

Year	Engine	Carburetor	Bore and Stroke	Piston Displacement, Cubic Inches	Compression Ratio	Maximum Brake H.P. @ R.P.M.	Maximum Torque Lbs. Ft. @ R.P.M.	Normal Oil Pressure Pounds
1974	4-122②③	2 Barrel	3.575 x 3.029	122②	8.2	80 @ 5400	98 @ 3000	45–65
	4-140③⑤	2 Barrel	3.781 x 3.126	140⑤	8.4	82 @ 4600	113 @ 2600	40–60
	4-140③⑤	2 Barrel	3.781 x 3.126	140⑤	8.4	88 @ 5000	116 @ 2600	40–60
	V6-171③⑥	2 Barrel	3.66 x 2.70	171⑥	8.2	105 @ 4600	140 @ 3200	40–55
1975	4-140③⑤	2 Barrel	3.781 x 3.126	140⑤	8.4	85.5 @ 4800	113 @ 2600	40–60
	V6-171③⑥	2 Barrel	3.66 x 2.70	171⑥	8.2	110 @ 5000	135 @ 2600	40–60
	V8-302③⑦	2 Barrel	4.00 x 3.00	302	8.0	140 @ 3800	228 @ 2600	40–60
1976	4-140③⑤	2 Barrel	3.781 x 3.126	140⑤	9.0	92 @ 5000	121 @ 5000	40–60
	V6-171③⑥⑧	2 Barrel	3.66 x 2.70	171⑥	8.7	⑨	⑩	40–60
	V6-171③⑥⑪	2 Barrel	3.66 x 2.70	171⑥	8.7	⑫	⑬	40–60
	V8-302③⑦	2 Barrel	4.00 x 3.00	302	8.0	134 @ 3600	⑭	40–60
1977	4-140③⑤⑮	2 Barrel	3.781 x 3.126	140⑤	9.0	89 @ 4800	120 @ 3000	40–60
	4-140③⑤⑯	2 Barrel	3.781 x 3.126	140⑤	9.0	⑰	119 @ 3000	40–60
	V6-171③⑥⑲	2 Barrel	3.66 x 2.70	171⑥	8.7	90 @ 4200	139 @ 2600	40–55
	V6-171③⑥⑳	2 Barrel	3.66 x 2.70	171⑥	8.7	90 @ 4000	139 @ 2600	40–55
	V6-171③⑥㉑	2 Barrel	3.66 x 2.70	171⑥	8.7	88 @ 4000	138 @ 2600	40–55
	V6-171③⑥⑱	2 Barrel	3.66 x 2.70	171⑥	8.7	93 @ 4200	140 @ 2600	40–55
	V8-302③⑦㉓	2 Barrel	4.00 x 3.00	302	8.4	129 @ 3400	242 @ 2000	40–60
	V8-302③⑦㉔	2 Barrel	4.00 x 3.00	302	8.1	132 @ 3600	228 @ 1600	40–60
	V8-302③⑦㉒	2 Barrel	4.00 x 3.00	302	8.4	139 @ 3600	247 @ 1800	40–60
1978	4-140⑤	2 Barrel	3.781 x 3.126	140⑤	9.0	88 @ 4800	118 @ 2800	50
	V6-171⑥	2 Barrel	3.66 x 2.70	171⑥	8.7	90 @ 4200	143 @ 2200	40–55
	V8-302⑦	2 Barrel	4.00 x 3.00	302	8.4	㉕	㉖	40–60
1979	4-140⑤㉗	2 Barrel	3.781 x 3.126	140⑤	—	—	—	40–60
	4-140⑤㉘	2 Barrel	3.781 x 3.126	140⑤	—	—	—	40–60
	V6-171⑥	2 Barrel	3.66 x 2.70	171⑥	—	—	—	40–60
	V8-302⑦	2 Barrel	4.00 x 3.00	302	—	—	—	40–65

①—1600 cc engine.
②—2000 cc engine.
③—Net Rating—as installed in vehicle.
④—Exc. station wagon, 85 @ 5600; station wagon, 83 @ 5200.
⑤—2300 cc engine.
⑥—2800 cc engine.
⑦—Refer to the Ford & Mercury—Compact & Intermediate Chapter for Service procedures on this engine.
⑧—Bobcat, Mustang II and Pinto with auto. trans.
⑨—Exc. Calif.; 100 @ 4600. Calif.; 100 @ 4400.
⑩—Exc. Calif.; 143 @ 2600. Calif.; 144 @ 2200.
⑪—Mustang II with manual trans.
⑫—Exc. Calif.; 103 @ 4400. Calif.; 99 @ 4400.
⑬—Exc. Calif.; 149 @ 2800. Calif.; 144 @ 2200.
⑭—Exc. Calif.; 247 @ 1800. Calif.; 243 @ 1800.

⑮—Exc. Calif.
⑯—Calif. only.
⑰—Sedan 88 @ 4800; Station wagon 85 @ 4800.
⑱—Sedans, exc. Calif.
⑲—Station Wagons exc. Calif.
⑳—Sedans Calif. only.
㉑—Station wagons Calif. only.
㉒—Auto. trans. exc. Calif.
㉓—Man. trans. exc. Calif.
㉔—Auto. trans. Calif. only.
㉕—Exc. Calif.; 139 @ 3600. Calif.; 133 @ 3600.
㉖—Exc. Calif.; 250 @ 1600. Calif.; 243 @ 1600.
㉗—Non-turbocharged.
㉘—Turbocharged.

BRAKE SPECIFICATIONS

Year	Model	Brake Drum Inside Diameter	Wheel Cylinder Bore Diameter			Master Cylinder Bore Diameter		
			Front Disc Brakes	Front Drum Brakes	Rear Brakes	With Disc Brakes	With Drum Brakes	With Power Brakes
1974	Mustang II & Pinto	9.0	2.60	—	.875	.9375	—	.9375
1975–78	Mustang II, Pinto & Bobcat	9.0	2.60	—	.875	.938	—	.938

①—Sta. Wagon .875.

TUNE UP SPECIFICATIONS

The following specifications are published from the latest information available. This data should be used only in the absence of a decal affixed in the engine compartment.

★When using a timing light, disconnect vacuum hose or tube at distributor and plug opening in hose or tube so idle speed will not be affected.

●When checking compression, lowest cylinder must be within 75 percent of highest.

▲Before removing wires from distributor cap, determine location of the No. 1 wire in cap, as distributor position may have been altered from that shown at the end of this chart.

| Year | Spark Plug | | Distributor | | Ignition Timing★ | | | Carb. Adjustments | | | | | |
| | Type | Gap Inch | Point Gap Inch | Dwell Angle Deg. | Firing Order Fig. ▲ | Timing BTDC ① | Mark Fig. | Hot Idle Speed③ | | Air Fuel Ratio | | Idle "CO" % | |
								Std. Trans.	Auto. Trans.②	Std. Trans.	Auto. Trans.	Std. Trans.	Auto. Trans.
1974													
4-122, 2000 cc	BRF-42	.034	.025	35–41	⑩	6	D	750	650	⑥	⑥	—	—
4-140, 2300 cc	AGRF-52	.034	.027	35–41	G	6	E	850	750	11 to 1	11 to 1	.15	.15
V6-171, 2800 cc	AGR-42	.034	.027	35–41	H	12	F	750	650	12.7 to 1	12.7 to 1	.7	.4
1975													
4-140, 2300 cc	AGRF-52	.034	—	—	G	⑦	E	850	750D	—	—	—	—
V6-171, 2800 cc	AGR-42	.034	—	—	H	⑧	F	850	700D	—	—	—	—
V8-302⑨	ARF-42	.044	—	—	I	6°	J	—	700D	—	—	—	—
1976													
4-140, 2300 cc	AWRF-42	.034	—	—	G	⑦	E	750	650D	—	—	—	—
V6-171, 2800 cc	AWRF-42	.034	—	—	H	⑧	F	850	700D	—	—	—	—
V8-302⑨	ARF-42	.044	—	—	I	6°	J	—	700D	—	—	—	—
1977													
4-140, 2300 cc	AWRF-42	.034	—	—	G	⑪	E	850	⑫	—	—	—	—
V6-171, 2800 cc⑱	㉓	.034	—	—	H	⑬	F	—	⑭	—	—	—	—
V6-171, 2800 cc④⑳	⑲	.034	—	—	H	⑲	F	850	—	—	—	—	—
V6-171, 2800 cc④㉑	AWSF-42	.034	—	—	H	12°	F	—	㉒	—	—	—	—
V8-302⑨⑮	⑲	⑲	—	—	K	⑲	J	—	⑲	—	—	—	—
V8-302⑨⑯	ARF-52-6	.060	—	—	K	12°	J	—	700D	—	—	—	—
1978													
4-140, 2300 cc⑳	AWSF-42	.034	—	—	G	6°⑲	E	850	—	—	—	—	—
4-140, 2300 cc㉕㉑	AWSF-42	.034	—	—	G	20°⑲	E	—	800D	—	—	—	—
4-140, 2300 cc㉖	AWSF-42	.034	—	—	G	⑰⑲	E	—	750D	—	—	—	—
V6-171, 2800 cc⑳	AWSF-42	.034	—	—	H	10°	F	850	—	—	—	—	—
V6-171, 2800 cc㉑	AWSF-42	.034	—	—	H	⑱⑲	F	—	650/750D㉚	—	—	—	—
V8-302㉑	ARF-52	.050	—	—	K	㉛⑲	J	—	⑲	—	—	—	—
V8-302⑳	ARF-52	.050	—	—	K	10°	J	800/875D㉚	—	—	—	—	—
1979													
4-140, 2300 cc㉑⑬	AWSF-42	.034	—	—	G	20°	E	—	800	—	—	—	—
4-140, 2300 cc⑱⑳	AWSF-42	.034	—	—	G	6°	E	850	—	—	—	—	—
V6-171 2800 cc	AWSF-42	.034	—	—	H	9°	F	—	650/750D㉚	—	—	—	—
V8-302⑳	ASF-52	.050	—	—	K	12°	J	—	800/875㉚	—	—	—	—

①—BTDC: Before top dead center.

②—D: Drive.

③—Headlamps on Hi Beam—Air Conditioner OFF. Where two speeds are listed, lower speed indicates solenoid disconnected.

④—Mustang.

⑤—Auto. trans., 9° BTDC; man. trans., 6° BTDC.

⑥—11.7:1 Except Calif.; 10:1 Calif.

⑦—Exc. Calif. Auto. Trans., 6° BTDC; Calif. Auto. Trans., 10° BTDC.

⑧—Manual Trans., 6° BTDC; Exc. Calif. Auto. Trans., 10° BTDC; Calif. Auto. Trans., 8° BTDC.

⑨—Refer to the Ford & Mercury—Compact & Intermediate Chapter for service procedures on this engine.

⑩—Since there are two alternate ignition wiring possibilities, be sure that the ignition wires are reinstalled in their proper locations referring to Fig. B.

⑪—Man. trans., 6° BTDC; auto. trans., 20° BTDC.

⑫—Except Calif. & high altitude, 800D RPM; Calif. & high altitude, 750D RPM.

⑬—Except Calif., 12° BTDC; Calif., 6° BTDC.

Continued

TUNE UP NOTES—Continued

⑭—Except Calif. less A/C, 700D RPM; except Calif. with A/C & Calif. 750D RPM.

⑮—Except Calif.

⑯—Calif.

⑰—Early production, 20° BTDC; Late production Pinto & Bobcat, 17° BTDC; Mustang, 20° BTDC.

⑰—The distributor cap retaining clip locations have been changed in Fig. I. The new locations are between wire towers 3 & 7, 4 & 5.

⑱—Pinto and Bobcat.

⑲—Must refer to engine decal due to running production changes.

⑳—Manual trans.

㉑—Auto. trans.

㉒—With A/C, 750D RPM; less A/C, 700D RPM.

㉓—Exc. Calif., AWSF-42; Calif., AWRF-42.

㉔—Manual trans., 10° BTDC; Auto. trans. exc. Calif., 12° BTDC; Auto trans., Calif., 6° BTDC.

㉕—Exc. Calif.

㉖—Calif.

㉗—Exc. high altitude, 4° BTDC; High altitude, 16° BTDC.

㉘—Exc. Calif., 800 RPM; Calif., 750 RPM.

㉙—Exc. Calif., 650 RPM; Calif., 600 RPM.

㉚—High RPM is for A/C, A/C on.

㉛—Exc. High altitude, 10° BTDC; High altitude, 14° BTDC.

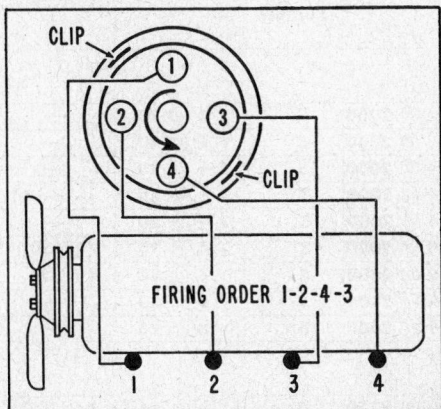

Fig. A

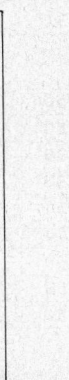

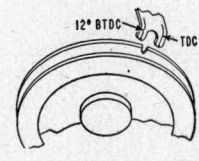

Fig. C

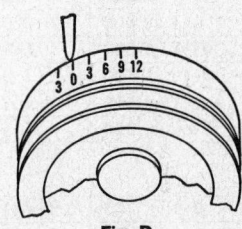

Fig. D

Fig. B

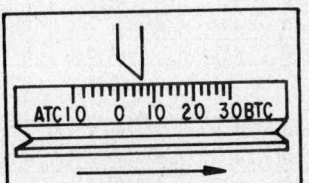

Fig. E

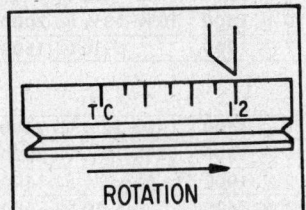

Fig. F

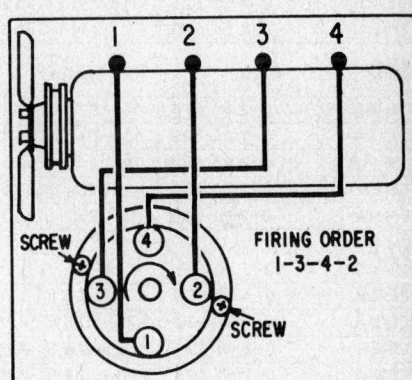

Fig. G

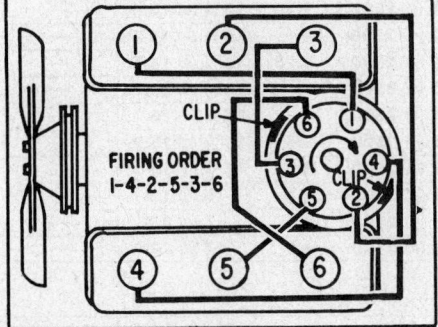

Fig. H

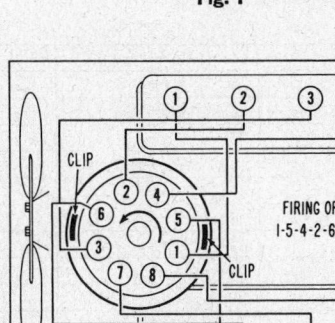

Fig. I

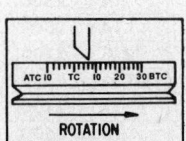

Fig. J

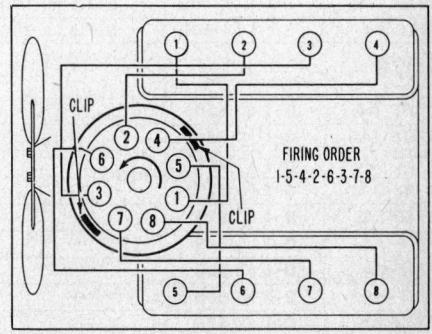

Fig. K

DISTRIBUTOR SPECIFICATIONS

★If unit is checked on vehicle double the RPM and degrees to get crankshaft figures.

Breaker arm spring tension—17–21.

Distributor Part No.	Centrifugal Advance Degrees @ RPM of Distributor					Vacuum Advance		Distributor Retard
	Advance Starts	Intermediate Advance			Full Advance	Inches of Vacuum To Start Plunger	Max. Adv. Dist. Deg. @ Vacuum	Max. Ret. Dist. Deg. @ Vacuum
1974								
74HF-EA	1–3 @ 500	5–7 @ 750	6½–8½ @ 1000	9½–11½ @ 1500	12–14 @ 2000	5	6 @ 20	—
74HF-LA	0–1 @ 500	1–3 @ 750	4–6 @ 1000	7–9 @ 1500	9½–11½ @ 2000	5	6 @ 20	—
D4ZE-AA	0–1 @ 500	4–6 @ 750	4–6 @ 1000	9½–11½ @ 1500	11½–14 @ 2000	5	7½ @ 20	—
D4ZE-BA	0–1 @ 500	4–6 @ 750	7–9 @ 1000	9¼–11½ @ 1500	11½–14 @ 2000	5	7½ @ 20	—
D4ZF-DA	0–1 @ 500	1½–3½ @ 750	6–8 @ 1000	9½–11½ @ 1500	11½–14 @ 2000	5	4½ @ 20	—
74TF-LA	0–½ @ 500	1–3 @ 750	3½–5½ @ 1000	7½–9½ @ 1500	8–10 @ 2000	5	4 @ 20	7 @ 20
74FT-MA	0–½ @ 500	1–3 @ 750	3½–5½ @ 1000	7½–9½ @ 1500	8–10 @ 2000	5	4 @ 20	4 @ 20
D4ZE-KA	0–1 @ 500	4–6½ @ 750	7–9 @ 1000	9¼–11½ @ 1500	12¾ @ 2000	5	6 @ 20	—
74TF-SA	0–½ @ 500	1–3 @ 750	3½–5½ @ 1000	7½–9½ @ 1500	9 @ 2000	5	3 @ 20	—
1975								
D5DE-KA	0–2 @ 775	2¾–4¾ @ 950	4¾–7 @ 1500	6¾–9¼ @ 2000	10¾ @ 2350	4	11¼ @ 14½	3 @ 7
D5DE-NA	0–2 @ 550	2½–4½ @ 675	3¾–6 @ 1100	7–9½ @ 2000	11½ @ 2500	4	11¼ @ 14½	—
D5ZE-AA	0–2 @ 600	1–3 @ 650	2¾–5 @ 1000	5¼–7½ @ 1500	13 @ 2500	4.8	5¾ @ 7½	—
D52E-EA	0–2 @ 675	5¼–7¼ @ 1025	7½–9¾ @ 1500	10–12½ @ 2000	14 @ 2250	4	5¼ @ 7	—
D52E-FA	0–2 @ 725	5½–7½ @ 1125	7¾–10 @ 1500	10¾–13¼ @ 2000	14 @ 2150	4	5¼ @ 7½	3 @ 7½
75TF-EA	0–2 @ 650	2–4 @ 800	5–7 @ 1200	8–10[1] @ 1600	10 @ 2000	4¼	3 @ 6¾	6 @ 6¾
1976								
D52E-EA	0–2 @ 675	5¼–7¼ @ 1025	7½–9¾ @ 1500	10–12½ @ 2000	14 @ 2250	4	5¼ @ 7	—
D52E-FA	0–2 @ 725	5½–7½ @ 1125	7¾–10 @ 1500	10¾–13¼ @ 2000	14 @ 2150	4	5¼ @ 7½	4 @ 7½
D5ZE-AA	0–2 @ 600	1.3 @ 650	2¼–5 @ 1000	5¼–7½ @ 1500	10¼–13 @ 2500	4.8	5¼ @ 7½	—
75TF-EA	0–2 @ 650	2.4 @ 800	5–7 @ 1600	8–10 @ 1600	7½–10 @ 2000	4¼	3 @ 6¾	7 @ 10
75TF-NA	0–2 @ 650	2.4 @ 800	5¼–7¾ @ 1200	7–9½ @ 1500	9–12 @ 2500	4¼	7 @ 9½	—
1977								
D7EE-CA	0–1 @ 800	1–3.5 @ 1500	—	—	7.5 @ 2500	2.3	13¼ @ 15.75	—
D7EE-DA	0–1 @ 510	3.75–5.75 @ 725	—	—	14 @ 2500	1.75	13¼ @ 12.4	—
D7EE-EA	0–1 @ 525	3.6–5.6 @ 725	—	—	14 @ 2500	2	13¼ @ 15.75	—
D7EE-GA	0–1 @ 525	3.75–5.75 @ 740	—	—	14 @ 2500	2.25	13¼ @ 15.75	—
D7EE-HA	0–1 @ 775	1.75–3.7 @ 1500	—	—	7.5 @ 2500	2	13¼ @ 15.75	—
D7OE-GA	0–1 @ 425	6–8 @ 650	—	—	16 @ 2500	3	13¼ @ 16	—
D7ZE-BA	0–1 @ 425	6–8 @ 650	—	—	16 @ 2500	3.5	13¼ @ 15.2	—
D7ZE-CA	0–1 @ 575	6.25–8.25 @ 1250	—	—	12 @ 2500	2.2	15¼ @ 16	—
77TF-AA	0–1 @ 625	5–7.5 @ 1000	—	—	10.5 @ 2100	4	10 @ 12	—
77TF-CA	0–1 @ 600	5–7.5 @ 1000	—	—	10.5 @ 2100	3.5	7 @ 8.5	—
77TF-DA	0–1 @ 600	5–7.5 @ 900	—	—	10.5 @ 2100	4.5	7 @ 10	—
1978								
D7DE-AA	0–1 @ 550	—	—	1¾–4 @ 750	12½ @ 2500	3	15¼ @ 11	—
D7DE-JA	0–1 @ 550	—	—	3½–5½ @ 650	10¾ @ 2500	3	13¼ @ 16	—
D7EE-CA	0–1 @ 800	—	—	1–3½ @ 1500	7½ @ 2500	2.3	13¼ @ 15.75	—
D7EE-DA	0–1 @ 510	—	—	3¾–5¾ @ 725	14 @ 2500	1.75	13¼ @ 12.4	—
D7EE-EA	0–1 @ 525	—	—	3⅝–5⅝ @ 725	14 @ 2500	2	13¼ @ 15.75	—
77TF-AA	0–1 @ 625	—	—	5–7½ @ 1000	10½ @ 2100	4	10 @ 12	—
77TF-CA	0–1 @ 600	—	—	5–7½ @ 900	10½ @ 2100	4.5	7 @ 10	—
77TF-HA	0–1 @ 600	—	—	5–7 @ 900	12 @ 2100	4.5	7 @ 10	—
D8ZE-BA	0–1 @ 425	—	—	6–8 @ 650	16 @ 2500	3.5	13¼ @ 14	—
D8ZE-CA	0–1 @ 575	—	—	6–7¾ @ 1200	11½ @ 2500	2.5	12¼ @ 15.7	—

STARTING MOTOR SPECIFICATIONS

Year	Engine Model	Ident. No.	Brush Spring Tension, Ounces	No Load Test			Torque Test		
				Amperes	Volts	R.P.M.	Amperes	Volts	Torque Lbs. Ft.
1974	4-122, 140	D42F-AA, AB, BA	40 Min.	70	—	—	460	5	9
	6-171	D4ZF-AA	40 Min.	70	—	—	460	5	9
1975	4-140	D42F-BA	40 Min.	70	—	—	460	5	9
	V6-171	D4ZF-BA	40 Min.	70	—	—	460	5	9
	V8-302	D5OF-BA	80 Min.	80	—	—	670	5	15.5
1976–77	4-140	D6EF-BA	40 Min.	70	—	—	460	5	9.0
	V6-171	D6EF-AA	40 Min.	70	—	—	460	5	9.0
	V8-302	D6OF-AA	80 Min.	80	—	—	670	5	15.5
1978	4-140	D8EF-AA	40 Min.	70	—	—	460	5	9.0
	V6-171	D8ZF-AA	40 Min.	70	—	—	460	5	9.0
	V8-302	D8OF-AA	80 Min.	80	—	—	670	5	15.5

ALTERNATOR & REGULATOR SPECIFICATIONS

Year	Make or Model	Current Rating		Field Current @ 75°F.		Voltage Regulator				Field Relay	
		Amperes	Volts	Amperes	Volts	Make or Model	Voltage @ 75°F.	Contact Gap	Armature Air Gap	Armature Air Gap	Closing Voltage @ 75°F.
1974	Purple①	38	15	2.9	12	D4AF-AA	13.5–15.3	—	—	—	2.5–4.0
	Green①	61	15	2.9	12	D4TF-AA	13.5–15.3	—	—	—	2.5–4.0
	All	70	15	2.9	12	D4TF-AA	13.5–15.3	—	—	—	2.5–4.0
	Orange①	42	15	2.9	12	D4AF-AA	13.5–15.3	—	—	—	2.5–4.0
	Red①	55	15	2.9	12	D4AF-AA	13.5–15.3	—	—	—	2.5–4.0
	All	70	15	2.9	12	D4AF-AA	13.5–15.3	—	—	—	2.5–4.0
	All	90	15	2.9	12	D4TF-AA	13.5–15.3	—	—	—	2.5–4.0
1975–77	Orange①	40	15	2.9	12	D4AF-AA	13.5–15.3	—	—	—	2.5–4.0
	Green①	60	15	2.9	12	D4AF-AA	13.5–15.3	—	—	—	2.5–4.0
	All	70	15	2.9	12	D4TF-AA	13.5–15.3	—	—	—	2.5–4.0
	All	90	15	2.9	12	D4TF-AA	13.5–15.3	—	—	—	2.5–4.0
1978	D7AF-AA	40	—	—	—	—	13.5–15.3	—	—	—	—
	D7AF-BA	40	—	—	—	—	13.5–15.3	—	—	—	—
	D7AF-CA	60	—	—	—	—	13.5–15.3	—	—	—	—
	D7AF-JA	40	—	—	—	—	13.5–15.3	—	—	—	—
	D7AF-LA	60	—	—	—	—	13.5–15.3	—	—	—	—
	D7EF-BA	70	—	—	—	—	13.5–15.3	—	—	—	—
	D7TF-AA	65	—	—	—	—	13.5–15.3	—	—	—	—
	D7ZF-AA	65	—	—	—	—	13.5–15.3	—	—	—	—
	D8ZF-AA	40	—	—	—	—	13.5–14.85	—	—	—	—
	D8ZF-BA	60	—	—	—	—	13.5–14.85	—	—	—	—
	D8ZF-CA	60	—	—	—	—	13.5–14.85	—	—	—	—
	D8ZF-EA	40	—	—	—	—	13.5–14.85	—	—	—	—
	D8ZF-FA	70	—	—	—	—	13.5–14.85	—	—	—	—
	D8ZF-HA	65	—	—	—	—	13.5–14.85	—	—	—	—

①—Color of identification tag.

REAR AXLE SPECIFICATIONS

| Year | Model | Carrier Type | Ring Gear & Pinion Backlash Inch | Nominal Pinion Locating Shim, Inch | Pinion Bearing Preload | | | | Differential Bearing Preload | Pinion Nut Torque Ft.-Lbs. |
					New Bearings With Seal Inch-Lbs.	Used Bearings With Seal Inch-Lbs.	New Bearings Less Seal Inch-Lbs.	Used Bearings Less Seal Inch-Lbs.		
1974–78	All	Integral	.008–.012	.030	17–27	6–12	—	—	.004–.008①	140
	All	Removable	.008–.012	.022	17–27	8–14	—	—	.004–.008①	170

①—Case spread with new bearings; with used bearings, .003–.005".

PISTONS, PINS, RINGS, CRANKSHAFT & BEARINGS

| Year | Engine | Piston Clearance | Ring End Gap① | | Wrist-pin Diameter | Rod Bearings | | Main Bearings | | Thrust on Bear. No. | Shaft End Play |
			Comp.	Oil		Shaft Diameter	Bearing Clearance	Shaft Diameter	Bearing Clearance		
1974	4-122	.0010–.0020	.015	.016	.9448	2.0468	.0006–.0026	2.2446	.0006–.0016	3	.003–.011
	4-140	.0013–.0021	.010	.015	.9120	2.0468	.0009–.0027	2.3996	.0008–.0015	3	.004–.008
	6-171	.0010–.0020	.015	.015	.9447	2.1268	.0006–.0022	2.2437	.0006–.0019	3	.003–.011
1975	4-140	.0014–.0022	.010	.015	.9121	2.0468	.0008–.0015	2.3986	.0008–.0015	3	.004–.008
	V6-171	.0011–.0019	.015	.015	.9448	2.1256	.0005–.0015	2.2437	.0005–.0016	3	.004–.008
	V8-302③	.0018–.0026	.015	.016	.9121	2.1232	.0008–.0015	2.2486	④	3	.004–.008
1976	4-140	.0010–.0020	.010	.015	.9121	2.0468	.0008–.0015	2.3986	.0008–.0015	3	.004–.008
	V6-171	.0011–.0019	.015	.015	.9448	2.1256	.0006–.0015	2.2437	.0008–.0015	3	.004–.008
	V8-302③	.0018–.0026	.010	.015	.9121	2.1232	.0008–.0015	2.2486	.0008–.0015	3	.004–.008
1977	4-140	.0014–.0022	.010	.015	.9121	2.0468	.0008–.0015	2.3986	.0008–.0015	3	.004–.008
	V6-171	.0011–.0019	.015	.015	.9448	2.1256	.0006–.0015	2.2437	.0008–.0015	3	.004–.008
	V8-302③	.0018–.0026	.010	.015	.9121	2.1232	.0008–.0015	2.2486	⑤	3	.004–.008
1978	4-140	.0014–.0022	.010	.015	.9121	2.0468	.0008–.0015	2.3990	.0008–.0015	3	.004–.008
	V6-171	.0011–.0019	.015	.015	.9448	2.1256	.0006–.0015	2.2437	.0008–.0015	3	.004–.008
	V8-302③	.0018–.0026	.010	.015	.9121	2.1232	.0008–.0015	2.2486	⑤	3	.004–.008
1979	4-140	.0014–.0022	.010	.015	.9121	2.0468	.0008–.0015	2.3990	.0008–.0015	3	.004–.008
	V6-171	.0011–.0019	.015	.015	.9448	2.1256	.0006–.0016	2.2437	.0008–.0015	3	.004–.008
	V8-302③	.0018–.0026	.010	.015	.9121	2.1232	.0008–.0015	2.2486	⑥	3	.004–.008

①—Fit rings in tapered bores for clearance listed in tightest portion of ring travel.
②—No. 1, 2 & 3 bore, .0016–.0022, No. 4 bore, .0019–.0025.
③—Refer to the Ford & Mercury—Compact & Intermediate chapter for service procedures on this engine.
④—No. 1, .0001–.0005; others, .0005–.0015.
⑤—No. 1, .0001–.0015"; others, .0005–.0015.
⑥—No. 1, .0001–.0015; others, .0004–.0015.

ENGINE TIGHTENING SPECIFICATIONS

★Torque specifications are for clean and lightly lubricated threads only. Dry or dirty threads produce increased friction which prevents accurate measurement of tightness.

Year	Engine	Spark Plugs Ft. Lbs.	Cylinder Head Bolts Ft. Lbs.	Intake Manifold Ft. Lbs.	Exhaust Manifold Ft. Lbs.	Rocker Arm Shaft Bracket Ft. Lbs.	Rocker Arm Cover Ft. Lbs.	Connecting Rod Cap Bolts Ft. Lbs.	Main Bearing Cap Bolts Ft. Lbs.	Flywheel to Crankshaft Ft. Lbs.	Vibration Damper or Pulley Ft. Lbs.
1974	4-122	14-20	65-80	12-15	15-18	③	4-6	29-34	65-75	47-51	39-43
	4-140	10-15	80-90	14-21	16-23	—	4-7	30-36	80-90	54-64	80-114
	6-171	15-22	65-80	15-18	14-18	43-49	3-5	21-25	65-75	47-51	92-104
1975	4-140	10-15	80-90	14-21	16-23	—	4-7	30-36	80-90	54-64	80-114
	V6-171	15-20	65-80	15-18	16-23	43-49	3-5	21-25	65-75	47-51	92-103
1975-79	V8-302⑤	⑧	65-72	23-25	18-24	17-23④	3-5	19-24	60-70	75-85	70-90
1976-79	4-140	5-10	80-90	14-21	16-23	—	⑨	30-36	80-90	54-64	100-120
	V6-171	10-15	65-80	⑥	⑦	43-49	3-5	21-25	65-75	47-51	92-103

①—Studs 9-12 ft.-lbs., nuts 12-15 ft.-lbs., bolts 12-15 ft.-lbs.
②—Studs 9-12 ft.-lbs., nuts 15-18 ft.-lbs.
③—Rocker arm ball stud nut 32-36 ft.-lbs.
④—Rocker arm stud nut.

⑤—Refer to the Ford & Mercury—Compact & Intermediate Chapter for service procedures on this engine.
⑥—Bolt/nut, 15-18 ft. lbs.; stud, 10-12 ft. lbs.
⑦—1976, 16-23 ft. lbs.; 1977-79, 20-30 ft. lbs.
⑧—1975-76, 15-20 ft. lbs.; 1977-79, 10-15 ft. lbs.
⑨—1976-78, 4-7; 1979, 6-8.

VALVE SPECIFICATIONS

Year	Engine	Valve Lash		Valve Angles		Valve Spring Installed Height	Valve Spring Pressure Lbs. @ In.	Stem Clearance		Stem Diameter, Standard	
		Int.	Exh.	Seat	Face			Intake	Exhaust	Intake	Exhaust
1974	4-122	.008①	.010①	45	44	1.406	176 @ 1.02	.0008-.0025	.0018-.0035	.3159-.3167	.3149-.3156
	4-140	.008C②	.010C②	45	44	1.56	210 @ 1.16	.0010-.0027	.0015-.0022	.3416-.3423	.3418-.3411
	6-171	.014H	.016H	45	44	1.593	144 @ 1.222	.0008-.0025	.0018-.0035	.3167-.3159	.3156-.3149
1975	4-140	.008C②	.010C②	45	44	1.531	189 @ 1.16	.0010-.0027	.0015-.0032	.3416-.3423	.3411-.3418
	V6-171	.014H	.016H	45	44	1.593	150 @ 1.222	.0008-.0025	.0018-.0035	.3158-.3167	.3149-.3156
	V8-302⑤	.115—	.130⑥	45	44	③	④	.0017-.0027	.0015-.0032	.3416-.3423	.3411-.3418
1976	4-140	.008C	.010C	45	44	1.563	189 @ 1.16	.0010-.0027	.0015-.0032	.3416-.3423	.3411-.3418
	V6-171	.015C	.018C	45	44	1.594	144 @ 1.222	.0008-.0025	.0018-.0035	.3159-.3167	.3149-3.156
	V8-302⑤	.115-.165⑥		45	44	③	⑦	.0010-.0027	.0015-.0032	.3416-.3423	.3441-.3418
1977	4-140	.040-.050⑥		45	44	1.560	189 @ 1.16	.0010-.0027	.0015-.0032	.3416-.3423	.3411-.3418
	V6-171	.014C	.016C	45	44	1.593	144 @ 1.222	.0008-.0025	.0018-.0035	.3159-.3167	.3149-.3156
	V8-302⑤	.096-.168⑥		45	44	③	⑦	.0010-.0027	.0015-.0032	.3416-.3423	.3411-.3418
1978	4-140	.040-.050⑥		45	44	1.560	189 @ 1.16	.0010-.0027	.0015-.0032	.3416-.3423	.3411-.3418
	V6-171	.014C	.016C	45	44	1.593	144 @ 1.222	.0008-.0025	.0018-.0035	.3159-.3167	.3149-.3156
	V8-302⑤	.096-.168⑥		45	44	③	⑦	.0010-.0027	.0015-.0032	.3416-.3423	.3411-.3418
1979	4-140	.040-.050⑥		45	44	1.56	187 @ 1.16	.0010-.0027	.0015-.0032	.3416-.3423	.3411-.3418
	V6-171	.014C	.016C	45	44	1.593	144 @ 1.222	.0008-.0025	.0018-.0035	.3159-.3167	.3149-.3156
	V8-302⑤	.096-.165⑥		45	44	③	⑧	.0010-.0027	.0015-.0032	.3416-.3423	.3411-.3418

①—Set Hot or Cold.
②—With hydraulic valve lash adjuster completely collapsed.
③—Intake 1.69; Exhaust 1.60.
④—Intake 200 @ 1.31; Exhaust 200 @ 1.22.
⑤—Refer to the Ford & Mercury—Compact & Intermediate Chapter for service procedures on this engine.

⑥—Clearance is obtained at valve stem tip with hydraulic lifter collapsed. If clearance is less than the minimum install an undersize push rod; if clearance is greater than the maximum install an oversize push rod.
⑦—Intake 200 @ 1.31; exhaust 200 @ 1.20.
⑧—Intake, 201 @ 1.36; exhaust, 200 @ 1.20.

WHEEL ALIGNMENT SPECIFICATIONS

| Year | Model | Caster Angle, Degrees | | Camber Angle, Degrees | | | | Toe-In. Inch | Toe-Out on Turns, Deg. | |
| | | Limits | Desired | Limits | | Desired | | | Outer Wheel | Inner Wheel |
				Left	Right	Left	Right			
1974	Mustang II	−¼ to +1¾	+¾	−½ to +1½	−½ to +1½	+½	+½	⅛	18.84	20
	Pinto	−¾ to +3¼	+1¼	−¼ to +1¾	−¼ to +1¾	+¾	+¾	¼	18.84	20
1975–76	Bobcat & Pinto①	+½ to +2	+1¼	0 to +1½	0 to +1½	+¾	+¾	⅛–⅜	18.84	20
	Bobcat & Pinto②	+¾ to +2¼	+1½	0 to +1½	0 to +1½	+¾	+¾	⅛–⅜	18.84	20
	Mustang II	+⅛ to +1⅝	+⅞	−¼ to +1¼	−¼ to +1¼	+½	+½	0–¼	18.84	20
1977–78	Bobcat & Pinto①	+¼ to +1¾	+1	−¼ to +1¼	−¼ to +1¼	+½	+½	⅛	18.84	20
	Bobcat & Pinto②	−½ to +1	+¼	−¼ to +1¼	−¼ to +1¼	+½	+½	⅛	18.84	20
	Mustang II	+⅛ to +1⅝	+⅞	−¼ to +1¼	−¼ to +1¼	+½	+½	⅛	18.84	20

①—Exc. sta. wag. ②—Sta. wag.

COOLING SYSTEM & CAPACITY DATA

| Year | Model or Engine | Cooling Capacity, Qts. | | | Radiator Cap Relief Pressure, Lbs. | | Thermo. Opening Temp. | Fuel Tank Gals. | Engine Oil Refill Qts. | Transmission Oil | | | Rear Axle Oil Pints |
		No Heater	With Heater	With A/C	With A/C	No A/C				3 Speed Pints	4 Speed Pints	Auto. Trans. Qts. ⑧	
1974	4-122	7½	8½	8½	13	13	186	③	5①	—	2.8	8	3
	4-140	7½	8½	9½	13	13	186	③	5①	—	⑤	8	3
	6-171	11½	12½	12½	13	13	186	13	5②	—	4.5	8	3
1975	4-140	—	⑨	9	13	13	191	④	5①	—	⑤	⑥	⑦
	V6-171	—	⑪	13¼	13	13	191	④	5①	—	⑤	⑥	⑦
	V8-302	—	16.3	16.3	13	13	191	16½	5①	—	—	8¾	4
1976	4-140	7.9	⑨	9	13	13	191	④	5①	—	⑤	⑥	⑦
	V6-171	11.7	⑪	13.2	13	13	191	④	5②	—	⑤	⑥	⑦
	V8-302	15½	16.3	16.3	13	13	191	16½	5①	—	—	8¾	4
1977	4-140	7.9	⑨	9.1	13	13	191	⑫	5①	—	⑤	⑥	⑦
	V6-171	7.7	⑩	9.2	13	13	191	④	5②	—	⑤	⑥	⑦
	V8-302	15.5	16.3	16.3	13	13	191	16.5	5①	—	⑤	⑥	4
1978	4-140⑬	7.8	8.6	9.0	13	13	191	⑯	5①	—	2.8	⑰	⑱
	4-140⑭	8.0	8.8	9.1	13	13	191	13	5①	—	3.5	⑰	⑱
	V6-171⑬	7.7	8.5	9.2	13	13	191	⑯	5②	—	2.8	⑰	⑱
	V6-171⑭	8.0	⑮	9.0	13	13	191	13	5②	—	3.5	⑰	⑱
	V8-302	—	14.6	14.6	13	13	191	16.5	5①	—	3.5	7	⑱
1979	4-140⑬	—	8.6	9.0	13	13	191	㉒	4½②	—	—	—	—
	4-140⑲⑳	—	8.6	10	13	13	191	11.5	4½②	—	—	—	—
	4-140⑲㉑	—	8.6	10.2	13	13	191	12.25	4½②	—	—	—	—
	V6-171⑬	—	8.5	9.1	13	13	195	㉒	5②	—	—	—	—
	V6-171⑲	—	9.2	9.4	13	13	195	12.25	5②	—	—	—	—
	V8-302	—	14	14.6	13	13	195	12.25	5①	—	—	—	—

①—Includes 1 qt. for filter.
②—Includes ½ qt. for filter.
③—Pinto: sedan, 13 gals.; wagon, 12 gals.
④—Exc. Sta. Wag., 13 gals.; Sta. Wag. 14 gals. Add 3½ gals. with auxiliary fuel tank.
⑤—Bobcat & Pinto, 2.8 pts.; Mustang, 3½ pts.
⑥—C3 trans., 8 qts.; C4 trans., 7¼ qts.
⑦—With 6¾" ring gear Bobcat & Pinto, 2.2 pts.; Mustang, 3 pts.; units with 8 inch ring gear, 4 pts.
⑧—Approximate. Make final check with dipstick.
⑨—Bobcat & Pinto, 8.7 qts.; Mustang, 8.5 qts.
⑩—Bobcat & Pinto, 8.5 qts.; Mustang w/man. trans., 8.3 qts.; Mustang w/auto. trans., 8.8 qts.
⑪—Bobcat & Pinto, 12.5 qts.; Mustang, 12.3 qts.

⑫—Bobcat Calif. 11.7 gals.; Exc. Sta. Wag., 13 gals.; Sta. Wag., 14 gals. Add 3½ gals. with auxiliary fuel tank.
⑬—Bobcat & Pinto.
⑭—Mustang.
⑮—Man. trans., 8.3 qts.; Auto. trans., 8.8 qts.
⑯—Exc. Sta. Wag., 13 gals.; Sta. Wag., 14 gals.
⑰—C3 trans., 8 qts.; C4 trans., 7 qts.
⑱—6¾" axle—Pinto & Bobcat 2.2 pts., Mustang, 3 pts., 8" axle 4 pts.
⑲—Capri & Mustang.
⑳—Non-turbocharged.
㉑—Turbocharged.
㉒—Exc Sta. Wag. & Calif. auto. sedan, 13 gals.; Calif. auto. sedan, 11.7 gals.; Sta. Wag., 14 gals.

Electrical Section

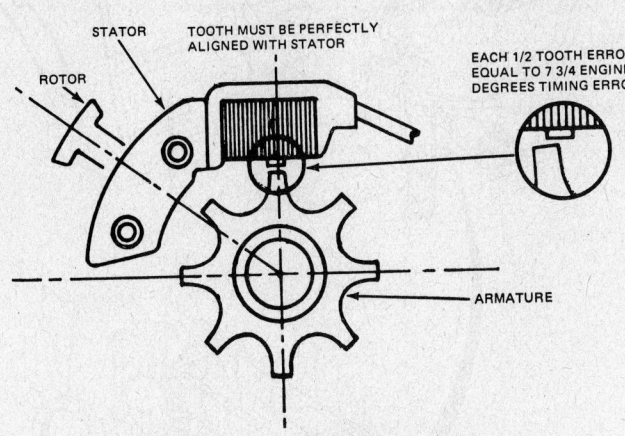

Fig. 1 Static timing position (typical)

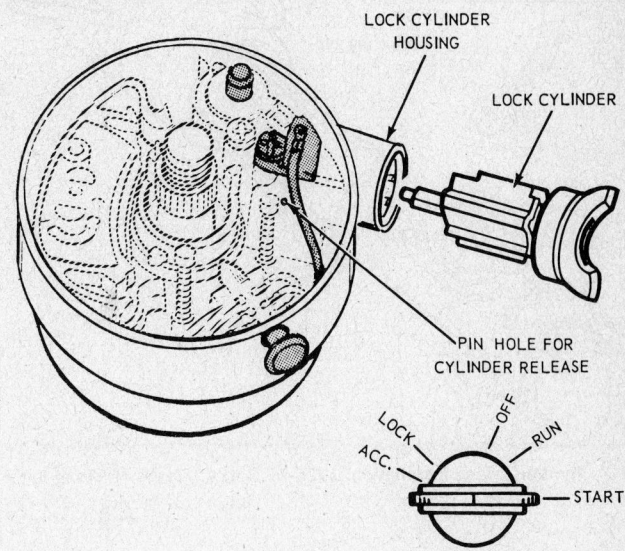

Fig. 1A Ignition lock

DISTRIBUTOR, REPLACE

1974 2000 & 2300 cc Engine

NOTE: On some engines, it may be necessary to position Thermactor pump aside to gain access to distributor.

1. Remove distributor cap and disconnect vacuum lines from distributor. Make sure that rotor is aligned with index mark on top edge of distributor body.

2. Remove hold down bolt and remove distributor.

   NOTE: *The hex shaft that drives the oil pump may stick in the distributor and be withdrawn from the pump.*

3. When installing distributor, make sure alignment marks are properly aligned, then install distributor and hold down bolt.

4. Check engine timing and adjust as necessary.

1975-79 2300 & 2800 cc Engine

1. On 2800 cc engine, remove air cleaner.

2. Remove Thermactor pump mounting bolt and drive belt, then move pump aside to permit access for distributor removal.

3. Rotate engine to position proper timing mark on engine crankshaft damper with timing pointer, then remove distributor cap and check that rotor and armature are aligned with stator.

4. Disconnect hose(s) from advance unit and electrical connector from harness.

5. Remove distributor hold down bolt and remove distributor.

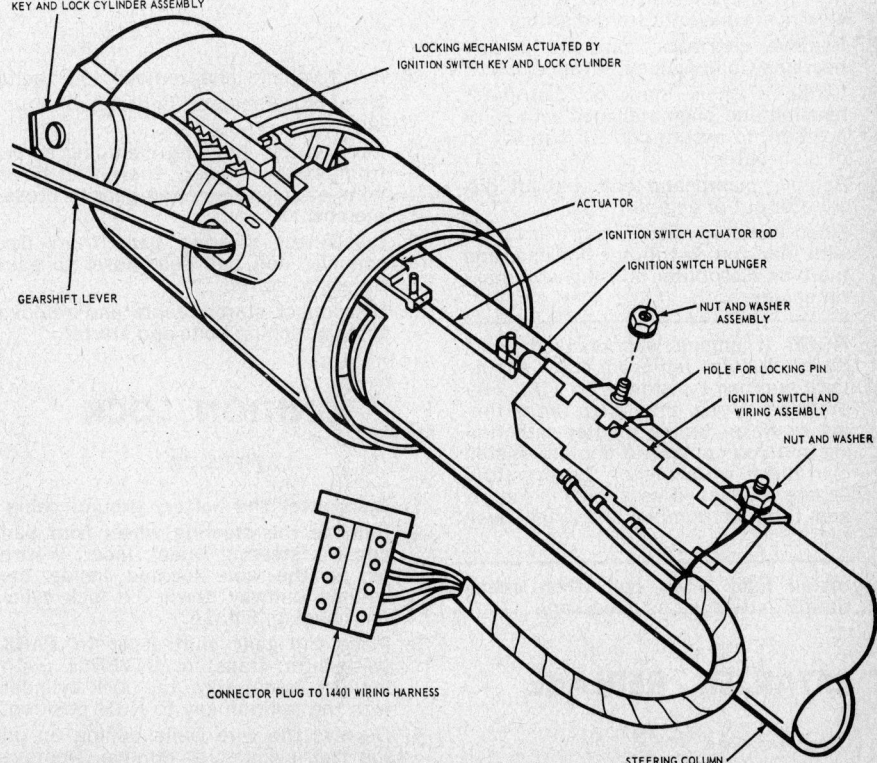

Fig. 1B Ignition switch installation. 1974 Pinto & 1974 Mustang

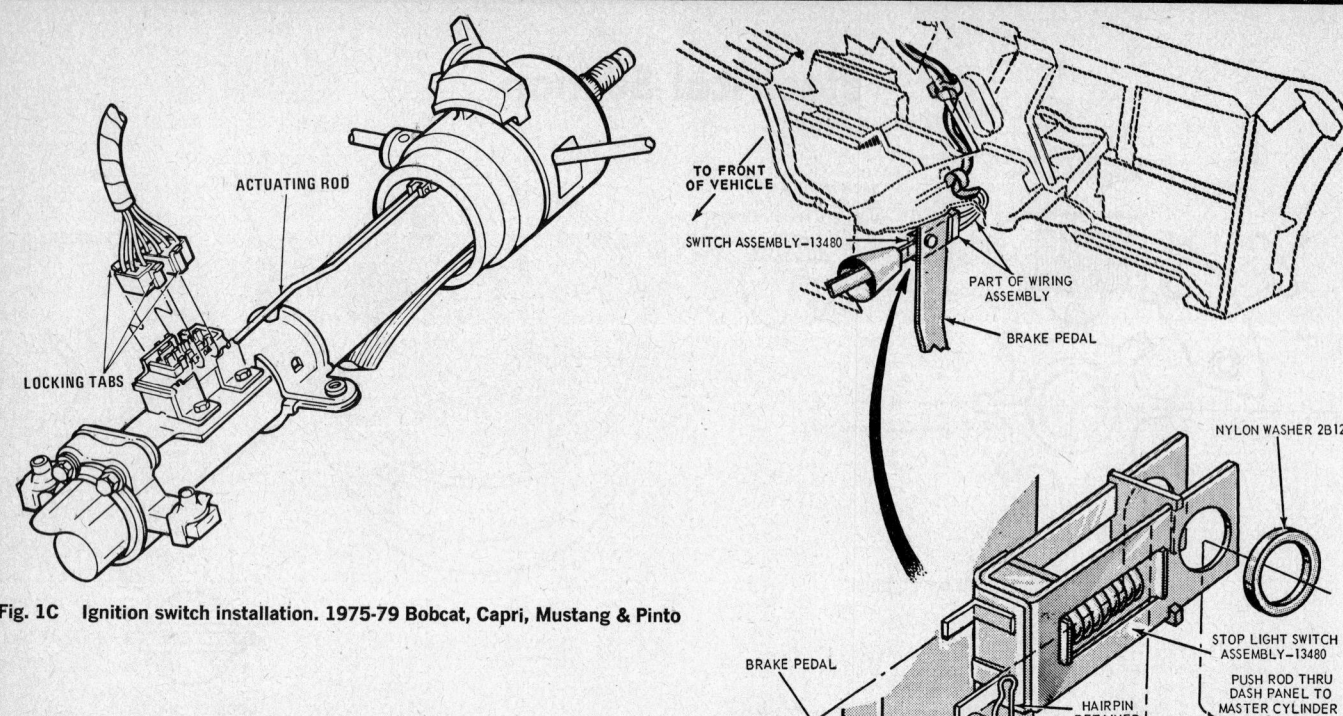

Fig. 1C   Ignition switch installation. 1975-79 Bobcat, Capri, Mustang & Pinto

Fig. 2   Stoplight switch installation

6. When installing distributor, make sure engine timing marks are properly aligned, and that rotor is aligned with mark on distributor housing and armature is perfectly aligned with stator, Fig. 1.
7. Install distributor and hold down bolt, then check engine timing and adjust as necessary.

V8-302 Engine

1. Remove air cleaner, then disconnect electrical connector from distributor.
2. Remove distributor cap and disconnect line from vacuum advance unit.
3. Scribe a chalk mark on distributor housing and engine aligned with rotor position, to assure correct installation of distributor.
4. Remove clamp and bolt and lift distributor out of engine.
5. When installing distributor, align rotor with mark on distributor housing, and mark on distributor housing with mark on engine.

NOTE: If engine was cranked while distributor was removed, crank engine until number 1 piston is on TDC compression stroke, then align initial timing mark on timing pointer with timing mark on crankshaft damper. Install distributor with one of the armature segments aligned as shown in Fig. 1, and rotor at number one firing position.

6. Install hold down bolt, then check timing and adjust as necessary.

STARTER, REPLACE

1974-79

1. Disconnect battery ground cable.
2. Raise vehicle and remove four bolts from crossmember under bell housing.
3. Remove flex coupling clamping screw from steering gear, then the three bolts attaching steering gear to crossmember.
4. Disconnect steering gear from flex coupling and pull gear down to gain access to starter.
5. Disconnect starter cable and remove three attaching bolts and starter.

IGNITION LOCK

1974-78

1. Disconnect the battery ground cable.
2. Remove the steering wheel trim pad and the steering wheel. Insert a wire pin in the hole located inside the column halfway down the lock cylinder housing, Fig. 1A.
3. Place the gear shift lever in *PARK* (with auto. trans) or *REVERSE* (with manual trans) turn the lock cylinder with the ignition key to *RUN* position.
4. Depress the wire while pulling up on the lock cylinder to remove. Remove the wire pin.

5. To install insert the lock cylinder into the housing in the flange casting, and turn the key to *OFF* position. This action will extend the cylinder retaining pin into the cylinder housing.
6. Turn the key to check for correct operation in all positions.
7. Install the steering wheel and trim pad. Reconnect the battery ground cable.

IGNITION SWITCH, REPLACE

1979 Capri & Mustang

1. Disconnect battery ground cable.
2. Rotate ignition key to "Lock" position.
3. Remove steering column trim shroud.
4. Using a 1/8 inch twist drill, drill out the bolt heads securing the switch to the lock cylinder. Then, remove the bolts using an "Easy Out" or equivalent.
5. Disengage the actuator rod from switch.
6. Disconnect electrical connector from switch.

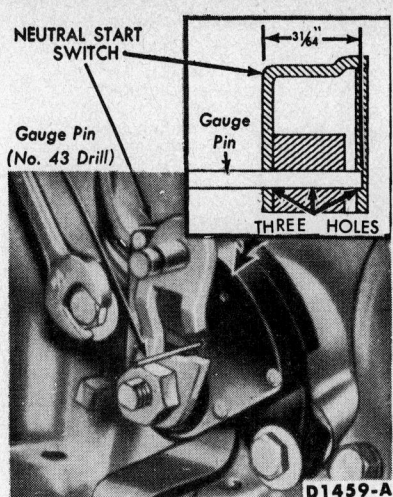

Fig. 3 Neutral safety switch adjustment

umn to locate the mid-position of rod lash and then tighten nuts.

11. Remove the plastic or substitute locking pin, connect battery and check switch for proper start in PARK or NEUTRAL.

LIGHT SWITCH, REPLACE

1974-78 Mustang

1. Disconnect battery ground cable.
2. Depress shaft release button by inserting a screwdriver through hole in underside of instrument panel, then remove knob and shaft.
3. Remove bezel nut, lower switch, disconnect electrical connector and remove switch.

1974-79 Bobcat & Pinto

1. Disconnect battery ground cable.
2. Remove instrument cluster as described further on.
3. Remove headlight switch knob and shaft assembly and retaining nut.
4. Disconnect connector plug from switch and remove switch from cluster opening.

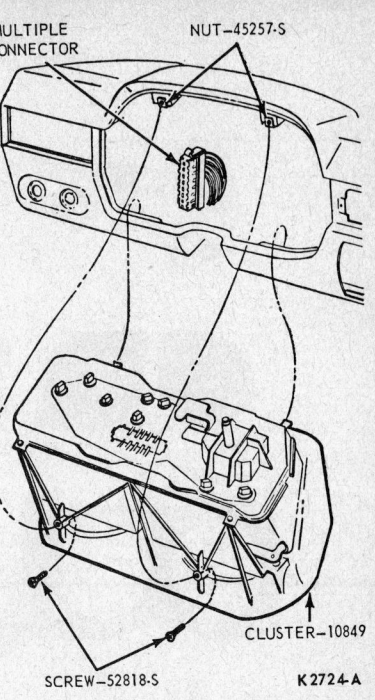

Fig. 4 Instrument-cluster removal (Typical). 1974-79 Bobcat & Pinto

7. Remove switch from vehicle.
8. With ignition key in "Lock" position, place switch on actuator rod.
9. Secure the switch with two new "Break-Off Head" bolts. Tighten the bolts until the heads shear.
10. Remove locking pin from new switch, if installed.
11. Connect switch electrical connector.
12. Connect battery ground cable.
13. Check for proper operation.

Exc. 1979 Capri & Mustang

1. Remove shrouding from steering column and detach and lower steering column from brake support bracket.
2. Disconnect battery ground cable.
3. Disconnect switch wiring at plug, Figs. 1B and 1C.
4. Remove two nuts that retain switch to column.
5. On 1974 models remove pin that connects switch directly to actuator and remove switch. On 1975-79 models, lifting switch vertically upward will disengage actuator rod from switch.
6. To install switch, both the locking mechanism at top of column and the switch must be in LOCK position for correct adjustment.
7. Move shift lever into Park (with automatic transmission) or Reverse (with manual transmission), turn the key to LOCK position and remove the key.

NOTE: New switches, when received, are already pinned in LOCK position by a plastic shipping pin inserted in a locking hole on top of switch.

8. Position the hole in the end of switch plunger to the hole in the actuator and install the connecting pin.
9. Position switch on column and install retaining nuts, but do not tighten them.
10. Move switch up and down along col-

STOP LIGHT SWITCH, REPLACE

1. Disconnect wires at connector.
2. Remove hairpin retainer, slide switch, push rod and nylon washers and bushing away from the pedal and remove the switch, Fig. 2.

NEUTRAL SAFETY SWITCH, REPLACE

Removal

1. Remove downshift linkage rod from transmission downshift lever.
2. Remove downshift outer lever retaining nut and lever.
3. Remove two switch attaching bolts.
4. Disconnect wire connector and remove switch.

Installation

1. Install switch on transmission and replace attaching bolts.
2. With transmission manual lever in neutral, rotate switch and install gauge pin (No. 43 drill) into gauge pin hole, Fig. 3.
3. Tighten switch attaching bolts and remove gauge pin.
4. Install outer downshift lever and attaching nut.
5. Install downshift linkage rod to downshift lever.
6. Install switch wire connector and check operation of switch. The engine should start only with lever in Neutral or Park.

TURN SIGNAL SWITCH, REPLACE

1. Disconnect battery ground cable.
2. Remove steering wheel.
3. Unscrew turn signal switch lever from column.
4. Remove shroud from under steering column.
5. Disconnect steering column wiring connector plugs from bracket.
6. Remove turn signal switch attaching screws.
7. Remove plastic cover sleeve from wiring harness.
8. Pull switch and wiring up from steering columns.
9. Reverse procedure to install.

HORN SOUNDER

The horn sounder can be removed by depressing it and turning counter-clockwise or by removing retaining screws from under steering wheel spokes.

INSTRUMENT CLUSTER

1979 Capri & Mustang

1. Disconnect battery ground cable.
2. Remove three upper retaining screws from instrument cluster trim cover, then the trim cover.
3. Remove two upper and two lower screws retaining instrument cluster to instrument panel.
4. Pull cluster from panel slightly and disconnect speedometer cable and the printed circuit electrical connectors.
5. Remove instrument clusters from instrument panel.
6. Reverse procedure to install.

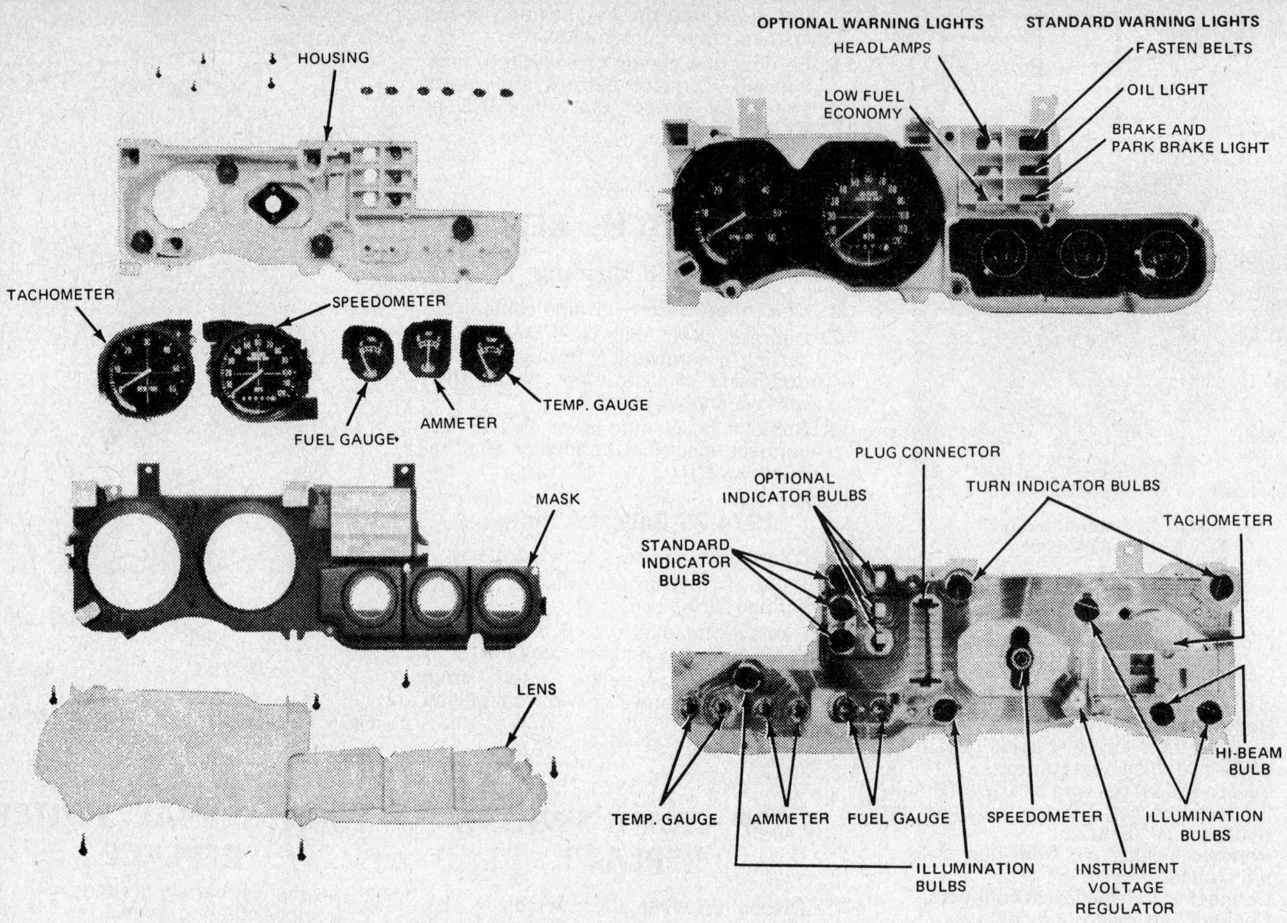

Fig. 4A   Instrument cluster (Typical). 1974-78 Mustang

1977-79 Bobcat & Pinto

Main Cluster
1. Remove two screws attaching upper half to lower half of steering column shroud, then remove lower half shroud.
2. Loosen forward steering column attaching nuts one or two turns.
3. Loosen rearward steering column attaching nuts $3/8$ to $1/2$ inch.
4. Disconnect wire connectors at printed circuit board and tachometer.
5. Disconnect speedometer cable.
6. Remove four cluster attaching screws and pull cluster out along angle of steering column, Fig. 4.

Auxiliary Cluster
1. Remove main cluster as described above.
2. Remove two screws attaching auxiliary cluster to instrument panel.
3. Remove auxiliary cluster mask from front of instrument panel.
4. Disconnect wire connector from printed circuit board, then remove auxiliary cluster through access provided by removal of main instrument cluster.

1974-78 Mustang

1. Disconnect battery ground cable.

2. On 1974 and early 1975 models, remove wiper switch and light switch knobs, then light switch bezel.
3. On all models, remove instrument cluster trim cover.
4. Disconnect speedometer cable by pressing on flat section of quick disconnect.
5. Remove cluster retaining screws, pull cluster from instrument panel, disconnect electrical connectors, then remove cluster, Fig. 4A.

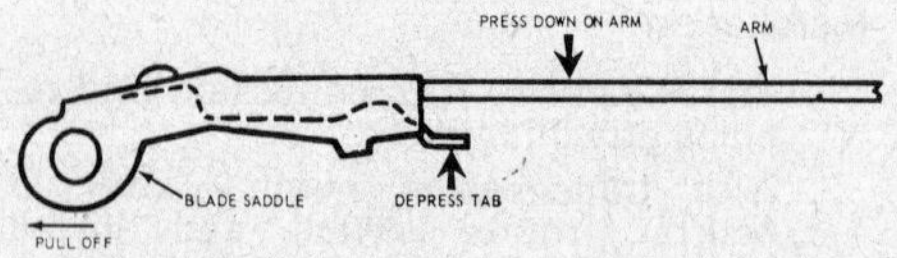

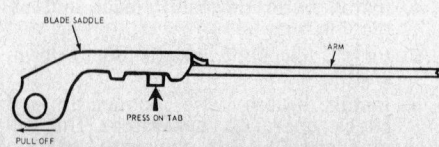

Fig. 5   Trico bayonet type blade

Fig. 6   Anco bayonet type blade

1974-76 Bobcat & Pinto

1. Disconnect battery ground cable.
2. From under instrument panel, disconnect speedometer cable.
3. Remove two retaining screws at top of cluster and swing cluster down away from panel, Fig. 4.
4. Disconnect connector from printed circuit, then disengage brackets on lower edge of panel and remove cluster.

W/S WIPER BLADES

NOTE: Trico and Anco Blades are used and both come in two types Bayonet type and Side Saddle Pin Type.

Bayonet Type: To remove the *Trico* type press down on the arm to unlock the top stud. Depress the tab on the saddle, Fig. 5, and pull the blade from the arm. To remove the *Anco* type press inward on the tab, Fig. 6, and pull the blade from the arm. To install a new blade assembly slide the blade saddle over the end of the wiper arm so that the locking stud snaps into place.

Side Saddle Pin Type: To remove the pin type (Trico or Anco) insert an appropriate tool into the spring release opening of the

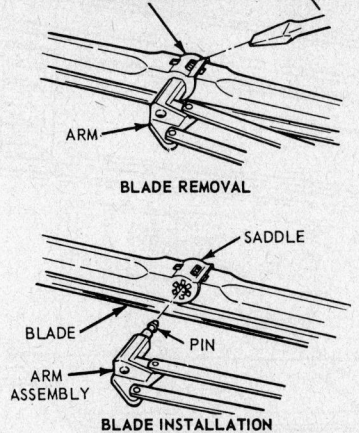

BLADE SADDLE

ARM

BLADE REMOVAL

SADDLE

BLADE

PIN

ARM ASSEMBLY

BLADE INSTALLATION

Fig. 7 Pin type blade

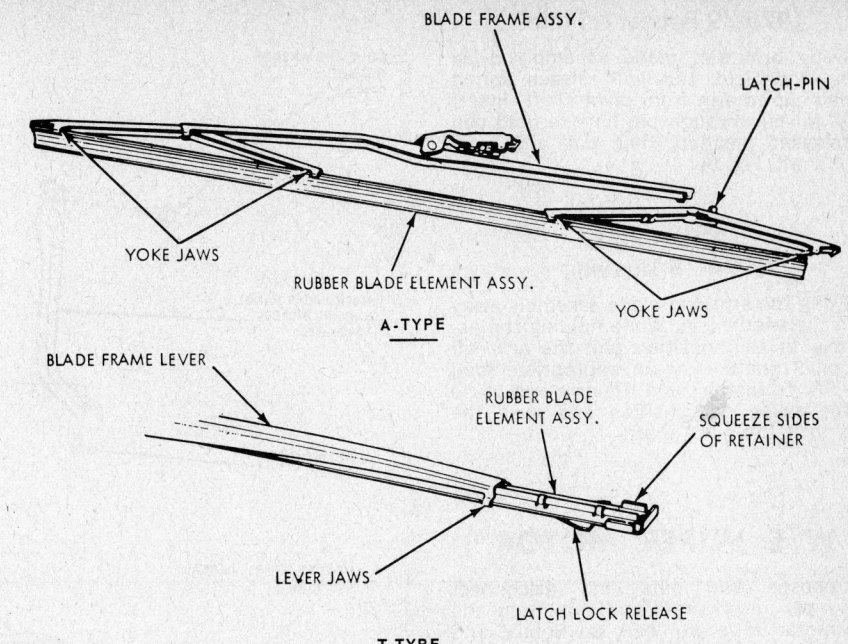

BLADE FRAME ASSY.

LATCH-PIN

YOKE JAWS

RUBBER BLADE ELEMENT ASSY.

YOKE JAWS

A-TYPE

BLADE FRAME LEVER

RUBBER BLADE ELEMENT ASSY.

SQUEEZE SIDES OF RETAINER

LEVER JAWS

LATCH LOCK RELEASE

T-TYPE

Fig. 8 Wiper blade element

blade saddle, depress the spring clip and pull the blade from the arm, Fig. 7. To install, push the blade saddle on to the pin so that the spring clip engages the pin. To replace the rubber element in a *Trico* blade squeeze the latch lock release and pull the element out of the lever jaws, Fig. 8. Remove *Anco* element by depressing the latch pin, Fig. 8, and sliding the element out of the yoke jaws. To install insert the element through the yoke or lever jaws. Be sure the element is engaged at all points.

W/S WIPER ARMS

1979 Capri & Mustang

Raise the blade end of the arm off the windshield and move the slide latch, Fig. 8A, away from the pivot shaft. This action will unlock the wiper arm from the pivot shaft and hold the blade end of the arm off the glass at the same time. The wiper arm can now be pulled off the pivot shaft without the aid of any tools.

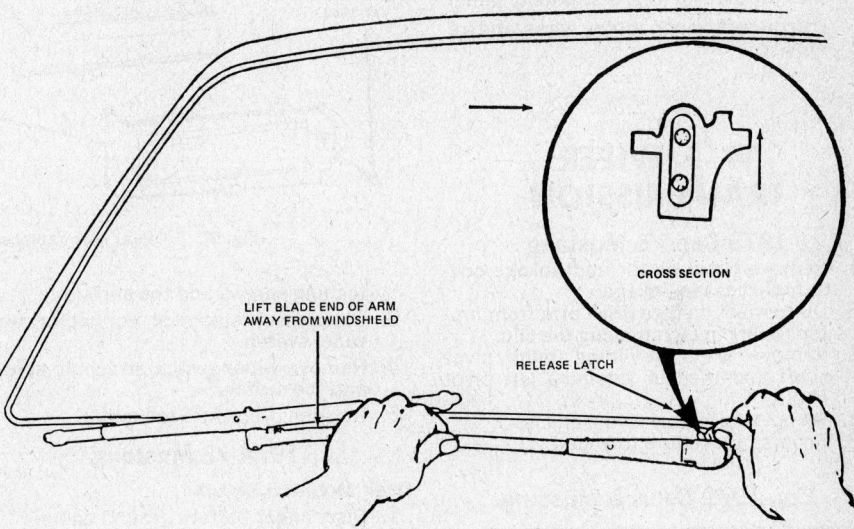

CROSS SECTION

LIFT BLADE END OF ARM AWAY FROM WINDSHIELD

RELEASE LATCH

Fig. 8A Wiper arm. 1979 Capri & Mustang

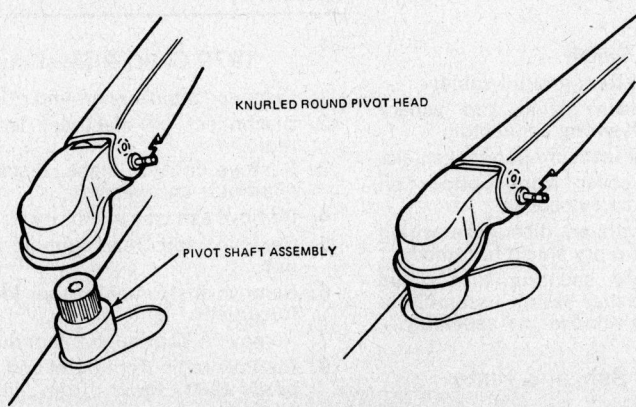

KNURLED ROUND PIVOT HEAD

PIVOT SHAFT ASSEMBLY

Fig. 9 Wiper arm removal. 1975-79 Bobcat & Pinto

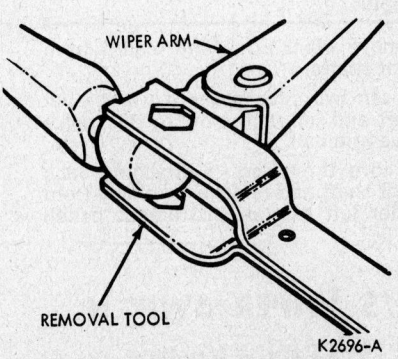

WIPER ARM

REMOVAL TOOL

K2696-A

Fig. 9A Wiper arm removal. 1974 Pinto & 1974-78 Mustang

1975-79 Bobcat & Pinto

Swing arm and blade assembly away from windshield, this will release spring loaded clip in arm from pivot shaft. Insert a 3/32 in. pin through pin hole to hold clip in released position, then pull arm from pivot shaft, Fig. 9.

1974 Pinto & 1974-78 Mustang

Swing the arm and blade assembly away from the windshield. While holding the assembly in this position pull the arm off the pivot shaft using an appropriate tool, Fig. 9A. To install, hold the arm and blade in the swing out position and push the arm on to the pivot shaft.

W/S WIPER MOTOR

1. Loosen two nuts and disconnect wiper pivot shaft and link from the motor drive arm ball, on Bobcat and Pinto models. A link retaining clip is used on Capri & Mustang models.
2. Remove three motor attaching screws and lower motor away from under the left side of the instrument panel.
3. Disconnect wiper motor wires and remove motor.

W/S WIPER TRANSMISSION

1979 Capri & Mustang

1. Remove wiper motor and linkage cover for access to linkage.
2. Disconnect linkage drive arm from motor crank pin by removing the clip.
3. Remove bolts retaining right pivot shaft and the nut retaining left pivot shaft.
4. Remove assembly from vehicle.
5. Reverse procedure to install.

Exc. 1979 Capri & Mustang

NOTE: On 1974-79 Bobcat & Pinto equipped with air conditioning, remove blower motor to gain access to wiper transmission as described further on in this chapter.

1. Remove wiper arms and blades from pivot shafts.
2. Loosen two nuts retaining wiper pivot shaft and link assembly to the motor drive arm ball.
3. Remove three screws attaching each pivot shaft and remove assembly from under left side of instrument panel.

W/S WIPER SWITCH

1979 Capri & Mustang

1. Disconnect battery ground cable.
2. Remove steering column shroud at-

taching screws and the shroud.
3. Disconnect electrical connector from wiper switch.
4. Remove wiper switch attaching screws and the switch.
5. Reverse procedure to install.

1974-78 Mustang

Dash Mounted Switch
1. Disconnect battery ground cable.
2. Remove switch knob and bezel nut, pull switch from panel, disconnect electrical connector and remove switch.

Column Mounted Switch
1. Disconnect battery ground cable.
2. Disconnect turn signal and wiper/washer switch wiring connector.
3. Remove lower instrument panel shield.
4. Pull wiring cover from bottom on column and remove cover.
5. With a screwdriver, disengage wiring shield tang and pry shield to remove.
6. Remove screw securing turn signal and wiper/washer switch assembly to column, then remove the assembly.

1974-79 Bobcat & Pinto

1. Remove instrument cluster as outlined previously.

2. Insert a thin bladed screwdriver into the slot in the switch knob and depress the spring. Then pull the knob from the switch shaft.
3. Remove wiper switch bezel nut. Then unplug wires and remove switch.

RADIO, REPLACE

NOTE: When installing radio, be sure to adjust antenna trimmer for peak performance.

1979 Capri & Mustang

1. Disconnect battery ground cable.
2. Disconnect all electrical leads from radio.
3. Remove control knobs, discs, control shaft nuts and washers.
4. Remove ash tray and bracket.
5. Remove radio rear support attaching nut.
6. Remove instrument panel lower reinforcement.
7. Remove A/C or heater floor ducts.
8. Remove radio from bezel and rear support, then lower from instrument panel.
9. Reverse procedure to install.

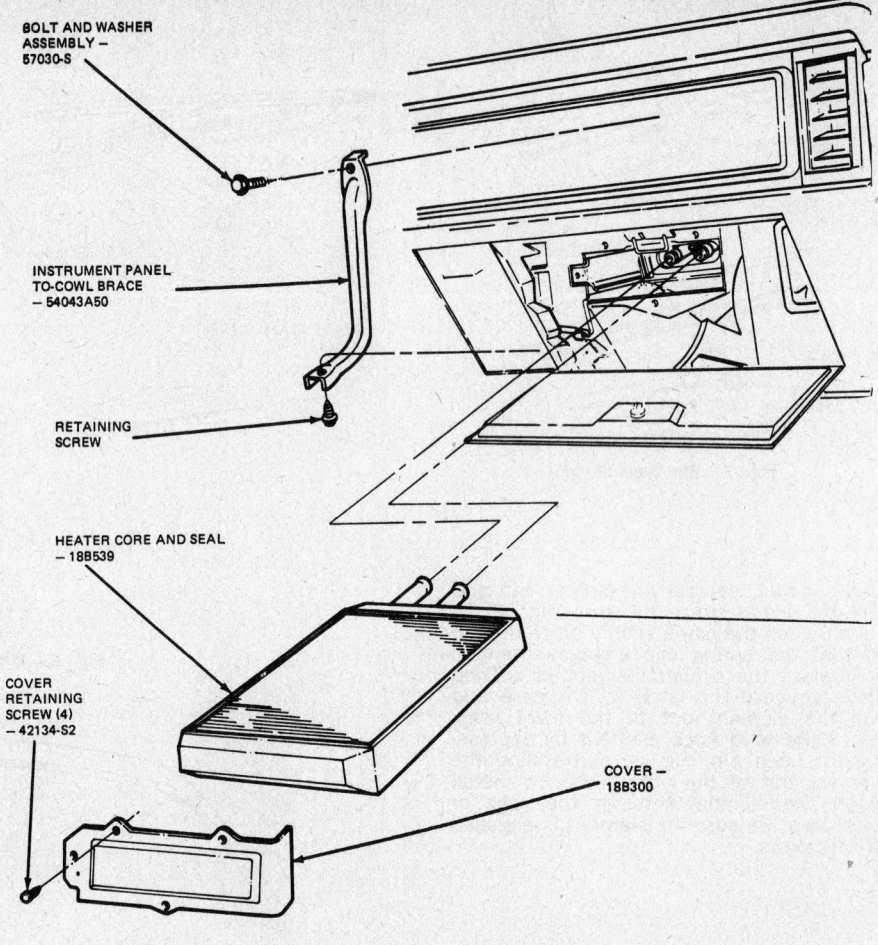

BOLT AND WASHER ASSEMBLY — 57030-S

INSTRUMENT PANEL TO-COWL BRACE — 54043A50

RETAINING SCREW

HEATER CORE AND SEAL — 18B539

COVER RETAINING SCREW (4) — 42134-S2

COVER — 18B300

Fig. 9B   Heater core replacement. 1979 Capri & Mustang less A/C

1974-78 Mustang

1. Disconnect battery ground cable.
2. Remove radio knobs, discs, shaft nuts and washers. On 1975-78 models, remove ash tray.
3. Remove radio rear support to instrument panel nut.
4. Lower radio, disconnect wiring and remove radio.

1974-79 Bobcat & Pinto

1. Disconnect battery ground cable.
2. Remove instrument panel trim brace cover.
3. Remove rear support to radio attaching bolt.
4. Remove four screws attaching the bezel to the instrument panel opening.
5. Pull radio out from instrument panel and disconnect speaker, power and antenna wires and remove radio.

HEATER CORE REMOVAL

Less Air Conditioning

1979 Capri & Mustang

1. Drain cooling system and disconnect battery ground cable.
2. Disconnect heater hoses from heater core and plug core openings.
3. Remove glove box liner.
4. Remove instrument panel to cowl brace retaining screws and the brace.
5. Move temperature control lever to warm position.
6. Remove the four heater core cover retaining screws, then the cover through the glove box opening.
7. Remove heater core assembly mounting stud nuts from engine compartment.
8. Push core tubes and seal toward passenger compartment to loosen core from case assembly.
9. Remove heater core from case through the glove box opening, Fig. 9B.
10. Reverse procedure to install.

Exc. 1979 Capri & Mustang

1. Drain coolant and disconnect battery.
2. Disconnect blower motor ground wire at engine side of dash.
3. Disconnect heater hoses at engine block.
4. Remove four heater assembly-to-dash mounting nuts from the engine side of the dash.
5. Remove the glove box.
6. Disconnect control cables from heater. Remove mounting bracket clips and disconnect cables from door crank arms.
7. Remove radio as outlined previously.
8. Working inside car, remove snap rivet that attaches the forward side of the defroster air duct to the plenum chamber. Move the air duct back into the defroster nozzle to disengage it from the tabs on the plenum cham-

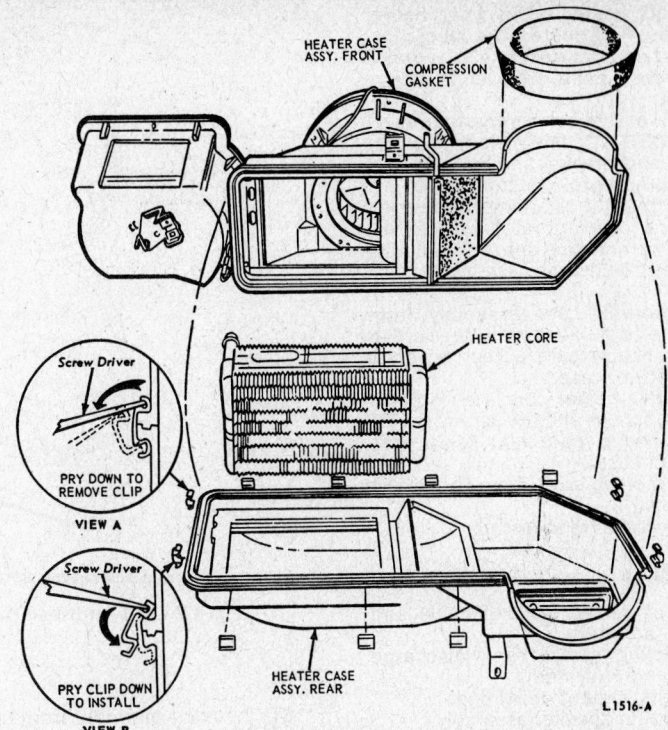

Fig. 10   Heater core removal 1974-78 Mustang & 1974-79 Bobcat & Pinto less A/C

ber. Now, tilt the forward edge of the duct up and forward to disengage it from the nozzle and remove it from the left side of the heater assembly.

9. Remove heater case-to-instrument panel support bracket mounting screw and remove the heater case. At the same time, pull the two heater hoses in through the dash panel. Then disconnect the hoses from the heater core in the case.
10. Remove compression gasket from cowl air inlet.
11. Remove eleven clips from around the front and rear case flanges and separate the front and rear halves of the case, Fig. 10.
12. Lift heater core from front half of case.

With Air Conditioning

1979 Capri & Mustang

1. Disconnect battery ground cable.
2. Remove screws securing the left side of instrument panel pad retaining tabs to the instrument panel, in the upper right and left corners of the instrument panel cluster area.
3. Remove screws securing the right side of instrument panel pad retaining tabs to instrument panel, located in the two openings at the top edge of the right instrument panel trim applique, above the glove box.
4. Remove screws securing leading edge of instrument panel pad to defroster openings. Use a magnetic or locking tang type phillips screwdriver. Do not let screws drop into defroster openings since plenum door damage may result.
5. Raise the overhanging edge of the instrument panel pad to clear retaining tabs and pull pad rearward to remove

from top of instrument panel.

6. Remove screws attaching steering column opening lower cover to instrument panel, then the cover.
7. Remove steering column trim shrouds.
8. Remove nuts securing steering column to brake pedal support and lower steering column for access to gearshift selector lever and cable assembly.
9. Reach between steering column and instrument panel and lift selector lever cable off selector lever. Then, remove cable clamp from steering column tube.
10. Rest steering column of front seat.
11. Remove screw attaching instrument panel to brake pedal support at steering column opening.
12. Remove screw attaching lower brace to lower edge of instrument panel, below the radio.
13. Remove screw attaching brace to lower edge of instrument panel.
14. Disconnect temperature control cable from temperature blend door and evaporator case bracket.
15. Disconnect seven-port vacuum hose connectors at evaporator case.
16. Disconnect blower resistor wire connector from resistor and the blower motor feed wire at in-line connector near the blower resistor wire connector.
17. Support instrument panel and remove three screws securing top of instrument panel to the cowl.
18. Remove screw at each side of instrument panel securing instrument panel to cowl side panels.
19. Move instrument panel rearward and disconnect speedometer cable and any wiring that will not permit the panel to lay on the front seat.
21. Drain cooling system.

22. Disconnect heater hoses from heater core tubes. Plug heater core tubes.
23. Remove two nuts securing evaporator case to dash panel from engine compartment.
24. From the passenger compartment, remove screws attaching the evaporator case support bracket and air inlet duct support bracket to cowl top panel.
25. Remove one nut retaining the bracket at left end of evaporator case to the dash panel and the one nut securing the bracket below the case to the dash panel.
26. Pull evaporator case assembly from dash panel to gain access to the screws retaining heater core access cover to the evaporator case.
27. Remove five heater core access cover attaching screws and the access cover.
28. Remove heater core and seals from evaporator case.
29. Remove the two seals from the heater core tubes.
30. Reverse procedure to install.

1975-78 Mustang

1. Disconnect battery ground cable and remove the battery.
2. Drain cooling system and discharge A/C refrigerant system.
3. Remove instrument panel pad.
4. Remove radio speaker assembly.
5. Remove both "A" pillar mouldings.
6. Remove both side kick panel pad assemblies.
7. Remove the lower steering column cover.
8. Remove the steering column to cowl panel shake brace.
9. Remove accelerator pedal assembly and disconnect the two cables.
10. Remove the bottom bolt retaining center shake brace to instrument panel assembly.
11. Disconnect antenna lead from radio.
12. Disconnect the five connectors at the left cowl panel.
13. Disconnect electrical connector from wiper switch.
14. Disconnect the five connectors from the right cowl panel.
15. Disconnect electrical connector from dimmer switch assembly.
16. Disconnect the heater blower motor resistor.
17. Disconnect temperature control cable.
18. Remove the two evaporator to upper cowl bracket screws.
19. Disconnect the main wiring harness in the engine compartment and push the connectors into the passenger compartment.
20. Disconnect the three remaining connectors and push the connectors into the passenger compartment.
21. Disconnect the turn signal switch assembly.
22. Lower the steering column.
23. Disconnect electrical connectors from ignition switch.
24. Disconnect electrical connector from stop light switch assembly.
25. Remove instrument panel to steering column center support bracket.
26. Remove instrument panel retaining bolts and the instrument panel.
27. Disconnect heater hoses from heater core.
28. Remove the two screws attaching evaporator manifold plate to expansion valve body.
29. Separate expansion valve body and

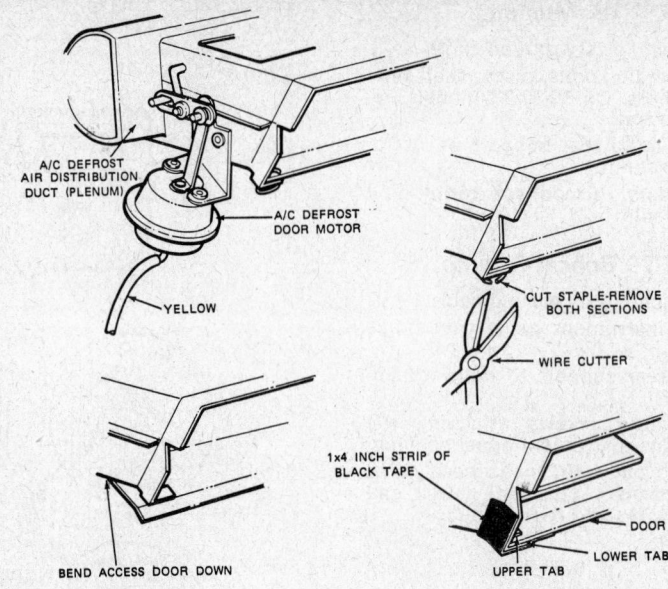

Fig. 11   A/C defrost air distribution duct fold down door. 1974-79 Bobcat & Pinto

STV housing manifold from evaporator manifold plate.
30. Remove four nuts retaining evaporator to dash panel and the evaporator assembly.
31. Remove the eight upper to lower case attaching screws.
32. Remove rubber seal from heater core tubes.
33. Remove upper half from evaporator case.
34. Remove air deflector mounting screw on lower case to left of heater core, then the air deflector and heater core.
35. Reverse procedure to install.

1974 Mustang & 1974-79 Bobcat & Pinto

1. Disconnect battery ground cable, drain radiator and discharge refrigerant from A/C system.
2. Remove refrigerant lines and the front half of refrigerant manifold.

NOTE: Remove manifold mounting stud to ensure clearance for removal of evaporator case.

3. Disconnect heater hoses from core tubes and remove condensation drain hose in engine compartment.
4. Remove glove box.
5. Disconnect vacuum hoses from evaporator case and temperature control cable from blend door crank arm.
6. Remove heat distribution duct.

NOTE: On Mustang, remove mode door vacuum motor.

7. On Mustang remove lower section of the air conditioning defrost plenum.
8. On Bobcat and Pinto, remove staples retaining fold down door on plenum, Fig. 11. Bend fold down door from locating tabs on plenum and remove adapter duct.

NOTE: During installation, position

fold down door between locating tabs and tape in place with two pieces of black tape, Fig. 11.

9. On all models, remove blower motor and wheel from blower scroll.
10. Install a ¼-20 hex washer head screw in mounting tab of inlet duct to upper cowl bracket, holding inlet duct in place.

NOTE: Leave screw in position during installation of case assembly.

11. Remove inlet duct to evaporator case screws.

NOTE: One upper case to inlet duct screw is located under outside-recirc. motor mounting bracket.

12. Remove evaporator to cowl bracket screws and the evaporator to dash panel nuts in engine compartment. Rotate evaporator down and away from instrument panel and remove from under panel.
13. Remove upper to lower case screws and rubber seal from heater core tubes.
14. Remove upper half of evaporator case and move rubber seal on evaporator core forward and pull evaporator core from lower case.
15. Remove heater core upper straps, air deflector mounting screw, then remove air deflector and heater core.

BLOWER MOTOR, REMOVE

Less Air Conditioning

1979 Capri & Mustang

1. Disconnect battery ground cable.

2. Remove right ventilator assembly.
3. Disconnect blower lead wire connector from spade terminal of resistor assembly and push back through hole in case.
4. Remove right side trim panel for access to blower ground terminal lug, then remove the ground terminal lug retaining screw.
5. Remove blower motor flange retaining screws from inside the blower housing.
6. Remove blower motor from housing.
7. Reverse procedure to install.

Exc. 1979 Capri & Mustang

1. Follow procedure to remove the heater core as described previously.
2. Disconnect the blower motor lead wire (orange) from the resistor.
3. Remove the four blower mounting plate nuts and remove the motor and wheel assembly, Fig. 12.
4. Reverse procedure to install.

With Air Conditioning

1979 Capri & Mustang

1. Disconnect battery ground cable.
2. Remove glove box and disconnect hose from outside-recirculation door vacuum motor.
3. Remove instrument panel lower right to side cowl attaching bolt.
4. Remove screw attaching support brace to top of air inlet duct.
5. Disconnect blower motor feed wire at connector.
6. Remove nut retaining blower housing lower support bracket to evaporator case.
7. Remove side cowl trim panel.
8. Remove blower motor ground wire screw.
9. Remove screw attaching top of air inlet duct to evaporator case.
10. Pull air inlet duct and blower housing assembly downward and away from evaporator case.
11. Remove four blower motor mounting plate screws, then the blower motor assembly from blower housing.
12. Reverse procedure to install.

Exc. 1979 Capri & Mustang

1. Remove glove box.
2. Remove four screws retaining blower motor and wheel to blower scroll.

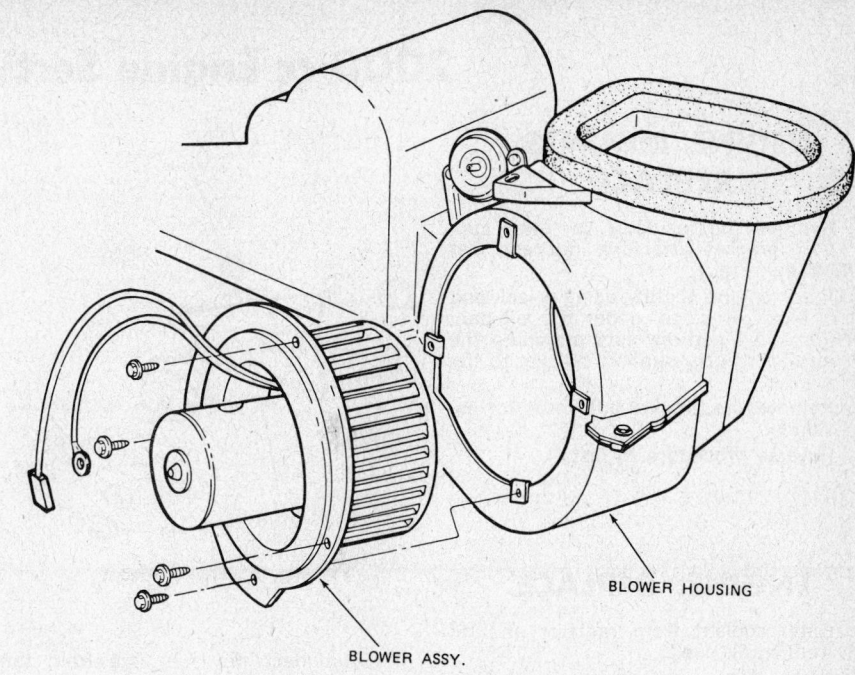

BLOWER HOUSING

BLOWER ASSY.

Fig. 12   Blower motor. 1974-78 All (Typical)

3. Remove blower motor and wheel assembly.

NOTE: On 1977-78 models, it may be necessary to remove bolt securing instrument panel to right side cowl and pull instrument panel rearward to provide clearance for blower motor removal.

SPEED CONTROL

1979

Bead Chain Adjustment

Adjust bead chain to obtain a taut chain with the engine at hot idle. The adjustment should be made as to remove as much slack as possible from the bead chain without restricting the carburetor lever from returning to idle. On vehicles equipped with a solenoid throttle positioner, perform adjustment with throttle positioner deactivated.

Actuator Cable Adjustment

1. Deactivate the throttle positioner.
2. Set carburetor at hot idle.
3. Pull the actuator cable to remove slack.
4. While maintaining light tension on the cable, insert the cable retaining clip.

Vacuum Dump Valve

The vacuum dump valve is mounted on a moveable mounting bracket. The valve should be adjusted so that it is closed when the brake pedal is not depressed and opens when the brake pedal is depressed.

2000 cc Engine Section

ENGINE MOUNTS, REPLACE

1. Remove the insulator to lower support bracket attaching nut and flat washer, Fig. 1.
2. Raise engine slightly using a jack and a block of wood under the oil pan. Remove the three nuts attaching the insulator upper-support bracket to the engine.
3. Remove the bracket and insulator assembly.
4. Reverse procedure to install.

ENGINE, REPLACE

1. Drain coolant from radiator and oil from crankcase.
2. Raise hood and secure in vertical position.
3. Remove air cleaner and exhaust manifold shroud.
4. Disconnect battery ground cable.
5. Remove radiator hoses and remove radiator and fan.
6. Disconnect heater hoses from water pump and carburetor choke fitting.
7. Disconnect wires from alternator and starter and disconnect accelerator cable from carburetor. On A/C vehicles, remove compressor from bracket and position it out of way with lines attached.

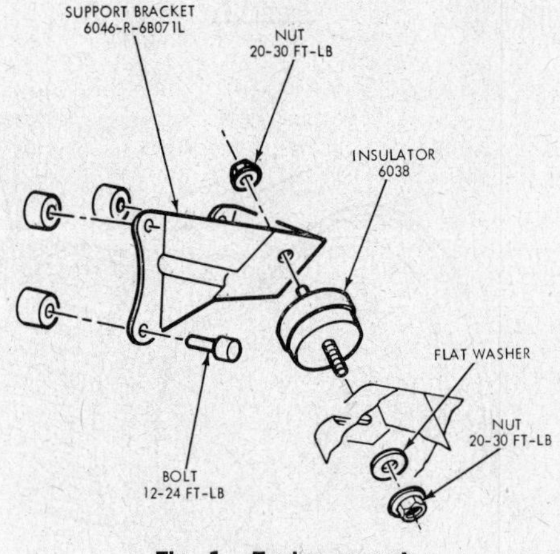

8. Disconnect flex fuel line from tank line and plug tank line.
9. Disconnect primary wire at coil and disconnect oil pressure and temperature sending unit wires at sending units.
10. Remove starter and raise vehicle to remove the flywheel or converter housing upper attaching bolts.
11. Disconnect inlet pipe at exhaust manifold. Disconnect engine mounts at underbody bracket and remove flywheel or converter housing cover.
12. On vehicle with manual shift, remove flywheel housing lower attaching bolts.
13. On vehicle with automatic transmission, disconnect converter from flywheel and remove converter housing lower attaching bolts.
14. Lower vehicle and support transmission and flywheel or converter housing with a jack.
15. Attach engine lifting hooks to brackets and carefully lift engine out of engine compartment.

Fig. 1 Engine mount

SUPPORT BRACKET
6046-R-6B071L

NUT
20-30 FT-LB

INSULATOR
6038

FLAT WASHER

NUT
20-30 FT-LB

BOLT
12-24 FT-LB

2. Remove exhaust manifold and remove intake manifold, carburetor and decel valve as an assembly.
3. Remove camshaft drive belt cover.
4. Loosen drive belt tensioner and remove drive belt.
5. Remove water outlet elbow from head.
6. Remove cylinder head attaching bolts.

NOTE: The cylinder head retaining bolts have 12 point heads.

7. Lift head and camshaft assembly from engine.
8. Reverse procedure to install. Torque cylinder head bolts in sequence shown in Fig. 2 and intake manifold bolts in sequence shown in Fig. 3.

NOTE: Do not overtighten the valve cover retaining screws, also make certain the valve cover gasket is aligned properly. It is possible to block the oil return hole on the right side of the front camshaft bearing support if the above cautions are not adhered to. If the oil return hole becomes blocked, sufficient oil pressure can build up in the front camshaft bearing area and push the oil seal out of position.

VALVE ARRANGEMENT

Front to Rear

2000 cc Engine . . . . E-I-E-I-E-I-E-I

VALVE LIFT SPECS.

Engine	Year	Intake	Exhaust
2000 cc	1974	.3993	.3993

Fig. 2 Cylinder head tightening sequence. 2000 cc engine

← FRONT

CYLINDER HEAD, REPLACE

1. Drain cooling system and remove air cleaner and rocker arm cover.

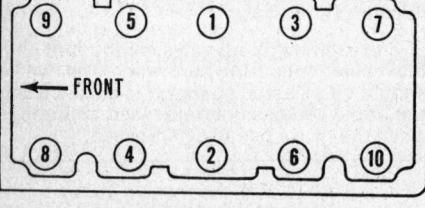

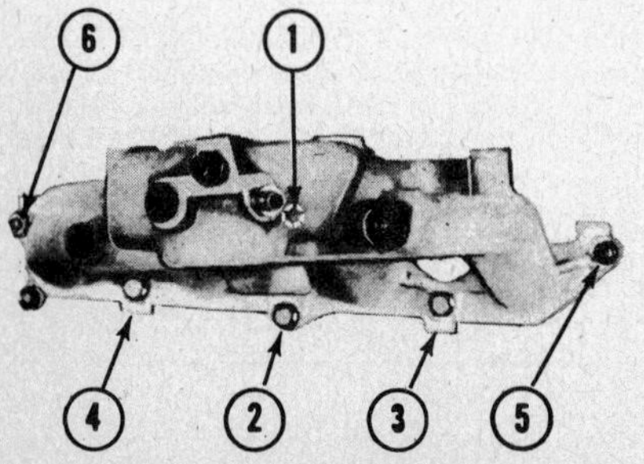

Fig. 3 Intake manifold tightening sequence

2000 cc Engine — Set at Any Temperature

| Valve Depressed | Valves to Adjust to | |
	.008	.010
no. 1	no. 6	no. 7
no. 2	no. 8	no. 3
no. 3	no. 2	no. 5
no. 6	no. 4	no. 1

Fig. 4 Valve adjustment table

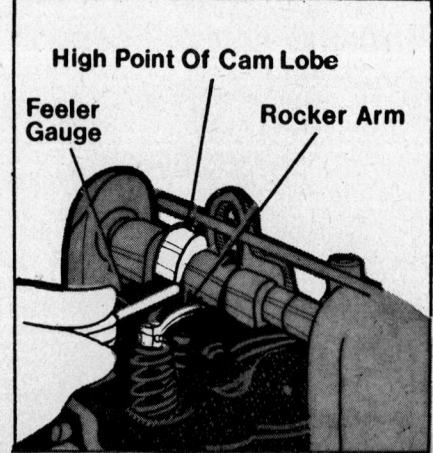

High Point Of Cam Lobe

Feeler Gauge

Rocker Arm

Fig. 5 Checking valve clearance

SEAL

Tool T71P-6150-A

A3423-A

Fig. 6   Removing crankshaft oil seal 2000 cc engine

ROCKER ARM SERVICE

1. Remove air cleaner.
2. Remove rocker arm cover.
3. Rotate crankshaft as required to place the low side of the camshaft lobe next to the rocker arm that is being replaced.
4. Remove the rocker arm retaining spring.
5. Depress the valve spring with Tool T71P6565-A just enough to remove the rocker arm.

NOTE: Refer to "NOTE" under "Cylinder Head, Replace" before installing valve cover.

TIMING CASE COVER

It is not necessary to remove the front cover to replace the crankshaft oil seal. Proceed as follows:
1. Remove alternator belt.
2. Remove crankshaft pulley bolt and slide pulley off shaft.
3. Remove camshaft drive belt and slide sprocket and belt guide off the crankshaft. If sprocket cannot be slid off shaft use a puller.
4. Install tool T71P-6150A over end of crankshaft and remove seal, Fig. 6.
5. Install a new seal with tool T71P-6150B, Fig. 7.

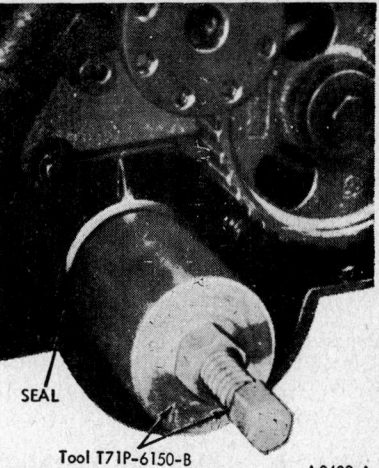

SEAL

Tool T71P-6150-B

A3422-A

Fig. 7   Installing crankshaft oil seal 2000 cc engine

VALVE TIMING

Intake Opens Before TDC

Engine	Year	Degrees
2000 cc	1974	24

TIMING BELT

1. Place crankshaft on TDC.
2. Remove the three camshaft drive belt cover screws and remove cover.
3. Loosen camshaft drive belt tensioner adjustment bolt, Fig. 8 and force the tensioner toward the exhaust manifold side of engine to relax belt tension, then tighten the bolt.
4. Lift the belt off the sprockets.

NOTE: Do not rotate the crankshaft or the camshaft after the belt is removed. Rotating either one will impair valve timing.

5. To install, make sure timing marks are aligned as in Fig. 8 and place the belt over the sprockets.
6. Loosen the tensioner adjustment bolt to place tension on the belt.
7. Rotate the crankshaft two complete turns to place the timing marks in the proper position and to remove all slack from the belt. Torque the adjustment bolt and the pivot bolt.
8. Position camshaft drive belt cover and install screws.
9. Start engine and check ignition timing and adjust as required.

VALVES, ADJUST

1. If there is a clamp between heat shroud pipe and air cleaner duct and valve assembly, loosen the clamp.
2. Disconnect crankcase ventilation hose and carbon cannister hose at air cleaner.
3. Remove wing nuts and unsnap wire clips on air cleaner cover and lift air cleaner off carburetor.
4. Remove screws (11 mm) from rocker cover.
5. Remove spark plug wires from retainer and move out of way.
6. Remove rocker cover.
7. Rotate the crankshaft clockwise by hand until the high point of the number 1 cam lobe is pointing down. Check clearances on valves 6 and 7. Consult Fig. 4 and continue on through sequence until all valves are adjusted, Fig. 5.

VALVE GUIDES

Valve guides consist of holes bored in the cylinder head. For service, the guides can be reamed oversize to accommodate valves with oversize stems. Valves with oversize stems are available in oversizes of .008", .016" and .032".

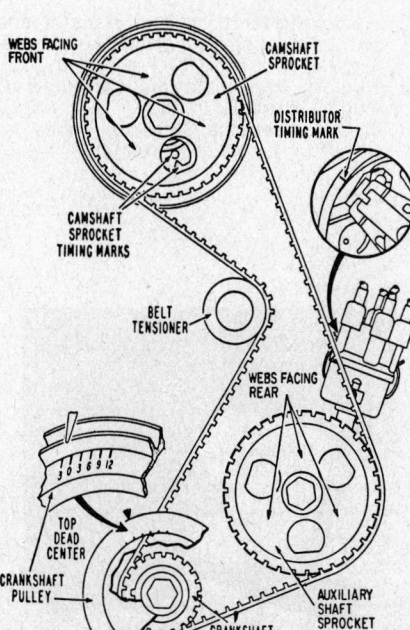

WEBS FACING FRONT

CAMSHAFT SPROCKET

DISTRIBUTOR TIMING MARK

CAMSHAFT SPROCKET TIMING MARKS

BELT TENSIONER

WEBS FACING REAR

TOP DEAD CENTER

CRANKSHAFT PULLEY

CRANKSHAFT SPROCKET

AUXILIARY SHAFT SPROCKET

Fig. 8   Timing marks 2000 cc engine

CAMSHAFT, REPLACE

After removal of cylinder head, proceed as follows:
1. Remove rocker arms.
2. Remove camshaft gear bolt and washer, and slide the gear and the belt guide plate off the shaft.
3. Remove camshaft thrust plate from rear of head and carefully slide camshaft from the rear of the head.

PISTON & ROD, ASSEMBLE

Assemble the piston to the rod with the oil squirt hole in the rod positioned to the right side of the engine. The arrow on the piston must face forward, Fig. 9.

PISTONS, PINS & RINGS

Oversize pistons and rings are available in .003, .020, .030 and .040". Oversize pins are not available.

MAIN & ROD BEARINGS

Undersize main bearings are available in .010, .020 and .030". Rod bearing undersizes are available in .010, .020, .030 and .040" on the 1600 cc engine. Only .010 and .020" undersizes are available on the 2000 cc engine.

CRANKSHAFT OIL SEAL

1. Remove transmission, clutch and flywheel or the automatic transmission, converter and flywheel.
2. Remove crankshaft rear seal with a sheet metal screw as shown in Fig. 10.
3. Install new seal with tool T71P-6701A as shown in Fig. 11.

OIL PAN, REPLACE

1. Drain crankcase and remove oil dipstick and flywheel inspection cover.
2. Disconnect steering cable from rack and pinion.
3. Disconnect rack and pinion from crossmember and move it forward to provide clearance.
4. Unfasten and remove the oil pan.

ARROW TOWARD FRONT OF ENGINE

OIL SPURT HOLE

NUMBERED SIDE OF ROD

Fig. 9   Piston and rod 2000 cc engine

OIL PUMP, REPLACE

The oil pump, Fig. 12, is easily removed after removal of the pan.

OIL PUMP REPAIRS

1. Remove filter body and element and extract sealing ring from the groove, Fig. 12.
2. Remove end plate and withdraw O ring from groove in body.
3. Check clearance between lobes of

inner and outer rotors. This should not exceed .006". Rotors are supplied only in a matched pair.
4. Check clearance between outer rotor and the housing. This should not exceed .010".
5. Place a straightedge across face of pump body. Clearance between face of rotors and straightedge should not exceed .005".
6. If necessary to replace rotor or drive shaft, remove outer rotor and then drive out retaining pin securing the skew gear to drive shaft and pull off the gear.

BELT TENSION DATA

	New	Used
1974 All	140	110

WATER PUMP, REPLACE

1. Drain cooling system and disconnect heater hose and radiator lower hose from the pump.
2. Loosen alternator and remove the belt.
3. Remove the fan, spacer and pulley.
4. Remove the camshaft drive belt cover.
5. Unfasten and remove the pump.

FUEL PUMP PRESSURE

Year	Engine	Pressure, Lbs.
1974	4 cyl	3½-4½

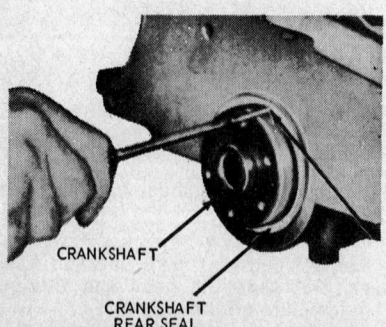

Fig. 10   Removing crankshaft rear oil seal. 2000 cc engine

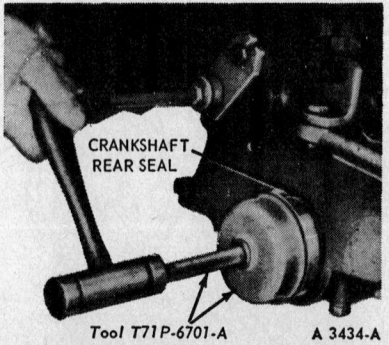

Tool T71P-6701-A   A 3434-A

Fig. 11   Installing crankshaft rear oil seal. 2000 cc engine

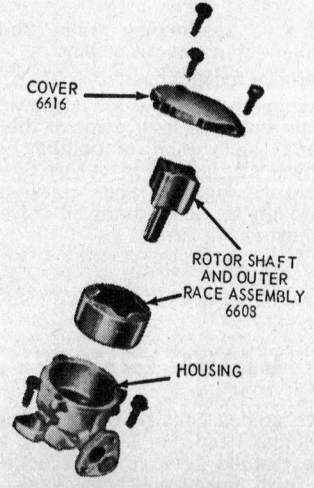

COVER 6616

ROTOR SHAFT AND OUTER RACE ASSEMBLY 6608

HOUSING

Fig. 12   Oil pump assembly. 2000 cc engine

FUEL PUMP, REPLACE

1. Disconnect inlet and outlet lines at pump.
2. Unfasten and remove the fuel pump.
3. Remove the actuator rod.

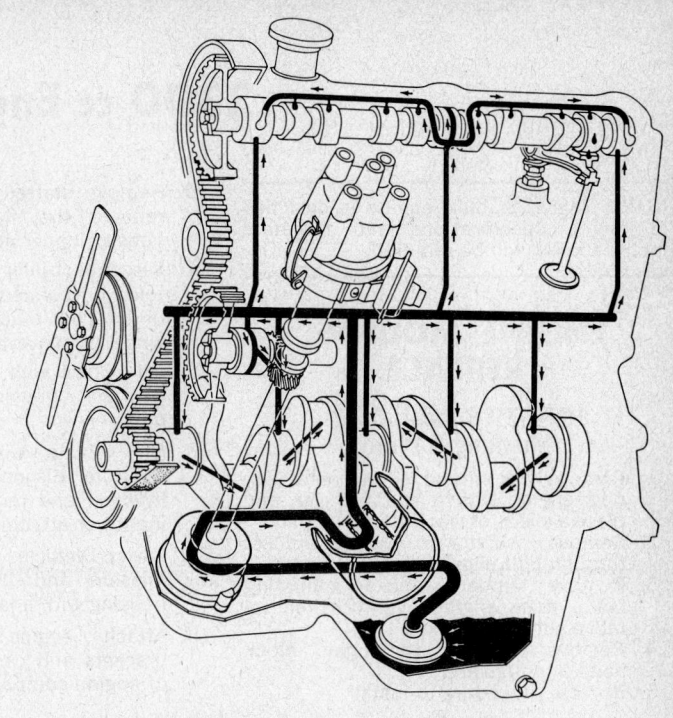

Engine oiling system. 2000 cc engine

2300 cc Engine Section

NOTE: This U.S. built engine is designed to metric specifications and therefore metric tooling will be required.

ENGINE MOUNTS, REPLACE

1974-79 Bobcat, Capri Mustang & Pinto

1. Remove fan shroud screws and support engine with a suitable jack and place a piece of wood under oil pan.
2. Remove insulator to support bracket through bolt, Figs. 1 and 2.
3. Remove support bracket mounting bolts, raise engine slightly, then remove support bracket.
4. Remove insulator to engine block bolts and insulator.
5. Reverse procedure to install.

ENGINE, REPLACE

1. Drain coolant from radiator and oil from crankcase.
2. Raise hood and secure in vertical position.
3. Remove air cleaner and exhaust manifold shroud.
4. Disconnect battery ground cable.
5. Remove radiator hoses and remove radiator and fan.
6. Disconnect heater hoses from water pump and carburetor choke fitting.
7. Disconnect wires from alternator and starter and disconnect accelerator cable from carburetor. On A/C vehicles, remove compressor from bracket and position it out of way with lines attached.
8. Disconnect flex fuel line from tank line and plug tank line.
9. Disconnect primary wire at coil and disconnect oil pressure and temperature sending unit wires at sending units.

10. Remove starter and raise vehicle to remove the flywheel or converter housing upper attaching bolts.
11. Disconnect inlet pipe at exhaust manifold. Disconnect engine mounts at underbody bracket and remove flywheel or converter housing cover.
12. On vehicle with manual shift, remove flywheel housing lower attaching bolts.
13. On vehicle with automatic transmission, disconnect converter from flywheel and remove converter housing lower attaching bolts.
14. Lower vehicle and support transmission and flywheel or converter housing with a jack.
15. Attach engine lifting hooks to brackets and carefully lift engine out of engine compartment.

CYLINDER HEAD, REPLACE

1. Drain cooling system and remove air cleaner and rocker arm cover.
2. Remove intake and exhaust manifolds and carburetor.
3. Remove timing case cover and drive belt.
4. Remove water outlet elbow from head.
5. Remove cylinder head bolts, then remove cylinder head.

NOTE: The cylinder head retaining bolts have 12 point heads.

6. Reverse procedure to install. Torque cylinder head bolts in sequence shown in Fig. 3 and intake manifold bolts in sequence shown in Fig. 3A.

CAUTION: When installing cylinder head, position camshaft at 5 o'clock position, Fig. 3, allowing minimal protrusion of the valves from the cylinder head.

VALVE ARRANGEMENT

Front to Rear

2300 cc Engine . . . . E-I-E-I-E-I-E-I

VALVE LIFT SPECS.

Engine	Year	Intake	Exhaust
2300 cc	1974-79	.400	.400

VALVE TIMING

Intake Opens Before TDC

Engine	Year	Degrees
2300 cc	1974-78	22

VALVES, ADJUST

The valve lash on this engine cannot be adjusted due to the use of hydraulic valve lash adjusters, Fig. 4. However, the valve train can be checked for wear as follows:

1. Crank engine to position camshaft with flat section of lobe facing rocker arm of valve being checked.
2. Remove rocker arm retaining spring.

NOTE: Late models do not incorporate the retaining spring.

3. Collapse lash adjuster with tool T74P-6565B and insert correct size feeler gauge between rocker arm and camshaft lobe, Fig. 5. If clearance is not as listed in the "Valve Specifications" chart in front of this chapter, remove rocker arm and check for wear and replace as necessary. If rocker arm is found satisfactory, check valve spring assembled height and adjust as needed. If valve spring assembled

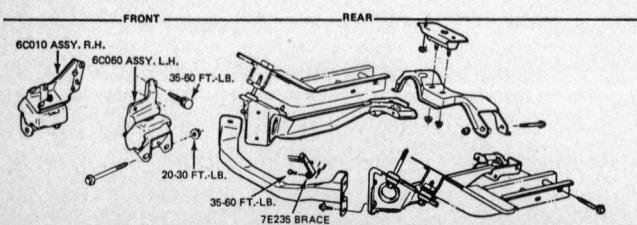

Fig. 1 Engine mount installation (typical). 1974-79 Capri Mustang

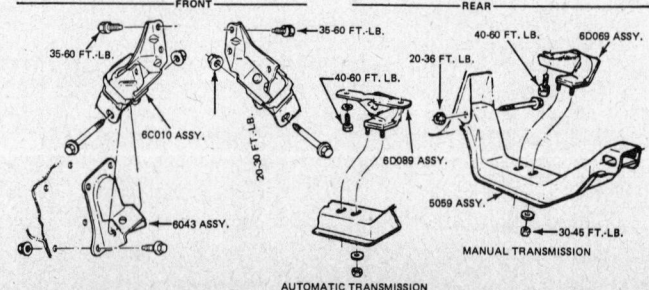

Fig. 2 Engine mount installation (typical). 1974-79 Bobcat & Pinto

TORQUE THE CYLINDER HEAD BOLTS TO SPECIFICATIONS IN TWO PROGRESSIVE STEPS IN THE SEQUENCE SHOWN.

FRONT OF ENGINE

WHEN INSTALLING CYLINDER HEAD, POSITION THE CAMSHAFT AS SHOWN TO AVOID DAMAGE TO PROTRUDING VALVES.

PIN

Fig. 3   Cylinder head installation. 2300 cc engine

GASKET

FITTINGS

FRONT OF ENGINE

LIFTING EYE

TORQUE THE MANIFOLD BOLTS TO SPECIFICATIONS IN TWO PROGRESSIVE STEPS IN THE SEQUENCE SHOWN

Fig. 3A   Intake manifold tightening sequence. 2300 cc engine.

height is within specifications listed in the front of this chapter, remove lash adjuster and clean or replace as necessary.

VALVE GUIDES

Valve guides consist of holes bored in the cylinder head. For service the guides can be reamed oversize to accommodate valves with oversize stems of .003, .015 and .030".

ROCKER ARM SERVICE

1. Remove rocker arm cover.
2. Rotate camshaft until flat section of lobe faces rocker arm being removed.
3. With tool T74P-6565B, collapse lash adjuster and, if necessary, valve spring and slide rocker arm over lash adjuster.
4. Reverse procedure to install.

NOTE: Before rotating camshaft, ensure

that lash adjuster is collapsed to prevent valve train damage.

LASH ADJUSTER, REPLACE

The hydraulic valve lash adjusters can be removed after rocker arm removal. There are two types of lash adjusters available, Type I, being the standard lash adjuster, Fig. 6, and Type II, having a .020 inch oversize outside diameter, Fig. 7.

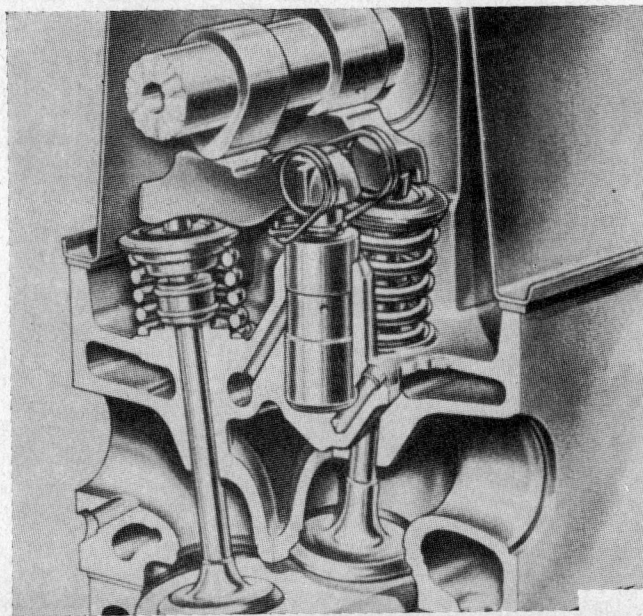

Fig. 4   Valve train installation. 2300 cc engine

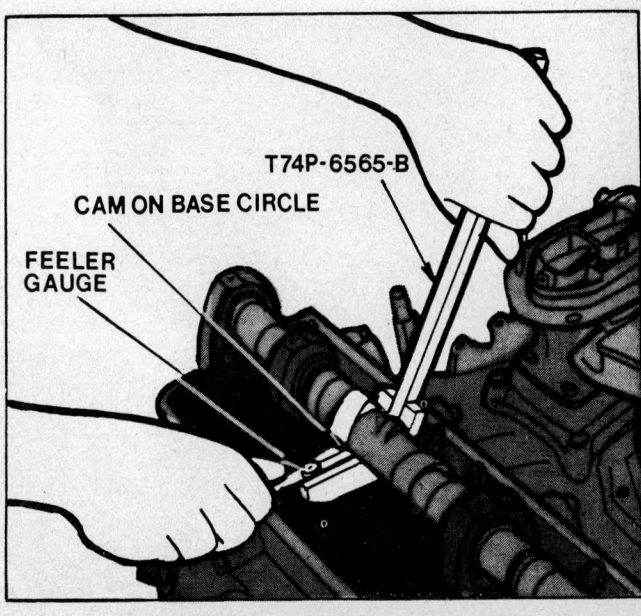

T74P-6565-B

CAM ON BASE CIRCLE

FEELER GAUGE

Fig. 5   Checking valve clearance. 2300 cc engine

FRONT ENGINE SEALS, REPLACE

To gain access to the front engine seals, remove the timing belt cover and proceed as follows:

Crankshaft Oil Seal

1. Without removing cylinder front cover, remove crankshaft sprocket with tool T74P-6306A, Fig. 8.
2. Remove crankshaft oil seal with tool T74P-6700B, Fig. 9.
3. Install a new crankshaft oil seal with tool T74P-6150A, Fig. 10.
4. Install crankshaft sprocket with recess facing engine block, Fig. 11.

Camshaft & Auxiliary Shaft Oil Seals

1. Remove camshaft or auxiliary shaft sprocket with tool T74P-6256A, Fig. 12.
2. Remove oil seal with tool T74P-6700B, Fig. 13.
3. Install a new oil seal with tool T74P-6150A, Fig. 10.
4. Install camshaft or auxiliary shaft sprocket with tool T74P-6256A with center arbor removed.

TIMING BELT

1. Position crankshaft at TDC, No. 1 cylinder compression stroke.
2. Remove timing belt cover, loosen belt tensioner, and remove belt from sprockets, Fig. 14. Tighten tensioner bolt, holding tensioner in position.

NOTE: Do not rotate crankshaft or

Fig. 6 Valve lash adjuster, Type I. 2300 cc engine

Fig. 7 Valve lash adjuster, Type II. 2300 cc engine

camshaft after belt is removed. Rotating either component will result in improper valve timing.

3. To install belt, ensure timing marks are aligned, Fig. 15, and place belt over sprockets.
4. Loosen tensioner bolt, allowing tensioner to move against belt.
5. Rotate crankshaft two complete turns, removing slack from belt. Torque tensioner adjustment and pivot bolts and check alignment of timing marks, Fig. 15.
6. Install timing belt cover.

CAMSHAFT, REPLACE

1. Remove rocker arm cover and rocker arms.
2. Remove timing belt cover, camshaft sprocket bolt and washer, then slide sprocket and belt guide off camshaft.
3. Remove camshaft retaining plate from

rear of head, then remove camshaft from front of head.

PISTON & ROD, ASSEMBLE

Assemble the rod to the piston with the arrow on top of piston facing front of engine, Fig. 16.

PISTONS, PINS & RINGS

Oversize pistons are available in oversizes of .003", .020", .030" and .040". Oversize rings are available in .020", .030" and .040" oversizes. Oversize pins are not available.

MAIN & ROD BEARINGS

Undersize main bearings are available in .002", .020", .030" and .040" undersizes. Undersize rod bearings are available in undersizes of .002", .010", .020", .030" and .040".

The crankshaft and main bearings are installed with arrows on main bearing caps facing front of engine, Fig. 17. Install PCV baffle between bearing journals No. 3 and 4.

CRANKSHAFT OIL SEAL

1. Remove oil pan.
2. Remove rear main bearing cap.
3. Loosen remaining bearing caps, allowing crankshaft to drop down about 1/32".
4. Install a sheet metal screw into seal and pull screw to remove seal.
5. Carefully clean seal groove in block with a brush and solvent. Also clean seal groove in bearing cap.
6. Dip seal halves in clean engine oil.
7. Carefully install upper seal half in its groove with locating tab toward rear of engine, Fig. 18, by rotating it on shaft journal of crankshaft until approximately 3/8" protrudes be-

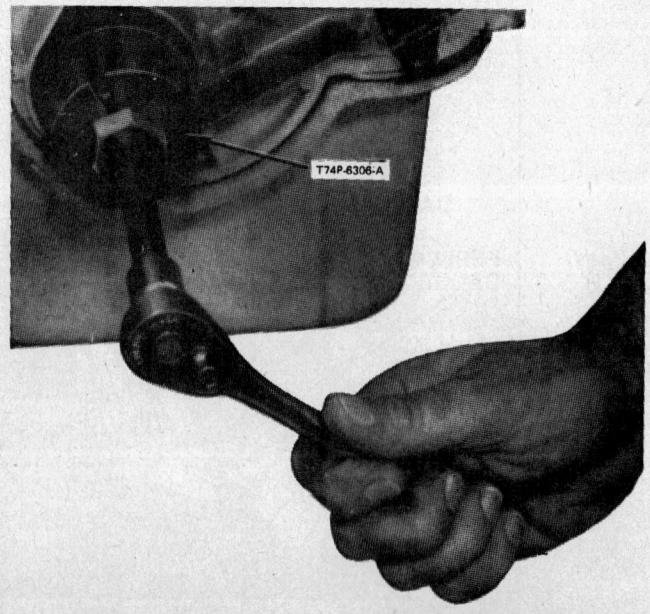

Fig. 8 Crankshaft sprocket removal. 2300 cc engine

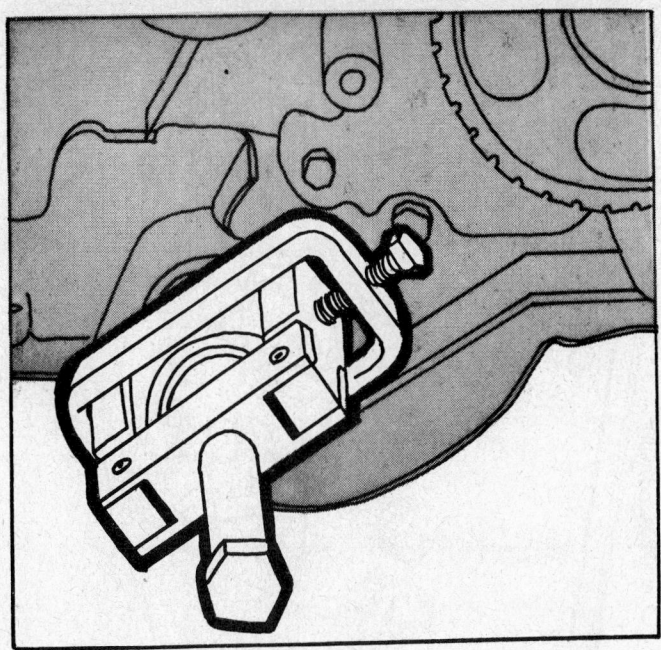

Fig. 9   Crankshaft front oil seal removal. 2300 cc engine

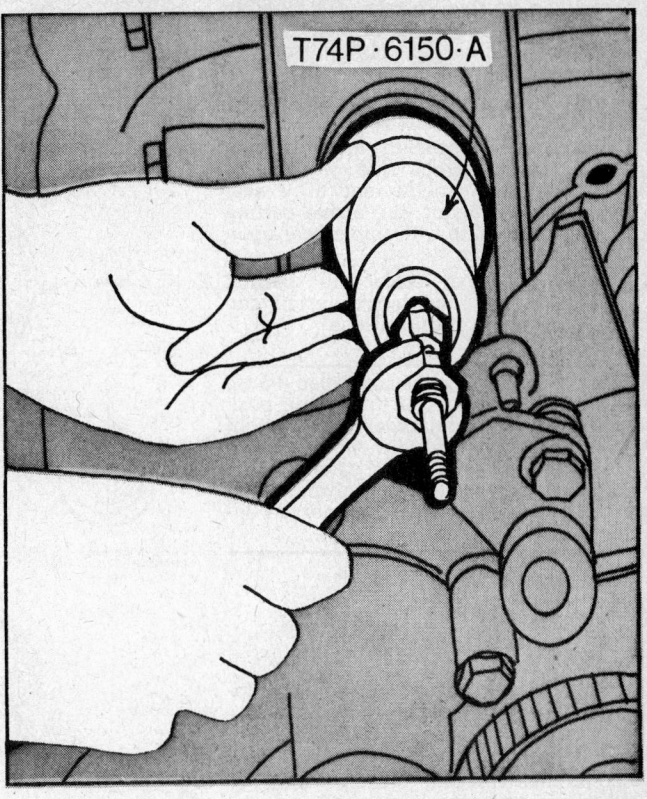

T74P·6150·A

Fig. 10   Engine front seals installation. 2300 cc engine

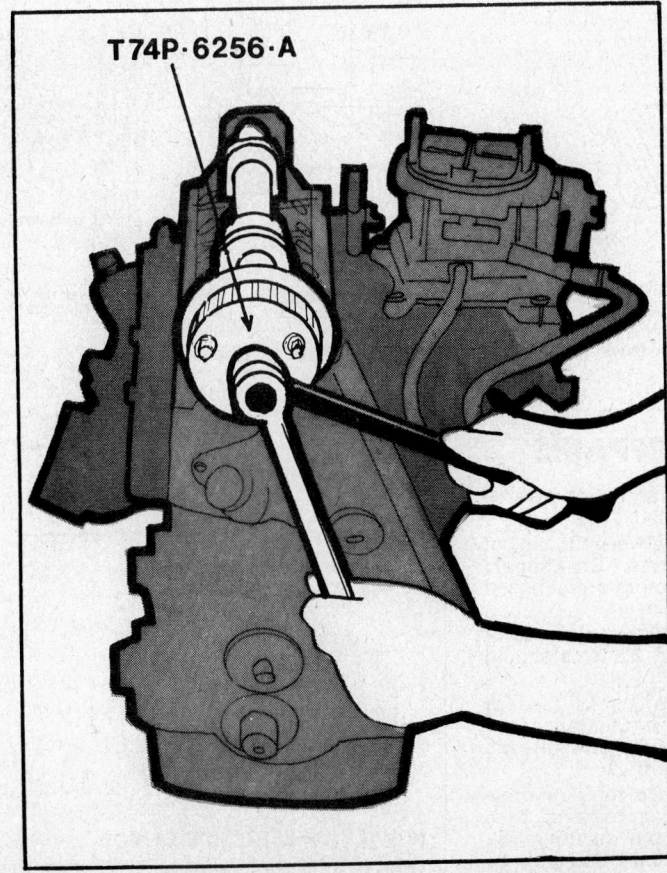

T74P·6256·A

Fig. 12   Camshaft & auxiliary shaft sprockets removal.
2300 cc engine

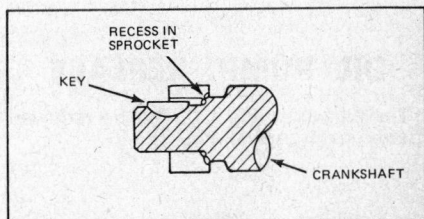

RECESS IN SPROCKET

KEY

CRANKSHAFT

Fig. 11   Crankshaft sprocket installation.
2300 cc engine

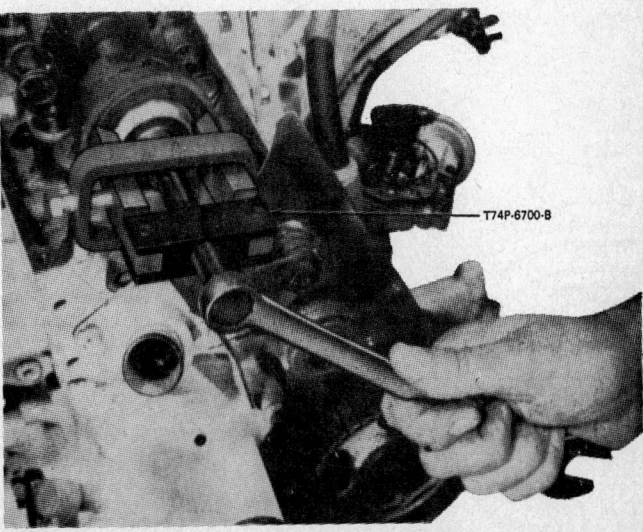

T74P-6700-B

Fig. 13   Camshaft & auxiliary shaft seals removal.
2300 cc engine

low the parting surface. *Be sure no rubber has been shaved from outside diameter of seal by bottom edge of groove.*

8. Retighten main bearing caps and torque to specifications.
9. Install lower seal in main bearing cap with undercut side of seal toward front of engine, and allow seal to protrude about 3/8" above parting surface to mate with upper seal upon cap installation.
10. Apply suitable sealer to parting faces of cap and block. Install cap and torque to specifications.

NOTE: If difficulty is encountered in installing the upper half of the seal in position, lightly lap (sandpaper) the side of the seal opposite the lip side using a medium grit paper. After sanding, the seal must be washed in solvent, then dipped in clean engine oil prior to installation.

OIL PAN

1. Drain crankcase and remove oil dipstick and flywheel inspection cover.
2. Disconnect steering cable from rack and pinion, then rack and pinion from crossmember and move forward to provide clearance.
3. Unfasten and remove oil pan. To install oil pan, refer to Fig. 19.

OIL PUMP, REPLACE

The oil pump, Fig. 20, can be removed after oil pan removal, Fig. 21.

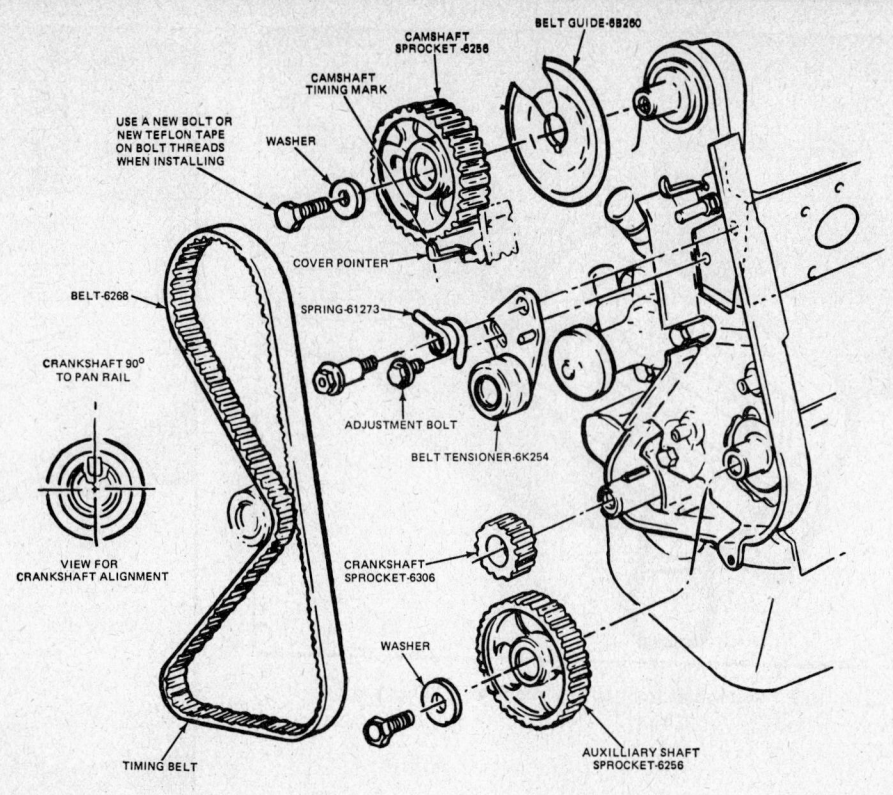

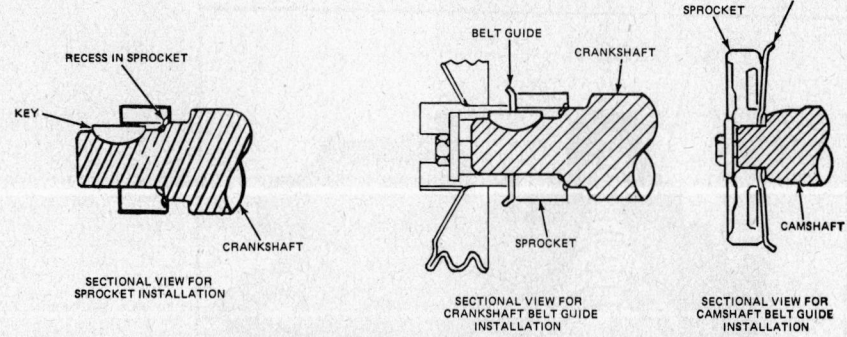

Fig. 14 Drive belt & sprockets installation. 2300 cc engine

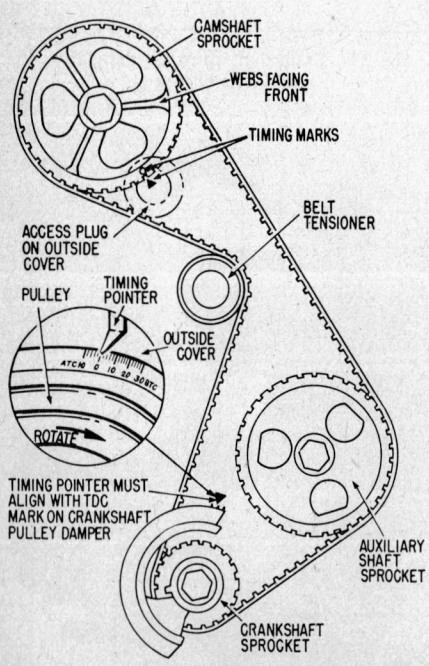

Fig. 15 Valve timing marks. 2300 cc engine

OIL PUMP REPAIRS

1. Remove end plate and withdraw O ring from groove in body.
2. Check clearance between lobes of inner and outer rotors. This should not exceed .006". Rotors are supplied only in a matched pair.
3. Check clearance between outer rotor and the housing, Fig. 22. This should not exceed .010".
4. Place a straightedge across face of pump body, Fig. 23. Clearance between face of rotors and straightedge should not exceed .005".
5. If necessary to replace rotor or drive shaft, remove outer rotor and then drive out retaining pin securing the skew gear to drive shaft and pull off the gear.
6. Withdraw inner rotor and drive shaft.

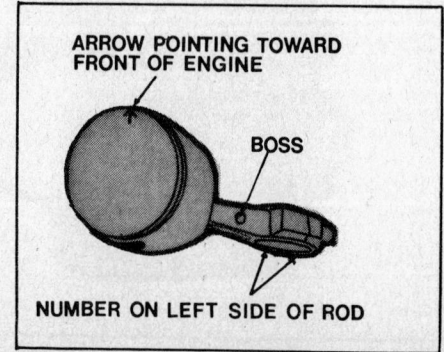

Fig. 16 Piston & rod. 2300 cc engine

BELT TENSION DATA

	New Ft. Lbs.	Used Ft. Lbs.
1974-79 Exc. ¼ inch	140	110
¼ inch	65	50

WATER PUMP, REPLACE

1. Drain cooling system and disconnect hoses from pump.
2. Loosen alternator and remove drive belt.
3. Remove fan, spacer and pulley.
4. Remove water pump attaching bolts and water pump after removing drive belt cover.

FUEL PUMP PRESSURE

Year	Engine	Pressure Lbs.
1974	2300 cc	3½-4½
1975	2300 cc	3½-5½
1976-79	2300 cc	5-7

FUEL PUMP, REPLACE

1. Disconnect fuel lines from pump.
2. Remove fuel pump attaching bolts and fuel pump.

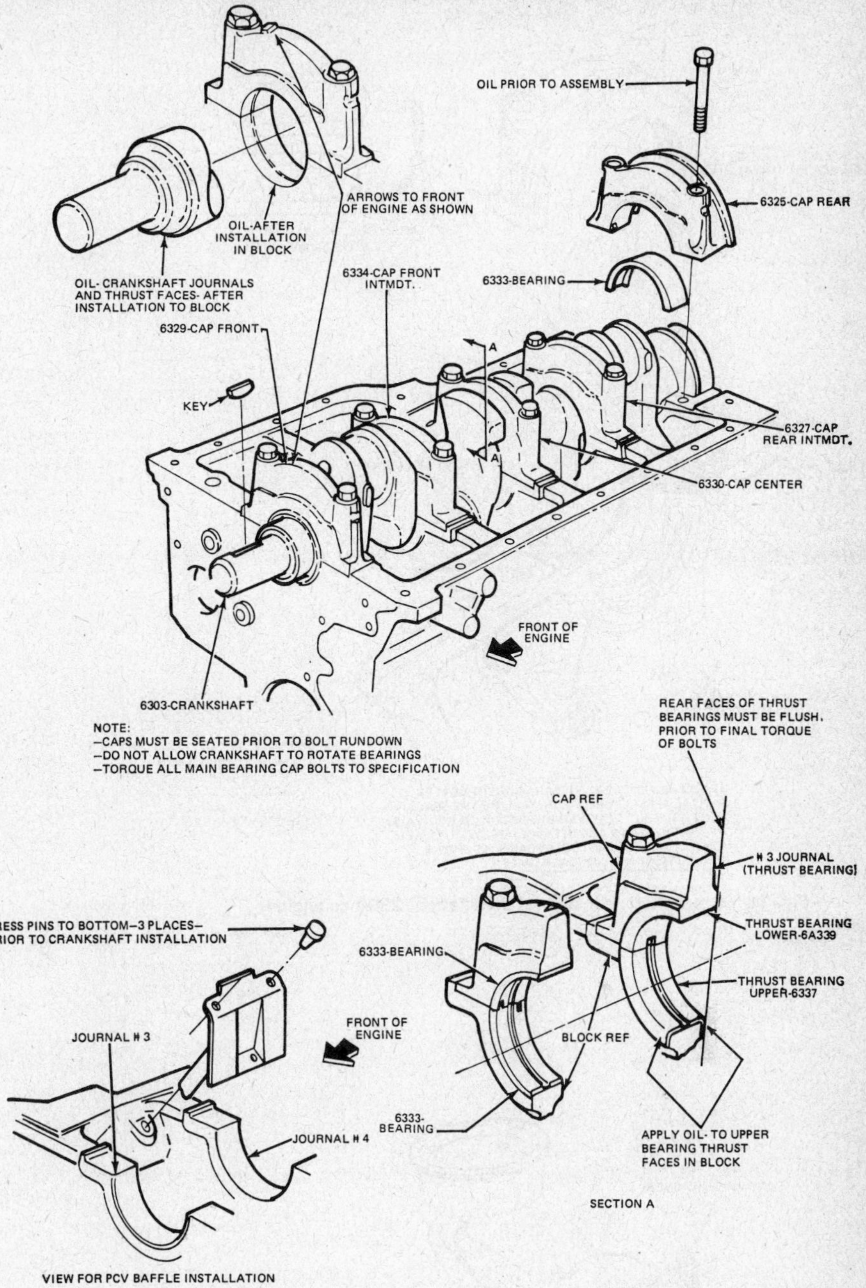

OIL PRIOR TO ASSEMBLY

6325-CAP REAR

ARROWS TO FRONT OF ENGINE AS SHOWN

OIL-AFTER INSTALLATION IN BLOCK

6334-CAP FRONT INTMDT.

6333-BEARING

OIL-CRANKSHAFT JOURNALS AND THRUST FACES- AFTER INSTALLATION TO BLOCK

6329-CAP FRONT

KEY

6327-CAP REAR INTMDT.

6330-CAP CENTER

FRONT OF ENGINE

6303-CRANKSHAFT

NOTE:
-CAPS MUST BE SEATED PRIOR TO BOLT RUNDOWN
-DO NOT ALLOW CRANKSHAFT TO ROTATE BEARINGS
-TORQUE ALL MAIN BEARING CAP BOLTS TO SPECIFICATION

REAR FACES OF THRUST BEARINGS MUST BE FLUSH, PRIOR TO FINAL TORQUE OF BOLTS

CAP REF

N 3 JOURNAL (THRUST BEARING)

THRUST BEARING LOWER-6A339

THRUST BEARING UPPER-6337

6333-BEARING

BLOCK REF

PRESS PINS TO BOTTOM-3 PLACES- PRIOR TO CRANKSHAFT INSTALLATION

FRONT OF ENGINE

JOURNAL N 3

6333-BEARING

JOURNAL N 4

APPLY OIL- TO UPPER BEARING THRUST FACES IN BLOCK

SECTION A

VIEW FOR PCV BAFFLE INSTALLATION

Fig. 17   Crankshaft & main bearing installation. 2300 cc engine

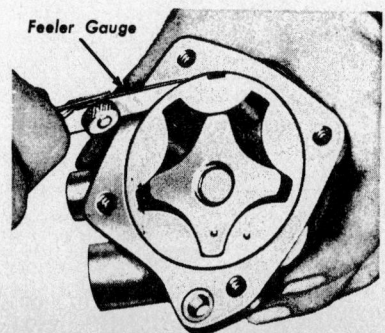

Feeler Gauge

Fig. 22   Checking outer rotor to housing clearance. 2300 cc engine

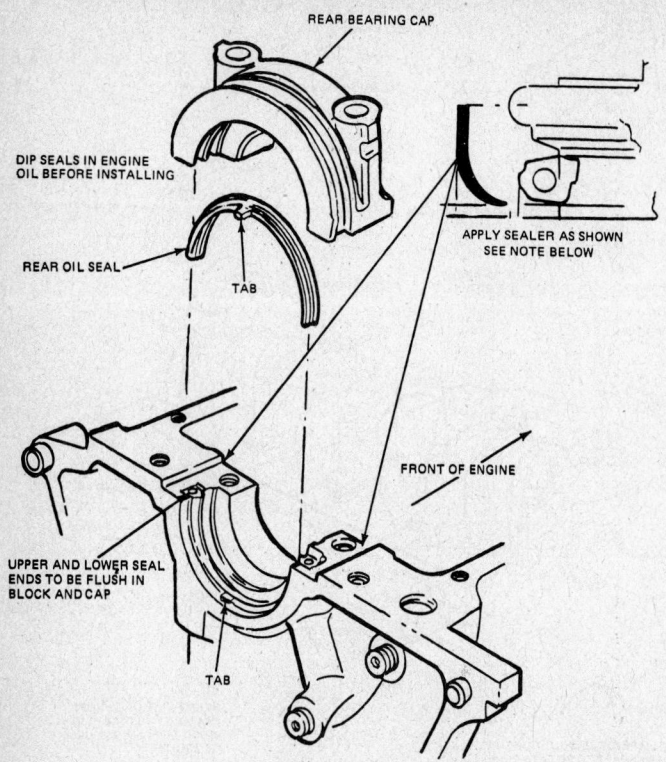

REAR BEARING CAP

DIP SEALS IN ENGINE
OIL BEFORE INSTALLING

APPLY SEALER AS SHOWN
SEE NOTE BELOW

REAR OIL SEAL

TAB

FRONT OF ENGINE

UPPER AND LOWER SEAL
ENDS TO BE FLUSH IN
BLOCK AND CAP

TAB

SEALER NOTE: CLEAN THE AREA WHERE SEALER
IS TO BE APPLIED BEFORE INSTALLING THE SEALS.
USE FORD SPOT REMOVER B7A-19521-A OR EQUIVALENT.
AFTER THE SEALS ARE IN PLACE, APPLY A 1/16 INCH
BEAD OF C3AZ-19562-A OR -B SEALER AS SHOWN.
SEALER MUST NOT CONTACT SEALS.

Fig. 18   Crankshaft rear oil seal installation. 2300 cc engine

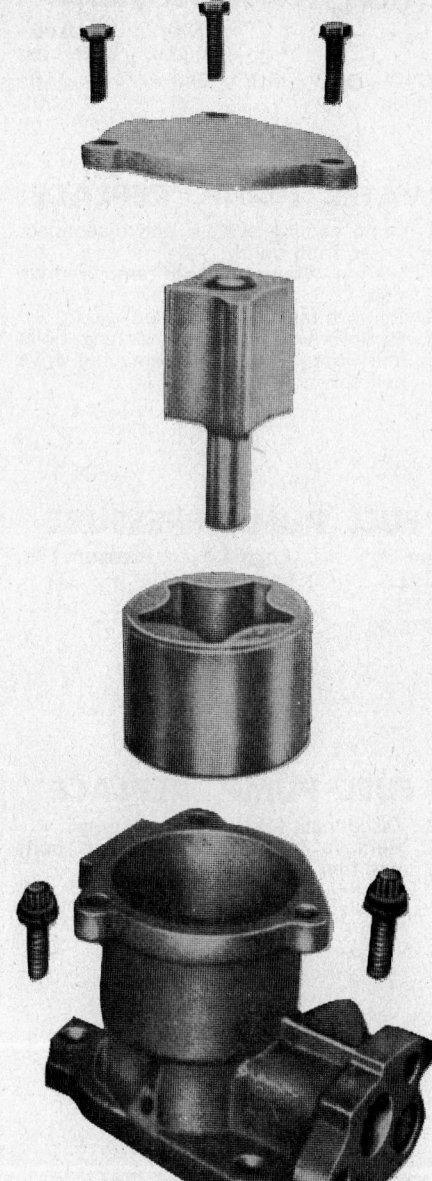

Fig. 20   Oil pump. 2300 cc engine

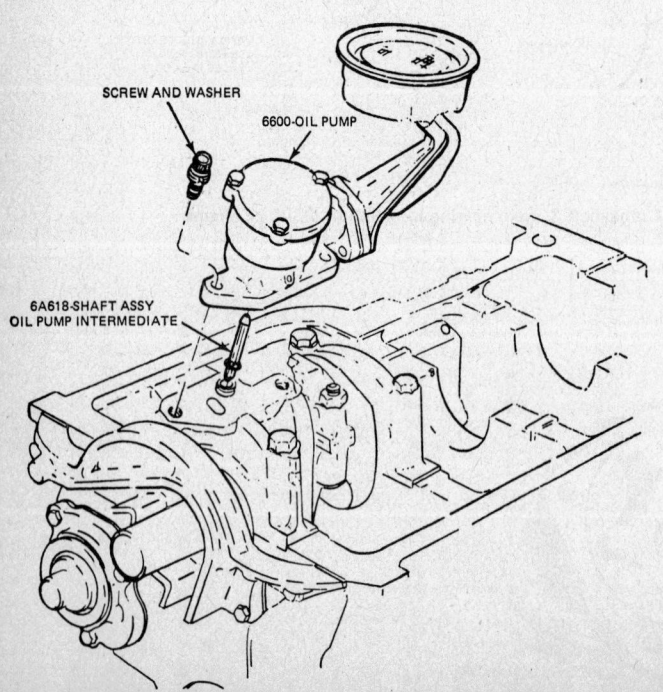

SCREW AND WASHER

6600-OIL PUMP

6A618-SHAFT ASSY
OIL PUMP INTERMEDIATE

**Fig. 21   Oil pump installation.
2300 cc engine**

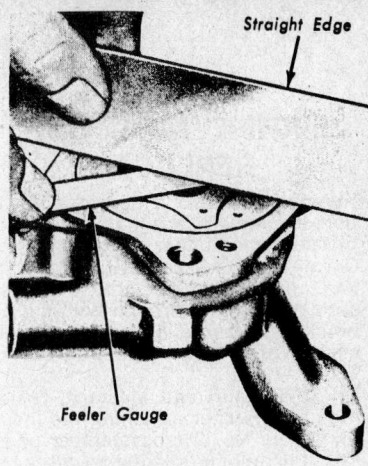

Fig. 23 Checking rotor end play. 2300 cc engine

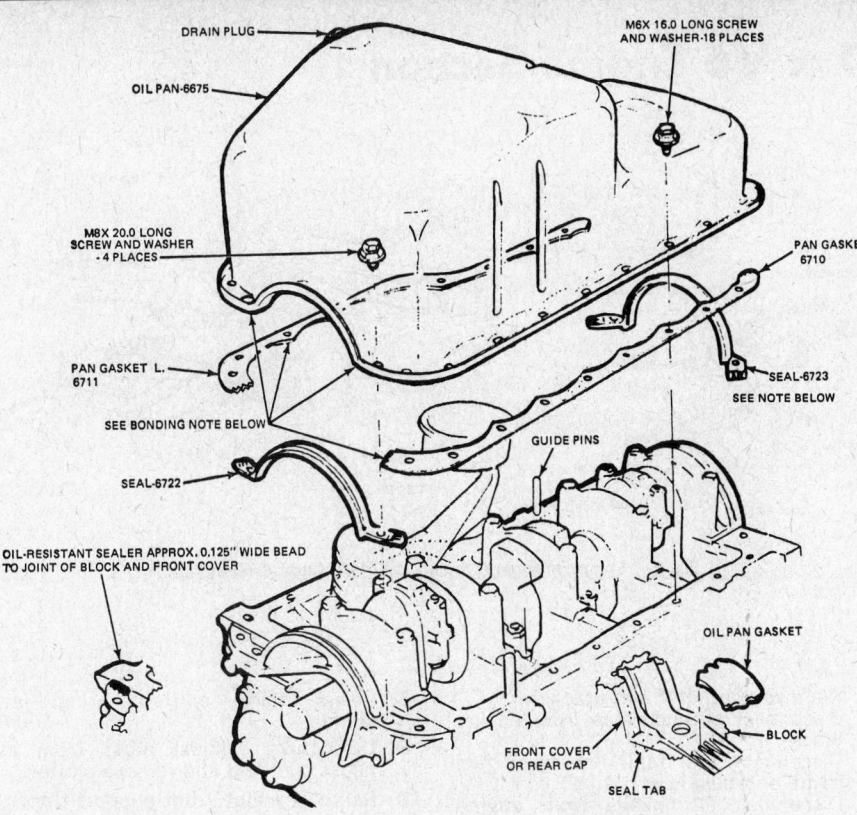

1. APPLY GASKET ADHESIVE EVENLY TO OIL PAN FLANGE AND TO PAN SIDE GASKETS. ALLOW ADHESIVE TO DRY PAST WET STAGE, THEN INSTALL GASKETS TO OIL PAN.
2. APPLY SEALER TO JOINT OF BLOCK AND FRONT COVER. INSTALL SEALS TO FRONT COVER AND REAR BEARING CAP AND PRESS SEAL TABS FIRMLY INTO BLOCK. BE SURE TO INSTALL THE REAR SEAL BEFORE THE REAR MAIN BEARING CAP SEALER HAS CURED.
3. POSITION 2 GUIDE PINS AND INSTALL THE OIL PAN. SECURE THE PAN WITH THE FOUR M8 BOLTS SHOWN ABOVE.
4. REMOVE THE GUIDE PINS AND INSTALL AND TORQUE THE EIGHTEEN M6 BOLTS, BEGINNING AT HOLE A AND WORKING CLOCKWISE AROUND THE PAN.

Fig. 19 Oil pan installation. 2300 cc engine

Engine oiling system. 2300 cc engine

2800 cc V6 Engine Section

ENGINE MOUNTS, REPLACE

1. Remove fan shroud screws and support engine with a suitable jack and a block of wood under the oil pan.
2. On all models except 1979 Capri and Mustang remove insulator to insulator support bracket through bolt, support bracket to frame bolts, raise engine slightly, then remove support bracket, Figs. 1 & 1 A.
3. On 1979 Capri and Mustang, remove nuts and washer attaching the insulator to the No. 2 crossmember pedestals. Lift engine slightly to disengage insulator stud from cross member, Fig. 1.
4. Remove bolt attaching fuel pump shield to left hand engine bracket, if equipped.
5. Remove insulator assembly to engine block bolts, then remove insulator and heat shield.

ENGINE, REPLACE

1. Disconnect battery cables and remove hood.
2. Remove air cleaner and intake duct.
3. Drain cooling system, disconnect radiator hoses from radiator, then remove radiator. Disconnect heater hoses from engine block and water pump.

NOTE: Remove fan shroud and position shroud over fan before removing radiator.

4. Remove alternator and bracket.
5. Disconnect ground wires from engine block.
6. Disconnect fuel tank line from fuel pump and plug line.
7. Disconnect all linkage from engine and wires from ignition coil.

NOTE: If equipped with Thermactor system, remove or disconnect system components interfering with engine removal.

8. Raise vehicle and place on jack stands.
9. Disconnect exhaust pipes from exhaust manifold and remove starter.
10. Remove engine front support through bolts or attaching nuts.
11. On vehicles equipped with automatic transmission, disconnect converter from flywheel, remove downshift rod, then remove converter housing to engine bolts and adapter plate to converter housing bolt.

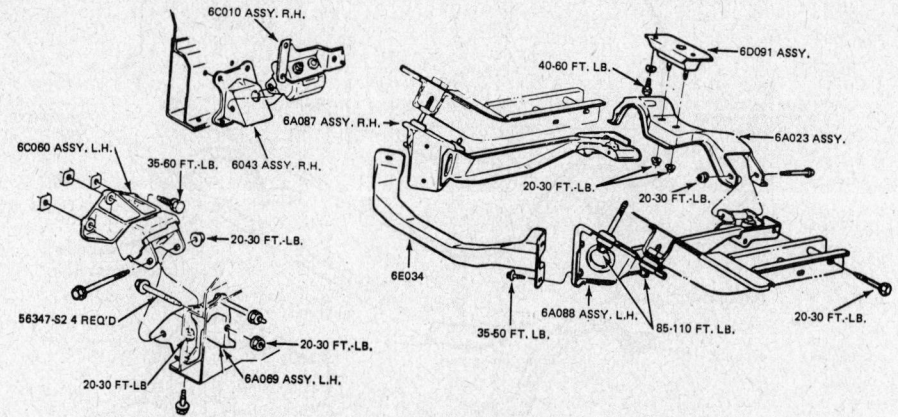

Fig. 1   Engine mounts (typical). 1974-79 Capri & Mustang

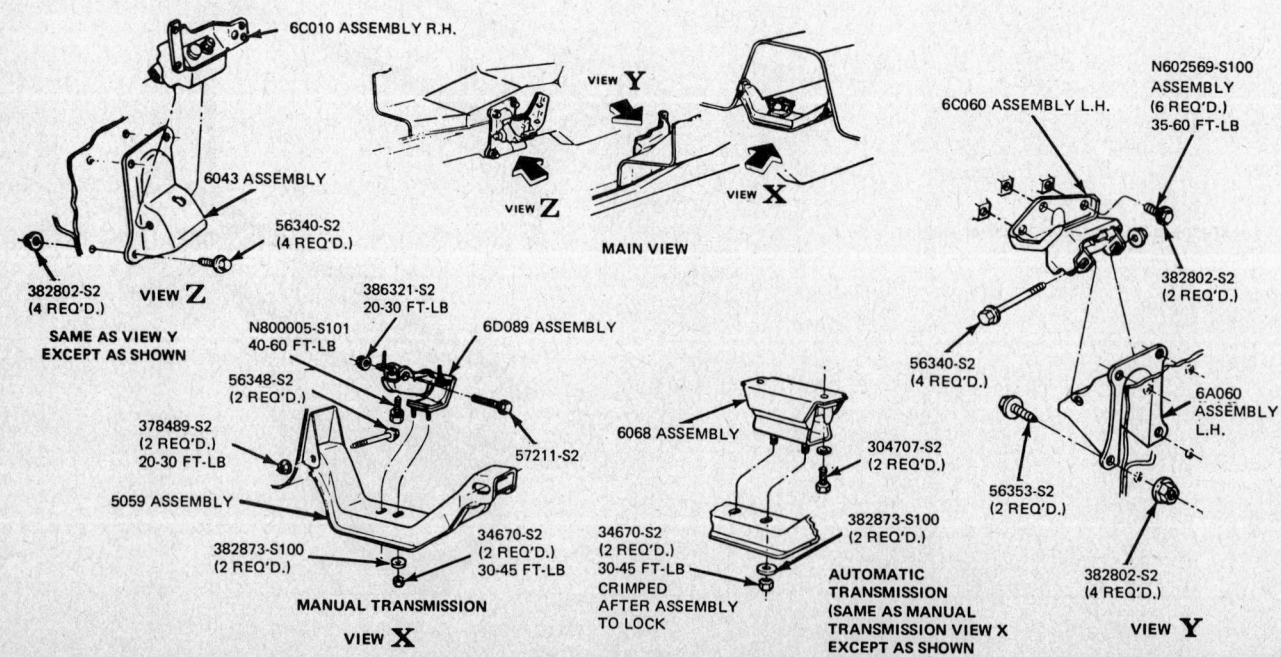

Fig. 1A   Engine mounts (typical). 1975-79 Bobcat & Pinto

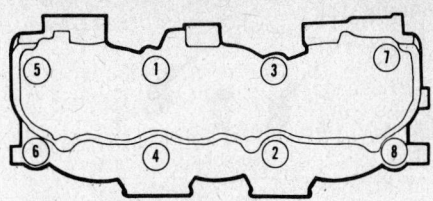

Fig. 2 Cylinder head tightening sequence. 2800 cc engine

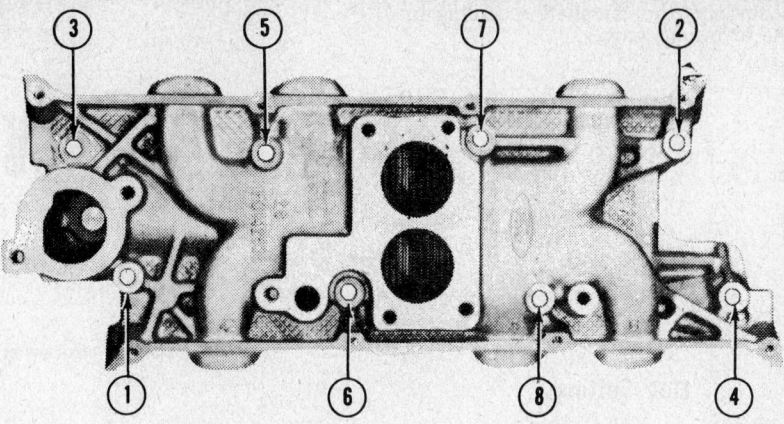

Fig. 2A Intake manifold tightening sequence. 2800 cc engine

12. On vehicles equipped with manual transmission, remove clutch linkage and bell housing to engine bolts.
13. On all models, lower vehicle and attach a suitable lifting sling to brackets on exhaust manifold.
14. Support transmission with a suitable jack, raise engine slightly and pull from transmission, then lift engine from engine compartment.

CYLINDER HEAD, REPLACE

1. Disconnect battery ground cable, disconnect linkage and drain coolant.
2. Remove distributor, coolant hoses, rocker arm covers, fuel line and filter, carburetor and intake manifold.
3. Remove rocker arm shaft, oil baffles and push rods.
4. Remove exhaust manifold.
5. Remove cylinder head bolts and cylinder head.
6. Reverse procedure to install. Torque cylinder head bolts in sequence shown in Fig. 2, and intake manifold bolts in sequence shown in Fig. 2A.

VALVE ARRANGEMENT

Front to Rear

2800 cc engine—
Right . . . . I-E-I-E-E-I
Left . . . . I-E-E-I-E-I

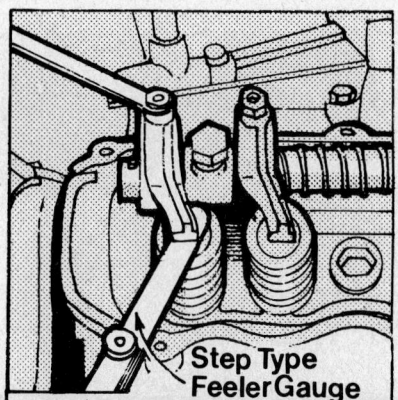

Fig. 3 Adjusting valve lash. 2800 cc engine

VALVE LIFT SPECS.

Engine	Year	Intake	Exhaust
2800 cc	1976-79	.3730	.3730

VALVE TIMING

Intake Opens Before TDC

Engine	Year	Degrees
2800 cc	1974-78	20

VALVES, ADJUST

Cold Setting

1974-75

1. Remove rocker arm cover bolts and torque rocker arm support bolts to 43-49 ft. lbs., before adjusting valves.
2. Rotate crankshaft until No. 1 cylinder is at TDC, compression stroke, and set valve lash on No. 1 cylinder to specifications as listed in the "Valve Specifications" table, Fig. 3.
3. Rotate crankshaft 120 degrees and set valve lash on No. 4 cylinder.
4. Rotate crankshaft an additional 120 degrees and set valve lash on No. 2 cylinder. The remaining valves are adjusted in the same manner as above, following the firing order found in the front of this chapter.

1976-79

1. Remove all necessary components to allow removal of valve covers, then remove valve covers.
2. Slowly crank engine until intake valve for number 5 cylinder just starts to open. The camshaft is now correctly positioned to adjust valves on number 1 cylinder.

3. Refer to "Valves Specifications" chart, then using a feeler gauge of the specified clearance, adjust number 1 cylinder intake valve so that feeler gauge has a light to moderate drag, and a feeler gauge .001 inch greater is very tight.

NOTE: Do not use a step-type "go/no-go" gauge shown in Fig. 3. Also, when checking valve lash, insert gauge between rocker arm and front or rear of valve tip and move gauge toward opposite edge with a rearward or forward motion parallel to the crankshaft centerline. Inserting gauge at outboard edge, and moving inward toward carburetor, will produce an erroneous "feel" and result in excessively tight valves.

4. Using the same procedure as in step 3, adjust the number 1 cylinder intake valve using a feeler gauge of the specified clearance.
5. Adjust the remaining valves in sequence of firing order (1-4-2-5-3-6), by

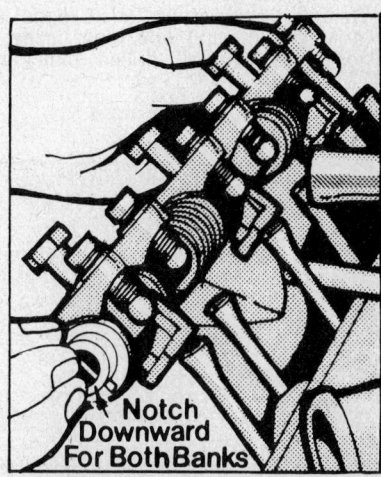

Fig. 4 Rocker arm replacement. 2800 cc engine

positioning the camshaft according to the following chart:

	With Intake Valve Just Opening for Cyl. No.					
	5	3	6	1	4	2
Adjust Both Valves For Cyl. No.	1	4	2	5	3	6

Fig. 5   Rocker arm shaft assembly. 2800 cc engine

Hot Setting

1974-75

With engine at operating temperature and idling, set valve lash with a step type feeler gauge, Fig. 3, to specifications as listed in the "Valve Specifications" table.

VALVE GUIDES

Valve guides consist of holes bored in the cylinder head. For service the guides can be reamed oversize to accommodate valves with oversize stems of .003, .015 and .030".

ROCKER ARM SERVICE

1. Disconnect throttle rod from carburetor and remove rocker arm cover.
2. Remove rocker arm shaft stand bolts, rocker arm shaft assembly and oil baffle, Fig. 4.
3. Remove cotter pin and spring washer from ends of rocker shaft and slide rocker arms, springs and shaft supports off shaft, marking components for proper reassembly, Fig. 5.
4. Remove plugs from shaft ends by drilling a hole in one plug, insert a long rod through drilled plug and

knock the opposite plug from shaft. Remove the drilled plug in same manner.

5. With a blunt tool, install plugs in end of rocker shafts with cup side out.
6. Install spring washer and cotter pin on one end of shaft and install components in proper sequence as marked during disassembly.

NOTE: Oil holes in rocker shaft must face downward during installation.

VALVE LIFTERS, REPLACE

Remove cylinder head as outlined previously and using a magnet, remove lifters from their bores.

TIMING CASE COVER

1. Remove oil pan as described further on.
2. Drain coolant and remove radiator, then remove any other components as necessary to obtain clearance.
3. If equipped, disconnect A/C compressor and bracket and place aside.
4. Remove alternator, Thermactor pump, drive belts, fan, water pump, hoses and harmonic balancer or pulley.
5. Remove cover retaining bolts and remove cover.

TIMING GEARS

1. Drain, then remove radiator and oil pan.
2. Remove cylinder front cover and water pump.
3. Align timing marks, Fig. 8.
4. Using a suitable gear puller, remove crankshaft gear and key.
5. Remove camshaft gear with a suitable gear puller.

NOTE: Do not rotate crankshaft or camshaft with gears removed as rotation of either component can result in improper valve timing.

6. Install key in camshaft, then press camshaft gear onto camshaft.
7. Install key in crankshaft, then press crankshaft gear onto crankshaft with tool T72C-6150, Fig. 9, and make sure timing marks are aligned, Fig. 8.
8. Install cylinder front cover, water pump, radiator and oil pan.
9. Refill cooling system and oil pan. Start engine and adjust ignition timing, if necessary.

CRANKSHAFT FRONT OIL SEAL

The crankshaft front oil seal may be serviced without removing the cylinder front cover as follows:
1. Drain coolant and remove radiator, crankshaft pulley and water pump drive belt.
2. Pull oil seal from front cover, Fig. 6.
3. Install new oil seal with tool T72C-6150, Fig. 7.
4. Install crankshaft pulley, water pump drive belt, radiator, then refill cooling system.

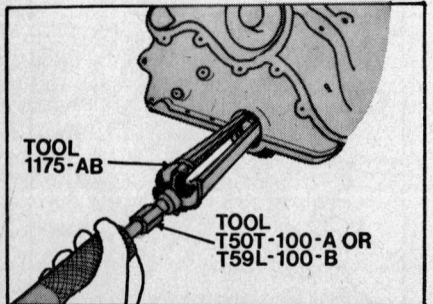

Fig. 6   Removing crankshaft front oil seal. 2800 cc engine

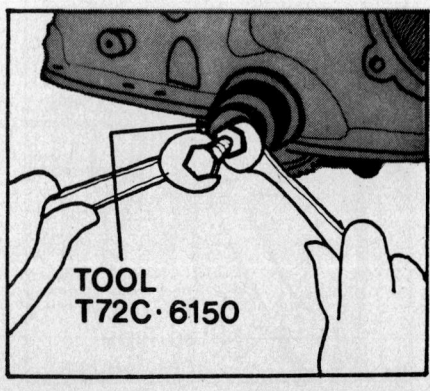

Fig. 7   Installing crankshaft front oil seal. 2800 cc engine

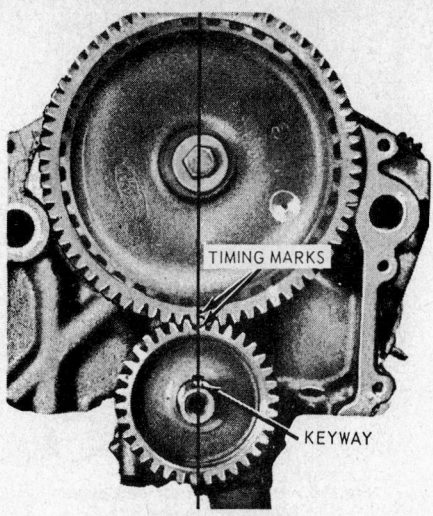

Fig. 8   Valve timing marks.
2800 cc engine

CAMSHAFT, REPLACE

1. Drain coolant, then remove radiator, fan, water pump pulley and belt.
2. Remove distributor, alternator, Thermactor pump, fuel line, filter, carburetor and intake manifold.
3. Remove rocker arm covers, rocker arm assemblies, pushrods and lifters. Identify pushrods and lifters so they can be reinstalled in their original location.
4. Remove oil pan as described further on.
5. Remove timing case cover as described previously.
6. Remove camshaft gear retaining bolt and slide gear off shaft and remove camshaft thrust plate.
7. Carefully remove camshaft from engine using care to avoid damage to camshaft bearings.

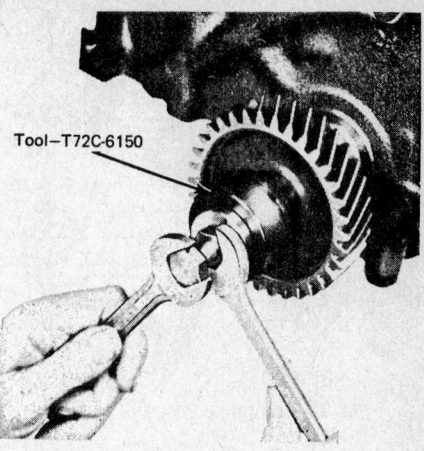

Fig. 9   Crankshaft gear installation.
2800 cc engine

PISTON & ROD ASSEMBLY

Assemble the piston to the rod with the notches facing front of engine and the numbered side of the rod toward left side of engine, Fig. 11.

PISTONS, PINS & RINGS

Oversize pistons and rings are available in .020″ and .040″ oversizes. Oversize pins are not available.

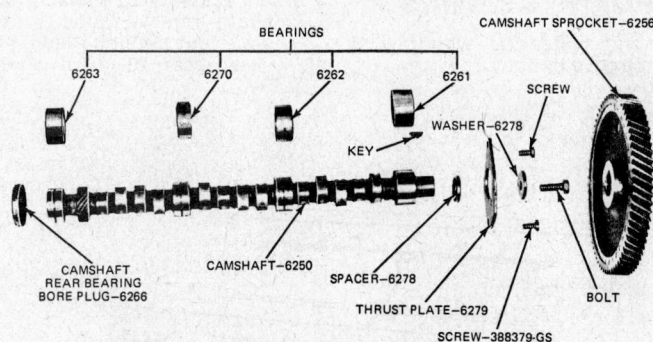

Fig. 10   Camshaft components. 2800 cc engine

CRANKSHAFT REAR OIL SEAL

1. Remove transmission assembly.
2. On automatic transmission vehicles, remove flywheel.
3. On manual transmission vehicles, remove clutch assembly, flywheel, clutch housing and rear plate.
4. Punch two holes on opposite sides of seal just above bearing cap to cylinder block split line and install a sheet metal screw in each hole. Using two large screwdrivers, pry evenly on both screws to remove seal, Fig. 12.

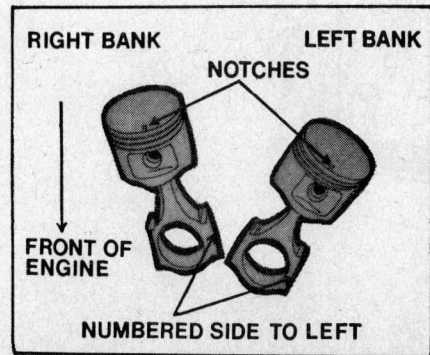

Fig. 11   Piston & rod. 2800 cc engine

Fig. 12   Removing crankshaft rear oil seal. 2800 cc engine

Fig. 13   Installing crankshaft rear oil seal. 2800 cc engine

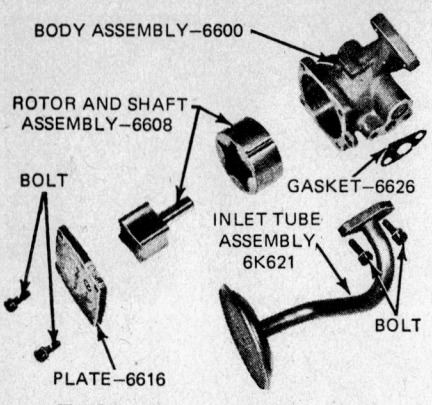

BODY ASSEMBLY—6600

ROTOR AND SHAFT ASSEMBLY—6608

BOLT

GASKET—6626

INLET TUBE ASSEMBLY 6K621

BOLT

PLATE—6616

Fig. 14   Oil pump. 2800 cc engine

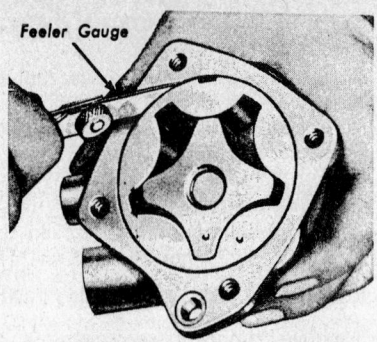

Fig. 15   Checking outer rotor to housing clearance. 2800 cc engine

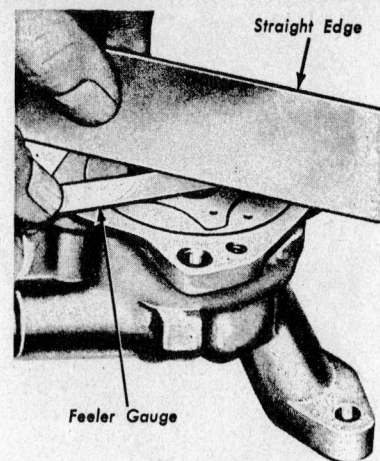

Straight Edge

Feeler Gauge

Fig. 16   Checking rotor end play. 2800 cc engine

NOTE: Use care to avoid damaging the crankshaft oil seal surface.

5. Install new seal with tool T72C-6165, Fig. 13.

OIL PAN, REPLACE

1979 Capri & Mustang

1. Disconnect battery ground cable.
2. Remove fan shroud attaching screws and position shroud over fan.
3. Raise and support vehicle, then drain oil pan.
4. Remove two bolts attaching steering gear to main crossmember and rest steering gear on frame away from oil pan.
5. Remove engine mount attaching nuts.
6. Raise engine with a suitable jack and place wood blocks between the engine mounts and the frame.
7. Remove rear "K" braces.
8. Remove oil pan attaching bolts and lower oil pan to frame.
9. Remove oil pump attaching bolts and lower oil pump into oil pan.
10. Remove oil pan. It may be necessary to rotate crankshaft to provide adequate clearance.
11. Reverse procedure to install.

Exc. 1979 Capri & Mustang

1. Disconnect battery ground cable.
2. Remove oil level dipstick.
3. On 1975-79 vehicles, drain cooling system and disconnect upper and lower radiator hoses.
4. Remove fan shroud attaching bolts and place shroud over fan.
5. On 1974 vehicles, loosen alternator bracket and adjustment bolt.
6. Raise vehicle and drain crankcase, then remove splash shield and starter.
7. If equipped with automatic transmission, disconnect cooler lines at radiator.
8. On 1975-79 vehicles, disconnect steering gear and power steering hoses (if equipped) and position gear aside, then disconnect sway bar and rotate to allow clearance.

9. Remove engine front support nuts, then raise engine and place wood blocks between engine front supports and chassis.
10. Remove converter or clutch housing cover.
11. Remove oil pan bolts and oil pan.

OIL PUMP, REPLACE

The oil pump, Fig. 14, can be removed after oil pan removal.

OIL PUMP REPAIRS

1. Remove end plate and withdraw O ring from groove in body.

2. Check clearance between lobes of inner and outer rotors. This should not exceed .006". Rotors are supplied only in a matched pair.
3. Check clearance between outer rotor and the housing, Fig. 15. This should not exceed .010".
4. Place a straightedge across face of pump body, Fig. 16. Clearance between face of rotors and straightedge should not exceed .005".
5. If necessary to replace rotor or drive shaft, remove outer rotor and then drive out retaining pin securing the skew gear to drive shaft and pull

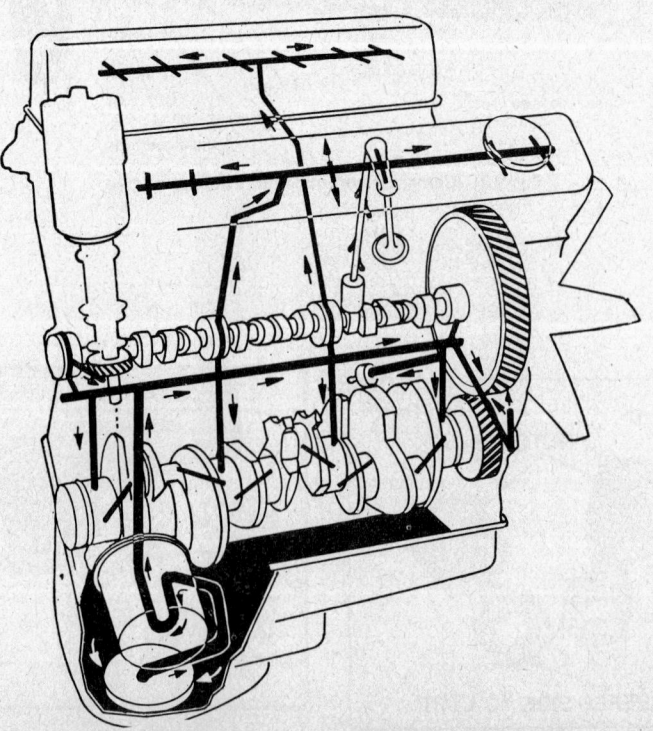

Engine oiling system. 2800 cc engine

off the gear.

6. Withdraw inner rotor and drive shaft.

BELT TENSION DATA

	New Ft. Lbs.	Used Ft. Lbs.
1974-78 Exc. ¼ inch	140	110
¼ inch	65	50

WATER PUMP, REPLACE

1. Drain coolant and disconnect heater hose and lower radiator hose from pump.
2. Loosen alternator and remove drive belt.
3. Remove fan and pulley.
4. Remove water pump mounting bolts, water pump, water inlet housing and thermostat.

FUEL PUMP PRESSURE

Year	Engine	Pressure Lbs.
1974-75	2800 cc	3½-5½
1976	2800 cc	3½-5¾
1977-79	2800 cc	3-6

FUEL PUMP, REPLACE

1. Disconnect fuel lines from pump.
2. Remove fuel pump attaching bolts and fuel pump.

V8 Engine Section

NOTE: Refer to the Ford & Mercury—Compact & Intermediate chapter for detailed service on this engine.

ENGINE MOUNTS, REPLACE

1979 Capri & Mustang

1. Remove fan shroud attaching screws.
2. Remove nuts attaching insulators to lower bracket, Fig. 1.
3. Raise engine with a suitable jack and a block of wood placed under oil pan.
4. Remove insulator to engine block attaching bolts.
5. Remove insulator from vehicle.
6. Reverse procedure to install.

1975-78 Mustang

1. Remove fan shroud screws and support engine with a suitable jack and a block of wood under the oil pan.
2. Remove insulator to frame through bolt, Fig. 2.
3. Remove insulator to engine block attaching bolts.
4. Raise engine slightly, then remove insulator and heat shield, if equipped.
5. Reverse procedure to install.

SERPENTINE DRIVE BELT

1979 Capri & Mustang

These models are equipped with a serpentine drive belt, Fig. 3, to drive the accessories in place of the usual arrangement. This "V" ribbed belt drives the fan/water pump, alternator, secondary air pump, optional A/C compressor and op-

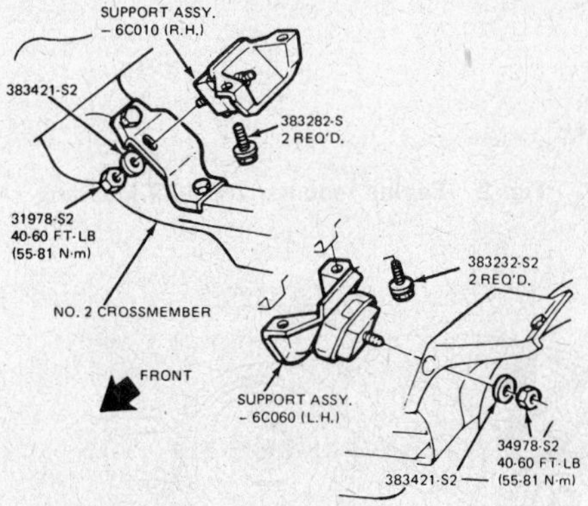

Fig. 1 Engine mount. 1979 Capri & Mustang

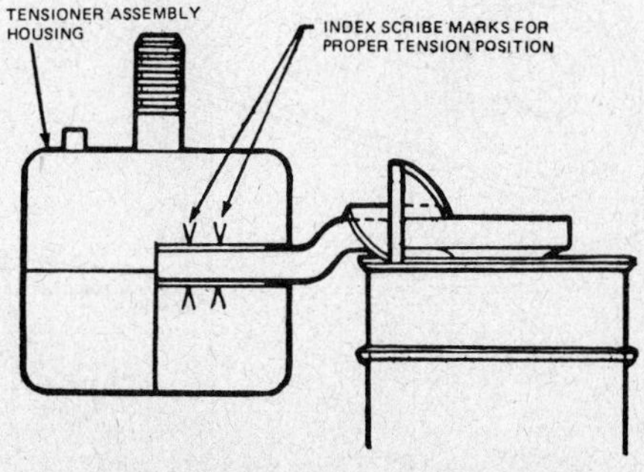

Fig. 4 Serpentine drive belt tensioner alignment marks

tional power steering pump.

The tensioner arm should be checked to ensure that the top edge of the arm is located between the two index marks scribed on the circumference next to the slot of the tensioner housing, Fig. 4. If the tensioner arm is not properly aligned, the drive belt and pulleys should be inspected for wear and binding. If the drive belt and pulleys are satisfactory, the tensioner must be replaced as outlined in the following procedure.

Drive belt & Tensioner, Replace

1. Insert a 16 inch pry bar or equivalent in the slot of the tensioner bracket, and using the tensioner housing as a fulcrum, push the pry bar downward to force the tensioner pulley upward, relieving tension on belt, Fig. 3.
2. Remove drive belt.
3. Remove bolt securing tensioner assembly to alternator bracket.
4. Remove tensioner assembly.
5. Position tensioner assembly so the tang, located on the rear of the assembly, is placed to fit in the hole or slot in alternator bracket.
6. Install the tensioner assembly bolt through the hole in the alternator bracket and torque bolt to 55-80 ft. lbs.
7. Install drive belt by inserting the pry bar as outlined in Step 1. Refer to decal located on top of the windshield washer/coolant expansion reservoir for proper belt routing.
8. Remove pry bar.
9. The drive belt is automatically tensioned when the tensioner arm is located between the two index marks, Fig. 4.

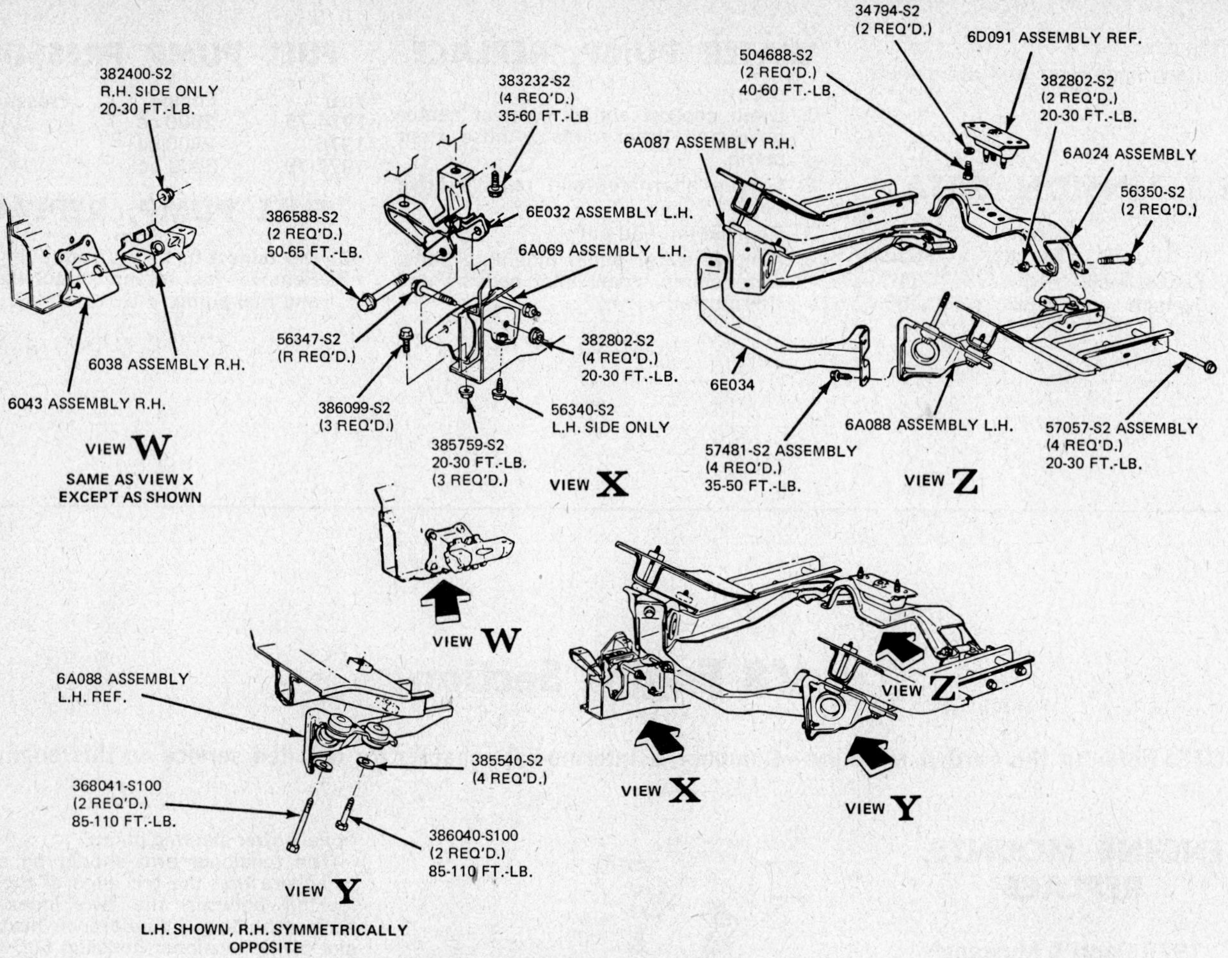

382400-S2
R.H. SIDE ONLY
20-30 FT.-LB.

34794-S2
(2 REQ'D.)

6D091 ASSEMBLY REF.

504688-S2
(2 REQ'D.)
40-60 FT.-LB.

382802-S2
(2 REQ'D.)
20-30 FT.-LB.

383232-S2
(4 REQ'D.)
35-60 FT.-LB

6A087 ASSEMBLY R.H.

6A024 ASSEMBLY

386588-S2
(2 REQ'D.)
50-65 FT.-LB.

6E032 ASSEMBLY L.H.

56350-S2
(2 REQ'D.)

6A069 ASSEMBLY L.H.

56347-S2
(R REQ'D.)

382802-S2
(4 REQ'D.)
20-30 FT.-LB.

6038 ASSEMBLY R.H.

386099-S2
(3 REQ'D.)

56340-S2
L.H. SIDE ONLY

6E034

6A088 ASSEMBLY L.H.

57057-S2 ASSEMBLY
(4 REQ'D.)
20-30 FT.-LB.

6043 ASSEMBLY R.H.

385759-S2
20-30 FT.-LB.
(3 REQ'D.)

57481-S2 ASSEMBLY
(4 REQ'D.)
35-50 FT.-LB.

VIEW W

SAME AS VIEW X
EXCEPT AS SHOWN

VIEW X

VIEW Z

VIEW W

6A088 ASSEMBLY
L.H. REF.

385540-S2
(4 REQ'D.)

368041-S100
(2 REQ'D.)
85-110 FT.-LB.

386040-S100
(2 REQ'D.)
85-110 FT.-LB.

VIEW Y

VIEW X

VIEW Y

L.H. SHOWN, R.H. SYMMETRICALLY
OPPOSITE

Fig. 2   Engine mounts. 1975-78 Mustang

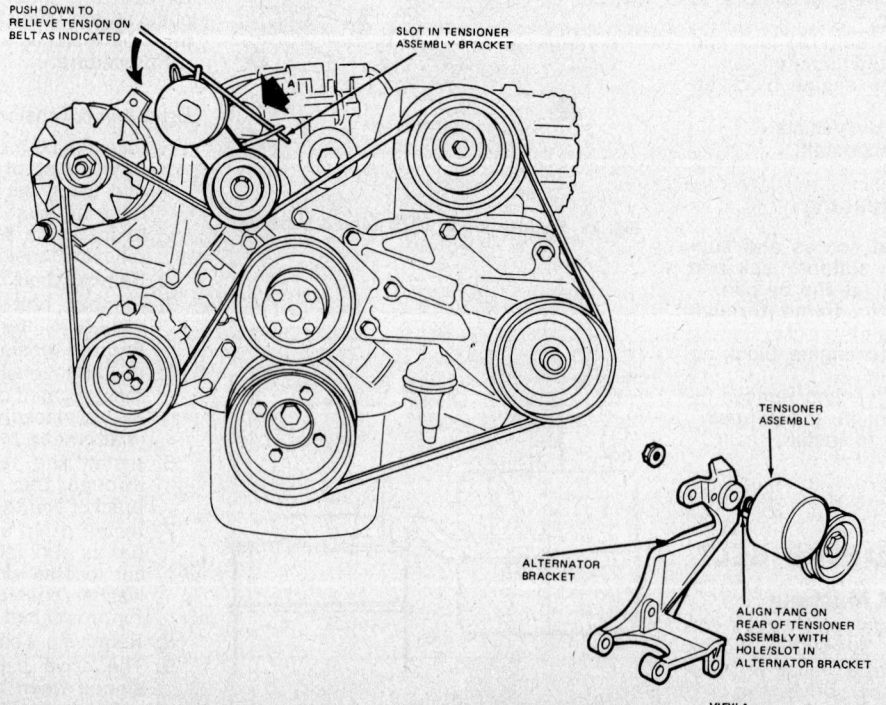

PUSH DOWN TO
RELIEVE TENSION ON
BELT AS INDICATED

SLOT IN TENSIONER
ASSEMBLY BRACKET

TENSIONER
ASSEMBLY

ALTERNATOR
BRACKET

ALIGN TANG ON
REAR OF TENSIONER
ASSEMBLY WITH
HOLE/SLOT IN
ALTERNATOR BRACKET

VIEW-A

Fig. 3   Serpentine drive belt. 1979 Capri & Mustang

Turbocharger Section

Fig. 1 Turbocharger. 1979 4-140 (2300cc) engine, Capri & Mustang

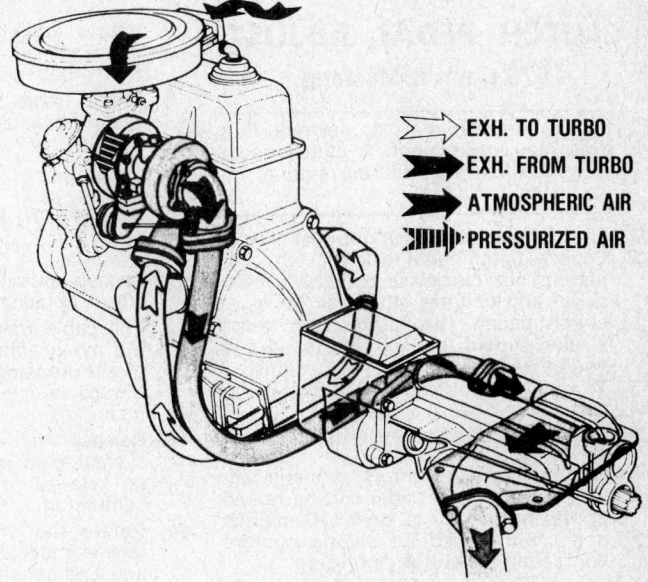

⇨ EXH. TO TURBO
➤ EXH. FROM TURBO
➤ ATMOSPHERIC AIR
⇛ PRESSURIZED AIR

Fig. 2 Turbocharger air flow

An optional turbocharger is available on the 1979 Capri and Mustang equipped with the 4-140 (2300cc) engine, Fig. 1.

A turbine in the exhaust gas flow is connected, through a shaft, to the impeller (compressor) near the carburetor, Fig. 2. During normal, steady operation, the turbine does not rotate with sufficient speed to boost pressure or fuel economy. However, when the accelerator is depressed, the engine speed increases, thereby increasing exhaust gas flow. This action accelerates the turbine, in turn, the impeller, increasing the density of the air/fuel mixture delivered to the engine.

The resulting increase in engine power and exhaust pressure further increases turbine speed and boost pressure. This cycle is self-perpetuating and could result in engine damage if not controlled.

A wastegate is used to bypass a portion of the exhaust gasses around the turbine at a predetermined point in the cycle, limiting the boost pressure. The wastegate starts to open when the turbocharger boost pressure reaches approximately 5 PSI and routes a sufficient portion of the exhaust gasses around the turbine to limit maximum boost to 5½ PSI.

A green light on the instrument panel indicates that the turbocharger is in a safe boost condition. A red light and buzzer is used to indicate a malfunction or if boost pressure rises above 5½ PSI. If the oil temperature exceeds a predetermined level, just the warning light will flash.

The high cylinder temperature created by boosted combustion can result in detonation, therefore, two spark retardation points have been designed into the electronic ignition system.

At approximately 1 PSI of boost pressure, a switch in the intake manifold, Fig. 3, sends an electrical signal to the ignition

module which electronically retards the ignition timing six degrees. At 4 PSI of boost pressure, another manifold switch sends a signal and timing is retarded an additional six degrees.

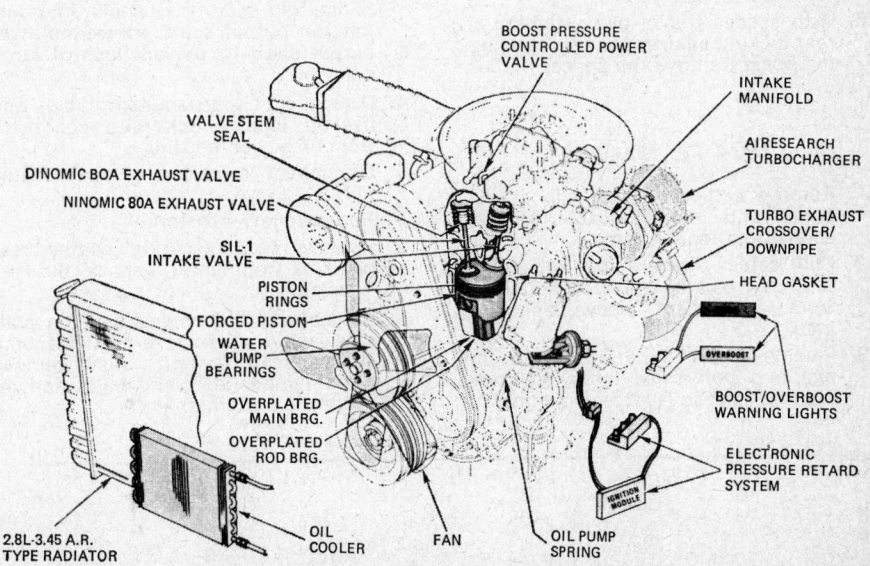

BOOST PRESSURE CONTROLLED POWER VALVE

INTAKE MANIFOLD

AIRESEARCH TURBOCHARGER

TURBO EXHAUST CROSSOVER/ DOWNPIPE

HEAD GASKET

VALVE STEM SEAL

DINOMIC BOA EXHAUST VALVE

NINOMIC 80A EXHAUST VALVE

SIL-1 INTAKE VALVE

PISTON RINGS

FORGED PISTON

WATER PUMP BEARINGS

OVERPLATED MAIN BRG.

OVERPLATED ROD BRG.

2.8L-3.45 A.R. TYPE RADIATOR

OIL COOLER

FAN

OIL PUMP SPRING

OVERBOOST

BOOST/OVERBOOST WARNING LIGHTS

ELECTRONIC PRESSURE RETARD SYSTEM

IGNITION MODULE

Fig. 3 Turbocharger system

Clutch & Transmission Section

CLUTCH PEDAL, ADJUST

1979 Capri & Mustang

NOTE: These models do not require a free play adjustment. A clutch pedal height adjustment will be required instead.

1. From under vehicle remove dust shield.
2. Loosen clutch cable lock nut. Turn adjusting nut clockwise to raise clutch pedal and counter clockwise to lower clutch pedal. The total clutch pedal stroke should be 5.3 in. for 4-140 engine and 6.5 in. for V8-302 engine.
3. Torque lock nut to 5 to 8 ft. lbs., using care not to disturb adjustment.
4. Cycle clutch pedal several times, then recheck pedal height.
5. When clutch system is properly adjusted the clutch pedal can be raised approximately 2.7 in. on 4-140 engines and 1.5 in. for V8-302 engines, before contacting the clutch pedal stop.

1974 Pinto

1. From under car, loosen cable locknuts and adjusting nut at flywheel housing.
2. Pull cable toward front of car until all free movement of the release lever is eliminated.
3. Holding cable in this position, place a 1/4" spacer block against the flywheel housing boss (on engine side). Run adjusting nut against the spacer finger tight.
4. Tighten the front locknut against the adjusting nut, being careful not to disturb the adjustment. Torque locknut to 40-60 ft. lbs.
5. With spacer still in place, tighten the rear locknut against the flywheel housing boss. Remove the spacer.

1974-78 Mustang

1. Remove cable retaining clip at dash panel and remove cable retaining screw from fender apron.
2. Pull cable toward front of vehicle until nut can be rotated. Rotate nut from adjustment sleeve about 1/4 inch.
3. Release cable to neutralize the linkage and pull cable until free movement of release lever is eliminated.

4. Rotate adjusting nut toward adjustment sleeve until contact is made, then index into the next notch.
5. Install cable retaining clip, cable retaining bracket and retaining screw.

1975-79 Bobcat & Pinto

1. Loosen clutch cable lock nut at flywheel housing.
2. Pull cable toward front of vehicle so the nylon adjuster nut tabs are clear of the housing boss, then rotate nut toward vehicle front approximately 1/4 inch.
3. Release the cable, neutralizing the system, and pull cable forward again so release lever free movement is eliminated.
4. Rotate the adjusting nut until contact is made between index tab face and the housing, then index the tabs to engage the nearest housing groove.
5. Torque lock nut to 15 ft. lbs.

CLUTCH, REPLACE

1974-79 Bobcat & Pinto

1. Remove shift lever by removing knob and boot, then compress rubber spring and remove retaining snap ring. Bend shift lever lock tabs up and remove plastic dome nut from extension housing.
2. Raise vehicle on a hoist.
3. Disconnect drive shaft from U joint flange and slide drive shaft off transmission output shaft. Insert tool over output shaft to prevent loss of lubricant.
4. Disconnect speedometer cable and backup light switch wire connector from extension housing.
5. Disconnect lower end of clutch cable at release lever.
6. Remove starter motor.
7. Remove bolts securing engine rear plate to front lower part of flywheel housing.
8. Support rear of engine using a suitable jack, then remove bolt attaching engine rear support. Also remove crossmember attaching bolts and remove the crossmember.

9. Remove bolts attaching flywheel housing to engine block.
10. Move transmission and flywheel housing assembly rearward until housing clears the clutch pressure plate. Lower transmission and remove.
11. Unfasten and remove the pressure plate, marking same to assure correct assembly.

1974-78 Mustang & 1979 Capri & Mustang

1. Loosen clutch cable adjusting nut to allow slack in cable.
2. Position gear shift lever in neutral, then remove the three lever attaching screws and remove lever.
3. Remove driveshaft then cover extension housing to prevent lubricant leakage.
4. Disconnect electrical leads and speedometer cable from transmission.
5. Support rear of engine and remove crossmember, then lower engine as necessary and remove transmission attaching bolts and transmission.
6. Disconnect clutch release cable from lever and flywheel housing.
7. Disconnect starter cable and remove starter motor.
8. On models with V6 engine, remove number 2A crossmember. This crossmember is located behind the number 2 crossmember which supports the engine.
9. Remove flywheel housing.
10. Evenly loosen and remove pressure plate attaching screws to prevent distortion of pressure plate. If pressure plate is to be reused, mark pressure plate and flywheel to assure correct assembly.

FOUR SPEED TRANS., REPLACE

The transmission is removed as described under "Clutch Replace".

1979 AUTO. TRANS. LINKAGE, ADJUST

Linkage adjustment procedures for 1979 models are the same as those for 1978 models as outlined elsewhere in this manual.

Rear Axle, Propeller Shaft & Brakes

REAR AXLE

Integral Type

This rear axle, Fig. 1, is an integral design hypoid with the centerline of the pinion set below the centerline of the ring gear. The semi-floating axle shafts are retained in the housing by ball bearings and bearing retainers at axle ends.

The differential is mounted on two opposed tapered roller bearings which are retained in the housing by removable caps. Differential bearing preload and drive gear backlash is adjusted by nuts located behind each differential bearing cup.

The drive pinion assembly is mounted on two opposed tapered roller bearings. Pinion bearing preload is adjusted by a collapsible spacer on the pinion shaft. Pinion and ring gear tooth contact is adjusted by shims between the rear bearing cone and pinion gear.

Removable Carrier Type

In these axles, Fig. 2, the drive pinion is straddle-mounted by two opposed tapered roller bearings which support the pinion shaft in front of the drive pinion

gear, and a straight roller bearing that supports the pinion shaft at the rear of the pinion gear. The drive pinion is assembled in a pinion retainer that is bolted to the differential carrier. The tapered roller bearings are preloaded by a collapsible spacer between the bearings. The pinion is positioned by a shim or shims located between the drive pinion retainer and the differential carrier.

The differential is supported in the carrier by two tapered roller side bearings. These bearings are preloaded by two threaded ring nuts or sleeves between the bearings and the pedestals. The differential assembly is positioned for proper ring gear and pinion backlash by varying the adjustment of these ring nuts. The differential case houses two side gears in mesh with two pinions mounted on a pinion shaft which held in place by a pin. The side gears and pinions are backed by thrust washers.

The axle shafts are of unequal length, the left shaft being shorter than the right. The axle shafts are mounted in sealed ball bearings which are pressed on the shafts.

Rear Axle, Replace

1. Raise vehicle and support at rear frame members.
2. Drain lubricant from axle.
3. Mark drive shaft and pinion flanges for reassembly, then disconnect drive shaft at rear axle U-joint and remove drive shaft from transmission extension housing. Install seal replacer tool in extension housing to prevent leakage.
4. Disconnect shock absorbers at lower mountings.
5. Remove rear wheels and brake drums, then disconnect brake lines at wheel cylinders.
6. Disconnect vent hose from vent tube, then remove vent tube from brake junction and axle housing.
7. Remove clips retaining brake lines to axle housing.
8. Support rear axle housing using a suitable jack.
9. On models with coil springs, disconnect upper control arms from mount-

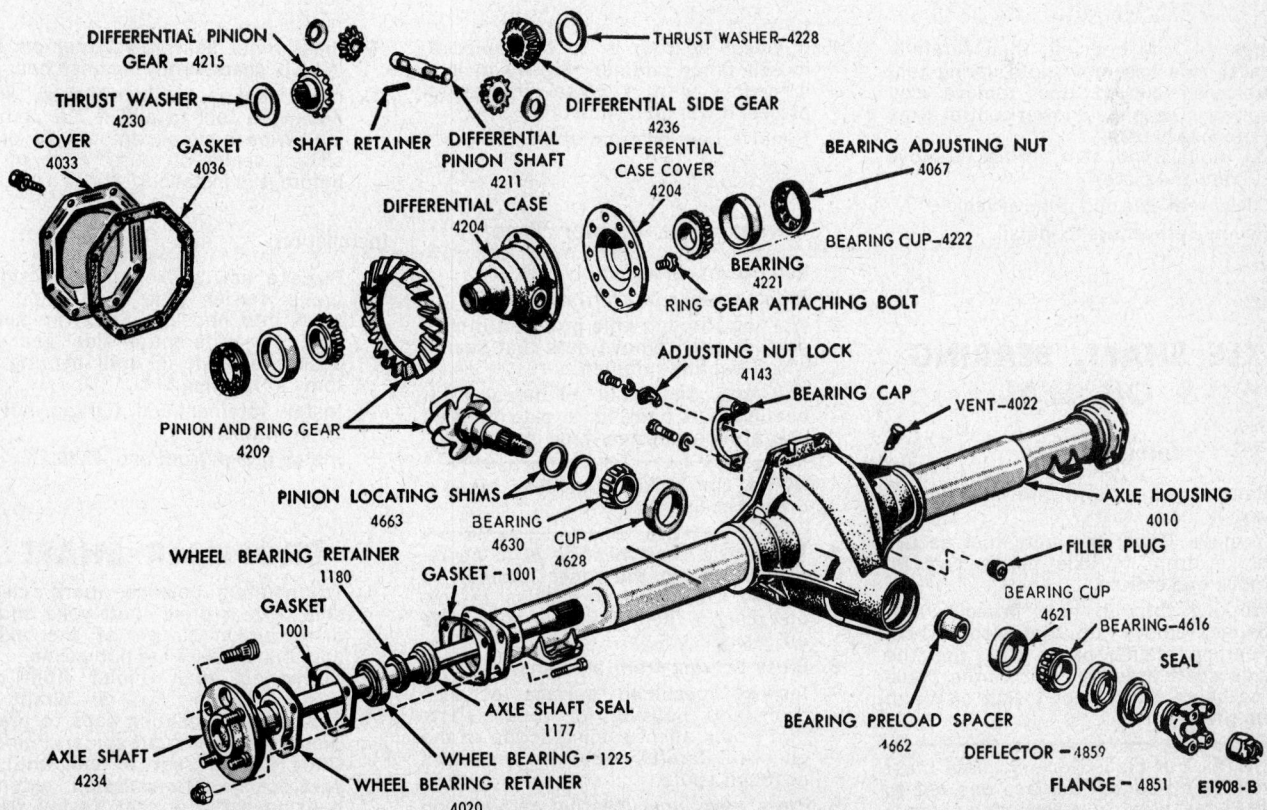

Fig. 1 Disassembled integral rear axle (typical)

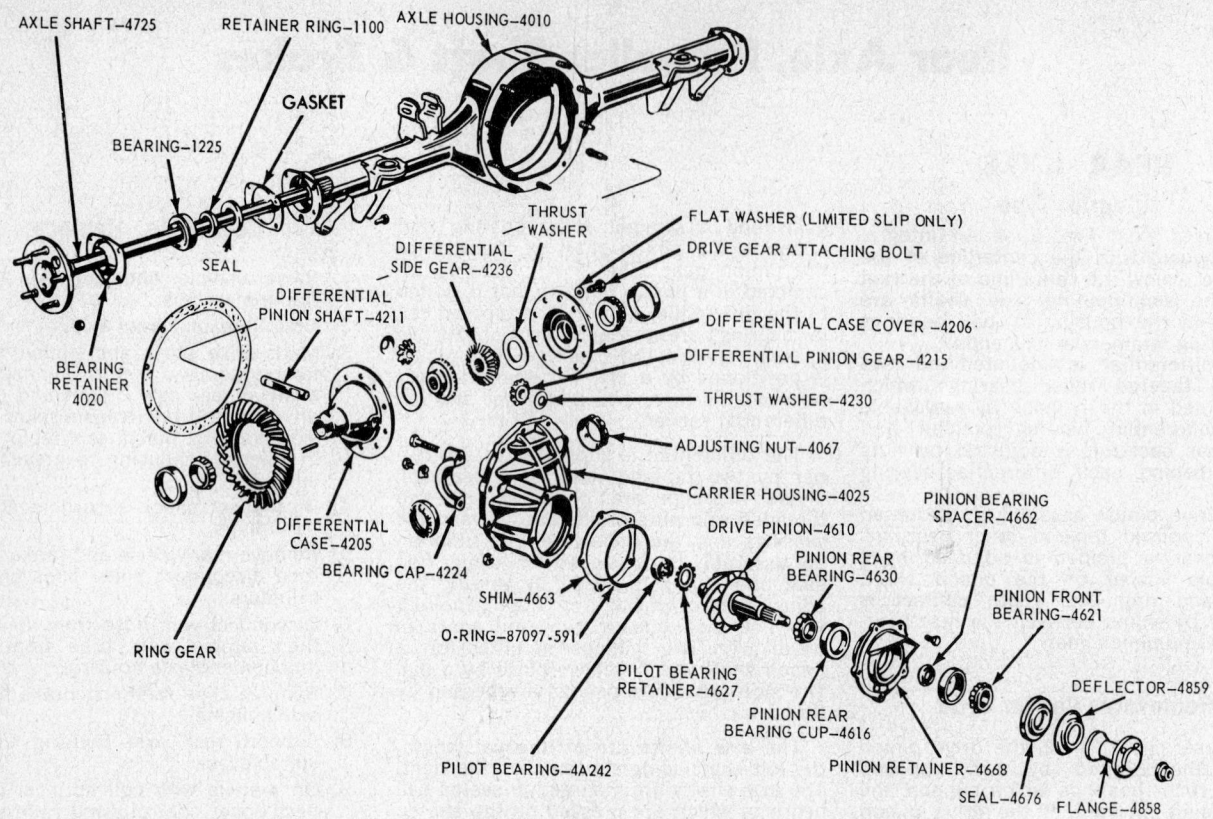

Fig. 2   Disassembled rear axle with removable carrier (typical)

ings on axle housing, then carefully lower axle assembly until spring tension is relieved and remove coil springs. Disconnect lower control arms from axle housing.

10. On models with leaf springs, remove U-bolts and plates.

11. Lower rear axle and remove vehicle.

12. Reverse procedure to install.

AXLE SHAFT, BEARING & OIL SEAL

Integral Type

1. Remove wheel and tire from brake drum.

2. Remove Tinnerman nuts that secure brake drum to axle flange and remove brake drum.

3. Working through hole in each axle flange, remove nuts that secure wheel bearing retainer plate. Then pull the axle shaft assembly out of the housing being careful not to cut or rough up the seal.

NOTE: *The brake backing plate must not be dislodged. Replace one nut to hold the plate in place after shaft is removed.*

4. If wheel bearing is to be replaced, loosen inner retainer ring by nicking it deeply with a chisel in several places. It will then slide off.

5. Remove bearing from shaft.

Removable Carrier Type

1. Remove wheel assembly.

2. Remove brake drum from flange.

3. Working through hole provided in axle shaft flange, remove nuts that secure wheel bearing retainer.

4. Pull axle shaft out of housing. If bearing is a tight fit in axle housing use a slide hammer-type puller.

NOTE: On 1974-79 models, remove brake backing plate.

5. If the axle shaft bearing is to be replaced, loosen the inner retainer by nicking it deeply with a chisel in several places. The bearing will then slide off easily.

6. Press bearing from axle shaft.

7. Inspect machined surface of axle shaft and housing for rough spots that would affect sealing action of the oil seal. Carefully remove any burrs or rough spots.

8. Press new inner bearing retainer on shaft until it seats firmly against shoulder on shaft.

9. Press inner bearing retainer on shaft until it seats firmly against bearing.

10. If oil seal is to be replaced, use a hook-type tool to pull it out of housing. Wipe a small amount of oil resistant sealer on outer edge of seal before it is installed.

Installation

1. Place a new gasket on each side of brake carrier plate and slide axle shaft into housing. Start the splines into the differential side gear and push the shaft in until bearing bottoms in housing.

2. Install retainer and tighten nuts to 20-40 ft. lbs.

3. Install brake drum and wheel.

PROPELLER SHAFT

1. To maintain balance, mark relationship of rear drive shaft yoke and the drive pinion flange of the axle if alignment marks are not visible.

2. Disconnect rear U-joint from companion flange, Fig. 3. Wrap tape around loose bearing caps to prevent them from falling off spider. Pull drive shaft toward rear of car until slip yoke clears transmission extension housing and the seal. Install tool in extension housing to prevent lubricant leakage.

BRAKE ADJUSTMENTS

The hydraulic drum brakes, Fig. 4, are self-adjusting and require a manual adjustment only after brake shoes have been replaced. The adjustment is made as follows:

1. Using tool HRE 8650, Fig. 5, determine inside diameter of brake drum.
2. Reverse tool and adjust brake shoes to fit the gauge. Hold automatic adjusting lever out of engagement while rotating adjusting screw, to prevent burring slots in screw.

PARKING BRAKE, ADJUST

1. Release parking brake.
2. Place transmission in Neutral and raise vehicle until rear wheels clear floor.
3. Tighten adjusting nut on equalizer rod at the control, Fig. 6, to cause the rear wheel brakes to drag.
4. Loosen adjusting nut until rear brakes are just free.

MASTER CYLINDER, REPLACE

Exc. Power Brakes

1. Disconnect stoplight switch wires at connector. Remove spring retainer and slide stop light switch off brake pedal pin just far enough to clear end of pin, then lift switch straight upward from the pin.
2. Slide master cylinder push rod and nylon washers and bushings off brake pedal pin.
3. Remove brake tubes from master cylinder ports.
4. Unfasten and remove master cylinder by lifting forward and upward from vehicle.

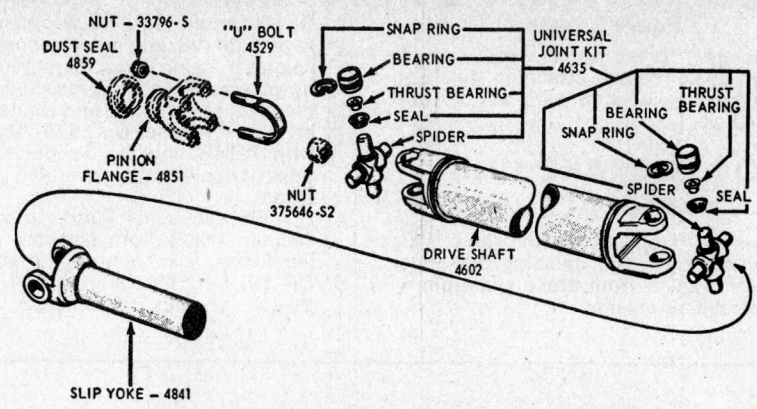

Fig. 3 Drive shaft and universal joints disassembled

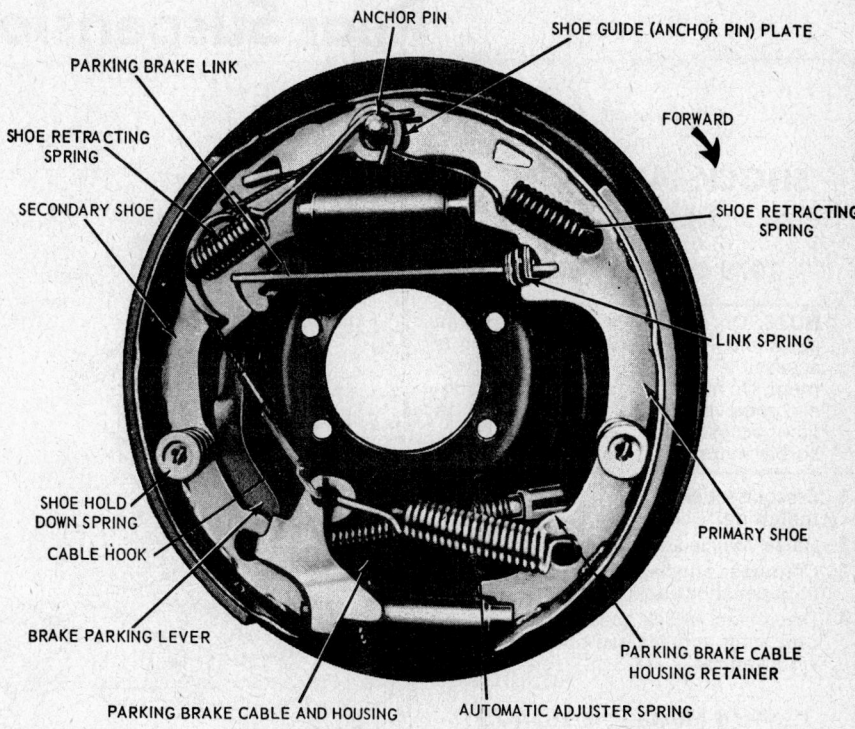

Fig. 4 Self-adjusting brake assembly. Rear shown

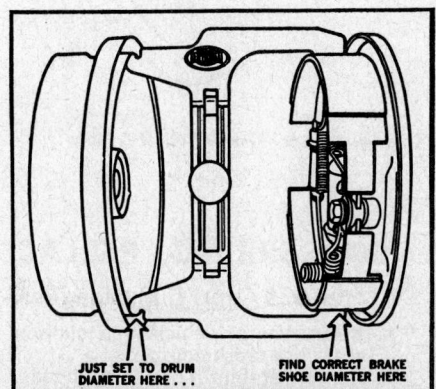

Fig. 5 Brake adjustment

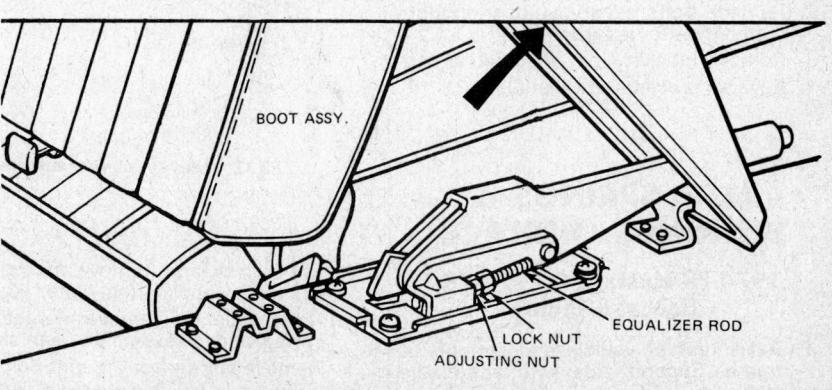

Fig. 6 Parking brake adjustment

Power Brakes

Disconnect brake tubes from master cylinder, then remove attaching nuts and slide master cylinder forward and upward from vehicle.

POWER BRAKE UNIT, REPLACE

1. Remove stoplight switch and slide booster push rod, bushing and inner nylon washer from brake pedal pin.
2. Remove air cleaner.

3. On all except Capri, Mustang and Mustang with V8 engine, disconnect accelerator cable from carburetor. Remove screws securing accelerator cable bracket to engine and rotate bracket toward engine. On 1974-79 models with 4-140 engine, disconnect inlet hose of choke water cover and position aside.
4. On Bobcat and Pinto, disconnect vacuum hoses from solenoid on fender apron, then remove the solenoid.
5. On 1974-78 Mustang with 4-140 or V6-171 engines, disconnect vacuum

hose from EGR vacuum reservoir.
6. On all models, disconnect vacuum hose from power brake unit.
7. Disconnect hydraulic lines from master cylinder and cap open lines and ports.
8. Remove master cylinder.
9. From inside vehicle, remove power brake unit to dash panel attaching nuts.
10. From engine compartment, pull power brake unit forward until push rod clears panel, raise front of unit and remove from vehicle.

Rear Suspension

SHOCK ABSORBER, REPLACE

1979 Capri & Mustang

NOTE: On hatchback models, the upper shock absorber upper mounting is accessible from the luggage compartment. On hatchback and fastback models, remove side panel trim covers to gain access to the upper shock absorber mounting.

1. Disconnect shock absorber from upper mounting.
2. Raise vehicle and support rear axle.
3. Compress shock absorber to clear hole in upper shock absorber tower.
4. Disconnect shock absorber from lower mounting and remove shock absorber from vehicle.

1974-78 Mustang & 1974-79 Bobcat & Pinto

1. With rear axle supported properly disconnect shock absorber from lower mounting.
2. Remove bolts securing upper mounting bracket to underbody.
3. Remove bracket from shock absorber.
4. Reverse procedure to install.

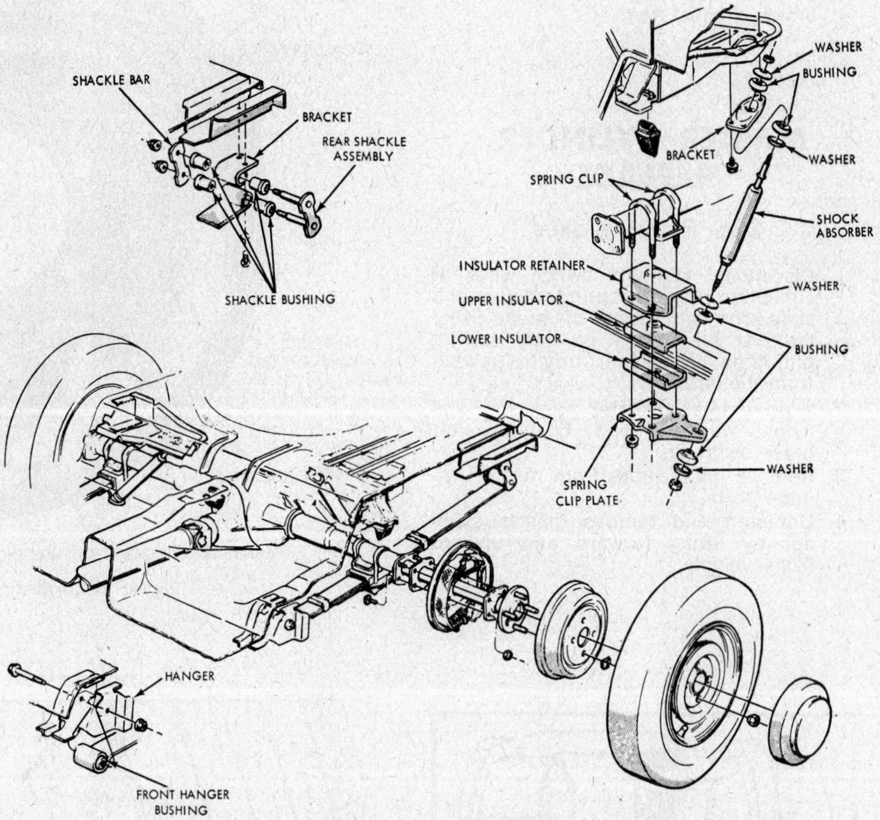

Fig. 1   Leaf spring rear suspension. 1974-78 Mustang & 1974-79 Bobcat & Pinto

LEAF SPRINGS & BUSHINGS, REPLACE

1974-78 Mustang & 1974-79 Bobcat & Pinto

1. Raise rear of vehicle and support at frame. Support axle with a suitable jack.
2. Disconnect shock absorbers from lower mountings.

3. Lower jack and remove spring plate "U" bolts and spring plate, Fig. 1.
4. Raise axle to remove weight from spring and disassemble rear shackle.
5. Remove spring front mount bolt.
6. Replace spring front eye bushing as necessary, Figs. 2 and 3.
7. Reverse procedure to install.

COIL SPRING, REPLACE

1979 Capri & Mustang

1. Raise rear of vehicle and support at rear body crossmember.
2. Remove stabilizer bar, if equipped.
3. Lower axle housing until shock absorbers are fully extended.

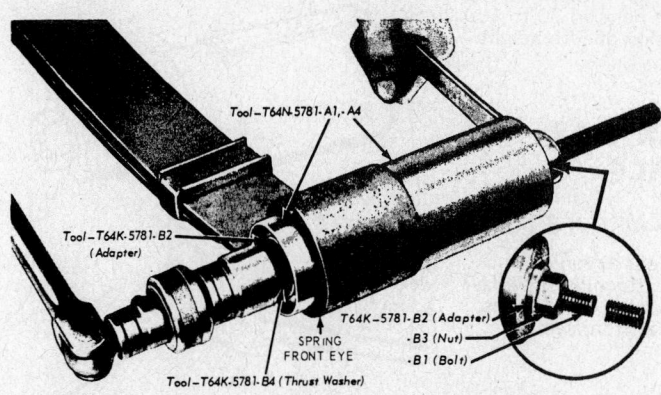

Fig. 2   Spring, front bushing removal. 1974-78 Mustang & 1974-79 Bobcat & Pinto

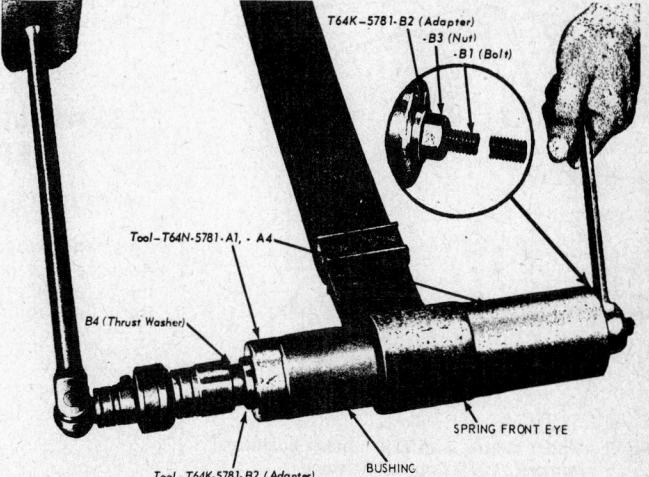

Fig. 3   Spring, front bushing installation. 1974-78 Mustang & 1974-79 Bobcat & Pinto

NOTE: The axle housing must be supported with a suitable jack.

4. Position a suitable jack under lower control arm rear pivot bolt to support control arm, then remove pivot bolt.
5. Carefully lower the lower control arm until spring tension is relieved, then remove coil spring and insulator.
6. Reverse procedure to install. Torque lower control arm pivot bolt to 70 to 100 ft. lbs. with suspension at curb height.

CONTROL ARMS & BUSHINGS, REPLACE

1979 Capri & Mustang

Upper Control Arm

1. Raise rear of vehicle and support at rear body crossmember.
2. Remove upper control arm rear and front pivot bolts, then remove control arm.
3. If control arm axle bracket bushings are to be replaced, refer to Figs. 5 and 6.

4. Position upper control arm into side rail bracket, then install front pivot bolt. Do not tight bolt at this time.
5. Raise rear axle until upper control arm rear pivot bolt hole is aligned with hole in axle housing, then install rear pivot bolt. Do not tighten bolt at this time.
6. Position suspension at curb height, then torque control arm pivot bolts to 70 to 100 ft. lbs.

Lower Control Arms

1. Remove coil spring as described under Coil Spring, Replace.

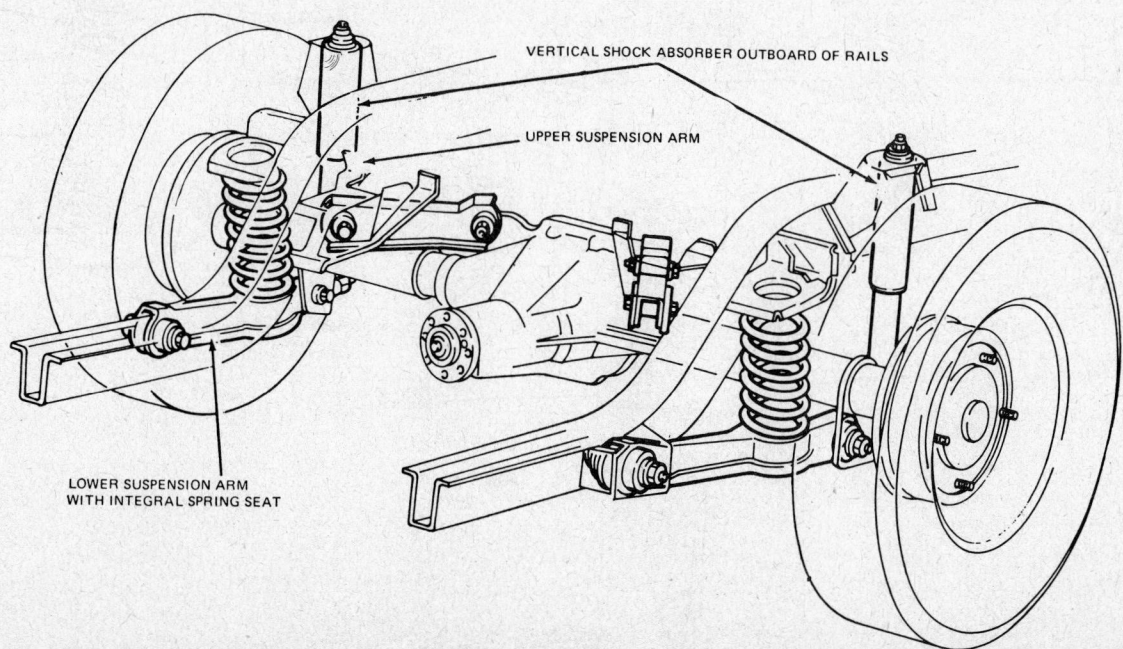

Fig. 4   Coil spring rear suspension. 1979 Capri & Mustang

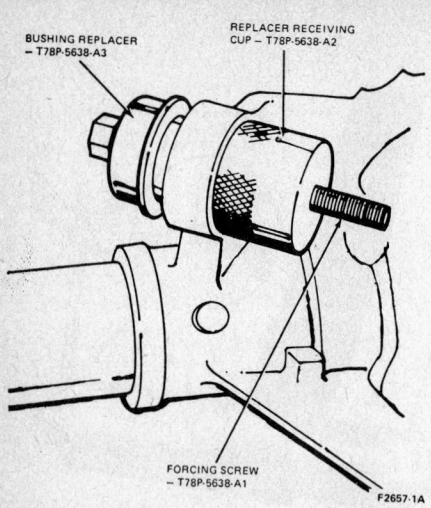

Fig. 5 Upper control arm axle bracket bushing removal. 1979 Capri & Mustang

2. Remove lower control arm front pivot bolt and nut, then remove control arm.
3. Reverse procedure to install. Torque front and rear pivot bolts to 70 to 100 ft. lbs. with suspension at curb height.

STABILIZER BAR, REPLACE

1979 Capri & Mustang

1. Raise and support rear of vehicle.
2. Remove four bolts attaching stabilizer bar to brackets on lower control arms.
3. Remove stabilizer bar from vehicle.

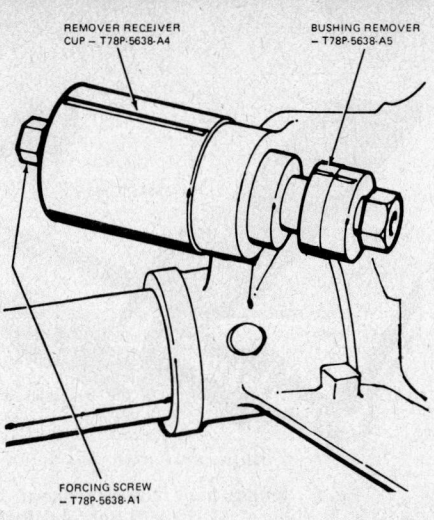

Fig. 6 Upper control arm axle bracket bushing installation. 1979 Capri & Mustang

Front End & Steering Section

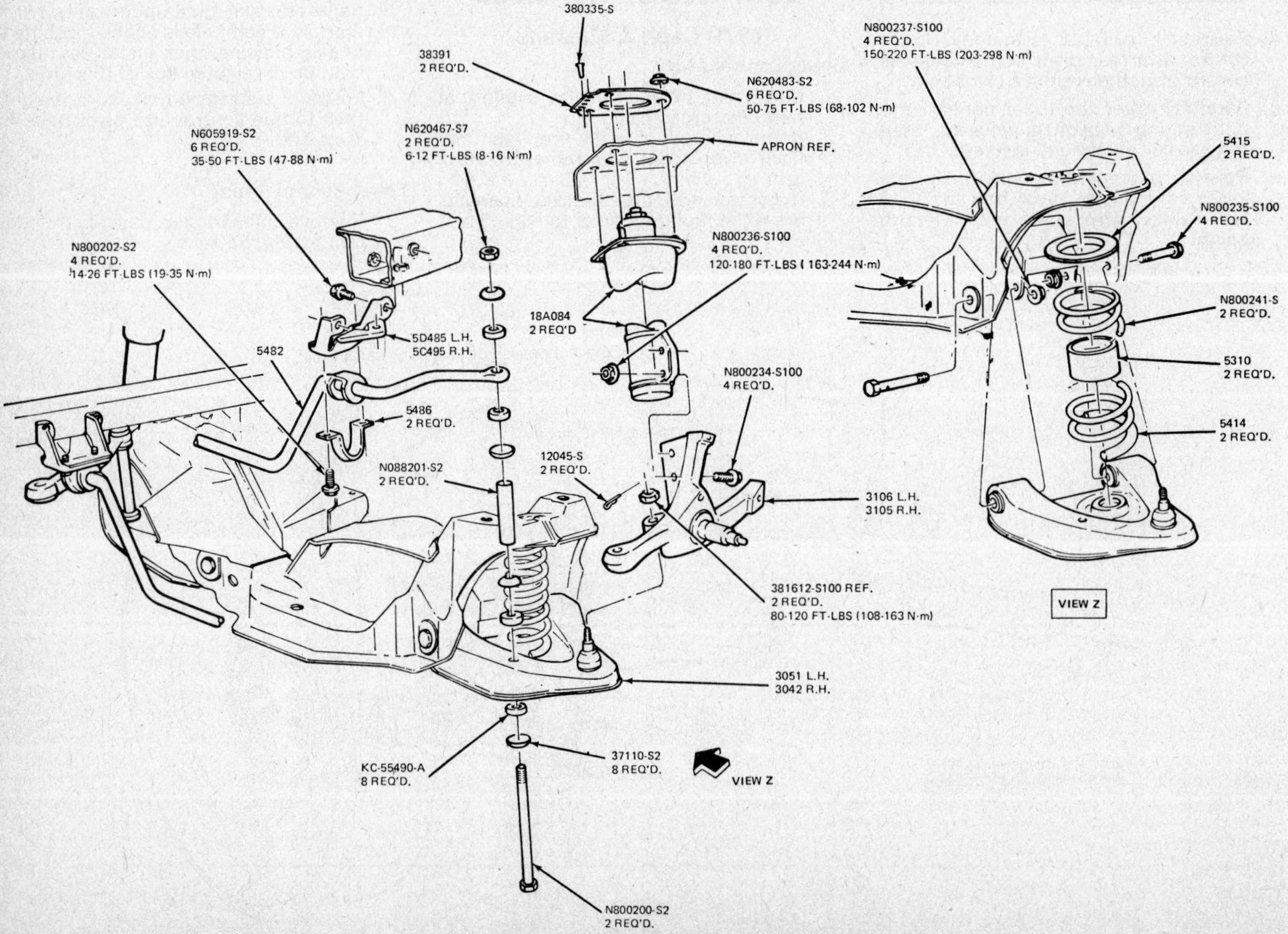

Fig. 1 Front suspension assembly. 1979 Capri & Mustang

FRONT SUSPENSION

1979 Capri & Mustang

The front suspension is of the modified McPherson strut design, which uses shock struts and coil springs. The springs are mounted between the lower control and a spring pocket in the crossmember.

1974-78 Mustang & 1974-79 Bobcat & Pinto

The upper and lower ends of the spindle are attached to upper and lower ball joints which are mounted in upper and lower arms. The upper arm pivots on a bushing and shaft assembly which is bolted to the frame. The lower arm pivots on a bolt in the front crossmember, Fig. 1A.

WHEEL ALIGNMENT

1979 Capri & Mustang

Caster & Camber

The caster and camber angles of this suspension are factory pre-set and can not be adjusted.

1974-78 Mustang & 1974-79 Bobcat & Pinto

Caster and Camber

1. Working inside front wheel housing, install special tool, one at each end of the upper arm inner shaft. Turn the special tool bolts inward until the bolt ends contact the body metal, Fig. 2.
2. Loosen the two upper arm inner shaft-to-body bolts. The upper shaft will move inboard until stopped by

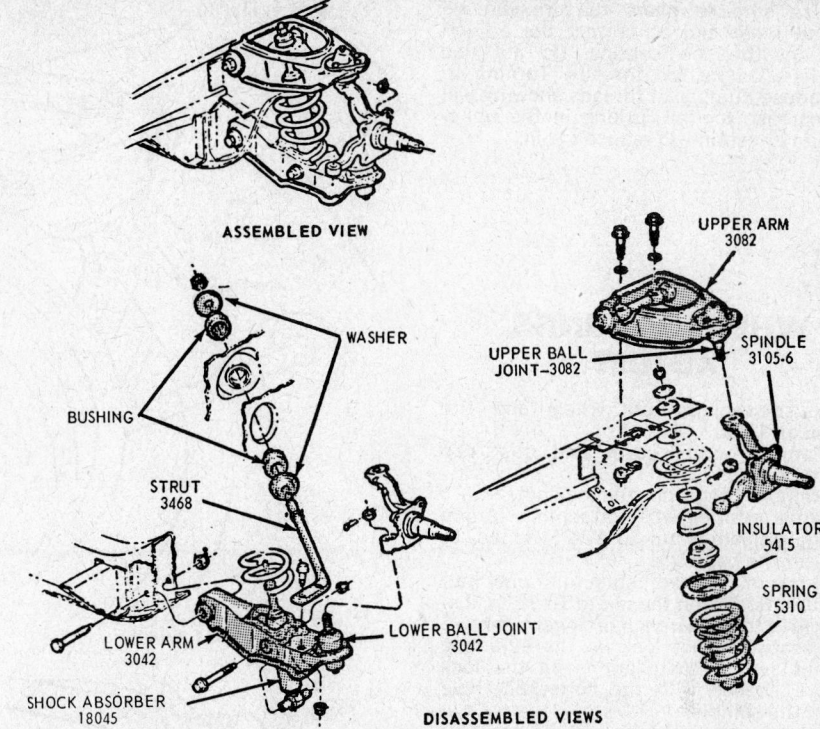

ASSEMBLED VIEW

DISASSEMBLED VIEWS

Fig. 1A   Front suspension assembly (typical). 1974-78 Mustang & 1974-79 Bobcat & Pinto

the tool bolt ends solidly contacting the body metal.
3. Turn the special tool bolts inward or outward until caster and camber are within specifications. Tightening these bolts on the special tool force the arm outward; while loosening the bolts on the tools permits the arm and inner shaft to move inboard due to weight force.

4. When properly adjusted, torque shaft-to-body bolts to 75-105 ft. lbs. on 1973-74 models and 95-120 ft. lbs. on 1975-78 models, then remove the special tools.

TOE-IN, ADJUST

1. Check to see that steering shaft and steering wheel marks are in alignment and in the top position.
2. Loosen clamp screw on the tie rod bellows and free the seal on the rod to prevent twisting of the bellows, Fig. 3.
3. Loosen tie rod jam nut.

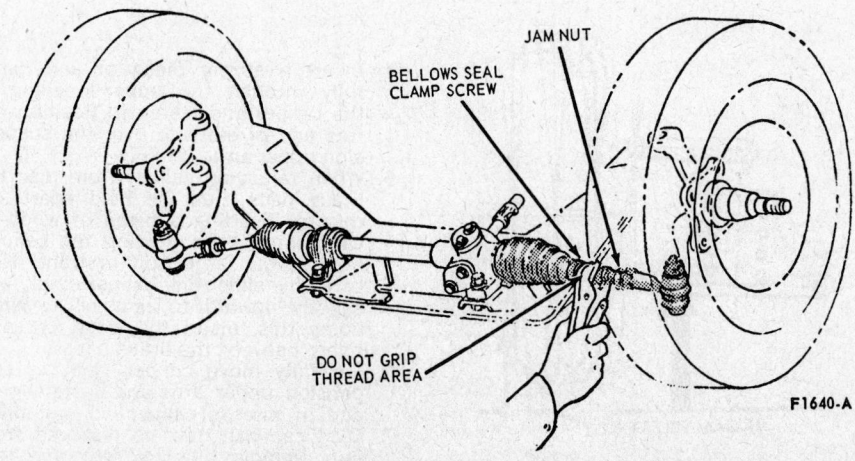

Fig. 3   Toe-in adjustment (typical)

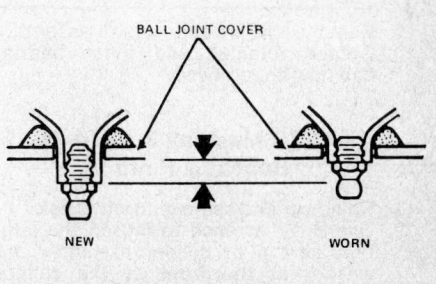

Fig. 4   Checking lower ball joint for wear. 1979 Capri & Mustang

4. Use suitable pliers to turn the tie rod inner end to correct the adjustment to specifications. Do not use pliers on tie rod threads. Turning to reduce number of threads showing will increase toe-in. Turning in the opposite direction will reduce toe-in.

WHEEL BEARINGS, ADJUST

1. Raise vehicle until wheel and tire clear floor.
2. Remove wheel cover and dust cap from hub.
3. Remove cotter pin and lock nut.
4. While rotating wheel assembly, torque the adjusting nut to 17-25 ft. lbs. to seat the bearings.
5. Back off the adjusting nut one half turn. Retighten the nut to 10-15 in. lbs. with a torque wrench or finger tight.
6. Locate the nut lock on the adjusting nut so the castellations on the lock are aligned with the cotter pin hole in the spindle.
7. Install new cotter pin and replace dust cap and wheel cover.

WHEEL BEARINGS, REPLACE

(Disc Brakes)

1979 Capri & Mustang

1. Raise vehicle and remove front wheels.
2. Remove caliper mounting bolts.

NOTE: It is not necessary to disconnect the brake lines for this operation.

3. Slide caliper off of disc, inserting a clean spacer between the shoes to hold them in their bores after the caliper is removed. Position caliper out of the way.

NOTE: Do not allow caliper to hang by brake hose.

4. Remove hub and disc assembly. Grease retainer and inner bearing can now be removed.

1974-78 Mustang & 1974-79 Bobcat & Pinto

1. Raise car and remove front wheels.
2. Use a ¾" wrench to loosen the large bolt at top of caliper assembly and washer at the front of the caliper. Loosen it until it can be turned with the fingers.
3. Remove the smaller bolt at bottom of caliper with a ⅝" wrench.

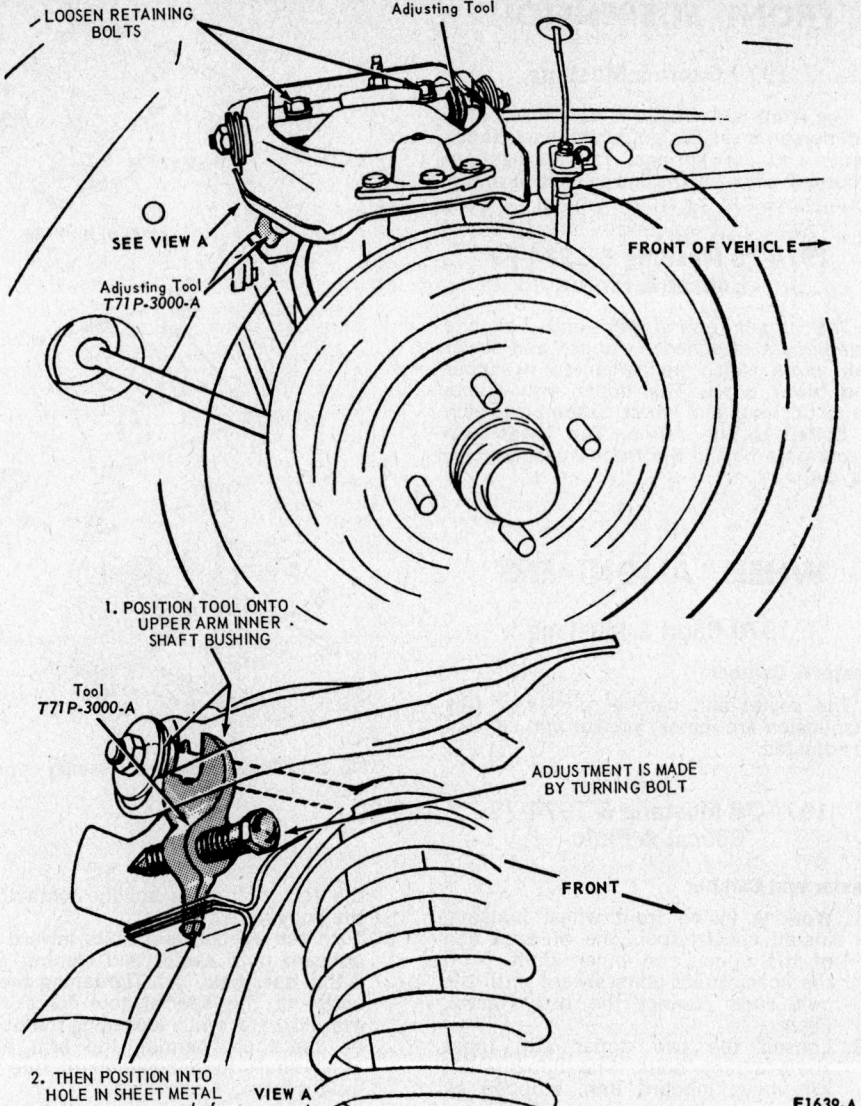

Fig. 2   Caster and camber adjustment. 1974-78 Mustang & 1974-79 Bobcat & Pinto

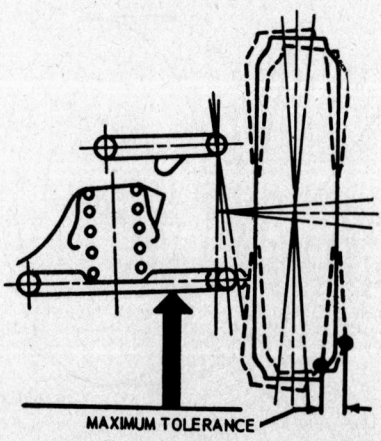

Fig. 4A   Measuring lower ball joint play

4. Insert a strong piece of wire carefully through the upper opening in the caliper and fasten it. Position the free end of the wire over the suspension upper arm.
5. When removing caliper from disc the brake pads must be held apart. Do this by inserting a piece of wood or cardboard. While holding the caliper, remove the large bolt in front. Now carefully slide the caliper back and slightly upward to remove it. While doing this, insert the wood or cardboard between the brake pads.
6. Carefully move caliper back to suspension upper arm and fasten loose end of wire so caliper will not drop.
7. Dust cap can now be removed from hub. Remove nut lock, etc. and rock disc to ease out washer and outer bearing. Disc can now be removed to service grease seal or inner bearing.

CHECKING BALL JOINTS FOR WEAR

Upper Ball Joint

1974-78 Mustang & 1974-79 Bobcat & Pinto

1. Raise car and place floor jacks beneath lower arms.
2. Grasp lower edge of tire and move wheel in and out.
3. As the wheel is being moved, notice any movement between the upper end of the spindle and the upper arm. If movement is present, replace the ball joint.

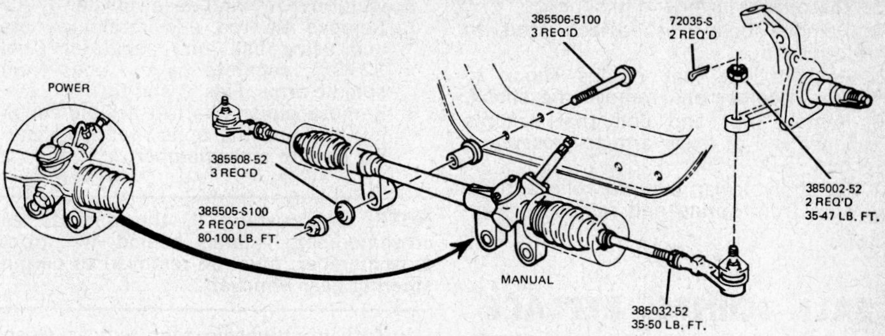

Fig. 5   Steering gear installation (typical)

Lower Ball Joint

1979 Capri & Mustang

Support vehicle in normal driving position with both ball joints loaded. Clean area around grease fitting and checking surface. The checking surface is the round boss into which the grease fitting is installed. The checking surface should project outside the ball joint cover Fig. 4. If checking surface is inside the cover replace the lower control arm assembly.

1974-78 Mustang & 1974-79 Bobcat & Pinto

1. Raise vehicle and place jacks under lower arms as shown in Fig. 4.
2. Be sure wheel bearings are properly adjusted.
3. Attach a dial indicator to lower arm and position indicator so that plunger rests against inner side of wheel rim near lower ball joint.
4. Grasp tire at top and bottom and slowly move tire in and out. If the reading exceeds .250", replace the joint.

SHOCK ABSORBER, REPLACE

1974-78 Mustang & 1974-79 Bobcat & Pinto

1. Disconnect upper end of the shock.
2. Raise vehicle and install safety stands.
3. Disconnect lower end of shock. It may be necessary to use a pry bar to free "T" shaped end of the shock from the lower end.

COIL SPRING, REPLACE

1979 Capri & Mustang

1. Raise front of vehicle and place safety stands under jack pads located rearward of wheels, then remove wheel and tire assembly.
2. Disconnect stabilizer bar link from lower control arm.
3. Remove steering gear attaching bolts and position gear out of way.
4. Using tool 3290-C, disconnect tie rod from spindle.

5. Install spring compressor D78P-5310-A and compress coil spring until it is free of the spring seat.

NOTE: Ensure spring compressor is properly installed before compressing spring. Also ensure spring is sufficiently compressed to permit removal of lower control arm pivot bolts.

6. Remove two lower control arm pivot bolts, then disengage lower control arm and remove spring assembly, Fig. 1.

NOTE: Measure compressed length of spring and amount of curvature to aid in compressing and installing spring.

7. Reverse procedure to install. Ensure lower spring end is positioned between two holes in lower control arm spring pocket.

1974-78 Mustang & 1974-79 Bobcat & Pinto

1. Raise vehicle and support front end with safety stands.
2. Place a jack under lower arm to support it.

SHOCK STRUT, REPLACE

1979 Capri & Mustang

1. Place ignition switch in the unlocked position.
2. From engine compartment, upper shock absorber mounting nut.
3. Raise front of vehicle and support lower control arms. Position safety stands under frame jacking pads located rearward of wheels.
4. Remove wheel and tire assembly.
5. Remove caliper, rotor and dust shield.
6. Remove two bolts attaching shock absorber to spindle.
7. Lift strut upward from spindle to compress rod, then pull downward and remove shock absorber.
8. Reverse procedure to install. Torque upper mounting nut to 50 to 75 ft. lbs. Torque lower mounting nuts to 120 to 180 ft. lbs.

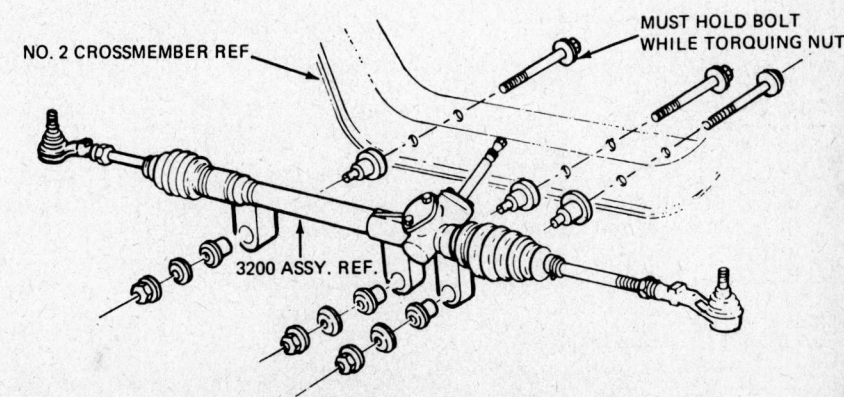

NO. 2 CROSSMEMBER REF.

MUST HOLD BOLT WHILE TORQUING NUT

3200 ASSY. REF.

* ATTACHING STANDARD PARTS (BOLTS, NUTS AND DISHED WASHERS) SHOULD BE RE-USED AFTER CLEANING AND OILING THREADS.

Fig. 6   Installation and positioning of two piece steering gear insulators

3. Disconnect lower end of shock.
4. Remove bolts that attach strut to lower arm.
5. Remove nut that retains shock to crossmember and remove the shock.
6. Remove nut and bolt that secures inner end of lower arm to crossmember.
7. Carefully lower jack to relieve pressure from spring and remove spring.

BALL JOINTS, REPLACE

NOTE: Ford Motor Company recommends that new ball joints should not be installed on used control arms and that the control arm be replaced if ball joint replacement is required. However, aftermarket ball joint repair kits which do not require control arm replacement, are available and can be installed using the following procedure.

The ball joints are riveted to the control arms. The ball joints can be replaced on the car by removing the rivets and replacing them with new attaching bolts, nuts and washers furnished with the kit.

When removing a ball joint, use a suitable pressing tool to force the ball joint out of the spindle.

STEERING GEAR, REPLACE

1974-78 Mustang, 1974-79 Bobcat, Pinto & 1979 Capri & Mustang

Manual Steering Gear

1. Disconnect battery ground cable, turn ignition "On" and raise vehicle.
2. Remove tie rod end retaining nuts and using ball joint separator (tool 3290C), separate tie rod ends from spindle arms, Figs. 5 and 6.
3. Remove pinion shaft to flexible coupling bolt and the bolts securing steering gear to crossmember.

NOTE: On Mustang II, the number 2A crossmember, located behind the front crossmember, must be removed to permit steering gear removal.

---

4. Turn front wheels, then remove steering gear from left side of vehicle.

Power Steering Gear

1. Disconnect battery ground cable.
2. Remove bolt retaining flexible coupling to input shaft.
3. Turn ignition key "ON" and raise vehicle.
4. Remove the two tie rod end retaining nuts, then separate studs from spindle arms, using a suitable tool.
5. On Mustang II models, remove the number 2A crossmember located behind the front crossmember to allow removal of steering gear retaining bolts.
6. Support gear and remove attaching bolts, then lower gear enough to gain access to pressure and return lines, and remove bolt attaching the hose bracket to the gear.
7. Disconnect pressure and return lines and remove steering gear. Plug lines and ports to prevent entry of dirt.

SERVICE BULLETIN

Two piece ribbed steering gear insulators have been released to overcome steering wheel shimmy on 1974-76 Mustang II with manual rack and pinion steering and equipped with radial tires. All three insulators from kit must be used. On steering gears with two point attachment, another nut, bolt and washer must be obtained prior to installation of kit.

Installation

1. Remove bolt securing flexible coupling to steering gear input shaft and discard.
2. Remove No. 2A crossmember from behind front crossmember, then remove nuts, bolts and washers securing steering gear to No. 2 crossmember.
3. Position steering gear assembly away from No. 2 crossmember and leave gear suspended by tie rods.
4. Remove one piece insulators from gear assembly.

NOTE: On steering gears mounted with two point attachment, remove plastic plug from center gear mounting boss.

---

5. Install three sets of two piece insulators from kit, Fig. 6.

NOTE: The rubber flange of both insulator halves should be seated against gear boss surface prior to torquing nuts. Ensure serrated steel washer face of insulator is adjacent to No. 2 crossmember.

---

6. Install steering gear assembly on No. 2 crossmember and torque nuts to 90-100 ft. lbs.
7. Install No. 2 crossmember on front crossmember.
8. Install flexible coupling to steering gear input shaft. Hand tighten bolt, then torque to 20-30 ft. lbs.

INDEX OF SERVICE OPERATIONS

ENGINE & SERIAL NUMBER LOCATION

Vehicle Warranty Plate On Left Front Door Pillar.

ENGINE IDENTIFICATION
*Serial number on vehicle Warranty Plate.

1974

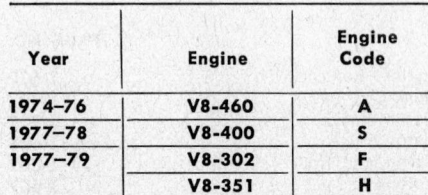

1978

Year	Engine	Engine Code
1974–76	V8-460	A
1977–78	V8-400	S
1977–79	V8-302	F
	V8-351	H

1975-76

1977

1979

GENERAL ENGINE SPECIFICATIONS

Year	Engine	Carburetor	Bore and Stroke	Piston Displacement, Cubic Inches	Compression Ratio	Maximum Brake H.P. @ R.P.M.	Maximum Torque Lbs. Ft. @ R.P.M.	Normal Oil Pressure Pounds
1974	220 Horsepower① V8-460	4 Barrel	4.36 x 3.85	460	8.0	220 @ 4000	355 @ 2600	35–65
1975	216 Horsepower① V8-460	4 Barrel	4.36 x 3.85	460	8.0	216 @ 4000	366 @ 2600	40–65
1976	202 Horsepower① V8-460	4 Barrel	4.36 x 3.85	460	8.0	202 @ 3800	352 @ 3800	40–65
1977	130 Horsepower① V8-302	2 Barrel	4.00 x 3.00	302	8.4	130 @ 3400	243 @ 1800	40–60
	149 Horsepower① V8-351W②	2 Barrel	4.00 x 3.50	351	8.3	149 @ 3200	291 @ 1600	40–60
	161 Horsepower① V8-351M②	2 Barrel	4.00 x 3.50	351	8.0	161 @ 3600	285 @ 1800	50–75
	161 Horsepower① V8-351M③	2 Barrel	4.00 x 3.50	351	8.0	161 @ 3600	286 @ 1800	50–75
	161 Horsepower① V8-351M④	2 Barrel	4.00 x 3.50	351	8.0	161 @ 3600	285 @ 1800	50–75
	173 Horsepower① V8-400②	2 Barrel	4.00 x 4.00	400	8.0	173 @ 3800	326 @ 1600	45–75
	168 Horsepower① V8-400③	2 Barrel	4.00 x 4.00	400	8.0	168 @ 3800	323 @ 1600	45–75
	173 Horsepower① V8-400④	2 Barrel	4.00 x 4.00	400	8.0	173 @ 3800	326 @ 1600	45–75
1978	134 Horsepower① V8-302②	2 Barrel	4.00 x 3.00	302	8.4	134 @ 3400	248 @ 1600	40–60
	144 Horsepower① V8-351W②	2 Barrel	4.00 x 3.50	351	8.3	144 @ 3200	277 @ 1600	40–60
	152 Horsepower① V8-351M②	2 Barrel	4.00 x 3.50	351	8.0	152 @ 3600	278 @ 1800	50–75
	166 Horsepower① V8-351M③	2 Barrel	4.00 x 3.50	351	8.0	152 @ 3600	278 @ 1800	50–75
	Horsepower① V8-351M④	2 Barrel	4.00 x 3.50	351	8.0	—	—	50–75
	166 Horsepower① V8-400②	2 Barrel	4.00 x 4.00	400	8.0	166 @ 3800	319 @ 1800	35–65
	166 Horsepower① V8-400③	2 Barrel	4.00 x 4.00	400	8.0	166 @ 3800	319 @ 1800	35–65
	Horsepower① V8-400④	2 Barrel	4.00 x 4.00	400	8.0	—	—	35–65
1979	Horsepower① V8-302	2 Barrel	4.00 x 3.00	302				
	Horsepower① V8-351W	2 Barrel	4.00 x 3.50	351				

①—Ratings are NET—as installed in the vehicle.   ③—Calif.
②—Except Calif. & high altitude.   ④—High altitude.

TUNE UP SPECIFICATIONS

The following specifications are published from the latest information available. This
data should be used only in the absence of a decal affixed in the engine compartment.

★When using a timing light, disconnect vacuum hose or tube at distributor and plug opening in hose or tube so idle speed will not be affected.
●When checking compression, lowest cylinder must be within 75 percent of highest.
▲Before removing wires from distributor cap, determine location of the No. 1 wire in cap, as distributor position may have been altered from that shown at the end of this chart.

| Year | Spark Plug | | Distributor | | Ignition Timing ★ | | | Carb. Adjustments | | | | | |
| | Type | Gap Inch | Point Gap Inch | Dwell Angle Deg. | Firing Order Fig. ▲ | Timing BTDC ①⑤ | Mark Fig. | Hot Idle Speed | | Air Fuel Ratio | | Idle "CO" % | |
								Std. Trans.	Auto. Trans.②⑤	Std. Trans.	Auto. Trans.	Std. Trans.	Auto. Trans.
1974													
8-460	ARF-52	③	⑧	—	A	14°	C	—	650D⑥	—	—	—	—
1975													
8-460	ARF-52	③	⑧	—	A	14°	C	—	650D	—	—	—	—
1976													
8-460⑪	ARF-52	.044	⑧	—	A	8°	C	—	650D⑬	—	—	—	—
8-460⑭	ARF-52	.044	⑧	—	A	14°	C	—	650D⑬	—	—	—	—
1977													
V8-302	ARF-52	.050	⑧	—	D	2°	C	—	600D	—	—	—	—
V8-351④⑪	ARF-52	.050	⑧	—	E	⑦	C	—	625D	—	—	—	—
V8-351⑪⑮	ARF-52	.050	⑧	—	E	⑦	C	—	650D	—	—	—	—
V8-351⑭⑮	ARF-52-6	.060	⑧	—	E	⑦	C	—	600D	—	—	—	—
V8-400⑪	ARF-52	.050	⑧	—	E	⑦	C	—	⑦	—	—	—	—
V8-400⑭	ARF-52-6	.060	⑧	—	E	6°	C	—	600D	—	—	—	—
1978													
V8-302	ARF-52	.050	⑧	—	D	14°	C	—	600D	—	—	—	—
V8-351④	ARF-52	.050	⑧	—	E	14°	C	—	600/675D⑲	—	—	—	—
V8-351⑭⑮	ASF-52	.050	⑧	—	E	16°	C	—	600/650D⑲	—	—	—	—
V8-351⑨⑮	ASF-52	.050	⑧	—	E	12°	C	—	650D	—	—	—	—
V8-351⑩⑫⑬	ASF-52	.050	⑧	—	E	14°	C	—	600/650D⑲	—	—	—	—
V8-351⑩⑮⑯	ASF-52	.050	⑧	—	E	⑰	C	—	600/675D⑲	—	—	—	—
V8-400⑭	ASF-52	.050	⑧	—	E	14°	C	—	600/675D⑲	—	—	—	—
V8-400⑨	ASF-52	.050	⑧	—	E	8°	C	—	650D	—	—	—	—
V8-400⑩	ASF-52	.050	⑧	—	E	⑱	C	—	575/650D⑲	—	—	—	—
1979													
V8-302	ASF-52	.050	⑧	—	D	8°	C	—	600/675⑲	—	—	—	—
V8-351④	ASF-42	.050	⑧	—	E	15°	C	—	600/650⑲	—	—	—	—
V8-351⑬	ASF-52	.050	⑧	—	E	12°	C	—	600/650⑲	—	—	—	—

Continued

TUNE-UP NOTES

①—BTDC: Before top dead center.
②—D: Drive. N: Neutral.
③—Exc. Calif., .054 inch; Calif. .044 inch.
④—Windsor engine.
⑤—On models equipped w/vacuum release parking brake, whenever adjusting ignition timing or idle speed, vacuum line to brake release mechanism must be disconnected and plugged to prevent parking brake from releasing when selector is moved to Drive.
⑥—With lights and A/C off.
⑦—Must refer to engine decal due to running production changes.
⑧—Breakerless distributor.
⑨—High altitude.
⑩—Exc. Calif. & high altitude.
⑪—Exc. Calif.
⑫—Engines less air pump.
⑬—With A/C "On".
⑭—Calif.
⑮—Modified engine.
⑯—Engine with air pump.
⑰—Early production models, 12° BTDC; Mid production models, 9° BTDC; Late production Models, 14° BTDC.
⑱—Early production models, 14° BTDC; Late production models, 13° BTDC.
⑲—Higher RPM is for A/C, A/C on.

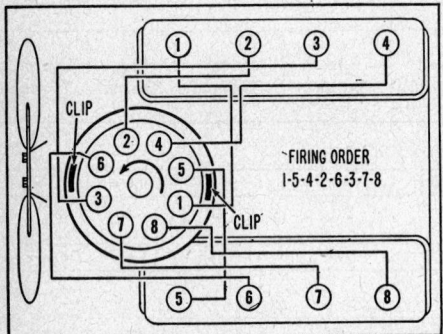
Fig. A

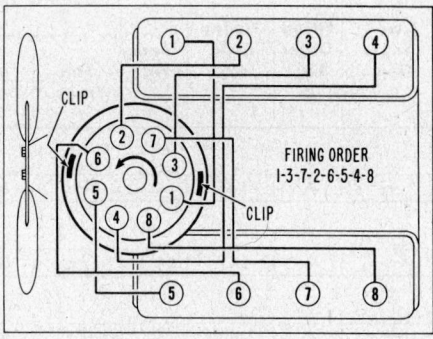
Fig. B

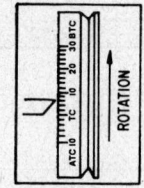
Fig. C

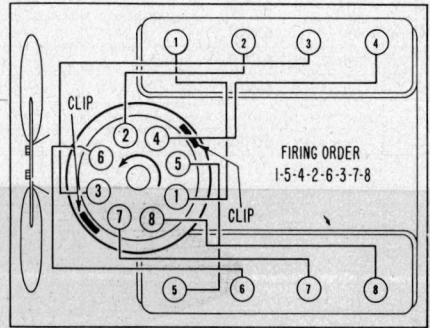
Fig. D

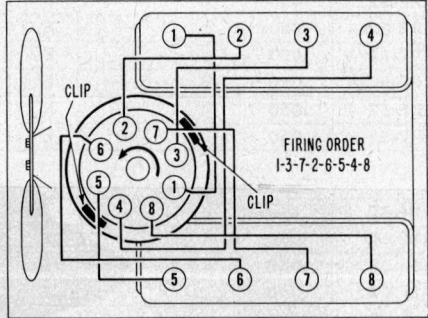
Fig. E

ENGINE TIGHTENING SPECIFICATIONS

★Torque specifications are for clean and lightly lubricated threads only. Dry or dirty threads produce increased friction which prevents accurate measurement of tightness.

Year	Engine	Spark Plugs Ft. Lbs.	Cylinder Head Bolts Ft. Lbs.	Intake Manifold Ft. Lbs.	Exhaust Manifold Ft. Lbs.	Rocker Arm Shaft Bracket Ft. Lbs.	Rocker Arm Cover Ft. Lbs.	Connecting Rod Cap Bolts Ft. Lbs.	Main Bearing Cap Bolts Ft. Lbs.	Flywheel to Crankshaft Ft. Lbs.	Vibration Damper or Pulley Ft. Lbs.
1974–76	V8-460	10–15	130–140	22–32④	28–33	18–25②	5–6	40–45	95–105	75–85	70–90
1977–78	V8-302	10–15	65–72	23–25	18–24	①	3–5	19–24	60–70	75–85	70–90
	V8-351⑤	10–15	105–112	23–25	18–24	①	3–5	40–45	95–105	75–85	70–90
	V8-351⑥	10–15	95–105	③	18–24	18–25②	3–5	40–45	95–105	75–85	70–90
	V8-400	10–15	95–105	③	18–24	18–25②	3–5	40–45	95–105	75–85	70–90

①—1977 & Early 1978, rocker arm stud nut 17-23 ft. lbs.; late 1978, rocker arm fulcrum bolt to cyl. head 18-25 ft. lbs.
②—Rocker arm fulcrum bolt to cyl. head.
③—5/16" bolts 19-25 ft. lbs.; 3/8" bolts 22-32 ft. lbs.
④—1975 models, 25-30 ft. lbs.
⑤—Windsor Engine.
⑥—Modified Engine.

DISTRIBUTOR SPECIFICATIONS

★If unit is checked on vehicle, double the RPM and degrees to get crankshaft figures.

Distributor Part No.①	Centrifugal Advance Degrees @ RPM of Distributor					Vacuum Advance		Distributor Retard
	Advance Starts	Intermediate Advance			Full Advance	Inches of Vacuum to Start Plunger	Max. Adv. Dist. Deg. @ Vacuum	Max. Retard Dist. Deg. @ Vacuum
1974-75								
D4VE-CA	0–½ @ 500	0–½ @ 750	3–5 @ 1000	7–9 @ 1500	10½ @ 2000	5	11¼ @ 20	—
D5VE-BA	—	—	—	—	—	—	—	—
1976								
D4VE-CA	−¾–½ @ 500	−1¼–½ @ 700	—	—	5 @ 1000	5	11¼ @ 15	
D5VE-CA	−1–½ @ 500	½–2½ @ 700	—	—	6½ @ 1000	5	13¼ @ 15	
D6VE-AA	0–2½ @ 500	4½–6½ @ 700	—	—	9 @ 1000	5	13½ @ 15	
D6VE-BA	−1–2¾ @ 500	6–9½ @ 700	—	—	11¾ @ 1000	5	13¼ @ 15	
D6VE-CA	−½–3 @ 500	6–9½ @ 700	—	—	10¼ @ 1000	5	13¼ @ 15	
1977-78								
D6AE-AA	0–2 @ 500	4–6 @ 700	—	—	14 @ 2500	4.3	15¼ @ 11½	—
D7AE-BA	0–1 @ 425	2¾–4¾ @ 625	—	—	13½ @ 2250	3½	15¼ @ 12	—
D7AE-CA	0–1 @ 700	3½–6 @ 1600	—	—	10¾ @ 2500	3	15¼ @ 11	—
D7AE-DA	0–1 @ 450	3¾–5¾ @ 675	—	—	14 @ 2500	3.2	15¼ @ 14½	—
D7DE-CA	0–1 @ 450	4¾–6¾ @ 700	—	—	15½ @ 2500	3	15¼ @ 11	—
D7OE-CA	0–1 @ 450	2¾–4¾ @ 575	—	—	16 @ 2500	3½	15¼ @ 14½	—

①—Basic part No. 12127

VALVE SPECIFICATIONS

Year	Engine Model	Valve Lash		Valve Angles		Valve Spring Installed Height	Valve Spring Pressure Lbs. @ In.	Stem Clearance		Stem Diameter	
		Int.	Exh.	Seat	Face			Intake	Exhaust	Intake	Exhaust
1974	8-460	.075–.125①	45	44	1¹³⁄₁₆	252 @ 1.33	.0010–.0027	.0010–.0027	.3416–.3423	.3416–.3423
1975	8-460	.100–.150①	45	44	1¹³⁄₁₆	252 @ 1.33	.0010–.0027	.0010–.0027	.3416–.3423	.3416–.3423
1976	8-460	.100–.150①	45	44	1¹³⁄₁₆	229 @ 1.33	.0010–.0027	.0010–.0027	.3416–.3423	.3416–.3423
1977	8-302	.071–.168①	45	44	②	③	.0010–.0027	.0015–.0032	.3416–.3423	.3411–.3418
	8-351④	.071–.168①	45	44	⑤	⑥	.0010–.0027	.0015–.0032	.3416–.3423	.3411–.3418
	8-351⑦	.125–.175①	45	44	1⁵³⁄₆₄	226 @ 1.39	.0010–.0027	.0015–.0032	.3416–.3423	.3411–.3418
	8-400	.125–.175①	45	44	1⁵³⁄₆₄	226 @ 1.39	.0010–.0027	.0015–.0032	.3416–.3423	.3411–.3418
1978	8-302⑧	.096–.168①	45	44	②	③	.0010–.0027	.0015–.0032	.3416–.3423	.3411–.3418
	8-302⑨	①⑩		45	44	②	③	.0010–.0027	.0015–.0032	.3416–.3423	.3411–.3418
	8-351④⑧	.096–.168①	45	44	⑤	⑥	.0010–.0027	.0015–.0032	.3416–.3423	.3411–.3418
	8-351④⑨	.142①		45	44	⑤	⑥	.0010–.0027	.0015–.0032	.3416–.3423	.3411–.3418
	8-351⑦	.125–.175①	45	44	1⁵³⁄₆₄	226 @ 1.39	.0010–.0027	.0015–.0032	.3416–.3423	.3411–.3418
	8-400	.125–.175①	45	44	1⁵³⁄₆₄	226 @ 1.39	.0010–.0027	.0015–.0032	.3416–.3423	.3411–.3418

①—Clearance specified is obtained at valve stem with lifter collapsed. See "Valves, Adjust" text.
②—Intake; 1¹¹⁄₁₆; exhaust, 1³⁹⁄₆₄.
③—Intake, 200 @ 1.31; exhaust, 200 @ 1.20.
④—Windsor engine.
⑤—Intake, 1⁵¹⁄₆₄; exhaust, 1³⁹⁄₆₄.
⑥—Intake, 200 @ 1.34; exhaust, 200 @ 1.20.
⑦—Modified engine.
⑧—Early 1978 engines.
⑨—Late 1978 engines.
⑩—Exc. Calif., .121; Calif., .142.

PISTONS, PINS, RINGS, CRANKSHAFT & BEARINGS

| Year | Engine Model | Piston Clearance | Ring End Gap① | | Wrist-pin Diameter | Rod Bearings | | Main Bearings | | | |
			Comp.	Oil		Shaft Diameter	Bearing Clearance	Shaft Diameter	Bearing Clearance	Thrust on Bear. No.	Shaft End Play
1974	8-460	.0022–.0030	.010	.015	1.0400	2.4992–2.5000	.0008–.0015	2.9994–3.0002	③	3	.004–.008
1975	8-460	.0014–.0022	.010	.015	1.0400	2.4992–2.5000	.0008–.0015	2.9994–3.0002	④	3	.004–.008
1976	8-460	.0014–.0022	.010	.015	1.0400	2.4992–2.5000	.0008–.0015	2.9994–3.0002	.0008–.0015	3	.004–.008
1977–78	8-302	.0018–.0026	.010	.015	.9121	2.1228–2.1236	.0008–.0015	2.2482–2.2490	②	3	.004–.008
	8-351⑤	.0018–.0026	.010	.015	.9121	2.3103–2.3111	.0008–.0015	2.9994–3.0002	.0008–.0015	3	.004–.008
	8-351⑥	.0014–.0022	.010	.015	.9751	2.3103–2.3111	.0008–.0015	2.9994–3.0002	.0008–.0015	3	.004–.008
	8-400	.0014–.0022	.010	.015	.9751	2.3103–2.3111	.0008–.0015	2.9994–3.0002	.0008–.0015	3	.004–.008

①—Fit rings in tapered boxes for clearance listed in tightest portion of ring travel.
②—No. 1, .0001–.0015; all others, .0005–.0015.
③—No. 1, .0004–.0015; No. 2, 3, 4 & 5, .0012–.0015.
④—No. 1, .0004–.0015; No. 2, 3, 4 & 5, .0009–.0015.
⑤—Windsor engine.
⑥—Modified engine.

STARTING MOTOR SPECIFICATIONS

| Year | Model | Ident. | Rotation ① | Brush Spring Tension, Ounces | No Load Test | | | Torque Test | | |
					Amperes	Volts	R.P.M.	Amperes	Volts	Torque Ft. Lbs.
1974	V8-460	D5AF-AB	C	80	90	12	—	—	—	—
1975–76	V8-460	D5AF-AB	C	40	70	12	—	—	—	—
1977–78	V8-302	D60F-AA	C	80	80	12	—	—	—	—
	V8-351②	D60F-AA	C	80	80	12	—	—	—	—
	V8-351③	D5AF-EA	C	80	80	12	—	—	—	—
	V8-400	D60F-AA	C	80	80	12	—	—	—	—

①—As viewed from the drive end. C—Clockwise.
②—Windsor engine.
③—Modified engine.

ALTERNATOR & REGULATOR SPECIFICATIONS

Year	Ident. No. (10300)	Current Rating[1]		Field Current @ 75°F.		Voltage Regulator				Field Relay	
		Amperes	Volts	Amperes	Volts	Ident. No. (10316) [2]	Voltage @ 75°F.	Contact Gap	Armature Air Gap	Armature Air Gap	Closing Voltage @75°F.
1974-76	Green[6]	61	15	2.9	12	D4AF-AA	13.5-15.3	[3]	[3]	[3]	2.5-4.0
1974-77	All	70	15	2.9	12	D4TF-AA	13.5-15.3	[3]	[3]	[3]	2.5-4.0
1975-77	All	90	15	2.9	12	D4TF-AA	13.5-15.3	[3]	[3]	[3]	2.5-4.0
1977	Orange[6]	40	15	2.9	12	D4AF-AA	13.5-15.3	[3]	[3]	[3]	2.5-4.0
	Green[6]	60	15	2.9	12	D4AF-AA	13.5-15.3	[3]	[3]	[3]	2.5-4.0
1978	Orange[1]	40	15	2.9	12	D4AF-AA	13.5-15.3	[3]	[3]	[3]	—
	Green[1]	60	15	2.9	12	D4AF-AA	13.5-15.3	[3]	[3]	[3]	—
	Green[1][4]	60	15	4.0	12	D8BF-AA[5]	14.0-14.4	[3]	[3]	[3]	—
	Black[1]	70	15	2.9	12	D4AF-AA	13.5-15.3	[3]	[3]	[3]	—
	Red[1]	90	15	2.9	12	D4TF-AA	13.5-15.3	[3]	[3]	[3]	—
	Red[1][4]	90	15	4.0	12	D8BF-AA[5]	14.0-14.4	[3]	[3]	[3]	—

[1]—Stamped on housing.
[2]—Stamped on cover.
[3]—Not adjustable.
[4]—Solid state alternator.
[5]—Electronic voltage regulator. These units are color coded black for systems w/warning indicator lamp and blue for systems w/ammeter.
[6]—Stamp color code.

BRAKE SPECIFICATIONS

Year	Model	Brake Drum Inside Diameter	Wheel Cylinder Bore Diameter			Master Cylinder Bore Diameter		
			Front Disc Brakes	Front Drum Brakes	Rear Brakes	With Disc Brakes	With Drum Brakes	With Power Brakes
1974	All	11.03	3.10	—	1.00	1.00	—	1.00
1975	All	11.03	3.10	—	[1]	[2]	—	[2]
1976	All	11.03	3.10	—	[1]	[2]	—	[2]
1977-79	All	11.03	3.10	—	15/16	1.00	—	1.00

[1]—Drum brakes; 1. Disc Brakes; 2.6.
[2]—Front wheel disc brakes only; 1. With 4-wheel disc brakes; 1⅛.

WHEEL ALIGNMENT SPECIFICATIONS

Year	Model	Caster Angle, Degrees		Camber Angle, Degrees				Toe-In. Inch	Toe-Out on Turns, Deg.	
		Limits	Desired	Limits		Desired			Outer Wheel	Inner Wheel
				Left	Right	Left	Right			
1974	All	+½ to +3½	+2	0 to +2	−½ to +1½	+1	+½	3/16	18.07	20
1975-76	All	+3¼ to +4¾	+4	−¼ to +1¼	−½ to +1	+½	+¼	3/16	18.09	20
1977-79	All	+3¼ to +4¾	+4	−¼ to +1¼	−½ to +1	+½	+¼	⅛	18.06	20

REAR AXLE SPECIFICATIONS

Year	Model	Carrier Type	Ring Gear & Pinion Backlash Inch	Nominal Pinion Locating Shim, Inch	Pinion Bearing Preload				Differential Bearing Preload	Pinion Nut Torque Ft.-Lbs.
					New Bearings With Seal Inch-Lbs.	Used Bearings With Seal Inch-Lbs.	New Bearings Less Seal Inch-Lbs.	Used Bearings Less Seal Inch-Lbs.		
1974-78	All	Removable	.008–.012	.015	17–27②	8–14②	—	—	.008–.012④	①③

①—If torque is not possible, install new spacer.
②—With collapsible spacer. With solid spacer 13–33 inch-lbs.
③—With collapsible spacer 170 ft.-lbs., with solid spacer 200 ft.-lbs.
④—Case spread with new bearings. With used bearings, .005–.008″.

COOLING SYSTEM & CAPACITY DATA

Year	Model or Engine	Cooling Capacity, Qts.			Radiator Cap Relief Pressure, Lbs.		Thermo. Opening Temp. ①	Fuel Tank Gals.	Engine Oil Refill Qts. ②	Transmission Oil			Rear Axle Oil Pints
		No Heater	With Heater	With A/C	With A/C	No A/C				3 Speed Pints	4 Speed Pints	Auto. Trans. Qts. ③	
1974	V8-460	—	19½	19½	12–16	12–16	191	26½	4	—	—	12½	5
1975–76	V8-460	—	19.3	19.3	12–16	12–16	191	26½	4	—	—	12½	5
1977	V8-302	—	14.8	15.1	14–18	14–18	191	26	4	—	—	10.3	5
	V8-351⑤	—	15.9	16.2	12–16	12–16	191	26④	4	—	—	⑥	5
	V8-351⑦	—	17.1	17.1	12–16	12–16	191	26④	4	—	—	⑥	5
	V8-400	—	17.1	17.1	12–16	12–16	191	26	4	—	—	⑧	5
1978	V8-302	—	14.3	14.6	14–18	14–18	191	21	4	—	—	10¼	5
	V8-351⑥	—	15.4	15.7	12–16	12–16	191	21	4	—	—	11	5
	V8-351⑦	—	16.5	16.5	12–16	12–16	191	21	4	—	—	11	5
	V8-400	—	16.5	16.5	12–16	12–16	191	21	4	—	—	12½	5

①—For permanent type anti-freeze.
②—Add one quart with filter change.
③—Approximate. Make final check with dipstick.
④—Calif, 22 gals.
⑤—Windsor engine.
⑥—C4, 10.3 qts.; FMX, 11 qts.; C6, 12.2 qts.
⑦—Modified engine.
⑧—FMX, 11 qts.; C6, 12.2 qts.

Electrical Section

DISTRIBUTOR, REPLACE
Removal

1. On vehicles with conventional ignition systems, disconnect primary wire from ignition coil. On vehicles with breakerless ignition systems, disconnect distributor wiring from connector from main wiring harness. On some models the work may be made easier if the accelerator pull back spring is disconnected.
2. Disconnect vacuum advance lines and remove distributor cap.
3. Scribe a mark on the distributor body indicating the position of the rotor, and scribe another mark on the body and engine block indicating position of distributor body in block. These marks can be used as guides when installing distributor in a correctly timed engine.
4. Remove hold down screw and screws and lift distributor out of block. *Do not crank engine while distributor is removed or the initial timing operation will have to be performed.*

Installation

If the crankshaft has not been disturbed, install the distributor, using the scribed marks previously made on the distributor body and engine block as guides.

If the crankshaft has been rotated while the distributor was removed from the engine, it will be necessary to retime the engine. Crank the engine to bring No. 1 piston on top dead center of its compression stroke. Align the timing mark on the vibration damper or pulley with the timing pointer (see *Tune Up* chart). Install the distributor so that the rotor points to the No. 1 spark plug wire terminal in the distributor cap.

NOTE: If equipped with breakerless ignition system, the distributor must be installed with one of the armature segments aligned with the stator, Fig. 1, and the rotor at the number 1 firing position.

NOTE: Make sure the oil pump intermediate shaft properly engages the distributor shaft. It may be necessary to crank the engine with the starter, after the distributor drive gear is properly engaged, in order to engage the oil pump intermediate shaft.

Check ignition timing and adjust to specifications.

NOTE: When using an inductive timing light on 1977-79 Dura Spark ignition systems, it is recommended that a split piece of vacuum hose be placed on the ignition wire where the inductive pick-up is placed.

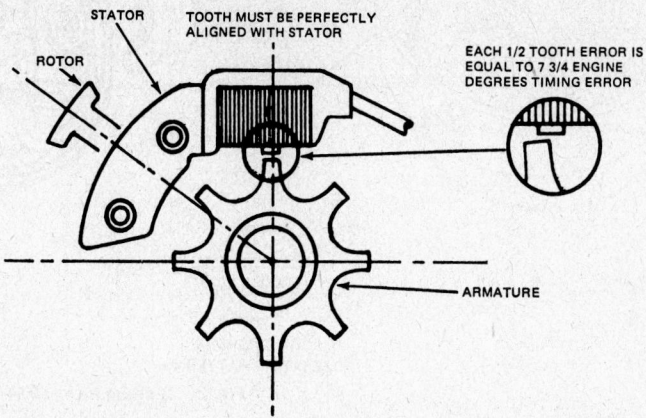

Fig. 1 Distributor stator & armature segment alignment. Breakerless distributor installation

STARTER, REPLACE
1974-79

1. Disconnect battery ground cable.
2. Disconnect cable and wiring at starter or solenoid.
3. Loosen two front brace attaching bolts, then remove all other attaching bolts and allow brace to hang.
4. Turn wheels to full right position, then remove two steering idler arms to frame attaching bolts.
5. Remove starter mounting bolts and the starter from vehicle.

NOTE: On some vehicles, it is necessary to turn the front wheels to the right or left to gain clearance between starter & steering linkages and allow for starter removal.

IGNITION LOCK, REPLACE
1974-78

1. Disconnect the battery ground cable.

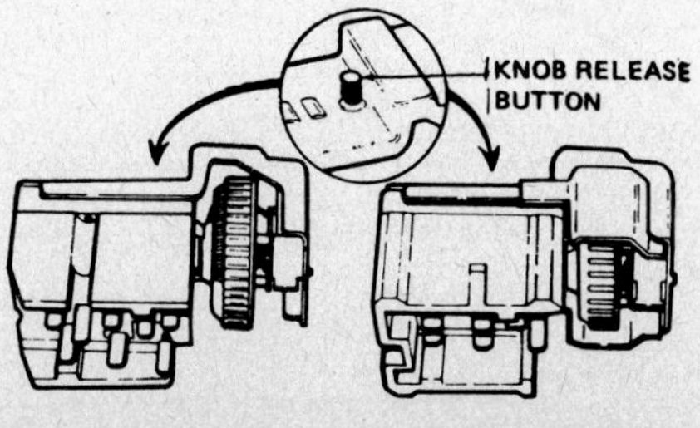

Fig. 4 Light switch (typical)

2. **Units With Fixed Steering Columns:** Remove the steering wheel and trim pad. Insert a wire pin in the hole located inside the column halfway down to lock cylinder housing, Fig. 2. **Units With Tilt Steering Columns:** Insert wire pin in the hole located on the outside of the flange casting next to the emergency flasher button, Fig. 2.
3. Place the gear shift lever in *PARK* position, and turn the lock cylinder with the ignition key to *RUN* position.
4. Depress the wire pin while pulling up on the lock cylinder to remove. Remove the wire pin.
5. To install insert the lock cylinder into the housing in the flange casting, and turn the key to *OFF* position. Be certain that the cylinder is fully inserted before turning to the *OFF* position. This action will extend the cylinder retaining pin into the cylinder housing.
6. Turn the key to check for correct operation in all positions.
7. Install the steering wheel and trim pad on fixed column units.
8. Connect the battery ground cable.

IGNITION SWITCH, REPLACE
1974-79

1. On 1977-79 models, remove instrument cluster.
2. On all models, to gain access, remove shrouding from steering column and detach and lower the steering column from the brake support bracket.
3. Disconnect battery cable.

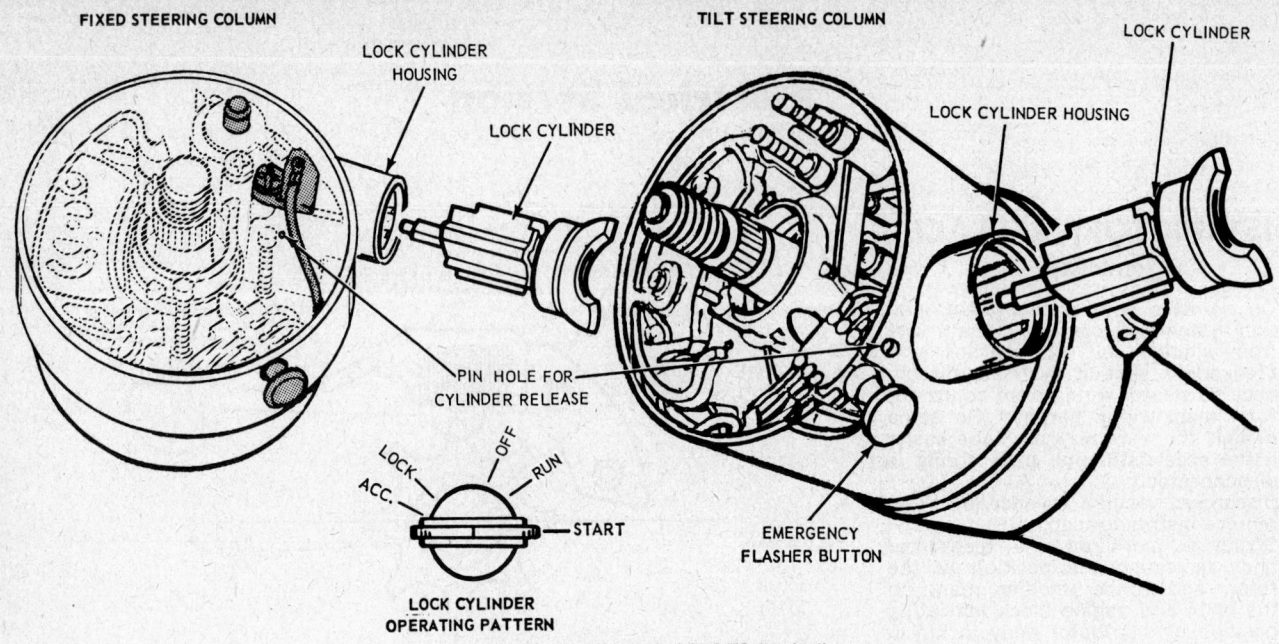

FIXED STEERING COLUMN

TILT STEERING COLUMN

LOCK CYLINDER
HOUSING

LOCK CYLINDER

LOCK CYLINDER

LOCK CYLINDER HOUSING

LOCK CYLINDER

PIN HOLE FOR
CYLINDER RELEASE

LOCK

OFF

ACC.

RUN

START

LOCK CYLINDER
OPERATING PATTERN

EMERGENCY
FLASHER BUTTON

Fig. 2   Ignition lock, 1974-79 (typical)

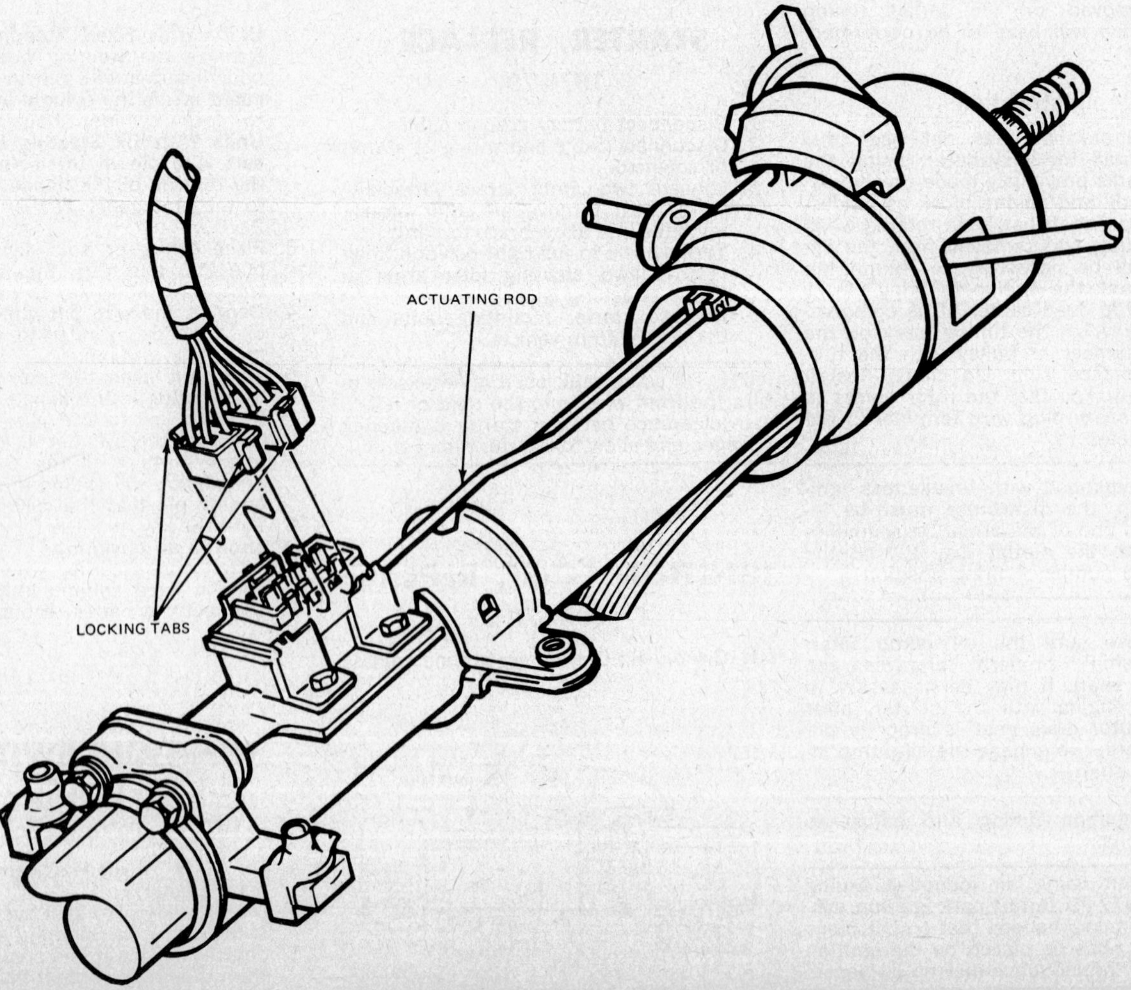

ACTUATING ROD

LOCKING TABS

Fig. 3   Ignition switch installation. 1974-79 (typical)

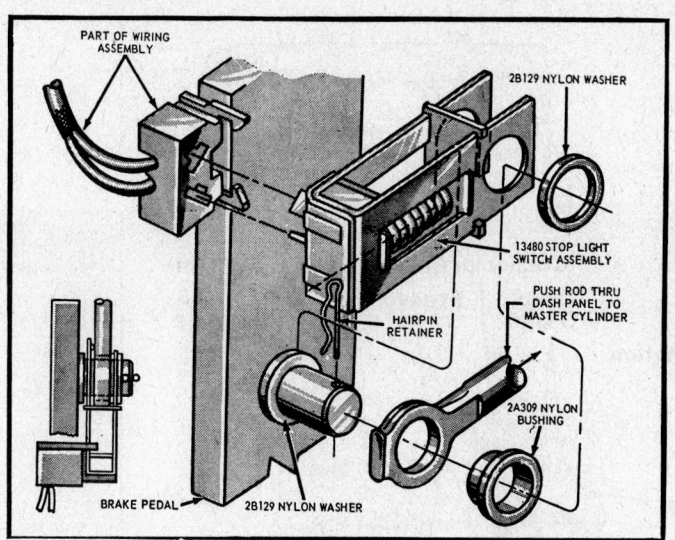
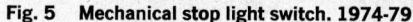

Fig. 5   Mechanical stop light switch. 1974-79

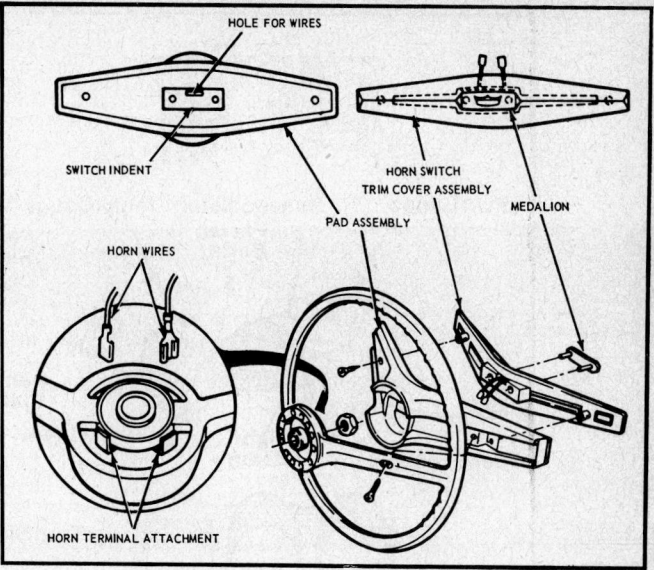

Fig. 6   Steering wheel and horn switch. 1974-79 (typical)

4. Disconnect switch wiring at multiple plug, Fig. 3.
5. Remove nuts that retain switch to column.
6. Detach switch plunger from actuator rod and remove switch.
7. When installing switch, both the switch and the locking mechanism at top of column must be in the "LOCK" position. New replacement switches are already pinned in the "LOCK" position when received by a shipping pin inserted in a locking hole on top of switch.

LIGHT SWITCH, REPLACE

1977-79

1. Disconnect battery ground cable.
2. Remove instrument panel trim cover.
3. Pull knob to "On" position and from beneath instrument panel, depress release button on switch and pull knob and shaft from switch, Fig. 4.
4. Remove switch bezel nut and lower switch from instrument panel.
5. Disconnect electrical connector and remove switch.
6. Reverse procedure to install.

1974-76

1. Disconnect battery ground cable.
2. Remove instrument cluster trim panel.
3. Remove switch mounting plate.
4. Remove bezel nut and disconnect multiple connector.
5. Reverse procedure to install.

STOP LIGHT SWITCH, REPLACE

1974-79

1. Disconnect wires at connector.
2. Remove hairpin retainer. Slide stop light switch, push rod and nylon washers and bushing away from pedal, and remove switch, Fig. 5.
3. Position switch, push rod, bushing and washers on brake pedal pin in the order shown, and install hairpin retainer.
4. Connect wires and install wires in clip.

NEUTRAL SAFETY SWITCH

1974-79

The neutral start switch has been eliminated from all column shift vehicles. A series of steps have been designed into the steering column selector lever hub casting which eliminates the need for a switch.

HORN SOUNDER & STEERING WHEEL

1974-79

A two spoke steering wheel with a pressure sensitive horn switch built into the trim cover is used, Fig. 6. If the switch needs to be replaced, the entire horn switch/trim cover assembly will have

to be replaced.
1. Disconnect battery ground cable.
2. From underside of steering wheel, remove screws attaching steering wheel horn cover.
3. Lift cover upward and disconnect horn wires and speed control wiring, if equipped.
4. Remove steering wheel attaching nut.
5. Using a suitable puller, remove steering wheel from upper shaft.

CAUTION: Do not use a knock-off type puller and do not strike the end of the steering shaft since damage to the collapsible steering column will result.

TURN SIGNAL SWITCH, REPLACE

1974-79

1. Remove retaining screw from underside of steering wheel spoke and lift off the pad horn switch/trim cover and medallion as an assembly. Disconnect horn switch wires from terminals.
2. Remove steering wheel retaining nut and steering wheel.
3. Remove turn signal switch lever by unscrewing it from column.
4. Remove shroud from under steering column.
5. Disconnect steering column wiring connector plugs and remove screws that secure switch assembly to column.
6. On vehicles with tilt column, remove wires and terminals from steering column connector plug.

NOTE: Record the color code and location of each wire before removing it from connector. A hole provided in the flange casting on fixed

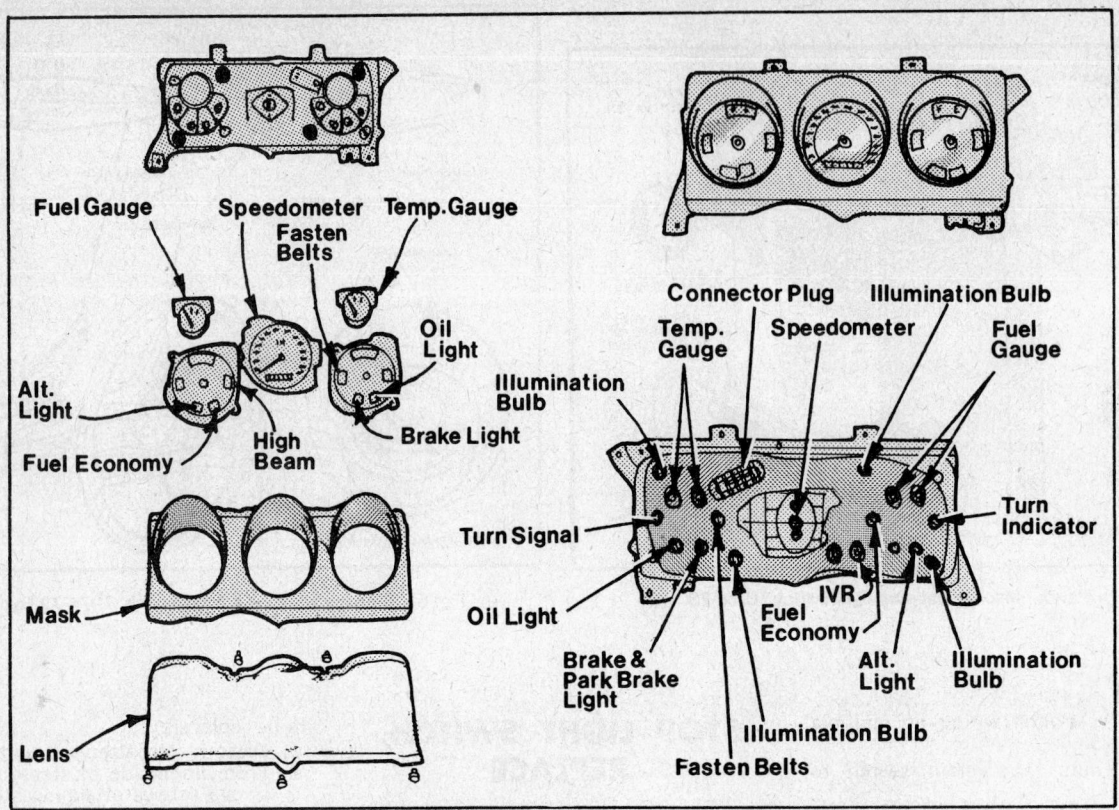

Fig. 7   Instrument cluster (typical). 1977-79 models with standard cluster

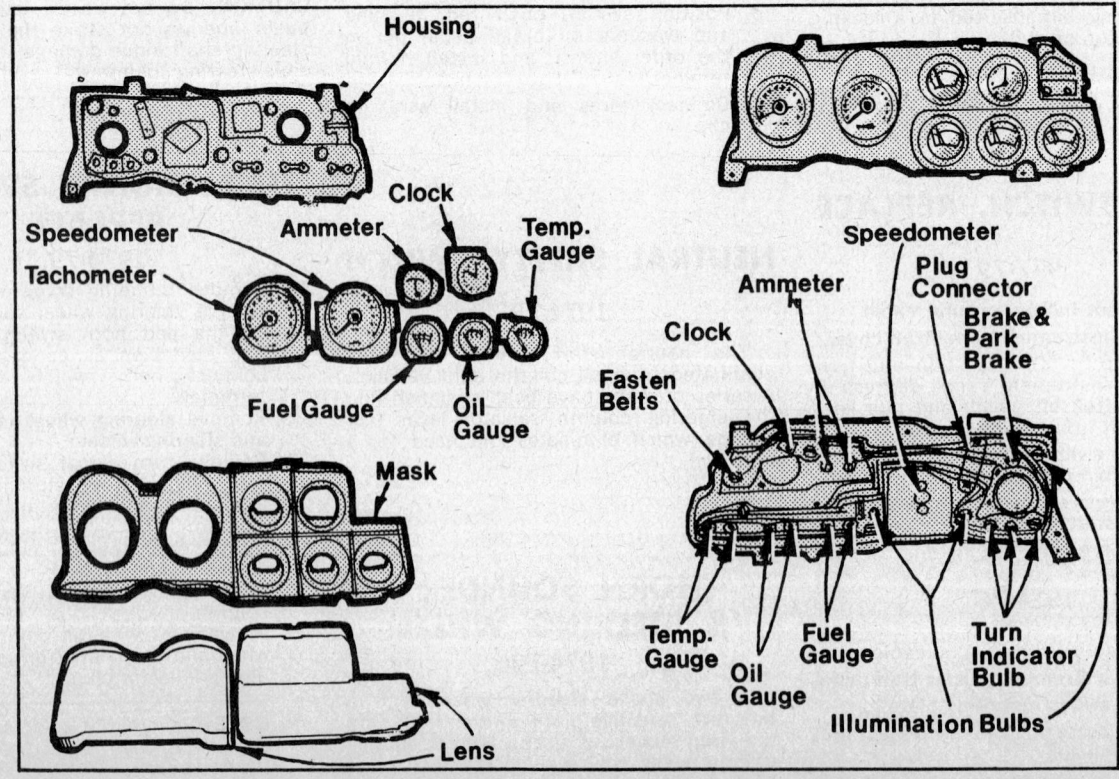

Fig. 8   Instrument cluster (typical). 1977-79 models with performance cluster

columns makes it unnecessary to separate the wires from the connector. The plug with wires installed can be guided through the hole.

7. Remove plastic cover sleeve from wiring harness and remove the switch and wires from top of column.
8. Reverse procedure to install.

INSTRUMENT CLUSTER

1977-79

1. Disconnect battery ground cable.
2. Remove upper and lower retaining screws from cluster trim cover and remove the cover, Fig. 7 and 8A.
3. With standard cluster, remove clock or cover to cluster attaching screw and clock or cover to instrument panel retaining screws. Disconnect wire connector from clock, then remove clock or cover.
4. On all models, remove two upper and two lower screws retaining cluster to the panel.
5. Pull cluster away from panel and disconnect speedo cable.
6. Disconnect cluster feed plug from receptable in printed circuit.
7. Disconnect overlay harness connector.
8. Remove cluster.

1974-76

1. Disconnect battery ground cable.
2. Remove screw retaining lower cluster applique cover below steering column.
3. Squeeze the lower half of the column shroud together and separate the lower half from the upper.
4. Remove upper half of shroud from column.
5. Remove screw attaching PRNDL control cable wire to the column.
6. Remove heated backlite control knob.
7. Reach under instrument panel and depress the button on side of headlight switch while withdrawing switch con-

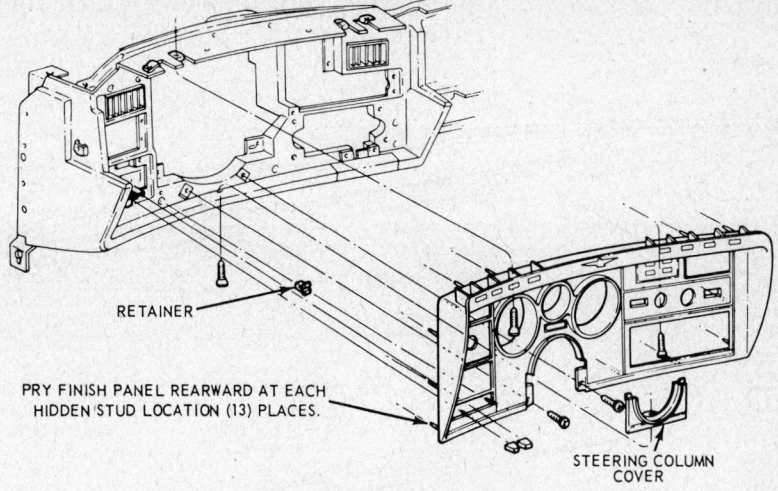

Fig. 9   Instrument cluster panel. 1974-76

trol knob and shaft assembly.
8. Reach under panel and disconnect speedo cable.
9. Remove threaded headlight switch bezel.
10. Remove windshield wiper/washer control knob and bezel.
11. Remove cigar lighter from its receptacle.
12. Remove four screws retaining cluster front cover.
13. Remove screw attaching shift control cable bracket to steering column and disconnect shift cable loop.
14. Insert a right angle standard tip screwdriver along edges of the finish panel withdrawing studs in sequence gradually around the periphery of the panel, Fig. 9.
15. Remove four screws retaining cluster to panel.
16. Pull cluster away from panel; disconnect cluster feed plug from its receptacle in the printed circuit.
17. Tilt cluster out, top first, and move the cluster toward center of car.

W/S WIPER BLADES

NOTE: Trico and Anco blades are used and both come in two types; Bayonet type and Side Saddle Pin type.

Bayonet Type: To remove the *Trico* type press down on the arm to unlock the top stud. Depress the tab on the saddle, Fig. 10, and pull the blade from the arm. To remove the *Anco* type press inward on the tab, Fig. 11, and pull the blade from the arm. To install a new blade assembly slide the blade saddle over the end of the wiper arm so that the locking stud snaps into place.
Side Saddle Pin Type: To remove the pin type insert an appropriate tool into the spring release opening of the blade saddle, depress the spring clip and pull the blade from the arm, Fig. 12. To install, push the

blade saddle on to the pin so that the spring clip engages the pin. To replace the rubber element in a *Trico* blade squeeze the latch lock release and pull the element out of the lever jaws, Fig. 13. Remove the *Anco* element by depressing the latch pin, Fig. 13, and sliding the element out of the yoke jaws. To install insert the element through the yoke or lever jaws. Be sure the element is engaged at all points.

W/S WIPER ARMS
1974-79

Raise the blade end of the arm off the windshield and move the slide latch, Fig. 14, away from the pivot shaft. This action will unlock the wiper arm from the pivot shaft and hold the blade end of the arm

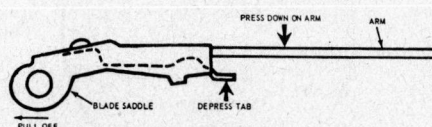

Fig. 10   Trico bayonet type blade

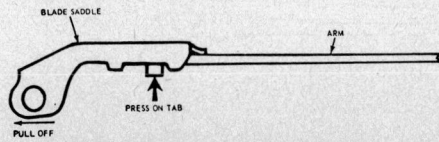

Fig. 11   Anco bayonet type blade

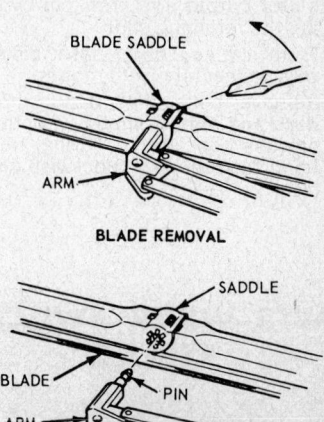

BLADE REMOVAL

BLADE INSTALLATION

Fig. 12   Pin type blade

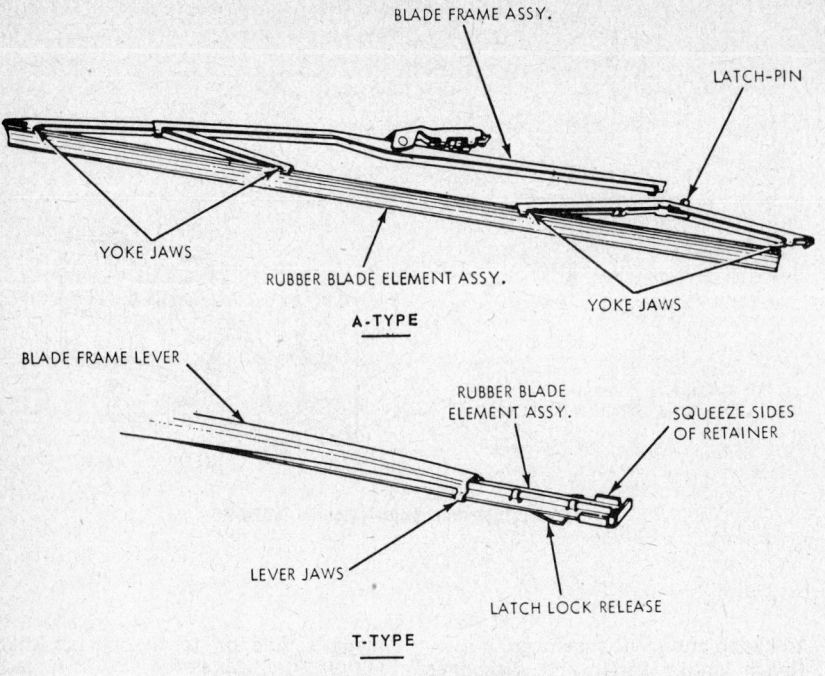

BLADE FRAME ASSY.

LATCH-PIN

YOKE JAWS

RUBBER BLADE ELEMENT ASSY.

YOKE JAWS

A-TYPE

BLADE FRAME LEVER

RUBBER BLADE ELEMENT ASSY.

SQUEEZE SIDES OF RETAINER

LEVER JAWS

LATCH LOCK RELEASE

T-TYPE

Fig. 13 Wiper blade element

off the glass at the same time. The wiper arm can now be pulled off the pivot shaft without the aid of any tools.

W/S WIPER MOTOR, REPLACE

1974-79

1. Disconnect battery ground cable.
2. Remove wiper arm and blade assemblies.
3. Remove left cowl screen for access through cowl opening.
4. Disconnect linkage drive arm from motor output arm crankpin by removing the retaining clip.
5. From engine side of dash, disconnect wire connectors from motor.
6. Remove bolts that retain motor to dash and remove motor. If output arm catches on dash during removal, hand turn the arm clockwise so it will clear.

W/S WIPER SWITCH, REPLACE

1977-79

1. Disconnect battery ground cable.
2. Remove switch knob and the bezel nut, then pull switch from panel.
3. Disconnect electrical connector and

remove switch from vehicle.
4. Reverse procedure to install.

1974-76

1. Remove instrument cluster finish panel.
2. Remove wiper switch mounting plate.
3. Disconnect cigar lighter and wiper switch wires.
4. Remove switch bezel nut and remove switch.

W/S WIPER TRANSMISSION, REPLACE

1977-79

1. Disconnect battery ground cable.
2. Remove wiper arm and blade assemblies.
3. Remove cowl top left vent screen.
4. Remove drive arm to pivot retaining clip and the three retaining screws from each pivot.
5. Remove pivot shaft and link assembly.
6. Reverse procedure to install.

1974-76

1. Disconnect battery ground cable and remove wiper arm and blade assemblies.
2. Remove cowl screen and left arm and blade stop.
3. Disconnect linkage drive arm from motor by removing retaining clip.
4. Remove pivot shaft retaining bolts and remove linkage and pivot shaft assemblies.

NOTE: When installing, be sure to force the linkage connecting clip into the locked position.

RADIO, REPLACE

NOTE: When installing radio, be sure to adjust antenna trimmer for peak per-

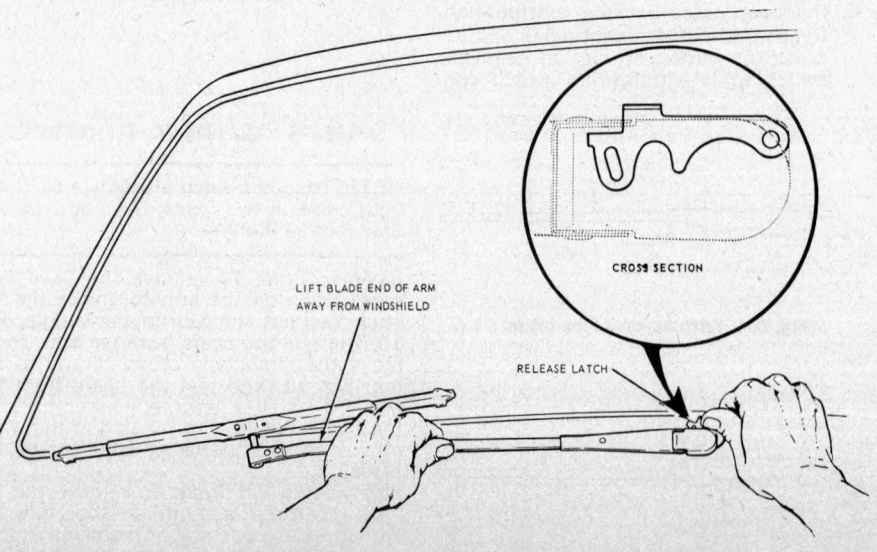

CROSS SECTION

LIFT BLADE END OF ARM AWAY FROM WINDSHIELD

RELEASE LATCH

Fig. 14 Wiper arm. 1974-79

formance.

1974-76

1. Disconnect battery ground cable.
2. Pull radio knobs, discs and nuts from shafts.
3. Remove twilight sentinel amplifier.
4. Remove air conditioning duct located under radio.
5. Remove radio rear support to panel screw and disconnect radio electrical leads, then remove radio.

1977-79

1. Disconnect battery ground cable.
2. Pull radio knobs off shafts.
3. Remove nut from radio control shafts.
4. Remove radio rear support attaching screw at instrument panel.
5. Disconnect power and speaker wires at connectors.
6. Disconnect antenna lead and remove radio.

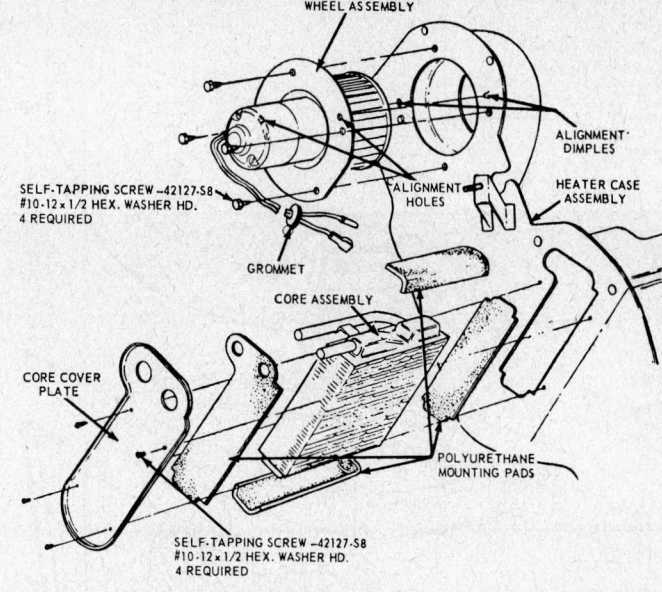

Fig. 15   Heater core & blower motor installation (typical). 1977-79 models less air conditioning

BLOWER MOTOR REMOVE

1977-79

Less Air Conditioning

1. Remove heater assembly as outlined under "Heater Core Removal", 1977-79 procedure.
2. Remove blower motor retaining screws and the blower motor, Fig. 15.

With Air Conditioning

1. Disconnect battery ground cable.
2. Remove instrument panel pad, glove box and the side cowl trim panel.
3. Remove instrument panel attachment on right side of vehicle.
4. From engine compartment, remove the one blower housing to dash nut.
5. From passenger compartment, remove the one blower housing to dash nut.
6. Remove blower housing mounting bracket and the cowl top inner screw.
7. Disconnect outside-recirculating air door vacuum motor vacuum hose.
8. Disconnect electrical leads from blower motor, then remove blower assembly.
9. Remove blower motor from the assembly.

1974-76

1. Disconnect the battery ground cable.
2. Remove the glove box for access.
3. Remove the recirc air register and duct assembly from the blower lower housing to the dash panel.
4. Disconnect the white hose from the outside-recirc air door vacuum motor and remove the vacuum motor from the blower lower housing. Leave the motor actuator connected to the door crank arm, Fig. 16.
5. Disconnect the blower lead wire (orange) from the harness connector,

disconnect the motor ground wire (black).
6. Remove the six upper to lower blower housing flange screws.
7. Separate the blower lower housing and motor assembly from the upper housing and remove it from under the instrument panel.
8. Remove the blower motor and wheel assembly from the lower housing.
9. Reverse the above to install.

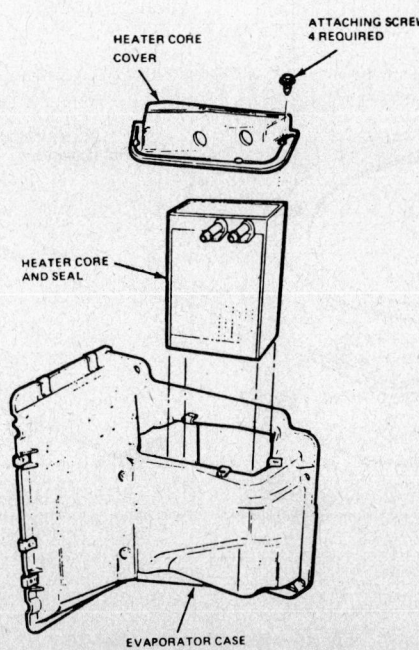

Fig. 17   Heater core installation. 1977-79 models with air conditioning

uum motor hose from the vacuum motor and remove the duct assembly.
5. Disconnect the lead wire to the blower motor.
6. Remove one screw on the motor mounting plate. Rotate the motor mounting plate counterclockwise to un-lock the mounting plate from the case. Remove the motor and wheel assembly through the opening in the cowl side panel.
7. Reverse above to install.

HEATER CORE REMOVAL

1977-79

Less Air Conditioning

1. Disconnect battery ground cable and drain cooling system.
2. Disconnect heater hoses from heater core and plug core openings.
3. Remove heater assembly to dash retaining nuts, Fig. 15.
4. Disconnect control cables from door crank arms.
5. Disconnect electrical wiring from resistor and blower motor.
6. Remove glove box.
7. Remove right air duct control to instrument panel retaining nuts and bolts and the screws securing the right air duct, then remove the duct.
8. Remove heater assembly from vehicle.
9. Remove heater core cover pad and slide heater core from case.

With Air Conditioning

1. Disconnect battery ground cable and drain cooling system.
2. Disconnect heater hoses from heater core and plug core openings.
3. Remove heater core cover plate retaining screws and the plate, Fig. 17.

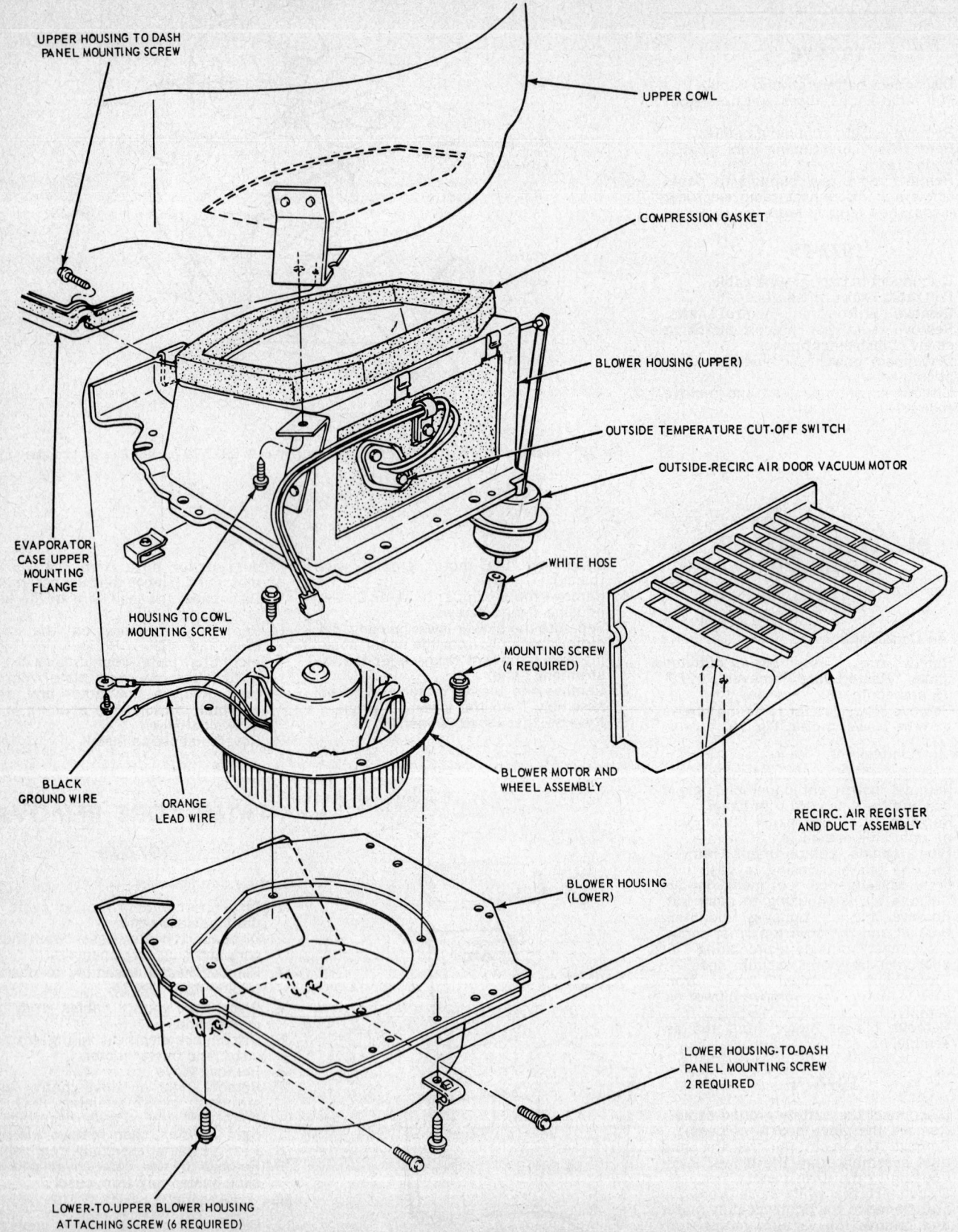

UPPER HOUSING TO DASH
PANEL MOUNTING SCREW

UPPER COWL

COMPRESSION GASKET

BLOWER HOUSING (UPPER)

OUTSIDE TEMPERATURE CUT-OFF SWITCH

OUTSIDE-RECIRC AIR DOOR VACUUM MOTOR

WHITE HOSE

EVAPORATOR
CASE UPPER
MOUNTING
FLANGE

HOUSING TO COWL
MOUNTING SCREW

MOUNTING SCREW
(4 REQUIRED)

BLACK
GROUND WIRE

ORANGE
LEAD WIRE

BLOWER MOTOR AND
WHEEL ASSEMBLY

RECIRC. AIR REGISTER
AND DUCT ASSEMBLY

BLOWER HOUSING
(LOWER)

LOWER HOUSING-TO-DASH
PANEL MOUNTING SCREW
2 REQUIRED

LOWER-TO-UPPER BLOWER HOUSING
ATTACHING SCREW (6 REQUIRED)

Fig. 16   Blower motor. 1974-76

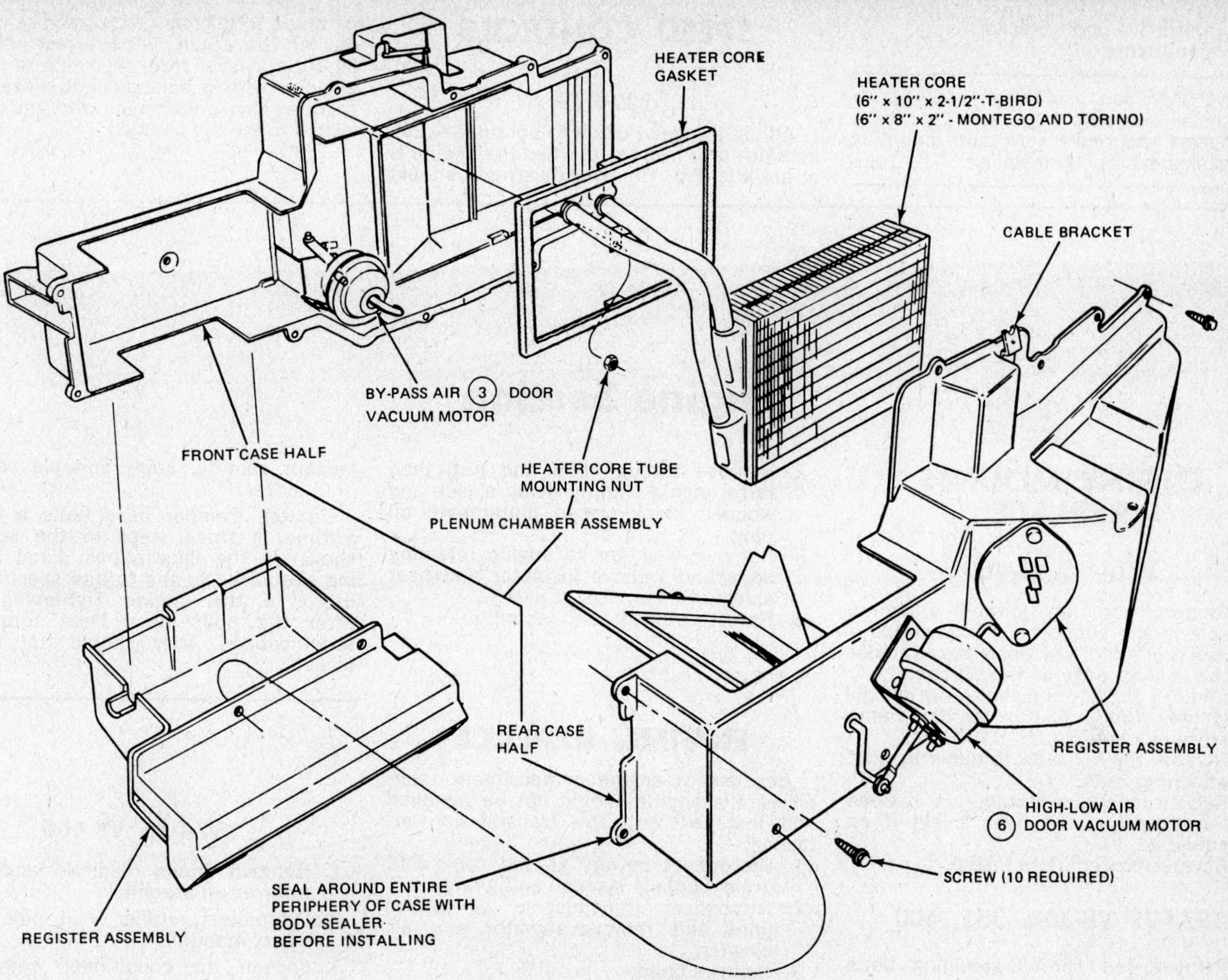

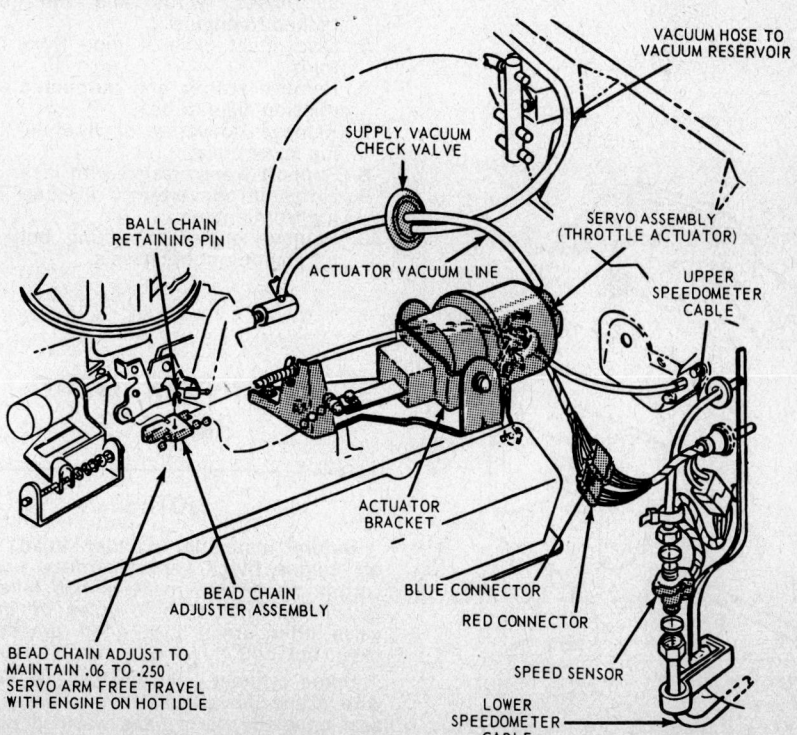

HEATER CORE GASKET

HEATER CORE
(6" x 10" x 2-1/2"-T-BIRD)
(6" x 8" x 2" - MONTEGO AND TORINO)

CABLE BRACKET

BY-PASS AIR ③ DOOR VACUUM MOTOR

FRONT CASE HALF

HEATER CORE TUBE MOUNTING NUT

PLENUM CHAMBER ASSEMBLY

REAR CASE HALF

REGISTER ASSEMBLY

HIGH-LOW AIR ⑥ DOOR VACUUM MOTOR

SCREW (10 REQUIRED)

REGISTER ASSEMBLY

SEAL AROUND ENTIRE PERIPHERY OF CASE WITH BODY SEALER BEFORE INSTALLING

Fig. 18 Heater core. 1974-76

4. Press downward on heater core and tip toward front of vehicle to release the heater core seal from housing.
5. Lift heater core from case and remove from vehicle.

1974-76

1. Drain coolant and disconnect heater hoses from core.
2. Remove glove box.
3. Remove heater air outlet register from plenum assembly (2 snap clips).
4. Remove temperature control cable assembly mounting screw and disconnect end of cable from blend door crank arm (1 spring nut).
5. Remove the blue and red vacuum hoses from the high-low door vacuum motor; the yellow hose from the panel-defrost door motor, and the brown hose at the inline tee connector to the temperature by-pass door motor, Fig. 18.
6. Disconnect wiring connector from resistor.
7. Remove ten screws from around flange of plenum case and remove the rear case half of the plenum.
8. Remove mounting nut from heater

VACUUM HOSE TO VACUUM RESERVOIR

SUPPLY VACUUM CHECK VALVE

BALL CHAIN RETAINING PIN

ACTUATOR VACUUM LINE

SERVO ASSEMBLY (THROTTLE ACTUATOR)

UPPER SPEEDOMETER CABLE

ACTUATOR BRACKET

BLUE CONNECTOR

RED CONNECTOR

SPEED SENSOR

BEAD CHAIN ADJUSTER ASSEMBLY

BEAD CHAIN ADJUST TO MAINTAIN .06 TO .250 SERVO ARM FREE TRAVEL WITH ENGINE ON HOT IDLE

LOWER SPEEDOMETER CABLE

Fig. 19 Servo assembly & throttle linkages (typical). 1974-79 (typical)

core tube support bracket.
9. Remove core.

NOTE: When installing, apply body sealer between front and rear case halves and make sure core mounting gasket is properly installed.

SPEED CONTROLS

1974-79

Adjust the bead chain to obtain .06-.25″ actuator arm free travel when the engine is at hot idle, Fig. 19. The adjustment should be made to take as much slack as possible out of the chain without restricting the carburetor lever from returning to idle. On vehicles with a solenoid anti-diesel valve, perform this adjustment with the ignition switch in the ON position.

Engine Section

ENGINE MOUNTS REPLACE

1974-76 V8-460

1. Remove the fan shroud attaching screws and support the engine with a jack and a block of wood placed under the leading edge of the oil pan.
2. Remove the through bolt and nut attaching the insulator to the frame crossmember, Fig. 1.
3. Remove the insulator to upper bracket attaching nuts.
4. Raise the engine enough to remove the insulator and heat shield if so equipped.
5. Reverse procedure to install.

1977-79 V8-302, 351, 400

1. Remove fan shroud retaining bolts and position shroud over fan.

2. Remove through bolt and nut, then raise engine slightly using a jack and wooden block placed underneath oil pan.
3. Remove insulator to engine retaining bolts and remove insulator and heat shield, if used, Figs. 2 and 3.
4. Reverse procedure to install.

ENGINE, REPLACE

Because of engine compartment tolerances, the engine should not be removed and installed with the transmission attached.
1. Disconnect battery ground cable and drain cooling system and crankcase.
2. Disconnect transmission oil cooler lines and remove radiator and air cleaner.
3. Remove hood.
4. Remove fuel and vacuum lines and all hoses, wires and linkage attached to engine.
5. Disconnect exhaust pipe from manifolds.
6. Remove starter and automatic transmission filler tube.
7. Remove converter or flywheel housing lower cover.
8. Support transmission with jack.
9. Unfasten converter or flywheel housing from engine.
10. Remove engine mounting bolts and lift engine out of chassis.

CYLINDER HEAD REPLACE

NOTES

Before installing cylinder head, wipe off engine block gasket surface and be certain no foreign material has fallen into cylinder bores, bolt holes or in the valve lifter area. It is good practice to clean out bolt holes with compressed air.

Some cylinder head gaskets are coated with a special lacquer to provide a good seal once the parts have warmed up. Do not use any additional sealer on such gaskets. If the gasket does not have this lacquer coating, apply suitable sealer to both sides.

Tighten cylinder head bolts a little at a time in three steps in the sequence shown in the illustrations. Final tightening should be to the torque specifications listed in the *Engine Tightening* table. After the bolts have been torqued to specifications, *they should not be disturbed.*

1974-76 V8-460

1. Remove intake manifold and carburetor as an assembly.
2. Disconnect muffler inlet pipe at exhaust manifold.
3. Loosen air conditioner compressor belt if so equipped.
4. Loosen alternator retaining bolts and remove bolt retaining alternator bracket to right head.
5. If air conditioned, isolate compressor

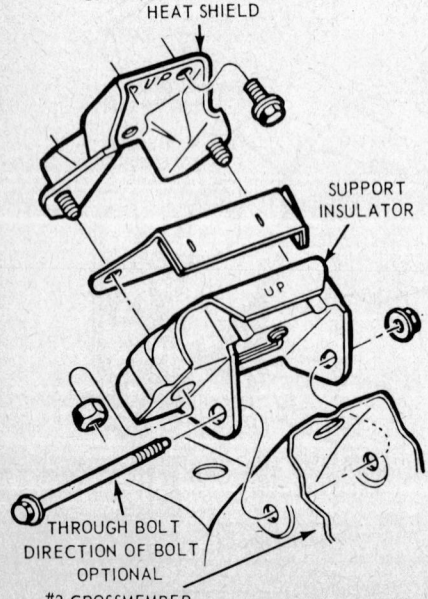

UPPER BRACKET ASSEMBLY
HEAT SHIELD

SUPPORT INSULATOR

UP

THROUGH BOLT
DIRECTION OF BOLT
OPTIONAL
#2 CROSSMEMBER

Fig. 1 Engine mount. 1974-76 V8-460

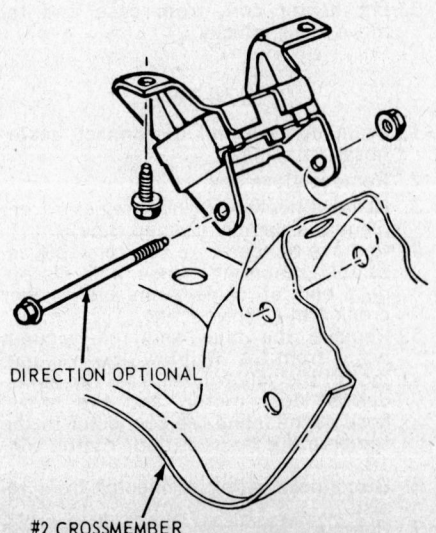

DIRECTION OPTIONAL

#2 CROSSMEMBER

**Fig. 2 Engine mount.
1977-79 V8-302, 351W (typical)**

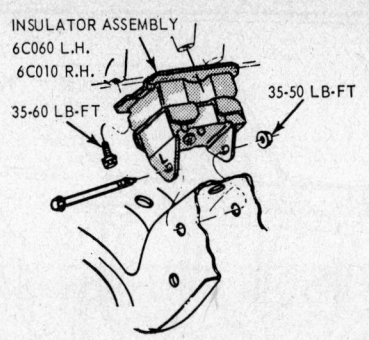

Fig. 3 Engine mounts. 1977-79 V8-351M, 400

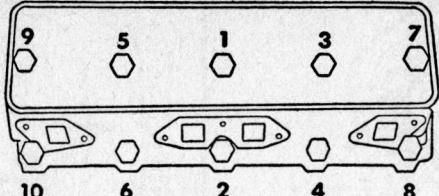

Fig. 4 Cylinder head tightening sequence

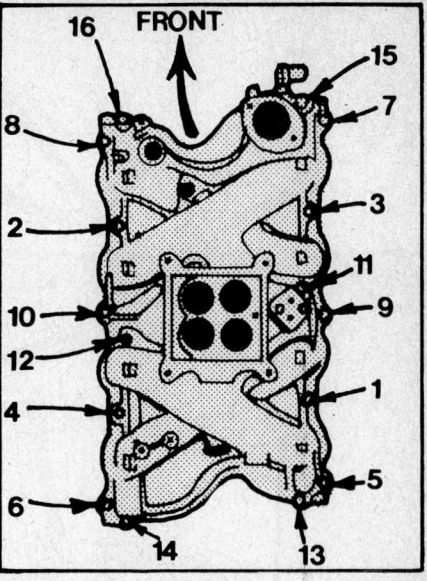

Fig. 5 Intake manifold tightening sequence. V8-460

at service valves and hoses from compressor. Remove nuts retaining compressor bracket to water pump. Remove bolts retaining compressor to upper mounting bracket and lay compressor out of way. Remove compressor upper bracket from head.

6. If not air conditioned, remove bolts retaining power steering reservoir bracket to left head and position reservoir out of way.

7. Remove rocker arm covers and rocker arms. Remove push rods in sequence so they can be installed in their positions.

8. Remove head retaining bolts and lift head with exhaust manifold.

NOTE: If necessary to break gasket seal,

pry at forward corners of cylinder heads against casting bosses provided on cylinder block. Avoid damaging machined surfaces on head and block.

9. Reverse procedure to install. Torque cylinder head bolts in sequence shown in Fig. 4 and intake manifold bolts in sequence shown in Fig. 5.

NOTE

The cylinder head gaskets are marked "Top" or "Front" stamped near the front end of the gasket. The gasket is properly installed when the word is at the forward end of the engine and water passage holes line up. This results in the sealing beads on the right head gasket being inverted with respect to the left head gasket.

1977-79 V8-302, 351, 400

1. Remove intake manifold and carburetor as an assembly.

2. Disconnect battery ground cable at cylinder head.

3. If left head is being removed, remove A/C compressor (if equipped). Also remove and wire power steering pump out of the way. If equipped with Thermactor System, disconnect hose from air manifold on left cylinder head.

4. If right head is to be removed, remove alternator mounting bracket bolt and spacer, ignition coil and air cleaner inlet duct.

5. If right head is to be removed on an engine with Thermactor System, remove air pump from bracket. Discon-

nect hose from air manifold.

6. Disconnect exhaust manifolds at exhaust pipes.

7. Remove rocker arm covers. If equipped with Thermactor System, remove check valve from air manifold.

8. On 1977 and early 1978 V8-302 and 351W engines, loosen rocker arm stud nuts so that rocker arms can be rotated to one side. On V8-351M, 400 and late 1978 and 1979 V8-302, 351W, remove fulcrum bolts, oil deflector (if used), fulcrum and rocker arms. On all engines, remove push rods. Keep push rods and rocker arm components in order so they can be installed in the same position.

9. Remove head bolts and lift head off block.

10. Reverse procedure to install. Torque cylinder head bolts in sequence shown in Fig. 4, and intake manifold bolts in sequence shown in Figs. 6 and 6A.

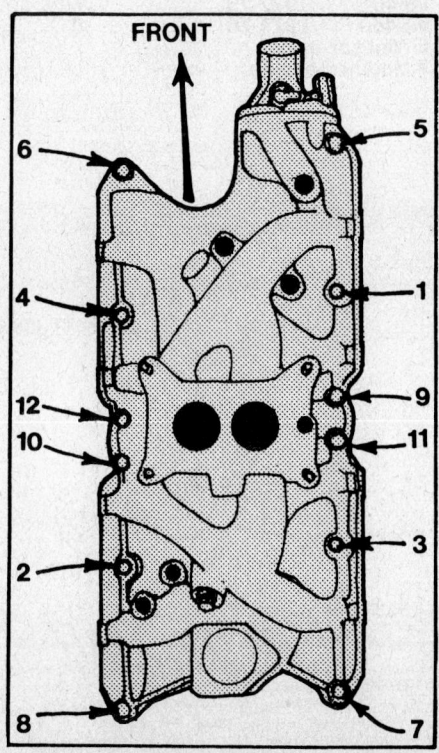

Fig. 6 Intake manifold tightening sequence. V8-302, 351W

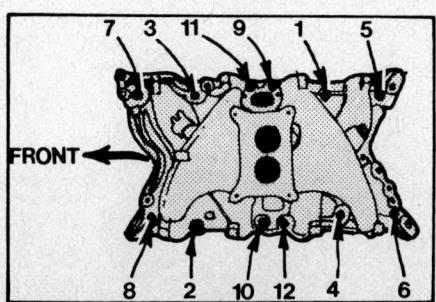

Fig. 6A Intake manifold tightening sequence. V8-351M, 400

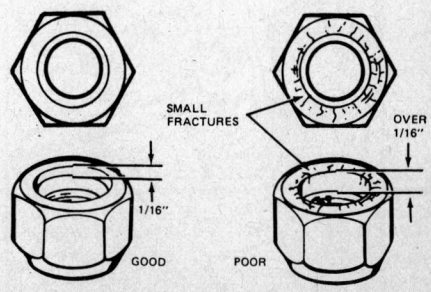

Fig. 7 Rocker arm stud nut inspection. 1977 & early 1978 V8-302, 351W

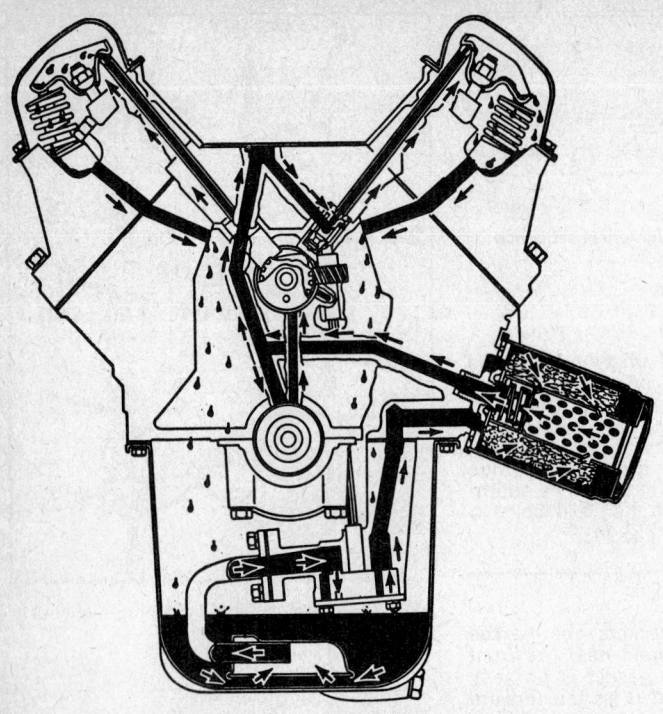

Engine oiling system. V8-302, 351, 400

Engine lubrication system. V8-460

TO LOW PRESSURE
WARNING LIGHT

VALVE LIFT SPECS.

Engine	Year	Intake	Exhaust
V8-302	1977-79	.382	.398
V8-351①	1977-79	.418	.418
V8-351②	1977-79	.406	.406
V8-400	1977	.427	.433
V8-400	1978-79	.428	.432
V8-460	1974	.437	.480
V8-460	1975-76	.437	.451

①Windsor engine.
②Modified engine.

VALVE TIMING

Intake Opens Before TDC

Engine	Year	Degrees
V8-302	1977-79	16
V8-351①	1977-79	23
V8-351②	1977-79	19½
V8-400	1977-79	17
V8-460	1974-76	8

①Windsor engine.
②Modified engine.

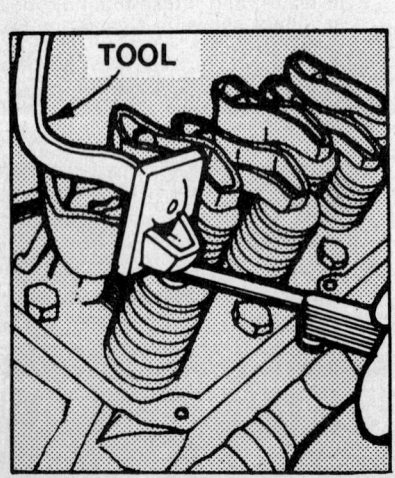

Fig. 7A Checking valve clearance

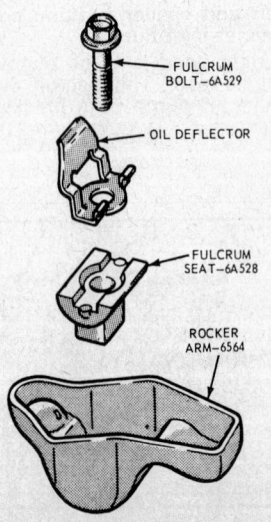

FULCRUM
BOLT—6A529

OIL DEFLECTOR

FULCRUM
SEAT—6A528

ROCKER
ARM—6564

**Fig. 8   Rocker arm and related parts.
1974-76 V8-460, 1977-79 V8-351M, 400**

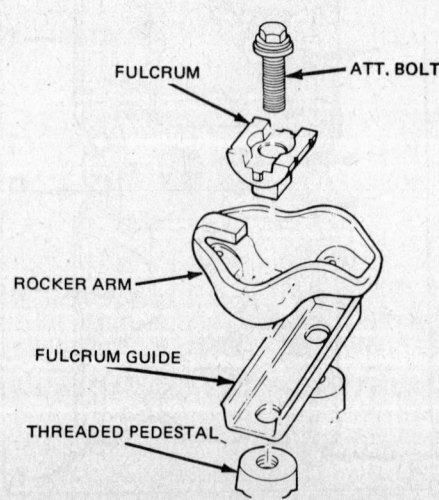

FULCRUM

ATT. BOLT

ROCKER ARM

FULCRUM GUIDE

THREADED PEDESTAL

**Fig. 8A   Rocker arm & related components.
Late 1978 & 1979 V8-302, 351W**

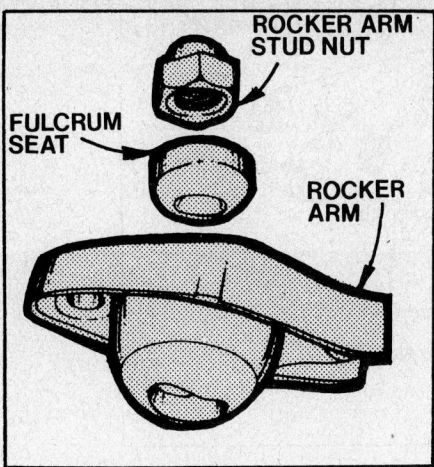

Fig. 9   Rocker arm and related parts.
1977 & early 1978 V8-302, 351W

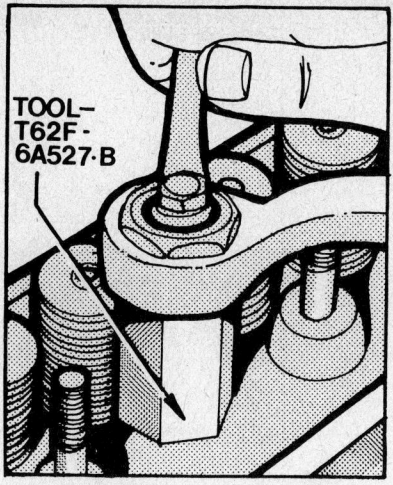

Fig. 10   Rocker arm stud removal.
1977 & early 1978 V8-302, 351W

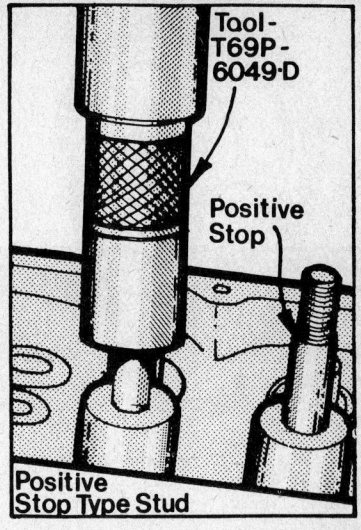

Fig. 11   Positive stop type rocker arm stud
installation. 1977 & early 1978 V8-302, 351W

VALVE ARRANGEMENT

Front to Rear

V8-302, 351, 400, 460 Right . I-E-I-E-I-E-I-E
V8-302, 351, 400, 460 Left . . E-I-E-I-E-I-E-I

VALVES, ADJUST

To eliminate the need of adjusting valve lash, a positive stop rocker arm stud and nut is used on 1977 and early 1978 V8-302 and 351W engines, Fig. 9, and a positive stop fulcrum bolt and seat is used on V8-351M, 400, 460 and late 1978 and 1979 V8-302 and 351W engines, Figs. 8 and 8A.

It is very important that the correct push rod be used and all components be installed and torqued as follows:
1. Position the piston of the cylinder being worked on at TDC of its compression stroke.
2. On 1977 and early 1978 V8-302 and 351W engines, lubricate and install rocker arm and fulcrum seat on the stud. Thread nut onto the stud until it contacts the shoulder and torque to 18-22 ft. lbs.

NOTE: Each rocker arm stud nut should be inspected when adjusting valve clearance, Fig. 7.

3. On V8-351M, 400, 460 and late 1978 and 1979 V8-302 and 351W engines, install rocker arm, fulcrum seat and oil deflector, if used. Install fulcrum bolt and torque to 18-25 ft. lbs.

A .060″ shorter push rod or a .060″ longer rod are available for service to provide a means of compensating for dimensional changes in the valve mechanism. Valve stem-to-rocker arm clearance should be as listed in the *Valve Specifications* table, with the hydraulic lifter completely collapsed, Fig. 7A. Repeated valve grind jobs will decrease this clearance to the point that if not compensated for the lifters will cease to function.

When checking valve clearance, if the clearance is less than the minimum, the .060″ shorter push rod should be used. If clearance is more than the maximum, the .060″ longer push rod should be used. (See *Valve Specifications* table). To check valve clearance, proceed as follows:

V8-302 & All 351, 400 & 460

1. Mark crankshaft pulley at three locations, with number 1 location at TDC timing mark (end of compression stroke), number 2 location one half turn (180°) clockwise from TDC and number 3 location three quarter turn clockwise (270°) from TDC.

2. Turn the crankshaft to the number 1 location and check the clearance on the following valves;
V8-302 & 460

No. 1 Intake	No. 1 Exhaust
No. 7 Intake	No. 5 Exhaust
No. 8 Intake	No. 4 Exhaust

V8-351, 400

No. 1 Intake	No. 1 Exhaust
No. 4 Intake	No. 3 Exhaust
No. 8 Intake	No. 7 Exhaust

3. Turn the crankshaft to the number 2 location and check the clearance on the following valves:
V8-302 & 460

No. 4 Intake	No. 2 Exhaust
No. 5 Intake	No. 6 Exhaust

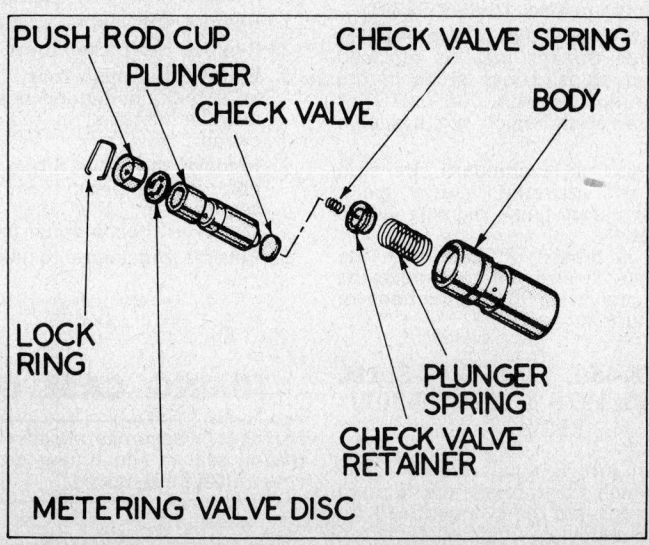

Fig. 12   Hydraulic valve lifter (typical)

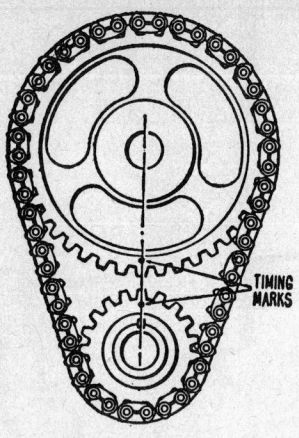

Fig. 13   Valve timing marks

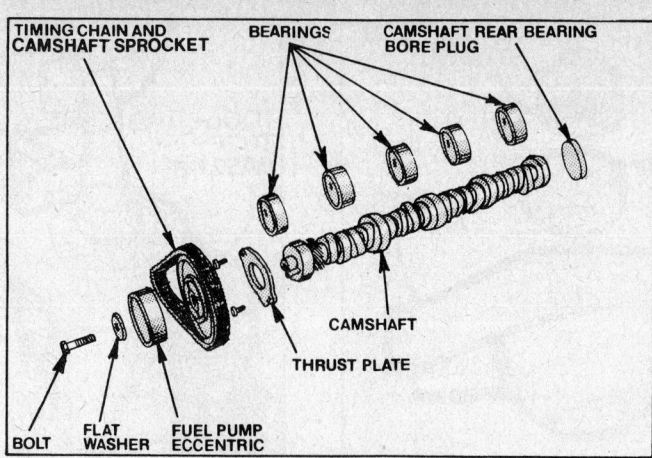

Fig. 14   Camshaft and related parts

V8-351, 400
    No. 3 Intake   No. 2 Exhaust
    No. 7 Intake   No. 6 Exhaust

4. Turn the crankshaft to the number 3 location and check the clearance on the following valves:

V8-302 & 460
    No. 2 Intake   No. 3 Exhaust
    No. 3 Intake   No. 7 Exhaust
    No. 6 Intake   No. 8 Exhaust

V8-351, 400
    No. 2 Intake   No. 4 Exhaust
    No. 5 Intake   No. 5 Exhaust
    No. 6 Intake   No. 8 Exhaust

ROCKER ARM STUD
1977 & Early 1978 V8-302, 351W

If necessary to replace a rocker arm stud, a rocker arm stud kit is available and contains a stud remover, Fig. 10, a stud installer, Fig. 11, and two reamers, one .006″ and the other .015″. For .010 in. studs use reamer No. T66P-6A527-B.

Rocker arm studs that are broken or have damaged threads may be replaced with standard studs. Loose studs in the head may be replaced with .006″, .010″ or .015″ oversize studs which are available for service.

When going from a standard size stud to a .015″ oversize stud, always use a .006″ reamer before finish reaming with a .015″ reamer.

If a stud is broken off flush with the stud boss, use an easy-out to remove the broken stud, following the instructions of the tool manufacturer.

1974-76 V8-460, 1977-79 V8-351M, 400 & Late 1978 & 1979 V8-302, 351W

The rocker arm is supported by a fulcrum bolt which fits through the fulcrum seat and threads into the cylinder head. To disassemble, remove the bolt, oil deflector, fulcrum seat and rocker arm. Figs. 8 and 8A.

VALVE GUIDES

Valve guides in these engines are an integral part of the head and, therefore, cannot be removed. For service, guides can be reamed oversize to accommodate one of three service valves with oversize stems (.003″, .015″ and .030″).

Check the valve stem clearance of each valve (after cleaning) in its respective valve guide. If the clearance exceeds the service limits of .0055″, ream the valve guides to accommodate the next oversize diameter valve.

HYDRAULIC VALVE LIFTERS

The internal parts of each hydraulic valve lifter assembly are a matched set. If these are mixed, improper valve operation may result. Therefore, disassemble, inspect and test each assembly separately to prevent mixing the parts, Fig. 12.

1. Remove the intake manifold.
2. Remove the rocker arms.
3. Remove the push rods, keeping them in a rack in sequence so that they may be installed in their original location.
4. Remove the valve lifters with a magnet rod and place them in a rack in sequence so that they may be installed in their original location.
5. Reverse procedure to install.

TIMING CASE COVER

NOTE: If it becomes necessary to replace the oil seal in the timing case cover the cover must be removed.

1974-79

1. Drain cooling system and crankcase.

2. Remove fan and shroud.
3. Remove radiator.
4. Remove drive belts and water pump pulley. Remove compressor support if so equipped.
5. Remove bolt and washer attaching crankshaft damper. Remove damper with suitable puller. Remove Woodruff key from crankshaft.
6. Remove power steering pump.
7. Remove fuel pump.
8. Remove front cover to cylinder block bolts. Cut the oil pan seal flush with cylinder block face prior to separating cover from cylinder block. Remove front cover and water pump as a unit.

TIMING CHAIN
1974-79

1. To remove the chain, first take off the front cover as outlined previously.
2. Crank engine until timing mark on camshaft sprocket is adjacent to timing mark on crankshaft sprocket, Fig. 13.
3. Remove camshaft sprocket cap screw and fuel pump eccentric.
4. Slide both sprockets and chain forward and remove as an assembly.
5. Reverse procedure to install the chain, being sure to align the timing marks as shown.

CAMSHAFT, REPLACE
1974-79

1. Drain cooling system and remove radiator.
2. If equipped with air conditioning:
    a. On 302, 351W and 460 engines, remove condensor retaining bolts and position condensor aside without disconnecting refrigerant lines.

b. On 351M and 400 engines, purge refrigerant from system and remove condensor.

3. On vehicles equipped with 460 engines, remove grille.
4. Remove front cover, timing chain and sprockets.
5. Remove intake manifold.
6. Remove push rods and lifters.

NOTE: On 351M and 400 engines, make sure that number one cylinder is at top dead center position.

7. Remove thrust plate, then carefully remove camshaft by pulling toward front of engine, Fig. 14.

CAUTION: Use care to avoid damaging camshaft bearings.

8. Reverse procedure to install.

CAMSHAFT BEARINGS

When necessary to replace camshaft bearings, the engine will have to be removed from the vehicle and the plug at the rear of the cylinder block will have to be removed in order to utilize the special camshaft bearing removing and installing tools required to do this job. If properly installed, camshaft bearings require no reaming—nor should this type bearing be reamed or altered in any manner in an attempt to fit bearings.

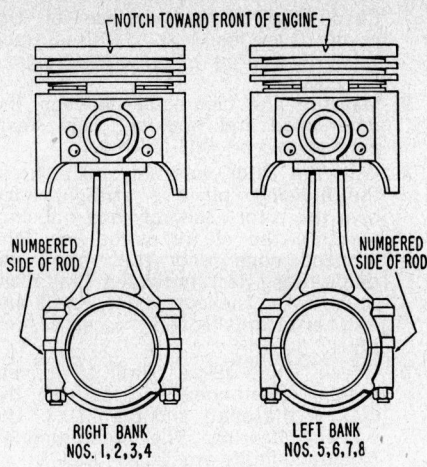

Fig. 15 Piston and rod assembly

PISTON & ROD, ASSEMBLE

All V8's

Assemble the pistons to the rods as shown in Fig. 15.

PISTONS, PINS & RINGS

Pistons are available in oversizes of .003, .020, .030 and .040".

Piston pins are available in oversizes of .001 and .002".

Rings are available in oversizes of .002, .010, .020, .030 and .040".

MAIN & ROD BEARINGS

Main and rod bearings are available in undersizes of .002, .010, .020, .030 and .040".

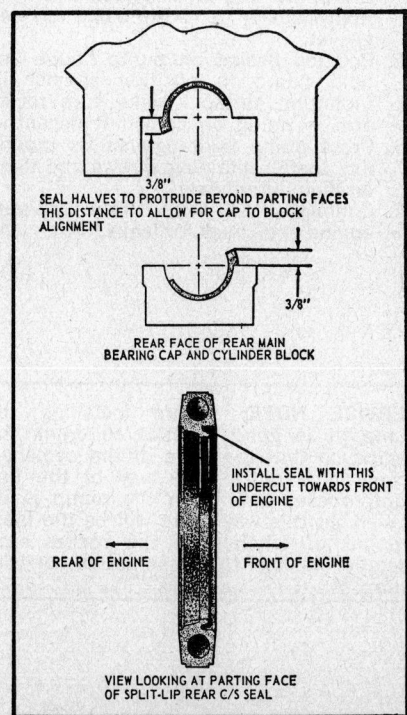

Fig. 16 Split-lip rear crankshaft seal installation

CRANKSHAFT OIL SEAL

1. Remove oil pan.
2. Remove rear bearing cap.
3. Loosen remaining bearing caps, allowing crankshaft to drop down about 1/32".
4. Remove old seals from both cylinder block and rear main bearing cap. Use a brass rod to drift upper half of seal from cylinder block groove. Rotate crankshaft while drifting to facilitate removal.
5. Carefully clean seal groove in block with a brush and solvent. Also clean seal groove in bearing cap. Remove the oil seal retaining pin from the bearing cap if so equipped. *The pin is not used with the split-lip seal.*
6. Dip seal halves in clean engine oil.

7. Carefully install upper seal half in its groove with undercut side of seal toward front of engine, Fig. 16, by rotating it on shaft journal of crankshaft until approximately 3/8" protrudes below the parting surface. *Be sure no rubber has been shaved from outside diameter of seal by bottom edge of groove.*
8. Retighten main bearing caps and torque to specifications.
9. Install lower seal in main bearing cap with undercut side of seal toward front of engine, and allow seal to protrude about 3/8" above parting surface to mate with upper seal upon cap installation.
10. Apply suitable sealer to parting faces of cap and block. Install cap and torque to specifications.

NOTE: If difficulty is encountered in installing the upper half of the seal in position, lightly lap (sandpaper) the side of the seal opposite the lip side using a medium grit paper. After sanding, the seal must be washed in solvent, then dipped in clean engine oil prior to installation.

SERVICE BULLETIN

A new crankshaft rear oil seal has been released for service. This new seal may be received when ordering an oil pan gasket kit and is installed in the same manner as described above, Fig. 17.

OIL PAN, REPLACE

V8-302, 351, 400

1. Remove oil level dipstick, then remove

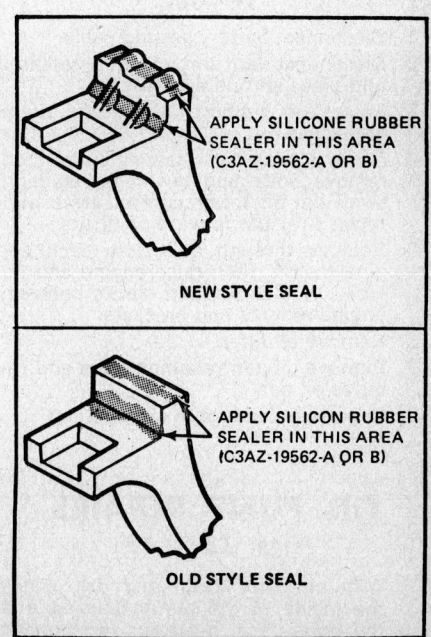

Fig. 17 Crankshaft rear oil seals

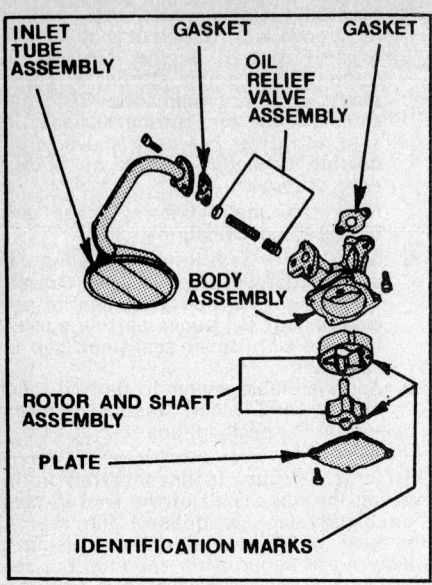

INLET TUBE ASSEMBLY — GASKET — GASKET — OIL RELIEF VALVE ASSEMBLY — BODY ASSEMBLY — ROTOR AND SHAFT ASSEMBLY — PLATE — IDENTIFICATION MARKS

Fig. 18 Oil pump assembly. V8-302, 351W, 460

2. Check the mating surface of the pump cover for wear. If this surface is worn, scored or grooved, replace the cover.
3. Measure the clearance between the outer race and housing. This clearance should be .001-.013".
4. With the rotor assembly installed in the housing, place a straight edge over the rotor assembly and housing. Measure the clearance between the straight edge and the rotor and outer race. Recommended limits are .001-.004". *The outer race, shaft and rotor are furnished only as an assembly.*
5. Check the drive shaft-to-housing bearing clearance by measuring the O.D. of the shaft and the I.D. of the housing bearing. The recommended clearance limits are .0015-.0029".
6. Inspect the relief valve spring for a collapsed or worn condition.
7. Check the relief valve piston for scores and free operation in the bore. The specified piston clearance is .0015-.0029".

GASKET-6659 — OIL RELIEF VALVE ASSEMBLY — 6A616 — 6674 — 6670 — BODY & SCREEN ASSEMBLY — INLET TUBE ASSEMBLY 6622 — I.D. MARKS — ROTOR & SHAFT ASSEMBLY 6608 — PLATE 6616

Fig 19 Oil pump assembly. V8-351M, 400

fan shroud retaining screws and position shroud over fan.
2. Raise vehicle and drain crankcase.
3. On 351M and 400 engines, remove starter.
4. Remove stabilizer retaining bolts and lower sway bar.
5. Remove engine mount through bolts, then raise engine and insert wooden blocks between engine mounts and brackets.
6. Position transmission oil cooler lines aside.
7. Remove oil pan retaining bolts and oil pan.
8. Reverse procedure to install.

V8-460

1. Disconnect battery ground cable.
2. Disconnect fan shroud from radiator and place shroud over fan.
3. Raise and support vehicle and drain crankcase.
4. Remove sway bar retaining bolts, then remove bolts and bushings retaining sway bar to lower control arms and move sway bar forward on struts.
5. Remove through bolt from each engine mount, then raise engine and insert 1¼ inch wooden blocks between engine mounts and brackets.
6. Remove oil filter.
7. Remove oil pan retaining bolts and remove oil pan.
8. Reverse procedure to install.

OIL PUMP REPAIRS
Figs. 18 & 19

1. With all parts clean and dry, check the inside of the pump housing and the outer race and rotor for damage or excessive wear.

BELT TENSION DATA

	New	Used
1974-78 All	140	110

WATER PUMP, REPLACE
V8-302, 351W

1. Drain cooling system.
2. Remove power steering drive belt (if equipped). If air conditioned, remove compressor belt.
3. Disconnect radiator lower hose and heater hose at water pump.
4. Remove drive belt, fan, spacer or fan drive clutch and pulley.
5. Unfasten and remove water pump from cylinder front cover.
6. Reverse procedure to install.

V8-351M, 400, 460

1. Drain cooling system, remove fan shroud, fan and all belts.
2. Disconnect alternator bracket and position bracket out of way.
3. Remove power steering pump, A/C compressor and position units out of way.
4. Remove A/C compressor bracket and disconnect hoses from water pump.
5. Remove water pump and remove separator plates from pump.
6. Reverse procedure to install.

FUEL PUMP PRESSURE

Year	Engine	Pressure Lbs.
1974	All [1]	5½-6½
1974	All [2]	6½-7½

1975-76	All	5.7-7.7
1977-79	V8-302	6-8
	V8-351W	6-8
	V8-351M, 400	6-8

[1] Exc. Calif.
[2] Calif.

FUEL PUMP, REPLACE

1. Remove all gasket material from the pump and block gasket surfaces. Apply sealer to both sides of new gasket.
2. Position gasket on pump flange and hold pump in position against its mounting surface. Make sure rocker arm is riding on camshaft eccentric.
3. Press pump tight against its mounting. Install retaining screws and tighten them alternately.
4. Connect fuel lines. Then operate engine and check for leaks.

SERVICE NOTE: Before installing the pump, it is good practice to crank the engine so that the nose of the camshaft eccentric is out of the way of the fuel pump rocker arm when the pump is installed. In this way there will be the least amount of tension on the rocker arm, thereby easing the installation of the pump.

Transmission Section

> NOTE: 1979 linkage adjustment information is in this section. Repair procedures on both automatic and manual shift transmissions are covered elsewhere in this manual. Procedures for removing automatic transmissions as well as linkage adjustments on 1974-78 models are included in the automatic transmission chapters. See Chapter Index.

1979 AUTO TRANS. LINKAGE, ADJUST

Linkage adjustment procedures for 1979 models are the same as those for 1978 models as outlined elsewhere in this manual.

Rear Axle, Propeller Shaft & Brakes

REAR AXLES

Fig. 1 illustrates the rear axle assembly used on these cars. When necessary to overhaul the unit, refer to the *Rear Axle Specifications* table in this chapter.

Description

In these axles, Fig. 1, the drive pinion is straddle-mounted by two opposed tapered roller bearings which support the pinion shaft in front of the drive pinon gear, and straight roller bearing that supports the pinion shaft at the rear of the pinion gear. The drive pinion is assembled in a pinion retainer that is bolted to the differential carrier. The tapered roller bearings are preloaded by a collapsible spacer between the bearings. The pinion is positioned by a shim or shims located between the drive pinion retainer and the differential carrier.

The differential is supported in the carrier by two tapered roller side bearings. These bearings are preloaded by two threaded ring nuts or sleeves between the bearings and pedestals. The differential assembly is positioned for proper ring gear and pinion backlash by varying the adjustment of these ring nuts. The differential case houses two side gears in mesh with two pinions mounted on a pinion shaft which is held in place by a pin. The side gears and pinions are backed by thrust washers. With high performance engines, an optional rear axle having a four-pinion differential is also used.

The axle shafts are of unequal length, the left shaft being shorter than the right. On 1974-78 units, the axle shafts are mounted on tapered roller bearings. The ball and tapered roller bearings are pressed onto the axle shafts.

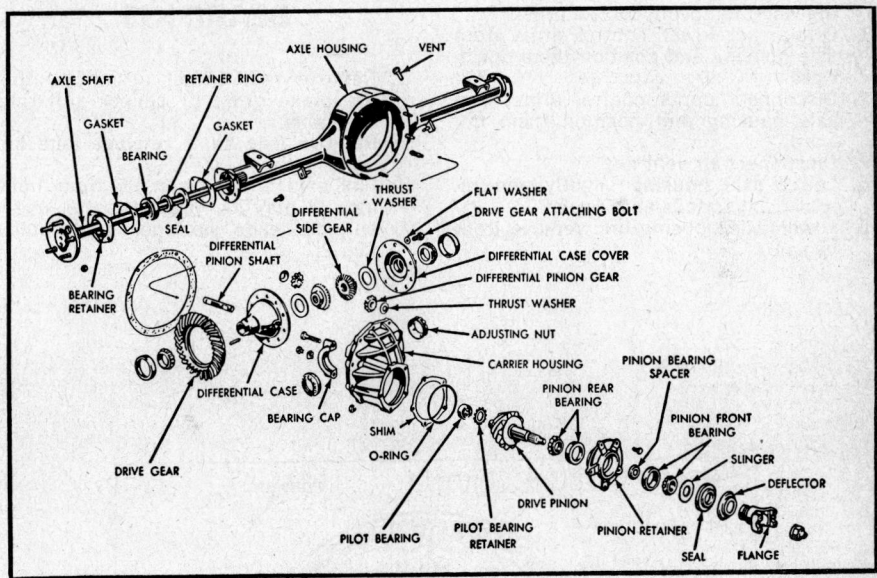

Fig. 1 Rear axle disassembled (Typical)

REAR AXLE, REPLACE

1. Raise rear of vehicle and remove wheel and tire assembly.
2. On models equipped with rear drum brakes, remove brake drums and disconnect brake lines at wheel cylinders.
3. On models equipped with rear disc brakes, remove calipers from anchor plates, then remove two retaining nuts and slide rotors off axle shafts.

NOTE: Secure calipers to frame with wire.

4. Make marks on drive shaft yoke and pinion flange for reassembly, then disconnect drive shaft at rear axle U-joint and remove drive shaft from transmission extension housing. Install seal replacer tool in extension

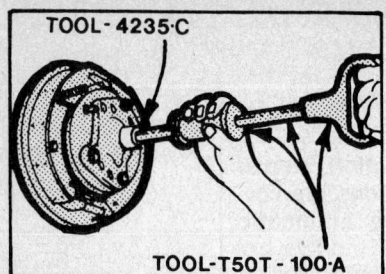

TOOL-4235-C

TOOL-T50T-100-A

Fig. 2   Removing axle shaft

Diff. Carrier Assy.

Service Bulletin

All Ford Built Rear Axles: Recent manufacturing changes have eliminated the need for marking rear axle drive pinions for individual variations from nominal shim thicknesses. In the past, these pinion markings, with the aid of a shim selection table, were used as a guide to select correct shim thicknesses when a gear set or carrier assembly replacement was performed.

With the elimination of pinion markings, use of the shim selection table is no longer possible and the methods outlined below must be used.

1. Measure the thickness of the original pinion depth shim removed from the axle. Use the same thickness upon installation of the replacement carrier or drive pinion. If any further shim change is necessary, it will be indicated in the tooth pattern check.
2. If the original shim is lost, substitute a nominal shim for the original and use the tooth pattern check to determine if further shim changes are required.

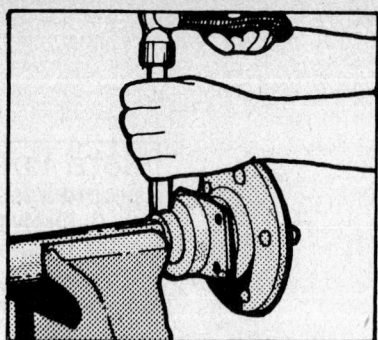

Fig. 3   Loosening or breaking inner bearing retainer with cold chisel

housing to prevent leakage.

5. Position a drain pan under differential carrier, then remove carrier attaching bolts and allow axle to drain.
6. Disconnect anti-skid sensor wire connector from differential carrier, then remove mounting bracket and sensor wiring from axle, if equipped.
7. Disconnect stabilizer, if equipped.
8. Disconnect shock absorber from lower mounting.
9. Remove brake line from retaining clips on rear axle housing, then remove brake line junction block retaining screw.
10. Position a suitable jack under axle housing to prevent housing from tilting when removing control arms.
11. Disconnect lower control arms from axle housing and position them downward.
12. Disconnect upper control arms from axle housing and position them upward.
13. Disconnect air vent line.
14. Lower axle housing slightly and remove coil springs and insulators.
15. Lower axle housing and remove from vehicle.

AXLE SHAFTS & BEARINGS

1. Remove rear wheel assembly, then the brake drum or caliper and rotor assembly.
2. Remove axle shaft retainer nuts and bolts.
3. Pull axle shaft assembly from housing. It may be necessary to use a suitable slide hammer type puller, Fig. 2.

4. On 1974-79 units, tapered roller bearing type:
   a. Drill a $\frac{1}{4}$ inch hole in inner bearing retainer approximately $\frac{3}{4}$ of the thickness of the bearing retainer deep.

NOTE: Do not drill completely through the bearing retainer since damage to the axle shaft may result.

   b. Place a cold chisel across the drilled hole and strike with a hammer to break retainer, then discard retainer, Fig. 3.
   c. Press bearing from axle shaft. Do not apply heat since the heat will weaken the axle shaft bearing journal area.
   d. Install lubricated seal and bearing on axle shaft, ensuring the cup rib ring faces toward the axle flange.

NOTE: The lubricated seal of the bearing assembly used with drum brake installations is of a different length than the seal used on disc brake installations and are not interchangeable. For identification, the seal used on drum brake installations has a grey color outer rim and on disc brake installations, the seal has a black oxide appearance.

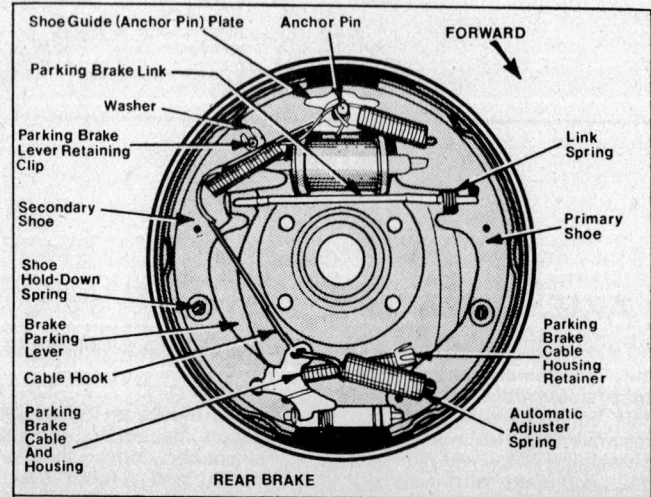

Shoe Guide (Anchor Pin) Plate
Anchor Pin
FORWARD
Parking Brake Link
Washer
Parking Brake Lever Retaining Clip
Link Spring
Secondary Shoe
Primary Shoe
Shoe Hold-Down Spring
Brake Parking Lever
Cable Hook
Parking Brake Cable Housing Retainer
Parking Brake Cable And Housing
Automatic Adjuster Spring
REAR BRAKE

Fig. 4   Rear drum type brake 1974-79

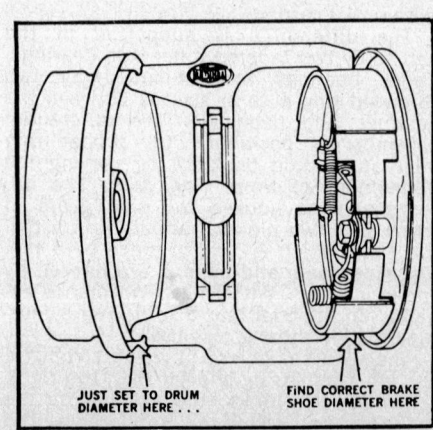

JUST SET TO DRUM DIAMETER HERE...
FIND CORRECT BRAKE SHOE DIAMETER HERE

Fig. 5   Brake adjustment with gauge

e. Press new bearing into place, then the bearing retainer firmly against the bearing.

f. Remove bearing cup from axle housing with a suitable puller and place on bearing. Apply lubricant to outside diameter of seal and bearing cup.

5. On all units, slide axle shaft assembly into housing, engaging axle shaft splines in the side gear.

6. Install and torque axle shaft retainer nuts and bolts to 50-75 ft. lbs. on 1975-76 models. 35-55 ft. lbs. on 1974 and 1977 models, 20 to 40 ft. lbs. on 1978 models.

7. Install brake drum or rotor and caliper.

8. Install wheel assembly.

PROPELLER SHAFT
Remove & Replace

NOTE: To maintain propeller shaft balance, mark relationship between rear yoke and pinion flange, and the front yoke and slip yoke before disassembling universal joints.

1. Disconnect rear U-joint from drive pinion flange.

2. Pull drive shaft toward rear of car until front U-joint yoke clears transmission extension housing and output shaft.

3. Install a suitable tool, such as a seal driver, in seal to prevent lube from leaking from transmission.

4. Before installing, check U-joints for freedom of movement. If a bind has resulted from misalignment after overhauling the U-joints, tap the ears of the drive shaft sharply to relieve the bind.

5. If rubber seal installed on end of transmission extension housing is damaged, install a new seal.

6. Lubricate yoke spline with special spline lubricant. *This spline is sealed so that transmission fluid does not "wash" away spline lubricant.*

7. Install yoke on transmission output shaft.

8. Install U-bolts and nuts which attach U-joint to pinion flange. Tighten U-bolts evenly to prevent binding U-joint bearings.

BRAKE ADJUSTMENTS
1974-79
Self-Adjusting Brakes

These brakes, Fig. 4, have self-adjusting shoe mechanisms that assure correct lining-to-drum clearances at all times. The automatic adjusters operate only when the brakes are applied when the car is moving rearward.

Although the brakes are self-adjusting, an initial adjustment is necessary when the brake shoes have been relined or replaced, or when the length of the star wheel adjuster has been changed during some other service operation.

Frequent usage of an automatic transmission forward range to halt reverse vehicle motion may prevent the automatic adjusters from functioning, thereby in-

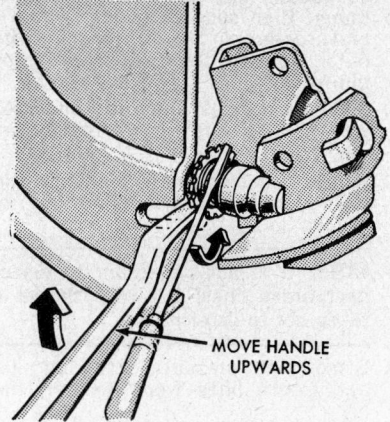

Fig. 6 Backing off brake adjustment by disengaging lever with screwdriver

MOVE HANDLE UPWARDS

ducing low pedal heights. Should low pedal heights be encountered, it is recommended that numerous forward and reverse stops be made until satisfactory pedal height is obtained.

If a low pedal height condition cannot be corrected by making numerous reverse stops (provided the hydraulic system is free of air) it indicates that the self-adjusting mechanism is not functioning. Therefore, it will be necessary to remove the brake drum, clean, free up and lubricate the adjusting mechanism. Then adjust the brakes as follows, being sure the parking brake is fully released.

Adjustment

NOTE: If after removing brake drum retaining nuts, the brake drum can not be removed, pry rubber plug from backing plate. Insert a narrow screwdriver through hole in backing plate and disengage lever from adjusting screw. While holding lever away from adjusting screw, back off adjusting screw using a suitable tool to retract brake shoes, Fig. 6.

The adjustment is made with the drums removed, using the brake gauge shown in Fig. 5. With the gauge, determine the inside diameter of the drum braking surface. Reverse the tool as shown and adjust the brake shoe diameter to fit the gauge. Hold the automatic adjusting lever out of engagement while rotating the adjusting screw to prevent burring the screw slots. Rotate the gauge around the brake shoes to be sure of the setting. After the brake drums and wheels have been installed, complete the adjustment by applying the brakes several times while backing the vehicle.

PARKING BRAKE, ADJUST
1974-79 Vacuum Release Unit

The vacuum power unit will release

the parking brake automatically when the transmission selector lever is moved into any driving position with the engine running. The brakes will not release automatically, however, when the selector lever is in neutral or park position with the engine running, or in any other position with the engine off.

The lower end of the release handle extends out for alternate manual release in the event of vacuum power failure or for optional manual release at any time.

1974-79
Rear Drum Brakes

1. Make sure parking brake is released.
2. Place transmission in neutral and raise the vehicle.
3. Tighten the adjusting nut against the cable equalizer to cause rear brakes to drag.
4. Then loosen the adjusting nut until the rear wheels are fully released. There should be no drag.
5. Lower vehicle and check operation.

1975-76
Rear Disc Brakes

1. Fully release parking brake, then place transmission in neutral and support vehicle at rear axle.
2. Tighten adjuster nut until levers on calipers just begin to move, then loosen adjuster nut until levers just return to stop position.
3. Apply and release parking brake. Check levers on caliper to determine if they are fully returned by attempting to pull lever rearward. If lever moves, the adjustment is too tight and must be readjusted.

MASTER CYLINDER, REPLACE

1. Disconnect brake lines from master cylinder.
2. Remove two nuts attaching master cylinder to power brake unit.
3. Slide master cylinder forward and remove from vehicle.

POWER BRAKE UNIT, REPLACE
1974-79 Except Hydro-Boost

1. Disconnect vacuum hose at booster.
2. Remove master cylinder from booster. It is not necessary to disconnect brake lines.
3. Working under instrument panel, disconnect booster push rod link from brake pedal as follows: 1) disconnect stop light switch wires at connector and remove hairpin clip, 2) slide stop light switch off pedal just

far enough for switch outer hole to clear pin, then tilt switch straight upward from pin, 3) slide master cylinder push rod and nylon washer and bushing from brake pedal pin.

4. Unfasten and remove booster from dash panel, sliding push rod link out from engine side of dash panel.

5. Remove dust seal from push rod link and place it in slot of dash panel for installation.

6. Reverse procedure to install.

1975-76 Hydro-Boost

1. Disconnect stoplight switch wires at connector and remove hairpin retainer, then slide stoplight switch off brake pedal pin far enough for switch outer hole to clear pin and remove pin from switch.

2. Slide hydro-boost push rod and nylon washers and bushing off brake pedal pin.

3. Remove master cylinder and position to one side without disturbing hydraulic lines.

NOTE: It is not necessary to disconnect brake lines, but care should be taken not to deform lines.

4. Disconnect pressure, steering gear and return lines from booster, then plug lines and ports in hydro-boost to prevent entry or dirt.

5. Remove hydro-boost retaining nuts, and remove assembly sliding push rod link from engine side of dash panel.

6. Reverse procedure to install. To purge system, disconnect coil wire so that engine will not start. Fill power steering pump reservoir, then while engaging starter, pump brake pedal. Do not cycle steering wheel until all residual air has been purged from the hydro boost unit. Check fluid level, then connect coil wire and start engine. Apply brakes with a pumping action and cycle steering wheel, then check system for leaks.

Rear Suspension

SHOCK ABSORBER, REPLACE

1. With rear axle supported properly disconnect shock absorber at upper mounting and compress it to clear hole in spring seat.
2. Disconnect shock absorber from stud on axle bracket.
3. Reverse procedure to install.

COIL SPRINGS, REPLACE

1. Raise rear of vehicle and support at frame. Support rear axle with a suitable jack.
2. Disconnect shock absorbers at lower mountings.
3. Lower axle to remove springs.
4. Reverse procedure to install. On 1974-79, an insulator is installed only between upper seat and the spring, Fig. 1.

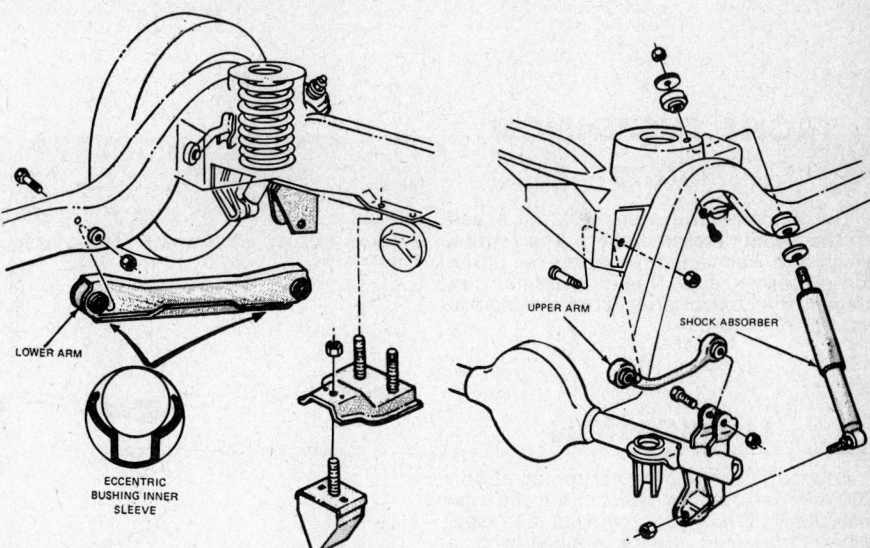

Fig. 1   Rear suspension, 1974-79 models (typical)

CONTROL ARMS, REPLACE

NOTE: On 1974-79 models, upper and lower control arms must be replaced in pairs.

1. Raise rear of vehicle and support at frame. Support axle with a suitable jack.
2. On all models lower axle and install a second jack under differential pinion nose.
3. Disconnect control arm from axle bracket. On upper arms, disconnect arm from crossmember and on lower arms, disconnect arm from frame attachment bracket.
4. Reverse procedure to install.

STABILIZER BAR, REPLACE

1. Remove bolts securing stabilizer bar to rear link assemblies on both sides, Fig. 2.
2. Remove nuts securing mounting bracket to lower mounting clamp and remove bar.
3. Reverse procedure to install.

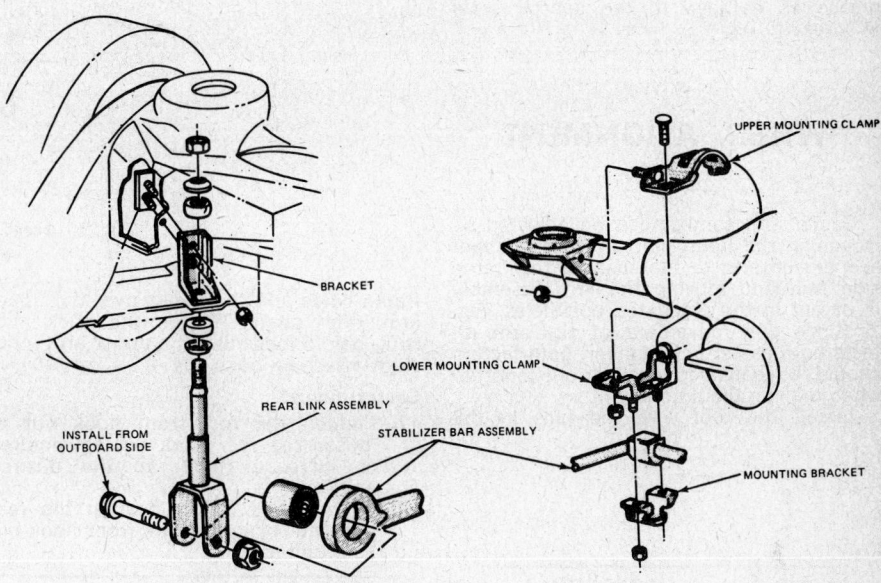

Fig. 2   Stabilizer bar installation, 1974-79 models (typical)

Front End & Steering Section

FRONT SUSPENSION

1974-79

The lower control arm pivots on a bolt in the front crossmember. The struts, which are connected between the lower control arms and frame crossmember, prevent the control arms from moving forward or backward.

LUBRICATION

Lubrication should be performed at 36,000-mile intervals at which time the special plugs should be removed and specially formulated grease applied with a hand-operated gun. This extended lubrication interval is made possible by a special type chassis lubricant combined with special seals and bearing materials. Under no circumstances should the special plugs be removed and fittings installed to accommodate conventional type grease as damage to the special seals may result.

WHEEL ALIGNMENT

1974-79

Caster and camber can be adjusted by loosening the bolts that attach the upper suspension arm to the shaft at the frame side rail, and moving the arm assembly in or out in the elongated bolt holes, Fig. 2. Since any movement of the arm affects both caster and camber, both factors should be balanced against one another when making the adjustment.

Install the tool with the pins in the frame holes and the hooks over the upper arm inner shaft. Tighten the hook nuts snug before loosening the upper arm inner shaft attaching bolts, Fig. 2.

Caster, Adjust

1. Tighten the tool front hook nut or loosen the rear hook nut as required to increase caster to the desired angle.
2. To decrease caster, tighten the rear hook nut or loosen the front hook nut as required.

NOTE: The caster angle can be checked without tightening the inner shaft retaining bolts.

3. Check the camber angle to be sure it did not change during the caster adjustment and adjust if necessary.
4. Tighten the upper arm inner shaft retaining bolts and remove tool.

Camber, Adjust

1. Install as previously outlined.
2. Loosen both inner shaft retaining bolts.
3. Tighten or loosen the hook nuts as necessary to increase or decrease camber.
4. Recheck caster angle.

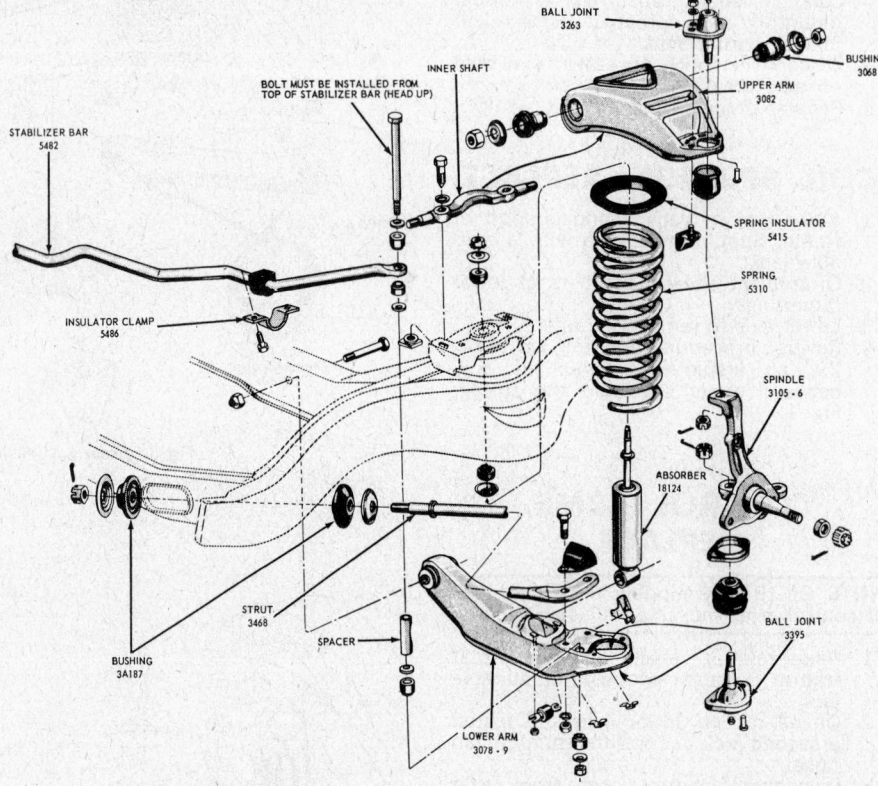

Fig. 1   Front suspension (typical)

TOE-IN, ADJUST

Check the steering wheel spoke position when the front wheels are in the straight ahead position. If the spokes are

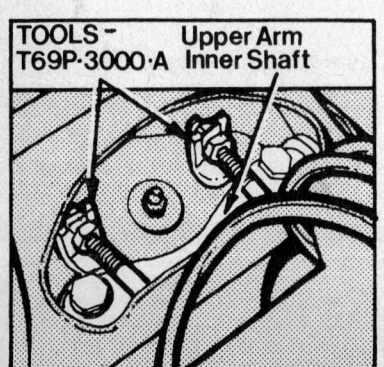

Fig. 2   Caster thand camber adjustment

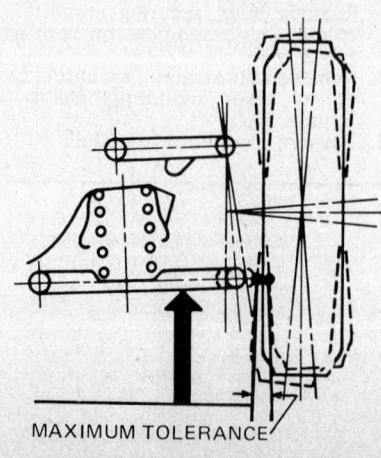

Fig. 3   Measuring lower ball joint radial play

not in the normal position, they can be adjusted while toe-in is being adjusted.

1. Loosen clamp bolts on each tie rod end sleeve.
2. Adjust toe-in. If steering wheel spokes are in their normal position, lengthen or shorten both rods equally to obtain correct toe-in. If spokes are not in normal position, make necessary rod adjustments to obtain correct toe-in and steering wheel spoke alignment.

WHEEL BEARINGS, ADJUST

1974-79

1. With wheel rotating, tighten adjusting nut to 17-25 ft. lbs.
2. Back off adjusting nut ½ turn and retighten nut to 10-15 inch lbs.
3. Place nut lock on nut so that castellations on lock are aligned with cotter pin hole in spindle and install cotter pin.
4. Check front wheel rotation, if it rotates noisily or rough, clean, inspect or replace wheel bearings as necessary.

WHEEL BEARINGS, REPLACE

(Disc Brakes)

1. Raise car and remove front wheels.
2. Remove caliper mounting bolts.

NOTE: It is not necessary to disconnect brake lines for this operation.

3. Slide caliper off of disc, inserting a spacer between the shoes to hold pistons in their bores after the caliper is removed. Position caliper assembly out of the way.

NOTE: Do not allow caliper to hang by the brake line.

4. Remove hub and disc assembly. Grease retainer and inner bearing can now be removed.

CHECKING BALL JOINTS FOR WEAR

Upper Ball Joint

1. Raise vehicle and place floor jacks beneath lower control arms.
2. Grasp the lower edge of tire and move the wheel in and out.
3. While the wheel is being moved observe any movement between the upper end of the spindle and upper arm. If any movement is observed replace the ball joint.

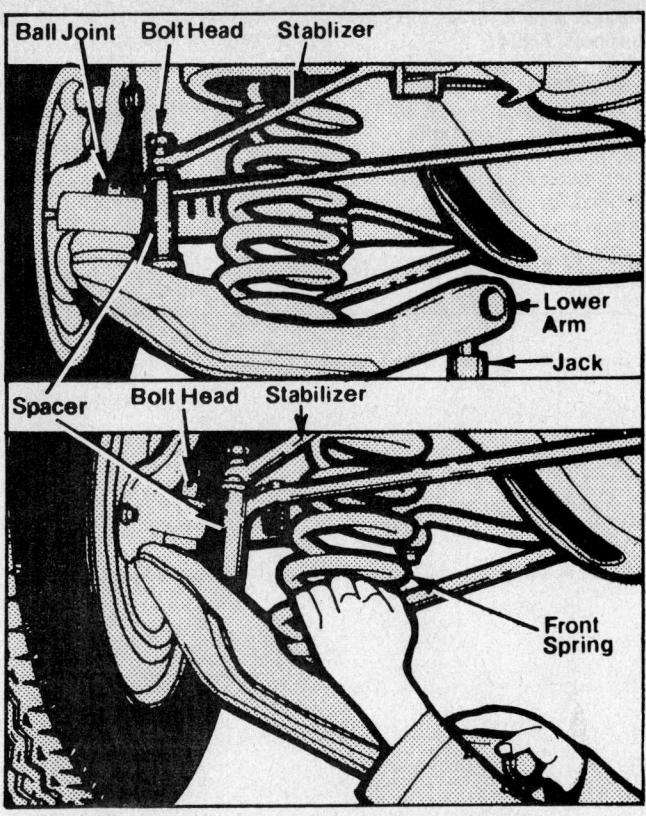

Fig. 4   Coil spring removal & installation

Lower Ball Joint

1. Raise vehicle and place floor jacks under lower control arms, Fig. 3.
2. Adjust wheel bearings and place a dial indicator to the lower arm and position the indicator so that the plunger rests against the inner side of the wheel rim adjacent to the lower ball joint.
3. Grasp tire at top and bottom and move it slowly in and out. Reading on dial will indicate the amount of radial play. If reading exceeds ¼ inch replace the ball joint.

BALL JOINTS, REPLACE

NOTE: Ford Motor Company recommends that new ball joints should not be installed on used control arms and that the control arm be replaced if ball joint replacement is required. However, aftermarket ball joint repair kits which do not require control arm replacement, are available and can be installed using the following procedure.

The upper and lower ball joints are riveted to the control arms. On later models, the upper ball joint is pressed into the upper control arm whereas the lower ball joint is riveted to the lower control arm.

When replacing a riveted ball joint, remove the rivets and retain the ball joint to its control arm with the bolts, nuts and washers furnished with the ball joint kit. Also, use a suitable pressing tool to force the ball joint studs out of the spindle.

SHOCK ABSORBER, REPLACE

1974-79

To remove a shock absorber, disconnect it from the frame at its upper end. Remove the two cap screws that retain the shock absorber mounting plate to the lower control arm and lower the shock absorber unit.

To install, reverse the removal procedure and tighten the two lower cap screws to 13-18 lbs. ft. torque.

COIL SPRING, REPLACE

1974-79

1. Raise vehicle and support front end of frame with jack stands.
2. Disconnect shock absorber from lower

arm and place a jack under the lower arm for support, Fig. 4.

3. Remove strut and rebound bumper bolts and disconnect lower end of sway bar stud from lower arm.

4. Remove the nut and bolt that retains the inner end of the lower arm to the crossmember.

5. Carefully lower jack to relieve the spring pressure on the lower arm, then remove the spring.

STEERING GEAR, REPLACE

1974-79

1. Disconnect pressure and return lines from steering gear. Cap each line and plug each port to prevent entry of dirt.

2. Remove bolt that secures flex joint to steering gear.

3. Raise the vehicle and remove sector shaft nut and pitman arm.

NOTE: Do not damage seals.

4. Support steering gear and remove three retaining bolts. Remove flex coupling clamp bolt and work steering gear free of coupling and remove from vehicle.

INDEX OF SERVICE OPERATIONS

SERIAL & ENGINE NUMBER LOCATION
Vehicle Warranty Plate on Left Front Door Pillar

1974 Lincoln

ENGINE IDENTIFICATION

*Serial number on vehicle Warranty Plate.

Engine code for 1974–79 is the last letter in the serial number.

Year	Engine	Engine Code*
1974–78	V8-460	A
1974–79	V8-400	S
1977	V8-351W	H
1977–79	V8-302	F

1977-79 Continental

1974 Mark IV

1977-79 Mark V

1975-76 Mark IV

1975-76 Continental

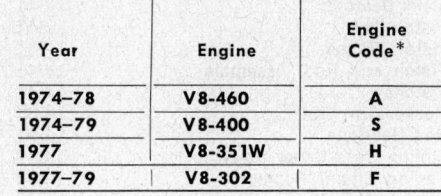
1977-79 Versailles

GENERAL ENGINE SPECIFICATIONS

Year	Engine	Car-buretor	Bore and Stroke	Piston Dis-place-ment, Cubic Inches	Com-pres-sion Ratio	Maximum Brake H.P. @ R.P.M.	Maximum Torque Lbs. Ft. @ R.P.M.	Normal Oil Pressure Pounds
1974	215 Horsepower①..........V8-460	4 Barrel	4.362 x 3.850	460	8.0	215 @ 4000	350 @ 2600	35–65
	220 Horsepower①..........V8-460	4 Barrel	4.362 x 3.850	460	8.0	220 @ 4000	355 @ 2600	35–65
1975	216 Horsepower①..........V8-460	4 Barrel	4.362 x 3.850	460	8.0	216 @ 4400	386 @ 2600	40–65
1976	202 Horsepower①..........V8-460	4 Barrel	4.362 x 3.850	460	8.0	202 @ 3800	352 @ 1600	40–65
1977	122 Horsepower............V8-302	2 Barrel	4.00 x 3.00	302	8.1	122 @ 3400	222 @ 1400	40–60
	135 Horsepower............V8-351	2 Barrel	4.00 x 3.50	351	8.1	135 @ 3200	275 @ 1600	45–65
	179 Horsepower①②.........V8-400	2 Barrel	4.00 x 4.00	400	8.0	179 @ 4000	329 @ 1600	45–75
	181 Horsepower①③.........V8-400	2 Barrel	4.00 x 4.00	400	8.0	181 @ 4000	331 @ 1600	45–75
	208 Horsepower①..........V8-460	4 Barrel	4.362 x 3.850	460	8.0	208 @ 4000	356 @ 2000	35–65
1978	133 Horsepower①..........V8-302	2 Barrel	4.00 x 3.00	302	8.1	133 @ 3600	243 @ 1600	40–60
	166 Horsepower①..........V8-400	2 Barrel	4.00 x 3.00	400	8.0	166 @ 3800	319 @ 1800	50–75
	210 Horsepower①..........V8-460	4 Barrel	4.362 x 3.850	460	8.0	210 @ 4200	357 @ 2200	35–65
1979	Horsepower................V8-302	2 Barrel						
	Horsepower................V8-400	2 Barrel						

①—Ratings are NET—as installed in the vehicle.　②—Exc. Calif.　③—Calif. only.

TUNE UP SPECIFICATIONS

The following specifications are published from the latest information available. This data should be used only in the absence of a decal affixed in the engine compartment.

★When using a timing light, disconnect vacuum hose or tube at distributor and plug opening in hose or tube so idle speed will not be affected.
●When checking compression, lowest cylinder must be within 75 percent of highest.
▲Before removing wires from distributor cap, determine location of No. 1 wire in cap, as distributor position may have been altered from that shown at the end of this chart.

| Year | Spark Plug | | Distributor | | Ignition Timing ★ | | | Carb. Adjustments | | | | | |
| | Type | Gap Inch | Point Gap Inch | Dwell Angle Deg. | Firing Order Fig. ▲ | Timing BTDC ① | Mark Fig. | Hot Idle Speed | | Air Fuel Ratio | | Idle CO % | |
								Std. Trans.	Auto. Trans.③	Std. Trans.	Auto. Trans.	Std. Trans.	Auto. Trans.
1974													
V8-460	ARF-52	.054	⑨	⑨	A	14°	B	—	650D	—	—	—	—
1975													
V8-460	ARF-52	.044	⑨	⑨	A	14°	B	—	650D	—	—	—	—
1976													
V8-460⑩	ARF-52	.044	⑨	⑨	A	8°③	B	—	650D⑤	—	—	—	—
V8-460④	ARF-52	.044	⑨	⑨	A	14°③	B	—	650D⑤	—	—	—	—
1977													
V8-302④	ARF-52	—	⑨	⑨	D	—	B	—	—	—	—	—	—
V8-302⑩	ARF-52	.050	⑨	⑨	D	12°	B	—	650	—	—	—	—
V8-351	ARF-52	.050	⑨	⑨	E	4°	B	—	625	—	—	—	—
V8-400⑩	ARF-52	.050	⑨	⑨	E	10°	B	—	600D	—	—	—	—
V8-460⑩	ARF-52	.050	⑨	⑨	D	10°	B	—	650D	—	—	—	—
1978													
V8-302⑦	ARF-52	.050	⑨	⑨	D	⑪⑫	B	—	⑬	—	—	—	—
V8-302④	ARF-52	.050	⑨	⑨	D	⑪⑮	B	—	600/625D⑭	—	—	—	—
V8-302⑧	ARF-52	.050	⑨	⑨	D	30°⑪⑰	B	—	625D	—	—	—	—
V8-400	ARF-52	.050	⑨	⑨	E	⑪⑯	B	—	⑱	—	—	—	—
V8-460	ARF-52	.050	⑨	⑨	D	⑪⑲	B	—	580/650D⑭	—	—	—	—
1979													
V8-302	ASF-52	.050	⑨	⑨	D	30°⑰	B	—	625D	—	—	—	—
V8-400	ASF-52	.050	⑨	⑨	E	14°	B	—	600/675D⑭	—	—	—	—

①—BTDC-Before top dead center.
②—D-Drive. N-Neutral.
③—In Drive with service & parking brakes applied.
④—California.
⑤—With A/C "On".
⑥—Exc. high altitude.
⑦—High altitude.
⑧—Exc. Calif. & high altitude.
⑨—Breakerless distributor.
⑩—Exc. Calif.
⑪—Must refer to engine decal due to running production changes.
⑫—Early production, 14° BTDC; Late production, 15° BTDC set in drive.
⑬—Early production, 650/725D⑭; Late production, 625D with A/C on.
⑭—Higher RPM is for A/C, A/C on.
⑮—Early production, 12° BTDC; Late production, 15° BTDC set in drive.
⑯—Exc. Calif. & High altitude, 13° BTDC; Calif., 16° BTDC; High altitude, 8° BTDC.
⑰—Set in drive.
⑱—Exc. Calif. & High altitude, 575/650D⑭; Calif. 600/650D⑭; High altitude, 650D.
⑲—Early production 16° BTDC; Late production 10° BTDC.

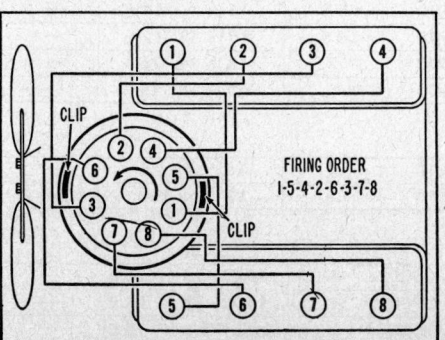

FIRING ORDER 1-5-4-2-6-3-7-8

Fig. A

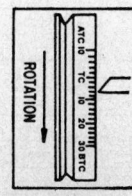

Fig. B

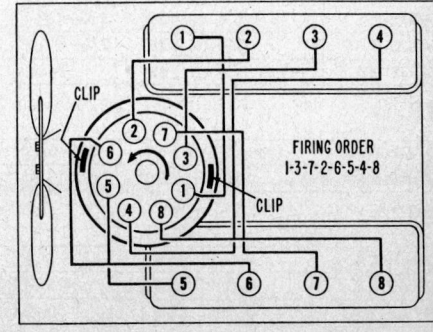

FIRING ORDER 1-3-7-2-6-5-4-8

Fig. C

TUNE UP NOTES—Continued

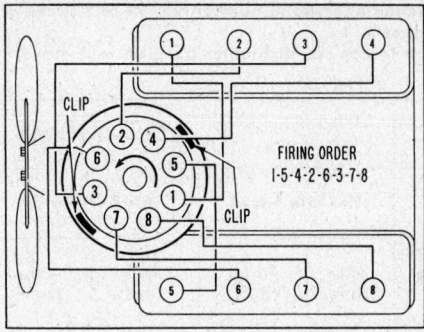

Fig. D

FIRING ORDER
1-5-4-2-6-3-7-8

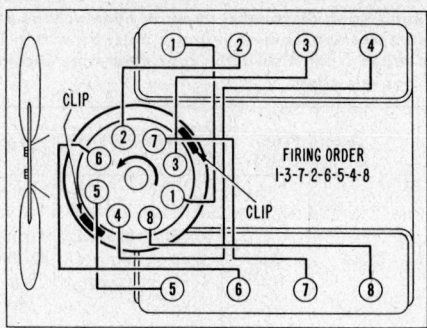

Fig. E

FIRING ORDER
1-3-7-2-6-5-4-8

DISTRIBUTOR SPECIFICATIONS

★Note: If unit is checked on vehicle, double the RPM and degrees to get crankshaft figures.

Breaker arm spring tension—17–21.

Distributor Ident. No.①	Centrifugal Advance Degrees @ RPM of Distributor					Vacuum Advance		Distributor Retard
	Advance Starts	Intermediate Advance			Full Advance	Inches of Vacuum to Start Plunger	Max. Adv. Dist. Deg. @ Vacuum	Max. Retard Dist. Deg. @ Vacuum
1974-75								
D4VE-CA	0–½ @ 500	0–½ @ 750	3–5 @ 1000	7–9 @ 1500	9½ @ 2000	5	11¼ @ 20	—
D5VE-BA	—	—			—	—	—	—
1976								
D4VE-CA	−¾ to +½ @ 500	−1¼–+½ @ 700	—		5 @ 1000	5	11¼ @ 15	—
D5VE-CA	−1 to +½ @ 500	½–2½ @ 700	—		6½ @ 1000	5	13¼ @ 15	—
D6VE-AA	0–2½ @ 500	4½–6½ @ 700	—		9 @ 1000	5	13½ @ 15	—
D6VE-BA	−1 to +2¾ @ 500	6–9½ @ 700	—		11¾ @ 1000	5	13¼ @ 15	—
D6VE-CA	−½ to +3 @ 500	6–9½ @ 700	—		10¼ @ 1000	5	13¼ @ 15	—
1977								
D6AE-AA	0–2 @ 500	4–6 @ 700	7¼–9½ @ 1500		14 @ 2500	3	15¼ @ 11½	—
D6VE-CA	0–1 @ 450	7½–9½ @ 725	—		14 @ 2500	3.5	13¼ @ 15	—
D7AE-DA	0–1 @ 450	3¾–5¾ @ 675	—		14 @ 2500	3.2	15¼ @ 14½	—
D7DE-FA	−1 to +1½ @ 450	1¾–4½ @ 550	—		13¾ @ 2500	4.5	15¼ @ 12½	—
D7DE-GA	0–1 @ 525	2¼–4¼ @ 700	—		7¼ @ 2500	3	13½ @ 16	—
D7DE-HA	−1 to +½ @ 550	2–4 @ 750	—		6½ @ 2500	5	12½ @ 15	—
1978								
D7DE-AA	−1 to +½ @ 500	2¾–5 @ 1000	—		12½ @ 2500	3	15½ @ 16	—
D8DE-EA	0–3 @ 500	4–6½ @ 1000	—		12¼ @ 2500	3	13¼ @ 16	—
1979								
D6VE-CA	0–1 @ 450	7.5–9.5 @ 725	—		11.25–14 @ 2500	4	10.75–13 @ 15.5	—
D7VE-CA	0–1 @ 450	4.5–7 @ 725	—		7.25–10 @ 2500	4	10.75–13 @ 15.5	—
D7AE-VA	0–1 @ 650	0–2 @ 700	—		7.5–10.5 @ 2500	1	10.75–13.5 @ 15.5	—
D8AE-BA	0–1 @ 450	4–6 @ 700	—		11.25–14 @ 2500	4	15.75–17 @ 14.5	—

①—Basic part No. 12127.

STARTING MOTOR SPECIFICATIONS

Year	Car Model	Ident. No.	Brush Spring Tension Ounces	No Load Test			Torque Test		
				Amperes	Volts	R.P.M.	Amperes	Volts	Torque Lbs. Ft.
1974	All	D4VF-AB	80	90	12	—	—	—	—
1975	All	D5AF-AB	40	70	12	—	—	—	—
1976	All	D6AF-AA	40	70	12	—	—	—	—
1977	V8-302, 351	D80F-AA	80	80	12	—	670	5.0	15½
	V8-400	D5AF-EA	80	80	12	—	670	5.0	15½
	V8-460	D6AF-AA	40	70	12	—	—	—	—
1978–79	V8-302	D80F-AA	80	80	12	—	670	5.0	15½
	V8-400	D8AF-AA	80	80	12	—	670	5.0	15½
	V8-460	D8AF-BA	—						

ALTERNATOR & REGULATOR SPECIFICATIONS

Year	Ident. No.①	Current Rating②		Field Current @ 75°F.		Voltage Regulator				Field Relay	
		Amperes	Volts	Amperes	Volts	Ident. No. ③⑥	Voltage @ 75°F.	Contact Gap	Armature Air Gap	Armature Air Gap	Closing Voltage @ 75°F.
1974	All Red④	55	15	2.9	12	D4TZ-A	—	—	—	—	—
	All Green④	61	15	2.9	12	D4TZ-A	—	—	—	—	—
	All	70	15	2.9	12	D4TZ-A	—	—	—	—	—
	All	90	15	2.9	12	D4TZ-A	—	—	—	—	—
1975–76	Green④	60	15	2.9	12	D4AF-AA	13.5–15.3	—	—	—	2.5–4.0
	All	70	15	2.9	12	D4TF-AA	13.5–15.3	—	—	—	2.5–4.0
	All	90	15	2.9	12	D4TF-AA	13.5–15.3	—	—	—	2.5–4.0
1977	Orange④	40	15	2.9	12	D4AF-AA	13.5–15.3	—	—	—	—
	Green④	60	15	2.9	12	D4AF-AA	13.5–15.3	—	—	—	—
	70 All	70	15	2.9	12	D4AF-AA	13.5–15.3	—	—	—	—
	90 All	90	15	2.9	12	D4TF-AA	13.5–15.3	—	—	—	—
1978	Orange④	40	15	2.9	12	D4AF-AA	13.5–15.3	—	—	—	—
	Green④	60	15	2.9	12	D4AF-AA	13.5–15.3	—	—	—	—
	Green④⑦	60	15	4.0	12	D8BF-AA⑧	14.0–14.4	—	—	—	—
	Black④	70	15	2.9	12	D4AF-AA	13.5–15.3	—	—	—	—
	Red④	90	15	2.9	12	D4TF-AA	13.5–15.3	—	—	—	—
	Red④⑦	90	15	4.0	12	D8BF-AA⑧	14.0–14.4	—	—	—	—
1979	D9UF-BA	60				D8BF-AA⑧	13.8–14.6	—	—	—	—
	D8VF-AA	60				D8BF-AA⑧	14.0–14.4	—	—	—	—
	D94F-AA	65				D8BF-AA⑧	13.8–14.6	—	—	—	—
	D9VF-AA	65				D8BF-AA⑧	14.0–14.4	—	—	—	—
	D8VF-BA	70				D8BF-AA⑧	14.0–14.4	—	—	—	—
	D8VF-CA	70				D8BF-AA⑧	14.0–14.4	—	—	—	—

①—Basic No. 10300.
②—Stamped on housing.
③—Stamped on cover.
④—Stamp color code.
⑥—Basic No. 10316.
⑦—Solid state alternator.
⑧—Electronic voltage regulator. These units are color coded black for system w/warning indicator lamp & blue for systems w/ammeter.

VALVE SPECIFICATIONS

Year	Engine Model	Valve Lash		Valve Angles		Valve Spring Installed Height	Valve Spring Pressure Lbs. @ In.	Stem Clearance		Stem Diameter	
		Int.	Exh.	Seat	Face			Intake	Exhaust	Intake	Exhaust
1974-75	V8-460	①	②	45	44	1¹³⁄₁₆	252 @ 1.33	.0010–.0027	.0010–.0027	.3416–.3423	.3416–.3423
1976	V8-460	.100–.150②		45	44	1¹³⁄₁₆	229 @ 1.33	.0010–.0027	.0010–.0027	.3416–.3423	.3416–.3423
1977	V8-302	.096–.168②		45	44	⑥	⑦	.0010–.0027	.0015–.0032	.3416–.3423	.3411–.3418
	V8-351	.096–.168②		45	44	⑥	⑧	.0010–.0027	.0015–.0032	.3416–.3423	.3411–.3418
	V8-400	.100–.200②		45	44	1¹³⁄₁₆	226 @ 1.39	.0010–.0027	.0015–.0032	.3416–.3423	.3411–.3418
	V8-460	.075–.175②		45	44	1¹³⁄₁₆	④	.0010–.0027	.0010–.0027	.3416–.3423	.3416–.3423
1978	V8-302③	.096–.168③		45	44	⑤	⑦	.0010–.0027	.0015–.0032	.3416–.3423	.3411–.3418
	V8-302⑧	②⑨		45	44	⑥	⑦	.0010–.0027	.0015–.0032	.3416–.3423	.3411–.3418
	V8-400	.125–.175②		45	44	1⁵³⁄₆₄	226 @ 1.39	.0010–.0027	.0015–.0032	.3416–.3423	.3411–.3418
	V8-460	.100–.150②		45	44	1¹³⁄₁₆	229 @ 1.33	.0010–.0027	.0010–.0027	.3416–.3423	.3416–.3423

①—1974, .075–.125; 1975, .100–.150.
②—Clearance is obtained at valve stem tip with hydraulic lifter collapsed. If clearance is less than minimum, install an undersize push rod; if clearance is greater than maximum, install an oversize push rod.
③—Early 1978 engines.
④—Intake, 229 @ 1.33; exhaust, 253 @ 1.33.
⑤—Intake; 1¹¹⁄₁₆; exhaust, 1³⁹⁄₆₄.
⑥—Intake, 1⁵¹⁄₆₄; exhaust, 1³⁹⁄₆₄.
⑦—Intake, 190–210 @ 1.31; exhaust, 190–210 @ 1.20.
⑧—Late 1978 engines.
⑨—Exc. Calif., .121; Calif., .142.

BRAKE SPECIFICATIONS

Year	Model	Brake Drum Inside Diameter	Wheel Cylinder Bore Diameter			Master Cylinder Bore Diameter		
			Front Disc Brakes	Front Drum Brakes	Rear Brakes	With Disc Brakes	With Drum Brakes	With Power Brakes
1974	Lincoln	11.030	3.100	—	1.000	1	—	1
	Mark IV	11.030	3.100	—	1.000	1	—	1
1975	Lincoln	11.030	3.100	—	1.000②	1①	—	1①
	Mark IV	③	3.100	—	2.6	1⅛	—	1⅛
1976	Lincoln	11.030	3.100	—	1.000②	1①	—	1①
	Mark IV	③	3.100	—	2.6	1⅛	—	1⅛
1977	Lincoln	11.030	3.100	—	1.000②	1.00①	—	1.00①
	Mark V	③	3.100	—	2.6	1⅛	—	1⅛
	Versailles	③	2.6	—	2.125	1.00	—	1.00
1978	Lincoln	11.030	3.1	—	1.000③	1.25	—	1.25
	Mark V	③	3.1	—	2.6	1.25	—	1.25
	Versailles	③	2.6	—	2.125	1.00	—	1.00

①—With 4 wheel disc brakes, 1⅛".
②—On models with 4 wheel disc brakes, 2.6".
③—4 wheel disc brakes.

ENGINE TIGHTENING SPECIFICATIONS★

★Torque specifications are for clean and lightly lubricated threads only. Dry or dirty threads produce increased friction which prevents accurate measurement of tightness.

Year	Model	Spark Plugs Ft. Lbs.	Cylinder Head Bolts Ft. Lbs.	Intake Manifold Ft. Lbs.	Exhaust Manifold Ft. Lbs.	Rocker Arm Shaft Bracket Ft. Lbs.	Rocker Arm Cover Ft. Lbs.	Connecting Rod Cap Bolts Ft. Lbs.	Main Bearing Cap Bolts Ft. Lbs.	Flywheel to Crankshaft Ft. Lbs.	Vibration Damper or Pulley Ft. Lbs.
1974	V8-460	15–20	130–140	22–32	28–33	18–25①	5–6	40–45	95–105	75–85	70–90
1975	V8-460	10–15	130–140	25–30	28–33	18–25①	5–6	40–45	95–105	75–85	70–90
1976	V8-460	10–15	130–140	22–32	28–33	18–25①	5–6	40–45	95–105	75–85	70–90
1977–78	V8-302	10–15	65–72	25–32	18–24		③	3–5	19–24	60–70	75–85	70–90
	V8-351	10–15	105–112	25–32	18–24		③	3–5	40–45	95–105	75–85	70–90
	V8-400	10–15	95–105	②	18–24	18–25①	3–5	40–45	95–105	75–85	70–90
	V8-460	10–15	130–140	22–32	28–33	18–25①	5–6	40–45	95–105	75–85	70–90

①—Rocker arm fulcrum bolt to cyl. head.
②—5/16″ bolts, 17–25 ft. lbs.; 3/8″ bolts, 22–32 ft. lbs.
③—1977 & early 1978, rocker arm stud nut 17–23 ft. lbs.; late 1978, rocker arm fulcrum bolt to cyl. head 18–25 ft. lbs.

PISTONS, PINS, RINGS, CRANKSHAFT & BEARINGS

Year	Model	Piston Clearance	Ring End Gap① Comp.	Ring End Gap① Oil	Wrist-pin Diameter	Rod Bearings Shaft Diameter	Rod Bearings Bearing Clearance	Main Bearings Shaft Diameter	Main Bearings Bearing Clearance	Thrust on Bear. No.	Shaft End Play
1974	V8-460	.0022–.0030	.010	.015	1.040	2.4992–2.5000	.0008–.0028	2.9994–3.0002	②	3	.004–.008
1975	V8-460	.0014–.0022	.010	.015	1.040	2.4992–2.5000	.0008–.0015	2.9994–3.0002	③	3	.004–.008
1976	V8-460	.0014–.0022	.010	.015	1.040	2.4992–2.5000	.0008–.0015	2.9994–3.0002	.0008–.0015	3	.004–.008
1977	V8-302	.0018–.0026	.010	.015	.9121	2.1232–2.1240	.0008–.0026	2.2482–2.2490	.0005–.0024	3	.004–.008
	V8-351	.0018–.0026	.010	.015	.9121	2.3103–2.3111	.0008–.0026	2.9996–3.0002	.0008–.0026	3	.004–.008
	V8-400	.0014–.0022	.010	.015	.9752	2.3103–2.3111	.0008–.0015	2.9994–3.0002	.0009–.0015	3	.004–.008
	V8-460	.0014–.0022	.010	.015	1.040	2.4992–2.5000	.0008–.0028	2.9994–3.0002	④	3	.004–.008
1978	V8-302	.0018–.0026	.010	.015	.9121	2.1232	.0007–.0024	2.2486	⑤	3	.004–.008
	V8-400	.0014–.0022	.010	.015	.9752	2.3107	.0008–.0025	2.9998	.0008–.0026	3	.004–.008
	V8-460	.0014–.0022	.010	.015	1.040	2.4992–2.5000	.0008–.0026	2.9998	④	3	.004–.008

①—Fit rings in tapered bores for clearance listed in tightest portion of ring travel.
②—#1 .0004–.002; others .0012–.0028.
③—#1 .0004–.0015; others, .0009–.0015.
④—#1 .0004–.0020; others, .0009–.0027.
⑤—#1 .0001–.002; others, .0005–.0024.

REAR AXLE SPECIFICATIONS

Year	Model	Carrier Type	Ring Gear & Pinion Backlash Inch	Nominal Pinion Locating Shim, Inch	Pinion Bearing Preload New Bearings With Seal Inch-Lbs.	Pinion Bearing Preload Used Bearings With Seal Inch-Lbs.	Pinion Bearing Preload New Bearings Less Seal Inch-Lbs.	Pinion Bearing Preload Used Bearings Less Seal Inch-Lbs.	Differential Bearing Preload	Pinion Nut Torque Ft.-Lbs.
1974–78	All	Removable	.008–.012	.015	17–27①	8–14①	—	—	.008–.012②	③

①—Bearing set with collapsible spacer; with solid spacer 13–33 inch-lbs.
②—Case spread with new bearings; with used bearings .005–.008″.
③—With collapsible spacer 170 ft. lbs., with solid spacer 200 ft. lbs.

LINCOLN CONTINENTAL & VERSAILLES

WHEEL ALIGNMENT SPECIFICATIONS

| Year | Model | Caster Angle, Degrees | | Camber Angle, Degrees | | | | Toe-In. Inch | Toe-Out on Turns, Deg.[1] | |
| | | Limits | Desired | Limits | | Desired | | | Outer Wheel | Inner Wheel |
				Left	Right	Left	Right			
1974	Lincoln	−½ to +3½	+1½	−½ to +1½	−½ to +1½	+½	+½	⅛	18.16	20
1971	Mark III	−1 to +3	+1	−½ to +1½	−½ to +1½	+½	+½	3/16	19.28	20
1972	Mark IV	−1 to +3	+1	−¼ to +1¾	−¼ to +1¾	+¾	+¾	3/16	17.74	20
1973	Mark IV	−½ to +3½	+1½	−¼ to +1¾	−¼ to +1¾	+¾	+¾	3/16	17.74	20
1974	Mark IV	+¼ to +3¼	+1¾	−¼ to +1¾	−¾ to +1¼	+¾	+¼	3/16	18.07	20
1975–76	Lincoln	+1¼ to +2¾	+2	−¼ to +1¼	−½ to +1	+½	+¼	⅛	18.16	20
	Mark IV	+1¼ to +2¾	+4	−¼ to +1¼	−½ to +1	+½	+¼	3/16	18.09	20
1977	Versailles	−1¼ to +¼	−½	−½ to +1	−½ to +1	+¼	+¼	⅛	[2]	20
	Lincoln	+1¼ to +2¾	+2	−¼ to +1¼	−½ to +1	+½	+¼	⅛	18.16	20
	Mark V	+1¼ to +2¾	+2	−¼ to +1¼	−½ to +1	+½	+¼	3/16	18.09	20
1978	Lincoln	+1¼ to 2¾	+2	−¼ to 1¼	−½ to +1	+½	+¼	⅛	18.16	20
	Mark V	+3¼ to +4¾	+4	−¼ to +1¼	−½ to +1	+½	+¼	3/16	18.09	20
	Versailles	−1¼ to +¼	−½	−½ to +1	−½ to +1	+¼	+¼	⅛	[2]	20

[1]—Incorrect toe-out, when other adjustments are correct, indicates bent steering arms.
[2]—With power steering; 18.20 & Without 18.43.

COOLING SYSTEM & CAPACITY DATA

| Year | Model or Engine | Cooling Capacity, Qts. | | | Radiator Cap Relief Pressure, Lbs. | | Thermo. Opening Temp. [1] | Fuel Tank Gals. | Engine Oil Refill Qts. [3] | Transmission Oil | | | Rear Axle Oil Pints |
		No Heater	With Heater	With A/C	With A/C	No A/C				3 Speed Pints	4 Speed Pints	Auto. Trans. Qts. [5]	
1974	Lincoln	—	20½	20½	12–16	12–16	191	22	4	—	—	12½	5
	Mark IV	—	20½	20½	12–16	12–16	191	26½	4	—	—	12½	5
1975	Lincoln	—	—	19¾	12–16	12–16	191	24¼	4	—	—	12½	5
	Mark IV	—	—	20	12–16	12–16	191	26½	4	—	—	12½	5
1976	Lincoln	—	—	19.7	12–16	12–16	191	24¼[6]	4	—	—	12½	5
	Mark IV	—	—	19.8	12–16	12–16	191	26½	4	—	—	12½	5
1977	Lincoln	—	[8]	[8]	12–16	12–16	191	24.2[9]	4	—	—	[7]	5
	Mark V	—	[11]	[11]	12–16	12–16	191	24.2[9]	4	—	—	[7]	5
	Versailles	[4]	[10]	[10]	14–18	14–18	191	19.2	4	—	—	10	5
1978	Lincoln	[12]	[13]	[13]	14–18	14–18	191	24.2	4	—	—	12½	5
	Mark V	[14]	[5]	[5]	14–18	14–18	191	25	4	—	—	[7]	5
	Versailles	13.8	14.2	14.3	14–18	14–18	191	19.2	4	—	—	10¼	5

[1]—With permanent type anti-freeze.
[2]—Add one quart with filter change.
[3]—Approximate. Make final check with dipstick.
[4]—V8-302, 13.8; V8-351, 14.9.
[5]—V8-400, 16.9; V8-460, 18.9.
[6]—Add 8 gals. with auxiliary tank.
[7]—FMX, 11 qts.; C6, 12½ qts.
[8]—V8-400, 17.1; V8-460, 18.5.
[9]—Calif. V8-400, 20.0.
[10]—V8-302, 14.6; V8-351, 15.7.
[11]—V8-400, 17.5; V8-460, 19.4.
[12]—V8-400, 16.2; V8-460, 17.9.
[13]—V8-400, 17.0; V8-460, 18.7.
[14]—V8-400, 16.7; V8-460, 18.2.

Electrical Section

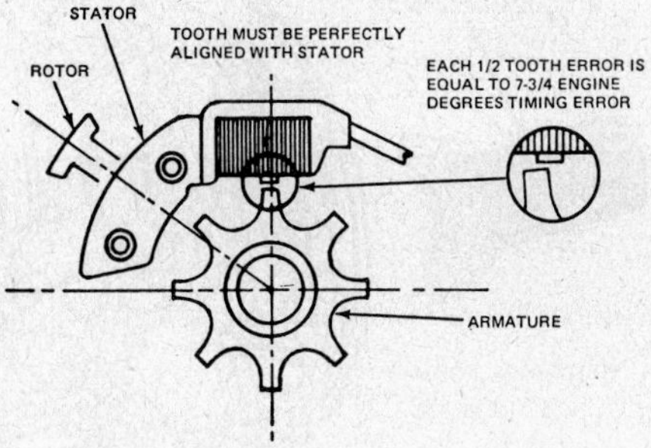

DISTRIBUTOR, REPLACE

Removal

1. On vehicles with conventional ignition systems, disconnect primary wire from ignition coil. On vehicles with electronic ignition, disconnect harness connector from engine wiring.
2. Disconnect vacuum control line and remove distributor cap.
3. Scribe a mark on the distributor body indicating the position of the rotor, and scribe another mark on the body and engine block indicating position of distributor body in block. These marks can be used as guides when installing distributor in a correctly timed engine.
4. Remove hold down screw or screws and lift distributor out of block. *Do not crank engine while distributor is removed or the initial timing operation will have to be performed.*

Installation

If the crankshaft has not been disturbed, install the distributor, using the scribed marks previously made on the distributor body and engine block as guides.

If the crankshaft has been rotated while the distributor was removed from the engine, it will be necessary to retime the engine. Crank the engine to bring No. 1 piston on top dead center of its compression stroke. Align the timing mark on the vibration damper or pulley with the timing pointer (see *Tune Up* chart). On models with electronic ignition, install distributor so that armature tooth is aligned with stator and rotor is pointing to No. 1 spark plug wire, Fig. 1. On models with breaker type ignition, install the distributor so that the rotor points to the No. 1 spark plug wire terminal in the distributor cap.

NOTE: Make sure the oil pump intermediate shaft properly engages the distributor shaft. It may be necessary to crank the engine with the starter, after the distributor drive gear is properly engaged, in order to engage the oil pump intermediate shaft.

CAUTION: When checking ignition timing on 1977-79 models using an inductive pickup type timing light, a length of split vacuum hose should be installed around the plug wire.

STARTER, REPLACE

1977-79 Versailles

1. Disconnect battery ground cable, then raise vehicle on a hoist.
2. Disconnect starter cable at starter terminal.
3. Remove through bolt and nut attach-

Fig. 1   Distributor stator & armature alignment. Breakerless distributor installation

ing motor mount insulator to mounting bracket.
4. Using a suitable jack raise engine.
5. Remove starter mounting bolts, then remove starter.

1974-79 Except Versailles

1. Disconnect battery ground cable and support vehicle on hoist.
2. Disconnect cable and wires from solenoid.
3. On 1974-76 Mark IV models and 1977-79 Mark V, loosen the two front brace retaining bolts, then remove all other brace retaining bolts and allow brace to hang.
4. Turn wheels fully to the right and remove the two bolts attaching the steering idler arm to the frame.
5. Remove starter attaching bolts and remove starter.

IGNITION LOCK, REPLACE

1974-78

1. Disconnect the battery ground cable.
2. **Units With Fixed Steering Columns:** Remove the steering wheel trim pad and steering wheel. Insert a wire pin in the hole located inside the column halfway down the lock cylinder housing, Fig. 2. **Units With Tilt Steering Columns:** Insert wire pin in the hole located on the outside of the flange casting next to the emergency flasher button, Fig. 2.
3. Place the gear shift lever in *Park* position, and turn the lock cylinder with the ignition key to the *Run* position.
4. Depress the wire pin while pulling up on the lock cylinder to remove. Remove the wire pin.
5. To install insert the lock cylinder into the housing in the flange casting, and turn the key to the *Off* position. Be certain that the cylinder is fully inserted before turning to the *Off* position. This action will extend the cylinder retaining pin into the cylinder housing.
6. Turn the key to check for correct operation in all positions.

7. Install the steering wheel and trim pad on fixed column units.
8. Connect the battery ground cable.

IGNITION SWITCH, REPLACE

1977-79 Mark V & Versailles

1. On 1977-79 Mark V, remove instrument cluster as described under "Instrument Cluster, Replace".
2. On all models, disconnect battery ground cable.
3. Remove steering column shroud, then detach and lower steering column from brake support bracket.
4. Disconnect switch wiring, then remove two nuts retaining switch to steering column, Fig. 3.
5. Lift switch vertically upward to disengage actuator rod, then remove switch.
6. When installing ignition switch, both locking mechanism at top of column and ignition switch must be in Lock position for correct adjustment. To hold mechanical parts in column in Lock position, move shift lever to Park, then turn key to Lock position and remove key.

NOTE: New replacement switches are pinned in Lock position by a metal pin inserted in locking hole located on side of switch. For existing switch, move switch carrier using a .010 in. diameter rod to lock detent. Insert a 5/64 in. drill bit into lock hole on side of switch to hold switch in Lock position.

7. Connect switch plunger to actuator rod.
8. Position switch on column and install retaining nuts, but do not tighten.
9. Move switch up and down along column to locate mid-position of rod lash, then tighten switch retaining nuts.
10. Remove locking pin, then connect battery ground cable and check switch for proper operation.
11. Attaching steering column to brake support and install steering column shroud.
12. On 1977-79 Mark V models, install instrument cluster.

1974-76 All & 1977-79 Continental

1. Disconnect battery ground cable.
2. On 1978-79 models, remove instrument cluster as described under Instrument Cluster, Replace.
3. On all models, remove shrouding from steering column and detach and lower steering column from brake support bracket.
4. Disconnect switch wiring at multiple plug, Figs. 3 and 4.
5. Remove two nuts that retain switch to column.
6. Detach switch plunger from actuator rod and remove the switch.

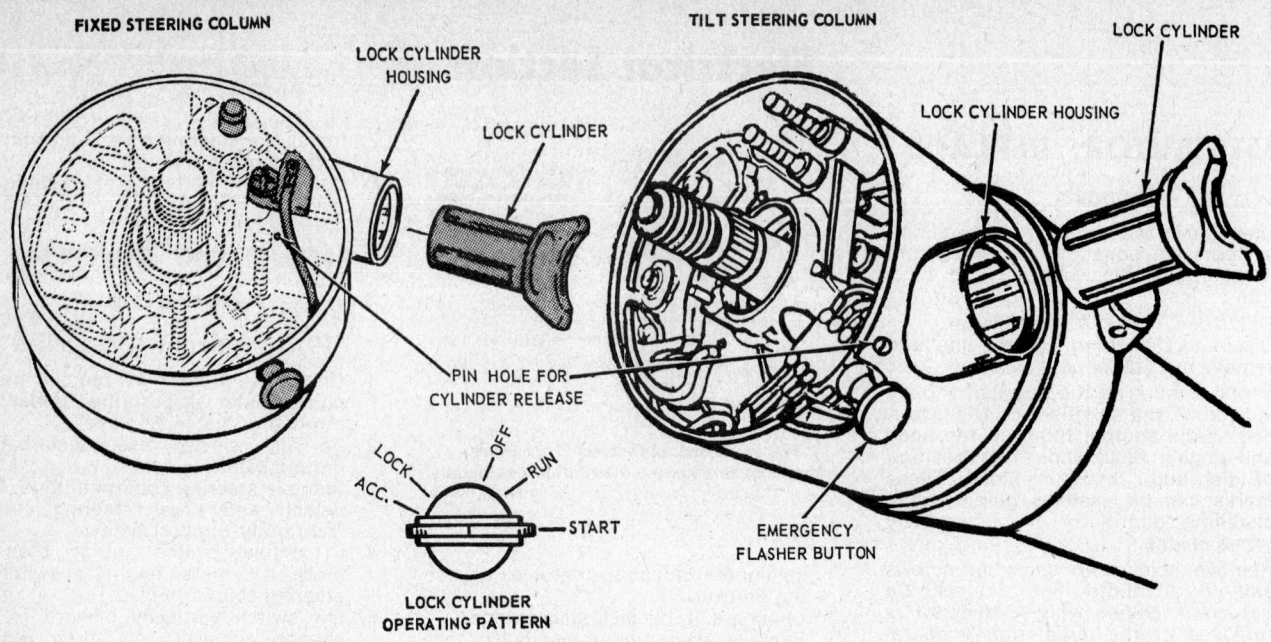

FIXED STEERING COLUMN

LOCK CYLINDER HOUSING

LOCK CYLINDER

TILT STEERING COLUMN

LOCK CYLINDER HOUSING

LOCK CYLINDER

PIN HOLE FOR CYLINDER RELEASE

LOCK
ACC.
OFF
RUN
START

LOCK CYLINDER OPERATING PATTERN

EMERGENCY FLASHER BUTTON

Fig. 2   Ignition lock cylinder

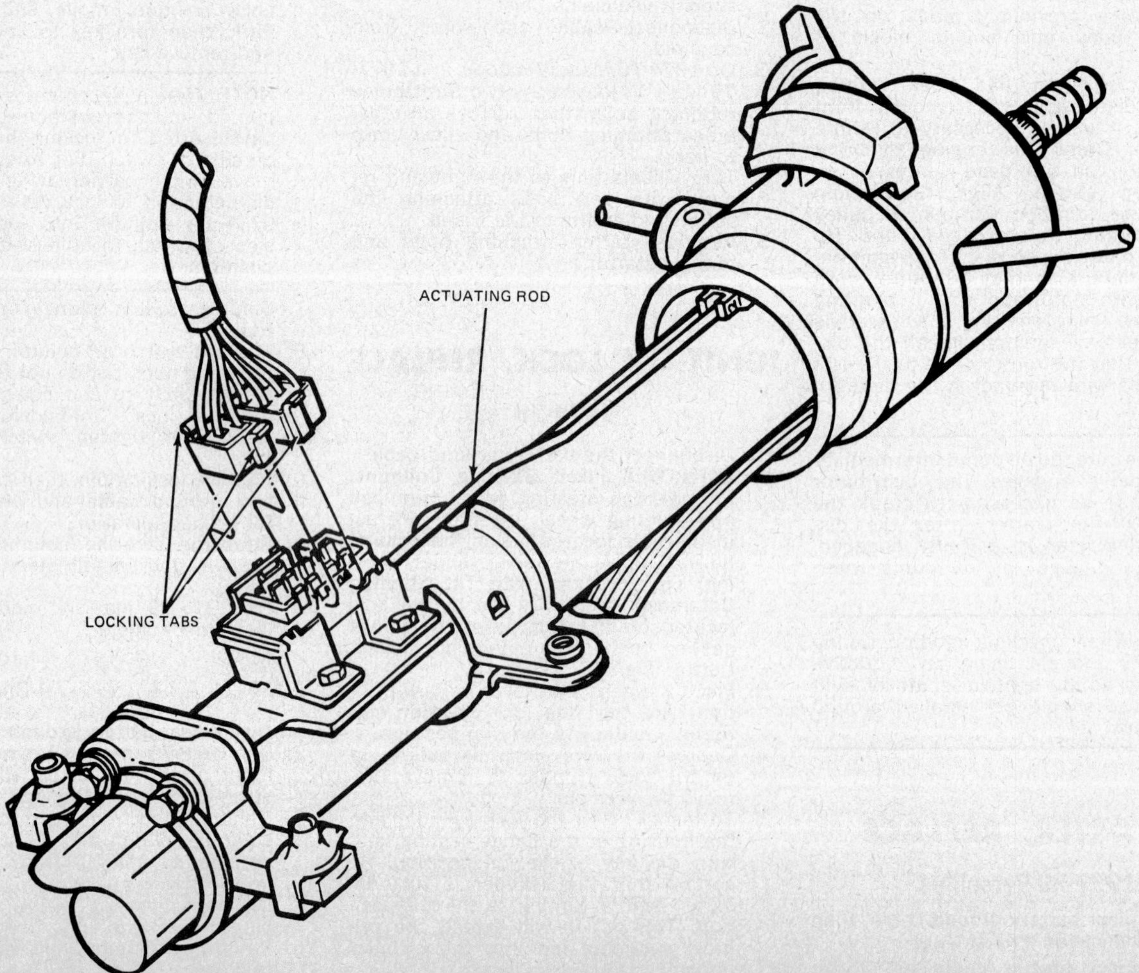

ACTUATING ROD

LOCKING TABS

Fig. 3   Ignition switch installation. 1974-76 Mark IV & 1977-79 Mark V & Versailles

6. Move shift lever to Park position. Place ignition key in Lock position and remove the key.

NOTE: New replacement switches are pinned in the Lock position by a plastic shipping pin inserted in a locking hole in the switch. For an existing switch, pull plunger out as far as it will go then back one detent to Lock position and insert a 3/32" drill in locking hole to retain switch in Lock position.

7. With locking pin in place, install switch on steering column, determine mid position of actuator lash and tighten retaining bolts.
8. Remove locking pin.
9. Attach steering column to brake support and install shrouding.
10. On 1978-79 models, install instrument cluster.

LIGHT SWITCH, REPLACE

1974-76 Mark IV & 1977-79 Mark V

1. Disconnect battery ground cable.
2. Remove instrument cluster trim panel.
3. Remove the headlight switch mounting plate.
4. Remove bezel nut and disconnect multiple connector.
5. Remove vacuum lines, if so equipped.
6. Remove the switch.

1974-79 Continental & 1977-79 Versailles

1. Disconnect battery ground cable.
2. Remove control knob and shaft by pressing knob release button and pulling it out of switch housing, Fig. 5.
3. Remove bezel nut and lower switch assembly.
4. Disconnect multiple plug and vacuum hoses at switch body and remove switch.
5. Reverse procedure to install.

STOP LIGHT SWITCH, REPLACE

1974-79

1. Disconnect wires at switch connector.

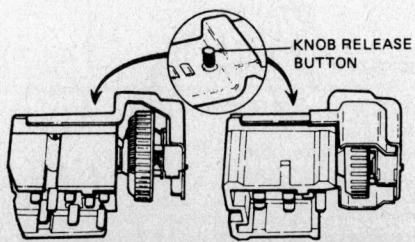

Fig. 5   Light switch. 1974-79 (typical)

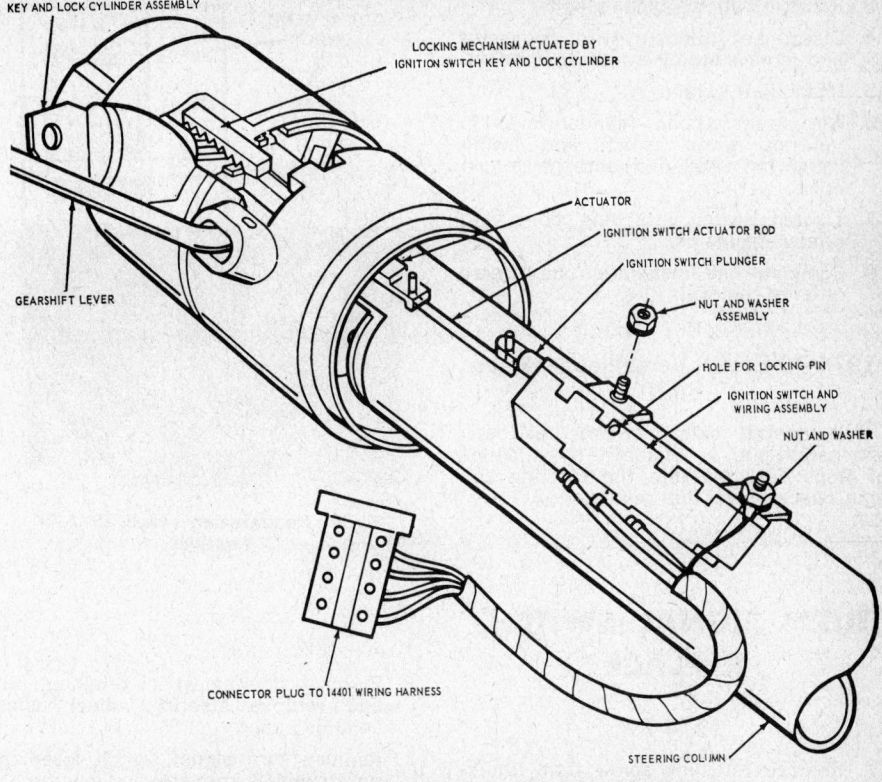

Fig. 4   Ignition switch installation. 1974-79 Continental

2. Remove hairpin retainer, slide switch, push rod and nylon washers and bushing away from brake pedal, and remove switch, Fig. 6.

NOTE: On 1977-79 Versailles models, loosen brake booster nuts at pedal support approximately 1/4 inch so booster is free to move to eliminate binding during switch removal.

3. Reverse above procedure to install.

NEUTRAL SAFETY SWITCH

1977-79 Versailles W/Floor Shift

Transmission Mounted Switch, Fig. 7

1. Remove downshift linkage rod from transmission downshift lever.
2. Apply penetrating oil to downshift lever shaft and nut; then remove downshift outer lever.

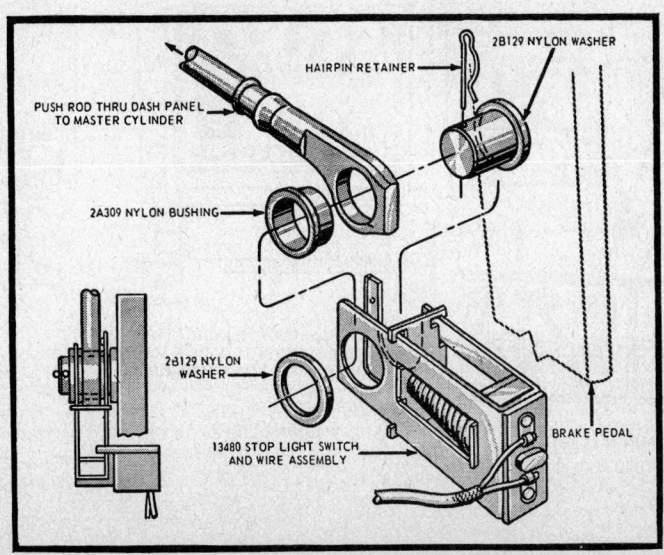

Fig. 6   Stop light switch. 1974-79

3. Remove switch attaching bolts.

4. Disconnect multiple wire connector and remove switch from transmission.

5. Install new switch.

6. With transmission manual lever in neutral, rotate switch and install gauge pin (#43 drill) into gauge pin holes.

7. Tighten switch attaching bolts and remove gauge pin.

8. Complete the installation in reverse order of removal.

1974-79 Except Versailles W/Floor Shift

The neutral safety switch has been eliminated and is replaced by a series of steps designed into the steering column selector lever hub casting.

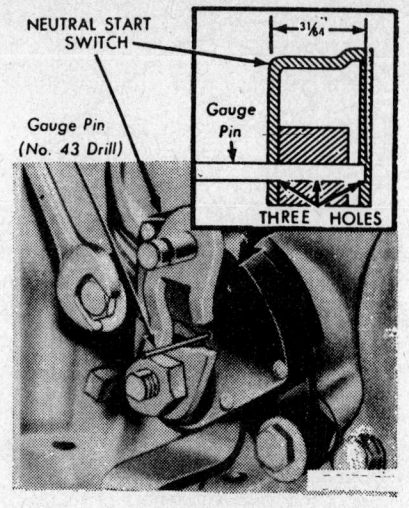

Fig. 7   Neutral safety switch. 1977-79 Versailles

TURN SIGNAL SWITCH, REPLACE

1974-79

1. Remove retaining screw from underside of steering wheel spoke and lift off the pad horn switch/trim cover and medallion as an assembly.

2. Disconnect horn switch wires from terminals.

3. Remove steering wheel retaining nut and remove steering wheel using suitable puller.

4. Remove turn signal switch lever by unscrewing it from steering column.

5. Remove shroud from under steering column.

6. Disconnect steering column wiring connector plugs and remove the screws that secure switch assembly to the column.

7. On vehicles with tilt column, remove wires and terminals from steering column wiring connector plug.

NOTE: *Record the color code and location of each wire before removing it from connector. A hole provided in the flange on fixed columns makes it unnecessary to separate the wires from the connector plug. The plug with wires installed can be guided through the hole.*

8. Remove the plastic cover sleeve from the wiring harness and remove the switch and wires from the top of the column.

HORN SOUNDER & STEERING WHEEL

1974-79 All

1. Disconnect battery ground cable.

2. Remove screws from behind wheel spoke holding crash pad to wheel. Lift pad and disconnect horn wires. Disconnect speed control wires if used and remove pad.

3. Remove steering wheel nut. Install a suitable puller and remove steering wheel.

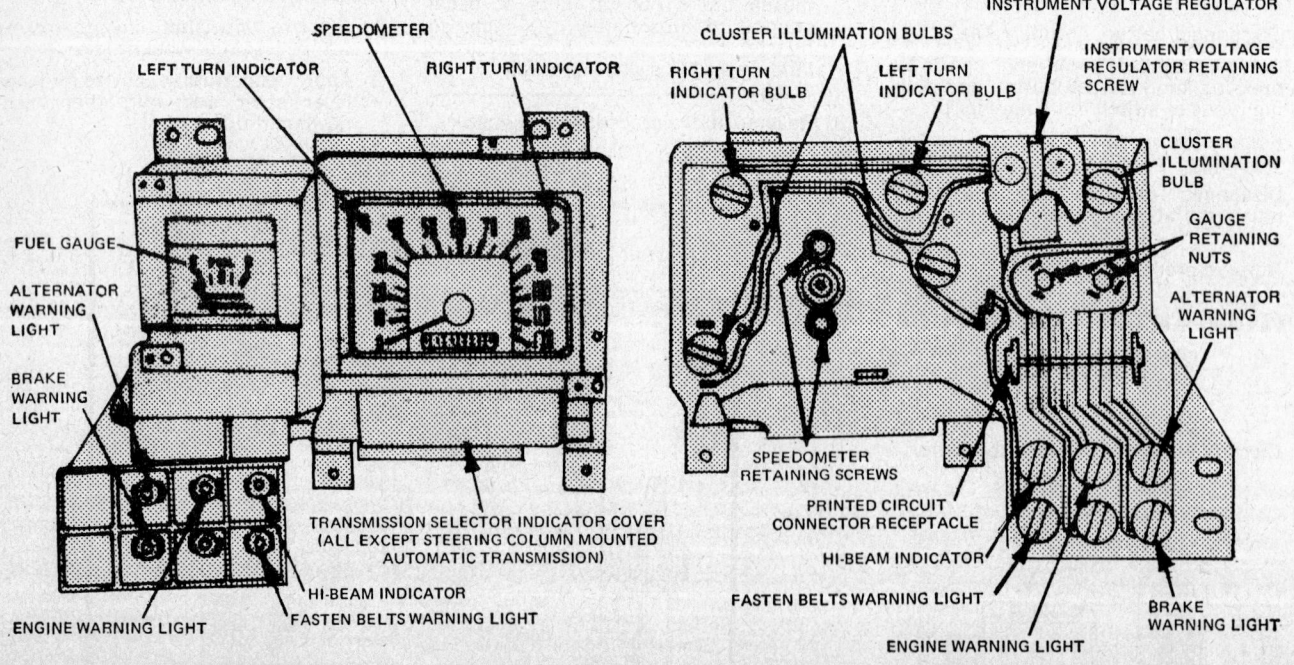

FRONT ASSEMBLED VIEW   BACK ASSEMBLED VIEW

Fig. 8   Instrument cluster. 1977-78 Versailles

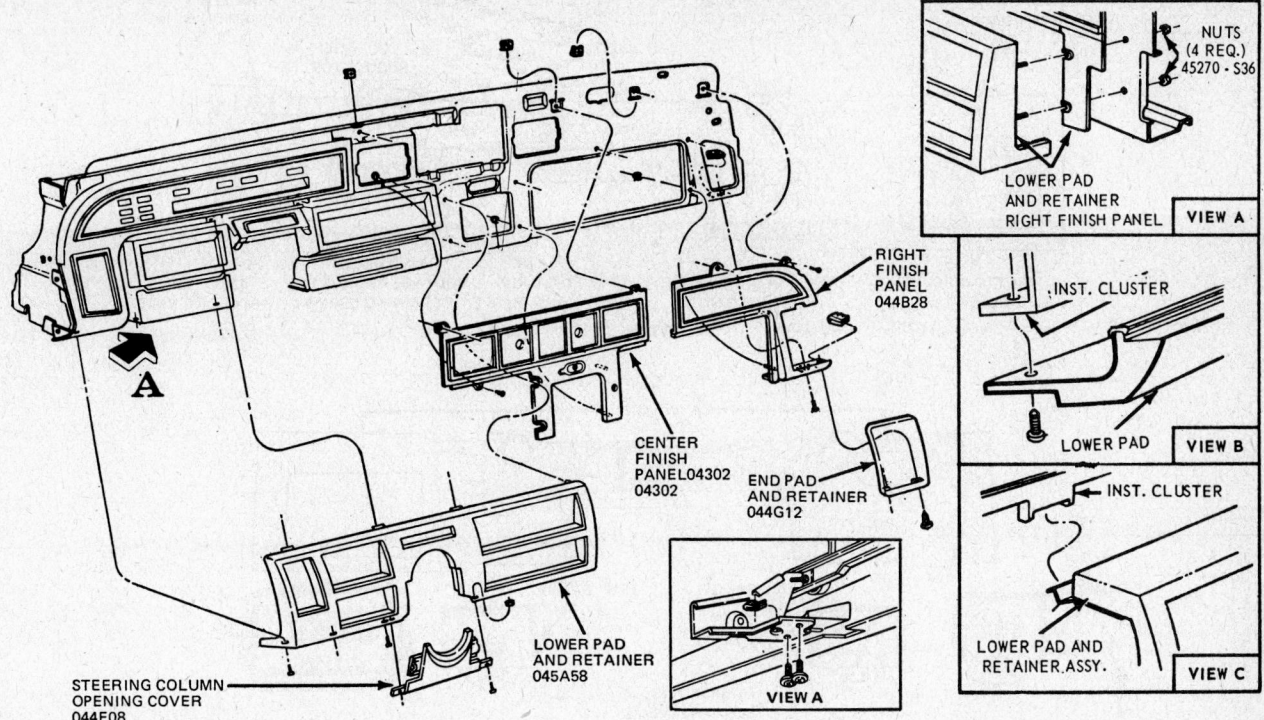

Fig. 9   Instrument panel lower pad removal (typical). 1974-78 Continental

INSTRUMENT CLUSTER

1977-78 Versailles

1. Disconnect battery ground cable.
2. Remove screws securing lower cluster applique beneath steering column.
3. Remove steering column shroud.
4. Remove headlamp switch knob and shaft assembly, then the switch bezel.
5. Remove four screws from cluster front cover.
6. Using a right angle screwdriver, pry along edges of finish panel, thereby removing studs from retainers and remove finish panel.
7. Pull front cover slightly outward at top, then rearward at bottom to disengage cover to panel retainers.
8. Remove cluster front cover.
9. Remove screw attaching transmission indicator cable bracket to steering column and detach cable loop from pin on column.
10. Disconnect speedometer cable connector.
11. Remove four screws securing cluster to instrument panel.
12. Pull cluster from instrument panel and disconnect electrical connectors, Fig. 8.
13. Remove cluster from vehicle.
14. Reverse procedure to install.

1974-78 Continental

1. Disconnect battery ground cable.

2. Remove steering column trim shroud, then remove instrument panel lower pad as follows Fig. 9:
   a. From behind panel, remove the two nuts retaining right end of panel to instrument panel.
   b. From bottom edge, remove the five pad to instrument cluster screws.
   c. Remove the three left hand end finish panel retaining screws, then swing pad assembly outward to disengage tabs at top of cluster and remove pad assembly.
3. Disconnect lower instrument cluster electrical connector from printed circuit.
4. Remove PRND21 control cable to steering column screw.
5. Remove instrument cluster retaining screws, pull cluster from panel and disconnect electrical connector.
6. Remove instrument cluster, Fig. 10.

1974-76 Mark IV & 1977-78 Mark V

1. Disconnect battery ground cable.
2. Remove three screws attaching upper access cover to instrument panel pad.
3. Remove one screw retaining lower cluster applique cover below steering column.
4. Squeeze lower half of steering column shroud together and separate lower half from upper.
5. Remove upper half of shroud from column.
6. Remove one screw attaching PRNDL control cable to steering column.
7. Remove heated backlite control knob.
8. Reach under panel and depress the button on side of headlight switch while withdrawing switch control knob

and shaft. Remove headlight switch bezel.
9. Reach under panel and disconnect speedo cable.
10. Remove wiper/washer control knob.
11. Remove threaded wiper/washer bezel.
12. Remove cigar lighter from its receptacle.
13. Remove four screws retaining cluster front cover.
14. Insert a right angle standard tip screwdriver along edges of finish panel withdrawing studs in sequence gradually around periphery of panel.
15. Remove two screws from cluster light baffle at cluster top.
16. Remove four screws retaining cluster to instrument panel.
17. Pull cluster away from panel and disconnect printed circuit feed plug.
18. Tilt cluster out, bottom first, and move cluster toward center of vehicle, Fig. 11.

W/S WIPER BLADES

NOTE: Trico and Anco blades are used and come in two types; Bayonet type and Side Saddle Pin type.

Bayonet Type: To remove the *Trico* type press down on the arm to unlock the top stud. Depress the tab on the saddle, Fig. 12, and pull the blade from the arm. To remove the *Anco* type press inward on the tab, Fig. 13, and pull the blade from the arm. To install a new blade assembly slide the blade saddle over the arm so that the locking stud snaps veto place.

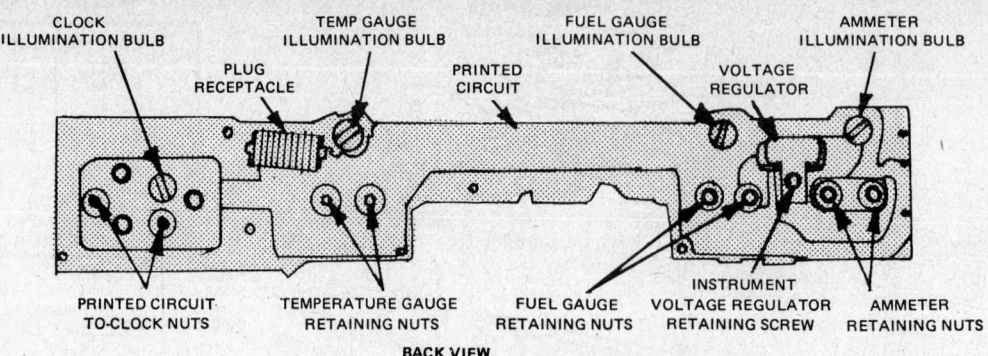

CLOCK ILLUMINATION BULB — TEMP GAUGE ILLUMINATION BULB — FUEL GAUGE ILLUMINATION BULB — AMMETER ILLUMINATION BULB — PLUG RECEPTACLE — PRINTED CIRCUIT — VOLTAGE REGULATOR

PRINTED CIRCUIT TO-CLOCK NUTS — TEMPERATURE GAUGE RETAINING NUTS — FUEL GAUGE RETAINING NUTS — INSTRUMENT VOLTAGE REGULATOR RETAINING SCREW — AMMETER RETAINING NUTS

BACK VIEW

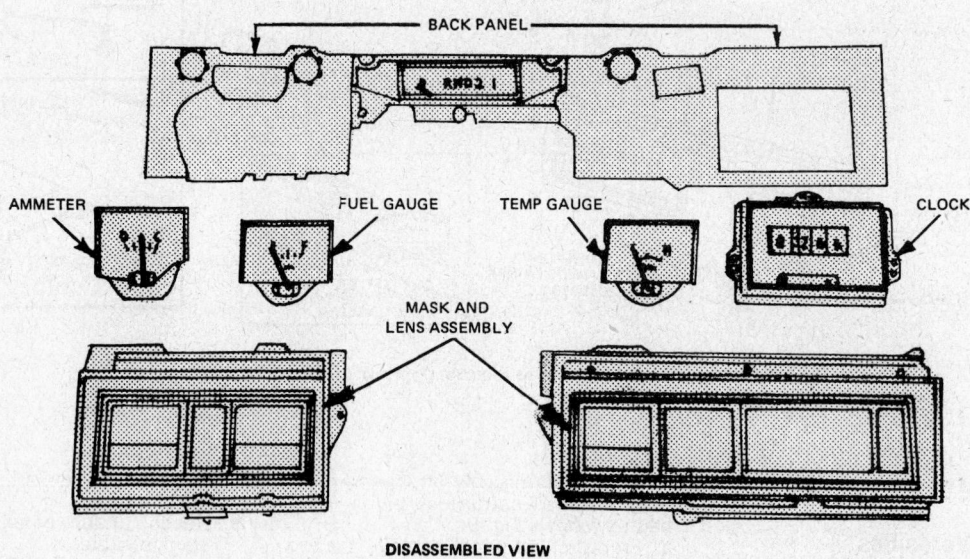

BACK PANEL

AMMETER — FUEL GAUGE — TEMP GAUGE — CLOCK

MASK AND LENS ASSEMBLY

DISASSEMBLED VIEW

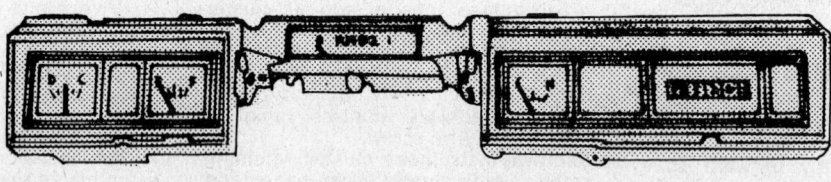

ASSEMBLED VIEW

Fig. 10   Instrument cluster (typical). 1974-78 Continental

Side Saddle Pin Type: To remove the pin type insert an appropriate tool into the spring release opening of the blade saddle, depress the spring clip and pull the blade from the arm, Fig. 14. To install, push the blade saddle onto the pin so that the spring clip engages the pin. To replace the rubber element in a *Trico* blade squeeze the latch lock release and pull the element out of the lever jaws, Fig. 15. Remove the *Anco* element by depressing the latch pin,

Fig. 15, and sliding the element out of the yoke jaws. To install, insert the element through the yoke or lever jaws. Be sure the element is engaged at all points.

W/S WIPER ARMS
1974-79

NOTE: On all models except Versailles, disconnect windshield washer hose from

wiper arm before attempting to remove arm.

Raise the blade end of the arm off the windshield and move the slide latch, Fig. 16, away from the pivot shaft. This action will unlock the wiper arm from the pivot shaft and hold the blade end of the arm off the glass at the same time. The wiper arm can now be pulled off the pivot shaft without the aid of any tools.

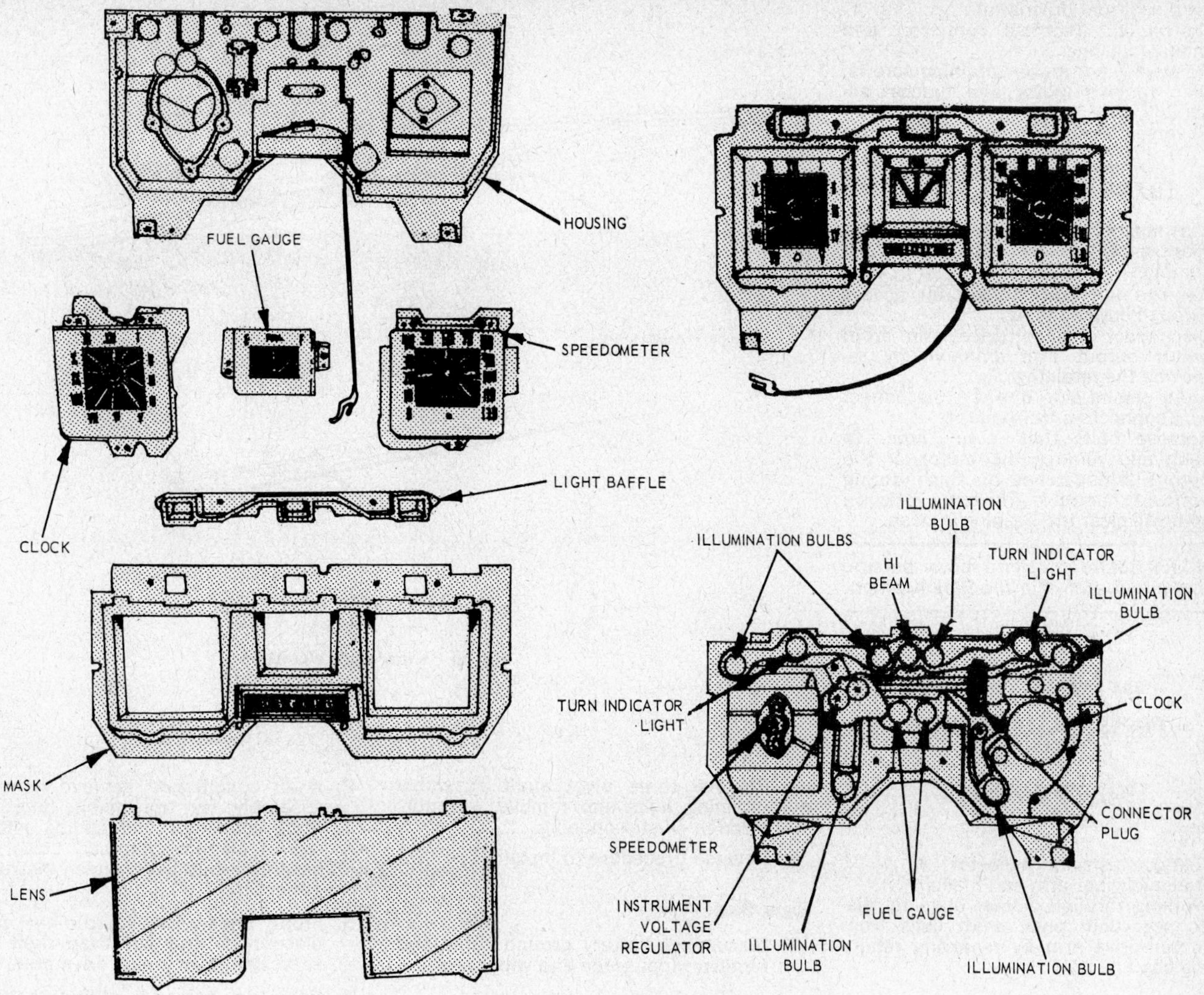

Fig. 11 Instrument cluster. 1974-78 Mark IV & V

W/S WIPER MOTOR, REPLACE

1978-79 Versailles

1. Disconnect battery ground cable.
2. Remove eight instrument panel pad attaching screws, then remove pad.
3. Remove speaker mounting bracket, then disconnect wire connector and remove speaker.
4. Remove defroster nozzle and air distribution duct.
5. Remove wiper bracket to cowl attaching bolts and drive arm clip, then remove wiper motor.

1977 Versailles

1. Disconnect battery ground cable.
2. Remove accelerator pedal and instrument panel to floor brace.
3. Remove drive arm clips and discon-

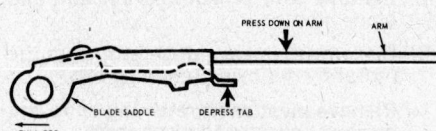

Fig. 12 Trico Bayonet wiper blade

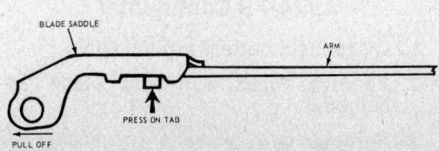

Fig. 13 Anco Bayonet wiper blade

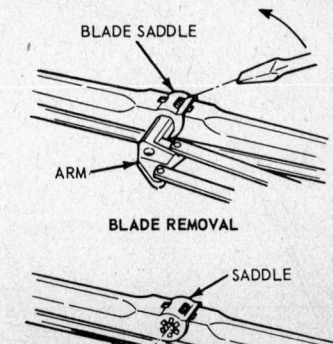

BLADE REMOVAL

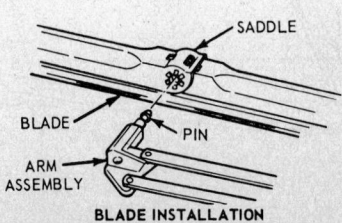

BLADE INSTALLATION

Fig. 14 Pin type wiper blade

nect rod from drive arm.
4. Disconnect electrical connector and manual linkage.
5. Remove wiper motor retaining screws, then remove motor and bracket assembly.
6. Reverse procedure to install.

1974-79 Exc. Versailles

1. Disconnect battery ground cable.
2. Remove wiper arm and blade assemblies.
3. Remove left cowl screen for access through cowl opening.
4. Disconnect linkage drive arm from motor output arm crankpin by removing the retaining clip.
5. From engine side of dash, disconnect wire connectors from motor.
6. Remove bolts that retain motor to dash and remove the motor. If the output arm catches on dash during removal, handturn the arm clockwise so it will clear the opening in dash.

NOTE: *Before installing motor be sure the output arm is in the Park position.*

W/S WIPER TRANSMISSION

1977-79 Versailles

Left Side:

1. Remove instrument cluster.
2. Remove wiper arm and blade.
3. Working through cluster opening, disconnect both pivot shaft links from motor drive arm by removing retaining clip.

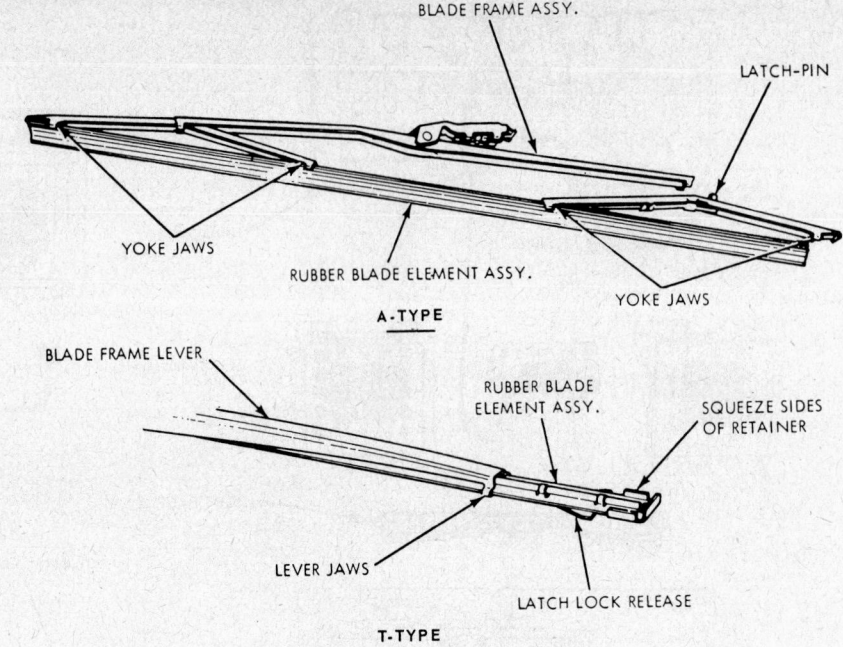

Fig. 15 Wiper blade element

4. Remove three pivot shaft assembly retaining bolts and remove assembly through cluster opening.
5. Reverse procedure to install.

Right Side:

1. Disconnect battery ground cable and remove wiper blade and wiper arm.

2. If air conditioned, remove right duct assembly by unclipping duct from right connector and sliding left end out of plenum chamber. Lower duct assembly out from under instrument panel.
3. From under the instrument panel, disconnect first left then right pivot shaft link from motor drive arm.
4. Reaching between utility shelf and instrument panel, remove pivot shaft retaining bolts and lower assembly out from under panel.
5. Reverse procedure to install.

1974-76 Mark IV & 1977-79 Mark V

1. Disconnect battery ground cable and remove wiper arm and blades.
2. Remove cowl screen and left arm and blade stop.
3. Disconnect linkage drive arm from the motor by removing retaining clip.
4. Remove pivot shaft retaining bolts and remove linkage and pivot shaft.

NOTE: When installing pivot shaft assemblies, be sure to force the linkage connecting clip into the locked position.

1974-79 Continental

1. Disconnect battery ground cable.
2. Remove wiper arm and blade assemblies.
3. Remove cowl screens for access to linkage.

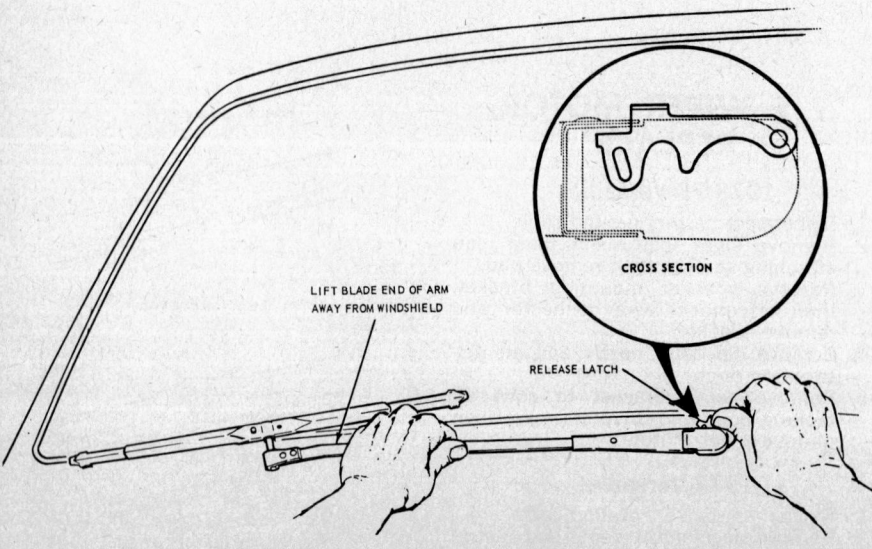

Fig. 16 Wiper arm. 1974-79

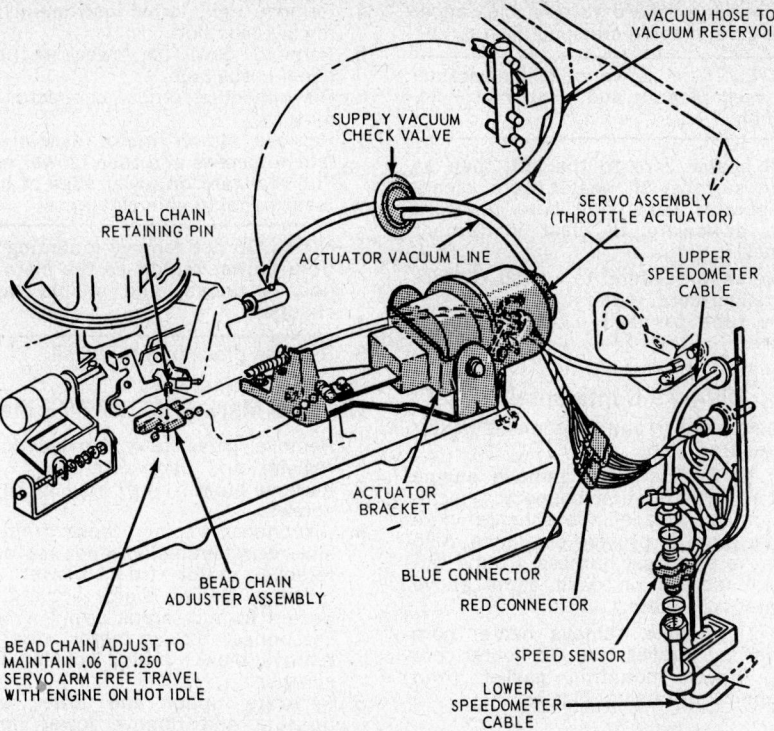

Fig. 17 Servo assembly & throttle linkage installation. 1974-78 (typical)

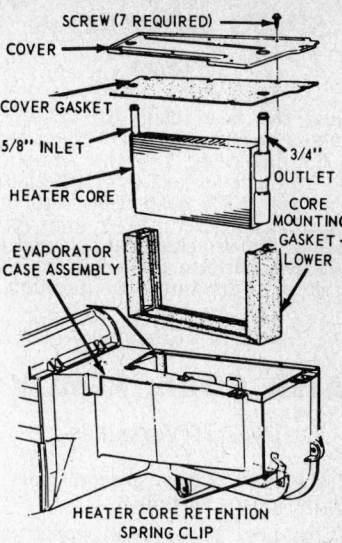

Fig. 18 Heater core removal. 1974-79 Continental

4. Disconnect left linkage arm from the drive arm by removing the clip.
5. Remove three bolts retaining left pivot shaft assembly to the cowl and remove the left arm and pivot shaft assembly through cowl opening.
6. Disconnect linkage drive arm from motor crankpin by removing the clip.
7. Remove three bolts that connect the drive arm pivot assembly to the cowl and remove the pivot shaft drive arm and right arm as an assembly.

W/S WIPER SWITCH

1977-79 Versailles

NOTE: The wiper/washer switch is an integral part of the turn signal arm and cannot be replaced separately.

1. Disconnect battery ground cable.
2. Disconnect wiper/washer and turn signal electrical connector from under instrument panel.
3. Remove lower instrument panel shield retaining screws and shield.
4. Remove steering column cover screws and separate cover halves.
5. Remove wiring cover by pulling it, then remove wiring shield by prying out.
6. Using an internal bit screwdriver, remove wiper/washer and turn signal arm assembly.

7. Reverse procedure to install.

1974-76 Mark IV & 1977-79 Mark V

1. Disconnect battery ground cable.
2. Remove instrument cluster finish panel.
3. Remove switch mounting plate and disconnect cigar lighter and wiper switch wires.
4. Remove switch bezel nut and remove switch.

1974-79 Continental

1. Disconnect battery ground cable.
2. Pull the knob and remove retaining nut and gasket from switch shaft.
3. Lower switch from behind instrument panel and disconnect the multiple connector.

RADIO REMOVAL

NOTE: When installing radio, be sure to adjust antenna trimmer for peak performance.

1977-79 Versailles

1. Disconnect battery ground cable.
2. Remove headlamp switch.
3. Remove knobs from heater and A/C control, windshield wiper switch and radio.

4. Remove instrument panel applique.
5. Remove radio bezel to instrument panel screws, then pull radio and bezel out to disconnect antenna lead and electrical leads, then remove radio from panel.
6. Remove rear support bracket and bezel from radio.
7. Reverse procedure to install.

1974-76 Mark IV & 1977-79 Mark V

1. Disconnect battery ground cable.
2. Pull radio knobs and discs from shafts.
3. Remove twilight sentinel amplifier.
4. Remove air conditioning duct located under radio.
5. Remove radio rear support to panel screw, disconnect radio electrical leads and remove radio.

1974-79 Continental

1. Disconnect battery ground cable.
2. Remove radio knobs and discs, then map light assembly.
3. Remove steering column shroud, ash tray door pad and instrument cluster panel pad.
4. Remove center register applique, then disconnect cigar lighter and glove box light switch electrical connectors.
5. Remove radio bracket to instrument panel tab nut and radio mounting bracket to instrument panel screws.
6. Pull radio out, disconnect wiring and remove radio.

SPEED CONTROLS

1974-79

Adjust the bead chain to obtain .06-.25" actuator arm free travel when engine is at hot idle, Fig. 17. The adjustment should be made to take as much slack as possible out of the bead chain without restricting the carburetor lever from returning to idle. On vehicles with solenoid anti-diesel valve, perform the adjustment with the ignition switch in the ON position.

HEATER CORE, REMOVAL

1977-79 Versailles

1. Disconnect battery ground cable and drain cooling system.

2. Disconnect hoses from heater core. Plug heater core tubes to prevent coolant leakage.

3. Remove washer nut from plenum assembly mounting stud on engine side of dash panel.

4. Remove floor duct, seat belt interlock module and bracket, glove box liner and shields.

5. Loosen right door sill scuff plate, right A-pillar trim cover and right cowl side trim panel.

6. Loosen instrument panel to right cowl side bolt and remove instrument panel brace at lower rail below glove box opening.

7. If used, remove tunnel to cowl brace located on left side of plenum assembly.

8. Disconnect vacuum hoses from A/C-Defrost and Heat/Defrost door motors. Remove screw from clip retaining vacuum harness to plenum.

9. Remove the two Heat/Defrost door motor mounting nuts and swing motor rearward on door crankarm.

10. Remove the two screws retaining plenum to left mounting bracket, then remove the two screws and three clips retaining plenum to evaporator case.

11. Swing bottom of plenum away from evaporator case to disengage S-clip on forward flange of plenum, then raise plenum to clear tabs on top of evaporator case.

12. Move plenum to left while pulling instrument rearward to gain clearance. Use care to avoid cracking plastic.

NOTE: There is very little clearance between plenum and wiper motor assembly.

13. Pull heater core to the left, then as rear surface of heater core clears evaporator case, pull core rearward and downward to clear instrument panel.

14. Reverse procedure to install. Before installing core, make sure that heater core tube to dash panel seal is in place.

1974-79 Continental

1. Drain radiator and disconnect heater hoses from core.

2. On 1978-79 models, remove engine vacuum distribution connector, located on dash panel above heater core cover plate to provide clearance. Also remove electrical harness ground terminal located on dash panel above heater core plate.

3. On all models, remove heater core cover and gasket, then lift heater core and lower mounting gasket from evaporator housing, Fig. 18.

1974-76 Mark IV & 1977-78 Mark V

1. Drain radiator and disconnect heater hoses from core.

2. Remove glove box, then heater air outlet register from plenum assembly by disengaging the snap clips.

3. Disconnect temperature control cable from blend door crank arm.

4. Remove vacuum hoses from high-low door motor, panel-defrost door motor and the in-line tee connector to temperature by-pass door motor.

5. Disconnect resistor wiring and remove plenum case flange screws, then remove plenum case rear half.

BLOWER MOTOR, REMOVAL

1977-79 Versailles

1. Disconnect battery ground cable.
2. Remove glove box.
3. Loosen right door sill scuff plate, right A-pillar trim cover and remove right cowl side trim panel.

4. Remove right lower instrument panel to cowl side bolt.
5. Remove cowl to lower instrument panel brace bolt.
6. Disconnect electrical connector from motor.
7. Remove blower motor assembly retaining screws and then blower motor. Pull rearward on lower edge of instrument panel to gain clearance.

NOTE: Do not remove mounting plate from blower motor, as the plate location is critical and should not be changed.

8. Reverse procedure to install.

1974-76 Mark IV & 1977-78 Mark V

1. Remove glove box, recirculating air register and duct assembly.
2. Remove blower lower housing to dash screws.
3. Disconnect vacuum hose from outside-recirculating air door motor and remove motor from blower lower housing, leaving motor actuator connected to door crank arm.
4. Disconnect blower motor wiring and remove blower motor housing flange screws.
5. Separate upper and lower blower housing and remove lower housing and motor from under instrument panel.
6. Remove blower motor from lower housing.

1974-79 Continental

1. Remove the hood.
2. Remove the right hood hinge and right fender inner support brace as an assembly.
3. Disconnect the blower motor air cooling tube from the motor.
4. Disconnect the motor lead wire from the harness and the ground wire from the dash panel.
5. Disconnect the rear section of the right front fender apron from the fender around the wheel opening (7 screws) and remove the two lower fender-to-cowl mounting screws.
6. Separate the fender apron from the fender wheel opening so that the apron can be pushed downward away from the blower motor.
7. Remove the four blower motor mounting plate screws. Move the motor and wheel forward out of the blower scroll and remove the assembly through the opening while applying pressure to the fender apron to enlarge the opening

Engine Section

ENGINE MOUNTS, REPLACE

CAUTION: Whenever self-locking mounting bolts and nuts are removed, they must be replaced with new self-locking bolts and nuts.

1977-79 Versailles

1. Support engine using a jack and block of wood placed under oil pan.
2. Remove through bolt attaching insulator to insulator support bracket, Fig. 1.
3. Raise engine slightly and remove insulator and support bracket to engine attaching bolts.
4. Remove insulator and support bracket assembly.

1974-79 Continental V8-400

1. Remove fan shroud attaching bolts, then disconnect transmission oil cooler lines from retaining bracket on block.
2. Remove through bolt attaching insulator support bracket, Fig. 2.
3. Raise engine slightly using a jack and block of wood placed under oil pan.
4. Remove insulator to engine attaching bolts.
5. Remove insulator and heat shield, if equipped.

V8-460

1. Block the rear wheels and set the parking brake. Raise front of vehicle and install safety stands.

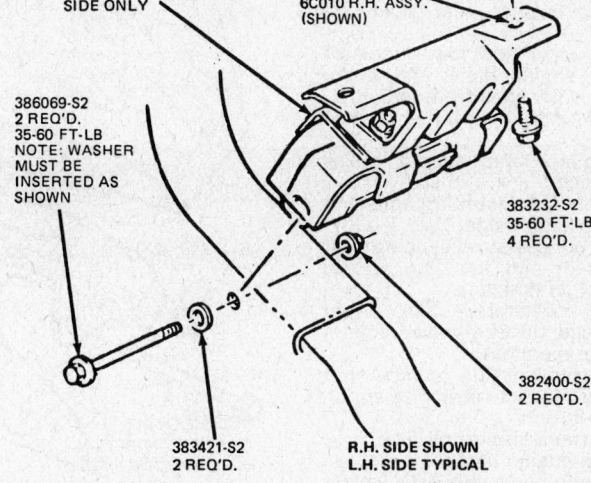

Fig. 1   Engine mount. 1977-79 Versailles

2. Remove the bolts that attach the support bracket to the cylinder block, Fig. 3.
3. Place a block of wood between a jack and the front edge of the oil pan. Raise the engine high enough to provide clearance to remove the support and not damage the radiator.
4. Remove the through bolts from the support insulator. Lift the insulator from the number 2 crossmember.
5. Remove the bracket-to-insulator attaching bolt and separate the units.

1974-76 Mark IV & 1977-79 Mark V

1. Remove the fan shroud attaching

screws and support the engine using a jack and a block of wood under the oil pan.
2. Remove the through bolt and nut attaching the insulator to the frame crossmember, Figs. 4 and 5.
3. Remove the insulator to upper bracket attaching nuts.
4. Raise the engine enough to remove the insulator and heat shield if so equipped.
5. If required, the upper bracket can now be removed by removal of the three screws holding the bracket to the cylinder block.

ENGINE, REPLACE

1977-79 Versailles

NOTE: On models equipped with Thermactor system, remove or disconnect components that will interfere with engine removal or installation.

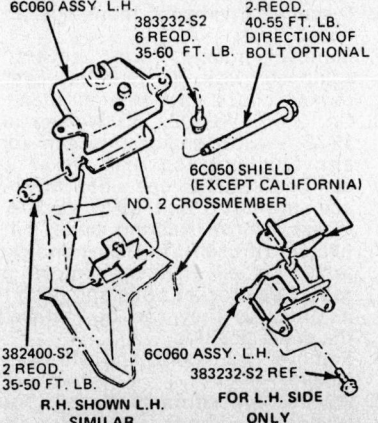

Fig. 2   Engine mount. 1977-79 Continental V8-400

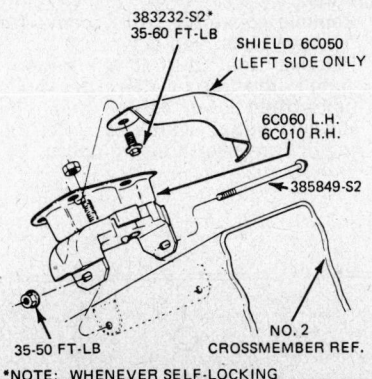

Fig. 3   Engine mount. 1974-78 Continental V8-460

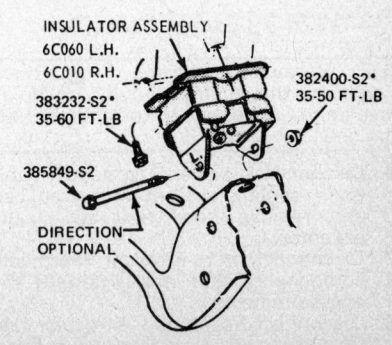

Fig. 4   Engine mount. 1977-79 Mark V V8-400

1. Drain cooling system and crankcase.
2. Remove hood, then disconnect battery and alternator ground cables from cylinder block.
3. Remove air cleaner and duct assembly.
4. Disconnect upper and lower radiator hoses from engine block and transmission oil cooler lines from radiator.
5. Remove bolts attaching fan shroud to radiator.
6. Remove radiator, fan, spacer, pulley and fan shroud.
7. Remove alternator mounting bolts and position alternator aside.
8. Disconnect oil pressure sending unit wire connector and fuel line at fuel pump. Plug fuel tank line.
9. Disconnect accelerator cable from carburetor and throttle valve vacuum line at intake manifold.
10. Disconnect transmission manual shift rod, then disconnect retracting spring at shift rod stud.
11. Disconnect transmission oil filler tube bracket from engine block.
12. On models equipped with A/C, isolate and remove compressor.
13. Remove power steering pump bracket from cylinder head and position pump aside. Position pump so that fluid will not drain from reservoir.
14. Disconnect heater hoses from water pump and intake manifold and temperature sending unit wire connector.
15. Remove converter housing to engage upper attaching bolts.
16. Disconnect primary wire connector from ignition coil, then remove wiring harness from left rocker arm cover and position out of way. Disconnect ground strap from block.
17. Raise front of vehicle and remove starter.
18. Disconnect exhaust pipes from exhaust manifold, then remove engine support insulators from brackets on frame.
19. Disconnect transmission oil cooler lines from retainer and remove converter housing inspection cover.
20. Disconnect flywheel from converter, secure converter to converter housing.
21. Remove remaining converter housing to engine attaching bolts, then lower vehicle and support transmission using a suitable jack.
22. Attach engine lifting device to lifting brackets on intake manifold, then raise engine slightly and disconnect from transmission.
23. Carefully lift engine from engine compartment.

1974-79 Except Versailles

NOTE: Because of engine compartment tolerances, the engine should not be removed and installed with the transmission attached.

1. Disconnect battery ground cable, drain cooling system and crankcase and remove hood and air cleaner assembly.
2. Disconnect or remove all Thermactor components that may interfere with engine removal.
3. Disconnect hoses and oil cooler lines from radiator, then remove radiator, fan shroud and fan.

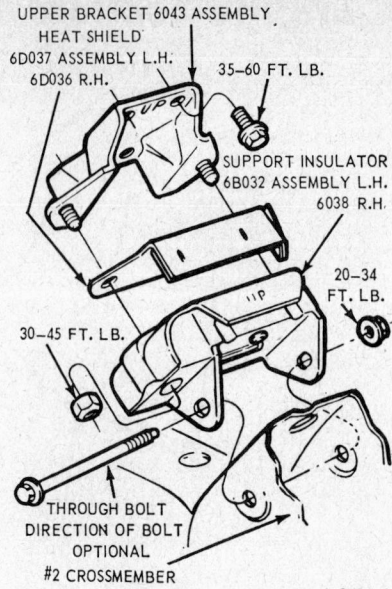

UPPER BRACKET 6043 ASSEMBLY
HEAT SHIELD
6D037 ASSEMBLY L.H.
6D036 R.H.
35—60 FT. LB.
SUPPORT INSULATOR
6B032 ASSEMBLY L.H.
6038 R.H.
20—34 FT. LB.
30—45 FT. LB.
THROUGH BOLT
DIRECTION OF BOLT
OPTIONAL
#2 CROSSMEMBER
A 3499-A

Fig. 5 Engine Mount. 1974-76 Mark IV & 1977-78 Mark V V8-460

4. Remove all drive belts.
5. Disconnect power steering pump and alternator and position units out of the way.
6. If equipped with air conditioning, isolate and remove compressor.
7. Disconnect all hoses, lines and wiring from engine. Make certain to remove ground wires from block and right cylinder head.
8. Disconnect fuel line from pump and plug line.
9. Disconnect speed control at carburetor, if equipped.
10. Disconnect engine wiring harness at dash panel.
11. Disconnect accelerator cable or linkage, then disconnect downshift linkage (if used).
12. Raise and properly support vehicle, then disconnect exhaust system from engine and remove starter.
13. Remove engine front support through bolts.
14. Remove converter cover, converter to flywheel bolts, and downshift rod.
15. Remove the four lower engine to clutch housing or converter housing bolts, then lower vehicle and remove the two upper engine to clutch housing or converter housing bolts.

16. Position jack under transmission, then using a suitable hoist, carefully remove engine from vehicle.
17. Reverse procedure to install.

CYLINDER HEAD, REPLACE

NOTES

Before installing cylinder head, wipe off engine block gasket surface and be certain no foreign material has fallen into cylinder bores, bolt holes or in the valve lifter area. It is good practice to clean out bolt holes with compressed air.

Some cylinder head gaskets are coated with a special lacquer to provide a good seal once the parts have warmed up. Do not use any additional sealer on such gaskets. If the gasket does not have this lacquer coating, apply suitable sealer to both sides.

Tighten cylinder head bolts at little at a time in three steps in the sequence shown in the illustrations. Final tightening should be to the torque specifications listed in the *Engine Tightening* table. After the bolts have been torqued to specifications, *they should not be disturbed*.

V8-302, 351 & 400

1. Remove intake manifold and carburetor as an assembly.
2. Disconnect battery ground cable at cylinder head.
3. If left head is being removed, remove A/C compressor (if equipped). Also remove and wire power steering pump out of the way. If equipped with Thermactor System, disconnect hose from air manifold on left cylinder head.
4. If right head is to be removed, remove alternator mounting bracket bolt and spacer, ground wire and air cleaner inlet duct.
5. If right head is to be removed on an engine with Thermactor System, remove air pump from bracket. Disconnect hose from air manifold.
6. Disconnect exhaust manifolds at exhaust pipes.
7. Remove rocker arm covers. If equipped with Thermactor System, remove check valve from air manifold.
8. On 1977 V8-302, 351W and early 1978 V8-302 engines, loosen rocker arm stud nuts so that rocker arms can be rotated to one side. On V8-400 and late 1978 and 1979 V8-302 engines, remove fulcrum bolts, oil deflectors (if used), fulcrums and rocker arms. On all engines, remove push rods. Keep rocker arms and push rods in order so they can be installed in the same position.
9. Remove head bolts and lift head off block.
10. Reverse procedure to install. Torque cylinder head bolts in sequence shown in Fig. 6, and torque intake manifold bolts in sequence shown in Figs. 7 and 8.

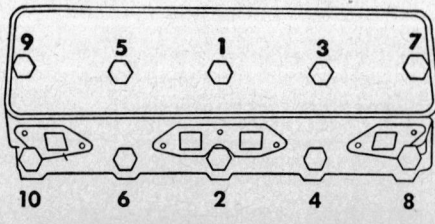

Fig. 6 Cylinder head tightening

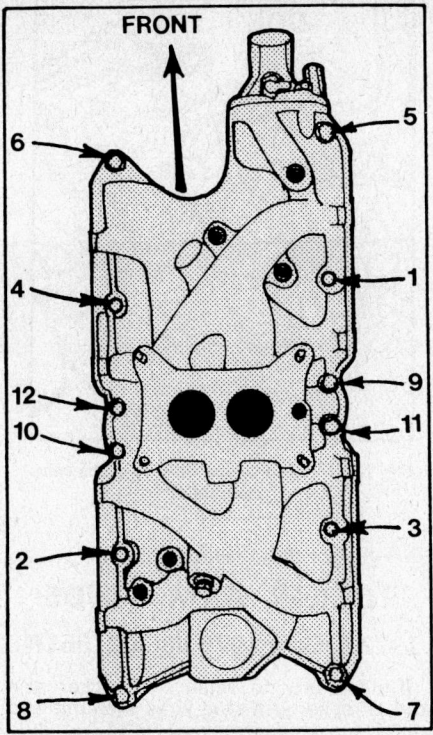

Fig. 7   Intake manifold tightening sequence. V8-302 & 351W

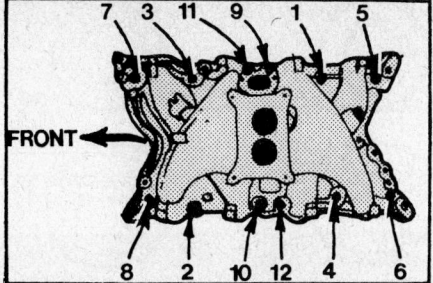

Fig. 8   Intake manifold tightening sequence, V8-400

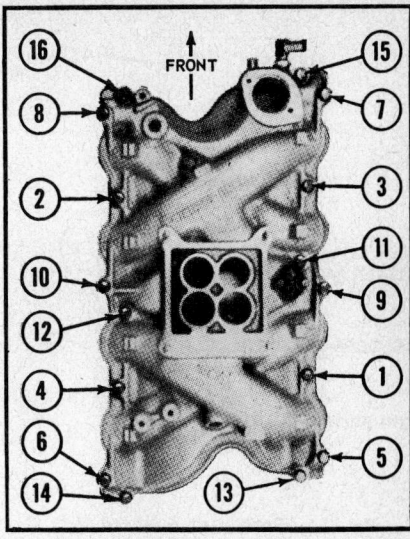

Fig. 9   Intake manifold tightening sequence. V8-460

V8-460

1. Remove intake manifold and carburetor as an assembly.
2. Disconnect muffler inlet pipe at exhaust manifold.
3. Loosen air conditioner compressor belt if so equipped.
4. Loosen alternator retaining bolts and remove bolt retaining alternator bracket to right head.
5. If air conditioned, purge system of refrigerant, then remove nuts retaining compressor bracket to water pump. Remove bolts retaining compressor

to upper mounting bracket and lay compressor out of way. Remove compressor upper bracket from head.
6. If not air conditioned, remove bolts retaining power steering reservoir bracket to left head and position reservoir out of way.
7. Remove rocker arm covers and rocker arms. Remove push rods in sequence so they can be installed in their positions.
8. Remove head retaining bolts and lift head with exhaust manifold.

NOTE: If necessary to break gasket seal, pry at forward corners of cylinder heads against casting bosses provided on cylinder block. Avoid damaging machined surfaces on head and block.

9. Reverse procedure to install. Torque cylinder head bolts in sequence shown in Fig. 6, and torque intake manifold bolts in sequence shown in Fig. 9.

NOTE

The cylinder head gaskets are marked "Top" or "Front" stamped near the front end of the gasket. The gasket is properly installed when the word is at the forward end of the engine and water passage holes line up. This results in the sealing beads on the right head gasket being inverted with respect to the left head gasket.

VALVES, ADJUST

To eliminate the need of adjusting valve lash, a positive stop rocker arm stud and nut is used on 1977 and early 1978 V8-302 and 351W engines, Fig. 10, and a positive stop fulcrum bolt and seat is used on V8-400 and 460 and late 1978 and 1979 V8-302 engines, Figs. 11 and 11A.

It is very important that the correct push rod be used and all components be installed and torqued as follows:
1. Position the piston of the cylinder being worked on at TDC of its compression stroke.
2. On 1977 and early 1978 V8-302 and 351 engines, lubricate and install rocker arm and fulcrum seat on the stud. Thread nut onto the stud until it contracts the shoulder and torque to 17-23 ft. lbs.

NOTE: Each rocker arm stud nut should be inspected when adjusting valve clearance, Fig. 12.

3. On V8-400, 460 and late 1978 and 1979 V8-302 engines, install rocker arm, fulcrum seat and oil deflector. Install fulcrum bolt and torque to 18-25 ft. lbs.

A .060″ shorter push rod or a .060″ longer rod are available for service to provide a means of compensating for dimensional changes in the valve mechanism. Valve stem-to-rocker arm clearance should be as listed in the *Valve Specifications* table, with the hydraulic lifter completely collapsed, Fig. 12A. Repeated valve grind jobs will decrease this clearance to the point that if not compensated for the lifters will cease to function.

When checking valve clearance, if the clearance is less than the minimum, the .060″ shorter push rod should be used. If clearance is more than the maximum, the

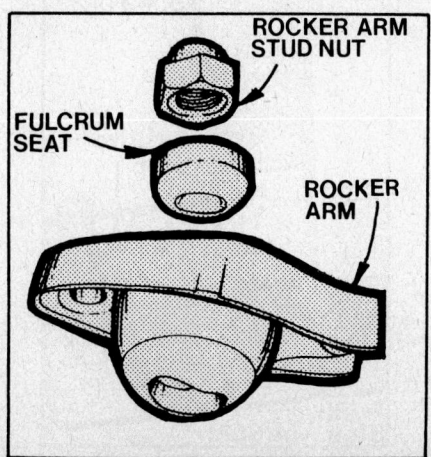

Fig. 10   Rocker arm assembly. 1977 & early 1978 V8-302 & 351W

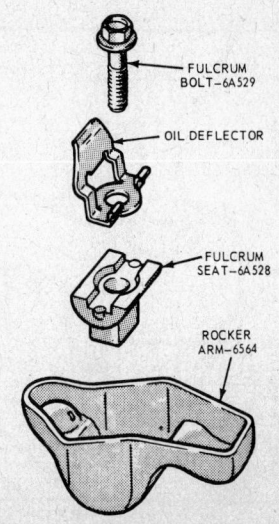

Fig. 11   Rocker arm & related parts. V8-400, 460

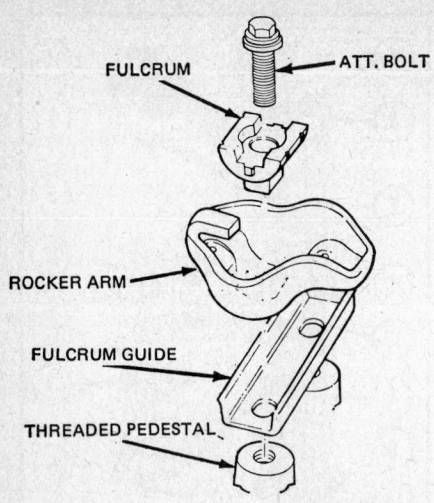

Fig. 11A   Rocker arm & related parts. Late 1978 & 1979 V8-302

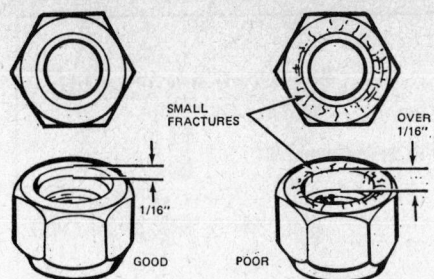

Fig. 12   Inspection of rocker arm stud nut. 1977 & early 1978 V8-302, 351W

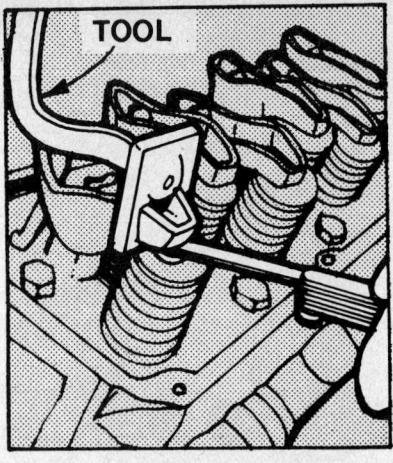

Fig. 12A   Compressing lifter to check valve clearance

.060″ longer push rod should be used. (See *Valve Specifications* table.) To check valve clearance, proceed as follows:

V8-302 & 351, 400 & 460

1. Mark crankshaft pulley at three locations, with number 1 location at TDC timing mark (end of compression stroke), number 2 location one half turn (180°) clockwise from TDC and number 3 location three quarter turn clockwise (270°) from TDC.

2. Turn the crankshaft to the number 1 location and check the clearance on the following valves:

V8-302 & 460	
No. 1 Intake	No. 1 Exhaust
No. 7 Intake	No. 5 Exhaust
No. 8 Intake	No. 4 Exhaust
V8-351 & 400	
No. 1 Intake	No. 1 Exhaust
No. 4 Intake	No. 3 Exhaust
No. 8 Intake	No. 7 Exhaust

3. Turn the crankshaft to the number 2 location and check the clearance on the following valves:

V8-302 & 460	
No. 4 Intake	No. 2 Exhaust
No. 5 Intake	No. 6 Exhaust
V8-351 & 400	
No. 3 Intake	No. 2 Exhaust
No. 7 Intake	No. 6 Exhaust

4. Turn the crankshaft to the number 3 location and check the clearance on the following valves:

V8-302 & 460	
No. 2 Intake	No. 3 Exhaust
No. 3 Intake	No. 7 Exhaust
No. 6 Intake	No. 8 Exhaust
V8-351 & 400	
No. 2 Intake	No. 4 Exhaust
No. 5 Intake	No. 5 Exhaust
No. 6 Intake	No. 8 Exhaust

VALVE ARRANGEMENT

Front to Rear

Right Bank	I-E-I-E-I-E-I-E
Left Bank	E-I-E-I-E-I-E-I

VALVE LIFT SPECS.

Engine	Year	Intake	Exhaust
V8-302	1977	.416	.434
	1978-79	.382	.398
V8-351W	1977	.416	.416
V8-400	1978-79	.427	.433
V8-460	1974	.437	.480
	1975-78	.437	.481

VALVE TIMING

Intake Opens Before TDC

Engine	Year	Degrees
V8-302	1977-79	16
V8-351W	1977	23
V8-400	1974-79	17
V8-460	1974-78	8

ROCKER ARM STUDS

1977 & Early 1978 V8-302, 351W

If necessary to replace a rocker arm stud, a rocker arm stud kit is available and contains a stud remover, Fig. 13, a stud installer, Fig. 13A, and two reamers, one .006″ and the other .015″. For .010″ oversize studs, use reamer T66P-6A527-B.

Rocker arm studs that are broken or have damaged threads may be replaced with standard studs. Loose studs in the head may be replaced with .006″, .010″ or .015″ oversize studs which are available for service.

When going from a standard size stud to a .015″ oversize stud, always use a .006″ reamer before finishing reaming with a .015″ reamer.

If a stud is broken off flush with the stud boss, use an easy-out to remove the broken stud, following the instructions of the tool manufacturer.

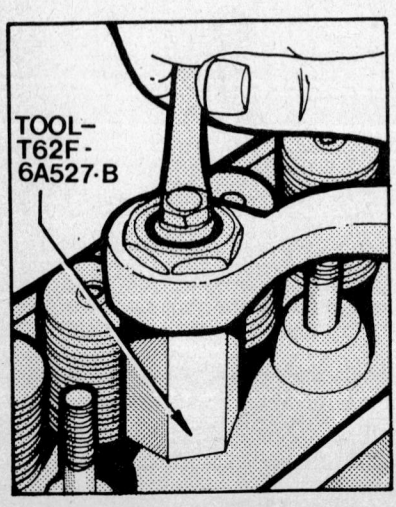

Fig. 13   Rocker arm stud removal. 1977 & early 1978 V8-302 & 351W

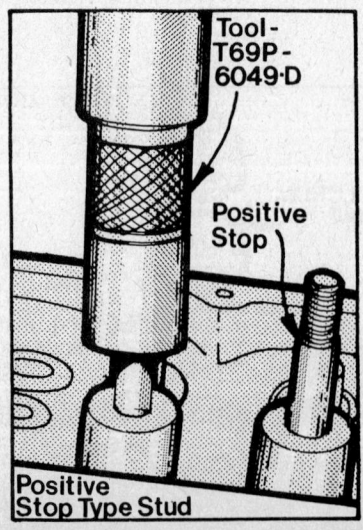

Fig. 13A   Positive stop type rocker arm stud installation. 1977 & early 1978 V8-302 & 351W

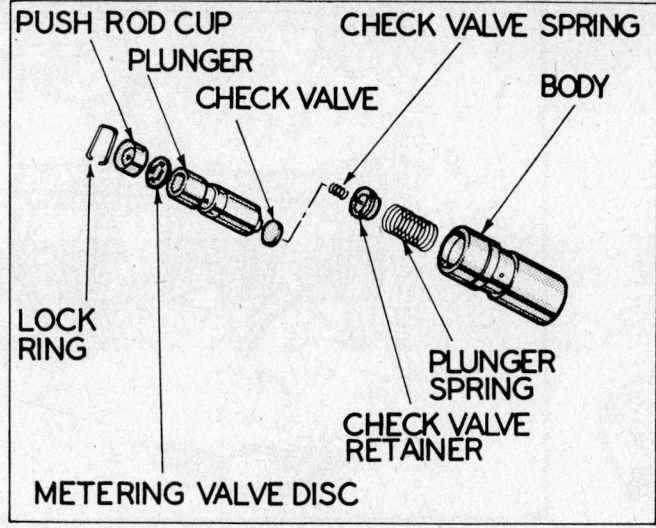

Fig. 14   Hydraulic valve lifter disassembled (typical)

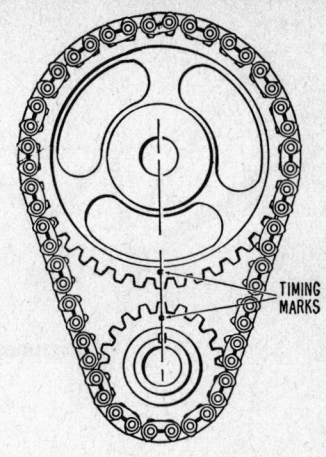

Fig. 15   Valve timing marks

Installation

1. Position the piston of the cylinder to be worked on at TDC compression stroke.
2. Locate stud properly with tool T69P-6049D. Make sure tool bottoms on the head.
3. Lubricate rocker arm components and place rocker arm and fulcrum on the stud.
4. Thread nut onto the stud until it contacts the shoulder then tighten nut to 17-23 ft-lbs.

V8-400, 460 & Late 1978 & 1979 V8-302

The rocker arm is supported by a fulcrum bolt which fits through the fulcrum seat and threads into the cylinder head. To disassemble, remove the bolt, oil deflector, fulcrum seat and rocker arm, Figs. 11 and 11A.

VALVE GUIDES

Valve guides in these engines are an integral part of the head and, therefore, cannot be removed. For service, guides can be reamed oversize to accommodate one of three service valves with oversize stems (.003", .015" and .030").

Check the valve stem clearance of each valve (after cleaning) in its respective valve guide. If the clearance exceeds the service limits of .0055," ream the valve guides to accommodate the next oversize diameter valve.

HYDRAULIC VALVE LIFTERS

The internal parts of each hydraulic valve lifter assembly are a matched set. If these are mixed, improper valve operation may result. Therefore, disassemble,

inspect and test each assembly separately to prevent mixing the parts.

Fig. 14, illustrates the type of hydraulic lifter used. See the *Trouble Shooting Chapter* under the heading *Engine Noises* for causes of hydraulic valve lifter noise.

Hydraulic Lifters, Replace

1. Remove intake manifold and related parts.
2. Remove rocker arm covers.
3. Loosen rocker arm stud nuts or bolts and rotate rocker arms to the side.
4. Lift out push rods, keeping them in sequence in a rack so they may be installed in their original location.
5. Using a magnet rod, remove valve lifters and place them in sequence in a rack so they may be installed in their original location.

TIMING CASE COVER

NOTE: If necessary to replace the cover oil seal the cover must first be removed.

V8-302, 351W

1. Drain cooling system and crankcase.
2. Remove fan shroud attaching bolts and position shroud over engine fan.
3. Remove engine fan, spacer and shroud.
4. Remove drive belts and A/C idler pulley bracket.
5. Remove power steering pump and position aside.
6. Remove all accessory brackets attached to water pump, then remove water pump pulley.
7. Disconnect lower radiator hose, heater hose and by-pass hose from water pump.
8. Remove crankshaft pulley from vibration damper.
9. Remove damper attaching screw and

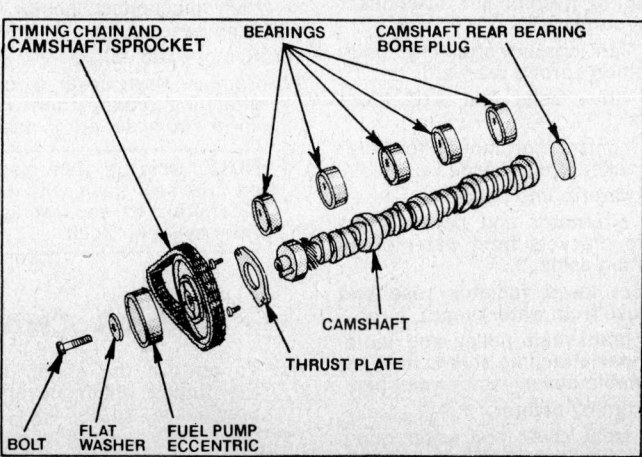

Fig. 16   Camshaft and related parts (typical)

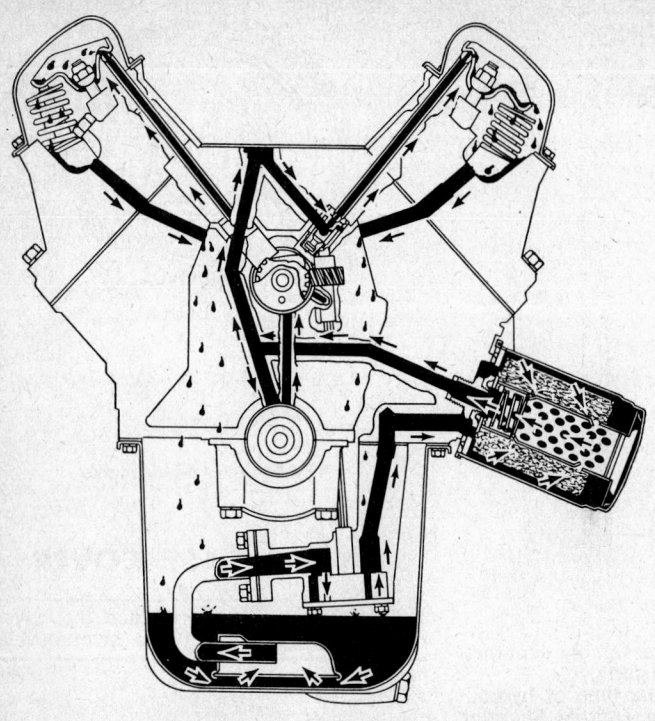

Engine lubrication. V8-302, 351W & 400

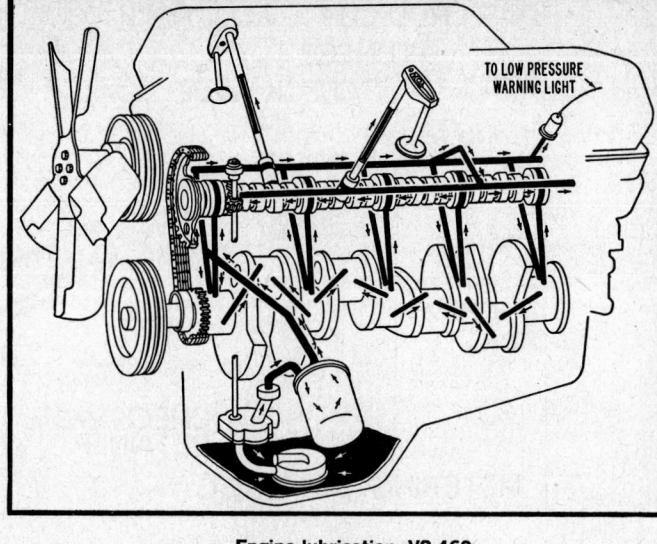

TO LOW PRESSURE
WARNING LIGHT

Engine lubrication. V8-460

washer, then using a suitable puller, remove damper.

10. Disconnect fuel pump outlet line, then remove fuel pump attaching bolts and position pump aside.
11. Remove oil level dip stick.
12. Remove oil pan to front cover attaching bolts.
13. Remove front cover to engine block attaching bolts, then remove front cover and water pump as an assembly.

NOTE: Use a thin blade knife to cut oil pan gasket flush with cylinder block face prior to separating front cover from cylinder block.

V8-400

1. Drain cooling system and disconnect battery ground cable.
2. Remove fan shroud attaching bolts then position shroud rearward.
3. Remove drive belts and A/C lower idler pulley.
4. Remove compressor mount to water pump bracket, if equipped.
5. Remove water pump pulley.
6. Remove alternator and power steering pump brackets from water pump and position aside.
7. Disconnect lower radiator hose and heater hose from water pump.
8. Remove crankshaft pulley and vibration damper attaching screw, then using a suitable puller, remove damper.
9. Remove timing pointer.
10. Remove front cover and water pump to engine block attaching bolts, then remove front cover and water pump as an assembly.

V8-460

1. Drain cooling system and crankcase.
2. Remove engine fan and radiator shroud.
3. Disconnect upper and lower radiator hoses and transmission oil cooler lines from radiator.
4. Remove radiator upper support and radiator.
5. Remove drive belts and water pump pulley.
6. Remove A/C compressor support, if equipped.
7. Remove crankshaft pulley and vibration damper attaching screw, then remove damper using a suitable puller.
8. Remove woodruff key from crankshaft.
9. Loosen by-pass hose at water pump, then disconnect heater return hose from water pump.
10. Remove fuel pump.
11. Remove front cover to cylinder block attaching bolts, then remove front cover and water pump assembly.

NOTE: Using a thin blade knife, cut oil pan seal flush with cylinder block face prior to separating front cover from cylinder block.

TIMING CHAIN

1. To remove the chain, first take off the timing chain cover as outlined previously.
2. Crank the engine until the timing mark on the camshaft sprocket is adjacent to the timing mark on the crankshaft sprocket, Fig. 15.

3. Remove cap screws, lock plate and fuel pump eccentric from front of camshaft.
4. Place a screwdriver behind the camshaft sprocket and carefully pry the sprocket and chain off the camshaft.
5. Reverse the foregoing procedure to install the chain, being sure to align the timing marks as shown in Fig. 15.

CAMSHAFT, REPLACE

If it is necessary to replace the camshaft only it may be accomplished without removing the engine from the chassis. But if the camshaft bearings are to be replaced the engine will have to be removed. To remove the camshaft, proceed as follows:

V8-302, 351W

1. Remove hood latch assembly, then disconnect A/C ambient temperature sensor wire connector and remove hood latch support brackets.
2. Remove condenser to radiator support attaching bolts, then remove fender to radiator support braces at each side of engine compartment.
3. Remove air dam and gasket located between radiator support and grille opening panel.
4. Carefully lift condenser upward until clearance is obtained to remove camshaft.
5. Remove cylinder front cover and timing chain as outlined previously.
6. Remove intake manifold and carburetor as an assembly.
7. Remove rocker covers. On 1977 and early 1978 engines, loosen rocker arm stud nuts and rotate rocker arms to the side. On late 1978 and 1979 engines, remove rocker arms.
8. Remove push rods and valve lifters in sequence so they can be installed in the same position.
9. Remove camshaft thrust plate, then

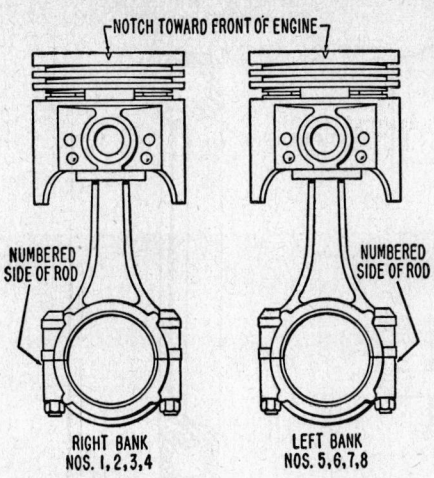

Fig. 17 Piston and rod assembly

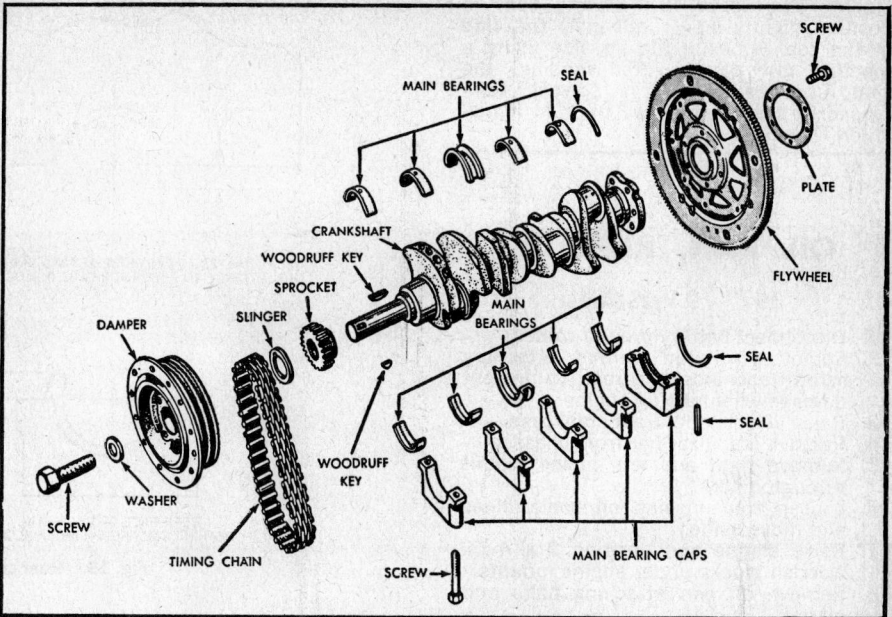

Fig. 18 Crankshaft and related parts

carefully remove camshaft from engine, Fig. 16.

NOTE: When removing camshaft, use care not to damage camshaft bearings.

10. Reverse procedure to install.

V8-400

1. Drain cooling system, then disconnect upper and lower radiator hose and transmission oil cooler lines from radiator.
2. If equipped with A/C, remove condenser.
3. Remove front cover and timing chain as outlined previously.
4. Remove fuel pump.
5. Remove intake manifold and carburetor as an assembly.
6. Remove rocker covers, then loosen fulcrum bolts and rotate rocker arms to the side.
7. Remove push rods and valve lifters in sequence so they can be installed in the same position.
8. Position No. 1 piston at TDC, then remove thrust plate and withdraw camshaft from engine, Fig. 16.

NOTE: When removing camshaft, use care not to damage camshaft bearings.

9. Reverse procedure to install.

V8-460

1. Drain crankcase and cooling system.
2. Remove timing cover, chain and sprockets as outlined previously.
3. Remove intake manifold and carburetor as an assembly.
4. Remove rocker arm covers. Back off rocker arm bolts, turn rocker arms sideways and remove push rods in sequence.
5. Remove valve lifters.

6. If air conditioned, unbolt and lay condenser on left fender. Secure in this position.
7. Remove grille.
8. Remove camshaft thrust plate bolts and carefully remove camshaft from front of engine, Fig. 16.
9. Reverse procedure to install.

PISTON & ROD, ASSEMBLE

If the old pistons are serviceable, make certain that they are installed on the rods from which they were removed. The assembly must be assembled as shown in Fig. 17.

PISTONS, RINGS & PINS

Pistons are available in oversizes of .003, .020, .030 and .040″.

Piston pins are available in oversizes of .001 and .002″.

Rings are available in oversizes of .020, .030 and .040″.

MAIN & ROD BEARINGS

Main and rod bearings are available in standard size and undersizes of .001, .002, .010, .020, .030 and .040″.

CRANKSHAFT OIL SEAL

1. Remove oil pan and oil pump, if necessary.
2. Remove rear bearing cap.
3. Loosen remaining bearing caps, allowing crankshaft to drop down about 1/32″.
4. Remove old seals from both cylinder block and rear main bearing cap. Use a brass rod to drift upper half of seal from cylinder block groove. Rotate crankshaft while drifting to facilitate removal.
5. Carefully clean seal groove in block with a brush and solvent. Also clean seal groove in bearing cap. Remove the oil seal retaining pin from the bearing cap if so equipped. *The pin is not used with the split-lip seal.*
6. Dip seal halves in clean engine oil.
7. Carefully install upper seal half in its groove with undercut side of seal toward front of engine, Fig. 19, by rotating it on shaft journal of crankshaft until approximately 3/8″ protrudes below the parting surface. *Be sure no rubber has been shaved from outside diameter or seal by bottom edge of groove.*
8. Retighten main bearing caps and torque to specifications.
9. Install lower seal in main bearing cap with undercut side of seal toward front of engine, and allow seal to protrude about 3/8″ above parting surface to mate with upper seal upon cap installation.
10. Apply suitable sealer to parting faces of cap and block. Install cap and torque to specifications.

NOTE: If difficulty is encountered in installing the upper half of the seal in position, lightly lap (sandpaper) the side of the seal opposite the lip side using a medium grit paper. After sanding, the seal must be washed in solvent, then dipped in clean engine oil prior to installation.

OIL PAN, REPLACE

1977-79 Versailles

1. Disconnect battery ground cable.
2. Remove two fan shroud attaching screws and loosen shroud to prevent damage when raising engine.
3. Raise vehicle and drain crankcase.
4. Remove stabilizer bar from chassis.
5. Remove right and left engine mount through bolts.
6. Loosen transmission oil cooler lines and move aside.
7. Raise engine and position 2 x 4 in. wooden blocks under engine mounts.
8. Remove oil pan attaching bolts and oil pan.

NOTE: It will be necessary to rotate the crankshaft during removal so that rear crankshaft throw is in horizontal position to clear rear oil pan flange.

9. Reverse procedure to install.

1978-79—Continental & Mark V

1. Disconnect battery ground cable. Also disconnect transmission oil cooler lines from radiator and position aside.
2. Remove fresh air intake duct and radiator shroud attaching bolts, then position radiator shroud over fan.
3. Raise vehicle and drain crankcase.
4. On Mark V models, remove "X" brace located below oil pan.
5. On all models, remove end attachments of front stabilizer bar and ro-

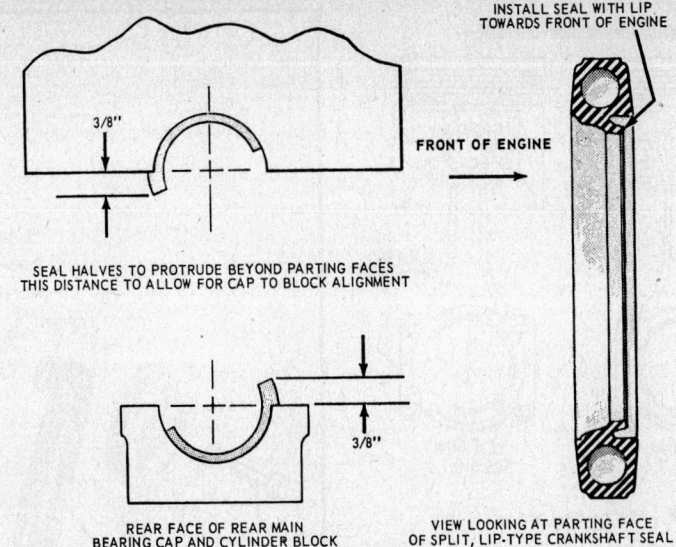

Fig. 19 Rear crankshaft seal installation

tate ends of bar downward to raise center of bar.
6. Support engine using a suitable jack, then remove engine support through bolts.
7. Raise engine and position wooden blocks 3 in. high between each engine support bracket and frame, then lower engine.
8. Remove oil pan attaching bolts, then lower pan to crossmember.
9. On models equipped with V8-400 engines, loosen oil pump and inlet tube and allow assembly to drop into the oil pan.
10. On all models, position rear crankshaft throw horizontally, then remove oil pan.

1974-77 Continental

1. Disconnect battery ground cable.
2. Disconnect radiator shroud from radiator.
3. Support vehicle on hoist and drain crankcase.
4. Remove starter retaining bolts.
5. Using a floor jack and wooden block under oil pan, raise engine enough to remove weight of engine from supports and remove through bolts from each support.
6. Remove the two forward support bolts from the right support insulator, then loosen the rear support bolt and pivot the insulator upward to gain access to the converter support bolts. Remove converter support bolts and remove bracket from each side of oil pan.
7. Position a 1 inch wooden block under each engine support bracket and remove jack.
8. Remove front stabilizer bar end attachments and rotate ends of bar down to raise center of bar.
9. Remove oil filter.
10. Remove oil pan attaching bolts and remove oil pan.

11. Reverse removal procedure for installation.

1974-77 Mark IV & V

1. Disconnect battery ground cable.
2. Disconnect transmission oil cooler lines from radiator, then remove radiator shroud attaching bolts and position shroud over fan.
3. Support vehicle on hoist, then drain crankcase and remove oil filter.
4. Remove end attachments of front stabilizer bar and rotate ends of bar down to raise center of bar.
5. Support engine with floor jack and re-

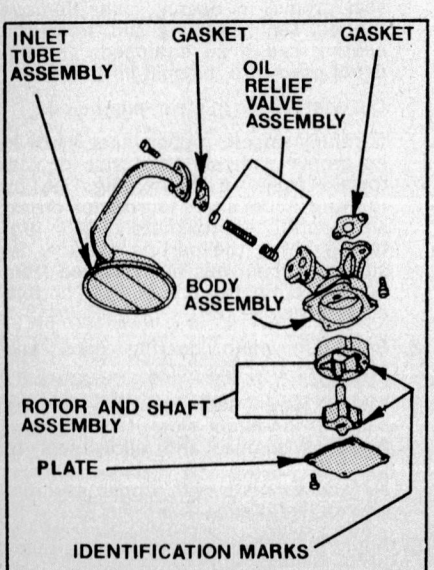

Fig. 20 Oil pump assembly. V8-302, 351W & 460

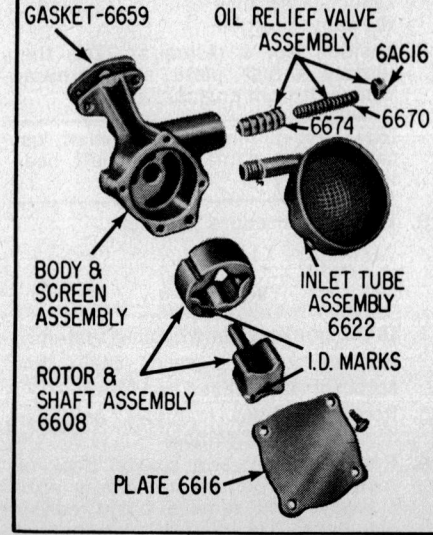

Fig. 21 Oil pump assembly. V8-400

move engine support through bolts.

6. Remove transmission oil cooler line attaching bolt from engine block and remove starter attaching bolts.

7. Raise engine enough to allow removal of right insulator heat shield, then position a wooden block 3 inches high between each engine support bracket and exhaust manifold. Lower engine allowing blocks to support engine.

8. Remove converter housing to cylinder block support attaching bolts and remove brackets.

9. Remove oil pan attaching bolts and lower pan to crossmember, then move transmission oil cooler lines upward and remove oil pan.

10. Reverse removal procedure for installation.

OIL PUMP

To remove the pump, remove oil pan as outlined above. Then remove the two bolts that attach the pump to the crankcase and remove pump, gasket and intermediate shaft.

To disassemble, remove the pump cover plate, Figs. 20 and 21, and lift out the rotor and shaft. Remove cotter pin that secures relief valve plug in pump housing. Drill a small hole and insert a self-tapping screw into plug, then using pliers remove plug from pump housing. Then remove the retainer spring and relief valve from the pump housing. Inspect the pump as follows:

1. With all parts clean and dry, check the inside of the pump housing and the outer race and rotor for damage or excessive wear.

2. Check the mating surface of the pump cover for wear. If this surface is worn, scored or grooved, replace the cover.

3. Measure the clearance between the outer race and housing. This clearance should be .001-.013.

4. With the rotor assembly installed in the housing, place a straight edge over the rotor assembly and housing. Measure the clearance between the straight edge and the rotor and outer race. Recommended limits are .0016-.004".

5. Check the drive shaft-to-housing bearing clearance by measuring the O.D. of the shaft and the I.D. of the housing bearing. The recommended clearance limits are .0015-.0030".

6. Inspect the relief valve spring for a collapsed or worn condition.

7. Check the relief valve piston for scores

and free operation in the bore. The specified clearance is .0015-.0030.

BELT TENSION DATA

	New	Used
1974-78	140	110

WATER PUMP, REPLACE

V8-302, 351W

1. Drain cooling system, then remove fan shroud attaching bolts and position shroud over fan.

2. Remove fan, spacer and shroud.

3. Remove drive belts, then remove A/C idler pulley bracket.

4. Remove power steering pump and position aside.

5. Remove all accessory brackets which attach to water pump, then remove water pump pulley.

6. Remove lower radiator hose, heater hose and by-pass hose from water pump.

7. Remove water pump to front cover attaching bolts, then remove water pump.

V8-400

1. Drain cooling system, then disconnect battery ground cable.

2. Remove fan shroud attaching bolts and position shroud rearward.

3. Remove fan and spacer from water pump shaft.

4. Remove drive belts, then remove A/C lower idler pulley.

5. Remove A/C compressor mount from water pump bracket.

6. Remove water pump pulley.

7. Remove alternator and power steering bracket from water pump and position aside.

8. Disconnect lower radiator and heater hose from water pump.

9. Remove water pump attaching bolts and water pump.

V8-460

1. Drain cooling system and remove fan,

fan shroud and drive belts.

2. Disconnect alternator bracket and position out of way.

3. Remove air pump pulley and pivot bolt, then disconnect adjusting bracket at pump. Remove upper bracket bolt and swing bracket out of way.

4. Remove power steering pump attaching bolts and position pump aside.

5. Remove A/C compressor and power steering pump and position aside.

NOTE: Secure compressor to left fender brace.

6. Remove A/C compressor bracket, then disconnect, radiator, heater and by-pass hoses from water pump.

7. Remove water pump attaching bolts and water pump.

FUEL PUMP PRESSURE

Year	Engine	Pressure, Lbs.
1974-75	V8-460	5.7-7.7
1976	V8-460	6.7-8.7
1977-79	V8-302, 351W	6-8
	V8-400	6-8
	V8-460	5.7-7.7

FUEL PUMP, REPLACE

1. Remove all gasket material from the pump and block gasket surfaces. Apply sealer to both sides of new gasket.

2. Position gasket on pump flange and hold pump in position against its mounting surface. Make sure rocker arm is riding on camshaft eccentric.

3. Press pump tight against its mounting. Install retaining screws and tighten them alternately.

4. Connect fuel lines. Then operate engine and check for leaks.

NOTE: Before installing the pump, it is good practice to crank the engine so that the nose of the camshaft eccentric is out of the way of the fuel pump rocker arm when the pump is installed. In this way there will be the lease amount of tension on the rocker arm, thereby easing the installation of the pump.

Transmission, Rear Axle, Propeller Shaft & Brakes

1979 AUTO. TRANS. LINKAGE ADJUST

The control linkage adjustment procedures are the same as described for the 1978 models in the rear of this manual.

REAR AXLES

Fig. 1 illustrates the rear axle assembly used on these cars. When necessary to overhaul either of these units, refer to the *Rear Axle Specifications* table in this chapter.

1974-79 Removable Carrier Type

In these axles, Fig. 1, the drive pinion is straddle-mounted by two opposed tapered roller bearings which support the pinion shaft in front of the drive pinion gear, and straight roller bearing that supports the pinion shaft at the rear of the pinion gear. The drive pinion is assembled in a pinion retainer that is bolted to the differential carrier. The tapered roller bearings are preloaded by a collapsible spacer between the bearings. The pinion is positioned by a shim or shims located between the drive pinion retainer and the differential carrier.

The differential is supported in the carrier by two tapered roller side bearings. These bearings are preloaded by two threaded ring nuts or sleeves between the bearings and pedestals. The differential assembly is positioned for proper ring gear and pinion backlash by varying the adjustment of these ring nuts. The differential case houses two side gears in mesh with two pinions mounted on a

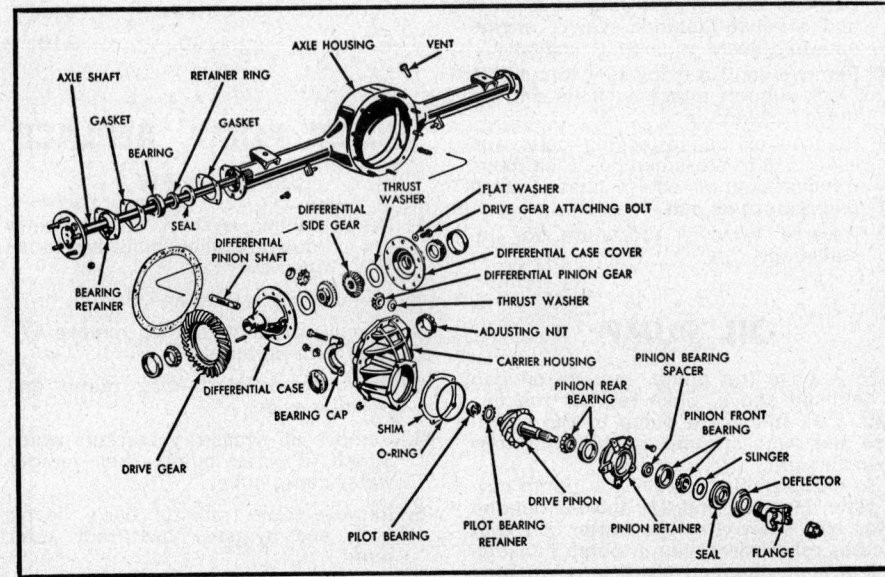

Fig. 1   Rear axle assembly. 1974-79

pinion shaft which is held in place by a pin. The side gears and pinions are backed by thrust washers. With high performance engines, an optional rear axle having a four-pinion differential is also used.

The axle shafts are of unequal length, the left shaft being shorter than the right. The axle shafts are mounted in sealed ball bearings that are pressed on the shafts.

Service Bulletin

All Ford Built Rear Axles: Recent manufacturing changes have eliminated the need for marking rear axle drive pinions for individual variations from nominal shim thicknesses. In the past, these pinion markings, with the aid of a shim selection table, were used as a guide to select correct shim thicknesses when a gear set or carrier assembly replacement was performed.

With the elimination of pinion markings, use of the shim selection table is no longer possible and the methods outlined below must be used.

1. Measure the thickness of the original pinion depth shim removed from the axle. Use the same thickness upon installation of the replacement carrier or drive pinion. If any further shim change is necessary, it will be indicated in the tooth pattern check.

2. If the original shim is lost, substitute a nominal shim for the original and

use the tooth pattern check to determine if further shim changes are required.

REAR AXLE, REPLACE

1977-79 Versailles

1. Raise vehicle and position safety stands under rear frame members.

2. Make marks on drive shaft yoke and pinion flange for reassembly, then dis-

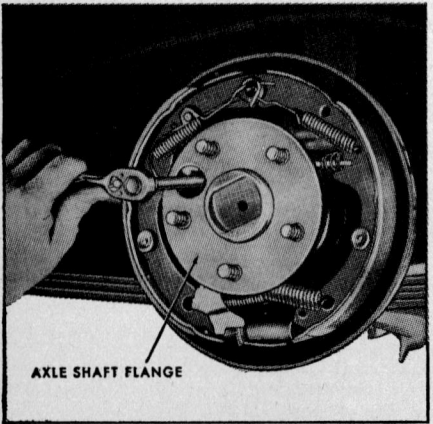

Fig. 2   Removing nuts from rear bearing retainer

Fig. 3   Removing axle shaft with slide hammer-type puller

Fig. 4 Splitting bearing inner retainer for bearing removal

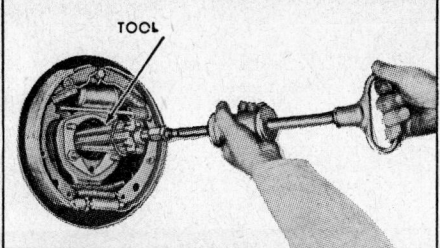

Fig. 5 Using hook-type tool to remove oil seal

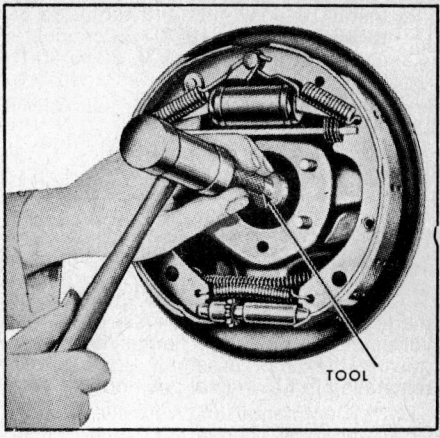

Fig. 6 Using special driver to install oil seal

connect drive shaft at rear axle U-joint and remove drive shaft from transmission extension housing. Install seal replacer tool in extension housing to prevent leakage.
3. Disconnect shock absorbers from lower mountings.
4. Remove wheel and tire assembly.
5. Remove calipers from anchor plates, then remove two retaining nuts and slide rotors off axle shafts.

NOTE: Secure calipers to frame with wire.

6. Remove vent tube from axle housing.
7. Remove brake lines from axle housing clips.
8. Support axle housing using a suitable jack, then remove spring clip nuts and plates.
9. Lower rear axle assembly and remove vehicle.

1974-79 Continental

1. Raise rear of vehicle and remove wheel and tire assembly.
2. On models equipped with rear drum brakes, remove brake drums, disconnect brake lines at wheel cylinders.
3. On models equipped with rear disc brakes, remove calipers from anchor plates, then remove two retaining nuts and slide rotors off axle shafts.

NOTE: Secure calipers to frame with wire.

4. Make marks on drive shaft yoke and pinion flange for reassembly, then disconnect drive shaft at rear axle U-joint and remove drive shaft from transmission extension housing. Install seal replacer tool in extension housing to prevent leakage.
5. Position a drain pan under differential carrier, then loosen carrier attaching bolts and allow axle to drain.
6. Disconnect anti-skid sensor wire connector from differential carrier, if equipped.
7. Position safety stands under frame rear members, then support axle housing using a suitable jack.
8. Disconnect brake lines from axle housing retaining clips.

9. Disconnect vent tube from rear housing.
10. Disconnect shock absorbers from lower mounting brackets.
11. Disconnect track bar from mounting stud on rear axle housing bracket.

NOTE: The axle housing mounting bracket has two holes; the track bar should be attached to the upper hole.

12. Lower rear axle housing until coil springs are released, then remove springs and insulators.
13. Disconnect suspension lower arms from axle housing, then disconnect suspension upper arms from housing.
14. Lower axle housing and remove from vehicle.

1974-79 Mark IV & V

1. Raise rear of vehicle and remove wheel and tire assembly.
2. On models equipped with rear drum brakes, remove brake drums and disconnect brake lines at wheel cylinders.
3. On models equipped with rear disc brakes, remove calipers from anchor plates, then remove two retaining nuts and slide rotors off axle shafts.

NOTE: Secure calipers to frame with wire.

4. Make marks on drive shaft yoke and pinion flange for reassembly, then disconnect drive shaft at rear axle U-joint and remove drive shaft from transmission extension housing. Install seal replacer tool in extension housing to prevent leakage.
5. Position a drain pan under differential carrier, then remove carrier attaching bolts and allow axle to drain.
6. Disconnect anti-skid sensor wire connector from differential carrier, then remove mounting bracket and sensor wiring from axle, if equipped.
7. Disconnect stabilizer, if equipped.
8. Disconnect shock absorber from lower mounting.
9. Remove brake line from retaining clips on rear axle housing, then remove brake line junction block retaining screw.
10. Position a suitable jack under axle housing to prevent housing from tilting when removing control arms.
11. Disconnect lower control arms from axle housing and position them downward.
12. Disconnect upper control arms from

axle housing and position them upward.
13. Disconnect air vent line.
14. Lower axle housing slightly and remove coil springs and insulators.
15. Lower axle housing and remove from vehicle.

AXLE SHAFTS

1. Remove wheel assembly.
2. Remove brake drum or caliper and rotor.
3. Working through hole provided in axle shaft flange, Fig. 2, remove nuts that secure wheel bearing retainer.
4. Pull axle shaft out of housing with a slide hammer-type puller, Fig. 3. *Brake carrier plate must not be dislodged. Install one nut to hold the plate in place after axle shaft is removed.*
5. If axle shaft bearing is to be replaced, loosen inner retainer by nicking it deeply with a chisel in several places, Fig. 4. The bearing will then slide off easily.
6. Press bearing from axle shaft.
7. Inspect machined surface of axle shaft and housing for rough spots that would affect the sealing action of the oil seal. Carefully remove any burrs or rough spots.
8. Press new bearing on shaft until it seats firmly against shoulder on shaft.
9. Press inner bearing retainer on shaft until it seats firmly against bearing.
10. If oil seal is to be replaced, use a hook-type tool to pull it out of the housing, Fig. 5. Wipe a small amount of oil resistant sealer on outer edge of seal before it is installed, Fig. 6.

Installation

1. Place a new gasket on each side of brake carrier plate and slide axle shaft into housing. Start splines into differential side gear and push the shaft in until bearing bottoms in housing.

2. Install retainer nuts and torque to 50 to 75 ft. lbs. for 1974-77 Continental and Mark IV and Mark V, 20 to 40 ft. lbs. for 1977-79 Versailles and 50 to 70 ft. lbs. for 1978-79 Continental and Mark V.

3. Install brake drum and wheel.

PROPELLER SHAFT

To maintain proper drive line balance, mark the drive shaft, universal joints, slip yoke and companion flange before removing the shaft assembly so it can be reinstalled in its original position.

1. On Continental and Versailles remove companion flange to drive pinion flange attaching bolts.

2. On 1974-76 Mark IV and 1977-79 Mark V, disconnect rear U joint from companion flange. Tape loose bearing caps to spider.

3. On all models, pull drive shaft rearward until slip yoke clears transmission extension housing.

4. Reverse procedure to install.

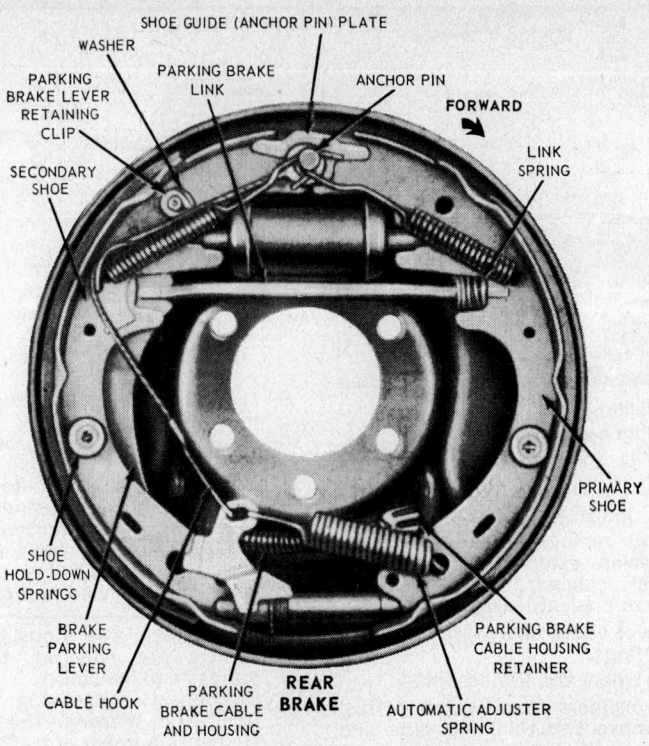

Fig. 7   Rear only on 1974-79

BRAKE ADJUSTMENTS

NOTE: For 1974-79 a new self-centering pressure differential valve is used which no longer requires bleeding at the opposite end of the car to cause the brake warning light to go out. To center the new valve, after any brake repair or bleeding, it is only necessary to turn the ignition switch on and depress the brake pedal. This action will center the piston and the light will go out.

These brakes, Fig. 7, have self-adjusting shoe mechanisms that assure correct lining-to-drum clearances at all times. The automatic adjusters operate only when the brakes are applied when the car is moving rearward.

Although the brakes are self-adjusting, an initial adjustment is necessary when the brake shoes have been relined or replaced, or when the length of the star wheel adjuster has been changed during some other service operation.

Frequent usage of an automatic transmission forward range to halt reverse vehicle motion may prevent the automatic adjusters from functioning, thereby inducing low pedal heights. Should low pedal heights be encountered, it is recommended that numerous forward and reverse stops be made until satisfactory pedal height is obtained.

Adjustment

SERVICE BULLETIN

When servicing a vehicle requiring a brake adjustment, the metal knock-out plugs should NOT be removed. Rather the drums should be removed and brakes inspected for a malfunction.

Although the brakes are self-adjusting, an initial adjustment will be necessary after a brake repair, such as relin-

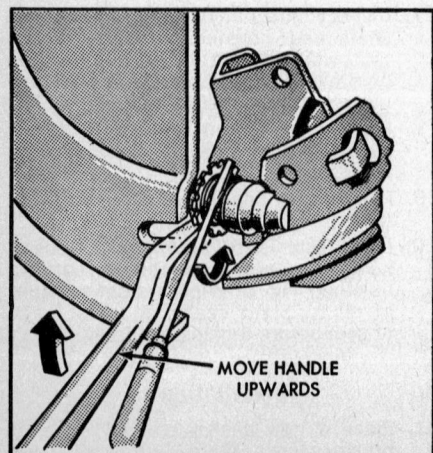

Fig. 8   Backing off brake adjustment by disengaging adjuster lever with screwdriver

NOTE

If a low pedal height condition cannot be corrected by making numerous reverse stops (provided the hydraulic system is free of air) it indicates that the automatic adjusting mechanism is not functioning. Therefore, it will be necessary to remove the brake drum, clean, free up and lubricate the adjusting mechanism. Then adjust the brakes, being sure the parking brake is fully released.

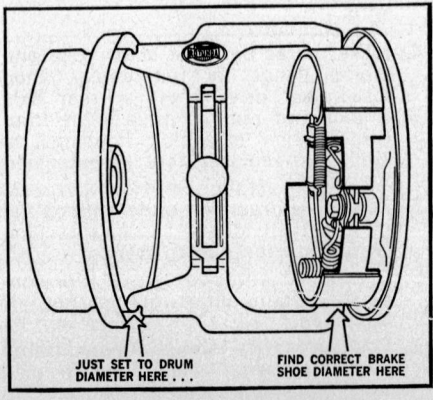

Fig. 9   Brake adjustment with gauge

ing or replacement. The initial adjustment can be obtained by the new procedure which follows:

NOTE: If after removing brake drum retaining nuts, the brake drum cannot be removed, pry rubber plug from backing plate. Insert a narrow screwdriver through hole in backing plate and disengage lever from adjusting screw. While holding lever away from adjusting screw, back off adjusting screw using a suitable tool to retract brake shoes, Fig. 6.

1. Use the brake shoe adjustment gauge shown in Fig. 9 to obtain the drum inside diameter as shown. Tighten the adjusting knob on the gauge to hold this setting.
2. Place the opposite side of the gauge over the brake shoes and adjust the shoes by turning the adjuster screw until the gauge just slides over the linings. Rotate the gauge around the lining surface to assure proper lining diameter adjustment and clearance.
3. Install brake drum and wheel. Final adjustment is accomplished by making several firm reverse stops, using the brake pedal.

PARKING BRAKES, ADJUST

1975-79 Rear Disc Brakes

1. Fully release parking brake, then place transmission in neutral and support vehicle at rear axle.
2. Tighten adjuster nut until levers on calipers just begin to move, then loosen adjuster nut until levers just return to stop position.
3. Apply and release parking brake. Check levers on caliper to determine if they are fully returned by attempting to pull lever rearward. If lever moves, the adjustment is too tight and must be readjusted.

1974-79 Rear Drum Brakes

1. Make sure the parking brake is fully released.

2. Place transmission in neutral and raise the vehicle.
3. Tighten the adjusting nut against the cable equalizer to cause rear wheel brake drag. Then loosen the adjusting nut until the rear brakes are fully released. There should be no brake drag.
4. Lower the vehicle and check operation.

1974-79 Vacuum Release Unit

The vacuum power unit will release the parking brake automatically when the transmission selector lever is moved into any driving position with the engine running. The brakes will not release automatically, however, when the selector lever is in neutral or park position with the engine running, or in any other position with the engine off.

The lower end of the release handle extends out for alternate manual release in the event of vacuum power failure or for optional manual release at any time.

MASTER CYLINDER, REPLACE

1. Disconnect brake lines from master cylinder.
2. Remove two nuts attaching master cylinder to power brake unit.
3. Slide master cylinder off mounting studs and remove from vehicle.

POWER BRAKE UNIT, REPLACE

Vacuum Booster

1974

1. Disconnect battery ground cable.

2. Disconnect stop light switch wires and remove switch retaining pin. Slide switch off pin so switch outer hole clears pin, then remove switch. Slide booster push rod, nylon washers and bushing off brake pedal pin.
3. Remove master cylinder and position aside without damaging hydraulic lines.
4. Disconnect vacuum hose from booster and remove booster attaching nuts and booster.
5. Reverse procedure to install.

1975-79 Hydro Boost

1. Disconnect stoplight switch wires at connector and remove hairpin retainer, then slide stoplight switch off brake pedal pin far enough for switch outer hole to clear pin and remove pin from switch.
2. Slide hydro-boost push rod and nylon washers and bushing off brake pedal pin.
3. Remove master cylinder and position to one side without disturbing hydraulic lines.

NOTE: It is not necessary to disconnect brake lines, but care should be taken not to deform lines.

4. Disconnect pressure, steering gear and return lines from booster, then plug lines and ports in hydro-boost to prevent entry of dirt.
5. Remove hydro-boost retaining nuts, and remove assembly sliding push rod link from engine side of dash panel.
6. Reverse procedure to install. To purge system, disconnect coil wire so that engine will not start. Fill power steering pump reservoir, then while engaging starter, pump brake pedal. Do not cycle steering wheel until all residual air has been purged from the hydro boost unit. Check fluid level, then connect coil wire and start engine. Apply brakes with a pumping action and cycle steering wheel, then check system for leaks.

Rear Suspension

SHOCK ABSORBER, REPLACE

1. With the rear axle supported properly disconnect shock absorber at upper mounting and compress it to clear hole in spring seat.
2. Disconnect shock absorber from stud on axle bracket.
3. Reverse procedure to install.

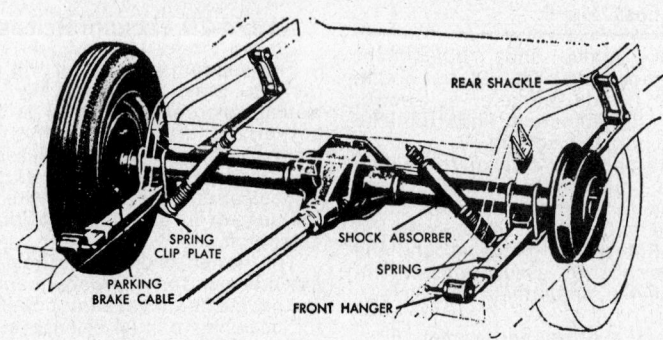

Fig. 1   Rear suspension (typical). 1977-79 Versailles

LEAF SPRINGS & BUSHINGS, REPLACE

1977-79 Versailles

1. Raise rear of vehicle and support at frame. Support axle with a suitable jack.
2. Disconnect shock absorbers from lower mountings.
3. Lower jack and remove spring plate "U" bolts and spring plate, Fig. 1.
4. Raise axle to remove weight from spring and disassemble rear shackle.
5. Remove spring front mount bolt.
6. Replace spring front eye bushings as necessary, Figs. 2 and 3.
7. Reverse procedure to install.

COIL SPRINGS, REPLACE

1974-79 Except Versailles

1. Raise rear of vehicle and support at frame. Support rear axle with a suitable jack.
2. Disconnect shock absorbers at lower mountings.
3. On 1974-79 Lincoln Continental models, disconnect brake hose at rear crossmember and remove hose to bracket clip.
4. Lower axle to remove springs.
5. Reverse procedure to install. On all models except 1974-76 Mark IV and 1977-79 Mark V, install an insulator between upper seats and the spring, Fig. 4. On 1974-76 Mark IV and 1977-79 Mark V, an insulator is installed only between upper seat and the spring, Fig. 5.

CONTROL ARMS, REPLACE

1974-79 Except Versailles

NOTE: The 1974-76 Mark IV and 1977-79 Mark V upper and lower control arms are replaced in pairs.

1. Raise rear of vehicle and support at frame. Support axle with a suitable jack.
2. On all models except 1974-76 Mark IV and 1977-79 Mark V, disconnect track bar from frame mounting bracket.
3. Lower axle and install a second jack under differential pinion nose.
4. Disconnect control arm from axle bracket. On upper arms, disconnect arm from crossmember and on lower arms, disconnect arm from frame attachment bracket.
5. Reverse procedure to install.

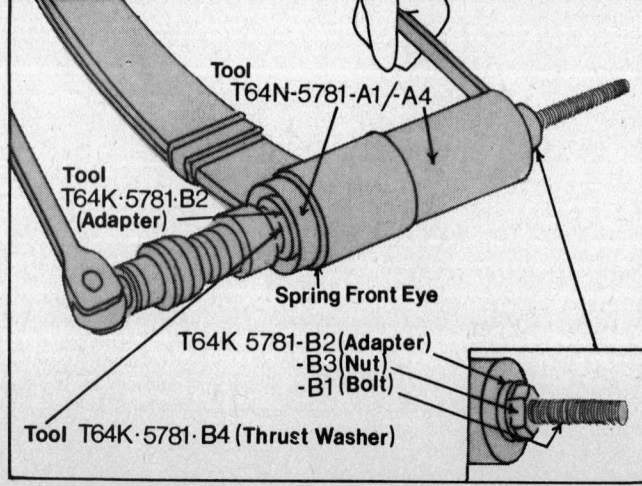

Fig. 2   Spring front bushing removal. 1977-79 Versailles

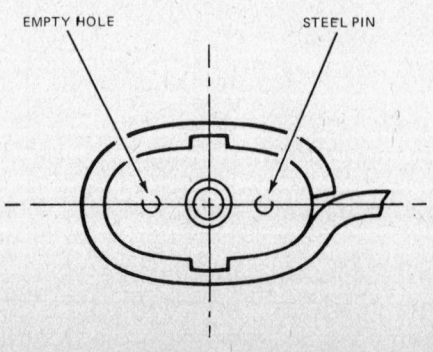

Fig. 3   Spring front bushing installation. 1977-79 Versailles

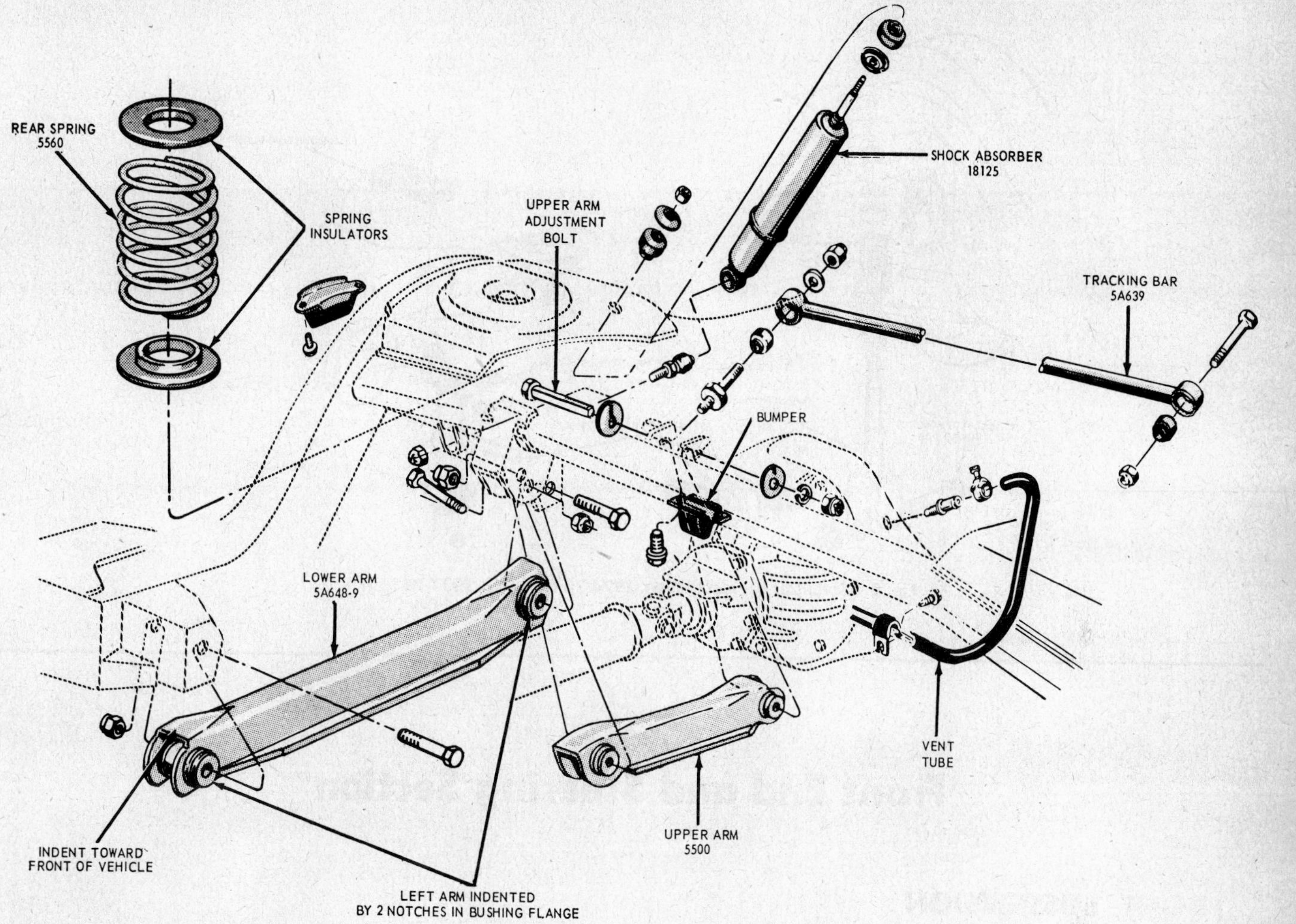

REAR SPRING
5560

SPRING
INSULATORS

UPPER ARM
ADJUSTMENT
BOLT

SHOCK ABSORBER
18125

TRACKING BAR
5A639

BUMPER

LOWER ARM
5A648-9

VENT
TUBE

INDENT TOWARD
FRONT OF VEHICLE

UPPER ARM
5500

LEFT ARM INDENTED
BY 2 NOTCHES IN BUSHING FLANGE

Fig. 4   Rear suspension (typical). 1974-79 Continental

STABILIZER BAR, REPLACE

1974-76 Mark IV & 1977-79 Mark V

1. Remove bolts securing stabilizer bar to rear link assemblies on both sides, Fig. 6.
2. Remove nuts securing mounting bracket to lower mounting clamp and remove bar.
3. Reverse procedure to install.

TRACK BAR & BUSHINGS, REPLACE

1974-79 Continental

1. Remove cover from track bar axle attachment, then disconnect track bar from mounting stud.
2. Disconnect track bar from frame side rail.
3. Reverse procedure to install.

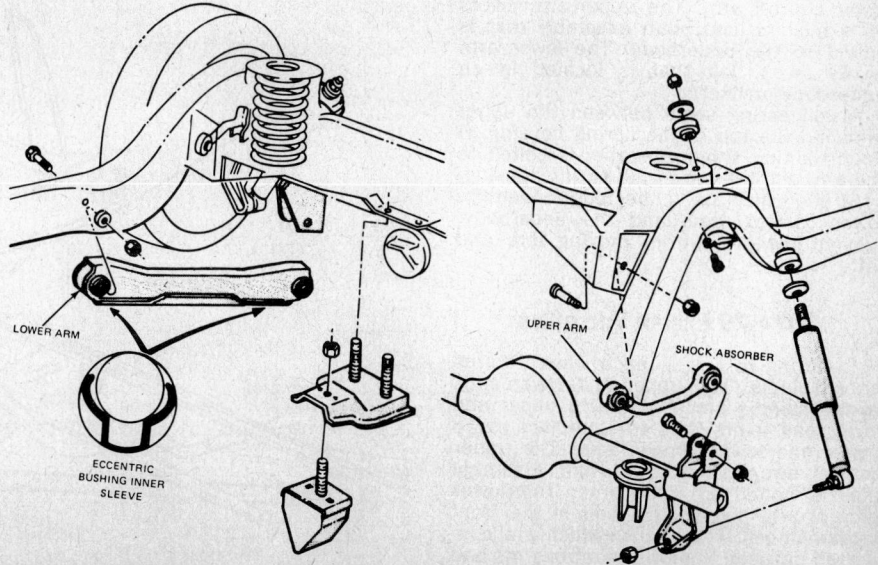

LOWER ARM

ECCENTRIC
BUSHING INNER
SLEEVE

UPPER ARM

SHOCK ABSORBER

Fig. 5   Rear suspension (typical). 1974-76 Mark IV & 1977-79 Mark V

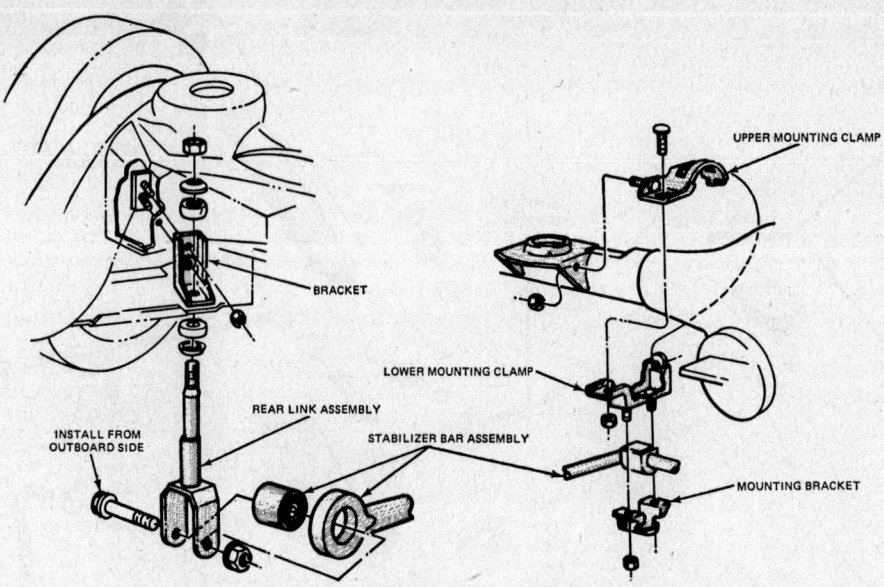

Fig. 6   Stabilizer bar installation. 1974-76 Mark IV & 1977-79 Mark V

Front End and Steering Section

FRONT SUSPENSION

1977-79 Versailles

Referring to Fig. 1, each front wheel rotates on a spindle. The upper and lower ends of the spindle are attached to ball joints that are mounted to an upper and lower control arm. The upper arm pivots on a bushing and shaft assembly that is bolted to the underbody. The lower arm pivots on a bolt that is located in an underbody bracket.

A coil spring seats between the upper arm and the top of the spring housing. A double-acting shock absorber is bolted to the arm and the top of the spring housing.

Struts, which are connected between the lower control arms and the underbody, prevent the arms from moving fore and aft.

1974-79 Except Versailles

Referring to Fig. 2, each wheel rotates on a spindle. The upper and lower ends of the spindle are attached to upper and lower ball joints that are mounted to an upper and lower control arm. The upper control arm pivots on a shaft assembly that is bolted to the frame. The lower control arm pivots on a bolt in the front crossmember. The struts, which are connected between the lower control arms and frame crossmember, prevent the control arms from moving forward or backward.

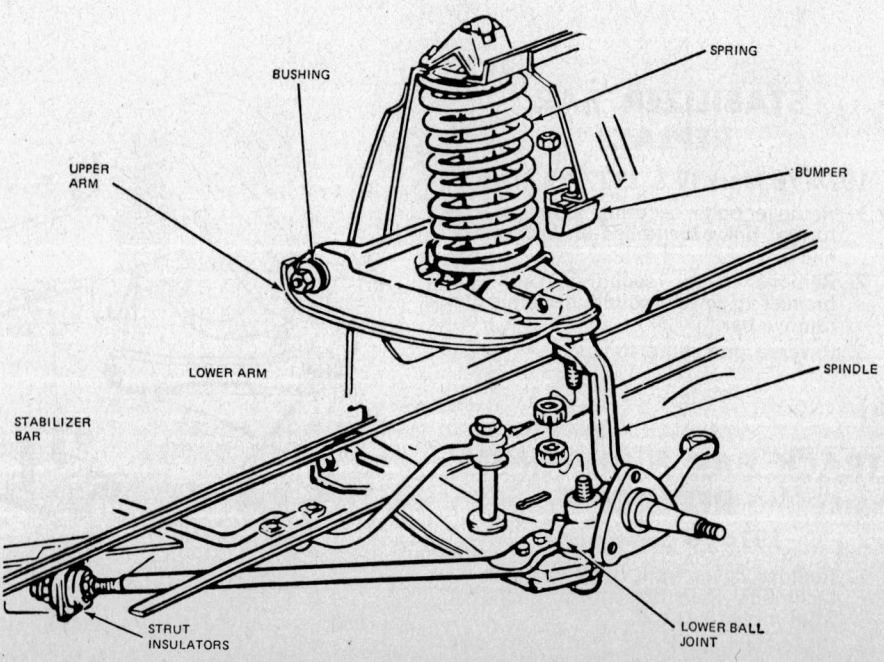

Fig. 1   Front suspension (typical). 1977-79 Versailles

LUBRICATION

1974-79 STEERING LINKAGE: The steering linkage should be lubricated at 30,-000 mile intervals. Normal breathing of socket joints permits moisture condensation within the joint. Moisture inside the joint assembly will cause no appreciable damage and the joint will function normally. However, if the moisture is concentrated in the bearing grease grooves and is frozen at the time of attempted lubrication, grease cannot flow and pressure greasing may damage the joint assembly.

Do not attempt to lubricate the steering linkage if it has set in temperatures lower than 20 deg. above zero F. The vehicle should be allowed to warm up in a heated garage for 30 minutes or until the joints accept lubrication.

IMPORTANT: A torch must not be used to heat joints because this quantity of heat will melt the nylon bearing within the joint.

Ball Joint Lubrication

Ball joints should be lubricated with special grease formulated just for this purpose every 30,000 miles.

Lubrication points are fitted with screw plugs. The plugs should be removed, grease fittings installed and, after applying the grease, remove the fittings and reinstall the plugs.

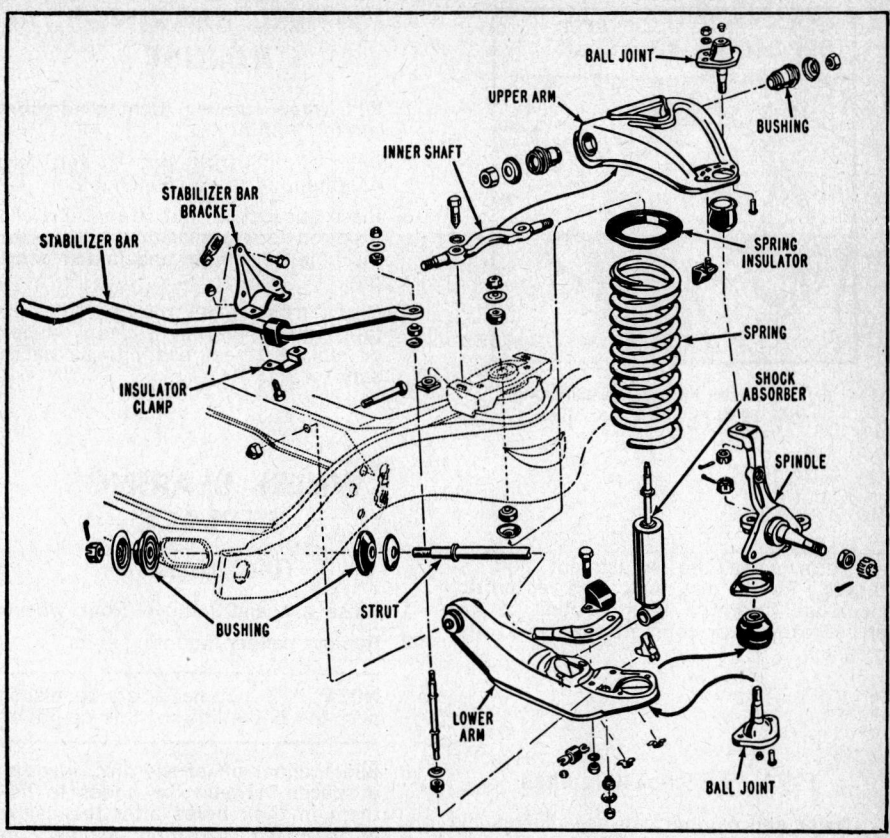

Fig. 2   Front suspension. 1974-79 Except Versailles

WHEEL ALIGNMENT

SERVICE BULLETIN

WHEEL BALANCING DIFFERS: On cars with disc brakes, dynamic balancing of the wheel-and-tire assembly on the car should not be attempted without first pulling back the shoe and lining assemblies from the rotor. If this is not done, brake drag may burn out the motor on the wheel spinner.

The drag can be eliminated by removing the wheel, taking out the two bolts holding the caliper splash shield, and detaching the shield. Then push the pistons into their cylinder bores by applying steady pressure on the shoes on each side of the rotor for at least a minute. If necessary, use waterpump pliers to apply the pressure.

After the pistons have been retracted, reinstall the splash shield and wheel. The wheel-and-tire assembly can then be dynamically balanced in the usual way. After the balancing job has been completed, be sure to pump the brake pedal several times until the shoes are seated and a firm brake pedal is obtained.

1977-79 Versailles

Caster & Camber

As shown in Fig. 3, caster is controlled by the front suspension strut. To obtain positive caster, loosen the strut rear nut and tighten the strut front nut against the bushing. To obtain negative caster, loosen the strut front nut and tighten the strut rear nut against the bushing.

Camber is controlled by the eccentric cam located at the lower arm attachment to the side rail. To adjust camber, loosen the camber adjustment bolt nut at the rear of the body bracket. Spread the body bracket at the camber adjustment bolt area just enough to permit lateral travel of

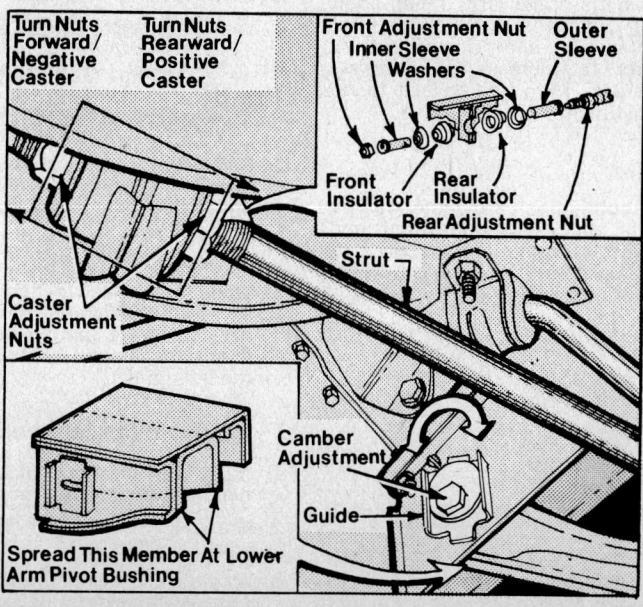

Fig. 3   Caster & camber adjustment. 1977-79 Versailles

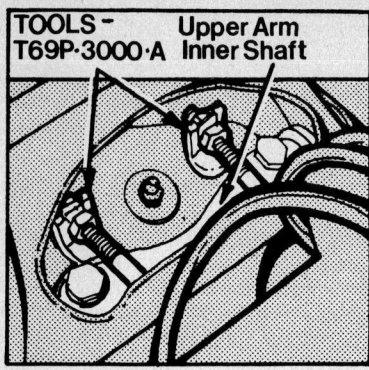

Fig. 4 Caster and camber adjusting tool. 1974-79 except Versailles

WHEEL BEARINGS, ADJUST

1. With wheel rotating, tighten adjusting nut to 17-25 ft. lbs.
2. Back off adjusting nut ½ turn and retighten nut to 10-15 inch lbs.
3. Place nut lock on nut so that castellations on lock are aligned with cotter pin hole in spindle and install cotter pin.
4. Check front wheel rotation, if it rotates noisily or rough, clean, inspect or replace wheel bearings as necessary.

WHEEL BEARINGS, REPLACE

(Disc Brakes)

1. Raise car and remove front wheels.
2. Remove caliper mounting bolts.

NOTE: It is not necessary to disconnect the brake line for this operation.

---

3. Slide caliper off of the disc, inserting a spacer between the shoes to hold them in their bores after the caliper is removed. Position caliper assembly out of the way.

NOTE: Do not allow caliper to hang by brake hose.

---

4. Remove hub and disc. Grease retainer and inner bearing can now be removed.

CHECKING BALL JOINTS FOR WEAR

Upper Ball Joint

1977-79 Versailles

1. Raise car on frame contact hoist or by floor jacks placed beneath underbody until wheel falls to full down position.
2. Grasp the lower edge of tire and move the wheel in and out.
3. While the wheel is being moved observe any movement between the upper end of the spindle and upper arm. If any movement is observed replace the ball joint.

1974-79 Except Versailles

1. Raise car on floor jacks placed beneath lower control arms.
2. Grasp lower edge of tire and move wheel in and out.
3. As wheel is being moved in and out, observe upper end of spindle and upper arm.

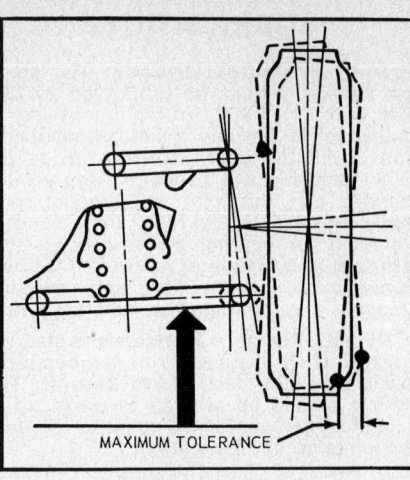

Fig. 5 Checking lower ball joint for wear. Exc. Versailles

4. Any movement between upper end of spindle and upper arm indicates ball joint wear and loss of preload. If such movement is observed, replace upper ball joint.

NOTE: During the foregoing check, the lower ball joint will be unloaded and may move. Disregard all such movement of the lower joint. Also, do not mistake loose wheel bearings for a worn ball joint.

Lower Ball Joint

1977-79 Versailles

1. With car jacked up as directed above, grasp the lower edge of the tire and move it in and out.
2. As wheel is being moved in and out, observe lower end of spindle and lower arm.
3. Any movement between lower end of spindle and lower arm indicates ball joint wear and loss of preload. If such movement is observed, replace lower arm and/or ball joint.

NOTE: During the foregoing check, the ball joints will be unloaded and may move. Therefore disregard any movement of the upper ball joint when checking the lower ball joint and any movement of the lower ball joint when checking the upper ball joint. Also, do not mistake loose wheel bearings for a worn ball joint.

1974-79 Except Versailles

1. Raise car on jacks placed under lower control arms as shown in Fig. 5.
2. With a dial indicator attached to the lower arm, position indicator so that the plunger rests against inner side

---

the arm when the adjustment bolt is turned. Rotate the bolt and eccentric clockwise from the high position to increase camber or counterclockwise to decrease it.

1974-79 Except Versailles

Caster and camber can be adjusted by loosening the bolts that attach the upper suspension arm to the shaft at the frame side rail, and moving the arm assembly in or out in the elongated bolt holes, Fig. 4. Since any movement of the arm affects both caster and camber, both factors should be balanced against one another when making the adjustment.

Caster, Adjust

1. To adjust caster, install the adjusting tool as shown in Fig. 4.
2. Loosen both upper arm inner shaft retaining bolts and move either front or rear of the shaft in or out as necessary to increase or decrease caster angle. Then tighten bolt to retain adjustment.

Camber, Adjust

1. Loosen both upper arm inner retaining bolts and move both front and rear ends of shaft inward or outward as necessary to increase or decrease camber angle.
2. Tighten bolts and recheck caster and readjust if necessary.

TOE-IN ADJUST

Position the front wheels in their straight-ahead position. Then turn both tie rod adjusting sleeves an equal amount until the desired toe-in setting is obtained.

of wheel rim adjacent to lower ball joint.

3. Grasp tire at top and bottom and slowly move tire in and out. Note reading on dial, which is the radial play. If the reading exceeds ¼", replace lower ball joint.

BALL JOINTS, REPLACE

NOTE: Ford Motor Company recommends that new ball joints should not be installed on used control arms and that the control arm be replaced if ball joint replacement is required. However, aftermarket ball joint repair kits which do not require control arm replacement, are available and can be installed using the following procedure.

When replacing a riveted joint, remove the rivets and retain the new joint in its control arm with the bolts, nuts and washers furnished with the ball joint kit.

Use a suitable pressing tool to force the ball joint from the spindle.

SHOCK ABSORBER, REPLACE

1977-79 Versailles

1. Raise hood and remove upper mounting bracket-to-spring tower retaining nuts.
2. Raise front of car and place safety stands under lower control arms.
3. Remove shock absorber lower retaining nuts and washers.
4. Lift shock absorber from spring tower.
5. Reverse procedure to install.

1974-79 Except Versailles

1. Remove nut, washer and bushing from upper end of shock absorber.
2. Raise vehicle and support on stands.
3. Remove screws retaining shock absorber to lower control arm and remove shock absorber.
4. Reverse procedure to install.

COIL SPRING, REPLACE

1977-79 Versailles

1. Remove shock absorber and upper mounting bracket as an assembly.
2. Raise car on hoist and install safety stands.
3. Remove wheel, tire, rotor and caliper assembly from spindle.
4. Install a suitable spring compressor and compress spring.

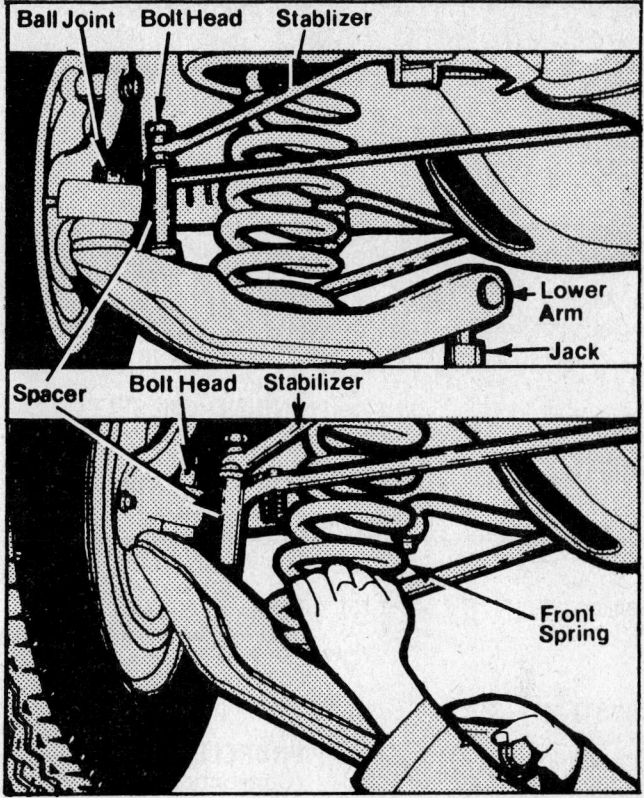

Fig. 6 Front spring replacement. Exc. Versailles

5. Remove two upper-arm-to-spring tower retaining nuts and swing upper arm outward from spring.
6. Release spring compressor, then remove spring.
7. Reverse procedure to install.

1974-79 Except Versailles

1. Raise vehicle and support front end of frame with jack stands.
2. Disconnect shock absorber from lower arm and place a jack under the lower arm to support it, Fig. 6.
3. Remove strut and rebound bumper bolts and disconnect lower end of sway bar stud from lower arm.
4. Remove the nut and bolt retaining inner end of the lower arm to crossmember.
5. Carefully lower jack relieving spring pressure on the lower arm, then remove spring.

POWER STEERING UNIT, REPLACE

1974-79 Integral Power Steering Gear

1. Disconnect lines from steering gear and plug lines and ports to prevent entry of dirt.

2. Remove the two bolts securing flex coupling to steering gear and to column.
3. Raise vehicle and remove sector shaft nut and pitman arm.

NOTE: Do not damage the seals.

4. Support steering gear and remove three attaching bolts. Remove flex coupling clamp bolt and work steering gear free of coupling, then remove steering gear from vehicle.

Control Valve Removal

1977-79 Non-Integral Power Steering

1. Disconnect fluid fittings at control valve and drain fluid from lines by turning wheels to left and right several times.
2. Loosen clamp at right-hand end of sleeve. Remove roll pin from steering arm-to-idler arm rod through slot in sleeve.
3. Using tool 3290-C, remove ball stud from sector shaft arm.

NOTE: The use of any other tool may result in damage to the control valve assembly.

4. Turn wheels fully to left and unthread control valve from idler arm rod.

OLDSMOBILE (Exc. Starfire)

TORONADO: Service procedures that apply to the Toronado only will be found starting on page 1-744.

INDEX OF SERVICE OPERATIONS

Vehicle Identification Plate: 1974-79 on left upper dash.

ENGINE NUMBER LOCATION

1973–76 6-250: Right side of engine block directly to rear of distributor.
1974 V8s: Stamped on oil filler tube.
1975 V8-400, 1975–76 Omega V8-350, 1977–78 V6-231, V8-350 & Omega V8-350 with distributor located at rear of engine, clockwise

distributor rotor rotation. Front right side of cylinder block.
1975–76 V8-455, 1975–78 V8-260, V8-350 Except Omega, 1977–78 Omega V8-350 with distributor located at rear of engine, counterclockwise distributor rotor rotation & V8-403: Stamped on engine oil filler tube

---

ENGINE IDENTIFICATION CODE

YEAR	ENGINE	ENGINE PREFIX
1974	6-250 Std. Tr.	CCC, CCD
	6-250 Auto. Tr.	CCA, CCB
	V8-350 2 Bar. Carb.	QS, QT
	V8-350 4 Bar. Carb.	QB, QC, QL
	V8-350 4 Bar. Carb.	QO, QU, QW
	V8-350 4 Bar. Carb.	TB, TC, TL, TO
	V8-455 2 Bar. Carb.	UU, UW
	V8-455 4 Bar. Carb.	UA, UB, UC
	V8-455 4 Bar. Carb.	UD, UI, UO
	V8-455 4 Bar. Carb.	UP, UN, UR
	V8-455 4 Bar. Carb.	UV, UX, VP
	V8-455 4 Bar. Carb.	VA, VB, VC
	V8-455 4 Bar. Carb.	VD, VL, VO
1975	6-250 Std. Tr. [1]	CJU
	6-250 Auto. Tr. [1]	CJT
	6-250 Auto. Tr. [2]	CJL
	V8-260 Std. Tr. [1]	QA, QK
	V8-260 Std. Tr. a/c [1]	QD, QN
	V8-260 Std. Tr. [2]	TA, TK
	V8-260 Std. Tr. a/c [2]	TD, TN
	V8-260 Auto. Tr. [1]	QE, QP
	V8-260 Auto. Tr. a/c [1]	QJ, QQ
	V8-260 Auto. Tr. [2]	TE, TP
	V8-260 Auto. Tr. a/c [2]	TJ, TQ
	V8-350 Auto. Tr. [1]	RW, QL
	V8-350 Auto. Tr. a/c [1]	RX, QO, QX
	V8-350 Auto. Tr. [2]	RN, TL
	V8-350 Auto. Tr. a/c [2]	RO, TO, TX
	V8-400 Auto. Tr. [1]	YM, YT
	V8-455 Auto. Tr. [1]	UB, UE, UP
	V8-455 Auto. Tr. a/c [1]	UC, UD, UP
	V8-455 Auto. Tr. [2]	VB, VE, VP
	V8-455 Auto. Tr. a/c [2]	VC, VD, VP
1976	6-250 Std. [1]	CCD, CCJ
	6-250 Auto. Tr. [1]	CCF, CCH
	6-250 Auto. Tr. [2]	CCC
	V8-260 Std. Tr. [1]	QA, QK
	V8-260 Std. Tr. a/c [1]	QD, QN
	V8-260 Std. Tr. [2]	TA, TD, TK, TN
	V8-260 Auto. Tr. [1]	QB, QP, Q7, Q8
	V8-260 Auto. Tr. a/c [1]	QC, QT

YEAR	ENGINE	ENGINE PREFIX
	V8-260 Auto. Tr. [2]	TE, TP, T-2, T-3, T-4, T-5, T-7, T-8
	V8-260 Auto Tr. a/c [2]	TJ, TT
	V8-350 2 Bar. Carb. Auto. Tr. [1]	PA
	V8-350 2 Bar. Carb. Auto. Tr. a/c [1]	PB
	V8-350 4 Bar. Carb. Auto. Tr. [1]	PE, Q2, Q4, Q6
	V8-350 4 Bar. Carb. Auto. Tr. a/c [1]	PF, Q3, Q5
	V8-350 4 Bar. Carb. Auto. Tr. [2]	PM, TL, TY
	V8-350 4 Bar. Carb. Auto. Tr. a/c [2]	PN, TO, TW, TX
	V8-455 Auto. Tr. [1]	UB, UE, U5, U6, U7, U8
	V8-455 Auto. Tr. a/c [1]	UC, UD, U3, U4
	V8-455 Auto. Tr. [2]	VB, VE, V5
	V8-455 Auto. Tr. a/c [2]	VD, V3, V4
1977	V6-231 Std. Tr. [1]	SG
	V6-231 Std. Tr. [2]	SU
	V6-231 Auto. Tr. [1]	SI
	V6-231 Auto. Tr. [1]	SK, SL
	V6-231 Auto. Tr. [2]	SM, SN
	V8-260 Std. Tr. [1]	QS, QT
	V8-260 Auto. Tr. [1]	QC, QD, QE, QJ, QU, QV
	V8-305 Std. Tr. [1]	CPA
	V8-305 Auto. Tr. [1]	CPY
	V8-350 4 Bar. Carb. Auto. Tr. [1]	QK, QL, QN, QO, QP, QQ
	V8-350 4 Bar. Carb. Auto. Tr. [2]	CKR, TK, TL, TN, TO, TP, TQ, TX, TY
	V8-350 4 Bar. Carb. Auto. Tr. [3]	Q2, Q3, Q6, Q7, Q8, Q9
	V8-403 Auto. Tr. [1]	UA, UB, UC, UD, UE
	V8-403 Auto. Tr. [2]	VA, VB, VE, VJ, VK
	V8-403 Auto. Tr. [3]	U2, U3, U6
1978	V6-231 Std. Tr. [4]	EA
	V6-231 Auto. Tr. [4]	EC, EK, EL, OH
	V6-231 Auto. Tr. [2]	EE, EK, EL, OK

YEAR	ENGINE	ENGINE PREFIX
	V6-231 Auto. Tr. [3]	EG
	V8-260 Std. Tr. [4]	QD, QE
	V8-260 Auto. Tr. [4]	QJ, QL, QK, QN, QT, QU
	V8-260 Auto. Tr. [2]	TK, TJ
	V8-305 Std. Tr. [4]	CTH, CRW
	V8-305 Auto. Tr. [4]	CPF, CTJ
	V8-305 Auto. Tr. [2]	CRY, CRZ
	V8-305 Auto. Tr. [3]	CPZ
	V8-350 Auto. Tr. [2]	TO, TP, TQ, TS, CHJ
	V8-350 Auto. Tr. [3]	Q2, Q3, CHL, CMC
	V8-350 Auto. Tr. [4]	QO, QP, QQ, QS, MA, MB
	V8-350 Diesel	QB, QC
	V8-403 Auto. Tr. [2]	VA, VB, VC
	V8-403 Auto. Tr. [3]	U2, U3, U4
	V8-403 Auto. Tr. [4]	UA, UB, UC, UD, UE
1979	V6-231 Auto. Tr. [2]	RG, RW, RY
	V6-231 Auto. Tr. [3]	RJ
	V6-231 Auto. Tr. [4]	NJ, NK, NL, RB, RC, RX
	V6-231 Std. Tr. [4]	NG, RA
	V8-260 Auto. Tr. [2]	VC
	V8-260 Auto. Tr. [3]	U5
	V8-260 Auto. Tr. [4]	UE, UJ, UK, UL, UN, UO
	V8-260 Std. Tr. [4]	UC, UD
	V8-260 Auto. Tr. [6]	UP, UQ
	V8-260 Std. Tr. [6]	UW, UX
	V8-301 Auto. Tr. [4]	XP, XR
	V8-305 Auto. Tr. [2]	DNX, DNY
	V8-305 Auto. Tr. [3]	DTA
	V8-305 Auto. Tr. [4]	DNJ, DNT, DNW, DTX
	V8-305 Std. Tr. [4]	DNS, DTM
	V8-350 Auto. Tr. [2]	VA, VK, DRJ
	V8-350 Auto. Tr. [3]	U2, U9, DRX, DRY
	V8-350 Auto. Tr. [4]	SA, SB, UA, US, UT, UU, UV
	V8-350 Diesel [3]	U3, V4, V6
	V8-350 Diesel [6]	UB, VN, VO, VP, VQ
	V8-403 Auto. Tr. [2]	TB
	V8-403 Auto. Tr. [3]	Q3
	V8-403 Auto. Tr. [4]	QB

[1]—Except California.
[2]—California.
[3]—High altitude.
[4]—Exc. Calif. & High altitude.
[6]—Exc. high altitude.

GRILLE IDENTIFICATION—Continued

1974 Omega

1974 Cutlass, Supreme & Vista Cruiser

1974 88

1974 98

1974 Toronado

1975 Omega & F-85

1975 Cutlass Supreme

1975 Cutlass Salon

1975 Cutlass "S"

1975 Delta 88

1975 98

1975 Toronado

1976 Delta 88

1976 Cutlass Supreme

1976 Cutlass "S" & "4-4-2"

1976 Omega

1976 Delta Royale

1976 98

1976 Toronado

1977 Omega

1977 Cutlass Supreme

GRILLE IDENTIFICATION—Continued

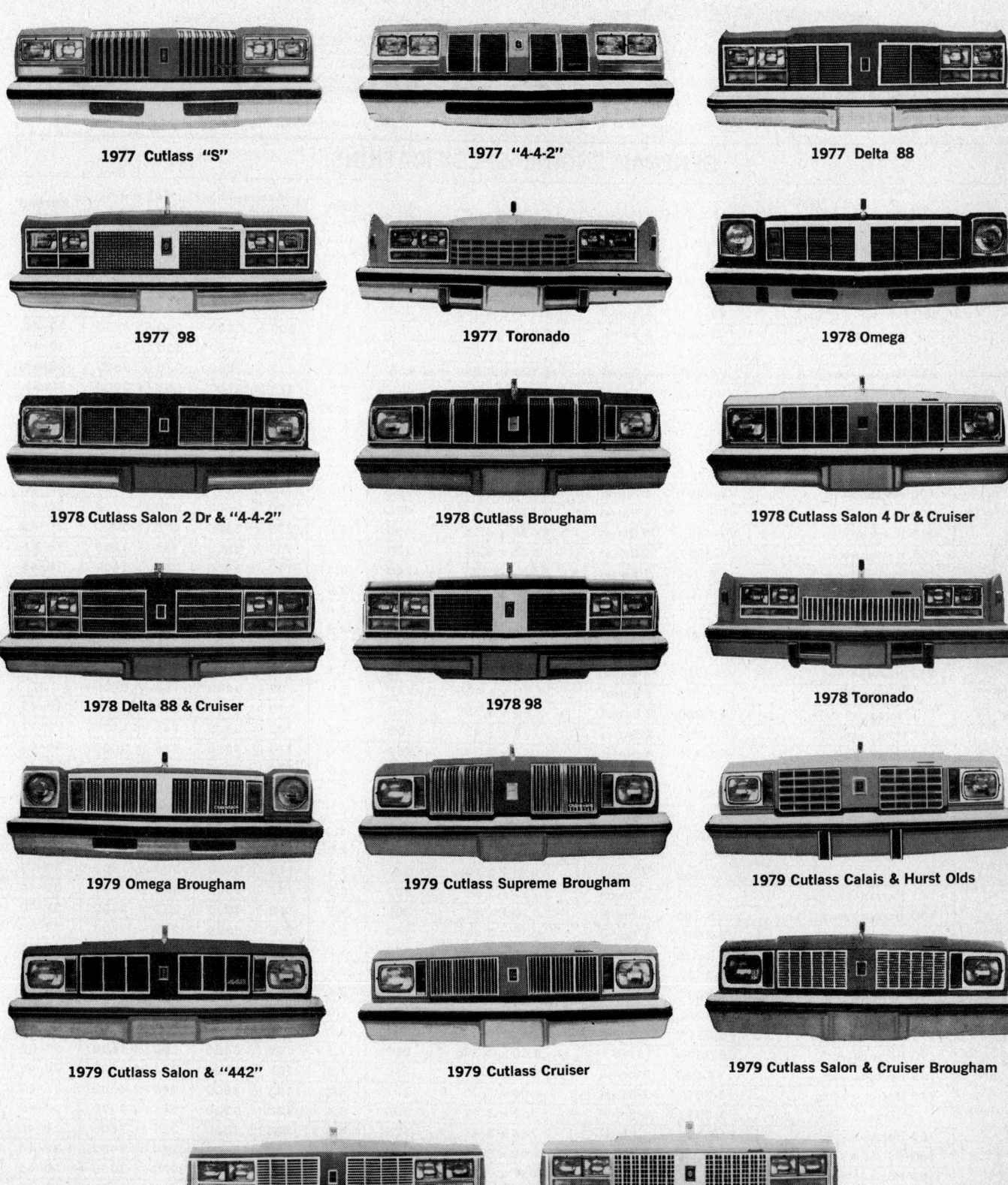

1977 Cutlass "S"

1977 "4-4-2"

1977 Delta 88

1977 98

1977 Toronado

1978 Omega

1978 Cutlass Salon 2 Dr & "4-4-2"

1978 Cutlass Brougham

1978 Cutlass Salon 4 Dr & Cruiser

1978 Delta 88 & Cruiser

1978 98

1978 Toronado

1979 Omega Brougham

1979 Cutlass Supreme Brougham

1979 Cutlass Calais & Hurst Olds

1979 Cutlass Salon & "442"

1979 Cutlass Cruiser

1979 Cutlass Salon & Cruiser Brougham

1979 Delta 88 Royale

1979 98 Regency

GRILLE IDENTIFICATION—Continued

1979 Custom Cruiser   1979 Toronado Brougham

GENERAL ENGINE SPECIFICATIONS

Year	Engine	Car- buretor	Bore and Stroke	Piston Dis- place- ment, Cubic Inches	Com- pres- sion Ratio	Maximum Brake H.P. @ R.P.M.	Maximum Torque Lbs. Ft. @ R.P.M.	Normal Oil Pressure Pounds
1974	100 Horsepower①..........6-250②	1 Barrel	3.87 x 3.53	250	8.5	100 @ 3600	175 @ 1800	40
	180 Horsepower①..........V8-350	4 Barrel	4.057 x 3.385	350	8.5	180 @ 3800	275 @ 2800	30–45
	200 Horsepower①..........V8-350	4 Barrel	4.057 x 3.385	350	8.5	200 @ 4200	300 @ 3200	30–45
	210 Horsepower①..........V8-455	4 Barrel	4.126 x 4.250	455	8.5	210 @ 3600	350 @ 2400	30–45
	230 Horsepower①..........V8-455	4 Barrel	4.126 x 4.250	455	8.5	230 @ 3800	370 @ 2800	30–45
	275 Horsepower①..........V8-455	4 Barrel	4.126 x 4.250	455	8.5	275 @ 4200	395 @ 3200	30–45
1975	105 Horsepower①..........6-250②	1 Barrel	3.87 x 3.53	250	8.25	105 @ 3800	185 @ 1200	36–41
	110 Horsepower①..........V8-260	2 Barrel	3.50 x 3.385	260	8.5	110 @ 3400	205 @ 1600	30–45
	165 Horsepower①..........V8-350③	4 Barrel	3.80 x 3.85	350	8.0	165 @ 3800	260 @ 2200	37
	170 Horsepower①..........V8-350	4 Barrel	4.057 x 3.385	350	8.5	170 @ 3800	275 @ 2400	30–45
	190 Horsepower①..........V8-400④	4 Barrel	4.1212 x 3.75	400	7.6	190 @ 3400	350 @ 2000	55–60
	190 Horsepower①..........V8-455	4 Barrel	4.126 x 4.25	455	8.5	190 @ 3600	350 @ 2400	30–45
	215 Horsepower①..........V8-455⑥	4 Barrel	4.126 x 4.25	455	8.5	215 @ 3600	370 @ 2400	30–45
1976	105 Horsepower①..........6-250②	1 Barrel	3.87 x 3.53	250	8.25	105 @ 3800	185 @ 1200	36–41
	110 Horsepower①..........V8-260	2 Barrel	3.50 x 3.385	260	8.5	110 @ 3400	205 @ 1600	30–45
	140 Horsepower①..........V8-350③	2 Barrel	3.80 x 3.85	350	8.0	140 @ 3200	280 @ 1800	37
	155 Horsepower①..........V8-350③	4 Barrel	3.80 x 3.85	350	8.0	155 @ 3400	280 @ 1800	37
	170 Horsepower①..........V8-350	4 Barrel	4.057 x 3.385	350	8.5	170 @ 3800	275 @ 2400	30–45
	190 Horsepower①..........V8-455⑤	4 Barrel	4.126 x 4.25	455	8.5	190 @ 3400	350 @ 2000	30–45
	215 Horsepower①..........V8-455⑥	4 Barrel	4.126 x 4.25	455	8.5	215 @ 3600	370 @ 2400	30–45
1977	105 Horsepower①..........V6-231⑨	2 Barrel	3.80 x 3.40	231	8.0	105 @ 3400	185 @ 2000	37
	110 Horsepower①..........V8-260	2 Barrel	3.50 x 3.385	260	8.0	110 @ 3400	205 @ 1600	30–45
	145 Horsepower①..........V8-305②	2 Barrel	3.736 x 3.48	305	8.5	145 @ 3800	245 @ 2400	32–40
	170 Horsepower①..........V8-350	4 Barrel	4.057 x 3.385	350	8.0	170 @ 3800	275 @ 2400	30–45
	170 Horsepower①..........V8-350⑦	4 Barrel	4.057 x 3.385	350	8.0	170 @ 3800	275 @ 2400	30–45
	170 Horsepower①..........V8-350②⑧	4 Barrel	4.00 x 3.48	350	8.5	170 @ 3800	270 @ 2400	32–40
	185 Horsepower①..........V8-403⑤	4 Barrel	4.351 x 3.385	403	8.0	185 @ 3600	320 @ 2000	30–45
	200 Horsepower①..........V8-403⑥	4 Barrel	4.351 x 3.385	403	8.0	200 @ 3600	330 @ 2400	30–45
1978	105 Horsepower① V6-231⑨	2 Barrel	3.80 x 3.40	231	8.0	105 @ 3400	185 @ 2000	37
	110 Horsepower①..........V8-260	2 Barrel	3.50 x 3.385	260	7.5	110 @ 2400	205 @ 1800	30–45
	145 Horsepower①..........V8-305②	2 Barrel	3.736 x 3.48	305	8.5	145 @ 3800	245 @ 2400	32–40
	160 Horsepower①..........V8-305②	4 Barrel	3.736 x 3.48	305	8.5	160 @ 4000	235 @ 2400	32–40
	160 Horsepower①..........V8-350②	4 Barrel	4.00 x 3.48	350	8.5	160 @ 3800	260 @ 2400	32–40
	170 Horsepower①..........V8-350	4 Barrel	4.057 x 3.385	350	8.0	170 @ 3800	275 @ 2000	30–45
	120 Horsepower①..........V8-350⑩	Fuel Inj.	4.057 x 3.385	350	22.5	120 @ 3600	220 @ 1600	30–45
	185 Horsepower①..........V8-403⑤	4 Barrel	4.351 x 3.385	403	8.0	185 @ 3600	320 @ 2200	30–45
	190 Horsepower①..........V8-403⑥	4 Barrel	4.351 x 3.385	403	8.0	190 @ 3600	325 @ 2000	30–45
1979	115 Horsepower①..........V6-231⑨	2 Barrel	3.80 x 3.40	231	8.0	115 @ 3600	190 @ 2000	37
	90 Horsepower①.........V8-260⑩	—	3.50 x 3.385	260	22.5	90 @ 3600	160 @ 1600	30–45
	105 Horsepower①..........V8-260	2 Barrel	3.50 x 3.385	260	7.5	105 @ 3600	205 @ 1800	30–45
	135 Horsepower①..........V8-301④	2 Barrel	4.00 x 3.00	301	8.2	135 @ 3800	240 @ 1600	35–40
	130 Horsepower①..........V8-305②	2 Barrel	3.736 x 3.48	305	8.5	130 @ 3200	245 @ 2000	32–40
	160 Horsepower①..........V8-305②	4 Barrel	3.736 x 3.48	305	8.5	160 @ 4000	235 @ 2400	32–40
	160 Horsepower①..........V8-350②	4 Barrel	4.00 x 3.48	350	8.5	160 @ 3600	260 @ 2400	32–40
	160 Horsepower①..........V8-350	4 Barrel	4.057 x 3.385	350	8.0	160 @ 3600	270 @ 2400	30–45
	125 Horsepower①..........V8-350⑩	—	4.057 x 3.385	350	22.5	125 @ 3600	225 @ 1600	30–45
	175 Horsepower①..........V8-403	4 Barrel	4.351 x 3.385	403	7.8	175 @ 3600	310 @ 2000	30–45

①—All horsepower and torque ratings are net.
②—See Chevrolet Chapter for service procedure on this engine.
③—Omega only. See Buick Chapter for service procedures on this engine.
④—See Pontiac Chapter for service procedures on this engine.
⑤—Exc. Toronado.
⑥—Toronado.
⑦—Cutlass.
⑧—Omega.
⑨—See Buick Chapter for service procedures on this engine.
⑩—Diesel.

TUNE UP SPECIFICATIONS

The following specifications are published from the latest information available. This data should be used only in the absence of a decal affixed in the engine compartment.

★When using a timing light, disconnect vacuum hose or tube at distributor and plug opening in hose or tube so idle speed will not be affected.

●When checking compression, lowest cylinder must be within 80 percent of highest.

▲Before removing wires from distributor cap, determine location of the No. 1 wire in cap, as distributor position may have been altered from that shown at the end of this chart.

| Year | Spark Plug | | Distributor | | Ignition Timing★ | | | Carb. Adjustments | | | | | |
| | Type | Gap Inch | Point Gap Inch | Dwell Angle Deg. | Firing Order Fig. ▲ | Timing BTDC ① | Mark Fig. | Hot Idle Speed | | Air Fuel Ratio | | Idle "CO" % | |
								Std. Trans.	Auto. Trans. ②	Std. Trans.	Auto. Trans.	Std. Trans.	Auto. Trans.
1974													
6-250(14)	R46TS	.035	.019	31–34	N	8°(7)	C	850	600D	—	—	0.3	0.3
8-350 4 Bar.	R46S	.040	.019	30	(20)	12°(16)	H	—	650D	—	—	0.2	0.2
8-455, 275 H.P.	R45S	.040	.019	30	(20)	14°(16)	H	—	650D	—	—	0.2	0.2
8-455 4 Bar.	R46S	.040	.019	30	(20)	8°(16)	H	—	650D	—	—	0.2	0.2
8-455 4 Bar.(8)	R46SX	.080	—	—	(20)	8°(16)	H	—	650D	—	—	0.2	0.2
8-455 4 Bar.(13)	R46S	.040	.019	30	(20)	10°(16)	H	—	650D	—	—	0.2	0.2
8-455 4 Bar.(8)(13)	R46SX	.080	—	—	(20)	10°(16)	H	—	650D	—	—	0.2	0.2
1975													
6-250(14)	R46TX	.060	—	—	I	10°	C	850	(19)	—	—	—	—
V8-260	R46SX	.080	—	—	J	(17)	G	750	650D	—	—	—	—
V8-350(10)	R45TSX	.060	—	—	K	12°	D	—	600D	—	—	—	—
V8-350	R46SX	.080	—	—	J	20°(16)	G	—	650D	—	—	—	—
V8-400(18)	R45TSX	.060	—	—	L	16°(16)	E	—	650D	—	—	—	—
V8-455	R46SX	.080	—	—	J	16°(16)	G	—	650D	—	—	—	—
V8-455(13)	R46SX	.080	—	—	J	12°(16)	G	—	650D	—	—	—	—
1976													
6-250(14)(21)	R46TS	.035	—	—	I	6°	C	850	—	—	—	—	—
6-250(14)(22)	R46TS	.035	—	—	I	10°	C	—	(19)	—	—	—	—
V8-260(23)	R46SZ	.060	—	—	J	(11)	G	750	650D(9)	—	—	—	—
V8-260(5)(24)	R46SZ	.060	—	—	J	(12)	G	—	650D(9)	—	—	—	—
V8-260(10)(24)	R46SZ	.060	—	—	J	(25)	G	—	650D(9)	—	—	—	—
V8-260(24)(26)	R46SZ	.060	—	—	J	14°(16)	G	750	—	—	—	—	—
V8-350	R46SZ	.060	—	—	J	20°(16)	G	—	(19)	—	—	—	—
V8-350(23)(27)	R46SZ	.060	—	—	J	22°(16)	G	—	650D(9)	—	—	—	—
V8-350(10)	R46TSX	.060	—	—	K	12°	D	—	600D	—	—	—	—
V8-455	R46SZ	.060	—	—	J	16°(16)	G	—	650D	—	—	—	—
V8-455	R46SZ	.060	—	—	J	18°(16)	G	—	650D(9)	—	—	—	—
V8-455(13)(23)	R46SZ	.060	—	—	J	14°(16)	G	—	650D(9)	—	—	—	—
V8-455(13)(24)	R46SZ	.060	—	—	J	12°(16)	G	—	650D(9)	—	—	—	—
1977													
V6-231(34)	R46TS	.040	—	—	(49)	12°	(50)	—	600N	—	—	—	—
V8-260	R46SZ	.060	—	—	J	(11)	G	750	650D(9)	—	—	—	—
V8-305(14)	R45TS	.045	—	—	O	8°(28)	C	700	650D	—	—	—	—
V8-350(14)(29)	R45TS	.045	—	—	O	(30)	C	—	650D	—	—	—	—
V8-350(35)	R46SZ	.060	—	—	J	20°(16)	G	—	650D(9)	—	—	—	—
V8-403	R46SZ	.060	—	—	J	(31)(32)	G	—	(9)(33)	—	—	—	—
1978													
V6-231(34)	R46TSX	.060	—	—	A	15°	P	800	670D(9)	—	—	—	—
V8-260	R46SZ	.060	—	—	J	(4)(18)	G	800	650D	—	—	—	—
V8-305(14)(36)	R45TS	.045	—	—	O	4°	C	700	600D	—	—	—	—
V8-305(14)(37)	R45TS	.045	—	—	O	8°	C	—	700D	—	—	—	—

Continued

TUNE UP SPECIFICATIONS—Continued

The following specifications are published from the latest information available. This
data should be used only in the absence of a decal affixed in the engine compartment.

★ When using a timing light, disconnect vacuum hose or tube at distributor and plug opening in hose or tube so idle speed will not be affected.
● When checking compression, lowest cylinder must be within 70 percent of highest.
▲ Before removing wires from distributor cap, determine location of the No. 1 wire in cap, as distributor position may have been altered from that shown at the end of this chart.

| Year | Spark Plug | | Distributor | | Ignition Timing ★ | | | Carb. Adjustments | | | | | |
| | Type | Gap Inch | Point Gap Inch | Dwell Angle Deg. | Firing Order Fig. ▲ | Timing BTDC ① | Mark Fig. | Hot Idle Speed | | Air Fuel Ratio | | Idle "CO" % | |
								Std. Trans.	Auto. Trans. ②	Std. Trans.	Auto. Trans.	Std. Trans.	Auto. Trans.
1978—Continued													
V8-350 [14][29]	R45TS	.045	—	—	O	8°	C	—	650D	—	—	—	—
V8-350 [35]	R46SZ	.060	—	—	J	20°[16]	G	—	650D	—	—	—	—
V8-350 [39]	—	—	—	—	[51]	[40]	—	—	650D	—	—	—	—
V8-403 [36]	R46SZ	.060	—	—	J	[41][16]	G	—	650D	—	—	—	—
V8-403 [37]	R46SZ	.060	—	—	J	20°[16]	G	—	650D[43]	—	—	—	—
V8-403 [13]	R46SZ	.060	—	—	J	[22][42][16]	G	—	650D[43]	—	—	—	—
1979													
V6-231 [34]	R46TSX	.060	—	—	A	15°	P	600/800[45]	[44]	—	—	—	—
V8-260 [21]	R46SZ	.060	—	—	J	18°[16]	G	600/800N[46]	—	—	—	—	—
V8-260 [5][22]	R46SZ	.060	—	—	J	[47][16]	G	—	[48]	—	—	—	—
V8-260 [6]	R46SZ	.060	—	—	J	20°[18]	G	—	500/625[46]	—	—	—	—
V8-260 [39]	—	—	—	—	[51]	[40]	—	—	640	—	—	—	—
V8-301 [18]	R46TSX	.060	—	—	L	12°	Q	—	500/625[46]	—	—	—	—
V8-305 [15]	R45TS	.045	—	—	O	4°	C	600/700N[46]	500/600[46]	—	—	—	—
V8-305 [3]	R45TS	.045	—	—	O	8°	C	—	600/650[46]	—	—	—	—
V8-350 [38][35]	R46SZ	.060	—	—	J	20°[16]	G	—	550/650[46]	—	—	—	—
V8-350 [14][24][29]	R45TS	.045	—	—	O	8°	C	—	500/600[46]	—	—	—	—
V8-350 [14][29][3]	R45TS	.045	—	—	O	8°	C	—	600/650[46]	—	—	—	—
V8-350 [3][5]	R46SZ	.060	—	—	J	20°[16]	G	—	600/700[46]	—	—	—	—
V 8-350 [24][35]	R46SZ	.060	—	—	J	20°[16]	G	—	500/600[46]	—	—	—	—
V8-350 [39]	—	—	—	—	[51]	[40]	—	—	650	—	—	—	—
V8-403 [36]	R46SZ	.060	—	—	J	20°[16]	G	—	550/650[46]	—	—	—	—
V8-403 [24]	R46SZ	.060	—	—	J	20°[16]	G	—	500/600[46]	—	—	—	—
V8-403 [3]	R46SZ	.060	—	—	J	20°[16]	G	—	600/700[46]	—	—	—	—

① —BTDC: Before top dead center.
② —D: Drive. N: Neutral. Add 50 R.P.M. to slow idle speed for air conditioned cars with A/C off.
③ —High altitude.
④ —Exc. Calif. & Manual trans., 20° BTDC; Calif. & manual trans., 18° BTDC.
⑤ —Cutlass.
⑥ —Full size cars.
⑦ —At 600 rpm with auto. trans. and 850 rpm with manual trans.
⑧ —With High Energy Ignition system.
⑨ —With A/C on and compressor clutch wires disconnected.
⑩ —Omega only. See Buick Chapter for service procedures on this engine.
⑪ —Manual trans., 16° BTDC; Auto. trans., 18° BTDC; at 1100 R.P.M.
⑫ —Early production with EFE/EGR-TVS 16° BTDC, Late production less EFE/EGR-TVS 14° BTDC; at 1100 R.P.M.
⑬ —Toronado.
⑭ —See Chevrolet Chapter for service procedures on this engine.
⑮ —Exc. High altitude.
⑯ —At 1100 R.P.M.

⑰ —Exc. Calif., 16° BTDC; Calif., 18° BTDC. At 1100 R.P.M.
⑱ —See Pontiac Chapter for service procedures on this engine.
⑲ —Exc. Calif., 550D; Calif., 600D.
⑳ —Exc. H.E.I., Fig. F; H.E.I., Fig. J.
㉑ —Manual trans.
㉒ —Auto. trans.
㉓ —Exc. California.
㉔ —California.
㉕ —Early production with EFE/EGR-TVS 14° BTDC, Late production less EFE/EGR-TVS 16° BTDC; at 1100 R.P.M.
㉖ —5 speed transmission.
㉗ —With 2.41 axle ratio.
㉘ —Manual trans., at 700D R.P.M.; auto. trans. at 500D R.P.M.
㉙ —Distributor rotor rotation—clockwise.
㉚ —Calif., 6° at 500D R.P.M.; high altitude, 8° at 600D R.P.M.
㉛ —Except Calif. & high altitude, 24° BTDC; Calif. & high altitude, 20° BTDC. At 1100 R.P.M.
㉜ —On models with EST, see text for procedure.
㉝ —Except Toronado & high altitude, 650D; Toronado high altitude, 700D.

㉞ —See Buick Chapter for service procedures on this engine.
㉟ —Distributor rotor rotation—counter-clockwise.
㊱ —Exc. Calif. and high altitude.
㊲ —Calif. and high altitude.
㊳ —Distributor at front of engine.
㊴ —Diesel.
㊵ —See text for procedure.
㊶ —98 & 88 Exc. wagon, 18° BTDC; 88 wagon, 20° BTDC.
㊷ —Exc. Calif., 20° BTDC; Calif., 22° BTDC.
㊸ —High altitude, 700 RPM.
㊹ —Ex. Calif. & High altitude—Less A/C, 550D; with A/C 550/670D, see note ㊻. Calif. & Hi. Alt., 600D.
㊺ —Where two idle speeds are listed, the higher speed is listed with idle solenoid energized.
㊻ —Where two idle speeds are listed, the higher speed is with A/C solenoid energized & A/C "ON".
㊼ —Exc. Calif.; 20° BTDC; Calif. 18° BTDC.
㊽ —Exc. wagon & Calif.—Less A/C 500D; with A/C. 550/625 see note ㊻. Wagon & Calif. 500/625D see note ㊻.
㊾ —Exc. even fire, Fig. M; Even fire, Fig. A.
㊿ —Exc. even fire, Fig. B; Even fire, Fig. P.
[51] —Firing order, 1, 8, 4, 3, 6, 5, 7, 2.

Continued

TUNE UP NOTES—Continued

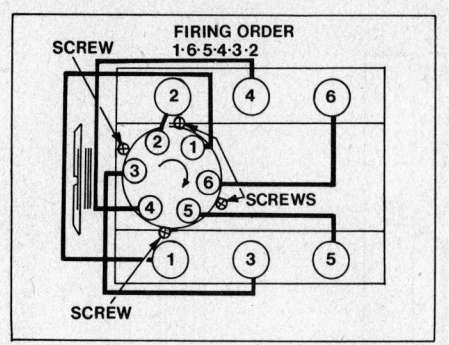

Fig. A

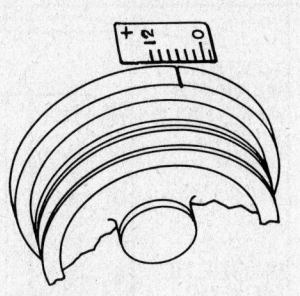

Fig. B

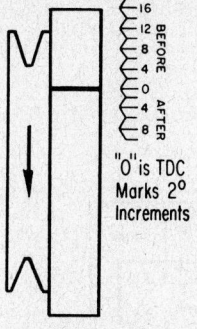

Fig. C

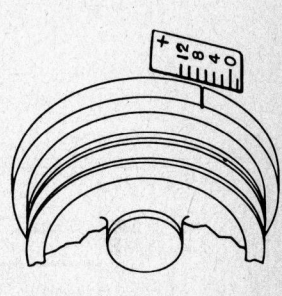

Fig. D

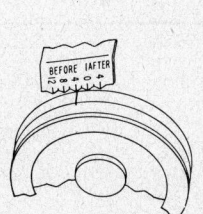

Fig. E

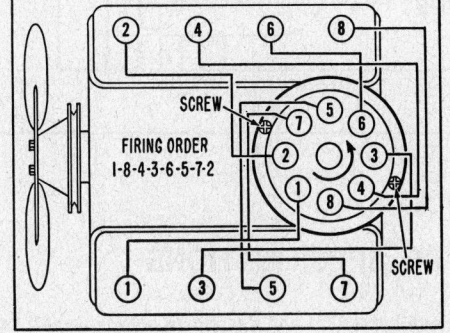

Fig. F

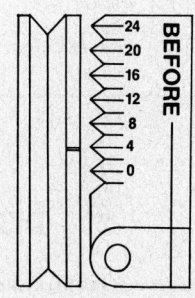

Fig. G

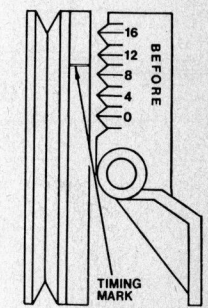

Fig. H

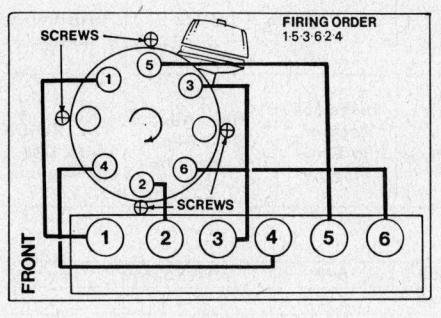

Fig. I

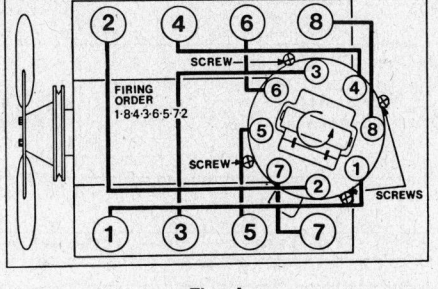

Fig. J

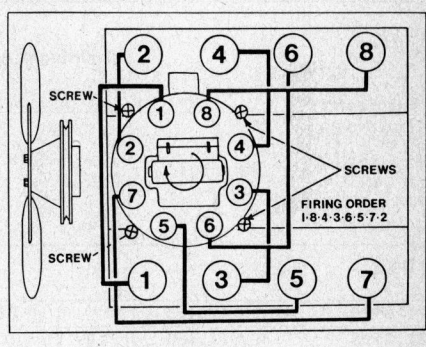

Fig. K

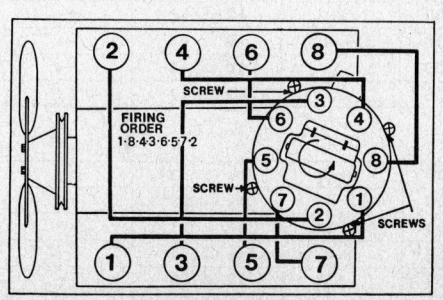

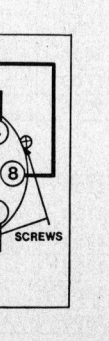

Fig. L

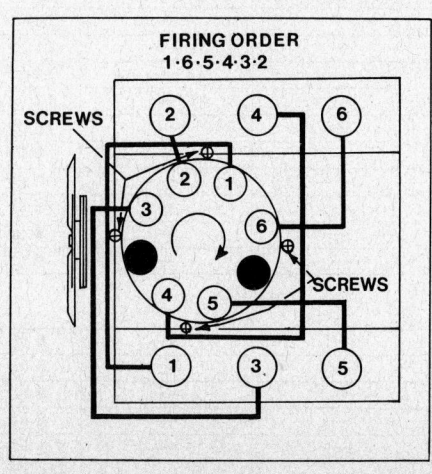

Fig. M

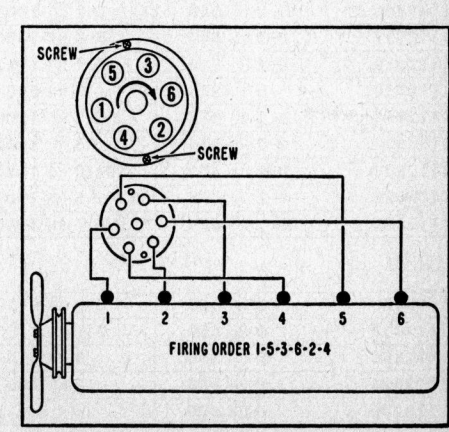

Fig. N

Continued

TUNE UP NOTES—Continued

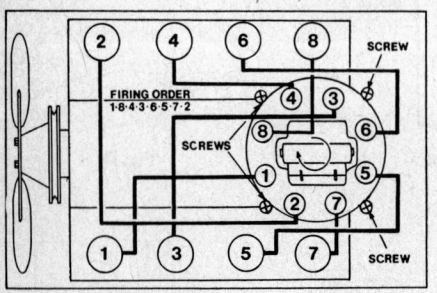

Fig. O

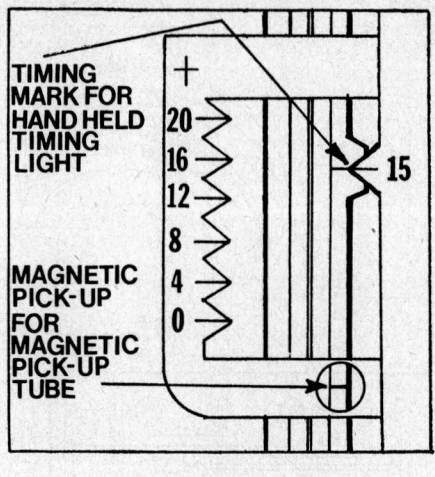

Fig. P

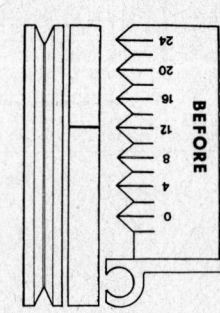

Fig. Q

DISTRIBUTOR SPECIFICATIONS

★Note: If unit is checked on vehicle, double the RPM and degrees to get crankshaft figures.
Breaker arm spring tension—19–23.

| Distributor Part No.① | Centrifugal Advance Degrees @ RPM of Distributor | | | | Vacuum Advance | | Distributor Retard |
	Advance Starts	Intermediate Advance		Full Advance	Inches of Vacuum to Start Plunger	Max. Adv. Dist. Deg. @ Vacuum	Max. Retard Dist. Deg. @ Vacuum
1974							
1110499	0 @ 465	1 @ 635	7 @ 1150	12 @ 2050	6–8	6 @ 15½	—
1112195	0–2 @ 400	8–10 @ 1050	—	16 @ 2000	5–7	8 @ 12	—
1112197	0–2 @ 540	5–7 @ 1000	—	11 @ 1800	7–9	9 @ 16.6	—
1112225	0–2 @ 380	5–7 @ 550	11–13 @ 1050	19 @ 2000	5–7	8 @ 12	—
1112226	0–2 @ 400	8–10 @ 1050	—	16 @ 2000	3½–4½	10 @ 13	—
1112506	0–2 @ 540	5–7 @ 1000	—	11 @ 1800	7–9	9 @ 16.6	—
1112531	0–2 @ 540	5–7 @ 1000	—	11 @ 1800	6	9 @ 10	—
1112532	0–2 @ 540	5–7 @ 1000	—	11 @ 1800	4	10 @ 13	—
1112550	0 @ 375	7 @ 600	—	13 @ 1500	12	8 @ 18	—
1112825	0–2 @ 575	3.5–5.5 @ 1000	—	9 @ 1700	6	9 @ 10	—
1112827	0–2 @ 575	3.5–5.5 @ 1000	—	9 @ 1700	7	12 @ 17	—
1112828	0–2 @ 400	8–10 @ 1050	—	16 @ 2000	3½–4½	10 @ 13	—
1112829	0–2 @ 575	3.5–5.5 @ 1000	—	9 @ 1700	4	10 @ 13	—
1112830	0–2 @ 575	3.5–5.5 @ 1000	—	9 @ 1700	7	12 @ 17	—
1975							
1110650	0 @ 550	3½ @ 1150	—	8 @ 2100	3–5	8¼ @ 12½	—
1112863	0 @ 550	3½ @ 1150	—	8 @ 2100	3–5	8¾ @ 12½	—
1112896	0 @ 550	3 @ 1150	—	6 @ 2250	6½–8½	7 @ 11½	—
1112928	0 @ 600	2 @ 700	—	8 @ 2200	6–8	12½ @ 12	—
1112936	0 @ 500	—	—	9½ @ 2000	6½	12 @ 16	—
1112937	0 @ 500	—	—	6½ @ 1800	8	9 @ 13	—

Continued

DISTRIBUTOR SPECIFICATIONS—Continued

★Note: If unit is checked on vehicle, double the RPM and degrees to get crankshaft figures.
Breaker arm spring tension—19–23.

Distributor Part No.①	Centrifugal Advance Degrees @ RPM of Distributor					Vacuum Advance		Distributor Retard
	Advance Starts	Intermediate Advance			Full Advance	Inches of Vacuum to Start Plunger	Max. Adv. Dist. Deg. @ Vacuum	Max. Retard Dist. Deg. @ Vacuum
1975—Continued								
1112951	0 @ 325	9½ @ 1200	—	—	14 @ 2200	4	12 @ 15	—
1112952	0 @ 500	3½ @ 1050	—	—	7 @ 1800	8	9 @ 13	—
1112953	0 @ 500	—	—	—	9½ @ 2000	8	9 @ 16	—
1112956	0 @ 325	9½ @ 1200	—	—	14 @ 2200	—	—	—
1112958	0 @ 600	2 @ 700	—	—	8 @ 2200	5	12½ @ 11	—
1976								
1103204	0 @ 325	9½ @ 1200	—	—	14 @ 2200	6	10 @ 14.8	—
1103208	0 @ 325	9½ @ 1200	—	—	14 @ 2200	6	9 @ 10.2	—
1103210	0 @ 500	—	—	—	9½ @ 2000	6	12 @ 13.7	—
1103211	0 @ 325	9½ @ 1200	—	—	14 @ 2200	6	7 @ 9.2	—
1103212	0 @ 500	—	—	—	6½ @ 1800	8	12 @ 15	—
1110666	0 @ 500	3½ @ 800	—	—	10 @ 2100	3	12 @ 15	—
1112863③	0 @ 550	3½ @ 1150	—	—	8 @ 2100	3	9 @ 13	—
1112863④	0 @ 550	3½ @ 1150	—	—	8 @ 2100	6	12 @ 16	—
1112936	0 @ 500	—	—	—	9½ @ 2000	6.5	12 @ 16	—
1112937	0 @ 500	—	—	—	6½ @ 1800	8	9 @ 13	—
1112952	0 @ 550	3½ @ 1050	—	—	7 @ 1800	8	9 @ 13	—
1112953	0 @ 500	—	—	—	9½ @ 2000	8	9 @ 16	—
1112956	0 @ 325	9½ @ 1200	—	—	14 @ 2200	—	—	—
1112988	0 @ 500	—	—	—	6½ @ 1800	8	9 @ 13	—
1112991	0 @ 872	8.9–11 @ 2212	—	—	11 @ 2500	6.9	10¼ @ 14.3	—
1112994	0 @ 325	9½ @ 1200	—	—	14 @ 2200	4.5	12 @ 10.5	—
1112995	0 @ 455	8½ @ 1188	—	—	13 @ 2233	4	15 @ 11	—
1977								
1103239	0–2 @ 700	7½–8½ @ 1350	—	—	11 @ 2100	3	8½ @ 11	—
1103246	0 @ 600	5–7 @ 1000	—	—	12 @ 2100	3	9½ @ 13	—
1103248	0 @ 600	5–7 @ 1000	—	—	12 @ 2100	3	6 @ 9	—
1103259	0 @ 500	—	—	—	9½ @ 2000	6	12 @ 13	—
1103260	0 @ 500	—	—	—	9½ @ 2000	6	12 @ 13	—
1103262	0 @ 455	8½ @ 1188	—	—	13 @ 2233	4	15 @ 11	—
1103264	0 @ 500	—	—	—	6½ @ 1800	5	8 @ 11	—
1103266	0 @ 500	—	—	—	9½ @ 2000	5	8 @ 11	—
1110677	0–2.2 @ 765	8.9–11 @ 1800	—	—	11 @ 2500	6	12¾ @ 20	—
1110686	0–2.2 @ 890	3.2–5.5 @ 1300	—	—	11 @ 2500	6	4¾ @ 20	—
1112990②	—	—	—	—	—	—	—	—
1978								
1103313②	—	—	—	—	—	—	—	—
1103337	0 @ 550	6 @ 800	8 @ 1200	—	11 @ 2300	4	12 @ 10	—
1110731	0–2 @ 1000	—	—	—	9 @ 1800	4	8 @ 9	—
1978-79								
1103281	0 @ 500	5 @ 850	—	—	10 @ 1900	4	9 @ 12	—
1103282	0 @ 500	5 @ 850	—	—	10 @ 1900	4	10 @ 10	—

Continued

DISTRIBUTOR SPECIFICATIONS—Continued

★Note: If unit is checked on vehicle, double the RPM and degrees to get crankshaft figures.

Distributor Part No.①	Centrifugal Advance Degrees @ RPM of Distributor				Vacuum Advance		Distributor Retard
	Advance Starts	Intermediate Advance		Full Advance	Inches of Vacuum to Start Plunger	Max. Adv. Dist. Deg. @ Vacuum	Max. Retard Dist. Deg. @ Vacuum
1978-79—Continued							
1103285	0 @ 600	6 @ 1000	—	—	11 @ 2100	4	12 @ 8	—
1103320	0 @ 455	8½ @ 1190	—	—	13 @ 2230	4	15 @ 11	—
1103322	0 @ 300	5½ @ 600	—	—	14½ @ 2000	6	12 @ 13	—
1103323	0 @ 500	—	—	—	9½ @ 2000	5	8 @ 11	—
1103324	0 @ 300	5½ @ 600	—	—	11½ @ 1800	6	12 @ 13	—
1103325	0 @ 500	—	—	—	6½ @ 1800	5	8 @ 11	—
1103342	0–2 @ 1000	—	—	—	9½ @ 2200	5–7	12 @ 13	—
1103346	0 @ 500	—	—	—	9½ @ 2000	6	12 @ 13	—
1103347	0 @ 500	—	—	—	6½ @ 1800	6	12 @ 13	—
1103353	0–1¾ @ 625	2½–3½ @ 850	—	3½–4½ @ 2000	5½–6 @ 2250	3	10 @ 12	—
1103355	0 @ 455	8½ @ 1190	—	—	13 @ 2230	4	15 @ 9	—
1110695	0–3 @ 1000	—	—	—	9 @ 1800	7	12 @ 13	—
1979							
1103259	0 @ 500	—	—	—	10½ @ 2000	4	15 @ 11	—
1103260	0 @ 500	—	—	—	6¾ @ 1600	6	12 @ 13	—
1103262	0 @ 550	—	—	8½ @ 1175	14 @ 2500	4½	15½ @ 20	—
1103264	0 @ 500	—	—	—	8½ @ 1700	5	8 @ 11	—
1103266	0 @ 500	—	—	—	10½ @ 2000	5	8 @ 11	—
1103314	0 @ 412½	5 @ 900	—	—	10½ @ 1700	4	12½ @ 12	—
1103368	0 @ 500	5 @ 850	—	—	10 @ 1900	4	5 @ 8	—
1103379	0 @ 500	5 @ 850	—	—	10 @ 1900	3	10 @ 7.5	—
1103396	0 @ 455	8½ @ 1190	—	—	13 @ 2230	5	15 @ 12	—
1110677	0 @ 640	—	—	—	10 @ 1800	5	12 @ 9.5	—
1110683	—	—	—	—	—	—	—	—
1110731	0 @ 950	—	—	7¼ @ 1800	8½ @ 2500	5	12¾ @ 20	—
1110766	0 @ 840	—	—	—	7½ @ 1800	4	12 @ 11	—
1110768	0 @ 500	2½ @ 800	—	3 @ 1200	7½ @ 1800	3	10 @ 12	—
1110769	0 @ 500	2½ @ 800	—	3 @ 1200	7½ @ 1800	4	12 @ 11	—
1110770	0 @ 840	—	—	—	7½ @ 1800	3	10 @ 9	—
1112995	0 @ 455	—	—	8½ @ 1185	23 @ 2232	4	15 @ 11	—
1113246	0 @ 600	—	—	6 @ 600	11 @ 2100	4	9 @ 12	—
1113248	0 @ 600	—	—	6 @ 600	11 @ 2100	4	5 @ 8	—

①—Stamped on distributor housing plate.
②—On models with EST, refer to text for specifications.
③—With Vacuum advance unit No. 1973505.
④—With Vacuum advance unit No. 1973517.

BRAKE SPECIFICATIONS

Year	Model	Brake Drum Inside Diameter	Wheel Cylinder Bore Diameter			Master Cylinder Bore Diameter		
			Disc Brake	Front Drum Brake	Rear Drum Brake	Disc Brakes	Drum Brakes	Power Brakes
1974	Omega	9 1/2	2 15/16	1 1/8	7/8	1 1/8	1	1
	Cutlass	9 1/2	2 15/16	—	7/8	1 1/8	—	1 1/8
	Vista Cruiser	11	2 15/16	—	15/16	1 1/8	—	1 1/8
	Custom Cruiser	12	2 15/16	—	1	1 1/8	—	1 1/8
	88, 98 & Toronado	11	2 15/16	—	15/16	1 1/8	—	1 1/8
1975	Omega, Cutlass	9 1/2	2 15/16	—	7/8	1 1/8	—	1 1/8
	Vista Cruiser	11	2 15/16	—	7/8	1 1/8	—	1 1/8
	Custom Cruiser	12	2 15/16	—	1	1 1/8	—	1 1/8
	88, 98, Toronado	11	2 15/16	—	15/16	1 1/8	—	1 1/8
1976	Omega	9 1/2①	2 15/16	—	15/16	1	—	1 1/8
	Cutlass	11	2 15/16	—	②	15/16	—	1 1/8
	Vista Cruiser	11	2 15/16	—	15/16	15/16	—	1 1/8
	Custom Cruiser	12	2 15/16	—	1	1 1/8	—	1 1/8
	88, 98	11	2 15/16	—	1	1 1/8	—	1 1/8
	Toronado	11	2 15/16	—	15/16	1 1/8	—	1 1/8
1977–78	Omega	9 1/2①	2 15/16	—	④	1	—	1 1/8
	Cutlass	11	2 1/2	—	3/4	13/16	—	③
	Vista Cruiser	11	2 15/16	—	15/16	1 1/8	—	1 1/8
	Custom Cruiser	11	2 15/16	—	15/16	1 1/8	—	1 1/8
	88, 98	11	2 15/16	—	⑤	1 1/8	—	1 1/8
	Toronado	11	2 15/16	—	15/16	1 1/8	—	1 1/8
1979	Omega	9 1/2	2 15/16	—	29/32	1 1/8	—	1 1/8
	Cutlass	9 29/64	2 7/16	—	3/4	7/8	—	15/16
	88	9 1/2	2 15/16	—	15/16	1 1/8	—	1 1/8
	Custom Cruiser, 98	11	2 15/16	—	15/16	1 1/8	—	1 1/8
	Toronado	9.5	2 1/2	—	3/4	15/16	—	15/16

①—With 5 speeds trans., 11″.
②—Non-power, 1″; power, 15/16″.
③—1977, 1 1/8″; 1978, 7/8″.
④—Exc. 5 speed, 15/16; 5 speed, 1″.
⑤—88 Exc. 403 7/8″; 88 with 403 & 98, 15/16″.

REAR AXLE SPECIFICATIONS

Year	Model	Carrier Type	Ring Gear & Pinion Backlash		Pinion Bearing Preload			Differential Bearing Preload		
			Method	Adjustment	Method	New Bearings Inch-Lbs.	Used Bearings Inch-Lbs.	Method	New Bearings Inch-Lbs.	Used Bearings Inch-Lbs.
1974–78	Toronado	Removable	Shims	.005–.009	Shims	2–15	2–5	Shims	10–15①	5–7①
	Others	Integral	Shims	.005–.009	Spacer	24–32	8–12	Shims	—	—

①—Over pinion bearing preload.

VALVE SPECIFICATIONS

Year	Model	Valve Lash Int.	Valve Lash Exh.	Valve Angles Seat	Valve Angles Face	Valve Spring Installed Height	Valve Spring Pressure Lbs. @ In.	Stem Clearance Intake	Stem Clearance Exhaust	Stem Diameter Intake	Stem Diameter Exhaust
1974	6-250(8)	1 Turn(3)		46	45	1.66	186 @ 1.27	.001-.0027	.0015-.0032	.3410-.3417	.3410-.3417
	V8-350	Hydraulic(6)		(2)	(13)	1.67	187 @ 1.27	.001-.0027	.0015-.0032	.3425-.3432	.3420-.3427
	V8-455	Hydraulic(6)		(2)	(13)	1.67	187 @ 1.27	.001-.0027	.0015-.0032	.3425-.3432	.3420-.3427
1975-76	6-250(8)	1 Turn(3)		46	45	1.66	(17)	.001-.0027	.0015-.0032	.3410-.3417	.3410-.3417
	V8-260	Hydraulic(6)		(2)	(13)	1.67	187 @ 1.27	.001-.0027	.0015-.0032	.3425-.3432	.3420-.3427
	V8-350(14)	Hydraulic(6)		45	45	1.727	(18)	.0015-.0035	.0015-.0032	.3720-.3730	.3723-.3730
	V8-350	Hydraulic(6)		(2)	(13)	1.67	187 @ 1.27	.001-.0027	.0015-.0032	.3425-.3432	.3420-.3427
	V8-400 2 B. C.(15)	Hydraulic(6)		45	44	1.54	135 @ 1.13	.0016-.0033	.0021-.0038	.3412-.3419	.3407-.3414
	V8-400 4 B. C.(15)	Hydraulic(6)		(4)	(16)	1.54	135 @ 1.13	.0016-.0033	.0021-.0038	.3412-.3419	.3407-.3414
	V8-455	Hydraulic(6)		(2)	(13)	1.62	187 @ 1.27	.0010-.0027	.0015-.0032	.3425-.3432	.3420-.3427
1977	V6-231(11)	Hydraulic(6)		45	45	1.727	(19)	.0015-.0035	.0015-.0032	.3402-.3412	.3405-.3412
	V8-260	Hydraulic(6)		(2)	(13)	1.67	187 @ 1.27	.0010-.0027	.0015-.0032	.3425-.3432	.3420-.3427
	V8-305(8)	¾ Turn(3)		46	45	(12)	200 @ 1.25	.0010-.0027	.0010-.0027	.3410-.3417	.3410-.3417
	V8-350	Hydraulic(6)		(2)	(13)	1.67	187 @ 1.27	.0010-.0027	.0015-.0032	.3425-.3432	.3420-.3427
	V8-350(8)	¾ Turn(3)		46	45	(12)	200 @ 1.25	.0010-.0027	.0010-.0027	.3410-.3417	.3410-.3417
	V8-403	Hydraulic(6)		(2)	(13)	1.67	187 @ 1.27	.0010-.0027	.0015-.0032	.3425-.3432	.3420-.3427
1978	V6-231(11)	Hydraulic(6)		45	45	1.727	168 @ 1.33	.0015-.0035	.0015-.0032	.3401-.3412	.3405-.3412
	V8-260	Hydraulic(6)		(2)	(13)	1.670	187 @ 1.27	.0010-.0027	.0015-.0032	.3425-.3432	.3420-.3427
	V8-305(8)	1 Turn(3)		46	45	1.718	200 @ 1.25	.0010-.0027	.0010-.0027	.3410-.3417	.3410-.3417
	V8-350	Hydraulic(6)		(2)	(13)	1.67	187 @ 1.27	.0010-.0027	.0015-.0032	.3425-.3432	.3420-.3427
	V8-350(8)	1 Turn(3)		46	45	1.718	200 @ 1.25	.0010-.0027	.0010-.0027	.3410-.3417	.3410-.3417
	V8-350(1)	Hydraulic(6)		(2)	(13)	1.670	151 @ 1.30	.0010-.0027	.0015-.0032	.3425-.3432	.3420-.3427
	V8-403	Hydraulic(6)		(2)	(13)	1.670	187 @ 1.27	.0010-.0027	.0015-.0032	.3425-.3432	.3420-.3427
1979	V6-231(11)	Hydraulic(6)		45°	45°	1.727	168 @ 1.33	.0015-.0035	.0015-.0032	.3402-.3412	.3405-.3412
	V8-260	Hydraulic(6)		(9)	(10)	1.270	187 @ 1.270	—	—	.3425-.3432	.3420-.3427
	V8-260(1)	Hydraulic(6)		(9)	(10)	1.670	152 @ 1.295	.0010-.0027	.0015-.0032	.3425-.3432	.3420-.3427
	V8-301(15)	Hydraulic(6)		46	45	1.66	166 @ 1.296	.0010-.0027	.0010-.0027	.3418-.3425	.3418-.3425
	V8-305(8)	1 Turn(3)		46	45	(5)	(20)	.0010-.0027	.0010-.0027	.3410-.3417	.3410-.3417
	V8-350	Hydraulic(6)		(9)	(10)	1.670	187 @ 1.270	.0010-.0027	.0015-.0032	.3425-.3432	.3427-.3420
	V8-350(8)	1 Turn(3)		46	45	(5)	(20)	.0010-.0027	.0010-.0027	.3410-.3417	.3410-.3417
	V8-350(1)	Hydraulic(6)		(9)	(10)	1.670	152 @ 1.295	.0010-.0027	.0015-.0032	.3425-.3432	.3420-.3427
	V8-403	Hydraulic(6)		(9)	(10)	1.670	187 @ 1.270	.0010-.0027	.0015-.0032	.3425-.3432	.3420-.3427

(1)—Diesel.

(2)—Intake 45°, exhaust 31°.

(3)—Tighten rocker arm adjusting screw to eliminate all push rod end clearance. Then tighten screw the number of turns listed.

(4)—Intake 30°, exhaust 45°.

(5)—Intake, 1.70; Exhaust, 1.61.

(6)—No adjustment.

(7)—Intake, 180 @ 1.25; Exhaust, 190 @ 1.16.

(8)—See Chevrolet Chapter for service procedures on this engine.

(9)—Intake, 45°; Exhaust, 59°.

(10)—Intake, 46°; Exhaust, 60°.

(11)—See Buick Chapter for service procedures on this engine.

(12)—Intake, 1 21/32; exhaust, 1 19/32.

(13)—Intake 44°, exhaust 30°.

(14)—Omega only. See Buick Chapter for service procedures.

(15)—See Pontiac Chapter for service procedures.

(16)—Intake 29°; Exhaust 44°.

(17)—1975: 186 @ 1.27; 1976: 175 @ 1.26.

(18)—Intake, 180 @ 1.34; exhaust, 177 @ 1.45.

(19)—Intake, 164 @ 1.34; exhaust, 182 @ 1.34.

(20)—Intake, 200 @ 1.25"; Exhaust 200 @ 1.16".

ENGINE TIGHTENING SPECIFICATIONS★

★Torque specifications are for clean and lightly lubricated threads only. Dry or dirty threads produce increased friction which prevents accurate measurement of tightness.

Year	Engine Model	Spark Plugs Ft. Lbs.	Cylinder Head Bolts Ft. Lbs.	Intake Manifold Ft. Lbs.	Exhaust Manifold Ft. Lbs.	Rocker Arm Shaft Bracket Ft. Lbs.	Rocker Arm Cover Ft. Lbs.	Connecting Rod Cap Bolts Ft. Lbs.	Main Bearing Cap Bolts Ft. Lbs.	Flywheel to Crankshaft Ft. Lbs.	Vibration Damper or Pulley Ft. Lbs.
1974	6-250④	15	95	⑤	⑤	—	5	35	65	60	60
	V8-350	35	85	35-40⑦	25	25②	7	42	70-80⑧	⑨	160③
	V8-400	35	85	35-40⑦	25	25②	7	42	100-120	⑨	160③
	V8-455	35	85	35-40⑦	25	25②	7	42	100-120	⑨	160③
1975-76	6-250④	15	95	—	⑤	—	⑬	35	65	60	60
	V8-260	25	85⑦	40⑦	25	25②	7	42	80⑫	⑭	310
	V8-350⑩	15	80	45	⑮	30	4	40	115	60	⑯
	V8-350	25	85⑦	40⑦	25	25②	7	42	80⑫	⑭	310
	V8-400⑪	15	95	40	30	20②	8	43	100⑫	95	160
	V8-455	25	85⑦	40⑦	25	25②	7	42	120	⑭	310
1977	V6-231⑰	20	80	45	25	30	4	40	100	60	175
	V8-260	25	85⑦	40	25	25②	7	42	80⑫	⑭	310
	V8-305④⑱	15	65	30	20	50⑳	45㉑	45	70	60	60
	V8-350④⑱㉒	15	65	30	20⑲	50⑳	45㉑	45	70	60	60
	V8-350㉓	25	130	40⑦	25	25②	7	42	80⑫	⑭	310
	V8-403	25	130	40⑦	25	25②	7	42	80⑫	⑭	310
1978	V6-231⑰	20	80	45	25	30	4	40	100	60	175
	V8-260	25	85⑦	40⑦	25	25②	7	42	80⑫	⑭	310
	V8-305④	15	65	30	20	50⑳	45㉑	45	70	60	60
	V8-350④㉒	15	65	30	20⑲	50⑳	45㉑	45	70	60	60
	V8-350㉓	25	130	40⑦	25	25②	7	42	80⑫	⑭	310
	V8-350㉕	—	130	40⑦	25	25②	—	42	120	60	200-310
	V8-403	25	130	40⑦	25	25②	7	42	80⑫	⑭	310

②—Rocker arm pivot bolt to head.
③—Minimum.
④—See Chevrolet Chapter for service procedures on this engine.
⑤—Outer clamp 20 ft.-lbs., all others 30 ft.-lbs.
⑦—Clean and dip entire bolt in engine oil before tightening.
⑧—Rear 100-120 ft.-lbs.
⑨—Auto. trans. 60, std. trans. 80.
⑩—Omega only. See Buick chapter for service.
⑪—See Pontiac Chapter for service.
⑫—Rear 120 ft.-lbs.
⑬—1975: 60 in lb.; 1976: 80 in lb.
⑭—Auto. trans., 60 ft. lbs.; manual trans., 90 ft. lbs.
⑮—1975: 28 ft. lb.; 1976: 25 ft. lb.
⑯—1975: 140 ft. lb. minimum; 1976: 175 ft. lb.
⑰—See Buick Chapter for service.
⑱—Omega.
⑲—Inner bolts, 30 ft. lb.
⑳—Rocker arm stud.
㉑—In. lb.
㉒—Distributor at rear of engine, rotor rotation clockwise.
㉓—Distributor at rear of engine, rotor rotation counter-clockwise.
㉔—Distributor at front of engine.
㉕—Diesel.

ALTERNATOR & REGULATOR SPECIFICATIONS

Year	Model	Alternator		Output @ 14 Volts		Regulator	Field Relay			Voltage Regulator		
		Rated Hot Output Amps.	Field Current 12 Volts @ 80° F.	2000 R.P.M. Amps.	5000 R.P.M. Amps.	Model	Air Gap In.	Point Gap In.	Closing Voltage	Air Gap In.	Point Gap In.	Voltage @ 125° F.
1974	1100497	37	4-4.5	—	36①	Integral	—	—	—	—	—	13.8-14.8
	1100573	42	4-4.5	—	37	Integral	—	—	—	—	—	—
	1100934	37	4-4.5	—	32	Integral	—	—	—	—	—	—
	1102367	55	—	—	—	Integral	—	—	—	—	—	—
	1102368	61	—	—	—	Integral	—	—	—	—	—	—

Continued

ALTERNATOR & REGULATOR SPECIFICATIONS—Continued

Year	Model	Alternator		Output @ 14 Volts		Regulator	Field Relay			Voltage Regulator		
		Rated Hot Output Amps.	Field Current 12 Volts @ 80° F.	2000 R.P.M. Amps.	5000 R.P.M. Amps.	Model	Air Gap In.	Point Gap In.	Closing Voltage	Air Gap In.	Point Gap In.	Voltage @ 125° F.
1975–76	1102399	37	4–4.5	—	37②	Integral	—	—	—	—	—	—
	1102481	37	4–4.5	—	37②	Integral	—	—	—	—	—	—
	1102483	37	4–4.5	—	37②	Integral	—	—	—	—	—	—
	1102488	57	—	—	—	Integral	—	—	—	—	—	—
	1102493	42	4–4.5	—	38	Integral	—	—	—	—	—	—
	1102549	61	—	—	—	Integral	—	—	—	—	—	—
	1102550	63	—	—	—	Integral	—	—	—	—	—	—
1976	1101016	80	4–4.9	—	76	Integral	—	—	—	—	—	—
	1102388	37	4–4.5	—	33	Integral	—	—	—	—	—	13.6–14.2
	1102394	37	4–4.5	—	33	Integral	—	—	—	—	—	—
	1102491	37	4–4.5	—	33	Integral	—	—	—	—	—	13.8–14.8③
	1102841	42	—	—	—	Integral	—	—	—	—	—	—
	1102842	63	—	—	—	Integral	—	—	—	—	—	—
	1102843	61	4–4.5	—	57	Integral	—	—	—	—	—	—
	1102844	63	—	—	—	Integral	—	—	—	—	—	—
	1101016	80	—	—	—	Integral	—	—	—	—	—	—
	1101034	80	—	—	—	Integral	—	—	—	—	—	—
1977–78	1102394	37	4–4.5	—	33	Integral	—	—	—	—	—	—
	1102479	55	—	—	—	Integral	—	—	—	—	—	—
	1102840	55	—	—	—	Integral	—	—	—	—	—	—
	1102841	42	—	—	—	Integral	—	—	—	—	—	—
	1102842	63	—	—	—	Integral	—	—	—	—	—	—
	1102843	61	4–4.5	—	57	Integral	—	—	—	—	—	—
	1102844	63	—	—	—	Integral	—	—	—	—	—	—
	1102881	37	—	—	—	Integral	—	—	—	—	—	—
	1102913	61	—	—	—	Integral	—	—	—	—	—	—
	1103033	42	—	—	—	Integral	—	—	—	—	—	—
1979	1101016	80	—	—	—	Integral	—	—	—	—	—	—
	1101028	80	—	—	—	Integral	—	—	—	—	—	—
	1101043	80	—	—	—	Integral	—	—	—	—	—	—
	1102394	37	—	—	—	Integral	—	—	—	—	—	—
	1102479	55	—	—	—	Integral	—	—	—	—	—	—
	1102840	55	—	—	—	Integral	—	—	—	—	—	—
	1102841	42	—	—	—	Integral	—	—	—	—	—	—
	1102842	63	—	—	—	Integral	—	—	—	—	—	—
	1102843	61	—	—	—	Integral	—	—	—	—	—	—
	1102844	63	—	—	—	Integral	—	—	—	—	—	—
	1102881	37	—	—	—	Integral	—	—	—	—	—	—
	1103042	63	—	—	—	Integral	—	—	—	—	—	—

①—At 7000 RPM.
②—At 5500 RPM.
③—At 85° F.

PISTONS, PINS, RINGS, CRANKSHAFT & BEARINGS

Year	Model	Piston Clearance	Ring End Gap①		Wrist-pin Diameter	Rod Bearings		Main Bearings			
			Comp.	Oil		Shaft Diameter	Bearing Clearance	Shaft Diameter	Bearing Clearance	Thrust on Bear. No.	Shaft End Play
1974	6-250⑧	.0005-.0016	.010	.015	.9271	1.999-2.000	.0007-.0027	2.3004	.0003-.0029	7	.002-.006
	V8-350	.001-.002	.010	.015	.9805	2.1238-2.1248	.0004-.0033	③	.0005-.0021⑤	3	.004-.008
	V8-455	.001-.002	.010	.015	.9805	2.4988-2.4998	.0004-.0033	2.9993-3.0003	.0005-.0021⑥	3	.004-.008
1975-76	6-250⑧	⑨	.010	.015	.9271	1.999-2.000	.0035	2.2983-2.2993	⑩	7	.002-.006
	V8-260	.0007-.0017	.010	.015	.9805	2.1238-2.1248	.0004-.0033	③	.0005-.0021⑤	3	.004-.008
	V8-350④⑫	.0008-.0014	.010	.015	.9392	1.991-2.000	.0005-.0026	3.000	.0004-.0015	3	.003-.009
	V8-350	.001-.002	.010	.015	.9805	2.1238-2.1248	.0004-.0033	③	.0005-.0021⑤	3	.004-.008
	V8-400⑦	.0029-.0037	②	.035	.9802	2.25	.0005-.0025	3.00	.0002-.0017	4	.003-.009
	V8-455	.001-.002	.010	.015	.9805	2.4988-2.4998	.0004-.0033	2.9993-3.0003	.0005-.0021⑥	3	.004-.008
1977	V6-231⑫	.0008-.0014	.013	.015	.9393	2.000	.0002-.0023	2.4995	.0004-.0015	2	.004-.008
	V8-260	.0007-.0017	.010	.015	.9805	2.1238-2.1248	.0004-.0033	③	⑪	3	.0035-.0135
	V8-305⑧	.0007-.0017	.010	.015	.9272	2.099-2.100	.0013-.0035	⑬	⑭	5	.002-.006
	V8-350	.0007-.0017	.010	.015	.9805	2.1238-2.1248	.0004-.0033	③	⑪	3	.0035-.0135
	V8-350⑧	.0007-.0017	.010	.015	.9272	2.099-2.100	.0013-.0035	⑬	⑭	5	.002-.006
	V8-403	.0003-.0005	.010	.015	.9805	2.1238-2.1248	.0004-.0033	③	.0005-.0026	3	.0035-.0135
1978	V6-231⑫	.0008-.0020	.010	.015	.9392	2.2487-2.2495	.0005-.0026	2.4995	.0003-.0017	2	.004-.008
	V8-260	.0007-.0017	.010	.015	.9805	2.1238-2.1248	.0004-.0033	③	⑪	3	.0035-.0135
	V8-305⑧	.0007-.0017	.010	.015	.9272	2.099-2.100	.0013-.0035	⑲	㉑	5	.002-.006
	V8-350⑧⑮	.0007-.0017	.010	.015	.9272	2.099-2.100	.0013-.0035	⑲	㉑	5	.002-.006
	V8-350⑰	.001-.002	.010	.015	.9805	2.1238-2.1248	.0005-.0026	⑳	⑪	3	.0035-.0135
	V8-350⑱	.005-.006	.015	.015	1.0951	2.1238-2.1248	.0005-.0026	2.9993-3.0003	⑪	3	.0035-.0135
	V8-403	.001-.002	.010	.015	.9805	2.1238-2.1248	.0005-.0026	⑳	⑪	3	.0035-.0135
1979	V6-231⑫	.0009-.0014	.013	.015	.9392	2.000	.0002-.0023	2.4995	.0004-.0015	2	.004-.008
	V8-260	—	.010	.015	.9805	2.1238-2.1248	.0005-.0026	2.50	⑪	3	.004-.008
	V8-260⑱	—	.010	.015	.9805	2.1238-2.1248	.0005-.0026	3.00	—	3	.0035-.0135
	V8-305⑧	.0017-.0042	.010	.010	.9271	2.099-2.100	.0013-.0035	⑲	—	5	.002-.007
	V8-350	—	.010	.015	.9805	2.1238-2.1248	.0005-.0026	2.50	—	3	—
	V8-350⑧	.0007-.0017	.010	.015	.9271	2.099-2.100	.0013-.0035	⑲	—	5	.002-.007
	V8-350⑱	—	.015	.015	1.0951	2.1238-2.1248	.0005-.0026	3.00	—	3	.0035-.0135
	V8-403	—	.010	.015	.9805	2.1238-2.1248	.0005-.0026	2.50	—	3	—

①—Fit rings in tapered bores for clearance listed in tightest portion of ring travel.
②—Top—.019, #2—.015.
③—No. 1: 2.4988-2.4998; Nos. 2, 3, 4, 5: 2.4985-2.4995.
④—Omega only.
⑤—Rear .0015-.0031.
⑥—Rear .002-.0034.
⑦—See Pontiac Chapter for service procedures.
⑧—See Chevrolet Chapter for service procedures on this engine.
⑨—.0025 maximum.
⑩—No. 1: .002 maximum; others: .0035 maximum.
⑪—No. 1, 2, 3, 4: .0005-.0021; No. 5: .0015-.0031.

⑫—See Buick Chapter for service procedures on this engine.
⑬—No. 1: 2.4484-2.4493; No. 2, 3, 4: 2.4481-2.4490; No. 5: 2.4479-2.4488.
⑭—No. 1: .0008-.0020; No. 2, 3, 4: .0011-.0023; No. 5: .0017-.0032.
⑮—Distributor at rear of engine, rotor rotation clockwise.
⑯—Distributor at front of engine.
⑰—Distributor at rear of engine, rotor rotation counter-clockwise.
⑱—Diesel.
⑲—No. 1, 2.4484-2.4493; No. 2, 3 & 4 2.4481-2.4490 & No. 5, 2.4479-2.4488.
⑳—No. 1, 2.4988-2.4998; No. 2, 3, 4 & 5, 2.4985-2.4995.
㉑—No. 1, .001-.0015; No. 2, 3 & 4, .001-.0025; No. 5, .0025-.0035.

STARTING MOTOR SPECIFICATIONS

Year	Model	Starter Number	Brush Spring Tension Oz.①	Free Speed Test			Resistance Test③	
				Amps.	Volts	R.P.M.	Amps.	Volts
1974	6-250	1108365	35	50–80②	9	5510–10500	—	—
	8-350	1108516	35	—	—	—	—	—
	8-455	1108517	35	—	—	—	—	—
	Toronado	1108518	35	—	—	—	—	—
1975	6-250	1108365	35	50–80	9	5500–10500	—	—
	6-250	1108774⑤	35	50–80	9	5500–10500	—	—
	8-260	1108765	35	55–80	9	3500–6000	—	—
	8-350④	1108762	35	55–80	9	3500–6000	—	—
	8-350	1108765	35	55–80	9	3500–6000	—	—
	8-400	1108758	35	65–95	9	7500–10500	—	—
	8-455	1108766	—	—	—	—	—	—
1976	6-250	1109024	35	—	—	—	—	—
	6-250	1109025	35	—	—	—	—	—
	8-260, 350	1108519	35	—	—	—	—	—
	8-350④	1108763	35	—	—	—	—	—
	8-455	1109026	35	—	—	—	—	—
	Toronado	1109027	35	—	—	—	—	—
1977	6-231	1108797	—	—	—	—	—	—
	8-260	1108765	—	—	—	—	—	—
	8-305④	—	—	—	—	—	—	—
	8-350④	—	—	—	—	—	—	—
	8-350	1108765	—	—	—	—	—	—
	8-403	1108794	—	—	—	—	—	—
1978	6-231	1109061	—	—	—	—	—	—
	8-260	1109523	—	—	—	—	—	—
	8-305④	1109064	—	—	—	—	—	—
	8-305⑥	1109524	—	—	—	—	—	—
	8-350⑦	1109065	—	—	—	—	—	—
	8-350⑧	1109067	—	—	—	—	—	—
	8-350⑨	1109072	—	—	—	—	—	—
	8-350 Diesel	1109213	—	—	—	—	—	—
	8-403⑨	1109072	—	—	—	—	—	—
	8-403	1109070	—	—	—	—	—	—
1979	6-231	110961	—	—	—	—	—	—
	6-231⑨	1108797	—	—	—	—	—	—
	8-260⑥	1109523	—	—	—	—	—	—
	8-260⑨	1108765	—	—	—	—	—	—
	8-260⑦	1109523	—	—	—	—	—	—
	8-350⑨	110865	—	—	—	—	—	—
	8-350⑩	1109214	—	—	—	—	—	—
	8-350 Diesel	1998205	—	—	—	—	—	—
	8-403	1108794	—	—	—	—	—	—

①—Minimum.
②—Includes solenoid.
③—Check capacity of motor by using a 500 ampere meter and a carbon pile rheostat to control voltage. Apply volts listed across motor with armature locked. Current should be as listed.
④—Omega only.
⑤—Has "R" terminal removed.
⑥—Cutlass
⑦—Auto. trans.
⑧—Manual trans.
⑨—88 & 98.
⑩—Toronado.

WHEEL ALIGNMENT SPECIFICATIONS

Year	Model	Caster Angle, Degrees		Camber Angle, Degrees				Toe-In. Inch	Toe-Out on Turns, Deg.①	
				Limits		Desired				
		Limits	Desired	Left	Right	Left	Right		Outer Wheel	Inner Wheel
1974	Omega	0 to +1	+½	−¼ to +¾	−¼ to +¾	+¼	+¼	⅛−¼	—	—
	Cutlass Exc. Sal.⑥	−½ to +½	0	+½ to +1½	0 to +1	+1	+½	0−⅛	—	—
	Cutlass Salon⑤	+1½ to +2½	+2	+½ to +1½	0 to +1	+1	+½	0−⅛	—	—
	88, 98⑤	+½ to +1½	+1	+½ to +1½	0 to +1	+1	+½	−1/16 to +3/16	—	—
	Toronado⑥	−1½ to −2½	−2	−¼ to +¾	−¾ to +¼	+¼	−¼	0	—	—
1975	Omega③	−1½ to −½	−1	+¼ to +1¼	+¼ to +1¼	+¾	+¾	0 to ⅛	—	—
	Omega④	+½ to +1½	+1	+¼ to +1¼	+¼ to +1¼	+¾	+¾	0 to ⅛	—	—
	Cutlass⑤	+1½ to +2½	+2	+½ to +1½	0 to +1	+1	+½	0 to ⅛	—	—
	88, 98⑤	+1 to +2	+1½	+½ to +1½	0 to +1	+1	+½	0 to ⅛	—	—
	Sta. Wagons⑤	+1 to +2	+1½	+½ to +1½	0 to +1	+1	+½	0 to ⅛	—	—
	Toronado⑤	−1 to +1	0	−¼ to +¾	−¾ to +¼	+¼	−¼	0 to 1/16	—	—
1976	Omega③	−½ to −1½	−1	+¼ to +1¼	+¼ to +1¼	+¾	+¾	0 to ⅛	—	—
	Omega④	+½ to +1½	+1	+¼ to +1¼	+¼ to +1¼	+¾	+¾	0 to ⅛	—	—
	Cutlass⑤	+1½ to +2½	+2	+½ to +1½	0 to +1	+1	+½	0 to ⅛	—	—
	88, 98⑥	+1 to +2	+1½	+½ to +1½	0 to +1	+1	+½	0 to ⅛	—	—
	Toronado⑤	−1 to +1	0	−¼ to +¾	−¾ to +¼	+¼	−¼	−1/16 to +1/16	—	—
1977	Omega③	−½ to −1½	−1	+¼ to +1¼	+¼ to +1¼	+¾	+¾	0 to ⅛	—	—
	Omega④	+½ to +1½	+1	+¼ to +1¼	+¼ to +1¼	+¾	+¾	0 to ⅛	—	—
	Cutlass⑤	+1½ to +2½	+2	+½ to +1½	0 to +1	+1	+½	0 to ⅛	—	—
	88, 98	+2½ to +3½	+3	+¼ to +1¼	+¼ to +1¼	+¾	+¾	1/16 to 3/16	—	—
	Toronado⑤	−1 to +1	0	−¼ to +¾	−¾ to +¼	+¼	−¼	−1/16 to +1/16	—	—
1978	Toronado	—	0	−¼ to +¾	−¾ to +¼	+¼	−¼	−1/16 to +1/16	—	—
1978-79	Omega③	−½ to −1½	−1	+¼ to +1¼	+¼ to +1¼	+¾	+¾	+1/16 to +3/16	—	—
	Omega④	+½ to +1½	+1	+¼ to +1¼	+¼ to +1¼	+¾	+¾	+1/16 to +3/16	—	—
	Cutlass③	+½ to +1½	+1	0 to +1	0 to +1	+½	+½	+1/16 to +3/16	—	—
	Cutlass④	+2½ to +3½	+3	0 to +1	0 to +1	+½	+½	+1/16 to +3/16	—	—
	88, 98	+2½ to +3½	+3	+¼ to +1¼	+¼ to +1¼	+¾	+¾	+1/16 to +3/16	—	—
1979	Toronado	+2 to +3	+2½	−½ to +½	−½ to +½	0	0	−1/16 to +1/16	—	—

①—Incorrect toe-out, when other adjustments are correct, indicates bent steering arms.
⑥—Manual Steering.
④—Power Steering.
⑤—Left and right side "camber" should be different at least ¼° and no more than ¾° with the left side having the greater (+) reading.

COOLING SYSTEM & CAPACITY DATA

Year	Model or Engine	Cooling Capacity, Qts.		Radiator Cap Relief Pressure, Lbs.		Thermo. Opening Temp. ①	Fuel Tank Gals.	Engine Oil Refill Qts. ②	Transmission Oil				Rear Axle Oil Pints
		With Heater	With A/C	With A/C	No A/C				3 Speed Pints	4 Speed Pints	5 Speed Pints	Auto. Trans. Qts. ⑫	
1974	6-250	15½	—	15	15	195	21	4	3.5	—	—	⑩	4¼
	8-350 Omega	18½	19½	15	15	195	21	4	3.5	—	—	⑩	4¼
	8-350 Cutlass	20④	20④	15	15	195	22	4	—	—	—	⑩	4¼
	8-350⑬	21⑥	21⑥	15	15	195	26	4	—	—	—	⑩	4¼
	8-350 Sta. Wagon	20④	20④	15	15	195	22	4	—	—	—	⑩	5½
	8-455 Cutlass	21	21½⑥	15	15	195	22	4	—	—	—	⑩	4¼
	8-455⑬	21	21½⑥	15	15	195	26	4	—	—	—	⑩	5½
	8-455 Sta. Wagon	21	21½⑥	15	15	195	22	4	—	—	—	⑩	5½
	Toronado	21	21½	15	15	195	26	5	—	—	—	⑰	4

Continued

COOLING SYSTEM & CAPACITY DATA—Continued

Year	Model or Engine	Cooling Capacity, Qts.		Radiator Cap Relief Pressure, Lbs.		Thermo. Opening Temp. [1]	Fuel Tank Gals.	Engine Oil Refill Qts. [2]	Transmission Oil				Rear Axle Oil Pints
		With Heater	With A/C	With A/C	No A/C				3 Speed Pints	4 Speed Pints	5 Speed Pints	Auto. Trans. Qts. [12]	
1975	6-250 Omega	15½	19½	15	15	195	21	4	3½	—	—	[10]	[9]
	6-250 Cutlass	17	17	15	15	195	22	4	3½	—	—	[10]	[9]
	8-260 Omega	18½	19½	15	15	195	21	4	3½	—	—	[10]	[9]
	8-260 Cutlass	23½	23½[4]	15	15	195	22	4	3½	—	—	[10]	[9]
	8-350 Omega	18½	19½	15	15	195	21	4	—	—	—	[10]	[9]
	8-350[7]	20	20[4]	15	15	195	26[8]	4	—	—	—	[10]	[9]
	8-400	21½	22[6]	15	15	195	26[8]	4	—	—	—	[10]	[9]
	8-455	21	21½[8]	15	15	195	26[8]	4	—	—	—	[10]	[9]
	Toronado	21	21½	15	15	195	26	5	—	—	—	[17]	4
1976	6-250 Omega	15½	16½	15	15	195	21	4	3½	—	—	[10]	5½
	6-250 Cutlass	17	17	15	15	195	22	4	3½	—	3½	[10]	4¼
	8-260 Omega	18½	19½	15	15	195	21	4	3½	—	3½	[10]	5½
	8-260 Cutlass	23½	23½[4]	15	15	195	22	4	3½	—	3½	[10]	4¼
	8-350 Omega	18½	19½	15	15	195	21	4	—	—	—	[10]	5½
	8-350[7]	20	20[4]	15	15	195	26[8]	4	—	—	—	[10]	[18]
	8-455	21	21½[8]	15	15	195	26[8]	4	—	—	—	[10]	[18]
	Toronado	21	21½[6]	15	15	195	26	5	—	—	—	[17]	4
1977	6-231 Omega	12.7	13.7	15	15	195	21	4	3	—	—	[14]	3½
	6-231 Cutlass	16.9	17.0	15	15	195	22	4	3	—	—	[10]	4¼
	6-231[13]	11.5	11.4	15	15	195	[15][16]	4	—	—	—	[14]	3½
	8-260 Omega	16.8	17.8	15	15	195	21	4	—	—	3½	[14]	3½
	8-260 Cutlass	16.9	17.0	15	15	195	22	4	—	—	3½	[14]	4¼
	8-260[13]	15.5	15.3	15	15	195	[15][16]	4	—	—	—	[14]	3½
	8-305 Omega	—	—	15	15	195	21	4	3	—	—	[14]	3½
	8-350 Omega	15.6	16.6	15	15	195	21	4	—	—	—	[14]	3½
	8-350 Cutlass	15.1	15.3	15	15	195	22	4	—	—	—	[14]	4¼
	8-350[13]	13.8	13.7	15	15	195	[15][16]	4	—	—	—	[14]	4¼
	8-403 Cutlass	16.3	16.4	15	15	195	22	4	—	—	—	[14]	4¼
	8-403[13]	14.9	14.8	15	15	195	24½[19]	4	—	—	—	[14]	4¼
	8-403 Toronado	17.2	17.4	15	15	195	26	5	—	—	—	[17]	4
1978	V6-231 Omega	12.75	12.75	15	15	195	21	4	3.5	—	3.5	[14]	[27]
	V6-231 Cutlass	12	12	15	15	195	18[24]	4	3.5	—	3.5	[14]	[27]
	V6-231 88, 98	12.25	12.25	15	15	195	25.25	4	—	—	—	[14]	[27]
	V8-260 Cutlass	16.25[19]	16.25[19]	15	15	195	18[24]	4	—	—	3.5	[14]	[27]
	V8-260 88, 98	16.25[20]	16.25[20]	15	15	195	25.25	4	—	—	—	[14]	[27]
	V8-305 Omega	15.75[19]	16.0[19]	15	15	195	21	4	—	2.5	—	[14]	[27]
	V8-305 Cutlass	15.5[21]	15.5[21]	15	15	195	18[24]	4	—	2.5	—	[14]	[27]
	V8-350 Omega	16.0	16.75	15	15	195	21	4	—	—	—	[14]	[27]
	V8-350 Cutlass	15.5	16.25	15	15	195	18[24]	4	—	—	—	[14]	[27]
	V8-350 Diesel	18	18	15	15	195	27.25[25]	7[26]	—	—	—	[14]	[27]
	V8-350 88, 98	14	15.5	15	15	195	25.25	4	—	—	—	[14]	[27]
	V8-403 88, 98	15.75	16.5	15	15	195	25.25	4	—	—	—	[14]	[27]
	V8-403 Toronado	17.5[23]	17.5[23]	15	15	195	26	5	—	—	—	[17]	4
1979	V6-231 Omega	13.5	13.4	15	15	195	21	4	3	3	—	[14]	[22]
	V6-231 Cutlass	13.3	13.3	15	15	195	19¾	4	3	3	—	[14]	[22]
	V6-231 88 & 98	13.3	13.3	15	15	195	21	4	—	—	—	[14]	[22]
	V8-260 Cutlass	16.2	16.6	13	13	195	19¾	4	—	—	3½	[14]	[22]
	V8-260 88 & 98	16.4	16.3	13	13	195	25¼	4	—	—	—	[14]	[22]
	V8-305 Omega	16.6	17	15	15	195	21	4	3	3	—	[14]	[22]
	V8-350 Omega	16.9	17.6	15	15	195	21	4	—	—	—	[14]	[22]
	V8-350 Cutlass	17.9	17.9	15	15	195	19¾	4	—	—	—	[14]	[22]
	V8-350 88 & 98[22]	18.0	17.9	15	15	195	22	6	—	—	—	[14]	[22]
	V8-350 88 & 98	14.6	15.2	15	15	195	25¼	4	—	—	—	[14]	[22]

Continued

COOLING SYSTEM & CAPACITY DATA—Continued

Year	Model or Engine	Cooling Capacity, Qts.		Radiator Cap Relief Pressure, Lbs.		Thermo. Opening Temp. ①	Fuel Tank Gals.	Engine Oil Refill Qts. ②	Transmission Oil				Rear Axle Oil Pints
		With Heater	With A/C	With A/C	No A/C				3 Speed Pints	4 Speed Pints	5 Speed Pints	Auto. Trans. Qts. --	
1979	V8-350 Toronado	14.9	15.6	15	15	195	20	4	—	—	—	⑰	3¼
	V8-350 Toronado㉒	18.4	18.4	15	15	195	22¾	6	—	—	—	⑰	3¼
	V8-403 88, 98	15.7	16.4	15	15	195	25¼	4	—	—	—	⑭	㉒

①—For Permanent type anti-freeze.
②—Add one quart with filter change.
③—Diesel, 6 pts.
④—With heavy duty cooling system add 2½ qts.
⑤—With heavy duty cooling system add 1½ qts.
⑥—With heavy duty cooling system add 2 qts.
⑦—Intermediate and full size.
⑧—Intermediate and station wagons 22 gallons.
⑨—8½" ring gear 4¼ pts., 8⅞" ring gear 5½ pts., 9⅜ ring gear 5½ pts.
⑩—Oil pan only 3 qts. After overhaul 10 qts.

⑫—Approximate; make final check with dipstick.
⑬—Full size cars.
⑭—Turbo Hydro-matic 200: Oil pan only, 3 qts.; after overhaul, 9 qts. T.H. 250, 350 & 400: par only, 3 qts.; after overhaul, 10 qts.
⑮—Delta 88 except Calif. V8-350: 21 gals.; Calif. V8-350 & Ninety-Eight models: 24½ gals.
⑯—Custom Cruiser 22 gallons.
⑰—Oil pan only 4 qts. after overhaul 12 qts.
⑱—8½" ring gear, 4¼ pts.; 8⅞" ring gear, 5½ pts.

⑲—Heavy duty & trailer towing, 16.75 qts.
⑳—Trailer towing, 17.0 qts.; Heavy duty, 17.25 qts.
㉑—Heavy duty & trailer towing, 16.25 qts.
㉒—Diesel engine.
㉓—Trailer towing, 17.25 qts.
㉔—Cutlass Cruiser, 18.25 gals.
㉕—Custom Cruiser, 22 gals.
㉖—Includes filter.
㉗—Exc. 7.5" ring gear, 4.25 pts.; 7.5" ring gear, 3.5 pts.

Electrical Section

DISTRIBUTOR, REPLACE
Except 1977 Toronado

1. On vehicles with point type ignition systems, disconnect primary lead from ignition coil.
2. On vehicles with H.E.I. system, disconnect electrical connector from distributor cap (V6 and V8 engines) or from ignition coil (6-250 engine).
3. On 1978 Toronado with E.S.T. system, disconnect electrical connector from distributor cap.
4. Remove distributor cap, then on all except 1978 Toronado with E.S.T. system, disconnect hose from vacuum advance unit.
5. Remove distributor clamp and screw.
6. Using chalk, make alignment marks on rotor, distributor housing and engine to ensure proper installation of distributor.
7. Pull distributor up until rotor just stops turning counterclockwise and make a second mark on distributor housing aligned with rotor.
8. Before installing distributor, align rotor with second mark made on distributor housing, then install distributor with first mark made on distributor housing aligned with mark on engine.

NOTE: It may be necessary to lift distributor slightly to align gears and oil pump drive shaft.

9. Install clamp and clamp bolt finger tight, then install distributor cap and reconnect all electrical connectors.

10. Check engine timing and adjust as necessary, then tighten clamp bolt and connect vacuum hose.

1977 Toronado

1. Release spark plug cable latches and lift cables out of the way, then disconnect wiring connectors from distributor and 2-wire connector near distributor cap.
2. Remove distributor cap.
3. Crank engine until rotor points toward rear of engine and number one piston is almost at TDC (0 degrees on timing indicator).
4. Using a socket on crankshaft bolt, turn crankshaft to 0 degrees.

NOTE: White mark on rotor should be aligned with pointer in distributor housing, if distributor was correctly positioned in engine.

5. Pull distributor up until rotor just stops turning and note position of rotor in relation to distributor, then remove distributor.
6. To install, turn rotor to position noted in step 5, then install distributor. Rotor will point near rear of engine.
7. Install clamp and bolt and leave loose, then rotate distributor to align white pointer in distributor housing with

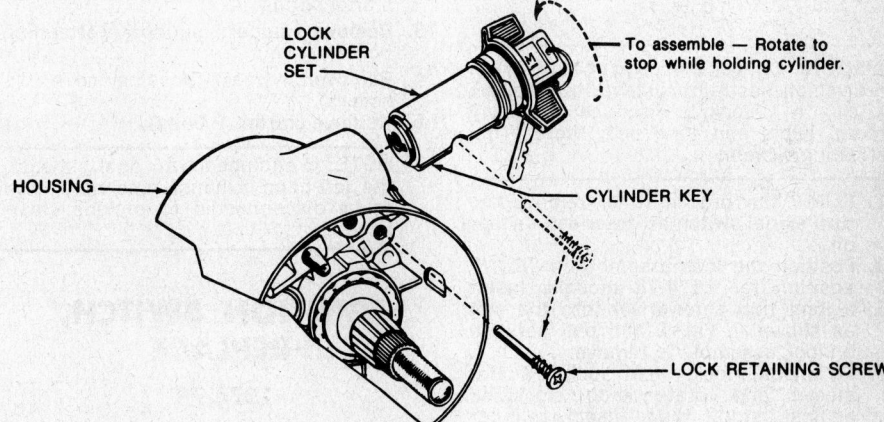

Fig. 1   Ignition lock removal. 1979

(Labels: LOCK CYLINDER SET, HOUSING, To assemble — Rotate to stop while holding cylinder, CYLINDER KEY, LOCK RETAINING SCREW)

white mark on side of rotor, and tighten clamp bolt.

NOTE: This is the final distributor position.

8. Install distributor cap and spark wires, and reconnect electrical connectors.
9. Check and adjust timing as required. Refer to "Adjusting Reference Timing" as described in the Tune-Up Chapter, Electronic Ignition Section.

IGNITION LOCK REPLACE

1979

1. Remove steering wheel as described under Horn Sounder and Steering Wheel.
2. Remove turn signal switch as described under Turn Signal Switch, Replace, then remove buzzer switch.
3. Place ignition switch in Run position, then remove lock cylinder retaining screw and lock cylinder.
4. To install, rotate lock cylinder to stop while holding housing, Fig. 1. Align cylinder key with keyway in housing, then push lock cylinder assembly into housing until fully seated.
5. Install lock cylinder retaining screw. Torque screw to 40 in. lbs. for standard columns. On adjustable columns, torque retaining screw to 22 in. lbs.
6. Install buzzer switch, turn signal switch and steering wheel.

1974-78

CAUTION: On vehicles equipped with an Air Cushion Restraint system, turn ignition switch to "Lock," disconnect battery ground cable and tape end, thereby deactivating system.

1. Follow the procedure to remove the turn signal switch as described further on.
2. Position the lock assembly in "RUN" position for 1974-78 models. Insert a long thin screwdriver into the slot as shown in Fig. 2 and pull outward on lock assembly to remove.
3. To install lock, hold lock cylinder sleeve and rotate knob clockwise against stop, then insert cylinder with key on cylinder sleeve aligned with keyway in housing. Push in to abutment of cylinder and sector, then rotate knob counterclockwise, maintaining a light inward push on cylinder until drive section of cylinder mates with drive shaft. Push in until ring snaps into groove and lock cylinder is secured.

STARTER, REPLACE

1979 V8-260 Diesel

1. Disconnect battery ground cable.
2. Remove fan shroud attaching screws and leave shroud loose.
3. Remove clutch equalizer shaft, if equipped.

Fig. 2   Ignition lock remove. 1974-78

4. Support engine with a suitable jack, disconnect engine mounts and raise engine approximately 1½ inches.
5. Disconnect starter wiring.
6. Remove starter attaching bolts and the starter.
7. Reverse procedure to install.

1974-79 Exc. V8-260 Diesel

1. Disconnect battery.
2. Noting position of wires, disconnect starter wiring.
3. Remove upper support attaching bolt.
4. Remove flywheel housing cover (4 screws).
5. Remove starter (2 bolts).

NOTE: If equipped with dual exhaust, the left-hand exhaust pipe may have to be disconnected to provide clearance.

IGNITION SWITCH, REPLACE

1974-79

CAUTION: On vehicles equipped with an Air Cushion Restraint system, turn ignition switch to "Lock," disconnect battery ground cable and tape end, thereby deactivating system.

1. Disconnect battery ground cable.
2. On models with regular steering column, turn ignition lock to "Off-Unlock" position. On models with tilt and telescope steering column, turn ignition lock to "Accessory" position.
3. Remove cover attaching bolts, loosen toe pan clamp bolts and remove trim cap from lower part of panel.
4. Remove bracket retaining nuts and lower steering column to the seat.
5. Disconnect and remove switch.
6. On models equipped with column mounted dimmer switch, remove two switch attaching screws, then remove

switch and disconnect wire connector.
6. Be sure that lock is in same position as when switch was removed then install switch onto actuator and column.
7. Connect wiring and reinstall column. On models with column mounted dimmer switch, install and adjust dimmer switch as described under Column Mounted Dimmer Switch.

LIGHT SWITCH, REPLACE

1979 Toronado

1. Disconnect battery ground cable.
2. Remove headlamp switch knob, radio knobs and steering column trim cover.
3. Remove four screws from underside of left hand trim cover.
4. Remove left hand sound absorber, then carefully pull left hand trim cover from instrument panel.

NOTE: It may be necessary to disconnect shift indicator cable clip and lower steering column slightly to remove left hand trim cover.

5. Remove two screws attaching switch to instrument cluster carrier, then pull switch rearward to remove.
6. To disconnect wire connector, remove two connector attaching screws, then pry connect at locations shown in Fig. 3.
7. Reverse procedure to install.

1978-79 Cutlass

1. Disconnect battery ground cable.
2. Remove cluster pad assembly.
3. Remove two headlight switch mounting screws, then pull switch away from panel adapter.
4. To disconnect wire connector, pry connector at locations indicated by arrows as shown in Fig. 4. Pull connector out, then slide to left and push forward to remove.
5. Reverse procedure to install. Refer to Fig. 4, to install wire connector.

1977-79 88 & 98

1. Disconnect battery ground cable.
2. Rotate headlight switch so notch on switch faces downward. Bend a ⅛ inch hook on a piece of stiff wire. Use the wire hook in the notch to pull the knob retainer clip and pull knob off shaft.
3. Remove twilight sentinel knob.
4. Position steering column collar upward and remove column lower trim cover.
5. Remove two screws securing trim cover to cluster carrier.
6. Pull trim cover from clips.
7. Remove light switch mounting plate screws.
8. Pull switch through opening and disconnect electrical connector.
9. Remove nut and switch from mounting plate.
10. Reverse procedure to install.

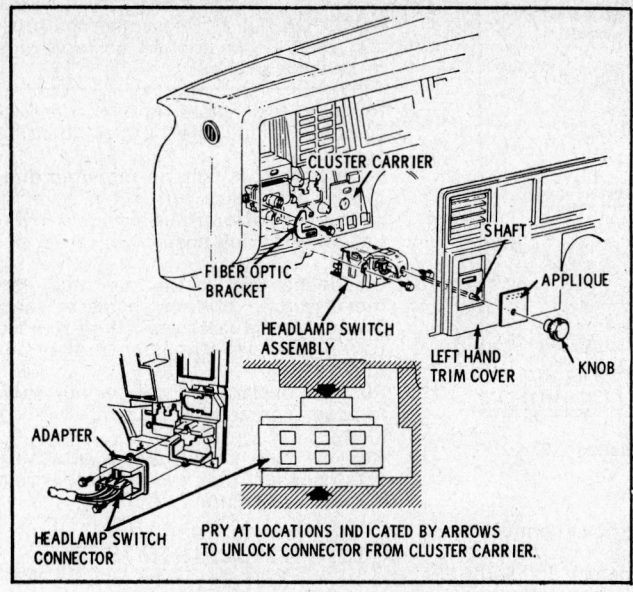

Fig. 3   Headlight switch. 1979 Toronado

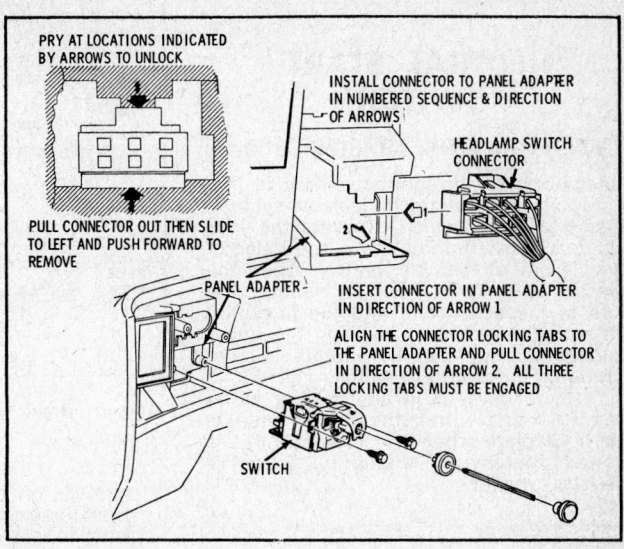

Fig. 4   Headlight switch. 1978-79 Cutlass

1974-76 Full Size & 1977-78 Toronado

CAUTION: On vehicles equipped with an Air Cushion Restraint system, turn ignition switch to "Lock," disconnect battery ground cable and tape end, thereby de-activating system.

1. Disconnect battery ground cable.
2. Without disconnecting vacuum hoses or electrical connectors, remove heater or air conditioning control.
3. Remove switch escutcheon and pull switch through heater or air conditioning control opening in cluster and disconnect electrical connector.
4. Reverse procedure to install.

1974-77 Cutlass

Less Air Conditioning

1. Disconnect battery ground cable.
2. Remove steering column trim cover.
3. Pull switch to "On" and push in button on switch rear, then pull switch knob and shaft from switch.
4. Remove switch escutcheon, pull switch from panel and disconnect electrical connector.
5. Reverse procedure to install.

With Air Conditioning

1. Disconnect battery ground cable.
2. Remove steering column trim cover and disconnect A/C outlet hose.
3. Disconnect parking brake release cable.
4. Remove screws securing left hand control panel and pull control panel from instrument panel.
5. Disconnect switch electrical connector.
6. Pull switch to "On" and push in but-

ton on switch rear, then pull switch knob and shaft from switch.
7. Remove switch escutcheon and switch.
8. Reverse procedure to install.

1974-79 Omega

1. Disconnect battery ground cable.
2. Disconnect multiple connector from switch.
3. Pull knob out to headlight ON position, then depress spring-loaded button on switch body and pull knob out of switch assembly, Fig. 5.
4. Remove switch escutcheon.
5. Remove switch from rear of panel.

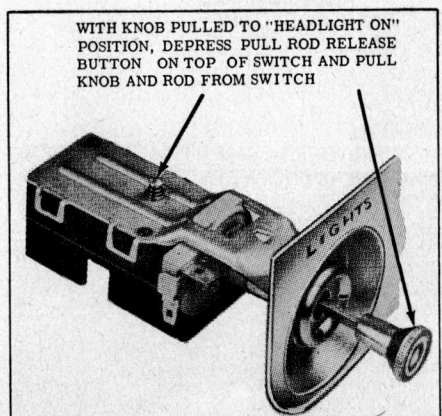

WITH KNOB PULLED TO "HEADLIGHT ON" POSITION, DEPRESS PULL ROD RELEASE BUTTON ON TOP OF SWITCH AND PULL KNOB AND ROD FROM SWITCH

Fig. 5   Light switch with release button (typical)

STOP LIGHT SWITCH

1974-79

The stop light switch is attached to the brake pedal bracket and is actuated by the brake pedal arm, Fig. 6. When installing the switch, insert switch into tubular clip until switch body seats on tube clip. Pull brake pedal rearward until it contacts brake pedal stop. This moves the switch in the tubular clip providing proper adjustment.

CLUTCH START SWITCH

1974-79

All cars equipped with a manual transmission use a clutch start switch which is mounted on the pedal bracket. The switch closes when the clutch is depressed and completes solenoid connection. When installing switch, no adjustment is necessary.

NEUTRAL START & BACK-UP LIGHT SWITCH

All Exc. 1977-79 88, 98 & 1978-79 Cutlass

1. On automatic transmission vehicles, place selector in "Neutral" for column shift, or "Park" for console shift vehicles. On manual transmission vehicles, place selector in "Reverse".
2. Install a .090 inch gauge pin into outer hole in switch cover, Figs. 7 & 8.
3. On all automatic transmission vehicles, rotate switch until pin fits into alignment hole in inner plastic slide.

4. On all models, tighten switch to column screws and remove gauge pin.

NEUTRAL START SWITCH

1977-79 88 & 98; 1978-79 Cutlass

Actuation of the ignition switch is prevented by a mechanical lockout system, Figs. 9 and 10, which prevents the lock cylinder from rotating when the selector lever is out of Park or Neutral. When the selector lever is in Park or Neutral, the slots in the bowl plate and the finger on the actuator rod align allowing the finger to pass through the bowl plate in turn actuating the ignition switch, Fig. 11. If the selector lever is in any position other than Park or Neutral, the finger contacts the bowl plate when the lock cylinder is rotated, thereby preventing full travel of the lock cylinder.

TURN SIGNAL SWITCH

CAUTION: On vehicles equipped with an Air Cushion Restraint system, turn ignition switch to "Lock," disconnect battery ground cable and tape end, thereby deactivating system.

1975-79 Tilt & Telescope

1. Disconnect battery ground cable and remove steering wheel.
2. Remove instrument panel lower trim panel, then disconnect turn signal

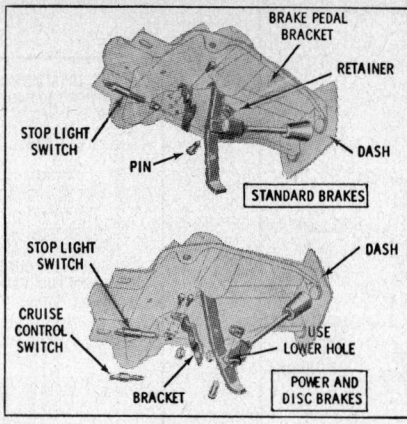

Fig. 6   Brake switch installation. 1974-79

harness connector. Remove connector from packet mounting bracket and wrap tape around connector and wires to prevent wires from snagging when removing switch, Fig. 12.
3. Remove four bolts securing column bracket assembly to mast jacket.
4. Disconnect shift indicator.
5. Hold column in position and remove two nuts securing column bracket assembly. Then, remove bracket and turn signal wiring connector. Loosely re-install bracket to hold column in place.
6. Remove rubber bumper and plastic retainer.
7. Using a suitable compressor, Fig. 13, depress lock plate far enough to remove "C" ring from shaft.

NOTE: On Tilt & Telescope, compressor must be positioned on large lips of cancelling cam.

8. Remove lock plate and carrier assembly, then the upper bearing spring.
9. On models less column mounted dimmer switch, place turn signal lever in right turn position and unscrew lever. Lift tilt lever and position in center position.
10. On models with column mounted dimmer switch, remove actuator arm screw and actuator arm, then remove turn signal lever by pulling straight out to disengage.
11. Push in hazard warning knob, then remove screw and hazard warning knob.
12. Remove turn signal switch attaching screws, then pull switch and wiring from top of column.

1974-79 Exc. 1975-79 Tilt & Telescope

1. Disconnect battery ground cable.
2. Remove steering wheel.
3. Remove cover screws and cover.
4. Using suitable compressor, depress lock plate far enough to remove the "C" ring from shaft.
5. Remove lock plate, cancelling cam, spring and signal lever.
6. Depress hazard warning knob then unscrew knob and remove.
7. On models less column mounted dimmer switch, position lever in right turn position and remove three switch attaching screws.
8. On models with column mounted dimmer switch, remove actuator arm screw and actuator arm, then remove turn signal lever by pulling straight out to disengage.
9. Remove panel lower trim cap, disconnect switch harness and remove bolts attaching bracket to column jacket.
10. Disconnect shift indicator if equipped.
11. Remove two nuts holding column in position, remove bracket and wire protector while holding column in position then loosely install bracket to hold column in place.
12. Tape switch wires at connector keeping wires flat, then carefully remove wires and switch.

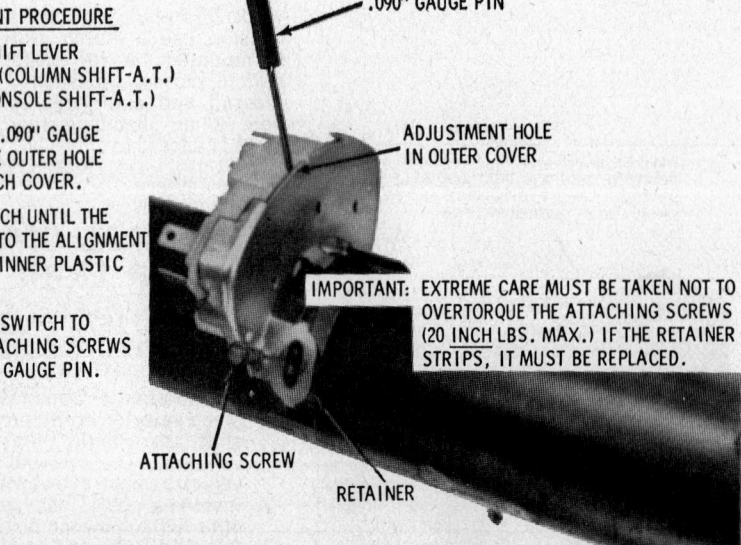

ADJUSTMENT PROCEDURE

1. POSITION SHIFT LEVER
   A. NEUTRAL (COLUMN SHIFT-A.T.)
   B. PARK (CONSOLE SHIFT-A.T.)
2. INSTALL THE .090" GAUGE PIN INTO THE OUTER HOLE IN THE SWITCH COVER.
3. ROTATE SWITCH UNTIL THE PIN GOES INTO THE ALIGNMENT HOLE IN THE INNER PLASTIC SLIDE.
4. TIGHTEN THE SWITCH TO COLUMN ATTACHING SCREWS AND REMOVE GAUGE PIN.

.090" GAUGE PIN

ADJUSTMENT HOLE IN OUTER COVER

IMPORTANT: EXTREME CARE MUST BE TAKEN NOT TO OVERTORQUE THE ATTACHING SCREWS (20 INCH LBS. MAX.) IF THE RETAINER STRIPS, IT MUST BE REPLACED.

ATTACHING SCREW

RETAINER

Fig. 7   Neutral safety switch adjustment. 1974-79 Auto. Trans.

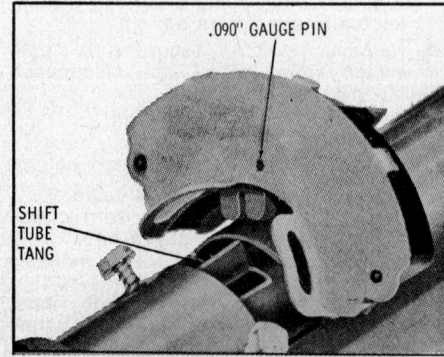

.090" GAUGE PIN

SHIFT TUBE TANG

Fig. 8   Neutral safety switch adjustment. 1974-79 manual trans. (typical)

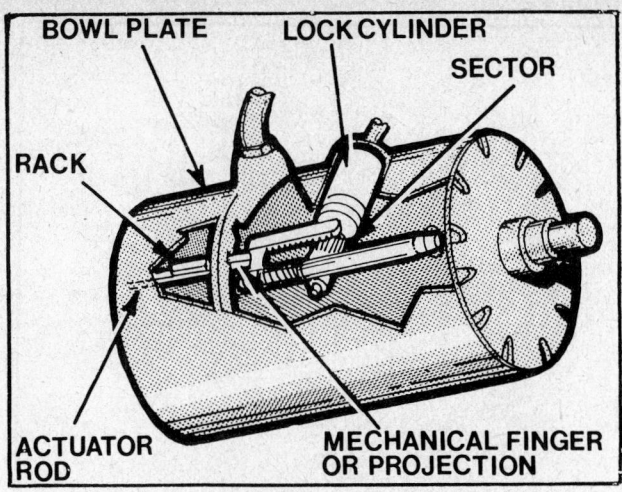

Fig. 9 Mechanical neutral start system with standard column. 1977-79 88, 98 & 1978-79 Cutlass

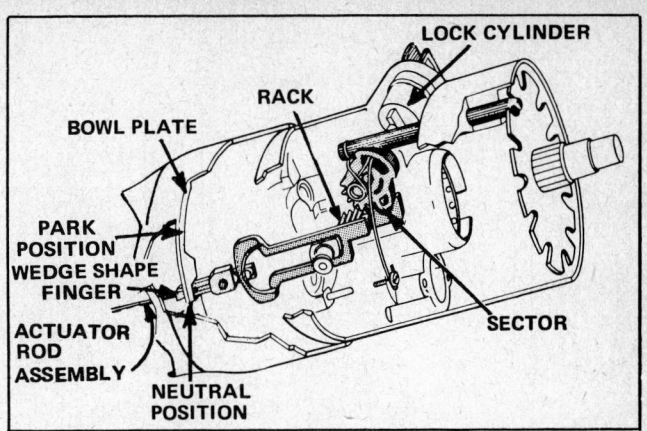

Fig. 10 Mechanical neutral start system with tilt column. 1977-79 88, 98 & 1978-79 Cutlass

COLUMN-MOUNTED DIMMER SWITCH

1977-79 88, 98 & 1978-79 Cutlass

1. Disconnect battery ground cable.
2. Remove instrument panel lower trim and on models with A/C, remove A/C duct extension at column.
3. Disconnect shift indicator from column and remove toe-plate cover screws.
4. Remove two nuts from instrument panel support bracket studs and lower steering column, resting steering wheel on front seat.
5. Remove dimmer switch retaining screw and the switch. Tape actuator rod to column and separate switch from rod.

NOTE: On 1978-79 models, two screws are used to retain dimmer switch to steering column.

6. Reverse procedure to install. To adjust switch, depress dimmer switch slightly and install a 3/32 inch twist drill to lock the switch to the body. Force switch upward to remove lash between switch and pivot. Torque switch retaining screw to 35 inch lbs. and remove tape from actuator rod. Remove twist drill and check for proper operation.

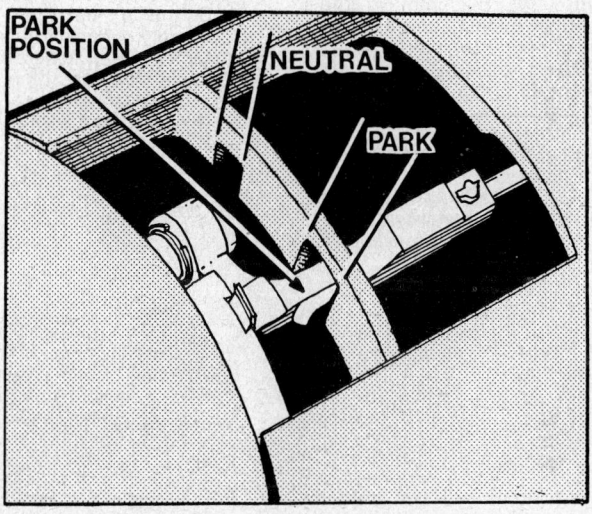

Fig. 11 Mechanical neutral start system in Park position. 1977-79 88, 98 & 1978-79 Cutlass

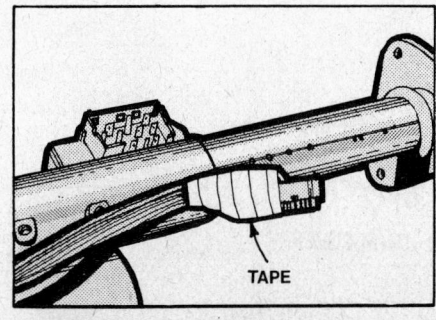

Fig. 12 Taping turn signal connector and wires

HORN SOUNDER & STEERING WHEEL
1974-79 All

CAUTION: On vehicles equipped with an Air Cushion Restraint System, turn ignition switch to "Lock," disconnect battery ground cable and tape end, thereby de-activating system. Also, on these vehicles, it is necessary to remove the drivers cushion module before removing steering

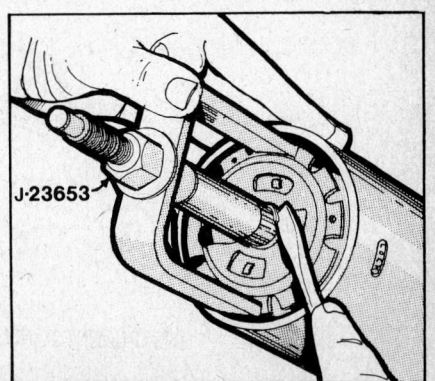

Fig. 13 Compressing lock plate and removing retaining ring

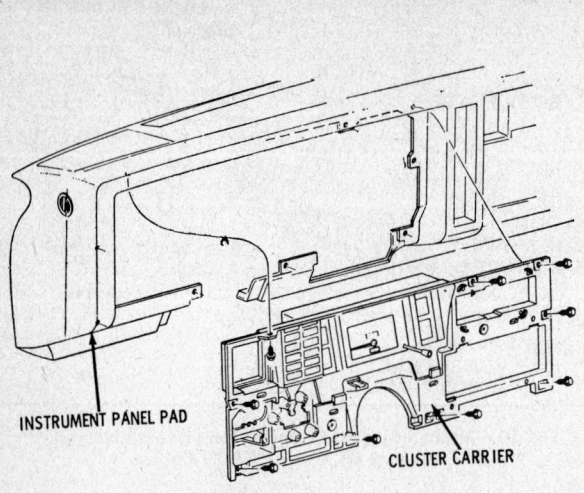

Fig. 14   Instrument cluster. 1979 Toronado

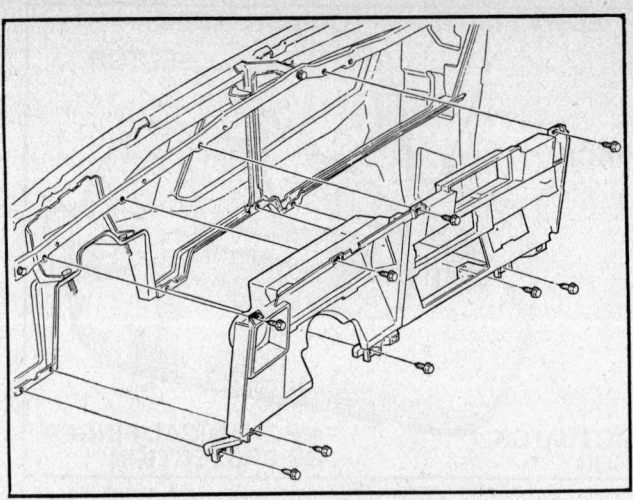

Fig. 15   Instrument cluster. 1977-79 88 & 98

wheel. With tool J-24628-2, remove the module to steering wheel screws, lift module and disconnect horn wire. Then, with tool J-24628-3, disconnect module wire connector from slip ring.

1. Disconnect battery ground cable.
2. For tilt and telescope steering column proceed as follows:
   a. On 1974-79 models, remove pad assembly retaining screws, disconnect connector and remove pad assembly.
   b. Move locking lever counterclockwise until full release is obtained. Scribe a mark on the plate assembly where the two screws attach plate assembly to locking lever (for ease of installation) and remove the two screws.
   c. Unscrew and remove plate assembly.
3. For standard wheel, pull up on horn cap retainer assembly and disconnect horn contacts.
4. For Deluxe wheel, remove three screws from pad assembly and disconnect connectors.
5. On sport wheel, pull up on and remove emblem and horn contact assembly from wheel.

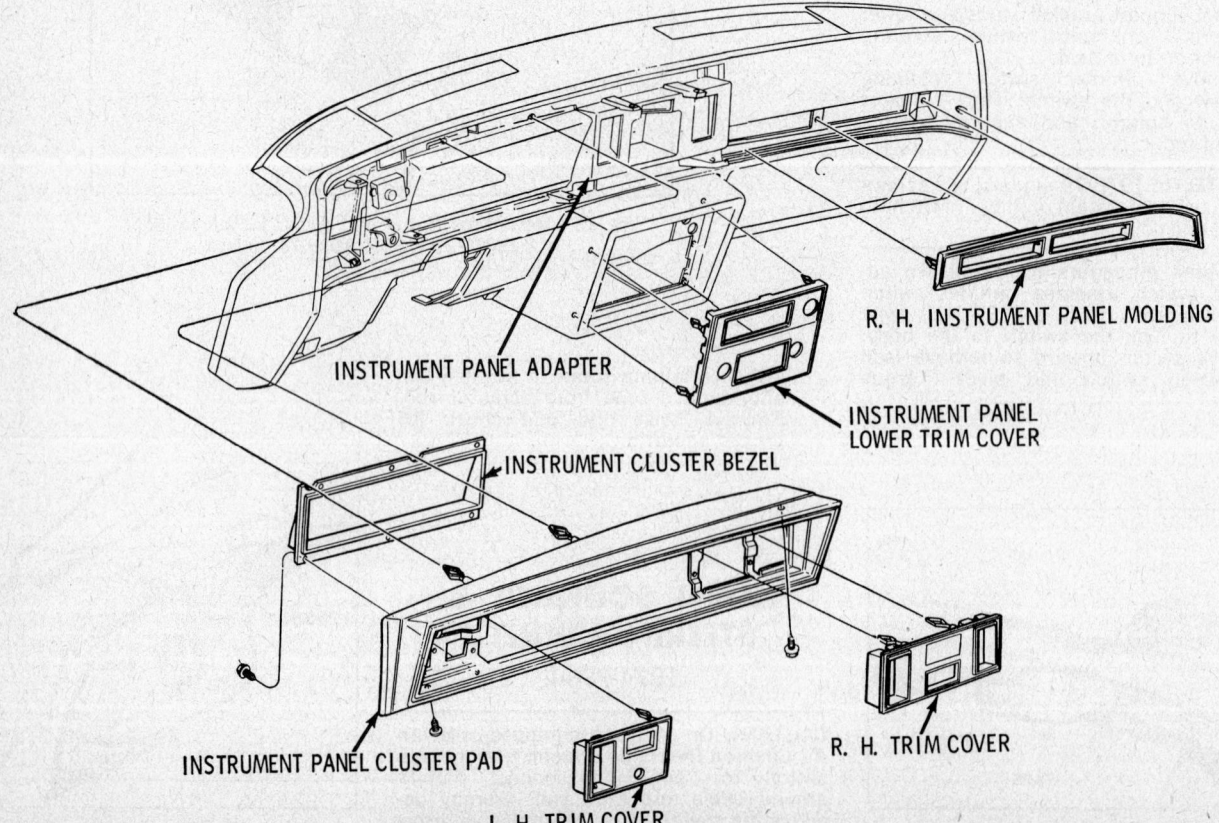

Fig. 14A   Instrument panel cluster pad. 1978-79 Cutlass

6. On Wood Grain wheel, carefully pry horn cap assembly from wheel.
7. On all models, remove steering wheel nut and using a suitable puller, remove steering wheel.

NOTE: Some vehicles have a snap ring on the end of the steering shaft which must be removed before removing steering wheel nut.

8. Reverse procedure to install.

INSTRUMENT CLUSTER

1979 Toronado

1. Disconnect battery ground cable.
2. Remove headlamp switch knob, radio knobs and steering column trim cover.
3. Remove four screws from underside of left hand cover.
4. Remove left hand sound absorber, then pull left hand trim cover from instrument panel.

NOTE: It may be necessary to disconnect shift indicator cable clip and lower steering column slightly to remove left hand trim cover.

5. Remove two screws attaching headlamp switch to cluster carrier, then pull switch from carrier.

6. Remove windshield wiper switch, then remove radio from instrument panel.
7. Remove four screws attaching heater-A/C control to cluster. Pull control out of cluster and disconnect wiring, vacuum lines and temperature control cable, then remove control assembly.
8. Unlock headlamp switch, windshield wiper, cruise control and defogger switch connectors from cluster carrier, then disconnect speedometer cable.
9. Remove nine cluster carrier attaching screws, then remove cluster carrier, Fig. 14.

1978-79 Cutlass

1. Disconnect battery ground cable.
2. Remove right hand and left hand trim panels, Fig. 14A.
3. Remove the 7 screws retaining cluster pad to panel adapter.
4. Pull panel pad to disengage it from retaining clips and remove pad assembly, Fig. 14A.
5. Remove steering column trim cover, then disconnect shift indicator clip from shift bowl.
6. Remove the 4 screws retaining cluster assembly, then disconnect speedometer cable and electrical connectors and remove cluster assembly.
7. Reverse procedure to install.

1977-79 88 & 98

1. Disconnect battery ground cable.
2. Rotate headlight switch so notch on switch faces downward. Bend a 1/8 inch hook on a piece of stiff wire. Use the wire hook in the notch to pull the knob retainer clip and pull knob off shaft.
3. Remove twilight sentinel knob.
4. Position steering column collar upward and remove column lower trim cover.
5. Remove two screws securing trim cover to cluster carrier, Fig. 15.
6. Pull trim cover from clips.
7. Remove radio knobs and cigar lighter.
8. Remove two screws securing to panel, Fig. 15.
9. Pull trim cover from panel clips.
10. Remove radio as outlined under "Radio, Removal."
11. Remove A/C-heater control attaching screws, pull control outward and disconnect control cables and electrical connectors.
12. Remove switches, clock and disconnect ash tray lamp.
13. Remove right hand outside remote mirror control screws.
14. Disconnect shift indicator cable clip.
15. Remove steering column bolts at floor pan and the nuts from the steer-

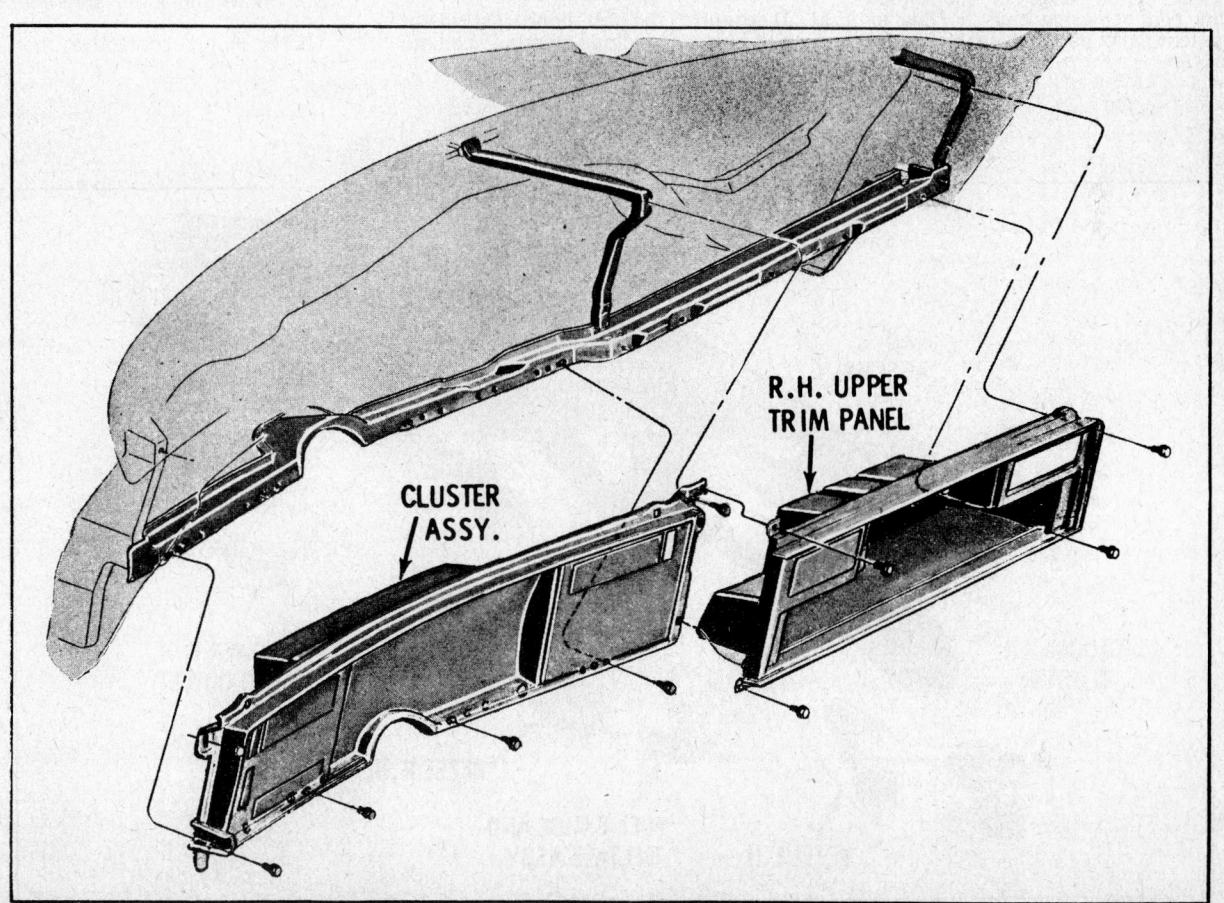

Fig. 16   Instrument cluster. 1974-76 Full Size & 1977-78 Toronado

ing column bracket. Then, lower the steering column and rest steering wheel on seat.

16. Disconnect speedometer cable.
17. Remove instrument panel cluster carrier bolts and the two instrument panel screws, Fig. 15.
18. Remove center air duct screws.
19. Pull cluster outward to disconnect electrical connectors.
20. Remove cluster carrier, Fig. 15.

1974-76 Full Size & 1977-78 Toronado

CAUTION: On vehicles equipped with an Air Cushion Restraint system, turn ignition switch to "Lock," disconnect battery ground cable and tape end, thereby deactivating system.

1. Disconnect battery ground cable.
2. Disconnect electrical connections at flood lamp or map lamp and remove lamp.
3. Carefully pry speakers from clips, disconnect electrical connections and remove speakers.
4. Remove instrument panel pad screws through speaker openings.
5. Remove screws from lower left outside edge of instrument panel pad, instrument cluster above speedometer, lower right hand corner of glove box and glove box top edge.
6. Pull at center edge of instrument panel pad, releasing clips holding instrument panel pad to windshield edge

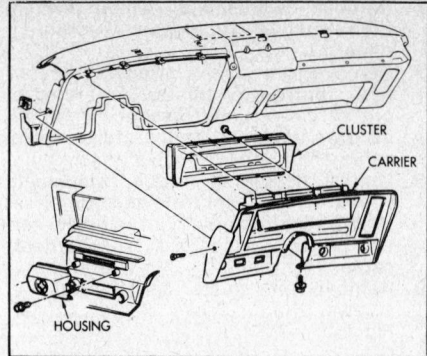

Fig. 17 Instrument cluster (Typical). 1974-79 Omega

and remove instrument panel pad.
7. Disconnect the right hand instrument panel cover from lower trim panel and remove glove box door.

NOTE: Cover is secured by one screw and five studs pushed through clips mounted in lower panel.

8. If equipped with air conditioning, disconnect upper right hand air hose from duct.
9. On all models, disconnect electrical connectors from clock, trunk release and glove box lamp.
10. Remove the upper trim panel.
11. Disconnect the left hand instrument panel cover, slide steering column

cover up the column and pull the left hand instrument panel cover from lower trim panel.

NOTE: Cover is secured by six studs pushed through clips mounted in lower panel.

12. If equipped with air conditioning, disconnect upper left hand air hose from duct.
13. On all models, disconnect temperature and defroster cables from heater case and remove radio to radio support nut.
14. Remove instrument cluster attaching screws, Fig. 16, pull cluster outward and disconnect speedometer cable.
15. Disconnect electrical connectors from instrument cluster and the vacuum harness from air conditioning or heater control.
16. Disconnect radio electrical connectors, pull fiber optic element from washer fluid indicator lens and remove screw from windshield wiper switch ground.
17. Remove three screws securing wiring harness to lower corners of instrument cluster, then disconnect harness from three retaining clips.
18. Remove instrument cluster assembly.

1974-79 Omega

1. Disconnect battery ground cable.
2. Remove shift indicator needle from shift bowl and lower steering column.

NOTE: Apply protective material to

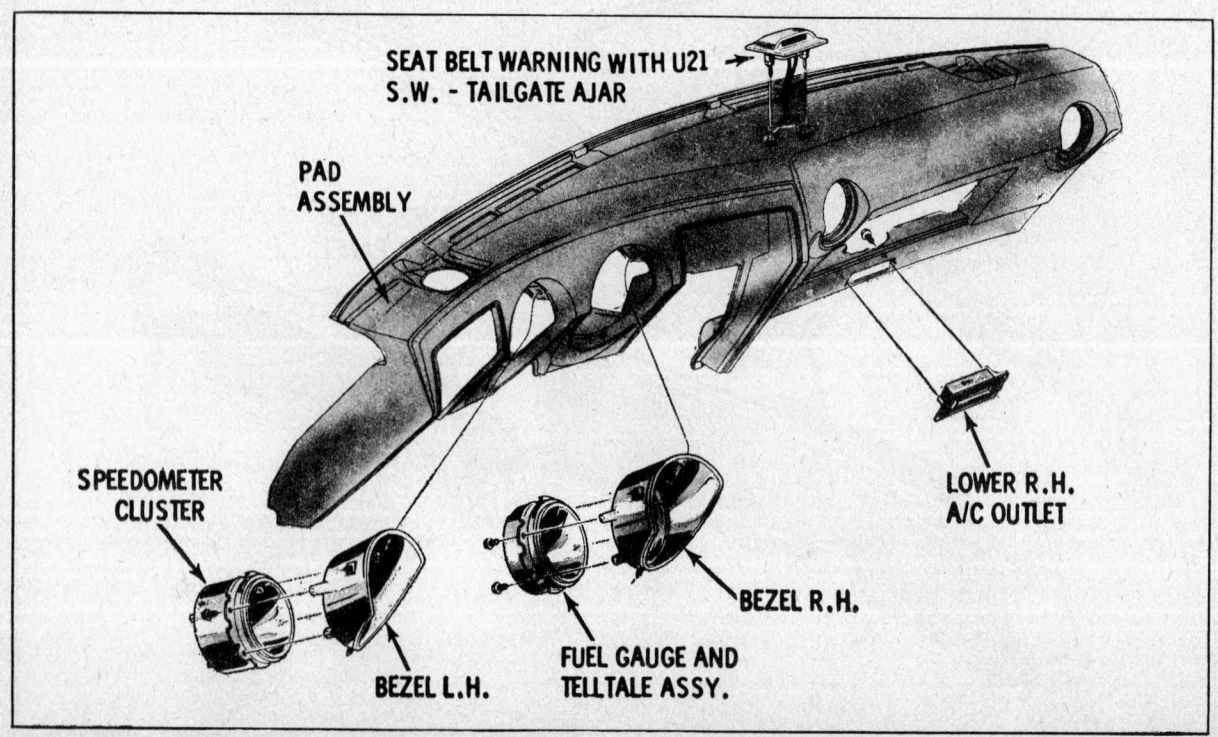

Fig. 18 Instrument cluster. 1974-77 Cutlass

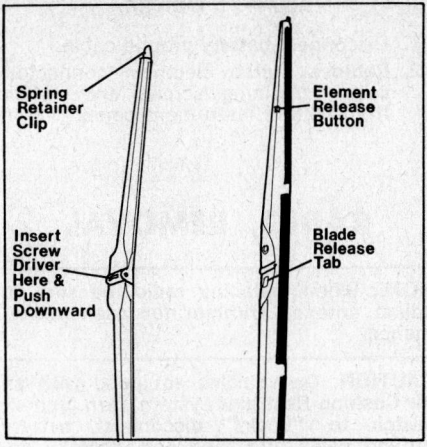

Fig. 19   Wiper blade retainers

blades to wiper arms, Fig. 19. One method uses a press type release tab. When the release tab is depressed the blade assembly can be slid off the wiper arm pin. The other method uses a coil spring retainer. A screwdriver must be inserted on top of the spring and the spring pushed downward. The blade assembly can then be slid off the wiper arm pin. Two methods are also used to retain the blade element in the blade assembly, Fig. 19. One method uses a press type release button. When the button is depressed, the two piece blade assembly can be slid off the blade element. The other method uses a spring type retainer clip in the end of the blade element. When the retainer clip is squeezed together, the blade element can be slid out of the blade assembly.

NOTE: To be sure of correct installation, the element release button, or the spring element retaining clip should be at the end of the wiper blade assembly nearest the wiper transmission.

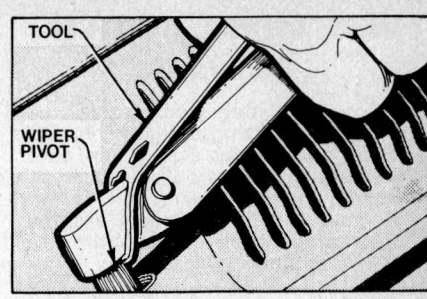

Fig. 20   Wiper arm removal

6. Remove motor while guiding crankarm through opening.

mast jacket to prevent damage to painted surfaces.

3. Remove three screws from front of heater control securing it to cluster.
4. Remove radio knobs, washers, bezel nuts and front support at lower edge of instrument cluster. This allows radio to remain in the panel.
5. Remove screws at top, bottom and side of cluster securing it to instrument panel, Fig. 17.
6. Tilt cluster forward and reach behind to disconnect speedo cable, speedminder and electrical connectors and lift cluster out of carrier after removing screws.

1974-77 Cutlass

Speedometer Cluster

1. Disconnect battery ground cable.
2. With automatic transmission column shift, remove lower trim cover (below steering column) then disconnect shift indicator clip on shift bowl.
3. On all models, lower steering column.
4. Disconnect speedo cable from speedometer.
5. Remove three cluster attaching screws and pull cluster out carefully so shift indicator needle is not damaged. Disconnect wiring connector and remove cluster.

Fuel Gauge & Telltale Assembly

1. Perform steps 1 through 3 as outlined under "Speedometer Cluster" procedure.
2. Remove three assembly attaching screws and pull assembly out of pad, Fig. 18.
3. Disconnect wiring connectors and remove assembly.

W/S WIPER BLADES

Two methods are used to retain wiper

W/S WIPER ARMS

Models w/Rectangular Motor

1. Wiper motor must be in park position.
2. Use suitable tool to minimize the possibility of windshield or paint finish damage during arm removal.
3. Remove arm by prying up with tool to disengage arm from serrated transmission shaft, Fig. 20.
4. To install arm to transmission rotate the required distance and direction so that blades rest in proper position.

Models w/Round Motor

1. Wiper motor must be in park position.
2. Raise hood to gain access to wiper arm.
3. On 1974-77 Intermediate Models: Lift arm off transmission shaft. On left arm, slide articulating arm lock clip, Fig. 21 away from transmission pivot pin and lift arm off pin. On 1978-79 intermediates, lift wiper arm and slide latch clip out from under wiper arm, Fig. 23. On Full Size Models: Lift arm and slide latch clip, Figs. 22 and 23 out from under wiper arm.
4. Release wiper arm and lift arm assembly off transmission shaft.

W/S WIPER MOTOR, REPLACE

1974-79

1. Raise hood and remove cowl screen or grille.
2. Reach through cowl opening and loosen transmission drive link attaching nuts to motor crankarm.
3. Disconnect wiring and washer hoses.
4. Disconnect transmission drive link from motor arm.
5. Remove motor attaching screws.

W/S WIPER TRANSMISSION, REPLACE

1974-79

Rectangular Motor

1. Remove wiper arms and blades.
2. Raise hood and remove cowl vent screen or grille.
3. Disconnect wiring from motor.
4. Loosen, do not remove, transmission drive link to motor crankarm attaching nuts and disconnect drive link from crankarm.
5. Remove right and left transmission to body attaching screws and guide transmission and linkage out through cowl opening.

Round Motor

1. Raise hood and remove cowl vent screen.
2. On 1974-76 Intermediate models and 1977-79 except Toronado, remove right and left wiper arm and blade assemblies. On 1974-76 Full Size models and 1977-79 Toronado, remove arm and blade only from transmission to be removed.
3. Loosen, do not remove, attaching nuts securing transmission drive link to motor crankarm.

NOTE: On 1974-76 models and 1977-79 Toronado, if only the left transmission is to be removed, it will not be necessary to loosen attaching nuts securing the right transmission drive link to the motor.

4. Disconnect drive link from motor crankarm.
5. On 1974-76 Intermediate models and 1977-79 except Toronado, remove right and left transmission to body attaching screws. On 1974-76 Full Size models and 1977-79 Toronado, remove the attaching screws securing only the transmission to be removed.
6. Remove transmission and linkage by guiding it through opening.

W/S WIPER SWITCH

1979 Toronado

1. Disconnect battery ground cable.
2. Remove headlamp switch knob, radio knobs and steering column trim cover.
3. Remove four screws from under side of left hand trim cover.
4. Remove left hand sound absorber, then carefully pull left hand trim cover from instrument panel.

NOTE: It may be necessary to disconnect shift indicator cable clip and lower steering column slightly to remove left hand trim cover.

5. Remove two screws attaching switch to cluster, then pull switch rearward to remove, Fig. 24.

1978-79 Cutlass

1. Disconnect battery ground cable.
2. Remove cluster pad assembly.
3. Remove switch retaining screws, then pull switch out to remove, Fig. 24A.
4. Reverse procedure to install.

1977-79 88 & 98

1. Disconnect battery ground cable.
2. Rotate headlight switch knob so that notch on back of switch knob is down. Bend a 1/8 in. hook on paper clip wire and use in notch to pull knob retainer clip while pulling knob off shaft.
3. Remove twilight sentinel knob, if equipped.
4. Move steering column collar up and snap out lower trim cover.
5. Remove two trim cover attaching screws, then pull trim cover out of clips.
6. Remove switch mounting plate screws, then pull switch through opening, disconnect wire connector and remove switch.

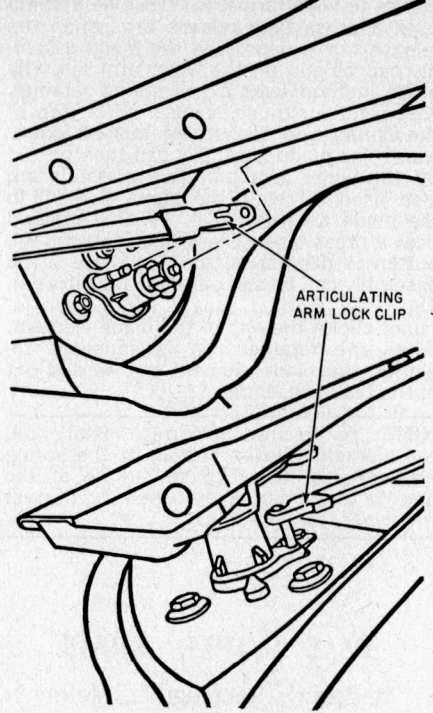

ARTICULATING ARM LOCK CLIP

Fig. 21   Wiper articulating lock clip 1974-77 Intermediates

1974-76 Full Size & 1977-78 Toronado

CAUTION: On vehicles equipped with an Air Cushion Restraint system, turn ignition switch to "Lock," disconnect battery ground cable and tape end, thereby deactivating system.

1. Disconnect battery ground cable.
2. Remove air conditioning or heater control without disconnecting vacuum harness or electrical connectors.
3. Remove headlamp switch escutcheon and pull headlamp switch through air conditioning or heater control opening without removing electrical connector.
4. Remove windshield wiper switch knob and two switch attaching nuts through air conditioning or heater control opening, then pull switch through opening, disconnect electrical connector and remove switch.

1974-77 Cutlass

1. Disconnect battery ground cable.
2. Remove steering column trim cover screws and if equipped with air conditioning, disconnect outlet hose.
3. Disconnect parking brake cable.
4. Remove left hand control panel screws, pull control panel from instrument panel and disconnect wiring.
5. Remove electrical connector from wiper switch, wiper switch knob, switch retaining screws and switch.

1974-79 Omega

1. Disconnect battery ground cable.
2. Remove switch electrical connector, switch retaining screws and switch from behind instrument panel.

RADIO, REMOVAL

NOTE: When installing radio, be sure to adjust antenna trimmer for peak performance.

CAUTION: On vehicles equipped with an Air Cushion Restraint system, turn ignition switch to "Lock," disconnect battery ground cable and tape end, thereby deactivating system.

1979 Toronado

1. Disconnect battery ground cable.
2. Remove headlamp switch knob, radio knobs and steering column trim cover.
3. Remove four screws from underside of left hand trim cover.
4. Remove left hand sound absorber, then pull left hand trim cover from instrument panel.

NOTE: It may be necessary to disconnect shift indicator cable clip and lower steering column slightly to remove left hand trim cover.

5. Remove right hand sound absorber.
6. Remove switch attaching instrument panel wiring harness to radio bracket and screw attaching radio to tie bar. Move tone generator aside, if equipped.

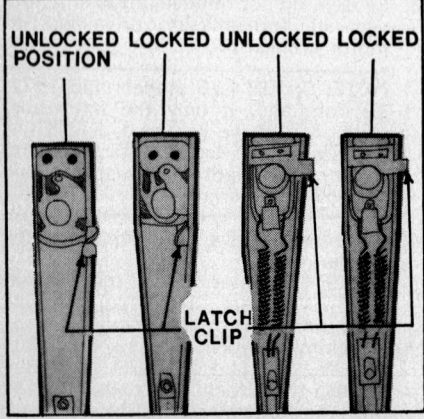

UNLOCKED LOCKED UNLOCKED LOCKED POSITION

LATCH CLIP

Fig. 22   Wiper arms. Except 1977-79 88 & 98 & 1978-79 Intermediates

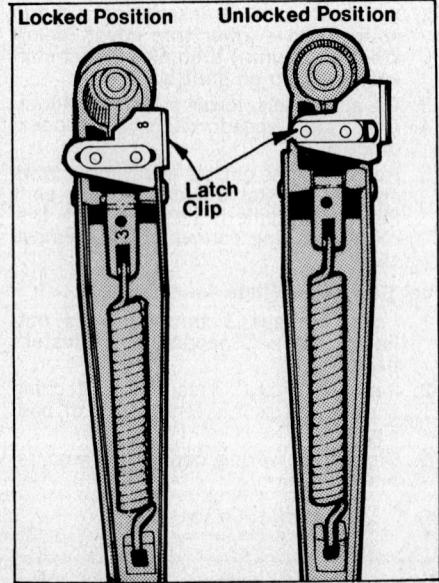

Locked Position   Unlocked Position

Latch Clip

Fig. 23   Wiper arms. 1977-79 88 & 98 & 1978-79 Intermediates

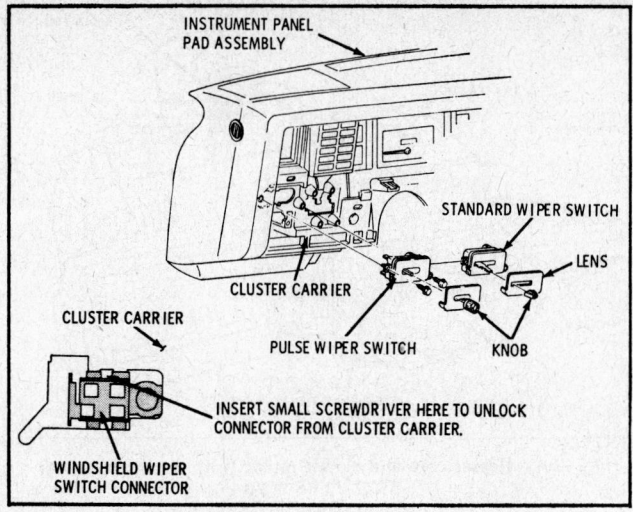

Fig. 24   Windshield wiper switch. 1979 Toronado

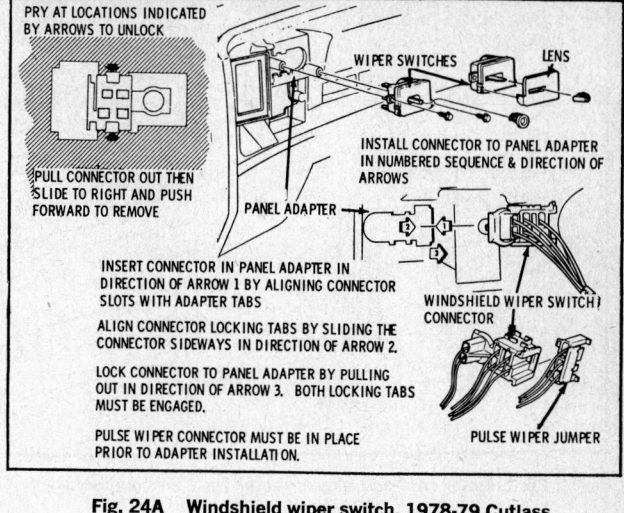

Fig. 24A   Windshield wiper switch. 1978-79 Cutlass

7. Remove four screws attaching radio mounting plate to cluster carrier.
8. Disconnect antenna lead and radio wiring.
9. Pull radio and mounting plate rearward to remove.

1978-79 Cutlass

1. Disconnect battery ground cable.
2. Remove instrument panel lower trim cover.
3. Remove the 4 radio mounting plate screws, and the screw from radio support bracket on lower instrument panel tie bar.
5. Pull radio outward, then disconnect antenna and electrical connectors and remove radio.
6. Reverse procedure to install.

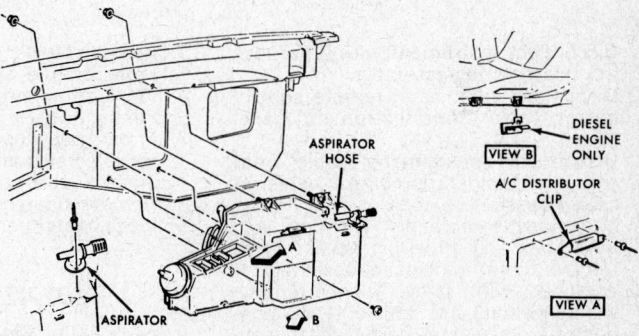

Fig. 25   Heater core. 1979 Toronado

1977-79 88 & 98

1. Disconnect battery ground cable.
2. Remove radio knobs, cigar lighter and right hand trim panel cover.
3. Remove radio bracket to lower tie bar screw and the four mounting plate screws.
4. Pull radio out, then disconnect the electrical connectors and antenna lead, and remove radio.
5. Reverse procedure to install.

1974-76 Full Size & 1977-78 Toronado

1. Disconnect battery ground cable.
2. Disconnect all wiring from radio.
3. Disconnect throttle cable, then remove throttle lever and reinforcement.
4. Remove radio support bracket to tie-bar screw.
5. Remove radio knobs and two nuts securing radio to instrument cluster.
6. Lower radio and remove from behind instrument panel.

1974-79 Omega

1. Disconnect battery cable.
2. Remove ash tray and housing as necessary.
3. Remove knobs, controls, washers, trim plate and nuts from radio.
4. Remove hoses from center A/C distribution duct as necessary.
5. Disconnect all leads to radio.
6. Remove screws or nuts from radio rear mounting bracket and remove radio.

1974-77 Cutlass

1. Disconnect battery ground cable.
2. Remove four screws from steering column trim cover and remove cover.
3. Remove knobs from radio by pulling outward on knobs.
4. Remove nuts from front of radio.
5. Remove four screws holding R.H. Control Panel to dash and gently pull panel outward and up.
6. Remove screw from radio support bracket.

7. Remove four screws holding ash tray housing to tie bar and remove housing assembly.
8. Disconnect all leads and remove radio.

HEATER CORE, REMOVAL

1979 Toronado

1. Disconnect battery ground cable, then drain cooling system.
2. Disconnect heater hoses at heater core, then install plugs in core outlets to prevent spillage.
3. Remove instrument panel sound absorbers, then lower steering column.
4. Remove instrument cluster as described under Instrument Cluster, Replace.
5. Remove radio front speakers.
6. Remove three screws attaching manifold to heater case.
7. Remove four upper and three lower instrument panel attaching screws.
8. Disconnect parking brake release cable.

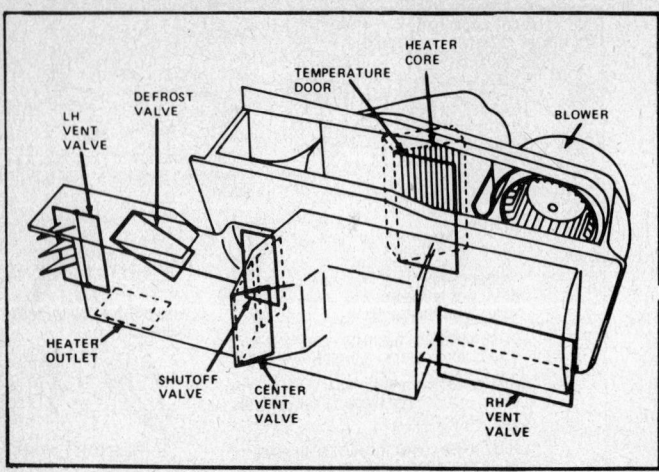

Fig. 26 Heater core and blower motor (less air conditioning). 1977-79 88 & 98

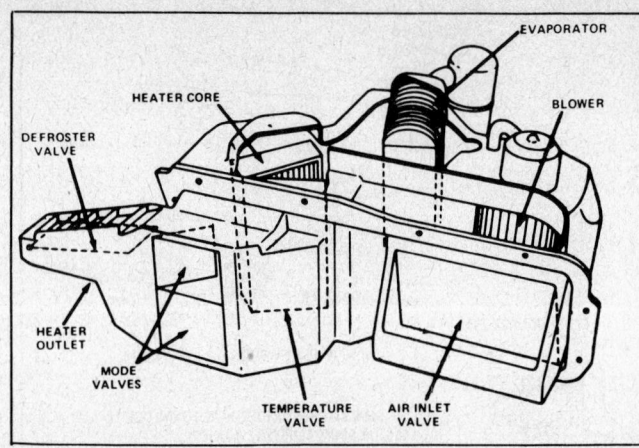

Fig. 26A Heater core and blower motor (with air conditioning). 1977-79 88 & 98

9. Disconnect instrument wiring harness from dash wiring assembly.
10. Disconnect right hand remote control mirror cable from instrument panel pad.
11. Disconnect speedometer cable from clip and temperate control cable at heater case.
12. Disconnect radio and A/C wiring, vacuum lines and all wiring necessary to remove instrument panel assembly. If equipped with pulse wiper, remove wiper switch and unlock wire connector from cluster carrier, then separate pulse wiper jumper harness from wiper switch wire connector.
13. Remove instrument panel and wiring harness assembly.
14. Remove defroster ducts, then disconnect vacuum lines from actuators.

15. Remove blower motor resistor.
16. From engine side of dash panel, remove three heater and A/C case retaining nuts.
17. From passenger compartment, remove screws and clip retaining heater and A/C case to dash panel.
18. Remove heater and A/C case, then remove heater core from case, Fig. 25.

1977-79 88 & 98

1. Disconnect battery ground cable.
2. Remove right half of hood seal from air inlet screen.
3. Remove air inlet screen.
4. Remove screws securing top of module, then disconnect electrical connectors from electrical components

on top of module.
5. Remove thermostatic switch mounting screws from top of module.
6. Remove A/C diagnostic connector mounting screws and position aside.
7. Remove top of module.
8. Disconnect and remove heater core from module, Figs. 26 and 26A.
9. Reverse procedure to install.

1974-76 Full Size & 1977-78 Toronado

CAUTION: On vehicles equipped with an Air Cushion Restraint system, turn ignition switch to "lock," disconnect battery ground cable and tape end, thereby deactivating system.

1. Disconnect battery ground cable and drain radiator.
2. Disconnect heater hoses and plug hoses and core openings to prevent coolant loss.
3. Remove heater case to dash panel attaching nuts, Fig. 27.
4. Remove instrument panel trim cover and the heater case to cowl bolts.
5. Remove lower air duct.
6. Remove instrument panel pad, then

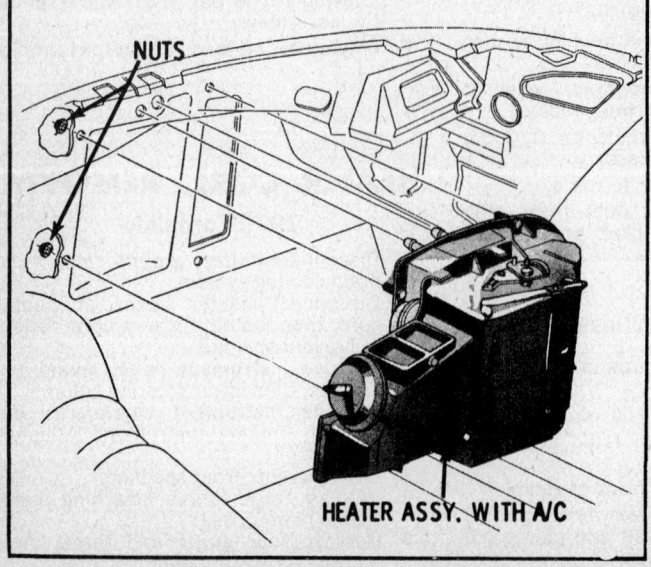

Fig. 27 Heater core. 1974-76 Full Size, 1977-78 Toronado & 1974-77 Cutlass (Typical)

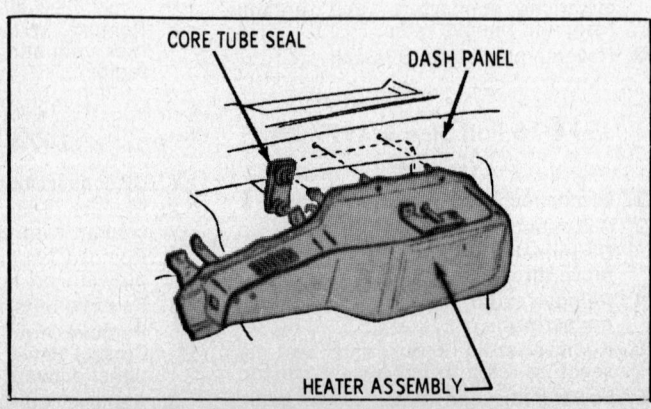

Fig. 28 Heater core. 1974-79 Omega (Typical)

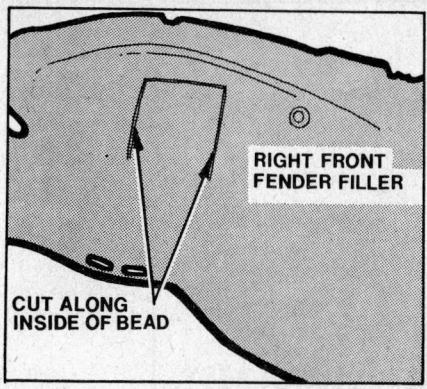

Fig. 29 Blower motor access hole location. 1975-76 Full size & 1977-78 Toronado

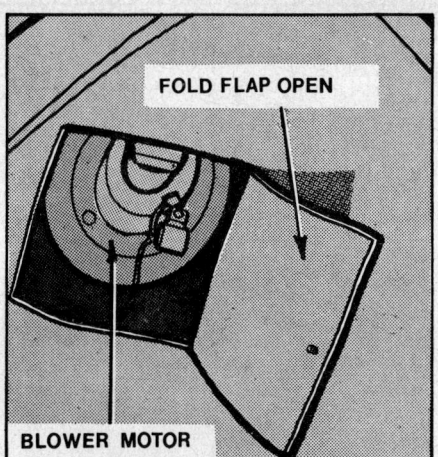

Fig. 30 Removing blower motor. 1975-76 Full size & 1977-78 Toronado

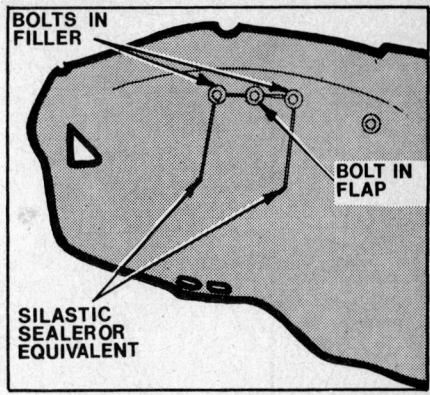

Fig. 31 Sealing blower motor access hole. 1975-76 Full size & 1977-78 Toronado

electrical connectors from glovebox light and clock.
7. Remove right hand upper trim panel and on models equipped with A/C, remove manifold from heater case.
8. On all models, remove defroster duct from heater case and disconnect lower dash trim panel.
9. Disconnect temperature and defroster cables, then the vacuum hose from heater case. Remove heater case from dash, then core from case.

Intermediate Models
Less Air Conditioning
1978-79 Cutlass
1. Disconnect battery ground cable and drain cooling system.
2. Disconnect heater hoses.
3. Disconnect electrical connectors from heater module.
4. Remove module front cover screws.
5. Remove heater core from module.
6. Reverse procedure to install.

1974-77 Cutlass
1. Disconnect battery ground cable and drain radiator.
2. Disconnect heater hoses and plug hoses and core openings to prevent coolant loss.
3. Remove heater case attaching nuts and screws, disconnect control cables and remove case from dash, then core from case, Fig. 27.

1974-79 Omega
1. Disconnect battery ground cable and drain radiator.
2. Disconnect heater hoses and plug hoses and core openings to prevent coolant loss.
3. Remove heater case retaining nuts from engine side of dash, Fig. 28.
4. Remove glove box and door, then pull heater case from dash.
5. Disconnect blower resistor electrical connector and control cables from

case, then remove heater case from dash and core from case.

With Air Conditioning
1978-79 Cutlass
1. Disconnect battery ground cable and drain cooling system.
2. Disconnect heater hoses from core.
3. Remove retention bracket and ground strap.
4. Remove module rubber seal and screen.
5. Remove right hand W/S wiper arm.
6. Remove attaching screws from the diagnostic connector, hi-blower relay and thermostatic switch.
7. Disconnect all electrical connectors from top of module.
8. Remove top cover from module.
9. Remove heater core from module.
10. Reverse procedure to install.

1974-77 Cutlass
1. Disconnect battery ground cable and drain radiator.
2. Remove glove box and the center A/C manifold.
3. Disconnect vacuum hoses and temperature cable from heater case.
4. Disconnect heater hoses and plug hoses and core openings to prevent coolant loss.
5. Remove heater case to dash panel attaching bolts, then heater case from dash and core from case, Fig. 27.

1974-79 Omega
1. Disconnect battery and drain coolant.
2. Disconnect upper heater hose from core.
3. Remove right front fender skirt bolts and lower skirt to gain access to lower heater hose clamp. Disconnect lower hose and remove lower right hand heater core and case attaching nut.
4. Remove glove box and door.

5. Remove recirculation vacuum diaphragm at right kick panel.
6. Remove heater outlet (at bottom of heater case).
7. Remove cold air distributor duct from heater case.
8. Remove heater case extension screws and separate extension from case.
9. Disconnect cables and wiring and remove case and core assembly, Fig. 28.
10. Separate core from case.

BLOWER MOTOR REMOVE

1979 Toronado
1. Disconnect battery ground cable.
2. Remove right hand side fender skirt.
3. Disconnect wire connector and cooling hose from blower motor.
4. Remove five blower motor mounting screws, then remove blower motor.

1977-79 88 & 98
1. Disconnect battery ground cable.
2. Disconnect blower motor ground and feed wires.
3. Remove six blower motor attaching screws and blower motor, Figs. 26 and 26A.

1975-76 Full Size & 1977-78 Toronado
1. Disconnect battery ground cable.
2. Raise vehicle and remove right front wheel.
3. Referring to Fig. 29, cut along inside of bead.
4. Fold flap over to expose blower motor, Fig. 30.
5. Remove blower motor attaching screws and the blower motor through

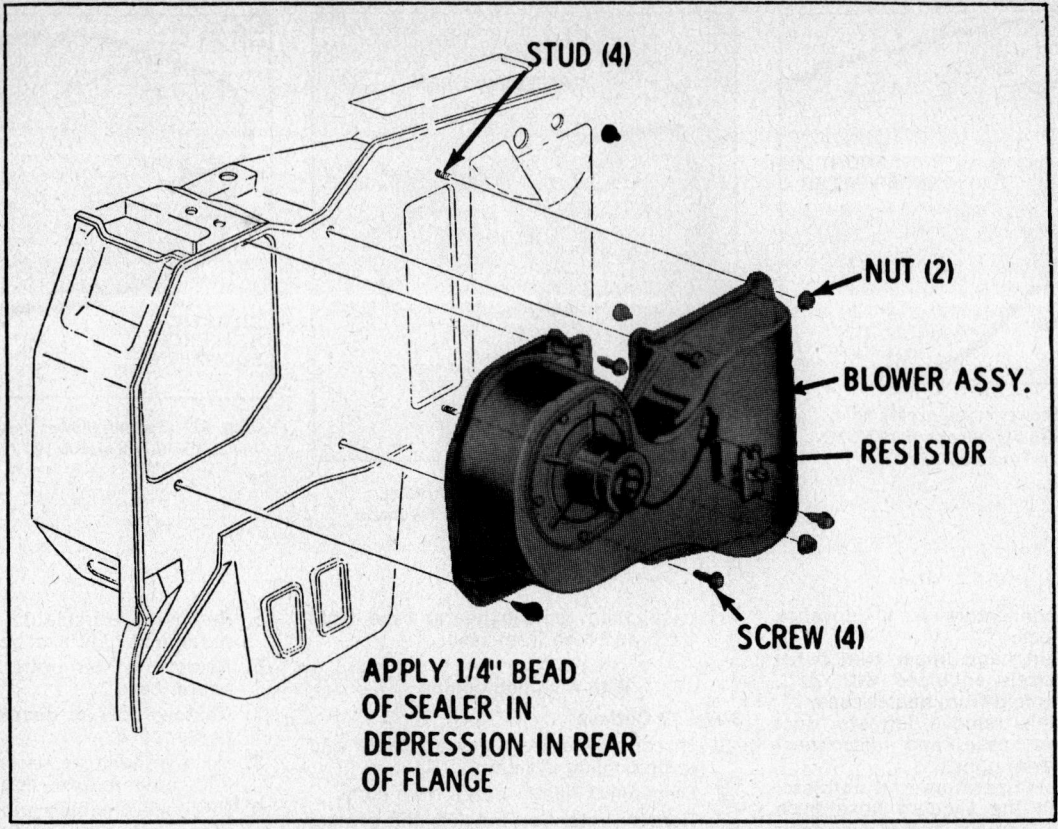

STUD (4)

NUT (2)

BLOWER ASSY.

RESISTOR

SCREW (4)

APPLY 1/4" BEAD
OF SEALER IN
DEPRESSION IN REAR
OF FLANGE

Fig. 32   Blower motor. 1974-76 Full Size, 1974-77 Cutlass & 1977-78 Toronado

opening.

NOTE: After blower motor installation, the access hole must be sealed as follows:

a. Drill a hole in flap and install a 5/16 inch self tapping bolt with a large flat washer, Fig. 31.
b. Close flap and drill two holes in inner filler panel and install two 5/16 inch self tapping bolts with large flat washers, Fig. 31.
c. With a suitable sealer, seal edge of flap. Do not use weatherstrip adhesive.

1974 Full Size Models

CAUTION: On vehicles equipped with an Air Cushion Restraint system, turn ignition switch to "Lock," disconnect battery ground cable and tape end, thereby deactivating system.

1. Disconnect battery.
2. Remove the right front wheel.
3. Remove canister or battery.
4. Remove the three filler plates to radiator support screws.
5. Remove the filler plate to wheelhouse attaching screws. Remove filler plate.
6. Remove the blower motor attaching screws and connector, Fig. 32.
7. Remove the blower motor.

1974-79 Intermediate Models

1978-79 Cutlass

1. Disconnect battery ground cable.
2. If equipped with air conditioning, disconnect cooling tube from blower motor.
3. On all models, disconnect electrical connector from blower motor.
4. Remove blower motor retaining screws and the blower motor.
5. Reverse procedure to install.

Less Air Conditioning

1974-77 Cutlass

1. Remove the right front fender filler panel.
2. Disconnect the blower motor wiring.
3. Remove the five nuts and two screws securing the inlet assembly to dash.
4. Disengage the inlet assembly from the studs and remove from the car. The blower motor can be removed from the inlet assembly by removing the attaching screws, Fig. 32. The fan is held to the motor shaft by a nut and lock-washer.

1974-79 Omega

1. Disconnect battery and detach hoses from clips on right fender skirt.
2. Raise vehicle on hoist.
3. Remove fender skirt attaching bolts except those retaining the skirt to radiator support.
4. Pull out then down on skirt and place block of wood between skirt and fender to allow clearance for blower motor removal.
5. Disconnect blower motor cooling tube and electrical connections at blower motor.
6. Remove blower motor attaching screws and remove blower motor, Fig. 33. Gently pry motor flange if sealer acts as an adhesive.

With Air Conditioning

1974-77 Cutlass

1. Disconnect battery ground cable and blower motor feed wire.
2. Remove screws securing blower motor to dash, then the blower motor, Fig. 32.
3. Reverse procedure to install.

1974-79 Omega

1. Disconnect the battery cable.
2. Remove the fender filler plate attaching bolts and position it forward and inboard.
3. Disconnect the blower feed wire.
4. Remove the blower motor attaching screws and blower motor.

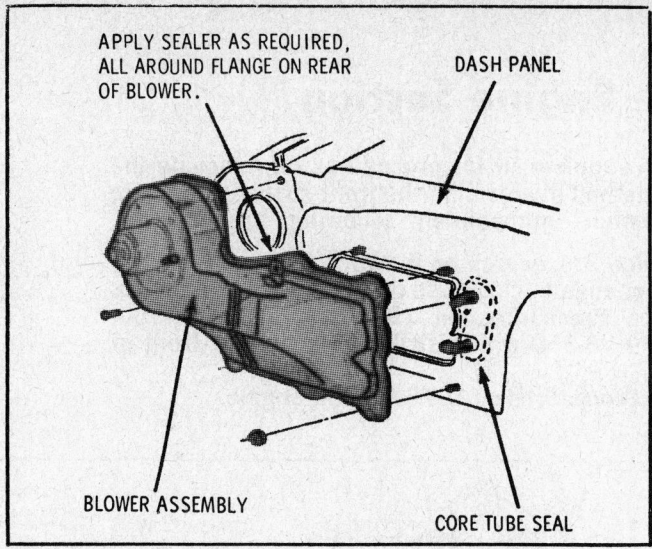

Fig. 33 Blower motor. 1974-79 Omega (Typical)

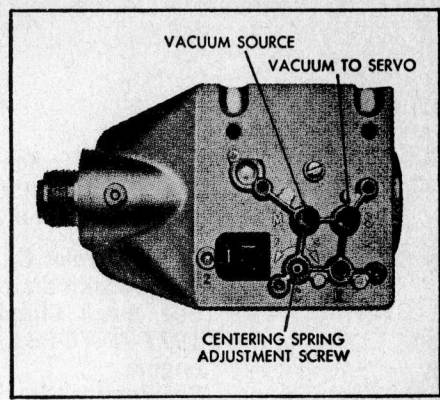

Fig. 34 Centering spring adjustment
Except Omega, 1977-79 88 & 98 &
1978-79 Cutlass

CRUISE CONTROLS

System Release Switches, Adjust

Insert switches into tubular clip until the switch seats on clip. Then, pull brake pedal rearward against stop. The switches will be moved in the clip, thereby providing the proper adjustment.

Servo Linkage, Adjust

Units With Servo Rod

With curb idle speed properly adjusted and the carburetor in curb idle position with the engine off, install servo rod retained in hole that provides clearance between retainer and servo bushing. Some clearance is required, however, not to exceed the width of one hole.

1974

With curb idle properly adjusted and the carburetor in curb idle position with the engine static, adjust servo rod to provide minimum slack.

Units With Beed Chain

Adjust chain to be taut with the carburetor in curb idle position and the engine static.

Units With Cable

With throttle closed, ignition and fast idle cam off, adjust cable jam nuts until free play is removed from cable sleeve at carburetor without holding throttle open. Torque jam nuts to 50 in. lbs. Ensure servo boot is over cable washer.

Centering Spring, Adjust

Except Omega, 1977-79 88 & 98 & 1978-79 Cutlass

1. If speed control system holds speed three or more mph higher than selected speed, turn centering spring adjusting screw (C) toward (S) $1/32''$ or less, Fig. 34.
2. If speed control system holds speed three or more mph below selected speed, turn centering spring adjusting screw (C) toward (F) $1/32''$ or less. *Do not move adjustment screw (R).*

Engagement-Cruising Speed Zeroing

1975-78 Omega, 1977-78 88 & 98 & 1978-79 Cutlass

If the cruising speed is lower than the engagement speed, loosen the orifice tube locknut and turn the tube outward; if higher turn the tube inward. Each $1/4$ turn will alter the engagement-cruising speed difference one mph. Tighten locknut after adjustment and check the system operation.

Gasoline Engine Section

IMPORTANT: See the Toronado supplement for procedures on removing the engine and transmission, and method of servicing the front suspension, drive axles and final drive (differential) immediately following this chapter.

See Chevrolet Chapter for Service Procedures on 6-250, V8-305 & 1977-79 V8-350 with distributor at rear of engine, clockwise distributor rotor rotation.
See Buick Chapter for Service Procedures on 1975-76 Omega V8-350, 1977-79 V6-231 Engine & 1979 V8-350 with distributor located at front of engine.
See Pontiac Chapter for Service Procedures on 1975 V8-400 Engine.

ENGINE MOUNTS

1974-76 Six

1. Remove engine mount nut and through bolt.
2. Raise engine and remove mount from frame.

   Install new mount on frame, lower engine and install through bolt.

1974-79 V8

Removal or replacement of a motor mount can be accomplished by supporting the weight of the engine at the area of the mount to be replaced, Figs. 1 thru 1C.

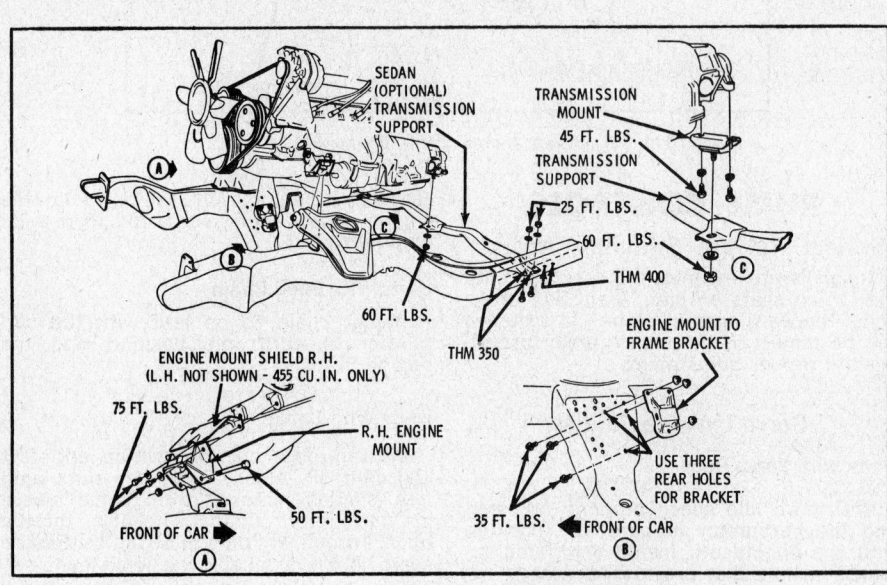

Fig. 1   Engine mounts. 1974-79 Cutlass (Typical)

ENGINE, REPLACE

1974-78 V8s

1. Mark hood hinge before removing to aid in proper alignment upon reassembly.
2. Drain radiator and disconnect battery.
3. Disconnect radiator hoses, heater hoses, vacuum hoses, power steering pump hoses (if necessary), starter cable at junction block, engine-to-body ground strap, fuel hose from fuel line, wiring and accelerator linkage.
4. Remove fan blade and pulley, coil and upper radiator support.
5. Raise car.
6. Disconnect exhaust pipes at manifolds.
7. Remove torque converter cover and the three bolts securing converter to flywheel.
8. Remove engine mount bolts, then three transmission to engine bolts on right side.
9. Remove starter with wiring attached and position aside.
10. Lower vehicle and support engine with suitable lifting equipment.

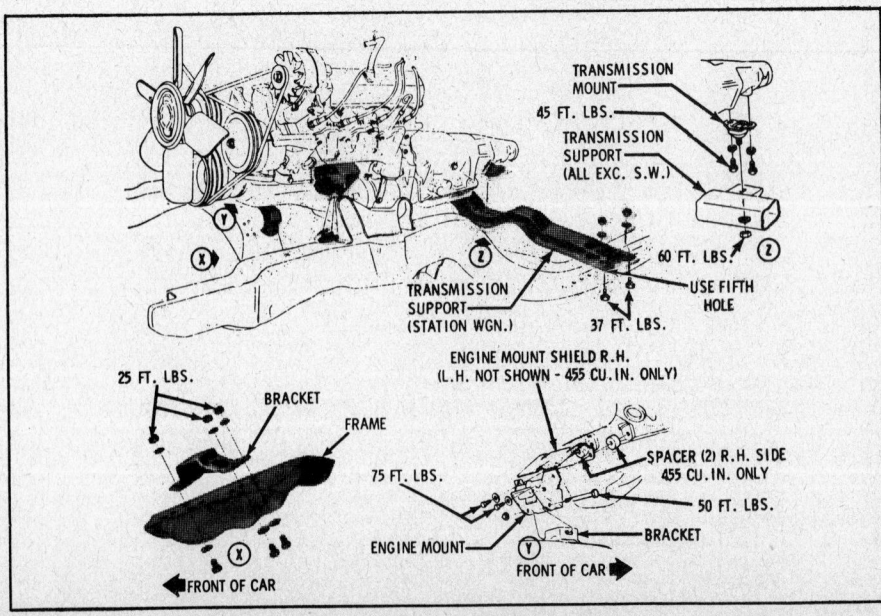

Fig. 1A   Engine mounts. 1974-79 88 & 98 (Typical)

11. Support transmission with a suitable jack and remove three left hand transmission to engine bolts.
12. Remove engine from vehicle.

NOTE

On V8 engines, whenever installation of a front engine mounting becomes necessary, the cap screws fastening the mounting to the frame or bracket should first be screwed finger tight, then tightened alternately, one at a time. *Do not tighten one cap screw in position independently of the other.* This is extremely important since the lower portion of the assembly would not seat evenly in the upper portion. The front mounting must be properly positioned and tightened, otherwise the mounting will not properly function as an insulator.

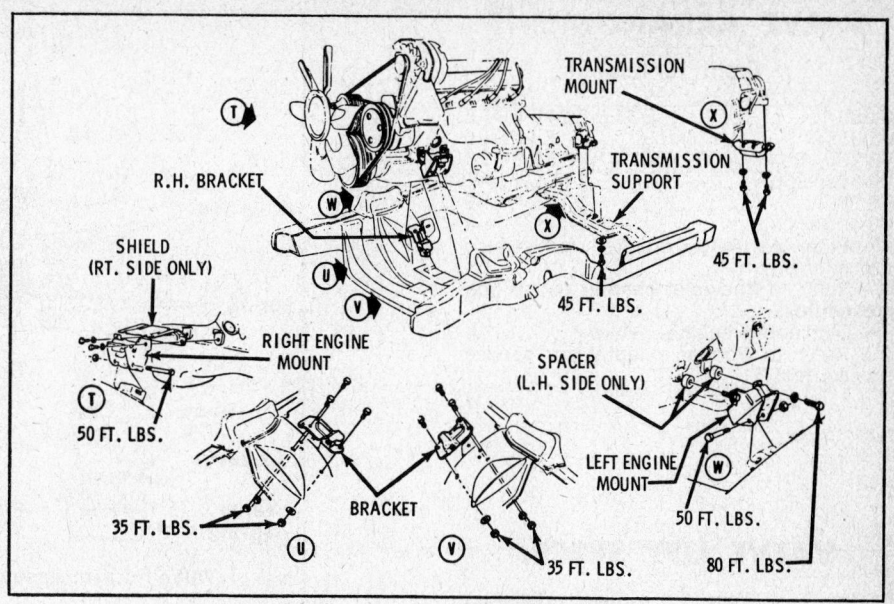

Fig. 1B   Engine Mounts. 1974-75 Omega & F85 (Typical)

CYLINDER HEAD, REPLACE

Some cylinder head gaskets are coated with a special lacquer to provide a good seal once the parts have warmed up. Do not use any additional sealer on such gaskets. If the gasket does not have this lacquer coating, apply suitable sealer to both sides.

Tighten cylinder head bolts a little at a time in three steps in the sequence shown in the illustrations. Final tightening should be to the torque specifications listed in the *Engine Tightening* table.

V8-260, 350, 403, 455

1. Disconnect battery ground cable.
2. Drain radiator and cylinder block.
3. Remove intake and exhaust manifolds.
4. On 1974-76 models, remove ground strap from right cylinder head. On 1977-79 models, remove ground strap from left cylinder head.
5. Remove rocker arm bolts, pivots, rocker arms and push rods. Keep rocker arms, pivots and push rods in order so they can be installed in the same position.
6. Remove cylinder head attaching bolts and remove cylinder head.
7. Reverse procedure to install. Torque cylinder head bolts in sequence shown in Fig. 2 and torque intake manifold bolts in sequence shown in Fig. 2A.

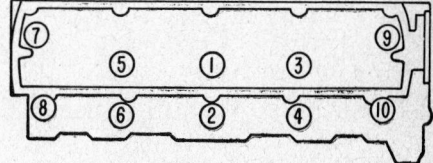

Fig. 2   Cylinder head tightening sequence. V8-260, 350, 403, 455

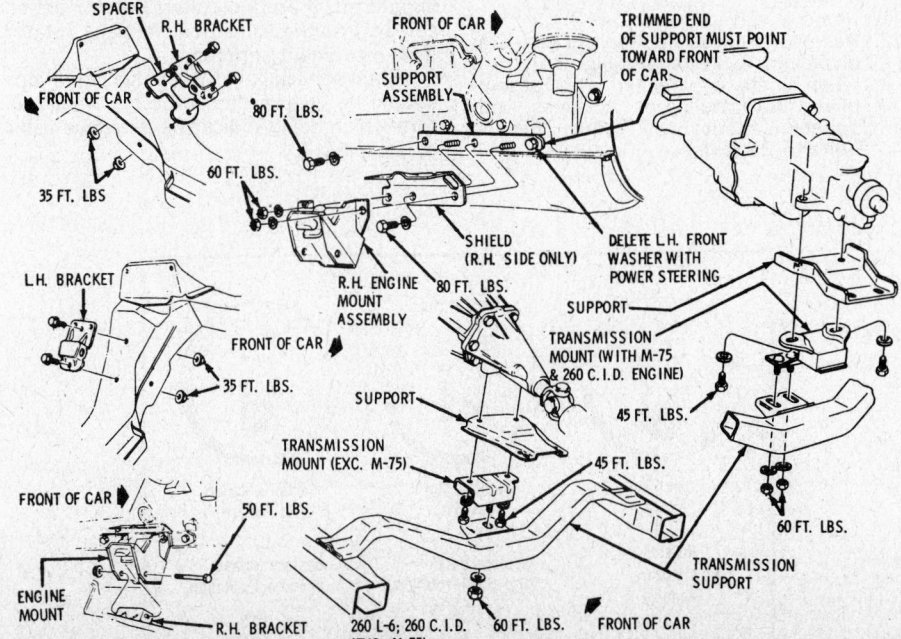

Fig. 1C   Engine mounts. 1976-77 Omega (Typical)

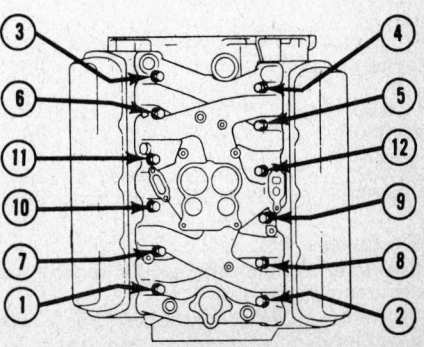

Fig. 2A   Intake manifold tightening sequence. V8-260, 350, 403, 455

VALVE ARRANGEMENT

Front to Rear

6-250	E-I-I-E-E-I-I-E-E-I-I-E
V6-231①	E-I-I-E-I-E
V8-260, 350③, 403, 455	I-E-I-E-E-I-E-I
V8-305, 350②	E-I-I-E-E-I-I-E
V8-350①	E-I-I-E-E-I-I-E
V8-400④	E-I-I-E-E-I-I-E

①—Refer to Buick chapter for service procedures.
②—Refer to Chevrolet chapter for service procedures.
③—Oldsmobile engine.
④—Refer to Pontiac chapter for service procedures.

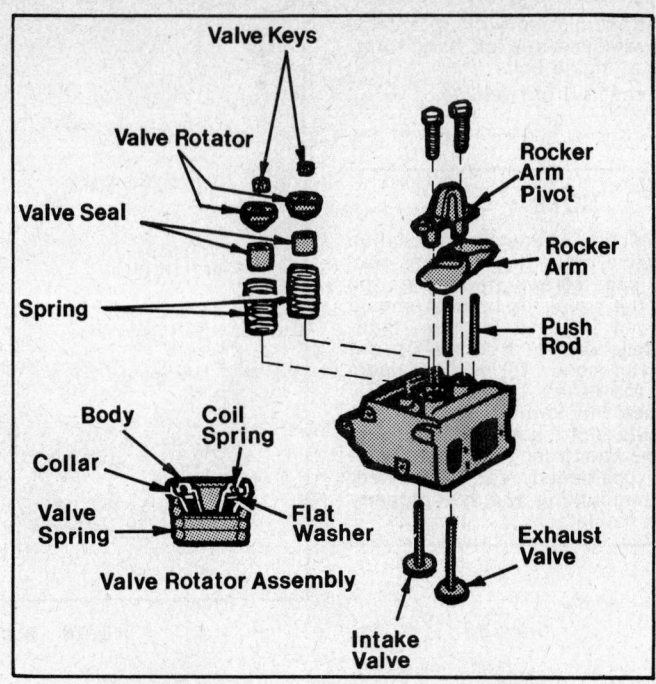

Fig. 3   Cylinder head exploded. 1974-79 V8

VALVE LIFT SPECS.

Engine	Year	Intake	Exhaust
6-250	1974-76	.388	.388
V6-231④	1975-79	.4011	.3768
V8-260	1975-79	.395	.400
V8-305⑥	1977-79	.3727	.4100
V8-350	1974-79	.400	.400
	1975-76	.382	.382
V8-350④	1979	.323	.339
V8-350⑥	1977-79	.390	.410
V8-400⑤	1975	.410	.410
V8-403	1977	.400	.400
V8-455	1974③	.474	.472
	1974-76	.435	.435

①—4 bar. carb. ②—2 bar. carb.
③—Cutlass
④—Refer to Buick chapter for service procedures.
⑤—Refer to Pontiac chapter for service procedures.
⑥—Refer to Chevrolet chapter for service procedures.

ROCKER ARMS

NOTE

V8 engines use valve rotators, Fig. 3. The rotator operates on a sprag clutch principle utilizing the collapsing action of a coil spring to give rotation to the rotor body which turns the valve.

1974-78 V8-260, 350, 403, 455

1. Remove valve cover.
2. Remove flanged bolts, rocker arm pivot and rocker arms, Fig. 3.
3. When installing rocker arm assemblies, lubricate wear surfaces with suitable lubricant. Torque flanged bolts to 25 ft. lbs.

VALVE ROTATORS

The rotator operates on a Sprag clutch principle utilizing the collapsing action of coil spring to give rotation to the rotor body which turns the valve, Fig. 3.

To check rotator action, draw a line across rotator body and down the collar. Operate engine at 1500 rpm, rotator body should move around collar. Rotator action can be in either direction. Replace rotator if no movement is noted.

When servicing valves, valve stem tips should be checked for improper wear pattern which could indicate a defective valve rotator, Fig. 4.

VALVE TIMING

Intake Opens Before TDC

Engine	Year	Degrees
6-250	1974-76	16
V6-231②	1975-78	17
V8-260	1975-79	14
V8-305⑥	1977-79	28
V8-350	1974	22
	1975-79	16
V8-350②	1975-76	19
V8-350③	1977-79	28
V8-400④	1975	30
V8-403	1977-79	16
V8-455	1974-76	20
	1974①	28

①—Cutlass
②—Refer to Buick chapter for service procedures.
③—Refer to Pontiac chapter for service procedures.
④—Refer to Chevrolet chapter for service procedures.

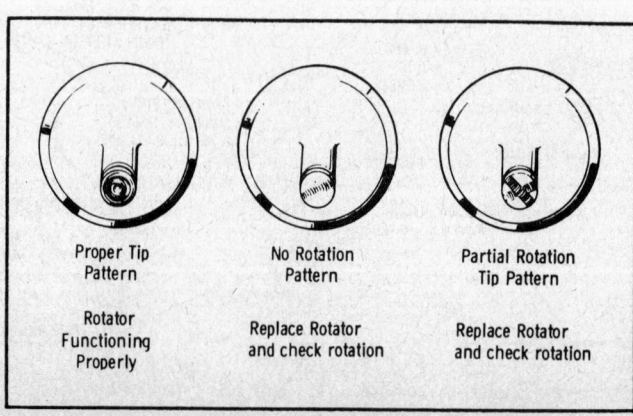

Fig. 4   Checking valve stems for rotator malfunction

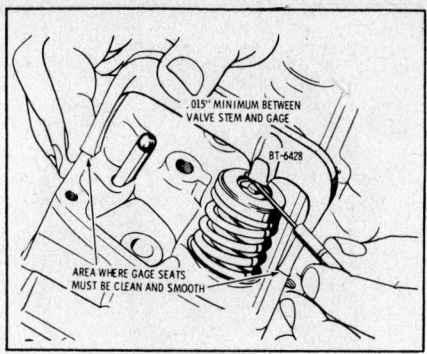

Fig. 5 Measuring valve stem height. V8-260, 350, 403, 455

VALVES, REMOVE

NOTE

Whenever a new valve is installed or after grinding valves, it will be necessary to measure valve stem height using the Special Tool shown in Figs. 5 and 6.

On 1975-79 V8-260, 350, 403 and 455 engines, there should be a minimum clearance of .015 inch between gauge surface and the valve stem, Fig. 5. On 1974 V8-350 engines, there should be .035 inch clearance between gauge surface and valve stem, Fig. 5. On 1974 455 engines, the minimum clearance is .005 inch.

Check valve rotator height, Fig. 6. If valve stem tip extends less than .005 inch above rotator, replace the valve.

Lacking this tool the only alternative is to lay flat feeler gauges on the retainer and check the distance between the retainer and valve stem tip.

VALVE GUIDES

V8-260, 350, 403, 455

Valve stem guides are not replaceable, due to being cast in place. If valve guide bores are worn excessively, they can be reamed oversize.

If a standard valve guide bore is being

reamed, use a .003" or .005" oversize reamer. For the .010" oversize valve guide bore, use a .013" oversize reamer. If too large a reamer is used and the spiraling is removed, it is possible that the valve will not receive the proper lubrication.

NOTE: Occasionally a valve guide will be oversize as manufactured. These are marked on the cylinder head as shown in Fig. 7. If no markings are present, the guide bores are standard. If oversize markings are present, any valve replacement will require an oversize valve. Service valves are available in standard diameters as well as .003", .005", .010" and .013" oversize.

VALVE LIFTERS

Valve lifters are available in standard size and an oversize of .010 inch. An "O" is etched on the side of the .010 inch oversize lifter for identification. Also, the cylinder block near the valve lifter bore is marked with an "O". Ensure valve lifters are re-installed in original bores.

Plungers are not interchangeable because they are selectively fitted to the bodies at the factory.

If plunger and body appear satisfactory blow off with air to remove all particles of dirt. Install the plunger in the body without other parts and check for free movement. A simple test is to be sure that the plunger will drop of its own weight in the body, Fig. 8.

TIMING CASE COVER

NOTE: When it becomes necessary to replace the cover oil seal, the cover need not be removed.

1977-79 V8-260, 350 & 403

1. Disconnect battery ground cable.
2. Drain cooling system and disconnect radiator hoses and bypass hose.
3. Remove all drive belts, fan and pul-

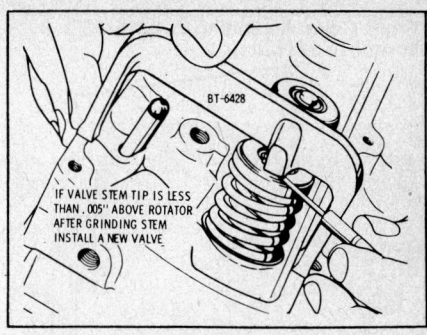

Fig. 6 Measuring valve retaining or valve rotor height. V8-260, 350, 403, 455

ley, crankshaft pulley and harmonic balancer, and accessory brackets.
4. Remove timing indicator and water pump.
5. Remove remaining front cover attaching bolts and the front cover. Also, remove the dowel pins. It may be necessary to grind a flat on the dowel pin to provide a rough surface for gripping.
6. Grind a chamfer on one end of each dowel pin.
7. Cut excess material from front end of oil pan gasket on each side of cylinder block.
8. Trim approximately 1/8 inch from each end of new front pan seal.
9. Install new front cover gasket and apply suitable sealer to gasket around coolant holes.
10. Apply RTV sealer to mating surfaces of cylinder block, oil pan and front cover.
11. Place front cover on cylinder block and press downward to compress seal. Rotate cover right and left and guide oil pan seal into cavity with a small screwdriver.
12. Apply engine oil to bolts.
13. Install two bolts finger tight to retain cover.
14. Install the two dowel pins, chamfered end first.

Fig. 7 Valve guide bore marking. V8-260, 350, 403, 455

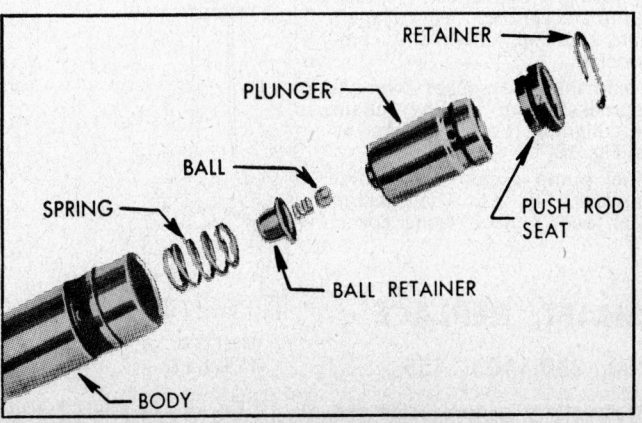

Fig. 8 Hydraulic valve lifter (typical)

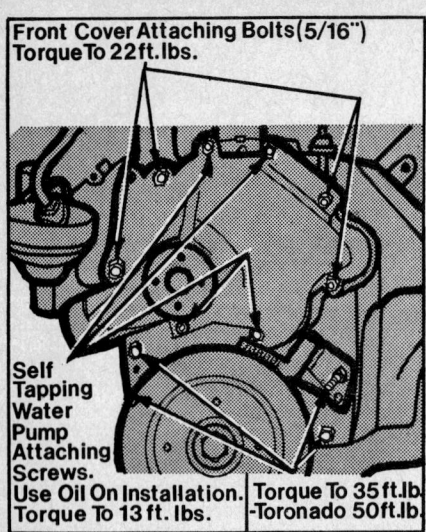

Front Cover Attaching Bolts (5/16")
Torque To 22 ft. lbs.

Self Tapping Water Pump Attaching Screws. Use Oil On Installation. Torque To 13 ft. lbs.

Torque To 35 ft. lb. -Toronado 50 ft. lb.

Fig. 9   Engine front cover bolts. V8-260, 350, 403, 455

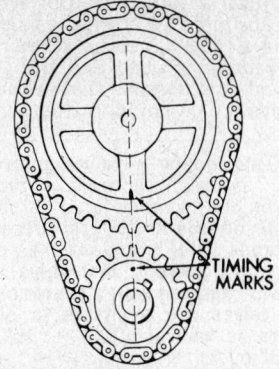

TIMING MARKS

Fig. 10   Timing chain position. V8-260, 350, 403, 455

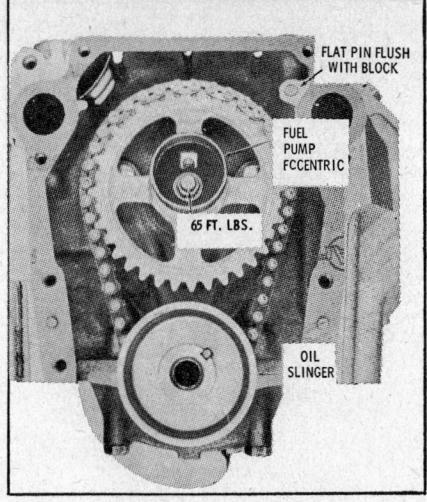

FLAT PIN FLUSH WITH BLOCK

FUEL PUMP ECCENTRIC

65 FT. LBS.

OIL SLINGER

Fig. 11   Fuel pump eccentric. V8-260, 350, 403, 455

15. Install timing indicator and water pump and torque bolts as shown in Fig. 9.
16. Install harmonic balancer and crankshaft pulley.
17. Install accessory brackets.
18. Install fan and pulley and drive belts.
19. Connect radiator hoses and bypass hose.
20. Connect battery ground cable.

1974-76 V8-260, 350 & 455

1. Drain cooling system and disconnect heater hose, by-pass hose and both radiator hoses.
2. Remove all belts, fan and pulley, crankshaft pulley and pulley hub.
3. Remove oil pan.
4. Unfasten and remove cover, timing pointer and water pump assembly.

TIMING CHAIN

V8-260, 350, 403, 455

1. After removing front cover, remove fuel pump eccentric, oil slinger, crankshaft sprocket, chain and camshaft sprocket.
2. Install camshaft sprocket, crankshaft sprocket and timing chain together, aligning timing marks as shown in Fig. 10.
3. Install fuel pump eccentric with flat side rearward, Fig. 11. Then install oil slinger and replace front cover.

CAMSHAFT, REPLACE

V8-260, 350, 403, 455

1. Disconnect battery ground cable and drain radiator.

2. Remove upper radiator baffle and disconnect upper radiator hose from water outlet.
3. Disconnect transmission oil cooler lines at radiator.
4. Remove radiator fan shroud, then the radiator.
5. Disconnect fuel lines from fuel pump.
6. Remove air cleaner and disconnect throttle cable.
7. Remove all drive belts and position alternator, power steering pump and air conditioning compressor aside.
8. Disconnect by-pass hose from water pump and all electrical and vacuum connections from engine.
9. Remove distributor.
10. Raise vehicle and drain oil pan.
11. Remove exhaust cross-over pipe and the starter.
12. Disconnect exhaust pipe from manifold.
13. Install engine support bar.
14. Remove engine mount to bracket bolts, raise engine and remove engine mounts.
15. Remove flywheel cover and engine oil pan.

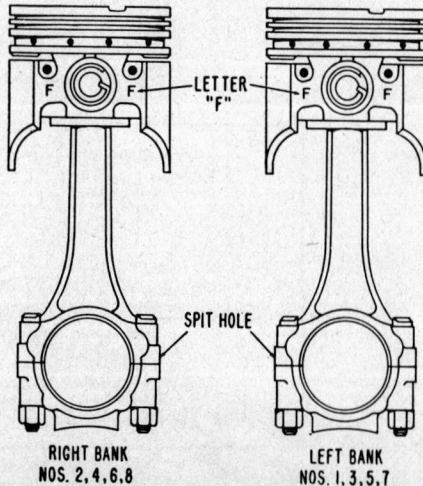

F   F   LETTER "F"   F   F

SPIT HOLE

RIGHT BANK NOS. 2, 4, 6, 8

LEFT BANK NOS. 1, 3, 5, 7

Fig. 12   Assembly of piston to rod. 1974-76 V8-260, 350

16. Place wood blocks between exhaust manifolds and cross-member to support engine, then remove engine support bar.
17. Remove crankshaft pulley and balancer, then the engine front cover.
18. Lower vehicle and remove valve covers, intake manifold, rocker arms, push rods and valve lifters.

NOTE: Note position of valve train components to ensure installation in original location.

19. If equipped with A/C, discharge refrigerant and remove condenser.
20. Remove fuel pump eccentric, camshaft sprocket, oil slinger and timing chain.
21. Slide camshaft from front of engine.
22. Reverse procedure to install.

NOTE: *To insure proper camshaft installation, and to provide initial lubrication, it is extremely important that the camshaft be coated with GM Concentrate (Part No. 582099).*

PISTON & ROD, ASSEMBLE

Lubricate the piston pin hole and piston pin to facilitate installation of pin, then position the connecting rod with its respective piston as shown in Figs. 12 through 14.

PISTONS, RINGS & PINS

Pistons are available in standard sizes and oversizes of .010 and .030".
Rings are available in standard sizes and oversizes of .010 and .030".

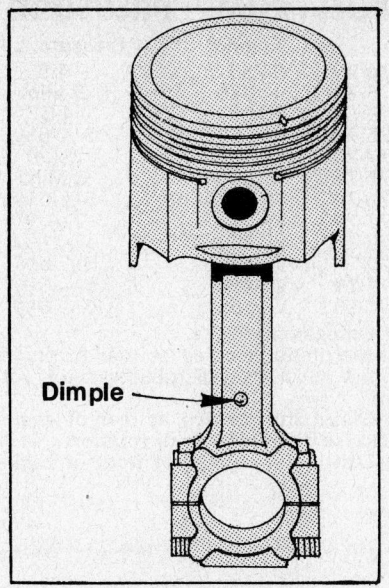

**Fig. 12A   Assembly of piston to rod.
1977-79 V8-260 & 350**

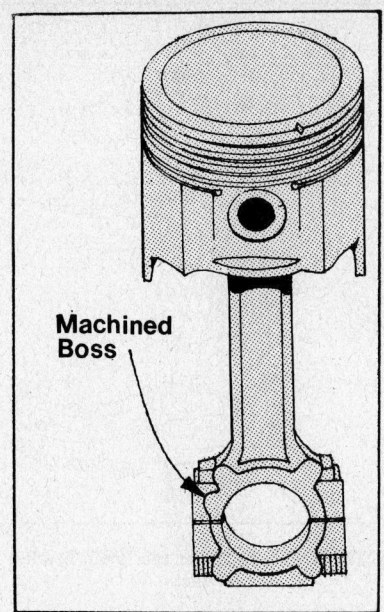

**Fig. 13   Assembly of piston to rod.
1977-79 V8-403**

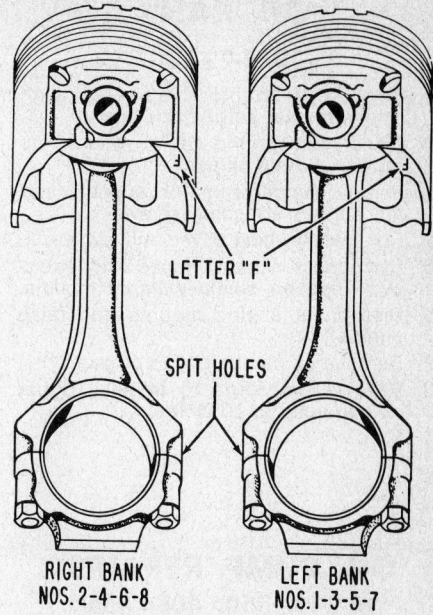

**Fig. 14   Assembly of piston to rod.
1974-76 V8-455**

MAIN & ROD BEARINGS

Main bearings are available in standard sizes and undersizes of .0005, .001, .0015, .002, .010 and .020".

Rod bearings are available in standard sizes and undersizes of .001, .002, .005, .010, .012 and .020 inch.

NOTE

Main bearing clearances not within specifications must be corrected by the use of selective upper and lower shells. Figs. 15 and 15A illustrate the undersize identification marking on the bearing tang.

REAR CRANKSHAFT SEAL SERVICE

Since the braided fabric seal used on these engines can be replaced only when the crankshaft is removed, the following repair procedure is recommended.

1. Remove oil pan and bearing cap.
2. Drive end of old seal gently into groove, using a suitable tool, until packed tight. This may vary between $\frac{1}{4}$ and $\frac{3}{4}$ inch depending on amount of pack required.
3. Repeat previous step for other end of seal.
4. Measure and note amount that seal was driven up on one side. Using the old seal removed from bearing cap, cut a length of seal the amount previously noted plus $\frac{1}{16}$ inch.
5. Repeat previous step for other side of seal.
6. Pack cut lengths of seal into appropriate side of seal groove. A packing tool, BT-6433, Fig. 16, may be used since the tool has been machined to provide a built-in stop. Use tool BT-6436 to trim the seal flush with block, Fig. 17.
7. Install new seal in lower bearing cap.

**Fig. 15   Main bearing size location.
1974-76 V8-260, 350, 455**

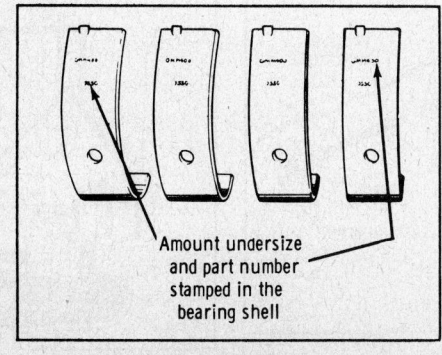

**Fig. 15A   Main bearing size location.
V8-260, 350, 403**

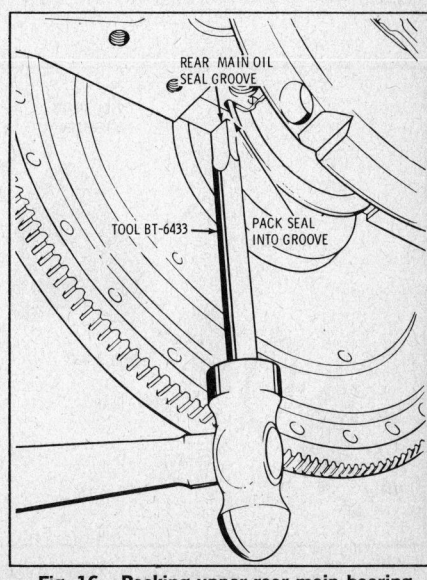

**Fig. 16   Packing upper rear main bearing
oil seal**

OIL PAN

1974-79 V8

1. Remove distributor cap and align rotor with No. 1 firing position.
2. Disconnect ground cable, remove dip stick and drain oil pan.
3. Remove upper radiator support and fan shroud attaching screws.
4. Remove flywheel cover and starter.
5. Disconnect exhaust pipes and cross-over pipe on single exhaust models.
6. Disconnect engine mounts and raise engine.
7. Remove oil pan bolts and oil pan.
8. Reverse procedure to install. Torque oil pan bolts to 10 ft. lbs.

OIL PUMP REPAIRS

V8-260, 350, 403, 455

1. Remove oil pan and pump baffle. Remove attaching screws and remove pump and drive shaft extension.
2. To service the pump, refer to Fig. 18.
3. To install, insert the drive shaft extension through the opening in the block until the shaft mates into the distributor drive gear. Position pump onto rear main bearing cap and torque the attaching bolts to 35 ft-lbs.
4. Install oil pump baffle and pan.

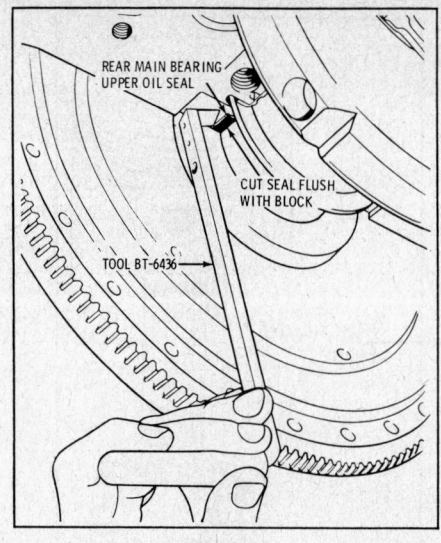

Fig. 17   Trimming upper rear main bearing oil seal

WATER PUMP, REPLACE

V8-260, 350, 403, 455

1. Drain cooling system and remove heater and lower hoses from pump.
2. Loosen pulley belts and remove fan and pulley. On air conditioned cars, remove clutch fan assembly and pulley.
3. Unfasten and remove pump from front cover.

FUEL PUMP PRESSURE

Year	Engine	Pressure, Lbs.
1974-75	6-250	4-5
1976-78	V6-231	3 Min.
1979	V6-231	4-5
1975-79	V8-260	$5\frac{1}{2}$-$6\frac{1}{2}$
1977-79	V8-305	$7\frac{1}{2}$-9
1975-76	V8-350 [1]	3 Min.
1975-79	V8-350 [2]	$5\frac{1}{2}$-$6\frac{1}{2}$
1977-79	V8-350 [3]	$7\frac{1}{2}$-9
1979	V8-350 [4]	6-$7\frac{1}{2}$
1975	V8-400	$5\frac{1}{2}$-$6\frac{1}{2}$
1977-79	V8-403	$5\frac{1}{2}$-$6\frac{1}{2}$
1974-76	V8-455	$5\frac{1}{2}$-$6\frac{1}{2}$

[1]—Omega only.
[2]—Distributor located at rear of engine, counter clockwise distributor rotor rotation.
[3]—Distributor located at rear of engine, clockwise distributor rotor rotation.
[4]—Distributor located at front of engine.

FUEL PUMP, REPLACE

1. Disconnect fuel lines from fuel pump.
2. Remove fuel pump mounting bolts and the fuel pump.
3. Remove all gasket material from the pump and block gasket surfaces. Apply sealer to both sides of new gasket.
4. Position gasket on pump flange and hold pump in position against its mounting surface. Make sure rocker arm is riding on camshaft eccentric.
5. Press pump tight against its mounting. Install retaining screws and tighten them alternately.
6. Connect fuel lines. Then operate engine and check for leaks.

BELT TENSION DATA

	New Lbs.	Used Lbs.
1974-79—		
V8 All	110-140	70

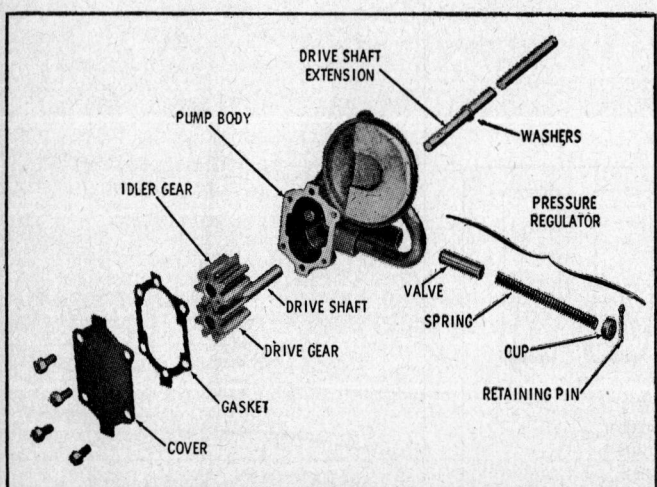

Fig. 18   Oil pump disassembled.
V8-260, 350, 403, 455 (Typical)

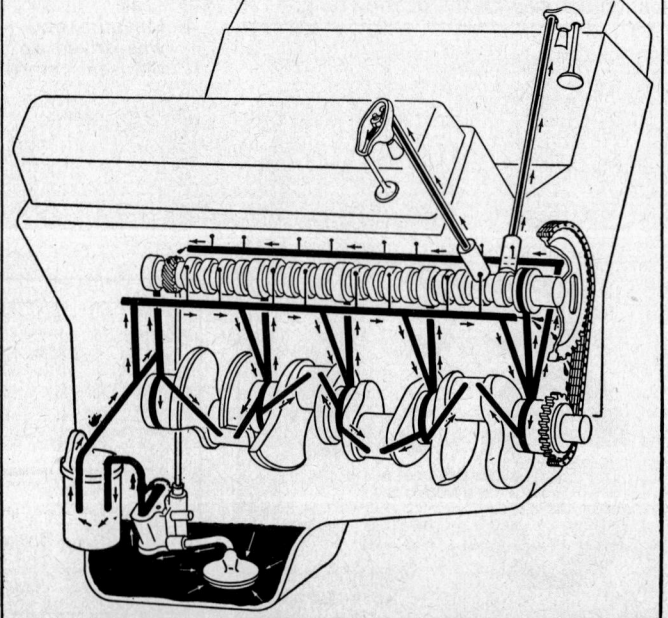

Engine lubrication. V8-260, 350, 403, 455

Diesel Engine Section

DIESEL ENGINE SECTION INDEX

DESCRIPTION

Engine Construction

The Oldsmobile four stroke cycle diesel engine is basically the same in construction as the Oldsmobile gasoline engine. The cylinders are numbered 1,3,5,7 on the left bank and 2,4,6,8 on the right bank. The firing order is 1-8-4-3-6-5-7-2. The major differences between the diesel and gasoline versions is in the cylinder heads, combustion chamber, fuel distribution system, air intake manifold and method of ignition. The cylinder block, crankshaft, main bearings, connecting rods, pistons and pins are of heavy construction due to the high compression ratio required to ignite the diesel fuel. The diesel fuel is ignited when the heat developed in the combustion chamber during the compression stroke reaches a certain temperature.

The valve train operates the same as in the gasoline engine, but are of special design and material for diesel operation. The stainless steel pre-chamber inserts in the cylinder head combustion chambers are serviced separately from the cylinder head. With the cylinder head removed, these pre-chamber inserts can be driven from the cylinder head after removing the glow plugs or injection nozzles. The glow plugs are threaded into the cylinder head and the injection nozzles are retained by a bolt and clamp. The injection nozzles are spring loaded and calibrated to open at a specified fuel pressure.

Fuel System

The fuel injection pump is mounted on top of the engine and is gear driven by the camshaft and rotates at camshaft speed. This high pressure rotary pump injects a metered amount of fuel to each cylinder at the proper time. Eight high pressure fuel delivery pipes from the injection pump to the injection nozzles, Fig. 1, are the same length to prevent any difference in timing from cylinder to cylinder. The fuel injection pump provides the required timing advance under all operating conditions. Engine speed is controlled by a rotary fuel metering valve, Fig. 2. When the accelera-tor is depressed, the throttle cable opens the metering valve and allows more fuel to be delivered to the engine. The injection pump also incorporates a low pressure transfer pump to deliver fuel to the fuel line to the high pressure pump, Fig. 2.

The fuel filter is located between the mechanical fuel pump and the injection pump. The diaphragm type mechanical fuel pump is mounted on the right side of the engine and is driven by a cam on the crankshaft. The fuel tank at the rear of the vehicle is connected by fuel pipes to the mechanical fuel pump. Excess fuel returns from the fuel injection pump and injection nozzles to the fuel tank through pipes and hoses.

Engine Lubrication System

The diesel engine lubrication system is basically the same as the gasoline engine. The fuel injection pump driven gear is lubricated by oil directed through a passage from the top of the camshaft bearing, Fig. 3. An angled passage in the shaft portion of the driven gear directs the oil to the rear driven gear bearing. At the front of the right oil gallery, a small orifice sprays oil to lubricate the fuel pump eccentric cam on the crankshaft and timing chain.

Engine Cooling System

The diesel engine cooling system is the same as the gasoline engine except the radiator incorporates two oil coolers. One cooler is used to cool the transmission fluid and the other cooler is used to cool the engine oil.

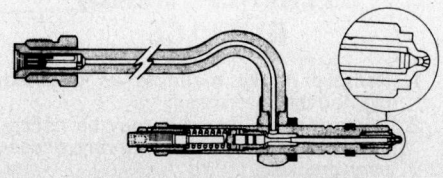

Fig. 1   Fuel injection nozzle

Engine Electrical System

Eight glow plugs are used to pre-heat the pre-chamber to aid in starting. The 1978 type 1 glow plugs are 12 volt heaters and are activated when the ignition key is turned to the "Run" position. The 1978 type 1 system, Fig. 4, uses steady current applied to 12 volt glow plugs. The 1978-79 type 2 glow plug system, Figs. 8, 9 and 9A, uses 6 volt glow plugs with a controlled pulsating current applied to them for starting. The 6 volt and 12 volt glow plugs are not interchangeable and can be identified by the wire connector spade. The 6 volt glow plugs have a 5/16 in. wire connector spade, while the 12 volt glow plugs have a 1/4 in. wire connector spade. The glow plugs remain activated for a short time after starting then are automatically turned "Off". Two 12 volt batteries are connected in parallel are required for the higher electrical load due to the glow plugs and starter motor. The diesel starter motor is larger than the gasoline engine starter and is designed to crank the engine at least the 100 RPM required for starting. An alternator supplies charging current to both batteries at the same time and there are no switches or relays in the charging circuit.

DIESEL ENGINE ELECTRICAL DIAGNOSIS

Refer to Figs. 4 through 10D for diesel engine electrical diagnosis.

ENGINE MOUNTS

Refer to Fig. 11 for engine mount installation.

ENGINE, REPLACE

1. Disconnect ground cable from batteries and drain cooling system.

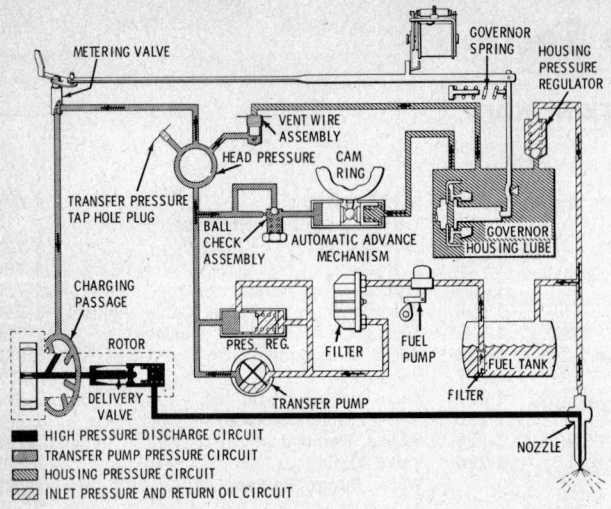

High Pressure Discharge Circuit
Transfer Pump Pressure Circuit
Housing Pressure Circuit
Inlet Pressure and Return Oil Circuit

Fig. 2   Fuel injection pump circuit

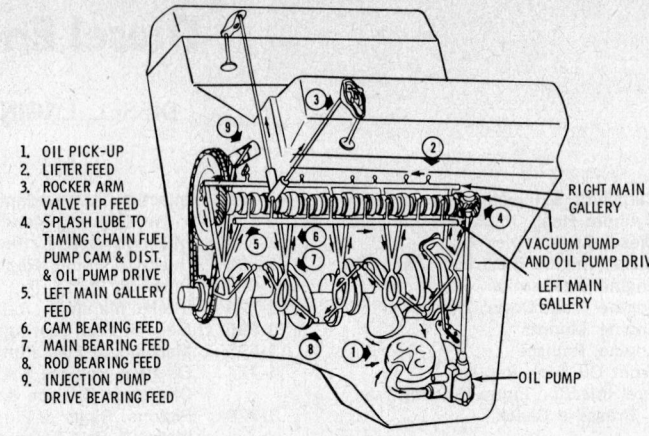

1. OIL PICK-UP
2. LIFTER FEED
3. ROCKER ARM VALVE TIP FEED
4. SPLASH LUBE TO TIMING CHAIN FUEL PUMP CAM & DIST. & OIL PUMP DRIVE
5. LEFT MAIN GALLERY FEED
6. CAM BEARING FEED
7. MAIN BEARING FEED
8. ROD BEARING FEED
9. INJECTION PUMP DRIVE BEARING FEED

Fig. 3   Engine lubricating system

2. Remove air cleaner.
3. Scribe hood hinge locations and remove hood.
4. Disconnect ground wires at inner fender and the engine ground strap at right cylinder head.
5. Disconnect radiator hoses, oil cooler lines, heater hoses, vacuum hoses, power steering hoses from gear, A/C compressor with brackets and hoses attached, fuel pump hose from fuel pump and the wiring.
6. Remove hairpin clip from bellcrank.
7. Remove throttle and throttle valve cables from intake manifold brackets and position cables aside.
8. Remove upper radiator support and the radiator.
9. Raise vehicle.
10. Disconnect exhaust pipes from exhaust manifold.
11. Remove torque converter cover and the three bolts securing torque converter to flywheel.
12. Remove engine mount bolts or nuts.
13. Remove three engine to transmission bolts on the right side.
14. Disconnect starter wiring and remove starter.
15. Lower vehicle.
16. Attach suitable engine lifting equipment to engine. Support transmission with a suitable jack.
17. Remove the three engine to transmission bolts on the left side.
18. Remove engine from vehicle.
19. Reverse procedure to install.

INTAKE MANIFOLD, REPLACE

1. Disconnect ground cables from batteries.
2. Remove air cleaner assembly.
3. Drain cooling system, then disconnect upper radiator hose and thermostat bypass hose from water pump outlet. Disconnect heater hose and vacuum hose from water control valve.
4. Remove breather pipes from valve covers and air crossover, Fig. 12.
5. Remove air crossover and cap intake manifold, Fig. 13.
6. Disconnect throttle rod and return spring. If equipped with Cruise Control, remove servo.
7. Remove hairpin clip from bellcrank and disconnect the cables. Remove throttle and throttle valve cables from intake manifold brackets and position cables aside.
8. Disconnect wiring as necessary.
9. Disconnect or remove alternator and A/C compressor brackets as necessary.
10. Disconnect fuel line from fuel pump and filter and remove fuel filter and bracket.
11. Disconnect lines from injector nozzles and remove injection pump. Cap all open fuel line lines and fittings.
12. Disconnect fuel return line from injection pump.
13. Disconnect vacuum lines at vacuum pump. Remove vacuum pump, if equipped with A/C, or oil pump drive assembly, if less A/C, Fig. 14.
14. Remove intake manifold drain tube, Fig. 15.
15. Remove intake manifold bolts and the intake manifold.
16. Remove adapter seal and injection pump adapter.
17. Remove procedure to install. Torque intake manifold bolts in sequence, Fig. 16, to specifications.

CYLINDER HEAD, REPLACE

1. Remove intake manifold as outlined previously.
2. Remove valve cover. It may be necessary to remove any interfering accessory brackets.
3. Disconnect glow plug wiring.
4. Remove ground strap from right cylinder head, if removing.
5. Remove rocker arm bolts, pivots, rocker arms and push rod. Note locations of valve train components so they can be installed in original locations.
6. Remove fuel return lines from injection nozzles.
7. Remove exhaust manifold.
8. Remove engine block drain plug on side of block that cylinder head is being removed.
9. Remove cylinder head bolts and cylinder head.
10. If necessary to remove pre-chamber, remove a glow plug or injection nozzle, then tap out pre-chamber with a suitable drift, Fig. 17.
11. Reverse procedure to install. **Do not use any sealing compound on cylinder head gasket.** Torque cylinder head bolts in sequence, Fig. 18, to 100 ft. lbs., then 130 ft. lbs.

ROCKER ARMS

NOTE

This engine uses valve rotators, Fig. 19. The rotator operates on a sprag clutch principle utilizing the collapsing action of a coil spring to give rotation to the rotor body which turns the valve.

1. Remove valve cover.
2. Remove flanged bolts, rocker arm pivot and rocker arms, Fig. 19.
3. When installing rocker arm assemblies, lubricate wear surfaces with suitable lubricant. Torque flanged bolts to 25 ft. lbs.

VALVE ARRANGEMENT

V8-260, 350 Diesel . . . . I-E-I-E-E-I-E-I

DIESEL ENGINE DIAGNOSIS

CONDITION	POSSIBLE CAUSE	CORRECTION
Engine Will Not Crank	1. Loose or corroded battery cables	1. Check connections at battery, engine block and starter solenoid.
	2. Discharged batteries	2. Check charging system.
	3. Starter Inoperative	3. Check starting system.
Engine Cranks Slowly— Will Not Start (Minimum Engine Crank Speed— 100 RPM)	1. Battery cable connections loose or corroded	1. Check connections at battery, engine block and starter.
	2. Batteries undercharged	2. Check charging system.
	3. Wrong engine oil	3. Drain and refill with recommended oil.
Engine Cranks Normally— Will Not Start	1. Incorrect starting procedure	1. Use recommended starting procedure.
	2. Incorrect or contaminated fuel	2. Flush fuel system and install correct fuel.
	3. No fuel to nozzles	3. Loosen injection line at a nozzle. Do not disconnect. Use care to direct fuel away from sources of ignition. Wipe connection to be sure it is dry. Crank 5 seconds. Fuel should flow from injection line. Tighten connection. If fuel does not flow, check fuel solenoid operation as follows: Connect a 12 volt test lamp from wire at injection pump solenoid to ground. Turn ignition to "ON". Lamp should light. If lamp does not light, check wiring to solenoid.
	4. No fuel to injection pump	4. Remove line at inlet to injection pump fuel filter. Connect hose from line to metal container. Crank engine. If no fuel is discharged, test the fuel supply pump. If the pump is OK, check the injection pump fuel filter and replace if plugged. If filter and inlet line to injection pump are OK, replace injection pump.

CONDITION	POSSIBLE CAUSE	CORRECTION
Engine Cranks Normally—Will Not Start (Cont'd)	5. Plugged fuel return system	5. Disconnect fuel return line at injection pump and route hose to a metal container. Connect a hose to the injection pump connection and route it to the metal container. Crank the engine; if engine starts and runs, correct restriction in fuel return system.
	6. Pump timing incorrect	6. Make certain that pump timing mark is aligned with mark on adapter.
	7. Glow plug control system inoperative	7. Refer to Diesel Engine Electrical System Diagnosis
	8. Glow plugs inoperative	8. Refer to Diesel Engine Electrical System Diagnosis
	9. Internal engine problems	9. Correct as necessary.
Engine Starts But Will Not Continue To Run At Idle	1. No fuel in tank	1. Install correct fuel in tank.
	2. Incorrect or contaminated fuel	2. Flush fuel system and install correct fuel.
	3. Limited fuel to injection pump	3. Test the fuel supply pump. Replace as necessary.
	4. Fuel solenoid disengaged with ignition switch in the "ON" position	4. Connect a 12 volt test lamp from wire at injection pump solenoid to ground. Turn ignition to "ON". Lamp should light. Turn ignition to "START". Lamp should light. If lamp does not light in both positions, check wiring to solenoid.
	5. Restricted fuel return system	5. Disconnect fuel return line at injection pump and route hose to a metal container. Connect a hose to the injection pump connection and route it to the metal container. Crank the engine; if engine starts and runs, correct restriction in fuel return system.

CONDITION	POSSIBLE CAUSE	CORRECTION
Engine Starts But Will Not Continue To Run At Idle (Cont'd)	6. Fast idle solenoid inoperative	6. With engine cold, start car; solenoid should move to support injection pump lever in "fast idle position" for about 5 seconds. If solenoid does not move, refer to Electrical System Diagnosis.
	7. Low idle incorrectly adjusted	7. Adjust idle screw to specification.
	8. Pump timing incorrect	8. Make certain that timing mark, on injection pump, is aligned with mark on adapter.
	9. Glow plug control system malfunction	9. Refer to Diesel Engine Electrical System Diagnosis.
	10. Injection pump malfunction	10. Install replacement pump.
	11. Internal engine problems	11. Correct as necessary.
Engine Starts, Idles Rough, Without Abnormal Noise or Smoke	1. Low idle incorrectly adjusted	1. Adjust idle screw to specification.
	2. Injection line leaks	2. Wipe off injection lines and connections. Run engine and check for leaks. Correct leaks.
	3. Restricted fuel return system	3. Disconnect fuel return line at injection pump and route hose to a metal container. Connect a hose to the injection pump connection and route it to the metal container. Crank the engine; if engine starts and runs, correct restriction in fuel return system.
	4. Incorrect or contaminated fuel	4. Flush fuel system and install correct fuel.
	5. Nozzle(s) inoperative	5. With engine running, loosen injection line fitting at each nozzle in turn. Use care to direct fuel away from sources of ignition. Each nozzle should contribute to rough running. If nozzle is found that does not change idle quality, it should be replaced.

CONDITION	POSSIBLE CAUSE	CORRECTION
Engine Starts, Idles Rough, Without Abnormal Noise or Smoke (Cont'd)	6. Internal fuel leak at nozzle(s)	6. Disconnect fuel return system from nozzles on one bank at a time. With the engine running, observe the normal fuel seepage at the nozzles. Replace any nozzle with excessive fuel leakage.
	7. Fuel supply pump malfunctions	7. Test the fuel supply pump. Replace if necessary.
	8. Uneven fuel distribution to cylinders	8. Install new or reconditioned nozzles, one at a time, until condition is corrected as indicated by normal idle.
Engine Starts And Idles Rough With Excessive Noise and/or Smoke	1. Injection pump timing incorrect	1. Be sure timing mark on injection pump is aligned with mark on adapter.
	2. Nozzle(s) inoperative	2. With engine running, crack injection line at each nozzle, one at a time. Use care to direct fuel away from sources of ignition. Each nozzle should contribute to rough running. If a nozzle is found that does not affect idle quality or changes noise and/or smoke, it should be replaced.
	3. High pressure lines incorrectly installed	3. Check routing of each line. Correct as required.
Engine Misfires But Idles Correctly	1. Plugged fuel filter	1. Replace filter.
	2. Incorrect injection pump timing	2. Be sure that timing mark on injection pump and adapter are aligned.
	3. Incorrect or contaminated fuel	3. Flush fuel system and install correct fuel.
	4. Internal engine damage	4. Correct as necessary.
Engine Will Not Return To Idle	1. External linkage misadjustment or failure	1. Reset linkage or replace as required.
	2. Internal injection pump malfunction	2. Install replacement injection pump.

CONDITION	POSSIBLE CAUSE	CORRECTION
Fuel Leaks On Ground— No Engine Malfunction	1. Loose or broken fuel line or connection	1. Examine complete fuel system, including tank, supply, injection and return system. Determine source and cause of leak and repair.
	2. Internal injection pump failure	2. Install replacement injection pump.
Significant Loss of Power	1. Incorrect or contaminated fuel	1. Flush fuel system and install correct fuel.
	2. Pinched or otherwise restricted return system	2. Examine system for restriction and correct as required.
	3. Plugged fuel tank vent	3. Remove fuel cap. If "hissing" noise is heard, vent is plugged and should be cleaned.
	4. Restricted supply	4. Examine fuel supply system to determine cause of restriction. Repair as required.
	5. Plugged fuel filter	5. Remove and replace filter.
	6. External compression leaks	6. Check for compression leaks at all nozzles and glow plugs, using "Leak-Tec" or equivalent. If leak is found, tighten nozzle clamp or glow plug. If leak persists at a nozzle, remove it and reinstall with a new carbon stop seal and compression seal.
	7. Plugged nozzle(s)	7. Remove nozzles, check for plugging and have repaired or replaced.
	8. Internal engine problem	8. Correct as necessary.
Noise—"Rap" From One or More Cylinders	1. Air in fuel system	1. Check for leaks and correct.
	2. Air in high pressure line(s)	2. Crack line at nozzle(s) and bleed air at each cylinder determined to be causing noise. Use care to direct fuel away from sources of ignition and be sure to carefully retighten lines.
	3. Nozzle(s) sticking open or with very low blowoff pressure	3. Replace the nozzle(s) causing the problem.
	4. Internal engine problem	4. Correct as necessary.

CONDITION	POSSIBLE CAUSE	CORRECTION
Noise—Significant Overall Combustion Noise Increase With Excessive Black Smoke	1. Timing not set to specification	1. Align timing marks on adapter and injection pump.
	2. Internal engine problem	2. Check for presence of oil in the air crossover. If present, determine cause and correct.
	3. Injection pump housing pressure out of specifications.	3. Check housing pressure. If incorrect, replace fuel return line connector assembly.
	4. Internal injection pump problem	4. Replace pump.
Noise—Internal or External	1. Fuel supply pump, alternator, water pump, valve train, short block, etc.	1. Inspect and correct as necessary.
Engine Overheats	1. Coolant system leak or oil cooler system leak	1. Check for leaks and correct as required.
	2. Belt failure	2. Replace.
	3. Thermostat malfunction, head gasket failure or internal engine problem	3. Inspect and correct as necessary.
Instrument Panel Oil Warning Lamp "ON" at Idle	1. Oil cooler or oil cooler line restricted	1. Remove restriction in cooler or cooler line.
	2. Internal engine problem	2. Correct as necessary.
Odor or Smoke— Excessive and Not Previously Covered	1. Same as Gasoline Engines	1. Correct as necessary. Refer to Trouble-Shooting Chapter.
Engine Will Not shut Off With Key NOTE: With engine at idle, pinch the fuel return line at the injection pump to shut off engine.	1. Injection pump solenoid does not drop out	1. Refer to electrical diagnosis. If problem is determined to be internal with the injection pump, replace the injection pump.
	2. Injection pump solenoid return spring failed	2. Replace injection pump.

DIESEL ENGINE GLOW PLUG ELECTRONIC CONTROL

1	2	3	4	5	6
IGN. SWITCH -"OFF"-	IGN. SWITCH -"RUN"-	IGN. SWITCH -"RUN"-	IGN. SWITCH -"START"-	IGN. SWITCH -"RUN"-	IGN. SWITCH -"RUN"-
WAIT LAMP - OFF	WAIT LAMP - ON	WAIT LAMP - OFF	WAIT LAMP - OFF	WAIT LAMP - OFF	WAIT LAMP - OFF
START LAMP - OFF	START LAMP - OFF	START LAMP - ON	START LAMP - OFF	START LAMP - OFF	START LAMP - OFF
GLOW PLUGS - OFF	GLOW PLUGS - ON	GLOW PLUGS - ON	GLOW PLUGS - ON	GLOW PLUGS - ON	GLOW PLUGS - OFF
		↓ SEE NOTE 1		↓ SEE NOTES 2 & 3	

NOTE 1: If the ignition is left in the "RUN" position 2-5 minutes before turning it to "START", the Glow Plugs and Lamps turn off. This prevents discharging the battery. Turn ignition "OFF" then to "RUN" and wait for Start Lamp. (Voltage to the starter solenoid is also directed to the module and is the signal that the ignition switch was turned to the Start position).

NOTE 2: Engine Running - Generator voltage to turn off the "GEN" lamp is also directed to the module. 9 volts or more indicates the engine is running. Glow plugs remain on the same length of time between No. 5 and 6 as they did between No. 2 and 3.

NOTE 3: Engine did not start. Ign. switch still in "RUN" position. "GEN" lamp on. Electronic control starts over after 2-4 second delay (step 2). Wait lamp on, Start lamp off, and Glow Plugs on.

NOTE 4: The extra light bulb is behind the I. P. and located so it cannot be seen. It's purpose is to provide more current to the generator field coil when starting and idling the engine.

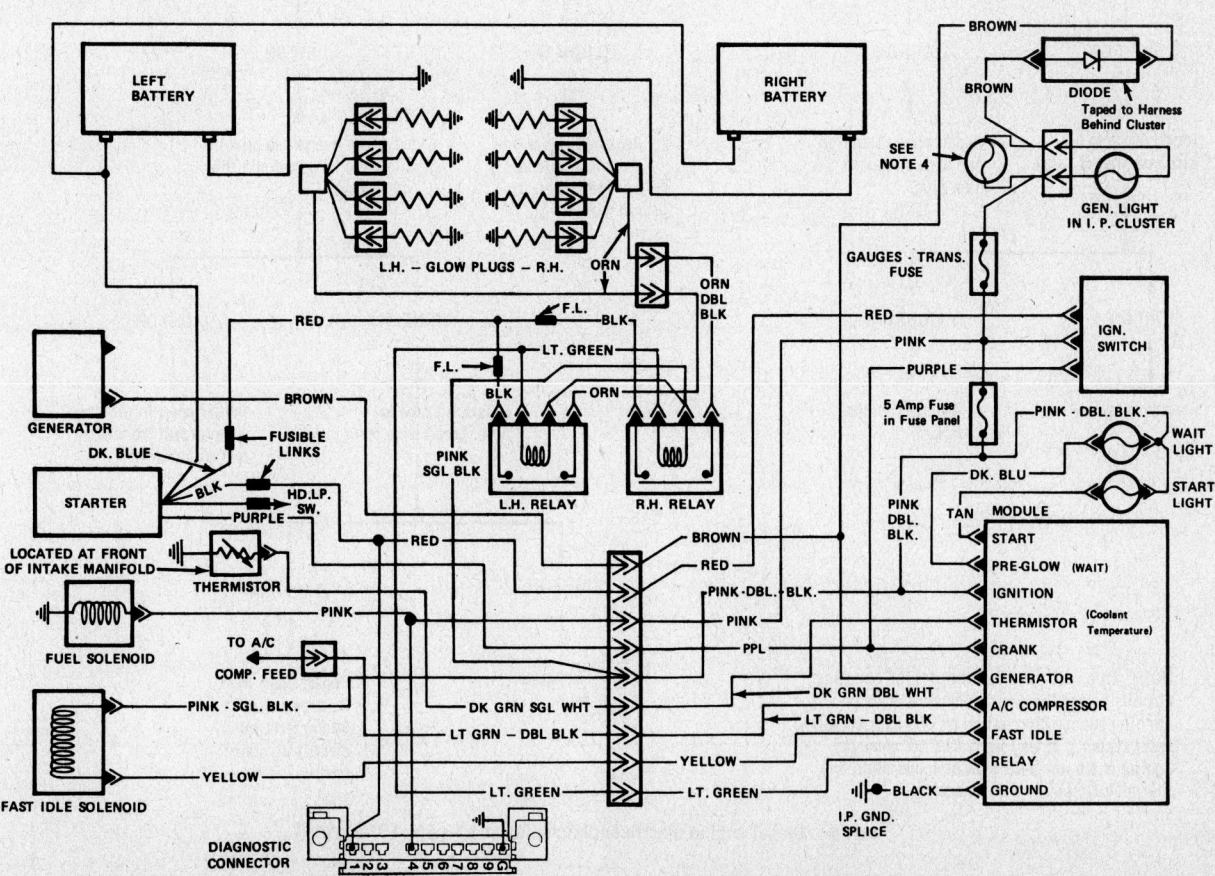

Fig. 4   Diesel engine electrical system. 1978 type 1

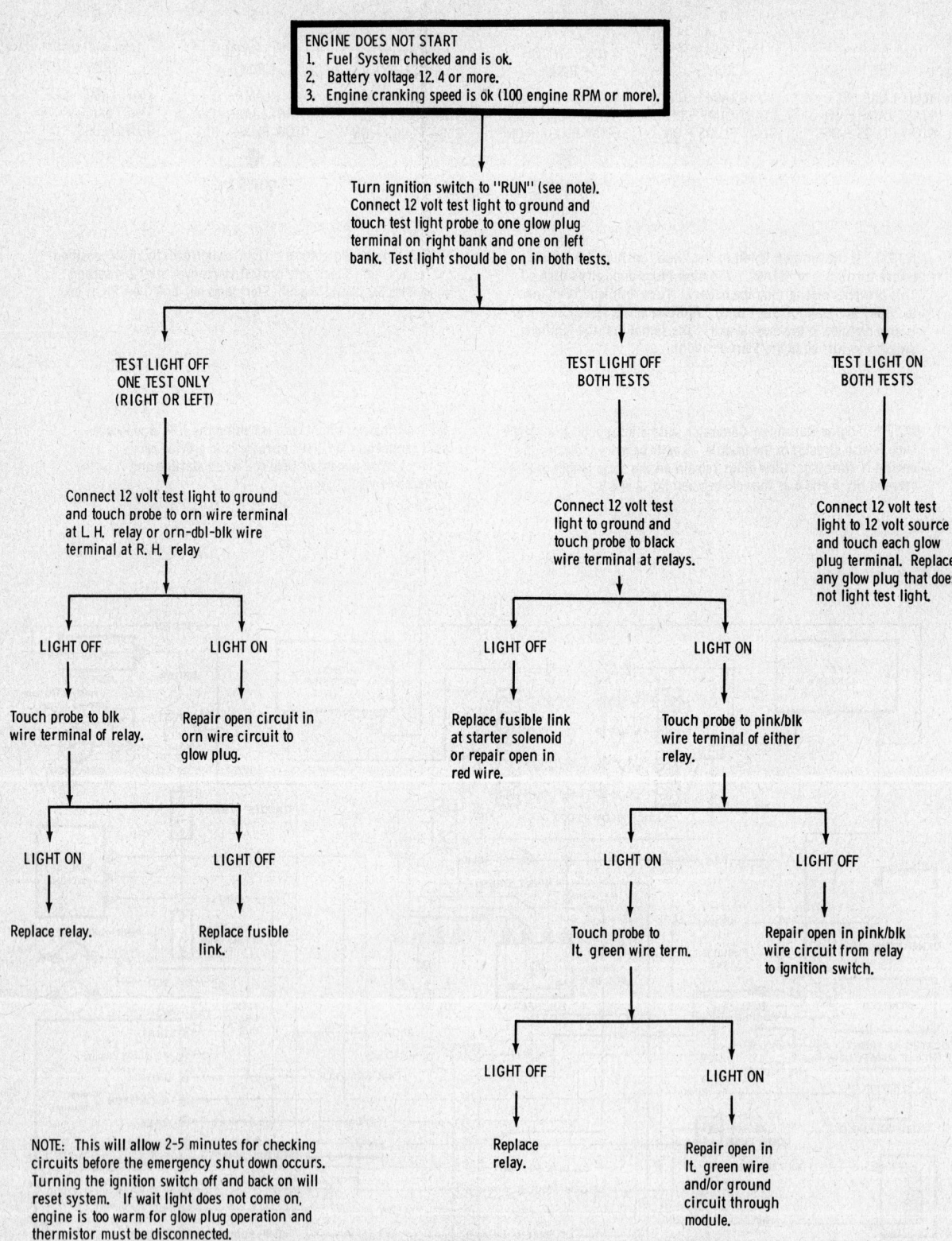

ENGINE DOES NOT START
1. Fuel System checked and is ok.
2. Battery voltage 12. 4 or more.
3. Engine cranking speed is ok (100 engine RPM or more).

Turn ignition switch to "RUN" (see note).
Connect 12 volt test light to ground and
touch test light probe to one glow plug
terminal on right bank and one on left
bank. Test light should be on in both tests.

TEST LIGHT OFF
ONE TEST ONLY
(RIGHT OR LEFT)

TEST LIGHT OFF
BOTH TESTS

TEST LIGHT ON
BOTH TESTS

Connect 12 volt test light to ground
and touch probe to orn wire terminal
at L. H. relay or orn-dbl-blk wire
terminal at R. H. relay

Connect 12 volt test
light to ground and
touch probe to black
wire terminal at relays.

Connect 12 volt test
light to 12 volt source
and touch each glow
plug terminal. Replace
any glow plug that does
not light test light.

LIGHT OFF

LIGHT ON

LIGHT OFF

LIGHT ON

Touch probe to blk
wire terminal of relay.

Repair open circuit in
orn wire circuit to
glow plug.

Replace fusible link
at starter solenoid
or repair open in
red wire.

Touch probe to pink/blk
wire terminal of either
relay.

LIGHT ON

LIGHT OFF

LIGHT ON

LIGHT OFF

Replace relay.

Replace fusible
link.

Touch probe to
lt. green wire term.

Repair open in pink/blk
wire circuit from relay
to ignition switch.

LIGHT OFF

LIGHT ON

Replace
relay.

Repair open in
lt. green wire
and/or ground
circuit through
module.

NOTE: This will allow 2-5 minutes for checking
circuits before the emergency shut down occurs.
Turning the ignition switch off and back on will
reset system. If wait light does not come on,
engine is too warm for glow plug operation and
thermistor must be disconnected.

Fig. 5   Diesel engine electrical diagnosis, part 1 of 5. 1978 type 1

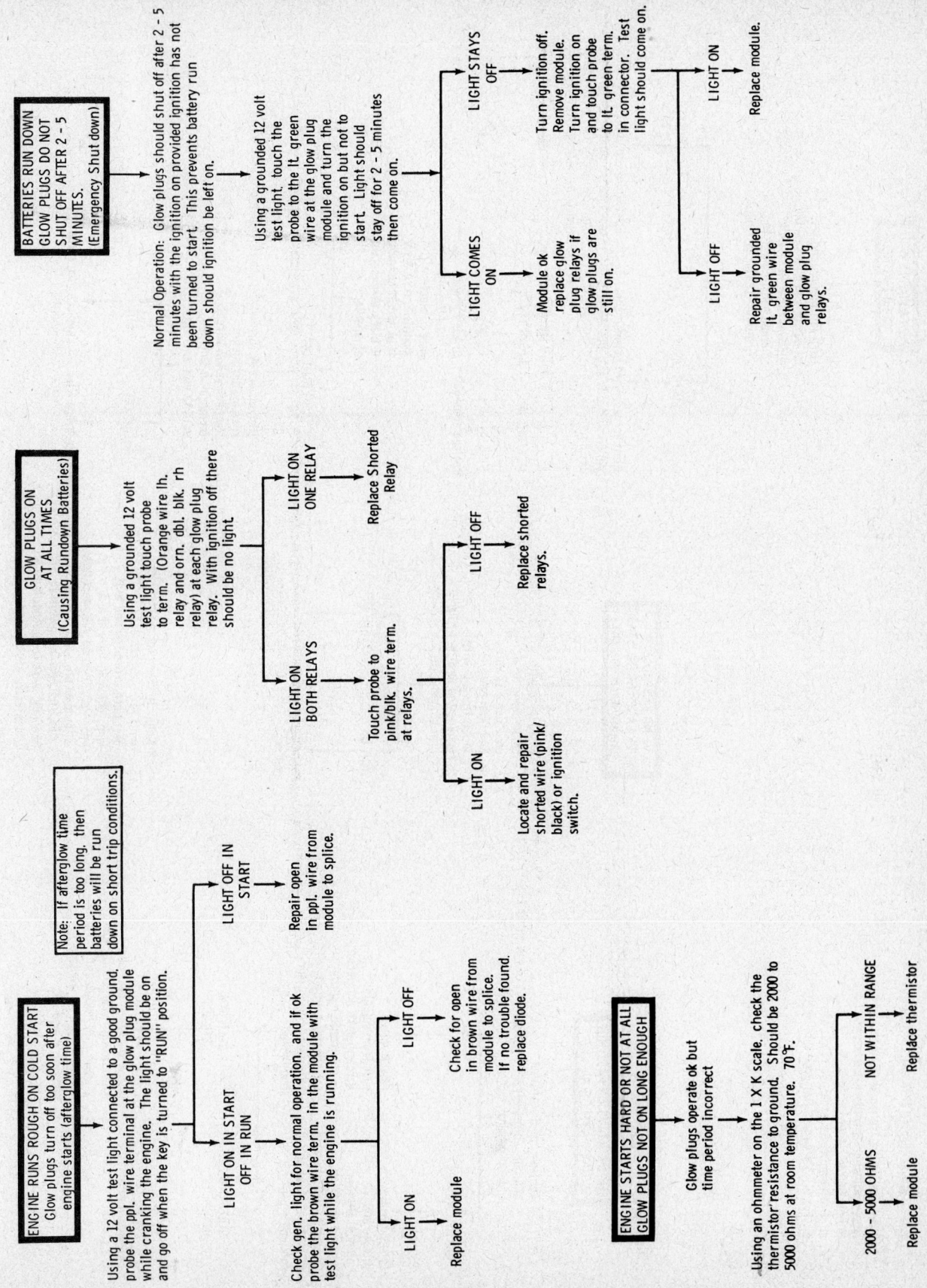

BATTERIES RUN DOWN GLOW PLUGS DO NOT SHUT OFF AFTER 2 - 5 MINUTES. (Emergency Shut down)

Normal Operation: Glow plugs should shut off after 2 - 5 minutes with the ignition on provided ignition has not been turned to start. This prevents battery run down should ignition be left on.

Using a grounded 12 volt test light, touch the probe to the lt. green wire at the glow plug module and turn the ignition on but not to start. Light should stay off for 2 - 5 minutes then come on.

LIGHT STAYS OFF → Turn ignition off. Remove module. Turn ignition on and touch probe to lt. green term. in connector. Test light should come on.

LIGHT ON → Replace module.

LIGHT OFF → Repair grounded lt. green wire between module and glow plug relays.

LIGHT COMES ON → Module ok replace glow plug relays if glow plugs are still on.

GLOW PLUGS ON AT ALL TIMES (Causing Rundown Batteries)

Using a grounded 12 volt test light touch probe to term. (Orange wire lh. relay and orn. dbl. blk. rh relay) at each glow plug relay. With ignition off there should be no light

LIGHT ON ONE RELAY → Replace Shorted Relay

LIGHT ON BOTH RELAYS → Touch probe to pink/blk. wire term. at relays.

LIGHT OFF → Replace shorted relays.

LIGHT ON → Locate and repair shorted wire (pink/black) or ignition switch.

Note: If afterglow time period is too long. then batteries will be run down on short trip conditions.

ENGINE RUNS ROUGH ON COLD START Glow plugs turn off too soon after engine starts (afterglow time)

Using a 12 volt test light connected to a good ground. probe the ppl. wire terminal at the glow plug module while cranking the engine. The light should be on and go off when the key is turned to "RUN" position.

LIGHT OFF IN START → Repair open in ppl. wire from module to splice.

LIGHT ON IN START OFF IN RUN → Check gen. light for normal operation. and if ok probe the brown wire term. in the module with test light while the engine is running.

LIGHT OFF → Check for open in brown wire from module to splice. If no trouble found. replace diode.

LIGHT ON → Replace module

ENGINE STARTS HARD OR NOT AT ALL GLOW PLUGS NOT ON LONG ENOUGH

Glow plugs operate ok but time period incorrect

Using an ohmmeter on the 1 X K scale. check the thermistor resistance to ground. Should be 2000 to 5000 ohms at room temperature. 70°F.

NOT WITHIN RANGE → Replace thermistor

2000 - 5000 OHMS → Replace module

Fig. 5A   Diesel engine electrical diagnosis, part 2 of 5. 1978 type 1

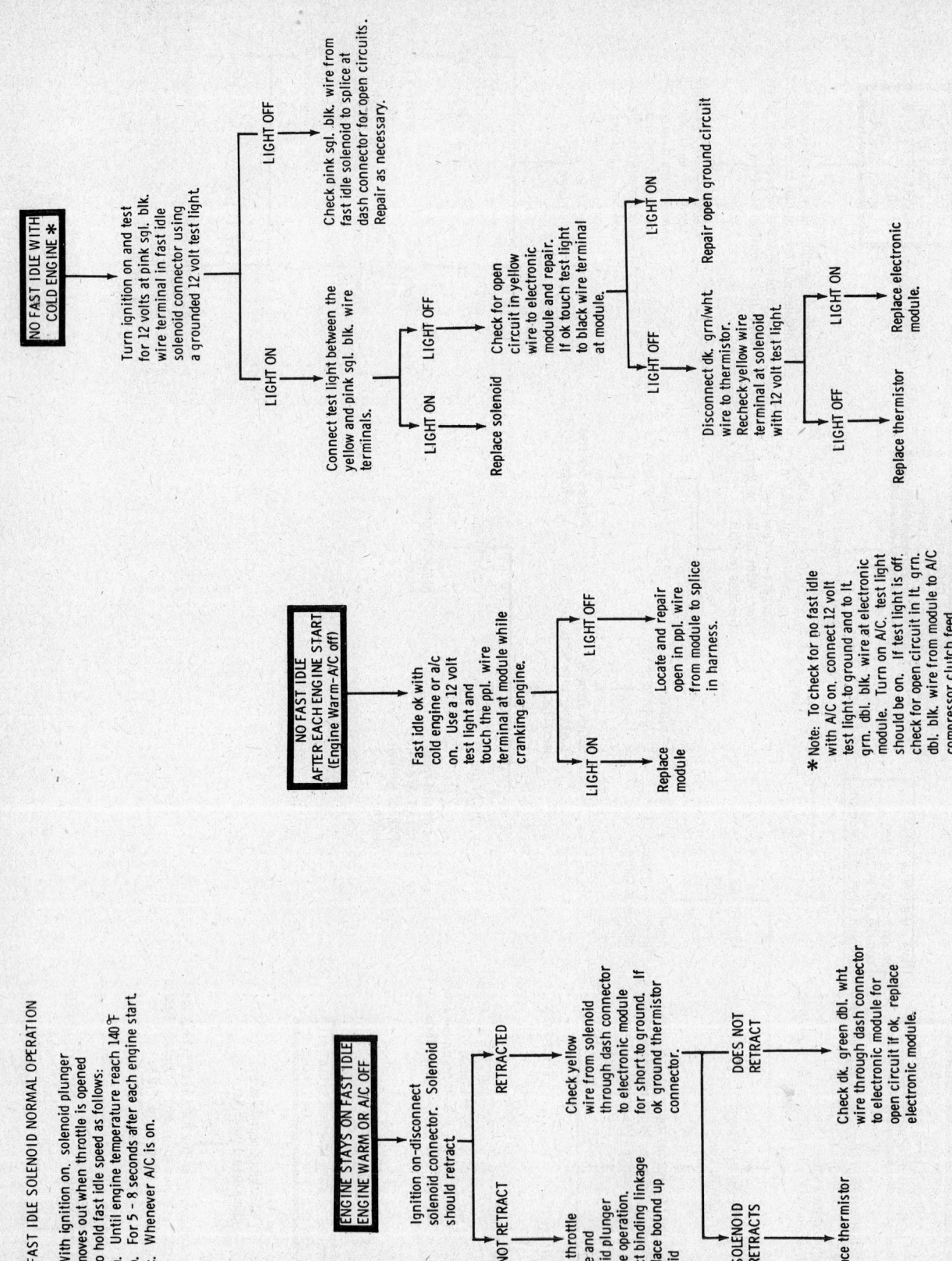

Fig. 5B   Diesel engine electrical diagnosis, part 3 of 5. 1978 type 1

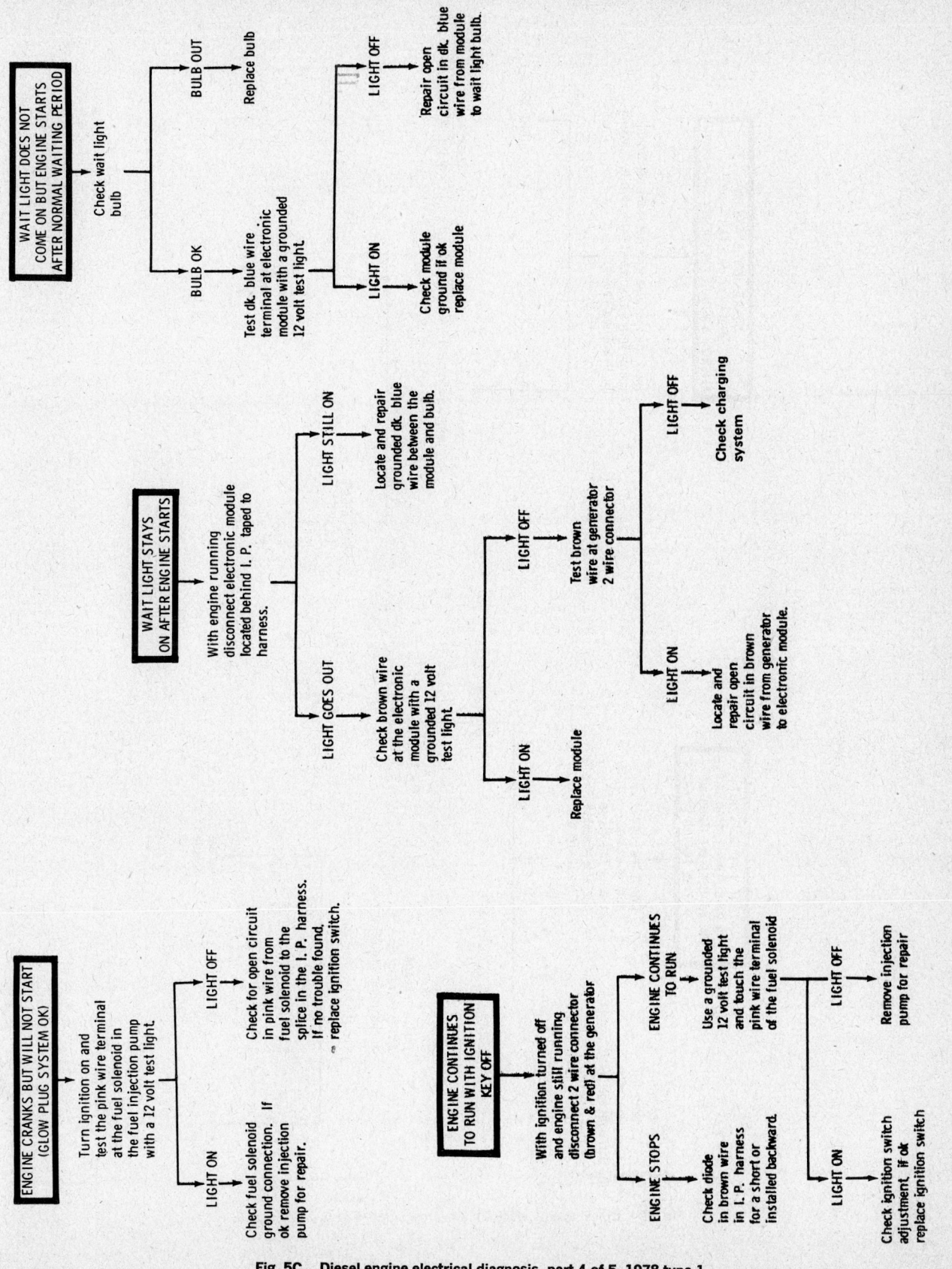

WAIT LIGHT DOES NOT COME ON BUT ENGINE STARTS AFTER NORMAL WAITING PERIOD

Check wait light bulb

- **BULB OUT** → Replace bulb
- **BULB OK** → Test dk. blue wire terminal at electronic module with a grounded 12 volt test light
  - **LIGHT OFF** → Repair open circuit in dk. blue wire from module to wait light bulb.
  - **LIGHT ON** → Check module ground if ok replace module

WAIT LIGHT STAYS ON AFTER ENGINE STARTS

With engine running disconnect electronic module located behind I. P. taped to harness.

- **LIGHT STILL ON** → Locate and repair grounded dk. blue wire between the module and bulb.
- **LIGHT GOES OUT** → Check brown wire at the electronic module with a grounded 12 volt test light
  - **LIGHT ON** → Replace module
  - **LIGHT OFF** → Test brown wire at generator 2 wire connector
    - **LIGHT OFF** → Check charging system
    - **LIGHT ON** → Locate and repair open circuit in brown wire from generator to electronic module.

ENGINE CRANKS BUT WILL NOT START (GLOW PLUG SYSTEM OK)

Turn ignition on and test the pink wire terminal at the fuel solenoid in the fuel injection pump with a 12 volt test light.

- **LIGHT OFF** → Check for open circuit in pink wire from fuel solenoid to the splice in the I. P. harness. If no trouble found, replace ignition switch.
- **LIGHT ON** → Check fuel solenoid ground connection. If ok remove injection pump for repair.

ENGINE CONTINUES TO RUN WITH IGNITION KEY OFF

With ignition turned off and engine still running disconnect 2 wire connector (brown & red) at the generator

- **ENGINE CONTINUES TO RUN** → Use a grounded 12 volt test light and touch the pink wire terminal of the fuel solenoid
  - **LIGHT OFF** → Remove injection pump for repair
  - **LIGHT ON** → Check ignition switch adjustment. if ok replace ignition switch
- **ENGINE STOPS** → Check diode in brown wire in I.P. harness for a short or installed backward

Fig. 5C   Diesel engine electrical diagnosis, part 4 of 5. 1978 type 1

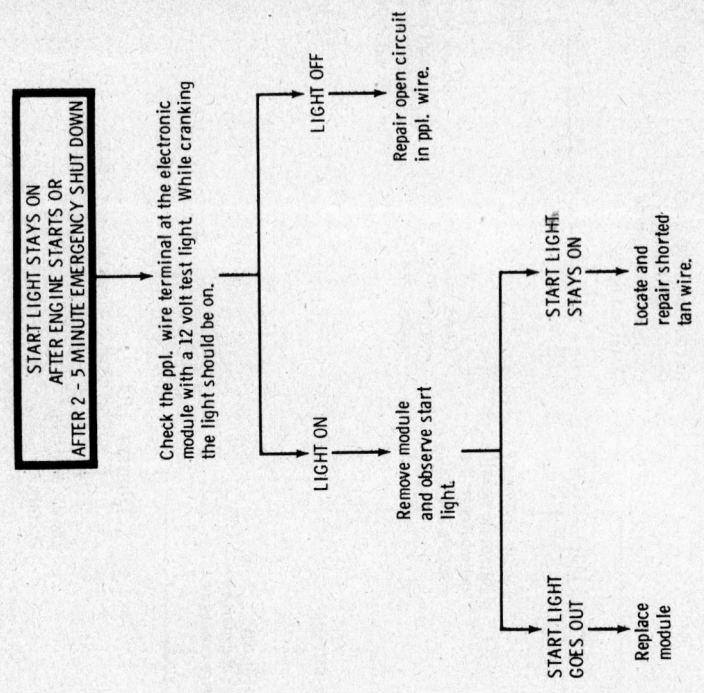

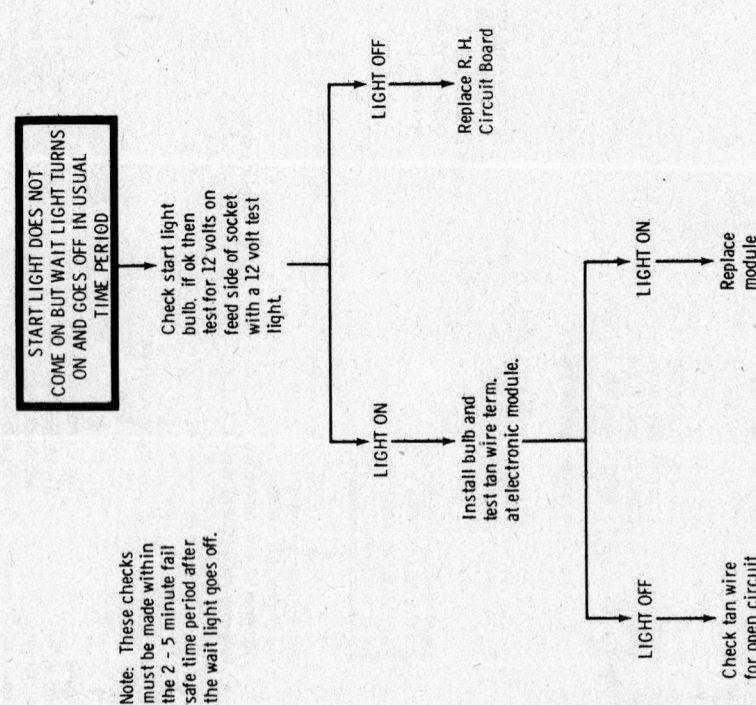

Fig. 5D Diesel engine electrical diagnosis, part 5 of 5. 1978 type 1

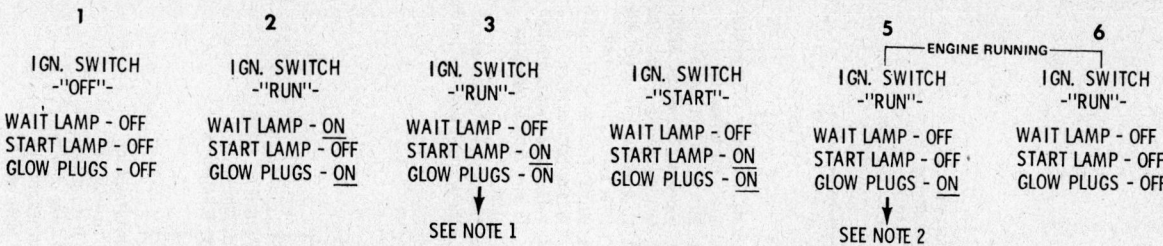

1	2	3		5	6
				ENGINE RUNNING	
IGN. SWITCH -"OFF"-	IGN. SWITCH -"RUN"-	IGN. SWITCH -"RUN"-	IGN. SWITCH -"START"-	IGN. SWITCH -"RUN"-	IGN. SWITCH -"RUN"-
WAIT LAMP - OFF	WAIT LAMP - ON	WAIT LAMP - OFF	WAIT LAMP - OFF	WAIT LAMP - OFF	WAIT LAMP - OFF
START LAMP - OFF	START LAMP - OFF	START LAMP - ON	START LAMP - ON	START LAMP - OFF	START LAMP - OFF
GLOW PLUGS - OFF	GLOW PLUGS - ON	GLOW PLUGS - ON	GLOW PLUGS - ON	GLOW PLUGS - ON	GLOW PLUGS - OFF
		SEE NOTE 1		SEE NOTE 2	

NOTE 1: If the ignition is left in the "Run" position without starting the engine, the glow plugs will continue to pulse on/off until batteries run down. (About 4 hours when coolant switch is open.)

NOTE 3: Do not manually energize or by-pass the glow plug relay as glow plugs will be damaged instantly.

NOTE 2: Glow plugs will pulse on/off for about 30 seconds after engine starts. Then turn off and remain off as long as engine temperature is above about 120° F (49° C).

NOTE 4: Diodes prevent glow plug operation when the engine is warm (above 120°) the engine is not running and key is in RUN.

IMPORTANT: Do Not use more than a 2–3 candle power test light when making circuit checks.

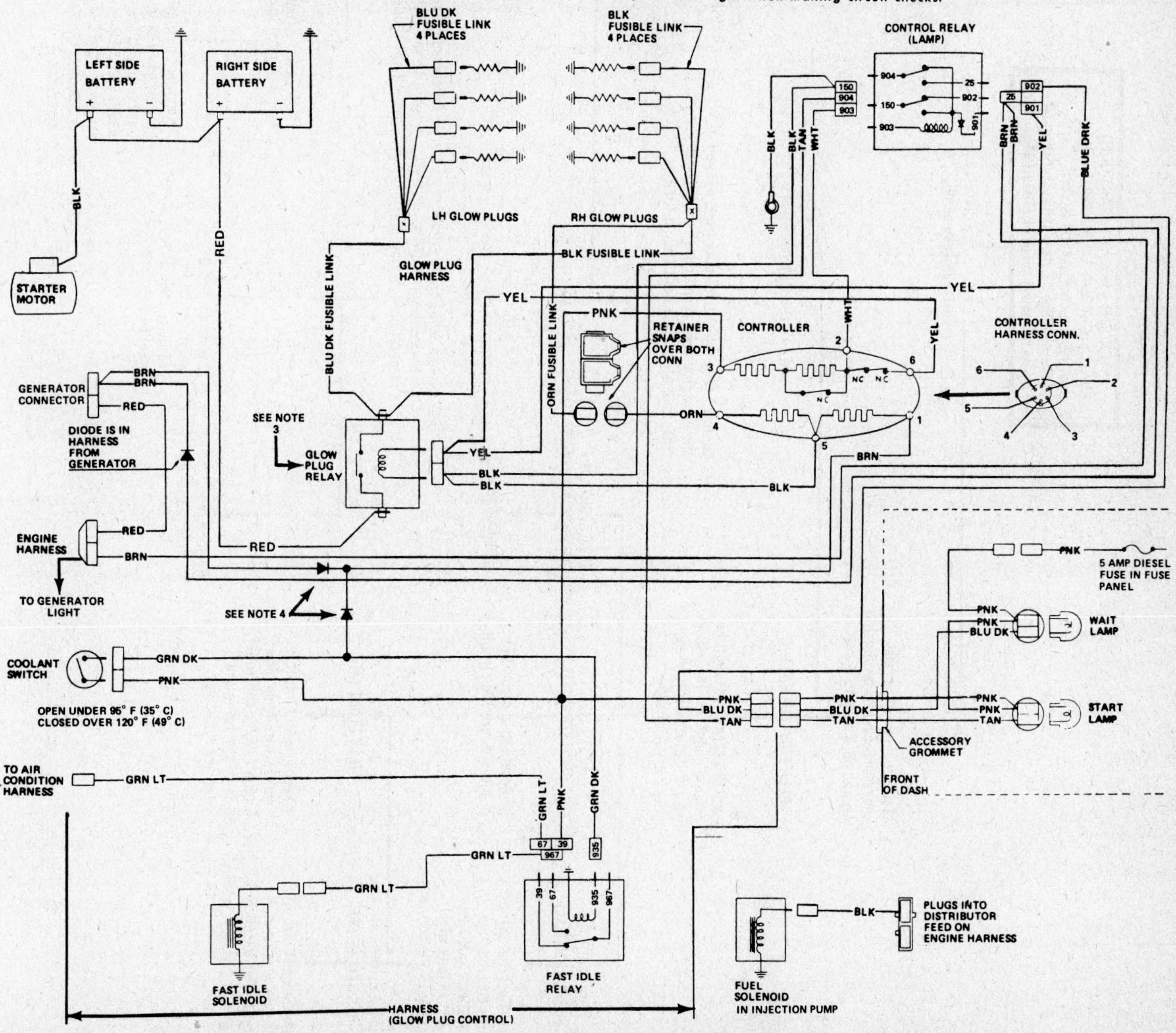

Fig. 6   Diesel engine electrical system. 1978 type 2

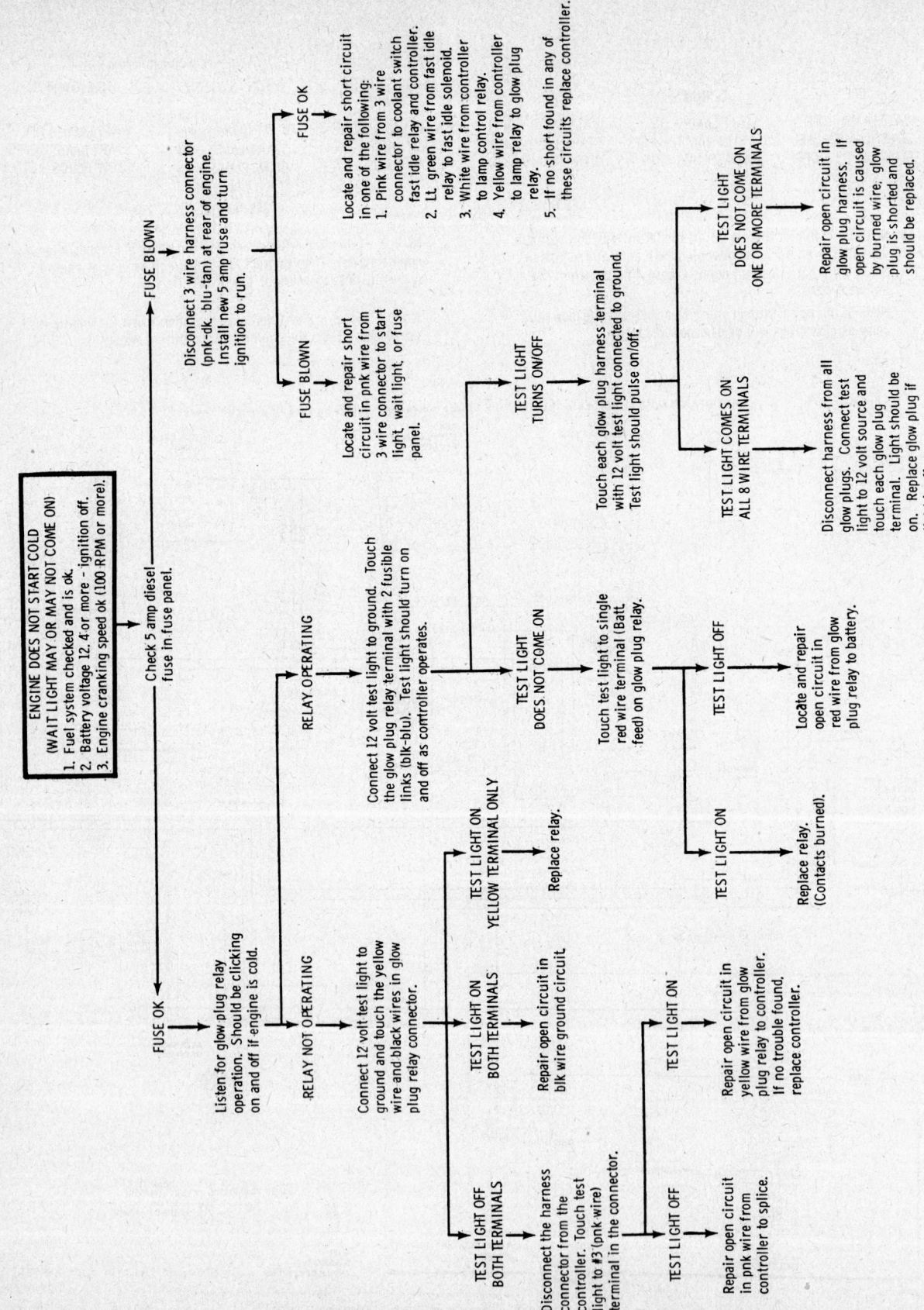

ENGINE DOES NOT START COLD
(WAIT LIGHT MAY OR MAY NOT COME ON)
1. Fuel system checked and is ok.
2. Battery voltage 12.4 or more - ignition off.
3. Engine cranking speed ok (100 RPM or more).

Check 5 amp diesel fuse in fuse panel.

FUSE OK

Listen for glow plug relay operation. Should be clicking on and off if engine is cold.

RELAY NOT OPERATING

Connect 12 volt test light to ground and touch the yellow wire and black wires in glow plug relay connector.

TEST LIGHT ON BOTH TERMINALS

Repair open circuit in blk wire ground circuit.

TEST LIGHT OFF BOTH TERMINALS

Disconnect the harness connector from the controller. Touch test light to #3 (pnk wire) terminal in the connector.

TEST LIGHT ON

Repair open circuit in yellow wire from glow plug relay to controller. If no trouble found, replace controller.

TEST LIGHT OFF

Repair open circuit in pnk wire from controller to splice.

TEST LIGHT ON YELLOW TERMINAL ONLY

Replace relay.

RELAY OPERATING

Connect 12 volt test light to ground. Touch the glow plug relay terminal with 2 fusible links (blk-blu). Test light should turn on and off as controller operates.

TEST LIGHT DOES NOT COME ON

Touch test light to single red wire terminal (Batt feed) on glow plug relay.

TEST LIGHT OFF

Locate and repair open circuit in red wire from glow plug relay to battery.

TEST LIGHT ON

Replace relay. (Contacts burned).

FUSE BLOWN

Disconnect 3 wire harness connector (pnk-dk. blu-tan) at rear of engine. Install new 5 amp fuse and turn ignition to run.

FUSE OK

Locate and repair short circuit in one of the following:
1. Pink wire from 3 wire connector to coolant switch fast idle relay and controller.
2. Lt. green wire from fast idle relay to fast idle solenoid.
3. White wire from controller to lamp control relay.
4. Yellow wire from controller to lamp relay to glow plug relay.
5. If no short found in any of these circuits replace controller.

FUSE BLOWN

Locate and repair short circuit in pnk wire from 3 wire connector to start light, wait light, or fuse panel.

TEST LIGHT TURNS ON/OFF

Touch each glow plug harness terminal with 12 volt test light connected to ground. Test light should pulse on/off.

TEST LIGHT DOES NOT COME ON ONE OR MORE TERMINALS

Repair open circuit in glow plug circuit. If open circuit is caused by burned wire, glow plug is shorted and should be replaced.

TEST LIGHT COMES ON ALL 8 WIRE TERMINALS

Disconnect harness from all glow plugs. Connect test light to 12 volt source and touch each glow plug terminal. Light should be on. Replace glow plug if light is off.

Fig. 7 Diesel engine electrical diagnosis, part 1 of 4. 1978 type 2

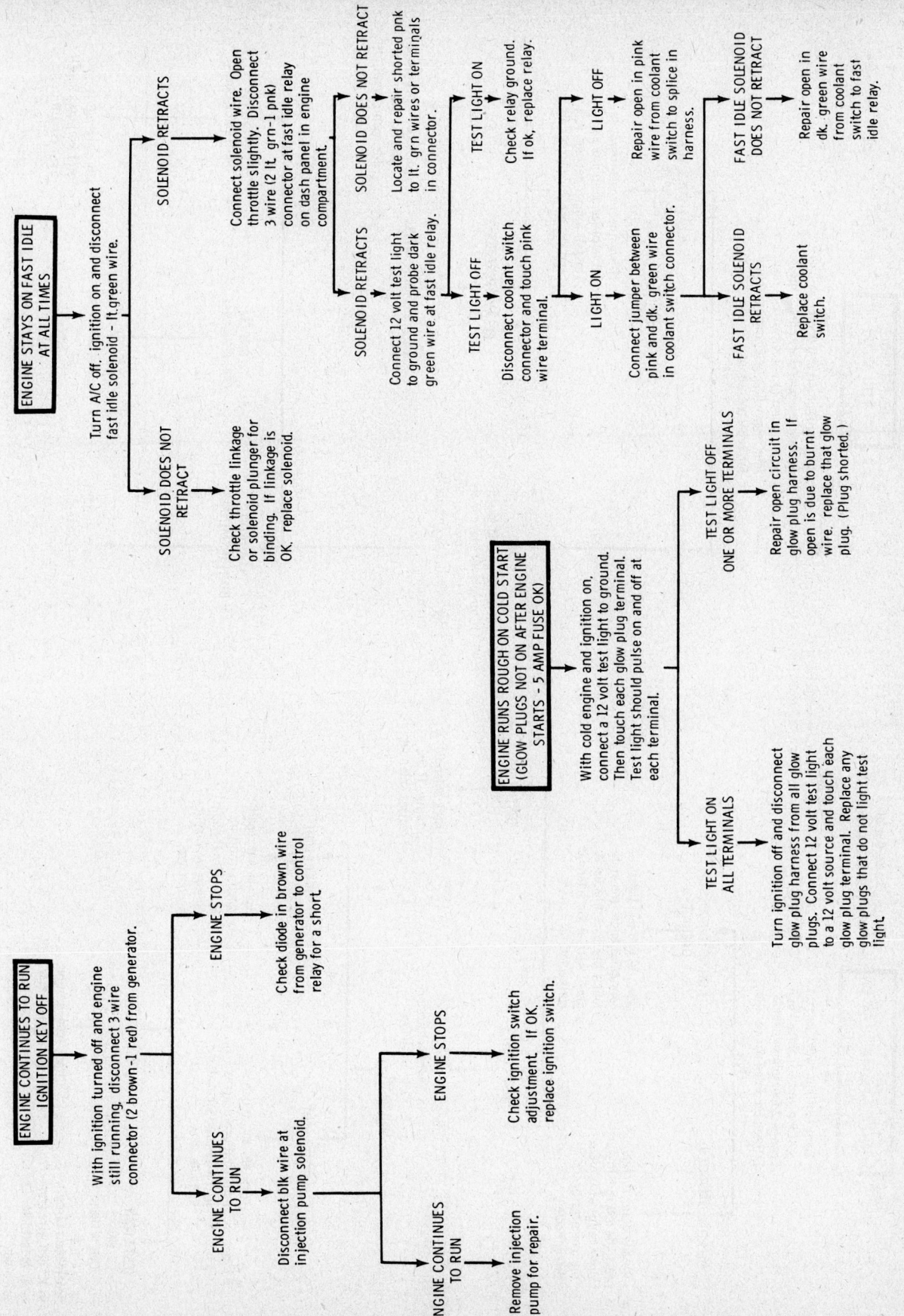

ENGINE STAYS ON FAST IDLE AT ALL TIMES

Turn A/C off, ignition on and disconnect fast idle solenoid - lt.green wire.

SOLENOID RETRACTS

Connect solenoid wire. Open throttle slightly. Disconnect 3 wire (2 lt. grn-1 pnk) connector at fast idle relay on dash panel in engine compartment.

SOLENOID DOES NOT RETRACT

Locate and repair shorted pnk to lt. grn wires or terminals in connector.

SOLENOID RETRACTS

Connect 12 volt test light to ground and probe dark green wire at fast idle relay.

TEST LIGHT ON

Check relay ground. If ok, replace relay.

LIGHT OFF

Repair open in pink wire from coolant switch to splice in harness.

FAST IDLE SOLENOID DOES NOT RETRACT

Repair open in dk. green wire from coolant switch to fast idle relay.

TEST LIGHT OFF

Disconnect coolant switch connector and touch pink wire terminal.

LIGHT ON

Connect jumper between pink and dk. green wire in coolant switch connector.

FAST IDLE SOLENOID RETRACTS

Replace coolant switch.

SOLENOID DOES NOT RETRACT

Check throttle linkage or solenoid plunger for binding. If linkage is OK, replace solenoid.

ENGINE RUNS ROUGH ON COLD START
(GLOW PLUGS NOT ON AFTER ENGINE STARTS - 5 AMP FUSE OK)

With cold engine and ignition on, connect a 12 volt test light to ground. Then touch each glow plug terminal. Test light should pulse on and off at each terminal.

TEST LIGHT OFF ONE OR MORE TERMINALS

Repair open circuit in glow plug harness. If open is due to burnt wire, replace that glow plug. (Plug shorted.)

TEST LIGHT ON ALL TERMINALS

Turn ignition off and disconnect glow plug harness from all glow plugs. Connect 12 volt test light to a 12 volt source and touch each glow plug terminal. Replace any glow plugs that do not light test light.

ENGINE CONTINUES TO RUN IGNITION KEY OFF

With ignition turned off and engine still running, disconnect 3 wire connector (2 brown-1 red) from generator.

ENGINE STOPS

Check diode in brown wire from generator to control relay for a short.

ENGINE CONTINUES TO RUN

Disconnect blk wire at injection pump solenoid.

ENGINE STOPS

Check ignition switch adjustment. If OK, replace ignition switch.

ENGINE CONTINUES TO RUN

Remove injection pump for repair.

Fig. 7A   Diesel engine electrical diagnosis, part 2 of 4. 1978 type 2

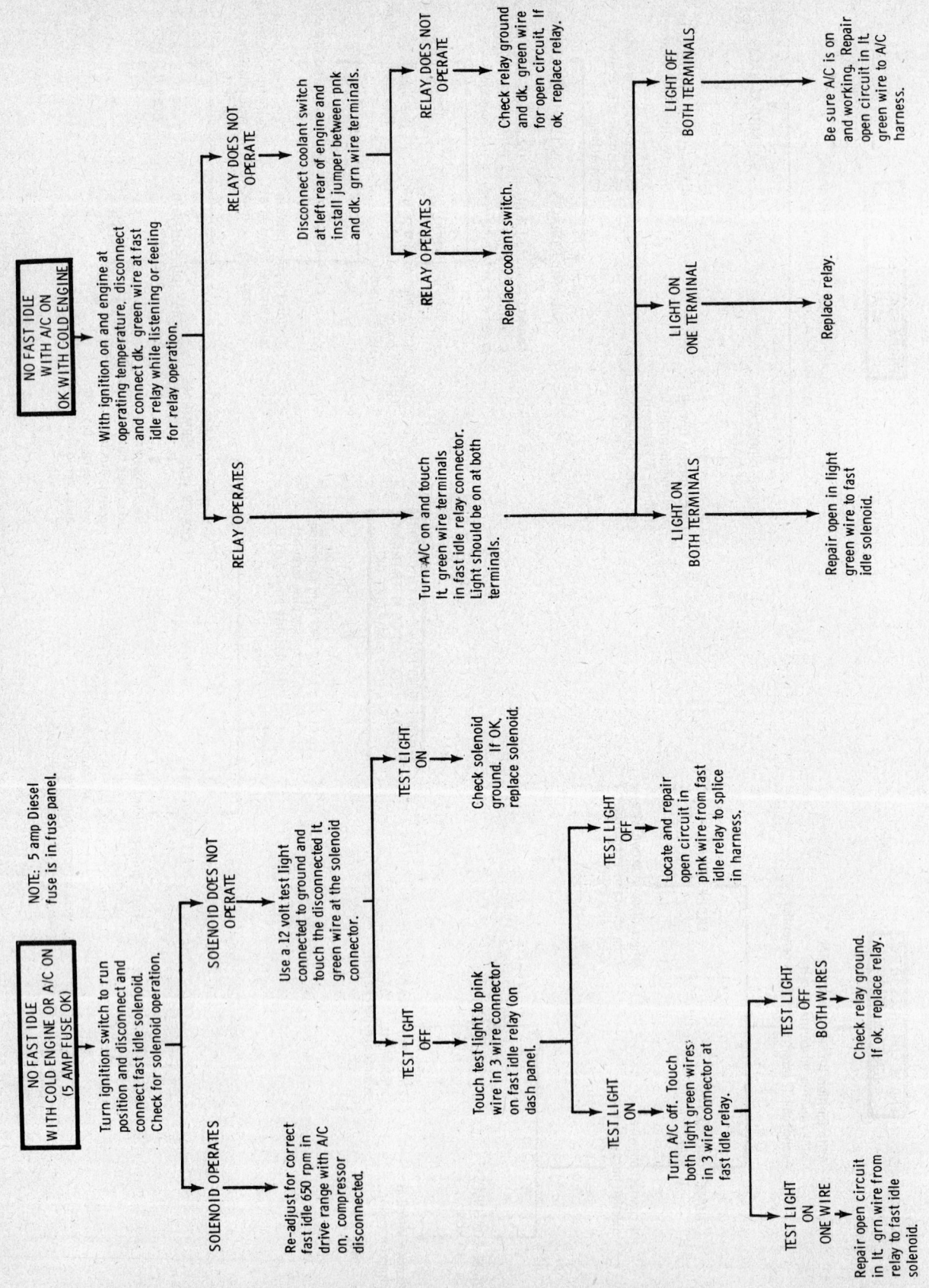

NO FAST IDLE WITH A/C ON OK WITH COLD ENGINE

With ignition on and engine at operating temperature, disconnect and connect dk. green wire at fast idle relay while listening or feeling for relay operation.

RELAY DOES NOT OPERATE

Disconnect coolant switch at left rear of engine and install jumper between pnk and dk. grn wire terminals.

RELAY DOES NOT OPERATE

Check relay ground and dk. green wire for open circuit. If ok, replace relay.

RELAY OPERATES

Replace coolant switch.

RELAY OPERATES

Turn A/C on and touch lt. green wire terminals in fast idle relay connector. Light should be on at both terminals.

LIGHT OFF BOTH TERMINALS

Be sure A/C is on and working. Repair open circuit in lt green wire to A/C harness.

LIGHT ON ONE TERMINAL

Replace relay.

LIGHT ON BOTH TERMINALS

Repair open in light green wire to fast idle solenoid.

NOTE: 5 amp Diesel fuse is in fuse panel.

NO FAST IDLE WITH COLD ENGINE OR A/C ON (5 AMP FUSE OK)

Turn ignition switch to run position and disconnect and connect fast idle solenoid. Check for solenoid operation.

SOLENOID DOES NOT OPERATE

Use a 12 volt test light connected to ground and touch the disconnected lt green wire at the solenoid connector.

TEST LIGHT ON

Check solenoid ground. If ok, replace solenoid.

TEST LIGHT OFF

Touch test light to pink wire in 3 wire connector on fast idle relay (on dash panel.

TEST LIGHT OFF

Locate and repair open circuit in pink wire from fast idle relay to splice in harness.

TEST LIGHT ON

Turn A/C off. Touch both light green wires in 3 wire connector at fast idle relay.

TEST LIGHT OFF BOTH WIRES

Check relay ground. If ok, replace relay.

TEST LIGHT ON ONE WIRE

Repair open circuit in lt. grn wire from relay to fast idle solenoid.

SOLENOID OPERATES

Re-adjust for correct fast idle 650 rpm in drive range with A/C on, compressor disconnected.

Fig. 7B   Diesel engine electrical diagnosis, part 3 of 4. 1978 type 2

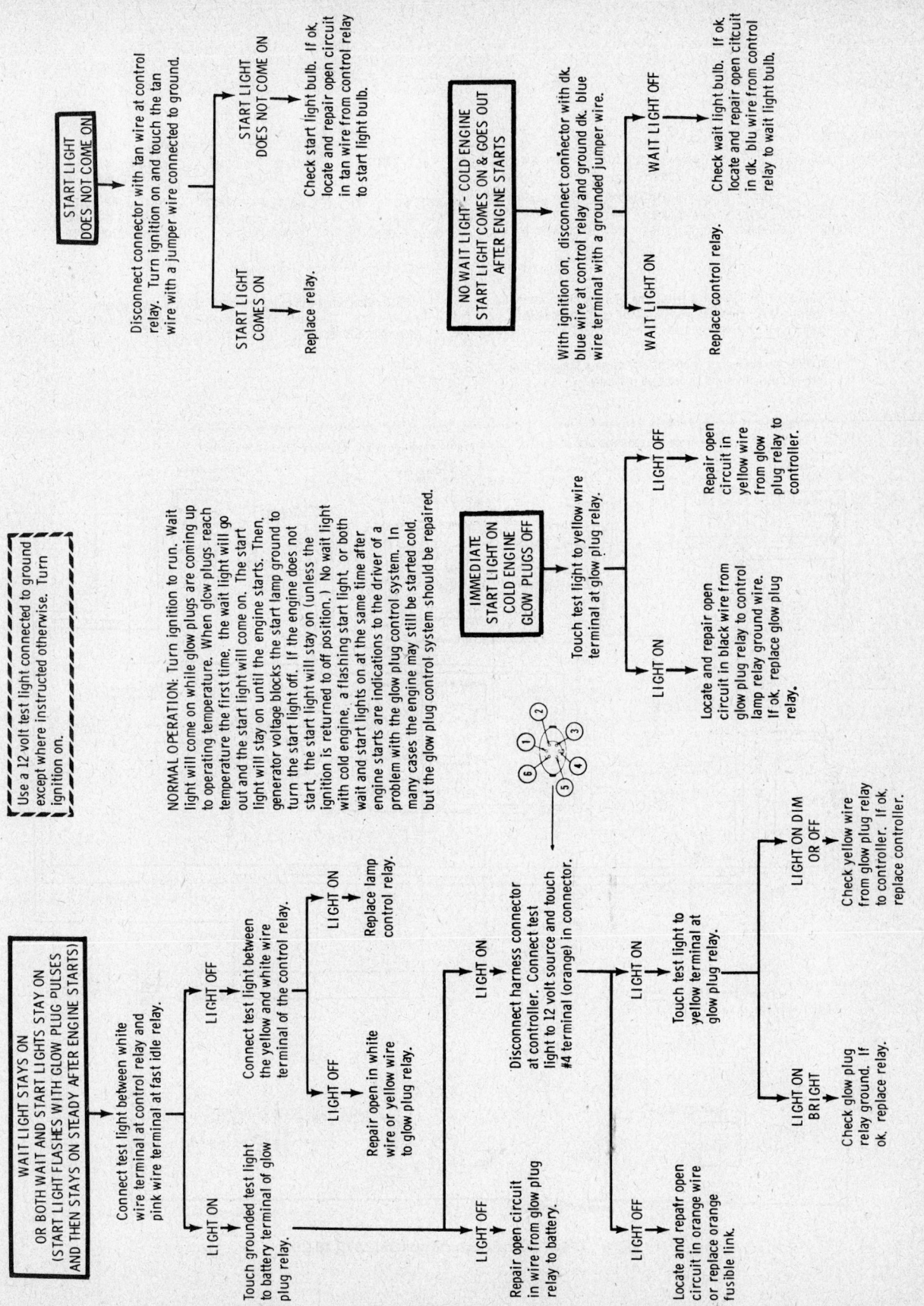

START LIGHT DOES NOT COME ON

Disconnect connector with tan wire at control relay. Turn ignition on and touch the tan wire with a jumper wire connected to ground.

START LIGHT DOES NOT COME ON

Check start light bulb. If ok, locate and repair open circuit in tan wire from control relay to start light bulb.

START LIGHT COMES ON

Replace relay.

NO WAIT LIGHT – COLD ENGINE START LIGHT COMES ON & GOES OUT AFTER ENGINE STARTS

With ignition on, disconnect connector with dk. blue wire at control relay and ground dk. blue wire terminal with a grounded jumper wire.

WAIT LIGHT OFF

Check wait light bulb. If ok, locate and repair open circuit in dk. blu wire from control relay to wait light bulb.

WAIT LIGHT ON

Replace control relay.

Use a 12 volt test light connected to ground except where instructed otherwise. Turn ignition on.

NORMAL OPERATION: Turn ignition to run. Wait light will come on while glow plugs are coming up to operating temperature. When glow plugs reach temperature the first time, the wait light will go out and the start light will come on. The start light will stay on until the engine starts. Then, generator voltage blocks the start lamp ground to turn the start light off. If the engine does not start, the start light will stay on (unless the ignition is returned to off position.) No wait light with cold engine, a flashing start light, or both wait and start lights on at the same time after engine starts are indications to the driver of a problem with the glow plug control system. In many cases the engine may still be started cold, but the glow plug control system should be repaired.

IMMEDIATE START LIGHT ON COLD ENGINE GLOW PLUGS OFF

Touch test light to yellow wire terminal at glow plug relay.

LIGHT OFF

Repair open circuit in yellow wire from glow plug relay to controller.

LIGHT ON

Locate and repair open circuit in black wire from glow plug relay to control lamp relay ground wire. If ok, replace glow plug relay.

WAIT LIGHT STAYS ON OR BOTH WAIT AND START LIGHTS STAY ON (START LIGHT FLASHES WITH GLOW PLUG PULSES AND THEN STAYS ON STEADY AFTER ENGINE STARTS)

Connect test light between white wire terminal at control relay and pink wire terminal at fast idle relay.

LIGHT OFF

Connect test light between the yellow and white wire terminal of the control relay.

LIGHT ON

Replace lamp control relay.

LIGHT OFF

Repair open in white wire or yellow wire to glow plug relay.

LIGHT ON

Touch grounded test light to battery terminal of glow plug relay.

LIGHT OFF

Repair open circuit in wire from glow plug relay to battery.

Disconnect harness connector at controller. Connect test light to 12 volt source and touch #4 terminal (orange) in connector.

LIGHT ON

Touch test light to yellow terminal at glow plug relay.

LIGHT OFF

Locate and repair open circuit in orange wire or replace orange fusible link.

LIGHT ON DIM OR OFF

Check yellow wire from glow plug relay to controller. If ok, replace controller.

LIGHT ON BRIGHT

Check glow plug relay ground. If ok, replace relay.

Fig. 7C   Diesel engine electrical diagnosis, part 4 of 4. 1978 type 2

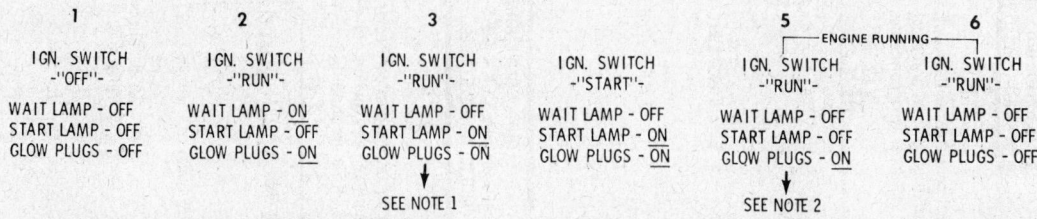

	1	2	3	5	6
	IGN. SWITCH -"OFF"-	IGN. SWITCH -"RUN"-	IGN. SWITCH -"RUN"-	IGN. SWITCH -"RUN"-	IGN. SWITCH -"RUN"-

ENGINE RUNNING (spanning columns 5 and 6)

IGN. SWITCH -"START"- (column 4)

WAIT LAMP - OFF   START LAMP - OFF   GLOW PLUGS - OFF

WAIT LAMP - ON   START LAMP - OFF   GLOW PLUGS - ON

WAIT LAMP - OFF   START LAMP - ON   GLOW PLUGS - ON

WAIT LAMP - OFF   START LAMP - ON   GLOW PLUGS - ON

WAIT LAMP - OFF   START LAMP - OFF   GLOW PLUGS - ON

WAIT LAMP - OFF   START LAMP - OFF   GLOW PLUGS - OFF

SEE NOTE 1

SEE NOTE 2

NOTE 1: If the ignition is left in the "Run" position without starting the engine, the glow plugs will continue to pulse on/off until batteries run down. (About 4 hours when coolant switch is open.)

NOTE 3: Do not manually energize or by-pass the glow plug relay as glow plugs will be damaged instantly.

NOTE 2: Glow plugs will pulse on/off for about 30 seconds after engine starts. Then turn off and remain off as long as engine temperature is above about 120° F (49° C).

IMPORTANT: Do Not use more than a 2–3 candle power test light when making circuit checks.

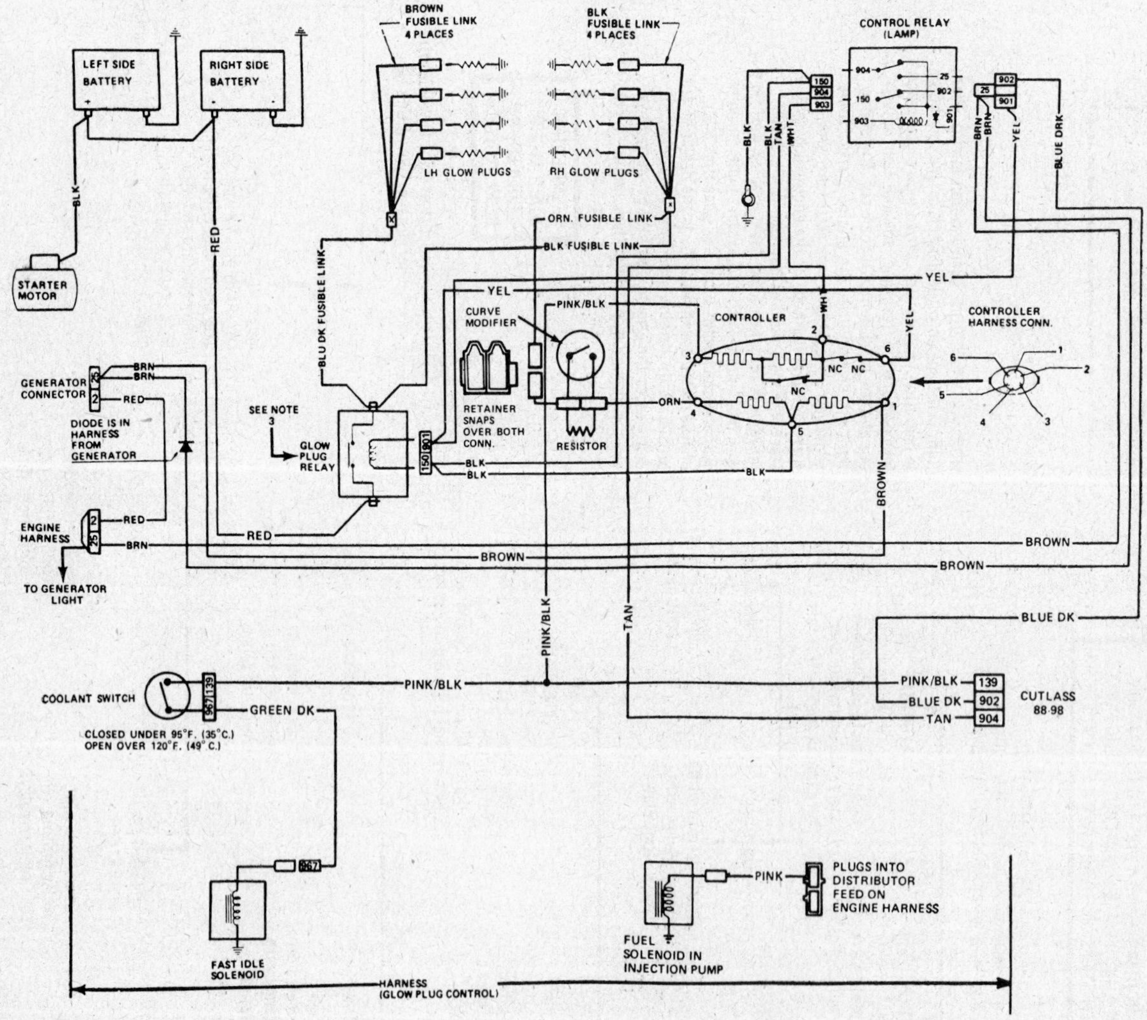

Fig. 8   Diesel engine electrical system. 1979 V8-260

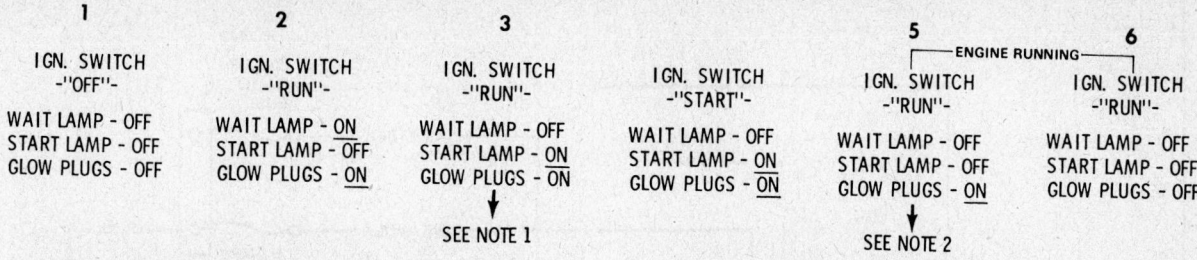

1	2	3		5	6
IGN. SWITCH -"OFF"-	IGN. SWITCH -"RUN"-	IGN. SWITCH -"RUN"-	IGN. SWITCH -"START"-	IGN. SWITCH -"RUN"-	IGN. SWITCH -"RUN"-
WAIT LAMP - OFF	WAIT LAMP - ON	WAIT LAMP - OFF	WAIT LAMP - OFF	WAIT LAMP - OFF	WAIT LAMP - OFF
START LAMP - OFF	START LAMP - OFF	START LAMP - ON	START LAMP - ON	START LAMP - OFF	START LAMP - OFF
GLOW PLUGS - OFF	GLOW PLUGS - ON	GLOW PLUGS - ON	GLOW PLUGS - ON	GLOW PLUGS - ON	GLOW PLUGS - OFF
		SEE NOTE 1		SEE NOTE 2	

— ENGINE RUNNING —

NOTE 1: If the ignition is left in the "Run" position without starting the engine, the glow plugs will continue to pulse on/off until batteries run down. (About 4 hours when coolant switch is open.)

NOTE 3: Do not manually energize or by-pass the glow plug relay as glow plugs will be damaged instantly.

NOTE 2: Glow plugs will pulse on/off for about 30 seconds after engine starts. Then turn off and remain off as long as engine temperature is above about 120° F (49° C).

NOTE 4: Diodes prevent glow plug operation when the engine is warm (above 120°) the engine is not running and key is in RUN.

IMPORTANT: Do Not use more than a 2—3 candle power test light when making circuit checks.

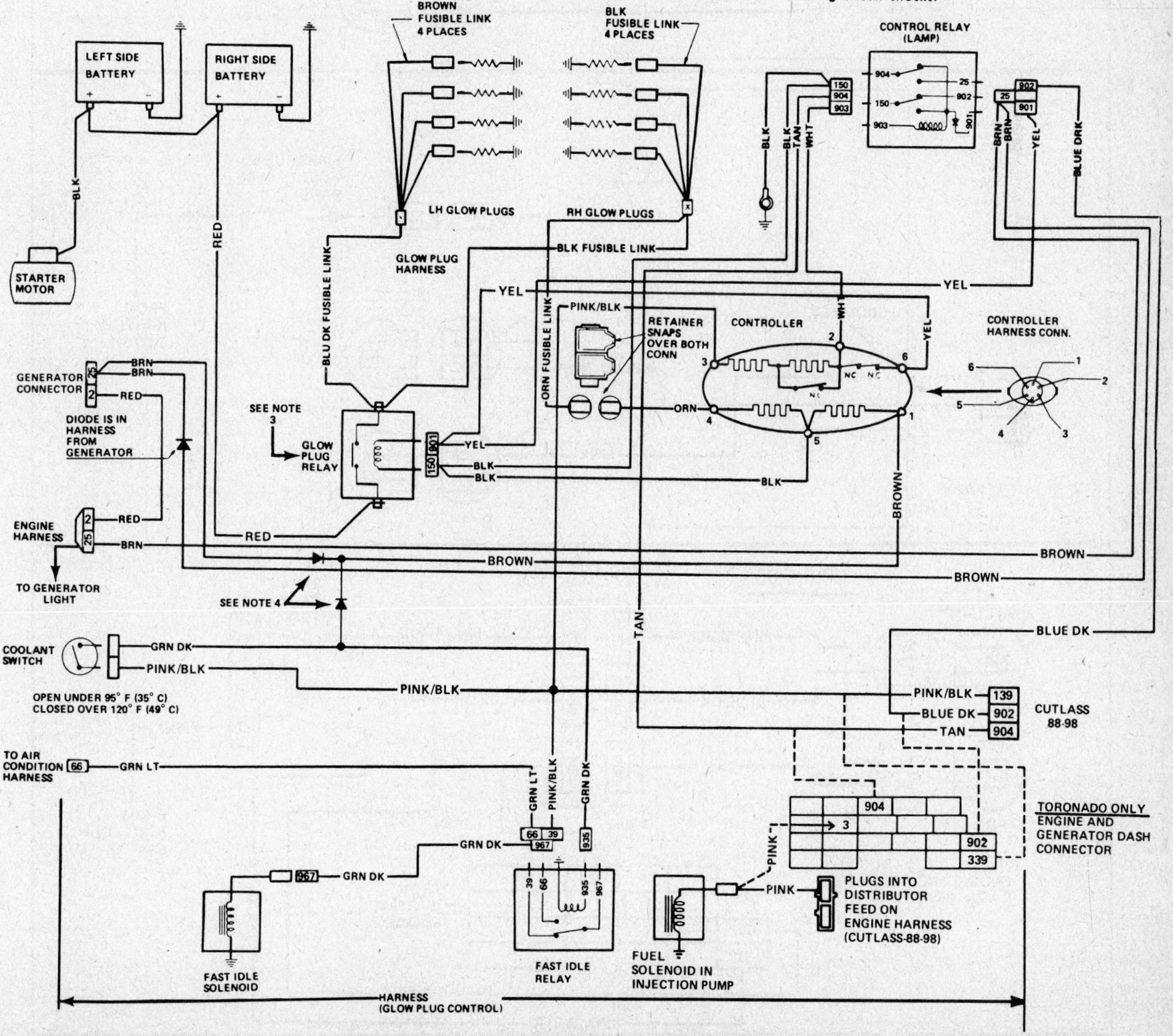

Fig. 9   Diesel engine electrical system, part 1 of 2. 1979 V8-350

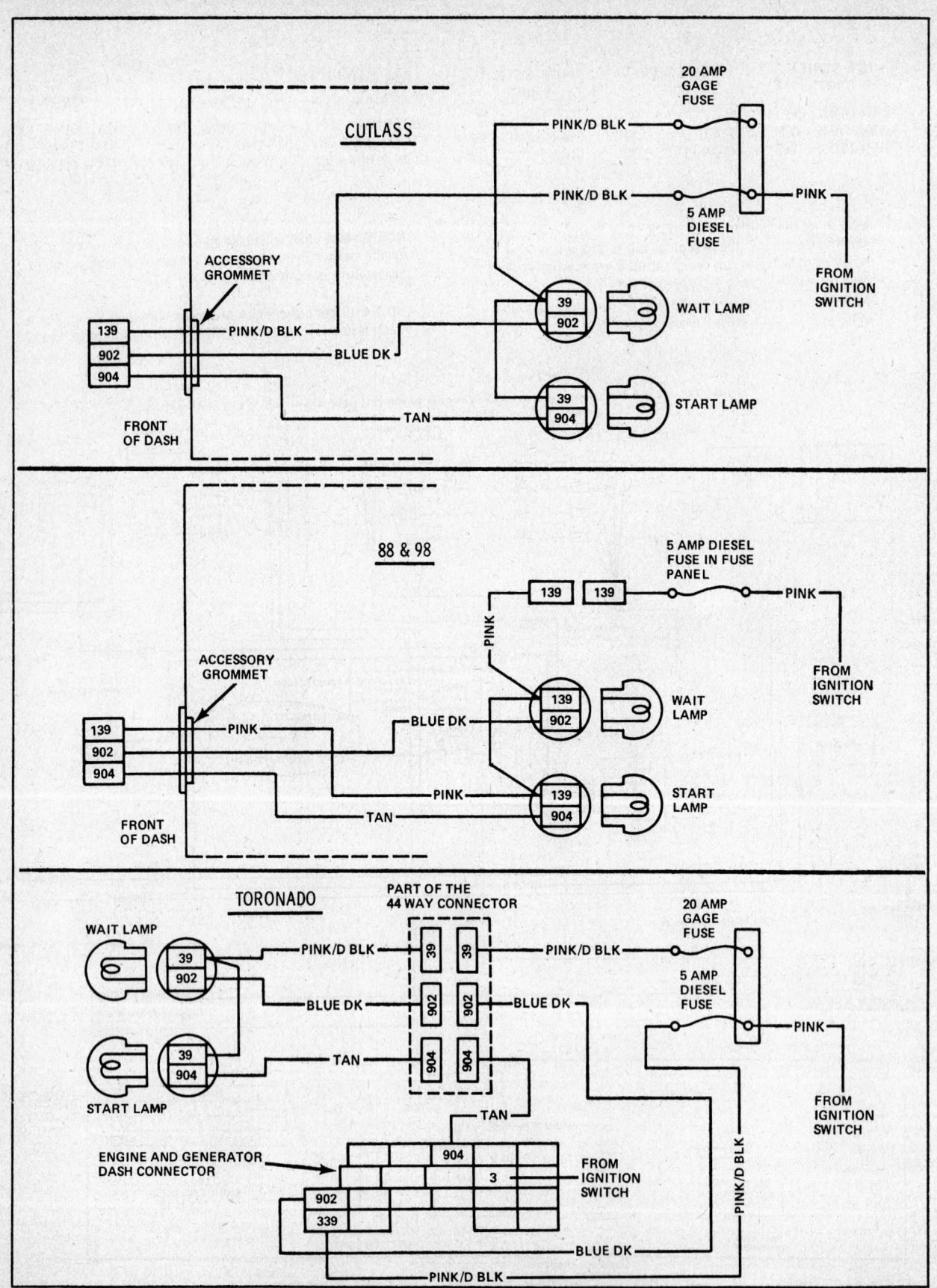

Fig. 9A   Diesel engine electrical system, part 2 of 2. 1979 V8-350

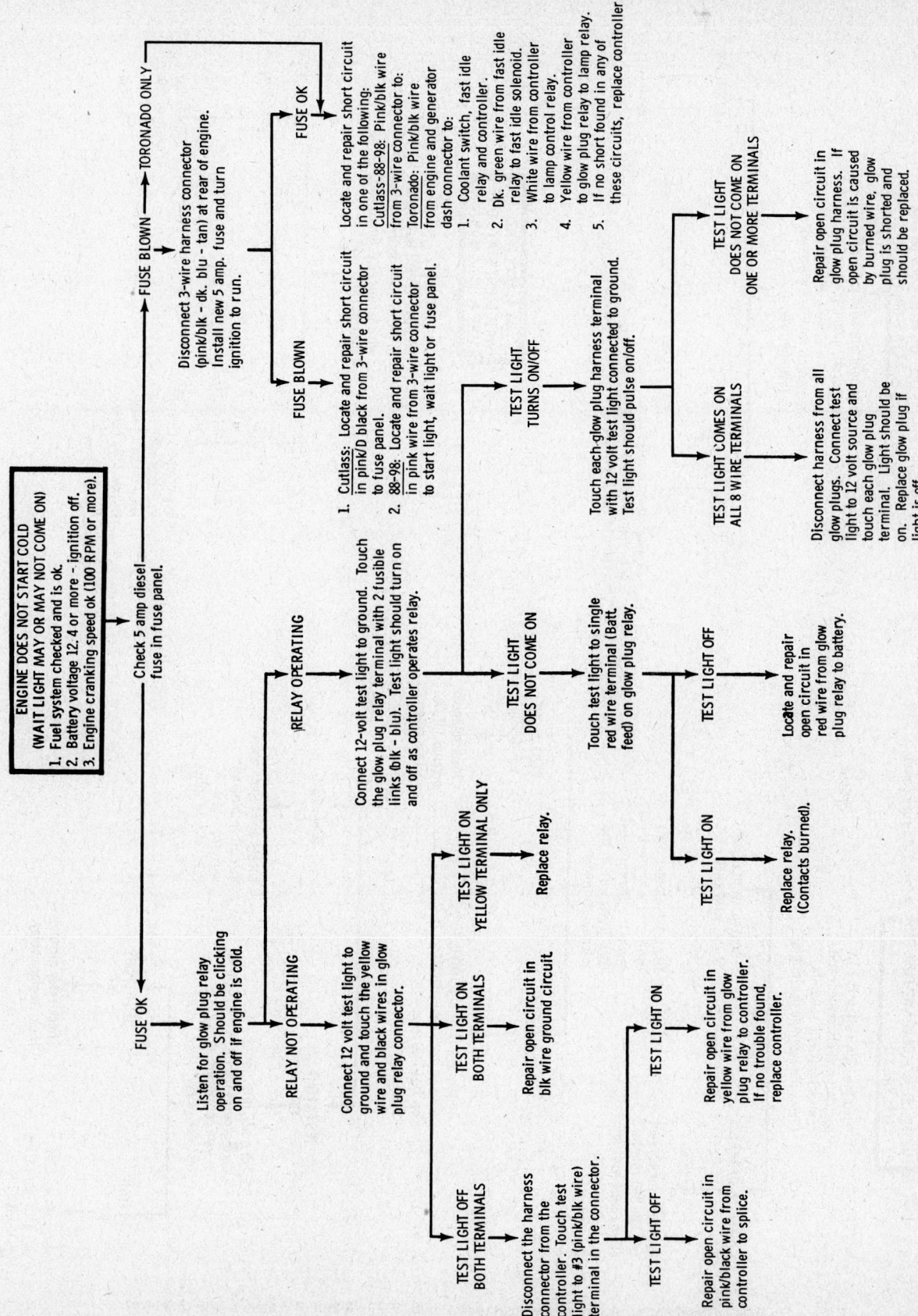

ENGINE DOES NOT START COLD
(WAIT LIGHT MAY OR MAY NOT COME ON)
1. Fuel system checked and is ok.
2. Battery voltage 12.4 or more - ignition off.
3. Engine cranking speed ok (100 RPM or more).

Check 5 amp diesel fuse in fuse panel.

FUSE BLOWN → TORONADO ONLY

Disconnect 3-wire harness connector (pink/blk - dk. blu - tan) at rear of engine. Install new 5 amp. fuse and turn ignition to run.

FUSE OK

Locate and repair short circuit in one of the following: Cutlass-88-98: Pink/blk wire from 3-wire connector to fuse panel. Toronado: Pink/blk wire from engine and generator dash connector to:

1. Coolant switch, fast idle relay and controller.
2. Dk. green wire from fast idle relay to fast idle solenoid.
3. White wire from controller to lamp control relay.
4. Yellow wire from controller to glow plug relay to lamp relay.
5. If no short found in any of these circuits, replace controller.

FUSE BLOWN

1. Cutlass: Locate and repair short circuit in pink/D black from 3-wire connector to fuse panel.
2. 88-98: Locate and repair short circuit in pink wire from 3-wire connector to start light, wait light or fuse panel.

TEST LIGHT TURNS ON/OFF

Touch each glow plug harness terminal with 12 volt test light connected to ground. Test light should pulse on/off.

TEST LIGHT DOES NOT COME ON ONE OR MORE TERMINALS

Repair open circuit in glow plug harness. If open circuit is caused by burned wire, glow plug is shorted and should be replaced.

TEST LIGHT COMES ON ALL 8 WIRE TERMINALS

Disconnect harness from all glow plugs. Connect test light to 12 volt source and touch each glow plug terminal. Light should be on. Replace glow plug if light is off.

FUSE OK

Listen for glow plug relay operation. Should be clicking on and off if engine is cold.

RELAY OPERATING

Connect 12-volt test light to ground. Touch the glow plug relay terminal with 2 fusible links (blk - blu). Test light should turn on and off as controller operates relay.

TEST LIGHT DOES NOT COME ON

Touch test light to single red wire terminal (Batt. feed) on glow plug relay.

TEST LIGHT OFF

Locate and repair open circuit in red wire from glow plug relay to battery.

TEST LIGHT ON

Replace relay. (Contacts burned).

RELAY NOT OPERATING

Connect 12 volt test light to ground and touch the yellow wire and black wires in glow plug relay connector.

TEST LIGHT ON BOTH TERMINALS

Repair open circuit in blk wire ground circuit.

TEST LIGHT ON YELLOW TERMINAL ONLY

Replace relay.

TEST LIGHT OFF BOTH TERMINALS

Disconnect the harness connector from the controller. Touch test light to #3 (pink/blk wire) terminal in the connector.

TEST LIGHT ON

Repair open circuit in yellow wire from glow plug relay to controller. If no trouble found, replace controller.

TEST LIGHT OFF

Repair open circuit in pink/black wire from controller to splice.

Fig. 10   Diesel engine electrical diagnosis, part 1 of 5. 1979 V8-260 (4.3 litre) & 350 (5.7 litre)

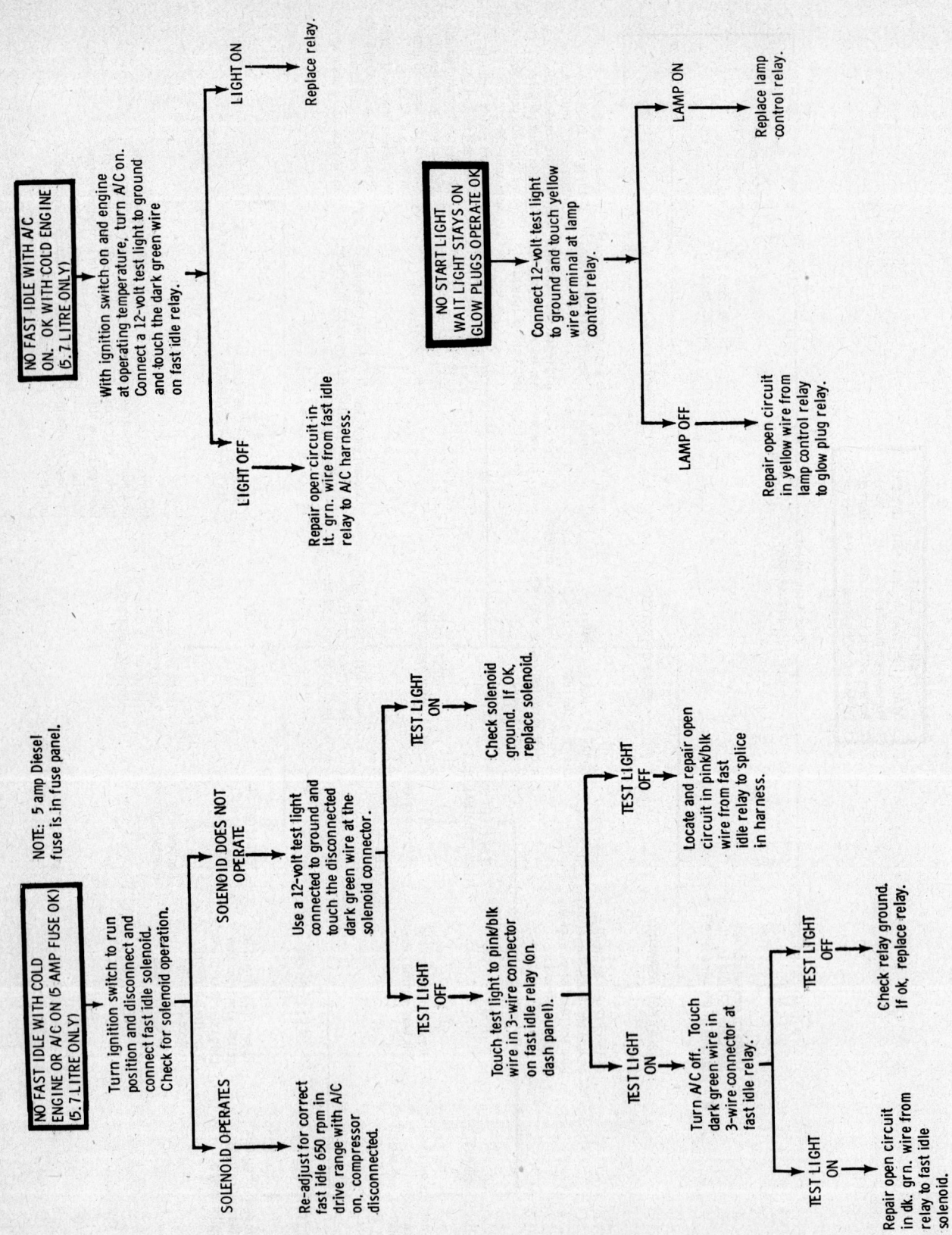

NO FAST IDLE WITH A/C ON. OK WITH COLD ENGINE (5.7 LITRE ONLY)

With ignition switch on and engine at operating temperature, turn A/C on. Connect a 12-volt test light to ground and touch the dark green wire on fast idle relay.

→ **LIGHT ON** → Replace relay.

→ **LIGHT OFF** → Repair open circuit in lt. grn. wire from fast idle relay to A/C harness.

NO START LIGHT WAIT LIGHT STAYS ON GLOW PLUGS OPERATE OK

Connect 12-volt test light to ground and touch yellow wire terminal at lamp control relay.

→ **LAMP ON** → Replace lamp control relay.

→ **LAMP OFF** → Repair open circuit in yellow wire from lamp control relay to glow plug relay.

NOTE: 5 amp Diesel fuse is in fuse panel.

NO FAST IDLE WITH COLD ENGINE OR A/C ON (5 AMP FUSE OK) (5.7 LITRE ONLY)

Turn ignition switch to run position and disconnect and connect fast idle solenoid. Check for solenoid operation.

→ **SOLENOID OPERATES** → Re-adjust for correct fast idle 650 rpm in drive range with A/C on, compressor disconnected.

→ **SOLENOID DOES NOT OPERATE** → Use a 12-volt test light connected to ground and touch the disconnected dark green wire at the solenoid connector.

→ **TEST LIGHT ON** → Check solenoid ground. If OK, replace solenoid.

→ **TEST LIGHT OFF** → Touch test light to pink/blk wire in 3-wire connector on fast idle relay (on dash panel).

→ **TEST LIGHT OFF** → Locate and repair open circuit in pink/blk wire from fast idle relay to splice in harness.

→ **TEST LIGHT ON** → Turn A/C off. Touch dark green wire in 3-wire connector at fast idle relay.

→ **TEST LIGHT OFF** → Check relay ground. If ok, replace relay.

→ **TEST LIGHT ON** → Repair open circuit in dk. grn. wire from relay to fast idle solenoid.

Fig. 10A   Diesel engine electrical diagnosis, part 2 of 5. 1979 V8-260 (4.3 litre) & 350 (5.7 litre)

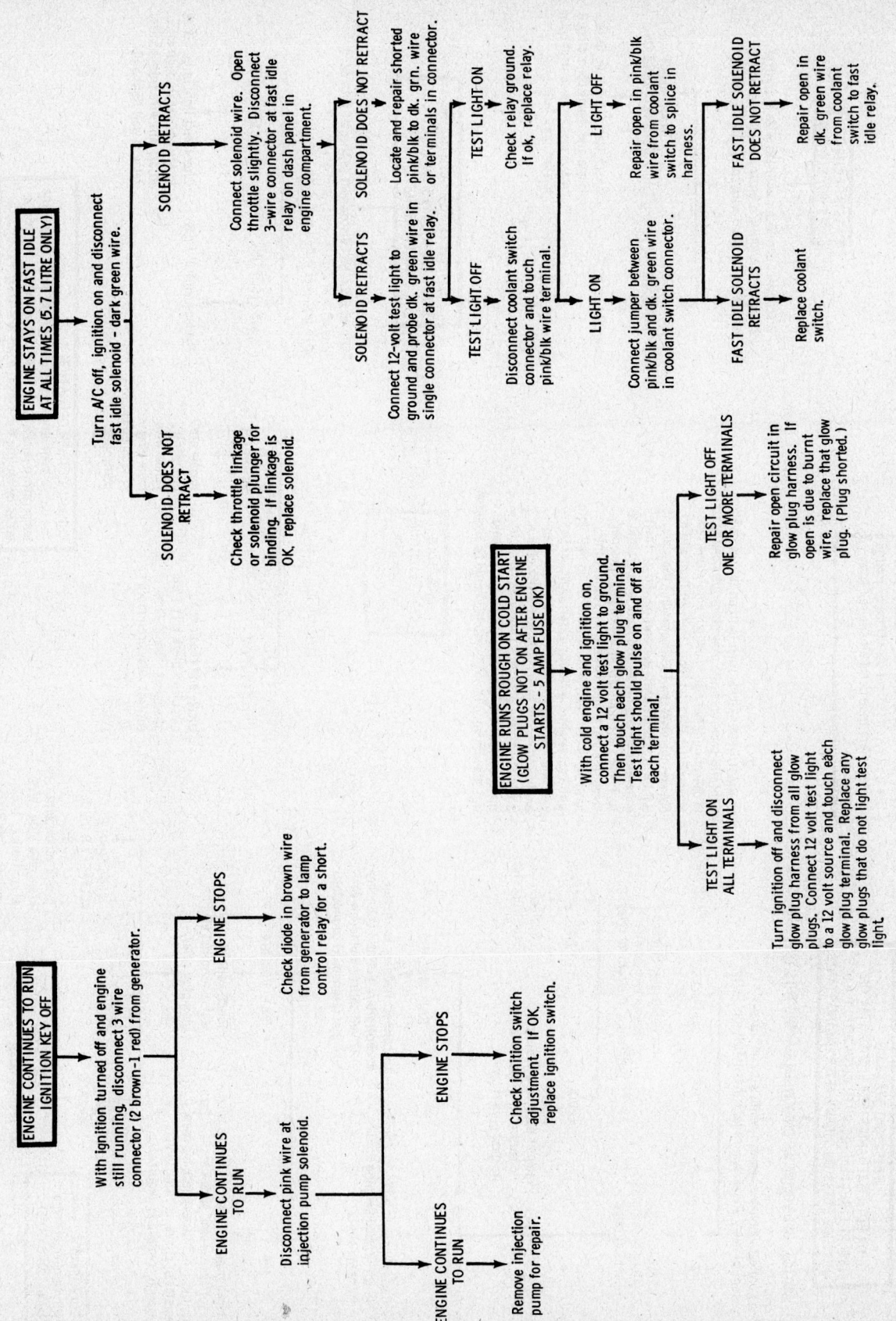

ENGINE STAYS ON FAST IDLE AT ALL TIMES (5.7 LITRE ONLY)

Turn A/C off, ignition on and disconnect fast idle solenoid - dark green wire.

SOLENOID RETRACTS

Connect solenoid wire. Open throttle slightly. Disconnect 3-wire connector at fast idle relay on dash panel in engine compartment.

SOLENOID DOES NOT RETRACT

Locate and repair shorted pink/blk to dk. grn. wire or terminals in connector.

SOLENOID RETRACTS

Connect 12-volt test light to ground and probe dk. green wire in single connector at fast idle relay.

TEST LIGHT ON

Check relay ground. If ok, replace relay.

TEST LIGHT OFF

Disconnect coolant switch connector and touch pink/blk wire terminal.

LIGHT OFF

Repair open in pink/blk wire from coolant switch to splice in harness.

LIGHT ON

Connect jumper between pink/blk and dk. green wire in coolant switch connector.

FAST IDLE SOLENOID DOES NOT RETRACT

Repair open in dk. green wire from coolant switch to fast idle relay.

FAST IDLE SOLENOID RETRACTS

Replace coolant switch.

SOLENOID DOES NOT RETRACT

Check throttle linkage or solenoid plunger for binding. If linkage is OK, replace solenoid.

ENGINE RUNS ROUGH ON COLD START (GLOW PLUGS NOT ON AFTER ENGINE STARTS - 5 AMP FUSE OK)

With cold engine and ignition on, connect a 12 volt test light to ground. Then touch each glow plug terminal. Test light should pulse on and off at each terminal.

TEST LIGHT ON ONE OR MORE TERMINALS

Repair open circuit in glow plug harness. If open is due to burnt wire, replace that glow plug. (Plug shorted.)

TEST LIGHT ON ALL TERMINALS

Turn ignition off and disconnect glow plug harness from all glow plugs. Connect 12 volt test light to a 12 volt source and touch each glow plug terminal. Replace any glow plugs that do not light test light.

ENGINE CONTINUES TO RUN IGNITION KEY OFF

With ignition turned off and engine still running, disconnect 3 wire connector (2 brown-1 red) from generator.

ENGINE STOPS

Check diode in brown wire from generator to lamp control relay for a short.

ENGINE CONTINUES TO RUN

Disconnect pink wire at injection pump solenoid.

ENGINE STOPS

Check ignition switch adjustment. If OK, replace ignition switch.

ENGINE CONTINUES TO RUN

Remove injection pump for repair.

Fig. 10B   Diesel engine electrical diagnosis, part 3 of 5. 1979 V8-260 (4.3 litre) & 350 (5.7 litre)

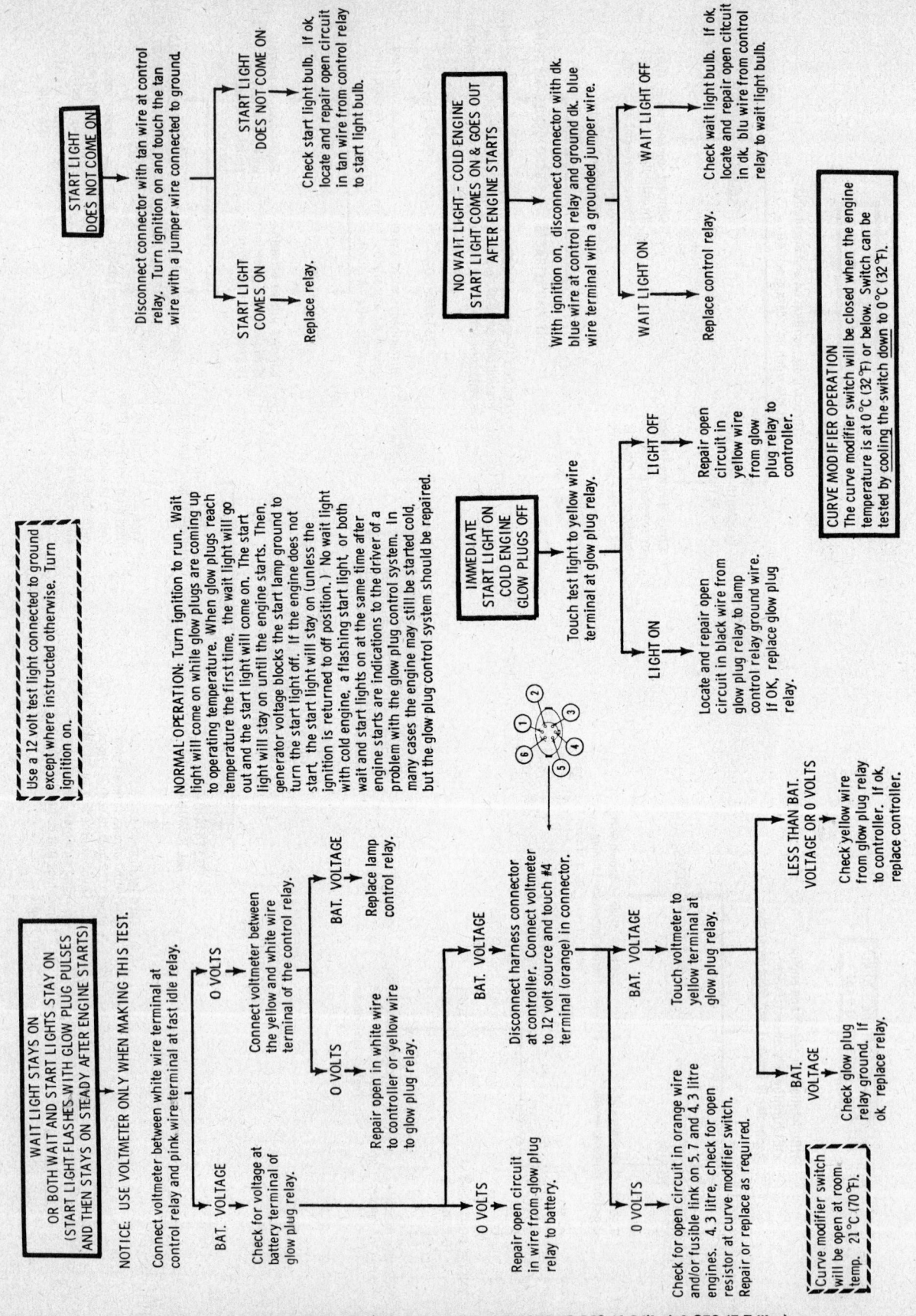

START LIGHT DOES NOT COME ON

Disconnect connector with tan wire at control relay. Turn ignition on and touch the tan wire with a jumper wire connected to ground.

- START LIGHT DOES NOT COME ON → Check start light bulb. If ok, locate and repair open circuit in tan wire from control relay to start light bulb.
- START LIGHT COMES ON → Replace relay.

NO WAIT LIGHT – COLD ENGINE START LIGHT COMES ON & GOES OUT AFTER ENGINE STARTS

With ignition on, disconnect connector with dk. blue wire at control relay and ground dk. blue wire terminal with a grounded jumper wire.

- WAIT LIGHT OFF → Check wait light bulb. If ok, locate and repair open circuit in dk. blu wire from control relay to wait light bulb.
- WAIT LIGHT ON → Replace control relay.

CURVE MODIFIER OPERATION
The curve modifier switch will be closed when the engine temperature is at 0°C (32°F) or below. Switch can be tested by cooling the switch down to 0°C (32°F).

Use a 12 volt test light connected to ground except where instructed otherwise. Turn ignition on.

NORMAL OPERATION: Turn ignition to run. Wait light will come on while glow plugs are coming up to operating temperature. When glow plugs reach temperature the first time, the wait light will go out and the start light will come on. The start light will stay on until the engine starts. Then, generator voltage blocks the start lamp ground to turn the start light off. If the engine does not start, the start light will stay on (unless the ignition is returned to off position.) No wait light with cold engine, a flashing start light, or both wait and start lights on at the same time after engine starts are indications to the driver of a problem with the glow plug control system. In many cases the engine may still be started cold, but the glow plug control system should be repaired.

IMMEDIATE START LIGHT ON COLD ENGINE GLOW PLUGS OFF

Touch test light to yellow wire terminal at glow plug relay.

- LIGHT OFF → Repair open circuit in yellow wire from glow plug relay to controller.
- LIGHT ON → Locate and repair open circuit in black wire from glow plug relay to lamp control relay ground wire. If OK, replace glow plug relay.

WAIT LIGHT STAYS ON OR BOTH WAIT AND START LIGHTS STAY ON (START LIGHT FLASHES WITH GLOW PLUG PULSES AND THEN STAYS ON STEADY AFTER ENGINE STARTS)

NOTICE: USE VOLTMETER ONLY WHEN MAKING THIS TEST.

Connect voltmeter between white wire terminal at control relay and pink wire terminal at fast idle relay.

- BAT. VOLTAGE → Check for voltage at battery terminal of glow plug relay.
- 0 VOLTS → Connect voltmeter between the yellow and white wire terminal of the control relay.
  - BAT. VOLTAGE → Replace lamp control relay.
  - 0 VOLTS → Repair open in white wire to controller or yellow wire to glow plug relay.

Check for voltage at battery terminal of glow plug relay.
- BAT. VOLTAGE → Disconnect harness connector at controller. Connect voltmeter to 12 volt source and touch #4 terminal (orange) in connector.
- 0 VOLTS → Repair open circuit in wire from glow plug relay to battery.

Disconnect harness connector at controller...
- BAT. VOLTAGE → Touch voltmeter to yellow terminal at glow plug relay.
- 0 VOLTS → Check for open circuit in orange wire and/or fusible link on 5.7 and 4.3 litre engines. 4.3 litre, check for open resistor at curve modifier switch. Repair or replace as required.

Touch voltmeter to yellow terminal at glow plug relay.
- LESS THAN BAT. VOLTAGE OR 0 VOLTS → Check yellow wire from glow plug relay to controller. If ok, replace controller.
- BAT. VOLTAGE → Check glow plug relay ground. If ok, replace relay.

Curve modifier switch will be open at room temp. 21°C (70°F).

Fig. 10C   Diesel engine electrical diagnosis, part 4 of 5. 1979 V8-260 (4.3 litre) & 350 (5.7 litre)

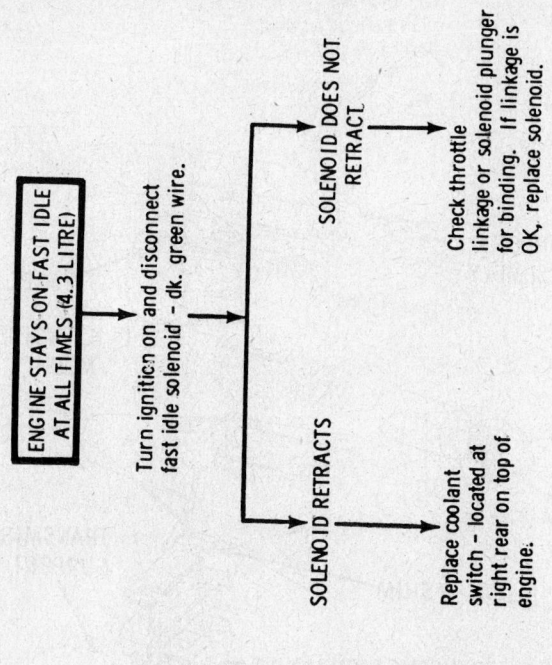

ENGINE STAYS ON FAST IDLE AT ALL TIMES (4.3 LITRE)

Turn ignition on and disconnect fast idle solenoid - dk. green wire.

SOLENOID DOES NOT RETRACT

Check throttle linkage or solenoid plunger for binding. If linkage is OK, replace solenoid.

SOLENOID RETRACTS

Replace coolant switch - located at right rear on top of engine.

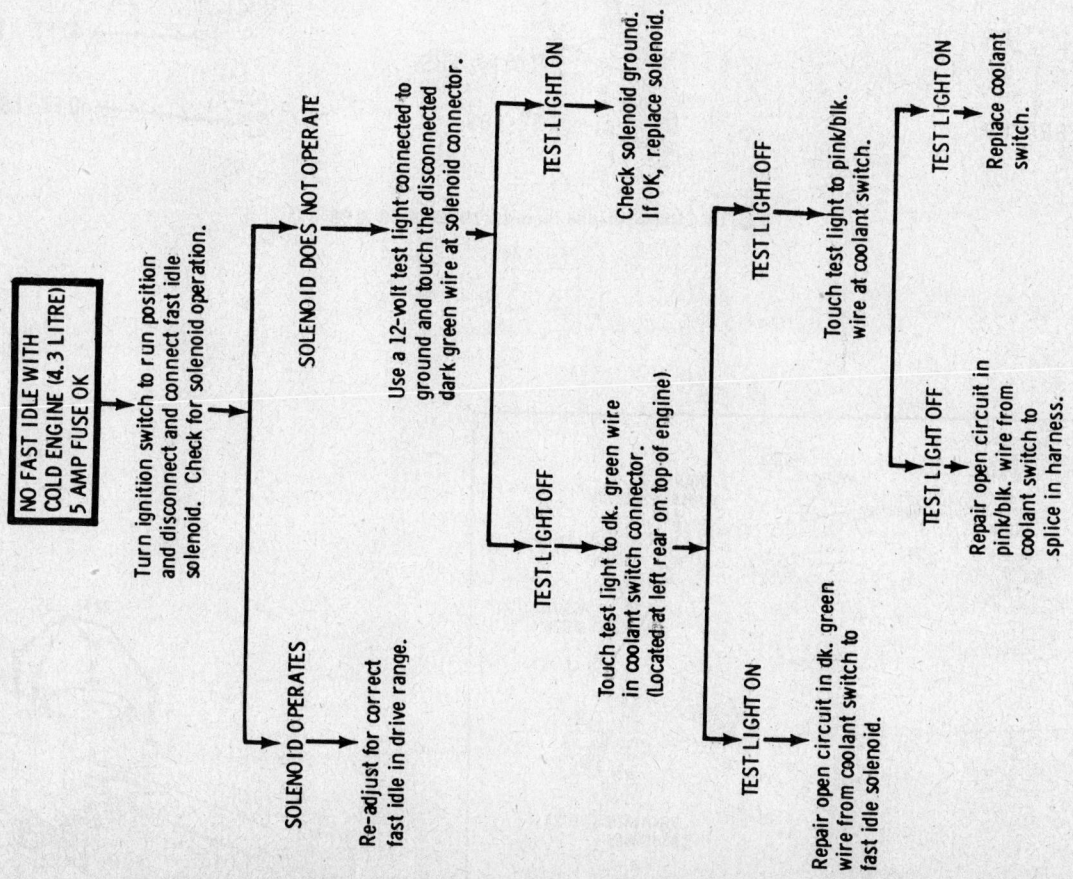

NO FAST IDLE WITH COLD ENGINE (4.3 LITRE) 5 AMP FUSE OK

Turn ignition switch to run position and disconnect and connect fast idle solenoid. Check for solenoid operation.

SOLENOID OPERATES

Re-adjust for correct fast idle in drive range.

SOLENOID DOES NOT OPERATE

Use a 12-volt test light connected to ground and touch the disconnected dark green wire at solenoid connector.

TEST LIGHT ON

Check solenoid ground. If OK, replace solenoid.

TEST LIGHT OFF

Touch test light to dk. green wire in coolant switch connector. (Located at left rear on top of engine)

TEST LIGHT ON

Repair open circuit in dk. green wire from coolant switch to fast idle solenoid.

TEST LIGHT OFF

Touch test light to pink/blk. wire at coolant switch.

TEST LIGHT ON

Replace coolant switch.

TEST LIGHT OFF

Repair open circuit in pink/blk. wire from coolant switch to splice in harness.

Fig. 10D   Diesel engine electrical diagnosis, part 5 of 5. 1979 V8-260 (4.3 litre)

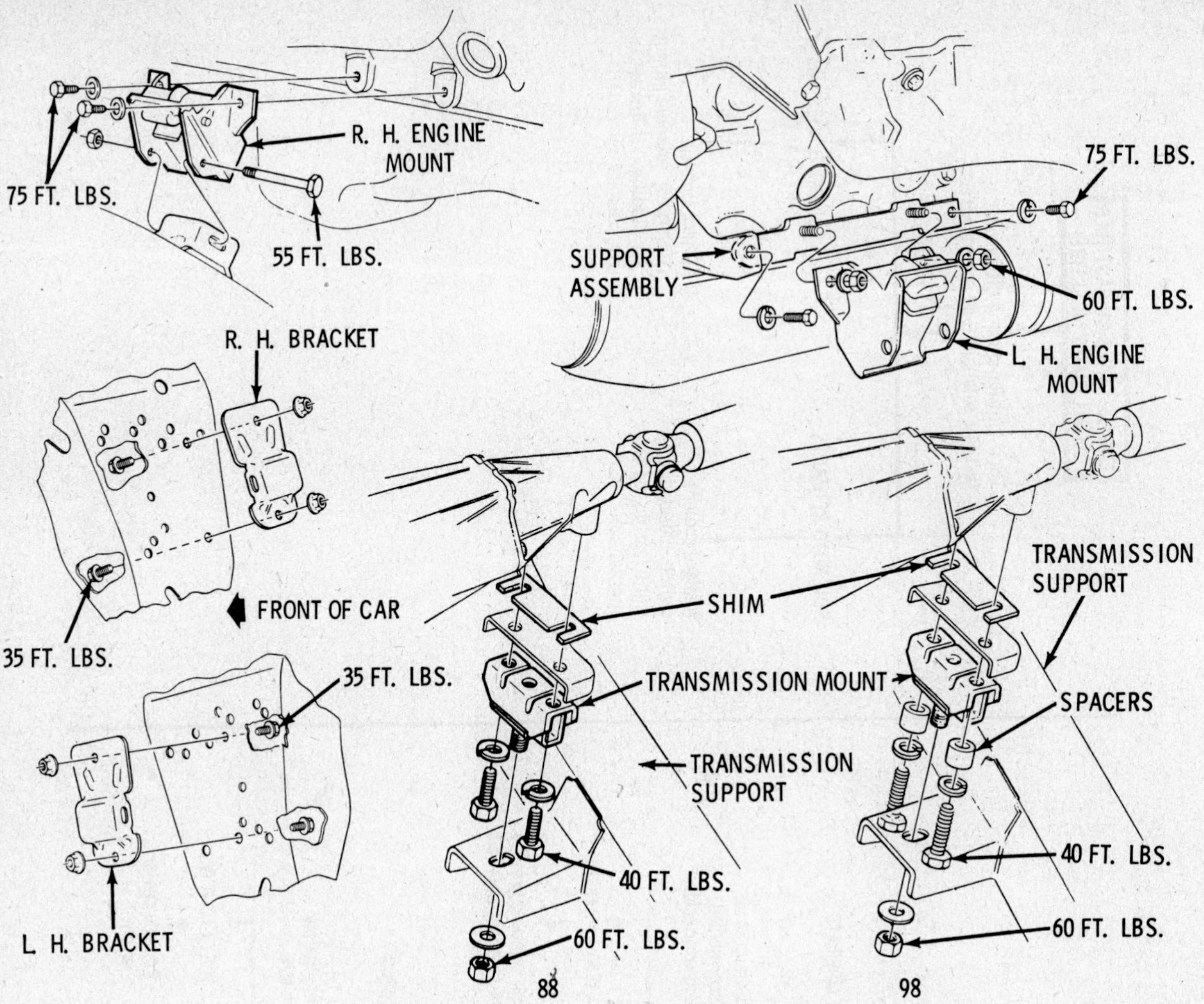

R. H. ENGINE MOUNT

75 FT. LBS.

55 FT. LBS.

75 FT. LBS.

SUPPORT ASSEMBLY

60 FT. LBS.

L. H. ENGINE MOUNT

R. H. BRACKET

FRONT OF CAR

35 FT. LBS.

35 FT. LBS.

L. H. BRACKET

SHIM

TRANSMISSION MOUNT

TRANSMISSION SUPPORT

TRANSMISSION SUPPORT

SPACERS

40 FT. LBS.

60 FT. LBS.

40 FT. LBS.

60 FT. LBS.

88

98

Fig. 11   Diesel engine mounts. 1978-79 88 & 98

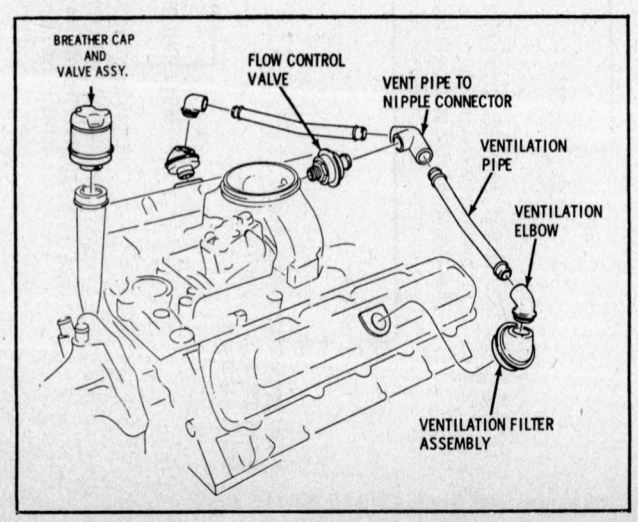

BREATHER CAP AND VALVE ASSY.

FLOW CONTROL VALVE

VENT PIPE TO NIPPLE CONNECTOR

VENTILATION PIPE

VENTILATION ELBOW

VENTILATION FILTER ASSEMBLY

Fig. 12   Crankcase ventilation system

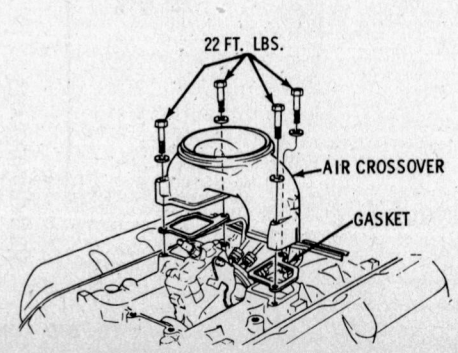

22 FT. LBS.

AIR CROSSOVER

GASKET

Fig. 13   Air crossover installation

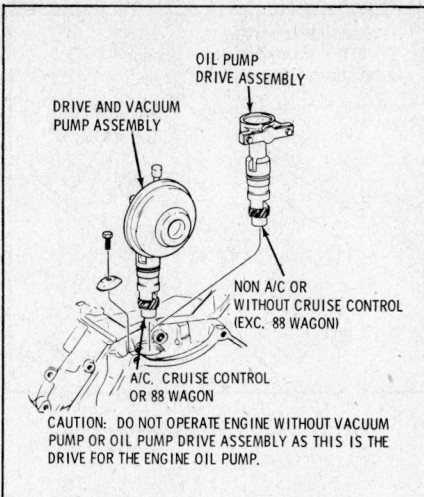

Fig. 14 Vacuum pump & oil pump drive assembly

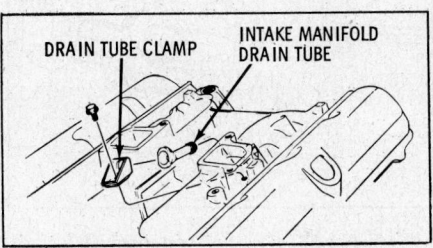

Fig. 15 Intake manifold drain tube installation

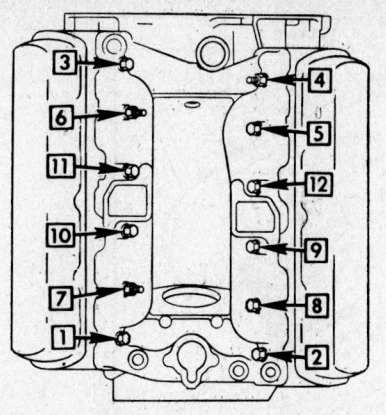

Fig. 16 Intake manifold tightening sequence

VALVE LIFT SPECS.

Engine	Year	Intake	Exhaust
V8-260, 350 Diesel	1978-79	.375	.376

VALVE TIMING

Intake Opens Before TDC

Engine	Year	Degrees
V8-260, 350 Diesel	1978-79	16

Fig. 17 Pre-chamber installation

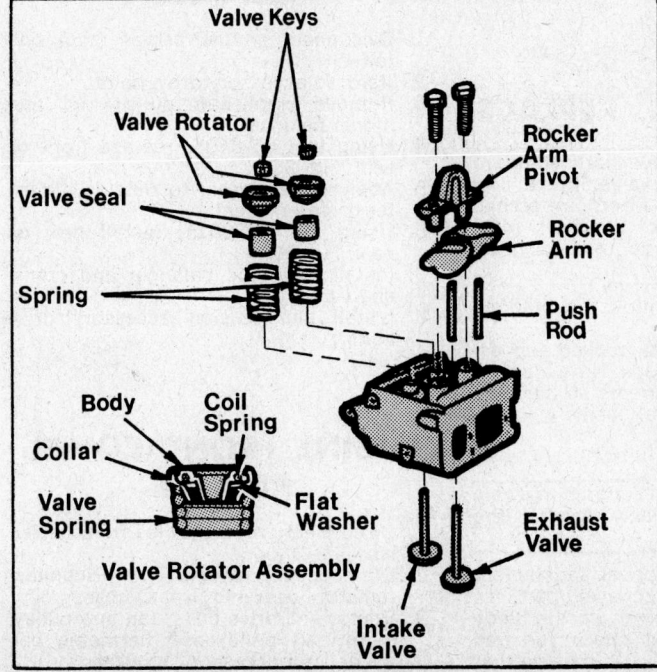

Fig. 18 Cylinder head tightening sequence

VALVES, REMOVE

Whenever a new valve is installed or after grinding valves, it is necessary to measure the valve stem height with the special tool as shown in Fig. 20.

There should be least .015 inch clearance between the gauge and end of valve stem. If clearance is less than .015 inch, remove valve and grind end of valve stem as required.

Check valve rotator height, Fig. 21. If valve stem end is less than .005 inch above rotator, the valve is too short and a new valve must be installed.

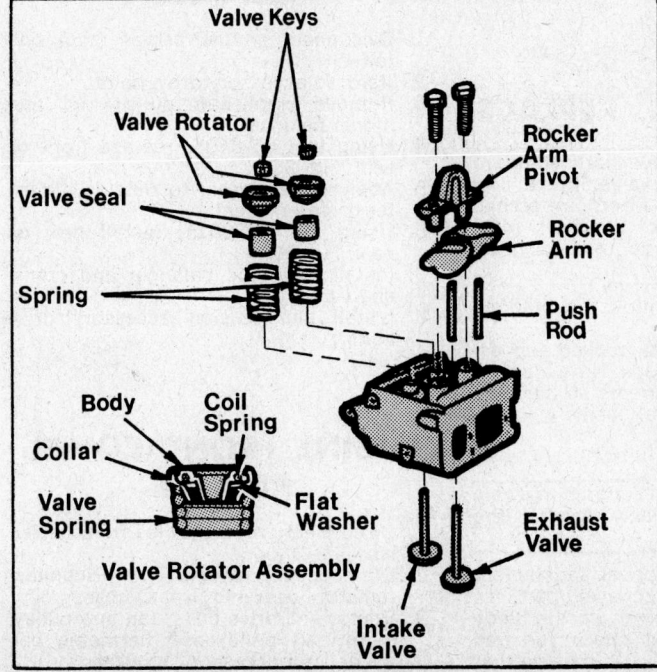

Fig. 19 Cylinder head exploded view

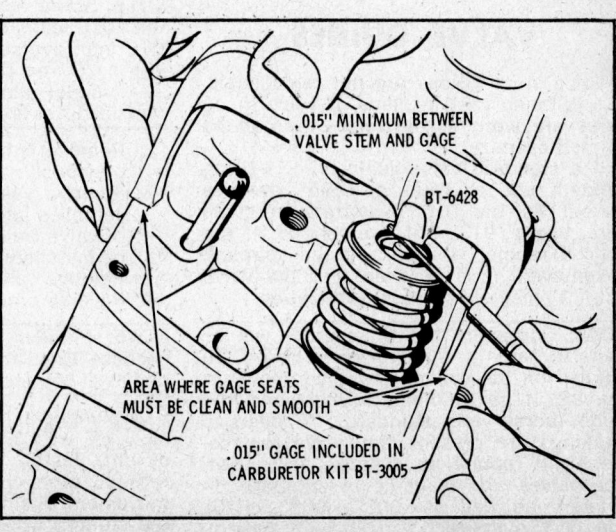

Fig. 20 Measuring valve stem height

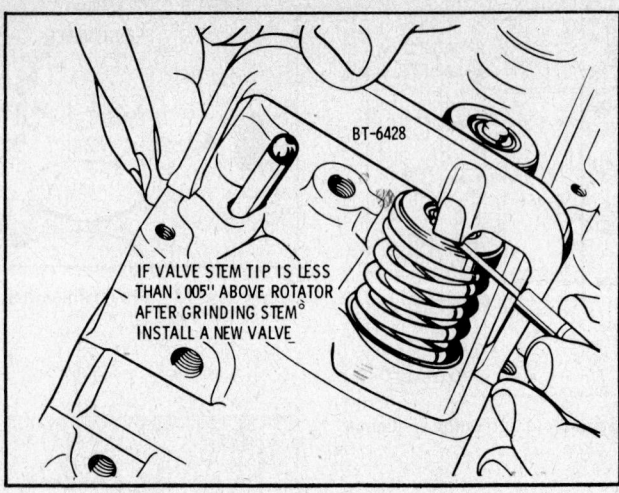

Fig. 21 Measuring valve rotator height

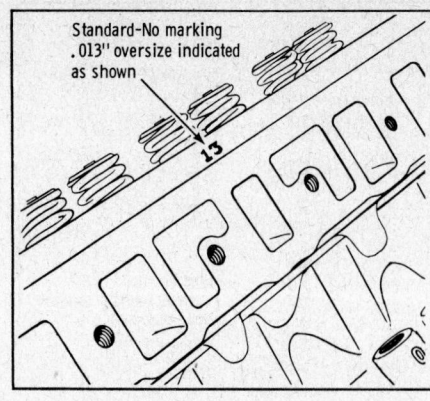

Fig. 22 Valve guide bore marking

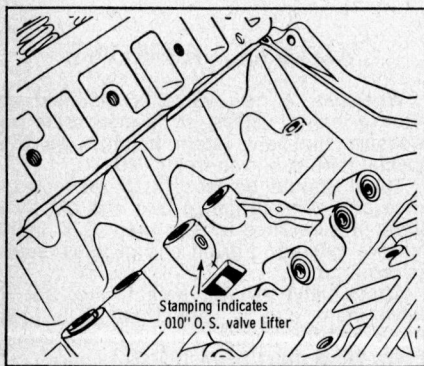

Fig. 23 Oversize valve lifter bore marking

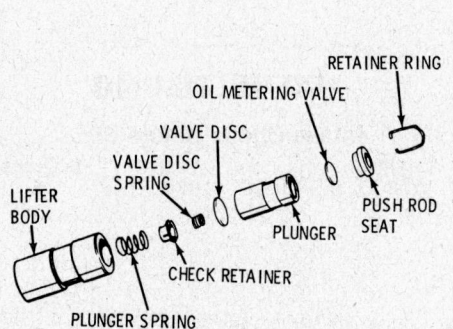

Fig. 24 Valve lifter exploded view

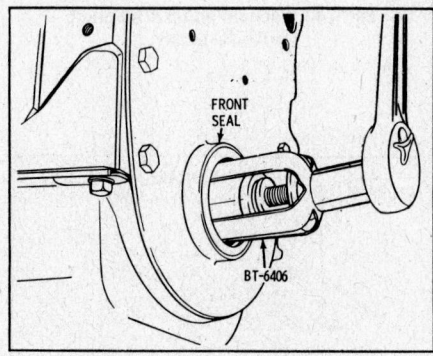

Fig. 25 Front oil seal removal

VALVE GUIDES

Valve stem guides are not replaceable, due to being cast in place. If valve guide bores are worn excessively, they can be reamed oversize.

If a standard valve guide bore is being reamed, use a .003" or .005" oversize reamer. For the .010" oversize valve guide bore, use a .013" oversize reamer. If too large a reamer is used and the spiraling is removed, it is possible that the valve will not receive the proper lubrication.

NOTE: Occasionally a valve guide will be oversize as manufactured. These are marked on the cylinder head as shown in Fig. 22. If no markings are present, the guide bores are standard. If oversize markings are present, any valve replacement will require an oversize valve. Service valves are available in standard diameters as well as .003", .005", .010" and .013" oversize.

VALVE LIFTERS, REPLACE

NOTE: Some engines have both standard and .010 inch oversize valve lifters. The .010 inch oversize valve lifters are etched with a "O" on the side of the lifter. Also, the cylinder block will be marked if an oversize lifter is used, Fig. 23.

1. Remove intake manifold as outlined previously.
2. Remove valve covers, rocker arm assemblies and push rods. Note location of valve train components so they can be installed in original position.
3. Remove valve lifters.
4. Reverse procedure to install.

NOTE: Plungers are not interchangeable because they are selectively fitted to the bodies at the factory.

If plunger and body appear satisfactory blow off with air to remove all particles of dirt. Install the plunger in the body without other parts and check for free movement. A simple test is to be sure that the plunger will drop of its own weight in the body, Fig. 24.

FRONT OIL SEAL, REPLACE

1. Disconnect ground cables from batteries.
2. Remove accessory drive belts.
3. Remove crankshaft pulley and harmonic balancer.
4. Using tool BT-6406, remove front oil seal, Fig. 25.
5. Apply suitable seal to outside diameter of new oil seal.
6. Using tool BT-6611, install new oil seal, Fig. 26.
7. Install harmonic balancer and crankshaft pulley.
8. Install and tension accessory drive belts.

ENGINE FRONT COVER, REPLACE

1. Disconnect ground cables from batteries.
2. Drain cooling system and disconnect radiator hoses and bypass hose.
3. Remove all drive belts, fan and pulley, crankshaft pulley and harmonic balancer, and accessory brackets.
4. Remove timing indicator and water pump.

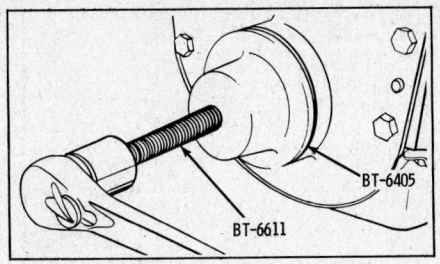

Fig. 26   Front oil seal installation

Fig. 27   Dowel pin chamfer

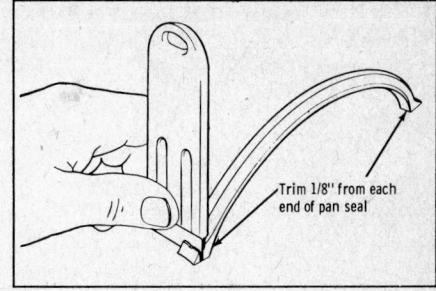

Trim 1/8" from each end of pan seal

Fig. 28   Trimming oil pan seal

5. Remove remaining front cover attaching bolts and the front cover. Also, remove the dowel pins. It may be necessary to grind a flat on the dowel pin to provide a rough surface for gripping.
6. Grind a chamfer on one end of each dowel pin, Fig. 27.
7. Cut excess material from front end of oil pan gasket on each side of cylinder block.
8. Trim approximately 1/8 inch from each end of new front pan seal, Fig. 28.
9. Install new front cover gasket and apply suitable sealer to gasket around coolant holes.
10. Apply RTV sealer to mating surfaces of cylinder block, oil pan and front cover.
11. Place front cover on cylinder block and press downward to compress seal. Rotate cover right and left and guide oil pan seal into cavity with a small screwdriver.
12. Apply engine oil to bolts.
13. Install two bolts finger tight to retain cover.
14. Install the two dowel pins, chamfered end first.
15. Install timing indicator and water pump and torque bolts as shown in Fig. 29.
16. Install harmonic balancer and crankshaft pulley.
17. Install accessory brackets.
18. Install fan and pulley and drive belts.
19. Connect radiator hoses and bypass hose.
20. Connect ground cables to batteries.

TIMING CHAIN & GEARS, REPLACE

1. Remove front cover as outlined previously.
2. Remove oil slinger, cam gear, crank gear and timing chain.
3. Remove fuel pump eccentric from crankshaft.
4. Install key in crankshaft, if removed.
5. Install fuel pump eccentric, if removed.
6. Install cam gear, crank gear and timing chain with timing marks aligned, Fig. 30.

NOTE: With the timing marks aligned in Fig. 30, No. 6 cylinder is in the firing position. To place No. 1 cylinder in the firing position, rotate crankshaft one complete revolution. This will bring the camshaft gear mark to top and No. 1 cylinder will be in the firing position.

7. Install oil slinger.
8. Install front cover.

CAMSHAFT & INJECTION PUMP DRIVE & DRIVEN GEARS

1. Disconnect ground cables from batteries.
2. Drain cooling system.
3. Remove radiator upper baffle.
4. Disconnect upper radiator hose at water outlet and hose support clamp.
5. Disconnect cooler lines at radiator.
6. Remove fan shroud and radiator.
7. Remove intake manifold as outlined previously.
8. Remove engine front cover as outlined previously.
9. Remove valve covers.
10. Remove rocker arm bolts, pivots, rocker arms and push rod. Note valve train

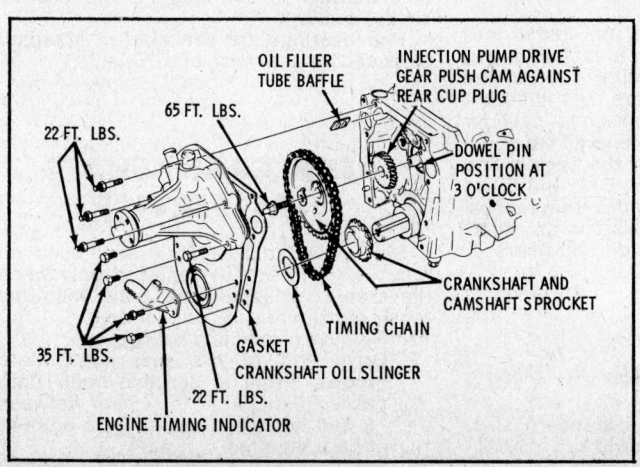

22 FT. LBS.

65 FT. LBS.

OIL FILLER TUBE BAFFLE

INJECTION PUMP DRIVE GEAR PUSH CAM AGAINST REAR CUP PLUG

DOWEL PIN POSITION AT 3 O'CLOCK

CRANKSHAFT AND CAMSHAFT SPROCKET

TIMING CHAIN

GASKET

CRANKSHAFT OIL SLINGER

35 FT. LBS.

22 FT. LBS.

ENGINE TIMING INDICATOR

Fig. 29   Engine front cover installation

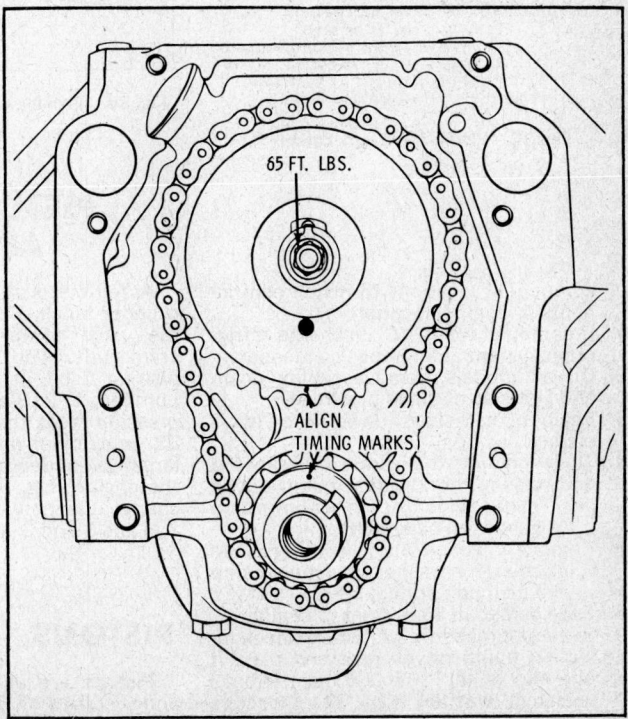

65 FT. LBS.

ALIGN TIMING MARKS

Fig. 30   Valve timing marks

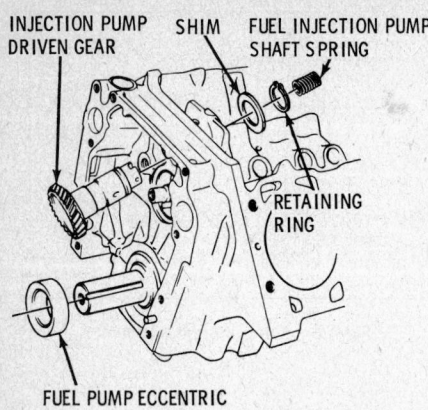

Fig. 31 Fuel injection pump driven gear installation

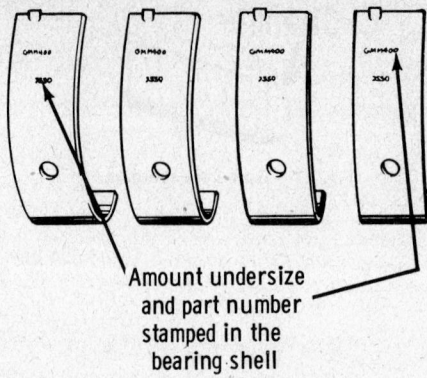

Amount undersize and part number stamped in the bearing shell

Fig. 33 Main bearing identification

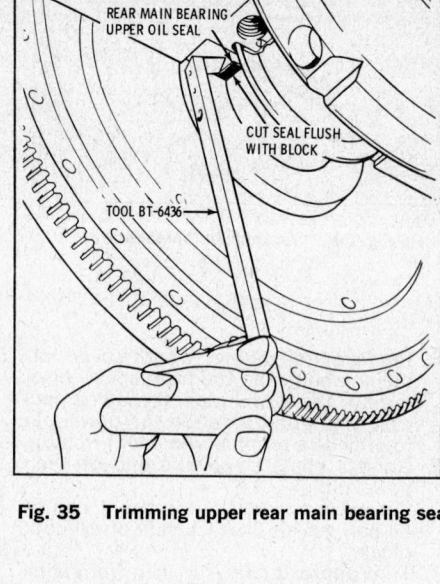

Fig. 35 Trimming upper rear main bearing seal

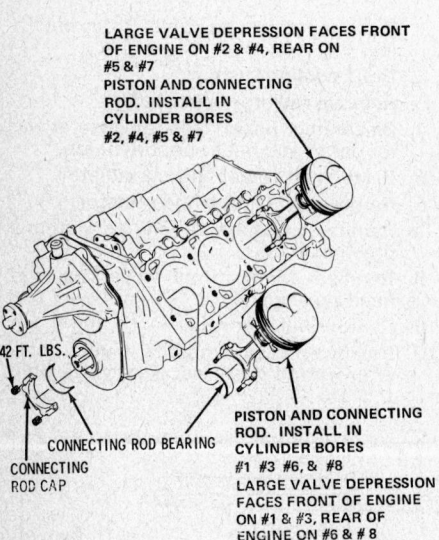

Fig. 32 Piston & rod installation

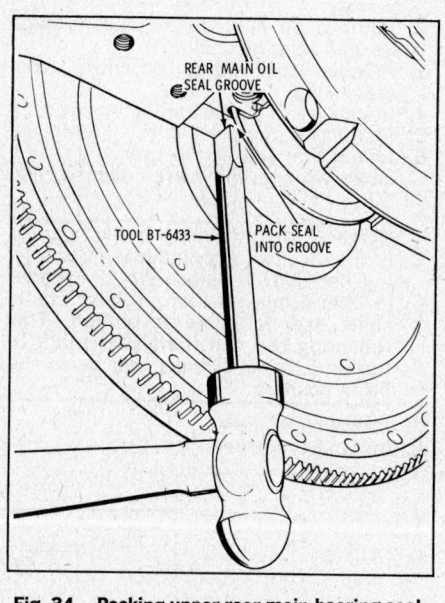

Fig. 34 Packing upper rear main bearing seal

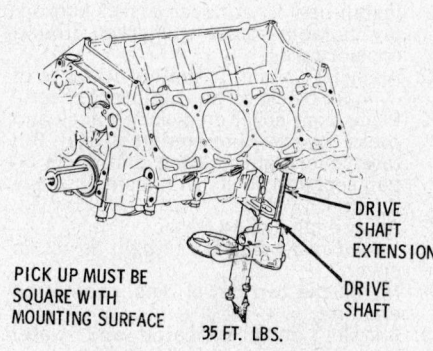

Fig. 36 Oil pump installation

component locations to install components in original locations.

11. If equipped with A/C, discharge refrigerant system and remove condenser.
12. On all models, remove timing chain and gears as outlined previously.
13. Position camshaft dowel pin at 3 o'clock position.
14. While holding the camshaft rearward and rocking the injection pump driven gear slide, slide the injection pump drive gear from camshaft.
15. Remove injection pump adapter, snap ring, selective washer, injection pump driven gear and spring, Fig. 31.
16. Slide camshaft from front of engine.
17. Reverse procedure to install. Check injection pump driven gear end play. If end play is not .002-.006 inch, replace selective washer, Fig. 31. Selective washers are available from .103 to .115 inch in increments of .003 inch.

PISTON & ROD ASSEMBLE

Assemble piston to rod and install into cylinder block. The piston is installed with the valve depression facing toward the crankshaft. Also, there are two different pistons used in this engine. In cylinder numbers 1, 2, 3 and 4, the large valve depression faces the front of the engine, Fig. 32. In cylinder numbers 5, 6, 7 and 8 the large valve depression faces the rear of the engine, Fig. 32. The pistons are interchangeable between cylinder numbers 1, 3, 6 and 8 and 2, 4, 5 and 7.

PISTONS, RINGS & PINS

Pistons are available in standard sizes and oversizes of .010 and .030".
Rings are available in standard sizes and oversizes of .010 and .030".

MAIN & ROD BEARINGS

Main bearings are available in standard sizes and undersizes of .0005, .0010 and .0015 inch. The amount of undersize and part number is stamped on the bearing shell, Fig. 33.
Rod bearings are available in standard sizes and an undersize of .010 inch.

REAR CRANKSHAFT SEAL SERVICE

Since the braided fabric seal used on these engines can be replaced only when the crankshaft is removed, the following repair procedure is recommended.

1. Remove oil pan and bearing cap.
2. Drive end of old seal gently into groove, using a suitable tool, until packed tight. This may vary between ¼ and ¾ inch depending on amount of pack required.
3. Repeat previous step for other end of seal.

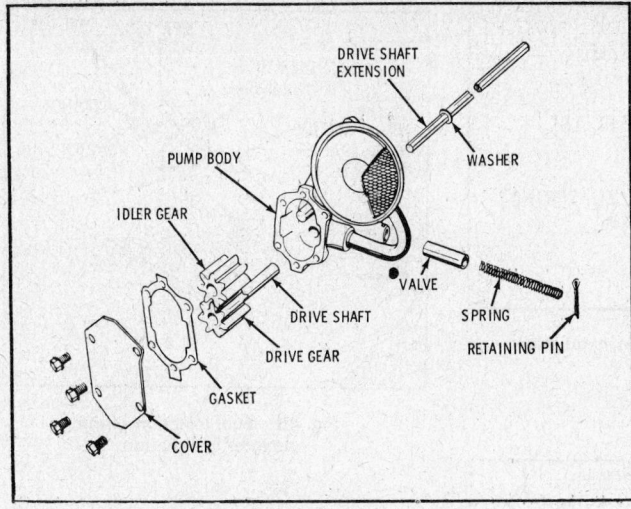

Fig. 37   Oil pump disassembled

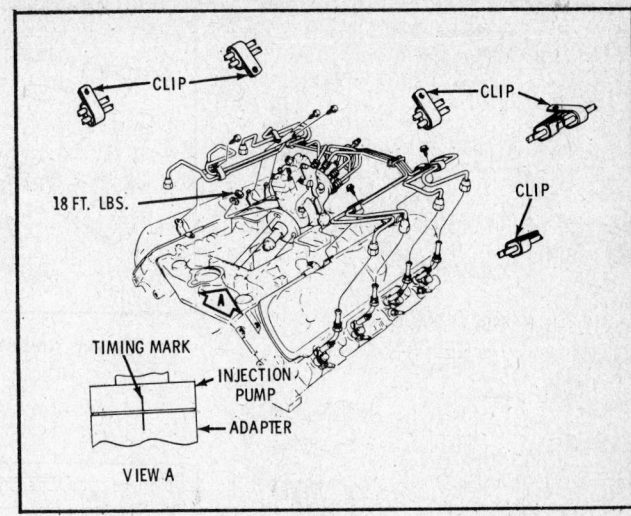

Fig. 39   Fuel injection pump timing marks

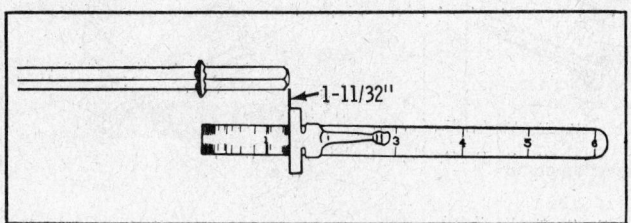

Fig. 38   Oil pump driveshaft extension

4. Measure and note amount that seal was driven up on one side. Using the old seal removed from bearing cap, cut a length of seal the amount previously noted plus $1/16$ inch.
5. Repeat previous step for other side of seal.
6. Pack cut lengths of seal into appropriate side of seal groove. A packing tool, BT-6433, Fig. 34, may be used since the tool has been machined to provide a built-in stop. Use tool BT-6436 to trim the seal flush with block, Fig. 35.
7. Install new seal in lower bearing cap.

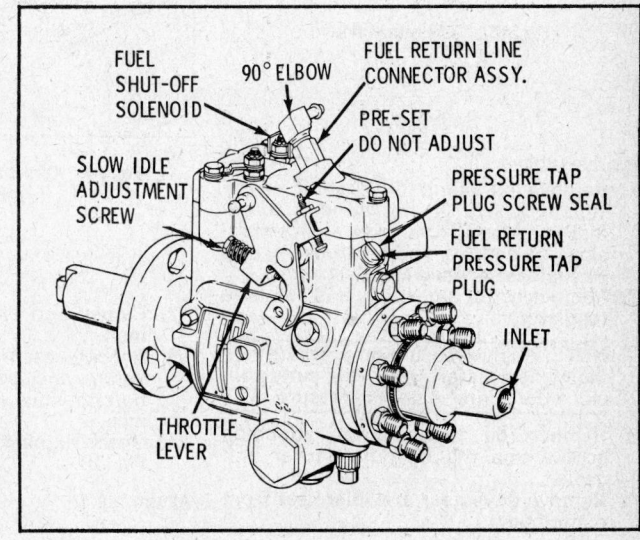

Fig. 40   Fuel injection pump connections

OIL PAN, REPLACE

1. Disconnect ground cables from batteries.
2. Remove drive and vacuum pump, if equipped with A/C, or oil pump drive, if less A/C.
3. Remove oil dipstick.
4. Remove radiator upper support and fan shroud attaching screws.
5. Raise vehicle and drain oil pan.
6. Remove flywheel cover.
7. Disconnect exhaust and crossover pipes from exhaust manifold.
8. Remove oil cooler lines at filter base.
9. Disconnect starter wiring and remove starter.
10. Remove engine mounts from engine block, then raise front of engine with

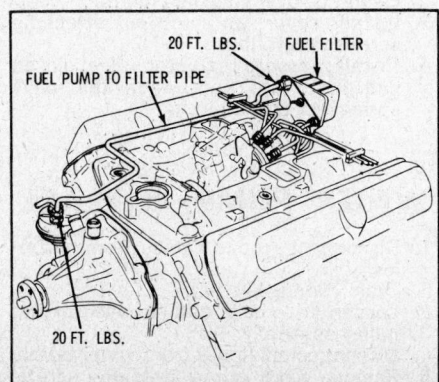

Fig. 41   Fuel filter & lines

suitable equipment.
11. Remove oil pan attaching bolts and the oil pan.
12. Reverse procedure to install. Torque oil pan attaching bolts to 10 ft. lbs.

OIL PUMP, REPLACE & SERVICE

Replacement

1. Remove oil pan as outlined previously.
2. Remove oil pump to rear main bearing cap attaching bolts, Fig. 36.
3. Remove oil pump and drive shaft extension.
4. Reverse procedure to install. Torque attaching bolts to 35 ft. lbs.

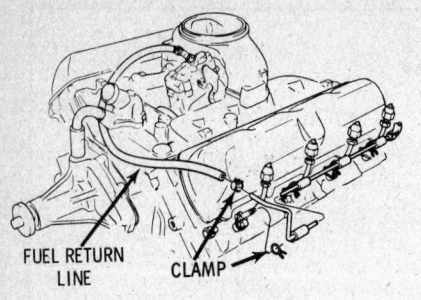

FUEL RETURN LINE   CLAMP

L. H. SIDE OF ENGINE

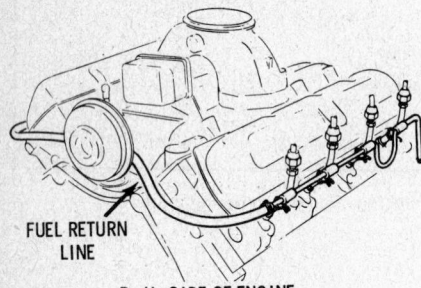

FUEL RETURN LINE

R. H. SIDE OF ENGINE

Fig. 42   Fuel return lines

Service

Dissassembly

1. Remove oil pump drive shaft extension, Fig. 37. Do not attempt to remove washers from drive shaft extension. The drive shaft extension and washers is serviced as an assembly.
2. Remove cotter pin, spring and pressure regulator valve.

NOTE: Apply pressure on pressure regulator bore before removing cotter pin since the spring is under pressure.

3. Remove oil pump cover attaching screws and the oil pump cover and gasket.
4. Remove drive gear and idler gear from pump body.

Inspection

1. Check gears for scoring or other damage, replace if necessary.

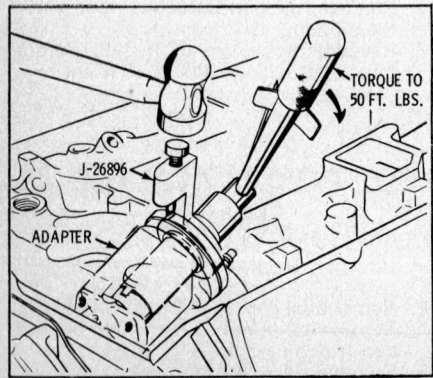

Fig. 47   Marking fuel injection pump adapter with new timing mark

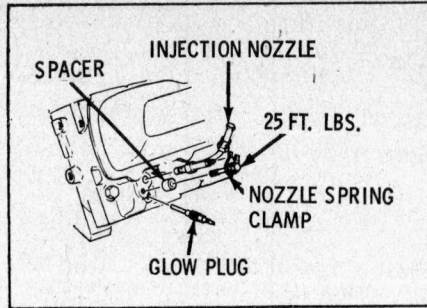

Fig. 43   Injection nozzle installation

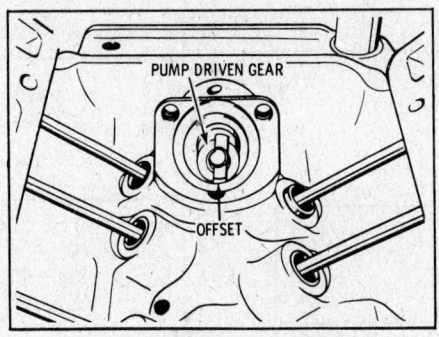

Fig. 44   Offset on fuel injection pump driven gear

2. Proper end clearance is .0005-.0075 inch.
3. Check pressure regulator valve, valve spring and bore for damage. Proper bore to valve clearance is .0025-.0050 inch.
4. Check extension shaft ends for wear, Fig. 38.

Assembly

1. Install gears and shaft in oil pump body.
2. Check gear end clearance by placing a straight edge over the gears and measure the clearance between the straight edge and gasket surface. If end clearance is excessive, check for scores in cover that would bring the clearance over specified limits.
3. Install cover and torque attaching screws to 8 ft. lbs.
4. Install pressure regulator valve, closed end first, into bore, then the valve spring and cotter pin.

WATER PUMP, REPLACE

1. Disconnect ground cables from batteries.
2. Drain cooling system.
3. Loosen drive belts and remove fan and pulley assembly.
4. Disconnect all hoses from water pump.
5. Remove water pump attaching screws and the water pump, Fig. 29.
6. Reverse procedure to install.

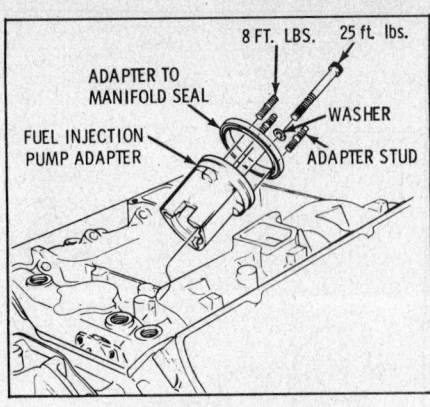

Fig. 45   Fuel injection pump adapter installation

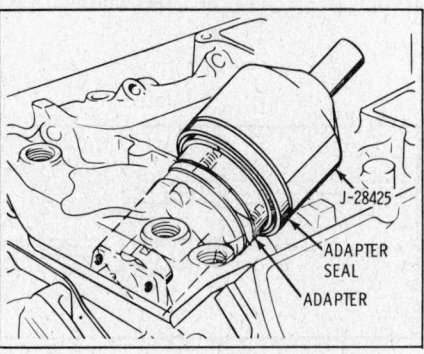

Fig. 46   Fuel injection pump adapter seal installation

MECHANICAL FUEL PUMP, REPLACE

1. Disconnect fuel lines from pump.
2. Remove fuel pump mounting bolts and the fuel pump.

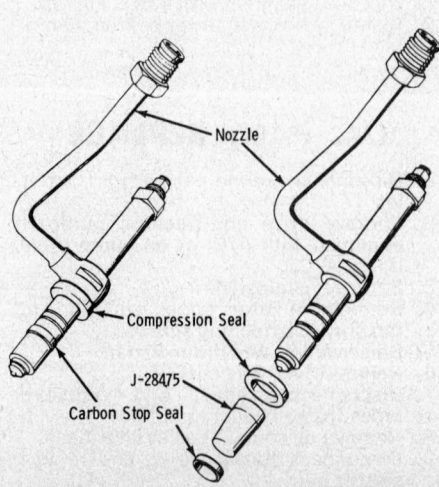

Fig. 48   Injection nozzle seal installation

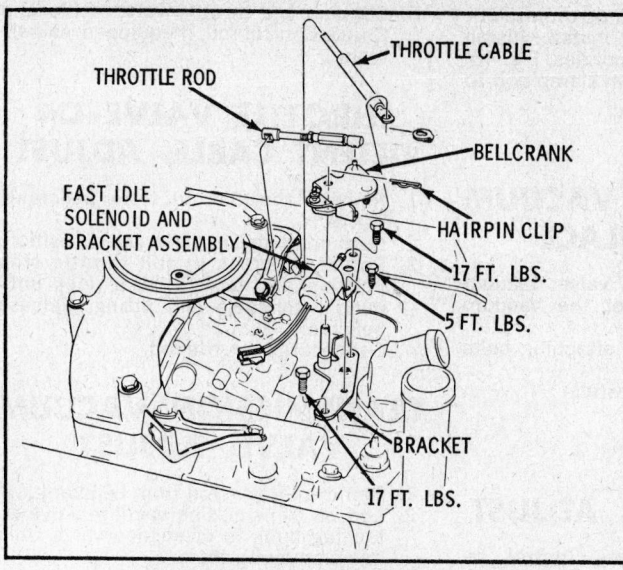

Fig. 49   Throttle linkage

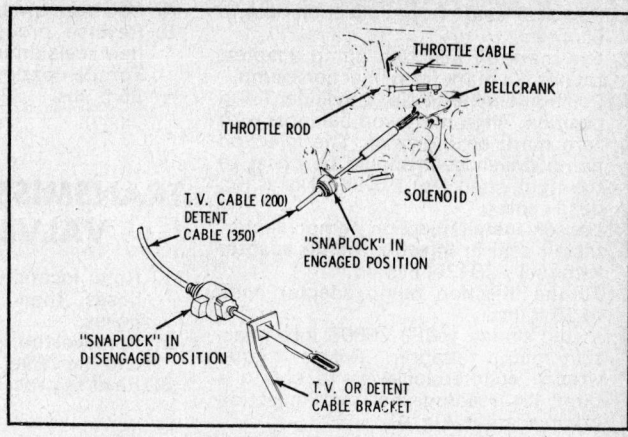

Fig. 50   Throttle valve or detent cable adjustment

3. Remove all gasket material from the pump and block gasket surfaces. Apply sealer to both sides of new gasket.
4. Position gasket on pump flange and hold pump in position against its mounting surface. Make sure rocker arm is riding on crankshaft eccentric.
5. Press pump tight against its mounting. Install retaining screws and tighten them alternately.
6. Connect fuel lines. Then operate engine and check for leaks.

SERVICE NOTE: Before installing the pump, it is good practice to crank the engine so that the nose of the crankshaft eccentric is out of the way of the fuel pump rocker arm when the pump is installed. In this way there will be the least amount of tension on the rocker arm, thereby easing the installation of the pump.

INJECTION PUMP TIMING

1. The mark on the injection pump adapter must be aligned with the mark on the injection pump flange, Fig. 39.
2. To adjust:
   a. Loosen the three injection pump retaining nuts with tool J-26987.
   b. Align the mark on the injection pump flange with the mark on the injection pump adapter, Fig. 39.
   c. Torque injection pump retaining nuts to 35 ft. lbs.

FUEL INJECTION PUMP HOUSING FUEL PRESSURE CHECK

1. Remove air crossover and install screened covers, tool J-26996-2 or equivalent.
2. Remove fuel return pressure tap plug, Fig. 40.

3. Install the seal from the pressure tap plug on the pressure tap adapter, tool J-28526, then install the adapter into pump housing.
4. Connect a low pressure gauge to the adapter.
5. Connect pick-up tachometer, tool J-26925, to the engine.
6. Check pressure with engine operating at 1000 RPM in Park. The pressure should be 4-10 PSI with no more than a 2 PSI fluctuation.
7. If the pressure is not within specifications, replace fuel return line connector assembly.
8. Remove tachometer, pressure gauge and adapter.
9. Install a new pressure tap plug seal on the pressure tap plug and install plug into housing.
10. Remove screened covers and install air crossover.

INJECTION PUMP, REPLACE

Removal

1. Disconnect ground cables from batteries.
2. Remove air cleaner.
3. Remove filters and pipes from valve covers and air crossover, Fig. 12.
4. Remove air crossover and plug intake manifold, Fig. 13.
5. Disconnect throttle rod and return spring.
6. Remove bellcrank.
7. Remove throttle and throttle valve cables from intake manifold brackets and position cables aside.
8. Remove fuel lines to fuel filter, then the fuel filter, Fig. 41.
9. Disconnect fuel line at fuel pump and remove fuel line. If equipped with A/C, remove rear compressor brace.
10. Disconnect fuel return line from injection pump, Fig. 42.

11. Slide clamp from fuel return lines at injector nozzles and remove fuel return lines from each bank.
12. Disconnect injection pump lines at injector nozzles, Fig. 43. It is necessary to use two wrenches.
13. Remove three nuts retaining injection pump with tool J-26987.
14. Remove injection pump and cap all lines and fittings.

Installation

1. Align offset tang on pump drive shaft with pump driven gear, Fig. 44, and install injector pump.
2. Loosely install the three injector pump retaining nuts and lock washers. Connect fuel lines to injector pump and torque line fittings to 25 ft. lbs., Fig. 43.
3. Connect fuel return lines to injector nozzles and injector pump.
4. Align mark on injection pump with line on adapter and torque retaining nuts to 18 ft. lbs.
5. Adjust throttle rod.
6. Install fuel line from fuel pump to fuel filter, Fig. 41. If equipped with A/C, install rear compressor brace.
7. Install bellcrank and hairpin clip.
8. Install throttle and throttle valve cables to intake manifold brackets and attach to bellcrank. Adjust throttle valve cable.
9. Connect throttle rod and return spring.
10. Crank engine and check for fuel leaks.
11. Remove plugs from intake manifold and install air crossover, Fig. 13.
12. Install tubes in flow control valve in air crossover and ventilation filters in valve covers, Fig. 12.
13. Install air cleaner.

INJECTION PUMP ADAPTER, ADAPTER SEAL & NEW TIMING MARK

1. Remove injection pump as outlined previously.
2. Remove injection pump adapter, Fig. 45.

3. Remove seal from injection pump adapter.
4. File mark off injection pump adapter. Do not file mark from injection pump.
5. Position engine to No. 1 cylinder firing position. Align marks on balancer with zero mark on indicator. The injection pump driven gear should be offset to the right when No. 1 cylinder is at top dead center.
6. Loosely install injection pump adapter.
7. Install seal in injection pump adapter with tool J-28425, Fig. 46.
8. Torque injection pump adapter bolts to 25 ft. lbs.
9. Install timing tool J-26896 into injection pump adapter. Rotate torque wrench counterclockwise to obtain a 50 ft. lbs. reading, then mark injection pump adapter, Fig. 47.
10. Install injection pump as outlined previously.

INJECTION NOZZLE, REPLACE

1. Remove fuel line from injector nozzle.
2. Remove fuel line clamps from all nozzles on bank where nozzle is being removed. Remove fuel return line from nozzle being replaced.
3. Remove nozzle hold down clamp and spacer, Fig. 43, then the nozzle with tool J-26952.

4. Cap nozzle inlet line and tip of nozzle.
5. Reverse procedure to install. Install new seals on injection nozzles, Fig. 48. Torque nozzle hold down clamp bolt to 25 ft. lbs.

TRANSMISSION VACUUM VALVE, REPLACE

1. Note location of the valve vacuum hoses, then disconnect the vacuum hoses.
2. Remove the two valve attaching bolts and the valve.
3. Reverse procedure to install.

THROTTLE ROD, ADJUST

1. If equipped with Cruise Control, remove clip from Cruise Control rod, then the rod from bellcrank.
2. Remove throttle valve cable from bellcrank, Fig. 49.
3. Loosen the throttle rod locknut and shorten the rod several turns.
4. Rotate the bellcrank to the full throttle stop, then lengthen the throttle rod until the injection pump lever contacts the injection pump full throttle stop. Release the bellcrank.
5. Tighten the throttle rod locknut.

6. Connect the throttle valve cable and Cruise Control rod, if equipped, to bellcrank.

THROTTLE VALVE OR DETENT CABLE, ADJUST

1. Remove throttle rod from bellcrank, Fig. 50.
2. Push snap lock to disengaged position.
3. Rotate bellcrank to full throttle stop position and push in snap lock until flush with cable end fitting. Release bellcrank.
4. Connect the throttle rod.

TRANSMISSION VACUUM VALVE, ADJUST

1. Remove throttle rod from bellcrank.
2. Loosen transmission vacuum valve attaching bolts to disengage valve from injection pump shaft.
3. Hold the injection pump lever against injection pump full throttle stop, rotate vacuum valve to full throttle position and insert a .090 inch diameter pin to hold the valve in the full throttle position.
4. Rotate assembly clockwise until the injection pump shaft lever is contacted, then tighten the valve attaching bolts.
5. Remove pin and release lever.
6. Connect throttle rod.

Clutch and Transmission Section

> NOTE: 1979 linkage adjustment information is in this section. Repair procedures on both automatic and manual shift transmissions are covered elsewhere in this manual. Procedures for removing automatic transmission as well as linkage adjustments on 1974-78 models are included in the automatic transmission chapters. See Chapter Index.

CLUTCH PEDAL, ADJUST

1974-79

Exc. 1978-79 Cutlass

1. Loosen lower push rod swivel lock nut, Figs. 1 and 2.
2. Disconnect pedal return spring.
3. Rotate clutch lever and shaft assembly until clutch pedal firmly contacts rubber bumper on dash brace.
4. Push outer end of clutch fork rearward until throwout bearing lightly contacts clutch plate.
5. Remove lower push rod swivel retaining clip and install swivel in the gage (Upper) hole. Reinstall retaining clip.
6. Increase length of push rod until lash is removed.
7. Install swivel in lower hole of lever and shaft assembly, then install retaining clip.
8. Tighten lock nut against swivel. Do not change rod length.
9. Connect pedal return spring.
10. Free pedal play should be 7/8 to 1 1/2 inch on 1974-79 Omega or 3/4 to 1 1/4 inch on 1975-77 Cutlass.

1978-79 Cutlass

1. Disconnect clutch return spring.

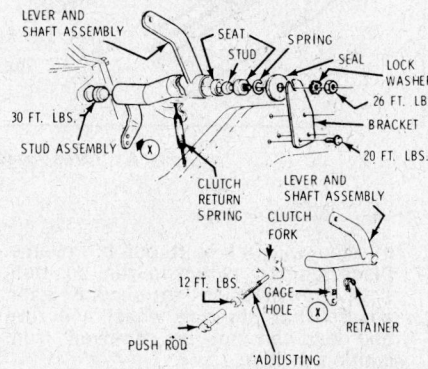

Fig. 1   Clutch linkage. 1974-79 Omega

2. Rotate clutch lever and shaft assembly until clutch pedal firmly contacts rubber bumper on bracket.
3. Push outer end of clutch fork rearward until release bearing lightly contacts clutch plate.
4. Install lower push rod "A", Fig. 3, in clutch fork and rod "B", Fig. 3, in gage (Upper) hole.
5. Increase length of push rod "A" until all lash is removed.

6. Install rod "B" in lower hole of lever and shaft, then the retaining clip.
7. Tighten lock nut "C" against rod "B", Fig. 3. Do not change rod length.
8. Connect return spring.
9. Free pedal play should be 11/16 to 5/8 inch.

CLUTCH, REPLACE

1974-79

1. Remove transmission.
2. Disconnect clutch release spring and clutch rod.
3. Remove clutch release bearing.
4. Remove flywheel housing, leaving starter attached to engine. Release yoke and ball stud will remain in housing.
5. Scribe mark on clutch cover to flywheel for correct assembly.
6. Unfasten and remove clutch cover and disc.

NOTE: Loosen pressure plate bolts alternately, one turn at a time.

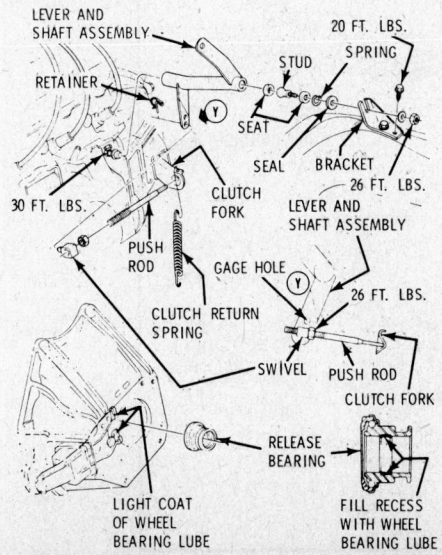

Fig. 2   Clutch linkage. 1975-77 Cutlass

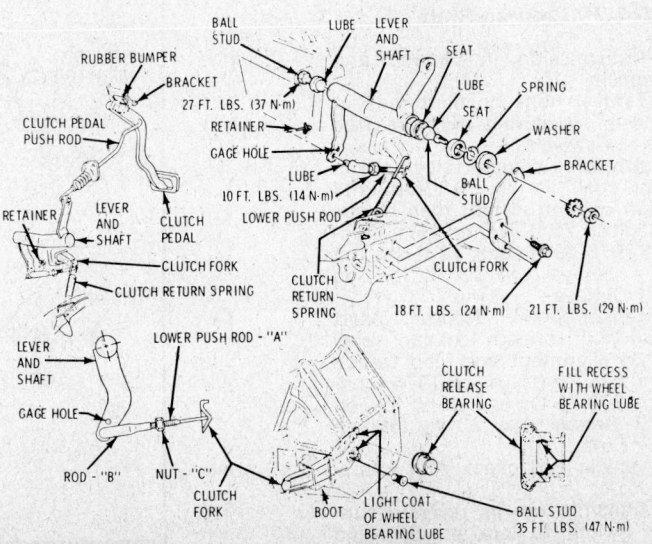

Fig. 3   Clutch linkage. 1978-79 Cutlass

7. Reverse removal procedure to install clutch and adjust clutch pedal free play.

THREE SPEED MANUAL TRANS., REPLACE

1974-79

1. On Omega models with floor shift, remove shift lever from shifter assembly.
2. Raise car and remove drive shaft.
3. Disconnect shift rods from shift levers and the TCS switch wiring, if equipped.
4. Support rear of engine.
5. Remove cross support bar-to-rear transmission mount attaching bolts.
6. Disconnect parking brake cables from cross support and remove cross support bar.
7. If equipped with dual exhaust it may be necessary to disconnect left-hand exhaust pipe at exhaust manifold to provide clearance.

NOTE: On 1975-79 models, remove catalytic converter support bracket.

8. Disconnect speedometer cable.
9. Remove transmission upper attaching bolts and install aligning studs in the bolt holes.
10. Remove lower bolts and remove transmission.
11. Reverse procedure to install.

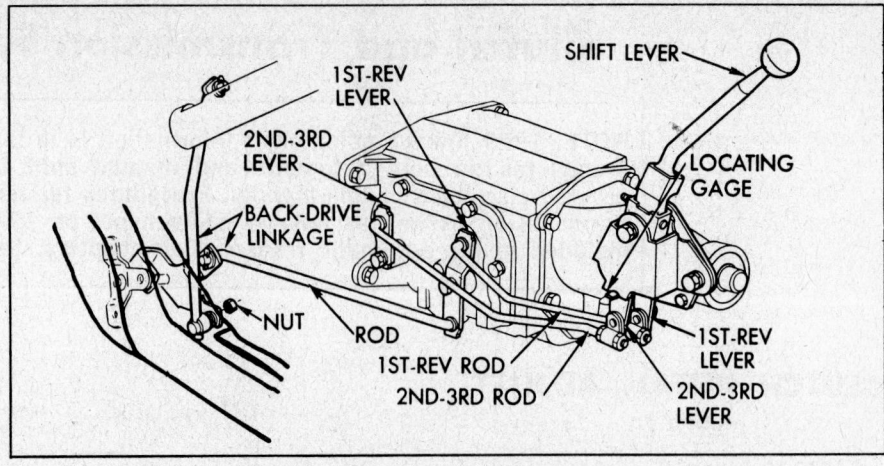

Fig. 4   Three speed shift linkage (typical)

mission will not shift out of reverse.
7. Place ignition switch in run position, shift transmission to second gear, ensure that steering wheel will turn and key can not be removed from ignition switch.

1973-76 Floor Shift

1978-79 Cutlass

1. Place ignition switch in "Off" position, then raise vehicle.
2. Remove retainers from shift rods, then place transmission shift levers in neutral.
3. Place control lever in neutral position. Align levers and insert gauge pin into levers and bracket.

4. Loosen nuts on 1st-reverse shift rod and adjust trunion and pin assembly, then tighten nuts.
5. Loosen nuts on 2nd-3rd shift rod and adjust trunion and pin assembly, then tighten nuts.
6. Remove gauge pin, then check linkage for proper operation.

1974-76

1. Place shift lever in Neutral and raise vehicle.
2. Loosen shift rod swivel nuts and disconnect rods from shifter, then insert a ¼ inch pin into shifter, Fig. 4.
3. Adjust swivel to obtain free pin length, tighten swivel nuts and connect shift rods to shifter.
4. With shift lever in Reverse and igni-

3 SPEED SHIFT LINKAGE, ADJUST

1974-79 Column Shift

1. Place transmission in reverse and raise vehicle.
2. Loosen swivel bolts on shift rods at transmission, ensuring rods are free to move in swivels.
3. Hold 1st-reverse column relay level in position, push up on shift rod until detent in column is felt, then torque swivel bolt to 20 ft. lbs. on 1974 models and 1978-79 Omega, 26 ft. lbs. on 1975-77 Omega and 23 ft. lbs. on 1975-77 Cutlass.
4. Place transmission in Neutral, insert ³⁄₁₆ inch rod through column relay lever into alignment hole and torque swivel nut to 20 ft. lbs. on 1974 models and 1978-79 Omega, 26 ft. lbs. on 1975-77 Omega and 23 ft. lbs. on 1975-77 Cutlass.
5. Lower vehicle and check shift operation.
6. Place transmission in reverse, turn ignition switch to lock position and ensure that the key can be removed, steering wheel will not turn and trans-

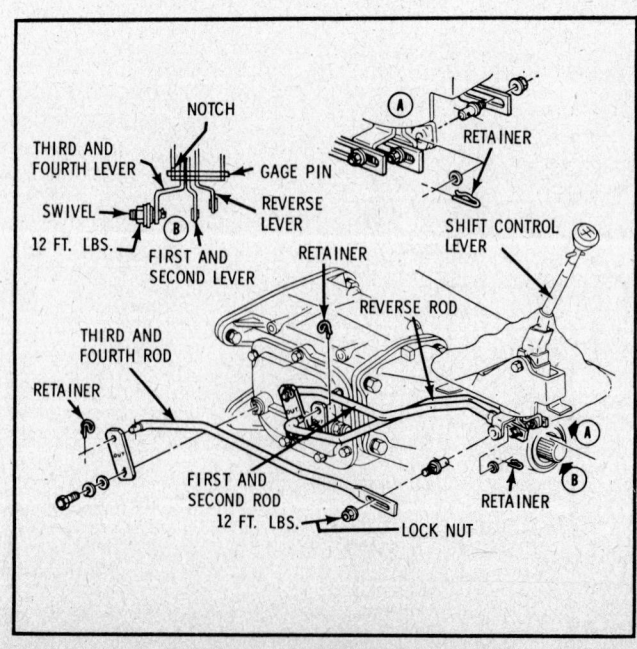

Fig. 5   Four speed shift linkage. 1975-78

tion key in Lock, loosen equalizer clamp and lightly pull back drive rod against stop. Torque equalizer clamp screw to 23 ft. lbs.

5. To check for proper operation:
   a. Place ignition key in Lock and shift lever in Reverse and ensure that key can be removed and steering wheel is locked.
   b. Place ignition key in Off and shift lever in Neutral and ensure that key cannot be removed and steering wheel is unlocked.

4 SPEED TRANS., REPLACE

1975-79

1. Raise vehicle and drain transmission.
2. Remove propeller shaft.
3. Disconnect speedometer cable and back-up light switch from transmission.
4. Disconnect transmission control rod and lever assemblies from shifter shafts. Position rods aside.
5. Remove crossmember to transmission mount bolts.
6. Remove catalytic converter support bracket.
7. Support engine with a suitable jack and remove crossmember to frame bolts, then the crossmember.
8. Remove transmission to clutch housing upper retaining bolts and install guide pins in holes.

9. Remove the transmission to clutch housing lower retaining bolts, slide transmission rearward and remove from vehicle.
10. Reverse procedure to install.

4 SPEED SHIFT LINKAGE, ADJUST

1975-79

1. Turn ignition switch to "Off" position and raise vehicle.
2. Loosen lock nuts on shift rod swivels, Fig. 5. The rods should pass freely through the swivels.
3. Place transmission shift levers in neutral.
4. Place shift control lever in neutral. Align control levers and install a suitable pin into levers and bracket.
5. Tighten 1st.-2nd. shift rod nut against swivel.
6. Tighten 3rd.-4th. shift rod nut against swivel.
7. Tighten reverse shift control rod nut.
8. Remove pin from control lever assembly and check for proper operation.

5 SPEED TRANS., REPLACE

1976-78

1. Remove Shifter assembly.

2. Raise vehicle and remove propeller shaft.
3. Disconnect speedometer cable from transmission.
4. Remove crossmember to transmission bolts.
5. Remove catalytic converter support bracket.
6. Support engine and remove crossmember.
7. Remove transmission to clutch housing upper retaining bolts and install guide pins.
8. Remove transmission to clutch housing lower bolts and slide transmission rearward, then remove from vehicle.
9. Remove back-up lamp switch and fill plug. Tilt transmission and drain fluid.
10. Reverse procedure to install.

1979 AUTO. TRANS. LINKAGE, ADJUST

1979 Toronado

For linkage adjustment procedures for the Turbo Hydra-Matic 325 automatic transmission, refer to Main Index.

Except 1979 Toronado

Adjustment procedures for the 1979 models are essentially the same as those for the 1978 units as outlined elsewhere in this manual.

Rear Axle, Propeller Shaft & Brakes

REAR AXLE

Figs. 1 and 2 illustrate the rear axle assemblies used on conventional models. When necessary to overhaul any of these units, refer to the *Rear Axle Specifications* table in this chapter.

Integral Carrier 1974-78
Type "B" & "O" (Except 7½")

As shown in Fig. 1, the drive pinion is mounted on two tapered roller bearings that are preloaded by two selected spacers. The drive pinion is positioned by shims located between a shoulder on the pinion and the rear bearing. The front bearing is held in place by a large nut.

The differential is supported in the carrier by two tapered roller side bearings. These are preloaded by inserting shims between the bearings and the pedestals. The differential assembly is positioned for ring gear and pinion backlash by varying these shims.

1974-78
Type C, G, K, M, O(7½") & P

In these rear axles, Fig. 2, the rear axle housing and differential carrier are cast into an integral assembly. The drive pinion assembly is mounted in two opposed tapered roller bearings. The pinion bearings are preloaded by a spacer behind the front bearing. The pinion is positioned by a washer between the head of the pinion and the rear bearing.

The differential is supported in the carrier by two tapered roller side bearings. These bearings are preloaded by spacers located between the bearings and carrier housing. The differential assembly is positioned for proper ring gear and pinion backlash by varying these spacers. The differential case houses two side gears in mesh with two pinions mounted on a pinion shaft which is held in place by a lock pin. The side gears and pinions are backed by thrust washers.

REAR AXLE ASSEMBLY, REPLACE

Construction of the axle assembly is such that service operations may be performed with the housing installed in the vehicle or with the housing removed and installed in a holding fixture. The following procedure is necessary only when the housing requires replacement.

1974-79 Omega

1. Raise vehicle and support axle using a suitable jack.
2. Disconnect shock absorbers from axle housing.
3. Disconnect propeller and support out of way.
4. Remove rear wheel, brake drums and axle shafts.
5. Disconnect brake lines from clips on axle tubes.

6. Remove backing plates and support from frame using wire.
7. Remove lower spring pad brackets, then shift axle to clear springs.
8. Reverse procedure to install.

1974-79 Except Omega

1. Raise car and remove rear wheels, drums and axle shafts.
2. Disconnect brake line from wheel cylinders.
3. Unfasten and support backing plates with wire hooks to frame kickup.
4. Disconnect shock absorbers at housing.
5. Position jack stands under frame rear torque boxes, then disconnect upper control arms and slowly lower axle housing to stands.
6. Remove springs.
7. Remove propeller shaft and support front of axle housing at companion flange to prevent assembly from rotating when the lower control arms are disconnected.
8. Remove lower control arm bolts at axle housing.
9. Remove support at companion flange and lower axle housing.
10. Remove assembly to bench and transfer parts to new axle housing.
11. Reverse procedure to install.

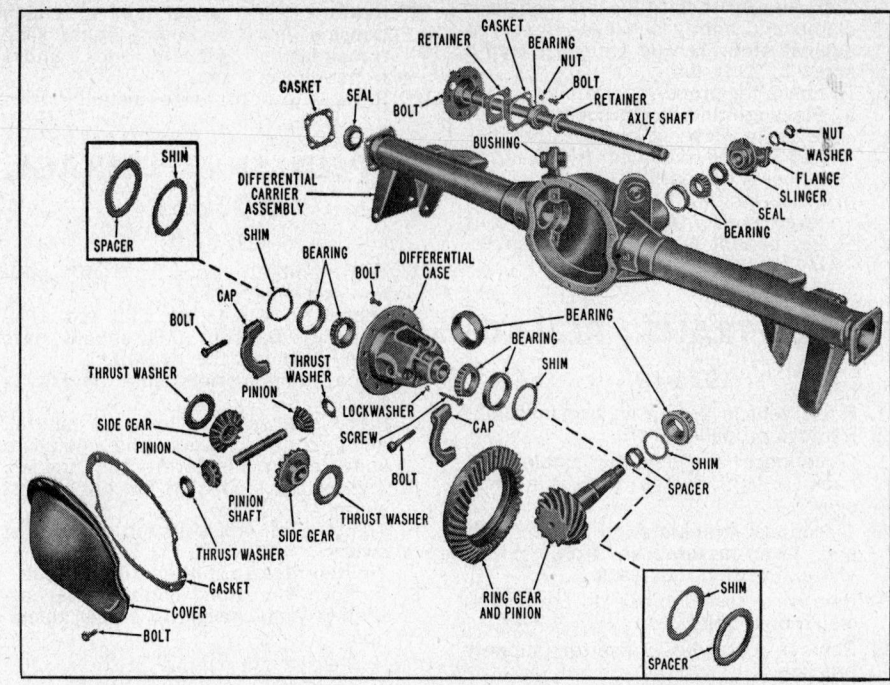

Fig. 1   Integral carrier type rear axle. 1974-78 Type B & O (Except 7½") axle

AXLE SHAFT, REPLACE

1974-79
Type C, G, K, M, O(7½") & P

1. Raise vehicle and remove wheel and brake drum.
2. Clean all dirt from area of carrier cover.
3. Drain lubricant from carrier by removing cover.
4. Remove differential pinion shaft lock screw and shaft.
5. Push flanged end of axle shaft toward center of vehicle and remove "C" lock from button end of shaft.
6. Remove axle shaft from housing, being careful not to damage oil seal.
7. Reverse procedure to install.

1974-78 Type B & O (Except 7½")

Removal

1. Remove wheel and brake drum.

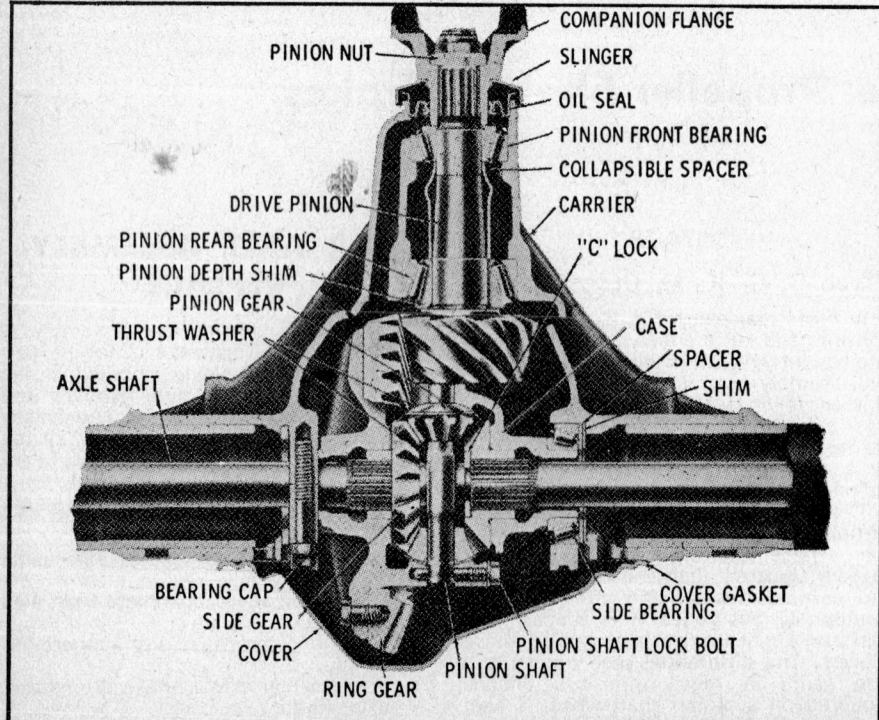

Fig. 2   Integral carrier type differential. 1974-79 Types C, G, K, M, O (7½") & P axle

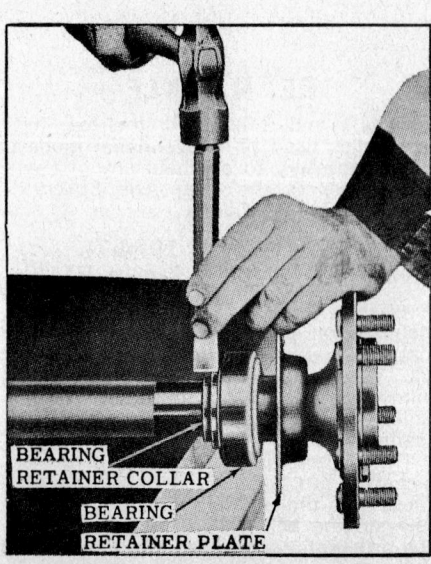

Fig. 3   Removing axle shaft bearing retainer

2. Remove axle bearing retainer (4 nuts).

NOTE: On 1976-79 8½ inch axles, new retainers are used and can be identified by a raised area around the axle shaft opening. This raised area provides proper seating of the seal and bearing.

3. Pull axle shaft from housing. If bearing is a tight fit in housing, use a slide hammer-type puller. Do not drag shaft over seal as this may damage seal.
4. Attach one axle bearing retainer nut to hold brake backing plate in position.
5. Before installing axle shaft, examine oil seal. The seals have feathered edges which form a tight seal around the shaft. If these edges are damaged in any way, seal must be replaced. Examine seal surface on shaft; if it is not smooth, dress it down with very fine emery cloth.
6. Reverse removal procedure to install axle shaft, being sure to grease outside of axle bearing, seal surface on axle shaft and bore of axle housing with differential lubricant. Place new gasket and bearing retainer over studs, install nuts and tighten to 35 ft. lbs. on 1974 Cutlass, 50 ft. lbs. on 1974 full size models, 40 ft. lbs. on 1975-76 Cutlass, 60 ft. lbs. on 1975-76 full size, 40 ft. lbs. on all 1977 models and 35 ft. lbs. on all 1978-79 models.

Installation

Bearings should be replaced if found to be rough or have greater than .020" end play. Remove bearing only when new bearing is to be installed; once removed it must not be reused.

1. With axle shaft removed from housing, split bearing retainer with a chisel, Fig. 3.
2. Press bearing off shaft.
3. Press new bearing on shaft up against shoulder on shaft.
4. Press retainer on shaft up against bearing.
5. Reverse removal procedure to install axle shaft.

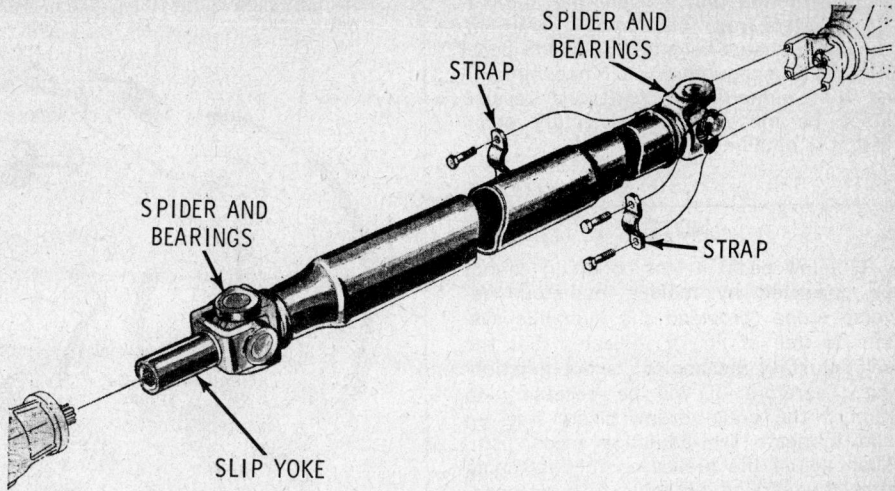

Fig. 4   Propeller shaft installation. 1974-76 Cutlass, Omega & station wagons & 1977-79 all (Typical)

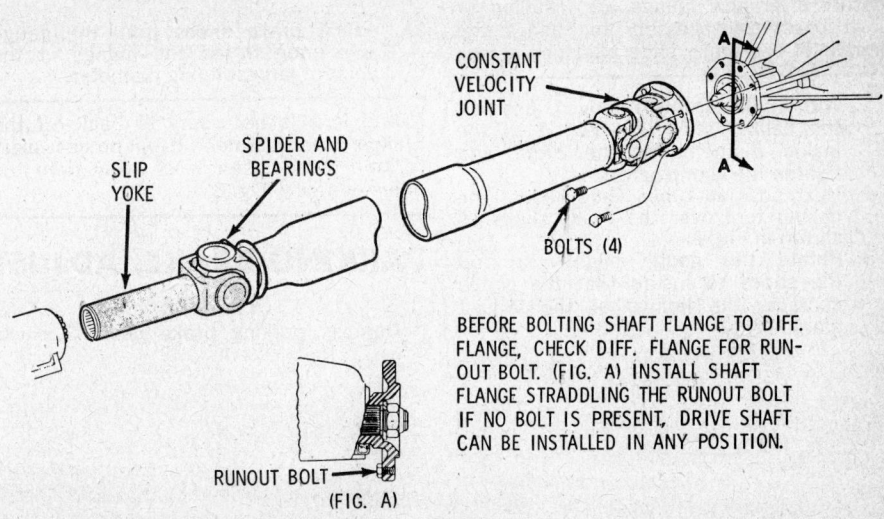

BEFORE BOLTING SHAFT FLANGE TO DIFF. FLANGE, CHECK DIFF. FLANGE FOR RUN-OUT BOLT. (FIG. A) INSTALL SHAFT FLANGE STRADDLING THE RUNOUT BOLT IF NO BOLT IS PRESENT, DRIVE SHAFT CAN BE INSTALLED IN ANY POSITION.

Fig. 4A   Propeller shaft installation. 1974-76 full size models except station wagon

PROPELLER SHAFT
1974-78

The propeller shaft is of one or two piece construction with a single or double U-joint securing the shaft to the companion flange, Figs. 4 and 4A.

1. Mark propeller shaft and companion flange so they can be installed in the same position.
2. On 1974-76 Cutlass, Omega, all station wagons and 1977-78 all models, remove strap bolts, Fig. 4. On 1974-76 full size models except station wagon, remove flange yoke to companion flange attaching bolts, Fig. 4A.

Use a piece of tape or wire to hold universal joint bearing caps in place.
3. Lower rear of shaft and side rearward.
4. Reverse procedure to install. If drive shaft yokes do not have vent holes, lubricate internal splines with engine oil. If drive shaft yokes have vent holes apply lubricant No. 1050169 or equivalent to internal splines prior to installation. On Cutlass, intermediate and full size station wagons, Omega and 1977-79 all models, torque strap bolts to 14 ft. lbs. for 1974, 20 ft. lbs. for 1975-77 and 16 ft. lbs. for 1978-79 models. On 1974-76 full size models except station wagon, torque flange yoke to companion flange attaching bolts to 75 ft. lbs. for 1974 and 95 ft. lbs. for 1975-76.

BRAKE ADJUSTMENTS
1974-79

These brakes, Figs. 5, 5A and 5B, have self adjusting shoe mechanisms that assure correct lining-to-drum clearances at all times. The automatic adjusters operate only when the brakes are applied as the car is moving rearward.

Although the brakes are self-adjusting, an initial adjustment is necessary after the brake shoes have been relined or replaced, or when the length of the star wheel adjuster has been changed during some other service operation.

Frequent usage of an automatic transmission forward range to halt reverse vehicle motion may prevent the automatic adjusters from functioning, thereby inducing low pedal heights. Should low pedal heights be encountered, it is recommended that numerous forward and reverse stops be made until satisfactory pedal height is obtained.

NOTE

If a low pedal height condition cannot be corrected by making numerous reverse stops (provided the hydraulic system is free of air) it indicates that the self-adjusting mechanism is not functioning. Therefore, it will be necessary to remove the brake drum, clean, free up and lubricate the adjusting mechanism. Then adjust the brakes as follows, being sure the parking brake is fully released.

Adjustment

NOTE: Inasmuch as there is no way to adjust these brakes with the drums installed, the following procedure is mandatory after new linings are installed or if it becomes necessary to change the length of the brake shoe adjusting screw.

1. With brake drums removed, position the caliper shown in Fig. 6 to the inside diameter of the drum and tighten the clamp screw.
2. Next position brake shoe end of the caliper tool over the brake shoes as shown in Fig. 7.
3. Rotate the gauge slightly around the shoes to insure that the gauge contacts the linings at the largest diameter.

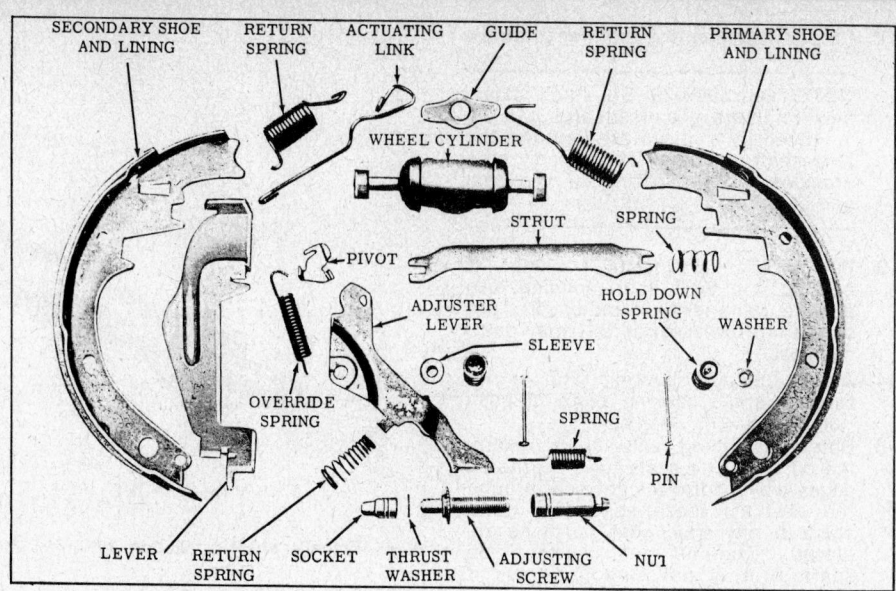

Fig. 5   Drum brake assembly exploded. Except 1978-79 Cutlass & 1979 Toronado

4. Adjust brake shoes until the gauge is a snug fit on the linings at the point of largest lining diameter.

NOTE: If it is necessary to back off the brake shoe adjustment, it will be necessary to hold the adjuster lever away from the adjuster screw, Fig. 8.

PARKING BRAKE, ADJUST

1974-78
Depress parking brake pedal 3 clicks

on all models except 1974-79 Omega and 1977 88 and 98 and all 1978-79 models. Depress parking brake pedal 2 clicks on 1974-77 Omega and 6 clicks on 1977 88 and 98 and 2 clicks on all 1978-79 models. Tighten adjusting nut until left rear wheel can just be rotated rearward using both hands and can not be rotated forward. Release parking brake, rear wheels should turn freely in either direction with no brake drag.

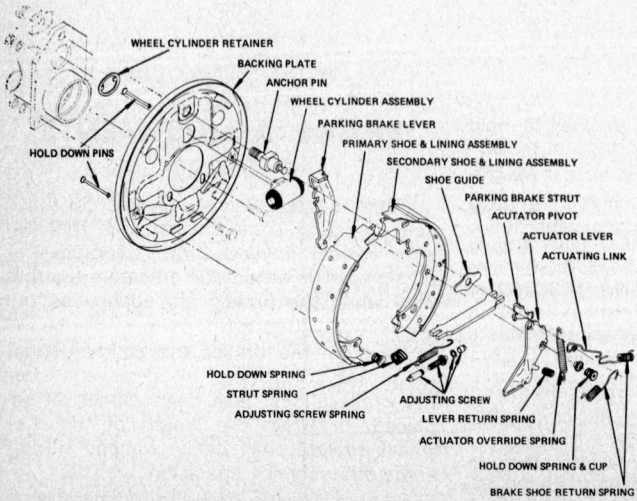

Fig. 5A   Left rear drum brake exploded. 1978-79 Cutlass

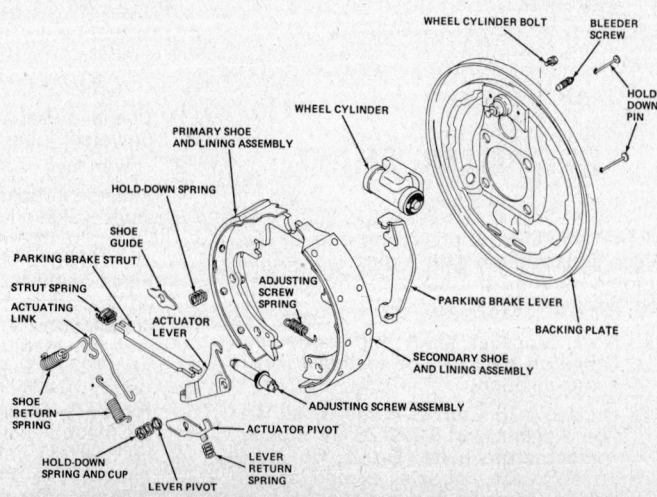

Fig. 5B   Left rear drum brake exploded. 1979 Toronado

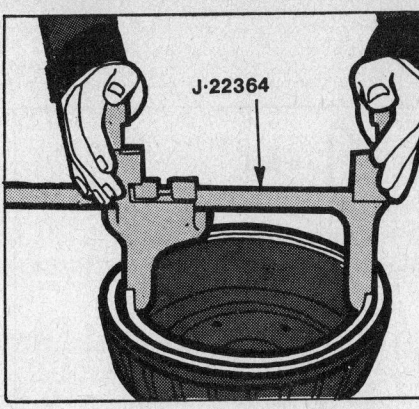

Fig. 6   Brake shoe gauge measuring inside diameter of brake drum. 1974-79

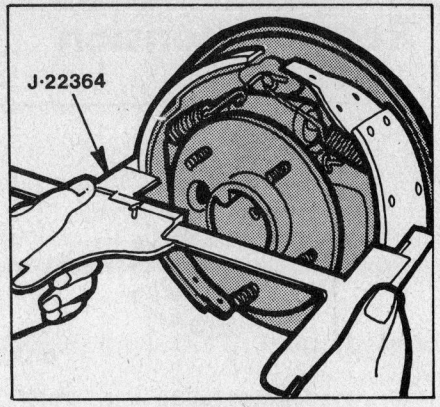

Fig. 7   Brake shoe gauge measuring outside diameter of brake shoes. 1974-79

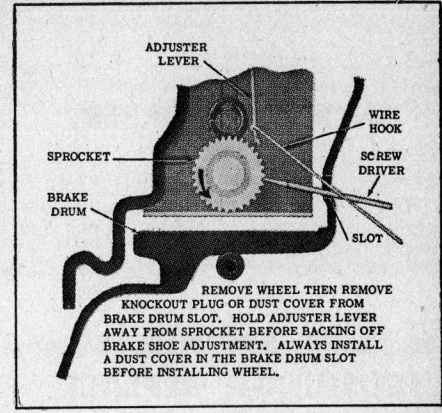

Fig. 8   Backing off brake shoe adjustment

POWER BRAKE UNIT, REPLACE
Hydro-Boost

1978-79

NOTE: Pump brake pedal several times with engine off to deplete accumulator of fluid.

1. Remove two nuts attaching master cylinder to booster, then move master cylinder away from booster with brake lines attached.
2. Remove three hydraulic lines from booster. Plug and cap all lines and outlets.
3. Remove retainer and washer securing booster push rod to brake pedal arm.
4. Remove four nuts attaching booster unit to dash panel.
5. From engine compartment, loosen booster from dash panel and move booster push rod inboard until it disconnects from brake pedal arm. Remove spring washer from brake pedal arm.
6. Remove booster unit from vehicle.
7. Reverse procedure to install. To purge system, disconnect feed wire from injection pump. Fill power steering pump reservoir, then crank engine for several seconds and recheck power steering pump fluid level. Connect injection pump feed wire and start engine, then cycle steering wheel from stop to stop twice and stop engine. Discharge accumulator by depressing brake pedal several times, then check fluid level. Start engine, then turn steering wheel from stop to stop and turn engine off. Check fluid level and add fluid as necessary. If foaming occurs, stop engine and wait for approximately one hour for foam to dissipate, then recheck fluid level.

Vacuum Booster

1974-79

1. Disconnect vacuum hose from vacuum cylinder and cover openings to prevent entrance of dirt.
2. Disconnect pipes from master cylinder outlets and cover openings in master cylinder and end of pipes to prevent entrance of dirt.
3. Disconnect push rod from brake pedal.

4. Unfasten and remove power brake unit.
5. Reverse procedure to install.

BRAKE MASTER CYLINDER, REPLACE

1974-79

NOTE: On models with power brakes, it is not necessary to disconnect the push rod from the brake pedal.

1. Be sure area around master cylinder is clean, then disconnect the hydraulic lines at master cylinder. Plug or tape end of line to prevent entrance of dirt or loss of brake fluid.
2. On Omega models with manual brakes, remove push rod to brake pedal clevis pin.
3. On Cutlass models with manual brakes, remove push rod to brake pedal pin.
4. Remove master cylinder retaining nuts and the master cylinder.
5. Reverse procedure to install.

Rear Suspension

SHOCK ABSORBER, REPLACE

With rear axle properly supported, disconnect shock absorber from upper and lower mountings.

LEAF SPRINGS & BUSHINGS, REPLACE

1974-79 Omega

1. Support vehicle at frame and support rear axle, relieving tension from spring.
2. Disconnect shock absorbers from lower mountings and loosen spring front mounting bolt.
3. Remove spring retainer bracket to underbody screws, lower rear axle and remove retainer bracket.
4. Disconnect parking brake cable from spring plate bracket.
5. Remove "U" bolts and spring plate, Fig. 1.
6. Support spring, remove spring front mounting bolt and rear shackle bolts.
7. Replace spring eye bushings and rear shackle frame bushings as necessary, Figs. 2 and 3.
8. Reverse procedure to install.

1974-76 Custom Cruiser

1. Support vehicle at frame and support rear axle, relieving tension from spring.
2. Disconnect shock absorbers from lower mountings and if removing right hand leaf spring, loosen tailpipe and resonator assembly.
3. Remove rear shackle bolts, "U" bolts and spring plate, Fig. 4.
4. Support spring and remove spring front mount bolt.

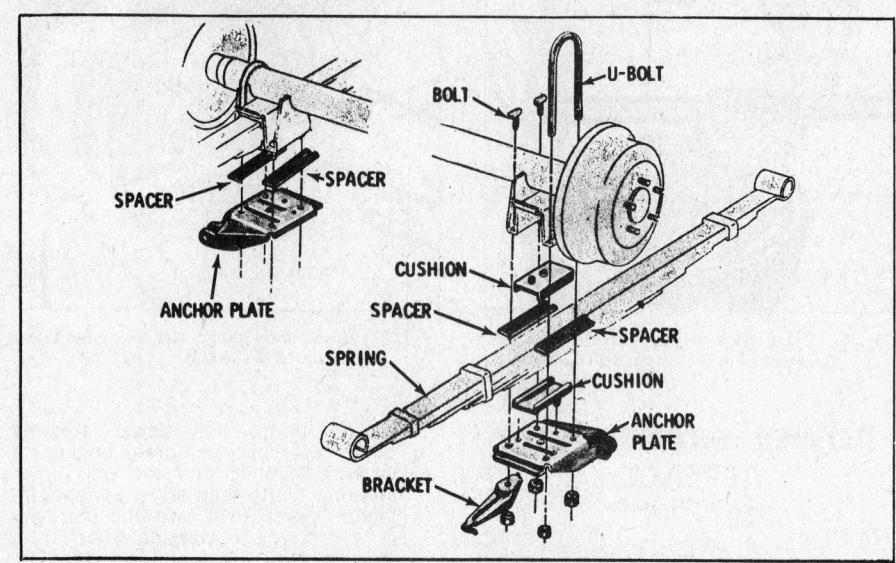

Fig. 1 Rear suspension (typical). 1974-79 Omega

5. Replace spring front bushing as necessary, Figs. 5, 6 and 7.
6. Reverse procedure to install.

COIL SPRING, REPLACE

1977-79 Except Omega

1. Position a suitable jack under rear axle housing and raise rear of vehicle, then support frame side rails with support stands. Do not lower jack.
2. Disconnect brake line at axle housing.
3. Disconnect upper control arms at axle housing.
4. Disconnect shock absorber at lower mounting, then carefully lower rear axle assembly.

NOTE: Use care not to stretch or kink brake hoses.

5. Remove coil spring from vehicle.

1974-76 Exc. Omega & Custom Cruiser

1. Raise rear of vehicle and support at frame and rear axle.
2. Disconnect shock absorber from lower mounting.
3. Compress coil spring using a suitable spring compressor.
4. Lower rear axle. Use caution not to damage or stretch brake hose.
5. Remove coil spring. It may be necessary to further compress spring and remove wheel.
6. Reverse procedure to install. Ensure spring is properly indexed, Fig. 8.

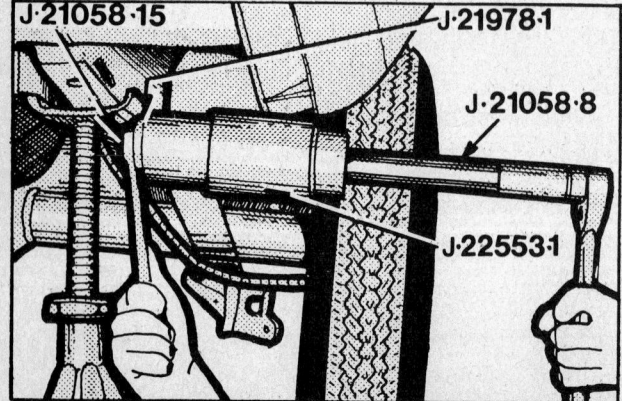

Fig. 2 Leaf spring bushings removal. 1974-79 Omega

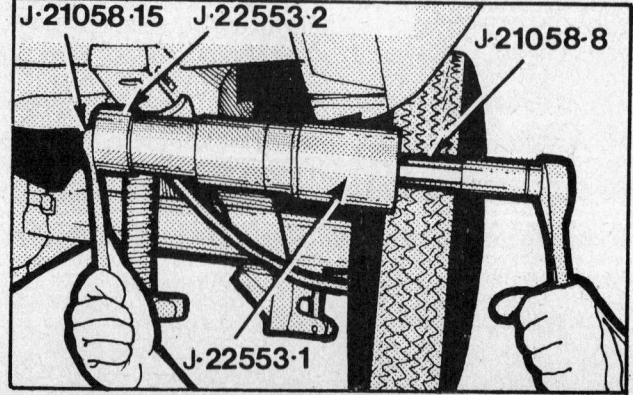

Fig. 3 Leaf spring bushings installation. 1974-79 Omega

CONTROL ARMS & BUSHINGS, REPLACE

NOTE: Replace control arms one at a time to prevent axle assembly misalignment, making installation difficult.

Upper Control Arms

1. Support vehicle at frame and rear axle.
2. Remove control arm front and rear mount bolts.
3. Replace axle housing bushing as necessary, Figs. 9 thru 12.
4. On 1978-79 models, replace control arm bushings as necessary, Figs. 13 and 14.
5. Reverse procedure to install. Tighten

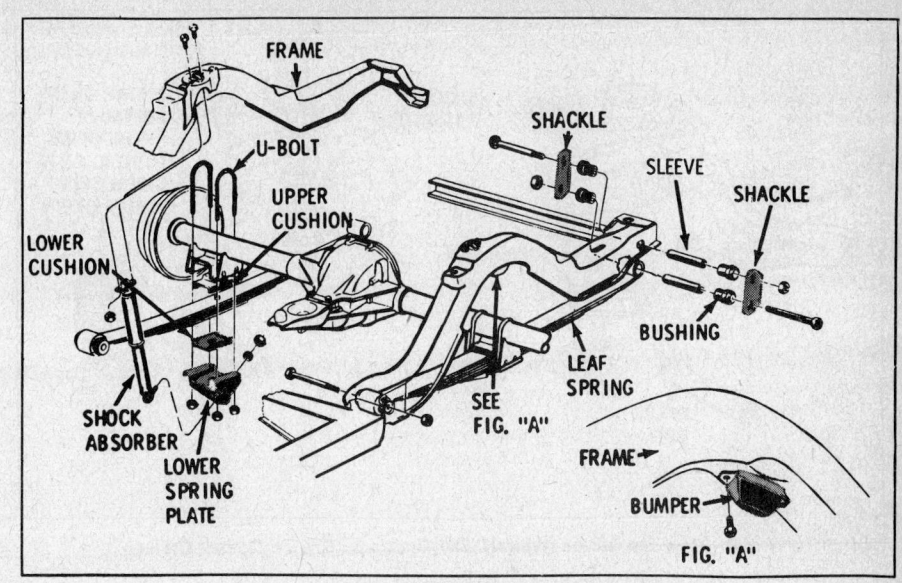

Fig. 4   Rear suspension. 1974-76 Custom Cruiser

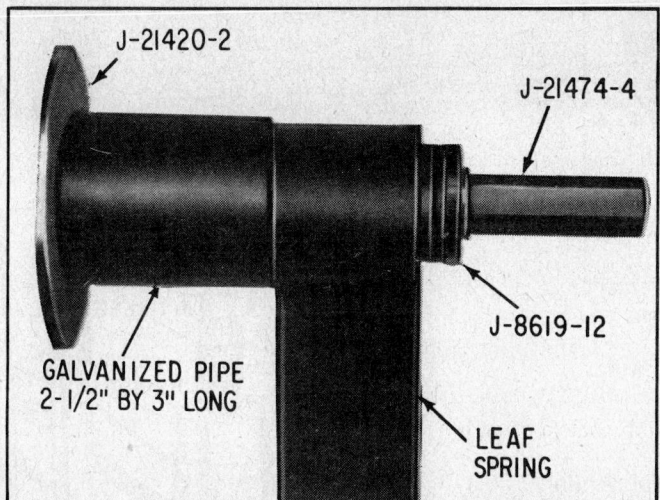

Fig. 5   Spring front bushing removal. 1974-76 Custom Cruiser

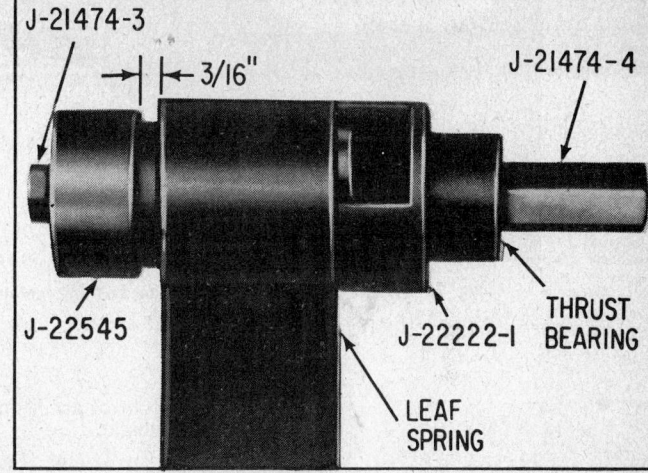

Fig. 7   Spring front bushing complete installation.
1974-76 Custom Cruiser

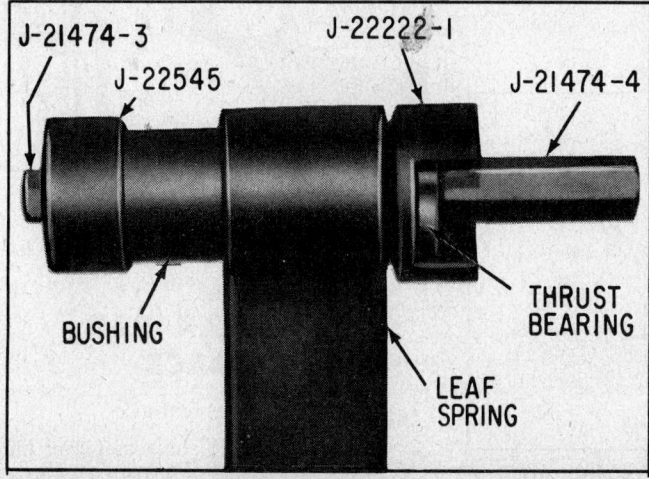

Fig. 6   Spring front bushing partial installation.
1974-76 Custom Cruiser

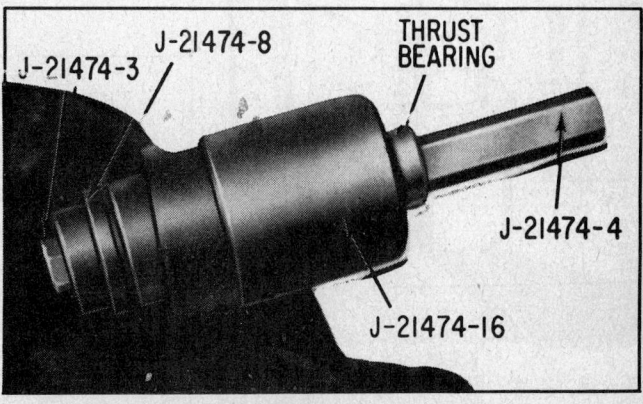

Fig. 9   Upper control arm axle bracket bushing removal.
1974-77 models

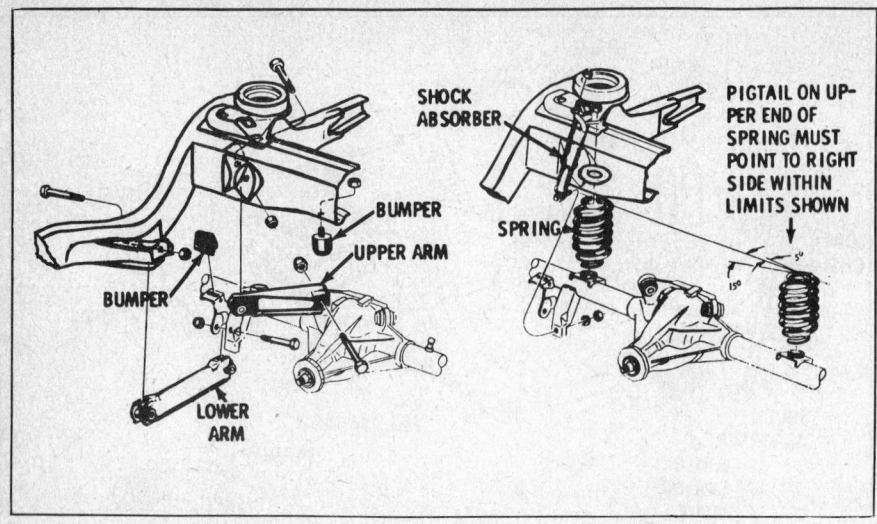

Fig. 8   Rear suspension (typical). Exc. Omega & 1974-76 Custom Cruiser

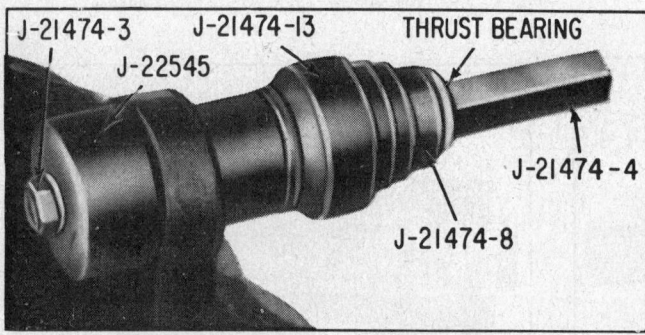

Fig. 10   Upper control arm axle bracket bushing installation. 1974-77 models

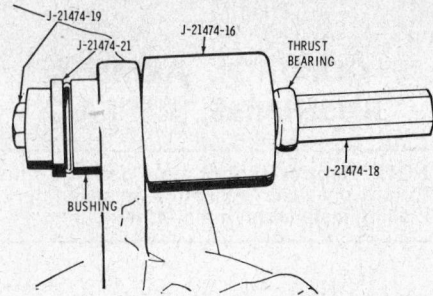

Fig. 11   Upper control arm axle bracket bushing removal. 1978-79 models

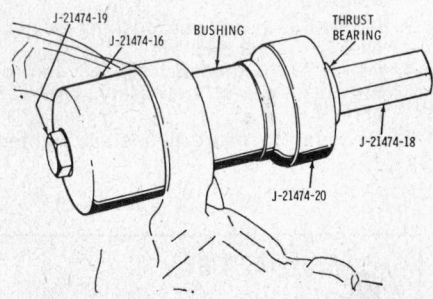

Fig. 12   Upper control arm axle bracket bushing installation. 1978-79 models

control arm bolts with vehicle at curb height.

Lower Control Arms

Follow "Upper Control Arms" procedure for replacement of lower control arms. On 1974-77 models, control arm bushings are not serviceable. On 1978-79 models, replace control arm bushings as shown in Figs. 13 and 14.

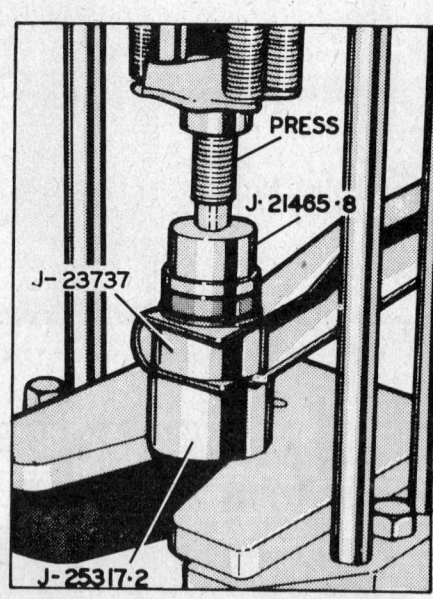

Fig. 13   All front & lower control arm rear bushing removal. 1978-79 models

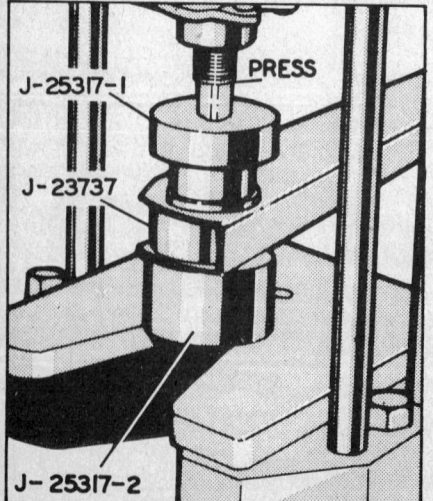

Fig. 14   All front & lower control arm rear bushing installation. 1978-79 models

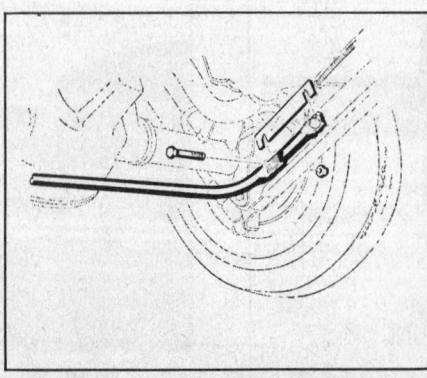

Fig. 15   Stablizer bar installation (typical)

STABILIZER BAR, REPLACE

1. Support vehicle at rear axle.
2. Remove bolts attaching stabilizer bar to the lower control arms, Fig. 15.
3. Reverse procedure to install.

Front End and Steering Section

FRONT SUSPENSION

As shown in Figs. 1 and 2, the front suspension is of the conventional "A" frame design with ball joints. Double acting shock absorbers are mounted within the coil springs. Caster and camber are controlled by shims.

LUBRICATION

Front suspension lubrication is recommended every 4 months or 6,000 miles on 1974 models, 6 months or 7,500 miles on 1975-76 models and 12 months or 7,500 miles on 1977-79 models, whichever occurs first. The ball joints are fitted with plugs which must be removed and grease fittings installed. After applying the approved type of grease, remove the fittings and reinstall the plugs.

WHEEL ALIGNMENT

1974-79

Camber and caster are adjusted by shims placed between the upper pivot shafts and the frame. In order to remove or install shims, *do not remove weight from front wheels.* Loosen pivot shaft-to-

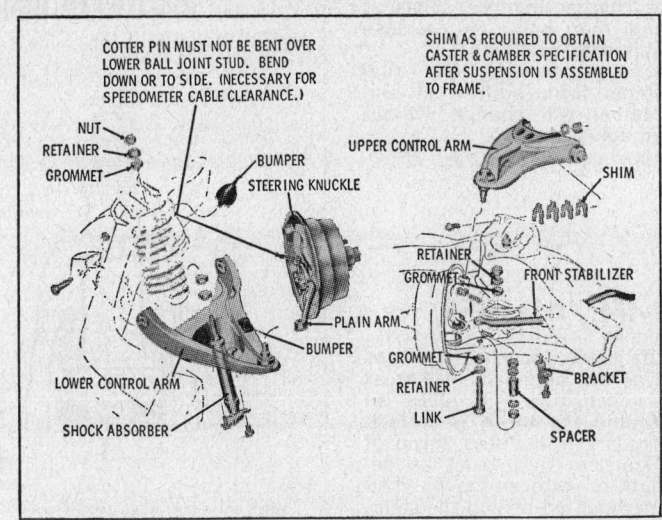

Fig. 1 Front suspension. 1974-79 Full Size Car (Typical)

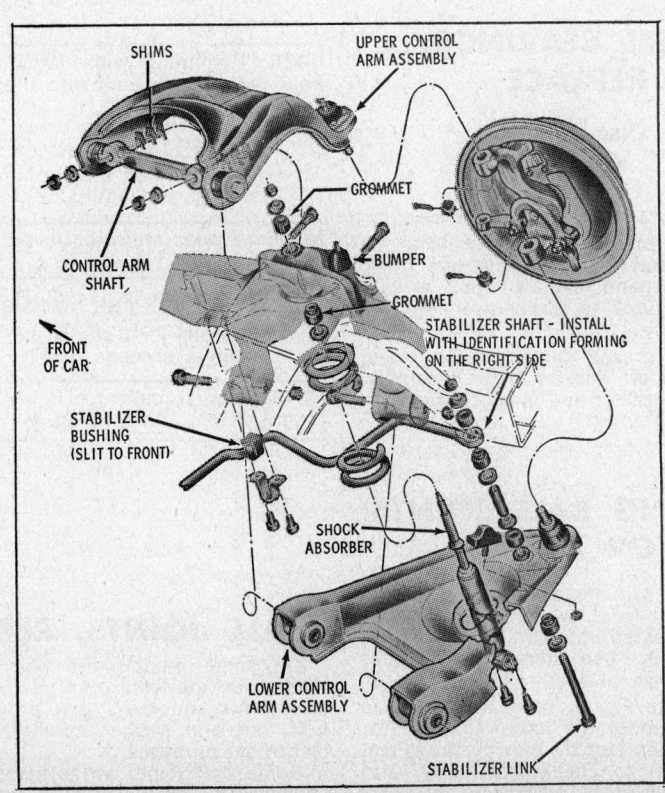

Fig. 2 Front suspension. 1974-79 Intermediate Models (Typical)

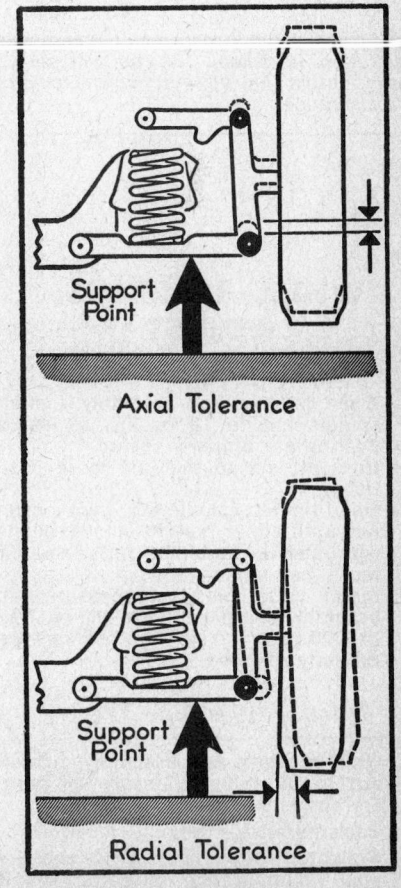

Fig. 3 Checking ball joints for wear

frame bolts. To gain access to these bolts, loosen top and rear fasteners on fender filler plate aprons.

To decrease positive caster, add shim at the front bolt. To increase positive caster, remove shim at the front bolt.

To increase camber, remove shims at both front and rear bolt. To decrease camber, add shims at both bolts.

By adding or subtracting an equal amount of shims from both front and rear bolts, camber will change without affecting caster adjustment.

TOE-IN, ADJUST

To adjust the toe-in, loosen the clamps at both ends of the adjustable tubes at each tie rod. Then turn the tubes an equal amount until the toe-in is correct. When the tie rods are mounted ahead of the steering knuckle, they must be decreased in length to increase toe-in. When the tie rods are mounted behind the steering knuckle, they must be increased in length to increase toe-in.

The steering knuckle and steering arm "rock" or tilt as front wheel rises and falls. Therefore, it is vitally important to position the bottom face of the tie rod end parallel with the machined surface at the outer end of the steering arm when tie rod length is adjusted. Severe damage and possible failure can result unless this precaution is taken. The tie rod sleeve clamps must be straight down to provide clearance.

WHEEL BEARINGS, ADJUST

1978-79

1. While rotating hub assembly, tighten spindle nut to 12 ft. lbs. to insure bearing are properly seated.
2. Back off nut to the just loose position.
3. Hand tighten spindle nut, then loosen nut until either hole in spindle aligns with slot in nut. Do not back off more than $\frac{1}{2}$ flat.
4. Install cotter pin, then measure hub assembly end play. There will be .001 to .005 in. end play when bearings are properly adjusted.

1974-77

1. While rotating hub assembly, tighten nut to 30 ft-lbs to insure all parts are properly seated.
2. Back off nut $\frac{1}{2}$ turn.
3. Retighten nut finger tight and install retaining ring or cotter key if possible. If unable to install retaining ring or cotter key, back off nut

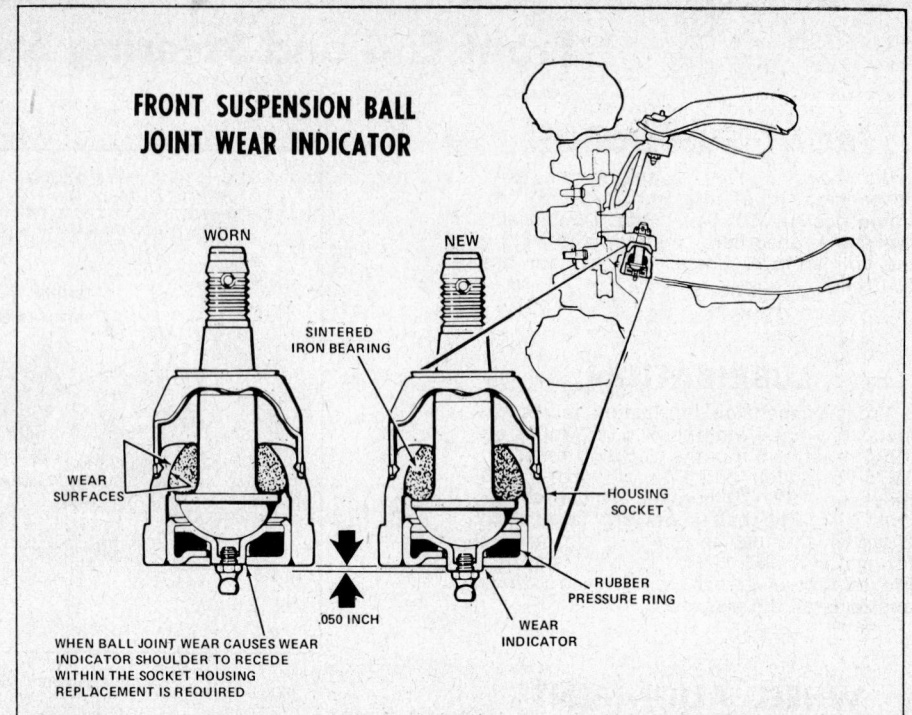

FRONT SUSPENSION BALL JOINT WEAR INDICATOR

WORN

NEW

SINTERED IRON BEARING

WEAR SURFACES

HOUSING SOCKET

.050 INCH

RUBBER PRESSURE RING

WEAR INDICATOR

WHEN BALL JOINT WEAR CAUSES WEAR INDICATOR SHOULDER TO RECEDE WITHIN THE SOCKET HOUSING REPLACEMENT IS REQUIRED

Fig. 4   Ball joint wear indicator. 1974 Exc. Omega & 1975-79 All

(not to exceed $\frac{1}{12}$ of a turn) until tabs on clip align with serrations in nut.

WHEEL BEARINGS, REPLACE

Disc Brakes
1974-79

1. Raise car and remove front wheels.
2. Remove brake pads and caliper assembly but do not disconnect brake line. Suspend caliper from a wire loop or hook to avoid strain on the brake hose.
3. Remove grease cap, cotter pin and nut. Pull off hub and disc assembly. Grease retainer and inner bearing can now be removed.

CHECKING BALL JOINTS FOR WEAR

If loose ball joints are suspected, first be sure the front wheel bearings are properly adjusted and that the control arms are tight. Then check ball joints for wear as follows:

Referring to Fig. 3, raise wheel with a jack placed under the lower control arm as shown. Then test by moving the wheel up and down to check axial play, and rocking it at the top and bottom to measure radial play.

1974-79 Omega

1. Upper ball joint should be replaced if looseness exceeds .125".
2. On 1974 models, lower ball joint should be replaced if looseness exceeds $\frac{1}{16}$".

NOTE: Beginning with 1975 models, a wear indicator is built into the lower ball joint, Fig. 4.

1974-79 Cutlass

1. Upper ball joint should be replaced if looseness exceeds .125".

NOTE: A wear indicator is built into the lower ball joint, Fig. 4.

1974-79 Full Size Cars

1. Upper ball joint should be replaced if looseness exceeds .125".

NOTE: A wear indicator is built into the lower ball joint. Refer to Fig. 4.

BALL JOINTS, REPLACE

On some models the ball joints are riveted to the control arms. All service ball joints, however, are provided with bolt, nut and washer assemblies for replacement purposes.

Some ball joints are pressed into the control arms, in which case they may be pressed out and new ones installed.

Fig. 5 Removing upper & lower ball joint stud from knuckle

Torque ball joint stud nut to the following specifications:

Year	Model	Ft. Lbs.
1974	Omega	50 Min.
	Cutlass, 88 & 98	60 Min.
1975-77	All	70 Min.
1978-79	All	60 Min.

SHOCK ABSORBER REPLACE

1. Remove upper attaching nut, retainer and grommet from shock absorber.
2. Remove two bolts and washers attaching shock absorber to lower control arm and remove shock absorber.
3. To install, position grommet and retainer over shock and slide shock up through spring and frame. Install and tighten attaching nut and lower capscrews.

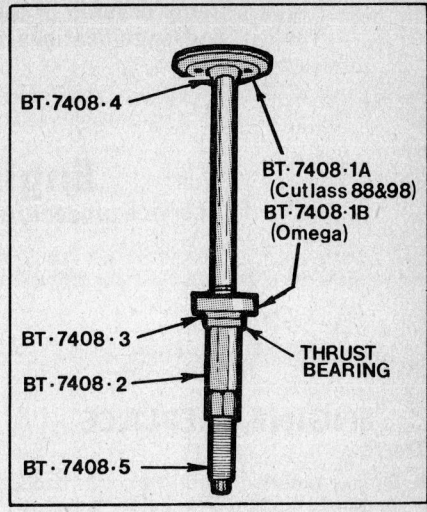

Fig. 6 Replacing coil spring 1974-79

Lower Ball Joint

1. Raise vehicle and support at frame. Remove wheel.
2. Support lower control arm with a suitable jack.
3. Remove cotter pin and loosen ball joint stud nut 2-3 turns. Then, remove ball joint stud from knuckle, Fig. 5.
4. Remove stud nut and lower the control arm. Position knuckle assembly aside.
5. Pry ball joint seal retainer from joint and remove seal.
6. Press ball joint from lower control arm with suitable tools.
7. Reverse procedure to install. Torque ball joint stud nut to the following specifications:

Year	Model	Ft. Lbs.
1974	88, 98	90 Min.
	Omega	80 Min.
1975-77	Cutlass, Omega	95 Min.
	88, 98	105 Min.
1978-79	All	83 Min.

Upper Ball Joint

1. Raise vehicle and support at frame. Remove wheel.
2. Support lower control arm with suitable jack or jack stand.
3. Remove cotter pin and loosen upper ball joint stud nut 2-3 turns. Then, remove ball joint stud from knuckle, Fig. 5.
4. Remove stud nut and support knuckle assembly to prevent damage to brake hose.
5. Using a 1/8 inch twist drill, drill the 4 ball joint rivets approximately 1/4 inch. Then, drill off rivets heads using a 1/2 inch twist drill.
6. Punch out rivets and remove lower ball joint.
7. Install new ball joint in lower control arm and torque attaching bolts to 8 ft. lbs.
8. Reverse procedure to assemble.

COIL SPRING, REPLACE

IMPORTANT: Left and right coil springs should not be interchanged. Spring part number is stamped on outer side of end coil.

1974-79

1. Place transmission in Neutral.
2. Disconnect shock absorber from upper mounting.
3. Raise vehicle and support at frame. Remove wheel.
4. Disconnect stabilizer bar from lower control arm.
5. Remove shock absorber.
6. Install lower plate BT-7408-1A or 1B, Fig. 6, with pivot ball seat facing downward into spring coils. Rotate plate to fully it in lower control arm spring seat.
7. Install upper plate BT-7408-1A or 1B, Fig. 6, with pivot ball seat facing upward into spring coils. Insert ball nut BT-7408-4 through spring coils and onto upper plate.
8. Install rod BT-7408-5 through shock absorber opening in lower control arm and through the upper and lower plates. Depress lock pin on shaft and thread into upper ball nut BT-7408-4. Ensure lock pin is fully extended above ball nut upper surface.
9. With ball nut tang engaged in slot in upper plate, rotate upper plate until it contacts upper spring seat.
10. Install lower pivot ball, thrust bearing and nut on rod and rotate nut until coil spring is compressed enough to be free in the seat.
11. Remove lower control arm pivot bolts. Move control arm rearward and remove coil spring.
12. Reverse procedure to install.

MANUAL STEERING GEAR, REPLACE

1. Remove two flex coupling flange nuts.

NOTE: On 1974-79 models, remove coupling shield.

2. Hoist and support car with stands under outer ends of lower control arms.
3. Remove nut and use a puller to remove pitman arm.
4. Remove gear-to frame bolts.
5. Position steering linkage out of the way and withdraw gear assembly from under car.
6. Reverse procedure to install unit.

POWER STEERING GEAR, REPLACE

1. Remove coupling flange hub bolt.

NOTE: On 1974-79 models, remove coupling shield.

2. Disconnect hoses from gear and cap gear and hose fittings.
3. Remove pitman arm nut and, using a suitable puller, remove pitman arm.
4. Remove gear-to-frame bolts. Permit lower shaft to slide free of coupling flange, then remove gear with hoses attached.

TORONADO SUPPLEMENT

Items covered in this section apply to the Toronado only. For service procedures and specifications not covered here, refer to the conventional Oldsmobile section of this chapter.

Engine & Transmission Section

For service procedure on 1979 Toronado Turbo Hydra-Matic 325 refer to Main Index

ENGINE, REPLACE

1974-78

1. Drain radiator and remove hood, marking hinge as a guide for reassembly.
2. If equipped with venturi shroud, unhook strap, removve seal to venturi ring clips and move towards radiator.
3. Remove air cleaner and hot air pipe.
4. Disconnect engine ground strap, upper and lower radiator hoses, transmission oil cooler lines and heater hoses.
5. Remove upper radiator baffle, radiator, fan shroud and venturi components, if equipped.
6. Disconnect power steering pump bracket from engine without disconnecting oil lines. Position pump and bracket assembly aside.
7. Disconnect A/C compressor bracket from engine without disconnecting refrigerant lines. Position compressor and bracket assembly aside.
8. Disconnect fuel lines at fuel pump, throttle cable, vacuum hoses and electrical connections.
9. Disconnect exhaust pipes from manifolds.
10. Raise vehicle.
11. Loosen upper left hand flywheel cover bolt.
12. Remove starter, then the remaining flywheel cover bolts and pivot cover from upper left hand bolt slot.
13. Mark relationship between converter and flywheel, then remove converter to flywheel bolts.
14. Remove engine front mounting attaching nuts.
15. Remove right hand output shaft support bracket bolts. Mark position of bracket to assist assembly.
16. From vehicle left side, remove final drive to engine through bolt and bracket.
17. Remove lower right hand transmission to engine attaching bolts.
18. Attach final drive support chain, Fig. 1, and lower vehicle.
19. Install suitable engine lifting equipment and remove remaining engine to transmission bolts.

NOTE: It may be necessary to raise or lower the transmission using a suitable jack with a wood block placed between the jack and transmission.

20. Remove engine from vehicle and place on support stand, Fig. 2.
21. Reverse procedure to install.

ENGINE FRONT COVER

With Engine & Oil Pan Removed

1974-78

1. Disconnect by-pass hose from water pump.
2. Remove cover-to-block bolts and remove cover, timing pointer and water pump.
3. Install cover and torque as shown in Fig. 3.

Oil Pan

1974-78

1. Remove engine as outlined.
2. Remove dipstick, drain oil and remove mount from front cover.
3. Unfasten and remove oil pan.
4. Apply sealer to both sides of pan gaskets (cork) and install on block.
5. Install front and rear rubber seals.
6. Wipe lube on seal area and install pan. Torque $5/16''$ bolts to 15 ft-lbs and $1/4''$ bolts to 10 ft-lbs.
7. Install mount on front cover and install engine.

1974-78 TRANSMISSION

Less Final Drive

Removal

1. Disconnect battery.
2. Disconnect oil cooler lines at transmission and radiator and speedometer cable at governor. Then, remove governor assembly and cover hole to prevent entry of dirt.
3. Install a suitable engine support, Fig. 2.
4. Remove the upper final drive to transmission attaching bolts, Fig. 4.
5. Remove bolts, Fig. 5.
6. Loosen, DO NOT REMOVE bolt A, Fig. 5A.
7. Hoist car and remove starter.
8. Remove bolts, B, C and D and remove flywheel cover. Remove cover by pivot-

ing the cover out of the upper bolt (A) slot, Fig. 5B.
9. Remove flywheel to converter bolts E, Fig. 5B. Rotate flywheel until bolts are removed.
10. Disconnect vacuum modulator line and detent switch wiring.
11. Install transmission lift.
12. Remove shift linkage.
13. Remove bolts E, F, G and nut H, Fig. 4.
14. Remove bolts A and B, Fig. 7.
15. Remove two upper engine mount bracket-to-transmission bolts.
16. Remove four bracket-to-engine mount bolts.
17. Slide transmission rearward and down. Remove two R. H. output shaft bracket to engine bolts. Final drive will now swing down to allow clearance to remove transmission.
18. Attach converter holding strap to housing to prevent converter from falling out when transmission is being removed.
19. After transmission is removed from vehicle, the link assembly cover insulator can be removed or installed.

Link Belt or Sprockets

Removal

1. Remove sprocket housing cover attaching bolts and cover.
2. Remove sprocket bearing retaining snap rings from retaining grooves in support housing located under drive and driven sprockets, Fig. 8.

NOTE: Do not remove the snap rings from beneath the sprockets, leave them in a loose position between the sprockets and the bearing assemblies.

3. Remove drive and driven sprockets, link belt, bearings and shafts simultaneously by alternately pulling upwards and driven support housing, Fig. 9.

NOTE: If sprockets and link belt are difficult to remove, place a small piece of masonite, or similar material between the sprocket and a short pry bar. Alternately pry upward under each sprocket. Do not pry on links or aluminum case, Fig. 10.

4. Remove link belt from drive and driven sprockets.

NOTE: REVISE CONVERTER HOLDING TOOL J-21654. DRILL A 3/8" HOLE 15-5/8" FROM ONE EXISTING HOLE.

FINAL DRIVE SUPPORT BT-6322

Fig. 1   Final drive supporting tool

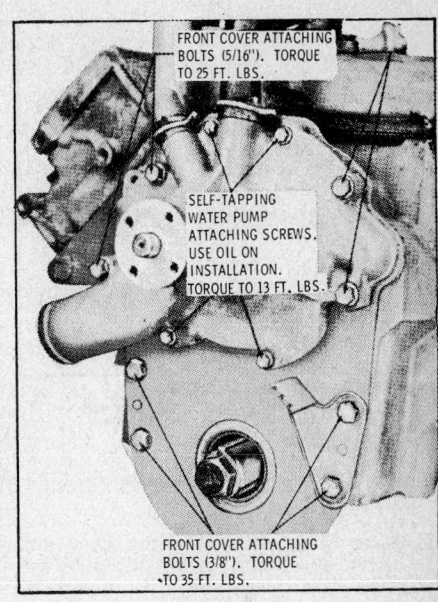

FRONT COVER ATTACHING BOLTS (5/16"). TORQUE TO 25 FT. LBS.

SELF-TAPPING WATER PUMP ATTACHING SCREWS. USE OIL ON INSTALLATION. TORQUE TO 13 FT. LBS.

FRONT COVER ATTACHING BOLTS (3/8"). TORQUE TO 35 FT. LBS.

Fig. 3   Engine front cover bolts

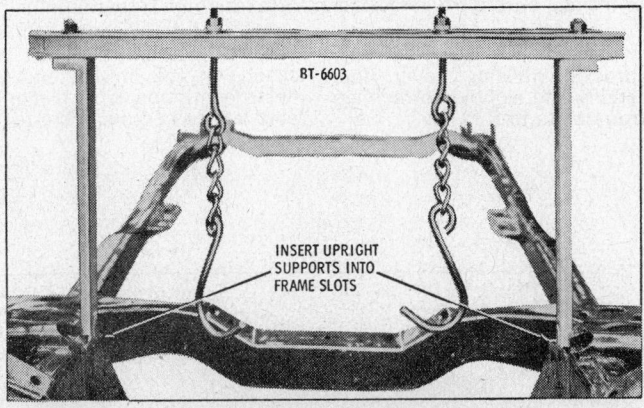

BT-6603

INSERT UPRIGHT SUPPORTS INTO FRAME SLOTS

Fig. 2   Installing support bars

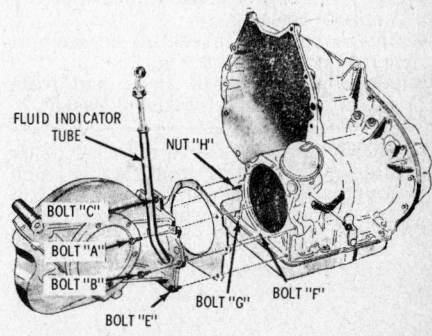

FLUID INDICATOR TUBE

NUT "H"

BOLT "C"

BOLT "A"

BOLT "B"

BOLT "E"

BOLT "G"

BOLT "F"

Fig. 4   Transmission attachment. 1974-78

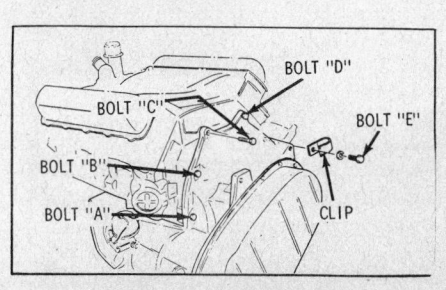

BOLT "D"

BOLT "C"

BOLT "E"

BOLT "B"

BOLT "A"

CLIP

Fig. 5   Transmission to engine attachment. 1974-78

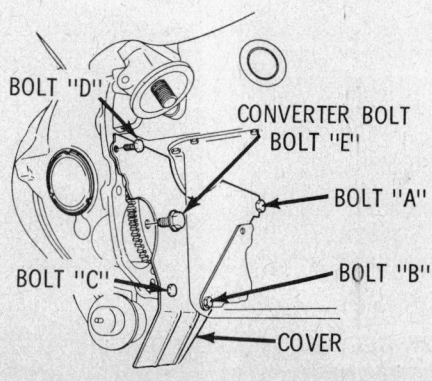

BOLT "D"

CONVERTER BOLT
BOLT "E"

BOLT "A"

BOLT "C"

BOLT "B"

COVER

Fig. 5A   Converter attachment. 1974-78

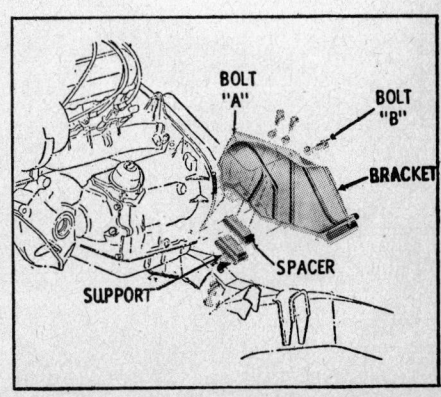

BOLT "A"

BOLT "B"

BRACKET

SPACER

SUPPORT

Fig. 6   Transmission-to-engine attachment

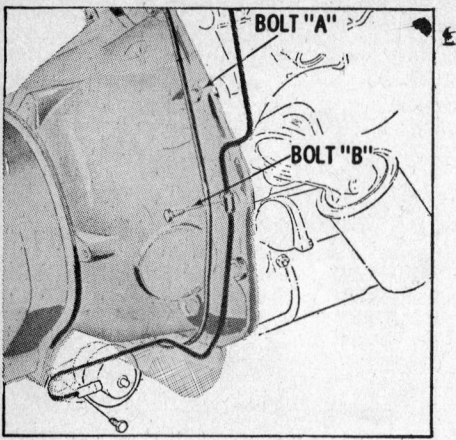

Fig. 7   Engine mount attachment

Fig. 8   Removing or installing retaining rings

Installation

1. Place link belt around the drive and driven sprockets so that the links engage the teeth of the sprockets, colored guide link which has etched numerals facing link cover.
2. Simultaneously place link belt, drive and driven sprockets into support housing, Fig. 8.
3. Using a plastic mallet, gently seat the sprocket bearing assemblies into the support housings.
4. Install sprocket assembly to support housing snap rings, Fig. 9.
5. Install new case to cover and plate assembly sprocket housing gasket.

NOTE: Important: One sprocket cover housing attaching bolt is ¼ inch longer. This bolt must be installed in the tapped hole located directly over

the cooler fittings on the transmission case.

6. Install sprocket housing cover and plate assembly and eighteen attaching bolts. Torque bolts to 8 ft. lbs.

Installation of Transmission

When installing the transmission, the motor mount bracket must be positioned loosely on the link assembly cover until the transmission is in place; then reverse removal procedure. Torque bolts to ft-

Fig. 9   Removing or installing suprockets and link assembly

Fig. 10   Removing tight sprockets

lbs as follows:

Engine to converter housing 30

Engine bracket to transmission—
1974 55
1975-78 60

Engine bracket to rubber mount—
1974 55
1975-78 60

Oil cooler lines to transmission—
1974 20
1975-78 12

Final drive to transmission—
1974 25
1975-78 30

Adjust shift linkage as directed in Fig. 11.

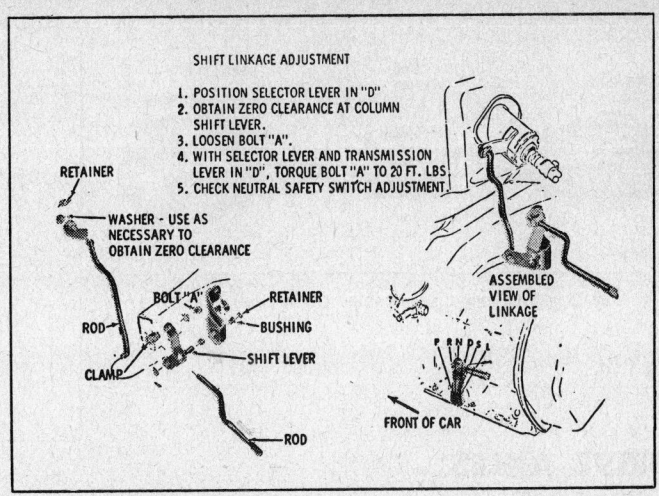

SHIFT LINKAGE ADJUSTMENT

1. POSITION SELECTOR LEVER IN "D"
2. OBTAIN ZERO CLEARANCE AT COLUMN SHIFT LEVER.
3. LOOSEN BOLT "A".
4. WITH SELECTOR LEVER AND TRANSMISSION LEVER IN "D", TORQUE BOLT "A" TO 20 FT. LBS.
5. CHECK NEUTRAL SAFETY SWITCH ADJUSTMENT.

Fig. 11   Shift linkage adjustment

Drive Axles & Final Drive Section

For service procedures on 1979 Toronado refer to Main Index

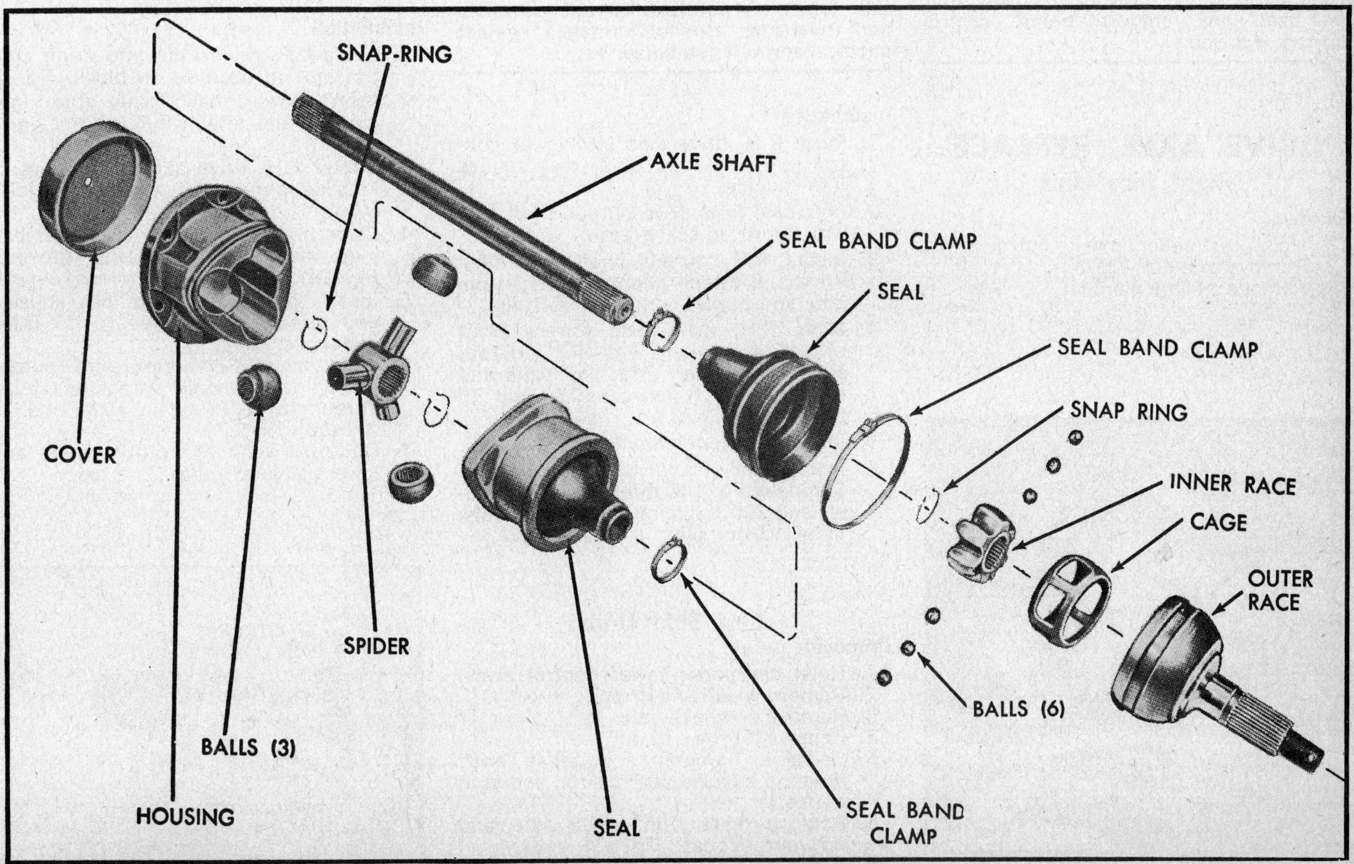

Fig. 1   Drive axle assembly. 1974-78

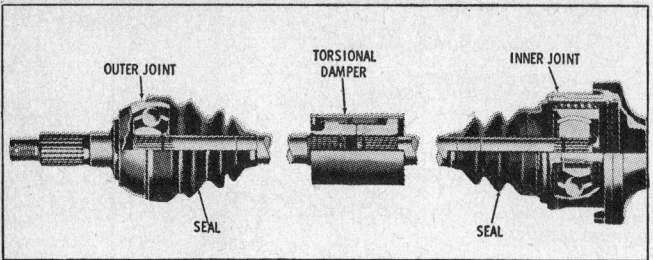

Fig. 2   Drive axle disassembled (right side)

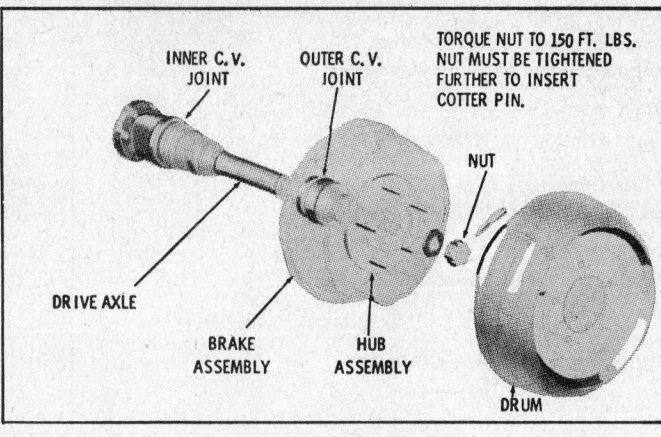

Fig. 3   Drive axle installed

DRIVE AXLES
Description

Drive axles are a complete flexible assembly and consist of an axle shaft and an inner and outer constant velocity joint, Fig. 1. The right axle shaft has a torsional damper mounted in the center. The inner constant velocity joint has complete flexibility plus inward and outward movement. The outer constant velocity joint has complete flexibility only.

NOTE: Whenever any operations call for disconnecting, connecting, removal or installation of the drive axles, care must be used to prevent damage to constant velocity joint seals. Seals may be wrapped with floor mat rubber or old inner tube, etc. Make sure rubber protective covers that are used are removed before car is started or driven.

DRIVE AXLE, REPLACE
Right Side Unit
Removal
1. Hoist car under lower control arms.
2. Remove axle nut, Fig. 3.
3. Remove oil filter element.

4. Remove inner constant velocity (C.V.) joint attaching bolts.
5. Push inner C.V. joint outward enough to disengage from R.H. final drive output shaft and move rearward.
6. Remove R.H. output shaft bracket bolts to engine and final drive.
7. Remove R.H. final drive output shaft.
8. Remove drive axle assembly.

NOTE: Care must be used to see that C.V. joints do not turn to full extremes and that seals are not damaged against shock absorber or stabilizer bar.

Installation
1. Place R.H. drive axle into lower control arm and enter outer race splines into knuckle.
2. Lubricate final drive output shaft seal with approved seal grease.
3. Install R.H. output shaft into final drive and attach support bolts to engine and brace. Torque to 55 ft-lbs.
4. Move R.H. drive axle toward front of car and align with R.H. output shaft. Install new attaching bolts and torque to 65 ft-lbs. on 1974 and 75 ft-lbs. on 1975-78.
5. Install oil filter element.
6. Install washer and nut on drive axle. Torque nut to 140 ft-lbs. on 1974 models and 200 ft-lbs. on 1975-78 models. Install cotter pin.

Left Side Unit
Removal
1. Hoist car under lower control arms.
2. Remove wheel and drum.
3. Remove drive axle nut.
4. Remove tie-rod end nut.
5. Using a hammer and brass drift, drive on knuckle until tie-rod end stud is free.
6. Remove bolts from drive axle and L.H. output shaft, Fig. 5.
7. Remove upper control arm ball joint nut. Using hammer and brass drift,

drive on knuckle until upper ball joint stud is free, Fig. 6.
8. Remove ball joint, Fig. 7, being careful not to damage drive axle seal.
9. Remove knuckle and support so that brake hose is not damaged.
10. Carefully guide drive axle out.

NOTE: Care must be used to see that C.V. joints do not turn to full extremes and that seals are not damaged against shock absorber or stabilizer bar.

Installation
1. Guide L.H. drive axle onto lower control arm in position on block, Fig. 5.
2. Insert lower ball joint stud into knuckle and attach nut (do not tighten).
3. Center L.H. drive axle in opening of knuckle and insert upper ball joint stud.
4. Place brake hose clip over upper ball joint stud and install nut (do not tighten).
5. Insert tie-rod end stud into knuckle and attach nut. Torque to 45 ft-lbs and insert cotter pin.
6. Align inner C.V. joint with output shaft and install attaching nuts. Torque to 65 ft-lbs on 1974 and 75 ft-lbs. on 1975-78.
7. On 1974 vehicles, torque upper and lower ball joint nut to 50 ft. lbs.

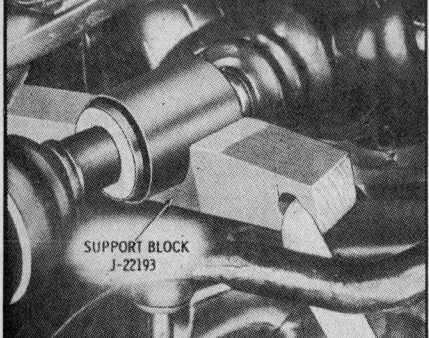

Fig. 5   Installing support block

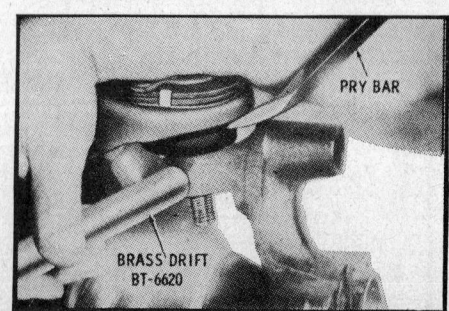

Fig. 6   Removing upper ball joint

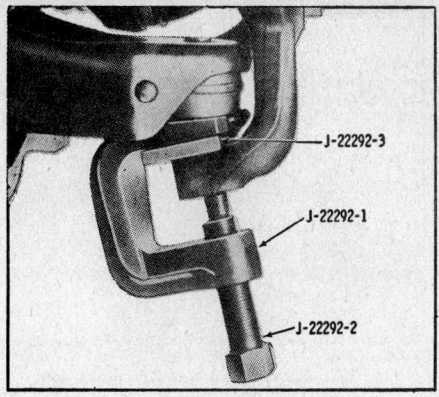

Fig. 7   Removing lower ball joint

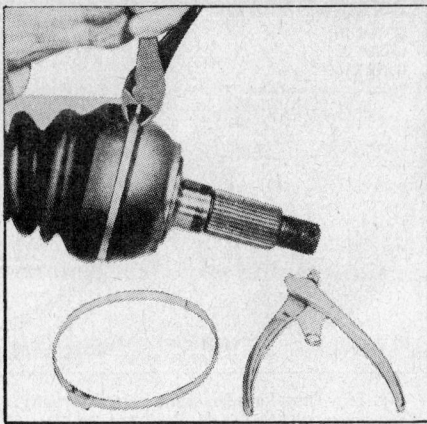

Fig. 8   Cutting seal clip

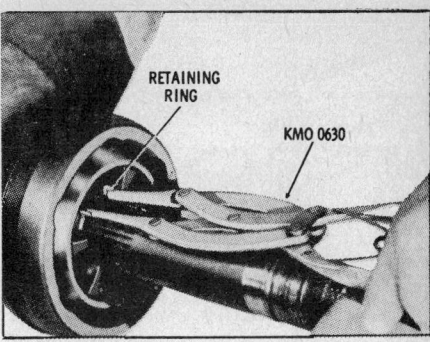

Fig. 9   Removing retaining ring

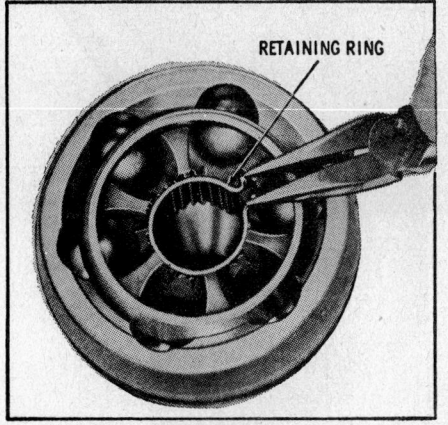

Fig. 10   Removing or installing retaining ring

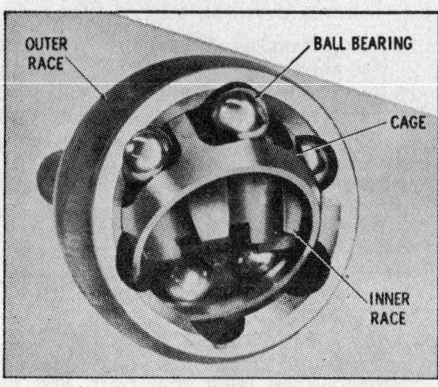

Fig. 11   Removing balls from outer race

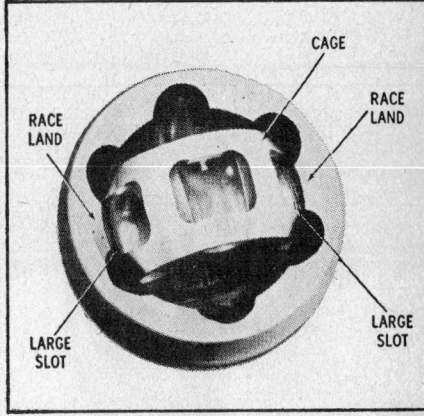

Fig. 12   Positioning cage for removal

minimum. On 1975-78 vehicles, torque upper ball joint nut to 60 ft. lbs. minimum, and lower ball joint nut to 95 ft. lbs. minimum.

NOTE: Upper ball joint cotter pin must be crimped toward upper control arm to prevent interference with outer C.V. joint seal.

8. Install drive axle washer and nut. Torque nut to 140 ft. lbs. on 1974 models and 200 ft. lbs. on 1975-78 models. Install cotter pin.
9. Install drum and wheel.
10. Lower car and check wheel alignment.

C.V. JOINT SERVICE

NOTE: The C.V. joints are to be replaced as a unit and are only disassembled for repacking and replacement of seals.

Outer C.V. Joint 1974-78
Disassemble
1. Insert axle in vise, clamping on mid-portion only.
2. Remove inner and outer seal clamps, Fig. 8.
3. Slide seal down axle shaft to gain access to C.V. joint.
4. Referring to Fig. 9, spread retaining ring until C.V. joint can be removed from axle spline.
5. Remove retaining ring, Fig. 10.
6. Slide seal from axle shaft.
7. Remove grease from C.V. joint.
8. Holding C.V. joint with one hand, tilt cage and inner race so that one ball can be removed. Continue until all six balls are removed, Fig. 11.
9. Turn cage 90° and with large slot in cage aligned with land in inner race, lift out, Fig. 12.
10. Turn inner race 90° in line with large hole in case, lift land on inner race up through large hole in cage and turn up and out to separate parts, Fig. 13.

Inspection
Wash all metal parts in cleaning solvent and dry with compressed air. Rubber seal should be replaced whenever joint is disassembled for service. Inspect all metal parts for nicks, cracks, breaks or scores. If any defects are found the joint

assembly will have to be replaced as a unit.

Reassemble
1. Insert land of inner race into large hole in cage and pivot to install in cage, Fig. 13.
2. Align inner race as shown in Fig. 12 and pivot inner race 90° to align in outer race as shown in Fig. 14.
3. Insert balls one at a time until all six are installed. Inner race and cage will have to be tilted as shown in Fig. 14 so that each ball can be inserted.
4. Pack joint full of approved lubricant. Pack inside of seal with approved lubricant until folds of seal are full.
5. Place small keystone clamp on axle shaft.
6. Install seal on axle shaft.
7. Install retaining ring into inner race, Fig. 10.
8. Insert axle shaft into splines of outer C.V. joint until retaining ring secures shaft.
9. Position seal in slot of outer race.
10. Install large keystone clamp over seal and secure, Fig. 15. Then install small keystone clamp over seal and secure, Fig. 16.

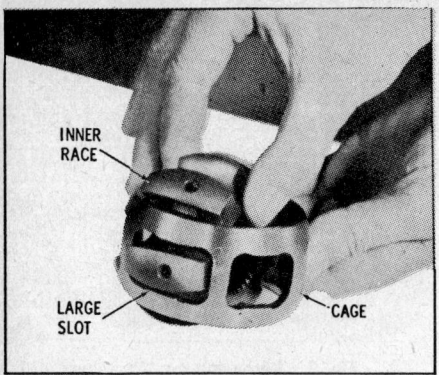

Fig. 13   Removing inner race from ball cage

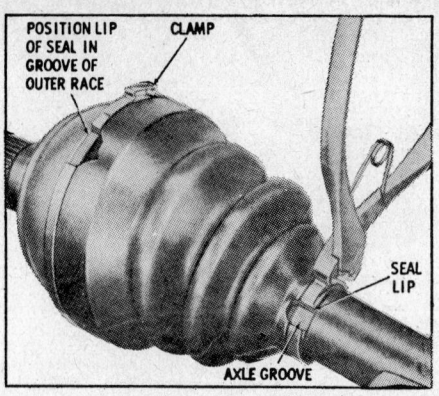

Fig. 16   Installing keystone clamp (small)

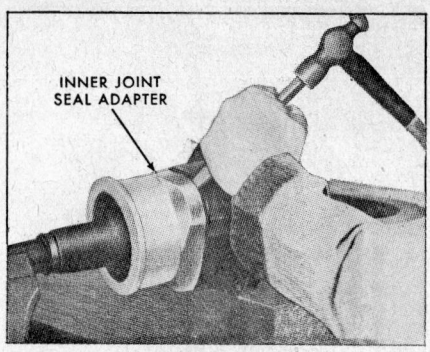

Fig. 17   Removing inner C.V. joint seal

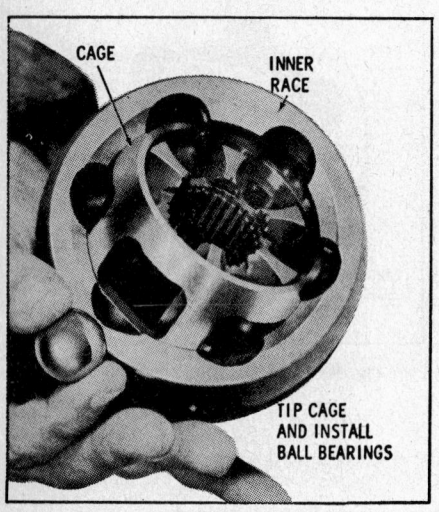

Fig. 14   Installing balls in outer race

Inner C.V. Joint 1974-78

1. Clamp mid portion of axle shaft in vise and remove small seal clamp.
2. Remove large end of seal from C.V. joint by prying out peened spots and driving off with hammer and chisel, Fig. 17.
3. Carefully slide seal down axle shaft.
4. Carefully lift housing from spider assembly and remove "O" ring from housing outer surface.

NOTE: Place a rubber band over ends of spider to retain the three balls and needle bearings.

5. Remove retaining ring from end of axle.
6. Remove spider assembly from axle.

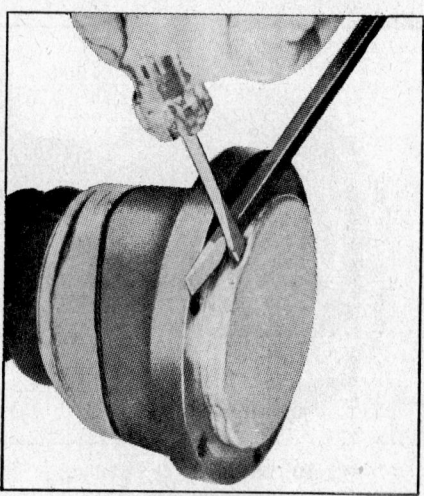

Fig. 18   Removing housing cover

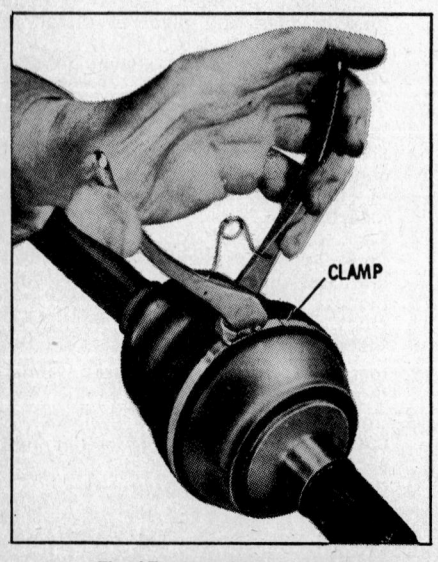

Fig. 15   Installing keystone clamp (large)

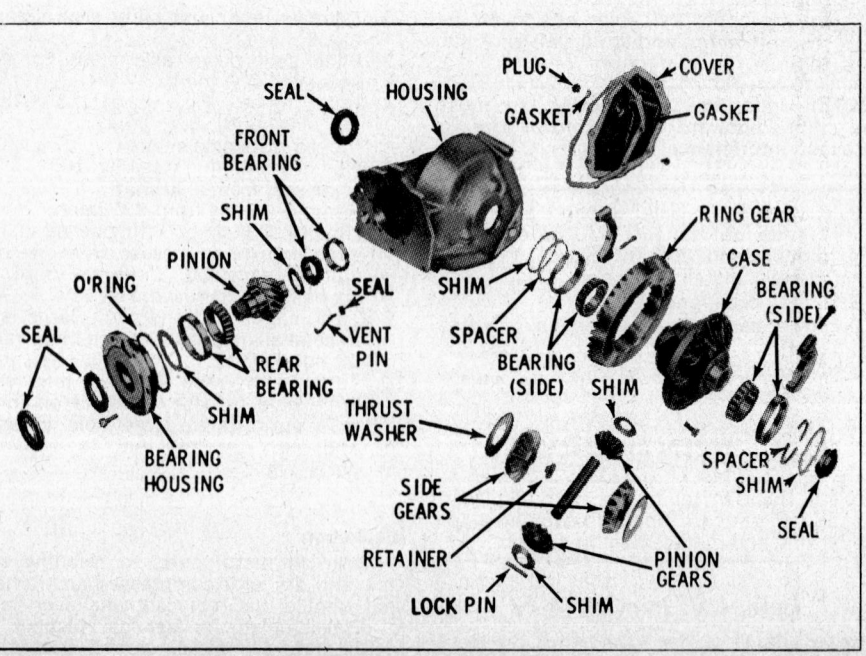

Fig. 19   Final drive disassembled. 1974-78

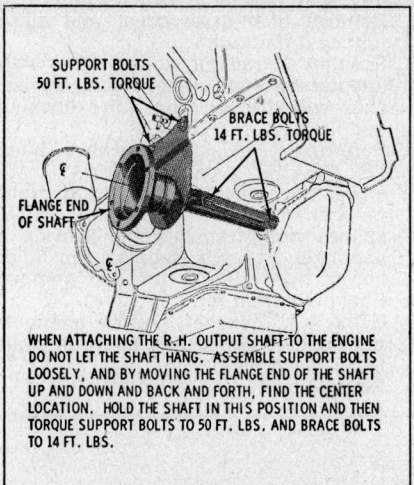

When attaching the R.H. output shaft to the engine do not let the shaft hang. Assemble support bolts loosely, and by moving the flange end of the shaft up and down and back and forth, find the center location. Hold the shaft in this position and then torque support bolts to 50 ft. lbs. and brace bolts to 14 ft. lbs.

Fig. 21 Aligning right output shaft

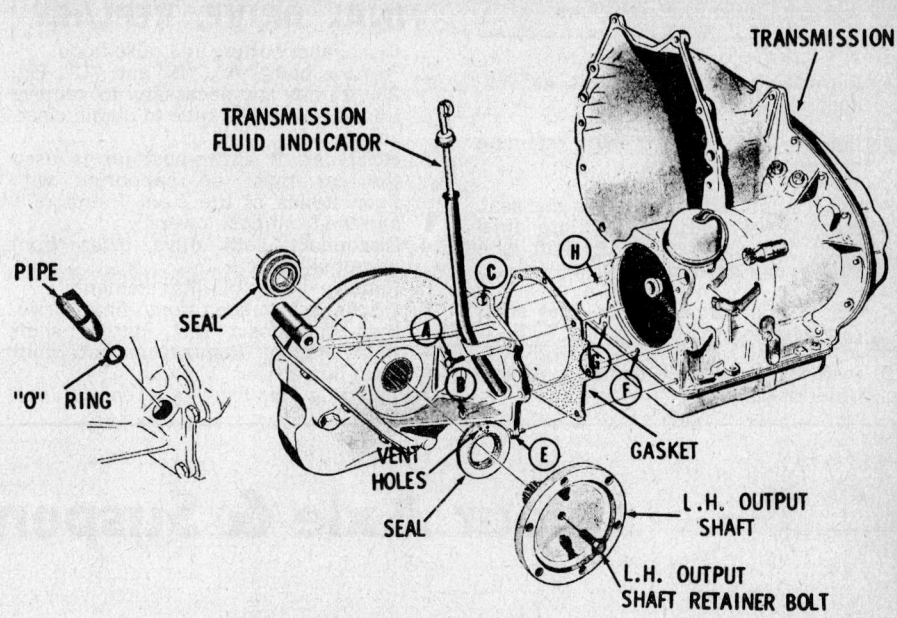

Fig. 23 Final drive attachment. 1974-78

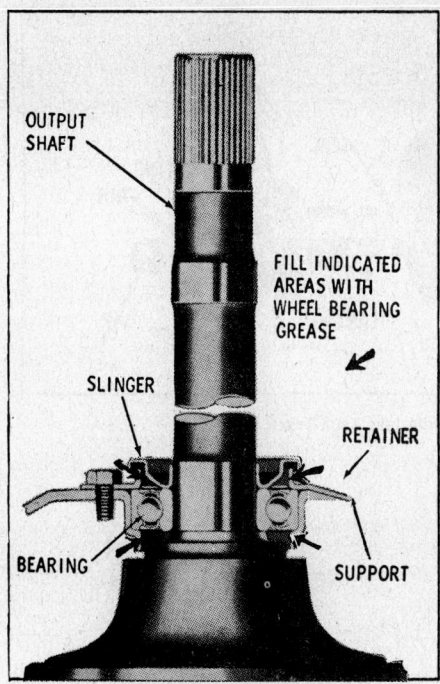

Fig. 22 Output shaft assembled (right side)

7. Remove inner retaining ring, seal and cover, Fig. 18.
8. Remove balls from spider, being careful not to lose any needles.
9. Reverse procedure to assemble, being sure to stake housing in six evenly spaced places after reassembly.

FINAL DRIVE, 1974-78

Description, Fig. 19

The final drive assembly, mounted and splined directly to the automatic transmission, consists of a pinion drive gear, a ring gear (bolted to the case), case assembly with two side gears and two pinion gears that are retained to the case with a pinion shaft. A lock pin is used instead of a bolt to lock the pinion shaft to the case. There are thrust washers used behind the side gears and shims behind the pinion gears the same as in a conventional differential. The left side gear is different than the right side gear in that it has a threaded retainer plate to which the left output shaft bolts. The two side bearings are the same and the preload shims are identical for the right and left side. The carrier is identical in external appearance and mounts to the transmission the same as in the past models.

The output shafts remain identical in external appearance as in the past. The left output shaft has the retainer bolt going through the shaft to the side gear.

OUTPUT SHAFT & SEALS

R.H. Shaft, Bearing & Seal

Removal

1. Disconnect battery. Hoist car.
2. Remove engine oil filter element.
3. Disconnect R.H. drive axle.
4. Disconnect support from engine and brace.
5. Remove output shaft assembly.

Installation Figs. 21 and 22

1. If removed, assemble bearing and related parts. Position assembly in a press and install bearing until seated against shoulder on shaft. Pack area between bearing and retainer with wheel bearing grease, then install

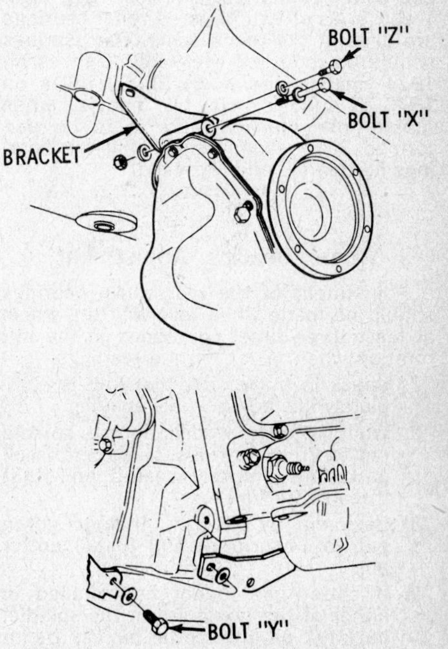

Fig. 24 Disconnecting final drive from engine

slinger. Install seal if removed.
2. Install remaining parts removed in reverse order of removal.

L.H. Output Shaft, Bearing & Seal

NOTE: The L.H. output shaft can normally be removed only after removing the final drive assembly from the car. However, if the L.H. drive axle has been removed for any reason, the output shaft and seal can be removed as follows:

1. Remove R.H. output shaft as outlined above.

2. Remove L.H. output shaft retaining bolt and remove shaft.

3. Apply approved lubricant to the seal, then insert output shaft into final drive, indexing splines of shaft with splines on final drive.

4. Install and torque L.H. output shaft retaining bolt to 45 ft-lbs.

5. Install R.H. output shaft in reverse order of removal.

FINAL DRIVE, REPLACE

1. Disconnect battery and raise hood.
2. Remove bolts "A", "B" and "C", Fig. 23. It may be necessary to remove transmission filler tube to obtain clearance.
3. Hoist car. If a two-post lift is used the car must be supported with floor stands at the front frame rails and the front post lowered.
4. Disconnect both drive axles from output shafts.
5. Remove engine oil filter element.
6. Disconnect brace from final drive, then disconnect R.H. output shaft from engine. Remove output shaft from final drive.
7. Referring to Fig. 24, remove bolt

"X" and loosen bolts "Y" and "Z".
8. Remove final drive cover and allow lubricant to drain.
9. Position transmission lift with adapter for final drive. Install an anchor bolt through final drive housing and lift pad.
10. Referring to Fig. 23, remove bolts "E", "F", "G" and nut "H".
11. Move transmission lift toward front of car to disengage final drive splines from transmission. Provide a container to catch transmission fluid.
12. Lower transmission lift and remove final drive from lift.
13. Using a ⁹⁄₁₆" socket, remove L.H. output shaft retaining bolt and pull shaft from final drive.
14. Reverse procedure to install.

Rear Axle & Suspension

REAR AXLE

NOTE: For service procedures on 1979 Toronado rear axle, refer to Main Index.

The rear wheel spindles are a press fit and bolted to the rear axle assembly, Figs. 1 and 2. As shown, tapered roller bearings are used in the rear wheels. The bearings should be repacked every 24000 miles on 1974 models and every 30000 miles on 1975-78 models. On all models, when major brake service work is to be performed, it is recommended that the bearings be cleaned and repacked.

Wheel Bearing Adjustment

Adjustment of the rear wheel bearings should be made while revolving the wheel at least three times the speed of the nut rotation when taking torque readings.

1. Check to make sure that hub is completely seated on wheel spindle.
2. While rotating wheel, tighten spindle nut to 25 to 30 ft-lbs. Make certain all parts are properly seated and that threads are free.
3. Back nut off ½ turn, then retighten nut to finger-tight and install cotter pin.
4. If cotter pin cannot be installed in either of the two holes in the spindle, back nut off until cotter pin can be installed.
5. The rear hub must be rotated at least three revolutions during tightening of spindle nut. The final adjustment to be finger-tight to provide .001-.005" bearing end play.
6. Peen end of cotter pin snug against side of nut. If it can be moved with a finger, vibration may cause it to wear and break.

Wheel Spindle, Replace

1. Raise and support rear of car and remove hub.

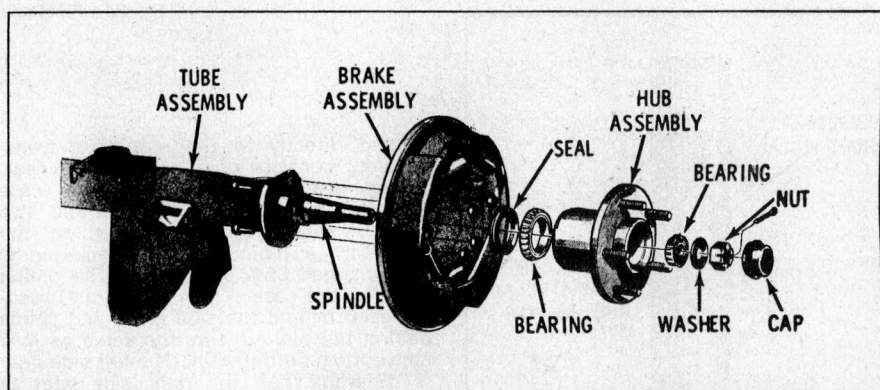

Fig. 1   Rear wheel hub & spindle less True-Track brake

2. Disconnect brake line at wheel cylinder.
3. Unfasten and remove brake backing plate and position out of the way.
4. Remove bolts securing spindle to axle.
5. Use a suitable puller to remove spindle from axle tube.

Installation

1. Start spindle into axle tube assembly with keyway facing up and install backing plate to spindle attaching bolts. Using a suitable slide hammer, drive spindle into tube while tightening bolts until spindle is fully seated.
2. Remove slide hammer and bolts.
3. Install new gasket on wheel spindle.
4. Install brake backing plate and tighten nuts to 40 ft-lbs.
5. Connect brake line to wheel cylinder, tightening fitting to 14 ft-lbs.
6. Install rear hub.

Rear Axle, Replace

1974-78

1. Raise and support rear of car with jack stands at rear frame pads ahead of rear wheel opening.
2. Remove rear wheels and hubs.
3. Disconnect brake lines at wheel cylinders.
4. Disconnect parking brake cable at equalizer.
5. Disconnect rubber brake hose at underbody, connector.
6. Support axle with a suitable jack.
7. If equipped with True Track brakes, disconnect wiring connector from underbody connector.
8. Disconnect shock absorbers from lower mountings.
9. Lower axle and remove coil spring.
10. Remove brake backing plate attaching bolts and position plates aside.
11. Disconnect upper and lower control arms from axle.
12. Lower axle from vehicle.
13. Reverse procedure to install.

SHOCK ABSORBER, REPLACE

1. With rear axle properly supported, disconnect shock absorber from upper mounting.
2. Disconnect shock absorber from lower mounting.
3. Reverse procedure to install.

COIL SPRINGS, REPLACE

1979

1. Raise and support rear of vehicle, then remove wheel and tire assembly.
2. Remove stabilizer bar as described under Stabilizer Bar, Replace.
3. Using a suitable jack support lower control arm.
4. Disconnect automatic level air line at shock absorber. If removing left hand spring from vehicle, disconnect automatic level control link from ball pivot at control arm.
5. Disconnect shock absorber from upper and lower mountings and remove shock absorber.
7. Carefully lower control arm until spring tension is relieved, then remove spring and insulator, Fig. 3.
8. Reverse procedure to install. Locate bottom end of spring between dimples on lower control arm assembly.

1974-78

1. Support vehicle at frame.
2. With rear axle properly supported, disconnect shock absorbers from lower mountings, Fig. 3A.
3. Carefully lower rear axle and remove springs.

NOTE: On 1974-78 models, it may be necessary to compress springs, using a suitable spring compressor, to facilitate removal.

4. Reverse procedure to install. On 1974-78 models, springs must be properly indexed, Fig. 4.

CONTROL ARMS & BUSHINGS, REPLACE

1974-79

NOTE: Replace one control arm at a time

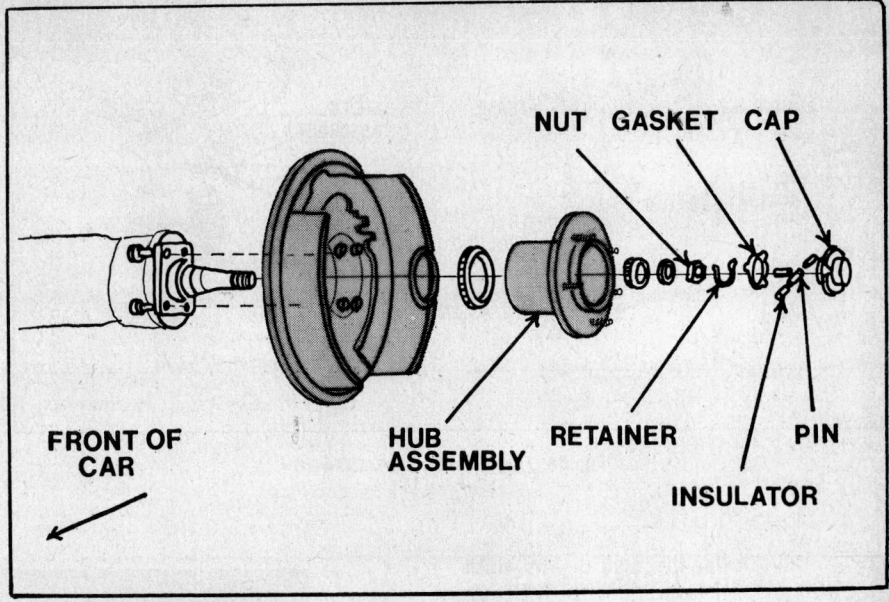

Fig. 2   Rear wheel hub & spindle with True-Track brake

to prevent rear axle misalignment, making installation difficult.

Upper Control Arms

1974-78

1. Support vehicle at frame and rear axle.
2. Remove control arm front and rear mounting bolts.
3. Replace control arm bushings as necessary, Fig. 5.

NOTE: When installing upper control arm rear bushing, reverse tool # J-21474-13.

4. Reverse procedure to install. Tighten control arm bolts with vehicle at curb height.

Lower Control Arms

1979

1. Raise and support rear of vehicle, then remove wheel and tire assembly.
2. Remove stabilizer bar as described under Stabilizer Bar, Replace.
3. Disconnect brake line bracket from control arm, then remove caliper assembly.
4. Mark a wheel stud and a corresponding point of the rotor for alignment, then remove rotor.
5. If left hand control arm is to be removed, disconnect automatic level control link from ball pivot on control arm.
6. Using a suitable jack support control arm.
7. Disconnect air line from shock absorber, then disconnect shock absorber from upper and lower mountings and remove shock absorber.

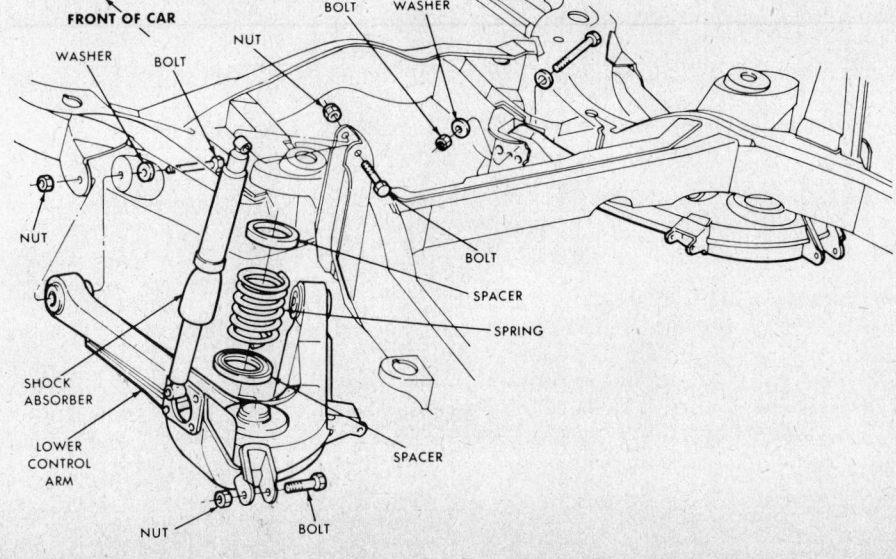

Fig. 3   Rear suspension. 1979

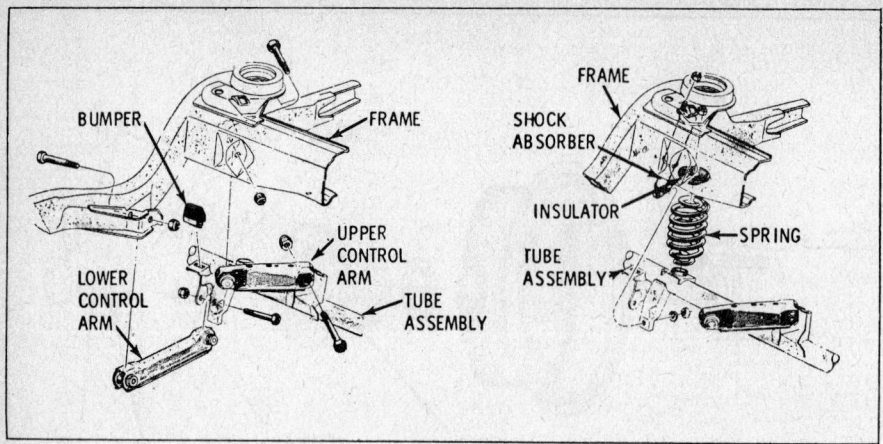

Fig. 3A Rear suspension. 1974-78

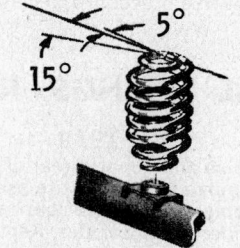

PIGTAIL ON FRAME END OF SPRING MUST POINT TO RIGHT SIDE OF CAR WITHIN LIMITS SHOWN

Fig. 4 Rear coil spring installation. 1974-78 models

8. Carefully lower the control arm until spring tension is relieved, then remove spring and insulator.

9. Remove two bolts mounting control arm to frame and remove control arm, Fig. 3.

10. Reverse procedure to install.

1974-78

Follow "Upper Control Arms" procedure for replacement of lower control arms.

STABILIZER BAR, REPLACE

1979

1. Raise and support rear of vehicle.

2. Remove nuts and bolts securing front of stabilizer bar to control arms.

3. Remove inside nut and bolt from each side of stabilizer bar link, then loosen outside nut and bolt on the stabilizer link.

4. Rotate bottom parts of link to one side and slip stabilizer out of bushings.

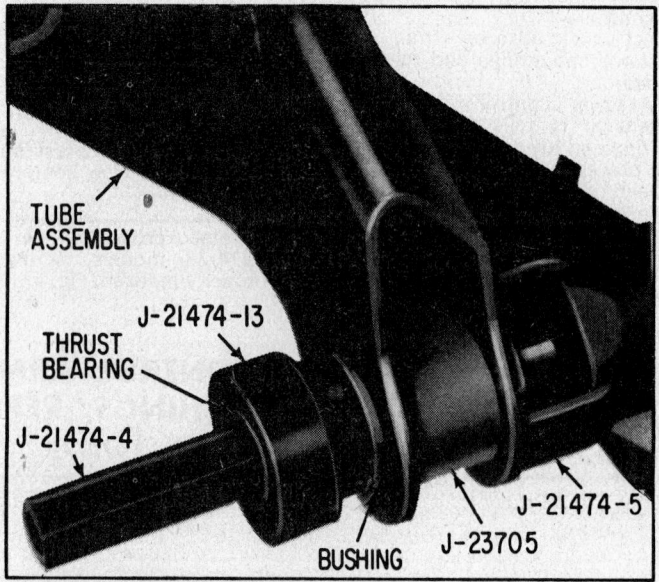

Fig. 5 Upper control arm bushing removal. 1974-78 models

Front Suspension & Steering Section

FRONT SUSPENSION

The front suspension consists of control arms, stabilizer bar, shock absorbers and a right and left torsion bar, Figs. 1, 2 and 3. Torsion bars are used instead of conventional coil springs. The front end of the torsion bar is attached to the lower control arm. The rear of the torsion bar is mounted into an adjustable arm at the torsion bar cross member. The riding height of the car is controlled by this adjustment.

LUBRICATION

Front suspension lubrication is recommended every 4 months or 6,000 miles on 1974 models, 6 months or 7,500 miles on 1975-76 models or 12 months or 7500 miles on 1977-79 models, whichever occurs first.

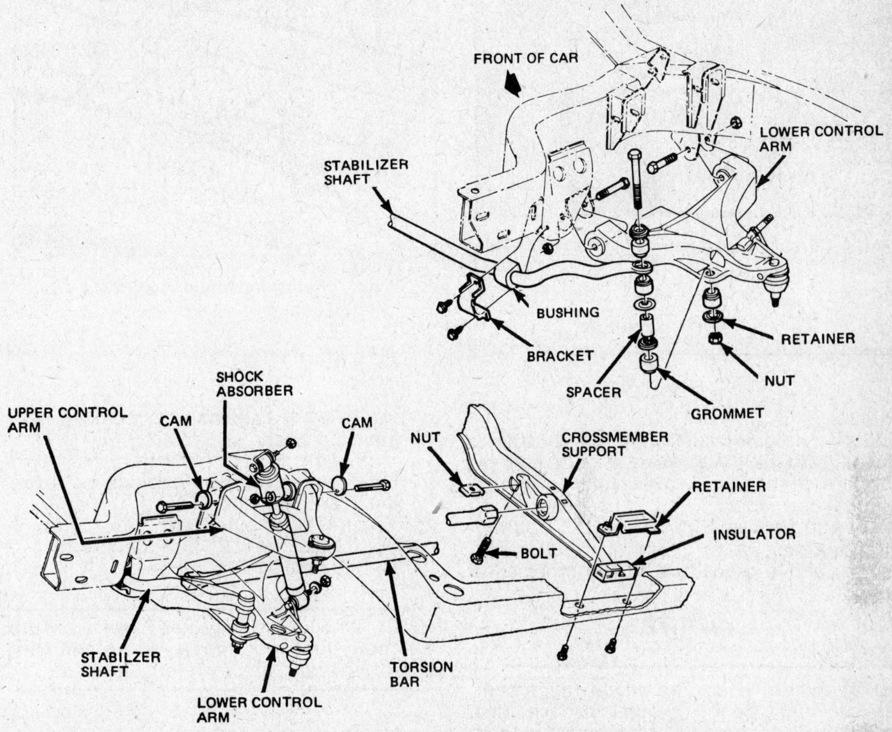

Fig. 1   Front suspension. 1979 models

STANDING HEIGHT ADJUSTMENT

1974-79

The standing height is controlled by the adjustment setting of the torsion bar adjusting bolt. To increase standing height, rotate the bolt clockwise. To decrease standing height rotate the bolt counter clockwise.

WHEEL ALIGNMENT

1979

Caster

Record camber reading, then hold front cam bolt and loosen nut. Turn front cam bolt to obtain 1/4 of the desired caster change. At front cam bolt a positive camber change produces a positive caster change and a negative camber change produces a negative caster change. Hold cam bolt in position and tighten nut. Loosen rear cam bolt nut and rotate cam bolt to return camber to setting recorded previously. When adjustment has been completed hold rear cam bolt and tighten nut.

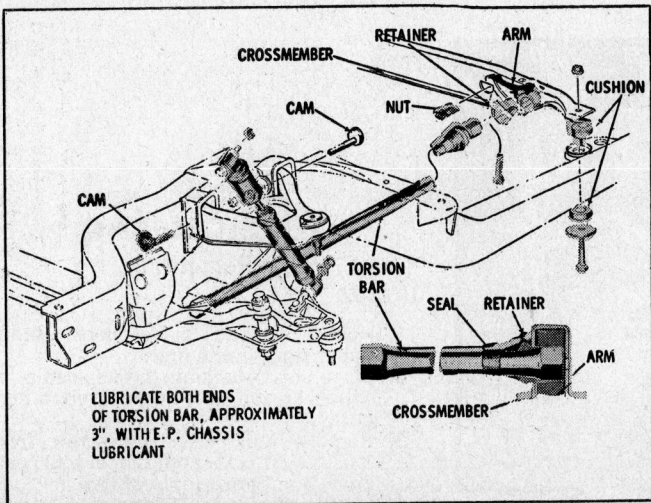

LUBRICATE BOTH ENDS OF TORSION BAR, APPROXIMATELY 3", WITH E.P. CHASSIS LUBRICANT

Fig. 2   Front suspension. 1974-78 models

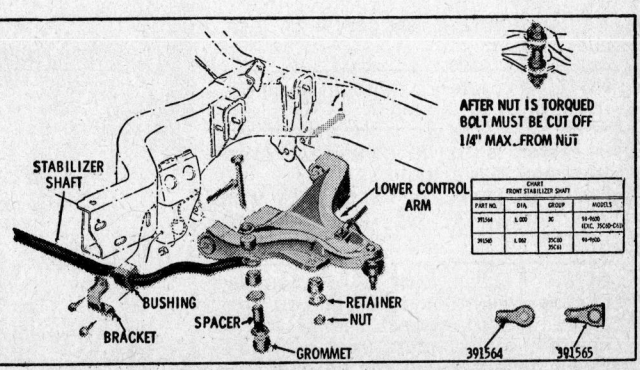

Fig. 3   Front suspension. 1974-78 models

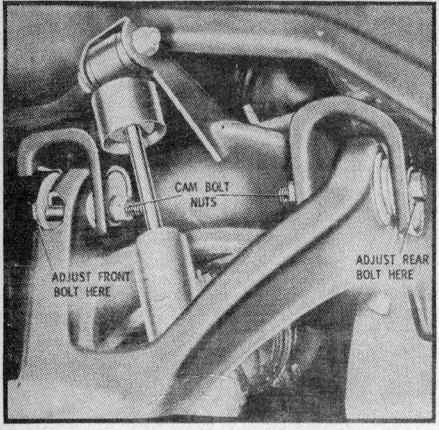

Fig. 4   Front wheel alignment cams. 1974-78

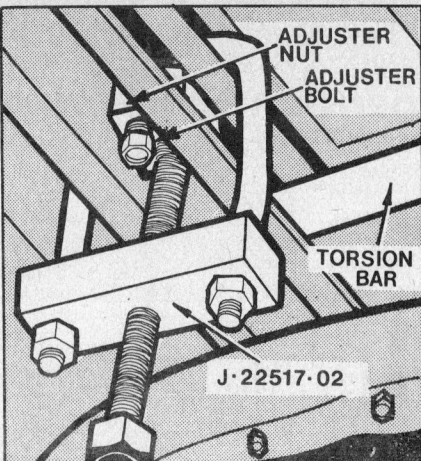

Fig. 5   Removing torsion bar. 1974-78

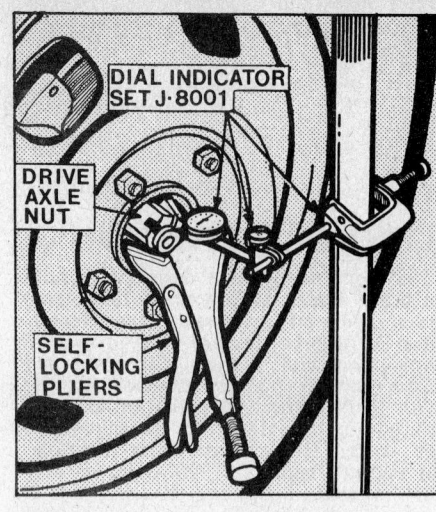

Fig. 6   Ball joint vertical check. 1974-79 models

Camber

While holding cam bolt in position, loosen cam bolt nut. Rotate cam bolt to obtain a change in camber equal to ½ the needed correction. Hold cam bolt in position and tighten cam bolt nut. To obtain the remaining ½ of needed correction apply the above procedure to the other cam bolt.

1974-78

NOTE: When checking wheel alignment the car must be on a level surface, gas tank full or a compensating weight added and front seat all the way to the rear. All doors must be closed and no passengers or additional weight should be in the car or trunk.

Caster and camber can be adjusted from under hood or under car. If under hood method is used, adjustments must be rechecked due to the change in weight distribution. After checking vehicle standing height adjust caster and camber as follows:

1. Loosen front and rear adjusting cam nuts, Fig. 4.
2. Rotate front cam to correct for ½ of incorrect camber reading.
3. Turn rear cam bolt in same direction as front cam bolt to correct for remaining ½ of incorrect camber reading.
4. Tighten front and rear cam nuts, then check caster.

NOTE: If caster is within specifications, proceed to step 7.

5. If caster is to be adjusted, lossen front and rear cam nuts.
6. Rotate front cam bolt so that camber will change ¼ of desired caster change.

NOTE: A change of 1° in camber reading will change caster reading about 2°. To correct for excessive negative caster rotate front cam bolt to increase positive camber. To correct for excessive positive caster,

rotate front cam bolt to increase negative camber.

7. Set camber to specifications by rotating rear cam bolt.
8. Torque front and rear cam nuts to 95 ft. lbs. on 1974 models and 110 ft. lbs. on 1975-78 models.

NOTE: When torquing cam nuts ensure cam bolt does not move, any movement of cam bolt will effect wheel alignment.

NOTE: If a problem exists where you should run out of cam to gain the correct reading, first turn front cam bolt so high part of cam is pointing up. Then turn rear cam bolt so high part of cam is pointing down. This is a location to start from and a correct setting can be obtained with the foregoing procedure.

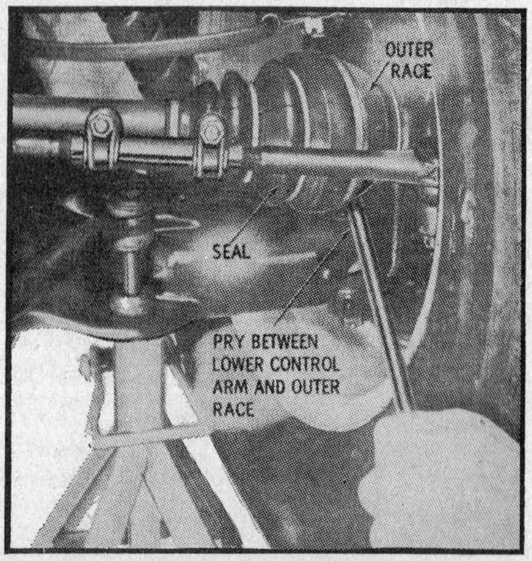

Fig. 7   Pry bar installation. 1974-79

TOE-IN, ADJUST
1979

Toe-in is adjusted by turning the tie rod adjusting tubes at outer ends of each tie rod after loosening clamp bolts. Reading should only be taken when front wheels are in the straight ahead position and steering gear is on its high spot.

1. Loosen clamp bolts at each end of tie rod adjusting sleeve.
2. Turn tie rod adjusting sleeve to obtain the proper toe-in adjustment.
3. After completing adjustment, check to ensure that the number of threads at each end of sleeve are equal and tie rod end housings and clamps are properly positioned. Torque clamp bolt to 15 ft. lbs.

1974-78

1. Center steering wheel.
2. Loosen tie-rod nuts and adjust to proper setting.
3. Torque tie-rod clamp bolts to 20 ft-lbs. on 1974 models, 24 ft-lbs. on 1975-76 models and 16 ft. lbs. on 1977-78 models. Position clamps so openings are facing upward.

TORSION BAR
Removal

1974-78

1. Hoist car and place floor stands under front frame horns.
2. Disconnect parking brake cable at equalizer and pull cable through support.
3. Remove four nuts and screw from tool J22517-02 and place tool over crossmember with pin of tool in crossmember hole, Fig. 5. Install two nuts and screw on tool, then install re-

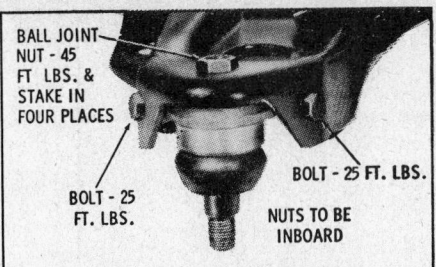

Fig. 7A   Installing service ball joint. 1974-78 models

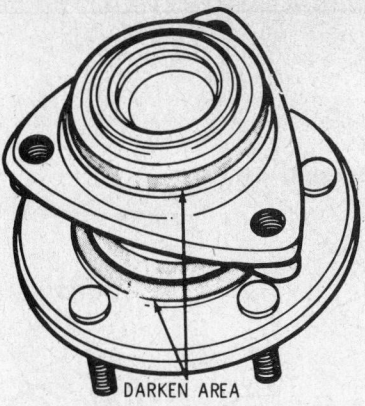

Fig. 8   Wheel bearing unit. 1979 models

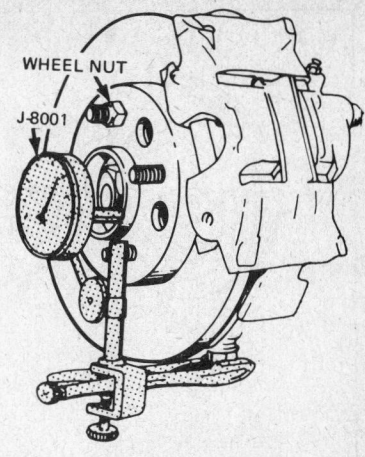

Fig. 8A   Checking wheel bearing for looseness. 1979 models

maining nuts and tighten.

NOTE: It may be necessary to pry up on underbody and down on cross-member to install tool.

4. Turn screw until seated in dimple of torsion bar adjusting arm, then remove torsion adjusting bolt and nut.

NOTE: Count and record number of turns required to remove adjusting bolt. This is required to obtain original riding height when installing torsion bar.

5. Turn center screw until tension on torsion bar is completely removed and remove tool.
6. Repeat steps 3 and 4 on other torsion bar.
7. Remove bolts and retainer from torsion bar crossmember at frame.
8. Move crossmember rearward until torsion bars are free and adjusting arms can be removed.

NOTE: It may be necessary to move both torsion bars forward until they bottom in lower control arm.

9. Disconnect hangers at muffler and tail pipes.
10. Move torsion bar crossmember sideways to the extreme right or left side. Insert a wooden block between body and frame, then move crossmember upward and outward until opposite end clears crossmember frame bracket.
11. Reverse procedure to install.

BALL JOINT CHECKS

Vertical Check

1974-79

1. Raise car and place jack stands under both lower control arms as near as possible to lower ball joints.
2. Install dial indicator, Fig. 6.
3. Place a pry bar as shown in Fig. 7 and push down on bar. Use care to see that drive axle seal is not damaged. Reading must not exceed .125".

BALL JOINTS, REPLACE

Lower Ball Joint

1979

1. Remove lower control arm and cut off two rivet heads from sides of control arm. Grind off head of rivet at bottom of control arm, then drive rivet out of arm.
2. Install service ball joint, securing it to control arm with bolts and nuts contained in kit.

1974-78

1. Remove knuckle.
2. Using a 5/8 in drill bit, drill just deep enough to remove rivet head on top side of control arm.
3. Using 1/8 in. drill bit, drill center of side rivets 1/2 in. deep, then using 1/2 in. drill bit, drill deep enough to remove rivet heads on each side of

control arm.

4. Using a hammer and punch, drive rivets out and remove ball joint.
5. Install service ball joint into control arm and torque bolts and nuts as shown in Fig. 7A.

Upper Ball Joint

1979

1. Remove upper control arm and grind head off three rivets. Using a hammer and punch, drive out rivets.
2. Install new ball joint, securing it in place with three bolts and nuts contained in the kit.
3. Install upper control arm and lubricate ball joint fitting.

1974-78

1. Raise vehicle and support under lower

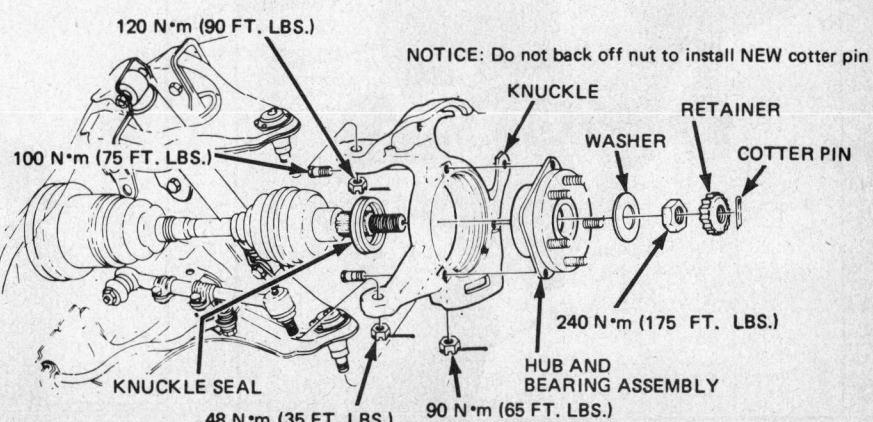

Fig. 9   Bearing & steering knuckle assembly. 1979 models

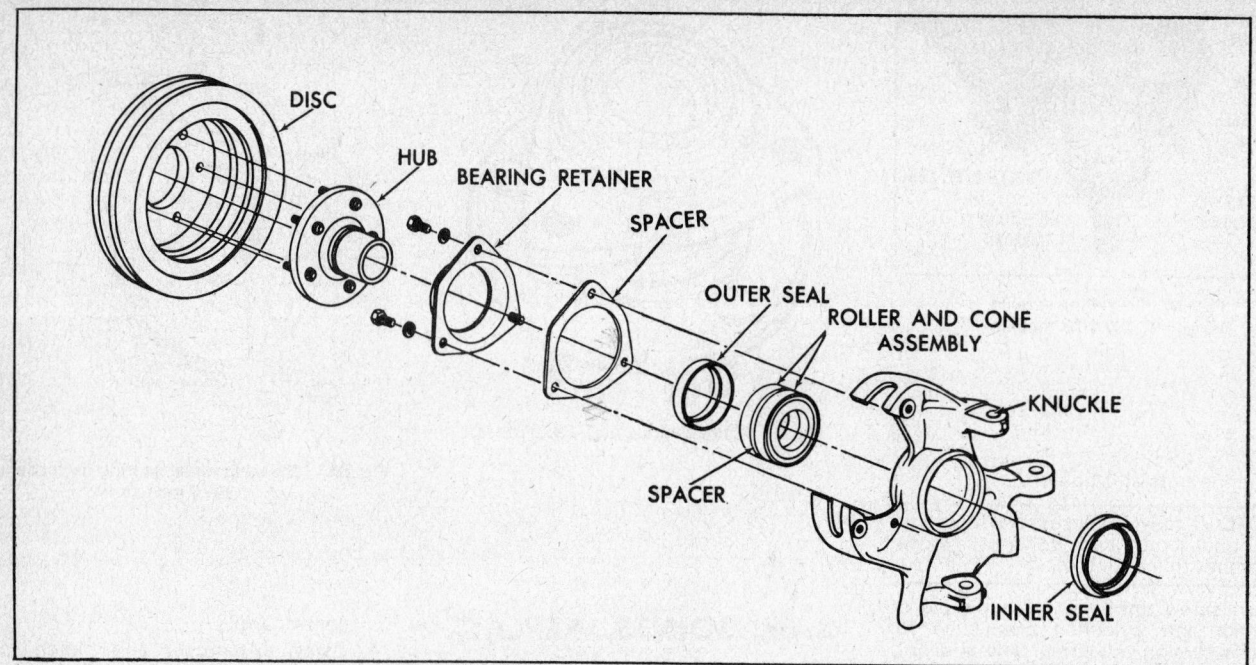

Fig. 9A Wheel bearing & steering knuckle assembly. 1974-78 models

control arms.
2. Remove wheel and tire assembly.
3. Remove cotter pin and nut from upper ball joint stud, then disconnect brake hose clip from stud.
4. Using a hammer and brass drift, disengage ball joint stud from steering knuckle.
5. Place a block of wood between con-

trol arm and frame, then drill rivets with a ⅛ in. drill bit ⅜ in. deep from top side of control arm.
6. Drill rivet heads off using a ½ inch drill bit. Do not drill into control arm.
7. Using a hammer and punch, drive rivets out and remove ball joint.
8. Install ball joint into control arm and torque nuts and bolts as shown in Fig. 8.

WHEEL BEARING INSPECTION

1979

The front wheel bearing is a sealed unit bearing. The bearing cannot be adjusted or repacked. There are darkened areas on the bearing assembly. These darkened areas are from a heat treatment process and do

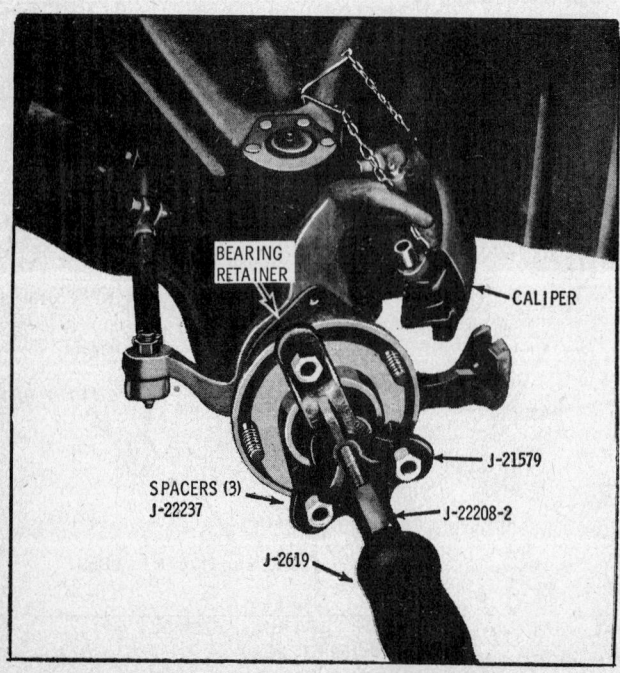

Fig. 10 Removing hub assembly. 1974-78 models

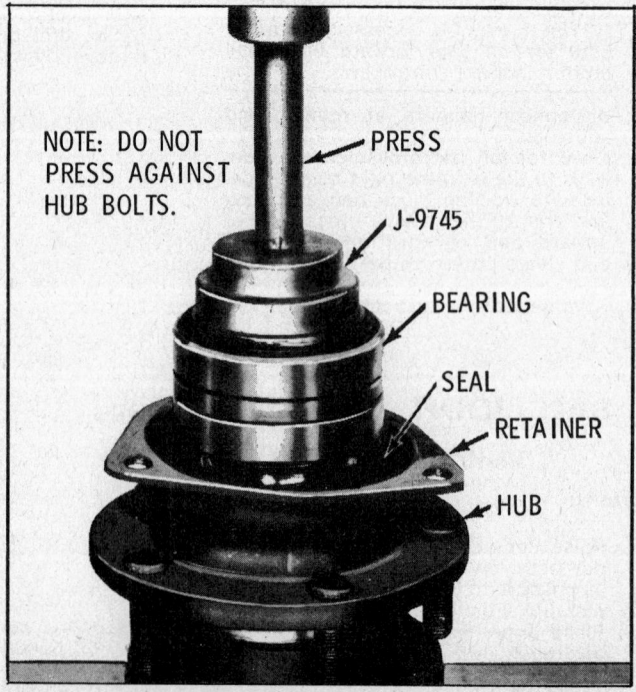

Fig. 11 Removing bearing from hub. 1974-78 models

Fig. 12   Bearing installation. 1974-78 models

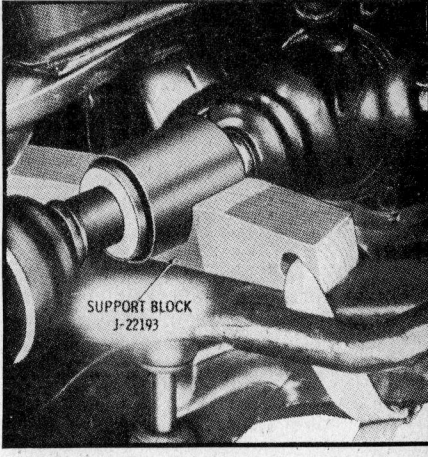

Fig. 13   Drive axle support block. 1974-78 models

not indicate need for bearing replacement, Fig. 8.

To check wheel bearing assembly for looseness, free brake pads from disc or remove calipers. Install two lug nuts to secure disc to bearing. Mount dial indicator as shown in Fig. 8A, then rock disc and note indicator reading. If looseness exceeds .005 in. replace hub and bearing assembly.

CAUTION: Use extreme care to prevent striking and damaging brake hose or ball joint seal.

5. Place a short length of rubber hose over lower control arm torsion bar connector to avoid damage to inboard tri-pot joint seal when hub and knuckle are removed.
6. Using appropriate puller, disconnect tie rod end, upper and lower ball joints and remove steering knuckle and hub assembly.

HUB & BEARING, REPLACE
1974-78

1. Remove cotter pin, retainer, nut and washer from drive axle.
2. Remove caliper and rotor assembly.

NOTE: When removing caliper use care not to damage brake tubing or hose. Secure caliper to frame with wire.

3. Remove three bolts attaching bearing retainer to knuckle, Fig. 9.
4. Using a suitable slide hammer remove hub and bearing retainer, Fig. 10.
5. Insert quarter circles of tool BT-6906 between outer seal and bearing.
6. Position tool over retainer and press bearing from hub, Fig. 11.
7. Lubricate seal lips with lubricant No. 1050169 or equivalent, then position seal over hub with metal end toward retainer.

WHEEL BEARING & STEERING KNUCKLE, REPLACE
1979

1. Raise and support vehicle under lower control arms.
2. Remove drive axle nut and washer and remove wheel and tire assembly, Fig. 9.
3. Remove brake hose clip from ball joint and replace nut, then remove brake caliper off disc, and using a length of wire support caliper on suspension.

NOTE: Do not allow caliper to hang from brake hose as this could cause damage and premature failure of hose.

4. Mark hub and disc assembly for alignment during assembly and remove disc, then strike steering knuckle in area of upper ball joint until upper ball joint is loose.

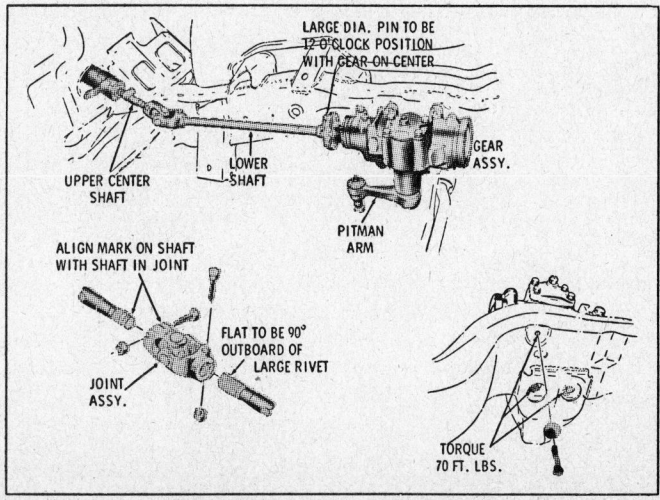

Fig. 14   Steering gear and shaft. 1974-78 models

8. Position bearing on retainer, then press bearing and seal into hub, Fig. 12.
9. Lubricate bearing with chassis grease, then install hub assembly over drive splines.

NOTE: Ensure hub and axle splines are in correct alignment.

10. Install bearing retainer to knuckle attaching bolts, torque bolts to 35 ft. lbs.
11. Install drive axle washer, nut, retainer and cotter pin. Torque nut to 140 ft. lbs. on 1974-76 models and 200 ft. lbs. on 1977-78 models.

NOTE: Tighten nut if cotter pin cannot be installed. Do not loosen nut to align cotter pin slot.

12. Install rotor, caliper and wheel assembly.

STEERING KNUCKLE, REPLACE
1974-78

1. Remove hub assembly.
2. Remove ball joint stud cotter pin and nut, then disconnect brake hose clip from stud.
3. Position support block under drive axle, Fig. 13.
4. Using hammer and brass drift, loosen upper ball joint stud.
5. Using a suitable puller, disconnect tie rod end from knuckle.
6. Remove cotter pin and nut from lower ball joint stud, then using tool No. J-22292 remove ball joint from knuckle.

Installation

1. Install lower ball joint and tie rod end on knuckle. Do not tighten attaching nuts.
2. Install upper ball joint on steering knuckle, then attach brake hose clip.
3. Torque upper ball joint stud nut to 50 ft. lbs. on 1974 models, 60 ft. lbs. on 1975-76 models, and 105 ft. lbs. on 1977-78 models, then install cotter pin.
4. Torque lower ball joint stud nut to 85 ft. lbs. on 1974 models, 95 ft. lbs. on 1975-76 models, and 95 ft. lbs. on 1977-78 models, then install cotter pin.
5. Torque tie rod end nut to 35 ft. lbs. on 1974 models and 40 ft. lbs. on 1975-78 models, then install cotter pin.

NOTE: Tighten nut if cotter pin cannot be installed. Do not loosen nut to align cotter pin slot.

6. Install hub assembly.

SHOCK ABSORBER, REPLACE

1. Remove upper shock attaching bolt.
2. Remove lower attaching nut and guide shock through upper control arm.
3. Reverse procedure to install.

STEERING GEAR, REPLACE
1974-78

1. Referring to Fig. 14, remove coupling flange hub bolt.

NOTE: On 1974-78 models, remove coupling shield.

2. Disconnect hoses from power steering pump and cap pump and hose fittings. On cars equipped with a cooler disconnect return hose from cooler inlet pipe.
3. Raise vehicle and disconnect pitman arm from relay rod.
4. Unfasten gear from frame, permit lower shaft to slide free of coupling flange, then remove gear with hoses attached.

NOTE: Before installing steering gear, apply a sodium soap fibre grease to gear mounting pads to prevent squeaks between gear housing and frame. Make sure alignment pin on gear housing enters hole provided in frame side rail. Make sure there is a minimum of .040" clearance between coupling hub and steering gear upper seal.

Install coupling hub bolt and torque to 30 ft-lbs. Before torquing gear retaining bolts, position gear so the flexible coupling will not be distorted. Torque gear retaining bolts to 70 ft-lbs. Torque pitman arm to relay rod nut to 45 ft-lbs. on 1974 models and 85 ft-lbs. on 1975-78 models.

5. After hoses are connected to pump, add power steering fluid as necessary to bring the fluid level to the full mark. Run engine at idle for 30 seconds, then run at a fast idle for a minute before turning steering wheel. With engine running, turn steering wheel through its full travel two or three times to bleed air from system. Recheck oil level and add oil if necessary.

PONTIAC

(Exc. Astre & Sunbird)

INDEX OF SERVICE OPERATIONS

SERIAL NUMBER LOCATION

1974-79: On plate fastened to upper left instrument
panel area, visible through windshield.

ENGINE IDENTIFICATION

The V8 Pontiac manufactured engine code is located beneath the production engine number on a machined pad on the right-hand bank of the engine block.

The V8-260, 350 and 403 Oldsmobile manufactured engine code is located on the oil filler tube.

The V6-231 and 1975-76 Ventura V8 engine codes are located on the front right hand of cylinder block.

The 6-250 engine code is stamped on the pad at front right-hand side of cylinder block at rear of distributor.

CODE	TRANS.	ENGINE	CODE	TRANS.	ENGINE	CODE	TRANS.	ENGINE
1974			**1975**			**1976 (Cont'd)**		
CCR	(4)	6-250(9)	JT	(6)	6-250(9)	T4	(6)	V8-260(1)(12)
CCX	(6)	6-250(9)	JL	(6)	6-250(9)	T5	(6)	V8-260(1)(12)
CCW	(6)	6-250(9)	QA	(4)	V8-260(1)	PA	(6)	V8-350(1)(13)
AA	(6)	V8-350(1)(10)	QD	(4)	V8-260(1)	PB	(6)	V8-350(1)(13)
WB	(4)	V8-350(1)	QE	(6)	V8-260(1)	PO	(6)	V8-350(1)(13)
WA	(4)	V8-350(1)	QJ	(6)	V8-260(1)	XH	(6)	V8-350(1)
YB	(6)	V8-350(1)	TE	(6)	V8-260(1)	XN	(6)	V8-350(1)
YA	(6)	V8-350(1)	TJ	(6)	V8-260(1)	YA	(6)	V8-350(1)
YC	(6)	V8-350(1)	RS	(6)	V8-350(1)	YB	(6)	V8-350(1)
YS	(6)	V8-350(2)(10)	RI	(6)	V8-350(13)	YK	(6)	V8-350(1)
AD	(6)	V8-400(1)(10)	YA	(6)	V8-350(1)	YL	(6)	V8-350(1)
ZB	(6)	V8-350(1)	YB	(6)	V8-350(1)	YP	(6)	V8-350(1)
ZA	(6)	V8-350(1)	RW	(6)	V8-350(1)	YR	(6)	V8-350(1)
WP	(6)	V8-350(2)	RX	(6)	V8-350(13)	PE	(6)	V8-350(2)(13)
WN	(4)	V8-350(2)	RN	(6)	V8-350(13)	PF	(6)	V8-350(2)(13)
YP	(6)	V8-350(2)	RO	(6)	V8-350(13)	PM	(6)	V8-350(2)(13)
YN	(6)	V8-350(2)	WN	(6)	V8-350(2)	PN	(6)	V8-350(2)(13)
ZP	(6)	V8-350(2)	YN	(6)	V8-350(2)	PP	(6)	V8-350(2)(13)
AH	(6)	V8-400(1)(10)	ZP	(6)	V8-350(2)	X3	(6)	V8-350(2)
AT	(6)	V8-400(2)(10)	YH	(6)	V8-400(1)	YD	(6)	V8-350(2)
A3	(3)	V8-400(2)(10)	YT	(6)	V8-400(1)	ZC	(6)	V8-350(2)
YH	(6)	V8-400(1)	ZT	(6)	V8-400(1)	ZX	(6)	V8-350(2)
YJ	(6)	V8-400(1)	YM	(6)	V8-400(2)	X3	(6)	V8-350(1)
ZH	(6)	V8-400(1)	WT	(4)	V8-400(2)	XM	(6)	V8-350(1)
WR	(4)	V8-400(2)	YS	(6)	V8-400(2)	XP	(6)	V8-350(1)
WT	(4)	V8-400(2)	YW	(6)	V8-455(2)	XR	(6)	V8-350(1)
YF	(6)	V8-400(1)(10)	YU	(6)	V8-455(2)	XU	(6)	V8-350(1)
YK	(6)	V8-400(1)(10)	ZU	(6)	V8-455(2)	XW	(6)	V8-350(1)
YL	(6)	V8-400(1)(10)	ZW	(6)	V8-455(2)	XX	(6)	V8-350(1)
YM	(6)	V8-400(2)(10)	WX	(5)	V8-455(2)	ZF	(6)	V8-350(1)
YZ	(6)	V8-400(2)(10)				ZH	(6)	V8-350(1)
Y3	(4)	V8-400(2)(10)	**1976**			XA	(6)	V8-400(1)
YT	(6)	V8-400(2)	CC	(6)	6-250(9)(14)	XB	(6)	V8-400(1)
ZD	(6)	V8-400(1)(10)	CD	(4)	6-250(9)(14)	XC	(6)	V8-400(1)
ZJ	(6)	V8-400(1)(10)	CF	(6)	6-250(9)(14)	XJ	(6)	V8-400(1)
ZK	(6)	V8-400(1)(10)	CH	(6)	6-250(9)(14)	YC	(6)	V8-400(1)
ZS	(6)	V8-400(3)(10)	CJ	(6)	6-250(9)(14)	YJ	(6)	V8-400(1)
ZT	(6)	V8-400(2)	QA	(7)	V8-260(1)(12)	Z8	(6)	V8-400(1)
AW	(6)	V8-455(2)(10)	QB	(6)	V8-260(1)(12)	WT	(6)	V8-400(2)
A4	(6)	V8-455(2)(10)	QC	(6)	V8-260(1)(12)	YS	(6)	V8-400(2)
YR	(6)	V8-455(2)(10)	QD	(7)	V8-260(1)(12)	YT	(6)	V8-400(2)
YW	(6)	V8-455(2)(10)	QK	(7)	V8-260(1)(12)	YY	(6)	V8-400(2)
YX	(6)	V8-455(2)(10)	QN	(7)	V8-260(1)(12)	YZ	(6)	V8-400(2)
YY	(6)	V8-455(2)(10)	QP	(6)	V8-260(1)(12)	Y6	(6)	V8-400(2)
Y4	(6)	V8-455(2)(10)	QT	(6)	V8-260(1)(12)	Y7	(6)	V8-400(2)
Y6	(6)	V8-455(2)(10)	TA	(7)	V8-260(1)(12)	ZA	(6)	V8-400(2)
Y9	(6)	V8-455(2)(10)	TD	(7)	V8-260(1)(12)	ZK	(6)	V8-400(2)
YU	(6)	V8-455(2)	TE	(6)	V8-260(1)(12)	X4	(6)	V8-400(1)
ZU	(6)	V8-455(2)	TJ	(7)	V8-260(1)(12)	X6	(6)	V8-400(1)
ZW	(6)	V8-455(2)(10)	TK	(7)	V8-260(1)(12)	X7	(6)	V8-400(1)
ZX	(6)	V8-455(2)(10)	TN	(7)	V8-260(1)(12)	X9	(6)	V8-400(1)
Z4	(6)	V8-455(2)(10)	TP	(6)	V8-260(1)(12)	X8	(6)	V8-400(1)
Z6	(6)	V8-455(2)(10)	TT	(6)	V8-260(1)(12)	XS	(6)	V8-400(1)
W8	(4)	V8-455(8)	T2	(6)	V8-260(1)(12)	XT	(6)	V8-400(1)
Y8	(6)	V8-455(2)	T3	(6)	V8-260(1)(12)	XY	(6)	V8-400(1)
JU	(4)	6-250(9)				XZ	(6)	V8-400(1)

ENGINE IDENTIFICATION—Continued

CODE	TRANS.	ENGINE
ZJ	[6]	V8-400 [11]
ZL	[6]	V8-400 [11]
WX	[5]	V8-455 [2]
Y3	[6]	V8-455 [2]
Y4	[6]	V8-455 [2]
Y8	[6]	V8-455 [2]
ZB	[6]	V8-455 [2]
Z3	[6]	V8-455 [2]
Z4	[6]	V8-455 [2]
Z6	[6]	V8-455 [2]

1977

CODE	TRANS.	ENGINE
WF	[7]	4-151 [1]
WH	[7]	4-151 [1]
YR	[6]	4-151 [1]
YS	[6]	4-151 [1]
SG	[4]	V6-231 [1][13]
SI	[6]	V6-231 [1][13]
SJ	[6]	V6-231 [1][13]
SK	[6]	V6-231 [1][13]
SL	[6]	V6-231 [1][13]
SM	[6]	V6-231 [1][13]
SN	[6]	V6-231 [1][13]
SU	[4]	V6-231 [1][13]
HK	[6]	V8-301 [1]
WB	[5]	V8-301 [1]
YH	[6]	V8-301 [1]
YW	[6]	V8-301 [1]
YX	[6]	V8-301 [1]
Q2	[6]	V8-350 [2][12]
Q3	[6]	V8-350 [2][12]
Q6	[6]	V8-350 [2][12]
Q7	[6]	V8-350 [2][12]
Q8	[6]	V8-350 [2][12]
Q9	[6]	V8-350 [2][12]
QP	[6]	V8-350 [2][12]
QQ	[6]	V8-350 [2][12]
TK	[6]	V8-350 [2][12]
TL	[6]	V8-350 [2][12]
TN	[6]	V8-350 [2][12]
TO	[6]	V8-350 [2][12]
TX	[6]	V8-350 [2][12]
TY	[6]	V8-350 [2][12]
Y9	[6]	V8-350 [2]

CODE	TRANS.	ENGINE
YA	[6]	V8-350 [2]
YB	[6]	V8-350 [2]
WA	[5]	V8-400 [2]
XA	[6]	V8-400 [2]
Y4	[6]	V8-400 [2]
Y6	[6]	V8-400 [2]
Y7	[6]	V8-400 [2]
YC	[6]	V8-400 [2]
YD	[6]	V8-400 [2]
YU	[6]	V8-400 [2]
U2	[6]	V8-403 [2][12]
U3	[6]	V8-403 [2][12]
UA	[6]	V8-403 [2][12]
UB	[6]	V8-403 [2][12]
VA	[6]	V8-403 [2][12]
VB	[6]	V8-403 [2][12]
VJ	[6]	V8-403 [2][12]
VK	[6]	V8-403 [2][12]

1978

CODE	TRANS.	ENGINE
YB	[6]	4-151 [1]
YC	[6]	4-151 [1]
EA	[4]	V6-231 [1][13]
EC	[6]	V6-231 [1][13]
EE	[6]	V6-231 [1][13]
EI	[6]	V6-231 [1][13]
EJ	[6]	V6-231 [1][13]
EK	[6]	V6-231 [1][13]
EL	[6]	V6-231 [1][13]
OE	[6]	V6-231 [1][13]
OH	[6]	V6-231 [1][13]
OK	[6]	V6-231 [1][13]
OR	[6]	V6-231 [1][13]
XA	[6]	V8-301 [1]
XB	[6]	V8-301 [1]
XC	[6]	V8-301 [1]
XD	[6]	V8-301 [1]
XF	[6]	V8-301 [2]
XH	[6]	V8-301 [2]
XU	[6]	V8-301 [2]
XW	[6]	V8-301 [2]
CPF	[6]	V8-305 [2][14]
CPH	[6]	V8-305 [1][14]

CODE	TRANS.	ENGINE
CPZ	[6]	V8-305 [1][14]
CRU	[6]	V8-305 [1][14]
CRY	[6]	V8-305 [1][14]
CRZ	[6]	V8-305 [1][14]
CTH	[4]	V8-305 [1][14]
CTJ	[6]	V8-305 [1][14]
CTK	[6]	V8-305 [1][14]
CTM	[6]	V8-305 [1][14]
CTS	[6]	V8-305 [1][14]
CTT	[6]	V8-305 [1][14]
CTU	[6]	V8-305 [1][14]
CTW	[6]	V8-305 [1][14]
CTX	[6]	V8-305 [1][14]
CTY	[6]	V8-305 [1][14]
CTZ	[6]	V8-305 [1][14]
MA	[6]	V8-350 [2][13]
MB	[6]	V8-350 [2][13]
TO	[6]	V8-350 [2][12]
TP	[6]	V8-350 [2][12]
TQ	[6]	V8-350 [2][12]
TS	[6]	V8-350 [2][12]
Q2	[6]	V8-350 [2][12]
Q3	[6]	V8-350 [2][12]
CHJ	[6]	V8-350 [2][14]
CHL	[6]	V8-350 [2][14]
CHR	[4]	V8-350 [2][14]
CMC	[6]	V8-350 [2][14]
WC	[4]	V8-400 [2]
XJ	[6]	V8-400 [2]
XK	[6]	V8-400 [2]
X7	[6]	V8-400 [2]
X9	[6]	V8-400 [2]
Y	[6]	V8-400 [2]
YA	[6]	V8-400 [2]
YH	[6]	V8-400 [2]
YJ	[6]	V8-400 [2]
YK	[6]	V8-400 [2]
U2	[6]	V8-403 [2][12]
U3	[6]	V8-403 [2][12]
U5	[6]	V8-403 [2][12]
U6	[6]	V8-403 [2][12]
VA	[6]	V8-403 [2][12]
VB	[6]	V8-403 [2][12]
VD	[6]	V8-403 [2][12]
VE	[6]	V8-403 [2][12]

[1]—Two barrel carburetor.
[2]—Four barrel carburetor.
[4]—Manual trans.
[5]—Four speed manual trans.
[6]—Automatic trans.
[7]—Five speed manual trans.
[8]—Super Duty engine.
[9]—One barrel carburetor.
[10]—High Energy Ignition System (H.E.I.).
[11]—Does not use harmonic balancer.
[12]—See Oldsmobile chapter for service procedures.
[13]—See Buick chapter for service procedures.
[14]—See Chevrolet chapter for service procedures.

GRILLE IDENTIFICATION

1974 Ventura Custom

1974 GTO

1974 Firebird

1974 LeMans Sport

1974 Luxury LeMans

1974 Grand Am

1974 Catalina

1974 Bonneville

1974 Grand Prix

1974 Grand Ville

1975 Ventura

1975 Grand Am

1975 Firebird

1975 LeMans

1975 Grand LeMans

1975 Catalina

1975 Bonneville

1975 Grand Prix

1975 Grand Ville & Grand Safari

1976 Ventura

1976 Firebird

GRILLE IDENTIFICATION—Continued

1976 LeMans

1976 Grand LeMans

1976 Catalina

1976 Grand Prix

1976 Bonneville & Grand Safari

1977 Ventura

1977 LeMans, Sports Cpe. & GT

1977 Grand LeMans

1977 Grand Prix

1977-78 Firebird Trans Am

1977-78 Formula Firebird

1977-78 Firebird, Esprit

1977 Catalina

1977 Bonneville & Grand Safari

1977-79 Phoenix

1978 Bonneville & Grand Safari

1978 Catalina

1978-79 Grand Am

1978 Grand LeMans, LeMans Safari

1978 Grand Prix

1979 Grand Prix

GRILL IDENTIFICATION—Continued

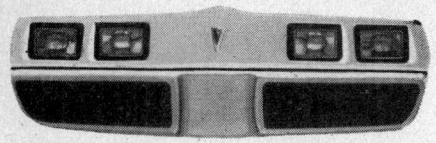

1979 Firebird Formula

1979 Firebird Trans Am

1979 Grand LeMans, Grand LeMans
Safari & Grand Am 4 Dr.

1979 Bonneville Brougham &
Safari

1979 Catalina

GENERAL ENGINE SPECIFICATIONS

Year	Engine	Car-buretor	Bore and Stroke	Piston Displacement, Cubic Inches	Compression Ratio	Maximum Brake H.P. @ R.P.M.	Maximum Torque Lbs. Ft. @ R.P.M.	Normal Oil Pressure Pounds
1974	100 Horsepower③............①6-250	1 Barrel	3.88 x 3.53	250	8.2	100 @ 3600	175 @ 1600	30-45
	155 Horsepower③.............8-350	2 Barrel	3.88 x 3.75	350	7.6	155 @ 3600	275 @ 2400	55-60
	170 Horsepower③.........④8-350	2 Barrel	3.88 x 3.75	350	7.6	170 @ 4000	290 @ 2400	55-60
	170 Horsepower③.............8-350	4 Barrel	3.88 x 3.75	350	7.6	170 @ 4000	280 @ 2000	55-60
	200 Horsepower③.........④8-350	4 Barrel	3.88 x 3.75	350	76	200 @ 4400	295 @ 2800	55-60
	175 Horsepower③.............8-400	2 Barrel	4.12 x 3.75	400	8.0	175 @ 3600	315 @ 2000	55-60
	190 Horsepower③.........④8-400	2 Barrel	4.12 x 3.75	400	8.0	190 @ 4000	330 @ 2400	55-60
	200 Horsepower③.............8-400	4 Barrel	4.12 x 3.75	400	8.0	200 @ 4000	320 @ 2400	55-60
	225 Horsepower③.........④8-400	4 Barrel	4.12 x 3.75	400	8.0	225 @ 4000	330 @ 2800	55-60
	215 Horsepower③.............8-455	4 Barrel	4.15 x 4.21	455	8.0	215 @ 3600	355 @ 2400	55-60
	250 Horsepower③.........④8-455	4 Barrel	4.15 x 4.21	455	8.0	250 @ 4000	380 @ 2800	55-60
	290 Horsepower③.........④8-455	4 Barrel	4.15 x 4.21	455	8.4	290 @ 4000	395 @ 3200	75-80
1975	105 Horsepower③............6-250①	1 Barrel	3.87 x 3.53	250	8.25	105 @ 3800	185 @ 1200	36-41
	110 Horsepower③.........V8-260⑥	2 Barrel	3.50 x 3.385	260	8.5	110 @ 3400	205 @ 1600	30-45
	155 Horsepower③.........V8-350	2 Barrel	3.88 x 3.75	350	7.6	155 @ 4000	—	55-60
	175 Horsepower③.........V8-350	4 Barrel	3.88 x 3.75	350	7.6	175 @ 4000	—	55-60
	145 Horsepower③........V8-350②⑥	2 Barrel	3.80 x 3.85	350	8.0	145 @ 3200	270 @ 3000	37
	165 Horsepower③........V8-350②⑥	4 Barrel	3.80 x 3.85	350	8.0	165 @ 3800	260 @ 2200	37
	170 Horsepower③.........V8-400	2 Barrel	4.12 x 3.75	400	7.6	170 @ 4000	—	55-60
	185 Horsepower③.........V8-400	4 Barrel	4.12 x 3.75	400	7.6	185 @ 3600	—	55-60
	200 Horsepower③.........V8-455	4 Barrel	4.15 x 4.21	455	7.6	200 @ 3500	—	55-60
1976	110 Horsepower③............6-250①	1 Barrel	3.87 x 3.53	250	8.3	110 @ 3600	185 @ 1200	36-41
	110 Horsepower③.........V8-260⑥	2 Barrel	3.50 x 3.385	260	7.5	110 @ 3400	205 @ 1600	30-45
	160 Horsepower③.........V8-350	2 Barrel	3.8762 x 3.75	350	7.6	160 @ 4000	280 @ 2000	35-40
	165 Horsepower③.........V8-350	4 Barrel	3.8762 x 3.75	350	7.6	165 @ 4000	260 @ 2400	35-40
	140 Horsepower③........V8-350②⑥	2 Barrel	3.80 x 3.85	350	8.0	140 @ 3200	280 @ 1600	37
	155 Horsepower③........V8-350②⑥	4 Barrel	3.80 x 3.85	350	8.0	155 @ 3400	280 @ 1800	37
	170 Horsepower③.........V8-400	2 Barrel	4.1212 x 3.75	400	7.6	170 @ 4000	310 @ 1600	35-40
	185 Horsepower③.........V8-400	4 Barrel	4.1212 x 3.75	400	7.6	185 @ 3600	310 @ 1600	35-40
	200 Horsepower③.........V8-455	4 Barrel	4.1522 x 4.21	455	7.6	200 @ 3500	330 @ 2000	55-60

Continued

GENERAL ENGINE SPECIFICATIONS—Continued

Year	Engine	Car-buretor	Bore and Stroke	Piston Dis-place-ment, Cubic Inches	Com-pres-sion Ratio	Maximum Brake H.P. @ R.P.M.	Maximum Torque Ft. Lbs. @ R.P.M.	Normal Oil Pressure Pounds
1977	88 Horsepower③............4-151	2 Barrel	4.00 x 3.00	151	8.3	88 @ 4400	128 @ 2400	30–45
	105 Horsepower③.........V6-231②	2 Barrel	3.80 x 3.40	231	8.0	105 @ 3200	185 @ 2000	37
	135 Horsepower③...........V8-301	2 Barrel	4.00 x 3.00	301	8.2	135 @ 4000	⑦	38–42
	145 Horsepower②.........V8-305①	2 Barrel	3.736 x 3.48	305	8.5	145 @ 3800	245 @ 2400	32–40
	170 Horsepower③........V8-350①	4 Barrel	4.00 x 3.48	350	8.5	170 @ 3800	270 @ 2400	32–40
	170 Horsepower②..........V8-350	4 Barrel	3.88 x 3.75	350	7.6	170 @ 4000	280 @ 1800	55–60
	170 Horsepower③........V8-350⑤	4 Barrel	4.057 x 3.385	350	8	170 @ 3800	275 @ 2000	37
	180 Horsepower③..........V8-400	4 Barrel	4.12 x 3.75	400	7.6	180 @ 3600	325 @ 1600	55–60
	200 Horsepower③.........V8-400⑩	4 Barrel	4.12 x 3.75	400	8.0	200 @ 3600	⑪	55–60
	185 Horsepower③........V8-403⑤	4 Barrel	4.351 x 3.385	403	8.0	185 @ 3600	320 @ 2200	30–45
1978	85 Horsepower③............4-151	2 Barrel	4.00 x 3.00	151	8.3	85 @ 4400	123 @ 2800	36–41
	105 Horsepower③.........V6-231②	2 Barrel	3.80 x 3.40	231	8.0	105 @ 3400	185 @ 2000	37
	140 Horsepower③...........V8-301	2 Barrel	4.00 x 3.00	301	8.2	140 @ 3600	235 @ 2000	35–40
	150 Horsepower③...........V8-301	4 Barrel	4.00 x 3.00	301	8.2	150 @ 4000	240 @ 2000	35–40
	135 Horsepower③⑨........V8-305①	2 Barrel	3.736 x 3.48	305	8.4	135 @ 3800	240 @ 2000	32–40
	145 Horsepower③⑧........V8-305①	4 Barrel	3.736 x 3.48	305	8.4	145 @ 3800	245 @ 2400	32–40
	155 Horsepower③.........V8-350②	4 Barrel	3.80 x 3.85	350	8.0	155 @ 3400	280 @ 1800	—
	160 Horsepower③.........V8-350①	4 Barrel	4.00 x 3.48	350	8.2	160 @ 3800	260 @ 2400	32–40
	170 Horsepower③........V8-350⑤	4 Barrel	4.057 x 3.385	350	7.9	170 @ 3800	275 @ 2000	30–45
	170 Horsepower③........V8-350①	4 Barrel	4.00 x 3.48	350	8.2	170 @ 3800	270 @ 2400	32–40
	180 Horsepower③..........V8-400	4 Barrel	4.12 x 3.75	400	7.7	180 @ 3600	325 @ 1600	35–40
	220 Horsepower③.........V8-400⑩	4 Barrel	4.12 x 3.75	400	8.1	220 @ 4000	320 @ 2800	55–60
	185 Horsepower③.........V8-403⑤	4 Barrel	4.351 x 3.385	403	7.9	185 @ 3600	320 @ 2000	30–45

①—See Chevrolet chapter for service procedures.
②—See Buick chapter for service procedures.
③—Ratings are NET—as installed in the vehicle.
④—With dual exhausts.
⑤—See Oldsmobile Chapter for service procedures.
⑥—Ventura only.

⑦—Manual trans., 235 @ 2000. Auto. trans., 245 @ 2000.
⑧—Exc. high altitude.
⑨—High altitude.
⑩—High performance Trans Am engine.
⑪—Manual trans., 325 @ 2400; auto. trans., 325 @ 2200.

TUNE UP SPECIFICATIONS

The following specifications are published from the latest information available. This data should be used only in the absence of a decal affixed in the engine compartment.

★When using a timing light, disconnect vacuum hose or tube at distributor and plug opening in hose or tube so idle speed will not be affected.

●When checking compression, lowest cylinder must be within 80% of the highest.

▲Before removing wires from distributor cap, determine location of the No. 1 wire in cap, as distributor position may have been altered from that shown at the end of this chart.

| Year | Spark Plug | | Distributor | | Ignition Timing ★ | | | Carb. Adjustments | | | | | |
| | Type | Gap Inch | Point Gap Inch | Dwell Angle Deg. | Firing Order Fig. ▲ | Timing BTDC ① | Mark Fig. | Hot Idle Speed ② | | Air Fuel Ratio | | Idle CO % | |
								Std. Trans.	Auto. Trans.	Std. Trans.	Auto. Trans.	Std. Trans.	Auto. Trans.
1974													
6-250(14)	R46T	.035	(15)	32½	E	6°	H	850	600	—	—	0.2	0.2
V8-350 2 Bar. Carb.	R46TS	.040	(15)	30	D	(18)	I	900	650	—	—	0.2	0.2
V8-350 2 Bar. Carb.(4)	R46TS	.040	(15)	30	D	10°	I	—	625	—	—	—	0.2
V8-350 4 Bar. Carb.	R46TS	.040	(15)	30	D	(18)	I	1000	650	—	—	0.2	0.2
V8-350 4 Bar. Carb.(4)	R46TS	.040	(15)	30	D	10°	I	—	625	—	—	—	0.2
V8-400 2 Bar. Carb.	R46TS	.040	(15)	30	(10)	(18)	I	—	650	—	—	—	0.2
V8-400 2 Bar. Carb.(4)	R46TS	.040	(15)	30	(10)	10°	I	—	625	—	—	—	0.2
V8-400 4 Bar. Carb.	R45TS	.040	(15)	30	(10)	(18)	I	1000	650	—	—	0.2	0.2
V8-400 4 Bar. Carb.(4)	R45TS	.040	(13)	30	(10)	10°	I	—	625	—	—	—	0.2
V8-455	R45TS	.040	(15)	30	(10)	(18)	I	—	650	—	—	—	0.2
V8-455(4)	R45TS	.040	(15)	30	(10)	10°	I	—	625	—	—	—	0.2
V8-455 S.D.	R44TS	.040	(15)	30	(10)	12°	I	1000	750	—	—	0.2	0.2
1975													
6-250(14)	R46TX	.060	—	—	L	10°	H	850	(20)	—	—	—	—
V8-260(5)(21)	R46SX	.080	—	—	M	16°(9)	J	750	650	—	—	—	—
V8-260(5)(22)	R46SX	.080	—	—	M	18°(9)	J	750	650	—	—	—	—
V8-350(6)	R45TSX	.060	—	—	N	12°	K	800	600	—	—	—	—
V8-350(21)	R46TSX	.060	—	—	O	12°	I	775	(23)	—	—	—	—
V8-350(22)	R46TSX	.060	—	—	O	16°	I	775	(23)	—	—	—	—
V8-400(21)	(24)	.060	—	—	O	12°	I	775	(25)	—	—	—	—
V8-400(22)	(24)	.060	—	—	O	16°	I	775	(25)	—	—	—	—
V8-455(28)	R45TSX	.060	—	—	O	16°	I	775	650D	—	—	—	—
V8-455(4)	R45TSX	.060	—	—	O	10°	I	—	675D	—	—	—	—
1976													
6-250(14)	R46T	.035	—	—	L	(27)	H	850	(20)	—	—	—	—
V8-260(5)(28)	R46SX	.080	—	—	M	(13)	J	750	550	—	—	—	—
V8-260(5)(4)	R46SX	.080	—	—	M	(17)	J	—	600	—	—	—	—
V8-350(6)	R45TSX	.060	—	—	N	12°	K	—	600D	—	—	—	—
V8-350	R46TSX	.060	—	—	O	16°	I	—	550D	—	—	—	—
V8-400 2 Bar. Carb.	R46TSX	.060	—	—	O	16°	I	—	550D	—	—	—	—
V8-400 4 Bar. Carb.	R45TSX	.060	—	—	O	(8)	I	775	575D	—	—	—	—
V8-455(4)	R45TSX	.060	—	—	O	12°	I	—	600D	—	—	—	—
V8-455(28)	R45TSX	.060	—	—	O	16°	I	775	550D	—	—	—	—
1977													
4-151(18)(26)	R44TSX	.060	—	—	F	14°	Q	500/1000(3)	500/650(3)	—	—	—	—
4-151(19)(26)	R44TSX	.060	—	—	F	14°	Q	500/1200(3)	650/850(3)	—	—	—	—
4-151(4)	R44TSX	.060	—	—	F	12°	Q	—	650/850(28)	—	—	—	—
V6-231(31)	R44TS	.040	—	—	G	12°	R(47)	600/800(28)	600/670(28)	—	—	—	—
V6-231(48)	R46TSX	.060	—	—	S	15°	T(47)	500/1000(3)	500/650D(3)	—	—	—	—
V8-301	R46TSX	.060	—	—	O	(32)	A	750/875(28)	550/650(28)	—	—	—	—
V8-305(14)	R45TS	.045	—	—	P	8°	H	700	500/650(28)	—	—	—	—

Continued

TUNE UP SPECIFICATIONS—Continued

The following specifications are published from the latest information available. This data should be used only in the absence of a decal affixed in the engine compartment.

★When using a timing light, disconnect vacuum hose or tube at distributor and plug opening in tube or hose so idle speed will not be affected.

●When checking compression, lowest cylinder must be within 80% of the highest.

▲Before removing wires from distributor cap, determine location of the No. 1 wire in cap, as distributor position may have been altered from that shown at the end of this chart.

| Year | Spark Plug | | Distributor | | Ignition Timing★ | | | Carb. Adjustments | | | | | |
| | Type | Gap Inch | Point Gap Inch | Dwell Angle Deg. | Firing Order Fig. ▲ | Timing BTDC ① | Mark Fig. | Hot Idle Speed② | | Air Fuel Ratio | | Idle CO % | |
								Std. Trans.	Auto. Trans.	Std. Trans.	Auto. Trans.	Std. Trans.	Auto. Trans.
1977—Continued													
V8-350㊴⑭	R45TS	.045	—	—	P	8°	H	700	500/650㉘	—	—	—	—
V8-350㉝㉟㊵	R45TSX	.060	—	—	O	16°	I	—	575/650㉘	—	—	—	—
V8-350⑤㉞㊶	R46SZ	.060	—	—	M	20°⑨	J	—	550/650㉘	—	—	—	—
V8-350㊱⑤㊶	R46SZ	.060	—	—	M	20°⑨	J	—	600/700㉘	—	—	—	—
V8-400㉙	R45TSX	.060	—	—	O	18°	I	775	—	—	—	—	—
V8-400㉚㊲	R45TSX	.060	—	—	O	16°	I	—	575/650㉘	—	—	—	—
V8-400㊳	R45TSX	.060	—	—	O	18°	I	—	600/700㉘	—	—	—	—
V8-403㉝⑤	R46SZ	.060	—	—	M	22°⑨	J	—	550/650㉘	—	—	—	—
V8-403④⑤	R46SZ	.060	—	—	M	20°⑨	J	—	550/650㉘	—	—	—	—
V8-403㊱⑤	R46SZ	.060	—	—	M	20°⑨	J	—	600/700㉘	—	—	—	—
1978													
4-151	R43TSX	.060	—	—	F	14°⑨	Q	—	650/850㉘	—	—	—	—
V6-231㊽	R46TSX	.060	—	—	S	15°	T㊼	800	600/670㉘	—	—	—	—
V8-301	R45TSX	.060	—	—	O	12°	A	—	550/650㉘	—	—	—	—
V8-305⑭㉟	R45TS	.045	—	—	P	4°	H	600/700㉘	500/600㉘	—	—	—	—
V8-305⑭④	R45TS	.045	—	—	P	6°	H	—	500/650㉘	—	—	—	—
V8-305⑭㊱	R45TS	.045	—	—	P	8°	H	—	600/700㉘	—	—	—	—
V8-350⑭㊴	R45TS	.045	—	—	P	㊷	H	700	㊸㉘	—	—	—	—
V8-350⑤⑦	R46SZ	.060	—	—	M	20°⑨	J	—	550/650㉘	—	—	—	—
V8-350⑪⑫	R46TSX	.060	—	—	N	15°	T㊼	—	550D	—	—	—	—
V8-400⑭	R45TSX	.060	—	—	O	16°	I	—	575/650㉘	—	—	—	—
V8-400㊺	R45TSX	.060	—	—	O	18°	I	775	600/700㉘	—	—	—	—
V8-403	R46SZ	.060	—	—	M	20°⑨	J	—	㊻㉘	—	—	—	—
1979													
V6-231㊽	㊾	.060	—	—	—	15°	T㊼	800	600	—	—	—	—
V8-301	㉔	.060	—	—	O	12°	A	—	550	—	—	—	—
V8-305⑭㉟	R45TS	.045	—	—	P	4°	H	700	500	—	—	—	—
V8-305⑭④	R45TS	.045	—	—	P	6°	H	—	600	—	—	—	—
V8-305⑭㊱	R45TS	.045	—	—	P	8	H	—	600	—	—	—	—

①—BTDC: Before top dead center.
②—Idle speed on manual trans. equipped vehicles is adjusted in neutral. Idle speed on auto. trans. equipped vehicles is adjusted in drive.
③—Where two idle speeds are listed, the higher speed is with idle solenoid energized.
④—California.
⑤—See Oldsmobile Chapter for service procedure.
⑥—Ventura only. See Buick Chapter for service procedures.
⑦—Distributor rotor rotation counter-clockwise.
⑧—Std. Trans. 12°, Auto. Trans. 16°.
⑨—At 1100 RPM.
⑩—Exc. H.E.I., Fig. D; H.E.I., Fig. O.
⑪—For service on this engine see Buick chapter.
⑫—Distributor at front of engine.

⑬—Manual trans., 16° BTDC; auto. trans., 18° BTDC.
⑭—For service on this engine, see Chevrolet Chapter.
⑮—New points .019", used points .016".
⑯—Std. trans. 10° BTDC. Auto. trans. 12° BTDC.
⑰—Engine codes TE, TJ, T4, T5, TK, TN, TA, & TD, 14° BTDC. Engine codes TP, TT, T2 & T3, 16° BTDC.
⑱—Less A/C.
⑲—With A/C.
⑳—Exc. Calif., 550 RPM; Calif. 600 RPM.
㉑—Std. trans. & all California models.
㉒—Auto. trans. exc. California.
㉓—2 bbl. carb., 600 RPM; 4 bbl. carb.—Exc. Calif., 650 RPM; Calif., 625 RPM.
㉔—2 bbl. carb., R46TSX; 4 bbl. carb., R45TSX.
㉕—2 bbl. carb., 650 RPM; 4 bbl. carb.—Exc.

Calif. & Grand Safari sta. wag., 650 RPM; Grand Safari sta. wag. exc. Calif., 625 RPM; All Calif. models, 600 RPM.
㉖—Exc. California.
㉗—Std. trans., 6° BTDC; auto. trans., 10° BTDC.
㉘—Where two idle speeds are listed, the higher speed is with A/C solenoid energized & A/C "On".
㉙—Std. trans.
㉚—Auto. trans.
㉛—Exc. even fire engine.
㉜—Auto. trans., 12° BTDC @ 550 RPM. Manual trans., 16° BTDC @ 850 RPM.
㉝—Firebird, LeMans & Grand Prix.
㉞—Exc. High Altitude.
㉟—Exc. Calif. & high altitude.

Continued
1—769

TUNE UP NOTES—Continued

㊱—High altitude vehicles.
㊲—Exc. Firebird engine code Y6.
㊳—Firebird engine code Y6.
㊴—Distributor rotor rotation, clockwise.
㊵—Distributor rotor rotation, counter-clockwise. Fuel pump located at left side of engine.
㊶—Distributor rotor rotation, counter-clockwise. Fuel pump located at right side of engine.

㊷—Auto. trans., 8 BTDC; Manual trans., 6 BTDC.
㊸—Calif. 500/600; High altitude, 600/650.
㊹—Exc. high performance engine.
㊺—High performance engine.
㊻—Calif. 550/650; High altitude, 600/700.
㊼—The harmonic balancer on these engines has two timing marks. The mark measuring 1/16

inch is used when setting timing with a hand held timing light. The mark measuring 1/8 inch is used when setting timing with magnetic timing equipment.
㊽—Even fire engine.
㊾—Exc. Calif. & High altitude, R46TSX; Calif. & High altitude, R45TSX.

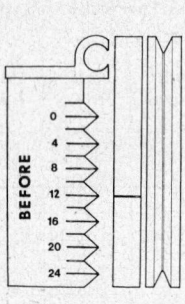

Fig. A

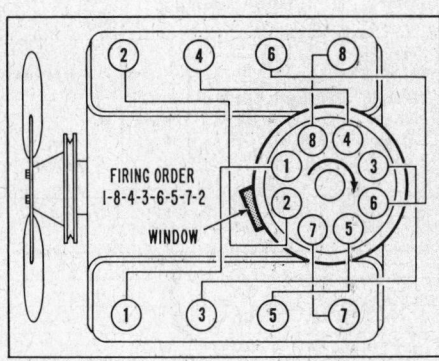

Fig. B

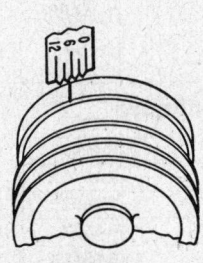

Fig. C

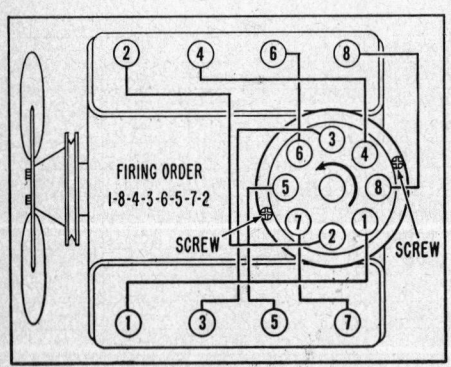

Fig. D

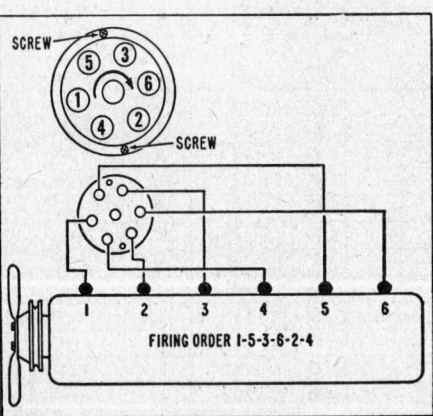

Fig. E

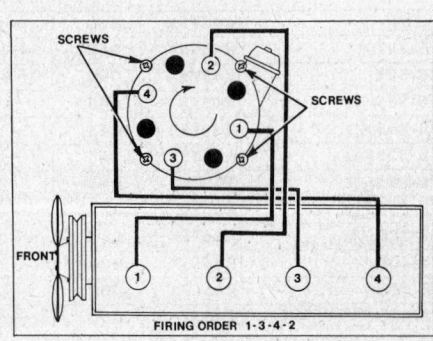

Fig. F

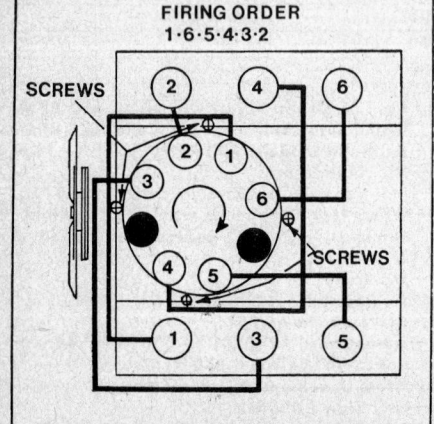

Fig. G

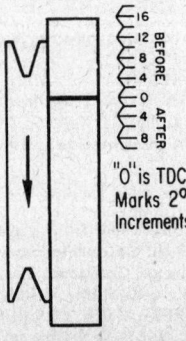

Fig. H

Fig. I

Continued

TUNE UP NOTES—Continued

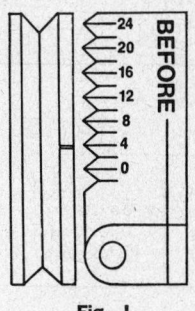

Fig. J

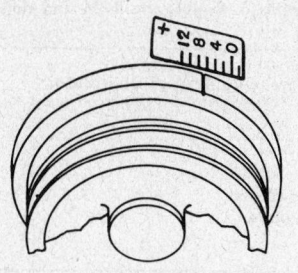

Fig. K

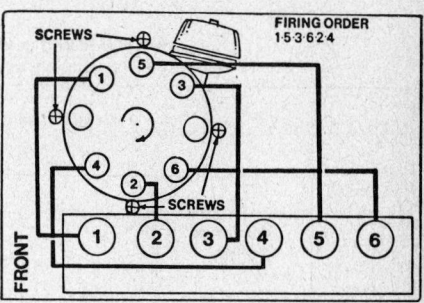

Fig. L

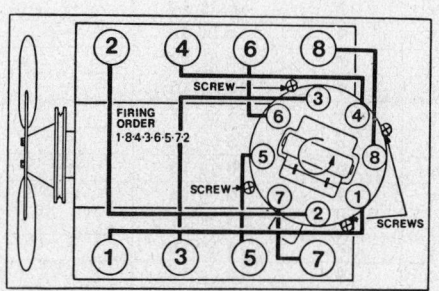

Fig. M

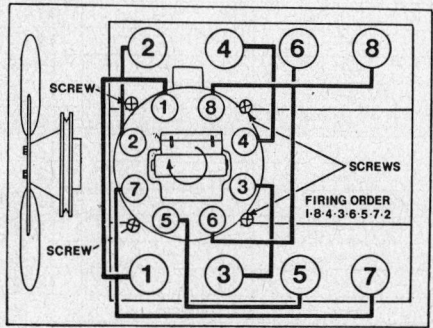

Fig. N

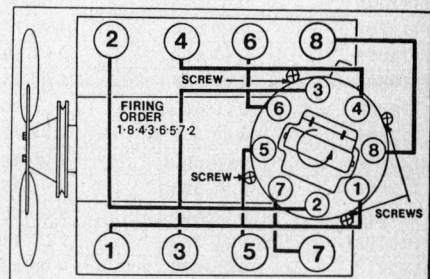

Fig. O

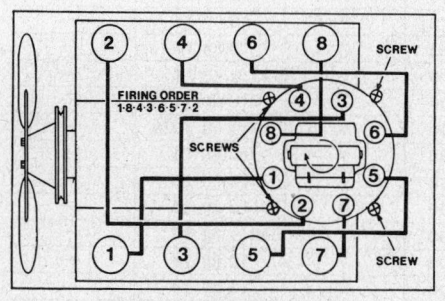

Fig. P

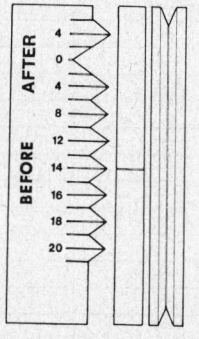

Fig. Q

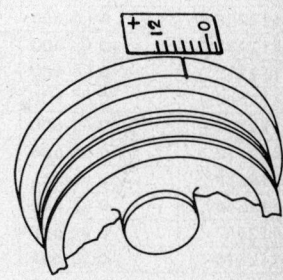

Fig. R

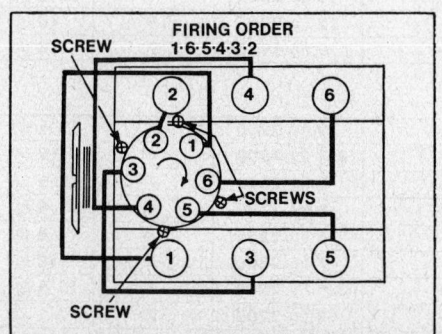

Fig. S

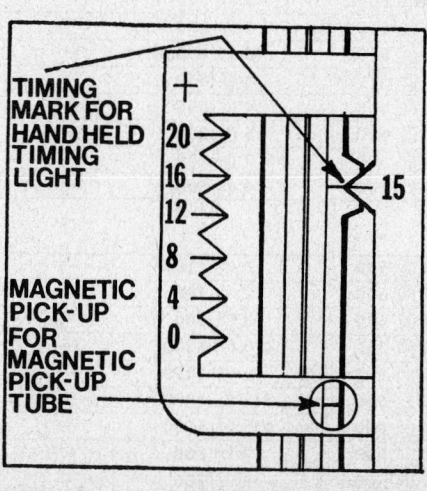

Fig. T

DISTRIBUTOR SPECIFICATIONS

★Note: If unit is checked on vehicle, double the RPM and degrees to get crankshaft figures.

Distributor Part No.①	Centrifugal Advance Degrees @ RPM of Distributor					Vacuum Advance		Distributor Retard
	Advance Starts	Intermediate Advance			Full Advance	Inches of Vacuum to Start Plunger	Max. Adv. Dist. Deg. @ Vacuum	Max. Retard Dist. Deg. @ Vacuum
1974								
1112205	0 @ 600	5 @ 850	—	—	11 @ 2300	9	12.5 @ 14	—
1112231	0 @ 600	5 @ 850	—	—	11 @ 2300	9	12.5 @ 13.5	—
1112804	0 @ 600	6.5 @ 1065	—	—	12 @ 1790	7	10 @ 14	—
1112805	0 @ 600	4 @ 775	—	—	12 @ 1875	9	10 @ 16	—
1112806	0 @ 650	8 @ 1050	—	—	13 @ 1725	7	10 @ 14	—
1112807	0 @ 575	4.5 @ 850	—	—	9 @ 1950	9	10 @ 16	—
1112808	0 @ 600	6.5 @ 1075	—	—	12 @ 1790	5	12.5 @ 11	—
1112809	0 @ 600	4 @ 790	—	—	12 @ 1875	7	12.5 @ 12	—
1112812②	0 @ 600	5 @ 850	—	—	11 @ 2300	9	10 @ 16	—
1112813	0 @ 600	5 @ 850	—	—	11 @ 2300	9	10 @ 16	—
1112814	0 @ 600	5 @ 850	—	—	11 @ 2300	7	12.5 @ 11.5	—
1110499	0 @ 550	7 @ 1150	—	—	12 @ 2050	7	12 @ 15	—
1112210	0 @ 600	4 @ 850	—	—	9 @ 1950	9	10 @ 16	—
1112212	0 @ 600	5 @ 850	—	—	11 @ 2300	9	10 @ 16	—
1112213	0 @ 600	5 @ 850	—	—	11 @ 2300	7	12½ @ 12	—
1122341③	0 @ 600	6.5 @ 1065	—	—	12 @ 1790	7	10 @ 14	—
1112235③	0 @ 600	6.5 @ 1075	—	—	13 @ 1725	5	12½ @ 11	—
1112236③	0 @ 650	8 @ 1050	—	—	13 @ 1725	7	10 @ 14	—
1112237③	0 @ 600	4 @ 775	—	—	12 @ 1875	9	10 @ 16	—
1112238③	0 @ 600	4 @ 790	—	—	12 @ 1875	7	12 @ 12	—
1112239③	0 @ 600	5 @ 850	—	—	11 @ 2300	9	12½ @ 14	—
1112240③	0 @ 600	5 @ 850	—	—	11 @ 2300	9	12½ @ 11½	—
1112243③	0 @ 600	5 @ 850	—	—	11 @ 2300	9	12½ @ 13½	—
1112512③	0 @ 600	5 @ 850	—	—	11 @ 2300	9	10 @ 16	—
1112513③	0 @ 575	4.5 @ 850	—	—	9 @ 1950	9	10 @ 16	—
1112546	0 @ 600	4 @ 800	—	—	12 @ 1800	9	10 @ 16	—
1112547	0 @ 600	4 @ 800	—	—	12 @ 1800	7	12½ @ 12	—
1112810②	0 @ 600	4 @ 800	—	—	9 @ 2000	9	10 @ 16	—
1112821	0 @ 500	4 @ 700	—	—	12 @ 1900	7	10 @ 14	—
1112822③	0 @ 500	4 @ 700	—	—	12 @ 1900	7	10 @ 14	—
1112833	0 @ 600	3 @ 825	—	—	12 @ 2000	9	10 @ 16	—
1112834③	0 @ 600	3 @ 825	—	—	12 @ 2000	9	10 @ 16	—
1112856③	0 @ 610	5 @ 800	—	—	12 @ 1900	—	10 @ 14	—
1112857	0 @ 610	5 @ 800	—	—	12 @ 1900	—	10 @ 14	—
1112859	0 @ 575	4 @ 850	—	—	9 @ 1950	7	10 @ 14.5	—
1112860③	0 @ 575	4 @ 850	—	—	9 @ 1950	7	10 @ 14.5	—
1112871	0 @ 600	5 @ 875	—	—	11 @ 2300	9	12½ @ 16	—
1112876	0 @ 600	3 @ 775	—	—	12 @ 900	9	10 @ 16	—
1112878	0 @ 600	4 @ 800	—	—	9 @ 1950	7	10 @ 14	—
1975								
1112495	0 @ 550	7 @ 1100	—	—	9 @ 2200	7	12½ @ 12	—
1112498	0 @ 600	2 @ 700	—	—	8½ @ 1800	6	12 @ 13	—
1112500	0 @ 600	3 @ 800	—	—	8 @ 2000	7	12½ @ 12	—
1112863	0 @ 362	4½ @ 1300	—	—	8 @ 2100	4	9 @ 12	—
1112896	0 @ 525	3 @ 1050	—	—	6 @ 2250	7	8 @ 12	—
1112918	0 @ 500	5½ @ 1000	—	—	7 @ 2200	7	10 @ 11	—
1112923	0 @ 500	2½ @ 1000	—	—	3½ @ 2200	7	12½ @ 12	—
1112928	0 @ 600	2 @ 700	—	—	8 @ 2200	7	12½ @ 12	—
1112929	0 @ 500	4 @ 700	—	—	10 @ 2200	7	10 @ 14	—

Continued

DISTRIBUTOR SPECIFICATIONS—Continued

★Note: If unit is checked on vehicle, double the RPM and degrees to get crankshaft figures.

Distributor Part No.①	Centrifugal Advance Degrees @ RPM of Distributor					Vacuum Advance		Distributor Retard
	Advance Starts	Intermediate Advance			Full Advance	Inches of Vacuum to Start Plunger	Max. Adv. Dist. Deg. @ Vacuum	Max. Retard Dist. Deg. @ Vacuum
1975—Continued								
1112930	0 @ 700	3½ @ 1000	—	—	5 @ 2200	7	12½ @ 12	—
1112946	0 @ 500	4 @ 700	—	—	10½ @ 1800	7	12 @ 15	—
1112947	0 @ 600	2 @ 700	—	—	10 @ 1900	8	10 @ 15	—
1112948	0 @ 500	4 @ 700	—	—	10 @ 2200	8	10 @ 15	—
1112949	0 @ 500	5½ @ 1000	—	—	7 @ 2200	7	10 @ 14	—
1112950	0 @ 600	2 @ 700	—	—	10 @ 1700	7	10 @ 11	—
1112951	0 @ 325	9½ @ 1200	—	—	14 @ 2200	4	12 @ 15	—
1112956	0 @ 325	9½ @ 1200	—	—	14 @ 2200	—	—	—
1112500	0 @ 600	3 @ 800	—	—	10 @ 2200	7	12½ @ 12	—
1976								
1103204	0 @ 325	9½ @ 1200	—	—	14 @ 2200	6	10 @ 15	—
1103205	0 @ 600	2 @ 700	—	—	8 @ 2200	7	10 @ 11	—
1103206	0 @ 600	2 @ 700	—	—	8½ @ 1800	7	10 @ 11	—
1103208	0 @ 325	9½ @ 1200	—	—	14 @ 2200	6	9 @ 10	—
1103211	0 @ 325	9½ @ 1200	—	—	14 @ 2200	6	7 @ 9	—
1103214	0 @ 600	3 @ 800	—	—	10 @ 2200	8	10 @ 15	—
1103216	0 @ 600	2 @ 700	—	—	10 @ 1900	5	10 @ 12	—
1103223	0 @ 350	2 @ 500	—	—	8 @ 1800	5	12½ @ 12	—
1110666	0 @ 500	3½ @ 800	—	—	10 @ 2100	4	12 @ 15	—
1112495	0 @ 550	7 @ 1100	—	—	9 @ 2200	7	12½ @ 12	—
1112497	0 @ 600	2 @ 700	—	—	10 @ 1900	5	12½ @ 11	—
1112500	0 @ 600	3 @ 800	—	—	10 @ 2200	7	12½ @ 12	—
1112863	0 @ 363	4½ @ 1300	—	—	8 @ 2200	4	9 @ 12	—
1112923	0 @ 500	2½ @ 1000	—	—	3½ @ 2200	7	12½ @ 12	—
1112928	0 @ 600	2 @ 700	—	—	8 @ 2200	7	12½ @ 12	—
1112930	0 @ 700	3½ @ 1000	—	—	5 @ 2200	7	12½ @ 12	—
1112950	0 @ 600	2 @ 700	—	—	10 @ 1900	7	10 @ 11	—
1112956	0 @ 325	9½ @ 1200	—	—	14 @ 2200	—	—	—
1112958	0 @ 600	2 @ 700	—	—	8 @ 2200	5	12½ @ 11	—
1112960	0 @ 500	5½ @ 1000	—	—	7 @ 2200	9	10 @ 16	—
1112991	0 @ 713	—	—	—	10 @ 2213	7	10 @ 13	—
1112992	0 @ 450	—	—	—	10 @ 2200	8	7 @ 11	—
1112994	0 @ 325	9½ @ 1200	—	—	14 @ 2200	5	12 @ 11	—
1112995	0 @ 450	8½ @ 1200	—	—	13 @ 2225	4	15 @ 11	—
1977								
1103231	0 @ 600	—	—	—	10 @ 2200	3.5	10 @ 12	—
1103257	0 @ 600	2 @ 700	—	—	8.5 @ 1800	5	10 @ 10	—
1103259	0 @ 500	—	—	—	9.5 @ 2000	6	12 @ 13	—
1103260	0 @ 500	—	—	—	6.5 @ 1800	6	12 @ 13	—
1103263	0 @ 600	—	—	—	10 @ 2200	3.5	10 @ 9	—
1103264	0 @ 500	—	—	—	6.5 @ 1800	5	8 @ 11	—
1103266	0 @ 500	—	—	—	9.5 @ 2000	5	8 @ 11	—
1103269	0 @ 500	4.5 @ 1000	—	—	8.5 @ 2300	5	10 @ 10	—
1103271	0 @ 500	4 @ 700	—	—	10 @ 2200	5	12.5 @ 11	—
1103272	0 @ 413	5 @ 900	—	—	10¾ @ 1715	4	12.5 @ 12	—
1103273	0 @ 500	8.5 @ 1300	—	—	9.5 @ 1800	4	12.5 @ 12	—
1103276	0 @ 400	2 @ 500	—	—	—	5	10 @ 10	—
1103278	0 @ 600	2 @ 700	—	—	8 @ 2200	5	10 @ 10	—
1110677	—	—	—	—	—	—	—	—
1110686	—	—	—	—	—	—	—	—

Continued

DISTRIBUTOR SPECIFICATIONS—Continued

★Note: If unit is checked on vehicle double the RPM and degrees to get crankshaft figures.

Distributor Part. No.①	Centrifugal Advance Degrees @ RPM of Distributor					Vacuum Advance		Distributor Retard
	Advance Starts	Intermediate Advance			Full Advance	Inches of Vacuum to Start Plunger	Max. Adv. Dist. Deg. @ Vacuum	Max. Retard Dist. Deg. @ Vacuum
1978								
1103281	0 @ 500	5 @ 850	—	—	10 @ 1900	4	9 @ 12	—
1103282	0 @ 500	5 @ 850	—	—	10 @ 1900	4	10 @ 10	—
1103285	0 @ 600	6 @ 1000	—	—	11 @ 2100	4	5 @ 8	—
1103310	0 @ 500	5.5 @ 1000	—	—	7 @ 2200	4	12.5 @ 12	—
1103314	0 @ 413	5 @ 900	—	—	10.7 @ 1700	4	12.5 @ 12	—
1103315	0 @ 500	4 @ 700	—	—	10 @ 2200	5	12.5 @ 11	—
1103316	0 @ 500	4.5 @ 1000	—	—	8.5 @ 2300	4	12.5 @ 12	—
1103323	0 @ 500	—	—	—	9.5 @ 2000	5	8 @ 11	—
1103325	0 @ 500	—	—	—	6.5 @ 1800	5	8 @ 11	—
1103329	0 @ 600	—	—	—	10 @ 2200	3.5	10 @ 9	—
1103337	0 @ 550	6 @ 800	—	—	8 @ 1200	4	12 @ 10	—
1103342	—	2 @ 1000	—	—	9.5 @ 2200	7	12 @ 13	—
1103343	0 @ 400	2.25 @ 508	—	—	8.25 @ 1820	4	12.5 @ 11	—
1103346	0 @ 500	—	—	—	9.5 @ 2000	6	12 @ 13	—
1103347	0 @ 500	—	—	—	6.5 @ 1800	6	12 @ 13	—
1103359	0 @ 500	4.5 @ 1000	—	—	8.5 @ 2300	5	10 @ 10	—
1110695	0-3 @ 1000	—	—	—	9 @ 1800	6	12 @ 13	—
1110731	0-2 @ 1000	—	—	—	9 @ 1800	6	8 @ 9	—
1979								
1103281	0 @ 500	5 @ 850	—	—	10 @ 1900	4	9 @ 12	—
1103282	0 @ 500	5 @ 850	—	—	10 @ 1900	4	10 @ 10	—
1103285	0 @ 600	6 @ 1000	—	—	11 @ 2300	4	5 @ 8	—
1103310	0 @ 500	5½ @ 100	—	—	7 @ 2200	4	12½ @ 12	—
1103314	0 @ 410	5 @ 900	—	—	10½ @ 1700	4	12½ @ 12	—
1103315	0 @ 500	4 @ 700	—	—	10 @ 2200	5	12½ @ 11	—
1103323	—	—	—	—	—	—	—	—
1103325	0 @ 500	—	—	—	6½ @ 1800	5	8 @ 11	—
1103337	0 @ 550	6 @ 800	—	—	8 @ 1200	4	12 @ 10	—
1103346	0 @ 500	—	—	—	9½ @ 2000	6	12 @ 13	—
1103347	0 @ 500	—	—	—	6½ @ 1800	6	12 @ 13	—
1103353	—	—	—	—	—	—	—	—
1103731	0 @ 840	—	—	—	7½ @ 1800	—	—	—
1110695	0-3 @ 1000	—	—	—	9 @ 1800	6	12 @ 13	—
1110713	0-2 @ 1000	—	—	—	9 @ 1800	6	8 @ 9	—
1110731	0-2 @ 1500	—	—	—	9 @ 1800	6	8 @ 9	—
1110766	—	—	—	—	—	—	—	—
1110768	—	—	—	—	—	—	—	—
1110769	—	—	—	—	—	—	—	—
1110772	—	—	—	—	—	—	—	—

①—Stamped on distributor housing plate. ②—Transistorized Unitized distributor. ③—Uni-Set ignition points.

STARTING MOTOR SPECIFICATIONS

Year	Model	Starter Number	Brush Spring Tension Oz[1]	Free Speed Test			Resistance Test[3]	
				Amps.[1]	Volts	R.P.M.[1]	Amps.[1]	Volts
1974	6-250	1108365	35	50[2]	9	5500–10500	—	—
	V8-350	1108224	35	—	—	—	—	—
	V8-400, 455	1108225	35	—	—	—	—	—
	V8-455[4]	1108226	35	65[2]	9	7500–10500	—	—
1975	6-250	1108365	35	50[2]	9	5500–10500	—	—
	6-250	1108745	35	—	—	—	—	—
	V8-260[6]	1108516	35	55–80	9	3500–6000	—	—
	V8-350[3][5]	1108762	35	—	—	—	—	—
	V8-350	1108758	35	65–95	9	7500–10500	—	—
	V8-400, 455	1108759	35	—	—	—	—	—
1976	6-250 Std. Trans.	1108365	35	50[2]	9	5500–10500	—	—
	6-250 Auto. Trans.	1108745	35	—	—	—	—	—
	V8-260[6]	1108516	35	55–80	9	3500–6000	—	—
	V8-260[6][7]	1108765	35	55–80	9	3500–6000	—	—
	V8-350[3][5]	1108762	35	55–80	9	3500–6000	—	—
	V8-350	1108758	35	65–95	9	7500–10500	—	—
	V8-400, 455	1108759	35	—	—	—	—	—
1977	4-151	1109412	—	—	—	—	—	—
	V6-231[8]	1108797	—	—	—	—	—	—
	V8-301	1108758	35	65–95	9	7500–10500	—	—
	V8-305[9]	1108776	—	—	—	—	—	—
	V8-350[9]	1108776	—	—	—	—	—	—
	V8-350[6]	1108765	35	55–80	9	3500–6000	—	—
	V8-350, 400	1108759	35	—	—	—	—	—
	V8-403[6]	1108794	—	—	—	—	—	—
1978	4-151	1109521	—	45–75	9	6500–9700	—	—
	V6-231[8]	1109061	—	60–85	9	6800–10300	—	—
	V8-301	1109523	—	45–70	9	7000–11900	—	—
	V8-305[3][12]	1109524	—	45–70	9	7000–11900	—	—
	V8-305[3][13][14]	1109064	—	60–85	9	6800–10300	—	—
	V8-305[3][13][15]	1109074	—	60–85	9	6800–10300	—	—
	V8-350[3][14]	1109065	—	65–95	9	7500–10500	—	—
	V8-350[3][15]	1109067	—	65–95	9	7500–10500	—	—
	V8-350[8]	1109061	—	60–85	9	6800–10300	—	—
	V8-350, 403[6]	1109072	—	65–95	9	7500–10500	—	—
	V8-400	1108759	—	65–95	9	7500–10500	—	—
1979	V6-231	1109061	—	60–85	9	6800–10300	—	—
	V8-301	1109523	—	45–70	9	7000–11900	—	—
	V8-305[3][9]	1109064[11]	—	60–85	9	6800–10300	—	—
	V8-305[3][10]	1109524	—	45–70	9	7000–11900	—	—
	V8-350[3]	1109065	—	65–95	9	7500–10500	—	—
	V8-350[8]	1109061	—	60–85	9	6800–10300	—	—
	V8-350, 403[6]	1109072	—	65–95	9	7500–10500	—	—
	V8-400	1108759	—	65–95	9	7500–10500	—	—

[1]—Minimum. [2]—Includes solenoid.
[3]—See Chevrolet for service procedures.
[4]—With super-duty engine.
[5]—Ventura models only.
[6]—See Oldsmobile Chapter for service procedures.
[7]—LeMans.
[8]—See Buick chapter for service procedures.
[9]—Two barrel Carb.
[10]—Four barrel Carb.
[11]—With high output option, 1102844.
[12]—LeMans & Grand Prix.
[13]—Firebird & Phoenix.
[14]—Auto trans.
[15]—Manual trans.

VALVE SPECIFICATIONS

Year	Model	Valve Lash		Valve Angles		Valve Spring Installed Height	Valve Spring Pressure Lbs. @ In.	Stem Clearance		Stem Diameter	
		Int.	Exh.	Seat	Face			Intake	Exhaust	Intake	Exhaust
1974	6-250[1]	1 Turn[2]		46	45	1.66	186 @ 1.27	.0010–.0027	.0015–.0032	.3410–.3417	.3410–.3417
	8-350	Hydraulic[7]		[16]	[13]	—	—	.0016–.0033	.0021–.0038	.3400	.3400
	8-400 2 Bar. Carb.	Hydraulic[7]		[16]	[13]	—	—	.0016–.0033	.0021–.0038	.3400	.3400
	8-400 4 Bar. Carb.	Hydraulic[7]		[16]	[13]	—	—	.0016–.0033	.0021–.0038	.3400	.3400
	8-455	Hydraulic[7]		[16]	[13]	—	—	.0016–.0033	.0021–.0038	.3400	.3400
1975	6-250[1]	1 Turn[2]		46	45	1.66	186 @ 1.27	.0010–.0027	.0010–.0027	.3410–.3417	.3410–.3417
	V8-260[17]	Hydraulic[21]		[11]	[12]	1.67	187 @ 1.27	.0010–.0027	.0015–.0032	.3425–.3432	.3420–.3427
	V8-350[20]	Hydraulic[21]		45	45	1.727	[22]	.0015–.0035	.0015–.0032	.3720–.3730	.3723–.3730
	V8-350	Hydraulic[7]		[16]	[13]	1.727	180 @ 1.34	.0016–.0033	.0021–.0038	.3412–.3419	.3407–.3414
	V8-400	Hydraulic[7]		[16]	[13]	1.54	135 @ 1.13	.0016–.0033	.0021–.0038	.3412–.3419	.3407–.3414
	V8-455	Hydraulic[7]		[16]	[13]	1.57	135 @ 1.16	.0016–.0033	.0021–.0038	.3412–.3419	.3407–.3414
1976	6-250[1]	1 Turn[2]		46	45	1.66	186 @ 1.27	.0010–.0027	.0010–.0027	.3410–.3417	.3410–.3417
	V8-260[17]	Hydraulic[21]		46	45	1.67	187 @ 1.27	.0010–.0027	.0015–.0032	.3425–.3432	.3420–.3427
	V8-350[20]	Hydraulic[21]		45	45	1.727	[23]	.0015–.0035	.0015–.0032	.372–.373	.3723–.3730
	V8-350	Hydraulic[7]		[16]	[13]	1.56	[24]	.0016–.0033	.0021–.0038	.3412–.3419	.3407–.3414
	V8-400 2 Bar. Carb.	Hydraulic[7]		[16]	[13]	1.54	[25]	.0016–.0033	.0021–.0038	.3412–.3419	.3407–.3414
	V8-400 4 Bar. Carb.	Hydraulic[7]		[16]	[13]	1.54	[26]	.0016–.0033	.0021–.0038	.3412–.3419	.3407–.3414
	V8-455	Hydraulic[7]		[16]	[13]	1.57	[9]	.0016–.0033	.0021–.0038	.3412–.3419	.3407–.3414
1977	4-151	Hydraulic[7]		46	45	1.66	176 @ 1.254	.0017–.0030	.0017–.0030	.3400	.3400
	V6-231[6]	Hydraulic[21]		45	45	1.727	168 @ 1.327	.0015–.0032	.0015–.0032	.3405–.3412	.3405–.3412
	V8-301	Hydraulic[7]		46	45	1.69	170 @ 1.26	.0017–.0020	.0017–.0020	.3400	.3400
	V8-305[1]	¾ Turn[2]		46	45	[10]	[5]	.0010–.0027	.0010–.0027	.3410–.3417	.3410–.3417
	V8-350[1]	¾ Turn[2]		46	45	[10]	[5]	.0010–.0027	.0010–.0027	.3410–.3417	.3410–.3417
	V8-350[17]	Hydraulic[21]		[11]	[12]	1.67	187 @ 1.27	.0010–.0027	.0015–.0032	.3425–.3432	.3420–.3427
	V8-350	Hydraulic[7]		[3]	[8]	1.549	131 @ 1.185	.0016–.0033	.0021–.0038	.3412–.3419	.3407–.3414
	V8-400	Hydraulic[7]		[3]	[8]	1.549	131 @ 1.185	.0016–.0033	.0021–.0038	.3412–.3419	.3407–.3414
	V8-403[17]	Hydraulic[21]		[11]	[12]	1.67	187 @ 1.27	.0010–.0027	.0015–.0032	.3425–.3432	.3420–.3427
1978	4-151	Hydraulic[7]		46	45	1.66	176 @ 1.254	.0010–.0027	.0010–.0027	.3425–.3418	.3425–.3418
	V6-231	Hydraulic[21]		45	45	1.727	182 @ 1.340	.0015–.0035	.0015–.0032	.3402–.3412	.3405–.3412
	V8-301	Hydraulic[7]		46	45	1.66	166 @ 1.296	.0010–.0027	.0010–.0027	.3425–.3418	.3425–.3418
	V8-305[1]	1 Turn[2]		46	45	1.70	200 @ 1.25	.0010–.0027	.0010–.0027	.3410–.3417	.3410–.3417
	V8-350[1]	1 Turn[2]		46	45	1.70	200 @ 1.25	.0010–.0027	.0010–.0027	.3410–.3417	.3410–.3417
	V8-350[17]	Hydraulic[21]		45	46	1.67	187 @ 1.270	.0010–.0027	.0015–.0032	.3432–.3425	.3427–.3420
	V8-350[6]	Hydraulic[21]		45	45	1.727	175 @ 1.34	.0015–.0035	.0015–.0032	.3720–.3730	.3730–.3723
	V8-400	Hydraulic[7]		[3]	[8]	1.549	131 @ 1.185	.0016–.0033	.0021–.0038	.3425	.3425
	V8-403[17]	Hydraulic[21]		[11]	[12]	1.670	187 @ 1.270	.0010–.0027	.0015–.0032	.3432–.3425	.3427–.3420
1979	V6-231	Hydraulic[21]		45	45	1.727	164 @ 1.340	.0015–.0035	.0015–.0032	.3402–.3412	.3405–.3412
	V8-301	Hydraulic[7]		46	45	1.66	166 @ 1.296	.0010–.0027	.0010–.0027	.3418–.3425	.3418–.3425
	V8-305[1]	Hydraulic[21]		46	45	[10]	[5]	.0010–.0027	.0010–.0027	.3410–.3417	.3410–.3417
	V8-350[1]	Hydraulic[21]		46	45	[10]	[5]	.0010–.0027	.0010–.0027	.3410–.3417	.3410–.3417
	V8-350[17]	Hydraulic[21]		45	46	1.67	187 @ 1.270	.0010–.0027	.0015–.0032	.3425–.3432	.3420–.3427
	V8-350[6]	Hydraulic[21]		45	45	1.727	175 @ 1.34	.0015–.0035	.0015–.0032	.3720–.3730	.3730–.3723
	V8-400	Hydraulic[7]		[3]	[8]	1.549	131 @ 1.185	.0016–.0033	.0021–.0038	.3412–.3419	.3407–.3414
	V8-403	Hydraulic[21]		[18]	[19]	1.670	187 @ 1.270	.0010–.0027	.0015–.0032	.3425–.3432	.3420–.3427

[1]—For service on this engine, see Chevrolet Chapter.
[2]—Turn rocker arm stud nut until all lash is eliminated, then tighten nut the additional turns listed.
[3]—Intake 30°, exhaust 45°.
[4]—Outer spring.
[5]—Intake 174–186 @ 1.25; Exhaust 184–196 @ 1.16.
[6]—See Buick chapter for service procedures.
[7]—No adjustment. On V8's, rocker arms are correctly positioned when ball retainer nuts are tightened to 20 ft.-lbs.
[8]—Intake 29°, exhaust 44°.
[9]—Intake, 135.8 @ 1.16; Exhaust, 141.6 @ 1.15.
[10]—Intake 1.7 inches; Exhaust 1.61 inches.
[11]—Intake, 45°; exhaust, 31°.
[12]—Intake, 44°; exhaust, 30°.

[13]—Small valve engines, intake 44° and exhaust 44°. Large valve engines, intake 29° and exhaust 44°.
[16]—Small valve engines, intake 45° and exhaust 45°. Large valve engines, intake 30° and exhaust 45°.
[17]—See Oldsmobile Chapter for service procedures.
[18]—Intake 45°, exhaust 59°.
[19]—Intake 46°, exhaust 60°.
[20]—Ventura only. See Buick Chapter for service procedures.
[21]—No adjustment.
[22]—Intake, 180 @ 1.34; Exhaust, 177 @ 1.45.
[23]—Intake, 180 @ 1.34; Exhaust, 175 @ 1.34.
[24]—Intake, 131.7 @ 1.18; Exhaust, 137.8 @ 1.15.
[25]—Intake, 134.5 @ 1.16; Exhaust, 135.1 @ 1.13.
[26]—Intake, 135.1 @ 1.13; Exhaust, 140.8 @ 1.12.

PISTONS, PINS, RINGS, CRANKSHAFT & BEARINGS

Year	Model	Piston Skirt Clearance	Ring End Gap① Comp.	Ring End Gap① Oil	Wrist-pin Diameter	Rod Bearings Shaft Diameter	Rod Bearings Bearing Clearance	Main Bearings Shaft Diameter	Main Bearings Bearing Clearance	Thrust on Bear. No.	Shaft End Play
1974	6-250	.0005-.0015	.010	.015	.9272	2.00	.0007-.0027	2.30	.0003-.0029	7	.002-.006
	V8-350	.0029-.0037	⑥	.035	.9802	2.25	.0005-.0025	3.00	.0002-.0017	4	.003-.009
	V8-400	.0029-.0037	⑥	.035	.9802	2.25	.0005-.0025	3.00	.0002-.0017	4	.003-.009
	V8-455	⑩	⑦	.035	.9802	2.25	⑪	3.25	⑫	4	.003-.009
1975	6-250⑧	.0005-.0015	.010	.015	.9272	2.000	.0007-.0027	2.30	.0003-.0029	7	.002-.006
	V8-260⑬	.001-.002	.010	.015	.9805	2.1238-2.1248	.0005-.0026	⑮	⑯	3	.004-.008
	V8-350⑭	.0008-.0020	.010	.015	.9393	2.000	.0005-.0026	3.000	.0004-.0015	3	.003-.009
	V8-350	.0029-.0037	⑥	.035	.9802	2.25	.0005-.0025	3.00	.0002-.0017	4	.003-.009
	V8-400	.0029-.0037	⑥	.035	.9802	2.25	.0005-.0025	3.00	.0002-.0017	4	.003-.009
	V8-455	.0021-.0029	⑦	.035	.9802	2.25	.0005-.0025	3.25	.0005-.0021	4	.003-.009
1976	6-250⑧	.0005-.0015	.010	.035	.9272	2.00	.0007-.0027	2.30	.0003-.0029	7	.002-.006
	V8-260⑬	.00075-.00175⑰	.010	.015	.9805	2.124	.0005-.0026	⑮	⑯	3	.004-.008
	V8-350⑭	.0008-.0014	.013	.015	.9396	2.00	.0005-.0026	2.9995	.0004-.0015	3	.003-.009
	V8-350	.0029-.0037	.019	.035	.9802	2.25	.0005-.0025	3.00	.0002-.0017	4	.0035-.0085
	V8-400	.0029-.0037	⑥	.035	.9802	2.25	.0005-.0025	3.00	.0002-.0017	4	.0035-.0085
	V8-455	.0021-.0029	⑦	.035	.9802	2.25	.0005-.0025	3.25	.0005-.0021	4	.0035-.0085
1977	4-151	.0025-.0033	.010	.010	.940	2.000	.0005-.0026	2.2983-2.2993	.0002-.0022	5	.0015-.0085
	V6-231⑱	.0008-.0020	.010	.015	.93925	1.991-2.000	.0005	2.4995	.0004-.0015	2	.004-.008
	V8-301	.0025-.0033	.010	.035	.927	2.000	.0005-.0025	3.00	.0004-.0020	5	.003-.009
	V8-305⑧	.0007-.0027	.010	.015	.9270	2.199-2.200	.0013-.0035	②	③	5	.002-.006
	V8-350⑧	.0007-.0027	.010	.015	.9270	2.199-2.200	.0013-.0035	②	④	5	.002-.006
	V8-350	.0025-.0023	.010	.035	.980	2.25	.0005-.0025	3.00	.0004-.0015	5	.003-.009
	V8-350⑬	.0005-.0015	.010	.015	.9805	2.1238-2.1248	.0004-.0033	⑮	⑯	3	.0035-.0135
	V8-400	.0025-.0033	.010	.035	.980	2.25	.0005-.0025	3.00	.0004-.0015	5	.003-.009
	V8-403⑬	.0003-.0017	.010	.015	.9805	2.1238-2.1248	.0004-.0033	⑮	⑯	3	.0035-.0135
1978	4-151	.0025-.0033	⑨	.015	.940	2.00	.0005-.0026	2.30	.0002-.0022	5	.0035-.0085
	V6-231⑱	.0008-.0020	.013	.015	.93925	2.2491	.0005-.0026	2.4995	.0004-.0015	2	.003-.009
	V8-301	.0025-.0033	.010	.015	.940	2.25	.0005-.0025	3.00	.0002-.0020	4	.003-.009
	V8-305⑧	.0007-.0017	.010	.010	.92715	2.009-2.100	.0013-.0035	②	⑲	5	.002-.007
	V8-350⑧	.0007-.0017	⑨	.015	.92715	2.009-2.100	.0013-.0035	②	⑲	5	.002-.007
	V8-350⑱	.008-.0020	.010	.015	.93915	1.991-2.000	.0005-.0026	2.9995	.0004-.0015	3	.003-.009
	V8-350⑬	.001-.002	.010	.015	.9805	2.1238-2.1248	.0005-.0026	⑮	⑯	3	.0035-.0135
	V8-400	.0025-.0033	.010	.015	.9802	2.25	.0005-.0025	3.00	.0002-.0017	4	.003-.009
	V8-403⑬	.001-.002	.010	.015	.9805	2.1238-2.1248	.0005-.0026	⑮	⑯	3	.0035-.0135
1979	V6-231⑱	.0008-.0020	.015	.015	.9392	2.2491	.0005-.0026	2.4995	.0004-.0015	2	.003-.009
	V8-301	.064-.084	.015	.015	.940	2.25	.0005-.0026	3.00	.0002-.0020	4	.0035-.0085
	V8-305⑧	.0017-.0042	.010	.010	.92715	2.009-2.100	.0013-.0035	②	⑲	5	.002-.007
	V8-350⑧	.0007-.0008	⑨	.015	.92715	2.009-2.100	.0013-.0035	②	⑲	5	.002-.007
	V8-350⑬	—	.010	.015	.9805	2.1238-2.1248	.0005-.0026	2.50	—	3	—
	V8-350⑮	.0008-.0020	.013	.015	.9392	1.991-2.000	.0005-.0026	2.9995	.0004-.0015	3	.002-.006
	V8-400	.0025-.0033	⑥	.015	.9802	2.25	.0005-.0026	3.000	.0002-.0017	4	—
	V8-403	—	.010	.015	.9805	2.1238-2.1248	.0005-.0026	2.50	—	3	—

①—Fit rings in tapered bores for clearance listed in tightest portion of ring travel.
②—No. 1, 2.4484-2.4493; Nos. 2, 3, 4, 2.4481-2.4490; No. 5, 2.4479-2.4488.
③—No. 1, .0010-.0015; Nos. 2, 3, 4, .0011-.0035; No. 5, .0017-.0035.
④—No. 1, .0008-.0020; Nos. 2, 3, 4, .0011-.0035; No. 5, .0017-.0035.
⑤—V8-400 Ram Air IV use .0055-.0061".
⑥—Top ring .019", second ring .015".
⑦—Top ring .021", second ring .015".
⑧—For service on this engine, see Chevrolet Chapter.
⑨—No. 1, .013"; No. 2, .010".
⑩—1973 exc. super-duty .0025"-.0033", super-duty; .0064"-.0072"; 1974 exc. super-duty .0021"-.0029", super-duty .0064"-.0072".
⑪—Exc. super-duty .0005"-.0025", super-duty .0015"-.0031".
⑫—Exc. super-duty .0005"-.0021", super-duty .0010"-.0026".
⑬—See Oldsmobile Chapter for service procedures.
⑭—Ventura only. See Buick Chapter for service procedures.
⑮—No. 1—2.4988-2.4998; No. 2, 3, 4, 5, 2.4985-2.4995.
⑯—No. 1, 2, 3, 4 .0005-.0021; No. 5—.0015-.0031.
⑰—Measured .77 below piston pin centerline.
⑱—See Buick chapter for service procedures.
⑲—No. 1, .001-.0015; No. 2, 3, 4, .001-.0025; No. 5, .0025-.0035.
⑳—Measured .75 inch below piston pin centerline.

ALTERNATOR & REGULATOR SPECIFICATIONS

Year	Alternator					Regulator						
				Output @ 14 Volts			Field Relay			Voltage Regulator		
	Model	Rated Hot Output Amps.	Field Current 12 Volts @ 80° F.	2000 R.P.M. Amps.	5000 R.P.M. Amps.	Model	Air Gap In.	Point Gap In.	Closing Voltage	Air Gap In.	Point Gap In.	Voltage @ 125° F.
1974	1100497	37	4.0–4.9	—	36①	Integral	—	—	—	—	—	—
	1100927	37	4.0–4.5	—	32	Integral	—	—	—	—	—	—
	1100928	55	4.0–4.5	—	50	Integral	—	—	—	—	—	—
	1101015	80	4.0–4.5	—	74	Integral	—	—	—	—	—	—
1975	1100497	37	4.0–4.5	—	33	Integral	—	—	—	—	—	—
	1101016	80	4.0–4.9	—	76	Integral	—	—	—	—	—	—
	1101027	80	4.0–4.9	—	76	Integral	—	—	—	—	—	—
	1102347	61	4.0–4.5	—	57	Integral	—	—	—	—	—	—
	1102384	37	4.0–4.5	—	33	Integral	—	—	—	—	—	—
	1102385	55	4.0–4.5	—	51	Integral	—	—	—	—	—	—
	1102388	37	4.0–4.5	—	33	Integral	—	—	—	—	—	—
	1102390	55	4.0–4.5	—	51	Integral	—	—	—	—	—	—
	1102394	37	4.0–4.5	—	33	Integral	—	—	—	—	—	—
	1102399	37	4.0–4.5	51	53	Integral	—	—	—	—	—	—
	1102457	55	4.0–4.5	—	51	Integral	—	—	—	—	—	—
	1102481	37	4.0–4.5	—	33	Integral	—	—	—	—	—	—
	1102482	55	4.0–4.5	—	51	Integral	—	—	—	—	—	—
	1102483	37	4.0–4.5	—	33	Integral	—	—	—	—	—	—
	1102486	61	4.0–4.5	—	57	Integral	—	—	—	—	—	—
	1102488	55	4.0–4.5	—	51	Integral	—	—	—	—	—	—
	1102491	37	4.0–4.5	—	33	Integral	—	—	—	—	—	—
	1102840	55	4.0–4.5	—	51	Integral	—	—	—	—	—	—
1976	1101016	80	4–4.9	—	76	Integral	—	—	—	—	—	—
	1102384	37	4–4.5	—	33	Integral	—	—	—	—	—	—
	1102385	55	4–4.5	—	51	Integral	—	—	—	—	—	—
	1102388	37	4–4.5	—	33	Integral	—	—	—	—	—	—
	1102390	55	4–4.5	—	51	Integral	—	—	—	—	—	—
	1102394	37	4–4.5	—	33	Integral	—	—	—	—	—	—
	1102486	61	4–4.5	—	57	Integral	—	—	—	—	—	—
	1102491	37	4–4.5	—	33	Integral	—	—	—	—	—	—
	1102840	55	4–4.5	—	51	Integral	—	—	—	—	—	—
1977	1101016	80	4.0–4.9	—	76	Integral	—	—	—	—	—	—
	1102389	42	—	—	—	Integral	—	—	—	—	—	—
	1102394	37	4–4.5	—	33	Integral	—	—	—	—	—	—
	1102478	55	—	—	—	Integral	—	—	—	—	—	—
	1102479	55	—	—	—	Integral	—	—	—	—	—	—
	1102485	42	—	—	—	Integral	—	—	—	—	—	—
	1102486	61	4–4.5	—	57	Integral	—	—	—	—	—	—
	1102491	37	4–4.5	—	33	Integral	—	—	—	—	—	—
	1102840	55	4–4.5	—	51	Integral	—	—	—	—	—	—
	1102841	42	—	—	—	Integral	—	—	—	—	—	—
	1102842	63	—	—	—	Integral	—	—	—	—	—	—
	1102843	61	—	—	—	Integral	—	—	—	—	—	—
	1102844	63	—	—	—	Integral	—	—	—	—	—	—
	1102854	63	—	—	—	Integral	—	—	—	—	—	—
	1102881	37	—	—	—	Integral	—	—	—	—	—	—
	1102906	61	—	—	—	Integral	—	—	—	—	—	—
	1102908	63	—	—	—	Integral	—	—	—	—	—	—
	1102909	61	—	—	—	Integral	—	—	—	—	—	—
1978-79	1101016	80	—	—	—	Integral	—	—	—	—	—	—
	1102389	42	—	—	—	Integral	—	—	—	—	—	—
	1102391	61	—	—	—	Integral	—	—	—	—	—	—
	1102392	63	—	—	—	Integral	—	—	—	—	—	—

Continued

ALTERNATOR & REGULATOR SPECIFICATIONS—Continued

Year	Alternator					Regulator							
				Output @ 14 Volts			Field Relay			Voltage Regulator		
	Model	Rated Hot Output Amps.	Field Current 12 Volts @ 80° F.	2000 R.P.M. Amps.	5000 R.P.M. Amps.	Model	Air Gap In.	Point Gap In.	Closing Voltage	Air Gap In.	Point Gap In.	Voltage @ 125° F.
1978-79	1102394	37	—	—	—	Integral	—	—	—	—	—	—
	1102478	55	—	—	—	Integral	—	—	—	—	—	—
	1102479	55	—	—	—	Integral	—	—	—	—	—	—
	1102480	61	—	—	—	Integral	—	—	—	—	—	—
	1102485	42	—	—	—	Integral	—	—	—	—	—	—
	1102486	61	—	—	—	Integral	—	—	—	—	—	—
	1102495	37	—	—	—	Integral	—	—	—	—	—	—
	1102841	42	—	—	—	Integral	—	—	—	—	—	—
	1102842	63	—	—	—	Integral	—	—	—	—	—	—
	1102843	61	—	—	—	Integral	—	—	—	—	—	—
	1102844	63	—	—	—	Integral	—	—	—	—	—	—
	1102854	63	—	—	—	Integral	—	—	—	—	—	—
	1102901	61	—	—	—	Integral	—	—	—	—	—	—
	1102909	61	—	—	—	Integral	—	—	—	—	—	—
	1102910	63	—	—	—	Integral	—	—	—	—	—	—
	1102913	61	—	—	—	Integral	—	—	—	—	—	—
	1103033	61	—	—	—	Integral	—	—	—	—	—	—
1979	1101024	80	—	—	—	Integral	—	—	—	—	—	—
	1102860	63	—	—	—	Integral	—	—	—	—	—	—
	1102908	63	—	—	—	Integral	—	—	—	—	—	—
	1103055	42	—	—	—	Integral	—	—	—	—	—	—
	1103056	63	—	—	—	Integral	—	—	—	—	—	—
	1103058	63	—	—	—	Integral	—	—	—	—	—	—
	1103076	63	—	—	—	Integral	—	—	—	—	—	—

①—At 7000 R.P.M.

ENGINE TIGHTENING SPECIFICATIONS★

★Torque specifications are for clean and lightly lubricated threads only. Dry or dirty threads produce increased friction which prevents accurate measurement of tightness.

Year	Model	Spark Plugs Ft. Lbs.	Cylinder Head Bolts Ft. Lbs.	Intake Manifold Ft. Lbs.	Exhaust Manifold Ft. Lbs.	Rocker Arm Ft. Lbs.	Rocker Arm Cover Ft. Lbs.	Connecting Rod Cap Bolts Ft. Lbs.	Main Bearing Cap Bolts Ft. Lbs.	Flywheel to Crankshaft Ft. Lbs.	Vibration Damper or Pulley Ft. Lbs.
1974	6 Cyl.④	15	95	②	25	—	55⑤	35	65	60	—
	V8's	15	95	40	30	20	8	①	100③	95	160
1975-76	6 Cyl.④	15	95	35	30	—	55⑤	35	65	60	60
	V8-260⑧	25	85	40	15–20	25	7	42	80③	⑩	200–310
	V8-350⑨⑫	15	80	45	28	30⑪	4	40	115	60	140 Min.
	V8's	15	95	40	30	20	8	43	100③	95	160
1977	4-151	15	95	⑬	⑬	20	85⑤	30	65	55	160
	V6-231	20	75	45	25	30⑪	5	40	100	55	150
	V8-301	15	90	35	40	20	7	30	70⑦	95	160
	V8-305④	15	65	30	20⑥	—	45⑤	45	70	60	60
	V8-350④	15	65	30	20⑥	—	45⑤	45	70	60	60
	V8-350	15	95	35	40	20	7	40	100③	95	160
	V8-350⑧	25	130	40	25	25	—	42	80③	60	260
	V8-400	15	95	35	40	20	7	40	100③	95	160
	V8-403	25	130	40	25	25	—	42	80③	60	260

Continued

ENGINE TIGHTENING SPECIFICATIONS*—Continued

★Torque specifications are for clean and lightly lubricated threads only. Dry or dirty threads produce increased friction which prevents accurate measurement of tightness.

Year	Model	Spark Plugs Ft. Lbs.	Cylinder Head Bolts Ft. Lbs.	Intake Manifold Ft. Lbs.	Exhaust Manifold Ft. Lbs.	Rocker Arm Ft. Lbs.	Rocker Arm Cover Ft. Lbs.	Connecting Rod Cap Bolts Ft. Lbs.	Main Bearing Cap Bolts Ft. Lbs.	Flywheel to Crank-shaft Ft. Lbs.	Vibration Damper or Pulley Ft. Lbs.
1978	4-151	15	95	⑱	⑬	20	85⑤	30	65	55	160
	V6-231⑫	15	80	45	25	30⑪	4	40	100	60	225
	V8-301	15	95	35	40	20	6	30	70⑭	95	160
	V8-305④	15	65	30	20⑥	—	45⑤	45	70	60	60
	V8-350④	15	65	30	20⑥	—	45⑤	45	70	60	60
	V8-350⑧	25	130	40	25	25	—	42	80③	⑩	260
	V8-350⑫	15	80	45	25	30	4	40	100	60	225
	V8-400	15	95	35	40	20	6	40	100③	95	160
	V8-403	25	130	40	25	25	—	42	80③	⑩	260

①—Exc. V8-455 Super Duty, 43 ft. lbs. On V8-455 Super Duty, torque in 10 ft. lbs. steps until 60 lbs. measure for .006"–.008" bolt elongation from original length, if less then .006" proceed with 5 ft. lb. steps as necessary to obtain proper elongation.
②—Outer 20, all others 30.
③—Rear 120.
④—For service on this engine, see Chevrolet Chapter.
⑤—Inch pounds.
⑥—Inside bolts 30 ft. lbs.

⑦—Rear, 100 ft. lbs.
⑧—For service on this engine, see Oldsmobile Chapter.
⑨—Ventura only.
⑩—Exc. manual trans. 60 ft. lbs.; manual trans. 90 ft. lbs.
⑪—Rocker arm shaft to cylinder head.
⑫—See Buick chapter for service procedures.
⑬—Intake to exhaust manifold bolts, 40 ft. lbs.; manifold to cylinder head nuts, 30 ft. lbs.; manifold to cylinder head bolts, 40 ft. lbs.
⑭—Rear 100.

BRAKE SPECIFICATIONS

Year	Model	Brake Drum Inside Diameter	Wheel Cylinder Bore Diameter			Master Cylinder Bore Diameter		
			Disc Brake	Front Drum Brake	Rear Drum Brake	Disc Brakes	Drum Brakes	Power Brakes
1974	①	9½③	2¹⁵⁄₁₆	1⅛	1⅛④	1⅛	1	1
	Pontiac	11⑤	2¹⁵⁄₁₆	—	¹⁵⁄₁₆	1⅛	1	1
1975	Ventura	9½	2¹⁵⁄₁₆	—	⅞	1	—	1⅛
	⑥	9½③	2¹⁵⁄₁₆	—	⅞⑦	1	—	1⅛
	Grand Prix	11	2¹⁵⁄₁₆	—	¹⁵⁄₁₆	—	—	1⅛
	Pontiac	11⑤	2¹⁵⁄₁₆	—	¹⁵⁄₁₆⑧	—	—	1⅛
1976	Firebird & Ventura	9½	2¹⁵⁄₁₆	—	¹⁵⁄₁₆	1	—	1⅛
	LeMans	11	2¹⁵⁄₁₆	—	¹⁵⁄₁₆	¹⁵⁄₁₆	—	1⅛
	Grand Prix	11	2¹⁵⁄₁₆	—	¹⁵⁄₁₆	—	—	1⅛
	Pontiac	11⑥	2¹⁵⁄₁₆	—	1	—	—	1⅛
1977	Firebird & Ventura	9.5	2.9375	—	.938	1	—	1.125
	LeMans	11	2.9375	—	.937	.9375	—	1.125
	Grand Prix	11	2.9375	—	.937	—	—	1.125
	Pontiac	11	2.9375	—	⑨	—	—	1.125
1978	Firebird	9.5	2.9375	—	.938	1	—	1.125
	Grand Prix	11	2.5	—	.75	.86614	—	.94488
	LeMans	11	2.5	—	.75	.86614	—	.94488
	Phoenix	9.5	2.9375	—	.938	1	—	1.125
	Pontiac	11	2.9375	—	.937	1.125	—	1.125
1979	Firebird	9.5	2.9375	—	.938	1	—	1.125
	Grand Prix	9.5	2.5	—	.75	.86614	—	.94488
	LeMans	9.5	2.5	—	.75	.86614	—	.94488
	Phoenix	9.5	2.9375	—	.938	1	—	1.125
	Pontiac	—	2.9375	—	.937	1.125	—	1.125

①—Intermediates, Ventura II, Firebird and Grand Prix.
③—Wagon, 11".
④—Wagon, ¹⁵⁄₁₆".
⑤—Wagon 12".
⑥—Firebird and intermediates.
⑦—Wagon ¹⁵⁄₁₆".
⑧—Wagon 1".
⑨—Exc. Sta. Wag. & V8-403, .875"; Sta. Wag. & V8-403 .9375".

REAR AXLE SPECIFICATIONS

Year	Model	Carrier Type	Ring Gear & Pinion Backlash		Pinion Bearing Preload			Differential Bearing Preload		
			Method	Adjustment	Method	New Bearings Inch-Lbs.	Used Bearings Inch-Lbs.	Method	New Bearings Inch-Lbs.	Used Bearings Inch-Lbs.
1974–76	All	Integral	Shims	.005–.009	①	24–32	8–12	Shims	②	②
1977–78	All	Integral	Shims	.006–.008	①	20–25	10–15	Shims	.001–.008	.001–.008

①—Tighten pinion shaft nut with inch-pound torque wrench. ②—Slip fit plus .008″ tight.

WHEEL ALIGNMENT SPECIFICATIONS

Year	Model	Caster Angle, Degrees		Camber Angle, Degrees				Toe-In. Inch	Toe-Out on Turns, Deg.	
		Limits	Desired	Limits		Desired			Outer Wheel	Inner Wheel
				Left	Right	Left	Right			
1974	Firebird	−½ to +½	Zero	+½ to +1½	+½ to +1½	+1	+1	⅛ to ¼	—	—
	Ventura	0 to +1	+½	−¼ to +¾	−¼ to +¾	+¼	+¼	⅛ to ¼	—	—
	Grand Prix	+2½ to +3½	+3	+½ to +1½	0 to +1	+1	+½	0 to ⅛	—	—
	Intermediates	④	⑤	+½ to +1½	0 to +1	+1	+½	0 to ⅛	—	—
	③	+½ to +1½	+1	+½ to +1½	0 to +1	+1	+½	0 to ⅛	—	—
1975	Ventura⑥	−½ to −1½	−1	+¼ to +1¼	+¼ to +1¼	+¾	+¾	0 to ⅛	—	—
	Ventura⑦	+½ to +1½	+1	+¼ to +1¼	+¼ to +1¼	+¾	+¾	0 to ⅛	—	—
	Firebird	−½ to +½	Zero	+½ to +1½	+½ to +1½	+1	+1	0 to ⅛	—	—
	Intermediate⑥	+½ to +1½	+1	+½ to +1½	0 to +1	+1	+½	0 to ⅛	—	—
	Intermediate⑦	+1½ to +2½	+2	+½ to +1½	0 to +1	+1	+½	0 to ⅛	—	—
	Grand Prix	+2½ to +3½	+3	+½ to +1½	0 to +1	+1	+½	0 to ⅛	—	—
	Pontiac	+½ to +2½	+1½	+½ to +1½	0 to +1	+1	+½	0 to ⅛	—	—
1976	Ventura⑥	−½ to −1½	−1	+¼ to +1¼	+¼ to +1¼	+¾	+¾	0 to ⅛	—	—
	Ventura⑦	+½ to +1½	+1	+¼ to +1¼	+¼ to +1¼	+¾	+¾	0 to ⅛	—	—
	Firebird	−½ to +½	Zero	+½ to +1½	+½ to +1½	+1	+1	0 to ⅛	—	—
	Intermediate⑥	+½ to +1½	+1	+½ to +1½	0 to +1	+1	+½	0 to ⅛	—	—
	Intermediate⑦	+1½ to +2½	+2	+½ to +1½	0 to +1	+1	+½	0 to ⅛	—	—
	Grand Prix	+2½ to +3½	+3	+½ to +1½	0 to +1	+1	+½	0 to ⅛	—	—
	Pontiac	+1 to +2	+1½	+½ to +1½	0 to +1	+1	+½	0 to ⅛	—	—
1977	Ventura⑥	−1½ to −½	−1	+.3 to +1.3	+.3 to +1.3	+.8	+.8	0 to ⅛	—	—
	Ventura⑦	+½ to +1½	+1	+.3 to +1.3	+.3 to +1.3	+.8	+.8	0 to ⅛	—	—
	Firebird	+½ to +1½	+1	+½ to +1½	+½ to +1½	+1	+1	0 to ⅛	—	—
	LeMans⑥	+½ to +1½	+1	+½ to +1½	0 to +1	+1	+½	0 to ⅛	—	—
	LeMans⑦	①	+2	+½ to +1½	0 to +1	+1	+½	0 to ⅛	—	—
	Grand Prix	①	+3	+½ to +1½	0 to +1	+1	+½	0 to ⅛	—	—
	Pontiac	+2½ to +3½	+3	+.3 to +1.3	+.3 to +1.3	+.8	+.8	⅛ to ¼	—	—
1978	Phoenix⑥	−1.5 to −.5	−1	+.3 to +1.3	+.3 to +1.3	+.8	+.8	1/16 to 3/16	—	—
	Phoenix⑦	+.5 to +1.5	+1	+.3 to +1.3	+.3 to +1.3	+.8	+.8	1/16 to 3/16	—	—
	Firebird	+.5 to +1.5	+1	+.5 to +1.5	+.5 to +1.5	+1	+1	1/16 to 3/16	—	—
	Intermediate⑥	+.5 to +1.5	+1	0 to +1	0 to +1	+.5	+.5	1/16 to 3/16	—	—
	Intermediate⑦	+2.5 to +3.5	+3	0 to +1	0 to +1	+.5	+.5	1/16 to 3/16	—	—
	Pontiac	+2.5 to +3.5	+3	+.3 to +1.3	+.3 to +1.3	+.8	+.8	1/16 to 3/16	—	—
1979	Phoenix⑥	−1.5 to −5	−1	+.5 to +1.5	+.5 to +1.5	+1	+1	0° to .12°	—	—
	Phoenix⑦	+.5 to +1.5	+1	+.5 to +1.5	+.5 to +1.5	+1	+1	0° to .12°	—	—
	Firebird	+.5 to +1.5	+1	+.5 to +1.5	+.5 to +1.5	+1	+1	0° to .12°	—	—
	LeMans⑥	+.5 to +1.5	+1	0 to +1	0 to +1	+.5	+.5	.06° to .18°	—	—
	LeMans⑦	+2.5 to +3.5	+3	0 to +1	0 to +1	+.5	+.5	.06° to .18°	—	—
	Grand Prix	+2.5 to +3.5	+3	0 to +1	0 to +1	+.5	+.5	.06° to .18°	—	—
	Pontiac	+2.5 to +3.5	+3	.3 to 1.3	.3 to 1.3	+.8	+.8	0 to .24°	—	—

①—Exc. radial tires, +½ to +1½; Radial tires +1½ to +2½.
②—Exc. radial tires; +1; Radial tires +2.
③—Catalina, Grand Ville and Bonneville.
④—Manual steering −1½ to −½, Power steering −½ to +½.
⑤—Manual steering −1°, Power steering 0°.
⑥—Manual Steering.
⑦—Power steering.

COOLING SYSTEM & CAPACITY DATA

Year	Model or Engine	Cooling Capacity, Qts.		Radiator Cap Relief Pressure, Lbs.		Thermo. Opening Temp. [1]	Fuel Tank Gals.	Engine Oil Refill Qts. [2]	Transmission Oil				Rear Axle Oil Pints
		With Heater	With A/C	With A/C	No A/C				3 Speed Pints	4 Speed Pints	5 Speed Pints	Auto. Trans. Qts. [12]	
1974	6-250 Ventura	13.1	—	14–17	14–17	195	21.5	4	3½	—	—	4½[20]	3¾
	6-250 Firebird	13.5	—	14–17	14–17	195	21.5	4	3½	—	—	4½[20]	4¼
	6-250 Le Mans	14.7	—	14–17	14–17	195	22	4	3½	—	—	4½[20]	3[28]
	8-350 Ventura	20.0	20.0	14–17	14–17	195	21.5	5	3½	2½	—	4½[20]	3¾
	8-350 Firebird	22.0	22.9	14–17	14–17	195	21.5	5	3½	2½	—	4½[20]	4¼
	8-350 Le Mans	21.3	23.6	14–17	14–17	195	22	5	3½[26]	2½	—	4½[20]	3[28]
	8-350 Pontiac	21.6	22.4	14–17	14–17	195	25.8	5	—	—	—	4½[11]	4¼[29]
	8-400 Firebird	21.9	22.9	14–17	14–17	195	21.5	5	—	2½	—	4½[11]	4¼
	8-400 Le Mans	21.3	22.8	14–17	14–17	195	22[24]	5	—	2½	—	4½[11]	3[28]
	8-400 Grand Prix	21.6	24.0	14–17	14–17	195	25	5	—	—	—	4½[11]	3[30]
	8-400 Pontiac	21.6	22.4	14–17	14–17	195	25.8	5	—	—	—	4½[11]	4¼[29]
	8-455 Firebird	20.3	21.3	14–17	14–17	195	21.5	5	—	2½	—	4½[11]	4¼
	8-455 Le Mans	21.1	21.6	14–17	14–17	195	22[24]	5	—	—	—	4½[11]	3[28]
	8-455 Grand Prix	20.2	22.2	14–17	14–17	195	25	5	—	—	—	4½[11]	3[30]
	8-455 Pontiac	19.8	22.3	14–17	14–17	195	25.8	5	—	—	—	4½[11]	4¼[29]
1975	6-250 Ventura	13.1	—	14–17	14–17	195	20.5	4	3½	—	—	2½[27]	3¾
	6-250 Firebird	13.1	—	14–17	14–17	195	21.5	4	3½	—	—	4[8]	4¼
	6-250 LeMans	14.7	—	14–17	14–17	195	21	4	3½	—	—	4[8]	3[28]
	V8-260 Ventura	22.4	22.9	14–17	14–17	195	20.5	4	3½	2½	—	2½[27]	3¾
	V8-350 Ventura	20	20	14–17	14–17	195	20.5	4	—	2½	—	2½[27]	3¾
	V8-350 Firebird	22	23.3	14–17	14–17	195	21.5	5	3½	2½	—	4[27]	4¼
	V8-350 LeMans	21.3	23.6	14–17	14–17	195	21	5	—	—	—	4[8]	3[28]
	V8-400 Firebird	21.3	[9]	14–17	14–17	195	21.5	5	—	2½	—	4[27]	4¼
	V8-400 LeMans	21.3	[10]	14–17	14–17	195	21[13]	5	—	—	—	3¾[8]	3[28]
	V8-400 Grand Prix	21.5	24	14–17	14–17	195	25	5	—	—	—	3¾[8]	3[28]
	V8-400 Pontiac	21.6	22.4	14–17	14–17	195	25.8	5	—	—	—	3¾[8]	5½
	V8-455 LeMans	19.9	21.6	14–17	14–17	195	21[13]	5	—	—	—	3¾[8]	3[28]
	V8-455 Grand Prix	20.2	22.5	14–17	14–17	195	25	5	—	—	—	3¾[8]	3[28]
	V8-455 Pontiac	19.8	22.3	14–17	14–17	195	25.8[14]	5	—	—	—	3¾[8]	5½
1976	6-250 Ventura	13.0	—	14–17	14–17	195	20.5	4	3.5	—	—	2½[27]	3¾
	6-250 Firebird	13.5	—	14–17	14–17	195	21.5	4	3.5	—	—	4[8]	4¼
	6-250 LeMans	15.0	—	14–17	14–17	195	21	4	3.5	—	—	4[8]	3[28]
	V8-260 Ventura	20.6	21.3	14–17	14–17	195	20.5	4	3.5	—	3.0	2½[27]	3¾
	V8-260 LeMans	23.5	26.0	14–17	14–17	195	21	4	3.5	—	3.0	4[8]	3[28]
	V8-350 Ventura	17.3	18.0	14–17	14–17	195	20.5	4	—	—	—	2½[27]	3¾
	V8-350 Firebird	21.2	21.6	14–17	14–17	195	21.5	5	—	—	—	4[27]	4¼
	V8-350 LeMans	21.4	22.0	14–17	14–17	195	21	5	—	—	—	4[8]	3[28]
	V8-350 Grand Prix	21.6	22.0	14–17	14–17	195	25	5	—	—	—	3¾[8]	3[28]
	V8-400 Firebird	21.6	23.3	14–17	14–17	195	21.5	5	—	2.5	—	4[27]	4¼
	V8-400 Le Mans	21.4	22.0	14–17	14–17	195	21[14]	5	—	—	—	3¾[8]	3[28]
	V8-400 Grand Prix	22.2	22.2	14–17	14–17	195	25	5	—	—	—	3¾[8]	3[28]
	V8-400 Pontiac	21.6	22.4	14–17	14–17	195	25.8[14]	5	—	—	—	3¾[8]	5½
	V8-455 Firebird	23.3	23.3	14–17	14–17	195	21.5	5	—	2.5	—	4[27]	4¼
	V8-455 LeMans	21.6	21.6	14–17	14–17	195	21[14]	5	—	—	—	3¾[8]	3[28]
	V8-455 Grand Prix	22.2	22.2	14–17	14–17	195	25	5	—	—	—	3¾[8]	3[28]
	V8-455 Pontiac	22.1	22.1	14–17	14–17	195	25.8[14]	5	—	—	—	3¾[8]	5½
1977	4-151 Ventura	12.4	12.4	14–17	14–17	195	21	4	3.5	2.4	3.5	3[15]	3½
	V6-231 Ventura	13.8	13.8	14–17	14–17	195	21	4	3.5	2.4	3.5	3[15]	3½
	V6-231 LeMans	14.5	14.5	14–17	14–17	195	22	4	3.5	—	—	4[8]	4.25
	V6-231 Firebird	13.2	13.2	14–17	14–17	195	21	4	3.5	2.5	—	4[8]	4.25
	V6-231 Pontiac	12.9	12.9	14–17	14–17	195	21	4	—	—	—	[16]	[17]
	V8-301 Ventura	19.8	20.2[23]	14–17	14–17	195	21	5½	3.5	2.4	3.5	3[18]	3½
	V8-301 LeMans	20.2	20.8[23]	14–17	14–17	195	22	5½	3.5	—	—	[16]	4.25
	V8-301 Firebird	19.5	19.5	14–17	14–17	195	21	5½	3.5	2.5	—	4[8]	4.25
	V8-301 Pontiac	18.6	19.8[28]	14–17	14–17	195	21	5½	—	—	—	[16]	
	V8-301 Grand Prix	20½	21.1[23]	14–17	14–17	195	25	5½	—	—	—	3¾[8]	4.25

Continued

COOLING SYSTEM & CAPACITY DATA—Continued

Year	Model or Engine	Cooling Capacity, Qts.		Radiator Cap Relief Pressure, Lbs.		Thermo. Opening Temp. ①	Fuel Tank Gals.	Engine Oil Refill Qts. ②	Transmission Oil				Rear Axle Oil Pints
		With Heater	With A/C	With A/C	No A/C				3 Speed Pints	4 Speed Pints	5 Speed Pints	Auto. Trans. Qts. ⑫	
1977	V8-305 Ventura	17	18	14–17	14–17	195	21	4	3.5	2.4	3.5	3⑱	3½
	V8-350 Ventura	16.6	16.6	14–17	14–17	195	21	4	3.5	2.4	3.5	3⑧	3½
	V8-350 LeMans⑲	21.7	23.9⑧	14–17	14–17	195	22	5	3.5	—	—	⑯	4.25
	V8-350 LeMans⑳	16.7	17.5⑧	14–17	14–17	195	22	4	3.5	—	—	⑯	4.25
	V8-350 Firebird⑲	20.3	23⑳	14–17	14–17	195	21	5	3.5	2.5	—	4⑧	4.25
	V8-350 Firebird⑳	16	18.2⑧	14–17	14–17	195	21	4	3.5	2.5	—	4⑧	4.25
	V8-350 Pontiac⑲	15	16.2⑧	14–17	14–17	195	21	5	—	—	—	⑱	⑰
	V8-350 Pontiac⑳	15	16.2⑧	14–17	14–17	195	21	4	—	—	—	⑯	⑰
	V8-350 Grand Prix⑦	21.9	24.1⑧	14–17	14–17	195	25	5	—	—	—	3¾⑧	4.25
	V8-350 Grand Prix⑳	17	17.8⑧	14–17	14–17	195	25	4	—	—	—	3¾⑧	4.25
	V8-400 LeMans	21.7	23.9⑧	14–17	14–17	195	22	5	3.5	—	—	⑯	4.25
	V8-400 Firebird㉑	21.1	22.9	14–17	14–17	195	21	5	3.5	2.5	—	4⑧	4.25
	V8-400 Firebird㉒	20.4	21.2	14–17	14–17	195	21	5	3.5	2.5	—	4⑧	4.25
	V8-400 Firebird	—	23⑧	14–17	14–17	195	21	5	3.5	2.5	—	4⑧	4.25
	V8-400 Pontiac	21.7	23.9⑧	14–17	14–17	195	21	5	—	—	—	⑯	⑰
	V8-400 Grand Prix	21.9	24.1⑧	14–17	14–17	195	25	5	—	—	—	3¾⑧	4.25
	V8-403 LeMans	17.9	18.7⑧	14–17	14–17	195	22	4	3.5	—	—	⑯	4.25
	V8-403 Firebird	17.1	19.4⑧	14–17	14–17	195	21	4	3.5	2.5	—	4⑧	4.25
	V8-403 Pontiac	16.1	17.3⑧	14–17	14–17	195	21	4	—	—	—	⑯	⑰
	V8-403 Grand Prix	18.2	19.0⑧	14–17	14–17	195	25	4	—	—	—	3¾⑧	4.25
1978	4-151 Phoenix	11.8	11.8	14–17	14–17	195	21	3	3.5	2.5	3.5	3③	3½
	V6-231 Phoenix	14.0	14.1	14–17	14–17	195	21	4	3.5	2.5	—	3③	3½
	V6-231 LeMans	14.3	14.2	14–17	14–17	195	17⑤	4	3.5	2.4	—	3③	3½
	V6-231 Firebird	14.0	14.0	14–17	14–17	195	21	4	3.5	2.5	—	3④	4¼
	V6-231 Grand Prix	14.3	14.2	14–17	14–17	195	15	4	3.5	—	—	3③	3½
	V6-231 Pontiac	14.2	14.1	14–17	14–17	195	21	4	—	—	—	3③	⑰
	V8-301 LeMans	20.3	20.2	14–17	14–17	195	15⑤	5	—	—	—	3③	3½
	V8-301 Grand Prix	20.3	20.2	14–17	14–17	195	15	5	—	—	—	3③	3½
	V8-301 Pontiac	20.2	20.1	14–17	14–17	195	21	5	—	—	—	3③	⑰
	V8-305 Phoenix	16.8	17.0	14–17	14–17	195	21	4	—	2.5	—	3③	3½
	V8-305 LeMans	17.7	17.4	14–17	14–17	195	15⑤	4	—	—	—	3③	3½
	V8-305 Firebird	17.2	17.2	14–17	14–17	195	21	4	—	3.5	—	3④	4¼
	V8-305 Grand Prix	17.7	17.4	14–17	14–17	195	15	4	—	—	—	3③	3½
	V8-350 Phoenix	17.1	17.8	14–17	14–17	195	21	4	—	—	—	3③	4¼
	V8-350 LeMans	17.7	18.1	14–17	14–17	195	15⑤	4	—	—	—	3③	3½
	V8-350 Firebird	17.2	17.2	14–17	14–17	195	21	4	—	3.5	—	3④	4¼
	V8-350 Pontiac⑥	16.6	18.5	14–17	14–17	195	21	4	—	—	—	3③	4¼
	V8-350 Pontiac⑦	16.5	19.1	14–17	14–17	195	21	4	—	—	—	3③	4¼
	V8-400 Firebird	19.7	22.0	14–17	14–17	195	21	5	—	2.4	—	3④	4¼
	V8-400 Pontiac	26.3	20.3	14–17	14–17	195	21	5	—	—	—	3③	4¼
	V8-403 Firebird	17.4	18.0	14–17	14–17	195	21	4	—	—	—	3④	4¼
	V8-403 Pontiac	17.7	23.0	14–17	14–17	195	21	4	—	—	—	3③	4¼
1979	V6-231 Phoenix	13.7	13.7	14–17	14–17	195	21	4	—	—	—	3	3½
	V6-231 LeMans	13.6	13.6	14–17	14–17	195	18	4	3.5	3.5	—	3	—
	V6-231 Firebird	15.8	15.8	14–17	14–17	195	21	4	3.5	—	—	3	4¼
	V6-231 Grand Prix	13.6	13.6	14–17	14–17	195	18	4	3.5	—	—	3	3½
	V6-231 Pontiac	12.8	12.8	14–17	14–17	195	21	4	—	—	—	—	㉛
	V8-301 Firebird	—	—	14–17	14–17	195	—	—	—	—	—	—	—
	V8-301 LeMans	21.8	21.8	14–17	14–17	195	18	5	—	—	—	3	—
	V8-301 Grand Prix	21.8	21.8	14–17	14–17	195	18	5	—	—	—	3	3½
	V8-301 Pontiac	20.9	20.9	14–17	14–17	195	21	5	—	—	—	—	㉛
	V8-305 Phoenix	16.6	16.6	14–17	14–17	195	21	4	—	—	—	2.25	3½
	V8-305 LeMans	16.1	16.1	14–17	14–17	195	18	4	—	—	—	3	—
	V8-305 Firebird	17.5	17.5	14–17	14–17	195	21	4	—	3.5	—	3	4¼
	V8-305 Grand Prix	16.1	16.1	14–17	14–17	195	18	4	—	—	—	3	3½
	V8-350 Phoenix	16.6	16.6	14–17	14–17	195	21	4	—	—	—	3	4¼
	V8-350 LeMans	16.1	16.1	14–17	14–17	195	18	4	—	—	—	3	—

Continued

COOLING SYSTEM & CAPACITY DATA—Continued

Year	Model or Engine	Cooling Capacity Qts.		Radiator Cap Relief Pressure, Lbs.		Thermo. Opening Temp. ①	Fuel Tank Gals.	Engine Oil Refill Qts. ②	Transmission Oil				Rear Axle Oil Pints
		With Heater	With A/C	With A/C	No A/C				3 Speed Pints	4 Speed Pints	5 Speed Pints	Auto. Trans. Qts. ⑫	
1979	V8-350 Firebird	17.5	17.5	14–17	14–17	195	21	4	—	3.5	—	3	4¼
	V8-350 Pontiac	—	—	14–17	14–17	195	21	4	—	—	—	—	㉛
	V8-400 Firebird	18.4	18.4	14–17	14–17	195	21	5	—	3.5	—	3.75	4¼
	V8-403 Firebird	20.4	20.4	14–17	14–17	195	21	4	—	—	—	3.75	4¼
	V8-403 Pontiac	16.3	16.3	14–17	14–17	195	21	4	—	—	—	—	㉛

①—With permanent type anti freeze.
②—Add one quart with filter change.
③—Oil pan only. After overhaul; THM 200, 9 qts., THM 350, 10 qts.
④—Oil pan only. After overhaul 10 qts.
⑤—Station Wagons, 18 gals.
⑥—Distributor located at front of engine.
⑦—Station Wagons 24 gals.
⑧—Oil pan only. After overhaul 9½ qts.
⑨—2 BBl. Carb. 22.5 qts., 4 BBl. Carb. 23.3 qts.
⑩—2 BBl. Carb. 21.9 qts., 4 BBl. Carb. 23.6 qts.
⑪—Oil pan only. After overhaul 12 qts.
⑫—Approximate. Make final check with dipstick.

⑬—Grand Am 25 gals., Sta. Wagon 22 gals.
⑭—Station Wagons 22 gals.
⑮—Oil pan only. After overhaul 6¾ qts.
⑯—THM 200, oil pan only 3 qts.; after overhaul 8¾ qts. THM 350, oil pan only 4 qts.; after overhaul 9.6 qts. THM 400, oil pan only 3¾ qts.; after overhaul 9½ qts.
⑰—7½ inch axle 3½ pints. 8½ & 8¾ inch axle 4¼ pints.
⑱—Oil pan only. After overhaul 8¾ qts.
⑲—With fuel pump located on driver side of engine.
⑳—With fuel pump located on passenger side of engine.

㉑—Manual trans.
㉒—Auto. trans.
㉓—Vehicles equipped with A/C and/or heavy duty cooling system.
㉔—Grand Am 25 gals.
㉕—Muncie 2¾ pints.
㉖—Oil pan only. After overhaul 11 qts.
㉗—Oil pan only. After overhaul 10½ qts.
㉘—"C" Type 4.9 pints.
㉙—"C" Type 4¼ pints.
㉚—"C" Type 3.9 pints.
㉛—Exc. Station Wagon, 3.5 pts.; Station Wagon, 4.25 pts.

Electrical Section

DISTRIBUTOR, REPLACE

1. Disconnect distributor-to-coil primary wire.

   NOTE: On H.E.I. systems, disconnect feed and module connectors from distributor cap.

2. Remove distributor cap.
3. Crank engine so rotor is in position to fire No. 1 cylinder and timing mark on vibration damper is indexed with pointer.
4. Remove vacuum line from distributor.
5. Remove distributor clamp.
6. Lift distributor from engine.

Installation

1. Check to see that engine is at firing position for No. 1 cylinder.
2. Install new gasket on block.
3. Install distributor so vacuum unit faces right side of engine and rotor points toward contact in cap for No. 1 cylinder.
4. Install distributor clamp, leaving screw loose enough to allow distributor to be turned for adjustment.
5. Attach vacuum line to distributor.
6. Install wires in distributor cap.
7. Attach distributor primary wire.
8. Adjust point gap, replace cap and set ignition timing.

NOTE: When using a timing light to adjust ignition timing, the connection should be made at the No. 1 spark plug. Forcing foreign objects through the boot at the No. 1 terminal of the distributor cap will damage the boot and could cause engine misfiring.

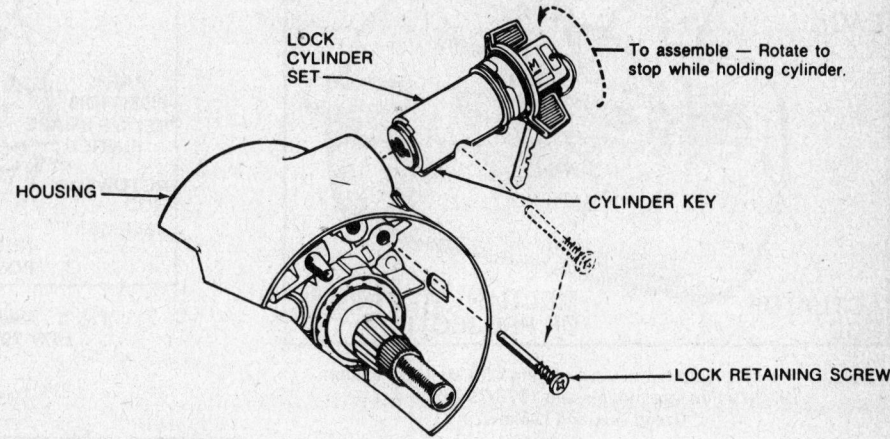

Fig. 1   Ignition lock replacement. 1979 models

STARTER, REPLACE

1. Disconnect battery ground cable.
2. Disconnect brace from starter and swing brace forward, then remove heat shields, if used.
3. On 4-151 and 6-250, disconnect wiring from starter, then remove retaining bolts and starter.
4. On all other engines, remove starter retaining bolts, then lower starter, disconnect wiring and remove starter.

   NOTE: If any shims are used between starter and engine, make sure that they are reinstalled in the same location and in the same thickness.

5. Reverse procedure to install.

IGNITION LOCK REPLACE
1979

1. Remove steering wheel as described under Horn Sounder and Steering Wheel.
2. Remove turn signal switch as described under Turn Signal Switch, Replace, then remove buzzer switch.
3. Place ignition switch in Run position, then, remove lock cylinder retaining screw and lock cylinder.
4. To install, rotate lock cylinder to stop while holding housing, Fig. 1. Align cylinder key with keyway in housing, then push lock cylinder assembly into housing until fully seated.
5. Install lock cylinder retaining screw. Torque screw to 40 in. lbs. for standard columns. On adjustable columns, torque retaining screw to 22 in. lbs.
6. Install buzzer switch, turn signal switch and steering wheel.

1974-78

1. Follow the procedure to remove the turn signal switch as described further on.
2. Remove the lock cylinder in "RUN" position by inserting a thin tool (screwdriver or knife blade), Fig. 2, into the slot next to the switch mounting screw boss (right hand slot) and depress spring latch at bottom of slot, which releases lock. Remove lock by pulling out of housing.

   NOTE: If this is the first time the lock cylinder is being removed, the slot will be covered by a thin casting "flash" which is easily broken when inserting thin tool.

3. To install, hold lock cylinder sleeve and rotate knob clockwise against stop, then insert cylinder into housing with key on lock cylinder sleeve aligned with keyway in housing. Push into abutment of cylinder and lock sector.
4. Push in until latch snaps into groove and lock cylinder is secured in housing.

Fig. 2A   Ignition lock replace. 1974-78

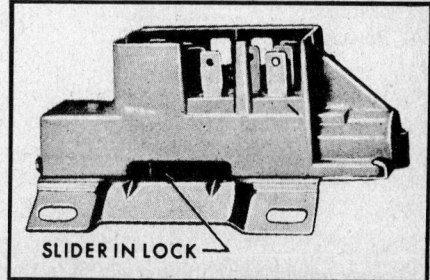

Fig. 3   Ignition switch. 1974-79 (typical)

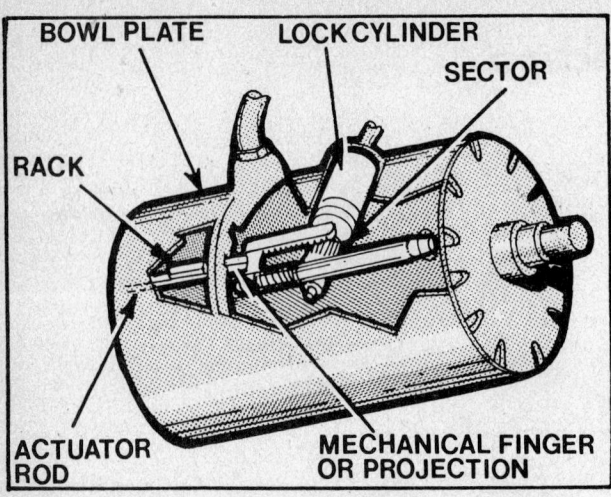

Fig. 4 Mechanical neutral start system with standard column. 1977-79 Full size models and 1978-79 Grand Am, Grand Prix and LeMans

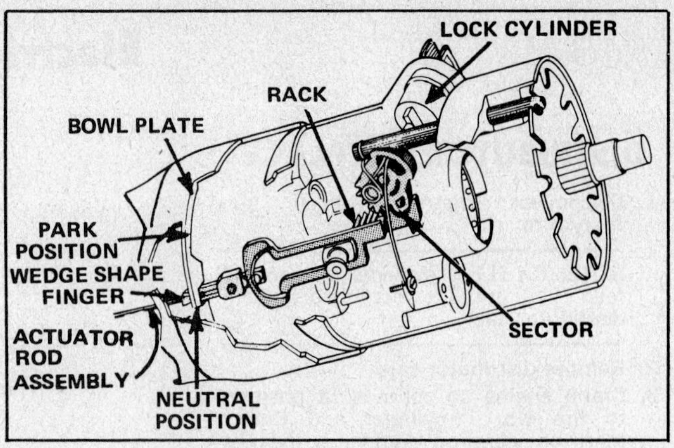

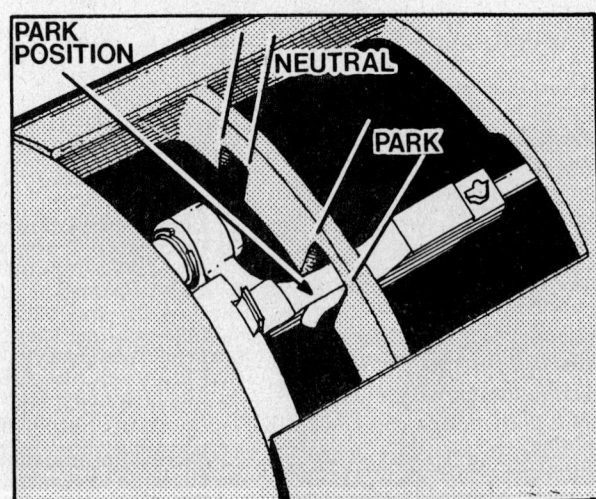

Fig. 5 Mechanical neutral start system with tilt column. 1977-79 Full size models and 1978-79 Grand Am, Grand Prix and LeMans

IGNITION SWITCH, REPLACE

1974-79

1. Disconnect battery and loosen toe pan screws.
2. Remove column to instrument panel trim plates.
3. Lower steering column from instrument panel.

NOTE: On some models it may be necessary to remove the upper column mounting bracket if it hinders the servicing of switch.

4. Disconnect switch wires and remove switch.
5. To replace switch move key lock to OFF-LOCK position.
6. Move actuator rod hole in switch to OFF-LOCK position, Fig. 3.
7. Install switch with rod in hole.

LIGHT SWITCH, REPLACE

1. Remove battery cable, pull knob to "On" position, depress latch button and remove knob and shaft.
2. Remove retaining nut.
3. Remove wire connector and remove switch.
4. Reverse procedure to install.

Fig. 6 Mechanical neutral start system in Park position. 1977-79 Full size models and 1978-79 Grand Am, Grand Prix and LeMans

firmly against the stop. The pedal arm forces the switch body to slip in the mounting sleeve bushing to position the switch properly.

1. Disconnect wires from switch and remove switch from bracket.
2. Position switch in bracket and push in to maximum distance. Brake pedal arm moves switch to correct distance on rebound. Check if pedal is in full return position by lifting slightly by hand.
3. Connect switch wires by inserting plug on switch.

tral" on automatic transmission models.

2. Rotate switch until alignment hole in outer cover aligns with hole in inner contact carrier. Insert a .089 inch gauge pin into alignment hole on manual transmission models. On models with automatic transmission, insert a .096 inch guage pin on 1974 models and .090 inch gauge pin on 1975-79 models, into alignment hole on top of switch. On all models, guage pin is inserted approximately ⅜ inch.
3. Tighten switch retaining screws and remove gauge pin.

STOP LIGHT SWITCH, REPLACE

1974-79

The stop light switch has a slip fit in the mounting sleeve which permits positive adjustment by pulling the brake pedal up

NEUTRAL SAFETY SWITCH

1974-79

1. Loosen switch retaining screws and place selector lever in "Reverse" on manual transmission models or "Neu-

MECHANICAL NEUTRAL START SYSTEM

1977-79 Full Size & 1978-79 Grand Am, Grand Prix & LeMans

Actuation of the ignition switch is pre-

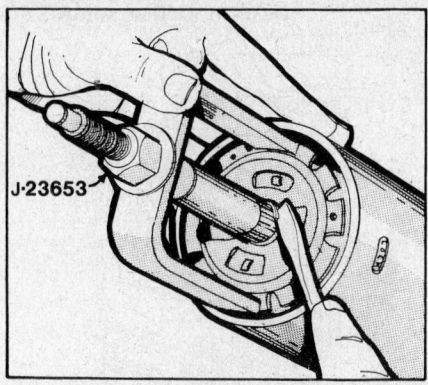

Fig. 7 Compressing lock plate and removing retaining ring.

vented by a mechanical lockout system, Figs. 4 and 5, which prevents the lock cylinder from rotating when the selector lever is out of Park or Neutral. When the selector lever is in Park or Neutral, the slots in the bowl plate and the finger on the actuator rod align allowing the finger to pass through the bowl plate in turn actuating the ignition switch, Fig. 6. If the selector lever is in any position other than Park or Neutral, the finger contacts the bowl plate when the lock cylinder is rotated, thereby preventing full travel of the lock cylinder.

CLUTCH START SWITCH
1974-79

All cars equipped with a manual transmission use a clutch start switch which is mounted on the pedal bracket. The switch closes when the clutch is depressed and completes solenoid connection. When installing switch, no adjustment is necessary.

TURN SIGNAL SWITCH
1974-79

NOTE: *On tilt column, the column must first be lowered from panel.*

1. Remove steering wheel using puller.

   CAUTION: *Do not hammer on end of shaft as hammering could collapse shaft or loosen plastic injections which maintain column rigidity.*

2. Remove three cover screws and lift cover off shaft.

   NOTE: *Screw retainers will be lost if screws are removed completely from cover.*

3. Depress lock plate and pry round wire lock ring out of shaft groove, Fig. 7.

   NOTE: *On 1976-79 models, remove lock plate cover with a suitable screwdriver.*

4. Slide upper bearing preload spring and turn signal cancelling cam off shaft.
5. Slide thrust washer off shaft and remove turn signal lever.

   NOTE: On models with column mounted dimmer switch, remove actuator arm screw and actuator arm before removing turn signal lever.

6. Push hazard warning switch in and unscrew knob.
7. Pull turn signal wiring connector out of bracket on jacket and disconnect.
8. Remove three turn signal switch screws.
9. On models equipped with column shift automatic transmission, loosen shift indicator needle attaching screw.
10. Lower steering column from instrument panel and remove wire protector, then pull switch straight up with wire protector and remove housing.

NOTE: Place tape around upper part of connector and wires to prevent snagging when switch is being removed, Fig. 8.

COLUMN-MOUNTED DIMMER SWITCH
1977-79 Full Size & 1978-79 Grand Prix & LeMans

1. Disconnect battery ground cable.
2. Remove instrument panel lower trim and on models with A/C, remove A/C duct extension at column.
3. Disconnect shift indicator from column and remove toe-plate cover screws.
4. Remove two nuts from instrument panel support bracket studs and lower steering column, resting steering wheel on front seat.
5. Remove dimmer switch retaining screw(s) and the switch. Tape actuator rod to column and separate switch from rod.
6. Reverse procedure to install. To adjust switch, depress dimmer switch slightly and install a 3/32 inch twist drill to lock the switch to the body. Force switch upward to remove lash between switch and pivot. Torque switch retaining screws to 35 inch lbs. and remove tape from actuator rod. Remove twist drill and check for proper operation.

HORN SOUNDER & STEERING WHEEL
1974-79

1. Lift ornament out of wheel hub.
2. Remove nut and washer from shaft.
3. Remove horn bar (deluxe wheel) or extension and switch assembly (standard wheel).
4. Use a suitable puller to remove wheel.
5. Reverse procedure to install, making sure wheel is in straight ahead position.

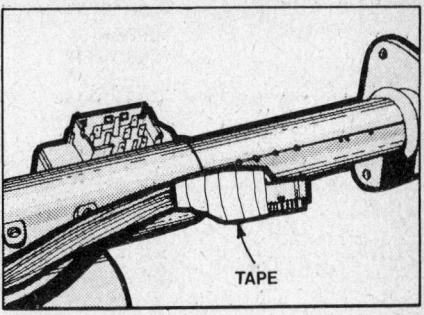

Fig. 8 Taping turn signal connector & wires

INSTRUMENT CLUSTER
Except 1974 GTO, 1974-77 Ventura & 1977-79 Phoenix

1. Disconnect battery ground cable.
2. Remove upper and lower instrument panel trim plates, Figs. 9 thru 14.
3. Remove shift indicator cable.
4. On Firebird, loosen steering column nuts and lower column approximately ½ inch.
5. On all models, remove cluster retaining screws, pull cluster outward and disconnect speedometer cable and printed circuit connector, then remove cluster, Figs. 14 thru 19.
6. Reverse procedure to install.

1974-GTO, 1974-77 Ventura & 1977-79 Phoenix

1. Disconnect battery ground cable.
2. Remove steering column trim panel, Figs. 20 and 21.
3. On 1977-79 models, remove hush panel.
4. Remove three screws retaining heater or A/C control panel to instrument panel carrier.
5. Remove radio control knobs, bezels and nuts.
6. Remove screws at top, bottom and side of carrier securing it to instrument panel pad.
7. Disconnect shift quadrant indicator cable at shaft bowl (if automatic), remove two steering column to panel nuts.
8. Remove toe plate cover and five toe plate to cowl screws, lower column from panel and protect it with shop towels or tape.
9. Remove ground wire screw from under left side of panel pad above kick pad and disconnect speedo cable from under dash.
10. Tilt carrier and cluster rearward, disconnect printed circuit and cluster ground connectors and rest assembly on top of column.
11. Remove screws from cluster to carrier assembly and remove cluster.
12. Reverse procedure to install.

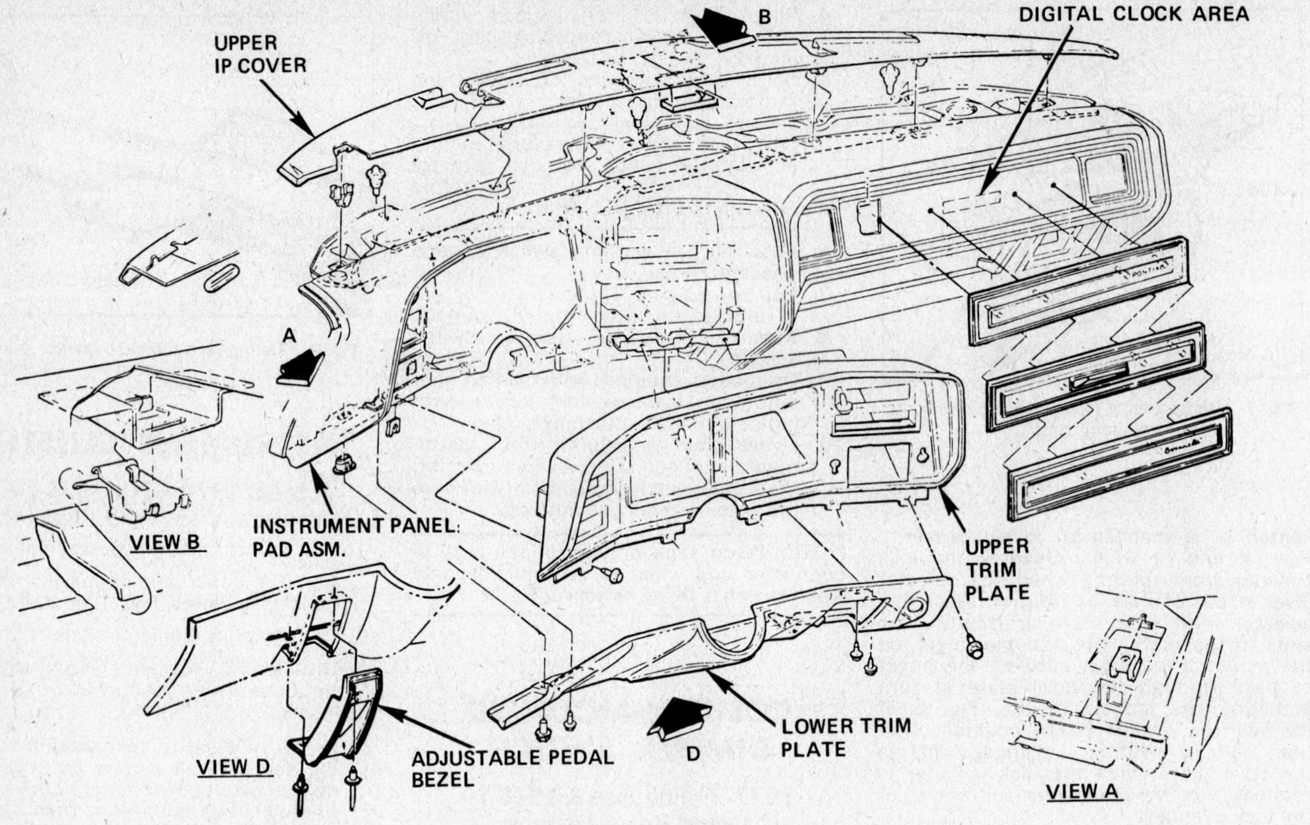

UPPER
IP COVER

B

DIGITAL CLOCK AREA

A

INSTRUMENT PANEL:
PAD ASM.

VIEW B

UPPER
TRIM
PLATE

VIEW D

ADJUSTABLE PEDAL
BEZEL

D

LOWER TRIM
PLATE

VIEW A

Fig. 9   Instrument panel. 1974-76 Full Size

W/S WIPER BLADES

Two methods are used to retain wiper blades to wiper arms, Fig. 22. One method uses a press type release tab. When the release tab is depressed the blade assembly can be slid off the wiper arm pin. The other method uses a coil spring retainer. A screwdriver must be inserted on top of the spring and the spring pushed downward. The blade assembly can then be slid off the wiper arm pin. Two methods are also used to retain the blade element in the blade assembly, Fig. 22. One method uses a press type release button. When the button is depressed, the two piece blade assembly can be slid off the blade element. The other method uses a spring type retainer clip in the end of the blade element. When the retainer clip is squeezed together, the blade element can be slid out of the blade assembly.

NOTE: To be sure of correct installation, the element release button, or the spring element retaining clip should be at the end of the wiper blade assembly nearest the wiper transmission.

W/S WIPER ARMS
With Rectangular Motor

1. Wiper motor must be in park position.
2. Use suitable tool to minimize the pos-

sibility of windshield or paint finish damage during arm removal.

3. Remove arm by prying up with tool to disengage arm from serrated transmission shaft, Fig. 23.

4. To install arm to transmission rotate the required distance and direction so that blades rest in proper position.

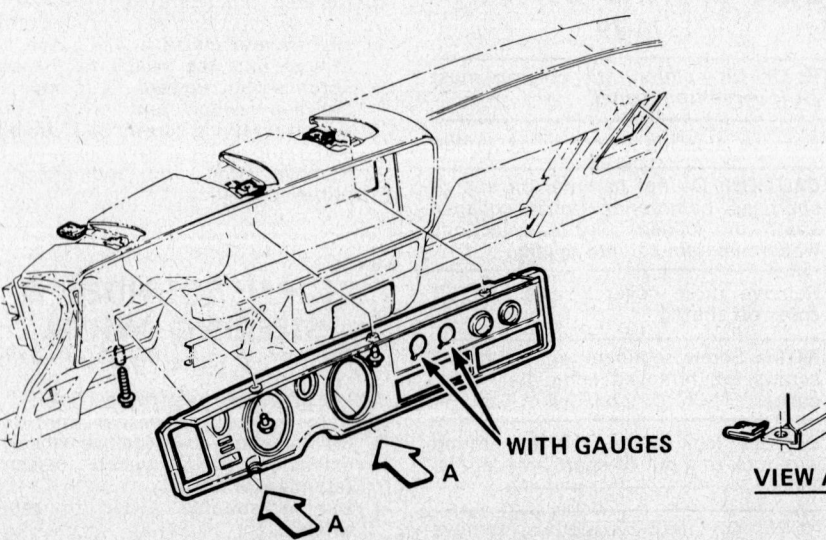

WITH GAUGES

A

A

VIEW A

Fig. 10   Instrument panel. 1974-79 Firebird

With Round Motor

1. Wiper motor must be in park position.

2. Raise hood to gain access to wiper arm.

3. **On Intermediate Models:** On 1974-77 models, use tool No. J-8966 to lift arm off transmission shaft. On left arm, slide articulating arm lock clip, Fig. 24, away from transmission pivot pin and lift arm off pin. On 1978-79 models, lift wiper arm and slide latch clipout from under arm, Fig. 26. **On Full Size Models:** Lift arm and slide latch clip, Figs. 25 and 26 out from under wiper arm.

4. Release wiper arm and lift arm assembly off transmission shaft.

W/S WIPER MOTOR, REPLACE

1974-79

1. Raise hood and remove cowl screen or grille.

2. Disconnect wiring and washer hoses.

3. Reaching through opening, loosen transmission drive link to crankarm attaching nuts.

4. Remove drive link from motor crank-arm.

5. Remove three motor attaching screws and remove motor while guiding crankarm through opening.

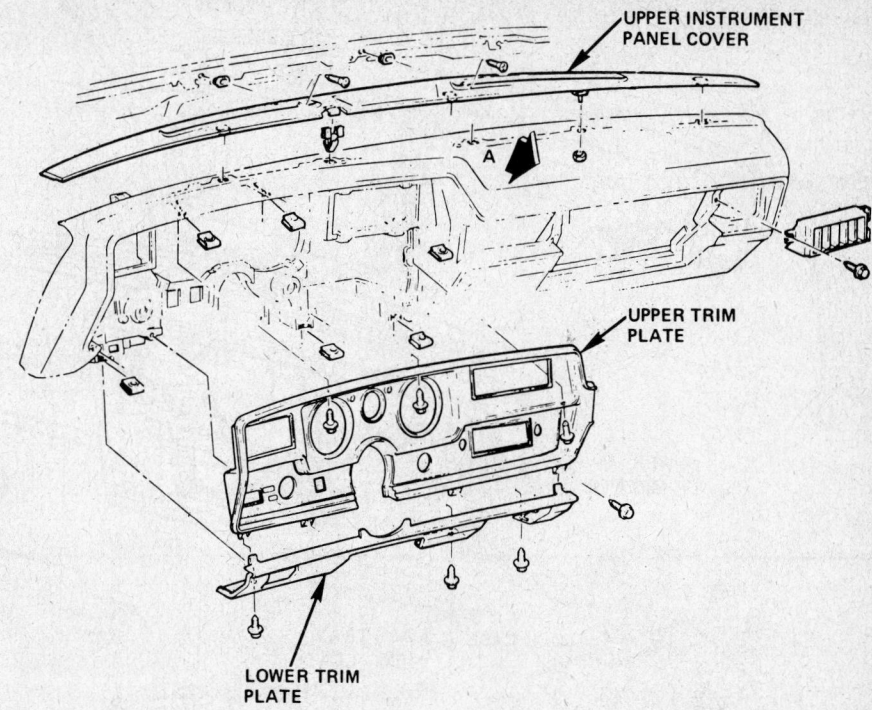

Fig. 11   Instrument panel. 1974-77 LeMans less optional instrument cluster

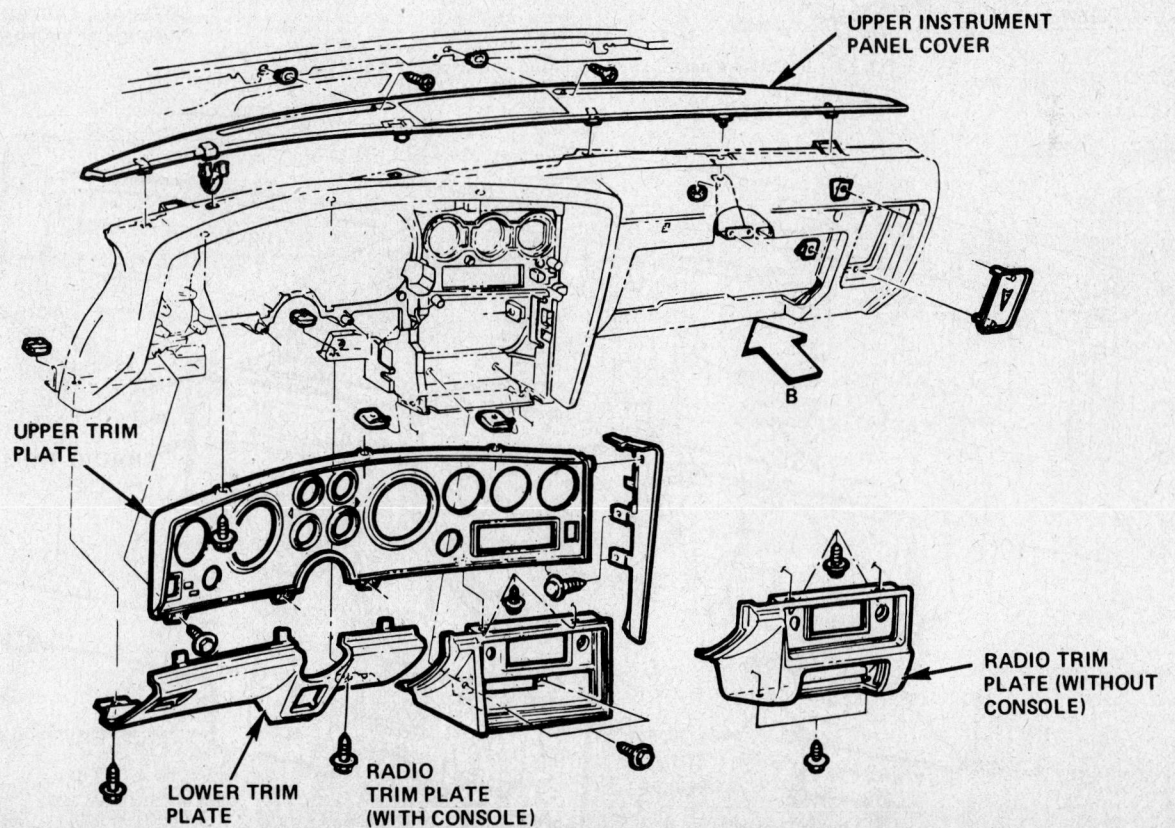

Fig. 12   Instrument panel. 1974-77 Grand Am, Grand Prix and LeMans with optional instrument cluster

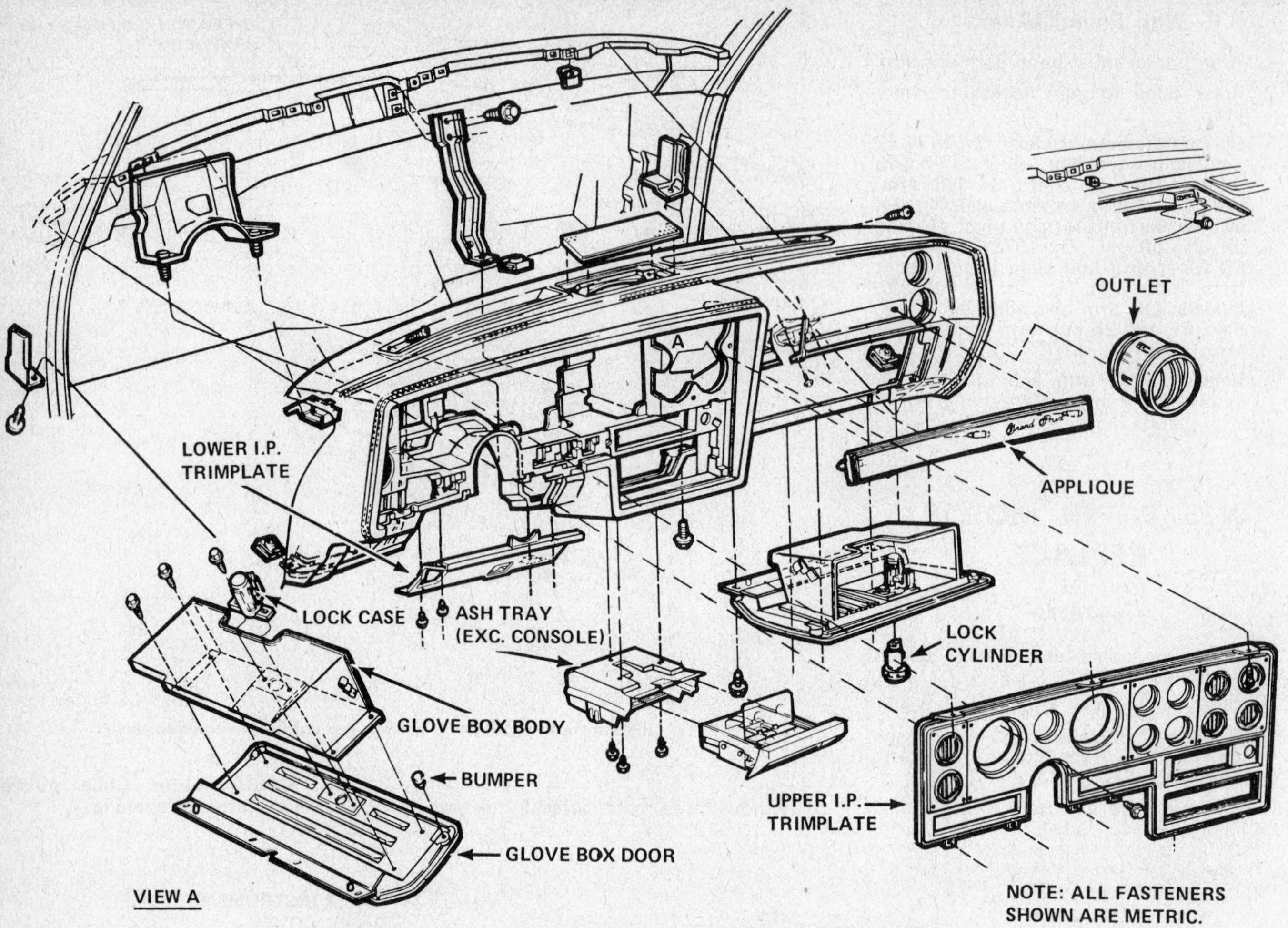

OUTLET

LOWER I.P.
TRIMPLATE

APPLIQUE

LOCK CASE

ASH TRAY
(EXC. CONSOLE)

LOCK
CYLINDER

GLOVE BOX BODY

BUMPER

UPPER I.P.
TRIMPLATE

GLOVE BOX DOOR

VIEW A

NOTE: ALL FASTENERS
SHOWN ARE METRIC.

Fig. 13   Instrument panel. 1978-79 Grand Am, Grand Prix and LeMans

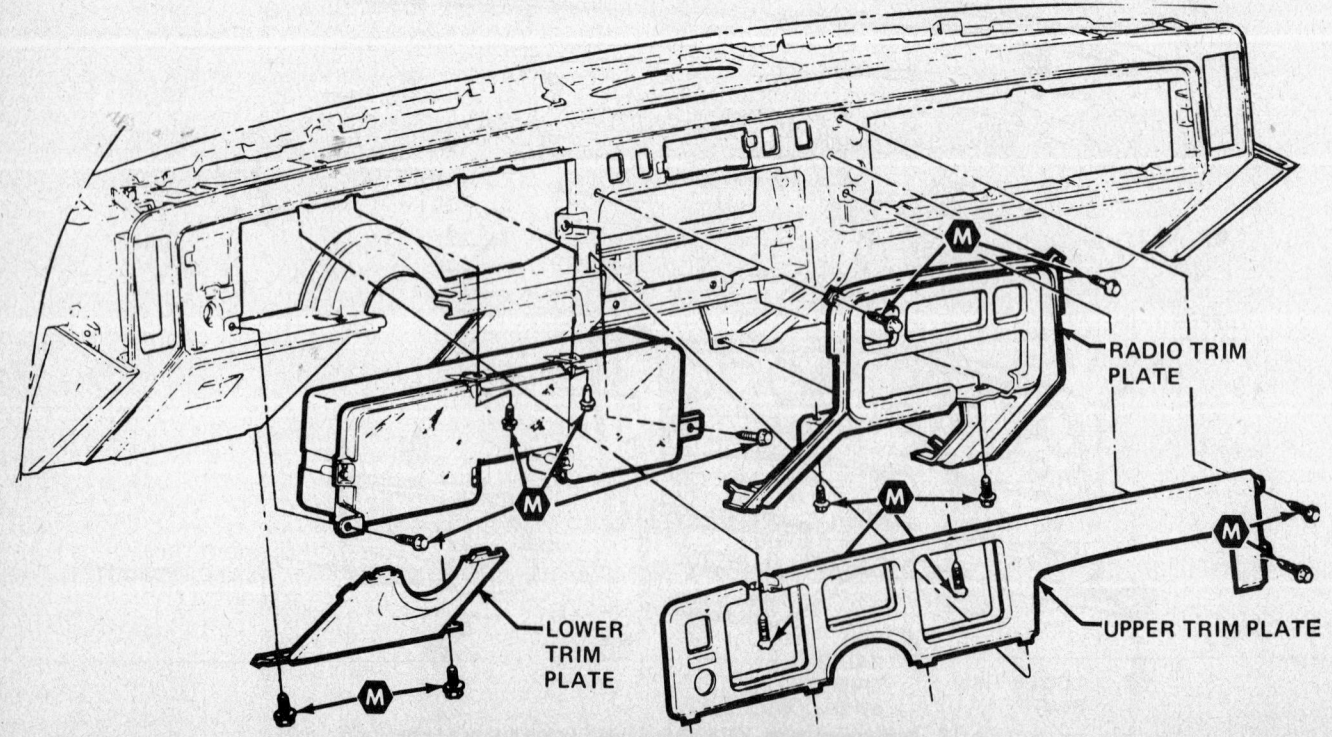

RADIO TRIM
PLATE

LOWER
TRIM
PLATE

UPPER TRIM PLATE

Fig. 14   Instrument panel and cluster. 1977-79 Full Size

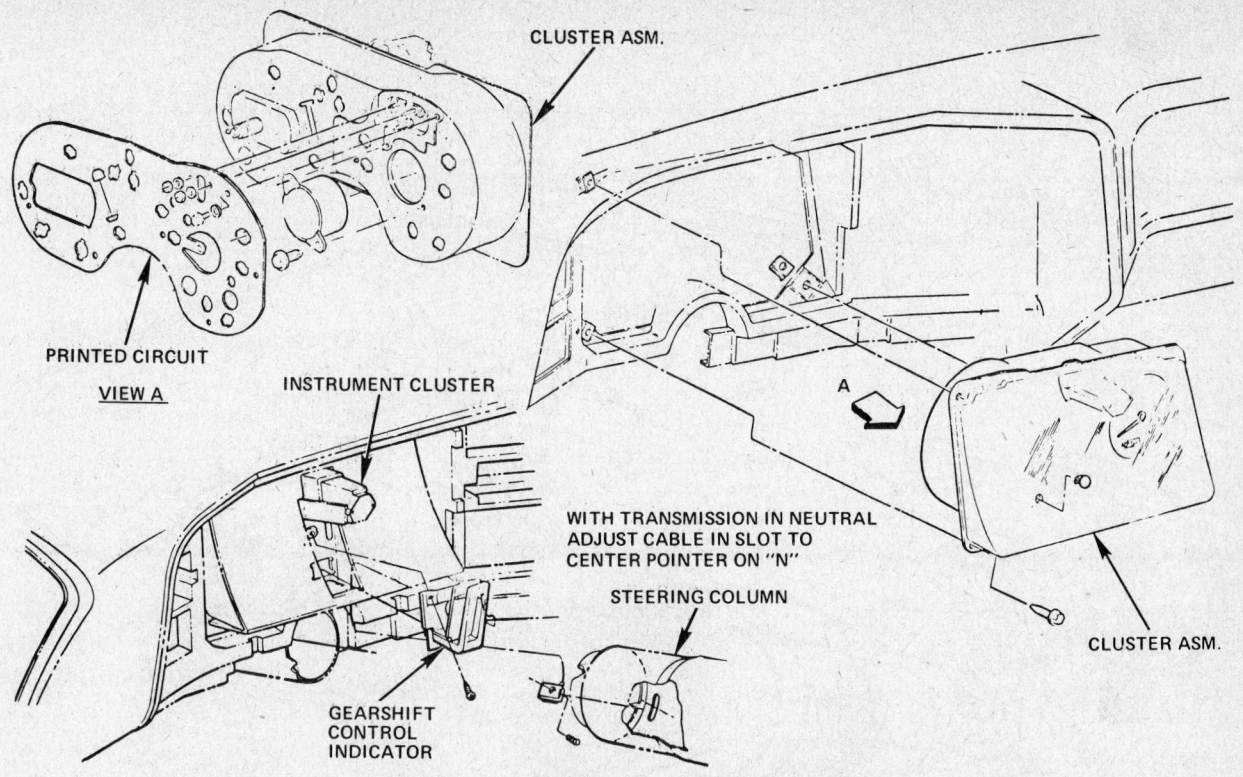

CLUSTER ASM.

PRINTED CIRCUIT

VIEW A

INSTRUMENT CLUSTER

WITH TRANSMISSION IN NEUTRAL
ADJUST CABLE IN SLOT TO
CENTER POINTER ON "N"

STEERING COLUMN

CLUSTER ASM.

GEARSHIFT
CONTROL
INDICATOR

A

Fig. 15   Instrument cluster. 1974-76 Full Size

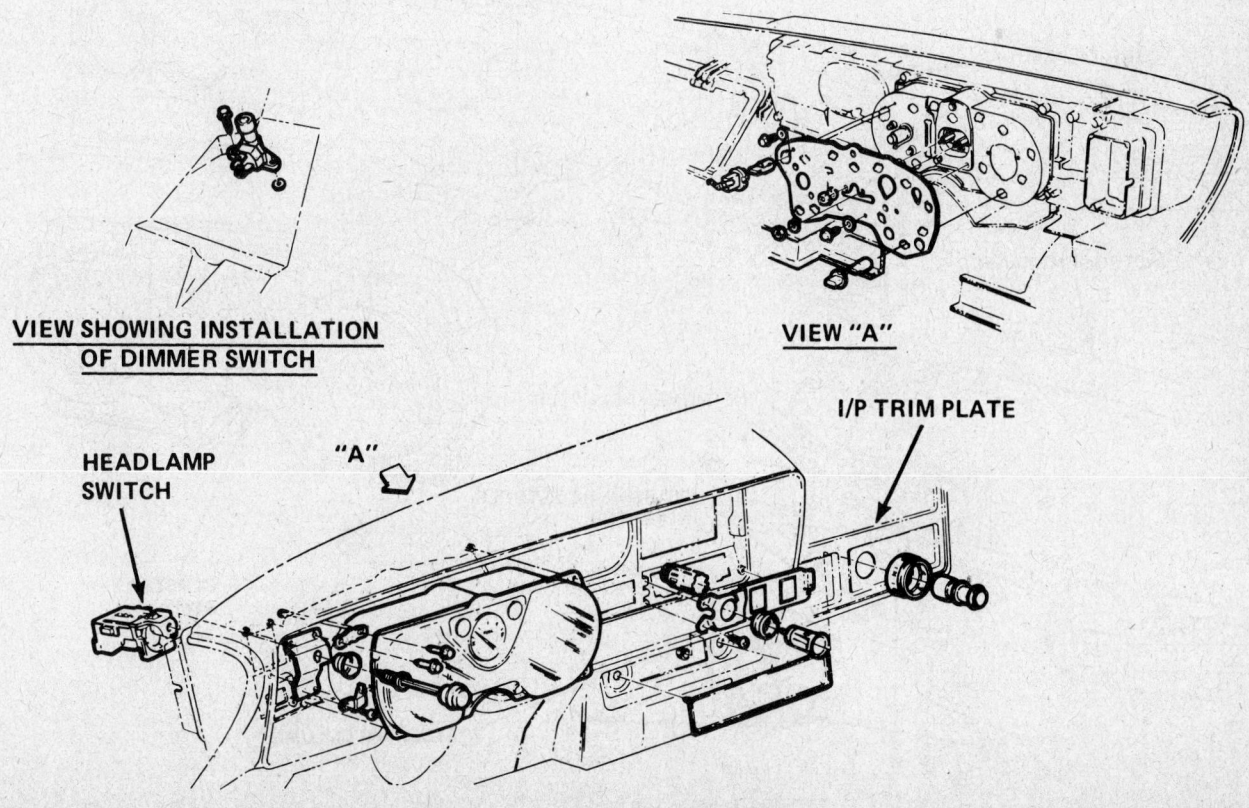

VIEW SHOWING INSTALLATION
OF DIMMER SWITCH

VIEW "A"

I/P TRIM PLATE

HEADLAMP
SWITCH

"A"

Fig. 16   Instrument cluster. 1974-79 Firebird

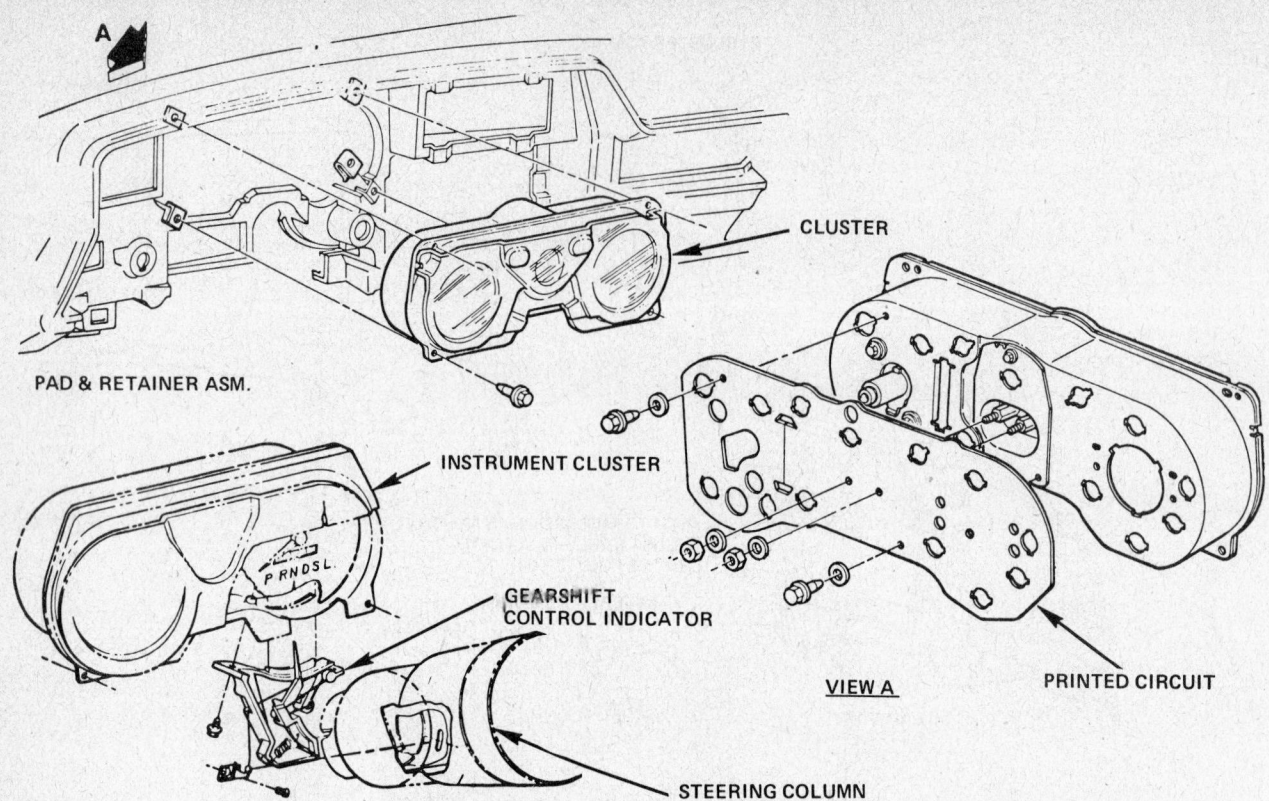

A
CLUSTER
PAD & RETAINER ASM.
INSTRUMENT CLUSTER
P R N D S L
GEARSHIFT
CONTROL INDICATOR
VIEW A
PRINTED CIRCUIT
STEERING COLUMN

Fig. 17 Instrument cluster. 1974-77 LeMans less optional instrument cluster

CARRIER ASM.
INSTRUMENT PANEL
INSTRUMENT CLUSTER
P R N D S L
GEARSHIFT CONTROLS
INDICATOR
CLUSTER
ASM.
STEERING COLUMN

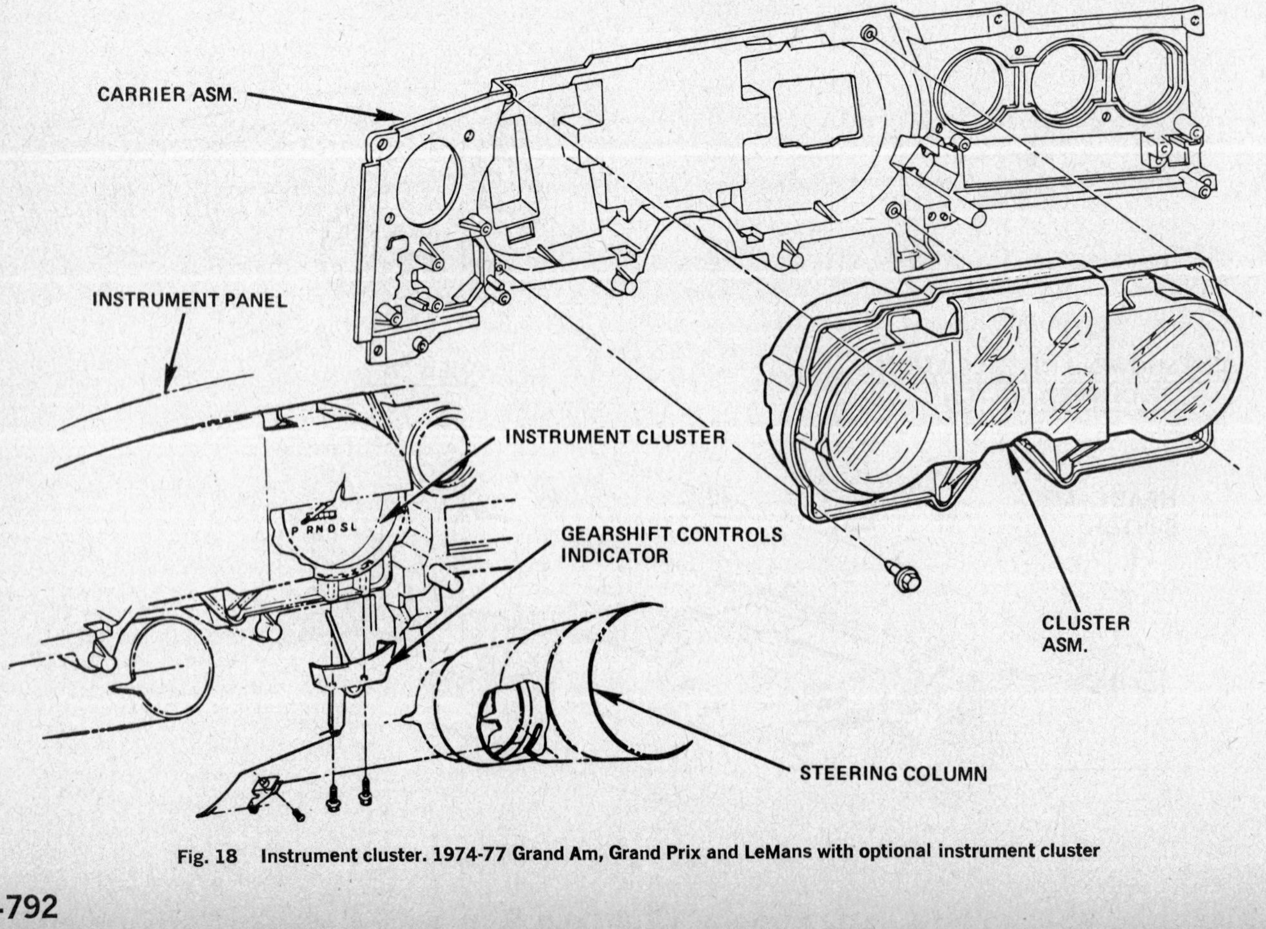

Fig. 18 Instrument cluster. 1974-77 Grand Am, Grand Prix and LeMans with optional instrument cluster

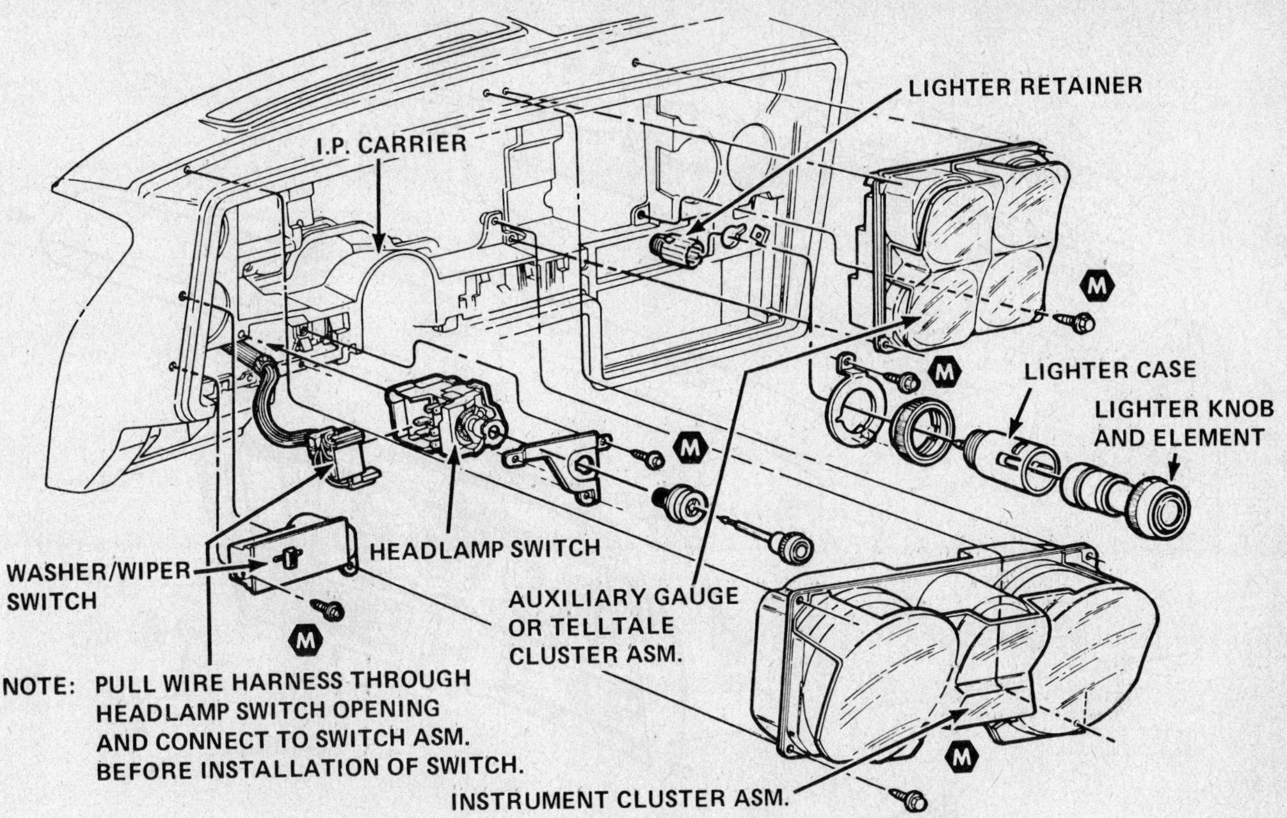

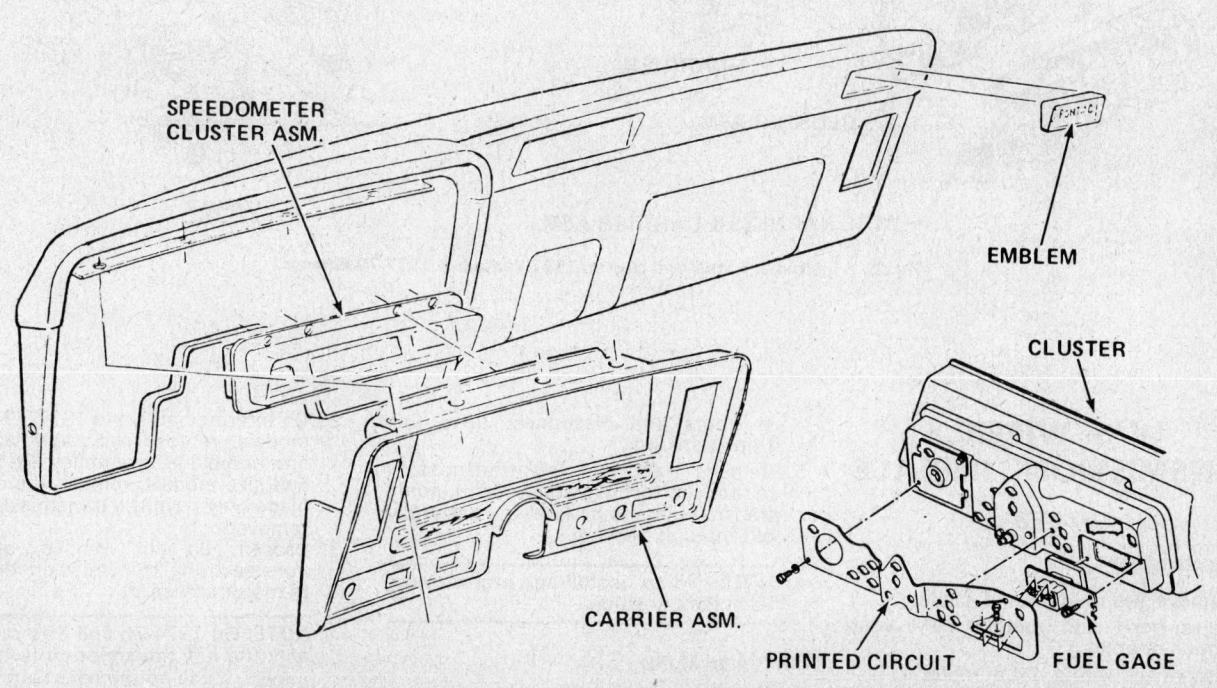

LIGHTER RETAINER

I.P. CARRIER

LIGHTER CASE

LIGHTER KNOB
AND ELEMENT

WASHER/WIPER
SWITCH

HEADLAMP SWITCH

AUXILIARY GAUGE
OR TELLTALE
CLUSTER ASM.

NOTE: PULL WIRE HARNESS THROUGH
HEADLAMP SWITCH OPENING
AND CONNECT TO SWITCH ASM.
BEFORE INSTALLATION OF SWITCH.

INSTRUMENT CLUSTER ASM.

Fig. 19   Instrument cluster. 1978-79 Grand Am, Grand Prix and LeMans

SPEEDOMETER
CLUSTER ASM.

EMBLEM

CLUSTER

CARRIER ASM.

PRINTED CIRCUIT

FUEL GAGE

Fig. 20   Instrument panel and cluster. 1974 GTO and 1974-76 Ventura

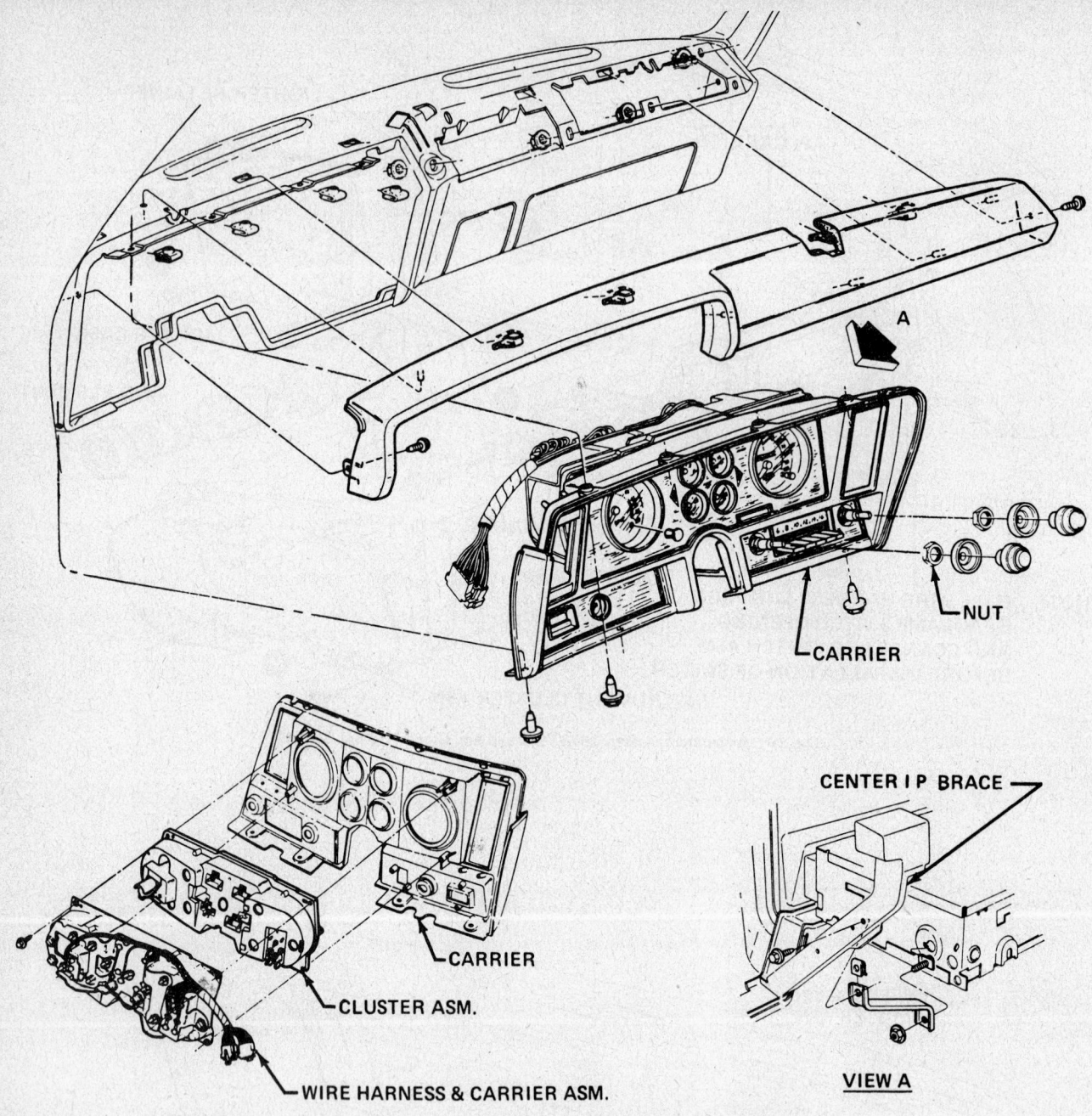

CARRIER

NUT

CENTER I P BRACE

CARRIER

CLUSTER ASM.

WIRE HARNESS & CARRIER ASM.

VIEW A

Fig. 21   Instrument panel and cluster. 1977 Ventura & 1977-79 Phoenix

W/S WIPER TRANSMISSION, REPLACE

1974-78

With Rectangular Motor

1. Remove wiper arms and blades.
2. Raise hood and remove cowl vent screen or grille.
3. Disconnect wiring from motor.
4. Loosen, do not remove, transmission drive link to motor crankarm attach-ing nuts and disconnect drive link from crankarm.
5. Remove right and left transmission to body attaching screws and guide transmission and linkage assembly out through opening.

NOTE: When installing, motor must be in Park position.

With Round Motor

1. Raise hood and remove cowl vent screen.

2. On Intermediates and 1977-79 full size models, remove right and left wiper arm and blade assemblies. On 1974-76 Full size models, remove the arm and blade only from the transmission to be removed.
3. Loosen, do not remove, attaching nuts securing transmission drive link to motor crankarm.

NOTE: On 1974-76 Full Size models, if only the left transmission is to be re-moved, it will not be necessary to loos-en nuts securing the right assembly.

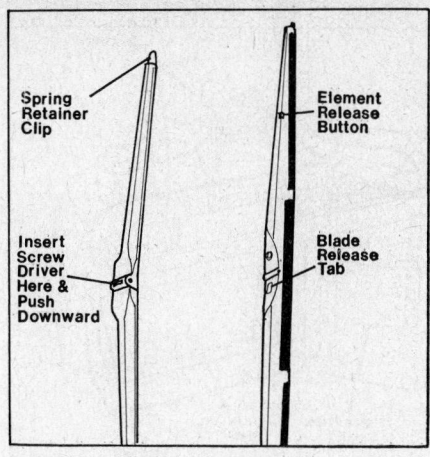

Fig. 22   W/S wiper blades

4. Disconnect transmission drive link from motor crankarm.

5. On Intermediate and 1977-79 full size models, remove right and left transmission to body attaching screws. On 1974-76 full size models, remove the attaching screw securing the transmission to be removed.

6. Remove transmission and linkage as-

sembly by guiding it through opening.

NOTE: When installing, motor must be in Park position.

W/S WIPER SWITCH

1974-79 Exc. Phoenix, Ventura & 1974 GTO

1. Disconnect battery ground cable. Remove upper and lower instrument panel trimplates.
2. Remove switch mounting plate and disconnect connector.
3. Remove switch retaining screws and remove switch.

1974-79 Phoenix, Ventura & 1974 GTO

1. Disconnect battery ground cable.
2. From under dash, disconnect wiring from switch.
3. Remove screws retaining switch to lower instrument panel and remove switch from panel.

RADIO, REPLACE

NOTE: When installing radio, be sure to adjust antenna trimmer for peak performance.

1978-79 Grand Am, Grand LeMans, Grand Prix & LeMans

1. Disconnect battery ground cable.
2. Remove upper and lower trim plates.
3. If equipped with console, move shift lever fully rearward.
4. On all models, remove four radio attaching screws from front of radio.
5. Open glove box door and lower by releasing spring clip.

Fig. 23   Wiper arm removal

6. Loosen radio rear attaching nut and pull radio outward slightly.
7. Disconnect electrical leads from radio and remove radio from vehicle.
8. Reverse procedure to install.

1977-79 Full Size

1. Disconnect battery ground cable.
2. Remove upper trim plate.
3. Remove radio trim plate by removing the two top screws and ash tray assembly, then disconnect cigar lighter electrical connector and remove the two small screws and large screw retaining ash tray bracket.
4. Remove two screws securing radio.
5. Pull radio from instrument panel opening and disconnect electrical leads from radio.
6. Remove radio from vehicle. Remove bezel nuts from front of radio to remove front trim plate if new radio is installed.
7. Reverse procedure to install.

1974-77 LeMans

1. Disconnect battery and remove radio

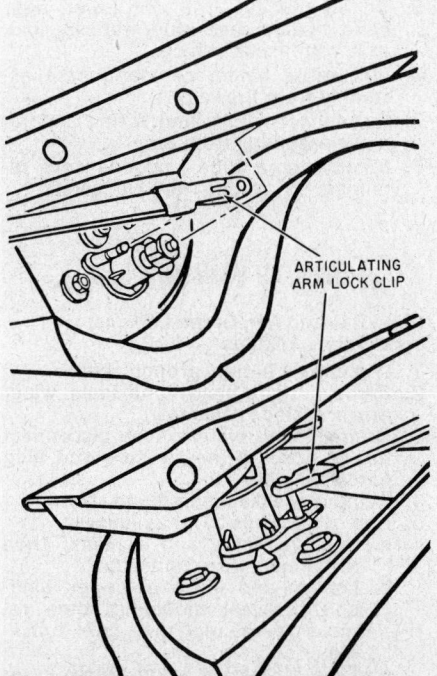

Fig. 24   W/S wiper articulating arm. 1974-77 intermediate models

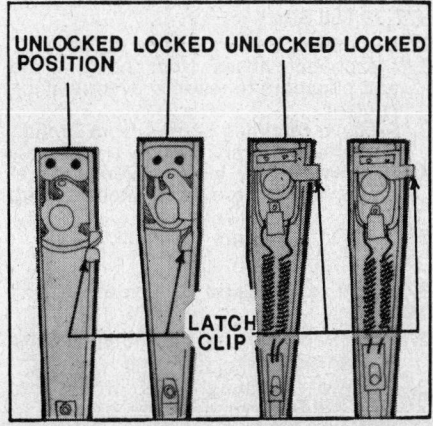

Fig. 25   W/S wiper arms. 1974-77 Full size

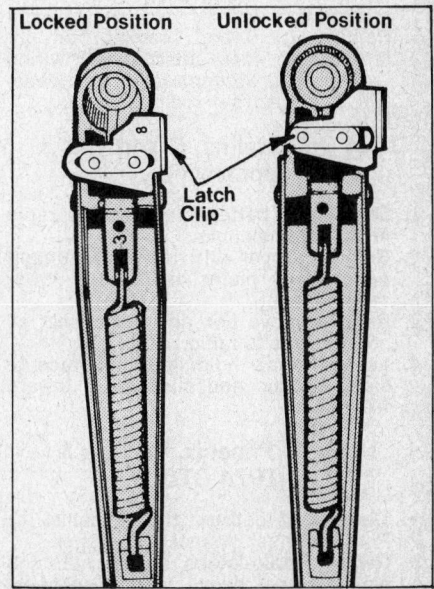

Fig. 26   W/S wiper arms. 1978-79 Full Size & intermediate models

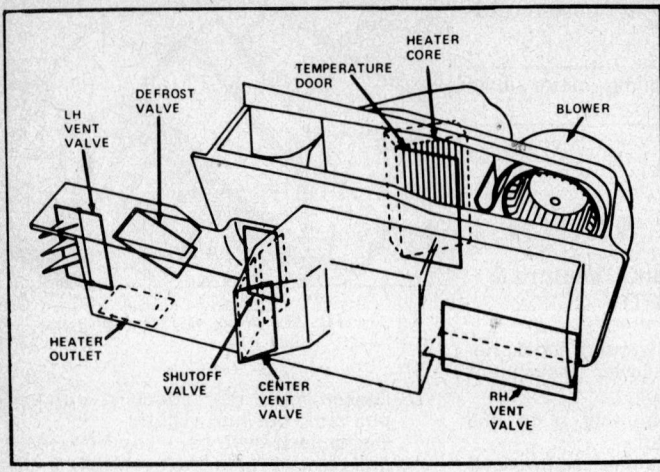

Fig. 27   Heater core and blower motor (less air conditioning).
1977-79 Full size

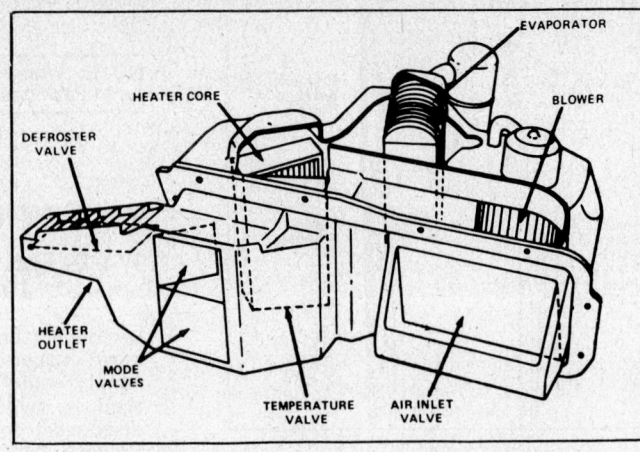

Fig. 28   Heater core and blower motor (with air conditioning).
1977-79 Full size

knobs and bezels.
2. Remove upper and lower trimplates.
3. Remove radio retaining screws.
4. Remove radio from opening, disconnect connections and antenna lead-in while radio is being pulled out.
5. If new unit is being installed, remove bushing from old unit and install on replacement unit.

1974-77 Grand Am, Grand Prix & 1975-77 Grand LeMans

1. Disconnect battery ground cable.
2. Remove radio knobs and bezels, then the hex nut from right hand tuning shaft.
3. Remove radio trim plate.
4. Remove radio and radio bracket to instrument panel retaining screws.

NOTE: Radio and bracket must be removed as an assembly.

5. Remove radio and bracket from instrument panel, disconnect wiring harness and antenna lead, then separate bracket from radio.

1974-76 Catalina, Grand Ville & Bonneville

1. Disconnect battery and remove radio knobs and hex nuts.
2. Remove upper and lower instrument panel trim plates and front lower radio bracket.
3. Remove glove box and disconnect all connections to radio.
4. Loosen screw holding radio brace to side of radio and slide radio toward front seat.

1974-79 Phoenix, Ventura & 1974 GTO

1. Disconnect battery ground cable.
2. Remove "hush" panel, if equipped.
3. Remove radio knobs, bezels, nuts and side braces screw and disconnect wiring and antenna.
4. Remove radio from under dash.

1974-79 Firebird

1. Disconnect battery ground cable.
2. Remove glove box and door and right lower A/C duct if equipped.
3. Remove radio knobs and hex nuts and trim plate.
4. Disconnect all leads to radio.
5. Remove radio bracket and radio from passenger side of instrument panel.

HEATER CORE REMOVAL

1974-79 Without Air Cond.

1978-79 Grand Am, Grand LeMans, Grand Prix & LeMans
1. Disconnect battery ground cable and drain cooling system.
2. Disconnect heater hoses.
3. Disconnect electrical connectors from heater module.
4. Remove module front cover screws.
5. Remove heater core from module.
6. Reverse procedure to install.

1977-79 Full Size
1. Disconnect battery ground cable.
2. Disconnect hoses from heater core and plug core tubes to prevent spilling coolant.
3. Remove retaining screws from around heater core cover.
4. Remove heater core cover and remove heater core from module, Fig. 27.
5. Reverse procedure to install.

1974-77 Exc. Phoenix & Ventura; 1974 GTO
1. Drain radiator and disconnect heater hoses from core.
2. Remove retaining nuts from core case studs on engine side of dash.
3. Inside car, remove glove box and

door on Firebird and heater outlet from case on Firebird.
4. Remove defroster duct retaining screw from heater case and pull entire heater assembly from firewall.
5. Disconnect control cables and wiring and remove assembly.
6. Remove core tube seal and core retaining strips and remove core.

1974-79 Phoenix & Ventura; 1974 GTO
1. Drain radiator and disconnect heater hoses from core.
2. Disconnect battery ground cable.
3. Remove retaining nuts from core case studs on engine side of dash.
4. Remove glove box and door.
5. On all models, drill out lower right hand heater case stud with 1/4 inch drill from inside vehicle.
6. Pull entire heater core and case assembly from firewall.
7. Disconnect cables and wiring and remove assembly from car.
8. Remove core tube seal and core retaining strips and remove core.

1974-79 With Air Cond.

1978-79 Grand Am, Grand LeMans, Grand Prix & LeMans
1. Disconnect battery ground cable.
2. Remove right hand windshield wiper arm and blade assembly.
3. Drain cooling system, then disconnect heater hoses at heater core and plug core openings.
4. Remove bracket and ground strap.
5. Remove module cover as follows:
   a. Remove seals and screens, then disconnect wire connector.
   b. Loosen and move up lower windshield reveal moulding, then remove reveal moulding cowl brackets.
   c. Tape a strip of wood below lower edge of windshield over module to prevent damage to windshield.

d. Remove all cover attaching screws, then cut through sealing material along cowl.

e. Carefully pry cover off from side, then lift cover away from flange of fender cowl brace.

f. Remove heater core and seal from module.

1977-79 Full Size

1. Disconnect battery ground cable.
2. Remove right half of hood seal from air inlet screen.
3. Remove air inlet screen.
4. Remove screws securing top of module, then disconnect electrical connectors from electrical components on top of module.
5. Remove thermostatic switch mounting screws from top of module.
6. Remove A/C diagnostic connector mounting screws and position aside.
7. Remove top of module.
8. Disconnect and remove heater core from module, Fig. 28.
9. Reverse procedure to install.

1974-76 Catalina, Grand Ville & Bonneville

1. Drain radiator and disconnect heater hoses from core.
2. Remove three nuts and one screw retaining core and case to dash.
3. Remove glove box and upper and lower instrument panel trim plates.
4. Remove radio.
5. Remove cold air duct and heater outlet duct.
6. Remove defroster duct to heater case screw.
7. Disconnect A/C temperature cable at heater case.
8. Disconnect vacuum hoses from diaphragms on heater case and remove core and case assembly.
9. Remove core from case (three screws).

1974-77 LeMans, Grand Am & Grand Prix GTO

1. Drain radiator and disconnect heater hoses from core.
2. Remove glove box, cold air duct and heater outlet and defroster duct screw.
3. Disconnect heater core case from dash. Remove blower motor resistor to gain access to case upper retaining nut.
4. Move case assembly rearward, freeing case studs from cowl and remove assembly.
5. Disconnect temperature cable and vacuum hoses from case and remove screws securing core inside of case.

1974-79 Firebird

1. Drain radiator.
2. Remove glove box and door.
3. Remove cold air duct (lower right hand duct) and remove left and center lower A/C ducts.
4. Jack right front area of car and place on safety stand.
5. Remove rocker panel trim on right side and remove screws holding forward portion of rocker panel trim attaching bracket.

6. Remove three lower fender bolts at rear of fender.
7. Remove four fender to skirt bolts at rear of wheel opening.
8. Remove two fender skirt bolts near blower motor area.
9. Pry rear portion of fender out at bottom to gain access to hose clamp on lower core hose and disconnect hose.
10. Disconnect water pump to core hose at core.
11. Remove heater case retaining nuts under hood at dash.
12. Remove two heater case retaining bolts (inside car).
13. Remove console, if equipped. If equipped with tape player, remove console with tape player intact. If equipped with tape player and no console, remove tape player.
14. Disconnect temperature cable at heater case.
15. Remove heater outlet duct.
16. Remove lower defroster duct screw at heater case.
17. Remove right kick panel.
18. Remove heater core and case.
19. Disconnect vacuum hoses from heater case.
20. Remove core from case.

1974-79 Phoenix & Ventura; 1974 GTO

1. Disconnect battery and drain coolant.
2. Disconnect upper heater hose from core.
3. Remove right front fender skirt bolts and lower skirt to gain access to lower heater hose clamp. Disconnect lower hose and remove lower right hand heater core and case attaching nut.
4. Remove glove box and door.
5. Remove recirculation vacuum diaphragm at right kick panel.
6. Remove heater outlet (at bottom of heater case).
7. Remove cold air distributor duct from heater case.
8. Remove heater case extension screws and separate extension from case.
9. Disconnect cables and wiring and remove case and core assembly.
10. Separate core from case.

BLOWER MOTOR REMOVE

1978-79 Grand Am, Grand LeMans, Grand Prix & LeMans

1. Disconnect battery ground cable.
2. If equipped with air conditioning, disconnect cooling tube from blower motor.
3. On all models, disconnect electrical connector from blower motor.
4. Remove blower motor retaining screws and the blower motor.
5. Reverse procedure to install.

1977-79 Full Size Without Air Cond.

1. Disconnect battery ground cable.
2. Disconnect blower motor electrical lead.
3. Remove blower motor retaining screws and remove blower motor, Fig. 27.
4. Reverse procedure to install.

1977-79 Full Size With Air Cond.

1. Disconnect battery ground cable.

2. Remove right half of hood seal from air inlet screen.
3. Remove air inlet screen.
4. Remove screws securing top of module, then disconnect electrical connectors from electrical components on top of module.
5. Remove thermostatic switch mounting screws from top of module.
6. Remove A/C diagnostic connector mounting screws and position aside.
7. Remove top of module.
8. Disconnect and remove blower motor from module, Fig. 28.
9. Reverse procedure to install.

1977-79 Firebird

1. Disconnect battery ground cable.
2. Disconnect wire connector. On models with A/C, disconnect cooling tube.
3. Remove motor attaching screws and nuts, then remove blower motor assembly from case.

1974-76 Full Size & Firebird

1. Raise car and remove right front wheel.
2. Cut access hole approx. $3/4$ of the way along the outline stamped on the right hand fender skirt. Bend cut section of skirt outward for access to blower motor.
3. Disconnect blower motor feed wire.

1974-77 Grand Prix & LeMans

1. Disconnect blower motor feed wire.
2. Remove blower motor retaining screws.
3. Remove blower motor.

1974-79 Phoenix & Ventura; 1974 GTO

1. Disconnect battery and detach hoses from clips on right fender skirt.
2. Raise vehicle on hoist.
3. Remove fender skirt attaching bolts except those retaining the skirt to radiator support.
4. Pull out then down on skirt and place block of wood between skirt and fender to allow clearance for blower motor removal.
5. Disconnect blower motor cooling tube and electrical connections at blower motor.
6. Remove blower motor attaching screws and remove blower motor. Gently pry motor flange if sealer acts as an adhesive.

SPEED CONTROLS
1974-79 Cruise Control

Brake Release Switches, Adjust

Apply brake pedal and push both switches forward as far as possible. Pull pedal forcibly rearward to adjust switches.

Centering Spring Adjustment Exc. Cruise Master Units

If speed control holds speed three or more mph higher than selected speed, turn centering screw (C) clockwise 1/8 turn or less, Fig. 29.

If speed control holds speed three or more mph below selected speed, turn centering adjustment screw (C) counterclockwise 1/8 turn or less. *Do not move adjustment screw (R).*

Orifice Tube Adjustment, Cruise Master Units

To check engagement speed, engage the system at 55 mph. If vehicle cruises below the engagement speed, loosen the locknut and screw the orifice tube outward. If vehicle cruises above the engagement speed, loosen the locknut and screw the orifice tube inward.

NOTE: Each 1/4 turn of the orifice tube will change the cruise speed about 1 mph. Also, do not remove orifice tube as it cannot be reinstalled once removed.

Bead Chain Adjustment, 1976 Firebird & Ventura

Pull rubber boot and hold it rearward, then with engine off and choke set to hot idle position, adjust cable jam nuts until servo chain is almost tight (allow some slack). Tighten jam nuts and pull rubber boot over washer.

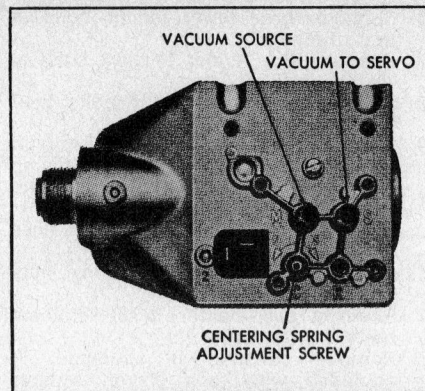

Fig. 29 Centering spring adjustment 1974-79 Cruise Control

Bead Chain Adjustment, 1977-79 Buick Built Engines

Assemble chain to be taut with carburetor in hot idle position and the idle solenoid deenergized. Place chain into swivel cavities which permits chain to have slight slack. Place retainer over swivel and chain assembly. Retainer must be made to rest between balls. Cut off chain flush with side of swivel to remove excess length. Chain slack should not exceed one half diameter of ball stud, .150 inch, when measured at hot idle position.

Cable Adjustment, 1975 All, 1976 Exc. Firebird & Ventura & 1977-79 Pontiac Built Engines

1. Set carburetor choke to hot idle position.
2. With cable connected to vacuum servo, pull steel tube of servo as far as it will go and check if one of the cross holes in the steel tube aligns with carburetor lever pin.
3. If one of the cross holes in the steel tube aligns with carburetor lever pin, install the tube, washer and cotter pin.
4. If none of the cross holes in the steel aligns with carburetor lever pin, move tube rearward to align the next closest hole and install cable, washer and cotter pin.

CAUTION: Do not stretch cable to make adjustment, as this will prevent carburetor from returning to normal idle.

Rod Adjustment, 1977-79 Oldsmobile Built Engines

Adjust length of rod to minimum slack with carburetor in hot idle position and the engine static.

Rod Adjustment, 1977-79 Chevrolet Built Engines

Screw rod into link with ignition "Off" and fast idle cam off and throttle closed. Hook rod through tab on servo. Adjust length so link assembles over end of stud, then install retainer.

Engine Section

For service on V6-231, 1975-76 V8-350 Ventura & 1978 V8-350 engines with distributor located at front of engine, see Buick Chapter
For service on 6-250, V8-305 & all 1977-79 V8-350 engines with distributor located at rear of engine and fuel pump located on right side of engine, see Chevrolet Chapter.

For service on V8-260 & all 1977-78 V8-350 & 403 engines with distributor located at rear of engine, fuel pump located on right side of engine and oil filler tube located on engine front cover, see Oldsmobile Chapter.

ENGINE MOUNTS REPLACE

4-151

1. Remove insulator to engine bracket through bolt(s), Fig. 1.
2. Raise engine to release weight off front mounts.
3. Remove insulator and separate from engine bracket.

1977-79 V8-301, 350 & 400

1. Disconnect battery ground cable.
2. Raise engine to release weight off front mounts.
3. Remove bolts fastening engine insulators to engine, Fig. 2.
4. Raise engine just clear of insulator.
5. Remove insulator.

1974-76 V8-350, 400 & 455

1. Disconnect battery ground cable.
2. Raise engine to release weight off front mounts.
3. On **Intermediate Models** remove stabilizer bracket to frame bolts. **On Grand Prix Models** remove the idler arm to frame bolts and disconnect pitman arm from shaft.
4. Remove bolts securing insulators to frame and engine, Fig. 2.
5. Remove insulators.

ENGINE, REPLACE

1974-79

1. Disconnect battery cables at battery and drain cooling system.
2. Scribe alignment marks on hood and

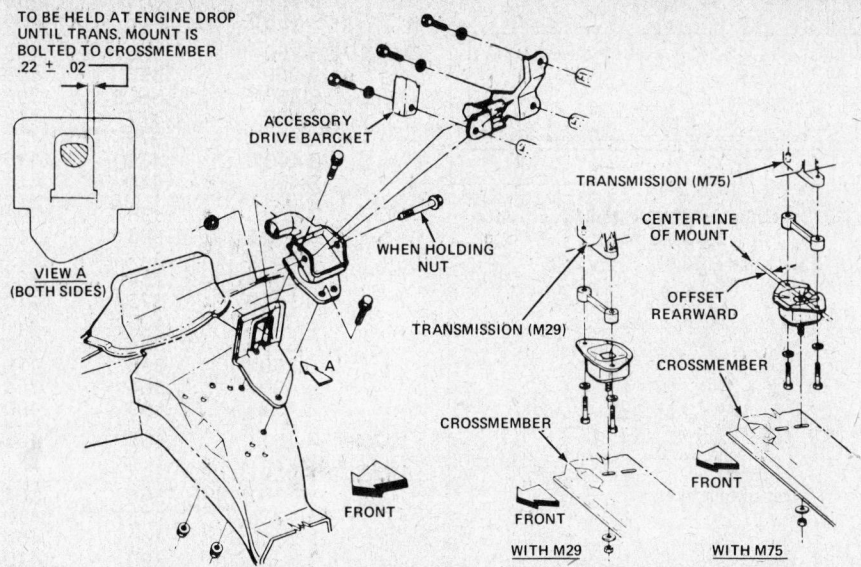

Fig. 1   Engine mounts. 1977-78 4-151

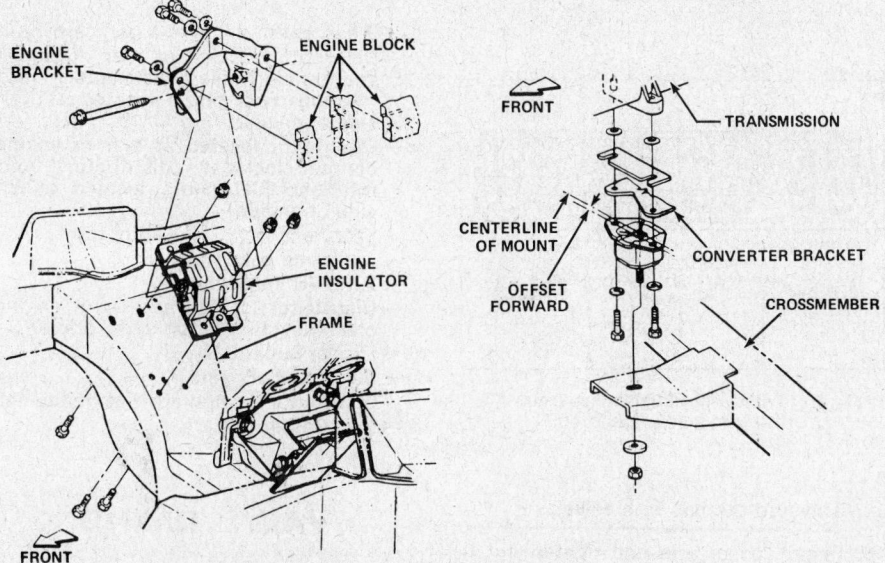

Fig. 2   Engine mounts (typical). V8-301, 350, 400 & 455

remove hood from hinges.

3. Disconnect all wiring, ground straps, fuel lines and vacuum hoses from engine.

NOTE: On 1974-79 V8's remove thermal feed switch, located on rear of left cylinder head on all models except Ventura. On Ventura models, switch is located on the right cylinder head.

4. Remove air cleaner and upper radiator shield assembly.
5. Disconnect radiator hoses and heater hoses at engine.
6. Remove fan and disconnect accelerator linkage.
7. If equipped with power steering or air conditioning, remove pump and/or compressor from mountings and set aside. Do not disconnect hoses.
8. On V8, disconnect transmission vacuum modulator line and power brake

vacuum line at carburetor and fold back out of way.

9. Raise vehicle on hoist and drain crankcase.
10. Disconnect exhaust pipe from manifold and remove starter.
11. If equipped with automatic transmission, remove converter cover and three converter retaining bolts and slide converter to rear.
12. With manual transmission, disconnect clutch linkage and remove clutch cross shaft.
13. Remove four lower bell housing bolts.
14. Disconnect transmission filler tube support and starter wire harness shield from cylinder head.
15. Remove two front motor mount to frame bracket bolts.
16. Lower vehicle and using a jack and block of wood, support transmission.
17. Support weight of engine with suitable lifting device.
18. Remove two remaining bell housing bolts.
19. Raise transmission slightly.
20. Position engine forward to free it from transmission and remove from car by tilting front of engine up.

CYLINDER HEAD, REPLACE

4-151

1. Drain cooling system and remove air cleaner.
2. Disconnect accelerator and fuel and vacuum lines at carburetor.
3. Remove intake and exhaust manifolds.
4. Remove bolts attaching alternator bracket to cylinder head.
5. If equipped with power steering or A/C, remove right side front bracket.
6. Disconnect temperature sending unit wiring harness, battery ground cable and radiator and heater hoses.
7. Disconnect spark plug wires and remove spark plugs.
8. Remove rocker cover, then back off rocker arm nuts.
9. Pivot rocker arms to clear push rods and remove push rods.

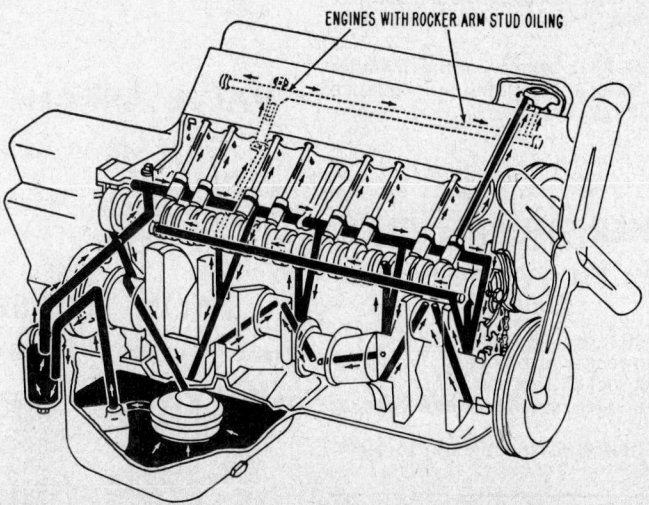

Engine oiling system. V8s

10. Remove cylinder head attaching bolts cylinder head.
11. Reverse procedure to install. Coat cylinder head bolts with sealer. Torque bolts in sequence as shown in Fig. 3. When installing intake manifold, refer to Fig. 3B, for bolt tightening sequence.

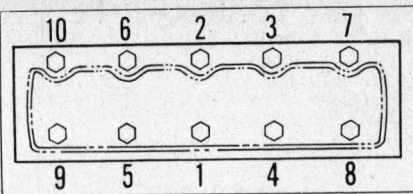

Fig. 3 Cylinder head tightening sequence. 1977-78 4-151

V8 Engines

NOTE: Pontiac recommends no numerical sequence for tightening cylinder heads on 1974-76 V8 except 301 engines. However, they may be tightened by starting at the center bolts and then working alternately from side to side and outward toward the ends.

1. Drain cooling system and remove air cleaner.
2. Remove intake manifold, push rod cover and rocker arm cover.
3. Loosen all rocker arm nuts and move rocker arms off push rods.
4. Remove push rods, keeping them in order so they may be installed in their original locations.
5. Detach exhaust crossover pipe from manifolds.
6. Remove battery ground strap and engine ground strap on left head or engine ground strap.
7. Unfasten and remove head with exhaust manifold attached.

NOTE: To remove left cylinder head on 1974-76 V8-455 HO, SD engines, it is necessary to remove the exhaust manifold and the inner panel of the carburetor heat stove from the cylinder head.

CAUTION: Use extreme care when handling heads as the rocker arm studs are hardened and may crack if struck.

NOTE: If left head is being removed, it will be necessary to raise head off dowel pins, move it forward and maneuver it in order to clear power steering and power brake equipment if so equipped.

8. Reverse procedure to install. On V8-301, coat cylinder head bolts with sealer.
9. On 1977-79 engines, orque cylinder heads to specifications in sequence shown in Fig. 3C.

ROCKER ARM STUDS

1974-79 4-151 & V8 With Screw in Stud

1. On V8-301, drain cooling system.
2. Remove rocker arm cover.
3. Remove rocker arm and nut.
4. Using a deep socket, remove rocker stud.
5. Install new stud and tighten to 50 ft. lbs.

NOTE: On V8-301, coat lower rocker

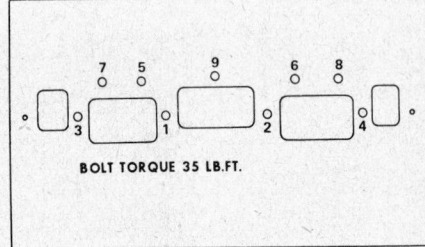

Fig. 4 Manifold tightening sequence. 1977-78 4-151

BOLT TORQUE 35 LB.FT.

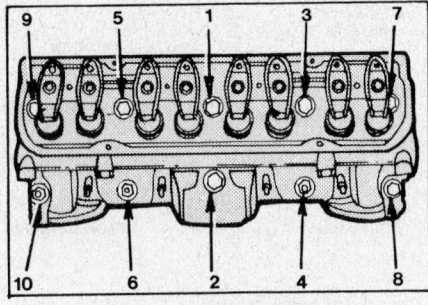

Fig. 5 Cylinder head tightening sequence. 1977-79 V8-301, 350 & 400

arm stud threads with sealer.

6. Install rocker arm and tighten nut to 20 ft. lbs.
7. Install rocker cover using new gasket.

VALVE ARRANGEMENT

Front to Rear

Four Cyl.	E-I-I-E-I-I-E
V8s	E-I-I-E-I-I-E

VALVE LIFT SPECS.

Year	Engine	Intake	Exhaust
1974	6-250[13]	.388	.388
	6-250[7]	.388	.405
	8-350	.374	.407
	8-350[5]	.403	.406
	8-400[6][2]	.404	.408
	8-400[6][1]	.374	.407
	8-455[10]	.403	.406
	8-455[11]	.406	.406
1975-76	6-250	.388	.405
	8-260	.395	.400
	8-350[8]	.3818	.3984
	8-350	.377	.413
	8-400[1]	.377	.415
	8-400[2]	.410	.415
	8-455	.410	.414
1977	4-151	.398	.398
	V6-231	.383	.366
	8-301[5]	.377	.377
	8-301[6]	.364	.364
	8-305[9]	.3727	.410
	8-350[3]	.400	.400
	8-350[4]	.364	.364
	8-350[9]	.390	.410
	8-400	.364	.364
	8-403	.400	.400
1978	4-151	.406	.406
1978-79	V6-231	.383	.366
	V8-301	.364	.364
	V8-305	.3727	.410
	V8-350[3]	.400	.400
	V8-350[9]	.390	.410
	V8-350[12]	.323	.339
	V8-400	.364	.364
	V8-403	.400	.400

[1]—2 bar. carb. [2]—4 bar. carb.
[3]—Distributor located at rear of engine, counter-clockwise distributor rotor rotation. Fuel pump located at right side of engine.
[4]—Distributor located at rear of engine, counter-clockwise distributor rotor rotation. Fuel pump located at left side of engine.
[5]—Std. trans. [6]—Auto. trans.
[7]—California cars.
[8]—1975-76 Ventura only.
[9]—Distributor located at rear of engine, clockwise distributor rotor rotation.
[10]—Except Super Duty.
[11]—Super Duty Engine.
[12]—Distributor located at front of engine.
[13]—Exc. California cars.

VALVE TIMING

Intake Opens Before TDC

Engine	Year	Degrees
4-151	1977	23
	1978	33
V6-231	1977-79	17
6-250	1974-76	16
8-260	1975-76	14
8-301	1977[5]	31
	1977[6]	27
	1978[1]	27
	1978[2]	14
	1979[1]	16
	1979[2][5]	27
	1979[2][6]	16
8-305	1977-79	28
	1974-75	26
8-350[8]	1975	19
8-350[8]	1976	13.5

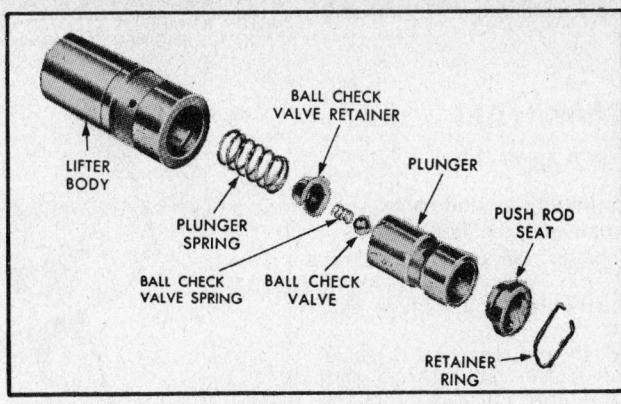

Fig. 6 Hydraulic valve lifter. Some lifters do not have the ball check valve spring shown

Fig. 7 Front of engine with timing case cover removed. V8 engines

8-350①	1976	22
8-350②	1976	26
8-350③	1977	29
8-350④	1977-79	16
8-350⑦	1977-79	28
8-350⑨	1978-79	13.5
8-400	1974②⑥	30
	1974①⑥	38
	1975-76①	26
	1975-76②	30
	1977-78⑤⑫	21
	1977-78⑥⑫	29
	1977-79⑬	16
8-403	1977-79	16
8-455	1974⑩	23
	1974⑥②	30
	1974⑪	38
	1975-76	23

①—2 bar. carb.   ②—4 bar. carb.

③—Distributor located at rear of engine, counter clockwise distributor rotor rotation. Fuel pump located at left side of engine.

④—Distributor located at rear of engine, counter clockwise distributor rotor rotation. Fuel pump located at right side of engine.

⑤—Std. trans.   ⑥—Auto. trans.

⑦—Distributor located at rear of engine, clockwise distributor rotor rotation.

⑧—1975-76 Ventura only.

⑨—Distributor located at front of engine.

⑩—Except Super Duty.

⑪—Super Duty Engine.

⑫—Except T/A engine.

⑬—T/A engine.

VALVE GUIDES

Valve guides are cast integral with the cylinder head. Valves with oversize stems are available in .001", .003" and .005" larger than standard.

Oversize reamers are required to enlarge valve guide holes to fit the oversize stems. For best results when installing .005" oversize valve stem use a .003" oversize reamer first and then ream to .005" oversize. Always reface the valve and valve seat after reaming valve guide. Valves are marked .001, .003 or .005 with colored ink.

VALVE LIFTERS

1. On V8 engines, remove intake manifold
2. Remove push rod cover and valve cover.
3. Loosen rocker arm, then rotate rocker arm off push rod and remove push rod.
4. Remove lifter, Fig. 6

NOTE: If more than one lifter is to be removed, identify lifters and push rods, so they can be reinstalled in their original locations.

5. Reverse procedure to install. Torque rocker arm ball nut to 20 ft. lbs.

TIMING COVER

NOTE: If necessary to replace the cover oil seal it can be accomplished without removing the timing chain cover.

1974-79 V8s

1. Drain cooling system.
2. Loosen alternator adjusting bolts.
3. Remove fan and accessory drive belts.
4. Remove fan and pulley.
5. Remove water pump.
6. Disconnect radiator hoses.
7. Remove fuel pump.
8. Remove vibration damper.
9. Remove front four oil pan-to-timing chain cover screws.
10. Remove cover attaching screws.
11. Pull cover forward to clear studs and remove.

1977-78 4-151

1. Disconnect battery ground cable.
2. Remove torsional damper and the two oil pan to front cover screws.

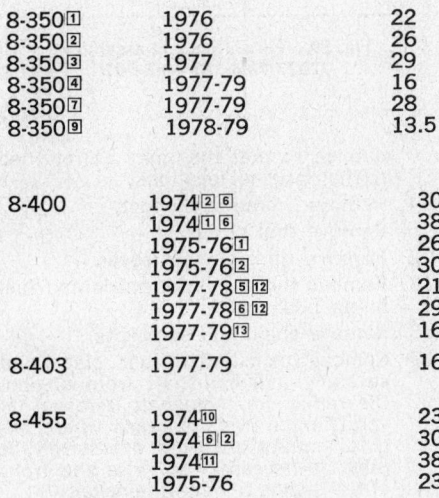

Fig. 8 Valve timing marks. V8 engines

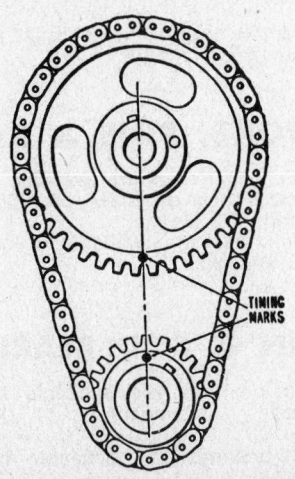

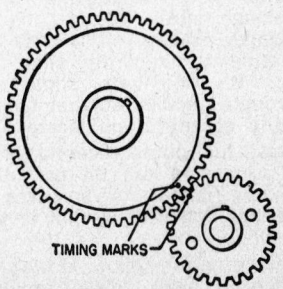

Fig. 8A Valve timing marks. 1977-78 4-151

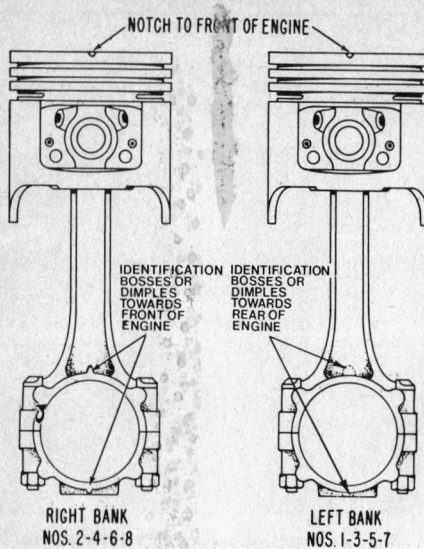

Fig. 9 Piston and rod assembly. 1974-79 V8-350, 400, 455 (Oil spurt hole toward camshaft)

3. Remove front cover retaining screws.
4. Pull cover forward just enough to permit cutting of oil pan front seal, then cut oil pan front seal flush with cylinder block at both sides and remove front cover.
5. Reverse procedure to install.

TIMING CHAIN

V8 Engines

1. Remove timing chain cover.
2. Remove fuel pump eccentric, bushing and timing chain cover oil seal, Fig. 7.
3. Align timing marks to simplify proper positioning of sprockets during assembly, Fig. 8.

NOTE: The valve timing marks, Fig. 8, does not indicate TDC, compression stroke for No. 1 cylinder for use during distributor installation. When installing the distributor, rotate engine until No. 1 cylinder is on compression stroke and the camshaft timing mark is 180° from the valve timing position shown in Fig. 8.

4. Slide off chain and sprockets.
5. Install new chain and sprockets, making sure timing marks are aligned exactly on a straight line passing through the shaft centers, Fig. 8. Camshaft should extend through sprocket so that hole in fuel pump eccentric will locate on shaft.
6. Install fuel pump eccentric and bushing, indexing tab on eccentric with keyway cutout in sprocket. Install retainer bolt with washer and tighten securely.
7. Making sure hollow dowels are in place in block, place timing chain cover gasket over studs and dowels.

8. Install cover, making sure O-ring seal is in place.

CAMSHAFT

1977-78 4-151

1. Disconnect battery ground cable.
2. Drain oil pan and radiator.
3. Remove radiator, fan and water pump pulley.
4. Remove distributor, spark plugs and fuel pump.
5. Remove push rod cover and valve cover, then loosen rocker arms and rotate rocker arms off push rods.
6. Remove push rods and valve lifters.

NOTE: Identify push rods and lifters so they can be reinstalled in their original locations.

7. Remove harmonic balancer and timing gear cover.
8. Remove camshaft thrust plate retaining screws and carefully pull camshaft out of engine.

NOTE: Use care to avoid damaging camshaft bearings.

9. Reverse procedure to install making sure to properly align gears, Fig. 8A. Torque thrust plate retaining screws to 75 inch lbs.

All V8s

The camshaft and camshaft bearings can be replaced with the engine installed in the car or with engine removed and disassembled for overhaul. However, to replace the rear camshaft bearing without removing and completely disassembling the engine, the propeller shaft, transmission and clutch housing must first be removed. The procedure for removing the camshaft is as follows:

1. Drain cooling system and remove air cleaner.
2. Disconnect radiator and heater hoses, distributor vacuum hose and spark plug wires.
3. Disconnect carburetor linkage, fuel lines and wire connector from temperature sending unit.
4. Remove hood latch brace.
5. Remove radiator, fan and pulleys.
6. On air conditioned cars, remove alternator and its mounting bracket.
7. Remove crankcase ventilator hose or outlet pipe.
8. Remove distributor.
9. Remove rocker arm covers.
10. Remove intake manifold. *Make certain "O" ring seal between intake manifold and timing chain cover is retained and installed during assembly.*
11. Remove push rod cover.
12. Loosen rocker arm ball retaining nuts so that rocker arms can be disengaged from push rods and turned sideways.
13. Remove push rods and hydraulic lifters, keeping them in proper se-

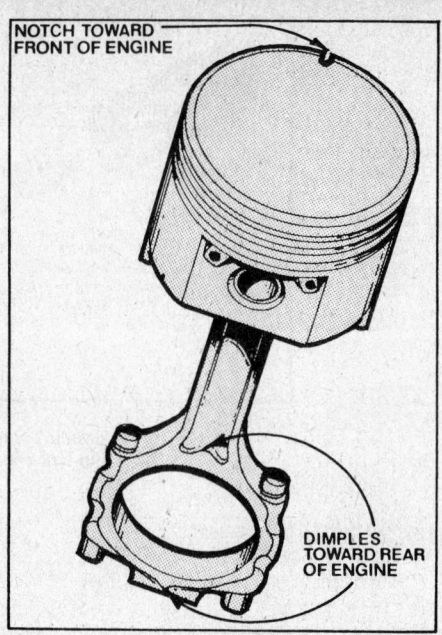

Fig. 9A Piston and rod assembly. 1977-79 4-151 & V8-301

quence so that they may be returned to their original locations.
14. Remove vibration damper.
15. Remove fuel pump.
16. Remove timing chain cover.
17. Remove fuel pump eccentric and fuel pump bushing.
18. Remove chain and sprockets.
19. Remove camshaft thrust plate and carefully pull camshaft from engine. *Clearance for camshaft removal is very limited and, in cases where engine mounts are worn excessively, it may be necessary to raise the front of the engine to permit removal.*

PISTON & ROD, ASSEMBLE

Assemble pistons and rods as indicated in Figs. 9 and 9A.

PISTONS, PINS & RINGS

Pistons and rings are available in standard sizes and oversizes of .005, .010, .020 and .030 inch.
Piston pins are available in oversizes of .001 and .003".

MAIN & ROD BEARINGS

Main bearings are available in standard sizes and undersizes of .001 and .002".
Rod bearings are available in standard sizes and undersizes of .001 and .002".

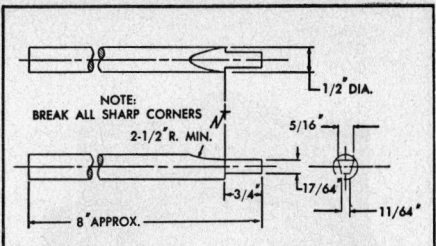

Fig. 10 Rear main bearing oil seal tool. V8-301, 350, 400

CRANKSHAFT REAR OIL SEAL

1974-79 V8

1. Remove oil pan, oil pump and pump drive shaft.
2. Remove oil baffle and cylinder block-to-oil baffle tube.
3. Remove rear main bearing cap.
4. Use tool shown in Figs. 10 & 11 made from brass bar stock to pack upper seal as follows:
   a. Insert tool against one end of oil seal in cylinder block and drive seal gently into groove until tool bottoms.
   b. Remove tool and repeat at other end of seal in cylinder block.
5. Clean block and bearing cap parting line thoroughly.
6. Form a new seal in cap.
7. Remove newly formed seal from cap and cut four pieces about $\frac{3}{8}$" long from this seal.
8. Work two $\frac{3}{8}$" pieces into each end of the gaps which have been made at the end of seal in cylinder block.

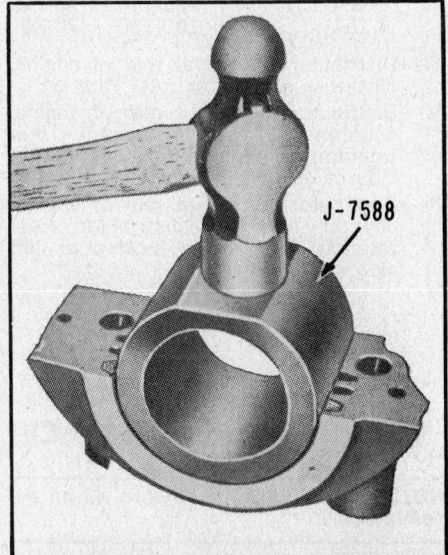

Fig. 12. Installing rear main bearing oil seal. V8-301, 350, 400, 455 engines

J-7588

Without cutting off the ends, work these seal pieces in until flush with parting line, being sure that no fibers are protruding over the metal adjacent to the groove.

9. Form another new seal in the cap.
10. Assemble the cap to the block and torque to specifications.
11. Remove cap and inspect parting line to insure that no seal material has been compressed between the block and cap.
12. Apply a $\frac{1}{16}$" bead of sealer from the center of the seal to the external cork groove.
13. Reassemble the cap and torque to specifications.

1977-78 4-151

1. Remove oil pan and rear main bearing cap.
2. Remove upper half of seal by tapping on one end with a blunt punch until other end of seal protrudes far enough to be removed with pliers. Remove lower half of seal by prying out with a small screwdriver.
3. Install upper half of seal by pushing into place with lip toward front of engine. Install lower half of seal by pushing with a hammer handle until seal is rolled into place.
4. Torque bearing cap bolts to specifications and install oil pan.

OIL PAN

1977-78 4-151

1. Disconnect battery ground cable and remove engine fan.
2. Raise vehicle and drain oil pan.
3. Disconnect exhaust pipe at manifold and loosen hanger bracket.
4. Remove starter and place aside, then remove flywheel housing inspection cover.
5. Raise engine slightly to remove weight from engine mounts and remove both brackets to engine mount bolts.
6. Remove oil pan bolts, then raise engine to allow oil pan removal and remove oil pan.
7. Reverse procedure to install.

1977-79 V8-301, 350 & 400 Pontiac Built Engines

1. Disconnect battery ground cable and remove fan.
2. Make sure that all hoses and wiring are properly rounted to avoid binding or stretching when engine is raised.
3. On some air conditioned vehicles, it will be necessary to remove A/C compressor from mounting brackets and placed aside for clearance.
4. Remove distributors cap, then raise vehicle and drain engine oil.
5. Disconnects exhaust pipes from manifolds, then remove starter and flywheel housing cover.
6. Rotate crankshaft until number on cylinder is at bottom dead center.

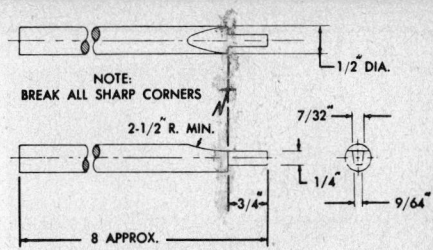

Fig. 11 Rear main bearing oil seal tool. V8-455

7. Remove engine mount through bolts.
8. Remove oil pan bolts, then raise engine just enough to allow oil pan removal and remove oil pan.
9. Reverse procedure to install.

1974 Ventura V8-350 Pontiac Manufactured Engines

1. Disconnect battery ground cable.
2. If equipped with power steering, remove drive belt and tilt pump upward.
3. Remove two fan shroud screws and position shroud so it will swing up with engine and remove fan.

NOTE: Ensure all hoses and wires are routed properly to avoid binding when engine is raised.

4. On 1974 models, remove thermal override switch from right cylinder head.
5. Raise car and drain oil.
6. Disconnect exhaust pipe to manifold bolts and let exhaust pipes hang down.
7. Remove flywheel dust cover.
8. Remove starter with wiring attached and position out of way.
9. Remove both frame bracket to engine mount thru bolts.
10. Attach a suitable engine lifting tool to engine.
11. Remove oil pan bolts.
12. Raise engine until pan can be removed.

1974-76 V8 Pontiac Manufactured Engines Exc. Ventura

1. Disconnect battery cable at battery

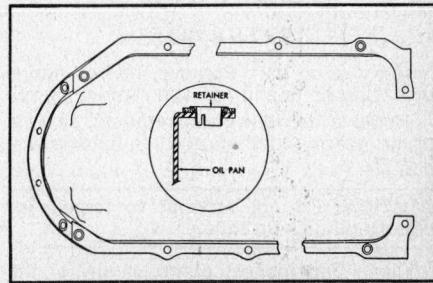

Fig. 13 Installing oil pan gasket retainers. V8-301, 350, 400, 455 engines

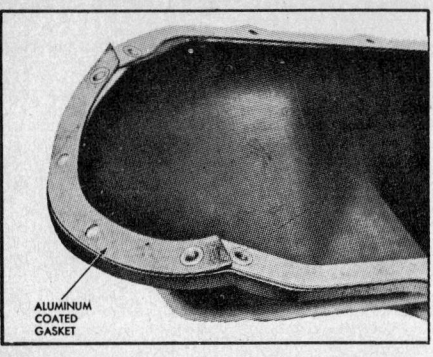

Fig. 14 Front oil pan gasket overlapping side gaskets. V8-301, 350, 400, 455 engines

2. Inspect gears for excessive wear or damage.
3. Inspect shaft for looseness in housing.
4. Inspect inside of cover for wear which may permit oil to leak past the ends of the gears.
5. Inspect oil pick-up screen.

To assemble, install drive gear and shaft in housing, then install idler gear with smooth side facing cover. Install cover and screws and torque screws to 105 inch lbs. Make sure that shaft turns freely. Install regulatory valve spring, retainer and pin.

To install pump, align drive shaft with distributor tang, then position pump on engine and install retaining bolts and nut. Torque bolts and nut to 115 inch lbs.

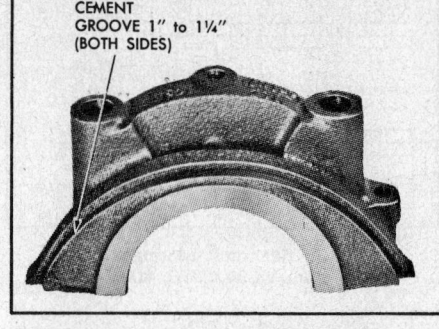

CEMENT GROOVE 1" to 1¼" (BOTH SIDES)

Fig. 15 Rear oil pan gasket positioned in bearing cap. V8-301, 350, 400, 455 engines

and remove fan.
2. On 1974-76 models equipped with power steering, remove pump adjusting bolt and drive belt, then tilt pump upward.
3. Remove fan shroud attaching screws and position shroud so it will swing up with engine.
4. On 1974-76 models, remove thermal switch from left cylinder head.
5. Make sure all hoses and wiring are routed properly to avoid bind when engine is raised.
6. Raise vehicle and drain crankcase.
7. On 1974-76 Firebird and Grand Prix, disconnect steering idler arm at frame and pitman arm from shaft.
8. Disconnect exhaust pipes from manifolds.
9. Remove starter assembly (set to one side with wires attached), starter motor bracket and flywheel inspection cover.
10. On 1974-76 LeMans, Grand Prix and Grand Am, remove stabilizer shaft to frame bracket attaching bolts to insure free movement of lifting device. It may also be necessary to loosen the fuel pump to timing cover bolts for clearance.
11. On all models, attach lifting tool, loosen oil pan bolts and raise engine until oil pan can be removed.

NOTE: On Firebird and Grand Prix models it may be necessary to loosen steering gear to frame attaching bolts to install lifting tool.

OIL PUMP
1977-78 4-151

Remove oil pan. Remove the two flange mounting bolts and nut and remove pump.

Remove the four cover retaining screws, cover, gears and shaft and regulator parts, Fig. 16.

CAUTION: Do not attempt to remove or disturb oil pick-up tube.

Clean and inspect pump. If any of the following conditions are found, the oil pump should be replaced:
1. Inspect pump body for cracks or wear.

V8 Engines

Remove oil pan. While holding pump in place, remove attaching screws. Lower the pump away from the block with one hand while removing the oil pump drive shaft with the other.

Remove oil screen and pressure regulator parts. Detach cover from pump body and take out gears, Fig. 16A.

Examine all parts for damage and assemble. Do not attempt to change oil pressure by varying length of pressure regulator spring.

Position drive shaft in distributor and oil pump drive gear. Place pump in position in the block, indexing the drive shaft with pump drive gear shaft. Install attaching screws with lock washers and tighten securely.

Removal and installation of pump does not affect distributor timing since the oil pump and distributor drive gear are mounted on the distributor shaft.

BELT TENSION DATA

	New Lbs.	Used Lbs.
1974-76—		
Six Cylinder—		
Air Pump	100-125	70-90
Alternator	100-125	70-90
Power Steering	100-130	70-90
1974—		
V8 Models—		
Air Condition	135-165	100-105
Air Pump	110-140	70-75
Alternator—		
With A/C	110-140	70-75
Without A/C	135-165	100-105
Power Steering	135-165	100-105
1975-76—		
V8 Models—		
Air Conditioning		
Ex. V8-260	135-165	100-105
V8-260	110-140	70
Air Pump		
Exc. Ventura		
V8-350	110-140	70
Ventura V8-350	65-80	50-70
Alternator		
Exc. 80 amp.	110-140	70
80 amp.	135-165	100-105
Power Steering		
Exc. V8-260	135-165	100-105
V8-260	110-140	70

	New Lbs.	Used Lbs.
1977—		
Air Conditioning		
Exc. 4-151 &		
V8-305, 350①	135-165	100-105
4-140	110-140	75-80
V8-305, 350①	135-165	80
Air Pump		
V6-231	60-80	50-55
V8-305, 350①	120-150	55
V8-350②, 403	110-140	75-80
Alternator		
Exc. V8-305, 350①	110-140	75-80
V8-305, 350①	120-150	55
Power Steering		
V6-231, V8-301, 350③, 400	135-165	100-105
4-151, V8-350②, 403	110-140	75-80
V8-305, 350①	120-150	55
1978-79—		
Air Conditioning		
Exc. 4-151	135-145	90-100
4-151	120-130	70-80
Air Pump		
Exc. V6-231	120-130	70-80
V6-231	65-75	45-55
Alternator		
All	120-130	70-80
Power Steering		
Exc. 4-151	135-145	90-100
4-151	120-130	70-80

①—Distributor located at rear of engine, clockwise distributor rotor rotation.

②—Distributor located at rear of engine, counter clockwise distributor rotor rotation. Fuel pump located at right side of engine.

③—Distributor located at rear of engine, counter clockwise distributor rotor rotation. Fuel pump located at left side of engine.

WATER PUMP, REPLACE

NOTE: Water pump is serviced as an assembly only.

1. Disconnect battery cable and drain cooling system.
2. Loosen alternator adjusting bolt and

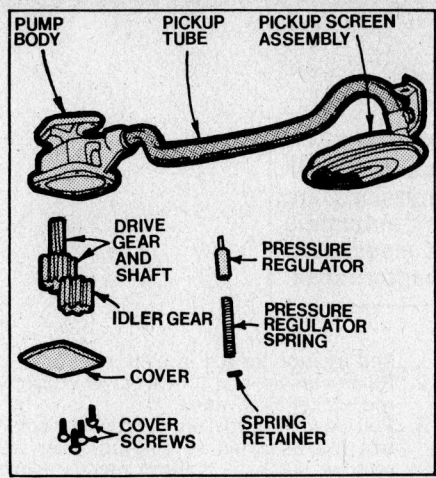

Fig. 16   Oil pump disassembled. 1977-78 4-151

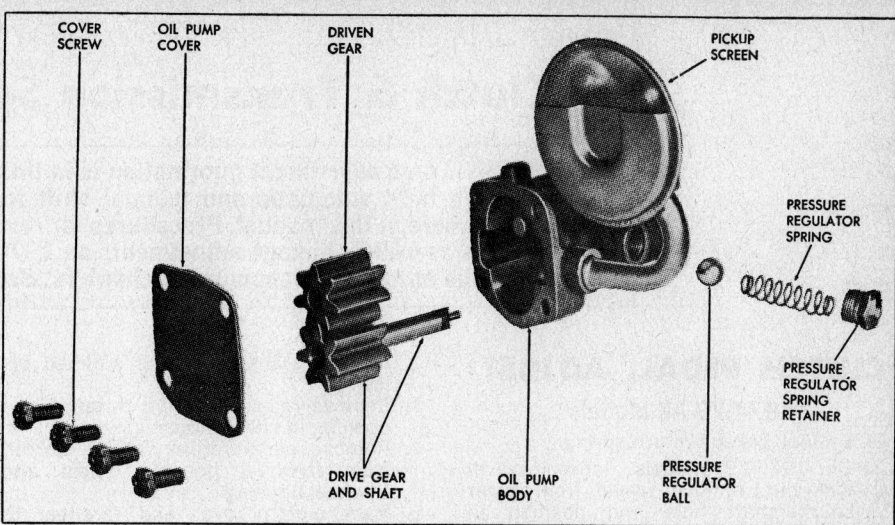

Fig. 16A   Oil pump disassembled. V8 Pontiac engines

remove fan belt.

3. Remove fan and pulley.
4. On 1974-78 V9 engine, remove alternator front bracket.
5. Disconnect radiator and heater hose at pump, then remove water pump retaining bolts and pump.
6. Reverse procedure to install. Torque water pump retaining bolts to 15 ft. lbs. on all engines except 4-151. On 4-151 engines torque water pump retaining bolts to 20 ft. lbs.

FUEL PUMP PRESSURE

Year	Engine	Pressure Lbs.
1974	Six	3-5
	V8	3-6½
1975-76	Six	4-5
	V8[1]	5-6½
	V8-350[2]	[7]
1977	4-151	4-5½
	V8-301, 350[3], 400	7-8½
	V-8-305, 350[4]	7½-9
	V8-350[5], 403	5½-6½

1978-79	4-151	4½-5
	V6-231	4½-6
	V8-301, 400	7-8½
	V8-305, 350[4]	7½-9
	V8-350[6][8]	5-6½
	V8-350[6][9]	6-7½
	V8-350[5], 403	5½-6½

[1]—Except Ventura V8-350.
[2]—Ventura V8-350.
[3]—Distributor located at rear of engine, counter clockwise distributor rotor rotation. Fuel pump located left side of engine.
[4]—Distributor located at rear of engine, clockwise distributor rotor rotation.
[5]—Distributor located at rear of engine, counter clockwise distributor rotor rotation. Fuel pump located right side of engine.
[6]—Distributor located front of engine.
[7]—3 lbs. minimum.
[8]—With A/C.
[9]—Less A/C.

FUEL PUMP, REPLACE

1. Remove all gasket material from the pump and block gasket surfaces. Apply sealer on both sides of new gasket.
2. Position gasket on pump flange and hold pump in position against its mounting surface. Make sure rocker arm is riding on camshaft eccentric.
3. Press pump tight against its mounting. Install retaining screws and tighten them alternately.
4. Connect fuel lines. Then operate engine and check for leaks.

SERVICE NOTE: Before installing the pump, it is good practice to crank the engine so that the nose of the camshaft eccentric is out of the way of the fuel pump rocker arm when the pump is installed. In this way there will be the least amount of tension on the rocker arm, thereby easing the installation of the pump.

Clutch & Transmission Section

> **NOTE:** 1979 linkage adjustment information is in this section. Repair procedures on both automatic and manual shift transmissions are covered elsewhere in this manual. Procedures for removing automatic transmissions as well as linkage adjustments on 1974-78 models are included in the automatic transmission chapters. See Chapter Index

CLUTCH PEDAL, ADJUST

1974-79 All Models

1. Unhook linkage return spring.
2. On 1975-79 models, loosen swivel lock nut, remove swivel from lower countershaft hole and position in countershaft upper gauge hole.
3. With clutch pedal against stop, loosen lock nut enough to allow adjusting rod to be turned out of swivel (V8) or push rod (6-cyl.) and rearward against clutch fork until clutch release bearing contacts pressure plate fingers lightly.
4. On 1974 models rotate adjustable rod into swivel or push rod 3½ turns and tighten lock nut.
5. On 1975-78 models rotate push rod until all lash is removed, remove swivel from gauge hole and position in countershaft lower hole, tighten lock nut.

NOTE: Use care when transfering push rod from gauge hole to lower hole to ensure push rod length does not change.

6. Install return spring and check clutch pedal free travel. Clutch pedal free travel when measured at center of pedal pad should be as follows:
   1974 All . . . . .1-1½"
   1975-76 All . . . . ¾-1¼"
   1977 LeMans . . . . ¾-1⁵⁄₁₆"
     Firebird, Phoenix &
     Ventura . . . . ⅞-1⁷⁄₁₆"
   1978 All . . . . ⁴⁵⁄₆₄-1⁵⁄₁₆"

CLUTCH, REPLACE

1974-79

1. Remove transmission as described under "Transmission, Replace."
2. Disconnect clutch fork push rod and spring.
3. Remove flywheel housing lower cover, then remove flywheel housing from engine.
4. Slide clutch fork from ball stud and remove fork from dust boot.
5. Install a dummy shaft to support clutch assembly during removal.
6. Mark clutch plate and flywheel to ensure reassembly in the same position.
7. Loosen clutch cover to flywheel bolts one turn at a time until spring pressure is relieved, then remove mounting bolts and clutch cover and disc.

1974-76 All

1. Disconnect battery-to-starter cable.

2. Remove transmission as outlined below.
3. Remove release bearing through rear opening in clutch housing.
4. Remove pedal return spring, starter, front flywheel housing shield and flywheel housing.
5. Mark clutch cover and flywheel to insure reassembly in the same position as balanced at the factory.
6. Loosen bolts holding clutch cover to flywheel a little at a time until all tension is relieved. Then remove clutch and driven disc.
7. Reverse removal procedure to install the clutch and adjust pedal free travel.

THREE-SPEED MANUAL TRANS., REPLACE

1974-79

1. Disconnect battery ground cable.
2. Raise vehicle and drain lubricant from transmission.
3. Scribe mark on companion flange and drive shaft yoke, then remove drive shaft.
4. Disconnect speedometer cable and backup light switch wire connector.
5. On models with column shift, disconnect transmission shift levers from transmission shifter shafts. On models with floor shift, it will also be necessary to remove shifter assembly to shifter support bolts and remove shifter assembly from transmission.
6. Remove crossmember to transmission mount bolts and catalytic converter to transmission bracket, if equipped, then remove crossmember to frame bolts.
7. Raise transmission and remove crossmember.
8. Remove transmission to clutch housing upper attaching bolts and install guide pins.
9. Remove transmission to clutch housing lower attaching bolts, then slide transmission straight back on guide pins until main drive splines are clear of clutch plate and remove transmission from vehicle.

SHIFT LINKAGE 3 SPEED TRANS.

1977-79

Column Shift

1. Place shift lever in reverse position

and ignition switch in Lock position.
2. Raise vehicle and loosen shift control rod swivel lock nuts.
3. Pull down slightly on 1st-reverse control rod attached to column lever to remove slack in column mechanism, then tighten lock nut at transmission.
4. Unlock ignition switch and position shift lever in neutral position. Position column lower levers in neutral, then align gauge holes in levers and inserts ³⁄₁₆ in. gauge pin.

NOTE: Alignment holes are located on lower side of levers.

5. Support rod and swivel to prevent movement of assembly and tighten 2nd-3rd control rod lock nut.
6. Remove alignment tool from column levers and check shifter operation. Place shift lever in reverse and check interlock control.

NOTE: With shift lever in reverse, ignition key must move freely to Lock position. It must not be possible to obtain Lock position in any other selector position than reverse.

Floor Shift

1. Place ignition switch in off position, then raise vehicle.
2. Loosen lock nuts at swivels on shift rods. Rods should pass freely through swivels.
3. Shift shift levers into neutral at transmission.
4. Place shift control lever in neutral detent, then align control assembly levers and insert a ³⁄₁₆ in. gauge pin into lever alignment slot.
5. Tighten locknuts at shift rod swivels and remove gauge pin.
6. Place shift control lever in reverse position and ignition switch in Lock position. Loosen lock nut at back drive control rod swivel, then pull down on rod slightly to remove slack in column mechanism and tighten clevis jam nut.
7. Check interlock control, ignition key should move freely to and from Lock position.
8. Lower vehicle and check adjustment.

1974-76

Column Shift

1. Set gearshift lever in Reverse and lock ignition.
2. Loosen swivel clamp screw at 1st & Rev. transmission shifter lever (both levers on Ventura) and loosen screw to swivel clamp at cross shaft assembly.

3. Position 2nd & 3rd transmission shifter levers in Neutral and 1st & Rev. shifter lever in Reverse.
4. Tighten swivel clamp screw at 1st & Rev. shifter level to 20 ft. lbs, unlock steering column and shift into Neutral. *On Ventura models*, pull down slightly on 1st & Rev. gearshift control rod to remove any slack in column mechanism before tightening clamp screw.
5. Align steering column lower levers in Neutral (unlock steering column on Ventura) and insert a .186" dia. pin through hole in steering column lower levers.
6. Tighten swivel clamp screw at cross shaft to 20 ft. lbs. *On Ventura models* position 2 & 3 shifter lever in Neutral and tighten swivel clamp nut at 2nd & 3rd shifter lever to 20 ft. lbs.
7. Remove gauge pin and check complete shift pattern.

Floor Shift (Exc. 1974 Muncie)

1. With steering column unlocked, position the shaft control lever into Neutral.
2. Loosen swivel clamp nut retaining the gearshift control rod to the idler lever.
3. Loosen trunnion jam nuts on 1st & Rev control rod, loosen jam nuts on 2nd & 3rd control rod and insert a .250" gauge pin into shifter assembly.
4. Manually position both transmission shifter levers in Neutral and torque jam nuts to 25 ft. lbs.
5. Remove gauge pin from shifter assembly and check operation.
6. Adjust backdrive by shifting into Reverse gear, set gearshift control rod in Lock position and lock the steering column.
7. Push up on gearshift control rod to take up clearance in column lock mechanism and torque adjusting swivel clamp nut to 20 ft. lbs.

Floor Shift (1974 Muncie)

1. Place shift control lever in Neutral

and insert a .250" pin into shifter assembly alignment holes. Be sure pin engages notch in far side of shifter housing.
2. Loosen swivel clamp screw to upper rod, loosen jam nuts at shifter assembly control rod trunnions, and disconnect 2nd & 3rd and 1st & Rev. trunnion and pin assemblies from both shifter levers.
3. With control rods disconnected, manually move shifter levers to check that transmission gears are in Neutral.
4. With gears and shifter assemblies in Neutral, adjust pin assemblies on their control rods so they align with and enter freely into their holes in shifter levers. Retain each with a plain washer and retainer clip and tighten jam nuts to 20 ft. lbs.
5. Remove gauge pin and check complete pattern for smooth operation.
6. Position shaft lever in Reverse, set steering column upper rod in Lock position and lock ignition. With transmission in Reverse, the ignition key must turn freely to its lock position.
7. Push up on upper rod to take up clearance in steering column lock mechanism and torque screw of adjusting swivel clamp to 20 ft. lbs.

4 SP. TRANS., REPLACE

1974-79

Follow procedure outlined for 1974-79 three-speed model.

SHIFT LINKAGE 4 SPEED TRANS.

1. Place selector lever in neutral.
2. Loosen trunnion nuts on transmission control rod.
3. Place transmission lever and bracket assembly in neutral and install a

gauge pin through hole and slot provided in bracket.
4. Position lever on transmission in neutral.
5. Tighten trunnion nuts and remove gauge pin.
6. Position shift lever in Reverse, set steering column lever in Lock position and lock ignition. Push up on control rod to remove clearance and tighten nut of adjusting swivel.

5 SP. TRANS., REPLACE

1. Disconnect battery ground cable.
2. From inside vehicle, remove screws attaching bezel to tunnel, then remove bezel by slipping over boot and shift lever.
3. With shift lever in neutral, hold boot out of way and remove four bolts attaching shift lever to transmission, then remove shift lever assembly.
4. Raise vehicle and scribe a mark on companion flange and drive shaft yoke, then remove drive shaft.
5. Remove bolts attaching catalytic converter support bracket to transmission.
6. Remove two bolts attaching transmission mount to support.
7. Raise transmission and remove two long end bolts, then remove transmission support.
8. Disconnect speedometer cable and backup light switch wire connector.
9. Remove transmission to clutch housing upper attaching bolts and install guide pins.
10. Remove transmission to clutch housing lower attaching bolts, then slide transmission back on guide pins until main drive gear splines clear clutch plate and remove transmission from vehicle.

1979 AUTO. TRANS. LINKAGE, ADJUST

Adjustment procedures for the 1979 linkages are essentially the same as those for 1978 units which are outlined elsewhere in this manual.

Rear Axle, Propeller Shaft & Brake Section

REAR AXLES

Figs. 1 and 2 illustrate the rear axle assemblies used on 1974-79 conventional models. When necessary to overhaul either of these units, refer to the *Rear Axle Specifications* table in this chapter.

1974-79

In this rear axle, Fig. 1, the rear axle housing and differential carrier are cast into an integral assembly. The drive pinion assembly is mounted in two opposed tapered roller bearings. The pinion bearings are preloaded by a spacer behind the front bearing. The pinion is positioned by a shim between the head of the pinion and the rear bearing.

The differential is supported in the carrier by two tapered roller side bearings. These bearings are preloaded by shims located between the bearings and carrier housing. The differential assembly is positioned for proper ring gear and pinion backlash by varying these shims. The differential case houses two side gears in mesh with two pinions mounted on a pinion shaft which is held in place by a lock screw. The side gears and pinions are backed by thrust washers.

Rear Axle, Replace

1974-79

Construction of the axle assembly is such that service operations may be performed with the housing installed in the vehicle or with the housing removed and installed in a holding fixture. The following procedure is necessary only when the housing requires replacement.

1. Raise car and place a floor jack under center of axle housing so it starts to raise rear axle assembly. Place jack stands solidly under frame members

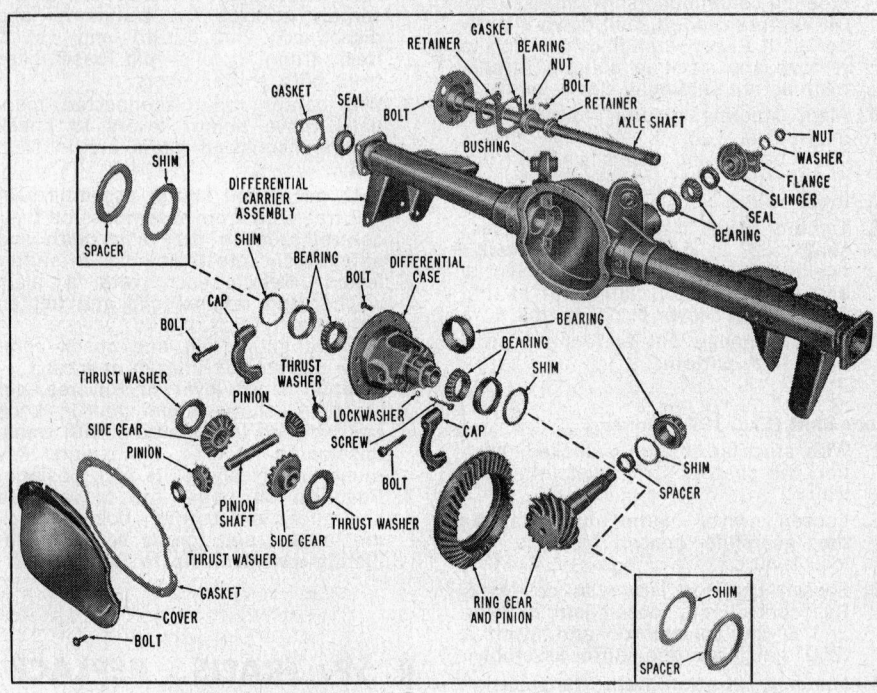

Fig. 1   Rear Axle assembly exploded. 1974-79 type "B & O" (Except 7½")

on both sides.
2. Disconnect rear U-joint from drive pinion flange and support propeller shaft out of the way.
3. Remove both axle shafts.
4. Support both brake backing plates out of the way.
5. Disconnect rear brake hose bracket by removing top cover bolt. Remove

brake line from housing by bending back tabs.
6. Loosen remaining cover bolts, break loose cover about ⅛" and allow lube to drain.
7. Disconnect shock absorbers at axle housing.
8. On models with coil springs,
   a. Disconnect upper control arms at axle housing.
   b. Slowly lower jack until all spring tension is relieved and remove springs.
   c. Disconnect lower control arms and remove axle assembly.
9. On models with leaf springs,
   a. While supporting spring, remove rear shackle from spring.
   b. Lower spring and remove nut and bolt from spring front bushing, remove spring.
   c. Remove axle assembly.

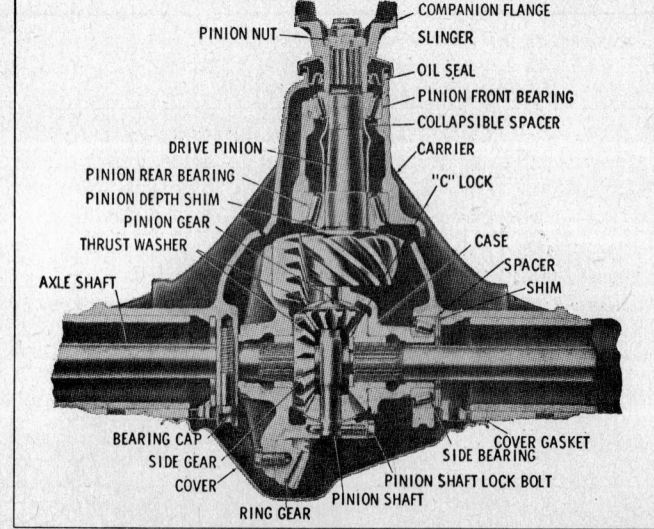

Fig. 2   1974-79 type "C", "G" "K" "O" (7½") & "P" differential case

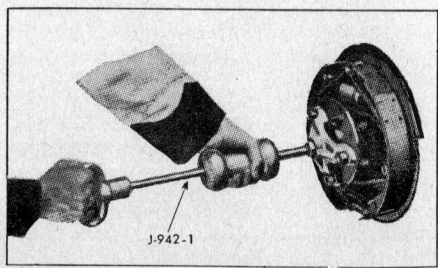

Fig. 3   Removing axle shaft with slide hammer-type puller

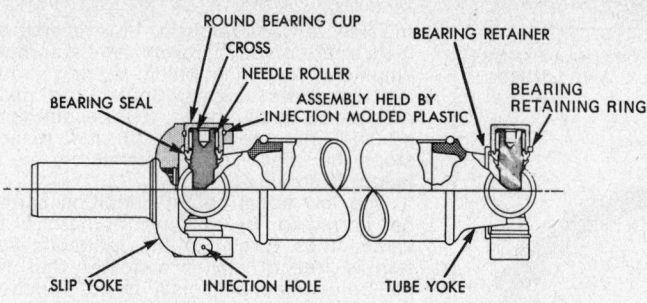

Fig. 4   Propeller shaft with single cardan U-joints. 1974-79

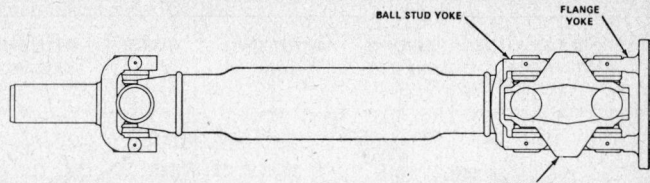

Fig. 5   Propeller shaft with rear double cardan U-joint. 1974-79

Axle Shaft, Replace

NOTE: Design allows for axle shaft end play of .018" max. on 1974-77 "B" and "O" (except 7½"), .002-.020" on 1978-79 "B" axles, .022" max. on 1974-79 "C", "G", "K", "O" (7½") and 1978-79 "P" (7½ & 8½") axles and .032" max. on 1974-79 "P" (except 7½ & 8½") axles. This end play can be checked with the wheel and brake drum removed by measuring the difference between the end of the housing and the axle shaft flange while moving the axle shaft in and out by hand.

On 1974-79 "C" axles, excessive end play can be compensated for by using selective thickness "C" locks. On all other 1974-79 axles, excessive end play cannot be compensated for by inserting a shim inboard of the bearing in the housing since it ignores the end play of the bearing itself, and may result in improper seating of the gasket or backing plate against the housing. If end play is excessive, the axle shaft and bearing should be removed and the cause of the excessive end play corrected.

1974-79 Type "B & O" (Except 7½")
1. To remove, take off wheels and brake drums.
2. Remove nuts holding retainer plates and brake backing plates. Pull retainers clear of bolts and reinstall two lower nuts finger tight to hold backing plate in position.
3. Use a slide hammer-type puller to remove axle shaft, Fig. 3.

Axle Shaft Bearing
1. Press axle shaft bearing off shaft.
2. Press new bearing against shoulder on shaft.

CAUTION: Outer retainer plate which retains bearing in housing must be on axle shaft before bearing is installed. A new outer retainer gasket can be installed after bearing. Use care not to wedge outer retainer between bearing and shoulder of shaft. Do not press bearing and inner retainer on in one operation.

3. Press new inner retainer ring against bearing.

Axle Shaft Seal
1. Insert suitable tongs behind seal and pull straight out to remove seal.
2. Apply sealer to outside diameter of new seal.
3. Position seal over a suitable installer and drive straight into axle housing until tool bottoms on bearing shoulder in housing.

Axle Shaft, Install
1. Apply a coat of wheel bearing grease in bearing recess of housing. Also lightly lubricate the axle shaft with rear axle lube from the sealing surface to about 6" inboard.
2. Install *new* axle housing-to-brake backing plate gasket.
3. Install brake assembly with backing plate in proper position.
4. With a *new* outer retainer gasket in proper position, insert axle shaft until splines engage differential. *Do not allow shaft to drag on seal.*
5. Drive axle shaft into position.
6. Place new outer retainer gasket and retainer over studs and install nuts.
7. Install brake drums and wheels.

1974-78 Type "C", "G", "K", "O" (7½") & "P" axle
1. Raise and support car leaving the rear wheels and differential suspended.
2. Remove rear wheels and brake drums.
3. Remove differential cover and drain lubricant.
4. Remove pinion shaft lock bolt and pinion shaft.
5. Push axle shaft inward to permit removal of "C" locks then remove axle shaft.
6. Install axle shaft bearing and seal remover and remove the bearing and seal.

PROPELLER SHAFT, REPLACE

Two types of propeller shafts are used. The first is a single cardan U-joint type, Fig. 4, and the second is a double cardan U-joint type, Fig. 5. The double cardan U-joint type is necessary on some vehicles because of the extreme angle of the differential pinion nose.

Two methods of retention are used at the rear of the propeller shaft. The first method uses a pair of straps retained by bolts, while the second method uses a set of bolted flanges.

1. Raise and properly support vehicle, then mark relationship of propeller shaft to companion flange in order to insure correct alignment during reassembly.
2. Disconnect rear U-joint by removing strap bolts of flange bolts.

NOTE: If U-joint bearing cups are loose, tape them together to avoid dropping and loosing needle rollers.

3. Remove propeller shaft by pulling rearward.

CAUTION: Support propeller shaft during removal. Do not allow propeller shaft to drop or allow universal joints to bend to an extreme angle.

4. Reverse procedure to install, making sure that alignment marks are properly aligned. Torque strap retaining bolts to 15 ft. lbs. Torque flange bolts to 85 ft. lbs.

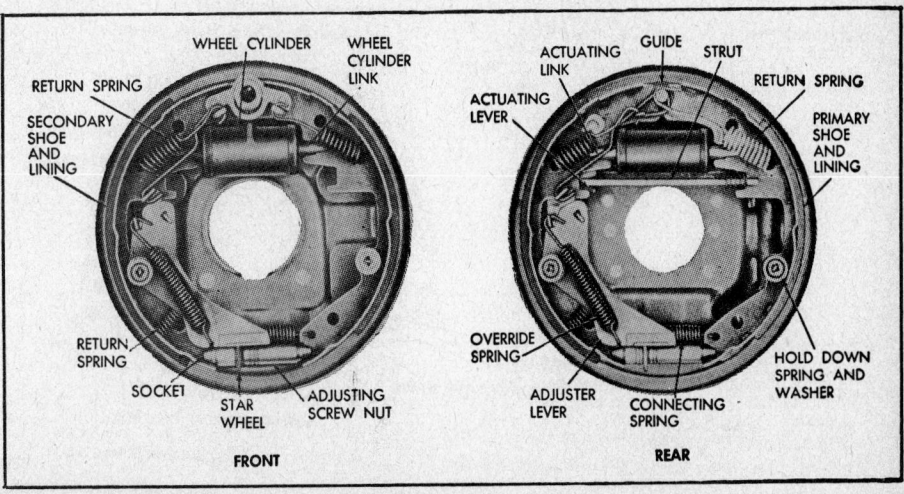

Fig. 6   Right front and rear brake. 1974-79 (typical)

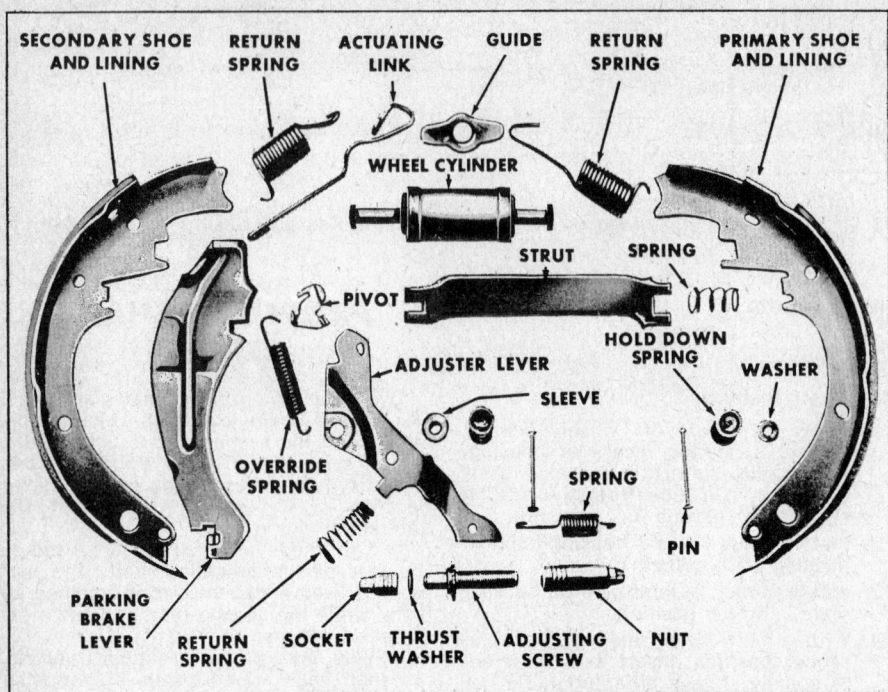

Fig. 7   Right rear self adjusting brake (Typical).
Except 1978-79 Grand Am, Grand Prix and LeMans

BRAKE ADJUSTMENTS
1974-79 Self-Adjusting Brakes

These brakes, Figs. 6, 7 and 8 have self-adjusting shoe mechanisms that assure correct lining-to-drum clearances at all times. The automatic adjusters operate only when the brakes are applied as the car is moving rearward.

Although the brakes are self-adjusting, an initial adjustment is necessary after the brake shoes have been relined or replaced, or when the length of the star wheel adjuster has been changed during some other service operation.

Frequent usage of an automatic transmission forward range to halt reverse vehicle motion may prevent the automatic adjusters from functioning, thereby inducing low pedal heights. Should low pedal heights be encountered, it is recommended that numerous forward and reverse stops be made until satisfactory pedal height is obtained.

If a low pedal height condition cannot be corrected by making numerous reverse stops (provided the hydraulic system is free of air) it indicates that the self-adjusting mechanism is not functioning. Therefore, it will be necessary to remove the drum, clean, free up and lubricate the adjusting mechanism. Then adjust the brakes as follows, being sure the parking brake is fully released.

Adjustment

1. Remove adjusting hole cover from brake backing plate and, from backing plate side, turn adjusting screw upward with a screwdriver or other suitable tool to expand the shoes until a slight drag is felt when the drum is rotated.
2. Remove brake drum.
3. While holding adjusting lever out of engagement with the adjusting screw, Fig. 9, back off the adjusting screw one full turn with the fingers.

NOTE: *If finger movement will not turn the screw, free it up. If this is not done, the adjusting lever will not turn the screw during subsequent vehicle operation. Lubricate the screw with oil and coat with wheel bearing grease. Any other adjustment procedure may cause damage to the adjusting screw with consequent self-adjuster problems.*

4. Install wheel and drum, and adjusting hole cover. Adjust brakes on remaining wheels in the same manner.
5. If pedal height is not satisfactory, drive the vehicle and make sufficient reverse stops until proper pedal height is obtained.

NOTE: The recommended method of ad-

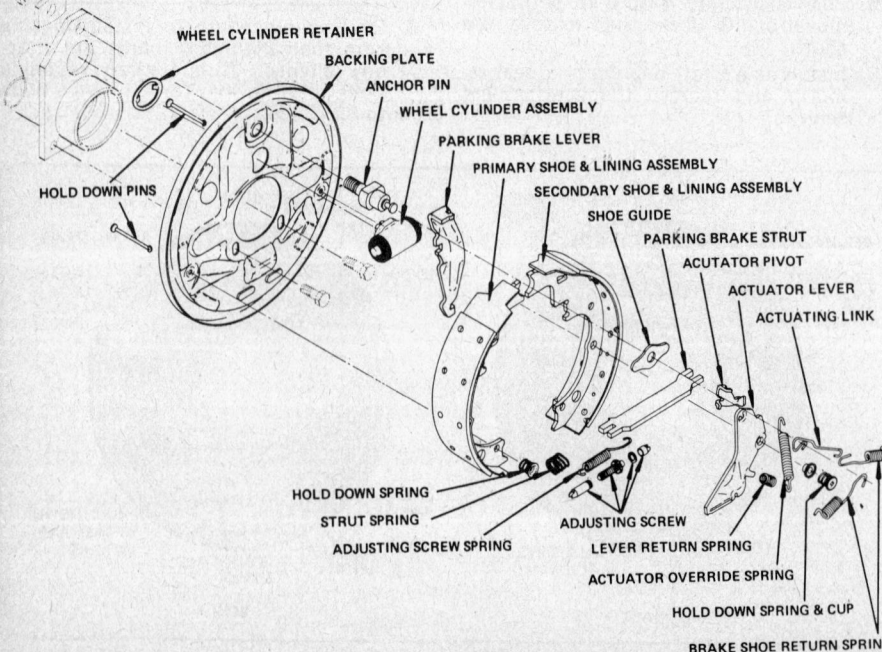

Fig. 8   Left rear self adjusting brake (Typical). 1978-79 Grand Am, Grand Prix & LeMans

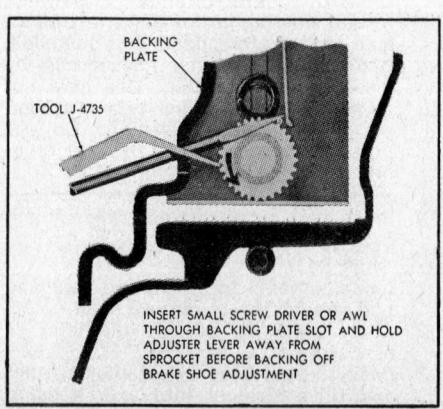

Fig. 9   Backing off adjusting screw. 1974-79

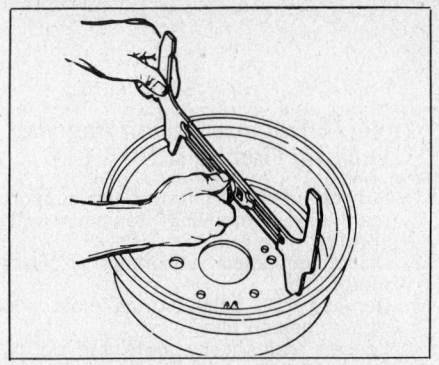

Fig. 10 Measuring brake drum inside diameter

justing the brakes is by using the Drum-to-Brake Shoe Clearance Guage shown in Fig. 10 to check the diameter of the brake drum inner surface. Turn the tool to the opposite side and fit over the brake shoes by turning the star wheel until the gauge just slides over the linings, Fig. 11. Rotate the gauge around the brake shoe lining surface to assure proper clearance.

PARKING BRAKE, ADJUST

CAUTION: It is very important that parking brake cables are not adjusted too tightly causing brake drag. With automatic brake adjusters, a tight cable causes brake drag and also positions the secondary brake shoe, hence the adjuster lever, so that it continues to adjust to compensate for wear caused by the drag. The result is a cycle of wear and adjustment that can wear out linings very rapidly.

1976-79

1. Raise and support rear of vehicle.
2. Apply parking brake pedal exactly two rachet clicks on Firebird, Phoenix and

Ventura, three rachet clicks on Grand Am, Grand Prix, LeMans and 1976 full size except station wagon and 6 rachet clicks on 1976 full size station wagon and 1977-79 all full size models.
3. Tighten adjusting nut until left rear wheel can just be rotated rearward but is locked when forward rotation is attempted.
4. Release parking brake and check to ensure that rear wheels rotate freely in either direction with no brake drag.

1974-75

1. Jack up both rear wheels.
2. Depress parking brake 8 rachet clicks on 1974 models, 2 rachet clicks on 1975 Firebird and Ventura, 3 rachet clicks on 1976 full size station wagon wagon, Grand Am, Grand Prix, LeMans and 6 rachet clicks on 1975 full size station wagon.
3. On 1974 models, loosen equalizer year lock nut. Adjust forward nut until a light to moderate drag is felt when rear lock nut. Adjust forward nut until nut.
4. On 1975 models, tighten adjusting nut until rear wheels can just be turned rearward using both hands but are locked when forward rotation is attempted.
5. With parking brake fully released, rear wheels should turn freely in either direction with no brake drag.

POWER BRAKE UNIT, REPLACE
1974-79 All Models

1. Remove vacuum check valve.
2. If brake booster and master cylinder are being removed as an assembly,

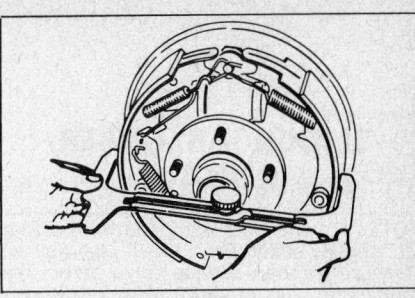

Fig. 11 Checking brake shoe lining clearance

disconnect hydraulic lines and cover openings in master cylinder and lines to avoid entry of dirt. If only brake booster is to be removed, remove master cylinder retaining nuts and position master cylinder aside.

CAUTION: Be careful not to bend or kink hydraulic lines.

3. Remove clevis pin retainer from brake pedal.
4. Remove brake booster retaining nuts and remove brake booster.
5. Reverse procedure to install.

BRAKE MASTER CYLINDER, REPLACE
1974-79

1. Disconnect brake lines from two outlets on master cylinder and tape end of lines to prevent entrance of dirt.
2. On models less power brakes, disconnect master cylinder push rod from brake pedal.
3. Remove two nuts attaching master cylinder to dash or power brake unit and remove master cylinder from vehicle.

Rear Suspension

SHOCK ABSORBER, REPLACE

NOTE: If vehicle is equipped with Super-lift shock absorbers, bleed system air pressure through service valve before disconnecting lines at shock absorber fittings.

1. With rear axle supported properly, disconnect shock absorber from lower mounting stud. Use a wrench to prevent mounting stud rotation.
2. Disconnect shock absorber from upper mounting.
3. Reverse procedure to install.

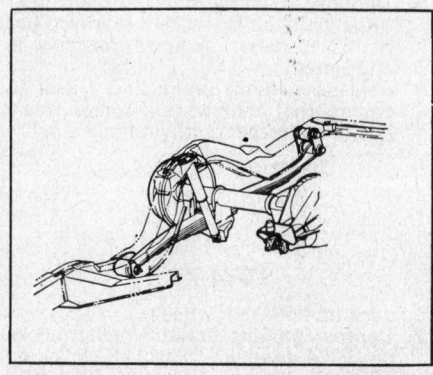

Fig. 1   Leaf spring suspension (typical). 1974-76 full size station wagon, 1974-77 Ventura, 1974-79 Firebird, 1974 GTO & 1977-79 Phoenix

1974-76 Full Size Station Wagons, Ventura, Firebird & 1974 GTO

1. Support vehicle at frame and support rear axle, removing tension from spring.
2. Disconnect shock absorbers at lower mountings.
3. Remove "U" bolts, spring plate and upper cushion pad.
4. Loosen rear shackle nuts and spring front mounting bolt, Fig. 1.
5. On all except station wagons, disconnect spring front mounting bracket from underbody, drop spring and remove bracket from spring. On station wagons, remove spring front mount bolt.
6. Support spring and remove lower rear

LEAF SPRING & BUSHINGS, REPLACE

1. Raise and support vehicle so that axle can be raised and lowered.
2. Lower axle assembly to relieve tension from spring.
3. Disconnect shock absorber from lower mounting, Fig. 1.
4. Loosen spring eye to bracket retaining bolt.
5. Remove bolts attaching spring retainer bracket to under body.
6. Lower axle assembly to permit access to spring retainer bracket, and remove bracket from spring.
7. Pry parking brake cable out of retainer bracket mounted on anchor plate.
8. Remove lower spring plate to axle bracket retaining nuts.
9. Remove upper and lower cushions and anchor plate.
10. Support spring, then remove lower bolt from spring rear shackle. Separate shackle and remove spring from vehicle.
11. To replace bushings, refer to Figs. 2 and 3.
12. Reverse procedure to install.

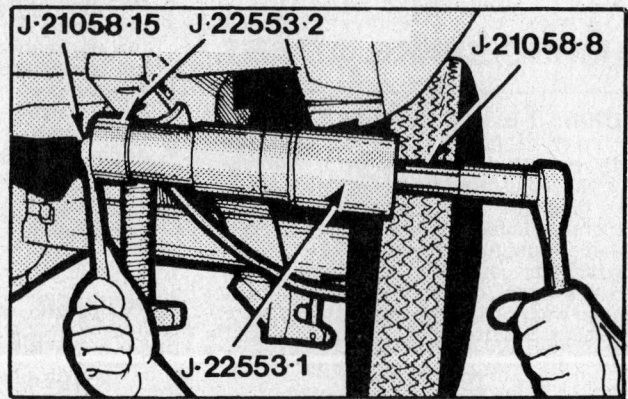

Fig. 3   Leaf spring front bushing installation

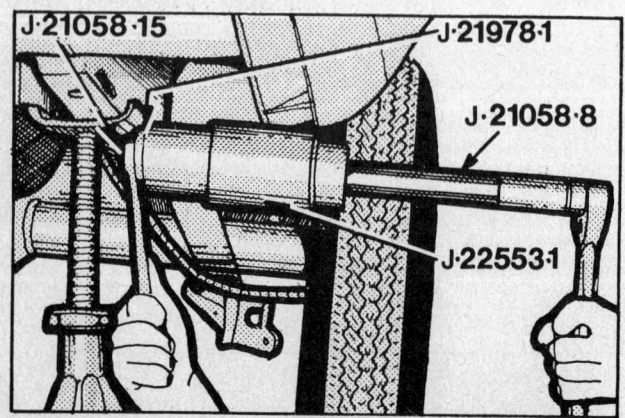

Fig. 2   Leaf spring front bushing removal

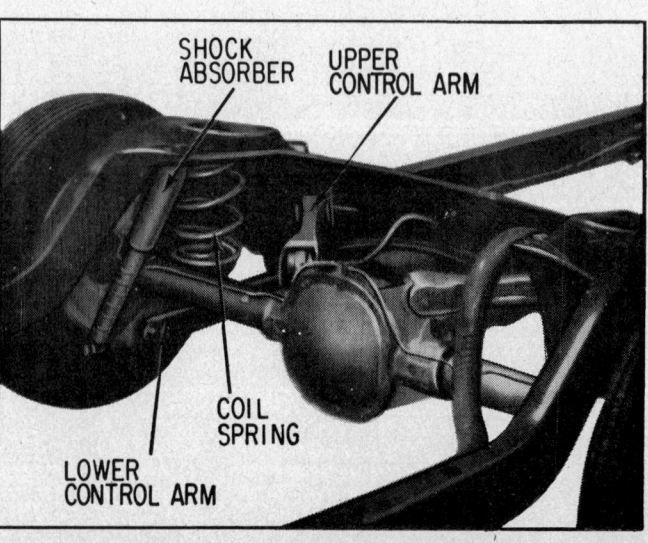

Fig. 4   Coil spring suspension (typical)

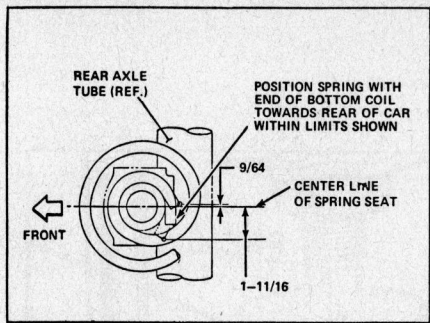

Fig. 5 Indexing coil springs. 1974-76 Intermediates exc. Firebird, Ventura & 1974 GTO

shackle bolt.
7. To replace bushings, refer to Figs. 2 and 3.
8. Reverse procedure to install.

Leaf Spring Service

NOTE: The main leaf may be serviced separately, however, if any of the smaller leaves require replacement, the entire assembly must be replaced.

1. Clamp spring in a vise, remove spring clips and center bolt, then carefully open vise, allowing spring to expand.
2. Replace main leaf and use a drift to align center bolt holes, compress spring in a vise, remove drift and install new center bolt.
3. Align spring leaves and bend spring clips into position.

NOTE: Overtightening spring clips will bind spring action.

COIL SPRING, REPLACE

1977-79 All Exc. Firebird, Phoenix & Ventura

1. Support vehicle at frame rails and support rear axle with a suitable jack.
2. Remove brake line connector block bolt at axle housing.
3. Release brake line from clips on axle housing as necessary.
4. Disconnect upper control arms from axle housing.
5. Disconnect shock absorbers from lower mountings.
6. Lower rear axle. Do not permit the rear brake hose to kink or stretch.
7. When the axle has been lowered sufficiently to provide clearance for coil spring removal, remove coil spring.
8. Reverse procedure to install. Ensure that coil springs are properly indexed, Fig. 6.

1974-76 Full Size

1. Support vehicle at frame side rails and support rear axle with a suitable jack.
2. Remove clip retaining brake hose to frame crossmember.

NOTE: Do not disconnect brake line from connector.

3. Disconnect shock absorber from axle housing bracket and carefully lower axle housing.

CAUTION: Avoid contact between rear lower control arm upper flange and rear lower control arm axle housing bracket when lowering axle.

4. Remove spring.
5. Reverse procedure to install making sure that springs are properly indexed, Figs. 5 and 6.

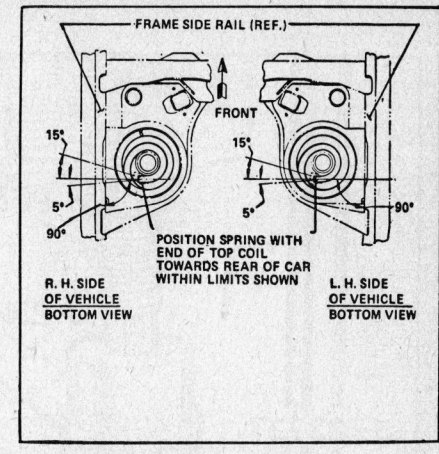

Fig. 6 Indexing coil springs. 1974-79 Full Size exc. 1974-76 station wagons; 1977-79 Intermediates

1974-76 Intermediate Models

1. Raise and support vehicle at frame side rails.
2. Disconnect brake hose at rear crossmember and remove clip.
3. Support nose of axle housing with suitable jack to prevent axle from rolling when upper arms are disconnected.
4. Disconnect upper control arms and shock absorbers from axle housing.
5. Carefully lower axle housing and remove spring.
6. Reverse procedure to install making sure that springs are properly indexed, Figs. 5 and 6.
7. Bleed both rear brakes.

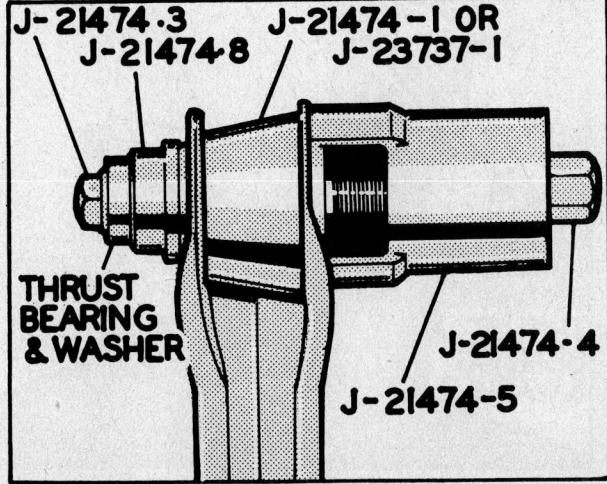

Fig. 7 All front bushings & lower control arm rear bushing removal, 1974-76 models

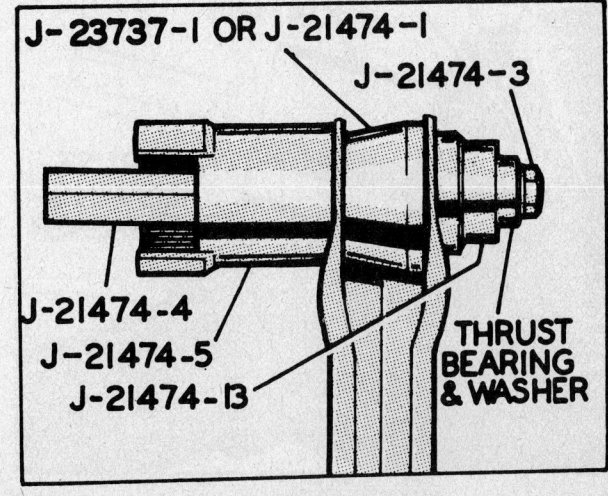

Fig. 8 All front bushings & lower control arm rear bushing installation, 1974-76 models

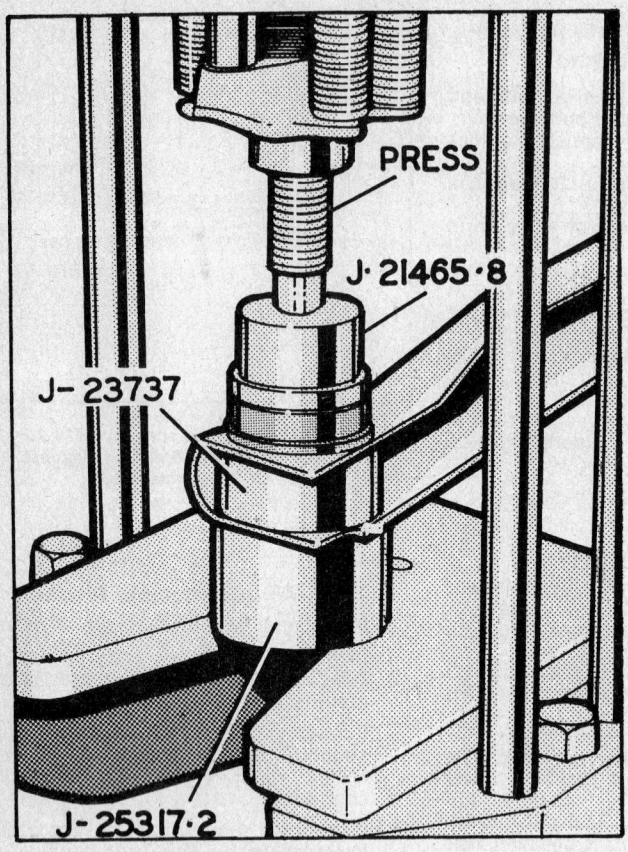

Fig. 9 All front & lower control arm rear bushing removal. 1978-79 models

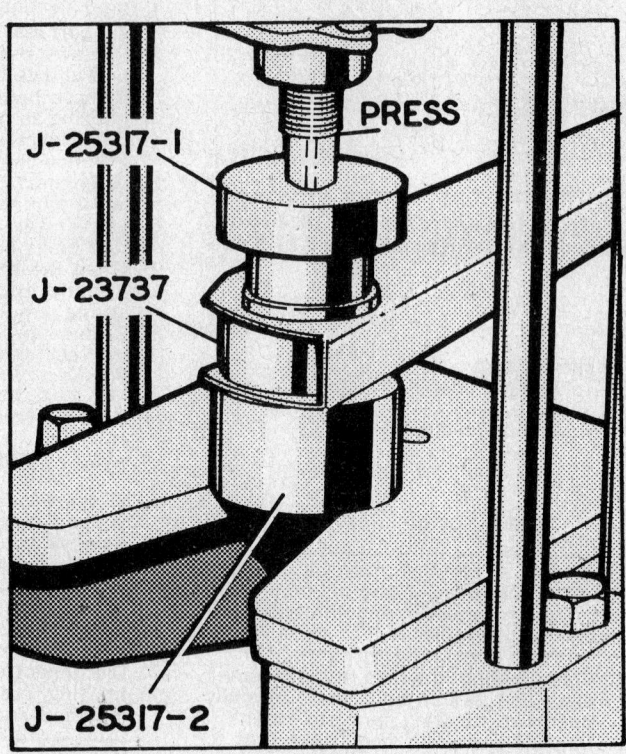

Fig. 10 All front & lower control arm rear bushing installation. 1978-79 models

Fig. 11 Upper control arm rear bushing removal. 1974-77 models (Typical)

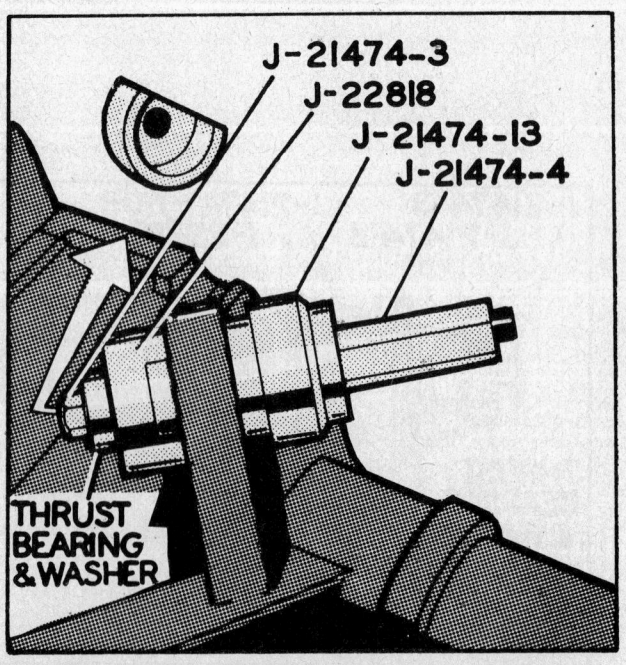

Fig. 12 Upper control arm rear bushing installation. 1974-77 models (Typical)

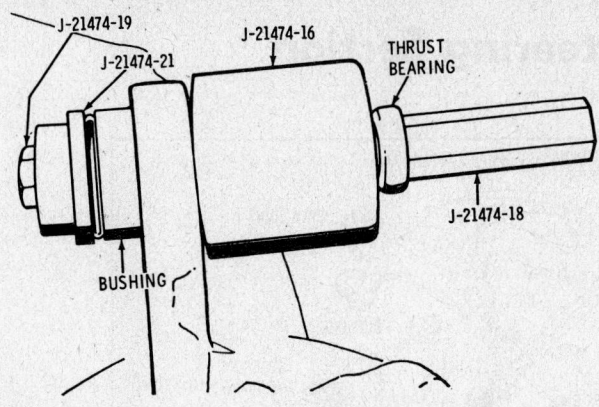

Fig. 13   Upper control arm rear bushing removal. 1978-79 models

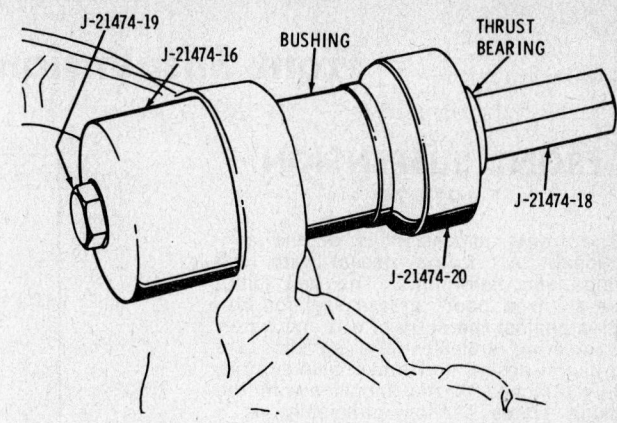

Fig. 14   Upper control arm rear bushing installation. 1978-79 models

CONTROL ARMS & BUSHINGS, REPLACE

NOTE: Replace control arms one at a time to prevent axle misalignment, making installation difficult.

Upper Control Arms

1. Support vehicle at frame and rear axle.

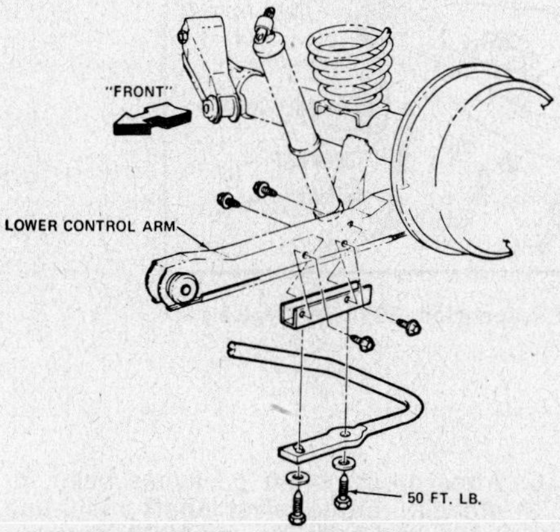

2. Remove control arm front and rear mounting bolts.

NOTE: On some vehicles, disconnect the shock absorber lower mounting stud to provide clearance. Also, use a suitable jack under the nose of differential housing to aid bolt removal.

3. Replace bushings as necessary, Figs. 7 thru 14.

NOTE: On 1977 models, bushings in control arms can only be serviced by replacing control arms.

4. Reverse procedure to install. Tighten control arm bolts with vehicle at curb height.

Lower Control Arms

Follow "Upper Control Arms" procedure for replacement of lower control arms. Lower control arm bushings are serviceable, Figs. 7 thru 10.

NOTE: On models equipped with a stabilizer bar, remove stabilizer bar outlined under "Stabilizer Bar & Bushings, Replace" procedure before removing lower control arm mounting bolts.

STABILIZER BAR & BUSHINGS, REPLACE

Models With Coil Springs

1. With vehicle supported at rear axle, remove bolts attaching stabilizer bar to lower cnotrol arms, Fig. 15.

2. Replace bushings as necessary.
3. Reverse procedure to install. Tighten attaching bolts with vehicle at curb.

Models With Leaf Springs

1. Raise and support rear of vehicle.
2. Remove clamping bolts to disconnect lower end of each support assembly from stabilizer shaft, Fig. 16.
3. Remove insulator and bracket from below each spring and shock absorber anchor plate.
4. Reverse procedure to install making sure that slit in insulators are positioned toward front of vehicle.

Fig. 15   Stabilizer bar installation. 1974-79 Intermediate models & 1974-79 full size models

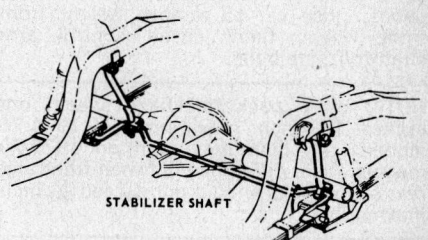

Fig. 16   Stabilizer bar installation. 1974-77 Ventura, 1974-79 Firebird & 1977-79 Phoenix

Front Suspension & Steering Section

FRONT SUSPENSION
1974-79

The front suspension is of the conventional "A" frame design with coil springs and ball joints. The ball joints have a "fixed boot" grease seal for protection against the entry of dirt and water. The steering knuckles and spindles are of integral design and brake cylinders are rigidly attached to the knuckles with the backing plates serving principally as a support for brake shoes and as a protective cover.

On most 1974-79 models, an integral steering knuckle which is a combination steering knuckle, brake caliper support and steering arm is used. On other models, the steering knuckle is of the conventional type with a separate steering arm.

Rubber bushings at the inner ends of the upper control arms pivot on shafts attached to the car frame. Caster and camber adjustments are made with shims at this point, Fig. 1. Direct acting shock absorbers operate within the coil springs.

LUBRICATION

Under normal driving conditions, lubrication is required every 4 months or 6000 miles on 1974 models, 6 months or 7500 miles on 1975-76 models and 12 months or 7500 miles on 1977-79 models.

WHEEL ALIGNMENT
1974-79 All Models

Caster and camber adjustments are made by placing shims between the upper pivot shafts and frame, Fig. 2. Both adjustments can be made at the same time. In order to remove or install shims, raise car to remove weight from front wheel, then loosen control arm shaft-to-frame bolts.

NOTE: Shim pack thickness should not exceed ¾ inch maximum on 1974-76 models, .40 inch maximum on 1977-79 models. Also, difference between front and rear shim packs should not exceed ⅜ inch maximum.

1. To increase negative caster, add shims to front bolt or remove shims from rear bolt.
2. To decrease negative caster (increase positive caster), remove shims from front bolt or add shims to rear bolt.
3. To increase positive camber, remove shims from both front and rear bolts.
4. To decrease positive camber (increase negative camber), add shims to both front and rear bolts.

NOTE: *By adding or subtracting an equal amount of shims from front and rear bolts, camber will be changed without affecting caster.*

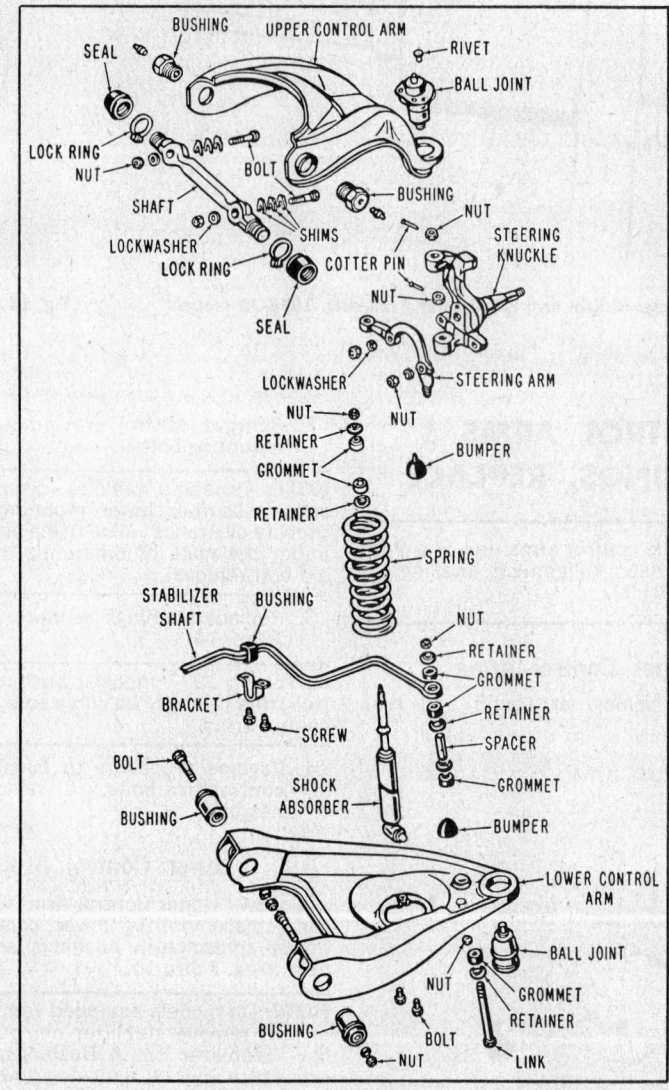

Fig. 1   Disassembled view of front suspension. 1974-79 (typical)

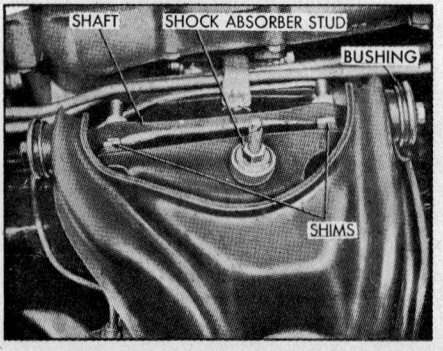

Fig. 2   Caster and camber shim location

6. After proper shim pack has been installed, torque pivot shaft mounting bolts to 50 ft. lbs. on 1974 Ventura, 80 ft. lbs. on 1974-75 full size models and Firebird, 1974-75 Grand Prix and LeMans and 1975 Ventura, 75 ft. lbs. on 1976-77 models, 70 ft. lbs. on 1978-79 Firebird, Grand Am, Grand Prix and LeMans, 74 ft. lbs. on 1978-79 full size and 74 ft. lbs. on 1978-79 Phoenix.

TOE-IN, ADJUST

1. Remove steering wheel trim cover or horn button and set gear on high point by turning steering wheel until

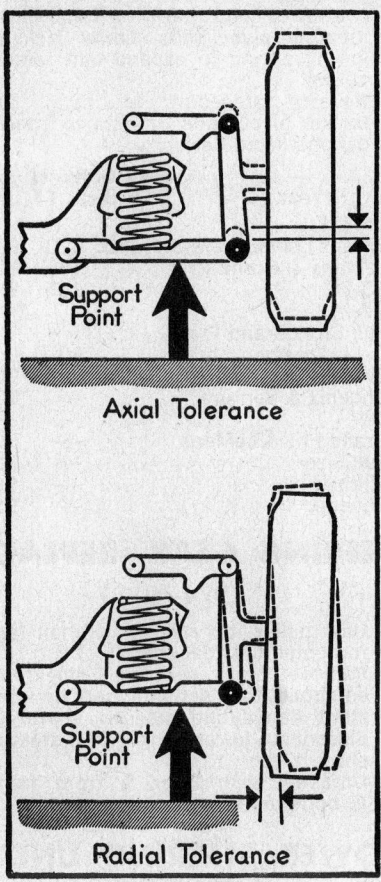

Fig. 3 Checking ball joints for wear

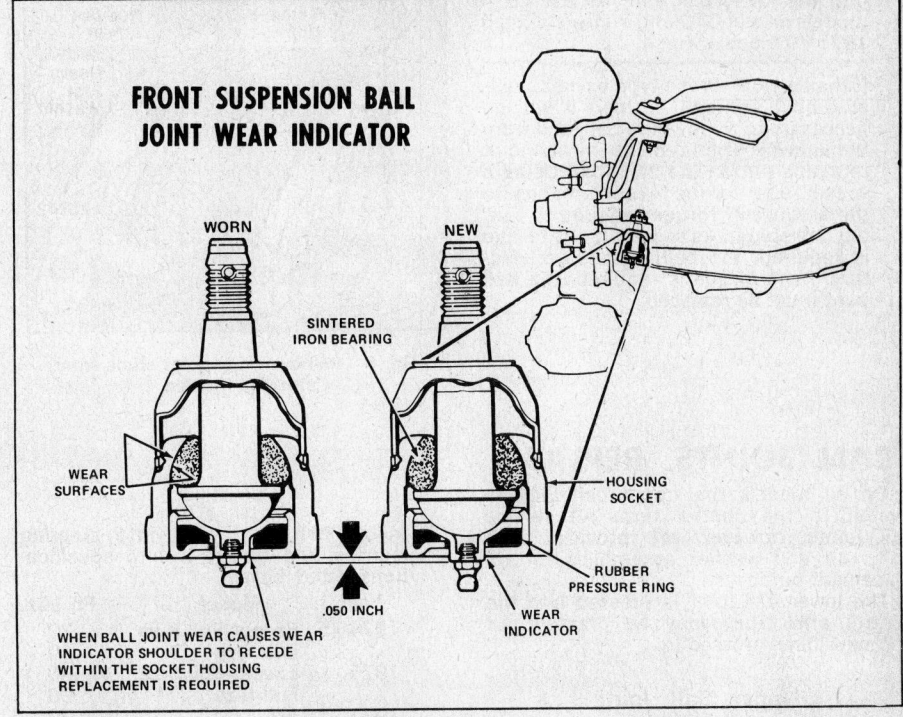

Fig. 4 Ball joint wear indicator. 1974 models exc. GTO & Ventura & all 1975-79

mark on end of shaft is exactly at top. This mark locates high point or middle travel of steering gear.

2. Loosen tie rod clamp bolts and turn both adjuster sleeves an equal amount until toe-in is set to specifications. To increase toe-in, turn left tie rod adjuster sleeve in direction of foward rotation of wheels. Turn right tie rod adjuster sleeve in opposite direction.

3. Make sure front wheels are straight ahead by measuring from a reference point at same place on each side of frame center to front of wheel rims. If measurements are unequal, turn both tie rod adjuster sleeves in same direction (so as not to change toe-in) until measurements become equal. Recheck toe-in and re-adjust as necessary.

4. Torque tie rod clamp bolts to 12 ft. lbs. on 1974 Ventura, 20 ft. lbs. 1974 except Ventura and 1975-76 all and 14 ft. lbs. on 1977-79 models.

NOTE: Open end of clamps should be located 0-45° from a vertical "down" position.

WHEEL BEARINGS, ADJUST

1974-79

1. While rotating wheel, torque spindle nut to 12 ft. lbs.
2. Back off spindle nut until just loose, then retighten by hand.
3. Loosen spindle nut until cotter pin can be inserted, however, do not loosen spindle nut more than ½ flat.
4. With bearing properly adjusted, there should be .001-.005 inch end play.

WHEEL BEARINGS, REPLACE

(Disc Brakes)

1. Raise vehicle and remove front wheels.
2. Remove brake hose support to caliper mounting bracket screw.
3. Remove caliper to mounting bracket bolts.

NOTE: Do not place strain on brake hose.

4. Remove spindle nut, and disc and hub assembly. Grease retainer and inner bearing can now be removed.

CHECKING BALL JOINTS FOR WEAR

Before checking ball joints for wear, make sure the front wheel bearings are properly adjusted and that the control arms are tight.

Referring to Fig. 3, raise wheel with a jack placed under the lower control at the point shown. Then test by moving the wheel up and down to check axial play, and rocking it at the top and bottom to measure radial play.

1. Upper ball joint should be replaced if there is any noticeable looseness at this joint.
   If the ball joint is the type using a built in rubber pre-load cushion it will be necessary to remove the ball stud from the knuckle. Then replace the ball joint retaining nut on the ball stud. Using a socket and torque wrench, measure amount of torque required to turn the ball stud in its socket. If any torque is required, the ball joint is satisfactory. If no torque is required, the ball joint must be replaced.
2. Lower ball joint should be replaced if radial play exceeds .250".
3. Lower ball joint should be replaced if axial play between lower control arm and spindle exceeds the following:
   1974 . . . . .050"

NOTE: A visual wear indicator is built

into the lower ball joint on the 1974 models except GTO and Ventura and all 1975-79 models, Fig. 4.

If the ball joint is the type using a built-in rubber pre-load cushion it will be necessary to remove the ball stud from the knuckle. Then replace the ball joint retaining nut on the ball stud. Using a socket and torque wrench, measure the amount of torque required to turn the ball stud in its socket. If any torque is required, the ball joint is satisfactory. If no torque is required, the ball joint must be replaced.

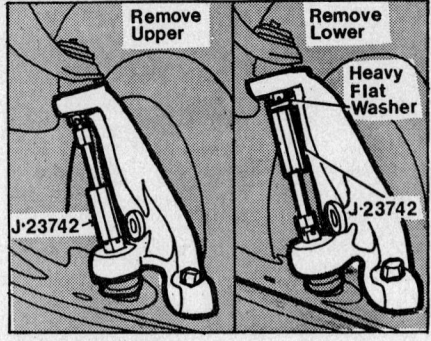

Fig. 5 Removing ball joint studs from steering knuckle.

BALL JOINTS, REPLACE

On all models the upper ball joint is riveted to the control arm. All service ball joints, however, are provided with bolt, nut and washer assemblies for replacement purposes.

The lower ball joint is pressed into the control arm. They may be pressed out and new joints pressed in.

Upper Ball Joint

1. Raise vehicle and support lower control arm.
2. Remove wheel assembly.
3. Remove upper ball joint stud from steering knuckle, Fig. 5.
4. Drill or chisel rivet heads from ball joint rivets. Then, drive rivets from control arm with a suitable punch.
5. Install new ball joint and torque retaining bolts to 9 ft. lbs.
6. Install ball joint stud into steering knuckle and torque nut to specifications listed below:

Year	Ft. Lbs.
1974	40
1975	50
1976	60
1977	50
1978	64

Install cotter pin.

7. Install wheel assembly and lower vehicle.

Lower Ball Joint

1. Raise vehicle and support lower control arm under spring seats.
2. Remove brake drum and backing plate or caliper.
3. Remove lower ball joint stud from steering knuckle, Fig. 5.
4. With a screwdriver, pry ball joint seal and retainer from ball joint.
5. Press lower ball joint from control arm.
6. Press new ball joint into lower control arm.

7. Install ball joint stud into steering knuckle and torque nut to specifications listed below:

Year	Model	Ft. Lbs.
1974-75	Except Full Size	70
	Full Size	80
1976	Except Full Size	80
	Full Size	90
1977	All	70
1978		83

8. Install cotter pin.
9. Install brake backing plate and drum or caliper, then the wheel assembly.

SHOCK ABSORBER, REPLACE

Hold the shock absorber upper stem from turning with a suitable wrench and remove the nut and grommet. Remove the lower shock absorber pivot from the lower control arm and pull the shock absorber and mounting out at the bottom of the spring housing.

To install, reverse the removal procedure. Torque upper retaining nut to 10 ft. lbs. Torque shock absorber lower retaining bolts to 20 ft. lbs.

COIL SPRING, REPLACE

1974-79

1. Support vehicle at frame and remove wheel.
2. Disconnect shock absorber from lower control arm and push shock absorber through hole in lower control arm up into spring.
3. Remove stabilizer link nut, link, spacer, grommets and retainer.
4. Support lower control arm with tool J-23028 bolted onto a suitable jack.
5. Install a safety chain through spring and lower control arm, remove the

two lower control arm to frame crossmember pivot bolts. Lower jack, allowing spring to expand and remove spring.
6. Reverse procedure to install and torque pivot bolts or nuts to specifications listed below:

Year	Pivot Bolts, Ft. lbs.	Nuts, Ft. lbs.
1974-		
Except LeMans & Grand Prix	120	90
LeMans & Grand Prix	100	80
1975-76	105	95
1977-		
Full Size, Grand Prix & LeMans	90	95
Firebird	—	90
Phoenix & Ventura	—	105
1978—		
Grand Prix & LeMans	—	70
Full Size	—	124
Firebird	—	90
Phoenix	—	92

STEERING GEAR, REPLACE

1974-79

1. Use puller to remove pitman arm from steering gear shaft.
2. Remove flex coupling shield, if equipped, then scribe a mark on worm shaft flange and steering shaft and disconnect lower flange from steering shaft.
3. Unfasten gear housing from frame (3 bolts) and remove from car.

POWER STEERING UNIT, REPLACE

1974-79

1. Remove flex coupling shield if equipped, then scribe mark on worm shaft flange and steering shaft and disconnect lower flange from steering shaft.
2. Disconnect pressure and return hoses from gear housing.
3. Raise vehicle and disconnect pitman arm from shaft.
4. Remove gear housing to frame bolts and remove steering gear assembly.

NOTE: On 1974-76 Pontiac models, remove brake hose bracket before removing frame bolts.

5. Reverse procedure to install.

NOTE: *Metal-to-metal contact between flanges of stub shaft and steering shaft will transmit and amplify gear noise to driver. Therefore, when installing the gear, align steering column jacket, shaft and steering gear so head of lower coupling bolt has 1/4" clearance from flange on steering shaft. Adjust mast jacket up or down to avoid metal-to-metal contact.*

GM ENGINE ELECTRICAL PLUG-IN DIAGNOSIS

1977-79 Full Size Models Except Cadillac

NOTE: The following models are equipped with the engine electrical diagnostic connector: 1977-78 Buick Riviera, 1977-79 Buick Electra, and LeSabre, Chevrolet Caprice and Impala, Oldsmobile 88 and 98, Pontiac Bonneville and Catalina and all 1977-79 full size station wagons.

1977-79 full size models are equipped with two electrical diagnostic connectors, Figs. 1 and 2. The A/C connector is located on top of the A/C module and the engine electrical connector is located on the left fender panel. The following diagnostic procedures require the use of a jumper wire and a voltmeter.

Engine Electrical Diagnosis

Some diagnostic connector wires are spliced into the individual unit feed wire, instead of being connected directly to the connector on the unit. The connector on the unit should be checked before starting a repair. The splice can be checked by connecting a voltmeter to the connector on the unit and the voltage should be the same as at the terminal at the diagnostic connector.

Cranking tests are performed with the engine at any temperature, however, if the engine is extremely hot or cold, the voltage readings obtained will be lower than specified. To determine which of the following problems apply, turn the ignition key to "Start".

a. Poor cranking, or solenoid clicks or chatters.

b. Solenoid makes no sound, no cranking.

c. Starter runs (spins), engine does not crank.

For all cranking problems, check for a damaged battery, loose or corroded terminals and cables and repair as necessary. If satisfactory, check battery state or charge indicator or specific gravity. If state of charge indicator is "Green" or the specific gravity is 1.200 or more, select condition in the following charts and perform checks with a voltmeter. The parking brakes should be applied with automatic transmission in "Park" and manual transmission in "Neutral", clutch released and the ignition key in the "Start" position. If the state of charge indicator is "Dark" or the specific gravity is less than 1.200, charge battery and recheck condition. Check charging system condition and also for a battery drain.

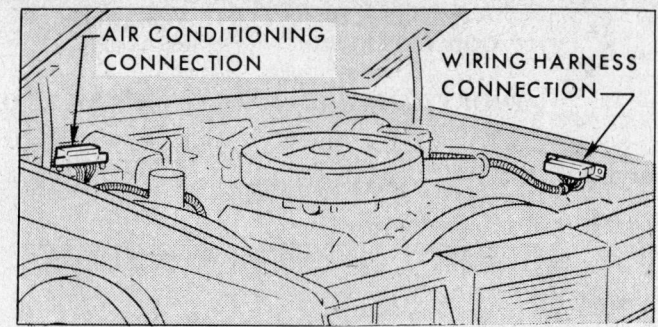

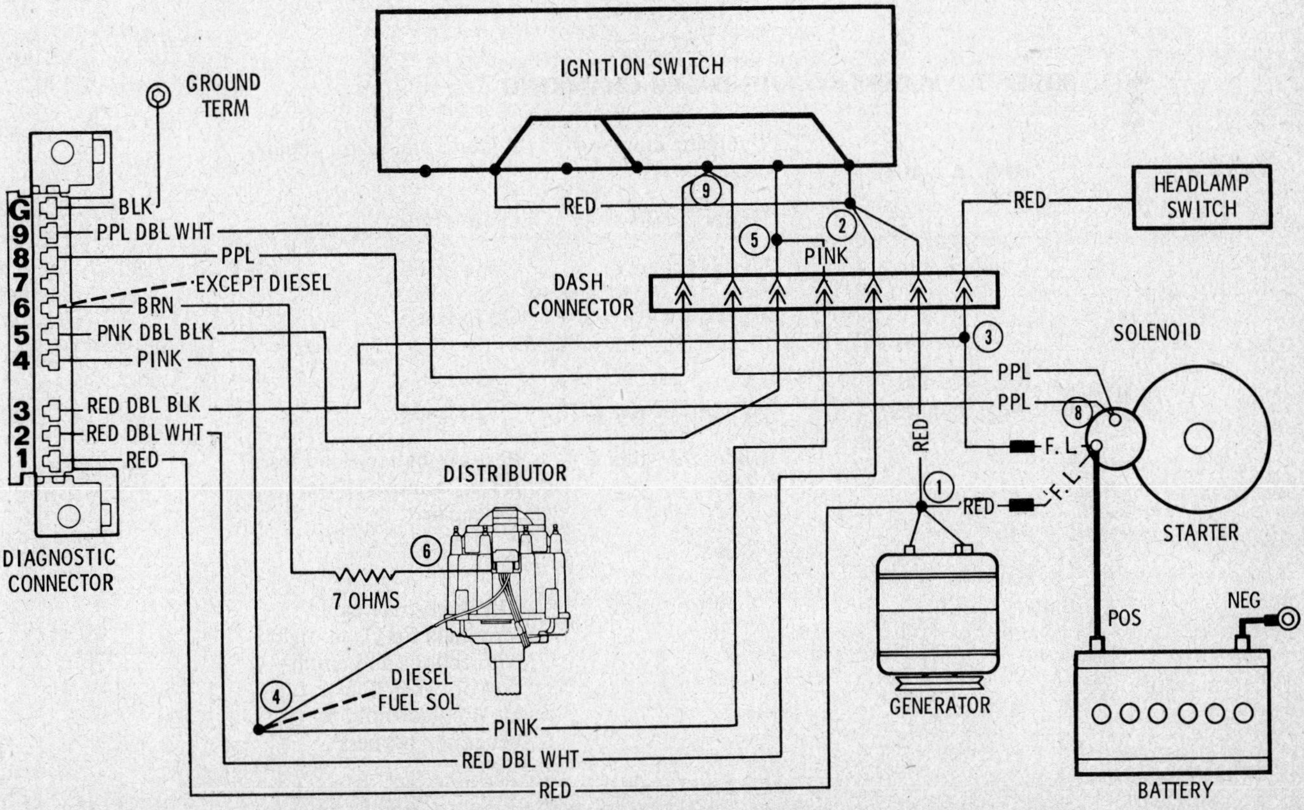

Fig. 1 Diagnostic connector location. 1977-79 models

Fig. 2 Engine electrical wiring circuit 1977-79 models

GM ENGINE ELECTRICAL PLUG-IN DIAGNOSIS

VOLTMETER CONNECTIONS	VOLTAGE READING	CORRECTION
POOR CRANKING, OR SOLENOID CLICKS OR CHATTERS		
1. 1 and G	9 volts or more	Move voltmeter lead from G to engine block, key in "Start". 9 volts or more - Remove starter for repair. Under 9 volts - Check battery ground cable connections at engine block and at battery.
	Under 9 volts	Go to test 2.
2. Bat. Pos. and Bat. Neg. at battery	9.6 volts or more	Go to test 3.
	Under 9.6 volts	Perform battery load test. If OK, remove starter for repair.
3. Bat. Pos. at Battery and 1	.7 volts or more	Check positive cable terminals for clean, tight connections and condition of cable. Check fusible link (solenoid to generator harness).
	Under .7 volts	Check battery ground cable condition and connections.
SOLENOID MAKES NO SOUND—NO CRANKING		
1. 8 and G (Key in Start)	7 volts or more	Remove starter for repair.
	Under 7 volts	Go to test 2.
2. 1 and G	9 volts or more	Go to test 5.
	Under 9 volts	Go to test 3.
3. Bat. Pos. and Bat. Neg. at Battery	9.6 volts or more	Go to test 4.
	Under 9.6 volts	Perform battery load test. If OK, remove starter for repair.
4. Bat. Pos. at Battery and 1	.7 volts or more	Check positive cable terminals for clean, tight connections and condition of cable. Check fusible link (solenoid to generator harness).
	Under .7 volts	Check battery ground cable condition and connections.

VOLTMETER CONNECTIONS	VOLTAGE READING	CORRECTION
5. 9 and G (Key in Start)	7 volts or more	Check purple wire from ignition switch through engine/generator dash connector to starter solenoid for open/loose connections.
	Under 7 volts	Go to test 6.
6. 2 and G	7 volts or more	Replace ignition switch.
	Under 7 volts	Check battery wire (red) from ignition switch through engine/generator dash connector to splice for open/loose connection.

STARTER RUNS (SPINS), ENGINE DOES NOT CRANK

Check flywheel gear teeth. If OK, remove starter for repair.

IGNITION MISS OR WILL NOT START (CRANKS OK)

Make a secondary output check (except diesel) using a calibrated spark gap or output meter. HEI system should produce at least 25,000 volts (25KV) cranking or engine idling. If not, follow procedure below. If satisfactory, check spark plugs, spark plug cables, distributor cap and rotor.

If car will not start, make voltage checks cranking. If it will start, make checks running. Both cranking and running voltages are given.

VOLTMETER CONNECTIONS	VOLTS CRANKING	VOLTS IDLING
1. 6 and G (Except Diesel)	7 or more	9.6 or more—Check HEI distributor.
	Under 7	Under 9.6—Go to test 2.
2. 4 and G	7 or more	9.6 or more—7 volts or more at HEI battery terminal, check the HEI distributor (fuel solenoid on diesel).
	Under 7	Under 9.6—Go to test 3.
3. 5 and G	7 or more	9.6 or more—Check for open circuit or loose connection in wire from bat. terminal on distributor (fuel solenoid on diesel) through engine dash connector to ignition switch.
	Under 7	Under 9.6—Replace ignition switch.

ALTERNATOR WARNING LIGHT "ON" ENGINE RUNNING

1. Check alternator belt, adjust or replace as needed.
2. Check gauges/trans. fuse, if blown check for short circuit in pink dbl. wht. str. wire from fuse panel to instrument cluster and/or trunk release.
3. Remove 2 wire connector from alternator, if warning light turns off remove alternator for repair. If warning light stays on, check for short circuit in brown wire from alternator connector through engine dash connector to instrument cluster connector (alternator warning, light circuit).

VOLTMETER CONNECTIONS	VOLTAGE READING	CORRECTION

LOW BATTERY, BUT ALTERNATOR LIGHT INDICATES NO PROBLEM

1. Adjust or replace alternator belt as needed.
2. Charge battery.
3. Run engine at 1500 to 2000 RPM for one minute with lights on high beam, heater on high, radio and defogger blower on.

1 and G	Under 12.5 volts	Remove alternator for repair.
	12.5 volts or more	Check for battery drain and driving habits. If no defect is found, make alternator output check.

OVERCHARGING

1. Connect voltmeter to terminal 1 and G. Run engine at 1500 to 2000 RPM until voltmeter reaches maximum, do NOT run engine more than one minute.

1 and G	15.5 or more	Remove alternator for repair.
	Under 15.5 volts	Check for extended driving conditions in hot weather.

TURBO HYDRA-MATIC 325

TRANSMISSION IDENTIFICATION

This transmission may be identified by the following codes located on the serial number plate attached to the left side of the converter housing.

Buick

1979 Riviera V6-231	6BJ
Riviera V8-350	6OJ

Cadillac

1979 Eldorado	AJ

Oldsmobile

1979 Toronado V8-350①	OJ
Toronado V8-350②	OK

①—Except diesel engine.
②—Diesel engine.

GENERAL DESCRIPTION

This transmission is a fully automatic front wheel drive unit consisting primarily of a three-element hydraulic torque converter and a compound planetary gear set, Fig. 1. Three multiple disc clutches, a roller clutch and a band provide the friction elements required to obtain the desired function of the compound planetary gear set. The compound planetary gear set provides three forward speeds and reverse.

The torque converter couples the engine to the planetary gears through oil and provides torque multiplication. It consists of a pump or driving member, a turbine or driven member and a stator assembly. The stator is mounted on a one-way roller clutch which allows the stator to turn clockwise but not counterclockwise.

The torque converter housing is filled with oil and rotates at engine speed. The converter pump is an integral part of the converter housing, therefore the pump blades rotating at engine speed set the oil within the converter into motion and direct it to the turbine causing the turbine to rotate. As the oil passes through the turbine it travels in such a direction that if it were not redirected by the stator it would strike the rear of the converter pump blades and impede its pumping action. Therefore at low turbine speeds, the oil is redirected by the stator to the converter pump in such a manner that it actually assists the converter pump to deliver power or multiply engine torque. As turbine speed increases, the direction of the oil leaving the turbine changes and flows against the rear side of the stator vanes in a clockwise direction. Since the stator is now impeding the smooth flow of oil, its roller clutch releases and it revolves freely on its shaft. Once the stator becomes inactive, there is no further multiplication of torque within the converter. At this point the converter is acting as a fluid coupling since the converter pump and turbine are being driven at about the same speed, or at a one-to-one ratio.

The hydraulic system in this transmission is pressurized by a gear type pump to provide the working pressures required to operate the friction elements and automatic controls.

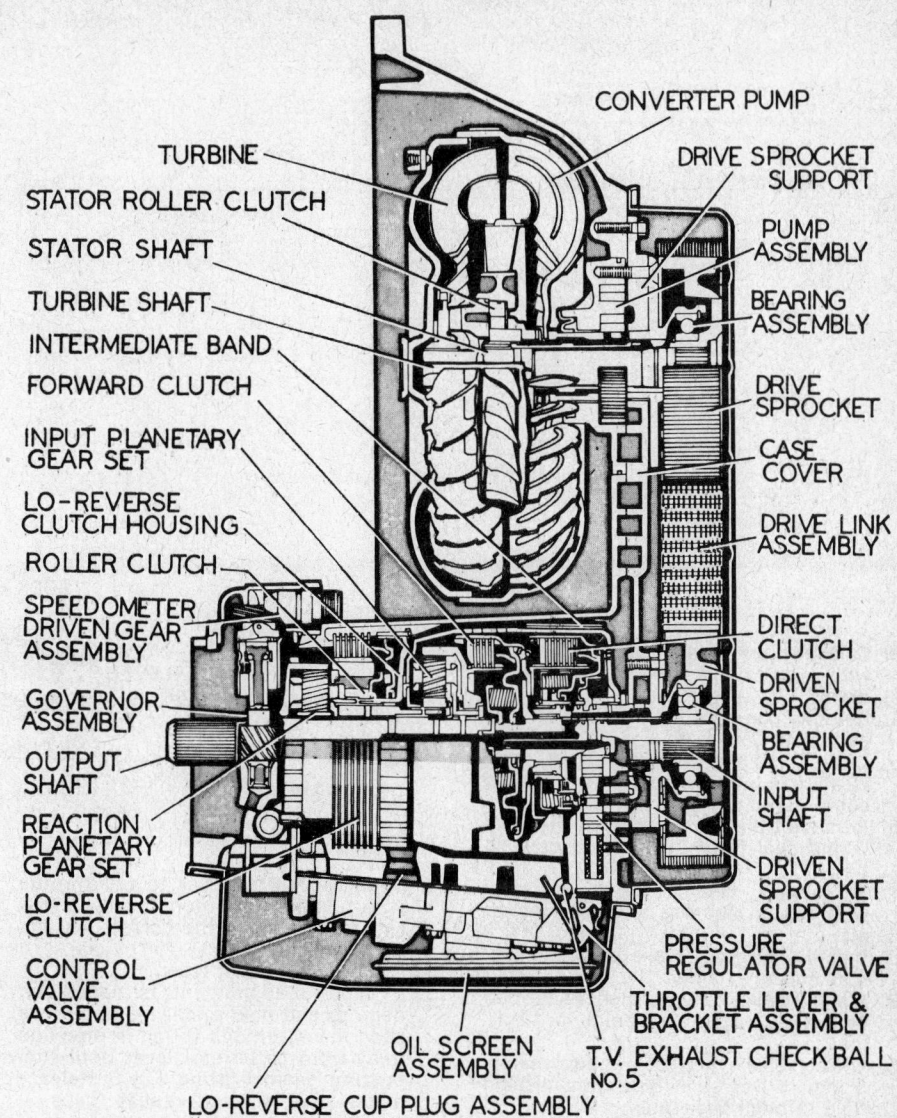

Fig. 1 Sectional view of Turbo Hydra-Matic 325 automatic transmission

MAINTENANCE
Adding Oil

To check fluid, drive vehicle for at least 15 minutes to bring fluid to operating temperature (190°-200° F). With vehicle on a level surface and engine idling in Park and parking brake applied, the level on the dipstick should be at the Full Hot mark. To bring the fluid level from the ADD mark to the FULL mark requires one pint of fluid. If vehicle cannot be driven sufficiently to bring fluid to operating temperature, the level on the dipstick should be between the two dimples on the dipstick with fluid temperature at 65°-85° F.

If additional fluid is required, use only Dexron II automatic transmission fluid.

NOTE: An early change to a darker color from the usual red color and or a strong odor that is usually associated with overheated fluid is normal and should not be considered as a positive sign of required maintenance or unit failure.

CAUTION: When adding fluid, do not over fill, as foaming and loss of fluid through the vent may occur as the fluid heats up. Also, if fluid level is too low, complete loss of drive may occur especially when cold, which can cause transmission failure.

Every 100,000 miles, the oil should be drained, the oil pan removed, the screen cleaned and fresh fluid added. For vehicles subjected to more severe use such as heavy city traffic especially in hot weather, prolonged periods of idling or towing, this maintenance should be performed every 15,000 miles.

Changing Oil

1. Raise vehicle and position drain pan under transmission pan.
2. Loosen rear pan attaching bolts approximately four turns.

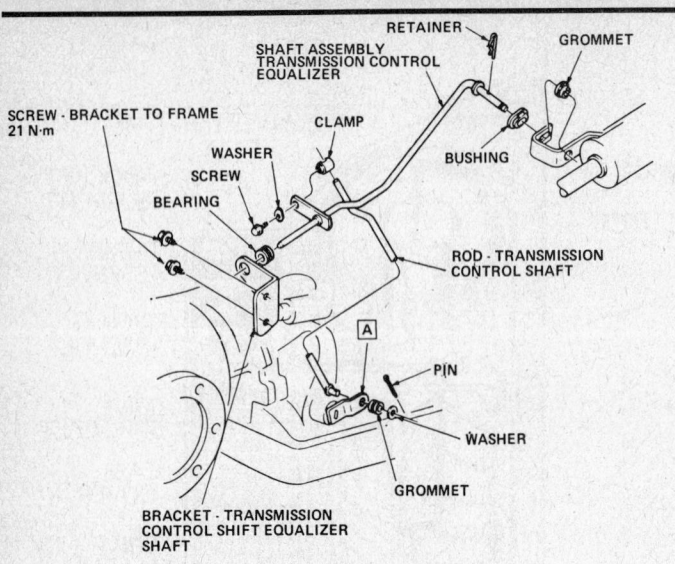

Fig. 2 Manual linkage

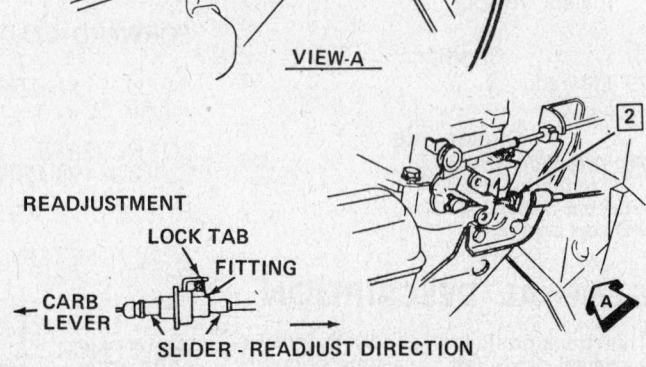

READJUSTMENT

VIEW-B

Fig. 3 Downshift linkage adjustment

3. Carefully pry transmission pan loose with a screwdriver and allow fluid to drain.
4. Remove pan attaching bolts, pan and pan gasket.
5. Drain remaining fluid from pan, then clean pan with solvent and dry with compressed air.
6. Remove transmission screen. Remove O-ring seal from intake pipe or case bore.
7. Thoroughly clean screen assembly with solvent and dry with compressed air.
8. Install O-ring on intake pipe, then install screen retainer.
9. Install gasket on pan, then install pan and torque attaching bolts to 12 ft. lbs.
10. Lower vehicle and add approximately 5 qts. of Dexron II type transmission fluid through filler tube.
11. Start engine and operate at idle speed, then move selector lever through each range.
12. Place transmission in Park position and check fluid level.

MANUAL LINKAGE, ADJUST

1. Loosen transmission control shaft rod clamp, Fig. 2.
2. Place shift lever in Neutral position.
3. Place transmission lever in Neutral position.
4. While holding clamp flush against control equalizer shaft assembly, tighten screw against rod finger tight.
5. Tighten clamp screw to 20 ft. lbs. No force should be exerted on in either direction on the rod or equalizer shaft assembly when tighten clamp screw.
6. Check neutral start switch adjustment and adjust as necessary.

DOWNSHIFT CABLE, ADJUST

1. After assembling cable to transmission install cable fitting into engine bracket.

2. Install cable terminal on carburetor lever.
3. Open carburetor lever to full throttle stop position to automatically adjust slider on cable to the correct setting, Fig. 3.
4. Release carburetor lever.
5. If cable readjustment is necessary, depress and hold metal tab and move slider back through fitting in direction away from carburetor lever until slider stops against fitting, Fig. 3. Release metal lock tab and repeat steps 3. and 4.

IN-VEHICLE REPAIRS

Valve Body, Replace

1. Drain transmission fluid and remove oil pan and screen.
2. Remove screw and disconnect downshift cable.
3. Remove throttle lever and bracket assembly. Use care not to bend throttle lever link.
4. Remove manual detent roller and spring assembly.
5. Support valve body and remove attaching bolts.
6. While holding manual valve with fingers, remove valve body spacer plate and gaskets together to prevent dropping of four check balls located in valve body and fifth check ball located on spacer plate.

NOTE: After removing valve body, intermediate band anchor pin and reverse clutch cup plug may come out.

7. Place valve body on bench with spacer plate side facing upward and remove check ball from spacer plate.

8. Reverse procedure to install. Torque valve body attaching bolts to 8 ft. lbs.

NOTE: Intermediate band anchor pin must locate on intermediate band or damage to transmission may result.

Intermediate Servo, Replace

1. Install tool No. J-28493 on transmission case and tighten bolt to depress servo cover.
2. Using a small screwdriver, remove servo cover retaining ring, then remove tool.
3. Remove servo cover, then remove servo piston and band apply pin assembly.
4. Reverse procedure to install.

Speedometer Gears, Replace

1. Disconnect speedometer cable, then remove driven gear attaching bolt, retainer and driven gear.
2. Remove governor cover attaching screws and governor cover.
3. Remove governor and speedometer drive gear assembly.
4. Remove speedometer drive gear from governor assembly.
5. Reverse procedure to install.

Pressure Regulator Valve, Replace

1. Drain transmission fluid and remove oil pan and screen.
2. Push in on pressure regulator valve, compress valve spring with a small screwdriver.

3. Remove retaining ring, then slowly release spring tension and remove pressure regulator guide.

DRIVE LINK BELT OR SPROCKETS

Refer to Cadillac Section, Eldorado Drive Link Belt, for removal and installation procedures.

TRANSMISSION, REPLACE

1. Disconnect downshift cable from carburetor linkage and remove from bracket. Position cable out of way.
2. Disconnect speedometer cable.
3. Install a suitable engine holding fixture so that engine can be lowered approximately 1 inch at time of transmission removal.

4. Remove air intake assembly from top of carburetor.
5. Remove exhaust heated air intake from exhaust manifold.
6. Remove accessible transmission to engine attaching bolts. Lower right hand attaching bolts are removed from under vehicle.
7. Remove bolt from inspection cover, then place transmission shift lever to low position.
8. Remove accessible bolts from left and right transmission mounts.
9. Raise vehicle and remove cotter pin from shift linkage at transmission, then disconnect shift linkage.
10. On models equipped with V8-350, loosen left hand exhaust pipe to crossover pipe clamp and position clamp with bolts at top and bottom.
11. Disconnect transmission cooler lines at transmission and install plugs in lines.

12. Remove starter motor.
13. Remove flywheel inspection cover.
14. Remove three flywheel to converter attaching bolts.
15. Position a suitable jack under transmission.
16. Remove bolts from right axle bearing support.
17. Remove remaining bolts at left transmission mount and one nut at frame, then remove mount.
18. Remove remaining bolts at right transmission mount and one nut at frame bracket.
19. Remove remaining transmission to engine attaching bolts.
20. Remove bolts attaching final drive to transmission.
21. Loosen final drive to engine support bracket.
22. Remove transmission from vehicle. It may be necessary to wiggle final drive to disengage splines.

GM FRONT WHEEL DRIVE

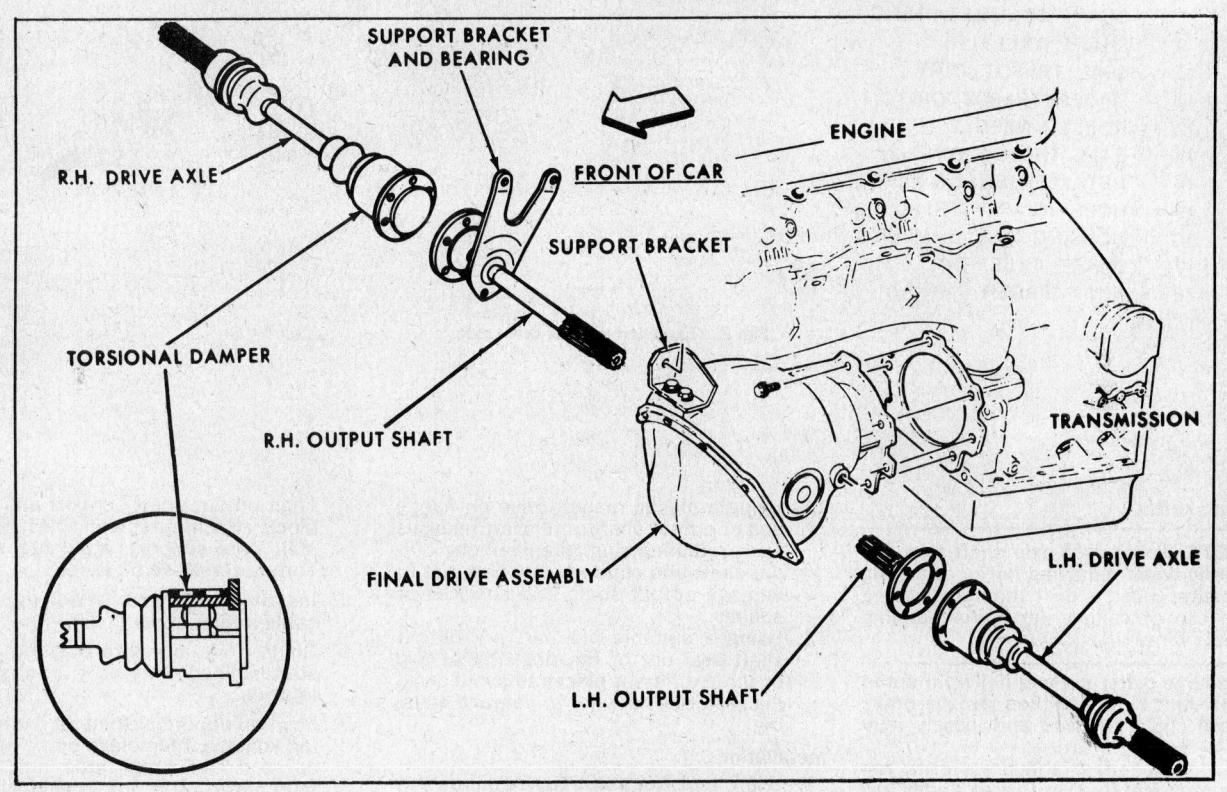

Fig. 1 Front wheel drive components

1979 BUICK RIVIERA, CADILLAC ELDORADO & OLDSMOBILE TORONADO
Description

The front wheel drive system, Fig. 1, consists of a final drive unit, left and right hand output shafts and drive axles. The output shafts are splined to the side gears and are retained by a retaining ring. Each drive axle, Fig. 2, consists of an axle shaft, with a ball type constant velocity at the outboard end and a tri-pot joint at the inboard end.

Right Hand Drive Axle, Output Shaft & Seal, Replace
Removal
1. Disconnect battery ground cable.

2. Raise front of vehicle and place jack stands under front frame horns.
3. Remove wheel and tire assembly.
4. Remove cotter pin, nut and shield from tie rod pivot, then using puller J-24319, detach tie rod end from steering knuckle.
5. Install drive shaft seal protector J-28712, then remove cotter pin, nut and washer from drive axle, then remove six screws attaching drive axle to out-

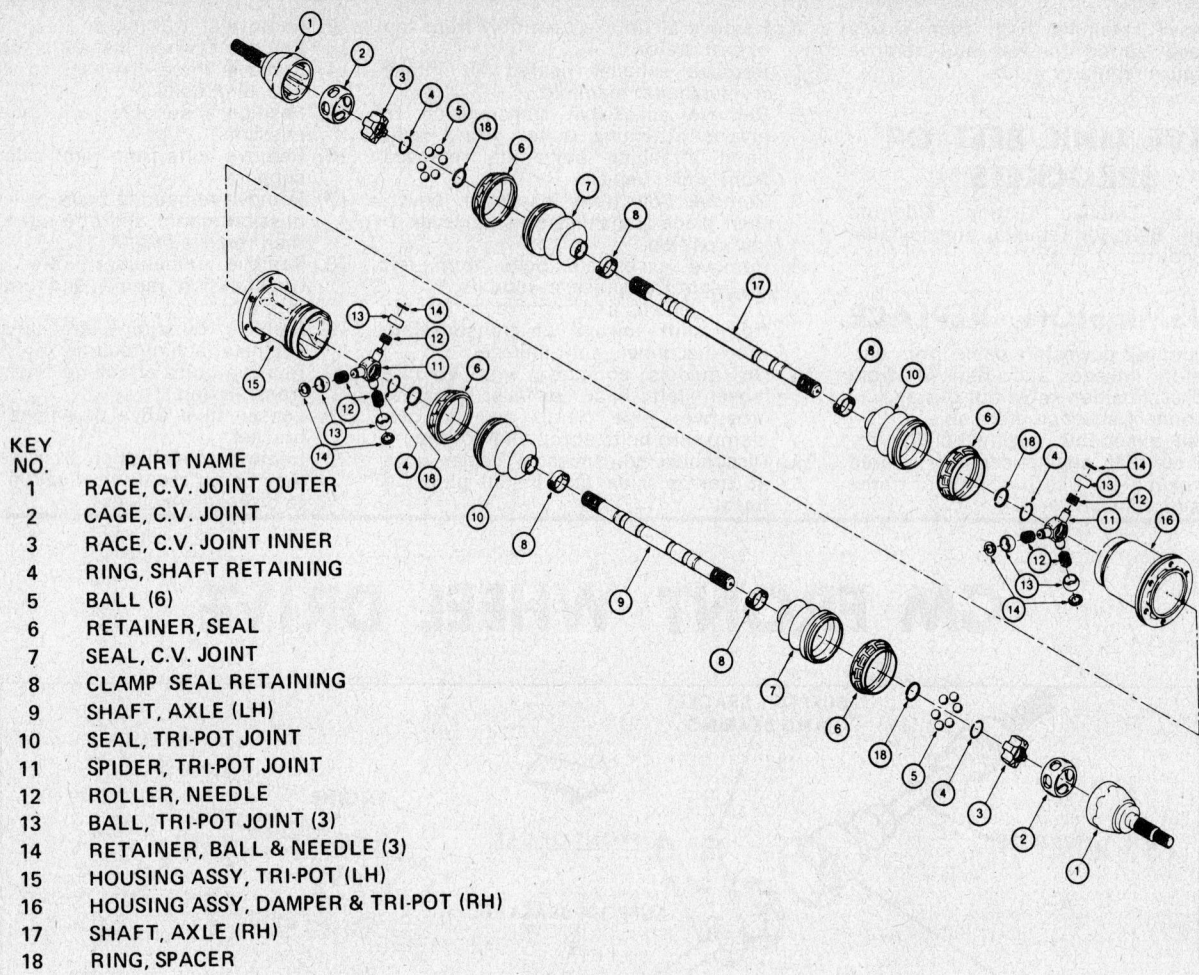

KEY NO.	PART NAME
1	RACE, C.V. JOINT OUTER
2	CAGE, C.V. JOINT
3	RACE, C.V. JOINT INNER
4	RING, SHAFT RETAINING
5	BALL (6)
6	RETAINER, SEAL
7	SEAL, C.V. JOINT
8	CLAMP SEAL RETAINING
9	SHAFT, AXLE (LH)
10	SEAL, TRI-POT JOINT
11	SPIDER, TRI-POT JOINT
12	ROLLER, NEEDLE
13	BALL, TRI-POT JOINT (3)
14	RETAINER, BALL & NEEDLE (3)
15	HOUSING ASSY, TRI-POT (LH)
16	HOUSING ASSY, DAMPER & TRI-POT (RH)
17	SHAFT, AXLE (RH)
18	RING, SPACER

Fig. 2 Exploded view of drive axle

put shaft.

NOTE: To prevent axle shaft from rotating when removing nut or attaching screws, insert a drift through opening on top of caliper into corresponding rotor vane.

6. Remove cotter pin and nut from upper ball joint stud nut, then remove brake hose clip from stud and loosely reinstall nut.
7. Using a hammer and brass drift, rap on steering knuckle to free upper ball joint stud. Use care not to damage brake hose or steering knuckle.
8. Remove nut and separate upper ball joint from steering knuckle.
9. Guide drive axle out of steering knuckle and remove from vehicle.
10. Remove two screws attaching battery cable retainer to support and remove two screws attaching output support to engine, then rotate support downward.
11. Remove front nut and bolt from right hand frame brace, then pivot brace outward to provide clearance.

12. Using a plastic mallet, drive on flange end of output shaft until shaft releases from retaining ring, then remove output shaft and support. Use care not to damage output shaft seal surfaces or splines.
13. Using a suitable pry bar, pry output shaft seal out of housing. Pry at two or three different places to avoid cocking seal. Use care not to damage housing.

Installation

1. Using tool No. J-28518, install output shaft seal. Rotate tool to maintain proper alignment when installing seal.
2. Apply wheel bearing grease between lips of seal.
3. Index splines of output shaft with splines of side gear in final drive assembly, then install shaft by tapping on flange end with a soft faced mallet until retaining ring snaps into shaft groove. Ensure shaft is securely locked into position.

NOTE: When installing output shaft, use care not to damage seal.

4. Align output shaft support and engine block attaching screw holes, then install two support attaching screws. Torque screws to 50 ft. lbs.
5. Install two screws attaching battery cable retainer to support.
6. Guide drive axle into position and install splined end axle into steering knuckle.
7. Position upper ball joint stud into steering knuckle, then place brake hose clip on stud and install stud nut. Torque stud nut to 60 ft. lbs., then install cotter pin. The nut may be tightened an additional 1/6 turn to align cotter pin slots.
8. Install six screws attaching output shaft to drive axle. Torque screws to 60 ft. lbs.
9. Install drive axle washer, nut, retainer and cotter pin. Torque nut to 175 ft. lbs. Align cotter pin slot by rotating retainer and bend cotter pin so that retainer is held snugly.
10. Install tie rod pivot on steering knuckle. Torque nut to 44 ft. lbs. The nut

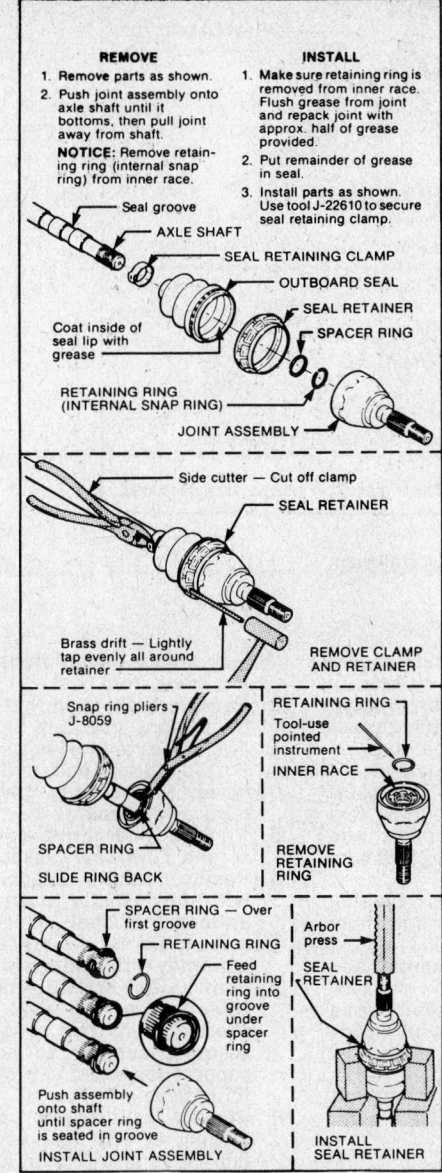

Fig. 3 Outer constant velocity joint seal removal & installation

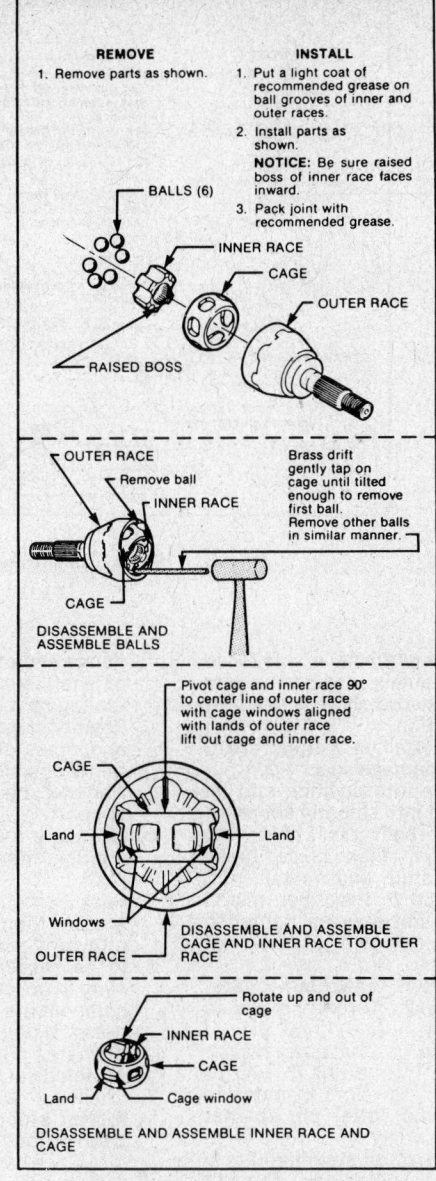

Fig. 4 Outer constant velocity joint disassembly & assembly

may be tightened an additional $\frac{1}{6}$ turn to align cotter pin slots.

11. Install right hand frame brace bolt and nut. Torque belt to 50 ft. lbs.
12. Install wheel and tire assembly, then lower vehicle and connect battery ground cable.
13. Check output shaft seal for leakage.

Left Hand Drive Axle, Output Shaft & Seal, Replace

Removal

1. Raise front of vehicle and place jack stands under front frame horns.
2. Remove wheel and tire assembly.
3. Remove cotter pin, nut and shield from tie rod pivot, then using puller J-24319, detach tie rod end from steering knuckle.
4. Remove cotter pin, nut and washer from drive axle, then remove six screws attaching drive axle to output shaft.

NOTE: To prevent drive axle from rotating when removing nut or attaching screws, insert a drift through opening on top of caliper into corresponding rotor vane.

5. Remove cotter pin and nut from upper ball joint stud nut, then remove brake hose clip from stud and loosely reinstall nut.
6. Using a hammer and brass drift, rap on steering knuckle to free upper ball joint stud. Use care not to damage brake hose or steering knuckle.
7. Remove nut and separate upper ball joint from steering knuckle.
8. Guide drive axle out of steering knuckle and remove from vehicle.

9. Remove front nut and bolt from left hand frame brace, then pivot brace outward to provide clearance.
10. Using a hammer and brass drift, drive on flange end of output shaft until shaft releases from retaining ring, then remove output shaft.
11. Using a suitable pry bar, pry output shaft seal from houing. Pry at two or three locations to avoid cocking seal. Use care not to damage housing.

Installation

1. Using tool No. J-28518, install output shaft seal. Rotate tool to maintain proper alignment when installing seal.
2. Apply wheel bearing grease between lips of seal.
3. Index splines of output shaft with splines of side gear in final drive assembly then install shaft by tapping

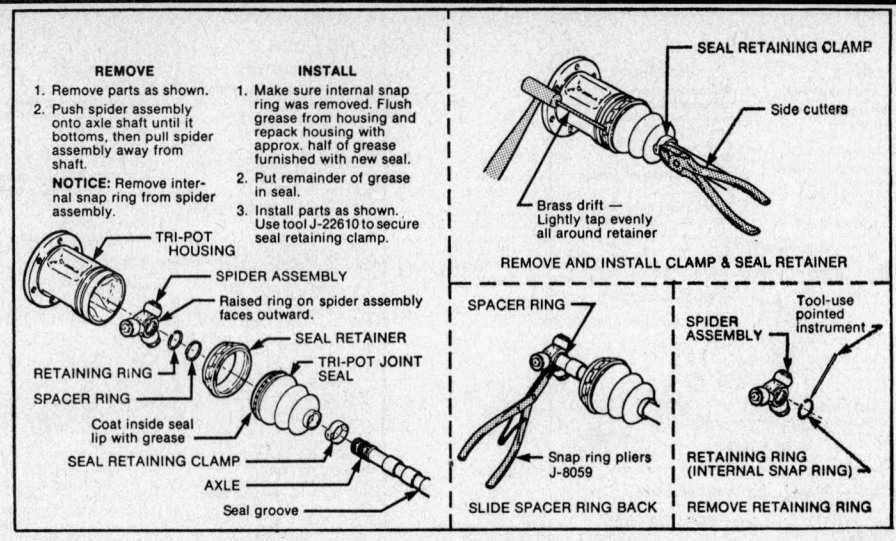

Fig. 5   Inner tri-pot seal removal & installation

center of flange end with a soft faced mallet until retaining ring snaps into shaft groove. Ensure shaft is securely locked into position.
NOTE: When installing output shaft, use care not to damage seal.

4. Guide drive axle into position and install splined end into steering knuckle.
5. Position upper ball joint stud into steering knuckle, then place brake hose clip on stud and install nut. Torque nut to 60 ft. lbs., then install cotter pin. The nut may be tightened an additional 1/6 turn to align cotter pin slots.
6. Install six screws attaching output shaft to drive axle. Torque screws to 60 ft. lbs.
7. Install drive axle washer, nut, retainer and cotter pin. Torque nut to 175 ft. lbs. Align cotter pin slots by rotating retainer and bend cotter pin so that retainer is held snugly.
8. Install tie rod pivot on steering knuckle. Torque nut to 44 ft. lbs. The nut may be tightened an additional 1/6 turn to align cotter pin slots.
9. Install left hand frame brace bolt and nut. Torque bolt to 50 ft. lbs.
10. Install wheel and tire assembly, then lower vehicle and check output shaft seal for leakage.

Right Hand Output Shaft Bearing, Replace

1. Remove right hand output shaft as described under Right Hand Drive Axle, Output Shaft and Seal, Replace.
2. Install tool No. J-22912 between

flange end of output shaft and flat area of shaft support, with flat surface of tool against flat area of shaft support. Position assembly on a suitable press and press shaft support, bearing, retainer and slinger from output shaft.
3. Remove bearing from output shaft support.
4. Lubricate output shaft support and bearing, then position bearing into support.
5. Pack bearing with wheel bearing grease, then install retainer and three attaching screws.
6. Place assembled components and slinger on output shaft, then position components and output shaft on a press. Using a standard 1 1/4 in. inside diameter pipe, press bearing and assembled components onto shaft.
7. Check to ensure bearing and support rotate smoothly, then install right hand output shaft.

Outer Constant Velocity Joint & Seal, Replace

For removal and installation procedures refer to Figs. 3 and 4.

Inner Tri-Pot Seal, Replace

For removal and installation procedures refer to Fig. 5.

FINAL DRIVE, REPLACE

1. Disconnect battery ground cable.
2. Raise front of vehicle and position

jack stands under front frame horns and lower front post.
3. Remove right and left hand frame brace front attaching blots, then position braces to provide clearance.
4. Position drain pan under final drive cover, then loosen cover and allow lubricant to drain.
5. Remove final drive cover attaching screws, cover and gasket.
6. Remove screws attaching right and left output shafts to drive axles. Separate output shaft flanges from drive axles to permit clearance of final drive assembly with shafts installed.
7. Remove two screws attaching battery cable retainer to right hand output shaft support, then remove two screws securing support to engine. Rotate support downward to provide clearance for removal.
8. Remove final drive to transmission attaching screws that secures rear of final drive shield, then loosen support bracket screw that secure front of shield and remove shield.
9. Remove five remaining final drive to transmission attaching screws,
10. Remove screws attaching final drive support bracket to engine block.
11. Slide final drive assembly forward, off transmission splined shaft and remove unit with output shafts attached. Use care not to damage output shaft seal or splines.
12. Reverse procedure to install. Torque final drive to transmission attaching bolts to 30 ft. lbs. and output shaft to drive shaft attaching bolts to 60 ft. lbs.

1979 CARBURETOR ADJUSTMENT SPECIFICATIONS

NOTE: For 1979 carburetor adjustment specifications not listed on these pages, refer to the "Carburetor Section" elsewhere in this manual.

CARTER TQ ADJUSTMENT SPECIFICATIONS

CHRYSLER, DODGE & PLYMOUTH

Year	Carb. Model	Air/Fuel Ratio	Float Setting	Secondary Throttle Linkage	Secondary Air Valve Opening	Secondary Air Valve Spring	Pump Travel	Choke Control Lever (Off Car)	Choke Vacuum Kick	Choke Unloader	Fast Idle R.P.M.	Choke Setting
1979	9195S	①	29/32	②	3/8	2 Turn	33/64 ③	3 3/8	.100	.310	1600	Fixed
	9196S	①	29/32	②	1/2	2 Turn	33/64 ③	3 3/8	.100	.310	1600	Fixed
	9198S	①	29/32	②	1/2	2 Turn	33/64 ③	3 3/8	.100	.310	1600	Fixed
	9202S	①	29/32	②	1/2	2 Turn	33/64 ③	3 3/8	.100	.310	1600	Fixed

①—For Air/Fuel ratio & Idle @ CO%, see Tune-Up Chart in car chapter.   ②—Adjust link so primary & secondary stops both contact at same time.   ③—Secondary stage pickup adjustment, 5/16 inch

MOTORCRAFT MODEL 2100, 2150-2V ADJUSTMENT SPECIFICATIONS

AMERICAN MOTORS

Year	Carb. Model (Code 9510)	Idle Mixture Turns Open	Float Level (Dry)	Fuel Level (Wet)	Pump Setting Hole No. ④	Choke Plate Clearance (Pull down)	Fast Idle Cam Linkage Clearance	Fast Idle Speed (Hot Engine)	Dechoke Clearance	Dashpot Setting	Choke Setting
1979	9DA2	①	5/16	25/32	—	.125	.113	1600	.300	—	1 Rich

①—For Air/Fuel ratio & Idle @ CO%, see Tune-Up chart in car chapter.

ROCHESTER 2SE ADJUSTMENT SPECIFICATIONS

Year	Carb. Production No.	Float Level	Accel. Pump	Choke Coil Lever	Choke Rod	Vacuum Break		Air Valve Rod	Choke Setting	Unloader	Fast Idle R.P.M.
						Primary	Secondary				
1979	17059640, 642	1/8	—	.085	17°	20°	37°	.040	1 Rich	49°	2000
	17059641, 643	1/8	—	.085	17°	23 1/2°	37°	.040	1 Rich	49°	1800
	17059674, 676	13/64	—	.085	18°	22°	—	.025	2 Rich	32°	—
	17059675, 677	13/64	—	.085	18°	22°	—	.025	1 Rich	32°	—
	17059740, 742	1/8	—	.085	17°	20°	37°	.040	1 Rich	49°	2000
	17059741, 764	1/8	—	.085	17°	20°	37°	.040	1 Rich	49°	2100
	17059765	1/8	—	.085	17°	23 1/2°	37°	.040	1 Rich	49°	2100
	17059767	1/8	—	.085	17°	23 1/2°	37°	.040	1 Rich	49°	2100

1979 CARBURETOR ADJUSTMENT SPECIFICATIONS

ROCHESTER MONOJET 1ME ADJUSTMENT SPECIFICATIONS

Year	Carb. Part No.	Float Level	Metering Rod	Choke Coil Lever	Choke Rod	Vacuum Break	Unloader	Choke Setting	Fast Idle R.P.M.
1979	17059013	⅜	.095	.120	.180	.200	.400	Index	1800
	17059014	⅜	.095	.120	.180	.200	.400	Index	2000
	17059020	⅜	.095	.120	.180	.200	.400	Index	2000
	17059314	⅜	.100	.120	.190	.245	.400	Index	2000

ROCHESTER QUADRAJET M4M SERIES ADJUSTMENT SPECIFICATIONS

Year	Carb. Production No.	Float Level	Pump Rod Hole	Pump Rod Adj.	Bowl Vent	Fast Idle (Bench)	Choke Coil Lever	Choke Rod	Vacuum Break Front	Vacuum Break Rear	Air-Valve Dash-pot	Choke Setting	Choke Unloader	Air-Valve Valve Spring Wind-Up
1979	17058263	17/32	Outer	⅜	—	3	.120	23°	28°	38°	.030	Index	35°	⅝
	17059202, 204	15/32	Inner	¼	—	2	.120	38°	27°	—	.015	1 Lean	38°	⅞
	17059203	15/32	Inner	¼	—	2	.120	38°	27°	—	.015	2 Lean	38°	⅞
	17059208, 209	15/32	Inner	9/32	—	—	.120	46°	—	23°	.015	1 Lean	42°	⅞
	17059210, 228	15/32	Inner	9/32	—	2	.120	38°	27°	—	.015	1 Lean	38°	1
	17059211	15/32	Inner	9/32	—	2	.120	38°	27°	—	.015	2 Lean	38°	1
	17059230	13/32	Inner	9/32	—	1½	.120	16°	25°	39°	.030	2 Rich	25°	½
	17059232	13/32	Inner	9/32	—	2¼	.120	16°	26°	28°	.030	2 Rich	25°	½
	17059240, 243	7/32	Inner	9/32	—	—	.120	14½°	21°	21°	.015	1 Rich	30°	¾
	17059241	5/16	Outer	⅜	—	—	.120	18°	21½°	20½°	.015	1 Rich	38°	¾
	17059250, 253	13/32	Inner	9/32	—	—	.120	18°	23°	30½°	.030	2 Rich	35°	½
	17059259	13/32	Inner	9/32	—	3	.120	18°	23°	30½°	.030	2 Rich	35°	—
	17059271	9/16	Outer	⅜	—	—	.120	20°	25°	36°	.030	1 Rich	33°	⅝
	17059272	15/32	Outer	⅜	—	—	.120	14½°	24°	32°	.030	2 Rich	35°	⅝
	17059502, 504	15/32	Inner	¼	—	2	.120	38°	28°	—	.015	2 Lean	38°	⅞
	17059530, 532	13/32	Inner	9/32	—	2¼	.120	16°	26°	28°	.030	2 Rich	25°	½
	17059540, 543	7/32	Inner	9/32	—	—	.120	14½°	21°	23°	.015	1 Rich	38°	¾
	17059553	13/32	Inner	9/32	—	—	.120	19°	24°	36½°	.030	2 Rich	35°	½
	17059555	13/32	Inner	9/32	—	—	.120	19°	26°	36½°	.030	2 Rich	35°	½
	17059582, 584	15/32	Outer	11/32	—	2	.120	38°	33°	—	.015	1 Lean	46°	⅞

HOLLEY 5210 ADJUSTMENT SPECIFICATIONS

Year	Carb. Part No.	Float Level (Dry)	Float Drop	Pump Position	Fast Idle Cam Index	Vacuum Plate Pulldown	Vacuum Break Primary	Vacuum Break Secondary	Fast Idle Setting	Unloader Setting	Choke Setting

CHEVROLET CHEVETTE

Year	Carb. Part No.	Float Level (Dry)	Float Drop	Pump Position	Fast Idle Cam Index	Vacuum Plate Pulldown	Vacuum Break Primary	Vacuum Break Secondary	Fast Idle Setting	Unloader Setting	Choke Setting
1979	466361, 362	.500	—	—	.110	—	—	—	2500	.350	2 Rich
	466363, 364	.500	—	—	.110	—	—	—	2500	.350	2 Rich
	466365, 366	.500	—	—	.130	—	—	—	2500	.350	1 Rich
	466367, 368	.500	—	—	.130	—	—	—	2500	.350	1 Rich
	466369, 370	.500	—	—	.110	—	—	—	2500	.350	2 Rich
	466371, 372	.500	—	—	.110	—	—	—	2500	.350	2 Rich
	466373, 374	.500	—	—	.130	—	—	—	2500	.350	1 Rich
	466375, 376	.500	—	—	.130	—	—	—	2500	.350	1 Rich

HOLLEY MODEL 6500 ADJUSTMENT SPECIFICATIONS

Year	Carb. Model	Float Level	Pump Level Hole No.	Choke Plate Pulldown	Fast Idle Cam Clearance	Dechoke	Choke Setting
FORD & MERCURY							
1979	D9EE-AFC	15/32	#2	.24	.12	.24	2 Rich
	D9EE-AGC	15/32	#2	.24	.12	.24	2 Rich
	D9EE-AJC	15/32	#2	.24	.12	.24	1 Rich
	D9EE-AKC	15/32	#2	.24	.12	.24	1 Rich

Flasher Locations

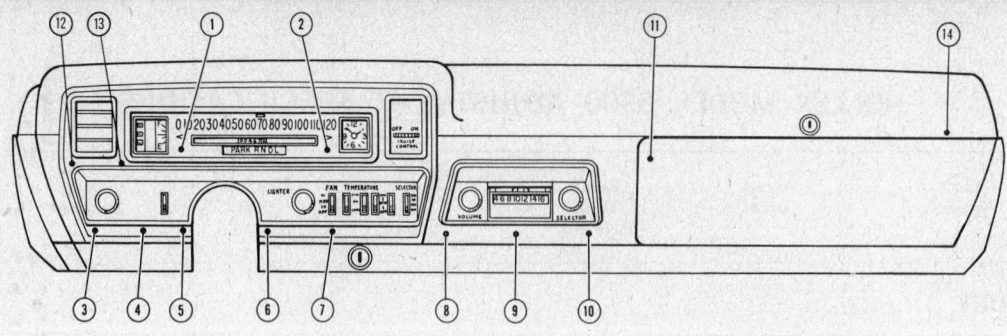

CAR	1974 TSF	1974 HWF	1975 TSF	1975 HWF	1976 TSF	1976 HWF	1977 TSF	1977 HWF	1978 TSF	1978 HWF
American Motors	3	⑧	3	⑨	3	⑨	3	⑨	3	③
Astre & Vega	5	3	5	3	5	3	5	3	—	—
Barracuda & Challenger	④	⑤	—	—	—	—	—	—	—	—
Buick, Special & Century	3	3	3	3	4	3	4	3	3	3
Buick Apollo & Skylark	10	3	10	3	10	3	10	3	10	3
Cadillac Exc. Seville	②	3	②	3	②	3	3⑪	3	3⑪	3
Cadillac Seville	—	—	—	—	4	3	4	3	4	3
Camaro	8	3	8	3	4	3	4	3	4	3
Chevelle, Malibu & Monte Carlo	4	3	4	3	4	3	4	3	3	3
Chevette	—	—	—	—	13	3	13	3	13	3
Chevrolet	6	3	6	3	7	3	3	3	3	3
Chevrolet Nova	10	3	10	3	10	3	10	3	10	3
Chrysler & Imperial	5	5	5	5	5	3	5	3	5	3
Comet & Maverick	11	11	4	3	4	3	4	3	—	—
Cordoba	—	—	3	6	13	⑤	13	⑤	13	4
Corvette	①	3	①	3	①	3	①	3	①	3
Cougar & LTD II	5	5	5	5	3	3	4	4	4	4
Dart & Valiant	④	⑤	4	5	5	5	—	—	—	—
Dodge & Plymouth Full Size	④	⑤	5	5	5	5	5	3	5	3
Dodge & Plymouth Intermediate	④	⑤	13	⑤	⑩	4⑦	⑫	3⑬	⑫	3
Dodge Omni & Plymouth Horizon	—	—	—	—	—	—	—	—	3	3
Firebird & LeMans	3	3	3	3	3	3	4	3	3	3
Ford & Mercury Full Size	3	4	3	4	3	4	3	3	3	3
Ford Fairmont & Mercury Zephyr	—	—	—	—	—	—	—	—	14	11
Ford Pinto & Mercury Bobcat	11	11	11	11	11	11	11	11	11	11
Granada, Monarch & Versailles	—	—	8	4	10	4	6	4	10	4
Grand Am & Grand Prix	3	3	3	3	3	3	3	3	3	3
Lincoln Continental	7⑥	7⑥	11⑥	3	10⑥	3	10⑥	3	10⑥	3
Montego, Torino & Elite	5	5	3	3	3	3	—	—	—	—
Monza, Skyhawk, Starfire & Sunbird	—	—	5	3	12	12	12	12	12⑭	4
Mustang II	7	7	7	7	7	7	7	7	7	7
Oldsmobile	4	3	4	3	4	3	3	3	3	3
Oldsmobile Cutlass	4	3	4	3	4	3	4	3	3	3
Olds. Omega	10	3	10	3	10	3	10	3	10	3
Oldsmobile Toronado	4	3	4	3	4	3	4	3	4	3
Pontiac	3	3	3	3	3	5	3	3	3	3
Pont. Phoenix & Ventura	10	3	10	3	10	3	10	3	10	3
Thunderbird	3	3	3	3	3	3	4	4	4	4

TSF: Turn Signal Flasher.　　　　HWF: Hazard Warning Flasher.

①—Extreme lower right corner of instrument panel.
②—On the underside of steering column lower cover.
③—Location 3 on Concord & Gremlin. Location 4 on Matador. Location 5 on Pacer.
④—Behind instrument panel, on right side of ash tray.
⑤—On right side of brake pedal support.
⑥—Location 3 on Mark IV & V.
⑦—On right side of brake pedal support on Charger, Coronet & Fury models.
⑧—Location 6 on Gremlin & Hornet. Location 4 on Ambassador & Matador.

⑨—Location 6 on Gremlin & Hornet. Location 4 on Matador. Location 5 on Pacer.
⑩—Location 3 on Aspen & Volaré. Location 13 on Charger, Coronet & Fury.
⑪—On underside of steering column lower cover on Eldorado models.
⑫—Location 3 on Aspen, Diplomat, LeBaron & Volaré. Location 13 on Charger, Fury, Magnum & Monaco.
⑬—On right side of brake pedal support on Charger, Fury & Monaco.
⑭—Location 5 on Monza "S" Coupe, Sunbird Coupe & all Sta. Wag.

Auto Care Guide

INTRODUCTION

This chapter has been compiled for the absolute novice in auto care. It will enable you to perform routine chores on your car that will result in dollar savings and provide the satisfaction of knowing that you have had a hand in keeping your car in a safe operating condition. Many of the parts required to perform these chores are available at mass merchandisers and certainly at automotive supply stores. Things such as anti-freeze and engine oil can even be found on the shelves of many supermarket food stores. Using this information, you can join the millions of car owners who are doing some of their own car maintenance.

BATTERY SERVICE

Construction & Operation

To understand why batteries malfunction, some knowledge of batteries is important. Simply stated, the battery is constructed of two unlike materials, a positive plate and a negative plate and a porous separator between the two plates, Fig. 1. This assembly placed in a suitable battery case and filled slightly above the top of the plates with electrolyte (sulphuric acid and distilled water) forms a cell. The 12 volt battery is composed of 6 cells interconnected by plate straps. Note that batteries have varying number of plates per cell, but each cell in any given battery has the same number of plates.

The battery performs the following four basic functions in a vehicle:
1. Supplies electrical energy to the starter motor to crank and start the engine and also to the ignition system while the engine is being started.
2. Supplies electrical energy for accessories such as radio, tape deck, heater and also lights when engine is not running and the ignition switch is in the "OFF" or the "Accessory" position.
3. Supplies additional electrical energy for accessories while the engine is running when the output of the alternator is exceeded by the various accessories.
4. The battery also stabilizes voltage in the electrical system. Satisfactory operation of the ignition system and any other electrical device is impossible with a damaged or weak or even underpowered (low rating) battery.

Sealed Batteries

Sealed batteries, otherwise called "Maintenance Free" or "Freedom" batteries, Fig. 2, are available on some vehicles, and can also be purchased from other sources.

The sealed batteries have unique chemistry and construction methods which provide the following advantages:

Water never needs to be added to the battery.

The battery is completely sealed except for two small vent holes on the side. The vent holes allow what small amount of gases are produced in the battery to escape. The special chemical composition inside the battery reduces the production of gas to an extremely small amount at normal charging voltages.

The battery has a very strong ability to withstand damaging effects of overcharge.

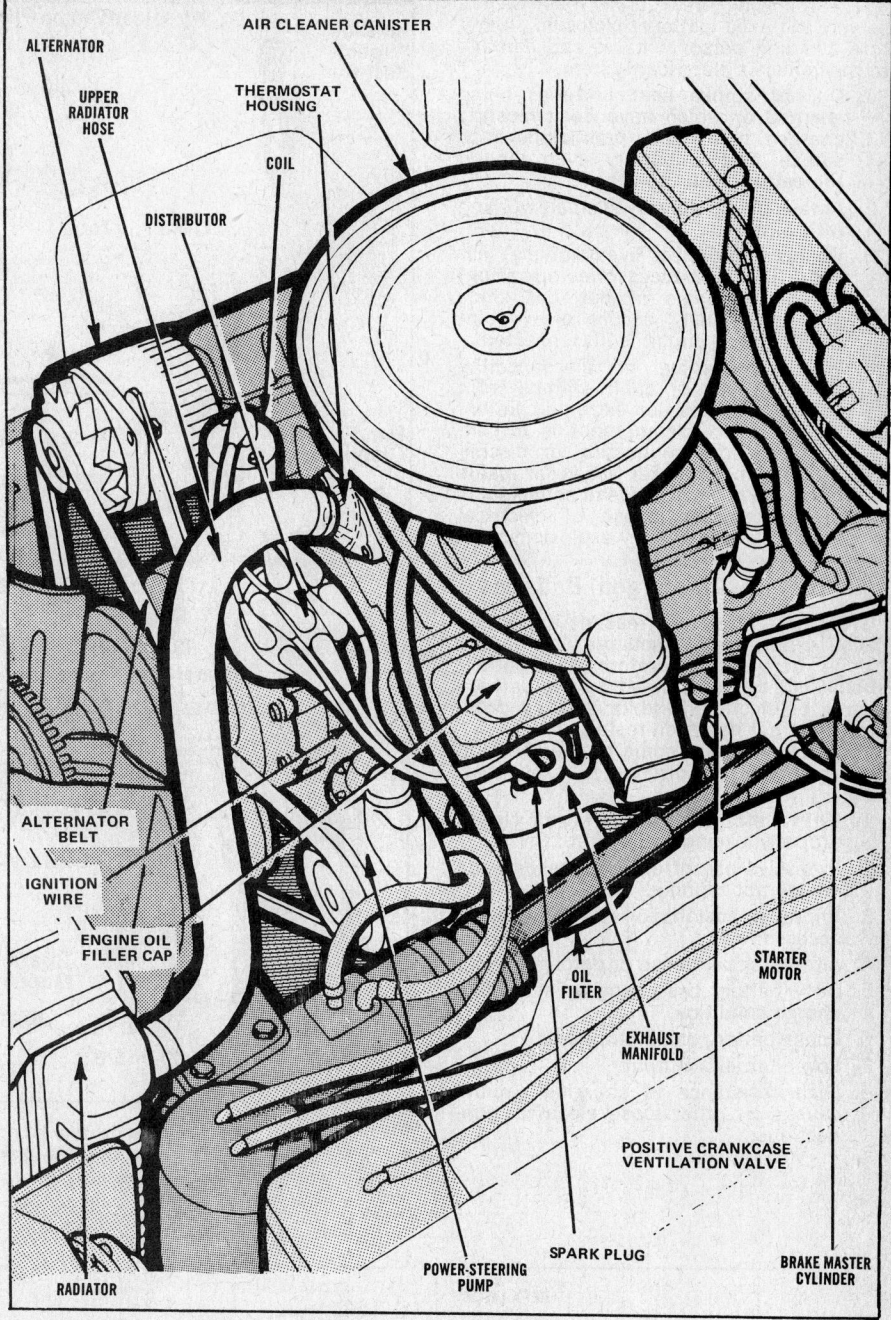

Typical engine compartment

Also, the terminals are sealed tightly to minimize leakage. A charge indicator in the cover indicates state of charge.

Compared to a conventional battery whose performance decreases steadily with age, the sealed battery delivers more available power at any time during its life. The battery has reduced tendency to self-discharge as compared to a conventional battery.

Safety Precautions

CAUTION:

Electrolyte solution in the battery is a strong and dangerous acid. It is extremely harmful to eyes, skin and clothing. If acid contacts any part of the body, flush immediately with water for a period not less then 15 minutes. If acid is accidentally swallowed, drink large quantities of milk or water, followed by milk of magnesia, a beaten raw egg or vegetable oil and call physician immediately.

Also when batteries are being charged, highly explosive hydrogen and oxygen gases form in each battery cell. Some of this gas escapes through the vent holes in the plugs on top of battery case and forms an explosive atmosphere surrounding the battery. This explosive gas will remain in and/or around the battery for several hours after the battery has been charged. Sparks or flames can ignite this gas and cause a dangerous battery explosion.

Auto Care Guide

The following precautions must be observed to avoid battery explosion, therefore avoiding personal harm and damage to the vehicle's electrical system.

1. Do not smoke near batteries being charged or which have been recently charged. It is a good practice never to smoke near a battery even though the battery is in the vehicle.
2. Always shield your eyes when working with batteries.
3. Do not disconnect live (working) circuits (lights or accessories operating) at the terminals of batteries since sparking usually occurs at a point where such a circuit is disconnected.
4. When connecting or disconnecting booster leads or cable clamps from battery chargers use extreme caution. Make sure the equipment is disconnected before connecting or disconnecting the booster leads or cable clamps. Poor booster lead connections are a common cause of electrical arcing causing battery explosions.

Causes of Discharged Batteries

There are numerous reasons that could cause a battery to discharge and appear to be defective, therefore the battery should not be condemned as the primary source of electrical and/or starting problems before it has been tested.

The following are some of the common causes that could discharge a good battery.

1. Lights left "ON" or doors not closed properly leaving dome light "ON".
2. Excessive use of accessories with the engine not running.
3. Improper installation of aftermarket accessories.
4. Alternator belt loose or damaged.
5. Dirty battery case causing a self-discharge condition.
6. Loose battery cable terminals.
7. Low alternator output.
8. High resistance in charging circuits caused by other loose electrical connections.

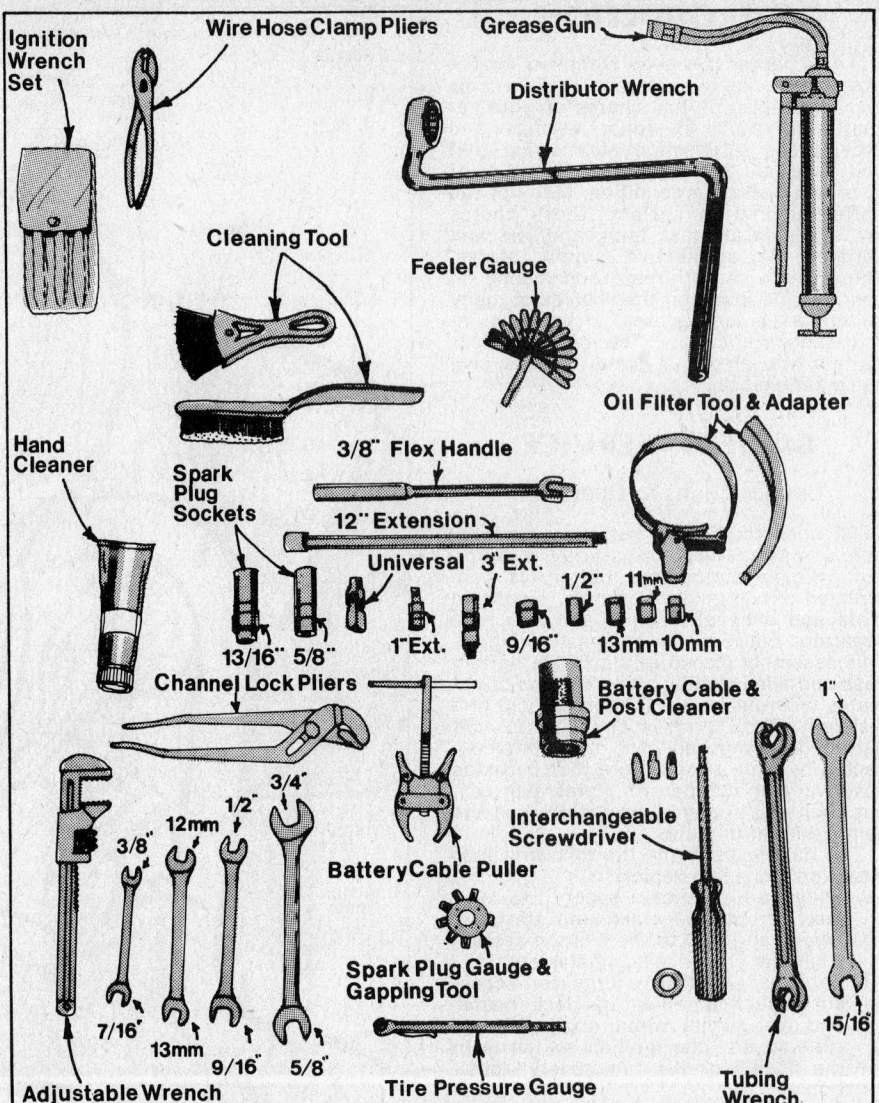

Typical tool kit necessary to perform the maintenance procedures in this section

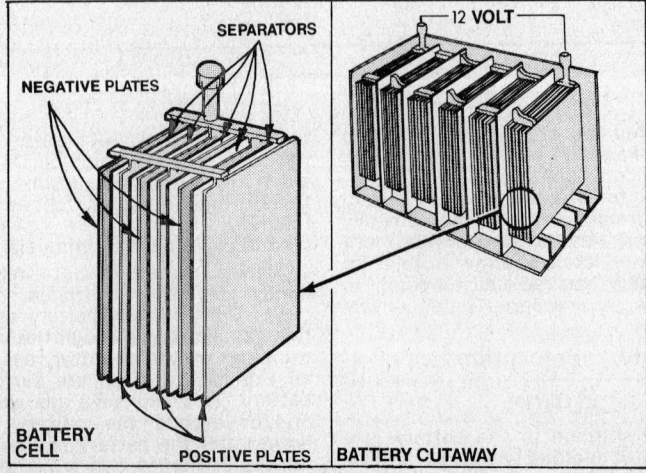

Fig. 1   Battery construction

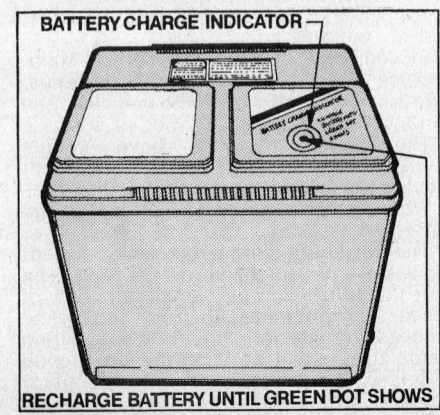

Fig. 2   Typical maintenance free battery

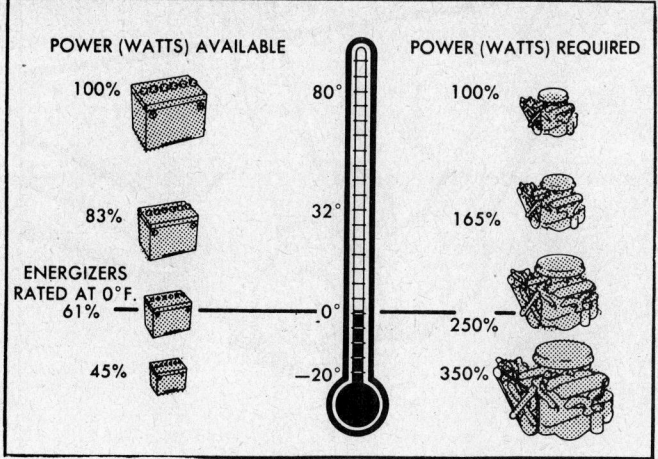

Fig. 3 Battery energy versus falling
temperature comparison chart

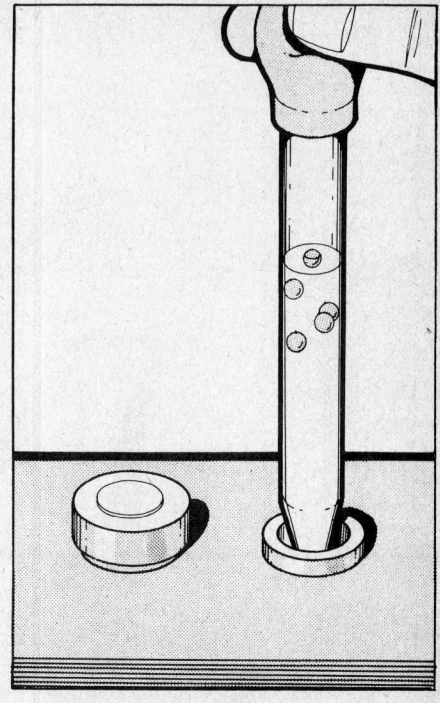

Fig. 4 Checking specific gravity
of electrolyte

Fig. 6 Cleaning battery terminal and post

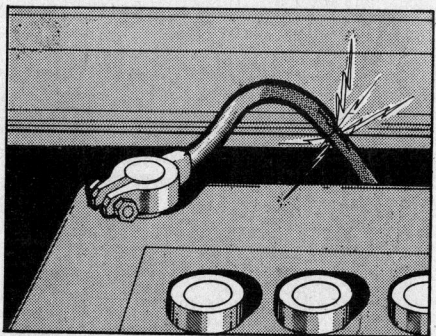

Fig. 7 Frayed insulation causing short circuit
between battery cable and body of vehicle

a battery at 0°F., batteries with the same Ampere-Hour ratings can have various 0°F. cranking capacities. The higher quality battery will have a higher Ampere-Hour rating and a higher cranking capacity rating at 0°F. Note that battery capacity will increase with: 1) larger number of plates per cell 2) larger size of plates 3) larger battery case size allowing for more electrolyte solution.

Selecting A Replacement Battery

Long and troublefree service can be more assured when the capacity or wattage rating of the replacement battery is at least equal to the wattage rating of the battery originally engineered for the application by the manufacturer.

The use of an undersize battery may result in poor performance and early failure. Fig. 3 shows how battery power shrinks while the need for engine cranking power increases with falling temperatures. Sub-zero temperatures reduce capacity of a fully charged battery to 45% of its nor-

Battery Rating & Capacity

The two most commonly used ratings are the 20 hour rating at 80°F. and the cold cranking load capacity of the battery at 0°F, specified in amps. Batteries are also rated by watts (PWR) Peak Watt Rating which is actually the cold cranking ability of the battery at 0°F.

Yet another battery rating method is the reserve capacity rating in minutes. The purpose of this rating is to determine the length of time a vehicle can be operated

with a faulty charging system (malfunctioning alternator or regulator). Batteries are normally marketed by the Ampere-Hour rating which is based on the 20 hour rating. The Ampere-Hour rating is also normally stamped on the battery case or on a label attached to the battery. A battery capable of furnishing 4 amps for a period of 20 hours is classified as a 80 ampere hour battery (4 amps x 20 hours = 80).

The Ampere-Hour rating should not be confused with the cranking performance of

Watt Rating	5 Amperes	10 Amperes	20 Amperes	30 Amperes	40 Amperes	50 Amperes
Below 2450	10 Hours	5 Hours	2½ Hours	2 Hours		
2450–2950	12 Hours	6 Hours	3 Hours	2 Hours	1½ Hours	
Above 2950	15 Hours	7½ Hours	3¼ Hours	2 Hours	1¾ Hours	1½ Hours

Fig. 5 Battery charging guide

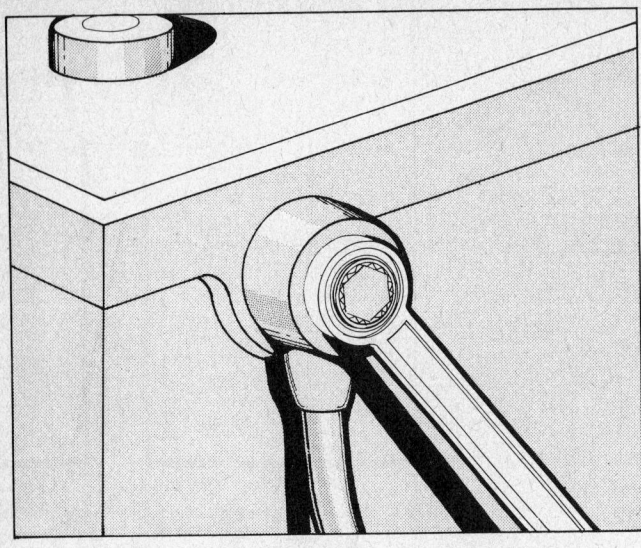

Fig. 8   Removing side type battery terminal

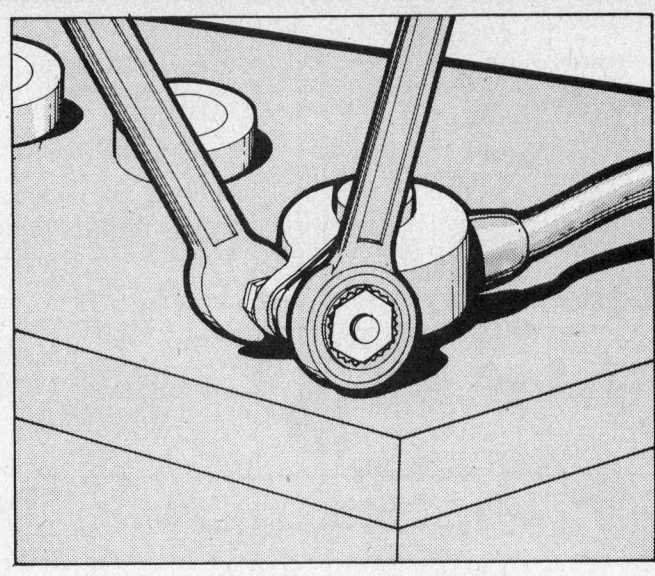

Fig. 9   Removing bolt type terminal

mal power and at the same time increase cranking load to 3½ times the normal warm weather load.

Hot weather can also place excessive electrical loads on the battery. Difficulty in starting may occur when cranking is attempted shortly after a hot engine has been turned off or stalls. High compression engines can be as difficult to start under such conditions as on the coldest winter day. Consequently, good performance can be obtained only if the battery has ample capacity to cope with these conditions.

A battery of greater capacity should be considered if the electrical load has been increased through the addition of accessories or if driving conditions are such that the generator cannot keep the battery in a charged condition.

On applications where heavy electrical loads are encountered, a higher output generator that will supply a charge during low speed operation may be required to increase battery life and improve battery performance.

Testing Battery (Specific Gravity)

A hydrometer can be used to measure the specific gravity of the electrolyte in each cell. There a several types of hydrometers available, the least expensive consists of a glass tube, a rubber bulb at the end of the tube and several balls within

the tube Fig. 4. To use this type, the specific gravity of the battery must be interpreted by the number of balls which float to the surface of the electrolyte and following the manufacturers instructions.

The hydrometer indicates the concentration of the electrolyte.

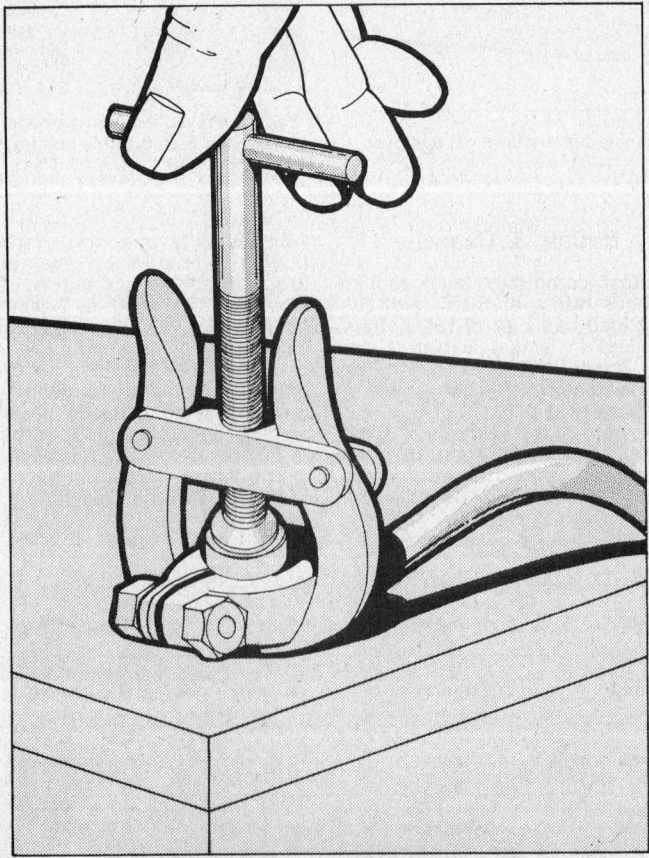

Fig. 11   Removing battery terminal using battery terminal puller

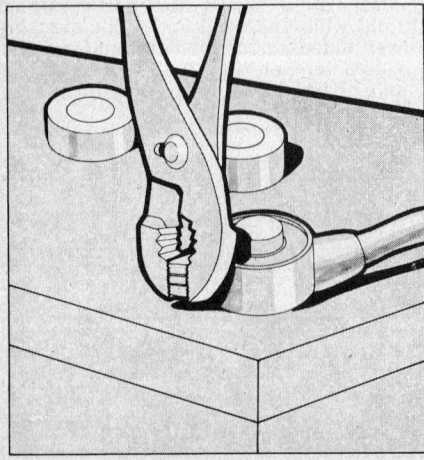

Fig. 10   Removing spread type terminal

Boost Starting A Vehicle With A Discharged Battery

1. Be sure that the ignition key is in the off position and that all accessories and lights are off.
2. Shield eyes. Use goggles or similar eye protection.
3. Connect the booster cables from the positive (+) battery terminal of the discharged battery (vehicle to be started) to the positive (+) battery terminal of the vehicle used as the booster.
4. Connect one end of the other cable to negative (−) terminal of the good battery.
5. Connect the other end of the cable to engine bolthead or similar good contact spot on the vehicle being started.

CAUTION: Never connect to negative terminal of dead battery.

NOTE: To prevent damage to other electrical components on the vehicle being started, make certain that engine is at idle speed before disconnecting jumper cables.

Charging The Battery

There are two separate methods of recharging batteries which differ basically in the rate of charge.

Slow Charging Method

Slow charging is the best and only method of completely recharging a battery. This method, when properly applied, may be used safely under all possible conditions of the battery providing the electrolyte is at proper level and the battery is capable of being fully charged. The normal charging rate is 5 amperes.

A fully charged battery is indicated when all cell specific gravities do not increase when checked at three one hour intervals and all cells are gassing freely.

Charge periods of 24 hours or more may be required because of the low charging rate. See charging guide Fig. 5.

Quick Charging Method

In order to get a car back on the road in the least amount of time, it is sometimes necessary to quick charge a battery. The battery cannot be brought up to a full charged condition by the quick charge method. It can be substantially recharged or boosted but, in order to bring it to a fully charged condition, the charging cycle must be finished by charging at a low or normal rate. Some quick chargers have a provision for finishing the charging cycle at a low rate to bring the battery up to a fully charged condition.

CAUTION: Too high a current during quick charging will damage battery plates.

Battery Cable Service

NOTE: At regular intervals, perform a visual inspection of the battery.

This inspection should be performed when any of the underhood maintenance items such as engine oil, transmission fluid or radiator coolant level are checked.

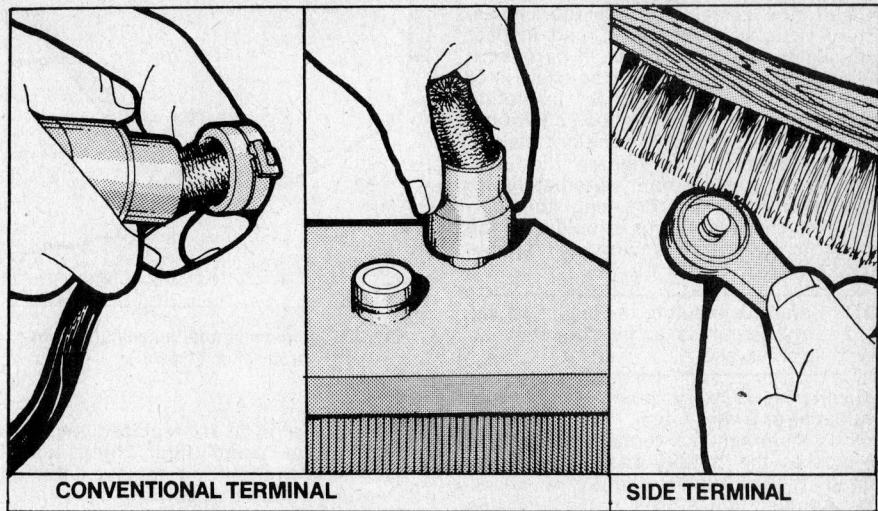

CONVENTIONAL TERMINAL · SIDE TERMINAL

Fig. 12 Cleaning battery terminals

1. Clean any heavy accumulation of dirt or corrosion on the battery terminals and battery tray with a wire brush, Fig. 6. Finish cleaning with a solution of baking soda and water. Diluted ammonia can also be used as a washing agent. Throughly flush battery with clean water.

NOTE: Baking soda and ammonia neutralize battery acid. Therefore make sure that these agents are kept out of the battery by keeping the battery caps tightly in place.

2. Check for damaged cable insulation, Fig. 7. Damaged insulation can cause the cable to short out against the body of the vehicle or other accessories. Cables in this condition should be replaced immediately.
3. Check level of electrolyte. If required, add water as described further on.
4. Make sure that battery is securely held in place. A loose or broken bracket can result in battery damage (both internally and externally) from excessive vibration.

Battery Cable, Replace

NOTE: When disconnecting battery cables, first make sure that all accessories are off, disconnect the negative battery cable and then the positive cable. Make sure to reconnect cables in the reverse order of removal.

1. On side terminal batteries, loosen the retaining bolts using a 5/16-inch wrench and disconnect the cable from the battery, Fig. 8.
2. On all other type batteries, loosen the cable retaining bolt using a 1/2-inch or 9/16-inch box wrench, Fig. 9 and lift the cable off the battery posts. Some cables can be removed by squeezing the tabs on the cable terminal using a pair of pliers, Fig. 10, and lifting the cable off the battery posts.
3. If the battery terminals are difficult to remove, use a terminal puller, Fig. 11. Place the legs of the puller underneath the terminal and tighten the puller screw until the terminal is re-

moved.

4. Clean the cable terminals and battery posts using a terminal and post wire brush, Fig. 12.
5. Clean the battery top using a solution of soda and water. Make sure that the battery is thoroughly cleaned and dried. Make sure that you cover the battery caps to avoid entry of the soda and water solution into the battery.
6. To install the cables on a side terminal battery, place the cables onto the battery and tighten the retaining screws using a 5/16-inch wrench.
7. To install the cables on all other types of batteries, place the cables on the battery post and force them all the way down. If the cable is not completely bottomed, spread the cable terminal slightly with a screwdriver, until the terminal is properly positioned.
8. Tighten the terminal bolts using a 1/2-inch or 9/16-inch box wrench.
9. Coat the outside of the terminals with petroleum jelly to prevent corrosion.

Replacing Battery

Careless installation of a new battery can ruin the battery. In removing the old battery, note the location of the positive battery post so the new battery can be installed in the same position. Always remove the negative (ground) cable first.

Use an open-end wrench to loosen the clamp. If the nut is very tight, use one wrench on the head of the bolt and the other on the nut, to avoid straining and possibly cracking the battery cover. A pair of battery pliers can be used to loosen the nut, but a wrench should always be used on the head of the bolt.

If a cable terminal is corroded to the post, don't try to loosen it by hammering, or by resting a tool on the battery and prying—either method can break the battery container. Use a screw type terminal puller, Fig. 11, or spread the cable terminals slightly with a screwdriver.

Clean any corrosion from the cables, battery case, or hold-downs, and inspect them. Paint any corroded steel parts with acid-proof paint. Make sure the cable is of the correct size and that its insulation and clamp terminal are in good condition.

Put the new battery in position, making sure it sits level, and tighten the hold-downs a little at a time, alternately, to avoid distorting and breaking the battery case. The hold-downs should be snug enough to prevent bouncing, but should not be too tight.

NOTE: Before connecting the cables, check the battery terminals to be sure the battery is not reversed.

Clean the battery posts bright with sandpaper or a wire brush.

Don't hammer the terminals down on the posts—the battery case may crack. Spread the terminals slightly if necessary. Connect the starter cable first and the negative (ground) cable last, tightening the terminal bolts after making sure that the cables don't interfere with the vent plugs or rub against the hold-downs.

LUBRICATION, OIL CHANGE, FILTERS & PCV VALVE SERVICE

Engine Oil & Filter Change

NOTE: Engine oil and filter should be changed at intervals recommended by the vehicle manufacturer.

1. Operate engine and allow to reach operating temperature, then turn ignition off.
2. Place drain pan under engine oil pan, then using a suitable wrench remove drain plug, Fig. 13.
3. Allow engine oil to thoroughly drain into pan, then replace drain plug.

NOTE: Do not overtighten drain plug, it can strip the threads in oil pan very easily.

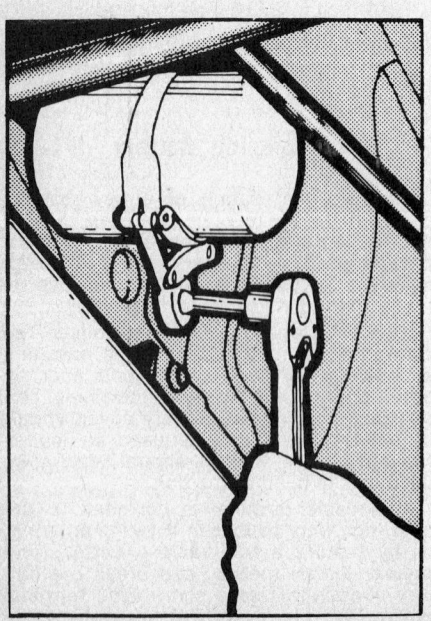

Fig. 14   Oil filter removal (typical)

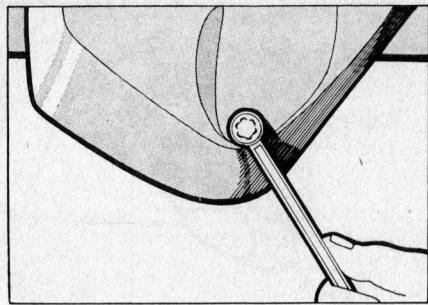

Fig. 13   Removing and installing oil pan drain plug (typical)

4. If oil filter is to be replaced, position drain pan under filter, then install oil filter wrench and remove filter by turning counter clockwise, Fig. 14.

NOTE: Ensure old oil filter gasket is not on the filter adapter on the engine. Clean adapter before installing new filter.

5. Coat new oil filter gasket with engine oil, then position filter on adapter, Fig. 15. Hand tighten filter until gasket contacts adapter face, then tighten filter one additional turn. Wipe filter and adapter with a clean cloth.

NOTE: Ensure gasket is in position on filter before tightening. Do not use oil filter wrench to tighten filter, hand tighten only.

6. Remove oil filler cap and add quantity of oil specified by manufacturer. Then install filler cap.

NOTE: Only add oil that meets the vehicle manufacturers specifications.

7. Start engine and check to ensure that oil filter and drain plug are not leaking, then turn ignition off.
8. Check oil level to ensure crankcase is full but not overfilled, add oil as necessary.

NOTE: Do not bring oil level above "Full" mark on dipstick, overfilling could result in damage to engine gaskets or seals causing leaks.

Air Filter, Replace

All Exc. General Motors 4-140 Engine
1. Remove wing nut, hex nut or other attaching hardware that secures the air cleaner lid. On some models, the air cleaner lid is also secured by clips on the sides of the housing that must be disengaged, Fig. 16.
2. Remove air cleaner lid from housing assembly and lift out air filter element.

NOTE: To check air filter condition, hold a light behind the element, Fig. 17. If no light can be seen through the element, the filter is excessively dirty and must be replaced.

3. Wipe out housing with a clean rag. Be sure not to allow dirt or other foreign material to enter the carburetor.
4. Install new air filter element, Fig. 16.

5. Install lid onto housing assembly and secure with the attaching hardware previously removed.

General Motors 4-140 Engine
1. Remove bolt or nuts securing air cleaner assembly to carburetor.
2. Pull vent pipe from air cleaner. This is the pipe running between the air cleaner and the cam cover (rocker cover).
3. Remove air cleaner assembly from carburetor and discard.
4. Install new air cleaner assembly and secure with bolt or nuts previously removed.

Crankcase Emission Filter

American Motors 6 Cyl. & All Ford Motor Co., Fig. 18.
1. Remove top of air cleaner housing.
2. Remove filter pack from filter retainer and clean out retainer.
3. Install new filter in retainer.
4. Install top of air cleaner.

American Motors V8

This filter is located in the sealed oil filler cap. The filter must be cleaned at mileage intervals recommended by the manufacturer by applying light air pressure in reverse direction of normal flow then lightly oil the filter with clean engine oil. If the filter is deteriorated, the oil filler cap must be replaced.

Chrysler Corp.

This filter must be cleaned at mileage intervals recommended by the manufacturer. Disconnect hose from filter and remove filter by pulling it out of the valve cover. Clean filter in kerosene or similar solvent, then lubricate filter by filling it with clean SAE 30 engine oil and inverting it to allow excess oil to drain out. Reinstall filter in valve cover and reconnect hose.

General Motors, All, Fig. 18
1. Remove top of air cleaner housing.
2. Disconnect hose from filter which leads to valve cover.
3. Remove clip which retains filter to air cleaner housing and remove filter.

Coat Gasket With Engine Oil

Fig. 15   Oil filter installation (typical)

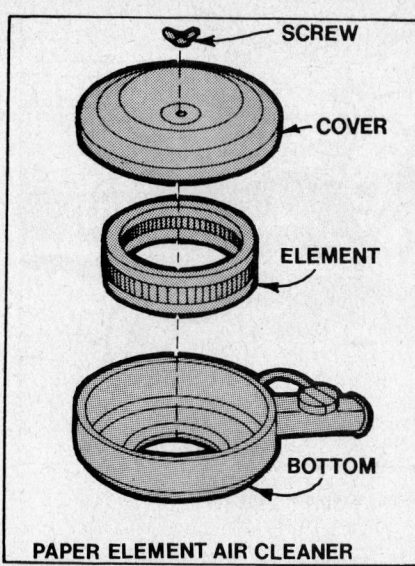

PAPER ELEMENT AIR CLEANER

Fig. 16   Replacing air filter (typical)

4. Position new filter in air cleaner housing and install retaining clip.
5. Connect hose to filter and install top of air cleaner housing.

Fuel Filter, Replace

Inline

NOTE: Inline fuel filter is located between fuel pump and carburetor Fig. 19.

1. Remove air cleaner, if necessary.

NOTE: On Pinto models with 1600cc engine, remove battery.

2. Loosen fuel hose clamps, then disconnect hoses and remove fuel filter Fig. 20.

NOTE: On some models, fuel filter may be attached to carburetor of fuel line tubing. On these models use suitable wrench to remove filter.

3. Reverse procedure to install, then start engine and check for fuel leaks.

NOTE: Before installing, refer to fuel filter body markings, which indicate the direction in which the fuel filter should be installed.

In-Carburetor

NOTE: The carburetor fuel filter is located in carburetor housing where fuel inlet line is connected to carburetor.

1. Remove air cleaner.
2. Position back up wrench on fuel filter fitting, then using a suitable wrench disconnect fuel inlet line Fig. 21.
3. Remove fuel filter fitting, filter and spring from carburetor.
4. Position spring and filter into carburetor, then install gasket and fitting.

NOTE: Position fuel filter in carburetor with open end facing fitting.

5. With back up wrench on fuel filter fitting, carefully connect and tighten fuel inlet line using a suitable wrench Fig. 21.
6. Start engine and check for leaks, then

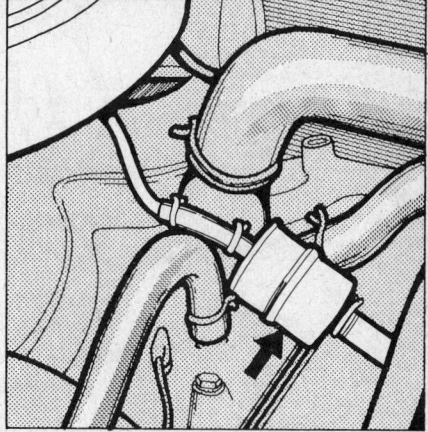

Fig. 19   Typical location of in-line fuel filter

install air cleaner.

PCV Valve, Replace

NOTE: To check PCV valve, remove valve from grommet and shake valve. A metallic clicking noise should be heard, indicating valve is free. If valve does not move freely, it should be replaced. Do not attempt to clean valve.

1. Remove PCV valve from grommet, then disconnect hose, Fig. 22.

NOTE: On American Motors models, PCV valve is located on valve cover on 6 cylinder engine and on intake manifold on V8 engine. On Chrysler Corp. models, valve is located on valve cover. On Ford Motor Co. models, valve is located on crankcase oil separator on 1600cc and 2000cc engines, in PCV valve hose on 2300cc engine, on carburetor spacer on V6 engine, on valve cover on inline 6 cylinder engine and in oil filler cap on V8 engine. On General Motors Corp. models, valve is located on valve cover on 4 cylinder and inline 6 cylinder engines, on intake manifold on V6 engines and on valve cover or intake manifold on V8 engines, depending on model.

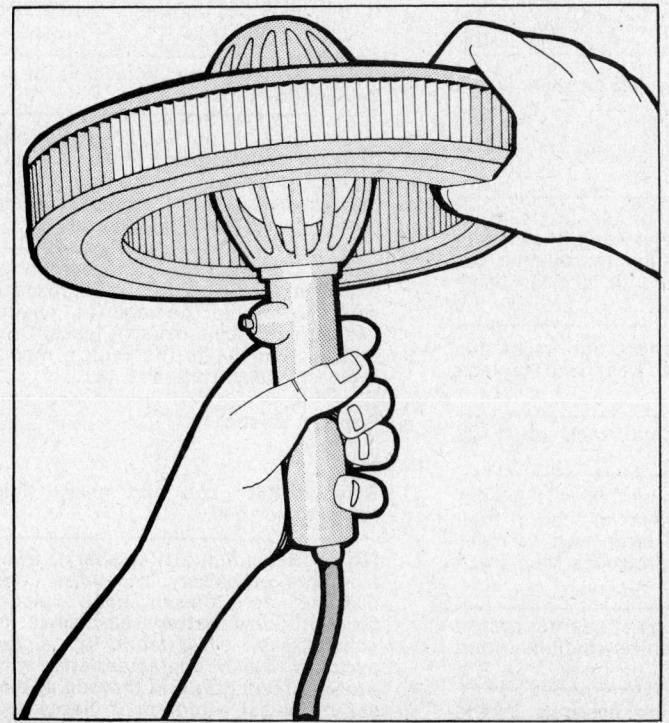

Fig. 17   Checking air filter condition

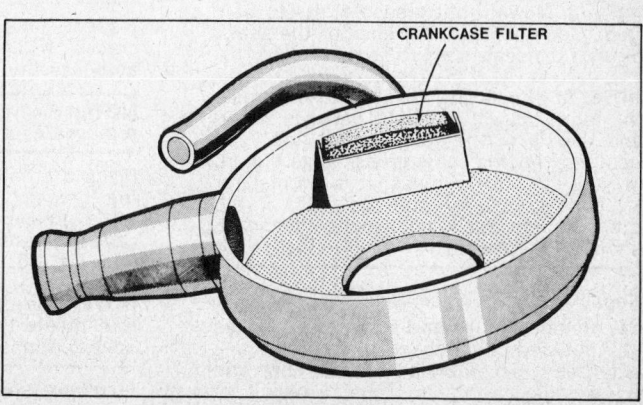

Fig. 18   Typical crankcase filter

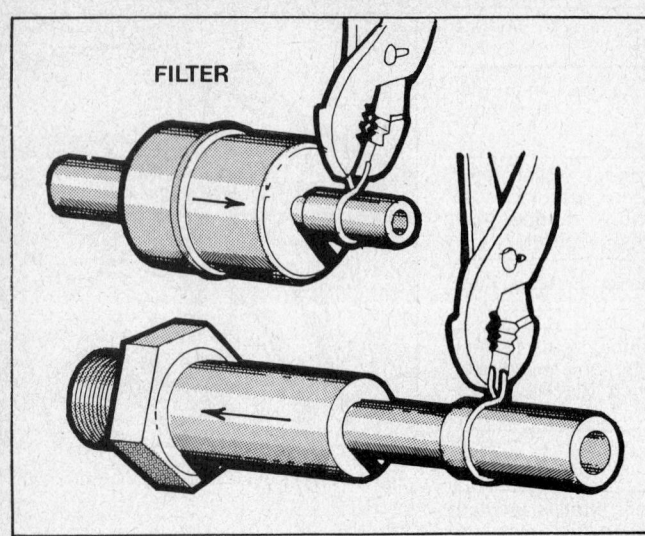

Fig. 20   Removing fuel hose from fuel filter (typical)

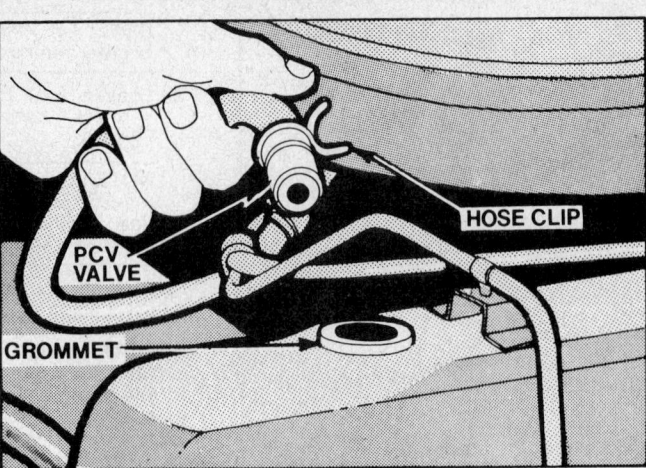

Fig. 22   PCV valve replacement (typical)

2. Install new PCV valve on grommet and connect hose.

   NOTE: Ensure valve is properly seated in grommet.

Chassis Lubricating

The first time you do a grease job you will spend much of the time looking for the fittings Figs. 23 and 24.

As you find a fitting, wipe it off with a clean rag. This will help you spot it later and also prevent you from injecting dirt with the grease.

The injection tip of the grease gun should be a catch fit on the fitting nipple. That is, once in place it will not slip off. Slight, straight-on pressure is all that is necessary for the gun tip to engage the fitting. Once that is done, pump the handle. Follow the recommendations below to ensure proper lubrication and also prevent damage to the seals:

American Motors and Ford:

Pump slowly until the rubber boot can be felt or seen to swell slightly.

Chrysler Corp. and General Motors:

Pump slowly until grease starts to flow from bleed holes at the base of the seals, or until the seals start to swell.

NOTE: If the fitting fails to take grease, the lubricant will ooze out between fitting and the tip of the gun. Do not just keep pumping, hoping some grease is getting in, or you will have a mess. It is normal for a bit of grease to seep out. But if the fitting is obviously not taking grease, it should be replaced.

Repacking Front Wheel Bearings

1. Remove inner and outer bearings as outlined in car chapters.
2. Clean old lubricant from hub and spindle.
3. Clean inner and outer bearings and bearing races with kerosene.

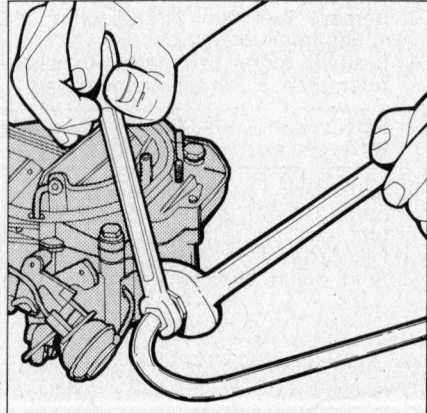

Fig. 21   Disconnecting fuel line

NOTE: Ensure all of old lubricant is removed before repacking. Allow bearings and races to dry thoroughly. Do not use compressed air to clean bearings.

4. Inspect cones, rollers and races for cracks, nicks and wear and replace as necessary.

   NOTE: Bearings and race must be replaced as a unit.

5. Place a small amount of wheel bearing grease in palm of hand, then force grease into large end of roller cage until grease protrudes from small end, Fig. 25.

   NOTE: Use only wheel bearing grease that meets the vehicle manufacturers specifications.

6. Lubricate remaining bearings in the same manner, then install and adjust bearings as outlined in car chapter.

NOTE: Apply a light film of grease to lips of grease retainer before installing.

Checking & Maintaining Fluid Levels

NOTE: When checking fluid levels, ensure vehicle is on a level surface. If vehicle is not level, an accurate fluid level reading cannot be obtained.

Engine Oil Level

1. Warm up engine, then turn ignition off and allow a few minutes for oil to return to crankcase.
2. Remove dipstick and wipe off.
3. Replace dipstick and ensure it is seated in tube.
4. Remove dipstick and inspect to see if oil level is between "Add" and "Full" marks.

   NOTE: Add oil only if level is at or below Add mark.

5. If oil level is at "Add" mark, one quart of oil will bring level to "Full" mark. If oil level is below "Add" mark, add oil as necessary to bring level between Add & Full marks.

   NOTE: Do not bring oil level above "Full" mark, overfilling of crankcase could result in damage to engine gaskets and seals causing leaks. Only add oil that meets the vehicle manufacturers specifications.

6. Replace dipstick.

Battery

1. Remove filler cap and check fluid level in each cell.

   NOTE: Keep flame and sparks away from top of battery, otherwise combustible gases present may explode. Do not allow battery electrolyte to contact skin, eyes, fabric or painted surfaces. Flush contacted area with water immediately and thoroughly and seek medical attention if necessary. Wear eye protection when working on or near battery. Do not wear rings or

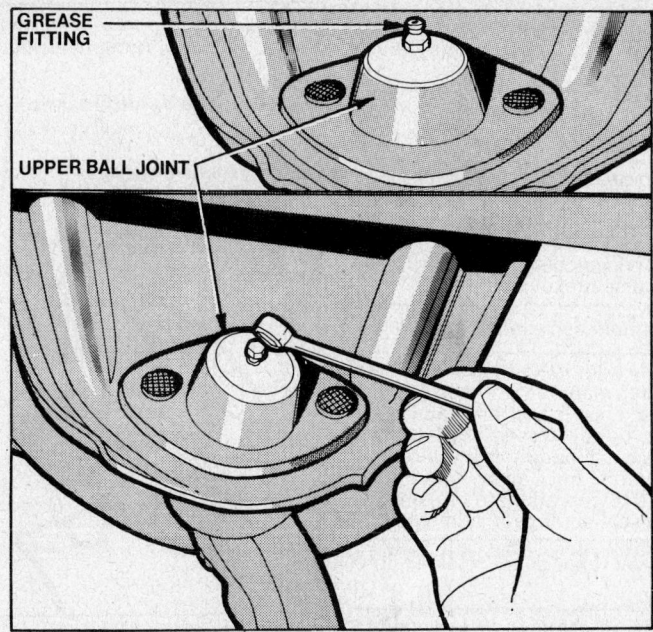

Fig. 23 Identifying fittings (typical). If vehicle is equipped with plugs, the plugs must be removed and a grease fitting installed prior to lubricating

Fig. 25 Repacking front wheel bearings

other metal jewelry when working on or near battery.

2. Add water as required to bring fluid level of each cell up to split ring located at bottom of filler well.

NOTE: In areas where water is known to be hard or have a high mineral or alkali content, distilled water must be used. If water is added during freezing weather, the vehicle should be driven several miles afterwards to mix the water and battery electrolyte.

3. Install filler caps.

Cooling System

NOTE: Add only permanent type anti-freeze that meets the vehicle manufacturers specifications.

CAUTION: Never add large quantities of water into radiator if car has overheated without the engine cooled off or if necessary to service at this time start engine and add water to coolant slowly. This will avoid damage to the engine.

Less Coolant Recovery System

NOTE: Avoid checking coolant level if engine is hot. If coolant level must be checked when engine is hot, muffle radiator cap with a thick cloth, then turn cap counter clockwise until pressure starts to escape. After pressure has been completely relieved, finish removing cap.

1. With engine cold, remove radiator cap and inspect coolant level.
2. Coolant level should be approximately 1 inch below bottom of filler neck.
3. Add solution of 50% water-50% anti-freeze as required.
4. Install radiator cap.

With Coolant Recovery System

NOTE: On these type systems do not remove radiator cap to check coolant level.

1. Start engine and allow to reach operating temperature.
2. Visually inspect coolant level in plastic reservoir.

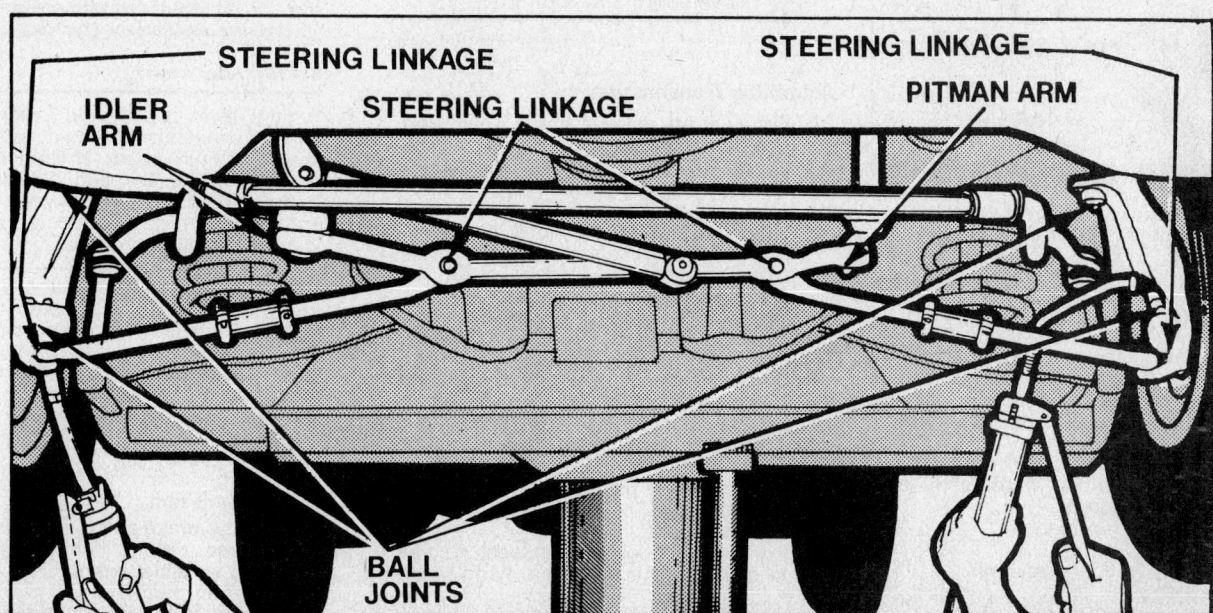

Fig. 24 Typical fitting locations

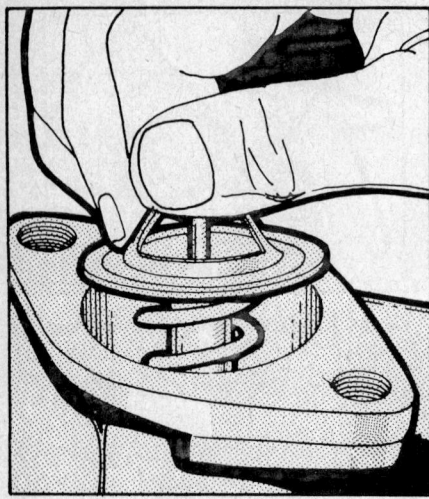

Fig. 26   Replacing thermostat (typical)

Hold Tube Vertical

Do Not Suck In Too Much Coolant

Fig. 27   Checking anti-freeze protection level (typical)

3. On all models except Chrysler Corp. vehicles, coolant level should be between Full and Add marks or at Full Hot mark, depending on reservoir. On Chrysler Corp. vehicles, coolant level should be between the one and two quart marks with engine operating at idle speed.
4. Remove reservoir filler cap and add solution of 50% water-50% anti-freeze as required.
5. Install reservoir filler cap.

Brake Master Cylinder Reservoir

1. Clean master cylinder reservoir cover, then using a screw driver unsnap retainer(s) and remove cover.

NOTE: Do not hold cover over vehicle, otherwise brake fluid may damage finish.

2. Brake fluid level should be 1/4 inch from top of master cylinder reservoir.

NOTE: If brake fluid level is excessively low, the brake linings should be inspected for wear and brake system checked for leaks. Fluid level in reservoirs servicing disc brakes will decrease as disc brake pads wear.

3. Add brake fluid as required.

NOTE: Only add brake fluid that meets the vehicle manufacturers specifications. Use only brake fluid that has been in a tightly closed container to prevent contamination from dirt and moisture. Do not allow petroleum base fluids to contaminate brake fluid, otherwise seal damage may result.

4. Install cover and snap retainer into place.

NOTE: Ensure retainer is locked into cover grooves.

Power Steering Pump Reservoir

1. Start engine and allow to reach operating temperature, and turn ignition off.
2. Clean area around filler cap or dipstick, then remove filler cap or dipstick and inspect fluid level.
3. Fluid level should be between "Full" mark and end of dipstick.

NOTE: On models without dipstick, fluid level should be half way up filler neck.

2. Add fluid as necessary, then install filler cap or dipstick.

NOTE: Only add fluid recommended by the vehicle manufacturer.

Automatic Transmission

1. Firmly apply parking brake, then start and run engine for approximately 10 minutes to bring transmission fluid to operating temperature.

NOTE: Do not run engine in unventilated area. Exhaust gases contain carbon monoxide which could be deadly in unventilated areas.

2. With engine running at idle speed, shift selector lever through all positions, then place lever in Neutral on American Motors and Chrysler Corp. vehicles and in Park on Ford Motor Co. and General Motors Corp. vehicles.
3. Clean dipstick cap, then remove dipstick and wipe off.
4. Replace dipstick and ensure it is seated in tube.
5. Remove dipstick and inspect to see if fluid level is between "Add" and "Full" marks.

NOTE: Add fluid only if level is at or

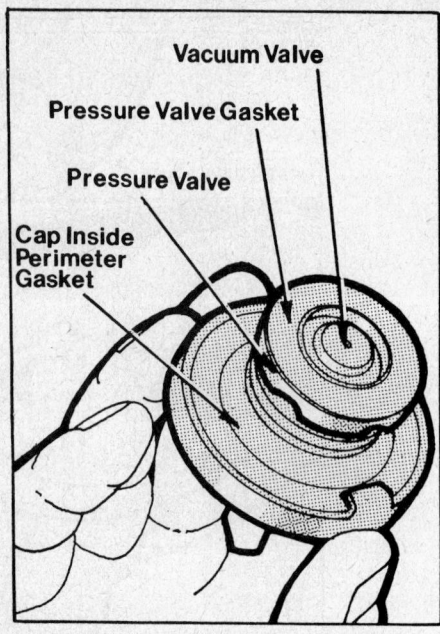

Vacuum Valve

Pressure Valve Gasket

Pressure Valve

Cap Inside Perimeter Gasket

Fig. 28   Radiator cap (typical)

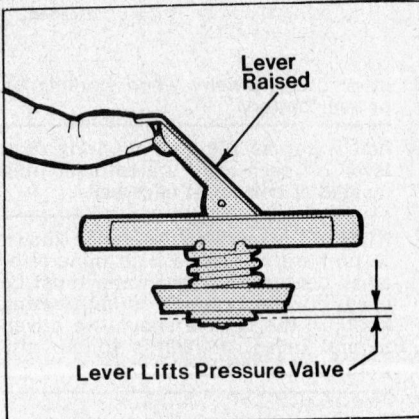

Lever Raised

Lever Lifts Pressure Valve

Fig. 29   Radiator cap with pressure release mechanism (typical)

below "Add" mark.

6. If fluid level is at "Add" mark, one pint of transmission fluid will bring level to "Full" mark. If fluid level is below "Add" mark, add fluid as necessary to bring level between "Add" and "Full" marks. Transmission fluid is added through the dipstick tube.

NOTE: Do not bring level above "Full" mark, overfilling could result in damage to transmission. Only add automatic transmission fluid of type and specification recommended by the vehicle manufacturer.

7. Replace dipstick and ensure it is seated in tube.

Manual Transmission

1. Set Parking brake and block wheels.
2. Clean area around filler plug, then using a suitable wrench or ratchet remove filler plug.
3. Fluid should be level with bottom of filler plug hole.

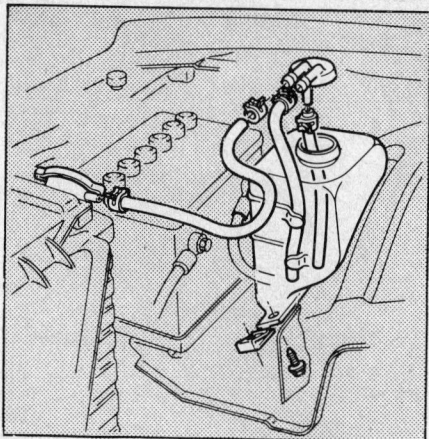

Fig. 30 Factory installed coolant recovery system (typical)

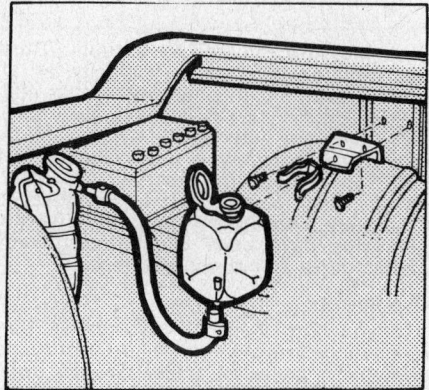

Fig. 31 Aftermarket coolant recovery system installation (typical)

4. Add fluid as required, then install filler plug.

NOTE: Only add lubricant recommended by the vehicle manufacturer.

Rear Axle

1. Set parking brake and block wheels.
2. Clean area around filler plug, then using a suitable ratchet remove filler plug.
3. Fluid level should be approximately ½ inch below bottom of filler plug hole.
4. Add fluid as required, then install filler plug.

Only add lubricant recommended by the vehicle manufacturer. Do not add conventional axle type lubricant to models equipped with Anti Spin, Controlled, Limited Slip, Positraction, Sure Grip, Traction Lok or Twin Grip axles. A special lubricant must be added to these type axles, refer to vehicle manufacturers recommendations.

COOLING SYSTEM SERVICE

CAUTION: Do not attempt to perform any system servicing when the engine is hot or the cooling system is pressurized. Even a simple operation such as removing the radiator cap should be avoided since per-

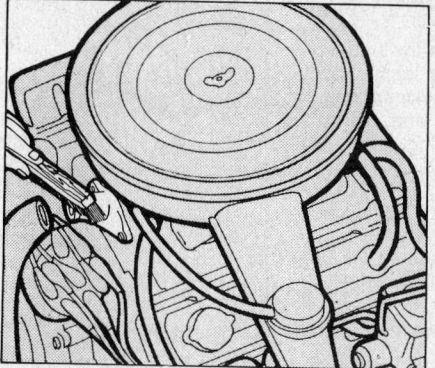

Fig. 32 Cleaning hose connections

sonal injury and loss of coolant may result.

Draining The System

Most cooling systems incorporate a radiator petcock usually located on the engine side of the radiator at either of the lower corners. Some radiator petcocks are located on the side of the radiator. Also, some cooling systems are not equipped with a radiator petcock.

1. Place a suitable container under radiator to catch coolant.
2. On systems equipped with a radiator petcock, turn the tangs (ears) to open the petcock. However, do not apply excessive pressure in either direction since damage to the petcock may result as some petcocks turn clockwise and others counter-clockwise to open.
3. On systems not equipped with a radiator petcock, it will be necessary to remove the lower hose from the radiator.
4. Dispose of coolant.

Flushing The System

There are two flushing methods which can be performed without the use of special equipment. One method outlined below requires the use of a garden hose only. The second method requires the use of the garden hose and a "Tee" fitting spliced into one of the heater hoses. The "Tee" fitting and other items and instructions needed to perform this type of flushing are available by aftermarket manufacturers.

1. With cooling system drained, remove thermostat as outlined below:
   a. To locate the thermostat housing on all engines except on Ford V6 engines, follow the upper radiator hose from the radiator to the engine block. On Ford V6 engines, follow the lower radiator hose from the radiator to the engine block. The point at which these hoses connect is the thermostat housing.
   b. The thermostat housing is usually retained by two bolts or nuts. Remove these bolts or nuts and remove the housing.
   c. Lift the thermostat from the mounting flange, Fig. 26, noting the position that it was installed. This is important to avoid reinstalling the thermostat upside down.
   d. Reinstall thermostat housing, how-

Core Plug Leaks

Fig. 33 Core plug locations (typical)

Belt Tension Gauge

Drive Belt

Fig. 34 Checking belt tension with a tension gauge.

ever, do not reinstall thermostat. Tighten retaining bolts.
2. Insert garden hose into radiator filler opening, open radiator petcock and turn on water.
3. Start engine and run engine for a few minutes. This should flush out any loose particles in the system.
4. Turn off engine and remove the garden hose.
5. Remove thermostat housing. Thoroughly clean the thermostat housing and engine surfaces of old gasket and sealer. This is necessary to prevent leakage between the housing and engine surfaces.
6. Install new thermostat housing gasket and the thermostat. Make certain that the thermostat is installed exactly in the same position as it was removed.
7. Install thermostat housing and tighten retaining bolts and nuts.
8. Allow radiator to drain.
9. Close radiator petcock, if equipped.
10. Remove coolant overflow tank, if equipped. Thoroughly clean the inside of the tank and reinstall.

Refilling The System

1. Determine the amount of anti-freeze required to achieve a 50/50 solution in the cooling system. Refer to the "Cooling System & Capacity Data" tables in the individual car chapters. Take the total number of quarts listed

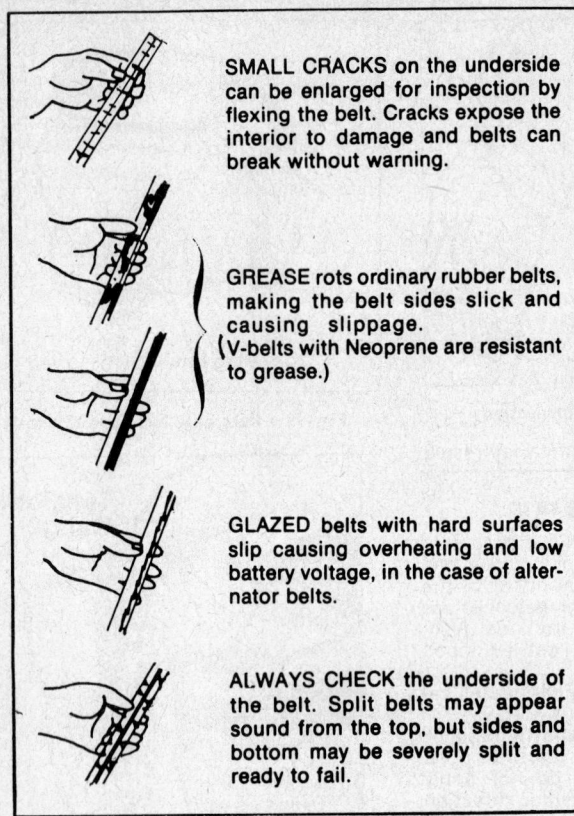

SMALL CRACKS on the underside can be enlarged for inspection by flexing the belt. Cracks expose the interior to damage and belts can break without warning.

GREASE rots ordinary rubber belts, making the belt sides slick and causing slippage.
(V-belts with Neoprene are resistant to grease.)

GLAZED belts with hard surfaces slip causing overheating and low battery voltage, in the case of alternator belts.

ALWAYS CHECK the underside of the belt. Split belts may appear sound from the top, but sides and bottom may be severely split and ready to fail.

Fig. 35   Drive belt inspection

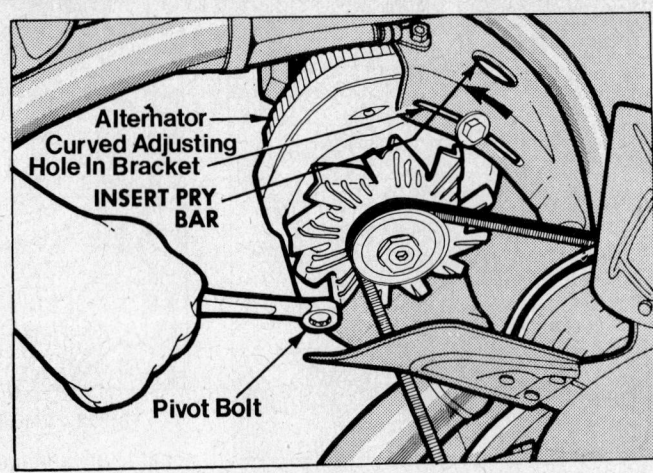

Fig. 38   Loosening adjusting bolt and pivot bolt

in the tables and divide by two. This number is the amount of anti-freeze, in quarts, required to achieve the 50/50 solution. This solution will generally provide protection to −35 degrees F. Fig. 27 illustrates a typical anti-freeze hydrometer.

2. Add the amount of anti-freeze to the radiator that was determined in the preceding step. If radiator fills before required amount of anti-freeze is installed, start engine and turn on heater. Add the anti-freeze as the coolant level sinks in the radiator.
3. Continue to run engine with the radiator cap removed until the upper radiator hose becomes hot to the touch.
4. Top up the coolant level in the radiator to the bottom of the filler neck

with a 50/50 mixture of anti-freeze and water.
5. If equipped with an overflow tank, add a 50/50 mixture of anti-freeze and water to the cold level as marked on the side of the tank.

Radiator Cap

The radiator filler cap contains a pressure relief valve and a vacuum relief valve, Fig. 28. The pressure relief valve is held against its seat by a spring, which when compressed, allows excessive pressure to be relieved out the radiator overflow. The vacuum valve is also held against its seat by a spring which when compressed opens the valve to relieve the vacuum created when the system cools.

NOTE: Some aftermarket radiator caps incorporate a pressure release mechanism to relieve cooling system pressure before rotating cap, Fig. 29.

The radiator cap should be washed with clean water and pressure checked at regular tune-up intervals. Inspect rubber seal on cap for tears or cracks. If the pressure cap will not hold pressure or does not release at the proper pressure replace the cap.

Coolant Recovery System

The coolant recovery system supplements the standard cooling system in that additional coolant is available from a plastic reservoir, Fig. 30.

As the coolant is heated it expands within the cooling system and overflows into the plastic reservoir. As the engine cools the coolant contracts and is drawn

back into the radiator by vacuum. Thus, the radiator is filled to capacity at all times, resulting in increased cooling efficiency.

Air or vapor entering the system will be forced to the reservoir under the coolant and exits through the reservoir cap.

A special radiator cap is designed to discourage inadvertent removal. The finger grips have been eliminated thereby presenting a round configuration.

Overflow Kit

If your car does not have an overflow reservoir, it is easy enough to retrofit one. Many kits prices at under $5 are available, Fig. 31. A kit should include the following:

1. A clear pastic reservoir with quart markings to indicate fluid level.
2. A replacement radiator cap, with an air sealing gasket in the cap's inside perimeter.
3. Necessary hoses and fittings.

Hose Replacement

The radiator, heater and the coolant by-pass hoses are held at each end by a clamp. All clamps but the spring design can be loosened with a screwdriver. To save yourself a long walk after you have removed the hose from your radiator or heater, buy the replacement hose and any necessary clamps before starting the job.

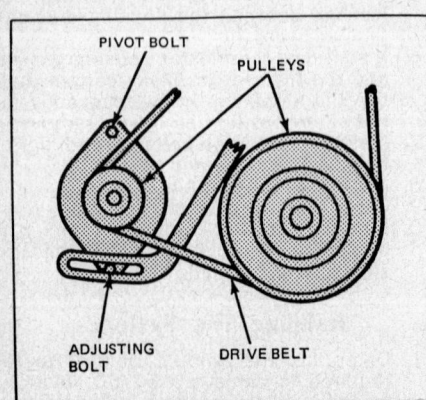

Fig. 36   Pivot bolt and adjusting bolt arrangement

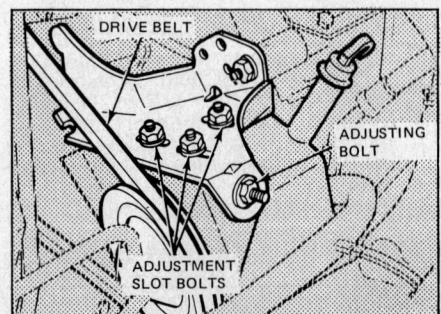

Fig. 37   Adjustment bolt and adjustment slot bolt arrangement

Removal

1. Drain the radiator as outlined previously. Use a clean container, large enough to hold the coolant from your cooling system, to save the coolant for refilling the system after replacing the hose. If you are removing the radiator upper hose or heater hoses, you need only drain the radiator. If you are removing the lower hose, also drain the block as follows: disconnect the lower hose at the radiator. Bend it down and use it as a drain spout.
2. Loosen the clamps at each end of the hose to be removed. You can do this quite easily with a screwdriver. If the clamps are old and corroded, they may be stuck to the hose, loosening the screw may not be enough on some designs, in which case you'll have to pry the clamp a bit.

CAUTION: Be very careful when prying under the clamp. The fittings are extremely fragile and might bend or break if too much force is exerted.

If the hose is held by spring clamps, you may be in for a struggle unless you have spring clamp pliers. There are many types of pliers designed for these clamps, including ordinary slip-joint pliers with recesses cut into the jaws to grip each end of the clamp. To release the clamp you must squeeze the ends together, and if you try to use ordinary pliers, the ends may slip off. The best procedure is to discard the spring type and install a worm-drive band clamp, but if you insist on re-using the one you have, at least invest in a pair of special pliers.

3. Twist the hose back and forth to loosen it from the connector. Slide the hose off the connections. If the hose is stuck, shove in a screwdriver and try to pry loose. If the working angle is poor for the screwdriver, or if the hose is really stuck, cut the hose off the neck with a single-edge razor blade. If the hose being removed is dried and cracked and remnants of it remain on either connection, clean the connection thoroughly with a scraper or putty knife.

Installation

1. With the old hose removed, wire brush the hose connections to remove foreign material, Fig. 32.
2. To ease installation, coat hose neck with a soap solution.
3. Slide the hose in position so that it is completely on the neck at each end, to avoid possibility of kinking and to provide room for proper positioning of the clamp. Except for the worm-drive clamp, which can be opened completely, the clamp must be loosely placed over the hose prior to fitting its end on the neck.
4. Make sure the clamps are beyond the head and placed in the center of the clamping surface of the connections.
5. Tighten the clamps.
6. Refill the cooling system as outlined in the previous procedure on refilling the cooling system.

Cooling System Leaks

If the coolant level must be adjusted

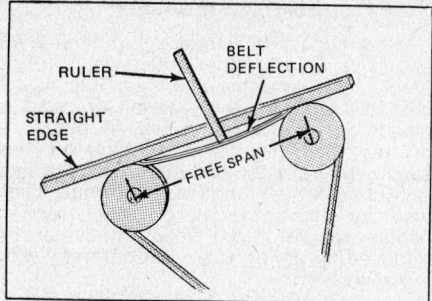

Fig. 39 Checking belt tension without belt tension gauge.

frequently, the cooling system may be leaking either internally or externally. To determine if the system is leaking internally, special equipment must be used such as a pressure tester. To determine if the system is leaking externally, check for leakage in the following locations: radiator and its seams, hoses and their connections, heater core, water pump, coolant temperature sending unit, thermostat housing, hot water choke housing, heater water valve, coolant recovery tank and core plugs, Fig. 33.

DRIVE BELTS

Proper belt tension is important not only to minimize noise and prolong belt life, but also to protect the accessories being driven.

Belts which are adjusted too tight may cause failure to the bearing of the accessory which it drives. Also premature wear and breakage of the belt may result. Belts which are too loose will slip on their pulleys and cause a screeching sound. Loose belts can also cause the battery to go dead, the engine to overheat, hard steering (if equipped with power steering) and air conditioner to malfunction.

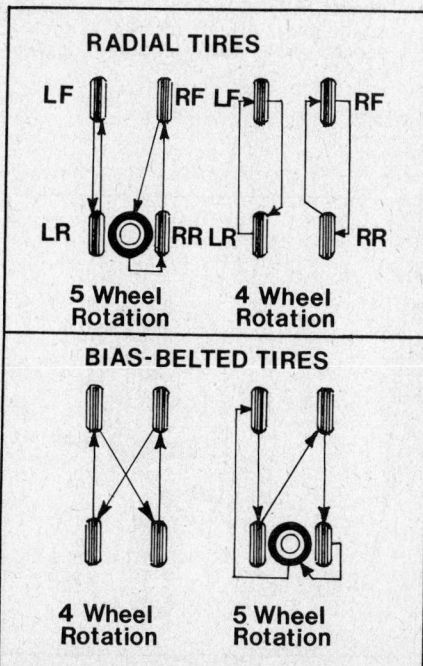

Fig. 40 Tire rotation chart

Drive Belt Tension Gauge

The use of a belt tension gauge will quickly indicate whether a belt is properly adjusted or not. Low cost tension gauges give spot readings while the more expensive ones give continuous readings as the belt tension is adjusted, Fig. 34.

Drive Belt Inspection

All drive belts should be inspected at regular intervals. Inspect condition of belts for uneven wear, cuts, fraying and glazing, Fig. 35.

CAUTION: Engine must be off when checking belts.

Drive Belt Tension Adjustment

1. Run engine until it reaches normal operating temperature, then turn engine off.

CAUTION: Do not attempt to check or adjust any drive belt while engine is running. Turn engine off.

2. Using belt tension gauge following manufacturers instructions, check tension of each belt, one at a time, Fig. 34. Refer to individual vehicle chapter for belt tension specifications.
3. If adjustment is necessary, proceed as follows:
   a. Pivot Bolt and Adjusting Bolt, Figs. 36 and 38. Using a suitable wrench, loosen adjusting bolt and pivot bolt, then using a pry bar, move accessory toward or away from engine until tension gauge reaches specified reading. Make sure to tighten bolts before relieving force applied to pry bar.

CAUTION: Do not pry against power steering housing or air pump housing.

   b. Adjusting Bolt and Adjusting Bolt Slots Fig. 37. Loosen adjusting slot bolts, then loosen or tighten adjusting bolt until tension gauge reaches specified reading. Make sure to tighten adjusting slot bolts.
   c. Idler Pulley Pivot Bolt and Adjusting Bolt. Loosen idler pulley pivot bolt and adjusting bolt, then insert a 1/2 inch flex handle into pulley arm slot and apply force on handle until tension gauge reaches specified reading. Make sure to tighten pivot and adjusting bolt before relieving force on handle.
4. To check tension on a belt without a belt tension gauge, proceed as follows:
   a. Place a straight edge along the belt from pulley to pulley, Fig. 39.
   b. Using a ruler, depress belt at midpoint between pulleys and measure amount of deflection. For belt with a free span of less than 12 inches between pulleys, the amount of deflection should be 1/4 inch. For belts with a free span of more than 12 inches between pulleys, the amount of deflection should be 1/2 inch.
   c. Adjust belt tension, if necessary as described previously.
5. Recheck belt tension. Readjust if necessary.

Drive Belt Replacement

To replace a belt, loosen the adjusting bolt and pivot bolt. Move accessory as required to obtain maximum slack on belt. Remove belt by lifting off the pulleys and working it around the fan or other accessories, as necessary. Sometimes, on multiple belt arrangements, it will be necessary to remove one or more additional belts in order to remove the defective belt. To install belt, reverse the removal procedure and adjust belt tension as described previously.

NOTE: On accessories which are driven by dual belts, it is advisable to replace both belts even if only one needs replacement.

TIRE CARE
Tire Rotation

The purpose of rotation is to equalize normal tire wear. There is such a thing as normal wear. Nothing lasts indefinitely. By equalizing this wear evenly over the entire tread surface, you extend tire life. Recommended rotation patterns are shown in Fig. 40.

It is wise to provide snow tires with rims of their own, so they do not have to be removed from rims in the late fall. They can be kept on rims of their own during both storage and use. In this way, you will protect tires from the bead damage which becomes a possibility when you break a tire away from a rim.

A studded snow tire should always be mounted on the same wheel of the car year after year after year. When storing studded snow tires mark each tire in chalk with either an R for Right or an L for Left, depending upon which side of the car the tire was mounted.

When storing tires, lay them flat, off the tread, and keep them away from electricity-producing machinery. Laying the tire flat keeps the flat spots from developing over the tread. Electricity-producing machinery creates ozone. Ozone damages rubber.

Tire Maintenance

Tires should be inspected regularly for excessive or abnormal tread wear, fabric breaks, cut or other damage, Fig. 41. A bulge or bump in the sidewall or tread is reason for discarding a tire. A bulge indicates that the tread or sidewall has separated from the tire body. The tire is a candidate for an imminent blowout. Look also for small stones or other foreign bodies wedged in the tread. These can be removed by prying them out carefully with a screwdriver.

TUNE-UP
Spark Plug, Replace

Removal
1. Mark all ignition wires since they must be replaced in the same sequence. This can be accomplished in several ways.
   a. Marking tags and attaching them to the ignition wires, according to the engine firing order, front to rear on inline engines, or D1 through D4 on driver's side and P1 through P4 on the passenger side on V8 engines.
   b. Use a white magic marker or nail polish to mark each ignition wire with a white spot. One spot for the first wire, two spots for the second and so on.
2. Remove the spark plug wires from the spark plugs by twisting the boot approximately 1/4-turn, and freeing it from spark plug.
3. Pull wire off by the boot only. Pulling on wires may cause internal breakage.
4. Before loosening plug, blow out loose dirt adjacent to spark plug. If a compressed air supply is not available, you can accomplish this by blowing through a soda straw or a rubber hose.
5. Install the proper size spark plug socket (13/16-inch or 5/8-inch) onto a spark plug. Attach ratchet wrench to socket and turn counterclockwise.

Loosen all spark plugs approximately one turn, breaking loose any accumulated carbon adjacent to the spark plugs.

Installation
The spark plug should be regapped to the exact specification given by the auto manufacturer. Always use a round wire type gauge. Refer to the "Tune-Up Service" section elsewhere in this book.

Torque spark plug to specifications as listed in the "Engine Tightening Specification" tables in the individual car chapters.

Distributor Cap, Replace

Remove the distributor cap. The distributor cap is retained either by latches, or bale clips, Fig. 41. To remove the first type, depress the latches using a flat screwdriver, then turn the latches one half turn in either direction and lift the cap off the distributor. To remove the second type, insert a flat screwdriver between the bale clip and distributor cap, and pry the clips to disengage them from the cap and lift the cap off the distributor. Inspect condition of cap, Fig. 42, and clean or replace as necessary.

Distributor Rotor, Replace

All distributor rotors except those used on General Motors and American Motors V8 engines may be removed by simply pulling them upward from the shaft. On General Motors V8 engines, it is necessary to remove the two screws that secures the rotor to the top of the shaft and advance mechanism.

When installing the rotor on all distributors except those used on General Motors V8 engines, align the notch on the shaft with the locating tab inside the open end of the rotor, then slide the rotor onto the shaft. Make sure that the rotor is firmly seated on the shaft.

Rotors used on General Motors and American Motors V8 engines incorporate two locating dowels on the underside of the rotor. Note that one dowel is square while the other one is round. When installing the rotor, be sure to engage these locating dowels in the proper locating holes, square hole for square dowel and round hole for round dowel. Tighten the retaining screws, however, not too tight since the rotor may crack.

Breaker Points, Replace

American Motors & General Motors Six Cylinder Engines
1. Pull primary and condenser leads from breaker point quick disconnect, Fig. 43 and 44.
2. Remove breaker point retaining screw and lift points out.
3. Clean all dirt and grease from breaker plate and distributor cam.
4. Install breaker points, making sure that pilot on breaker points base is inserted in corresponding hole in breaker plate. Install and tighten retaining screw.
5. Connect primary and condenser leads to breaker points.
6. Apply a light coat of cam lubricant to

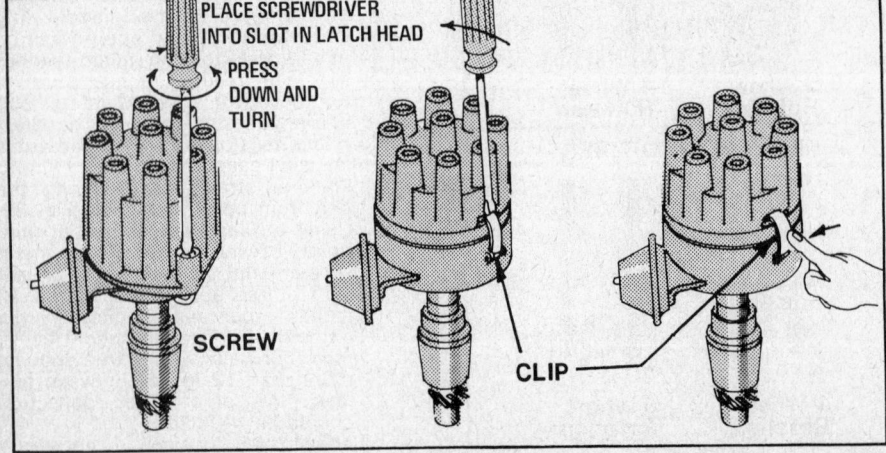

PLACE SCREWDRIVER INTO SLOT IN LATCH HEAD

PRESS DOWN AND TURN

SCREW

CLIP

Fig. 41 Distributor cap removal

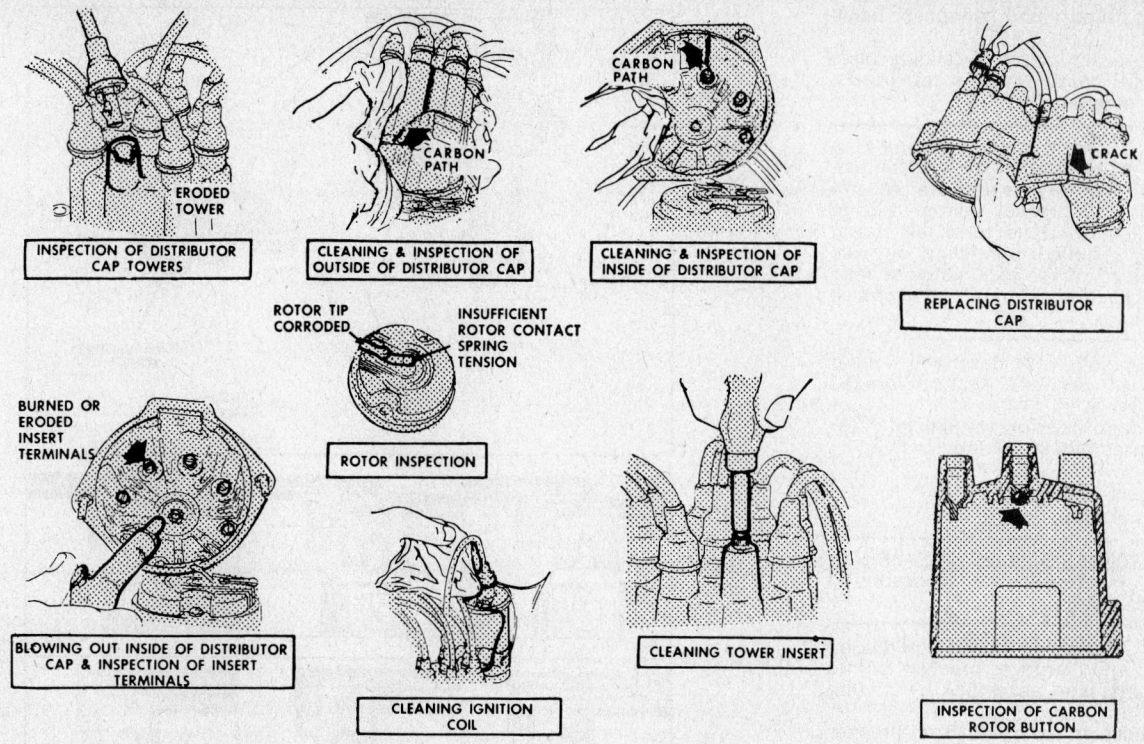

Fig. 42   Inspecting and cleaning distributor cap

distributor cam.

NOTE: This lubricant is usually supplied with new breaker points.

7. Adjust points as outlined in the "Tune Up Service" section of this manual.
8. Install rotor and cap as described previously.

American Motors & General Motors V8 Engines, except Uni-Set Points

NOTE: On these engines, the breaker points and condenser are two individual assemblies.

1. If used, remove radio interference shield retaining screws and shield.
2. Loosen breaker points retaining screw and remove breaker points by sliding out, Fig. 44.
3. Disconnect primary and condenser leads from breaker points. If the leads are retained by a screw, loosen screw to remove. If the leads are retained by a push-in type terminal, pull leads out.
4. Remove condenser retaining screw and condenser.
5. Clean all dirt and grease from breaker plate and distributor cam.
6. Apply a light coat of cam lubricant to distributor cam.

NOTE: This lubricant is usually supplied with new breaker points. Also, the cam lubricator should be rotated every 12,000 miles and replaced every 24,000 miles.

7. Install condenser and retaining screw.

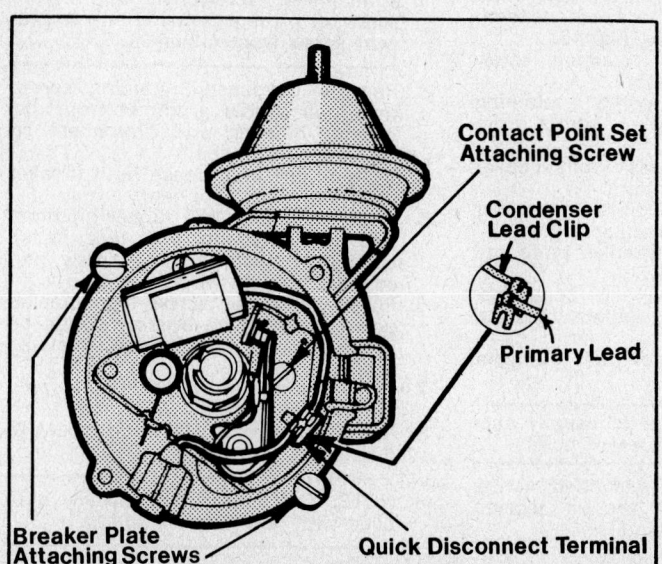

Fig. 43   Breaker points and condenser installation. American Motors and General Motors 6 cylinder engines

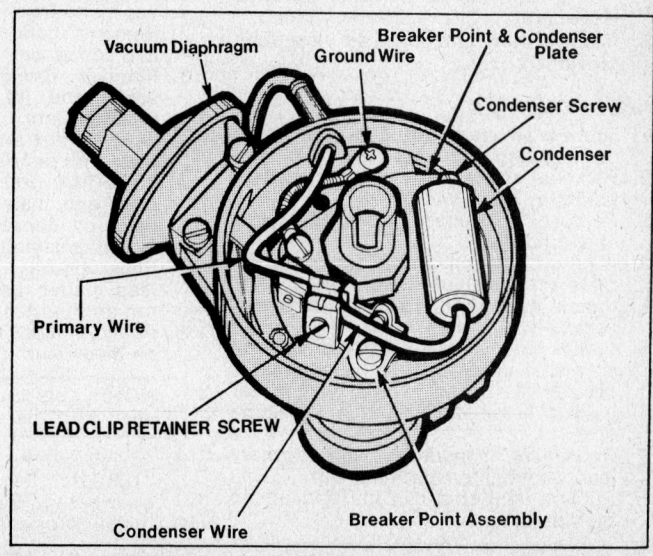

Fig. 45   Breaker points and condenser installation. Ford Motor Co. exc. 2000cc engine (typical)

8. Connect primary and condenser leads to breaker points.
9. Install breaker points by sliding base of breaker points under screw heads. Tighten screws.

NOTE: Breaker points utilizing the push-in type terminal for the condenser and primary leads are recommended. The breaker points utilizing the lock screw type terminal, if not carefully installed, may short out due to the head of the lock screw or lead clips contacting the radio interference shield.

10. Adjust points as described under "Tune Up Service" section located elsewhere.
11. Install radio interference shield, rotor and cap as described previously.

General Motors V8 Engines, With Uni-Set Points

NOTE: On these engines, the breaker points and condenser are incorporated into one assembly.

1. Loosen breaker points retaining screws and remove breaker points and condenser assembly by sliding out.
2. Disconnect primary lead from breaker points.
3. Wipe all dirt and grease from breaker plate and distributor cam.
4. Apply a light coat of cam lubricant to distributor cam.

NOTE: This lubricant is usually supplied with new breaker points. Also, the cam lubricator should be rotated every 12,000 miles and replaced every 24,000 miles.

5. Connect primary lead to breaker points.
6. Install breaker point and condenser assembly by sliding base of breaker points under screw heads. Tighten screws.
7. Adjust points as described under "Tune Up Service" section located elsewhere.
8. Install rotor and cap as described previously.

Chrysler Corp.

1. Loosen terminal nut and disconnect primary and condenser leads.
2. Remove screw and remove breaker points by lifting out.
3. Remove condenser retaining screw and condenser.
4. Wipe all dirt and grease from breaker plate and distributor cam.
5. Install new condenser and retaining screw.
6. Install new breaker points, making sure that sleeve at end of adjustable bracket fits over pivots on breaker plate. Install and tighten retaining screw.
7. Reconnect condenser and primary lead and tighten terminal nut.
8. Apply a light coat of cam lubricant to distributor cam.

NOTE: This lubricant is usually supplied with new breaker points.

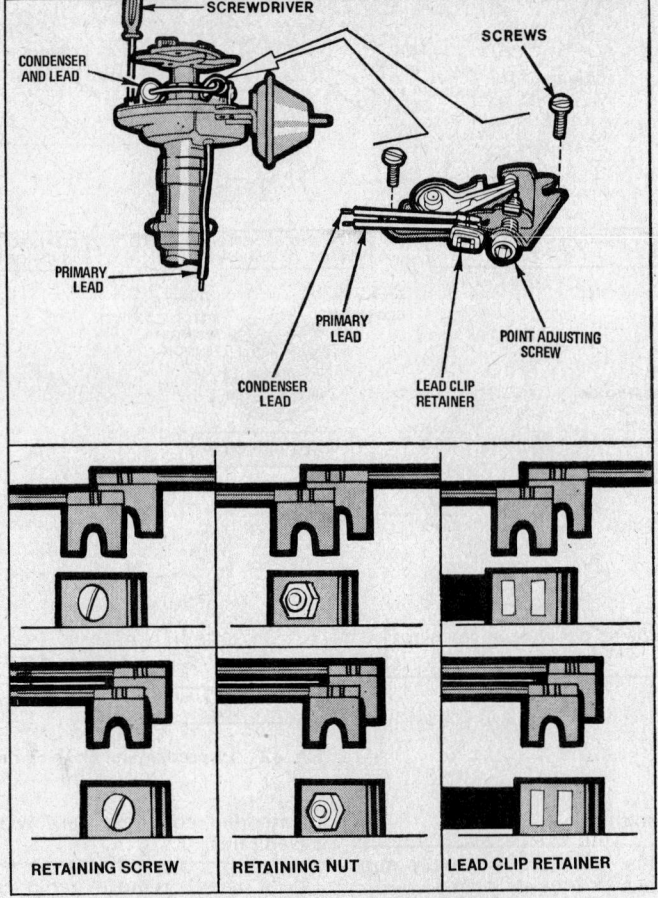

Fig. 44   Breaker points and condenser installation. American Motors and General Motors V8 engines less Uni-Set points

9. Adjust points as described under "Tune Up Service" section located elsewhere in this manual.
10. Install rotor and cap.

Ford Motor Co., Exc. 2000cc Engine

1. Loosen terminal nut on breaker points and disconnect primary and condenser leads from points, Fig. 45.
2. Remove condenser retaining screw and condenser, Fig. 45.
3. Remove breaker points retaining screw and lift breaker points from breaker plate.
4. Wipe all dirt and grease from breaker plate and distributor cam.
5. Place new breaker points on breaker plate and install retaining screws.
6. Place condenser on breaker plate and install retaining screw.
7. Slide primary lead and condenser lead under breaker points terminal nut and tighten nut.
8. Apply a light coat of cam lubricant on distributor cam.

NOTE: This lubricant is usually supplied with the new breaker points.

9. Adjust points as described under "Tune-Up Service" section located elsewhere in this manual.
10. Install rotor and cap.

Ford Motor Co., 2000cc Engine

1. Pull breaker points lead from clip in rubber grommet.

2. Remove breaker points retaining screw and remove points by lifting out.

NOTE: Use care to avoid dropping screw into hole in breaker plate. Use a magnetic screwdriver to remove screw, or place a pencil in hole to prevent screw from falling in.

3. Remove condenser retaining screw, then pull rubber grommet from distributor housing and disconnect ignition wire from coil.
4. Wipe all dirt and grease from breaker plate and distributor cam.
5. Work condenser lead rubber grommet into distributor housing, then install condenser and retaining screw and connect ignition wire to coil.
6. Place retaining screw on breaker points, then place breaker points on breaker plate and tighten retaining screw.
7. Connect breaker points lead to plug in rubber grommet.
8. Apply a light coat of cam lubricant to distributor cam.

NOTE: This lubricant is usually supplied with new breaker points.

9. Adjust point as described under "Tune-Up Service" section located elsewhere in this manual.
10. Install rotor and cap.

TROUBLE SHOOTING
Index of Symptoms

TROUBLE SHOOTING

INTRODUCTION

STARTING A STALLED ENGINE

When an engine fails to start the chances are that 90 per cent of the cases will involve the ignition system and seldom the fuel system or other miscellaneous reasons. If a systematic procedure is followed the trouble can almost always be found without the use of special equipment.

To begin with, turn on the ignition switch and if the ammeter shows a slight discharge (or if the telltale lamp lights) it indicates that current is flowing. A glance at the gas gauge will indicate whether or not there is fuel in the tank.

Operate the starter and if the engine turns over freely, both the battery and starter are functioning properly. On the other hand, if the starter action is sluggish it may be due to a discharged or defective battery, loose, corroded or dirty battery terminals, mechanical failure in the starter, starter switch or starter drive. If the starter circuit is okay, skip this phase of the discussion and proceed to ignition.

Starter Circuit Checkout

To determine which part of the starter circuit is at fault, turn on the light switch and again operate the starter. Should the lights go out or become dim, the trouble is either in the battery, its connections or cables. A hydrometer test of the battery should indicate better than 1.250 specific gravity, while a voltmeter, placed across the positive and negative posts, should indicate about 12 volts. If either of these tests prove okay, clean and tighten the battery connections and cable terminals or replace any cable which seems doubtful.

If the lights remain bright when the starter is operated, the trouble is between the battery and the starter, or the starter switch is at fault, since it is evident that there is no electrical connection between these points. If these connections are clean and tight, it is safe to assume that the starter or starter switch is defective.

Neutral Safety Switch

If the ammeter shows a slight discharge (or if the telltale lamp lights) when the ignition is turned on, but the system goes dead when the starting circuit is closed, the neutral safety switch may be at fault. To check, bypass the switch with a suitable jumper. If the engine now starts, adjust or replace the switch.

CAUTION: With the safety switch bypassed, the car can be started in any gear. *Be sure the transmission is in neutral or park and the parking brake is applied.*

Primary Ignition Checkout

Let's assume that the battery and starter are doing their job, and that fuel is reaching the carburetor, but the car does not start, then the trouble must be somewhere in the ignition circuit. But first, before starting your diagnosis, it is advisable to give the whole system a visual inspection which might uncover obvious things such as broken or disconnected wires etc.

The best way to start tracking down ignition troubles is to begin with the primary circuit since this is where troubles show up most frequently. First remove the distributor cap and block the points open with a piece of cardboard, then turn on the ignition and with a test bulb or voltmeter check to see if there is current at the terminal on the distributor. If you do not get a reading at this point, the current is cut off somewhere in the connections leading back to the ignition switch or it may be that the condenser has an internal short to the ground. The latter possibility can be eliminated if you can restore current at the distributor terminal by disconnecting the condenser from the distributor plate so that its outside shell is not grounded. With the possibility of a bad condenser out of the way, work toward the ignition switch and test for current at each connection until you get to one where you get a reading. Between this connection and the distributor lies the trouble.

The foregoing steps in checking the primary circuit should include checking the ignition coil resistor for defects or loose connections. As this is done, bear in mind that while the starter cranks the engine, the resistor is by-passed by the starter switch on Ford and Delco-Remy systems (see Tune Up Chapter for details). This means that while the circuit through the resistor may be satisfactory, a broken connection or high resistance between the starter switch by-pass terminal and the coil would prevent starting. On the other hand, a satisfactory by-pass circuit might start the engine while the engine would stall immediately upon releasing the starter switch if there was a defect in the coil resistance circuit.

If, to begin with, the test equipment shows a current reading at the distributor terminal, it is safe to assume that the trouble is in the unit itself, most likely burned or dirty breaker points. A final positive test for defective breaker points can be made very simply by removing the cardboard from between the points, and positioning the distributor cam by turning the engine to where the points are closed. With the points closed there should be no current at the distributor terminal. If there is current, replace the points.

In an emergency, the points can be cleaned by using the sanded side of a match box, a knife blade, or the sharp edge of a screwdriver to scrape the scale from the contact faces. After cleaning the points, if a gauge is not available to set the gap, a quick adjustment can be made by using four layers of a piece of newspaper. The thickness of the paper is equivalent to about .020", which is the approximate gap setting for most distributors. Of course, at the earliest opportunity, a precise point adjustment should be made.

If the procedure outlined under "Primary Ignition Checkout" does not uncover the trouble then it will be necessary to continue the tests into the secondary ignition circuit.

Secondary Ignition Checkout

First of all, remove the wire from one of the spark plugs, turn on the ignition and operate the starter. While the engine is cranking, hold the terminal of the spark plug wire about ¼" away from the engine or spark plug base. If the spark is strong and jumps the gap, the trouble is confined to either the spark plugs or lack of fuel. Before going any further, wipe the outside of the plugs to remove any dirt or dampness which would create an easy path for the current to flow, then try to start the engine again. If it still fails to start, remove one of the spark plugs and if it is wet around the base, it indicates that the fuel system is okay, so it naturally follows that the spark plugs are at fault. Remove all the plugs, clean them and set the gaps. An emergency adjustment of spark plug gaps can be made by folding a piece of newspaper into 6 or 7 layers. When changing the gap, always bend the side (ground) electrode and never the center one as there is danger of breaking the insulation.

Fuel System Checkout

If the spark plug that was removed showed no indication of dampness on its base, check the fuel system. A quick check can be made by simply removing the carburetor air cleaner and looking down into the carburetor. Open and close the throttle manually and if fuel is present in the carburetor, the throttle will operate the accelerating pump, causing it to push gasoline through the pump jet. If it does, check the choke valve. If the engine is cold, the choke valve should be closed. If the choke won't close, the engine can be started by covering the carburetor throat while the engine is cranking, provided, of course, that fuel is reaching the carburetor.

Check the operation of the fuel pump by disconnecting the fuel lines from the pump to the carburetor. Crank the engine and if the pump is working, fuel will pulsate out of the line. If not, either the pump isn't working or the line from the tank to the pump is clogged. Before blaming the pump, however, disconnect the line at the inlet side of the pump which leads to the tank and, while a companion listens at the tank, blow through the line. If a gurgling sound is heard back in the tank, the line is open and the trouble is in the pump. Remove the sediment bowl, if so equipped and clean the screen, then replace the bowl and screen, being sure that you have an air-tight fit. If the pump still refuses to function, it should be removed and repaired.

The foregoing discussion will, in most cases, uncover the cause of why an engine won't start. However, if further diagnosis is necessary, the following list will undoubtedly provide the answer.

ENGINE NOISE TESTS
Loose Main Bearing

A loose main bearing is indicated by a powerful but dull thud or knock when the engine is pulling. If all main bearings are loose a noticeable clatter will be audible.

The thud occurs regularly every other revolution. The knock can be confirmed by shorting spark plugs on cylinders adjacent to the bearing. Knock will disappear or be less when plugs are shorted. This test should be made at a fast idle equivalent to 15 mph in high gear. If bearing is not quite loose enough to produce a knock by itself, the bearing may knock if oil is too thin or if there is no oil at the bearing.

Loose Flywheel

A thud or click which is usually irregular. To test, idle the engine at about 20 mph and shut off the ignition. If thud is heard, the flywheel may be loose.

Loose Rod Bearing

A metallic knock which is usually loudest at about 30 mph with throttle closed. Knock can be reduced or even eliminated by shorting spark plug. If bearing is not loose enough to produce a knock by itself, the bearing may knock if oil is too thin or if there is no oil at the bearing.

Piston Pin

Piston pin, piston and connecting rod noises are difficult to tell apart.

A loose piston pin causes a sharp double knock which is usually heard when engine is idling. Severity of knock should increase when spark plug to this cylinder is short-circuited. However, on some engines the knock becomes more noticable at 25 to 35 mph on the road.

Piston pin rubs against cylinder wall, caused by lock screw being loose or snap ring broken.

Hydraulic Lifters

The malfunctioning of a hydraulic valve lifter is amost always accompanied by a clicking or tapping noise. More or less hydraulic lifter noise may be expected when the engine is cold but if lifters are functioning properly the noise should disappear when the engine warms up.

If all or nearly all lifters are noisy, they may be stuck because of dirty or gummy oil.

If all lifters are noisy, oil pressure to them may be inadequate. Foaming oil may also cause this trouble. If oil foams there will be bubbles on the oil level dipstick. Foaming may be caused by water in the oil or by too high an oil level or by a very low oil level.

If the hydraulic plungers require an initial adjustment, they will be noisy if this adjustment is incorrect.

If one lifter is noisy the cause may be:
1. Plunger too tight in lifter body.
2. Weak or broken plunger spring.
3. Ball valve leaks.
4. Plunger worn.
5. Lock ring (if any) improperly installed or missing.
6. Lack of oil pressure to this plunger.

If ball valve leaks, clean plunger in special solvent such as acetone and reinstall. Too often, plungers are condemned as faulty when all they need is a thorough cleaning.

Gum and dirty oil are the most common causes of hydraulic valve lifter trouble. Engine oil must be free of dirt. Select a standard brand of engine oil and use no other. Mixing up one standard brand with another may cause gummy oil and sticking plungers. Do not use any special oils unless recommended by the car manufacturer and change oil filter or element as recommended intervals.

Loose Engine Mountings

Occasional thud with car in operation. Most likely to be noticed at the moment the throttle is opened or closed.

Excessive Crankshaft End Play

A rather sharp rap which occurs at idling speed but may be heard at higher speeds also. The noise should disappear when clutch is disengaged.

Fuel Pump Noise

Diagnosis of fuel pumps suspected as noisy requires that some form of sounding device be used. Judgment by ear alone is not sufficient, otherwise a fuel pump may be needlessly replaced in attempting to correct noise contributed by some other component. Use of a stethoscope, a long screwdriver, or a sounding rod is recommended to locate the area or component causing the noise. The sounding rod can easily be made from a length of copper tubing $\frac{1}{4}$ to $\frac{3}{8}$ inch in diameter.

If the noise has been isolated to the fuel pump, remove the pump and run the engine with the fuel remaining in the carburetor bowl. If the noise level does not change, the source of the noise is elsewhere and the original fuel pump should be reinstalled. On models using a fuel pump push rod, check for excessive wear and/or galling of the push rod.

VAPOR LOCK

The term vapor lock means the flow of fuel to the mixing chamber in the carburetor has been stopped (locked) by the formation of vaporized fuel pockets or bubbles caused by overheating the fuel by hot fuel pump, hot fuel lines or hot carburetor.

The more volatile the fuel the greater the tendency for it to vapor lock. Vapor lock is encouraged by high atmospheric temperature, hard driving, defective engine cooling and high altitude.

A mild case of vapor lock will cause missing and hard starting when engine is warm. Somewhat more severe vapor lock will stop the engine which cannot be started again until it has cooled off enough so that any vaporized fuel has condensed to a liquid.

SERVICE NOTE: Some cars equipped with air conditioning have a vapor bypass system. These cars have a special fuel filter which has a metering outlet in the top. Any vapor which forms is bled off and returned to the fuel tank through a separate line alongside the fuel supply line. This system greatly reduces the possibility of vapor lock. However, if vapor lock is suspected examine the bypass valve to see if it is functioning.

PERCOLATION

Percolation means simply that gasoline in the carburetor bowl is boiling over into the intake manifold. This condition is most apt to occur immediately after a hot engine is shut off. Most carburetors have a provision for relieving the vapor pressure of overheated fuel in the carburetor bowl by means of ports. If, however, percolation should take place, the engine may be started by allowing it to cool slightly and then holding the throttle wide open while cranking to clear the intake manifold of excess fuel.

CARBURETOR ICING

The carburetor discharges liquid fuel into the air stream in the form of an atomized spray which evaporates readily. The heat required to evaporate the gasoline is drawn from the entering air, thereby lowering its temperature. The cooler air chills the interior of the carburetor and may cause the moisture in the air to condense into droplets.

Under certain conditions of atmospheric temperature and humidity, the liberated moisture actually collects and freezes on the chilled carburetor surfaces, especially on the throttle plate and surrounding throttle body. When the throttle is almost completely closed for idling, this ice tends to bridge the gap between the throttle plate and throttle body, thereby cutting off the air supply and causing the engine to stall. Opening the throttle for restarting breaks the ice bridge but does not eliminate the possibility of further stalling until the engine and carburetor have warmed up.

For carburetor icing to occur, the outside air must be cool enough so that the refrigerating effect of fuel evaporation in the carburetor will lower the temperatures of the throttle plate and body below both the dew point of moist air and the freezing point of water. The air must also contain sufficient moisture for appreciable condensation of water to occur when it is chilled in the carburetor.

Generally speaking, carburetor icing occurs when winter grade gasoline (more volatile than summer grade) is used and when the atmospheric temperature ranges from 30° to 50° F. at relative humidities in excess of 65%.

Carburetor icing problems can be reduced by the use of anti-icing additives, such as alcohols, in the fuel. Some fuel refiners use anti-stalling additives in their gasolines which have proved effective in combating carburetor icing.

Another form of carburetor icing has been observed in some engines during high-speed driving on cool, moist days. When certain cars are driven steadily at 60 to 80 mph, the large quantities of cool air passing through the carburetor may result in gradual ice formation within the carburetor's venturi. Since this ice restricts the venturi passage, the resultant increased vacuum in the venturi tends to increase the rate of fuel flow. The fuel-air mixture thus becomes excessively rich, causing loss of power and high fuel consumption.

SPARK KNOCK, PING, DETONATION

All three expressions mean the same thing. It is a sharp metallic knock caused by vibration of the cylinder head and block. The vibration is due to split-second high-pressure waves resulting from almost instantaneous abnormal combustion instead of the slower normal combustion.

The ping may be mild or loud. A mild ping does no harm but a severe ping will reduce power. A very severe ping may shatter spark plugs, break valves or crack pistons.

Pinging is most likely to occur on open throttle at low or moderate engine speed. Pinging is encouraged by:
1. Overheated engine.
2. Low octane fuel.
3. Too high compression.
4. Spark advanced too far.
5. Hot mixture due to hot engine or hot weather.
6. Heavy carbon deposit which increases the compression pressure.

Tendency to ping increases with mixture temperature including high atmospheric temperature; intake manifold heater valve "on" when engine is warm; hot cooling water; hot interior engine surfaces due to sluggish water circulation or water jackets clogged with rust or dirt especially around exhaust valves. Some of these troubles may be confined to one or two cylinders.

If an engine pings objectionably because of too low octane fuel, retard the spark setting but first be sure that the cooling system is in good condition, the mixture not too lean and the combustion chambers free of carbon deposit.

PRE-IGNITION

Pre-ignition means that the mixture is set on fire before the spark occurs, being ignited by a red hot spot in the combustion chamber such as an incandescent particle of carbon; a thin piece of protruding metal; an overheated spark plug, or a bright red hot exhaust valve. The result is reduction of power and overheating accompanied by pinging. The bright red hot exhaust valve may be due to a leak, to lack of tappet clearance, to valve sticking, or a weak or broken spring.

Pre-ignition may not be noticed if not severe. Severe pre-ignition results in severe pinging. The most common cause of pre-ignition is a badly overheated engine.

When the engine won't stop when the ignition is shut off, the cause is often due to red hot carbon particles resting on heavy carbon deposit in a very hot engine.

AFTER-BURNING

A subdued put-putting at the exhaust tail pipe may be due to leaky exhaust valves which permit the mixture to finish combustion in the muffler. If exhaust pipe or muffler is red hot, better let it cool, as there is some danger of setting the car on fire. Most likely to occur when mixture is lean.

ENGINE CONTINUES TO RUN AFTER IGNITION IS TURNED OFF

This condition, known as "dieseling," "run on," or "after running," is caused by improper idle speed and/or high temperature. Idle speed and engine temperature are affected by:

Carburetor Adjustment: High idle speed will increase the tendency to diesel because of the inertia of the engine crankshaft and flywheel. Too low an idle speed, particularly with a lean mixture, will result in an increase in engine temperature, especially if the engine is allowed to idle for long periods of time.

Ignition Timing: Because advanced ignition timing causes a corresponding increase in idle speed and retarded timing reduces idle speed, ignition timing influences the tendency to diesel in the same manner as Carburetor Adjustment.

Fuel Mixture: Enriching the idle fuel mixture decreases the tendency to diesel by causing the engine to run cooler.

Fuel Content: High octane fuels tend to reduce dieseling. Increased fuel content of lead alkyl increases the tendency to diesel. Phosphates and nickel fuel additives help prevent dieseling.

Spark Plugs: Plugs of too high a heat range for the engine in question can cause dieseling.

Throttle Plates: If the throttle plates are not properly aligned in the carburetor bore, a resulting leanness in fuel mixture occurs, contributing to dieseling.

Electrical System: Normally, during dieseling, ignition is self-supplied by a "hot spot," self-igniting fuel, etc. However, there is a possibility of the vehicle's electrical system supplying the necessary ignition. When the ignition switch is turned off, a small amount of current can flow from the generator into the primary of the ignition coil through the generator tell-tale light. This is particularly true when the warning light bulb has been changed for one of increased wattage.

NOTE: "Run on" is more prevalent in an engine when the ignition is turned off before the engine is allowed to return to idle. Therefore, it can be reduced by letting the engine return to idle before shutting off the ignition. "Run on" incidence can be reduced on automatic transmission units by turning off the engine when in gear.

A certain amount of "run on" can be expected from any gasoline engine regardless of make, size or configuration. (Diesel engines operate on this principle.) However, if the above suggestions are correctly employed, "run on" will be reduced to an unnoticeable level.

ENGINE

Condition	Possible Cause	Correction
ENGINE WILL NOT START	1. Weak battery.	1. Test battery specific gravity. Recharge or replace as necessary.
	2. Corroded or loose battery connections.	2. Clean and tighten battery connections. Apply a coat of petroleum to terminals.
	3. Faulty starter.	3. Repair starter motor.
	4. Moisture on ignition wires and distributor cap.	4. Wipe wires and cap clean and dry.
	5. Faulty ignition cables.	5. Replace any cracked or shorted cables.
	6. Open or shorted primary ignition circuit.	6. Trace primary ignition circuit and repair as necessary.
	7. Malfunctioning ignition points or condensor.	7. Replace ignition points & condensor as necessary.
	8. Faulty coil.	8. Test and replace if necessary.
	9. Incorrect spark plug gap.	9. Set gap correctly.
	10. Incorrect ignition timing.	10. Reset timing.
	11. Dirt or water in fuel line or carburetor.	11. Clean lines and carburetor. Replace filter.
	12. Carburetor flooded.	12. Adjust float level—check seats.
	13. Incorrect carburetor float setting.	13. Adjust float level—check seats.
	14. Faulty fuel pump.	14. Install new fuel pump.
	15. Carburetor percolating. No fuel in the carburetor.	15. Measure float level. Adjust bowl vent. Inspect operation of manifold heat control valve.
ENGINE STALLS	1. Idle speed set too low.	1. Adjust carburetor.
	2. Incorrect choke adjustment.	2. Adjust choke.
	3. Idle mixture too lean or too rich.	3. Adjust carburetor.
	4. Incorrect carburetor float setting.	4. Adjust float setting.
	5. Leak in intake manifold.	5. Inspect intake manifold gasket and replace if necessary.
	6. Worn or burned distributor rotor.	6. Install new rotor.
	7. Incorrect ignition wiring.	7. Install correct wiring.
	8. Faulty coil.	8. Test and replace if necessary.
	9. Incorrect tappet lash.	9. Adjust to specifications.
ENGINE LOSS OF POWER	1. Incorrect ignition timing.	1. Reset timing.
	2. Worn or burned distributor rotor.	2. Install new rotor.
	3. Worn distributor shaft.	3. Remove and repair distributor.
	4. Dirty or incorrectly gapped spark plugs.	4. Clean plugs and set gap.
	5. Dirt or water in fuel line, carburetor or filter.	5. Clean lines, carburetor and replace filter.
	6. Incorrect carburetor float setting.	6. Adjust float level.
	7. Faulty fuel pump.	7. Install new pump.
	8. Incorrect valve timing.	8. Check and correct valve timing.
	9. Blown cylinder head gasket.	9. Install new head gasket.
	10. Low compression.	10. Test compression of each cylinder.
	11. Burned, warped or pitted valves.	11. Install new valves.
	12. Plugged or restricted exhaust system.	12. Install new parts as necessary.
	13. Faulty ignition cables.	13. Replace any cracked or shorted cables.
	14. Faulty coil.	14. Test and replace as necessary.
ENGINE MISSES ON ACCELERATION	1. Dirty, or gap too wide in spark plugs.	1. Clean spark plugs and set gap.
	2. Incorrect ignition timing.	2. Reset timing.
	3. Dirt in carburetor.	3. Clean carburetor and replace filter.
	4. Acceleration pump in carburetor.	4. Install new pump.
	5. Burned, warped or pitted valves.	5. Install new valves.
	6. Faulty coil.	6. Test and replace if necessary.
ENGINE MISSES AT HIGH SPEED	1. Dirty or gap set too wide in spark plug.	1. Clean spark plugs and set gap.
	2. Worn distributor shaft.	2. Remove and repair distributor.
	3. Worn or burned distributor rotor.	3. Install new rotor.
	4. Faulty coil.	4. Test and replace if necessary.
	5. Incorrect ignition timing.	5. Reset timing.
	6. Dirty jets in carburetor.	6. Clean carburetor, replace filter.
	7. Dirt or water in fuel line, carburetor or filter.	7. Clean lines, carburetor and replace filter.
NOISY VALVES	1. High or low oil level in crankcase.	1. Check for correct oil level.
	2. Thin or diluted oil.	2. Change oil.
	3. Low oil pressure.	3. Check engine oil level.
	4. Dirt in valve lifters.	4. Clean lifters.
	5. Bent push rods.	5. Install new push rods.

TROUBLE SHOOTING

ENGINE—Continued

Condition	Possible Cause	Correction
NOISY VALVES, continued	6. Worn rocker arms.	6. Inspect oil supply to rockers.
	7. Worn tappets.	7. Install new tappets.
	8. Worn valve guides.	8. Ream and install new valves with O/S Stems.
	9. Excessive run-out of valve seats or valve faces.	9. Grind valve seats and valves.
	10. Incorrect tappet lash.	10. Adjust to specifications.
CONNECTING ROD NOISE	1. Insufficient oil supply.	1. Check engine oil level.
	2. Low oil pressure.	2. Check engine oil level. Inspect oil pump relief valve and spring.
	3. Thin or diluted oil.	3. Change oil to correct viscosity.
	4. Excessive bearing clearance.	4. Measure bearings for correct clearance.
	5. Connecting rod journals out-of-round.	5. Replace crankshaft or regrind journals.
	6. Misaligned (bent) connecting rods.	6. Replace bent connecting rods.
MAIN BEARING NOISE	1. Insufficient oil supply.	1. Check engine oil level.
	2. Low oil pressure.	2. Check engine oil level. Inspect oil pump relief valve and spring.
	3. Thin or diluted oil.	3. Change oil to correct viscosity.
	4. Excessive bearing clearance.	4. Measure bearings for correct clearances.
	5. Excessive end play.	5. Check thrust bearing for wear on flanges.
	6. Crankshaft journal worn out-of-round.	6. Replace crankshaft or regrind journals.
	7. Loose flywheel or torque converter.	7. Tighten to correct torque.
OIL PUMPING AT RINGS	1. Worn, scuffed, or broken rings.	1. Hone cylinder bores and install new rings.
	2. Carbon in oil ring slot.	2. Install new rings.
	3. Rings fitted too tight in grooves.	3. Remove the rings. Check grooves. If groove is not proper width, replace piston.
OIL PRESSURE DROP	1. Low oil level.	1. Check engine oil level.
	2. Faulty oil pressure sending unit.	2. Install new sending unit.
	3. Clogged oil filter.	3. Install new oil filter.
	4. Worn parts in oil pump.	4. Replace worn parts or pump.
	5. Thin or diluted oil.	5. Change oil to correct viscosity.
	6. Excessive bearing clearance.	6. Measure bearings for correct clearance.
	7. Oil pump relief valve stuck.	7. Remove valve and inspect, clean, and reinstall.
	8. Oil pump suction tube loose, bent or cracked.	8. Remove oil pan and install new tube if necessary.
NO OIL PRESSURE	1. Low oil level.	1. Add oil to correct level.
	2. Oil pressure gauge or sending unit inaccurate.	2. Replace defective unit.
	3. Oil pump malfunction.	3. Repair oil pump.
	4. Oil pressure relief valve sticking.	4. Remove and inspect oil pressure relief valve assembly.
	5. Oil passages on pressure side of pump obstructed.	5. Inspect oil passages for obstructions.
	6. Oil pickup screen or tube obstructed.	6. Inspect oil pickup for obstructions.
LOW OIL PRESSURE	1. Low oil level.	1. Add oil to correct level.
	2. Oil excessively thin due to dilution, poor quality, or improper grade.	2. Drain and refill crankcase with recommended oil.
	3. Oil pressure relief spring weak or sticking.	3. Remove and inspect oil pressure relief valve assembly.
	4. Oil pickup tube and screen assembly has restriction or air leak.	4. Remove and inspect oil inlet tube and screen assembly. (Fill pickup with lacquer thinner to find leaks.)
	5. Excessive oil pump clearance.	5. Check clearances.
	6. Excessive main, rod, or camshaft bearing clearance.	6. Measure bearing clearances, repair as necessary.
HIGH OIL PRESSURE	1. Improper grade oil.	1. Drain and refill crankcase with correct grade oil.
	2. Oil pressure gauge or sending unit inaccurate.	2. Replace defective unit.
	3. Oil pressure relief valve sticking closed.	3. Remove and inspect oil pressure relief valve assembly.

ENGINE—Continued

Condition	Possible Cause	Correction
EXTERNAL OIL LEAK	1. Fuel pump gasket broken or improperly seated.	1. Replace gasket.
	2. Cylinder head cover gasket broken or improperly seated.	2. Replace gasket; check cylinder head cover gasket flange and cylinder head gasket surface for distortion.
	3. Oil filter gasket broken or improperly seated.	3. Replace oil filter.
	4. Oil pan side gasket broken or improperly seated.	4. Replace gasket; check oil pan gasket flange for distortion.
	5. Oil pan front oil seal broken or improperly seated.	5. Replace seal; check timing chain cover and oil pan seal flange for distortion
	6. Oil pan rear oil seal broken or improperly seated.	6. Replace seal; check oil pan rear oil seal flange; check rear main bearing cap for cracks, plugged oil return channels, or distortion in seal groove.
	7. Timing chain cover oil seal broken or improperly seated.	7. Replace seal.
	8. Oil pan drain plug loose or has stripped threads.	8. Repair as necessary and tighten.
	9. Rear oil gallery plug loose.	9. Use appropriate sealant on gallery plug and tighten.
	10. Rear camshaft plug loose or improperly seated.	10. Seat camshaft plug or replace and seal, as necessary.
EXCESSIVE OIL CONSUMPTION	1. Oil level too high.	1. Lower oil level to specifications.
	2. Oil too thin.	2. Replace with specified oil.
	3. Valve stem oil seals are damaged, missing, or incorrect type.	3. Replace valve stem oil seals.
	4. Valve stems or valve guides worn.	4. Check stem-to-guide clearance and repair as necessary.
	5. Piston rings broken, missing.	5. Replace missing or broken rings.
	6. Piston rings incorrect size.	6. Check ring gap, repair as necessary.
	7. Piston rings sticking or excessively loose in grooves.	7. Check ring side clearance, repair as necessary.
	8. Compression rings installed upside down.	8. Repair as necessary.
	9. Cylinder walls worn, scored, or glazed.	9. Repair as necessary.
	10. Piston ring gaps not properly staggered.	10. Repair as necessary.
	11. Excessive main or connecting rod bearing clearance.	11. Check bearing clearance, repair as necessary.

OIL PRESSURE INDICATOR

Condition	Possible Cause	Correction
LIGHT NOT LIT, IGNITION ON AND ENGINE NOT RUNNING.	1. Bulb burned out.	1. Replace bulb.
	2. Open in light circuit.	2. Locate and correct open.
	3. Defective oil pressure switch.	3. Replace oil pressure switch.
LIGHT ON, ENGINE RUNNING ABOVE IDLE SPEED.	1. Grounded wiring between light and switch.	1. Locate and repair ground.
	2. Defective oil pressure switch.	2. Replace oil pressure switch.
	3. Low oil pressure.	3. Locate cause of low oil pressure and correct.

IGNITION, STARTER & FUEL

Condition	Possible Cause	Correction
NOTHING HAPPENS WHEN START ATTEMPT IS MADE	1. Undercharged or defective battery.	1. Check condition of battery and recharge or replace as required.
	2. Loose battery cables.	2. Clean and tighten cable connections.
	3. Burned fusible link in starting circuit.	3. Check for burned fusible link. Correct wiring problem.
	4. Incorrectly positioned or defective neutral start switch.	4. Check neutral start switch adjustment. If O.K., replace switch.
	5. Loose or defective wiring between neutral start switch and ignition switch.	5. Check for loose connections and opens between battery, horn relay, ignition switch, and solenoid "S" terminal. Check battery ground cable. Replace or repair defective item.

TROUBLE SHOOTING

IGNITION, STARTER & FUEL—Continued

Condition	Possible Cause	Correction
NOTHING HAPPENS WHEN START ATTEMPT IS MADE, continued	6. Defective starter motor. 7. Defective starter interlock system.	6. Repair or replace starter motor. 7. Use emergency button under hood. If car starts, repair circuit in interlock system. If car does not start, check and repair starter circuit.
SOLENOID SWITCH CLICKS BUT STARTER DOES NOT CRANK	1. Undercharged or defective battery. 2. Loose battery cables. 3. Loose or defective wiring at starter. 4. Defective solenoid. 5. "Hot stall" condition. 6. Excessive engine rotational torque caused by mechanical problem within engine. 7. Defective starter motor.	1. Test battery. Recharge or replace battery. 2. Check and tighten battery connections. 3. Tighten connections or repair wiring as required. 4. Replace solenoid. 5. Check engine cooling system. 6. Check engine torque for excessive friction. 7. Repair or replace starter motor.
SLOW CRANKING	1. Vehicle is overheating. 2. Undercharged or defective battery. 3. Loose or defective wiring between battery and engine block. 4. Loose or defective wiring between battery and solenoid "Bat" terminal. 5. Defective starter motor.	1. Check engine cooling system and repair as required. 2. Recharge or replace battery. 3. Repair or replace wiring. 4. Repair or replace wiring. 5. Repair or replace starter.
STARTER SPINS AND/OR MAKES LOUD GRINDING NOISE BUT DOES NOT TURN ENGINE	1. Defective starter motor. 2. Defective ring gear.	1. Repair or replace starter motor. 2. Replace ring gear.
STARTER KEEPS RUNNING AFTER IGNITION SWITCH IS RELEASED—FROM "START" TO "RUN" POSITION	1. Defective ignition switch. 2. Defective solenoid.	1. Replace ignition switch. 2. Replace solenoid.
STARTER ENGAGES ("CLUNKS") BUT ENGINE DOES NOT CRANK	1. Open circuit in solenoid armature or field coils. 2. Short or ground in field coil or armature.	1. Repair or replace solenoid or starter motor. 2. Repair or replace starter motor.
HARD STARTING (ENGINE CRANKS NORMALLY)	1. Binding linkage, choke valve or choke piston. 2. Restricted choke vacuum and hot air passages. 3. Improper fuel level. 4. Dirty, worn or faulty needle valve and seat. 5. Float sticking. 6. Exhaust manifold heat valve stuck. 7. Faulty fuel pump. 8. Incorrect choke cover adjustment. 9. Inadequate unloader adjustment. 10. Faulty ignition coil. 11. Improper spark plug gap. 12. Incorrect initial timing. 13. Incorrect valve timing.	1. Repair as necessary. 2. Clean passages. 3. Adjust float level. 4. Repair as necessary. 5. Repair as necessary. 6. Repair as necessary. 7. Replace fuel pump. 8. Adjust choke cover. 9. Adjust unloader. 10. Test and replace as necessary. 11. Adjust gap. 12. Adjust timing. 13. Check valve timing; repair as necessary.
ROUGH IDLE OR STALLING	1. Incorrect curb or fast idle speed. 2. Incorrect initial timing. 3. Improper idle mixture adjustment. 4. Damaged tip on idle mixture screw(s). 5. Improper fast idle cam adjustment. 6. Faulty PCV valve air flow. 7. Exhaust manifold heat valve inoperative. 8. Choke binding. 9. Improper choke setting. 10. Vacuum leak. 11. Improper fuel level.	1. Adjust curb or fast idle speed. 2. Adjust timing to specifications. 3. Adjust idle mixture. 4. Replace mixture screw(s). 5. Adjust fast idle. 6. Test PCV valve and replace as necessary. 7. Lubricate or replace heat valve as necessary. 8. Locate and eliminate binding condition. 9. Adjust choke. 10. Check manifold vacuum and repair as necessary. 11. Adjust fuel level.

IGNITION, STARTER & FUEL—Continued

Condition	Possible Cause	Correction
ROUGH IDLE OR STALLING, continued	12. Faulty distributor rotor or cap.	12. Replace rotor or cap.
	13. Leaking engine valves.	13. Check cylinder leakdown rate or compression and repair as necessary.
	14. Incorrect ignition wiring.	14. Check wiring and correct as necessary.
	15. Faulty coil.	15. Test coil and replace as necessary.
	16. Clogged air bleed or idle passages.	16. Clean passages.
	17. Restricted air cleaner.	17. Clean or replace air cleaner.
	18. Faulty EGR valve operation if equipped.	18. Test EGR system and replace as necessary if equipped.
FAULTY LOW-SPEED OPERATION	1. Clogged idle transfer slots.	1. Clean transfer slots.
	2. Restricted idle air bleeds and passages.	2. Clean air bleeds and passages.
	3. Restricted air cleaner.	3. Clean or replace air cleaner.
	4. Improper fuel level.	4. Adjust fuel level.
	5. Faulty spark plugs.	5. Clean or replace spark plugs.
	6. Dirty, corroded, or loose secondary circuit connections.	6. Clean or tighten secondary circuit connections.
	7. Faulty ignition cable.	7. Replace ignition cable.
	8. Faulty distributor cap.	8. Replace cap.
FAULTY ACCELERATION	1. Improper pump stroke.	1. Adjust pump stroke.
	2. Incorrect ignition timing.	2. Adjust timing.
	3. Inoperative pump discharge check ball or needle.	3. Clean or replace as necessary.
	4. Worn or damaged pump diaphragm or piston.	4. Replace diaphragm or piston.
	5. Leaking main body cover gasket.	5. Replace gasket.
	6. Engine cold and choke too lean.	6. Adjust choke.
	7. Faulty spark plug(s).	7. Clean or replace spark plug(s).
	8. Leaking engine valves.	8. Check cylinder leakdown rate or compression, repair as necessary.
	9. Faulty coil.	9. Test coil and replace as necessary.
FAULTY HIGH-SPEED OPERATION	1. Incorrect ignition timing.	1. Adjust timing.
	2. Faulty distributor centrifugal advance.	2. Check centrifugal advance and repair as necessary.
	3. Faulty distributor vacuum advance.	3. Check vacuum advance and repair as necessary.
	4. Low fuel pump volume.	4. Replace fuel pump.
	5. Improper spark plug gap.	5. Adjust gap.
	6. Faulty choke operation.	6. Adjust choke.
	7. Partially restricted exhaust manifold, exhaust pipe, muffler, or tailpipe.	7. Eliminate restriction.
	8. Clogged vacuum passages.	8. Clean passages.
	9. Improper size or obstructed main jets.	9. Clean or replace as necessary.
	10. Restricted air cleaner.	10. Clean or replace as necessary.
	11. Faulty distributor rotor or cap.	11. Replace rotor or cap.
	12. Worn distributor shaft.	12. Replace shaft.
	13. Faulty coil.	13. Test coil and replace as necessary.
	14. Leaking engine valve(s).	14. Check cylinder leakdown or compression and repair as necessary.
	15. Faulty valve spring(s).	15. Inspect and test valve spring tension and replace as necessary.
	16. Incorrect valve timing.	16. Check valve timing and repair as necessary.
	17. Intake manifold restricted.	17. Pass chain through passages.
MISFIRE AT ALL SPEEDS	1. Faulty spark plug(s).	1. Clean or replace spark plug(s).
	2. Faulty spark plug cable(s).	2. Replace as necessary.
	3. Faulty distributor cap or rotor.	3. Replace cap or rotor.
	4. Faulty coil.	4. Test coil and replace as necessary.
	5. Primary circuit shorted or open intermittently.	5. Trace primary circuit and repair as necessary.
	6. Leaking engine valve(s).	6. Check cylinder leakdown rate or compression and repair as necessary.
	7. Faulty hydraulic tappet(s).	7. Clean or replace tappet(s).
	8. Faulty valve spring(s).	8. Inspect and test valve spring tension, repair as necessary.
	9. Worn lobes on camshaft.	9. Replace camshaft.
	10. Vacuum leak.	10. Check manifold vacuum and repair as necessary.
	11. Improper carburetor settings.	11. Adjust carburetor.
	12. Fuel pump volume or pressure low.	12. Replace fuel pump.
	13. Blown cylinder head gasket.	13. Replace gasket.
	14. Intake or exhaust manifold passage(s) restricted.	14. Pass chain through passages.

TROUBLE SHOOTING

IGNITION, STARTER & FUEL—Continued

Condition	Possible Cause	Correction
POWER NOT UP TO NORMAL	1. Incorrect ignition timing. 2. Faulty distributor rotor. 3. Worn distributor shaft. 4. Incorrect spark plug gap. 5. Faulty fuel pump. 6. Incorrect valve timing. 7. Faulty coil. 8. Faulty ignition cables. 9. Leaking engine valves. 10. Blown cylinder head gasket. 11. Leaking piston rings.	1. Adjust timing. 2. Replace rotor. 3. Replace shaft. 4. Adjust gap. 5. Replace fuel pump. 6. Check valve timing and repair as necessary. 7. Test coil and replace as necessary. 8. Test cables and replace as necessary. 9. Check cylinder leakdown rate or compression and repair as necessary. 10. Replace gasket. 11. Check compression and repair as necessary.
INTAKE BACKFIRE	1. Improper ignition timing. 2. Faulty accelerator pump discharge. 3. Improper choke operation. 4. Lean fuel mixture.	1. Adjust timing. 2. Repair as necessary. 3. Repair as necessary. 4. Check float level or manifold vacuum for vacuum leak.
EXHAUST BACKFIRE	1. Vacuum leak. 2. Faulty A.I.R. diverter valve. 3. Faulty choke operation. 4. Exhaust leak.	1. Check manifold vacuum and repair as necessary. 2. Test diverter valve and replace as necessary. 3. Repair as necessary. 4. Locate and eliminate leak.
PING OR SPARK KNOCK	1. Incorrect ignition timing. 2. Distributor centrifugal or vacuum advance malfunction. 3. Excessive combustion chamber deposits. 4. Carburetor set too lean. 5. Vacuum leak. 6. Excessively high compression. 7. Fuel octane rating excessively low. 8. Heat riser stuck in heat on position.	1. Adjust timing. 2. Check advance and repair as necessary. 3. Use combustion chamber cleaner. 4. Adjust carburetor. 5. Check manifold vacuum and repair as necessary. 6. Check compression and repair as necessary. 7. Try alternate fuel source. 8. Free-up or replace heat riser.
SURGING (CRUISING SPEEDS TO TOP SPEEDS)	1. Low fuel level. 2. Low fuel pump pressure or volume. 3. Improper PCV valve air flow. 4. Vacuum leak. 5. Dirt in carburetor. 6. Undersize main jets. 7. Clogged fuel filter screen. 8. Restricted air cleaner.	1. Adjust fuel level. 2. Replace fuel pump. 3. Test PCV valve and replace as necessary. 4. Check manifold vacuum and repair as necessary. 5. Clean carburetor, replace filter. 6. Replace main jet(s). 7. Replace fuel filter. 8. Clean or replace air cleaner.

CHARGING SYSTEM

Condition	Possible Cause	Correction
ALTERNATOR FAILS TO CHARGE (No Output or Low Output)	1. Alternator drive belt loose. 2. Regulator base improperly grounded. 3. Worn brushes and/or slip rings. 4. Sticking brushes. 5. Open field circuit. 6. Open charging circuit. 7. Open circuit in stator windings. 8. Open rectifiers.	1. Adjust drive belt to specifications. 2. Connect regulator to a good ground. 3. Install new brushes and/or slip rings. 4. Clean slip rings and brush holders. Install new brushes if necessary. 5. Test all the field circuit connections, and correct as required. 6. Inspect all connections in charging circuit, and correct as required. 7. Remove alternator and disassemble. Test stator windings. Install new stator if necessary. 8. Remove alternator and disassemble. Test the rectifiers. Install new rectifier assemblies if necessary.

CHARGING SYSTEM—Continued

Condition	Possible Cause	Correction
LOW, UNSTEADY CHARGING RATE	1. High resistance in body to engine ground lead. 2. Alternator drive belt loose. 3. High resistance at battery terminals. 4. High resistance in charging circuit. 5. Open stator winding.	1. Tighten ground lead connections. Install new ground lead if necessary. 2. Adjust alternator drive belt. 3. Clean and tighten battery terminals. 4. Test charging circuit resistance. Correct as required. 5. Remove and disassemble alternator. Test stator windings. Install new stator if necessary.
LOW OUTPUT AND A LOW BATTERY	1. High resistance in charging circuit. 2. Shorted rectifier. Open rectifier. 3. Grounded stator windings. 4. Faulty voltage regulator.	1. Test charging circuit resistance and correct as required. 2. Perform current output test. Test the rectifiers and install new rectifier heat sink assembly as required. Remove and disassemble the alternator. 3. Remove and disassemble alternator. Test stator windings. Install new stator if necessary. 4. Test voltage regulator. Replace as necessary.
EXCESSIVE CHARGING RATE TO A FULLY CHARGED BATTERY	1. Faulty ignition switch. 2. Faulty voltage regulator.	1. Install new ignition switch. 2. Test voltage regulator. Replace as necessary.
NOISY ALTERNATOR	1. Alternator mounting loose. 2. Worn or frayed drive belt. 3. Worn bearings. 4. Interference between rotor fan and stator leads. 5. Rotor or rotor fan damaged. 6. Open or shorted rectifier. 7. Open or shorted winding in stator.	1. Properly install and tighten alternator mounting. 2. Install a new drive belt and adjust to specifications. 3. Remove and disassemble alternator. Install new bearings as required. 4. Remove and disassemble alternator. Correct interference as required. 5. Remove and disassemble alternator. Install new rotor. 6. Remove and disassemble alternator. Test rectifiers. Install new rectifier heat sink assembly as required. 7. Remove and disassemble alternator. Test stator windings. Install new stator if necessary.
EXCESSIVE AMMETER FLUCTUATION	1. High resistance in the alternator and voltage regulator circuit.	1. Clean and tighten all connections as necessary.

CHARGING SYSTEM INDICATOR

LIGHT ON, IGNITION OFF.	1. Shorted positive diode.	1. Locate and replace shorted diode.
LIGHT NOT ON, IGNITION ON AND ENGINE NOT RUNNING.	1. Bulb burned out. 2. Open in light circuit. 3. Open in field.	1. Replace bulb. 2. Locate and correct open. 3. Replace rotor.
LIGHT ON, ENGINE RUNNING ABOVE IDLE SPEED.	1. No generator output. 2. Shortened negative diode. 3. Loose or broken generator belt.	1. Check and correct cause of no output. 2. Locate and replace shorted diode. 3. Tighten or replace and tighten generator belt.

TROUBLE SHOOTING

COOLING SYSTEM

Condition	Possible Cause	Correction
HIGH TEMPERATURE INDICATION- OVERHEATING	1. Coolant level low. 2. Fan belt loose. 3. Radiator hose(s) collapsed. 4. Radiator blocked to airflow. 5. Faulty radiator cap. 6. Car overloaded. 7. Ignition timing incorrect. 8. Idle speed low. 9. Air trapped in cooling system. 10. Car in heavy traffic. 11. Incorrect cooling system component(s) installed. 12. Faulty thermostat. 13. Water pump shaft broken or impeller loose. 14. Radiator tubes clogged. 15. Cooling system clogged. 16. Casting flash in cooling passages. 17. Brakes dragging. 18. Excessive engine friction. 19. Car working beyond cooling system capacity. 20. Antifreeze concentration over 68%. 21. Low anti-freeze concentration.	1. Replenish coolant level. 2. Adjust fan belt. 3. Replace hose(s). 4. Remove restriction. 5. Replace cap. 6. Reduce load. 7. Adjust ignition timing. 8. Adjust idle speed. 9. Purge air. 10. Operate at fast idle intermittently to cool engine. 11. Install proper component(s). 12. Replace thermostat. 13. Replace water pump. 14. Flush radiator. 15. Flush system. 16. Repair or replace as necessary. Flash may be visible by removing cooling system components or removing core plugs. 17. Repair brakes. 18. Repair engine. 19. Install heavy-duty cooling fan and/or radiator. 20. Lower antifreeze content. 21. Add anti-freeze to provide a minimum 50% concentration.
LOW TEMPERATURE INDICATION—OVERCOOLING	1. Improper fan being used. 2. Improper radiator. 3. Thermostat stuck open. 4. Improper fan pulley (too small).	1. Install proper fan. 2. Install proper radiator. 3. Replace thermostat. 4. Install proper pulley.
COOLANT LOSS—BOILOVER **NOTE:** Immediately after shutdown, the engine enters a period known as heat soak. This is caused because the cooling system is inoperative but engine temperature is still high. If coolant temperature rises above boiling point, it may push some coolant out of the radiator overflow tube. If this does not occur frequently, it is considered normal.	Refer to Overheating Causes in addition to the following: 1. Overfilled cooling system. 2. Quick shutdown after hard (hot) run. 3. Air in system resulting in occasional "burping" of coolant. 4. Insufficient antifreeze allowing coolant boiling point to be too low. 5. Antifreeze deteriorated because of age or contamination. 6. Leaks due to loose hose clamps, loose nuts, bolts, drain plugs, faulty hoses, or defective radiator. 7. Faulty head gasket. 8. Cracked head, manifold, or block.	 1. Reduce coolant level to proper specification. 2. Allow engine to run at fast idle prior to shutdown. 3. Purge system. 4. Add antifreeze to raise boiling point. 5. Replace coolant. 6. Pressure test system to locate leak then repair as necessary. 7. Replace head gasket. 8. Replace as necessary.
COOLANT ENTRY INTO CRANKCASE OR CYLINDER	1. Faulty head gasket. 2. Crack in head, manifold or block.	1. Replace head gasket. 2. Replace as necessary.
COOLANT RECOVERY SYSTEM INOPERATIVE	1. Coolant level low. 2. Leak in system. 3. Pressure cap not tight or gasket missing or leaking. 4. Pressure cap defective. 5. Overflow tube clogged or leaking. 6. Recovery bottle vent plugged.	1. Replenish coolant. 2. Pressure test to isolate leak and repair as necessary. 3. Repair as necessary. 4. Replace cap. 5. Repair as necessary. 6. Remove restriction.
NOISE	1. Fan contacting shroud. 2. Loose water pump impeller. 3. Dry fan belt. 4. Loose fan belt. 5. Rough surface on drive pulley. 6. Water pump bearing worn.	1. Reposition shroud and check engine mounts. 2. Replace pump. 3. Apply belt dressing or replace belt. 4. Adjust fan belt. 5. Replace pulley. 6. Remove belt to isolate. Replace pump.

COOLING SYSTEM—Continued

Condition	Possible Cause	Correction
NO COOLANT FLOW THROUGH HEATER CORE	1. Plugged return pipe in water pump. 2. Heater hose collapsed or plugged. 3. Plugged heater core. 4. Plugged outlet in thermostat housing. 5. Heater bypass hole in cylinder head plugged.	1. Remove obstruction. 2. Remove obstruction or replace hose. 3. Remove obstruction or replace core. 4. Remove flash or obstruction. 5. Remove obstruction.

COOLANT TEMPERATURE INDICATOR

Condition	Possible Cause	Correction
"HOT" INDICATOR; LIGHT NOT LIT WHEN CRANKING ENGINE.	1. Bulb burned out. 2. Open in light circuit. 3. Defective ignition switch.	1. Replace bulb. 2. Locate and correct open. 3. Replace ignition switch.
LIGHT ON, ENGINE RUNNING.	1. Wiring grounded between light and switch. 2. Defective temperature switch. 3. Defective ignition switch. 4. High coolant temperature.	1. Locate and correct grounded wiring. 2. Replace temperature switch. 3. Replace ignition switch. 4. Locate and correct cause of high coolant temperature.

EXHAUST SYSTEM

Condition	Possible Cause	Correction
LEAKING EXHAUST GASES	1. Leaks at pipe joints. 2. Damaged or improperly installed seals or packing. 3. Loose exhaust pipe heat tube extension connections. 4. Burned or rusted out exhaust pipe heat tube extensions.	1. Tighten U-bolt nuts at leaking joints. 2. Replace seals or packing as necessary. 3. Replace seals or packing as required. Tighten stud nuts or bolts. 4. Replace heat tube extensions as required.
EXHAUST NOISES	1. Leaks at manifold or pipe connections. 2. Burned or blown out muffler. 3. Burned or rusted out exhaust pipe. 4. Exhaust pipe leaking at manifold flange. 5. Exhaust manifold cracked or broken. 6. Leak between manifold and cylinder head.	1. Tighten clamps at leaking connections to specified torque. Replace gasket or packing as required. 2. Replace muffler assembly. 3. Replace exhaust pipe. 4. Tighten attaching bolt nuts. 5. Replace manifold. 6. Tighten manifold to cylinder head stud nuts or bolts.
LOSS OF ENGINE POWER AND/OR INTERNAL RATTLES IN MUFFLER	1. Dislodged turning tubes and or baffles in muffler.	1. Replace muffler.
LOSS OF ENGINE POWER	1. Imploding (inner wall collapse) of exhaust pipe.	1. Replace exhaust pipe.
ENGINE HARD TO WARM UP OR WILL NOT RETURN TO NORMAL IDLE	1. Heat control valve frozen in the open position.	1. Free up manifold heat control using a suitable manifold heat control solvent.
MANIFOLD HEAT CONTROL VALVE NOISE	1. Thermostat broken. 2. Broken, weak or missing anti-rattle spring.	1. Replace thermostat. 2. Replace spring.

CLUTCH & SYNCHRO-MESH TRANSMISSION

Condition	Possible Cause	Correction
CLUTCH CHATTER	1. Worn or damaged disc assembly. 2. Grease or oil on disc facings. 3. Improperly adjusted cover assembly. 4. Broken or loose engine mounts. 5. Misaligned clutch housing.	1. Replace disc assembly. 2. Replace disc assembly and correct cause of contamination. 3. Replace cover assembly. 4. Replace or tighten mounts. 5. Align clutch housing.

TROUBLE SHOOTING

CLUTCH & SYNCHRO-MESH TRANSMISSION—Cont'd

Condition	Possible Cause	Correction
CLUTCH SLIPPING	1. Insufficient pedal free play. 2. Burned, worn, or oil soaked facings. 3. Weak or broken pressure springs.	1. Adjust release fork rod. 2. Replace disc assembly and correct cause of contamination. 3. Replace cover assembly.
DIFFICULT GEAR SHIFTING	1. Excessive pedal free play. 2. Excessive deflection in linkage or firewall. 3. Worn or damaged disc assembly. 4. Improperly adjusted cover assembly. 5. Clutch disc splines sticking. 6. Worn or dry pilot bushing. 7. Clutch housing misaligned.	1. Adjust release fork rod. 2. Repair or replace linkage. 3. Replace disc assembly. 4. Replace cover assembly. 5. Remove disc assembly and free up splines or replace disc. 6. Lubricate or replace bushing. 7. Align clutch housing.
CLUTCH NOISY	1. Dry clutch linkage. 2. Worn release bearing. 3. Worn disc assembly. 4. Worn release levers. 5. Worn or dry pilot bushing. 6. Dry contact-pressure plate lugs in cover.	1. Lubricate where necessary. 2. Replace release bearing. 3. Replace disc assembly. 4. Replace cover assembly. 5. Lubricate or replace bushing. 6. Lubricate very lightly.
TRANSMISSION SHIFTS HARD	1. Incorrect clutch adjustment. 2. Clutch linkage binding. 3. Gearshift linkage incorrectly adjusted, bent, or binding. 4. Bind in steering column, or column is misaligned. 5. Incorrect lubricant. 6. Internal bind in transmissions - e.g. shift rails, interlocks, shift forks, synchronizer teeth. 7. Clutch housing misalignment.	1. Adjust clutch pedal free-play. 2. Lubricate or repair linkage as required. 3. Adjust linkage - correct any bind. Replace bent parts. 4. Disconnect shift rods at column. Check for bind/misalignment between tube and jacket by shifting lever into all positions. Correct as required. 5. Drain and refill transmission. 6. Remove transmission and inspect shift mechanism. Repair as required. 7. Check runout at rear face of clutch housing.
GEAR CLASH WHEN SHIFTING FROM ONE FORWARD GEAR TO ANOTHER	1. Incorrect clutch adjustment. 2. Clutch linkage binding. 3. Gear shift linkage incorrectly adjusted, bent or binding. 4. Clutch housing misalignment. 5. Damaged or worn transmission components: shift forks, synchronizers, shift rails and interlocks. Excessive end play due to worn thrust washers.	1. Adjust clutch. 2. Lubricate or repair linkage as required. 3. Adjust linkage, correct binds, replace bent parts. 4. Check runout at rear face of clutch housing. 5. Inspect components. Repair or replace as required.
TRANSMISSION NOISY	1. Insufficient lubricant. 2. Incorrect lubricant. 3. Clutch housing to engine or transmission to clutch housing bolts loose. 4. Dirt, chips in lubricant. 5. Gearshift linkage incorrectly adjusted, or bent or binding. 6. Clutch housing misalignment. 7. Worn transmission components: front-rear bearings, worn gear teeth, damaged gear teeth or synchronizer components.	1. Check lubricant level and replenish as required. 2. Replace with proper lubricant. 3. Check and correct bolt torque as required. 4. Drain and flush transmission. 5. Adjust linkage, correct binds, replace bent parts. 6. Check runout at rear face of clutch housing. 7. Inspect components and repair as required.
JUMPS OUT OF GEAR	1. Gearshift linkage incorrectly adjusted. 2. Gearshift linkage bent or binding. 3. Clutch housing misaligned. 4. Worn pilot bushing. 5. Worn or damaged clutch shaft roller bearings.	1. Adjust linkage. 2. Correct bind, replace bent parts. 3. Check runout at rear face of clutch housing. 4. Replace bushing. 5. Replace bearings.

CLUTCH & SYNCHRO-MESH TRANSMISSION—Cont'd

Condition	Possible Cause	Correction
JUMPS OUT OF GEAR, continued	6. Worn, tapered gear teeth; synchronizer parts worn.	6. Inspect and replace as required.
	7. Shifter forks, shift rails, or detent-interlock parts worn, missing, etc.	7. Inspect and replace as required.
	8. Excessive end play of output shaft gear train, countershaft gear or reverse idler gear.	8. Replace thrust washers, and snap rings (output shaft gear train).
WILL NOT SHIFT INTO ONE GEAR—ALL OTHERS OK	1. Gearshift linkage not adjusted correctly.	1. Adjust linkage.
	2. Bent shift rod at transmission.	2. Replace rod.
	3. Transmission shifter levers reversed.	3. Correctly position levers.
	4. Worn or damaged shift rails, shift forks, detent-interlock plugs, loose setscrew in shifter fork, worn synchronizer parts.	4. Inspect and repair or replace parts as required.
LOCKED IN ONE GEAR—CAN NOT BE SHIFTED OUT OF THAT GEAR	1. Gearshift linkage binding or bent.	1. Correct bind, replace bent components.
	2. Transmission shifter lever attaching nuts loose or levers are worn at shifter fork shaft hole.	2. Tighten nuts, replace worn levers.
	3. Shift rails worn or broken, shifter fork bent, setscrew loose, detent-interlock plug missing or worn.	3. Inspect and replace worn or damaged parts.
	4. Broken gear teeth on countershaft gear, clutch shaft, or reverse idler gear.	4. Inspect and replace damaged part.

BRAKES

Condition	Possible Cause	Correction
LOW BRAKE PEDAL (Excessive pedal travel required to apply brake)	1. Excessive clearance between linings and drums caused by inoperative automatic adjusters.	1. Make 10 to 15 firm forward and reverse brake stops to adjust brakes. If brake pedal does not come up, repair or replace adjuster parts as necessary.
	2. Worn brake lining.	2. Inspect and replace lining if worn beyond minimum thickness specification.
	3. Bent, distorted brakeshoes.	3. Replace brakeshoes in axle sets.
	4. Caliper pistons corroded.	4. Repair or replace calipers.
	5. Power unit push rod height incorrect.	5. Check height with gauge (only). Replace power unit if push rod height is not within specifications.
LOW BRAKE PEDAL (Pedal may go to floor under steady pressure)	1. Leak in hydraulic system.	1. Fill master cylinder to within 1/4-inch of rim; have helper apply brakes and check calipers, wheel cylinders combination valve, tubes, hoses and fittings for leaks. Repair or replace parts as necessary.
	2. Air in hydraulic system.	2. Bleed air from system. Refer to Brake Bleeding.
	3. Incorrect or non-recommended brake fluid (fluid boils away at below normal temp.).	3. Flush hydrauilc system with clean brake fluid. Refill with correct-type fluid.
LOW BRAKE PEDAL (Pedal goes to floor on first application—Ok on subsequent applications)	1. Disc brakeshoe (pad) knock back; shoes push caliper piston back into bore. Caused by loose wheel bearings or excessive lateral runout of rotor (rotor wobble).	1. Adjust wheel bearings and check lateral runout of rotor(s). Refinish rotors if runout is over limits. Replace rotor if refinishing would cause rotor to fall below minimum thickness limit.
	2. Calipers sticking on mounting surfaces of caliper and anchor. Caused by buildup of dirt, rust, or corrosion on abutment.	2. Clean mounting surfaces and lubricate surfaces with molydisulphide grease or equivalent.
FADING BRAKE PEDAL (Pedal falls away under steady pressure)	1. Leak in hydraulic system.	1. Fill master cylinder reservoirs to within 1/4-inch of rim; have helper apply brakes, check master cylinder, calipers, wheel cylinders combination valve, tubes, hoses, and fittings for leaks. Repair or replace parts as necessary.

BRAKES—Continued

Condition	Possible Cause	Correction
FADING BRAKE PEDAL, continued	2. Master cylinder piston cups worn, or master cylinder bore is scored, worn or corroded.	2. Repair or replace master cylinder.
DECREASING BRAKE PEDAL TRAVEL (Pedal travel required to apply brakes decreases, may be accompanied by hard pedal)	1. Caliper or wheel cylinder pistons sticking or seized. 2. Master cylinder compensator ports blocked (preventing fluid return to reservoirs) or pistons sticking or seized in master cylinder bore. 3. Power brake unit binding internally. 4. Incorrect power unit push rod height.	1. Repair or replace calipers, or wheel cylinders. 2. Repair or replace master cylinder. 3. Test unit as follows: (a) Raise hood, shift transmission into neutral and start engine. (b) Increase engine speed to 1500 RPM, close throttle and fully depress brake pedal. (c) Slowly release brake pedal and stop engine. (d) Remove vacuum check valve and hose from power unit. Observe for backward movement of brake pedal or power unit-to-brake pedal push rod. (e) If pedal or push rod move backward, power unit has internal bind—replace power brake unit. 4. Adjust push rod height.
SPONGY BRAKE PEDAL (Pedal has abnormally soft, springy, spongy feel when depressed)	1. Air in hydraulic system. 2. Brakeshoes bent or distorted. 3. Brake lining not yet seated to drums and rotors.	1. Bleed brakes. 2. Replace brakeshoes. 3. Burnish brakes.
HARD BRAKE PEDAL (Excessive pedal pressure required to stop car. May be accompanied by brake fade)	1. Loose or leaking power brake unit vacuum hose. 2. Brake lining contaminated by grease or brake fluid. 3. Incorrect or poor quality brake lining. 4. Bent, broken, distorted brakeshoes. 5. Calipers binding or dragging on anchor. Rear brakeshoes dragging on support plate. 6. Rear brake drum(s) bell mouthed, flared or barrel shaped (distorted). 7. Caliper, wheel cylinder, or master cylinder pistons sticking or seized. 8. Power brake unit vacuum check valve malfunction. 9. Power brake unit has internal bind or incorrect push rod height (too long).	1. Tighten connections or replace leaking hose. 2. Determine cause of contaminations and correct. Replace contaminated brake lining in axle sets. 3. Replace lining in axle sets. 4. Replace brakeshoes and lining. 5. Sand or wire brush anchors and caliper mounting surfaces and lubricate surfaces lightly. Clean rust or burrs from rear brake support plate ledges and lubricate ledges. NOTE: If ledges are deeply grooved or scored, do not attempt to sand or grind them smooth—replace support plate. 6. Replace rear drum(s). 7. Repair or replace parts as necessary. 8. Test valve as follows: (a) Start engine, increase engine speed to 1500 RPM, close throttle and immediately stop engine. (b) Wait at least 90 seconds then try brake action. (c) If brakes are not vacuum assisted for 2 or more applications, check valve is faulty. 9. Test unit as follows: (a) With engine stopped, apply brakes several times to exhaust all vacuum in system. (b) Shift transmission into neutral, depress brake pedal and start engine. (c) If pedal falls away under foot pressure and less pressure is required to hold pedal in applied position, power unit vacuum system is working. Test power unit as outlined in item (3) under

BRAKES—Continued

Condition	Possible Cause	Correction
HARD BRAKE PEDAL, continued		Decreasing Brake Pedal Travel. If power unit exhibits bind condition, replace power unit. (d) If power unit does not exhibit bind condition, disconnect master cylinder and check push rod height with appropriate gauge. If height is not within specifications, replace power unit.
	10. Master cylinder compensator ports (at bottom of reservoirs) blocked by dirt, scale, rust, or have small burrs (blocked ports prevent fluid return to reservoirs).	10. Repair or replace master cylinder. CAUTION: Do not attempt to clean blocked ports with wire, pencils, or similar implements.
	11. Brake hoses, tubes, fittings clogged or restricted.	11. Use compressed air to check or unclog parts. Replace any damaged parts.
	12. Brake fluid contaminated with improper fluids (motor oil, transmission fluid, or poor quality brake fluid) causing rubber components to swell and stick in bores.	12. Replace all rubber components and hoses. Flush entire brake system. Refill with recommended brake fluid.
GRABBING BRAKES **(Severe reaction to brake pedal pressure)**	1. Brake lining(s) contaminated by grease or brake fluid.	1. Determine and correct cause of contamination and replace brakeshoes and linings in axle sets.
	2. Parking brake cables incorrectly adjusted or seized.	2. Adjust cables. Free up or replace seized cables.
	3. Power brake unit binding internally or push rod height incorrect.	3. Test unit as outlined in item (3) under Decreasing Brake Pedal Travel. If o.k., check push rod height. If unit has internal bind or incorrect push rod height, replace unit.
	4. Incorrect brake lining or lining loose on brakeshoes.	4. Replace brakeshoes in axle sets.
	5. Brakeshoes bent, cracked, distorted.	5. Replace brakeshoes in axle sets.
	6. Caliper anchor plate bolts loose.	6. Tighten bolts.
	7. Rear brakeshoes binding on support plate ledges.	7. Clean and lubricate ledges. Replace support plate(s) if ledges are deeply grooved. Do not attempt to smooth ledges by grinding.
	8. Rear brake support plates loose.	8. Tighten mounting bolts.
	9. Caliper or wheel cylinder piston sticking or seized.	9. Repair or replace parts as necessary.
	10. Master cylinder pistons sticking or siezed in bore.	10. Repair or replace master cylinder.
BRAKES GRAB, PULL, OR WON'T HOLD IN WET WEATHER	1. Brake lining water soaked.	1. Drive car with brakes lightly applied to dry out lining. If problem persists after lining has dried, replace brakeshoe lining in axle sets.
	2. Rear brake support plate bent allowing excessive amount of water to enter drum.	2. Replace support plate.
DRAGGING BRAKES **(Slow or incomplete release of brakes)**	1. Brake pedal binding at pivot.	1. Free up and lubricate.
	2. Power brake unit push rod height incorrect (too high) or unit has internal bind.	2. Replace unit if push rod height is incorrect. If height is o.k., check for internal bind as outlined in item (3) under Decreasing Brake Pedal Travel.
	3. Parking brake cables incorrectly adjusted or seized.	3. Adjust cables. Free up or replace seized cables.
	4. Brakeshoe return springs weak or broken.	4. Replace return springs. Replace brakeshoe if necessary in axle sets.
	5. Automatic adjusters malfunctioning.	5. Repair or replace adjuster parts as required.
	6. Caliper, wheel cylinder or master cylinder pistons sticking or seized.	6. Repair or replace parts as necessary.
	7. Master cylinder compensating ports blocked (fluid does not return to reservoirs).	7. Use compressed air to clear ports. Do not use wire, pencils, or similar objects to open blocked ports.
CAR PULLS TO ONE SIDE WHEN BRAKES ARE APPLIED	1. Incorrect front tire pressure.	1. Inflate to recommended cold (reduced load) inflation pressures.

BRAKES—Continued

Condition	Possible Cause	Correction
CAR PULLS TO ONE SIDE WHEN BRAKES ARE APPLIED, continued	2. Incorrect front wheel bearing adjustment or worn—damaged wheel bearings.	2. Adjust wheel bearings. Replace worn, damaged bearings.
	3. Brakeshoe lining on one side contaminated.	3. Determine and correct cause of contamination and replace brakeshoe lining in axle sets.
	4. Brakeshoes on one side bent, distorted, or lining loose on shoe.	4. Replace brakeshoes in axle sets.
	5. Support plate bent or loose on one side.	5. Tighten or replace support plate.
	6. Brake lining not yet seated to drums and rotors.	6. Burnish brakes.
	7. Caliper anchor plate loose on one side.	7. Tighten anchor plate bolts.
	8. Caliper or wheel cylinder piston sticking or seized.	8. Repair or replace caliper or wheel cylinder.
	9. Brakeshoe linings watersoaked.	9. Drive car with brakes lightly applied to dry linings. Replace brakeshoes in axle sets if problem persists.
	10. Loose suspension component attaching or mounting bolts, incorrect front end alignment. Worn suspension parts.	10. Tighten suspension bolts. Replace worn suspension components. Check and correct alignment as necessary.
CHATTER OR SHUDDER WHEN BRAKES ARE APPLIED (Pedal pulsation and roughness may also occur)	1. Front wheel bearings loose.	1. Adjust wheel bearings.
	2. Brakeshoes distorted, bent, contaminated, or worn.	2. Replace brakeshoes in axle sets.
	3. Caliper anchor plate or support plate loose.	3. Tighten mounting bolts.
	4. Excessive thickness variation or lateral rim out of rotor.	4. Refinish or replace rotor.
	5. Rear drum(s) out of round, sharp spots.	5. Refinish or replace drum.
	6. Loose suspension component attaching or mounting bolts, incorrect front end alignment. Worn suspension parts.	6. Tighten suspension bolts. Replace worn suspension components. Check and correct alignment as necessary.
NOISY BRAKES (Squealing, clicking, scraping sound when brakes are applied)	1. Bent, broken, distorted brakeshoes.	1. Replace brakeshoes in axle sets.
	2. Brake lining worn out—shoes contacting drum or rotor.	2. Replace brakeshoes and lining in axle sets. Refinish or replace drums or rotors.
	3. Foreign material imbedded in brake lining.	3. Replace brake lining.
	4. Broken or loose holdown or return springs.	4. Replace parts as necessary.
	5. Rough or dry drum brake support plate ledges.	5. Lubricate support plate ledges.
	6. Cracked, grooved, or scored rotor(s) or drum(s).	6. Replace rotor(s) or drum(s). Replace brakeshoes and lining in axle sets if necessary.
PULSATING BRAKE PEDAL	1. Out of round drums or excessive thickness variation or lateral runout in disc brake rotor(s).	1. Refinish or replace drums or rotors.
	2. Bent rear axle shaft.	2. Replace axle shaft.

SUSPENSION & STEERING

Condition	Possible Cause	Correction
HARD OR ERRATIC STEERING	1. Incorrect tire pressure.	1. Inflate tires to recommended pressures.
	2. Insufficient or incorrect lubrication.	2. Lubricate as required.
	3. Suspension, steering or linkage parts damaged or misaligned.	3. Repair or replace parts as necessary.
	4. Improper front wheel alignment.	4. Adjust wheel alignment angles.
	5. Incorrect steering gear adjustment.	5. Adjust steering gear.
	6. Sagging springs.	6. Replace springs.
PLAY OR LOOSENESS IN STEERING	1. Steering wheel loose.	1. Inspect splines and repair as necessary. Tighten steering wheel nut.
	2. Steering linkage or attaching parts loose or worn.	2. Tighten, adjust, or replace faulty components.

SUSPENSION & STEERING—Continued

Condition	Possible Cause	Correction
PLAY OR LOOSENESS IN STEERING, continued	3. Pitman arm loose.	3. Inspect shaft splines and repair as necessary. Torque attaching nut and stake in place.
	4. Steering gear attaching bolts loose.	4. Tighten bolts.
	5. Loose or worn wheel bearings.	5. Adjust or replace bearings.
	6. Steering gear adjustment incorrect or parts badly worn.	6. Adjust gear or replace defective parts.
WHEEL SHIMMY OR TRAMP	1. Improper tire pressure.	1. Inflate tires to recommended pressures.
	2. Wheels, tires, or brake drums out-of-balance or out-of-round.	2. Inspect parts and replace unacceptable out-of-round parts. Rebalance parts.
	3. Inoperative, worn, or loose shock absorbers or mounting parts.	3. Repair or replace shocks or mountings.
	4. Loose or worn steering or suspension parts.	4. Tighten or replace as necessary.
	5. Loose or worn wheel bearings.	5. Adjust or replace bearings.
	6. Incorrect steering gear adjustments.	6. Adjust steering gear.
	7. Incorrect front wheel alignment.	7. Correct front wheel alignment.
TIRE WEAR	1. Improper tire pressure.	1. Inflate tires to recommended pressures.
	2. Failure to rotate tires.	2. Rotate tires.
	3. Brakes grabbing.	3. Adjust or repair brakes.
	4. Incorrect front wheel alignment.	4. Align incorrect angles.
	5. Broken or damaged steering and suspension parts.	5. Repair or replace defective parts.
	6. Wheel runout.	6. Replace faulty wheel.
	7. Excessive speed on turns.	7. Make driver aware of condition.
CAR LEADS TO ONE SIDE	1. Improper tire pressures.	1. Inflate tires to recommended pressures.
	2. Front tires with uneven tread depth, wear pattern, or different cord design (i.e., one bias ply and one belted tire on front wheels).	2. Install tires of same cord construction and reasonably even tread depth and wear pattern.
	3. Incorrect front wheel alignment.	3. Align incorrect angles.
	4. Brakes dragging.	4. Adjust or repair brakes.
	5. Faulty power steering gear valve assembly.	5. Replace valve assembly.
	6. Pulling due to uneven tire construction.	6. Replace faulty tire.

HEADLAMPS

Condition	Possible Cause	Correction
ONE HEADLAMP INOPERATIVE OR INTERMITTENT	1. Loose connection.	1. Secure connections to sealed beam including ground.
	2. Defective sealed beam.	2. Replace sealed beam.
ONE OR MORE HEADLIGHTS ARE DIM	1. Open ground connection at headlight.	1. Repair ground wire connection between sealed beam and body ground.
	2. Ground wire mislocated in headlight connector (type 2 sealed beam).	2. Relocate ground wire in connector.
ONE OR MORE HEADLIGHTS SHORT LIFE	1. Voltage regulator maladjusted.	1. Readjust regulator to specifications.
ALL HEADLIGHTS INOPERATIVE OR INTERMITTENT	1. Loose connection.	1. Check and secure connections at dimmer switch and light switch.
	2. Defective dimmer switch.	2. Check voltage at dimmer switch with test lamp. If test lamp bulb lights only at switch "Hot" wire terminal, replace dimmer switch.

HEADLAMPS—Continued

Condition	Possible Cause	Correction
ALL HEADLAMPS INOPERATIVE OR INTERMITTENT, continued	3. Open wiring - light switch to dimmer switch.	3. Check wiring with test lamp. If bulb lights at light switch wire terminal, but not at dimmer switch, repair open wire.
	4. Open wiring - light switch to battery.	4. Check "Hot" wire terminal at light switch with test lamp. If lamp does not light, repair open wire circuit to battery (possible open fusible link).
	5. Shorted ground circuit.	5. If, after a few minutes operation, headlights flicker "ON" and "OFF" and/or a thumping noise can be heard from the light switch (circuit breaker opening and closing), repair short to ground in circuit between light switch and headlights. After repairing short, check for headlight flickering after one minute operation. If flickering occurs, the circuit breaker has been damaged and light switch must be replaced.
	6. Defective light switch.	6. Check light switch. Replace light switch, if defective.
UPPER OR LOWER BEAM WILL NOT LIGHT OR INTERMITTENT	1. Open connection or defective dimmer switch.	1. Check dimmer switch terminals with test lamp. If bulb lights at all wire terminals, repair open wiring between dimmer switch and headlights. If bulb will not light at one of these terminals, replace dimmer switch.
	2. Short circuit to ground.	2. Follow diagnosis above (all headlights inoperative or intermittent).

SIDE MARKER LAMPS

Condition	Possible Cause	Correction
ONE LAMP INOPERATIVE	1. Turn signal bulb burnt out (front lamp). 2. Side marker bulb burnt out. 3. Loose connection or open in wiring.	1. Switch turn signals on. If signal bulb does not light, replace bulb. 2. Replace bulb. 3. Using test lamp, check "Hot" wire terminal at bulb socket. If test lamp lights, repair open ground circuit. If lamp does not light, repair open "Hot" wire circuit.
FRONT OR REAR LAMPS INOPERATIVE	1. Loose connection or open ground connection.	1. If associated tail or park lamps do not operate, secure all connectors in "Hot" wire circuit. If park and turn lamps operate, repair open ground connections.
	2. Multiple bulbs burnt out.	2. Replace burnt out bulbs.

SIDE MARKER LAMPS—Continued

Condition	Possible Cause	Correction
ALL LAMPS INOPERATIVE	1. Blown fuse.	1. If park and tail lamps do not operate, replace blown fuse. If new fuse blows, check for short to ground between fuse panel and lamps.
	2. Loose connection.	2. Secure connector to light switch.
	3. Open in wiring.	3. Check tail light fuse with test lamp. If test lamp lights, repair open wiring between fuse and light switch. If not, repair open wiring between fuse and battery (possible open fusible link).
	4. Defective light switch.	4. Check light switch. Replace light switch, if defective.

TAIL, PARK AND LICENSE LAMPS

Condition	Possible Cause	Correction
ONE SIDE INOPERATIVE	1. Bulb burnt out.	1. Replace bulb.
	2. Open ground connection at bulb socket or ground wire terminal.	2. Jump bulb base socket connection to ground. If lamp lights, repair open ground circuit.
BOTH SIDES INOPERATIVE	1. Tail lamp fuse blown.	1. Replace fuse. If new fuse blows, repair short to ground in "Hot" wire circuit between fuse panel through light switch to lamps.
	2. Loose connection.	2. Secure connector at light switch.
	3. Open wiring.	3. Using test light, check circuit on both sides of fuse. If lamp does not light on either side, repair open circuit between fuse panel and battery (possible open fusible link). If test lamp lights at light switch terminal, repair open wiring between light switch and lamps.
	4. Multiple bulb burnout.	4. If test lamp lights at lamp socket "Hot" wire terminal, replace bulbs.
	5. Defective light switch.	5. Check light switch. Replace light switch, if defective.

TROUBLE SHOOTING

TURN SIGNAL AND HAZARD WARNING LAMP

Condition	Possible Cause	Correction
TURN SIGNALS INOPERATIVE ONE SIDE	1. Bulb(s) burnt out (flasher cannot be heard).	1. Turn hazard warning system on. If one or more bulbs are inoperative replace necessary bulbs.
	2. Open wiring or ground connection.	2. Turn hazard warning system on. If one or more bulbs are inoperative, use test lamp and check circuit at lamp socket. If test lamp lights, repair open ground connection. If not, repair open wiring between bulb socket and turn signal switch.
	3. Improper bulb or defective turn signal switch.	3. Turn hazard warning system on. If all front and rear lamps operate, check for improper bulb. If bulbs are OK, replace defective turn signal switch.
	4. Short to ground (flasher can be heard, no bulbs operate).	4. Locate and repair short to ground by disconnecting front and rear circuits separately.
TURN SIGNALS INOPERATIVE	1. Blown turn signal fuse.	1. Turn hazard warning system on. If all lamps operate, replace blown fuse. If new fuse blows, repair short to ground between fuse and lamps.
	2. Defective flasher.	2. If turn signal fuse is OK and hazard warning system will operate lamps, replace defective turn signal flasher.
	3. Loose connection.	3. Secure steering column connector.
HAZARD WARNING LAMPS INOPERATIVE	1. Blown fuse.	1. Switch turn signals on. If lamps operate, replace fuse if blown. If new fuse blows, repair short to ground. (could be in stop light circuit).
	2. Defective hazard warning flasher.	2. If fuse is OK, switch turn signals on. If lamps operate, replace defective hazard flasher.
	3. Open in wiring or defective turn signal switch.	3. Using test lamp, check hazard switch feed wire in turn signal steering column connector. If lamp does not light on either side of connector, repair open circuit between flasher and connector. If lamp lights only on feed side of connector, clean connector contacts. If lamp lights on both sides of connector, replace defective turn signal switch assembly.

BACK-UP LAMP

Condition	Possible Cause	Correction
ONE LAMP INOPERATIVE OR INTERMITTENT	1. Loose or burnt out bulb. 2. Loose connection. 3. Open ground connections.	1. Secure or replace bulb. 2. Tighten connectors. 3. Repair bulb ground circuit.
BOTH LAMPS INOPERATIVE OR INTERMITTENT	1. Neutral start or back-up lamp switch maladjusted. 2. Loose connection or open circuit. 3. Blown fuse. 4. Defective neutral start or back-up lamp switch. 5. Defective ignition switch.	1. Readjust neutral start or back-up lamp switch. 2. Secure all connectors. If OK, check continuity of circuit from fuse to lamps with test lamp. If lamp does not light on either side of fuse, correct open circuit from battery to fuse. 3. Replace fuse. If new fuse blows, repair short to ground in circuit from fuse through neutral start switch to back-up lamps. 4. Check switch. Replace neutral start or back-up lamp switch, if defective. 5. If test lamp lights at ignition switch battery terminal but not at output terminal, replace ignition switch.
LAMP WILL NOT TURN OFF	1. Neutral start or back-up switch maladjusted. 2. Defective neutral start or back-up lamp switch.	1. Readjust neutral start or back-up lamp switch. 2. Check switch. Replace neutral start or back-up lamp switch, if defective.

STOP LIGHTS

Condition	Possible Cause	Correction
ONE BULB INOPERATIVE	1. Bulb burnt out.	1. Replace bulb.
ONE SIDE INOPERATIVE	1. Loose connection, open wiring or defective bulbs. 2. Defective directional signal switch or cancelling cam.	1. Turn on directional signal. If lamp does not operate, check bulbs. If bulbs are OK, secure all connections. If lamp still does not operate, use test lamp and check for open wiring. 2. If lamp will operate by turning directional signal on, the switch is not centering properly during cancelling operation. Replace defective cancelling cam or directional signal switch.
ALL INOPERATIVE	1. Blown fuse. 2. Stop-switch maladjusted or defective.	1. Replace fuse. If new fuse blows, repair short to ground in circuit between fuse and lamps. 2. Check stop switch. Adjust or replace stop switch, if required.
WILL NOT TURN OFF	1. Stop switch maladjusted or defective.	1. Readjust switch. If switch still malfunctions, replace.

TROUBLE SHOOTING

HORNS

Condition	Possible Cause	Correction
HORNS WILL NOT OPERATE	1. Loose connections in circuit. 2. Defective horn switch. 3. Defective horn relay. 4. Defects within horn.	1. Check and tighten connections. Be sure to check ground straps. 2. Replace defective parts. 3. Replace relay. 4. Replace horn.
HORNS HAVE POOR TONE	1. Low available voltage at horn, or defects within horn.	1. Check battery and charging circuit. Although horn should blow at any voltage above 7.0 volts, a weak or poor tone may occur at operating voltages below 11.0 volts. If horn has weak or poor tone at operating voltage of 11.0 volts or higher, remove horn and replace.
HORNS OPERATE INTERMITTENTLY	1. Loose or intermittent connections in horn relay or horn circuit. 2. Defective horn switch. 3. Defective relay. 4. Defects within horn.	1. Check and tighten connections. 2. Replace switch. 3. Replace relay. 4. Replace horn.
HORNS BLOW CONSTANTLY	1. Sticking horn relay. 2. Horn relay energized by grounded or shorted wiring. 3. Horn button can be grounded by sticking closed.	1. Replace relay. 2. Check and adjust wiring. 3. Adjust or replace damaged parts.

SPEEDOMETER

Condition	Possible Cause	Correction
SPEEDOMETER NOT OPERATING PROPERLY	1. Noisy speedometer cable. 2. Pointer and odometer inoperative. Inaccurate reading. 3. Kinked cable. 4. Defective speedometer head. 5. Casing connector loose on speedometer case.	1. Loosen over-tightened casing nuts and snap-on at speedometer head. Replace housing and core. Replace broken cable. 2. Check tire size. Check for correct speedometer driven gear. 3. Replace cable. Reroute casing so that bends have no less than 6" radius. 4. Replace speedometer. 5. Tighten connector.

AIR CONDITIONING

NOTE: This chapter deals only with fundamentals and basic system tests. For complete air conditioning service details, Motor Air Conditioner & Heater Service Manual is available. It includes unit replacement, servicing, diagnosis and testing, vacuum and wiring diagrams, aftermarket hang-on units, & truck/trailer refrigeration and all 1970-77 specifications.

CONTENTS

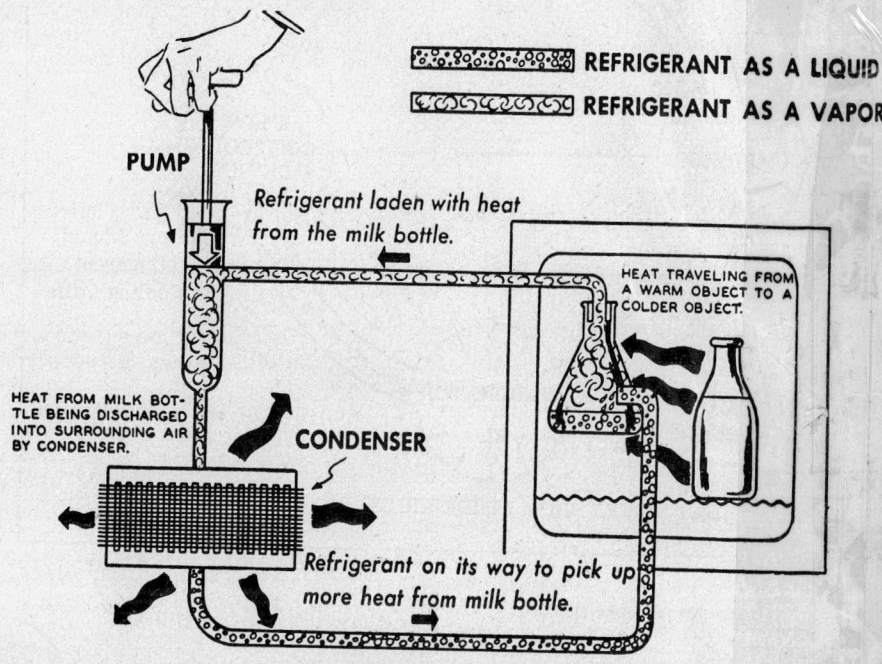

REFRIGERANT AS A LIQUID

REFRIGERANT AS A VAPOR

PUMP

Refrigerant laden with heat from the milk bottle.

HEAT TRAVELING FROM A WARM OBJECT TO A COLDER OBJECT.

HEAT FROM MILK BOTTLE BEING DISCHARGED INTO SURROUNDING AIR BY CONDENSER.

CONDENSER

Refrigerant on its way to pick up more heat from milk bottle.

Diagram showing refrigerant cycle

FUNDAMENTALS OF REFRIGERATION

In order to understand how an air conditioning system works, we must have a knowledge of the fundamentals of refrigeration. And since refrigeration is the process of removing heat from things, an air conditioner removes heat from the surrounding air. In both cases, the process is simplified by one of Nature's laws—heat always moves from a warm object to a cold object.

When we put milk or vegetables into an ice box, they are warmer than the ice. Since heat always travels from warmer to cooler objects, the heat in the milk and vegetables naturally travels to the cold ice. Then, of course, as heat is removed from these articles, they begin to grow cooler—they have less heat than before. Therefore, if refrigeration is the removal of heat, then anything can be made cooler by finding a method of absorbing heat from it.

In order to maintain cold temperatures, we have to have continuous refrigeration. This is accomplished in modern refrigerators and cooling systems (1) by using a refrigerant that will readily absorb heat and (2) by using the same refrigerant over and over.

Ice can refrigerate effectively only when it is changing from a solid to a liquid.

A liquid can refrigerate only when it is changing from a liquid to a vapor. A vapor cannot refrigerate since the absorption of heat will not change it to any other state. The only thing to do with a vapor is to change it back to a liquid—by removing heat from it.

In other words, if the ice didn't melt, it could absorb a little heat from the objects and the air around it but not enough to do an effective job of cooling. But when it begins to change to a liquid (water), then the ice is absorbing heat rapidly and effectively.

The same applies to a liquid refrigerant. No matter how cold the liquid is, it won't actually "refrigerate" until it is absorbing heat fast enough to change its form into a vapor.

Operating Cycle of Car Air Conditioning System

1. The compressor compresses heat-laden, low-pressure vaporous refrigerant and discharges it into the condenser.
2. In the condenser, the vapor changes into a liquid as the heat is dissipated into the surrounding air.
3. From the condenser, the liquid is forced into the reservoir or receiver, which is simply a storage container the function of which is to ensure a supply of liquid Freon to the expan-

sion valve. (The expansion valve functions in much the same manner as a hose nozzle).
4. From the reservoir, the liquid Freon passes through a combination strainer-drier, then through the expansion valve into the evaporator.
5. Being connected to the suction line of the compressor, the evaporator is a low-pressure region in which the refrigerant boils and reverts to a vapor, absorbing heat in the process and thereby cooling the evaporator coil and the air passing over it.
6. Upon leaving the evaporator, the vaporous refrigerant returns to the compressor inlet and completes the refrigeration cycle.

EXERCISE SYSTEM

An important fact most car owners ignore is that car coolers must be used periodically or they will go sour. Car manufacturers are emphatic on this point. They caution that, when the air conditioner is not used regularly, particularly during cold months, it should be turned on for a few minutes once every two or three weeks while the engine is running. This keeps the system in good operating condition.

Checking out the system for the ef-

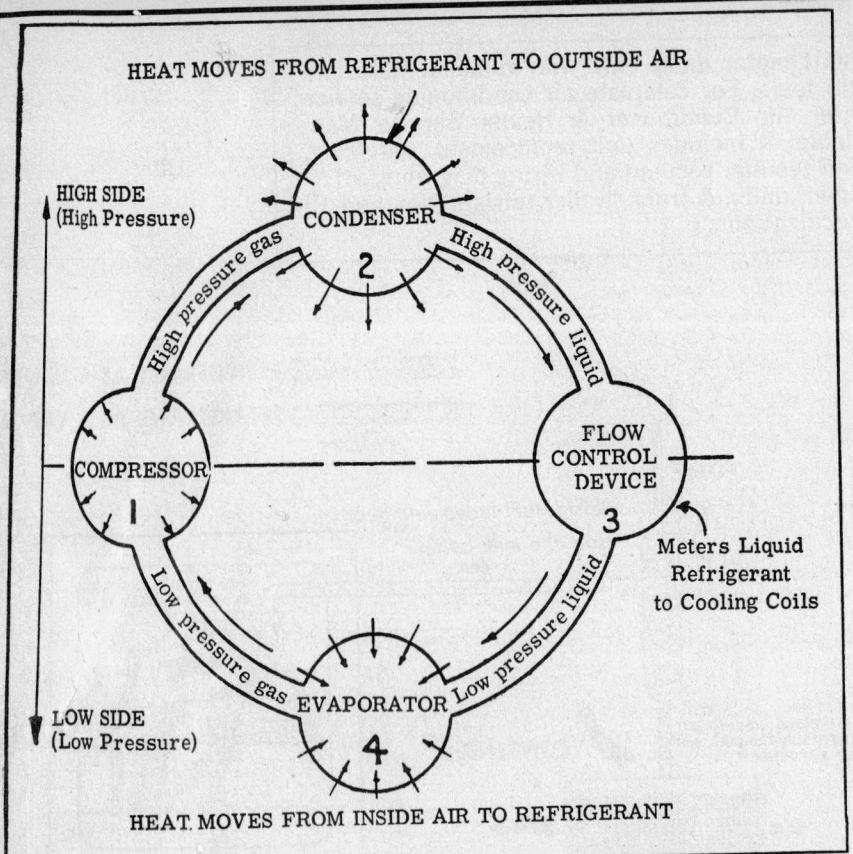

HEAT MOVES FROM REFRIGERANT TO OUTSIDE AIR

HIGH SIDE
(High Pressure)

CONDENSER
2

High pressure gas

High pressure liquid

COMPRESSOR
1

FLOW
CONTROL
DEVICE
3

Meters Liquid
Refrigerant
to Cooling Coils

Low pressure gas

Low pressure liquid

EVAPORATOR
4

LOW SIDE
(Low Pressure)

HEAT MOVES FROM INSIDE AIR TO REFRIGERANT

◄ Air conditioning cycle of operation

▼ How air conditioner works

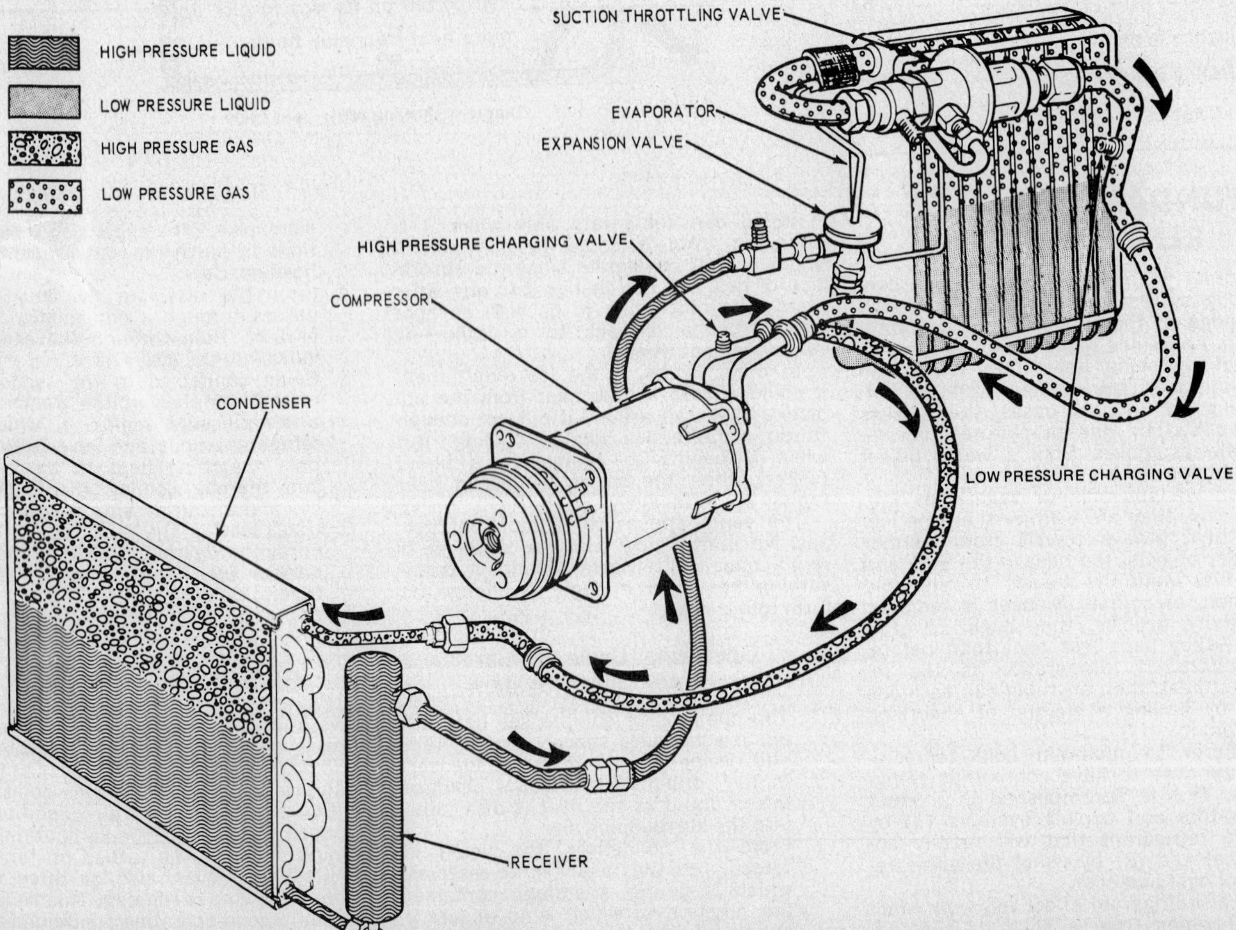

HIGH PRESSURE LIQUID

LOW PRESSURE LIQUID

HIGH PRESSURE GAS

LOW PRESSURE GAS

SUCTION THROTTLING VALVE

EVAPORATOR

EXPANSION VALVE

HIGH PRESSURE CHARGING VALVE

COMPRESSOR

LOW PRESSURE CHARGING VALVE

CONDENSER

RECEIVER

fects of disuse before the onset of summer is one of the most important aspects of car cooler servicing.

First on the list is to clean out the condenser core, mounted in all cases at the front of the car's radiator. All obstructions, such as leaves, bugs, dirt, and the like, must be removed, as these will reduce heat transfer and impair the efficiency of the system. Make sure the space between the condenser and the radiator also is free of foreign matter.

Make certain the evaporator water drain is open. Certain systems have two evaporators, one in the engine compartment and one in the trunk. The evaporator is the device which cools and dehumidifies the air before it enters the car, and the place where refrigerant is changed from a liquid to a vapor. As the core cools the air, moisture condenses on it but the moisture is prevented from collecting in the evaporator by means of the water drain.

TROUBLE DIAGNOSIS

Insufficient or No Cooling

The first unit to check is the blower mechanism and its air-distribution system, since the cooling is produced by a combination of a cool evaporator and a blower to circulate the cooled air. If the blower is inoperative, check for a broken switch, a blown fuse, a loose connection, a broken wire or a defective motor activating the blower mechanism.

In the event the blower is working but the air output is low, look for loose wire connections or shorts, low battery charge, dirty or loose switch contacts or binding of the blower shaft or blades. Also check the air-distribution system for closed air-output valves or obstructions in the flexible hoses.

If the blower is circulating the air efficiently but there is no cooling, the trouble lies in the refrigerating circuit. Beginning at the source of power, check the compressor driving belt. Is it loose, slipping or broken? If the belt is tight and the pulley is turning but the compressor shaft is not, check the magnetic clutch for lack of current or a faulty coil.

A steady, resonant noise from the compressor is normal but any clicking or rattling sounds should be investigated. Using a standard set of twin gauges, check the compressor inlet and outlet pressures according to manufacturer's specifications. If the normally high outlet pressure is not up to specs, it is probably due to a low charge of coolant, excess moisture in the system, or a restriction or kink in the circulation lines.

Be sure that there is sufficient compressor oil of the proper viscosity. At the same time, make certain that there is no excess oil from the compressor flowing through the system, slowing coolant circulation and reducing compressor outlet pressure.

If inlet-suction pressure is high but the outlet pressure is normal, there is probably trouble either at the expansion valve, which controls the amount of fluid entering the evaporator, or with the sensor bulb that controls the expansion valve. Other causes would include excess moisture in the system or a defective suction throttle valve (if used) on the compressor.

Excessive vibration of the compressor indicates loose mounting bolts or an out-of-true belt pulley. A thumping noise from the compressor or a cool and sweating suction line into it, is usually caused by too much coolant in the system. Should there be no moisture in the system, evacuate the excess coolant into the atmosphere.

Check Condenser

If the condenser unit, located in front of the radiator, is suspected, the first thing to look for is clogged coils that limit the cooling capacity of the unit. Any bugs, leaves or debris caught in the coils should be removed by air pressure. In the event there is any icy or frosty spots apparent on the exterior of the condenser, they usually indicate a partial restriction inside the condenser at that point.

Check Sight Glass

The next spot to check in the refrigerating circuit is the line sight glass (if used). This small transparent device permits a visual check of the condition of the high-pressure liquid coolant. A cloudy, foamy appearance, or the presence of bubbles in the fluid, indicates air or excess moisture in the lines, or a low charge of coolant.

Check Receiver-Dehydrator

Sometimes fault will be found in the receiver-dehydrator unit, usually located alongside the condenser. This small storage unit for the coolant also contains an element for removing small amounts of moisture from the refrigerant and has a filtering element for catching small dirt particles.

If the system has been in operation for a considerable period of time, this dehydrating element may lose its moisture-absorbing ability. This condition causes the constant presence of small bubbles in the sight glass. It is also indicated when the high-pressure line into the dehydrator has a distinctly different temperature from that of the outlet line. This receiver-dryer component should be replaced as a unit if the above symptoms are observed, if all other parts of the system are in good operating condition, and the system is fully charged.

Check Evaporator

The proper functioning of the evaporator is always dependent on an efficient expansion valve at the intake end and an efficient sensor bulb and (if used) a suction throttle valve at the outlet end of the coils. In normal operation, this unit should be cold and sweating, but not iced. Icing calls for a check of the expansion valve, sensor bulb, or the suction throttle valve (if used).

Since there is a constant condensation of atmospheric moisture on the outside of the evaporator coils, make sure that the draining system is free and clean and able to dispose of the collected water through the car floor.

NOTE: Some of the larger, more expensive cars have a supplementary evaporator unit in the luggage compartment. Don't forget to check the operation of this unit.

Testing System for Leaks

Testing the system for leaks is one of the most important over-all phases of trouble-shooting an air conditioning system. There are several methods of performing this operation which is explained elsewhere in this chapter.

Refrigerant Dangers

A final word of caution. The freon refrigerant used in car air-conditioners is also known as R-12 or F-12. It is colorless and odorless both as a gas and a liquid. Since it boils (vaporizes) at 21.7 deg. F., it will usually be in a vapor state when being handled in a repair shop. But if a portion of the liquid coolant should come in contact with the hands or face, remember that its temperature momentarily will be at least 22 deg. below zero!

Protective goggles should be worn when opening any refrigerant lines. If liquid coolant does touch the eyes, bathe the eyes quickly in cold water. Then apply a bland disinfectant oil to the eyes. See an eye doctor.

TROUBLE SHOOTING GUIDE

NOTE: When a unit must be removed from the system for replacement or repairs, the dehydrator must be replaced also, and the system must be purged, evacuated and recharged to remove excess moisture.

System Produces No Cooling

Electrical
1. Blown fuse.
2. Disconnected or broken wire.
3. Disconnected or broken ground wire.
4. Clutch coil disconnected or burned out.
5. Switch contacts in thermostat (if used) burned excessively, or sensing element defective.
6. Blower motor burned out or disconnected.

Mechanical
1. Loose or broken drive belt.
2. Compressor completely or partially frozen.
3. Compressor reed valves inoperative.
4. Expansion valve stuck open.

Refrigeration
1. Broken refrigeration line.
2. Fusable plug blown (if used).
3. Leak in system.
4. Compressor shaft seal leaking.
5. Clogged screen or screens in receiver-dehydrator or expansion valve.
6. Plugged coil or hose.

Insufficient Cooling

Electrical
1. Blower motor operates sluggishly.

Mechanical
1. Compressor clutch slipping.
2. Obstructed blower discharge passage.
3. Clogged air intake filter.
4. Outside air vents open.
5. Insufficient air circulation over condenser coils; fins clogged with dirt,

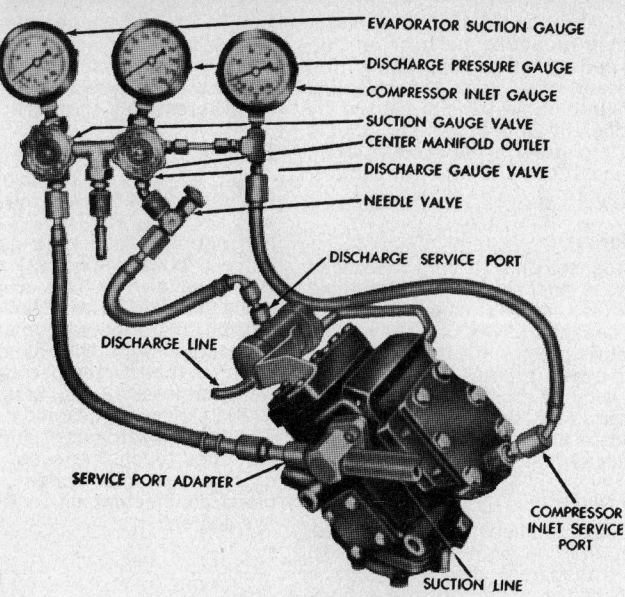

Fig. 1 Chrysler Air-Temp gauge set manifold connections (Typical)

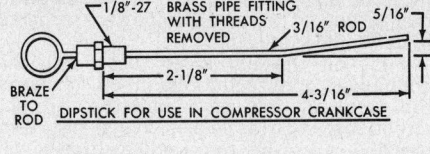

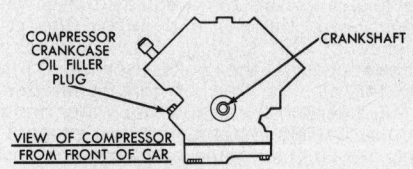

Fig. 2 Air Temp compressor oil level dipstick fabrication and filler plug location

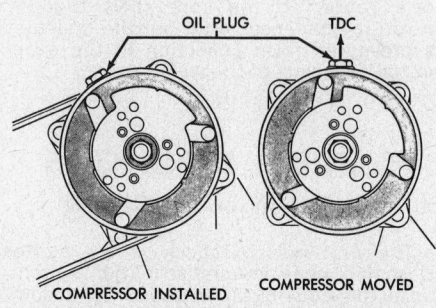

Fig. 2A Positioning compressor for oil level check. Sankyo compressor

leaves or insects.
6. Evaporator clogged.
7. Evaporator regulator defective or improperly adjusted.

NOTE: The evaporator regulator includes the suction throttling valve (STV) used on Ford cars, the Pilot-Operated Absolute (POA) valve or Valves In Receiver (VIR) used on General Motors cars, and the Chrysler Evaporator Pressure Regulator (EPR) or Evaporator Temperature Regulator (ETR) valve. When any of these devices is used in a system, it can be assumed that the system contains no thermostat control.

Refrigeration

1. Unit icing up; may be caused by excessive moisture in system, incorrect super-heat adjustment in expansion valve, or thermostat adjusted too low (if used).
2. Thermostat defective (if used).

3. Stuck hot gas by-pass valve, STV, POA or EPR valve.

OIL LEVEL CHECK

NOTE: The oil level of these compressors should be checked whenever refrigerant has been lost due to leakage or through normal system servicing.

Air Temp

RV2 Compressor

1. On 1974-75 Models, operate engine at 800-1000 rpm for approximately 15 minutes. If ambient temperature is above 85°F, position control on A/C high blower. If ambient temperature is below 85°F, position control on Max. A/C, high blower and temperature lever on warm.

NOTE: On 1974 Fury, 1974-75 Chrysler, Imperial, Monaco and 1975 Gran Fury, disconnect and plug water valve vacuum line in order to obtain re-heat in max. A/C mode.

Refrigeration

1. Insufficient refrigerant in system.
2. Clogged screen in expansion valve.
3. Expansion valve thermal bulb has lost its charge.
4. Clogged screen in receiver.
5. Excessive moisture in system.
6. Air in system.
7. Thermostat defective or improperly adjusted (if used).

System Cools Intermittently

Electrical

1. Defective circuit breaker, blower switch or blower motor.
2. Partial open, improper ground or loose connection in compressor clutch coil.

Mechanical

1. Compressor clutch slipping.

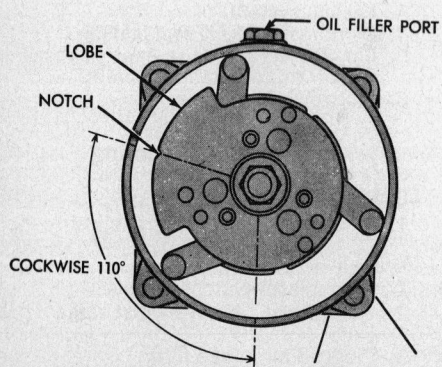

Fig. 2B Positioning front plate for oil level check. Sankyo compressor

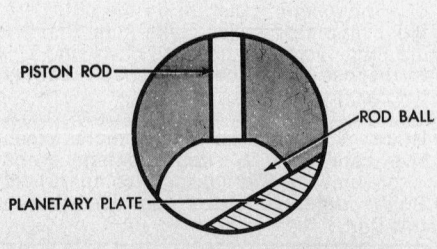

Fig. 2C Top piston rod as viewed through oil filler port. Sankyo compressor

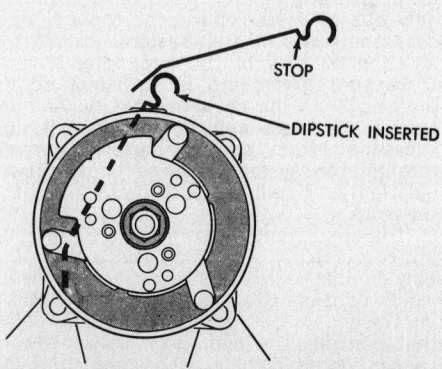

Fig. 2D Checking oil level. Sankyo compressor

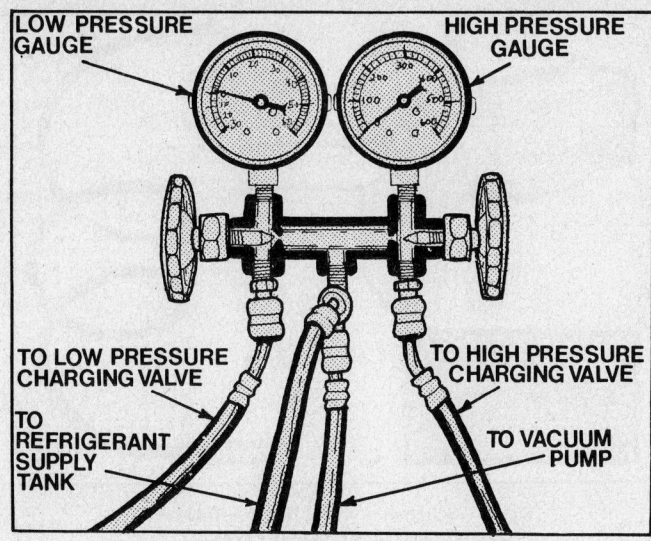

Fig. 3 Manifold gauge set for Frigidaire, Sankyo, Tecumseh and York compressors

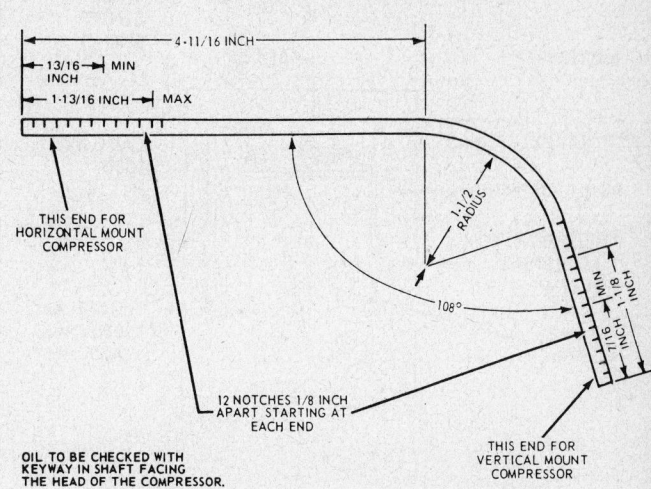

Fig. 4 York compressor oil level dipstick fabrication. Ford Motor Co. models

2. On all models, connect gauge and manifold assembly, Fig. 1, and slowly discharge refrigerant system. Near completion of discharge, flush dipstick with existing freon. This will ensure dipstick is clean and at approximately the same temperature as refrigerant oil in compressor sump.

3. Carefully remove compressor oil sump filler plug, then insert dipstick into hole until it bottoms in sump, Fig. 2.

   NOTE: When removing compressor oil sump filler plug a face shield should be worn. Refrigerant dissolved in compressor oil could cause oil to purcolate out through filler plug opening.

4. Remove dipstick and measure oil level, refer to A/C Specification Tables. Add refrigerant oil as necessary to bring oil level within limits.

   NOTE: Oil level should be checked only after refrigerant has boiled off and oil surface has stabilized.

5. On 1974-78 models, if any of the following components are to be replaced, it will be necessary to add

additional oil to system.
Evaporator . . . . 2 ounces
Condenser . . . . 1 ounce
Filter Drier . . . . 1 ounce

6. On all models, install filler plug, then evacuate and recharge system.

Sankyo Compressor

1. Disconnect and plug vacuum hose from water valve.

2. With engine at idle speed, operate A/C system for 10 minutes in Max A/C mode, high blower speed and temperature control set at maximum heat.

3. Shut off engine and reconnect water valve vacuum hose, then slowly discharge the A/C system.

4. Loosen compressor mounting bolts and remove belt, then rotate compressor so that oil filler tube is at top dead center position, Fig. 2A.

5. Thoroughly clean area around oil filler plug and remove plug.

   CAUTION: Use care when removing the filler plug to prevent the dissolved refrigerant in the crankcase oil from percolating out through the filler plug opening. This action will stop as soon as the refrigerant has boiled away. Also, the oil level should be measured only after the refrigerant has boiled away and the oil surface has stabilized.

6. Rotate front plate of clutch hub so that notch in center of lobe is indexed 110° from bottom, Fig. 2B. In this position, the ball end of the piston rod aligns with oil filler port, Fig. 2C.

7. Looking at front plate with lobe notch at upper left in the 110° position, insert dipstick (tool C-4504) diagonally from upper right to lower left until stop contacts the filler port surface, Fig. 2D.

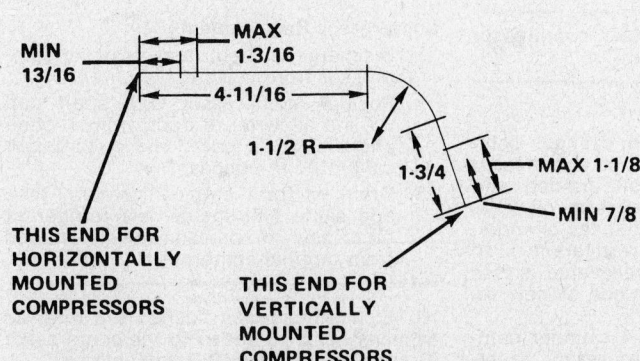

Fig. 5 York compressor oil level dipstick fabrication. American Motors

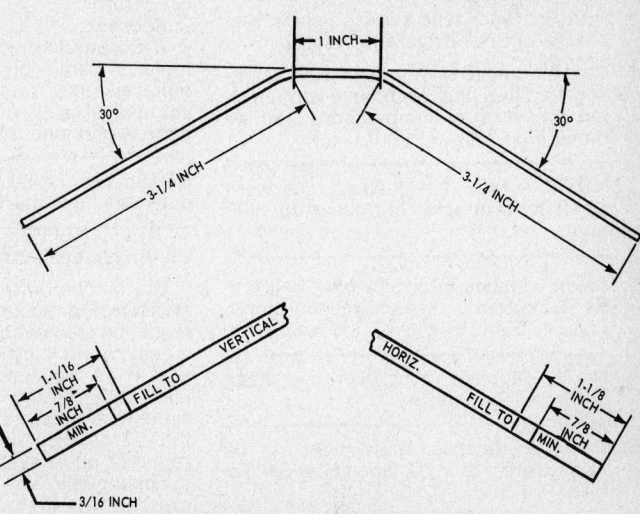

Fig. 6 Tecumseh compressor oil level dipstick fabrication. Ford Motor Co. models

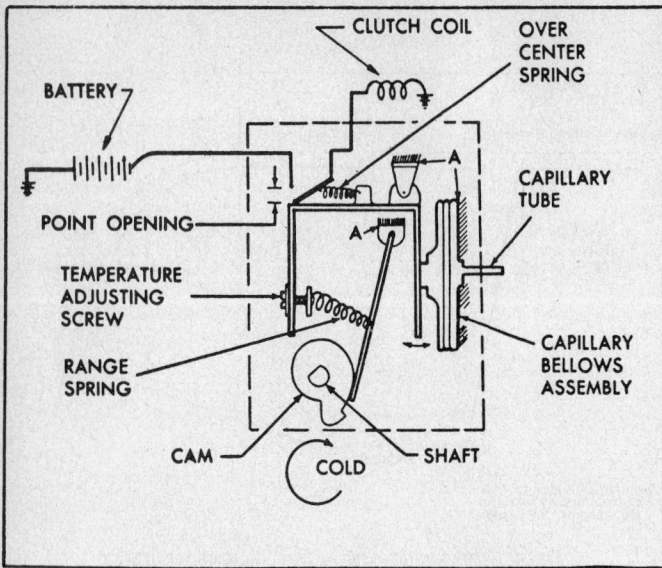

Fig. 7 Wiring diagram of a typical adjustable thermostatic switch (Typical)

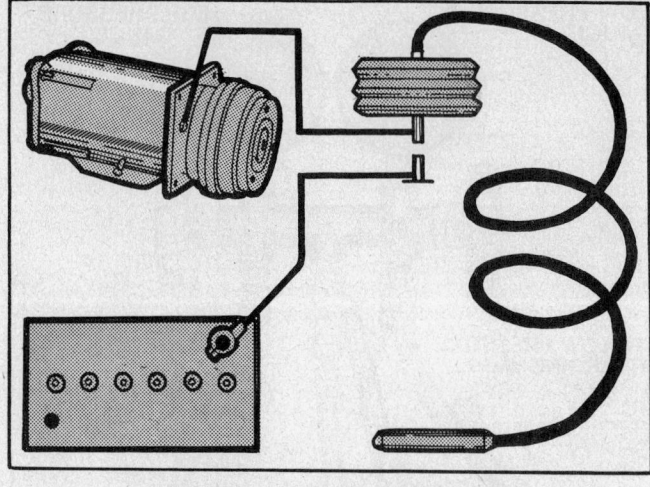

Fig. 8 Schematic layout of a thermostatic-controlled clutch circuit (Typical)

NOTE: Before inserting dipstick, clean and cool the dipstick with refrigerant.

8. Remove dipstick and note oil level. The dipstick is marked in eight increments and each increment represents one ounce of oil. Add oil if necessary to bring level within specifications.

Tecumseh & York

1. Connect pressure gauge and manifold set, Fig. 3, then operate system for approximately 10 minutes or until system pressures stabilize. This will allow oil entrained in system to return to compressor sump.

2. On models with manual service valves, isolate compressor from system as outlined under Isolating Compressor From System.

3. On 1974-78 Ford Motor Co. models, with Schrader type service valves, discharge entire refrigerant system.

4. On all models, slowly loosen compressor oil filler plug to relieve any internal pressure in compressor, then remove filler plug.

NOTE: A face shield should be worn when loosening or removing oil filler plug.

5. Insert dipstick into filler plug hole until it bottoms in compressor sump, Figs. 4, 5 and 6.

NOTE: Dipstick must be wiped clean before each insertion.

6. Remove dipstick and measure oil level, refer to A/C Specification Tables.

7. Add refrigerant oil as necessary to bring oil level within limits, then install filler plug and "O" ring.

8. On American Motors models with manual service valve, purge air from compressor.

9. On 1974-78 Ford Motor Co. models with Schrader type service valves, evacuate and recharge system.

FRIGIDAIRE OIL CHARGE

1976 Chevette, Late 1976 Grand Prix & 1977-78 Models With Cycling Clutch

Oil Charge-Component Replacement

If there are no signs of excessive leakage, add the following amount of oil depending on component to be replaced.

Evaporator . . . . 3 ounces
Condenser . . . . 1 ounce

If accumulator or compressor are to be replaced, drain oil from component to be replaced and measure, then add same amount of new oil to replacement component plus one additional ounce.

NOTE: The radial 4 cylinder compressor does not have an oil sump.

Oil Charge-Leak Condition

On models with axial 6 cylinder compressor, both accumulator and compressor must be removed and oil drained and measured in cases of excessive oil leakage. If oil recovered is 4 ounces or more, add same amount of new refrigerant oil to system. If amount of oil recovered is less than 4 ounces, add 6 ounces of new refrigerant oil to system.

On models with radial 4 cylinder compressor, it will only be necessary to remove and drain and measure oil from accumulator assembly in cases of excessive oil leakage. The radial 4 cylinder compressor does not have an oil sump, therefore it is not necessary to remove compressor in cases of oil leakage. If amount of oil recovered is 2 ounces or more, add same amount of new refrigerant oil to system. If amount of oil recovered is less than 2 ounces, add two ounces of new refrigerant oil to system.

NOTE: On all models, if accumulator is replaced one additional ounce of oil must be added to replace amount captured by desiccant in old accumulator.

1974-78 Models Less Cycling Clutch

RADIAL 4 CYLINDER COMPRESSOR

Component Replacement

When replacing a system component, oil should be added to the system as follows. If compressor is operating, idle engine for 10 minutes with A/C controls set for maximum cooling and high blower prior to discharging system.

Add additional oil as specified if any of components are replaced.

Condenser . . . . 1 ounce
Evaporator . . . . 1 ounce
VIR . . . . 3 ounce
Accumulator . . . . 1 ounce

Compressor Replacement

1. Discharge system and remove compressor from vehicle.

2. Position compressor with shaft end up and allow oil to drain from suction and discharge ports into a container calibrated in ounces.

3. Drain oil from new compressor, then add same amount of new refrigerant oil to new compressor as was drained from original compressor.

NOTE: If system was flushed the total oil capacity must be added to the compressor as specified in the A/C Data Table.

4. Install new compressor and charge system.

Temperature of Air Entering Condenser	70°	80°	90°	100°	110°
Engine rpm			1500		
Compressor out Pressure (before expansion tube)	150 205	185 235	215 270	250 300	280 335
Evaporator Pressure—at accumulator (psi)	20– 26	20– 28	21– 29	25– 33	30– 39
Discharge Air Temp.—Right Hand Center Outlet	35° 41°	36°– 43°	36°– 44°	42°– 52°	47°– 57°

Fig. 9   Performance test chart, 1974-76 Vega & 1975-76 Astre

Temperature of air entering condenser	70°F	80°F	90°F	100°F	110°F
Engine RPM			2000		
Compressor out pressure before expansion tube (psig)	110– 140	145– 175	185– 215	220– 250	265– 295
Evaporator pressure at accumulator (psig)	24– 30	25– 31	25– 31	26– 32	27– 33
Discharge air temp @ right hand outlet ①	38°F 44°F	39°F 45°F	39°F 45°F	40°F 46°F	41°F 47°F

①—Coldest temperature just prior to compressor cycling off.

Fig. 10   Performance test chart, 1976 Chevette

Component Rupture, Fast Discharge

1. Repair leak and flush system.
2. Remove compressor and drain oil.
3. Add total capacity as specified in A/C *Data Table* of new refrigerant oil to suction port of compressor.
4. Install compressor, charge system and perform leak check.

Slow Leak

1. If refrigerant loss has occurred over an extended period of time, add 3 ounces of refrigerant oil to system.
2. Recharge system.

System Performance Evaluation

When system performance, efficiency and proper oil charge are in doubt, the system should be flushed and the total capacity, as specified in the *A/C Data Table*, of new refrigerant oil be added to the compressor prior to any further checks of the system.

AXIAL 6 CYLINDER COMPRESSOR

Oil Charge

1. Idle engine for 10 minutes at 1250 rpm with system controls set for maximum cooling and high blower speed.
2. Stop engine, discharge system and remove compressor.
3. With compressor in a horizontal position and drain plug down, remove plug and drain oil into a measured container.
4. If 4 ounces or more of oil was drained, add the same amount to the compressor. If less than 4 ounces of oil was drained, add 6 ounces of oil to compressor.

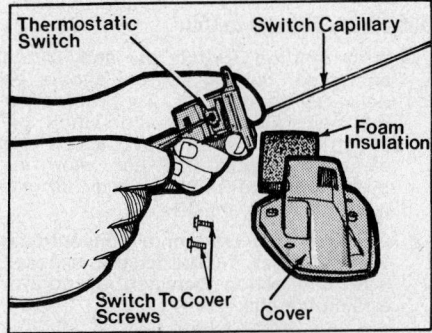

Fig. 11   Thermostatic switch adjustment, 1974-76 Vega, 1975-76 Astre & 1976 Chevette

Compressor Replacement

1. Idle engine for 10 minutes at approximately 1250 rpm at maximum cooling and high blower speed to distribute oil in system.
2. Remove compressor from vehicle.
3. Remove plug and allow oil to drain from compressor into a container calibrated in ounces.
4. Drain oil from new compressor.
5. If amount drained from original compressor is more than four ounces, add the same amount of new refrigerant oil to the new compressor plus amount lost during discharge.
6. If amount of oil drained from original compressor is less 4 ounces, add 6 ounces of new refrigerant oil to the new compressor plus amount lost during discharge.

Component Replacement

Whenever a component of the A/C system is replaced, if not pre-charged by factory, measured quantities of refrigeration oil should be added to the component to assure that the total oil charge in the system is correct before the unit is placed into operation.

The oil is poured directly into the replacement component. If an evaporator is installed, pour oil into the inlet pipe with the pipe held vertically so the oil will drain into the evaporator core. No additional oil is required if valves and hoses are replaced.

Add additional oil as specified if any of the following components are replaced.
Evaporator (front or rear) .... 3 ounces
Condenser .... 1 ounce
VIR .... 1 ounce
Accumulator .... 1 ounce
Receiver .... 1 ounce

NOTE: If the system is flushed with sufficient quantity of a flushing agent that would remove oil from the system, install the full amount specified in the *A/C Data Table*. On a newly installed system, install the full capacity of oil prior to operation. On systems containing metal particles in the oil, replace or overhaul the compressor, replace the receiver-dehydrator or VIR dessicant and install a high capacity, low pressure drop filter in the liquid line to the filter to protect the expansion valve and new compressor from damage

due to foreign particles.

THERMOSTAT CONTROL SWITCH

When an A/C system is not provided with a suction throttling valve (STV, POA or EPR), the pumping action of the compressor is stopped by a thermostatically-controlled switch, Figs. 7 and 8.

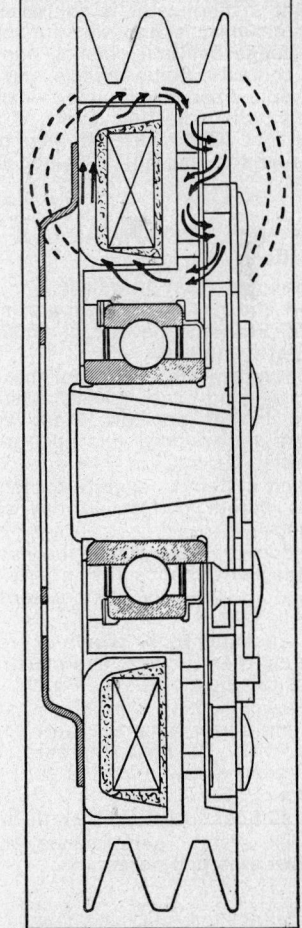

Fig. 12   Path of magnetic flow through compressor clutch

The opening and closing of the electrical contacts are controlled by a movement of a temperature sensitive diaphragm or bellows. The bellows has a capillary tube connected to it which is filled with Freon or CO_2. The capillary tube is positioned so that it may have either the cold air from the evaporator pass over it or it may be connected to the tail pipe of the evaporator. In either position, evaporator temperature will affect the temperature-sensitive compound in the capillary tube by causing it to contract as the evaporator becomes colder. The contraction of the gas will cause the bellows to contract. This action separates the electrical contacts and breaks the electrical circuit to the compressor clutch, which stops compressor operation.

The evaporator begins to warm which, in turn, causes the gas in the capillary tube to expand. The bellows will also begin to expand, moving the electrical contacts closer to each other. At a predetermined point, the expansion of the bellows will bring the contacts together, closing the circuit to the compressor clutch, energizing it and bringing the compressor into operation again. This cycling action will be repeated as long as air conditioning operation is required.

Thermostat, Adjust

Visual inspection must be made to determine if a thermostat is adjustable. All thermostats have a provision for regulating the range between opening and closing the contacts. Some models may have a removable fiber cover under which will be located the adjusting screw. If a set screw is not found here, it may be assumed that the thermostat is not adjustable.

1974-76 Vega, 1975-76 Astre & 1976 Chevette

1. Install gauge set on vehicle.
2. Start and run engine at approximately 2000 RPM on Chevette or 1500 RPM on Astre and Vega.
3. Set temperature control for maximum cooling and place blower switch in high blower position. Close vehicle doors and windows and open all A/C outlets.
4. Permit system to operate for ten minutes before performing any adjustments.
5. Suction pressure should be as listed in the Performance Test Charts, Figs. 9 and 10, when the compressor clutch disengages.
6. If adjustment is required, remove switch, then the fiber end plate for access to adjusting screw, Fig. 11.
7. To lower suction pressure, rotate adjusting screw a partial turn counterclockwise. To raise pressure, rotate adjusting screw a partial turn clockwise.
8. Install fiber end plate, then the switch.
9. Check system performance and readjust switch, if necessary.

COMPRESSOR CLUTCHES

The clutch units found on automotive

Evaporator Pressure Gauge Reading	Evaporator Temperature F°	High Pressure Gauge Reading	Ambient Temperature
0	-21°	45	20°
0.6	-20°	55	30°
2.4	-15°	72	40°
4.5	-10°	86	50°
6.8	-5°	105	60°
9.2	0°	126	70°
11.8	5°	140	75°
14.7	10°	160	80°
17.1	15°	185	90°
21.1	20°	195	95°
22.5	22°	220	100°
23.9	24°	240	105°
25.4	26°	260	110°
26.9	28°	275	115°
28.5	30°	290	120°
37.0	40°	305	125°
46.7	50°	325	130°
57.7	60°		
70.1	70°		
84.1	80°		
99.6	90°		
116.9	100°		
136.0	110°		
157.1	120°		
179.0	130°		

Fig. 13 Pressure-temperature relationship. Conditions equivalent to 30 mph or 1750 engine rpm

A/C systems are of two general types. The first type developed had the magnetic coil installed inside the pulley and rotated with it. This type is called the rotating coil type. The electrical current is carried to the coil by the use of brushes mounted to the compressor frame and contacting a slip ring mounted to the inside of the rotating pulley.

The second type has the magnetic coil mounted to the frame of the compressor and does not rotate. This is called the stationary coil type. This coil being stationary, correct spacing becomes important to prevent the rotating pulley from contacting the coil and still bring the hub and armature into position to obtain the maximum attraction of the magnetic force.

Each clutch manufacturer furnishes units to fit all models of compressors according to the required specifications for different applications. Therefore, when replacing either the clutch unit or the coil, note carefully that the replacement unit is correct for the vehicle on which it is to be installed.

All clutches operate on the same principle of magnetic attraction. The operation is the same whether the magnetic coil is so mounted that it rotates with the pulley or is solidly mounted to the compressor. Each has a wound core located within a metal cup acting in a manner

similar to a horseshoe magnet when the coil is energized magnetically, Fig. 12.

Testing Clutch Coil

To determine if a clutch coil is defective, the following general procedure is enough to meet all requirements regardless of variations of installation. Meter connections given are for negative ground systems; reverse connections for positive ground systems.

Determine Voltage to Coil

1. With ignition switch on and clutch energized, battery voltage should be delivered to the coil. To prepare for the test, expose the connection between the coil and evaporator for electrical checks. *Do not allow exposed wire to contact body of car while switches are ON.*
2. Connect RED lead of a conventional Volt-Ammeter Tester to the exposed wire connection between evaporator and clutch coil.
3. Connect BLACK lead of voltmeter to compressor body.
4. Voltmeter should register battery voltage. If there is no voltage indication,

check line fuse, voltage into evaporator, and to the "OFF-ON" switch to locate and repair voltage loss.

Determine Current Draw of Coil

1. Separate wires at connection between evaporator and coil.
2. Connect RED ammeter lead to exposed wire of evaporator.
3. Connect BLACK lead of ammeter to clutch coil wire.
4. Turn switches ON to energize clutch coil.
5. On all models except Chrysler Le Baron and Dodge Diplomat current draw at 11.8 to 12.7 volts and 80 F

should be approximately 3.2 to 4.2 amps for copper wire and 4.2 to 5.1 amps for aluminum wire. On Chrysler Le Baron and Dodge Diplomat models, current draw should be 4.1 to 4.9 amps for copper wire.
6. A zero ampere draw indicates an open circuit inside coil; excessive current draw indicates a short-circuit within the coil.

Determine Ground Circuit Resistance

Performance of the resistance test requires that the current draw of the coil be within specifications given above.

1. Connect evaporator and clutch coil wire.

2. Connect RED lead of voltmeter to compressor body.
3. Connect BLACK lead of voltmeter to battery post.
4. Turn switches ON to energize clutch coil.
5. Total resistance from compressor body to battery post cannot exceed .3 of a volt.
6. If resistance is excessive, clean all connections and metal-to-metal contacts, including engine-to-body and compressor-to-engine, to reduce resistance.

A/C System Testing

PERFORMANCE TEST

The system should be operated for at least 15 minutes to allow sufficient time for all parts to become completely stabilized. Determine if the system is fully charged by the use of test gauges and sight glass if one is installed on system. Head pressure will read from 180 psi to 220 psi or higher, depending upon ambient temperature and the type unit being tested. The sight glass should be free of bubbles if a glass is used in the system. Low side pressures should read approximately 15 psi to 30 psi, again depending on the ambient temperature and the unit being tested. It is not feasible to give a definite reading for all types of systems used, as the type control and component installation used on a particular system will directly influence the pressure readings on the high and low sides, Fig. 13.

The high side pressure will definitely be affected by the ambient or outside air temperature. A system that is operating normally will indicate a high side gauge reading between 150-170 psi with an 80° F ambient temperature. The same system will register 210-230 psi with an ambient temperature of 100°F. No two systems will register exactly the same, which requires that allowance for variations in head pressures must be considered. Following are the most important normal readings likely to be encountered during the season.

Ambient Temp.	High Side Pressure
80	150-170
90	175-195
95	185-205
100	210-230
105	230-250
110	250-270

Relative Temperature of High and Low Sides

The high side of the system should be uniformly hot to the touch throughout. A difference in temperature will indicate a partial blockage of liquid or gas at this point.

The low side of the system should be uniformly cool to the touch with no ex-

cessive sweating of the suction line or low side service valve. Excessive sweating or frosting of the low side service valve usually indicates an expansion valve is allowing an excessive amount of refrigerant into the evaporator. This condition will not necessarily be applicable to those units installed on General Motors vehicles that use the Suction Throttling valve. On these systems the line from the valve to the compressor will normally drop to a much lower reading than the evaporator pressure as the Suction Throttling Valve closes, resulting in the presence of moisture or frosting on this line. This is a normal reaction in this type system and is the result of the construction and operation of the STV or POA and the compressor, having approximately 35% more capacity than previous models of these vehicles that used the hot gas by-pass valve. These factors often cause the line from the STV or POA to the compressor to drop into a partial vacuum under normal operation.

Evaporator Output

At this point, provided all other inspec-

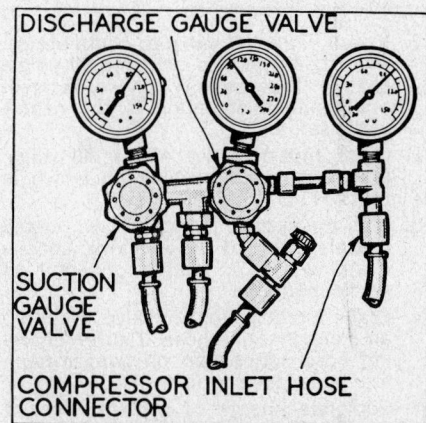

Fig. 14   Purge gauge hoses for Air-Temp compressors

tion tests have been performed, and components have been found to operate as they should, a rapid cooling down of the interior of the vehicle should result. The use of a thermometer is not necessary to determine evaporator output. Bringing all units to the correct operating specifications will insure that the evaporator performs as intended.

PURGING SYSTEM

1. Connect gauges into system, Figs. 14, 15, and adjust controls for maximum cooling. *This is necessary when the system has not been operating to return excess oil to the compressor.*
2. Operate engine for 10 to 15 minutes to stabilize the system at 1500-1750 rpm.
3. Shut off engine and controls. Adjust engine speed to slow idle to prevent "dieseling".
4. Open low side hand manifold valve slightly, using a rag or container to catch refrigerant. *Do not discharge the refrigerant near an open flame as a toxic gas (phosgene) can result.*
5. Open high side manifold hand valve. *Open hand valves only enough to bleed refrigerant from system. Too rapid purging will draw excessive oil from compressor and system.*
6. Close gauge manifold shut-off valves when refrigerant ceases to bleed from hose. Both gauges will read zero psi.

Evacuate System with Vacuum Pump

Vacuum pumps suitable for removing air and moisture from A/C systems are commercially available. A specification for system pump-down used here is 28 to 29½" vacuum. This reading can be attained at or near sea level only. For each 1000 feet of altitude this operation is being performed, the reading will be 1" vacuum lower. As an example, at 5000 feet elevation, only 23-24½" of vacuum can be obtained.

NOTE: On General Motors vehicles, disconnect wire connector from thermal limiter assembly. Connect a jumper wire between feed wire and clutch coil wire, if equipped.

1. Connect vacuum pump to gauge manifold. With gauges connected into system, remove cap from vacuum hose connector. Install center hose from gauge manifold to vacuum pump connector. Mid-position high and low side compressor service valves (if used). Open high and low side gauge manifold hand valves.

2. Operate vacuum pump a minimum of 30 minutes for air and moisture removal. Watch compound gauge that system pumps down into a vacuum. System will reach 28-29½" vacuum in not over 5 minutes. If system does not pump down, check all connections and leak-test if necessary.

3. Close gauge manifold hand valves and shut off vacuum pump.

4. Check ability of system to hold vacuum. Watch compound gauge to see that gauge does not rise at a faster rate than 1" vacuum every 4 or 5 minutes. If compound gauge rises at too rapid a rate, install partial charge and leak-test. Then purge system as outlined above.

5. If system holds vacuum, charge system with refrigerant.

Evacuate System Using Charging Station

A vacuum pump is built into the charging station and is constructed to withstand repeated and prolonged use without damage. Complete moisture removal from the system is possible only with a vacuum pump constructed for the purpose.

NOTE: On General Motors vehicles, disconnect wire connector from thermal limiter assembly. Connect a jumper wire between feed wire and compressor clutch coil wire, if equipped.

1. Operate vacuum pump. Connect hose to vacuum pump if system was purged through charging station.

2. Open high and low side gauge valves of charging station.

3. Connect station into 110-volt current.

4. Engage "Off-On" switch to vacuum pump according to directions of specific station being used.

5. System should pump down into a 28-29½" vacuum in not more than 5 minutes. If system fails to meet this specification, repair as necessary.

6. Operate pump a minimum of 30 minutes to remove all air and moisture.

7. Close high and low side gauge valves. Open switch to turn off pump.

8. Check ability of system to hold vacuum by watching compound gauge to see that it does not rise at a rate higher than 1" of vacuum every 4 or 5 minutes: If rise rate is not within specifications, repair system as necessary. If rise rate is within specifications, charge system with refrigerant.

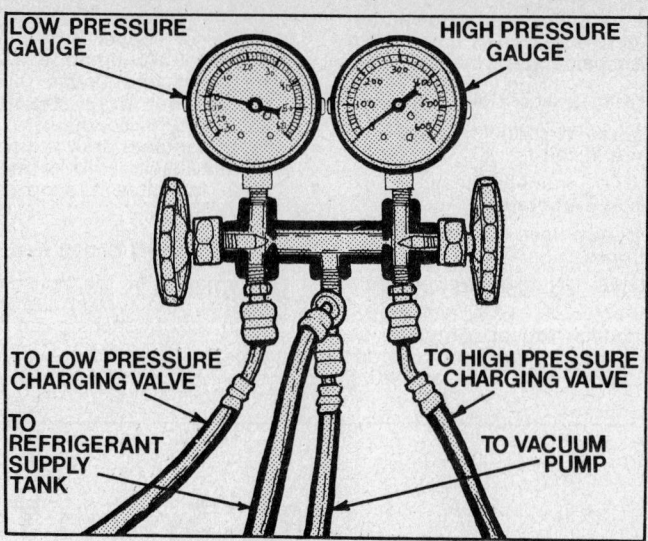

Fig. 15   Purge gauge hoses for Frigidaire, Sankyo, Tecumseh and York compressors

CHARGING THE SYSTEM
Except General Motors (C.C.O.T.) Cycling Clutch Orifice Tube System

Using 15-Ounce Containers

CAUTION: Do not use 15 ounce cans to charge into high pressure side of system or into a system that is at high temperature. High system pressures could cause charging can to explode.

To prevent waste and to aid in more accurate charging, refrigerant manufacturers package refrigerant in 15-ounce cans. The small containers are advantageous to small shops doing only a limited amount of A/C service work. The small containers are handled in the same manner as the larger drums except care must be taken not to overheat the cans because of the danger of explosion.

NOTE: On General Motors vehicles, disconnect wire connector from thermal limiter assembly. Connect a jumper wire between feed wire and compressor clutch coil wire, if equipped.

1. Install "Fitz-All" valve to container(s). The Fitz-All valve is available for single cans or three cans. Whichever is used, preliminary installation to the can(s) is the same.

2. Close shut-off valve of Fitz-All valve. Pierce can with mechanism which is part of Fitz-All valve.

3. With the system pumped-down, install charging hose to Fitz-All valve. Loosen charging hose at center connector on gauge manifold.

4. Crack Fitz-All shut-off valve to purge air from charging hose. Tighten charging hose connection on gauge manifold and close shut-off valve.

5. Complete charge of system. Do not overfill. Use A/C Data table to determine capacity of system being serviced. Close high side gauge manifold

hand valve. Start engine and adjust throttle to 1500-1750 rpm. Adjust A/C controls for maximum cooling. Open low side gauge manifold hand valve to allow Freon to be drawn into system. If single containers are used, it will be necessary to replace each as it becomes empty.

7. Bubbles may appear in sight glass even though system is fully charged. After system is fully charged, refer to A/C Data Table, test system for leaks and make functional check of system.

Using Charging Station

Most stations contain a charging cylinder into which the exact amount of refrigerant required for the system being serviced may be placed while system pump-down is being performed. The refrigerant charging cylinder contained in the station is heated to the correct temperature to insure proper refrigerant flow to all parts of the system as a gas during the charging operation. Following correct evacuation procedure as to length of time for complete moisture removal, the vacuum pump will so efficiently pump-down the system that opening the correct valves will completely charge the system from the high side, and the use of the compressor in the charging operation will not be required.

NOTE: On General Motors vehicles, disconnect wire connector from thermal limiter assembly. Connect a jumper wire between feed wire and compressor clutch coil wire, if equipped.

1. Prepare charging cylinder for filling: Open storage drum valve. Close all valves on station. Read storage tank gauge pressure. Rotate dial shroud on charging cylinder to correlate with pressure on gauge. Open cylinder fill valve.

2. Fill charging cylinder: Determine system capacity from A/C Data table. Intermittently open and close pres-

sure relief valve. *When pressure relief valve opens, Freon will enter cylinder and boil. Closing the valve will increase pressure on the Freon, changing it to a liquid to stabilize the refrigerant in the sight glass. Fill to specified level in sight glass and close pressure relief valve.*

3. Charge system: With gauges connected into system, open refrigerant control valve. Open high pressure valve. After full charge has entered system, close refrigerant control valve and high pressure valve. Reseat suction and discharge service valves and remove charging station hoses.

4. Test system for leaks and make functional check of system.

General Motors (C.C.O.T.) Cycling Clutch Orifice Tube System

NOTE: The following procedure applies to vehicles which have been discharged, oil level checked and corrected as necessary, and evacuated.

1. With engine running at normal idle speed, set A/C controls to OFF.

2. With refrigerant drums or cans inverted, open valves and allow 1 pound or 1-2 14 ounce cans of liquid refrigerant to enter system through low side service fitting on accumulator.

3. As soon as 1 pound or 1-2 14 ounce cans of liquid refrigerant enter the system, immediately engage the compressor, by setting the A/C control to NORM and blower speed on HI to draw in the remainder of the recommended refrigerant charge. Refer to specifications.

NOTE: To speed up the charging process, place a fan in front of the condenser so that the additional air flow will maintain the temperature of the condenser below that of the charging cylinder.

4. Close refrigerant source valve and run engine for 30 seconds to clear lines and gauges.

5. With engine running, quickly disconnect the charging hose adapter from the accumulator fitting.
   CAUTION: Disconnect charging hose adapter from accumulator fitting as

quickly as possible to avoid excess loss of refrigerant. Also, never disconnect charging line from adapter, as this will cause a total discharge of the system due to the depressed shrader valve in the service fitting.

6. Replace protective cap on accumulator fitting and leak check system.

7. Check system for proper system pressures.

LEAK TEST SYSTEM

The propane torch Halide Leak Detector is the most widely used of the detection devices. Therefore, only the procedure for this device will be given. The procedure is the same for any electronic detector, except that the pick-up device registers the presence of refrigerant by a flashing light or high pitched squeal instead of changing the color of the flame. All other steps in preparing the system and leak testing are the same and can be followed as outlined below:

1. Stabilize system at 1500-1750 rpm. If system is empty of refrigerant, it will be necessary to install a partial charge before continuing. With gauges connected into system, adjust A/C controls for maximum cooling. Operate for 10 to 15 minutes, then shut off car engine.

2. Light leak detector. Open valve to a low flame that will not blow itself out. Warm up until copper element turns cherry red. Lower flame until flame tip is even with or slightly below center of element. *For electronic tester, follow preparation procedure as given in operating instructions.*

3. Move leak detector pick-up under hoses, joints, seals, and any possible place for a leak to occur.

NOTE: Freon 12 refrigerant is heavier than air and will move downward. If concentration of refrigerant is located, move pick-up upward to locate leak. Do not inhale fumes produced by burning refrigerant.

4. Watch for color change of flame: Pale blue, no refrigerant; yellow, small amount of refrigerant; purplish-blue, large amount of refrigerant. Repair system as necessary if leaks are located.

5. Check sensitivity of reaction plate: Pass pick-up hose over empty can or crack open refrigerant container; flame

should show violent reaction. If no color change, replace reaction plate, following instructions accompanying leak detector. *Too high a flame will result in short life to reaction plate and poor reaction and will soon burn out element.*

6. Charge system if repairs were necessary.

ISOLATE COMPRESSOR FROM SYSTEM

On systems having both a high side and low side service valve, the compressor may be isolated and refrigerant retained in the system while service work is being performed on the compressor or in the engine compartment of the car.

1. Stabilize system at 1500-1750 rpm: With gauges connected into system, adjust A/C controls for maximum cooling. Operate system for 10 to 15 minutes.

2. Isolate compressor: Slowly close low side service valve until low side gauge reads zero psi. Then shut off car engine.

3. Return car engine to idle speed to prevent "dieseling". Completely close low side service valve. Close high side service valve. Purge refrigerant from compressor by cracking low side hand manifold until both gauges read zero psi. *Purge refrigerant slowly to prevent pulling oil from compressor.*

4. Remove gauges from service valves and service valves from compressor. Then perform service work as required.

5. Place compressor in system: Install service valves to compressor, using new gaskets or O-ring seals, whichever are required. Purge air from compressor by cracking high side service valve for 3 seconds with high side hose connector capped and low side hose connector open.

6. Install gauges to service valve connectors and purge air from hoses.

7. Mid-position service valves, continue testing system and adjust controls for maximum performance.

Each make and model of A/C system has its own type of construction. To cover service work on components of all models is beyond the scope of this manual.

AIR CONDITIONING

AIR CONDITIONING SPECIFICATIONS

Year	Model	Refrigerant Capacity, Lbs.		Refrigeration Oil				Temperature Control Device	Comp. Pulley to Clutch Plate Clearance (inch)
		With One Evaporator	With Two Evaporators	Viscosity	Capacity, Ounces		Oil Level Inches		
					With One Evaporator	With Two Evaporators			

AMERICAN MOTORS

1974–76	Ambassador, Matador	3¼	—	300	7	—	⑧	Thermo. Switch	—
	Others, Exc. Pacer	2	—	300	7	—	⑧	Thermo. Switch	—
1975–76	Pacer	2⅛	—	300	7	—	⑧	Thermo. Switch	—
1977	Matador	3	—	③	7	—	⑧	Thermo. Switch	—
	Gremlin, Hornet	2	—	③	7	—	⑧	Thermo. Switch	—
	Pacer	2⅛	—	③	7	—	⑧	Thermo. Switch	—
1978	AMX, Concord, Gremlin	2	—	③	7	—	⑧	Thermo. Switch	—
	Matador	3	—	③	7	—	⑧	Thermo. Switch	—
	Pacer	2⅛	—	③	7	—	⑧	Thermo. Switch	—

BUICK—FULL SIZE

1974–76	All	3¾	—	525	⑮	—	①	POA Valve	⑩
1977–78	All	3¾	—	525	10	—	①	Thermo. Switch	.031–.062

BUICK—COMPACT & INTERMEDIATE (EXC. SKYHAWK)

1974	All	3¾	—	525	10½	—	①	POA Valve	.031–.062
1975–76	Century, Regal	3¾	—	525	⑯	—	①	POA Valve	⑩
	Apollo, Skylark	3½	—	525	⑱	—	①	POA Valve	⑩
1977–78	Skylark	3½	—	525	④	—	①	Thermo. Switch	⑥
	Exc. Skylark	3¾	—	525	④	—	①	Thermo. Switch	⑥

CADILLAC

1974–76	All Exc. Seville	3¾	5	525	10½	13½	①	POA Valve	.031–.057
1976	Seville	3½	—	525	10½	—	①	POA Valve	.031–.057
1977–78	All Exc. Seville	3¾	5	525	10	13½	①	Thermo. Switch	.031–.057
	Seville	3½	—	525	10	—	①	Thermo. Switch	.031–.057

CAMARO, CHEVROLET, CHEVELLE, NOVA, MALIBU & MONTE CARLO

1974	Four Season	3¾	—	525	11	—	①	POA Valve	.022–.057
	Comfortron	3¾	—	525	11	—	①	POA Valve	.022–.057
1975–76	4 Cyl. Comp.	3¾	—	525	5½–6½	—	①	POA Valve	.020–.040
	6 Cyl. Comp.	3¾	—	525	⑰	—	①	POA Valve	.022–.057
1977–78	Exc. Camaro, Nova	3¾	—	525	㉗	—	①	Thermo. Switch	㉘
	Camaro	3¼	—	525	㉗	—	①	Thermo. Switch	㉘
	Nova	3½	—	525	㉗	—	①	Thermo. Switch	㉘

CHEVROLET CHEVETTE

1976–78	All	2¼	—	525	5½–6½	—	①	Thermo. Switch	.020–.040

AIR CONDITIONING SPECIFICATIONS—Continued

Year	Model	Refrigerant Capacity, Lbs.		Refrigeration Oil				Temperature Control Device	Comp. Pulley to Clutch Plate Clearance (Inch)
		With One Evaporator	With Two Evaporators	Viscosity	Total System Capacity, Ounces		Compressor Oil Level Check, Inches		
					With One Evaporator	With Two Evaporators			
CHEVROLET MONZA, BUICK SKYHAWK, OLDS STARFIRE & PONTIAC SUNBIRD									
1975-76	Monza	2¹³⁄₁₆	—	525	⑮	—	①	POA Valve	.022–.057
	Skyhawk	3	—	525	5½–6½	—	①	POA Valve	.020–.040
	Starfire	4	—	525	5½–6½	—	①	POA Valve	.020–.040
1976	Sunbird	2¹³⁄₁₆	—	525	5½–6½	—	①	POA Valve	.020–.040
1977	Sunbird	3¼	—	525	6	—	①	Thermo. Switch	.020–.040
1977-78	Monza	2¹³⁄₁₆	—	525	④	—	①	Thermo. Switch	⑯
	Skyhawk	3	—	525	6	—	①	Thermo. Switch	.020–.040
	Starfire	2½	—	525	6	—	①	Thermo. Switch	.020–.040
1978	Sunbird	2½	—	525	6	—	①	Thermo. Switch	.020–.040
CHEVROLET VEGA & PONTIAC ASTRE									
1974-75	All	2¹³⁄₁₆	—	525	11	—	①	Thermo. Switch	.022–.057
1976-77	All	⑨	—	525	5½–6½	—	①	Thermo. Switch	.020–.040
CHEVROLET CORVETTE									
1974-78	All	3	—	525	⑰	—	①	POA Valve	.022–.057
CHECKER MOTORS									
1974-75	All	2¾	4½	525	⑮	13½	①	Thermo. Switch	.022–.057
CHRYSLER & IMPERIAL									
1974	All	4¼	—	300	10–12	—	1⅝–2⅜②	EPR-2 Valve	—
1975	Exc. Cordoba	4¼	—	300	10–12	—	1⅝–2⅜②	EPR-2 Valve	—
	Cordoba	3¾	—	300	10–12	—	1⅝–2⅜②	EPR-2 Valve	—
1976	Exc. Cordoba	2¾	—	⑲	10–12	—	2⅜	EPR-2 Valve	—
	Cordoba	2⅝	—	⑲	10–12	—	2⅜	EPR-2 Valve	—
1977	Except Cordoba & LeBaron	2¾	—	500	10–12	—	2⅜	EPR-2 Valve	—
	Cordoba & LeBaron	2⅝	—	500	10–12	—	2⅜	EPR-2 Valve	—
1978	All	2⅝	—	500	㉙	—	㉚	㉛	.016–.032㉞
DODGE—FULL SIZE									
1974-75	All	4¼	—	300	10–12	10–12	1⅝–2⅜②	EPR-2 Valve	—
1976-77	All	2¾	—	⑲	10–12	—	2⅜	EPR-2 Valve	—
1978	All	2⅝	—	500	㉙	—	㉚	㉛	.016–.032㉞
DODGE—COMPACT & INTERMEDIATE									
1974	Exc. Dart	2¾	—	300	10–12	—	⑦	EPR-2 Valve	—
	Dart	3¼	—	300	10–12	—	⑦	EPR-2 Valve	—
1975	Exc. Dart	3¾	—	300	10–12	—	⑦	EPR-2 Valve	—
	Dart	3	—	300	10–12	—	⑦	EPR-2 Valve	—
1976-77	All	2⅝	—	⑲	10–12	—	2⅜	EPR-2 Valve	—
1978	All	2⅝	—	500	㉙	—	㉚	㉛	.016–.032㉞
DODGE OMNI & PLYMOUTH HORIZON									
1978	All	2¼	—	500	7–8	—	㉜	㉝	.016–.032

AIR CONDITIONING SPECIFICATIONS—Continued

| Year | Model | Refrigerant Capacity, Lbs. | | Refrigeration Oil | | | Compressor Oil Level Check, Inches | Temperature Control Device | Comp. Pulley to Clutch Plate Clearance (inch) |
| | | With One Evaporator | With Two Evaporators | Viscosity | Total System Capacity, Ounces | | | | |
					With One Evaporator	With Two Evaporators			
FORD—FULL SIZE									
1974	York Comp.	4¼	—	③	10	—	②⑧	STV Valve	—
	Tecumseh Comp.	4¼	—	③	11	—	②⑧	STV Valve	—
	V8-460 W/ATC	4¼	—	525	10½	—	①	STV Valve	.022–.057
1975–78	All	4¼	—	525	10½	—	①	STV Valve	.022–.057
FORD—COMPACT & INTERMEDIATE (EXC. MUSTANG II & PINTO)									
1974–76	York Comp.	⑩	—	③	10	—	②⑧	⑪	—
	Tecumseh Comp.	⑩	—	③	11	—	②⑧	⑪	—
1976–78	Granada	4¼	—	525	10½	—	①	STV Valve	.022–.057
1977–78	York Comp.	⑳	—	③	10	—	⑧	㉑	—
	Tecumseh Comp.	⑳	—	③	11	—	⑧	㉑	—
FORD MUSTANG II									
1974–78	York Comp.	3¼	—	③	10	—	⑧	STV Valve	—
	Tecumseh Comp.	3¼	—	③	11	—	⑧	STV Valve	—
FORD PINTO & MERCURY BOBCAT									
1974–78	York Comp.	2¼	—	③	10	—	②⑧	STV Valve	—
	Tecumseh Comp.	2¼	—	③	11	—	②⑧	STV Valve	—
LINCOLN CONTINENTAL, MARK IV, V & VERSAILLES									
1974–76	Lincoln	4¼	—	525	10½	—	—	STV Valve	.022–.057
	Mark IV	4½	—	525	10½	—	—	STV Valve	.022–.057
1977–78	All	4¼	—	525	10½	—	—	STV Valve	.022–.057
MERCURY—FULL SIZE									
1974	York Comp.	4¼	—	③	10	—	⑧	STV Valve	—
	Tecumseh Comp.	4¼	—	③	11	—	⑧	STV Valve	—
	V8-460 W/ATC	4¼	—	525	10½	—	①	STV Valve	.022–.057
1975–78	All	4¼	—	525	10½	—	①	STV Valve	.022–.057
MERCURY—COMPACT & INTERMEDIATE (EXC. BOBCAT)									
1974–76	York Comp.	⑫	—	③	10	—	⑧	Thermo. Switch⑬	—
	Tecumseh Comp.	⑫	—	③	11	—	⑧	Thermo. Switch⑬	—
1976–78	Monarch	4¼	—	525	10½	—	①	STV Valve	.022–.057
1977–78	York Comp.	㉒	—	③	10	—	⑧	㉓	—
	Tecumseh Comp.	㉒	—	③	11	—	⑧	㉓	—
OLDSMOBILE—FULL SIZE									
1974–76	All	4	—	525	10½	—	①	POA Valve	.022–.057
1977–78	All	3¾	—	525	10	—	①	㉔	.022–.057

AIR CONDITIONING SPECIFICATIONS—Continued

Year	Model	Refrigerant Capacity, Lbs.		Refrigeration Oil				Temperature Control Device	Comp. Pulley to Clutch Plate Clearance (inch)
		With One Evaporator	With Two Evaporators	Viscosity	Total System Capacity, Ounces		Compressor Oil Level Check, Inches		
					With One Evaporator	With Two Evaporators			

OLDSMOBILE—COMPACT & INTERMEDIATE (EXC. STARFIRE)

Year	Model	With One Evaporator	With Two Evaporators	Viscosity	With One Evaporator	With Two Evaporators	Oil Level	Temperature Control Device	Clearance
1974–76	All	4	—	525	⑮	—	①	POA Valve	⑯
1977–78	Omega	3½	—	525	④	—	①	Thermo. Switch	⑯
	Cutlass	3¾	—	525	④	—	①	Thermo. Switch	⑯

PLYMOUTH—FULL SIZE

1974–75	All	4¼	—	300	10–12	—	1⅝–2⅜	EPR-2 Valve	—
1976–77	All	2¾	—	⑲	10–12	—	2⅜	EPR-2 Valve	—
1978	All	2⅝	—	500	㉙	—	㉚	㉛	.016–.032㉞

PLYMOUTH—COMPACT & INTERMEDIATE

1974	Exc. Valiant	2¾	—	300	10–12	—	⑦	EPR-2 Valve	—
	Valiant	3¼	—	300	10–12	—	⑦	EPR-2 Valve	—
1975	Exc. Valiant	3¾	—	300	10–12	—	⑦	EPR-2 Valve	—
	Valiant	3	—	300	10–12	—	⑦	EPR-2 Valve	—
1976–77	All	2⅝	—	⑲	10–12	—	2⅜	EPR-2 Valve	—
1978	All	2⅝	—	500	㉙	—	㉚	㉛	.016–.032㉞

PONTIAC—FULL SIZE

1974–75	All	⑭	—	525	11	—	①	POA Valve	.022–.057
1976	All	3¾	—	525	10½	—	①	POA Valve⑱	.022–.057
1977	All	3¾	—	525	10	—	①	Thermo. Switch	.022–.057

PONTIAC—COMPACT & INTERMEDIATE (EXC. ASTRE & SUNBIRD)

1974–75	All	⑭	—	525	11	—	①	POA Valve	.022–.057
1976	Exc. Firebird	3¾	—	525	⑮	—	①	POA Valve	⑯
	Firebird	3¼	—	525	⑮	—	①	POA Valve	⑯
1977	All	㉕	—	525	④	—	①	Thermo. Switch	⑯

THUNDERBIRD

| 1974–78 | All | ㉖ | — | 525 | 10½ | — | ① | STV Valve | .022–.057 |

①—Note that "Oil level inches" cannot be checked. Refer to total capacity in ounces. See text for procedure.
②—Dipstick reading with compressor installed.
③—Suniso 5G or Capella E.
④—Axial comp., 10 oz.; radial comp., 6 oz.
⑤—Auto Temp uses ETR valve.
⑥—Axial comp., .031"–.062"; radial comp., .020"–.040".
⑦—Six cylinder engines, 1¾–2⅜; V8 engines, 1⅝–2⅜.
⑧—York Comp.—Vertical mount., ⅞–1⅛; horizontal mount., 1³⁄₁₆–1³⁄₁₆. Tecumseh Comp.—Vertical mount., ⅞–1⅜; horizontal mount., ⅞–1⅝.
⑨—Exc. 1977 Astre, 2¹³⁄₁₆; 1977 Astre, 2½.
⑩—Maverick, 1⅞; Elite & Torino, 4½; 1¾; 1975 Granada, 4.
⑪—Exc. Granada & Torino thermo. switch; Granada & Torino, STV valve.
⑫—Comet, 1⅞; 1974–75 Montego & 1974–76 Cougar, 4½; 1975 Monarch, 4.
⑬—1975 Monarch, 1974–76 Montego & 1974–76 Cougar, STV valve.
⑭—Refer to compressor decal when servicing these systems.
⑮—Axial comp., 10½ oz.; radial comp., 5½–6½ oz.
⑯—Axial comp., .022–.057"; radial comp., .020–.040".
⑰—1975, 11 oz.; 1976, 10½ oz.
⑱—Late 1976 Grand Prix, thermostatic switch.

⑲—1976, 300; 1977, 500.
⑳—Maverick, 1⅞; LTD II, 4¼; Fairmont, 3½.
㉑—Maverick, thermo. switch; LTD II, STV valve.
㉒—Comet, 1⅞; Cougar, 4¼; Zephyr, 3½.
㉓—Comet thermo switch; Cougar, STV valve.
㉔—Exc. Toronado, thermo. switch; Toronado, POA valve.
㉕—Firebird, 3¼; Ventura, 3½; Grand Prix & LeMans, 3¾.
㉖—1974–76, 4½; 1977–78, 4¼.
㉗—4 cylinder compressor, 6 ounces. 6 cylinder compressor, 10 ounces.
㉘—4 cylinder compressor, .020–.040 inch. 6 cylinder compressor, .022–.057 inch.
㉙—With RV2 compressor, 10–12 ounces. With Sankyo compressor, 7–8 ounces.
㉚—RV2 compressor, 2⅜ inches. On Sankyo compressors, the oil level should be at the third to fourth increment on the dipstick which represents 3 to 4 ounces of oil. Refer to text for procedure.
㉛—Vehicles with RV2 compressor use EPR-2 valve. Vehicles with Sankyo compressor use a cycling clutch switch.
㉜—Oil level should be at the third or fourth increment on the dipstick which represents 3 to 4 ounces of oil. Refer to text for procedure.
㉝—Cycling clutch switch.
㉞—Sankyo compressor only.

CHARGING VALVE LOCATIONS

Year & Model	High Press.	Low Press.
AMERICAN MOTORS		
1974–78	Compressor	Compressor
BUICK-FULL SIZE		
1974–76	Compressor	VIR
1977–78	⑤	Accumulator
BUICK COMPACT & INTERMEDIATE EXC. SKYHAWK		
1974—		
Exc. Apollo	Compressor	VIR
Apollo	Compressor	POA①
1975–76	Compressor	VIR
1977–78	⑤	Accumulator
CADILLAC		
1974–76③—		
Exc. Seville	Vapor Line	VIR
Seville	Compressor	VIR
1977–78	⑤	Accumulator
CAMARO, CHEVELLE, CHEVROLET NOVA, MALIBU & MONTE CARLO		
1974–76	④	VIR
1977–78	⑤	Accumulator
CHEVROLET CHEVETTE		
1976–78	Dis. Pres. Sw.	Accumulator
CHEVROLET VEGA & PONTIAC ASTRE		
1974–77	Dis. Pres. Sw.	Accumulator

Year & Model	High Press.	Low Press.
CHECKER MOTORS		
1974–75	④	VIR
CHRYSLER & IMPERIAL		
1974–77	Compressor	Compressor
1978	⑫	Compressor
CORVETTE		
1974–77	VIR	VIR
1978	⑤	Accumulator
DODGE (ALL)		
1974–77	Compressor	Compressor
1978	⑫	Compressor
FORD (ALL)		
1974–77⑩	Compressor	Compressor
1977–78⑪	Compressor	⑥
LINCOLN CONTINENTAL, MARK IV, V & VERSAILLES		
1974–76	Compressor	Compressor
1977–78	Compressor	⑥
MONZA, SKYHAWK, STARFIRE & SUNBIRD		
1975–76—		
Exc. Monza	Compressor	VIR
Monza	④	VIR
1977–78	⑦	⑧
MERCURY (ALL)		
1974–78⑩	Compressor	Compressor
1977–78⑪	Compressor	⑥

Year & Model	High Press.	Low Press.
OLDSMOBILE EXC. STARFIRE		
1973–74②	Compressor	POA①
1974–78③	Compressor	VIR
1977–78②	⑤	Accumulator
PLYMOUTH (ALL)		
1974–77	Compressor	Compressor
PONTIAC EXC. ASTRE & SUNBIRD		
1974②	Compressor	POA①
1974–76③	Compressor	VIR
1977–78	⑨	Accumulator,
THUNDERBIRD		
1974–78	Compressor	Compressor

①—Located at cowl, right side of engine.
②—Except VIR system.
③—With VIR.
④—Axial comp., VIR inlet line; radial comp., located on compressor.
⑤—On high pressure line from compressor.
⑥—On low pressure line from compressor.
⑦—4 cyl., on line from condenser; 6 cyl. & 8 cyl., Dis. Press. Switch.
⑧—4 cyl. & 6 cyl. on VIR; 8 cyl., on accumulator.
⑨—Liquid line or muffler.
⑩—2 cyl. compressor.
⑪—6 cyl. compressor.
⑫—With RV2 compressor, on compressor. With Sankyo compressor, on muffler.

VARIABLE SPEED FANS

The fan drive clutch, Fig. 1, is a fluid coupling containing silicone oil. Fan speed is regulated by the torque-carrying capacity of the silicone oil. The more silicone oil in the coupling the greater the fan speed, and the less silicone oil the slower the fan speed.

Two types of fan drive clutches are in use. On one, Fig. 2, a bi-metallic strip and control piston on the front of the fluid coupling regulates the amount of silicone oil entering the coupling. The bi-metallic strip bows outward with a decrease in surrounding temperature and allows a piston to move outward. The piston opens a valve regulating the flow of silicone oil into the coupling from a reserve chamber. The silicone oil is returned to the reserve chamber through a bleed hole when the valve is closed.

On the other type of fan drive clutch, Fig. 3, a heat-sensitive, bi-metal spring connected to an opening plate brings about a similar result. Both units cause the fan speed to increase with a rise in temperature and to decrease as the temperature goes down.

In some cases a Flex-Fan is used instead of a Fan Drive Clutch. Flexible blades vary the volume of air being drawn through the radiator, automatically increasing the pitch at low engine speeds.

Fig. 1 Typical variable-speed fan installed

Fan Drive Clutch Test

Run the engine at a fast idle speed (1000 rpm) until normal operating temperature is reached. This process can be speeded up by blocking off the front of the radiator with cardboard. Regardless of temperatures, the unit must be operated for at least five minutes immediately before being tested.

Stop the engine and, using a glove or a cloth to protect the hand, immediately check the effort required to turn the fan. If considerable effort is required, it can be assumed that the coupling is operating satisfactorily. If very little effort is required to turn the fan, it is an indication that the coupling is not operating properly and should be replaced.

Service Procedure

CAUTION: To prevent silicone fluid from draining into fan drive bearing, do not store or place drive unit on bench with rear of shaft pointing downward.

The removal procedure for either type of fan clutch assembly is generally the same for all cars. Merely unfasten the unit from the water pump and remove the assembly from the car.

The type of unit shown in Fig. 2 may by partially disassembled for inspection and cleaning. Take off the capscrews that hold the assembly together and separate the fan from the drive clutch. Next remove the metal strip on the front by pushing one end of it toward the fan clutch body so it clears the retaining bracket. Then push the strip to the side so that its opposite end will spring out of place. Now remove the small control piston underneath it.

Check the piston for free movement of the coupling device. If the piston sticks, clean it with emery cloth. If the bi-metal strip is damaged, replace the entire unit. These strips are not interchangeable.

When reassembling, install the control piston so that the projection on the end of it will contact the metal strip. Then install the metal strip with any identification numerals or letters facing the clutch. After reassembly, clean the clutch drive with a cloth soaked in solvent. Avoid dipping the clutch assembly in any type of liquid. Install the assembly in the reverse order of removal.

The coil spring type of fan clutch cannot be disassembled, serviced or repaired. If it does not function properly it must be replaced with a new unit.

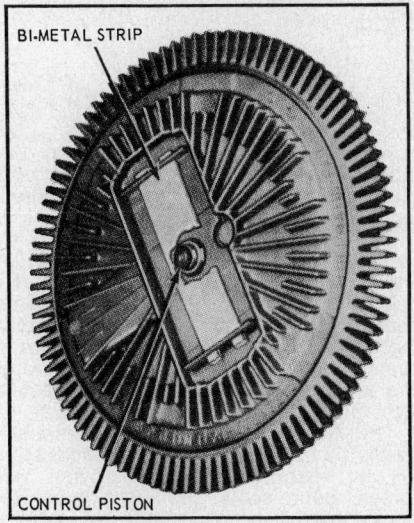

Fig. 2 Variable-speed fan with flat bi-metal thermostatic spring

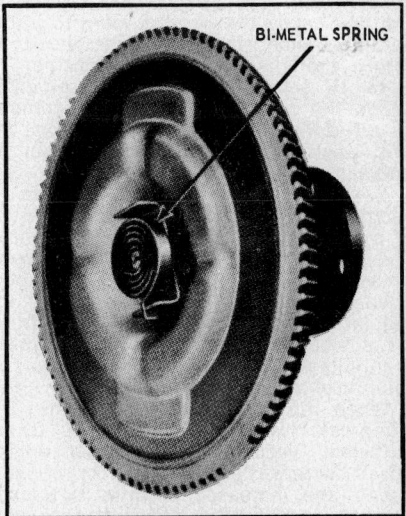

Fig. 3 Variable-speed fan with coiled bi-metal thermostatic spring

AUTOMATIC LEVEL CONTROL

SUPERLIFT SYSTEM

Description

This system, Fig. 1, combines the Superlift shock absorber option with an air compressor and a height control valve. When the Superlift option is used alone, the shocks are filled with (or deflated of) compressed air at any gas station through a fill valve. When used in this system, however, the air pressure is supplied by the compressor and the amount of pressure added or removed is controlled by a sensing valve.

The compressor, a two stage type requiring no lubrication, is designed to operate off engine vacuum to replenish air used from the reservoir which is part of the compressor. As the compressor cycles, the reservoir air pressure gradually increases, causing a back pressure on the secondary stage piston, until it equals the engine vacuum pull against the diaphragm and the unit stops operating until reservoir pressure drops again.

A pressure regulator is attached to the output side of the compressor to limit reservoir outlet pressure to 125 psi. The rear standing height is controlled by a valve which is mounted to the frame, and senses changes in vehicle loading through a link attached to the suspension upper control arm. Changes in the position of the link cause the control valve to either admit or exhaust air from the shocks to return the link to "neutral" position. A 4 to 18 second time delay mechanism inside the control valve prevents transfer of air during normal ride conditions. In this way the system only responds to actual changes in vehicle loading.

Some later systems incorporate a vacuum regulator valve which consists of a relay valve and a deceleration valve. The relay valve is connected to the compressor and the P.C.V. line by rubber hose. The spark advance port of the regulator is connected into the distributor advance vacuum line and the intake manifold port is tapped into the rear of the intake manifold.

When the engine is at slow idle, the compressor will not operate due to insufficient vacuum, Fig. 3. As engine speed increases to fast idle or cruising speed, the increased vacuum is applied through a .020-.025" orifice to the vacu-

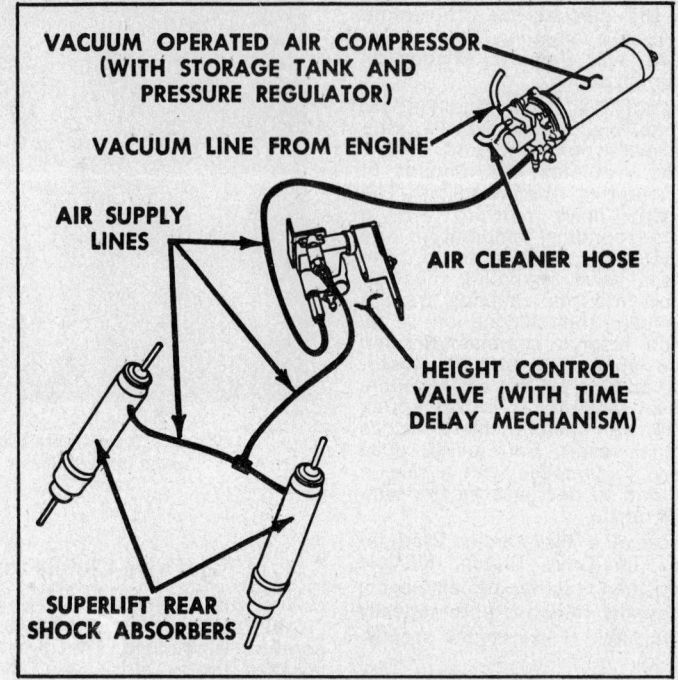

Fig. 1 Schematic diagram of Superlift Automatic Level Control System

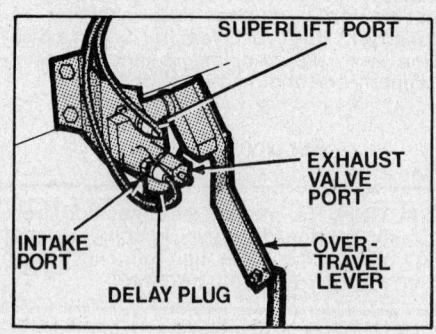

Fig. 2 Height control valve

um relay, overcoming valve spring tension and opening the relay valve. Vacuum from the P.C.V. line now acts upon the compressor and allows it to operate, Fig. 4.

During deceleration, vacuum at the rear of the intake manifold exceeds 17" and vacuum at the spark advance port is negligible. Manifold vacuum overcomes deceleration valve spring tension, opening the valve and permitting vacuum to overcome the relay valve spring and open the relay valve to admit P.C.V. vacuum and operate the compressor, Fig. 5.

The Superlift, Fig. 6, is essentially a conventional shock absorber enclosed in an air chamber. A pliable nylon reinforced boot seals the dust tube (air dome) to the reservoir tube (air piston).

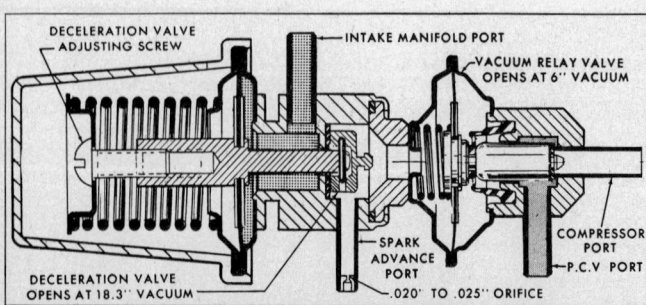

Fig. 3 Vacuum regulator valve in slow idle position

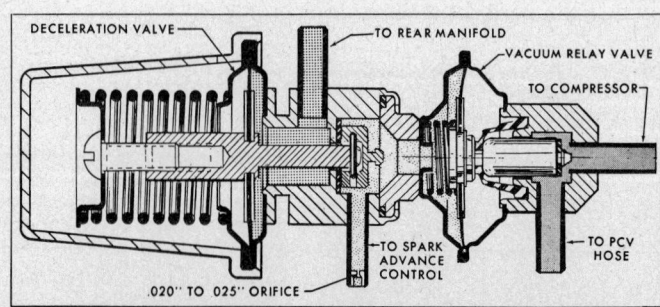

Fig. 4 Vacuum regulator valve in fast idle position

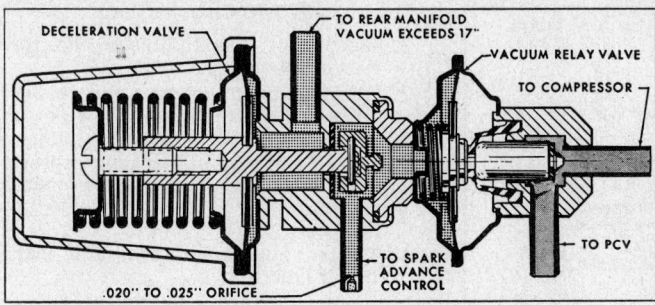

Fig. 5 Vacuum regulator valve in deceleration position

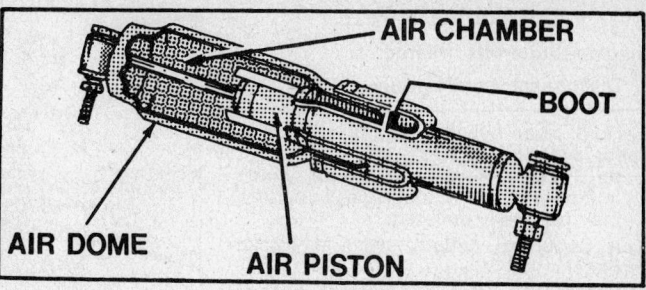

Fig. 6 Superlift shock absorber

The unit will extend when inflated and retract when deflated by the control valve. A 5 to 20 psi air pressure is maintained in the unit to minimize boot friction. This is accomplished by a check valve in the exhaust fitting of the control valve.

TROUBLE SHOOTING GUIDE

Car Loaded, Will Not Rise

1. External damage or breakage.
2. Line leak.
3. Linkage to overtravel lever in wrong hole.
4. Control valve setting incorrect.
5. Defective component.

Car Loaded, Raises to Level, Then Leaks Down

1. Line leak.
2. Control valve exhaust leak.
3. Superlift leak.
4. Control valve leak.

Car Loaded, Raises Partially

1. Load excessive (over 500 lbs at axle) on cars with special springs.
2. Control valve setting incorrect.
3. Low supply pressure.

Car Unloaded, Rides too High, Will Not Come Down

1. Control valve setting incorrect.

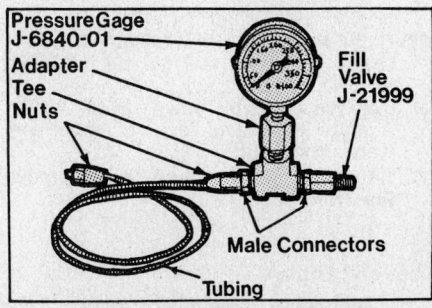

Fig. 7 Test gauge set (Kent-Moore No. J-22124)

2. Improper springs.
3. External damage or breakage.
4. Linkage to overtravel in wrong hole.
5. Defective control valve.

Car Rises When Loaded but Leaks Down While Driving

1. Time delay mechanism not functioning properly.

CHECKS & ADJUSTMENTS

Quick Check of System

1. Record rear trim height of empty car (measure from center of rear bumper to ground).
2. Add weight equivalent to two-passenger load to rear of car. Car should begin to level in 4 to 15 seconds, and final position should be (plus or minus) ½" of measured dimension.
3. Remove weight. After 4 to 18 seconds car should begin to settle. Final unloaded position should be within approximately (plus or minus) ½" of the original measured dimension.

NOTE: To service the system it will be necessary to secure the gauge set shown in Fig. 7 or make one out of the materials illustrated.

Compressor Output Test

1. With all accessories off, run engine until engine settles to hot idle speed. Then turn off ignition.
2. Deflate system through service valve, then remove high pressure line at regulator adapter and connect test gauge.
3. Inflate reservoir to 70 psi through service valve.
4. Observe test gauge for evidence of compressor air leak.
5. If leaking, proceed to leak-test compressor reservoir and regulator. If not leaking, continue this test.
6. With engine running at hot idle speed, observe reservoir build-up for five minutes. Reservoir pressure should build up to a minimum of 90 psi.
7. If compressor fails to cycle, make

sure vacuum and air intake lines are open and unobstructed before removing compressor for repair.
8. If build-up is too slow, repair compressor.
9. Satisfactory build-up indicates system problems to be in the control section. However, again observe the test gauge for evidence of an air leak and proceed accordingly.

Regulator Test & Adjustment General Motors

1. Performance test the regulator with a known good compressor on the car.
2. Deflate system through service valve, remove line at regulator and connect test gauge at regulator adapter.
3. Inflate reservoir through service valve to maximum pressure available. If less than 140 psi, start engine to build-up pressure.
4. Regulated pressure on test gauge should build up to 100-130 psi and hold steady within this range.
5. Recheck regulated pressure by momentarily depressing valve core on test gauge and observe reading.
6. If regulated pressure exceeds 130 psi, replace regulator as a unit.

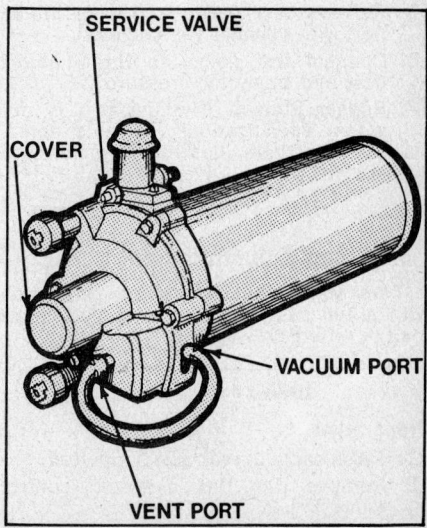

Fig. 8 Assembly leak test preparation

Control Valve Test

Exhaust—Superlifts Inflated

1. Disconnect control valve lever from link.
2. Hold lever down in exhaust position for a period of 15-18 seconds except on 1974-76 Ford and Mercury which is 2 minutes. If time allows, Superlifts may be totally deflated.
3. If Superlifts deflate, perform Intake Check.
4. If Superlifts do not deflate, remove exhaust adapter from control valve and hold lever down as in Step 2. Replace adapter, O-ring and filter if this deflates Superlifts.
5. Replace control valve if none of the above steps solve problem.

Intake Check—Reservoir Pressure, 125 psi Minimum (Ford, 90 psi Min.)

1. Disconnect overtravel lever from link.
2. Hold lever up in intake position for a period of 15-18 seconds except on 1974-76 Ford, Mercury which is a period of two minutes. If time allows, Superlifts may be totally inflated.
3. If Superlifts inflate and hold, proceed to Time Delay Test.
4. If Superlifts inflate and then leak down, perform leak test on lines and fittings and then on Superlifts and control valve. Repair or replace as required.

Time Delay Test Ford & GM
Reservoir Pressure 125 PSI Minimum

1. Disconnect overtravel lever from link.
2. Disconnect lines at Superlift and intake ports.
3. Connect test gauge to intake valve port and apply air pressure (95 lbs.).
4. Move overtravel lever down approximately one inch from neutral position then quickly move lever up two inches. Air should begin to escape from the Superlift port in 4 to 30 seconds. Repeat test.
5. Remove test gauge and plug intake port with fill valve (female end).
6. Connect test gauge to the Superlift port and apply air pressure (95 lbs.).
7. Repeat Step 4. If either test is not within specifications, valve is defective or there has been a loss of silicone fluid.

Trim Adjustment On Car

Trim adjustment should be performed with a full gas tank or the equivalent in load at rate of 6 lbs. per gallon.

1974-77 GM Models

Preparation

1. Raise car with rear axle supported.
2. Remove Superlift line at control valve, Fig. 2.
3. Connect a Fill Valve Assembly (see Fig. 7).

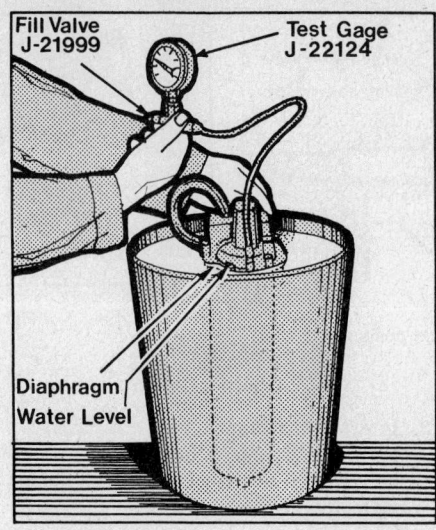

Fig. 9   Checking compressor, reservoir and regulator for leaks

4. Inflate Superlifts to 8 to 15 psi. Jounce car to neutralize suspension.
5. Connect test gauge to Superlift adapter on control valve and attach air pressure source (80 to 110 psi).

Adjustment

1. Loosen overtravel lever adjusting nut.
2. Hold overtravel body down in exhaust position until air escapes from exhaust valve port.
3. Slowly move overtravel body and tighten nut at the point of minimum air bleed. With nut tight, a slight continuous air bleed should be noticeable.

Restore System

1. Remove test gauge and air pressure source from Superlift adapter.
2. Remove Fill Valve Assembly from Superlift line and reconnect line to control valve.
3. Lower car and inflate reservoir through service valve.

1974-76 Ford & Mercury

1. Support vehicle by the front and rear suspensions.
2. Disconnect control valve link from rear upper control arm and manually exhaust air from Superlifts.
3. Loosen control valve lever adjusting nut.
4. On all models, adjust lever arm until link enters control arm hole. Or if a downward movement of lever arm of ¼ inch is required for a fit into the control arm hole.
5. Tighten adjusting nut and connect link to upper control arm.

1975-78 Chrysler Corp.

1. Disconnect U-bolt linkage clip from rear axle housing.
2. Loosen adjustment arm nut to allow arm to move freely.
3. Adjust lever valve arm to obtain a distance of 6¼ in. between center of adjustment arm linkage grommet to upper wheel housing, inside the flange.
4. Tighten adjustment arm and install U-bolt linkage clip.

Leak Tests

Compressor, Reservoir & Regulator

1. Remove assembly intact.
2. Connect test gauge to regulator. Inflate reservoir through service valve to 80-100 psi.
3. Route an 8" rubber hose between vacuum and vent ports, Fig. 8.
4. Submerge in water, Fig. 9, and observe for air leaks at: a) Reservoir weld seam. b) Reservoir-to-compressor O-ring. c) Regulator-to-compressor O-ring. d) Regulator boot defective. e) Boot internal O-ring defective. f) Diaphragm between 1st and 2nd stage housing. g) Tightening thru bolts may correct leak. h) Cover gasket and retainer screw. A few bubbles here is not a leak. A continuous stream indicates defective compressor check valves. i) Service valve. j) Test gauge connections.
5. Correct any leaks detected by either tightening screws or replacing parts.

Control Valve

1. Remove control valve from car.
2. Clean exterior of valve thoroughly.
3. Connect test gauge and air pressure source to intake adapter and open air pressure (80-110 psi).
4. Submerge unit in water. No air should escape if overtravel lever is in "neutral" position. If bubbles escape from Superlift port, replace control valve.
5. Shut off air pressure and detach test gauge from air intake port. Plug intake port with Fill Valve Assembly.
6. Connect test gauge to Superlift port and open air pressure.
7. With overtravel lever in "neutral" position, no air should escape. If bubbles escape from exhaust port, replace control valve.
8. If air escapes around edge of cover plate, tighten screws or replace gasket.
9. Remove control valve from water. Actuate overtravel lever to expel any water from unit.
10. Shut off air pressure and remove line from Superlift port.

Lines and Fittings

1. Disconnect overtravel lever from link.
2. Hold lever up in intake position for

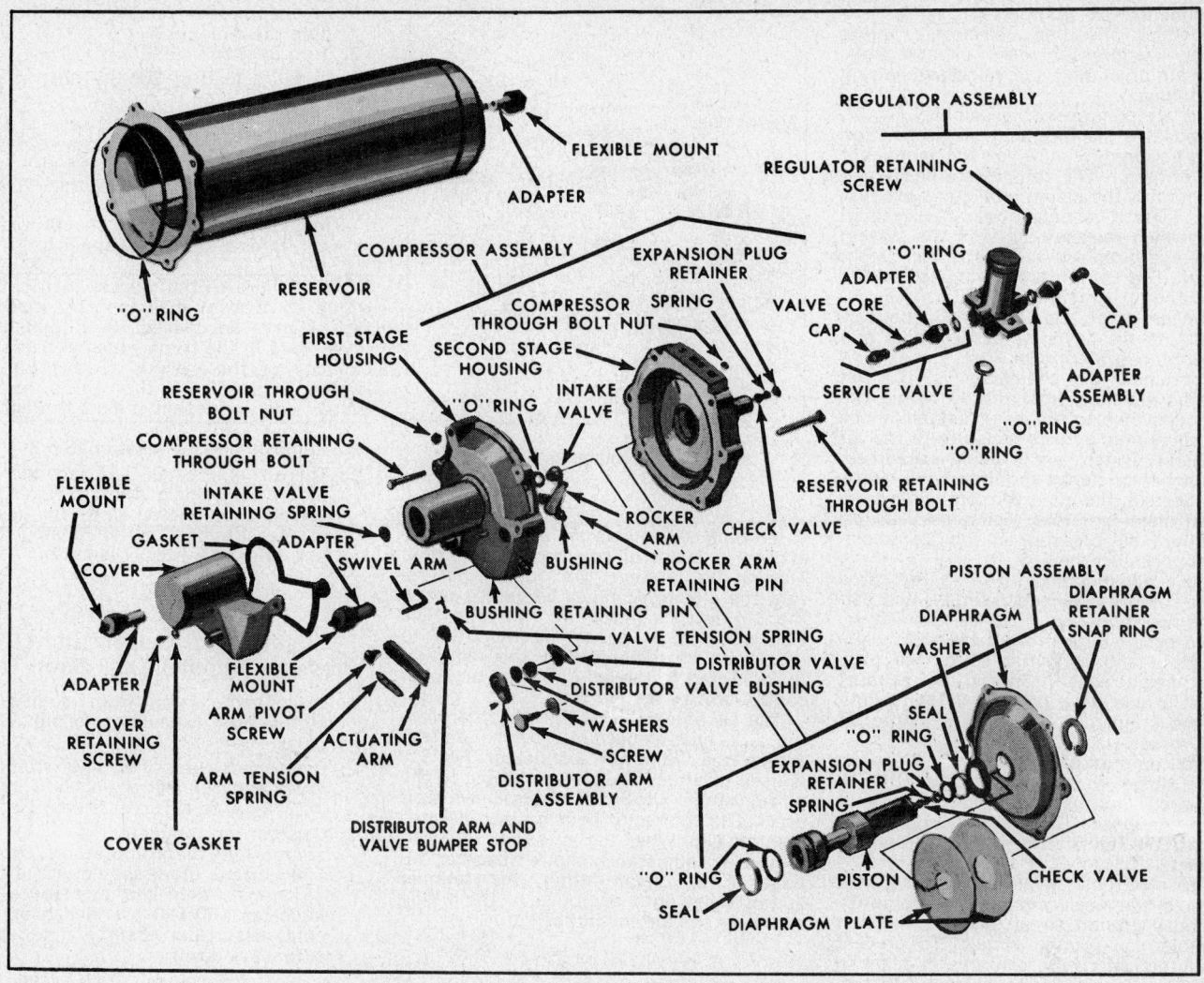

Fig. 10 Exploded view of General Motors compressor, reservoir and regulator

maximum Superlift inflation and release.

3. Leak check all connections with a soap and water solution.

Superlifts

1. Disconnect lines and remove unit from car.
2. Inflate individually to 50-60 psi, utilizing Fill Valve (see Fig. 7). Submerge in water and observe unit for leaks.
3. Install Superlifts.

COMPRESSOR SERVICE

Removal

1. Disconnect vacuum and air intake hoses.
2. Remove air intake and vacuum hoses.

3. Unfasten compressor brackets from mounting points.
4. Remove compressor with brackets attached.
5. Deflate system, using service valve, and remove high pressure fitting at pressure regulator.
6. Remove brackets from compressor.

NOTE: The compressor is a precision-built mechanism, Fig. 10. If an overhaul is contemplated, all parts should be handled carefully. Take care to prevent entrance of dirt or foreign matter. Do not lubricate as unit is designed to run dry.

Installation

1. Attach brackets to compressor.
2. Install compressor to its mounting.
3. Attach air intake and vacuum hoses.
4. Secure air line to compressor pres-

sure regulator.
5. Lower car.
6. Inflate reservoir to 140 psi through compressor service valve.
7. Be sure that vacuum and air intake lines are not rubbing against adjacent parts to prevent chafing.

1978 GENERAL MOTORS ELECTRONIC LEVEL CONTROL

Description

The Electronic Level Control (ELC) system used on 1978 Buick, Cadillac, Oldsmobile and Pontiac vehicles is a totally different type of leveling system from that used in previous models. The system performs the same function of adjusting the carrying height of the vehicle when weight is added to or removed from the vehicle. The ELC system consists of the following components: air compressor, air adjustable shock absorbers, electronic height sensor, compressor relay, exhaust solenoid, air dryer and the necessary wiring and tubing.

The air compressor assembly, Fig. 1, is a positive displacement single position pump powered by a 12 volt DC permanent magnet motor. The compressor head casting contains the piston intake and exhaust valves plus a solenoid operated exhaust valve which releases air from the system when energized by the electronic height sensor. The compressor is located in the engine compartment.

The air dryer, Fig. 11, is attached externally to the air compressor output and performs two functions. First, the air dryer contains a dry chemical, Fig. 12, that absorbs moisture from the air before the air is delivered to the air adjustable shock absorbers and returns moisture to the air when the system air is being exhausted. This action prolongs the life of the chemical. Second, the air dryer contains a valving arrangement that maintains 8-15 psi minimum air pressure in the air adjustable shock absorbers.

The exhaust solenoid, Fig. 13, is located in the compressor head assembly and performs two functions. First, the exhaust solenoid exhausts air from the system when energized and is controlled by the electronic height sensor. Second, the exhaust solenoid acts as a blow-off valve to limit the maximum output pressure of the air compressor.

The compressor relay is a single pole, single throw type that completes the 12 volt circuit to the air compressor motor when energized. The compressor relay is located on the air compressor mounting bracket.

The electronic height sensor, Fig. 14, controls two basic circuits: the compressor relay ground circuit and the exhaust solenoid coil ground circuit. To prevent falsely activating the compressor relay or exhaust solenoid during normal ride motions, the sensor circuitry provides an 8-14 second delay before the circuit can be completed. This sensor limits air compressor run time or exhaust solenoid energized time to a maximum of 3½ minutes. The time limit function is necessary

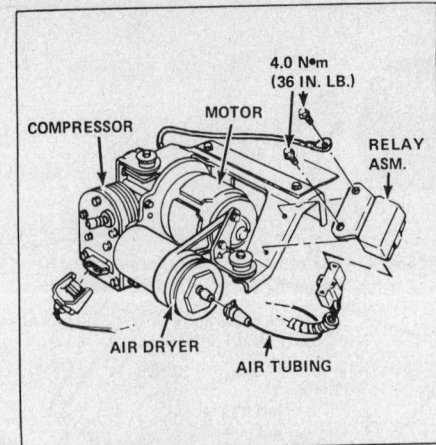

Fig. 11   Air compressor assembly

to prevent continuous air compressor operation in event of solenoid malfunction. Turning the ignition "On" and "Off" resets the electronic timer circuit to renew the 3½ minute maximum run time. The electronic height sensor is mounted to the frame crossmember in the rear and is connected to the axle housing or upper control arm by a short link.

The air adjustable shock absorbers are the same type as used in previous models. A new type "Snap-On" connector, Fig. 15, is used to attach the air line tubing to the air adjustable shock absorbers and the air dryer. The connector housing incorporates a spring clip. When the air line is attached to the air adjustable shock absorber fittings or air dryer fitting, the retainer spring snaps into a groove in the fitting and locks the air line in position.

DIAGNOSIS & TESTING

System Operation Test

1. Measure distance between a location

on rear bumper and the ground and note the dimension.
2. Turn ignition "On".
3. Install a load of 300-350 lbs. in rear of vehicle.
4. There should be an 8-14 second delay before the air compressor activates and the vehicle starts to rise. The vehicle should raise to within ¾ inch of measurement made in step 1 before the compressor deactivates. If not, refer to System Diagnosis.

NOTE: Failure of the vehicle to return to within ¾ inch of measurement made in step 1 may be caused by an unusually heavy load in the trunk which exceeds the capacity of the system. If this type of loading is installed in the vehicle, remove excess load and repeat steps 1 through 4.

5. Remove load installed in step 3.
6. There should be an 8-14 second delay before the vehicle starts to lower. The vehicle should lower to within ¾ inch of measurement made in step 1. If not, refer to System Diagnosis.

Compressor Current Draw, Pressure Output & Leak Down Test

1. Disconnect wiring from compressor motor and exhaust solenoid terminals.
2. Disconnect pressure line from air dryer and connect a pressure gauge, J-22124-A, to air dryer fitting, Fig. 16.
3. Connect an ammeter to a 12 volt source and the compressor, Fig. 16. The current draw should not exceed 14 amps. When the pressure gauge indicates 100-120 psi, deactivate the compressor and observe if the pressure leaks down.

    a. If the current draw exceeds 14 amps., replace the compressor.
    b. If compressor is inoperative, replace the compressor.
    c. If compressor output is less than 100 psi and current draw is normal, check air dryer "O" ring and replace, if necessary. Check for air leak at compressor service valve. If the air dryer "O" ring and the compressor service valve are satisfactory,

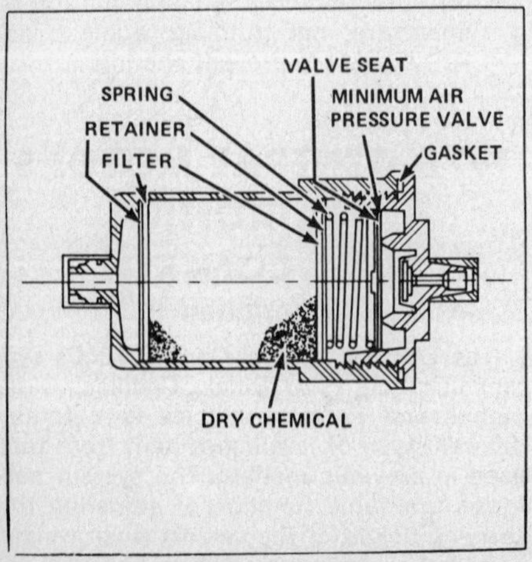

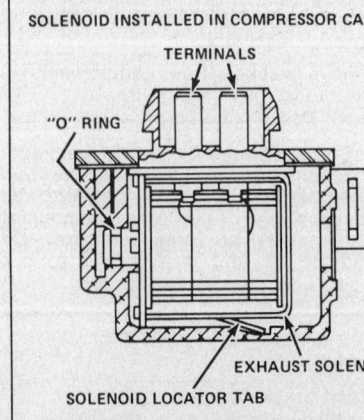

Fig. 12   Air dryer

Fig. 13   Exhaust solenoid

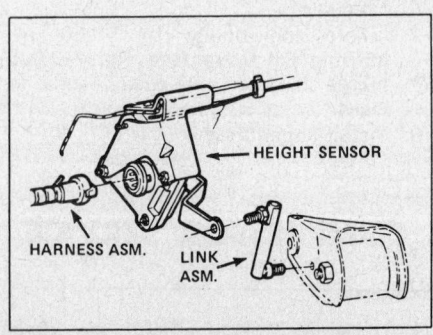

Fig. 14   Electronic height sensor

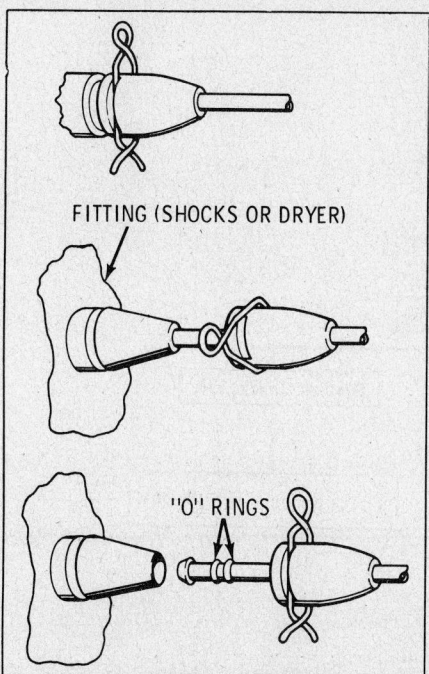

FITTING (SHOCKS OR DRYER)

"O" RINGS

Fig. 15 Airline fittings

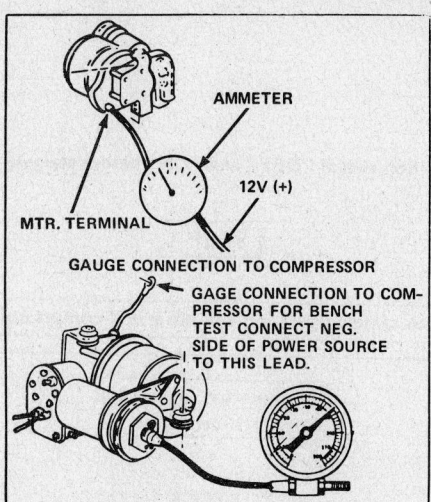

AMMETER

12V (+)

MTR. TERMINAL

GAUGE CONNECTION TO COMPRESSOR

GAGE CONNECTION TO COMPRESSOR FOR BENCH TEST CONNECT NEG. SIDE OF POWER SOURCE TO THIS LEAD.

Fig. 16 Compressor current draw, pressure output & leakdown test connections

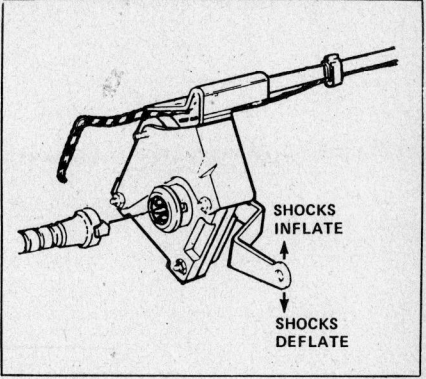

SHOCKS INFLATE

SHOCKS DEFLATE

Fig. 17 Electronic height sensor operational test

replace the compressor.

d. If the compressor pressure leaks down when the compressor is deactivated, check air dryer "O" and replace, if necessary. Check for an air leak at compressor service valve. If the air dryer "O" ring and the compressor service valve are satis-factory, replace the compressor.

Height Sensor Operational Test

1. Cycle ignition "Off" and "On". This will reset the height sensor timer circuits.
2. Raise and support vehicle. Be sure that the rear wheels or axle housing is supported and that the vehicle is at the proper carrying height.
3. Disconnect link from height sensor arm.
4. Check that wiring is properly connected to the height sensor and the harness ground wire is properly connected.
5. Move metal height sensor arm upward, Fig. 17. There should be an 8-14 second delay before the compressor activates and the shock absorbers inflate. After the shock absorbers inflate, deactivate the compressor by moving the height sensor arm downward.
6. Move metal height sensor arm downward below the point where the compressor deactivated. There should be an 8-14 second delay before the shock absorbers start to deflate.

System Diagnosis

Refer to the "Diagnostic Procedure Selection Chart", the "Diagnosis Procedures", Figs. 18 through 33, and the wiring diagrams, Figs. 34 through 37.

DIAGNOSIS PROCEDURE SELECTION CHART

NOTE: When certain tests require raising the vehicle on a hoist, the hoist should support the rear wheels or axle housing. When a frame type hoist is used, two additional jack stands should be used to support the rear axle housing in the normal curb weight position.

REPORTED CONDITION	USE PROCEDURE
System inoperative—compressor does not run.	1
Car stays low—will not raise or raises partially when load is added to rear	1
Car low—car raises and lowers OK when load is added or removed but normal carrying height seems low.	Adjust carrying height per height sensor adjustment.
Car raises OK but gradually leaks down, or compressor cycles on and off intermittently while driving.	1 Start with Step 9 on Oldsmobile. Start with Step 10 on Buick & Pontiac. Start with Step 12 on Cadillac.
Car high (if compressor runs continuously with ignition switch on, use Procedure No. 3).	2
Compressor runs continuously with ignition ON (Compressor does not shut off after 3½ minutes).	3
Compressor relay clicks on and off continuously while driving.	4

<u>IMPORTANT</u>: Always cycle ignition switch "OFF" and "ON" before starting tests.

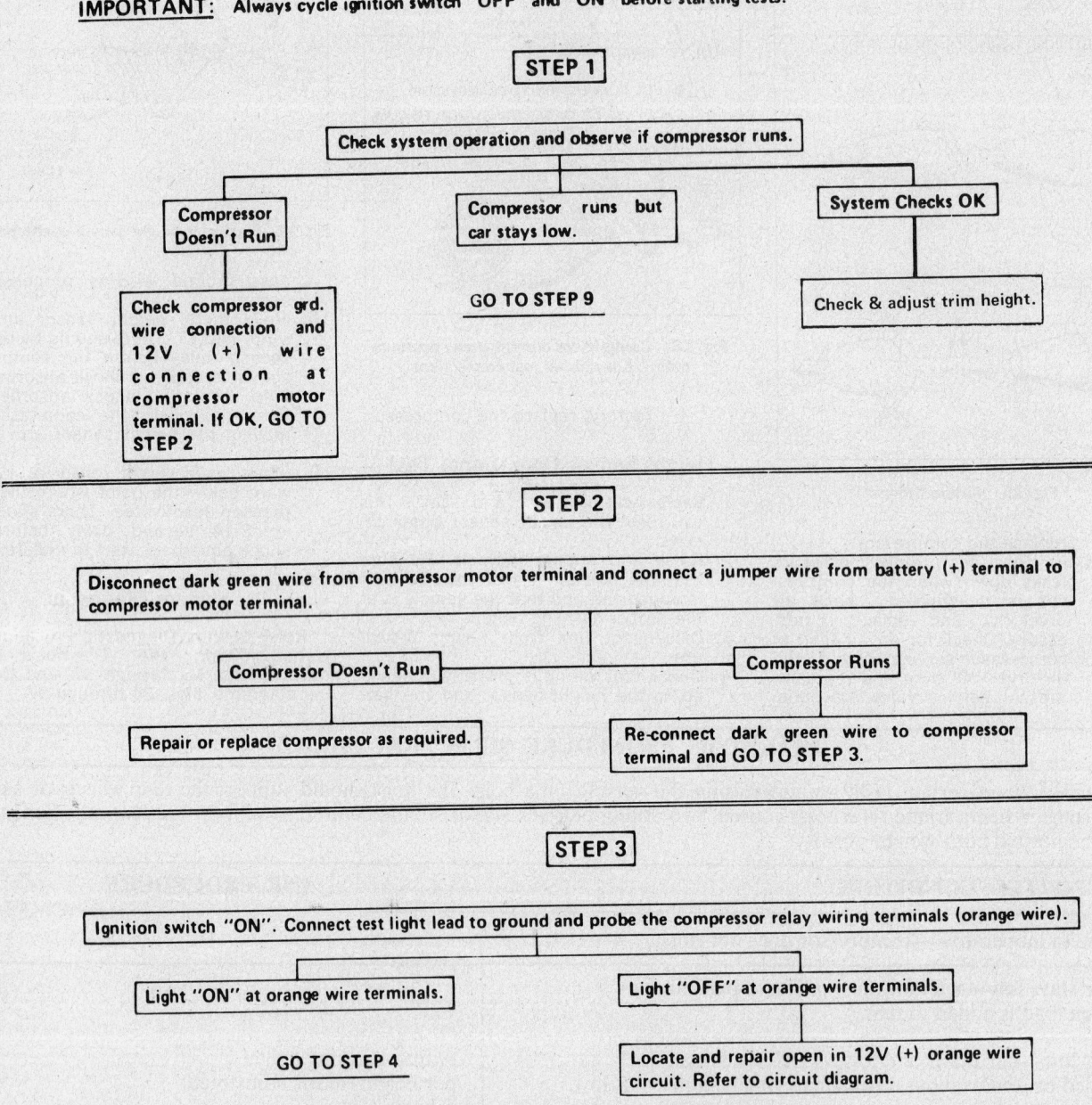

Fig. 18   System diagnosis procedure No. 1, part 1 of 3. Buick & Pontiac

STEP 4

Ignition switch "ON". Connect jumper wire from yellow wire terminal at compressor relay to ground. Observe if compressor runs. NOTE: Be sure motor ground wire is connected.

Compressor Doesn't Run	Compressor Runs
Replace relay.	Disconnect jumper wire and GO TO STEP 5.

STEP 5

Raise car on a hoist and check the following items:
a) Height sensor wiring ground wire securely connected.
b) Link attached to height sensor arm.
c) Height sensor arm adjusting nut tight.
d) Wiring to height sensor securely connected.
e) Check for correct height sensor on car. Refer to height sensor identification chart.

All Items Check OK	Defect Found
GO TO STEP 6	Repair defect and check system.

STEP 6

Ignition switch "ON". Check height sensor operation. Observe if compressor runs.

Compressor Doesn't Run	Compressor Runs
GO TO STEP 7	Re-connect link to height sensor and make adjustment as required.

STEP 7

Ignition switch "ON". Disconnect wiring from sensor. Connect test light lead to ground and probe harness connector terminals 5 and 6. Test light should be ON at both.

Test light "OFF" at one or both terminals.		Test Light "ON"
Locate and repair open circuit in brown wires. Refer to circuit diagram.		GO TO STEP 8

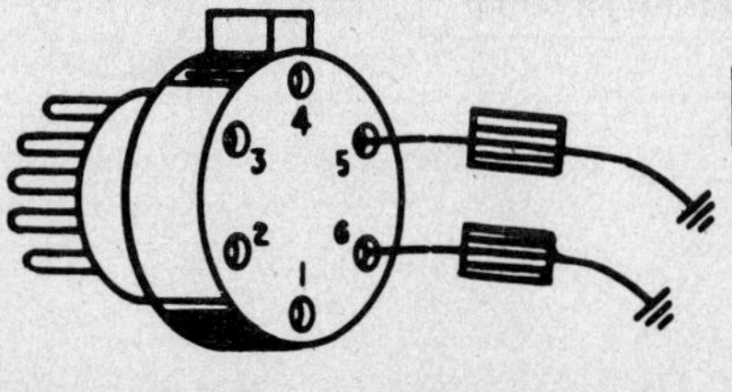

Fig. 19   System diagnosis procedure No. 1, part 2 of 3. Buick & Pontiac

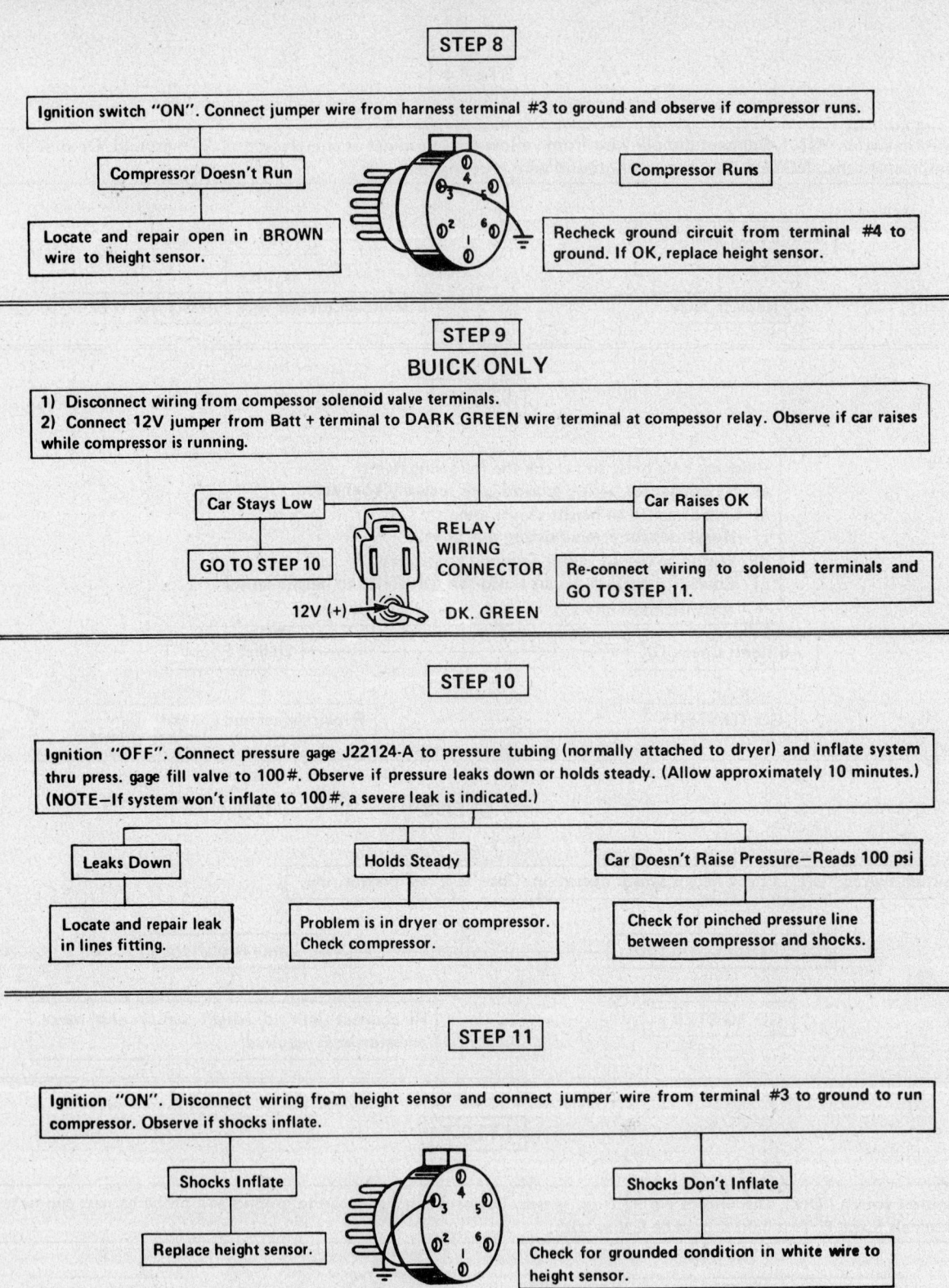

STEP 8

Ignition switch "ON". Connect jumper wire from harness terminal #3 to ground and observe if compressor runs.

Compressor Doesn't Run

Locate and repair open in BROWN wire to height sensor.

Compressor Runs

Recheck ground circuit from terminal #4 to ground. If OK, replace height sensor.

STEP 9

BUICK ONLY

1) Disconnect wiring from compressor solenoid valve terminals.
2) Connect 12V jumper from Batt + terminal to DARK GREEN wire terminal at compressor relay. Observe if car raises while compressor is running.

Car Stays Low

GO TO STEP 10

RELAY WIRING CONNECTOR

12V (+)   DK. GREEN

Car Raises OK

Re-connect wiring to solenoid terminals and GO TO STEP 11.

STEP 10

Ignition "OFF". Connect pressure gage J22124-A to pressure tubing (normally attached to dryer) and inflate system thru press. gage fill valve to 100#. Observe if pressure leaks down or holds steady. (Allow approximately 10 minutes.) (NOTE—If system won't inflate to 100#, a severe leak is indicated.)

Leaks Down

Locate and repair leak in lines fitting.

Holds Steady

Problem is in dryer or compressor. Check compressor.

Car Doesn't Raise Pressure—Reads 100 psi

Check for pinched pressure line between compressor and shocks.

STEP 11

Ignition "ON". Disconnect wiring from height sensor and connect jumper wire from terminal #3 to ground to run compressor. Observe if shocks inflate.

Shocks Inflate

Replace height sensor.

Shocks Don't Inflate

Check for grounded condition in white wire to height sensor.

Fig. 20   System diagnosis procedure No. 1, part 3 of 3. Buick & Pontiac

NOTE: ALWAYS CYCLE IGNITION OFF AND ON BEFORE STARTING TESTS.

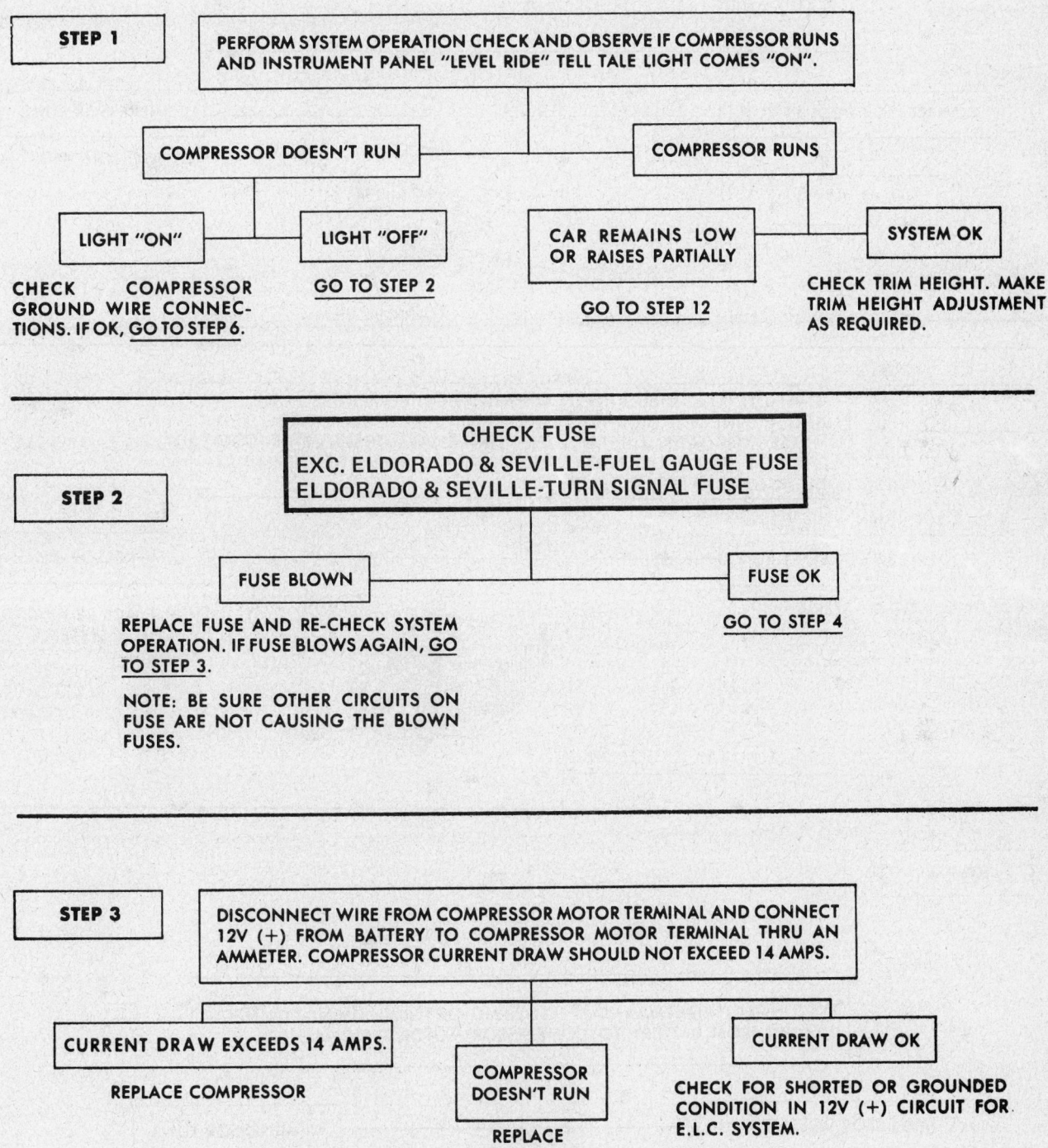

STEP 1

PERFORM SYSTEM OPERATION CHECK AND OBSERVE IF COMPRESSOR RUNS AND INSTRUMENT PANEL "LEVEL RIDE" TELL TALE LIGHT COMES "ON".

COMPRESSOR DOESN'T RUN

COMPRESSOR RUNS

LIGHT "ON"

CHECK COMPRESSOR GROUND WIRE CONNECTIONS. IF OK, GO TO STEP 6.

LIGHT "OFF"

GO TO STEP 2

CAR REMAINS LOW OR RAISES PARTIALLY

GO TO STEP 12

SYSTEM OK

CHECK TRIM HEIGHT. MAKE TRIM HEIGHT ADJUSTMENT AS REQUIRED.

STEP 2

**CHECK FUSE
EXC. ELDORADO & SEVILLE-FUEL GAUGE FUSE
ELDORADO & SEVILLE-TURN SIGNAL FUSE**

FUSE BLOWN

REPLACE FUSE AND RE-CHECK SYSTEM OPERATION. IF FUSE BLOWS AGAIN, GO TO STEP 3.

NOTE: BE SURE OTHER CIRCUITS ON FUSE ARE NOT CAUSING THE BLOWN FUSES.

FUSE OK

GO TO STEP 4

STEP 3

DISCONNECT WIRE FROM COMPRESSOR MOTOR TERMINAL AND CONNECT 12V (+) FROM BATTERY TO COMPRESSOR MOTOR TERMINAL THRU AN AMMETER. COMPRESSOR CURRENT DRAW SHOULD NOT EXCEED 14 AMPS.

CURRENT DRAW EXCEEDS 14 AMPS.

REPLACE COMPRESSOR

COMPRESSOR DOESN'T RUN

REPLACE COMPRESSOR

CURRENT DRAW OK

CHECK FOR SHORTED OR GROUNDED CONDITION IN 12V (+) CIRCUIT FOR E.L.C. SYSTEM.

Fig. 21   System diagnosis procedure No. 1, part 1 of 4. Cadillac

STEP 4

IGNITION "ON". LEAVE WIRING CONNECTED TO COMPRESSOR RELAY AND CONNECT A JUMPER WIRE FROM YELLOW WIRE TERMINAL TO GROUND. OBSERVE IF COMPRESSOR RUNS. TEST PIGTAIL CAN BE USED.

COMPRESSOR DOESN'T RUN

GO TO STEP 5

COMPRESSOR RUNS

GO TO STEP 7

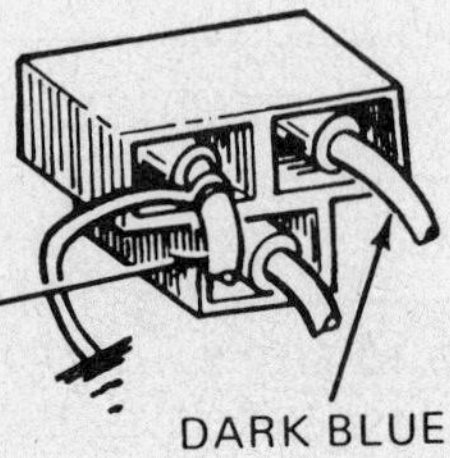

YELLOW

DARK BLUE

STEP 5

IGNITION "ON" DISCONNECT WIRING FROM COMPRESSOR RELAY AND CONNECT A JUMPER WIRE FROM DARK BLUE WIRE TERMINAL TO DARK GREEN WIRE TERMINAL. OBSERVE IF COMPRESSOR RUNS. DO NOT TOUCH DARK BLUE WIRE TERMINAL DURING THIS TEST.

COMPRESSOR DOESN'T RUN

GO TO STEP 6

COMPRESSOR RUNS

REPLACE RELAY AND CHECK SYSTEM.

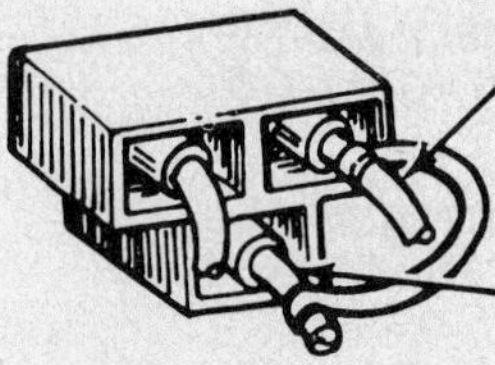

DARK BLUE

DARK GREEN

(DARK BLUE TO DARK GREEN ONLY)

STEP 6

DISCONNECT WIRE FROM COMPRESSOR MOTOR TERMINAL AND CONNECT 12V (+) FROM BATTERY TO COMPRESSOR MOTOR TERMINAL

COMPRESSOR DOESN'T RUN

REPLACE COMPRESSOR

COMPRESSOR RUNS

CHECK FOR OPEN 12V (+) CIRCUIT BETWEEN RELAY AND COMPRESSOR.

Fig. 22   System diagnosis procedure No. 1, part 2 of 4. Cadillac

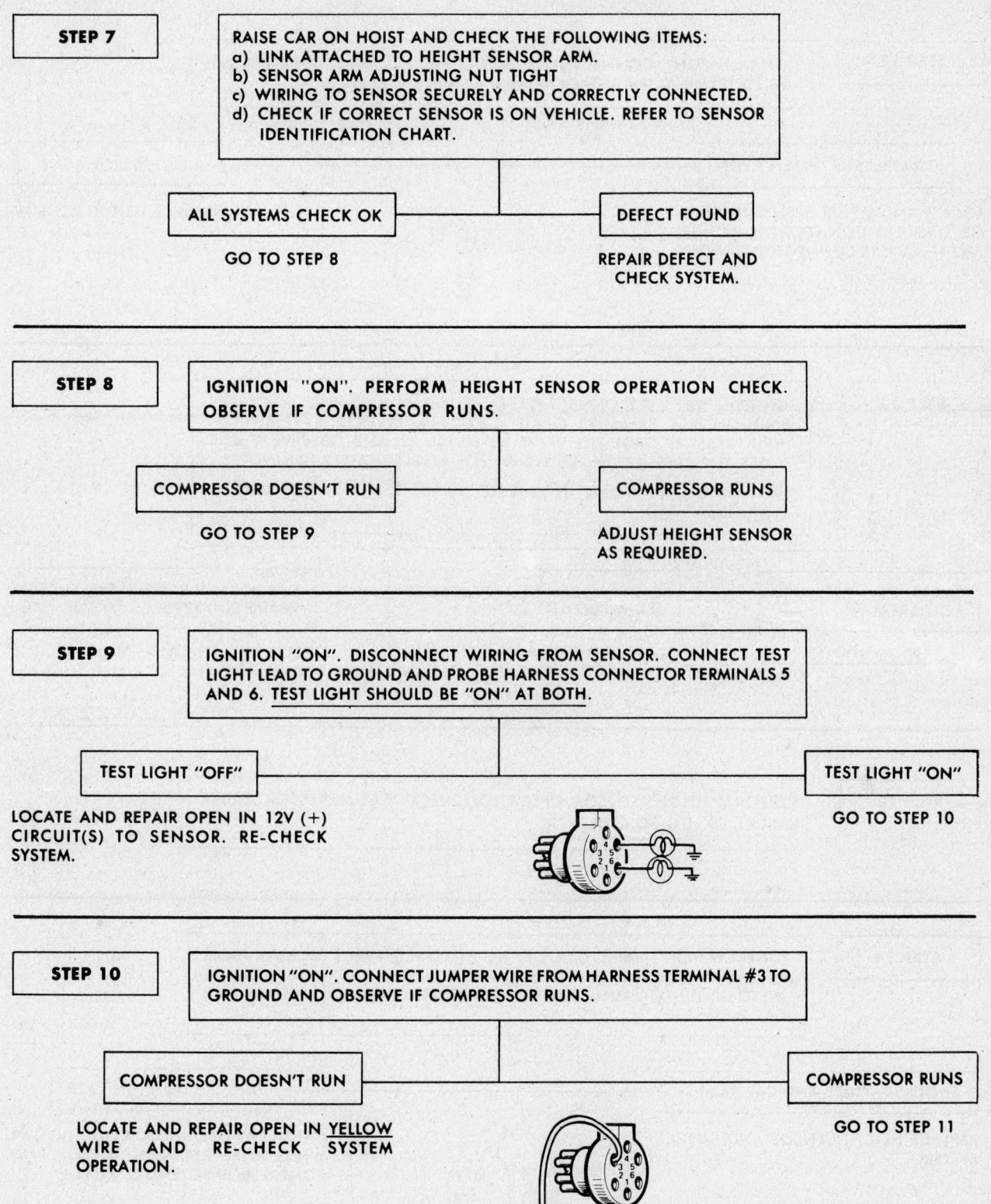

STEP 7

RAISE CAR ON HOIST AND CHECK THE FOLLOWING ITEMS:
a) LINK ATTACHED TO HEIGHT SENSOR ARM.
b) SENSOR ARM ADJUSTING NUT TIGHT
c) WIRING TO SENSOR SECURELY AND CORRECTLY CONNECTED.
d) CHECK IF CORRECT SENSOR IS ON VEHICLE. REFER TO SENSOR IDENTIFICATION CHART.

ALL SYSTEMS CHECK OK

GO TO STEP 8

DEFECT FOUND

REPAIR DEFECT AND CHECK SYSTEM.

STEP 8

IGNITION "ON". PERFORM HEIGHT SENSOR OPERATION CHECK. OBSERVE IF COMPRESSOR RUNS.

COMPRESSOR DOESN'T RUN

GO TO STEP 9

COMPRESSOR RUNS

ADJUST HEIGHT SENSOR AS REQUIRED.

STEP 9

IGNITION "ON". DISCONNECT WIRING FROM SENSOR. CONNECT TEST LIGHT LEAD TO GROUND AND PROBE HARNESS CONNECTOR TERMINALS 5 AND 6. TEST LIGHT SHOULD BE "ON" AT BOTH.

TEST LIGHT "OFF"

LOCATE AND REPAIR OPEN IN 12V (+) CIRCUIT(S) TO SENSOR. RE-CHECK SYSTEM.

TEST LIGHT "ON"

GO TO STEP 10

STEP 10

IGNITION "ON". CONNECT JUMPER WIRE FROM HARNESS TERMINAL #3 TO GROUND AND OBSERVE IF COMPRESSOR RUNS.

COMPRESSOR DOESN'T RUN

LOCATE AND REPAIR OPEN IN YELLOW WIRE AND RE-CHECK SYSTEM OPERATION.

COMPRESSOR RUNS

GO TO STEP 11

Fig. 23   System diagnosis procedure No. 1, part 3 of 4. Cadillac

STEP 11

IGNITION "ON". CONNECT JUMPER WIRE FROM CONNECTOR TERMINAL #3 TO TERMINAL #4 AND OBSERVE IF COMPRESSOR RUNS.

COMPRESSOR DOESN'T RUN

LOCATE AND REPAIR OPEN CONDITION OR GROUND CONNECTION IN WIRE FROM HARNESS CONNECTOR TERMINAL #4.

COMPRESSOR RUNS

REPLACE HEIGHT SENSOR

STEP 12

IGNITION "OFF". DISCONNECT PRESSURE LINE FROM COMPRESSOR DRYER AND CONNECT PRESSURE GAGE J-22124-A. INFLATE SYSTEM THRU PRESSURE GAGE FILL VALVE TO 80-100 PSI AND OBSERVE IF CAR RAISES AND PRESSURE HOLDS STEADY FOR APPROXIMATELY 10 MINUTES.

NOTE: IF SYSTEM WON'T INFLATE TO 80-100 PSI, A SEVERE LEAK IS INDICATED.

CAR RAISES — PRESSURE HOLDS READY.

GO TO STEP 13

CAR RAISES BUT PRESSURE LEAKS DOWN.

LOCATE AND REPAIR LEAK IN LINES, FITTINGS AND/OR SHOCKS.

CAR DOESN'T RAISE — PRESSURE READS 80-100 PSI.

CHECK FOR PINCHED PRESSURE LINE BETWEEN COMPRESSOR AND SHOCKS.

STEP 13

PERFORM HEIGHT SENSOR OPERATION CHECK. IF COMPRESSOR/DRYER CHECKS OK GO TO STEP 14.

STEP 14

IGNITION "ON". RAISE CAR ON HOIST. DISCONNECT WIRING FROM HEIGHT SENSOR AND CONNECT JUMPER WIRE FROM HARNESS TERMINAL #3 TO GROUND TO RUN COMPRESSOR. OBSERVE IF SHOCKS INFLATE AND CAR RAISES.

SHOCKS INFLATE AND CAR RAISES.

REPLACE HEIGHT SENSOR AND CHECK SYSTEM.

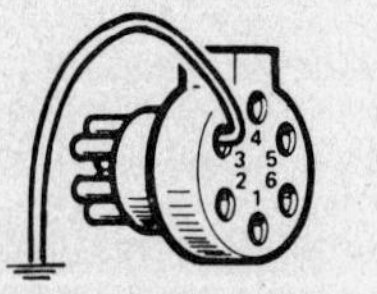

SHOCKS DON'T INFLATE

CHECK FOR GROUNDED CONDITION IN WHITE WIRE BETWEEN SENSOR AND COMPRESSOR SOLENOID VALVE.

Fig. 24   System diagnosis procedure No. 1, part 4 of 4. Cadillac

IMPORTANT: Always cycle ignition switch "OFF" and "ON" before starting tests.

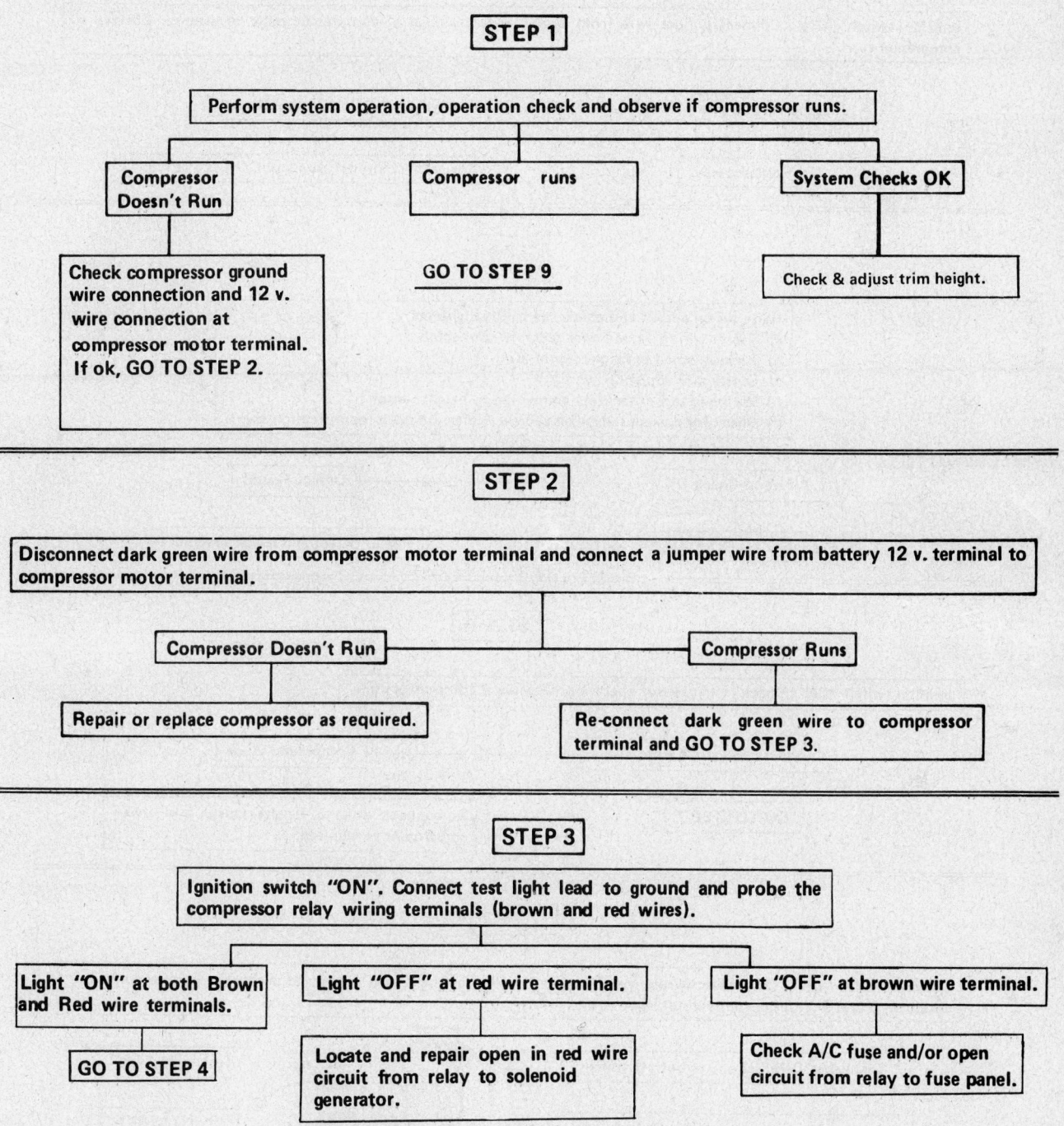

Fig. 25   System diagnosis procedure No. 1, part 1 of 3. Oldsmobile

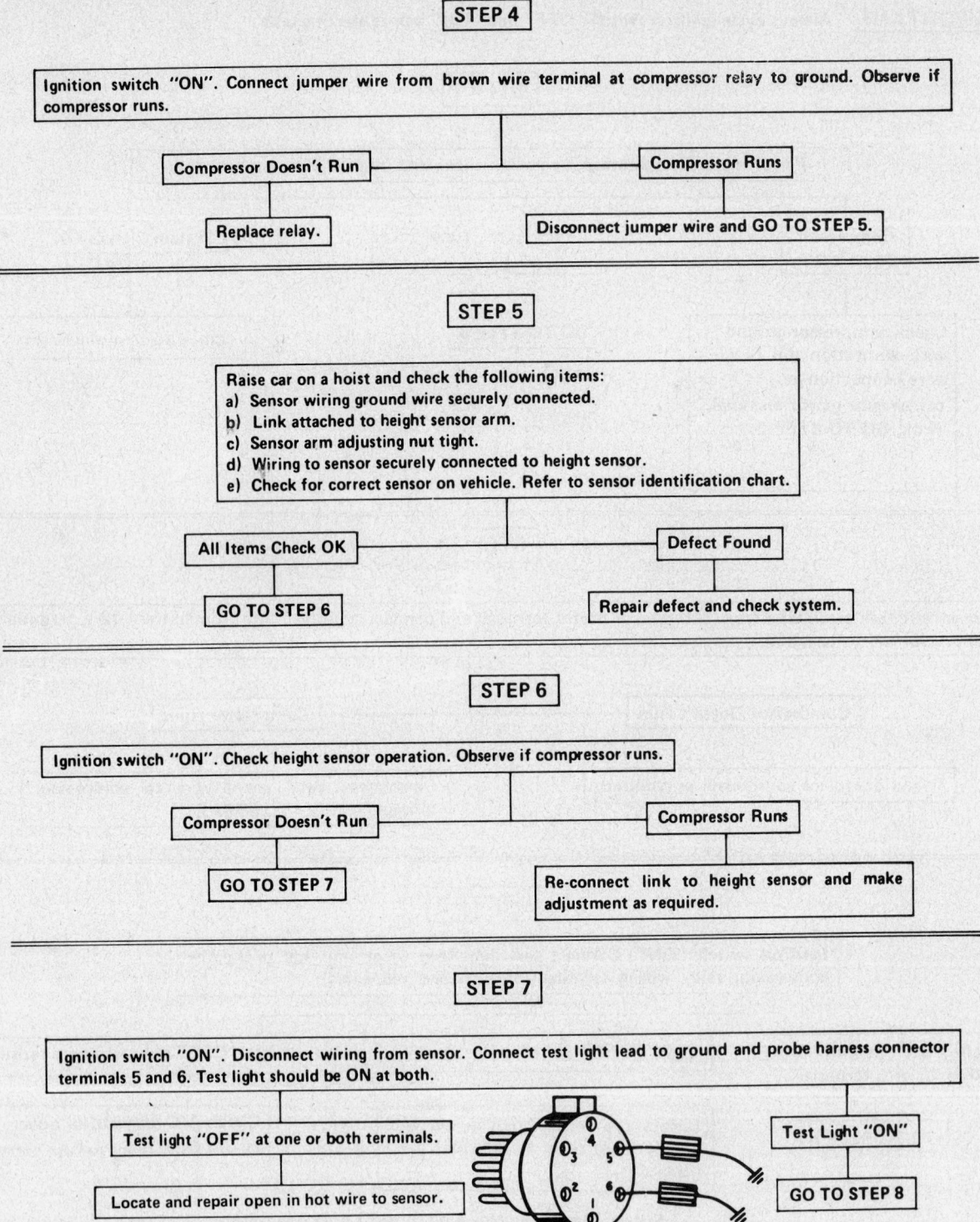

STEP 4

Ignition switch "ON". Connect jumper wire from brown wire terminal at compressor relay to ground. Observe if compressor runs.

Compressor Doesn't Run

Replace relay.

Compressor Runs

Disconnect jumper wire and GO TO STEP 5.

STEP 5

Raise car on a hoist and check the following items:
a) Sensor wiring ground wire securely connected.
b) Link attached to height sensor arm.
c) Sensor arm adjusting nut tight.
d) Wiring to sensor securely connected to height sensor.
e) Check for correct sensor on vehicle. Refer to sensor identification chart.

All Items Check OK

GO TO STEP 6

Defect Found

Repair defect and check system.

STEP 6

Ignition switch "ON". Check height sensor operation. Observe if compressor runs.

Compressor Doesn't Run

GO TO STEP 7

Compressor Runs

Re-connect link to height sensor and make adjustment as required.

STEP 7

Ignition switch "ON". Disconnect wiring from sensor. Connect test light lead to ground and probe harness connector terminals 5 and 6. Test light should be ON at both.

Test light "OFF" at one or both terminals.

Locate and repair open in hot wire to sensor.

Test Light "ON"

GO TO STEP 8

Fig. 26   System diagnosis procedure No. 1, part 2 of 3. Oldsmobile

STEP 8

Ignition switch "ON". Connect jumper wire from harness terminal #3 to ground and observe if compressor runs.

Compressor Doesn't Run

Locate and repair open circuit in yellow wire from height sensor to relay.

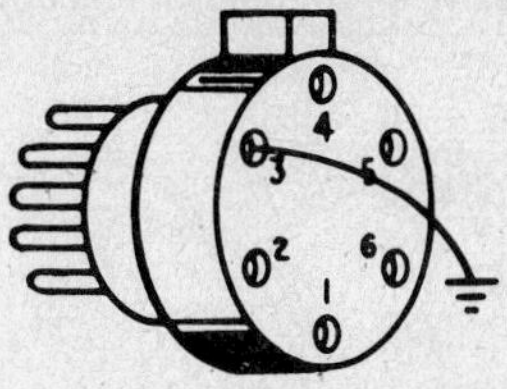

Compressor Runs

Recheck ground circuit from terminal #4 to ground. If OK, replace height sensor.

STEP 9

Ignition "OFF". Connect pressure gage J-22124-A to pressure tubing and inflate system thru pressure gage fill valve to 100 lbs. Observe if pressure leaks down or holds steady. (Allow approximately 10 minutes).
(NOTE—If system won't inflate to 100#, a severe leak is indicated.)

Leaks Down

Locate and repair leak in lines, fittings or shocks.

Holds Steady

Problem is in dryer or compressor. Check compressor.

Car doesn't raise, pressure gage reads 100 psi.

Check for pinched pressure line between compressor and shocks.

STEP 10

Ignition "ON" raise car on hoist and check height sensor operation. Observe if shocks inflate ok.

Shocks Inflate

1) Check for correct height sensor
2) Check adjustment

Shocks Don't Inflate

GO TO STEP 11.

STEP 11

Ignition "ON". Disconnect wiring from height sensor and connect jumper wire from terminal #3 to ground to run compressor. Observe if shocks inflate.

Shocks Inflate

1) Check for correct height sensor
2) Replace height sensor

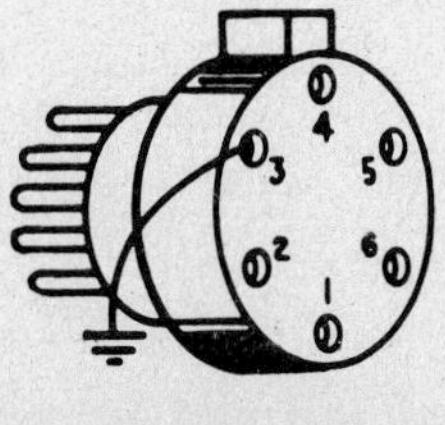

Shocks Don't Inflate

Check for grounded condition in white wire from height sensor to compressor assembly.

Fig. 27   System diagnosis procedure No. 1, part 3 of 3. Oldsmobile

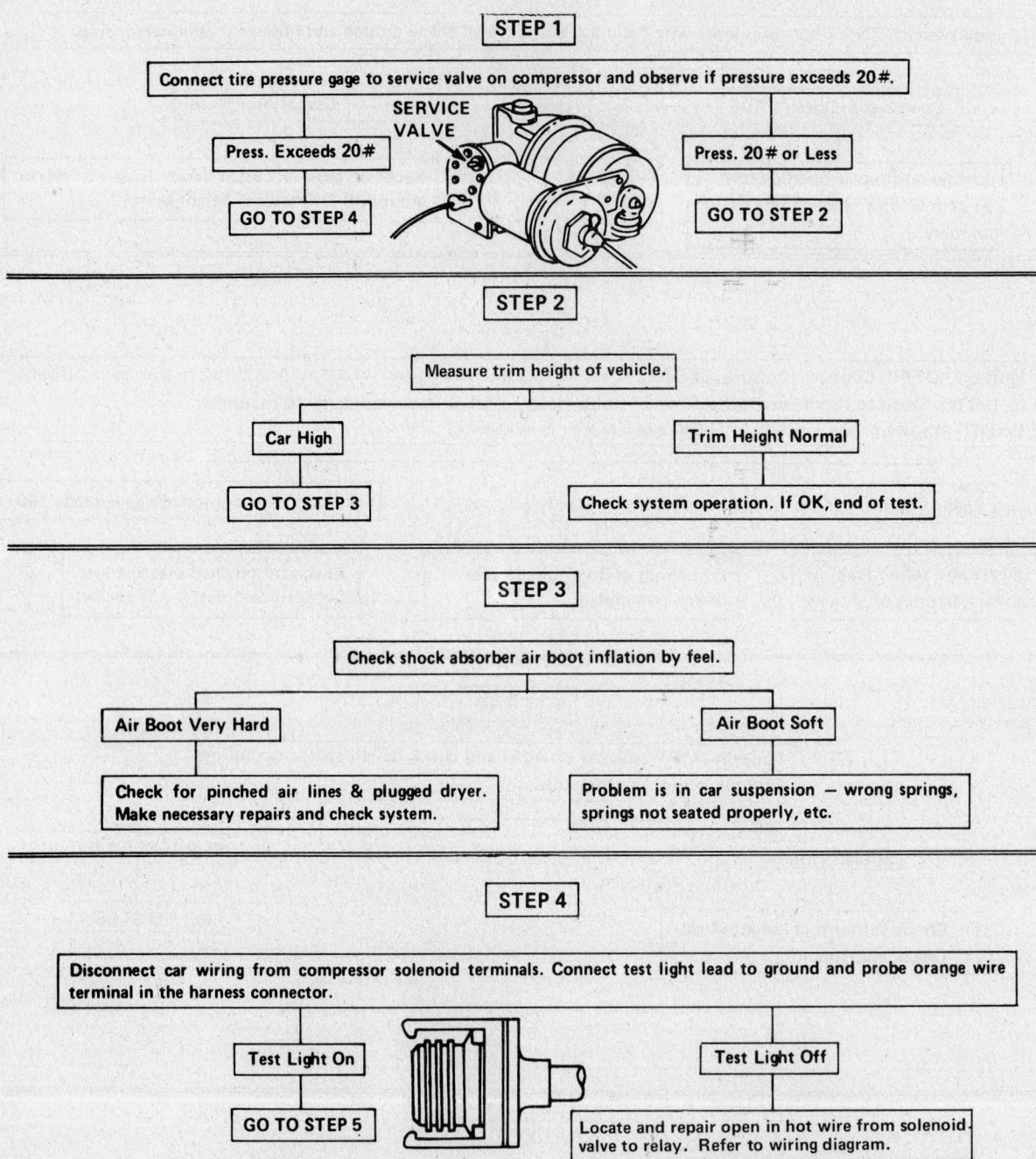

STEP 1

Connect tire pressure gage to service valve on compressor and observe if pressure exceeds 20#.

SERVICE VALVE

Press. Exceeds 20#

GO TO STEP 4

Press. 20# or Less

GO TO STEP 2

STEP 2

Measure trim height of vehicle.

Car High

GO TO STEP 3

Trim Height Normal

Check system operation. If OK, end of test.

STEP 3

Check shock absorber air boot inflation by feel.

Air Boot Very Hard

Check for pinched air lines & plugged dryer. Make necessary repairs and check system.

Air Boot Soft

Problem is in car suspension — wrong springs, springs not seated properly, etc.

STEP 4

Disconnect car wiring from compressor solenoid terminals. Connect test light lead to ground and probe orange wire terminal in the harness connector.

Test Light On

GO TO STEP 5

Test Light Off

Locate and repair open in hot wire from solenoid valve to relay. Refer to wiring diagram.

Fig. 28   System diagnosis procedure No. 2, part 1 of 2. Buick, Oldsmobile & Pontiac

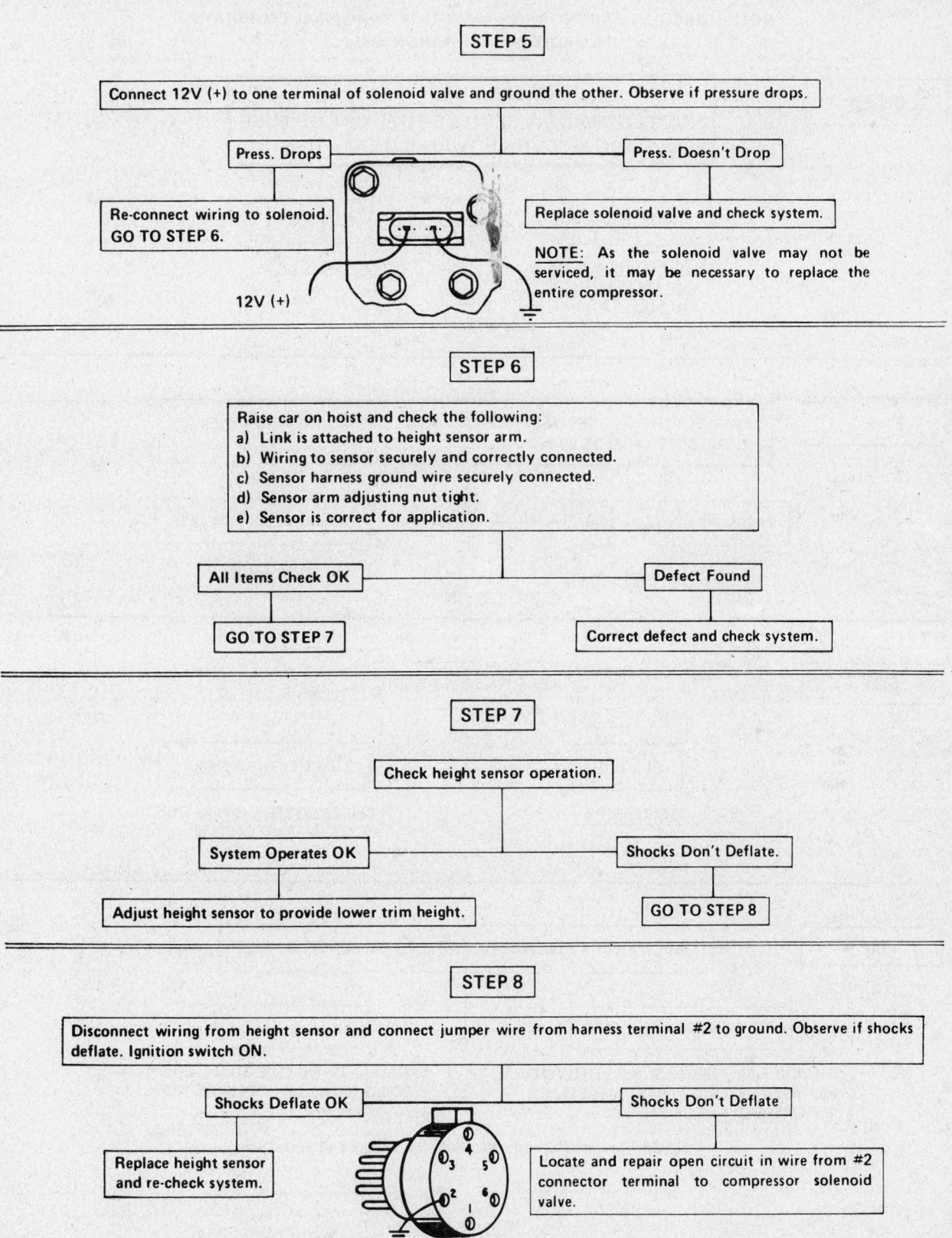

STEP 5

Connect 12V (+) to one terminal of solenoid valve and ground the other. Observe if pressure drops.

Press. Drops

Re-connect wiring to solenoid. GO TO STEP 6.

12V (+)

Press. Doesn't Drop

Replace solenoid valve and check system.

NOTE: As the solenoid valve may not be serviced, it may be necessary to replace the entire compressor.

STEP 6

Raise car on hoist and check the following:
a) Link is attached to height sensor arm.
b) Wiring to sensor securely and correctly connected.
c) Sensor harness ground wire securely connected.
d) Sensor arm adjusting nut tight.
e) Sensor is correct for application.

All Items Check OK

GO TO STEP 7

Defect Found

Correct defect and check system.

STEP 7

Check height sensor operation.

System Operates OK

Adjust height sensor to provide lower trim height.

Shocks Don't Deflate.

GO TO STEP 8

STEP 8

Disconnect wiring from height sensor and connect jumper wire from harness terminal #2 to ground. Observe if shocks deflate. Ignition switch ON.

Shocks Deflate OK

Replace height sensor and re-check system.

Shocks Don't Deflate

Locate and repair open circuit in wire from #2 connector terminal to compressor solenoid valve.

Fig. 29 System diagnosis procedure No. 2, part 2 of 2. Buick, Oldsmobile & Pontiac

AUTOMATIC LEVEL CONTROL

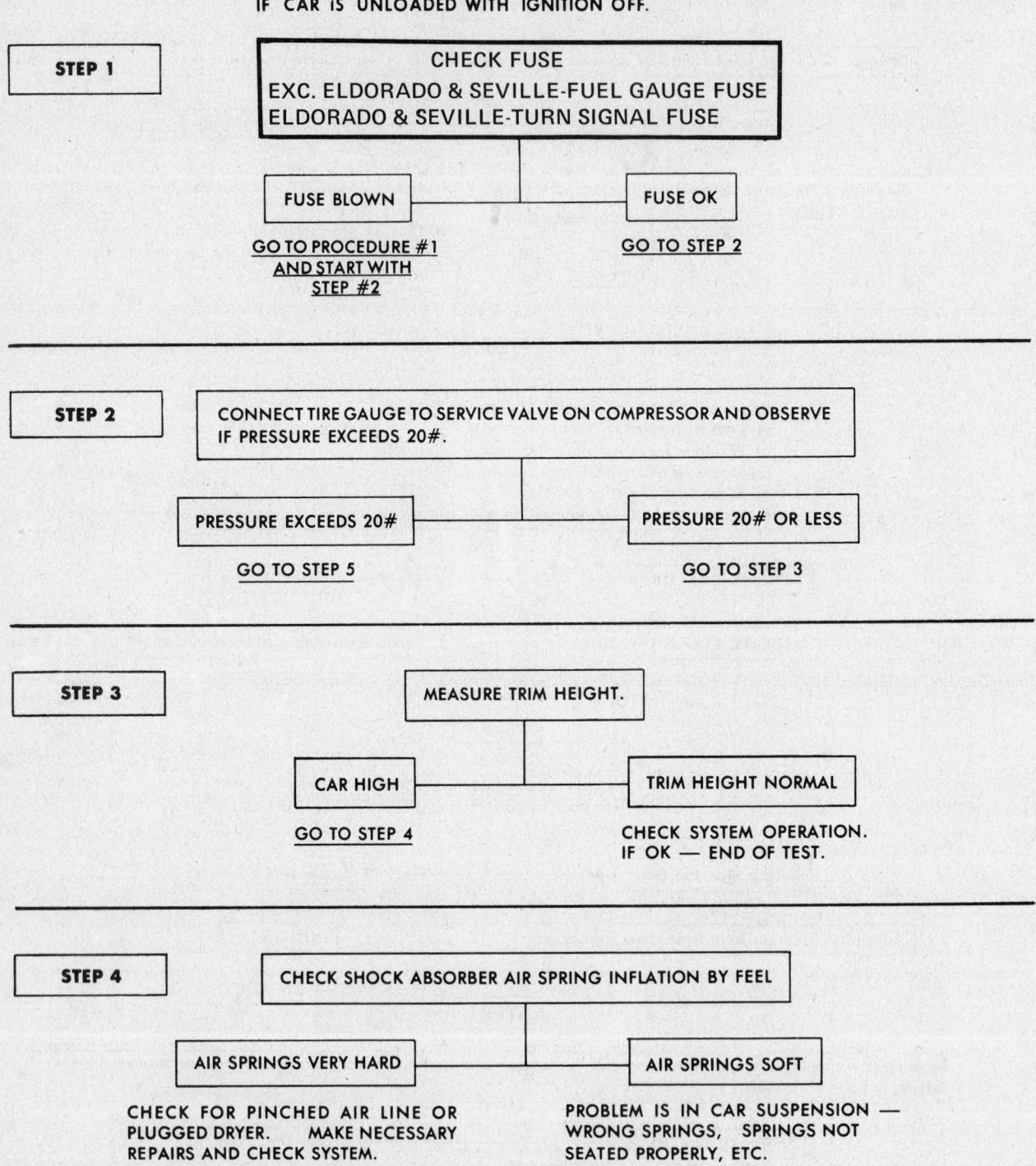

NOTE: VEHICLE REMAINING HIGH IN REAR IS A NORMAL CONDITION
IF CAR IS UNLOADED WITH IGNITION OFF.

STEP 1

CHECK FUSE
EXC. ELDORADO & SEVILLE-FUEL GAUGE FUSE
ELDORADO & SEVILLE-TURN SIGNAL FUSE

FUSE BLOWN

GO TO PROCEDURE #1
AND START WITH
STEP #2

FUSE OK

GO TO STEP 2

STEP 2

CONNECT TIRE GAUGE TO SERVICE VALVE ON COMPRESSOR AND OBSERVE
IF PRESSURE EXCEEDS 20#.

PRESSURE EXCEEDS 20#

GO TO STEP 5

PRESSURE 20# OR LESS

GO TO STEP 3

STEP 3

MEASURE TRIM HEIGHT.

CAR HIGH

GO TO STEP 4

TRIM HEIGHT NORMAL

CHECK SYSTEM OPERATION.
IF OK — END OF TEST.

STEP 4

CHECK SHOCK ABSORBER AIR SPRING INFLATION BY FEEL

AIR SPRINGS VERY HARD

CHECK FOR PINCHED AIR LINE OR
PLUGGED DRYER.   MAKE NECESSARY
REPAIRS AND CHECK SYSTEM.

AIR SPRINGS SOFT

PROBLEM IS IN CAR SUSPENSION —
WRONG SPRINGS,   SPRINGS NOT
SEATED PROPERLY, ETC.

Fig. 30 System diagnosis procedure No. 2, part 1 of 3. Cadillac

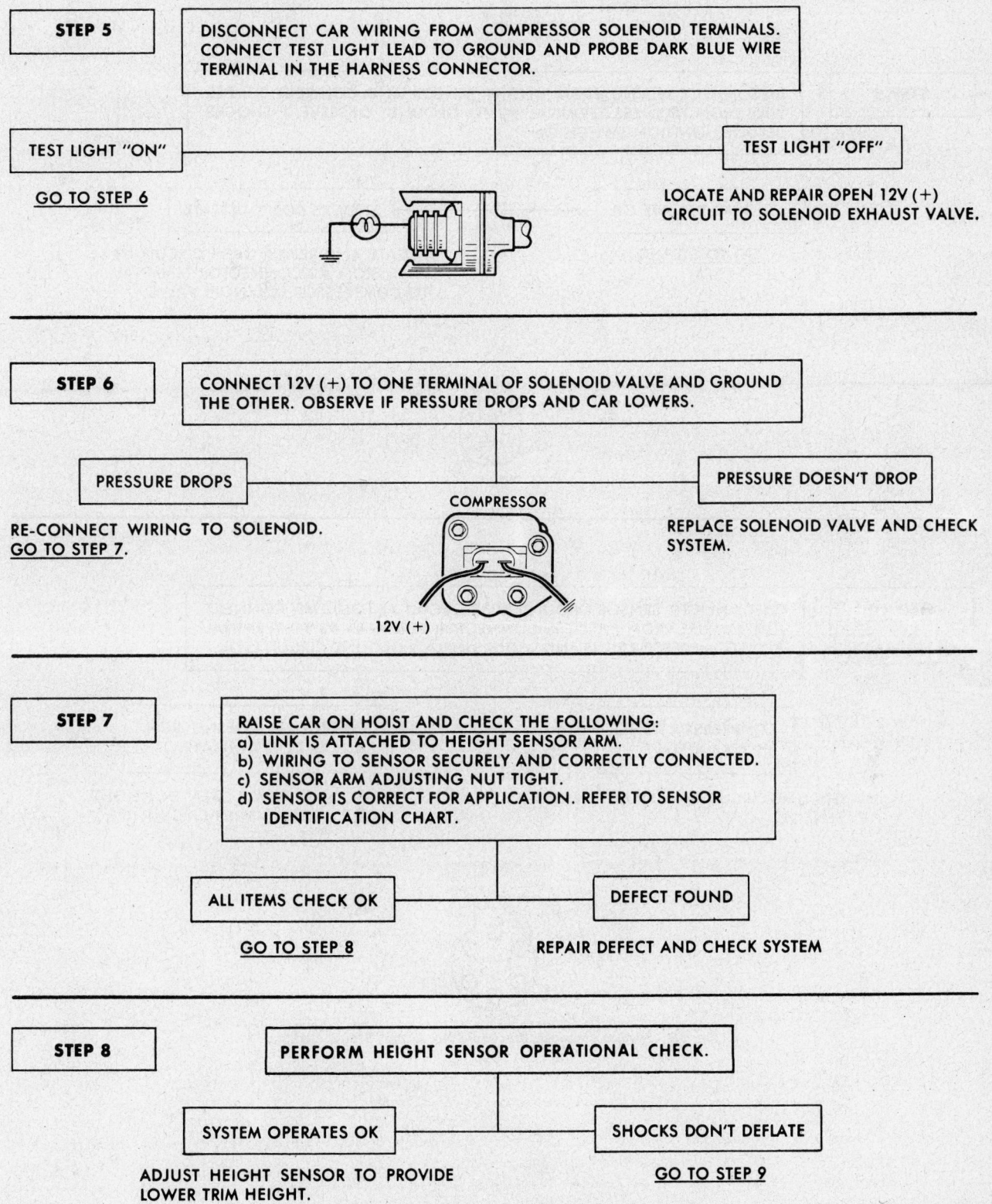

STEP 5

DISCONNECT CAR WIRING FROM COMPRESSOR SOLENOID TERMINALS. CONNECT TEST LIGHT LEAD TO GROUND AND PROBE DARK BLUE WIRE TERMINAL IN THE HARNESS CONNECTOR.

TEST LIGHT "ON"

GO TO STEP 6

TEST LIGHT "OFF"

LOCATE AND REPAIR OPEN 12V (+) CIRCUIT TO SOLENOID EXHAUST VALVE.

STEP 6

CONNECT 12V (+) TO ONE TERMINAL OF SOLENOID VALVE AND GROUND THE OTHER. OBSERVE IF PRESSURE DROPS AND CAR LOWERS.

PRESSURE DROPS

RE-CONNECT WIRING TO SOLENOID. GO TO STEP 7.

COMPRESSOR

12V (+)

PRESSURE DOESN'T DROP

REPLACE SOLENOID VALVE AND CHECK SYSTEM.

STEP 7

RAISE CAR ON HOIST AND CHECK THE FOLLOWING:
a) LINK IS ATTACHED TO HEIGHT SENSOR ARM.
b) WIRING TO SENSOR SECURELY AND CORRECTLY CONNECTED.
c) SENSOR ARM ADJUSTING NUT TIGHT.
d) SENSOR IS CORRECT FOR APPLICATION. REFER TO SENSOR IDENTIFICATION CHART.

ALL ITEMS CHECK OK

GO TO STEP 8

DEFECT FOUND

REPAIR DEFECT AND CHECK SYSTEM

STEP 8

PERFORM HEIGHT SENSOR OPERATIONAL CHECK.

SYSTEM OPERATES OK

ADJUST HEIGHT SENSOR TO PROVIDE LOWER TRIM HEIGHT.

SHOCKS DON'T DEFLATE

GO TO STEP 9

Fig. 31 System diagnosis procedure No. 2, part 2 of 3. Cadillac

STEP 9 | DISCONNECT WIRING FROM HEIGHT SENSOR AND CONNECT JUMPER WIRE FROM HARNESS TERMINAL #2 TO GROUND. OBSERVE IF SHOCKS DEFLATE. IGNITION SWITCH ON.

SHOCKS DEFLATE OK

GO TO STEP 10

SHOCKS DON'T DEFLATE

LOCATE AND REPAIR OPEN CIRCUIT IN WIRE FROM #2 CONNECTOR TERMINAL TO COMPRESSOR SOLENOID VALVE.

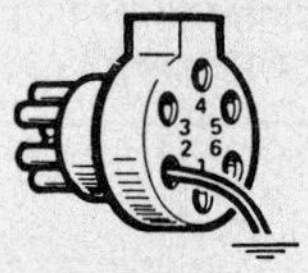

STEP 10 | CHECK HEIGHT SENSOR GROUND WIRE CIRCUIT AS FOLLOWS: CONNECT JUMPER WIRE FROM HARNESS CONNECTOR TERMINAL #3 TO TERMINAL #4. IF COMPRESSOR RUNS AND SHOCKS INFLATE GROUND CIRCUIT IS OK.

COMPRESSOR RUNS, SHOCKS INFLATE

GROUND CIRCUIT OK. REPLACE HEIGHT SENSOR.

COMPRESSOR DOESN'T RUN, SHOCKS DON'T INFLATE.

LOCATE AND REPAIR OPEN IN HEIGHT SENSOR GROUND WIRE CIRCUIT.

Fig. 32   System diagnosis procedure No. 2, part 3 of 3. Cadillac

STEP 1

Remove wire terminal from compressor to sensor wiring connector and plug connector back on relay. Turn ignition switch "ON".

Compressor Stops

Replace wire in connector; re-connect wiring to relay and GO TO STEP 2.

Compressor Still Runs

Replace relay and check system.

IMPORTANT: Be sure that 8-14 second delay functions correctly. If not, replace height sensor also.

STEP 2

a) Ignition switch ON. Raise car on hoist.
b) Disconnect wiring from height sensor.

Compressor Stops

Replace height sensor and check system.

Compressor Still Runs

Locate and repair grounded condition in wire from #3 terminal to compressor relay.

DIAGNOSIS PROCEDURE #4

STEP 1

Check height sensor time delay function (system check)

No Time Delay

Replace height sensor and relay and check system.

Time Delay OK

Check for the following:
1) Intermittent ground condition in circuit between compressor relay and height sensor
2) Defective compressor relay. This can be determined by tapping the relay and obersving if relay "clicks".

Fig. 33 System diagnosis procedures Nos. 3 & 4. Buick, Cadillac, Oldsmobile & Pontiac

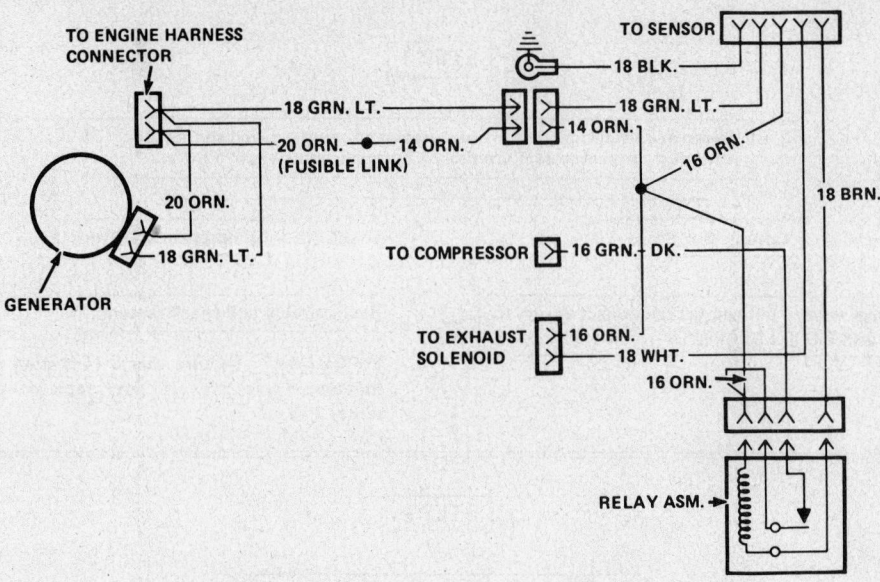

Fig. 34 Electronic level control system wiring diagram. Buick

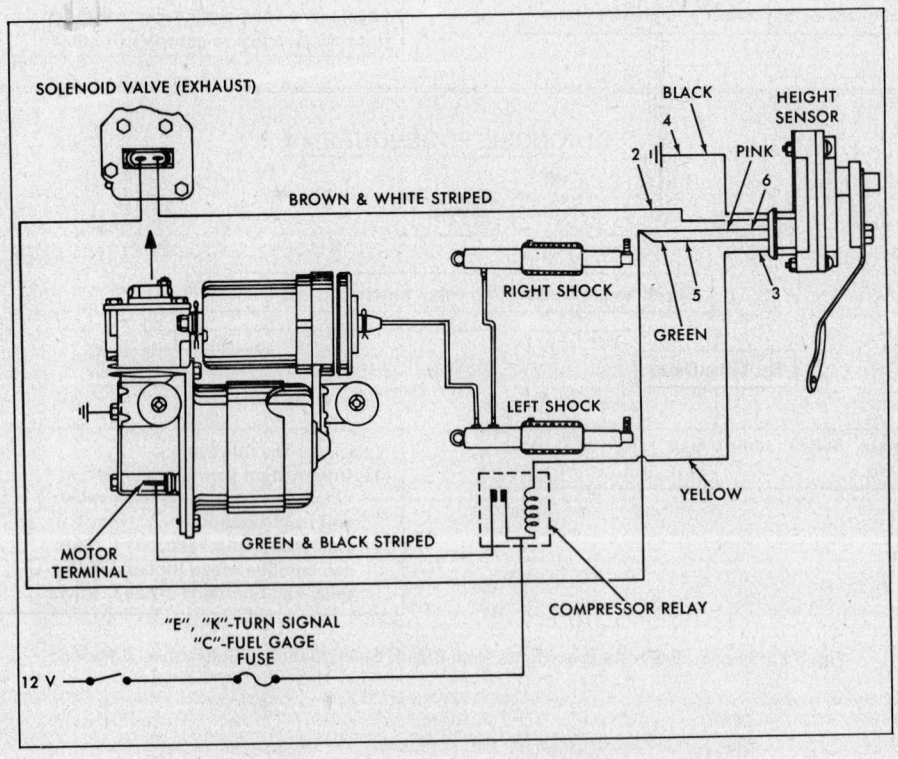

Fig. 35 Electronic level control system wiring diagram. Cadillac

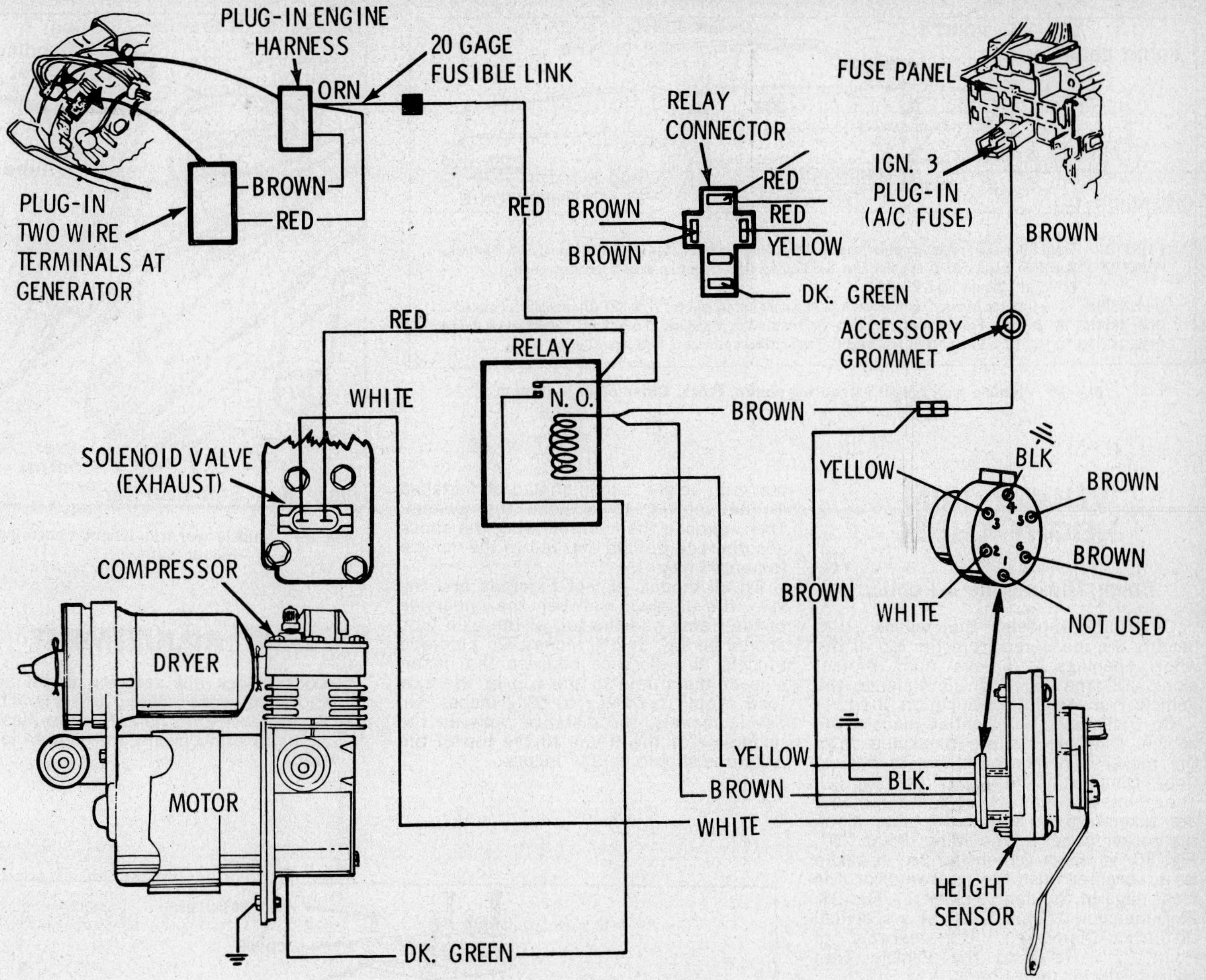

PLUG-IN ENGINE HARNESS

20 GAGE FUSIBLE LINK

ORN

PLUG-IN TWO WIRE TERMINALS AT GENERATOR

BROWN
RED

RED

RELAY CONNECTOR

BROWN
BROWN

RED
RED
YELLOW

DK. GREEN

FUSE PANEL

IGN. 3 PLUG-IN (A/C FUSE)

BROWN

ACCESSORY GROMMET

RED

WHITE

RELAY

N. O.

BROWN

SOLENOID VALVE (EXHAUST)

COMPRESSOR

DRYER

MOTOR

YELLOW

BROWN

BLK

BROWN

BROWN

WHITE

NOT USED

YELLOW
BROWN
WHITE

BLK.

HEIGHT SENSOR

DK. GREEN

Fig. 36   Electronic level control system wiring diagram. Oldsmobile

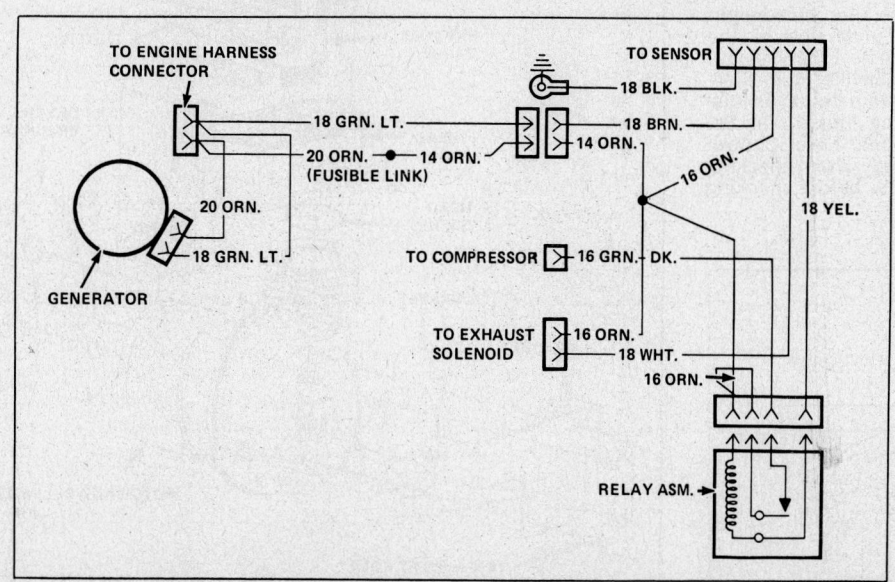

Fig. 37   Electronic level control system wiring diagram. Pontiac

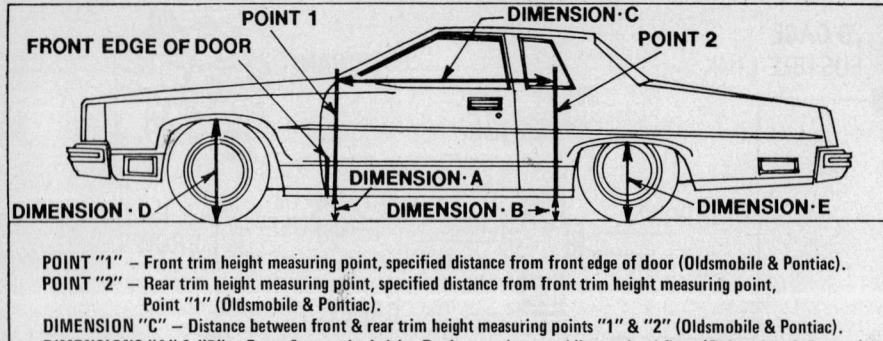

POINT "1" – Front trim height measuring point, specified distance from front edge of door (Oldsmobile & Pontiac).
POINT "2" – Rear trim height measuring point, specified distance from front trim height measuring point, Point "1" (Oldsmobile & Pontiac).
DIMENSION "C" – Distance between front & rear trim height measuring points "1" & "2" (Oldsmobile & Pontiac).
DIMENSIONS "A" & "B" – Front & rear trim height, Rocker panel or mouldings to level floor (Oldsmobile & Pontiac).
DIMENSIONS "D" & "E" – Front & rear trim height. Top of wheel openings to level floor (Buick).

Fig. 38   Vehicle trim height measuring points. Buick, Oldsmobile & Pontiac

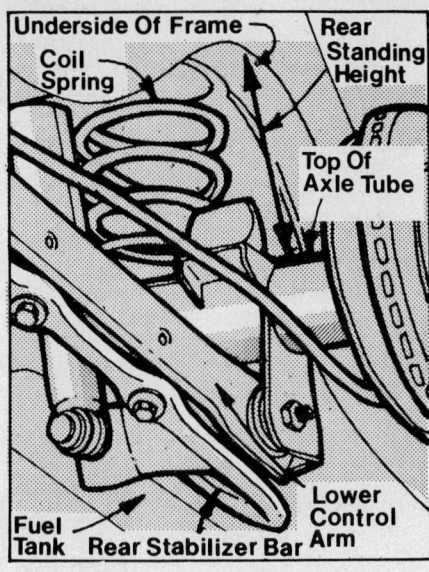

Fig. 39   Vehicle rear trim height measuring point. Cadillac

VEHICLE TRIM HEIGHT CHECK

Buick, Oldsmobile & Pontiac

On Buick models, the vehicle trim heights are measured from the top of the wheel openings to a level floor, Dimensions "D" and "E", Fig. 38. Refer to the Vehicle Trim Height Specification Chart.

On Oldsmobile and Pontiac models, the vehicle trim heights are measured from the rocker panel or moulding to a level floor, Dimensions "A" and "B", Fig. 38. The points at which these measurements are taken are at specified points along the rocker panel or moulding. Point "1", Fig. 38, at which Dimension "A" is taken is a specified distance rearward of the front edge of the door. Point "2", Fig. 38, at Dimension "B" is taken at a specified distance, Dimension "C", rearward of Point "1". Refer to the Vehicle Trim Height Specification Chart.

Cadillac

On these vehicles, the rear trim height is measured from the underside of the frame to the top of the axle tube, Fig. 39. On all models except Seville, the Electronic Level Control system must be disconnected when checking height. On Seville models, the Electronic Level Control system is left connected when checking height. On Seville models, before checking rear trim height, a load should be installed in the vehicle, to activate the system. Then, remove the load, allowing the shock absorbers to deflate and return the vehicle to normal height.

On all models except Eldorado and Seville, the distance between the underside of the frame and the top of the axle tube should be $5\frac{3}{8}$ to $6\frac{1}{8}$ inches. On Eldorado models, the distance between the underside of the frame to the top of the axle tube should be $4\frac{13}{16}$ to $5\frac{9}{16}$ inches. On Seville models, the distance between the underside of the frame to the top of the axle tube should be $3\frac{7}{8}$ inches.

TRIM ADJUSTMENT

1. Loosen lock nut securing metal arm to height sensor plastic arm, Fig. 41.
2. To increase trim height, move plastic actuator arm upward and tighten lock nut.

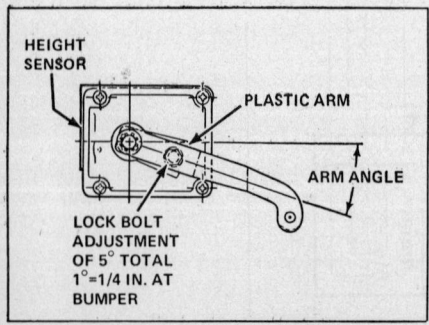

Fig. 40   Trim adjustment

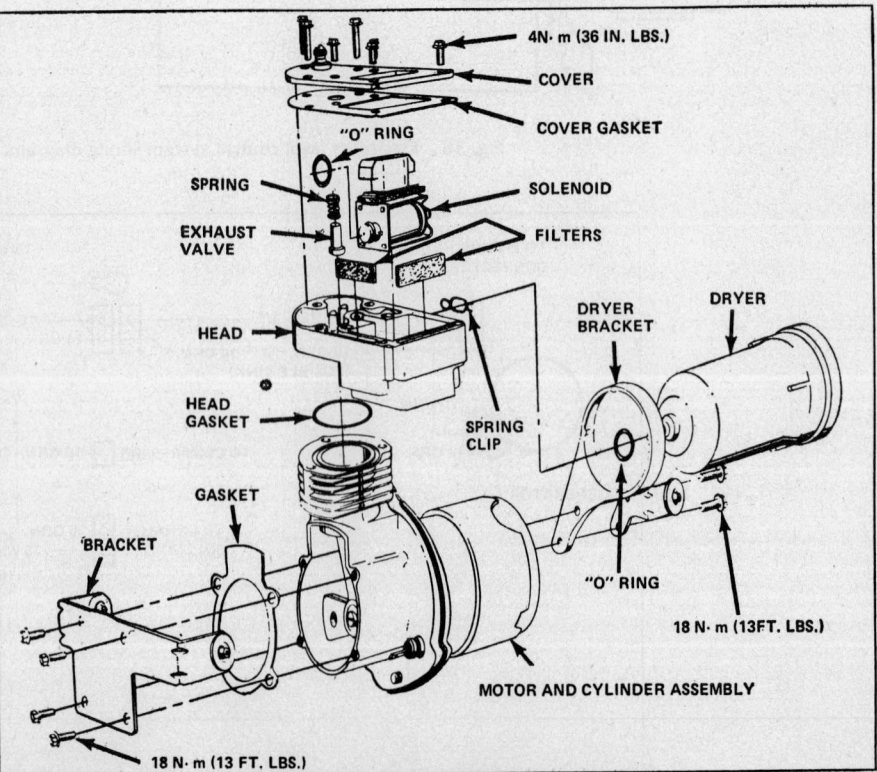

Fig. 41   Air compressor, disassembled

VEHICLE TRIM HEIGHT SPECIFICATION CHART

Refer to Fig. 38

Year & Model	Point "1"	Dimension "A"	Point "2"	Dimension "C"	Dimension "B"	Dimension "D"	Dimension "E"
1978 BUICK—							
Century & Regal exc. Sta. Wag.	—	—	—	—	—	26.7	26
Century Sta. Wag.	—	—	—	—	—	26.8	26.4
Skylark	—	—	—	—	—	27.1	25.3
LeSabre & Electra	—	—	—	—	—	28.9	28.5
Estate Wagon	—	—	—	—	—	28.9	28
Riviera	—	—	—	—	—	28.9	23.2
1978 OLDSMOBILE—							
Omega	1	9⅝	①	55⅛	9½	—	—
Cutlass exc. Sta. Wag.	1	10⅜	①	62⅝	10½	—	—
Cutlass Sta. Wag.	1	10½	①	62⅝	10⅝	—	—
88 & 98	1¾	10	①	67⅞	10¼	—	—
Toronado	6	9	①	60	9¼	—	—
1978 PONTIAC—							
Firebird & Phoenix	1	9⅝	①	55⅛	9½	—	—
LeMans, Grand LeMans, Grand Am & Grand Prix exc. Sta. Wag.	1	10⅜	①	62⅝	10½	—	—
LeMans Sta. Wag.	1	10½	①	62⅝	10⅝	—	—
Full Size	1¾	10	①	67⅞	10¼	—	—

①—See text for procedure.

3. To decrease trim height, move plastic actuator arm downward and tighten lock nut.

4. If proper adjustment cannot be made, check for correct height sensor outlined in the chart below:

Year 1978 Vehicle	Height Sensor Code
Buick—	
Century & Regal Full Size Exc. Sta. Wag.	AG
Sta. Wag.	AC
Full Size Sta. Wag.	AA
Cadillac—	
Exc. Eldorado & Seville	AB
Eldorado	AE
Seville	AF
Oldsmobile—	
Cutlass Salon & Brougham	AK
Cutlass Supreme & Supreme Brougham	AJ
Cutlass Wagon	AG
88 & 98 Exc. Sta. Wag.	AA
88 Sta. Wag.	AD
Pontiac—	
LeMans, Grand LeMans & Grand Am	AG
Grand Prix	AH
Full Size Exc. Sta. Wag.	AC
Full Size Sta. Wag.	AA

ELC SYSTEM SERVICE

Air Compressor, Replace

Exc. Cadillac

1. Disconnect battery ground cable.
2. Deflate system through service valve.
3. Disconnect high pressure line at air dryer by rotating spring clip 90° while holding connector end and removing tube assembly.
4. Remove two relay to compressor bracket screws and position relay aside.
5. Remove support bracket screws.
6. Remove two radiator support to compressor bracket screws.

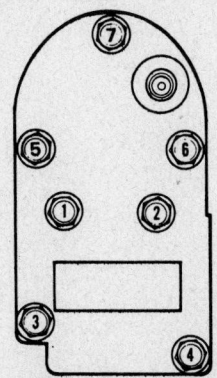

TORQUE BOLTS TO 4 N·m
(36 IN. LBS.) PER SEQUENCE

Fig. 42 Air compressor head tightening sequence.

7. Disconnect electrical connectors from exhaust solenoid and compressor motor.
8. Remove compressor and bracket assembly.
9. Remove compressor mounting bracket screws and the mounting bracket.
10. If replacing compressor assembly, remove air dryer and bracket.
11. Reverse procedure to install.

Cadillac

1. Disconnect battery ground cable.
2. Disconnect electrical connectors from exhaust solenoid and compressor motor.
3. Disconnect air line from air dryer.
4. Remove two screws securing compressor bracket to radiator cradle and on Seville, the wheelhouse.
5. Remove compressor from vehicle.
6. Remove compressor bracket mounting screws and the bracket.
7. Reverse procedure to install.

Air Compressor Service

Disassembly

1. Remove the seven compressor cover screws, then the compressor cover and gasket, Fig. 41.
2. Remove head and solenoid assembly.
3. Remove two filters, exhaust valve, spring and air dryer "O" ring from head assembly.
4. Remove solenoid from head by lifting slightly and sliding to the dryer outlet side.
5. Remove "O" ring from solenoid assembly.

6. Remove head gasket from cylinder assembly.
7. Remove four mounting bracket screws, then the bracket and gasket. Note position of ground wire for installation.

Assembly

1. Install gasket and mounting bracket, then the ground wire and screws. Torque screws to 13 ft. lbs.
2. Install head gasket on cylinder assembly.
3. Install "O" ring on solenoid assembly, then the solenoid in the head with valve opposite air dryer outlet.
4. Install two filters, exhaust valve and spring on head assembly.
5. Install gasket and cover on head assembly, then four short cover screws.

6. Install head and cover assembly to cylinder assembly using three long screws. Torque all seven screws in sequence, Fig. 42, to 36 inch lbs.
7. Install air dryer "O" ring on compressor.

Height Sensor, Replace

1. Raise and support vehicle.
2. Disconnect electrical connector from height sensor.
3. Disconnect link from height sensor arm.
4. Remove two screws securing height sensor to frame and the height sensor.
5. Reverse procedure to install.

Air Dryer, Replace

1. Deflate system through service valve.
2. Disconnect high pressure line at air dryer.
3. Remove air dryer from compressor by rotating spring clip and sliding air dryer from compressor head, through the bracket.

NOTE: On some models, the compressor is mounted on the right side of the engine compartment and the air dryer mounting bracket screws and bracket must be removed to facilitate removal of air dryer.

4. Remove "O" ring from compressor head.
5. Reverse procedure to install.

HEADLIGHT AIMING

All headlight adjustments should be made with a half-full tank plus or minus one gallon, with a person seated in the driver's seat and a person seated in the passenger seat, the car unloaded and the trunk empty except for the spare tire and jacking equipment, and recommended pressure in all tires. If necessary, compensate for unspecified gas capacity by adding or removing weight at the tank area at the rate of six pounds per gallon. Before each adjustment, bounce the car by pushing on the center of both the front and rear bumpers, then rock car side-to-side, to level the vehicle.

Headlights can be aimed mechanically or by means of a wall screen. When using a mechanical aimer, follow manufacturer's instructions. To align the No. 1 headlights by means of a wall screen, select a level portion of the shop floor. Lay out the floor and wall as shown in Fig. 1.

Establish the headlight horizontal centerline by subtracting 20 inches from the actual measured height of the headlight lens center from the floor and adding this difference to the 20-inch reference line obtained by sighting over the uprights to obtain dimension B (upper diagram Fig. 2). Draw a horizontal line 2 inches below, and parallel to the headlight horizontal centerline on the screen as measured on the vehicle (dimension A, upper diagram Fig. 2).

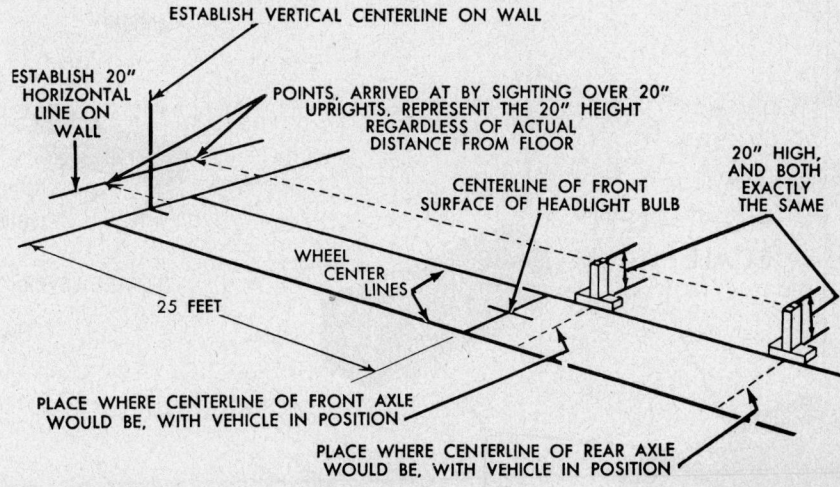

Fig. 1 Floor and wall layout

NO. 1 HEADLIGHT HIGH BEAM ADJUSTMENT

(Four Bulb Cars)

Adjust each No. 1 headlight beam as shown in Fig. 2 upper diagram. **Cover the No. 2 lights when making this adjustment.**

Some states may not approve of the 2-inch dimension for the No. 1 headlights. Check the applicable state law, as a 3-inch dimension may be required.

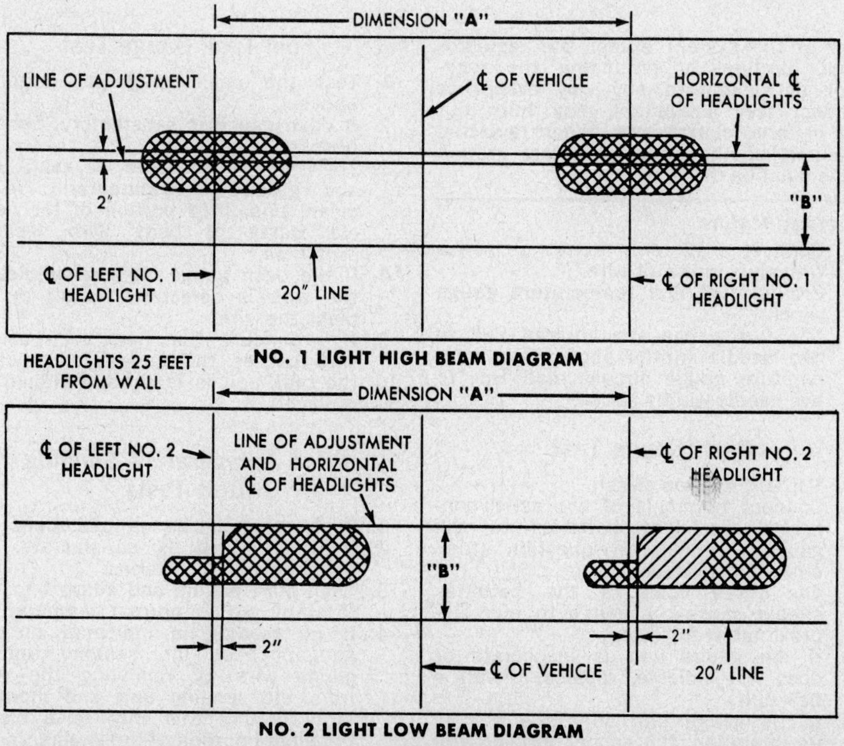

NO. 2 HEADLIGHT LOW BEAM ADJUSTMENT

(Four Bulb And All Two Bulb Cars)

To align the No. 2 headlights on four bulb cars or the headlights on two bulb cars, a different wall chart is used (lower diagram of Fig. 2). Dimension B for the No. 2 lights will be different than B for the No. 1 lights, but dimension A which is measured on the car will be the same as for the No. 1 lights. **Note that the line of adjustment of the No. 2 lights is the horizontal centerline of the No. 2 lights.** Turn the headlights to low beam and adjust each No. 2 light as shown in Fig. 2.

Each headlight can be adjusted by means of two screws located on the headlight adjusting ring. Always bring each beam into final position by turning the adjusting screws clockwise so that the headlights will be held against the tension springs when the operation is completed.

MECHANICAL AIMERS

NOTE: The rectangular headlamps used on some 1975-78 vehicles may be properly aimed using the mechanical aimer equipped with a special adapter that will fit these headlamps.

There are many different types of mechanical aiming equipment available one of which is shown in Figs. 3 and 4. Some may require a level floor whereas others have levelling devices which compensate for floor level variations.

When using this type of equipment, consult the equipment manufacturers instructions for its proper use.

NO. 1 LIGHT HIGH BEAM DIAGRAM

HEADLIGHTS 25 FEET FROM WALL

NO. 2 LIGHT LOW BEAM DIAGRAM

Fig. 2 Headlight wall screens

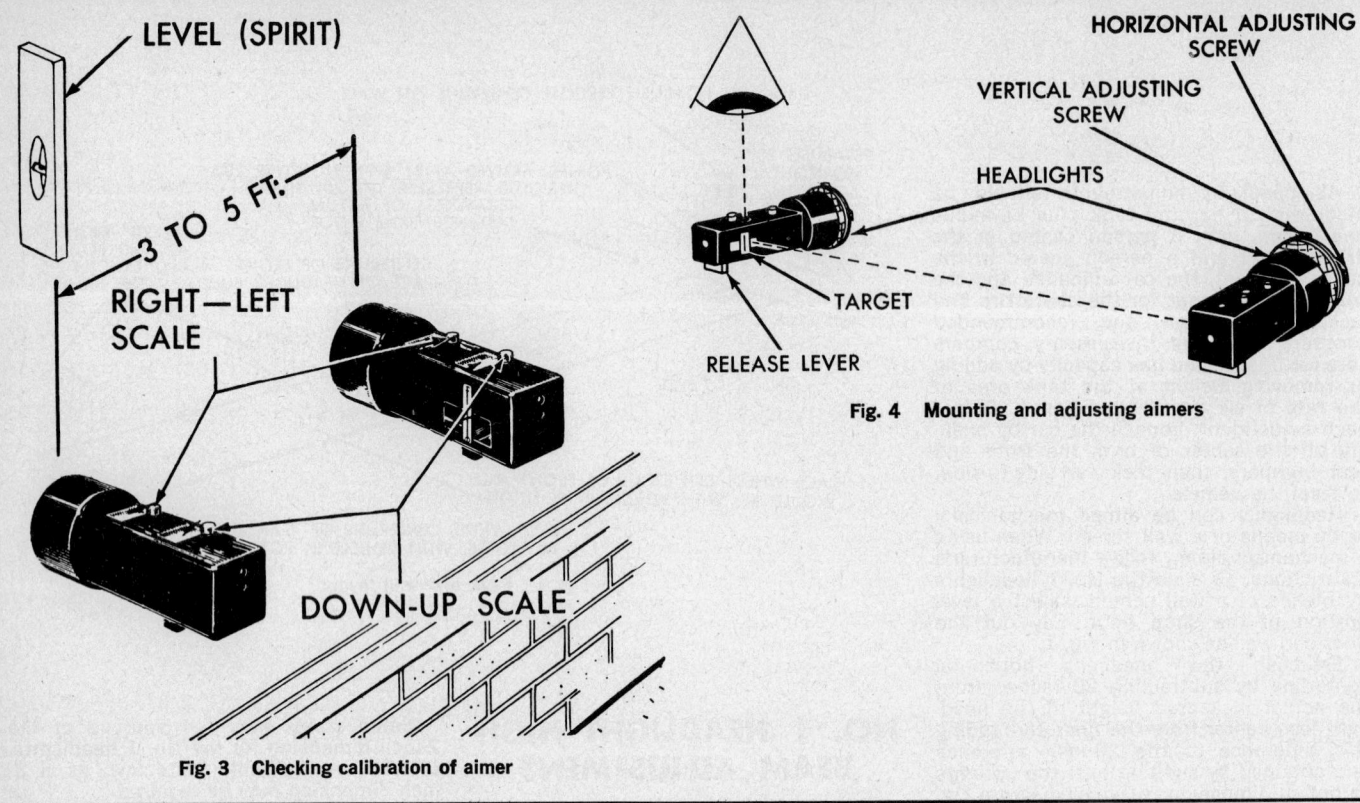

Fig. 3 Checking calibration of aimer

Fig. 4 Mounting and adjusting aimers

DASH GAUGES

TESTING

Gauge failures are often caused by defective wiring or grounds. Therefore, the first step in locating trouble should be a thorough inspection of all wiring and terminals. If wiring is secured by clamps, check to see whether the insulation has been severed thereby grounding the wire. In the case of a fuel gauge installation, rust may cause failure by corrosion at the ground connection of the tank unit.

CONSTANT VOLTAGE TYPE

Voltage Regulator Test

Except American Motors
1. Turn on ignition switch.
2. Connect one lead of a test light or positive lead of a voltmeter to the feed terminal of one of the gauges without disconnecting wire.
3. If regulator is okay, voltage will oscillate.
4. If it does not, voltage regulator is defective or there is a short or ground between regulator and gauges.

CAUTION: Applying 12 volts to any part of the system except the regulator input terminal or grounding the regulator or system in any way except to connect test equipment may burn out one or more components. When replacing any part of the system, battery ground cable must be disconnected.

American Motors
1. Connect a 10 ohm resistor in series with each indicator wire.
2. Ground fuel and temperature gauge wires.
3. The fuel gauge should read Full to two needle widths above. The temperature gauge should read Hot to two needle widths above.

Dash Gauge Test
1. Turn off ignition switch.
2. Connect terminals of two series-connected flashlight batteries to the gauge terminals in question (fuel, oil or temperature).
3. The three volts of the batteries should cause the gauge to read approximately full scale.
4. If the gauge unit is inaccurate or does not indicate, replace it with a new unit.
5. If the gauge unit still is erratic in its operation, the sender unit or wire to the sender unit is defective.

Fuel Tank Gauge Test
1. Test the dash gauge as outlined above.
2. If dash gauge is satisfactory, remove flashlight batteries.
3. Then disconnect wire at tank unit and ground it momentarily to a clean, unpainted portion of the vehicle frame or body *with ignition switch on.*
4. If the dash gauge does not indicate, the wire is defective. Repair or replace the wire.
5. If grounding the new or repaired wire causes the gauge to indicate, the tank unit is faulty and should be replaced.

Oil & Temperature Sending Unit Tests
1. Test dash gauge as outlined above.
2. If dash gauge is satisfactory, remove flashlight batteries.
3. Then start engine and allow it to run to warm up to normal temperature.
4. If no reading is indicated on the gauge, check the sending unit-to-gauge wire by removing the wire from the sending unit and momentarily ground this wire to a clean, unpainted portion of the engine.
5. If the gauge still does not indicate,

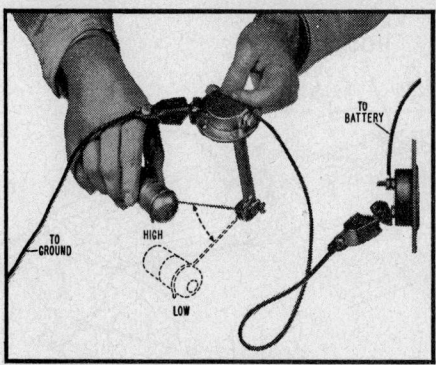

Fig. 1 Hook-up for testing dash gauge with a spare tank unit

ative ammeter should be given prompt attention.

The typical ammeter, Fig. 2, consists of a frame to which a permanent magnet is attached. The frame also supports an armature and pointer assembly.

When no current flows through the ammeter, the magnet holds the pointer armature so that the pointer stands at the center of the dial. When current passes in either direction through the ammeter, the resulting magnetic field attracts the armature away from the effect of the permanent magnet, thus giving a reading proportional to the strength of the current flowing.

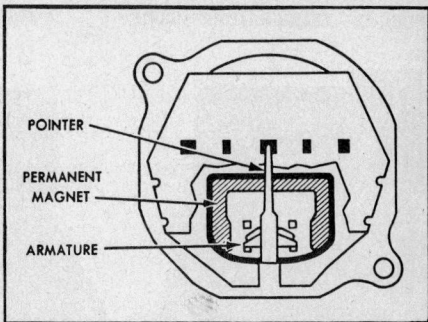

Fig. 2 Drawing of a typical automobile ammeter

Trouble Shooting

When the ammeter apparently fails to register correctly, there may be trouble in the wiring which connects the ammeter to the alternator and battery or in the alternator or battery itself.

To check the connections, first tighten the two terminal posts on the back of the ammeter. Then, following each wire from the ammeter, tighten all connections on the ignition switch, battery and alternator. Chafed, burned or broken insulation can be found by following each ammeter wire from end to end.

All wires with chafed, burned or broken insulation should be repaired or replaced. After this is done, and all connections are tightened, connect the battery cable and turn on the ignition switch. The needle should point slightly to the discharge (−) side.

Start the engine and speed it up a little above idling speed. The needle should then move to the charge side (+), and its movement should be smooth.

If the pointer does not behave correctly, the ammeter itself is out of order and a new one should be installed.

the wire is defective. Repair or replace the wire.
6. If grounding the new or repaired wire causes the dash gauge to indicate, the sending unit is faulty.

VARIABLE VOLTAGE TYPE

The procedure given herewith applies to AC, and Ford systems. Following is the method of quickly checking the gauge system to determine which component (sender or receiver) of a given system is defective.

Fuel Gauge Tank Unit Method

1. Use a spare gauge tank unit known to be correct.
2. To test whether the dash gauge in question (fuel, oil or temperature) is functioning, disconnect the wire at the gauge which leads to the sending unit.
3. Attach a wire lead from the dash gauge terminal to the terminal of the "test" tank gauge, Fig. 1.
4. Ground the test tank unit to an unpainted portion of the dash panel and move the float arm.
5. If the gauge operates correctly, the sending unit is defective and should be replaced.
6. If the gauge does not operate during this test, the dash gauge is defective and should be replaced.

ALTERNATOR INDICATOR LIGHT

Delcotron SI Integral Charging System

This system features an integral solid state regulator mounted inside the alternator slip ring end frame. The alternator indicator lamp is installed in the field wire circuit connected between the ignition "Ign." terminal and alternator No. 1 terminal, Fig. 3. The resistance provided by the alternator warning light circuit is needed to protect the diode trio. The alternator indicator lamp should light when the ignition switch is turned on before engine is started. If lamp does not light, either lamp is burned out or indicator lamp wiring has an open circuit. After engine is started, the indicator lamp should be out at all times. If indicator lamp comes on,

AMMETERS

This instrument shows whether the battery is being charged by the alternator or is being discharged by lights, radio, engine, etc. If a constant discharge is indicated on the ammeter, it is a signal that the battery is being run down. It is often a signal that the alternator is out of order. Since both a charged battery and a working alternator are very necessary—especially with vehicles equipped with many electricity-consuming devices, an inoper-

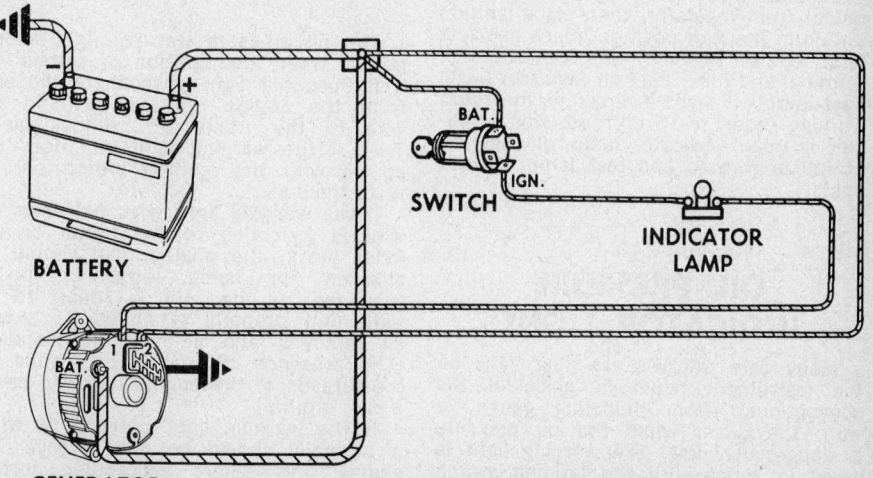

Fig. 3 Charge indicator switch wiring circuit. Delco SI integral charging system

DASH GAUGES

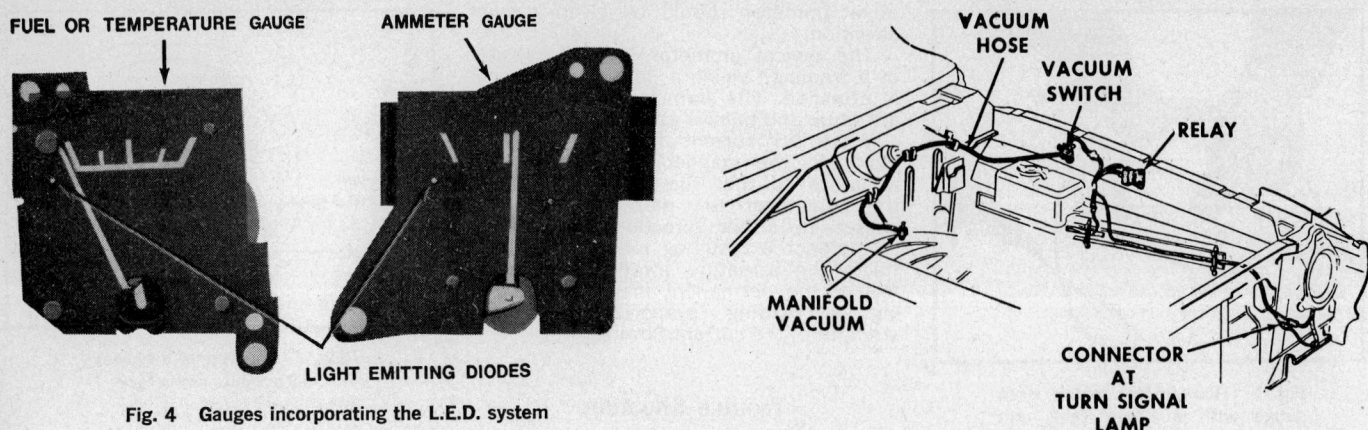

Fig. 4 Gauges incorporating the L.E.D. system

Fig. 5 Fuel pacer system. 1975-76 Dart & Valiant (Typical)

alternator belt may be loose, alternator or regulator may be defective, charging circuit may be defective or fuse may be blown.

Motorcraft Alternator

The indicator lamp glows when field relay fails to close. When ignition is in the On position, battery current flows through the charge indicator lamp and a parallel resistor, and through regulator to field, and the lamp comes on. Vehicles with electronic voltage regulator have a 500 ohm resistor. On all others the resistor is 15 ohms. When the alternator builds up enough voltage to close the field relay the charge indicator lamp will go out. Place ignition switch in the Run position with the engine stopped. The lamp should light. If not, the bulb is burned out or indicator lamp has an open circuit.

On vehicles with electro-mechanical or transistorized regulators, an open resistor wire in the alternator charging circuit will usually cause the indicator lamp to remain on until engine speed is increased to approximately 2000 rpm. In some cases the lamp will remain on above 2000 rpm. The charge indicator lamp may be tested using a test light containing a No. 67 or 1155 bulb. Disconnect regulator wire connector from regulator, then place ignition switch in the Run position. Place one test lamp lead on regulator wire connector "I" terminal and other lead on regulator base. Test lamp will light if circuit is in proper working order. If 15 ohm resistor or circuit is open, indicator lamp will operate at full brightness and test lamp will not light.

OIL PRESSURE INDICATOR LIGHT

Many cars utilize a warning light on the instrument panel in place of the conventional dash indicating gauge to warn the driver when the oil pressure is dangerously low. The warning light is wired in series with the ignition switch and the engine unit—which is an oil pressure switch.

The oil pressure switch contains a diaphragm and a set of contacts. When the ignition switch is turned on, the warning light circuit is energized and the circuit is completed through the closed contacts in the pressure switch. When the engine is started, build-up of oil pressure compresses the diaphragm, opening the contacts, thereby breaking the circuit and putting out the light.

Trouble Shooting

NOTE: On some 1978 General Motors models with V6-196, 231 engines, the oil pressure indicator light also serves as the electric choke defect indicator. If Oil or Eng. indicator light does not light, check to ensure electric choke is not disconnected at carburetor. Also check for defect in electric choke heater, blown gauge fuse or defect in lamp or wiring circuit. If indicator light stays on with engine running possible causes are: oil pressure is low, switch to indicator light wiring has an open circuit, oil pressure switch wire connector has disconnected or on some models, gauge or radio fuse has blown.

The oil pressure warning light should go on when the ignition is turned on. If it does not light, disconnect the wire from the engine unit and ground the wire to the frame or cylinder block. Then if the warning light still does not go on with the ignition switch on, replace the bulb.

If the warning light goes on when the wire is grounded to the frame or cylinder block, the engine unit should be checked for being loose or poorly grounded. If the unit is found to be tight and properly grounded, it should be removed and a new one installed. (The presence of sealing compound on the threads of the engine unit will cause a poor ground).

If the warning light remains lit when it normally should be out, replace the engine unit before proceeding further to determine the cause for a low pressure indication.

The warning light sometimes will light up or will flicker when the engine is idling, even though the oil pressure is adequate. However, the light should go out when the engine is speeded up. There is no cause for alarm in such cases; it simply means that the pressure switch is not calibrated precisely correct.

TEMPERATURE INDICATOR LIGHT

Trouble Shooting

If the red light is not lit when the engine is being cranked, check for a burned out bulb, an open in the light circuit, or a defective ignition switch.

If the red light is lit when the engine is running, check the wiring between light and switch for a ground, temperature switch defective, or overheated cooling system.

NOTE: As a test circuit to check whether the red bulb is functioning properly, a wire which is connected to the ground terminal of the ignition switch is tapped into its circuit. When the ignition is in the "Start" (engine cranking) position, the ground terminal is grounded inside the switch and the red bulb will be lit. When the engine is started and the ignition switch is in the "On" position, the test circuit is opened and the bulb is then controlled by the temperature switch.

CHRYSLER GAUGE ALERT SYSTEM

L.E.D. (Light Emitting Diode)

The fuel, temperature and ammeter gauges are equipped with a L.E.D. (Light Emitting Diode) mounted in each of the gauge dials, Fig. 4. This diode will illuminate and alert the driver that the system the gauge is monitoring is malfunctioning.

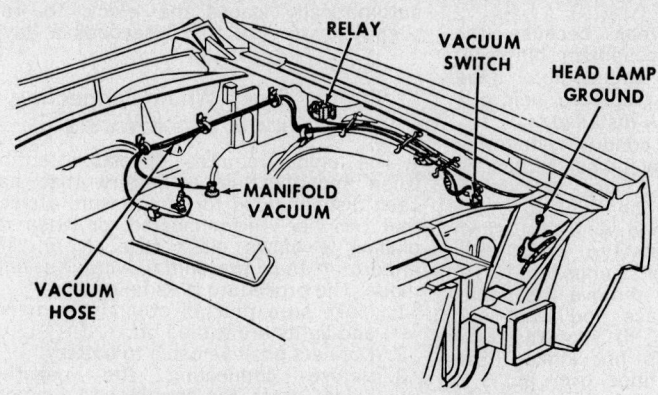

Fig. 6   Fuel pacer system. 1975-77 Charger, Cordoba, Coronet & Fury; 1977 Monaco (Typical)

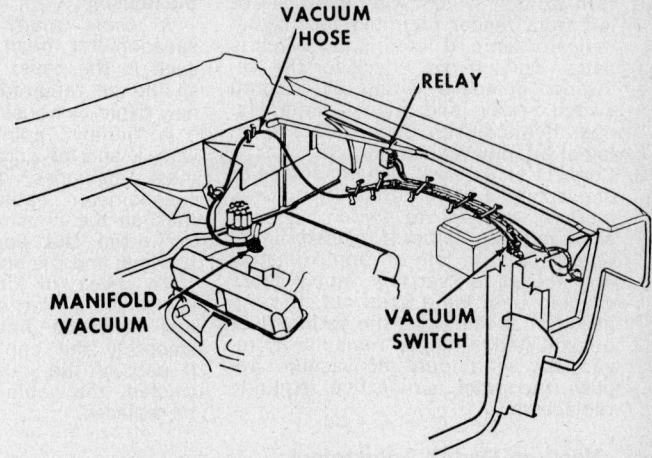

Fig. 7   Fuel pacer system. 1975-76 Monaco; 1975-77 Chrysler, Gran Fury & Imperial; 1977 Royal Monaco (Typical)

The electronic sensor circuit is mounted on the gauge housing. The printed circuit board is permanently attached and is not serviceable. If the L.E.D. is malfunctioning, the gauge and the printed circuit board must be replaced as an assembly.

Operation

Fuel Gauge

When gauge indicator shows approximately ⅛ of a tank of fuel remaining, the L.E.D. will light alerting the driver of a low fuel situation.

Temperature Gauge

When gauge indicator shows engine temperature approximately 240 to 260 degrees F. the L.E.D. will light alerting the driver of an overheat condition.

Ammeter Gauge

This L.E.D. operates independently of the gauge indicator and monitors system voltage. The L.E.D. will alert the driver of three charging system potential malfunctions.

1. A discharging condition, caused by excessive electrical demand on charging system, (engine at idle rpm).
2. A weak or defective battery with ignition switch in the "ON" position, (before the ignition switch is moved to the "START" position).
3. A weak or defective battery with minimum demand on charging system, while vehicle is being used in stop and go driving (intermittent L.E.D. illumination occurring).

Testing

Fuel And Temperature L.E.D.

Use testor C-3826 for diagnosing systems.

Ammeter L.E.D.

NOTE: Only if battery and charging system are functioning properly can the following

test be performed.

Turn ignition switch to the "ON" position and turn on headlights, windshield wipers and stoplights. This will cause excessive demand on charging system activating the L.E.D. immediately or within approximately one minute, if the L.E.D. does not light there is a malfunction in the system. If L.E.D. lights, run engine at approximately 2000 rpm, L.E.D. should stop emitting light, if the L.E.D. continues to emit light there is a malfunction in the system.

NOTE: In all cases of system malfunctions the complete gauge must be replaced.

CHRYSLER FUEL PACER SYSTEM

The Fuel Pacer system, Figs. 5, 6 and 7, incorporates a vacuum switch, relay on 1975 models, vacuum hoses, diodes and the use of the left front fender mounted turn signal indicator lamp. When engine vacuum falls below 4½ inches Hg., electrical contacts in the vacuum switch close, causing the indicator lamp to light, therefore indicating excessive fuel consumption by the engine.

On 1975 models, the relay dims the indicator lamp during night operations by routing the current through a resistor, in turn, dimming the indicator lamp. The relay is activated when the parking lamps or headlamps are "On."

The Fuel Pacer system overrides the blinking action of the fender mounted left turn indicator lamp. However, an in-line diode is incorporated in the circuit so the complete turn signal system is not affected. A second in-line diode is placed in the fender mounted indicator lamp feed wire, preventing feedback through the main harness and therefore avoiding some accessories from functioning when the hazard warning flashers are "On", with the ignition switch in the "Accessory" position.

1976-77 System Tests

Test 1

1. Disconnect vacuum hose from vacuum switch and connect an external vacuum source to the switch.
2. Turn ignition switch to "On" position and observe fender mounted turn indicator lamp. If indicator lamp is lit, the vacuum switch is satisfactory. If not, check the following: defective wiring or connections supplying current through vacuum switch to indicator lamp, burnt indicator bulb or a defective vacuum switch.

Test 2

1. With an external vacuum source connected to the vacuum switch and the ignition switch in the "On" position, apply increasing vacuum to the switch and observe fender mounted indicator lamp.
2. Indicator lamp should turn off at approximately 4½ inches of vacuum. If not, increase vacuum until switch does go out. If lamp goes out, the switch is out of adjustment, requiring readjustment. If lamp does not go out regardless of amount of vacuum applied, the switch is defective, requiring replacement.

1975 System Tests

Relay Tests

1. Turn ignition switch "On" and observe the left front fender mounted turn indicator lamp. If indicator lamp is lit, relay is satisfactory. If not, check for the following: defective wiring at the vacuum switch, relay and signal lamp, inoperative indicator bulb, open vacuum switch or a defective relay.
2. With ignition switch "On", turn headlamps "On". If indicator lampdims, relay is satisfactory. If not, check wiring at relay windings. If wiring is satisfactory, the relay is defective.

Vacuum Switch Tests

1. Disconnect the switch vacuum hose,

turn ignition switch "On" and observe left front fender mounted turn signal indicator lamp. If lamp is lit, switch is satisfactory. If not, check for the following: defective wiring at vacuum switch, relay and signal lamp, inoperative indicator bulb, defective relay or a faulty vacuum switch.

2. Connect an external vacuum source to the vacuum switch, turn ignition "On", increase vacuum to switch and observe indicator lamp. If indicator lamp does not turn off at approximately 4½ inches of vacuum, apply more vacuum until lamp goes out. If lamp goes out at this time, the switch must be adjusted. If lamp remains lit, regardless of amount of vacuum applied, the switch is defective, requiring replacement.

Vacuum Switch Adjustment

1976-77

1. Install a vacuum gauge on the engine.
2. Operate vehicle, noting the vacuum reading at which the indicator lamp glows. This also may be accomplished by carefully loading the engine with the brakes applied.
3. Remove vacuum switch adjusting screw cap.
4. To decrease vacuum setting, turn adjusting screw counter-clockwise. To increase vacuum setting, turn adjusting screw clockwise.
5. Install adjusting screw cap.
6. Operate vehicle or load engine, noting the vacuum reading at which the indicator lamp glows. It may be necessary to readjust switch to obtain desired setting.

1975

1. If 5.2 inches of vacuum or more was required to turn indicator lamp off, turn adjusting screw counter-clockwise to decrease amount of vacuum required.
2. If 3.8 inches of vacuum or less was required to turn vacuum switch off, turn adjusting screw clockwise to increase amount of vacuum required.

NOTE: If more than two turns of adjusting screw (in either direction) was required to adjust switch, the switch is defective, requiring replacement.

SPEEDOMETERS

The following material covers only that service on speedometers which is feasible to perform by the average service man. Repairs on the units themselves are not included as they require special tools and extreme care when making repairs and adjustments and only an experienced speedometer mechanic should attempt such servicing.

The speedometer has two main parts —the indicating head and the speedometer drive cable. When the speedometer fails to indicate speed or mileage, the cable or housing is probably broken.

Speedometer Cable

Most cables are broken due to lack of lubrication or a sharp bend or kink in the housing.

A cable might break because the speedometer head mechanism binds. If such is the case, the speedometer head should be repaired or replaced before a new cable or housing is installed.

A "jumpy" pointer condition, together with a sort of scraping noise, is due, in most instances, to a dry or kinked speedometer cable. The kinked cable rubs on the housing and winds up, slowing down the pointer. The cable then unwinds and the pointer "jumps".

To check for kinks, remove the cable, lay it on a flat surface and twist one end with the fingers. If it turns over smoothly the cable is not kinked. But if part of the cable flops over as it is twisted, the cable is kinked and should be replaced.

Lubrication

The speedometer cable should be lubricated with special cable lubricant every 10,000 miles.

Fill the ferrule on the upper end of the housing with the cable lubricant. Insert the cable in the housing, starting at the upper end. Turn the cable around carefully while feeding it into the housing. Repeat filling the ferrule except for the last six inches of cable. Too much lubricant at this point may cause the lubricant to work into the indicating hand.

Installing Cable

During installation, if the cable sticks when inserted in the housing and will not go through, the housing is damaged inside or kinked. Be sure to check the housing from one end to the other. Straighten any sharp bends by relocating clamps or elbows. Replace housing if it is badly kinked or broken. Position the cable and housing so that they lead into the head as straight as possible.

Check the new cable for kinks before installing it. Use wide, sweeping, gradual curves where the cable comes out of the transmission and connects to the head so the cable will not be damaged during its installation.

If inspection indicates that the cable and housing are in good condition, yet pointer action is erratic, check the speedometer head for possible binding.

The speedometer drive pinion should also be checked. If the pinion is dry or its teeth are stripped, the speedometer may not register properly.

The transmission mainshaft nut must be tight or the speedometer drive gear may slip on the mainshaft and cause slow speed readings.

ELECTRIC CLOCKS

Regulation of electric clocks used on automobiles is accomplished automatically by merely resetting the time. If the clock is running fast, the action of turning the hands back to correct the time will automatically cause the clock to run slightly slower. If the clock is running slow, the action of turning the hands forward to correct the time will automatically cause the clock to run slightly faster (10 to 15 seconds a day).

Winding Clock When Connecting Battery or Clock Wiring

The clock requires special attention when reconnecting a battery that has been disconnected for any reason, a clock that has been disconnected, or when replacing a blown clock fuse. *It is very important that the initial wind be fully made.* The procedure is as follows:

1. Make sure that all other instruments and lights are turned off.
2. Connect positive cable to battery.
3. Before connecting the negative cable, press the terminal to its post on the battery. Immediately afterward strike the terminal against the battery post to see if there is a spark. If there is a spark, allow the clock to run down until it stops ticking, and repeat as above until there is no spark. Then immediately make the permanent connection before the clock can again run down. The clock will run down in approximately two minutes.
4. Reset clock after all connections have been made. *The foregoing procedure should also be followed when reconnecting the clock after it has been disconnected, or if it has stopped because of a blown fuse. Be sure to disconnect battery before installing a new fuse.*

Trouble Shooting

If clock does not run, check for blown "clock" fuse. If fuse is blown check for short in wiring. If fuse is not blown check for open circuit.

With an electric clock, the most frequent cause of clock fuse blowing is low voltage at the clock which will prevent a complete wind and allow clock contacts to remain closed. This may be caused by any of the following: discharged battery, corrosion on contact surface of battery terminals, loose connections at battery terminals, at junction block, at fuse clips, or at terminal connection of clock. Therefore, if in reconnecting battery or clock it is noted that the clock is not ticking, always check for blown fuse, or examine the circuits at the points indicated above to determine and correct the cause.

FIBER OPTIC MONITORING SYSTEM

Fiber optics are non-electric light conductors made up of coated strands which, when exposed to a light source at one end, will reflect the light through their entire length, thereby illuminating a monitoring lens on the instrument panel or fender without the use of a bulb when the exterior lights are turned on.

LOW FUEL WARNING SYSTEM

There are two types of low fuel warning

systems, the thermistor and switch types. The thermistor type incorporates an indicator light, low fuel relay and a thermocouple assembly which is attached to the fuel sender outlet tube in the fuel tank. The thermistor temperature is low when submerged in fuel and, in turn, high electrical resistance is evident. When the fuel level drops and the thermistor is exposed to the air, the thermistor heat will increase thus decreasing its resistance allowing current to energize the low fuel relay and activate the indicator light. The switch type consists of an indicator light and a low fuel warning switch located on the instrument panel.

The warning switch contacts are closed by the difference in voltage potential between the fuel gauge terminals. This voltage differential will activate the warning switch when the fuel tank is less than $\frac{1}{4}$ full and, in turn, cause the indicator to light.

Trouble Shooting

Both systems incorporate an indicator light which may be checked in the same manner. With ignition switch turned to "ON", the indicator should light. If not, check bulb and all electrical connections. On General Motors switch type, replace warning switch if bulb and connections prove satisfactory. On Ford thermistor and switch type systems, perform additional tests outlined below.

On Ford thermistor system, using an ohmmeter and thermistor assembly out of the fuel, connect one lead to metal housing of sending unit and the other lead to thermistor terminal of sending unit. The ohmmeter should then indicate a resistance of 450 to 600 ohms. If resistance is not within above limits, replace fuel sender.

Improper operation of the warning switch will be indicated when the light remains "ON" when tank is more than $\frac{1}{4}$ full. To test system, disconnect connector on warning switch and turn ignition "ON". Starting with the terminal on the end opposite the blank position, connect a jumper wire between the battery positive terminal and connector terminal. The indicator on instrument panel should light. If not, replace warning switch. Skip the next connector terminal and connect a test lamp between the battery positive terminal and connector terminal. The test lamp should light. If not, trace wire from ignition switch for an open circuit. Test the remaining connector terminals with the test lamp making connections between ground and terminal connectors. If lamp fails to light, trace particular wire for an incomplete circuit.

LOW WASHER FLUID INDICATOR

There are two types of low washer fluid indicating systems used on GM cars. They are the mechanical type and electrically controlled type. The mechanical type of a float and rod assembly, sending unit and a fiber optic. The electrically controlled type consists of a float, magnet, contact points and a resistor.

On the mechanical type, the upper end of the rod extends into the sending unit

POWER RANGE   **DRIVING RANGE**

ECONOMY

Fig. 8   Typical vacuum gauge

and has colored red and green portions. When the windshield wipers are activated, a lamp bulb in the sending unit lights either the red or green sections of the rod. The colored light is then picked up by the fiber optic and is transmitted through it to the tell tale lens. The lens will show red or green depending upon washer fluid level.

The electrically controlled indicator is activated when the windshield wipers are engaged. A slight amount of current flows from the wiper motor to the washer bottle float unit. This current will either pass through the contact points or the resistor which is in parallel with the points. When the washer fluid level is high, the magnet holds the contact points open. The current will now flow through the resistor where it is reduced so the indicator will not light. When the washer fluid level is low, the float drops and the magnet will separate from the cap assembly allowing the current to pass through the contact points and activate the indicator light.

Trouble Shooting

On the mechanical indicating system, if the tell tale lens fails to glow when the windshield wipers are activated, check lamp bulb in sending unit and see that fiber optic is not broken.

On the electrically controlled system, the first item to check is the indicator bulb. With the windshield wipers "ON", connect a jumper wire between the two terminals on the washer bottle cap. The indicator should then light. If not, replace bulb. If the bulb is found to be satisfactory, remove cap and float assembly from washer bottle. Float should be able to move to the bottom of the stem and the magnet should separate from the cap. If not, replace float and cap assembly.

VACUUM GAUGE

This gauge, Fig. 8, measures intake manifold vacuum. The intake manifold vacuum varies with engine operating conditions, carburetor adjustments, valve

timing, ignition timing and general engine condition.

Since the optimum fuel economy is directly proportional to a properly functioning engine, a high vacuum reading on the gauge relates to fuel economy. For this reason some manufacturers call the vacuum gauge a "Fuel Economy Indicator." Most gauges have colored sectors the green sector being the "Economy" range and red the "Power" range. Therefore, the vehicle should be operated with gauge registering in the green sector or a high numerical number, Fig. 8, for maximum economy.

FUEL USAGE GAUGE

1978 Buick & Cadillac

Operation

This system consists of green and amber indicator lights located on the fuel gauge or telltale lamp cluster, a switch mounted on the instrument panel behind the gauges and an interconnecting vacuum hose and tee. The system operates on engine vacuum through a dual contact vacuum sensing switch. When the accelerator is operated slowly and smoothly, engine vacuum remains high and the switch passes current to the green indicator light which indicates economical fuel consumption. When the accelerator pedal is depressed rapidly, vacuum decreases and the switch passes current to the amber indicator light, which indicates high fuel consumption. The amber indicator light will glow when the ignition switch is in the "On" position with the engine stopped.

Functional Test

1. With ignition switch in the "On" position, ground each terminal at the economy switch. Both green and amber indicator lights should glow. If not check for burned out bulbs.
2. With ignition switch in "On" position, amber indicator light should glow. If not, check for loose or disconnected wires at fuel economy switch or for poor ground. If amber indicator light still does not glow, replace switch.
3. Start engine and allow to idle, the green indicator light should glow. If not, check for leaking, plugged or kinked vacuum hose between vacuum source and fuel economy switch. Check for loose or disconnected wires at economy switch or poor ground. If green indicator lamp still does not glow, replace switch.

TURBO-POWER INDICATOR

1978 Buick V6-231 Turbo-Charged Engine

Century models utilize two lights located in the lower right hand gauge area. The yellow light indicates moderate acceleration and the orange light indicates power or heavy acceleration. When neither light is illuminated, the indication visible is a green paint band signifying economy. LeSabre models utilize three lights located at the bottom of the fuel gauge. On light acceleration or cruising, a green light indicates economy. Moderate acceleration activates a yellow indicator light. The orange light is activated during heavy acceleration.

LOW COOLANT LEVEL INDICATOR

Some General Motors vehicles use a buzzer or indicator lamp to indicate a low coolant level condition. The buzzer or lamp is activated by a sensor, located in the radiator, when the coolant level becomes one quart or more low.

STARTING SWITCHES

MAGNETIC and SOLENOID SWITCHES are designed to perform mechanical jobs electromagnetically such as closing a heavy circuit or shifting the starter drive pinion with the engine flywheel ring gear for cranking. Switches of this type consist basically of contacts and a winding (or windings) around a hollow cylinder containing a movable core or plunger. When the winding (or windings) is energized by the battery through an external control circuit the plunger is pulled inward, producing the necessary mechanical movement.

MAGNETIC SWITCHES

The switch shown in Fig. 1 is not designed for disassembly and must be replaced if defective.

In the Delco-Remy switch shown in Fig. 1 the terminals are assembled into a molded terminal ring which is held in place on the switch case by the cover and screws. Gaskets on both sides of the ring seal the contact compartment as a protection against moisture and dirt. The winding assembly is not removable from the case on this unit although the contact disk, plunger and plunger return spring can be removed after the cover is taken off.

NOTE

On vehicles with overrunning clutch

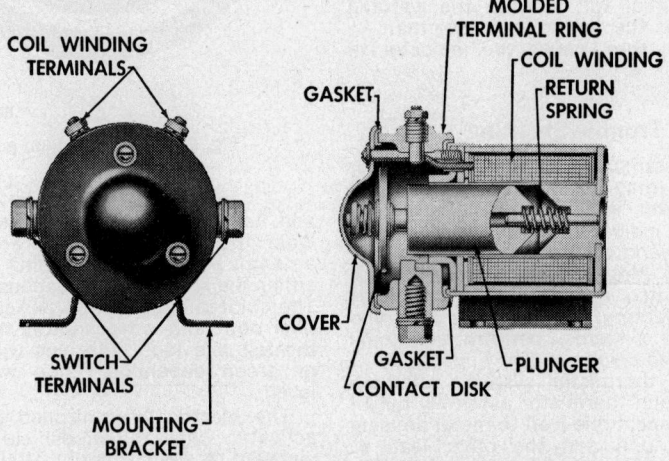

Fig. 1 End and sectional views of a sealed type magnetic switch which uses gaskets to seal the contact compartment

starting motors, a magnetic switch is normally used to shift the drive pinion into mesh and to close the starter circuit. There are two variations of three-terminal switches and also one type with four terminals. Any of these switches may be manufactured with either a grounded or insulated base. When installing a switch that is not marked "grounded base" or "insulated base", it must be checked out as follows, using a battery and test lamp in series.

Three Terminal Switches

1. If the switch has a grounded base the test lamp will light when con-

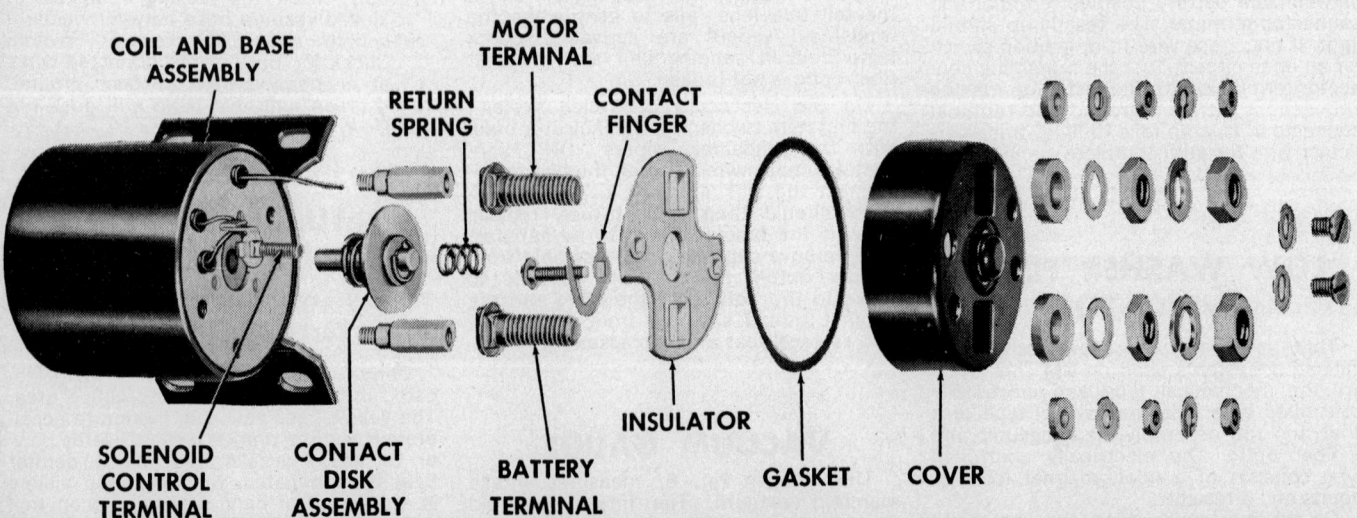

Fig. 2 Exploded view of a typical solenoid switch

nected between the starter ("S") terminal or ignition ("I") terminal and switch mounting bracket.

2. If the switch has an insulated base the test lamp will light when connected between the "S" and "I" terminals and either one of the $5/16$" threaded studs.

3. If the test lamp fails to light when connected between the "S" and "I" terminals and any external part of the switch, disassemble the switch to determine whether the base is grounded or insulated.

Four Terminal Switches

1. If the switch has a grounded base the test lamp will light when connected between the "S" terminal and switch mounting bracket.

2. If the switch has an insulated base the test lamp will light when connected between the "S" and "I" terminals.

3. If the test lamp fails to light when connected between the "S" terminal and any other external part of the switch, disassemble the switch to determine whether it has an insulated or grounded base.

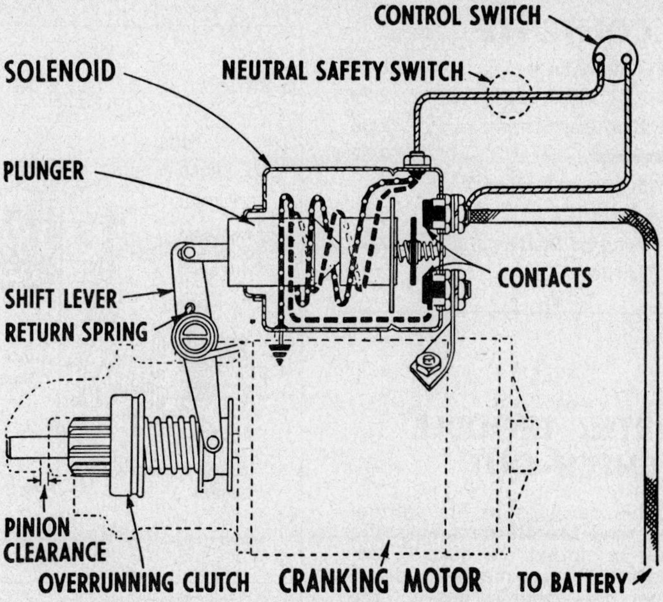

Fig. 3 Wiring circuit of a typical solenoid switch

SOLENOID SWITCHES

The solenoid switch on a cranking motor not only closes the circuit between the battery and the cranking motor but also shifts the drive pinion into mesh with the engine flywheel ring gear. This is done by means of a linkage between the solenoid switch plunger and the shift lever on the cranking motor (see *Starting Motors* chapter).

Fig. 2 shows a solenoid switch used on vehicles with 12-volt systems. Like other solenoid switches, this type is energized by the battery through a separate starting switch. Note, however, that the switch includes an additional small terminal and contact finger. This terminal has no functional duty in relation to the switch, but is used to complete a special ignition circuit during the cranking cycle only. When the solenoid is in the cranking position, the finger touches the contact disk and provides a direct circuit between the battery and ignition coil.

When reassembling the switch the contact finger should be adjusted to touch the contact disk before the disk makes contact with the main switch terminals. There should be $1/16$" to $3/32$" clearance between the contact disk and the main terminals when the finger touches.

Fig. 3 is a wiring circuit of a typical solenoid switch. There are two windings in the solenoid; a pull-in winding (shown as dashes) and a hold-in winding (shown dotted). Both windings are energized when the external control switch is closed. They produce a magnetic field which pulls the plunger in so that the drive pinion is shifted into mesh, and the main contacts in the solenoid switch are closed to connect the battery directly to the cranking motor. Closing the main switch contacts shorts out the pull-in winding since this winding is connected across the main contacts. The magnetism produced by the hold-in winding is sufficient to hold the plunger in, and shorting out the pull-in winding reduces drain on the battery. When the control switch is opened, it disconnects the hold-in winding from the battery. When the hold-in winding is disconnected from the battery, the shift lever spring withdraws the plunger from the solenoid, opening the solenoid switch contacts and at the same time withdrawing the drive pinion from mesh. Proper operation of the switch depends on maintaining a definite balance between the magnetic strength of the pull-in and hold-in windings.

This balance is established in the design by the size of the wire and the number of turns specified. *An open circuit in the hold-in winding or attempts to crank with a discharged battery will cause the switch to chatter.*

To disassemble the solenoid, remove nuts, washers and insulators from the switch terminal and battery terminal. Remove cover and take out the contact disk assembly.

STARTING MOTORS

CONTENTS

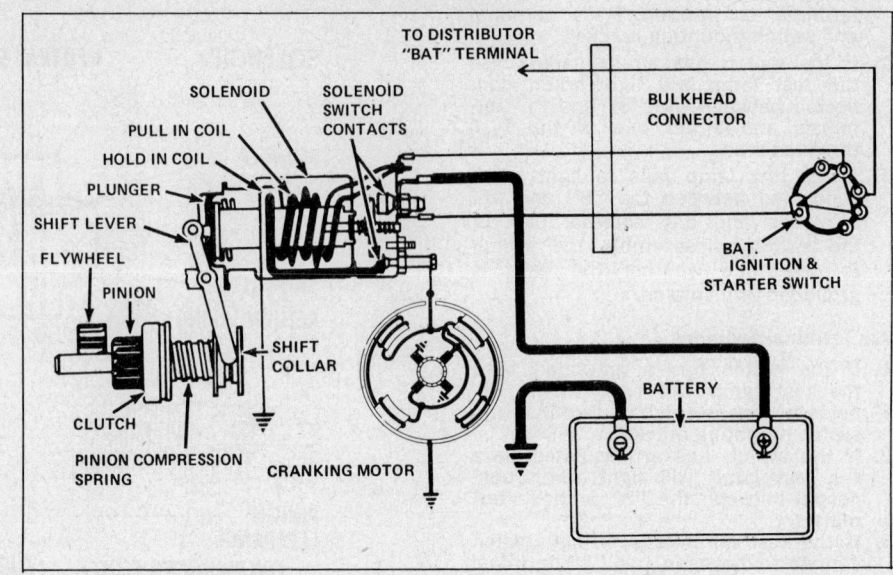

Fig. 1 Wiring diagram of a typical starting circuit

STARTER TROUBLE CHECK-OUT

When trouble develops in the starting motor circuit, and the starter cranks the engine slowly or not at all, several preliminary checks can be made to determine whether the trouble lies in the battery, in the starter, in the wiring between them, or elsewhere. Many conditions besides defects in the starter itself can result in poor cranking performance.

To make a quick check of the starter system, turn on the headlights. They should burn with normal brilliance. If they do not, the battery may be run down and it should be checked with a hydrometer.

If the battery is in a charged condition so that the lights burn brightly, operate the starting motor. Any one of three things will happen to the lights: (1) They will go out, (2) dim considerably or (3) stay bright without any cranking action taking place.

If Lights Go Out

If the lights go out as the starter switch is closed, it indicates that there is a poor connection between the battery and starting motor. This poor connection will most often be found at the battery terminals. Correction is made by removing the cable clamps from the terminals, cleaning the terminals and clamps, replacing the clamps and tightening them securely. A coating of corrosion inhibitor (vaseline will do) may be applied to the clamps and terminals to retard the formation of corrosion.

If Lights Dim

If the lights dim considerably as the starter switch is closed and the starter operates slowly or not at all, the battery may be run down, or there may be some mechanical condition in the engine or starting motor that is throwing a heavy burden on the starting motor. This imposes a high discharge rate on the battery which causes noticeable dimming of the lights.

Check the battery with a hydrometer. If it is charged, the trouble probably lies in either the engine or starting motor itself. In the engine, tight bearings or pistons or heavy oil place an added burden on the starting motor. Low temperatures also hamper starting motor performance since it thickens engine oil and makes the engine considerably harder to crank and start. Also, a battery is less efficient at low temperatures.

In the starting motor, a bent armature, loose pole shoe screws or worn bearings, any of which may allow the armature to drag, will reduce cranking performance and increase current draw.

In addition, more serious internal damage is sometimes found. Thrown armature windings or commutator bars, which sometimes occur on over-running clutch drive starting motors, are usually caused by excessive over-running after starting. This is the result of such conditions as the driver keeping the starting switch closed too long after the engine has started, the driver opening the throttle too wide in starting, or improper carburetor fast idle adjustment. Any of these subject the over-running clutch to extra strain so it tends to seize, spinning the armature at high speed with resulting armature damage.

Another cause may be engine backfire during cranking which may result, among other things, from ignition timing being too far advanced.

To avoid such failures, the driver should pause a few seconds after a false start to make sure the engine has come completely to rest before another start is attempted. In addition, the ignition timing should be reset if engine backfiring has caused the trouble.

Fig. 2 Checking voltage drop between vehicle frame and grounded battery terminal post

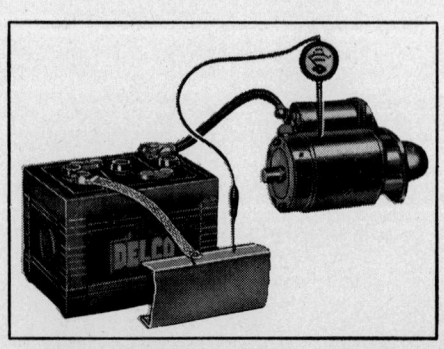

Fig. 3 Checking voltage drop between vehicle frame and starter field frame

Fig. 4 Checking voltage drop between ungrounded battery terminal post and battery terminal on solenoid

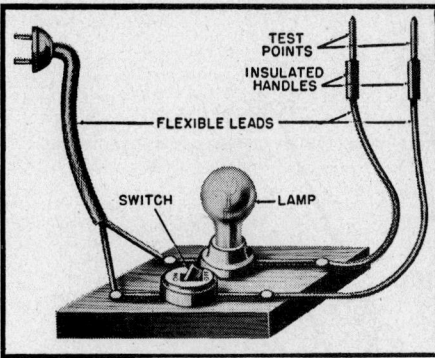

Fig. 5 A simple tester for use in making continuity and ground tests on armature and field windings

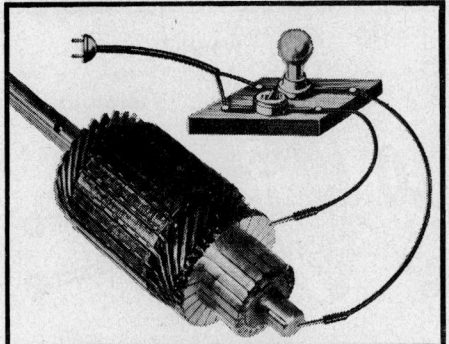

Fig. 6 Checking armature for grounds. If lamp lights armature is grounded and should be replaced

Fig. 7 Measuring commutator runout with dial indicator. Mount shaft in V blocks and rotate commutator. If runout exceeds .003", commutator should be turned in a lathe to make it concentric

Lights Stay Bright, No Cranking Action

This condition indicates an open circuit at some point, either in the starter itself, the starter switch or control circuit. The solenoid control circuit can be in

eliminated momentarily by placing a heavy jumper lead across the solenoid main terminals to see if the starter will operate. This connects the starter directly to the battery and, if it operates, it indicates that the control circuit is not functioning normally. The wiring and control units must be checked to locate the trouble, Fig. 1.

If the starter does not operate with the jumper attached, it will probably have to be removed from the engine so it can be examined in detail.

Checking Circuit With Voltmeter

Excessive resistance in the circuit between the battery and starter will reduce cranking performance. The resistance can be checked by using a voltmeter to measure voltage drop in the circuits while the starter is operated. There are three checks to be made:

1. Voltage drop between car frame and grounded battery terminal post (not cable clamp), Fig. 2.
2. Voltage drop between car frame and starting motor field frame, Fig. 3.
3. Voltage drop between insulated battery terminal post and starting motor terminal stud (or the battery terminal stud of the solenoid), Fig. 4.

Each of these should show no more than one-tenth (0.1) volt drop when the starting motor is cranking the engine. Do not use the starter for more than 30 seconds at a time to avoid overheating it.

If excessive voltage drop is found in any of these circuits, make correction by disconnecting the cables, cleaning the connections carefully, and then reconnecting the cables firmly in place. A coating of vaseline on the battery cables and terminal clamps will retard corrosion.

NOTE—On some cars, extra long battery cables may be required due to the location of the battery and starter. This may result in somewhat higher voltage drop than the above recommended 0.1 volt. The only means of determining the normal voltage drop in such cases is to check several of these vehicles. Then when the voltage drop is well above the normal figure for all cars checked, abnormal resistance will be indicated and correction can be made as already explained.

STARTING MOTOR SERVICE

To obtain full performance data on a starting motor or to determine the cause of abnormal operation, the starting motor should be submitted to a no-load and torque test. These tests are best performed on a starter bench tester with the starter mounted on it.

From a practical standpoint, however, a simple torque test may be made quickly with the starter in the car. Make sure the battery is fully charged and that the starter circuit wires and terminals are good condition. Then operate the

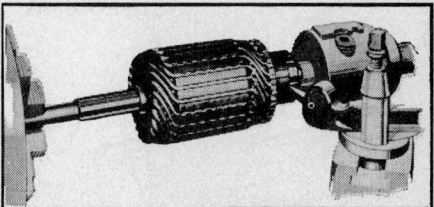

Fig. 8 Turning commutator in a lathe. Take light cuts until worn or bad spots are removed. Then remove burrs with No. 00 sandpaper

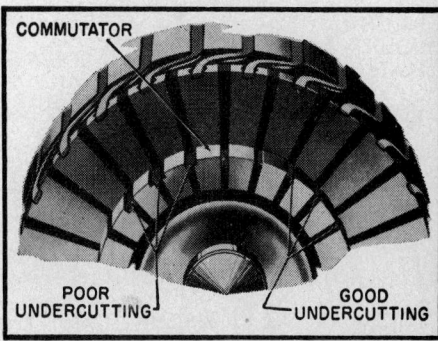

Fig. 9 Good undercutting should be .002" wider than mica insulation, 1/64" deep and exactly centered so that there are no burrs on the mica. Do not undercut molded commutators

Fig. 10 Checking armature for short circuit. As armature is rotated by hand, steel strip (hacksaw blade) will vibrate if short circuit exists

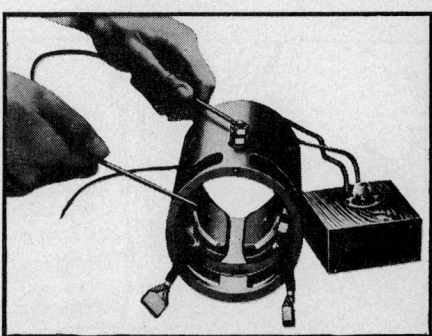

Fig. 11 Testing field coils for grounds. If a ground is present, lamp will light

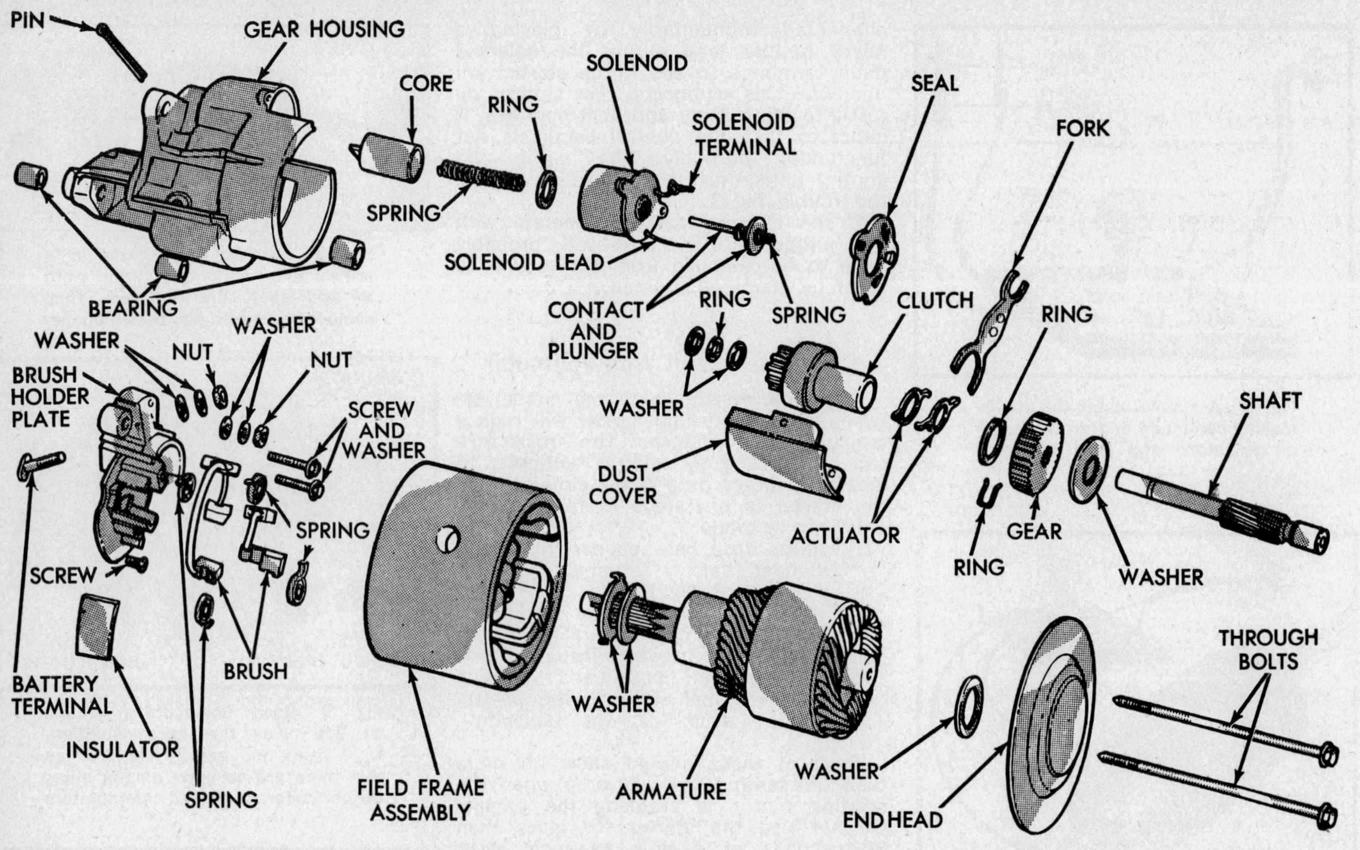

Fig. 13   Chrysler built reduction gear starting motor

starter to see if the engine turns over normally. If it does not, the torque developed is below standard and the starter should be removed for further checking.

Remove the starter from the engine as outlined in the vehicle chapters, disassemble it as outlined further on and make the tests as suggested in Figs. 6 through 11.

CHRYSLER REDUCTION GEAR STARTER

This reduction gear starting motor, Fig. 13, has an armature-to-engine crankshaft ratio of 45 to 1; 2 to 1 or a 3½ to 1 reduction gear set is built into the motor assembly. The starter utilizes a solenoid shift. The housing of the solenoid is integral with the starter drive end housing.

Disassembly

1. Place gear housing of starter in a vise with soft jaws. *Use vise as a support fixture only; do not clamp.*
2. Remove through bolts and starter end head assembly.
3. Pull field frame assembly from gear housing to expose terminal screw.

4. Support terminal screw with a finger, then remove terminal screw, Fig. 14.
5. Remove field frame assembly.
6. Remove nuts attaching solenoid and brush holder plate assembly to gear housing, then the solenoid and brush plate assembly.
7. Remove nut, steel washer and insulating washer from solenoid terminal.
8. Unwind solenoid lead wire from brush terminal, Fig. 15, and remove screws securing solenoid to brush plate, then the solenoid from brush plate.
9. Remove nut from battery terminal on brush plate, then the battery terminal.

Fig. 14   Terminal screw replacement

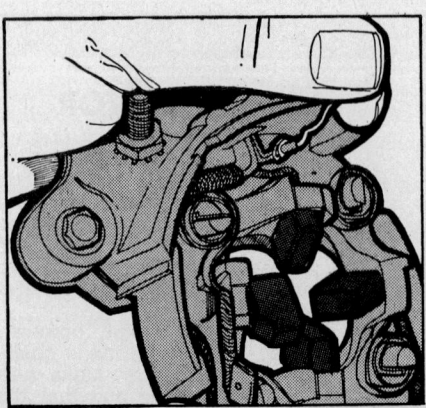

Fig. 15   Unwinding solenoid lead wire

Fig. 16   Solenoid contact & plunger

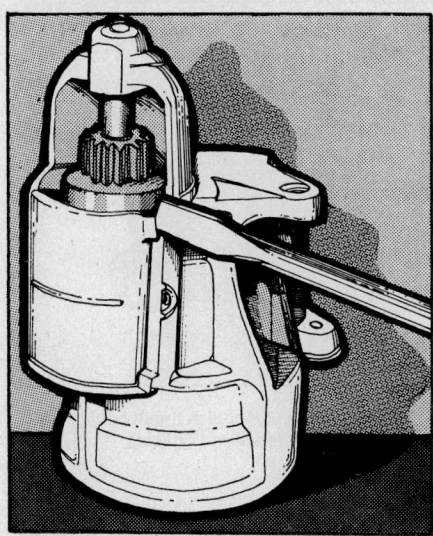

Fig. 17   Dust cover removal, all (Typical)

Fig. 18   Driven gear snap ring replacement, all (Typical)

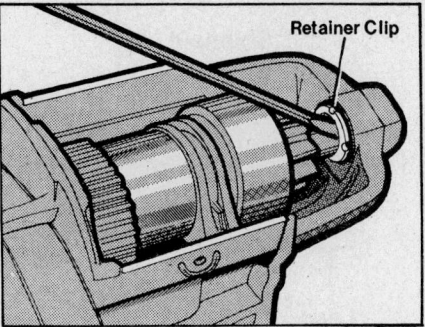

Fig. 19   Pinion shaft "C" clip replacement

Fig. 20   Removing pinion shaft

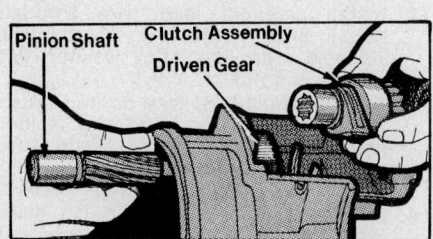

Fig. 21   Clutch assembly replacement (Typical)

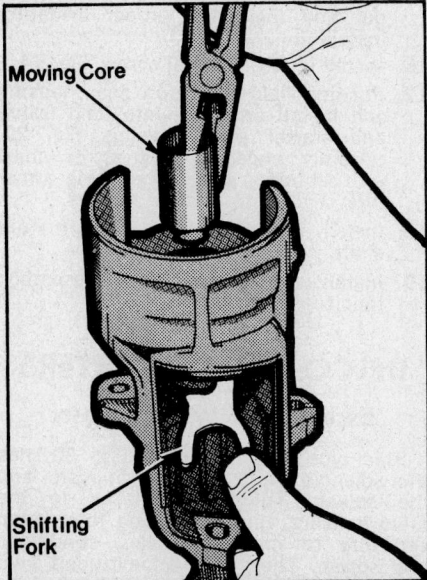

Fig. 22   Solenoid core replacement (Typical)

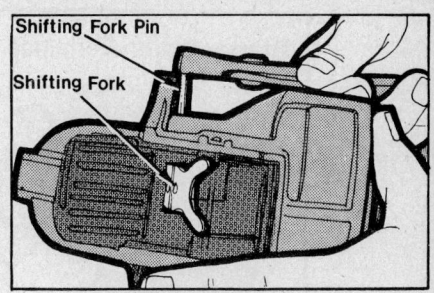

Fig. 23   Shifter fork pin replacement, all (Typical)

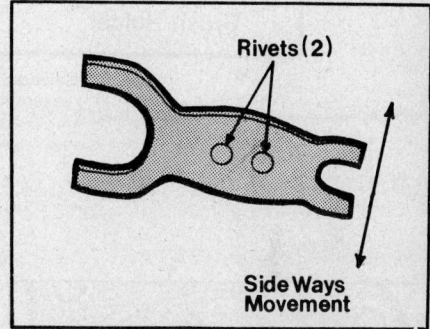

Fig. 24   Shifter fork assembly (Typical)

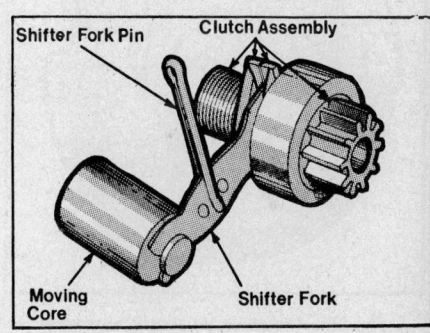

Fig. 25   Shifter fork & clutch assembly (Typical)

10. Remove solenoid contact and plunger assembly from solenoid, Fig. 16, then the return spring from the solenoid moving core.
11. Remove dust cover from gear housing, Fig. 17.
12. Release retainer clip positioning driven gear on pinion shaft, Fig. 18.

NOTE: The retainer clip is under tension. Therefore, it is recommended that a cloth be placed over the retainer clip when released, preventing it from spring away.

13. Remove pinion shaft "C" clip, Fig. 19.
14. Push pinion shaft toward rear of housing, Fig. 20, and remove retainer ring and thrust washers, clutch and pinion assembly, with the two shift fork nylon actuators as an assembly, Fig. 21.
15. Remove driven gear and thrust washer.
16. Pull shifting fork forward and remove solenoid moving core, Fig. 22.
17. Remove shifting fork retainer pin, Fig. 23, and remove clutch shifting fork assembly.

Reassembly

The shifter fork consists of two spring

steel plates assembled with two rivets, Fig. 24. There should be about 1/16" side movement to insure proper gear engagement. Lubricate between plates sparingly with SAE 10 engine oil.

1. Position shift fork in drive housing and install fork retaining pin, Fig. 23. One tip of pin should be straight, the other tip should be bent at a 15 degree angle away from housing. Fork and pin should operate freely after bending tip of pin.
2. Install solenoid moving core and engage shifting fork, Fig. 22.
3. Enter pinion shaft in drive housing and install friction washer and driven gear.
4. Install clutch and pinion assembly, Fig. 21, thrust washer, retaining ring, and thrust washer.
5. Complete installation of pinion shaft, engaging fork with clutch actuators, Fig. 25. *Friction washer must be*

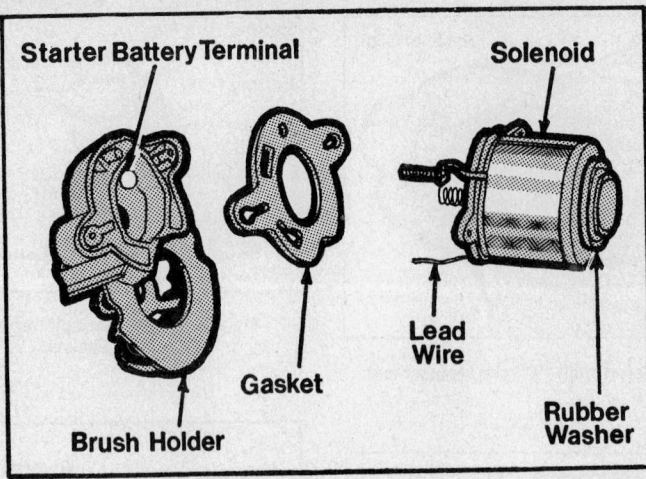

Fig. 26   Solenoid to brush holder plate assembly (Typical)

Fig. 27   Solenoid & brush holder installation (Typical)

Fig. 28   Installing brushes & armature thrust washer (Typical)

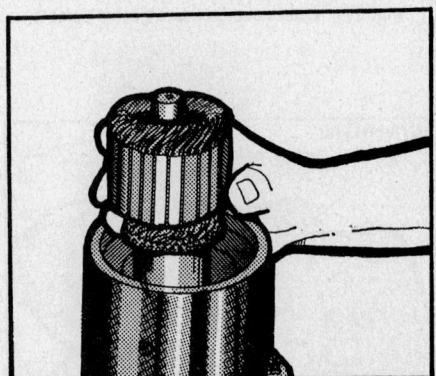

Fig. 29   Armature installation (Typical)

positioned on shoulder of splines of pinion shaft before driven gear is positioned.

6. Install driven gear snap ring, Fig. 18, then the pinion shaft retaining ring or "C" clip, Fig. 19.
7. Install starter solenoid return spring into movable core bore.

NOTE: Inspect starter solenoid switch contacting washer. If top of washer is burned, disassemble contact switch plunger assembly and reverse the washer.

8. Install solenoid contact plunger assembly into solenoid, Fig. 16. Ensure contact spring is properly positioned on shaft of solenoid contact plunger assembly.
9. Install battery terminal stud in brush holder.

NOTE: Inspect contacts in brush holder. If contacts are badly burned, replace brush holder with brushes and contacts as an

assembly.

10. Position seal on brush holder plate.
11. Install solenoid lead wire through hole in brush holder, Fig. 26, then the solenoid stud, insulating washer, flat washer and nut.
12. Wrap solenoid lead wire around brush terminal post, Fig. 15, and solder with a high temperature resin core solder and resin flux.
13. Install brush holder attaching screws.
14. Install solenoid coil and brush plate assembly into gear housing bore and position brush plate assembly into starter gear housing, Fig. 27. Then, install and tighten housing attaching nuts.
15. Install brushes with armature thrust washer, Fig. 28. This holds brushes out and facilitates proper armature installation.
16. Install brush terminal screw, Fig. 14.
17. Position field frame on gear housing and install armature into field frame and starter gear housing, Fig. 29, carefully engaging splines of shaft with reduction gear by rotating armature slightly to engage splines.
18. Install thrust washer on armature shaft.
19. Install starter end head assembly, then the through bolts.

DELCO-REMY STARTERS

Except 1978 V8-350 Diesel

This type staring motor, Fig. 30, has the solenoid shift lever mechanism and the solenoid plunger enclosed in the drive housing, thus protecting them from exposure to road dirt, icing conditions and splash. They have an extruded field frame and an overrunning clutch type of drive. The overrunning clutch is operated by a solenoid switch mounted to a flange on the drive housing.

Solenoid

The solenoid is attached to the drive end housing by two screws. The angle of the nose of the plunger provides a greater bearing area between the plunger and core tube. A molded push rod, Fig. 31, is assembled in the contact assembly. A shoulder molded on the push rod and a cup that can easily be assembled to the rod and locked into position over two molded bosses holds the contact assembly in place.

To disassemble the cup from the push rod, push in on the metal cup and rotate ¼ turn so the molded bosses on the rod are in line with openings in the cup; then slide the metal cup off the rod.

To assemble the metal cup on the rod, locate the parts on the rod as shown and align the large openings in the cup with the molded bosses on the rod; then push in on the cup and rotate it ¼ turn so the small bosses on the rod fall into the keyways of the cup.

Solenoid Terminals

The terminals of the solenoid are assembled in a molded cover. Some sole-

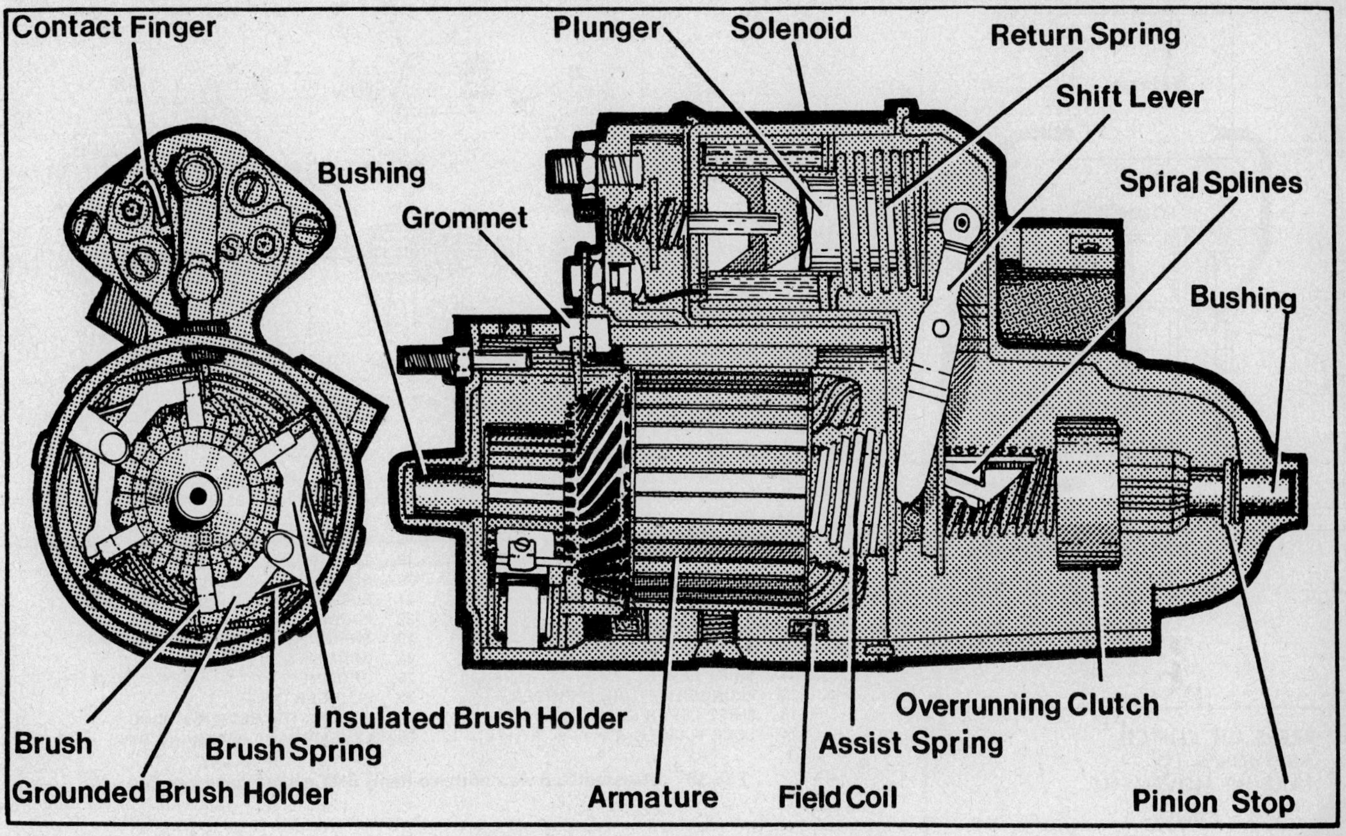

Contact Finger — Plunger — Solenoid — Return Spring

Bushing — Shift Lever

Grommet — Spiral Splines

Bushing

Brush — Insulated Brush Holder — Overrunning Clutch

Grounded Brush Holder — Brush Spring — Assist Spring — Pinion Stop

Armature — Field Coil

Fig. 30   Delco-Remy starter with enclosed shift lever

noids have an additional small terminal which is identified with the letter "R". To this terminal is attached a small metal finger which makes contact with a disc inside the solenoid when it is energized. On the vehicle, this terminal is connected to the battery side of the ignition coil. The purpose of this is to short out the ignition resistor during cranking and thereby provide high ignition coil output for starting the engine.

NOTE: On vehicles equipped with High Energy Ignition (HEI), the "R" terminal is eliminated since the resistance wire is not used.

Maintenance

Most motors of this type have graph-ite and oil impregnated bronze bearings which ordinarily require no added lubrication except at times of overhaul when a few drops of light engine oil should be placed on each bearing before reassembly.

Motors provided with hinge cap oilers should have 8-10 drops of light engine oil every 5000 miles, or every 300 hours of operation. Since the motor and brushes cannot be inspected without disassembling the unit, there is no service that can be performed with the unit assembled on the vehicle.

Free Speed Test

With the circuit connected as shown in Fig. 32, use a tachometer to measure armature revolutions per minute. Failure of the motor to perform to specifications may be due to tight or dry bearings, or high resistance connections.

Pinion Clearance

There is no provision for adjusting pinion clearance on this type motor. When the shift lever mechanism is correctly assembled, the pinion clearance should fall within the limits of .010 to .140". When the clearance is not within these limits, it may indicate excessive wear of the solenoid linkage or shift lever yoke buttons.

Pinion clearance should be checked after the motor has been disassembled and reassembled. To check, disconnect motor field coil connector from solenoid terminal and insulate end. Connect one battery lead to solenoid switch terminal and the other lead to the solenoid frame, Fig. 33. Using a jumper lead connected to the solenoid motor terminal, momentarily flash the lead to the solenoid frame. This will shift the pinion into the cranking position until the battery is disconnected.

After energizing the solenoid with the clutch shifted toward the pinion stop retainer, push the pinion back toward the commutator end as far as possible to take up any slack movement; then check the clearance with feeler gauge, Fig. 34.

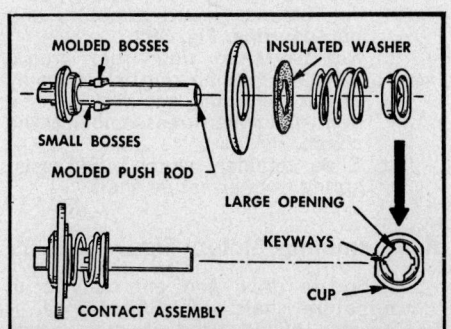

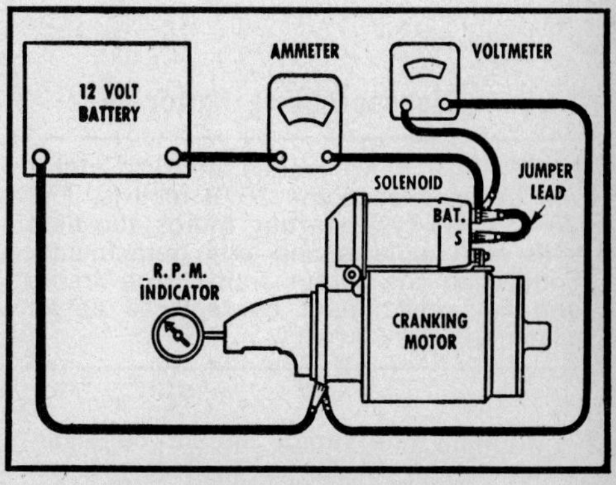

Fig. 31   Solenoid contact assembly

MOLDED BOSSES — INSULATED WASHER

SMALL BOSSES

MOLDED PUSH ROD

LARGE OPENING

KEYWAYS

CUP

CONTACT ASSEMBLY

12 VOLT BATTERY — AMMETER — VOLTMETER

SOLENOID — JUMPER LEAD

BAT. S

R.P.M. INDICATOR — CRANKING MOTOR

Fig. 32   Connections for checking free speed of motor

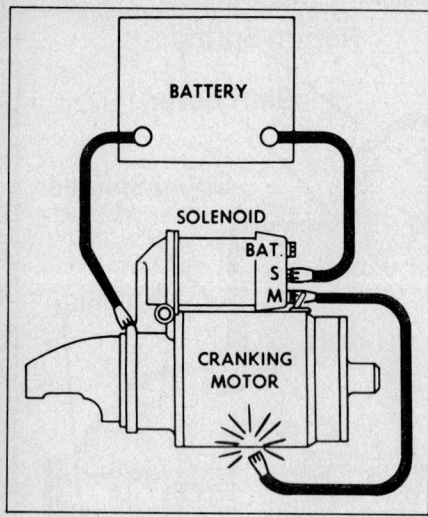

Fig. 33   Connections for checking pinion clearance

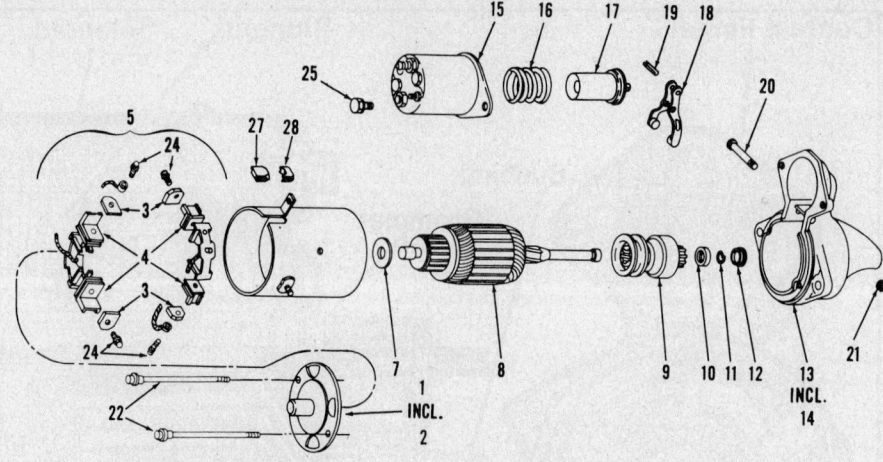

1.	FRAME—COMMUTATOR END	15.	SCREW—BRUSH ATTACHING
2.	BRUSH AND HOLDER PKG.	16.	SCREW—FIELD LEAD TO SWITCH
3.	BRUSH	17.	SCREW—SWITCH ATTACHING
4.	BRUSH HOLDER	18.	WASHER—BRAKE
5.	HOUSING—DRIVE END	19.	THRU BOLT
6.	FRAME AND FIELD ASM.	20.	BUSHING—COMMUTATOR END
7.	SOLENOID SWITCH	21.	BUSHING—DRIVE END
8.	ARMATURE	22.	PINION STOP COLLAR
9.	DRIVE ASM.	23.	THRUST COLLAR
10.	PLUNGER	24.	GROMMET
11.	SHIFT LEVER	25.	GROMMET
12.	PLUNGER RETURN SPRINGER	26.	PLUNGER PIN
13.	SHIFT LEVER SHAFT	27.	PINION STOP RETAINER RING
14.	LOCK WASHER	28.	LEVER SHAFT RETAINING RING

Fig. 35   Disassembled view of Delco-Remy 5MT series starting motor

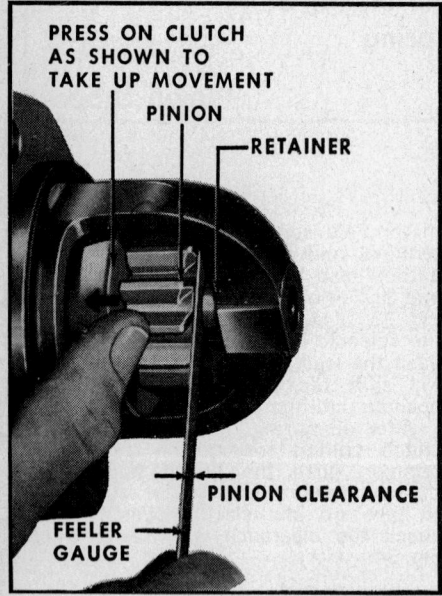

Fig. 34   Checking pinion clearance

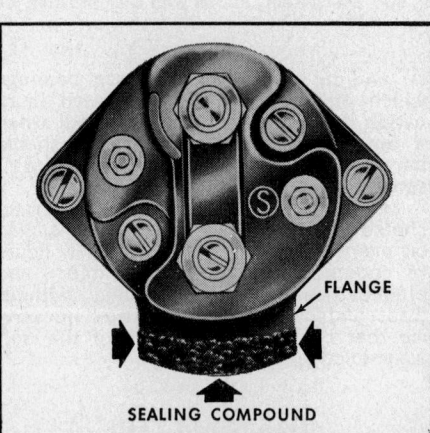

Fig. 36   Sealing solenoid housing to frame

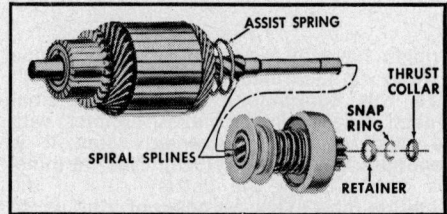

Fig. 37   View of armature and over-running clutch

a) Slide thrust collar off end of armature shaft, Fig. 37.
b) Slide a standard ½" pipe coupling, a ⅝" deep socket or other metal cylinder of suitable size onto shaft so end of coupling or cylinder butts against edge of retainer. Tap end of coupling with hammer, driving retainer toward armature and off snap ring, Fig. 38.
c) Remove snap ring from groove in shaft. If snap ring is too badly distorted during removal, use a new one when reassembling the clutch.
d) Slide retainer, clutch and assist spring from armature shaft.

Reassembling Motor, Figs. 35 & 39

1. Lubricate drive end and splines of armature shaft with SAE 10 oil. If heavier oil is used it may cause failure to mesh at low temperatures.

Disassembling Motor

NOTE: The 5 MT series starting motor will be used on some 1978 models, Fig. 35. On this type starting motor, the field coils and pole shoes are permanently bonded to the motor frame. The frame and field coils must be replaced as an assembly.

Normally the motor should be disassembled only so far as necessary to repair or replace defective parts.

1. Disconnect field coil connectors from solenoid "motor" terminal.
2. Remove thru bolts.
3. Remove commutator end frame and field frame assembly.
4. Remove armature assembly from drive housing. On some models it may be necessary to remove solenoid and shift lever assembly from the drive housing before removing the armature assembly. *Important: When solenoid is installed, apply sealing compound between field frame and solenoid flange, Fig. 36.*
5. Remove overrunning clutch from armature shaft as follows:

2. Place "assist" spring on drive end of shaft next to armature, with small end against lamination stack.

3. Slide clutch assembly onto armature shaft with pinion outward.

4. Slide retainer onto shaft with cupped surface facing end of shaft.

5. Stand armature on end on wood surface with commutator down. Position snap ring on upper end of shaft and hold in place with a block of wood. Hit wood block with a hammer forcing snap ring over end of shaft, Fig. 40. Slide snap ring into groove, squeezing it to ensure a good fit in groove.

6. Assemble thrust collar on shaft with shoulder next to snap ring.

7. Position retainer and thrust collar next to snap ring. With clutch pressed against assist spring, for clearance next to retainer, use two pairs of pliers at the same time (one pair on either side of shaft) to grip retainer and thrust collar. Then squeeze until snap ring is forced into retainer, Fig. 41.

8. Place 4 or 5 drops of SAE 10 oil in drive housing bushing. Make sure thrust collar is in place against snap ring and retainer; then slide armature and clutch assembly into place in drive housing.

9. Attach solenoid and shift lever assembly to drive housing. Be sure lever buttons are located between sides of clutch collar.

10. Position field frame over armature, *applying sealing compound between frame and solenoid flange* (Fig. 36). Position frame against drive housing, using care to prevent damage to brushes.

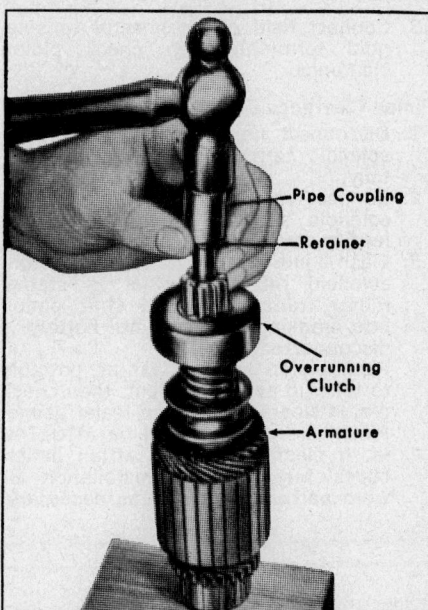

Fig. 38 Removing over-running clutch snap ring retainer

11. Place 4 or 5 drops of SAE 10 oil in bushing in commutator end frame. Make sure leather brake washer is on armature shaft; then slide commutator end frame onto shaft.

12. Install thru bolts and tighten securely.

13. Reconnect field coil connectors to solenoid "motor" terminal.

1978 V8-350 Diesel

Disassemble

1. Remove screw from field coil connector and solenoid mounting screws, then rotate solenoid 90° and remove solenoid with plunger return spring, Fig. 42.

2. Remove two through bolts, then commutator end frame with washer.

3. Remove end frame assembly from drive gear housing.

4. Remove shift lever pivot bolt.

5. Remove center bearing screws, then remove drive gear housing from armature shaft. Shift lever and plunger assembly, should fall from starter clutch.

6. Remove thrust washer or collar from armature shaft.

7. Position a 5/8 in. deep socket over shaft against retainer, then tap socket to move retainer off snap ring.

8. Remove snap ring from groove in shaft, then remove retainer, clutch assembly, fiber washer and center bearing from armature shaft.

9. Remove roll pin and separate shift lever and plunger.

10. Remove brush pivot pin and brush spring, then replace brushes as necessary.

Assemble

1. Lubricate drive end of armature with lubricant 1960954 or equivalent.

2. Install center bearing with bearing facing toward armature winding, then install fiber washer on armature shaft, Fig. 42.

3. Position clutch assembly on armature shaft with pinion facing away from armature.

4. Position retainer on armature shaft

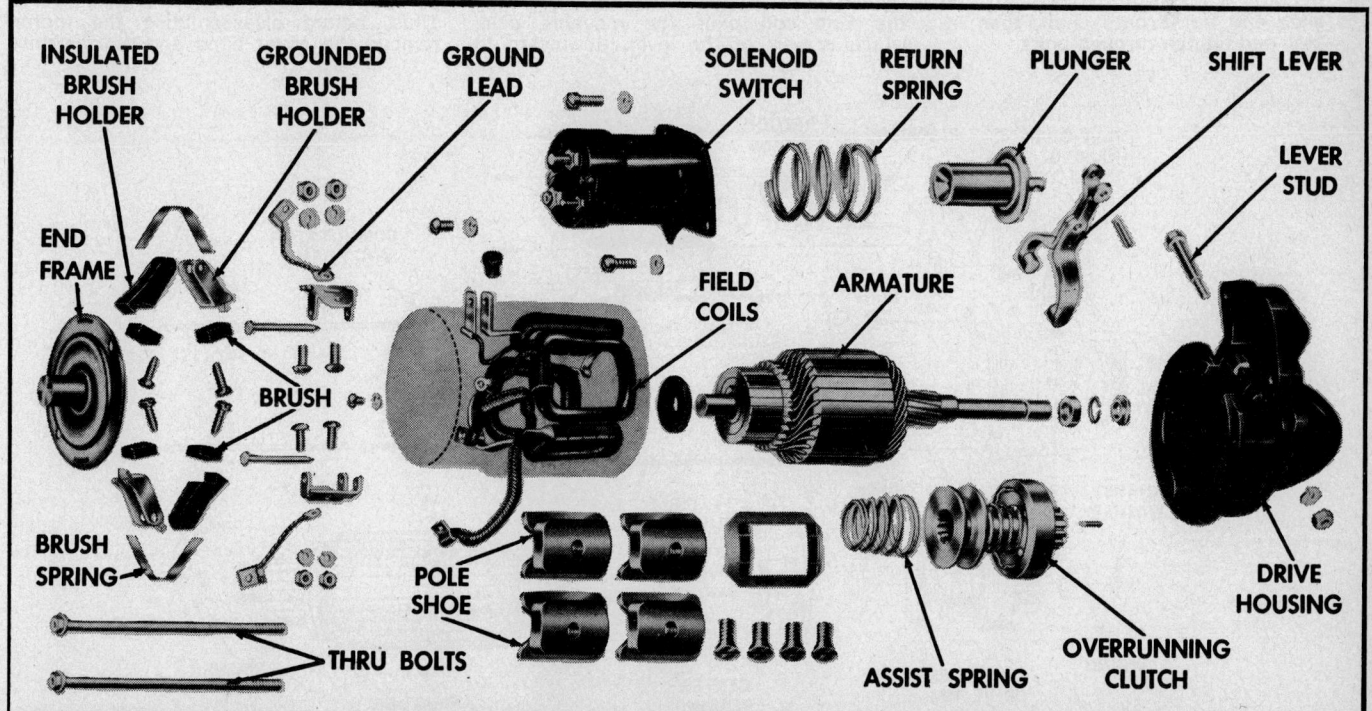

Fig. 39   Disassembled view of Delco-Remy 10MT series starting motor

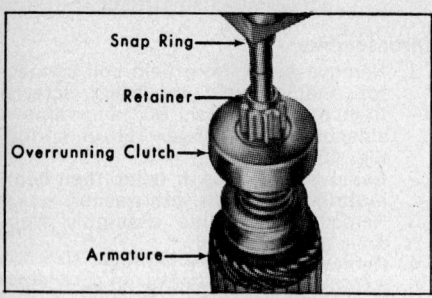

Fig. 40 Installing snap ring onto armature shaft

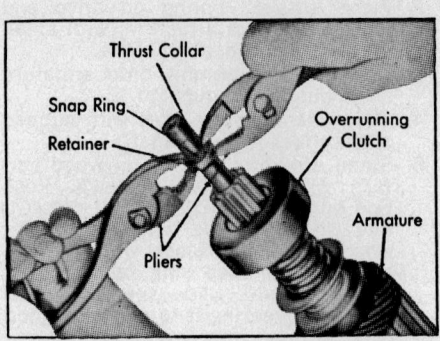

Fig. 41 Installing snap ring into retainer

15. Connect field coil connector to solenoid terminal, then check pinion clearance.

Pinion Clearance Check

1. Disconnect field coil connector from solenoid terminal and insulate carefully.
2. Connect one 12 volt battery lead to solenoid switch terminal and other lead to starter motor frame.
3. Flash a jumper lead momentarily from solenoid motor terminal to starter motor frame. This will shift pinion into cranking position until battery is disconnected.
4. Push pinion back as far as possible to take up any movement, then check pinion clearance using a feeler gauge. Pinion clearance should be .010-.140 in. If clearance is not within limits, check for improper installation or worn parts and replace as necessary.

with cupped side facing end of shaft.
5. Install snap ring into groove on armature shaft, then install trust washer.
6. Using two pliers, grip retainer and thrust washer or collar and squeeze until snap ring is forced into retainer and is held securely in groove on armature shaft.
7. Lubricate drive end housing bushing with lubricant 1960954 or equivalent.
8. Engage shift lever yoke with clutch and slide complete assembly into drive gear housing.
9. Install center bearing attaching screws and shift lever pivot bolt.
10. Install solenoid on drive gear housing.
11. Apply sealer No. 1050026 or equivalent to solenoid flange where field frame contacts solenoid.
12. Position field frame against drive gear housing on alignment pin, using care to prevent damage to brushes.
13. Lubricate commutator end frame bushing with lubricant 1960954 or equivalent.
14. Install washer on armature shaft and slide end frame onto shaft, then install and tighten through bolts.

FORD MOTORCRAFT STARTER WITH INTEGRAL POSITIVE ENGAGEMENT DRIVE

This type starting motor, Figs. 43 through 45A, is a four pole, series parallel unit with a positive engagement drive built into the starter. The drive mechanism is engaged with the flywheel by lever action before the motor is energized.

When the ignition switch is turned on to the start position, the starter relay is energized and supplies current to the motor. The current flows through one field coil and a set of contact points to ground. The magnetic field given off by the field coil pulls the movable pole, which is part of the lever, downward to

its seat. When the pole is pulled down, the lever moves the drive assembly into the engine flywheel, Fig. 46.

When the movable pole is seated, it functions as a normal field pole and opens the contact points. With the points open, current flows through the starter field coils, energizing the starter. At the same time, current also flows through a holding coil to hold the movable pole in its seated position.

When the ignition switch is released from the start position, the starter relay opens the circuit to the starting motor. This allows the return spring to force the lever back, disengaging the drive from the flywheel and returning the movable pole to its normal position, Fig. 47.

1974-77 Units

Disassemble, Figs. 43 & 44

It may not be necessary to disassemble the starter completely to accomplish repair or replacement of certain parts. Thus, before disassembling the motor, remove the cover band and starter drive

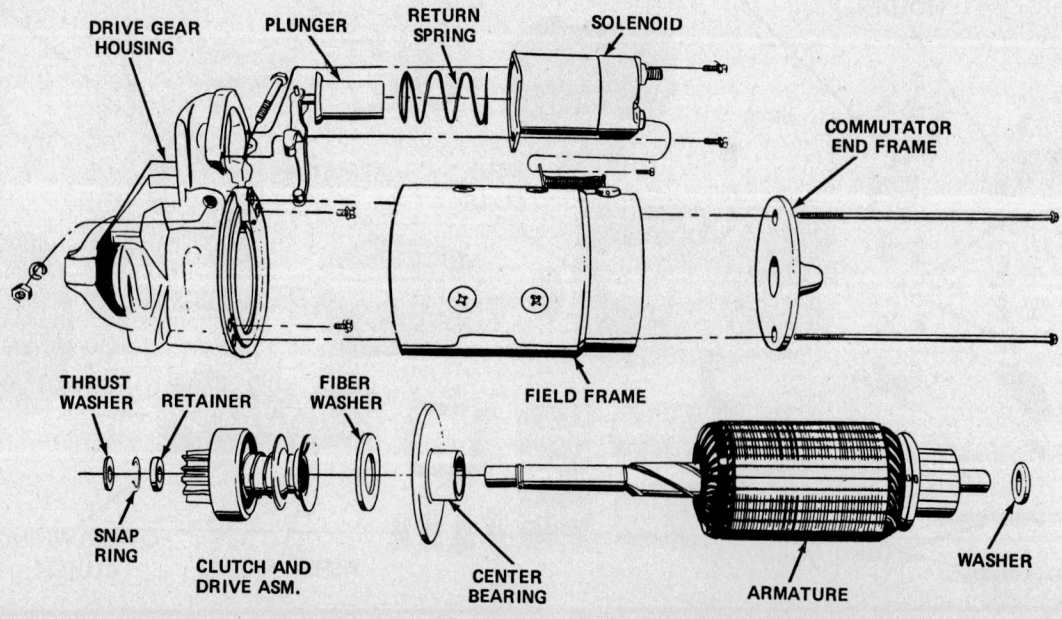

Fig. 42 Disassembled view of Delco-Remy 25 MT series starting motor. 1978 V8-350 diesel

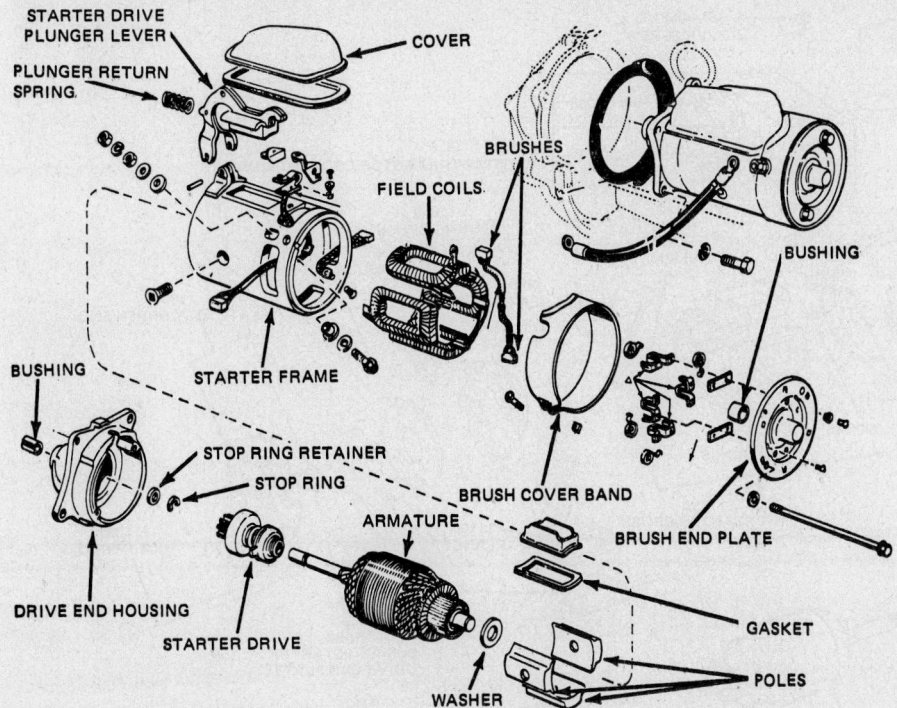

Fig. 43 Ford Motorcraft positive engagement starting motor. 1974-77 except V6-2800cc engine

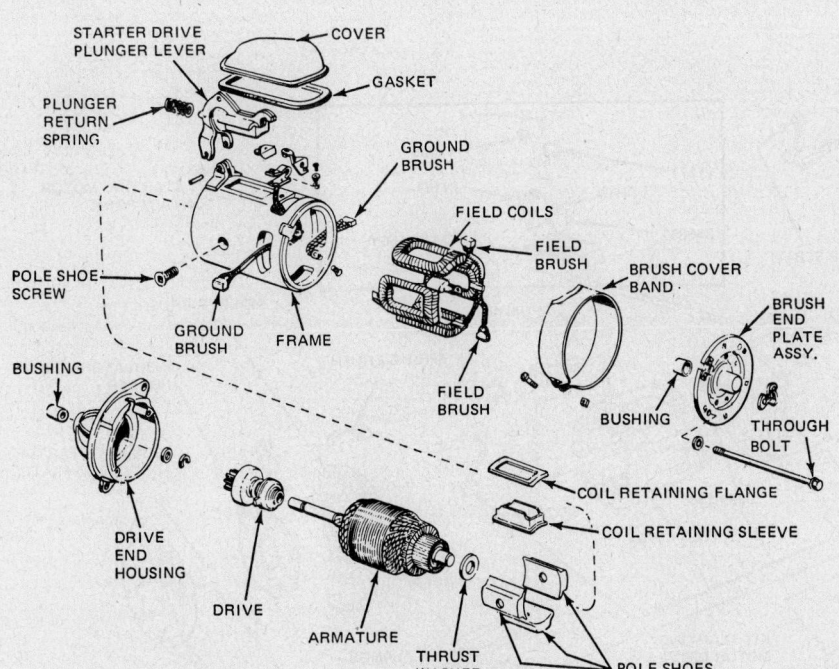

Fig. 44 Ford Motorcraft positive engagement starting motor. 1974-77 V6-2800cc engine

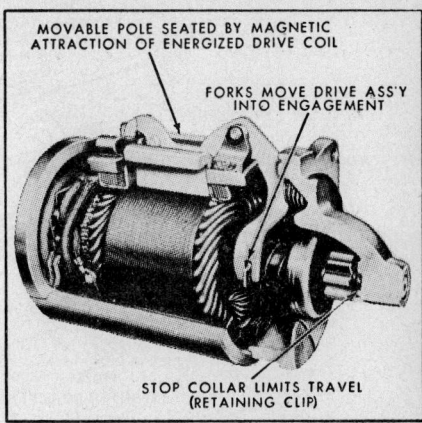

Fig. 46 Starter drive engaged

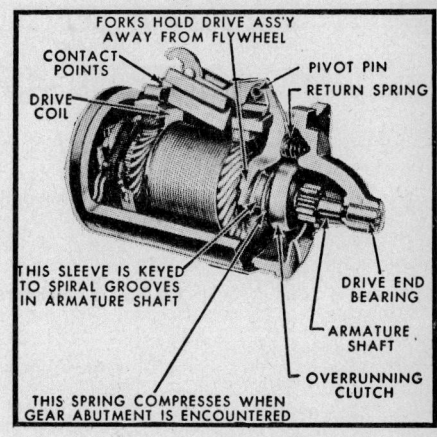

Fig. 47 Starter drive disengaged

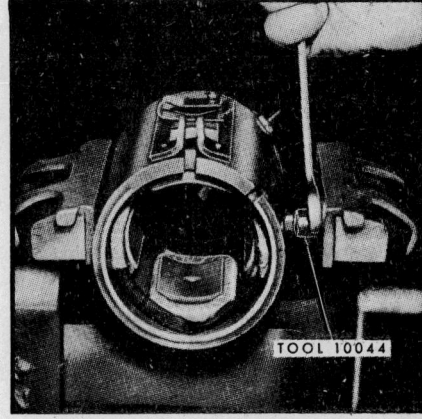

Fig. 48 Removing field coil pole shoe screws

actuating lever cover. Examine brushes to make sure they are free in their holders. Replace brushes if defective or worn beyond their useful limit. Check the tension of each brush spring with a pull scale. Spring Tension should not be less than 45 ounces. If disassembly is necessary, proceed as follows:

1. Remove cover band and starter drive actuating lever cover.
2. Remove through bolts, starter drive gear housing, drive gear retaining clip cup and starter drive actuating lever return spring.

3. Remove pivot pin retaining starter gear actuating lever and remove lever and armature.
4. Remove and discard spring clip retaining starter drive gear to end of armature shaft, and remove starter drive gear.

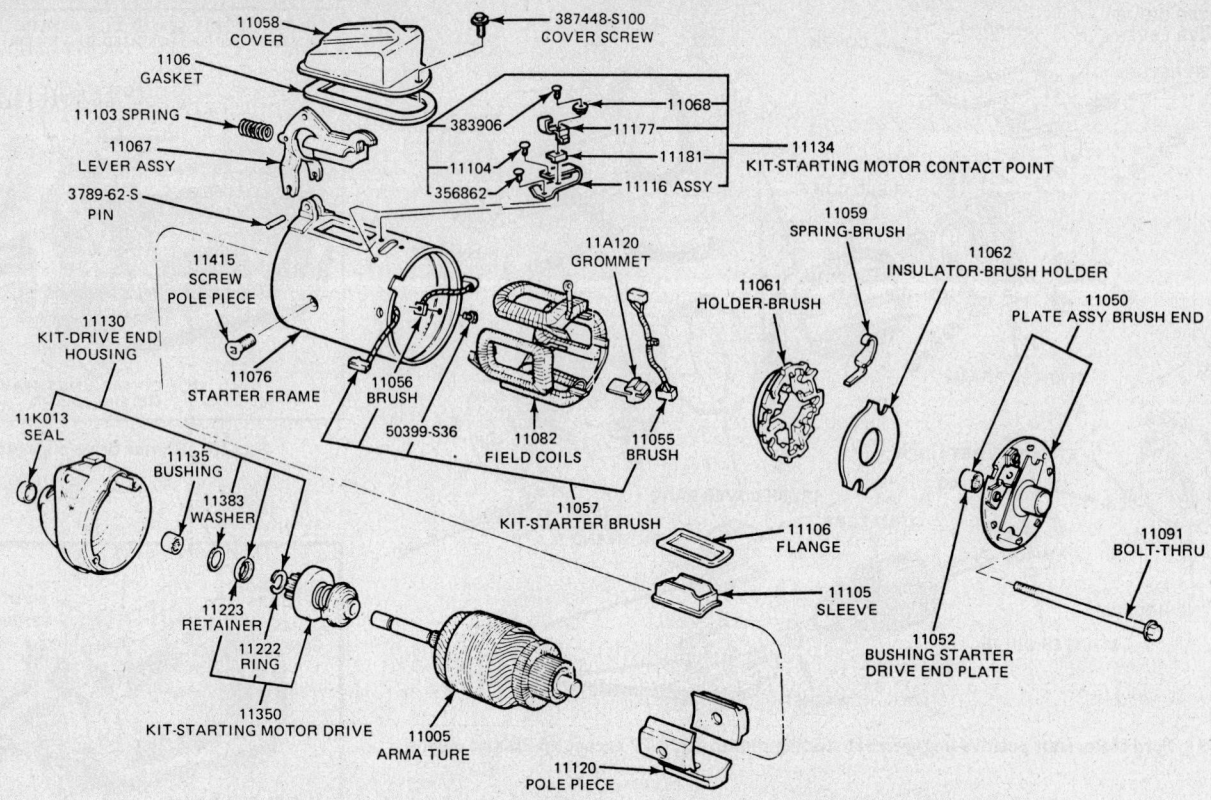

Fig. 45 Ford Motorcraft positive engagement starting motor. 1978 4-2300cc & V6-2800cc engines

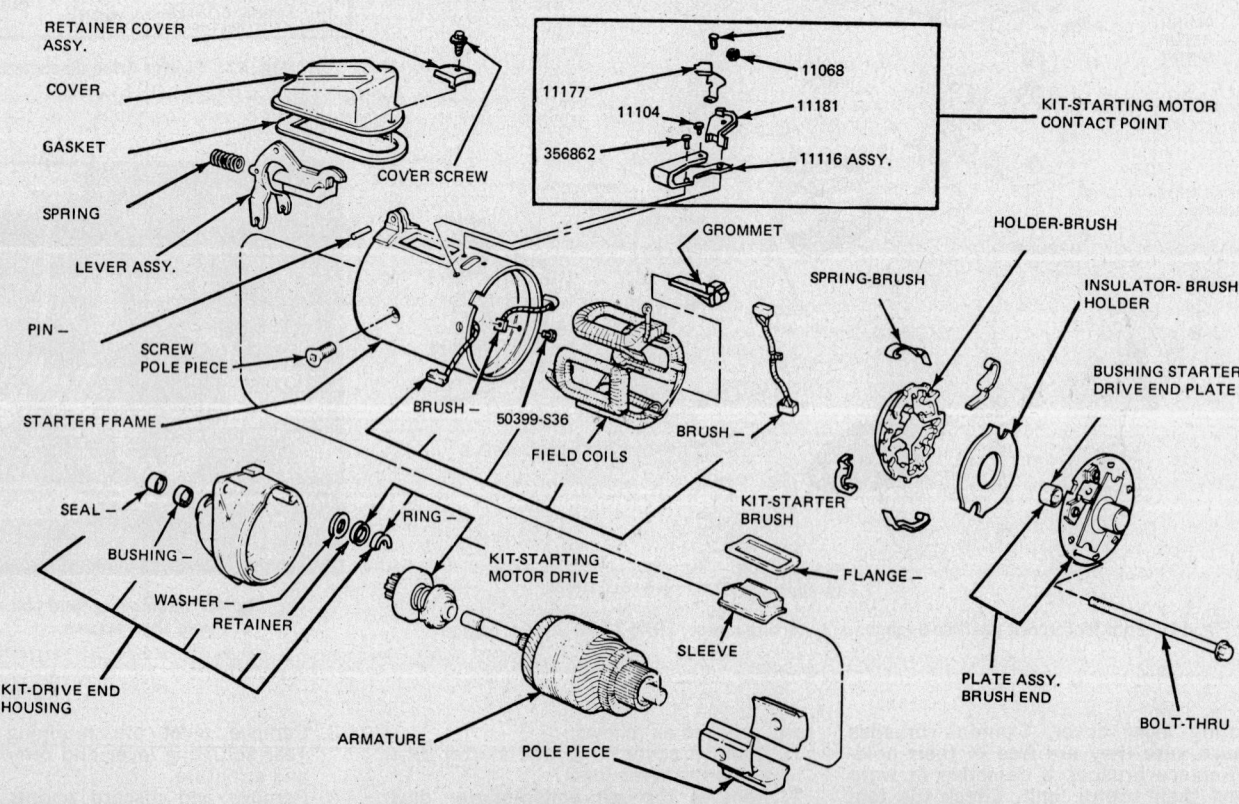

Fig. 45A Ford Motorcraft positive engagement starting motor. 1978 except 4-2300cc & V6-2800cc engines

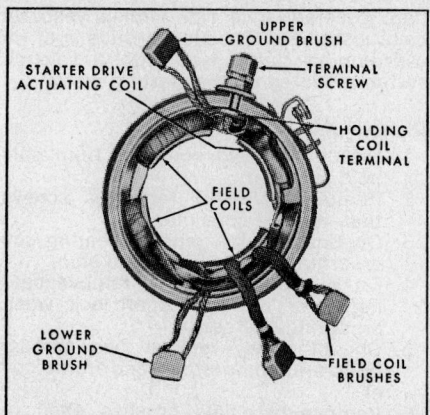

Fig. 49   Field coil assembly

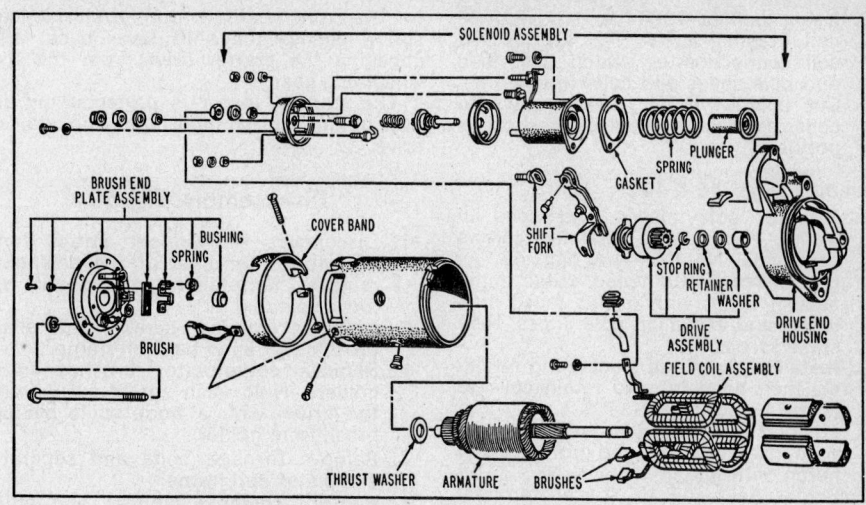

Fig. 50   Ford Motorcraft solenoid actuated starter, exploded

5. Remove commutator brushes from brush holders and remove brush end plate.
6. Remove two screws retaining ground brushes to frame.
7. On the field coil that operates the drive gear actuating lever, bend tab up on field retainer and remove retainer.
8. Remove field coil retainer screws, Fig. 48. Unsolder field coil leads from terminal screw, and remove pole shoes and coils from frame.
9. Remove starter terminal nut and related parts. Remove any excess solder from terminal slot.

Assemble, Figs. 43 & 44

1. Install starter terminal, insulator, washers and retaining nut in frame, Fig. 49. Be sure to position slot in screw perpendicular to frame end surface.

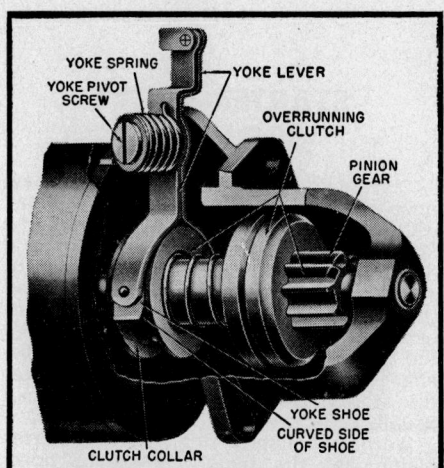

Fig. 51 Overrunning clutch drive. When assembling, make sure curved sides of yoke shoes are toward gear end of clutch. Reversed yoke shoes can cause improper meshing of pinion

2. Install field coils and pole pieces. As pole shoe screws are tightened, strike frame several sharp blows with a soft-faced hammer to seat and align pole shoes, then stake the screws.
3. Install solenoid coil retainer and bend tabs to retain tabs to frame.
4. Solder field coils and solenoid wire to starter terminal, using rosin core solder.
5. Check for continuity and grounds in the assembled coils.
6. Position solenoid coil ground terminal over ground screw hole nearest starter terminal.
7. Position ground brushes to starter frame and install retaining screws, Fig. 49.
8. Position starter brush end plate to frame with end plate boss in frame slot.
9. Install drive gear to armature shaft and install a new retaining spring clip.
10. Position fiber thrust washer on commutator end of armature shaft and install armature in frame.
11. Install starter drive actuating lever to frame and starter drive, and install pivot pin.
12. Position actuating lever return spring and drive gear housing to frame and install through bolts. Do not pinch brush leads between brush plate and frame.
13. Install brushes in holders, being sure to center brush springs on brushes.
14. Position drive gear actuating lever cover on starter and install brush cover band.

1978 Units

Disassemble, Figs. 45 & 45A

1. Remove cover screw, cover, through bolts, starter drive end housing and starter drive plunger lever return spring.
2. Remove plunger lever retaining pin, then remove lever and armature.

3. Remove stop ring retainer from armature shaft, then remove stop ring and starter drive gear assembly.
4. Remove brush end plate and insulator assembly.
5. Remove brushes from brush holder, then remove brush holder. Note position of brush holder to end terminal.
6. Remove two screws retaining ground brushes to frame.
7. Bend up edges of sleeve inserted in frame, then remove sleeve and retainer.
8. Detach field coil ground wire from copper tab on frame.

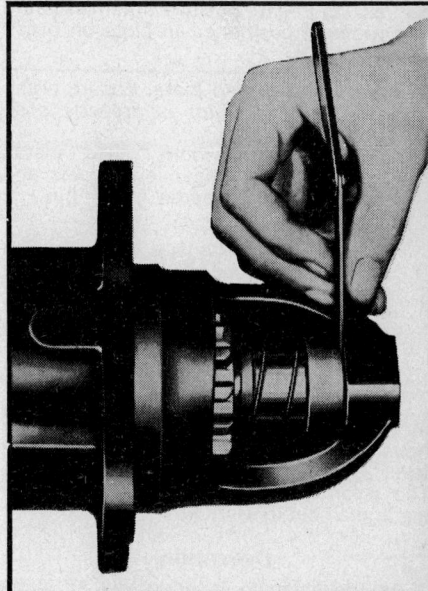

Fig. 52 Measuring overrunning clutch drive stop clearance. Do not compress anti-drift spring as this will give an incorrect clearance. If clearance is not present there is danger of the drive housing being broken as gear or collar slams back against it

9. Using tool No. 10044-A, remove three coil retaining screws, Fig. 48. Cut field coil connection at switch post lead and pole shoes and coils from frame.
10. Cut positive brush leads from field coils, as close to field connection as possible.

Assemble, Figs. 45 & 45A

1. Position pole pieces and coils in frame, then install retaining screws using tool No. 10044-A, Fig. 48. As pole shoes are tightened, strike frame several times with a soft faced mallet to seat and align pole shoes, then stake screws.
2. Install plunger coil sleeve and retainer, then bend tabs to retain coils to frame.
3. Position grommet on end terminal, then insert terminal and grommet into notch on frame.
4. Solder field coil to starter terminal post strap.

NOTE: Use 300 watt soldering iron and rosin core solder.

5. Check coils for continuity and grounds.
6. Position brushes to starter frame and install retaining screws.
7. Apply a thin coat of Lubriplate 777 or equivalent to armature shaft splines.
8. Install drive gear assembly on armature shaft, then install stop ring and stop ring retainer.
9. Install armature into starter frame.
10. Position starter drive gear plunger to frame and starter drive assembly, then install pivot assembly. Fill end housing bearing bore approximately ¼ full with grease, then position drive end housing to frame.
11. Install brush holder, then insert brushes into holder and install brush springs.

NOTE: Ensure positive brush leads are properly positioned in slots on brush holder.

12. Install brush end plate. Ensure brush end plate insulator is properly positioned.
13. Install through bolts, then install starter drive plunger lever cover and tighten retaining screw.

FORD MOTORCRAFT SOLENOID ACTUATED STARTER

Description

The solenoid assembly, in this unit, is mounted to a flange on the starter drive housing which encloses the entire shift lever and solenoid plunger mechanism The solenoid incorporates a pull-in winding and a hold-in winding.

Operation

As the solenoid is energized, it shifts the starting motor pinion into mesh with the engine flywheel ring gear.

At the same time, the solenoid contacts are closed and battery current flows to the motor, turning it and the engine.

After the engine starts, the starter drive is disengaged when the ignition switch is returned from the start position

to the run position and the solenoid spring pushes the shift lever back, disengaging the starter drive from the flywheel ring gear.

The starting motor is protected by an overrunning clutch built into the starter drive.

Disassembly, Fig. 50

1. Disconnect the copper strap from the starter terminal of the solenoid, remove the retaining screws and remove solenoid.
2. Loosen retaining screw and slide brush cover band back on frame.
3. Remove commutator brushes from holders. Hold each spring away from the brush with a hook while sliding brush from holder.
4. Remove through bolts and separate end plates and frame.
5. Remove solenoid plunger and shift fork assembly.
6. Remove armature and drive assembly from frame. Remove drive stop ring and slide drive assembly from shaft. Remove fiber thrust washer from commutator end of shaft.
7. Remove drive stop ring retainer from shaft.

Reassembly

1. Install drive assembly on shaft and install new stop ring.
2. Install solenoid plunger and shift fork.
3. Place new retainer in drive housing and install armature and drive in housing. Be sure shift lever tangs properly engage drive assembly.
4. Install fiber washer on commutator end of shaft and position frame to drive housing, being sure to index frame and drive housing correctly.
5. Install brush plate assembly being sure to index it properly, install through bolts and tighten to 55-75 in lbs.
6. Install brushes by pulling each spring away from holder with a hook to allow entry of the brush. Center the brush springs on the brushes. Press insulated brush leads away from all other components to prevent possible shorts.
7. Install rubber gasket and solenoid.
8. Connect copper strap to starter terminal of solenoid.
9. Position cover band and tighten retaining screw.
10. Connect starter to battery and check operation.

BOSCH & NIPPONDENSO STARTER MOTORS

Dodge Omni & Plymouth Horizon

Description

Four direct drive starting motors are used on the Dodge Omni & Plymouth Horizon. All the starting motors are almost identical except in the pinion housing area. Bosch units are painted black, while Nippondenso units have an alumi-

num covered drive side with a yellowish color elsewhere. The starter drive is of the overrunning clutch type with a solenoid switch mounted on the starting motor.

Disassembly

1. Disconnect field coil wire from solenoid terminal.
2. Remove solenoid retaining screws, then remove solenoid.
3. On Bosch units, remove bearing cover, armature shaft lock and shim.
4. On Nippondenso units, remove bearing cover, armature shaft lock, washer, spring and seal.
5. On all units, remove two through bolts and commutator end frame cover.
6. Remove two field brushes, then remove brush holder.
7. Remove field end frame.
8. Remove shift lever pivot bolt.
9. Remove rubber gasket and metal plate.
10. Remove armature and shift lever from drive end housing.
11. Press stop collar from snap ring, then remove snap ring, stop collar and clutch.

Assemble

1. Lubricate armature shaft and splines with SAE 10W or 30 engine oil.
2. Install starter clutch, stop collar and lock ring on armature shaft.
3. Position armature and shift fork into drive end housing.
4. Install shift lever pivot bolt.
5. Install rubber gasket and metal plate.
6. Install field end frame.
7. Install brush holder and brush.
8. Position commutator end frame, then install two through bolts.
9. On Bosch units, install shim and armature shaft lock, then check armature end play. End play should be .05 to .3 mm. Install bearing cover.
10. On Nippondenso units, install seal, spring, washer, armature shaft lock and bearing cover.
11. Position solenoid to shift lever, then install retaining screws.
12. Connect field coil wire to solenoid.

STARTER DRIVE TROUBLES

Starter drive troubles are easy to diagnose and they usually cannot be confused with ordinary starter difficulties. If the starter does not turn over at all or if it drags, look for trouble in the starter or electrical supply system. Concentrate on the starter drive or ring gear if the starter is noisy, if it turns but does not engage the engine, or if the starter won't disengage after the engine is started. After the starter is removed, the trouble can usually be located quickly.

Worn or chipped ring gear or starter pinion are the usual causes of noisy operation. Before replacing either or both of these parts try to find out what caused the damage. With the Bendix type drive, incomplete engagement of the pinion with the ring gear is a common cause of tooth damage. The wrong pinion clearance on starter drives of the overrunning clutch type leads to poor meshing of the pinion and ring gear and too rapid tooth wear.

A less common cause of noise with either type of drive is a bent starter armature shaft. When this shaft is bent, the pinion gear alternately binds and then only partly meshes with the ring gear. Most manufacturers specify a maximum of .003" radial run-out on the armature shaft.

When Clutch Drive Fails

The over-running clutch type drive seldom becomes so worn that it fails to engage since it is directly activated by a fork and lever, Fig. 51. The only thing that is likely to happen is that, once engaged, it will not turn the engine because the clutch itself is worn out. A much more frequent difficulty and one that rapidly wears ring gear and teeth is partial engagement. Proper meshing of the pinion is controlled by the end clearance between the pinion gear and the starter housing or pinion stop, if used.

The clearance is set with the starter off the car and with the drive in the engaged position. To check the clearance, supply current to the starter solenoid with the electrical connection between starter and solenoid removed. Supplying

current to the solenoid but not the starter will prevent the starter from rotating during the test. Take out all slack by pushing lightly on the starter drive clutch housing while inserting a feeler gauge between pinion and housing or pinion stop, Fig. 52.

On late model cars, the solenoids are completely enclosed in the starter housing and the pinion clearance is not adjustable. If the clearance is not correct, the starter must be disassembled and checked for excessive wear of solenoid linkage, shift lever mechanism, or improper assembly of parts.

Failure of the over-running clutch drive to disengage is usually caused by binding between the armature shaft and the drive. If the drive, particularly the clutch, shows signs of overheating it indicates that it is not disengaging immediately after the engine starts. If the clutch is forced to over-run too long, it overheats and turns a bluish color. For the cause of the binding, look for rust or gum between the armature shaft and the drive, or for burred splines. Excess oil on the drive will lead to gumming, and inadequate air circulation in the flywheel housing will cause rust.

Over-running clutch drives cannot be overhauled in the field so they must be replaced. In cleaning, never soak them

in a solvent because the solvent may enter the clutch and dissolve the sealed-in lubricant. Wipe them off lightly with kerosene and lubricate them sparingly with SAE 10 or 10W oil.

When Bendix Drive Fails

When a Bendix type drive doesn't engage the cause usually is one of three things: either the drive spring is broken, one of the drive spring bolts has sheared off, or the screwshaft threads won't allow the pinion to travel toward the flywheel. In the first two cases, remove the drive by unscrewing the set screw under the last coil of the drive spring and replace the broken parts. Gummed or rusty screwshaft threads are fairly common causes of Bendix drive failure and are easily cleaned with a little kerosene or steel wool, depending on the trouble. Here again, as in the case of over-running clutch drives, use light oil sparingly, and be sure the flywheel housing has adequate ventilation. There is usually a breather hole in the bottom of the flywheel housing which should be open.

The failure of a Bendix drive to disengage or to mesh properly is most often caused by gummed or rusty screwshaft threads. When this is not true, look for mechanical failure within the drive itself.

ALTERNATOR SYSTEMS

CONTENTS

INTRODUCTION

Alternators are composed of the same functional parts as the conventional D.C. generator but they operate differently: The field is called a rotor and is the turning portion of the unit. A generating part, called a stator, is the stationary member, comparable to the armature in a D.C. generator. The regulator, similar to those used in a D.C. system, regulates the output of the alternator-rectifier system.

The power source of the system is the alternator. Current is transmitted from

the field terminal of the regulator through a slip ring to the field coil and back to ground through another slip ring. The strength of the field regulates the output of the alternating current. This alternating current is then transmitted from the alternator to the rectifier where it is converted to direct current.

These alternators employ a three-phase stator winding in which the phase windings are electrically 120 degrees apart. The rotor consists of a field coil encased between interleaved sections producing a magnetic field with alternate north and south poles. By rotating the rotor inside the stator the alternating current is induced in the stator windings. This alternating current is rectified (changed to D.C.) by silicon diodes and brought out to the output terminal of the alternator.

Diode Rectifiers

Six silicon diode rectifiers are used and act as electrical one-way-valves. Three of the diodes have ground polarity and are pressed or screwed into a heat sink which is grounded. The other three diodes (ungrounded) are pressed or screwed into and insulated from the end head; these diodes are connected to the alternator output terminal.

Since the diodes have a high resistance to the flow of current in one direction and a low resistance in the opposite direction, they may be connected in a manner which allows current to flow from the alternator to the battery in the low resistance direction. The high resistance in the opposite direction prevents the flow of current from the battery to the alternator. Because of this feature no circuit breaker is required between the alternator and battery.

SERVICE PRECAUTIONS

1. Be certain that battery polarity is correct when servicing units. Reversed battery polarity will damage rectifiers and regulators.

2. If booster battery is used for starting, be sure to use correct polarity in hook up.

3. When a fast charger is used to charge a vehicle battery, the vehicle battery cables should be disconnected *unless the fast charger is equipped with a special Alternator Protector,* in which case the vehicle battery cables need not be disconnected. Also the fast charger should

never be used to start a vehicle as damage to rectifiers will result.

4. Lead connections to the grounded rectifiers (negative) on Chrysler units should never be soldered as the excessive heat may damage the rectifiers.

5. Unless the system includes a load relay or field relay, grounding the alternator output terminal will damage the alternator and/or circuits. This is true even when the system is not in operation since no circuit breaker is used and the battery is

applied to the alternator output terminal at all times. The field or load relay acts as a circuit breaker in that it is controlled by the ignition switch.

6. When adjusting the voltage regulator, do not short the adjusting tool to the regulator base as the regulator may be damaged. The tool should be insulated by taping or by installing a plastic sleeve.

7. Before making any "on vehicle" tests of the alternator or regulator, the battery should be checked and the circuit inspected for faulty wir-

ing or insulation, loose or corroded connections and poor ground circuits.

8. Check alternator belt tension to be sure the belt is tight enough to prevent slipping under load.

9. The ignition switch should be off and the battery ground cable disconnected before making any test connections to the system to prevent damage to the system.

10. The vehicle battery must be fully charged or a fully charged battery may be installed for test purposes.

Chrysler Alternators

All Chrysler alternators except the 100 amp units are equipped with six silicon rectifiers, Figs. C1 and C2. The 100 amp alternators are equipped with twelve silicon rectifiers, Figs. C3 and C4. The charging system on all 1975-76 Chrysler Corp. vehicles except Dart and Valiant incorporates a field-loads relay, Fig. C5. This protects the battery from overcharging and provides a more consistent voltage to the electrical accessories. This field-loads relay, located between the battery and voltage regulator, brings the regulator electrically closer to the battery, thereby reducing the voltage drop between these components and also makes the regulator more sensitive to battery requirements than the previous system.

TESTING SYSTEM ON VEHICLE

Charging Circuit Resistance Test

1. Disconnect battery ground cable. Disconnect "Batt" lead at the al-

ternator.

2. Complete test connections as per Figs. C6, C7 and C8.

NOTE: Use a 0-100 amp ammeter.

---

3. Connect battery ground cable, start engine and operate at idle.

4. Adjust engine speed and carbon pile to obtain 20 amps in the circuit and check voltmeter reading. Reading should not exceed .7 volts. If a voltage drop is indicated, inspect, clean and tighten all connections in the circuit. A voltage drop test at each connection can be performed to isolate the trouble.

Current Output Test

1. Disconnect battery ground cable, complete test connections as per Figs. C9, C10 and C11 and start engine and operate at idle. *Immedi-*

ately after starting, reduce engine speed to idle.

2. Adjust the carbon pile and engine speed in increments until a speed of 1250 RPM and 15 volts are obtained on all units except 100 amp alternators. On 100 amp alternators, obtain engine speed of 900 RPM and 13 volts.

CAUTION: While increasing speed, do not allow voltage to exceed 16 volts.

3. Check ammeter reading. Output current should be within specifications.

Voltage Regulator Test

NOTE: Battery must be fully charged for test to be accurate.

---

1. Connect test equipment, Figs. C12, C13 and C14.

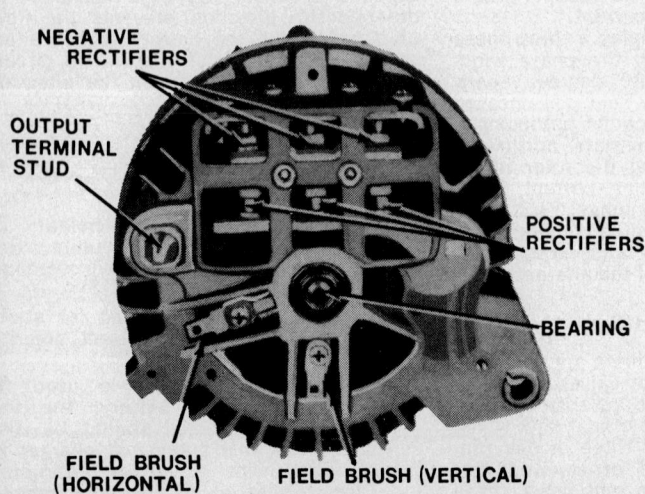

NEGATIVE RECTIFIERS

OUTPUT TERMINAL STUD

POSITIVE RECTIFIERS

BEARING

FIELD BRUSH (HORIZONTAL)

FIELD BRUSH (VERTICAL)

Fig. C1   Alternator assembly exc. 100 amp units. 1974-78

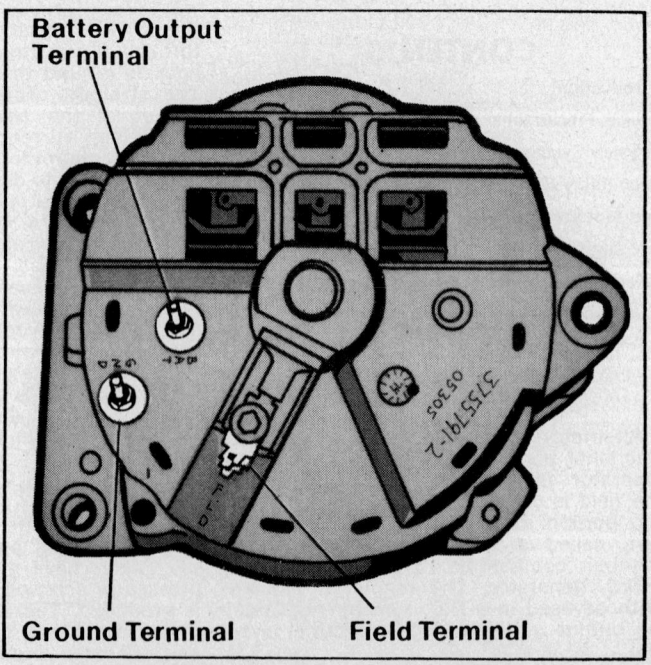

Battery Output Terminal

Ground Terminal

Field Terminal

Fig. C3   100 amp alternator assembly. 1975-78

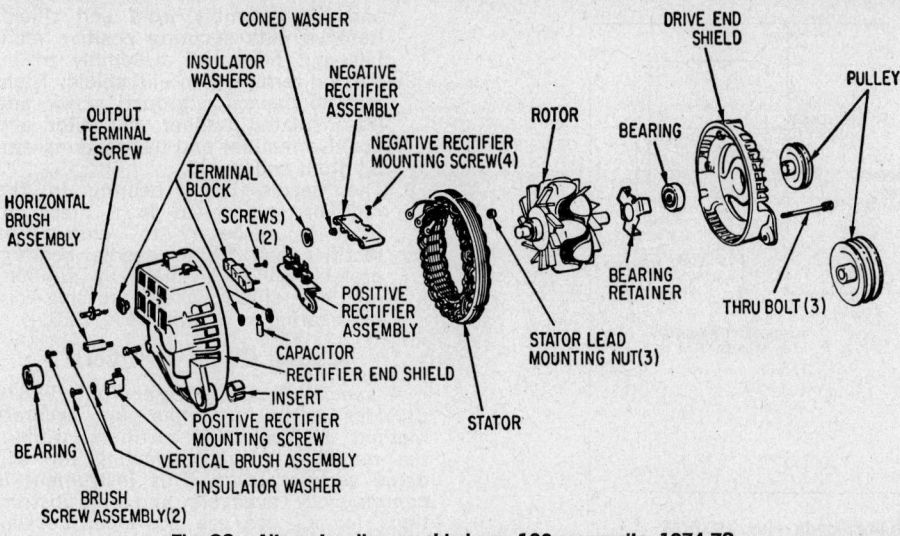

Fig. C2 Alternator disassembled exc. 100 amp units. 1974-78

BENCH TESTS

If the alternator performance does not meet current output specification limits, it will have to be disassembled for further tests and servicing.

To remove the alternator, disconnect the battery ground cable and the leads at the alternator. Then unfasten and remove the alternator from the vehicle.

Field Coil Draw

1. Connect jumper wire between one alternator field terminal and the positive terminal of a fully charged battery.
2. Connect test ammeter positive lead to the other alternator field terminal and the ammeter negative lead to the negative battery terminal.
3. Slowly rotate alternator rotor by hand. Field current at 12 volts should be 2.5-3.7 amps on 1974-75 units except

2. Start and run engine at 1250 RPM with all lights and accessories turned "Off". Voltage should be as specified in Fig. C15.
3. It is normal for the vehicle ammeter to indicate an immediate charge, then gradually return to the normal position.
4. If voltage is below limits or is fluctuating, proceed with the following:
   A. Check voltage regulator for proper ground. The ground is obtained through the regulator case to mounting screws, then to the vehicle sheet metal.
   B. With ignition switch "Off", disconnect voltage regulator connector. Turn ignition "On" and check for battery voltage at the wiring harness terminal. Both green and the blue leads should have battery voltage.
   C. If voltage regulator was grounded properly and battery voltage was present at the green and blue leads, replace voltage regulator except on systems incorporating a field-loads relay. On systems with a field-loads relay, test the relay as outlined under "Field-Loads Relay Test". If relay tests satisfactory, replace voltage regulator. On all systems, repeat test.
5. If voltage is above limits, refer to Steps 4B and 4C.

Field-Loads Relay Test
1975-76

1. Disconnect voltage regulator connector and turn ignition switch "On".
2. Using a voltmeter, check for battery voltage at terminals of disconnected connector.
3. If battery voltage is present, the field-loads relay is satisfactory.
4. If battery voltage is not measured at the terminals, check circuit wiring and connections. If wiring and connections are satisfactory, replace field-loads relay.

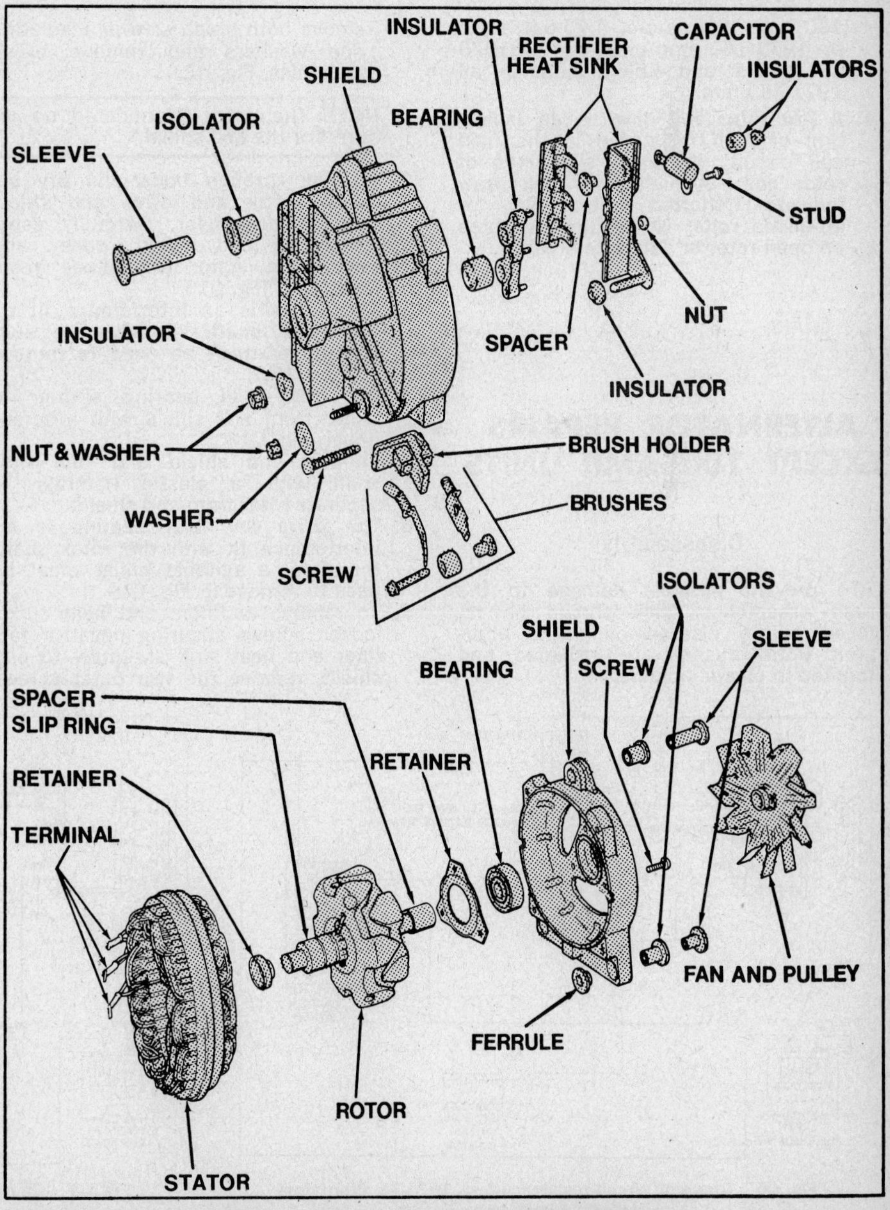

Fig. C4 100 amp alternator disassembled. 1975-78

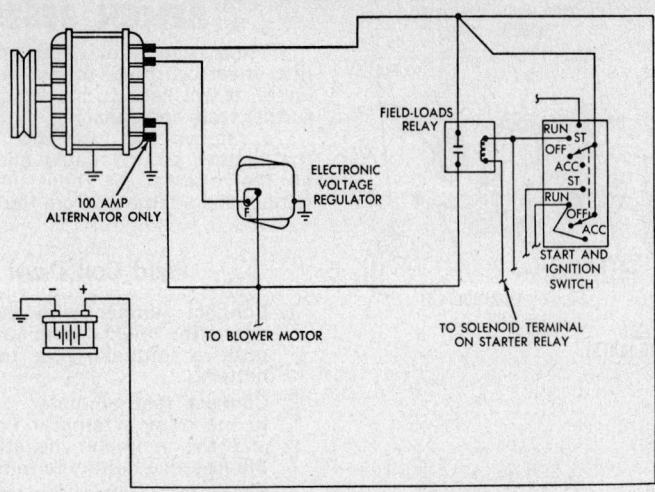

Fig. C5 Charging system with field-loads relay. 1975-76

100 amp alternators, 4.75-6.0 amps on 1975 100 amp units and all 1976 alternators, and 4.5-6.5 amps on all 1977-78 units.

4. A low rotor coil draw is an indication of high resistance in the field coil circuit, (brushes, slip rings or rotor coil). A high rotor coil draw indicates shorted rotor coil or grounded rotor. No reading indicates an open rotor or defective brushes.

ALTERNATOR REPAIRS EXCEPT 100 AMP UNITS

Disassembly

To prevent possible damage to the brush assemblies, they should be removed before disassembling the alternator. Both brushes are insulated and mounted in plastic holders.

1. Remove both brush screws, insulating nylon washers and remove brush assemblies, Fig. C2.

NOTE: The stator is laminated; do not burr it or the end shield.

2. Remove through bolts and pry between stator and drive end shield with a screwdriver. Carefully separate drive end shield, pulley and rotor from stator and diode rectifier shield, Fig. C16.
3. The pulley is an interference fit on the rotor shaft; therefore, a suitable puller must be used to remove it, Fig. C17.
4. Pry drive end bearing spring retainer from end shield with a screwdriver, Fig. C18.
5. Support end shield and tap rotor shaft with a plastic hammer to separate rotor from end shield.
6. The drive end ball bearing is an interference fit with the rotor shaft; therefore, a suitable puller must be used to remove it, Fig. C19.
7. To remove rectifiers and heat sinks, loosen screws securing negative rectifier and heat sink assembly to end shield, remove the two outer screws

and lift assembly from end shield. Remove nuts securing positive rectifier and heat sink assembly to insulated terminals in end shield. Then, remove capacitor ground screw and lift insulated washer, capacitor and positive rectifier and heat sink assembly from end shield.

8. The needle roller bearing in the rectifier end shield is a press fit. If it is necessary to remove the rectifier end frame needle bearing, protect the end shield by supporting the shield when pressing out the bearing as shown in Fig. C20.

Testing Diode Rectifiers

A special Rectifier Tester Tool C-3829 provides a quick, simple and accurate method to test the rectifiers without the necessity of disconnecting the soldered rectifier leads. This instrument is commercially available and full instructions for its use are provided. Lacking this tool, the rectifiers may be tested with a 12 volt battery and a test lamp having a No. 67 bulb. The procedure is as follows:

1. Remove nuts securing stator windings, positive and negative rectifier straps to terminal block. Remove stator winding terminals and pry stator from end shield.
2. Connect one side of test lamp to positive battery post and the other side of the test lamp to a test probe. Connect another test probe to the negative battery post, Fig. C21.
3. Contact heat sink with one probe and strap on top of rectifier with the other probe.
4. Reverse position of probes. If test lamp lights in one direction only, the rectifier is satisfactory. If test lamp lights in both directions, the rectifier is shorted. If test lamp lights in neither direction, the rectifier is open.

NOTE: Possible cause of an open or a blown rectifier is a faulty capacitor or a battery that has been installed on reverse polarity. If the battery is installed properly and the rectifiers are open, test the capacitor capacity, which should be .50 microfarad plus or minus 20%.

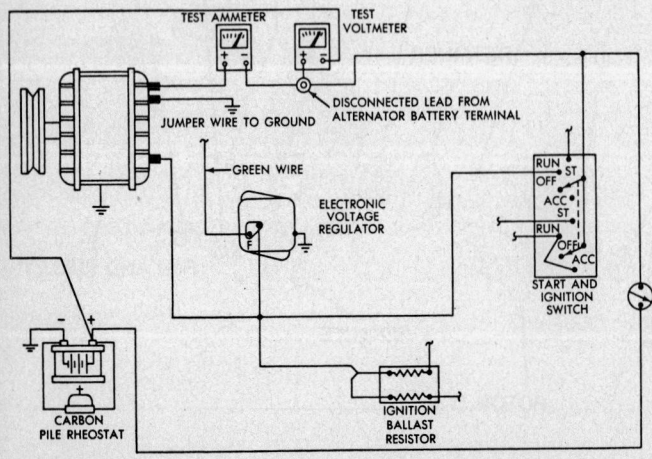

Fig. C6 Charging circuit resistance test. 1974-76 alternators less field-loads relay

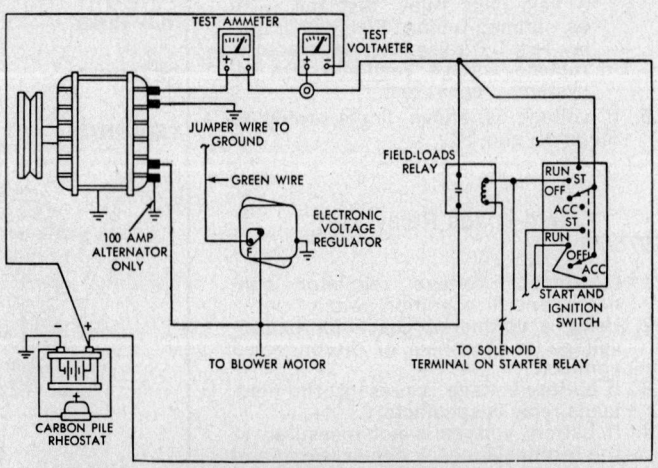

Fig. C7 Charging circuit resistance test. 1975-76 alternators with field-loads relay

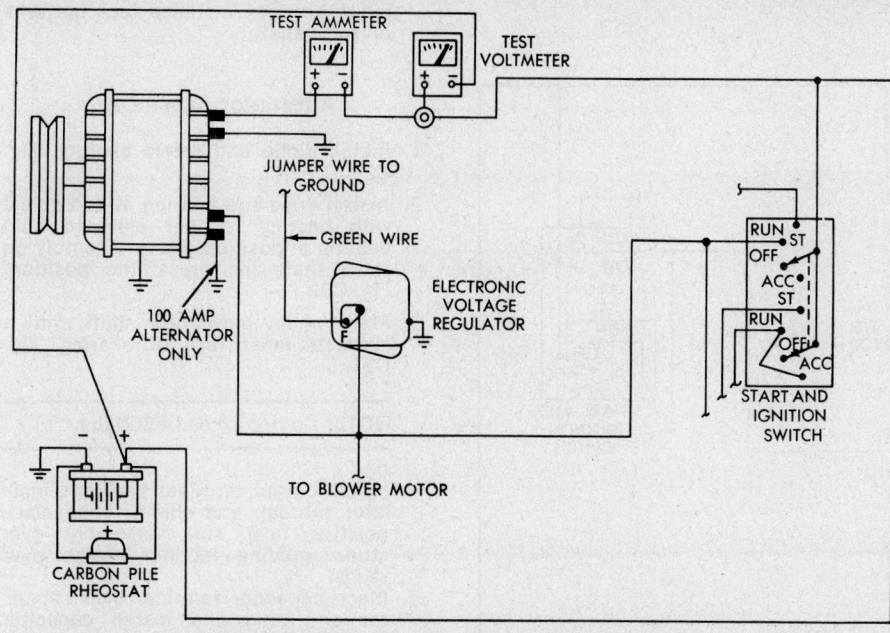

Fig. C8   Charging circuit resistance test. 1977-78 alternators

tory. Readings above 6.5 ohms on 1974-75 units or 3.5 ohms on 1976-78 units indicate a high resistance in the field coils and further testing or rotor replacement is required.

Replacing Slip Rings

NOTE: Slip rings on 1975-78 alternators are not serviced as a separate item. Rotor replacement is required when the slip rings are defective.

1. Cut through rotor grease retainer with a chisel and remove retainer and insulator.
2. Unsolder field coil leads at solder lugs, Fig. C24.
3. Cut through copper of both slip rings at opposite points with a chisel, Fig. C25.
4. Break insulator and remove old ring.
5. Clean away dirt and particles of old slip ring from rotor.
6. Scrape ends of field coil lead wires clean for good electrical contact.
7. Position field coil wires aside and place new slip ring on rotor shaft so slip ring lugs are properly positioned for field coil wire connections, Fig. C26.
8. Place installing tool over rotor shaft and with a suitable press, press slip ring onto shaft, Fig. C27.

NOTE: With slip ring bottomed against fan, the field lead wire should clear the access hole, fan and pole piece.

9. Tin field coil lead wires, then coil each lead wire around slip ring lug with first wrap against lug shoulder and wind-

Testing Stator

1. Separate stator from end shields.
2. Using a 12 volt test lamp, Fig. C22, test stator for grounds. Contact one test probe to any pin on stator frame and the other to each stator lead. If lamp lights, stator is grounded.

NOTE: Remove varnish from stator frame pin to ensure proper electrical connection.

3. Use a 12-volt test lamp to test stator for continuity. Contact one stator lead with one probe and the remaining two leads with the other probe, Fig. 23. If test lamp does not light, the stator has an open circuit.
4. Install new stator if one tested is defective.

Testing Rotor

The rotor may be tested electrically for grounded, open or shorted field coils as follows:

Grounded Field Coil Test: Connect an ohmmeter between each slip ring and the rotor shaft. The ohmmeter should indicate infinite resistance. If reading is zero or higher, rotor is grounded.

Open or Shorted Field Coil Test: Connect an ohmmeter between the slip rings. If the reading is below 3 ohms on 1974-75 units or 1.5 ohms on 1976-78 units, the field coil is shorted. A resistance of 3-4 ohms on 1974-75 units or 1.5-2 ohms on 1976-78 units at room temperature indicates the rotor is satisfactory. A reading of 4-6 ohms on 1974-75 units or 2.5-3 ohms indicates that the alternator was operated at a high underhood temperature, however, the rotor is still satisfac-

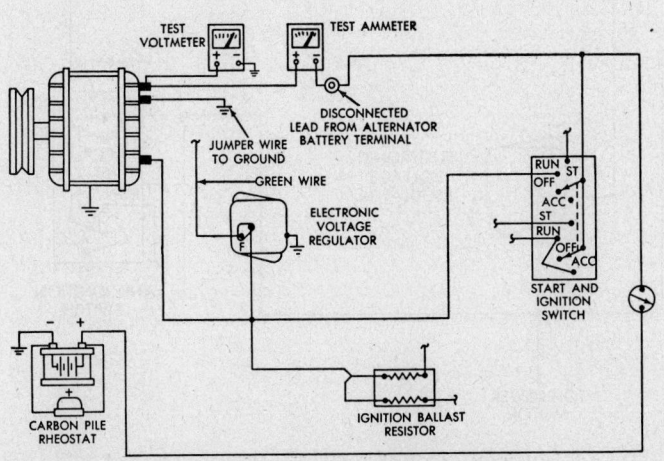

Fig. C9   **Current output test. 1974-76 alternators less field-loads relay**

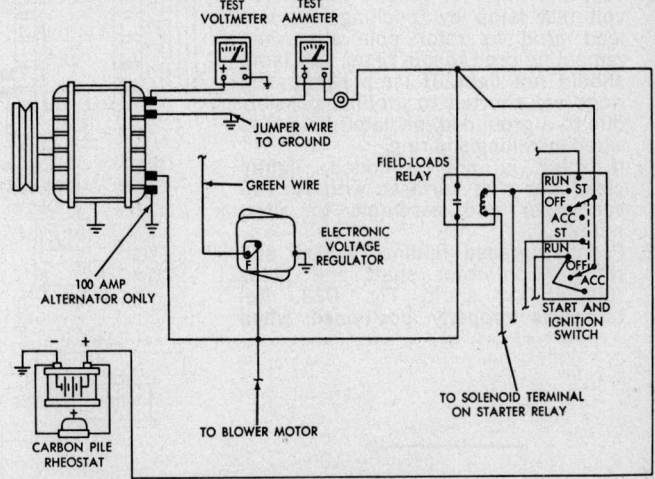

Fig. C10   **Current output test. 1975-76 alternators with field-loads relay**

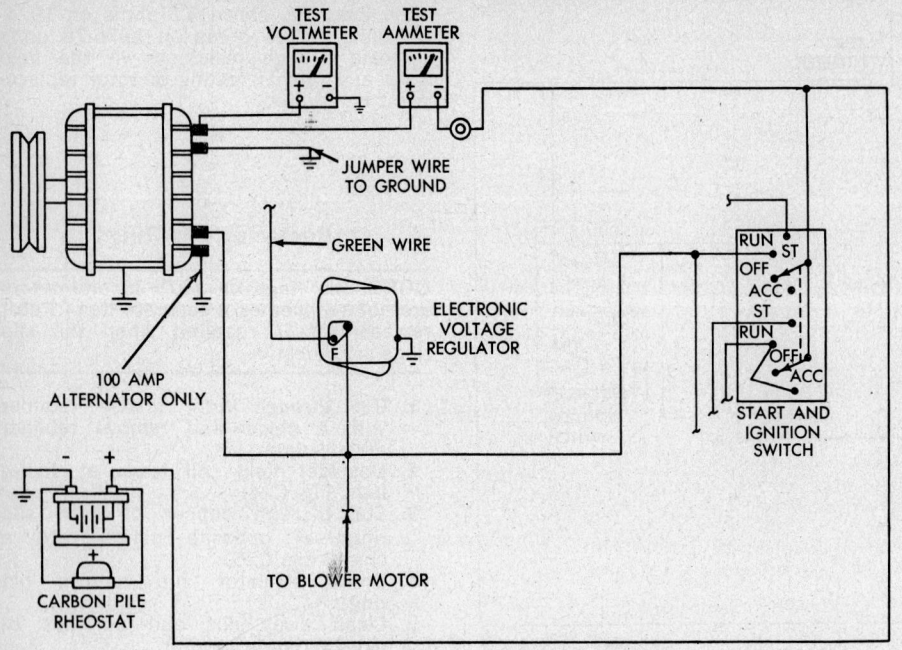

Fig. C11   Current output test. 1977-78 alternators

inner bore of installer tool bottoms on rotor shaft.

Alternator Assemble

1. Install diode end shield bearing, Fig. C29.
2. Install drive end bearing in end shield with bearing retainer plate to hold bearing in position. Place assembly on rotor shaft and press into position, Fig. C30.
3. Press pulley onto rotor shaft until it contacts inner race of bearing, Fig. C31.

NOTE: Do not exceed 6800 lbs.

---

4. Install output terminal stud and insulator through end shield. Then place positive heat sink assembly over studs, guiding rectifier straps over studs.
5. Place capacitor terminal over capacitor end stud and install capacitor shoulder insulator. Ground the capacitor bracket to end shield with a

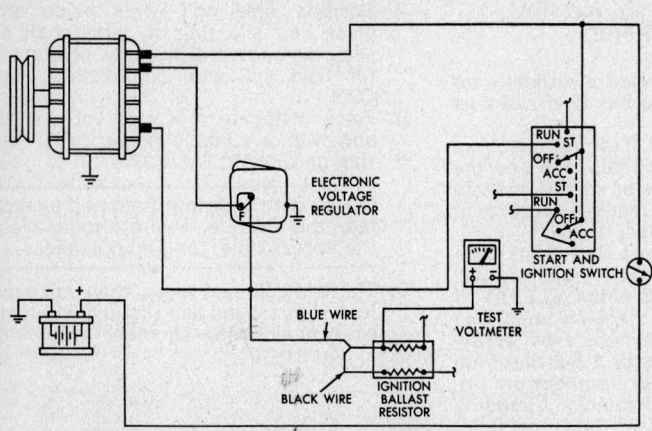

Fig. C12   Voltage regulator test. 1974-76 alternators less field-loads relay

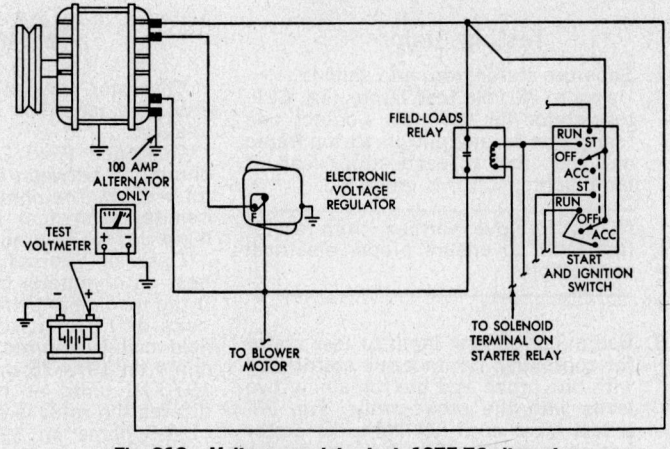

Fig. C13   Voltage regulator test. 1975-76 alternators with field-loads relay

ing outward. Solder leads with resin core solder.

10. Test slip rings for ground with a 110 volt test lamp by touching one test lead prod to rotor pole shoe and remaining prod to slip rings. The lamp should not light. If lamp lights, slip rings are shorted to ground, possibly due to a grounded insulated field lead when installing slip ring.
11. If rotor is not grounded, lightly clean slip ring surfaces with No. 00 sandpaper and assemble to alternator.
12. Position grease retainer gasket and retainer on rotor shaft and press retainer on shaft, Fig. C28. Retainer is properly positioned when

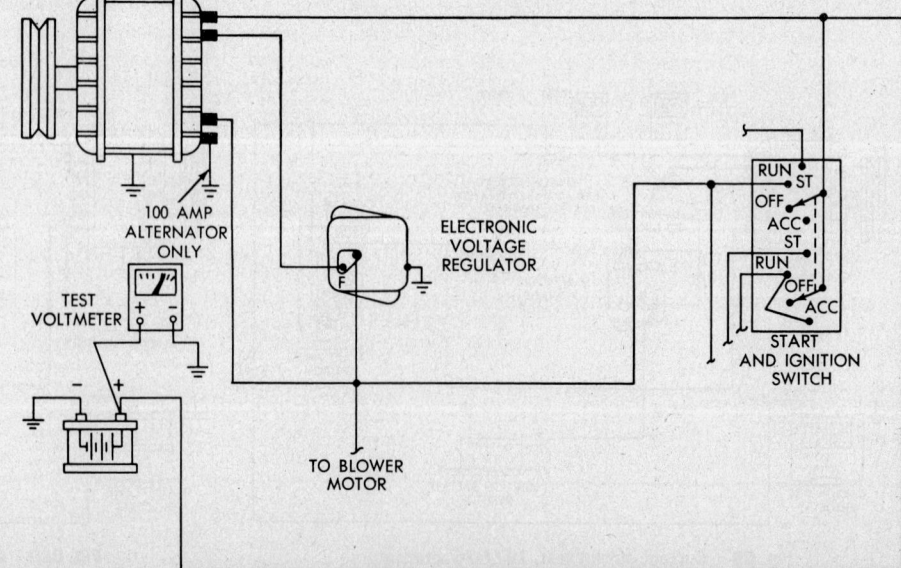

Fig. C14   Voltage regulator test. 1977-78 alternators

Ambient Temperature Near Regulator	−20°F	80°F	140°F	Above 140°F
1974	14.3–15.3	13.8–14.4	13.3–14.0	Less than 13.8
1975–78	14.9–15.9	13.9–14.6	13.3–13.9	Less than 13.6

Fig. C15   Voltage regulator test specifications

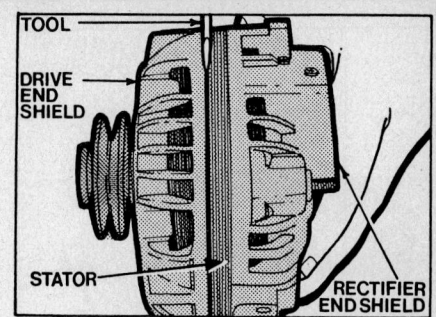

Fig. C16   Separating drive end shield from stator

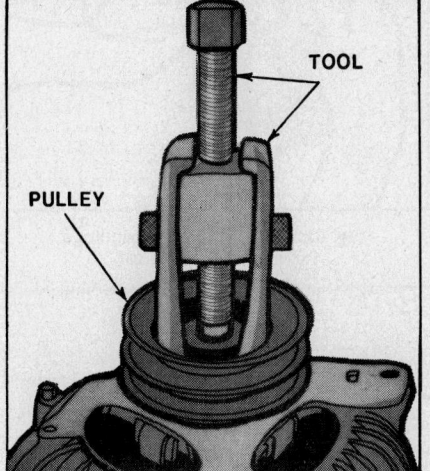

Fig. C17   Removing pulley

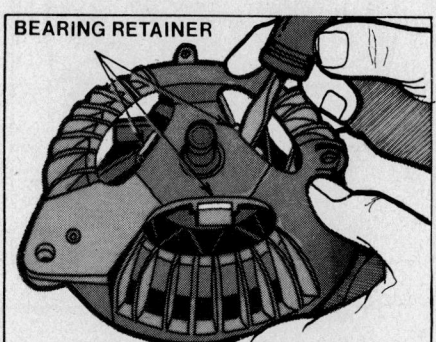

Fig. C18   Disengaging bearing retainer from end shield

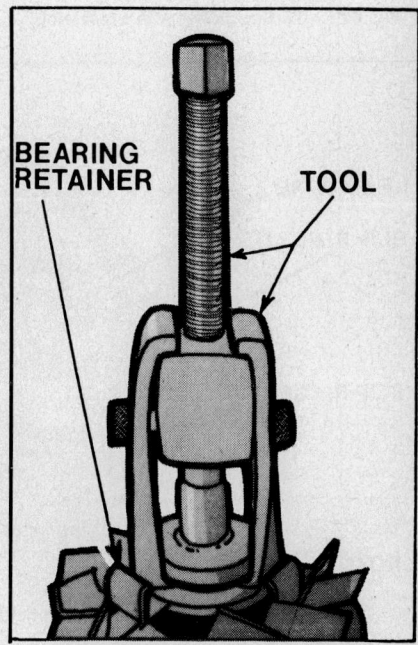

Fig. C19   Removing bearing from rotor shaft

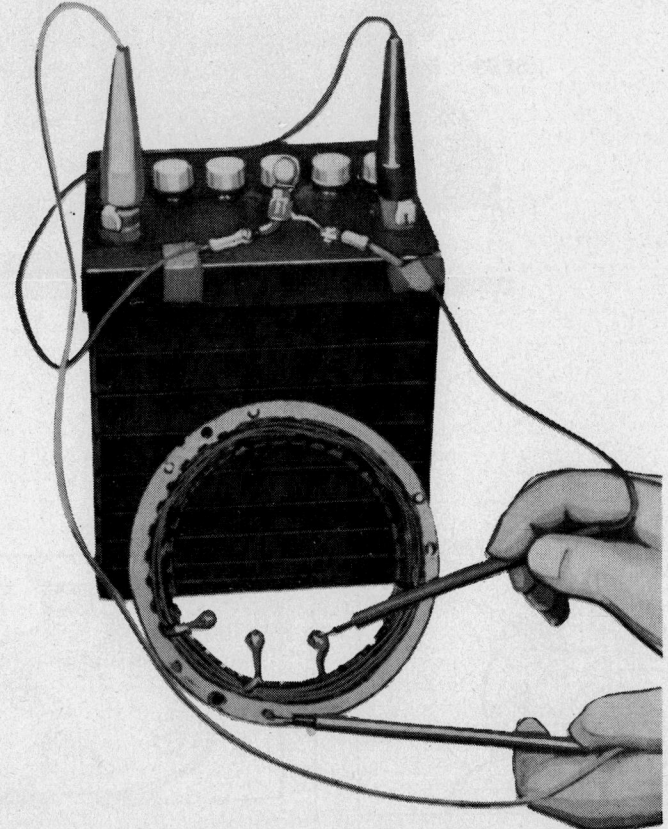

Fig. C22   Testing stator for grounds

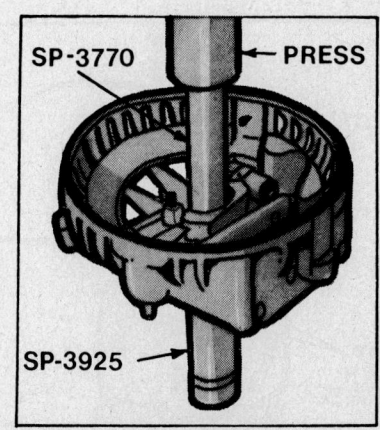

Fig. C20   Removing rectifier end shield bearing

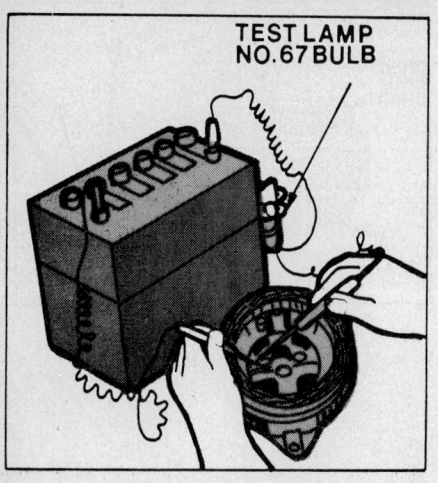

Fig. C21   Testing diodes with a test lamp

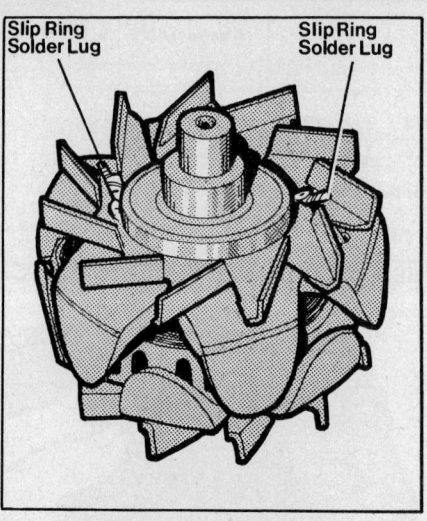

Fig. C24   Soldering points
with slip ring installed. 1974

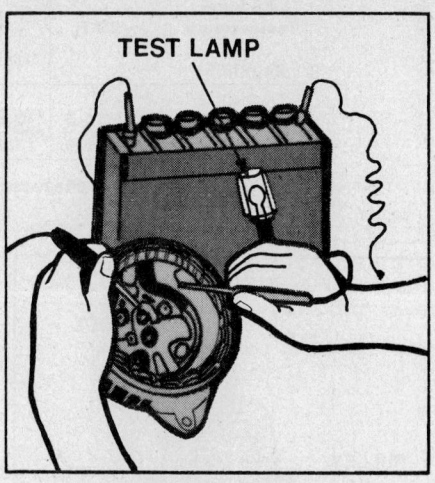

Fig. C23   Testing stator windings
for continuity (typical)

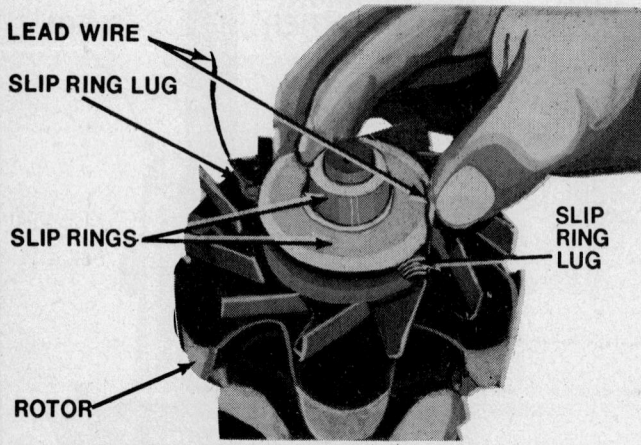

Fig. C26   Aligning slip ring with field lead wires. 1974

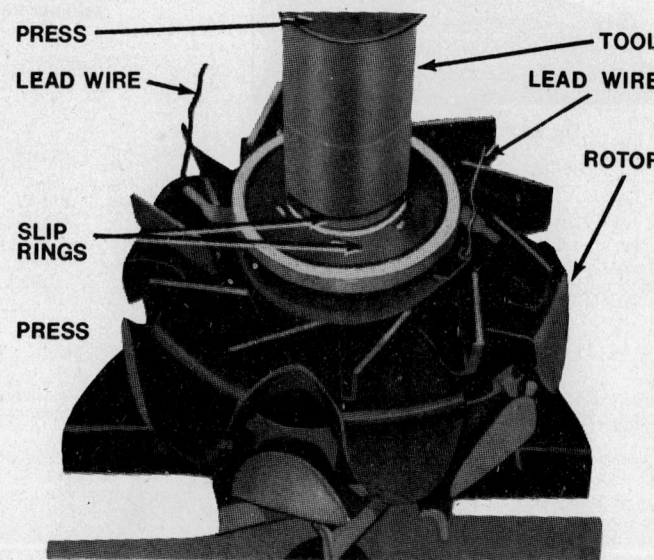

Fig. C27   Installing slip ring. 1974

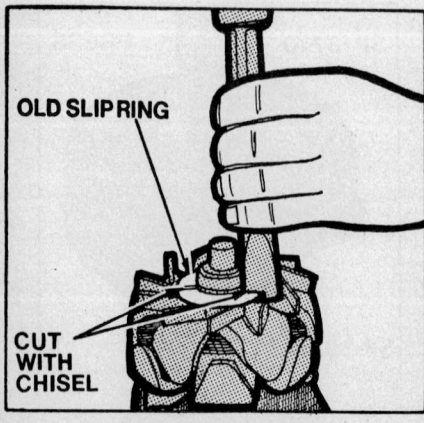

Fig. C25   Cutting old slip rings
for removal. 1974

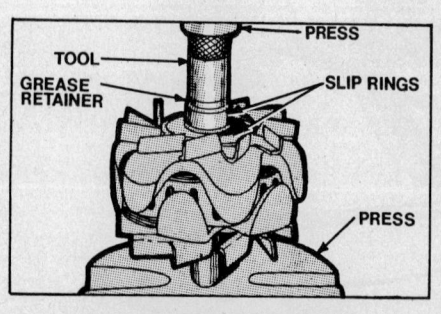

Fig. C28   Installing bearing
grease retainer

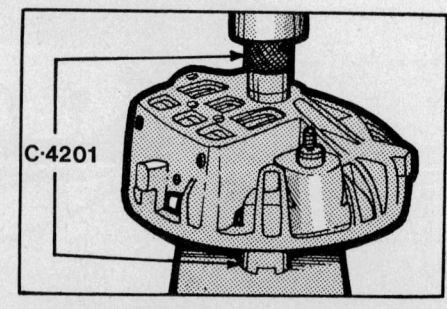

Fig. C29   Installing diode end shield bearing

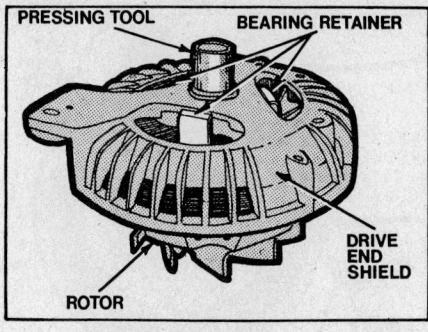

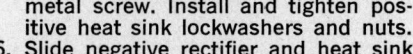

Fig. C30 Installing drive end shield and bearing

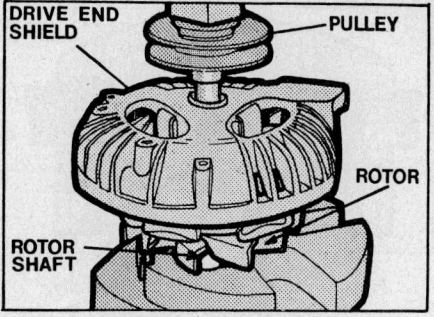

Fig. C31 Installing pulley

Fig. C32 Separating end shields. 100 amp units

metal screw. Install and tighten positive heat sink lockwashers and nuts.
6. Slide negative rectifier and heat sink assembly into place, position straps on terminal block studs, then install and tighten attaching screws.
7. Position stator on diode end shield.
8. Position rotor end shield on stator and diode end shield.
9. Align through bolt holes in stator, diode end shield and drive end shield.
10. Compress stator and both end shields by hand and install through bolts, washers and nuts.
11. Install field brush into vertical and horizontal holders. Place an insulating washer on each field brush terminal and install lock-washers and attaching screws.

NOTE: Ensure brushes are not grounded.

12. Rotate pulley slowly by hand to be sure rotor fans do not touch diodes, capacitor lead and stator connections.
13. Install alternator and adjust drive belt.

14. Connect leads to alternator.
15. Connect battery ground cable.
16. Start and operate engine and observe alternator operation.
17. If necessary, test current output and regulator voltage setting.

100 AMP ALTERNATOR

Disassembly & Testing

Separating End Shields
1. Remove brush holder screw and insulating washer, then lift brush holder from end shield.
2. Remove the through bolts, then using a screwdriver, pry between the stator and end shield in the slot provided to separate end shields, Fig. C32.

Rectifier Testing
1. Remove stator winding leads to terminal block stud nuts, Fig. C33.
2. Lift stator winding leads and pry stator

from end shield.
3. Using a 12 volt battery and a test lamp equipped with a #67 bulb, test rectifiers as follows:
   A. Connect one test probe to rectifier heat sink and the other test probe to the metal strap on top of rectifier, Fig. C34. Reverse the probes.
   B. If test lamp lights in one direction and does not light in the other, rectifier is satisfactory. If test lamp lights in both directions, rectifier is shorted. If test lamp does not light in either direction, rectifier is open.

Rectifier & Heat Sink Assembly Removal
1. Remove nut and insulator securing positive heat sink assembly to end shield stud.
2. Remove capacitor attaching screw.
3. Remove nut and insulator securing positive heat sink assembly stud to end shield, then remove positive heat sink assembly, Fig. C35, noting location of the insulators.
4. Remove screws securing negative heat sink assembly to end shield, then the negative heat sink assembly, Fig. C36.
5. Remove terminal block, then the capacitor and insulator.

Stator Testing
1. Contact one test lamp probe to outer

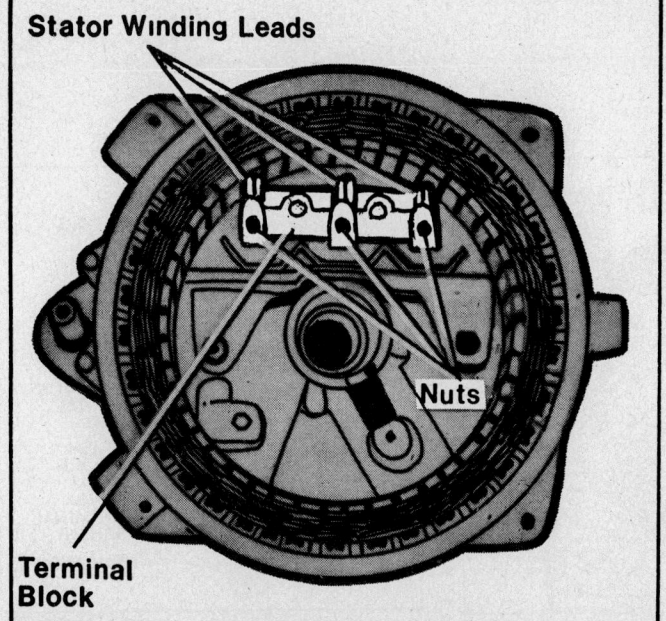

Stator Winding Leads

Nuts

Terminal Block

Fig. C33 Removing stator winding leads. 100 amp units

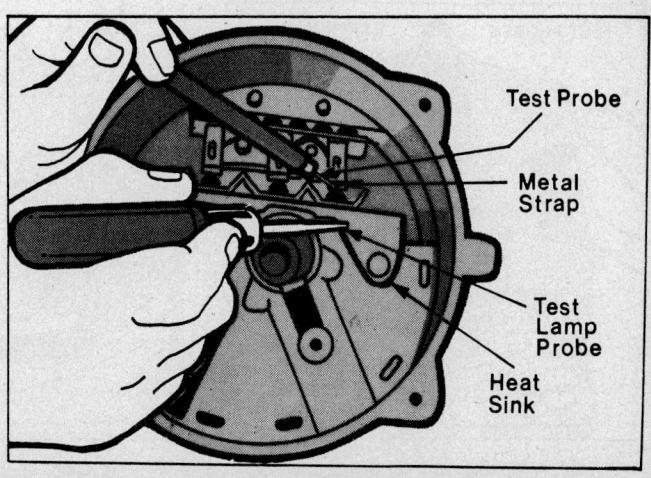

Test Probe

Metal Strap

Test Lamp Probe

Heat Sink

Fig. C34 Testing rectifiers with a test lamp. 100 amp units

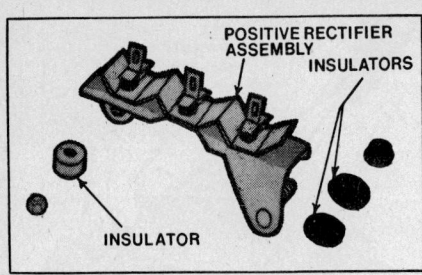

Fig. C35 Positive rectifier assembly. 100 amp units

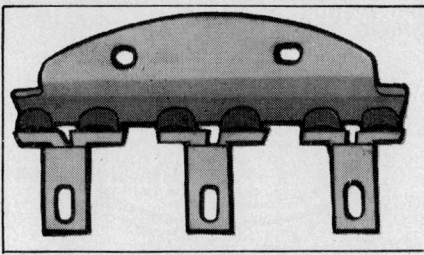

Fig. C36 Negative rectifier assembly. 100 amp units

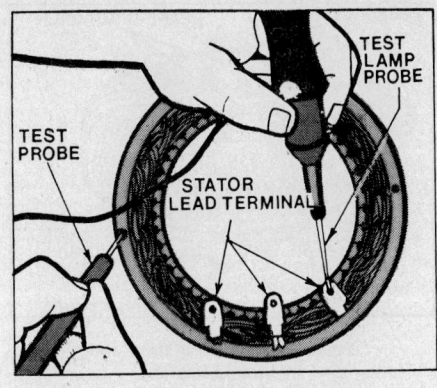

Fig. C37 Testing stator. 100 amp units

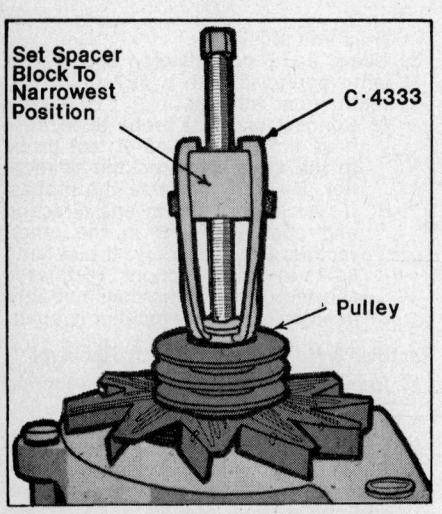

Fig. C38 Removing pulley. 100 amp units

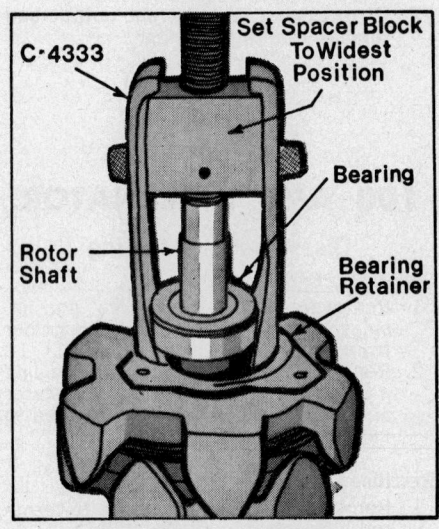

Fig. C39 Removing bearing from rotor shaft. 100 amp units

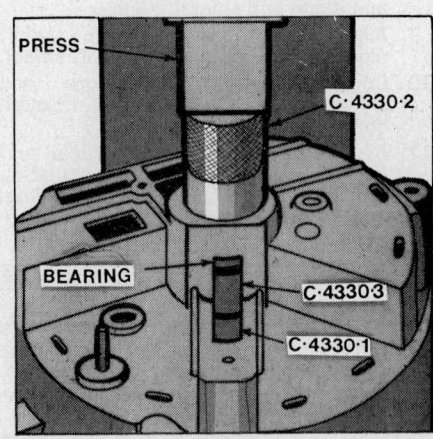

Fig. C40 Removing rectifier end shield bearing. 100 amp units

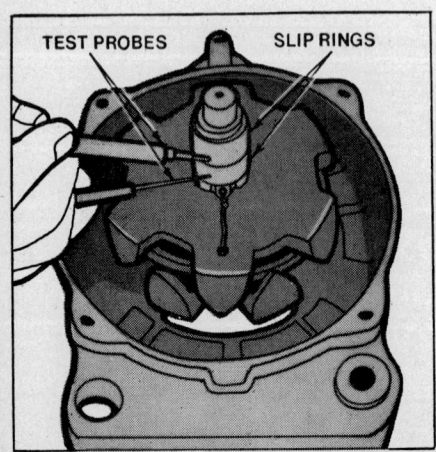

Fig. C41 Testing rotor for opens or shorts 100 amp units

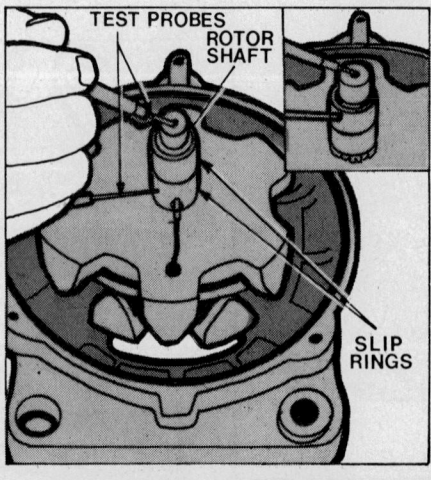

Fig. C42 Testing rotor for grounds 100 amp units

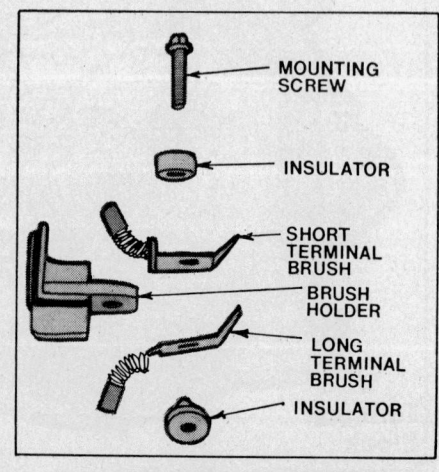

Fig. C43 Assembling field brushes. 100 amp units

diameter of stator frame and the other probe to each of the stator lead terminals, one at a time, Fig. C37.

2. If test lamp lights, the stator lead is grounded, requiring replacement.

NOTE: The stator windings are Delta Wound, therefore the windings cannot be tested for opens or shorts using a test lamp. If the stator is not grounded, and all other electrical circuits and alternator components test satisfactory, the stator may be open or shorted.

Pulley & Bearing Removal

1. Remove pulley with a suitable puller, Fig. C38.
2. Remove bearing retainer to drive end shield attaching screws.
3. Support end shield and using a mallet, tap rotor from end shield.
4. Remove bearing with a suitable puller, Fig. C39.
5. If necessary to remove needle roller bearing in rectifier end shield, use tool C-4330, Fig. C40.

Rotor Testing

Grounded Field Coil Test: Connect a test lamp between each slip ring and the rotor shaft, Fig. C41. If test lamp lights, the rotor is grounded, requiring replacement.

Open Field Coil Test: Connect a test lamp between the slip rings, Fig. C42. If test lamp does not light, the rotor is open, requiring replacement.

Shorted Field Coil Test: Connect an ohmmeter between the slip rings, Fig. C42. If reading is below 1.7 ohms, the rotor is shorted.

High Resistance Test: with an ohmmeter connected across the slip rings, reading should be between 1.7 and 2.1 ohms at 80° F. If not, replace rotor.

Assembly

1. Press grease retainer onto rotor shaft, Fig. C40 (Omit tool C-4330-3).
2. Place rectifier end shield bearing on base of tool C-4330-1, Fig. C40 (Omit tool C-4330-3), then place rectifier end shield on top of bearing. Using tool C-4330-2, press end shield onto bearing until end shield contacts press base.
3. Install drive end bearing and retainer in drive end shield.
4. Position bearing and drive end shield on rotor and while supporting base of rotor shaft, press end shield onto shaft. Ensure rotor spacer is in place before pressing bearing and end shield on shaft.
5. Press pulley onto rotor shaft until it contacts inner race of bearing.

NOTE: Do not exceed 6800 lbs.

6. Place insulator and capacitor on positive heat sink mounting stud, then install capacitor mounting screw.
7. Place terminal block into position in rectifier end shield and install mounting screws.
8. Place negative heat sink into position, ensuring metal straps are properly located over studs on terminal block, then install negative heat sink mounting screws.

9. Place insulator over positive heat sink stud and install positive heat sink assembly into position in end shield, ensuring metal straps are properly located over terminal block studs. From inside end shield, place insulator on positive heat sink mounting stud, then install mounting nut. From outside end shield, place insulator on positive heat sink stud, then install mounting nut.
10. Place stator over rectifier end shield and install terminals on terminal block. Then, press stator pins into end shield and install terminal nuts.

NOTE: Route leads to avoid contact with rotor or sharp edge of negative heat sink.

11. Place rotor and drive end shield assembly over stator and rectifier end shield assembly, aligning bolt holes. Compress stator and both end shields, then install and torque through bolts to 40-60 inch lbs.
12. Install field brushes into brush holder with long terminal on bottom and the short terminal on top, Fig. C43. Then, install insulators and mounting screw.
13. Place brush holder on end shield, ensure it is properly seated and tighten mounting screw.
14. Slowly rotate pulley to ensure rotor poles do not contact stator winding leads.

Delcotron Type SI Integral Charging System

DESCRIPTION

This unit, Fig. 1, features a solid state regulator mounted inside the alternator slip ring end frame, along with the brush holder assembly. All regulator components are enclosed in a solid mold with no need or provision for adjustment of the regulator. A rectifier bridge, containing six diodes and connected to the stator windings, changes A.C. voltage to D.C. voltage which is available at the output terminal. Generator field current is supplied through a diode trio which is also connected to the stator windings. The diodes and rectifiers are protected by a capacitor which is also mounted in the end frame.

NOTE: General Motors 1975-78 units incorporate a 40 ohm resistor in the warning indicator circuit. Fig. 2.

No maintenance or adjustments of any kind are required on this unit.

TROUBLE SHOOTING
Undercharged Battery

SERVICE NOTE: If inadequate charging is encountered on 1974 Camaro's Z28 with optional gauge package the cause could be an omitted wire in the engine wiring harness. If wire in Fig. 3 is missing the alternator will not charge below 2,000 engine rpm. Add this wire to the existing harness and connect as shown in Fig. 3.

1. Disconnect battery ground cable.
2. Disconnect wire at "BAT" terminal of alternator, connect ammeter, positive lead to "BAT" terminal and negative lead to wire.
3. Connect battery ground cable.
4. Turn on all accessories, then connect a carbon pile regulator across battery.
5. Operate engine at moderate speed,

adjust carbon pile regulator to obtain maximum current output.

6. If ammeter reading is within 10 percent of rated output, alternator is not at fault.

NOTE: Alternator rated output is stamped on alternator frame.

7. If ammeter reading is not within 10 percent of rated output, ground field winding by inserting screw driver in end frame hole, contacting tab. Fig. 4.

NOTE: Do not insert screwdriver deeper than one inch since tab is usually located within 3/4 inch of casing surface.

8. If reading is within 10 percent of rated output, regulator must be replaced. If reading is not within limits, check field winding, diode trio, recti-

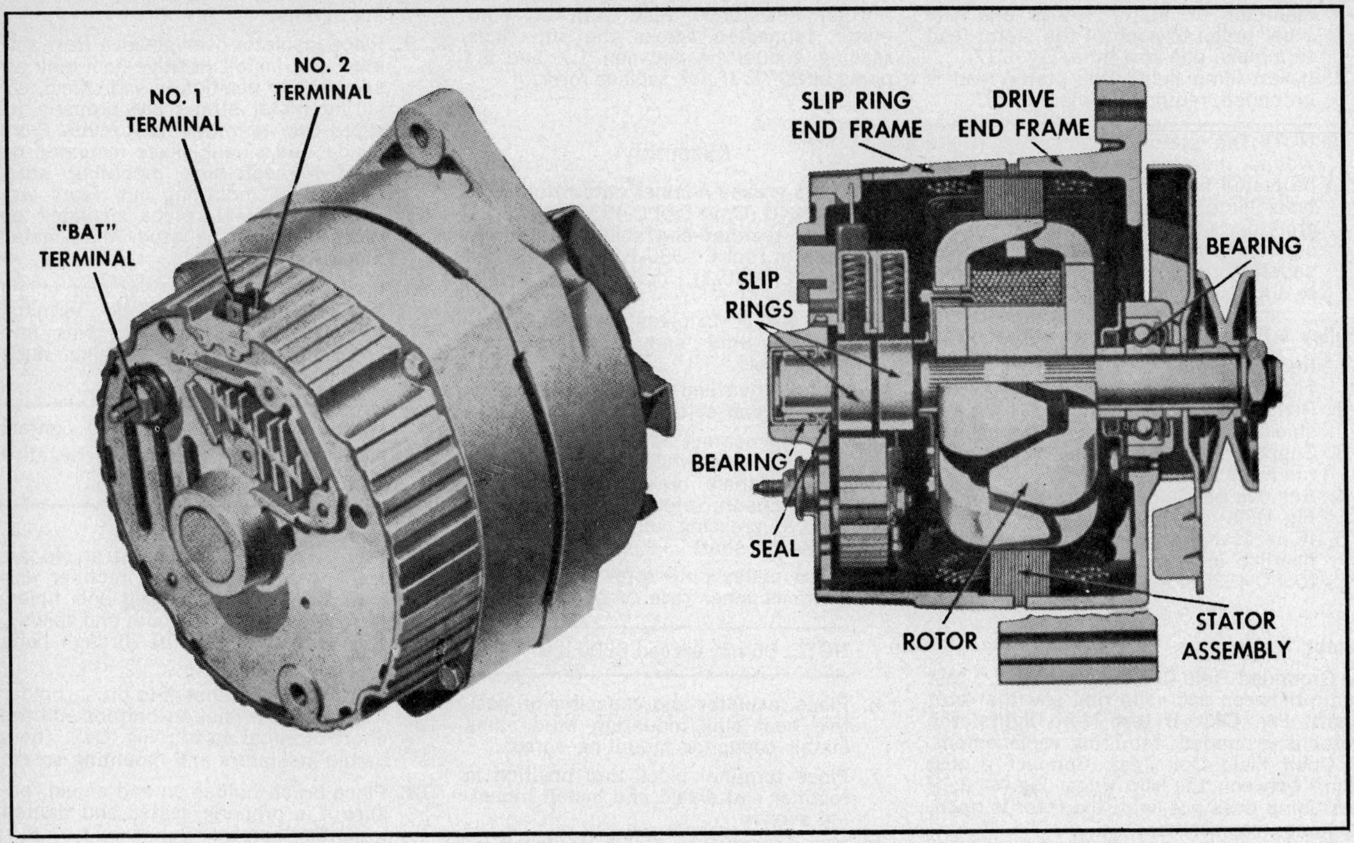

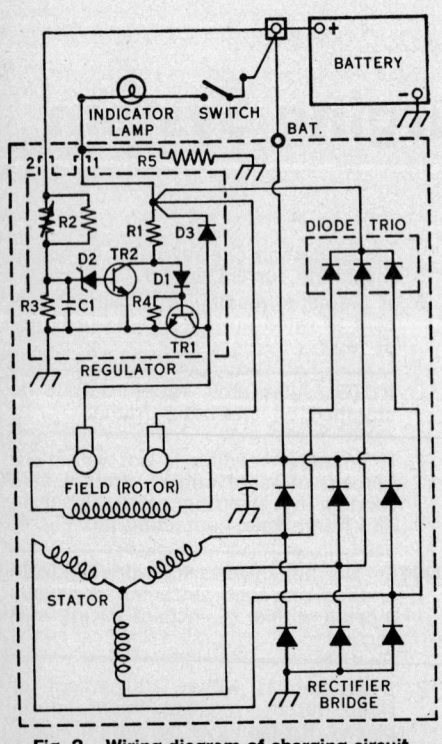

Fig. 1 Delcotron Type SI Integral Charging System

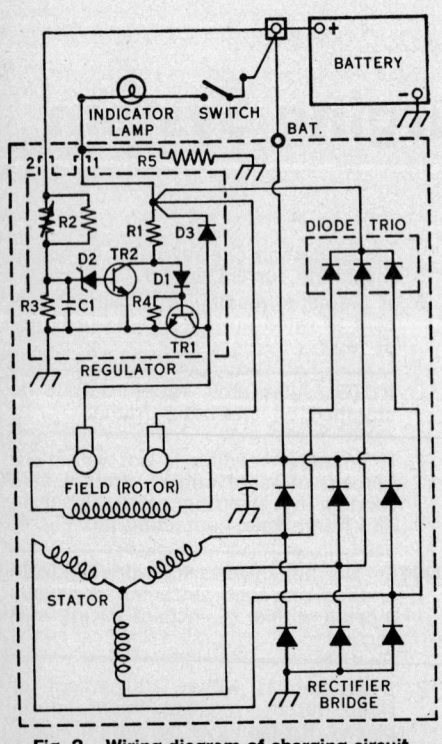

fier bridge and stator.
9. Turn off all accessories and disconnect ammeter and carbon pile regulator.

Overcharging Battery

1. Remove alternator from vehicle and separate end frames as outlined under "Alternator Disassembly."
2. Check field winding, if shorted replace rotor and regulator.
3. Connect ohmmeter from brush clip to end frame, set meter on low scale and note reading. Fig. 5.
4. Reverse leads, if both readings are zero remove screw from brush clip and inspect sleeve and insulator.

5. If sleeve and insulator are in good condition, then regulator is at fault and must be replaced.

ALTERNATOR DISASSEMBLY

NOTE: When pressing bearings or seals from end frames, support frames from inside.

1. Scribe mark across end frames and stator ring so parts can be installed in same position.
2. Remove four through bolts, then us-

Fig. 2 Wiring diagram of charging circuit. 1975-78 G.M. vehicles

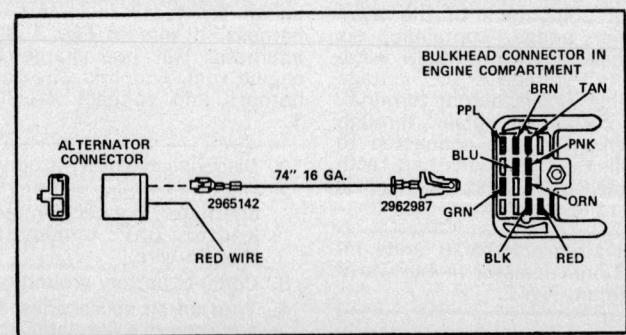

Fig. 3 Harness connections for omitted wire. 1974 Camaro Z-28

Fig. 4 Grounding field windings

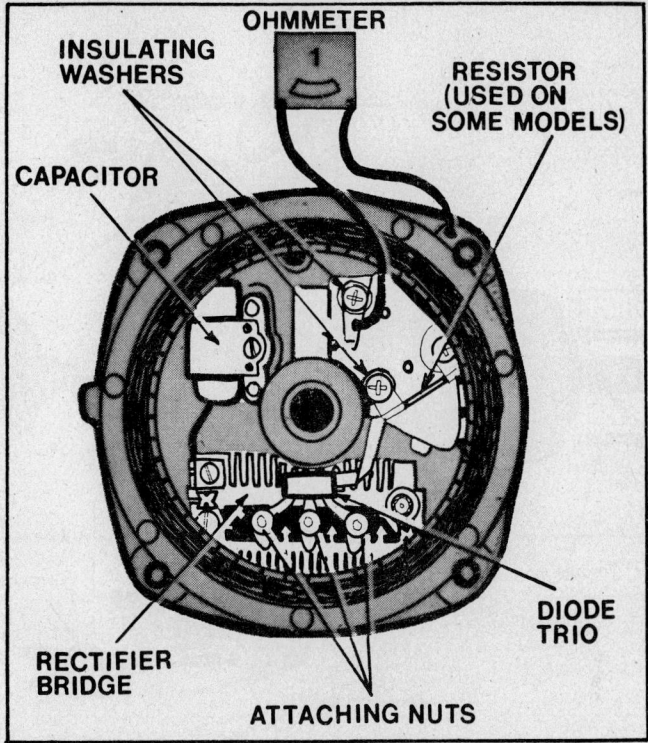

Fig. 5 Testing brush clip

ing screw driver in stator slot pry end frames apart. Fig. 6.

NOTE: Brushes may fall from holders and become contaminated with bearing grease, if so they must be cleaned prior to assembly.

3. Place tape over slip ring end frame bearing and shaft at slip ring end.
4. Remove nut, washer, pulley, fan and collar from rotor shaft, then slide drive end frame from shaft.
5. Remove bearing, retainer and seal from drive end frame.
6. Remove attaching bolts, then pry stator from slip ring end frame.
7. Remove capacitor, diode trio, rectifier bridge and battery terminal stud.
8. Remove resistor (if equipped), brush holder and regulator.
9. Remove bearing and seal from slip ring end frame.

BENCH TESTS

Rotor & Slip Ring Test

NOTE: Ohmmeter must be at low scale setting during this test.

1. Inspect rotor for wear or damage.
2. Touch ohmmeter leads to slip rings. Fig. 7.
3. If no reading is obtained an open circuit exists in windings.
4. If reading below 2.5 ohms is obtained winding is shorted.
5. If a reading above 3 ohms is obtained excessive resistance exists in windings.
6. Connect one ohmmeter lead to rotor shaft and touch slip rings with other lead, if any reading is obtained there is a ground in the circuit. Fig. 7.

NOTE: If any of the above problems are present the rotor assembly must be replaced.

Stator Winding Test

1. Inspect stator for discolored windings, loose connections and damage.

2. Connect an ohmmeter from stator lead to frame, if any reading is obtained windings are grounded. Fig. 8.
3. Connect ohmmeter between stator leads, if reading is high when connected between each pair of leads, an open circuit exists in windings.

NOTE: Shorted windings are difficult to locate without special equipment. If other tests indicate normal, but rated alternator output cannot be obtained the windings are probably shorted.

Diode Trio

1. With diode unit removed, connect an ohmmeter to the single connector and to one of the three connectors. Fig. 9.
2. Observe the reading. Reverse ohmmeter leads.
3. Reading should be high with one connection and low with the other. If both readings are the same, unit must be replaced.
4. Repeat between the single connector and each of the three connectors.

NOTE: There are two diode units differing in appearance. These are completely interchangeable.

The diode unit can be checked for a grounded brush lead while still installed in the end frame by connecting an ohmmeter from the brush lead clip to the end frame as in Steps 1 and 2 above. If both readings are zero, check for a grounded brush or brush lead.

Rectifer Bridge Test

1. Connect ohmmeter to the grounded heat sink and one of the three terminals. Fig. 10.
2. Observe the reading then reverse leads.
3. Reading should be high with one connection and low with the other. If both readings are the same, unit must be replaced.
4. Repeat test for each of the other terminals.

Voltage Regulator/Brush Lead Test

Connect an ohmmeter from the brush lead clip to the end frame, note reading, then reverse connections. If both readings are zero, either the brush lead clip is grounded or the regulator is defective.

ALTERNATOR ASSEMBLY

NOTE: When pressing bearings or seals, end frames must be supported from inside.

1. Lightly lubricate seal and position on slip ring end frame with lip facing toward rotor. Fig. 6.

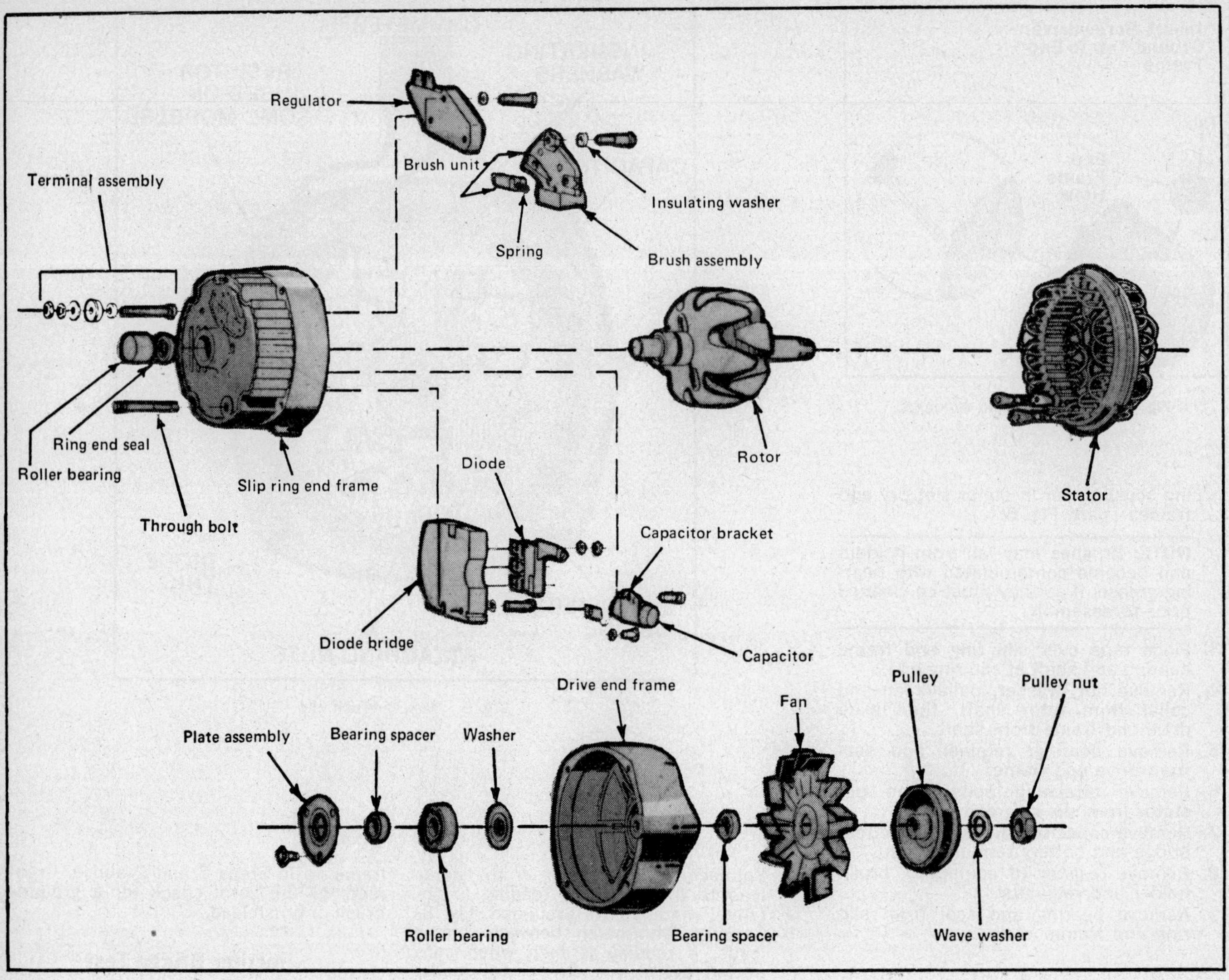

Regulator

Terminal assembly

Brush unit

Insulating washer

Spring

Brush assembly

Ring end seal

Roller bearing

Rotor

Slip ring end frame

Through bolt

Stator

Diode

Capacitor bracket

Diode bridge

Capacitor

Drive end frame

Fan

Pulley

Pulley nut

Plate assembly

Bearing spacer

Washer

Roller bearing

Bearing spacer

Wave washer

Fig. 6   Alternator disassembled

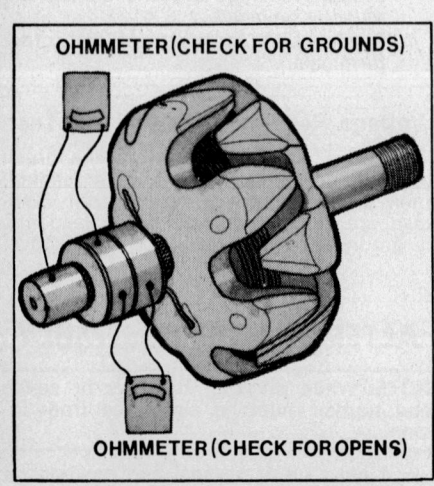

OHMMETER (CHECK FOR GROUNDS)

OHMMETER (CHECK FOR OPENS)

Fig. 7   Testing rotor & slip rings

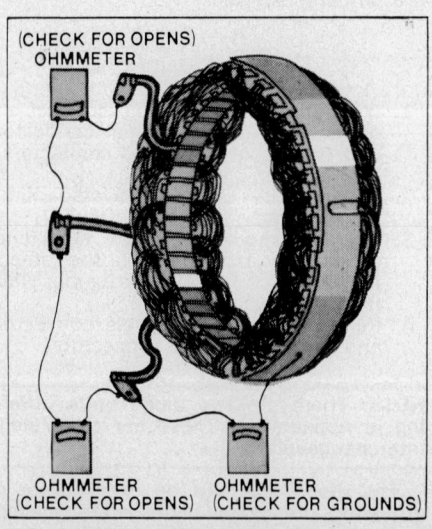

(CHECK FOR OPENS)
OHMMETER

OHMMETER
(CHECK FOR OPENS)

OHMMETER
(CHECK FOR GROUNDS)

Fig. 8   Testing stator winding

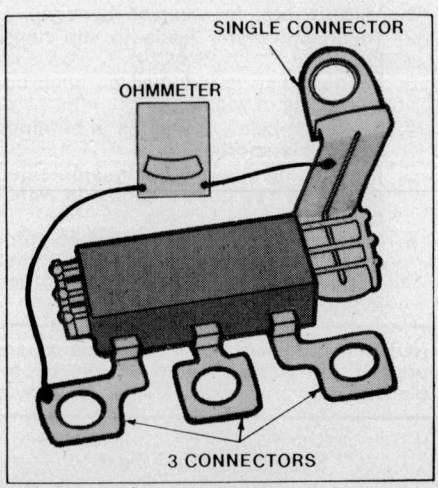

SINGLE CONNECTOR

OHMMETER

3 CONNECTORS

Fig. 9   Testing diode trio

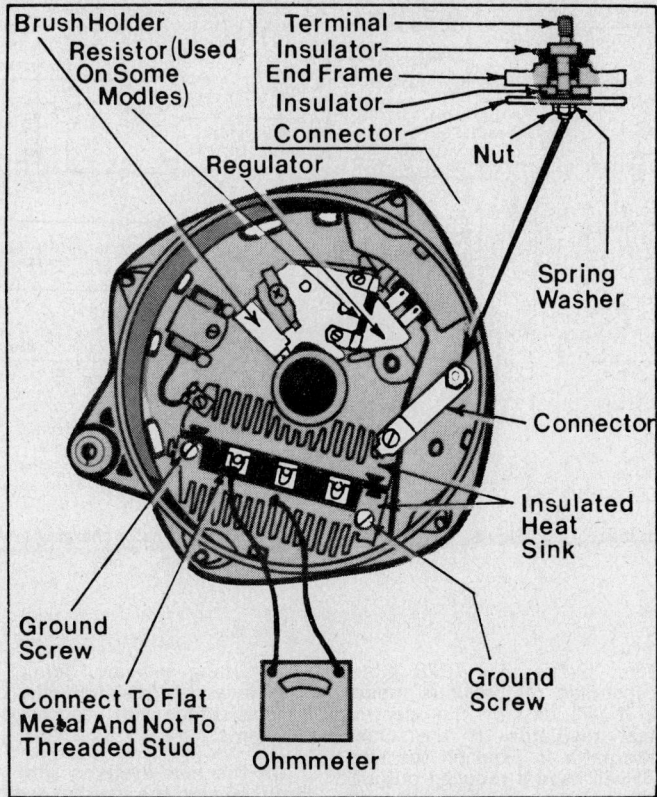

Fig. 10 Testing rectifier bridge diodes

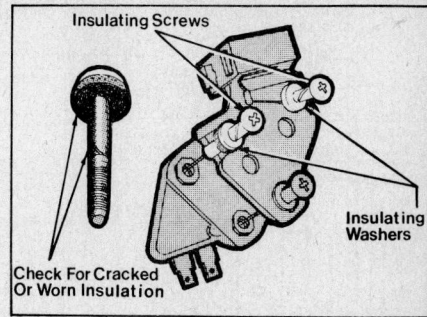

Fig. 11 Brush holder & regulator installation

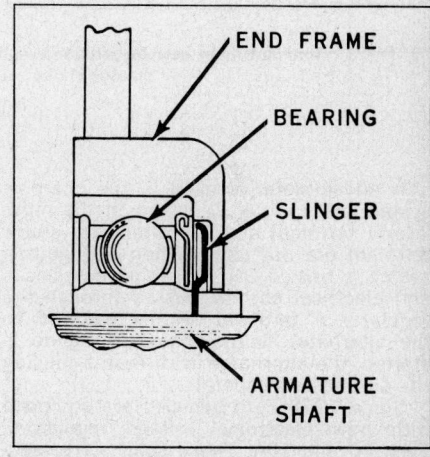

Fig. 12 Drive end frame bearing & slinger installed

2. Press seal part way into housing.
3. Position bearing and end plug on slip ring end frame, press bearing and plug in until flush with end frame.
4. Place regulator in end frame, install brushes and springs in brush holder, use pin to hold brushes in compressed position.

NOTE: Insulating washers are installed under two of the attaching screws, Fig. 11.

5. Install rectifier bridge and battery terminal stud.

6. Install diode trio, ensure current only flows one way through single connector.
7. Install capacitor.
8. Install stator, check the three leads for continuity, ensure stator is not grounded against case or holder.
9. Position slinger on drive end frame, then press ball bearing into end frame. Fig. 12.
10. Fill seal cavity ¼ full with special alternator lubricant, then install retainer.

11. Install rotor in drive end frame, then install collar, fan, pulley, washer and nut.
12. Align scribe marks on end frames and stator plate, install through bolts and remove brush retaining pins.

Ford Motorcraft Alternator

CONTENTS

GENERAL

A charge indicator lamp or ammeter can be used in charging system.

If a charge indicator lamp is used in the charging system, Figs. 1, 2, 5, 6 and 9A, the system operation is as follows: when the ignition switch is turned ON, a small electrical current flows through the lamp filament (turning the lamp on) and through the alternator regulator to the alternator field. When the engine is started, the alternator field rotates and produces a voltage in the stator winding. When the voltage at the alternator stator terminal reaches about 3 volts, the regulator field relay closes. This puts the same voltage potential on both sides of the charge indicator lamp causing it to go out. When the field relay has closed, current passes through the regulator A terminal and is metered to the alternator field.

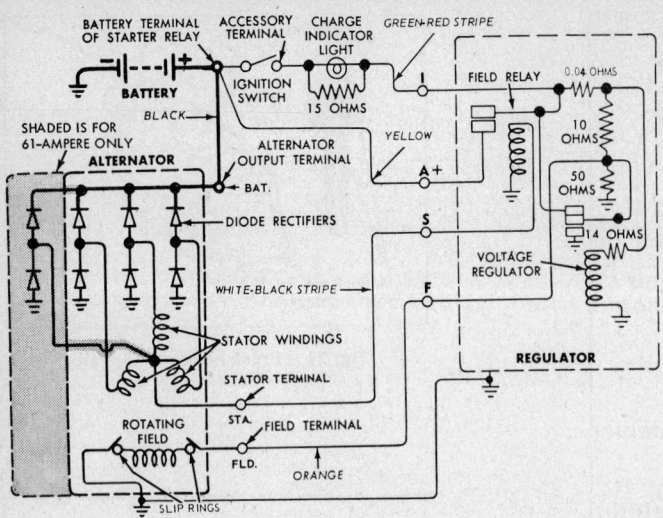

Fig. 1 Indicator light rear terminal alternator charging system less electric choke

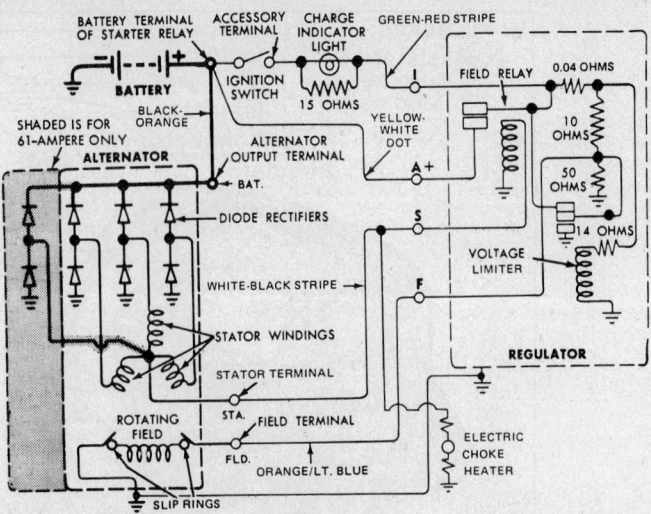

Fig. 2 Indicator light rear terminal alternator charging system with electric choke

If an ammeter is used in the charging system, Figs. 3, 4, 7, 8 and 9; the regulator I terminal and the alternator stator terminal are not used. When the ignition switch is turned ON, the field relay closes and electrical current passes through the regulator A terminal and is metered to the alternator field. When the engine is started, the alternator field rotates causing the alternator to operate.

Some 1978 Ford vehicles are equipped with new electronic voltage regulators, Figs. 10 and 10A. These solid state regulators are used in conjunction with other new components in the charging system such as an alternator with a higher field current requirement, a warning indicator lamp shunt resistor (500 ohms) and a new wiring harness with a new regulator connector. When replacing system components, note the following precautions:

1. Always use the proper alternator in the system. If the new 1978 alternator is installed on previous model systems, it will destroy the electro-mechanical regulator. If the older model alternator is used on the new system, it will have a reduced output.

2. Do not use an electro-mechanical regulator in the new system since the wiring harness connector will not index properly with this type of regulator.

3. The new electronic regulators are color coded for proper installation. The black color coded unit is installed in systems equipped with a warning indicator lamp. The blue color coded regulator is installed in systems equipped with an ammeter.

4. The new systems use a 500 ohm resistor on the rear of the instrument cluster on vehicles equipped with a warning indicator lamp. Do not replace this resistor with the 15 ohm resistance wire used on previous systems.

On the new systems with an indicator lamp, closing the ignition switch energizes the warning lamp and turns on the regulator output stage. The alternator receives maximum field current and is ready to generate an output voltage. As the alternator rotor speed increases, the output and stator terminal voltages increase from zero to the system regulation level determined by the regulator setting. When the ignition switch is turned off, the solid state relay circuit turns the output stage off, interrupting current flow through the regulator so there is not a current drain on the battery.

On vehicles equipped with an ammeter, the operating principle is similar.

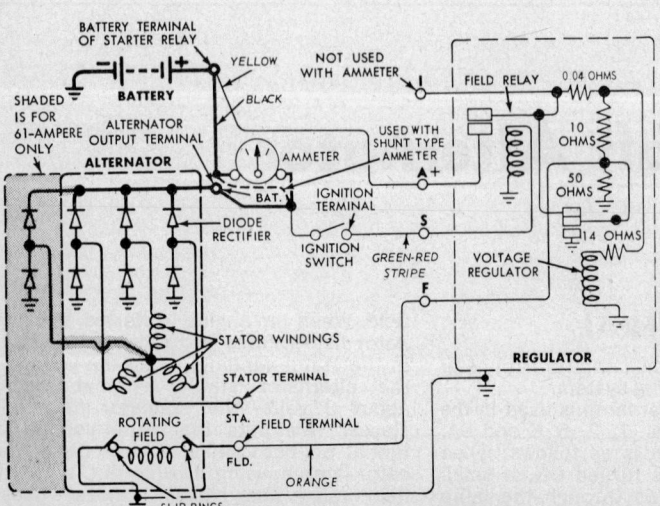

Fig. 3 Ammeter rear terminal alternator charging system less electric choke

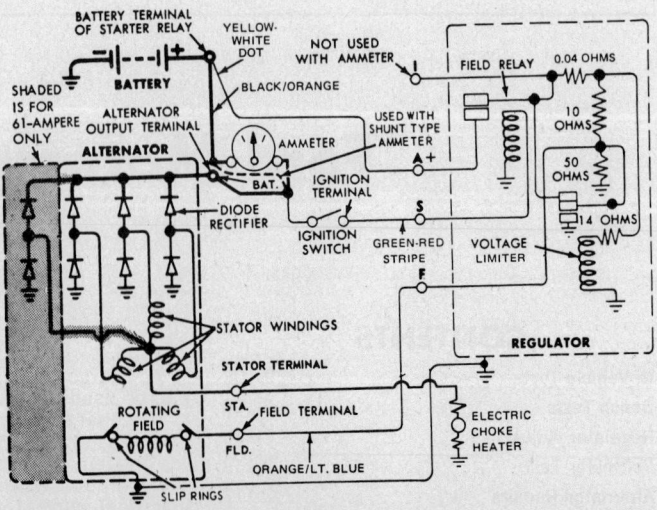

Fig. 4 Ammeter rear terminal alternator charging system with electric choke

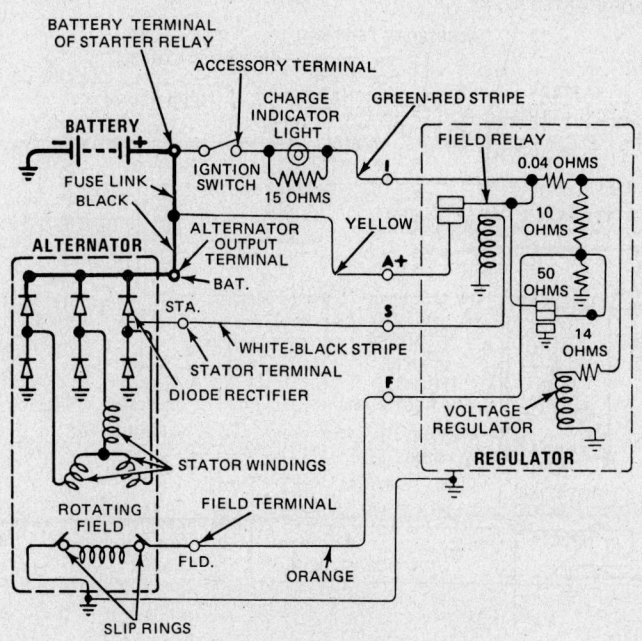

Fig. 5 Indicator light side terminal alternator charging system. 65 amp system

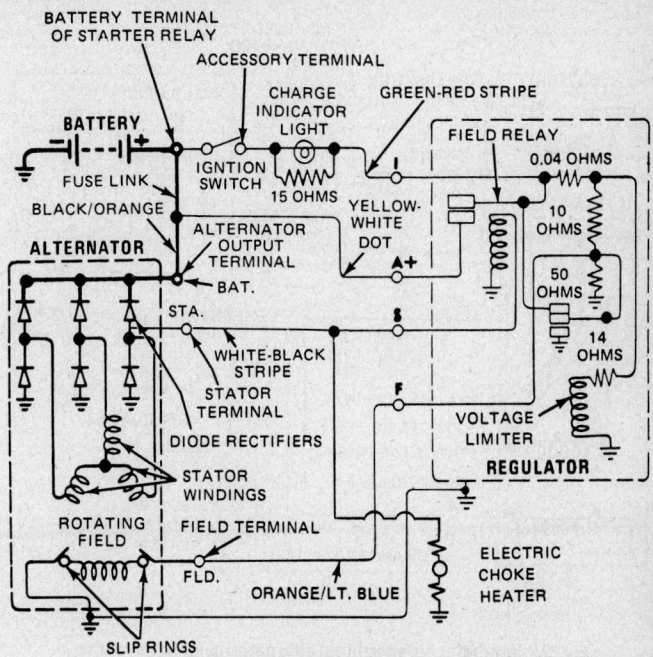

Fig. 6 Indicator light side terminal alternator charging system. 70 amp system

NOTE: The ammeter indicates current flow into (charge) or out of (discharge) the vehicle battery.

SYSTEM TESTING

NOTE: The operations and on vehicle test procedures for the side terminal alterna-

tor are same as for rear terminal alternator. However, the internal wiring, Figs. 5 through 9A, and bench test procedures differ.

Alternator In-Vehicle Tests
Alternator Output Test

When the alternator output test is con-

ducted off the car, a test bench must be used. Follow the procedure given by the test bench equipment manufacturer.

NOTE: When the alternator is removed from the vehicle for this purpose, always disconnect the battery ground cable as the alternator output connector is connected to the battery at all times.

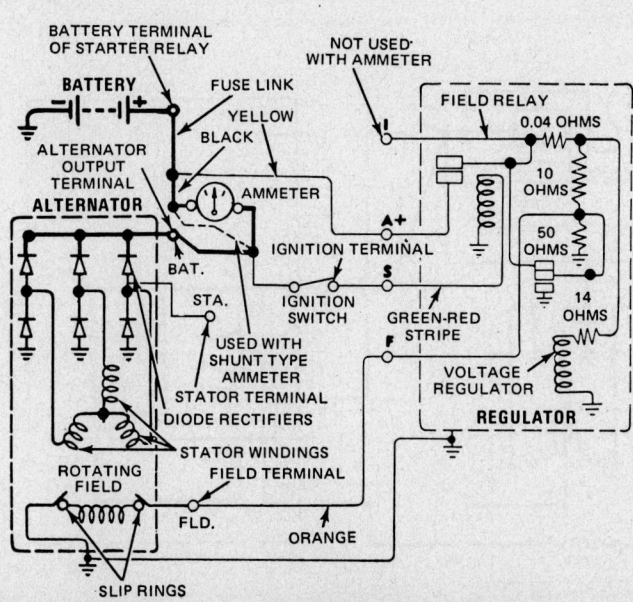

Fig. 7 Ammeter side terminal alternator charging system. 65 amp system

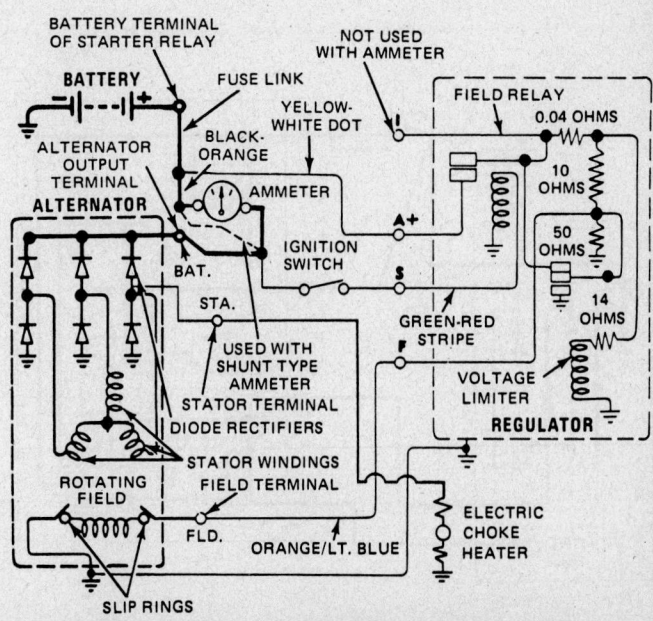

Fig. 8 Ammeter side terminal alternator charging system. 70 amp system

FORD MOTORCRAFT ALTERNATOR

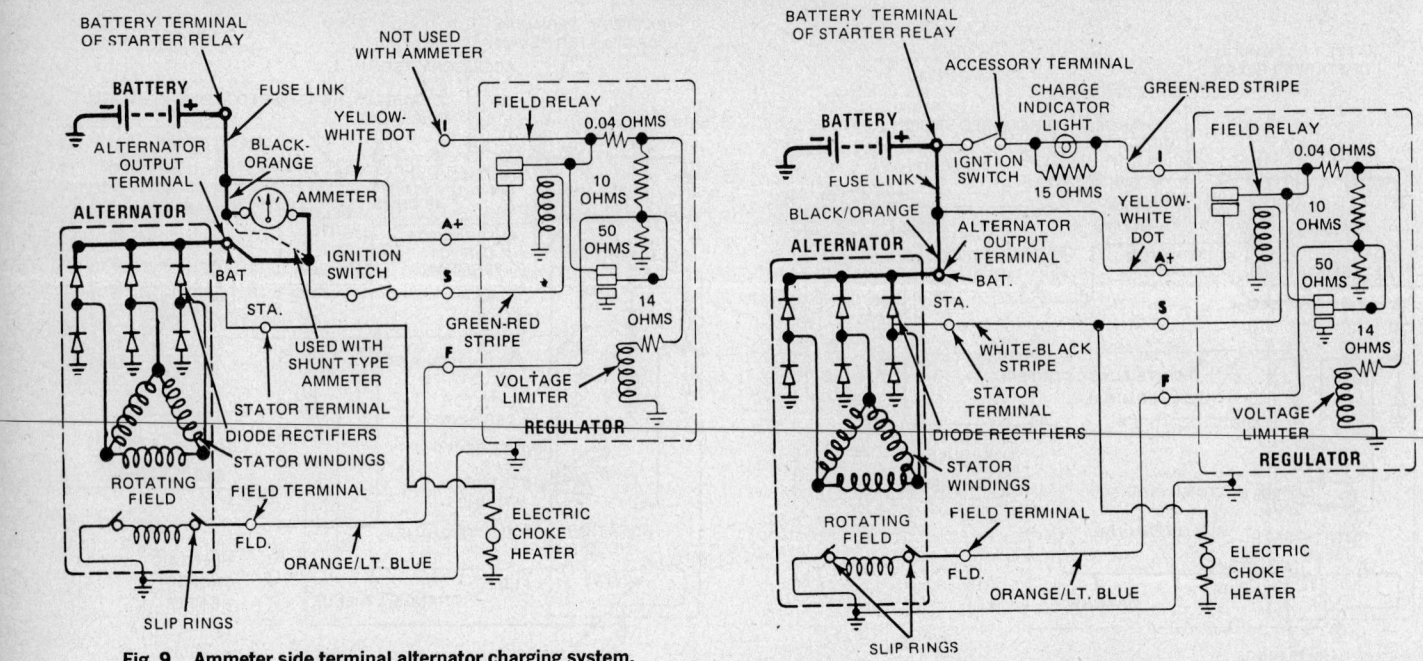

Fig. 9   Ammeter side terminal alternator charging system. 90 amp system

Fig. 9A   Indicator light side terminal alternator charging system. 90 amp system

Test Procedure

CAUTION: On vehicles equipped with breakerless ignition systems, it is recommended that the following test not be performed with the equipment described since possible damage may occur to the breakerless ignition electronic module and other electronic devices. Refer to the "In-Vehicle Voltmeter Test" procedure for vehicles equipped with breakerless ignition.

1. Make the connections and tester knob adjustments, Fig. 11 (Output Test).

Be sure that the field rheostat knob is at the OFF position at the start of this test.

2. Close the battery adapter switch. Start the engine, then open the battery adapter switch.
3. Increase the engine speed to approximately 2000 rpm (use a tachometer following the manufacturers instructions). Turn off all lights and electrical accessories.
4. Turn the field rheostat clockwise until 15 volts is indicated on the voltmeter upper scale. Turn the master control

clockwise until the voltmeter indicates between 11 and 12 volts. Holding the master control in this position, turn the field rheostat clockwise to its maximum rotation. Turn the master control counter clockwise until the voltmeter indicates 15 volts. Observe the ammeter reading. Add 2 amperes to this reading to obtain alternator output. If rated output cannot be obtained, increase the engine speed to 2900 rpm and repeat this step.

5. Return the field rheostat knob to OFF, release the master control knob, and

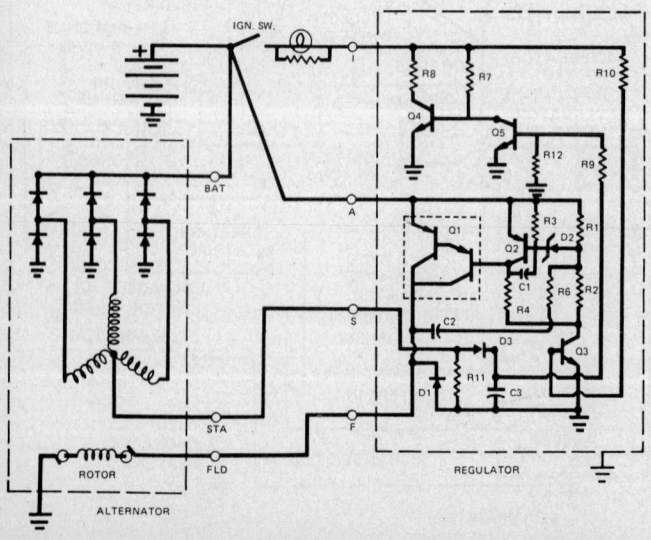

Fig. 10   Indicator light charging system with electronic voltage regulator

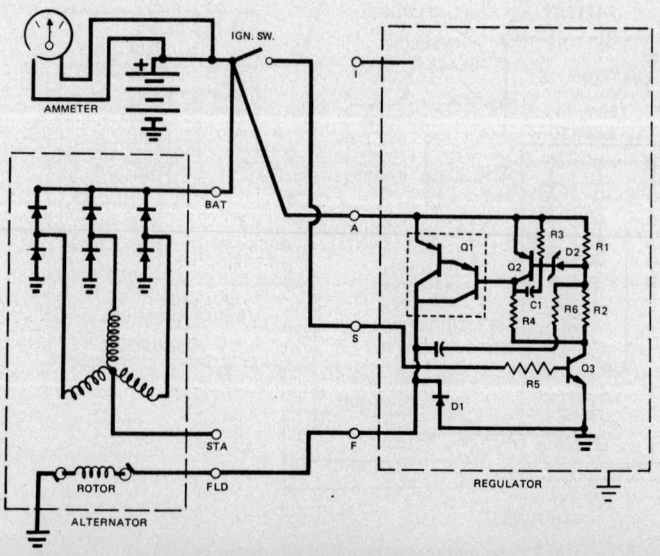

Fig. 10A   Ammeter charging system with electronic voltage regulator

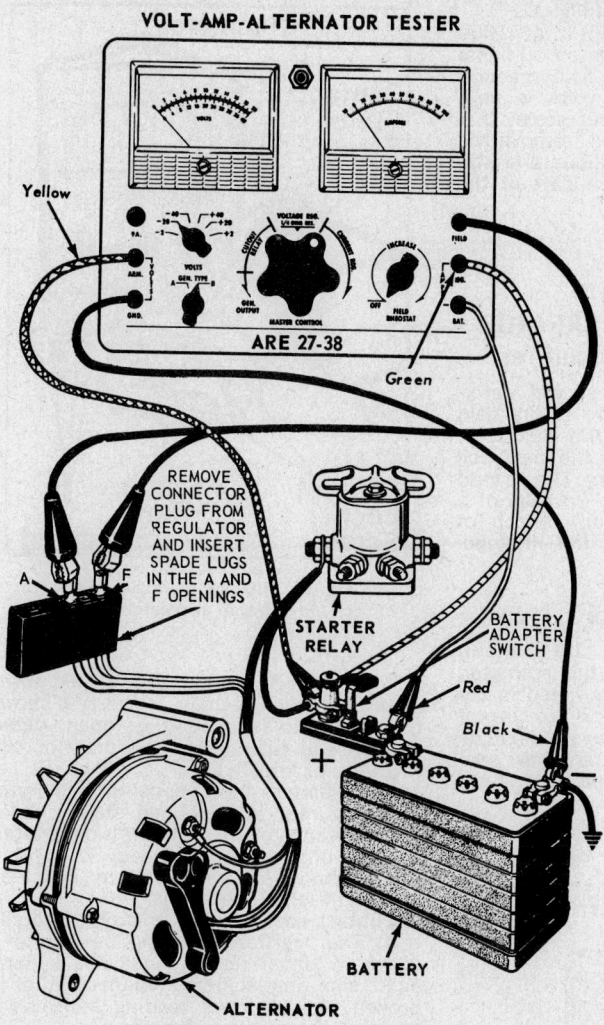

VOLT-AMP-ALTERNATOR TESTER

Yellow

REMOVE CONNECTOR PLUG FROM REGULATOR AND INSERT SPADE LUGS IN THE A AND F OPENINGS

A F

STARTER RELAY

BATTERY ADAPTER SWITCH

Red

Black

Green

+

−

BATTERY

ALTERNATOR

ARE 27-38

Fig. 11 Alternator output test

VOLT-AMP-ALTERNATOR TESTER

Green

ALTERNATOR

Red

+

BATTERY

−

FIELD

REG.

BAT.

ARE 27-38

FIELD TERMINAL

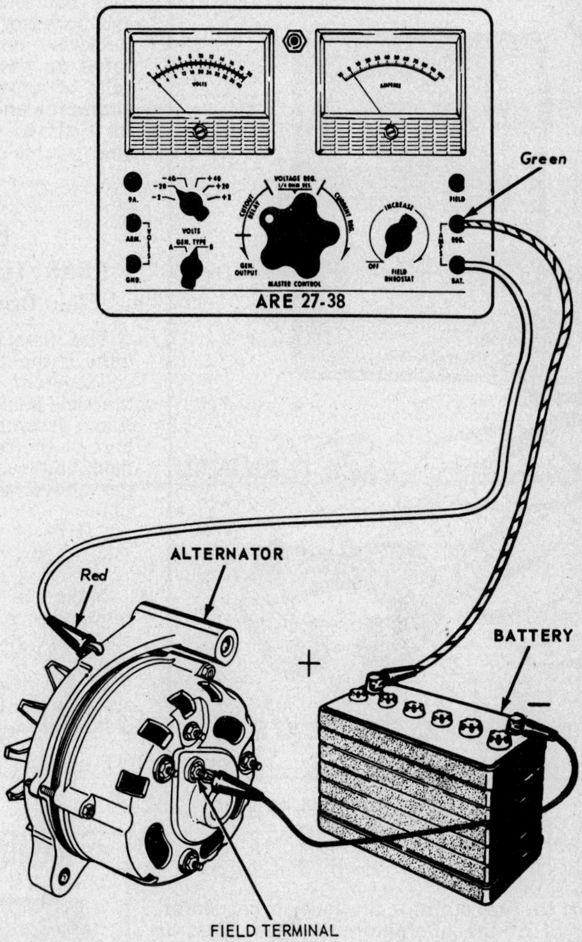

Fig. 13 Alternator field open or short circuit test

stop the engine. Disconnect the test equipment, if no further tests are to be made.

If the alternator output is not O.K., it will be necessary to remove the alternator from the vehicle and perform the necessary bench tests to locate the defect.

An output of approximately 2 to 5 amperes below specification usually indicates an open alternator diode. An output of approximately 10 to 14 amperes below specification usually indicates a shorted alternator diode. An alternator with a shorted diode will usually whine, which will be most noticeable at idle speeds.

Stator Neutral Voltage Test

CAUTION: On vehicles equipped with breakerless ignition systems, it is recommended that the following test not be performed with the equipment described since possible damage may occur to the breakerless ignition electronic module and other electronic devices. Refer to the "In-Vehicle Voltmeter Test" procedure for vehicles equipped with breakerless ignition systems.

The alternator STA terminal is connect-

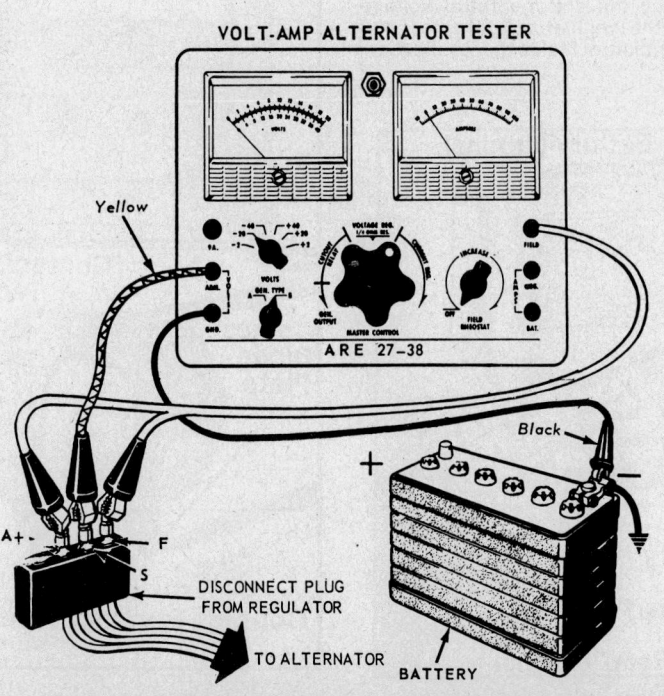

VOLT-AMP ALTERNATOR TESTER

Yellow

FIELD

REG.

BAT.

ARE 27-38

Black

A+ − F
S

DISCONNECT PLUG FROM REGULATOR

TO ALTERNATOR

+

−

BATTERY

Fig. 12 Typical stator neutral voltage test

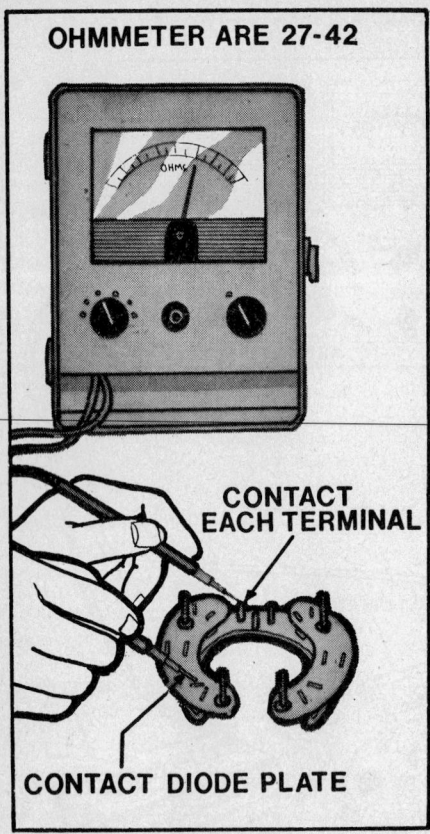

OHMMETER ARE 27-42

CONTACT EACH TERMINAL

CONTACT DIODE PLATE

Fig. 14   Diode test. 38, 42 & 55 amp alternators

ed to the stator coil neutral or center point of the alternator windings, Figs. 1 thru 10. The voltage generated at this point is used to close the field relay in the charge indicator light system.

To test for the stator neutral voltage, disconnect the regulator connector plug from the regulator. Make the connections

and tester knob adjustments, Fig. 12.

Start the engine and run it at 1000 rpm (use a tachometer). Turn off all lights and accessories. Rotate the field rheostat clockwise until at least 6 volts is indicated on the voltmeter upper scale. If 6 volts or more is not obtained, remove the alternator and perform the diode and stator tests to determine which part of the alternator is damaged.

Bench Tests
REAR TERMINAL ALTERNATOR
Field Open Or Short Circuit Test

The first part of this test will determine if the alternator portion of the field coil system, consisting of the field coil, the field coil slip rings and the field coil brush assembly is satisfactory. The second part of the test will indicate (in case of a field coil system malfunction), which of the above items is causing the malfunction.

Test Procedure

Make the connection, Fig. 13. The current draw, as indicated by the ammeter, should be to specification as listed in car chapters. If there is little or no current flow, the field or brushes have a high resistance or are open. A current flow considerably higher than that specified above

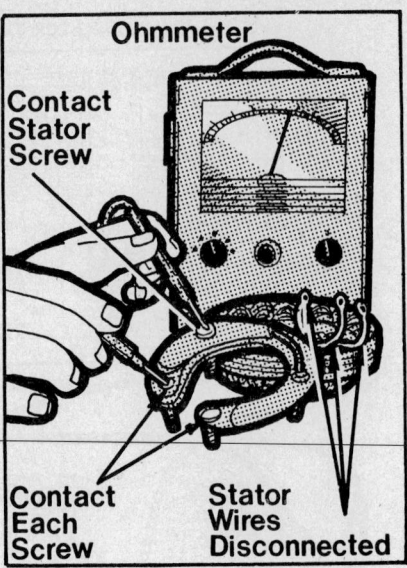

Ohmmeter

Contact Stator Screw

Contact Each Screw

Stator Wires Disconnected

Fig. 15   Booster plate diode test. 61-amp alternator

indicates shorted or grounded field turns or brush leads touching. If the test shows that the field is shorted or open, determine if the field brush assembly or slip rings are at fault.

Disassemble front housing and rotor from the rear housing and stator, check the resistance of the rotor with ohmmeter. Set the ohmmeter multiply-by knob at 1 and calibrate the ohmmeter as indicated inside the ohmmeter cover.

Contact each ohmmeter probe to a slip ring. The resistance should be 3.5 to 5 ohms. A higher reading indicates a damaged slip ring soldered connection or a broken wire. A lower reading indicates a shorted wire or slip ring assembly.

Contact one ohmmeter probe to a slip ring and the other probe to the rotor shaft. The resistance should be infinite. Any reading other than infinite indicates

Battery Terminal

OhmmeterProbes

Stator (Rear) Terminal

Fig. 16   Rectifier short or grounded and stator grounded test

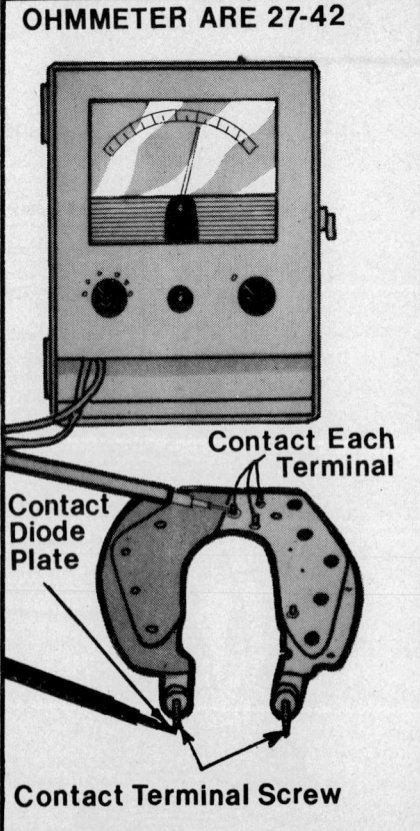

OHMMETER ARE 27-42

Contact Each Terminal

Contact Diode Plate

Contact Terminal Screw

Fig. 17   Side terminal alternator diode test

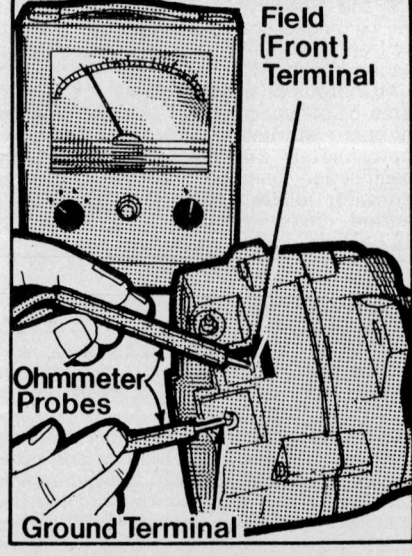

Field (Front) Terminal

Ohmmeter Probes

Ground Terminal

Fig. 16A   Field open or short circuit test

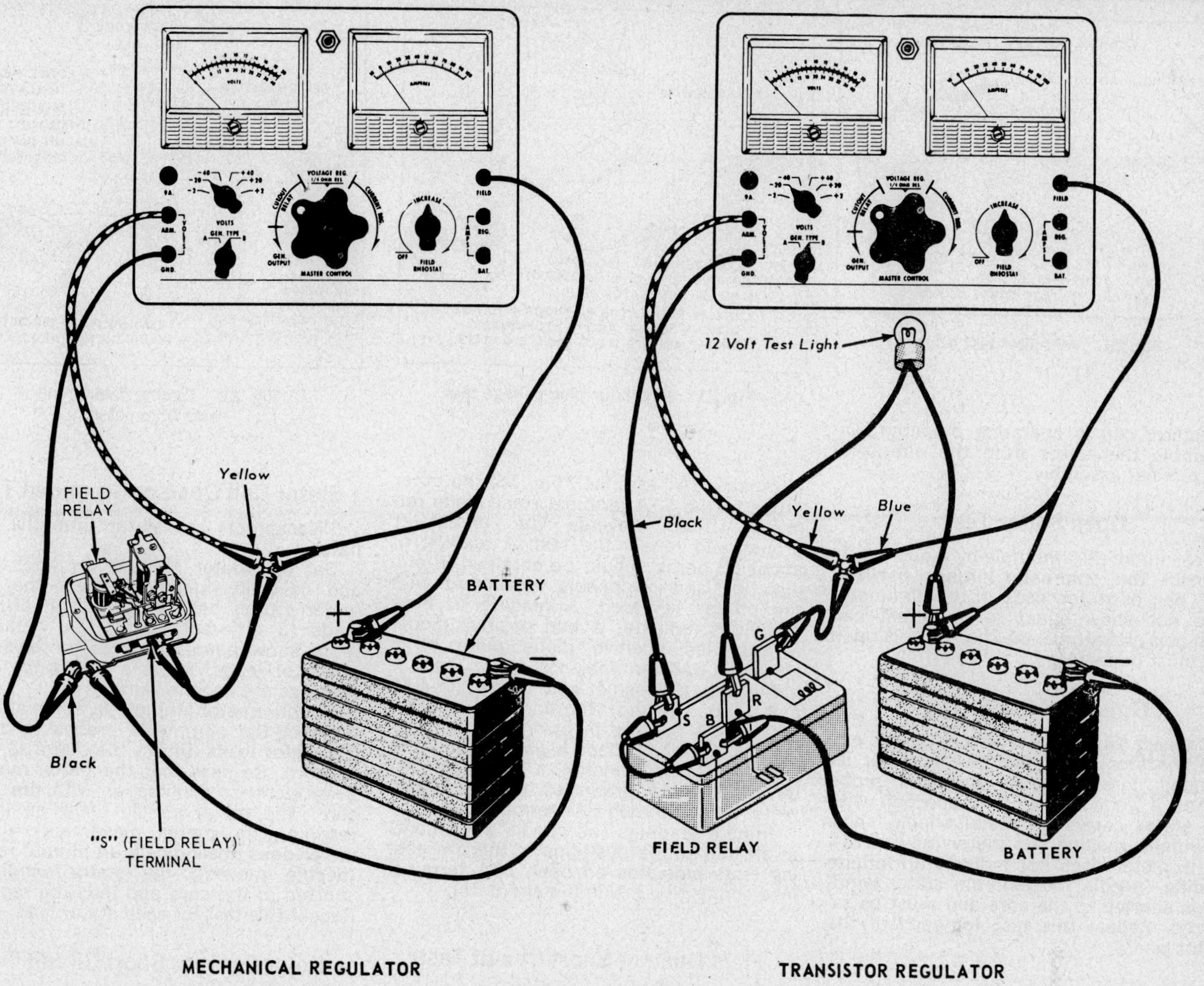

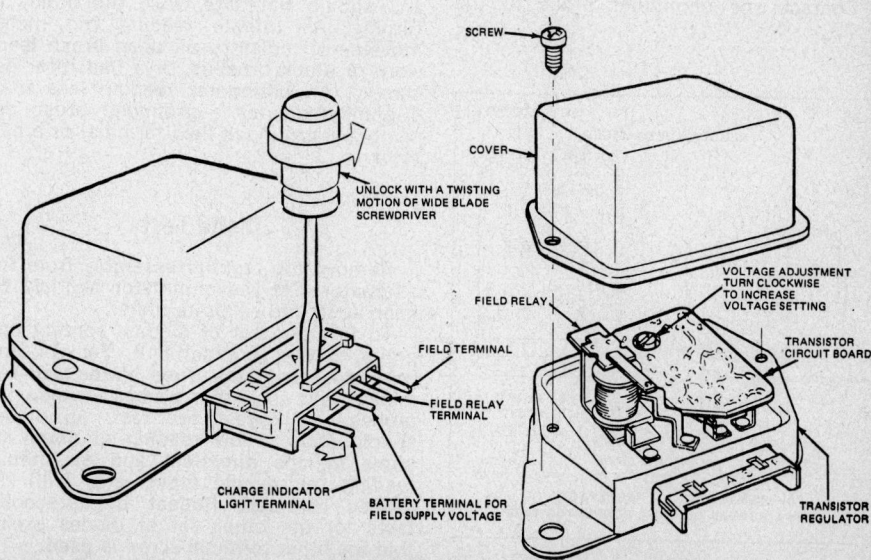

MECHANICAL REGULATOR   TRANSISTOR REGULATOR

Fig. 18   Autolite regulators field relay test

a short to ground. Inspect the slip ring soldered terminals to make certain that they are not bent and touching the shaft, or the excess solder is not grounding the rotor coil.

If the rotor checks indicate that it is in proper operating condition but the overall test, Fig. 13, indicates trouble, the brushes or brush assembly are the cause.

Diode Tests

Disassemble the alternator. Disconnect the rectifier assembly from the stator and connect leads, Fig. 14. To test one set of diodes, contact one probe to the diode plate and contact each of the three stator lead terminals with the other probe. Reverse the probes and repeat the test. Test the other set of diodes in the same way. On 61-ampere alternators, test the two additional diodes, Fig. 15.

All 6 tests (8 tests on 61-ampere alternator) should show a low reading of approximately 60 ohms in one direction and an infinite reading (no needle movement) with the probes reserved.

Open Or Grounded Stator Coil Tests

These tests are made to determine if

Fig. 19   Transistorized regulator adjustment, 1974-77

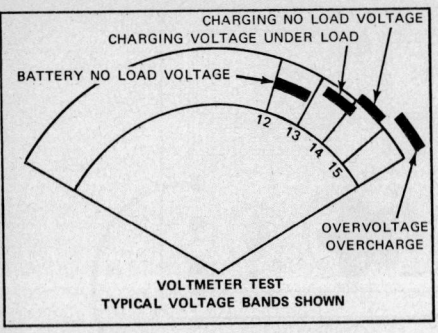

Fig. 20 Voltmeter test scale

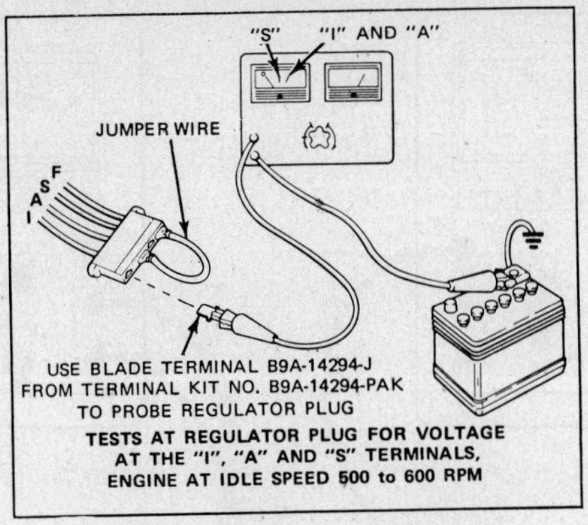

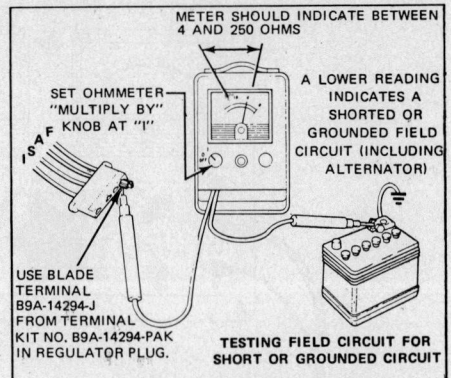

Fig. 21 Regulator plug voltage test

**Fig. 22 Testing field circuit
with Ohmmeter**

the stator coil is operating properly. Disassemble the stator from the alternator and rectifier assembly.

Open Stator Test

Set ohmmeter multiple-by knob at 1. Connect the ohmmeter probes between each pair of stator leads. If the ohmmeter does not show equal readings between each pair of stator leads, the stator is open and must be replaced.

Grounded Stator Test

Connect the ohmmeter probes to one of the stator leads and to the stator laminated core. Be sure that the probe makes a good electrical connection with the stator core. The metal should show an infinite reading (no meter movement). If the meter does not indicate an infinite reading (needle moves), the stator winding is shorted to the core and must be replaced. Repeat this test for each of the stator leads.

SIDE TERMINAL ALTERNATOR
Rectifier Short or Grounded and Stator Grounded Test

Set ohmmeter Multiply By knob at 10, and calibrate meter.

Contact one ohmmeter probe to the

alternator BAT terminal, Fig. 16, the other probe to the STA terminal (rear blade terminal). Then, reverse the ohmmeter probes and repeat the test. A reading of about 60 ohms should be obtained in one direction and no needle movement with the probes reversed. A reading in both directions indicates a bad positive diode, a grounded positive diode plate or a grounded BAT terminal.

Perform the same test using the STA and GND (ground) terminals of the alternator. A reading in both directions indicates either a bad negative diode, a grounded stator winding, a grounded stator terminal, a grounded positive diode plate, or a grounded BAT terminal.

Infinite readings (no needle movement) in all four probe positions in the preceeding tests indicates an open STA terminal lead connection inside the alternator.

Field Open or Short Circuit Test

Set the ohmmeter Multiply By knob at 1 and calibrate meter.

Contact the alternator field terminal with one probe and the ground terminal with the other probe, Fig. 16A. Then, spin the alternator pulley. The ohmmeter reading should be between 4 and 200 ohms, and should fluctuate while the pulley is turning. An infinite reading (no meter movement) indicates an open brush lead, worn or stuck brushes, or a bad rotor assembly. An ohmmeter reading less than 4 ohms indicates a grounded brush assembly, a grounded field terminal or a bad rotor.

Diode Test

Remove the rectifier assembly from the alternator. Set the ohmmeter Multiply By knob at 10 and calibrate meter.

To test one set of diodes, contact one probe to the terminal bolt, Fig. 17 and contact each of the three stator lead terminals with the other probe. Reverse the probes and repeat the test. All diodes should show a low reading of about 60 ohms in one direction, and an infinite reading (no needle movement) with the probes reversed. Repeat the preceding tests for the other set of diodes except that the other terminal screw is used.

If the meter readings are not as specified, replace the rectifier assembly.

Stator Coil Open or Grounded Test

Disassemble the stator from the alternator.

Set ohmmeter Multiply By knob at 1, and calibrate meter. Connect the ohmmeter probes between each pair of stator leads (3 different ways). The ohmmeter must show equal readings for each pair or stator leads. Replace the stator if the readings are not the same.

Set ohmmeter Multiply By Knob at 1000. Connect the ohmmeter probes to one of the stator leads and to the stator laminated core. Be sure that the probe makes a good electrical connection with the stator core. The meter should show an infinite reading (no meter movement). If the meter does not indicate an infinite reading (needle moves), the stator winding is shorted to the core and must be replaced. Repeat this test for each stator lead.

Rotor Open or Short Circuit Test

Disassemble the front housing and rotor from the rear housing and stator. Set the ohmmeter, multiply By knob at 1 and calibrate meter.

Contact each ohmmeter probe to a rotor slip ring. The meter reading should be 3 to 5½ ohms. A higher reading indicates a damaged slip ring solder connection or a broken wire. A lower reading indicates a shorted wire or slip ring.

Contact one ohmmeter probe to a slip ring and the other probe to the rotor shaft. The meter reading should be infinite (no

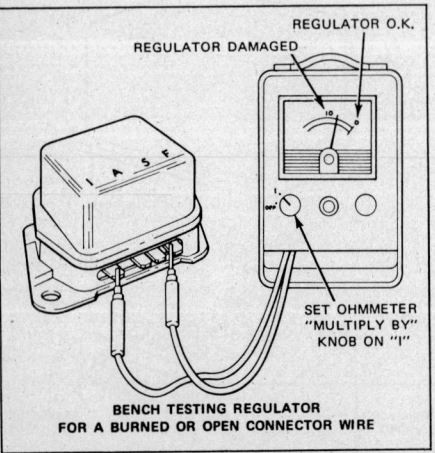

Fig. 23 Testing regulator for a burned or open connector wire

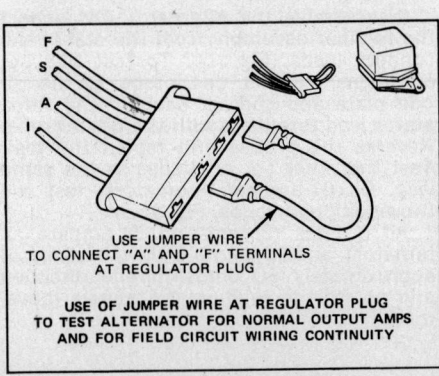

**Fig. 24 Regulator plug.
Jumper wire connection**

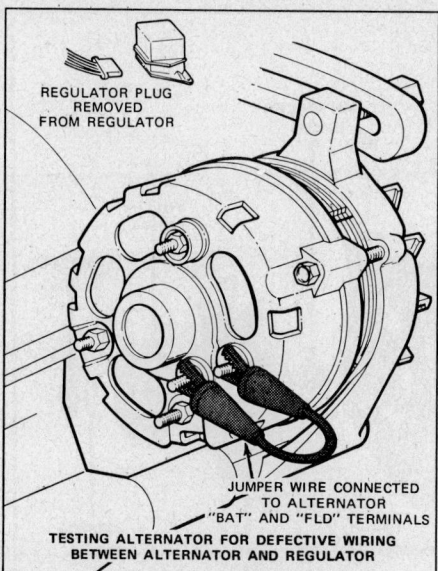

Fig. 25 Rear terminal alternator. Jumper wire connection

tight before testing the regulator.

Test Procedure

Connect the voltmeter positive lead to the battery positive terminal, and the negative lead to the battery negative terminal. Turn off all electrical loads. Then, check and record the voltmeter reading. Connect the red lead of a tachometer to the distributor terminal of the coil and the block tachometer lead to a good ground.

Place the transmission shift lever in the neutral or park position and start the engine. Increase the engine speed to 1800-2200 rpm for 2 or 3 minutes. Check and record the voltmeter reading., it should be 1 to 2 volts higher than the first reading. If the reading is less than 1 volt or greater than 2½ volts, replace the voltage regulator. If the reading is between 1 and 2 volts, turn on the headlights and heater blower. The voltage should not decrease more than ½ volt. Replace the regulator if the voltage drop is greater than ½ volt.

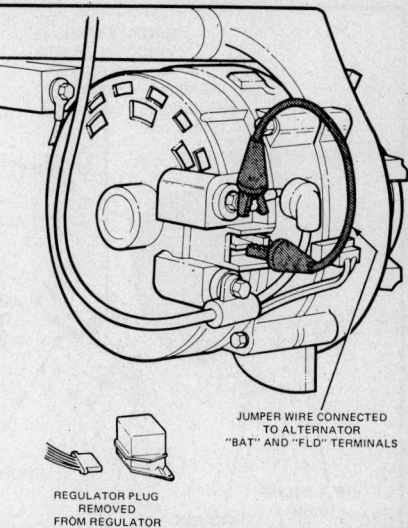

Fig. 26 Side terminal alternator. Jumper wire connection

deflection). A reading other than infinite indicates the rotor is shorted to the shaft. Inspect the slip ring soldered terminals to be sure they are not bent and touching the rotor shaft, or that excess solder is not grounding the rotor coil connections to the shaft. Replace the rotor if it is shorted and cannot be repaired.

Field Relay Test Electro-Mechanical Regulator

Remove the regulator from the car, and remove the regulator cover. Make the connections Fig. 18. Slowly rotate the field rheostat control clockwise from the maximum counterclockwise position until the field relay contacts close. Observe the voltmeter reading at the moment that the relay contacts close. This is the relay closing voltage. If the relay closes immediately, even with the field rheostat close to the maximum counterclockwise position, push the red button between the two meters, and repeat the test. If the closing voltage is not within specification, unit must be replaced.

Field Relay Test-Transistor Regulator

Disconnect the relay connector plug. Make the connections, Fig. 18. Slowly rotate the field rheostat control clockwise from the maximum counterclockwise position until the test light comes on. Observe the voltmeter reading at the moment that the light comes on. This is the relay closing voltage. If the relay closes immediately, even with the field rheostat close to the maximum counterclockwise position, push the red button between the two meters, and repeat the test. If the closing voltage is not to specification as listed in car chapters, replace the relay.

1974-78 UNITS

The alternator must be adjusted within specification, and the charging system electrical connections must be clean and

REGULATOR ADJUSTMENTS

1974-78 Transistorized Regulator

The only adjustment of this regulator is the voltage limiter adjustment. This adjustment is made with regulator at normal operating temperature. Remove the regulator cover and using a fiber rod, turn voltage adjusting screw clockwise to raise voltage setting or counter-clockwise to lower voltage setting, Fig. 19. Refer to the "Alternator & Regulator Specifications" as listed in the individual car chapters for proper voltage setting.

1974-78 Electro-Mechanical & 1978 Electronic Regulators

These regulators are factory calibrated and sealed and no adjustment is possible. If regulator calibration values are not within specifications, the regulator must be replaced.

IN-VEHICLE VOLTMETER TEST

NOTE: *All lights and electrical systems in the off position, parking brake applied, transmission in neutral and a charged battery (at least 1200 specific gravity).*

1. Connect the negative lead of the voltmeter to the negative battery cable clamp (not bolt or nut).
2. Connect the positive lead of the voltmeter to the positive battery cable clamp (not bolt or nut).
3. Record the battery voltage reading shown on the voltmeter scale.
4. Connect the red lead of a tachometer to the distributor terminal of the coil and the black tachometer lead to a good ground.
5. Then, start and operate the engine at approximately 1500 rpm. With no other electrical load (foot off brake

pedal and car doors closed), the voltmeter reading should increase (1 volt) and not exceed (2 volts) above the first recorded battery voltage reading. The reading should be taken when the voltmeter needles stops moving.

6. With the engine running, turn on the heater and/or air conditioner blower motor to high speed and headlights to high beam.
7. Increase the engine speed to 2000 rpm. The voltmeter should indicate a reading of 0.5 to 1.0 volts above the battery voltage, Fig. 20.

NOTE: *If the above tests indicate proper voltage readings, the charging system is operating normally. Proceed to "Test Results" if a problem still exists.*

Test Results

1. If voltmeter reading indicates *over voltage* (2.0 volts above battery voltage), stop the engine and check the ground connections between the regulator and alternator and/or regulator to engine. Clean and tighten connections securely and repeat the *Voltmeter Test Procedures.*
2. If *over voltage* condition still exists, disconnect the regulator wiring plug from the regulator and repeat the *Voltmeter Test Procedures.*
3. If *over voltage* still exists with the regulator wiring plug disconnected, repair the short in the wiring harness between the alternator and regulator. Then, replace the regulator and connect the regulator wiring plug to the regulator and repeat the *Voltmeter Test Procedures.*
4. If voltmeter does not increase (One volt on 1974 systems or ½ volt on 1975-78 systems), check for presence of battery voltage at alternator BAT terminal and the regulator plug A terminal, Fig. 21. Repair the wiring if no voltage is present at these terminals, and repeat the *Voltmeter Test Procedures.*

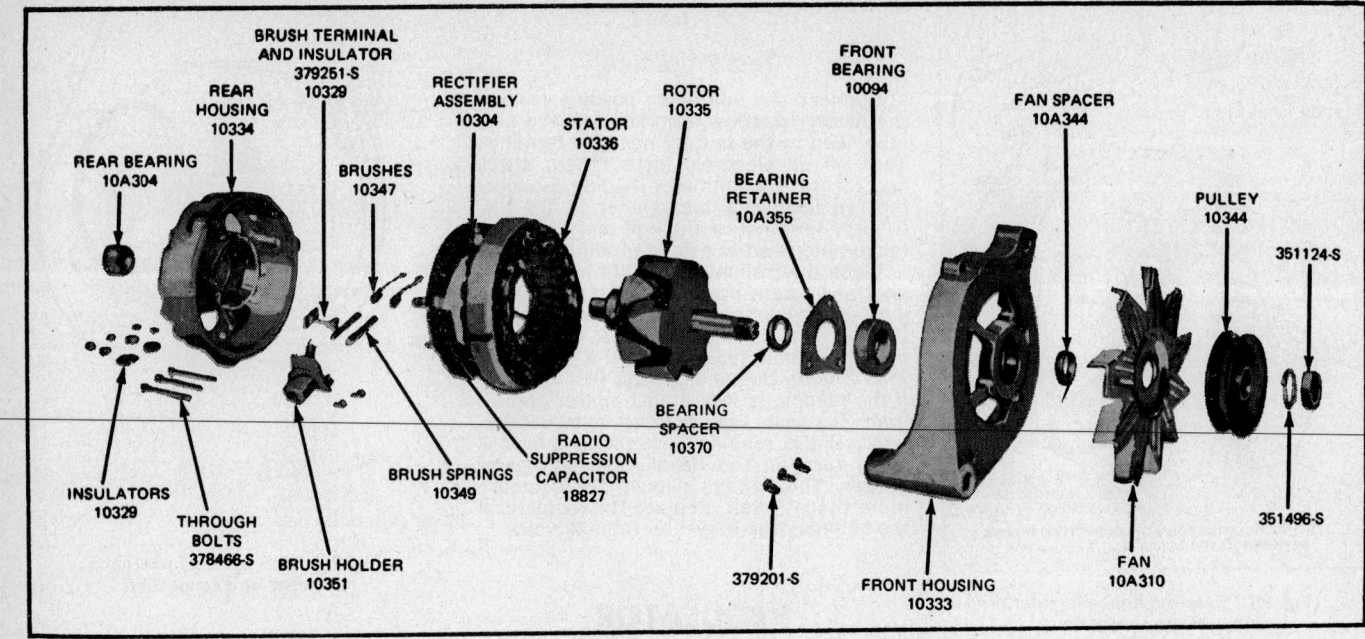

Fig. 27 Disassembled rear terminal alternator

5. If voltmeter reading does not increase (One volt on 1974 systems or ½ volt on 1975-78 systems) above battery voltage, proceed to next step.

6. Before performing other tests, the field circuit (regulator plug to alternator) must be checked for a grounding condition. If the field circuit is grounded and the jumper wire is used as a check at the regulator wiring plug from the A to F terminals, Fig. 21, excessive current will cause heat damage to the regulator wiring plug terminals and may burn the jumper wire, Fig. 21. Also, if the field circuit was grounded, the connector wire inside the regulator will be burned open and an under voltage condition will result.

7. The field circuit should be checked with the regulator wiring plug disconnected and an ohmmeter connected from the F terminal of the regulator wiring plug to the battery ground. The ohmmeter should indicate between 4 and 250 ohms, Fig. 22.

8. A check for the regulator burned-open wire is made by connecting an ohmmeter from the I to F terminals of the regulator, Fig. 23. The reading should indicate O (no resistance). If the reading indicates approximately 10 ohms, the connector wire inside the regulator is burned open. *The field circuit grounded condition must be found and repaired before installing a new regulator.*

Field Circuit and Alternator Tests

1. If the field circuit is satisfactory, disconnect the regulator wiring plug at the regulator and connect the jumper wire from the A to the F terminals on the regulator wiring plug, Fig. 24.
2. Repeat the *Voltmeter Test Procedures.*
3. If the *Voltmeter Test Procedures* still indicate a problem of under voltage, remove the jumper wire at the regulator plug and leave the plug disconnected from the regulator, Figs. 25 and 26. Connect a jumper wire to the *FLD* and *BAT* terminals on the alternator, Figs. 25 and 26.
4. Repeat the *Voltmeter Test Procedures.*
5. If the *Voltmeter Test* are now satisfactory, repair the wiring harness from the alternator to the regulator. Then, remove the jumper wire at the alternator and connect the regulator wiring plug to the regulator.
6. Repeat the *Voltmeter Test Procedures,* to be sure the charging system is operating normally.
7. If the *Voltmeter Test* results still indicate under voltage, repair or replace the alternator. With the jumper wire removed, connect the wiring to the alternator and regulator.
8. Repeat the *Voltmeter Test Procedures.*

REGULATOR TESTS

S Circuit Test—With Ammeter

1. Connect the positive lead of the voltmeter to the S terminal of the regulator wiring plug Fig. 21. Turn the ignition switch to the ON position. *Do not start the engine.*
2. The voltmeter reading should indicate battery voltage.
3. If there is *no* voltage reading, disconnect the positive voltmeter lead from the positive battery clamp and repair the S wire lead from the ignition switch to the regulator wiring plug.
4. Connect the positive voltmeter lead to the positive battery cable terminal and repeat the *Voltmeter Test Procedures.*

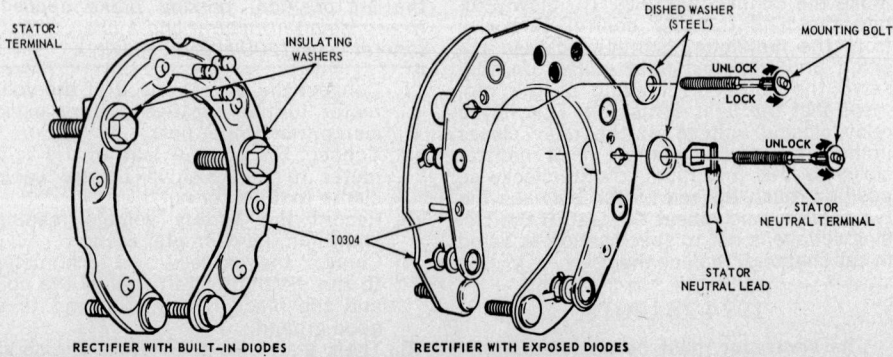

Fig. 28 Rectifier assembly

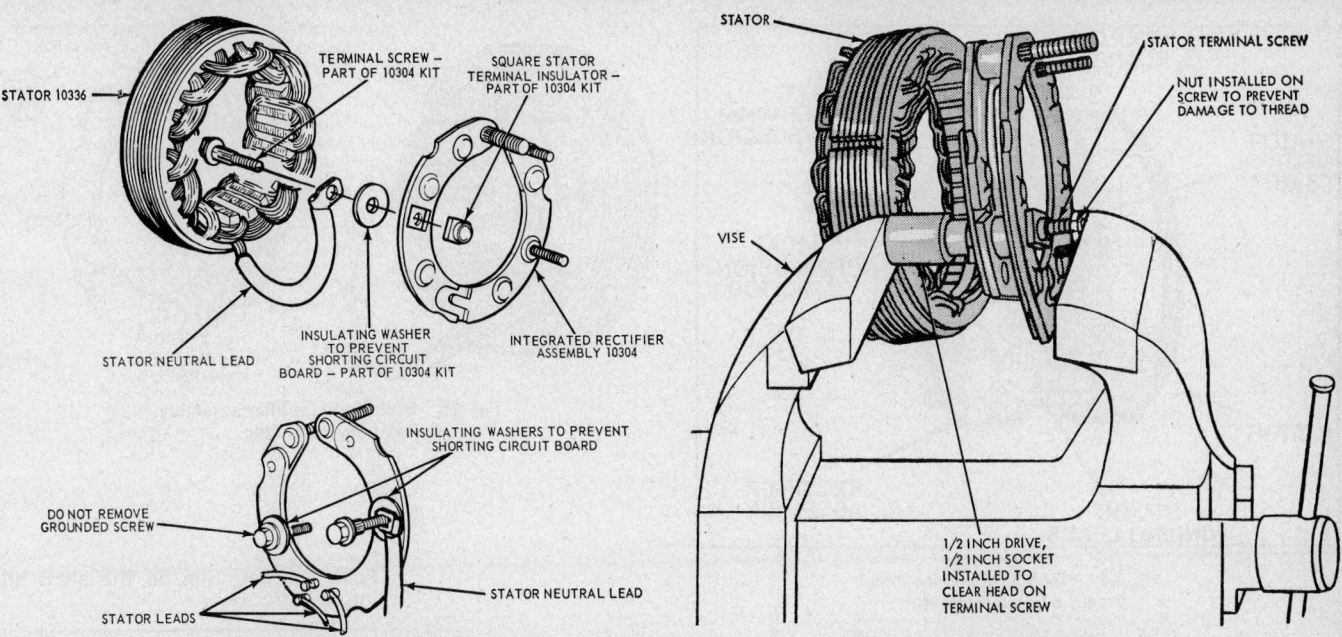

Fig. 29 Stator terminal installation. Integral rectifier circuit board

Fig. 30 Stator terminal screw removal. 61-amp alternator

S and I Circuit Test—With Indicator Light

1. With the engine idling, connect the positive lead of the voltmeter to the S terminal and then to the I terminal of the regulator wiring plug, Fig. 21. The voltage of the S circuit should read approximately 1/2 of the I circuit.
2. If no voltage is present, repair the alternator or the wiring circuit at fault. Reconnect the positive voltmeter lead to the positive battery cable terminal and repeat the *Voltmeter Test Procedures.*
3. If the above tests are satisfactory, install a new regulator.
4. Then, remove the jumper wire from the regulator wiring plug and connect the wiring plug to the regulator. Repeat the *Voltmeter Test Procedures.*

Diode Test

Test Procedure

1. Disconnect electric choke, if equipped.
2. Disconnect voltage regulator wiring connector.
3. Connect a jumper wire between the "A" and "F" terminals of the voltage regulator wiring connector, Fig. 24.
4. Connect voltmeter to battery clamps. Then, start and idle engine.
5. Observe and note voltmeter reading.
6. Move the voltmeter positive lead to the alternator "S" terminal and note voltage reading.

Test Results

1. If voltmeter reading is within 1/2 of battery voltage, the diodes are satisfactory.
2. If voltmeter reading is approximately 1.5 volts, the alternator has a shorted negative diode or a grounded stator winding.
3. If voltmeter reading is approximately 1.5 volts less than battery voltage, the alternator has a shorted positive diode.
4. If voltage reading is approximately 1 to 1.5 volts less than 1/2 battery voltage, the alternator has an open positive diode.
5. If voltage reading is 1 to 1.5 volts above 1/2 battery voltage, the alternator has an open negative diode.
6. Reconnect electric choke into circuit after tests are completed, if equipped.

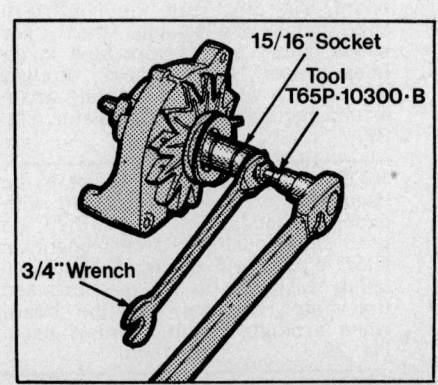

Fig. 31 Typical pulley removal

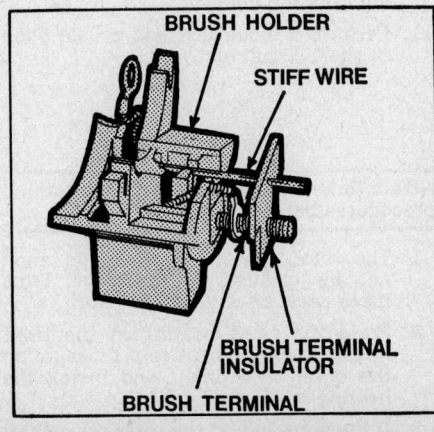

Fig. 32 Brush holder assembly

Fig. 33 Typical brush lead positions

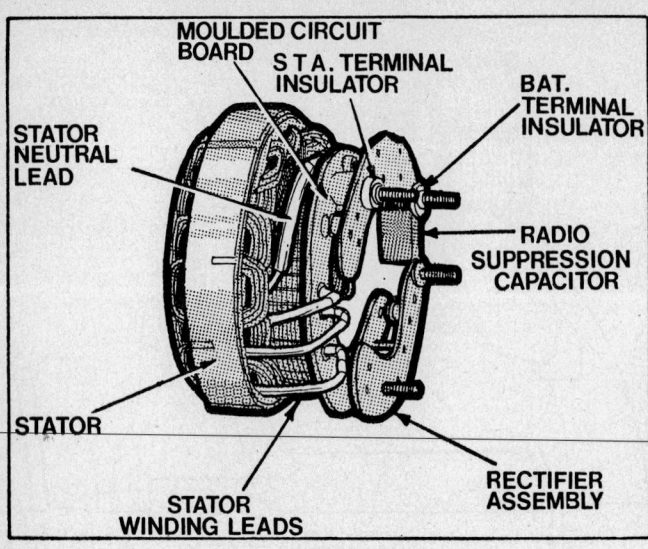

MOULDED CIRCUIT BOARD
S T A. TERMINAL INSULATOR
BAT. TERMINAL INSULATOR
STATOR NEUTRAL LEAD
RADIO SUPPRESSION CAPACITOR
STATOR
STATOR WINDING LEADS
RECTIFIER ASSEMBLY

Fig. 34   Stator lead connections. Except 61-amp alternator

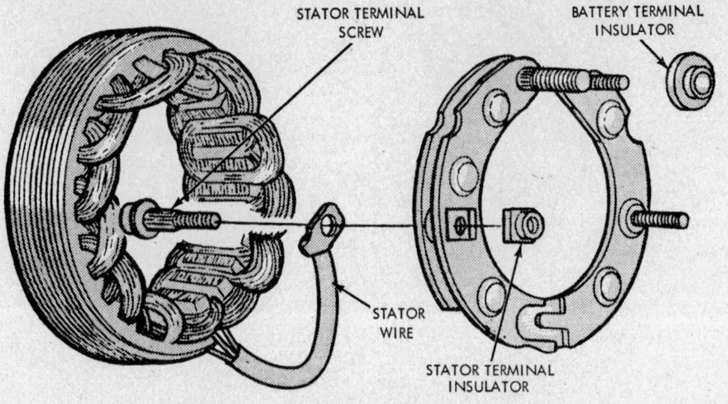

STATOR TERMINAL SCREW
BATTERY TERMINAL INSULATOR
STATOR WIRE
STATOR TERMINAL INSULATOR

Fig. 35   Stator and rectifier assembly. 61-amp alternator

ALTERNATOR REPAIRS
Rear Terminal Alternator

NOTE: Use a 100 watt soldering iron.

Disassembly

1. Mark both end housings and the stator with a scribe mark for assembly, Fig. 27.
2. Remove the three housing through bolts.
3. Separate the front housing and rotor from the stator and rear housing.
4. Remove all the nuts and insulators from the rear housing and remove the rear housing from the stator and rectifier assembly.
5. Remove the brush holder mounting screws and remove the holder, brushes, brush springs, insulator and terminal.
6. If replacement is necessary, press the bearing from the rear housing, supporting the housing on the inner boss.
7. If the rectifier assembly is being replaced, unsolder the stator leads from the printed-circuit board terminals, and separate the stator from the rectifier assembly.
8. Original production alternators will have one of three types of rectifier assembly circuit boards, Fig. 28; one has the circuit board spaced away from the diode plates with the diodes exposed. Another type is a single circuit board with built-in diodes. The third type circuit board has built-in diodes with an additional booster diode plate containing two diodes. This circuit board is used only in the 61-ampere alternator.

   If the alternator rectifier has an exposed diode circuit board, remove the screws from the rectifier by rotating the bolt heads 1/4 turn clockwise to unlock them and then remove the screws, Fig. 28. Push the stator terminal screw straight out on a rectifier with the diodes built into the circuit board, Fig. 28. Avoid turning the screw while removing to make certain that the straight knurl will engage the insulators when installing. Do not remove the grounded screw, Fig. 29.

   On 61-ampere alternator rectifier, press the stator terminal screw from the circuit board, Fig. 30. When the terminal screw has moved about 1/4 inch, remove the nut from the end of the screw and lift the screw from the circuit board.

NOTE: Do not twist the screw in the circuit board.

9. Remove the drive pulley nut, Fig. 31. Then, pull the lockwasher, pulley, fan, fan spacer, front housing and rotor stop from the rotor shaft.
10. Remove the three screws that hold the front end bearing retainer, and remove the retainer. If the bearing is damaged or has lost its lubricant, support the housing close to the bearing boss and press out the old bearing from the housing.
11. Perform a diode test and a field open or short circuit test.

Assembly

NOTE: Refer to "Cleaning and Inspection" procedures before reassembly.

1. The rotor, stator and bearings must not be cleaned with solvent. Wipe these parts off with a clean cloth.
2. Press the front bearing in the front housing bearing boss (put pressure on the outer race only), and install the bearing retainer, Fig. 27.
3. If the stop-ring on the rotor drive shaft was damaged, install a new stop-ring.

Push the new ring on the shaft and into the groove.

NOTE: Do not open the ring with snap ring pliers as permanent damage will result.

4. Position the rotor stop on the drive shaft with the recessed side against the stop-ring.
5. Position the front housing, fan spacer, fan, pulley and lock washer on the drive shaft and install the retaining nut. Torque the retaining nut, Fig. 31, to 60-100 ft lbs.
6. If the rear housing bearing was removed, support the housing on the inner boss and press in a new bearing flush with the outer end surface.
7. Place the brush springs, brushes, brush terminal and terminal insulator in the brush holder and hold the brushes in position by inserting a piece of stiff wire in the brush holder, Fig. 32.
8. Position the brush holder assembly in the rear housing and install the mounting screws. Position the brush leads in the brush holder, Fig. 33.
9. Wrap the three stator winding leads around the circuit board terminals and solder them. Position the stator neutral lead eyelet on the stator terminal screw and install the screw in the rectifier assembly, Fig. 34.
10. For a rectifier with the diodes exposed insert the special screws through the wire lug, dished washers and circuit board, Fig. 28. Turn them 1/4 turn counterclockwise to lock them. For single circuit boards with built in diodes, insert the screws straight through the wire lug, insulating washer and rectifier into the insulator, Fig. 29.

NOTE: The dished washers are to be used only on the circuit board with exposed diodes, Fig. 28. If they are used on the single circuit board, a short circuit will occur. A flat insulating washer is to be used between the stator terminal and the board when a single circuit board is used, Fig. 29.

11. For a rectifier with a booster diode plate (61-Ampere Alternator only),

proceed as follows:

a. Position the stator wire terminal on the stator terminal screw and position the screw into the rectifier. Position the square insulator over the screw and into the square hole in the rectifier, Fig. 35.

b. Rotate the terminal screw until it locks in position. Then, press the screw in finger tight.

c. Position the stator wire, Fig. 36. Press the terminal screw into the rectifier and insulator, Fig. 37.

12. Position the radio noise suppression capacitor on the rectifier terminals. On the circuit board with exposed diodes, install the STA and BAT terminal insulators, Fig. 34. On the single circuit board, position the square stator-terminal insulator in the square hole in the rectifier assembly, Fig. 29. Position the BAT terminal insulator, Fig. 38.

Position the stator and rectifier assembly in the rear housing. Make certain that all terminal insulators are seated properly in the recesses, Fig. 34. Position the STA (black), BAT (red) and FLD (orange) insulators on the terminal bolts, and install the retaining nuts, Fig. 39.

13. Wipe the rear end bearing surface of the rotor shaft with a clean lint-free rag.

14. Position the rear housing and stator assembly over the rotor and align the scribe marks made during disassembly. Seat the machined portion of the stator core into the step in both end housings. Install the housing through bolts. Remove the brush retracting wire, and put a daub of water-proof cement over the hole to seal it.

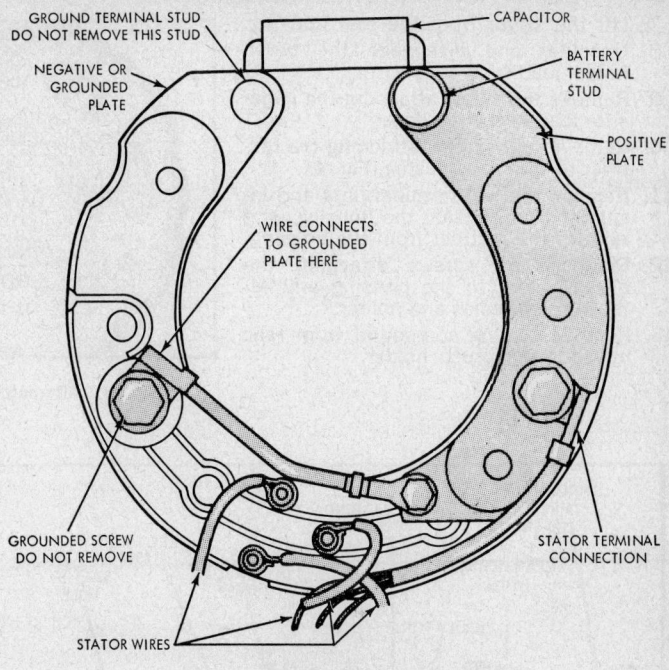

Fig. 36   Rectifier terminal locations. 61-amp alternator

Side Terminal Alternator

Disassembly

NOTE: Use a 200 watt soldering iron.

1. Mark both end housings and the stator with a scribe mark for use during assembly, Fig. 40.

2. Remove the four housing through bolts, and separate the front housing and rotor from the rear housing and stator. Slots are provided in the front housing to aid in disassembly. *Do not separate the rear housing from the stator at this time.*

3. Remove the drive pulley nut, Fig. 31. Remove the lockwasher, pulley, fan and fan spacer from the rotor shaft.

4. Pull the rotor and shaft from the front housing, and remove the spacer from the rotor shaft, Fig. 40.

5. Remove three screws retaining the bearing to the front housing. If the bearing is damaged or has lost its lubricant, remove the bearing from the housing. To remove the bearing, support the housing close to the bearing boss and press the bearing from the housing.

6. Unsolder and disengage the three stator leads from the rectifier, Fig. 41.

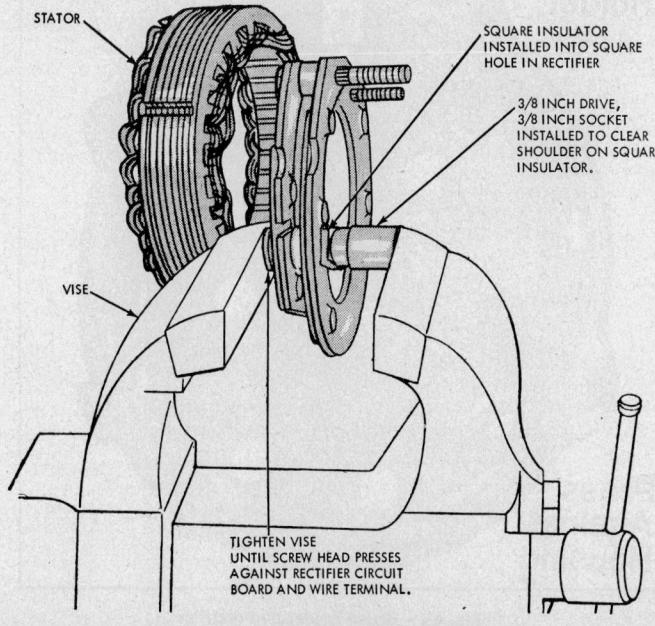

Fig. 37   Stator terminal screw installation. 61-amp alternator

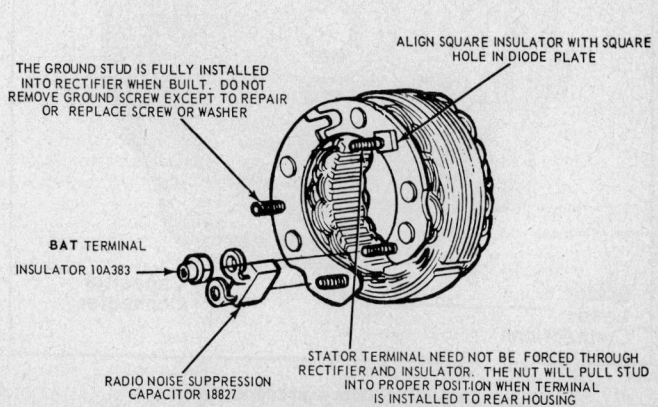

Fig. 38   Fiber-glass circuit board terminal insulators

7. Lift the stator from the rear housing.
8. Unsolder and disengage the brush holder lead from the rectifier.
9. Remove the screw attaching the capacitor lead to the rectifier.
10. Remove four screws attaching the rectifier to the rear housing, Fig. 41.
11. Remove the two terminal nuts and insulator from outside the housing, and remove the rectifier from the housing.
12. Remove two screws attaching the brush holder to the housing and remove the brushes and holder.
13. Remove sealing compound from rear housing and brush holder.

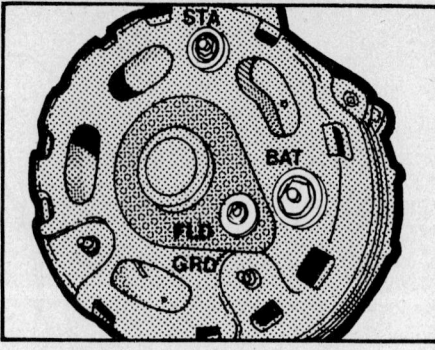

Fig. 39   Alternator terminal locations

14. Remove one screw attaching the capacitor to the rear housing and remove the capacitor.
15. If bearing replacement is necessary, support the rear housing close to the bearing boss and press the bearing out of the housing from the inside.

Assembly

NOTE: Refer to "Cleaning and Inspection" procedures before reassembly.

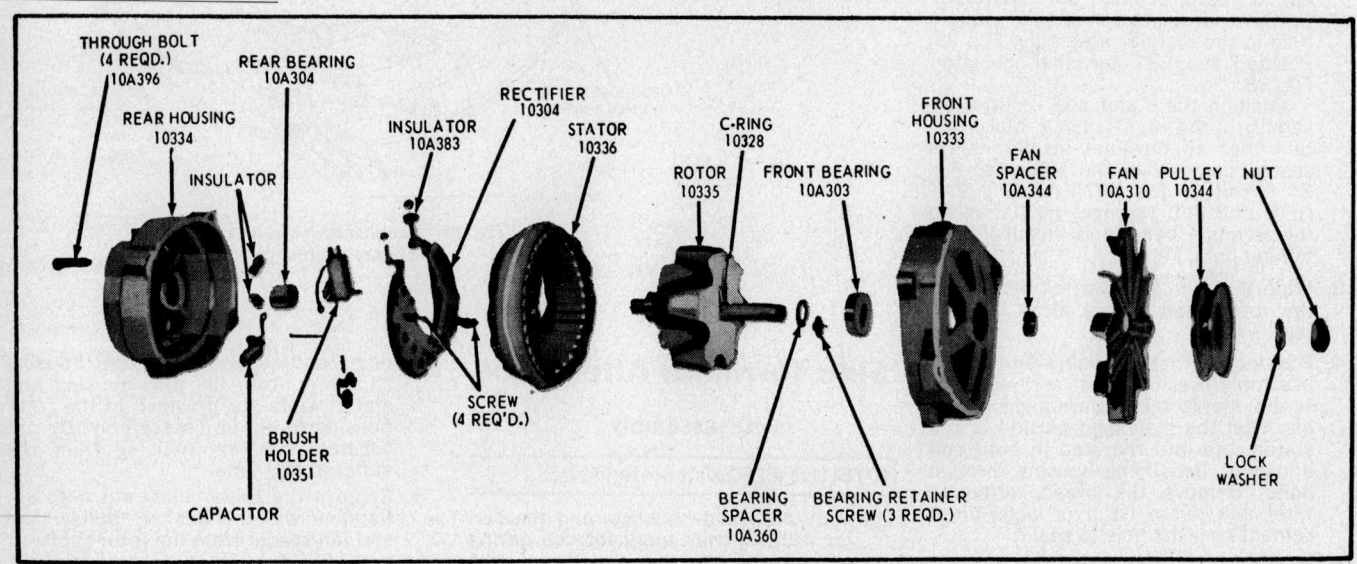

Fig. 40   Disassembled side terminal alternator

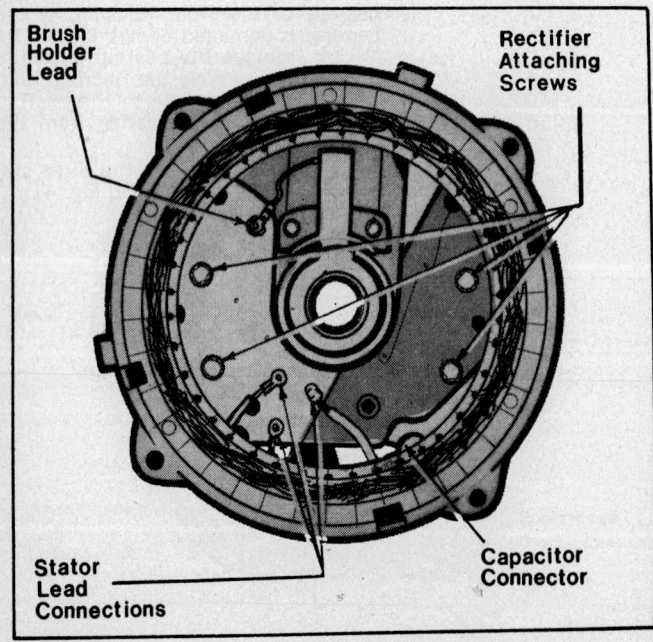

Fig. 41   Stator lead connections

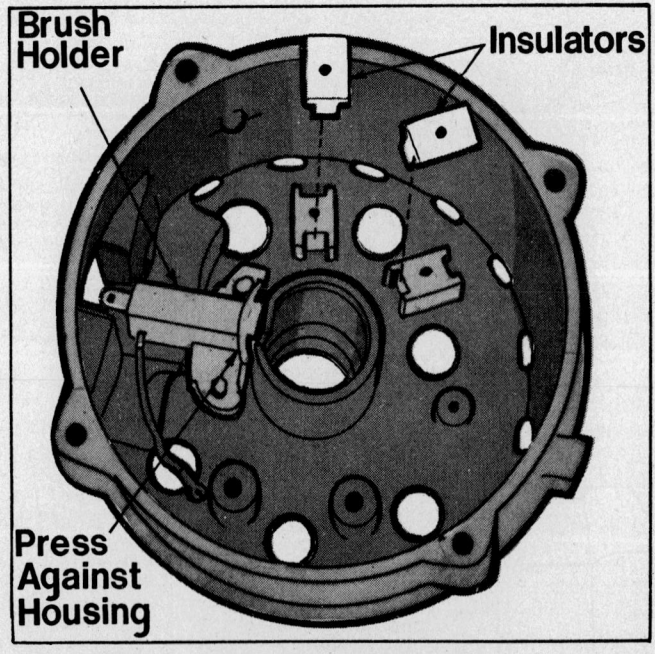

Fig. 43   Brush holder and rectifier insulators installed

1. If the front housing bearing is being replaced, press the new bearing in the housing.

   NOTE: *Put pressure on the bearing outer race only.* Then, install the bearing retaining screws.

2. Place the inner spacer on the rotor shaft and insert the rotor shaft into the front housing and bearing.

3. Install the fan spacer, fan, pulley, lockwasher and nut on the rotor shaft, Fig. 31. Torque nut to 60-100 ft. lbs.

4. If the rear bearing is being replaced, press a new bearing in from inside the housing until it is flush with the boss outer surface.

5. Position the brush terminal on the brush holder, Fig. 42. Install the springs and brushes in the brush holder, and insert a piece of stiff wire to hold the brushes in place, Fig. 42.

6. Position the brush holder in the rear housing and install the attaching screws. Push the brush holder toward the rotor shaft opening and tighten the brush holder attaching screws.

7. Position the capacitor to the rear housing and install the attaching screw.

8. Place the two cup shaped (rectifier) insulators on the bosses inside the housing, Fig. 43.

9. Place the insulator on the BAT (large) terminal of the rectifier, and position the rectifier in the rear housing. Place the outside insulator on the BAT terminal, and install the nuts on the BAT and GRD terminals *finger tight.*

10. Install but do not tighten the four rectifier attaching screws.

11. Tighten the BAT and GRD terminal nuts on the outside of the rear housing. Then, tighten the four rectifier attaching screws.

12. Position the capacitor lead to the rectifier and install the attaching screw.

13. Press the brush holder lead on the rectifier pin and solder securely, Fig. 41.

14. Position the stator in the rear housing and align the scribe marks. Press the three stator leads on the rectifier pins and solder securely, Fig. 41.

15. Position the rotor and front housing into the stator and rear housing. Align the scribe marks and install the four through bolts. Tighten two opposing bolts and then the two remaining bolts.

16. Spin the fan and pulley to be sure nothing is binding within the alternator.

17. Remove the wire retracting the brushes, and place a daub of waterproof cement over the hole to seal it.

Brush Replacement

Removal

1. Mark both end housings and the stator with a scribe mark for use during assembly.

2. Remove the four housing through bolts, and separate the front housing and rotor from the rear housing and stator. Slots are provided in the front

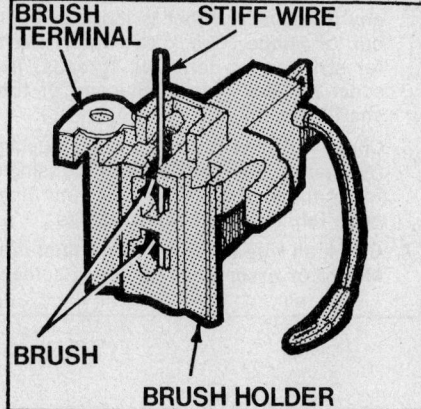

Fig. 42 Brush holder assembly

housing to aid in disassembly.

NOTE: Do not separate the rear housing and stator.

3. Unsolder and disengage the brush holder lead from the rectifier.

4. Remove the two brush holder attaching screws and lift the brush holder from the rear housing.

5. Remove the brushes from the brush holder.

Installation

1. Insert the brushes into the brush holder and position the terminal on the brush holder.

2. Depress the brushes and insert a 1½ inch piece of stiff wire, Fig. 42, to hold the brushes in the retracted position.

3. Position the brush holder to the rear housing, inserting the wire used to retract the brushes through the hole in the rear housing.

4. Install the brush holder attaching screws. Push the brush holder toward the rotor shaft opening and tighten the attaching screws.

5. Press the brush holder lead on the rectifier pin and solder securely.

6. Position the rotor and front housing into the stator and rear housing. Align the scribe marks and install the four through bolts. Tighten two opposing bolts and then the two remaining bolts.

7. Spin the fan and pulley to be sure nothing is binding within the alternator.

8. Remove the wire retracting the brushes, and place a daub of waterproof cement over the hole to seal it.

Rectifier Replacement

Removal

1. Mark both end housings and the stator with a scribe mark for use during assembly, Fig. 40.

2. Remove the four housing through bolts, and separate the front housing and rotor from the rear housing and stator. Slots are provided in the front housing to aid in disassembly.

NOTE: *Do not separate the rear housing and stator at this time.*

3. Unsolder and disengage the three stator leads from the rectifier, Fig. 41. Lift the stator from the rear housing.

4. Unsolder and disengage the brush holder lead from the rectifier.

5. Remove the screw attaching the capacitor lead to the rectifier.

6. Remove four screws attaching the rectifier to the rear housing, Fig. 41.

7. Remove two terminal nuts and insulator from outside the housing, and remove the rectifier from the housing.

Installation

1. Insert a piece of wire through the hole in the rear housing to hold the brushes in the retracted position.

2. Place the two cup shaped (rectifier) insulators on the bosses inside the housing, Fig. 43.

3. Place the insulator on the BAT (large) terminal of the rectifier, and position the rectifier in the rear housing. Place the outside insulator on the BAT terminal, and install the nuts on the BAT and GRD terminals finger tight.

4. Install but do not tighten the four rectifier attaching screws.

5. Tighten the BAT and GRD terminal nuts on the outside of the rear housing. Then, tighten the four rectifier attaching screws.

6. Position the capacitor lead to the rectifier and install the attaching screw.

7. Press the brush holder lead on the rectifier pin and solder securely, Fig. 41.

8. Position the stator in the rear housing and align the scribe marks. Press the three stator leads on the rectifier pins and solder securely, Fig. 41.

9. Position the rotor and front housing into the stator and rear housing. Align the scribe marks and install the four through bolts. Partially tighten all four through bolts. Then, tighten two opposing bolts and then the two remaining bolts.

10. Spin the fan and pulley to be sure nothing is binding within the alternator.

11. Remove the wire retracting the brushes in the brush holder, and place a daub of waterproof cement over the hole in the rear housing to seal it.

Cleaning and Inspection Procedures

1. The rotor, stator, and bearings must not be cleaned with solvent. Wipe these parts off with a clean cloth.

2. Rotate the front bearing on the drive end of the rotor drive shaft. Check for any scraping noise, looseness or roughness that will indicate that the bearing is excessively worn. Look for excessive lubricant leakage. If any of these conditions exist, replace the bearing.

3. Inspect the rotor shaft at the rear bearing surface for roughness or severe chatter marks. Replace the rotor

assembly if the shaft is not smooth.

4. Place the rear end bearing on the slip-ring end of the shaft and rotate the bearing on the shaft. Make the same check for noise, looseness or roughness as was made for the front bearing. Inspect the rollers and cage for damage. Replace the bearing if these conditions exist, or if the lubricant is lost or contaminated.

5. Check the pulley and fan for excessive looseness on the rotor shaft. Replace any pulley or fan that is loose or bent out of shape. Check the rotor shaft for stripped or damaged threads. Inspect the hex hole in the end of the shaft for damage.

6. Check both the front and rear housing for cracks. Check the front housings for stripped threads in the mounting gear. Replace defective housings.

7. Check all wire leads on both the stator and rotor assemblies for loose soldered connections, and for burned insulation. Resolder poor connections. Replace parts that show burned insulation.

8. Check the slip rings for nicks and surface roughness. If the slip rings are badly damaged, the entire rotor will have to be replaced, as it is serviced as a complete assembly.

9. Replace any parts that are burned or cracked. Replace brushes and brush springs that are not to specification.

Ford Sierracin
High Voltage Alternator

DESCRIPTION

This alternator, used with the Ford Sierracin system, Figs. 1 and 1A delivers approximately 120 volts to heat the front and rear windows on some Ford Co. vehicles. This system is completely isolated from the main vehicle system to prevent high voltage feed into the main system. Plastic shielded wiring is used between the alternator output terminals and the window heating elements, Fig. 2. Note that a high voltage warning tag is attached to the wiring at each junction.

ALTERNATOR TESTING

CAUTION: Since this is a 120 volt system and danger of electrical shock is present, all testing must be done with the field lead disconnected, using an ohmmeter and the engine stopped. Do not attempt to check alternator output voltage at the output terminal.

Field Coil Test

Connect an ohmmeter to the field terminal stud and the rear housing, avoiding contact with epoxy on housing since this will act as an insulator, Fig. 3. Field coil resistance is 2.8 ohms, however, reading will vary with brush contact resistance. A resistance between 3 and 250 ohms indicates the field circuit is satisfactory.

Stator Coil Tests

Check stator coil resistance by connecting an ohmmeter between two of the three output terminals in the connector, Fig. 4. Resistance should be approximately one ohm.

Check stator coils for grounds by connecting an ohmmeter to one output terminal and the rear housing. Hands should not contact probes or terminals during this test. A reading of infinity indicates coil is satisfactory. Check all three coils in this manner.

Field Circuit Voltage Test

Remove field terminal connector and connect a voltmeter between metal termination and rear housing. A voltage of 12 to 13 volts should be noted with the system control switch in the "On" position and zero volts in the "Off" position.

ALTERNATOR REPAIRS

Disassembly

1. Scribe reference marks between end housings to aid reassembly.
2. Remove through bolts and separate front end housing and rotor assembly from rear housing.
3. Remove outlet plug retaining nuts, then separate stator from rear end housing.
4. Remove brush holder attaching screws, brush holder, insulator and terminal.
5. If necessary, press out rear housing bearing while supporting housing on inner boss.
6. Remove drive pulley nut, lockwasher, pulley fan, fan spacer, front housing and rotor stop from rotor shaft.
7. If necessary, remove front bearing retainer and press bearing from housing while supporting housing on the bearing boss.

Assembly

1. If removed, press front bearing into housing putting pressure on outer race. Install bearing retainer.
2. To replace stop ring, if damaged, push new stop ring into groove in rotor shaft.

NOTE: Do not spread stop ring with snap ring pliers since permanent damage will result.

3. Position rotor stop on shaft with recessed side against stop ring, then install front housing, fan spacer, fan, pulley, lockwasher and retaining nut.
4. If removed, press rear housing bearing into bearing while supporting housing on inner boss. Bearing is

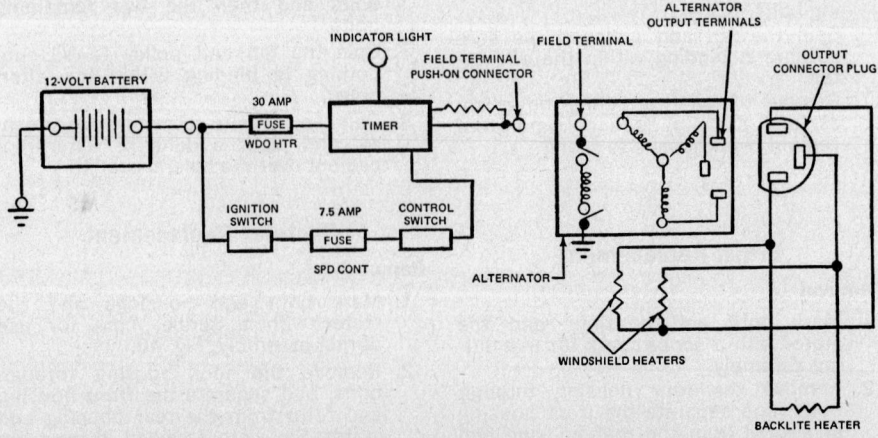

Fig. 1 High voltage alternator system circuit. 1974

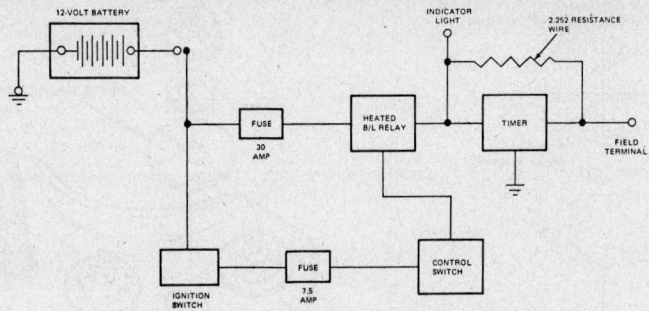

Fig. 1A   High voltage system circuit. 1975-76

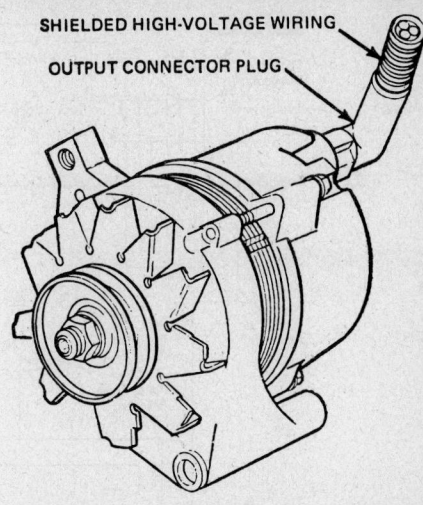

Fig. 2   High voltage alternator assembly

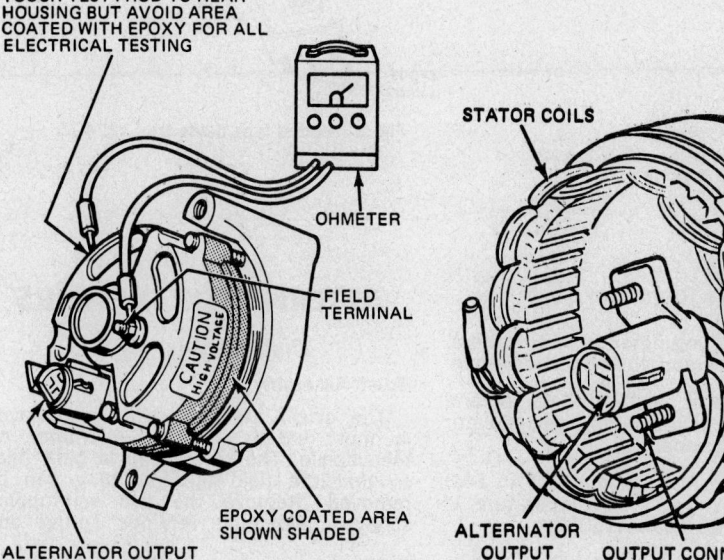

Fig. 3   Field coil test

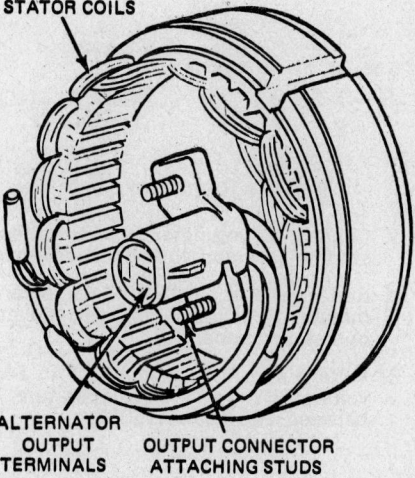

Fig. 4   Stator assembly

properly installed when bearing is flush with outer end surface.
5. Assemble brush holder and insert a stiff wire to hold brushes in position. Place assembly in rear housing and install brush holder mounting screws and the output connector retaining nuts.
6. Place rear housing and stator assembly over front housing and rotor assembly, aligning reference marks, and seat the machined portion of stator core into the step in both end housings. Remove brush retracting wire.
7. Install alternator into vehicle and check for proper operation.

Motorola Alternator

DESCRIPTION
1974-75

The electrical circuit, Fig. 1, of these units differ from previous units in that a field diode assembly is used. Also, on alternators used in American Motors cars equipped with a four barrel carburetor, an extra terminal is used on the rear housing which provides about seven volts of alternating current to the heating element of the electric assisted choke.

The field diode (diode trio) assembly incorporates three diodes mounted on a circuit board or, on some 1974-75 units, a potted type diode trio is used, Fig. 2. The input leads are connected to the stator windings in parallel with the positive diodes. The diode output leads are connected to a metal grommet in the circuit board and is secured to the insulated regulator terminal.

A portion of the alternating current and voltage developed in the stator windings is rectified by the field diode assembly. This voltage is sensed by the voltage regulator to provide current to the field windings. Fig. 3 shows the charging circuit.

Voltage Regulator

The voltage regulator is an electrical switching device sealed at the factory, requiring no adjustments. It senses the voltage appearing at the regulator terminal of the alternator and supplies the necessary field current for maintaining the system voltage at the output terminal.

TESTING SYSTEM IN VEHICLE

Alternator Output Test

1. Connect a voltmeter to the battery, start engine and turn on headlamps.

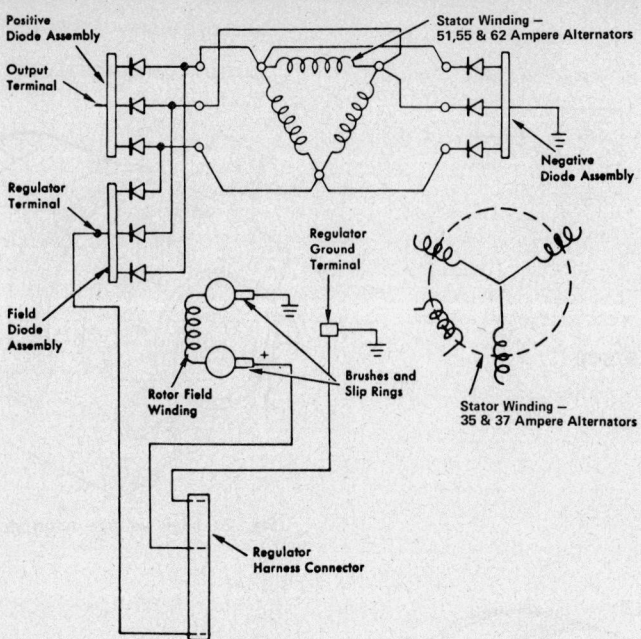

Fig. 1   Alternator circuit. 1974-75 35, 37, 51, 55 & 62 amp

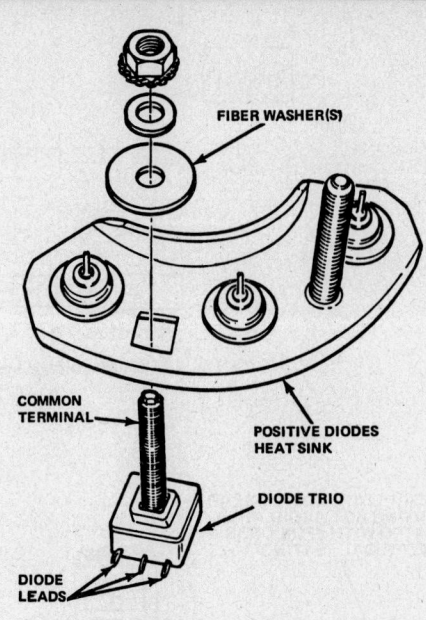

Fig. 2   Potted type diode trio. 1974-75

2. Run engine for two minutes at 1000 RPM and observe voltmeter. If voltage remains above 13 volts, alternator and regulator are satisfactory.

Rectifier Diode Tests

Any commercial in-circuit diode tester will suffice to make the test. Follow Test Equipment Manufacturer's instructions.

Check diodes individually after the diodes have been disconnected from the stator. A shorted stator coil or shorted insulating washers or sleeves on positive diodes would make diodes appear to be shorted.

A test lamp will not indicate an open condition unless all three diodes of either assembly are open. However, a shorted diode can be detected. This test is not 100% effective but can be used if so desired when an in-circuit diode tester is not available.

The test lamp should light in one direction but not in the other direction. If the test lamp lights in both directions, one or more of the diodes of the assembly being tested is shorted. If the test lamp does not light in either direction, *all three diodes in the assembly are open.* Check diodes individually after disassembly to ascertain findings.

NOTE: *A shorted stator coil would appear as a shorted negative diode. Also check stator for shorts after disassembly.*

Field Diode (Diode Trio) Test

1. Using a voltmeter, connect positive lead to alternator output terminal and negative lead to regulator terminal.
2. Start and run engine at idle speed. The voltmeter should then read .6 volt or less. If reading is over .6 volt, replace field diode assembly.

Voltage Regulator Test

1. Connect a voltmeter to the battery, start engine and turn on headlamps.
2. Run engine at 1000 RPM for several minutes to establish voltage regulator operating temperature.
3. Voltage should be within 13.1 to 14.3 volts when regulator temperature is between 100°F and 150°F.

ALTERNATOR REPAIRS

Disassembly, Fig. 4

Brush Assembly

The brush assembly can be removed in most cases with the alternator on the vehicle. The spring clip is bent back so that the field terminal plug can be removed. Remove the two self-tapping screws, field plug retainer spring and

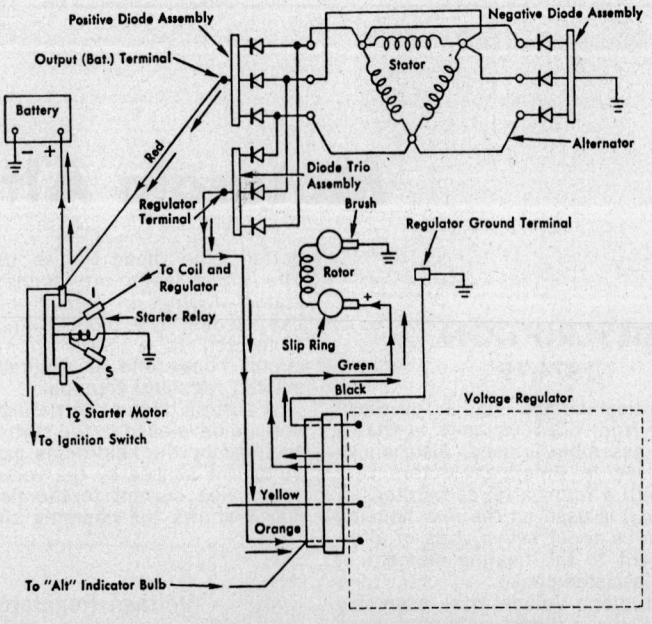

Fig. 3   Charging circuit diagram. 1974-75 (typical)

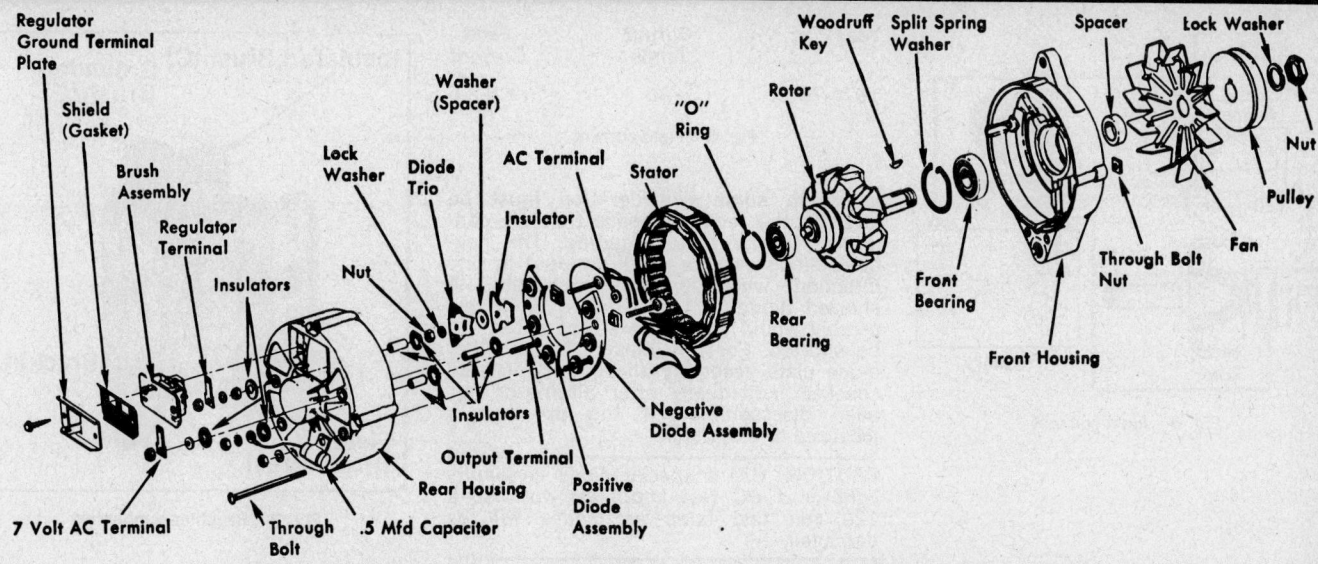

Fig. 4 Alternator disassembled. 1974-75 NOTE: model shown has AC terminal for electric choke

cover. Pull brush assembly straight out far enough to clear locating pins, then lift brush assembly out. The complete brush assembly is available for replacement.

Rear Housing

Remove the 4 through bolts and nuts. Carefully separate the rear housing and stator from the front housing by using 2 small screwdrivers and prying the stator from the front housing at 2 opposing slots where the "through bolts" are removed. Do not burr the stator core which would make assembly difficult.

Caution: *Do not insert screwdriver blade deeper than* $1/16"$ *to avoid damaging stator winding.*

Stator and Diode Assembly

Do not unsolder stator-to-diode wire junction. Remove stator and diode as an assembly. Avoid bending stator wire at junction holding positive and negative diode assembly from housing.

Remove 4 lock nuts and insulating washers. The insulating washers and nylon sleeves are used to insulate the positive plate studs from the housing. With the 4 nuts removed, the stator can be separated from rear housing by hand.

Diode Replacement

To replace field diode assembly, remove nylon sleeve, insulating washer and holddown nut from regulator stud. Unsolder field diode wires from positive diodes. *When replacing positive or negative diodes, make note of diode assembly to stator connections, and make sure replacement diode assembly connections are the same. The positive diode assembly has red markings, the negative black markings.*

In soldering and unsoldering leads from diodes, grasp the diode lead with pliers between the diode and stator lead to be

removed. This will give better heat dissipation and protect the diode. Do not exert excessive stress on diode lead.

ROTOR

The rotor should only require removal from the front housing if there is a defect in the field coil itself or in the front bearing. Front and rear bearings are permanently sealed, self-lubricating type. If the front housing must be removed from the rotor, use a two jaw puller to remove the pulley. The split spring washer must be loosened with snap ring pliers through the opening in the front housing. Remove the washer only after the housing is removed. The rotor and front bearing can be removed from the front housing by tapping the rotor shaft slightly.

NOTE: *Make certain that the split spring washer has been removed from its groove before attempting to remove the front housing from the bearing.*

Alternator Bench Tests

Field Coil Test

The rotor should be tested for grounds and for shorted turns in the winding. The ground test is made with test probes connected in series with a 110 volt test lamp. Place one test probe on the slip ring and the other probe on the rotor core. If the bulb lights the rotor is grounded.

To test for shorted turns, check rotor field current draw as shown in Fig. 5. Slowly reduce resistance of rheostat to zero. With full battery voltage applied to the field coil, field current should be as shown in Fig. 6. Excessive current draw indicates shorted turn in field winding.

Brush Insulation Test

Connect an ohmmeter or a test lamp to the field terminal and bracket. Resist-

ance should be high (infinite) or test lamp should not light. If resistance is low or if test lamp lights, brush assembly is shorted and must be replaced.

Continuity Test

Connect an ohmmeter to field terminal and brush. Use an alligator clip to assure good contact to brush, test points "A" and "C" in Fig. 7.

CAUTION: *Do not chip brush.*

Resistance reading should be zero. Move brush and brush lead wire to make certain that brush lead wire connections are not intermittent. Resistance reading should not vary when brush and lead wire are being moved around. Connect ohmmeter to bracket and grounded brush, test points "E" and "D", Fig. 7. Resistance reading should be zero.

1974-75 Diode Tests

Diode Trio: Unsolder diode trio leads and using a 12 volt meter which draws a one amp maximum load, connect test leads providing current path, Fig. 8. Hold this connection for at least two minutes, then reverse test leads immediately. Test each diode in this manner. If current flows in both directions, neither direction or flows intermittently, the diode trio must be replaced.

Rectifier Diodes: The same method of testing is used for the rectifier diodes as for the diode trio, Fig. 9. However, a 20 amp load is used when testing the rectifier diodes.

NOTE: A diode can be tested for opens or shorts using an ohmmeter. Reason for applying an electrical load to the diodes, in turn generating heat, is to detect intermittent diode failures.

Stator In-Circuit Test

When making the in-circuit stator leak-

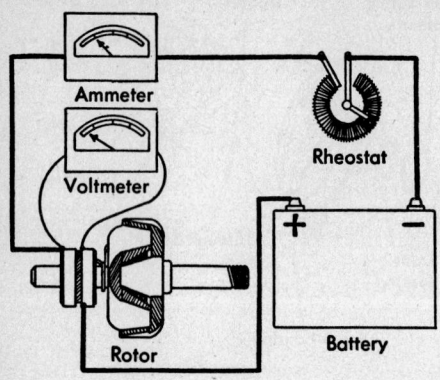

Fig. 5   Field coil test

Year	Output Amps	Field Current
1974-75	All	1.8-2.5

Fig. 6   Field current

age test, some consideration must be given to the rectifier diodes that are connected to the stator winding. The negative diode assembly will conduct in one direction when properly polarized. A shorted diode in the negative diode assembly would make the stator appear to be shorted. For this reason, the rectifier diode plate assembly and stator must be checked individually after alternator has been disassembled if the problem is localized to the stator.

CAUTION: *Use a special diode continuity light or a DC test lamp. Do not use a 120 volt test lamp as diodes will be damaged.*

1. Connect the test lamp to a diode

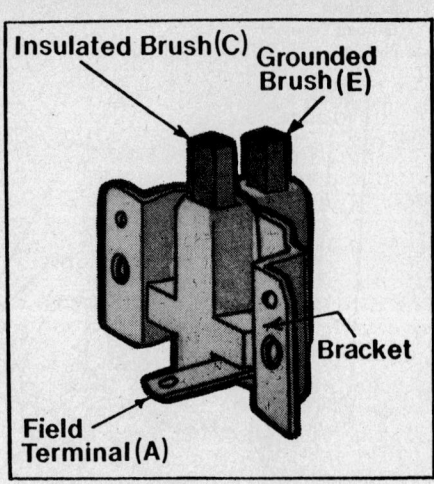

Fig. 7   Brush assembly test

terminal of the negative assembly and ground terminal.
2. Reverse test probes. The lamp should light in one direction but not in the other.
3. If the test lamp does not light in either direction, this indicates that all three rectifiers in the negative diode assembly are open.
4. If the test lamp lights in both directions, the stator winding is shorted to stator or one of the negative diodes is shorted.
5. Check stator again when it is disassembled from diode assemblies.

Unsolder All Diode Trio Wires From Positive Diodes

Diode Trio Common Terminal

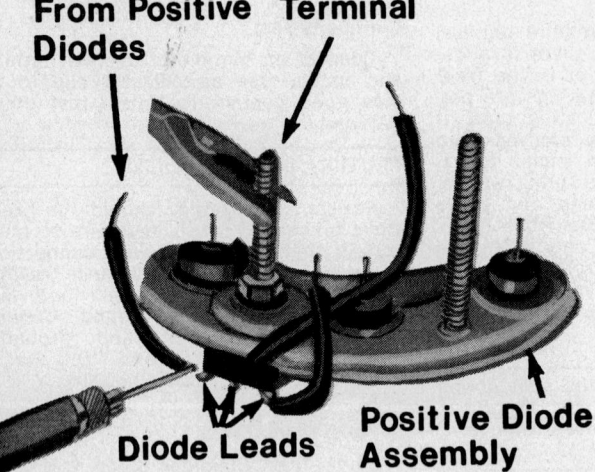

Diode Leads

Positive Diode Assembly

Potted Type

Center Mount Eyelet (Common Diode Connection)

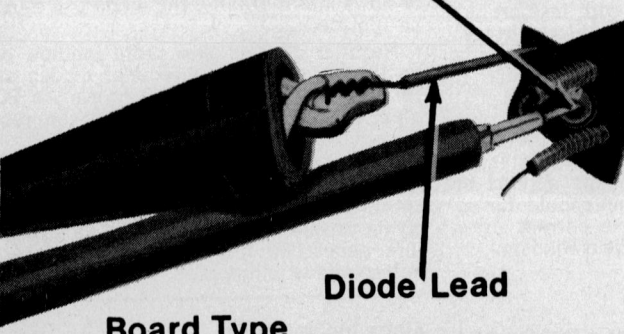

Diode Lead

Board Type

Fig. 8   Diode trio bench test. 1974-75 alternators

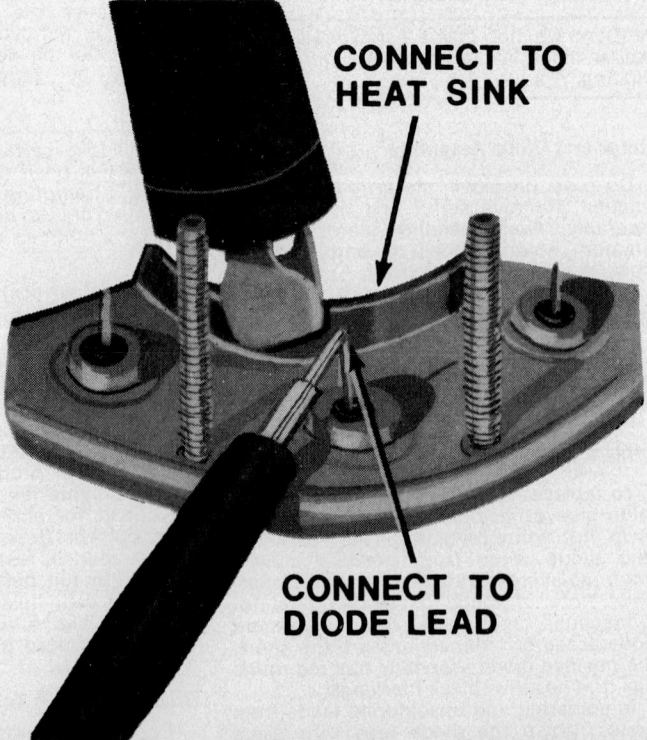

CONNECT TO HEAT SINK

CONNECT TO DIODE LEAD

Fig. 9   Rectifier diodes bench test. 1974-75 alternators

6. With alternator disassembled, connect an ohmmeter or test lamp probes to one of the diode terminals and to stator.
7. Resistance reading should be infinite or test lamp should not light.
8. If resistance reading is not infinite or test lamp lights, high leakage or a short exists between stator winding and stator. In either case, stator should be replaced.

Stator Coil Shorts Test

1. This test checks for shorts between stator coil windings. The winding junctions must be separated as shown in Fig. 10. An ohmmeter or test lamp may be used.
2. Connect one of the test probes to test point "U" and the other to test point "V" and then to test point "W". Resistance should be infinite or test lamp should not light.
3. Connect test probes to test points V and W. Resistance should be infinite or test lamp should not light. In either test, if resistance reading is not infinite or test lamp lights, high leakage or a short exists between stator windings. Stator should be replaced.

Continuity Test

1. Measure resistance of each winding in stator between test points U and U1, V and V1, W and W1, Fig. 10. Resistance should be a fraction of an ohm (approximately .1 Ohm). An extremely accurate instrument would be necessary to ascertain shorted turns. Only an open condition can be detected with a commercial type ohmmeter.
2. If the alternator has been disassembled because of an electrical malfunction, replace stator only after

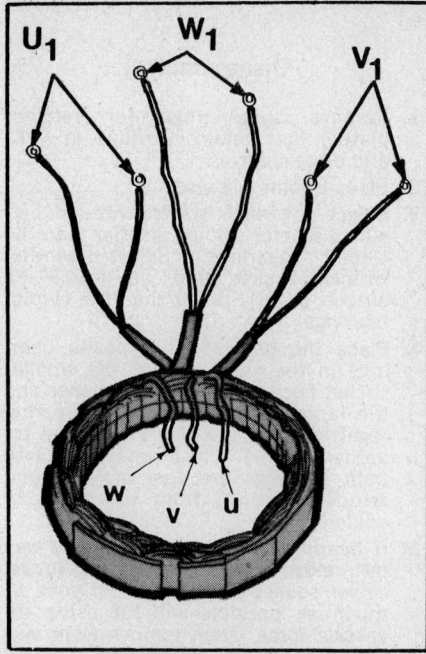

Fig. 10 Stator coil shorts and continuity tests

all other components have been checked and found to be satisfactory.

Assemble Alternator

1. Clean bearing and inside of bearing hub of front housing. Support front housing and, using a suitable driver, apply sufficient pressure to outside race of bearing to seat bearing.
2. Insert split spring washer hub of front housing, seating washer into groove of hub.

NOTE: *Do not use a screwdriver or any small object to compress washer that can slip off and damage bearing seal. Make certain that split spring washer has been installed prior to assembling front housing and rotor.*

3. Use sufficient pressure to seat front bearing against shoulder on rotor shaft. The bearing drive tool must fit the inner race of bearing.
4. Install fan and pulley.
5. Use a $7/16''$ socket to fit inside race of rear bearing and apply sufficient pressure to drive bearing against shoulder of rotor shaft.
6. Assemble front and rear housings.
7. Make certain that rear bearing is properly seated in rear housing hub and that diode wires are properly dressed so that rotor will not contact diode wires.
8. Align stator slots with rear housing through bolt holes, then align front housing through bolt holes with respect to rear housing.

NOTE: *The position of the brush and belt adjusting screw boss must be in the same relative position to each other.*

9. Spin rotor to make certain that rotor is not contacting diode wires. Install bolts and tighten evenly.
10. Before mounting isolation diode, make certain that positive rectifier diode plate has been properly insulated from housing.
11. Install brush assembly, cover and field plug retainer spring.

SERVICE NOTES

Before disassembling any universal joint, examine the assembly carefully and note the position of the grease fitting (if used). Also, be sure to mark the yokes with relation to the propeller shaft so they may be reassembled in the same relative position. Failure to observe these precautions may produce rough car operation which results in rapid wear and failure of parts, and place an unbalanced load on transmission, engine and real axle.

When universal joints are disassembled for lubrication or inspection, and the old parts are to be reinstalled, special care must be exercised to avoid damage to universal joint spider or cross and bearing cups.

NOTE: Some late model cars use an injected nylon retainer on the universal joint bearings. When service is necessary, pressing the bearings out will sheer the nylon retainer. Replacement with the conventional steel snap ring type is then necessary.

CROSS & ROLLER TYPE

Figs. 1, 2 and 3 illustrate typical examples of universal joints of this type. They all operate on the same principle and similar service and replacement procedures may be applied to all.

Disassembly

1. Remove snap rings (or retainer plates) that retain bearings in yoke and drive shaft.
2. Place U-joint in a vise.
3. Select a wrench socket with an outside diameter slightly smaller than the U-joint bearings. Select another wrench socket with an inside diameter slightly larger than the U-joint bearings.
4. Place the sockets at opposite bearings in the yoke so that the smaller socket becomes a bearing pusher and the larger socket becomes a bearing receiver when the vise jaws come together, Fig. 4. Close vise jaws until both bearings are free of yoke and remove bearings from the cross or spider.
5. If bearings will not come all the way out, close vise until bearing in receiver socket protrudes from yoke as much as possible without using excessive force. Then remove from vise and place that portion of bearing which protrudes from yoke between vise jaws. Tighten vise to hold bearing and drive yoke off with a soft hammer.
6. To remove opposite bearing from yoke, replace in vise with pusher socket on exposed cross journal with receiver socket over bearing cup. Then tighten vise jaws to press bearing back through yoke into receiving socket.

7. Remove yoke from drive shaft and again place protruding portion of bearing between vise jaws. Then tighten vise to hold bearing while driving yoke off bearing with soft hammer.
8. Turn spider or cross ¼ turn and use the same procedure to press bearings out of drive shaft.

Reassembly

1. If old parts are to be reassembled, pack bearing cups with universal joint grease. *Do not fill cups completely or use excessive amounts as over-lubrication may damage seals during reassembly.* Use new seals.
2. If new parts are being installed, check new bearings for adequate grease before assembling.
3. With the pusher (smaller) socket, press one bearing part way into drive shaft. Position spider into the partially installed bearing. Place second bearing into drive shaft. Fasten drive shaft in vise so that bearings are in contact with faces of vise jaws, Fig. 5. *Some spiders are provided with locating lugs which must face toward drive shaft when installed,* Fig. 6.
4. Press bearings all the way into position and install snap rings or retainer plates.
5. Install bearings in yoke in same manner. When installation is completed,

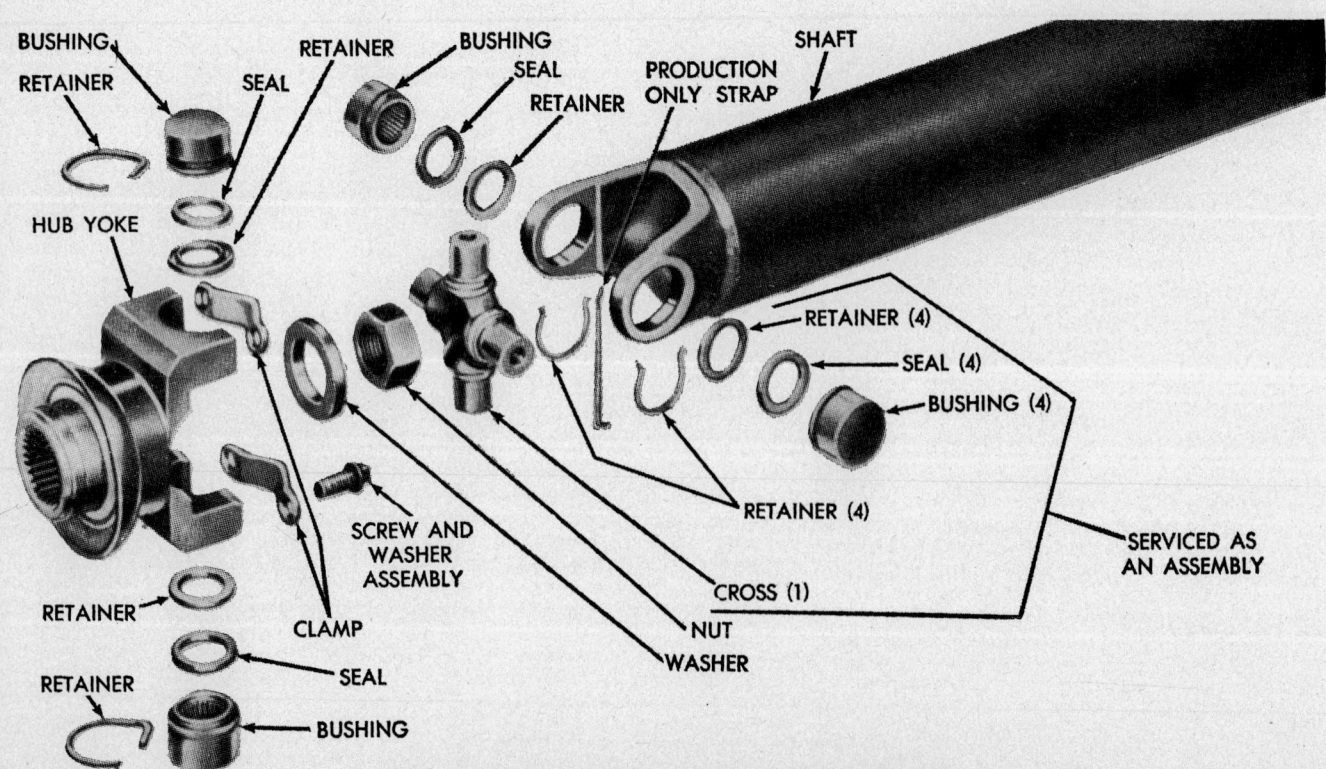

Fig. 1 Cross and roller type universal joint. Chrysler-built cars

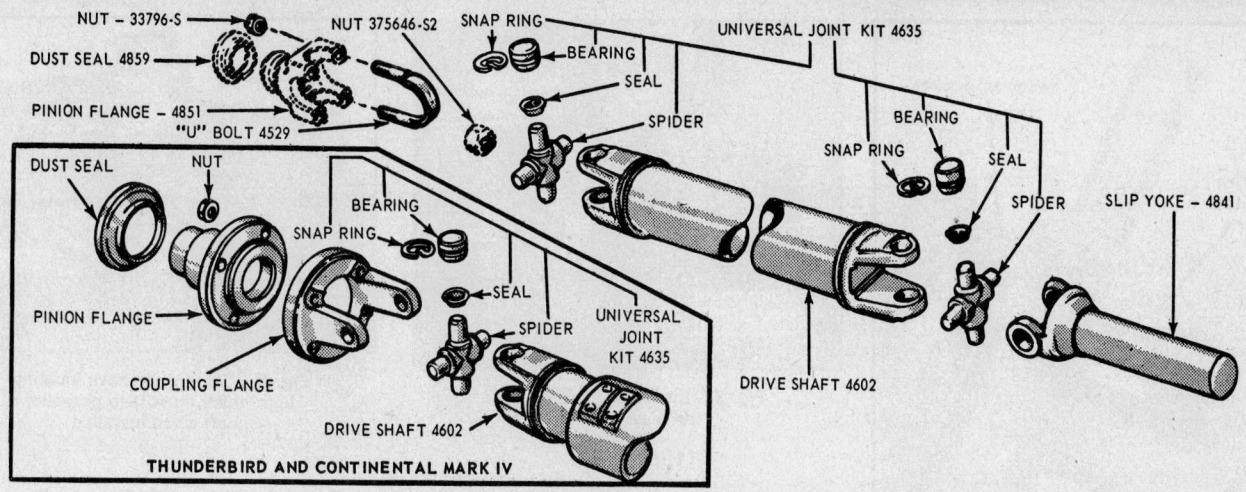

Fig. 2 Cross and roller universal joints and propeller shaft. Ford-built cars

check U-joint for binding or roughness. If free movement is impeded, correct the condition before installation in vehicle.

CONSTANT VELOCITY TYPE

This type of U-joint, Fig. 7, is composed of two conventional cross and roller joints connected with a special link yoke. Because the two joint angles are the same, even though the usual U-joint fluctuation is present within the unit, the acceleration of the front joint (within the yoke) is always neutralized by the deceleration of the rear joint (within the yoke) and vice versa. The end result is the front and rear propeller shafts always turn at a constant velocity.

General Motors

For ease of handling and to prevent damage to the constant velocity U-joints, the front and rear propeller shafts must be separated at the slip joint before any service is attempted.

Disassemble Slip Joint

1. Pry lockwasher from flats on bearing locknut.
2. Loosen locknut until free of threads and slide locknut and seal against constant velocity joint.
3. Slide rear propeller shaft from front propeller shaft, making sure that index spring wire in splines is not lost.

Disassemble Constant Velocity U-Joint

1. Mark yokes before disassembly to be

sure reassembly is made in same relative position of components, Fig. 8.
2. Disassemble rear section of constant velocity U-joint first as follows:
3. Remove snap rings from bearings using a punch.
4. Place rear propeller shaft yoke in a vise. Shaft must be supported horizontally and link yoke must be free to move vertically, Fig. 9.
5. Using a pipe coupling or a wrench socket with the inside diameter slightly larger than outside diameter of bearing, Fig. 9, drive link yoke downward until about 1/4" of bearing projects from yoke. *Do not attempt to drive yoke down farther than ball socket will allow easily.*
6. Rotate shaft 180 degrees and repeat Steps 3, 4 and 5.

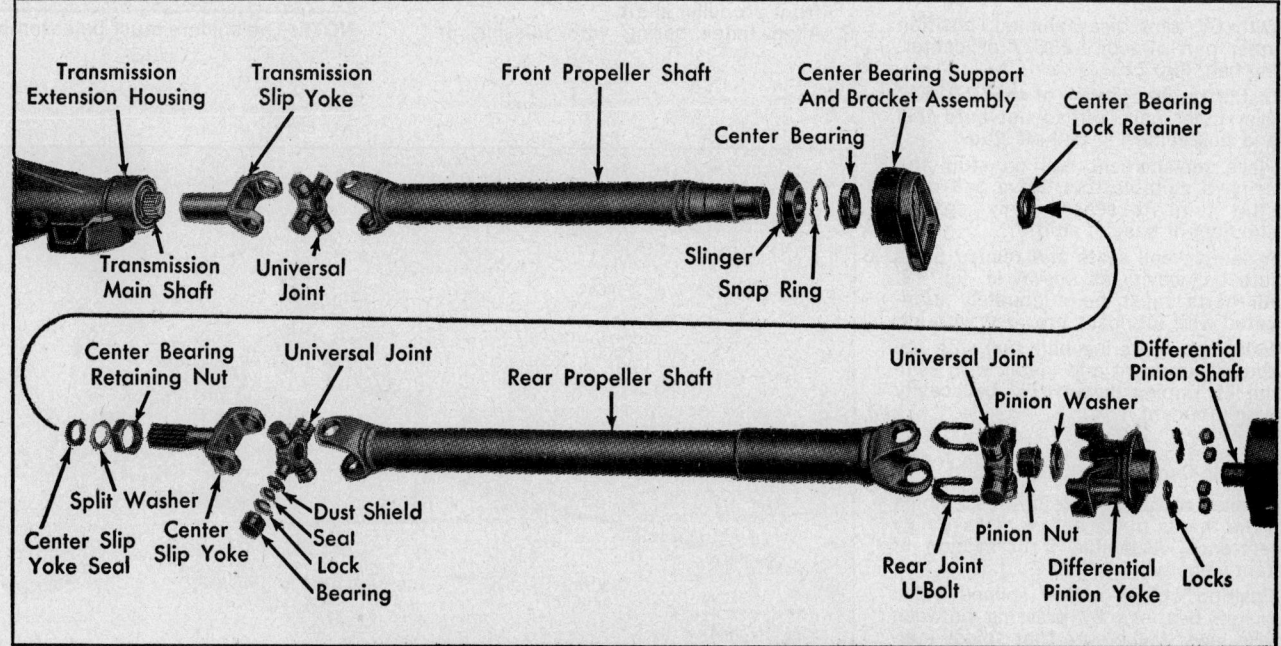

Fig. 3 Example of a two-piece propeller shaft with three cross and roller universal joints and center bearing support assembly. Cadillac

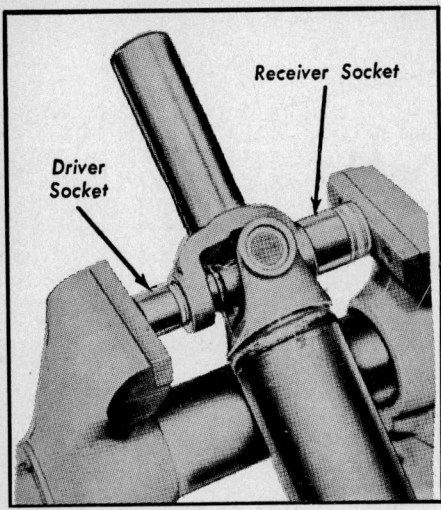

Fig. 4   Removing bearings from yoke using small and large wrench sockets as pusher and receiver tools, respectively

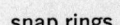

Fig. 5   Installing bearings into drive shaft yoke

Fig. 6   Some units have locating lugs which must face propeller shaft when installed

7. Clamp 1/4" projecting portion of either bearing in vise and remove bearing by driving link yoke upward. Remove other bearing in same manner, Fig. 10.
8. Separate spider, shaft yoke and shaft from link yoke.
9. To remove bearings from shaft yoke, clamp spider in vise with its jaws bearing against ends of spider journals. Yoke must be free to move vertically between jaws of vise.
10. Using the same bearing remover tool as in Step 5, apply force on shaft yoke around bearing. Drive yoke downward until bearing is free of yoke.

Centering Ball Replacement

1. With CV joint disassembled, position inner part of tool J-23677 on centering ball, Fig. 11.
2. Install outer cylinder of tool J-23677 over inner part, thread nut onto tool and pull centering ball off stud.
3. Place replacement ball on stud and using a suitable tool, drive ball onto stud until it seats firmly against shoulder at base of stud.
4. Assemble ball seats and related parts into ball cavity as shown in Fig. 12. All parts must be adequately lubricated with lubricant provided with kit.
5. Lubricate centering ball seal with approved lubricant and install with sealing lip tipping inward. Fill ball cavity with lubricant.

Reassemble Constant Velocity U-Joint

All yokes must be carefully assembled using the marks made before disassembly for reference. Assemble front section of constant velocity joint first.
1. Position spider inside splined yoke. Install bearings by pressing between vise jaws. Make sure that spider journals enter bearings squarely to avoid damage, Fig. 13.
2. Fully install bearings and install

snap rings.
3. Position splined yoke and spider inside link yoke and install bearings into link yoke in same manner as for splined yoke.
4. Position spider inside rear propeller shaft yoke and install bearings.
5. Lubricate ball and socket with a high grade of extreme pressure grease.
6. Position spider of rear propeller shaft assembly in link yoke.
7. Engage socket with ball of splined yoke assembly. *Make sure that all reference marks are properly aligned.*
8. Install bearings into link yoke in same manner as above while holding spring loaded ball and socket assembly together to make sure that spider journals enter bearings squarely.

Reassemble Slip Joint

1. Make sure locknut, seal and split washer are in place on smooth part of spline shaft. Also make sure that index spring wire is in place in splines and that spacer washer and large lockwasher are in place on rear end of front propeller shaft.
2. Align index spring with missing in-

ternal spline in rear end of propeller shaft and slide slip joint together, Fig. 14.
3. Install locknut and tighten securely. Bend in rim of lockwasher to engage flat of locknut firmly.

1974-78 Lincoln

These vehicles incorporate a double cardan type constant velocity joint at each end of the drive shaft, Fig. 15. Each double cardan has a center yoke (cage), a centering socket yoke and a stud yoke which is welded to each end of the tube assembly. The splines on the yoke and transmission output shaft permit the drive shaft to move in and out as the axle moves up and down. All drive shaft assemblies are balanced and should be kept free of undercoating.

Disassembly

1. Mark location of spiders, center yoke and centering socket yoke as related to stud yoke.

NOTE: The spiders must be assembled

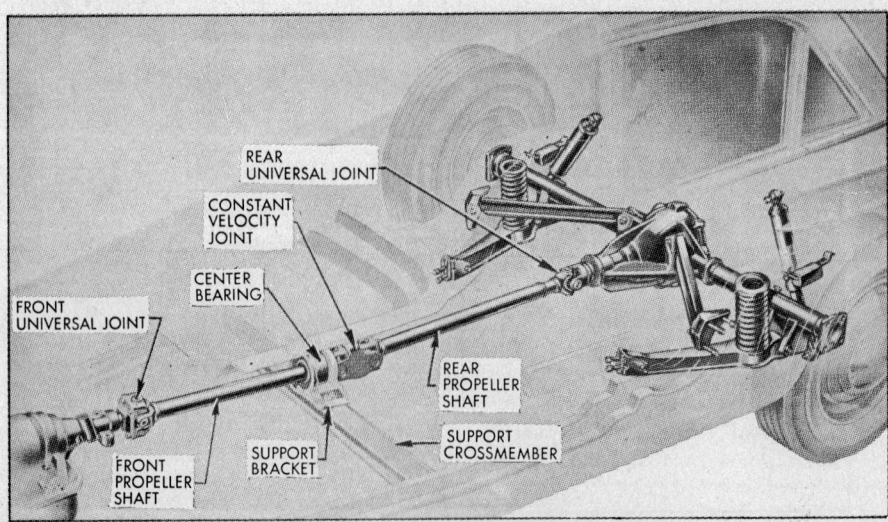

Fig. 7   Two piece propeller shaft with constant velocity universal joint. General Motors (Typical)

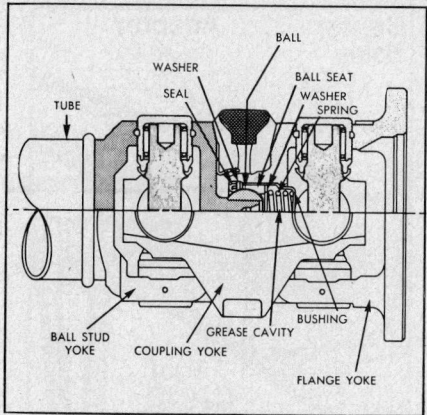

Fig. 8 Cross-section of typical GM constant velocity U-joint

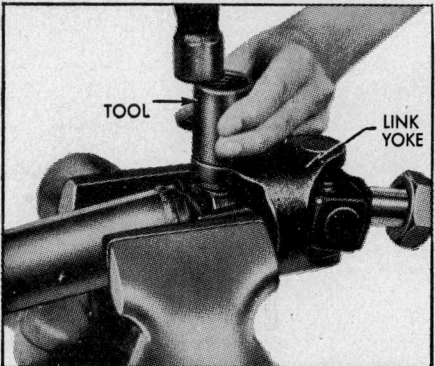

Fig. 9 Driving bearing from link yoke

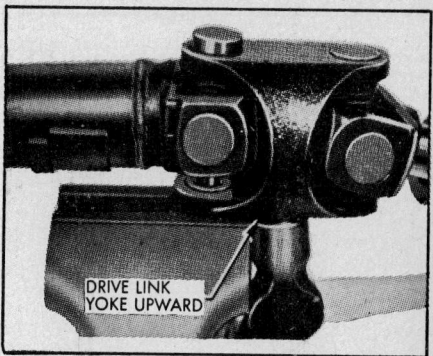

Fig. 10 Removing bearing

with bosses in their original position to provide proper clearance.

2. Remove snap rings that secure bearings in front of center yoke, then position tool, Fig. 16, and thread clockwise until bearing protrudes about ⅜-inch out of yoke.

3. Remove drive shaft from vise and tighten bearing in vise then tap the center yoke, Fig. 17, to free it from bearing.

4. Remove the two bearings from the spider, Fig. 18, then reposition the tool on the yoke and move the remaining bearing in the opposite direction so that it protrudes about ⅜ inch out the yoke.

5. Grip bearing in a vise, then drive the center yoke freeing it from bearing, Fig. 17, and remove spider from center yoke.

6. Pull centering socket yoke off center stud, Fig. 19, then remove rubber seal from centering ball stud.

7. Remove the snap rings from center and drive shaft yokes, then position tool on drive shaft yoke, Fig. 20, and press bearing outward until inside of center yoke almost contacts the slinger ring at the front of the drive shaft yoke.

NOTE: Pressing beyond this point can distort the slinger ring. Fig. 21 shows the interference point.

8. Clamp exposed end of bearing in a vise and drive the center yoke with a soft face hammer freeing it from bearing, then reposition tool and press on spider to remove opposite bearing.

9. Remove center yoke from spider and remove spider from drive shaft yoke in same manner.

10. Clean all serviceable parts in cleaning solvent. If using a repair kit, use all parts supplied in kit. If driveshaft is damaged, it should be replaced to insure a balanced assembly.

Assembly

1. Position spider in shaft yoke making sure that spider bosses (or lubrication plugs) will be in original position. Press in bearing cups and install snap rings.

2. Position center yoke over spider ends then press in bearing cups and install snap rings.

3. Install new seal on centering stud and position centering socket yoke on stud.

4. Place front spider in center yoke making sure that spider bosses (or lubrication plugs) are properly positioned. Press in bearing cups and install snap rings.

5. Applying pressure on centering socket, install remaining bearing cup.

6. If using a repair kit, remove plug from each spider and lubricate universal joints. Reinstall plug.

1977-78 Versailles

These models use a one-piece driveshaft with a constant velocity universal joint between the driveshaft and companion flange, Fig. 22.

Disassembly

1. Mark relative positions of the spiders, center yoke and centering socket yoke to the companion flange.

2. Install tool CJ91B, Fig. 16. Thread tool clockwise until bearing protrudes approximately ⅜ inch from yoke.

3. Remove driveshaft from vise.

4. Tighten the bearing in a vise and tap on yoke to free bearing from center yoke, Fig. 17. Do not tap on driveshaft tube.

5. Repeat steps 2 through 4 on remaining bearings.

6. Remove spider from center yoke.

Fig. 11 Removing centering ball with tool J-23677

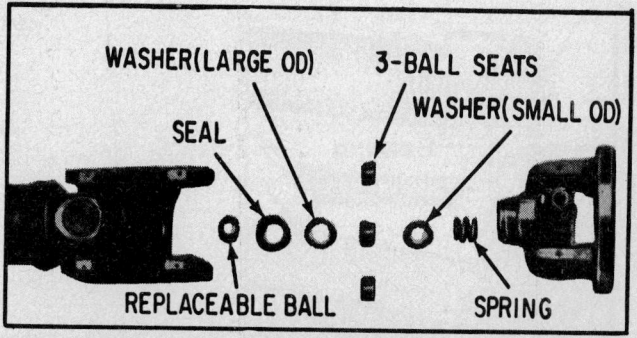

Fig. 12 Centering ball assembly

Fig. 13   Installing bearings

PRESS BEARING INTO PLACE

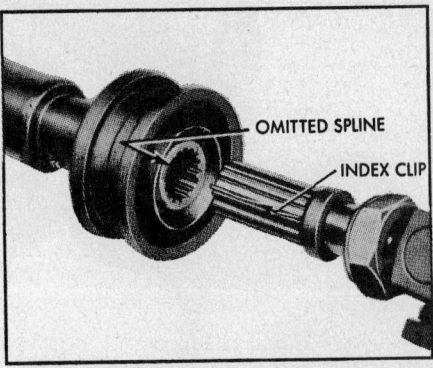

Fig. 14   Aligning index spring with missing internal spline on propeller shaft

OMITTED SPLINE

INDEX CLIP

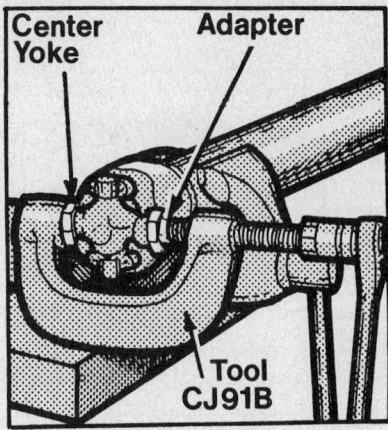

Center Yoke

Adapter

Tool CJ91B

Fig. 16   Partially pressing bearing from center yoke

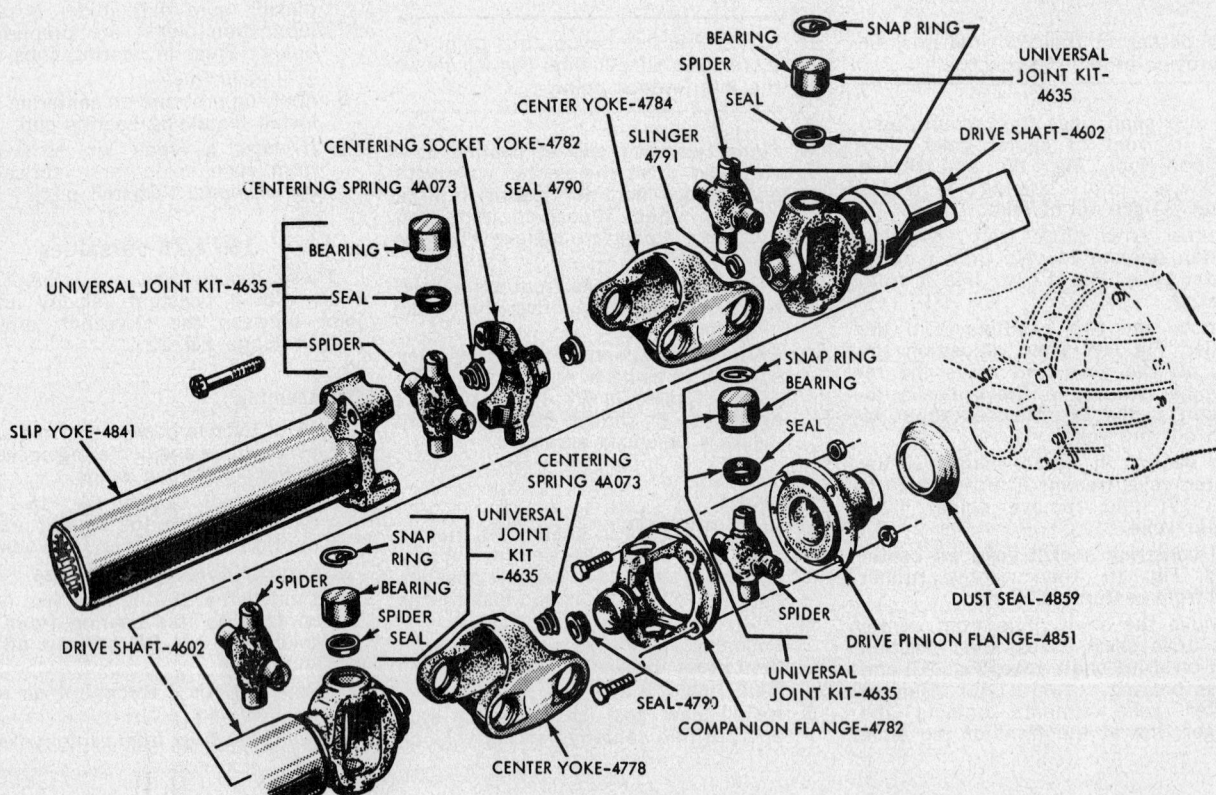

Fig. 15   Constant velocity type universal joint 1974-78 Lincoln

Fig. 17   Removing bearing from center yoke

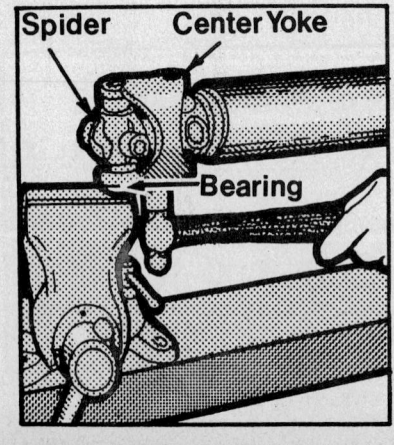

Spider   Center Yoke

Bearing

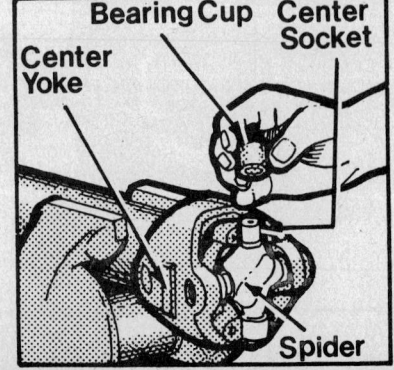

Bearing Cup   Center Socket

Center Yoke

Spider

Fig. 18   Removing bearing cup from centering yoke

Fig. 19 Removing center socket yoke

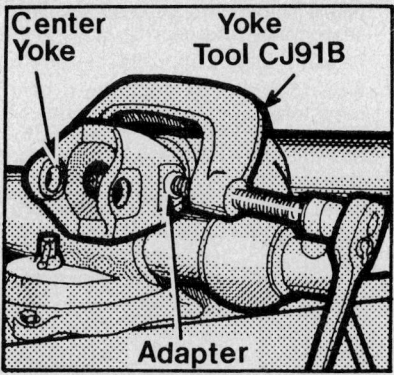

Fig. 20 Removing bearing from rear of center yoke

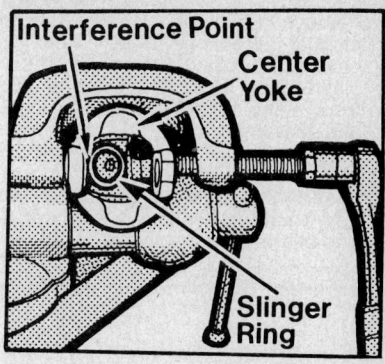

Fig. 21 Center yoke interference point

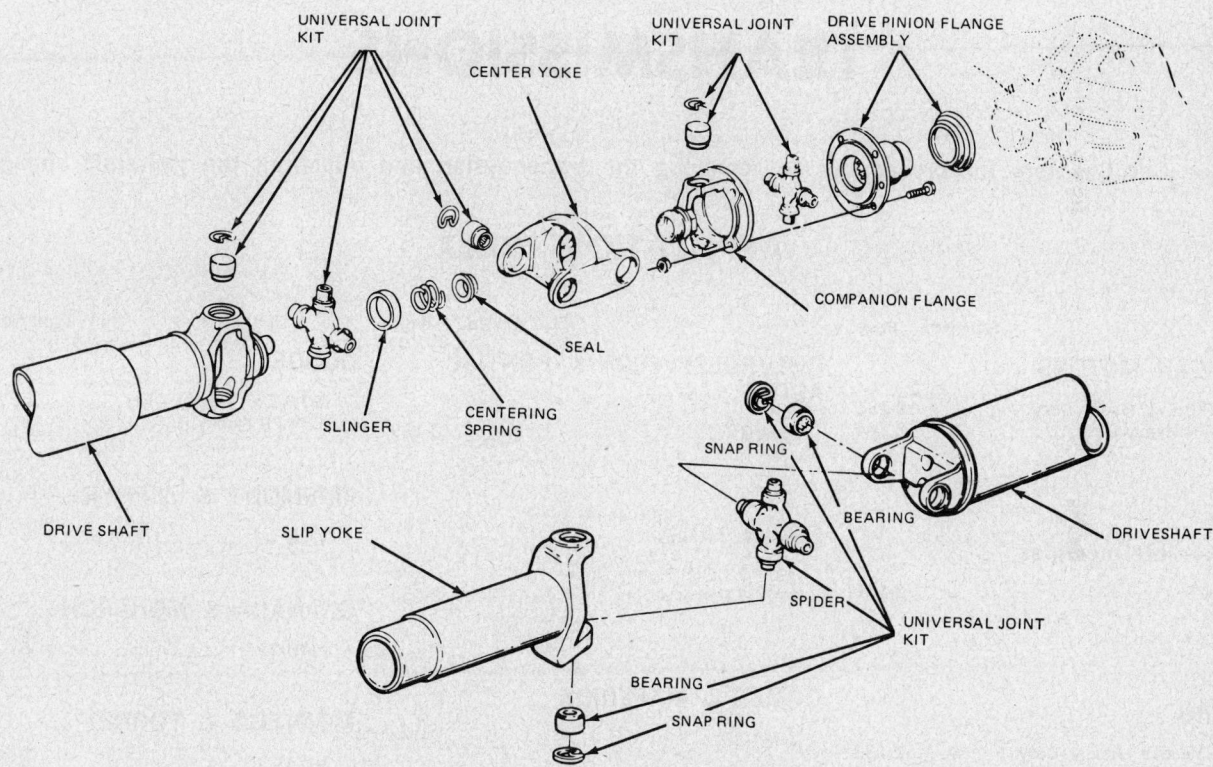

Fig. 22 Constant velocity universal joint. 1977-78 Versailles

7. Remove bearings from driveshaft yoke as outlined in steps 2 through 4. Remove spider from yoke.

8. Insert a screwdriver into centering ball socket, located in companion flange, and pry out rubber seal. Remove retainer, three piece ball seat, washer and spring from ball socket.

Assembly

1. Inspect centering ball socket assembly for worn or damaged components and replace the assembly if necessary.

2. Insert spring, washer, three piece ball seat and retainer into ball socket.

3. With a suitable tool, install centering ball socket seal.

4. Place spider in driveshaft yoke. Ensure that spider bosses are in the original position. Press in bearing cups with tool CJ91B. Install snap rings.

5. Place center yoke over spider ends and press in bearing cups. Install snap rings.

6. Install spider in companion flange yoke. Ensure that spider bosses are in original positions. Press on bearing cups and install snap rings.

7. Place center yoke over spider ends and press in bearing cups. Install snap rings.

1978 Lincoln

Disassembly

1. Mark position of all yokes so that original positions can be maintained during assembly.

2. Support driveshaft in a suitable vise.

3. Install tool CJ91B, Fig. 16. Tighten tool clockwise until the plastic retaining the bearing is sheared and the bearing protrudes approximately 3/8 inch from yoke.

4. Remove driveshaft from vise and tighten bearing in vise, then tap the center yoke, Fig. 17, to free yoke from bearing.

5. Repeat steps 2 through 4 on opposite bearing.

6. Remove remainder of the sheared plastic retaining rings from the grooves in the yokes. The sheared plastic may prevent the bearing cups from being properly pressed in place and seated.

Assembly

1. Ensure all alignment marks are properly positioned, then partially install one bearing cup into yoke.

2. Insert spider into yoke so the journal seats freely into bearing cup.
3. Partially install opposite bearing cup.
4. With tool CJ91B, press both bearing cups into yoke. Move the spider when pressing in the bearing cups. If any binding is felt, check the needle bearings.
5. When one of the retaining ring grooves clears the inside of the yoke,

install the retaining ring.

6. Press in the remaining bearing cup until the retaining ring can be installed. If difficulty is encountered, tap the yoke with a hammer to aid in seating the retaining rings.

Centering Ball Replacement

Refer to the "General Motors, Centering Ball Replacement" procedure for centering ball service.

THREE SPEED TRANSMISSIONS

See Car Chapters for procedures on removing the transmission and adjusting the gearshift linkage

APPLICATION INDEX

Type One

DISASSEMBLE TRANS.

1. Remove transmission cover and shift levers.
2. Remove front retainer and gasket and front bearing snap rings.
3. Align notch in clutch shaft with 3rd speed gear and use suitable puller to remove clutch shaft using care not to lose rollers.
4. Remove front bearing with puller.
5. Remove extension case and remove snap rings that retain speedometer drive gear.
6. Remove speedometer gear using care not to lose drive ball.
7. Remove rear bearing snap rings and remove rear bearing with a puller.
8. Move mainshaft to side and remove shift forks.
9. Place front synchronizer in 2nd speed position and remove mainshaft by tilting front of shaft up and lifting through top of case, Fig. 3.
10. If equipped, remove transmission controlled spark switch assembly.
11. Use a punch to remove roll pins from shift shafts and push shafts into case. Detent assembly may now be removed from case.
12. Using a brass drift drive reverse idler gear shaft out of rear of case and remove idler gear. Do not lose rollers.
13. To retain rollers in countershaft gear, use a dummy shaft to drive countershaft out of rear of case.
14. After disassembling mainshaft carefully inspect all bearings and gears.

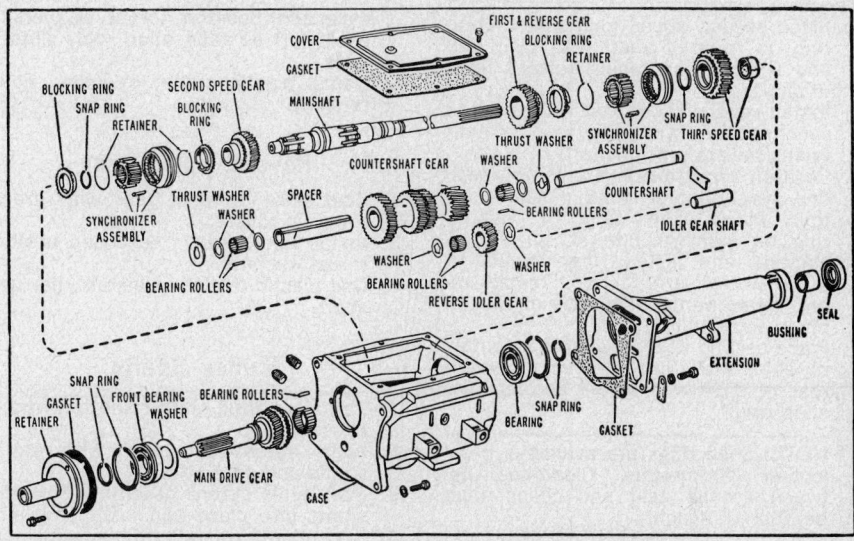

Fig. 1   Type 1 fully synchronized transmission exploded

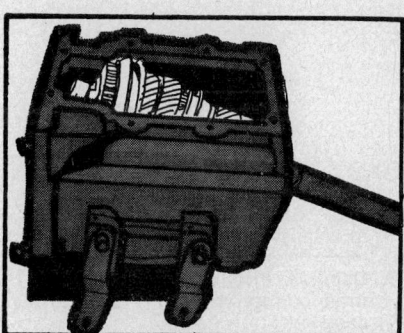

Fig. 3   Removing mainshaft

REASSEMBLE TRANS.
Mainshaft Assemble

1. Place low speed gear and friction ring on shaft with friction ring hub facing toward rear of shaft.
2. Insert low speed synchro-gear into synchro-collar with deep end of gear facing the low speed gear.

NOTE: Synchro-plates and retainer ring are installed with large end of plates facing toward groove in synchro-hub.

3. Place synchro-clutch assembly on shaft with groove in synchro-collar facing toward low speed gear and

Fig. 2   Removing clutch shaft with puller

Fig. 4   Installing mainshaft with Pilot End Support J-22994

install low speed synchro-clutch snap ring.

NOTE: Snap rings are available in selective thicknesses. Clearance between first gear and collar on mainshaft must be .003-.012 inch.

4. Place second speed gear and friction ring on front of shaft with gear hub and friction ring facing toward front of shaft.
5. Install second speed synchro-gear into synchro-collar with deep end of gear facing toward rear of shaft.
6. Position synchro-clutch assembly with one synchro-plate in 12 o'clock position. Place either tang of retainer ring on synchro-plate at 12 o'clock position and install ring, feeding it in a clockwise direction. Install retainer ring on opposite side of assembly in same manner.
7. Place second speed synchro assembly on shaft with deep end facing toward rear of shaft and install second gear snap ring.

NOTE: Snap rings are available in selective thicknesses. Clearance between second gear and collar must be .003-.018 inch.

8. Install reverse gear onto mainshaft.

Countergear

1. Coat bore at each end of counter gear with grease to hold rollers in place.
2. Install dummy shaft in countergear and install spacer, washers and rollers.
3. Place countergear in transmission case and position thrust washers at each end so tabs align with slots in case.
4. Use a plastic mallet to install countershaft.

Reverse Idler Gear

1. Coat bore of idler gear with grease to retain rollers.
2. Install idler gear in case and position thrust washers.
3. Use plastic mallet to install idler gear shaft.

Shifter Shafts

1. Partially install shifter shafts in transmission case.
2. Align detent assembly with shifter shafts and case stud.
3. Push shift detent assembly and shift shafts into place and install roll pins.
4. If equipped, install transmission controlled spark switch.

Mainshaft Installation

1. Place front synchronizer in 2nd speed position and place mainshaft in case.
2. Move mainshaft to side and install shift forks by pulling detent lever up and placing forks in the shifting assembly.
3. Position mainshaft assembly in center of case and install Pilot End Support J-22994, Fig. 4.
4. Place rear bearing on mainshaft and drive bearing into position and install snap ring.
5. Install speedometer gear and snap ring.

Final Assembly

1. Install rollers in clutch shaft using grease to retain them.
2. Slide clutch shaft into position through front of case.
3. Install front bearing, snap rings, gasket and retainer.
4. Replace seal if necessary and install extension housing, shift levers and case cover.
5. Fill transmission with lubricant and check operation.

Type Two

DISASSEMBLE TRANS.
Case Components, Fig. 1

1. With transmission in neutral, remove side cover and shift forks.
2. Remove extension housing bolts, then rotate extension housing 1/4 turn and using a suitable tool, drive reverse idler gear shaft out of case, Fig. 2.
3. Move 2nd-3rd synchronizer sleeve forward, then from rear of case, remove extension housing and mainshaft assemblies.
4. Remove reverse idler gear from case and 3rd speed blocker ring from main drive gear.
5. Using snap ring pliers, expand snap ring at front of extension housing and remove extension housing from mainshaft assembly, Fig. 3.
6. Remove main drive gear bearing retainer and gasket.
7. Remove bearing to main drive gear stem snap ring and remove main drive gear from inside of case by gently tapping on pilot end of main drive gear.
8. Remove oil slinger from main drive gear stem, then remove pilot bearings from main drive gear cavity.
9. Remove main drive gear from case.

NOTE: Since main drive gear bearing is a slip fit on main drive gear stem and case bore, it may be necessary to use a screwdriver between case

and bearing outer snap ring to aid in disassembly.

10. Using a drift or other suitable tool, drive countershaft and key out of rear case.
11. Remove countergear and tanged thrust washers from each end of countergear.

Mainshaft Disassembly, Fig. 4

1. Depress speedometer drive gear retaining clip and slide gear from mainshaft.
2. With front of mainshaft up, remove 3rd speed blocker ring, then using snap ring pliers, remove 2nd-3rd synchronizer hub snap ring from mainshaft.
3. Support 2nd speed gear on press plates and press on front of mainshaft to remove 2nd-3rd synchronizer assembly, 2nd speed blocker ring and 2nd speed gear from mainshaft.
4. With rear of mainshaft up, remove snap ring from mainshaft groove, then support reverse gear on press plates and press on rear of mainshaft to remove reverse gear, thrust washer and rear bearing from mainshaft.

NOTE: Make sure that reverse gear, thrust washer and rear bearing are centered on mainshaft when pressing.

5. Remove 1st-Reverse synchronizer hub snap ring from mainshaft.

6. Support 1st speed gear on press plates, then press on rear of mainshaft to remove 1st-Reverse synchronizer assembly, 1st speed blocker ring and 1st speed gear from mainshaft.

Mainshaft Reassemble

With front of mainshaft up:

1. Install 2nd speed gear with clutching teeth upward; the rear face of the gear will butt against the shoulder on the shaft.
2. Install blocker ring with teeth downward over gear. All three blocker rings used in this unit are identical.
3. Install 2nd and 3rd synchronizer assembly with fork slot downward and press onto splines until it bottoms. Install snap ring.

NOTE: Be sure the notches of the blocker ring align with the keys of the synchronizer assembly.

With rear of mainshaft up:

4. Install 1st speed gear with clutching teeth upward. Install a blocker ring with teeth downward over synchronizer surface of the gear.
5. Install 1st and Reverse synchronizer assembly with fork slot up.

NOTE: Be sure the notches of the blocker ring align with the keys of

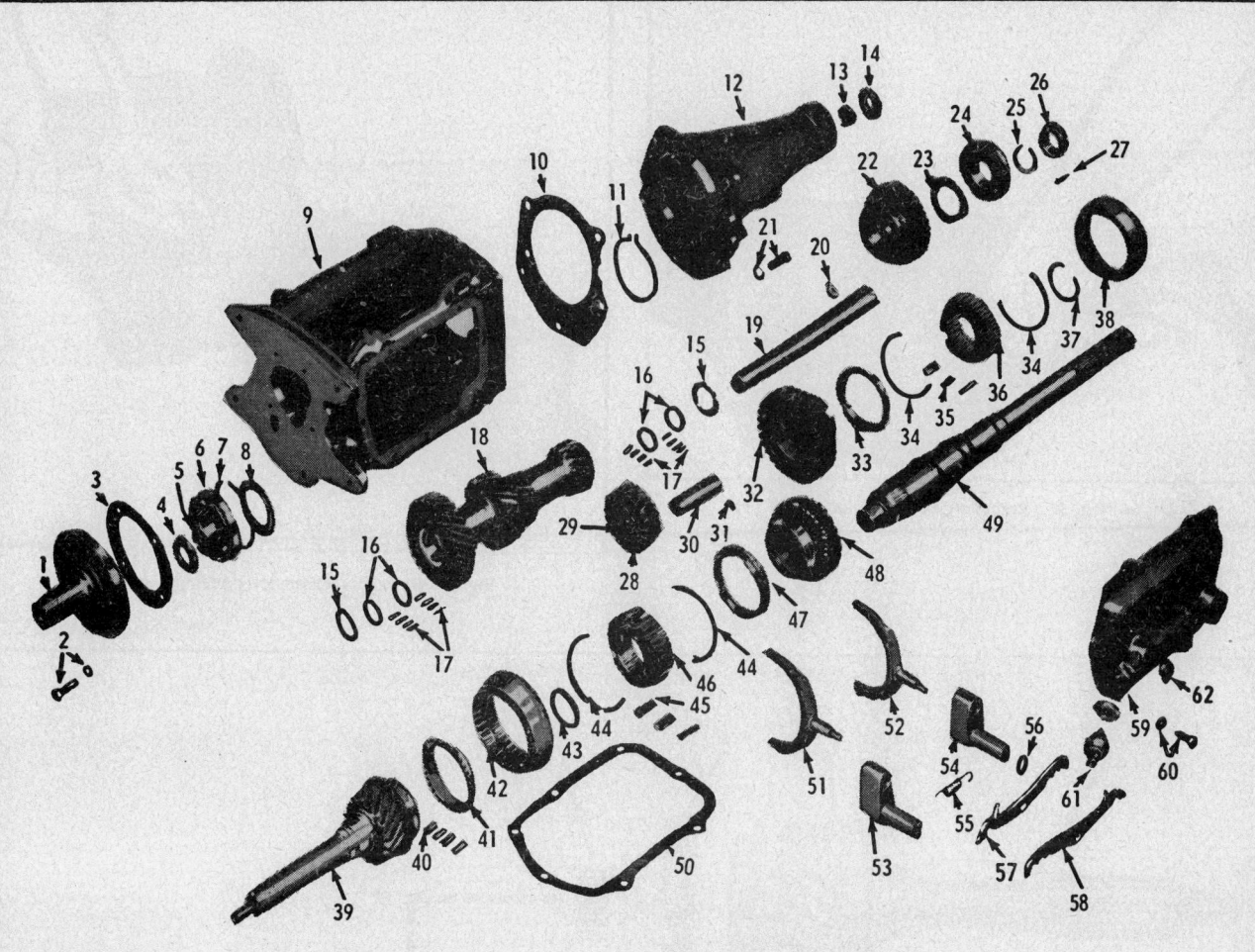

Fig. 1   Type two fully synchronized transmission. Exploded view

1. Bearing Retainer
2. Bolt and Lock Washer
3. Gasket
4. Oil Seal
5. Snap Ring (Bearing-to-Main Drive Gear)
6. Main Drive Gear Bearing
7. Snap Ring Bearing
8. Oil Slinger
9. Case
10. Gasket
11. Snap Ring (Rear Bearing-to-Extension)
12. Extension
13. Extension Bushing
14. Oil Seal
15. Thrust Washer
16. Bearing Washer
17. Needle Bearings

18. Countergear
19. Countershaft
20. Woodruff Key
21. Bolt (Extension-to-Case)
22. Reverse Gear
23. Thrust Washer
24. Rear Bearing
25. Snap Ring
26. Speedometer Drive Gear
27. Retainer Clip
28. Reverse Idler Gear
29. Reverse Idler Bushing
30. Reverse Idler Shaft
31. Woodruff Key
32. 1st Speed Gear
33. 1st Speed Blocker Ring
34. Synchronizer Key Spring

35. Synchronizer Keys
36. 1st and Reverse Synchronizer Hub Assembly
37. Snap Ring
38. 1st and Reverse Synchronizer Collar
39. Main Drive Gear
40. Pilot Bearings
41. 3rd Speed Blocker Ring
42. 2nd and 3rd Synchronizer Collar
43. Snap Ring
44. Synchronizer Key Spring
45. Synchronizer Keys
46. 2nd and 3rd Synchronizer Hub
47. 2nd Speed Blocker Ring
48. 2nd Speed Gear
49. Mainshaft

50. Gasket
51. 2nd and 3rd Shifter Fork
52. 1st and Reverse Shifter Fork
53. 2-3 Shifter Shaft Assembly
54. 1st and Reverse Shifter Shaft Assembly
55. Spring
56. O-Ring Seal
57. 1st and Reverse Detent Cam
58. 2nd and 3rd Detent Cam
59. Side Cover
60. Bolt and Lock Washer
61. TCS Switch and Gasket
62. Lip Seal

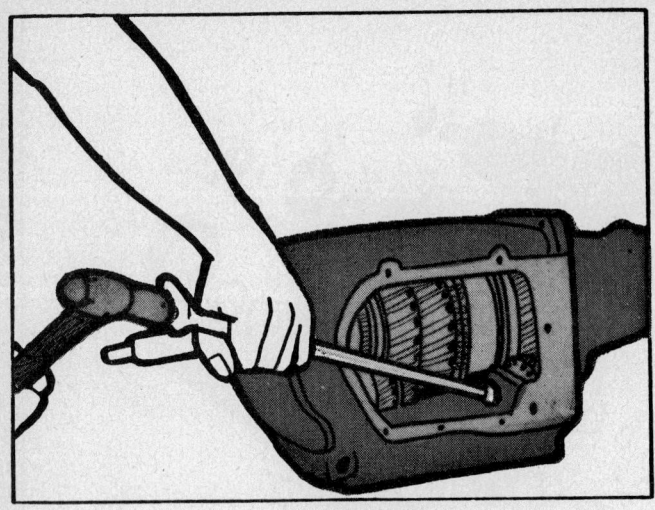

Fig. 2 Removing reverse idler shaft

Fig. 3 Removing extension housing snap ring

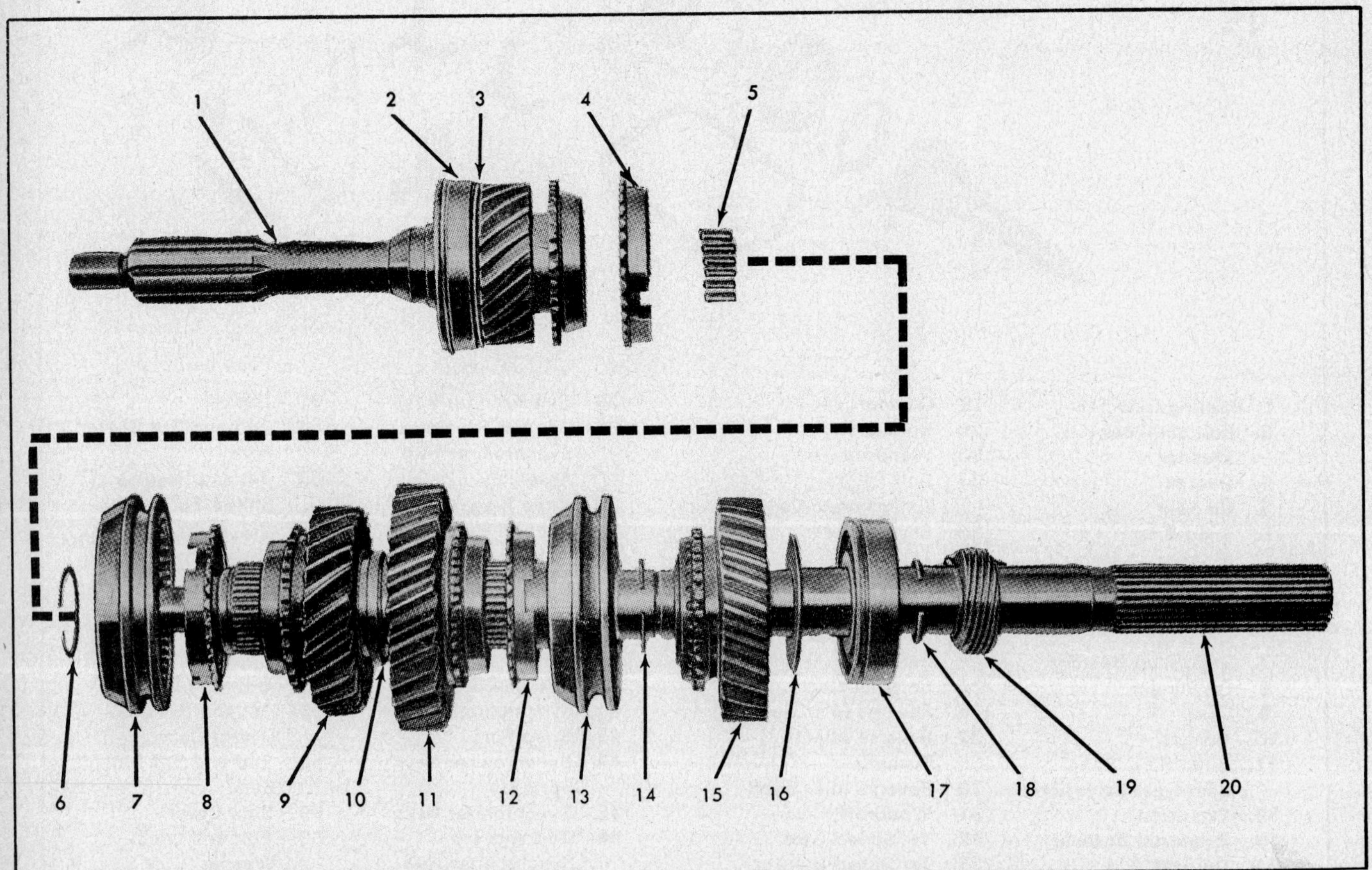

1. Clutch Gear
2. Clutch Gear Bearing
3. Oil Slinger
4. 3rd Speed Blocker Ring
5. Mainshaft Pilot Bearings (16)

6. Snap Ring
7. 2-3 Synchronizer Assembly
8. 2nd Speed Blocker Ring
9. 2nd Speed Gear
10. Shoulder (Part of Mainshaft)

11. 1st Speed Gear
12. 1st Speed Blocker Ring
13. 1st Speed Synchronizer Assembly
14. Snap Ring
15. Reverse Gear

16. Reverse Gear Thrust Washer
17. Rear Bearing
18. Snap Ring
19. Speedo Drive Gear
20. Mainshaft

Fig. 4 Mainshaft assembly

the synchronizer assembly and that both synchronizer sleeves face the front of the mainshaft.

6. Install snap ring.
7. Install Reverse gear with clutching teeth downward. Install bronze thrust washer.
8. Press rear bearing onto mainshaft with snap ring slot downward. Install snap ring.
9. Install speedometer drive gear and retaining clip.

REASSEMBLE TRANS.

1. Load a double row of roller bearings and a thrust washer at each end of the countergear. Use heavy grease to hold them in place.
2. Place countergear through case rear opening with tanged thrust washer (tang away from gear) at each end

and install countergear shaft and woodruff key from rear of case.

NOTE: Be sure countershaft picks up both thrust washers and that the tangs are aligned with their notches in the case.

3. Position reverse idler gear in case but do not install shaft.
4. Expand snap ring and install mainshaft assembly into rear extension housing.
5. Load roller bearings into clutch gear bore, install blocker ring onto clutch gear and install clutch gear assembly onto mainshaft.

NOTE: Be sure notches in blocker ring align with keys in synchronizer assembly.

6. Using new gasket, install the main-

shaft assembly through the rear of the case. Be sure the clutch gear engages the teeth of the countergear anti-lash plate and that the oil slinger is in place on the clutch gear.

7. Rotate extension housing and install reverse idler shaft and woodruff key. Install extension bolts.
8. Position oil slinger with inner lip facing forward on drive gear stem, then install snap ring on bearing.
9. Install front bearing on clutch gear stem, install snap ring and bearing retainer.

NOTE: Oil return hole in retainer should be at 6 o'clock.

10. With synchronizers in Neutral, install cover assembly. Be sure forks align with their synchronizer sleeve grooves.

Type Three

DISASSEMBLE TRANS.
Case Components

1. Shift transmission into 2nd gear for shift fork clearance and remove side cover and shifter assembly, Fig. 1.
2. Remove front bearing retainer.
3. Tap drive pinion forward with brass drift as far as possible to provide clearance for mainshaft removal, Fig. 2.
4. Rotate cut away part of second gear next to countergear for mainshaft removal clearance. Shift 2-3 synchronizer sleeve forward.
5. Remove speedometer gear.
6. Remove rear extension housing.
7. Using dummy shaft, push reverse idler shaft and key out of case.
8. Remove idler gear with dummy shaft in place to retain rollers. Remove thrust washers.
9. Remove mainshaft through rear case opening, Fig. 3.
10. Using dummy shaft to retain rollers, tap countershaft out rear of case and lower countergear to bottom of

case to permit removal of drive pinion.
11. Remove snap ring from pinion bearing outer race, drive pinion into case and remove through rear case opening, Fig. 4.
12. Remove countergear through rear case opening.

Mainshaft, Disassemble

1. Remove 2-3 synchronizer clutch gear retaining ring from front of mainshaft.
2. Slide 2-3 synchronizer and 2nd gear stop ring off of shaft. Remove 2nd gear.
3. Spread snap ring in mainshaft bearing retainer and slide retainer off bearing race, Fig. 5.
4. Remove snap ring securing bearing to mainshaft.
5. Support front side of the reverse gear in press and press bearing off shaft. *When bearing clears shaft, do not allow parts to drop through.*
6. Remove 1st-Reverse synchronizer retaining ring and remove synchronizer assembly from mainshaft, Fig. 6.
7. Remove 1st gear and stop ring.
8. Reverse procedure to assemble mainshaft.

Mainshaft, Reassemble

1. Slide 1st gear and stop ring onto mainshaft and against flange, Fig. 7.
2. Slide 1st-Reverse synchronizer over mainshaft, indexing hub slots to stop ring lugs.
3. Install clutch gear snap ring on mainshaft.
4. Install reverse gear and mainshaft bearing, support inner race of bearing and press shaft through to shoulder. *Be sure snap ring groove on outer race is forward.* Install bearing retaining ring on mainshaft.
5. Spread snap ring in mainshaft bearing retainer and slide retainer over bearing. Be sure snap ring seats in groove.
6. Referring to Fig. 1, install 2nd gear, stop ring and 2nd-3rd gear synchronizer. Install snap ring.

Transmission, Assemble

1. Using dummy shaft to hold rollers in place and heavy grease to hold thrust washers, carefully place countergear assembly in bottom of case.

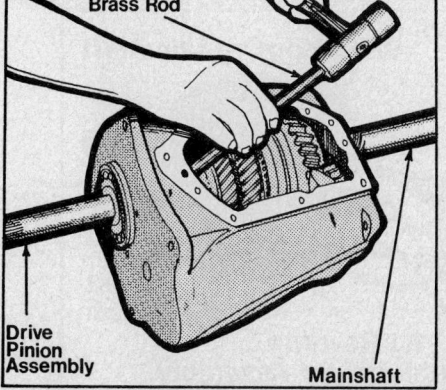

Fig. 2 Tapping drive pinion forward for mainshaft clearance

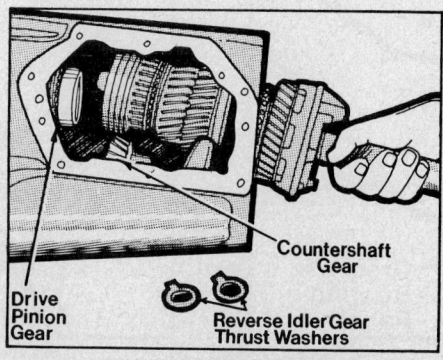

Fig. 3 Removing mainshaft assembly

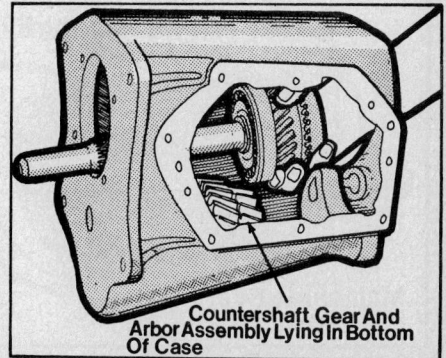

Fig. 4 Removing drive pinion

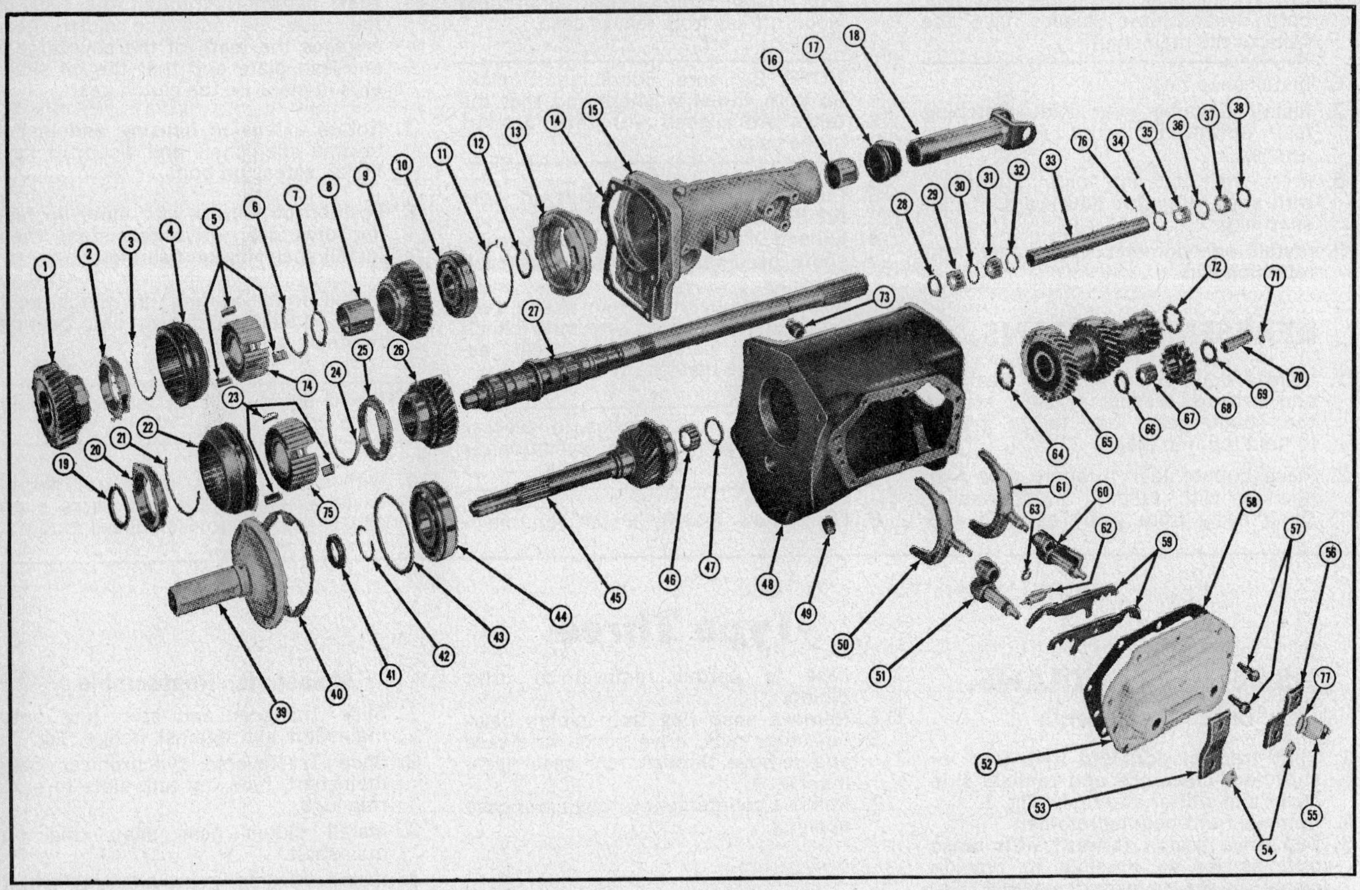

1. Gear, First	14. Gasket	27. Shaft, Output	40. Gasket	53. Lever	66. Washer
2. Ring	15. Extension	28. Washer	41. Seal	54. Nut Locking	67. Roller
3. Spring	16. Bushing	29. Roller	42. Snap Ring	55. Switch	68. Gear, Idler
4. Sleeve	17. Seal	30. Washer	43. Snap Ring	56. Lever	69. Washer
5. Struts (3)	18. Yoke	31. Roller	44. Bearing	57. Bolt	70. Shaft
6. Spring	19. Snap Ring	32. Washer	45. Pinion, Drive	58. Gasket	71. Key
7. Snap Ring	20. Ring	33. Countershaft	46. Roller	59. Lever, Interlock	72. Washer
8. Bushing	21. Spring	34. Washer	47. Snap Ring	60. Lever	73. Plug, Filler
9. Gear, Reverse	22. Sleeve	35. Roller	48. Case	61. Fork	74. Gear, Clutch
10. Bearing	23. Struts (3)	36. Washer	49. Plug, Drain	62. Spring	75. Gear, Clutch
11. Snap Ring	24. Spring	37. Roller	50. Fork	63. Snap Ring	76. Key
12. Snap Ring	25. Ring	38. Washer	51. Lever	64. Washer	77. Gasket
13. Retainer	26. Gear, Second	39. Retainer	52. Housing	65. Gear, Countershaft	

Fig. 1. Type 3 fully synchronized three speed transmission

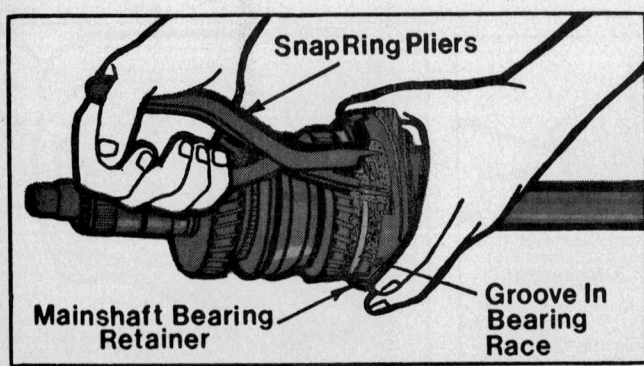

Fig. 5 Removing mainshaft bearing retainer

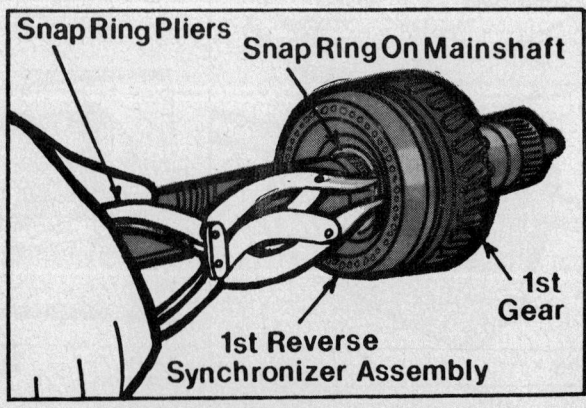

Fig. 6 Removing 1st-Reverse synchronizer snap ring

Do not finish installation until drive pinion is installed.

2. Load rollers and retaining ring in drive pinion bore and install drive pinion through rear case opening and into case bore. Install large snap ring on bearing and install front bearing retainer.
3. Align countergear with its shaft bore and install countershaft through gear, driving dummy shaft out as countershaft is installed. Install countershaft key.
4. Carefully tap drive pinion forward to provide mainshaft installation clearance.
5. With 2-3 synchronizer sleeve fully

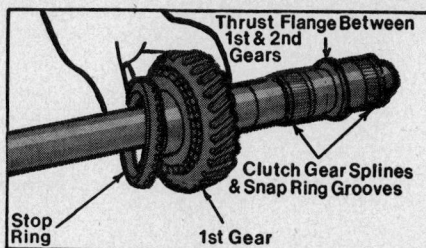

Fig. 7   First gear installation

forward and cut out on 2nd gear turned so it is toward countershaft, insert mainshaft assembly through

rear case opening.

NOTE: If installation is correct, the bearing retainer will bottom in the case without force. If not, check for strut, roller or stop ring is out of position.

6. Using dummy shaft to hold rollers, install reverse idler in case and install idler shaft and key.
7. Install rear extension housing, speedometer gear and with transmission shifted in 2nd gear, install cover and shifter assembly.

Type Four

Disassemble

1. Drain lubricant and remove damper assembly, if equipped.
2. Remove side cover and gasket.
3. Remove front bearing retainer.
4. Remove clutch gear bearing-to-stem snap ring then slide bearing off over clutch gear stem. The clutch gear bearing is a slip fit on the gear and into the case bore.
5. Remove extension-to-case bolts.
6. Remove reverse idler shaft-to-gear "E" ring, Fig. 2.
7. Remove clutch gear, mainshaft and extension assembly together through rear case opening.
8. Expand snap ring and remove rear bearing retainer and mainshaft from extension, Fig. 3.
9. Drive countershaft and woodruff key out through the rear of the case. Remove countergear and bearings.
10. Use a long drift and drive reverse idler shaft and key through rear of case.
11. Remove reverse idler gear tanged thrust washer.

Disassemble Mainshaft

1. Remove clutch gear, roller bearings

and blocking ring from mainshaft. Referring to Fig. 5, remove 2-3 synchronizer sleeve.
2. Remove speedometer gear.
3. Remove rear bearing snap ring, and press off rear bearing, spring washer, thrust washer and Reverse gear.
4. Remove 1st and Reverse sliding clutch hub snap ring and clutch assembly, 1st speed blocker ring and gear.

Synchronizers

NOTE: The synchronizer hubs and sliding sleeves are a selected assembly and should be kept together as originally assembled. The keys and springs may be replaced if worn or broken.

1. Mark hub and sleeve so they can be reassembled in same position.
2. Remove sleeve from synchronizer hub.
3. Remove keys and springs from hub.
4. Place three keys and two springs in position (one on each side of hub) so all three keys are engaged by both springs, Fig. 6. The tanged end of each synchronizer spring should be installed in different key cavities on

either side of hub. Slide sleeve onto hub, aligning marks made before disassembly.

NOTE: A chamfer or groove around the outside of synchronizer hub identifies the end that must be opposite the fork slot in the sleeve, Fig. 7.

Assemble Mainshaft

With front of mainshaft up:
1. Install second speed gear with clutching teeth upward.
2. Install blocking ring with clutching teeth downward. All blocking rings in this unit are identical.
3. Press 2-3 synchronizer onto mainshaft, Fig. 8. *Be sure notches in blocking ring align with keys in synchronizer.*
With rear of mainshaft up:
4. Install first speed gear with clutching teeth upward.
5. Install blocking ring on gear with teeth downward.
6. Press first and reverse synchronizer onto mainshaft. *Be sure notches in*

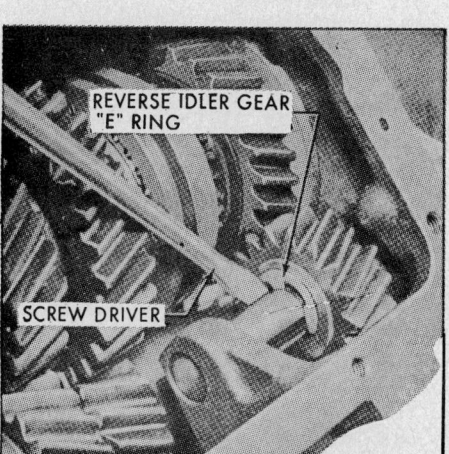

Fig. 2   Removing reverse idler "E" ring

Fig. 3   Removing rear bearing retainer after spreading snap ring as shown

Fig. 4   Removing countershaft, using aligning arbor to hold needle bearings in place

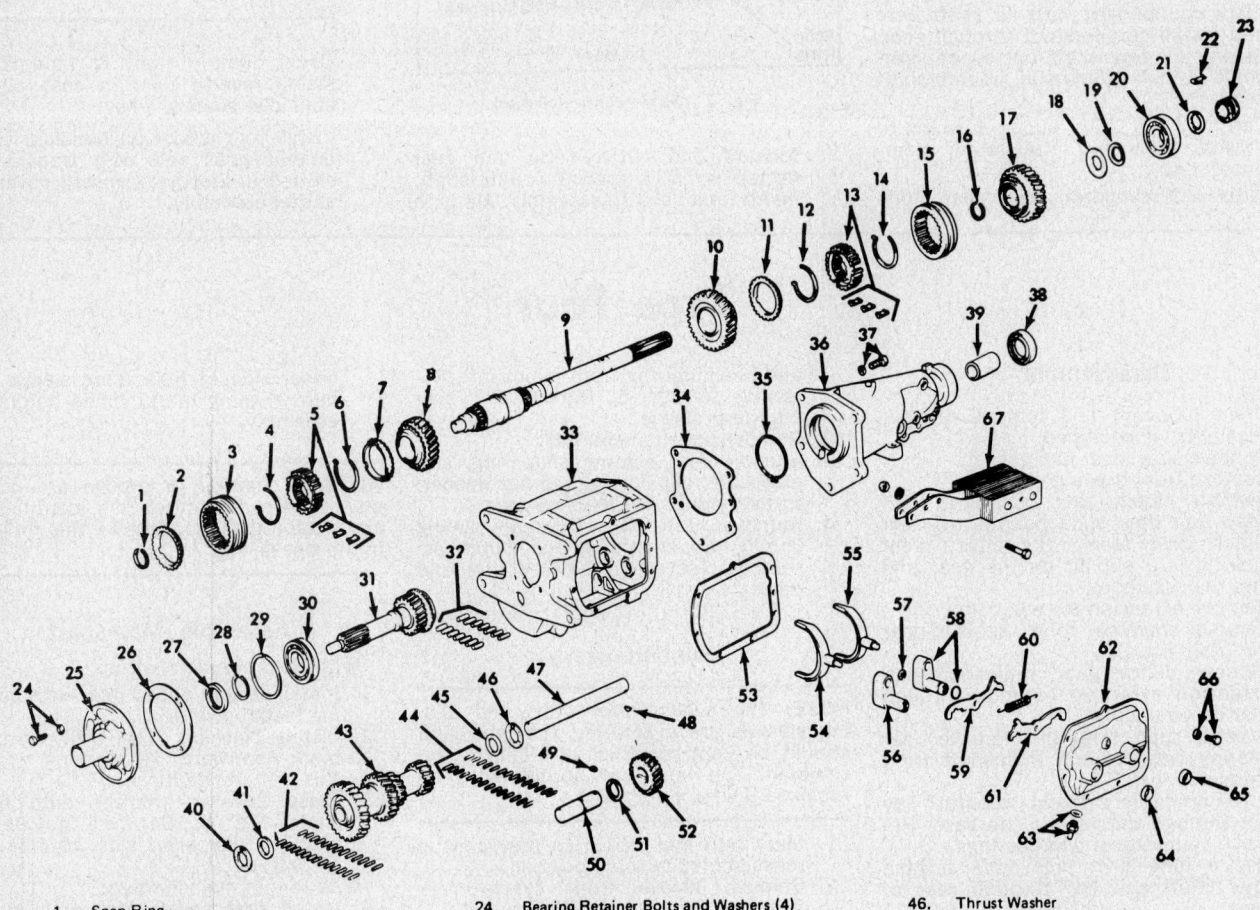

1.	Snap Ring	24.	Bearing Retainer Bolts and Washers (4)	46.	Thrust Washer
2.	Synchronizer Ring	25.	Front Bearing Retainer	47.	Countergear Shaft
3.	2-3 Synchronizer Sleeve	26.	Bearing Retainer Gasket	48.	Countergear Shaft Key
4.	Synchronizer Key Spring	27.	Bearing Retainer Oil Seal	49.	Idler Shaft Key
5.	Synchronizer Hub and Keys	28.	Snap Ring	50.	Reverse Idler Shaft
6.	Synchronizer Key Spring	29.	Bearing Snap Ring	51.	Snap Ring
7.	Synchronizer Ring	30.	Front Bearing	52.	Reverse Idler Gear
8.	Second Gear	31.	Drive Gear	53.	Side Cover Gasket
9.	Main Shaft	32.	Pilot Bearings	54.	2-3 Shift Fork
10.	First Gear	33.	Case	55.	1-Rev Shift Fork
11.	Synchronizer Ring	34.	Extension to Case Gasket	56.	2-3 Shifter Shaft
12.	Synchronizer Key Spring	35.	Rear Bearing to Extension Retaining Ring	57.	Retaining "E" Ring
13.	Synchronizer Hub and Keys	36.	Rear Extension	58.	1-Rev Shifter Shaft with "O" Ring
14.	Synchronizer Key Spring	37.	Extension to Case Retaining Bolts and Washers	59.	2-3 Detent Cam
15.	1-2 Synchronizer Sleeve	38.	Rear Extension Bushing	60.	Detent Cam Spring
16.	Snap Ring	39.	Rear Seal	61.	1-Rev Detent Cam
17.	Reverse Gear	40.	Thrust Washer	62.	Shift Cover
18.	Thrust Washer	41.	Spacer	63.	TCS Switch and Gasket
19.	Waved Washer	42.	Countergear Shaft Bearings	64.	Shifter Shaft Seal
20.	Rear Bearing	43.	Countergear	65.	Shifter Shaft Seal
21.	Snap Ring	44.	Countergear Shaft Bearings	66.	Shift Cover Bolts and Washers
22.	Speedometer Gear Clip	45.	Spacer	67.	Damper Assembly
23.	Speedometer Drive Gear				

Fig. 1   Type 4 three speed transmission

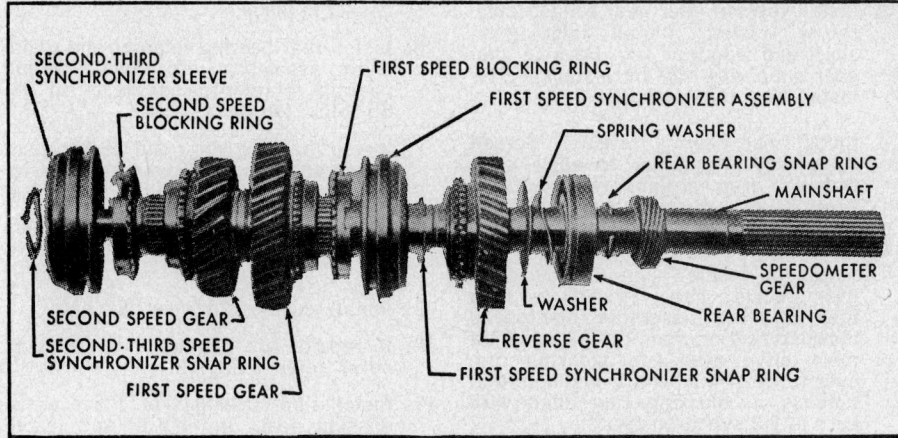

SECOND-THIRD SYNCHRONIZER SLEEVE
SECOND SPEED BLOCKING RING
FIRST SPEED BLOCKING RING
FIRST SPEED SYNCHRONIZER ASSEMBLY
SPRING WASHER
REAR BEARING SNAP RING
MAINSHAFT
SPEEDOMETER GEAR
REAR BEARING
WASHER
REVERSE GEAR
SECOND SPEED GEAR
SECOND-THIRD SPEED SYNCHRONIZER SNAP RING
FIRST SPEED GEAR
FIRST SPEED SYNCHRONIZER SNAP RING

Fig. 5 Mainshaft and related parts assembled loosely to show location of parts

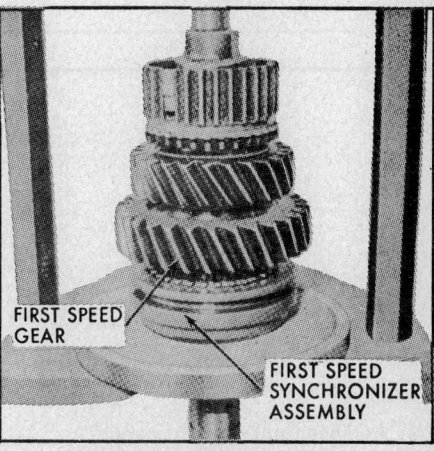

SLEEVE
SPRING
KEY
HUB

Fig. 6 Synchronizer assembly

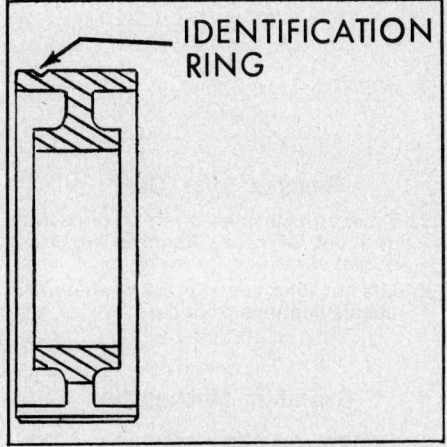

IDENTIFICATION RING

Fig. 7 Identification chamfer around synchronizer hub

SECOND SPEED GEAR

MAKE CERTAIN NOTCHES IN BLOCKING RING ALIGN WITH KEY IN SYNCHRONIZER

Fig. 8 Installing second speed gear

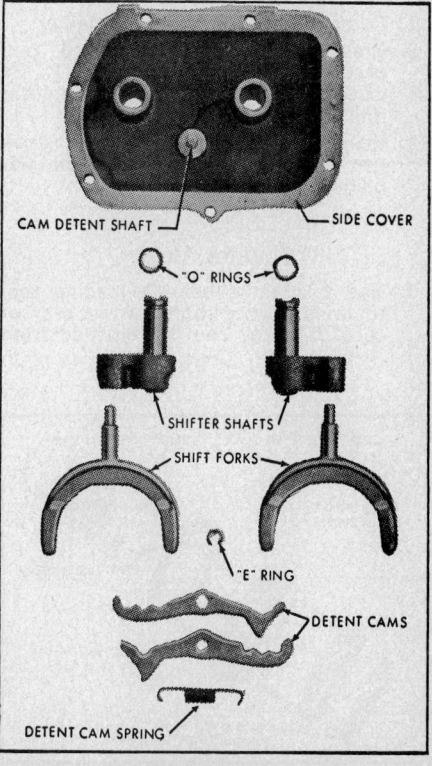

FIRST SPEED GEAR
FIRST SPEED SYNCHRONIZER ASSEMBLY

Fig. 9 Installing first speed gear

CAM DETENT SHAFT
SIDE COVER
"O" RINGS
SHIFTER SHAFTS
SHIFT FORKS
"E" RING
DETENT CAMS
DETENT CAM SPRING

Fig. 12 Disassembled view of side cover

Fig. 10 Countergear with riveted anti-rattle gear. Except Astre, Monza & Vega

Fig. 11 Astre, Monza & Vega counter-gear

2–141

blocking ring align with keys in syn-chronizer. Install snap ring.

7. Install reverse gear, thrust washer, spring washer, rear bearing and bearing snap ring.

8. Install speedometer gear.

Assemble Transmission

1. Install countergear-to-case thrust washers. Install countergear into case from rear. Make certain woodruff key is in place. Note that anti rattle gear is riveted to countergear in four places and is not serviced separately, Fig. 10.

NOTE: Astre, Monza and Vega trans-missions do not use an anti-rattle gear, Fig. 11.

---

2. Install reverse idler gear tanged steel thrust washer. Install idler gear, shaft and woodruff key. *Reverse idler gear snap ring will be installed after installation of mainshaft.*

3. Install rear bearing retainer. Spread snap ring in retainer to allow snap ring to drop around rear bearing. Press on end of mainshaft until snap ring engages groove in rear bearing.

4. Install 14 needle rollers in main drive gear pocket, using grease to hold them in place. Assemble third speed blocking ring on main drive gear. Pilot main drive gear and blocking ring over front of mainshaft. Make certain notches in blocking ring align with keys in 2-3 synchronizer.

5. Install rear bearing retainer-to-case gasket, using heavy grease to hold

gasket in place.

6. Install rear bearing retainer and main-shaft assembly into case. Torque bearing retainer-to-case bolts to 35-55 ft-lbs. torque.

7. Install bearing on main drive gear. Outer snap ring groove must be to-ward front of gear. Install snap ring.

8. Install front bearing retainer and gas-ket. Torque retainer bolts to 8-12 ft. lbs.

9. Install reverse idler gear "E" ring.

10. If repairs are required to the side cover, refer to Fig. 12.

11. Install side cover gasket. Place trans-mission gears in neutral and install side cover. Install attaching bolts and tighten evenly to avoid cover dis-tortion.

Type Five

DISASSEMBLE TRANS.

1. Pull flange from rear of mainshaft.
2. Slide extension housing off main-shaft.
3. Remove transmission cover.

Main Drive Gear

1. Remove drive gear bearing retainer.
2. Grasp drive gear shaft and pull assembly out of case, Fig. 1. *Be careful not to bind inner synchronizer ring on drive gear clutch teeth.*
3. Remove bearing rollers from drive gear pocket, using a hook or flat blade.

Counter Gear

1. Use a suitable bearing loading tool to drive countershaft toward rear of case until key can be removed from

countershaft. Then drive countershaft all the way out, keeping loading tool tight against end of countershaft to keep needle bearings in place.

Mainshaft

1. With transmission in reverse, remove outer center bearing snap ring, using a hook or flat blade, then partially remove mainshaft.
2. Cock mainshaft, then remove clutch sleeve, outer synchronizer rings, front inner ring and 2-3 shift fork, Fig. 2.
3. Remove clutch gear snap ring. Slide clutch gear off end of mainshaft.
4. Slide 2nd speed gear, stop ring and synchronizer spring off mainshaft.
5. Remove low-reverse sliding gear and shift fork as mainshaft is withdrawn from case.
6. Lift counter gear assembly from case.

Reverse Idler Gear

1. Drive reverse idler shaft towards rear and out of case. Remove key from end of shaft.
2. Lift out idler gear, thrust washers and needle bearings from case.

Gearshift Mechanism

1. Remove operating levers from shafts.
2. Drive out tapered pin from either of two lever shafts, Fig. 3, then with-draw shaft from inside of case. The detent balls are spring-loaded; as the shaft is being withdrawn, ball will drop to bottom of case.
3. Remove interlock sleeve, spring, pin and both balls from case. Then drive out remaining tapered pin and slide shaft out of transmission.
4. Drive out shaft seals and discard.

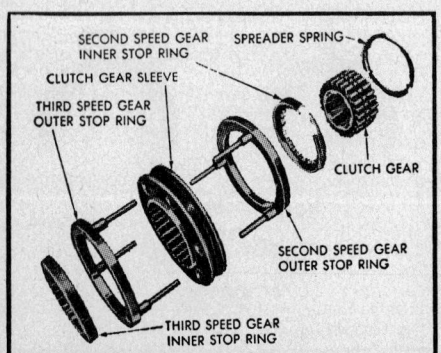

Fig. 2 Synchronizer unit

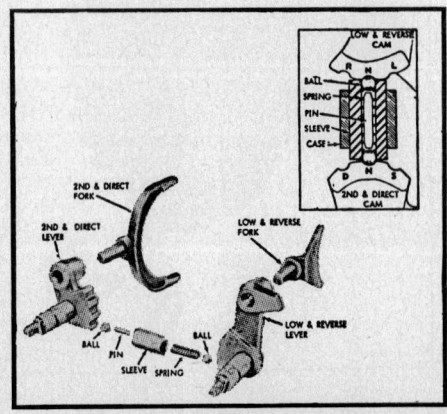

Fig. 3 Gearshift mechanism

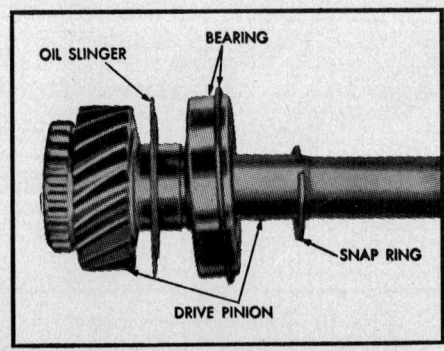

Fig. 4 Main drive gear components

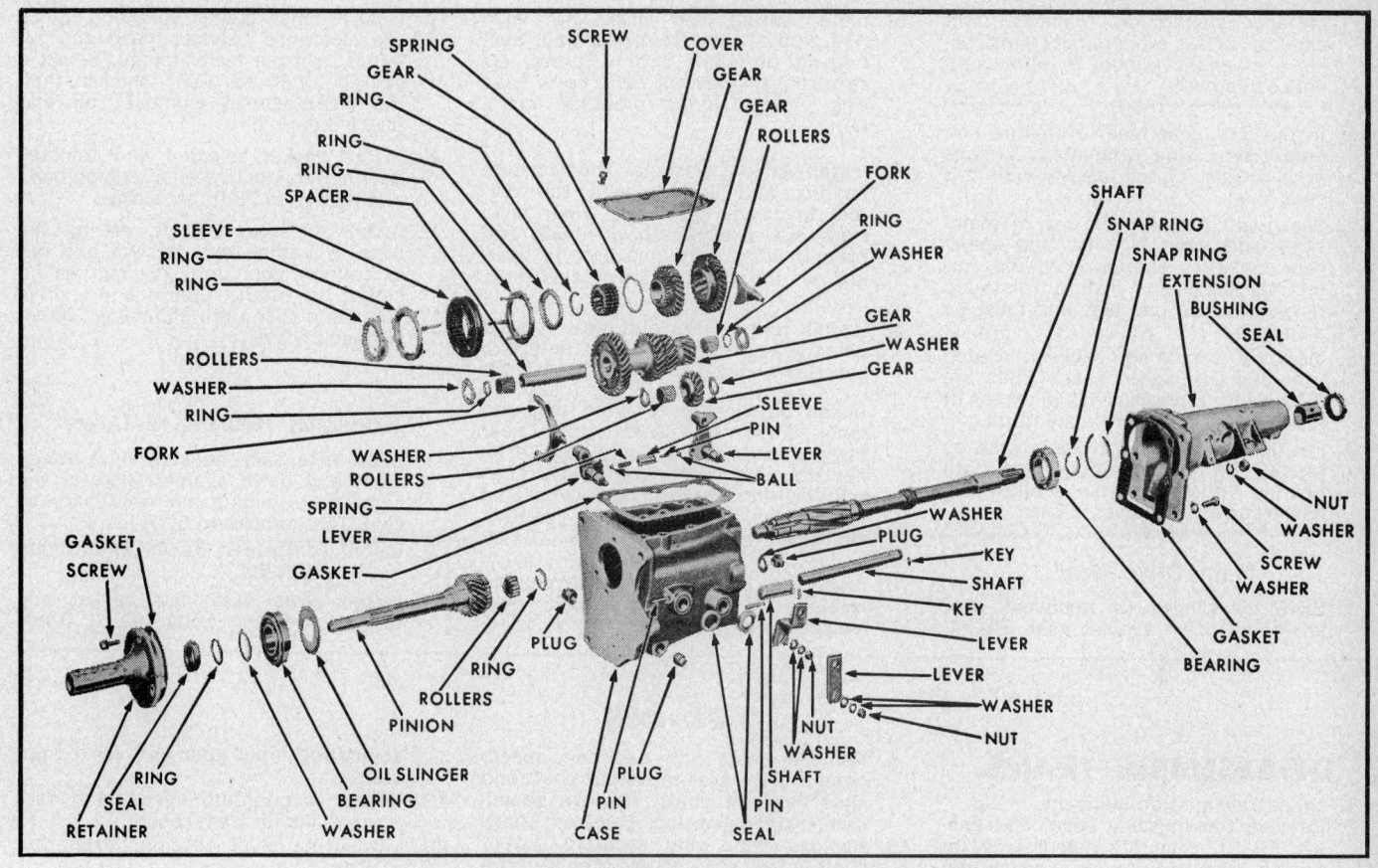

Fig. 1   Type 5 standard duty transmission disassembled. Note that low-reverse mainshaft gear shift fork groove goes to the front

REASSEMBLE TRANS.
Gearshift Mechanism

1. Center two new seals over holes in case, then drive both seals into case.
2. Slide low-reverse shaft into rear boss of case, through seal and into position. Lock with tapered pin. Turn lever until center (neutral) detent is in line with interlock bores. Use sealer on pins.
3. Slide interlock sleeve into its bore, followed by one interlock ball. Install interlock spring and pin.
4. Place remaining interlock ball on top of spring. Depress interlock ball and at the same time install 2-3 lever into fully seated position with center (neutral) detent aligned with detent ball. Secure shaft with tapered pin.

Counter Gear

1. Slide bearing spacer over bearing loading tool. Coat bore of gear with lubricant. Then slide tool and spacer into gear bore.
2. Lubricate needle bearings and install half the total of bearings at each end of gear around loading tool (44 total).

3. Install bearing retainer rings at each end of gear. Apply grease to hold bearings in place.
4. Thrust washers are available in two sizes, marked A and B. Make a selection to obtain .004-.012″ total end play of counter gear.
5. Install thrust washers at each end of assembly and over loading tool, using grease to hold washers in place.
6. Install counter gear assembly in case, making sure tabs on thrust washers slide into grooves in case.

Reverse Idler Gear

1. Coat bore of gear with grease and slide a suitable bearing loading tool into bore.
2. Lubricate 22 needle bearings and install around loading tool.
3. Install new thrust washer at each end of gear and over loading tool using grease to hold washers in place.
4. With bevelled ends of gear teeth forward, slide gear down into position in case.
5. Install gear shift in its opening at rear of case.
6. Install key in shaft, and position shaft with keyway.
7. Raise idler gear slightly to align with shaft, then drive shaft into case

through thrust washer and gear until end of shaft is about $1/64″$ below surface of case.

Mainshaft

1. If new bearing is to be installed, press it on mainshaft and install snap ring.
2. Install low-reverse fork with offset to rear. Engage fork in low-reverse sliding gear. Position in case by shifting into reverse.
3. Slide mainshaft into case and through low-reverse gear.
4. Install 2-3 shift fork with offset toward rear.
5. Install 2nd speed gear and spreader spring on mainshaft.

NOTE: *Synchronizer float should be .050″ to .090″ when measured between end of synchronizer outer ring pin and opposite synchronizer outer ring. This measurement must be made 180 degrees apart with equal gap on both pin ends for float determination. To be acceptable, the gauge should be a snug fit between pins and outer rings. In cases where float dimension is over .090″, synchronizer shims (part no. 2464724) should be installed to reduce float to .090″ or less. This shim is to be installed on the 2nd speed gear before the energizing spring is installed. In cases where float is below .050″,* *material should be removed from ends of all six synchronizer pins, using a magnetic grinder or other suitable equipment.*

6. Install 2nd gear inner stop ring and outer stop ring assembly. Engage synchronizer clutch sleeve with 2-3 shift fork.

7. Slide clutch gear over end of mainshaft and down against 2nd speed gear. Select a snap ring of the correct thickness and install. This snap ring eliminates end play and must be a snug fit.

8. Measure clearance between clutch gear and 2nd speed gear. Limits are .002-.011". If clearance is in excess of .011", "gear jump-out" may result.

9. Position mainshaft further in case by tapping on outer bearing race until bearing bottoms. Install a snap ring of the correct thickness in case.

Main Drive Gear

1. Slide oil slinger (if removed) over shaft and down against gear, Fig. 4.

2. Slide bearing over shaft with snap ring groove away from gear end. Seat bearing on shaft with a press. *Be sure slinger does not hang up in snap ring groove during pressing operation.*

3. Install keyed washer. Then secure bearing and washer with the correct thickness snap ring. Four snap rings are available to eliminate end play. If large snap ring around bearing was removed, install at this time.

4. Install rollers in drive gear pocket using grease to hold them in place, and retain with lock ring (14 rollers).

5. Install 3rd gear outer stop ring and inner stop ring. Guide drive gear through front of case and engage inner stop ring with clutch teeth. Then seat bearing. Bearing is fully seated when snap ring is in full contact with case.

6. Install new seal in drive gear bearing retainer. Slide bearing retainer (less gasket) down against case.

7. Hold retainer against case and measure clearance between case and retainer, using a feeler gauge. Select a gasket .003" to .004" thicker than the clearance to eliminate all end play in bearing.

8. Install gasket selected and reinstall bearing retainer. Install attaching bolts and tighten to 23 ft-lbs. torque.

9. Install the countershaft, driving the bearing loading tool forward and out of counter gear until key can be inserted in shaft. Continue to drive shaft into case until about 1/64" below surface of case.

Extension Housing & Cover

1. Slide extension housing over mainshaft and down against case, at the same time guiding mainshaft into oil seal. Torque bolts to 50 ft-lbs.

2. Install companion flange and torque nut to 175 ft-lbs.

3. Install cover with new gasket and torque attaching bolts to 12 ft-lbs.

Type Six

DISASSEMBLE TRANS.

1. Drain transmission lubricant.
2. Remove transmission cover and gasket, Fig. 1, then the detent plug retaining spring from case. Remove detent plug with a magnet.
3. Remove extension housing and gasket from case.
4. Remove front bearing retainer and gasket from case.
5. Working through filler plug opening, drive roll pin from countershaft with a 1/4 inch punch, Fig. 2.
6. On some models it is necessary to tap the countershaft from the rear of the case with a dummy shaft to remove the expansion plug from the countershaft bore at front of case.
7. On other models, hold countershaft gear with a hook and, with a dummy shaft push countershaft from rear of case, Fig. 3.
8. On all models, lower countershaft gear and thrust washers to bottom of case.

9. Remove snap ring securing speedometer drive gear to output shaft and slide gear off shaft. Remove speedometer drive gear lock ball from shaft.
10. Remove snap ring securing output shaft bearing on shaft, then remove bearing from case and shaft, Fig. 4.
11. Place both shift levers in neutral (Center) position. Remove set screw securing first-reverse shaft fork to shaft rail, then slide first-reverse shaft rail through rear of case.
12. Slide first-reverse synchronizer fully forward, then rotate and lift first-reverse shift fork from case.
13. Place the second-third speed shift fork to the second speed position, then remove set screw from fork. Rotate shift fork 90°.
14. If equipped, remove seat belt switch retaining clamp and bolt.
15. Remove detent plug with a magnet.
16. Tap on inner end of second-third speed shift rail to remove expansion plug, then slide shift rail from case, Fig. 5.
17. If equipped, remove seat belt sensor switch actuator plunger and spring with a magnet.
18. Pull input gear and shaft forward,

separating input gear and shaft from case.
19. Rotate second-third speed shift fork upward and lift from case.
20. Lift output shaft assembly from top of case.
21. Drive idler gear shaft from front of case.
22. Lift reverse idler gear and two thrust washers from case, then the countergear shaft, thrust washer and dummy shaft, Fig. 6. Remove detent plug and spring from bottom of detent hole.
23. Remove snap ring from front of output shaft and slide the synchronizer and second speed gear off shaft, Fig. 7.
24. Remove the next snap ring and tabbed thrust washer from output shaft, then slide first speed gear and

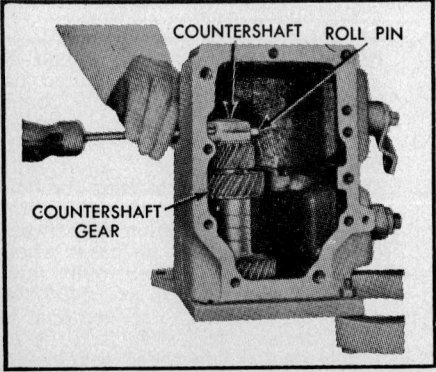

Fig. 2 Removing countershaft roll pin

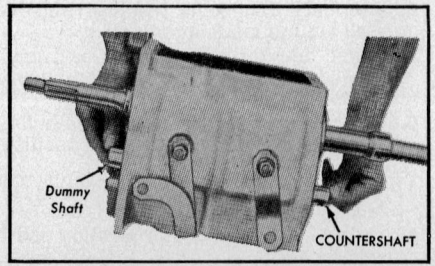

Fig. 3 Removing countershaft

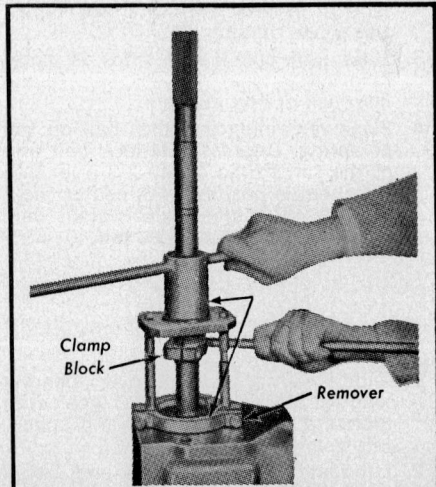

Fig. 4 Removing mainshaft bearing

blocking ring off shaft.

25. Remove the next snap ring from shaft and press first-reverse synchronizer hub off shaft.

NOTE: The synchronizer hub is a press fit on the shaft. Do not attempt to hammer or pry the synchronizer hub off the shaft since damage to the assembly may result.

Sub-Assembly Service

Shift Levers & Seals

1. Remove nut, lock washer and flat washer securing each shift lever to the shaft and lever in the transmission case, Fig. 8. Remove levers from shaft, then slide each lever and shaft from case. Remove and discard "O" rings from shafts.
2. Lubricate new "O" rings and install on shafts.
3. Install lever and shafts into case, then place shift lever on each shaft and secure with a flat washer, lock washer and nut.

Input Shaft Bearing

1. Remove input shaft bearing snap ring and press input shaft from bearing, Fig. 9.
2. Press input shaft bearing onto input shaft and install snap ring.

Synchronizers

1. Mark relationship between synchronizer hub and sleeve, then push hub from each sleeve.
2. Separate inserts and insert springs from hubs.
3. Install insert spring into first-reverse synchronizer hub. Ensure the spring covers all the insert grooves, Fig. 10. Then, start hub on sleeve ensuring the alignment marks are properly aligned. Position the three inserts in hub with the small end inside hub. Slide the sleeve and reverse gear onto hub.
4. Install one insert spring into second-third speed synchronizer hub groove, Fig. 11, ensuring the three insert slots are fully covered. With the hub and sleeve properly aligned, start hub into sleeve. Place three inserts on top of retaining spring and push assembly together. Install remaining insert spring with spring ends cover-do not stagger springs. Place a synchronizer blocking ring on each end of the synchronizer sleeve.

Countershaft Gear Bearings

1. Remove dummy shaft, fifty needle bearings and two bearing retainer washers from countershaft gear, Fig. 12.
2. Lubricate bore in each end of countershaft gear.
3. Insert dummy shaft into gear and install twenty-five needle bearings and a retainer washer into each end of gear.
4. Place countershaft gear assembly into case, then, with the case in the vertical position, align the gear bore and thrust washers with the

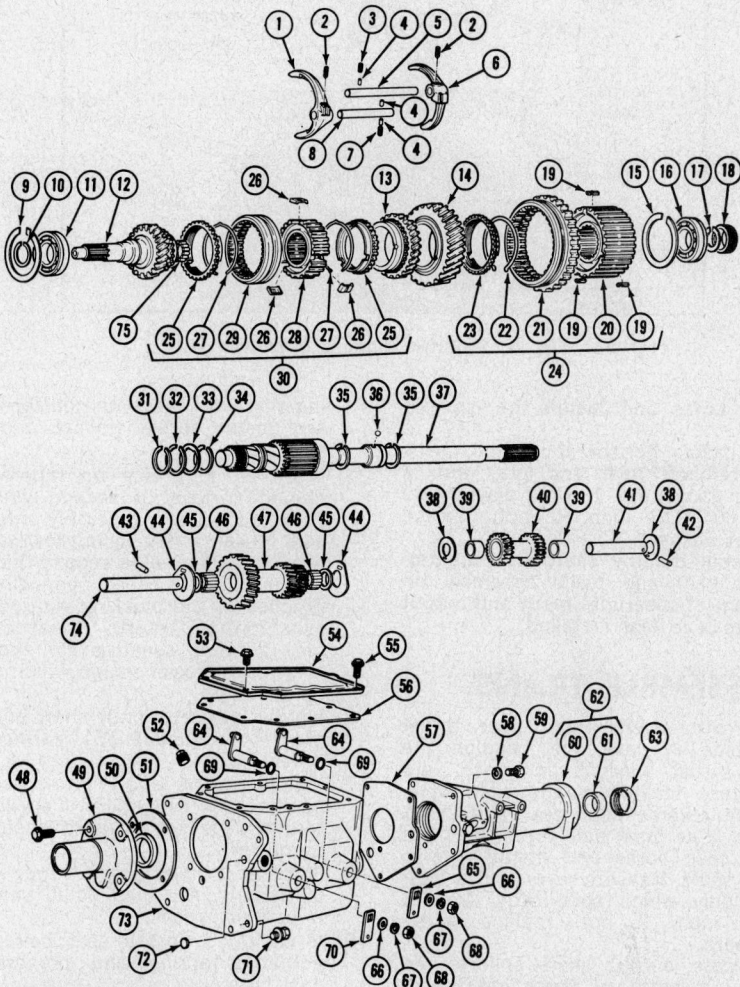

1. Fork, Second and Third Shifter
2. Setscrew, Shifter Fork (2)
3. Spring, Upper Detent (Long)
4. Plugs, Gear Shift Detent and Interlock (3)
5. Shift Rail, First and Reverse
6. Fork, First and Reverse Shifter
7. Spring, Lower Detent (Short)
8. Shift Rail, Second and Third
9. Ring, Locating (Snap) Front Bearing
10. Ring, Retaining (Snap) Front Bearing to Clutch Shaft
11. Bearing, Front
12. Shaft, Clutch
13. Gear, Second
14. Gear, First
15. Ring, Locating (Snap) Rear Bearing
16. Bearing, Rear
17. Ring, Retaining (Snap) Rear Bearing
18. Gear, Speedometer Drive
19. Insert, First and Reverse Synchronizer (3)
20. Hub, First and Reverse
21. Sleeve and Gear, First and Reverse
22. Spring, Insert, First and Reverse Synchronizer
23. Ring, Blocking, First and Reverse Synchronizer
24. Synchronizer Assembly, First and Reverse
25. Ring, Blocking, Second and Third Synchronizer (2)
26. Insert, Second and Third Synchronizer (3)
27. Spring, Insert, Second—Third Synchronizer (2)
28. Hub, Second and Third
29. Sleeve, Second and Third Synchronizer
30. Second—Third Synchronizer Assembly
31. Ring, Retaining (Snap) Output Shaft
32. Ring, Retaining (Snap) First Gear
33. Washer, Thrust (Tabbed) First Gear
34. Ring, Retaining (Snap) First-Reverse Hub
35. Ring, Retaining (Snap) (2) Rear Bearing and Speedometer Gear
36. Lock Ball, 1/4 Diameter—Speedometer Gear
37. Shaft, Output
38. Washer, Thrust, Reverse Idler Gear (2)
39. Bushing, Reverse Idler Gear (2)
40. Gear, Reverse Idler
41. Shaft, Reverse Idler Gear
42. Pin, Roll, Reverse Idler Gear Shaft
43. Pin, Roll, Countershaft
44. Washer, Thrust, Countershaft Gear (2)
45. Retainer, Countershaft Needle Bearing
46. Needle Bearing, Countershaft Gear (50)
47. Gear, Countershaft
48. Bolt, Front Bearing Cap
49. Cap, Front Bearing
50. Oil Seal, Front Bearing Cap
51. Gasket, Front Bearing Cap
52. Plug, Transmission Fill
53. Bolt, Top Cover
54. Top Cover, Case
55. Bolt, Top Cover
56. Gasket, Top Cover
57. Gasket, Extension Housing
58. Lockwasher, Extension Housing Bolt (5)
59. Bolt, Extension Housing
60. Extension Housing
61. Bushing, Extension Housing (Included with Housing)
62. Housing Assembly, Extension
63. Seal, Oil, Extension Housing
64. Shaft, Shifter Fork
65. Lever, First and Reverse Shifter
66. Flatwasher, Shifter Levers (2)
67. Lock, Washer Shifter Levers (2)
68. Nut, Hex, Shifter Levers (2)
69. O-Ring, Shifter Shaft (2)
70. Lever, Second and Third Shifter
71. Bolt, Transmission Mounting (4)
72. Plug, Expansion
73. Case, Transmission
74. Countershaft
75. Bearings, Clutch Shaft Roller

Fig. 1 Type 6 transmission disassembled

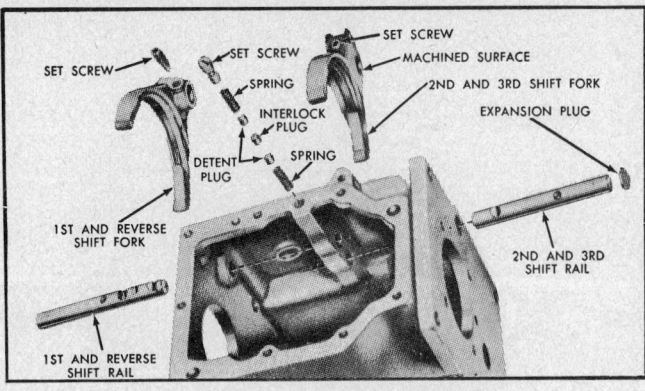

Fig. 5   Shift rails and forks disassembled

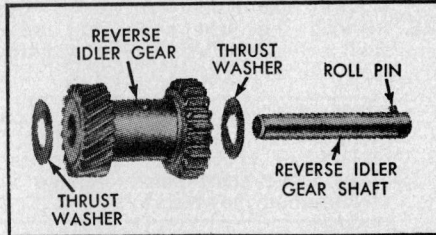

Fig. 6   Reverse idler gear disassembled

case bores and install the countershaft.

5. With case in horizontal position, check countershaft gear end play with a feeler gauge, Fig. 13. End play should be .004-.018 inch. If not, replace thrust washers.

6. Reinstall dummy shaft into countershaft gear and place assembly on bottom of case until input and output shafts have been installed.

ASSEMBLE TRANS.

1. Lubricate reverse idler gear thrust surfaces in case and position the two thrust washers in place with the tabs located in the case slots.

2. Install reverse idler gear and shaft. Align gear bore and thrust washers with case bores and install reverse idler shaft. Measure reverse idler gear end play which should be .004 to .018 inch. If not, replace thrust washers.

3. Lubricate output shaft splines and machined surfaces. Press first-reverse synchronizer hub with gear teeth facing toward rear of shaft. Install snap ring.

4. Place blocking ring on machined surface of first gear, then slide first gear onto shaft with blocking ring facing toward rear of shaft. Rotate gear to engage the three notches in the block-

ing ring with the synchronizer inserts and install thrust washer and snap ring.

5. Place blocking ring on tapered machined surface of second gear and slide second gear assembly onto shaft with blocking ring facing toward front of shaft. Then, slide second-third synchronizer onto shaft engaging the notches of the blocking ring with the synchronizer inserts. Measure end play between synchronizer and snap ring with a feeler gauge which should be .004 inch.

6. Lightly lubricate input shaft bore and gear, then install 15 bearings into bore.

7. Install output shaft into case and position the second-third speed shift fork on the second-third speed synchronizer.

8. Place the input shaft through front of transmission and install snap ring in bearing groove.

9. If equipped, install seat belt sensor actuating spring and plunger into case bore.

10. Align second-third speed shift fork with the shift rail bores and slide shift rail into place with the interlock pin in the horizontal position. Rotate the rail 90° until the three detents face toward the outside of the case. Then, place the second-third speed synchronizer in the second speed

position, toward the rear of case, and secure fork to rail with a set screw.

11. Place synchronizer in neutral position. If equipped, install seat belt sensor switch, ensuring switch oil seal is properly positioned. Then, install sensor switch retaining clamp and bolt.

12. Install interlock plug in case.

NOTE: If second-third speed shift rail is in the neutral position, the top of the interlock plug will be slightly lower than the surface of the first-reverse shift rail bore.

13. Place first-reverse shift fork in groove

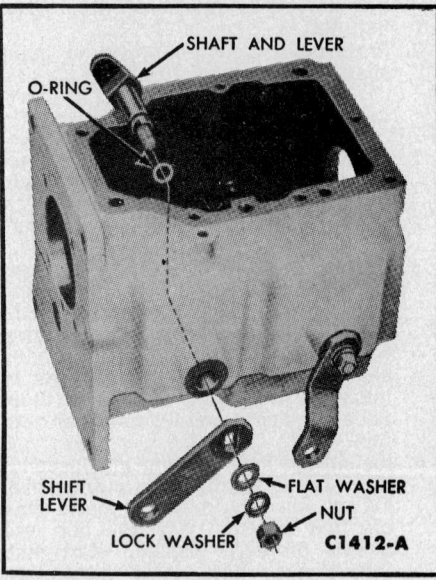

Fig. 8   Shift lever and related parts

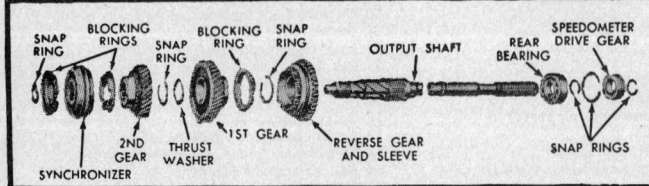

Fig. 7   Mainshaft disassembled

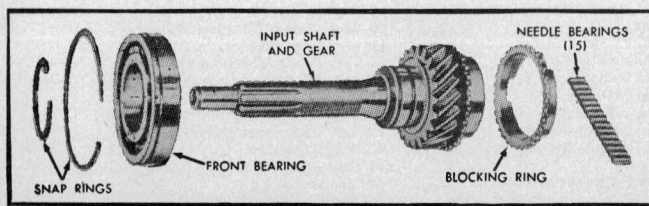

Fig. 9   Input shaft & gear disassembled

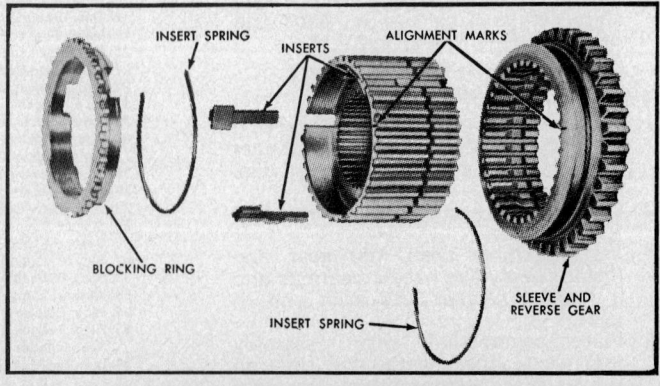

Fig. 10   Low-reverse synchronizer disassembled

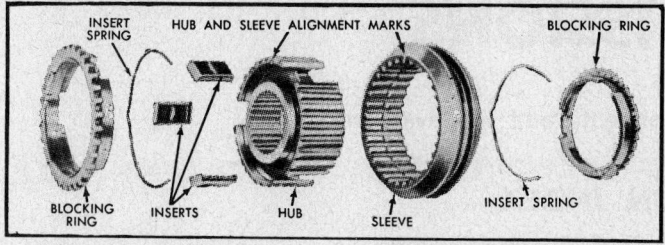

Fig. 11 Second-high synchronizer disassembled

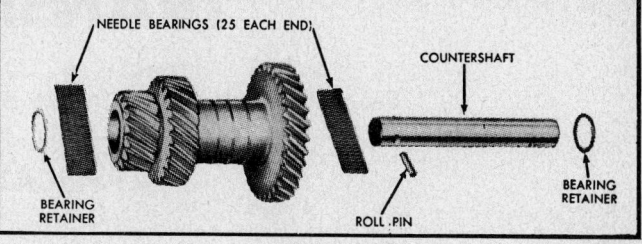

Fig. 12 Counter gear disassembled

of first-reverse synchronizer, then rotate fork into position and install first-reverse shift rail. Move rail inward until the center notch is aligned with detent bore. Install set screw securing fork to shaft.

14. Install a new shift rail expansion plug in front of case flush with the case face or a maximum of .60 inch below the face.

15. With input shaft and blocking ring in position, move output shaft forward to seat pilot in the roller bearings of the input gear.

16. Tap input gear bearing into position while holding the output shaft to hold the roller bearings in place. Install gasket and front bearing retainer, ensuring oil return slot is at bottom of case.

17. Install large snap ring on rear bearing, then place bearing on output shaft with snap ring facing toward rear of shaft. Press bearing into position and secure bearing to shaft with a snap ring.

18. Hold speedometer drive gear lock ball in the detent and slide the gear into place, then secure with a snap ring.

19. Place transmission in the vertical po-

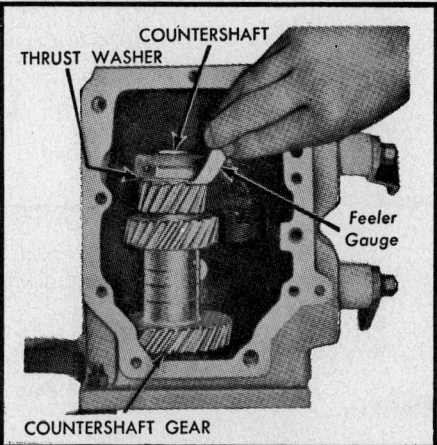

Fig. 13 Checking counter gear end play

sition. Working through drain hole in transmission case bottom, if equipped, align countershaft gear bore and thrust washers with bore of case. Push dummy shaft out the

front of case and countershaft gear with the countershaft. Before countershaft is fully inserted in bore, ensure roll pin hole in case and shaft are properly aligned. Drive countershaft into place and install roll pin.

NOTE: On some models, the countershaft is a press fit in the case. On other models, there is a countershaft to case clearance of .020 inch at the front bore and .010 inch at the rear bore, then install an expansion plug at front of countershaft bore. Install plug flush with case or .060 inch maximum below case face.

20. Install extension housing and gasket on case.

21. Install drain plug, if equipped, and the filler hole plug.

22. With transmission in gear, pour transmission lubricant over gear train while rotating input or output shaft.

23. Install remaining detent plug in case, then the long spring against detent plug.

24. Install transmission cover and gasket.

FOUR SPEED MANUAL SHIFT TRANSMISSIONS

See Car Chapters for Linkage Adjustments and Removal Procedures

APPLICATION INDEX

Type One Warner T-10

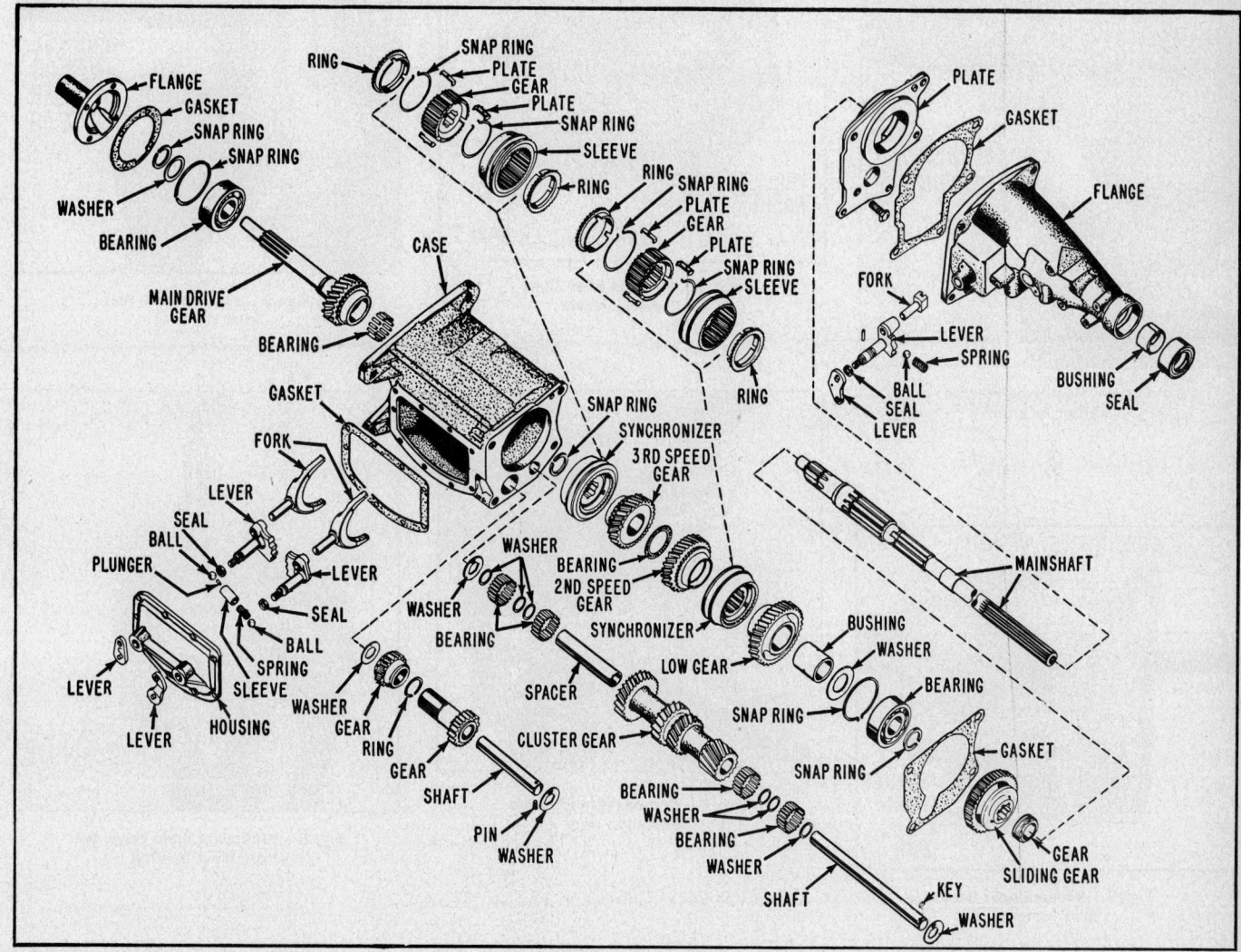

Fig. 1 Type 1 Warner T-10 four speed transmission. Some units do not have the mainshaft low gear bushing shown.

Side Cover, Remove

1. Disconnect control rods from levers.
2. Remove cover assembly from transmission and allow oil to drain.
3. Remove outer shift lever nuts and lockwashers and pull levers from shaft.
4. Carefully push shifter shafts into cover, allowing detent balls to fall free, then remove both shifter shafts.
5. Remove interlock sleeve, pin and poppet spring.

Side Cover, Install

1. Install interlock sleeve and one shifter shaft. Place detent ball into sleeve followed by poppet spring and interlock pin.
2. Start second shifter shaft into position and place second detent ball on poppet spring. Compress ball and spring with screwdriver and push shifter shaft fully in.
3. With transmission in neutral and shifter forks and levers in place, lower side cover into place. Install attaching bolts, using sealer on bolts to prevent leakage. Tighten bolts evenly.

Disassemble Transmission

1. Remove side cover as outlined above.
2. Remove front bearing retainer.
3. Drive lock pin from bottom side of reverse shifter lever boss, Fig. 3, and pull shifter out about ⅛". This disengages reverse shift fork from reverse gear.
4. Unfasten extension housing from rear bearing retainer (adapter). Tap extension with soft hammer in rearward direction to start. When reverse idler shaft is out as far as it will go, move extension to left so reverse fork clears reverse gear, and remove extension and gasket.
5. Remove speedometer drive gear with a suitable puller.
6. The rear reverse idler gear, tanged thrust washer and reverse gear may now be removed, Figs. 4 and 5.
7. Remove self-locking bolts attaching rear bearing retainer (adapter) to transmission case. Then carefully remove entire mainshaft assembly.
8. Lift front reverse idler gear and thrust washer from case, Fig. 6.

Fig. 3   Removing reverse
shifter lock pin

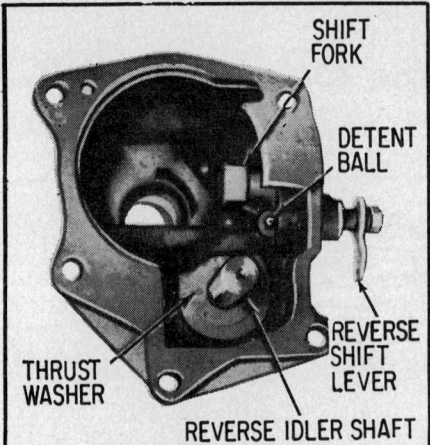

Fig. 4   Reverse idler shaft
and reverse shifter

Fig. 5   Reverse gear rear
idler removal

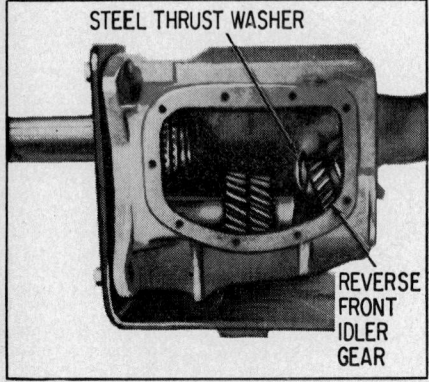

Fig. 6   Reverse gear front
idler removal

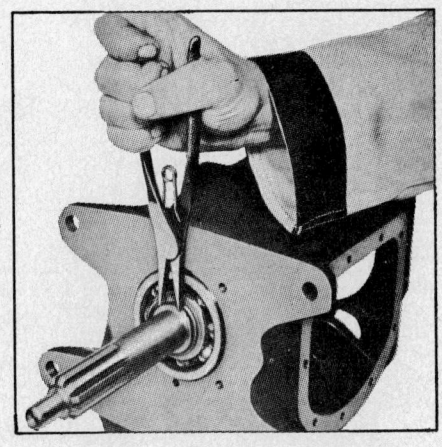

Fig. 7   Removing main drive
gear snap ring

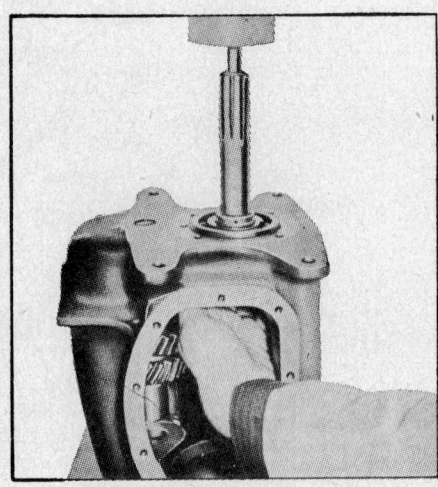

Fig. 8   Removing main drive gear
from front bearing

9. Unload bearing rollers from main drive gear and remove 4th speed synchronizing ring.
10. Remove main drive gear snap ring, Fig. 7, and remove spacer washer.
11. With soft hammer, tap main drive gear down from front bearing, Fig. 8.
12. From inside case, tap out front bearing and snap ring.
13. From front of case, tap out countershaft, Fig. 9, using a dummy shaft as shown. Remove countergear and both tanged thrust washers.
14. Remove dummy shaft, all 80 rollers and six spacers from countergear.
15. Remove mainshaft front snap ring, Fig. 10, and slide 3-4 speed synchronizer, 3rd speed gear and synchronizing ring, 2-3 speed gear thrust washer (needle roller bearing), 2nd speed gear and synchronizing ring from front of mainshaft.
16. Spread rear bearing snap ring and

press mainshaft out of retainer, Fig. 11.
17. Remove mainshaft rear snap ring. Support 1-2 speed synchronizer assembly Fig. 12, and press on rear of mainshaft to remove shaft from remaining parts on shaft.

Cleaning & Inspection

1. Wash transmission case inside and out with cleaning solvent and inspect for cracks. Inspect front face of case for burrs and, if present, dress them off with a fine cut mill file.
2. Wash front and rear bearings in cleaning solvent. Blow out bearings with compressed air. *Do not allow bearings to spin; turn them slowly by hand. Spinning bearings will damage race and balls.*
3. Make sure bearings are clean, then lubricate them with light engine oil and check them for roughness. Roughness may be determined by turning outer race by hand.
4. All main drive gear and countergear

bearing rollers should be inspected closely and replaced if they show wear. Inspect countershaft and replace if necessary. Replace all worn spacers.
5. Inspect all gears and first speed gear bushing (or sleeve) and, if necessary, replace all that are worn or damaged.

Synchronizers

Clutch hubs and sliding sleeves are a selected assembly and should be kept together as originally assembled, but the three keys and two springs may be replaced if worn or broken.

Push hub from sliding sleeve. Keys will fall free and springs may be easily removed. To assemble, place the two springs in position (one on each side of hub) so tanged end of each spring falls into same keyway in hub. Place keys in position and, holding them in place, slide hub into sleeve.

Assemble Mainshaft

1. From rear of mainshaft, assemble 1-

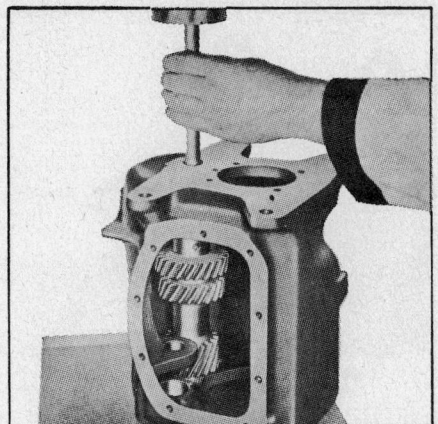

Fig. 9 Removing countershaft

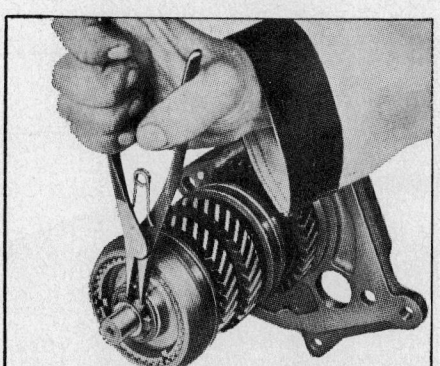

Fig. 10 Removing mainshaft front snap ring

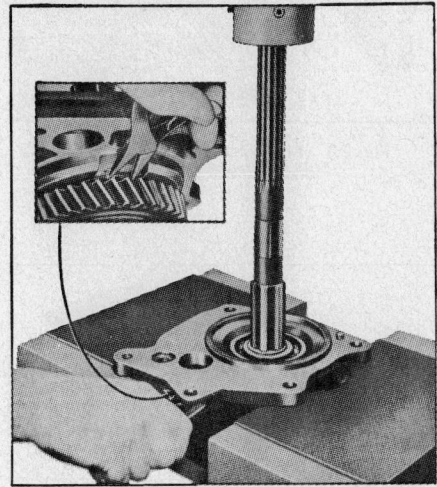

Fig. 11 Removing mainshaft from rear bearing retainer

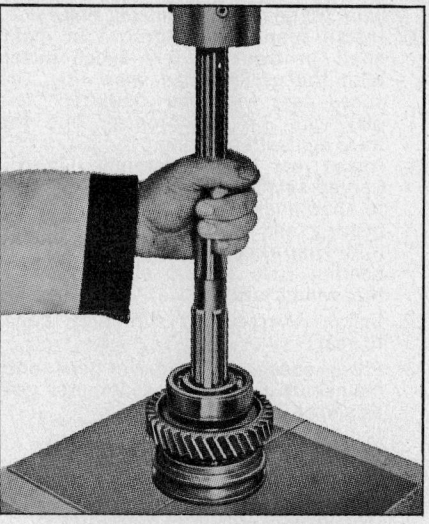

Fig. 12 Removing mainshaft from rear bearing and synchronizer

Fig. 13 Installing first speed gear bushing

Fig. 14 Installing synchronizer ring

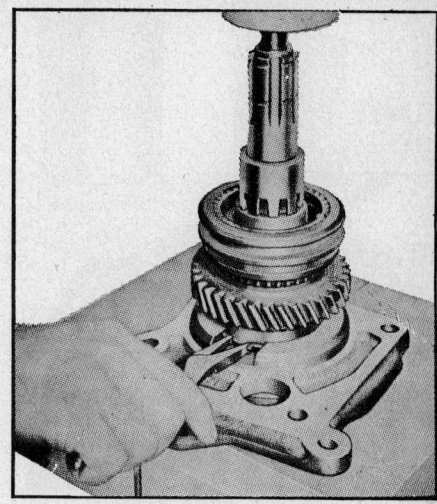

Fig. 15 Installing rear bearing retainer

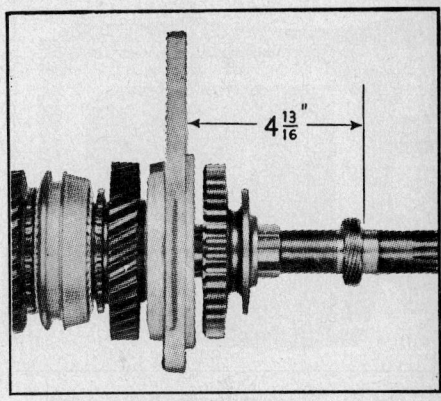

Fig. 16 Installing speedometer drive gear

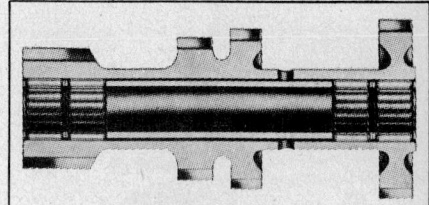

Fig. 17 Cross section of countergear assembly

2 speed synchronizer to mainshaft with sleeve taper toward rear. Press 1st gear bushing on shaft, Fig. 13.
2. Install 1st gear synchronizing ring so that notches in ring correspond to keys in hub, Fig. 14.
3. Install 1st gear with hub toward front, and 1st gear thrust washer. Make certain that grooves in washer are facing 1st gear.
4. Press on rear bearing with snap ring groove toward front of transmission.
5. Choose correct selective fit snap ring and install it in groove in mainshaft behind rear bearing. *Always use new snap ring and do not expand it further than necessary for assembly.*

6. From front of mainshaft, install 2nd gear synchronizing ring so notches in ring correspond to keys in hub.
7. Install 2nd gear with hub of gear toward back of transmission. Install 2-3 speed gear thrust washer (needle roller bearing).
8. Install 3rd gear with hub to front of transmission, and 3rd gear synchronizing ring with notches to front of transmission.
9. Install 3-4 synchronizer with sleeve taper toward front, making sure keys in hub correspond to notches

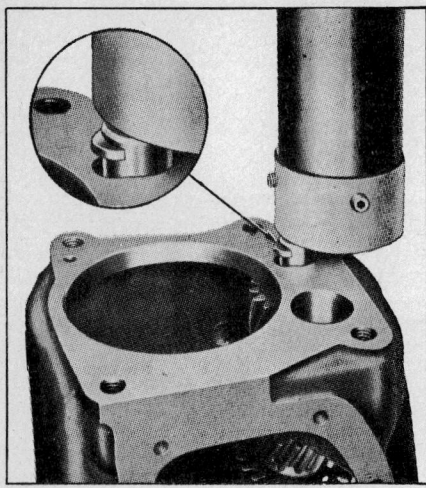

Fig. 18   Installing countershaft

Fig. 19   Checking countershaft end play

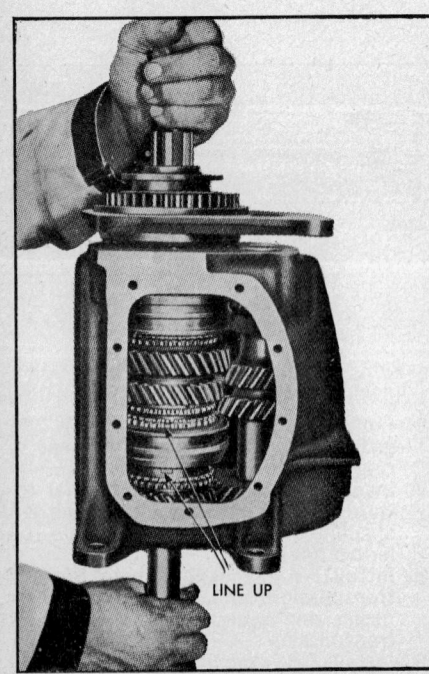

Fig. 20   Installing mainshaft assembly

with 3rd gear synchronizing ring.

10. Install snap ring in groove in mainshaft in front of 3-4 synchronizer. *With the correct size snap ring, 3rd speed gear will have .010-.015" end play with 3-4 synchronizer hub forward against snap ring.*

11. Install rear bearing retainer, Fig. 15. Spread selective fit snap ring in plate to allow snap ring to drop around rear bearing and press end of mainshaft until snap ring engages groove in rear bearing (use largest size snap ring that will fit into groove).

12. Install reverse gear with shift collar to rear.

13. Press speedometer drive gear onto mainshaft. Position speedometer gear as shown in Fig. 16.

Assemble Countergear

1. Install roller spacer in countergear.

2. Using heavy grease to retain rollers, install 20 rollers in either end of countergear, two spacers, 20 more rollers, then one spacer, Fig. 17.

3. Assemble rollers and spacers in the same manner in other end of countergear. Then insert dummy shaft in countergear to retain rollers.

Assemble Transmission

1. Rest case on its side with side cover opening toward you. Place countergear tanged thrust washers in place, retaining them with heavy grease, making sure that tangs are resting in notches in case.

2. Place countergear assembly in bottom of case, making sure that tanged thrust washers are not knocked out of place.

3. Press bearing onto main drive gear with snap ring groove to front.

4. Install spacer washer and selective fit snap ring in groove on gear stem.

5. Install main drive gear assembly through side cover opening and into position in transmission front bore. Tap lightly into place with a soft hammer, if necessary. Place snap ring in groove in front bearing.

6. With transmission resting on its front face, move countergear into mesh with main drive gear, making sure thrust washers remain in place. Install key in end of countershaft and, from front of case, tap or press shaft, Fig. 18, until end of shaft is flush with rear of case and dummy shaft is displaced.

7. Attach dial indicator as shown in Fig. 19 and check end play of countergear. End play must not be more than .025".

8. Install 14 rollers into main drive gear, using heavy grease to hold them in place. Place gasket in position on front face of rear bearing retainer, using heavy grease to hold it in position.

9. Install 4th gear synchronizing ring on main drive gear with clutch key notches toward rear of case.

10. Position reverse idler gear thrust washer (untanged) on machined face

Fig. 21   Self-locking bearing retainer-to-case bolt

Fig. 22   Installing extension housing on transmission case

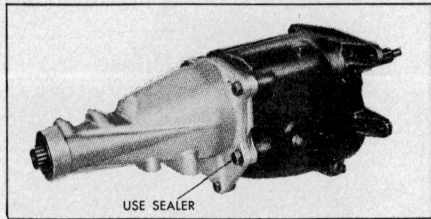

Fig. 23   Sealing lower right attaching bolt

of ear cast in case for reverse idler shaft. Position front reverse idler gear on top of thrust washer, with hub facing toward rear of case.

11. Lower mainshaft assembly into case, making certain that notches on 4th gear synchronizing ring correspond to keys in synchronizer, Fig. 20.

12. Install self-locking bolt attaching rear bearing retainer to case, Fig. 21.

13. From rear of case, insert rear reverse idler gear, engaging splines with portion of gear within case.

14. Using heavy grease, place gasket into position on rear face of rear bearing retainer.

15. Install remaining tanged thrust washer into place on reverse idler shaft, being sure tang on washer is in notch in idler thrust face of extension.

16. Place two synchronizers in neutral position. *If locking-up of gears is encountered, a small amount of petrolatum may be applied to the 1st speed gear synchronizing ring, en-*

abling it to turn freely on 1st speed gear hub.

17. Pull reverse shifter shaft to left side of extension and rotate shaft to bring reverse shift fork to extreme forward position in extension. Line up front and rear reverse idler gears, making sure front thrust washer is in place.

18. Start extension into case. Fig. 22, by carefully inserting reverse idler shaft through reverse idler gears. Slowly push it on shifter shaft until shift fork engages reverse gear shift collar. When fork engages, rotate shifter shaft to move reverse gear rearward, permitting extension to slide onto transmission case.

19. Install extension and retainer to case

attaching bolts, and extension to retainer attaching bolts. Use suitable sealer on the bolt indicated in Fig. 23.

20. Adjust reverse shifter shaft so that groove in shaft lines up with hole in boss and drive in lock pin from top of boss, Fig. 22.

21. Install main drive gear bearing retainer and gasket, being sure oil well lines up with oil outlet hole.

22. Install shift fork in each synchronizer sleeve. With both synchronizers in neutral, install side cover with gasket. Use suitable sealer when installing lower right cover bolt.

23. Install shifter levers, lock washers and nuts.

Type Two

Transmission Disassembly

1. Drain lubricant from transmission by removing the lower extension housing bolt.

2. Drive access plug from rear of extension housing and remove offset lever assembly, Fig. 2-1.

3. Remove extension housing from case.

4. Remove transmission cover, shifter fork and shift rod assembly.

5. Remove front bearing retainer and gasket.

6. Remove spring clip securing reverse lever assembly to pivot bolt, then remove pivot bolt and reverse level assembly.

7. Support countershaft gear with a wire hook. Drive a dummy countershaft through front of case until cluster gear drops to bottom of case, then remove counter shaft through rear of case and lower the cluster gear to bottom of case.

8. Remove input shaft, Fig. 2-2.

9. Remove speedometer drive gear snap ring, slide gear off output shaft and remove lock ball from output shaft.

10. Remove output shaft bearing retaining snap ring. Using the outer snap ring, pull output shaft bearing from case and off shaft, then remove output shaft assembly through top of case.

11. Slide reverse idler gear shaft through rear of case, then remove reverse gear and cluster gear from bottom of case.

Cover Disassembly

1. Remove detent screw, spring and plunger, Fig. 2-1.

2. Pull shifter rod shaft rearward and rotate counter-clockwise. Remove manual selector and interlock to shaft spring pin, shifter shaft, manual selector and the interlock from cover.

3. Remove the first-second shift fork, then the third-fourth shift fork.

4. Reverse procedure for reassembly.

Output Shaft Disassembly

1. Scribe alignment marks on sychronizer and blocker ring for alignment during installation, remove snap ring from front of shaft and slide third and fourth speed synchronizer assembly, blocker rings and third speed gear off shaft, Fig. 2-1.

2. Remove next snap ring, then second speed gear thrust washer, second speed gear and blocker ring from shaft.

NOTE: The first and second speed

synchronizer hub cannot be removed from output shaft.

3. Remove first gear thrust washer from rear of shaft, first gear spring pin retainer and slide first gear and blocker ring off shaft.

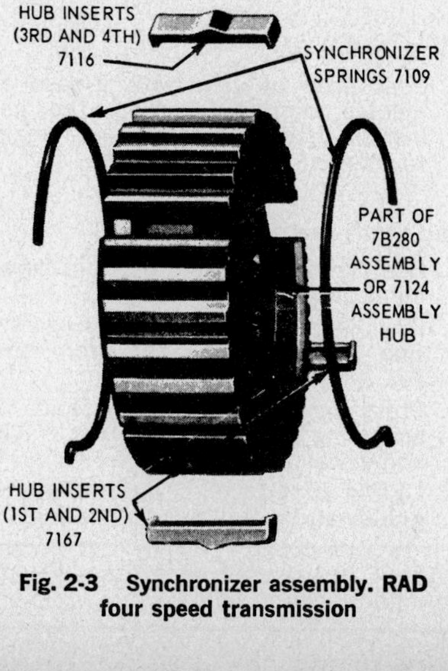

Output Shaft Reassembly

1. Place blocker ring on cone of first gear and slide assembly onto output shaft, engaging notches in blocker ring with inserts in synchronizer, Fig. 2-3 and install first gear spring pin.

2. Place blocker ring on cone of second gear and slide assembly onto output shaft, engaging notches in blocker ring with inserts in synchronizer. Install second gear thrust washer and new snap ring.

3. Place blocker ring on cone of third gear and slide assembly onto output shaft, install third and fourth speed synchronizer, engaging notches on blocker ring with inserts on synchronizer. Install new snap ring.

4. Install first gear thrust washer and first gear spring pin retainer onto shaft.

NOTE: Oil grooves in thrust washer must be positioned against gear.

Fig. 2-2 Removing input shaft. RAD four speed transmission

HUB INSERTS (3RD AND 4TH) 7116

SYNCHRONIZER SPRINGS 7109

PART OF 7B280 ASSEMBLY OR 7124 ASSEMBLY HUB

HUB INSERTS (1ST AND 2ND) 7167

Fig. 2-3 Synchronizer assembly. RAD four speed transmission

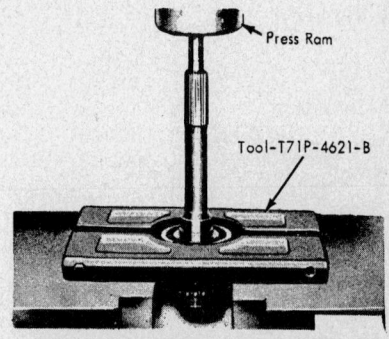

Press Ram

Tool-T71P-4621-B

Fig. 2-4 Input shaft bearing removal. RAD four speed transmission

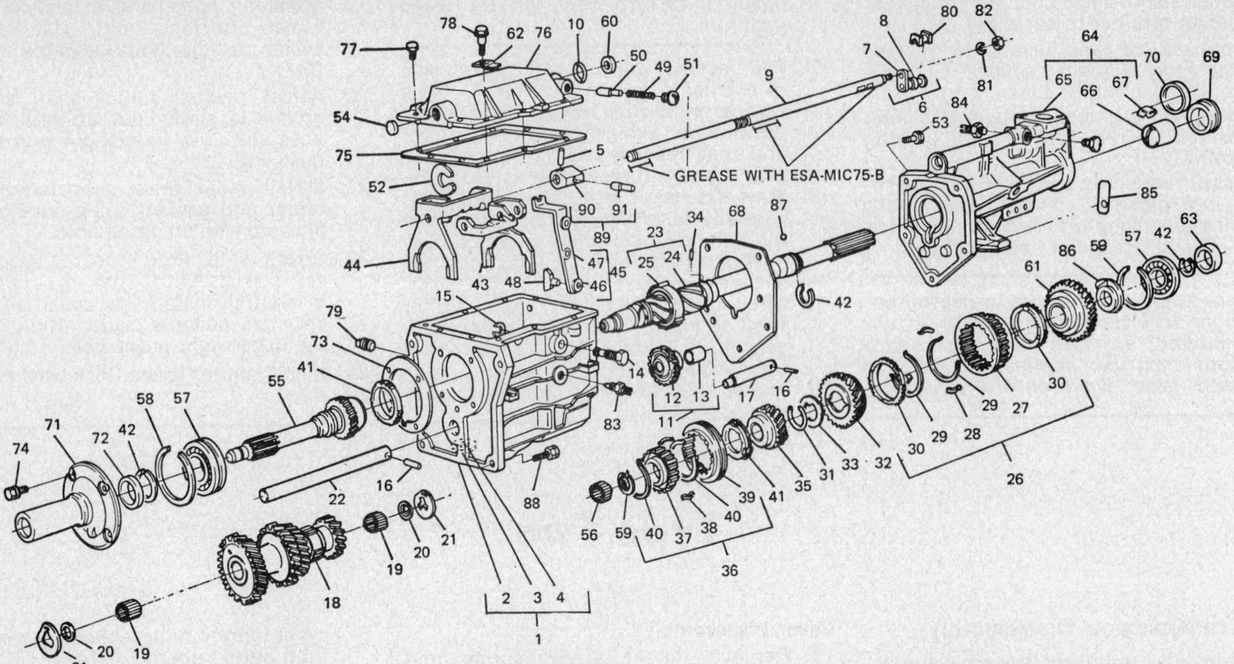

Fig. 2-1 RAD four speed transmission disassembled.

ITEM	PART NAME
1.	TRANS. CASE ASSY.
2.	CASE
3.	TRANS. CASE CHIP MAGNET
4.	SPRING NUT
5.	PIN
6.	LEVER ASSY.
7.	OFFSET LEVER
8.	PIN
9.	SHIFTER SHAFT
10.	O-RING SEAL
11.	REVERSE IDLER ASSY.
12.	REVERSE IDLER GEAR
13.	BUSHING
14.	REVERSE GEAR SELECTOR FORK PIVOT PIN
15.	RETAINING RING
16.	PIN
17.	REVERSE IDLER GEAR SHAFT
18.	COUNTERSHAFT GEAR
19.	COUNTERSHAFT ROLLER BEARINGS
20.	WASHER
21.	COUNTERSHAFT GEAR THRUST WASHERS
22.	COUNTERSHAFT
23.	OUTPUT SHAFT ASSY.
24.	OUTPUT SHAFT
25.	1ST & 2ND GEAR CLUSTER SYNCHRONIZER HUB
26.	OUTPUT SHAFT GEAR ASSY.
27.	REVERSE SLIDING GEAR
28.	SYNCHRONIZER HUB INSERT
29.	SYNCHRONIZER RETAINING SPRING
30.	SYNCHRONIZER BLOCKING RING

ITEM	PART NAME
31.	2ND SPEED GEAR RETAINING SNAP RING
32.	2ND SPEED GEAR
33.	2ND SPEED GEAR THRUST WASHER
34.	PIN
35.	3RD SPEED GEAR
36.	3RD & 4TH SPEED SYNCHRONIZER ASSY.
37.	SYNCHRONIZER CLUTCH HUB
38.	SYNCHRONIZER HUB INSERTS
39.	SYNCHRONIZER SLEEVE
40.	SYNCHRONIZER RETAINING SPRINGS
41.	SYNCHRONIZER BLOCKING RING
42.	SNAP RING
43.	1ST & 2ND GEAR SHIFT FORK
44.	3RD & 4TH GEAR SHIFT FORK
45.	REVERSE GEAR SHIFT RELAY LEVER ASSY.
46.	RELAY LEVER RING
47.	RELAY LEVER
48.	REVERSE GEAR SHIFT FORK
49.	SHIFTER INTERLOCK SPRING
50.	MESHLOCK PLUNGER
51.	SCREW
52.	GEAR SELECTOR INTERLOCK PLATE
53.	EXTENSION HOUSING RETAINING BOLT
54.	WELSH PLUG
55.	INPUT SHAFT
56.	MAINSHAFT ROLLER BEARINGS
57.	BALL BEARING
58.	BEARING RETAINING SNAP RING
59.	RETAINING RING
60.	SHIFT SHAFT SEAL
61.	1ST SPEED GEAR

ITEM	PART NAME
62.	SPARK CONTROL SWITCH WIRE RETAINING CLIP
63.	SPEEDOMETER DRIVE GEAR
64.	EXTENSION ASSY.
65.	EXTENSION HOUSING
66.	EXTENSION HOUSING BUSHING
67.	SHIFT LEVER REVERSE STOP
68.	EXTENSION HOUSING GASKET
69.	EXTENSION HOUSING OIL SEAL
70.	EXTENSION HOUSING PLUG
71.	INPUT SHAFT BEARING RETAINER
72.	INPUT SHAFT OIL SEAL
73.	INPUT SHAFT BEARING RETAINER GASKET
74.	INPUT SHAFT RETAINING BOLT
75.	CASE COVER GASKET
76.	CASE COVER
77.	CASE COVER RETAINING BOLT
78.	BOLT
79.	OIL FILLER PLUG
80.	GEAR SHIFT DAMPER BUSHING
81.	SPRING LOCK WASHER
82.	LEVER RETAINING NUT
83.	BACK-UP LAMP SWITCH
84.	SEAT BELT WARNING SENSOR SWITCH
85.	TRANSMISSION IDENTIFICATION TAG
86.	1ST GEAR THRUST WASHER
87.	BALL
88.	TRANS. RETAINING BOLT
89.	TRANS. CONTROL SELECTOR ARM ASSY.
90.	CONTROL SELECTOR ARM
91.	GEARSHIFT RETAINING PIN

Countershaft Gear Bearing, Replace

1. Remove dummy shaft, bearing retainer washers and needle bearings from gear.

2. Coat bore of gear with grease and holding dummy shaft in the gear, install needle bearings and retainer washers at each end of gear.

Input Shaft Bearing, Replace

1. Remove needle bearings from bore of input shaft.

2. Remove input shaft bearing snap ring and press bearing from shaft, Fig. 2-4.

3. Press new bearing onto shaft with snap ring groove facing front of shaft and install new snap ring.

4. Lightly coat bore of input shaft with grease and install needle bearings.

NOTE: A heavy coat of grease will plug bearing lubrication holes.

Extension Housing Bushing and Seal, Replace

1. Remove seal from extension housing, Fig. 2-5.

2. Using a suitable puller, remove bush-

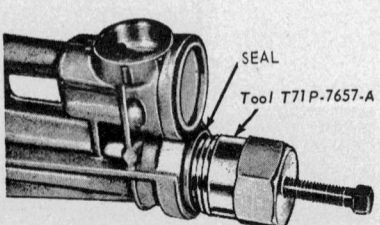

Fig. 2-5 Extension housing seal removal. RAD four speed transmission

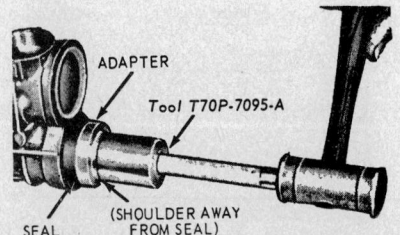

Fig. 2-6 Extension housing seal installation. RAD four speed transmission

ing from housing.

3. Drive new bushing into housing and install new extension housing seal, Fig. 2-6.

Transmission Reassembly

1. Place reverse idler gear and shaft in position.
2. Coat countershaft thrust washer with grease and place into case and position cluster gear assembly in bottom of case.
3. Install output shaft assembly into case through cover opening and place first gear thrust washer on roll pin and holding it securely. Install rear bearing, with snap ring groove facing rearward followed by the snap ring.
4. Install input shaft and fourth gear blocker ring through front of case, engaging notches in blocker ring with inserts on synchronizer.
5. Install front bearing gasket and re-

tainer and torque bolts to 11-15 ft. lbs.

NOTE: Apply a suitable sealer to bolt threads.

6. Align countershaft gear bore and thrust washers with case bore and install countershaft through rear of case.
7. Install reverse idle gear lever assembly with fork positioned in reverse idler gear groove. Apply a suitable sealer to threads of reverse lever pivot bolt and install bolt into case. Align lever on pivot bolt, torque bolt to 15-25 ft. lbs., and install reverse lever spring clip.
8. Install cover gasket and cover, wiring clips and torque bolts to 7-10 ft. lbs.

NOTE: The two (shouldered) locating bolts must be installed first and place

shift rail into first or third gear position.

9. Install speedometer drive gear lock ball into hole and holding the ball, slide speedometer drive gear into place and secure with a snap ring.

NOTE: On some models, the speedometer drive gear is secured with a clip.

10. Install extension housing gasket and extension housing onto case and with a suitable sealer applied to the threads of the attaching bolts, torque bolts to 18-27 ft. lbs.
11. Install offset lever onto shifter shaft and torque nut to 14-20 ft. lbs.
12. Install gearshift lever and check gear positions for proper operation.
13. Drive new access plug into rear of extension housing.

Type Three Muncie

SIDE COVER, REPLACE

1. Referring to Fig. 3-2 disconnect control rods from levers.
2. Shift transmisson into 2nd speed before removing cover by moving 1-2 shifter lever into forward detent position.
3. Remove cover from case.
4. Reverse procedure to install the cover, being sure first to shift the transmission into 2nd gear. Make sure shift forks are aligned with their respective grooves in synchronizer sliding sleeves.

DISASSEMBLE TRANSMISSION

1. Remove side cover.
2. Remove front bearing retainer.
3. Shift transmission into two gears at once to keep mainshaft from turning, then remove retainer nut from main drive gear.
4. With gears in neutral, drive lock pin from reverse shifter lever boss and pull shifter shaft out about ⅛". This disengages reverse shift fork from reverse gear.
5. Unfasten extension case from main case. Tap extension case rearward with a soft hammer to start. When reverse idler shaft is out as far as it will go, move extension to left so reverse fork clears reverse gear. Then remove extension and gasket.
6. Now remove rear reverse idler gear, shaft and plate thrust washer.
7. Use a suitable puller to remove speedometer gear from mainshaft, after which remove reverse gear.

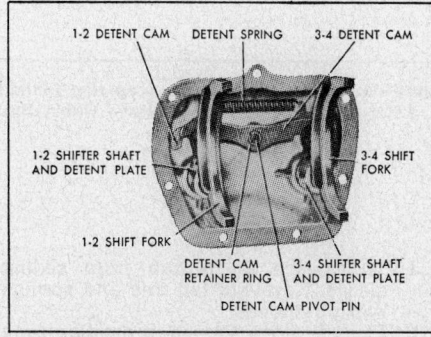

Fig. 3-2   Transmission side cover

8. Slide 3-4 synchronizer clutch sleeve to 4th gear position before trying to remove mainshaft assembly from case.
9. Remove rear bearing retainer and mainshaft assembly from case by tapping retainer with soft hammer.
10. Unload bearing rollers from main drive gear and remove 4th gear synchronizer blocking ring.
11. Lift front half of reverse idler gear and its tanged washer from case.
12. Press main drive gear down into case and remove. From inside of case, tap out front bearing and snap ring.
13. From front of case, press out countershaft. Then remove countergear and both tanged washers.
14. Remove mainshaft front snap ring and strip mainshaft of loose parts.
15. Spread rear bearing retainer snap ring and press mainshaft out of retainer.

NOTE: Early models of this transmission

use a snap ring behind the 1-2 synchronizer hub to retain the hub in position while later units have a sleeve within the 1st speed gear. This sleeve acts as a spacer between the rear bearing and 1-2 synchronizer hub.

16. Remove mainshaft rear snap ring. Support 1st gear in a press and press against rear of shaft to remove it from rear bearing, 1st gear thrust washer, 1st gear and synchronizing ring.
17. Remove 1-2 synchronizer snap ring and remove 1-2 synchronizer unit, 2nd gear synchronizer ring and 2nd gear from shaft, Fig. 3-3.

UNIT REPAIRS
Reverse Idler

Because of the high degree of accuracy to which the reverse idler gear bushings are machined, the bushings are not serviced separately. Check bushings for excessive wear by using a narrow feeler gauge between shaft and bushing. Proper clearance is from .003 to .005".

Reverse Shifter Shaft & Seal

1. With extension case removed as outlined previously, remove shift fork.
2. Drive shifter shaft into case extension, allowing ball detent to drop into case. Remove shaft and ball detent spring.
3. Place ball detent spring into its hole and, from inside extension, install shifter shaft fully into its opening until detent plate is butted against inside

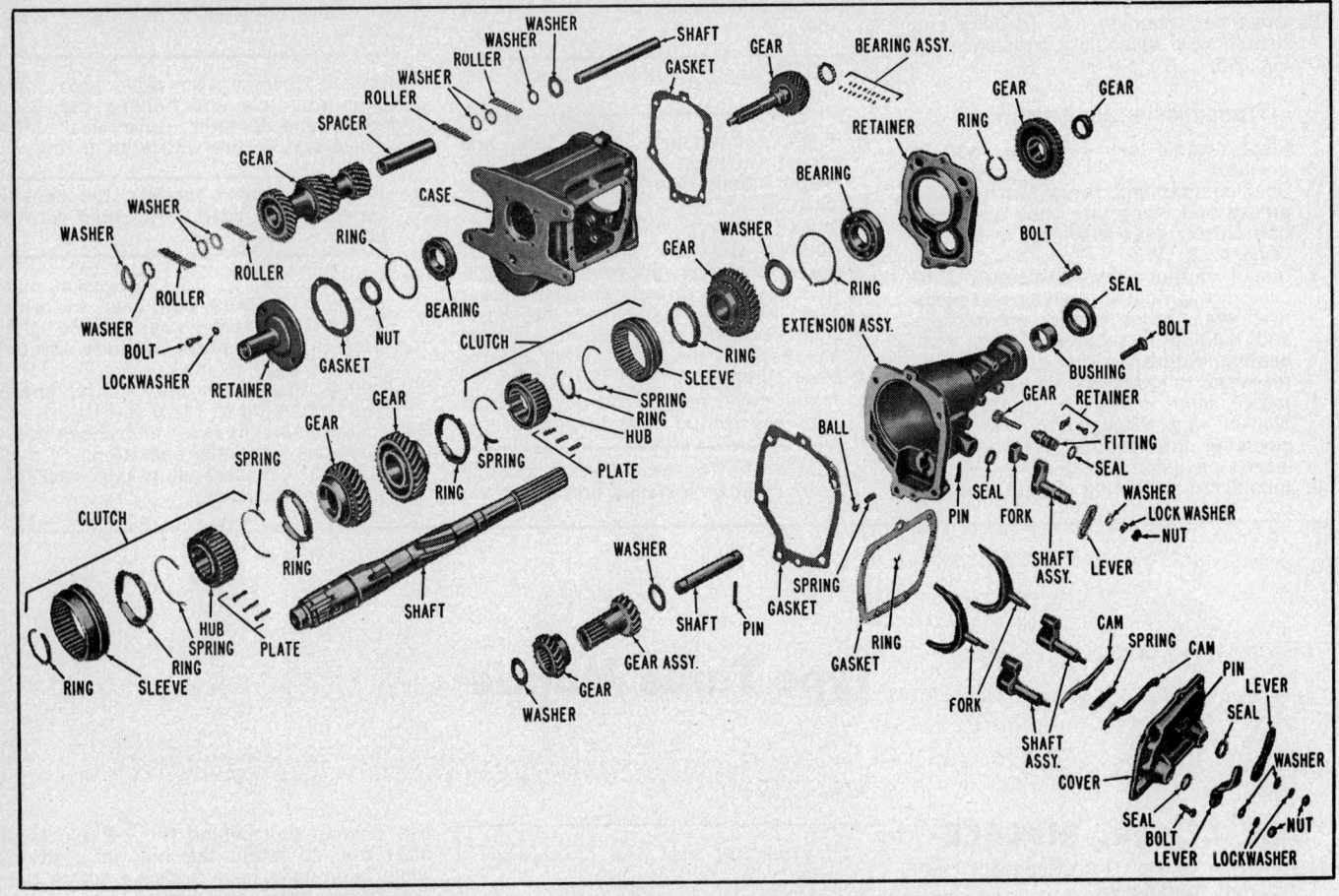

Fig. 3-1 Muncie four speed transmission. Early models use a snap ring (illustrated) behind the 1-2 synchronizer hub to retain the hub in position. Later units have a spacer sleeve within the 1st speed gear, (not illustrated)

of extension housing.

4. Place detent ball on spring, Fig. 3-4, and, holding ball down with thumb or a suitable tool, push shifter shaft back in, away from case until it is directly over ball and turn until ball drops into detent on shaft detent plate.
5. Install shift fork.

NOTE: Do not drive shifter shaft lock pin into place until extension has been installed on transmission case.

Extension Oil Seal or Bushing

If bushing in rear of extension requires replacement, remove oil seal and drive bushing into case extension. Drive new bushing in from the rear. Coat I.D. of bushing with transmission lubricant, then install new oil seal.

Clutch Keys & Springs

NOTE: The clutch hubs and sliding sleeves are a selected assembly and should be kept together as originally assembled. However, the three keys and two springs may be replaced if worn or broken.

1. To replace, push hub from sliding sleeve. Keys will fall free and springs easily removed.
2. Place the two springs in position (one on each side of hub) so all three keys are engaged by both springs. Place keys in position and, holding them in place, slide hub into sleeve.

Assemble Mainshaft

1. From rear of mainshaft, assemble 2nd gear with hub of gear toward rear of shaft.
2. Install 1-2 synchronizer clutch, with clutch sleeve taper to rear, together with a blocker ring on each side so their keyways line up with clutch keys, Fig. 3-5. On early units, install 1-2 synchronizer retainer snap ring (smaller of the two). On later units, install 1st gear spacer sleeve.
3. Install 1st gear (hub toward front) and 1st gear thrust washer.
4. Press rear bearing on mainshaft, Fig. 3-6, being sure to seat bearing firmly.
5. Choose correct selective fit snap ring and install it in groove of mainshaft behind rear bearing. (Snap rings of .084", .087", .090", .093", .096" are available.) With proper snap ring, maximum distance between ring and rear

face of bearing will be from zero to .005".
6. Install 3rd gear (hub to front) and 3rd gear synchronizing ring (notches to front).
7. Install 3-4 clutch assembly with both sleeve taper and hub toward front, making sure keys in hub correspond to notches in 3rd gear synchronizing ring.
8. Install snap ring in mainshaft groove in front of 3-4 synchronizer clutch with ends of snap ring seated behind spline teeth.
9. Install rear bearing retainer. Spread snap ring in plate to allow ring to drop around rear bearing and press on end of mainshaft until snap ring engages groove in rear bearing.
10. Install reverse gear with shift collar to rear.
11. Press speedometer drive gear on mainshaft to distance shown in Fig. 3-7.

Assemble Countergear

1. Install roller spacer in countergear.
2. Using heavy grease to retain rollers, install 28 rollers in either end of countergear, two .050" spacers, 28 more rollers, then one .050" spacer.

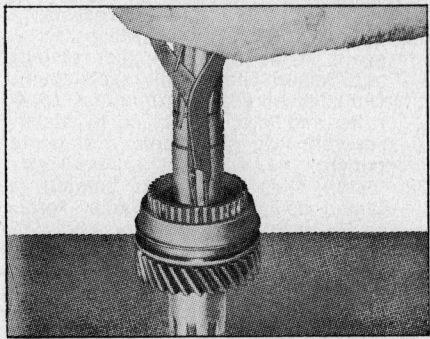

Fig. 3-3   Removing 1-2 synchronizer clutch snap ring

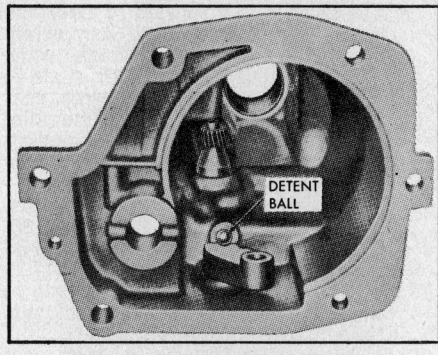

Fig. 3-4   Installing reverse shifter shaft and detent ball

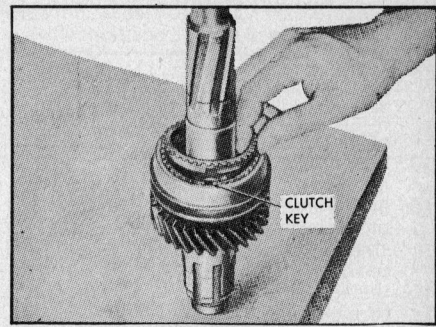

Fig. 3-5   Installing synchronizer ring

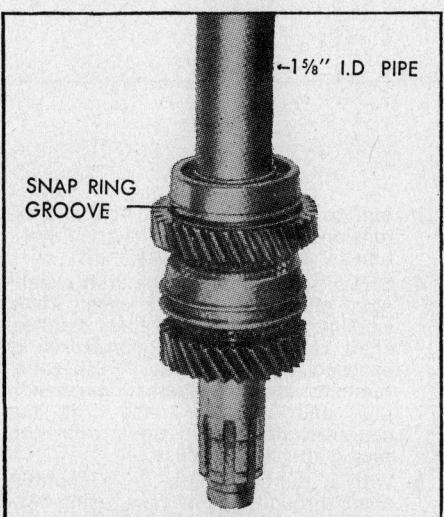

Fig. 3-6   Installing mainshaft rear bearing

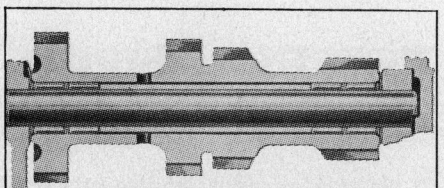

Fig. 3-8   Sectional view of countergear assembly

Fig. 3-10   Checking countergear end play

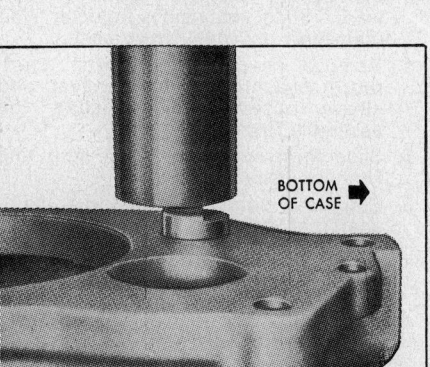

Fig. 3-9   Installing countershaft

Fig. 3-7   Installing speedometer drive gear

Make same installation at other end of countergear, Fig. 3-8.

ASSEMBLE TRANS.

1. With transmission case on its side, put countergear tanged thrust wash-ers in place, retaining them with heavy grease, and making sure tangs are resting in notches in case.
2. Set countergear in bottom of case.
3. Position transmission so it is resting on its front face.
4. Lubricate and insert countershaft through rear of case. Turn counter-shaft so flat on end of shaft is hori-zontal and facing bottom of case.
5. Align countergear with shaft in rear and hole in front of case. Press coun-tershaft into case until flat on shaft is flush with rear of case, Fig. 3-9. Be sure thrust washers remain in place.
6. Attach a dial indicator as shown in Fig. 3-10 and check end play of coun-tergear. If end play is greater than .025", new thrust washers must be installed.
7. Install 17 roller bearings in main drive gear, using heavy grease to hold bear-

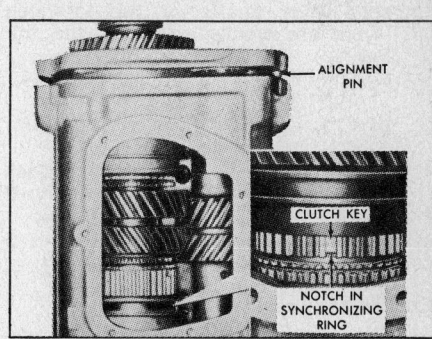

Fig. 3-11   Installing mainshaft assembly

ings and cage in place.
8. Install main drive gear and pilot bear-ings through side cover opening and into transmission front bore.
9. Place gasket in position of front face of rear bearing retainer.
10. Install 4th gear synchronizing ring on main drive gear with notches toward rear.
11. Position tanged reverse idler gear thrust washer on machined face of ear cast in case for reverse idler shaft and hold with heavy grease. Position front reverse idler gear next to thrust washer, with hub facing to-ward rear.

NOTE: Before attempting to install mainshaft assembly in case, slide 3-4 synchronizer clutch sleeve forward into 4th speed detent position.

12. Lower mainshaft into case making certain notches in 4th speed synchronizing ring correspond to keys in clutch, Fig. 3-11.
13. Tap rear bearing into position.
14. Insert rear reverse idler gear.
15. Install remaining flat thrust washer on reverse idler shaft. If new idler shaft is being used, drive out roll pin and press it into new shaft.
16. Install reverse idler shaft, making sure to pick up rear tanged thrust washer. *Roll pin should be in a vertical position.*
17. Pull reverse shifter shaft to left side of extension and rotate shaft to bring

reverse shift fork forward in extension (reverse detent position). Start extension onto transmission case, while slowly pushing in on shifter shaft to engage shift fork with reverse gear shift collar. Then pilot reverse idler shaft into extension housing, permitting extension to slide into transmission case.

18. Install extension attaching bolts. Torque upper three bolts to 15-25-ft-lbs, and lower three bolts to 25-35 ft-lbs.
19. Push or pull reverse shifter shaft to line up holes and drive in lock pin. Then install shifter lever.
20. Press bearing onto main drive gear (snap ring groove to front) and into case until several main drive gear

retaining nut threads are exposed.

21. Lock transmission by shifting into two gears. Install main drive gear retaining nut. Be sure bearing fully seats against shoulder of gear. Torque nut to 40 ft-lbs and lock it in place by staking securely into shaft hole with center punch.
22. Install main drive gear bearing retainer, using sealer on bolts. Torque to 15-20 ft-lbs.
23. Shift 3-4 sliding sleeve into neutral and 1-2 sliding sleeve into 2nd gear position. Shift side cover 3-4 shift lever into neutral and 1-2 shift lever into 2nd gear.
24. Install side cover with gasket. Torque attaching bolts evenly to avoid cover distortion and torque to 15-20 ft-lbs.

Type Four Chrysler

DISASSEMBLE TRANS.

Gearshift Housing

1. Remove reverse shift lever from shaft, Fig. 4-1, then the gearshift housing attaching bolts, Fig. 4-2.
2. With levers in neutral detent position, pull housing away from case. Remove forks from sleeves.
3. If oil leakage is present around gearshift lever shafts or the interlock levers are cracked, perform the following:
   a. Remove nuts and the shift operating levers from shafts.
   b. Remove gearshift lever shafts from housing.
   c. Remove "E" ring from interlock lever pivot pin, then the interlock levers and spring from housing.

Extension Housing & Mainshaft

Exc. Overdrive Units

1. Remove bolt and retainer securing speedometer pinion adapter in extension housing, then the adapter and pinion from housing.

2. Remove extension housing attaching bolts.
3. Slide third-fourth synchronizer sleeve slightly forward, slide reverse idler gear to center of shaft, then using a mallet, tap extension housing rearward. Slide extension housing and mainshaft assembly from case.
4. Remove snap ring retaining third-fourth synchronizer clutch gear and sleeve assembly, then slide the assembly from mainshaft.
5. Slide third speed gear and stop ring from mainshaft.
6. Compress snap ring retaining mainshaft ball bearing in extension housing and pull mainshaft assembly and bearing from extension housing, Fig. 4-3.
7. Remove mainshaft bearing retaining snap ring. Remove bearing by installing steel plates on the first speed gear, then press or drive mainshaft through bearing. Use caution not to damage gear teeth.
8. Remove bearing, bearing retainer ring, first speed gear and first speed stop ring from shaft.
9. Remove first-second clutch gear and sleeve assembly snap ring, Fig. 4-4, then slide assembly and the second speed gear from shaft.
10. Measure countershaft gear end play by inserting a feeler gauge between thrust washer and gear, Fig. 4-5. End play should be .015-.029. If not, install new thrust washers when reassembling transmission.

Overdrive Units

1. Remove bolt and retainer securing speedometer pinion adapter in extension housing, then the adapter and pinion from housing.
2. Remove extension housing attaching bolts.
3. Rotate extension housing on output shaft to expose the rear of countershaft. Clearance is provided on extension housing flange to permit one

bolt to be reinstalled to hold the extension housing in the inverted position for access to countershaft.

4. Drill a hole in the countershaft expansion plug at front of case. Then, working through hole, push countershaft rearward until woodruff key is exposed and remove key. Push countershaft forward against expansion plug and, using a brass drift, tap countershaft forward until expansion plug is driven from case.
5. With a dummy shaft, drive countershaft through rear of case, using caution so the countershaft washers do not fall out of position. Lower cluster gear to bottom of case.
6. Rotate extension housing back to normal position.
7. Remove drive pinion bearing retainer attaching bolts, then slide retainer and gasket from pinion shaft. Pry pinion or seal from retainer. Use caution not to nick or scratch seal bore in retainer or the surface on which the seal bottoms.
8. With a brass drift, drive the pinion and bearing assembly through the front of case.
9. Perform steps 3 through 9 as outlined under "Extension Housing & Mainshaft, Except Overdrive Units" procedure.

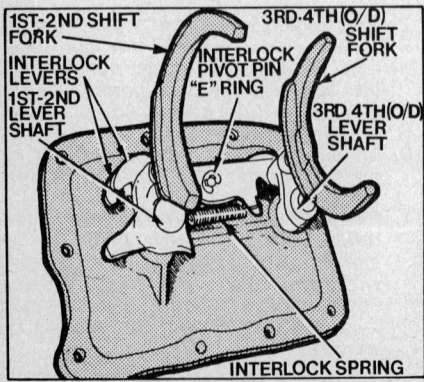

Fig. 4-2 Gearshift housing assembly

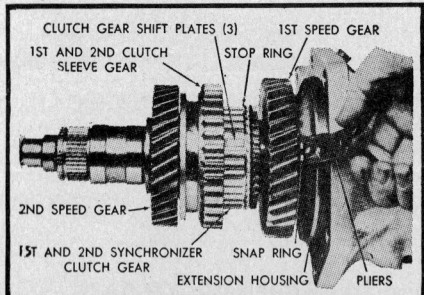

Fig. 4-3 Compressing center bearing snap ring

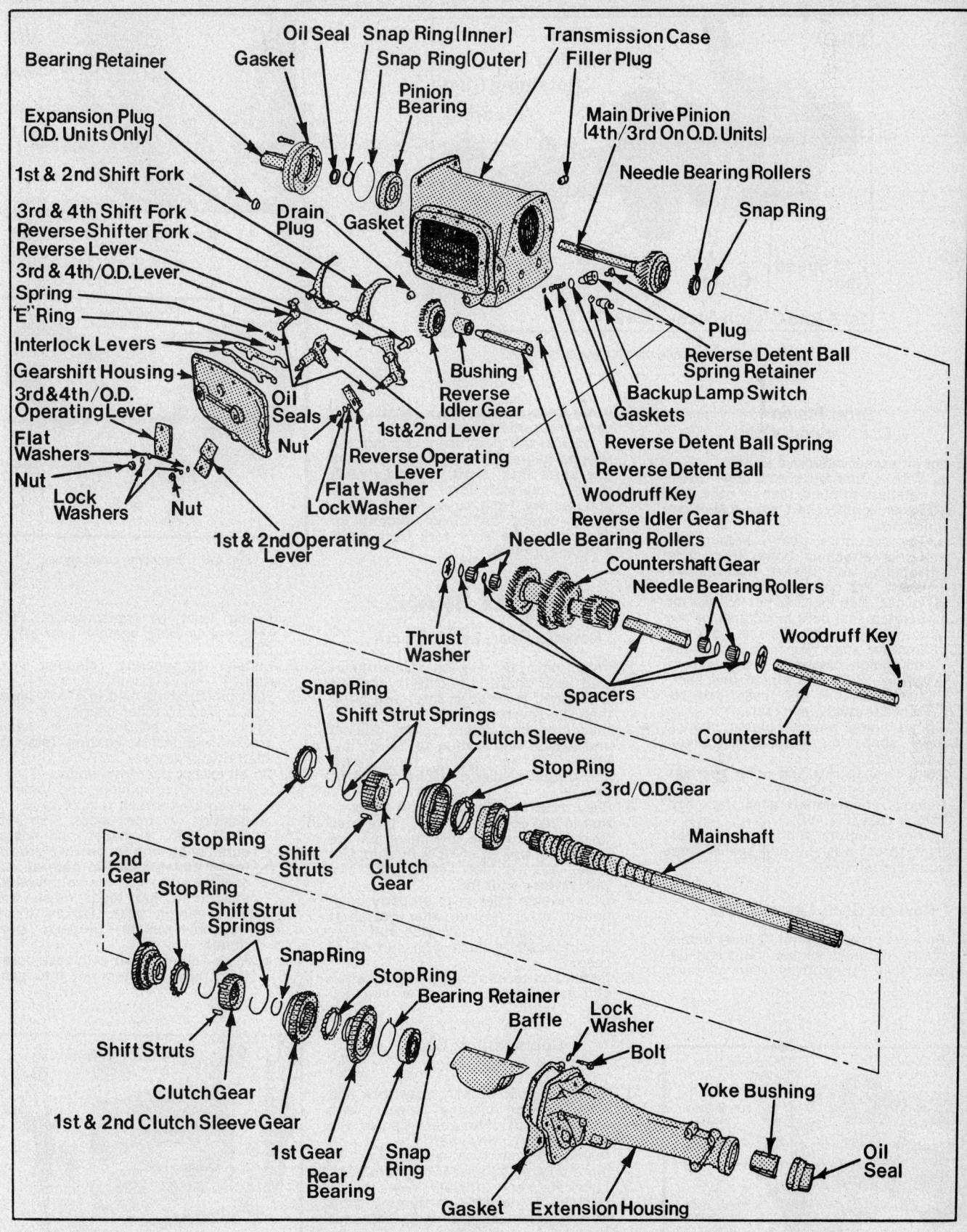

Fig. 4-1 Type Four Chrysler four-speed transmission.

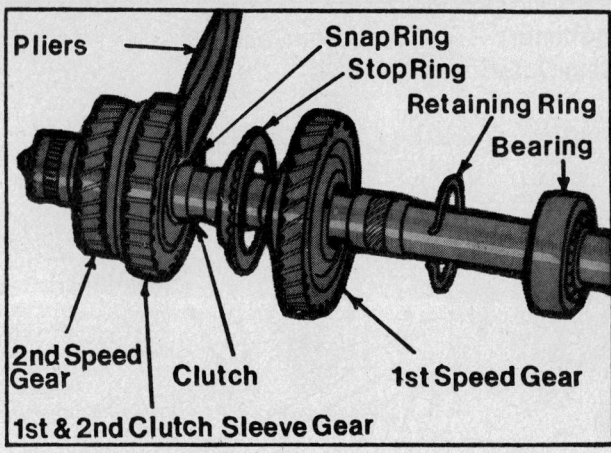

Fig. 4-4 Removing clutch gear snap ring

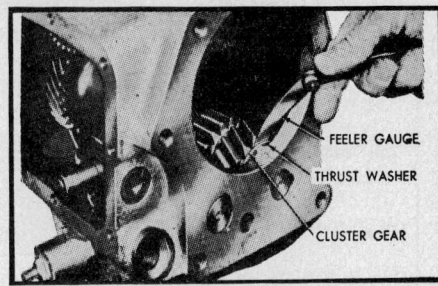

Fig. 4-5 Measuring countergear end play

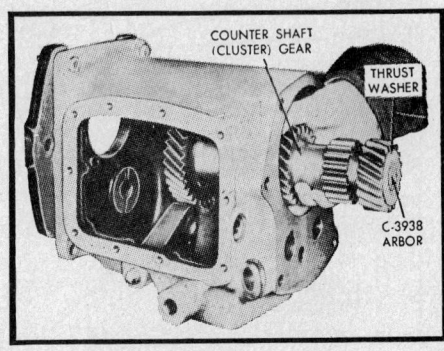

Fig. 4-6 Replacing countergear

Drive Pinion & Countershaft Gear

1. On all except overdrive units:
   a. With a dummy shaft, drive countershaft through rear of case and lower countershaft gear to bottom of case.
   b. Remove drive pinion bearing retainer attaching bolts, then slide retainer and gasket from pinion shaft. Pry pinion or seal from retainer. Use caution not to nick or scratch seal bore in retainer or the surface on which the seal bottoms.
   c. Remove snap ring from outer race of pinion bearing, then, with a mallet, drive the pinion and bearing assembly into case and remove through case rear.
2. On all units, remove pinion bearing inner snap ring, then press pinion from bearing.
3. Remove snap ring and roller bearings from drive pinion cavity.
4. Remove countershaft gear from bottom of case, Fig. 4-6.
5. Remove dummy shaft, needle bearings, thrust washers and spacer from countershaft gear.

Reverse Gear, Lever & Fork

1. Remove reverse gearshift lever detent spring retainer, gasket, plug and detent ball spring from rear of case, Fig. 4-7.

2. Press reverse idler gear shaft from case and remove woodruff key.
3. If oil leakage is present around the reverse gearshift lever shaft, remove any burrs from shaft. Carefully push reverse gearshift lever shaft inward and remove from case, Fig. 4-8. Remove detent ball from bottom of case, then the shift fork from shaft and detent plate.

ASSEMBLE TRANS.

Reverse Gear, Lever & Fork

1. Install new "O" ring on reverse gearshift lever shaft. Lubricate lever shaft and install lever shaft into case bore, then the reverse fork in lever.
2. Install reverse detent spring retainer and gasket and torque to 50 ft. lbs. Insert ball and spring, then install and torque gasket and plug to 24 ft. lbs.
3. Place reverse idler gearshaft in position in end of case and drive into case to position reverse idler gear on the protruding end of shaft with shift slot facing toward rear and engage slot with reverse shift fork.
4. With reverse idler gear properly positioned, drive reverse idler gearshaft into case and install woodruff key. Ensure shaft is flush with surface of case.
5. Install and torque back-up light switch and gasket to 15 ft. lbs. if removed.

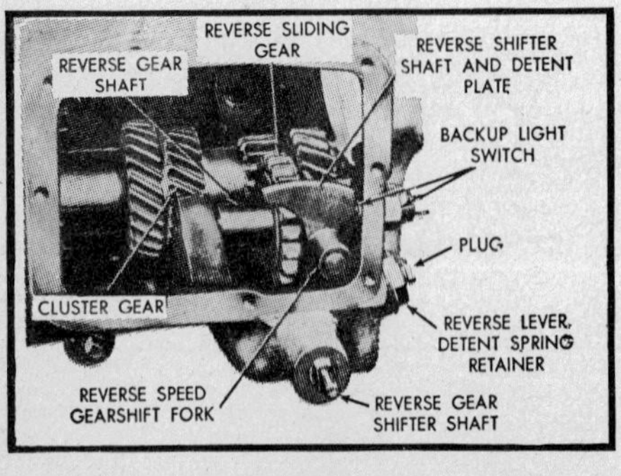

Countershaft Gear & Drive Pinion

1. Lubricate countershaft gear bore and install roller bearing spacer with dummy shaft into gear. Center the spacer and dummy shaft.
2. Install 19 rollers, a spacer ring, 19 more rollers and spacer ring into gear.
3. Lubricate and install new thrust washers, if needed, on dummy shaft with tanged side facing toward case boss.
4. Place countershaft gear assembly on bottom of case, Fig. 4-6.
5. Press drive pinion bearing onto pinion shaft with outer snap ring groove

facing front of transmission. Fully seat the bearing against gear shoulder.
6. Install new bearing retaining snap ring.
7. With pinion shaft held in a soft jawed vise, install 16 roller bearings in shaft cavity. Coat bearings with heavy grease and install bearing retaining snap ring in groove.
8. On all except overdrive units:
   a. Install drive pinion and bearing assembly through rear of case and position in front bore. Tap into place with a mallet and install outer snap ring in bearing groove.
   b. Insert countershaft in bore at rear of case and raise the countershaft gear until the teeth mesh with drive pinion gear. Ensure thrust washers remain properly positioned.
   c. Align dummy shaft with case bores, then push countershaft into gear.

Fig. 4-7 Reverse gearing and countergear

Fig. 4-8 Removing reverse shift fork and lever

Tap shaft into case until shaft end is flush with case surface. Remove dummy shaft.

9. On all units, install new oil seal in retainer bore.

Extension Housing Bushing, Replace

1. Remove extension housing yoke seal.
2. Drive bushing from housing.
3. Drive new bushing into housing, aligning bushing oil hole with housing oil slot.
4. Install new extension housing yoke seal.

Mainshaft

1. Partially assemble synchronizer components as follows:
   a. Place a stop ring flat on bench, then the clutch sleeve and gear.
   b. Place struts into slots and snap a strut spring into place with the tang inside one strut.
   c. Turn assembly over and install second strut spring with the tang in a different strut.
2. Slide second speed gear onto mainshaft with synchronizer cone facing toward rear against shoulder.
3. Slide first-second synchronizer with stop ring lugs indexed in slots onto mainshaft against second gear cone and secure with new snap ring. Slide next stop ring onto shaft and index lugs into clutch hub slots.
4. Slide first speed gear with synchronizer cone facing forward into position against clutch sleeve gear.
5. Install mainshaft bearing retaining ring, then the mainshaft rear bearing. Press bearing into place and install new snap ring to retain bearing.
6. Install partially assembled mainshaft into extension housing and compress bearing retaining ring so mainshaft ball bearing can move inward and bottom against thrust shoulder in extension housing. Release and seat ring in groove in the housing.
7. On all except overdrive units:
   a. Slide third speed gear onto mainshaft with synchronizer cone facing forward, then the third gear stop ring.
   b. Install third-fourth synchronizer clutch gear assembly on mainshaft with shift fork slot facing rearward against third speed gear.
   c. Install retaining snap ring, then, with grease, position front stop ring over clutch gear, indexing ring lugs with clutch struts.
8. On overdrive units:
   a. Slide overdrive gear onto mainshaft with synchronizer cone facing forward, then the overdrive gear stop ring.
   b. Install third-overdrive synchronizer clutch gear assembly on mainshaft with shift fork slot facing rearward against overdrive gear.
   c. Install retaining snap ring, then, with grease, position front stop ring over clutch gear, indexing ring lugs with clutch struts.
9. On all units, coat new extension housing to case gasket with grease, then place gasket on housing.
10. Slide reverse idler gear to center of the shaft, then move the third-fourth synchronizer sleeve or the third-overdrive synchronizer sleeve forward.
11. On all except overdrive units, move drive pinion forward to provide maximum clearance for mainshaft pilot end.
12. On all units, slowly insert mainshaft assembly into case, tilting the shaft as necessary to clear idler and cluster gears. On all except overdrive units, engage the mainshaft with the pilot rollers in the drive pinion gear.
13. On all except overdrive units:
    a. Place third-fourth synchronizer sleeve in neutral position.
    b. If all components are positioned properly the extension housing will bottom on the case without force. If not, check position of struts, pinion rollers and stop rings.
    c. Install and torque extension housing attaching bolts to 50 ft. lbs.
    d. Install drive pinion bearing retainer and gasket. Coat attaching bolt threads with a suitable sealing compound, then install and torque bolts to 30 ft. lbs.
14. On overdrive units:
    a. Place third-overdrive synchronizer sleeve in neutral position.
    b. Rotate extension housing on mainshaft to expose countershaft rear and install one extension housing attaching bolt, holding housing in inverted position and preventing housing from moving rearward.
    c. Install drive pinion and bearing assembly through front of case and into front bore. Install outer snap ring in bearing groove. Tap lightly into position with a mallet. If all components are positioned properly, the bearing outer snap ring will bottom onto case face without force. If not, check position of struts, pinion rollers and stop rings.
    d. Turn transmission upside down while holding countershaft gear assembly to prevent damage.
    e. Lower countershaft gear assembly into position with teeth meshed with drive pinion gear. Ensure thrust washers are positioned properly with the tangs aligned with case slots.
    f. Start countershaft into bore at rear of case and push until approximately halfway into case, then install woodruff key. Push shaft forward until end is flush with case surface. Remove dummy shaft.
    g. Properly align extension housing on case and install and torque extension housing attaching bolts to 50 ft. lbs.
    h. Install drive pinion bearing retainer and gasket. Coat attaching bolt threads with a suitable sealing compound, then install and torque bolts to 30 ft. lbs.
    i. Install new expansion plug in countershaft bore at front of case.

Gearshift Housing

1. Install interlock levers on pivot pin and retain with "E" ring, Fig. 4-2. Use pliers to install spring on interlock lever hangers.
2. Lubricate and install new "O" rings on shift lever shafts. Lubricate housing bores and push shafts into proper bore.
3. Install operating levers and torque retaining nuts to 18 ft. lbs. On overdrive units, ensure the third-overdrive points downward.
4. Rotate shift fork bores to neutral position and install the third-fourth shift fork or the third-overdrive shift fork in proper bore and under both interlock levers.
5. Position both synchronizer sleeves in neutral and place first-second shift fork in the first-second synchronizer sleeve groove.
6. Lay transmission on its right side and place gearshift housing gasket on case with grease to hold in position.
7. Lower gearshift housing into place, guiding the third-fourth shift fork or the third-overdrive shift fork into synchronizer groove, and lead the first-second shift fork into the first-second shift lever bore. Raise interlock lever against its spring tension with a screwdriver, allowing first-second shift fork shaft to slip under the levers. The gearshift housing should now seat against case gasket.
8. Install gearshift housing attaching bolts finger tight and shift transmission through all gears to insure proper operation.

NOTE: Eight gearshift housing attaching bolts are shoulder bolts used to accurately locate the mechanism on the transmission. One bolt shoulder is longer and acts as a dowel, passing through the cover and into the case at center of rear flange. Two bolts are of standard design, located at the lower rear of cover.

9. Torque gearshift housing attaching bolts to 15 ft. lbs.
10. The reverse shift lever and the first-second shift lever incorporate cam surfaces which mate in the reverse position to lock the first-second lever, fork and synchronizer in the neutral position. To check, place transmission in reverse, then, while turning input shaft, move first-second lever in each direction. If input shaft lock becomes difficult to turn, the synchronizer is partially engaged, caused by excessive cam clearance. Install a new first-second shift lever of different size. If insufficient cam clearance exists, it is difficult or impossible to shift into reverse.
11. Lubricate reverse shaft and install operating lever, then torque attaching nut to 18 ft. lbs.
12. Install speedometer drive pinion gear and adapter, ensuring range number (indicating number of teeth) is in the six o'clock position.

Type Five Ford

DISASSEMBLE TRANS.

1. Remove the lower extension housing to case attaching screw to drain lubricant.
2. Remove cover attaching screws and the cover from case.
3. Remove the long spring retaining detent plug in case, then, using a magnet, remove detent plug.
4. Remove extension housing to case screws and the extension housing.
5. Remove input shaft bearing retainer attaching screws and slide retainer from input shaft.
6. Support countershaft gear with a wire hook. Working from front of case, push countershaft out rear of case with a dummy shaft. Lower countershaft gear to bottom of case and remove the wire hook.
7. Remove set screw from first and second speed shift fork, then slide first and second speed shift rail out rear of case, Fig. 5-1.
8. With a magnet, remove interlock detent from between the first and second and the third and overdrive shift rails.
9. Shift transmission into overdrive position. Remove set screw from the third and overdrive shift fork. Remove the side detent bolt, detent plug and spring. Rotate the third and overdrive speed shift rail 90 degrees and tap rail out front of case with a suitable punch and hammer.
10. With a magnet, remove interlock plug from top of case.
11. Remove snap ring securing speedometer drive gear to output shaft, then slide gear from shaft. Remove speedometer gear drive ball.
12. Remove output shaft bearing retaining snap ring and the snap ring from

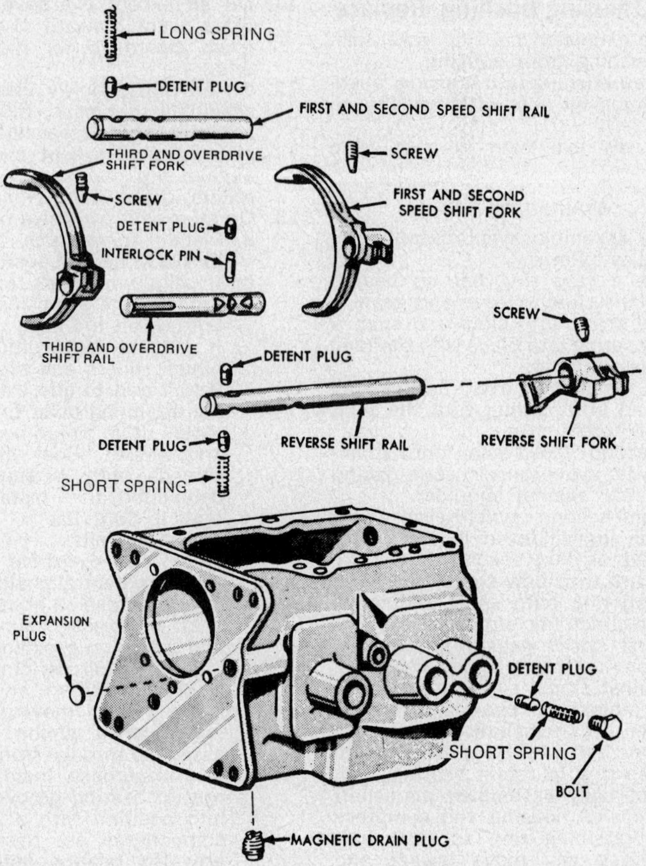

Fig. 5-1 Shift forks & rails, disassembled

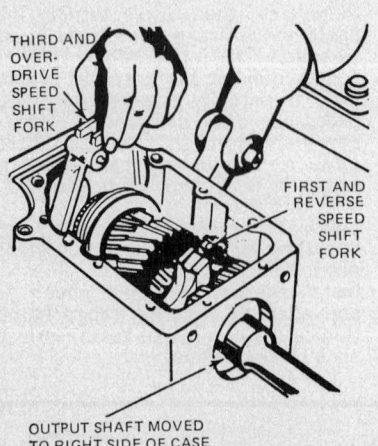

Fig. 5-2 Removing shift forks

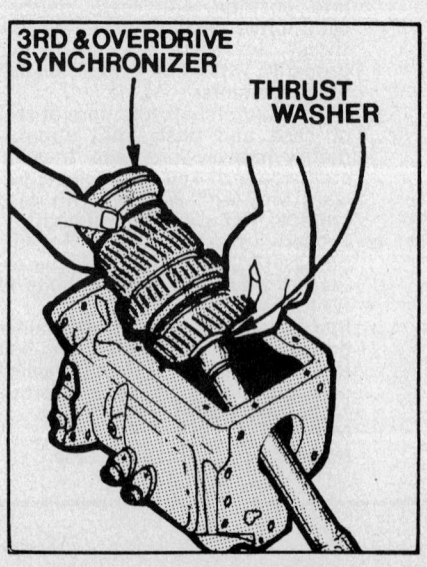

Fig. 5-3 Replacing output shaft assembly

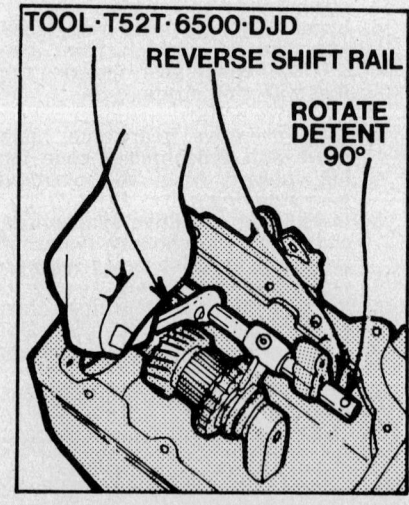

Fig. 5-4 Rotating reverse shift rail

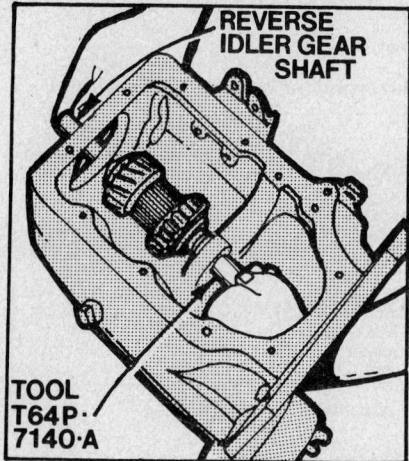

Fig. 5-5 Removing reverse idler gear shaft

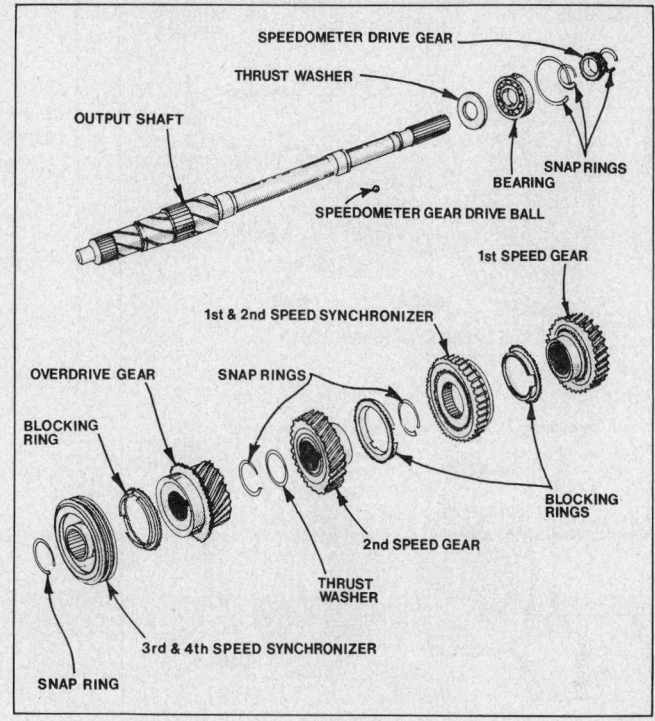

Fig. 5-6 Output shaft disassembled

outside diameter of output shaft bearing.

13. Remove output shaft bearing.
14. Remove input shaft bearing retaining snap ring and the snap ring from outside diameter of input shaft bearing.
15. Remove input shaft bearing from shaft and case, then the input shaft and blocking from front of case.
16. Position output shaft to right side of case and remove shift forks, Fig. 5-2.
17. Lift output shaft assembly from case, Fig. 5-3, support the thrust washer and first speed gear to prevent the washer and gear from sliding from shaft.
18. Remove reverse gear shift fork set screw, rotate reverse shift rail 90 degrees, Fig. 5-4, slide shift rail out rear of case and lift the reverse shift fork from case.
19. With a magnet, remove reverse detent plug and spring with a magnet.
20. Remove reverse idler gear shaft with a dummy shaft and lower reverse idler gear to bottom of case, Fig. 5-5.
21. Lift countershaft gear and thrust washers from bottom of case, using caution not to drop bearings or the dummy shaft from countershaft gear.
22. Lift reverse idler gear shaft from case, using caution not to drop bearings or the dummy shaft from reverse idler gear.
23. Remove snap ring from front of output shaft and slide the third and overdrive synchronizer, blocking and gear from output shaft, Fig. 5-6.
24. Remove the next snap ring and the second speed gear thrust washer, gear and blocking ring from output shaft.
25. Remove the next snap ring and the first speed gear thrust washer, gear and blocking ring from rear of output shaft.

Sub-Assembly Service

Cam & Shaft Seals

NOTE: To facilitate reassembly, note position of cams and shafts assemblies and levers before removal from transmission

case.

1. Remove three shift levers, Fig. 5-7.
2. Remove three cams and shafts from inside of case.
3. Remove O-ring from each cam and shaft.
4. Dip new O-rings in gear lubricant and install them on cam and shafts.
5. Slide each cam and shaft into its respective bore in case.
6. Secure each shift lever.

Synchronizers

1. Push synchronizer hub from each sleeve, Fig. 5-8.
2. Separate inserts and springs from hubs. Do not mix parts from one synchronizer to another.
3. Position hub in sleeve, being sure that alignment marks are properly indexed.
4. Place three inserts into hub. Install insert springs, making sure that ir-

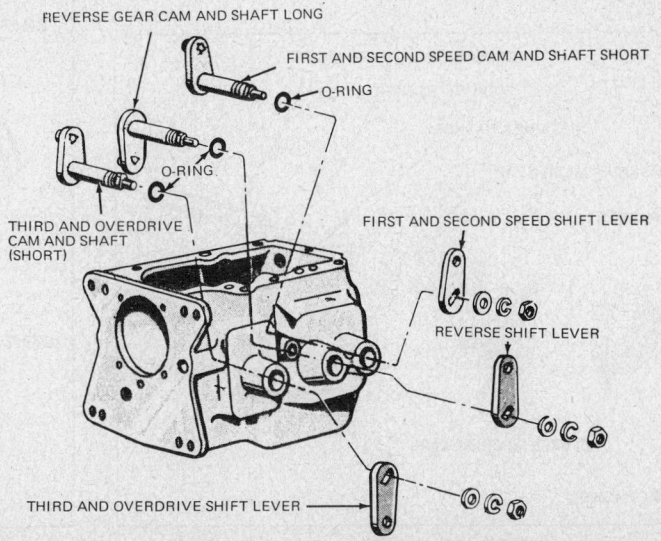

Fig. 5-7 Cams, shafts & levers

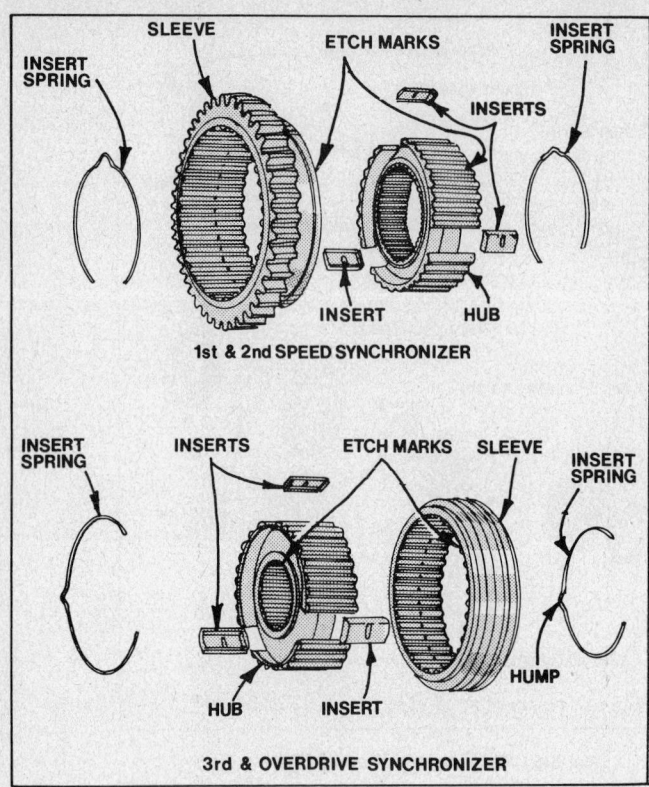

1st & 2nd SPEED SYNCHRONIZER

3rd & OVERDRIVE SYNCHRONIZER

Fig. 5-8   Synchronizer assemblies, disassembled

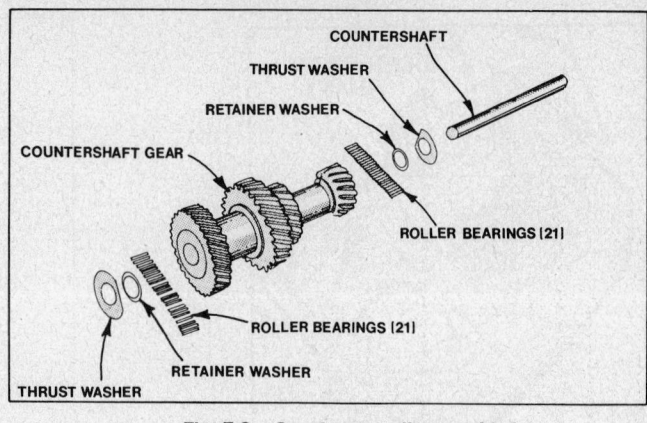

Fig. 5-9   Countergear, disassembled

regular surface (hump) is seated in one of inserts. Do not stagger springs.

Countershaft Gear Bearings

1. With unit disassembled, coat bore in each end of countergear with grease, Fig. 5-9.
2. Hold a suitable dummy shaft in gear and insert 21 rollers and a retainer washer in each end of gear.

Reverse Idler Gear Bearings

1. With unit disassembled, Fig. 5-10, coat bore at each end of gear with grease.
2. Hold a suitable dummy shaft in gear and insert 22 rollers and retainer washer at each end of gear.
3. Install sliding gear on reverse idler gear, making sure that shift fork groove is toward front.

Input Shaft Seal

1. Remove seal from input shaft bearing retainer.
2. Lubricate sealing surface and install new seal.

Transmission Assembly

1. Lubricate countershaft gear thrust surfaces and position a thrust washer at each end of case. Place countershaft gear, dummy shaft and roller bearings in the case.
2. Place case in the vertical position, align gear bore and thrust washers with case bores and install countershaft.
3. Place case in the horizontal position and, with a feeler gauge, check countershaft gear end play which should be .004-.018 inch. If not, replace thrust washers.
4. Reinstall dummy shaft in countershaft gear and place gear at bottom of case.

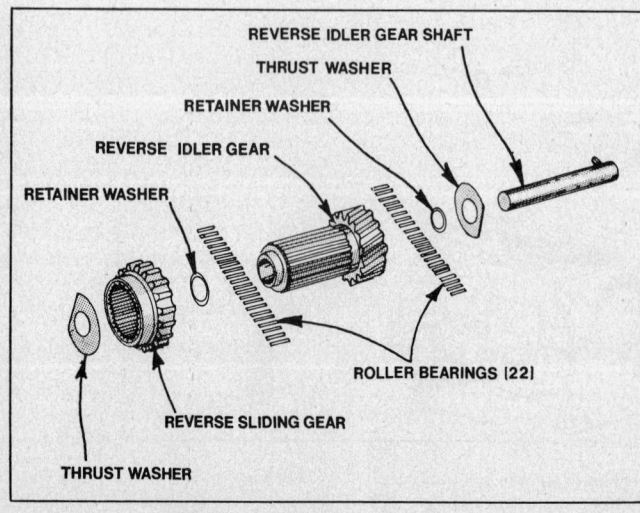

Fig. 5-10   Reverse idler gear, disassembled

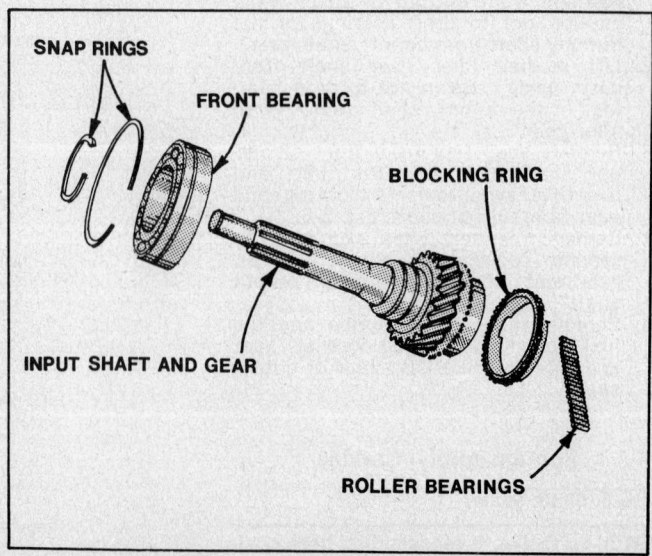

Fig. 5-11   Input shaft, disassembled

5. Lubricate reverse idler gear thrust surfaces and place the two thrust washers in position. Install reverse idler gear, sliding gear, dummy shaft and roller bearings in place, ensuring the sliding gear shift fork groove is facing toward front of case. Align gear bore and thrust washers with case bores and install the reverse idler shaft.

6. With a feeler gauge, check reverse idler gear end play which should be .004-.018 inch. If not, replace thrust washers. If end play is within limits, do not remove gear and shaft.

7. Install reverse gear shift rail detent spring and detent plug into case. Holding reverse shift fork in place on the reverse idler sliding gear, install the shift rail from rear of case. Install shift rail to fork set screw.

8. Place first and second speed synchronizer onto output shaft with shift fork groove facing toward rear of shaft. The synchronizer hub is installed with the teeth end of the gear facing toward rear of output shaft.

9. Place blocking ring on second speed gear, then slide the gear onto front of output shaft, ensuring synchronizer inserts engage the blocker ring notches.

10. Install second speed gear thrust washer and snap ring.

11. Slide overdrive gear onto shaft with coned surface facing toward front of output shaft, then install blocking ring on gear.

12. Slide third and overdrive gear synchronizer onto shaft, ensuring synchronizer inserts engage blocking ring notches and the thrust surface is facing toward overdrive gear.

13. Install snap ring at front of output shaft.

14. Place blocking ring on first speed gear, then slide first speed gear onto rear of output shaft, ensuring synchronizer inserts engage blocking ring notches.

15. Install the heavy thrust washer at rear of output shaft.

16. Support thrust washer and first speed gear to prevent washer and gear from sliding off shaft and lower assembly into case, Fig. 5-3.

17. Install first and second speed shift fork and the third and overdrive speed shift fork, rotating forks into place.

18. Install detent spring and plug into reverse shift rail, then place rail in neutral position.

19. Lubricate third and overdrive shift rail interlock pin and install in shift rail.

20. Align third and overdrive shift fork with shift rail bores and slide shift rail into position, ensuring the three detents are facing toward outside of case. Place front synchronizer into neutral nosition and install the third and overdrive shift fork set screw. Place synchronizer in neutral position and install the third and overdrive shift rail detent plug, spring and bolt into left side of case. Install detent plug into case bore.

21. Align first and second speed shift fork with case bores and slide shift rail into place, then install set screw.

22. Lubricate input gear bore and install 15 roller bearings into bore.

NOTE: Apply a thin coat of lubricant since a heavy application may plug the lubricant holes and restrict lubrication of the bearings.

---

23. Place front blocking ring in the third and overdrive synchronizer.

24. Place a dummy bearing on rear of output shaft to support and align shaft in case.

25. Install input shaft gear into case, ensuring output shaft pilot enters roller bearings in input gear pocket.

26. Place input shaft bearing on input shaft and press bearing onto shaft and into case bore, Fig. 5-11.

27. Install input shaft and bearing snap rings, Fig. 5-11.

28. Place new gasket on input shaft bearing retainer, apply sealer to attaching bolts and install and torque attaching bolts to 19-25 ft. lbs.

29. Remove dummy bearing from output shaft and install output shaft bearing onto shaft and press into case bore.

NOTE: Before pressing bearing onto output shaft, ensure the bearing is aligned with the case bore and the countershaft is not interfering with the output shaft assembly.

---

30. Install output shaft and bearing snap rings.

31. Place transmission in the vertical position. Align countershaft gear bore and thrust washers with case bore and install countershaft.

32. Install extension housing on case with a new gasket, apply sealer to attaching screws and install and torque to 42-50 ft. lbs.

33. Install filler plug.

34. Pour transmission lubricant over gear train while rotating input shaft.

35. Place each shift fork in all positions to ensure proper operation.

36. Install remaining detent plug in case and the long spring to secure detent plug.

37. Install cover with a new gasket, apply sealer to attaching screws and install and torque attaching screws to 20-25 ft. lbs.

38. Apply sealer to the third and overdrive shift rail plug bore and install new expansion plug.

Type Six

DISASSEMBLE TRANSMISSION

1. Remove side cover assembly and shift forks. On Vega transmissions, remove damper assembly which is bolted to extension housing.
2. Remove clutch gear bearing retainer.
3. Remove clutch gear bearing to gear stem snap ring, then remove bearing by pulling clutch gear outward until a screwdriver can be inserted between large snap ring and case to complete removal, Fig. 6-2. Do not remove clutch gear. The bearing is a slip fit on the gear and into the case bore.
4. Remove extension to case bolts and remove clutch gear, mainshaft and extension assembly through rear case opening. Remove clutch gear and

blocker ring from mainshaft.
5. Expand extension housing to rear mainshaft bearing snap ring and remove extension, Fig. 6-3.
6. Using a dummy shaft, drive countershaft and woodruff key out through rear of case, Fig. 6-4. Dummy shaft will hold roller bearings in position within countergear bore. Remove countergear.
7. Remove reverse idler gear stop ring and, using a long drift, drive idler shaft and woodruff key out through rear of case.

Disassemble Mainshaft

1. Remove snap ring and press 3-4 synchronizer clutch assembly, 3rd speed blocker ring and 3rd gear off main-

shaft, Fig. 6-5.
2. Depress speedometer gear retaining clip and remove gear.
3. Remove rear bearing to mainshaft snap ring, support 1st gear with press plates and press on rear of mainshaft to remove 1st speed gear, thrust washer, spring washer and rear bearing, Fig. 6-6.
4. Remove 1-2 sliding clutch hub snap ring, support 2nd speed gear and press clutch assembly, 2nd speed blocker ring and gear from mainshaft, Fig. 6-7.

Clutch Keys & Springs

NOTE: The clutch hubs and sleeves are a

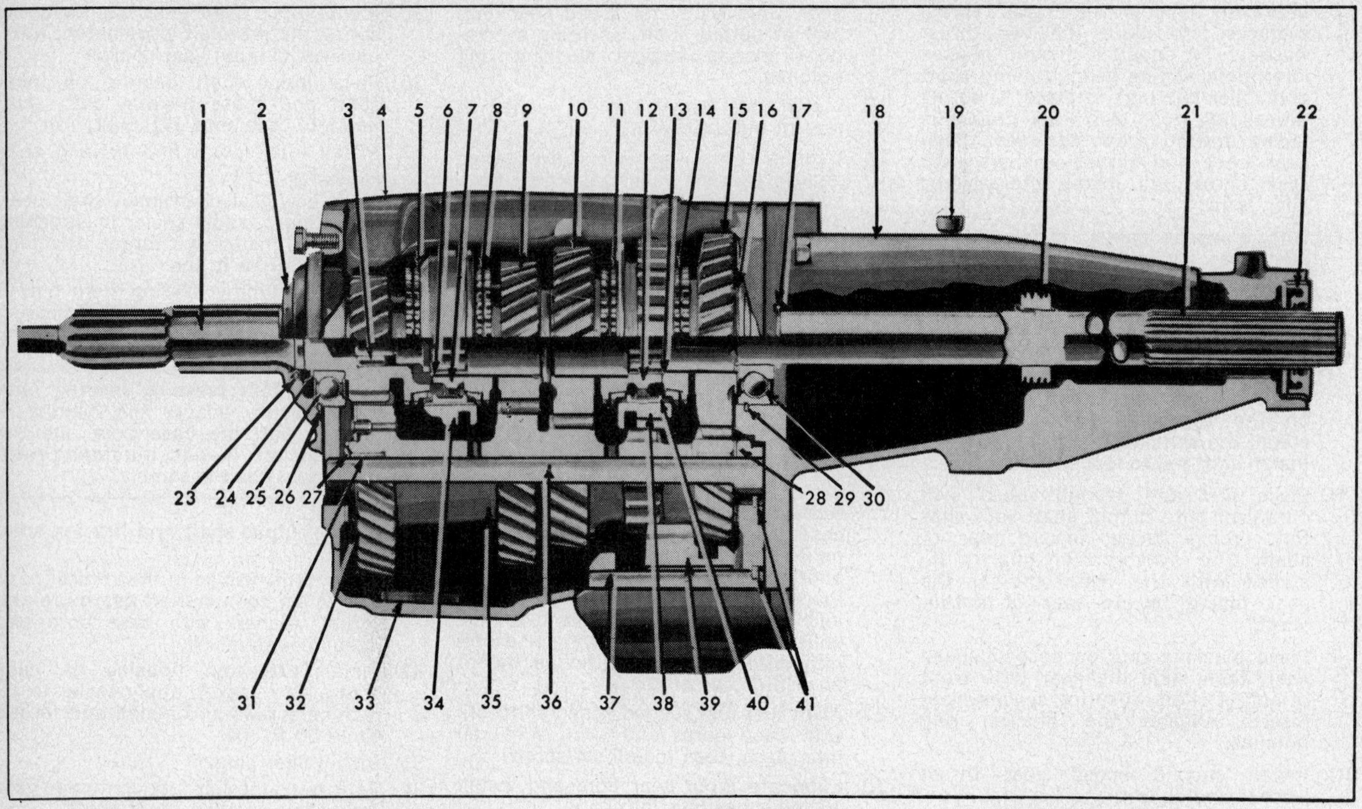

1	Clutch Gear	12. 1-2 Speed Synch. Hub	23. Retainer Oil Seal
2	Bearing Retainer	13. 1-2 Speed Synch. Snap Ring	24. Snap Ring-Bearing to Gear
3	Pilot Bearings	14. 1st Speed Blocker Ring	25. Clutch Gear Bearing
4	Case	15. First Gear	26. Snap Ring-Bearing to Case
5	4th Speed Blocker Ring	16. Reverse Gear Thrust and Spring Washers	27. Thrust Washer-Front
6	4-3 Snych. Snap Ring	17. Snap Ring-Bearing to Mainshaft	28. Thrust Washer-Rear
7	4-3 Synch. Hub	18. Extension	29. Snap Ring-Bearing to Extension
8	3rd Speed Blocker Ring	19. Vent	30. Rear Bearing
9	3rd Speed Gear	20. Speedometer Drive Gear and Clip	31. Countergear Roller Bearings
10.	2nd Speed Gear	21. Mainshaft	32. Anti-Lash Plate Assembly
11.	2nd Speed Blocker Ring	22. Rear Oil Seal	33. Magnet

34. 4-3Snych. Sleeve	
35. Countergear Assembly	
36. Counter Shaft	
37. Reverse Idler Shaft	
38. 1-2 Speed Synch. Sleeve and Reverse Gear	
39. Reverse Idler Gear (Sliding)	
40. Clutch Key	
41. Woodruff Key	

Fig. 6-1 Sectional view of Type Six four speed transmission

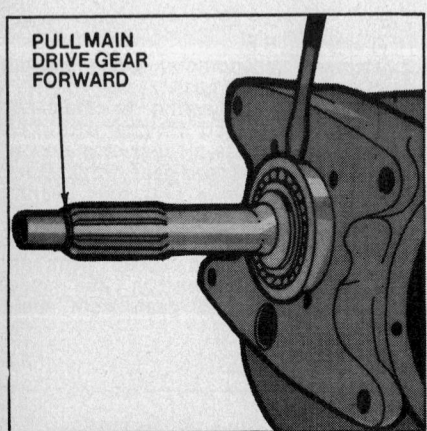

Fig. 6-2 Removing clutch gear bearing

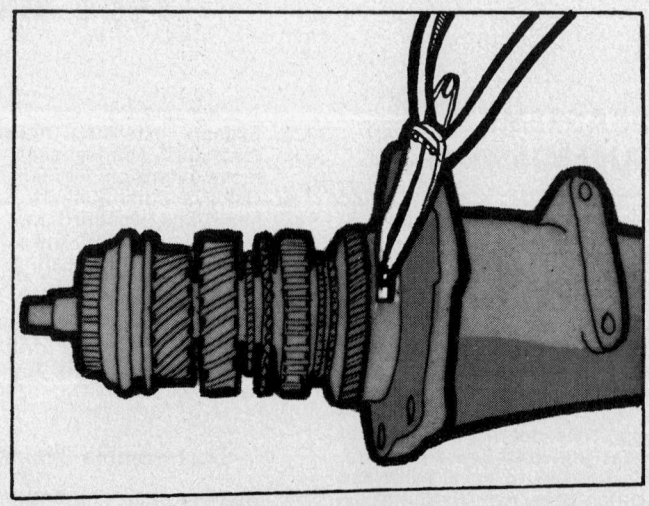

Fig. 6-3 Removing extension

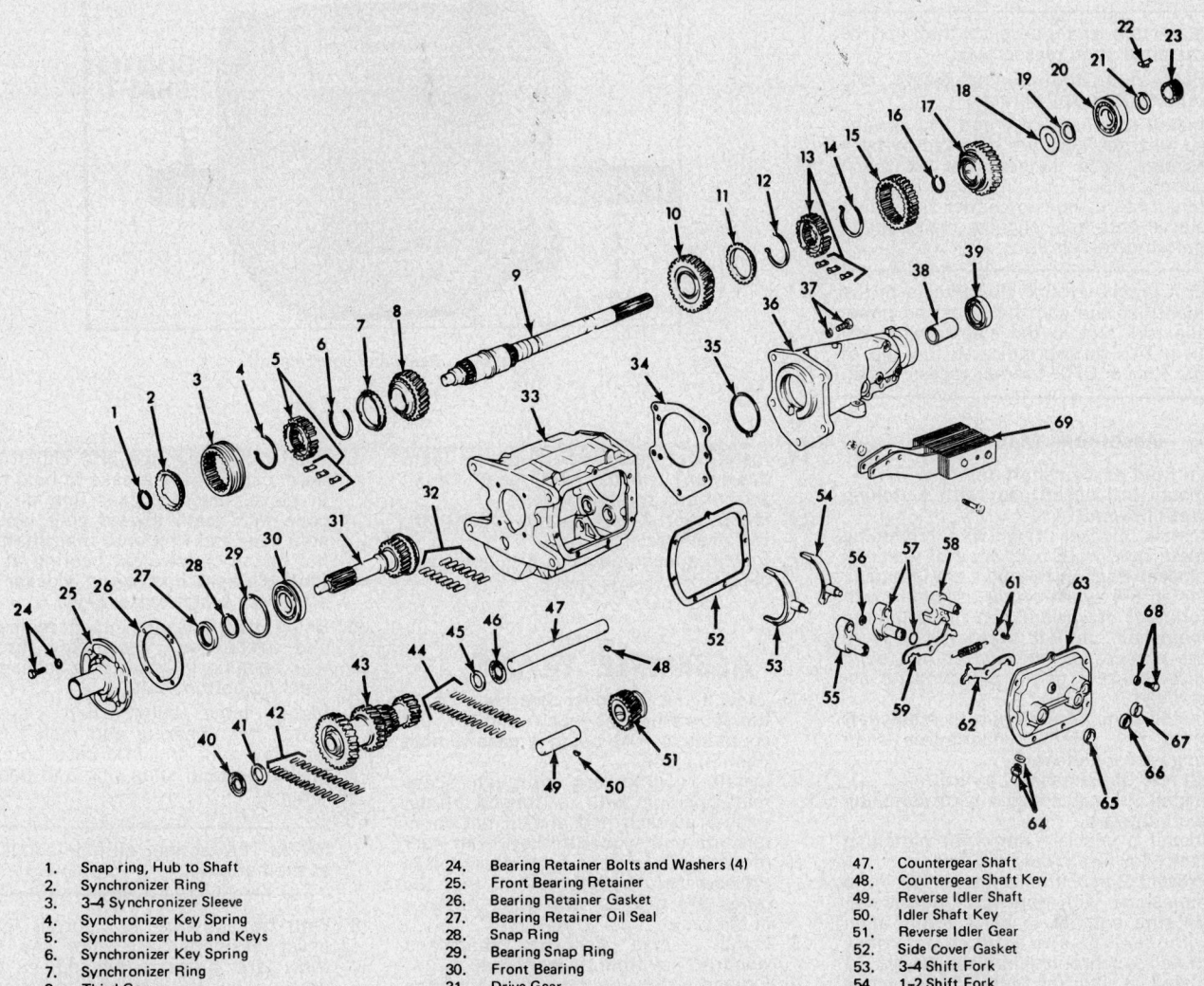

Fig. 6-1A   Disassembled view of Type Six four speed transmission

1.	Snap ring, Hub to Shaft	24.	Bearing Retainer Bolts and Washers (4)
2.	Synchronizer Ring	25.	Front Bearing Retainer
3.	3-4 Synchronizer Sleeve	26.	Bearing Retainer Gasket
4.	Synchronizer Key Spring	27.	Bearing Retainer Oil Seal
5.	Synchronizer Hub and Keys	28.	Snap Ring
6.	Synchronizer Key Spring	29.	Bearing Snap Ring
7.	Synchronizer Ring	30.	Front Bearing
8.	Third Gear	31.	Drive Gear
9.	Main Shaft	32.	Pilot Bearings
10.	Second Gear	33.	Case
11.	Synchronizer Ring	34.	Extension to Case Gasket
12.	Synchronizer Key Spring	35.	Rear Bearing to Extension Retaining Ring
13.	Synchronizer Hub and Keys	36.	Rear Extension
14.	Synchronizer Key Spring	37.	Extension to Case Retaining Bolts and Washers
15.	1-2 Synchronizer Sleeve & Rev. Gear	38.	Rear Extension Bushing
16.	Snap Ring, Hub to Shaft	39.	Rear Seal
17.	First Gear	40.	Thrust Washer
18.	Thrust Washer	41.	Spacer
19.	Waved Washer	42.	Countergear Shaft Roller Bearings
20.	Ring Bearing	43.	Countergear
21.	Snap Ring, Bearing to Shaft	44.	Countergear Shaft Roller Bearings
22.	Speedometer Gear Clip	45.	Spacer
23.	Speedometer Drive Gear	46.	Thrust Washer

47.	Countergear Shaft
48.	Countergear Shaft Key
49.	Reverse Idler Shaft
50.	Idler Shaft Key
51.	Reverse Idler Gear
52.	Side Cover Gasket
53.	3-4 Shift Fork
54.	1-2 Shift Fork
55.	3-4 Shifter Shaft
56.	Retaining "E" Ring
57.	1-2 Shifter Shaft with "O" Rings
58.	Reverse Shifter Shaft
59.	3-4 Detent Cam
60.	Detent Cam Spring
61.	Reverse Detent Ball & Spring
62.	1-2 Detent Cam
63.	Shift Cover
64.	TCS Switch and Gasket
65.	Shifter Shaft Seal
66.	Shifter Shaft Seal
67.	Shift Cover Bolts and Washers
68.	Shift Cover Attaching Bolts and Lock Washers
69.	Damper Assembly

selected assembly and should be kept together as originally assembled, but the keys and springs may be replaced separately.

1. Mark hub and sleeve so they can be matched upon reassembly.
2. Push hub from sliding sleeve and remove keys and springs.
3. Install the three keys and two springs so all three keys are engaged by both springs. The tanged end of each spring should be installed into different key cavities on either side. Slide sleeve onto hub, aligning marks made before disassembly.

NOTE: A groove around the outside of the hub identifies the end that must be opposite the fork slot in the sleeve when assembled. This groove indicates the end of the hub with a .070″ greater recess depth.

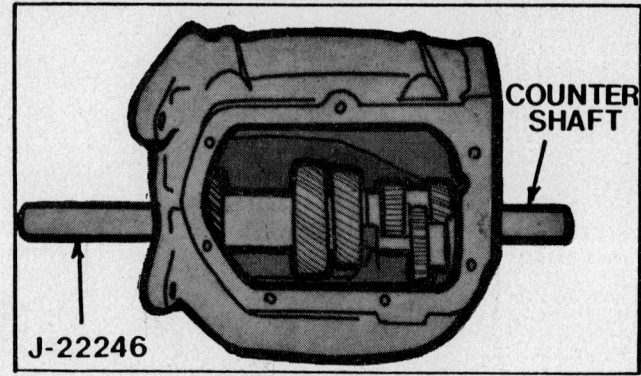

Fig. 6-4 Removing countershaft

Assemble Mainshaft

With front of mainshaft up:
1. Install 3rd speed gear with clutching teeth upward.
2. Install blocker ring with clutching teeth downward over cone of gear. All blocker rings in this unit are identical.
3. Install 3-4 synchronizer assembly with fork slot downward and press it onto mainshaft until it bottoms. *Be sure the notches of the blocker ring align with the keys of the synchronizer assembly.*
4. Install synchronizer hub to mainshaft snap ring. Both synchronizer snap rings are identical.

With rear of mainshaft upward:
5. Install 2nd speed gear with clutching teeth upward.
6. Install a blocker ring with clutching teeth downward over cone of gear.
7. Press 1-2 synchronizer assembly onto mainshaft with fork slot downward. *Be sure notches in blocker ring align with keys of synchronizer assembly.*
8. Install synchronizer hub snap ring.
9. Install a blocker ring with notches downward so they align with the synchronizer keys.

10. Install 1st gear with clutching teeth downward. Install 1st gear thrust washer and spring washer.
11. Press rear bearing onto mainshaft. Install snap ring.
12. Install speedometer drive gear and clip.

ASSEMBLE TRANS.

1. Load a row of roller bearings and a thrust washer at each end of the countergear. Use heavy grease to hold them in place.
2. Install countergear through case rear opening with a tanged thrust washer at each end and install countershaft and woodruff key from rear of case. *Be sure countershaft picks up both thrust washers and that the tangs are aligned with their notches in the case.*
3. Install reverse idler gear, shaft and woodruff key from rear of case.
4. Expand extension housing snap ring and assemble extension housing over mainshaft.

5. Load roller bearings into clutch gear bore, using heavy grease to hold them in place, place blocker ring on gear cone with teeth toward gear, and install gear and ring onto mainshaft. Do not install clutch gear bearing at this time. *Be sure notches in blocker ring align with synchronizer keys.*
6. Using new gasket, install mainshaft and extension assembly through rear opening in case. Use sealing cement on bottom bolt.
7. Install large outer snap ring on clutch gear bearing and install bearing onto gear and into case bore. Install gear stem snap ring and bearing retainer.

NOTE: The retainer oil hole should be at the bottom.

8. With transmission in neutral, install cover assembly. *Be sure the shift forks are properly aligned in their grooves in the synchronizer sleeves before attempting to tighten cover bolts.*

Fig. 6-5 Removing 3-4 synchronizer assembly

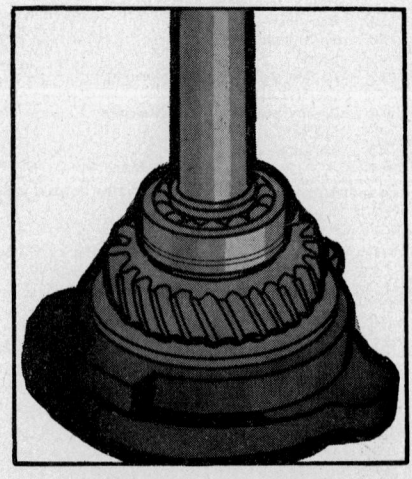

Fig. 6-6 Removing 1st gear and rear bearing

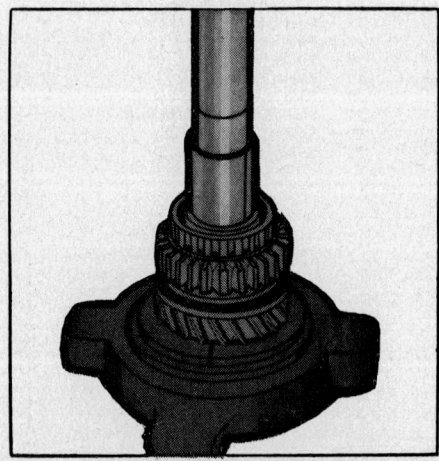

Fig. 6-7 Removing 1-2 synchronizer and 2nd speed gear

Type Seven

This section covers the English built unit which can be identified by having only 4 top cover bolts. The next section covers the German built unit which has 10 top cover bolts of 10 mm metric size.

DISASSEMBLE TRANS.

1. Remove clutch release bearing and lever from clutch housing.
2. Remove clutch housing to transmission bolts and remove housing.
3. Mount transmission in suitable holding fixture and remove top cover bolts.
4. Using a suitable tool, pry blanking plug from extension housing.
5. Using suitable punch, remove roll pin securing shift boss to rail. Be sure the pin can be punched through clear of any output shaft components. It may be necessary to position the synchronizer hub on the output shaft to suit.
6. Withdraw shift rail rearward, taking care not to let the shift boss and C-cam drop into case.
7. To remove shift forks, move 1st-2nd and 3rd-4th synchronizer hubs to their foremost position towards input shaft bearing.
8. Remove spring pin securing 3rd-4th shift fork to relay lever and remove fork.
9. Remove bolts securing extension housing to case.
10. Using a plastic faced mallet, tap the extension housing slightly rearward until it is possible to rotate it so countershaft aligns with cutaway in extension housing flange.
11. Tap countershaft rearward using a drift until it is just clear of front of case. Push countershaft out using a dummy countershaft. The countershaft gear will drop to bottom of case.
12. Remove extension housing and output shaft assembly. It is necessary to push 3rd-4th synchronizer sleeve forward to provide clearance between synchronizer and countershaft gear.

NOTE: Do not move synchronizer sleeve beyond 4th gear position or synchronizer inserts will fall out.

13. Unfasten bearing retainer from front of case and pry the oil seal from the retainer.
14. Remove needle bearing from recess in end of input shaft gear.
15. Remove outer snap ring from around input shaft bearing. Using a suitable drift, tap the outer race inward evenly until bearing is free of case. Lift assembly out of transmission.
16. Remove countershaft gear and two thrust washers from case. In both ends of gear there are 20 needle rollers retained by a washer on each

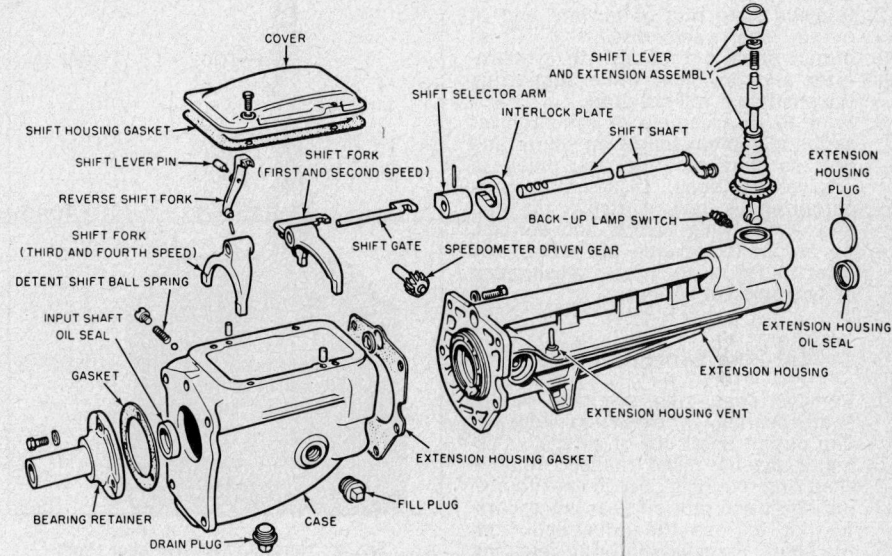

Fig. 1   Type 7 transmission case and related parts

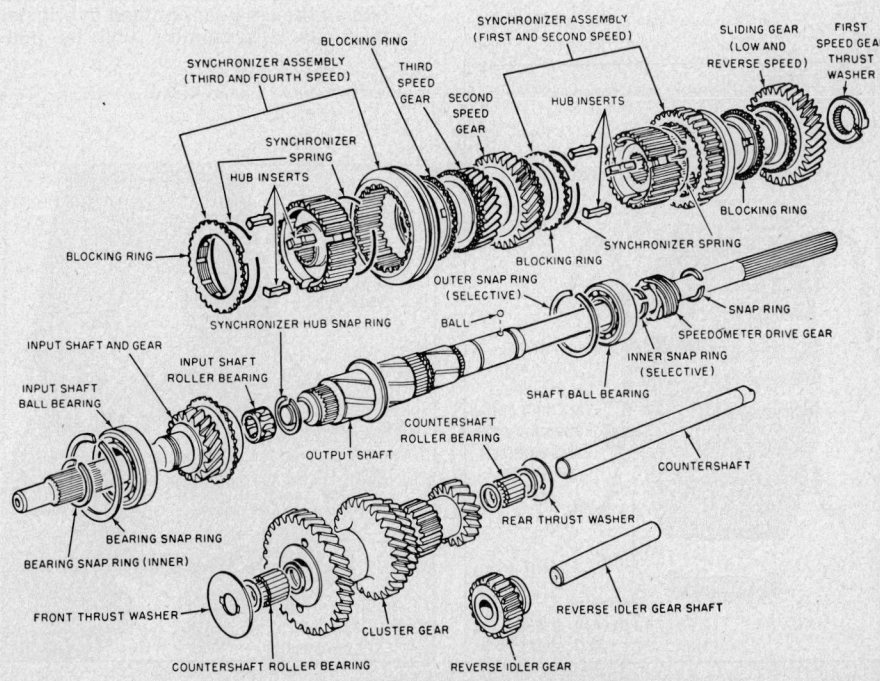

Fig. 2   Type 7 transmission internal parts

side of each set. Remove the rollers, washers and dummy shaft.

17. Withdraw reverse idler shaft, Fig. 3. Should these tools not be available, locate a nut, flat washer and a sleeve on a ⁵⁄₁₆" 24UNF threaded bolt. Screw bolt into reverse idler shaft and tighten nut to withdraw shaft.

18. Slide reverse relay lever from fulcrum pin on case. Do not remove pin.

3rd-4th Synchronizer

1. Lift 4th gear blocking ring from front of 3rd-4th synchronizer.
2. Remove snap ring at forward end of output shaft and discard it. Press output shaft out of 3rd-4th synchronizer and 3rd gear while supporting the shaft so it will not drop.
3. Prior to disassembly of synchronizer scribe alignment marks on sleeve and hub so they may be assembled in original positions. Disassemble synchronizer by pulling sleeve off hub and withdrawing inserts and springs.
4. To assemble, reverse procedure and refer to Fig. 4 for proper positioning of synchronizer springs.

1st-2nd Synchronizer

1. Remove snap ring securing output shaft bearing to extension housing. Tap output shaft out of extension using a plastic faced mallet. Remove snap ring retaining speedo gear to output shaft and pull off gear being careful not to lose the drive ball from the shaft. Remove snap ring retaining output shaft bearing.
2. Press low and reverse sliding gear, spacer, snap ring and output shaft bearing from the output shaft.
3. Remove snap ring securing 1st-2nd synchronizer to output shaft.
4. Press 2nd gear and 1st-2nd synchro-

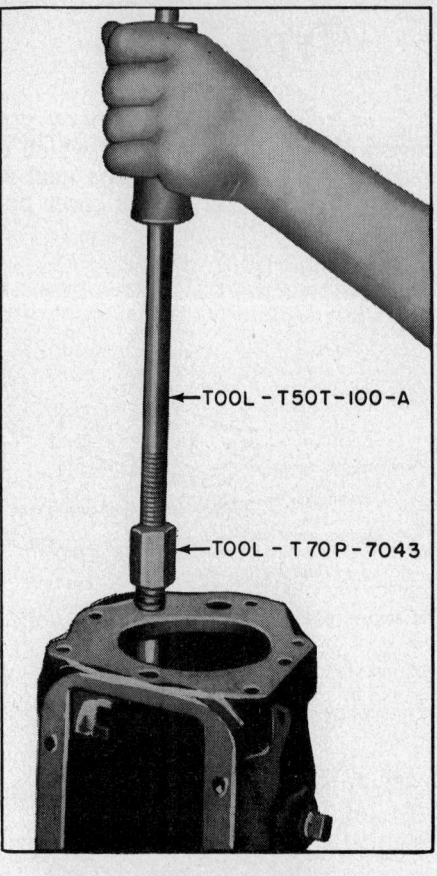

Fig. 3 Removing reverse idler shaft

nizer assembly complete with blocking rings off the output shaft.

5. Prior to disassembly of synchronizer, scribe alignment marks on sleeve and hub so they may assembled in original positions. Disassemble unit by pull-

ing sleeve off hub and withdrawing the inserts and springs.

6. To assemble, reverse the procedure and refer to Fig. 4 for proper positioning of synchronizer springs.

Output Shaft

1. When installing output shaft assembly into extension, place master spacer tool T70P-7154 in output shaft bearing bore of extension, Fig. 5.
2. Determine thickness of the snap ring required to remove all end play from the master gauge as follows:
   a. Measure width of shaft bearing outer race with micrometer. The difference in thickness between master gauge and bearing outer race will determine thickness of selective ring to be used.
   b. If bearing race thickness is more than that stamped on master gauge, the snap ring thickness must be decreased by that closest to available ring, Fig. 6.
   c. If the thickness is less, the snap ring thickness must be increased.
3. Position the selected snap ring and the bearing on the output shaft.
4. Position tool T71P-4621B on the shaft, then place assembly into press. Press the bearing into place, Fig. 7, and secure with the thickest snap ring that will fit the groove in the output shaft.
5. Locate drive ball in output shaft detent and push speedo gear onto shaft so it just clears the snap ring groove in the shaft. Install a new snap ring to shaft to retain the gear.
6. Heat the front end of the extension housing, using a suitable hot plate or by placing in hot water. This will expand the extension housing so that the shaft can easily be installed.

NOTE: Do not use a welding torch.

7. Secure the output shaft bearing in the extension housing with the snap ring selected previously.

Input Shaft and Gear

1. Remove snap ring from input shaft and discard snap ring.
2. The bearing should not be removed unless it is noisy, rough, spalled or cracked. Position input shaft bearing, Fig. 8, and press bearing off shaft.

HUB INSERTS
(FIRST AND SECOND SPEED)
(THIRD AND FOURTH SPEED)

SYNCHRONIZER SPRINGS

PART OF FIRST AND SECOND SPEED OR THIRD AND FOURTH SPEED SYNCHRONIZER ASSEMBLY

HUB INSERTS
(FIRST AND SECOND SPEED)
(THIRD AND FOURTH SPEED)

Fig. 4 Synchronizer spring rotation

SELECTIVE SNAP RING

TOOL 70P-7154

FEELER GAUGE

Fig. 5 Determining snap ring thickness

Part Number	Identification	Thickness
DORY-7030-A	Yellow	0.0726-0.0736
DORY-7030-B	Red	0.0715-0.0725
DORY-7030-C	Blue	0.0703-0.0713
DORY-7030-D	Violet	0.0691-0.0701
DORY-7030-E	Green	0.0679-0.0689
DORY-7030-F	Magenta	0.0677-0.0667
DORY-7030-G	Plain	0.0665-0.0655

Fig. 6 Output shaft bearing snap ring thickness chart

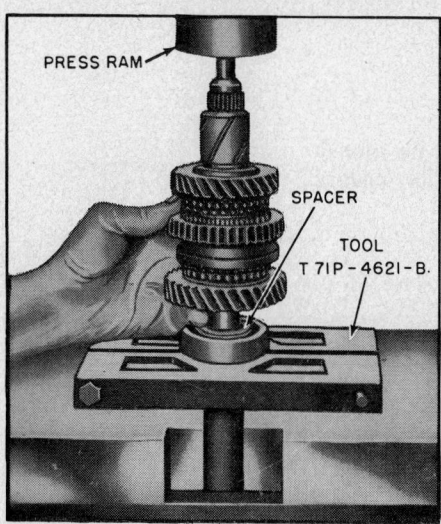

Fig. 7   Installing output shaft bearing

3. To assemble, press bearing on input shaft. The bearing must be placed on the shaft with the ring groove facing away from the gear. The tool used to replace the bearing insures that all the load is taken through the bearing inner race so the bearing will not be damaged in the pressing operation.
4. Install the thickest snap ring to secure the bearing to the shaft.

ASSEMBLE TRANS.

1. Slide reverse relay lever onto fulcrum pin on case.
2. Lubricate idler shaft and push it into case. Install reverse idler gear on shaft and locate reverse relay lever in groove in reverse idler gear.
3. Tap reverse idler shaft into position with copper mallet.
4. Slide dummy countershaft into countershaft gear. Install a retainer washer over dummy shaft and push it into the gear bore. Grease needle rollers and assemble 20 into the recess; install 2nd retaining washer and repeat procedure at other end of gear.
5. Grease thrust washers and locate them so their tab side seats into recess in case.
6. Position countershaft gear in bottom of case, taking care not to displace washers.
7. Assemble input shaft and gear into transmission. Using a copper drift on the bearing outer race, tap it into place until the snap ring groove appears on the outside of the case.

Take care that the dog teeth on the input shaft gear are not damaged by the countershaft gear.

NOTE: The bearing is an interference fit in the case, it is important that the outer race is tapped. Do not tap on input shaft gear as the bearing will be damaged.

8. Install snap ring to periphery of the bearing.
9. Lubricate input shaft needle bearing and position it in recess of input shaft gear.
10. Place a new oil seal on input shaft retainer and install so lips of seal face transmission. Drive seal into retainer until it bottoms.
11. Lubricate front bearing retainer seal and the seal journal area on input shaft. Place a new gasket on retainer. Fabricate a plastic sleeve and slide it over input shaft splines to prevent damage to seal lip. Be sure that oil groove in retainer is in line with oil passage in case and that gasket does not cover this passage. Coat attaching screws with suitable sealer and install them. Remove plastic sleeve. Apply a light film of grease to release bearing surface on bearing retainer.
12. Prior to installing output shaft and extension assembly, lubricate input shaft gear cone and position 4th gear blocking ring on input shaft gear cone.
13. If necessary, install a new seal in shaft rail aperture in rear of case and use a standard socket to drive in the seal.
14. Thread cord or suitable plastic covered wire under countershaft gear at each end to facilitate lifting into position later.
15. Install new gasket on extension using a sealer.
16. Slide extension and output shaft assembly into position after pulling the 3rd-4th synchronizer sleeve forward to clear countershaft gear.

NOTE: Do not move sleeve beyond 4th gear position as synchronizer inserts will drop out. Be sure 4th gear blocking ring locates correctly.

17. Align cutaway on extension housing with countershaft opening in rear face of transmission.
18. Carefully, with string or wire attached previously, lift countershaft gear into mesh with output shaft and input shaft gears. Take care that thrust washers in case at each end of gear are not displaced.
19. Check that countershaft gear bore aligns with apertures of countershaft. Push dummy shaft out of gear by in-

Fig. 8   Removing input shaft bearing

serting countershaft from rear. Finally, tap countershaft into position with suitable mallet. Be sure that lug on rear of countershaft is positioned horizontally so it will install into recess on extension housing flange. The front of the countershaft must be flush with front face of transmission case after installation.

20. Rotate extension so bolts align and push extension fully home onto the transmission. Secure housing to case using sealer on bolts.
21. Replace shift forks on relay lever and secure the 3rd and 4th fork to lever with new roll pin.
22. Position assembled shift forks on their synchronizer sleeves and move the synchronizer hubs into neutral position so that shift fork extension arms locate beneath the reverse idler shift arm mounted on side of case.
23. Grease shift rail oil seal in rear of case and slide the rail through the extension housing. Position the shift boss and the C-cam so that the cam locates the cutouts in the shift fork extension arms. Pass the rail through the boss and forks until the spring pin holes in the boss and rail align. Take care not to damage the shift rail seal.
24. Assemble detent ball and spring to their bore and install set screw using sealer.
25. Install roll pin to retain shift boss to shift rail.
26. Apply sealer to blanking plug and tap it into extension housing behind shift rail.
27. Using a new gasket and sealer, install top cover.
28. Remove transmission from holding fixture, install clutch housing, release lever and bearing. Refill with oil to proper level.

Type Eight

This section covers the German built unit which can be identified by having 10 top cover bolts. The previous section covers the English built unit which has only 4 top cover bolts.

DISASSEMBLE TRANS.

1. Remove clutch release bearing, lever and clutch housing.
2. Remove top cover bolts with 10mm wrench and drain lubricant.
3. Remove threaded plug, spring and shift rail detent plunger from case, Fig. 1.
4. Drive access plug from rear of case, Fig. 2, and drive the interlock plate retaining pin from case, Fig. 3. Lift interlock plate from case.
5. Remove roll pin from selector lever arm, Fig. 2.
6. Tap front end of shaft rail to displace plug at rear of extension housing.
7. Withdraw shift rail from extension and case, Fig. 4.
8. Lift selector arm and shift fork from case.
9. Remove extension housing bolts and tap extension housing with plastic mallet to loosen it from case so it may be rotated.
10. Rotate extension to align countershaft with cutaway in extension flange. Using a brass drift, drive countershaft rearward until it just clears front of case. Install a dummy shaft in the case and gear until the countershaft gear can be lowered to bottom of case, then remove the countershaft.
11. Lift extension housing and mainshaft from case as an assembly, Fig. 5.
12. Remove 10mm input shaft attaching bolts and remove the input shaft and bearing retainer from case as an assembly.
13. Remove reverse idler gear shaft from rear of case, Fig. 6. Remove reverse idler gear and on 74WT, 75WT and 78ET units, reverse idler gear spacer, Fig. 6A.
14. Remove countershaft bearing retaining washers, bearings (19 on each

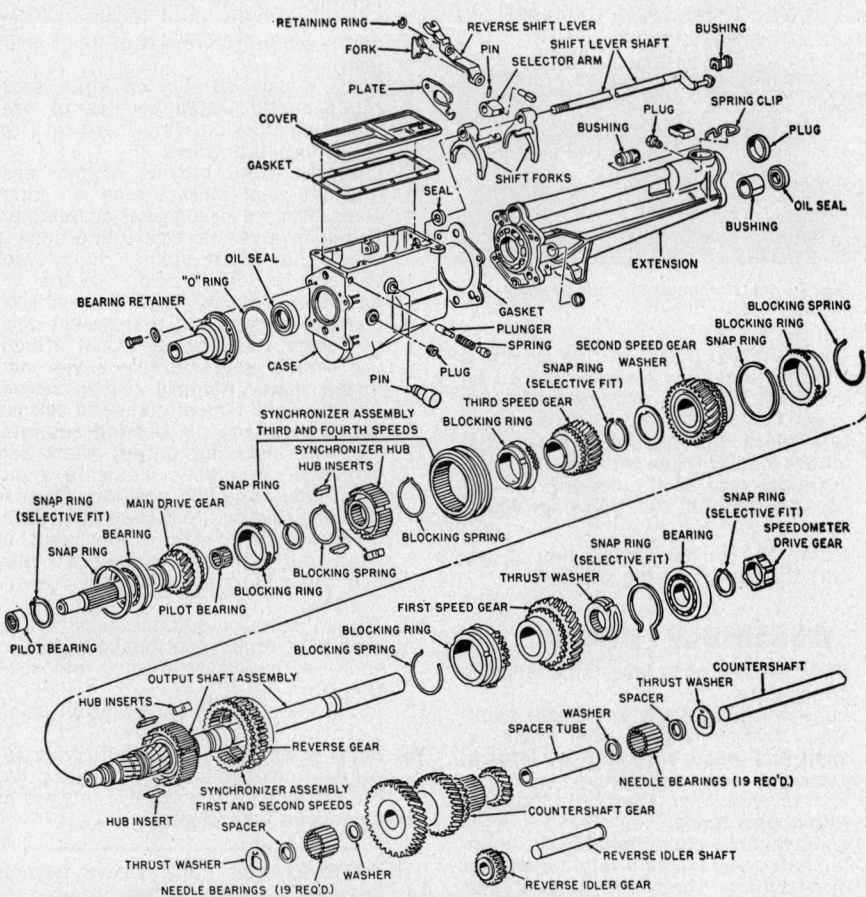

Exploded view of Type 8 transmission

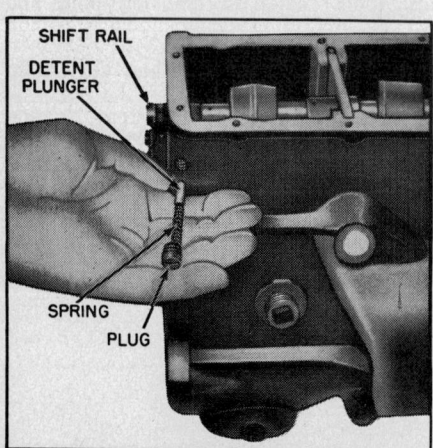

Fig. 1 Shift rail detent plunger

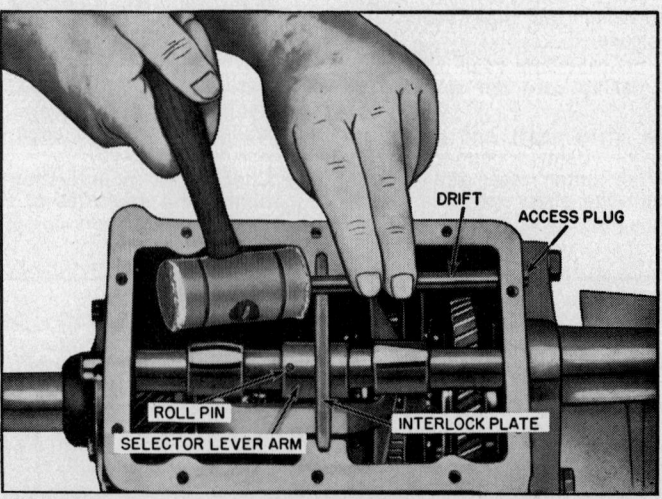

Fig. 2 Removing interlock plate access plug

end for 74WG transmissions and 21 for 74WT, 75WT & 78ET models), dummy shaft and spacer from countershaft gear, Fig. 7.

NOTE: 74WG, 75WT & 78ET transmissions have one thrust washer located at each end of the countershaft whereas, the 74WT transmissions have two thrust washers.

15. Remove bearing retainer and pilot bearing from input shaft gear.

NOTE: Do not remove the ball bearing from input shaft unless replacement is necessary. If so, remove snap ring from input shaft, Fig. 8, and press the shaft out of the bearing, Fig. 9.

16. Pry input shaft seal out of bearing retainer, Fig. 8.
17. Lift 4th gear blocker ring, Fig. 10, from front of output shaft.
18. Remove snap ring from forward end of output shaft and discard it.
19. Position tool T69P-4621A behind 3rd speed gear. Place output shaft and extension assembly in a press and press output shaft out of 3rd-4th synchronizer and the 3rd gear while supporting the extension housing and output shaft to prevent it from dropping.
20. Remove snap ring and washer, then slide 2nd gear and blocker ring off output shaft and discard snap ring.
21. Disassemble synchronizer assembly by pulling sleeve off hub and removing inserts and springs.
22. Remove snap ring that retains output shaft bearing in extension housing.
23. Tap output shaft assembly out of extension with a plastic hammer.
24. Position tool T69P-4621A behind 1st gear, then place assembly in press as shown in Fig. 11.
25. The 1st-2nd speed synchronizer and hub are serviced only as an assembly and no attempt should be made to separate the hub from the shaft. The sleeve, springs and inserts may be removed from the hub.

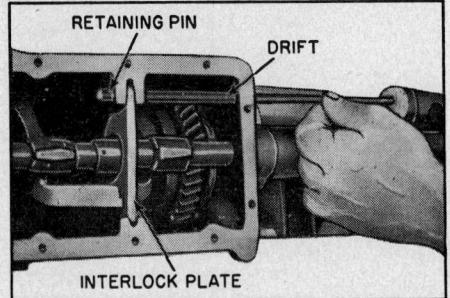

Fig. 3 Removing interlock plate retaining pin

26. Drive shift rail bushing from rear of extension with a ⁹/₁₆" socket and extension. Do not remove bushing if serviceable.
27. Pry shift rail seal from rear of transmission case.
28. Remove remaining linkage from case.

ASSEMBLE TRANS.

1. Seat new shift rail seal in rear of case, Fig. 12.
2. If shift rail bushing was removed, drive a new one into place with a ⁹/₁₆" socket and extension.
3. If 1st-2nd synchronizer was disassembled, slide the sleeve over the hub making sure the shift fork groove is toward front of shaft. The sleeve and hub are select fit and must be reassembled with etch marks in same lo-

cation. Locate an insert in each of three slots cut in the hub. Install insert spring inside the sleeve beneath the inserts. The tab on end of spring must locate in the section of an insert. Fit the other spring to the opposite face of the synchronizer unit, being sure the spring tab locates in the same insert as the spring just installed and is in the same rotational direction. Looking down at the synchronizer, the tab end of one spring should be in line with the tab of the spring on the opposite side.

NOTE: Oil all parts at time of assembly.

4. Assemble a blocker ring on the 1st gear side of the 1st-2nd synchronizer. Apply grease to the cone surface of the 1st gear. Slide 1st gear onto output shaft so that cone surface engages blocker ring.
5. Position spacer on shaft making certain the large diameter is toward rear of staff.
6. Place master spacer tool T70P-7154 in the output shaft bearing bore of the extension, Fig. 13. Determine thickness of snap ring required to remove all end play from master gauge. Then measure width of the output shaft bearing outer race with a micrometer. The difference in thickness between the master gauge and the bearing outer race will determine thickness of selective snap ring. If the bearing race thickness is more than that stamped on the master gauge, the snap ring thickness must be de-

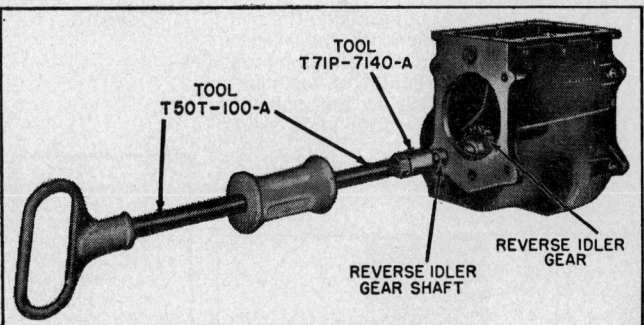

Fig. 6 Removing reverse idler gear shaft

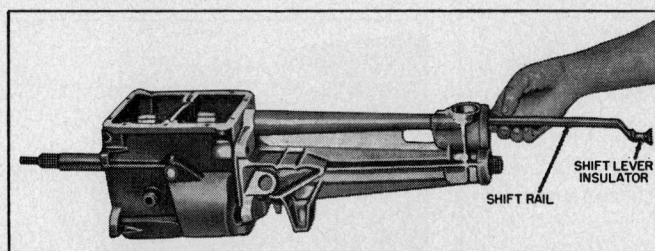

Fig. 4 Removing or installing shift rail

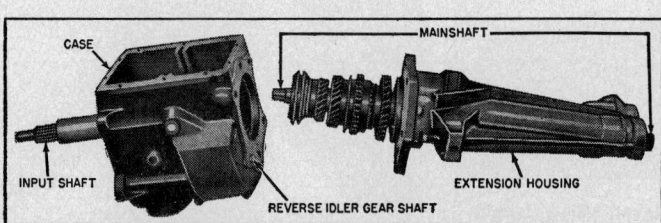

Fig. 5 Removing or installing extension and mainshaft

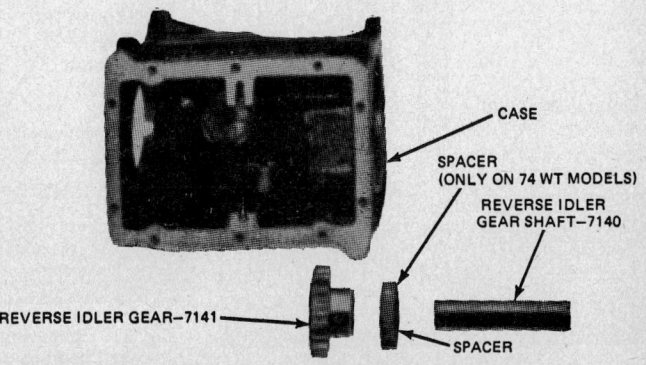

Fig. 6A Reverse idler gear spacer location

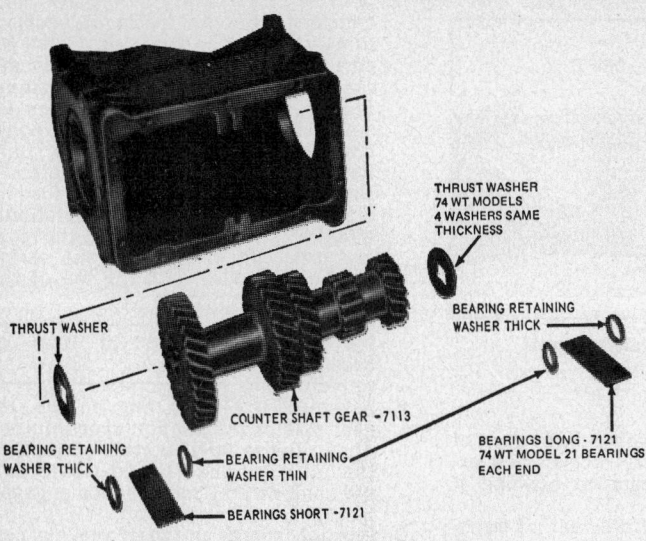

Fig. 7 Countershaft gear disassembled

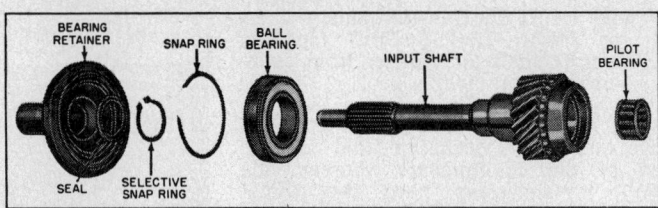

Fig. 8 Input shaft disassembled

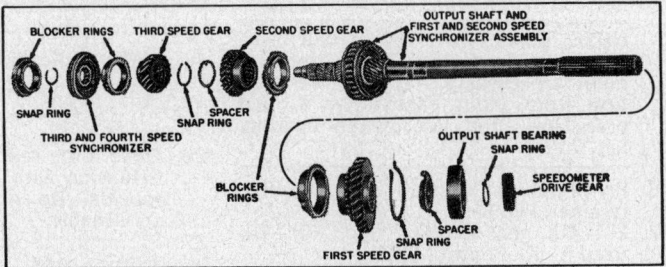

Fig. 10 Output shaft disassembled

creased to the closest available ring, Fig. 14. If the thickness is less, the snap ring thickness must be increased.

7. Position selected snap ring and the bearing on the output shaft. Position tool T69P-4621A on the shaft, then place assembly in a press and press bearing into place. Secure bearing with thickest snap ring that will fit the groove in the output shaft.

8. Slide the synchronizer sleeve over the hub and locate an insert in each of the three slots cut into sleeve. The sleeve and hub are select fit and must be reassembled with etch marks in same relative location.

9. Install an insert spring inside the synchronizer sleeve beneath the inserts. The tab on the end of the spring must locate in the U section of an insert. Fit the other spring to the opposite face of the synchronizer unit, being

sure that the spring tab locates in the same insert as the spring just installed and is in the same rotational direction. Looking down at the unit, the tab end of one spring should be in line with the tab of the spring on the opposite side.

10. Position the 2nd gear and blocker ring on output shaft so that dog teeth face rearward. Install washer and snap ring. Position 3rd gear on output shaft so dog teeth face forward. Apply grease to cones of the gears and assemble the blocker ring on the 3rd gear cone.

11. Position the 3rd-4th synchronizer on output shaft with the hub boss facing forward.

12. Position tool T69P-4621A so that it butts against the boss on the synchronizer hub.

13. Place entire unit, extension end up, in a press and push the synchronizer unit onto the output shaft as far as possible.

14. Retain the 3rd-4th synchronizer to output shaft with snap ring. Pull up on the synchronizer assembly so the snap ring is tight in its groove.

15. Prior to assembling output shaft and extension housing into the case, apply lubricant to the cone of the gear and place the 4th gear blocker ring on the input shaft gear cone.

16. Press the speedo gear onto the shaft with tools shown in Fig. 15, until dowels just contact bearing outer race.

NOTE: The dowels must contact the

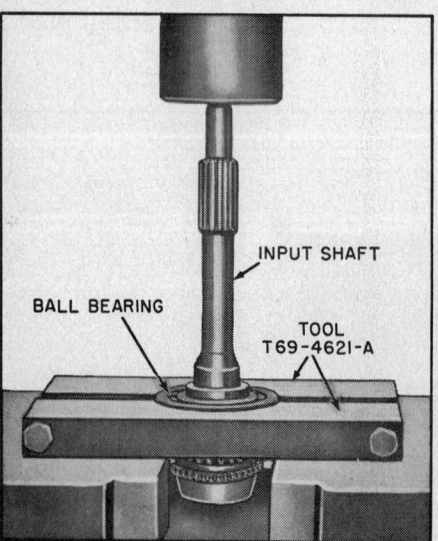

Fig. 9 Removing input shaft bearing

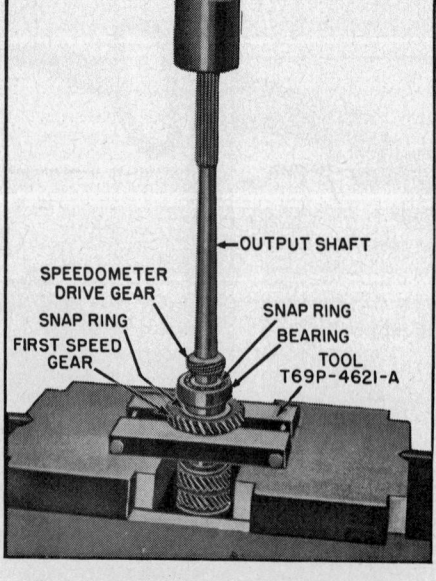

Fig. 11 Removing 1st gear, spacer, output shaft bearing, snap rings and speedo gear from output shaft

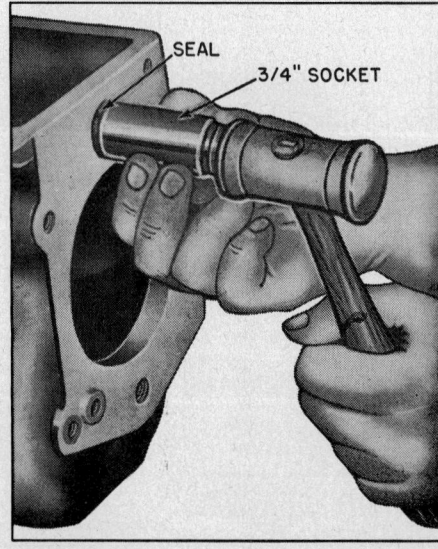

Fig. 12 Installing shift rail seal

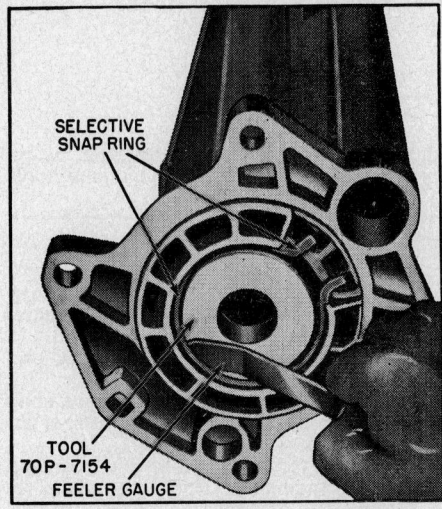

Fig. 13   Determining snap ring thickness

Part No.	Thickness	Identification
D1FZ-7030-A	0.0679-	Color Coded–Copper
D1FZ-7030-B	0.0689-	Letter–W
D1FZ-7030-C	0.0699-	Letter–V
D1FZ-7030-D	0.0709-	Letter–U
D1FZ-7030-E	0.0719-	None
D1FZ-7030-F	0.0728-	Color Coded–Blue
D1FZ-7030-G	0.0738-	Color Coded– Black
D1FZ-7030-H	0.0748-	Color Coded– Brown

Fig. 14   Output shaft bearing snap ring thickness chart

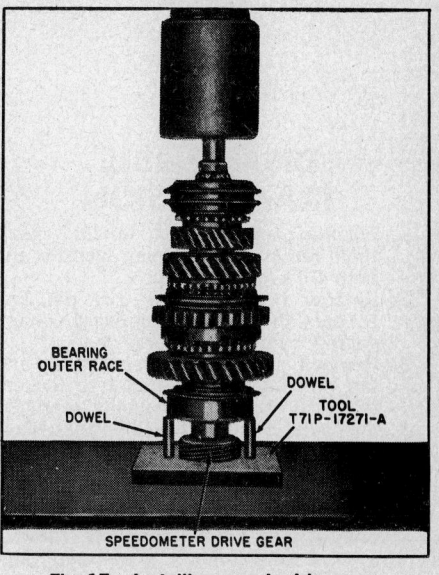

Fig. 15   Installing speedo drive gear

bearing outer race to properly locate the speedo gear on the shaft.

17. Coat the bearing bore of the extension housing with lubricant and install the output shaft in the housing. It may be necessary to tap the shaft with a plastic hammer while holding the two synchronizer sleeves firmly to prevent sleeve separation from the hubs. Secure it to the extension with the selective snap ring that was previously installed.

18. Press bearing on input shaft with snap ring groove toward front of shaft. Secure bearing to shaft with thickest selective snap ring.

19. Slide spacer and dummy shaft into countershaft gear. Position a thin bearing retaining washer at each end of dummy shaft. Coat the bearings with lubricant. Load long bearings into small end of countershaft gear and the short bearings into large end of gear. Note that the 74WG transmission has 19 bearings at each end and the 74WT, 75WT & 78ET transmissions, have 21 bearings at each end. Fit a thick retaining washer over each end of dummy shaft. Coat each thrust washer with lubricant and on 74WG, 75WT & 78ET models position one on each end of dummy shaft and on 74WT models, position two thrust washers on ends of dummy shaft. Make sure the tabs are in the same relative position so they may engage the slots in the case when the gear

is lowered into place. Loop a piece of rope or wire around each end of the gear. Carefully install the countershaft gear with rope through rear end of case being careful not to disturb thrust washers and making sure that the tabs engage slots in case.

20. Apply lubricant to reverse idler gear shaft. If selector lever relay was removed, position it on the pivot pin. Secure lever on pin with spring clip. Hold gear in the lever with long hub toward rear of case. Slide reverse idler gear shaft into place and seat the shaft in the case with a copper hammer.

21. Install a new seal in input shaft bearing retainer.

22. Assemble input shaft to case using a new retainer O ring, Fig. 16. If necessary, tap outer race of bearing with copper hammer evenly until outer snap ring is seated against case.

NOTE: Do not tap on input shaft as this may damage the races or bearings.

23. Carefully slide 3rd-4th speed synchronizer sleeve into 4th speed position (forward to provide clearance).

24. Position new gasket on extension housing.

25. Lubricate input shaft pilot bearing and install in shaft. Slide extension housing and output shaft into place being careful not to disturb 3rd-4th synchronizer.

26. Align cutaway in extension housing flange with countershaft bore in rear of case.

27. Lift countershaft gear into place with cord or wire, then slip countershaft into place making sure both thrust washers are in place. Make sure that the flat on the countershaft is toward top of case and in horizontal position, Fig. 17. Then tap it into case with brass hammer until front of shaft is flush with case.

28. Place shift forks in synchronizer sleeves. Position interlock lever and install new retaining pin. Lubricate shift rail oil seal and slide shift rail through extension housing, transmission case and the 1st and 2nd speed shift fork. Position selector arm on the rail, then slide the rail through the 3rd and 4th speed shift fork, then through the front of case until center detent is aligned with the detent plunger bore. Install new retaining pin in selector arm.

29. Install detent plunger, spring and plug with sealer.

30. Install new access plug in rear of case.

31. Rotate extension to align bolt holes, then install bolts loosely. Before tightening bolts make sure shift rail slides freely in bore.

32. Position new oil seal in input shaft retainer so tension spring and lip face the case. Drive seal into position.

33. Position new O ring in groove in face of case. Install input shaft bearing retainer to case. Be sure that oil passage in case is in line with oil groove in retainer, Fig. 16. Apply sealer to bolts and attach to case.

34. Reinstall clutch release bearing.

35. Apply sealer to new extension housing plug and install it.

36. Install top cover with vent toward rear. Make sure that sealer is applied to bolt over detent plunger bore.

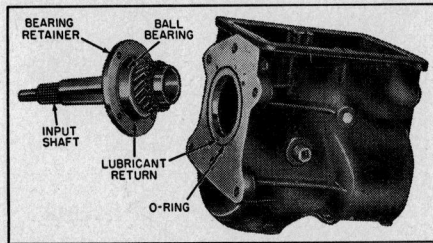

Fig. 16   Installing input shaft gear

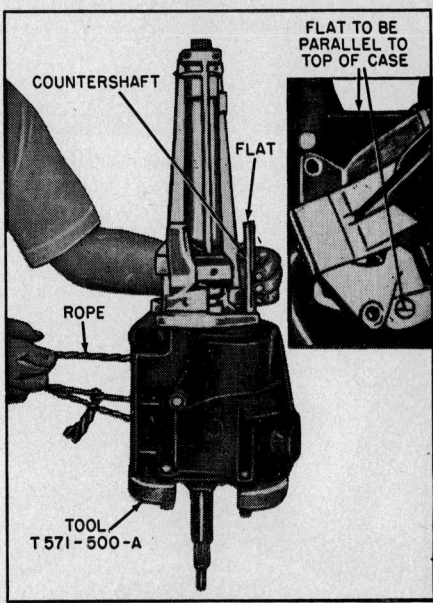

Fig. 17   Installing countershaft

Type Nine Warner

DISASSEMBLE TRANSMISSION

1. Position transmission in 2nd gear, then remove side cover, gasket and both shift forks. Fig. 1.
2. Remove reverse shifter lock pin, Fig. 2, pull shifter shaft outward, disengaging lever from reverse gear.
3. Remove extension housing bolts and tap housing with a mallet to loosen, then pull extension housing rearward until idler shaft clears idler gear. Turn housing to left thereby freeing reverse shift fork from collar and remove housing.
4. Remove snap ring, then slide speedometer gear from mainshaft, remove second speedometer gear snap ring. Fig. 3.
5. Remove reverse gear from mainshaft, then slide rear reverse idler gear from rear bearing retainer. Fig. 4.
6. Remove lock bolt from rear bearing retainer and drive locating pin from bearing retainer into case.
7. Rotate rear bearing retainer counterclockwise, providing access to rear of countershaft.
8. From front of case, using a dummy shaft, tap countershaft and key out the rear of case. Fig. 5.

9. Using a mallet, tap rear bearing retainer rearward, remove mainshaft through rear of transmission.
10. Remove bearing rollers and washer from main drive gear bore.
11. Remove front reverse idler gear and thrust washer from case.
12. Remove fourth gear synchronizing ring from main drive gear.
13. Remove main drive gear bearing retainer from case, remove snap ring and washer from main drive gear, then press gear from bearing, Fig. 6.
14. Tap drive gear bearing from case, remove countergear assembly and 2 washers, drive locating pin from case.

NOTE: It is not necessary to remove countershaft and main gear assemblies if only main drive gear bearing is to be replaced. This is accomplished by using tools J-22912 and J-8433-1. Fig. 7.

Disassemble Mainshaft

1. From rear of mainshaft, remove snap ring and slide rear bearing retainer from mainshaft. Fig. 8.
2. Remove rear bearing snap ring and washer.
3. From front of mainshaft, remove snap ring, then remove 3-4 synchronizer assembly and 3rd gear, Fig. 1.
4. Support forward face of 2nd gear and press mainshaft from rear then remove the rear bearing, thrust washer, 1st gear and bushing, 1-2 synchronizer and 2nd gear.

Disassemble Countergear

Remove dummy shaft, remove bearing rollers, spacers and tubular spacer, Fig. 9.

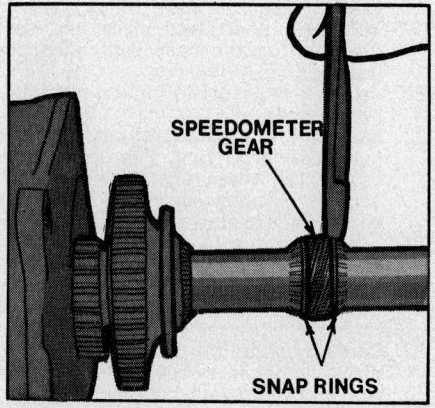

Fig. 3 Speedometer gear and snap rings

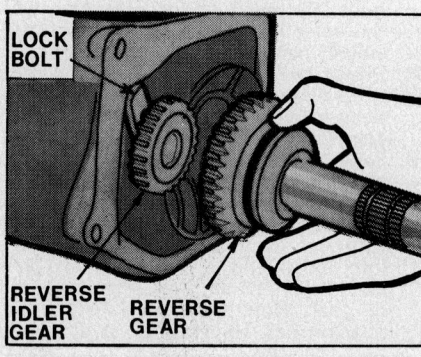

Fig. 4 Removing & installing reverse gear

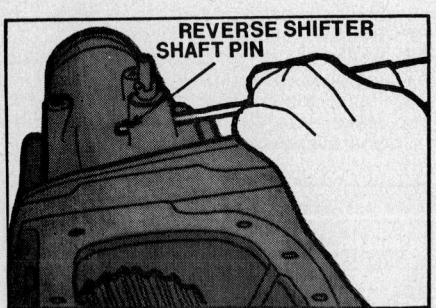

Fig. 2 Removing reverse shifter shaft lock pin

Fig. 5 Removing countershaft

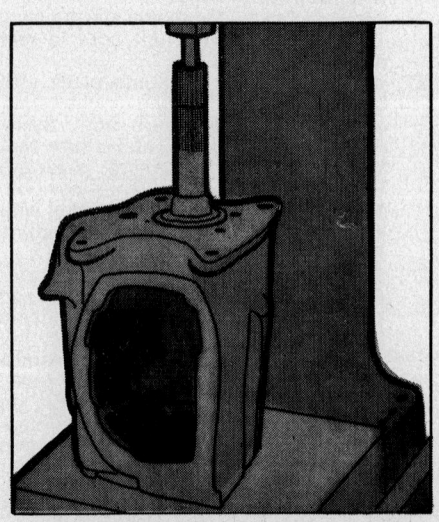

Fig. 6 Pressing drive gear from bearing

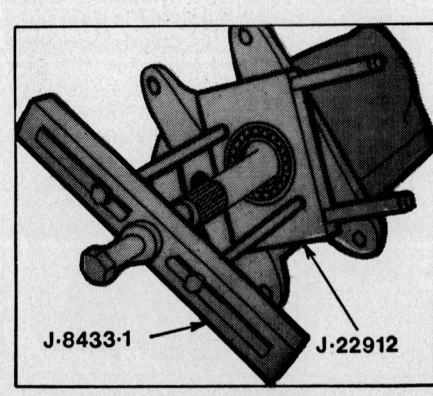

Fig. 7 Main drive gear bearing removal

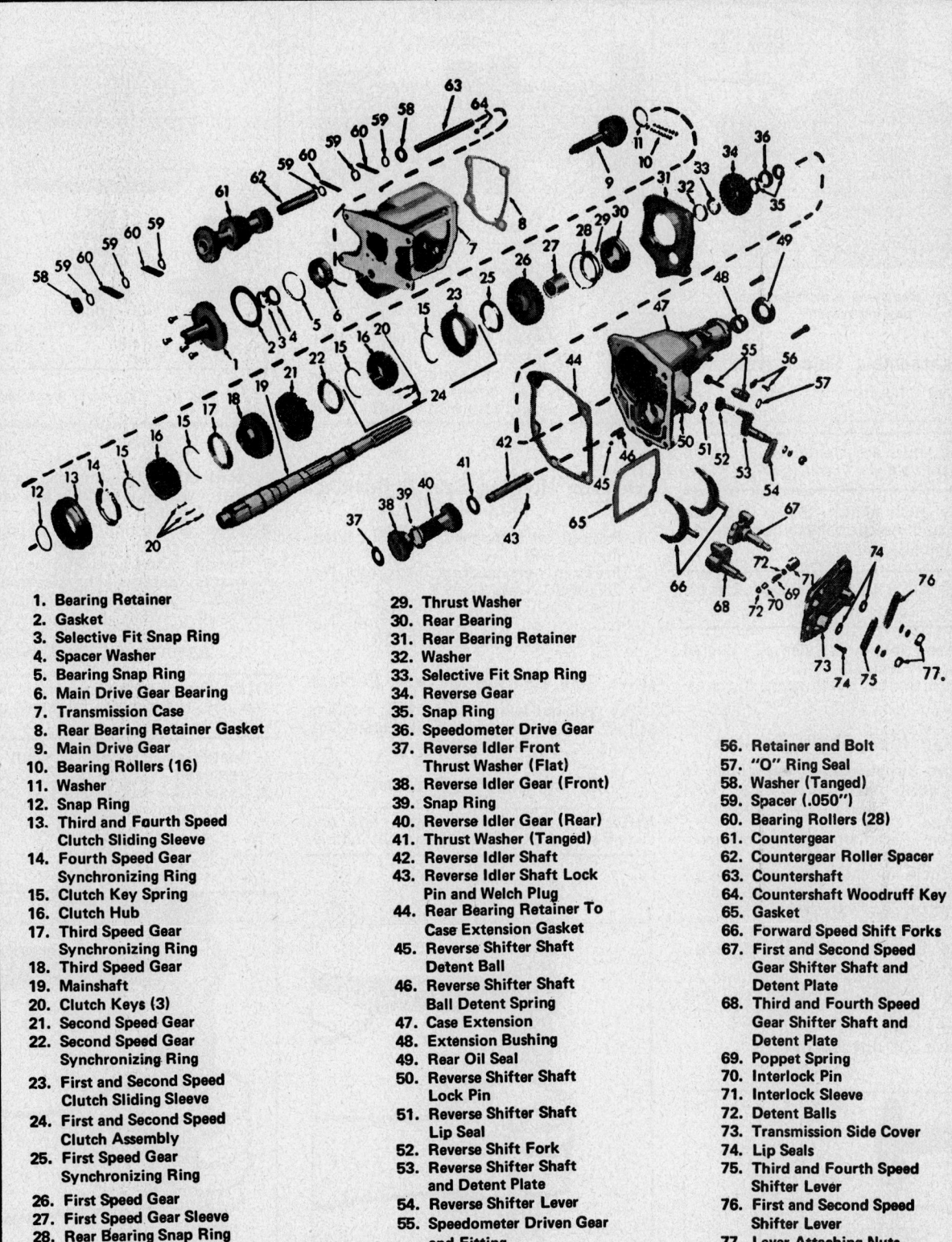

1. Bearing Retainer
2. Gasket
3. Selective Fit Snap Ring
4. Spacer Washer
5. Bearing Snap Ring
6. Main Drive Gear Bearing
7. Transmission Case
8. Rear Bearing Retainer Gasket
9. Main Drive Gear
10. Bearing Rollers (16)
11. Washer
12. Snap Ring
13. Third and Fourth Speed Clutch Sliding Sleeve
14. Fourth Speed Gear Synchronizing Ring
15. Clutch Key Spring
16. Clutch Hub
17. Third Speed Gear Synchronizing Ring
18. Third Speed Gear
19. Mainshaft
20. Clutch Keys (3)
21. Second Speed Gear
22. Second Speed Gear Synchronizing Ring
23. First and Second Speed Clutch Sliding Sleeve
24. First and Second Speed Clutch Assembly
25. First Speed Gear Synchronizing Ring
26. First Speed Gear
27. First Speed Gear Sleeve
28. Rear Bearing Snap Ring

29. Thrust Washer
30. Rear Bearing
31. Rear Bearing Retainer
32. Washer
33. Selective Fit Snap Ring
34. Reverse Gear
35. Snap Ring
36. Speedometer Drive Gear
37. Reverse Idler Front Thrust Washer (Flat)
38. Reverse Idler Gear (Front)
39. Snap Ring
40. Reverse Idler Gear (Rear)
41. Thrust Washer (Tanged)
42. Reverse Idler Shaft
43. Reverse Idler Shaft Lock Pin and Welch Plug
44. Rear Bearing Retainer To Case Extension Gasket
45. Reverse Shifter Shaft Detent Ball
46. Reverse Shifter Shaft Ball Detent Spring
47. Case Extension
48. Extension Bushing
49. Rear Oil Seal
50. Reverse Shifter Shaft Lock Pin
51. Reverse Shifter Shaft Lip Seal
52. Reverse Shift Fork
53. Reverse Shifter Shaft and Detent Plate
54. Reverse Shifter Lever
55. Speedometer Driven Gear and Fitting

56. Retainer and Bolt
57. "O" Ring Seal
58. Washer (Tanged)
59. Spacer (.050")
60. Bearing Rollers (28)
61. Countergear
62. Countergear Roller Spacer
63. Countershaft
64. Countershaft Woodruff Key
65. Gasket
66. Forward Speed Shift Forks
67. First and Second Speed Gear Shifter Shaft and Detent Plate
68. Third and Fourth Speed Gear Shifter Shaft and Detent Plate
69. Poppet Spring
70. Interlock Pin
71. Interlock Sleeve
72. Detent Balls
73. Transmission Side Cover
74. Lip Seals
75. Third and Fourth Speed Shifter Lever
76. First and Second Speed Shifter Lever
77. Lever Attaching Nuts

Fig. 1   Type 9 Warner four speed transmission

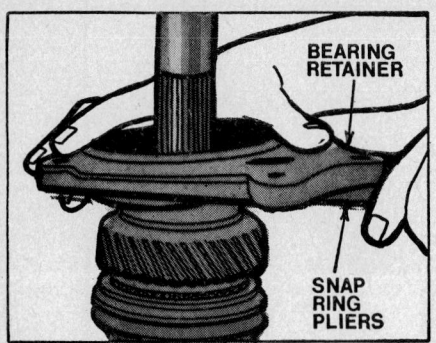

Fig. 8 Removing & installing rear bearing retainer

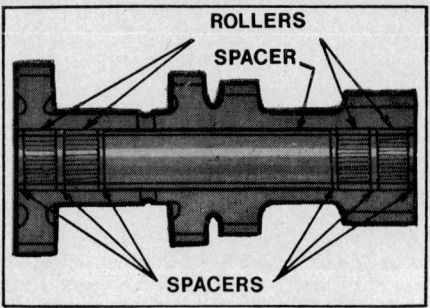

Fig. 9 Countergear assembly

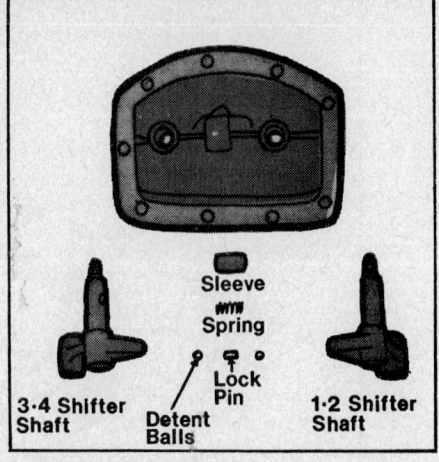

Fig. 10 Side cover assembly

Disassemble Side Cover

Remove forks from shifter shafts. Fig. 10.

NOTE: Forks are identical and are interchangable.

2. Slowly push shifter shafts into side cover until detent balls fall from cover, then remove shifter shafts.

NOTE: The 3-4 shifter shaft has a detent.

3. Remove interlock sleeve, poppet spring and lock pin.
4. Replace shifter shaft seals if necessary.

Reverse Idler Shaft, Replace

1. Remove thrust washer, use punch to drive welch plug and pin into idler shaft, Fig. 11, until idler shaft can be removed.
2. Position idler shaft in extension housing.
3. Align hole in shaft with hole in extension housing, drive in pin and install welch plug with sealer.

Reverse Shifter & Seal, Replace

1. Remove shifter fork, tap shaft into extension housing until detent ball falls from housing, then remove shaft and detent spring.
2. Remove "O" ring and discard.

3. Install detent spring, then position "O" ring on shaft.
4. Position ball on spring, then while pressing ball downward, slide shaft into place and rotate shaft until ball is seated.
5. Install shift fork.

Extension Housing Seal & Bushing, Replace

1. Pry out oil seal, then drive out bushing, Fig. 12.
2. Press in new bushing using tool No. J-21465-17 and J-8092.
3. Coat bushing and seal with transmission oil, then using tool No. J-21359 install oil seal. Fig. 13.

Drive Gear Bearing Oil Seal, Replace

Pry seal out with screw driver. Position seal in bore and tap in with flat plate, Fig. 14.

Synchronizers, Overhaul

NOTE: The synchronizer clutch hub and sliding sleeve are replaced as an assembly.

1. Mark clutch hub and sliding sleeve so they can be installed in the same position, Fig. 15.
2. Press clutch hub from sliding sleeve, remove clutch keys and springs.
3. Install clutch keys and springs, align marks, install sliding sleeve on clutch hub.

Assemble Side Cover

NOTE: When assembling transmission always use new gaskets, oil seals and snap rings.

1. Install seals in shifter shaft bores, if removed.
2. Install 3-4 shifter shaft in bore, position in neutral, then install detent ball,

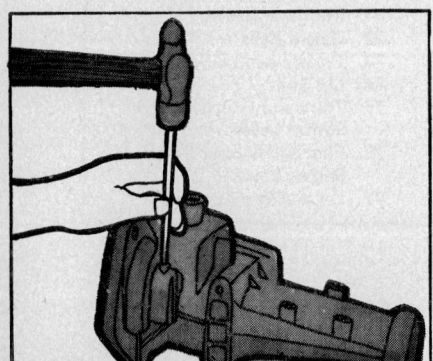

Fig. 11 Removing roll pin from reverse idler shaft

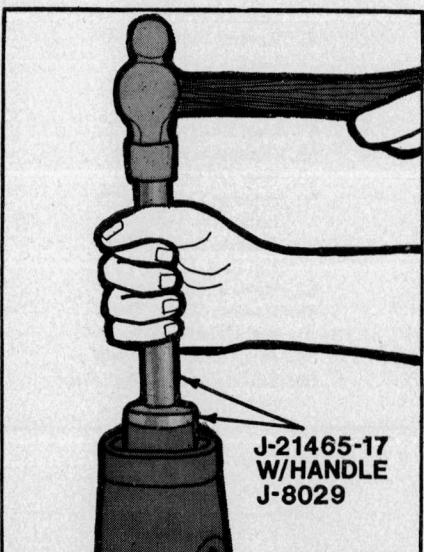

J-21465-17 W/HANDLE J-8029

Fig. 12 Removing & installing extension housing bushing

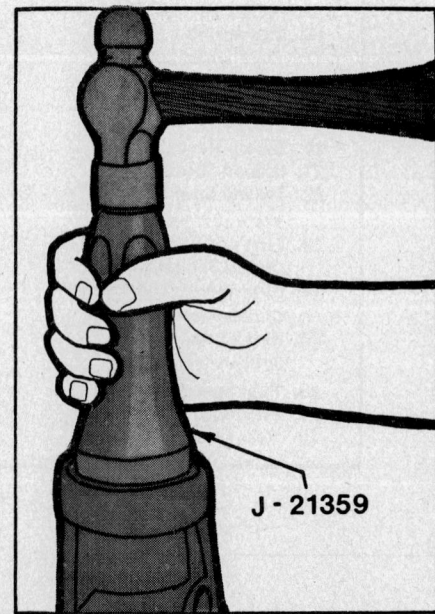

J-21359

Fig. 13 Installing extension housing oil seal

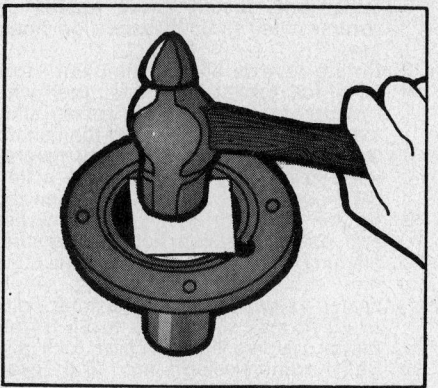

Fig. 14   Installing drive gear bearing retainer oil seal

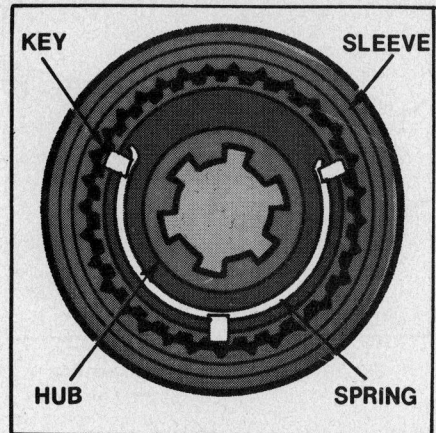

KEY   SLEEVE

HUB   SPRING

Fig. 15   Synchronizer assembly

Fig. 16   Countergear end play check

interlock sleeve, poppet spring and lock pin, Fig. 10.
3. Position detent ball in other end of interlock sleeve, depress ball and install 1-2 shifter shaft.
4. Position 1-2 shifter shaft in 2nd gear and install shift forks.

Countergear Assemble & Install

1. Position dummy shaft in countergear bore and install tubular spacer.
2. Install spacer in bore, then using heavy grease to hold rollers in place install 28 rollers. Fig. 9.
3. Install second spacer, then install 28 additional rollers and install third spacer.
4. Install rollers and spacers in other end of countergear using above procedure.
5. Install thrust washers in each end of transmission case with tangs inserted in case recesses, use grease to hold washers in place.
6. Insert countershaft through rear of case, in turn forcing dummy shaft

out through front of case. Install woodruff key on countershaft, tap countershaft until flush with rear of case.

Countergear End Play Check

Attach dial indicator, Fig. 16, check end play. If end play is greater than .025 in. new selective thrust washers must be installed.

Assemble Mainshaft

1. From rear of mainshaft, install 2nd gear with hub facing rearward.
2. Position sychronizing rings on 1-2 synchronizer, then install synchronizer on mainshaft with hub facing forward.
3. Press 1st gear bushing on mainshaft until 2nd gear, 1-2 synchronizer and bushing are against mainshaft shoulder, Fig. 17.
4. Install 1st gear and inner race with gear hub facing front, then press rear bearing on mainshaft with snap ring groove facing front. Fig. 18.
5. Install spacer and selective thickness snap ring.

NOTE: Use the thickest snap ring that will fit in mainshaft groove.

6. Install 3rd gear with hub facing front and the 3rd gear synchronizing ring with notches facing front.
7. Install 3rd and 4th gear clutch assembly with the taper facing front.

NOTE: Ensure that keys in hub mate with notches in 3rd gear synchronizing ring.

8. Install selective thickness snap ring, use thickness snap ring that will fit mainshaft groove.
9. Install locating pin in rear bearing retainer, then place bearing retainer over rear of mainshaft, spread retainer snap ring and align with groove in rear bearing. Fig. 18.
10. Using heavy grease, install 16 rollers and washer into bore of main drive gear, Fig. 19.
11. Position 4th gear synchronizer ring on 3-4 synchronizer, aligning ring notches with hub keys.
12. Install front drive gear on main shaft.

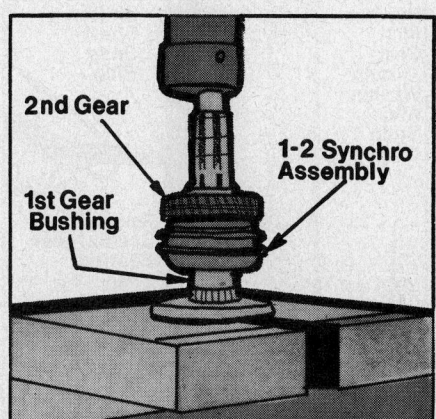

2nd Gear

1-2 Synchro Assembly

1st Gear Bushing

Fig. 17   Installing 2nd gear, 1-2 synchronizer assembly & 1st gear bushing

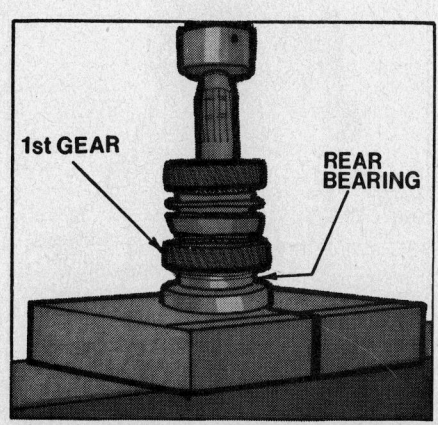

1st GEAR   REAR BEARING

Fig. 18   Installing 1st gear & rear bearing

MAIN DRIVE GEAR

Fig. 19   Installing main drive gear bearing rollers

ASSEMBLE TRANSMISSION

1. Install drain plug in transmission case.
2. Install thrust washer and front section of reverse idler gear with hub facing rear and position gasket on rear of transmission case.
3. Position synchronizers in neutral and install mainshaft in case. Install retainer locating pin and torque retainer lock bolt to 25 ft. lbs.
4. Tap main drive gear bearing into case using suitable tool, pull drive gear shaft forward, and tap bearing again until bearing bottoms on main drive gear and the washer and snap ring can be installed on main gear drive shaft, Fig. 20.
5. Install main drive gear bearing retainer and gasket, apply sealer to bolts and torque to 18 ft. lbs.
6. Install rear reverse idler gear, engaging splines with front section.

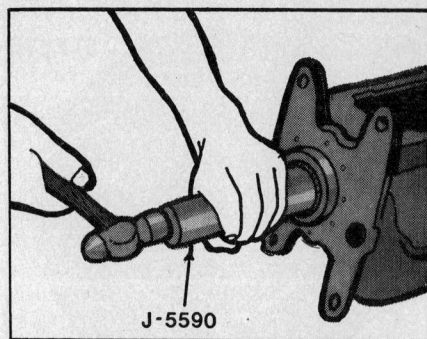

Fig. 20   Installing drive gear bearing

7. Install reverse sliding gear with hub facing rear, Fig. 4, then install the speedometer gear and two snap rings on mainshaft. Fig. 3.
8. Position gasket on rear bearing re-tainer and, install thrust washer on reverse idler shaft in extension housing.
9. Rotate reverse shifter shaft until fork is in full forward position, then with synchronizer sleeves in neutral, slide extension housing over mainshaft. Guide reverse idler shaft into reverse idler gears, engaging fork on collar, then position shifter shaft in neutral.
10. Rotate reverse shifter shaft clockwise and push extension housing forward, aligning rear bearing retainer locating pin with extension housing. Apply sealer to bolts and torque long bolts to 40 ft. lbs., short bolts to 25 ft. lbs.
11. Install reverse shifter shaft lock pin.
12. Shift transmission into 2nd gear. The front synchronizer sleeve should be in neutral and the rear sleeve in forward position to engage 2nd gear synchronizer teeth.
13. Position slide cover and gasket to transmission case and index shift forks to shift collars, then install and torque side cover bolts to 18 ft. lbs.

Type Ten

DISASSEMBLE TRANS.
Fig. 1

1. With transmission in a vertical position, drive roll pin out and remove shifter shaft lever assembly, Fig. 1A.
2. Using tools J-25295 and J-2619-01, remove reverse shifter shaft cover, shifter shaft detent cap, spring and ball and interlock lock pin, Fig. 2.
3. Remove extension housing retaining bolts and remove extension housing, then press down on speedometer gear retainer and remove gear and retainer from mainshaft.
4. Remove shifter shaft snap rings, Fig.

3, then using a pair of pliers, pull exposed end of reverse shifter shaft outward to disengage reverse lever from idler shaft. Remove idler shaft with gear attached.
5. Remove reverse gear and reverse countergear snap rings, Fig. 3, and remove gears.
6. With transmission in a horizontal position, remove clutch gear bearing retainer bolts, retainer and gasket, then remove snap ring retaining clutch gear ball bearing to housing, Fig. 4, and remove the bellhousing retaining bolts.
7. With transmission in a vertical position, expand snap ring in mainshaft bearing opening and remove case by lifting it off mainshaft. Assure that mainshaft, countergear and shifter shaft assemblies remain with bell-housing.

NOTE: It may be necessary to tap case with a plastic hammer to remove it.

8. As an assembly, remove from the bell-housing, the mainshaft with the shifter forks attached and the counter-gear meshed with gear teeth in the mainshaft.

Fig. 1A   Replacing roll pin

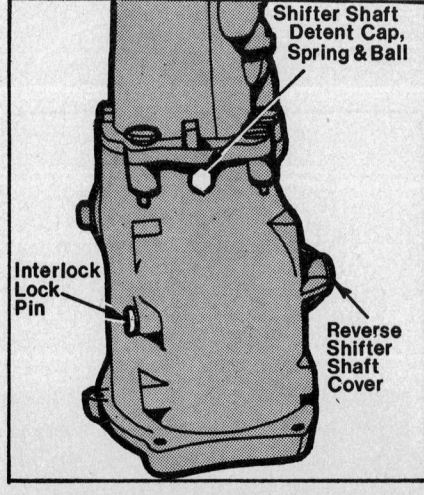

Fig. 2   Cover, cap, spring, ball and interlock pin removal

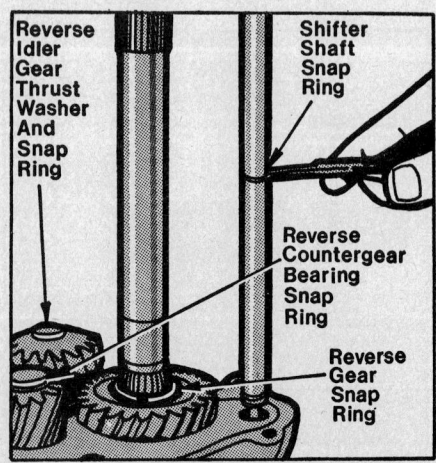

Fig. 3   Replacing snap rings

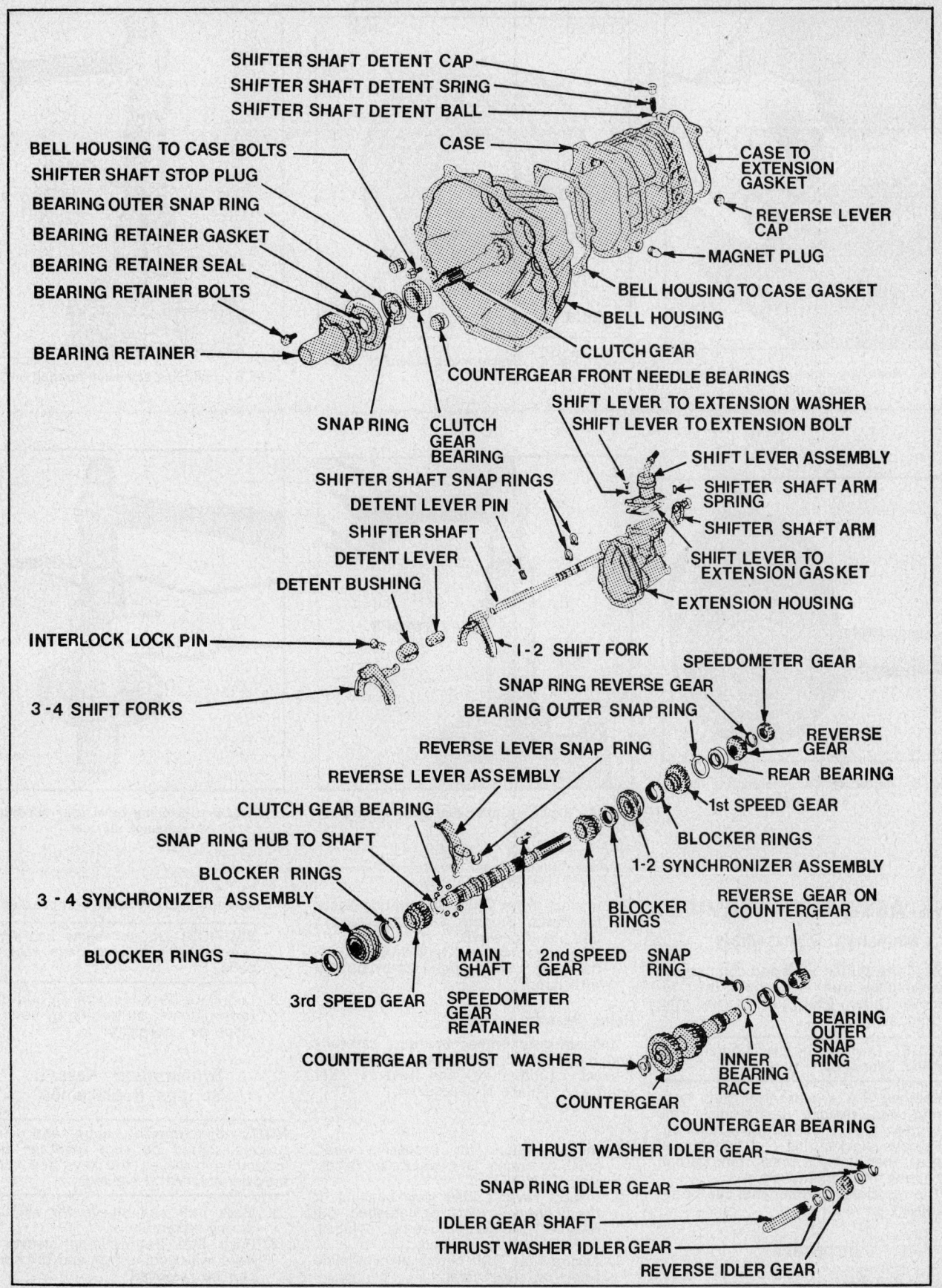

Fig. 1   Type 10 Four Speed Transmission

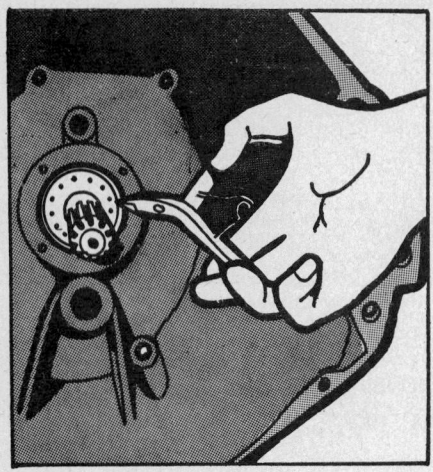

Fig. 4   Replacing clutch gear ball bearing snap ring

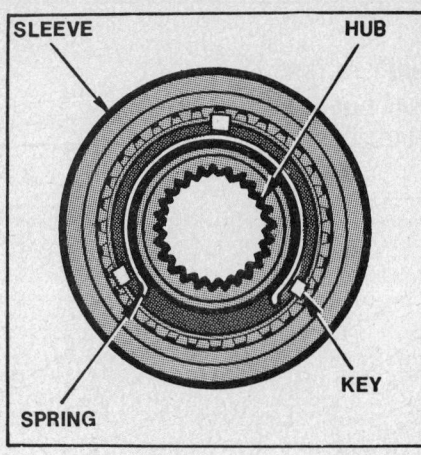

Fig. 6   Synchronizer assembly

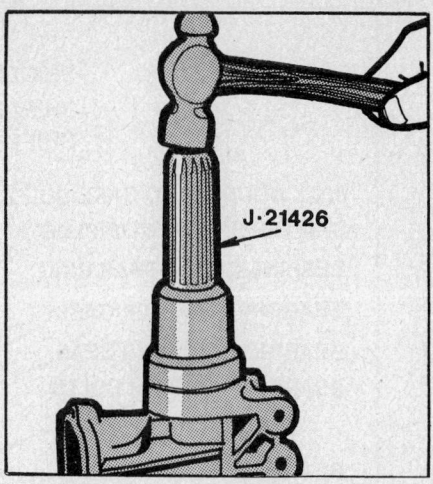

Fig. 8   Installing extension housing oil seal

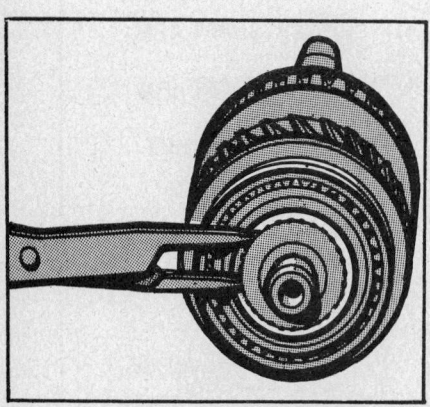

Fig. 5   Replacing 3-4 synchronizer hub snap ring

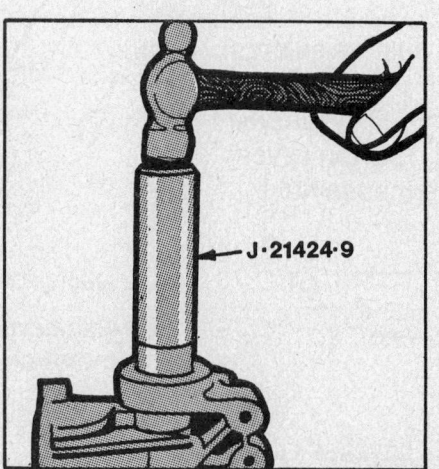

Fig. 7   Replacing extension housing bushing

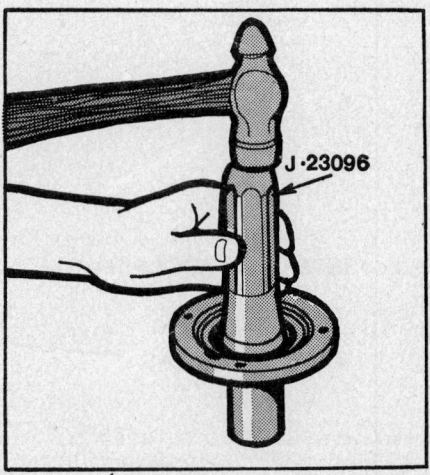

Fig. 9   Installing drive gear bearing retainer oil seal

SUB-ASSEMBLY SERVICE

Mainshaft Disassembly

1. Separate shifter shaft and countergear assemblies from mainshaft, then remove clutch gear and blocker ring from mainshaft.

   NOTE: The clutch gear contains 15 roller bearings.

2. Remove 3-4 synchronizer hub snap ring and remove synchronizer assembly, Fig. 5. Use press if required.
3. Remove blocker ring and third speed gear, then using a press, remove ball bearing from mainshaft.
4. The remaining components can be removed as required.

Inspection

Transmission Case

1. Thoroughly clean transmission case and inspect for cracks.

2. Inspect front and rear mating faces for burrs. Smooth surfaces using a fine file, if needed.
3. Clean bearings and lubricate with oil, then inspect for roughness by turning with hand.

Roller Bearing & Shafts

Inspect countergear bearings carefully and replace if signs of wear are evident. Inspect countershaft and reverse idler shaft and replace if necessary.

Gears

1. Inspect gears for excessive wear, chips or cracks and replace as necessary.
2. Inspect reverse idler gear bushing. If the bushing is worn or damaged, the reverse idler gear must be replaced, as it cannot be serviced.
3. Assure that both clutch sleeves slide freely on their hubs.

Front & Rear Bearings

1. Thoroughly clean bearings in clean solvent and dry with compressed air.

CAUTION: Do not allow bearings to spin as this will damage race and balls.

2. Lubricate bearings with oil and check for roughness by turning by hand. Replace as necessary.

Synchronizer Keys & Springs Replacement

NOTE: Synchronizer hubs and sliding sleeves should be kept together as an assembly, however, the keys and springs may be replaced, if needed.

1. Mark hub and sleeve for alignment during assembly.
2. Push hub from sliding sleeve. The keys will become free and the springs can be removed.
3. Position the two springs so that all three keys are engaged by both springs, Fig. 6.

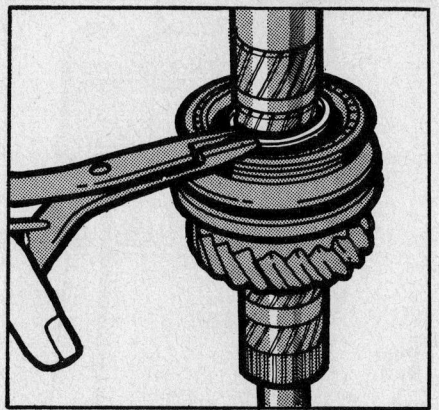

Fig. 10   Installing 1-2 synchronizer hub snap ring

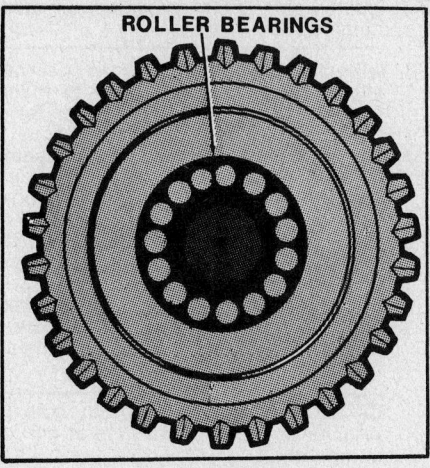

ROLLER BEARINGS

Fig. 12   Roller bearings installed in clutch gear

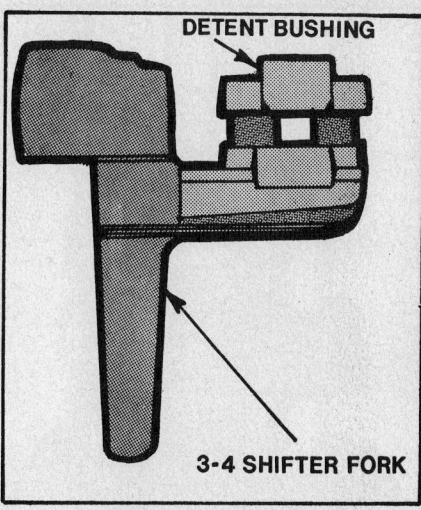

DETENT BUSHING

3-4 SHIFTER FORK

Fig. 14   Assembling detent bushing to 3-4 shifter fork

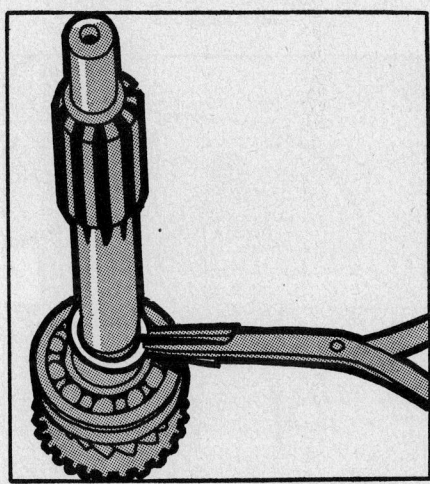

Fig. 11   Installing clutch gear ball bearing snap ring

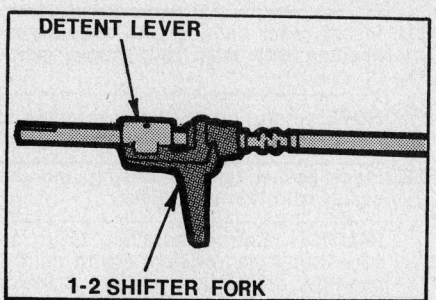

DETENT LEVER

1-2 SHIFTER FORK

Fig. 13   Engaging detent lever to 1-2 shifter fork

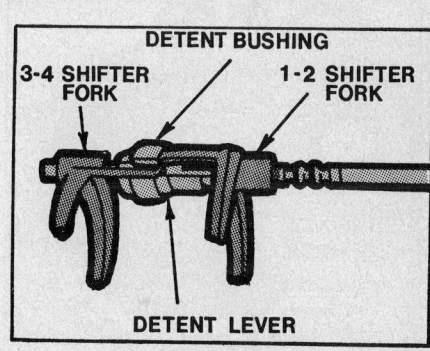

DETENT BUSHING

3-4 SHIFTER FORK   1-2 SHIFTER FORK

DETENT LEVER

Fig. 15   Assembling 1-2 and 3-4 shifter forks on shifter shaft

4. Position keys and hold in place, then slide sleeve onto hub aligning marks made during disassembly.

Extension Oil Seal & Bushing Replacement

1. Pry oil seal from extension.
2. Using tools J-21524-9 and J-8092, drive bushing out of extension housing, then using same tools, drive bushing into housing, Fig. 7.
3. Coat inside diameter of bushing and seal with transmission lubricant, then using tool J-21426, install new seal, Fig. 8.

Drive Gear Bearing Retainer Oil Seal Replacement

1. Pry out seal from retainer.
2. Position new seal into retainer, then using tool J-23096, drive seal until tool bottoms in bore. Lubricate inside diameter of seal, Fig. 9.

Mainshaft Assemble

1. With rear of mainshaft facing upward, install the second speed gear with clutching teeth upward. The rear face of gear will butt against flange of mainshaft.
2. Install blocker rings with clutching teeth downward over synchronizing surface of second speed gear.

NOTE: All blocker rings are identical.

3. Install first and second synchronizer assembly with fork slot downward and press it on the mainshaft splines until it bottoms.

NOTE: Both synchronizers are identical.

CAUTION: Assure that notches of blocker ring align with keys of synchronizer assembly.

4. Install 1-2 synchronizer hub to mainshaft snap ring, Fig. 10, then install blocker ring with notches downward, so that they are aligned with keys of first and second synchronizer assembly.
5. Install first speed gear with clutching teeth downward, then install rear ball bearing with snap ring groove downward and press onto shaft.

NOTE: The bearing used on the mainshaft is shielded and the one used on the clutch gear is not. These bearings should not be intermixed.

6. With front of mainshaft facing upward, install third speed gear with clutching teeth upward. The front face of gear will butt against mainshaft flange.
7. Install blocker ring with clutching teeth downward over synchronizer surface of third speed gear, then install third and fourth synchronizer assembly with fork slot facing downward.

CAUTION: Assure that notches of blocker ring align with keys of synchronizer assembly.

8. Install 3-4 synchronizer hub to mainshaft snap ring, Fig. 5, and install blocker ring with notches downward so they align with keys of the 3-4 synchronizer.

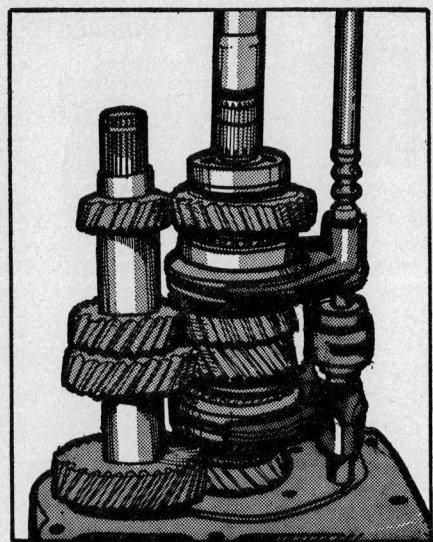

Fig. 16 Shifter shaft, mainshaft gears and countergear meshed and installed on bellhousing

Fig. 17 Reverse lever installation

ASSEMBLE TRANS.

1. Press shielded ball bearing onto clutch gear shaft with snap ring groove facing up, then install snap ring on clutch gear hub, Fig. 11.
2. Load the 15 pilot roller bearings into clutch gear cavity, Fig. 12. Use heavy grease to retain them in place.
3. Install clutch gear to mainshaft, then install detent lever to shifter shaft with roll pin and slide 1-2 shifter fork on shaft so its arm engages detent lever, Fig. 13.
4. Assemble 3-4 shifter fork onto detent bushing, Fig. 14, then slide assembly onto shifter shaft, with 3-4 shifter fork arm located below the 1-2 shifter fork arm, Fig. 15.
5. Place bellhousing on wooden blocks, place a thrust washer over hole for countergear shaft.

NOTE: Assure that thrust washers are

located in holes provided in bell-housing.

6. With both synchronizers in neutral, align shifter shaft assembly to mainshaft assembly, indexing shifter forks into synchronizer sleeve grooves.
7. Mesh countergears with mainshaft gears and install countergear, mainshaft and shifter shaft onto bellhousing as a complete assembly, Fig. 16.
8. With bellhousing positioned on its side, install snap ring onto ball bearing on clutch gear, Fig. 4.
9. Install gasket and bearing retainer onto bellhousing. Use sealer on the 4 retaining bolts. Reposition bellhousing on wooden blocks.

CAUTION: Assure that drain hole in retainer is aligned with hole at end of countershaft.

10. If removed, install reverse lever into case and install snap ring, Fig. 17.

NOTE: When reverse lever is installed, screwdriver slot should be parallel with front of case.

11. Install roller bearing into countergear opening with snap ring groove inside of case.

NOTE: Snap ring will be assembled to roller bearing.

12. Place gasket on bellhousing and use sealer to retain it in place.

CAUTION: Before installing case, assure that synchronizers are in neutral position, detent bushing slot is facing outward and reverse lever is flush with inside wall of case.

13. While installing case over mainshaft, countergear and shifter shaft, expand snap ring in mainshaft bearing and allow snap ring to pilot over mainshaft.

NOTE: It may be necessary to tap case using a plastic hammer to aid assembly.

14. Install interlock pin to hold detent bushing in place on shifter shaft, Fig. 2, then install idler shaft so that it engages reverse lever within case.
15. Install cover over reverse shifter shaft to retain reverse lever in place, then install detent ball, spring and cap, Fig. 2.
16. Install large reverse gear with chamfer on gear teeth upward, then push reverse gear onto mainshaft splines and retain with snap ring, Fig. 3.
17. Install small reverse gear with chamfer on gear teeth upward onto countershaft, with shoulder resting against countergear bearing and retain with snap ring, Fig. 3.
18. If removed, install snap ring, thrust washer and reverse idler gear with chamfer on gear teeth facing downward onto idler shaft. Retain thrust washer with snap ring, Fig. 3.
19. Install snap rings onto shifter shaft, Fig. 3.
20. Position speedometer gear retainer in hole in mainshaft with retainer loop

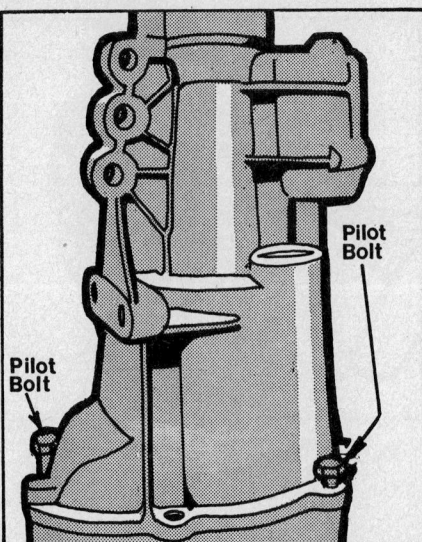

Fig. 18 Extension housing to case pilot bolt locations

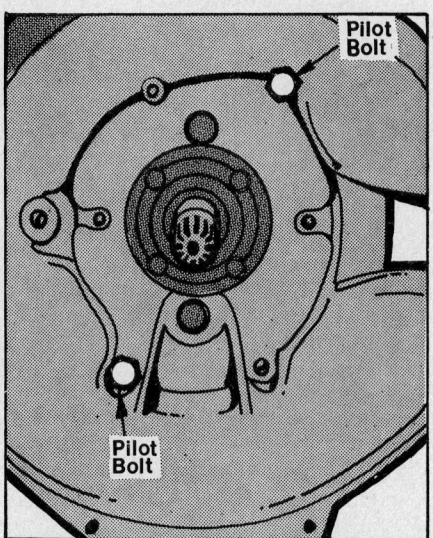

Fig. 19 Bellhousing to case pilot bolt locations

forward and slide speedometer gear over mainshaft and into place.

21. Position extension housing and gasket on case, then install the 2 pilot bolts followed by the 3 regular bolts, Fig. 18.

NOTE: Pilot bolts are partially threaded and are installed in the top right hand corner and bottom left hand corner of the case.

22. Install shifter shaft lever onto shifter shaft, aligning drilled hole near end of shaft. Drive roll pin into shifter shaft lever and shifter shaft, Fig. 1.
23. Install the 2 bellhousing retaining pilot bolts followed by the 4 regular bolts, Fig. 19.

NOTE: Pilot bolts are partially threaded and are installed in the right hand top corner and left hand bottom corner of the bellhousing.

FIVE SPEED MANUAL SHIFT TRANSMISSIONS

See Car Chapters for Linkage Adjustments and Removal Procedures

APPLICATION INDEX

DISASSEMBLE TRANS. FIG. 1

1. Remove selector lever pivot.
2. Remove plug and poppet spring, then using a magnet, remove plunger.
3. Drive roll pin from shifter head, Fig. 2, then remove extension housing to center support retaining bolts.
4. Slide transmission case forward and remove thrust bearing and races from input shaft or case.
5. Remove extension housing by sliding it rearward, then remove shifter head, shift rail and selector lever. The selector lever may be removed by removing retaining ring and pin.

NOTE: Catch loose needle bearings which may fall out, as they must be installed in original race.

6. Remove rail selector pin and rail selector.
7. Remove snap ring located behind speedometer gear, then remove gear and ball.
8. Remove snap ring, Fig. 3, thrust washer, 1st speed gear and blocker ring from output shaft.

NOTE: All snap rings are not identical. Therefore, make sure that correct snap ring is installed into correct groove during reassembly.

9. Remove snap ring located behind synchronizer hub, Fig. 4.
10. Turn shift rail to position interlock pawl to inboard position and remove 1st-reverse shift link.
11. Slide 1st-reverse synchronizer, shift fork, shift link and shift rail rearward from transmission.
12. Remove reverse idler from idler shaft and slide reverse gear rearward from output shaft.
13. Place interlock pawl to center position and remove 2nd-3rd shift link and shift fork.
14. Place interlock pawl to outboard position and remove 4th-5th shift link and fork.
15. Remove center support from output shaft and countergear, Fig. 5.

NOTE: Roller bearings may come out of center support.

16. Remove needle thrust bearings, Fig. 6, then remove countergear from gears on output shaft.
17. Remove input shaft from output shaft.

NOTE: Roller bearings may drop out of input shaft.

18. Remove thrust bearing from end of input shaft or synchronizer hub.
19. Remove 4th-5th speed synchronizer and blocker rings and 5th speed gear.

NOTE: Spacers and roller bearings may come out. Also, when correct number of needle bearings are installed, there should be enough space left for about one needle bearing.

20. Remove snap ring and thrust washer from output shaft and remove 2nd speed gear and blocker ring, Fig. 7.
21. Remove snap ring, then remove 2nd-3rd speed gear synchronizer assembly, blocker ring and 3rd speed gear.

SUB-ASSEMBLY SERVICE

Roller Bearings

Roller bearings in the center support, case and extension housing may be replaced if worn or damaged. All bearings can be removed with tool J-26225. Install

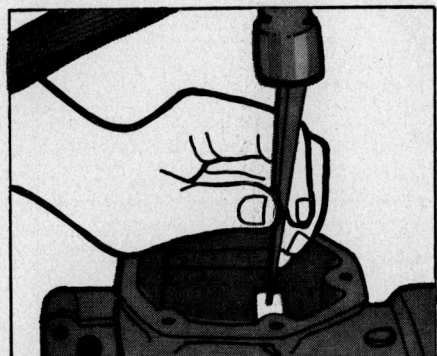

Fig. 2   Removing spring pin

Fig. 3   Removing first gear snap ring

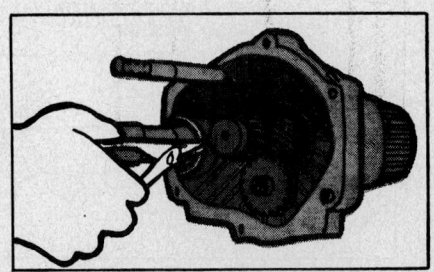

Fig. 4   Removing synchronizer hub snap ring

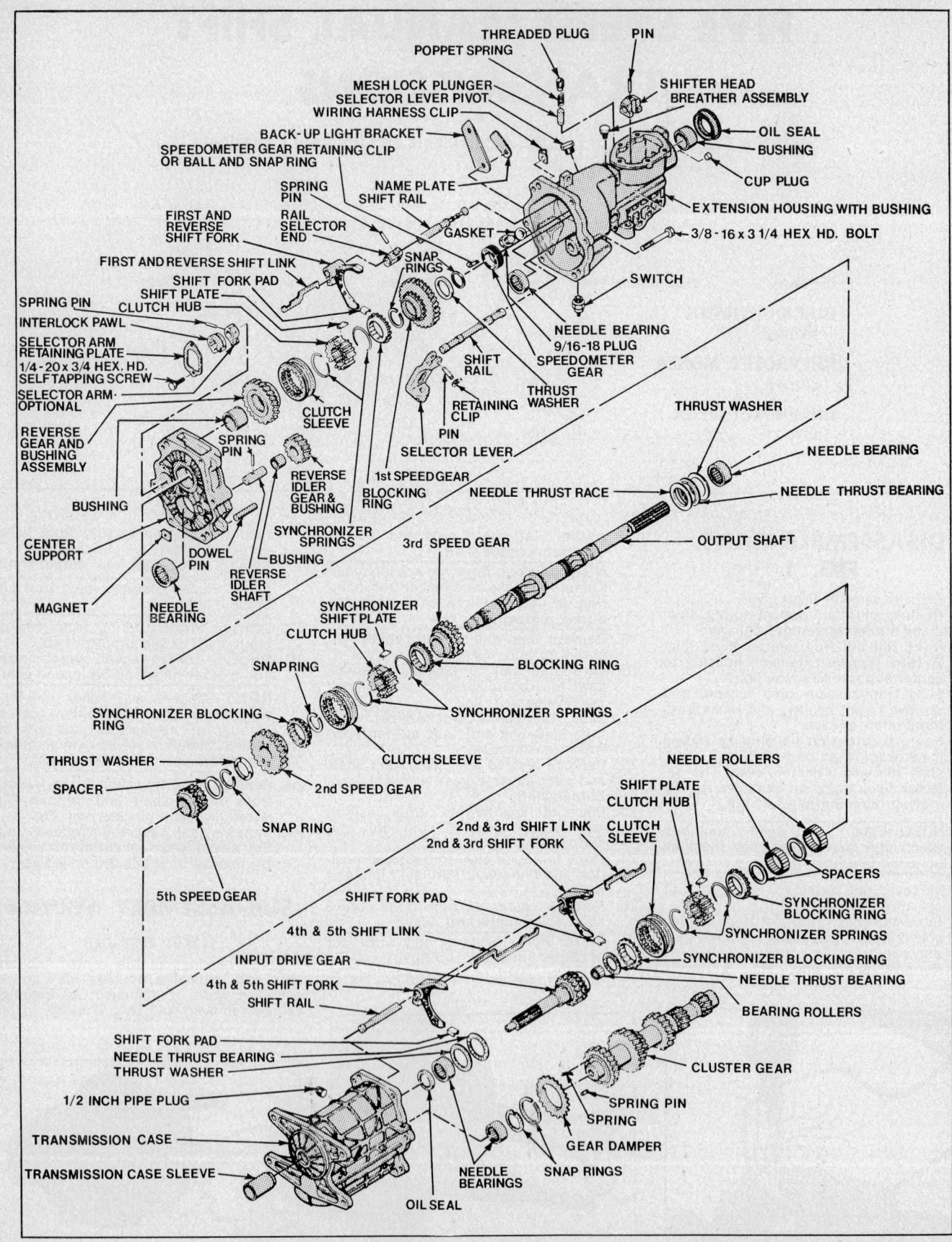

Fig. 1   GM five speed transmission, disassembled

Fig. 5 Removing center support

countergear bearings in case, Fig. 8, and center support with tools J-8092 and J-26223. Install input shaft bearings in center support, Fig. 9, and case with tools J-8092, J-26222-1 and J-26222-2.

Apply Loctite No. 601 or equivalent to bearing bore inside diameter for all bearings installed on case, center support and extension housing. The surfaces must be degreased and cleaned prior to applying the retaining compound.

Synchronizers

NOTE: The clutch hubs and sliding sleeves are a selected assembly and should be kept together as an assembly, but the keys and springs may be replaced if worn or broken.

1. Mark hub and sleeve so they can be reassembled in original position.
2. Push hub from sliding sleeve and remove keys and springs.
3. Place one spring on each side of hub so springs overlap slots in hub and opening and are not opposite each other.
4. Place shift keys in slots of hub with radius side out and springs in grooves in keys.
5. Install sliding sleeve onto hub aligning marks made before disassembly. Depress keys to ease installation, Fig. 10.

Clutch Bearing Retainer Oil Seal

To replace, pry seal from retainer with tool J-26243 and drive new seal into place with tool J-26224 or other similar tool.

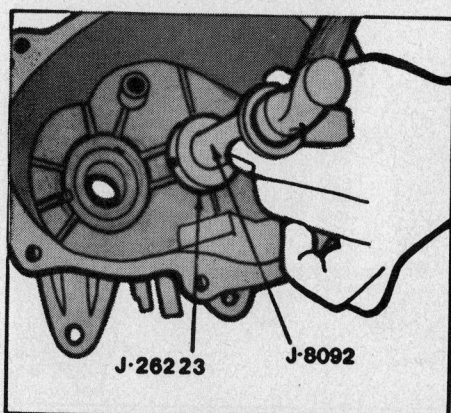

Fig. 8 Installing countergear bearing in case

Fig. 6 Removing needle thrust race & bearing

Extension Housing Oil Seal & Bushing

1. Pry oil seal out and using tool J-5778 or J-21424-9, drive bushing from extension housing.
2. Drive new bushing into housing from the rear using same tools.
3. Lubricate bushing and new seal and drive new seal into bushing using tool J-5154 or J-21426.

ASSEMBLE TRANS.

1. Install 3rd speed gear over output shaft with coned end toward front and against shaft shoulder.

   NOTE: Synchronizer assemblies are similar except hub splines differ. Hub and sleeve are a selective fit to obtain a free sliding fit with .002 inch maximum backlash. Make sure to keep mated parts together to insure correct sliding fit and backlash.

2. Install blocker ring with slots aligned with shift keys of synchronizer assembly.
3. Install synchronizer and blocker rings with chamfer on sleeve toward front of shaft and positioned on face of 3rd speed gear.
4. Install snap ring in shaft groove ahead of synchronizer hub.
5. Install 2nd speed gear with coned end into blocker ring.
6. Install thrust washer on face of 2nd speed gear and install snap ring in shaft groove in front of thrust washer, Fig. 7.
7. Install two rows of 46 needle bearings inside of 5th gear with a spacer in between and on each end of needle bearings. Fig. 11. Retain with petroleum jelly.

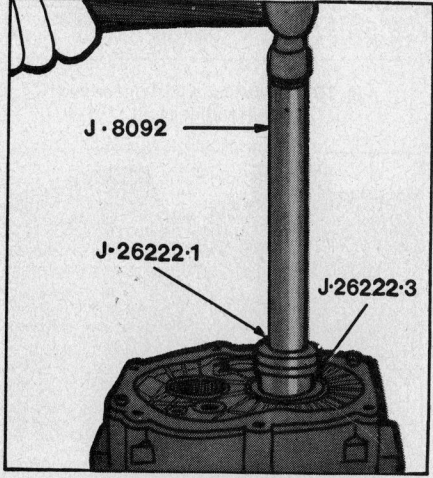

Fig. 9 Installing input shaft bearing in center support

J·8092

J·26222·1

J·26222·3

Fig. 7 Removing snap ring and 2nd speed gear

NOTE: Make sure to use correct needle bearings, as other bearings are similar in length but differ in diameter.

8. Install 5th speed gear on output shaft with coned end toward output shaft.

   NOTE: Make sure needle bearings do not come out.

9. Install blocker rings with slots aligned with shift keys of 4th-5th synchronizer assembly, Fig. 12.
10. Install 4th-5th speed synchronizer assembly on output shaft with chamfered edge of sleeve toward front of transmission.
11. Install thrust bearing on end of 4th-5th synchronizer assembly.
12. Install 19 needle rollers into 2nd step of input shaft bore and retain with petroleum jelly, Fig. 13, then install shaft over end of output shaft.

    NOTE: Make sure needle rollers do not fall out.

13. Install needle thrust bearing and races with inner race lip toward rear and over output shaft against shaft shoulder, Fig. 6.
14. Install needle rollers into center support and retain with petroleum jelly.
15. Mesh countergear teeth with teeth of input shaft gears assembled onto output shaft, then install center support over output shaft and countergear, Fig. 14.

    NOTE: Make sure needle rollers do not fall out.

16. Install reverse gear and bushing assembly over output shaft and against center support.
17. Install reverse idler gear and bushing assembly over reverse idler shaft meshing it with reverse gear, Fig. 15.

NOTE: Replace worn or damaged shift pads on all shift forks if necessary.

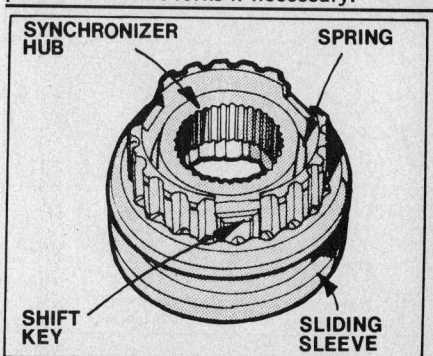

SYNCHRONIZER HUB

SPRING

SHIFT KEY

SLIDING SLEEVE

Fig. 10 Synchronizer assembly

Fig. 11   Fifth speed gear & bearings

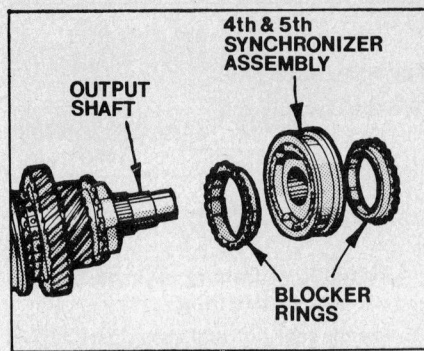

Fig. 12   Installing 4th-5th speed synchronizer

Fig. 13   Input shaft & bearings

18. Assemble 4th-5th shift fork on 4th-5th synchronizer sliding sleeve. Move interlock pawl to permit shift link to be installed through outboard slot of center support. Refer to Fig. 16 for shift fork identification.
19. Install 4th-5th shift link through slot and engage with shift fork.
20. Assemble 2nd-3rd shift fork on 2nd-3rd sliding sleeve. Move interlock pawl to permit shift link to be installed through center slot in center support.
21. Install 2nd-3rd shift link through slot and engage in shift fork.
22. Locate interlock pawl to permit first

and reverse shift link to be installed in inboard slot of center support, then install 1st-reverse shift link into shift fork.
23. If selector arm was removed during disassembly, install selector arm over shift rail aligning hole in selector arm with hole near middle of rail. Drive roll pin into arm and rail.
24. Install shift rail through shift fork from front to rear with poppet notches located towards rear of transmission.
25. Engage shift fork with 1st-reverse synchronizer sleeve and install these parts by sliding synchronizer hub over output shaft with chamfered edge of sleeve towards front, Fig. 17.
26. Guide shift rail through interlock pawl, 2nd-3rd shift fork and 4th-5th shift fork, making sure selector arm

is aligned with notch in shift link.
27. Install synchronizer hub snap ring, Fig. 4.
28. Install blocker ring and 1st speed gear over output shaft behind 1st speed gear over output shaft behind 1st-reverse synchronizer assembly.
29. Align notches on blocker ring with notches in synchronizer hub, then install thrust washer and snap ring behind 1st speed gear.
30. Install speedometer gear retainer with loop forward, then slide speedometer gear over shaft and retainer until retainer snaps into place.
31. Slide rail selector with hole in selector to rear of transmission and ball facing inboard and retain with roll pin.
32. Install selector lever and shift rail into hole in extension housing. Install shifter head on rail as rail becomes exposed in housing opening. Do not install roll pin.

CAUTION: Make sure to use correct needle bearings, as other bearings

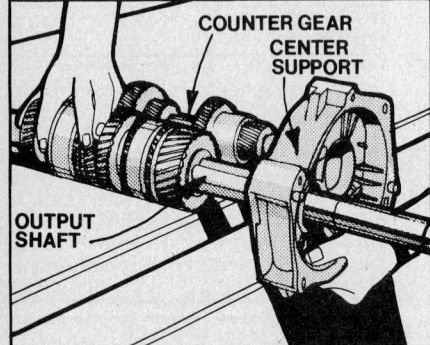

Fig. 14   Installing output shaft and cluster gear to center support

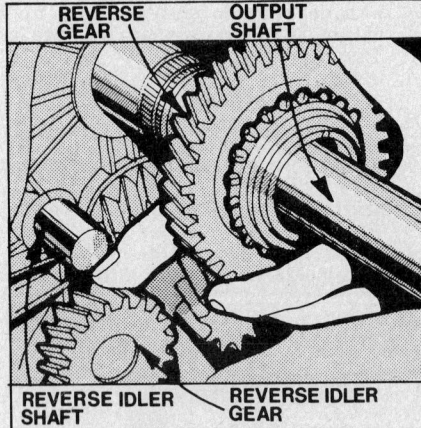

Fig. 15   Installing reverse gear and reverse idler gear

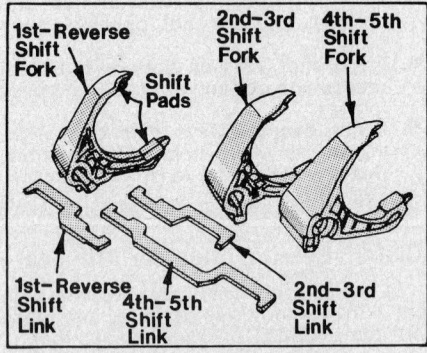

Fig. 16   Shift forks and links

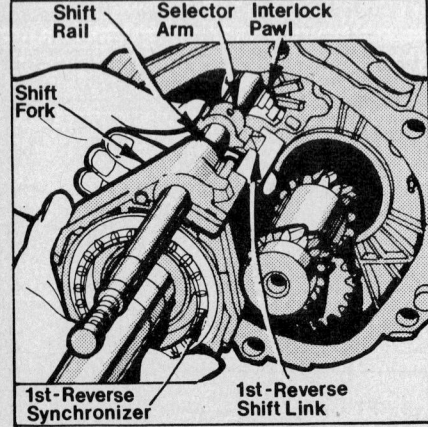

Fig. 17   Installing 1st-reverse synchronizer shift fork and rail

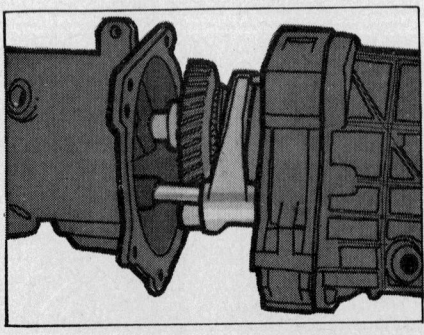

Fig. 18   Mating extension housing & center support

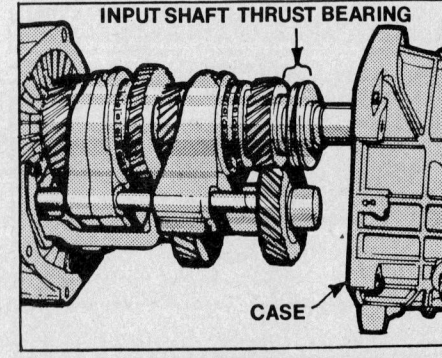

Fig. 19   Installing input shaft thrust bearing and case

are similar in length, but differ in diameter.

33. Apply a ⅟₃₂ inch bead of RTV sealer to transmission case and extension housing, then install extension housing while guiding selector lever to engage rail selector, Fig. 18.

34. Install thrust race with lip toward front, then install thrust bearing and flat thrust washer over input shaft, Fig. 19.

35. Install case to front side of center support, then install retaining bolts and torque to 40 ft. lbs.

NOTE: If case binds while it is being installed, check to make sure that 5th speed gear spacer for bearings did not fall between 5th gear and synchronizer.

36. Install roll pin into shifter head and shift rail.

37. Coat threaded plug with Loctite 92 or equivalent, then install plunger, poppet spring and threaded plug. Torque plug to 12 ft. lbs.

38. Coat selector lever pivot threads with Loctite 92 or equivalent, then align hole in selector lever with hole in extension housing and install pivot. Torque to 60 ft. lbs.

OVERDRIVE TRANSMISSIONS

INDEX

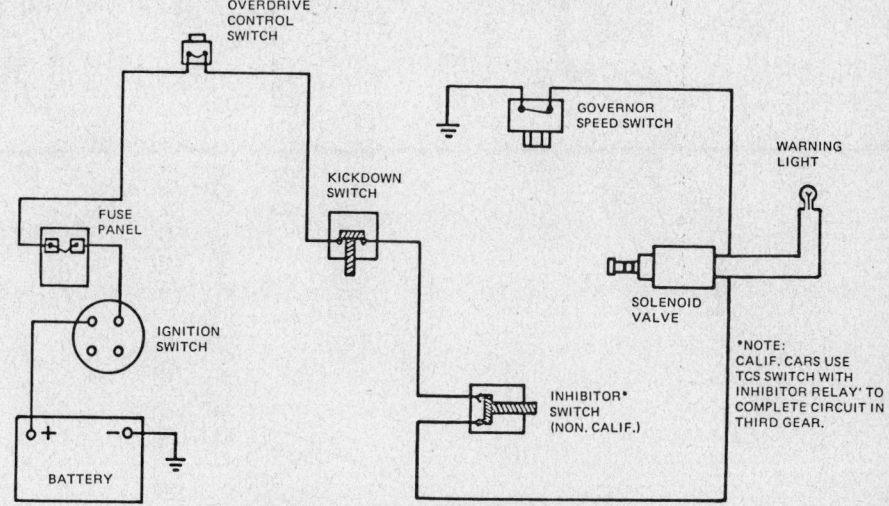

Fig. 2 Overdrive electrical control circuit

1975-76 AMERICAN MOTORS

The overdrive is an additional gear unit located between the transmission and propeller shaft, Fig. 1, and provides a higher overall gear ratio than normally provided by the drive gear and pinion. The overdrive permits highway cruising at a lower engine speed than in a normal third gear. This unit reduces engine-to-rear axle ratio approximately 25%, thus providing a transmission ratio in overdrive third gear of .75 to 1.00.

The overdrive is a hydraulically operated unit and its actuation is controlled by a solenoid valve. This solenoid valve is activated by a control switch mounted on the steering column. A governor speed switch, operated by the speedometer cable, determines cut-in and cut-out speeds for the unit. The overdrive may be engaged when the vehicle is above the governor cut-in speed of 38 MPH and in third gear. A third gear switch installed in the transmission prevents overdrive engagement in any other gear.

NOTE: California vehicles require a TCS switch which is open when the transmission is in third gear. To complete the overdrive control circuit, but also prevent overdrive operation in any gear except third gear, a third gear relay is connected to the TCS switch. This relay performs the same function as the third gear switch and is closed only when the transmission is in third gear.

The overdrive is engaged by activating the control switch and until the switch is deactivated or the vehicle decelerates to

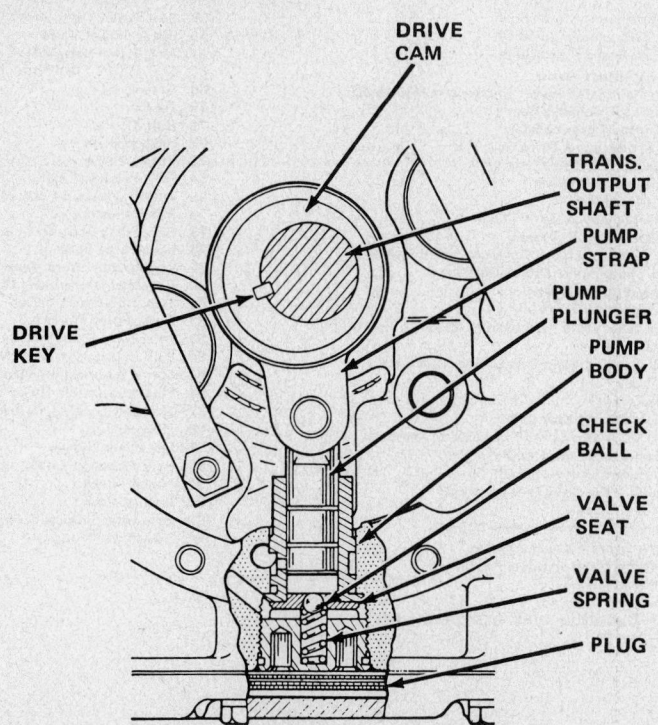

Fig. 3 Overdrive unit oil pump assembly

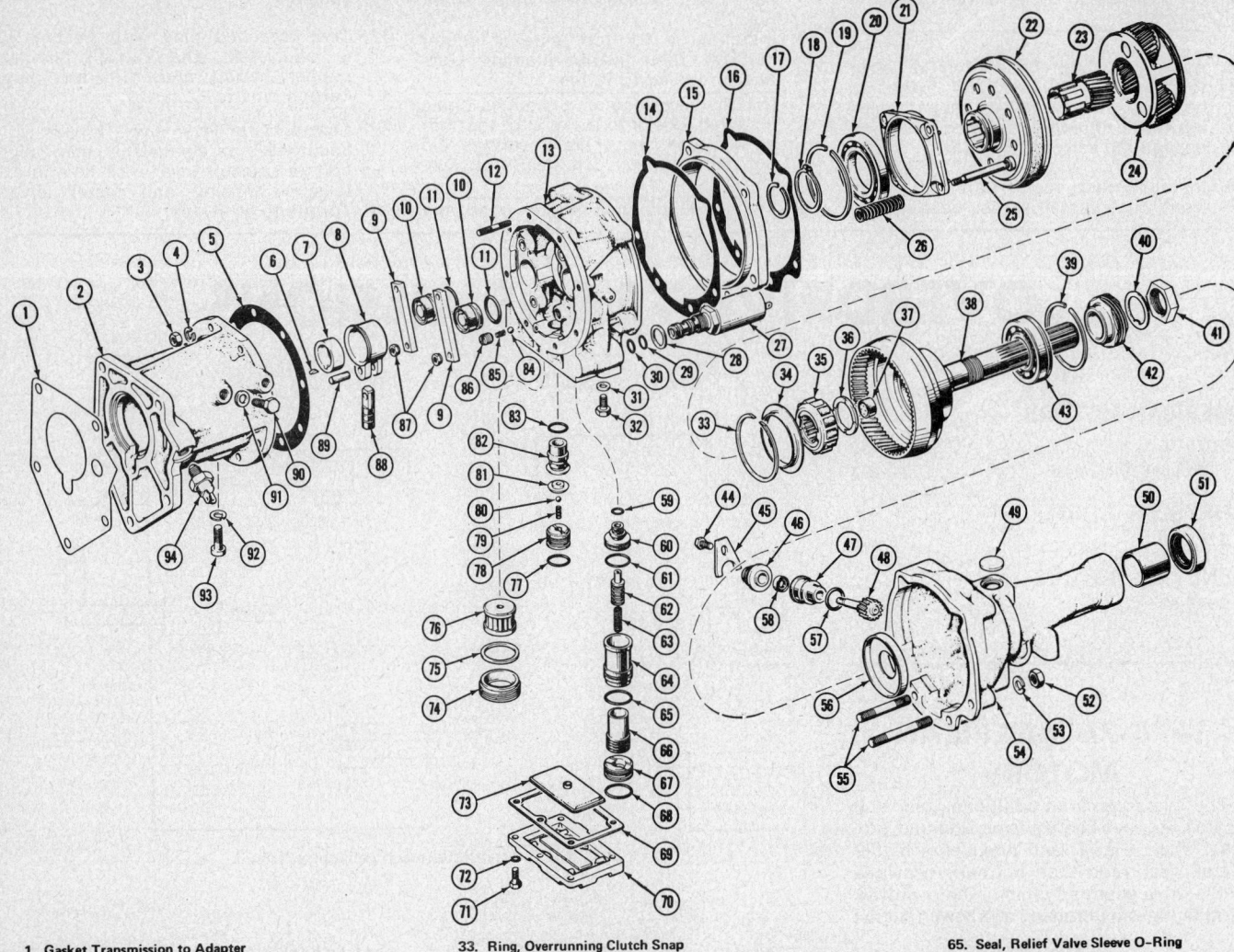

Fig. 1   Overdrive unit, exploded view

1. Gasket Transmission to Adapter
2. Adapter, Transmission
3. Nut, Self Locking, Main Case Stud
4. Washer, Lock
5. Gasket, Main Case to Transmission Adaptor
6. Key, Pump Strap Cam Drive
7. Cam, Pump Strap
8. Strap, Pump
9. Bar, Clutch Piston Apply
10. Piston, Clutch Apply
11. Seal, Clutch Apply Piston O-Ring
12. Stud, Main Case to Transmission Adapter
13. Main Case
14. Gasket, Clutch Brake Ring (front)
15. Brake Ring, Clutch
16. Gasket, Clutch Brake Ring (rear)
17. Ring, Sun Gear Snap
18. Ring Lock, Sliding Clutch
19. Ring, Thrust Bearing Snap
20. Bearing, Thrust
21. Cover, Thrust Bearing
22. Clutch, Sliding
23. Sun Gear
24. Assembly, Pinion Carrier
25. Bolt, Thrust Bearing Cover (4 reqd.)
26. Spring, Clutch Return (4 reqd.)
27. Solenoid Valve
28. Washer, Solenoid Valve
29. Seal, Solenoid Valve O-Ring
30. Seal, Solenoid Valve O-Ring
31. Gasket, Main Case Pressure Plug
32. Plug, Main Case Pressure

33. Ring, Overrunning Clutch Snap
34. Slinger, Overrunning Clutch Oil
35. Assembly, Overrunning Clutch
36. Washer, Mainshaft Thrust
37. Bushing, Mainshaft Support (Included in Mainshaft)
38. Main Shaft and Annulus Gear
39. Ring, Mainshaft Bearing Snap
40. Washer, Speedometer Drive Gear Tab
41. Nut, Speedometer Drive Gear Lock
42. Gear, Speedometer Drive
43. Bearing, Mainshaft
44. Bolt, Speedometer Adapter Clamp
45. Clamp, Speedometer Adapter
46. Adapter, Speedometer to Governor Speed Switch
47. Adapter, Speedometer Driven Gear
48. Gear, Speedometer Driven
49. Plug, Expansion
50. Bushing, Rear Case (Included in Case)
51. Seal, Rear Case Oil
52. Nut, Self Locking, Main Case to Rear Case Stud
53. Washer, Lock
54. Rear Case
55. Stud, Main Case to Rear Case
56. Washer, Disc (not removed: included in rear case)
57. Seal, Speedometer Adapter O-Ring
58. Seal, Speedometer Adaptor Oil
59. Seal, Relief Valve Body O-Ring (Inner)
60. Body, Relief Valve
61. Seal, Relief Valve Body O-Ring (Outer)
62. Assembly, Relief Valve and Spring
63. Spring, Relief Valve Residual Pressure
64. Sleeve, Relief Valve

65. Seal, Relief Valve Sleeve O-Ring
66. Piston, Relief Valve
67. Plug, Relief Valve Piston
68. Seal, Relief Valve Piston Plug O-Ring
69. Gasket, Oil Pan
70. Oil Pan
71. Bolt, Oil Pan
72. Washer, Lock
73. Filter, Oil Pan
74. Plug, Pressure Filter
75. Washer, Pressure Filter (Aluminum)
76. Filter, Pressure
77. Seal, Pump Body O-Ring
78. Plug, Pump Body
79. Spring, Non-return Valve Ball-seat
80. Ball, Non-return Valve Check
81. Seat, Non-return Valve
82. Body, Pump Plunger
83. Seal, Pump Plunger Body O-Ring
84. Ball, Lubrication Relief Valve Check
85. Spring, Lubrication Relief Valve
86. Plug, Lubrication Relief Valve
87. Nut, Self Locking, Clutch Piston Apply Bar
88. Plunger, Pump
89. Pin, Pump Plunger
90. Bolt, Gearshift Lever Retainer to Adapter
91. Washer, Lock
92. Washer, Lock
93. Bolt, Rear Support Cushion to Adapter
94. Switch, Back-up Light

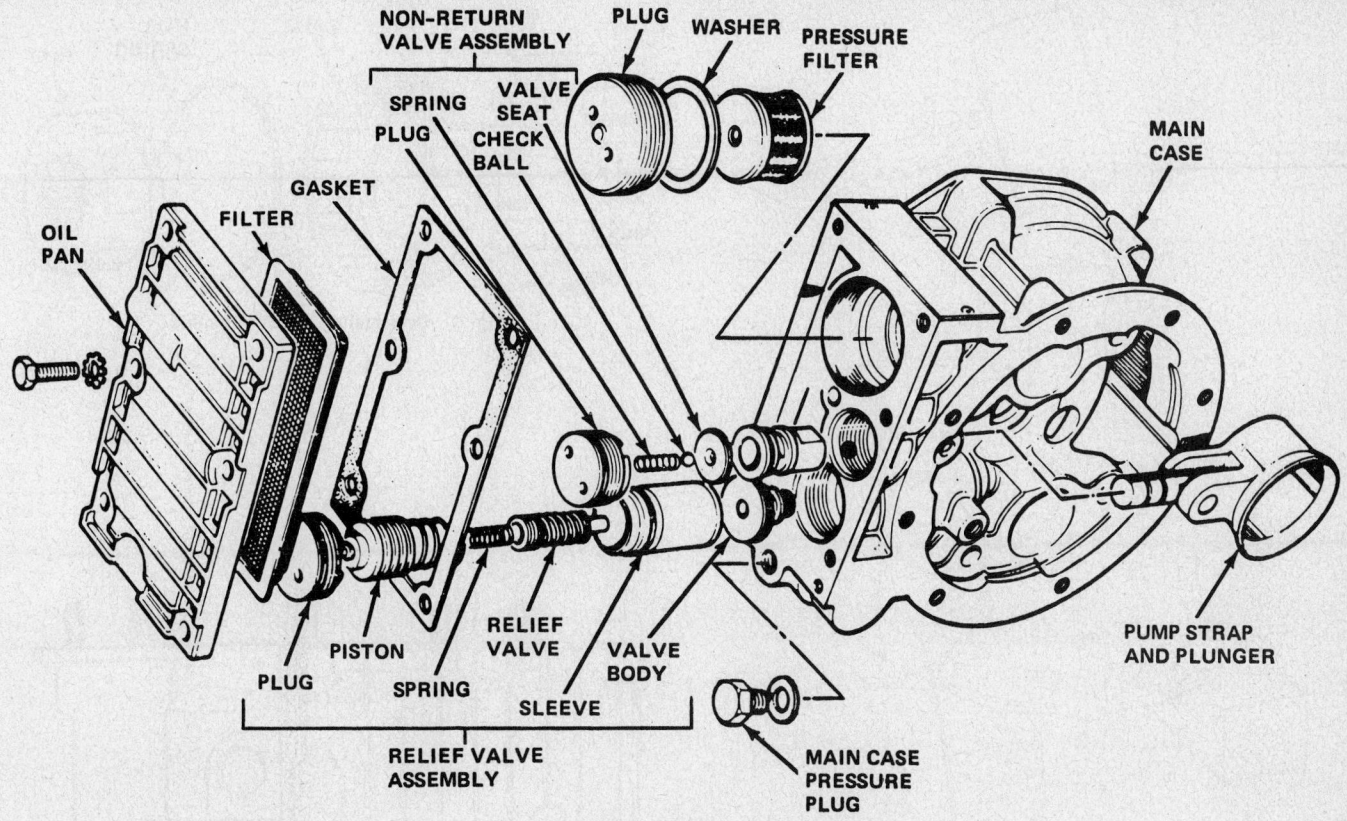

Fig. 4 Overdrive main case components

below the governor cut-out speed of 32 MPH, the overdrive remains engaged. A kickdown switch is incorporated into the control circuit, Fig. 2. This switch, mounted on the carburetor base, is actuated by throttle linkage. When the throttle is fully opened, the switch is actuated and "Opens" the control circuit, in turn de-energizing the solenoid valve and disengaging the overdrive. When the throttle returns from the wide open position, the switch "Closes" the control circuit, re-energizing the solenoid and re-engaging the overdrive.

An indicator lamp, connected electrically to the solenoid valve, is provided to indicate overdrive engagement.

Hydraulic system pressure is developed by a cam operated plunger-type pump, Fig. 3, and is driven by the transmission output shaft through a drive key. The pump obtains oil from the air cooled sump, through the oil pan filter, and pumps it through the non-return valve and pressure filter to the clutch apply pistons, solenoid valve and relief valve assembly. A spring loaded piston within the relief valve assembly provides smooth engagement and disengagement under all operating conditions. When the overdrive is disengaged, a residual system pressure of 20 to 40 PSI is maintained. The system pressure with the overdrive engaged is 520 to 540 PSI and is maintained by the relief valve.

DISASSEMBLY

1. Remove solenoid valve, Fig. 1, with tool J-25304. Use only specified tool since solenoid damage may result.

2. Remove and discard nuts securing clutch piston apply bars to thrust bearing cover pins.
3. Separate main case from rear case. Note location of copper gaskets used on main case to rear case studs.
4. Remove clutch return springs, clutch brake ring and gaskets from main case. If clutch brake ring is stuck, tap lightly with a mallet.
5. Remove oil pan, gasket, filter and main case pressure plug from main case, Fig. 4, then pressure filter plug, filter and aluminum washer.
6. Remove pump body plug, non-return valve ball seat spring, check ball and valve seat.
7. Remove clutch apply pistons from bores, then "O" rings from pistons.

NOTE: Do not remove lubrication relief valve plug, spring or ball from main case.

8. Remove pump assembly as follows:
   a. Push pump body upward until it unseats from case bore and slide pump plunger from pump body, then remove body from case bore.

NOTE: The pump body has a flat machined on one side which aligns with oil feed hole and slot in main case bore. Note location of oil feed hole and slot for proper reassembly.

   b. Remove drive cam and key from pump strap. Do not disassemble pump strap and plunger since they are serviced as an assembly.

9. Remove relief valve piston plug, piston and residual pressure spring.

NOTE: The residual pressure spring is the only loose spring in the relief valve assembly.

10. With a magnet or needlenose plier, remove relief valve and spring assembly. Do not remove calibrated spring from relief valve piston.
11. Using tool J-25307, remove relief valve sleeve and body as follows:
    a. Install hooked end of tool through relief valve body bore and hook tool over inner edge of body. Slide tool barrel downward, securing tool, and pull valve body and sleeve from case bore.
    b. Remove and discard "O" rings from valve body, sleeve and plug.
12. Remove sliding clutch, sun gear and thrust bearing cover from main shaft annulus gear in rear case, then remove pinion carrier from main shaft annulus gear.
13. Remove sun gear snap ring, sliding clutch ring lock and push sun gear from sliding clutch hub.
14. Install tool J-25315 into sliding clutch hub and tap end of tool to drive clutch hub from thrust bearing. Remove thrust bearing snap ring and press bearing from cover.
15. Remove overrunning clutch snap ring and brass oil slinger. Install tool J-25308 into main shaft annulus gear bore, reach through tool and pull overrunning clutch into tool and remove tool and overrunning clutch together. Remove main shaft thrust

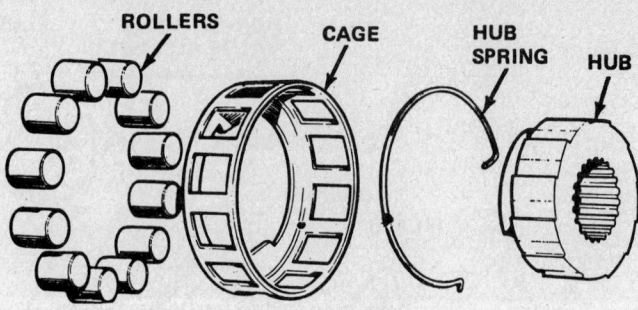

Fig. 6   Overrunning clutch assembly

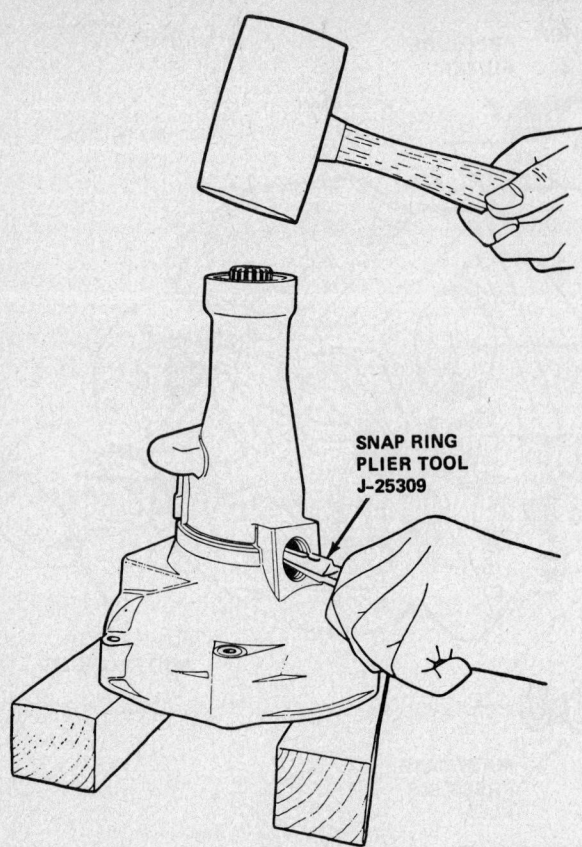

Fig. 5   Main shaft removal

washer from main shaft annulus gear recess. Remove overrunning clutch from tool and disassemble.

16. Remove rear case expansion plug.
17. Place rear case on wooden blocks, expand main shaft bearing snap ring and tap main shaft out from rear case, Fig. 5.
18. Remove speedometer drive gear lock nut, tab washer and drive gear, then main shaft bearing.
19. Pry rear case oil seal from case and remove main shaft bearing snap ring from machined groove in rear case.

NOTE: Do not remove disc washer or rear bushing from rear case since they are not serviceable and are available as part of the rear case.

ASSEMBLY

1. Lubricate and install main shaft bearing on main shaft with the groove facing toward rear of main shaft.
2. Install speedometer drive gear with shoulder side of gear facing toward main shaft bearing, tab washer and drive gear lock nut on main shaft. Torque lock nut to 55 ft. lbs. while holding main shaft secure, then bend drive gear washer against lock nut in two places, securing lock nut.
3. Install main shaft bearing snap ring into rear case machined groove, place main shaft in upright position and lower rear case onto main shaft. Tap end of case to start main shaft bear-

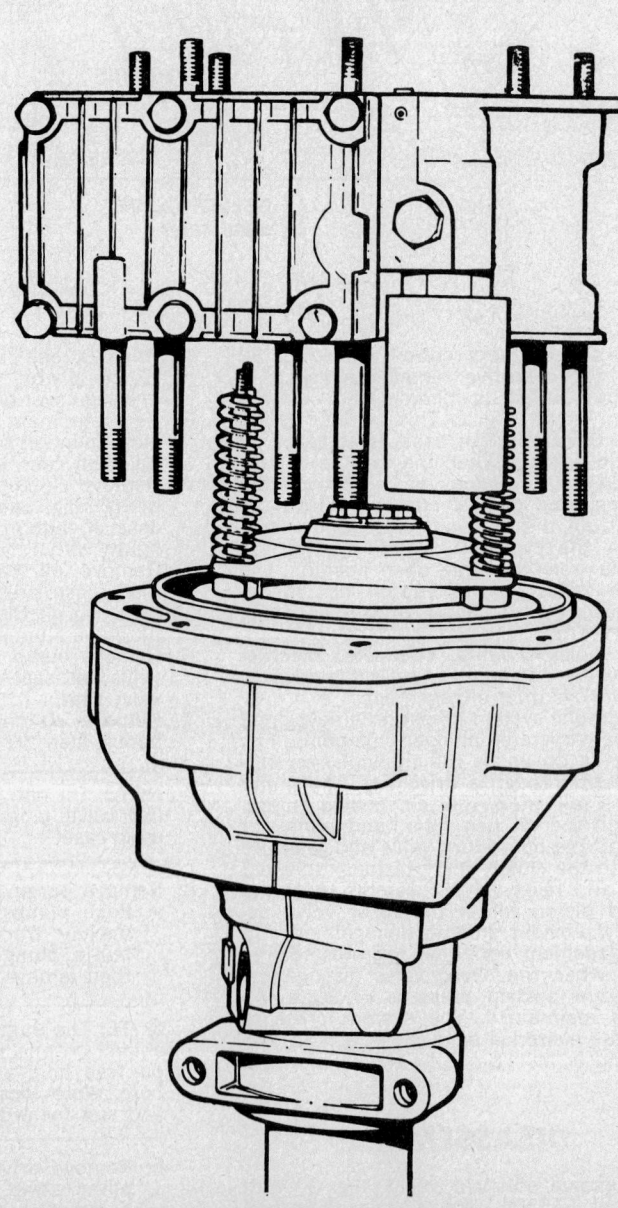

Fig. 7   Installing main case on rear case

ing into counterbore of case, expand snap ring and tap case until bearing fully seats in counterbore and snap ring in bearing groove.

4. Lubricate and install rear case oil seal, then new rear case expansion plug.
5. Lubricate and install main shaft thrust washer into main shaft annulus gear recess.
6. Assemble overrunning clutch, Fig. 6, as follows:
   a. Insert longest hub spring hooked end into cage locating hole.
   b. Hold cage stationary and rotate hub against spring.
7. Place assembled cage and hub into tool J-25308 with cage open end facing outward. Install clutch rollers into cage slots through gate in tool while rotating cage in clockwise direction.
8. Lubricate and install overrunning clutch assembly in main shaft annulus gear bore. Remove tool J-25308 and install brass oil slinger with shoulder facing outward, then overrunning clutch snap ring, ensuring snap ring fully seats in groove.
9. Lubricate and install pinion carrier into main shaft annulus gear.
10. Press thrust bearing into thrust bearing cover, then install thrust bearing snap ring.
11. Position thrust bearing and cover on sliding clutch hub and tap cover to start bearing onto hub. Invert assembly and install tool J-25315 into clutch hub and drive hub into thrust bearing.
12. Install sun gear into sliding clutch hub, then sliding clutch lock ring with sharp edge facing upward and sun gear snap ring.
13. Install sliding clutch assembly onto main shaft annulus gear while engaging sun gear in pinion gears. Ensure sliding clutch fully seats on the an-

nulus and the sun gear is fully engaged in pinion gears.

NOTE: To aid installation, rotate main shaft while engaging sun gear.

14. Lubricate and install clutch apply pistons with new "O" rings into main case bores with piston counterbored ends facing outward.
15. Install new "O" rings on relief valve body, sleeve and valve piston plug, then install relief valve assembly as follows:
    a. Install valve body into main case bore.
    b. Align valve sleeve oil hole with oil hole in bore and insert sleeve into bore with "O" ring end facing upward until sleeve and valve body are seated.
    c. Install relief valve and spring assembly into valve body, then residual pressure spring into the assembly.
    d. Install valve piston and relief valve piston plug and torque plug to 16 ft. lbs.
16. Install pressure filter into main case bore and install torque pressure filter plug with new aluminum washer to 16 ft. lbs.
17. Install new "O" rings on pump body and plug, then lubricate and install pump plunger, pump body and non-return valve components as follows:
    a. Align flat on pump body with oil hole in main case bore and install pump body halfway into bore.
    b. Insert pump plunger into pump body, then push pump body fully into main case.
    c. Place non-return valve seat on top of pump body with check ball seat facing upward, then place check ball onto valve seat.

d. Place non-return valve spring into pump body plug and install assembly. Torque plug to 16 ft. lbs.
18. Install main case pressure plug, gasket, oil pan filter, oil pan gasket and oil pump cover on main case. Torque oil pan bolts to 6 ft. lbs. and pressure plug to 13 ft. lbs.
19. Place rear case assembly in a soft jawed vise and install new clutch return springs on thrust bearing cover bolts.
20. Install first clutch brake ring gasket on rear case, then clutch brake ring into case with tapered surface facing rearward. Install second new clutch brake ring gasket on brake ring. Ensure gaskets and brake ring are aligned with rear case stud holes.
21. Apply a light coat of suitable sealer to main case studs, place main case over rear case, aligning studs, and lower onto rear case, Fig. 19. Align thrust bearing cover bolts as main case is being lowered.
22. Install copper gaskets on the upper main case to rear case studs, four lockwashers on remaining studs and nuts and all studs. Torque nuts to 11 ft. lbs.
23. Install clutch apply bars on thrust bearing cover bolts and torque attaching nuts to 8 ft. lbs.
24. Install solenoid valve with tool J-25304.
25. Lubricate and install oil pump drive cam and drive key on transmission output shaft and secure with snap ring.

TROUBLE DIAGNOSIS

A detailed trouble diagnosis chart follows.

Condition	Possible Cause	Correction
OVERDRIVE WILL NOT ENGAGE	1. Low lubricant level.	1. Check and correct level. Correct any oil leaks.
	2. Open switch or wire in electrical control circuit.	2. Check for loose, broken, shorted wires, blown fuse, or open switches (use 12V test lamp). Repair or replace parts as required.
	3. Solenoid valve sticking, grounded, open.	3. Remove, clean, and test solenoid valve. Replace solenoid valve if defective.
	4. Plugged oil pan or pressure filters. Plugged, or sticking pump non-return valve assembly. Sticking relief valve piston. Broken relief valve assembly or piston springs. Plugged control orifice.	4. Perform hydraulic pressure test with overdrive engaged. If pressures are below 520 psi with overdrive engaged, remove oil pan, main case plugs, and all valves and filters. Clean all parts thoroughly. Replace plugged filters, worn o-ring seals, scored or pitted valves, or valves with broken springs. Remove solenoid valve and clean control orifice with compressed air.
	5. Sticking sliding clutch. Worn sliding clutch friction lining. Broken or weak clutch return springs. Leaking clutch apply piston seals. Internal case leaks. Damaged or worn gear components. Pump body not aligned with oil feed slot in case bore. Pump plunger or pump body worn excessively.	5. Road test car with control switch on-at 40 to 45 mph-depress and release clutch pedal 3 or 4 times in rapid succession. If overdrive does not engage, remove and disassemble overdrive. Repair or replace defective parts as required.

OVERDRIVE TRANSMISSIONS

Condition	Possible Cause	Correction
OVERDRIVE WILL NOT DISENGAGE **CAUTION: This condition calls for immediate attention. Do not attempt to back up car—extensive damage to overdrive may result.**	1. Closed switch or shorted wire in electrical control circuit.	1. Check for shorted wires, sticking control switch pushbutton (at turn indicator lever) or closed switches.
	2. Solenoid valve stuck, or shorted.	2. Remove, clean, and test solenoid valve. Replace solenoid valve if defective.
	3. Relief valve piston stuck or spring broken. Relief valve assembly spring broken. Control orifice plugged.	3. Install pressure test gauge and check residual pressure at 25 to 30 mph. Pressure should be approximately 20 to 40 psi. If pressure is higher than 40 psi, remove oil pan, main case plugs and all valves and filters. Clean all components thoroughly. Replace plugged filters, worn o-ring seals, scored or pitted valves, or valves with broken springs. Remove solenoid valve and clean control orifice with compressed air.
	4. Sliding clutch sticking. Damaged or seized gear components.	4. Remove and disassemble overdrive. Repair or replace defective parts as required.
SLOW DISENGAGEMENT AND/OR OVERDRIVE FREEWHEELS ON OVERRUN	1. Relief valve piston sticking.	1. Remove and clean piston. Replace if scored, pitted or corroded. Check sleeve for pitting, scoring, or corrosion. Replace sleeve if damaged.
	2. Solenoid valve oil feed holes plugged or valve sticking.	2. Remove, clean, and test solenoid valve as outlined in Service Procedures-In Car. Replace solenoid valve if defective.
	3. Control orifice plugged.	3. Remove relief valve piston, valve assembly, sleeve, and valve body. Remove solenoid valve and clean control orifice with compressed air.
	4. Overrunning clutch worn, or seized. Worn, damaged sun gear, or sliding clutch hub. Worn or damaged friction material on sliding clutch hub. Worn, damaged brake ring.	4. Remove and disassemble overdrive. Repair or replace parts as required.
OVERDRIVE SLIPS WHEN ENGAGING	1. Low lubricant level.	1. Check and correct level. Correct any oil leaks.
	2. Plugged oil pan, or pressure filter.	2. Remove and clean filters. Replace filters if cleaning does not unplug them.
	3. Sticking or plugged non-return valve. Sticking relief valve piston. Broken spring on relief valve assembly. Control orifice plugged.	3. Perform hydraulic pressure test with overdrive engaged. If pressures are below 510 psi with overdrive engaged or pressure fluctuates rapidly, remove oil pan, main case plugs, and all valves and filters. Clean all parts thoroughly. Replace plugged filters, worn o-ring seals, scored, or pitted valves, or valves with broken springs. Remove solenoid valve and clean control orifice with compressed air.

Condition	Possible Cause	Correction
OVERDRIVE SLIPS WHEN ENGAGING (Continued)	4. Solenoid valve sticking, oil feed holes plugged, or loose wire at solenoid terminal.	4. Remove, clean, and test valve. Replace solenoid valve if defective. Repair loose connections at terminals.
	5. Worn clutch apply piston seals. Worn friction material on sliding clutch. Internal leak in case. Worn pump plunger or pump body. Damaged or worn gear components. Pump body not aligned with oil feed slot in case bore. Annulus gear clutch surface worn, burned, or galled.	5. Remove and disassemble overdrive. Repair or replace defective parts as required.
SHUDDERS-CHATTERS WHEN BACKING UP-(OVERDRIVE DISENGAGED)	1. Loose or defective engine and transmission support cushions. 2. Transmission clutch slipping (incorrectly adjusted). 3. Weak clutch return springs. Worn or damaged friction material on sliding clutch. Burned, or galled annulus gear clutch surface.	1. Inspect all support cushions. Tighten if loose; replace if defective. 2. Adjust clutch free play. 3. Remove and disassemble overdrive. Replace parts as required.
NO KICKDOWN	1. Kickdown switch not adjusted correctly. 2. Kickdown switch stuck, shorted, broken.	1. Adjust switch. 2. Check plunger and switch continuity. Replace if necessary.
NOISY WHEN ENGAGED	1. Sliding clutch slipping. All bearings worn, pitted, or galled. Rear bushing worn. Pinion gears or mainshaft annulus gear teeth chipped or broken, worn, chipped overrunning clutch rollers, or clutch race in annulus gear bore. Mainshaft thrust washer worn, broken, or missing. Sun gear teeth chipped or broken.	1. Remove and disassemble overdrive. Replace defective parts as required.
MAKES LIGHT KNOCKING SOUND	1. Pump body installed improperly. (Flat not aligned with oil hole.)	1. Remove pump body and align properly in case bore.

1975-78 CHRYSLER

This four speed overdrive transmission is basically the same transmission as the Chrysler four speed A-833 unit found in the "Four Speed Transmission" chapter, under "Type Four Chrysler".

The differences in these transmissions are as follows: second gear ratio changed from 1.92 to 1.67, third gear ratio changed from 1.40 to 1.00 (direct drive) and the fourth gear ratio changed from 1.00 (direct drive) to 0.73 (overdrive). Since the fourth gear ratio is less than 1 to 1, an overdrive condition is achieved.

1975-78 GENERAL MOTORS

The General Motors overdrive transmission is a five speed manual shift unit, fully synchronized in all forward gears. Fifth gear is the overdrive gear in which the engine RPM is approximately 20% lower than the RPM in direct drive.

Refer to the "Five Speed Transmission" chapter for service procedure on this unit.

AUTOMATIC TRANSMISSIONS

NOTE:—This chapter deals only with maintenance, adjustments and "in car" repairs. For major service work, Motor's Automatic Transmission Manual is available. Current edition is a 976 page volume that includes 326 pages of oil circuit diagrams, most in full color.

INDEX

NOTE: For 1979 linkage adjustment information, see car chapters.

TURBO HYDRA-MATIC 180

TRANSMISSION IDENTIFICATION

This transmission may be identified by the following codes located on the tag attached to the right side of the transmission.

CHEVETTE

1977-78 4-98 . . . . ND

GENERAL DESCRIPTION

This transmission is a fully automatic unit consisting primarily of a three-element hydraulic torque converter and a compound planetary gear set, Fig. 1. Three multiple disc clutches, a roller clutch and a band provide the friction elements required to obtain the desired function of the compound planetary gear set. The compound planetary gear set provides three forward speeds and reverse.

The torque converter couples the engine to the planetary gears through oil and provides torque multiplication. It consists of a pump or driving member, a turbine or driven member and a stator assembly. The stator is mounted on a one-way roller clutch which allows the stator to turn clockwise but not counterclockwise.

The torque converter housing is filled with oil and rotates at engine speed. The converter pump is an integral part of the converter housing, therefore the pump blades rotating at engine speed set the oil within the converter into motion and direct it to the turbine causing the turbine to rotate. As the oil passes through the turbine it travels in such a direction that if it were not redirected by the stator it would strike the rear of the converter pump blades and impede its pumping action. Therefore at low turbine speeds, the oil is redirected by the stator to the converter pump in such a manner that it actually assists the converter pump to deliver power or multiply engine torque. As turbine speed increases, the direction of the oil leaving the turbine changes and flows against the rear side of the stator vanes in a clockwise direction. Since the stator is now impeding the smooth flow of oil, its roller clutch releases and it revolves freely on its shaft. Once the stator becomes inactive, there is no further multiplication of torque within the converter. At this point the converter is acting as a fluid coupling since the converter pump and turbine are being driven at about the same speed, or at a one-to-one ratio.

The hydraulic system in this transmission is pressurized by a gear type pump to provide the working pressures required to operate the friction elements and automatic controls.

TROUBLE-SHOOTING

Low Fluid Level

1. Fluid coming out of filler tube.
2. External fluid leak.
3. Defective vacuum modulator.

Fluid Coming Out of Filler Tube

1. High fluid level.
2. Engine coolant in transmission fluid.
3. Clogged external vent.
4. Leak in pump suction circuit.

Low Fluid Pressure

1. Low fluid level.
2. Clogged screen.
3. Leak in oil pump suction or pressure circuit.
4. Stuck priming valve.
5. Faulty pressure regulator valve.
6. Missing sealing ball in valve body.

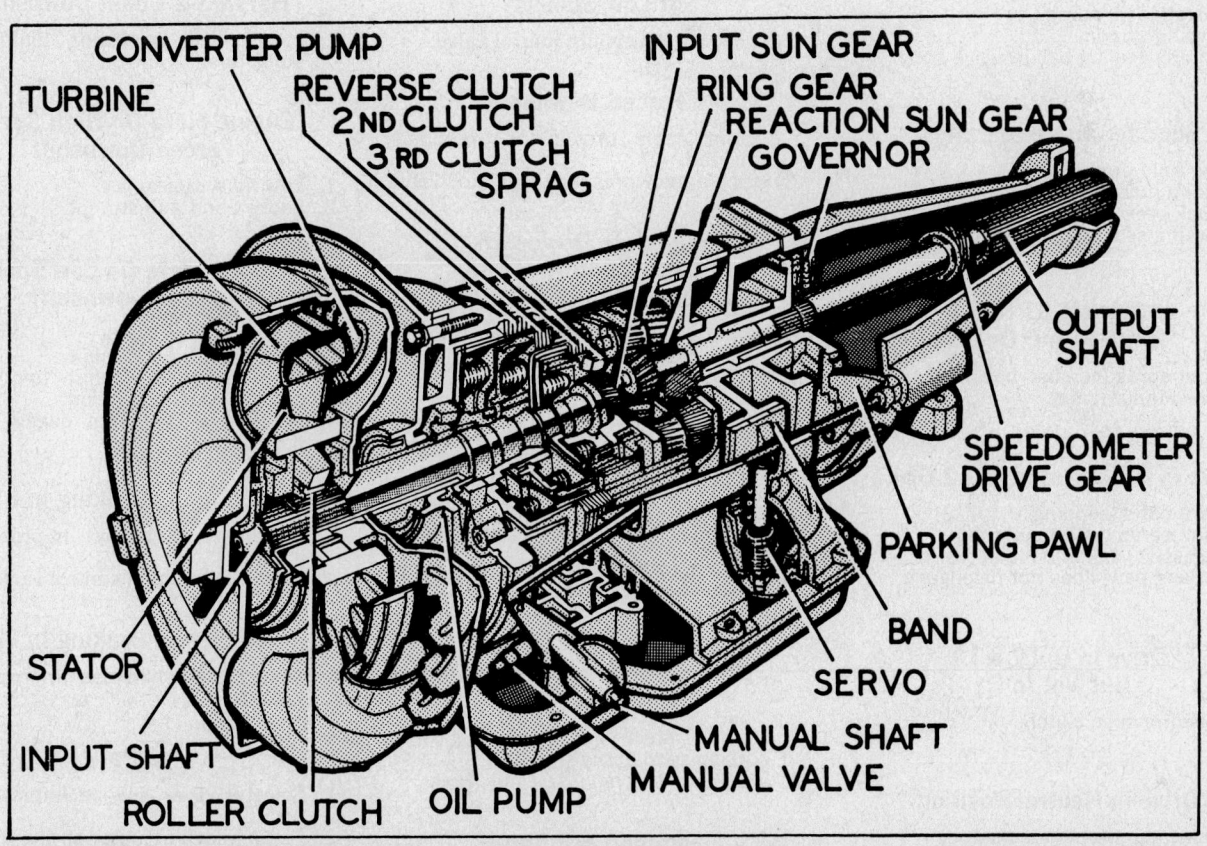

Fig. 1   Turbo Hydra-Matic 180 transmission

High Fluid Pressure

1. Modulator vacuum line leaking.
2. Defective vacuum modulator.
3. Leak in vacuum system.
4. Defective pressure regulator valve.

No Drive

1. Low fluid level.
2. Clogged screen.
3. Manual valve linkage or inner transmission selector lever disconnected.
4. Broken input shaft.
5. Pressure regulator valve stuck in open position.
6. Defective oil pump.

Delayed Engagement

1. Manual valve position does not coincide with valve body channels.
   a. Missing selector lever shaft retaining pin.
   b. Loose connecting rod to manual valve connection.
   c. Loose selector lever shaft nut.

No Drive When Shifting From P to D, L2 Or L1

1. Parking pawl does not engage.

Harsh Engagement

1. Band servo piston jamming.
2. Low fluid level.
3. Defective oil pump.
4. Missing screen.
5. Missing sealing ball in valve body.

Shudder on Acceleration

1. Low fluid pressure.
2. Wrong modulator valve installed.
3. Stuck pressure regulator valve.
4. Missing sealing ball in valve body.

Drive in L1 & R But Not In D Or L2

1. Input sprag installed backwards.
2. Failed input sprag.

Drive in R But Not In D, L2 Or L1

1. Worn band, slipping.
2. Band servo piston jamming.
3. Excessive leak in band servo.
4. Parking pawl does not disengage.

Drive In D, L2 & L1 But Not In R

1. Failed reverse clutch.

Drive In Neutral Position

1. Linkage improperly adjusted.
2. Broken planetary gear set.
3. Band inproperly adjusted.

No 1-2 Upshift In D & L2

1. Stuck governor valves.
2. 1-2 shift valve stuck in first gear position.
3. Leaking seal rings in oil pump hub.
4. Excessive leak in governor pressure circuit.
5. Clogged governor screen.

No 2-3 Upshift In D

1. 2-3 shift valve stuck.
2. Excessive leak in governor pressure circuit.

Upshifts In D & L2 Only At Full Throttle

1. Faulty vacuum modulator.
2. Modulator vacuum line leaking.
3. Leak in vacuum system.
4. Stuck detent valve or cable.

Upshifts In D Or L2 Only At Part Throttle No Detent Upshift

1. Stuck detent regulator valve.
2. Detent cable broken or adjusted improperly.

Drive In 1st. Gear of D Or L2

1. L1 and R control valve stuck in L1 or R position.

No Part Throttle 3-2 Downshift At Low Speeds

1. Stuck 3-2 downshift control valve.

No Forced Downshifts

1. Detent cable broken or improperly adjusted.
2. Stuck detent pressure regulator valve.

Immediate Downshift After Full Throttle Upshift & Releasing Accelerator

1. Detent valve stuck in open position.
2. Detent cable stuck.
3. Clogged or leaking vacuum modulator line.

Transmission Downshifts At High Vehicle Speeds

1. Missing selector lever shaft retaining pin.
2. Loose selector lever linkage to manual valve connection.
3. Pressure leak at governor.

Hard Disengagement From Park Position

1. Missing steel guide bushing from parking pawl actuating rod.
2. Stuck manual valve selector lever.

Slipping 1-2 Shift

1. Low fluid pressure.

2. Missing sealing ball in valve body.
3. Leaking second clutch piston seals.
4. Second clutch piston centrifugal ball stuck open.
5. Second clutch piston cracked or broken.
6. Second clutch plates worn.
7. Leaking oil pump hub sealing rings.

Slipping 2-3 Shift

1. Low fluid pressure.
2. Improper band adjustment.
3. Third clutch piston seals leaking.
4. Third clutch piston centrifugal ball stuck open.
5. Third clutch piston cracked or broken.
6. Worn input shaft bushing.
7. Missing sealing ball in valve body.

Harsh 1-2 Shift

1. High fluid pressure.
2. 1-2 accumulator valve stuck.
3. Second clutch spring cushion broken.
4. Second gear ball valve missing.

Harsh 2-3 Shift

1. High fluid pressure.
2. Improper band adjustment.

Harsh 3-2 Detent Downshift At High Vehicle Speeds

1. High speed downshift valve stuck open.
2. Improper band adjustment.

Harsh 3-2 Coast Downshift

1. Low speed downshift timing valve stuck open.

Engine Flare On High Speed Forced Downshift

1. Low fluid pressure.
2. Loose band adjustment.

Engine Flare On Low Speed Forced Downshift

1. Low fluid pressure.
2. Loose band adjustment.
3. High speed downshift timing valve stuck in closed position.
4. Sprag race does not engage on 3-1 downshift.

No Engine Braking In L1

1. Selector level linkage improperly adjusted.
2. Stuck low manual control valve.

No Engine Braking In L2

1. Selector lever linkage improperly adjusted.

No Park

1. Selector lever linkage improperly adjusted.
2. Parking lock actuator spring broken.
3. Parking pawl.
4. Governor hub.

Excessive Noises In All Drive Ranges

1. Excessive backlash between sun gear and planetary gears.
2. Lock plate on planetary carrier loose.
3. Defective thrust bearing.
4. Worn bearing bushings.
5. Excessive transmission axial play.
6. Unhooked parking pawl spring contacting governor hub.
7. Converter balancing weights loose.
8. Converter housing attaching bolts loose and contacting converter.

Screeching Noise On Acceleration

1. Converter failure.

Short Vibrating Hissing Noise Before 1-2 Upshift

1. Reverse clutch dampening cushion wearing into transmission case.

MAINTENANCE

To check fluid, drive vehicle for at least 15 minutes to bring fluid to operating temperature (200° F). With vehicle on a level surface and engine idling in Park and parking brake applied, the level on the dipstick should be at the "F" mark. To bring the fluid level from the ADD mark to the FULL mark requires one pint of fluid. If vehicle cannot be driven sufficiently to bring fluid to operating temperature, the level on the dipstick should be between the two dimples on the dipstick with fluid temperature at 70° F.

If additional fluid is required, use only Dexron II automatic transmission fluid.

NOTE: An early change to a darker color from the usual red color and or a strong odor that is usually associated with overheated fluid is normal and should not be considered as a positive sign of required maintenance or unit failure.

CAUTION: When adding fluid, do not over fill, as foaming and loss of fluid through the vent may occur as the fluid heats up. Also, if fluid level is too low, complete loss of drive may occur especially when cold, which can cause transmission failure.

Every 60,000 miles, the oil should be drained, the oil pan removed, the screen cleaned and fresh fluid added. For vehicles subjected to more severe use such as heavy city traffic especially in hot weather, prolonged periods of idling or towing, this maintenance should be performed every 15,000 miles.

Draining Bottom Pan

1. Raise vehicle, then remove drain plug and allow fluid to drain for at least 5 minutes.
2. If oil screen is to be serviced, remove oil pan bolts, oil pan and gasket.
3. Remove oil screen to valve body bolts, screen and gasket.
4. Thoroughly clean oil screen and oil pan with solvent.
5. Install oil screen using a new gasket and torque attaching bolts to 13-15 ft. lbs., then install oil pan using a new gasket and torque attaching bolts to 13-15 ft. lbs.
6. Add three quarts of fluid, then with engine idling and parking brake applied, move selector lever through each range and return selector lever to PARK.
7. Check fluid level and add fluid as required to bring level between the two dimples on the dipstick.

Adding Fluid To Dry Transmission

1. Add 4.9 quarts of fluid.
2. With transmission in PARK and parking brake applied, start engine and place carburetor on fast idle cam.
3. Move shifter lever through each range then with transmission in PARK, add additional fluid as required to bring the level between the two dimples on the dipstick.

IN-VEHICLE ADJUSTMENTS

Manual Linkage, Adjust

1. Place shifter assembly (A) in Neutral position, Fig. 2.
2. With link (B) loosely assembled to rod (F) and rod (F) attached to lever (G), place lever (G) in Neutral posi-

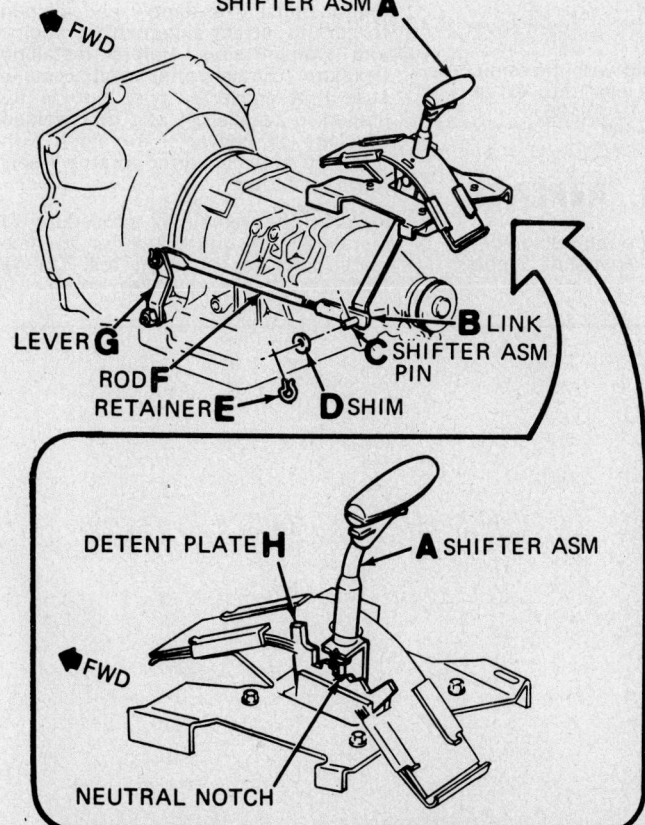

Fig. 2 Manual linkage adjustment. 1977-78 Turbo Hydra-Matic 180

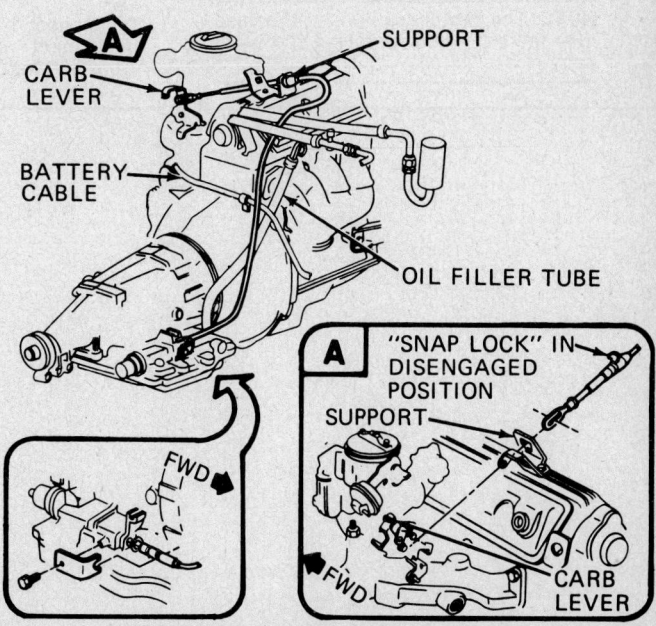

Fig. 3 Detent downshift cable adjustment. 1977-78 Turbo Hydra-Matic 180

tion. To obtain Neutral position, move lever (G) clockwise to maximum detent position (Park), then counterclockwise two detents to Neutral position.

3. While holding lever (G) in Neutral position, adjust link (B) until hole aligns with shifter assembly pin (C), then install link onto pin.

4. Install shim (D) and retainer (E). CAUTION: The above procedure must be followed exactly, since any inaccuracies may result in premature failure of the transmission due to operation without controls in full detent.

Detent Downshift Cable, Adjust

1. Disengage cable "Snap Lock" from support, Fig. 3.

   NOTE: Cable should be free to slide through "Snap Lock".

2. With cable installed in support and attached to transmission and carburetor lever, move carburetor lever to wide open throttle position.

3. Push "Snap Lock" flush and return carburetor lever to closed position.

IN-VEHICLE REPAIRS
Valve Body, Replace

1. Drain transmission and remove oil pan and screen.

2. Remove screw and retainer securing detent cable to transmission, then disconnect detent cable.

3. Remove throttle lever and bracket assembly. Use caution not to bend the throttle lever link.

4. Remove manual detent roller and spring assembly.

5. Remove transfer plate reinforcement attaching bolts and the reinforcement.

6. Remove servo cover and gasket.

7. Remove valve body attaching bolts, then the valve body and transfer plate.

   NOTE: The two check balls in the case may fall out when removing the valve body.

8. Remove transfer plate to valve body bolts, then the plate from valve body.

9. Reverse procedure to install.

Servo Assembly, Replace

1. Remove valve body from transmission as outlined previously.

2. Compress servo piston with tool J-23075.

3. With suitable pliers, remove servo piston snap ring and slowly loosen the tool. Remove tool, servo piston return spring and apply rod from transmission.

4. Install apply rod, return spring and piston into case.

5. Use tool J-23075 to compress spring and install snap ring. Remove tool.

6. With a 3/16 inch wrench on servo adjusting bolt, adjust apply rod by torquing bolt to 40 inch lbs, then back off bolt exactly 5 turns. Tighten lock nut while holding apply rod in position.

7. Install valve body.

Speedometer Driven Gear, Replace

1. Remove bolt securing driven gear housing retainer, then the retainer.

2. Pull speedometer driven gear from housing.

3. Install speedometer driven gear into housing, then the retainer into slot of driven gear housing.

4. Install retainer attaching bolt.

Rear Extension Oil Seal

1. Remove propeller shaft.

2. Remove oil seal with a screwdriver or suitable tool.

3. Lubricate new seal lip with transmission fluid and install seal into extension housing with tool J-21426.

4. Install propeller shaft.

TRANSMISSION, REPLACE

1. Disconnect battery ground cable then disconnect detent downshift cable from bracket.

2. Remove air cleaner and dipstick, then on vehicles with air conditioning, remove the 5 heater core retaining screws, disconnect connector and place heater core assembly aside.

3. Raise and support vehicle and remove propeller shaft.

4. Disconnect speedometer cable, electrical lead, oil cooler lines, and shift control linkage.

5. Support transmission with suitable jack and remove the crossmember retaining bolts.

6. Remove converter to bracket retaining nuts, then disconnect exhaust pipes from rear of catalytic converter and from exhaust manifolds and remove catalytic converter and converter bracket as an assembly.

7. Remove converter dust shield and remove converter to flywheel bolts.

8. Lower transmission until it is barely supported by jack and remove transmission to engine bolts.

9. Raise transmission to its normal position, then support engine with jack and lower and remove transmission from vehicle.

   NOTE: Use converter holding tool J-5384, or keep rear of transmission lower than the front to prevent the converter from sliding out.

10. Before installing transmission, place two inch blocks between rack and pinion housing assembly and oil pan to permit correct alignment of engine and transmission. Before installing flexplate to converter bolts, make sure that converter pilot hub is installed in crankshaft and that welded brackets on converter are flush with flexplate and converter rotates freely in this position.

11. Reverse the remaining procedure to install and torque converter to flexplate bolts to 20-30 ft. lbs. (27-41 Nm).

TURBO HYDRA-MATIC 200

TRANSMISSION IDENTIFICATION

This transmission may be identified by the following codes located on the serial number plate attached to the right side of the transmission.

BUICK

	CODE
1976 V6-231 Skyhawk	BH
V6-231 Skylark	BZ
V8-260 Skylark	OZ
1977 V6-231 Skyhawk Except Calif.	BH
V6-231 Skylark Calif.	BL
V6-231 Skylark Except Calif.	BZ
V8-350 LeSabre & Riviera	OS
V8-301 LeSabre & Riviera	PZ
1978 V6-231 Century Sta. Wag. & LeSabre	5BZ
V8-305 Century	5CO
V8-350 LeSabre	5BA, 5OS, 5PZ

CADILLAC

	CODE
1978 Seville	AS, AX

CHEVROLET

	CODE
1976 V8-305 Nova	CE
4-97 Chevette Except Calif.	CN
6-250 Nova	CQ
4-97 Chevette Calif.	CU
4-85 Chevette	CU
1977 V8-305 Nova	CE
V8-305 Monza	CD, CK
4-97 Chevette Less A/C	CN
8-305 Full Size	CO, CR
4-85 Chevette	CU
V8-350 Full Size	CY
4-97 Chevette With A/C	CZ
1978 Chevrolet	CO, CY
Malibu	BZ, CD, CS
Monza	CA

OLDSMOBILE

	CODE
1976 6-250 Omega	CQ
V8-260 Omega	CZ
1977 V6-231 Starfire Except Calif.	BH
V6-231 Omega Calif.	BL

OLDSMOBILE—Continued

	CODE
V6-231 Omega Except Calif.	BZ
V8-305 Starfire	CD
V8-350 Full Size	OS
V8-260 Omega	OZ
1978 Cutlass	BZ, CO, CR, OW
Full Size	BZ, OS, OT, OW
Starfire	PY

PONTIAC

	CODE
1977 V6-231 Sunbird Except Calif.	BH
V6-231 Phoenix & Ventura Calif.	BL
V6-231 Sunbird Calif.	BU
V6-231 Phoenix & Ventura Except Calif.	BZ
4-151 Sunbird	PY
4-151 Phoenix & Ventura Except Calif.	PY
V8-301 Full Size Except Calif.	PZ
V8-350 Full Size	OS
1978 4-151 Phoenix & Sunbird	PY
V6-231 LeMans Exc. Sta. Wag.	BZ
V6-231 Full Size	BZ
V8-301 LeMans & Grand Prix	PG, PH
V8-301 Full Size	PH
V8-305 LeMans	CO, CR
V8-305 Grand Prix	CO

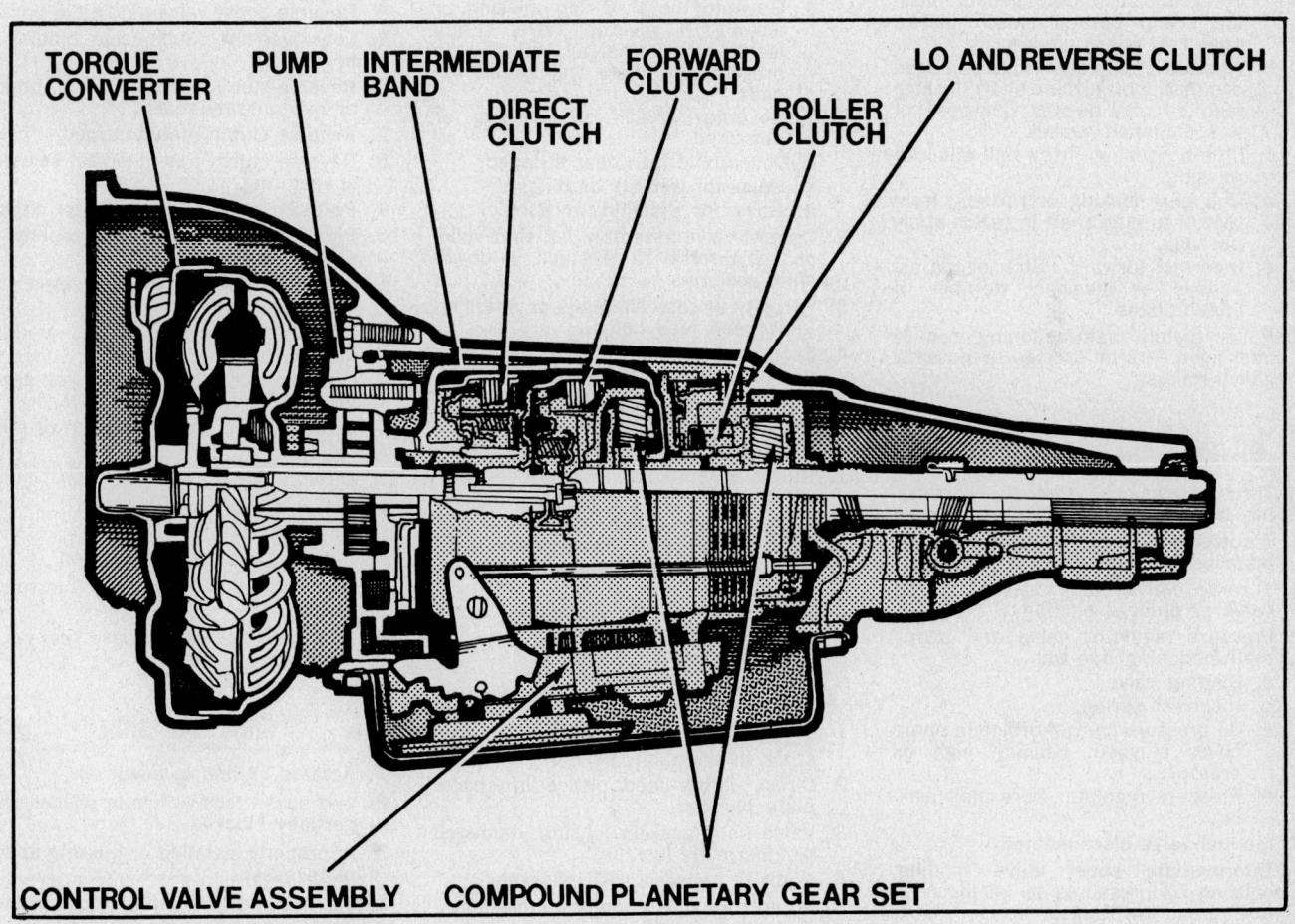

Fig. 1   Turbo Hydra-Matic 200 transmission

TURBO HYDRA-MATIC 200

Description

The Turbo Hydra-Matic 200 transmission, Fig. 1, is fully automatic and consists of a three element torque converter and a compound planetary gear set. Three multiple disc clutches, a roller clutch and a band provide the required friction elements to obtain the desired function of the planetary gear set.

TROUBLE SHOOTING GUIDE

No Drive in Drive Range

1. Low oil level.
2. Manual linkage maladjusted.
3. Low oil pressure due to:
   a. Restricted or plugged oil screen.
   b. Oil screen gasket improperly installed.
   c. Oil pump pressure regulator.
   d. Pump drive gear tangs damaged by converter.
   e. Case porosity in intake bore.
4. Forward clutch malfunctioning due to:
   a. Forward clutch not applying due to cracked piston, damaged or missing seals, burned clutch plates, snap ring not in groove.
   b. Forward clutch seal rings damaged or missing on turbine shaft, leaking feed circuits due to damaged or mispositioned gasket.
   c. Clutch housing check ball stuck or missing.
   d. Cup plug leaking or missing from rear of turbine shaft in clutch apply passage.
   e. Incorrect forward clutch piston assembly or incorrect number of clutch plates.
5. Roller clutch malfunctioning due to missing rollers or springs or possibly galled rollers.

Oil Pressure High Or Low

1. Throttle valve cable maladjusted, binding, disconnected or broken.
2. Throttle lever and bracket improperly installed, disconnected or binding.
3. Throttle valve shift valve, throttle valve or plunger binding.
4. Pressure regulator valve and spring malfunctioning due to:
   a. Binding valve.
   b. Incorrect spring.
   c. Oil pressure control orifice in pump cover plugged, causing high oil pressure.
   d. Pressure regulator bore plug leaking.
5. Manual valve disconnected.
6. Intermediate boost valve binding, causing oil pressures to be incorrect in 2nd and low ranges.
7. Orifice in spacer plate at end of intermediate boost valve plugged.
8. Reverse boost valve binding, causing pressure to be incorrect in reverse only.
9. Orifice in spacer plate at end of reverse boost valve plugged.

1-2 Shift At Full Throttle Only

1. Throttle valve cable maladjusted, binding, disconnected or broken.
2. Throttle lever and bracket assembly binding or disconnected.
3. Throttle valve exhaust ball lifter or number 5 check ball binding, mispositioned or disconnected.

NOTE: If number 5 ball is fully seated, it will cause full throttle valve pressure regardless of throttle valve position.

4. Throttle valve and plunger binding.
5. Valve body gaskets leaking, damaged or incorrectly installed.
6. Porous control valve assembly.

First Speed Only, No 1-2 Shift

1. Due to governor and governor feed passages:
   a. Plugged governor oil feed orifice in spacer plate.
   b. Plugged orifice in spacer plate that feeds governor oil to the shift valves.
   c. Balls missing in governor assembly.
   d. Governor cover O-ring missing or leaking. If governor cover O-ring leaks, an external oil leak will be present and there will be no up-shift.
   e. Governor shaft seal missing or damaged.
   f. Governor driven gear stripped.
   g. Governor weights binding.
   h. Governor assembly missing.
2. Control valve assembly 1-2 shift valve or 1-2 throttle valve stuck in downshift position.
3. Porosity in case channels or undrilled 2nd speed feed holes.
4. Excessive leakage between case bore and intermediate band apply ring.
5. Intermediate band anchor pin missing or disconnected from band.
6. Missing or broken intermediate band.
7. Due to intermediate servo assembly:
   a. Servo to cover oil seal ring damaged or missing.
   b. Porous servo cover or piston.
   c. Incorrect intermediate band apply pin.
   d. Incorrect cover and piston.

1st & 2nd Only, No 2-3, Shift

1. 2-3 shift valve or 2-3 throttle valve stuck in downshift position.
2. Direct clutch feed orifice in spacer plate plugged.
3. Valve body gaskets leaking, damaged or incorrectly installed.
4. Porosity between case passages.
5. Pump passages plugged or leaking.
6. Pump gasket incorrectly installed.
7. Rear seal on pump cover leaking or missing.
8. Direct clutch oil seals missing or damaged.
9. Direct clutch piston or housing cracked.

10. Direct clutch plates damaged or missing.
11. Direct clutch backing plate snap ring out of groove.
12. Intermediate servo to case oil seal broken or missing on intermediate servo piston.
13. Intermediate servo exhaust hole in case between servo piston seals plugged or undrilled.

Moves Forward In Neutral

1. Manual linkage maladjusted.
2. Forward clutch does not release.
3. Cross leakage between pump passages.
4. Cross leakage to forward clutch through clutch passages.

No Drive in Reverse or Slips in Reverse

1. Throttle valve cable binding or maladjusted.
2. Manual linkage maladjusted.
3. Throttle valve binding.
4. Reverse boost valve binding in bore.
5. Low overrun clutch valve binding in bore.
6. Reverse clutch piston cracked, broken or has missing seals.
7. Reverse clutch plates burned.
8. Reverse clutch has incorrect selective spacer ring.
9. Porosity in passages to direct clutch.
10. Pump to case gasket improperly installed or missing.
11. Pump passages cross leaking or restricted.
12. Pump cover seals damaged or missing.
13. Direct clutch piston or housing cracked.
14. Direct clutch piston seals cut or missing.
15. Direct clutch housing ball check, stuck, leaking or missing.
16. Direct clutch plates burned.
17. Incorrect direct clutch piston.
18. Direct clutch orifices plugged in spacer plate.
19. Intermediate servo to case seal cut or missing.

Slips 1-2 Shift

1. Aerated oil due to low level.
2. 2nd speed feed orifice in spacer plate partially blocked.
3. Improperly installed or missing spacer plate gasket.
4. 1-2 accumulator valve stuck, causing low 1-2 accumulator pressure.
5. Weak or missing 1-2 accumulator valve spring.
6. 1-2 accumulator piston seal leaking or spring missing or broken.
7. Leakage between 1-2 accumulator piston and pin.

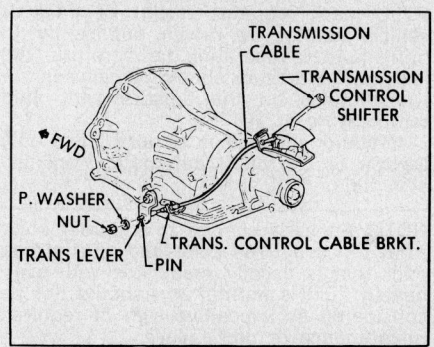

Fig. 2 Console shift manual linkage adjustment. Monza, Skyhawk, Starfire & Sunbird

8. Incorrect intermediate band apply pin.
9. Excessive leakage between intermediate band apply pin and case.
10. Porous intermediate servo piston.
11. Servo cover to servo seal damaged or missing.
12. Incorrect servo and cover.
13. Throttle valve cable improperly adjusted.
14. Shift throttle valve or throttle valve binding.
15. Intermediate band worn or burned.
16. Case porosity in 2nd clutch passages.

Rough 1-2 Shift

1. Throttle valve cable improperly adjusted or binding.
2. Throttle valve or plunger binding.
3. Shift throttle or 1-2 accumulator valve binding.

4. Incorrect intermediate servo pin.
5. Intermediate servo piston to case seal damaged or missing.
6. 1-2 accumulator oil ring damaged, piston stuck, bore damaged or spring broken or missing.

Slips 2-3 Shift

1. Low oil level.
2. Throttle valve cable improperly adjusted.
3. Throttle valve binding.
4. Direct clutch orifice in spacer plate partially blocked.
5. Spacer plate gaskets improperly installed or missing.
6. Intermediate servo to case seal damaged.
7. Porous direct clutch feed passages in case.
8. Pump to case gasket improperly installed or missing.
9. Pump passages cross feeding, leaking or restricted.
10. Pump cover oil seal rings damaged or missing.
11. Direct clutch piston or housing cracked.
12. Direct clutch piston seals cut or missing.
13. Direct clutch plates burned.

Rough 2-3 Shift

1. Throttle valve cable improperly installed or missing.
2. Throttle valve or throttle valve plunger binding.
3. Shift throttle valve binding.

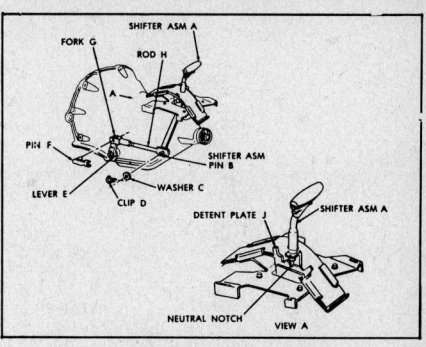

Fig. 3 Console shift manual linkage adjustment. Chevette

4. Intermediate servo exhaust hole undrilled or plugged between intermediate servo piston seals.
5. Direct clutch exhaust valve number 4 check ball missing or improperly installed.

No Engine Braking In 2nd Speed

1. Intermediate boost valve binding in valve body.
2. Intermediate-Reverse number 3 check ball improperly installed or missing.
3. Shift throttle valve number 3 check ball improperly installed or missing.
4. Intermediate servo to cover seal missing or damaged.
5. Intermediate band off anchor pin, broken or burned.

No Engine Braking In 1st Speed

1. Low overrun clutch valve binding in valve body.

NOTE: The following conditions will also cause no reverse.

2. Low-reverse clutch piston seals broken or missing.
3. Porosity in low-reverse piston or housing.
4. Low-reverse clutch housing snap ring out of case.
5. Cup plug or rubber seal missing or damaged between case and low-reverse clutch housing.

No Part Throttle Downshift

1. Throttle plunger bushing passages obstructed.
2. 2-3 throttle valve bushing passages obstructed.
3. Valve body gaskets improperly installed or damaged.
4. Spacer plate hole obstructed or undrilled.
5. Throttle valve cable maladjusted.
6. Throttle valve or shift throttle valve binding.

Low or High Shift Points

1. Throttle valve cable binding or dis-

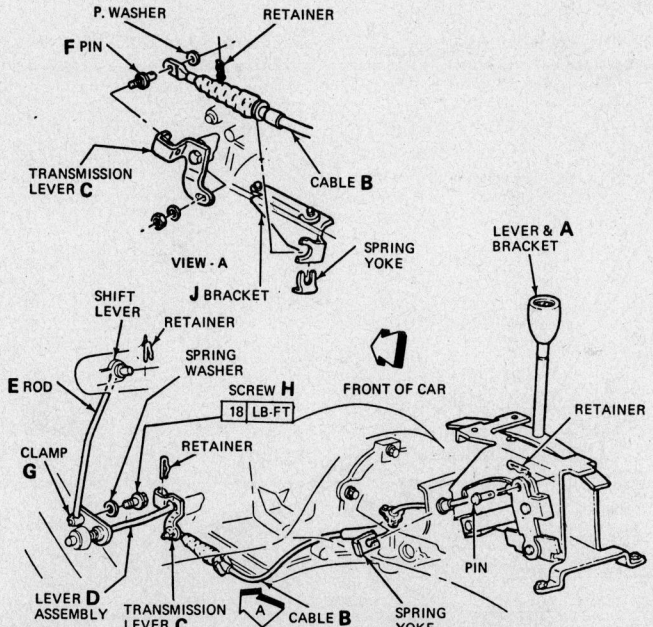

Fig. 4 Console shift manual linkage adjustment. Nova, Omega, Phoenix, Skylark & Ventura

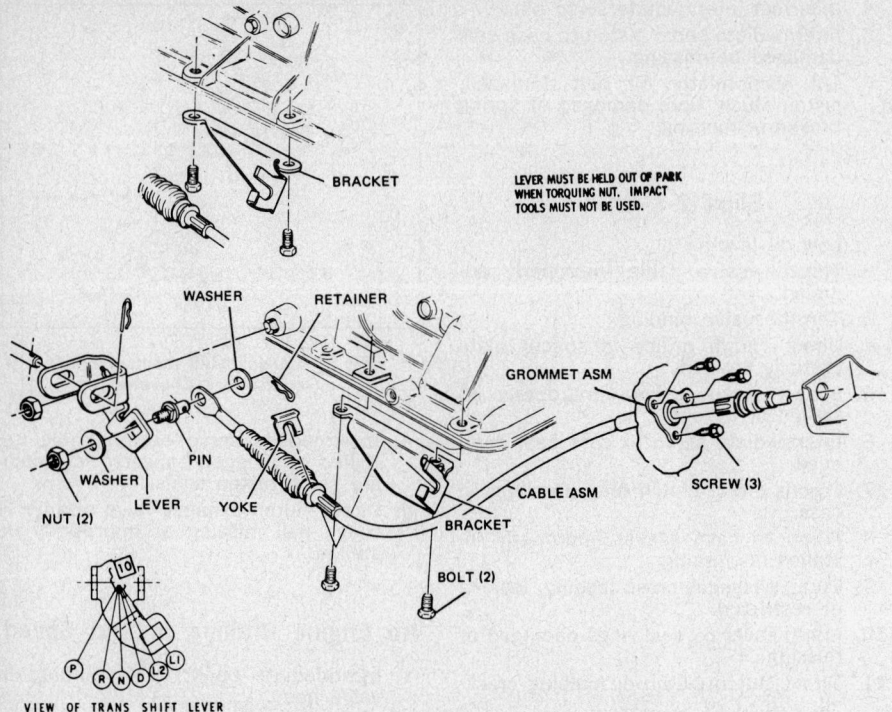

LEVER MUST BE HELD OUT OF PARK WHEN TORQUING NUT. IMPACT TOOLS MUST NOT BE USED.

VIEW OF TRANS SHIFT LEVER

Fig. 5   Console shift manual linkage adjustment. Century, Chevelle, Cutlass, Grand Prix, LeMans, Malibu, Monte Carlo & Regal

connected.

2. Throttle valve or shift throttle valve binding.
3. Number 1 throttle shift check ball improperly installed or missing.
4. Throttle valve plunger, 1-2 or 2-3 throttle valves binding.
5. Valve body gaskets improperly installed or missing.
6. Pressure regulator valve binding.
7. Throttle valve exhaust number 5 check ball and lifter, improperly installed, disconnected or missing.
8. Throttle lever binding, disconnected or loose at valve body mounting bolt or not positioned at the throttle valve plunger bushing pin locator.
9. Governor shaft to cover seal broken or missing.
10. Governor cover O-rings broken or missing.

NOTE: Outer ring will leak externally and the inner ring will leak internally.

11. Case porosity.

Will Not Hold In Park

1. Manual linkage maladjusted.
2. Parking pawl binding in case.
3. Actuator rod or plunger damaged.
4. Parking pawl damaged.
5. Parking bracket loose or damaged.
6. Detent lever nut loose.
7. Detent lever hole worn or damaged.
8. Detent roller to valve body bolt loose.
9. Detent roller or pin damaged, incorrectly installed or missing.

MAINTENANCE

To check fluid, drive vehicle for at least 15 minutes to bring fluid to operating temperature (200° F). With vehicle on a level surface and engine idling in Park and parking brake applied, the level on the dipstick should be at the "F" mark. To bring the fluid level from the ADD mark to the

FULL mark requires 1 pint of fluid. If vehicle cannot be driven sufficiently to bring fluid to operating temperature, the level on the dipstick should be between the two dimples on the dipstick with fluid temperature at 70° F.

If additional fluid is required, use only Dexron or Dexron II automatic transmission fluid.

NOTE: An early change to a darker color from the usual red color and or a strong odor that is usually associated with overheated fluid is normal and should not be considered as a positive sign of required maintenance or unit failure.

CAUTION: When adding fluid, do not overfill, as foaming and loss of fluid through the vent may occur as the fluid heats up. Also, if fluid level is too low, complete loss of drive may occur especially when cold, which can cause transmission failure.

Every 60,000 miles, the oil should be drained, the oil pan removed, the screen cleaned and fresh fluid added. For vehicles subjected to more severe use such as heavy city traffic especially in hot weather, prolonged periods of idling or towing, this maintenance should be performed every 15,000 miles.

Draining Bottom Pan

1. Remove front and side oil pan attaching bolts, then loosen the rear oil pan attaching bolts.
2. Carefully pry oil pan loose and allow fluid to drain into a suitable container.
3. Remove the oil pan and gasket, then remove the screen attaching bolts and remove screen.
4. Thoroughly clean oil screen and oil pan with solvent.
5. Install oil screen using a new gasket

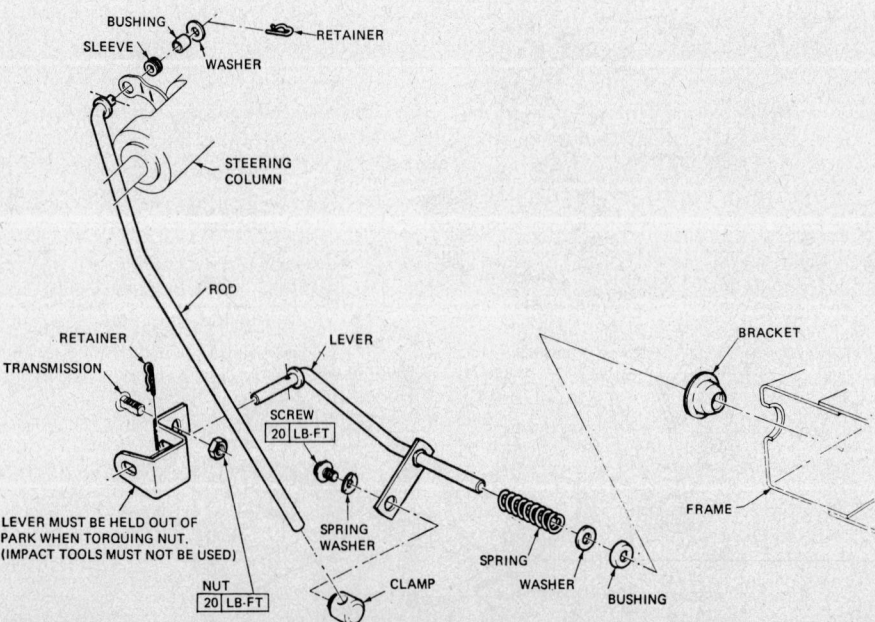

LEVER MUST BE HELD OUT OF PARK WHEN TORQUING NUT. (IMPACT TOOLS MUST NOT BE USED.)

Fig. 6   Column shift manual linkage adjustment. Nova, Omega, Phoenix, Skylark & Ventura

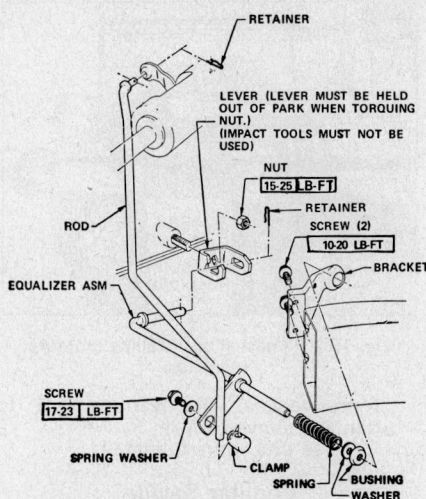

Fig. 7 Column shift manual linkage adjusment. Century, Chevelle, Cutlass, Grand Prix, LeMans, Malibu, Monte Carlo & Regal

and torque attaching bolts to 6-10 ft. lbs., then install oil pan using a new gasket and torque attaching bolts to 10-13 ft. lbs.

6. Add 3 quarts of fluid, then with engine idling and parking brake applied, move selector lever through each range and return selector lever to PARK.
7. Check fluid level and add fluid as required to bring level between the two dimples on the dipstick.

Adding Fluid To Dry Transmission and Converter

1. Add 4½ quarts of fluid.
2. With transmission in PARK and parking brake applied, start engine and place carburetor on fast idle cam.
3. Move shifter lever through each range, then with transmission in PARK, add additional fluid as required to bring the level between the two dimples on the dipstick.

MANUAL LINKAGE, ADJUST

Console Shift
Monza, Skyhawk, Starfire & Sunbird

1. Loosen nut on transmission lever, Fig. 2.
2. Place transmission control shifter in Neutral position.
3. Place transmission lever in Neutral position.
4. Torque transmission lever nut to 20 ft. lbs.
5. Check for proper operation.

Chevette

1. Place shift lever (A) in neutral position, Fig. 3.
2. Move lever (E) clockwise to maximum detent to PARK, then move lever counterclockwise two detent positions to NEUTRAL.
3. With lever (E) in NEUTRAL, insert pin

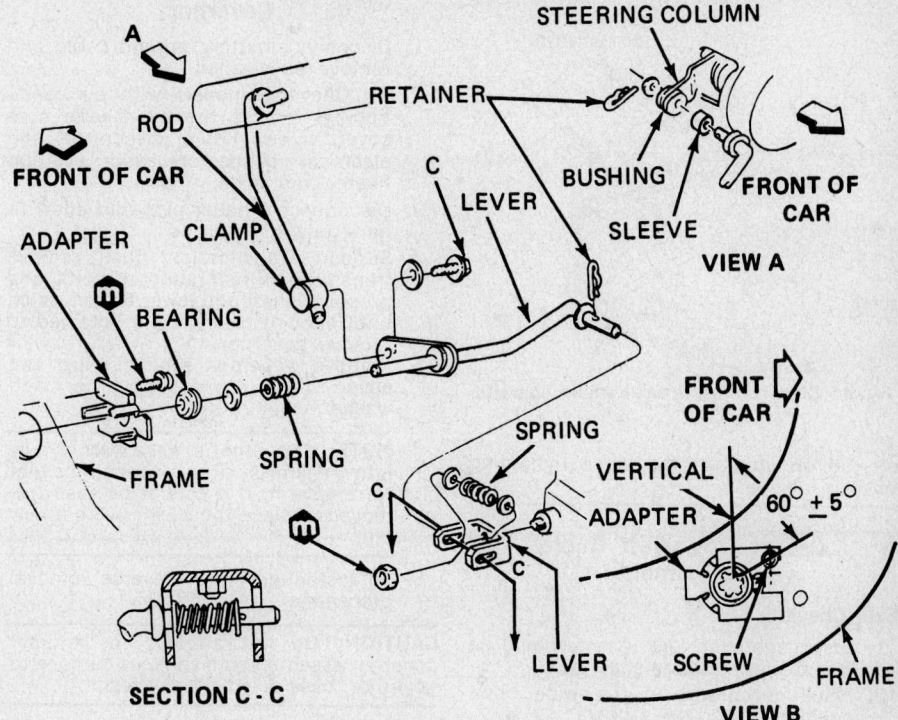

Fig. 7A Column shift manual linkage adjustment. 1978 Cadillac Seville

(F) on fork (G). Adjust rod (H) until hole in rod aligns with shifter assembly pin (B) and install rod on pin.

Nova, Omega, Phoenix, Skylark & Ventura, Fig. 4

1. Attach cable (B) to transmission lever (A) with pin, retainer and spring, yoke, then place transmission lever (A) in Drive position.
2. Install lever assembly (D), then place lever (D) in Drive position by turning lever (C) counterclockwise to Low and then clockwise three detent positions to Drive.
3. Install cable (B) to lever (C) with pin (F) and retainer and bracket (J) with spring yoke.
4. Place transmission lever (A) in Park position and turn ignition switch to Lock position.
5. Install rod (E) to shift lever with retainer, then slide clamp (G) onto rod

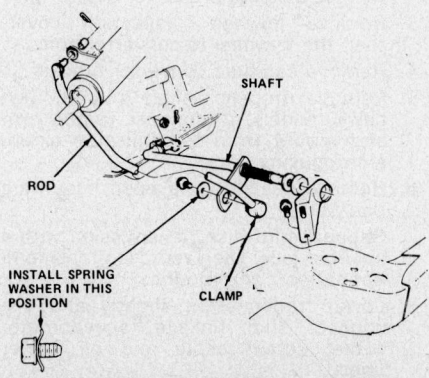

Fig. 8 Column shift linkage adjustment. All full size models except Grand Prix

(E) and loosely assemble clamp, spring washer and screw (H) to lever (D).
6. Remove column lash by rotating shift lever downward and retain rod (E) with screw (H).

Century, Chevelle, Cutlass, Grand Prix, Le-Mans, Malibu, Monte Carlo & Regal, Fig. 5

1. Place shift lever in Park position and transmission lever in Park position.
2. Move pin to obtain a "free pin" fit in transmission lever and torque retaining nut to 20 ft. lbs.

Column Shift

Intermediate Models Figs. 6, 7 & 7A

1. Place shift lever and transmission lever in Neutral position.
2. Assemble clamp, spring washer and screw to equalizer lever and control rod.
3. Hold clamp flush against equalizer lever and lightly tighten clamping screw against rod.
4. On all models except Cadillac Seville, torque clamp screw to 20 ft. lbs. On Cadillac Seville torque clamp screw to 23 ft. lbs.

NOTE: Do not exert force in either direction on rod or equilizer rod while tightening screw.

All Full Size Models Except Grand Prix, Fig. 8

1. Position shift lever and transmission lever in Neutral position.
2. Hold clamp flush against equalizer lever and lightly tighten.
3. Torque bolt to 20 ft. lbs.

NOTE: Do not exert force in either direction

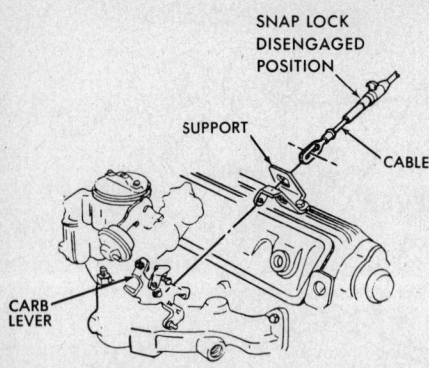

Fig. 9   Detent downshift cable adjust. Chevette

on rod or equalizer rod while tightening screw.

Detent Downshift Cable Adjustment

Exc. Chevette

1. Disengage snap lock. Cable should be free to slide through snap lock.
2. Place carburetor in the wide open position.
3. Engage snap lock and position flush with cable fitting.

Chevette

1. Disconnect cable from support, Fig. 9. and check that cable is free to slide through snap lock.
2. With cable installed in support and connected to transmission and carburetor lever, move throttle valve to wide open position.
3. Push snap lock until flush with support and throttle valve.

IN VEHICLE REPAIRS
Valve Body Assembly

1. Drain transmission fluid, then remove oil pan and screen.
2. Remove detent cable retaining bolt and disconnect cable.
3. Remove throttle lever and bracket assembly. Use care to avoid bending throttle lever link.
4. Remove detent roller and spring assembly.
5. Support valve body and remove retaining bolts, then while holding manual valve, remove valve assembly, spacer plate and gaskets as an assembly to prevent dropping the five check balls.

NOTE: After removing valve body assembly, the intermediate band anchor band pin, and reverse cup plug may be removed.

6. To install control valve, reverse removal procedure and torque all valve body bolts to 8 ft. lbs.

CAUTION: Assure that intermediate band anchor pin is located on intermediate band prior to installation of valve body, as damage will result.

Governor

1. Disconnect battery ground cable and remove air cleaner.
2. On Chevette models with air conditioning, remove the five heater core cover screws, then disconnect the electrical connectors and position heater core aside.
3. Disconnect exhaust pipe and allow to hang down.
4. Support transmission, then remove transmission rear support bolts and propeller shaft and lower transmission until enough clearance is obtained to remove governor.
5. Remove governor retainer ring and cover, then remove governor and washer.

NOTE: If governor to case washer falls into transmission, use a small magnet to remove it. If it cannot be easily removed, replace the washer with a new one.

6. To install governor, reverse removal procedure.

CAUTION: Do not attempt to hammer governor assembly into case, as damage to governor, case or cover may result.

Pressure Regulator Valve

1. Drain transmission fluid, then remove oil pan and screen.
2. Using a small screwdriver or tool J-24684, Fig. 10, compress regulator spring.
3. Remove retaining ring and slowly release spring tension.
4. Remove pressure regulator bore plug, valve, spring and guide.
5. To assemble, install pressure regulator spring, guide and valve with stem end first and bore plug with hole side out.
6. Using a small screwdriver or tool J-24684, Fig. 5, compress regulator spring and install retaining ring.

TRANSMISSION REPLACE
Buick

1. Disconnect battery ground cable and the detent cable at carburetor.
2. Raise vehicle and on Skyhawk models, remove exhaust crossover pipe.
3. Remove flywheel inspection cover, then the flywheel to converter bolts.
4. Remove catalytic converter bracket.
5. Remove propeller shaft and on Skyhawk models, disconnect torque arm and mount from transmission extension housing.
6. Remove rear transmission mounting pad bolts.
7. Support and raise transmission with a suitable jack, then remove crossmember support and mount.
8. Lower transmission slightly and disconnect shift linkage, speedometer cable, detent cable and oil cooler lines.
9. Remove transmission to engine bolts and the filler pipe.
10. Move transmission rearward and lower

Fig. 10   Removing or installing pressure regulator

from vehicle. Use caution not to damage converter.
11. Reverse procedure to install.

Cadillac Seville

1. From inside vehicle, hold sleeve and pull cable outward, then lift snap lock.
2. Remove transmission oil level dipstick and upper dipstick tube retaining bolt.
3. Raise vehicle, then remove detent cable retaining bolt.
4. Remove detent cable from link and plug hole.
5. Disconnect transmission cooler line at transmission.
6. Remove catalytic converter support bracket.
7. Support engine, then remove flywheel cover and three bolts attaching converter to flywheel.

NOTE: Mark flywheel and converter so they can be installed in the same position.

8. Disconnect speedometer cable, then remove cotter pin from shift linkage.
9. Remove propeller shaft.
10. Remove transmission support attaching bolts, then raise transmission using a suitable jack and remove support.
11. Lower transmission slightly and remove transmission to engine attaching bolts.
12. Move transmission rearward and carefully lower from vehicle.

NOTE: Use tool No. J-21366 to hold converter in position.

13. Reverse procedure to install.

Chevrolet
Exc. Chevette

1. Disconnect battery ground cable and the detent cable from carburetor. Remove filler tube.
2. Raise vehicle and remove propeller shaft.
3. Disconnect speedometer cable, electrical lead to case, oil cooler pipes and the shift linkage.
4. Support transmission with a suitable jack and remove the four rear transmission support bolts.
5. Remove nuts securing catalytic converter bracket to support.
6. On Monza and Vega models, disconnect torque arm from transmission and push toward left side of vehicle.
7. On all models, remove torque converter under pan.

8. Remove converter to flywheel bolts.
9. Lower transmission slightly and remove engine to transmission bolts.
10. Raise transmission and move rearward, then lower from vehicle.
11. Reverse procedure to install.

Chevette

1. Disconnect battery ground cable then disconnect detent downshift cable from bracket.
2. Remove air cleaner and dipstick, then on vehicles with air conditioning, remove the 5 heater core retaining screws, disconnect connector and place heater core assembly aside.
3. Raise and support vehicle and remove propeller shaft.
4. Disconnect speedometer cable, electrical lead, oil cooler lines, and shift control linkage.
5. Support transmission with suitable jack and remove the crossmember retaining bolts.
6. Remove converter to bracket retaining nuts, then disconnect exhaust pipes from rear of catalytic converter and from exhaust manifolds and remove catalytic converter and converter bracket as an assembly.
7. Remove converter dust shield and remove converter to flywheel bolts.
8. Lower transmission until it is barely supported by jack and remove transmission to engine bolts.
9. Raise transmission to its normal position, then support engine with jack

and lower and remove transmission from vehicle.

NOTE: Use converter holding tool J-5384, or keep rear of transmission lower than the front to prevent the converter from sliding out.

10. Before installing transmission, place two inch blocks between rack and pinion housing assembly and oil pan to permit correct alignment of engine and transmission.
11. Reverse removal procedure to install and torque converter to flywheel bolts to 30-40 ft. lbs. (40-54 N-m).

Oldsmobile

1. Disconnect battery ground cable and the detent cable from carburetor or accelerator lever. Remove filler tube.
2. Raise vehicle and disconnect detent cable, shift linkage and oil cooler pipes.
3. Remove catalytic converter support bracket and flywheel cover pan.
4. Remove flywheel to converter bolts.
5. Disconnect speedometer cable and remove propeller shaft.
6. On Starfire, disconnect torque arm from transmission.
7. On all models, remove transmission support to transmission bolts and the transmission support to frame bolts.
8. Support and raise transmission with a suitable jack, then remove support.

9. Lower transmission slightly and remove engine to transmission bolts.
10. Move transmission rearward and lower from vehicle.
11. Reverse procedure to install.

Pontiac

1. Disconnect battery ground cable.
2. Disconnect detent cable from carburetor, then remove dipstick and oil filler tube from transmission.
3. Remove detent cable retaining bolt and cable. Plug opening to prevent entry of dirt.
4. Disconnect transmission cooler lines and speedometer cable from transmission.
5. Disconnect shift linkage from selector lever. If equipped with console, remove spring clip and detent cable from transmission bracket.
6. Remove flywheel cover and then the flywheel to converter bolts.
7. Remove propeller shaft.
8. Remove transmission support to transmission mount bolts and transmission support to mount bolts.
9. Raise transmission with a suitable jack and remove support, then lower transmission and remove transmission to engine bolts.
10. Remove transmission being careful not to damage oil coller lines and detent cable.
11. Reverse procedure to install.

TURBO HYDRA-MATIC 250, 350, 375B

TRANSMISSION IDENTIFICATION

A production day and shift built number, transmission model and model year are stamped on the 1-2 accumulator cover, which is located on the middle lower right side of the transmission case.

BUICK	CODE
1974 6-250	JE
V8-350 Century	KA
V8-350 LeSabre	KL
1975 V6-231 Skyhawk Exc. Calif.	KX
V6-231 Skyhawk Calif.	KD
V6-231 Skylark	KC
V6-231 Century	KB
6-250 Apollo	JE
V8-260 Apollo/Skylark Exc. Calif.	LA
V8-260 Apollo/Skylark Calif.	NC
V8-350 Apollo/Skylark	KA
V8-350 Century	KE
V8-350 Le Sabre	KL
1976 V6-231 Skyhawk	KD
V6-231 Skylark	KC

BUICK—Continued	CODE
V6-231 Century	KB
V6-231 LeSabre	KM
V8-260 Skylark Exc. Calif.	LA
V8-260 Skylark Calif.	NC
V8-350 Skylark	KA
V8-350 Century	KE
V8-350 LeSabre	KL
V8-350 LeSabre & Electra	KK
1977 V6-231 Skyhawk	KD
V6-231 Skylark	KK
V6-231 Skylark	KS
V6-231 Century	KE
V6-231 Century	KW
V6-231 LeSabre, Estate Wag. & Riviera	KW
V8-301 Skylark	KC
V8-305 Skylark	KJ
V8-350 Skylark	KX
V8-350 Century	KA
V8-350 Century	LE
V8-350 LeSabre, Estate Wag. & Riviera	JB
V8-350 Electra	JB
V8-350 Rivera & Electra	LT
V8-350 Estate Wag. & Skylark	LC
V8-403 Century	LM
V8-403 LeSabre & Estate Wagon	LA

BUICK—Continued	CODE
1978 V6-196 Century	5KD
V6-231 Skyhawk	5KA
V6-231 Century, LeSabre & Skylark	5KE
V6-231 Century & LeSabre	5KJ
V6-231 Skyhawk	5KL
V8-301 LeSabre	5MO
V8-305 Century, LeSabre & Skylark	5JC
V8-305 Century & Skylark	5KC
V8-350 LeSabre	5KH, 5LA, 5LH
V8-350 Century, LeSabre & Skylark	5JD
V8-403 Century, LeSabre & Skylark	5JD
V8-403 LeSabre	5LC, 5LE, 5LK

CHEVROLET	CODE
1974 V8-400 2 Bar. Carb. Chevelle	AW
V8-350 Camaro Exc. Z28, Chevelle & Nova	FB
V8-400 4 Bar. Carb. Chevelle	FB
V8-400 4 Bar. Carb. Chevrolet	FD, FH
V8-350 Police & Taxi	FH
V8-400 2 Bar. Carb. Chevrolet	FH
V8-400 4 Bar. Carb. Chevrolet	FW
V8-350 Police & Taxi	HA
6-250 Camaro, Chevelle & Nova	TT
6-250 Nova	TZ

CHEVROLET—Continued	CODE
1975 4-140 Vega (T.H. 250)	DJ
6-250 All With T.H. 250	TZ
6-250 Chevelle	DE
V8-262 Monza 2+2 (T.H. 250)	FU
V8-262 Nova	DD
V8-350 4 Bar. carb. Nova	YA
V8-350 Chevelle	HB
V8-350 Monte Carlo	JA
V8-350 Chevrolet	YC
V8-350 Chevrolet Police	YD
V8-400 Chevelle	YB
1976 4-140 Monza & Vega	DJ
6-250 Chevelle	TA
6-250 Nova	JB
6-250 Camaro & Nova	TK
V8-262 Monza	FU
V8-305 Camaro & Nova	XE
V8-305 Chevelle	TH
V8-350 Camaro & Nova	TF
V8-350 Chevelle & Monte Carlo	XX
V8-350 Corvette	XH
V8-400 Chevelle & Monte Carlo Exc. Calif.	XB
V8-400 Chevelle & Monte Carlo Calif.	XA
V8-400 Chevelle & Monte Carlo Calif.	XX
Chevrolet Sta. Wag. Exc. Calif.	DG
Chevrolet Sta. Wag. Calif.	TB
Chevrolet W /2.73 rear axle Calif.	TC
Chevrolet W /3.08 rear axle	TD
1977 4-140 Monza & Vega Exc. Calif.	AP
4-140 Monza & Vega Calif.	AO
6-250 Chevelle & Monte Carlo Exc. Calif.	AD
6-250 Chevrolet Exc. Calif.	AD
6-250 Nova & Camaro Exc. Calif.	WK
6-250 Nova & Camaro Calif.	AN
V8-305 Chevelle & Monte Carlo	AF
V8-305 Chevrolet	AF
V8-305 Nova & Camaro	AG
V8-350 Chevelle & Monte Carlo	AH
V8-350 Chevrolet	AH
V8-350 Nova & Camaro Exc. Z-28	AJ
V8-350 Z-28 & Corvette	AM
1978 Monza	KK, KL, WC
Camaro & Nova	AG, AJ
Camaro	AN, WB, WK
Nova	AH, WL, WZ
Malibu & Monte Carlo	AG, AJ, AN
Malibu & Monte Carlo	KE, TE
Chevrolet	AG, AJ, AN
Chevrolet	KE, WK

OLDSMOBILE

	CODE
1974 6-250 Omega	JE
V8-350 Omega & Cutlass Exc. Calif.	LA
V8-350 Omega & Cutlass Calif.	LC
V8-350 Vista Cruiser Exc. Calif.	LE
1975 V6-231 Starfire	KD
V6-231 Starfire Exc. Calif.	KX
6-250 Omega	JB
6-250 Cutlass	JE
V8-260 Omega Exc. Calif.	LA
V8-260 Omega Calif.	NC
V8-260 Cutlass	LH
V8-350 Omega	KA
V8-350 Cutlass	LC
V8-350 Intermediate Wagons Calif.	LC
V8-350 Intermediate Wagons Exc. Calif.	LF
1976 V6-231 Starfire	KD
6-250 Omega	JB

OLDSMOBILE—Continued	CODE
6-250 Cutlass	JE
V8-260 Omega Exc. Calif.	LA
V8-260 Omega Calif.	NC
V8-260 Cutlass	LH
V8-350 Omega	KA
V8-350 Cutlass Exc. Calif.	LB
V8-350 Cutlass Calif.	LC
V8-350 Intermediate Wagons	LE
V8-350 88 Exc. Calif.	LL
1977 4-140 Starfire Exc. Calif.	AP
4-140 Starfire	AO
V6-231 Omega	KK
V6-231 Cutlass & 88	KE
V8-260 Cutlass	LH
V8-305 Omega	KJ
V8-350 Omega	KX
V8-350 Omega Hi Alt.	LK
V8-350 Omega Calif.	LL
V8-350 Cutlass Exc. Hi Alt. & Calif.	LX
V8-350 Cutlass Exc. Hi Alt.	LE
V8-350 Cutlass Hi Alt.	LD
V8-350 88 Exc. Hi Alt.	LC
V8-350 88 Wagon	LZ
V8-350 88 Wagon Hi Alt.	LK
V8-350 98	LC
V8-350 98 Exc. Hi Alt.	LT
V8-350 98 Hi Alt.	LK
V8-403 Cutlass Exc. Hi Alt.	LM
V8-403 Cutlass Hi Alt.	LP
V8-403 88 Exc. Hi Alt.	LA
V8-403 88 Hi Alt.	LJ
V8-403 98	LA
V8-403 98 Hi Alt.	LS
V8-403 98 Hi Alt.	LJ
1978 V6-231 Starfire	KA, KL
V6-231 Omega	KC
V6-231 Cutlass & 88	KE
V8-260 Cutlass & 88	LD
V8-305 Starfire	WC
V8-305 Omega & Cutlass	JC
V8-350 Omega & Cutlass	JD
V8-350 88	LA, LH
V8-350 Diesel Custom Cruiser	LJ
V8-403 88	LC, LE, LK

PONTIAC

	CODE
1974 6-250 Firebird & LeMans	JE
6-250 Ventura	TZ
V8-350 2 Bar. Carb. w/2.73 or 2.93 rear axle	MA
V8-350 w/3.08 rear axle	ME
1975 4-140 Astre	DJ
6-250 Exc. Le Mans	JB
6-250 Le Mans	JE
V8-260 Ventura	LA
V8-350 Ventura	KA
V8-350 Firebird	MA
V8-350 Le Mans	ME
V8-400 Firebird	MF
V8-400 Firebird	MG
1976 4-140 Astre & Sunbird	DJ
V6-231 Sunbird	KD
6-250 Firebird & Ventura	JB
6-250 LeMans	JE
V8-260 Ventura Exc. Calif	LA
V8-260 Ventura Calif	NC
V8-260 LeMans	LH
V8-350 Firebird	MA
V8-350 LeMans 2 Bar. Carb.	ME
V8-350 LeMans 4 Bar. Carb.	MB
V8-350 Ventura	KA
V8-400 Firebird	MG

PONTIAC—Continued	CODE
1977 4-140 Astre & Sunbird Exc. Calif. & Hi Alt.	AO
4-140 Astre & Sunbird Calif. & Hi Alt.	AP
V6-231 Astre & Sunbird	KD
V6-231 Astre & Sunbird (2.56 Ratio)	KL
V6-231 Astre & Sunbird (2.93 Ratio)	KP
V6-231 Firebird	MC
V6-231 LeMans	JB
V6-231 LeMans, Catalina & Bonneville	MD
V8-301 Ventura & Firebird	MX
V8-301 LeMans, Catalina & Bonneville	MM
V8-350 Firebird	MA
V8-350 Firebird	MJ
V8-350 LeMans, Catalina & Bonneville	ME
V8-350 LeMans & Grand Prix	LE
V8-350 LeMans & Grand Prix Alt. Perf. Pkg.	LD
V8-350 Catalina & Bonneville	ML
V8-350 Catalina, Bonneville & Ventura	LL
V8-400 Firebird	MG
V8-400 LeMans, Catalina & Bonneville Exc. Police & Trailer	MR
V8-400 Catalina & Bonneville Police & Trailer	MP
V8-400 Firebird	MZ
V8-403 LeMans & Grand Prix	LM
V8-403 Catalina & Bonneville Exc. Police & Trailer	LA
1978 V6-231 Sunbird	KA, KL
V6-231 Firebird & Phoenix	KC
V6-231 Grand Prix & LeMans	KE
V6-231 Catalina & Bonneville	KE
V8-301 Grand Prix & LeMans	MP
V8-301 Catalina & Bonneville	MD, MH, MP
V8-305 Firebird & Phoenix	JC
V8-305 Grand Prix & LeMans	JC
V8-350 Firebird, Phoenix & LeMans	JD
V8-350 Catalina & Bonneville	KH, LA, LH
V8-400 Firebird Exc. Trans Am	MC
V8-400 Firebird Trans Am	MK
V8-400 Catalina & Bonneville	ME, MJ
V8-403 Firebird	LP
V8-403 Catalina & Bonneville	LC, LE

DESCRIPTION

The Turbo Hydra-Matic 250, 350, 375B, Figs. 1 and 2, are fully automatic three speed transmissions consisting of a three element torque converter and a compound planetary gear set. The Turbo Hydra-Matic 350, 375B transmission has four multiple-disc clutches, two roller clutches and a band to provide the required friction elements to obtain the desired function of the planetary gear set. The Turbo Hydra-Matic 250 transmission uses an adjustable intermediate band in place of the intermediate clutch found in the Turbo Hydra-Matic 350. Also, the Turbo Hydra-Matic 250 has three multiple-disc clutches and one roller clutch.

The friction elements couple the engine to the planetary gears through oil pressure, providing three forward speeds and one reverse.

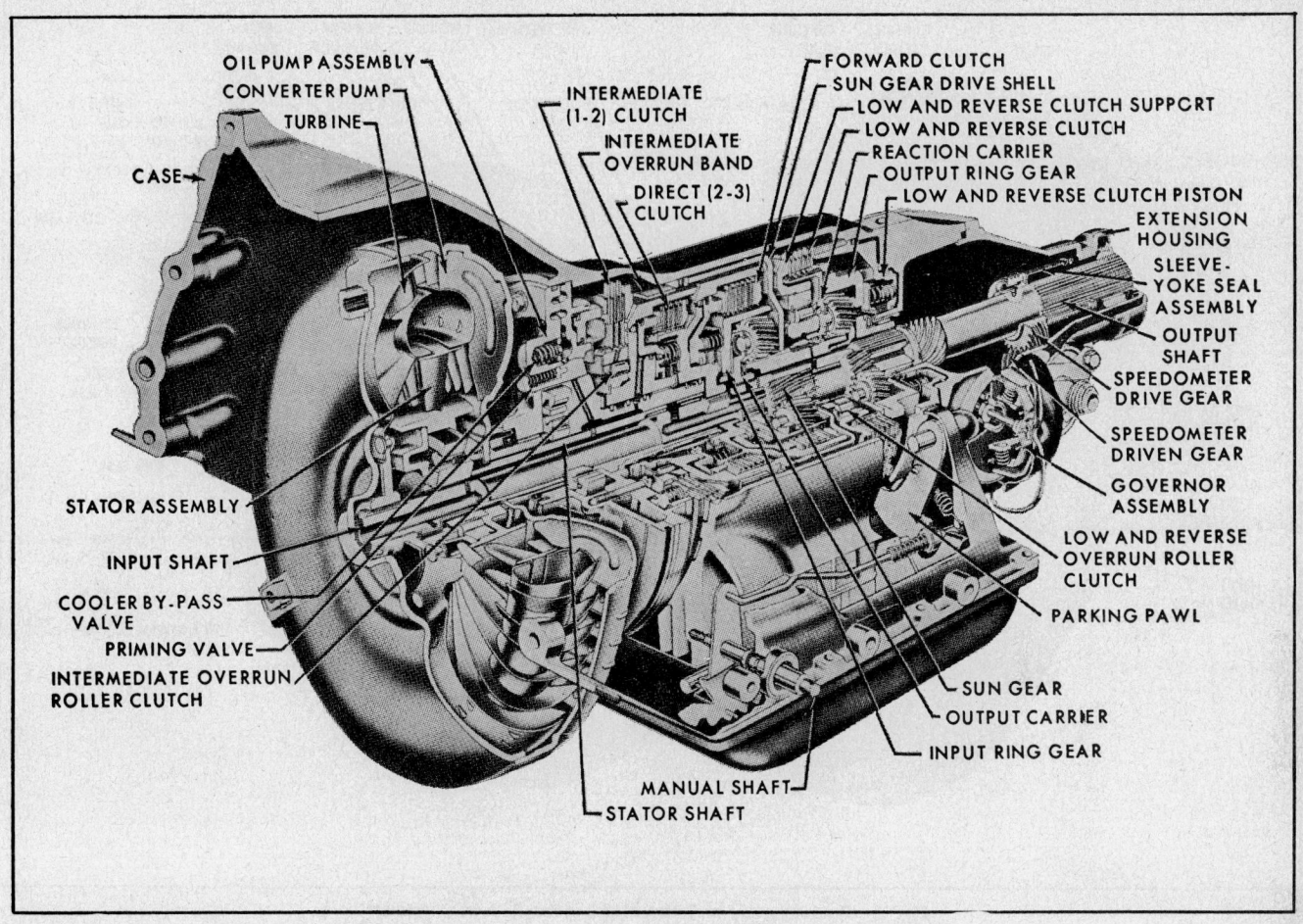

Fig. 1 Cutaway view of Turbo Hydra-Matic 350, 375B transmission

The three element torque converter is of welded construction and is serviced as an assembly. The unit consists of a pump or driving member, a turbine or driven member and a stator assembly. When required, the torque converter supplements the gears by multiplying engine torque.

TROUBLE SHOOTING GUIDE

No Drive In Drive Range

1. Low oil level (check for leaks).
2. Manual control linkage improperly adjusted.
3. Low oil pressure due to blocked strainer, defective pressure regulator, pump assembly or pump drive gear. See that tangs have not been damaged by converter. Check case for porosity in intake bore.
4. Check control valve assembly to be sure manual valve has not been disconnected from inner lever.
5. Forward clutch may be stuck or damaged. Check pump feed circuits to forward clutch, including clutch drum ball check.
6. Roller clutch assembly broken or damaged.

Oil Pressure High or Low

High Pressure:

1. Vacuum line or fittings leaking.
2. Vacuum modulator.
3. Modulator valve.
4. Pressure regulator.
5. Oil pump.

Low Pressure:

1. Vacuum line or fittings obstructed.
2. Vacuum modulator.
3. Modulator valve.
4. Pressure regulator.
5. Governor.
6. Oil pump.

1 - 2 Shift At Full Throttle Only

1. Detent valve may be sticking or linkage may be misadjusted.
2. Vacuum line or fittings leaking.
3. Control valve body gaskets leaking, damaged or incorrectly installed. Detent valve train or 1-2 valve stuck.
4. Check case for porosity.

First Speed Only, No 1 - 2 Shift

T.H.M. 250, 350 & 375B

1. Governor valve may be sticking.

2. Driven gear in governor assembly loose, worn or damaged. If driven gear shows damage, check output shaft drive gear for nicks or rough finish.
3. Control valve governor feed channel blocked or gaskets leaking. 1-2 shift valve train stuck closed.
4. Check case for blocked governor feed channels or for scored governor bore which will allow cross pressure leak. Check case for porosity.
5. Intermediate clutch or seals damaged.
6. Intermediate roller clutch damaged.

T.H.M. 250

1. Intermediate servo piston seals damaged, missing or installed improperly.
2. Intermediate band improperly adjusted.
3. Intermediate servo apply rod broken.

1st & 2nd Only, No 2 - 3 Shift

1. Control valve 2-3 shift train stuck. Valve body gaskets leaking, damaged or improperly installed.
2. Pump hub-to-direct clutch oil seal rings broken or missing.
3. Direct clutch piston seals damaged. Piston ball check stuck or missing.

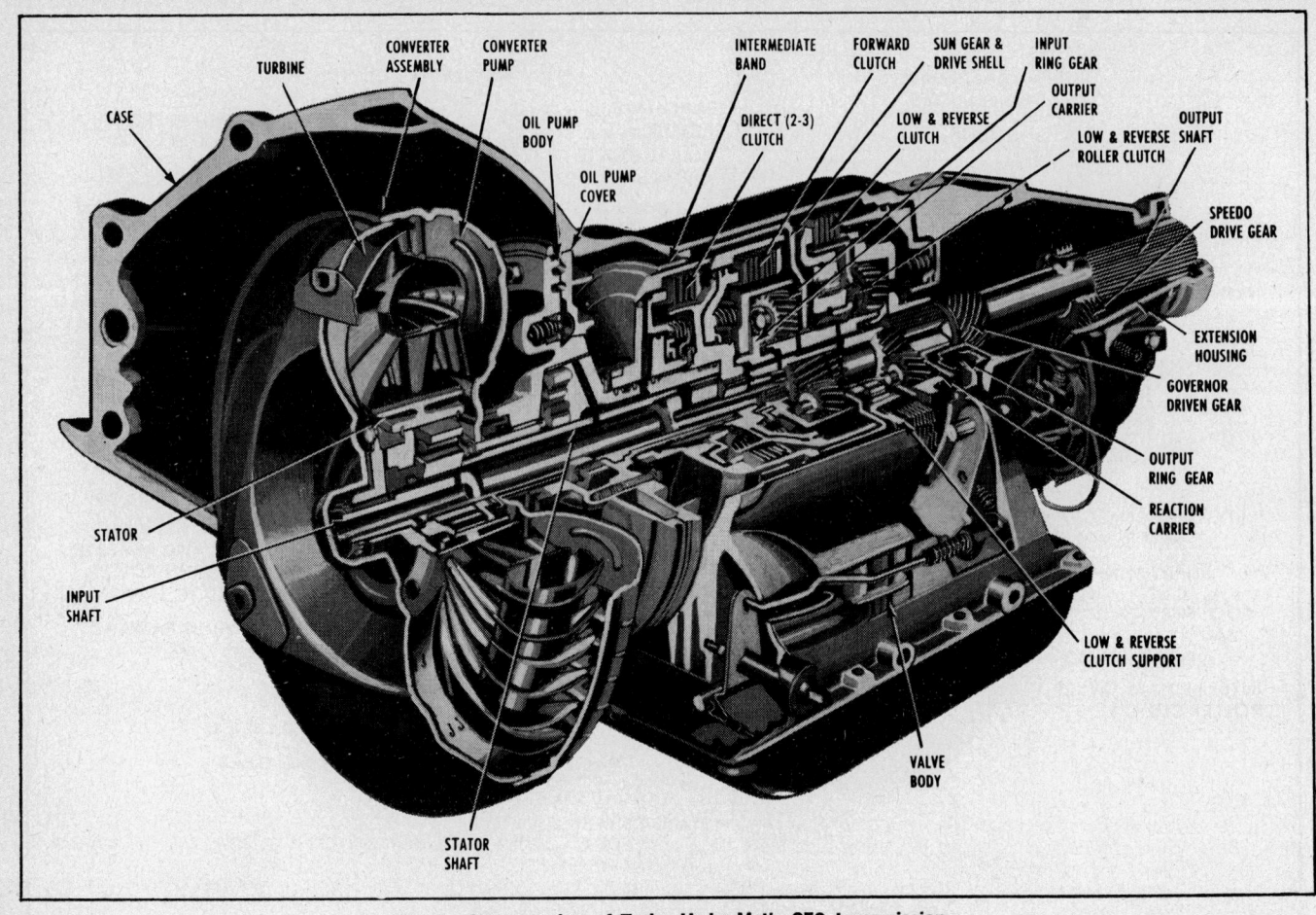

Fig. 2 Cutaway view of Turbo Hydra-Matic 250 transmission

No First Speed

T.H.M. 250

1. Intermediate band adjusted too tightly.
2. 1-2 shift valve stuck in upshift position.

T.H.M. 350, 375B

1. Excessive number of clutch plates in intermediate clutch pack.
2. Incorrect intermediate clutch piston.

Moves Forward In Neutral

1. Manual linkage misadjusted.
2. Forward clutch not releasing.

No Forward or Reverse Operation

1. Fatigue failure of forward clutch housing due to excessive pinion pin runout in output carrier.

No Drive In Reverse or Slips In Reverse

1. Low oil level.
2. Manual linkage misadjusted.
3. Modulator valve stuck.
4. Modulator and reverse boost valve stuck.

5. Pump hub-to-direct clutch oil seal rings broken or missing.
6. Direct clutch piston seal cut or missing.
7. Low and reverse clutch piston seal cut or missing.
8. Number 1 check ball missing.
9. Control valve body gaskets leaking or damaged.
10. 2-3 valve train stuck in upshifted position.
11. 1-2 valve train stuck in upshifted position.
12. Intermediate servo piston or pin stuck so intermediate band is applied.
13. Low and reverse clutch piston out or seal damaged.
14. Direct clutch plates burned — may be caused by stuck ball check in piston.
15. Forward clutch not releasing.

Slips In All Ranges

1. Low oil level.
2. Vacuum modulator valve defective or sticking.
3. Filter assembly plugged or leaking.
4. Pressure regulator valve stuck.
5. Pump to case gasket damaged.
6. Check case for cross leaks or porosity.
7. Forward clutch slipping.

Slips 1 - 2 Shift

T.H.M. 250, 350 & 375B

1. Low oil level.
2. Vacuum modulator assembly defective.
3. Modulator valve sticking.
4. Pump pressure regulator valve defective.
5. 1-2 accumulator oil ring damaged or missing. Case bore damaged.
6. Pump to case gasket mispositioned or damaged.
7. Check for case porosity.
8. Intermediate clutch piston seals damaged. Clutch plates burned.

T.H.M. 250

1. Intermediate servo piston seals damaged or missing.
2. Burned intermediate band.

T.H.M. 350, 375B

1. 2-3 accumulator oil ring damaged or missing.

Rough 1 - 2 Shift

T.H.M. 250, 350 & 375B

1. Vacuum modulator, check for loose fittings, restrictions in line or defective modulator assembly.

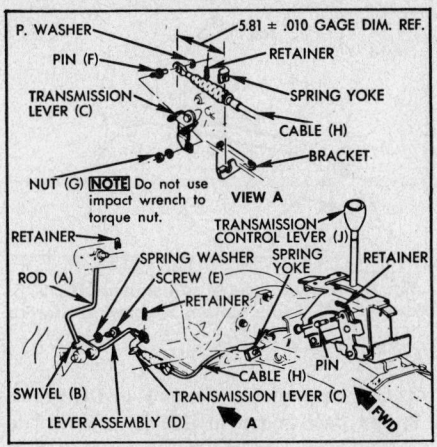

Fig. 3 Manual linkage adjustment. 1974-78 Camaro, Chevelle, Malibu & Monte Carlo. 1975-78 Nova, Buick Apollo & Skylark

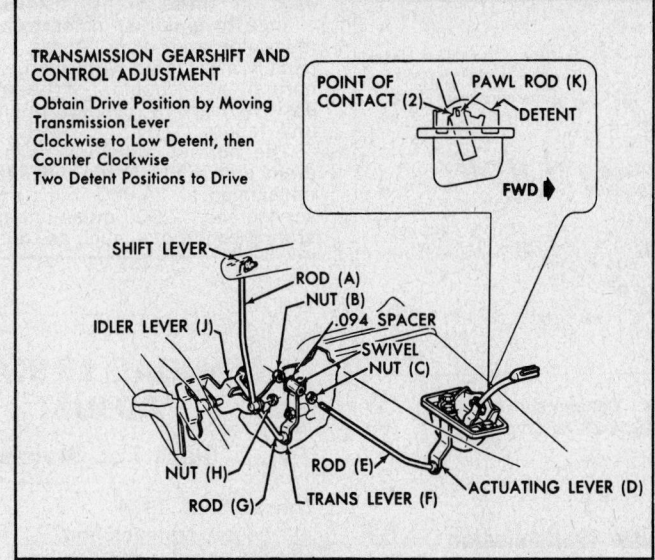

Fig. 4 Manual linkage. 1974 Nova console (typical)

2. Modulator valve stuck.
3. Valve body regulator or boost valve stuck.
4. Pump to case gasket mispositioned or damaged.
5. Check case for porosity.
6. Check 1-2 accumulator assembly for damaged oil rings, stuck piston, broken or missing spring, or damaged case bore.

T.H.M. 250

1. Intermediate band improperly adjusted.
2. Improper or broken servo spring.

T.H.M. 350, 375B

1. Burned intermediate clutch plates.
2. Improper number of intermediate clutch plates.

Slips 2 - 3 Shift

1. Low oil level.
2. Modulator valve or vacuum modulator assembly defective.
3. Pump pressure regulator valve or boost valve; pump to case gasket mispositioned.
4. Check case for porosity.
5. Direct clutch piston seals or ball check leaking.

Rough 2 - 3 Shift

1. High oil pressure. Vacuum leak, modulator valve sticking or pressure regulator or boost valve inoperative.
2. 2-3 accumulator piston stuck, spring broken or missing.

No Engine Braking In Second Speed

1. Intermediate servo or 2-3 accumulator oil rings or bores leaking or accumulator piston stuck.
2. Intermediate band burned or broken.
3. Low oil pressure: Pressure regulator and/or boost valve stuck.

No Engine Braking In 1st Speed

1. Manual low control valve assembly

stuck.
2. Low oil pressure: Pressure regulator and/or boost valve stuck.
3. Low and reverse clutch piston inner seal damaged.

No Part Throttle Downshift

1. Oil pressure: Vacuum modulator assembly, modulator valve or pressure regulator valve train malfunctioning.
2. Detent valve and linkage sticking, disconnected or broken.
3. 2-3 shift valve stuck.

No Detent Downshifts

1. 2-3 valve stuck.
2. Detent valve and linkage sticking, disconnected or broken.

Low or High Shift Points

1. Oil pressure: Check engine vacuum at transmission end of modulator pipe.
2. Vacuum modulator assembly, vacuum line connections at engine and transmission, modulator valve, pressure regulator valve train.
3. Check governor for sticking valve, restricted or leaking feed holes, damaged pipes or plugged feed line.
4. Detent valve stuck open.
5. 1-2 or 2-3 valve train sticking.
6. Check case for porosity.

Won't Hold In Park

1. Manual linkage misadjusted.
2. Parking brake lever and actuator assembly defective.
3. Parking pawl broken or inoperative.
4. Defective or improperly installed inner lever and actuating rod assembly.
5. Parking lock bracket loose, burred or rough edges, or improperly installed.

6. Parking pawl disengaging spring missing, broken or installed improperly.

Burned Forward Clutch Plates

1. Check ball in clutch drum damaged, stuck or missing.
2. Clutch piston cracked, seals damaged or missing.
3. Low line pressure.
4. Pump cover oil seal rings missing, broken or undersize; ring groove oversize.
5. Transmission case valve body face not flat or porosity between channels.

Burned Intermediate Clutch Plates

T.H.M. 350, 375B

1. Intermediate clutch piston seals damaged or missing.
2. Low line pressure.
3. Transmission case valve body face not flat or porosity between channels.

Burned Intermediate Band

T.H.M. 250

1. Intermediate servo piston seals damaged or missing.
2. Low line pressure.
3. Transmission case valve body face not flat or porosity between channels.

Burned Direct Clutch Plates

1. Restricted orifice in vacuum line to modulator.
2. Check ball in clutch drum damaged, stuck or missing.
3. Defective modulator.
4. Clutch piston cracked, seals damaged or missing.
5. Transmission case valve body face not flat or porosity between channels.

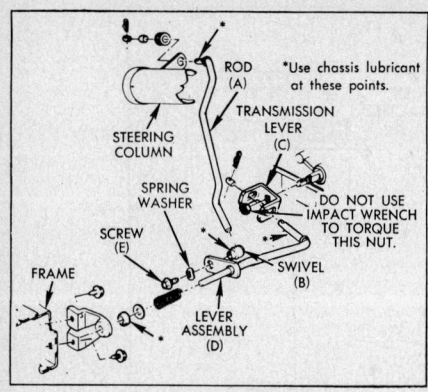

Fig. 5 Column shift linkage. 1974-78 All (Typical)

Noisy Transmission

NOTE: Before checking transmission for noise, ensure noise is not coming from water pump, alternator or any belt driven accessory.

Park, Neutral & All Driving Ranges
1. Low fluid level.
2. Plugged or restricted screen.
3. Damaged screen to valve body gasket.
4. Porosity in valve body intake area.
5. Transmission fluid contaminated with water.
6. Porosity at transmission case intake port.
7. Improperly installed case to pump gasket.
8. Pump gears damaged.
9. Driving gear assembled backwards.
10. Crescent interference in pump.
11. Damaged or worn pump oil seals.
12. Loose converter to flywheel bolts.
13. Damaged converter.

1st, 2nd And/Or Reverse Gear
1. Planetary gears or thrust bearings damaged.
2. Damaged input or output ring gear.

Acceleration In Any Gear
1. Transmission case or transmission oil cooler lines contacting underbody.
2. Broken or loose engine mounts.

Squeal At Low Vehicle Speed
1. Speedometer driven gear shaft seal requires lubrication or replacement.

MAINTENANCE

Fluid should be checked every 6,000 miles with engine idling, selector lever in neutral position, parking brake set and transmssion at operating temperature. Use only General Motors Dexron transmission fluid when adding oil. Do not overfill.

Every 24,000 miles, remove drain plug in transmission oil pan and drain transmission oil sump. Add 1½ quarts after replacing plug, check fluid and add enough fluid to bring level to the Full mark.

NOTE: A revised type Dexron fluid is

used in these transmissions. An early change to a darker color from the usual red color and or a strong odor that is usually associated with overheated fluid is normal, and should not be treated as a positive sign of needed maintenance or unit failure.

The normal maintenance schedule for drain and refill of this type fluid remains unchanged at 24,000 miles under normal service and 12,000 miles under severe operating conditions, such as trailer towing.

MANUAL LINKAGE, ADJUST

Buick Exc. Skyhawk

Console Shift, 1974
1. Loosen trunnion bolt.
2. Set selector lever against Drive stop.
3. Place transmission in Drive.
4. Tighten trunnion bolt to 6-9 ft-lbs.
5. Set selector lever in Park and set Back Drive Adjustment as outlined below.

Console Shift, 1975-78 Exc. Apollo & Skylark
1. Place selector lever in Park position.
2. Place transmission lever in Park position.
3. Position pin to obtain a free pin fit in the transmission lever and torque nut to 15-25 ft. lbs.
4. Check for proper operation.

Console Shift, 1975-78 Apollo & Skylark
Refer to Chevrolet for adjustment procedure.

Column Shift 1974-78
1. Loosen adjusting clamp bolt.
2. Place selector lever against Neutral stop.
3. Place transmission in Neutral.
4. Tighten clamp bolt to 17-23 ft. lbs.

Chevrolet Exc. Monza & Vega

Console Shift 1974-78 Camaro, Chevelle, Malibu & Monte Carlo; 1975-78 Nova & Buick Apollo & Skylark
1. Loosen swivel screw so rod is free to move in swivel, Fig. 3.
2. Place transmission control lever in Drive and loosen pin in transmission lever, so it moves in the slot.
3. Move transmission lever counterclockwise to L1 detent and then three detents clockwise to Drive position. Tighten nut on transmission lever to 20 ft. lbs.
4. Place transmission control lever in Park and ignition switch in the Lock position and pull lightly against lock stop, then tighten swivel screw to 20 ft. lbs. Check for proper operation.

Nova Console Shift, 1974
1. Loosen assembly nuts B and C on rod E, Fig. 4.

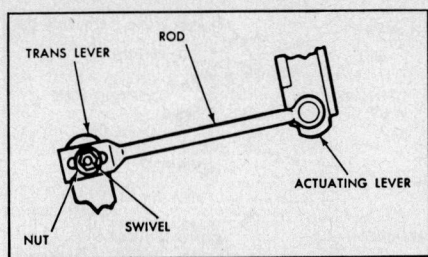

Fig. 6 Manual linkage adjustment. 1974-75 Vega & 1975 Astre, Monza, Skyhawk & Starfire

2. Set transmission lever F in DRIVE.
3. Set pawl rod K in DRIVE notch of detent.
4. Apply load in direction of arrow on actuating lever D until pawl rod K comes in contact with detent at contact point Z.
5. Place a .094" spacer between nut B and swivel, run nut B until it touches spacer. Remove spacer and tighten nut C against swivel and lock swivel between nuts B and C.
6. Set transmission lever F in PARK and turn ignition switch to LOCK.
7. Install rod G to idler lever J and lever F.
8. Install rod A to shift lever and idler lever J. Loosely attach clamp to idler lever.
9. Remove column lash by rotating shift lever in a downward direction and secure with attaching nut H. The foregoing provides .05" overtravel gap in notches of the detent.

Column Shift, 1974-78 All
1. Place transmission lever in Neutral by moving lever counter-clockwise to L1 detent then clockwise three detent positions to Neutral.
2. Place selecter lever in Neutral as determined by mechanical stop on steering column. Do not use indicator as reference.
3. Assemble swivel, spring washer and screw to lever assembly then tighten screw to 20 ft. lbs., Fig. 5.

Astre, Monza, Skyhawk, Starfire, Sunbird & Vega

1974-75
1. Place transmission lever in Neutral by rotating lever clockwise to Park, then two detents counter-clockwise to Neutral.
2. Place shift lever in Neutral.
3. Insert flats of swivel into slot in rod and tighten nut to 120 pound inches, Fig. 6.

1976-78
1. Loosen nut on transmission lever, Fig. 7.
2. Place transmission control shifter in Neutral position.
3. Place transmission lever in Neutral position.
4. Torque transmission lever nut to 20 ft. lbs.

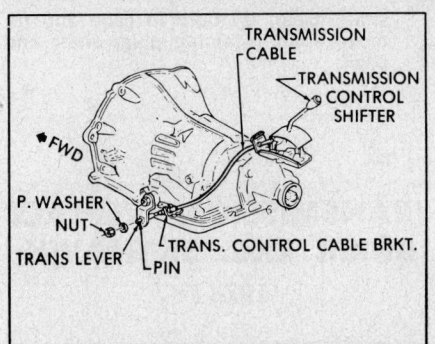

**Fig. 7 Manual linkage adjustment.
1976-78 Astre, Monza, Skyhawk, Starfire.
Sunbird & Vega**

5. Check for proper operation.

Oldsmobile Exc. Starfire

Console Shift, Exc. 1974 Omega

1. Loosen shift rod clamp screw and pin in transmission manual lever. Place shift handle and transmission manual lever in Park position.
2. With rod held lightly against Park stop, tighten screw in clamp at lower end of shift rod.
3. Move pin to give "free pin" fit in manual lever and tighten nut.

Console Shift, 1974 Omega

1. Transmission manual lever must be free in swivel.
2. Place shift and transmission levers in Neutral.
3. Holding the actuating rod rearward against stop, place a .094" spacer between rear nut and swivel. Tighten nut to contact spacer, remove spacer, hold rear nut and tighten forward nut to lock swivel in place.
4. Loosen shift rod clamp screw and move shift and transmission manual levers to Park position and ignition switch to Lock position.
5. Pull down lightly on shift rod to contact lock stop and tighten clamp screw.
6. Check operation.

NOTE: With ignition key in the Lock position and transmission selector lever in Park, the key can be removed and the steering wheel should be locked.

Column Shift, All 1974-78

1. Loosen shift rod clamp screw and place outer lever in the Neutral position. Hold column shift lever in Neutral position and tighten clamp. Check operation.

Pontiac Exc. Astre & Sunbird

Console Shift, 1974 Exc. Ventura

1. Place shift handle in Park and transmission manual lever in Park.
2. With rod held lightly against Park stop, tighten screw in clamp at lower end of rod.

---

3. Adjust pin in selector lever to freely enter the end of the shift cable and tighten pin nut.

Console Shift, 1975 & 1977-78

1. Disconnect shift cable at transmission lever.
2. Adjust back drive, as outlined under "Back Drive, Adjust" procedure.
3. Unlock ignition switch, move transmission lever two detents counter-clockwise, then place transmission shift lever against Neutral stop.
4. Assemble cable to transmission lever, torque nut to 20 ft. lbs.

Console Shift, 1976

1. Place shift lever in Park position.
2. Loosen pin from transmission selector lever, then place selector lever in Park position.
3. Set pin to obtain a free pin fit in selector lever and torque nut to 20 ft. lbs.
4. Check for proper operation.

Console Shift, 1974 Ventura

Refer to the Oldsmobile Omega "Console Shift" adjustment procedure to adjust the console shift linkage.

Column Shift, All 1974-78

With shift rod clamp and screw loosely assembled to shift rod, set transmission outer lever in Park position. Check to see that steering column lever is in Park position and tighten clamp on shift rod.

BACK DRIVE, ADJUST

1. Disconnect lower rod at transmission lever.
2. Move transmission lever to Park position.
3. Place transmission selector lever in Park position.
4. Attach lower rod to transmission lever and check for proper operation.

NOTE: Any inaccuracies in the above adjustments may result in premature failure of the transmission due to operation without the controls in full detent. Such operation results in reduced oil pressure and in turn partial engagement of the affected clutches.

THROTTLE LINKAGE, ADJUST

The flexible cable type linkage is used on all models and requires no adjustment.

DETENT CABLE, ADJUST

1974-76 Buick, Oldsmobile & Pontiac Except Apollo, Astre, Firebird, Omega, Skyhawk, Starfire, Sunbird, Ventura, Skylark & 1976 Cutlass 6-250

The detent cable is adjusted from inside

**Fig. 8 Detent cable adjustment.
1974-76 Buick, Oldsmobile & Pontiac
except Apollo, Astre, Firebird, Omega,
Skyhawk, Starfire, Sunbird, Ventura,
Skylark & 1976 Cutlass 6-250**

the driver's compartment as follows:

1. With engine off, throttle closed and fast idle off, position retainer clip against the insert on the detent cable, Fig. 8.
2. Grasp throttle pedal lever adjacent to the detent cable and pull the carburetor cable to the wide open position. By following this procedure, the detent cable will be adjusted properly.

1974-76 Apollo, Astre, Firebird, Omega, Skyhawk, Starfire, Sunbird, Ventura, Skylark, 1976 Cutlass 6-250, 1974-78 Camaro, Monza, Nova & Vega, 1977-78 Buick, Oldsmobile & Pontiac All

1. Release snap lock.
2. Place carburetor lever in the wide open throttle position, being sure that lever is against the stop, push snap lock down onto cable until the top is flush with the cable.

1974-78 Chevrolet, Chevelle, Malibu & Monte Carlo

NOTE: On Chevrolet units, the detent cable is adjusted at the carburetor.

1. With the accelerator and detent cables connected, depress accelerator pedal to the wide open throttle position. The ball will then slide into the cable sleeve and permanently adjust the cable length.

INTERMEDIATE BAND, ADJUST

Turbo Hydra-matic 250

Since the Turbo Hydra-matic 250 transmission uses an intermediate band instead of a clutch (used in the Turbo Hydra-matic 350 transmission) to control the operation of the planetary gear sets, it is necessary

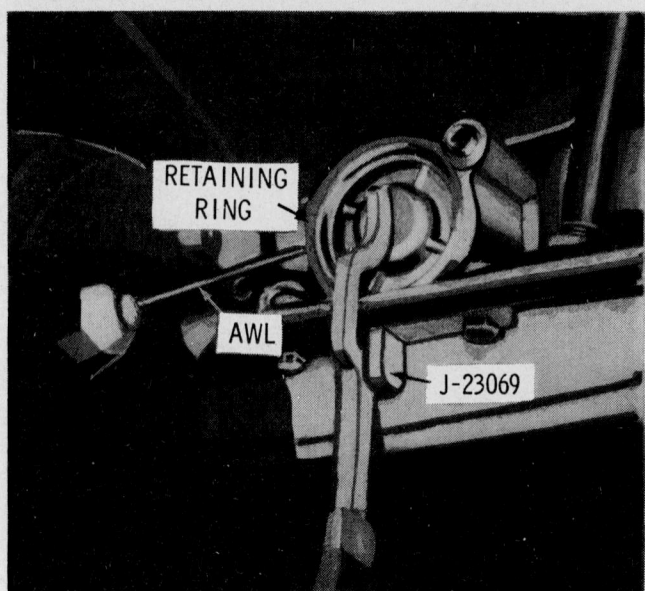

Fig. 9 Intermediate clutch accumulator piston removal

to adjust the intermediate band as follows:

1. Loosen adjusting screw lock nut, located on case right side, ½ turn.
2. Torque adjusting screw to 30 inch pounds, then back off screw 3 turns.
3. Torque adjusting screw lock nut to 15 foot pounds while holding adjusting screw in position.

IN CAR REPAIRS

Valve Body Assembly

1. Remove oil pan and strainer.
2. Remove retaining pin to disconnect downshift actuating lever bracket, remove valve body attaching bolts and detent roller and spring assembly.
3. Remove valve body assembly while disconnecting manual control valve link from range selector inner lever.

CAUTION: Do not drop valve.

4. Remove manual valve and link from valve body assembly.
5. Reverse procedure to install.

Governor

1. Remove governor cover retainer and cover.
2. Remove governor.

Intermediate Clutch Accumulator Piston Assembly

1. Remove two oil pan bolts adjacent to accumulator piston cover, install compressor on oil pan lip and retain with these two bolts, Fig. 9.

2. Compress intermediate clutch accumulator piston cover and remove retaining ring piston cover and O ring from case.
3. Remove spring and intermediate clutch accumulator piston.

Vacuum Modulator & Modulator Valve Assembly

1. Disconnect vacuum hose from modulator stem and remove vacuum modulator screw and retainer.
2. Remove modulator and its O ring.
3. Remove modulator valve from case.

Extension Housing Oil Seal

1. Remove propeller shaft.
2. Pry out lip seal with screwdriver or small chisel.

Manual Shaft, Range Selector Inner Lever & Parking Linkage Assemblies

1. Remove oil pan and strainer.
2. Remove manual shaft to case retainer and unthread jam nut holding range selector inner lever to manual shaft.
3. Remove jam nut and remove manual shaft from range selector inner lever and case. *Do not remove manual shaft lip seal unless replacement is required.*
4. Disconnect parking pawl actuating rod from range selector inner lever and remove bolt from case.
5. Remove bolts and parking lock bracket.
6. Remove pawl disengaging spring.
7. If necessary to replace pawl or

shaft, clean up bore in case and remove shaft retaining plug, shaft and pawl.

TRANSMISSION, REPLACE BUICK EXC. SKYHAWK
1974-78

1. Raise car and remove propeller shaft. If necessary, disconnect exhaust crossover pipe. Remove catalytic converter support bracket, if equipped.
2. Place suitable jack under transmission and fasten transmission securely to jack.
3. Remove vacuum line from vacuum modulator.
4. Loosen cooler line nuts and separate cooler lines from transmission.
5. Remove detent cable from accelerator or carburetor lever assembly. *Do not bend cable.* Remove plastic guide from bracket and slide cable out through slot.
6. Remove detent cable from detent valve link.
7. Remove crossmember.
8. Disconnect speedometer cable, shift linkage and filler pipe. Remove filler pipe.
9. Support engine at oil pan.
10. Remove transmission flywheel cover pan.
11. Mark flywheel and converter for reassembly and remove three flywheel to converter bolts.
12. Be sure transmission is supported by transmission jack and remove transmission case to engine block bolts.
13. Move transmission rearward to provide clearance between converter and crankshaft. Install converter holding tool, lower transmission and remove.

CHEVROLET EXC. MONZA & VEGA
1974-78

1. Disconnect negative battery cable and raise car.
2. Remove propeller shaft, disconnect speedometer cable, detent cable, modulator vacuum line and oil cooler lines. Disconnect catalytic converter support bracket from transmission.
3. Disconnect shift linkage.
4. Support transmission with suitable jack and remove crossmember.
5. Remove converter under pan.
6. Remove converter to flywheel bolts.
7. On all models except Nova, loosen exhaust pipe to manifold bolts approximately ¼ inch. Lower transmission until jack is barely supporting transmission.

NOTE: On V8 engines, care must be taken not to lower the rear of the transmission too far as the distributor housing may be forced against fire-wall causing damage to the distributor.

8. Remove transmission to engine mounting bolts and remove oil filler tube at transmission.
9. Raise transmission to its normal position, support engine with jack and slide transmission rearward from engine and lower it away from vehicle.
10. Reverse procedure to install.

OLDSMOBILE EXC. STARFIRE

1974-78

1. Disconnect detent cable from accelerator or carburetor lever assembly.
2. Remove transmission oil level dipstick. Remove catalytic converter support bracket, if equipped.
3. Raise car and remove detent cable from link. Plug hole.
4. Disconnect oil cooler lines at transmission.
5. Remove flywheel cover pan and mark converter and flywheel for reassembly. Remove three flywheel to converter bolts.
6. Disconnect vacuum modulator line. Remove speedometer clip and driven gear. Plug hole.
7. Disconnect shift linkage.
8. Remove propeller shaft.
9. Support transmission with a suitable jack and remove crossmember.
10. Lower transmission slightly and remove transmission to engine bolts.
11. Remove oil level indicator tube and

clip holding detent cable to tube.
12. Lower transmission being careful not to damage cooler lines, detent cable, modulator line and shift linkage.
13. Reverse procedure to install.

PONTIAC EXC. ASTE & SUNBIRD

1974-78

1. Disconnect battery ground cable and release parking brake.
2. Raise car and remove propeller shaft. Remove catalytic converter support bracket, if equipped.
3. Disconnect speedometer cable, vacuum hose at modulator, detent cable at transmission and shift linkage.

NOTE. When removing detent cable, be careful not to bend it.

4. Support transmission with a suitable jack and remove crossmember.
5. Remove converter dust pan, mark flywheel and converter for reassembly and remove flywheel to converter bolts. Make sure converter hub is free of converter.
6. Disconnect transmission filler pipe at engine and remove pipe from transmission.
7. Lower transmission and engine to gain access to cooler line fitting nuts and disconnect cooler lines. On some models it may be necessary to loosen the exhaust system.
8. With transmission in lowered position, remove the transmission to engine bolts.
9. Raise transmission to its normal position, support engine and slide trans-

mission rearward and lower it away from car.

NOTE: When lowering transmission, keep rear of transmission lower than the front so as not to lose the converter.

10. Reverse procedure to install.

ASTRE, MONZA, SKYHAWK, STARFIRE, SUNBIRD & VEGA

1974-78

1. Disconnect battery ground cable.
2. Remove air cleaner and disconnect downshift cable from carburetor. Release parking brake.
3. Raise vehicle and remove propeller shaft. Disconnect torque arm from transmission, if equipped.
4. On 1975-78 models, remove catalytic converter bracket from transmission and disconnect exhaust pipe and converter.
5. Disconnect speedo cable, modulator vacuum line, shift linkage and downshift cable from transmission.
6. Support transmission with a suitable jack and disconnect transmission rear mount from crossmember, then remove crossmember.
7. Remove converter cover, then converter to flywheel bolts.
8. Lower transmission until it is barely supported and remove transmission to engine bolts.
9. Remove oil filter tube and on V8 models, disconnect oil cooler lines.
10. Raise transmission, support engine with a suitable jack and slide transmission rearward and lower unit from vehicle.
11. Reverse procedure to install.

TURBO HYDRA-MATIC 375, 400

TRANSMISSION IDENTIFICATION

An identification plate is attached to the transmission. The plate indicates year of production, code letters, and serial number.

BUICK	CODE
1974 V8-455 Century, Regal less Stage 1	BS
V8-455 Century, Regal Stage 1	BB
All Others—	
Hi Perf.	BT
Exc. Hi. Perf.	BC
1975 V8-350 LeSabre	BK
V8-400	OC
V8-455	BC, BT
1976 V8-455	BC
V8-455	BT
1977-78 V8-350	BB
V8-350	OB
V8-403	OD

CADILLAC

	CODE
1974-76 Exc. Electronic Fuel Injection	AA
1975 Electronic Fuel Injection	AD
1976 Electronic Fuel Injection—	
Exc. Seville	AB
Seville	AC
1977-78 Fleetwood & DeVille Exc. E.F.I. & Hi. Alt.	AD
Fleetwood & DeVille E.F.I. Exc. Calif. Emiss.	AB
Fleetwood & DeVille Calif. Emiss. Exc. E.F.I.	AE
Fleetwood & DeVille Exc. E.F.I., Hi. Alt. & Calif. Emiss.	AA
Fleetwood & DeVille Hi. Alt.	AL
Seville (2:56 Axle)	AC
Seville (3:08 Axle)	AH
1978 Seville V8-350 Diesel	AT

CHECKER MOTORS

	CODE
1974-75 6-250	NA
V8-350	NB

CHEVROLET

	CODE
1974 V8-400 Chevrolet	CA
V8-400 2 Bar. Carb. Chevrolet	CB
V8-400 Chevrolet	CG
V8-350 Corvette 190 H.P.	CK
V8-454 Chevrolet	CR
V8-454 Corvette	CS
V8-350 Corvette 250 H.P.	CZ
1975 V8-350 Police	CR
V8-350 Corvette Exc. Sp. H/Perf.	CK
V8-350 Corvette Sp. H/Perf.	CZ
V8-400 Chevrolet with 3.08, 3.42	
Axles Exc. Calif.	CA

CHEVROLET—Continued	CODE
V8-400 Chevrolet with 2.56, 2.73	
Axles Exc. Calif.	CB
V8-454 Chevelle	CF
V8-454 Chevrolet	CR
1976 V8-350 Corvette	CZ
V8-400 Chevrolet	CA
V8-454 Chevrolet	CR
1977 V8-350 Corvette	CB

OLDSMOBILE

	CODE
1974 V8-350 88	OA
V8-455 Cutlass Exc. Calif.	OD
V8-455 Cutlass Calif.	OW
V8-455 Cutlass 275 H.P.	OX
V8-455 88 & 98 Single Exhaust Exc. Calif.	OR
V8-455 88 & 98 Single Exh. Calif.	OL
V8-455 88 & 98 Dual Exhaust	OK
V8-455 Custom Cruiser Exc. Calif.	OK
V8-455 Custom Cruiser Calif.	OE
1975 V8-350 88 Exc. Calif.	OA
V8-350 88 Calif.	OB
V8-400 Custom Cruiser	OC
V8-400 98	OF
V8-455 Cutlass Exc. Calif.	OD
V8-455 Cutlass Calif.	OW
V8-455 Custom Cruiser Exc. Calif.	OK
V8-455 Custom Cruiser Calif.	OE
V8-455 88 & 98 Exc. Calif.	OR
V8-455 88 & 98 Calif.	OL
1976 V8-350 88 Calif.	OB
V8-455 Cutlass Exc. Calif.	OD
V8-455 Cutlass Calif.	OW
V8-455 Custom Cruiser	OK
V8-455 88 & 98 Exc. Calif.	OR
V8-455 98 Exc. Calif.	OC
V8-455 88 & 98 Calif.	OL
1977-78 V8-350 Cutlass Wag. & 98	OB
V8-403 Cutlass Wag.	OC
V8-403 98	OD

PONTIAC

	CODE
1974 V8-400 2 Bar. Carb. Sta. Wag.	PA
V8-400 4 Bar. Carb. (Police & H.D.)	PA
V8-400 4 Bar. Carb. (Pontiac)	PB
V8-455 4 Bar. Carb. (Pontiac)	PC
V8-400 2 Bar. Carb. (Pontiac Exc. Calif.)	PD

PONTIAC—Continued	CODE
V8-400 2 Bar. Carb. (Pontiac Calif.)	PF
V8-400 4 Bar. Carb. (LeMans & Firebird, Exc. Calif.)	PG
V8-400 4 Bar. Carb. (LeMans & Firebird, Calif.)	PW
V8-455 4 Bar. Carb. (Police)	PH
V8-455 SD (Firebird)	PQ
V8-455 4 Bar. Carb. (LeMans & Grand Prix)	PR
V8-400 2 Bar. Carb. (LeMans & Firebird, Exc. Calif.)	PT
V8-400 2 Bar. Carb. (LeMans & Firebird, Calif.)	PL
V8-400 4 Bar. Carb. (Grand Prix)	PX
V8-455 4 Bar. Carb. (Firebird)	PZ
1975 V8-400 2 Bar. Carb. (Pontiac)	PD
V8-400 2 Bar. Carb. (LeMans & Grand Prix)	PT
V8-400 4 Bar. Carb. (Pontiac Exc. Calif.)	PB
V8-400 4 Bar. Carb. (Pontiac, Calif.)	PF
V8-400 4 Bar. Carb. (LeMans & Grand Prix Exc. Calif.)	PX
V8-400 4 Bar. Carb. (LeMans & Grand Prix, Calif.)	PG
V8-455 Pontiac Exc. Calif.	PC
V8-455 Pontiac, Calif.	PA
V8-455 LeMans & Grand Prix Exc. Calif.	PR
V8-455 LeMans & Grand Prix, Calif.	PL
1976 V8-350 Grand Prix	PS
V8-400 2 Bar. Carb. (Lemans & Grand Prix)	PT
V8-400 2 Bar. Carb. (Pontiac)	PD
V8-400 4 Bar. Carb. (LeMans & Grand Prix)	PX
V8-400 4 Bar. Carb. (Pontiac)	PB
V8-400 LeMans (Police)	PQ
V8-400 Pontiac (Police)	PA
V8-455 LeMans & Grand Prix (Exc. Trailer Option)	PR
V8-455 LeMans (Trailer Option)	PL
V8-455 Pontiac (Exc. Trailer Option)	PC
V8-455 Pontiac (Police or Trailer Option)	PH
1977 V8-301 LeMans & Grand Prix	PA
V8-350 4 Bar. Carb. (LeMans Sta. Wag.)	OB
V8-350 Grand Prix	PB
V8-400 LeMans & Grand Prix Police & Trailer	PD
V8-400 LeMans Sta. Wag. Exc. Trailer	PC
V8-400 Grand Prix Exc. Trailer	PC
V8-403 LeMans Sta. Wag. Exc. Trailer	OC

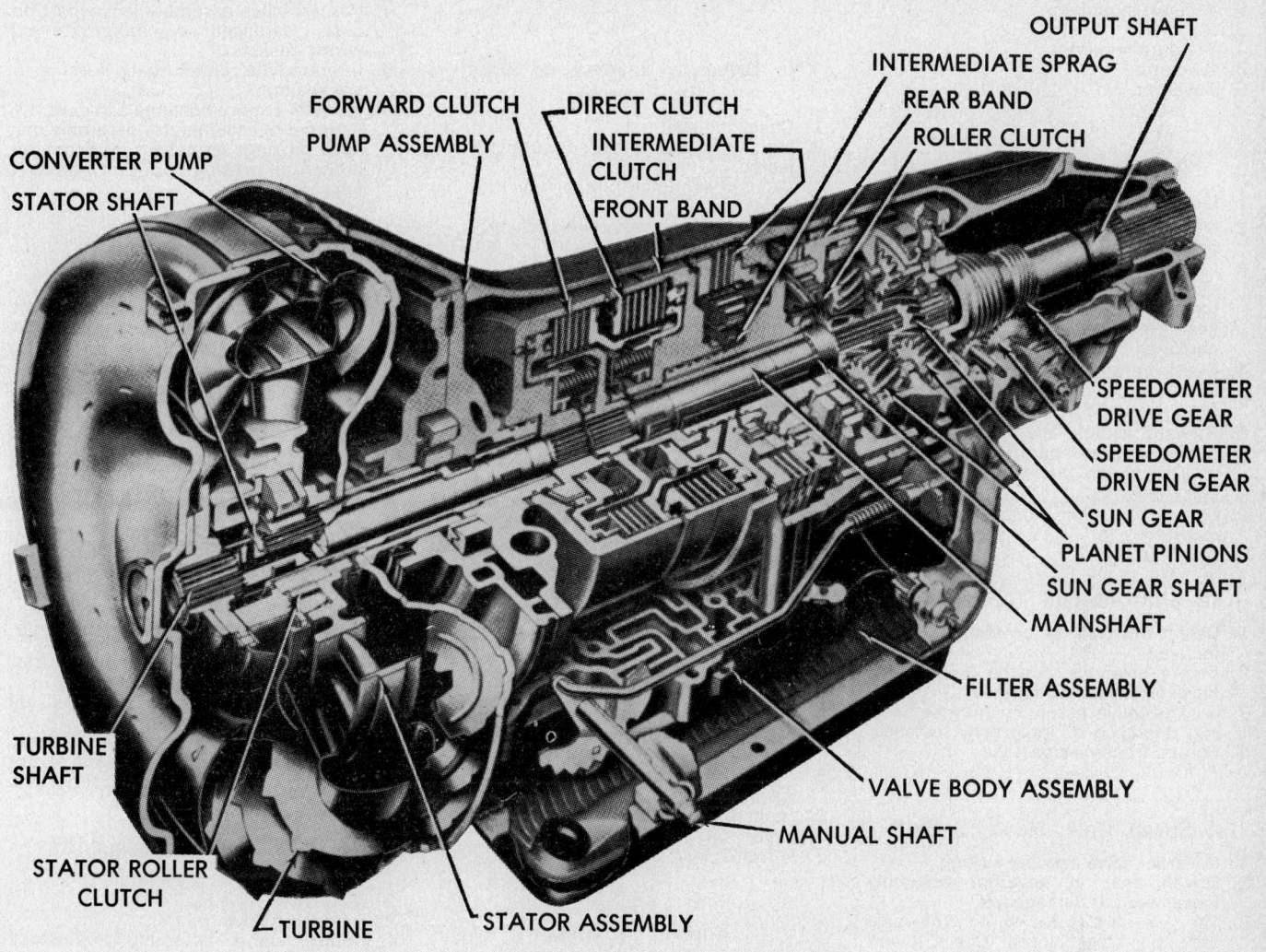

Fig. 1 Cutaway view of transmission assembly

GENERAL DESCRIPTION

This transmission, Fig. 1, is a fully automatic unit consisting primarily of a three-element hydraulic torque converter and a compound planetary gear set. Three multiple-disc clutches, two one-way clutches, and two bands provide the friction elements required to obtain the desired functions of the planetary gear set.

The torque converter, the multiple-disc clutches and the one-way clutches couple the engine to the planetary gears through oil pressure, providing three forward speeds and reverse. The torque converter, when required, supplements the gears by multiplying engine torque.

Torque Converter

The torque converter is of welded construction and is serviced as an assembly. The unit is made up of two vaned sections, or halves, that face each other in an oil-filled housing. The pump half of the converter is connected to the engine and the turbine half is connected to the transmission.

When the engine makes the converter

pump revolve, it sends oil against the turbine, making it revolve also. The oil then returns in a circular flow back to the converter pump, continuing this flow as long as the engine is running.

Stator

The converter also has a smaller vaned section, called a stator, that funnels the oil back to the converter pump through smaller openings, at increased speed. The speeded up oil directs additional force to the engine-driven converter pump, thereby multiplying engine torque. In other words, without the stator, the unit is nothing more than a fluid coupling.

External Controls

The external control connections to the transmission are:

1. Manual linkage to select the desired operating range.

2. Engine vacuum to operate the vacuum modulator unit.

3. An electrical signal to operate an electric detent solenoid.

Vacuum Modulator

A vacuum modulator is used to sense engine torque input to the transmission automatically. The vacuum modulator transmits this signal to the pressure regulator, which controls line pressure, so that all torque requirements of the transmission are met and proper shift spacing is obtained at all throttle openings.

Detent Solenoid

The detent solenoid is activated by an electric switch at the carburetor. When the throttle is opened sufficiently to close this switch, the solenoid in the transmission is activated, causing a downshift at speeds below 70 mph. At lower speeds, downshifts will occur at lesser throttle openings without use of the electric switch.

TROUBLE SHOOTING GUIDE

Oil Pressure High or Low

1. Vacuum line or fittings clogged or

leaking.
2. Vacuum modulator.
3. Modulator valve.
4. Pressure regulator.
5. Oil pump.
6. Governor.

No Drive In Drive Range

1. Low oil level (check for leaks).
2. Manual control linkage not adjusted properly.
3. Low oil pressure. Check for blocked strainer, defective pressure regulator, pump assembly or pump drive gear. See that tangs have not been damaged by converter.
4. Check control valve assembly to see if manual valve has been disconnected from manual lever pin.
5. Forward clutch may be struck or damaged. Check pump feed circuits to forward clutch including clutch drum ball check.
6. Sprag or roller clutch assembled incorrectly.

1 - 2 Shift At Full Throttle Only

1. Detent switch may be sticking or defective.
2. Detent solenoid may be stuck open, loose or have leaking gasket.
3. Control valve assembly may be leaking, damaged or incorrectly installed.
4. Porous transmission case.

1st Speed Only - No 1 - 2 Shift

1. Governor valve may be sticking.
2. Driven gear in governor assembly loose, worn or damaged.
3. The 1-2 shift valve in control valve assembly stuck closed. Check governor feed channels for blocks, leaks, and position. Also check control valve body gaskets for leaks and damage.
4. Intermediate clutch plug in case may be leaking or blown out.
5. Check for porosity between channels and for blocked governor feed channels in case.
6. Check intermediate clutch for proper operation.

No 2 - 3 Shift - 1st & 2nd Only

1. Detent solenoid may be stuck open.
2. Detent switch may not be properly adjusted.
3. Control valve assembly may be stuck, leaking, damaged, or incorrectly installed.
4. Check direct clutch case center support for broken, leaking or missing oil rings.
5. Check clutch piston seals and piston ball check in clutch assembly.

Moves Forward In Neutral

1. Manual control linkage improperly adjusted.
2. Forward clutch does not release.
3. Oil pump.

4. Internal linkage.

No Drive In Reverse or Slips In Reverse

1. Check oil level.
2. Manual control linkage improperly adjusted.
3. Vacuum modulator assembly may be defective.
4. Vacuum modulator valve sticking.
5. Strainer may be restricted or leaking at intake.
6. Regulator or boost valve in pump assembly may be sticking.
7. Control valve assembly may be stuck, leaking or damaged.
8. Rear servo and accumulator may have damaged or missing servo piston seal ring.
9. Reverse band burned out or damaged. Determine that apply pin or anchor pins engage properly.
10. Direct clutch may be damaged or may have stuck ball check in piston.
11. Forward clutch does not release.
12. Low-reverse ball check missing from case.

Slips In All Ranges & On Starts

1. Check oil level.
2. Vacuum modulator defective.
3. Modulator valve sticking.
4. Strainer assembly plugged or leaking at neck.
5. Pump assembly regulator or boost valve sticking.
6. Leaks from damaged gaskets or cross leaks from porosity of case.
7. Forward and direct clutches burned.

Slips 1 - 2 Shift

1. Incorrect oil level.
2. Vacuum modulator valve sticking.
3. Vacuum modulator defective.
4. Pump pressure regulator valve defective.
5. Porosity between channels in case.
6. Control valve assembly.
7. Pump-to-case gasket may be mispositioned.
8. Intermediate clutch plug in case may be missing or leaking excessively.
9. Intermediate clutch piston seal missing or damaged.
10. Intermediate clutch plates burned.
11. Front or rear accumulator oil ring may be damaged.

Slips 2 - 3 Shift

1. Items 1 through 6 under Slips 1-2 Shift will also cause 2-3 shift slips.
2. Direct clutch plates burned.
3. Oil seal rings on direct clutch may be damaged permitting excessive leaking between tower and bushing.

Rough 1 - 2 Shift

1. Modulator valve sticking.
2. Modulator assembly defective.
3. Pump pressure regulator or boost

valve stuck or inoperative.
4. Control valve assembly loosened from case, damaged or mounted with wrong gaskets.
5. Intermediate clutch ball missing or not sealing.
6. Porosity between channels in case.
7. Rear servo accumulator assembly may have oil rings damaged, stuck piston, broken or missing spring or damaged bore.

Rough 2 - 3 Shift

1. Items 1, 2 and 3 under Rough 1-2 Shift will also cause rough 2-3 shift.
2. Front servo accumulator spring broken or missing. Accumulator piston may be sticking.

No Engine Braking in Second Speed

1. Front servo or accumulator oil rings may be leaking.
2. Front band may be broken or burned out.
3. Front bank not engaged on anchor pin and/or servo pin.

No Engine Braking In Low Range

1. Low-reverse check ball may be missing from control valve assembly.
2. Rear servo may have damaged oil seal ring, bore or piston.
3. Rear servo apply pressure, leaking.
4. Rear band broken, burned out or not engaged on anchor pins or servo pin.

No Part Throttle Downshifts

1. Vacuum modulator assembly.
2. Modulator valve.
3. Regulator valve train.
4. Control valve assembly has stuck 3-2 valve or broken spring.

No Detent Downshifts

1. Detent switch needs fuse, connections tightened or adjustment.
2. Detent solenoid may be inoperative.
3. Detent valve train in control valve assembly malfunctioning.

Low or High Shift Points

1. Oil pressure. Check vacuum modulator assembly, vacuum line connections, modulator valve, and pressure regulator valve train.
2. Governor may have sticking valve or feed holes that are leaking, plugged or damaged.
3. Detent solenoid may be stuck open or loose.
4. Control valve assembly. Check detent, 3-2, and 1-2 shift valve trains, and check spacer plate gaskets for positioning.
5. Check case for porosity, missing or leaking intermediate plug.

Won't Hold In Park

1. Manual control linkage improperly ad-

juted.
2. Internal linkage defective; check for chamfer on actuator rod sleeve.
3. Parking pawl broken or inoperative.

Excessive Creep At Idle

NOTE: Transmissions have the variable pitch stator.

1. High idle speed.
2. Stator switch inoperative or defective.
3. Stator solenoid defective.
4. Pump may have stator valve train stuck.
5. Pump lead wires disconnected or grounded out.
6. Pump feed circuit to stator may be restricted or blocked.
7. Converter out check valve may be broken or stuck.
8. Turbine shaft may have defective oil seal ring.
9. Stator orifice plug in case may be blocked.
10. Converter assembly defective.

Poor Performance - ¾ Throttle

NOTE: Transmissions having the variable pitch stator.

1. Stator and detent switch inoperative.
2. Items 3 through 10 above will also cause poor performance at ¾ throttle.

Noisy Transmission

1. Pump noises caused by high or low oil level.
2. Cavitation due to plugged strainer, porosity in intake circuit or water in oil.
3. Pump gears may be damaged.
4. Gear noise in low gear of Drive Range.
5. Transmission contacting body.
6. Defective planetary gear set.
7. Clutch noises during application can be worn or burned clutch plates.

Forward Clutch Plates Burned

1. Check ball in clutch housing damaged, stuck or missing.
2. Clutch piston cracked, seals damaged or missing.
3. Low line pressure.
4. Manual valve mispositioned.
5. Restricted oil feed to forward clutch.
6. Pump cover oil seal rings missing, broken or undersize; ring groove oversize.
7. Case valve body face not flat or porosity between channels.
8. Manual valve bent and center land not properly ground.

Intermediate Clutch Plates Burned

1. Constant bleed orifice in center support missing.
2. Rear accumulator piston oil ring damaged or missing.
3. 1-2 accumulator valve stuck in control valve assembly.
4. Intermediate clutch piston seal dam-

aged or missing.
5. Center support bolt loose.
6. Low line pressure.
7. Intermediate clutch plug in case missing.
8. Case valve body face not flat or porosity between channels.
9. Manual valve bent and center land not ground properly.

Direct Clutch Plates Burned

1. Restricted orifice in vacuum line to modulator.
2. Check ball in direct clutch piston damaged, stuck or missing.
3. Defective modulator bellows.
4. Center support bolt loose.
5. Center support oil rings or grooves damaged or missing.
6. Clutch piston seals damaged or missing.
7. Front and rear servo pistons and seals damaged.
8. Manual valve bent and center land not cleaned up.
9. Case valve body face not flat or porosity between channels.
10. Intermediate sprag clutch installed backwards.
11. 3-2 valve, 3-2 spring or 3-2 spacer pin installed in wrong location in 3-2 valve bore.

MAINTENANCE

Checking & Adding Fluid

Fluid level should be checked at every engine oil change. The full ("F") and "ADD" marks on the transmission dipstick are one pint apart and determine the correct fluid level at normal operating temperature (170°F.). *Careful attention to transmission oil temperature is necessary as proper fluid level at low operating temperatures will be below the "ADD" mark on the dipstick. Proper fluid level at higher operating temperatures will rise above the "F" mark.*

Fluid level must always be checked with the car on a level surface, and with the engine running to make certain the converter is full. To determine proper fluid level, proceed as follows:

1. Operate engine at a fast idle for about 1½ minutes with selector lever in park ("P") position.
2. Reduce engine speed to slow idle and check fluid level.
3. With engine running, add Dexron fluid as required to bring it to the proper level.

NOTE: Beginning with 1974 models, Cadillac uses an extended-life Dexron transmission fluid. With this new fluid, strainer replacement and fluid change is now recommended at 100,000 miles under normal operating conditions and 50,000 miles under severe or abnormal service such as trailer towing.

This recommendation applies only to the improved fluid and its availability for

service. If the new fluid is not available, the former fluid can be used but then the 24,000 mile maintenance rule will apply.

Beginning with 1974 Chevrolet, Buick, Oldsmobile and Pontiac models, a revised type Dexron fluid is used in these transmissions. An early change to a darker color from the usual red color and or a strong odor that is usually associated with overheated fluid is normal, and should not be treated as a positive sign of needed maintenance or unit failure.

The normal maintenance schedule for drain and refill of this type fluid remains unchanged at 24,000 miles under normal service and 12,000 miles under severe operating conditions, such as trailer towing.

CAUTION: *Do not overfill as foaming might occur when the fluid heats up. If fluid level is too low, especially when cold, complete loss of drive may result after quick stops. Extremely low fluid level will result in damage to transmission.*

Draining Bottom Pan Only

1. Disconnect filler tube at bottom pan and allow fluid to drain. Remove and discard filler tube O-ring.
2. Use a new O-ring on filler tube and install tube on pan.
3. Lower car and add three quarts of Dexron transmission fluid through filler tube when replacing intake pipe and strainer assembly. When just draining bottom pan, add only two quarts.
4. Operate engine at a fast idle for about 1½ minutes with selector lever in park ("P") position.
5. Reduce engine speed to slow idle and check fluid level. Then add fluid as required to bring it to the proper level.

Adding Fluid to Fill Dry Transmission and Converter

1. Add seven quarts of fluid through filler tube.
2. Operate engine at a fast idle for about 1½ minutes with selector lever in park ("P") position.
3. Reduce engine speed to slow idle and add three more quarts of fluid.
4. Check fluid level and add as required to bring it to the proper level.

BACK DRIVE LINKAGE, ADJUST

Adjust back drive at trunnion so that:
1. Transmission is in full detent in each selector position.
2. With key in Run position and transmission in Reverse, key cannot be removed and steering wheel is not locked.
3. With key in Lock position and transmission in Park, key can be removed and steering wheel is locked.

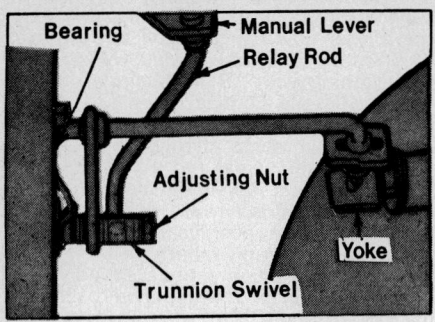

Fig. 2 Manual linkage adjustment. 1974-76 Cadillac (typical)

MANUAL LINKAGE, ADJUST

Buick Column Shift

1974-78

1. Loosen shift rod adjusting clamp bolts.
2. Place selector lever against Neutral stop.
3. Place transmission lever in Neutral.
4. Tighten clamp bolt to 17-23 ft. lbs.

Buick Console Shift

1974 All

1. Loosen trunnion bolt.
2. Set selector lever against Neutral stop.
3. Place transmission in Neutral.
4. Tighten trunnion bolt to 6-9 ft. lbs.
5. Set selector lever in Park and set back drive adjustment as described previously.

1975-78 All

1. Place selector lever and transmission lever in Park position.
2. Position pin to obtain "Free pin" fit in transmission lever and torque nut to 15-25 ft. lbs.
3. Adjust back drive as outlined previously.

1974-78 Cadillac

1. Loosen nut or screw on shift rod trunnion, Figs. 2, 3 and 4.
2. Pull trunnion lever upward to Park position, then downward to the third (Neutral) step.
3. Place steering column selector lever in Neutral position.
4. Tighten the shift rod trunnion nut or screw.
5. Check for proper operation.

Chevrolet Column Shift
1974-76

1. Place transmission lever in Neutral

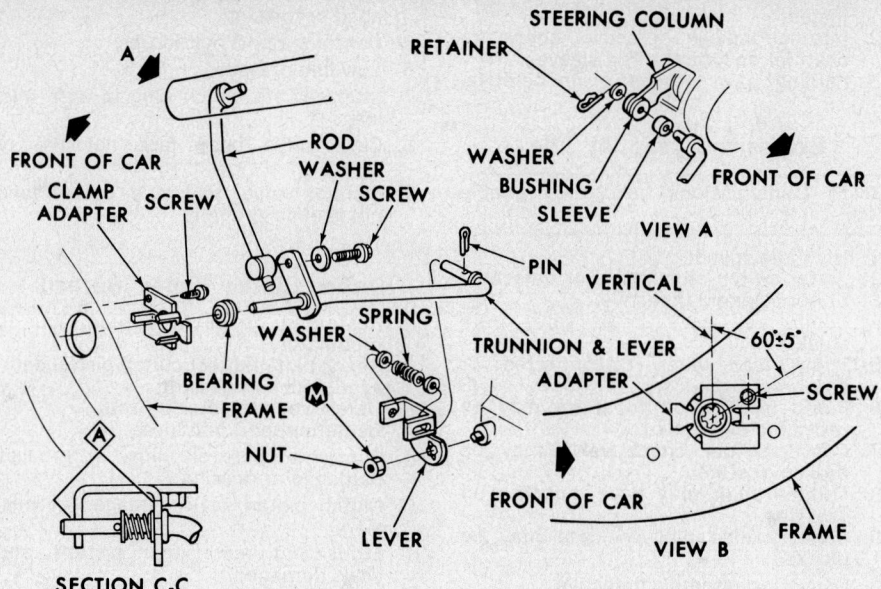

Fig. 3 Manual linkage adjustment. 1977-78 Seville

by moving lever counter-clockwise to L1 detent then clockwise three detent positions to Neutral.

2. Place selector lever in Neutral as determined by mechanical stop on steering column. Do not use indicator as reference.
3. Assemble swivel, spring washer and screw to lever assembly then tighten screw to 20 ft. lbs., Figs. 5 and 6.

Chevelle, Monte Carlo & Camaro 1974-76 Console Shift

1. Place shift lever (J) in Drive and loosen nut (G) so that pin (F) moves freely in slot of transmission lever (c). Fig. 7.
2. Place transmission lever (C) in Drive by moving lever counter-clockwise to L1 detent then clockwise three detent

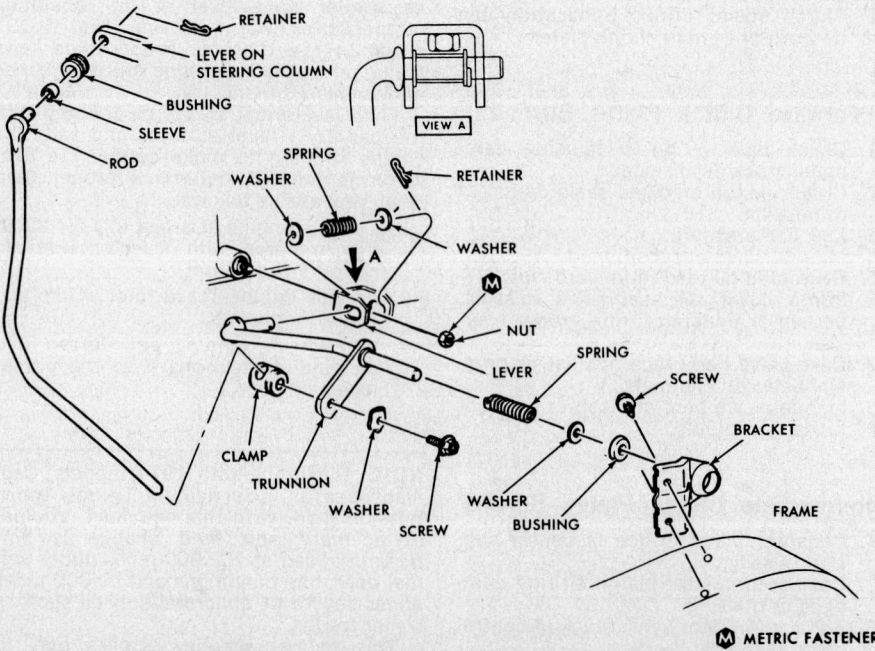

Ⓜ METRIC FASTENER

Fig. 4 Manual linkage adjustment. 1977-78 Cadillac except Seville

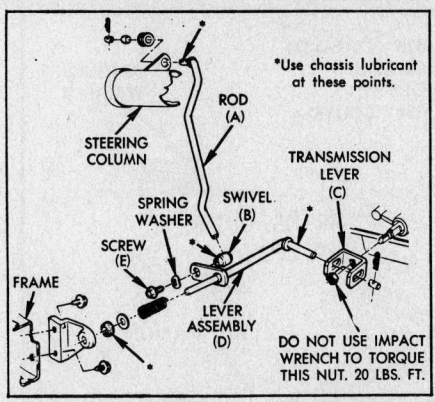

Fig. 5 Column shift linkage. 1974-76 Camaro, Chevrolet

positions to Drive.

3. Tighten nut (G) to 20 ft. lbs.

Corvette
1974-77

1. Loosen transmission lever nut.
2. Move transmission lever counterclockwise to its maximum position, then clockwise 5 detent positions to Park.
3. Place shift lever in Park and insert a .040″ spacer forward of pawl as shown in Fig. 8 and tighten nut to 20 ft. lbs.

Oldsmobile
Column Shift, 1974-78

1. Loosen shift rod clamp bolt and place transmission outer lever in Neutral position, Figs. 9 and 10.
2. Push on shift rod until selector lever is against Neutral position stop in upper steering column.

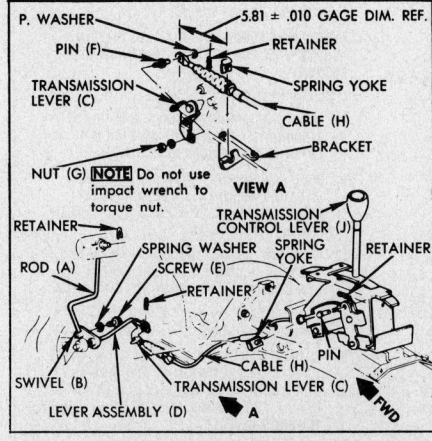

Fig. 7 Console shift adjustment. 1974-76 Camaro, Chevelle & Monte Carlo

3. Tighten bolt in clamp on lower end of shift rod to 20 ft. lbs.
4. Check for proper operation.

Console Shift, 1974-77

1. Loosen shift rod clamp bolt. Fig. 11.
2. Place selector lever in Park position. Place transmission lever in Park position with ignition key in Lock position.
3. Hold shift rod against Lock stop and tighten clamp screw.
4. Set pin to give free pin fit and tighten nut.
5. Check for proper operation.

Pontiac
Column Shift, 1974-75

1. Loosen screw on adjusting swivel clamp.
2. Set transmission selector lever in Park detent.
3. Set upper gearshift lever in Park position and lock ignition.
4. Push up on gearshift control rod to take up clearance in steering column lock mechanism and tighten screw on adjusting swivel clamp to 20 ft. lbs.

Column Shift, 1976-77

1. Place column shift lever in neutral gate notch, then loosen swivel clamp screw.
2. Place transmission shift lever in neutral detent.
3. Torque swivel clamp screw to 20 ft. lbs.
4. Check for proper operation.

Console Shift, 1974-77

1. Disconnect shift cable from transmission, Fig. 12.
2. Adjust back drive linkage as outlined at the front of this section.
3. After adjusting back drive, unlock ignition and set transmission and gear selector in Neutral position.
4. Install cable and tighten nut to 20 ft-lbs.

THROTTLE LINKAGE, ADJUST

The flexible cable type linkage is used on all models and requires no adjustment.

DOWNSHIFT SWITCHES
Buick

Detent Switch, 1974-78

Push switch lever all the way towards

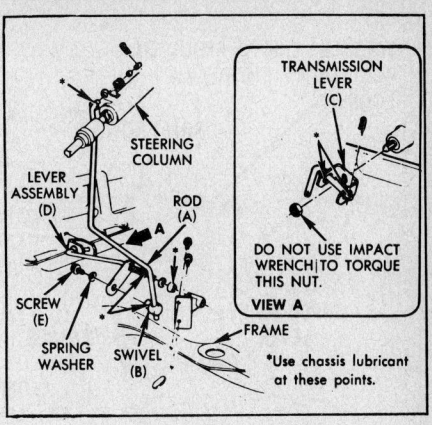

Fig. 6 Column shift linkage. 1974-76 Chevelle & Monte Carlo

dash. Final adjustment is made automatically the first time accelerator pedal is depressed to floor.

Cadillac
1974-78

1. Remove air cleaner.
2. Make certain carburetor is adjusted to specification and that linkage is at low speed idle setting.
3. Loosen two mounting screws and insert a #42 drill through calibrating hole below lower wire terminal extending through to carburetor side of switch, Fig. 13. Adjust position of switch so that lever just touches the carburetor adapter plate arm.
4. Tighten mounting screws and remove drill.
5. Install air cleaner.

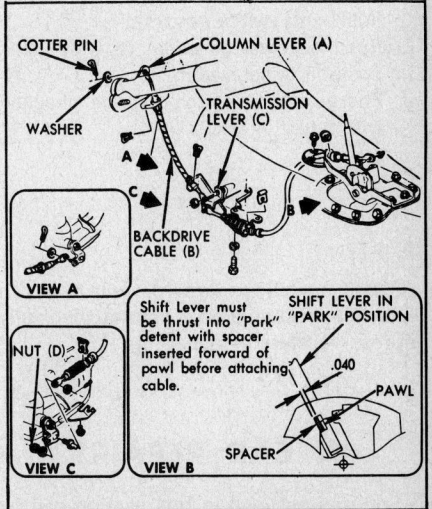

Fig. 8 Floor shift adjustment. 1974-77 Corvette

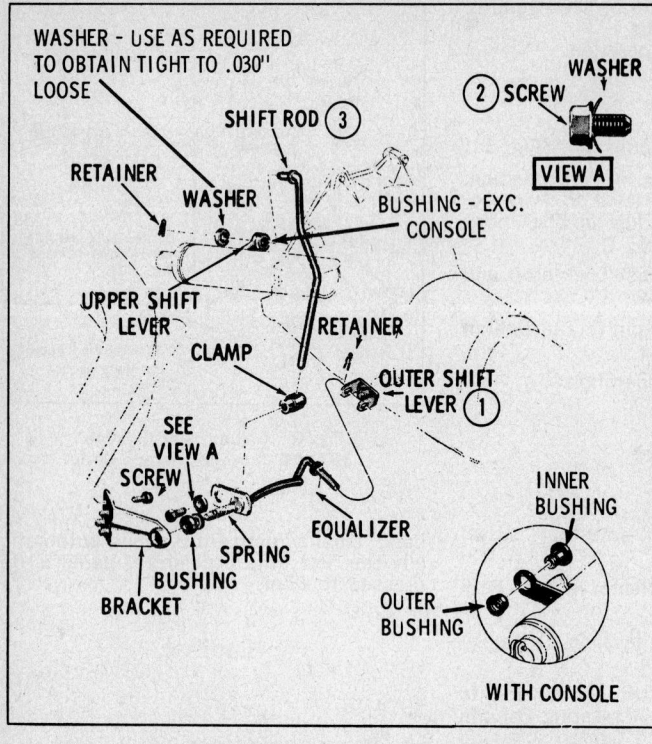

Fig. 9 Shift linkage adjustment. Oldsmobile full size (typical)

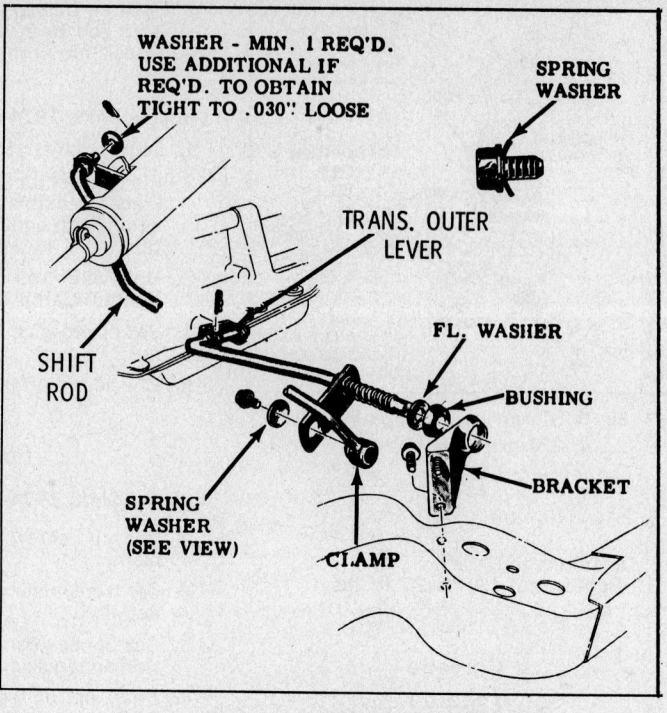

Fig. 10 Shift linkage. Oldsmobile intermediates (typical)

Chevrolet Line

1974-76

Install switch as shown in Fig. 14. After installing, press switch plunger as far forward as possible. This switch will then adjust itself the first time the accelerator pedal is pushed to floor.

Oldsmobile

1974-78

1. Push plunger of switch forward until flush with switch housing.
2. Push accelerator pedal to wide open position to set switch.
3. Energizing of switch can be checked with a test light.

Pontiac

1974-77

After installing switch, fully bottom plunger to insure proper setting then fully depress accelerator pedal, Fig. 15.

IN CAR REPAIRS

Services outlined in this section can be performed without removing the transmission from the vehicle.

Pressure Regulator Valve

NOTE: A solid type pressure regulator valve must be used only in a pump cover with a "Squared Off" (machined) pressure regulator boss, Fig. 16. A pressure regulator valve with oil holes and an orifice cup plug may be used with either type pump.

1. Remove bottom pan and strainer.
2. Using a screwdriver or steel rod, compress regulator boost valve bushing against pressure regulator spring, Fig. 17.

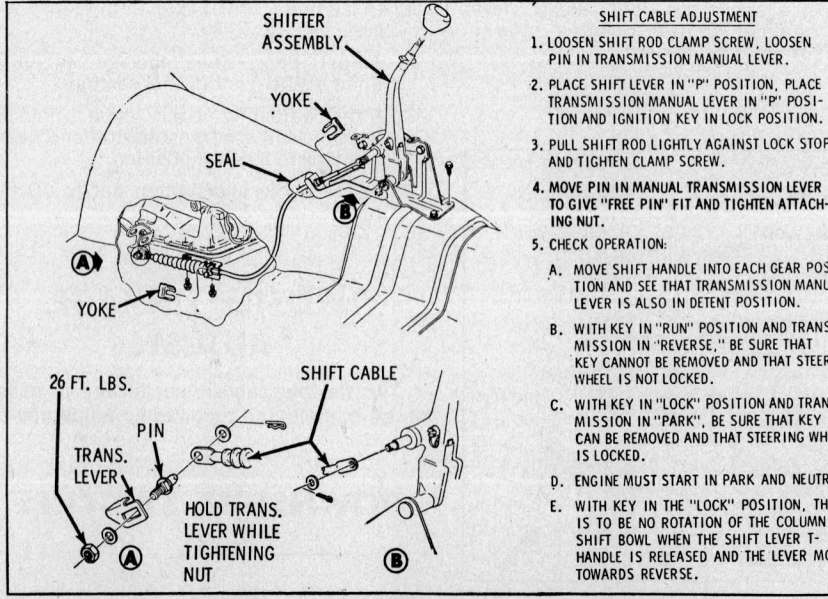

SHIFT CABLE ADJUSTMENT

1. LOOSEN SHIFT ROD CLAMP SCREW, LOOSEN PIN IN TRANSMISSION MANUAL LEVER.
2. PLACE SHIFT LEVER IN "P" POSITION, PLACE TRANSMISSION MANUAL LEVER IN "P" POSITION AND IGNITION KEY IN LOCK POSITION.
3. PULL SHIFT ROD LIGHTLY AGAINST LOCK STOP AND TIGHTEN CLAMP SCREW.
4. MOVE PIN IN MANUAL TRANSMISSION LEVER TO GIVE "FREE PIN" FIT AND TIGHTEN ATTACHING NUT.
5. CHECK OPERATION:
   A. MOVE SHIFT HANDLE INTO EACH GEAR POSITION AND SEE THAT TRANSMISSION MANUAL LEVER IS ALSO IN DETENT POSITION.
   B. WITH KEY IN "RUN" POSITION AND TRANSMISSION IN "REVERSE," BE SURE THAT KEY CANNOT BE REMOVED AND THAT STEERING WHEEL IS NOT LOCKED.
   C. WITH KEY IN "LOCK" POSITION AND TRANSMISSION IN "PARK", BE SURE THAT KEY CAN BE REMOVED AND THAT STEERING WHEEL IS LOCKED.
   D. ENGINE MUST START IN PARK AND NEUTRAL.
   E. WITH KEY IN THE "LOCK" POSITION, THERE IS TO BE NO ROTATION OF THE COLUMN SHIFT BOWL WHEN THE SHIFT LEVER T-HANDLE IS RELEASED AND THE LEVER MOVED TOWARDS REVERSE.

Fig. 11 Console shift adjustment. 1974-78 Oldsmobile

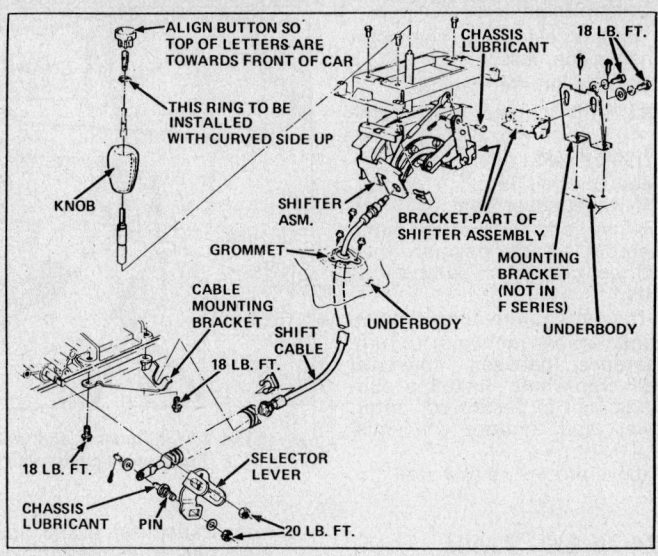

Fig. 12   Console shift adjustment. 1976-77 Pontiac (Typical)

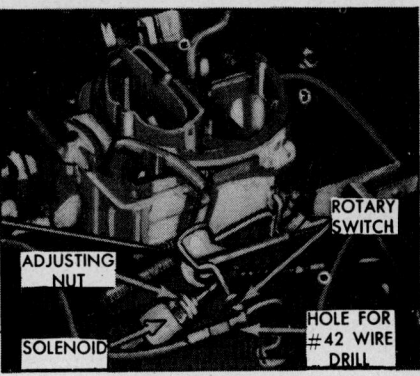

Fig. 13   Detent switch adjustment. 1974-78 Cadillac

taching screws.

4. Remove control valve body and governor pipes. If care is used in removing control valve body, the six check balls will stay in place above spacer plate.

5. Remove governor pipes and manual valve from control valve body.

6. Reverse procedure to install.

CAUTION: Pressure regulator spring is under extreme pressure and will force valve bushing out of bore when snap ring is removed if valve bushing is not held securely.

3. Continue to exert pressure on valve bushing and remove snap ring. Gradually release pressure on valve bushing until spring force is exhausted.

4. Carefully remove regulator boost valve bushing and valve, and pressure regulator spring. Be careful not to drop parts as they will fall out if they are not held.

5. Remove pressure regulator valve and spring retainer. Remove spacers if

present.

6. Reverse procedure to install.

Control Valve Body

1. Remove bottom pan and strainer.

2. Disconnect pressure switch lead wire.

3. Remove control valve body attaching screws and detent roller spring assembly. *Do not remove solenoid at-*

Governor

1. Remove governor cover and discard gasket.

2. Withdraw governor from case.

3. Reverse procedure to install, using a new gasket.

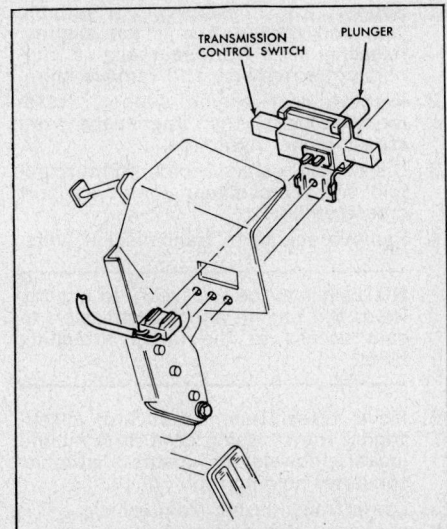

Fig. 14   Detent switch adjustment. 1974-76 Chevrolet Line

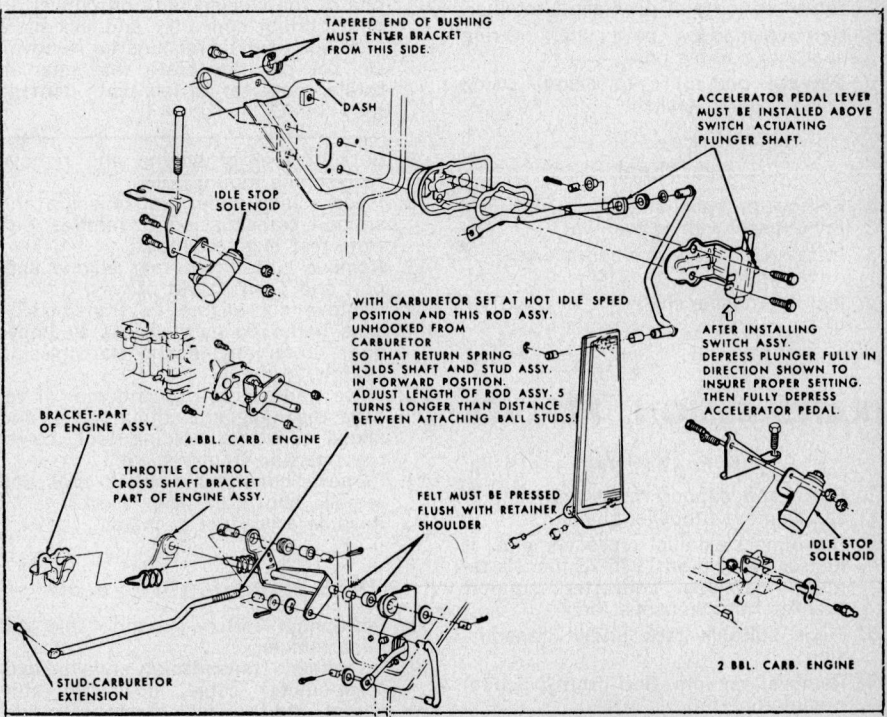

Fig. 15   Detent switch adjustment. 1974-77 Pontiac (Typical)

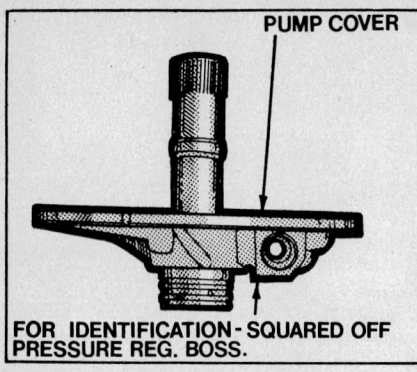

PUMP COVER

FOR IDENTIFICATION - SQUARED OFF PRESSURE REG. BOSS.

Fig. 16 Pressure regulator identification

Modulator & Modulator Valve

1. Remove modulator attaching screw and retainer.
2. Remove modulator assembly from case and discard O-ring seal.
3. Remove modulator valve from case.
4. Reverse procedure to install, using a new O-ring seal.

Parking Linkage

1. Remove bottom pan and oil strainer.
2. Unthread jam nut holding detent lever to manual shaft.
3. Remove manual shaft retaining pin from case.
4. Remove manual shaft and jam nut from case.
5. Remove O-ring seal from manual shaft.
6. Remove parking actuator rod and detent lever assembly.
7. Remove parking pawl bracket, pawl return spring and pawl shaft retainer.
8. Remove parking pawl shaft, O-ring seal and parking pawl.
9. Reverse procedure to install, using new seals and gasket.

Rear Seal

1. Remove propeller shaft.
2. Pry out seal with screwdriver.
3. Install new seal with a suitable seal driver.
4. Install propeller shaft.

TRANSMISSION, REPLACE

Buick, 1974-78

1. Raise and support front and rear of car. Remove propeller shaft.
2. Disconnect exhaust crossover pipe, if necessary, and on 1975-78 models remove catalytic converter support bracket from transmission.
3. Place suitable jack under transmission.
4. Remove vacuum line from vacuum modulator.
5. Separate cooler lines from transmission.

6. Remove transmission crossmember.
7. Remove detent electrical connector from transmission case.
8. Disconnect speedometer cable.
9. Disconnect shift linkage from transmission.
10. Remove transmission filler pipe.
11. Support engine at oil pan.
12. Remove flywheel cover pan.
13. Mark flywheel and converter pump for reassembly in same position, then remove three converter pump-to-flywheel bolts.
14. Remove transmission-to-engine bolts.
15. Move transmission rearward to provide clearance between converter pump and crankshaft. Install a suitable holding tool to secure converter. Then lower and remove transmission.
16. Reverse above procedure to install.

1974-76 Exc. Seville

1. Disconnect negative battery cable and raise vehicle on hoist.
2. Disconnect transmission linkage and remove speedometer drive cable.
3. Disconnect downshift solenoid connector and Track Master electrical harness, if equipped.
4. Disconnect oil cooler pipes at transmission and cap pipes and plug holes in transmission.
5. Disconnect vacuum modulator hose.
6. Remove starter mount bolts and starter bracket and slide starter forward.
7. Remove propeller shaft.
8. Remove lower flywheel housing cover and three converter to flex plate bolts.

NOTE: This is done by inserting a heavy screwdriver in open slot under one of the welded nuts on converter, and rotating converter and flex plate until bolts can be reached for removal. Do not pry flex plate ring gear to rotate converter as flex plate damage may result.

9. Support rear of engine and remove rear engine mount bolts.
10. Place a jack under transmission and support transmission to remove load from rear engine support.
11. Remove bolts from rear engine support and position out of way.
12. Remove six engine to transmission case bolts. To gain access to upper bolts, lower engine and transmission slightly.
13. Move transmission toward rear of vehicle, disengaging locating dowels and install converter holding tool. Lower transmission from vehicle.
14. Remove converter holding tool and remove converter from shaft.
15. Reverse procedure to install.

1976 Seville & 1977-78 All

1. Disconnect battery ground cable and raise vehicle.
2. Disconnect transmission shift linkage, speedometer cable, downshift connector, and the Track Master electrical connector, if equipped.
3. Disconnect and plug oil cooler lines

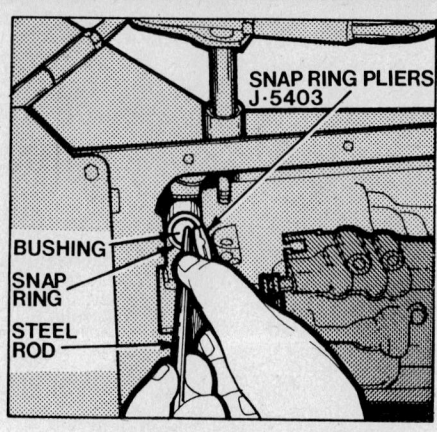

SNAP RING PLIERS J-5403

BUSHING
SNAP RING
STEEL ROD

Fig. 17 Removing and installing Pressure regulator valve

from transmission and position aside. Also, plug transmission ports.
4. Disconnect vacuum line from vacuum modulator and position aside.
5. Remove propeller shaft.
6. Remove lower flywheel housing cover and the three converter to flywheel attaching bolts.

NOTE: This is accomplished by inserting a heavy screwdriver in open slot under one of the converter weld nuts and rotating the converter with a 1¼ inch deep socket until the bolts are accessible. Do not pry on ring gear or transmission case to rotate converter as damage may result.

7. Support rear of engine with a suitable jack.
8. On Seville, remove lateral strut-rod from rear engine mount and crossmember. Also remove two nuts from tunnel strap, then the strap.
9. Remove two nuts from tunnel strap, then the strap.
10. Remove two rear engine mounts to extension housing screws.
11. Support transmission with a suitable jack and raise transmission slightly, releasing load from rear engine support crossmember, and remove shim.
12. Remove rear engine support crossmember bolts, then the space from crossmember right side.
13. Disconnect exhaust pipe from manifold and remove rear engine support crossmember.
14. Remove engine to transmission bolts.

NOTE: It may be necessary to slightly lower the engine and transmission to gain access to the upper attaching bolts.

15. Move transmission rearward, disengaging transmission case from engine locating dowels, and install a suitable converter holding tool.
16. Lower transmission from vehicle.
17. Reverse procedure to install. Torque engine to transmission case bolts to 35 ft. lbs. and the converter to flywheel bolts to 30 ft. lbs.

Chevrolet Line 1974-76

Before raising car, disconnect negative battery cable and release the parking brake.

1. Raise vehicle, remove propeller shaft and on 1975-76 models, remove catalytic converter support bracket from transmission.
2. Disconnect speedometer cable, electrical lead to case connector, vacuum modulator line and cooler lines.
3. Disconnect shift control linkage.
4. Support transmission with suitable jack.
5. Disconnect rear mount from frame crossmember.
6. Remove two bolts at each end of frame crossmember (plus through bolt at inside of frame and parking brake pulley on Corvette). Remove crossmember.
7. Remove converter underpan.
8. Remove converter to flywheel bolts.
9. On Chevrolet and Chevelle, loosen exhaust pipe to manifold bolts about ¼".
10. Lower transmission until jack is barely supporting it.
11. Remove transmission to engine mounting bolts and remove oil filler tube.
12. Raise transmission to its normal position, support engine with jack and slide transmission rearward from engine and lower it away from car.

NOTE: Use converter holding tool when lowering transmission or keep rear of transmission lower than front so as not to lose converter.

---

13. Reverse removal procedure to install transmission.

Oldsmobile 1974-78

1. Remove flywheel cover and torque converter attaching bolts.
2. Mark flywheel and converter so they can be installed in same position.
3. Support engine at rear.
4. Disconnect solenoid wires and manual shift linkage at side of transmission.
5. Disconnect oil cooler lines, vacuum modulator line and oil filler pipe.
6. Disconnect parking brake cable.
7. Before removing propeller shaft, scribe marks on drive shaft and companion flange for correct assembly.
8. Disconnect exhaust pipe bracket from rear of crossmember and on 1975-78 models, remove catalytic converter support bracket from transmission, if necessary.
9. Support transmission, then remove crossmember.
10. Unfasten transmission from engine.
11. Move transmission away from engine, then, before removing transmission, fasten a suitable piece of strap iron to housing to prevent converter from falling out as transmission is removed.

Pontiac 1974-78

1. Disconnect battery and release parking brake. Then raise car.
2. Remove propeller shaft and on 1975-78 models, remove catalytic converter support bracket from transmission.
3. Disconnect speedometer cable, electrical lead to case connector, vacuum line at modulator, and oil cooler pipes.
4. Disconnect shift control linkage.
5. Support transmission with jack.
6. Disconnect rear mount from transmission and crossmember.
7. Remove crossmember (2 bolts at each end).
8. Remove converter dust shield.
9. Remove converter-to-flex plate bolts.
10. Loosen exhaust pipe to manifold about ¼", and lower transmission until jack is barely supporting it.
11. Remove transmission - to - engine mount bolts.
12. Raise transmission to its normal position, slide it rearward and lower it away from vehicle.

NOTE: When lowering transmission, keep rear of unit lower than front so as not to drop converter.

---

13. Reverse procedure to install.

GM FRONT WHEEL DRIVE
TURBO HYDRA-MATIC

TRANSMISSION IDENTIFICATION

CADILLAC ELDORADO

1974-78 Exc. Electronic Fuel Injection . . . AJ

1975-78 Electronic Fuel Injection . . . . AK

OLDSMOBILE TORONADO

1974-78 Exc. Below . . . . OJ

1974-77 California . . . . OM

DESCRIPTION

This transmission is a fully automatic unit used for front wheel drive applications, Fig. 1. It consists primarily of a three-element hydraulic torque converter, dual sprocket and chain link assembly, compound planetary gear set, three multiple disc clutches, a sprag clutch, a roller clutch, two band assemblies, and a hydraulic control system.

Torque Converter

The torque converter consists of a pump or driving member, a turbine or driven member and a stator or reaction member.

The stator is mounted on a one-way roller clutch which allows it to overrun when not used as a reaction member.

The torque converter couples the engine to the planetary gear set through the use of a drive sprocket, a chain link assembly, and a driven sprocket. Clockwise engine torque turns the drive sprocket clockwise. This, in turn, drives the driven sprocket in a clockwise direction. This in effect is a reverse in the direction of engine torque due to the side mounting of the gear unit.

Planetary Gear Set

The gear set provides three forward ratios and reverse. The approximate gear ratios are: First 2½ to 1, second 1½ to 1, third 1.1 to 1, reverse 2.1 to 1. Second and third are also multiplied by a lesser degree.

Converter stall ratio, first gear (2½ x 2) equals 5 to 1. Converter stall ratio, reverse (2.1 x 2) equals 4.2 to 1.

External Controls

External control connections to the transmission are: a) Engine vacuum, b) 12-volt electrical signals, c) manual linkage control.

Engine vacuum is used to operate the vacuum modulator assembly. The vacuum modulator automatically senses any change in torque input to the transmission that the driver induces through a change in accelerator position.

On all models an electrical signal is used to operate an electrical solenoid. The solenoid is activated by a switch at the carburetor. When the throttle is opened sufficiently to close this switch, the solenoid in the transmission is activated, causing a downshift at speeds below approximately 70 mph. At lower speeds, downshifts will occur at lesser speeds without use of the switch.

TROUBLE SHOOTING GUIDE

NOTE: In many of the following diagnosis procedures, it is recommended that air pressure be applied to help in determining if the seal, rings or pistons are stuck, missing or damaged. Therefore, when air is applied, listen carefully for escaping air and piston action as air is applied to a particular area.

No Drive In "D" Range

1. Low oil level. Check for external leaks or vacuum modulator diaphragm leaking.
2. Manual linkage maladjusted. Correct alignment in manual lever shift quadrant.
3. Low oil pressure.
4. Oil strainer O-ring seal missing or damaged, neck weld leaking, strainer blocked.
5. Oil pump pressure regulator stuck or inoperative. Pump drive gear tangs damaged by converter.
6. Case porosity in intake bore.
7. Control valve. Manual valve disconnected from manual lever pin. (Other shift lever positions would also be affected.)
8. Forward clutch does not apply. Piston cracked; seals missing or damaged. These defects can be checked by removing the valve body and applying air pressure to the drive cavity in the case valve body face. Missing, damaged or worn oil rings on driven support housing can also be checked in this manner at the same time because they can also cause the forward clutch not to apply. Clutch plates burned.
9. Roller clutch inoperative. Rollers worn, damaged springs, or damaged races. May be checked by placing selector lever in "L" range.

No Drive In "R" or Slips In Reverse

1. Low oil level.
2. Manual linkage.
3. Oil pressure. Vacuum modulator defective, modulator valve sticking.
4. Restricted strainer, leak at intake pipe or O-ring seal. Pressure regulator or boost valve sticking.
5. Control valve body gaskets leaking or damaged (other malfunctions may also be indicated). Low-reverse check ball missing from case (this will cause no overrun braking in low range). The 2-3 valve train stuck open (this will also cause 1-3 upshifts in drive range). Reverse feed passage not drilled; also check case passages. Apply air to reverse passage in case valve body face.
6. Rear servo and accumulator. Servo piston seal ring broken or missing. Apply air pressure to drilled hole in intermediate clutch passage of case valve body face to check for piston operation and excessive leakage. Band apply pin too short (this may also cause no overrun braking or slip in overrun braking in low range).

7. Rear band burned, loose lining, apply pin or anchor pin not engaged; band broken.
8. Direct clutch outer seal damaged or missing. Clutch plates burned (may be caused by stuck ball check in piston).
9. Forward clutch does not release (will also cause drive in neutral range).

Drive In Neutral

1. Manual linkage maladjusted.
2. Forward clutch does not release (this condition will also cause no reverse).

1st Speed Only—No 1-2 Upshift

1. Governor valve sticking; driven gear loose, damaged or worn. If driven gear shows signs of wear or damage, check output flange drive gear for nicks or rough finish.
2. Control valve. The 1-2 shift valve train stuck closed. Dirt, chips or damaged valve in 1-2 shift valve train. Governor feed channels blocked or leaking; pipes out of position. Valve body gaskets leaking or damaged. Case porosity between oil channels. Governor feed passage blocked.
3. Intermediate clutch. Case center support oil rings missing, broken or defective. Clutch piston seals missing, improperly assembled, cut or damaged. Apply air to intermediate clutch passage located in case valve body face to check for these defects.

1-2 Shift Obtained Only At Full Throttle

1. Detent switch sticking or defective.
2. Detent solenoid loose, gasket leaking, sticks open, electrical wire pinched between cover and casting.
3. Control valve body gasket leaking or damaged. Detent valve train stuck.

1st & 2nd Speeds Only No 2-3 Shift

1. Detent solenoid stuck open (the 2-3 shift would occur at very high speeds) may be diagnosed as no 2-3 shift.
2. Detent switch sticking or defective.
3. Control valve body. The 2-3 valve train stuck with dirt or foreign material. Valve body gaskets leaking or damaged.
4. Direct clutch. Case center support oil rings missing or broken. Clutch piston seals missing, improperly assembled, cut or damaged; piston ball check stuck or missing. Apply air to direct clutch passage in case valve body face to check these conditions.

Slips In All Ranges

1. Oil level incorrect.
2. Low oil pressure. Vacuum modulator defective or valve sticking. Oil strainer plugged or leaks at neck; O-ring (case to strainer) missing or damaged. Pressure regulator or boost valve sticking.

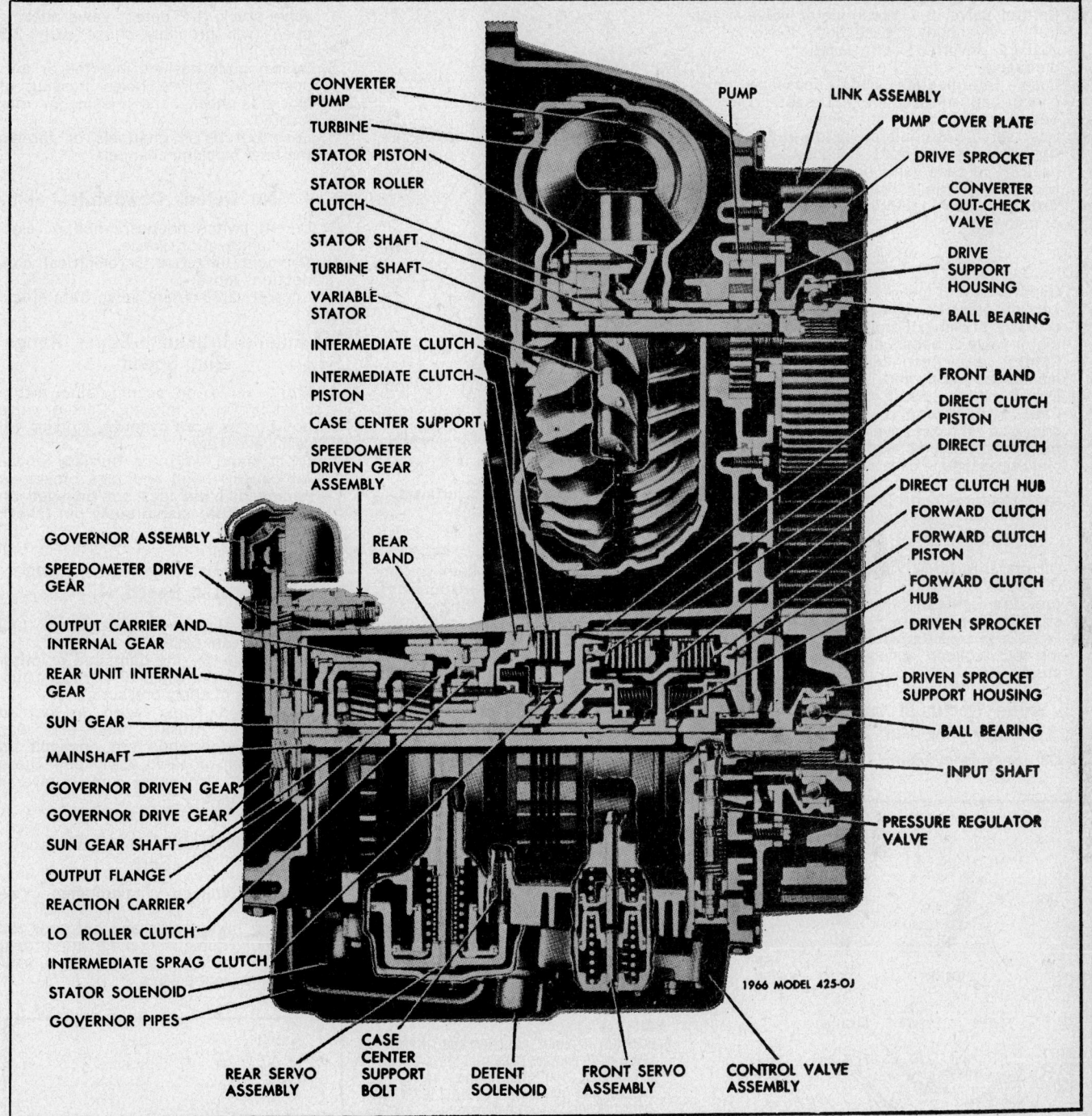

CONVERTER PUMP
TURBINE
STATOR PISTON
STATOR ROLLER CLUTCH
STATOR SHAFT
TURBINE SHAFT
VARIABLE STATOR
INTERMEDIATE CLUTCH
INTERMEDIATE CLUTCH PISTON
CASE CENTER SUPPORT
SPEEDOMETER DRIVEN GEAR ASSEMBLY
REAR BAND
GOVERNOR ASSEMBLY
SPEEDOMETER DRIVE GEAR
OUTPUT CARRIER AND INTERNAL GEAR
REAR UNIT INTERNAL GEAR
SUN GEAR
MAINSHAFT
GOVERNOR DRIVEN GEAR
GOVERNOR DRIVE GEAR
SUN GEAR SHAFT
OUTPUT FLANGE
REACTION CARRIER
LO ROLLER CLUTCH
INTERMEDIATE SPRAG CLUTCH
STATOR SOLENOID
GOVERNOR PIPES

PUMP
LINK ASSEMBLY
PUMP COVER PLATE
DRIVE SPROCKET
CONVERTER OUT-CHECK VALVE
DRIVE SUPPORT HOUSING
BALL BEARING
FRONT BAND
DIRECT CLUTCH PISTON
DIRECT CLUTCH
DIRECT CLUTCH HUB
FORWARD CLUTCH
FORWARD CLUTCH PISTON
FORWARD CLUTCH HUB
DRIVEN SPROCKET
DRIVEN SPROCKET SUPPORT HOUSING
BALL BEARING
INPUT SHAFT
PRESSURE REGULATOR VALVE

1966 MODEL 425-OJ

REAR SERVO ASSEMBLY
CASE CENTER SUPPORT BOLT
DETENT SOLENOID
FRONT SERVO ASSEMBLY
CONTROL VALVE ASSEMBLY

Fig. 1 General Motors Front Wheel Drive Turbo Hydra-Matic

3. Case cross channel leaks; porosity.
4. Forward, intermediate and direct clutches slipping. Clutch plates burned. Always look for a primary defect that would cause clutch plates to burn. (Missing feed holes, seals and oil rings, etc., are primary defects).
5. Roller clutch rollers worn; springs or cage damaged, and worn or damaged races (operates normally in low and reverse ranges).

Slips 1 - 2 Shift

1. Oil level incorrect.

2. Low oil pressure. Look for defective vacuum modulator or valve sticking. Pump pressure regulator valve stuck.
3. Front servo accumulator piston cracked or porous, oil ring damaged or missing.
4. Control valve. The 1-2 accumulator valve train (may cause a slip-bump shift). Porous valve body or case valve body face.
5. Rear servo accumulator oil ring missing or damaged; case bore damaged; piston cracked or damaged.
6. Case porous between oil passages.

7. Intermediate clutch lip seals missing, cut or damaged. Apply air pressure to intermediate clutch passage in case valve body face to check. Clutch plates burned. Case center support leaks in feed circuits (oil rings damaged or grooves damaged) or excessive leak between tower and bushing.

Rough 1 - 2 Shift

1. Oil pressure. Check vacuum modulator for loose fittings, restrictions in line; defective vacuum modulator. Modulator valve stuck. Pressure reg-

ulator boost valve stuck.
2. Control valve. 1-2 accumulator valve train; valve body-to-case bolts loose; gaskets inverted, off location, or damaged.
3. Case. Intermediate clutch passage check ball missing or not seating. Case porous between channels.
4. Rear servo accumulator piston stuck. Apply air pressure to 1-2 accumulator passage in case valve body face (you should hear the servo piston move). Broken or missing spring; bore scored or damaged.

Slips 2 - 3 Shift

1. Oil level high or low.
2. Low oil pressure. Modulator defective or valve sticking. Pump pressure regulator valve or boost valve sticking.
3. Control valve. Accumulator piston pin leak at valve body end.
4. Direct clutch piston seals leaking. Case center support oil seal rings damaged or excessive leak between tower and bushing. Apply air to direct clutch passage in case valve body face. If air comes out intermediate passage, center support is defective.

Rough 2 - 3 Shift

1. Oil pressure high. Vacuum modulator defective or valve sticking. Pump pressure regulator valve or boost valve stuck or inoperative.
2. Front servo accumulator spring missing or broken; accumulator piston stuck.

Shifts Occur at too High or too Low Car Speed

1. Oil pressure. Vacuum modulator de-

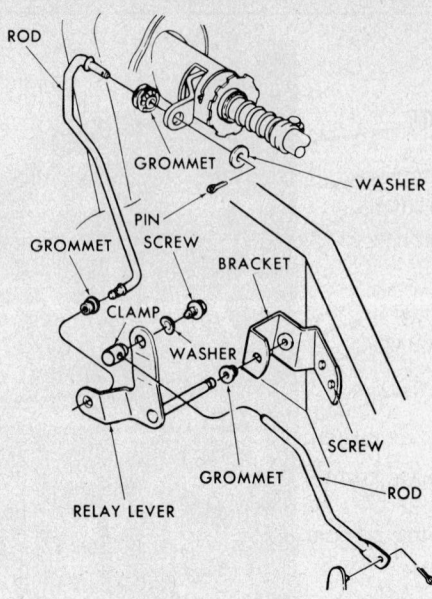

Fig. 2 Manual control linkage adjustment. Cadillac Eldorado (typical)

fective or valve sticking. Leak in vacuum line (engine to transmission). Vacuum modulator line fitting on carburetor blocked. Pump pressure regulator valve or boost valve train stuck.
2. Governor valve stuck or sticking. Feed holes restricted or leaking; pipes damaged or mispositioned.
3. Detent solenoid stuck open or loose on valve body (will cause late shifts).
4. Control valve. Detent valve train stick-

ing; 3-2 valve train sticking; 1-2 shift valve stuck; 1-2 detent valve sticking open (will probably cause early 2-3 shift).
5. Spacer plate gaskets inverted or mispositioned; orifice holes missing or blocked; check balls missing or mislocated.
6. Case porous in channels or foreign material blocking channels.

No Detent Downshift

1. Detent switch mispositioned or electrical connections loose.
2. Solenoid defective or electrical connections loose.
3. Control valve detent valve train stuck.

No Engine Braking—Super Range 2nd Speed

1. Front servo or accumulator piston rings broken or missing. Case or valve body bores worn oversize, causing excessive leakage.
2. Front band worn or burned (check for cause); band end lugs broken or damaged; band lugs not engaged on anchor pins or servo apply pin (check for cause).

No Engine Braking—Low Range 1st Speed

1. Control valve low-reverse check ball missing from case.
2. Rear servo oil ring damaged or missing; piston damaged or porous, causing a leak in apply pressure.
3. Rear band lining worn or burned (check for cause); band end lugs broken; band ends not engaged on anchor pin or servo apply pin. These items will also cause slip in reverse or no reverse.

Will Not Hold Car In Park Position

1. Manual linkage maladjusted (external).
2. Parking brake lever and actuator rod assembly defective (check for proper actuator spring action). Parking pawl broken or inoperative.

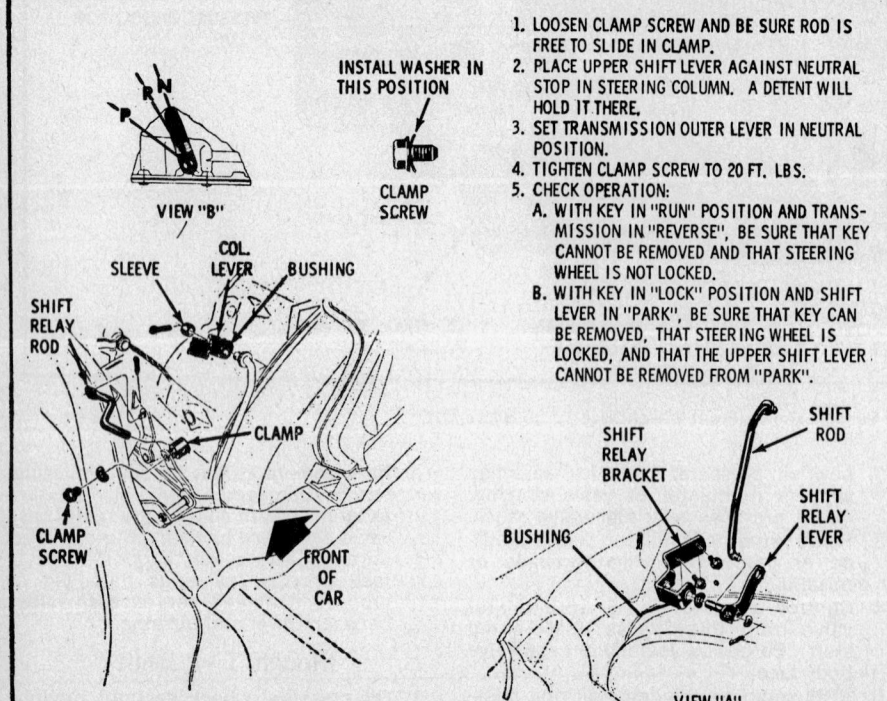

Fig. 3 Shift linkage adjustment. Toronado column shift, 1974-78

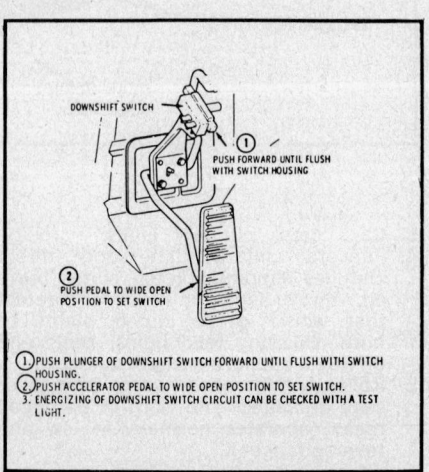

Fig. 4 Downshift switch adjustment. Oldsmobile Toronado

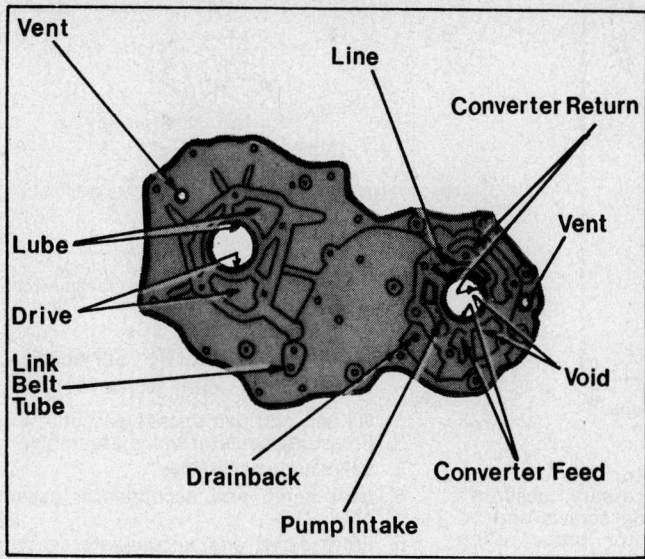

Fig. 5   Location of check balls

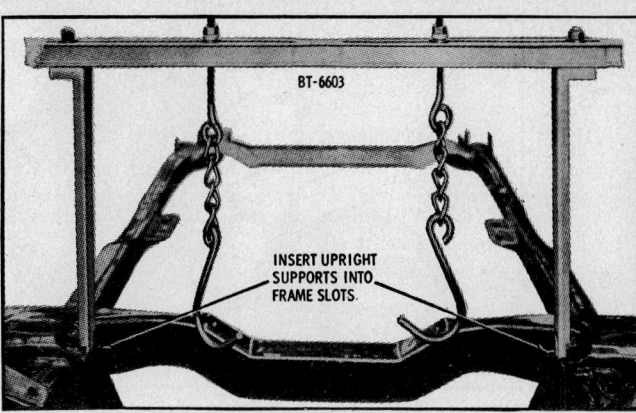

Fig. 6   Installing support bar. Olds Toronado

Poor Performance or Rough Idle

1. Stator switch defective or maladjusted.
2. Stator solenoid defective or wire ground to solenoid housing; electrical connection loose; stator valve train stuck (located in valve body); oil feed circuit to stator restricted or blocked (check feed hole in stator shaft); converter-out check valve broken or missing (reed valve located in cover plate under drive support housing).
3. Turbine shaft converter return passage not drilled; oil seal rings broken, worn or missing.
4. Case porous in feed circuit channels or foreign material blocking feed circuit.
5. Converter assembly defective.

Transmission Noise

1. Pump noise. Oil level high or low; water in oil, driving gear assembled upside down; driving or driven gear teeth damaged.
2. Gear noise (1st gear drive range). Check planetary pinions for tooth damage. Check sun gear and front and rear internal gears for tooth finish or damage.
3. Clutch noise during application. Check clutch plates.
4. Sprocket and chain link assembly. Chain link too long (sounds similar to popcorn popping). There will be a rough burr along teeth of drive sprocket if chain link is too long; replace chain link and drive sprocket. Drive or driven sprocket teeth damaged. Engine mounts worn or damaged.

Burned Forward Clutch Plates

1. Check ball in clutch housing damaged, stuck or missing.
2. Clutch piston cracked, seals damaged or missing.
3. Low line pressure.
4. Manual valve mispositioned.

5. Restricted oil feed to forward clutch.
6. Pump cover oil seal rings missing, broken or undersize or ring groove oversize.
7. Case valve body face not flat or porosity between channels.
8. Manual valve bent and center land not ground properly.

Burned Intermediate Clutch Plates

1. Rear accumulator piston oil ring damaged or missing.
2. 1-2 accumulator valve stuck in control valve assembly.
3. Intermediate clutch piston seals damaged or missing.
4. Center support bolt loose.
5. Low line pressure.
6. Intermediate clutch plug in case missing.
7. Case valve body face not flat or porosity between channels.
8. Manual valve bent and center land not ground properly.

Burned Direct Clutch Plates

1. Restricted orifice in vacuum line to modulator.
2. Check ball in direct clutch piston damaged, stuck or missing.
3. Defective modulator bellows.
4. Center support bolt loose.
5. Center support oil rings or grooves damaged or missing.
6. Clutch piston seals damaged or missing.
7. Front and rear servo pistons and seals damaged.
8. Manual valve bent and center land not cleaned up.
9. Case valve body face not flat or porosity between channels.
10. Intermediate sprag clutch installed backwards.

MAINTENANCE
Adding Oil

The fluid level should be checked at

every engine oil change interval, and should be changed at 24,000 mile intervals. The fluid level should be checked with the selector lever in PARK position, engine running at idle speed and car on a level surface. The oil indicator and filler tube are located under the hood at the left front corner of the engine. *The filler tube comes out from the final drive housing but it is for the transmission.*

NOTE: If any work is performed on the transmission, it will require the following amounts of oil to bring the oil to the correct level:
1. Pan removed 5½ qts.
2. Drive cover sprocket housing ½ qt.
3. Converter changed 3½ qts.
4. Total overhaul (total capacity) 13 qts.

Changing Oil

When changing transmission oil, first add 4 quarts, start the engine, and add oil to bring the fluid level to the FULL mark on the dipstick. Use only Dexron automatic transmission oil.

NOTE: Cadillac uses an extended-life Dexron transmission fluid. With this new fluid, strainer replacement and fluid change is now recommended at 100,000 miles under normal operating conditions and 50,000 miles under severe or abnormal service such as trailer towing.

This recommendation applies only to the improved fluid and its availability for service. If the new fluid is not available, the former fluid can be used but then the 24,000 mile maintenance rule will apply.

Oldsmobile is using a revised type Dexron fluid. An early change to a darker color from the usual red color and or a strong odor that is usually associated with overheated fluid is normal, and should not be treated as a positive sign of needed maintenance or unit failure.

The normal maintenance schedule for drain and refill of this type fluid remains unchanged at 24,000 miles under normal service and 12,000 miles under severe operating conditions, such as trailer towing. Also on Olds Toronado, the normal maintenance schedule for drain and refill is 30,000 miles on 1975 models and 60,000 miles on 1976-78 models.

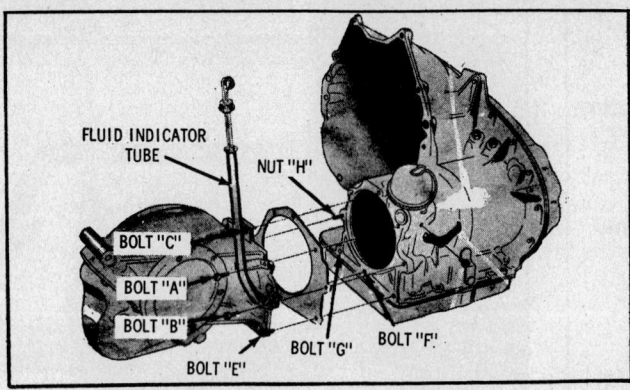

Fig. 7 Transmission attachment. 1974-78 Oldsmobile Toronado

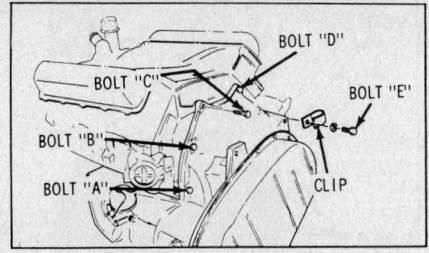

Fig. 8 Transmission to engine attachment

MANUAL LINKAGE, ADJUST

Cadillac Eldorado

1. Referring to Fig. 2, loosen adjusting screw on relay lever.
2. Pull relay rod up to position transmission shift valve in Park, then push rod down to the third (Neutral) step. Make sure rod is centered in this detent position.
3. Position selector lever in Neutral against quadrant stop in steering column.
4. Tighten relay rod adjusting screw, making sure shift lever is held against Neutral stop while this operation is being performed.

Olds Toronado

Make the adjustment as directed in Fig. 3.

DOWNSHIFT SWITCH, ADJUST

Cadillac Eldorado

1. Remove carburetor air cleaner.
2. Make sure that carburetor is properly adjusted and that throttle linkage is at low speed idle setting.
3. If the downshift switch is properly adjusted, a #42 (wire gauge size) drill can be inserted in the calibrating hole below lower wire terminal extending

through to carburetor side of switch.
4. If adjustment is necessary, loosen the two switch mounting screws and position the switch for proper alignment.
5. With switch positioned, tighten mounting screws, remove drill gauge and install air cleaner.

Olds Toronado

Adjust detent downshift switch as described in Fig. 4

NOTE: Trailer Hauling Switch (Y-73 option) is bronze colored. When checking the special throttle switches with a test lamp, the test lamp *should light* only when the throttle valves are at idle or at wide open throttle position. The test lamp *will not light* at the 40° throttle opening as it does when checking a regular switch.

IN CAR REPAIRS

Operations Not Requiring Transmission Removal

1. Oil cooler fitting replacement or adjustment.
2. Governor assembly service.
3. Vacuum modulator, bushing and valve service.
4. Speedometer drive gear service.
5. Cruise Control service.
6. Oil level check.
7. Oil pressure check with oil pressure gauge.

Units That Can Be Serviced After Oil Pan Removal

1. Oil pan and pan-to-case gasket.
2. Pressure regulator valve assembly.
3. Valve body assembly.
4. Rear servo and accumulator assembly.
5. Front servo and accumulator assembly.
6. Governor pipes.
7. Detent solenoid.
8. Stator solenoid.
9. Solenoid connector.
10. Manual linkage.
11. Parking linkage.
12. Valve body-to-case spacers and gaskets.
13. Check balls for proper location (7 balls), Fig. 5.
14. Detent roller and spring assembly.

TRANS., REPLACE

1974-78 Olds Toronado

Removal

1. Disconnect battery.
2. Disconnect oil cooler lines at transmission and speedometer cable at governor. Remove governor and cover opening to prevent entry of dirt.
3. Install a suitable engine support bar, such as shown in Fig. 6.
4. Remove three upper final drive to transmission attaching bolts, Fig. 7.

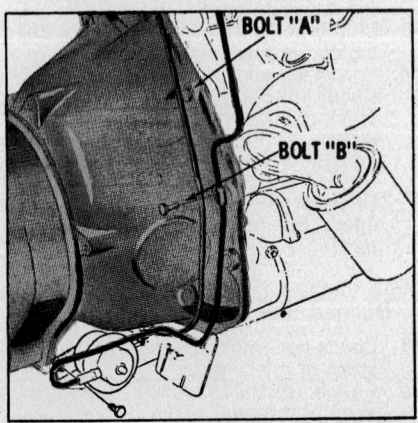

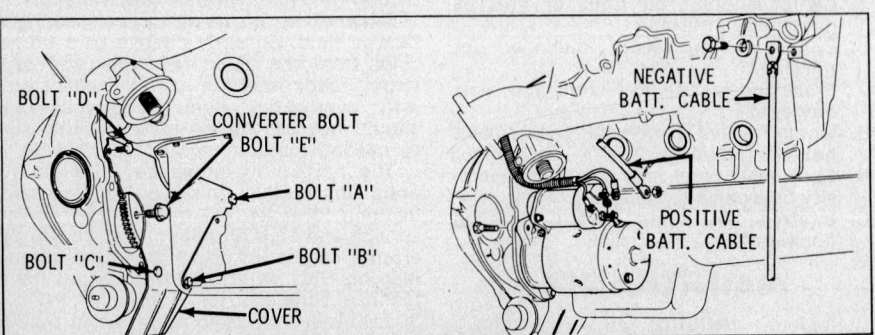

Fig. 9 Converter attachment

Fig. 10 Transmission to engine attachment

Fig. 11   Transmission attaching bolt
locations. Cadillac Eldorado

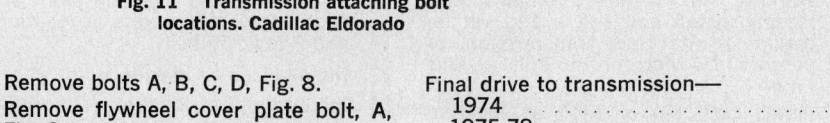

Fig. 12   Positioning transmission jack to
transmission. Cadillac Eldorado

5. Remove bolts A, B, C, D, Fig. 8.
6. Remove flywheel cover plate bolt, A, Fig. 9.
7. Hoist car and remove starter.
8. Remove bolts B, C and D from flywheel cover plate, Fig. 9.
9. Remove flywheel to converter bolt E, Fig. 9. Rotate flywheel until bolts are removed.
10. Disconnect vacuum modulator line and stator wiring.
11. Install transmission lift.
12. Remove shift linkage.
13. Remove bolts E, F, G and nut H, Fig. 7.
14. Remove bolts A and B, Fig. 10.
15. Remove two upper engine mount bracket-to-transmission bolts.
16. Remove four bracket-to-engine mount bolts.
17. Slide transmission rearward and down.
18. Attach converter holding strap to housing to prevent converter from falling out when transmission is being removed.
19. After transmission is removed from vehicle, the link assembly cover insulator can be removed or installed.

Installation

When installing the transmission the engine mount bracket must be positioned loosely on the link assembly cover until the transmission is in place. Then reverse removal procedure and torque bolts to ft-lb values as follows:
Engine to converter housing 30

Engine bracket to transmission—
    1974 55
    1975-78 60

Engine bracket to rubber mount—
    1974 55
    1975-78 60

Oil cooler lines to transmission—
    1974 20
    1975-78 12

Final drive to transmission—
    1974 25
    1975-78 30

1974-78 Cadillac Eldorado

Removal—Figs. 11 and 12

1. Disconnect ground cable at battery.
2. Remove transmission dipstick.
3. Remove filler tube.
4. Remove bolts at locations A, B and C, securing final drive case to transmission.
5. Disconnect speedometer cable from governor and detent solenoid connector from transmission case.
6. Disconnect oil cooler pipes from transmission.
7. Cap pipes and plug connector holes in transmission and radiator.
8. Remove bolt securing cooler pipe bracket to final drive bracket and position pipes away from governor.
9. Remove nut at location H, securing final drive case to transmission.
10. Remove bolts at locations I, J, K and L, securing transmission to engine and adapter plate.
11. Remove upper left bolt securing rear engine mount bracket to transmission.
12. Remove ground strap from cowl.
13. Remove upper left nut securing converter cover plate to transmission.

NOTE: Use a 7/16" universal socket and extension and reach underneath left exhaust manifold. Removal of this screw can be facilitated by having a helper under the car, verbally guiding socket onto nut.

14. Position safety chain over top of transmission.
15. Raise vehicle and place on jack stands.
16. Disconnect leads from starter motor.
17. Remove bolt at location O, securing

starter motor to transmission case and remove ground strap from bolt.
18. Remove bolt at location P and remove starter.
19. Remove three remaining screws securing converter cover plate to transmission and remove cover plate.
20. Position transmission jack.
21. Disconnect electrical connector from transmission connector.
22. Remove pipe from vacuum modulator.
23. Secure transmission to transmission jack adapter plate with safety chain.
24. Remove three flex plate-to-converter attaching bolts.

NOTE: This can be done by installing a 9/16-18 bolt and washer into end of crankshaft at vibration damper, after removing cork plug, and rotating converter and flex plate until bolts are accessible for removal. Do not pry on flex plate ring gear to rotate flex plate and converter as flex plate may be damaged.

25. Remove bolts at locations M and N securing transmission to engine and adapter plate.
26. On left side of transmission, separate relay rod from manual yoke.
27. Remove bolts at locations D. E and F, and nut at location G, securing final drive to transmission.

NOTE: Position drain pan under point where transmission and final drive meet as approximately 1½ quarts of transmission fluid will be lost when transmission and final drive are separated.

28. Remove five bolts and washers securing rear of acromat (cushion) to front cross bar and frame horns and allow acromat to hang free.
29. Through access holes in bottom of front cross bar, remove left bolt and loosen right bolt securing front engine mount to front cross bar. Turn wheels all the way to the left to provide maximum clearance.
30. Have a helper, using a large pry bar, shift engine forward, while you use a

small pry bar to help separate transmission from engine and final drive. *Select pry points with care to avoid damaging any components.*

31. After initial separation has been made, allow transmission oil to drain at final drive junction.

32. Remove two bolts on right side securing rear engine mount bracket to transmission.

33. Through access hole in bottom of transmission support bar, remove two bolts, one each side, securing rear mounts to transmission support bar, and position mounts and bracket rearward to underbody.

34. While a helper pries and holds engine forward, move transmission rearward to disengage transmission case from dowels on engine adapter and to disengage final drive from studs on transmission case. Top of transmission should be tilted slightly rearward.

35. Slowly lower transmission, making certain top of transmission case clears flex plate ring gear and splined input shaft of final drive, until converter is approximately half-way exposed from flex plate.

36. Install a suitable clamp to transmission case at location N to avoid possibility of converter becoming disengaged when transmission is removed.

37. Lower transmission from car.

CAUTION: Rear engine mount bracket will follow transmission from car; to avoid damage or injury, remove bracket as soon as there is sufficient clearance.

38. Remove and discard final drive gasket and clean mounting surface of final drive.

Installation

1. Position transmission, on jack, under car.

2. Install new gasket on final drive, after first soaking gasket with transmission fluid.

3. Position rear engine mount bracket on top of transmission support bar against underbody.

4. Raise transmission in place until converter is approximately half-way covered by flex plate, then remove converter holding clamp.

5. While a helper assists in holding engine forward with pry bar, continue raising transmission, making certain top of transmission case clears splined input shaft of final drive, and position to engine.

6. Position transmission to engine and final drive by aligning following points in the order listed, while a helper assists:
   a. Studs on transmission case to

mounting holes in final drive.
   b. Guide holes in transmission case to dowels on adapter.
   c. Internal flange on final drive to transmission.

NOTE: As engagement of splined final drive input shaft to transmission is hidden, extreme care must be taken to avoid damaging transmission and final drive.

To facilitate engagement of final drive splines, rotate one front wheel while a helper holds the other. When alignment is complete and proper, gap between final drive case and transmission should not exceed $\frac{1}{4}$".

7. Loosely install bolts ($\frac{3}{8}$ x 1$\frac{1}{4}$) at locations D and F attaching transmission to final drive and bolt ($\frac{3}{8}$ x 2$\frac{1}{2}$) at location N attaching transmission to engine adapter, alternately tightening bolts to avoid cocking transmission. *Do not torque bolts at this time.*

8. Working in engine compartment, loosely install bolt ($\frac{3}{8}$ x 1$\frac{3}{8}$) at location J attaching transmission to adapter. *Do not torque bolt at this time.*

9. Install bolt ($\frac{3}{8}$ x 1$\frac{3}{8}$) at location M attaching transmission to adapter plate. *Do not torque bolt at this time.*

10. Position rear engine mount bracket to transmission and loosely install bolts at locations K and L.

11. Position rear engine mounts and bracket to transmission support bar and loosely install bolts through access holes in bottom of bar, attaching mounts to bar.

12. Reposition engine if necessary and install left bolt securing front engine mount to front cross bar. Tighten both front mount bolts to 30-ft-lbs.

13. Remove transmission jack.

14. Torque rear engine mounts to transmission support bar bolts to 55 ft-lbs. Torque rear engine mount to bracket bolts to 25 ft. lbs. Torque transmission to adapter to engine bolts (located N) to 30 ft-lbs. Torque transmission to adapter bolts (location M) to 30 ft-lbs.

NOTE: The procedure for securing the converter to the flex plate outlined in steps 15 through 17 must be strictly followed, otherwise damage to the flex plate and transmission will result from improper installation.

15. Rotate converter until two of the three weld nuts on converter line up with two of the three bolt holes in flex plate. Position converter so that weld nuts are flush with flex plate, making certain converter is not cocked and that pilot in center of converter is properly seated in crankshaft.

16. Loosely install two flex plate to converter bolts through accessible holes in flex plate.

17. Rotate flex plate and converter by rotating bolt previously installed in forward end of crankshaft until third bolt hole is accessible. Install the third flex plate to converter bolt and torque all three bolts to 30 foot pounds. Remove bolt from crankshaft and install cork plug.

18. Install hose on vacuum modulator.

19. Install electrical connector to transmission connector.

20. Position converter cover plate to transmission case and install two lower and one upper right bolts securing cover plate to transmission, tightening to 5 ft-lbs.

21. Position starter to transmission case and install bolt at location P.

22. Position ground strap to transmission and install bolt securing ground strap and starter to transmission at location O. Tighten bolts at locations O and P to 25 ft-lbs.

23. Install leads on starter motor.

24. Install bolts at locations C and E and nut at location G, securing transmission to final drive.

25. Torque bolts at locations C through F to 35 foot pounds.

26. On all models, connect relay rod to manual yoke with a cotter pin.

27. Check operation of manual linkage and adjust.

28. Lower vehicle.

29. Install bolts at locations A and B and the nut at location H. Torque bolts to 35 foot pounds.

30. Install upper left bolt securing converter cover plate to transmission in the manner described for removing it in Step 13.

31. Install bolt at location I and torque bolts at locations I, J, K, and L to 25 foot pounds.

32. Torque oil cooler pipe connectors at transmission case to 20 foot pounds. Clean cooler pipe ends with a suitable solvent, connect pipes to transmission and torque pipe fittings to 20 foot pounds.

33. On all models, connect speedometer to governor and detent solenoid connector to transmission case.

34. Install new O-ring seal on transmission oil filler tube through hole in final drive case. Fasten filler tube bracket to exhaust manifold.

35. Install body ground strap to firewall.

36. Connect battery cable, fill transmission with fluid and install hood if previously removed.

CHRYSLER TORQUEFLITE &
AMERICAN MOTORS TORQUE-COMMAND

IDENTIFICATION

Transmission identification markings shown in the following application chart are cast in raised letters and numerals on the lower left side of the bell housing. NOTE: There are sufficient variations within each of the main categories listed below to make it necessary to service them by serial number—a stamped 7-digit number appearing on the oil pan side rail.

CHRYSLER CORPORATION

1977-78 6-225	A-904
6-225 Police & Taxi	A-904-HD
V8-318 Aspen, Volare, Diplomat & LeBaron	A-904-LA
V8-318 Exc. Aspen & Volare	A-727
V8-360 Aspen & Volare	A-904-LA
V8-360 Exc. Aspen & Volare	A-727
V8-360 H.P.	A-727
V8-400, 440	A-727
1974-76 6-198, 225 engine	A-904
6-225 engine, police & taxi	A-727

CHRYSLER CORP.—(Continued)

V8-318 engine	A-904-LA
V8-318 engine, police & taxi	A-727
V8-360, 400, 440 engines	A-727

AMERICAN MOTORS

1974-78 6-232, 258 engines	904
6-258, V8-304, 360, 401 Heavy Duty	727
V8-304 engine	998
V8-360, 401 engines	727
1977-78 4-121	904

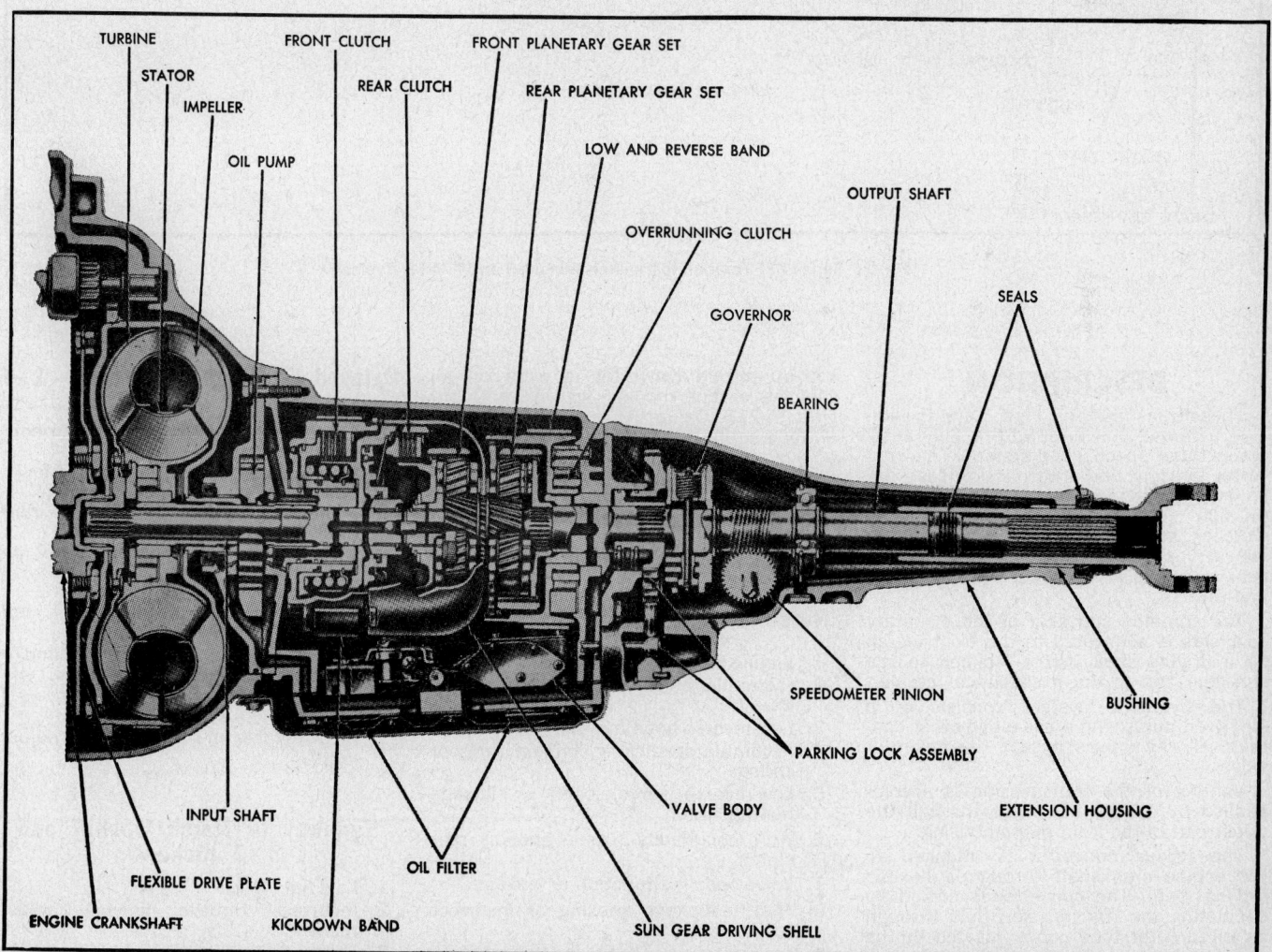

Fig. 1   Series 904 Torqueflite transmission used on 1974-78 (typical). 998 model is similar

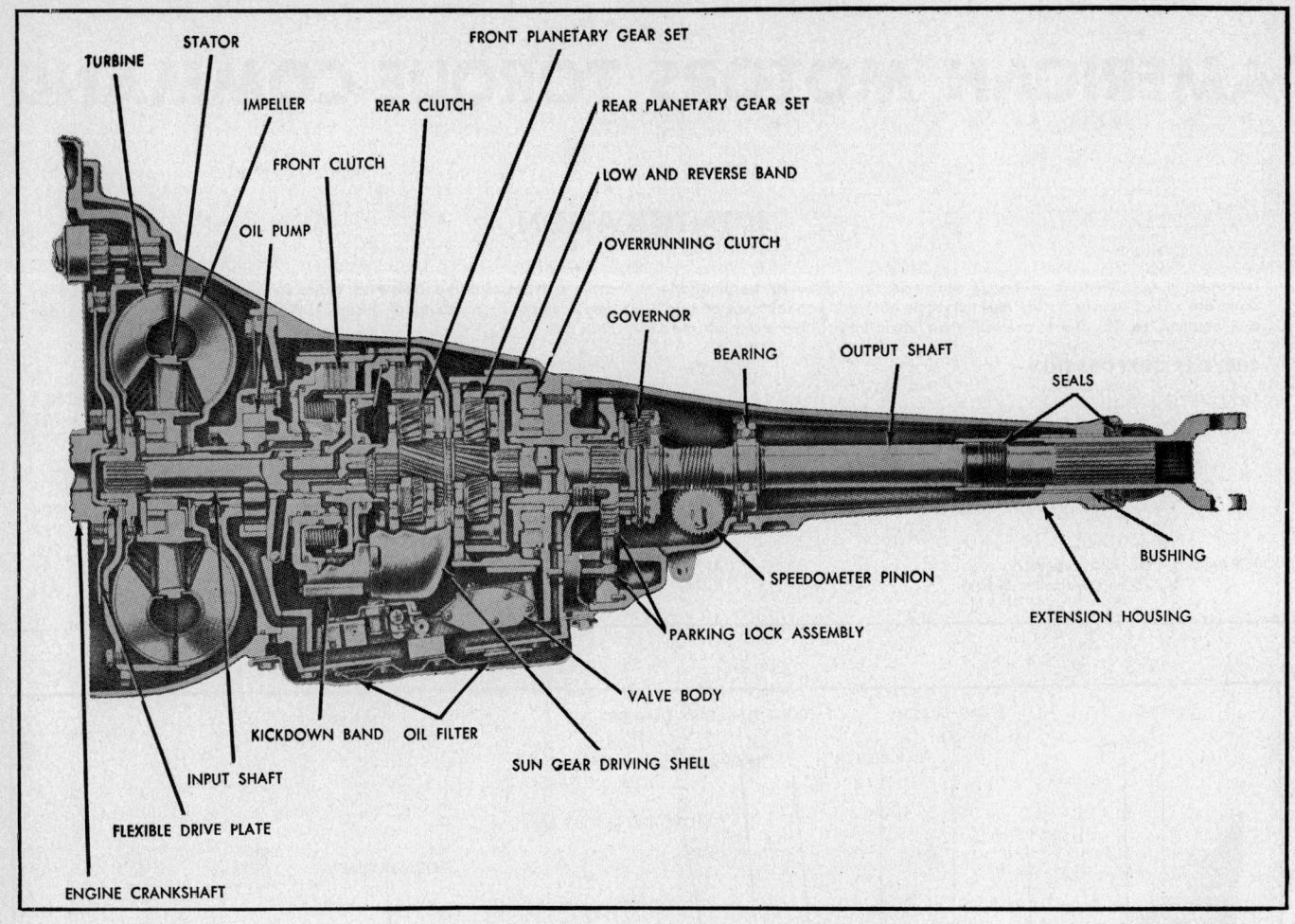

Fig. 2 Series 727 Torqueflite transmission used on 1974-78 (typical).

DESCRIPTION

These transmissions, Figs. 1 and 2, combine a torque converter with a fully automatic three speed gear system. The converter housing and transmission case are an integral aluminum casting. The transmission consists of two multiple disc clutches, an overrunning (one-way) clutch, two servos and bands and two planetary gear sets to provide three forward speeds and reverse.

The common sun gear of the planetary gear sets is connected to the front clutch by a driving shell that is splined to the sun gear and to the front clutch retainer.

The hydraulic system consists of a single oil pump and a valve body that contains all the valves except the governor valve.

Venting of the transmission is accomplished by a drilled passage through the upper part of the front pump housing.

The torque converter is attached to the engine crankshaft through a flexible driving plate. The converter is cooled by circulating the transmission fluid through an oil-to-water type cooler located in the radiator lower tank. The converter is a sealed assembly that cannot be disassembled. On 1978 Chrysler Corp models, the lock-up torque converter is used on all vehicles except models with V8-440 engine, 6-225 California engines, all high altitude and heavy duty applications.

TROUBLE SHOOTING GUIDE

Harsh Engagement In D - 1 - 2 - R

1. Engine idle speed too high.
2. Hydraulic pressures too high or too low.
3. Low-reverse band out of adjustment.
4. Accumulator sticking, broken rings or spring.
5. Low-reverse servo, band or linkage malfunction.
6. Worn or faulty front and/or rear clutch.
7. Valve body malfunction or leakage.
8. Throttle linkage sticking or incorrect adjustment.
9. Accumulator broken seal rings, scratched bore, broken or collapsed spring, cracked piston.

Delayed Engagement In D - 1 - 2 - R

1. Low fluid level.
2. Incorrect manual linkage adjustment.
3. Oil filter clogged.
4. Hydraulic pressures too high or low.
5. Valve body malfunction or leakage.
6. Accumulator sticking, broken rings or spring.
7. Clutches or servos sticking or not operating.
8. Faulty front oil pump.
9. Worn or faulty front and/or rear clutch.
10. Worn or broken input shaft and/or reaction shaft support seal rings.
11. Aerated fluid.
12. Incorrect idle adjustment.
13. Incorrect low and reverse band adjustment.

Runaway or Harsh Upshift and 3 - 2 Kickdown

1. Low fluid level.
2. Incorrect throttle linkage adjustment.
3. Hydraulic pressures too high or low.
4. Kickdown band out of adjustment.
5. Valve body malfunction or leakage.

6. Governor malfunction.
7. Accumulator sticking, broken rings or spring.
8. Clutches or servos sticking or not operating.
9. Kickdown servo, band or linkage malfunction.
10. Worn or faulty front clutch.
11. Worn or broken input shaft and/or reaction shaft support seal rings.
12. Aerated oil.
13. Clogged oil filter.

No Upshift

1. Low fluid level.
2. Incorrect throttle linkage adjustment.
3. Kickdown band out of adjustment.
4. Hydraulic pressures too high or low.
5. Governor sticking.
6. Valve body malfunction or leakage.
7. Accumulator sticking, broken rings or spring.
8. Clutches or servos sticking or not operating.
9. Faulty oil pump.
10. Kickdown servo, band or linkage malfunction.
11. Worn or faulty front clutch.
12. Worn or broken input shaft and/or reaction shaft support seal rings.
13. Incorrect gearshift linkage adjustment.
14. Governor support seal rings broken or worn.

Delayed Upshift

1. Incorrect throttle linkage adjustment.
2. Kickdown band out of adjustment.
3. Governor support seal rings broken or worn.
4. Worn or broken reaction shaft support seal rings.
5. Governor malfunction.
6. Kickdown servo band or linkage malfunction.
7. Worn or faulty front clutch.

No Kickdown or Normal Downshift

1. Incorrect throttle linkage adjustment.
2. Incorrect gearshift linkage adjustment.
3. Kickdown band out of adjustment.
4. Hydraulic pressure too high or low.
5. Governor sticking.
6. Valve body malfunction or leakage.
7. Accumulator sticking, broken rings or spring.
8. Clutches or servos sticking or not operating.
9. Kickdown servo, band or linkage malfunction.
10. Overrunning clutch not holding.
11. Low fluid level.

Erratic Shifts

1. Low fluid level.
2. Aerated fluid.
3. Incorrect throttle linkage adjustment.
4. Incorrect gearshift control linkage adjustment.
5. Hydraulic pressures too high or low.
6. Governor sticking.

7. Oil filter clogged.
8. Valve body malfunction or leakage.
9. Clutches or servos sticking or not operating.
10. Faulty oil pump.
11. Worn or broken input shaft and/or reaction shaft support rings.
12. Governor support seal rings broken or worn.
13. Kickdown servo band or linkage malfunction.
14. Worn or faulty front clutch.

Slips In Forward Drive Positions

1. Low oil level.
2. Aerated fluid.
3. Incorrect throttle linkage adjustment.
4. Incorrect gearshift control linkage adjustment.
5. Hydraulic pressures too low.
6. Valve body malfunction or leakage.
7. Accumulator sticking, broken rings or springs.
8. Clutches or servos sticking or not operating.
9. Worn or faulty front and/or rear clutch.
10. Overrunning clutch not holding.
11. Worn or broken input shaft and/or reaction shaft support seal rings.
12. Clogged oil filter.
13. Faulty oil pump.
14. Overrunning clutch worn, broken or seized.
15. Incorrect kickdown band adjustment.

Slips In Reverse Only

1. Low fluid level.
2. Aerated fluid.
3. Incorrect gearshift control linkage adjustment.
4. Hydraulic pressures too high or low.
5. Low-reverse band out of adjustment.
6. Valve body malfunction or leakage.
7. Front clutch or rear servo sticking or not operating.
8. Low-reverse servo, band or linkage malfunction.
9. Faulty oil pump.
10. Worn or broken reaction shaft support seal rings.
11. Worn or faulty front clutch.

Slips In All Positions

1. Low fluid level.
2. Hydraulic pressures too low.
3. Valve body malfunction or leakage.
4. Faulty oil pump.
5. Clutches or servos sticking or not operating.
6. Worn or broken input shaft and/or reaction shaft support seal rings.
7. Oil filter clogged.
8. Aerated oil.

No Drive In Any Position

1. Low fluid level.
2. Hydraulic pressures too low.
3. Oil filter clogged.
4. Valve body malfunction or leakage.
5. Faulty oil pump.
6. Clutches or servos sticking or not operating.
7. Planetary gear sets broken or seized.

8. Torque converter failure.
9. Incorrect gearshift linkage adjustment.

No Drive In Forward Drive Positions

1. Hydraulic pressures too low.
2. Valve body malfunction or leakage.
3. Accumulator sticking, broken rings or spring.
4. Clutches or servos, sticking or not operating.
5. Worn or faulty rear clutch.
6. Overrunning clutch not holding.
7. Worn or broken input shaft and/or reaction shaft support seal rings.
8. Low fluid level.
9. Planetary gear sets broken or seized.
10. Overrunning clutch worn, broken or seized.
11. Incorrect gearshift linkage adjustment.

No Drive In Reverse

1. Incorrect gearshift control linkage adjustment.
2. Hydraulic pressures too low.
3. Low-reverse band out of adjustment.
4. Valve body malfunction or leakage.
5. Front clutch or rear servo sticking or not operating.
6. Low-reverse servo, band or linkage malfunction.
7. Worn or faulty front and/or rear clutch.
8. Worn or broken reaction shaft support seal rings.
9. Planetary gear sets broken or seized.

Drives In Neutral

1. Incorrect gearshift control linkage adjustment.
2. Valve body malfunction or leakage.
3. Rear clutch worn, faulty, dragging or inoperative.
4. Insufficient clutch plate clearance.

Drags or Locks

1. Kickdown band out of adjustment.
2. Low-reverse band out of adjustment.
3. Kickdown and/or low-reverse servo, band or linkage malfunction.
4. Front and/or rear clutch faulty.
5. Planetary gear sets broken or seized.
6. Overrunning clutch worn, broken or seized.
7. Hydraulic pressure to low.
8. Valve body: nicks, scratches and burrs on valve and plugs. Rounded edges on valve lands. Scratches on bores, collapsed springs. Nicked or warped mating surfaces.
9. Accumulator, broken seal rings, scratched bore, broken or collapsed spring, cracked piston.

Grating, Scraping or Growling Noise

1. Kickdown band out of adjustment.
2. Low-reverse band out of adjustment.
3. Output shaft bearing and/or bushing damaged.
4. Governor support binding or broken seal rings.

5. Oil pump scored or binding.
6. Front and/or rear clutch faulty.
7. Planetary gear sets broken or seized.
8. Overrunning clutch worn, broken or seized.
9. Low fluid level.
10. Clogged oil filter.

Buzzing Noise

1. Low fluid level.
2. Pump sucking air.
3. Valve body malfunction.
4. Overrunning clutch inner race damaged.
5. Aerated oil.
6. Governor valve: burrs, nicks, scores or binding on weights, shaft and valve.
7. Collapsed or distorted springs or distorted snap ring. Cracked or warped body. Dirty filter.

Hard to Fill, Oil Flows Out Filler Tube

1. High fluid level.
2. Breather clogged.
3. Oil filter clogged.
4. Aerated fluid.
5. Clogged lines to cooler.

Transmission Overheats

1. Low fluid level.
2. Kickdown band adjustment too tight.
3. Low-reverse band adjustment too tight.
4. Faulty cooling system.
5. Cracked or restricted oil cooler line or fitting.
6. Faulty oil pump.
7. Insufficient clutch plate clearance in front and/or rear clutches.
8. Engine idle too low.
9. Hydraulic pressures too low.
10. Incorrect gearshift linkage adjustment.
11. Kickdown band adjustment too tight.
12. Clogged oil filter.
13. Valve body: Nicks, scratches and burrs on valve and plugs. Rounded edges on valve lands. Scratches on bores, collapsed springs. Nicked or warped mating surfaces.

Starter Will Not Energize in Neutral or Park

1. Incorrect gearshift control linkage adjustment.
2. Faulty or incorrectly adjusted neutral starting switch.
3. Broken lead to neutral switch.

Sluggish Acceleration, Excessive Throttle Needed To Maintain Speed

1. Low fluid level.
2. Sticking or incorrect throttle linkage adjustment.
3. Faulty torque converter or clutches.
4. Incorrect hydraulic pressures.

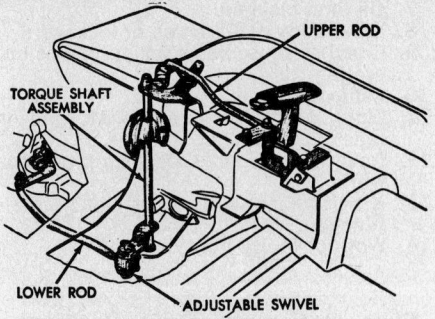

Fig. 3 Console gearshift linkage. 1974 Barracuda, Challenger & Satellite, 1974-76 Coronet, 1974-78 Charger, 1975-78 Aspen, Cordoba, Fury & Volare, 1977-78 Diplomat, LeBaron & Monaco & 1978 Magnum

MAINTENANCE

Adding Oil

To check the oil level, apply the parking brake and operate the engine at idle speed with the transmission in Neutral position. Add oil as necessary.

Changing Oil

Fluid and filter changes or band adjustments are not required for average passenger car use. Severe usage such as police, taxi, trailer towing or prolonged operation in city traffic, requires that fluid and filter be changed and bands adjusted every 24,000 miles.
Whenever the factory fill fluid is changed, only fluids of the type labeled DEXRON should be used.
1. Remove drain plug (if equipped) from transmission oil pan and allow oil to drain.

NOTE: *If the oil pan does not have a drain plug, loosen pan bolts and tap pan with a soft mallet to break it loose, permitting fluid to drain.*

2. Remove flywheel access plate, remove torque converter drain plug and allow to drain. Replace drain plug.
3. Remove transmission oil pan, replace filter or clean intake screen and pan, adjust bands and reinstall.
4. Install 6 quarts of approved automatic transmission fluid through filler tube.
5. Start engine.
6. Allow engine to idle for about two minutes. Then with parking brake applied, place transmission in neutral.
7. Add oil as necessary to bring to proper level.

BANDS, ADJUST
Kickdown Band

The kickdown band adjusting screw is located on the left side of the transmission case near the throttle lever shaft.

1. Loosen lock nut and back off approximately five turns. Check adjusting screw for free turning in transmission case.
2. Using an inch-pound torque wrench, tighten the band adjusting screw to a reading of 72 inch lbs.
3. Back off adjusting screw the number of turns indicated:

Chrysler Corp.
1974-78
A-904 & A-904LA model trans. .2 turns
A-727 model trans.
  Except V8-440 dual exhaust. 2½ turns
  V8-440 dual exhaust........2 turns

American Motors
1974-77
  904 model trans. ....2 turns
  998 & 727 model trans. .....2½ turns
1978
  904 & 998 model trans. ......2 turns
  727 model trans. ....2½ turns
Hold adjusting screw in this position and tighten locknut.

Low and Reverse Band

1. Raise vehicle, drain transmission and remove oil pan.
2. Inspect fluid for friction material or metal particles which indicate damaged or worn parts.
3. Loosen adjusting screw lock nut and back off nut approximately five turns. Check adjusting screw for free turning in lever.
4. Using an inch pound torque wrench, tighten band adjusting screw to 72 in. lbs. on all except 904 and 1978 998 series transmissions. On 904 and 1978 998 series transmissions, tighten adjusting screw to 41 in. lbs.
5. Back off adjusting screw the number of turns indicated:

American Motors
904 Series ....7 turns
998 Series ....4 turns
727 Series ....2 turns

Chrysler Corp.
A-904 ....7 turns
A-904-LA ....4 turns
A-727 ....2 turns

6. Hold adjusting screw and tighten to 35 ft. lbs., then install oil pan and refill transmission.

GEARSHIFT CONTROL LINKAGE, ADJUST
1974-78 Chrysler Corp.

1. Referring to Figs. 3 to 6, place selector lever in Park and loosen control rod swivel clamp screw a few turns.

2. Move transmission control lever all the way to rear (in Park detent).
3. With both levers still in Park position, tighten swivel clamp screw securely.

1974-78 American Motors

Place the selector lever in the Park position and place the transmission shift lever in the Park detent. Adjust the shift rod to obtain a "free pin" fit. Check steering column lock for ease of operation. Move selector lever to Neutral position and check safety switch operation.

THROTTLE LINKAGE, ADJUST

1974-78 American Motors

1. Disconnect throttle control spring, then use spring to hold transmission throttle control lever forward against stop, Fig. 7.
2. Block choke open and set throttle off fast idle.

   NOTE: On carburetors equipped with a throttle solenoid, energize solenoid and open throttle half way to allow solenoid to lock and return carburetor to idle.

3. Loosen retaining bolt on throttle control adjusting link. On 6 cylinder engines, do not remove spring clip and nylon washer. On V8 engines, remove spring clip and nylon washer from link.
4. On 6 cylinder engines, pull on end of link to eliminate lash and tighten retaining bolt, Fig. 8. On V8 engines, push on end of link to eliminate lash and tighten link retaining bolt, Fig. 9, then install nylon washer and spring clip.
5. Reconnect throttle control rod spring.

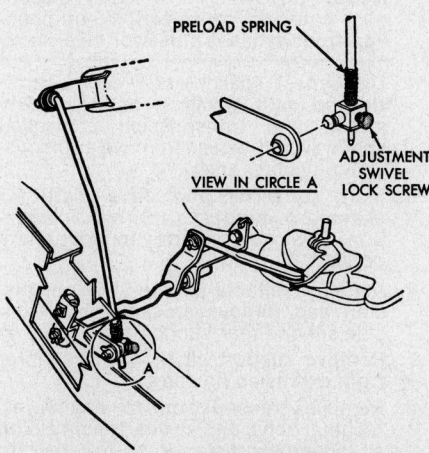

**Fig. 5   Column gearshift linkage.
1974-78 Exc. Aspen, Dart, Valiant, Volare, 1977-78 Diplomat & LeBaron**

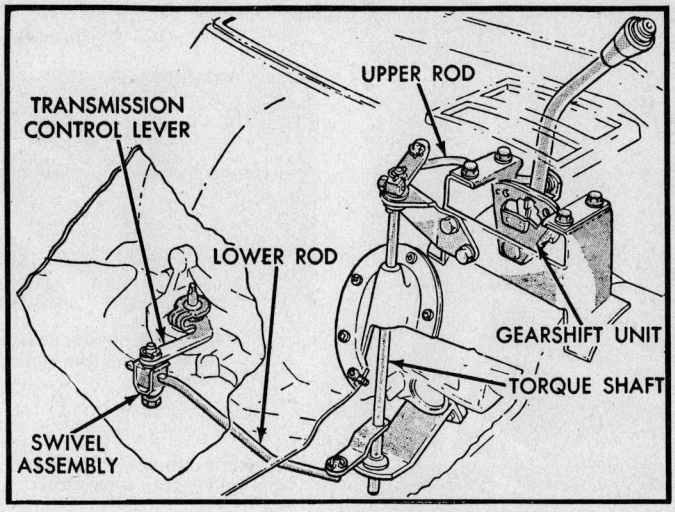

Fig. 4   Console gearshift linkage. 1974-76 Dart & Valiant

1974-78 Chrysler Corp.

NOTE: Before proceeding with the adjustment, disconnect the choke rod at the carburetor or block the choke valve wide open. Open the throttle slightly to release the fast idle cam, then return carburetor to the hot idle position.

Hold or fasten the transmission lever firmly forward against the stop while performing the adjustment to insure a proper adjustment.

1. Support vehicle on hoist and loosen swivel lock screw, Fig. 10.

   NOTE: To insure correct adjustment, swivel must be free to slide along flat end of throttle rod so that preload spring action is not restricted. If necessary, disassemble and clean or repair parts to assure free action.

2. Hold transmission lever firmly forward against its internal stop and tighten swivel lock screw to 125 inch lbs.

   NOTE: Adjustment is now finished. Linkage backlash was automatically removed by the preload spring.

3. Lower vehicle and test linkage operation by moving throttle rod rearward and slowly releasing it making certain that it returns fully.

EXTENSION HOUSING & PARKING LOCK CONTROL ROD

NOTE: Charger, Coronet, Imperial, Satellite and 1975-78 Cordoba, Fury, Magnum and Monaco models, require unloading of both torsion bars, and dropping one side of torsion bar crossmember to provide clearance for extension housing removal.

1. Mark parts for reassembly and remove propeller shaft.

2. Remove speedometer pinion and adapter assembly, then drain about two quarts of fluid from transmission.
3. Remove extension housing to crossmember bolts, then raise transmission with jack and remove crossmember.
4. Remove extension housing to transmission bolts. On console shift models, remove torque shaft lower bracket to extension housing bolts.

NOTE: In the following step, the gearshift must be in "low" therefore positioning the parking lock control rod rearward so it can be disengaged or engaged with the parking lock sprag.

5. Remove two screws, plate and gasket from bottom of extension housing mounting pad, then spread snap ring from output shaft bearing, Fig. 11, and carefully tap extension housing off output shaft bearing.
6. Slide extension housing off shaft to remove parking sprag and spring, then remove snap ring and slide reaction plug and pin assembly out of housing, Fig. 12.
7. To replace parking lock control rod, refer to "Valve Body".

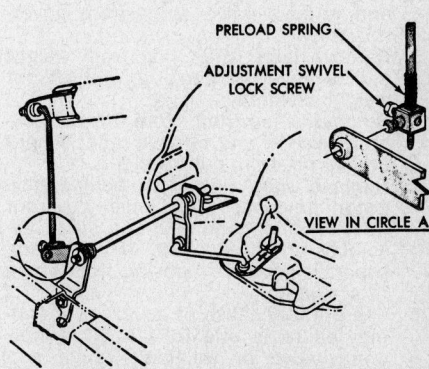

**Fig. 6   Column gearshift linkage.
1974-76 Dart & Valiant, 1975-78 Aspen & Volare, 1977-78 Diplomat & LeBaron**

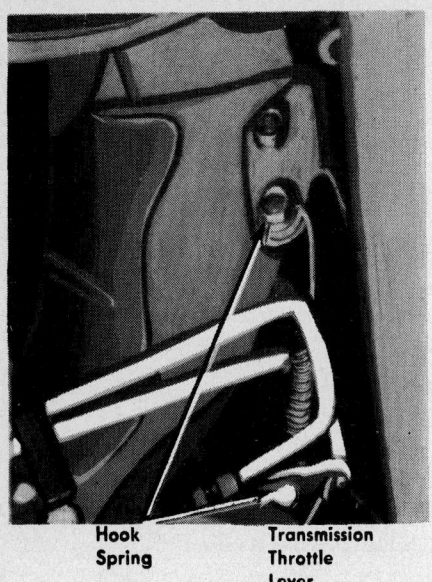

Hook Transmission
Spring Throttle
     Lever

**Fig. 7 Install spring on lever.
1974-78 American Motors**

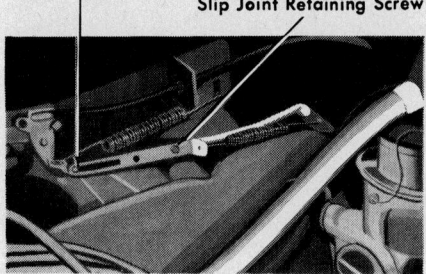

Shorten Rod to "O" Clearance
Slip Joint Retaining Screw

**Fig. 8 V8 throttle linkage.
1974-78 American Motors**

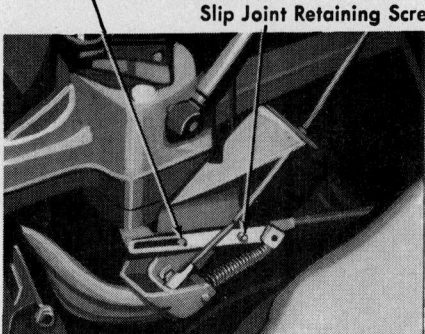

Lengthen Rod to "O" Clearance
Slip Joint Retaining Screw

**Fig. 9 Six cylinder throttle linkage.
1974-78 American Motors (Typical)**

OUTPUT SHAFT OIL SEAL

1. Mark propeller shaft to aid in reassembly and remove propeller shaft being careful not to scratch or nick surface on sliding spline yoke.
2. Using a screwdriver and hammer, drive between extension housing and seal and remove seal.
3. Position new seal and drive it into extension housing using tool C-3995 or C-3972.
4. Carefully install yoke into housing, then align marks made at removal and install propeller shaft.

GOVERNOR

1. Remove extension housing, then remove output shaft bearing rear snap ring and remove bearing. On 727 Series, remove remaining snap ring from shaft.
2. Remove snap ring, Fig. 13, from weight end of governor valve shaft and remove valve shaft from governor body.
3. Remove large snap ring from weight end of governor housing, and lift out weight assembly.
4. Remove snap ring from inside governor weight and remove inner weight and spring from outer weight.
5. Remove snap ring from behind governor housing, then slide governor housing and parking brake sprag assembly off input shaft. If necessary, separate governor housing from sprag (4 screws).
6. The primary cause of governor operating failure is due to a sticking governor valve or weights. Rough surfaces may be removed with crocus cloth. Thoroughly clean all parts and check for free movement before assembly.

7. Reverse above operations to assemble and install governor.

VALVE BODY

1. Drain transmission and remove oil pan.
2. Loosen clamp bolts and remove throttle and gear selector levers from manual lever, Fig. 14.
3. Remove neutral safety switch and oil filter.
4. Place a drain pan under transmission and remove the ten valve body to transmission bolts. Hold valve body in place while removing bolts.
5. Carefully lower valve body while pulling it forward to disengage parking control rod.

NOTE: It may be necessary to rotate output shaft to permit parking control

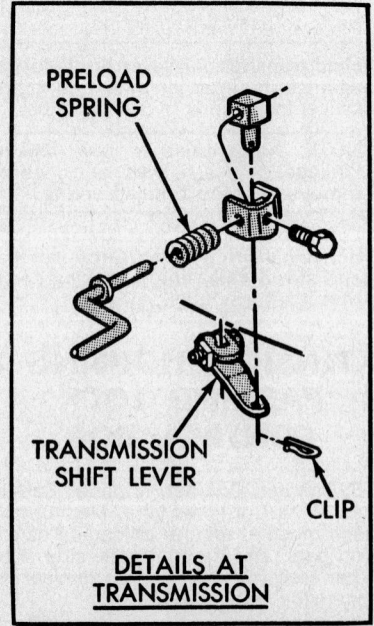

PRELOAD
SPRING

TRANSMISSION
SHIFT LEVER

CLIP

**DETAILS AT
TRANSMISSION**

**Fig. 10 Throttle linkage adjustment.
All 1974-78 Chrysler Corp. models**

rod to clear sprag.

6. Remove accumulator piston and spring from transmission case. Inspect piston for nicks, scores and wear. Inspect spring for distortion. Inspect rings for freedom in piston grooves and wear or breakage. Replace parts as necessary.

TRANSMISSION, REPLACE

American Motors
1974-78

CAUTION: The hood must be open to prevent damage to hood and air cleaner when removing rear crossmember.

1. Remove cover from front of bell housing, then turn converter until drain plug is at "6 o'clock" position.
2. Drain converter and transmission. Remove filler tube and starter.
3. Mark rear universal joint and yoke for alignment purposes during installation. Then remove propeller shaft.

NOTE: On 1975-78 models, disconnect catalytic converter, if equipped, and front exhaust pipes for clearance.

4. Disconnect speedometer cable, throttle and shift linkages, neutral safety switch and transmission controlled spark switch wires. Remove transmission oil cooler lines.
5. Mark converter and drive plate for alignment purposes during installation. Remove converter to drive plate bolts.
6. Install a suitable jack under transmission and remove crossmember from side sill and rear support cushion.
7. Remove support cushion and adapter from extension housing.
8. Remove transmission to engine attaching bolts and move transmission an adequate distance to the rear to clear crankshaft.
9. Lower transmission, maintaining pressure against converter, until transmis-

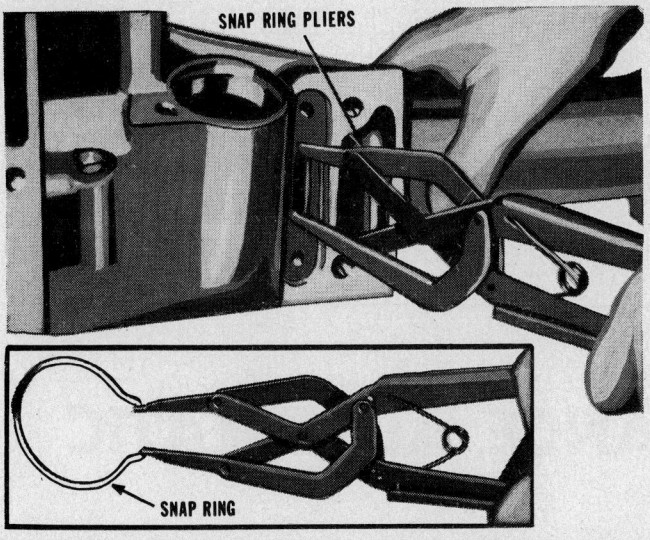

Fig. 11 Removing or installing extension housing snap ring

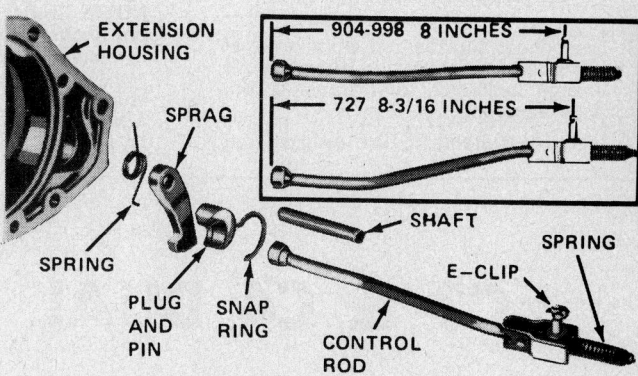

Fig. 12 Parking lock components

sion clears engine.

10. Reverse procedure to install.

Chrysler Corp.
1974-78

CAUTION: The transmission and converter must be removed as an assembly, otherwise, the converter drive plate, front pump bushing and oil seal will be damaged. The drive plate will not support the load; therefore, none of the weight of the transmission should be allowed to rest on the plate during removal.

NOTE: Some V8-400 and 440 engines were built with a forged crankshaft requiring a different torque converter and damper than the engines using the cast crankshaft.

This forged crankshaft is normally only used in the 400-4-BBL, HP engine with manual transmission.

If replacement of the crankshaft, torque converter, crankshaft damper or short engine is required, it is important that matching parts are used otherwise severe engine vibration will result, (Consult Chrysler Parts Dept.).

The cast crankshaft engine can be easily identified since it has the letter "E" stamped on the engine numbering pad following the built date.

1. Disconnect battery ground cable.

NOTE: Some models will require that the exhaust system be lowered for clearance.

2. Remove engine to transmission struts (if equipped), then disconnect transmission cooler lines and remove starter motor, cooler line bracket and converter access cover.
3. Using a socket wrench on vibration dampener bolt, rotate engine clockwise until converter drain plug is at bottom. Remove plug and drain converter, than loosen oil pan and drain transmission.
4. Mark converter and drive plate to aid in reassembly. The crankshaft flange bolt circle, inner and outer circle of holes in the drive plate, and the four tapped holes in front face of converter all have one hole offset so

these parts will be installed in the original position. This maintains balance of the engine and converter.

5. Remove converter to drive plate bolts. Rotate engine clockwise using socket wrench to gain access to all bolts.

CAUTION: Do not rotate converter or drive plate by prying with a screwdriver or similar tool as the drive plate might become distorted. Also, the starter should never be engaged if the drive plate is not attached to the converter with at least one bolt or if the transmission case-to-engine bolts have been loosened.

6. Mark drive shaft to aid in reassembly and remove drive shaft.
7. Disconnect neutral and back-up light switch and gearshift and torque shaft

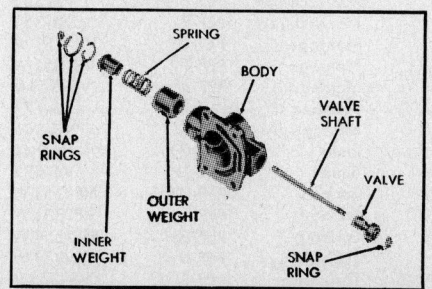

Fig. 13 Governor disassembled

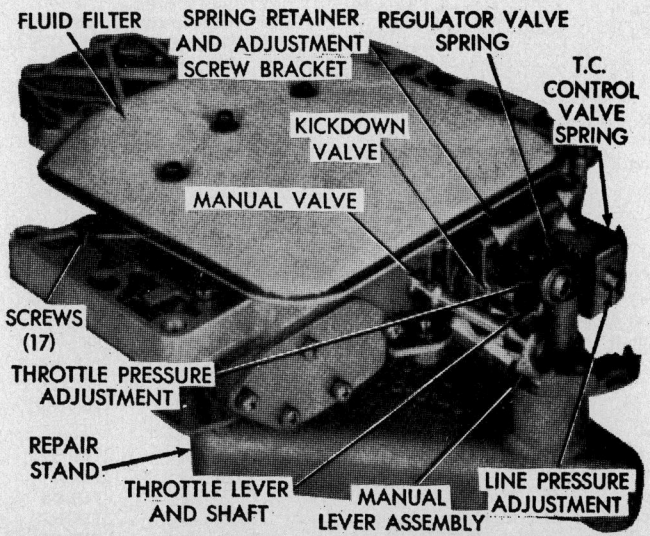

Fig. 14 Valve body external parts

assembly from transmission.

NOTE: When disassembling linkage rods from levers which use plastic grommets as retainers, the grommets should be replaced with new ones.

8. Disconnect throttle rod from lever at left side of transmission, then remove linkage bellcrank from transmission, if so equipped.
9. Install a suitable fixture or jack that will support engine, then raise transmission slightly with a jack to relieve the load on the supports, and remove the crossmember.

NOTE: Some models have a torsion bar anchor crossmember that remains in place and requires a careful downward tilt of front of transmission as it is being lowered. If these models have a vibration dampening weight bolted to rear of extension housing, it must be removed.

10. Remove transmission to engine bolts and carefully work transmission and converter assembly rearward off engine block dowels and disengage converter hub from end of crankshaft. Using a small C-clamp on edge of bell housing, hold converter in place during transmission removal.
11. Remove transmission assembly from under vehicle.
12. Reverse procedure to install.

C3 & C4 DUAL RANGE AUTOMATIC

TRANSMISSION IDENTIFICATION

Each transmission may be identified by the tag attached to the low-reverse servo cover bolt. The tag includes the model prefix and suffix, a service identification number and a build date code. The service identification number indicates changes to service details which affect interchangeability when the transmission model is not changed. For interpretation of this number the Ford Master Parts Catalog should be consulted.

YEAR	CAR MODEL	TRANS. MODEL	ENGINE MODEL
		C3 Transmission	
1974	Mustang II	74DT-BKB	4-140
	Pinto	74DT-BNA	4-140
1975	Bobcat	75DT-BB	4-140
	Bobcat	75DT-BC	4-140
	Bobcat①	75DT-EA	V6-171
	Bobcat②	75DT-FA	V6-171
	Mustang II	75DT-AA	4-140
	Mustang II	75DT-AD	4-140
	Pinto	75DT-BB	4-140
	Pinto	75DT-BC	4-140
1976	Bobcat	76DT-AA	4-140
	Bobcat	76DT-EA, FA	V6-171
	Mustang II	76DT-CA	4-140
	Pinto	76DT-AA	4-140
	Pinto	76DT-EA, FA	V6-171
1977	Bobcat	77DT-BA, CA	4-140
	Bobcat	77DT-GA	V6-171
	Mustang II	77DT-BA, CA	4-140
	Mustang II	77DT-DA, EA	4-140
	Mustang II	77DT-FA, GA	V6-171
	Pinto	77DT-BA, CA	4-140
	Pinto	77DT-FA, GA	V6-171
1978	Bobcat	78DT-ACA, ADA	4-140
	Bobcat	78DT-AGA	V6-171
	Fairmont	78DT-SA	4-140
	Fairmont	78DT-BAA, BCA	6-200
	Fairmont⑤	78DT-BJA	6-200
	Mustang II	78DT-ACA, ADA	4-140
	Mustang II	78DT-AGA	V6-171

YEAR	CAR MODEL	TRANS. MODEL	ENGINE MODEL
	Pinto	78DT-ACA, ADA	4-140
	Pinto	78DT-AGA	V6-171
	Zephyr	78DT-SA	4-140
	Zephyr	78DT-BAA, BCA	6-200
	Zephyr⑤	78DT-BJA	6-200
		C4 Transmission	
1974	Comet③	PEB-D7	6-200
	Comet④	PEB-H6	6-200
	Comet③	PEE-AK5	6-250
	Comet④	PEE-AM5	6-250
	Comet③	PEE-AH5	V8-302
	Comet④	PEE-AL5	V8-302
	Comet①③	PEE-BH	V8-302
	Comet①④	PEE-BJ	V8-302
	Cougar③	PEF-D6	V8-351
	Cougar④	PEF-E6, 7	V8-351
	Ford	PEF-A5	V8-351
	Maverick③	PEB-D7	6-200
	Maverick④	PEB-H6	6-200
	Maverick③	PEE-AK5	6-250
	Maverick④	PEE-AM5	6-250
	Maverick③	PEE-AH5	V8-302
	Maverick④	PEE-AL5	V8-302
	Maverick①③	PEE-BH	V8-302
	Maverick①④	PEE-BJ	V8-302
	Montego	PEE-V7	V8-302
	Montego	PEF-D6	V8-351
	Mustang II①	PEJ-H	4-140
	Mustang II	PEJ-E	6-171
	Mustang II①	PEJ-J	6-171
	Pinto	PEJ-B6	4-122
	Pinto①	PEJ-G	4-140
	Pinto	PEJ-C	4-140
	Torino③	PEE-V7	V8-302
	Torino④	PEE-M7, 8	V8-302
	Torino③	PEF-D6	V8-351
	Torino④	PEF-E6, 7	V8-351
1975	Bobcat	PEJ-G2	4-140
	Bobcat	PEJ-J1	V6-171
	Comet③	PEB-D8	6-200
	Comet④	PEB-H7	6-200
	Comet③	PEE-AK6	6-250
	Comet④	PEE-AM6	6-250

YEAR	CAR MODEL	TRANS. MODEL	ENGINE MODEL
	Comet③②	PEE-AH6	V8-302
	Comet③②	PEE-AH7	V8-302
	Comet③①	PEE-BH1	V8-302
	Comet④②	PEE-AL6	V8-302
	Comet④②	PEE-AL7	V8-302
	Comet④①	PEE-BJ1	V8-302
	Cougar	PEF-S	V8-351M
	Granada③	PEE-BT	6-250
	Granada④	PEE-AM6	6-250
	Granada③	PEE-CA	V8-302
	Granada④②	PEE-AL6	V8-302
	Granada④①	PEE-BJ1	V8-302
	Granada③②	PEF-Y	V8-351
	Granada③①	PEF-Q	V8-351
	Granada④②	PEF-Z	V8-351
	Granada④①	PEF-R	V8-351
	Maverick③	PEB-D8	6-200
	Maverick④	PEB-H7	6-200
	Maverick③	PEE-AK6	6-250
	Maverick④	PEE-AM6	6-250
	Maverick③②	PEE-AH6	V8-302
	Maverick③①	PEE-BH1	V8-302
	Maverick④②	PEE-AL6	V8-302
	Maverick④①	PEE-BJ1	V8-302
	Monarch④	PEE-BU	6-250
	Monarch③	PEE-BT	6-250
	Monarch④	PEE-AM6	6-250
	Monarch③	PEE-CA	V8-302
	Monarch③	PEE-CA1	V8-302
	Monarch④	PEE-AL6	V8-302
	Monarch④	PEE-AL7	V8-302
	Monarch④①	PEE-BJ1	V8-302
	Monarch③②	PEF-Y	V8-351
	Monarch③①	PEF-Q	V8-351
	Monarch④②	PEF-Z	V8-351
	Monarch④①	PEF-R	V8-351
	Montego	PEF-D7	V8-351W
	Montego	PEF-T	V8-351W
	Montego③	PEF-S	V8-351M
	Mustang II	PEJ-J1	V6-171
	Mustang II	PEE-CC	V8-302
	Pinto	PEJ-G2	4-140
	Pinto	PEJ-J1	V6-171
	Torino③	PEF-D7	V8-351W
	Torino③	PEF-T	V8-351W
	Torino④	PEF-E8	V8-351W
	Torino④	PEF-U	V8-351W
	Torino③	PEF-S	V8-351M
	Torino④	PEF-V	V8-351M
	Torino④	PEF-W	V8-351M

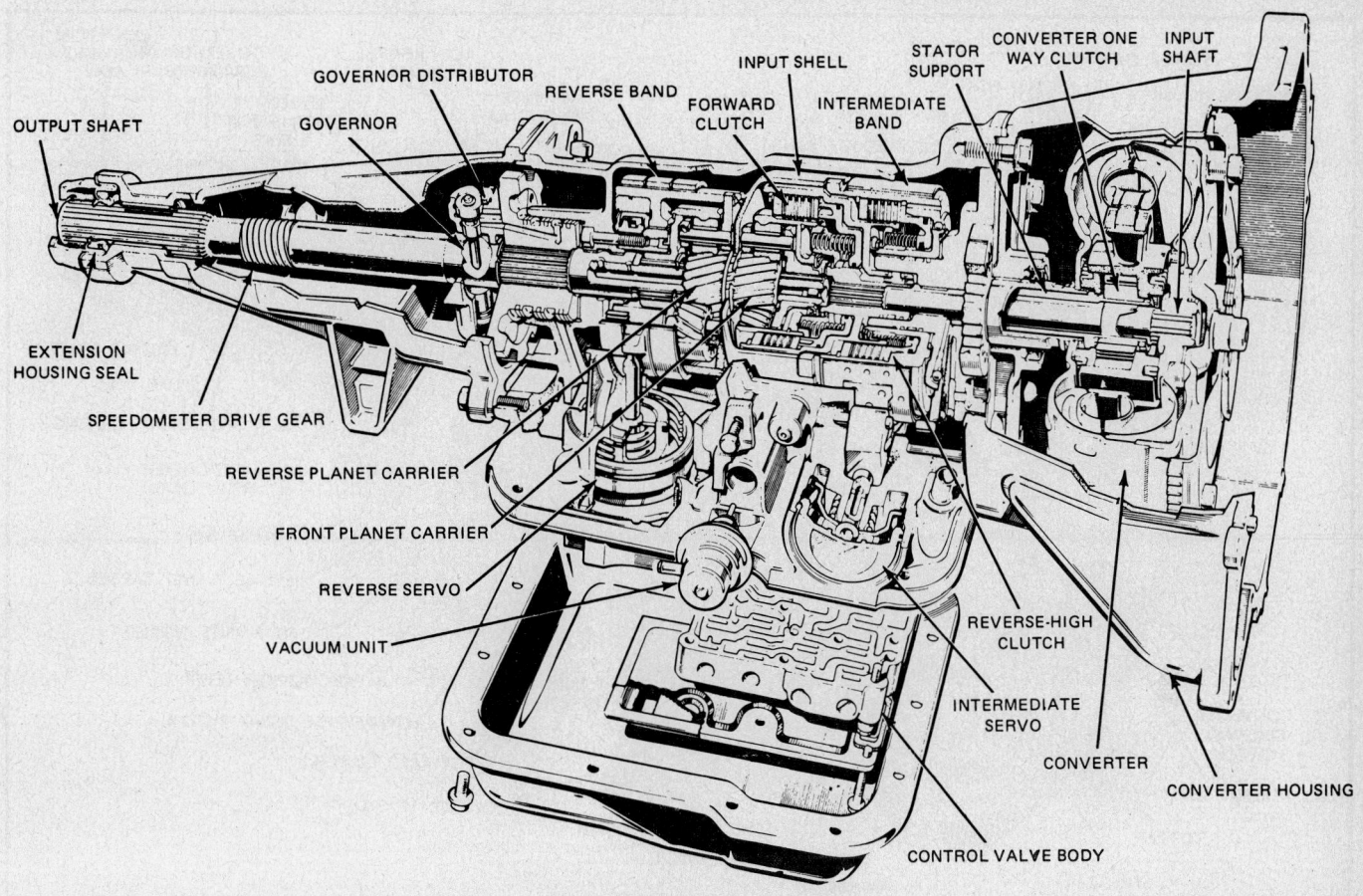

Fig. 2 C3 Dual Range Automatic

TRANSMISSION IDENTIFICATION—Continued

YEAR	CAR MODEL	TRANS. MODEL	ENGINE MODEL	YEAR	CAR MODEL	TRANS. MODEL	ENGINE MODEL	YEAR	CAR MODEL	TRANS. MODEL	ENGINE MODEL
1976	Bobcat	PEJ-G3	4-140		Maverick	PEE-AH7	V8-302	1977	Bobcat	PEJ-P	4-140
	Bobcat	PEJ-M1	V6-171		Maverick	PEE-AL7	V8-302		Bobcat	PEJ-L	6-171
	Bobcat	PEJ-N	V6-171		Maverick	PEE-CS	V8-302		Bobcat	PEJ-M2	6-171
	Comet②	PEB-N	6-200		Maverick	PEE-CT	V8-302		Comet	PEB-N1	6-200
	Comet②	PEB-P	6-200		Monarch	PEE-CH1	6-250		Comet	PEE-CJ2	6-250
	Comet	PEE-CH1	6-250		Monarch	PEE-CK1	6-250		Comet	PEE-CS1	V8-302
	Comet	PEE-CJ1	6-250		Monarch①	PEE-BV1	V8-302		Comet	PEE-CZ	V8-302
	Comet	PEE-AH7	V8-302		Monarch①	PEE-CB	V8-302		Cougar	PEE-V8	V8-302
	Comet	PEE-AL7	V8-302		Monarch②	PEE-CA2, 3	V8-302		Cougar	PEF-AA2	V8-351M
	Comet	PEE-CS	V8-302		Monarch②	PEE-CE, 1	V8-302		Cougar	PEF-AB2	V8-351M
	Comet	PEE-CT	V8-302		Monarch	PEF-AE, F	V8-351W		Cougar	PEF-K	V8-351W
	Cougar	PEF-S	V8-351M		Montego	PEF-S	V8-351M		Ford	PEA-CH	V8-302
	Cougar	PEF-V	V8-351M		Montego	PEF-AA1	V8-351M		Ford	PEF-AP1	V8-351W
	Cougar②	PEF-AA1	V8-351M		Montego①	PEF-AG	V8-351M		Granada	PEE-BU	6-250
	Cougar②	PEF-AB1	V8-351M		Montego	PEF-D8	V8-351W		Granada	PEE-CK2	6-250
	Cougar①	PEF-AG	V8-351M		Mustang II	PEJ-M1	V6-171		Granada	PEE-CD1	6-250
	Cougar	PEF-D8	V8-351W		Mustang II	PEJ-N	V6-171		Granada	PEE-CP1	6-250
	Cougar	PEF-E9	V8-351W		Mustang II	PEE-CC	V8-302		Granada	PEE-CA4	V8-302
	Granada	PEE-CH1	6-250		Pinto	PEJ-M1	V6-171		Granada	PEE-CE2	V8-302
	Granada	PEE-CK1	6-250		Pinto	PEJ-N	V6-171		Granada	PEE-CB2	V8-302
	Granada①	PEE-BV1	V8-302		Torino②	PEF-D8	V8-351W		Granada	PEE-DN	V8-302
	Granada②	PEE-CA1, 3	V8-302		Torino②	PEF-E9	V8-351W		Granada	PEE-CW	V8-302
	Granada①	PEE-CB	V8-302		Torino②	PEF-S	V8-351M		Granada	PEF-AE1	V8-351W
	Granada②	PEE-CE, 1	V8-302		Torino②	PEF-V	V8-351M		Granada	PEF-AE2	V8-351W
	Granada	PEF-AE	V8-351W		Torino②	PEF-W	V8-351M		Granada	PEF-AF1	V8-351W
	Granada	PEF-AF	V8-351W		Torino②	PEF-AA1	V8-351M		Granada	PEF-AF2	V8-351W
	Maverick②	PEB-N	6-200		Torino②	PEF-AB1	V8-351M		LTD II	PEE-M9	V8-302
	Maverick②	PEB-P	6-200		Torino②	PEF-AG	V8-351M		LTD II	PEE-V8	V8-302
	Maverick	PEE-CH1	6-250		Torino②	PEF-AH	V8-351M		LTD II	PEF-AA2, 3	V8-351M
	Maverick	PEE-CJ1	6-250								

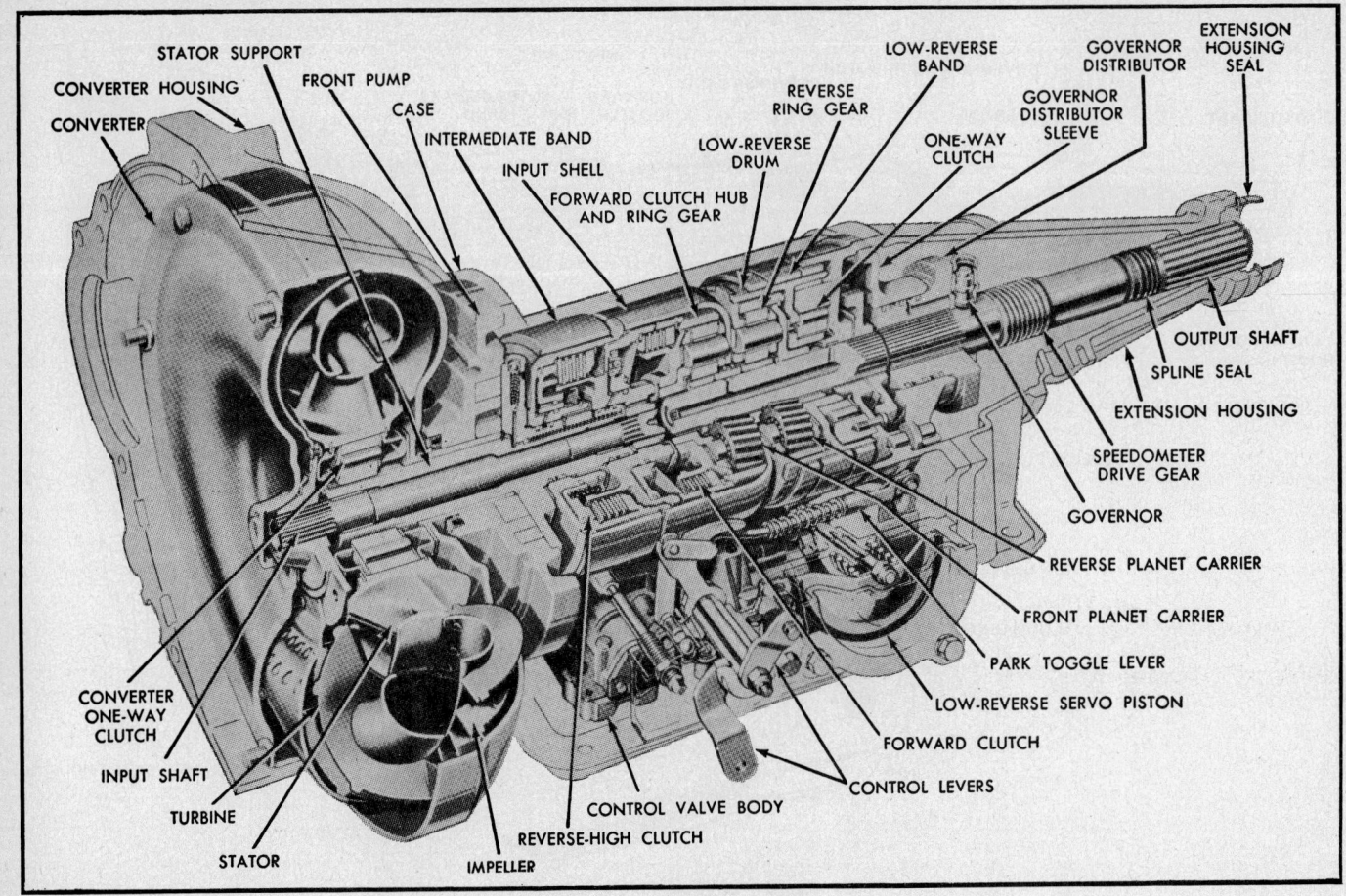

Fig. 1 C4 Dual Range Automatic

TRANSMISSION IDENTIFICATION—CONTINUED

YEAR	CAR MODEL	TRANS. MODEL	ENGINE MODEL	YEAR	CAR MODEL	TRANS. MODEL	ENGINE MODEL	YEAR	CAR MODEL	TRANS. MODEL	ENGINE MODEL
1977	LTD II	PEF-AB2, 3	V8-351M		Versailles	PEE-DH	V8-302		Monarch	PEE-CD3, CP3	6-250
	LTD II	PEF-K, 1	V8-351W		Versailles	PEE-DJ	V8-302		Monarch	PEE-CA6, CE4	V8-302
	Maverick	PEB-N1	6-250		Versailles	PEE-DV	V8-302		Monarch	PEE-CW2	V8-302
	Maverick	PEE-CJ2	6-250		Versailles	PEE-DW	V8-302		Mustang II	PEJ-P2	4-140
	Maverick	PEE-CS1	V8-302		Versailles	PEF-AM	V8-351W		Mustang II	PEJ-M4	V6-231
	Maverick	PEE-CZ	V8-302		Versailles	PEF-AN	V8-351W		Mustang II	PEE-BY2, CC3	V8-302
	Monarch	PEE-BU	6-250						Pinto	PEJ-P2	4-140
	Monarch	PEE-CD1	6-250	1978	Bobcat	PEJ-P2	4-140		Pinto	PEJ-M4	V6-231
	Monarch	PEE-CK2	6-250		Bobcat	PEJ-M4	V6-231		Thunderbird	PEE-M11, M12	V8-302
	Monarch	PEE-CPI	6-250		Cougar	PEE-M11, M12	V8-302		Thunderbird	PEE-V10, V11	V8-302
	Monarch	PEE-CA4	V8-302		Cougar	PEE-V10, V11	V8-302		Thunderbird	PEF-K3	V8-351W
	Monarch	PEE-CB2	V8-302		Cougar	PEE-DY	V8-302		Thunderbird	PEF-AA5, AB5	V8-351M
	Monarch	PEE-CE2	V8-302		Cougar	PEF-K3	V8-351W		Versailles	PEE-DH3, DJ3	V8-302
	Monarch	PEE-CW	V8-302		Cougar	PEF-AA5, AB5	V8-351M		Versailles	PEE-EF, EG	V8-302
	Monarch	PEE-DN	V8-302		Fairmont	PEB-N3, P1, R	6-200		Versailles	PEE-EH, EJ	V8-302
	Monarch	PEF-AE1	V8-351W		Fairmont⑤	PEB-S	6-200		Zephyr	PEB-N3, P1, R	6-200
	Monarch	PEF-AF1	V8-351W		Fairmont	PEE-CS3, CS4	V8-302		Zephyr⑤	PEB-S	6-200
	Mustang II	PEH-H	4-140		Fairmont	PEE-CT1, CT2	V8-302		Zephyr	PEE-CS3, CS4	V8-302
	Mustang II	PEJ-M2	6-171		Fairmont	PEE-DA, ED	V8-302		Zephyr	PEE-CT1, CT2	V8-302
	Mustang II	PEE-BY	V8-302		Ford	PEA-CH2, CL	V8-302		Zephyr	PEE-DA, ED	V8-302
	Mustang II	PEE-CC1	V8-302		Ford	PEF-AP3	V8-351W				
	Pinto	PEJ-P	4-140		Granada	PEE-CD3, CP3	6-250				
	Pinto	PEJ-L	6-171		Granada	PEE-CA6, CE4	V8-302		①—California.		
	Pinto	PEJ-M2	6-171		Granada	PEE-CW2	V8-302		②—Exc. Calif.		
	Thunderbird	PEE-M9	V8-302		LTD II	PEE-M11, M12	V8-302		③— Column shift.		
	Thunderbird	PEE-V8	V8-302		LTD II	PEE-V10, V11	V8-302		④—Floor shift.		
	Thunderbird	PEF-AA2	V8-351M		LTD II	PEE-DY	V8-302		⑤—Police & taxi.		
	Thunderbird	PEF-AB2	V8-351M		LTD II	PEF-K3	V8-351W				
	Thunderbird	PEF-K, 1	V8-351M		LTD II	PEF-AA5, AB5	V8-351M				

DESCRIPTION

The main control assembly incorporates a manually selective first and second gear range. The transmission features a drive range that provides for fully automatic upshifts and downshifts, and manually selected low and second gears.

The transmission consists essentially of a torque converter, a compound planetary gear train, two multiple disc clutches, a one-way clutch and a hydraulic control system, Figs. 1 and 2.

For all normal driving the selector lever is moved to the green dot under "Drive" on the selector quadrant on the steering column or on the floor console. As the throttle is advanced from the idle position, the transmission will upshift automatically to intermediate gear and then to high. The driver can force downshift the transmission from high to intermediate at speeds up to 65 mph. A detent on the downshift linkage warns the driver when the carburetor is wide open. Accelerator pedal depression through the detent will bring in the downshift.

With the throttle closed the transmission will downshift automatically as the car speed drops to about 10 mph. With the throttle open at any position up to the detent, the downshifts will come in automatically at speeds above 10 mph and in proportion to throttle opening. This prevents engine lugging on steep hill climbing, for example.

When the selector lever is moved to "L" with the transmission in high, the transmission will downshift to intermediate or to low depending on the road speed. At speed above 25 mph, the downshift will be from high to intermediate. At speeds below 25 mph, the downshift will be from high to low. With the selector lever in the "L" position the transmission cannot upshift.

TROUBLE SHOOTING GUIDE

Rough Initial Engagement In D1 or D2

1. Engine idle speed.
2. Vacuum diaphragm unit or tubes restricted, leaking or maladjusted.
3. Check control pressure.
4. Pressure regulator.
5. Valve body.
6. Forward clutch.

1-2 or 2-3 Shift Points Erratic

1. Check fluid level.
2. Vacuum diaphragm unit or tubes restricted, leaking or maladjusted.
3. Intermediate servo.
4. Manual linkage adjustment.
5. Governor.
6. Check control pressure.
7. Valve body.
8. Make air pressure check.

Rough 1-2 Upshifts

1. Vacuum diaphragm unit or tubes restricted, leaking or maladjusted.
2. Intermediate servo.

3. Intermediate band.
4. Check control pressure.
5. Valve body.
6. Pressure regulator.

Rough 2-3 Upshifts

1. Vacuum diaphragm unit or tubes restricted, leaking or maladjusted.
2. Intermediate servo.
3. Check control pressure.
4. Pressure regulator.
5. Intermediate band.
6. Valve body.
7. Make air pressure check.
8. Reverse-high clutch.
9. Reverse-high clutch piston air bleed valve.

Dragged Out 1-2 Shift

1. Check fluid level.
2. Vacuum diaphragm unit or tubes restricted, leaking or maladjusted.
3. Intermediate servo.
4. Check control pressure.
5. Intermediate band.
6. Valve body.
7. Pressure regulator.
8. Make air pressure check.
9. Leakage in hydraulic system.

Engine Overspeeds on 2-3 Shift

1. Manual linkage.
2. Check fluid level.
3. Vacuum diaphragm unit or tubes restricted, leaking or maladjusted.
4. Reverse servo.
5. Check control pressure.
6. Valve body.
7. Pressure regulator.
8. Intermediate band.
9. Reverse-high clutch.
10. Reverse-high clutch piston air bleed valve.

No 1-2 or 2-3 Shift

1. Manual linkage.
2. Downshift linkage, including inner lever position.
3. Vacuum diaphragm unit or tubes restricted, leaking or maladjusted.
4. Governor.
5. Check control pressure.
6. Valve body.
7. Intermediate band.
8. Intermediate servo.
9. Reverse-high clutch.
10. Reverse-high clutch piston air bleed valve.

No 3-1 Shift in D1 or 3-2 Shift in D2

1. Governor.
2. Valve body.

No Forced Downshifts

1. Downshift linkage, including inner lever position.
2. Valve body.
3. Vacuum diaphragm unit or tubes restricted, leaking or maladjusted.

Runaway Engine on Forced 3-2 Downshift

1. Check control pressure.

2. Intermediate servo.
3. Intermediate band.
4. Pressure regulator.
5. Valve body.
6. Vacuum diaphragm unit or tubes restricted, leaking or maladjusted.
7. Leakage in hydraulic system.

Rough 3-2 or 3-1 Shift at Closed Throttle

1. Engine idle speed.
2. Vacuum diaphragm unit or tubes restricted, leaking or maladjusted.
3. Intermediate servo.
4. Valve body.
5. Pressure regulator.

Shifts 1-3 in D1 and D2

1. Intermediate band.
2. Intermediate servo.
3. Vacuum diaphragm unit or tubes restricted, leaking or maladjusted.
4. Valve body.
5. Governor.
6. Make air pressure check.

No Engine Braking In 1st Gear —Manual Low

1. Manual linkage.
2. Reverse band.
3. Reverse servo.
4. Valve body.
5. Governor.
6. Make air pressure check.

Slips or Chatters in 1st Gear—D1

1. Check fluid level.
2. Vacuum diaphragm unit or tubes restricted, leaking or maladjusted.
3. Check control pressure.
4. Pressure regulator.
5. Valve body.
6. Forward clutch.
7. Leakage in hydraulic system.
8. Planetary one-way clutch.

Slips or Chatters in 2nd Gear

1. Check fluid level.
2. Vacuum diaphragm unit or tubes restricted, leaking or maladjusted.
3. Intermediate servo.
4. Intermediate band.
5. Check control pressure.
6. Pressure regulator.
7. Valve body.
8. Make air pressure check.
9. Forward clutch.
10. Leakage in hydraulic system.

Slips or Chatters in R

1. Check fluid level.
2. Vacuum diaphragm unit or tubes restricted, leaking or maladjusted.
3. Reverse band.
4. Check control pressure.
5. Reverse servo.
6. Pressure regulator.
7. Valve body.
8. Make air pressure check.
9. Reverse-high clutch.
10. Leakage in hydraulic system.
11. Reverse-high piston air bleed valve.

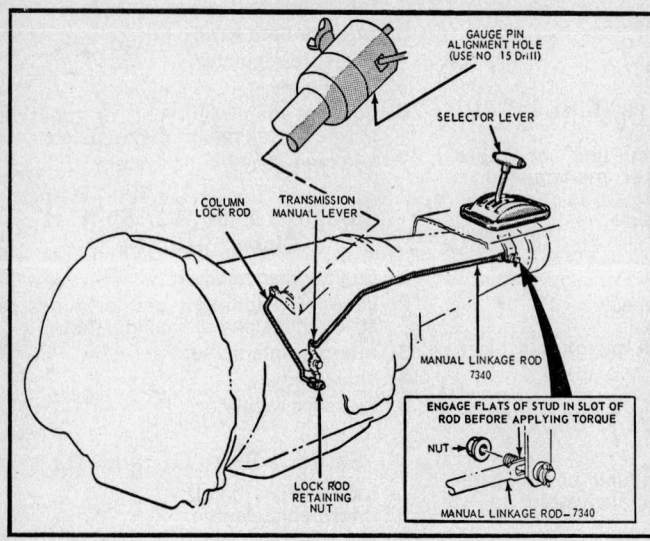

Fig. 3 Manual linkage, floorshift. Typical. Column lock rod is used on some models

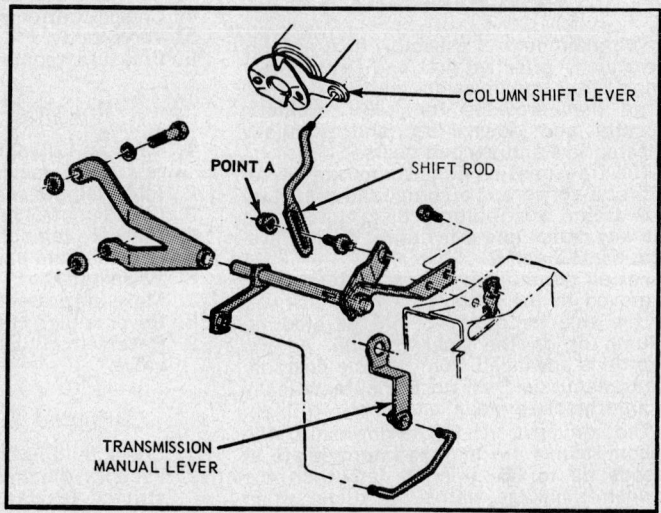

Fig. 4 Manual linkage. 1974-75 Ford & Mercury column shift. Typical

No Drive in D1 Only

1. Check fluid level.
2. Manual linkage.
3. Check control pressure.
4. Valve body.
5. Make air pressure check.
6. Planetary one-way clutch.

No Drive in D2 Only

1. Check fluid level.
2. Manual linkage.
3. Check control pressure.
4. Intermediate servo.
5. Valve body.
6. Make air pressure check.
7. Leakage in hydraulic system.
8. Planetary one-way clutch.

No Drive in L Only

1. Check fluid level.
2. Manual linkage.
3. Check control pressure.
4. Valve body.
5. Reverse servo.
6. Make air pressure check.
7. Leakage in hydraulic system.
8. Planetary one-way clutch.

No Drive in R Only

1. Check fluid level.
2. Manual linkage.
3. Reverse band.
4. Check control pressure.
5. Reverse servo.
6. Valve body.
7. Make air pressure check.
8. Reverse-high clutch.
9. Leakage in hydraulic system.
10. Reverse-high clutch piston air bleed valve.

No Drive in Any Selector Position

1. Check fluid level.
2. Manual linkage.
3. Check control pressure.

4. Pressure regulator.
5. Valve body.
6. Make air pressure check.
7. Leakage in hydraulic system.
8. Front pump.

Lockup in D1 Only

1. Reverse-high clutch.
2. Parking linkage.
3. Leakage in hydraulic system.

Lockup in D2 Only

1. Reverse band.
2. Reverse servo.
3. Reverse-high clutch.
4. Parking linkage.
5. Leakage in hydraulic system.
6. Planetary one-way clutch.

Lockup in L Only

1. Intermediate band.
2. Intermediate servo.
3. Reverse-high clutch.
4. Parking linkage.
5. Leakage in hydraulic system.

Lockup in R Only

1. Intermediate band.

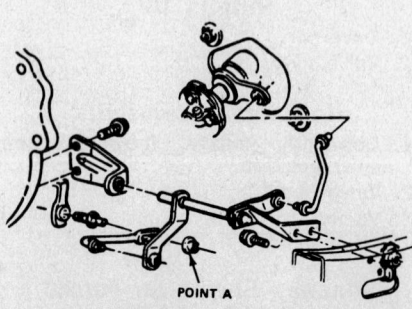

Fig. 4A Manual linkage (typical). 1976-78 Ford & Mercury column shift

2. Intermediate servo.
3. Forward clutch
4. Parking linkage.
5. Leakage in hydraulic system.

Parking Lock Binds or Won't Hold

1. Manual linkage.
2. Parking linkage.

Maximum Speed Too Low, Poor Acceleration

1. Engine performance.
2. Brakes bind.
3. Converter one-way clutch.

Noisy in N or P

1. Check fluid level.
2. Pressure regulator.
3. Front pump.
4. Planetary assembly.

Noisy in All Gears

1. Check fluid level.
2. Pressure regulator.
3. Planetary assembly.
4. Forward clutch.
5. Front pump.
6. Planetary one-way clutch.

Car Moves Forward in N

1. Manual linkage.
2. Forward clutch.

MAINTENANCE

Checking Oil Level

1. With transmission at operating temperature, park vehicle on a level surface.
2. Run engine at idle speed with service and parking brakes applied and move

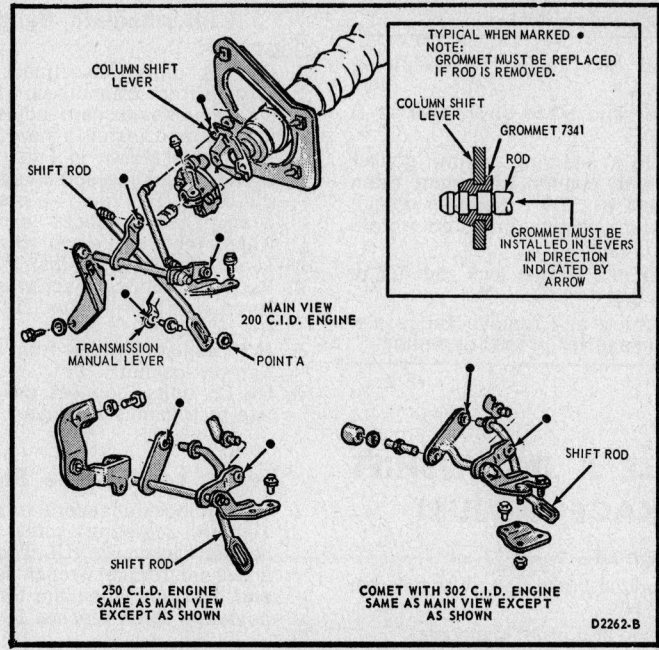

Fig. 5 Manual linkage. Maverick and Comet column shift

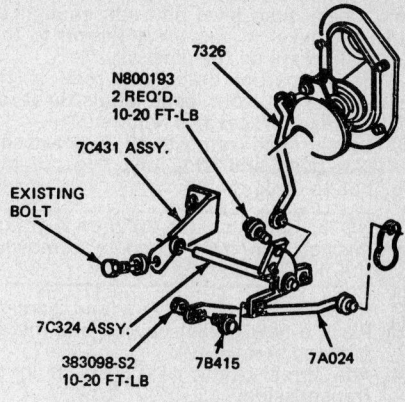

Fig. 5A Manual linkage (typical). 1978 Fairmont & Zephyr column shift

Drain & Refill

NOTE: *Normal maintenance and lubrication requirements do not necessitate periodic fluid changes. If a major failure has occurred in the transmission, it will have to be removed for service. At this time the converter must be thoroughly flushed to remove any foreign matter.*

When filling a dry transmission and converter, install five quarts of Type F fluid. Start engine, shift the selector lever through all ranges and place it at P posi-

selector lever through each range. Return selector lever to Park.

3. With engine idling, remove dipstick and check fluid level. Fluid level should be between the Add and Full marks.

4. Add Type F fluid as required to bring the fluid to the proper level.

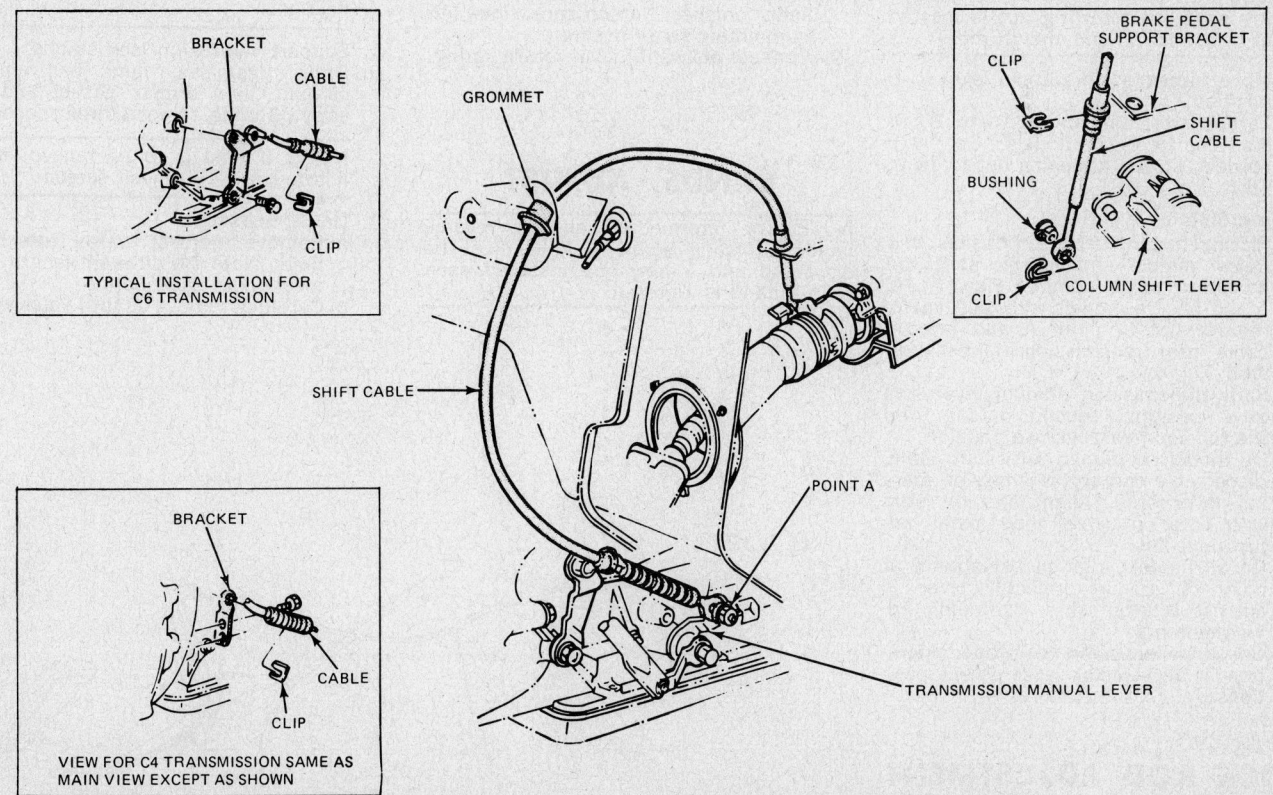

Fig. 6 Manual linkage. 1974-76 Torino & Montego; 1974-78 Cougar & Elite; 1975-78 Granada & Monarch; 1977-78 LTD II, Thunderbird & Versailles column shift

tion. Check fluid level and add enough to raise the level in the transmission to the "F" (full) mark on the dipstick.

When a partial drain and refill is required due to front band adjustment or minor repair, proceed as follows:

1. Loosen and remove all but two oil pan bolts and drop one edge of the pan to drain the oil.

NOTE: Some models of the C4 transmission can be drained by removing the filler tube from the pan.

2. Remove and clean pan and screen.
3. Place a new gasket on pan and install pan and screen.
4. Add three quarts of Type F fluid to transmission.
5. Run engine at idle speed for about two minutes.
6. Check oil level and add oil as necessary.
7. Run engine at a fast idle until it reaches normal operating temperature.
8. Shift selector lever through all ranges and then place it in P position.
9. Add fluid as required to bring the level to the full mark.

MANUAL LINKAGE, ADJUST

Floor Shift

1. Place transmission selector lever in D position.
2. Raise vehicle and loosen shift rod retaining nut, Fig. 3.

NOTE: On 1977-78 LTD II and Cougar, the shift rod retaining nut is located at transmission end of shift rod.

3. Move transmission manual lever to D position.
4. Torque attaching nut to 10 to 20 ft. lbs. on 1974-77 models. On 1978 models, torque attaching nut to 10 to 15 ft. lbs.

Column Shift

1. Place selector lever in D position.
2. Raise vehicle and loosen shift rod adjusting nut at point A, Figs. 4, 4A, 5 and 5A. On models with shift cable, remove nut at point A and remove cable from transmission manual lever stud, Fig. 6.
3. Shift transmission manual lever into drive position, second detent from the full counter clockwise position.
4. On models equipped with shift cable, place cable end on transmission manual lever stud. Align flats on stud with flats on cable, then install adjustment nut.
5. On all models, tighten adjustment at point A. Ensure selector lever is against D stop when tightening adjustment nut.
6. Check transmission for proper operation in all selector lever detent positions.

LOCK ROD ADJUSTMENT

1974-76 Comet & Maverick W/Floor Shift

NOTE: After adjusting manual linkage,

adjust lock rod as follows:

1. Raise car and loosen rod retaining nut, Fig. 3.
2. Lower car and place shift lever in D position.
3. Align hole in steering column socket casting with column alignment mark and insert a .180" diameter gauge pin. Column casting must not rotate with pin in place.
4. Raise car and torque lock rod nut to 10-20 ft. lbs.
5. Lower vehicle and remove gauge pin. Check linkage for proper operation.

THROTTLE & DOWNSHIFT LINKAGE, ADJUST

Figs. 7 through 10

1. Apply parking brake and place selector lever in "N".
2. Run engine at normal idle speed.
3. Connect tachometer to engine.
4. Adjust engine idle speed to specified RPM listed under Tune Up Specifications in individual car chapters.
5. Disconnect downshift lever return spring and hold throttle lever in wide open position.
6. Hold downshift rod against the through detent stop.
7. Adjust downshift screw to provide 0.01 to 0.08" clearance between screw and throttle arm.
8. On 1974 Montego and Torino six cylinder engines, tighten screw lock nut to maintain screw position.
9. Connect downshift lever return spring.

BANDS, ADJUST

NOTE: The intermediate and low-reverse bands adjusting screw locknut must be discarded and a new one installed each time a band is adjusted.

Intermediate Band

C3 & C4

1. On C3 units, disconnect downshift linkage from transmission lever.
2. On all units, discard adjusting screw locknut and install a new locknut.
3. With tools shown in Figs. 11 and 12 tighten adjusting screw until tool handle clicks. *This tool is a pre-set torque wrench which clicks and overruns when the torque on the adjusting screw reaches 10 ft-lbs.*
4. Back off adjusting screw exactly 1½ turns on C3 units and 1¾ turns on C4 units.
5. Hold adjusting screw from turning and tighten locknut.
6. On C3 units, connect downshift linkage to transmission lever.

C4 Low-Reverse Band

1. Loosen lock nut several turns.
2. Tighten adjusting screw until tool handle clicks, Fig. 13. *Tool shown is a pre-set torque wrench which clicks and overruns when the torque on the adjusting screw reaches 10 ft-lbs.*
3. Back off adjusting screw exactly 3 full turns.
4. Hold adjusting screw from turning and tighten lock nut.

CONTROL VALVE

NOTE: All fasteners used on C3 transmissions are designed to metric specifications.

1. Support vehicle on jack stands.
2. Drain transmission fluid, then remove oil pan, fluid screen, gasket and on early C3 units, remove three spacers.

NOTE: If fluid is to be reused, filter it through a 100 mesh screen.

3. On C3 units:
   a. Remove control valve attaching bolts. Note the different length and location of each bolt.
   b. Carefully remove control valve while

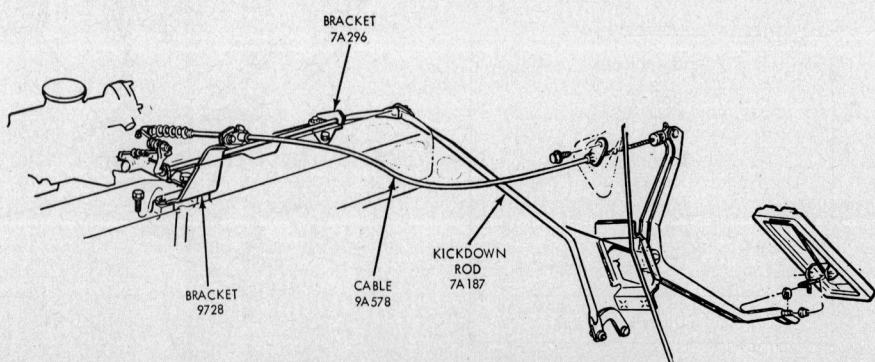

Fig. 7 Throttle & downshift linkage Ford & Mercury (typical)

unlocking and detaching selector lever connecting rod.

4. On C4 units:
   a. Shift selector lever into PARK and remove the two detent spring to control valve and case bolts.
   b. Remove remaining control valve to case bolts, then while holding manual valve inward, remove control valve.

NOTE: Failure to hold manual valve inward, while removing control valve, could cause manual valve to become damaged.

5. After installing valve, torque attaching bolts to 84-108 in. lbs. on C3 units and 80-120 in. lbs. on C4 units.

SERVO REPAIR
C4 Intermediate Servo

1. Support vehicle on jack stands.
2. On some models, it is necessary to remove crossmember to gain access to the servo.
3. Remove servo cover attaching screws, servo cover, gasket, piston and piston return spring.
4. Replace piston seals. Lubricate new seals with transmission fluid before installation.
5. Reverse procedure to install.

C4 Low-Reverse Servo

1. Support vehicle on jack stands.
2. Loosen reverse band adjusting screw locknut and torque adjusting screw to 10 foot pounds. With adjusting screw torqued, the band strut is forced against case, preventing the strut from falling out of position when removing servo piston.
3. Remove servo cover retaining bolts, servo cover, seal and servo piston from case.
4. On some models, the piston seal is

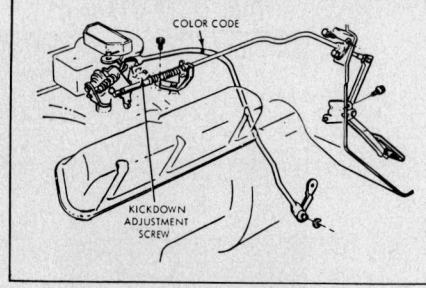

Fig. 8 Throttle and downshift linkage. Comet, Maverick, Granada & Monarch with V8 engine, Cougar, Elite, Montego. Torino & 1977-78 LTD II, Thunderbird & Versailles, 1978 Fairmont & Zephyr

bonded to the piston, requiring piston replacement. To remove piston from stem, insert a small screwdriver through hole in stem and remove piston retaining nut, piston, accumulator spring and spacer.
5. On all other models, replace piston seals. Lubricate new seals with transmission fluid before installation.
6. Reverse procedure to install.

C3 Rear Servo

1. Support vehicle on jack stands, then drain transmission.
2. Remove oil filter screws, gasket and on early models, three spacers.
3. Remove servo cover retaining screws, servo cover, piston and spring, Fig. 14.
4. Reverse procedure to install.

EXTENSION HOUSING

1. Support vehicle on jack stands and remove driveshaft.

NOTE: Scribe marks on driveshaft yoke and companion flange, to insure proper positioning of driveshaft during assembly.

2. Support transmission with suitable jack and disconnect speedometer cable.

NOTE: On some models, it will be necessary to disconnect the exhaust system from the exhaust manifolds to perform the following step.

3. Remove engine rear support to crossmember attaching bolts or nuts, then raise transmission slightly and remove rear support from extension housing.

NOTE: On some models, it will be necessary to remove crossmember in order to remove rear support from extension housing.

4. Loosen extension housing bolts and allow transmission fluid to drain and remove extension housing.

GOVERNOR

1. Remove extension housing as described previously.
2. On C3 units, remove governor retaining pin snap ring, then the retaining pin, Fig. 15.
3. On all units, remove governor to governor housing retaining bolts and slide governor off output shaft.
4. Reverse procedure to install. Torque governor retaining bolts to 7 to 10 foot pounds.

TRANSMISSION, REPLACE
All Models

1. Support vehicle on jack stands and remove converter housing lower cover.
2. Drain transmission oil pan and the converter. Use a wrench on crankshaft pulley nut to rotate crankshaft and converter to gain access to drain plug.

NOTE: Do not rotate 2000 cc or 2300 cc engines in opposite direction of

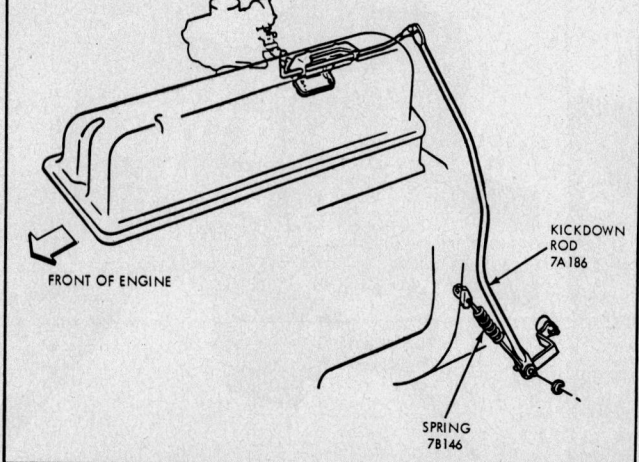

Fig. 9   Downshift linkage 1974-77 6 cyl. Comet, Maverick, Montego, Torino, 1975-78 Granada & Monarch, 1977-78 Versailles

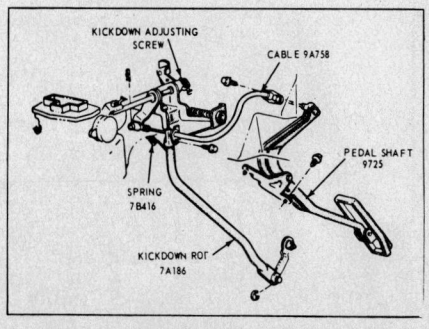

Fig. 10   Throttle & downshift linkage. 1974-78 Mustang II, 1974-78 Pinto & 1975-78 Bobcat (Typical)

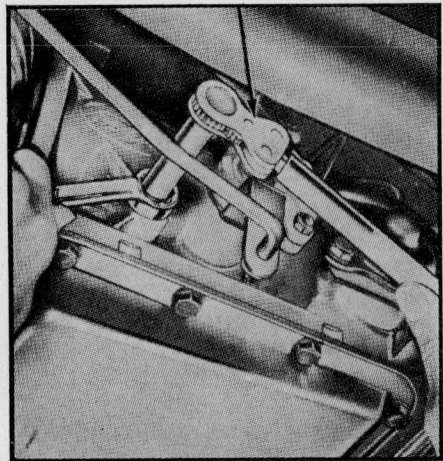

Fig. 11   Intermediate band adjustment. C4

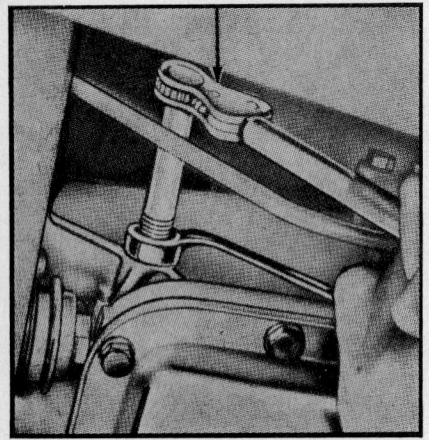

Fig. 13   Low-reverse band adjustment. C4

TOOL - T71P - 77370 - H

TOOL - T71P - 77370 - B

Fig. 12   Intermediate band adjustment. C3

normal rotation.

3. Remove converter to flywheel bolts or nuts.
4. Remove propeller shaft.
5. Remove vacuum line hose from transmission vacuum unit. Disconnect vacuum line from clip.
6. If equipped, disconnect TRS switch wire.
7. Remove two extension housing to crossmember bolts.
8. Remove speedometer cable from extension housing.
9. On Bobcat, Comet, Maverick, Mustang II, Granada, Monarch and Pinto mod-

Fig. 14   Rear servo removal. C3

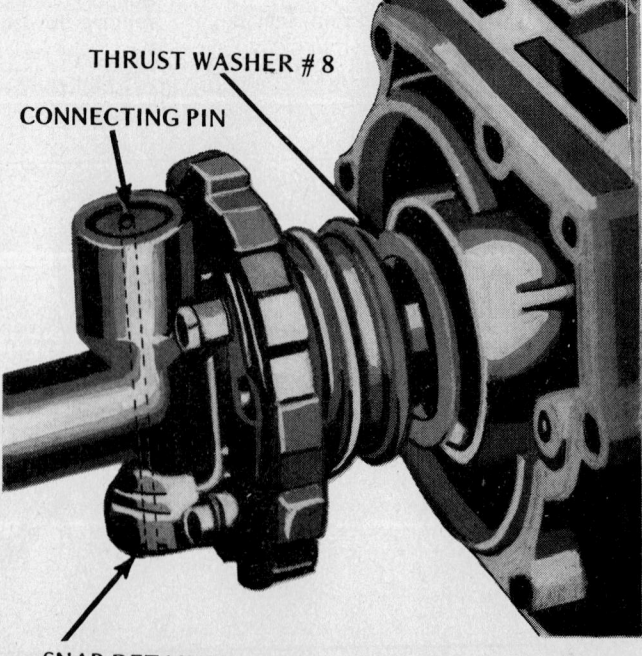

THRUST WASHER # 8

CONNECTING PIN

SNAP RETAINER

Fig. 15   Governor removal. C3

els, disconnect exhaust pipe from manifold.

NOTE: On Bobcat, Mustang II and Pinto with C3 transmission, remove exhaust support from pipe and rear engine support.

10. On all models, disconnect oil cooler lines from transmission.
11. Remove the manual and kickdown linkage rods from transmission shift levers.
12. Where necessary disconnect the neutral start switch wires.
13. Remove starter.
14. Remove transmission fluid filler tube.
15. On all models except Pinto, Mustang II and Bobcat:
    a. Support transmission with a suitable jack and remove crossmember.
    b. Remove converter housing to engine bolts and lower transmission from vehicle.
16. On Pinto, Mustang II and Bobcat:
    a. Raise transmission slightly with a suitable jack and remove engine rear support to crossmember nut.
    b. Remove crossmember attaching bolts and crossmember.
    c. Lower jack, allowing transmission to hang, and raise front of engine with a suitable jack, thereby gaining access to the two upper converter housing to engine bolts.
    d. Secure transmission to jack, remove the lower converter housing to engine bolts, then the two upper bolts, move transmission rearward and lower from vehicle.
17. Reverse procedure to install.

NOTE: Flywheel assemblies used with 1975-78 C3 transmissions have a pilot whole to ensure proper converter to flywheel alignment. Before installing transmission, position flywheel at 6 o'clock. Position transmission to engine, then install attaching bolt through pilot hole and torque to 27-37 ft. lbs. Install remaining bolts and torque to 27-37 ft. lbs.

C6 DUAL RANGE AUTOMATIC

TRANSMISSION IDENTIFICATION

An identification tag attached to the servo cover bolt, includes the model prefix and suffix

YEAR	CAR MODEL	TRANS. MODEL	ENGINE MODEL
1974	Cougar(1)(3)	PGA-AW	V8-351
	Cougar(1)(4)	PGA-AF3	V8-351
	Cougar(2)(3)	PGA-AY2, 3	V8-351
	Cougar(2)(4)	PGA-AG3, 4	V8-351
	Cougar(1)	PJA-G3	V8-400
	Cougar(2)	PJA-H3, 4	V8-400
	Cougar(1)	PJD-R	V8-460
	Cougar(2)	PJD-S, S1	V8-460
	Ford	PJA-C5	V8-400
	Ford(5)	PJC-H6	V8-460
	Ford	PJD-G3	V8-460
	Lincoln	PJD-F4	V8-460
	Mark IV	PJD-E4	V8-460
	Mercury	PJA-C5	V8-400
	Mercury(5)	PJC-H6	V8-460
	Mercury	PJD-G3	V8-460
	Montego(3)	PGA-AW2	V8-351
	Montego(4)	PGA-AF3	V8-351
	Montego	PJA-C3	V8-400
	Montego(6)	PJC-J2	V8-460
	Montego	PJD-R	V8-460
	Torino(1)(3)	PGA-AW2	V8-351
	Torino(2)(3)	PGA-AY2, 3	V8-351
	Torino(1)(4)	PGA-AF3	V8-351
	Torino(1)(4)	PGA-AG3, 4	V8-351
	Torino(1)(4)	PJA-C3	V8-400
	Torino(2)(4)	PJA-H3, 4	V8-400
	Torino(1)(5)	PJC-J2	V8-460
	Torino(1)	PJD-R	V8-460
	Torino(2)	PJD-S, S1	V8-460
	Thunderbird	PJD-E4	V8-460
1975	Cougar(1)	PJA-V-1	V8-351M
	Cougar(2)	PJA-W-1	V8-351M
	Cougar(1)	PJA-G4-5	V8-400
	Cougar(1)	PJA-R1	V8-400
	Cougar(2)	PJA-H5-6	V8-400
	Cougar(2)	PJA-S1	V8-400
	Cougar(1)(6)	PJD-R1-2	V8-460
	Cougar(1)(7)	PJD-T1-2	V8-460
	Cougar(2)(6)	PJD-S2-3	V8-460
	Cougar(2)(7)	PJD-U1-2	V8-460
	Ford(5)	PJA-C6-7	V8-400
	Ford(5)(6)	PJC-H7-8	V8-460
	Ford(5)(7)	PJC-K-1	V8-460
	Ford(6)	PJD-G4-5	V8-460
	Ford(7)	PJD-P-1-2	V8-460
	Lincoln(6)	PJD-F5-6	V8-460
	Lincoln(7)	PJD-N-1-2	V8-460
	Mark IV(6)	PJD-E5-6	V8-460
	Mark IV(7)	PJD-M-1-2	V8-460
	Mercury(5)	PJA-C6-7	V8-400
	Mercury(5)	PJA-P1	V8-400
	Mercury(5)(6)	PJC-H7-8	V8-460
	Mercury(5)(7)	PJC-K-1	V8-460
	Mercury(6)	PJC-G4-5	V8-460
	Mercury(7)	PJD-P-1-2	V8-460
	Montego(1)	PJA-V-1	V8-351M
	Montego	PJA-G4-5	V8-400
	Montego	PJA-R1	V8-400
	Montego(6)	PJD-R1-2	V8-460
	Montego(7)	PJD-T1-2	V8-460
	Torino(1)	PJA-V-1	V8-351M
	Torino(1)	PJA-W-1	V8-351M
	Torino(1)	PJA-G4-5	V8-400
	Torino(2)	PJA-H5-6	V8-400
	Torino(1)(6)	PJD-R1-2	V8-460
	Torino(1)(7)	PJD-T1-2	V8-460
	Torino(2)(6)	PJD-S2-3	V8-460
	Torino(2)(7)	PJD-U1-2	V8-460
	Thunderbird(6)	PJD-E5-6	V8-460
	Thunderbird(7)	PJD-M1-2	V8-460
1976	Cougar(6)	PJA-V3, 4	V8-351M
	Cougar(6)	PJA-W3, 4	V8-351M
	Cougar(6)	PJA-G5, 6, 7	V8-400
	Cougar(6)	PJA-H6, 7, 8	V8-400
	Cougar(7)	PJA-R, 1	V8-400
	Cougar(7)	PJA-S, 1	V8-400
	Cougar	PJD-R2, 3	V8-460
	Cougar	PJD-S3, 4	V8-460
	Cougar	PJD-AJ	V8-460
	Cougar	PJD-AK	V8-460
	Ford(6)	PJA-C7, 8, 9	V8-400
	Ford(7)	PJA-P, 1	V8-400
	Ford	PJD-G5, 6	V8-460
	Ford	PJD-AH	V8-460
	Ford(5)	PJD-H9, 10	V8-460
	Lincoln	PJD-F6, 7	V8-460
	Lincoln	PJD-AG	V8-460
	Mark IV	PJD-E6, 7	V8-460
	Mark IV	PJD-AF	V8-460
	Mercury(6)	PJA-C7, 8, 9	V8-400
	Mercury(7)	PJA-P, 1	V8-400
	Mercury	PJD-G5, 6	V8-460
	Mercury	PJD-AH	V8-460
	Mercury(5)	PJD-H9, 10	V8-460
	Montego(6)	PJA-V3, 4	V8-351M
	Montego(6)	PJA-G5, 6, 7	V8-400
	Montego(7)	PJA-R, 1	V8-400
	Montego	PJD-R2, 3	V8-460
	Montego	PJD-AJ	V8-460
	Montego(5)	PJC-J3, 4	V8-460
	Torino(6)	PJA-V3, 4	V8-351M
	Torino(6)	PJA-W3, 4	V8-351M
	Torino(6)	PJA-G5, 6, 7	V8-400
	Torino(6)	PJA-H6, 7, 8	V8-400
	Torino(7)	PJA-R, 1	V8-400
	Torino(7)	PJA-S, 1	V8-400
	Torino	PJD-R2, 3	V8-460
	Torino	PJD-S3, 4	V8-460
	Torino	PJD-AJ	V8-460
	Torino	PJD-AK	V8-460
	Torino(5)	PJC-J3, 4	V8-460
	Thunderbird	PJD-E6, 7	V8-460
	Thunderbird	PJD-AF	V8-460
1977	Cougar	PJA-AT, AU	V8-351M
	Cougar	PJA-G11, 13	V8-400
	Cougar	PJA-H12, 13	V8-400
	Cougar	PJA-R4, 5	V8-400
	Cougar	PJA-S4, 5	V8-400
	Cougar	PJA-BJ	V8-400
	Ford	PJA-PU, 1	V8-351M
	Ford	PJA-BH, 1	V8-400
	Ford	PJA-BV, 1	V8-400

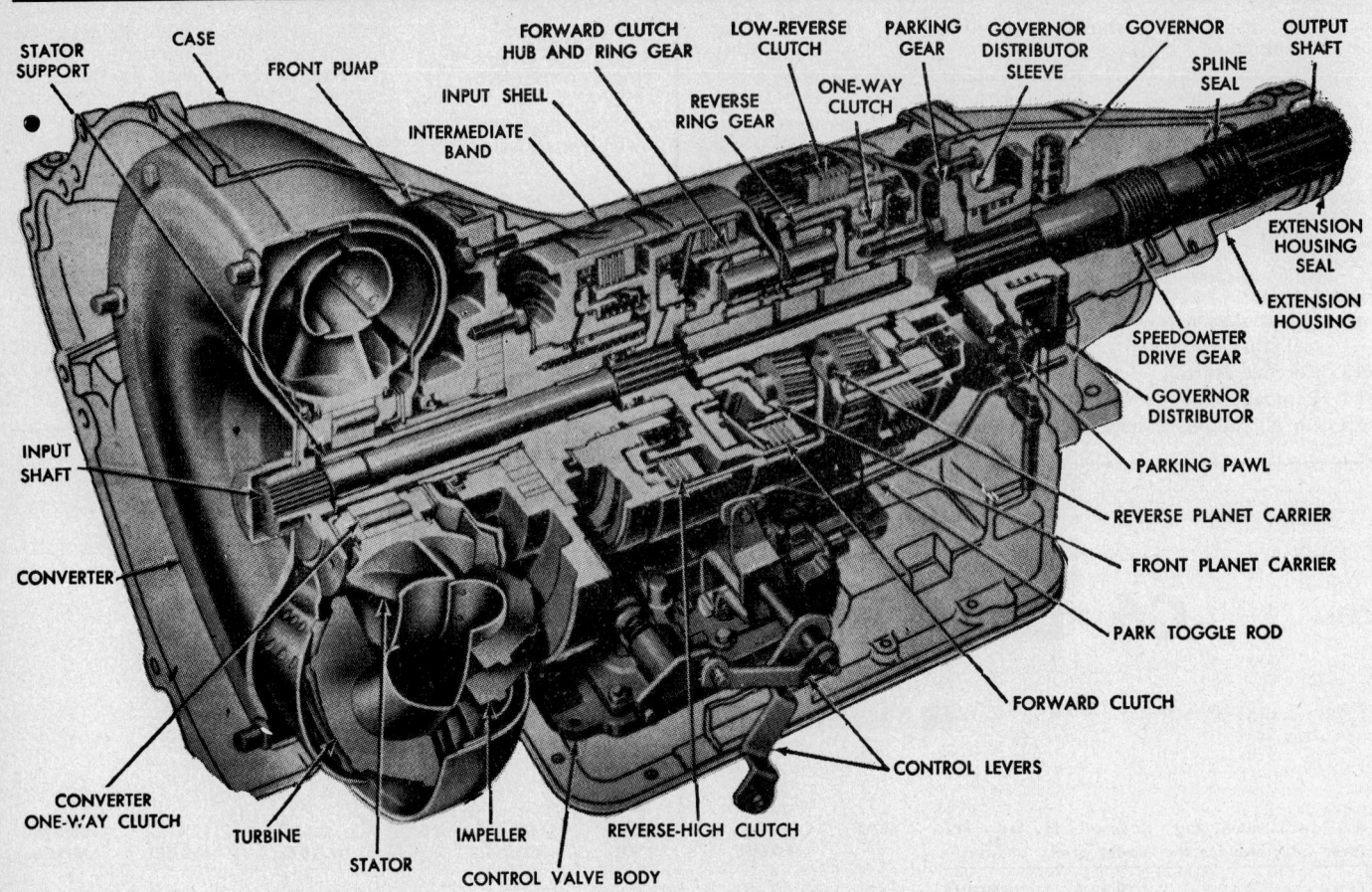

Fig. 1   Sectional view of C6 transmission

Labels: STATOR SUPPORT, CASE, FRONT PUMP, FORWARD CLUTCH HUB AND RING GEAR, INPUT SHELL, INTERMEDIATE BAND, REVERSE RING GEAR, LOW-REVERSE CLUTCH, ONE-WAY CLUTCH, PARKING GEAR, GOVERNOR DISTRIBUTOR SLEEVE, GOVERNOR, SPLINE SEAL, OUTPUT SHAFT, EXTENSION HOUSING SEAL, EXTENSION HOUSING, SPEEDOMETER DRIVE GEAR, GOVERNOR DISTRIBUTOR, PARKING PAWL, REVERSE PLANET CARRIER, FRONT PLANET CARRIER, PARK TOGGLE ROD, FORWARD CLUTCH, CONTROL LEVERS, REVERSE-HIGH CLUTCH, CONTROL VALVE BODY, IMPELLER, STATOR, TURBINE, CONVERTER ONE-WAY CLUTCH, CONVERTER, INPUT SHAFT

TRANSMISSION IDENTIFICATION—Continued

YEAR	CAR MODEL	TRANS. MODEL	ENGINE MODEL	YEAR	CAR MODEL	TRANS. MODEL	ENGINE MODEL	YEAR	CAR MODEL	TRANS. MODEL	ENGINE MODEL
1977	Ford	PJA-C13,14,15	V8-400		Mercury	PJA-BH	V8-400		Lincoln	PJA-CZ	V8-400
	Ford	PJD-G10,11,12	V8-460		Mercury	PJA-BV	V8-400		Lincoln	PJD-AN3, 4	V8-460
	Ford	PJD-AH2,3	V8-460		Mercury	PJC-H13	V8-460		LTD II	PJA-BJ3, 4	V8-351, 400
	Ford	PJD-AP,1	V8-460		Mercury	PJC-M	V8-460		LTD II	PJA-G15, 16	V8-400
	Ford	PJD-AR,1	V8-460		Mercury	PJD-G10,11	V8-460		LTD II	PJA-H16, 17	V8-400
	Ford	PJC-H13,14	V8-460		Mercury	PJD-AH2	V8-460		Mark V	PJA-BW3, 4	V8-400
	Lincoln	PJA-BL	V8-400		Mercury	PJD-AP	V8-460		Mark V	PJA-CY	V8-400
	Lincoln	PJD-F12,13	V8-460		Mercury	PJD-AR	V8-460		Mark V	PJA-CB, 1	V8-400
	Lincoln	PJD-AG2	V8-460		Thunderbird	PJA-AU,1	V8-351M		Mark V	PJD-AM3, 4	V8-460
	Lincoln	PJD-AN	V8-460		Thunderbird	PJA-G11,12,13	V8-400		Mercury	PJA-BU3, 4	V8-351M
	LTDII	PJA-AU1	V8-351M		Thunderbird	PJA-R4,5,6	V8-400		Mercury	PJA-C17, 18	V8-400
	LTDII	PJA-C11,12,13	V8-400		Thunderbird	PJA-S4,5,6	V8-400		Mercury	PJA-BH3, 4	V8-400
	LTDII	PJA-R4,5,6	V8-400		Thunderbird	PJA-H12,13,14	V8-400		Mercury	PJC-M3, 4	V8-460
	LTDII	PJA-S4,5,6	V8-400		Thunderbird	PJA-BJ,1	V8-400		Mercury	PJD-AP3, 4	V8-460
	LTDII	PJA-H12,13,14	V8-400	1978	Cougar	PJA-BJ3, 4	V8-351		Thunderbird	PJA-BJ3, 4	V8-351, 400
	LTDII	PJA-BJ1	V8-400		Cougar	PJA-G15, 16	V8-400		Thunderbird	PJA-G15	V8-400
	Mark V	PJA-BK,1	V8-400		Cougar	PJA-H16, 17	V8-400		Thunderbird	PJA-H16, 17	V8-400
	Mark V	PJA-BW	V8-400		Ford	PJA-BU3, 4	V8-351M				
	Mark V	PJD-F12,13	V8-460		Ford	PJA-C17, 18	V8-400				
	Mark V	PJD-AF2	V8-460		Ford	PJA-BH3, 4	V8-400				
	Mark V	PJD-AM	V8-460		Ford	PJD-AP3, 4	V8-460				
	Mercury	PJA-BU	V8-351M		Ford⑤	PJC-H16, 17	V8-460				
	Mercury	PJA-C13,14	V8-400		Lincoln	PJA-CA3, 4	V8-400				
					Lincoln	PJA-CC, 1	V8-400				

①—Column shift.
②—Floor shift.
③—Two barrel carburetor.
④—Four barrel carburetor.
⑤—Police or Fleet.
⑥—Exc. Calif.
⑦—Calif.

DESCRIPTION

As shown in Fig. 1, the transmission consists essentially of a torque converter, a compound planetary gear train controlled by one band, three disc clutches and a one-way clutch, and a hydraulic control system.

The transmission is made so that a system of manual and automatic shifting is provided.

Automatic & Manual Shifting

This unit has a shift pattern which is indicated on the selector as P-R-N-D-2-1. This refers respectively to Park, Reverse, Neutral, Full Automatic, Second Gear (manual), Low Gear (manual).

In this unit an overriding control is provided which enables the driver to exercise his own judgement with regard to the gear ratios to be selected and an understanding of what is possible greatly enhances the pleasure to be derived from driving the car. No automatic mechanism has the power of anticipation, but the driver can see ahead and has the means for over-riding the automatic mechanism.

Automatic Shift

In "D" position the shift sequence is fully automatic in that the transmission starts in low gear and upshifts through second gear to third or high gear.

Manual Shifting

The shift to 2 or 1 is done manually by shifting the lever from neutral to either position. In "1" position, the transmisson starts in 1st (low gear) and is retained. In "2" position it starts in 2nd gear and remains in 2nd gear, regardless of road speed.

Manual Shift To "1"

Manual shifting from "D" to "1" can also be accomplished any time. Here the transmission immediately shifts to second and remains in second until the predetermined governor control speed allows it to shift down to low gear where it remains. The governor speed control at this point eliminates the possibility of a direct down shift to low gear until the road speed is reduced.

Shift Lever Controls

A shift lever button control is used to shift from neutral to reverse or park, also when shifting from "D" to "2" or "1" position. However, the button control function is not required when shifting from neutral to "D", or to shift forward from "1" to "2" position.

Parking Pawl

The transmission gear train is in neutral in both P and N positions. There is no pressure to any clutch and only the transmission input shaft turns. In park, a pawl engages a parking gear which is splined to the transmission output shaft, Fig. 1, to lock the rear wheels to the transmission main case.

A neutral start switch, mounted on the transmission and operated by the selector linkage, completes the engine cranking circuit in P and N only so that the engine cannot be started in any drive gear.

Forced Downshifts

Forced downshifts (kickdown shifts) from high to second gear are possible at speeds as high as 65 mph. In D1 it is possible to force a downshift to 1st gear up to 30 mph.

The carburetor is at full throttle before the accelerator is floored. Up to full throttle, a "torque demand" downshift to 2nd is possible up to 40 mph. "Kickdown" shifts require depressing the accelerator to the floor to actuate the downshift valve in the transmission.

TROUBLE SHOOTING GUIDE

No Drive In Forward Speeds
1. Manual linkage adjustment.
2. Check control pressure.
3. Valve body.
4. Make air pressure check.
5. Forward clutch.
6. Leakage in hydraulic system.

Rough Initial Engagement in D, D1, D2 or 2
1. Engine idle speed too high.
2. Vacuum diaphragm unit or tubes restricted, leaking or maladjusted.
3. Check control pressure.
4. Valve body.
5. Forward clutch.

1-2 or 2-3 Shift Points Incorrect or Erratic
1. Check fluid level.
2. Vacuum diaphragm unit or tubes restricted, leaking or maladjusted.
3. Downshift linkage, including inner lever position.
4. Manual linkage adjustment.
5. Governor defective.
6. Check control pressure.
7. Valve body.
8. Make air pressure check.

Rough 1-2 Upshifts
1. Vacuum diaphragm unit or tubes restricted, leaking or maladjusted.
2. Intermediate servo.
3. Intermediate band.
4. Check control pressure.
5. Valve body.

Rough 2-3 Shifts
1. Vacuum diaphragm or tubes restricted leaking or maladjusted.
2. Intermediate servo.
3. Check control pressure.
4. Intermediate band.
5. Valve body.
6. Make air pressure check.
7. Reverse-high clutch.
8. Reverse-high clutch piston air bleed valve.

Dragged Out 1-2 Shift
1. Check fluid level.
2. Vacuum diaphragm unit or tubes restricted, leaking or maladjusted.
3. Intermediate servo.
4. Check control pressure.
5. Intermediate band.
6. Valve body.
7. Make air pressure check.
8. Leakage in hydraulic system.

Engine Overspeeds on 2-3 Shift
1. Manual linkage adjustment.
2. Check fluid level.
3. Vacuum diaphragm unit or tubes restricted, leaking or maladjusted.
4. Intermediate servo.
5. Check control pressure.
6. Valve body.
7. Intermediate band.
8. Reverse-high clutch.
9. Reverse-high clutch piston air bleed valve.

No 1-2 or 2-3 Shift
1. Manual linkage adjustment.
2. Downshift linkage including inner lever position.
3. Vacuum diaphragm unit or tubes restricted, leaking or malajusted.
4. Governor.
5. Check control pressure.
6. Valve body.
7. Intermediate band.
8. Intermediate servo.
9. Reverse-high clutch.
10. Leakage in hydraulic system.

No 3-1 Shift In D1, 2 or 3-2 Shift In D2 or D
1. Governor.
2. Valve body.

No Forced Downshifts
1. Downshift linkage, including inner lever position.
2. Check control pressure.
3. Valve body.

Runaway Engine on Forced 3-2 Shift
1. Check control pressure.
2. Intermediate servo.
3. Intermediate band.
4. Valve body.
5. Vacuum diaphragm unit or tubes restricted, leaking or maladjusted.
6. Leakage in hydraulic system.

Rough 3-2 Shift or 3-1 Shift at Closed Throttle
1. Engine idle speed.
2. Vacuum diaphragm unit or tubes restricted, leaking or maladjusted.
3. Intermediate servo.
4. Check control pressure.
5. Valve body.

Shifts 1-3 in D, D1, 2, D2
1. Intermediate band.
2. Intermediate servo.
3. Valve body.
4. Governor.
5. Make air pressure check.

No Engine Braking in 1st Gear—Manual Low Range

1. Manual linkage adjustment.
2. Low-reverse clutch.
3. Valve body.
4. Governor.
5. Make air pressure check.
6. Leakage in hydraulic system.

Creeps Excessively

1. Engine idle speed too high.

Slips or Chatters In 1st Gear, D1

1. Check fluid level.
2. Vacuum diaphragm unit or tubes restricted, leaking or maladjusted.
3. Check control pressure.
4. Valve body.
5. Forward clutch.
6. Leakage in hydraulic system.
7. Planetary one-way clutch.

Slips or Chatters In 2nd Gear

1. Check fluid level.
2. Vacuum diaphragm unit or tubes restricted, leaking or maladjusted.
3. Intermediate servo.
4. Intermediate band.
5. Check control pressure.
6. Valve body.
7. Make air pressure check.
8. Forward clutch.
9. Leakage in hydraulic system.

Slips or Chatters In Reverse

1. Check fluid level.
2. Vacuum diaphragm unit or tubes restricted, leaking or maladjusted.
3. Manual linkage adjustment.
4. Low-reverse clutch.
5. Check control pressure.
6. Valve body.
7. Make air pressure check.
8. Reverse-high clutch.
9. Leakage in hydraulic system.
10. Reverse-high clutch piston air bleed valve.

No Drive In D1 or 2

1. Manual linkage adjustment.
2. Check control pressure.
3. Valve body.
4. Planetary one-way clutch.

No Drive In D, D2

1. Check fluid level.
2. Manual linkage adjustment.
3. Check control pressure.
4. Intermediate servo.
5. Valve body.
6. Make air pressure check.
7. Leakage in hydraulic system.

No Drive In L or 1

1. Check fluid level.
2. Check control pressure.
3. Valve body.
4. Make air pressure check.
5. Leakage in hydraulic system.

No Drive In R Only

1. Check fluid level.
2. Manual linkage adjustment.
3. Low-reverse clutch.
4. Check control pressure.
5. Valve body.
6. Make air pressure check.
7. Reverse-high clutch.
8. Leakage in hydraulic system.
9. Reverse-high clutch piston air bleed valve.

No Drive In Any Selector Position

1. Check fluid level.
2. Manual linkage adjustment.
3. Check control pressure.
4. Valve body.
5. Make air pressure check.
6. Leakage in hydraulic system.
7. Front pump.

Lockup In D1 or 2

1. Valve body.
2. Parking linkage.
3. Leakage in hydraulic system.

Lockup In D2 or D

1. Low-reverse clutch.
2. Valve body.
3. Reverse-high clutch.
4. Parking linkage.
5. Leakage in hydraulic system.
6. Planetary one-way clutch.

Lockup In L or 1

1. Valve body.
2. Parking linkage.
3. Leakage in hydraulic system.

Lockup In R Only

1. Valve body.
2. Forward clutch.
3. Parking linkage.
4. Leakage in hydraulic system.

Parking Lock Binds or Does Not Hold

1. Manual linkage adjustment.
2. Parking linkage.

Transmission Overheats

1. Oil cooler and connections.
2. Valve body.
3. Vacuum diaphragm unit or tubes restricted, leaking or maladjusted.
4. Check control pressure.
5. Converter one-way clutch.
6. Converter pressure check valves.

Maximum Speed Too Low, Poor Acceleration

1. Engine performance.
2. Car brakes.
3. Forward clutch.

Transmission Noisy In N and P

1. Check fluid level.
2. Valve body.
3. Front pump.

Noisy In 1st, 2nd, 3rd or Reverse

1. Check fluid level.
2. Valve body.
3. Planetary assembly.
4. Forward clutch.
5. Reverse-high clutch.
6. Planetary one-way clutch.

Car Moves Forward In N

1. Manual linkage adjustment.
2. Forward clutch.

Fluid Leak

1. Check fluid level.
2. Converter drain plugs.
3. Oil pan gasket, filler tube or seal.
4. Oil cooler and connections.
5. Manual or downshift lever shaft seal.
6. 1/8" pipe plugs in case.
7. Extension housing-to-case gasket.
8. Extension housing rear oil seal.
9. Speedometer driven gear adapter seal.
10. Vacuum diaphragm unit or tubes.
11. Intermediate servo.
12. Engine rear oil seal.

MAINTENANCE
Checking Oil Level

1. Make sure car is on a level floor.
2. Apply parking brake firmly.
3. Run engine at normal idle speed. If transmission fluid is cold, run engine at a fast idle until fluid reaches normal operating temperature. When fluid is warm, slow engine to normal idle speed.
4. Shift selector lever through all positions, then place lever at "P". Do not shut down engine during fluid level checks.
5. Clean all dirt from dipstick cap before removing dipstick from filler tube.
6. Pull dipstick out of tube, wipe it clean and push it all the way back in tube.
7. Pull dipstick out of tube again and check fluid level. If necessary, add enough fluid to raise the level to the "F" mark on dipstick. Do not overfill.

Drain & Refill

NOTE: The Ford Motor Company recommends the use of an automatic transmission fluid with Qualification No. M2C-33F for 1974-76 models and M2C-138-CJ for 1977-78 models (on container). The recommended fluid is said to have a greater coefficient of friction and greater ability to handle maximum engine torques without band or clutch slippage.

Normal maintenance and lubrication requirements do not necessitate periodic

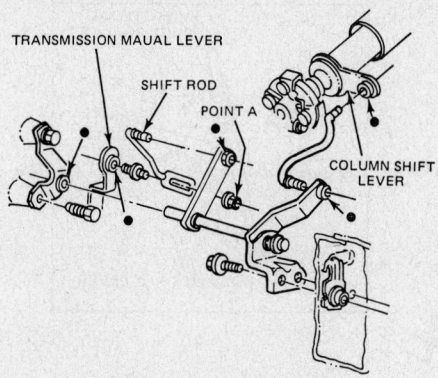

Fig. 2 Column shift linkage.
Lincoln Continental (Typical)

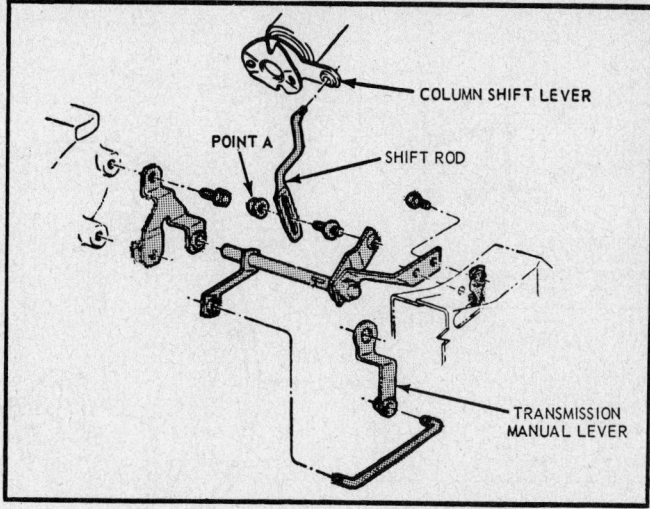

Fig. 3 Column shift linkage. 1974-75 Ford & Mercury (Typical)

fluid changes. If a major failure has occurred in the transmission, it will have to be removed for service. At this time the converter must be thoroughly flushed to remove any foreign matter.

1. To drain the fluid, loosen pan attaching bolts and allow fluid to drain.
2. After fluid has drained to the level of the pan flange, remove pan bolts working from rear and both sides of pan to allow it to drop and drain slowly.
3. When fluid has stopped draining, remove and clean pan and screen. Discard pan gasket.
4. Using a new gasket, install pan.
5. Add 3 quarts of recommended fluid to transmission through filler tube.
6. Run engine at idle speed for 2 minutes, and then run it at a fast idle until it reaches normal operating temperature.
7. Shift selector lever through all positions, place it at "P" and check fluid level.
8. If necessary, add enough fluid to transmission to bring it to the "F" mark on the dipstick.

MANUAL LINKAGE, ADJUST

All Models

Column Shift

1. Place selector lever in D position.
2. Loosen shift rod adjusting nut, point A in Figs. 2 through 4.
3. Shift transmission manual lever to D.
4. Make sure selector lever has not moved from D position then tighten adjusting nut to 10-20 ft. lbs.

Floor Shift

1. Place transmission selector lever in D position.
2. Raise car and loosen shift rod retaining nut, Fig. 5.
3. Move transmission manual lever to D position.
4. Tighten retaining nut to 10-20 ft. lbs.

THROTTLE & DOWNSHIFT LINKAGE

Adjusting the throttle linkage is important to be certain the throttle and kickdown systems are properly adjusted. The kickdown system should come in when the accelerator is pressed through detent, and not before detent. See Figs. 6 thru 8.

All Models

1. Hold carburetor lever in the wide open throttle position.
2. Hold downshift rod against through detent stop.
3. Adjust downshift screw to provide .01 to .08 inch clearance between screw and throttle arm.
4. Connect downshift lever return spring.

BAND ADJUSTMENT

NOTE: When making the intermediate

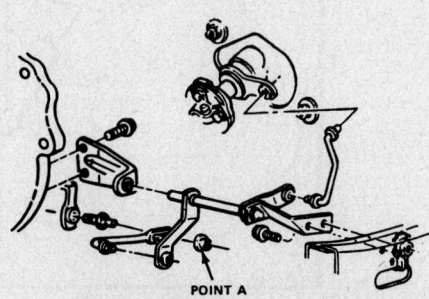

POINT A

Fig. 3A Manual linkage (Typical).
1976-78 Ford & Mercury column shift

band adjustment, the lock nut must be discarded and a new one installed each time the band is adjusted.

1. Loosen the locknut on the adjusting screw several turns, Fig. 9.
2. Torque the screw to 10 ft-lbs, or until the adjuster wrench overruns.
3. Back the screw off exactly 1½ turns.
4. Hold the adjustment and torque the locknut to the 35-45 ft-lbs.

OIL PAN & CONTROL VALVE

Removal

1. Raise car on hoist or jack stands.
2. Loosen and remove all but two oil pan bolts from front of case and drop rear edge of pan to drain fluid. Remove and clean pan and screen.
3. Unfasten and remove valve body.

Installation

1. Position valve body to case, making sure that selector and downshift levers are engaged, then install and torque attaching bolts to specifications.
2. Using a new pan gasket, secure pan to case and torque bolts to specifications.
3. Lower car and fill transmission to the correct level with specified fluid.

INTERMEDIATE SERVO

Removal, Exc. Continental

1. Raise car and remove engine rear support-to-extension housing bolts.
2. Raise transmission high enough to relieve weight from support.
3. Remove support (1 bolt).
4. Lower transmission.
5. Place drain pan beneath servo.
6. Remove servo cover-to-case bolts.

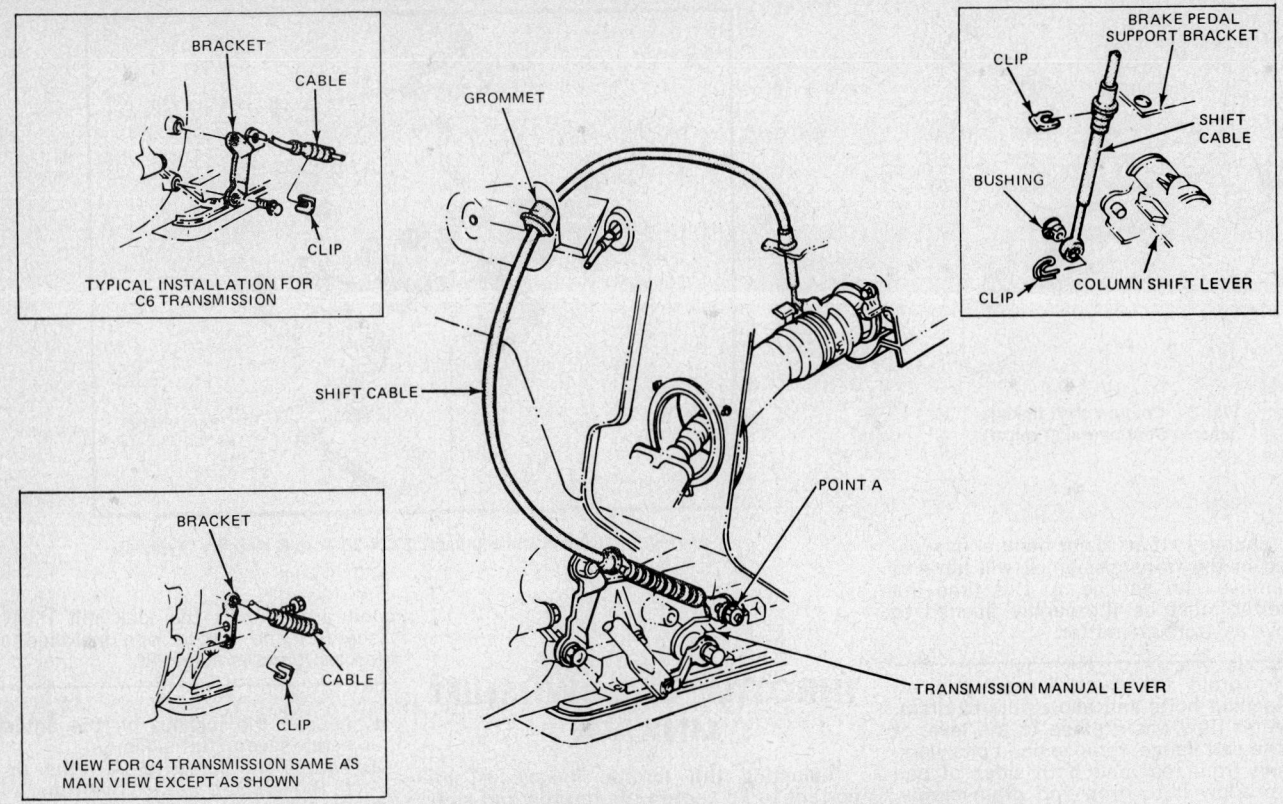

Fig. 4   Column shift linkage. 1974-76 Mark IV, Montego, Torino, 1974-78 Thunderbird, 1974-76 Elite, 1974-78 Cougar & 1977-78 LTD II & Mark V (Typical)

7. Loosen band adjusting screw locknut.
8. Remove servo cover, piston, spring and gasket from case, *screwing band adjusting screw inward as piston is removed. This insures that there will be enough tension on the band to keep the struts properly engaged in the band end notches while the piston is removed.*

Removal, Continental

1. Raise vehicle and remove servo cover retaining bolts.
2. Remove manual and downshift control rod splash shield from frame side rail and reinforcement plate from beneath transmission oil pan.
3. Loosen band adjusting screw locknut.
4. Remove engine rear mount to cross-member nuts and with a suitable jack, raise transmission to remove weight from crossmember.
5. Remove engine rear support to extension housing bolts, then the support.
6. Remove servo cover, piston, spring and gasket from case, turning adjusting screw inward as piston is removed. This places enough tension on the band to keep struts properly engaged in band end notches as piston is withdrawn.

Replacing Seal, Fig. 10

1. Apply air pressure to port in servo cover to remove piston and stem.
2. Remove seals from piston.

NOTE: On Continental Mark IV and all 1975-78 units, replace complete piston and rod assembly if piston or piston sealing lips are damaged.

3. Remove seal from cover.
4. Dip new seals in transmission fluid.
5. Install seals in piston and cover.
6. Dip piston in transmission fluid and install in cover.

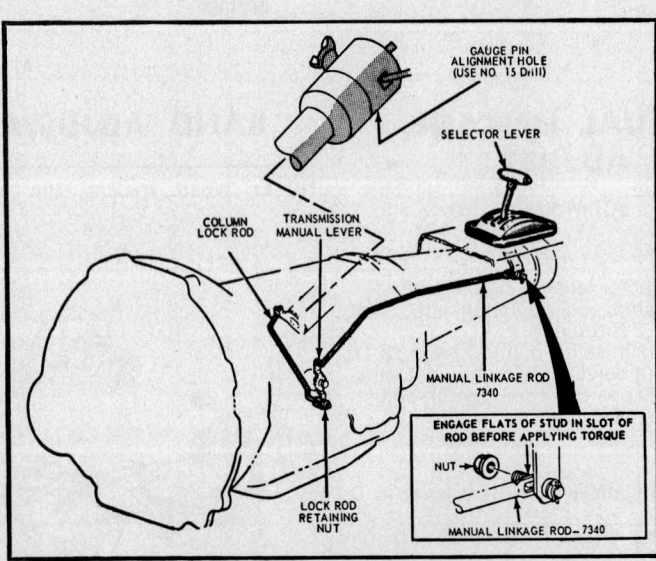

Fig. 5   Manual linkage, floor shift. Typical. Column lock rod is used on some models

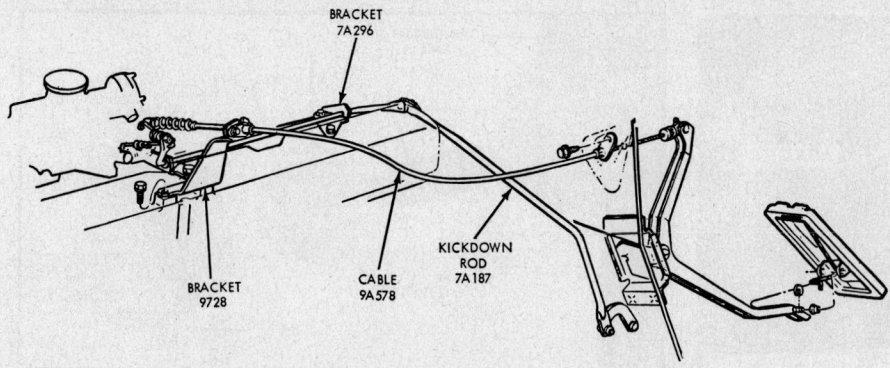

Fig. 6 Throttle & downshift linkage. Ford, Mercury, & Lincoln Continental (typical)

Installation, All

1. Position new gasket on servo cover and spring on piston stem.
2. Insert piston stem in case. Secure cover with bolts, taking care to back off band adjusting screw while tightening cover bolts. Make sure that vent tube retaining clip is in place.
3. Raise transmission high enough to install engine rear support. Secure support to extension housing. Lower transmission as required to install support-to-crossmember bolt.
4. On Continental models, secure manual and downshift rod splash shield to frame side rail.
5. Remove jack supporting transmission and adjust the band as outlined previously.
6. Lower car and replenish fluid as required.

EXTENSION HOUSING & GOVERNOR

Removal

1. Raise vehicle and disconnect parking brake cable from equalizer and on Continental models, remove the equalizer.
2. Disconnect drive shaft from rear axle flange and remove from transmission.
3. Disconnect speedometer cable from extension housing.
4. Remove engine rear support to extension housing bolts and on Continental models, remove reinforcement plate from beneath oil pan.
5. Raise transmission slightly with a suitable jack to remove weight from engine rear support.
6. Remove engine rear support to crossmember bolt and the support.

7. Lower transmission to permit access to extension housing bolts. Remove bolts and slide housing off output shaft.
8. Disconnect governor from distributor (4 bolts) and slide governor off output shaft.

Installation, Fig. 11

1. Secure governor to distributor flange.
2. Position new gasket on transmission.
3. Secure extension housing to case.
4. Raise transmission to position engine rear support on crossmember and install the support attaching bolt.
5. Lower transmission and remove jack. Install engine rear support to extension housing bolts and on Continental models, oil pan reinforcement plate.
6. Install speedometer cable.
7. On Continental models, install parking brake cable equalizer and on all models, connect parking brake cable to equalizer. Adjust parking brake.
8. Install drive shaft.
9. Correct transmission fluid level.

TRANSMISSION, REPLACE

NOTE: On models with the neutral safety switch wire harness connected at the dash panel, disconnect the harness before raising the vehicle.

1. Raise vehicle and drain transmission and converter.

   NOTE: On Continental models, disconnect idler arm from frame side rail.

2. Remove drive shaft and starter.
3. Remove four converter to flywheel attaching bolts.
4. Disconnect parking brake front cable from equalizer.
5. Disconnect speedometer cable and transmission linkage.

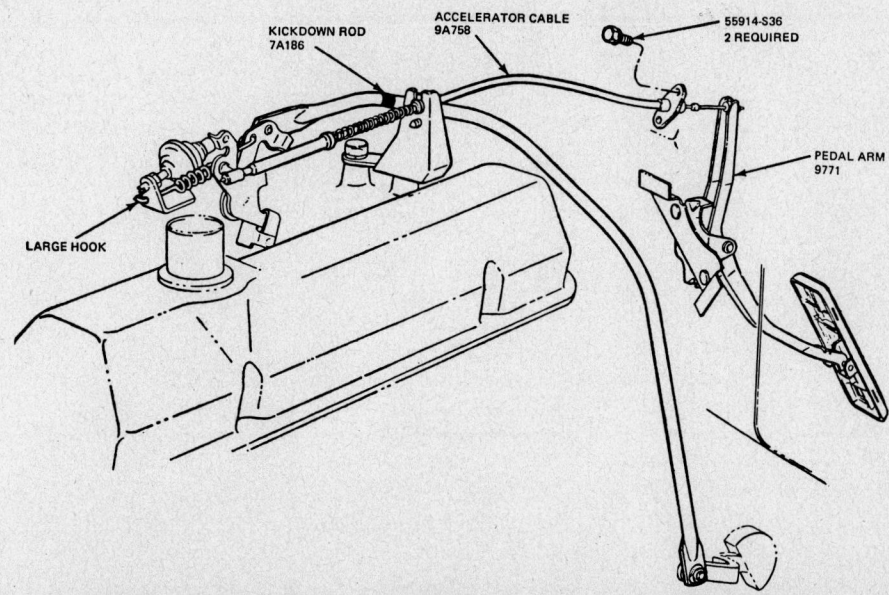

Fig. 7 Throttle & downshift linkage. Mark IV, V & 1974-76 Thunderbird (typical)

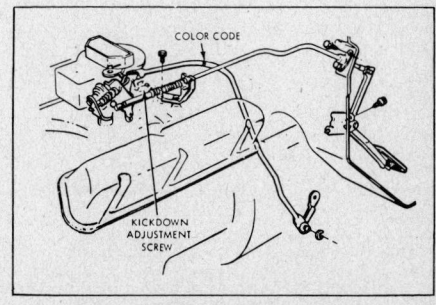

Fig. 8 Throttle & downshift linkage. 1974-76 Montego, Torino, 1974-76 Elite, 1974-77 Cougar & 1977 LTD II & Thunderbird

Fig. 9   Band adjustment

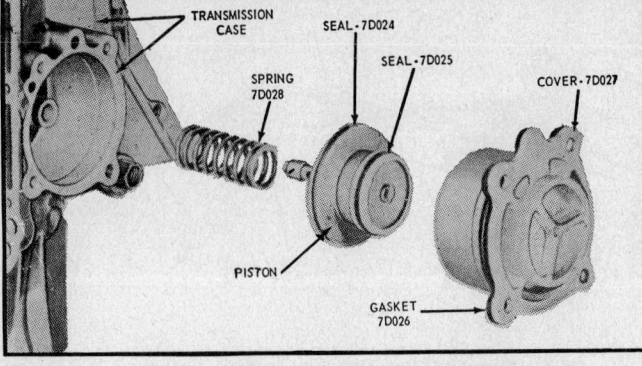

Fig. 10   Intermediate servo disassembled

6. Disconnect TRS switch wire, if equipped.

7. On 1974-78 Continental, remove lower shift rod bellcrank and pry upper shift rod bellcrank from converter housing and allow bellcrank to hang free.

8. Where necessary, disconnect muffler inlet pipes from exhaust manifold.

9. Support the transmission with a suitable jack, remove parking brake rear cables from the equalizer and remove the crossmember.

10. Lower transmission and remove oil cooler lines, vacuum line and transmission oil filler tube.

11. Secure the transmission to the jack with the chain, remove the converter housing to cylinder block bolts and carefully move the transmission away from the engine, at the same time lowering it to clear the underside of the vehicle.

12. Reverse procedure to install.

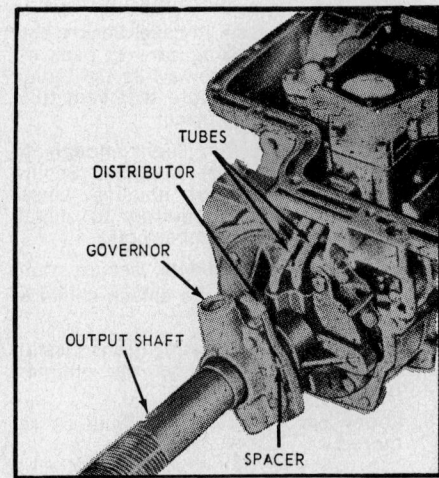

Fig. 11   Governor installed

CW & FMX DUAL RANGE AUTOMATIC

TRANSMISSION IDENTIFICATION

The identification tag on 1974–78 FMX units is on the lower right hand extension housing-to-case bolt. On CW units, the identification tag is attached to the transmission case.

CW Transmissions

FORD MODELS

YEAR	ENGINE MODEL	TRANS. MODEL
1974	8-400(2)(4)	PHE-A1

MERCURY MODELS

YEAR	ENGINE MODEL	TRANS. MODEL
1974	8-400(2)(4)	PHE-A1

TORINO & MONTEGO MODELS

YEAR	ENGINE MODEL	TRANS. MODEL
1974	V8-302	PHA-J3
	V8-351(2)	PHB-Z5
1975	8-351(3)	PHB-Z
	8-351(5)	PHB-AJ
	8-351(5)	PHB-AP
	8-400(6)	PHB-AL
	8-400(1)	PHB-AM
1976	8-351M(1)(5)	PHB-AP1
	8-351M(5)(6)	PHB-AT
	8-351W(3)(6)	PHB-Z7
	8-400(6)	PHB-AL1

FMX Transmissions

FORD MODELS

YEAR	ENGINE MODEL	TRANS. MODEL
1974	V8-351	PHB-AA1
	V8-351	PHB-L8
	V8-400	PHB-AC1
1975	8-351M(5)	PHB-AN
	8-400(6)	PHB-AC2
	8-400(1)	PHB-AK
1976	8-351M(5)	PHB-AR
	8-351M(5)(6)	PHB-AR1
	8-400	PHB-AC3
1977	8-351M(5)	PHB-AW
	8-400	PHB-AW
	8-400	PHB-AC4
1978	8-351M	PHB-BB
	8-400	PHB-BC, 1

LTD II MODELS

YEAR	ENGINE MODEL	TRANS. MODEL
1977	8-351W(3)	PHB-Z8
	8-351M(5)	PHB-AT1
	8-351M(5)	PHB-AY
	8-351M(5)	PHB-AL2
	8-400	PHB-AL2
1978	8-351W	PHB-Z9
	8-351M	PHB-AT2
	8-400	PHB-BD, BE

MERCURY MODELS

YEAR	ENGINE MODEL	TRANS. MODEL
1974	V8-351	PHB-AA1
	V8-400	PHB-AC1
1975	8-400(6)	PHB-AC2
	8-400(1)	PHB-AK
1976	8-351M(5)	PHB-AR
	8-351M(5)(6)	PHB-AR1
	8-400	PHB-AC3
1977	8-351M(5)	PHB-AW
	8-400	PHB-AW
	8-400	PHB-AC4
1978	8-351M	PHB-BB
	8-400	PHB-BC, 1

COUGAR MODELS

YEAR	ENGINE MODEL	TRANS. MODEL
1974	V8-351(2)	PHB-Z5
1975	8-351(5)	PHB-AP
	8-351(5)	PHB-AJ
	8-400(6)	PHB-AL
	8-400(1)	PHB-AM
1976	8-351M(1)	PHB-AP1
	8-351M(6)	PHB-AT
1977	8-351W(3)	PHB-Z8
	8-351M(5)	PHB-AT1
	8-351M(5)	PHB-AY
	8-351M(5)	PHB-AL2
	8-400	PHB-AL2
1978	8-351W	PHB-Z9
	8-351M	PHB-AT2
	8-400	PHB-BD, BE

THUNDERBIRD MODELS

YEAR	ENGINE MODEL	TRANS. MODEL
1977	8-351W(3)	PHB-Z8
	8-351M(5)	PHB-AT1
	8-351M(5)	PHB-AY
	8-351M(5)	PHB-AL2
	8-400	PHB-AL2
1978	8-351W	PHB-Z9
	8-351M	PHB-AT2
	8-400	PHB-BD, BE

(1)—California.
(2)—With 2 barrel carburetor.
(3)—Windsor engine.
(4)—Ford & Mercury sedans with 2.75 rear axle ratio only.
(5)—Modified engine.
(6)—Exc. California.

DESCRIPTION

Operation

This transmission, Fig. 1, features a drive range that provides for fully automatic upshifts and downshifts, and manually selected low and second gears. The six selector lever positions provided are P (park), R (reverse), N (neutral), D (automatic drive range), 2 (second gear hold) and 1 (low gear hold).

D is a fully automatic range providing for a first gear start with automatic upshifts to second and high gear occurring at appropriate intervals.

Second gear (2) is a manually selected second gear hold. When the selector lever is moved to 2, the transmission will engage and remain in second gear, regardless of throttle opening or road speed.

Low gear (1) is a manually selected first gear hold. When the selector lever is moved to this position the transmission will remain in first gear. To provide engine braking, moving the lever to this position will cause the transmission to downshift from 2nd when the car speed reaches about 22 to 39 mph depending on axle ratio and tire size.

D—Drive

The normal automatic driving range is indicated by D. In this range the car starts off in first gear and gives the best combination of automatic gear shifts to provide for economy and full power starts. As the accelerator is depressed and the

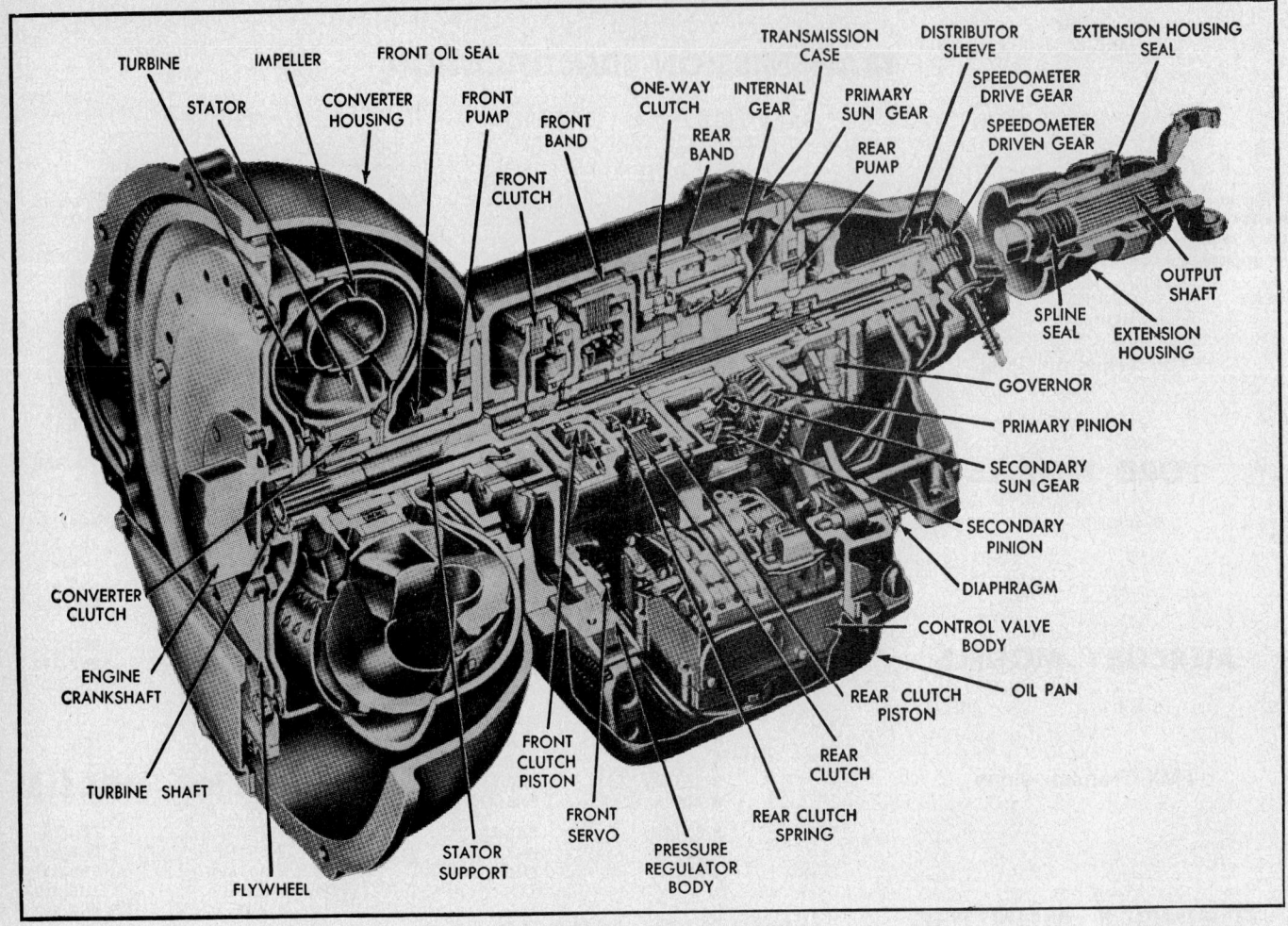

Fig. 1   Cruiseomatic and Mercomatic three speed dual range unit with cast iron case

car picks up speed, automatic shifts to second and high gears will occur. The transmission will automatically downshift as speed decreases. Forced downshifts in D are made by pressing the accelerator pedal all the way to the floor.

2—Second Gear Hold

When the car is started and the shift lever is moved to 2, the car will start off and remain in second gear, regardless of throttle opening or road speed. This range is especially useful for starting the car on icy pavements or other slippery surfaces. Similarly, when engine braking is required and the shift lever is moved from D to 2, the transmission will engage and remain in second gear.

Selector lever position 2 is not a cruising range in the usual sense of the term. While the transmission is capable of limited cruising in second gear, maximum fuel economy and best all-around performance are realized in D range.

1—Low Gear Hold

This range is identical in operation to manual low range except that when the shift lever is moved to 1 to provide engine braking, the automatic shift from second

to low gear will occur between 22 and 39 mph (exact shift point will vary with axle ratio and tire size).

TROUBLE SHOOTING GUIDE

Rough Initial Engagement

1. Idle speed.
2. Vacuum unit or tubes.
3. Front band.
4. Check control pressure.
5. Pressure regulator.
6. Valve body.

Shift Points High, Low or Erratic

1. Fluid level.
2. Vacuum unit or tubes.
3. Manual linkage.
4. Governor.
5. Check control pressure.
6. Valve body.
7. Downshift linkage.

Rough 2-3 Shift

1. Manual linkage.
2. Front band.
3. Vacuum unit or tubes.
4. Pressure regulator.
5. Valve body.
6. Front servo.

Engine Overspeeds, 2-3 Shift

1. Vacuum unit or tubes.
2. Front band.
3. Valve body.
4. Pressure regulator.

No 1-2 or 2-3 Shifts

1. Governor.
2. Valve body.
3. Manual linkage.
4. Rear clutch.
5. Front band.
6. Front servo.
7. Leakage in hydraulic system.
8. Pressure regulator.

No Forced Downshifts

1. Downshift linkage.
2. Check control pressure.
3. Valve body.

Rough 3-2 or 3-1 Shifts

1. Engine idle speed.
2. Vacuum unit or tubes.
3. Valve body.

Slips or Chatters in 2nd

1. Fluid level.
2. Vacuum unit or tubes.
3. Front band.
4. Check control pressure.
5. Pressure regulator.
6. Valve body.
7. Front servo.
8. Front clutch.
9. Leakage in hydraulic system.

Slips or Chatters in 1st

1. Fluid level.
2. Vacuum unit or tubes.
3. Check control pressure.
4. Pressure regulator.
5. Valve body.
6. Front clutch.
7. Leakage in hydraulic system.
8. Fluid distributor sleeve in output shaft.
9. Planetary one-way clutch.

Slips or Chatters in Reverse

1. Fluid level.
2. Rear band.
3. Check control pressure.
4. Pressure regulator.
5. Valve body.
6. Rear servo.
7. Rear clutch.
8. Vacuum unit or tubes.
9. Leakage in hydraulic system.
10. Fluid distributor sleeve in output shaft.

No Drive in D or D2

1. Valve body.
2. Make air pressure check.
3. Manual linkage.
4. Front clutch.
5. Leak in hydraulic system.
6. Fluid distributor sleeve in output shaft.

No Drive in D1

1. Manual linkage.
2. Valve body.
3. Planetary one-way clutch.

No Drive in L

1. Manual linkage.
2. Front clutch.
3. Valve body.
4. Make air pressure check.
5. Leak in hydraulic system.
6. Fluid distributor sleeve in output shaft.

No Drive in R

1. Rear band.
2. Rear servo.
3. Valve body.
4. Make air pressure check.
5. Rear clutch.
6. Leak in hydraulic system.
7. Fluid distributor sleeve in output shaft.

No Drive in Any Range

1. Fluid level.
2. Manual linkage.
3. Check control pressure.
4. Pressure regulator.
5. Valve body.
6. Make air pressure check.
7. Leak in hydraulic system.

Lockup in D or D1

1. Manual linkage.
2. Rear servo.
3. Front servo.
4. Rear clutch.
5. Parking linkage.
6. Leak in hydraulic system.

Lockup in D2

1. Manual linkage.
2. Rear band.
3. Rear servo.
4. Rear clutch.
5. Parking linkage.
6. Leak in hydraulic system.
7. Planetary one-way clutch.

Lockup in R

1. Front band.
2. Front servo.
3. Front clutch.
4. Parking linkage.
5. Leak in hydraulic system.

Lockup in L

1. Front band.
2. Pressure regulator.
3. Valve body.
4. Rear clutch.
5. Parking linkage.
6. Leak in hydraulic system.

Parking Lock Binds or Won't Hold

1. Manual linkage.
2. Parking linkage.

Transmission Overheats

1. Oil cooler and connections.
2. Pressure regulator.
3. Converter one-way clutch.

Engine Runaway on Forced Downshift

1. Front band.
2. Pressure regulator.
3. Valve body.

4. Front servo.
5. Vacuum unit or tubes.
6. Leak in hydraulic system.

Maximum Speed Below Normal, Acceleration Poor

1. Converter one-way clutch.

No 3-1 Downshift

1. Engine idle speed.
2. Vacuum unit or tubes.
3. Valve body.

Noise in Neutral

1. Pressure regulator.
2. Front clutch.
3. Front pump.

Noise in 1-2-3 or R

1. Pressure regulator.
2. Planetary assembly.
3. Front clutch.
4. Rear clutch.
5. Front pump.

Noise in Reverse

1. Pressure regulator.
2. Front pump.

Noise on Coast in Neutral

1. Rear pump.

MAINTENANCE

NOTE: Despite apparent similarities, the CW and FMX transmissions must be serviced as individual units. Although some CW parts are interchangeable with FMX parts, the majority of parts are not interchangeable.

Adding Fluid

The fluid level in the transmission should be checked at 1000-mile intervals Make sure that the car is standing level, and firmly apply the parking brake.

Run the engine at normal idle speed. If the transmission fluid is cold, run the engine at fast idle speed until the fluid reaches normal operating temperature. When the fluid is warm, slow the engine down to normal idle speed, shift the transmission through all ranges and then place the lever at P.

Clean all dirt from the transmission fluid dipstick cap before removing the dipstick from the filler tube. Pull the dipstick out of the tube, wipe it clean and push it all the way back into the tube.

Pull the dipstick out again and check the fluid level. If necessary, add enough Type F Automatic Transmission Fluid to the transmission to raise the fluid level to the F (full mark) on the dipstick.

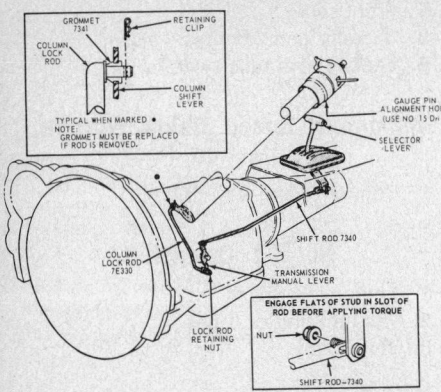

Fig. 2 Manual linkage. Floor shift (typical)

MANUAL LINKAGE, ADJUST

Cougar, Elite/Torino, Ford, LTD II Mercury, Montego & 1977-78 Thunderbird

Floor Shift, Fig. 2

1. Place selector lever in D.
2. Raise vehicle and loosen manual shift rod retaining nut.

NOTE: On 1977-78 Cougar and LTD II, the shift rod retaining nut is located at the transmission end of the shift rod.

3. Move transmission manual lever to D position.
4. Torque nut to 10-20 ft-lbs.

Column Shift

1. Place selector lever in D position.
2. Raise vehicle and loosen shift rod adjusting nut at point A, Figs. 3 and 3A. On models with shift cable, remove nut at point A and remove cable from transmission manual lever stud, Fig. 4.
3. Shift transmission manual lever into drive position, second detent from the full counter clockwise position.
4. On models equipped with shift cable, place cable end on transmission manual lever stud. Align flats on stud with flats on cable, then install adjustment nut.
5. On all models, tighten adjustment at point A. Ensure selector lever against D stop when tightening adjustment nut.
6. Check transmission for proper operation in all selector lever detent positions.

THROTTLE LINKAGE, ADJUST

All Models, Figs. 5 & 6

1. Disconnect downshift lever return

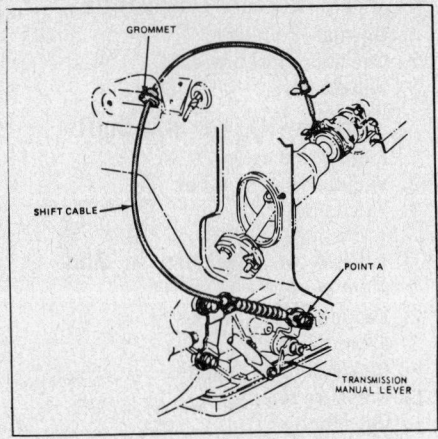

Fig. 4 Manual linkage. 1974-76, Torino & Montego; 1974-78 Cougar & Elite; 1977-78 LTD II & Thunderbird column shift.

spring and hold throttle lever in wide open position.
2. Hold downshift rod against the through detent stop.
3. Adjust downshift screw to provide .01 to .08 inch clearance between screw
4. Connect downshift lever return spring. and throttle arm.

BAND ADJUSTMENTS

NOTE: CW series transmissions incorporate a self-adjusting front band. It is adjusted at time of assembly and requires no further adjustment until unit is overhauled. The rear band should be adjusted at the first 12,000 miles. No further adjustment is required until unit is overhauled.

Front Band

FMX Units

1. Drain fluid from transmission, remove and clean oil pan and screen.
2. Loosen front servo adjusting screw locknut.
3. Pull back on actuating rod and insert a ¼ inch spacer between adjusting screw and servo piston stem, Fig. 7.

Changing Fluid

NOTE: Normal maintenance and lubrication does not require periodic transmission fluid changes. However, a major transmission repair will require that the fluid be drained and be replaced with type F "lifetime" fluid.

1. Raise and support vehicle on hoist, then place a drain pan under transmission.
2. Loosen pan bolts and drain fluid until it has reached level of pan flange, then remove bolts working from rear and both sides of pan allowing to drop and drain slowly.
3. When fluid has completely drained, remove and thoroughly clean pan and filter.
4. Install filter, then using a new gasket install oil pan and add three quarts of fluid.
5. With transmission at operating temperature and parking brake applied, move shift lever through each range, allowing time for transmission to engage, then return shift lever to Park.
6. Check fluid level and add fluid as necessary to bring level between ADD and FULL mark.

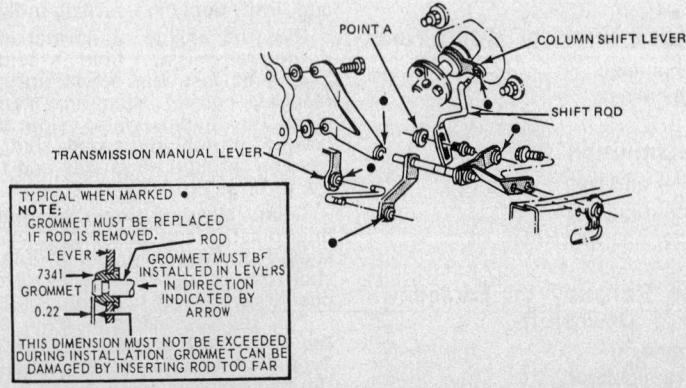

Fig. 3 Manual linkage. 1974-75 Ford & Mercury, column shift (Typical)

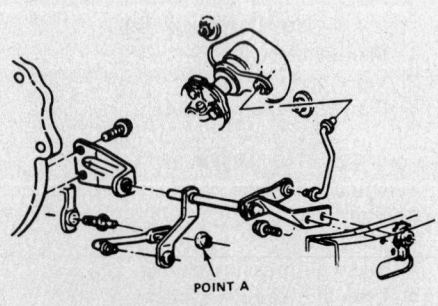

Fig. 3A Manual linkage (Typical). 1976-78 Ford & Mercury column shift

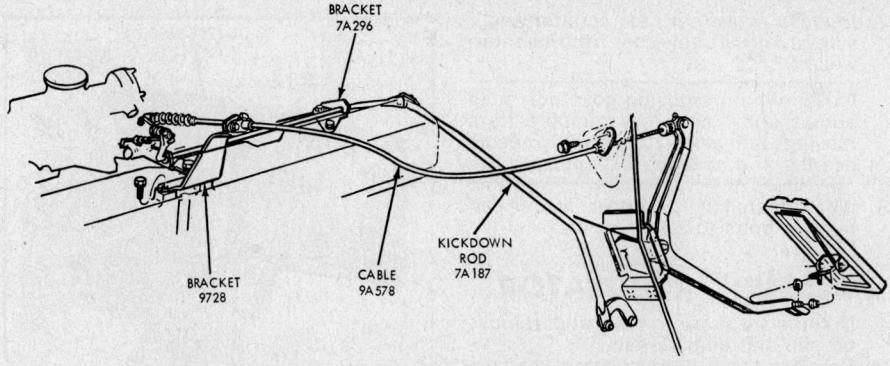

Fig. 5   Throttle & downshift linkage. Ford & Mercury (typical)

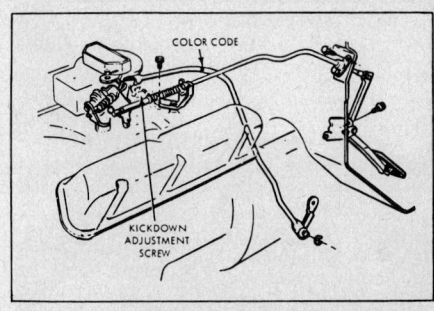

Fig. 6   Throttle & downshift linkage. 1974-76
Elite, Montego, Torino; 1974-78 Cougar; 1977-78
LTD II & Thunderbird

4. Tighten adjusting screw to 10 inch-lbs torque. Remove spacer and tighten adjusting screw an additional ¾ turn. Hold adjusting screw stationary and tighten locknut securely.
5. Install oil pan with new gasket and add fluid to transmission.

CW Units
1. Install a .250 inch thick spacer between adjusting screw and servo piston stem, Fig. 8.
2. Using an inch pound torque wrench and an 8 point socket torque adjusting screw to 10 in. lbs. and remove spacer.

NOTE: Adjusting screw has a left hand thread and is self adjusting. After initial adjustment, no further adjustment should be required.

3. Space one way clutch spring .125-.188 inch from lever, otherwise proper automatic adjustments cannot be made.

Rear Band

NOTE: There is no access hole in the floor pan to adjust the rear band. With the use of special tools this band can be adjusted externally as follows, Figs. 9, 10:
1. Loosen rear band adjusting screw locknut. A special tool is required to gain access in limited space.
2. Tighten adjusting screw until special tool clicks. It is preset to overrun when torque reaches 10 ft. lbs.

NOTE: If screw is found to be tighter than 10 ft. lbs., loosen screw and tighten until wrench clicks and breaks.

3. Back off adjusting screw 1½ turns on FMX units and 1¼ turns on CW units.

NOTE: Severe damage may result if adjusting screw is not backed off the exact amount of turns indicated.

4. Hold adjusting screw stationary and tighten locknut securely.

CONTROL VALVE BODY
1. Support vehicle on hoist, then drain transmission fluid and remove pan.

NOTE: If fluid is to be reused, filter it through a 100-mesh screen before replacing it in transmission.

2. Disconnect hoses from vacuum diaphragm unit, then using Snap-On tool S8696-A, remove vacuum diaphragm and push rod.
3. Remove fluid screen retaining clip and small compensator pressure tube.
4. Remove main pressure oil tube, by gently prying up end that connects to main control valve, then remove other end of tube from pressure regulator.

NOTE: Tube must be removed in this manner. Failure to do so, could kink or bend tube causing excessive internal transmission leakage.

5. Loosen front servo bolts three turns, then remove the three control valve body screws, and lower valve body while pulling it off front servo tubes, being careful not to damage valve body or tubes.
6. Before installing control valve, check for bent manual valve by rolling it on a flat surface.

NOTE: Before torquing control valve

attaching bolts, move valve toward center of case until clearance is less than .050 inch between manual valve and actuating pin.

7. After installing control valve, torque control valve attaching bolts to 8-10 ft. lbs., front servo bolts to 30-35 ft. lbs. and vacuum diaphragm to 15-23 ft. lbs.
8. After completing assembly, adjust front and rear bands. If valve body was replaced, adjust control linkage.

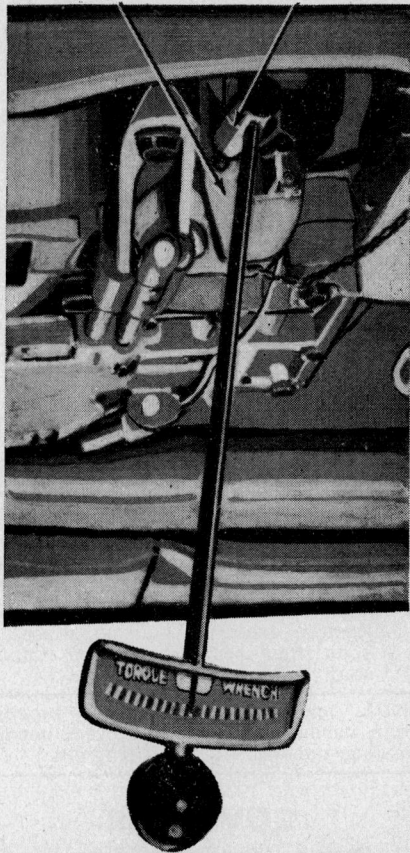

Fig. 8   Adjusting front servo band. CW

**TOOL-7225-C-13B
1/4 INCH SPACER**

FRONT SERVO

LOCK NUT

TOOL-7225-C

**ADJUSTING
SCREW**

ACTUATING LEVER

Fig. 7   Front band adjustment. Ford, Mercury and Thunderbird

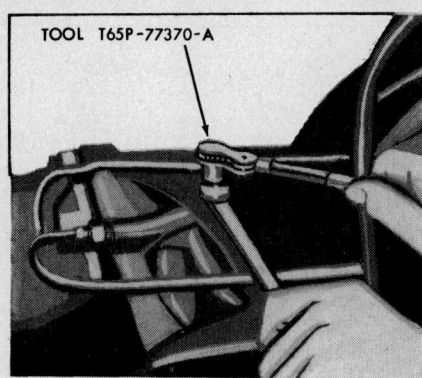

**Fig. 9   Rear band adjustment.
1974-78 Ford & Mercury full size**

FRONT & REAR SERVOS

1. Drain transmission fluid and remove oil pan and screen.
2. Remove vacuum diaphragm, then loosen control valve body attaching bolts.
3. Remove retaining bolts from servo, then hold actuating strut and remove servo.
4. After installation, if front servo was serviced, torque front servo attaching bolts to 30-35 ft. lbs. and adjust front band. If rear servo was serviced, torque rear servo attaching bolts to 40-45 ft. lbs., adjust rear bands and check for less than .050 inch clearance between manual lever actuating pin and manual lever as outlined under "Control Valve."

EXTENSION HOUSING BUSHING & REAR SEAL

Proper removal and installation of extension housing bushing and rear seal will necessitate the use of five specialty tools. When removing bushing and rear seal, the vehicle will have to be raised and driveshaft removed.

EXTENSION HOUSING

1. Drain transmission fluid and remove driveshaft.
2. Disconnect speedometer cable from housing and remove engine rear supports to crossmember nuts.
3. Raise transmission slightly with suitable jack, then remove crossmember to side rail bolts and position the crossmember out of way.
4. Remove the two engine rear support-to-extension housing bolts and remove support.
5. Remove extension housing attaching bolts, then slide housing off output shaft and remove gasket.

NOTE: Hold output shaft and rear support from moving rearward to prevent needle bearing and race from dropping out.

GOVERNOR

1. Remove extension housing as outlined previously.

2. Remove governor to counterweight screws and lift governor from counterweight.

NOTE: When removing governor, hold output shaft and rear support from moving rearward to prevent needle bearing and race from dropping out.

3. When installing governor torque attaching bolts to 50-60 in. lbs.

PRESSURE REGULATOR

1. Drain transmission fluid and remove oil pan and fluid screen.
2. Remove small compensator pressure tube from control valve body and pressure regulator.
3. Remove main pressure oil tube by gently prying up end that connects to main control valve assembly, then remove other end of tube from pressure regulator.

NOTE: Tube must be removed in this manner. Failure to do so, could kink or bend tube, causing excessive internal transmission leakage.

4. Remove pressure regulator spring retainer, springs and spacer.

NOTE: Maintain pressure on retainer to prevent springs from falling out.

5. Remove regulator attaching bolts and remove regulator.
6. After installing regulator, torque attaching bolts to 17-22 ft. lbs.

PARKING PAWL

1. Drain transmission fluid and remove driveshaft.
2. Support rear of transmission and remove crossmember, then remove the two engine rear support-to-extension housing bolts and remove support.
3. Disconnect speedometer cable and remove oil pan and screen.
4. Loosen rear band adjusting screw locknut and tighten adjusting screw to 24 in. lbs.

NOTE: This will hold planetary carrier and clutch assemblies in place during parking pawl removal.

5. Remove small compensator pressure tube from pressure regulator and control valve body.
6. Remove main pressure oil tube by gently prying up end that connects to main valve body assembly, then remove other end of tube from pressure regulator.

NOTE: Tube must be removed in this manner. Failure to do so could kink or bend tube, causing excessive internal transmission leakage.

7. Remove vacuum diaphragm and loosen front servo attaching bolts, then remove valve body attaching bolts and lower valve body while pulling it off servo tubes, being careful not to damage valve body or tubes.
8. Remove rear servo bolts and remove servo and struts.
9. Remove extension housing and output shaft rear support.
10. Using a magnet, remove parking pawl

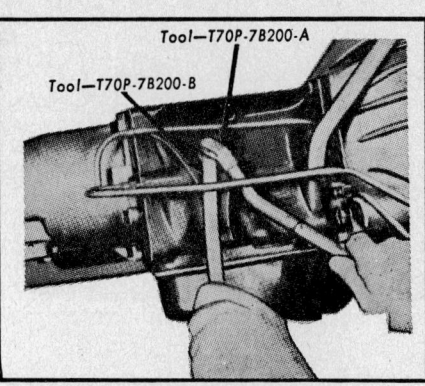

**Fig. 10   Rear band adjustment.
1974-78 Cougar; 1974-76 Elite, Montego & Torino; 1977-78 LTD II & Thunderbird**

pin from case, then working from inside of case, drive on shoulder of toggle lever pin with a small punch to move retaining plug part way out of case. Using a pair of pliers, remove plug.
11. Slide toggle lever toward front of case. Cock lever to one side to apply pressure on pin, then move toggle to rear of case to move pin outward.
12. Remove pawl and toggle lever as an assembly.
13. During assembly refer to "Control Valve Body" and "Front & Rear Servos" for installation. After assembly, adjust front and rear bands as outlined previously.

TRANSMISSION, REPLACE

NOTE: On some models, it is necessary to remove the two upper converter housing to engine bolts before raising vehicle.

1. Raise vehicle and place on jack stands, then drain transmission oil pan.
2. Remove converter access cover and remove converter drain plug.
3. Remove converter to flywheel attaching nuts, reinstall converter drain plugs and converter housing access cover to hold converter in place when transmission is removed.
4. Remove starter and propeller shaft.
5. Where necessary, disconnect exhaust pipes from manifold.
6. Disconnect oil cooler lines, speedometer cable, vacuum hose and manual downshift linkage.
7. Disconnect TRS switch wire, if equipped.
8. Support transmission with suitable jack and remove crossmember.

NOTE: On some models, it is necessary to remove the engine rear support to transmission bolts before crossmember removal.

9. Lower transmission and remove filler tube and dipstick.
10. Remove converter housing-to-engine bolts. Move transmission and jack rearward and lower away from vehicle.
11. Reverse procedure to install.

FORD (JATCO) AUTOMATIC

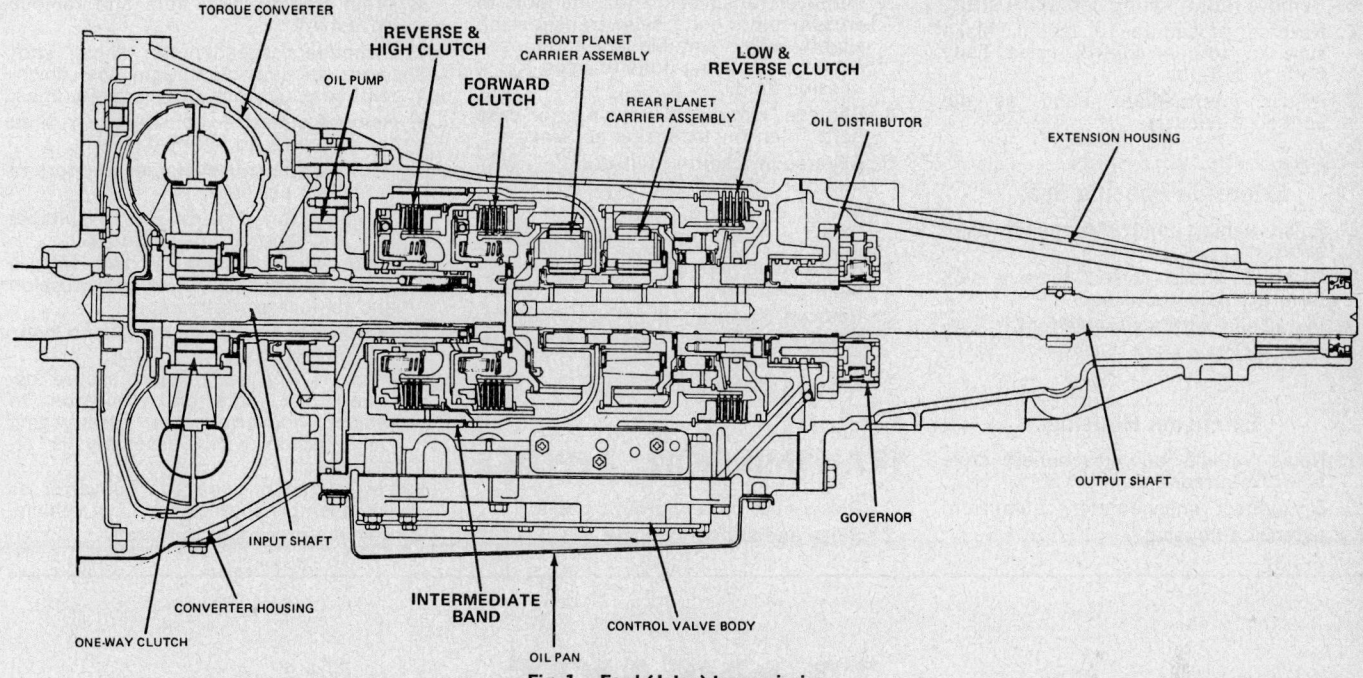

TORQUE CONVERTER

OIL PUMP

REVERSE & HIGH CLUTCH

FORWARD CLUTCH

FRONT PLANET CARRIER ASSEMBLY

REAR PLANET CARRIER ASSEMBLY

LOW & REVERSE CLUTCH

OIL DISTRIBUTOR

EXTENSION HOUSING

OUTPUT SHAFT

GOVERNOR

CONTROL VALVE BODY

OIL PAN

INTERMEDIATE BAND

CONVERTER HOUSING

INPUT SHAFT

ONE-WAY CLUTCH

Fig. 1   Ford (Jatco) transmission

TRANSMISSION IDENTIFICATION

Granada & Monarch

1977-78 6-250 . . . . PLA

DESCRIPTION

The Jatco transmission, Fig. 1, is a three speed unit capable of providing automatic upshifts and downshifts through the three forward gear ranges, also manual selection of first and second gears. This transmission consists of a torque converter, planetary gear train, two multiple disc clutches, one multiple disc brake, a one-way clutch and a hydraulic control system.

MAINTENANCE

NOTE: Use only fluid that meets Ford Motor Company specification ESP-M2C138-CJ. Use of a fluid other than specified may result in transmission malfunction or failure.

Checking Oil Level

1. With transmission at operating temperature, park vehicle on level surface.
2. Run engine at idle speed with service and parking brakes applied and move selector lever through all ranges and return to Park position.
3. With engine idling, remove dipstick and check fluid level. Fluid level should be between Add and Full marks.
4. Add specified fluid to bring fluid to proper level.

Drain & Refill

NOTE: Normal maintenance and lubrication requirements do not necessitate periodic fluid changes.

When filling a dry transmission and converter, add five quarts of specified fluid. Start engine, move selector lever through all ranges and return to Park position. Check fluid level and add fluid to bring level to Full mark.

When a partial drain and refill is required due to a minor repair, proceed as follows:

1. Loosen and remove all but two oil pan bolts and drop one edge of the pan to drain oil.
2. Remove and clean oil pan and screen.
3. Place a new gasket on pan and install pan and screen.
4. Add three quarts of specified fluid to transmission.
5. Operate engine at idle speed for approximately two minutes, then run at fast idle until transmission reaches operating temperature.
6. Move selector lever through all ranges and return to Park position, recheck

oil level and add fluid, if necessary, to bring level to between Add and Full marks.

INTERMEDIATE BAND, ADJUST

1. Raise and support vehicle.
2. Remove servo cover retaining bolts and cover, Fig. 2.
3. Loosen adjusting screw locknut and torque adjusting screw to 9-11 ft. lbs.
4. Back off adjusting screw two turns, then while holding adjusting screw stationary, torque adjusting screw locknut to 22-29 ft. lbs.
5. Install servo cover, gasket and bolts. Torque servo cover bolts to 5 ft. lbs.

IN VEHICLE REPAIRS
Control Valve Body

1. Raise vehicle, drain transmission and remove oil pan.
2. Remove downshift solenoid, vacuum diaphragm, vacuum diaphragm rod and O-rings.
3. Remove valve body to case attaching bolts. Hold manual valve to keep it from sliding out of the valve body, then remove valve body from the case.

NOTE: Failure to hold the manual valve while removing control assembly may result in valve damage.

4. Reverse procedure to install.

Servo

1. Raise and support vehicle.
2. Drain transmission fluid and remove oil pan.
3. Remove control valve body.
4. Remove servo cover bolts and cover.
5. Remove servo retainer to case bolts and remove retainer and servo piston as an assembly.

Stub Filler Tube

Intermediate Servo Adjusting Screw

Locknut

Line Pressure Port

ServoCover

Fig. 2   Intermediate band adjustment

6. Remove return spring and apply strut.
7. Reverse procedure to install. Make sure to torque control valve body bolts to 5 ft. lbs.
8. Adjust intermediate band as described previously.

Extension Housing Seal

1. Raise vehicle and disconnect drive shaft.
2. Using a sharp chisel, remove seal from extension housing.
3. Install seal with a suitable tool.
4. Connect drive shaft.

Extension Housing

1. Raise vehicle and disconnect drive shaft from rear axle.
2. Disconnect speedometer cable from extension housing.

3. Remove transmission rear support to crossmember bolts, raise transmission slightly with a suitable jack and loosen extension housing bolts to drain transmission fluid.
4. Remove extension housing to case bolts, then the extension housing.
5. Reverse procedure to install.

Governor

1. Remove the extension housing as outlined previously.
2. Remove governor housing to oil distributor bolts, then the governor housing from distributor.
3. Reverse procedure to install.

TRANSMISSION, REPLACE

1. Disconnect battery ground cable.
2. Raise and support vehicle.

3. Drain transmission fluid and remove driveshaft.
4. Disconnect speedometer cable, shift cable, vacuum diaphragm line, downshift solenoid wire and oil cooler lines.
5. Remove converter housing cover, then the converter to flywheel nuts.
6. Remove transmission rear support to crossmember nuts.
7. Support transmission with a suitable jack and remove crossmember.
8. Secure transmission to jack with a safety chain, then lower transmission and remove starter motor.
9. Remove transmission to engine bolts and oil filler tube.
10. Using a pry bar, exert pressure between flex plate and converter to prevent converter from disengaging transmission when assembly is removed.
11. Lower transmission and converter as an assembly and remove from vehicle.
12. Reverse procedure to install.

TRANSAXLE

A-412 Four Speed Manual Shift Unit

See Car Chapter for Linkage Adjustments and Removal Procedures

1978 DODGE OMNI & PLYMOUTH HORIZON

Description

Gear reduction, ratio selection and differential functions are combined into one unit, Fig. 1. The four speed transaxle uses a two piece magnesium case, one piece is the transmission housing and the other piece is the clutch and differential housing. Synchronizers are serviced as an assembly. Except for stop rings, synchronizer components should not be interchanged. Power is transmitted to the differential ring gear by means of a transfer gear on the transmission countershaft. From the ring gear, power is transmitted to the differential pinion gears by means of the differential cross shaft. Power is then directed from the pinion gears to the differential side gears, which

drive the output shafts to which the output flanges are joined.

Transmission Disassemble

1. Remove clutch input shaft.
2. Using a screwdriver, remove drive flange dust seal.
3. Remove drive flange snap ring, then using tool No. L-4443, remove drive flange, Fig. 2.
4. Using tool No. L-4445, remove drive flange oil seal.
5. Using tool No. L-4441, remove selector shaft plug, then using a plastic mallet, tap out selector shaft, Fig. 3.
6. Using tool No. L-4445, remove selector shaft oil seal.
7. Using a screwdriver, remove mainshaft bearing retainer nut rubber plugs.
8. Remove four attaching bolts and release bearing end cover.
9. Remove release bearing and sleeve.

10. Using two screwdrivers, disengage snap rings from torque shaft, Fig. 4.
11. Remove clutch torque shaft, return spring and release lever.
12. Using tool No. L-4445, remove clutch torque shaft oil seals.
13. Remove three mainshaft bearing retainer nuts. The three studs and clips will drop into the case.
14. Remove transmission case to differential and clutch housing attaching bolts.
15. Using tool No. L-4443, remove transmission case, Fig. 5. Note location of shims for reassembly.
16. Remove reverse shift fork support attaching bolts, supports and reverse shift fork.
17. Remove 4th speed gear snap ring from pinion shaft.
18. Using a suitable puller and tool No. L-4443-4, remove mainshaft bearings.

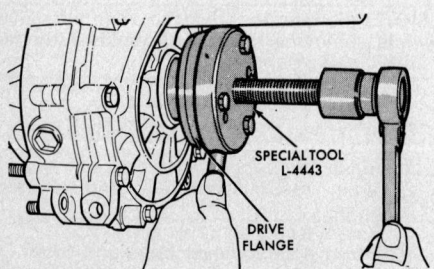

Fig. 2 Removing drive flange

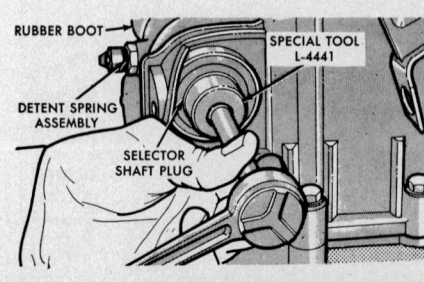

Fig. 3 Removing selector shaft plug

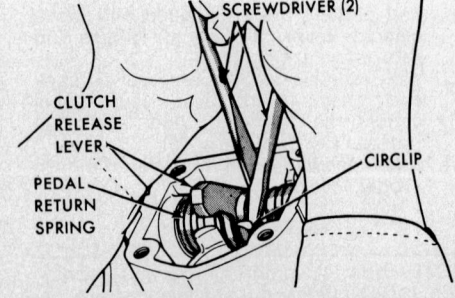

Fig. 4 Disengaging snap rings from torque shaft

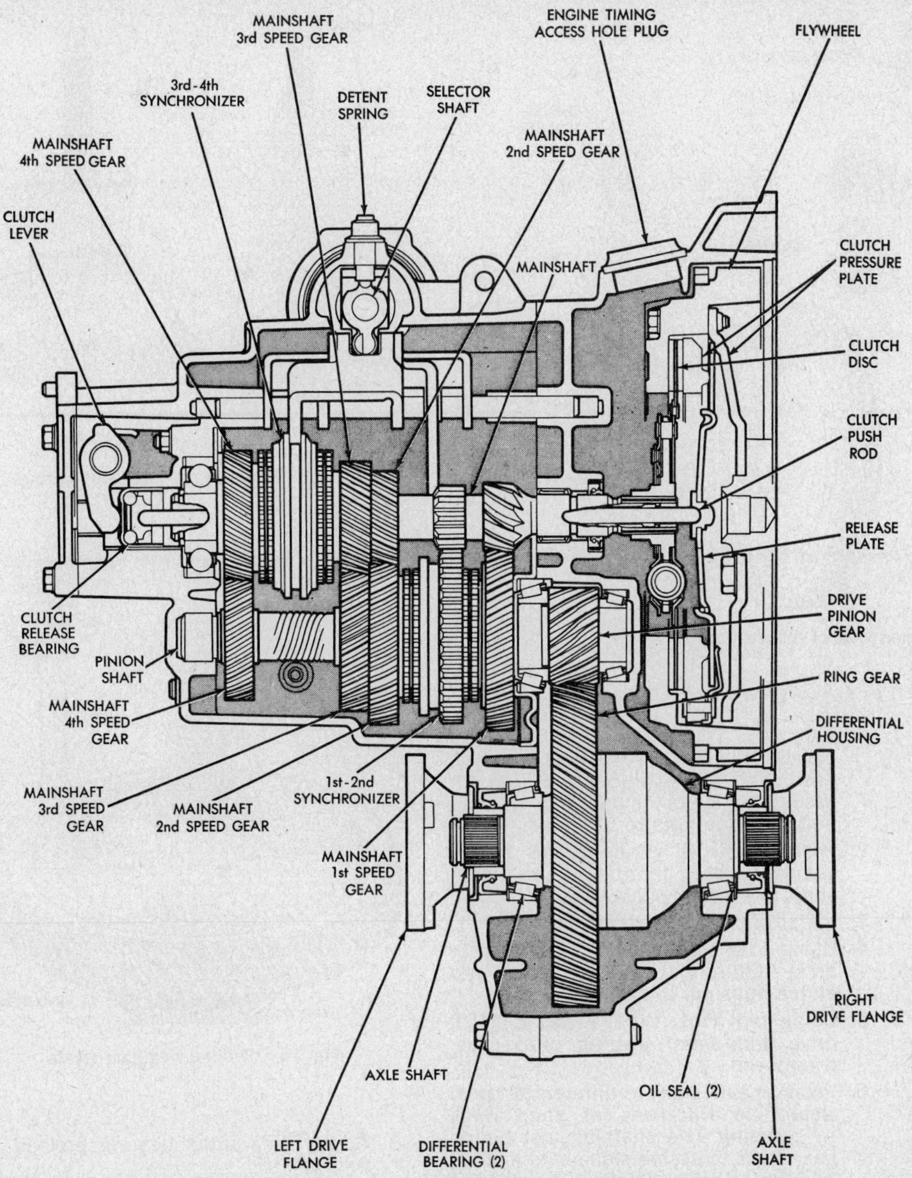

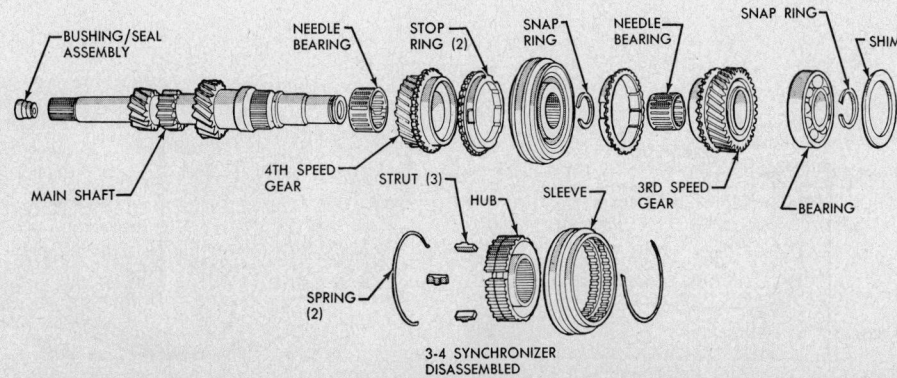

Fig. 1 Sectional view of A-412 4 speed manual shift transaxle

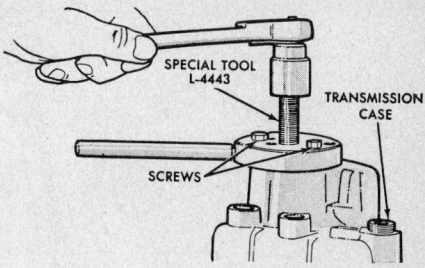

Fig. 5 Removing transmission case

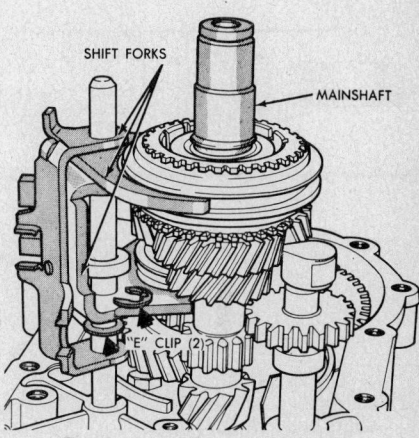

Fig. 6 Removing shift rail E-clips

19. Remove 4th speed gear and bearing from mainshaft.
20. Remove shift rail E-clips, then remove shift rail assembly, Fig. 6.
21. Remove mainshaft assembly from transmission case.
22. Referring to Fig. 7, disassemble mainshaft.
23. Using a 3/8 in. brass drift, drive out clutch push rod and bushing assembly.
24. Remove snap ring and 3rd speed gear from pinion shaft.
25. Remove 2nd speed gear and bearing from pinion shaft.
26. Using a suitable pry bar, remove reverse idler shaft, Fig. 8.
27. Using a suitable puller, remove 1st-2nd synchronizer assembly and 1st speed gear.
28. Remove pinion shaft retainer attaching bolts, then lift off pinion retainer.
29. Remove 1st gear thrust washer and lift pinion shaft from transmission case.

Fig. 7 Disassembled view of mainshaft assembly

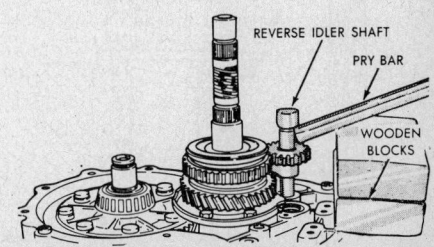

Fig. 8 Removing reverse idler gear shaft

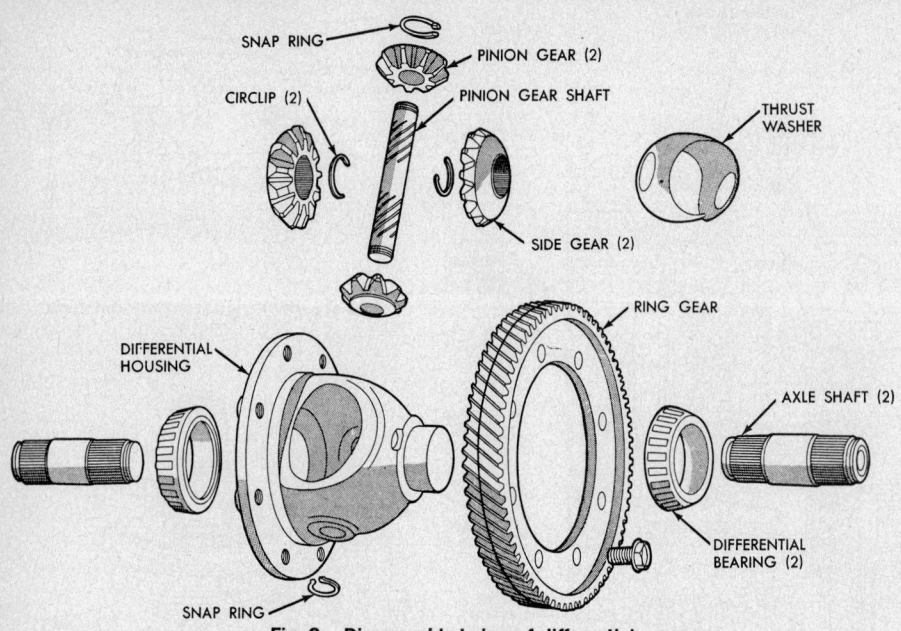

Fig. 9 Disassembled view of differential

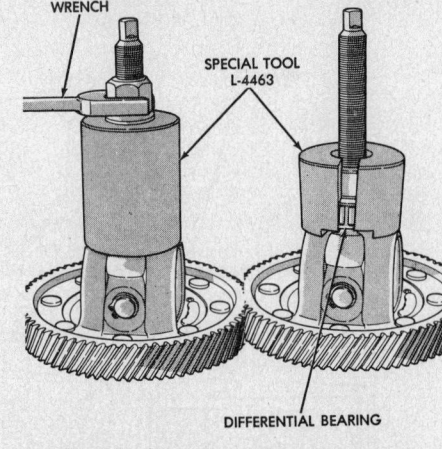

Fig. 10 Removing differential bearing

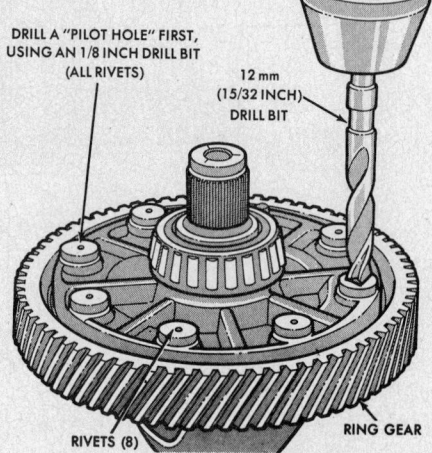

Fig. 11 Drilling ring gear rivets

Differential Disassemble

1. Using two screwdrivers, remove axle shaft snap rings, Fig. 9.
2. Using tool No. L-4463, remove differential bearings from case, if necessary, Fig. 10.
3. Using tool Nos. C-4171 and L-4449, drive differential bearing outer race out of differential housing, if necessary.
4. Remove side gears from differential case.
5. Remove pinion shaft snap rings, then drive out pinion shaft using a brass drift.
6. Remove pinion gears and thrust washers.
7. If ring gear is to be replaced, drill a pilot hole in rivet using a 1/8 in. drill, then drill out rivets using a 15/32 in. drill, Fig. 11. Using a suitable punch, drive out rivets. Use care when drilling, do not allow metal filings to come in contact with differential bearings. Clean differential housing after removing ring gear.

Differential Assemble

1. To install ring gear, if removed, special bolts, nuts and washers must be used, Fig. 12. Position ring gear on case, then install nuts, washers and bolts. Torque nuts to 51 ft. lbs.
2. Position thrust washers, and pinion gears in case, then drive in pinion shaft and install snap rings.
3. Install side gears into case.
4. Using tool Nos. C-4171 and L-4450, drive differential bearing race into clutch housing, if removed.
5. Using tool Nos. C-4171 and L-4510, drive differential bearing onto case, if removed.
6. Position axle shaft in differential case. Determine thickness of snap rings by pressing axle shaft against pinion gear shaft, pressing side gears against housing. Insert thickest snap ring possible, Fig. 13. Snap rings are available in thickness of .078 in. and .090 in.
7. If ring gear, drive pinion, transmission case, differential housing or bearings are replaced, adjust pinion shaft preload as described under Transmission Assemble.

8. Adjust differential bearing preload as follows:
   a. Install outer race of bearing opposite ring gear with shim into clutch and differential housing, Fig. 14. This shim is always .039 in. thick.
   b. Install outer race on ring gear side without shim into transmission housing.
   c. Install differential into differential housing.

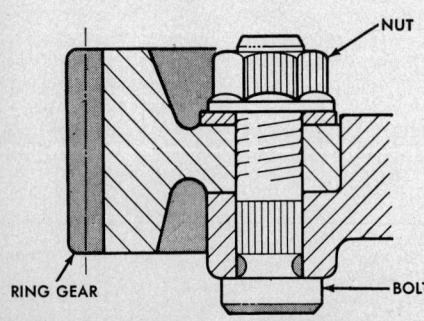

Fig. 12 Installing ring gear bolts & nuts

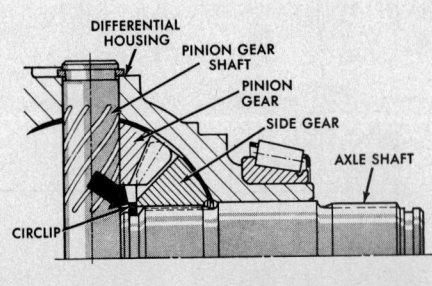

Fig. 13 Selecting snap ring of proper thickness

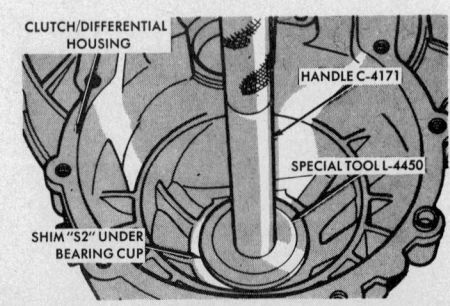

Fig. 14 Installing shim & differential bearing race

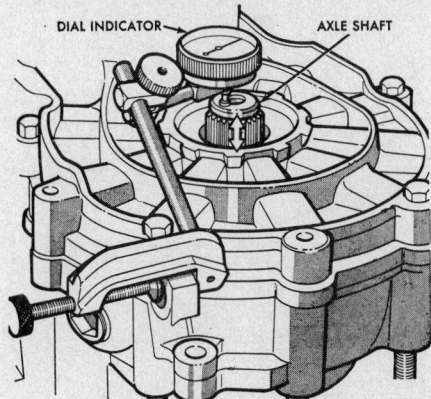

Fig. 15 Determining differential bearing preload shim thickness

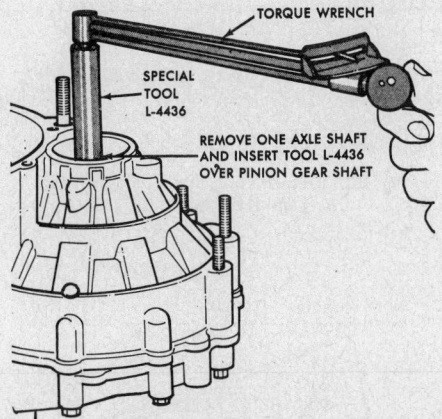

Fig. 16 Checking differential bearing preload

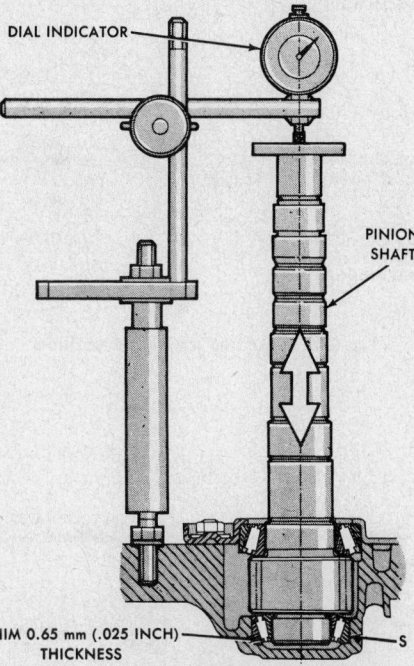

SHIM 0.65 mm (.025 INCH) THICKNESS

Fig. 17 Determining pinion shaft bearing preload shim thickness

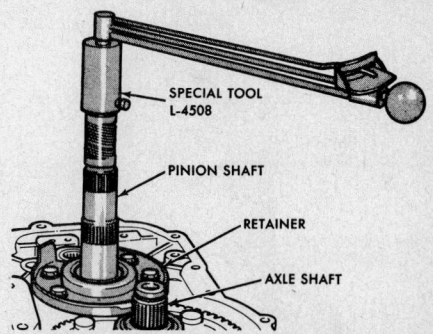

Fig. 18 Checking pinion shaft bearing preload

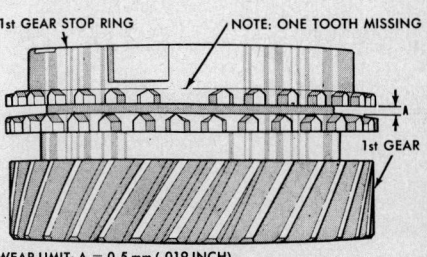

WEAR LIMIT: A = 0.5 mm (.019 INCH)

Fig. 19 Measuring clearance between 1st gear stop ring & 1st gear

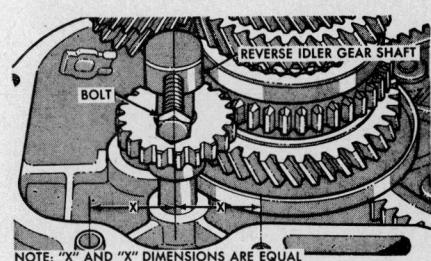

NOTE: "X" AND "X" DIMENSIONS ARE EQUAL

Fig. 20 Reverse idler gear shaft alignment

d. Place transmission housing in position with gasket, then install and torque attaching bolts to 14 ft. lbs.
e. Position dial indicator on case, then zero indicator on axle shaft, Fig. 15.
f. Move differential upward and downward and note reading. Do not turn differential when measuring, otherwise bearings will settle and give an incorrect indicator reading.
g. Correct bearing preload is obtained by adding a constant figure of .015 in. to the measured reading to obtain the thickness of shim to be installed. Shims are available in thickness of .006 in., .012 in., .024 in., .028 in. and .031 in.
h. Remove transmission case and drive out bearing cup.
i. Insert selected shim and if more than one shim is needed insert thickest shim first.
j. Drive in outer race and install gear carrier housing with gasket.

9. Check differential bearing preload, Fig. 16. Rotating torque should be 10.4 to 21.7 inch lbs. for new bearings and a minimum of 2.7 inch lbs. for used bearings.

NOTE: Lubricate bearings with transmission oil before measuring rotating torque.

Transmission Assemble

1. Install .025 in. shim, pinion shaft and bearing retainer on transmission case.
2. Install dial indicator on, Fig. 17, then move pinion shaft up and down and note reading. Do not turn pinion shaft while measuring, otherwise bearings may settle and give an incorrect reading. Determine thickness of shim to be installed by adding a constant figure of .008 in. to measured reading and .025 in. shim installed. Pinion shaft bearing preload shims are available in thicknesses of .025 in. to .055 in.
3. Lubricate bearings with transmission oil, then check pinion shaft bearing preload, Fig. 18. Rotating torque for new bearings should be 4.4 to 13.1 inch lbs. Used bearings do not require a rotating torque check. Remove pinion shaft retainer, pinion shaft and shim.
4. Install selected shim, pinion shaft and 1st gear thrust washer.

NOTE: Install 1st speed gear thrust washer with flat side facing toward 1st speed gear.

5. Install pinion shaft retainer. Torque attaching bolts to 29 ft. lbs.
6. Check clearance between first gear stop ring and first gear, Fig. 19. If clearance is less than .019 in., replace stop ring.
7. Install 1st gear and synchronizer stop ring.
8. Using tool No. L-4507, install 1st-2nd synchronizer on pinion shaft.
9. Using tool No. L-4462, install 2nd gear bearing inner race on pinion shaft.
10. Install reverse idler gear shaft on transmission case. Align reverse idler shaft as shown in Fig. 20.
11. Install 2nd gear bearing and 2nd gear on pinion shaft.

12. Install 3rd gear and snap ring on pinion shaft, Fig. 21.

NOTE: Collar on 3rd gear must face downward, toward 2nd gear.

13. Using a feeler gauge, measure clearance between 3rd gear and snap ring, Fig. 22. Clearance should be .000 to a maximum of .008 in. If not, select a snap ring that will provide a clearance as close to the lower limit as possible. Snap rings are available in thickness of .098 in. (brown), .102 in. (black), .106 in. (shiny), .110 in. (copper), .114 in. (brass) and .118 in. (blue).
14. Assemble mainshaft, Fig. 7.
15. Install mainshaft on transmission case.
16. Position shift rail assembly on transmission case, then install E-clips.
17. Install 4th gear bearing and 4th speed gear on mainshaft.
18. Install 4th speed gear and snap ring on pinion shaft.
19. Install reverse shift fork and brackets. Torque attaching bolts to 105 inch lbs.

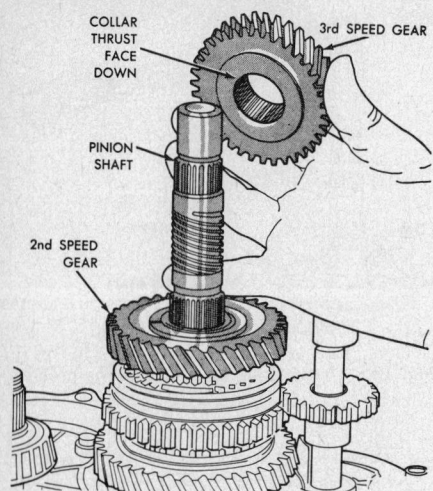

Fig. 21   Install 3rd speed gear

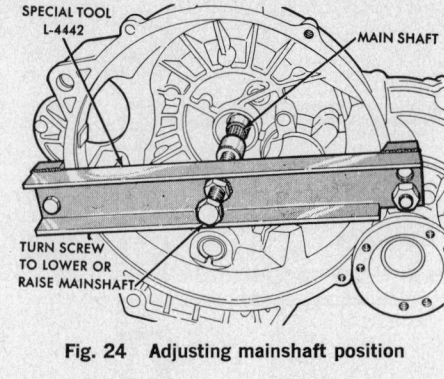

Fig. 24   Adjusting mainshaft position

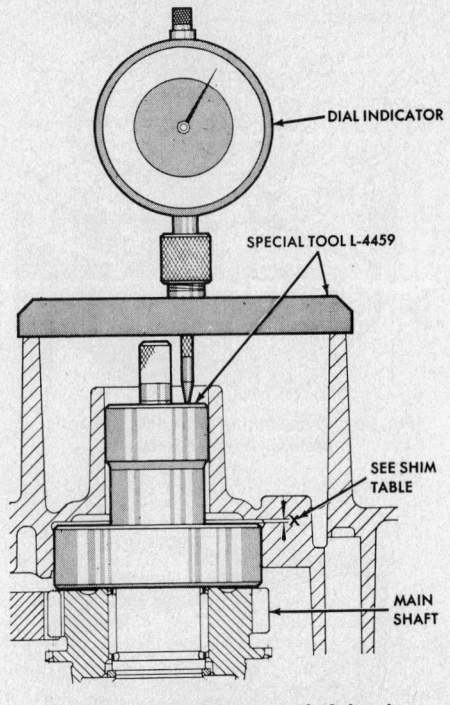

Fig. 26   Determining mainshaft bearing shim thickness

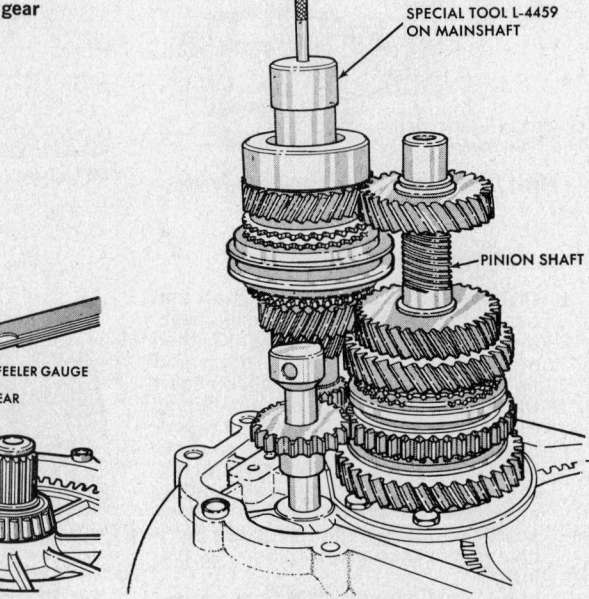

Fig. 22   Measuring clearance between third speed gear & snap ring

Fig. 25   Tool L-4459 installed on mainshaft

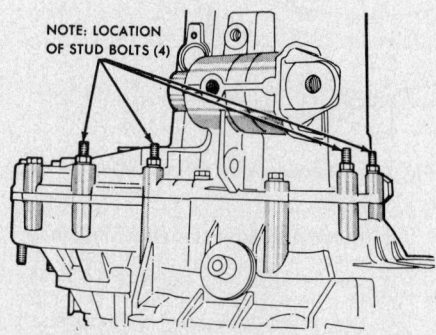

Fig. 27   Transmission case stud bolt locations

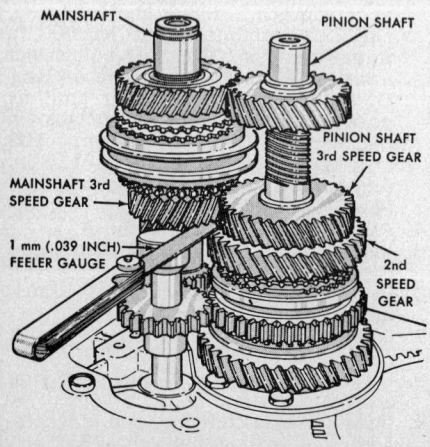

Fig. 23   Checking mainshaft position

20. Measure clearance between pinion shaft 2nd speed gear and mainshaft 3rd speed gear, Fig. 23. Clearance should be .039 in., if not use tool No. L-4442 to raise or lower mainshaft, Fig. 24.

21. Position tool No. 4459 on mainshaft, Fig. 25. Install transmission housing without bearing and torque attaching bolts to 14 ft. lbs. Install measuring sleeve and zero dial indicator, Fig. 26. Determine end play by moving sleeve upward and downward. If end play is .000 to .018 in. no shim is required. If shim thickness is not .000 to .018 in. select shim of proper thickness as follows: if end play is .019 to .029 in. use .012 in. thick shim, if end play is .030 to .041 in. use .024 in. thick shim and if end play is .042 to .057 in. shim thickness should be .035 in. Shims are available in thicknesses of .012 in. and .024 in. Insert shim between mainshaft bearing and transmission housing.

22. Install mainshaft shims and bearing in case. Install bolts, clips and nuts. Torque nuts to 155 in. lbs.

23. Using guide pins install transmission case on clutch housing. Torque attaching bolts to 250 in. lbs., Fig. 27.

24. Install clutch torque shaft oil seals, clutch torque shaft, return spring, release lever and snap rings.

25. Install release bearing and sleeve.

26. Install clutch release bearing cover. Torque bolts to 105 inch lbs.

27. Install mainshaft bearing retainer nut plugs.

28. Install selector shaft oil seal, then install selector shaft and plug.

29. Using tool Nos. C-4171 and L-4446, install drive flange oil seal.

30. Using tool No. L-4443, install drive flange, Fig. 2.

31. Install snap ring and drive flange dust plug.

32. Install clutch push rod.

A-404 Torqueflite Automatic Transaxle

IDENTIFICATION

A seven digit part number is stamped on a pad located at the rear of the transaxle on the transmission oil pan flange. This number must be referred to when servicing the transmission due to differences in some internal components.

DODGE OMNI & PLYMOUTH HORIZON

1978 4-105 . . . . A-404

DESCRIPTION

The transaxle combines a torque converter, 3 speed automatic transmission, final drive gearing and a differential into a front wheel drive unit, Fig. 1. There are three primary areas within the transaxle: the main centerline plus valve body, the transfer shaft center line which includes the governor and parking sprag and the differential centerline. The torque converter, transmission area and differential are housed in an integral aluminum housing. The differential oil sump is separate from the transmission oil sump.

The transmission consists of two multiple disc clothes, an overrunning clutch, two servos, a hydraulic accumulator, two bands and two planetary gear sets. The sun gear of the planetary gear sets is connected to the front clutch by a driving shell which is splined to the sun gear and front clutch retainer. The hydraulic system consists of an oil pump and a valve body which contains all the valve except the governor valve.

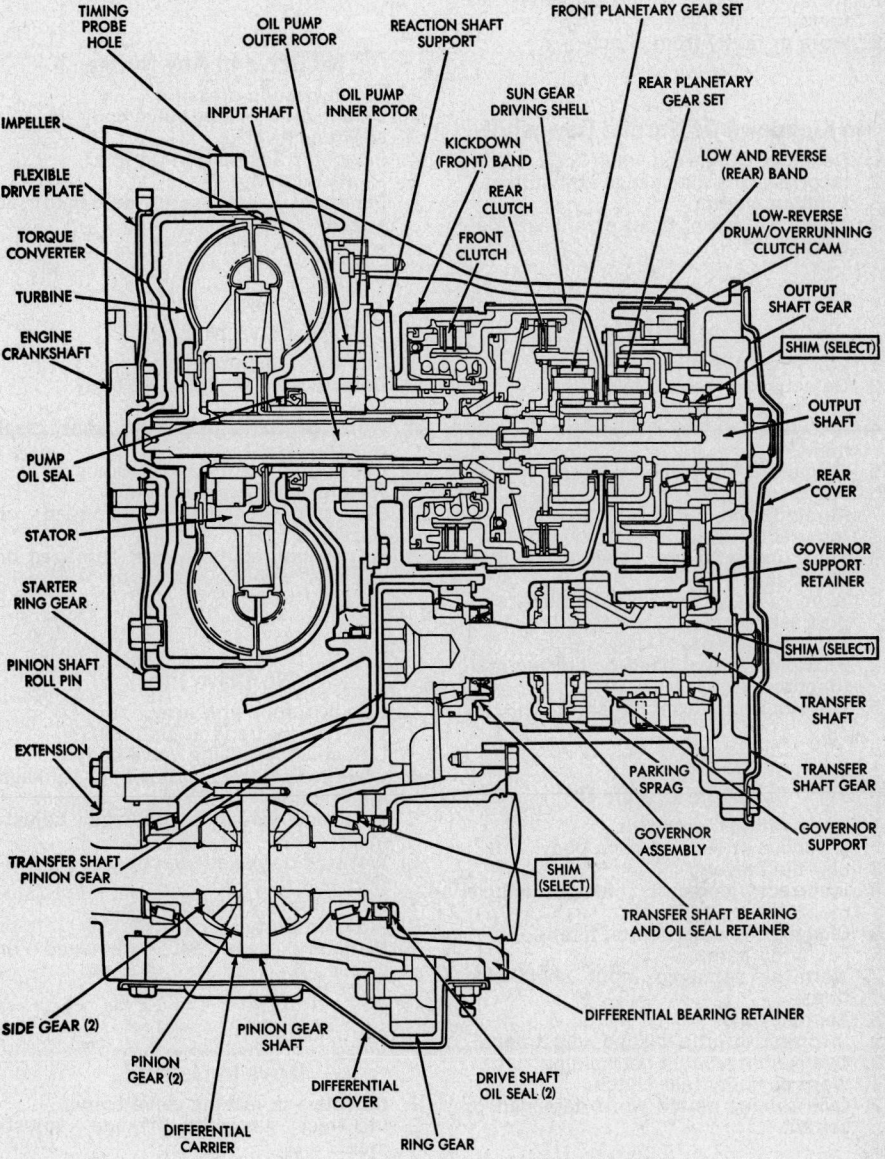

Fig. 1 Sectional view of automatic transaxle

TROUBLE SHOOTING GUIDE

Harsh Engagement From N to D Or R

1. High idle speed.
2. Defective or leaking valve body.
3. High hydraulic pressure.
4. Worn or damaged rear clutch.

Delayed Engagement From N to D Or R

1. Low hydraulic pressure.
2. Defective or leaking valve body.
3. Low-reverse servo, band or linkage malfunction.
4. Low fluid level.
5. Incorrect gearshift linkage adjustment.
6. Clogged transmission oil filter.
7. Faulty oil pump.
8. Worn or damaged input shaft seal rings.
9. Aerated fluid.
10. Low idle speed.
11. Worn or damaged reaction shaft support seal rings.
12. Worn or defective front clutch.
13. Worn or defective rear clutch.

Runaway Upshifts

1. Low hydraulic pressure.
2. Defective or leaking valve body.
3. Low fluid level.
4. Clogged transmission oil filter.
5. Aerated fluid.
6. Incorrect throttle linkage adjustment.
7. Worn or damaged reaction shaft support seal rings.
8. Kickdown servo, band or linkage malfunction.
9. Worn or faulty front clutch.

No Upshift

1. Low hydraulic pressure.
2. Defective or leaking valve body.
3. Low fluid level.

4. Incorrect gearshift linkage adjustment.
5. Incorrect throttle linkage adjustment.
6. Worn or damaged governor support seal rings.
7. Worn or damaged reaction shaft support seal rings.
8. Faulty governor.
9. Kickdown servo, band or linkage malfunction.
10. Worn or faulty front clutch.

3-2 Kickdown Runaway

1. Low hydraulic pressure.
2. Defective or leaking valve body.
3. Low fluid level.

4. Aerated fluid.
5. Incorrect throttle linkage adjustment.
6. Kickdown band adjustment.
7. Worn or damaged reaction shaft support seal rings.
8. Kickdown servo, band or linkage malfunction.
9. Worn or faulty from clutch.

No Kickdown Or Normal Downshift

1. Defective or leaking valve body.
2. Incorrect throttle linkage adjustment.
3. Faulty governor.
4. Kickdown servo, band or linkage malfunction.

Erratic Shifts

1. Low hydraulic pressure.
2. Defective or leaking valve body.
3. Low fluid level.
4. Incorrect gearshift linkage adjustment.
5. Clogged transmission oil filter.
6. Faulty oil pump.
7. Aerated fluid.
8. Incorrect throttle linkage adjustment.
9. Worn or damaged governor support seal rings.
10. Worn or damaged reaction shaft support seal rings.
11. Faulty governor.
12. Kickdown servo, band or linkage malfunction.
13. Worn or faulty front clutch.

Slips In 1, 2 Or D

1. Low hydraulic pressure.
2. Defective or leaking valve body.
3. Low fluid level.
4. Incorrect gearshift linkage adjustment.
5. Clogged transmission oil filter.
6. Faulty oil pump.
7. Worn or damaged input shaft seal rings.
8. Aerated fluid.
9. Incorrect throttle linkage adjustment.
10. Overrunning clutch not holding.
11. Worn or faulty rear clutch.
12. Overrunning clutch worn damaged or seized.

Slips In R Only

1. Low hydraulic pressure.
2. Low-reverse band adjustment.
3. Defective or leaking valve body.
4. Low-reverse servo, band or linkage malfunction.
5. Low fluid level.
6. Incorrect gearshift linkage adjustment.
7. Faulty oil pump.
8. Aerated fluid.
9. Worn or damaged reaction shaft seal rings.
10. Worn or faulty front clutch.

Slips In All Ranges

1. Low hydraulic pressure.
2. Defective or leaking valve body.
3. Low fluid level.
4. Clogged transmission oil filter.

5. Faulty oil pump.
6. Worn or damaged input shaft seal rings.
7. Aerated fluid.

No Drive In Any Range

1. Low hydraulic pressure.
2. Defective or leaking valve body.
3. Low fluid level.
4. Clogged transmission oil filter.
5. Faulty oil pump.
6. Planetary gear sets damaged or seized.

No Drive In 1, 2 or D

1. Low hydraulic pressure.
2. Defective or leaking valve body.
3. Low fluid level.
4. Worn or damaged input shaft seal rings.
5. Overrunning clutch not holding.
6. Worn or faulty rear clutch.
7. Planetary gear sets damaged or seized.
8. Overrunning clutch worn, damaged or seized.

No Drive In R

1. Low hydraulic pressure.
2. Low-reverse band adjustment.
3. Defective or leaking valve body.
4. Low-reverse servo, band or linkage malfunction.
5. Incorrect gearshift linkage adjustment.
6. Worn or damaged reaction shaft support seal rings.
7. Worn or faulty front clutch.
8. Worn or faulty rear clutch.
9. Planetary gear sets damaged or seized.

Drive In Neutral

1. Defective or leaking valve body.
2. Incorrect gearshift linkage adjustment.
3. Insufficient clutch plate clearance.
4. Worn or faulty rear clutch.
5. Rear clutch dragging.

Drags or Locks

1. Low-reverse band adjustment.
2. Kickdown band adjustment.
3. Planetary gear sets damaged or seized.
4. Overrunning clutch worn, damaged or seized.

Hard To Fill (Oil Blows Out Filler Tube)

1. Clogged transmission oil filter.
2. Aerated fluid.
3. High fluid level.
4. Breather clogged.

Transmission Overheats

1. Stuck switch valve.
2. High idle speed.
3. Low hydraulic pressure.
4. Low fluid level.
5. Incorrect gearshift adjustment.
6. Faulty oil pump.
7. Kickdown band adjustment too tight.
8. Faulty cooling system.
9. Insufficient clutch plate clearance.

Harsh Upshifts

1. Low hydraulic pressure.
2. Incorrect throttle linkage adjustment.
3. Kickdown band adjustment.
4. High hydraulic pressure.

Delayed Upshift

1. Incorrect throttle linkage adjustment.
2. Kickdown band adjustment.
3. Worn or damaged governor support seal rings.
4. Worn or damaged reaction shaft support seal rings.
5. Faulty governor.
6. Kickdown servo, band or linkage malfunction.
7. Worn or faulty front clutch.

Grating, Scraping Or Growling Noise

1. Low-reverse band out of adjustment.
2. Kickdown band adjustment.
3. Output shaft bearing or bushing damaged.
4. Planetary gear sets damaged or seized.
5. Overrunning clutch worn, damaged or seized.

Buzzing Noise

1. Defective or leaking valve body.
2. Low fluid level.
3. Aerated fluid.
4. Overrunning clutch inner race damaged.

MAINTENANCE
Adding Oil

To check fluid level, apply the parking brake and operate engine at idle speed with transmission in Neutral or Park position. Add fluid as necessary.

Changing Oil

Fluid and filter changes are not required for average passenger car use. Severe usage such as commercial type usage or prolonged operation in city traffic, requires that fluid be changed and bands adjusted every 15,000 miles.

Whenever factory fill fluid is changed, only fluid of the type labeled Dexron should be used.

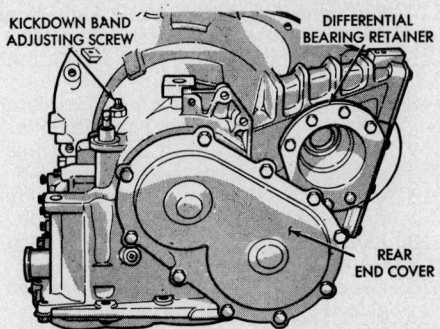

Fig. 2 Kickdown band adjusting screw location

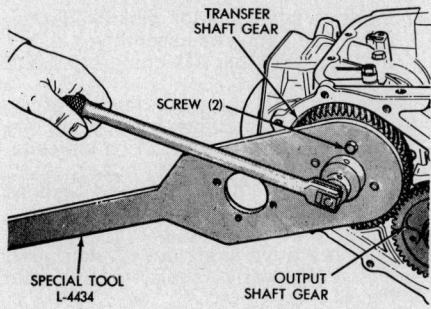

Fig. 3 Loosening transfer shaft gear retaining nut

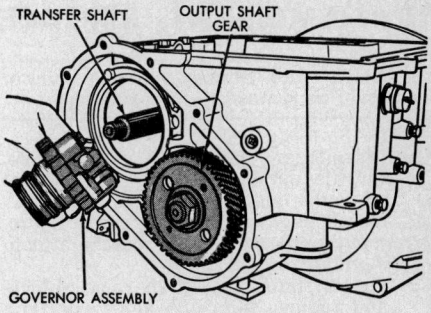

Fig. 5 Removing governor assembly

1. Raise vehicle and place a suitable drain pan under transmission oil pan.
2. Loosen transmission oil pan attaching bolts and allow fluid to drain, then remove oil pan.
3. Replace oil filter and adjust bands if necessary, then install oil pan and gasket.
4. Add four quarts of approved automatic transmission fluid through the filler tube.
5. Start engine and allow to idle for at least two minutes, then with parking brake applied move selector lever momentarily to each position. Place selector lever in Neutral or Park and check fluid level. Add fluid to bring level to Add mark.
6. Recheck fluid level after transmission has reached operating temperature. The level should be between Add and Full marks.

BANDS, ADJUST

Kickdown Band

1. Loosen lock nut and back off nut approximately five turns, Fig. 2.
2. Using tool No. C-3380-A and adapter C-3705, tighten band adjusting screw to 47 to 50 inch lbs. If adapter C-3705 is not used, tighten adjusting screw to 72 inch lbs.

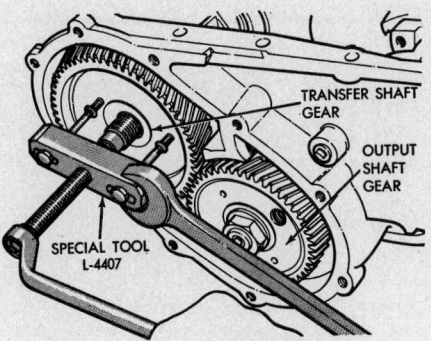

Fig. 4 Removing transfer shaft gear

3. Back off adjusting screw 2½ turns, then while holding adjusting screw in this position, torque lock nut to 35 ft. lbs.

GEARSHIFT LINKAGE, ADJUST

1. Place selector lever in Park position.
2. Raise vehicle, then loosen swivel lock bolt.
3. Move transmission lever to the rear detent position (Park).
4. Torque swivel lock bolt to 90 inch lbs., then check adjustment.

THROTTLE CABLE, ADJUST

1. Perform adjustment with engine at operating temperature, otherwise ensure carburetor is not on fast idle cam by disconnecting choke.
2. Loosen adjusting bracket lock screw.
3. Hold transmission lever rearward against internal stop and tighten adjusting bracket lock screw to 105 inch lbs.

VALVE BODY

1. Loosen transmission oil pan attaching bolts and allow transmission to drain, then remove oil pan.
2. Remove oil filter attaching screws and oil filter.
3. Using a screwdriver, remove E-clip, then remove parking rod.
4. Remove seven valve body attaching bolts, then remove valve body and governor oil tubes.

GOVERNOR & TRANSFER SHAFT OIL SEAL

1. Remove rear cover attaching bolts and rear cover.
2. Using tool No. L-4434, remove transfer shaft gear retaining nut, Fig. 3.
3. Using tool No. L-4407, remove transfer shaft gear and shim, Fig. 4.
4. Remove governor support retainer, then remove low-reverse band anchor pin.
5. Remove governor assembly.
6. Remove transfer shaft retainer snap ring, then using tool No. L-4512 and a suitable puller, remove transfer shaft and retainer assembly.
7. Remove transfer shaft retainer from shaft.
8. Using a screwdriver, remove oil seal from transfer shaft retainer.
9. Using tool No. L-4520 and C-4171, tap oil seal into shaft retainer, Fig. 5.
10. Reverse procedure to install. Torque transfer shaft gear retaining nut to 200 ft. lbs.

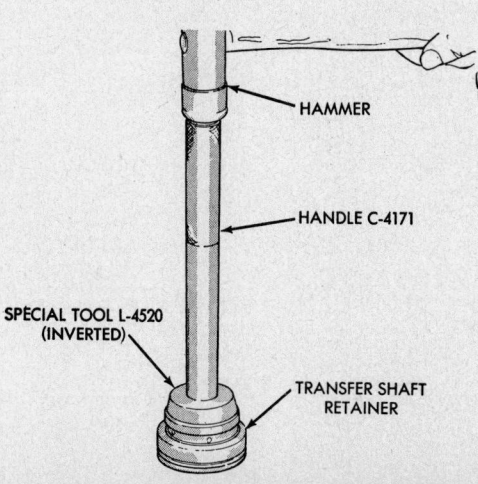

Fig. 6 Installing transfer shaft oil seal

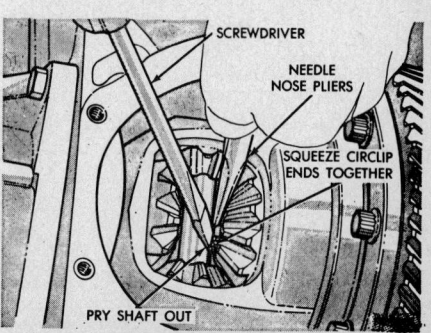

Fig. 7 Prying drive shaft out of side gear

TRANSAXLE

TRANSMISSION, REPLACE

NOTE: The transaxle and converter must be removed as an assembly.

1. Disconnect battery positive cable, throttle and shift linkage and upper oil cooler line.
2. Install engine support fixture, the remove upper converter housing attaching bolts.
3. Loosen hub nuts, then raise vehicle and remove hub nuts and wheel and tire assemblies.
4. Remove left splash shield.
5. Remove differential drain plug and allow differential to drain, then remove differential cover.
6. Remove speedometer pinion adapter, cable and pinion as assembly.
7. Remove sway bar attaching bolts and sway bar.
8. Remove both lower ball joint to steering knuckle retaining bolts, then pry lower ball joint from steering knuckle.
9. Remove drive shaft from hub.
10. Rotate both driveshafts to expose snap ring ends.
11. Squeeze ends of snap ring together, then pry drive shaft out of side gear, and remove drive shaft from vehicle, Fig. 6.
12. Mark converter and drive shaft so they can be installed in the same position, then remove torque converter mounting bolts.
13. Remove access plug in right splash shield to rotate engine.
14. Disconnect lower oil cooler tube and neutral safety switch wire connector.
15. Remove engine bracket from front crossmember.
16. Remove engine front mount insulator through bolt and bezel housing bolts.
17. Secure transaxle to a suitable transmission jack.
18. Remove left engine mount, then remove left engine mount through bolt.
19. Remove lower converter housing attaching bolts.
20. Lower transaxle from vehicle. Pry engine for clearance, if necessary.
21. Reverse procedure to install. Before lowering vehicle fill differential with Dexron automatic transmission fluid. Refer to car chapter when installing hub nut.

DISC BRAKES

CONTENTS

SERVICE PRECAUTIONS

Brake Lines & Linings

Remove one of the front wheels and inspect the brake disc, caliper and linings. (The wheel bearings should be inspected at this time and repacked if necessary).

Do not get any oil or grease on the linings. If the linings are worn to within .030" of the surface of the shoe, replace both sets of shoe and lining assemblies. It is recommended that both front wheel sets be replaced whenever a respective shoe and lining is worn or damaged. Inspect and, if necessary, replace rear brake linings also.

If the caliper is cracked or fluid leakage through the casting is evident, it must be replaced as a unit.

Shoe & Lining Wear

If visual inspection does not adequately determine the condition of the lining, a physical check will be necessary.

To check the amount of lining wear, remove a wheel from the car, the caliper from the steering knuckle, and the shoe and lining assemblies. Three thickness measurements should be taken (with a micrometer) across the middle section of the shoe and lining; one reading at each side and one reading in the center.

When a shoe and lining assembly has worn to a thickness of .180", it should be replaced. If shoes do not require replacement, reinstall them in their original inner and outer positions.

Brake Roughness

The most common cause of brake chatter on disc brakes is a variation in thickness of the disc. If roughness or vibration is encountered during highway operation

Fig. 1   Checking rotor for lateral runout

or if pedal puming is experienced at low speeds, the disc may have excessive thickness variation. To check for this condition, measure the disc at 12 points with a micrometer at a radius approximately one inch from edge of disc. If thickness measurements vary by more than .0005", the disc should be replaced with a new one.

Excessive lateral runout of braking disc may cause a "knocking back" of the pistons, possibly creating increased pedal travel and vibration when brakes are applied.

Before checking the runout, wheel bearings should be adjusted. The readjustment is very important and will be required at the completion of the test to prevent bearing failure. Be sure to make the adjustment according to the recommendations given under *Front Wheel Bearings, Adjust* in the car chapters.

Brake Disc Service

Servicing of disc brakes is extremely critical due to the close tolerances required in machining the brake disc to insure proper brake operation.

The maintenance of these close controls of the shape of the rubbing surfaces is necessary to prevent brake roughness. In addition, the surface finish must be non-directional and maintained at a micro inch finish. This close control of the rubbing surface finish is necessary to

Fig. 2. Checking rotor parallelism (Thickness variation)

Inspection of Caliper

Should it become necessary to remove the caliper for installation of new parts, clean all parts in alcohol, wipe dry using lint-free cloths. Using an air hose, blow out drilled passages and bores. Check dust boots for punctures or tears. If punctures or tears are evident, new boots should be installed upon reassembly.

Inspect piston bores in both housings for scoring or pitting. Bores that show light scratches or corrosion can usually be cleaned with crocus cloth. However, bores that have deep scratches or scoring may be honed, provided the diameter of the bore is not increased more than .002". If the bore does not clean up within this specification, a new caliper housing should be installed (black stains on the bore walls are caused by piston seals and will do no harm).

When using a hone, Fig. 3, be sure to install the hone baffle before honing bore. The baffle is used to protect the hone stones from damage. Use extreme care in cleaning the caliper after honing. Remove all dust and grit by flushing the caliper with alcohol. Wipe dry with clean lint-less cloth and then clean a second time in the same manner.

Bleeding Disc Brakes

NOTE: Pressure bleeding is recommended for all hydraulic disc brake systems.

The disc brake hydraulic system can be bled manually or with pressure bleeding equipment. On vehicles with disc brakes the brake pedal will require more pumping and frequent checking of fluid level in master cylinder during bleeding operation.

Never use brake fluid that has been drained from hydraulic system when bleeding the brakes. Be sure the disc brake pistons are returned to their normal positions and that the shoe and lining assemblies are properly seated. Before driving the vehicle, check brake operation to be sure that a firm pedal has been obtained.

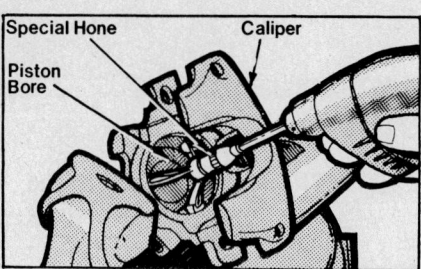

Fig. 3. Honing caliper piston bore

Proportioning Valve

The proportioning valve (when used), Fig. 4, provides balanced braking action between front and rear brakes under a wide range of braking conditions. The valve regulates the hydraulic pressure applied to the rear wheel cylinders, thus limiting rear braking action when high pressures are required at the front brakes. In this manner, premature rear wheel skid is prevented.

Testing Proportioning Valve

When a premature rear wheel slide is obtained on a brake application, it usually is an indication that the fluid pressure to the rear wheels is above the 50% reduction ratio for the rear line pressure and that a malfunction has occured within the proportioning valve.

To test the valve, install gauge set shown in Fig. 4 in brake line between master cylinder and proportioning valve, and at output end of proportioning valve and brake line as shown. Be sure all joints are fluid tight.

Have a helper exert pressure on brake pedal (holding pressure). Obtain a reading on master cylinder output of approximately 700 psi. While pressure is being held as above, reading on valve outlet should be 550-610 psi. If the pressure readings do not meet these specifications, the valve should be removed and a new valve installed.

avoid pulls and erratic performance and promote long lining life and equal lining wear of both left and right brakes.

In light of the foregoing remarks, refinishing of the rubbing surfaces should not be attempted unless precision equipment, capable of measuring in micro inches (millionths of an inch) is available.

To check lateral runout of a disc, mount a dial indicator on a convenient part (steering knuckle, tie rod, disc brake caliper housing) so that the plunger of the dial indicator contacts the disc at a point one inch from the outer edge, Fig. 1. If the total indicated runout exceeds specifications, install a new disc.

To check parallelism (thickness variation), mount dial indicators, Fig. 2, so the plunger contacts rotor approximately 1 inch from outer edge. If parallelism exceeds specifications, replace rotor.

General Precautions

1. Grease or any other foreign material must be kept off the caliper, surfaces of the disc and external surfaces of the hub, during service procedures. Handling the brake disc and caliper should be done in a way to avoid deformation of the disc and nicking or scratching brake linings.
2. If inspection reveals rubber piston seals are worn or damaged, they should be replaced immediately.
3. During removal and installation of a wheel assembly, exercise care so as not to interfere with or damage the caliper splash shield, the bleeder screw or the transfer tube.
4. Front wheel bearings should be adjusted to specifications.
5. Be sure vehicle is centered on hoist before servicing any of the front end components to avoid bending or damaging the disc splash shield on full right or left wheel turns.
6. Before the vehicle is moved after any brake service work, be sure to obtain a firm brake pedal.
7. The assembly bolts of the two caliper housings should not be disturbed unless the caliper requires service.

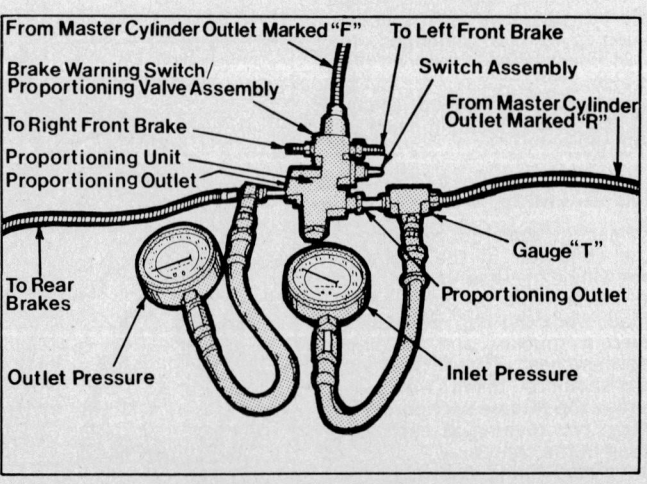

Fig. 4 Gauge hook-up for testing proportioning valve (typical)

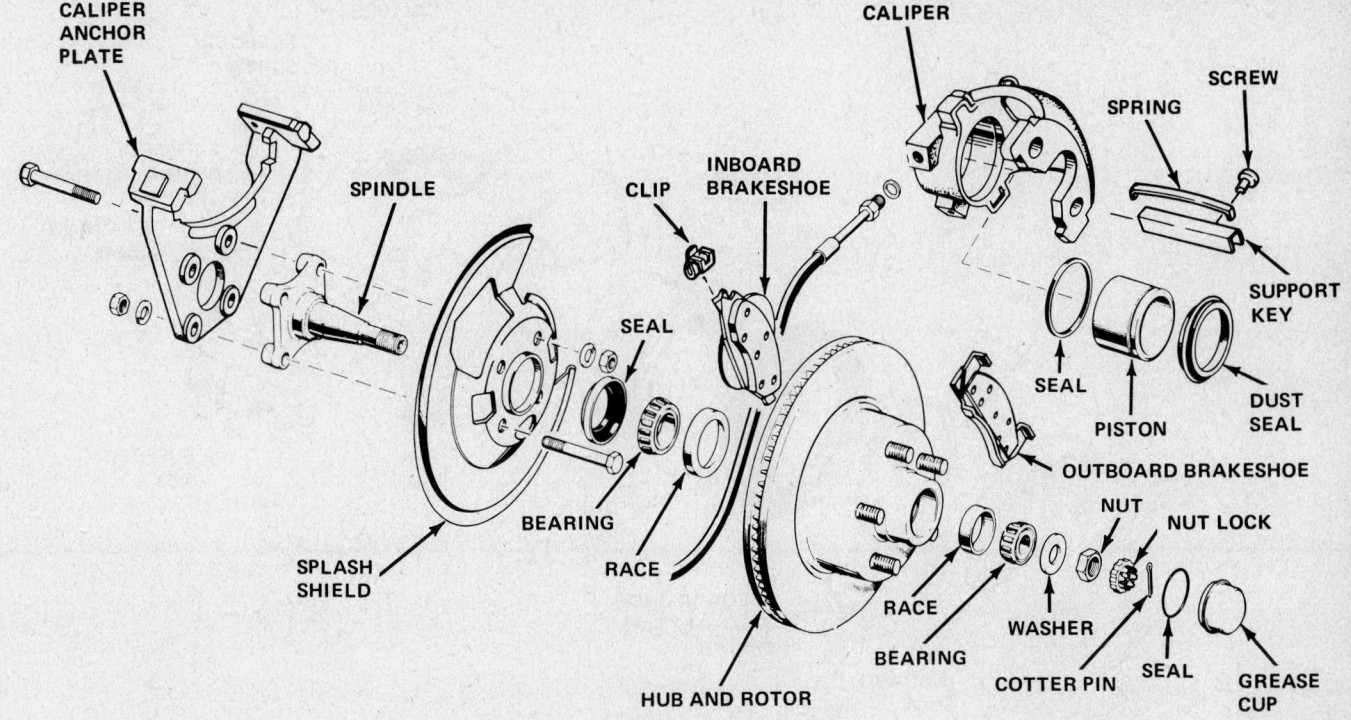

Fig. 5   Bendix sliding caliper disc brake (Typical)

BENDIX SLIDING CALIPER

This sliding caliper disc brake assembly incorporates a hub and rotor assembly, caliper, brake shoes and linings, caliper anchor plate and a splash shield, Fig. 5.

Cooling fins are cast into the rotor between the two braking surfaces to ventilate and cool the rotor. The sliding caliper is positioned in, and slides on, the abutment surfaces on the leading and trailing edges of the caliper anchor plate. A caliper support key, located between the forward edge of the caliper and abutment surface, is secured with a retaining screw. A support spring is installed between the support key and caliper to maintain tension on the support key.

The caliper is a one-piece casting containing the piston, piston seal and dust seal, Fig. 6. The hydraulic seal between the caliper piston and piston bore is achieved by a square cut piston seal, located in a machined groove in the piston bore. The dust seal seats in a recess machined on the edge of the piston bore and into a groove in the caliper piston.

Caliper Removal

1. Siphon two-thirds of brake fluid from master cylinder reservoir serving front disc brakes.
2. Raise vehicle, support on jackstands and remove front wheels.
3. Bottom the caliper piston in bore. Insert a screwdriver between inboard shoe and piston, then pry piston back into bore. The piston can also be bottomed in the bore with a large "C" clamp.
4. Using a 1/4 inch allen wrench, remove support key retaining screw, Fig. 7.
5. Drive caliper support key and spring from anchor plate with a suitable drift and hammer, Fig. 8.
6. Lift caliper from anchor plate and off rotor, Fig. 9. Hang caliper from coil spring with wire. Do not allow caliper to hang from brake hose.

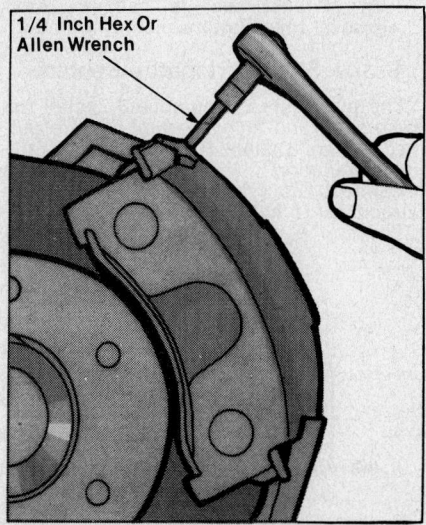

Fig. 7   Removing support key retaining screw

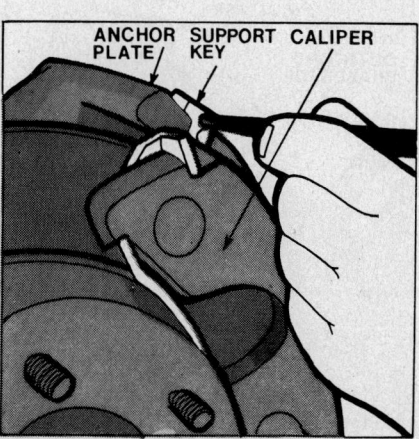

Fig. 8   Removing support key

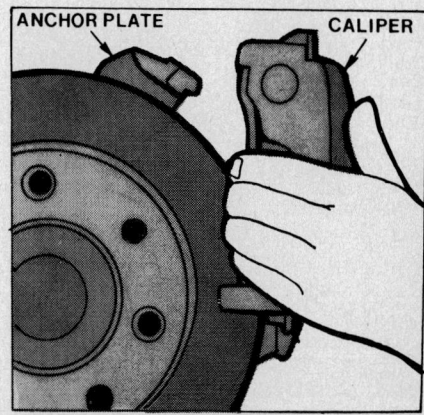

Fig. 9   Removing or installing caliper

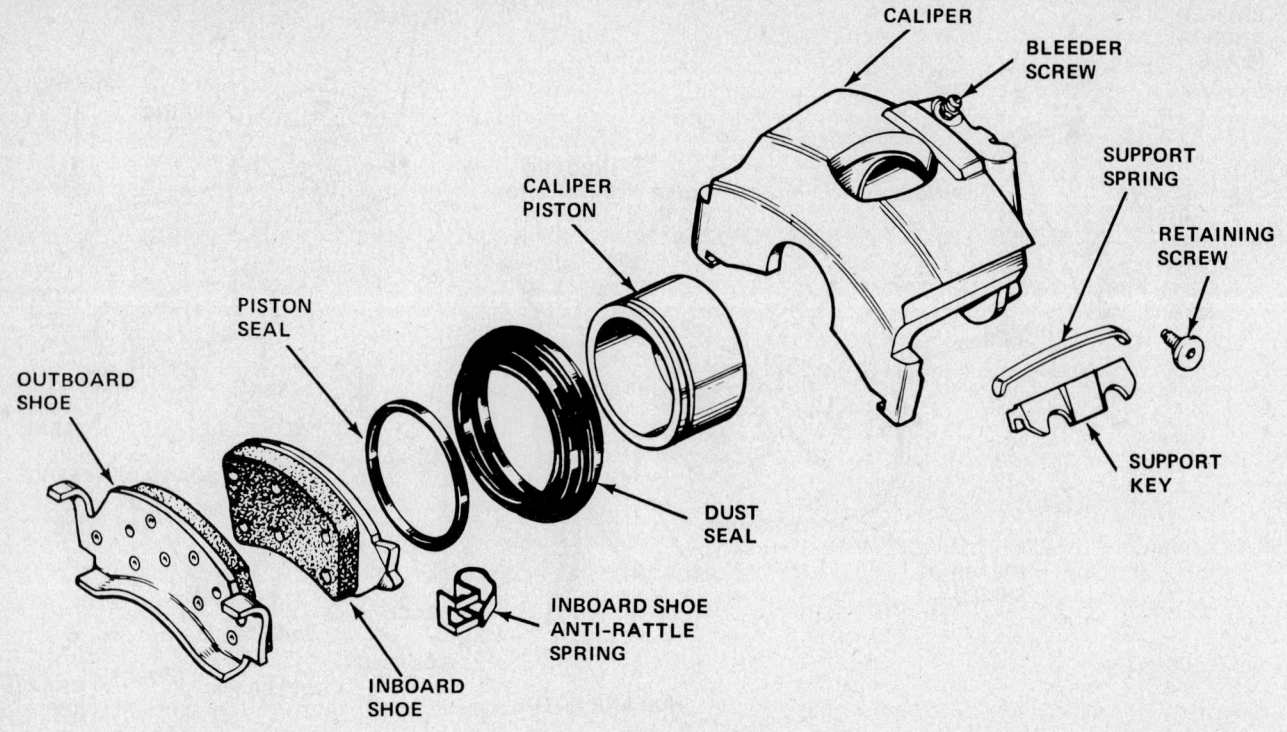

Fig. 6 Caliper assembly

7. Remove inboard brake shoe from anchor plate, then the anti-rattle spring from the brake shoe, Fig. 10.
8. Remove outboard brake shoe from caliper, Fig. 11. It may be necessary to loosen the brake shoe with a hammer to permit shoe removal.

Caliper Disassembly

1. Drain brake fluid from caliper.
2. Position caliper with shop cloths, Fig. 12, and apply compressed air to fluid inlet port to ease piston from bore.

NOTE: Do not attempt to catch piston or to protect it when applying compressed air since personal injury is possible.

3. Remove dust seal from piston, then the piston seal from bore, Fig. 6. Use wooden or plastic tool to remove piston seal since metal tools may damage piston.
4. Remove bleeder screw.

Caliper Assembly

1. Coat square cut piston seal with clean brake fluid, then install seal into piston bore. Work seal into groove with clean fingers.

2. Install and torque bleeder screw to 11 ft. lbs.
3. Lubricate dust seal and tool J-24387 with clean brake fluid, then place dust seal on tool, allowing 1/4 inch of tool to extend past small lip of dust seal, Fig. 13.
4. Place dust seal and tool over piston bore, then work large lip of dust seal into seal groove, Fig. 14. Ensure dust seal is fully seated.
5. Lubricate caliper piston and insert through tool. Center piston in bore and use a hammer handle to apply pressure to install piston halfway into bore, Fig. 14.
6. Remove tool J-24387 and seat small lip of dust seal in caliper piston groove, then bottom piston in bore.

Brake Shoe & Lining, Replace

The procedures to remove & install the brake shoe and lining assemblies are outlined under "Caliper Removal" and "Caliper Installation". It is not necessary to disconnect the brake hose, however, use caution not to twist or kink hose.

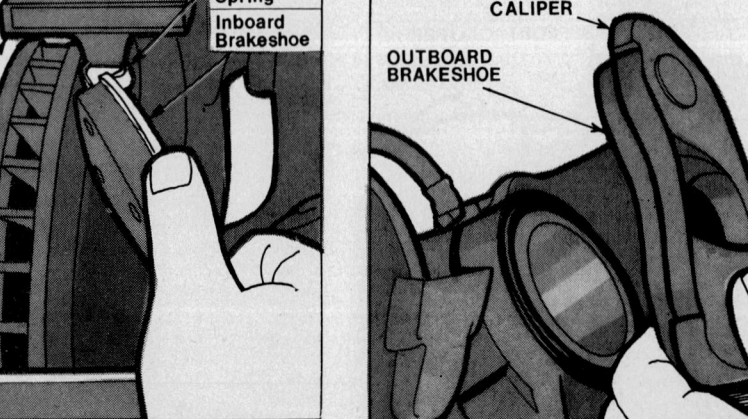

Fig. 10 Removing or installing inboard brake shoe

Fig. 11 Removing or installing outboard brake shoe

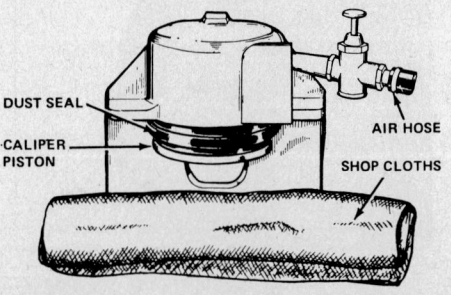

Fig. 12 Removing piston from caliper

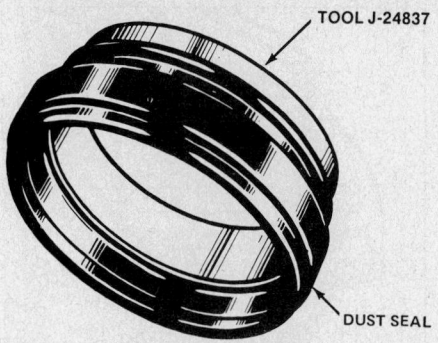

Fig. 13. Dust seal & installer tool assembly

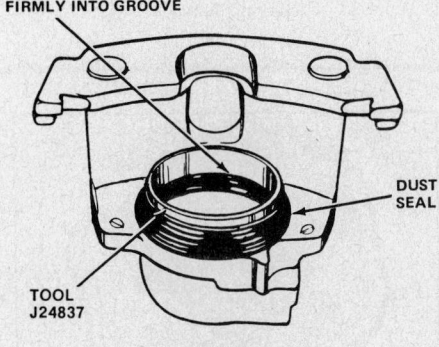

VIEW A

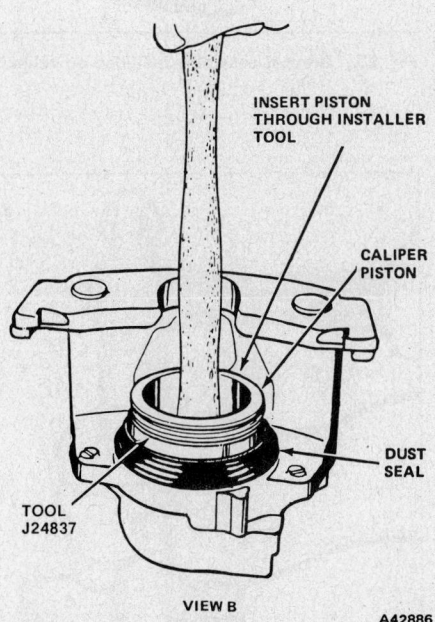

VIEW B   A42886

Fig. 14 Installing dust seal & caliper piston

Caliper Installation

1. Clean and lubricate abutment surfaces of caliper and the anchor plate with a suitable molydisulfide grease, Fig. 15.
2. Install inboard brake shoe anti-rattle

spring on brake shoe rear flange, ensure looped section of clip is facing away from rotor, Fig. 16.

3. Install inboard brake shoe on caliper anchor plate, Fig. 10.
4. Install outboard brake shoe in caliper, Fig. 11. Ensure the shoe flange is seated fully into outboard arms of caliper. It may be necessary to use a hammer to seat the shoe.
5. Place caliper assembly over rotor and position in caliper anchor plate. Ensure dust boot is not torn or mispositioned by inboard brake shoe during caliper installation.
6. Align caliper with anchor plate abutment surfaces, then insert support key and spring between abutment surfaces at the trailing end of caliper and anchor plate. With a hammer and brass drift, drive caliper support key and spring into position, then install and torque support key retaining screw to 15 ft. lbs.
7. Refill master cylinder to within one inch of rim. Press brake pedal several times to seat shoes.
8. Install front wheels and lower vehicle.

DELCO-MORAINE SINGLE PISTON

w/Single Mounting Bolt

This single piston sliding caliper assembly, Figs. 17 and 18, incorporates a one piece housing with the inboard side of the housing bored for the piston. A seal within the housing bore provides a hydraulic seal between the piston and housing wall.

A spring steel scraper (wear sensor) is incorporated on each inboard shoe. When shoe lining has worn to within .030 inch of the shoe, the sensor scrapes the rotor and emits an audible high frequency sound indicating that the linings should be replaced.

The caliper assembly slides on a mounting sleeve which is secured by a mounting bolt. Upon brake application fluid pressure against the piston forces the inboard shoe against the inboard side of the rotor. This action causes the caliper to slide until the outboard shoe comes in contact with the rotor.

Caliper Removal

1. Siphon brake fluid from master cylinder to bring level to 1/3 full, discard brake fluid removed.
2. Raise vehicle and remove wheel and tire assembly.
3. Install a 7 inch C-clamp on caliper with solid end of clamp on caliper housing and screw end on metal portion of outboard brake shoe. Tighten clamp until piston bottoms in caliper bore, then remove clamp.
4. Disconnect brake hose from caliper and remove copper gaskets, cap end of brake hose.

NOTE: If only brake shoes are to be

Fig. 15 Caliper & anchor plate abutment surfaces

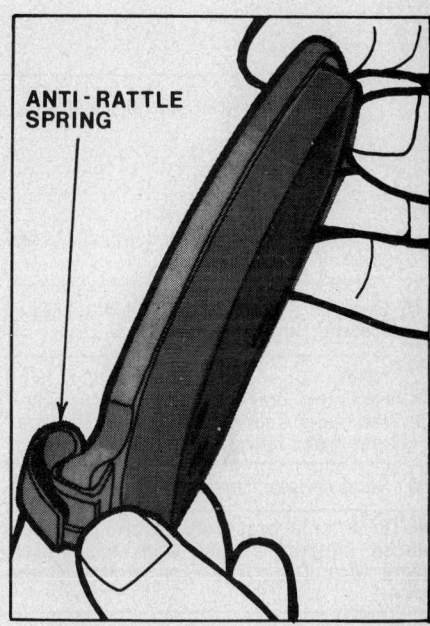

Fig. 16 Installing inboard brake shoe anti-rattle spring

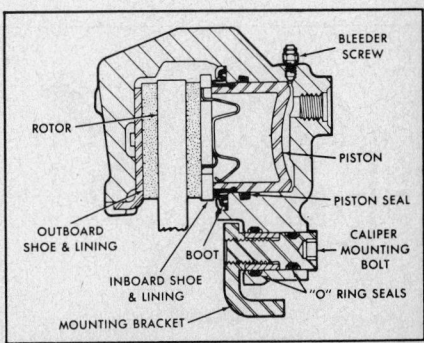

Fig. 17 Single piston disc brake assembly

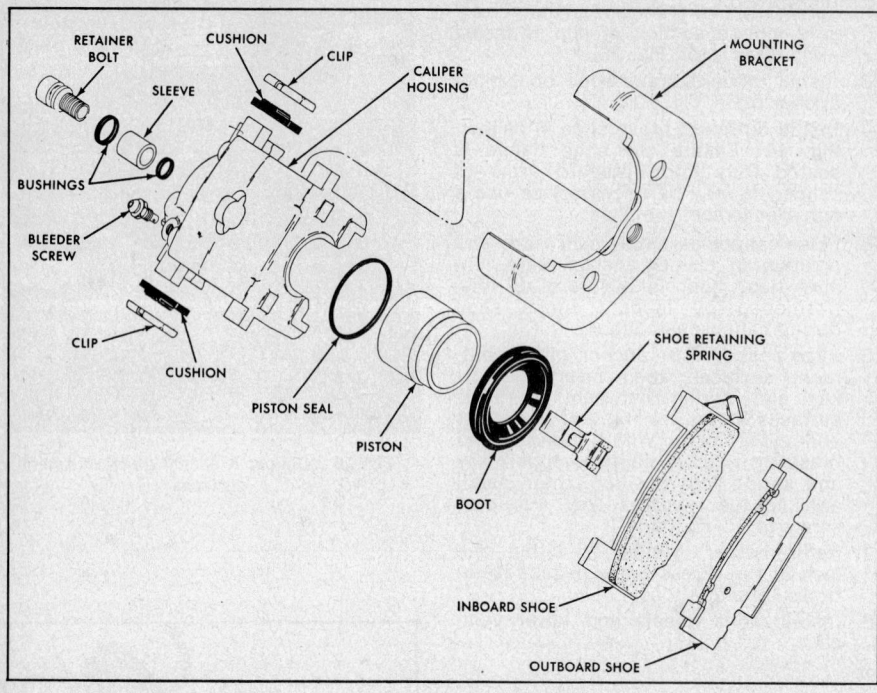

Fig. 18   Delco-Moraine single piston disc brake with single mounting bolt

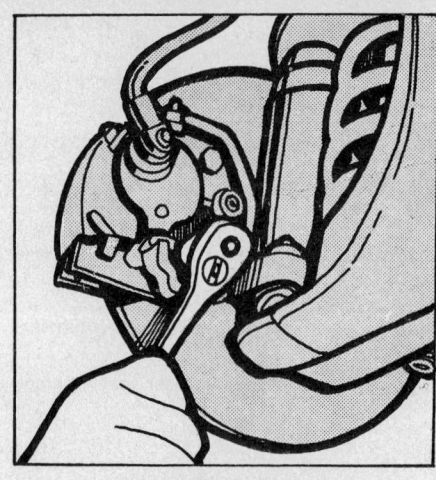

Fig. 19   Removing mounting bracket from steering knuckle

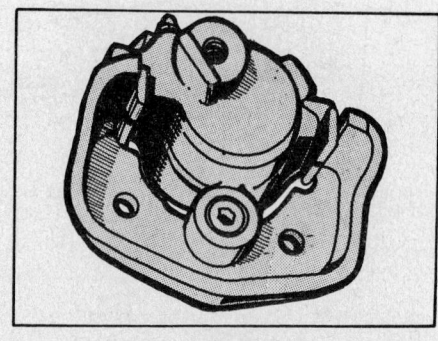

Fig. 20   Bracket assembly installed on caliper

replaced do not disconnect brake hose.

5. Remove the two mounting brackets to steering knuckle bolts, Fig. 19.

   NOTE: Do not remove socket head retaining bolt. Support caliper when removing second bolt to prevent caliper from falling.

6. Slide caliper from rotor.

NOTE: If only brake shoes are to be replaced support caliper from suspension using wire. Do not stretch or kink brake hose.

Brake Shoe Removal

1. Remove caliper as described under "Caliper Removal".

2. Remove brake shoes, if retaining spring does not come off with inboard shoe remove it from piston.

Caliper Disassembly

1. Using clean brake fluid clean exterior of caliper.
2. Drain brake fluid from caliper.
3. Remove caliper mounting bracket bolt and slide bracket from caliper, Fig. 20, then remove sleeve and bushing from bolt and bushing from caliper mounting hole, Fig. 18.
4. Remove clips if still in place, then remove cushions, Fig. 21.
5. Pad interior of caliper with clean shop towels, then direct compressed air through caliper inlet hole to remove piston.

NOTE: Use only enough air pressure to ease piston out of bore.

Fig. 21   Removing and installing cushions

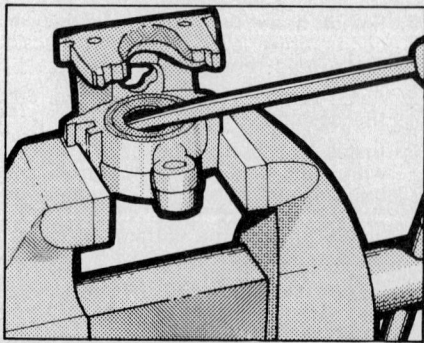

Fig. 22   Removing piston boot

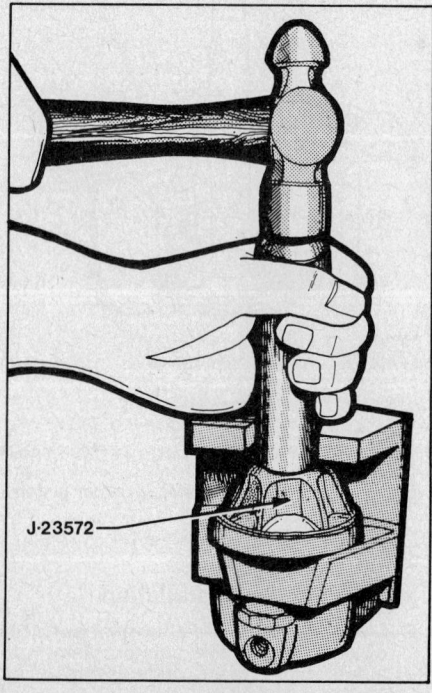

J-23572

Fig. 23   Installing boot on caliper

CAUTION: Do not place fingers in front of piston for any reason when applying compressed air. This could result in serious personal injury.

6. Using a screwdriver carefully pry boot from caliper, Fig. 22.
7. Remove piston seal from caliper bore using a piece of wood or plastic.

NOTE: Do not use metal tool to remove piston seal as it may damage caliper bore.

8. Remove bleeder valve.

Caliper Assembly

1. Lubricate caliper bore and piston seal with clean brake fluid, then position seal in caliper bore groove.
2. Lubricate piston with clean brake fluid and install boot into piston groove with fold facing the open end of piston, Fig. 18.
3. Insert piston into caliper, then using care to avoid unseating seal, force piston into caliper.

NOTE: To force piston into caliper a force of 50-100 pounds will be required.

4. Position outside diameter of boot into caliper counterbore and seat with tool J-23572, Fig. 23.

CAUTION: Assure that retaining ring molded into boot is not bent and that boot is installed fully and evenly below and around the caliper, as dirt and moisture may enter caliper and cause damage and corrosion.

5. Install bleeder screw.
6. Position and stretch cushions over caliper lugs, fitting the heavy section

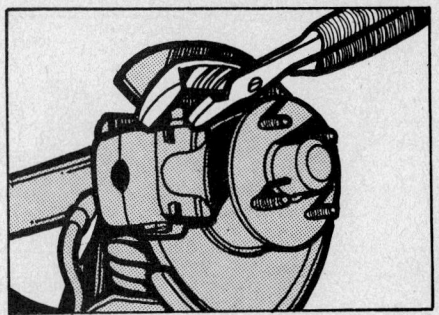

Fig. 24   Fitting brake pad to caliper

in the lug recess and saw-tooth edges of cushions facing out, Fig. 21.
7. Using silicone lubricant, liberally lubricate sleeve and bushings and the unthreaded portion of the retainer bolt. Install the larger bushing in the caliper hole groove and install the sleeve. Install the smaller bushing in the retainer bolt groove.
8. With caliper clamped in a vise, position clips over cushions and squeeze mounting bracket over clips, aligning the bolt hole. Move bracket against retainer boss on caliper and install retainer bolt. Torque bolt to 28 ft. lbs., (38 N·m).

NOTE: Considerable force may be required to squeeze bracket over cushions and clips on caliper. Start open end of bracket over ends of clips near the boot and move the bracket toward the closed end of caliper.

Brake Shoes Installation

1. Position retaining spring on inboard shoe, place single leg in brake shoe hole, then snap two other legs over notch in shoe.

NOTE: Some inboard replacement brake pads incorporate wear sensors and have a specific left and right hand assembly. Properly installed, the wear sensor will face toward the rear of caliper.

2. Install shoe in caliper.
3. Position caliper over rotor, align mounting holes, install and torque bolts to 70 ft. lbs., (95 N·m).
4. Using suitable pliers clinch outboard shoe to caliper, place lower jaw of pliers on bottom edge of shoe, place upper jaw of pliers on shoe tab, squeeze pliers and bend tab, Fig. 24. Clinch other end of shoe in same manner. Outboard end play should be zero to .005 inch., (zero to 0.127mm).
5. Install wheel and tire assembly and lower vehicle.
6. Add brake fluid to within ¼ inch from top of master cylinder.

NOTE: Pump brake pedal several times to ensure it is firm before moving vehicle.

Caliper Installation

1. Install caliper as described under "Brake Shoe Installation", then install brake hose with new copper gaskets, torque fitting to 21 ft. lbs., (29 N·m), if removed, bleed brake system.

NOTE: Brake hose fitting must be against machined surface on caliper to ensure proper hose positioning.

DELCO-MORAINE OPPOSED PISTONS

These brakes are used on all four wheels. The components of the disc brake system are shown in Fig. 25. The caliper assemblies replace the conventional wheel cylinder, brake shoes and linings, and the disc replaces the brake drum.

The caliper assembly contains four pistons, two acting on each shoe with one shoe on each side of the disc.

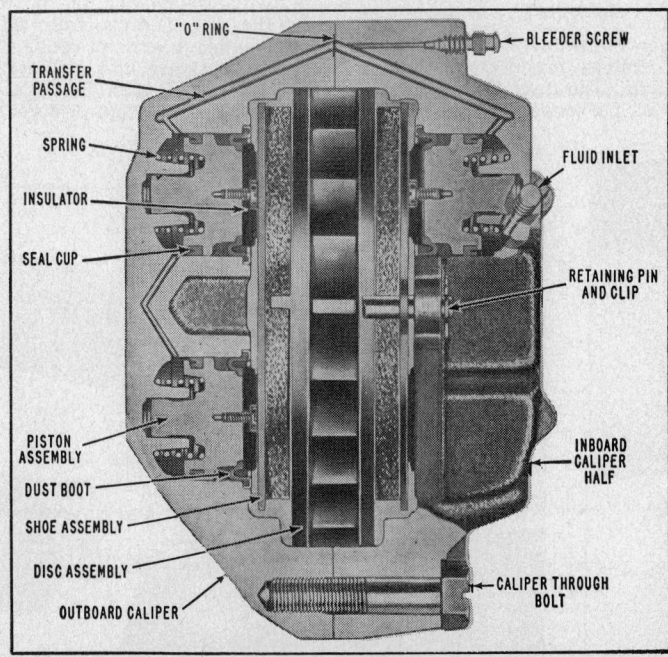

Fig. 25   Delco-Moraine disc brake assembly

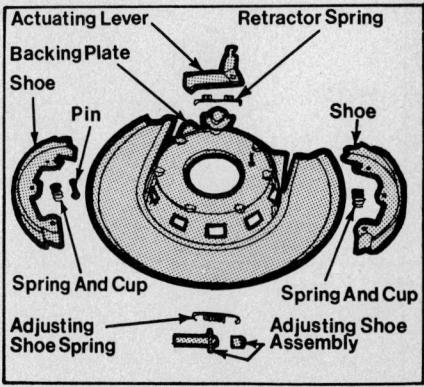

Fig. 26   Delco-Moraine parking brake components

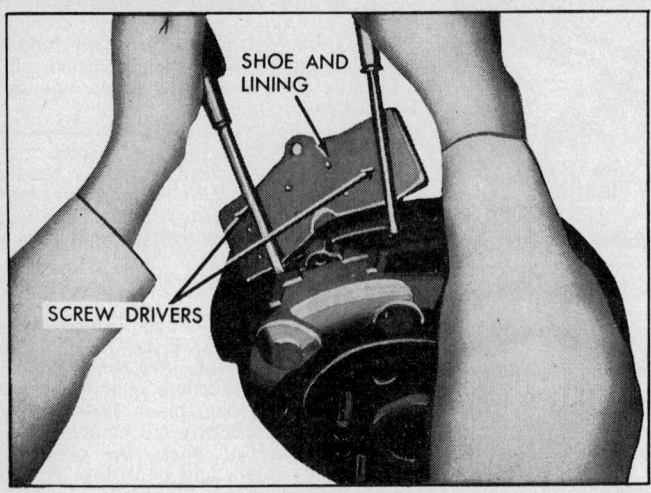

Fig. 27   Installing Delco Moraine disc brake shoes

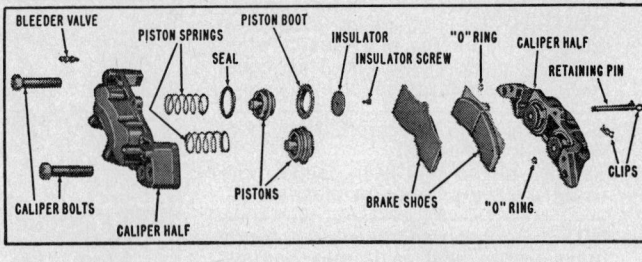

Fig. 28   Delco-Moraine disc brake caliper components

The brake disc is riveted to the hub flange at the front wheel and to the spindle flange at the rear wheel. The disc rotates through the caliper assembly, which is bolted to a support that is attached to the steering knuckle at the front wheel and the spindle support bolts at the rear wheel. The disc has cooling fins between the two shoe reacting surfaces. When a disc must be replaced, the rivets can be drilled out and then the wheel studs will be used for disc retension purposes.

A miniature set of brake shoes, mounted on a flange plate and shield assembly attached to the rear wheel spindle support bolts, are used for vehicle parking, Fig. 26.

Removing Lining

1. To prevent overflow, remove two thirds of brake fluid from master cylinder.
2. Support vehicle on hoist and remove wheel.
3. Remove cotter pin from inboard end of retaining pin.

4. Remove inboard and outboard shoe by pulling up.

Installing Lining

1. Install inboard and outboard shoe one at a time. Use two screwdrivers to push pistons back as shoes are inserted, Fig. 27.
2. Install retaining pin through outboard caliper half, outboard shoe, inboard shoe and inboard caliper half. Insert a new $3/32 \times 5/8$ inch plated cotter pin through retaining pin.
3. Repeat above procedure at each wheel where shoes are to be replaced.
4. Refill master cylinder, then install wheel and lower vehicle.

CAUTION: Do not move vehicle until a firm brake pedal has been obtained.

Calipers

The caliper assembly, Fig. 28, incorporates two halves retained by bolts at the flange end. The two halves contain fluid crossover passages from one to the other, sealed with "O" rings.

The bleeder screw is threaded into a passage drilled to intersect the fluid cross-over passage. The bleeder screws are located at the front of each caliper. There are two bleeder screws, one inboard, one outboard at the rear wheels, and one bleeder screw at the inboard side at the front wheel. It is necessary, therefore, to remove the rear wheel when bleeding the rear caliper.

Removing Caliper

1. Support vehicle on hoist and remove wheel.
2. On front caliper, disconnect brake hose from support bracket. On rear caliper, disconnect tubing from inboard caliper. Tape open tube or line end to prevent entry of dirt.
3. Remove caliper mounting bolts and remove caliper.

Disassembling Caliper

1. Remove brake hose from front caliper.
2. Remove cotter pin from retaining pin, then remove pin and shoe assembly from caliper.
3. Remove caliper retaining bolts and separate caliper halves, then remove the two O-rings from fluid transfer cavities in ends of caliper halves.
4. Push piston into caliper as far as it will move, then insert a screwdriver under inner edge of steel ring in boot

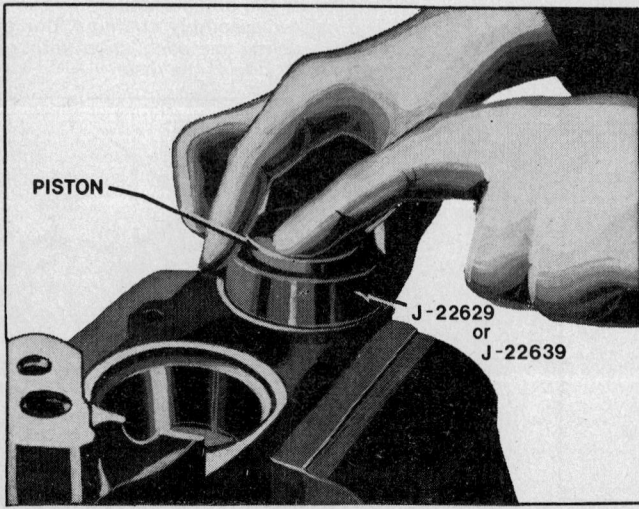

Fig. 29   Installing piston in caliper

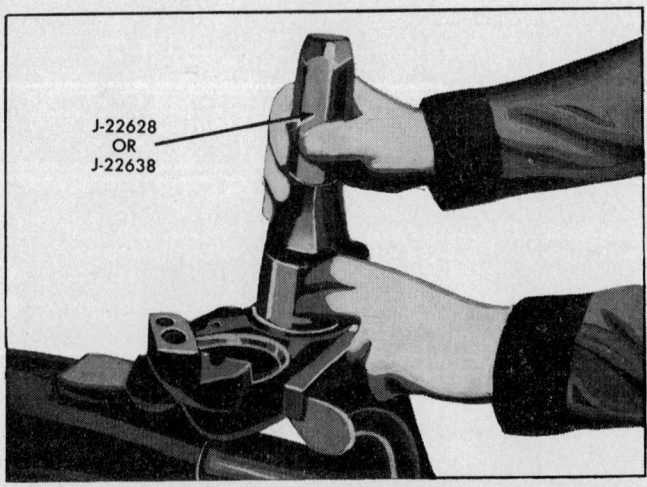

Fig. 30   Installing boot seal in caliper

and using piston as a fulcrum, pry piston boot from its seat in caliper half.

CAUTION: Use care not to puncture seal when removing pistons from caliper.

5. Remove pistons and springs from caliper half, then remove boot and seal from piston.

Cleaning & Inspection

1. Clean all metal parts using clean brake fluid, removing all traces of dirt and grease.

CAUTION: Never use mineral base cleaning solvents as they can cause deterioration of rubber parts or make them soft and swollen.

2. Using air pressure, blow out all fluid passages in caliper halves, making sure that these passages are not obstructed.
3. Discard all rubber parts and replace with new service kit parts.
4. Inspect piston bores. They must be free of scores and pits. A damaged bore will cause leaks and unsatisfactory brake operation. If either caliper half is damaged to the extent that polishing with fine crocus cloth will not restore to satisfactory condition, replace the caliper half.
5. Check fit of piston in bore using a feeler gauge. Clearance should be as follows:

$2\frac{1}{16}$ inch bore	.0045-.010
$1\frac{7}{8}$ inch bore	.0045-.010
$1\frac{3}{8}$ inch bore	.0035-.009

If bore is not damaged and clearance exceeds specifications, only a new piston will be required.

Assembling Caliper

1. Install seal in piston groove which is closest to flat end of piston. The seal lip must face toward large end of piston.

NOTE: Make certain seal lips are in piston groove and do not extend over step in end of groove.

2. Place spring in piston bore, then lubricate seal with brake fluid.
3. Install piston assembly in bore using tool J-22591, 22629 or 22639, Fig. 29. Use care not to damage seal lip as piston is pressed past edge of bore.
4. Install piston boot in groove closest to concave end of piston with fold in boot facing toward end of piston with seal attached.
5. Make certain that piston slides smoothly into bore until end of piston is flush with end of bore. If not, recheck piston assembly and position of piston spring and seal.
6. Using boot seal installer tool J-22592, J-22628 or J-22638, Fig. 30, over piston, seat steel boot retaining ring evenly into counterbore.

NOTE: Boot retaining ring must be flush or below machined face of caliper. Any distortion or uneven seating could allow corrosive elements to enter bore.

7. Install O-rings in cavities around brake fluid transfer holes at both ends of outboard caliper halves. Lubricate caliper bolts with Delco Brake Lube #540032 (or equivalent) or clean brake fluid, then secure caliper halves together and torque caliper bolts to 130 ft. lbs.

Installing Caliper

1. Mount caliper over disc, then using two screwdrivers, depress pistons so that caliper can be lowered into place.

NOTE: Use care not to damage boots on edge of disc as caliper is installed.

2. Install mounting bolts and torque to 70 ft. lbs.

CAUTION: If reusing old shoe assemblies, be sure to install shoes in same location from which removed.

3. Install disc pads as outlined previously.
4. Place a new copper gasket on male end of front wheel brake hose and install brake hose in calipers. With wheels straight ahead, pass female end of hose through support bracket, then making certain that tube seat is clean, connect brake line tube nut to caliper and tighten securely.
5. Allowing hose to seek a normal position, without twist, insert hose fitting in support bracket and secure with "U" shaped retainer, then while turning steering geometry from stop to stop, check that hose does not contact other parts at anytime. If contact does occur, remove "U" shaped retainer and twist hose in a direction that will eliminate hose contact. Reinstall retainer and recheck for hose contact. If satisfactory, place steel tube connecter in hose fitting and tighten securely.
6. If rear caliper is being serviced, connect brake line to caliper.
7. Bleed brakes and install wheels.

CAUTION: Do not move vehicle until a firm pedal has been obtained.

Service Summary

1. There is no brake shoe adjustment on the disc brakes.
2. The groove in the brake shoe is an indicator of brake wear. When the groove is just about gone it is time for shoe replacement.
3. When replacing shoes it is necessary to siphon fluid from master cylinder reservoir to make room for fluid to return to the reservoir when pushing the caliper pistons back into their bores to make room for the thickness

Fig. 31 Single piston disc brake (typical)

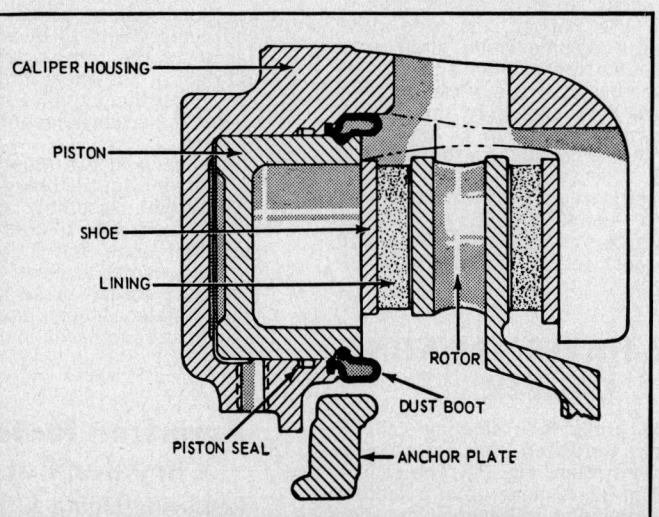

Fig. 32 Single piston disc brake caliper (typical)

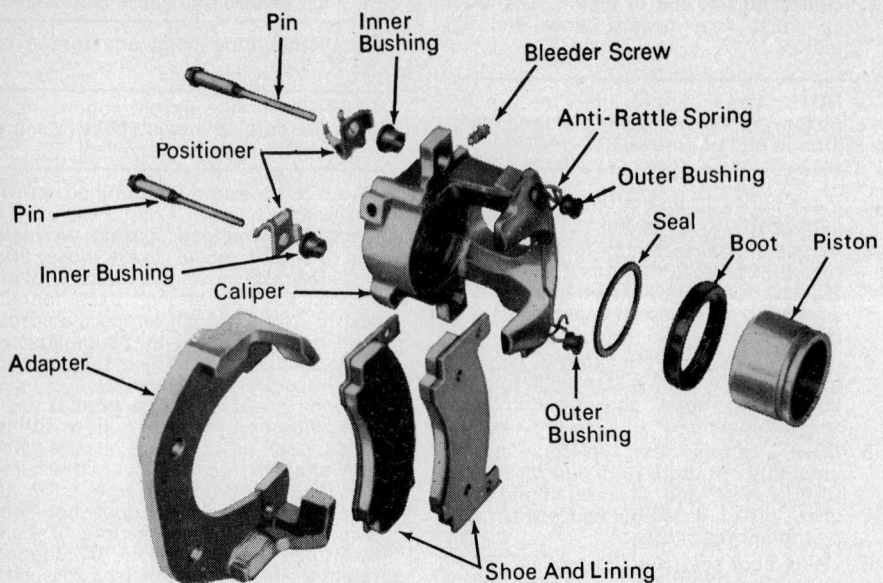

Fig. 33 Single piston disc brake caliper disassembled. (typical of American Motors and Chrysler Corp.)

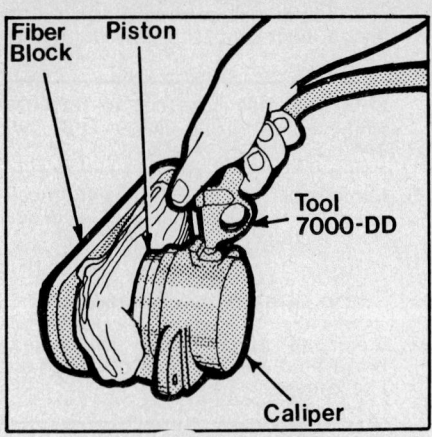

Fig. 34 Removing piston with air pressure

of the new shoes.

4. The shoes have a directional arrow on the back of the shoe plate. This arrow points to the forward rotation of the disc, and the purpose is for aligning the grain of the lining material in relation to the disc.

5. When bleeding the calipers, the rear wheel must be removed to reach the outboard bleeder screw.

6. A retaining clip of thin metal is used to hold the pistons into the bores while installing the new brake shoes.

7. The caliper assembly is removable, after disconnecting the brake line, by removing the two mounting bolts and lifting the assembly off the disc.

8. The disc is riveted to the spindle flange in production. However, the rivets may be drilled out and the wheel studs and nuts are sufficient to hold the new disc in place when replacing the disc.

9. The rear wheel spindle must be removed to gain access to the parking brake shoes. It is necessary then to remove the caliper, the axle drive shaft, the spindle drive shaft yoke and remove the spindle and disc as an assembly from the wheel support. You now have access to the parking brake shoes the same as any other conventional bendix type brake shoe, Fig. 26.

10. If the car is equipped with the special optional knock-off hub assemblies, the adapters must be removed to gain access to the parking brake adjustment.

KELSEY-HAYES FLOATING CALIPER

This type brake is a floating caliper, single piston, ventilated unit, actuated by the hydraulic system, Fig. 31. The caliper assembly, Fig. 32, is made up of a floating caliper assembly and an anchor plate. The anchor plate is bolted to the wheel spindle arm by two bolts. The caliper

is attached to the anchor plate through two spring steel stabilizers. The caliper slides on two guide pins which also attach to the stabilizers. A single piston is used. The cylinder bore contains a piston with a molded rubber dust boot to seal the cylinder bore from contamination and also to return the piston to the released position when hydraulic pressure is released. Also a rubber piston seal is used to provide sealing between cylinder and piston.

Service Precautions

In addition to the precautions described at the beginning of this chapter, the following must be observed.

1. If the piston is removed for any reason the piston seal must be replaced.

2. During removal and installation of a wheel assembly, use care not to interfere with and damage the caliper splash shield or the bleeder screw fitting.

3. Be sure the vehicle is centered on the hoist before servicing any front end components to avoid bending or damaging the rotor splash shield on full right or left wheel turns.

4. The proportioning valve should not be disassembled or adjustments attempted on it.

5. The wheel and tire must be removed separately from the brake rotor.

6. The caliper assembly must be removed from the spindle prior to removal of shoe and lining assembly.

7. Do not attempt to clean or restore oil or grease soaked brake linings. When contaminated linings are found, linings must be replaced in complete axle sets.

American Motors & Chrysler Corp.

Removing Lining & Caliper

1. Support vehicle on hoist and remove wheel assembly.

2. Remove two thirds of brake fluid from reservoir that serves disc brakes.

3. If caliper is to be removed, disconnect front brake hose from tube from mounting bracket and plug brake tube to prevent loss of fluid.

NOTE: If pistons are to be removed, leave flex brake line connected to tube at mounting bracket.

4. Remove caliper guide pins, Fig. 33. On American Motors models, remove positioners and anti-rattle clips.

5. Slide outboard and inboard shoe assembly out of caliper and adaptor.

6. Remove inner and outer bushings from caliper.

Installing Lining & Caliper

1. Install new inner and outer bushings Fig. 33, then slide shoe and lining assembly into place in caliper and adaptor making certain that metal portion of shoe is fully in recess of caliper and adaptor.

2. Holding inboard shoe assembly in place, carefully slide caliper down into position in adaptor and over rotor. Align guide pin holes of adaptor and inboard and outboard shoes.

3. On American Motors models, install positioners over guide pins with open ends up and anti-rattle spring.

4. Press in on end of guide pin and thread pin into adaptor using extreme care not to cross threads. Torque guide pins from 33 ft. lbs. making sure that tabs of positioners are over machined surfaces of caliper.

5. If caliper was removed, connect brake hose to caliper and tighten securely, then open bleeder screw and allow caliper to fill with fluid. Make certain that all air bubbles have escaped when bleeding caliper.

CAUTION: Do not move vehicle until a firm brake pedal has been obtained.

Caliper Disassembly

1. Open bleeder screw and drain brake

fluid from caliper then place caliper assembly in a soft jawed vice.

CAUTION: Do not overtighten vise as excessive pressure will cause bore distortion and binding of piston.

2. To remove piston place a cloth over piston and apply compressed air to fluid port in caliper, Fig. 34. Use extreme care to avoid damage to piston or bore. Allow dust boot to remain in caliper groove as piston is withdrawn.

3. Using a small wooden or plastic stick, work piston seal out of its groove and discard seal.

NOTE: Do not use screwdriver to remove piston seal as it could scratch bore or burr edges of seal groove.

4. Remove bleeder screw.

Cleaning & Inspection

1. Clean all parts with brake fluid and wipe dry, then blow out all drilled passages using compressor.

2. Inspect bore for scoring, pitting or corrosion. A deeply scored or corroded caliper should be replaced, although light scores and stains may be removed.

NOTE: If piston is pitted, scored or worn, replace piston.

3. Using crocus cloth, polish any discolored or stained area. Using finger pressure rotate crocus cloth in cylinder bore. Do not slide cloth in and out of bore under pressure or use any other form of abrasive or abrasive cloth. Black stains on bore wall are caused by piston seals and will do no harm.

4. Bores that have deep scratches or scores, should be honed providing that the diameter of the bore is not

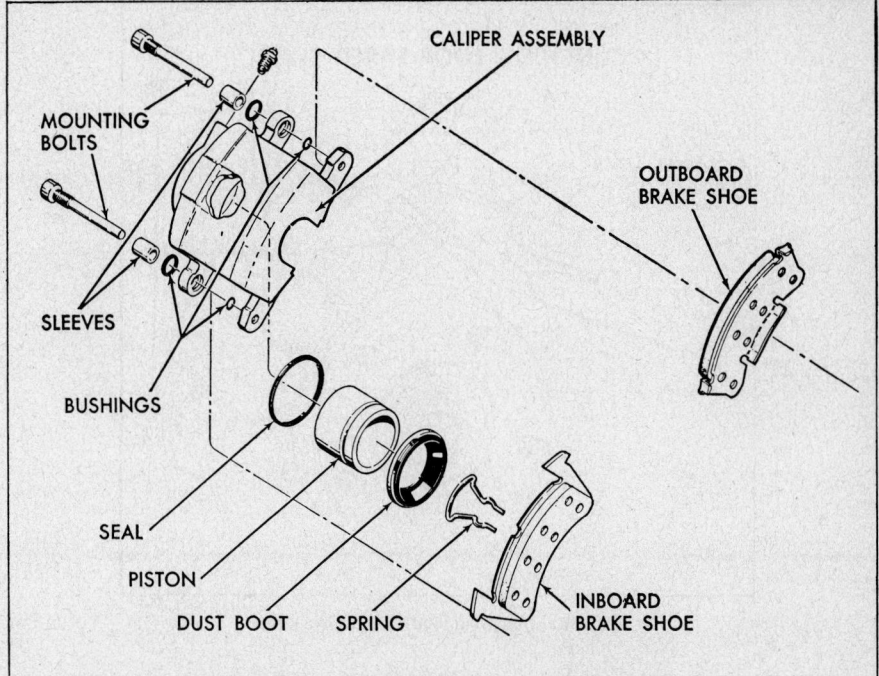

Fig. 35   Single piston caliper. Exploded (Typical)

increased more than .002 inch.

5. Using a feeler gauge, check clearance of piston in bore. Clearance should be .002-.006 inch. If clearance exceeds this specification, replace caliper assembly.

Caliper Assembly

1. Dip new piston seal in clean brake fluid and install in bore groove. Seal should be positioned and gently worked around groove until properly seated.

2. Dip new dust boot in clean brake fluid and install in caliper by working into outer groove. Boot will seem larger than diameter of groove but will snap into place when properly seated in groove. Slide forefinger around inside of boot to be sure it is seated.

3. Dip piston in clean brake fluid, then with fingers spreading boot, work piston into boot and carefully down the bore until bottomed.

CAUTION: To avoid cocking, force must be uniformly applied on piston.

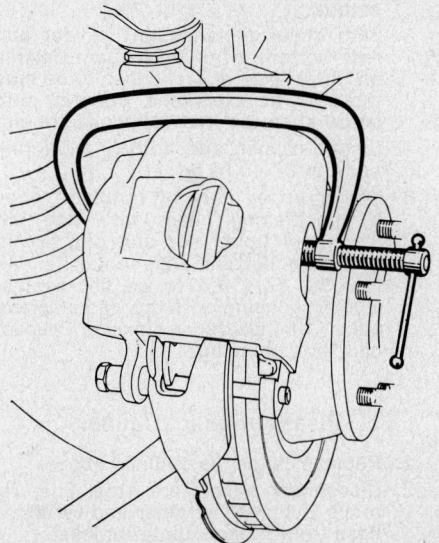

Fig. 36   Compressing piston and shoes with "C" clamp

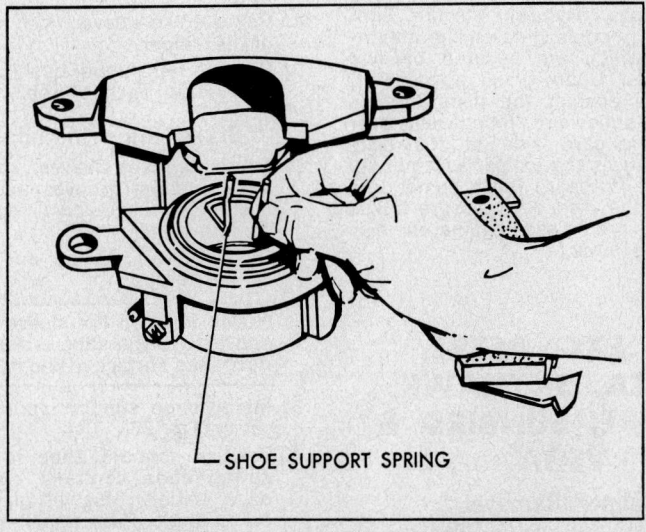

Fig. 37   Installing support spring

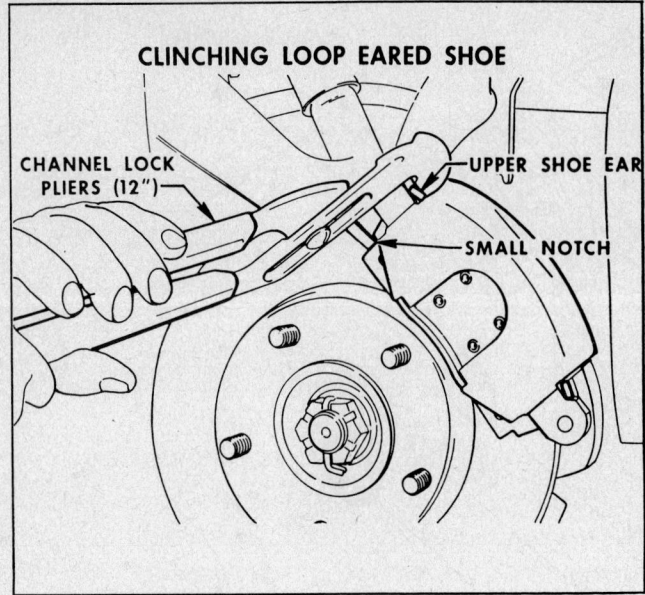

Fig. 38   Clinching loop eared brake shoe

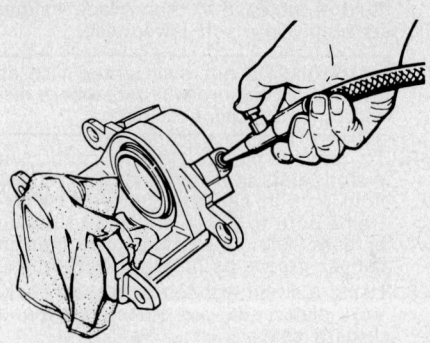

Fig. 39   Removing piston from caliper

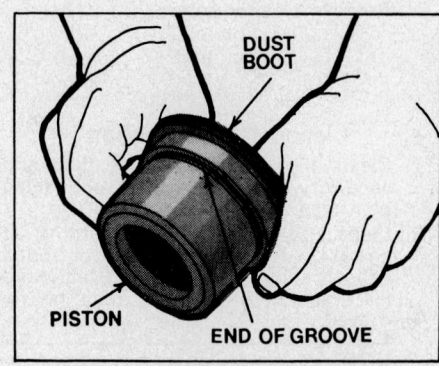

Fig. 40   Installing boot to piston

DELCO-MORAINE SINGLE PISTON

Dual Bolt Mounting

This single piston sliding caliper assembly, Fig. 35, incorporates a one piece housing with the inboard side of the housing bored for the piston. A seal within the housing bore provides a hydraulic seal between the piston and housing wall.

A spring steel scraper (wear sensor) is incorporated on each inboard shoe. When the shoe lining has worn to within .030 inch of the shoe, the sensor scrapes the rotor and emits an audible high frequency sound indicating that the linings should be replaced.

The caliper assembly used on all models except Astre, Monza, Skyhawk, Starfire, Sunbird and Vega, Fig. 35, slides on the mounting bolts. The caliper used on Astre, Monza, Skyhawk, Starfire, Sunbird and Vega models slide on the mounting sleeves which are secured by two mounting pins. Upon brake application, fluid pressure against the piston forces the inboard shoe and lining assembly against the inboard side of the disc. This action causes the caliper assembly to slide until the outboard lining comes into contact with the disc. As pressure builds up, the linings are pressed against the disc with increased force.

ALL EXC. ASTRE, MONZA, SKYHAWK, STARFIRE, SUNBIRD & VEGA

Caliper Removal

1. Siphon enough brake fluid out of the master cylinder to bring fluid level to 1/3 full to avoid fluid overflow when the caliper piston is pushed back into its bore.
2. Raise vehicle and remove front wheels.
3. Using a "C" clamp, as illustrated in Fig. 36, push piston back into its bore.
4. Remove two mounting bolts and lift caliper away from disc.

Brake Shoe Removal

1. Remove caliper assembly as outlined above.
2. Remove inboard shoe. Dislodge outboard shoe and position caliper on the front suspension so the brake hose will not support the weight of the caliper.
3. Remove shoe support spring from piston.
4. Remove two sleeves from inboard ears of the caliper.
5. Remove four rubber bushings from the grooves in each of the caliper ears.

Brake Shoe Installation

1. Lubricate new sleeves, rubber bushings, bushing grooves and mounting bolt ends with Delco Silicone Lube or its equivalent.
2. Install new bushings and sleeves in caliper ears.

NOTE: Position the sleeve so that the end toward the shoe is flush with the machined surface of the ear.

3. Install shoe support spring in piston cavity, Fig. 37.
4. Position inboard shoe in caliper so spring ends centrally contact shoe edge. Initially, this will place the shoe on an angle. Push upper edge of shoe down until shoe is flat against caliper. When properly seated, spring ends will not extend past shoe more than .100".

NOTE: Some inboard replacement brake pads incorporate wear sensors and have a specific left and right hand assembly. Properly installed, the wear sensor will face toward the rear of caliper.

5. Position outboard shoe in caliper with shoe ears over caliper ears and tab at bottom of shoe engaged in caliper cutout.
6. With shoes installed, lift caliper and rest bottom edge of outboard lining on outer edge of brake disc to be sure there is no clearance between outboard shoe tab and caliper abutment.
7. Install caliper and torque mounting bolts to 30-40 ft. lbs.
8. Clinch upper ears of outboard shoe by positioning pliers with one jaw on top of upper ear and one jaw in notch on bottom shoe opposite ear, Fig. 38. Ears are to be flat against caliper housing with no radial clearance. If clearance exists, repeat clinching procedure.

Disassembling Caliper

1. Remove caliper as outlined above.
2. Disconnect hose from steel line, remove U shaped retainer and withdraw hose from frame support bracket.
3. After cleaning outside of caliper, remove brake hose and discard copper gasket.

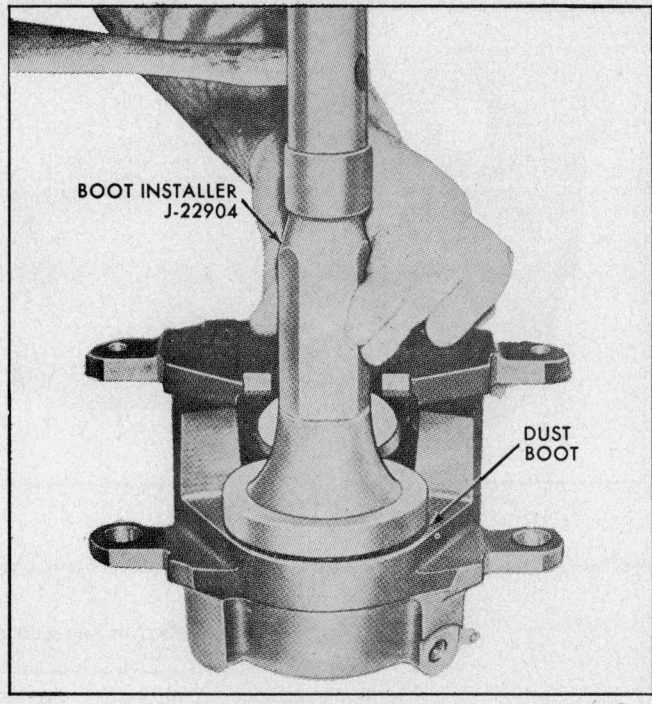

BOOT INSTALLER
J-22904

DUST
BOOT

Fig. 41   Installing boot to caliper

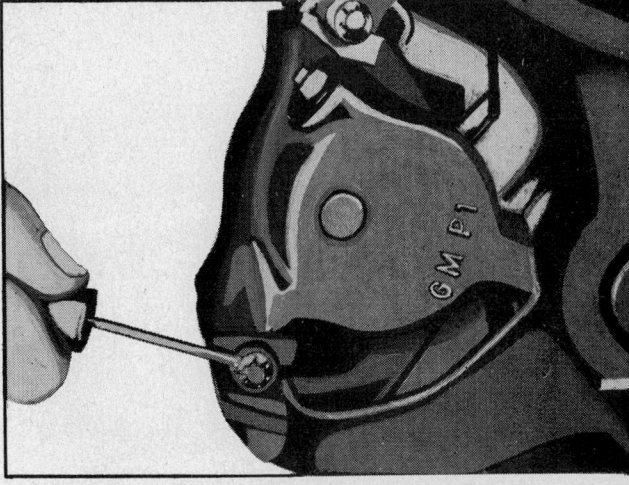

Fig. 42   Removing stamped nuts from mounting pins

4. Drain brake fluid from caliper.
5. Pad caliper interior with clean shop towels and use compressed air to remove piston, Fig. 39.

NOTE: Use just enough air pressure to ease piston out of bore. Do not blow piston out of bore.

CAUTION: Do not place fingers in front of piston in an attempt to catch or protect it when applying compressed air. This could result in serious injury.

6. Carefully pry dust boot out of bore.
7. Using a small piece of wood or plastic, remove piston seal from bore.

NOTE: Do not use a metal tool of any kind to remove seal as it may damage bore.

8. Remove bleeder valve.

Assembling Caliper

1. Lubricate caliper piston bore and new piston seal with clean brake fluid. Position seal in bore groove.
2. Lubricate piston with clean brake fluid and assemble a new boot into the groove in the piston so the fold faces the open end of the piston, Fig. 40.
3. Using care not to unseat the seal, insert piston into bore and force the piston to the bottom of the bore.
4. Position dust boot in caliper counter-

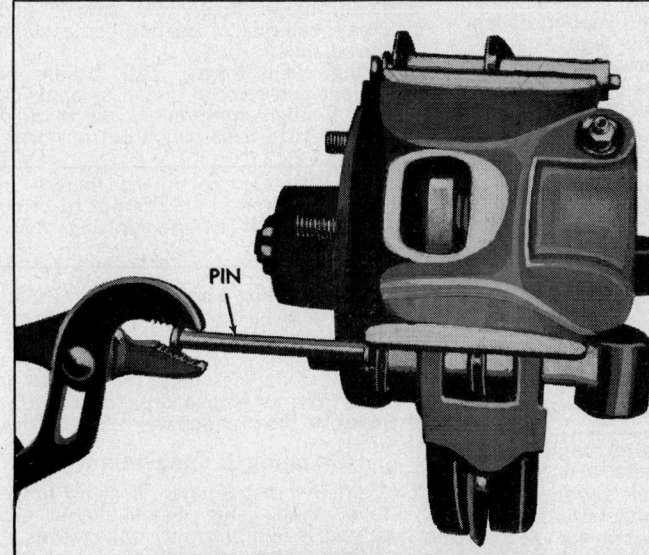

PIN

Fig. 43   Removing mounting pins

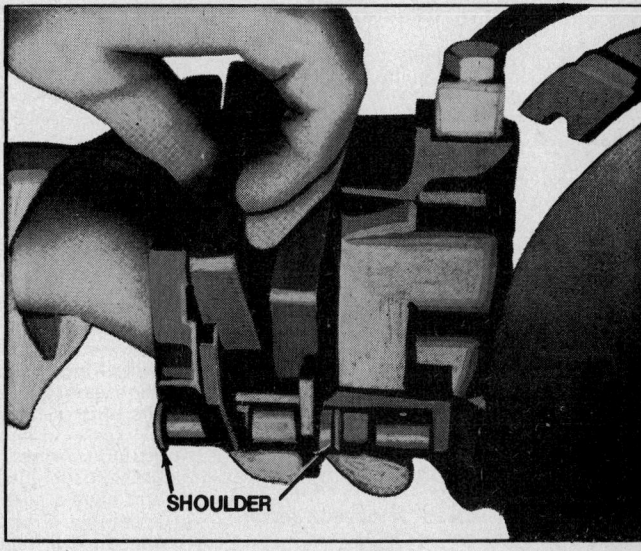

SHOULDER

Fig. 44   Mounting sleeves and brake shoe installation

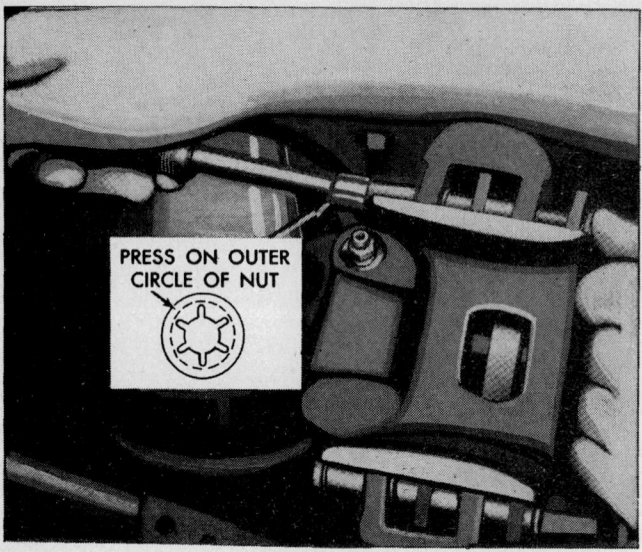

Fig. 45   Installing stamped nuts on mounting pins

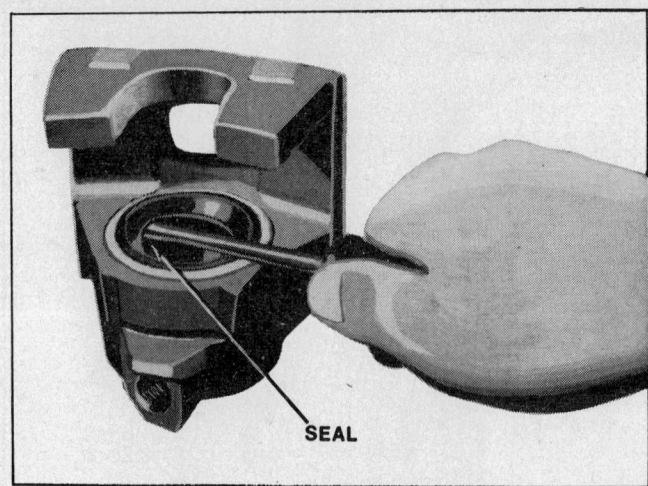

Fig. 46   Dust boot seal removal

bore and install, Fig. 41.

NOTE: Check the boot installation to be sure the retaining ring moulded into the boot is not bent and that the boot is installed below the caliper face and evenly all around. If the boot is not fully installed, dirt and moisture may enter the bore and cause corrosion.

5. Install the brake hose in the caliper using a new copper gasket.
6. Install shoes and re-install caliper assembly.

Caliper Installation

1. Position caliper over disc, lining up holes in caliper with holes in mounting bracket. If brake hose was not disconnected during removal, be sure not to kink it during installation.
2. Start mounting bolts through sleeves in inboard caliper ears and the mounting bracket, making sure ends of bolts pass under ears on inboard shoe.

NOTE: Right and left calipers must not be interchanged.

3. Push mounting bolts through to engage holes in the outboard ears. Then thread mounting bolts into bracket.
4. Torque mounting bolts to 30-40 ft. lbs.
5. If brake hose was removed, reconnect it and bleed the calipers.
6. Replace front wheels, lower vehicle and add brake fluid to master cylinder to bring level to 1/4" from

top.

NOTE: Before moving vehicle, pump brake pedal several times to be sure it is firm. Do not move vehicle until a firm pedal is obtained.

ASTRE, MONZA, SKYHAWK, STARFIRE, SUNBIRD & VEGA

Lining Removal

1. Support vehicle on hoist and remove wheel assembly.
2. Remove the two mounting pin stamped nuts, Fig. 42, and slide out the mounting pins, Fig. 43.
3. Lift caliper off disc and support caliper from suspension using wire.
4. Slide inboard and outboard shoes past mounting sleeve openings and remove mounting sleeves and bushing assemblies.
5. If caliper is to be removed, disconnect brake line.

Lining Installation

1. Install new sleeves with bushings on caliper grooves, Fig. 44.

NOTE: The "shouldered end" of sleeve must be installed toward outside.

2. Install inner shoe on caliper and slide shoe ears over sleeve, Fig. 44. Install the outer shoe in the same manner.

NOTE: Some inboard replacement brake pads incorporate wear sensors and have a specific left and right hand assembly. Properly installed, the wear sensor will face toward the rear of caliper.

CAUTION: If pads are being re-used,

they must be installed in same location as when removed.

3. Mount caliper on rotor. If brake line was disconnected, reconnect and torque bolt to 22 ft. lbs.

NOTE: To avoid overflow, it may be necessary to remove half of brake fluid capacity from master cylinder.

4. Install mounting pins from outside in and install stamped nuts, Fig. 45. Nuts should be pressed on as far as possible using a suitable size socket that just seats on outer edge of nut.
5. Install wheel assembly and lower vehicle.
6. Add brake fluid to within 1/4 inch from top of master cylinder and test brake operation to insure a firm brake pedal before moving vehicle.

Caliper Disassembly

1. Remove caliper as described under "Lining Removal".
2. Drain brake fluid from caliper and clean exterior of caliper using clean brake fluid.
3. Using clean towels, pad interior of caliper and remove piston by applying just enough compressed air to fluid inlet port to ease piston out of bore.

CAUTION: Do not place fingers in front of piston in an attempt to catch or protect it when applying compressed air.

4. Carefully using a screwdriver so as not to scratch piston bore, pry dust boot out of piston bore, Fig. 46.
5. Using a piece of wood or plastic so as not to damage bore, remove piston seal from its groove in caliper bore.
6. Remove bleeder screw.

Cleaning & Inspection

1. Clean all metal parts in clean brake fluid, then using clean filtered air, dry parts and blow out all passages in caliper and bleeder valve.

NOTE: Always use clean brake fluid to

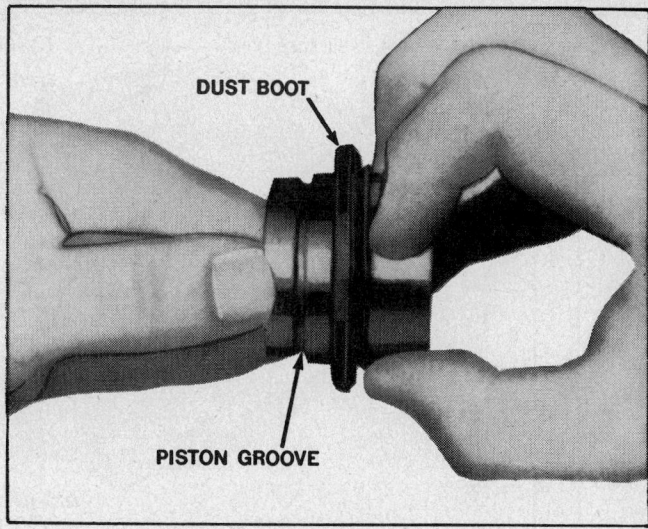

Fig. 47   Installing piston on boot

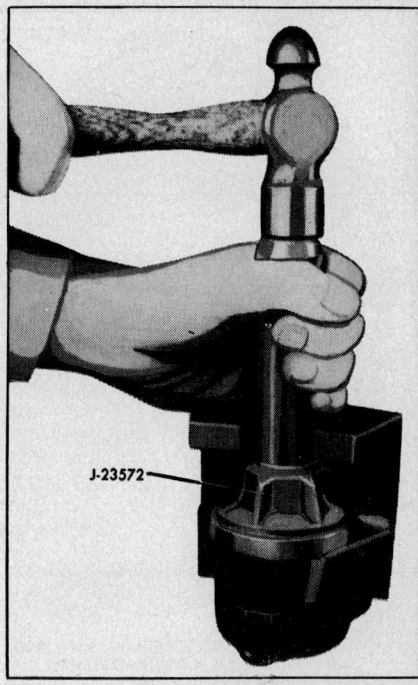

Fig. 48   Seating dust boot in caliper

clean caliper parts. Never use mineral base cleaning solvents as they can cause rubber parts to deteriorate and become soft and swollen, also the use of lubricated compressed air will leave a film of oil on metal parts that may damage rubber parts when they come in after reassembly.

2. Inspect piston surface for scoring, nicks, corrosion and worn or damaged plating. If any surface defects are detected, replace piston.

CAUTION: The piston outside surface is the primary sealing surface in the caliper. It is manufactured and plated to close tolerances, therefore refinishing by any means or the use of any abrasive is not recommended.

3. Check caliper bore for same defects as piston. The piston bore is not plated and stains or minor corrosion may be polished with crocus cloth.

CAUTION: Do not use emery cloth or any other form of abrasive and thoroughly clean caliper after use of crocus cloth. If caliper cannot be cleaned up in this manner, replace caliper.

Caliper Assembly

NOTE: The dust boot and piston seal are to be replaced each time that the caliper is disassembled.

1. Lubricate piston bore and new piston seal with clean brake fluid, then position seal in caliper bore groove.
2. Lubricate piston with clean brake fluid and assemble a new boot into groove in piston, Fig. 47.
3. Install piston into bore using care not to unseat seal, then force piston to bottom of bore.

NOTE: Approximately 50-100 pounds of force are required to push piston to bottom of bore.

4. Position dust boot in caliper counterbore and seat boot using tool shown in Fig. 48.

NOTE: Check boot installation to make sure that retaining ring moulded into boot is not bent and that boot is installed evenly all around. If boot is not fully installed, dirt and moisture may enter bore.

FORD
SLIDING CALIPER

The caliper assembly is made up of a sliding caliper housing assembly and an anchor plate, Fig. 49.

The anchor plate is bolted to the wheel spindle arm. Two angular machined surfaces on the upper end of the caliper housing contact mating machined surfaces of the anchor plate. A steel, plated key and a caliper support spring is fitted between the angular machined surfaces of the lower end of the caliper and the machined surface of the anchor plate. The key is held in position with a retaining screw. The caliper is held in position against the mating surfaces of the anchor plate by means of the caliper support spring. A brake shoe anti-rattle spring clip is provided on the anchor plate at the lower end of the inner brake shoe and lining assembly. The inner and outer brake shoe assemblies are not interchangeable.

The sliding caliper contains a single cylinder and a piston with a molded dust boot to seal the cylinder bore from contamination. A square section rubber piston seal is positioned in a groove in cylinder bore to provide sealing between cylinder and piston.

Caliper Removal

1. Raise car and support with safety stands. Block both rear wheels if a jack is used.
2. Remove wheel and tire assembly from hub.

3. Disconnect brake hose from caliper.
4. Remove retaining screw from caliper retaining key, Fig. 49.
5. Slide caliper retaining key and support spring either inward or outward from anchor plate. Use hammer and drift, if necessary, to remove the key and caliper support spring. Use care to avoid damaging the key.
6. Lift caliper assembly away from anchor plate by pushing caliper down against anchor plate and rotate upper end upward out of anchor plate, Fig. 50.
7. Remove inner shoe and lining from anchor plate. The brake shoe anti-rattle clip (inner shoe only) may become displaced at this time and if so, reposition it on anchor plate, Fig. 51. Tap lightly on outer shoe and lining to free it from caliper.
8. Clean caliper, anchor plate and rotor assemblies and inspect them for signs of fluid leakage, wear or damage. If either lining is worn to within 1/32" of any rivet head, both shoe and lining assemblies must be replaced. Also, if necessary to replace shoes and lining on one wheel, they must be replaced on both wheels to maintain equal brake action.

Caliper Disassembly

1. With caliper removed as described previously, disconnect brake hose. Cap hose and plug caliper inlet to prevent fluid loss.
2. With caliper on work bench, remove inlet plug and drain fluid from housing.

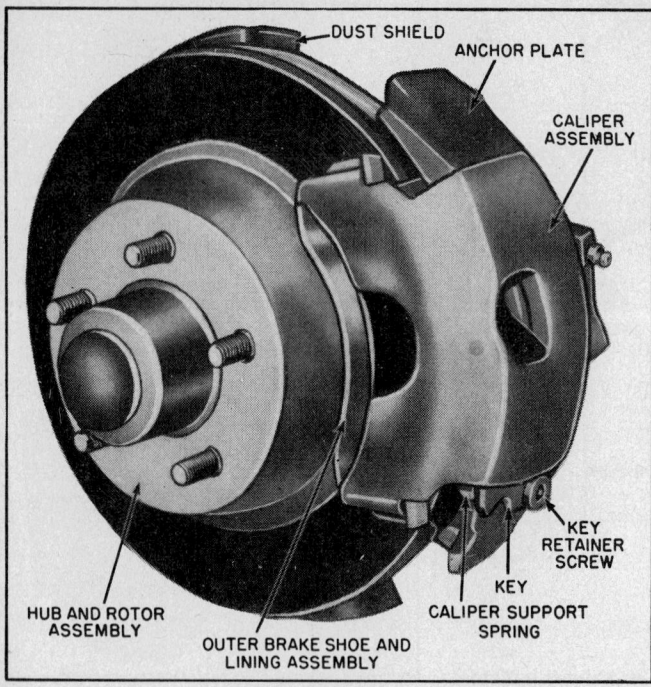

Fig. 49   Ford sliding caliper disc brake

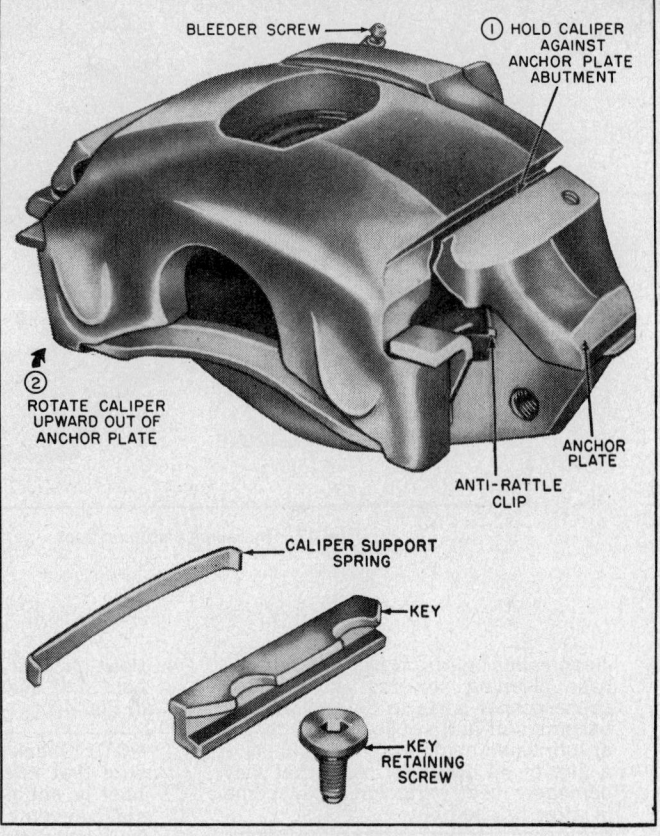

Fig. 50   Removing caliper assembly

3. Place a wooden block or an old brake pad into the caliper, then place a shop cloth between wooden block and piston.
4. Apply air pressure slowly to caliper inlet port to remove piston, Fig. 52.

NOTE: If high pressure is applied quickly, piston may pop out and cause injury. A cocked or seized piston can be eased out by rapping sharply on piston end with a soft brass hammer.

5. Remove boot from piston and seal from caliper cylinder bore.

Caliper Assembly

1. Lubricate piston seal with clean brake fluid and piston seal in its cylinder bore groove.
2. Assemble dust boot on caliper housing by seating boot flange in the outer groove of cylinder bore, making sure it is fully seated.
3. Coat piston with clean brake fluid and install in cylinder bore.
4. Spread dust boot over piston as piston is installed and then bottom piston in the bore. Seat dust boot in its piston groove.

Caliper Installation

1. If new shoe and lining assemblies are to be installed, use a 4" C-clamp and a block of wood $1\frac{3}{4}$" x 1" and about $\frac{3}{4}$" thick to seat the caliper piston in its bore. This must be done to provide clearance for the caliper to fit over new shoes when installed.
2. Be sure brake shoe anti-rattle clip is in place on lower inner brake shoe support on anchor plate with pigtail of clip toward inside of anchor plate. Position inner shoe and lining on anchor plate with lining toward rotor, Fig. 51.
3. Install outer shoe and lining with lower flange ends against the caliper leg abutments and the brake shoe upper flanges over the shoulders on caliper legs. The shoe upper flanges

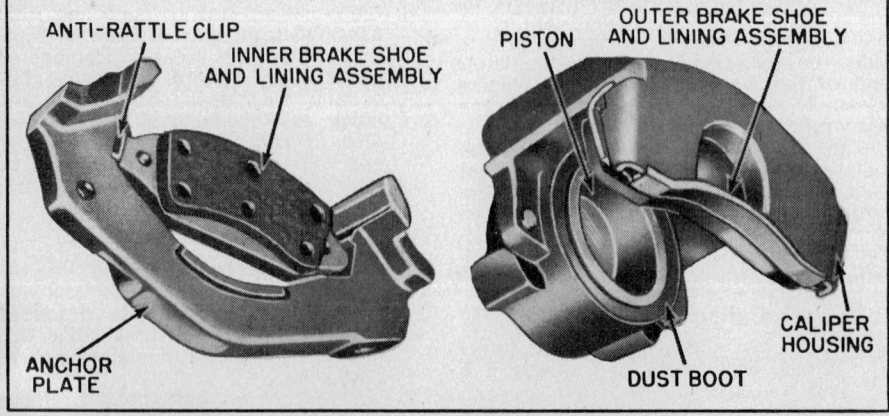

Fig. 51   Caliper and outer shoe removed from anchor plate

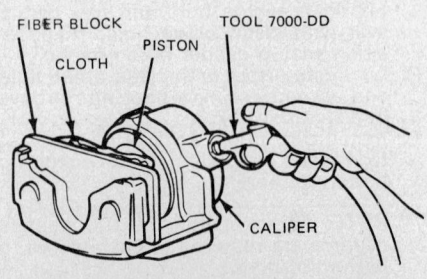

Fig. 52   Removing piston from caliper

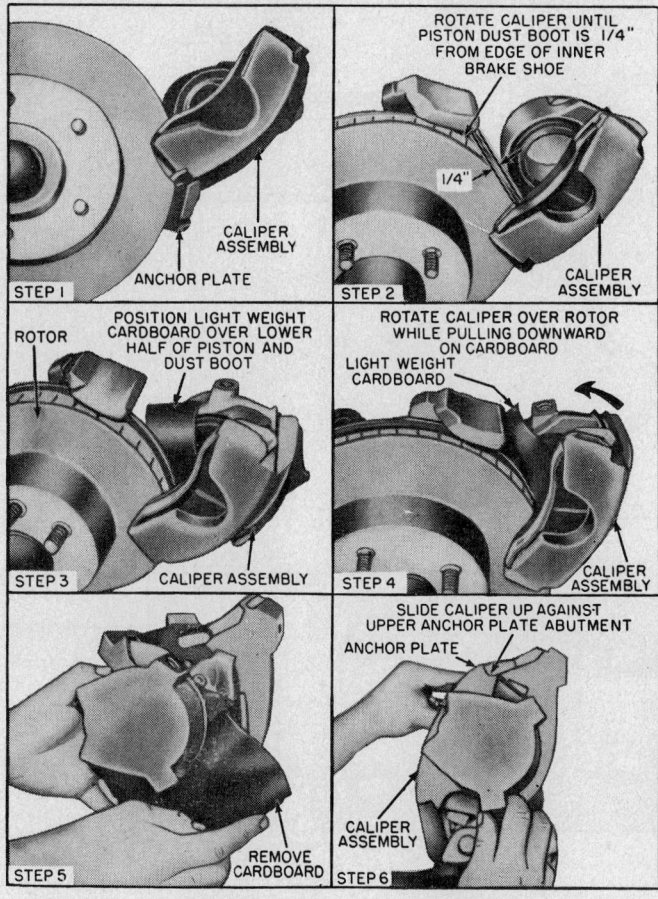

Fig. 53 Installing caliper assembly

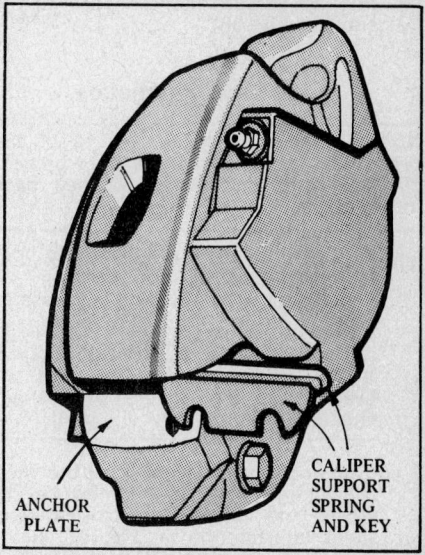

Fig. 54 Installing caliper support spring and retaining key

fit tightly against the shoulder machined surfaces. If the same brake shoes and linings are to be used, be sure they are installed in their original positions.

4. Remove C-clamp if used, from the caliper (the piston will remain seated in its bore).

5. Position caliper housing lower V groove on anchor plate lower abutment surface, Fig. 53. Refer to Figs. 53 and 54 to complete assembly following steps shown. Connect brake hose, bleed brakes and replace wheel.

6. Install key retaining screw and torque to 12-20 ft. lbs.

Brake Shoe & Lining, Replace

The procedure to replace the shoe and lining assemblies is the same as the caliper removal discussed previously with the exception that it is not necessary to disconnect the brake hose. Use care to avoid twisting or stretching the brake hose.

Hub & Rotor Removal

1. Remove caliper and shoes as previously described. If no repairs are necessary on the caliper it is not necessary to disconnect the brake hose. The caliper can be temporarily secured to the upper suspension arm. Do not remove the anchor plate and be careful not to stretch or twist the brake hose.

2. Remove grease cap from wheel spindle and remove cotter pin and nut lock from wheel bearing adjustment nut.

3. Remove wheel bearing adjusting nut and grasp the hub and rotor and pull it out far enough to loosen the washer and outer wheel bearing. Then push it back in and remove the washer, outer wheel bearing and remove the hub and rotor.

KELSEY-HAYES SLIDING CALIPER

This sliding caliper single piston system uses a one piece hub and is actuated by the hydraulic system and disc assembly, Fig. 55. Alignment and positioning of the caliper is achieved by two machined guides or "ways" on the adaptor, while caliper retaining clips allow lateral movement of the caliper, Fig. 56. Outboard shoe flanges are used to position and locate the shoe on the caliper fingers, Fig. 57, while the inboard shoe is retained by the adaptor, Fig. 58. Braking force applied onto the outboard shoe is transferred to the caliper, while braking force applied onto the inboard shoe is transferred directly to the adaptor.

A square cut piston seal provides a hydraulic seal between the piston and the cylinder bore, Fig. 55. A dust boot with a wiping lip installed in a groove in the cylinder bore and piston, prevents contamination in the piston and cylinder bore area. Adjustment between the disc and the shoe is obtain automaticaly by the outward relocation of the piston as the inboard lining wears and inward movement of the caliper as the outboard lining wears.

Caliper Removal

1. Raise the vehicle and remove front wheel.

2. Remove caliper retaining clips and anti-rattle springs, Fig. 56.

3. Remove caliper from disc by slowly sliding caliper assembly out and away from disc.

NOTE: Use some means to support caliper. Do not let caliper hang from hydraulic line.

Brake Shoe Removal

1. Remove caliper assembly as outlined above.

2. Remove outboard shoe by prying between the shoe and the caliper fingers, Fig. 59, since flanges on outboard shoe retain caliper firmly.

NOTE: Caliper should be supported to avoid damage to the flexible brake hose.

3. Remove inboard brake shoe from the adaptor, Fig. 58.

Brake Shoe Installation

NOTE: Remove approximately ⅓ of the brake fluid out of the reservoir to prevent overflow when pistons are pushed back into the bore.

1. With care, push piston back into bore until bottomed.
2. Install new outboard shoe in recess of caliper.

NOTE: No free play should exist between brake shoe flanges and caliper fingers, Fig. 60.

If up and down movement of the shoe shows free play, shoe must be removed and flanges bent to provide a slight interference fit, Fig. 57. Reinstall shoe after modification, if shoe can not be finger snapped into place, use light "C" clamp pressure, Fig. 61.

3. Position inboard shoe with flanges inserted in adaptor "ways," Fig. 58.
4. Carefully slide caliper assembly into adaptor and over the disc while aligning caliper on machined "ways" of adaptor.

NOTE: Make sure dust boot is not pulled out from groove when piston and boot slide over the inboard shoe.

5. Install anti-rattle springs and retaining clips and torque retaining screws to 180 inch-pounds.

NOTE: The inboard shoe anti-rattle spring is to be installed on top of the retainer spring plate, Fig. 56.

Caliper Disassembly

1. With caliper and shoes removed as described previously, place caliper onto the upper control arm and slowly depress brake pedal, in turn hydraulically pushing piston out of bore.

NOTE: Pedal will fall when piston passes bore opening.

2. Support pedal below first inch of pedal travel to prevent excessive fluid loss.
3. To remove piston from the opposite caliper, disconnect flexible brake line at frame bracket, from vehicle side where piston has been removed previously and plug tube to prevent pressure loss. By depressing brake pedal this piston can also be hydraulically pushed out.
   Important: Air pressure should never be used to remove piston from bore.
4. Mount caliper in a vise equipped with protector jaws.

NOTE: Excessive vise pressure will distort caliper bore.

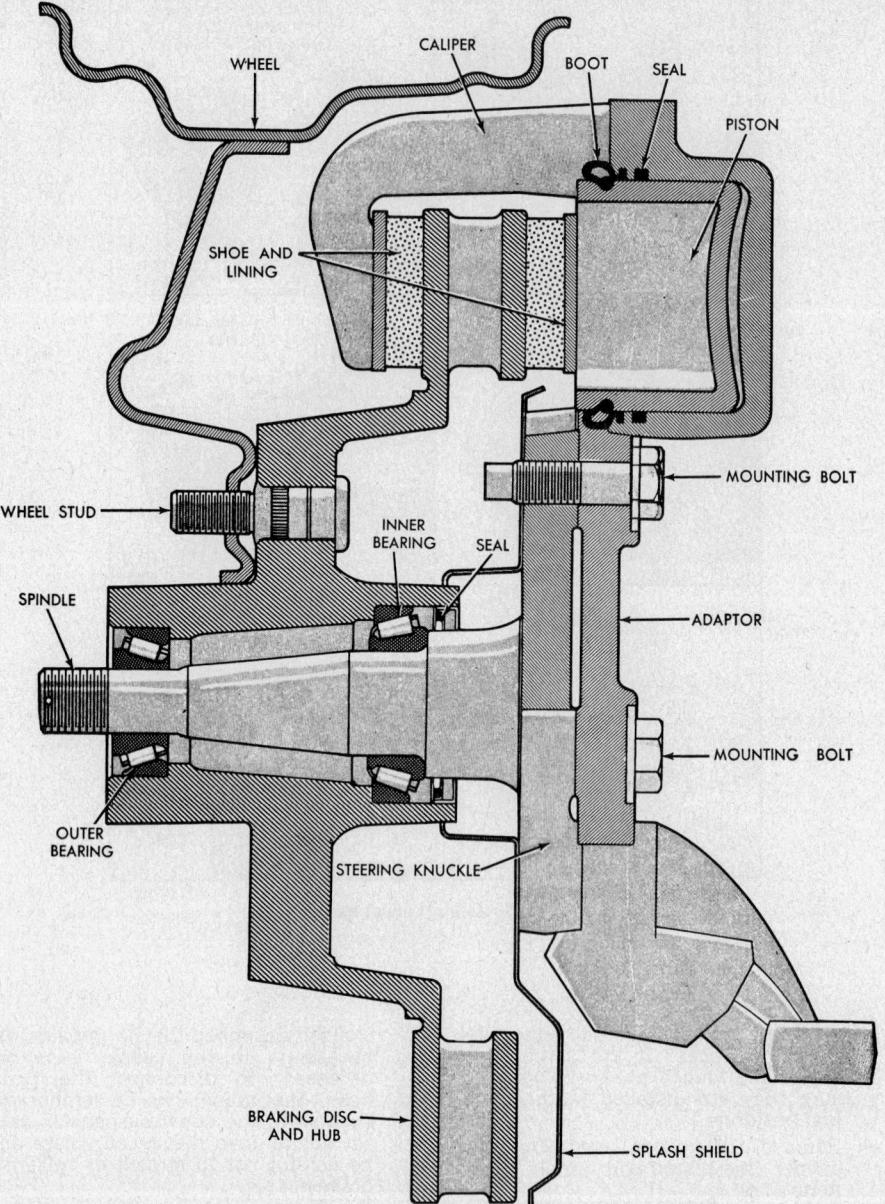

Fig. 55 Sectional view of Kelsey-Hayes sliding caliper front disc brake

5. Remove the dust boot, Fig. 62.
6. Insert a suitable tool such as a small, pointed wooden or plastic object between the cylinder bore and the seal and work seal out of the groove in the piston bore.

NOTE: A metal tool such as a screwdriver should not be used since it can cause damage to the piston bore or burr the edges of the seal groove.

Caliper Assembly

1. On 1974-76 models, before installing the new piston seal in groove of bore, dip seal in Ucon LB1145Y24 lubricant or equivalent. On 1977-78 models, dip new piston seals in clean brake fluid.

On all models, work seal gently into the groove (using clean fingers) until seal is properly seated, make sure that seal is not twisted or rolled.

NOTE: Old seals should never be reused.

2. On 1974-76 models, lubricate piston boot generously with Ucon LB1145-Y24 or equivalent. On 1977-78 models, lubricate piston boot generously with clean brake fluid. On all models, using finger pressure, install into caliper by pushing into outer groove of the caliper bore. When properly positioned in groove boot will snap into place. Double check to make sure boot is properly installed and seated

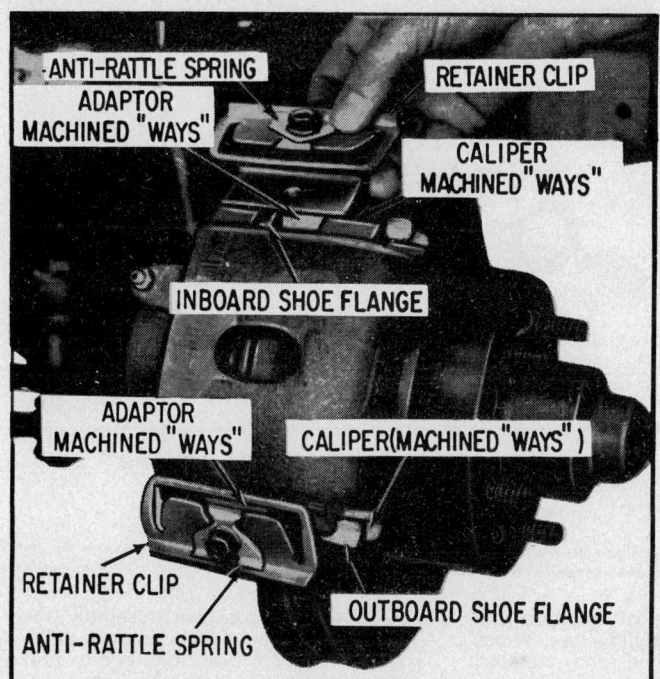

Fig. 56   Caliper machined "ways" and assembly retention

Fig. 58   Replacing inboard shoe

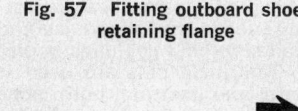

Fig. 57   Fitting outboard shoe retaining flange

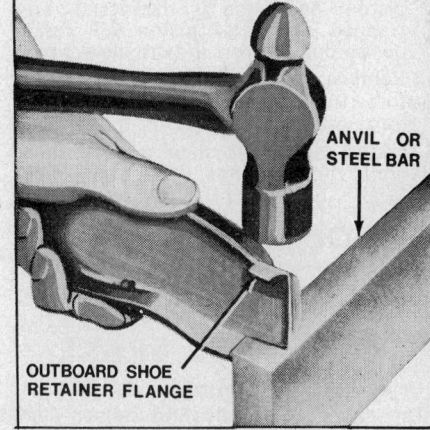

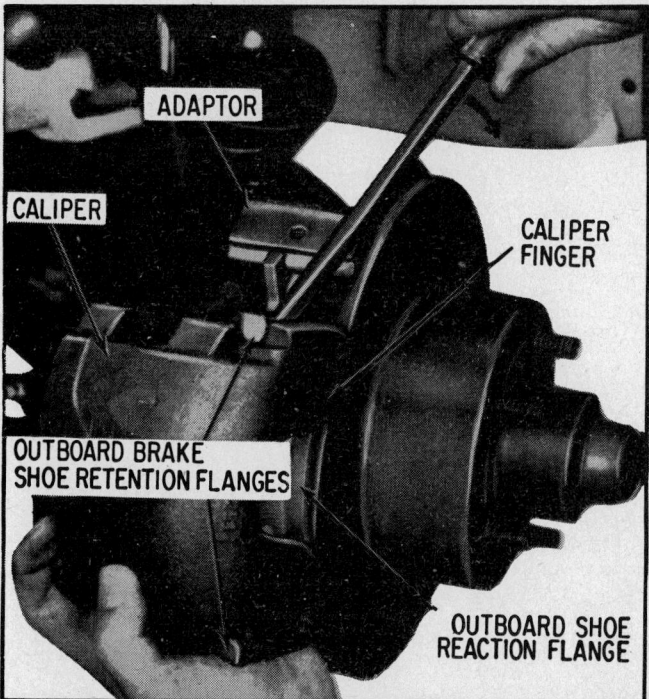

Fig. 59   Removing outboard shoe

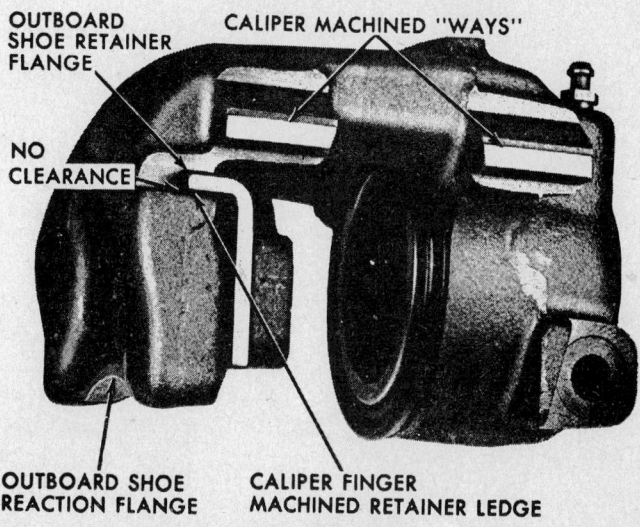

Fig. 60   Positioning outboard shoe onto caliper finger machined retainer ledge

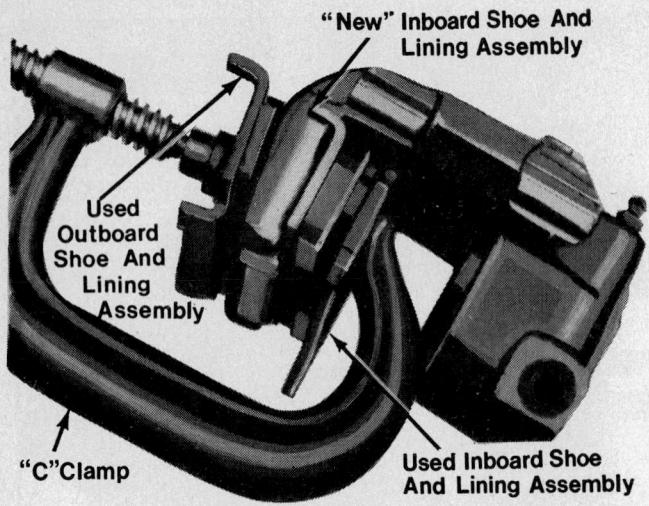

Fig. 61   Installing outboard shoe using "C" clamp

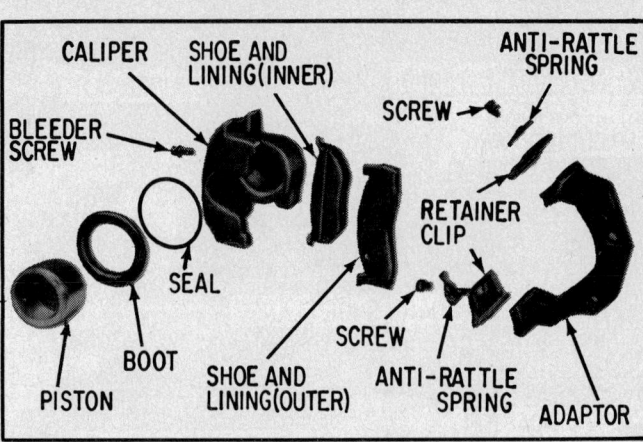

Fig. 62   Exploded view of a Kelsey-Hayes sliding caliper disc brake

by running finger around the inside of the boot.

3. Plug high pressure inlet to caliper and bleeder screw hole and coat piston with a generous amount of lubricant. Spread boot with finger and work piston into boot while pressing down on piston. As piston is depressed, entrapped air below piston will force boot around piston and into its groove.

4. Remove the plug and apply uniform force to the piston (avoid cocking piston) until piston bottoms in bore.

5. Install caliper and shoes as described under "Brake Shoe Installation."

DODGE OMNI & PLYMOUTH HORIZON FLOATING CALIPER DISC BRAKE

Operation

The single piston floating caliper disc brake assembly consists of the hub and disc brake rotor assembly, caliper, shoes and linings, splash shield and adapter, Fig. 63.

The caliper assembly floats on two rubber bushings riding on two steel guide pins threaded into the adapter. The bushings are inserted on the outboard portion of the caliper. Four machined abutments position and align the caliper fore and aft. Two positioners, installed over guide pins, control movement of the caliper along with piston seal, assist in maintaining proper shoe clearance and are also required to hold bushings in place.

The guide pins are used to radially locate and restrain both shoes, while all braking force is taken by the caliper on the outboard shoe and machined lug on adapter for inboard shoe.

Brake Shoe & Lining, Replace

Removal

1. Raise and support front of vehicle, then remove wheel and tire assembly.

2. Remove caliper guide pins and anti-rattle spring, Fig. 64.

3. Carefully slide caliper assembly away from disc, Fig. 65. Support caliper assembly to prevent damage to brake hose.

4. Remove outboard shoe and lining assembly from adapter, Fig. 66.

5. Remove rotor from drive axle flange and studs, Fig. 67.

6. Remove inboard shoe and lining assembly from adapter, Fig. 68.

Installation

1. Carefully push piston into caliper bore.

NOTE: Remove some brake fluid from reservoir to prevent overflowing when pushing piston into caliper bore.

2. Position inboard shoe and lining on adapter. Ensure metal portion of shoe is properly positioned in recess of adapter.

3. Install rotor over studs and drive flange.

4. While holding outboard shoe in position on adapter, carefully position adapter over disc brake rotor.

5. Carefully lower caliper over disc brake rotor and adapter.

6. Install guide pins through bushings, caliper and adapter.

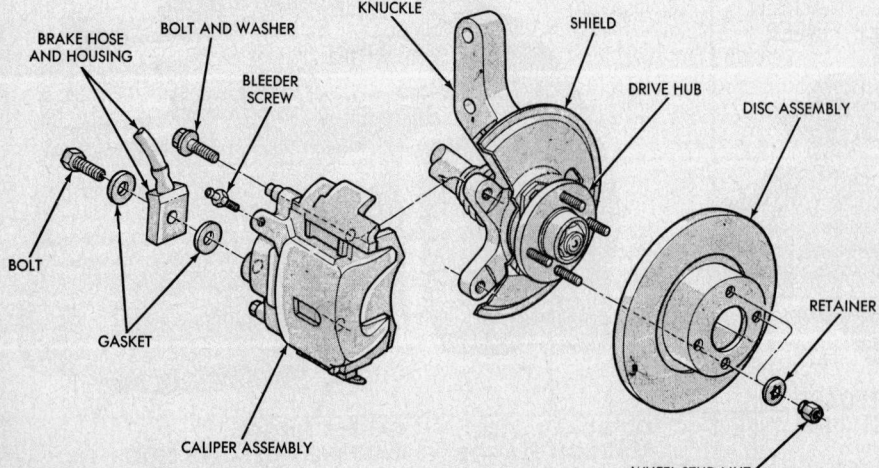

Fig. 63   Dodge Omni & Plymouth Horizon floating caliper disc brake

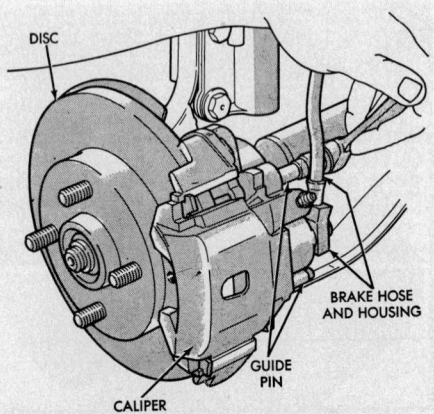

Fig. 64   Removing caliper guide pins

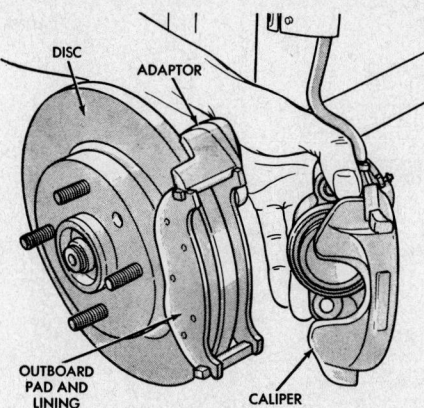

Fig. 65   Removing caliper

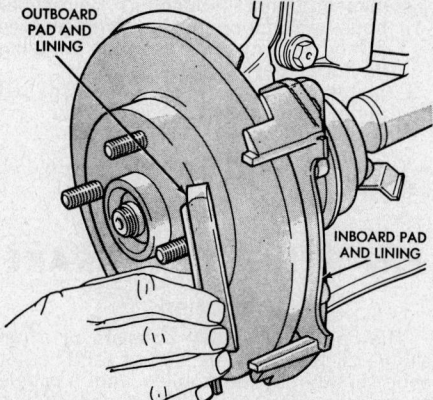

Fig. 66   Removing outboard pad & lining assembly

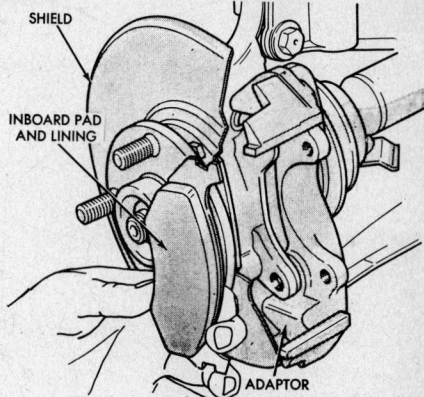

Fig. 68   Removing inboard pad & lining assembly

7. Press in on guide pins and thread pin into adapter. Torque pins to 25 to 40 ft. lbs.
8. Connect brake hose using seal washers, then bleed brake system. Check brake fluid level, then pump brake pedal until a firm pedal is obtained.
9. Install wheel and tire assembly, then lower vehicle.

Caliper Oerhaul

Disassemble, Fig. 69

1. Remove caliper assembly as described under Brake Shoe & Lining, Replace.
2. With brake hose attached to caliper, carefully depress brake pedal to push piston out of caliper bore. Prop brake pedal to any position below first inch of brake pedal travel to prevent brake fluid loss.
3. If pistons are to be removed from both calipers, disconnect brake hose at frame bracket after removing piston, then cap brake line and repeat procedure to remove piston from other caliper.

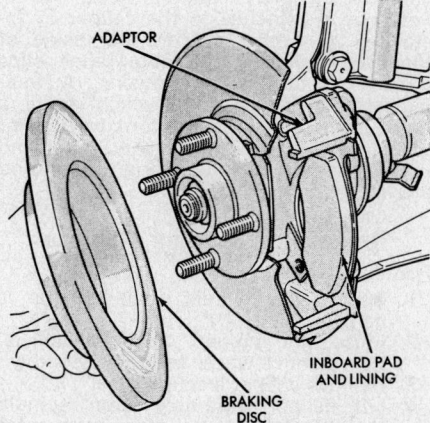

Fig. 67   Removing disc brake rotor from hub

4. Disconnect brake hose from caliper.
5. Mount caliper in a soft jawed vise.
6. Support caliper and remove dust boot and discard.
7. Using a small wooden or plastic stick, remove seal from groove in piston bore and discard.
8. Using a suitable tool, remove bushings from caliper.

Inspection

1. Clean all components using alcohol or other suitable cleaning solvent, then blow dry using compressed air. With compressed air blow out drilled passages and bores.
2. Inspect piston bore for pitting or scoring. Light scratches or corrosion can usually be cleared with crocus cloth. Bores that have deep scratches or scoring should be honed with tool No. C-4095, providing bore diameter is not increased by more than .001 in. If scratches or scoring cannot be cleared up, or if caliper bore is increased by more than .001 in., replace caliper housing.

NOTE: When using hone C-4095, coat hone and caliper bore with clean brake fluid. After honing carefully clean boot and seal grooves with a stiff non-metallic brush. Flush caliper with clean brake fluid and wipe dry with a clean lintless cloth, then flush and wipe caliper dry again.

3. Replace piston if found to be scored, pitted or if plating is severely worn

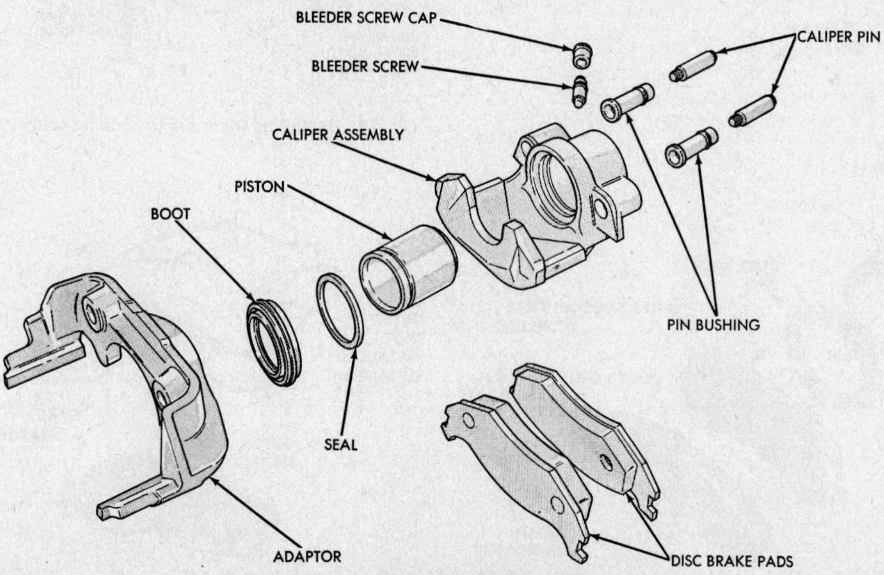

Fig. 69   Disassembled view of disc brake caliper

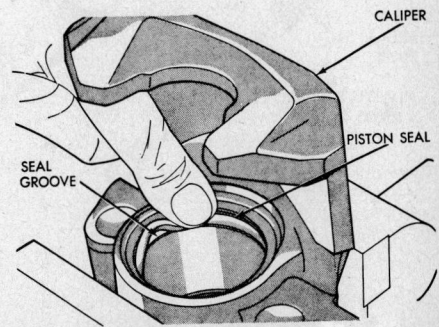

Fig. 70   Installing piston seal

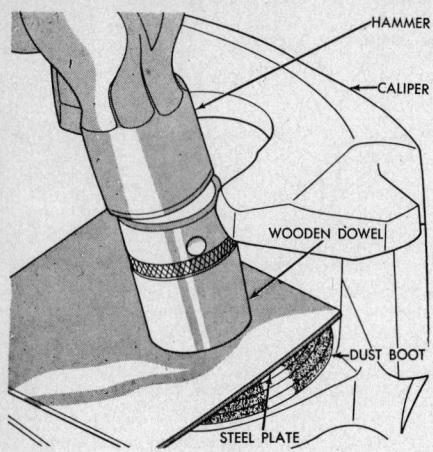

Fig. 71   Installing piston dust boot

or if caliper bore was honed. Black stains on piston are caused by piston seal and are not cause for replacing piston.

Assemble, Fig. 69

1. Mount caliper in a soft jawed vise.
2. Lubricate piston seal with clean brake fluid and install seal in caliper bore groove, Fig. 70. Ensure seal is properly seated.
3. Lubricate piston boot with clean brake fluid and install boot in caliper bore groove, Fig. 71.
4. Using a hammer and small steel plate or a suitable C-clamp, drive into caliper until seated, Fig. 72. Ensure boot is properly seated in caliper bore.
5. Plug brake hose inlet boss and bleeder screw hole, then lubricate piston with clean brake fluid.
6. Spread boot with finger and work piston into boot, then press down on piston.
7. Remove plug and carefully push piston down in bore until bottomed.
8. Compress flanges of guide pin bushings and install bushings on caliper housing. Ensure that bushing flanges extend evenly over caliper housing on both sides.
9. Install caliper on vehicle as described under Caliper, Replace.

KELSEY-HAYES PIN SLIDER DISK BRAKE

Operation

The caliper assembly consists of a pin slider caliper housing, inner and outer shoe and lining assemblies and a single piston, Fig. 73. The caliper slides on two pins which also act as attaching bolts between caliper and the combination anchor plate and spindle. The outer brake shoe and lining assembly is longer than the inner brake shoe and lining assembly. Inner and outer shoe and lining assemblies are attached to the caliper by spring clips riveted to the shoe surfaces. The inner shoe is attached to the caliper by installing the spring clip to the inside of the caliper piston. The outer shoe clips directly to the caliper housing. A wear indicator is incorporated which emits a noise when the lining is worn to a point when replacement is necessary. Inner and outer shoes are of left and right hand and are not interchangeable.

Brake Shoe & Lining, Replace

Removal

1. Remove brake fluid until reservoir is half full.
2. Raise and support front of vehicle, then remove wheel and tire assembly.
3. Remove caliper locating pins.
4. Lift caliper assembly from spindle and adapter plate, then remove outer shoe from caliper assembly.
5. Remove inner shoe and lining assembly.
6. Suspend caliper from inner fender housing with wire to avoid damaging brake hose.
7. Remove and discard locating pin insulators and plastic sleeves.

Installation

1. Using a 4 in. C-clamp and a block of wood 2¾ x 1 in. and approximately ¾ in. thick, seat caliper piston in bore, then remove C-clamp and wooden block.
2. Install locating pin insulators and plastic sleeves on caliper housing. Ensure insulators and sleeves are properly positioned.
3. Install inner shoe and lining assembly on caliper piston, Fig. 74.

NOTE: Inner brake shoes are marked LH (left hand) and RH (right hand)

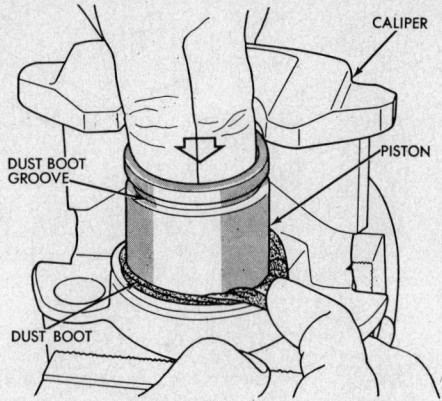

Fig. 73   Kelsey-Hayes pin slider disc brake caliper

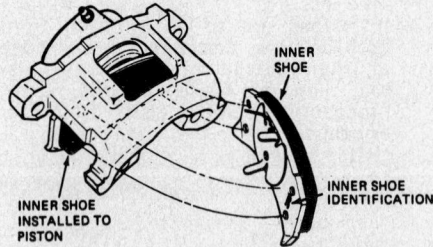

Fig. 74   Installing inner brake shoe on caliper

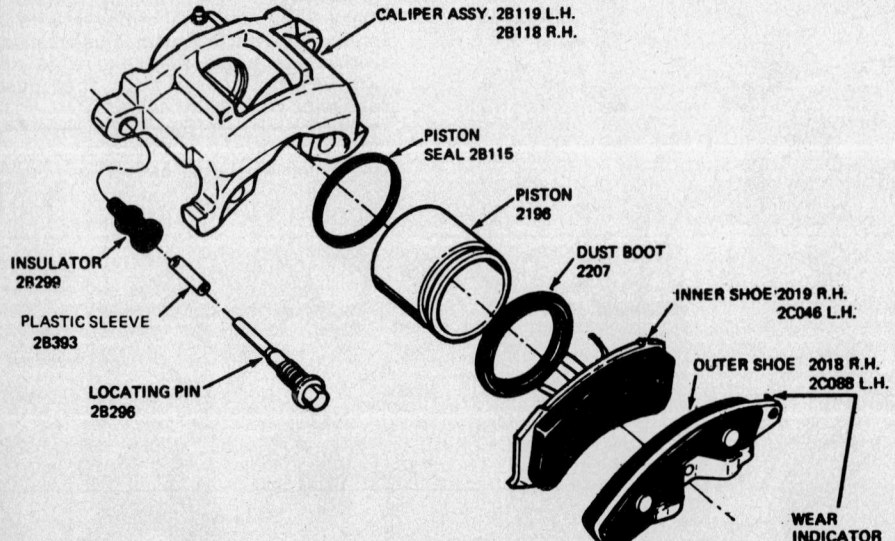

Fig. 72   Installing caliper piston

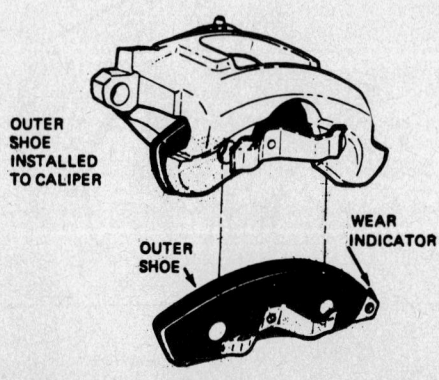

Fig. 75   Installing outer brake shoe on caliper

and must be installed on the proper caliper. Use care to not bend spring clips too far during installation in piston, otherwise distortion and rattles may result.

4. Install outer brake shoe and lining assembly, Fig. 75. Ensure that shoes are installed on proper caliper. Make sure that clip and buttons on shoe are properly seated.

NOTE: The outer shoe can be identified as left hand and right hand by the wear indicator which must be installed toward front of vehicle.

5. Refill master cylinder, then install wheel and tire assembly and lower vehicle.
6. Pump brake pedal several times to position brake linings before moving vehicle.

Caliper, Replace

Removal
1. Raise and support front of vehicle, then remove wheel and tire assembly.
2. Loosen brake tube fitting which connects brake tube to fitting on frame and plug brake tube. Remove retaining clip from brake hose and bracket, then disconnect brake hose from caliper.
3. Remove caliper locating pins.
4. Lift caliper from rotor and spindle anchor plate assembly.

NOTE: Before removing calipers, mark left and right hand calipers so they can be installed in the same position.

Installation
1. Install caliper assembly over rotor with outer shoe against rotor braking surface during installation on spindle and anchor plate to prevent pinching of piston boot between inner brake shoe and piston.

NOTE: Ensure calipers are installed in the correct position.

2. Install locating pins. Torque locating pins to 30 to 40 ft. lbs.
3. Connect brake hose to caliper. Torque hose fitting to 20 to 30 ft. lbs.
4. Position upper end of brake hose in bracket and install retaining clip. Remove plug from brake line, then connect brake hose fitting to brake line. Torque fitting to 10 to 18 ft. lbs.
5. Bleed brake system and centralize pressure differential valve.
6. Install wheel and tire assembly, then lower vehicle.
7. Pump brake pedal several times to position brake shoes before moving vehicle.

Caliper Overhaul

Disassemble, Fig. 73
1. Remove caliper assembly from vehicle as described under Caliper, Replace.
2. Position fiber block and shop towels between caliper piston and caliper housing, then apply compressed air to caliper brake line fitting bore to force piston from caliper.
3. Remove dust boot from caliper assembly.

4. Remove pistol seal from cylinder and discard.

Inspection
Clean all metal parts with isopropyl alcohol, then clean and dry passages and grooves with compressed air. Check caliper and piston for damage and wear and replace as necessary.

Assemble, Fig. 73
1. Lubricate piston seal with clean brake fluid, then install seal in caliper bore.

NOTE: Ensure seal is firmly seated in groove.

2. Install dust boot in outer groove of caliper bore.
3. Coat piston with clean brake fluid and install piston in caliper bore. Spread dust boot over piston as it is installed. Seat dust boot in piston groove.
4. Install caliper assembly as described under ''Caliper, Replace.''

REAR WHEEL DISC BRAKE & PARKING BRAKE SERVICE
1974-75 Imperial

The parking brake assembly of this system is mounted on the axle flange and intermediate disc brake adaptor. The rotor has an internal 7 inch drum surface for the internal expanding parking brake shoes, Fig. 76. Service to system should be performed as follows:

Disassembly
1. Support vehicle on a stand and remove rear wheel.
2. Remove caliper retaining screws and anti rattle spring assemblies, Fig. 56. Slide caliper from adaptor machined ways and position caliper on leaf spring for support, Fig. 77.
3. Remove inboard shoe from adaptor ways and remove parking brake adjusting access hole plug.
4. Using brake adjusting tool C-4223, release parking brake adjustment and remove disc/drum.
5. Remove lower shoe spring, Fig. 78. Spread brake shoes slightly and remove adjusting star wheel and upper shoe spring, Fig. 79.
6. Move brake shoes off support and remove brake shoe retainers, springs and nails and remove from support, Fig. 80.
7. Disconnect park brake cable from lever and snap ring retainer from shaft and remove lever, Fig. 81.
8. Remove inner snap ring from shaft and remove cam lever, cam and shaft, Fig. 82.

Cleaning & Inspection
1. Brush or wipe (dry) metal portions of the brake shoes. Inspect lining contact area, the lining should show contact marks across its entire area. Shoes showing contact on one side should be replaced.
2. Using a suitable solvent, clean brake

support. Inspect for burrs and remove as necessary.
3. Clean cam lever, cam, shaft and operating lever. Inspect for damaged or distorted parts, including O-rings and replace as necessary. Replace any parts that do not permit freedom of operation. Apply lubricant to threads, sockets and washers.

Drum Refacing
Check drum diameter and runout. Drum diameter should not vary more than .002 inch. Drum runout should not exceed .006 inch. If drum runout or diameter exceed these limits, the drum should be refaced. Remove only as much metal as necessary, but do not remove more than .060 inch over the standard brake diameter.

NOTE: Maximum allowable diameter of 7.090 inches, Fig. 83, includes the .030 inch allowable drum wear.

Assembling Parking Brake Mechanism
1. Lubricate shaft with Mopar Lubricant #2932524 or equivalent and install in intermediate shaft adaptor.
2. Install cam and cam lever and snap ring on shaft, Fig. 82.
3. Install inner operating lever and snap ring on shaft and connect parking brake cable to lever, Fig. 81.
4. Lubricate shoe tab contact area (6 places) with Mopar Lubricant #2932524 or equivalent.
5. Place brake shoes on support and install retaining nails, springs and retainers, Fig. 80.
6. Install upper shoe spring and adjuster wheel, Fig. 79.

NOTE: Adjuster star wheel is forward on left side of vehicle and to the rear on right side of vehicle.

7. Install lower shoe spring and install disc drum, Fig. 78.

Assembling Caliper
1. Place inboard shoe on adaptor with shoe flanges in adaptor ways, Fig. 77.
2. Carefully slide caliper assembly into

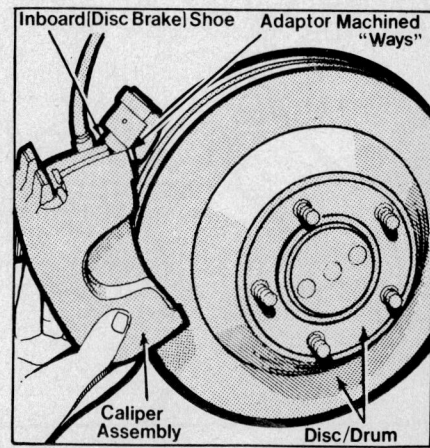

Fig. 77 Replacing caliper assembly

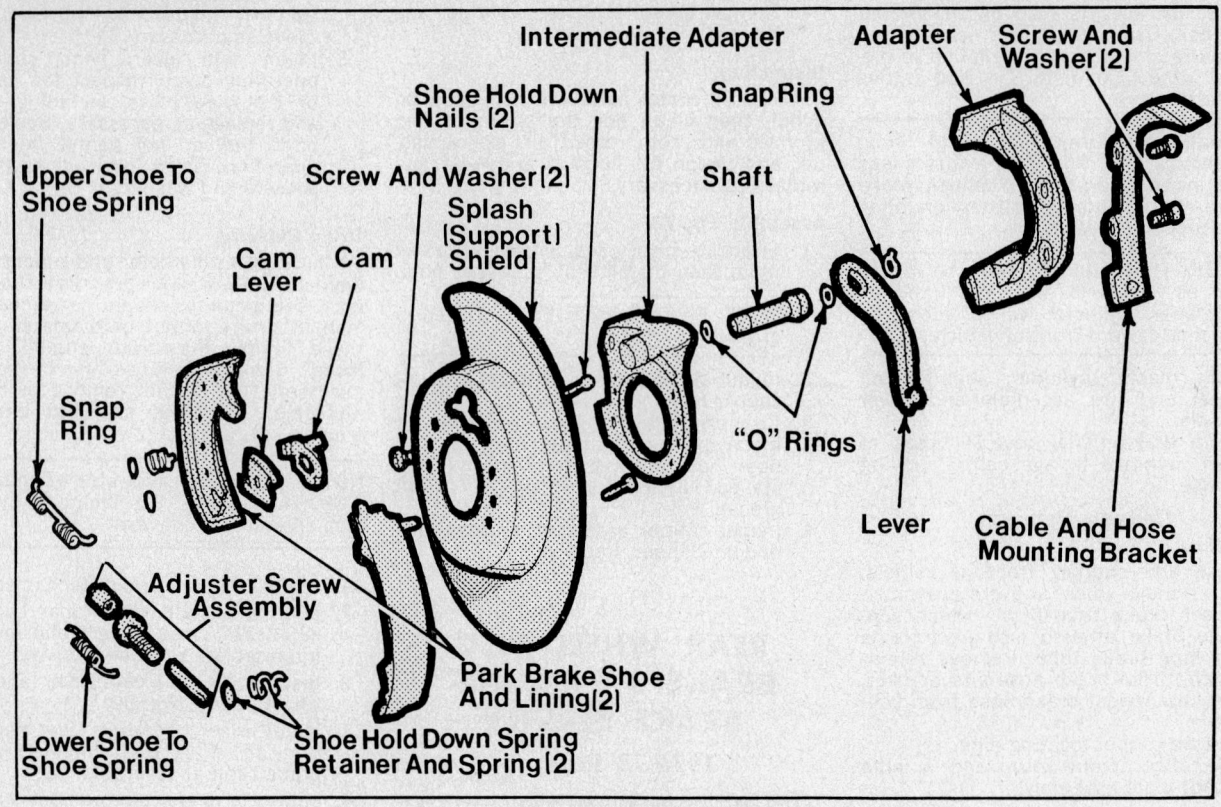

Fig. 76   Rear wheel parking brake assembly

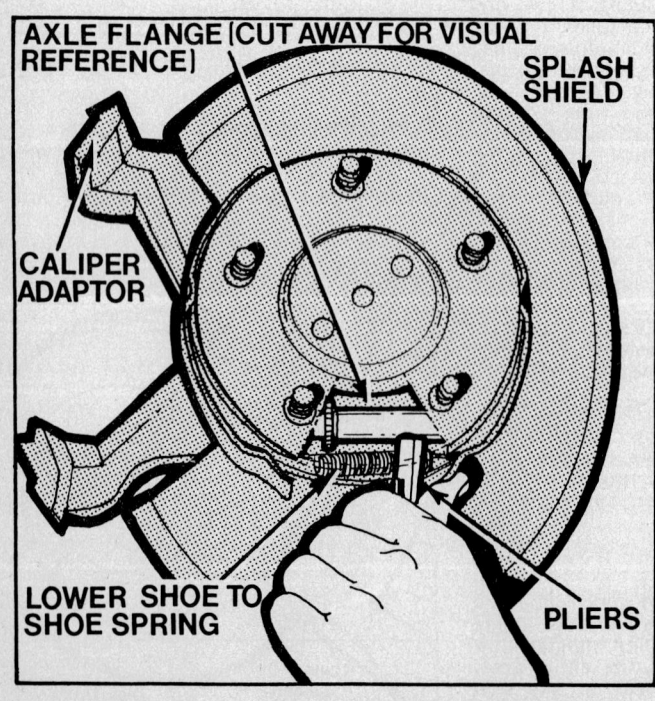

Fig. 78   Replacing lower shoe to shoe spring

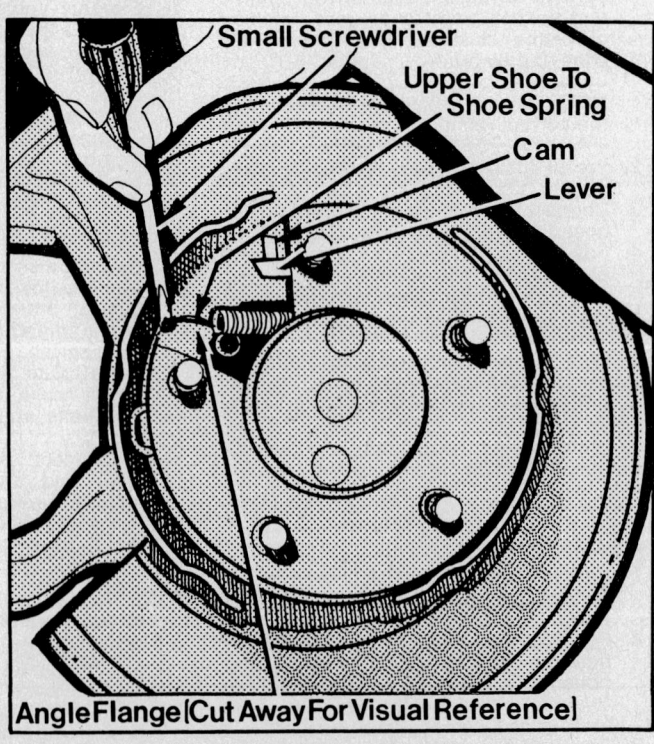

Fig. 79   Replacing upper shoe to shoe spring

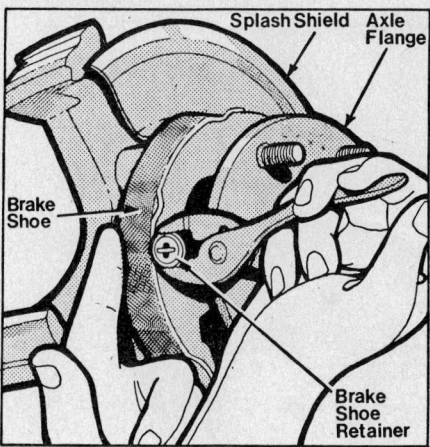

Fig. 80   Replacing brake shoe retainer, springs and nails

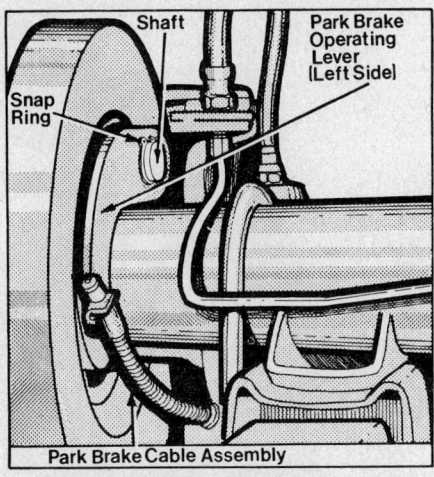

Fig. 81   Park brake operating lever location

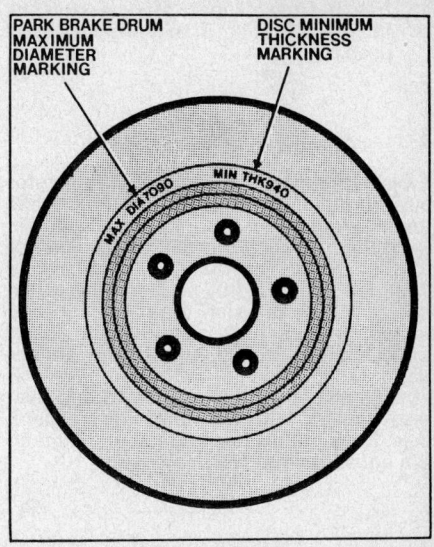

Fig. 83   Maximum drum diameter marking

place in adaptor and over disc, Fig. 77. Align caliper on machined ways of adaptor.

NOTE: Be careful not to pull dust boot from its grooves as the piston and boot slide over the inboard shoe.

3. Install anti rattle springs and retaining clips and torque screws, Fig. 56.

NOTE: Inboard shoe anti rattle spring must always be installed on top of retainer spring plate.

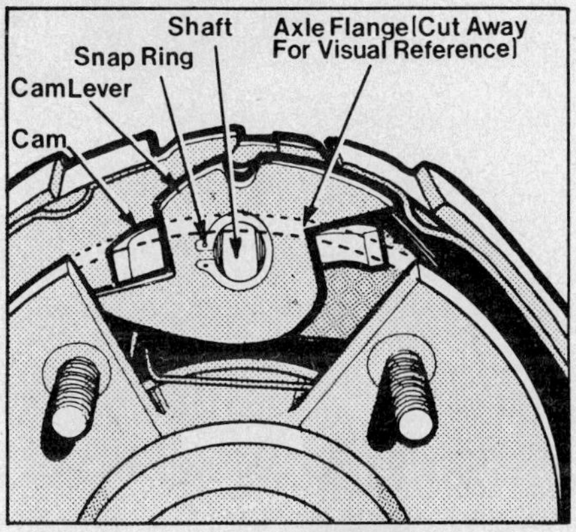

Fig. 82   Outer cam, cam lever, snap ring and shaft location

FORD REAR WHEEL DISC BRAKE & PARKING BRAKE

Sliding caliper rear disc brakes are used on some 1975-78 models, Fig. 84. The caliper is basically the same as the larger front wheel caliper, however, a parking brake mechanism and a larger inner brake shoe anti-rattle spring have been added, Fig. 85. A hydraulically powered brake booster (Hydroboost) provides the power assist for this four wheel disc brake system.

The parking brake lever, located at the rear of the caliper, is actuated by a cable system similar to rear drum brake applications. When the parking brake is applied, the cable rotates the lever and operating shaft. Three steel balls, placed in pockets between the opposing heads of the operating shaft and thrust screw, roll between ramps formed in the pockets and force the thrust screw away from the operating shaft, in turn, driving the caliper piston and brake shoe assembly against the rotor. An automatic adjuster in the assembly compensates for lining wear and maintains proper clearance in the parking brake mechanism.

The cast iron rotors are ventilated by curved fins located between the braking surfaces and are designed to cause the rotor to act as an air pump when the vehicle is traveling forward. The rotors are not interchangeable and are identified by a Right or Left marking cast inside the hat section of the rotor. The rotor is secured to the axle flange in the same manner as a rear brake drum. A splash shield is bolted to a forged axle adapter to protect the inboard rotor surface.

Caliper Removal

NOTE: After performing any service work, obtain a firm brake pedal before moving vehicle.

1. Raise vehicle and support on safety stands, then remove tire and wheel assemblies.
2. Disconnect fitting on rear brake tube from hose end fitting at frame mounted bracket and plug end of brake tube to prevent loss of fluid and entry of dirt. Remove horseshoe retaining clip from hose fitting and disengage hose from bracket.

NOTE: On Granada, Monarch and Versailles models, disconnect hose bracket

from axle spring seat. On Lincoln Continental, Ford and Mercury models, disconnect hose end fitting from caliper. On Granada, Mark IV, Mark V, Monarch, Thunderbird and Versailles models, remove hollow retaining bolt, connecting hose fitting to caliper.

3. Disconnect parking cable from lever, Fig. 86, using care to avoid kinking or cutting cable or return spring, then remove retaining screw from caliper retaining key, Fig. 87.
4. Slide caliper retaining key and support spring from anchor plate, Fig. 87. If necessary, use a hammer and brass drift, being careful to avoid damaging key on sliding ways or hitting parking brake lever.

NOTE: If caliper cannot be removed due to rust build-up on outer edge of rotor, scrape off loose scale, being careful not to damage braking surfaces. If rotor wear or scoring prevents removal of caliper, it will be necessary to loosen caliper end retainer ½ turn maximum, to allow piston to be forced back into its bore. To loosen end retainer, remove parking brake lever and mark or scribe end retainer and caliper housing to be sure that end retainer is not loosened more than ½ turn, then force piston back in its bore, Fig. 84, and move caliper back and forth to center rotor and remove caliper. If retainer must be loosened more than ½ turn, use caution, as the seal between the thrust screw and housing may be broken and brake fluid will enter parking brake mechanism chamber. In this case, the end retainer must be removed and the internal parts cleaned and lubricated.

5. Remove inner shoe and lining assembly from anchor plate, then tap lightly on outer shoe and lining assembly to

free it from caliper. Mark each shoe for identification if they are to be re-used.

Cleaning & Inspection

Clean caliper, anchor plate and rotor assembly and inspect for signs of brake fluid leakage, excessive wear or damage. The caliper must be inspected for leakage both in piston boot area and operating shaft seal area. Lightly sand or wire brush any rust or corrosion from caliper and anchor plate sliding surfaces and inner brake shoe abutment surfaces in anchor plate. Inspect brake shoes for wear. If either lining is within $1/32$ inch of any rivet head, replace both shoe and lining assemblies from both wheels in order to maintain equal brake action.

Caliper Installation

1. If end retainer has been loosened only $1/2$ turn, reinstall caliper in anchor plate using key. Do not install shoe and lining assembly. Torque end retainer to 75-95 ft. lbs. and install parking brake actuating lever on its keyed spline. Lever arm must point down and rearward so that parking brake cable will pass freely under axle. Torque retainer screw to 16-22 ft. lbs.

NOTE: Parking brake lever must rotate freely after torquing retainer screw.

---

2. Remove caliper from anchor plate. If new shoe and lining assemblies are to be installed, the piston must be bottomed in caliper bore using tool T75P-2588-B to provide clearance. Remove rotor and install caliper without lining and shoe assemblies in anchor plate using key only. Install tool and while holding shaft, rotate tool handle counterclockwise until the tool seats firmly against piston, Fig. 85. Loosen handle about $1/4$ turn, and while holding handle rotate tool shaft clockwise until piston is fully bottomed in bore (piston will continue to turn even after it is bottomed). Turn tool handle until there is no further inward movement of piston and there is a firm seating force, then remove caliper from mounting plate and re-install rotor.
3. Making certain that brake shoe anti-rattle clip is in place in lower inner brake shoe support on anchor plate with loop of clip toward inside of anchor plate, Fig. 87, position inner brake shoe and lining assembly on anchor plate.
4. Install outer brake shoe with lower flange ends against caliper abutments and brake shoe upper flanges over shoulders on caliper legs. The shoe upper flanges fit tightly against machined shoulder surfaces.

NOTE: If old brake shoes and lining assemblies are re-used, be certain the shoes are installed in their original positions as marked for identification

Fig. 84   Rear disc brake

Fig. 85   Caliper housing cutaway to show parking brake mechanism

Fig. 86 Parking lever & cable installation

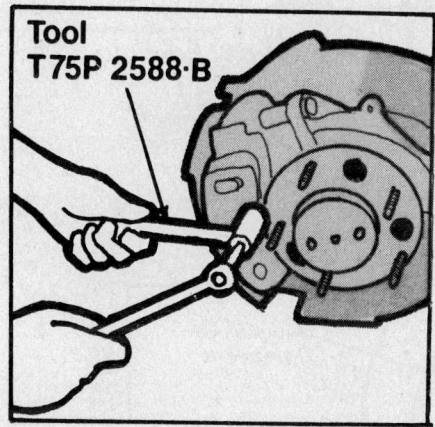

Tool T75P 2588·B

Fig. 88 Adjusting piston depth for lining installation

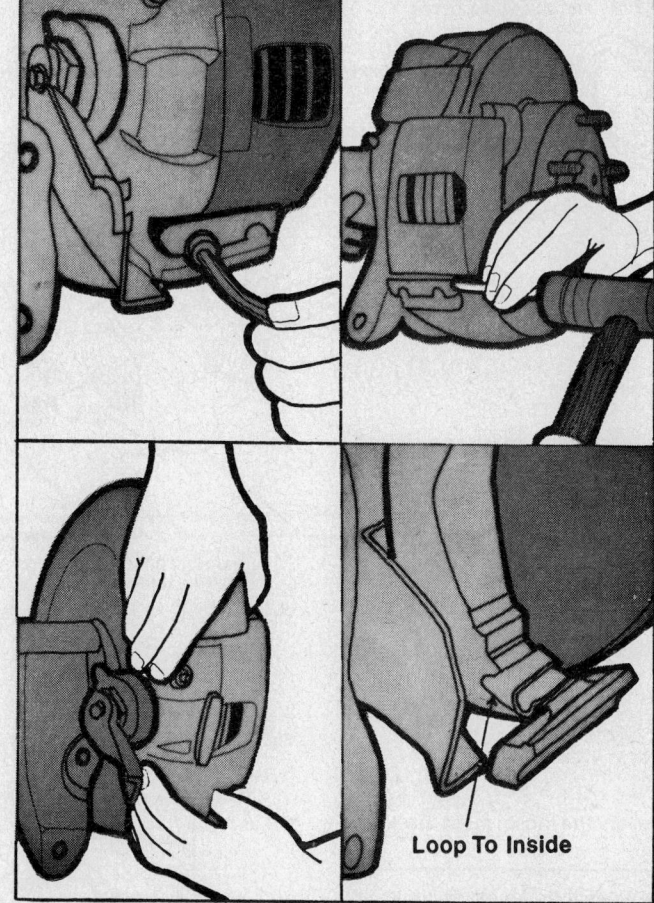

Loop To Inside

Fig. 87 Removing rear caliper assembly

during removal.

5. Lubricate caliper and anchor sliding ways with M1C-167-A (LPS-ESA-100) grease, using care to prevent lubricant from getting on braking surfaces, then position caliper housing lower V-groove on anchor plate lower abutment surfaces.

6. Rotate caliper until it is completely over rotor, being careful not to damage piston dust boot, then pull caliper outboard until inner shoe and lining is firmly seated against rotor. Measure clearance between outer lining and rotor which should be 1/16 inch or less, Fig. 89. If it is greater, remove caliper and move piston outward to narrow gap. Follow procedure in step 2 and note that 1/4 turn of the shaft counterclockwise, moves piston about 1/16 inch.

CAUTION: A clearance greater than 1/16 turn may allow adjuster to be pulled out of piston when service brake is applied, causing parking brake to fail to adjust. It will then be necessary to replace piston/adjuster assembly.

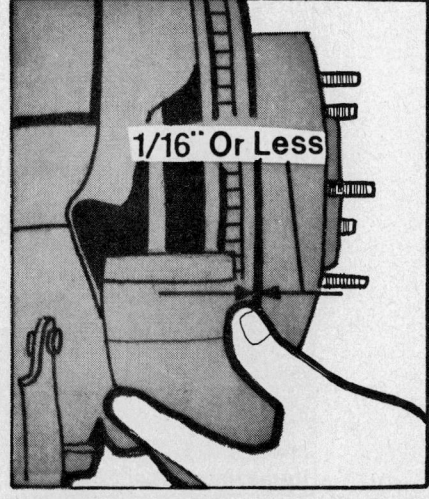

1/16" Or Less

Fig. 89 Checking lining clearance

7. While holding caliper against anchor plate upper abutment surfaces, center caliper over lower anchor plate abutment, then position caliper support spring and key in slot and slide them into opening between lower end of caliper and lower anchor plate abutment until key semi-circular slot is centered over retaining screw threaded hole in anchor plate.

8. Install key retaining screw and torque to 12-16 ft. lbs., then reinstall brake hose on caliper. On Lincoln and Ford Mercury models, place a new gasket on fitting and torque to 20-30 ft. lbs. On Granada, Mark IV, Mark V, Monarch, Thunderbird and Versailles models, place a new gasket on each side of the fitting outlet, then install the attaching bolt through the washers and fitting and torque to 17-25 ft. lbs.

NOTE: On Granada, Monarch and Versailles models, ensure the pin in the hose fitting engages the mating hole in the caliper before torquing the bolt.

9. Position upper end of flexible hose in bracket and install retaining clip, then connect brake tube to hose and torque fitting to 10-15 ft. lbs.

NOTE: Do not twist or coil brake hose,

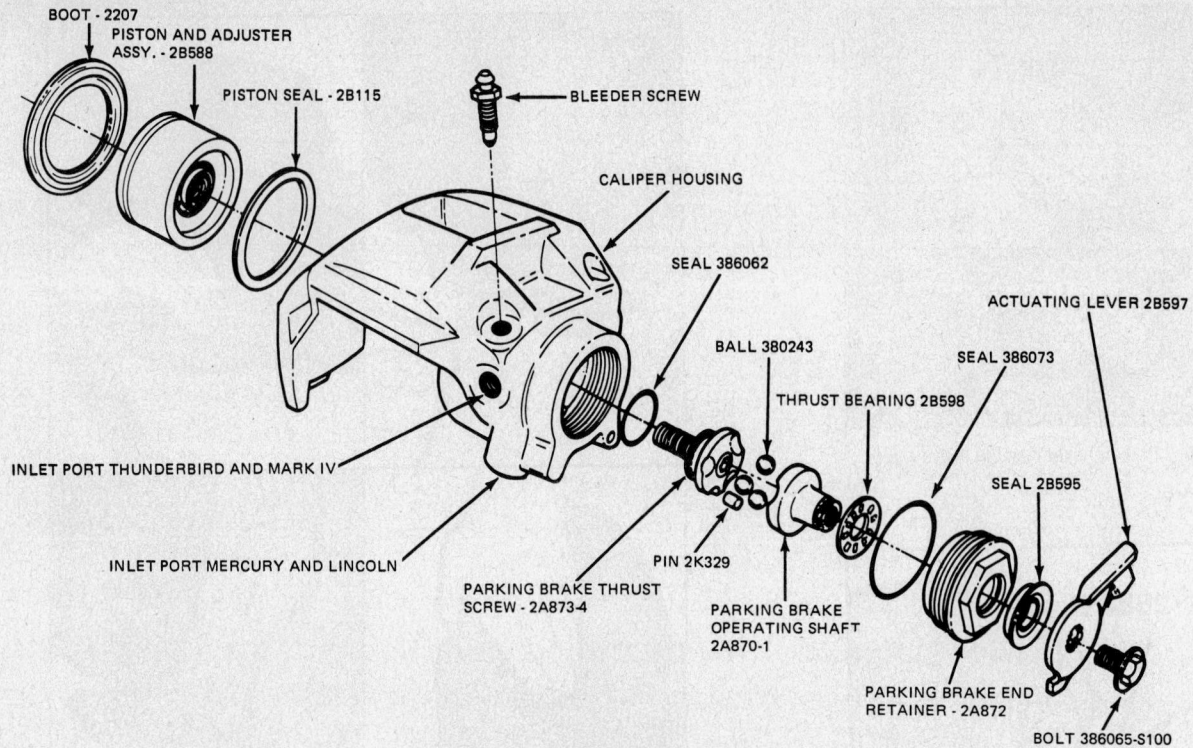

BOOT - 2207
PISTON AND ADJUSTER ASSY. - 2B588
PISTON SEAL - 2B115
BLEEDER SCREW
CALIPER HOUSING
SEAL 386062
BALL 380243
THRUST BEARING 2B598
ACTUATING LEVER 2B597
SEAL 386073
SEAL 2B595
INLET PORT THUNDERBIRD AND MARK IV
INLET PORT MERCURY AND LINCOLN
PIN 2K329
PARKING BRAKE THRUST SCREW - 2A873-4
PARKING BRAKE OPERATING SHAFT 2A870-1
PARKING BRAKE END RETAINER - 2A872
BOLT 386065-S100

Fig. 90   Rear disc brake caliper assembly

the stripe on the hose must be kept straight.

10. Connect parking brake lever to lever on caliper.
11. Bleed brake system, then with engine running pump brake pedal lightly about 40 times allowing 1 second between pedal applications. An alternate with engine off is to pump brake pedal lightly about 10 times to discharge accumulator, then pump brake pedal firmly about 30 times. Check parking brake for excessive travel or very light effort, if so, repeat pumping brake pedal, and if necessary check parking brake cable tension.
12. Install wheel and torque nuts to 70-115 ft. lbs.

NOTE: Before moving vehicle, make certain that a firm brake pedal has been obtained.

Shoe & Lining Removal & Installation

To remove shoe and lining assemblies, follow "Caliper Removal" procedure and omit step 2 as it is not necessary to disconnect brake hose. After removing caliper, support it with a length of wire to avoid damaging brake hose. To install shoe and lining assemblies, follow "Caliper Installation" procedure, making certain that proper parking brake adjustment is obtained.

Caliper Overhaul

Disassemble

1. Remove caliper assembly as described

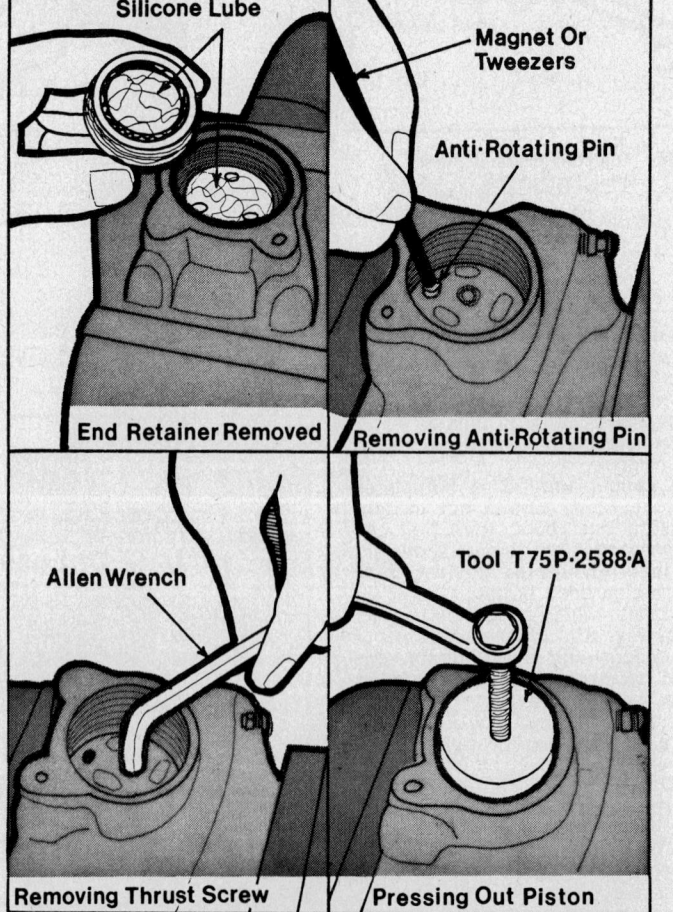

Silicone Lube

Magnet Or Tweezers

Anti-Rotating Pin

End Retainer Removed

Removing Anti-Rotating Pin

Allen Wrench

Tool T75P-2588-A

Removing Thrust Screw

Pressing Out Piston

Fig. 91   Disassembling rear disc brake caliper

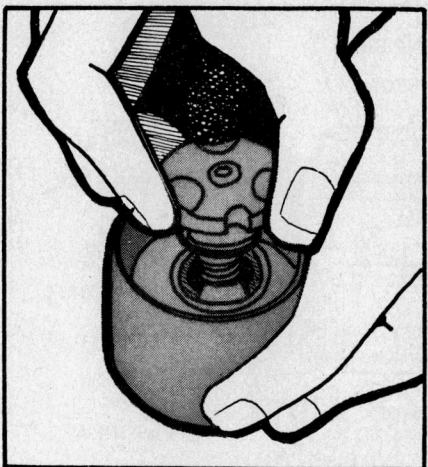

Fig. 92 Checking parking brake adjuster operation

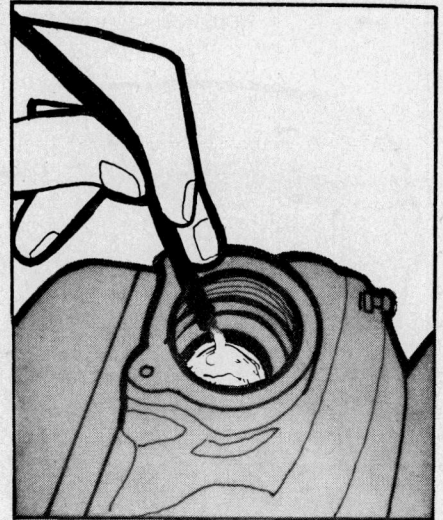

Fig. 93 Filling piston/adjuster assembly

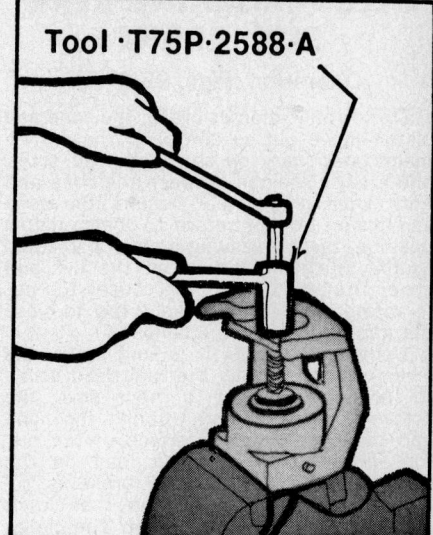

Tool·T75P·2588·A

Fig. 94 Bottoming piston in caliper

previously.
2. Remove caliper end retainer, operating shaft, thrust bearing and balls, Fig. 90.
3. Remove thrust screw anti-rotation pin with a magnet or tweezers. If pin cannot be removed with a magnet or tweezers, proceed with the following procedure:
   a. With tool T75P-2588B, force piston approximately one inch from caliper bore.
   b. Push piston back into caliper housing with tool, then with tool in position, hold tool shaft in place and rotate handle counter-clockwise until thrust screw clears anti-rotation pin. Remove thrust screw and anti-rotation pin.
4. Remove thrust screw by rotating with 1/4 inch allen wrench.

NOTE: On 1975 Granada and Monarch models, use a 1/4 inch drive socket.

5. Install tool T75P-2588-A through back of caliper housing and remove piston assembly, Fig. 91.

CAUTION: Use care not to damage polished surface in thrust screw bore and do not attempt to remove or press adjuster can, as it is a press fit in piston.

4. Remove and discard piston seal, boot, thrust O-ring seal, end retainer, O-ring and end retainer lip seal.

Cleaning & Inspection

1. Clean all metal parts with alcohol, then using clean, dry compressed air, blow out and dry all grooves and passages making sure the caliper bore and component parts are free of any foreign material.
2. Inspect caliper bore for damage or excessive wear. The thrust screw must be smooth and free of pits. If piston is pitted, scored or chrome plating is worn, replace piston and adjuster assembly.
3. Adjuster can must be bottomed in piston to be properly seated and provide consistent brake operation. If adjuster can is loose, appears high in piston, is damaged, or if brake adjustment is usually too tight, too loose or not functioning, replace piston/adjuster assembly. Check adjuster operation by assembling thrust screw into piston/adjuster assembly, then pull the two parts apart about 1/4 inch and release them, Fig. 92. When pulling on the two parts, the brass drive ring must remain stationary causing the nut to rotate. When releasing the two parts, the nut must remain stationary and drive ring must rotate. If action does not follow this pattern, replace piston/adjuster assembly.
4. Inspect ball pockets, threads, grooves, bearing surfaces of thrust screw, operating shaft, balls and anti rotation pin for wear, brinnelling or pitting. Replace operating shaft, balls, thrust screw and anti rotation pin if any of these parts are worn or damaged. A polished appearance on the ball paths is acceptable if there is no sign of wear into the surface.
5. Inspect thrust bearing for corrosion, pitting or wear and replace as necessary.
6. Inspect end plug bearing surface for wear or brinnelling and replace as necessary. A polished appearance on bearing surface is acceptable if there is no sign of wear into surface.
7. Inspect operating lever for damage and replace as necessary.

Assemble

1. Coat new caliper piston seal with clean brake fluid and install it in caliper making certain that seal is not twisted and is fully seated in groove.
2. Install new dust boot by seating flange squarely in outer groove of caliper bore, then coat piston/adjuster assembly with clean brake fluid and install it in caliper bore. Spread dust boot over piston as it is installed and seat dust boot in piston groove.
3. Install caliper in vise, Fig. 93, and fill piston/adjuster assembly with clean brake fluid.
4. Coat new thrust screw O-ring with clean brake fluid and install it in thrust screw groove, then install thrust screw into piston adjuster assembly until top surface of thrust screw is flush with bottom of threaded bore, being careful to avoid cutting O-ring seal. Index notches on thrust screw and caliper housing and install anti-rotation pin.

NOTE: The thrust screw and operating shafts are not interchangeable from side to side since the ramp direction in the ball pockets are different. The pocket surfaces of the operating shaft and thrust screws are stamped "R" (Right) and "L" (Left).

5. Place a ball in each of three pockets of thrust screw and apply a liberal amount of silicone grease M1C-169-A on parking brake components, then install operating shaft on balls.
6. Coat thrust bearing with silicone grease and install it on operating shaft, then install a new lip seal and O-ring on end retainer.
7. Lightly coat O-ring seal and lip seal with silicone grease and install end retainer in caliper. Firmly hold operating shaft against internal mechanism while installing end retainer to prevent mislocation of balls. If lip seal moves out of position, reseat seal. Torque end retainer to 75-95 ft. lbs.

NOTE: Parking brake lever must rotate freely after torquing.

8. Install parking brake lever on keyed spline facing down and rearward. Torque retaining screw to 16-22 ft. lbs.
9. Bottom piston using tool T75P-2588-B, Fig. 94, and install caliper as described previously.

DELCO-MORAINE REAR DISC BRAKE

Operation, Figs. 95 & 96

Upon application of brake, the cone and piston move out as one part. The nut remains stationary on the high lead screw and a gap develops between the cone and nut. When lining wear occurs, the cone and piston do not return to their original position, thereby leaving a small gap equal to the lining wear between the nut and cone. The adjusting spring causes the nut to rotate on the high lead screw to close the gap and adjust the caliper.

Upon application of parking brake, the lever rotation causes the high lead screw to turn and the nut to move down the screw, thereby loading through the cone and the cone-clutch interface of the piston, resulting in a clamp load on the linings. When the parking brake is released, the cone rotates on the clutch interface to adjust the caliper. The clutch interface prevents the cone from turning when the parking brake is applied.

Caliper Removal

CAUTION: Do not mix power steering fluid with brake fluid. If brake seals contact steering fluid or steering seals contact brake fluid, damage will result.

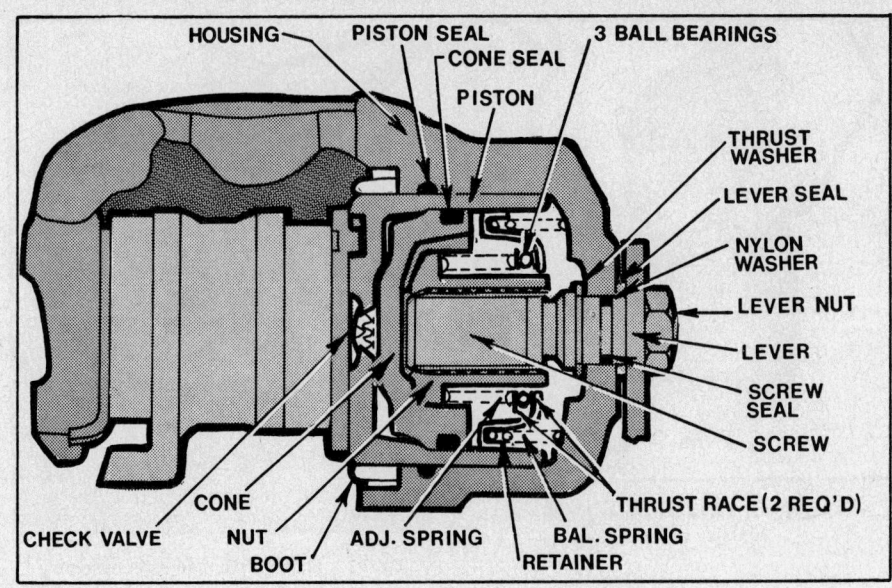

Fig. 95   Delco-Moraine rear disc brake

1. Remove two thirds of the total brake fluid capacity from the master cylinder front reservoir, to prevent overflow of brake fluid.

2. Support vehicle on a hoist and remove tire and wheel assembly.

3. Install one nut with flat side facing rotor to prevent rotor from falling out

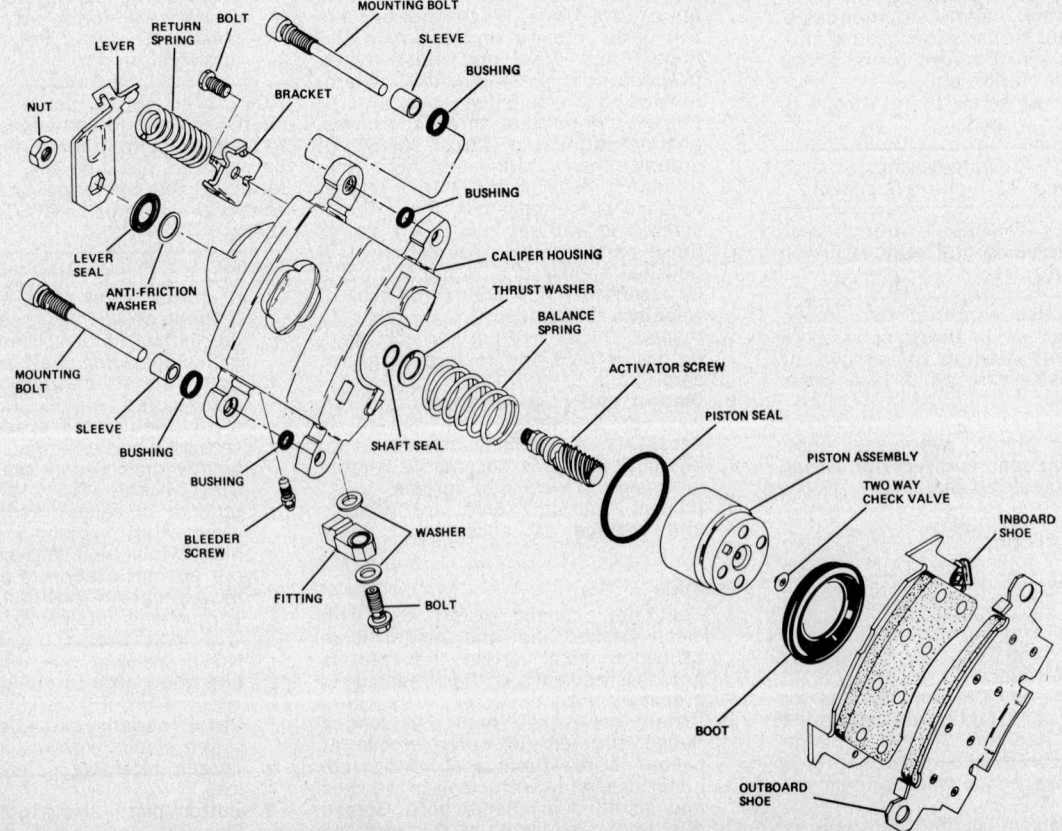

Fig. 96   Rear disc brake caliper disassembled. 1976-78 Eldorado & 1977-78 Riviera

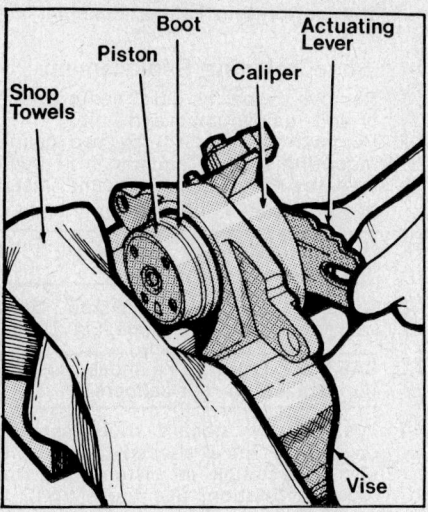

Fig. 97 Removing piston from bore

Fig. 98 Positioning piston in caliper

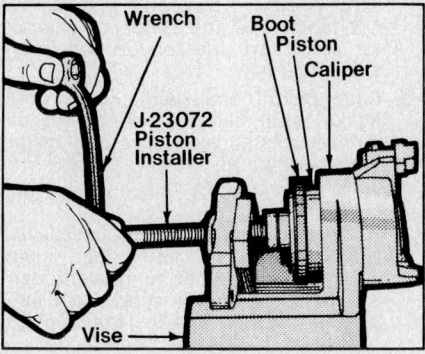

Fig. 99 Installing piston into caliper

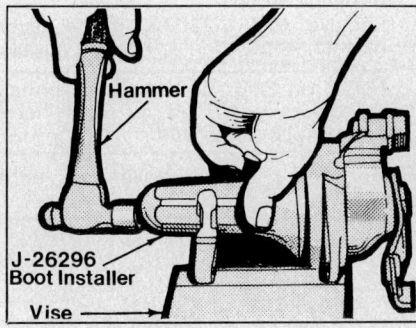

Fig. 100 Driving boot into caliper

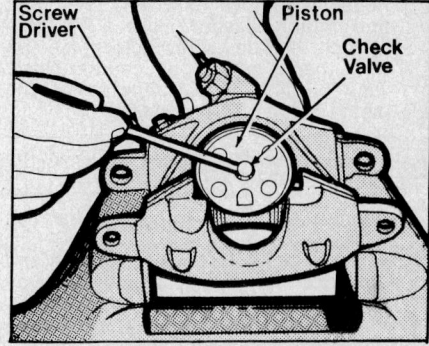

Fig. 101 Removing piston check valve

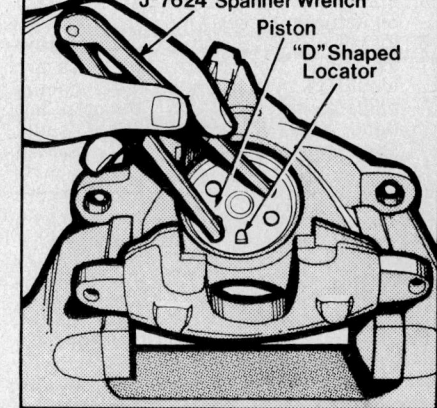

Fig. 102 Rotating piston in bore

when caliper is removed.

4. Loosen parking brake cable tension at equalizer, then remove cable from parking brake lever and remove return spring, lock nut, lever, lever seal and anti-friction washer.

NOTE: Lever must be held in place while removing nut.

5. Clean surface in area of lever seal, then using a 7 inch (or larger) C-clamp, with the solid end on lever stop and screw end on back of outboard lining, turn clamp until piston is bottomed in caliper.

NOTE: Do not position C-clamp on actuator screw.

6. Before removing clamp, lubricate housing surface under lever seal with silicone lubricant.
7. Install a new anti-friction washer, a new lever seal and lever.

NOTE: Install lever on hex with arm pointing downward.

8. Rotate lever toward front of vehicle and while holding in this position, in-stall nut and torque to 25 ft. lbs. and rotate lever back to stop.
9. Install lever return spring and remove C-clamp.

NOTE: On Eldorado springs are color coded, red for the right hand caliper and black for the left hand caliper.

10. Disconnect brake line from caliper and plug openings to prevent loss of fluid and entry of dirt.
11. On all calipers except Eldorado and right hand Brougham remove the brass bolt from the block.

NOTE: If brake line nut is seized, brass bolt and block can be removed with brake line attached by removing bolt. Plug openings to prevent loss of fluid and entry of dirt.

12. Remove caliper mounting bolts and remove caliper.
13. Reverse procedure to install and torque caliper mounting bolts to 30 ft. lbs.

NOTE: When installing brass bolt and block, use two new copper gaskets. Torque bolt or connector to 30 foot-pounds.

Inspection

1. Clean corrosion and dirt from face of piston. Inspect piston and check valve

area for fluid leakage, indicated by excessive moisture around boot area.
2. Inspect dust boot for cuts, cracks or other damage which may affect its sealing ability. If leaks are present, replace dust boot.

NOTE: Do not use compressed air to clean caliper as it may unseat the dust boot.

3. Inspect piston boot seal. Replace boot seal if leakage is indicated.
4. Inspect for leaks at threaded end of actuator screw. Replace seal if leakage is indicated. If bore is nicked or scratched, replace caliper.

Caliper Overhaul

Disassembly

1. Clamp caliper in a vise and remove the two mounting sleeves and four bushings, Fig. 96.
2. Remove brake shoes and lever return spring.
3. Rotate parking brake lever back and forth to remove piston from housing, Fig. 97. If piston will not move from

housing, remove lock nut, lever and anti-friction washer. With a $\frac{9}{16}$ inch wrench, rotate screw clockwise on right hand caliper or counter-clockwise on left hand caliper until the piston moves from housing.

NOTE: Pad caliper with shop cloths when removing piston.

4. Remove piston assembly and balance spring.
5. Remove lock nut, lever, lever seal and anti-friction washer if not removed previously.
6. Push screw from housing, then remove piston seal and boot.

Assembly

1. Install new piston seal.
2. Install new boot onto piston assembly with lip of boot located in piston groove.
3. Install new thrust washer and seal on actuator screw.
4. Install actuator screw into piston assembly. The piston assemblies are identified by a stamped letter on the adjuster nut end. "L" denotes left hand and "R" denotes right hand. The caliper housing is also marked with a letter. The parking brake will not function if the caliper and actuator screw are located on the wrong side of vehicle.
5. Coat piston seal with clean brake fluid. install balance spring into piston and install assembly into caliper housing, Fig. 98.
6. With tool J-23072, push piston fully into caliper housing, Fig. 99.

NOTE: The piston must be pushed straight into caliper to prevent damage to the actuator screw seal as it passes through hole in rear of piston bore.

7. Before removing tool J-23072, install lubricated anti-friction washer, new lever seal, lever and lock nut. Position lever away from stop, rotate forward and hold lever in position, then torque nut to 25 ft. lbs.
8. Remove tool J-23072, rotate lever back to stop and install return spring.

NOTE: On Eldorado the return springs are color coded red for right hand and black for left hand.

9. With tool J-26296, drive boot until seal bottoms in caliper housing, Fig. 100.

Shoe & Lining Replacement

1. Remove caliper as described previously and remove shoe and lining.
2. Remove and discard the two caliper mounting sleeves and the four bushings. Using silicone lubricant, install new bushings and seals.

NOTE: Sleeves are installed in inner bushings.

3. Remove and discard piston check valve and install a new one, Fig. 101.

CAUTION: Front brake shoes must not be installed on rear calipers.

4. Position new inboard shoe assembly on piston. The D-shaped tab must fit into indentation in piston. If piston requires rotation, use tool J-7642 to rotate it, Fig. 102.

NOTE: Install new spring retainers on all exc. Eldorado outboard shoe assembly.

5. Install new outboard shoe assembly onto caliper. Install caliper and torque mounting bolts to 30 ft. lbs.

DISC BRAKE ROTOR SPECIFICATIONS

CAR	Year	Nominal Thickness	Minimum Refinish Thickness	Thickness Variation Parallelism	Lateral Run-out (T.I.R.)	Finish (Micro-In.)
AMERICAN MOTORS						
All	1974	1.000	.940	.0005	.005	15–80
	1975–76	1.190	1.120	.0005	.003	20–60
Matador	1977–78	1.190	1.120	.0005	.003	15–80
Pacer, Gremlin & Hornet	1977–78	.880	.810	.0005	.003	15–80
BUICK (EXC. SKYHAWK)						
Full Size	1974–76	1.290	1.230	.0005	.005	30–80
	1977	1.040	.980	.0005	.005	30–80
	1978	1.040	.965	.0005	.005	30–80
Intermediate	1974–75	1.040	.980	.0005	[5]	30–80
	1976–77	1.040	.980	.0005	[11]	30–80
	1978	1.040	.965	.0005	[11]	30–80
CADILLAC						
Eldorado	1974–76	—	1.190	.0005	.008	—
Seville	1976	1.030	.980	.0005	.005	20–60
All others	1974–76	—	1.220	.0005	.005	
All[12]	1977	1.037	.980	.0005	.005	19.7–59
All[13]	1977	.974	.911	.0005	.003	15.7–78.7
All[12]	1978	1.0382	.981	.0005	.005	19.7–59.1
All[13]	1978	.975	.911	.0005	.003	15.76–78.8
CHECKER						
All	1974–75	1.290	1.215	.0007	.005	20–60
CHEVROLET (EXC. CHEVETTE, MONZA & VEGA)						
Camaro & Chevelle	1974–76	1.035	.980	.0005	.005	20–60
Nova	1974–76	1.035	.980	.0005	.005	20–60
Chevrolet	1974–76	1.285	1.230	.0005	.005	20–60
Corvette	1974–78	1.250	1.230	.0005	[14]	20–60
Exc. Corvette	1977–78	1.030	.980	.0005	.004	20–60
CHEVROLET CHEVETTE						
All	1976–77	.50 (12.7 mm)	[15]	.003 (.08mm)	.005 (.13 mm)	20–60 (.5–1.6 micro/m)
All	1978	.4334 (11mm)	.390 (9.9mm)	.003 (.08mm)	.005 (.13mm)	20–60 (.5–1.6 micro/m)
CHEVROLET VEGA & PONTIAC ASTRE						
All	1974–77	.500	.455	.0005	[14]	20–60
CHRYSLER, DODGE & PLYMOUTH						
Full Size Exc. Imperial	1974–78	1.250	1.180		.004	15–80
Imperial	1974–75	[3]	[4]	.0005	.004	15–80
Intermediate (Exc. Below)	1974–78	1.010	.940	.0005	.004	15–80
Aspen, Dart, Diplomat, LeBaron, Valiant & Volaré	1974–78	1.010	.940	.0005	.004	15–80
Challenger & Barracuda	1974	1.010	.940	.0005	.004	15–80
Omni, Horizon	1978	1.010	.940	.0005	.004	15–80

CAR	Year	Nominal Thickness	Minimum Refinish Thickness	Thickness Variation Parallelism	Lateral Run-out (T.I.R.)	Finish (Micro-In.)
FORD MOTOR COMPANY						
Ford & Mercury Full Size	1974–78	1.180[7]	1.120[8]	.0005[2]	.003[9]	15–80
Ford & Mercury Intermediate	1974–78[1]	1.180	1.120	..0005	.003	15–80
Comet & Maverick	1974–77	.870	.810	.0005	.003	15–80
Granada, Monarch & Versailles	1975–78	.870[7]	.810[8]	.0005	.003[9]	15–80
Lincoln	1974–78	1.180[7]	1.120[8]	.00025[10]	.003[9]	15–80
Mark IV & V	1974–78	1.180[7]	1.120[8]	.00025[10]	.003[9]	15–80
Mustang II, Pinto & Bobcat	1974–78	.870	.810	.0005	.003	15–80
Fairmont & Zephyr	1978	.870	.810	.0005	.003	15–80
MONZA, SKYHAWK, STARFIRE & SUNBIRD						
All	1975	.500	.455	.0005	.005	20–60
All	1976	.880	.830	.0005	.005	20–60
Monza & Sunbird	1977–78	.880	.830	.0005	.004	20–60
Skyhawk & Starfire	1977–78	.880	.830	.0005	.005	20–60
OLDSMOBILE (EXC. STARFIRE)						
Oldsmobile	1974–76	1.290	1.230	.0005	.005	30–50
	1977–78	1.040	.980	.0005	[6]	30–50
Olds F-85, Cutlass, Omega	1974–78	1.040	.980	.0005	.004	30–50
Olds Toronado	1974–78	1.245	1.185	.0005	.002	30–50
PONTIAC (EXC. ASTRE & SUNBIRD)						
Full Size Exc. Grand Prix	1974–75	1.285	1.230	.0007	.004	20–60
	1976	1.250	1.215	.0007	.004	20–60
	1977–78	1.040	.980	.0005	.004	20–60
Grand Prix & Intermediate Exc. Below	1974–75	1.035	.980	.0007	.004	20–60
	1976	1.00	.965	.0007	.004	20–60
	1977–78	1.040	.980	.0005	.004	20–60
Pontiac Firebird	1974–75	1.035	.980	.0007	.004	20–60
	1976	1.030	.965	.0007	.004	20–60
	1977–78	1.040	.980	.0005	.004	20–60
Phoenix & Ventura	1974–75	1.035	.980	.0007	.004	20–60
	1976	1.030	.965	.0007	.004	20–60
	1977–78	1.040	.980	.0005	.004	20–60

①—Montego, Torino & 1974-78 Cougar, Elite & LTD II.
②—1974-78 Mercury, front disc. .0004, 1975-78 rear disc. .0005.
③—Front, 1.250; Rear, 1.000.
④—Front, 1.180; Rear, .940.
⑤—Exc. Apollo .004; Apollo .005.
⑥—Exc. 88 w/V8-403 engine,.004; 88 w/V8-403 engine, .005.
⑦—1975-78 rear disc. .945.
⑧—1975-78 rear disc. .895.
⑨—1975-78 rear disc. .004.
⑩—1975-78 rear disc. .0004.
⑪—1976, .005; 1977-78 exc. Century & Regal, .005; Century & Regal, .004.
⑫—Front
⑬—Rear
⑭—Exc. 1977-78, .005; 1977-78, .004.
⑮—1976, .448(11.40 mm); 1977 .456(11.58 mm).

CARBURETORS

INDEX

CARBURETION

Since carburetion is dependent in several ways on both compression and ignition, it should always be checked last when tuning an engine. See the car chapter for adjustments for the unit you are interested in.

Before adjusting the carburetor, consider the factors outlined below and which definitely affect engine performance.

Performance Complaints

Flooding, flat spots or other performance complaints are often caused by dirt, or water in the carburetor. To aid in diagnosing the complaint, the carburetor should be carefully removed from the engine without draining the fuel from the bowl. The contents of the fuel bowl can then be examined for contamination as the carburetor is disassembled. A magnet moved through the fuel in the bowl will pick up any iron oxide dust that may have caused needle valve leakage.

Check float setting carefully. Too high a level will cause flooding while too low a level will starve the engine.

Before installing carburetor, fill the bowl with clean fuel and operate the throttle by hand several times to visually check the discharge from pump jets.

Inspect gasketed surfaces between body and air horn. Small nicks or burrs should be smoothed down to eliminate air or fuel leakage. On carburetors having a vacuum piston, be especially particular when inspecting the top surface of the inner wall of the bowl around the vacuum piston passage. A poor seal at this location may contribute to a "cutting out" on turns complaint.

Dirty or Rusty Choke Housing

In cases where it is found that the interior of the choke housing is dirty, gummed or rusty while the carburetor itself is comparatively clean, look for a punctured or eroded manifold heat tube (if one is used).

Manifold Heat Control Valve

An engine equipped with a manifold heat control valve can operate with the valve stuck in either the open or closed position. Because of this, an inoperative valve is frequently overlooked at vehicle lubrication or tune-up.

A valve stuck in the "heat-off" position can result in slow warm up, deposits in combustion chamber, carburetor icing, flat spots during acceleration, low gas mileage and spark plug fouling.

A valve stuck in the "heat-on" position can result in power loss, engine knocking, sticking or burned valves and spark plug burning.

To prevent the possibility of a stuck valve, check and lubricate the valve each time the vehicle is lubricated or tuned-up. Check the operation of the valve manually. To lubricate the valve, place a few drops of penetrating oil on the valve shaft where it passes through the manifold. Then move the valve up and down a few times to work the oil in. *Do not use engine oil to lubricate the valve as it will leave a residue which hampers valve operation.*

Carburetor Flange

Check the flange for looseness on the manifold. If one of the flange nuts is loose as little as one-half turn, a sufficient amount of air will enter the intake manifold below the throttle plate to destroy engine idle and all engine performance.

If a tight fit cannot be obtained by tightening the nuts, install a new gasket but be sure that all the old gasket material has been removed.

Throttle Linkage

If the throttle linkage is adjusted so

Internal idle mixture limiter

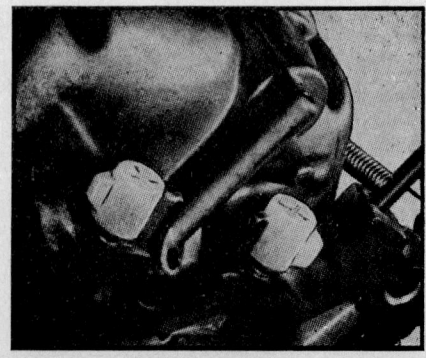

External idle mixture limiter

that the accelerator pedal will strike the floor board before the throttle plate is wide open, it will result in low top speed.

Fuel Lines

A restriction of the fuel line will result in an apparent vapor lock action or a definite cut-off of gasoline. This can generally be corrected by blowing out the line with compressed air. In some cases, it may be necessary to replace the line.

Fuel Pump

The pump should be tested to make sure that it will draw an adequate supply of fuel from the tank and deliver it to the carburetor under all conditions of operation. If the pump functions inefficiently, proper adjustment and operation of the carburetor is impossible because the fuel will not be maintained at the prescribed level in the idle passages and main discharge jet (or jets) of the carburetor under all operating conditions.

Fuel Tank

The fuel tank should not be overlooked as a possible source of trouble with carburetion. A shortage of fuel at the fuel pump or carburetor may be caused by pieces of filling station pump hose or other material obstructing the mouth of the feed pipe in the tank, or by a restriction of the air vents in the filler cap and neck.

An unusual amount of dirt, water or gum in the fuel filter indicates that the tank is contaminated with these substances, which should be cleaned out to prevent future failure of the pump or carburetor.

Intake Manifold Leaks

Leakage of air into the intake manifold at any point will affect carburetion and general engine performance. Air may leak into the manifold through the joints at the carburetor or cylinder head, cracks in the manifold, cracks or poor connections in the vacuum hoses or lines, or the connections of any accessories which may be connected to the manifold. All such joints should be tested for leaks.

To test the intake manifold for leaks, apply oil from an oil can along the gasket joints with the engine idling. An air leak is indicated when oil is drawn past the gaskets by the suction of the engine. Tighten the nuts or cap screws holding the manifold to the engine and retest for leaks. If tightening fails to stop the leaks, replace the manifold gaskets. If the new gaskets fail to stop the leaks, carefully inspect the manifold for cracks and test any suspicious area with oil.

Air Cleaner

An air cleaner with a dirty element, will restrict the air flow through the carburetor and cause a rich mixture at high speeds. In such a condition the air cleaner

likewise will not properly remove dirt from the air, and the dirt entering the engine will cause rapid formation of carbon, sticking valves, and wear of piston rings and cylinder bores.

Automatic Choke

The choke mechanism must be inspected and cleaned to make sure it is operating freely. Sluggish action or sticking of the choke will cause excessive fuel consumption, poor performance during warm-up, and possibly hard starting.

The choke thermostat should be set in accordance with the average air temperature as well as the volatility of the fuel being used. It is desirable to have the thermostat set as lean as operating conditions permit in order to avoid an over-rich mixture during engine warm up.

Choke Thermostat

If necessary to adjust the choke more than two marks from the specified setting, either rich or lean, it indicates that the thermostat spring may be bent or has lost its tension.

Carter Float Settings

When replacing a solid float needle and seat with the new type resilient seat, the float setting should be reduced $\frac{1}{32}''$ on AFB, WCFB, WGD and WCD carburetors.

Carburetor Ball Checks

Whenever it becomes necessary to dismantle a carburetor be sure to account for the ball checks that may be found under pump plungers and compensating or power valves.

CARBURETOR IDLE ADJUST

Cars Without Exhaust Emission Controls

There are two basic types of exhaust emission control systems—air injection type and engine modification type. With both types, the slow idle adjustment method, referred to as "Lean Roll" is to be used. This method insures proper idle, ignition timing and mixture settings for greatest possible exhaust emission reduction and proper engine operation. It should be noted here that smooth idle is extremely sensitive to vacuum leaks. If rough idle is noted, check for vacuum leaks at the carburetor, manifold, etc.

Carburetor Idle Limiters

Some carburetors are equipped with idle adjustment limiters which restrict the maximum idle richness of the air/fuel mixture and prevents overly rich adjustments. There are two types of idle

limiters: internal and external (see illustrations). The internal needle limiter is located in the idle channel and is not visible externally. This limiter is set and sealed at the factory and, under no circumstances, during normal service or during overhaul, should the seal be removed and adjustments made to this needle.

The other type of idle limiter is an external idle limiter cap installed on the knurled head of the idle mixture adjusting screw. Any adjustment to the idle fuel mixture on carburetors with this type of limiter must be made within the range of the limiter cap.

Under no circumstances may the limiter cap, the stop boss or the power valve cover, which the limiter caps stop against, be mutilated or deformed in any way to render the limiter inoperative. A satisfactory idle is obtainable within the range of the limiter cap.

The addition of idle limiters does not eliminate the need for adjusting idle speed and mixture. All the limiters do is prevent overly rich mixtures, which increase the amount of hydro-carbons emitted into the atmosphere.

1. With engine at operating temperature, set parking brake and block drive wheels.
2. Make sure choke valve is wide open.
3. On C.C.S. equipped vehicles, see that the air cleaner thermostatic valve is open.
4. On carburetors so equipped, hold hot idle compensator hole closed with eraser on pencil.
5. Turn air conditioner off or on according to directions given in *Tune Up Charts* in car chapters.
6. Set idle mixture screw(s) for maximum idle rpm.
7. Adjust speed screw (or idle stop solenoid screw on C.C.S.) to obtain the specified rpm in Drive or Neutral as specified.
8. Set ignition timing according to specifications with vacuum advance line disconnected and hole in manifold plugged.
9. Adjust mixture screw IN to obtain a 20 rpm drop (lean roll).
10. Adjust mixture screw OUT $\frac{1}{4}$ turn.
11. Repeat Steps 9 and 10 for second mixture screw (2 and 4 barrel carbs).
12. Readjust speed screw (or solenoid screw) if necessary to obtain specified rpm.
13. On C.C.S. with idle solenoid stop on carburetor, electrically disconnect solenoid and adjust carburetor idle speed screw to obtain 400 rpm in neutral, then reconnect wire to solenoid.

NOTE: Exact instructions for each C.C.S. equipped engine-transmission combination is given for this Lean Roll (low idle) speed method on a decal permanently affixed to the vicinity of the radiator support as well as in the *Tune Up Charts* in the car chapter of this manual.

SERVICE BULLETINS

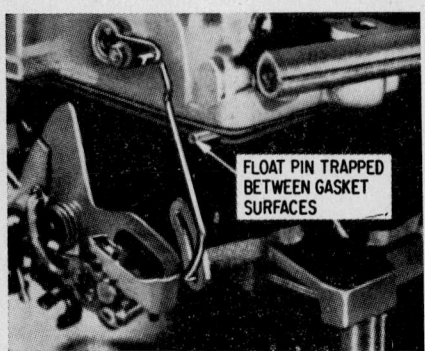

Fig. 1   Carter Thermo-quad float lever pins improperly placed

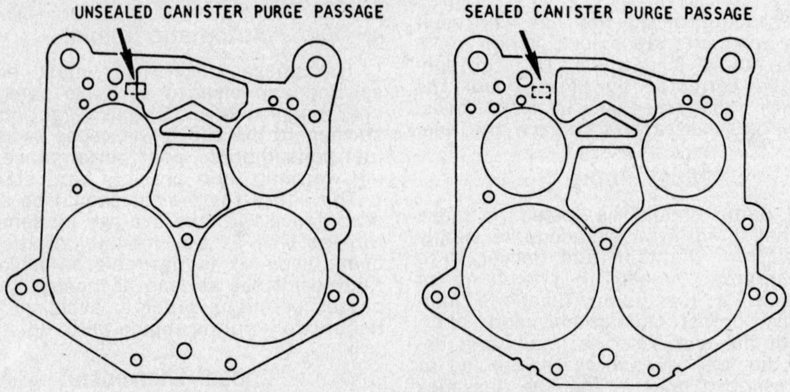

UNSEALED CANISTER PURGE PASSAGE   SEALED CANISTER PURGE PASSAGE

Fig. 2   Delco/Rochester Quadrajet throttle body to float bowl gaskets

Carter Thermo-Quad

When installing the bowl cover on Carter TQ carburetors, it is important that the float lever pins are correctly positioned (centered in their supports). If the pins are not properly placed, they may be trapped between the gasket surfaces. When the bowl cover screws are tightened, the bowl will crack, Fig. 1.

Rochester Quadrajet

Delco/Rochester advises the possibility exists that the wrong throttle body to float bowl gaskets are being used by servicemen on Quadrajet carburetors. When this wrong substitution is made, vacuum leaks occur and cause rough idle due to air bypassing the primary throttle valves through the canister purge passage in the throttle body because the gasket will not seal this passage.

The difference between the throttle body to bowl gaskets is shown in Fig. 2.

Carter Thermo-Quad

The metering rods are preset to specifications by the manufacturer. No additional adjustment should be attempted since an accurate adjustment cannot be made in the field. An improper adjustment may result in the exhaust emissions exceeding specifications. Also, maladjustment of the metering rods may prevent the carburetor from returning to the idle position from wide open throttle (WOT) due to throttle shaft binding, resulting in poor fuel economy.

Carter BBD

Some 1974 Carter 1¼″ BBD carburetors used on V8-318 engine may have been manufactured with the cluster cap gaskets reversed, Fig. 3. This causes fuel leakage into the manifold resulting in flooding, poor hot starting or poor fuel economy.

Holley 2245

Some difficulty may be encountered when adjusting curb idle speed on these carburetors. This condition may be caused by the side of the carburetor interfering with the throttle lever. To correct this condition, the throttle lever may be filed to remove excess metal causing the interference, Fig. 4.

Holley 5210-C

A possible cause of hard cold starting

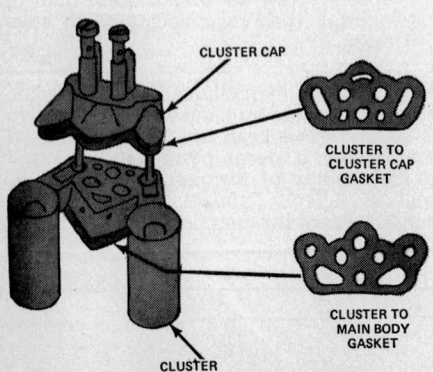

Fig. 3   Cluster cap gasket installation. Carter BBD carburetors

Fig. 4   Removing excess metal from throttle lever. Holley 2245 carburetors

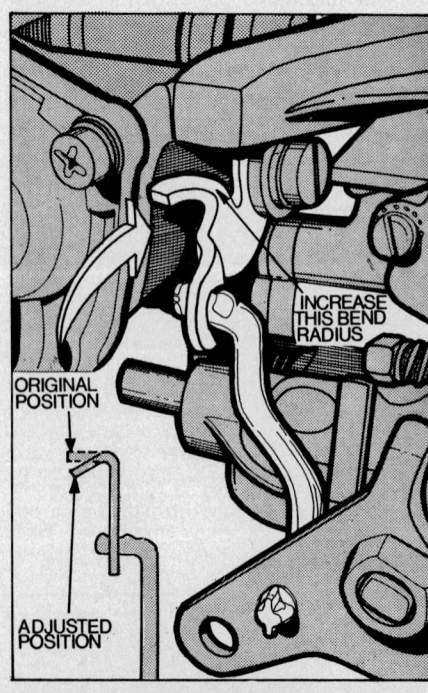

Fig. 5   Revised unloader (Dechoke) adjustment. Holley 5210

on vehicles equipped with this model carburetor may be binding choke linkage, preventing proper choke operation. To determine if binding choke linkage is the cause of hard starting, remove air cleaner with engine cold, then fully depress and release the accelerator pedal once. If choke blade does not fully close, the linkage is binding. This binding condition may occur at the contact point between the fast idle lever and fast idle cam. To correct this condition, proceed as follows:

1. Lubricate contact surface of fast idle lever tang with Lubriplate 1050520 or equivalent.
2. Reset dechoke adjustment to .300 inch instead of the production specification of .375 inch, listed in the Holley 5210 Specification Chart.
3. Bend tang at existing bend so tang slopes toward the choke housing, Fig. 5.

NOTE: Do not bend tang at tip since

this will not achieve the desired results.

Motorcraft 2150

On some applications, the clearance between the carburetor choke pulldown vacuum hose and the EGR spacer may be less than $1/4$ inch. If improper clearance exists, cut $1/2$ inch off hose and recheck clearance.

Carter Carburetor Section

CARTER YF SERIES ADJUSTMENT SPECIFICATIONS
See Tune Up Chart in car chapter for hot idle speed.

Year	Carb. Model	Idle Mixture Screw Setting	Float Level	Float Drop	Idle Vent Setting	Fast Idle Cam Setting	Dechoke or Unloader Setting	Pulldown Setting	Vacuum Break Setting	Choke Setting
AMERICAN MOTORS										
1974	6423, 6431	①	15/32	1⅜	—	.190	.275	.215	—	1 Rich
	6510	①	15/32	1⅜	—	.190	.275	.215	—	1 Rich
	6511	①	15/32	1⅜	—	.190	.275	.215	—	1 Rich
	7000	①	15/32	1⅜	—	.190	.275	.215	—	1 Rich
	7001	①	15/32	1⅜	—	.190	.275	.215	—	1 Rich
	7028	①	15/32	1⅜	—	.190	.275	.215	—	1 Rich
	7029	①	15/32	1⅜	—	.190	.275	.215	—	1 Rich
1975	7039	①	15/32	1⅜	—	.180②	.275	.205	—	1 Rich
	7041	①	15/32	1⅜	—	.180②	.275	.205	—	1 Rich
	7061	①	15/32	1⅜	—	.180②	.275	.205	—	1 Rich
	7062	①	15/32	1⅜	—	.180②	.275	.205	—	1 Rich
	7074	①	15/32	1⅜	—	.180②	.275	.205	—	1 Rich
1976	7083	①	15/32	1⅜	—	.185②	.275	.205	—	1 Rich
	7084	①	15/32	1⅜	—	.185②	.275	.205	—	2 Rich
	7085	①	15/32	1⅜	—	.185②	.275	.205	—	1 Rich
	7086	①	15/32	1⅜	—	.185②	.275	.205	—	2 Rich
	7112	①	15/32	1⅜	—	.185②	.275	.205	—	1 Rich
1977	7111	①	15/32	1⅜	—	.201③	.275	.221	—	2 Rich
	7151	①	15/32	1⅜	—	.195②	.275	.215	—	1 Rich
	7152	①	15/32	1⅜	—	.195③	.275	.215	—	1 Rich
	7153	①	15/32	1⅜	—	.195②	.275	.215	—	Index
	7189	①	15/32	1⅜	—	.201③	.275	.215	—	1 Rich
	7195	①	15/32	1⅜	—	.195②	.275	.221	—	1 Rich
	7223	①	15/32	1⅜	—	.195③	.275	.215	—	Index
1978	7201	①	15/32	1⅜	—	.195②	.275	.215	—	Index
	7232	①	15/32	1⅜	—	.201③	.275	.221	—	2 Rich
	7233	①	15/32	1⅜	—	.201③	.275	.221	—	1 Rich
	7235	①	15/32	1⅜	—	.195③	.275	.215	—	Index
	7267	①	15/32	1⅜	—	.195③	.275	.215	—	1 Rich
1978-79	7228	①	15/32	1⅜	—	.195②	.275	.215	—	1 Rich
	7229	①	15/32	1⅜	—	.195③	.275	.215	—	1 Rich

①—Air/fuel ratio or idle CO% rating is found in Tune Up Specification tables in car chapters.
②—1600 RPM hot on 2nd step of cam with TCS solenoid & EGR disconnected.
③—1500 RPM hot on 2nd stop of cam with TCS solenoid & EGR disconnected.

Continued

CARTER CARBURETORS

CARTER YF SERIES ADJUSTMENT SPECIFICATIONS—Continued

See Tune Up Chart in car chapter for hot idle speed.

Year	Carb. Model	Idle Mixture Screw Setting	Float Level	Float Drop	Idle Vent Setting	Fast Idle Cam Setting	Dechoke or Unloader Setting	Pulldown Setting	Vacuum Break Setting	Choke Setting
FORD										
1974	D4DE-ABA	②	⅜	1¼	—	.170	.250	.230	—	Index
	D4DE-EA	②	⅜	1¼	—	.140	.250	.200	—	Index
	D4DE-JA	②	⅜	1¼	—	.140	.250	.200	—	1 Rich
	D4DE-JB	②	⅜	1¼	—	.140	.250	.200	—	Index
	D4DE-KA	②	⅜	1¼	—	.140	.250	.200	—	1 Rich
	D4DE-KB	②	⅜	1¼	—	.140	.250	.200	—	Index
1975	D5DE-DA	②	①	③	—	.140	.250	.290	—	2 Rich
	D5DE-DB	②	23⁄32	1⅝	—	.140	.250	.290	—	2 Rich
	D5DE-EA	②	①	③	—	.140	.250	.290	—	2 Rich
	D5DE-GA	②	①	③	—	.140	.250	.290	—	2 Rich
	D5DE-MA	②	①	③	—	.140	.250	.290	—	2 Rich
	D5DE-MB	②	23⁄32	1⅝	—	.140	.250	.290	—	2 Rich
	D5DE-ZA	②	①	③	—	.140	.250	.290	—	2 Rich
1976	D5BE-BB	②	④	③	—	.140	.250	.260	—	2 Rich
	D5DE-DB	②	④	③	—	.140	.250	.290	—	2 Rich
	D5DE-MB	②	④	③	—	.140	.250	.290	—	2 Rich
	D6BE-AA	②	④	③	—	.140	.250	.260	—	1 Rich
	D6BE-BB	②	④	③	—	.140	.250	.260	—	2 Rich
	D6DE-AB	②	④	③	—	.140	.250	.290	—	Index
	D6DE-BB	②	④	③	—	.140	.250	.230	—	Index
1977	B7DF-ABA	②	25⁄32	1 19⁄32	—	.140	.250	.260	—	Index
	D7BE-BA	②	25⁄32	1 19⁄32	—	.140	.250	.260	—	1 Rich
	D7BE-BC	②	25⁄32	1 19⁄32	—	.140	.250	.260	—	1 Rich
	DDE-DA	②	25⁄32	1 19⁄32	—	.140	.250	.260	—	1 Rich
	D7DE-DD	②	25⁄32	1 19⁄32	—	.140	.250	.260	—	1 Rich
1978	D8DE-BA	②	25⁄32	1 19⁄32	—	.140	.250	.230	—	2 Rich
	D8DE-DA	②	25⁄32	1 19⁄32	—	.140	.250	.230	—	2 Rich
	D8DE-EA	②	25⁄32	1 19⁄32	—	.140	.250	.200	—	2 Rich
	D8KE-AA	②	25⁄32	1 19⁄32	—	.140	.250	.230	—	2 Rich
1979	D9BE-RA	②	25⁄32	—	—	.140	.250	.180	—	1 Rich
	D9DE-AA	②	25⁄32	—	—	.140	.250	.230	—	1 Rich
	D9DE-BA	②	25⁄32	—	—	.140	.250	.230	—	1 Rich
	D9DE-CA	②	25⁄32	—	—	.140	.250	.260	—	1 Rich
	D9DE-CB	②	25⁄32	—	—	.140	.250	.260	—	1 Rich
	D9DE-DB	②	25⁄32	—	—	.140	.250	.260	—	1 Rich
	D9DE-EA	②	25⁄32	—	—	.140	.250	.230	—	1 Rich

①—Straight float, ⅜ inch; tapered float, 23⁄32 inch.
②—Air/fuel ratio or idle CO% rating is found in Tune Up Specification tables in car chapters.
③—Straight float, 1¼ inch; tapered float, 1⅝ inch.
④—Straight float, 7⁄16 inch; tapered float, 25⁄32 inch.

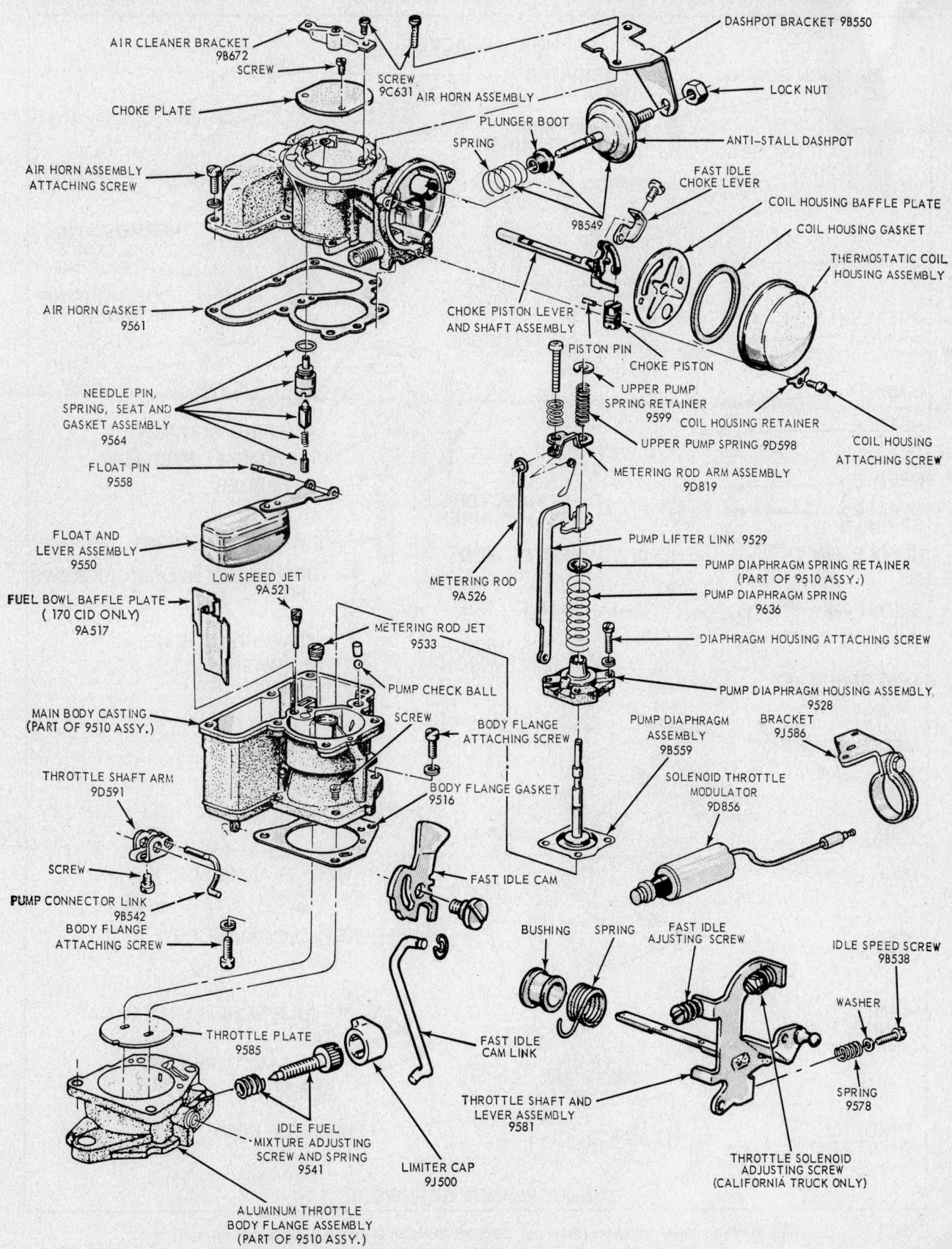

Fig. 1   Carter Model YF Series carburetor. 1974-78 Ford (Typical)

CARTER CARBURETORS

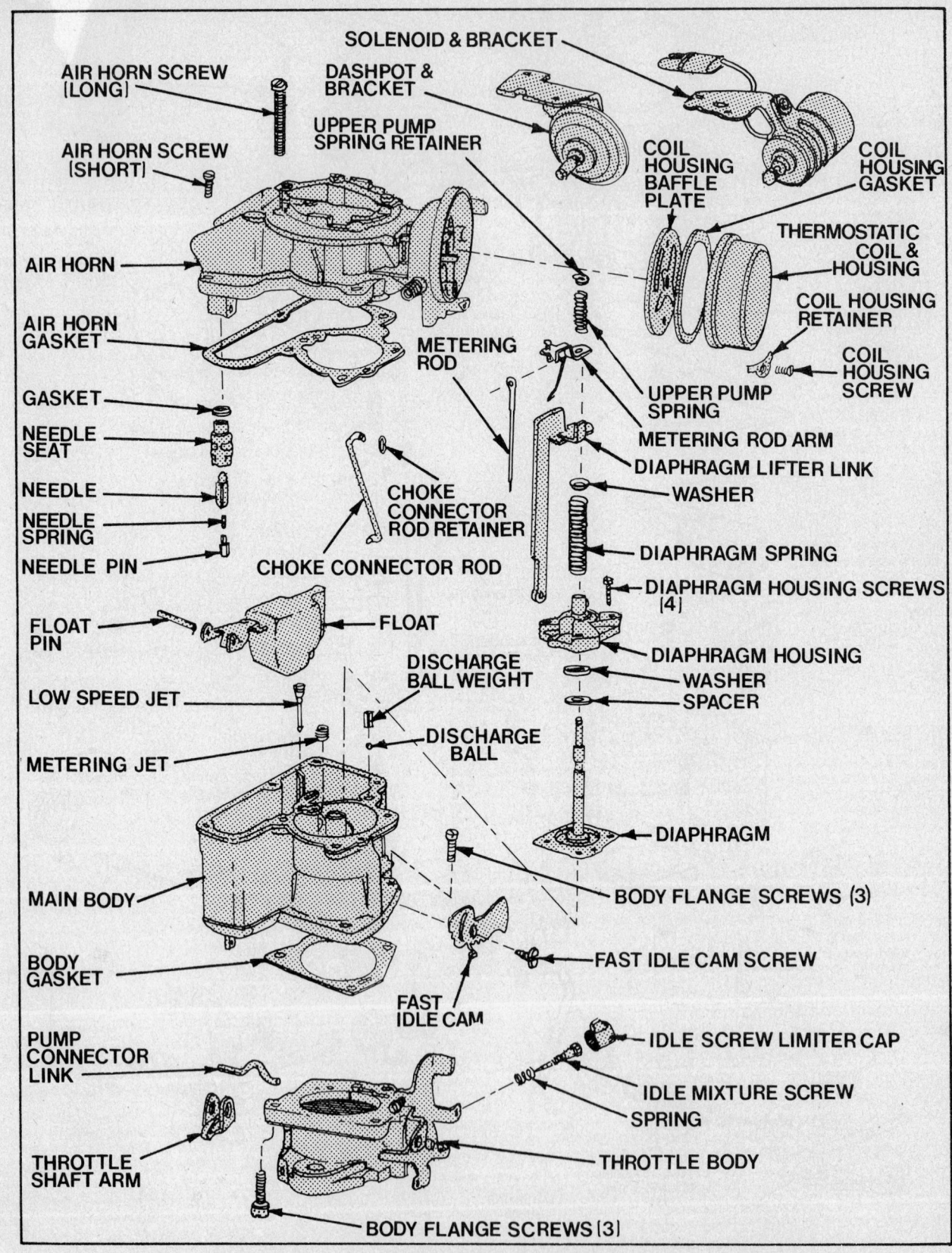

AIR HORN SCREW (LONG)
AIR HORN SCREW (SHORT)
AIR HORN
AIR HORN GASKET
GASKET
NEEDLE SEAT
NEEDLE
NEEDLE SPRING
NEEDLE PIN
FLOAT PIN
LOW SPEED JET
METERING JET
MAIN BODY
BODY GASKET
PUMP CONNECTOR LINK
THROTTLE SHAFT ARM

SOLENOID & BRACKET
DASHPOT & BRACKET
UPPER PUMP SPRING RETAINER
COIL HOUSING BAFFLE PLATE
COIL HOUSING GASKET
THERMOSTATIC COIL & HOUSING
COIL HOUSING RETAINER
COIL HOUSING SCREW
METERING ROD
UPPER PUMP SPRING
METERING ROD ARM
DIAPHRAGM LIFTER LINK
WASHER
DIAPHRAGM SPRING
DIAPHRAGM HOUSING SCREWS (4)
CHOKE CONNECTOR ROD RETAINER
CHOKE CONNECTOR ROD
DIAPHRAGM HOUSING
FLOAT
WASHER
SPACER
DISCHARGE BALL WEIGHT
DISCHARGE BALL
DIAPHRAGM
BODY FLANGE SCREWS (3)
FAST IDLE CAM SCREW
FAST IDLE CAM
IDLE SCREW LIMITER CAP
IDLE MIXTURE SCREW
SPRING
THROTTLE BODY
BODY FLANGE SCREWS (3)

Fig. 2   Carter Model YF Series carburetor. 1974-78 American Motors less altitude compensation

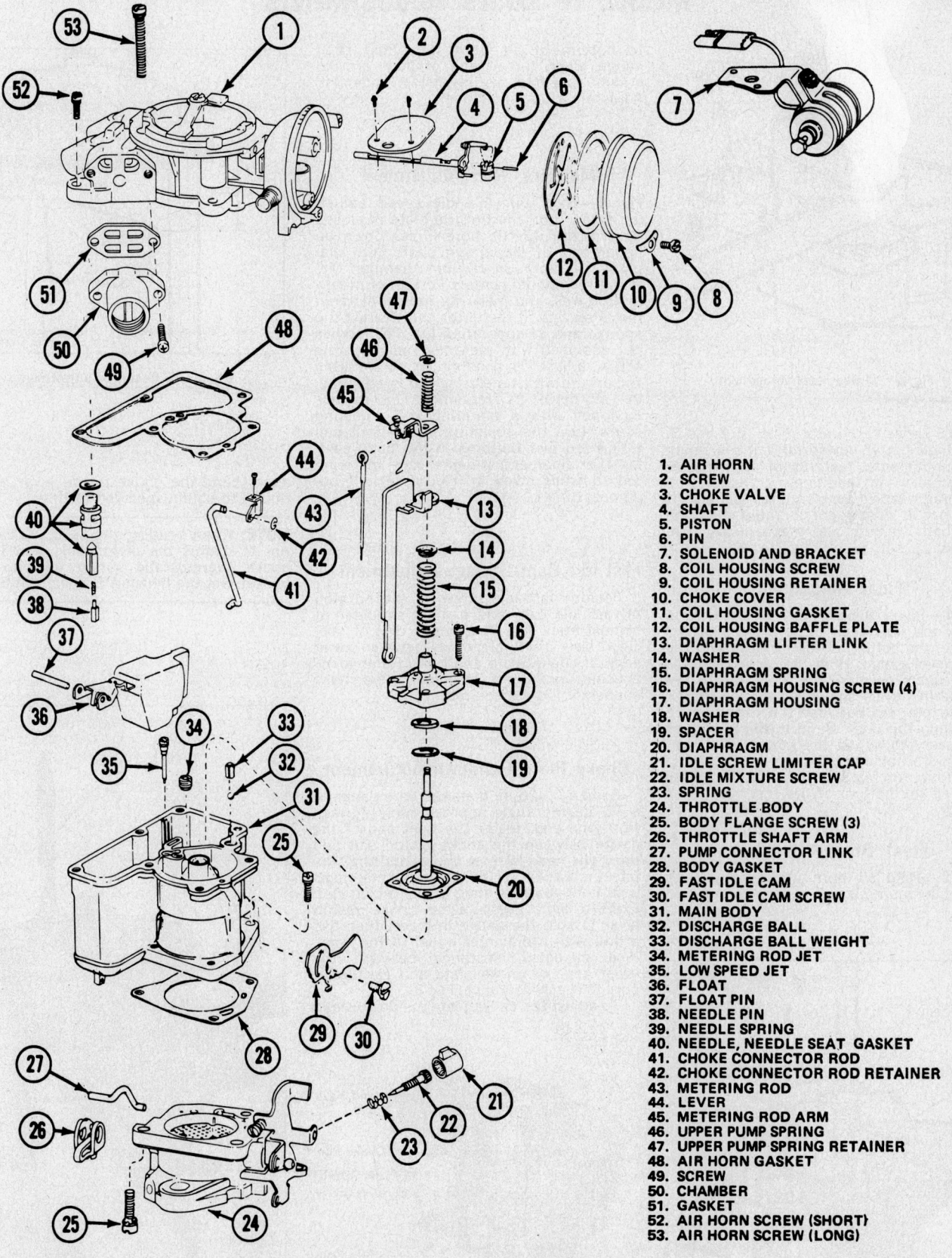

1. AIR HORN
2. SCREW
3. CHOKE VALVE
4. SHAFT
5. PISTON
6. PIN
7. SOLENOID AND BRACKET
8. COIL HOUSING SCREW
9. COIL HOUSING RETAINER
10. CHOKE COVER
11. COIL HOUSING GASKET
12. COIL HOUSING BAFFLE PLATE
13. DIAPHRAGM LIFTER LINK
14. WASHER
15. DIAPHRAGM SPRING
16. DIAPHRAGM HOUSING SCREW (4)
17. DIAPHRAGM HOUSING
18. WASHER
19. SPACER
20. DIAPHRAGM
21. IDLE SCREW LIMITER CAP
22. IDLE MIXTURE SCREW
23. SPRING
24. THROTTLE BODY
25. BODY FLANGE SCREW (3)
26. THROTTLE SHAFT ARM
27. PUMP CONNECTOR LINK
28. BODY GASKET
29. FAST IDLE CAM
30. FAST IDLE CAM SCREW
31. MAIN BODY
32. DISCHARGE BALL
33. DISCHARGE BALL WEIGHT
34. METERING ROD JET
35. LOW SPEED JET
36. FLOAT
37. FLOAT PIN
38. NEEDLE PIN
39. NEEDLE SPRING
40. NEEDLE, NEEDLE SEAT GASKET
41. CHOKE CONNECTOR ROD
42. CHOKE CONNECTOR ROD RETAINER
43. METERING ROD
44. LEVER
45. METERING ROD ARM
46. UPPER PUMP SPRING
47. UPPER PUMP SPRING RETAINER
48. AIR HORN GASKET
49. SCREW
50. CHAMBER
51. GASKET
52. AIR HORN SCREW (SHORT)
53. AIR HORN SCREW (LONG)

Fig. 3   Carter Model YF Series carburetor. 1977-78 American Motors with altitude compensation

MODEL YF SERIES ADJUSTMENTS

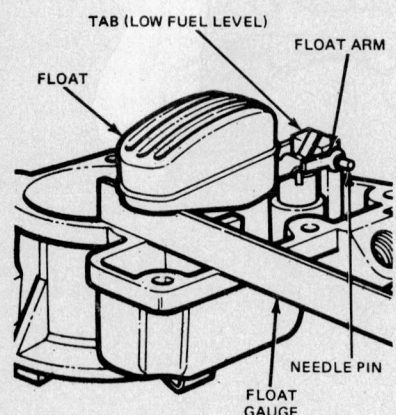

Fig. 4   YF float level adjustment

The YF Series carburetor, Figs. 1, 2 and 3, is a single-barrel, downdraft unit combining the fundamental features of other Carter carburetors. In addition, it features a diaphragm-type accelerating pump. It also has a diaphragm-operated metering rod, both vacuum and mechanically controlled.

Float Adjustment

Fig. 4—Invert the air horn assembly, and check the clearance from the top of the float to the bottom of the air horn with the float level gauge. Hold the air horn at eye level when gauging the float level. The float arm (lever) should be resting on the needle pin. Do not load the needle when adjusting the float. Bend the float arm as necessary to adjust the float level (clearance). Do not bend the tab at the end of the float arm. It prevents the float from striking the bottom of the fuel bowl when empty.

Float Drop Adjustment

Fig. 5—Hold air horn upright and measure maximum clearance from top of float

to bottom of air horn with float drop gauge. Bend tab at end of float arm to obtain specified setting listed under YF Adjustment Specifications.

Metering Rod Adjustment

Fig. 6—Back out the idle speed adjusting screw until the throttle plate is closed tight in the throttle bore. Press down on upper end of diaphragm shaft until diaphragm bottoms in vacuum chamber. Metering rod should contact bottom of metering rod well, and metering rod should contact lifter link at the outer end nearest the springs and at supporting lug. For models not equipped with metering rod adjusting screw, adjust by bending lip of metering rod arm to which metering rod is attached, up or down as required. For models equipped with a metering rod adjusting screw, turn the adjusting screw until metering rod just bottoms in the body casting. For final adjustments turn metering rod adjusting screw in (clockwise) one additional turn.

Fast Idle Cam Linkage Adjustment

Position fast idle screw on second step of fast idle cam and against shoulder of highest step, Fig. 7. Using a drill of specified size, check clearance between lower edge of choke plate and bore. Refer to YF Specifications Chart. To adjust, bend choke connector rod as required.

Choke Plate Pulldown Adjustment

Bend a 0.026 in. diameter wire gauge at a 90 degree angle approximately ⅛-inch from one end. Insert the bent end of the gauge between the choke piston slot and the right hand slot in choke housing. Rotate the choke piston lever counterclockwise until gauge is snug in the piston slot. Exert a light pressure on choke piston lever to hold the gauge in place, then use a drill with a diameter equal to the specified pulldown clearance between the lower edge of choke plate and carburetor bore to check clearance, Fig. 8.

To adjust the choke plate pulldown clear-

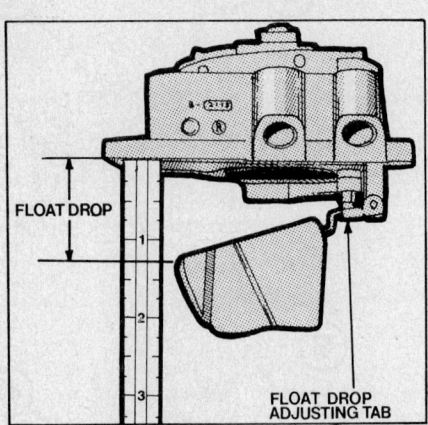

Fig. 5   YF float drop adjustment

ance, bend the choke piston lever as required to obtain specified setting.

NOTE: When bending the lever, be careful not to distort the piston link. Install the choke thermostatic spring housing and gasket. Set the housing to specifications.

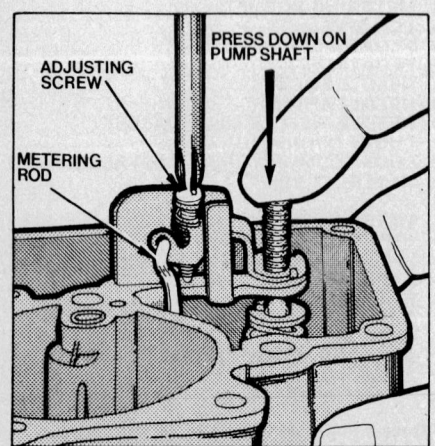

Fig. 6   YF metering rod adjustment

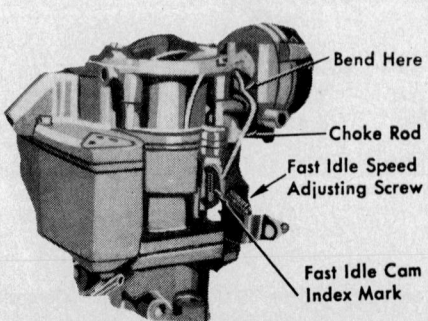

Fig. 7   YF fast idle cam linkage adjustment

Fig. 8   YF choke plate pulldown adjustment

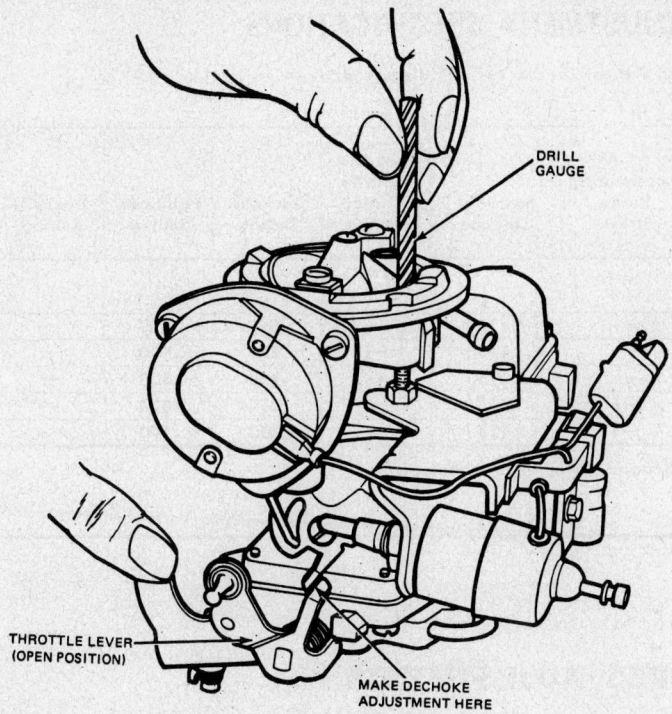

Fig. 9   YF dechoke adjustment

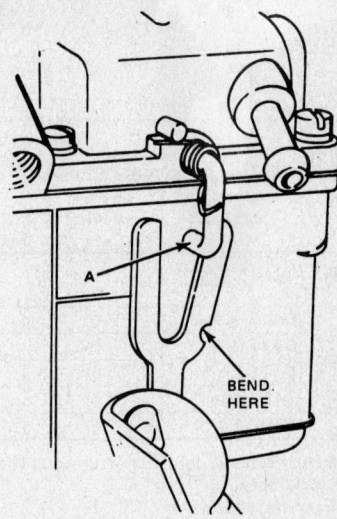

Fig. 10   YF fuel bowl vent adjustment. 1975 Ford

Dechoke Adjustment

Hold the throttle plate fully open and close the choke plate as far as possible without forcing it. Use a drill of specified diameter to check the clearance between choke plate and air horn, Fig. 9. If clearance is not within specification, adjust by bending arm on choke trip lever of the throttle lever. Bending the arm downward will decrease the clearance, bending it upward will increase the clearance.

If the choke plate clearance and fast idle cam linkage adjustment was performed with the carburetor on the engine, adjust the engine idle speed and fuel mixture. Adjust dashpot (if so equipped).

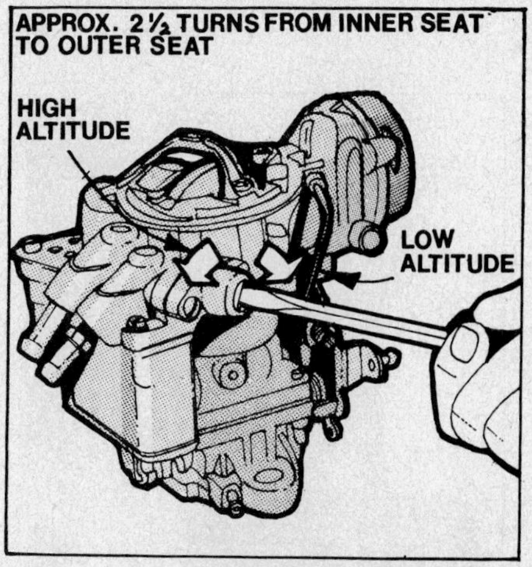

Fuel Bowl Vent Adjustment

1975 Ford

With curb idle adjusted properly, stop engine and turn ignition "On" to activate the solenoid with the engine "Off". Open the throttle so the throttle vent rod does not contact the fuel bowl vent rod, then close throttle and measure the fuel bowl vent rod travel at point "A", Fig. 10, from the open throttle position to the closed throttle position. Fuel bowl vent rod travel should be .010-.030 inch. To adjust, bend throttle vent lever at indentation to obtain specified travel.

Altitude Compensator Adjustment

1977-78 American Motors

For operation on vehicle above 4000 feet in altitude, rotate plug fully counterclockwise, Fig. 11. For operation on vehicles below 4000 feet in altitude, rotate plug fully clockwise, Fig. 11.

NOTE: Whenever the position of the altitude compensator plug is changed, the ignition timing must also be corrected. Refer to the "Tune-up Specifications" in the individual car chapter.

Dashpot Adjustment

With the engine idle speed and mixture properly adjusted, the engine at normal operating temperature, loosen the anti-stall dashpot lock nut, Fig. 12. Hold the throttle in the curb idle position and depress the dashpot plunger. Measure the clearance between the throttle lever and plunger tip. Turn the anti-stall dashpot to provide 7/64" ± 1/64" clearance between the tip of the plunger and the throttle lever. Tighten the locknut to secure the adjustment.

Automatic Choke Adjustment

Loosen choke cover retaining screws and turn choke cover so that line or Index mark on cover lines up with the specified mark listed in *YF Specifications Chart* on choke housing.

Fig. 12   YF dashpot adjustment

Fig. 11   Altitude compensator adjustment. 1977-78 American Motors

CARTER RBS ADJUSTMENT SPECIFICATIONS

See Tune Up Chart in car chapter for hot idle speed.

Year	Carb. Model	Idle Mixture Screw Setting	Float Level	Step-Up Rod	Accelerating Pump Stroke	Fast Idle Linkage	Fast Idle Throttle Plate Setting	Dechoke Setting	Pulldown Setting	Dashpot Setting	Choke Setting
FORD ENGINES											
1974	D4DE-AAA	①	⁹⁄₁₆	—	—	.115②	—	.250	.190	—	1 Lean
	D4DE-AB	①	⁹⁄₁₆	—	—	.115②	—	.250	.190	—	Index
	D4DE-BB	①	⁹⁄₁₆	—	—	.115②	—	.250	.300	—	Index
	D4DE-SB	①	⁹⁄₁₆	—	—	.115②	—	.250	.300	—	Index
	D4DE-TA	①	⁹⁄₁₆	—	—	.115②	—	.250	.190	—	Index

①—Air/fuel ratio or idle CO% rating is found in Tune Up Specification tables in car chapters.
②—At kickdown.
③—Closed throttle.

MODEL RBS ADJUSTMENTS

This carburetor, Fig. 1 incorporates a single aluminum casting with a pressed steel bowl. Adjustments are readily accessible and most calibration points are located in the single casting.

Fuel pickups are located near the centerline of the carburetor bore to gain the benefits of a concentric bowl carburetor, yet so located that engine heat being radiated through the bore is conducted through the casting but is not readily conducted to the fuel in the bowl. Two internal vapor vents allow rapid fuel vapor dissipation to help provide smooth idle conditions and to minimize hard starting when engine is hot. Also an external vent, mechanically controlled by the throttle, is used on 1974 California units.

A diaphragm-controlled step-up type metering rod controls the fuel supply. The accelerator pump is spring-actuated.

The carburetor is equipped with a vacuum piston automatic choke. On 1974 California units, an electric assist choke is used to open the choke plate within 1-1½ minutes after underhood temperatures reach approximately 60° F. For service procedures, refer to the "Emission Control System" chapter.

The 1974 RBS unit incorporates an Exhaust Gas Recirculation port, Fig. 2. The E.G.R. port connects to the primary bore and allows a metered amount of exhaust gas to be fed into the fuel-air mixture.

The carburetor model number is stamped on the side of the flange near the throttle lever.

Float Level Adjustment

Fig. 3—With carburetor inverted, bowl and bowl gasket removed, and only weight of float pressing needle into its seat, meas-ure vertical distance from casting to the small "bump" at outer ends of float. Gauge both ends of float. If the vertical distance is not as listed in the *RBS Specifications Chart*, adjustment can be made by removing float from casting, or by holding lip end of float bracket securely with needle-nose pliers. However, be sure to hold float lip away from needle when adjusting. To adjust, bend bracket at its narrowest portion, Fig. 4.

Float Drop Adjustment

With the air horn upright and the float hanging free measure the vertical distance from the main body casting surface for the fuel bowl to the outer ends of the float on the top side. Adjust by bending tab at the end of the float arm to obtain 1.250" setting.

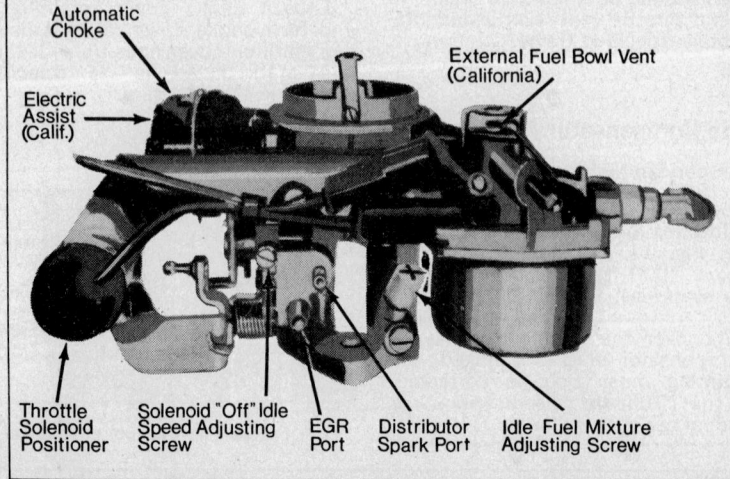

Fig. 2   Carter RBS carburetor side view

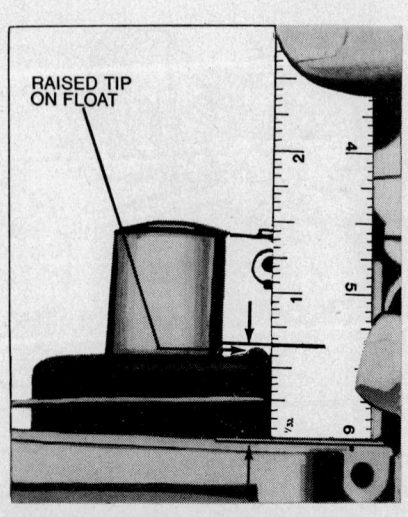

Fig. 3   RBS float level adjustment

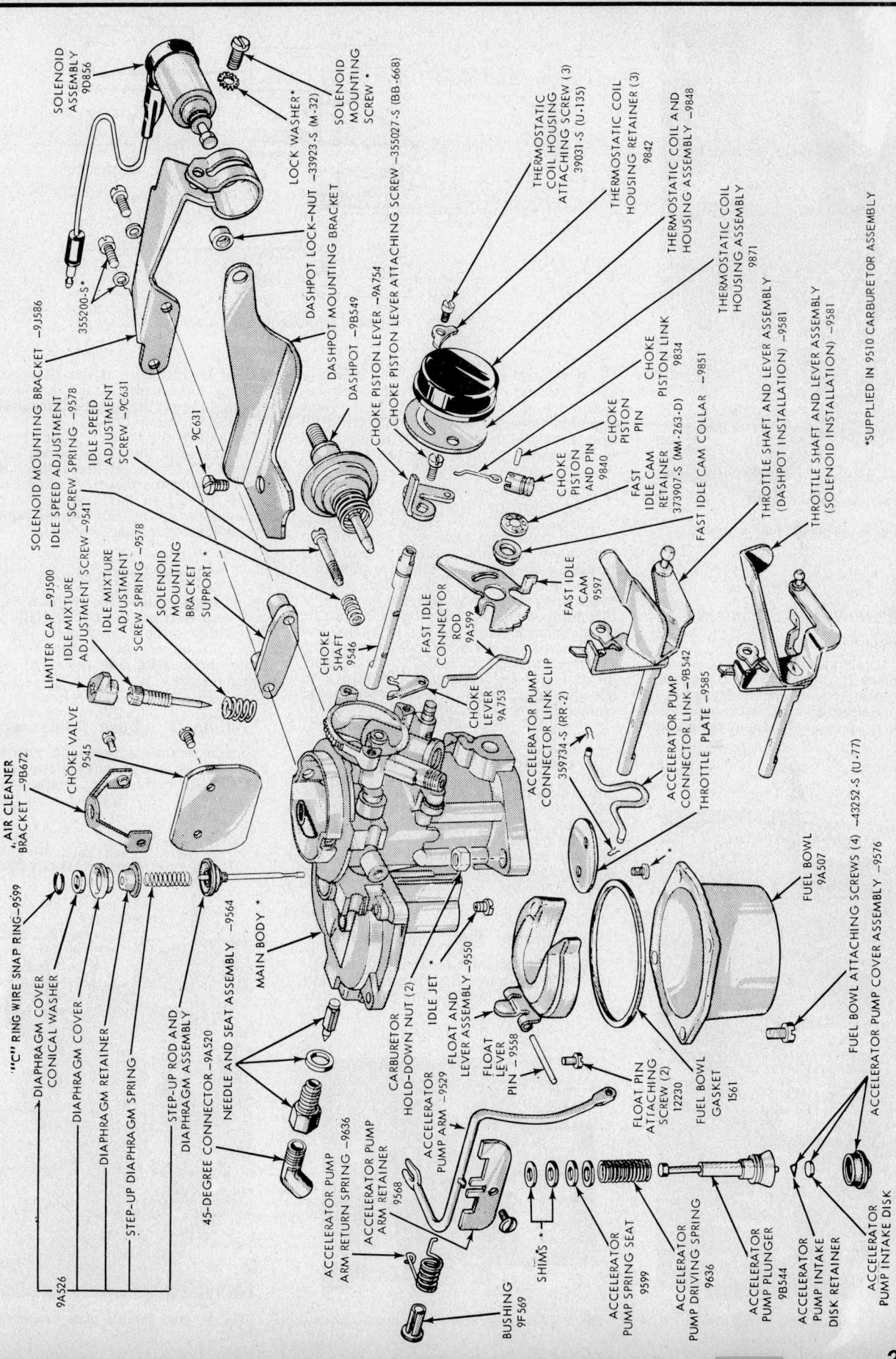

Fig. 1 Carter model RBS carburetor. (typical)

SOLENOID ASSEMBLY —9D856

LOCK WASHER *

SOLENOID MOUNTING SCREW *

THERMOSTATIC COIL HOUSING ATTACHING SCREW (3) 39031-S (U-135)

THERMOSTATIC COIL HOUSING RETAINER (3) 9842

THERMOSTATIC COIL AND HOUSING ASSEMBLY —9848

SOLENOID MOUNTING BRACKET —9J586

DASHPOT LOCK-NUT —33923-S (M-32)

SOLENOID MOUNTING BRACKET

CHOKE PISTON LEVER —9A754

CHOKE PISTON LEVER ATTACHING SCREW —355027-S (BB-668)

THERMOSTATIC COIL HOUSING ASSEMBLY 9871

355200-S *

IDLE SPEED ADJUSTMENT SCREW SPRING —9578

IDLE SPEED ADJUSTMENT SCREW —9C631

DASHPOT MOUNTING BRACKET

DASHPOT —9B549

9C631

CHOKE PISTON LINK 9834

CHOKE PISTON PIN 9840

CHOKE PISTON AND PIN 9840

THROTTLE SHAFT AND LEVER ASSEMBLY (DASHPOT INSTALLATION) —9581

THROTTLE SHAFT AND LEVER ASSEMBLY (SOLENOID INSTALLATION) —9581

LIMITER CAP —9J500

IDLE MIXTURE ADJUSTMENT SCREW —9541

IDLE MIXTURE ADJUSTMENT SCREW SPRING —9578

SOLENOID MOUNTING BRACKET SUPPORT *

FAST IDLE CAM RETAINER 373907-S (MM-263-D)

FAST IDLE CAM PIN

FAST IDLE CAM COLLAR —9851

*SUPPLIED IN 9510 CARBURETOR ASSEMBLY

*SUPPLIED IN 9510 CARBURETOR ASSEMBLY

CHOKE SHAFT 9546

FAST IDLE CONNECTOR ROD 9A599

FAST IDLE CAM 9597

AIR CLEANER BRACKET —9B672

CHOKE VALVE 9545

CHOKE LEVER 9A753

ACCELERATOR PUMP CONNECTOR LINK CLIP 359734-S (RR-2)

ACCELERATOR PUMP CONNECTOR LINK —9B542

ACCELERATOR PUMP —9B542

THROTTLE PLATE —9585

"C" RING WIRE SNAP RING —9599

DIAPHRAGM COVER CONICAL WASHER

DIAPHRAGM COVER

DIAPHRAGM RETAINER

STEP-UP DIAPHRAGM SPRING

STEP-UP ROD AND DIAPHRAGM ASSEMBLY

45-DEGREE CONNECTOR —9A520

NEEDLE AND SEAT ASSEMBLY —9564

MAIN BODY *

CARBURETOR HOLD-DOWN NUT (2)

IDLE JET *

FLOAT AND LEVER ASSEMBLY —9550

FLOAT LEVER PIN —9558

FLOAT PIN ATTACHING SCREW (2) 12230

FUEL BOWL GASKET 1561

FUEL BOWL 9A507

FUEL BOWL ATTACHING SCREWS (4) —43252-S (U-77)

ACCELERATOR PUMP COVER ASSEMBLY —9576

9A526

ACCELERATOR PUMP ARM RETURN SPRING —9636

ACCELERATOR PUMP ARM RETAINER 9568

ACCELERATOR PUMP ARM —9529

SHIMS *

ACCELERATOR PUMP SPRING SEAT 9599

ACCELERATOR PUMP DRIVING SPRING 9636

ACCELERATOR PUMP PLUNGER 9B544

ACCELERATOR PUMP INTAKE DISK RETAINER

ACCELERATOR PUMP INTAKE DISK

BUSHING 9F 569

2–317

Fig. 4   Adjusting fuel float level

HOLD FLOAT LEVER HERE

RAISE OR LOWER FLOAT

V1252-A

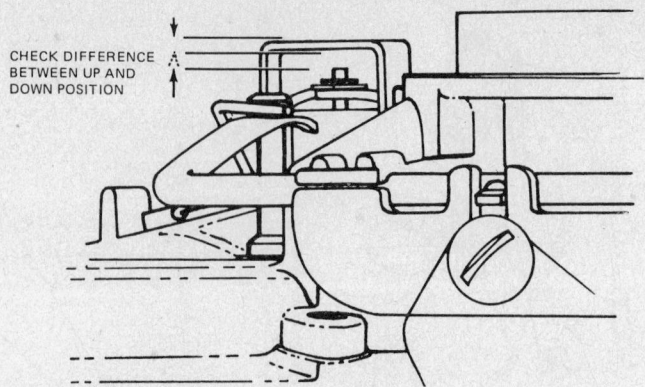

CHECK DIFFERENCE BETWEEN UP AND DOWN POSITION

Fig. 5   Bowl vent adjustment. 1974 California units

tle until vent valve seats and measure same distance again. The difference between the two measurements is the vent opening, Fig. 5. Refer to Carter RBS Specification Chart. Adjust by bending link at accelerator pump arm contact point.

Accelerator Pump Adjustment

Open the choke plate and back off the idle speed adjustment screw to allow the throttle plate to seat in the bore. Measure the height from the flat surface of the main body casting to the top surface of the pump stem, Fig. 6. Open the throttle wide, then measure the height again. The pump stroke is the difference between the two measurements. Refer to *RBS Specifications Chart*. To adjust the stroke to specifications, open or close the pump connector link at the offset portion, Fig. 7.

Fast Idle Cam Adjustment

Position the fast idle screw on the kickdown step of the fast idle cam against the shoulder of the high step. Adjust by bending the choke plate connecting rod to obtain the specified clearance between the lower edge of the choke plate and the carburetor bore.

Throttle Plate Clearance

Align the fast idle tang on the throttle lever with the index mark on the fast idle cam. Use a drill between the throttle plate

and the throttle bore at the idle port side to check the clearance, Fig. 8. Adjust by bending tang on the throttle lever. Refer to *R.B.S. Specification Chart*.

To adjust the choke plate pulldown clearance, bend the choke piston lever as required to obtain specified setting. NOTE: When bending the lever, be careful not to distort the piston link. Install the choke thermostatic spring housing and gasket. Set the housing to specifications.

Dechoke Clearance

Hold the throttle lever at the wide open position and close the choke plate as far as possible without forcing it. The clearance is measured between the lower edge of the choke plate and the inner wall of the main body.

Automatic Choke Adjustment

Loosen retainer screws and turn choke cover so that line or index mark on cover lines up with the specified mark on choke housing (see *RBS Specifications Chart*).

Bowl Vent Adjustment

1974 California Units

With accelerator pump properly adjusted, place throttle at curb idle position on the extended solenoid. Measure direction between top of vent guard and top of vent valve stem. Then, open throt-

PUMP STROKE

Fig. 6   Accelerator pump stroke

PUMP ARM

CONNECTOR LINK

Fig. 7   Adjusting accelerator pump stroke

DRILL GAUGE OF SPECIFIED CLEARANCE SIZE

FAST IDLE CAM

ALIGN FAST IDLE TANG WITH MARK ON CAM

FAST IDLE TANG

Fig. 8   RBS throttle plate clearance.

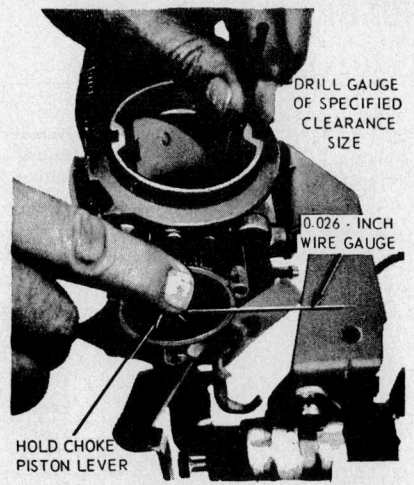

DRILL GAUGE OF SPECIFIED CLEARANCE SIZE

0.026 - INCH WIRE GAUGE

HOLD CHOKE PISTON LEVER

Fig. 9 Adjusting choke plate pulldown

Choke Plate Pulldown or Piston Linkage Adjustment

Bend a .026 in. diameter wire gauge at a 90 degree angle approximately ⅛-inch from one end. Insert the bent end of the gauge between the choke piston slot and the right hand slot in choke housing. Rotate the choke piston lever counter clockwise until gauge is snug in the piston slot. Exert a light pressure on choke piston lever to hold the gauge in place, then use a drill with a diameter equal to the specified pulldown clearance between the lower edge of choke plate and carburetor bore to check clearance, Fig. 9.

Dashpot Adjustment

Loosen the anti-stall dashpot lock nut, Fig. 10. Hold the throttle in the closed position and depress the plunger. The clearance between the throttle lever and the plunger tip is 7/32 inch. Tighten the locknut to secure the adjustment.

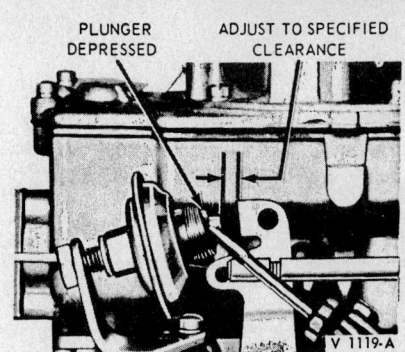

PLUNGER DEPRESSED   ADJUST TO SPECIFIED CLEARANCE

V 1119-A

Fig. 10 Typical anti-stall dashpot adjustment

CARTER BBD ADJUSTMENT SPECIFICATIONS

See Tune Up Chart in car chapter for hot idle speed.

Year	Carb. Model	Initial Idle Mix. Screws Turns Open	Float Level	Pump Travel Inch	Bowl Vent Clearance	Choke Unloader Clearance	Initial Choke Valve Clearance	Choke Vacuum Kick Clearance	Fast Idle Cam Position Clearance	Automatic Choke Setting
AMERICAN MOTORS										
1976	8067	①	¼	—	—	¼	.128	—	.095	2 Rich
	8073	①	¼	—	—	¼	.128	—	.095	1 Rich
1977	8103	①	¼	.496	—	.280	.150	—	.120	1 Rich
	8104	①	¼	.520	—	.280	.128	—	.095	1 Rich
	8117	①	¼	.480	—	.280	.152	—	.112	1 Rich
1978	8128	①	¼	.496	—	.280	.150	—	.110	Index
	8129	①	¼	.520	—	.280	.128	—	.095	1 Rich
1979	8185	①	¼	.470	—	.280	.140	—	.110	1 Rich
	8186	①	¼	.520	—	.280	.150	—	.110	1 Rich
	8187	①	¼	.470	—	.280	.140	—	.110	1 Rich
	8221	①	¼	.530	—	.280	.150	—	.110	1 Rich
CHRYSLER, DODGE & PLYMOUTH										
1974	6464S	①	¼	½③	—	.325	—	.150	.095	Fixed
	6465S	①	¼	½③	—	.325	—	.110	.095	Fixed
	6466S④	①	¼	½③	—	.325	—	.150	.095	Fixed
	6467S④	①	¼	½③	—	.325	—	.110	.095	Fixed
1975	8000S	①	¼	½③	—	.280	—	.130	.070	Fixed
	8001S	①	¼	½③	—	.310	—	.110	.070	Fixed
	8003S	①	¼	½③	—	.310	—	.110	.070	Fixed
	8062S	①	¼	½③	—	.310	—	.110	.070	Fixed
	8064S	①	¼	½③	—	.310	—	.070	.070	Fixed
	8066S	①	¼	½③	—	.280	—	.130	.070	Fixed
	8076S	①	¼	½③	—	.310	—	.070	.070	Fixed
1975–76	8077S	①	¼	½③	—	.280	—	.110	.070	Fixed
1976	8069S	①	¼	½③	—	.310	—	.070	.070	Fixed
	8070S	①	¼	½③	—	.310	—	.110	.070	Fixed
	8071S	①	¼	½③	—	.280	—	.130	.070	Fixed

Continued

CARTER BBD ADJUSTMENT SPECIFICATIONS

See Tune Up Chart in car chapter for hot idle speed.

Year	Carb. Model	Initial Idle Mix. Screws Turns Open	Float Level	Pump Travel Inch	Bowl Vent Clearance	Choke Unloader Clearance	Initial Choke Valve Clearance	Choke Vacuum Kick Clearance	Fast Idle Cam Position Clearance	Automatic Choke Setting
1977	8087S	①	¼	¹⁵⁄₃₂③	—	.280	—	.100	.070	Fixed
	8089S	①	¼	¹⁵⁄₃₂③	—	.280	—	.130	.070	Fixed
	8090S	①	¼	¹⁵⁄₃₂③	—	.280	—	.130	.070	Fixed
	8093S	①	¼	¹⁵⁄₃₂③	—	.310	—	.130	.070	Fixed
	8094S	①	¼	¹⁵⁄₃₂③	—	.310	—	.070	.070	Fixed
	8096S	①	¼	¹⁵⁄₃₂③	—	.310	—	.110	.070	Fixed
	8126S	①	¼	¹⁵⁄₃₂②	—	.310	—	.110	.070	Fixed
	8127S	①	¼	¹⁵⁄₃₂③	—	.280	—	.110	.070	Fixed
	8135S	①	¼	¹⁵⁄₃₂③	—	.310	—	.070	.070	Fixed
	8145S	①	¼	¹⁵⁄₃₂③	—	.310	—	.110	.070	Fixed
	8170S	①	¼	½③	.080③	.310	—	.110	.070	Fixed
	8171S	①	¼	½③	.080③	.310	—	.110	.070	Fixed
	8172S	①	¼	½③	.080③	.310	—	.110	.070	Fixed
1978	8136S	①	¼	½③	.080③	.280	—	.110	.070	Fixed
	8137S	①	¼	½③	.080③	.280	—	.100	.070	Fixed
	8143S	①	¼	½③	.080③	.280	—	.150	.070	Fixed
	8175S	①	¼	½③	.080③	.280	—	.160	.070	Fixed
	8177S	①	¼	½③	.080③	.280	—	.100	.070	Fixed
1979	8198S	①	¼	½③	.080	.280	—	.100	.070	Fixed
	8199S	①	¼	½③	.080	.280	—	.100	.070	Fixed

① —Air/fuel ratio or idle CO% rating is found in Tune Up Specification tables in car chapters.
② —Model less red tag, ¹⁵⁄₃₂ inch at idle; model with red tag, ½ inch at idle.
③ —At idle.
④ —With California Emission package.

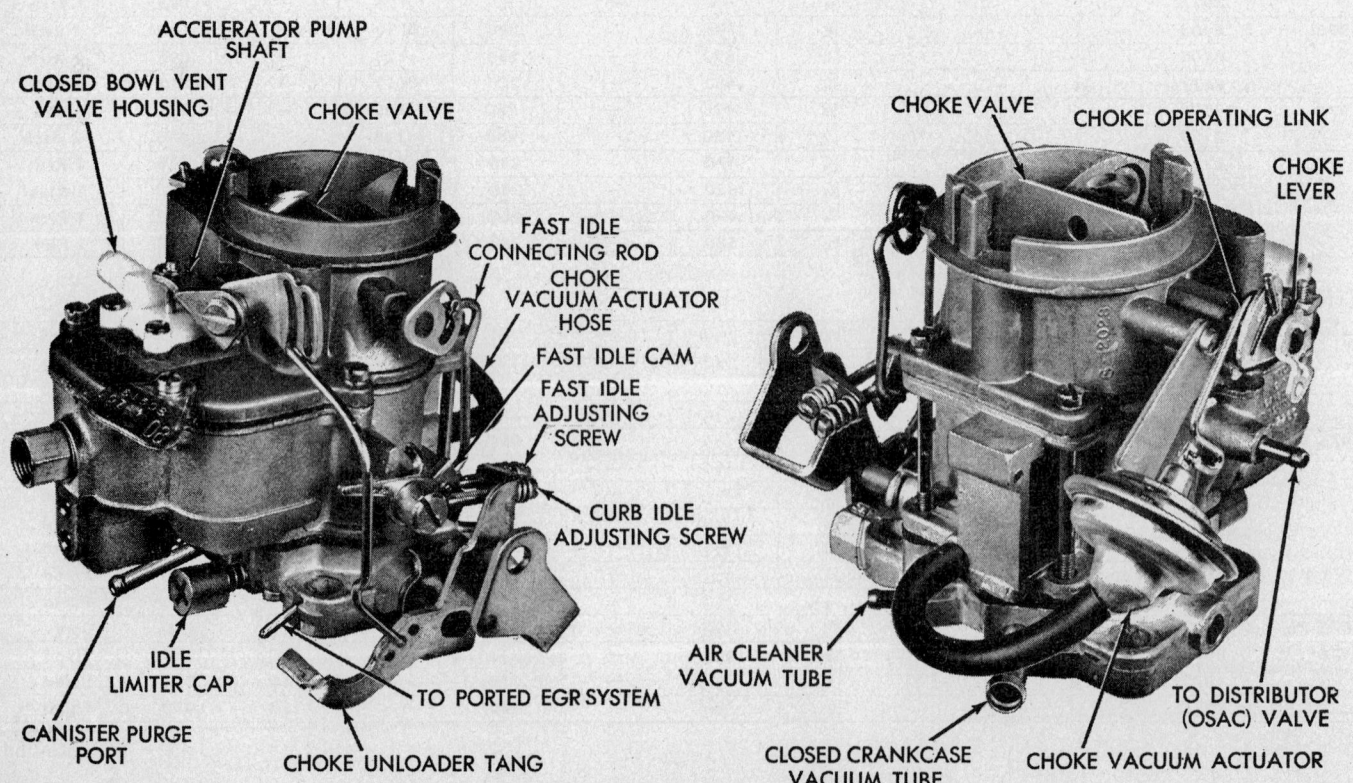

Fig. 2 BBD 1¼" carburetor assembly. 1974-77. (typical)

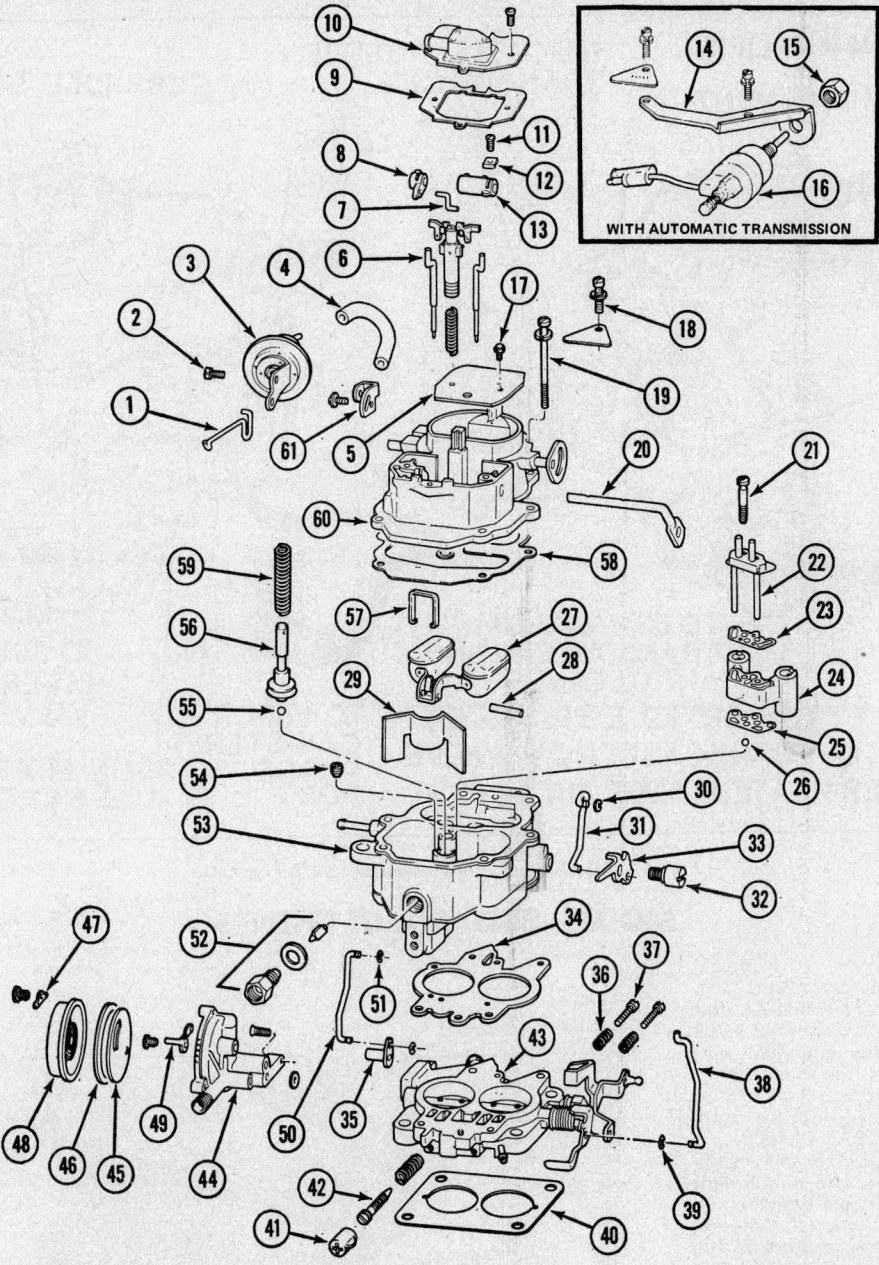

WITH AUTOMATIC TRANSMISSION

Fig. 1   Exploded view of Carter model BBD 1¼" two barrel carburetor. 1974-77 (typical)

1. DIAPHRAGM CONNECTOR LINK
2. SCREW
3. CHOKE VACUUM DIAPHRAGM
4. HOSE
5. VALVE
6. METERING ROD
7. S-LINK
8. PUMP ARM
9. GASKET
10. ROLLOVER CHECK VALVE
11. SCREW
12. LOCK
13. ROD LIFTER
14. BRACKET
15. NUT
16. SOLENOID
17. SCREW
18. AIR HORN RETAINING SCREW (SHORT)
19. AIR HORN RETAINING SCREW (LONG)
20. PUMP LEVER
21. VENTURI CLUSTER SCREW

22. IDLE FUEL PICK-UP TUBE
23. GASKET
24. VENTURI CLUSTER
25. GASKET
26. CHECK BALL (SMALL)
27. FLOAT
28. FULCRUM PIN
29. BAFFLE
30. CLIP
31. CHOKE LINK
32. SCREW
33. FAST IDLE CAM
34. GASKET
35. THERMOSTATIC CHOKE SHAFT
36. SPRING
37. SCREW
38. PUMP LINK
39. CLIP
40. GASKET
41. LIMITER CAP
42. SCREW

43. THROTTLE BODY
44. CHOKE HOUSING
45. BAFFLE
46. GASKET
47. RETAINER
48. CHOKE COIL
49. LEVER
50. CHOKE ROD
51. CLIP
52. NEEDLE AND SEAT ASSEMBLY
53. MAIN BODY
54. MAIN METERING JET
55. CHECK BALL (LARGE)
56. ACCELERATOR PUMP PLUNGER
57. FULCRUM PIN RETAINER
58. GASKET
59. SPRING
60. AIR HORN
61. LEVER

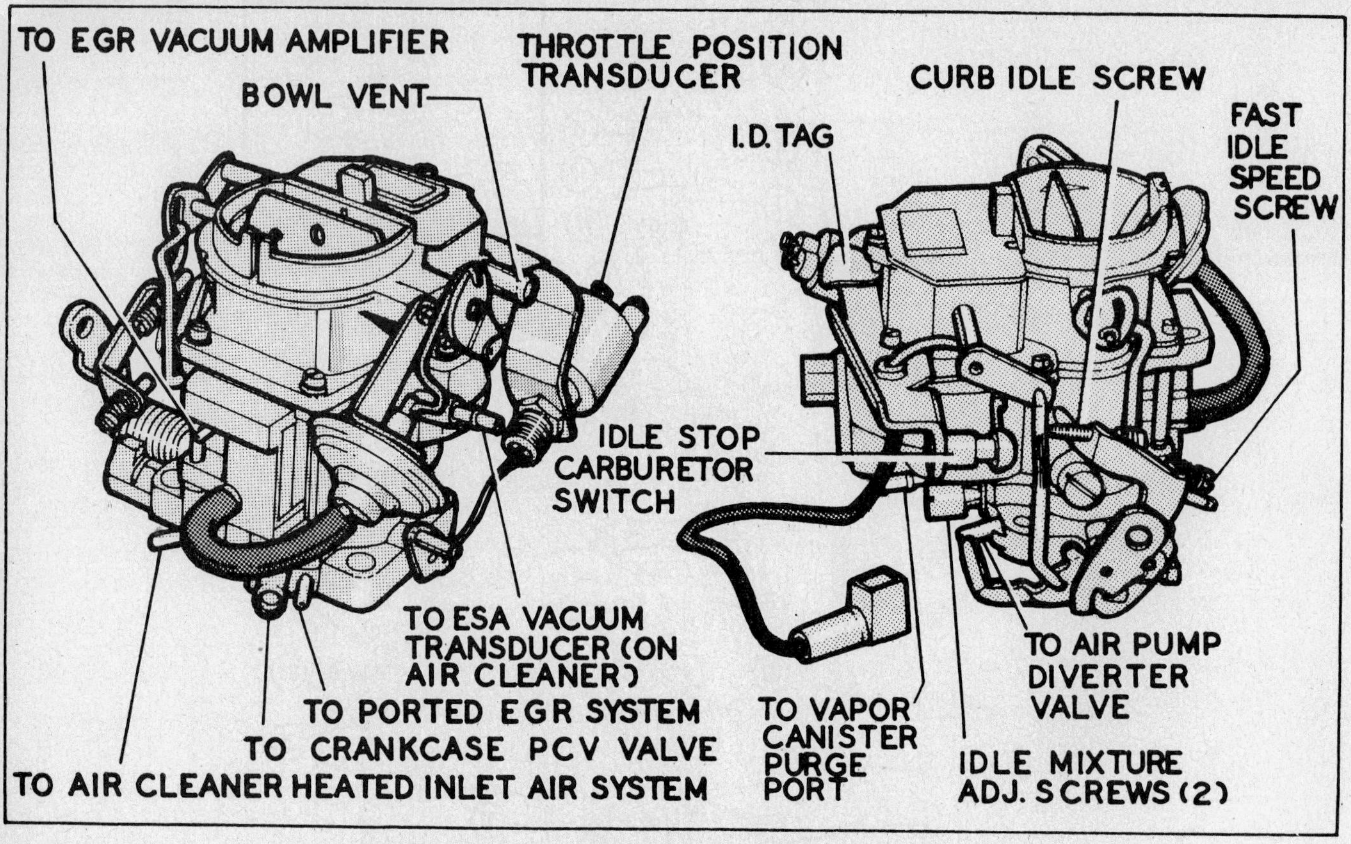

TO EGR VACUUM AMPLIFIER

BOWL VENT

THROTTLE POSITION TRANSDUCER

I.D. TAG

CURB IDLE SCREW

FAST IDLE SPEED SCREW

IDLE STOP CARBURETOR SWITCH

TO ESA VACUUM TRANSDUCER (ON AIR CLEANER)

TO PORTED EGR SYSTEM

TO CRANKCASE PCV VALVE

TO AIR CLEANER HEATED INLET AIR SYSTEM

TO VAPOR CANISTER PURGE PORT

TO AIR PUMP DIVERTER VALVE

IDLE MIXTURE ADJ. SCREWS (2)

Fig. 3   BBD 1¼″ carburetor assembly. 1978 (Typical)

MODEL BBD ADJUSTMENTS

Fig. 1 is an exploded view of a typical 1974-78 BBD two barrel carburetor. Fig. 2 is an external view of a 1974-77 unit and Fig. 3 is an external view of a 1978 unit. On Chrysler vehicles equipped with a manual transmission, a dashpot is mounted on the carburetor. On 1975-76 Chrysler vehicles equipped with an automatic transmission or 1978 Chrysler vehicles equipped with a V8-318 and an automatic transmission, an idle enrichment system is used to reduce cold engine stalling by the use of an additional metering system which enriches the mixture in the off idle position. This system is controlled by a vacuum diaphragm mounted near the top of the carburetor, Fig. 2.

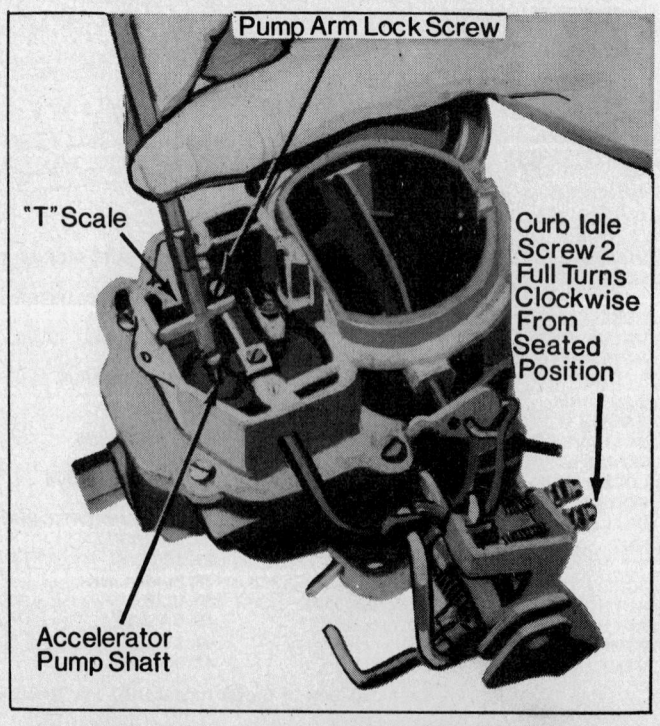

Pump Arm Lock Screw

"T" Scale

Curb Idle Screw 2 Full Turns Clockwise From Seated Position

Accelerator Pump Shaft

Fig. 5   Accelerator pump setting, 1974-78 BBD 1¼″

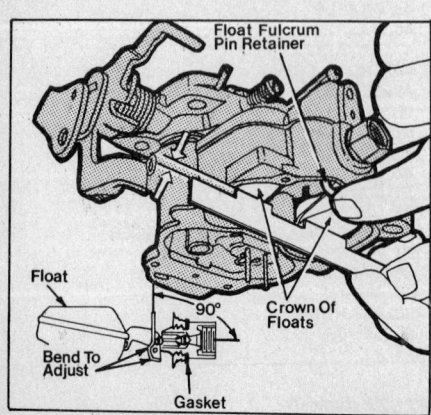

Float Fulcrum Pin Retainer

Float

Crown Of Floats

90°

Bend To Adjust

Gasket

Fig. 4   Checking float level. BBD carburetors

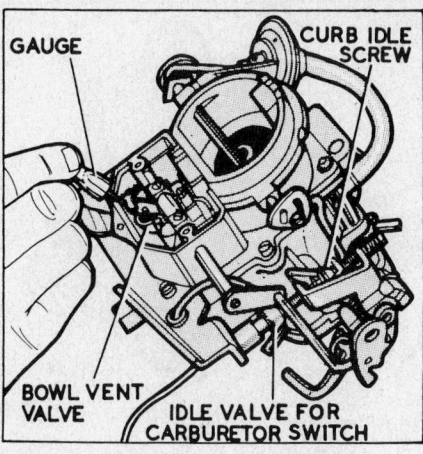

Fig. 6 Bowl vent valve adjustment. 1978 BBD carburetor

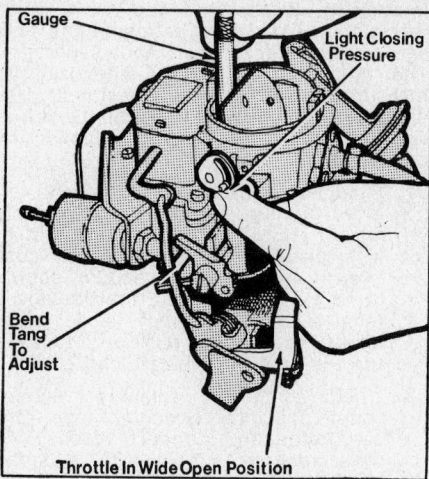

Fig. 7 Choke unloader setting. BBD carburetors

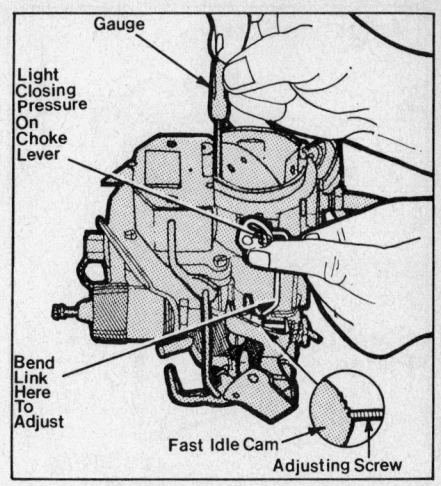

Fig. 8 Fast idle cam position adjustment. BBD 1¼" bore carburetors

Float Level Adjustment

Fig. 4—With carburetor body inverted so that weight of floats ONLY is forcing needle against its seat, use a T-scale or the tool shown, and check the float level from surface of fuel bowl to crown of each float at center.

If an adjustment is necessary, hold floats on bottom of bowl and bend float lip as required to give the specified dimension.

CAUTION: When bending the float lip, do not allow the lip to push against the needle as the synthetic rubber tip (if used) can be compressed sufficiently to cause a false setting which will affect correct level of fuel in bowl. After being compressed, the tip is very slow to recover its original shape.

Accelerator Pump

1974-78 1¼" Bore Units, Fig. 5

1. Back off curb idle adjusting screw, completely closing throttle valve, then open choke valve, allowing throttle valves to seat in bores. Ensure ac-

celerator pump "S" link is located in outer hole or pump arm.
2. Turn curb idle adjusting screw until screw contacts, stop, then rotate screw two additional turns.
3. Measure distance between air horn surface and top of accelerator pump shaft. Refer to BBD Specifications Chart.
4. Adjust by loosening pump arm adjusting screw and rotating sleeve until proper dimension is obtained. Tighten adjusting screw.

Bowl Vent Valve

Fig. 6

NOTE: The accelerator pump stroke and curb idle speed must be properly adjusted before making this adjustment.

1. Remove step-up piston cover plate and gasket.
2. Insert specified gauge between top of bowl vent valve and seat. Refer to the BBD Specifications Chart.
3. Adjust by bending bowl vent lever tab while supporting bowl vent lever assembly.
4. Install step-up piston cover gasket and cover.

Choke Unloader Adjustment

Fig. 7—The choke unloader is a mechanical device to partially open the choke valve at wide open throttle. It is used to eliminate choke enrichment during engine cranking. Engines that have been flooded or stalled by excessive choke enrichment can be cleared by the use of the unloader. Adjust as follows:

1. Hold throttle valve in wide open position. Insert the specified drill size between upper edge of choke valve and inner wall of air horn.
2. With a finger lightly pressing against choke valve, a slight drag should be felt as the drill is being withdrawn.
3. If an adjustment is necessary, bend unloader tang on throttle lever until specified opening has been obtained.

Fast Idle Cam Position

Fig. 8

1. With fast idle adjusting screw contacting second highest step on fast idle cam, move choke valve toward closed position with light pressure on choke shaft lever.
2. Insert the specified size drill between choke valve and air horn wall.

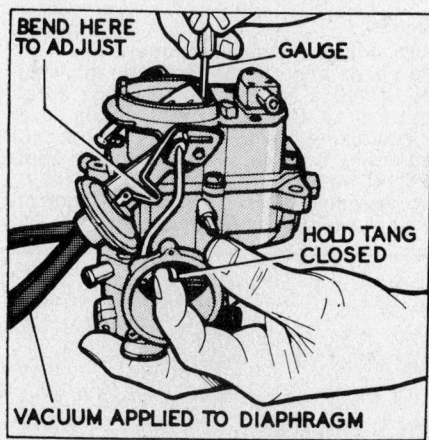

Fig. 9 Initial choke valve clearance adjustment. 1976 American Motors BBD unit

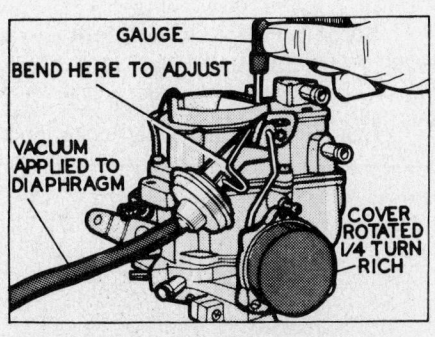

Fig. 10 Initial choke valve clearance adjustment. 1977-78 American Motors BBD unit

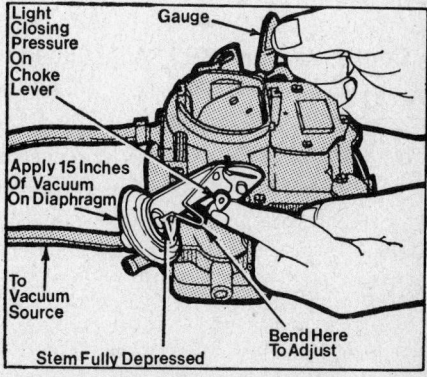

Fig. 11 Choke vacuum kick setting. BBD 1¼" bore carburetors

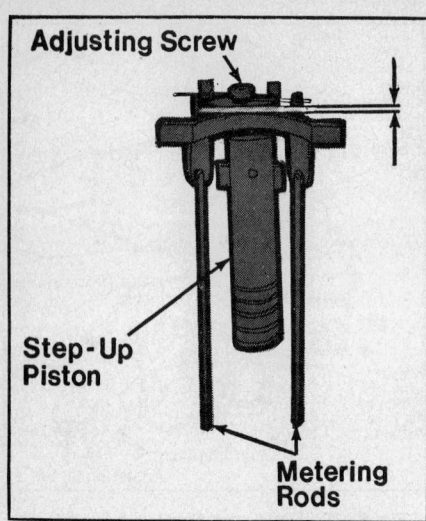

Fig. 12   Step-up piston adjustment

An adjustment will be necessary if a slight drag is not obtained as drill is being removed.

3. Adjust by bending fast idle connector rod at angle.

Initial Choke Valve Clearance

1976 American Motors

Fig. 9—Remove choke cover and using an external vacuum source, apply at least 19 inches of vacuum to pull diaphragm against stop. Open throttle valve slightly to place fast idle screw on high step of cam. Hold choke coil tang in closed position and measure clearance between choke plate and air horn wall. Adjust by bending diaphragm connecting link.

1977-78 American Motors

Fig. 10—Loosen choke cover and rotate ¼ turn rich, then tighten one screw. Open throttle valve slightly to place fast idle screw on high step of cam. Using an external vacuum source, apply at least 19 inches of vacuum to pull diaphragm against stop. Measure clearance between choke plate and air horn wall. Adjust by bending diaphragm connector link.

Choke Vacuum Kick Adjustment

Fig. 11 Chrysler

The choke diaphragm adjustment controls the fuel delivery while the engine

is running. It positions the choke valve within the air horn by action of the linkage between choke shaft and diaphragm. The diaphragm must be energized to measure the vacuum kick adjustment. Use either a distributor test machine with a vacuum source, or vacuum supplied by another vehicle.

1. If adjustment is to be made with engine running, disconnect fast idle linkage to allow choke to close to kick position with engine at curb idle. If an auxiliary vacuum source is to be used, open throttle valves (engine not running) and move choke to closed position. Release throttle first, then release choke.

2. When using an auxiliary vacuum source, disconnect vacuum hose from carburetor and connect it to hose from vacuum supply with a small length of tube to act as a fitting. Removal of hose from diaphragm may require forces which damage the system. Apply a vacuum of 15 or more inches of mercury.

3. Insert the specified drill size between choke valve and wall of air horn. Apply sufficient closing pressure on lever to which choke rod attaches to provide a minimum choke valve opening without distortion of diaphragm link. Note that the cylindrical stem of diaphragm will extend as internal spring is compressed. This spring must be fully compressed for proper measurement of vacuum kick adjustment.

4. An adjustment will be necessary if a slight drag is not obtained as drill is being removed. Shorten or lengthen diaphragm link to obtain correct choke opening. Length changes should be made carefully by bending (opening or closing) the bend provided in the diaphragm link. Do not apply twisting or bending force to diaphragm.

5. Reinstall vacuum hose on correct carburetor fitting. Return fast idle linkage to its original condition if it has been disturbed as in Step 1.

6. Check as follows: With no vacuum applied to diaphragm, choke valve should move freely between open and closed positions. If movement is not free, examine linkage for misalignment or interferences caused by bending operation. Repeat adjustment if necessary.

Step-up Piston Adjustment

1974-77 1¼" BBD Units, Figs. 12 & 13

1. On 1974 Chrysler units, adjust vacuum piston gap to .030 inch. On 1975 and 1978 Chrysler units and

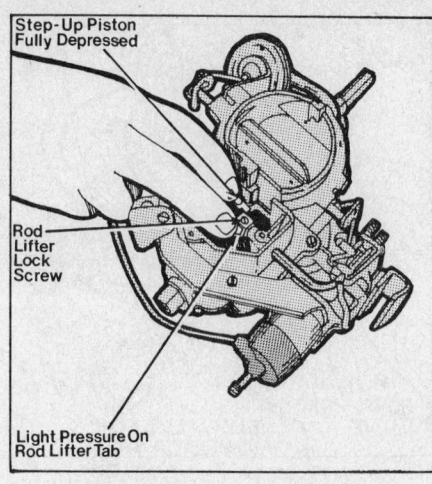

Fig. 13   Step-up piston adjustment. 1974-78 BBD 1¼" carburetors

1977 American Motors units, adjust vacuum piston gap to .035 inch. On 1976 and 1978 American Motors units, adjust vacuum piston gap to .040 inch. Rotate allen head screw on top of piston to adjust gap.

2. On all units, install step-up piston assembly into air horn bore, ensuring metering rods are positioned in the metering jets.

3. Back off curb idle screw until throttle valves are completely closed. Count number of turns so that screw can be returned to its original setting.

4. Fully depress piston and while applying moderate pressure on rod lifter, tighten rod lifter screw.

5. Release piston and rod lifter and reset curb idle screw.

Dashpot Adjustment

American Motors

With curb idle speed properly adjusted, hold dashpot plunger firmly against stop. Measure clearance between plunger and throttle lever with throttle in idle position. Clearance should be .104 inch. To adjust, loosen locknut and rotate dashpot.

Chrysler

To adjust the dashpot, have the curb idle speed and mixture properly adjusted, and install a tachometer. Position throttle lever so that actuating tab on lever is contacting stem of dashpot but not depressing it. Engine RPM should be 2500 RPM. If not correct, screw dashpot in or out as required, then tighten lock nut on dashpot against the bracket.

CARTER TQ ADJUSTMENT SPECIFICATIONS

See Tune Up Chart in car chapters for hot idle speeds.

Year	Carb. Model	Air/Fuel Ratio	Float Setting	Secondary Throttle Linkage	Secondary Air Valve Opening	Secondary Air Valve Spring	Pump Travel	Choke Control Lever (Off Car)	Choke Vacuum Kick	Choke Unloader	Fast Idle R.P.M.	Choke Setting
CHRYSLER, DODGE, IMPERIAL & PLYMOUTH												
1974	6452S	①	⑤	⑧	½	1¼ Turn	35/64⑧	3⅜	.210	.310	1900	Fixed
	6453S	①	⑤	②	½	1¼ Turn	31/64	3⅜	.160	.310	1900	Fixed
	6454S④	①	⑤	②	½	1¼ Turn	35/64⑧	3⅜	.210	.310	1900	Fixed
	6455S④	①	⑤	②	½	1¼ Turn	31/64	3⅜	.160	.310	1900	Fixed
	6456S	①	⑤	②	½	1¼ Turn	35/64⑧	3⅜	.210	.310	1700	Fixed
	6457S④	①	⑤	②	½	1¼ Turn	31/64	3⅜	.100	.310	1800	Fixed
	6459S④	①	⑤	②	½	1¼ Turn	31/64	3⅜	.100	.310	1800	Fixed
	6460S	①	⑤	②	½	1¼ Turn	31/64	3⅜	.100	.310	1700	Fixed
	6461S④	①	⑤	②	½	1¼ Turn	31/64	3⅜	.100	.310	1700	Fixed
	6462S	①	⑤	②	½	1¼ Turn	31/64	3⅜	.150	.310	1700	Fixed
	6463S④	①	⑤	②	½	1¼ Turn	31/64	3⅜	.100	.310	1700	Fixed
	6487S	①	⑤	②	½	1¼ Turn	35/64	3⅜	.100	.310	2000	Fixed
	6488S④	①	⑤	②	½	1¼ Turn	35/64	3⅜	.100	.310	1800	Fixed
	6489S	①	⑤	②	½	1¼ Turn	31/64	3⅜	.100	.310	2000	Fixed
	6496S	①	⑤	②	½	1¼ Turn	31/64	3⅜	.100	.310	2000	Fixed
	6498S	①	29/32	②	33/64	1¼ Turn	31/64	3⅜	.100	.310	1900	Fixed
	6499S④	①	29/32	②	33/64	1¼ Turn	35/64	3⅜	.100	.310	1900	Fixed
	9013S④	①	⑤	②	½	1¼ Turn	35/64	3⅜	.160	.310	1800	Fixed
	9014S	①	⑤	②	½	1¼ Turn	31/64	3⅜	.160	.310	2000	Fixed
	9015S	①	⑤	②	½	1¼ Turn	31/64	3⅜	.160	.310	1700	Fixed
	9016S④	①	⑤	②	½	1¼ Turn	31/64	3⅜	.160	.310	1700	Fixed
	9023S	①	⑤	②	½	1¼ Turn	31/64	3⅜	.160	.310	1700	Fixed
	9024S④	①	⑤	②	½	1¼ Turn	31/64	3⅜	.160	.310	1700	Fixed
1975	9002S	①	29/32	②	½	1¼ Turn	35/64	3⅜	—	.310	1600	Fixed
	9004S	①	29/32	②	½	1¼ Turn	35/64	3⅜	.160	.310	1600	Fixed
	9008S	①	29/32	②	½	1¼ Turn	35/64	3⅜	.160	.310	1800	Fixed
	9009S	①	29/32	②	½	1¼ Turn	35/64	3⅜	.160	.310	1600	Fixed
	9010S	①	29/32	②	½	1¼ Turn	35/64	3⅜	—	.310	1600	Fixed
	9011S	①	29/32	②	½	1¼ Turn	35/64	3⅜	—	.310	1600	Fixed
	9012S	①	29/32	②	½	1¼ Turn	35/64	3⅜	.160	.310	1800	Fixed
	9046S	①	29/32	②	½	1¼ Turn	35/64	3⅜	.160	.310	1800	Fixed
	9053S	②	29/32	②	½	1¼ Turn	35/64	3⅜	.160	.310	1800	Fixed
1976	9002S	①	29/32	②	33/64	1¼ Turn	33/64⑨	3⅜	.160	.310	1700	Fixed
	9054S	①	29/32	②	33/64	1¼ Turn	33/64⑨	3⅜	.160	.310	1800	Fixed
	9055S	①	29/32	②	33/64	1¼ Turn	33/64⑨	3⅜	.160	.310	1700	Fixed
	9058S	①	29/32	②	33/64	1¼ Turn	31/64	3⅜	.100	.310	1600	Fixed
	9059S	①	29/32	②	33/64	1¼ Turn	31/64	3⅜	.100	.310	1600	Fixed
	9062S	①	29/32	②	33/64	1¼ Turn	33/64⑨	3⅜	.100	.310	1600	Fixed
	9066S	①	29/32	②	33/64	1¼ Turn	33/64⑨	3⅜	.100	.310	1600	Fixed
	9074S	①	29/32	②	33/64	1¼ Turn	33/64⑨	3⅜	.100	.310	1600	Fixed
	9097S③	①	27/32	②	½	1¼ Turn	33/64⑨	3⅜	.100	.310	1150	Fixed
1977	9076S	①	27/32	②	½	⑥	⑩	3⅜	.100	.310	⑪	Fixed
	9077S	①	27/32	②	31/64	1½ Turn	33/64⑨	3⅜	.100	.310	1400	Fixed
	9078S	①	27/32	②	½	1¼ Turn	33/64⑨	3⅜	.100	.310	1400	Fixed
	9080S	①	27/32	②	½	1¼ Turn	33/64⑨	3⅜	.100	.310	1200	Fixed
	9081S	①	27/32	②	½	1¼ Turn	33/64⑨	3⅜	.100	.310	1600	Fixed
	9093S	①	27/32	②	17/32	1¼ Turn	33/64⑦	3⅜	.100	.310	1500	Fixed
	9101S	①	27/32	②	½	1¼ Turn	33/64⑨	3⅜	.100	.310	1600	Fixed
	9102S	①	27/32	②	31/64	1½ Turn	33/64⑨	3⅜	.100	.310	1400	Fixed
	9103S	①	27/32	②	31/64	1½ Turn	33/64⑨	3⅜	.100	.310	1400	Fixed
	9115S	①	27/32	②	½	2¼ Turn	31/64⑨	3⅜	.150	.310	1500	Fixed
	9119S	①	27/32	②	½	1¼ Turn	33/64⑨	3⅜	.100	.310	1600	Fixed

Continued

CARTER TQ ADJUSTMENT SPECIFICATIONS—Continued
See Tune Up Chart in car chapters for hot idle speeds.

Year	Carb. Model	Air/Fuel Ratio	Float Setting	Secondary Throttle Linkage	Secondary Air Valve Opening	Secondary Air Valve Spring	Pump Travel	Choke Control Lever (Off Car)	Choke Vacuum Kick	Choke Unloader	Fast Idle R.P.M.	Choke Setting
CHRYSLER, DODGE, IMPERIAL & PLYMOUTH—Continued												
1978	9104S	①	$\frac{29}{32}$	②	½	1½ Turn	$\frac{31}{64}$⑨	$3\frac{3}{8}$	.150	.310	1500	Fixed
	9109S	①	$\frac{27}{32}$	②	½	1½ Turn	$\frac{33}{64}$⑨	$3\frac{3}{8}$	.100	.310	1400	Fixed
	9110S	①	$\frac{27}{32}$	②	½	1½ Turn	$\frac{33}{64}$⑨	$3\frac{3}{8}$	.100	.310	1600	Fixed
	9112S	①	$\frac{29}{32}$	②	½	1½ Turn	$\frac{33}{64}$⑨	$3\frac{3}{8}$	.100	.310	1200	Fixed
	9134S	①	$\frac{29}{32}$	②	½	1½ Turn	$\frac{31}{64}$⑦	$3\frac{3}{8}$	.100	.310	1500	Fixed
	9140S	①	$\frac{29}{32}$	②	½	1½ Turn	$\frac{33}{64}$⑨	$3\frac{3}{8}$	.150	.310	1500	Fixed
	9147S	①	$\frac{29}{32}$	②	½	1½ Turn	$\frac{31}{64}$⑦	$3\frac{3}{8}$	.100	.310	1600	Fixed
	9148S	①	$\frac{29}{32}$	②	½	1½ Turn	$\frac{33}{64}$⑨	$3\frac{3}{8}$	.100	.310	1600	Fixed

①—For Air/Fuel ratio and idle CO%, see Tune-Up charts in car chapters.
②—Adjust link so primary and secondary stops both contact at same time.
③—With Electronic Lean Burn System.
④—With California Emission package.
⑤—Brass float, 1 inch; cellular plastic float, $\frac{29}{32}$ inch.
⑥—Models less red tag. 1½ turns; models with red tag, 2¼ turns.
⑦—Secondary stage pick/up adjustment $\frac{23}{64}$ inch.
⑧—Secondary stage pick/up adjustment $\frac{21}{64}$ inch.
⑨—Secondary stage pick/up adjustment $\frac{5}{16}$ inch.
⑩—Models less red tag, $\frac{33}{64}$ inch, refer to note ⑨.
  Models with red tag, $\frac{31}{64}$ inch, refer to note ⑦.
⑪—Models less red tag, 1700 rpm; models with red tag, 1500 rpm.

FORD & MERCURY

Year	Carb. Model	Air/Fuel Ratio	Float Setting	Secondary Throttle Linkage	Secondary Air Valve Opening	Secondary Air Valve Spring	Pump Travel	Choke Control Lever (Off Car)	Choke Vacuum Kick	Choke Unloader	Fast Idle R.P.M.	Choke Setting
1974	D4AE-BB,BC	①	$1\frac{1}{16}$	②	.468	—	$\frac{5}{16}$③	—	.250	1250	Index	

①—For Air/Fuel ratio and idle CO%, see Tune-Up charts in car chapters.
②—Adjust link so primary and secondary stops both contact at same time.
③—Measured bottom of "S" link to top of bowl cover.
On most 1975-78 California and all 1978 high altitude carburetors an altitude compensator is used to maintain proper air/fuel mixtures.

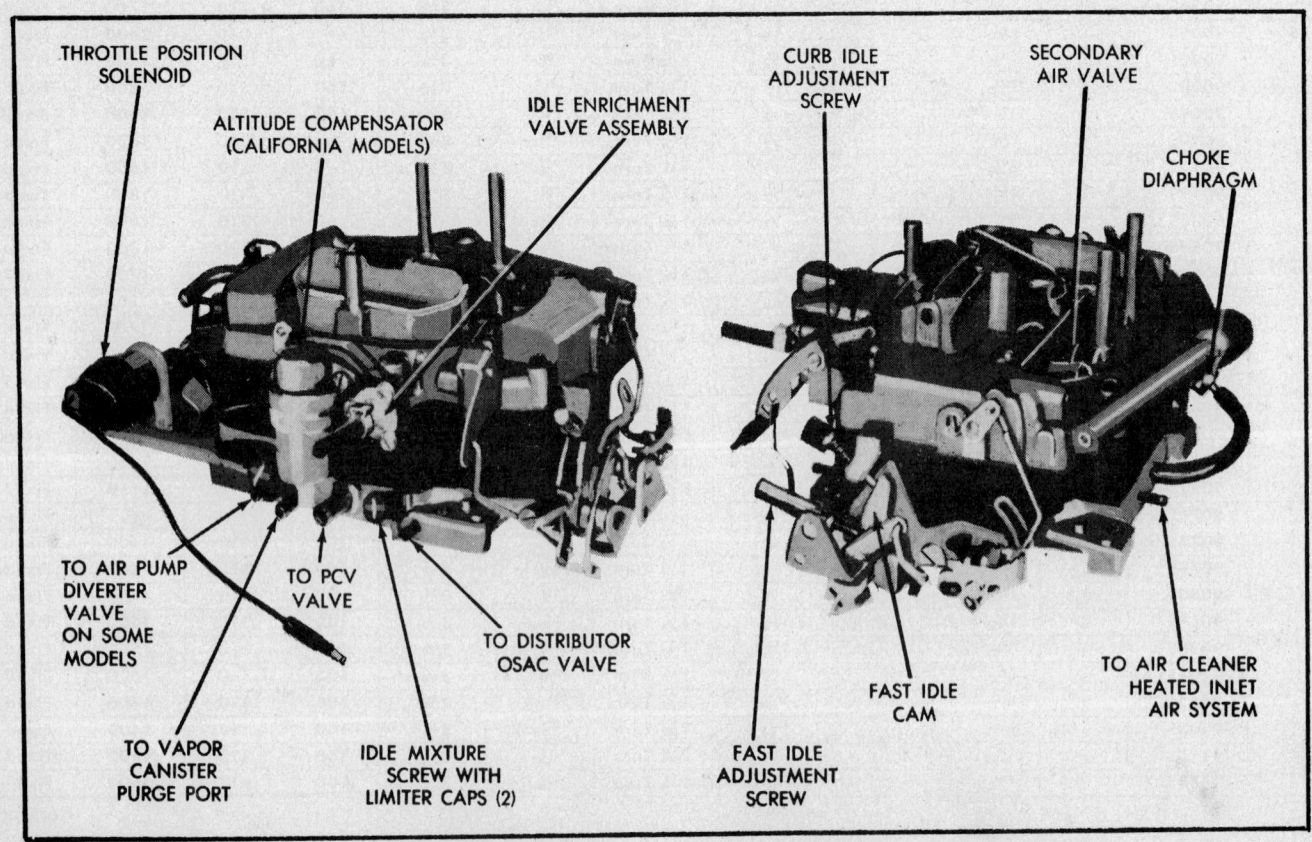

Fig. 1   TQ carburetor assembly. 1974-78 (typical)

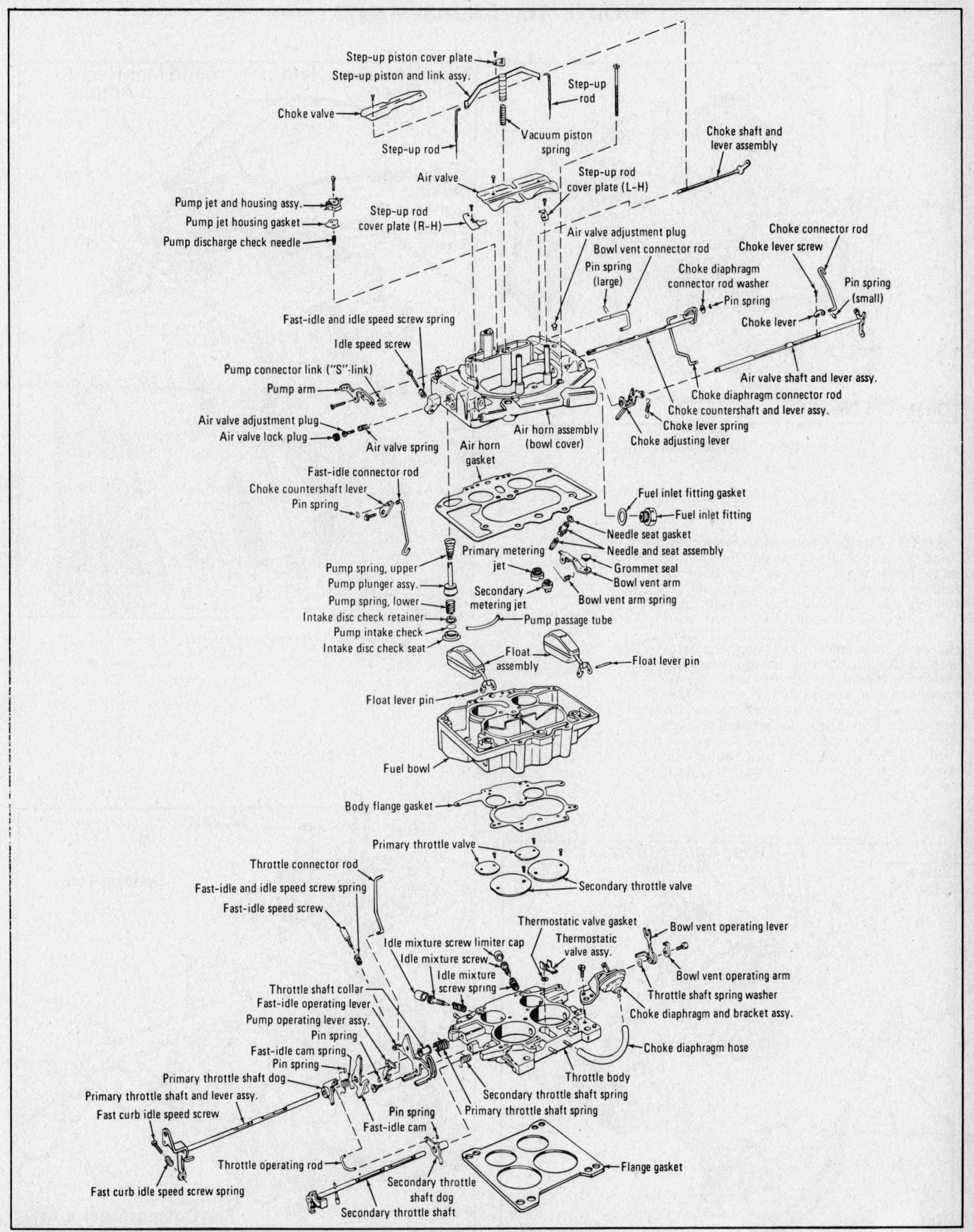

Fig. 2 Carter TQ model exploded view

MODEL TQ ADJUSTMENTS

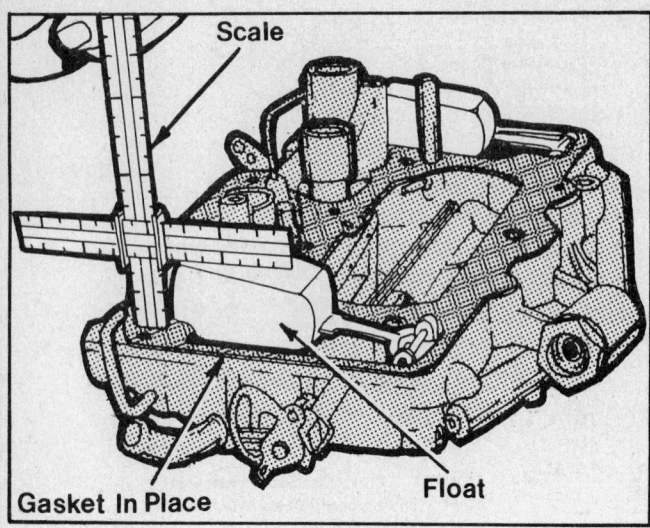

Fig. 3   TQ float setting

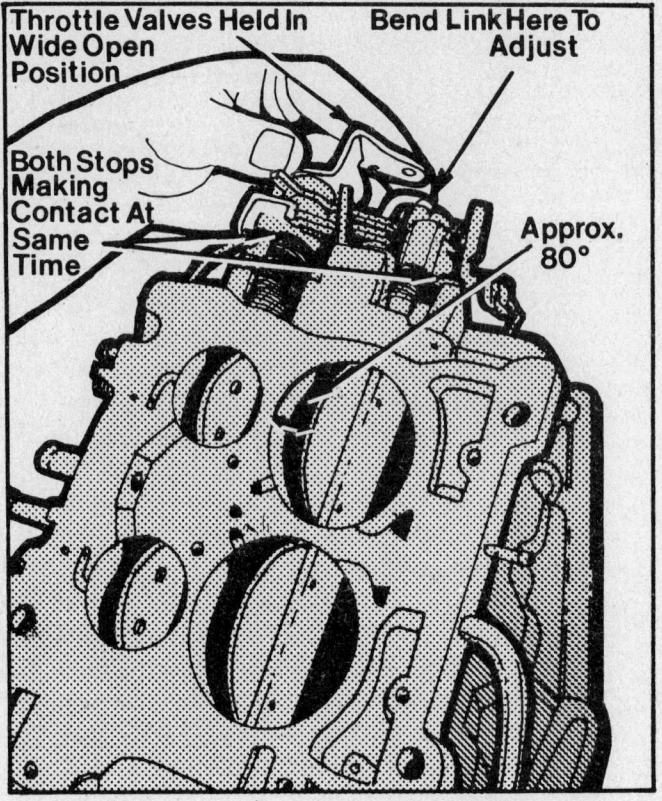

Fig. 4   TQ secondary throttle adjustment

The TQ (Thermo-Quad) carburetor, Figs. 1 and 2, is unique in design in that it has a black main body or fuel bowl of molded phenolic resin. This acts as an effective heat insulator. Fuel is kept cooler by about 20 degrees Fahrenheit than in carburetors of all metal design. Another reason for the lower operating temperatures is its suspended design metering system. All calibration points with the exception of the idle adjusting screws, are in the upper aluminum casting or air horn and are in effect suspended in cavities in the plastic main body.

On 1975-78 vehicles with automatic transmissions, an idle enrichment system

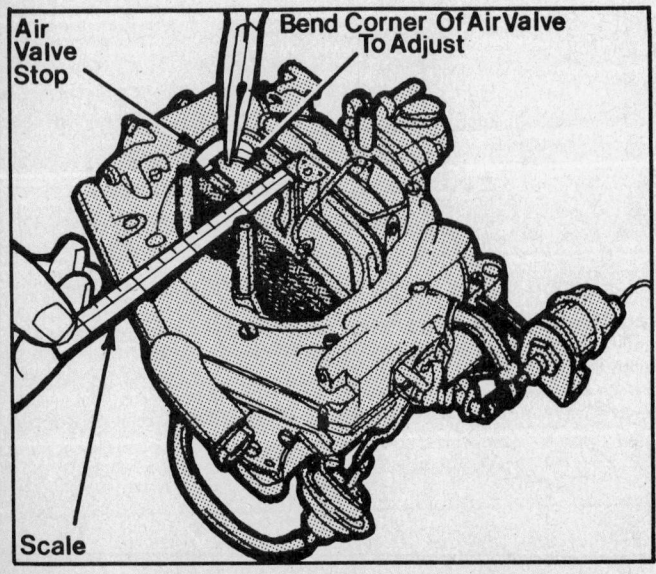

Fig. 5   TQ secondary air valve opening

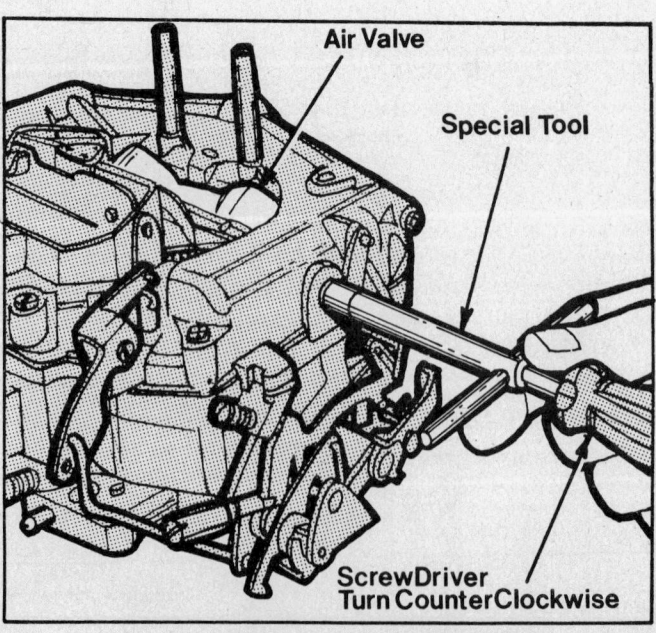

Fig. 6   TQ secondary air valve spring tension

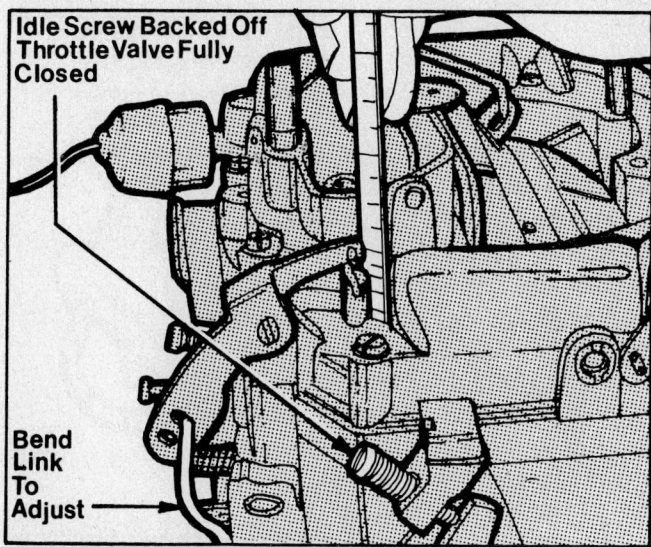

Fig. 7 TQ accelerator pump stroke adjustment, less staged pump system

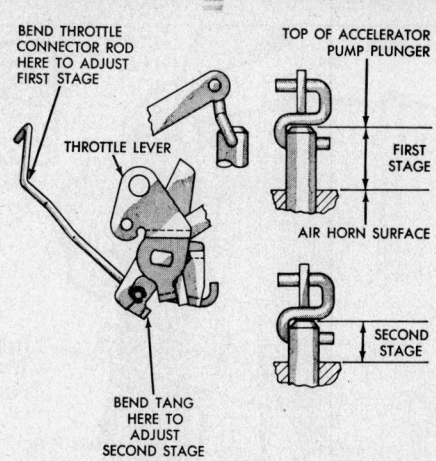

Fig. 8 TQ accelerator pump stroke adjustment, with staged pump system

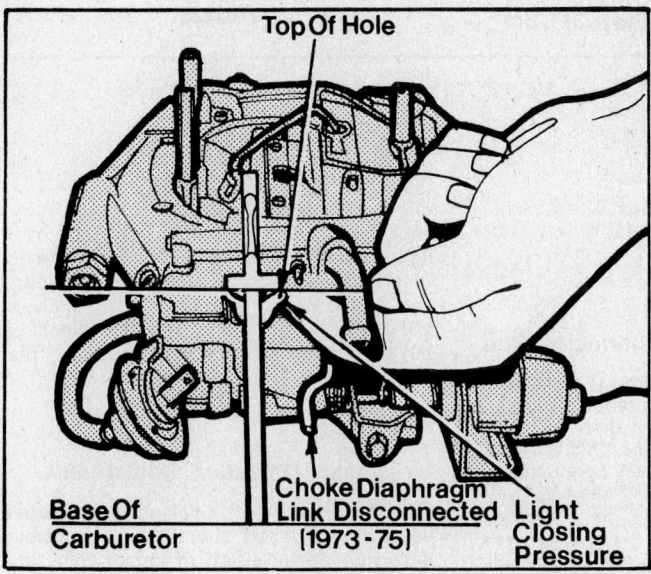

Fig. 9 TQ choke control lever adjustment

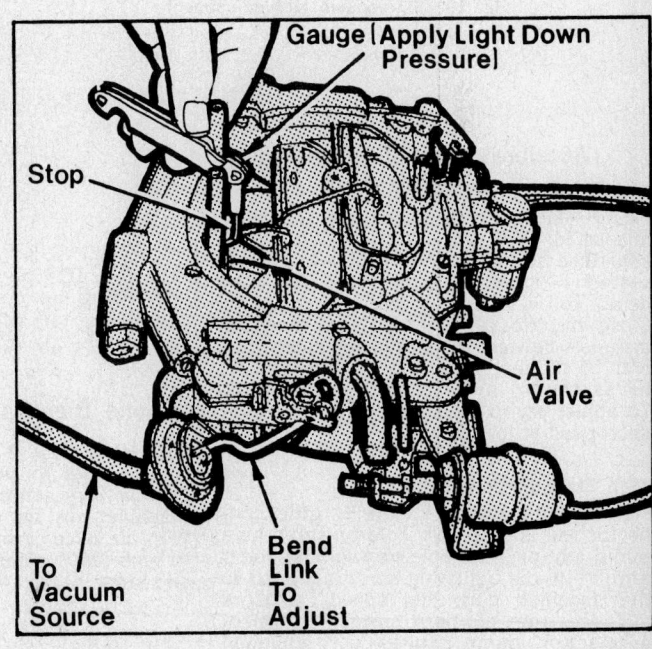

Fig. 10 TQ choke diaphragm connector rod

is used to reduce cold engine stalling by the use of an additional metering system, which enriches the mixture in the off idle position. This system is controlled by a vacuum diaphragm mounted near the top of the carburetor.

Some 1974 and all 1975-78 units incorporate cellular plastic floats. Note that the float level settings are different. Refer to TQ Specifications Chart.

Float Setting

Fig. 3—With bowl cover inverted, gasket installed and floats resting on seated needle, the dimension of each float from bowl cover gasket to bottom side of float should be as shown in *TQ Specifications Chart*. To adjust, bend float lever.

Secondary Throttle Linkage

Fig. 4—Hold fast idle lever in curb idle position and invert carburetor. Open primary throttle valve until the primary and secondary stops contact simultaneously. To adjust, bend secondary throttle operating rod at angle until correct adjustment is obtained.

Secondary Air Valve Opening

Fig. 5

1. With air valve in closed position, the opening along air valve at its long side must be at its maximum and parallel with air horn gasket surface.

2. With air valve wide open, the opening of the air valve at the short side and air horn must be as shown in *TQ Specifications Chart*. The corner of air valve is notched for adjustment. Bend the corner with a pair of pliers to give proper opening.

Secondary Air Valve Spring Tension

Fig. 6—Loosen air valve lock plug and allow air valve to position itself wide open. With a long screwdriver that will enter center of tool C-4152 positioned on air valve adjustment plug, turn plug counterclockwise until air valve contacts stop lightly, then turn additional turn as specified in *TQ Specifications Chart*. Hold plug with screwdriver and tighten lock plug securely with tool C-4152.

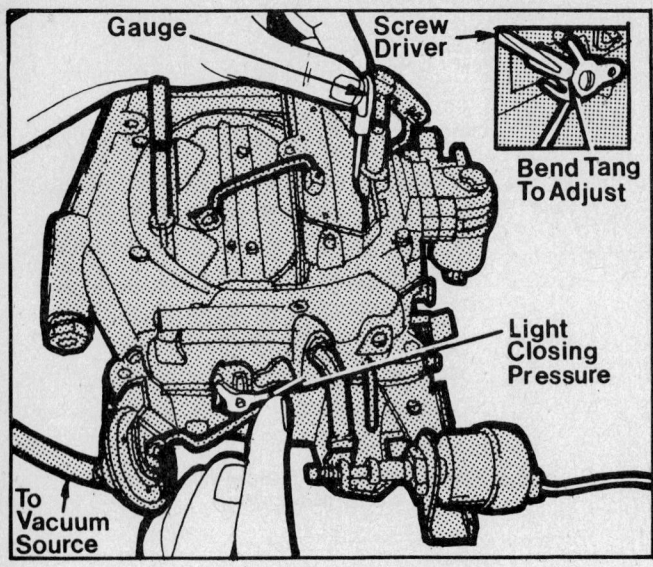

Fig. 10 TQ vacuum kick adjustment

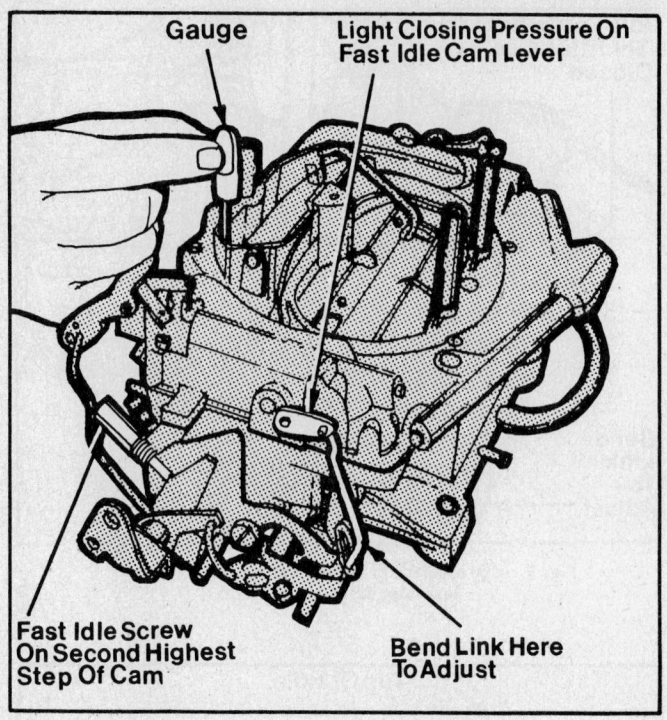

Fig. 12 TQ fast idle cam & linkage adjustment

Accelerator Pump Stroke

Less Staged Pump System

Fig. 7—Move choke valve wide open to release fast idle cam. Back off idle speed adjusting screw until throttle valves are seated in bores. Be sure throttle connector rod is in center hole of pump arm. Close throttle valve tightly and measure distance between top of bowl cover and end of plunger shaft. Dimension should be as shown in *TQ Specifications Chart*. To adjust pump stroke, bend throttle connector rod at lower angle.

With Staged Pump System

Fig. 8—**First Stage.** Ensure throttle connector rod is in center hole on three hole pump arm or inner hole on two hole pump arm. With idle adjusting screw adjusted to the specified curb idle speed, measure distance from air horn surface to top of accelerator pump plunger. If equipped with an idle stop solenoid the ignition switch must be in the on position. Dimensions should be as shown in the *TQ Specifications Chart*. Bend throttle connector rod at lower angle to adjust.

Second Stage. With choke in the open position, open throttle until secondary lockout latch is just applied. Plunger downward travel stops at this point. Measure distance from air horn surface to top of accelerator pump plunger. Dimension should be shown in the *TQ Specifications Chart*. Bend tang on throttle to adjust.

Choke Control Lever

Fig. 9—Place carburetor on a flat surface and on 1974-75 Chrysler units, disconnect choke diaphragm rod at diaphragm. On all units, close choke by pushing on choke lever with throttle partly open. Measure vertical distance between top of rod hole in control lever and base of carburetor (flat surface). Dimension should be as

shown in TQ Specifications Chart. Adjust by bending link connecting the two choke shafts.

Choke Diaphragm Connector Rod

Fig. 10—Apply a vacuum of 15 inches Hg or more to fully depress diaphragm. An auxilliary source like a distributor test machine can be used for this purpose. With air valve closed, adjust connector rod to give .040" clearance between air valve and stop.

Vacuum Kick Adjustment

Fig. 11—With engine running, back off fast idle speed screw until choke can be closed to kick position at idle. Note number of screw turns so fast idle can be turned back to original adjustment. Insert a gauge or drill of specified size between long side (lower edge) of choke valve and air horn wall. Apply sufficient pressure on choke control lever to provide a minimum choke valve opening. The spring connecting the control lever to the adjustment lever must be fully extended for proper adjustment. Bend tang as shown to change contact with end of diaphragm rod. Do not adjust diaphragm rod. A slight drag should be felt as drill is being removed.

Fast Idle Cam & Linkage

Fig. 12—With fast idle adjusting screw

on second step of fast idle cam, move choke valve toward closed position with light pressure on choke control lever. Clearance between choke valve lower edge and air horn wall should be .100 inch on 1974-78 Chrysler units and .099 inch on 1974 Ford units. Adjust by bending fast idle connector rod at angle.

Choke Unloader Adjustment

Fig. 13—Hold throttle valves in wide open position and insert specified drill between long side (lower edge) of choke valve and inner wall of air horn. With finger lightly pressing against choke valve control lever, a slight drag should be felt as drill is withdrawn. Refer to TQ Specification Chart for proper drill size or dimension. Adjust by bending tang on fast idle control lever.

Secondary Throttle Lockout

Fig. 14—Move choke control lever to open choke position. Measure clearance between lockout lever and stop. Clearance should be .060-.090 inch on 1974-77 units and .075 inch on 1978 units. Adjust by bending tang on fast idle control lever.

Bowl Vent Valve Adjustment

Fig. 15—Remove bowl vent valve checking hole plug in bowl cover. With throttle valves at curb idle, insert a narrow ruler

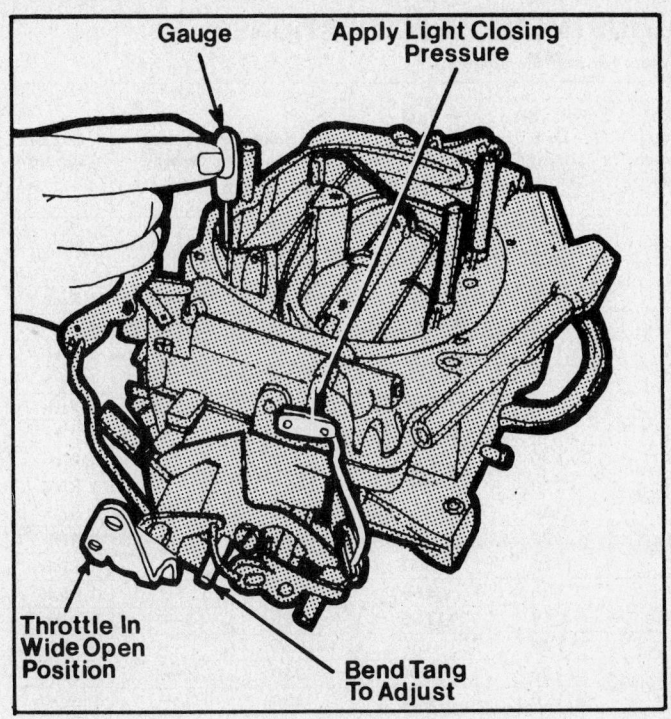

Fig. 13   TQ choke unloader adjustment

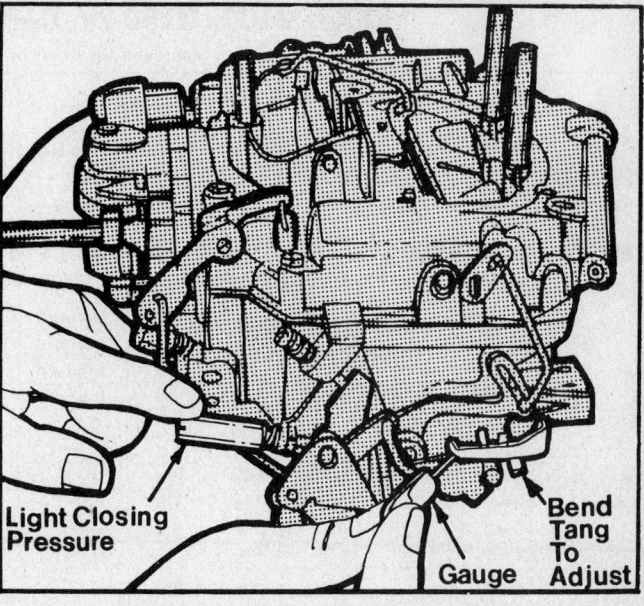

Fig. 14   TQ secondary throttle lockout

down through hole. Allow ruler to rest lightly on top of valve. Dimension should be .812 inch on 1974-78 Chrysler units and .900 inch on 1974 Ford units. Adjust by bending bowl vent operating lever at notch. Install a new plug.

Solenoid Bowl Vent Valve Check
Fig. 16
1. Remove air cleaner.
2. Disconnect vacuum hose from solenoid bowl vent diaphragm.
3. Connect an external vacuum source and apply 15 inches of vacuum to the diaphragm.
4. Observe valve movement through air horn vent tube. Valve should move when vacuum is applied.
5. Turn ignition switch "On" and disconnect external vacuum source. The valve should remain in the downward position until the ignition switch is turned "Off".
6. If the valve does not move when vacuum is applied, the diaphragm is defective and requires replacement. If the valve does not remain in the downward position when the ignition switch is turned "On" and the vacuum source removed, the solenoid or wiring is defective.
7. Install air cleaner.

Fast Idle Speed

NOTE: On 1974-77 Chrysler models without Electronic Lean Burn system, remove air cleaner and plug vacuum fittings to heated air control and OSAC valves. On 1978 Chrysler models without Electronic Lean Burn system, remove air cleaner and eliminate vacuum ignition advance and EGR signals, then cap or plug disconnected vacuum lines. On Chrysler models with Electronic Lean Burn system, remove top of air cleaner and lift air cleaner for access to carburetor. Also, use a jumper wire to ground carburetor idle stop switch. On Ford units, disconnect vacuum hoses at carburetor spark port and distributor primary diaphragm, then install a jumper hose between the two disconnected hoses. Disconnect and plug EGR vacuum line.

Fig. 17—With engine off and transmission in Park or Neutral, open throttle slightly. Close choke valve until fast idle screw is positioned on second step of cam against shoulder of first step. Start engine and stabilize RPM, then adjust fast idle speed. Refer to TQ Specification Chart.

NOTE: On models with Electronic Lean Burn system, if speed continues to rise slowly, the carburetor idle stop switch has not been properly grounded.

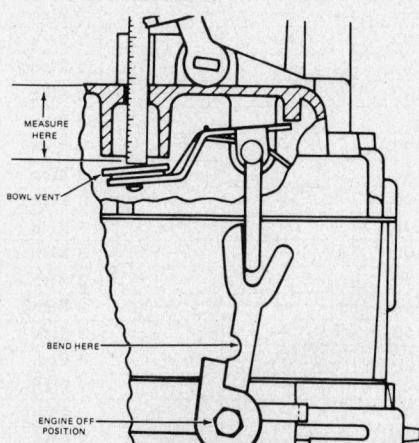

Fig. 15   TQ bowl vent valve adjustment

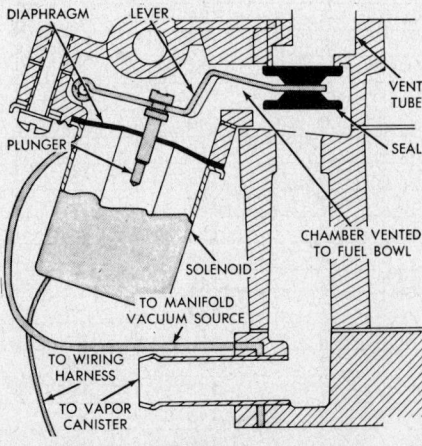

Fig. 16   TQ solenoid bowl vent check. 1978 units

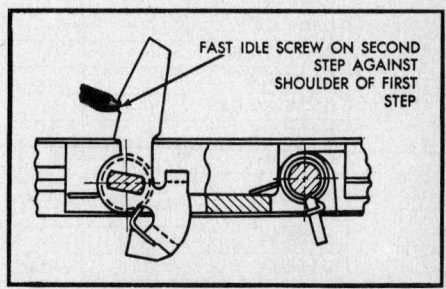

Fig. 17   TQ fast idle speed cam position

Ford Motorcraft Carburetors

MODEL 2100, 2150-2V CARB. ADJUSTMENT SPECIFICATIONS
See Tune Up Chart in car chapters for hot idle speeds.

Year	Carb. Model (Code 9510) ①	Idle Mixture Turns Open	Float Level (Dry)	Fuel Level (Wet)	Pump Setting Hole No. ④	Choke Plate Clearance (Pull down)	Fast Idle Cam Linkage Clearance	Fast Idle Speed (Hot Engine)	Dechoke Clearance ②	Dashpot Setting	Choke Setting
AMERICAN MOTORS											
1974	4DA2	③	13/32	25/32	Inboard	.140	.130	1600	.250	.140	1 Rich
	4DA2-E	③	13/32	25/32	Inboard	.140	.130	1600	.250	.140	1 Rich
	4DM2	③	13/32	25/32	Inboard	.130	.130	1600	.250	.140	2 Rich
	4RA2	③	13/32	25/32	Inboard	.140	.130	1600	.250	.140	1 Rich
	4RAC2	③	13/32	25/32	Inboard	.140	.130	1600	.250	.140	1 Rich
1975	5DA2	③	13/32	3/4	—	.140	.130	1600⑦	.250	—	1 Rich
	5DMS	③	13/32	3/4	—	.130	.130	1600⑦	.250	.093	2 Rich
	5RAS	③	13/32	3/4	—	.140	.130	1600⑦	.250	—	1 Rich
1976	6DA2	③	13/32	25/32	—	.140	.130	1600⑦	.250	—	1 Rich
	6DM2	③	35/64	15/16	—	.130	.120	1600⑦	.250	.075	2 Rich
	6RA2	③	13/32	25/32	—	.140	.130	1600⑦	.250	—	1 Rich
1977	7RA2	③	5/16	25/32	—	.136	.126	1600	.250	—	1 Rich
	7RA2A	③	5/16	25/32	—	.104	.089	1800	.250	—	1 Rich
	7RA2C	③	5/16	25/32	—	.130	.120	⑨	.250	—	1 Rich
	7RA2CP	③	5/16	25/32	—	.136	.126	1600	.250	—	1 Rich
	7DA2	③	5/16	25/32	—	.136	.126	1600	.250	—	Index
1978	8DA2	③	35/64	25/32	—	.136	.126	1600	.250	—	Index
	8DA2A	③	35/64	15/16	—	.089	.078	1600	.170	—	2 Rich
	8RA2	③	35/64	25/32	—	.136	.126	1600	.250	—	1 Rich
	8RA2A	③	35/64	25/32	—	.089	.078	1800	.170	—	2 Rich
	8RA2C	③	35/64	25/32	—	.136	.120	1800	.250	—	1 Rich
FORD AND MERCURY											
1974	D4AE-DA	③	7/16	13/16	No. 2A	⑩	—	—	—	—	1 Rich
	D4AE-EA	③	7/16	13/16	No. 2A	⑩	—	—	—	—	3 Rich
	D4AE-FA	③	7/16	13/16	No. 3A	⑩	—	—	—	—	3 Rich
	D4AE-GA	③	7/16	13/16	No. 3A	⑩	—	—	—	—	3 Rich
	D4AE-HB	③	7/16	13/16	No. 3A	⑩	—	—	—	—	3 Rich
	D4AE-KA	③	7/16	13/16	No. 2A	⑩	—	—	—	—	3 Rich
	D4DE-RB	③	7/16	13/16	No. 2	⑩	—	—	—	—	3 Rich
	D4DE-LA	③	7/16	13/16	No. 2	⑩	—	—	—	—	3 Rich
	D4DE-NB	③	7/16	13/16	No. 2	⑩	—	—	—	—	3 Rich
	D4DE-PA	③	7/16	13/16	No. 2	⑩	—	—	—	—	3 Rich
	D4DE-VA	③	7/16	13/16	No. 2A	⑩	—	—	—	—	3 Rich
	D4OE-CA,EA	③	7/16	13/16	No. 2	⑩	—	—	—	—	3 Rich
	D4OE-FA,PA	③	7/16	13/16	No. 2A	⑩	—	—	—	—	3 Rich
	D4ME-BA,CA	③	7/16	13/16	No. 3A	⑩	—	—	—	—	3 Rich
1975	D5AE-AA,EA	③	7/16	13/16	3	.125	—	1500	—	—	3 Rich
	D5DE-AA,BA	③	7/16	13/16	2	.140	—	⑧	—	—	3 Rich
	D5DE-AEA	③	7/16	13/16	2	.135	—	⑧	—	—	3 Rich
	D5DE-AFA	③	7/16	13/16	2	.135	—	⑧	—	—	3 Rich
	D5DE-HA	③	7/16	13/16	2	.140	—	1400	—	—	3 Rich
	D5DE-JA	③	7/16	13/16	2	.140	—	⑧	—	—	3 Rich
	D5DE-UA	③	7/16	13/16	2	.140	—	1400	—	—	3 Rich
	D5ME-BA,FA	③	7/16	13/16	2	.125	—	1500	—	—	3 Rich
	D5OE-AA	③	7/16	13/16	2	.140	—	1400	—	—	3 Rich
	D5OE-BA,CA	③	7/16	13/16	3	.125	—	1350	—	—	3 Rich
	D5OE-DA	③	7/16	13/16	2	.140	—	1400	—	—	3 Rich
	D5OE-GA	③	7/16	13/16	2	.125	—	1350	—	—	3 Rich
	D5WE-FA	③	7/16	13/16	2	—	—	⑧	—	—	3 Rich
	D5ZE-AC,BC	③	3/8	3/4	2	.145	—	1600	—	—	2 Rich
	D5ZE-BE	③	3/8	3/4	2	.105	.125	1600	—	—	3 Rich
	D5ZE-CC, DC	③	3/8	3/4	2	.145	—	1600	—	—	2 Rich
	D5ZE-JA	③	7/16	13/16	2	.140	—	⑧	—	—	3 Rich

Continued

MODEL 2100, 2150-2V CARB. ADJUSTMENT SPECIFICATIONS—Continued

See Tune Up Chart in car chapters for hot idle speeds.

Year	Carb. Model (Code 9510) ①	Idle Mixture Turns Open	Float Level (Dry)	Fuel Level (Wet)	Pump Setting Hole No. ④	Choke Plate Clearance (Pull down)	Fast Idle Cam Linkage Clearance	Fast Idle Speed (Hot Engine)	Dechoke Clearance ②	Dashpot Setting	Choke Setting
FORD AND MERCURY—Continued											
1976	D5DE-AEA	③	7/16	13/16	No. 2	.135	—	⑧	—	—	3 Rich
	D5DE-AFA	③	7/16	13/16	No. 2	.135	—	⑧	—	—	3 Rich
	D5WE-FA	③	7/16	13/16	No. 2	.135	—	⑧	—	—	3 Rich
	D5ZE-BE	③	3/8	3/4	No. 2	.105	.125	1600	—	—	3 Rich
	D6AE-HA	③	7/16	13/16	No. 2	.160	.180	1350	—	—	3 Rich
	D6AE-JA	③	7/16	13/16	No. 2	.160	.180	—	—	—	2 Rich
	D6AE-KA	③	7/16	13/16	No. 2	.160	.180	—	—	—	2 Rich
	D6ME-AA	③	7/16	13/16	No. 2	.160	.180	1400	—	—	3 Rich
	D6ME-BA	③	7/16	13/16	No. 2	.160	.180	—	—	—	2 Rich
	D6ME-CA	③	7/16	13/16	No. 4	.160	.180	—	—	—	3 Rich
	D6ME-DA	③	7/16	13/16	No. 4	.160	.180	—	—	—	3 Rich
	D6OE-AA	③	7/16	13/16	No. 3	.160	.180	1400	—	—	3 Rich
	D6OE-BA	③	7/16	13/16	No. 3	.160	.180	2000	—	—	3 Rich
	D6OE-CA	③	7/16	13/16	No. 3	.160	.180	1400	—	—	3 Rich
	D6WE-AA	③	7/16	13/16	No. 2	.160	.180	1150	—	—	3 Rich
	D6WE-BA	③	7/16	13/16	No. 2	.160	.180	1350	—	—	2 Rich
	D6WE-CA	③	7/16	13/16	No. 2	.160	.180	—	—	—	3 Rich
	D6WE-CB	③	7/16	13/16	No. 4	.160	.180	—	—	—	3 Rich
	D6WE-EA	③	7/16	13/16	No. 2	.160	.180	—	—	—	3 Rich
	D6WE-FA	③	7/16	13/16	No. 3	.160	.180	—	—	—	3 Rich
	D6ZE-AA	③	3/8	3/4	No. 2	.100	.120	1700	—	—	3 Rich
	D6ZE-BA	③	3/8	3/4	No. 2	.100	.120	1600	—	—	3 Rich
	D6ZE-CA	③	13/32	3/4	No. 2	.110	.130	1700	—	—	3 Rich
	D6ZE-DA	③	3/8	3/4	No. 2	.110	.130	1600	—	—	3 Rich
	D6ZE-JA	③	7/16	13/16	No. 2	.140	.160	⑧	—	—	3 Rich
	D6GE-AAA	③	3/8	3/4	No. 4	.110	.130	—	—	—	3 Rich
	D64E-AA	③	7/16	13/16	No. 2	.140	.160	—	—	—	3 Rich
	D64E-BA	③	7/16	13/16	No. 3	.160	.180	—	—	—	3 Rich
	D64E-DA	③	7/16	13/16	No. 2	.140	.160	—	—	—	3 Rich
	T67F-AA	③	3/8	3/4	No. 2	.100	.120	—	—	—	3 Rich
	T67F-BA	③	3/8	3/4	No. 2	.100	.120	—	—	—	3 Rich
	T67F-CA	③	3/8	3/4	No. 2	.110	.130	—	—	—	3 Rich
	T67F-DA	③	3/8	3/4	No. 2	.110	.130	—	—	—	3 Rich
1977	D7AE-ACA	③	7/16	13/16	No. 2	.156	.170	—	—	—	Index
	D7AE-AHA	③	7/16	13/16	No. 3	.179	.189	—	—	—	Index
	D7AE-AKA	③	7/16	13/16	No. 3	.179	.189	—	—	—	Index
	D7BE-YA	③	7/16	13/16	No. 2	.147	.167	—	—	—	1 Rich
	D7OE-LA	③	7/16	13/16	No. 4	.169	.189	—	—	—	3 Rich
	D7OE-RA	③	3/4	3/4	No. 3	.167	.187	—	—	—	2 Rich
	D7OE-TA	③	7/16	13/16	No. 3	.185	.205	—	—	—	2 Rich
	D7YE-EA	③	3/8	3/4	No. 3	.122	.142	—	—	—	2 Rich
1978	D8AE-JA	③	3/8	3/4	No. 3	.167	—	—	—	–	3 Rich
	D8BE-ACA	③	7/16	3/4	No. 4	.155	—	—	—	—	2 Rich
	D8BE-ADA	③	7/16	13/16	No. 2	.110	—	—	—	—	3 Rich
	D8BE-AEA	③	7/16	13/16	No. 2	.110	—	—	—	—	4 Rich
	D8BE-AFA	③	7/16	13/16	No. 2	.110	—	—	—	—	4 Rich
	D8BE-MB	③	3/8	13/16	No. 3	.122	—	—	—	—	Index
	D8DE-HA	③	7/16	13/16	No. 2	.157	—	—	—	—	Index
	D8KE-EA	③	7/16	13/16	No. 2	.135	—	—	—	—	3 Rich
	D8OE-BA	③	3/8	3/4	No. 3	.167	—	—	—	–	3 Rich
	D8OE-EA	③	7/16	13/16	No. 2	.136	—	—	—	—	Index
	D8OE-HA	③	7/16	13/16	No. 3	.180	—	—	—	—	2 Rich
	D8SE-CA	③	7/16	13/16	No. 3	.150	—	—	—	—	2 Rich

Continued

FORD MOTORCRAFT CARBURETORS

MODEL 2100, 2150-2V CARB. ADJUSTMENT SPECIFICATIONS—Continued
See Tune Up Chart in car chapters for hot idle speeds.

Year	Carb. Model (Code 9510) ①	Idle Mixture Turns Open	Float Level (Dry)	Fuel Level (Wet)	Pump Setting Hole No. ④	Choke Plate Clearance (Pull down)	Fast Idle Cam Linkage Clearance	Fast Idle Speed (Hot Engine)	Dechoke Clearance ②	Dashpot Setting	Choke Setting
FORD AND MERCURY—Continued										
1978	D8SE-DA	③	7/16	13/16	No. 3	.147	—	—	—	—	3 Rich
	D8SE-EA	③	7/16	13/16	No. 3	.147	—	—	—	—	3 Rich
	D8SE-FA	③	3/8	13/16	No. 3	.147	—	—	—	—	3 Rich
	D8SE-GA	③	3/8	13/16	No. 3	.147	—	—	—	—	3 Rich
	D8WE-DA	③	7/16	13/16	No. 4	.143	—	—	—	—	1 Rich
	D8YE-AB	③	3/8	13/16	No. 3	.122	—	—	—	—	Index
	D8ZE-TA	③	3/8	3/4	No. 4	.122	—	—	—	—	Index
	D8ZE-UA	③	3/8	3/4	No. 4	.135	—	—	—	—	Index
	D84E-EA	③	7/16	13/16	No. 2	.110	—	—	—	—	3 Rich

①—Stamped on left side of fuel bowl or on tag attached to bowl cover.
②—Minimum clearance between choke plate and air horn wall with throttle plates wide open.
③—Air/fuel ratio or idle CO% rating is found in Tune Up Specification tables in car chapters.
④—With link in inboard hole in pump lever.

⑤—Auto Trans. 1500; Manual Trans. 1400.
⑥—California 1 Rich; all others 2 Rich.
⑦—Hot on 2nd step of cam with TCS solenoid & EGR disconnected.
⑧—On high step of cam; Manual trans.: 2000; Auto. trans.: 2100.
⑨—V8-304, 1800; V8-360, 1600.
⑩—Refer to procedure in service section.

2100, 2150-2V ADJUSTMENTS

Models 2100, 2150-2V, Figs. 1 thru 3

These carburetors have two main bodies—the air horn and throttle body. The air horn assembly, which serves as a cover for the throttle body, contains the choke plate and vents for the fuel bowl. On 1975-77 Ford units and 1978 American Motors 2100 units, an external bowl vent valve is used. On 2150 units installed on V-6 engines, the air horn assembly contains a fuel deceleration system which consists of a metered pickup orifice in the fuel bowl and air/fuel mixing orifices and bleeds.

A choke modulator assembly is incorporated on 2100 units, Fig. 4. This system, through the use of a bimetal sensor and a series of diaphragms, pulls open the choke plate within 15-60 seconds. The system operates only during times when underhood temperatures are above 60 degrees F. On Ford units, an electric

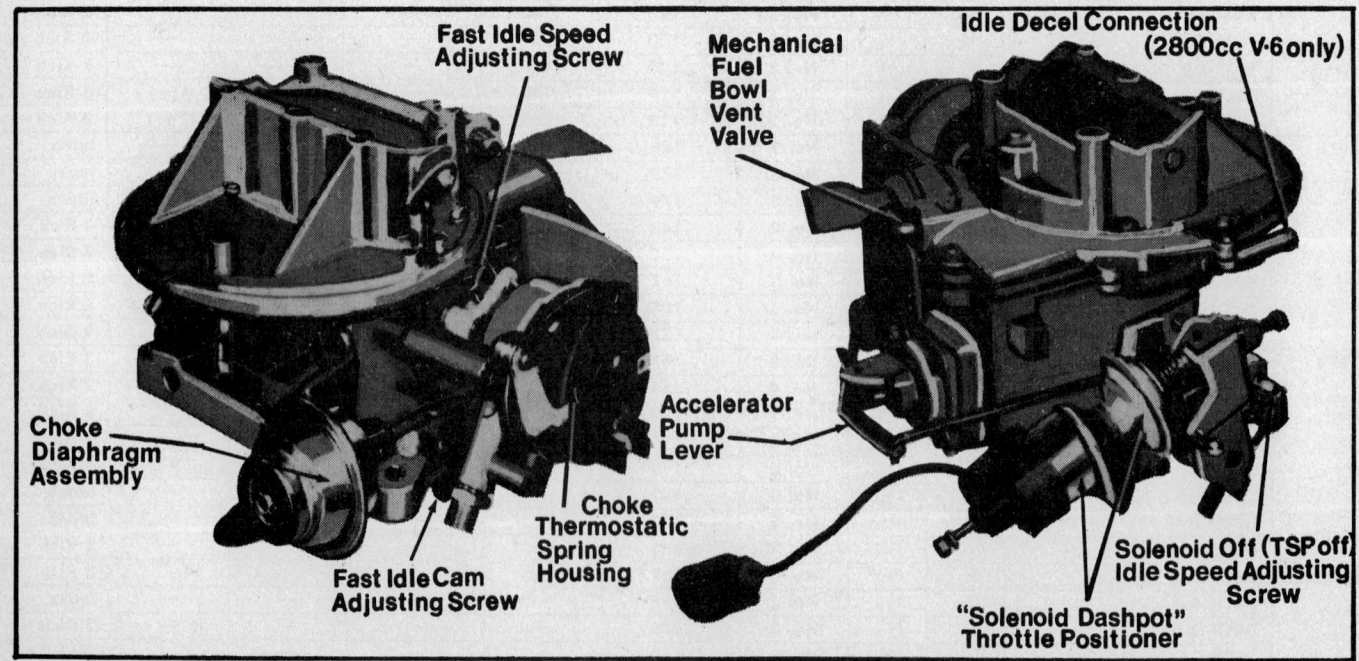

Fig. 1 Typical Motorcraft 2150 carburetor. 1975-78

choke system is incorporated which opens choke plate within 1-1½ minutes when underhood temperatures are above approximately 55° to 60°. On 1975-78 Ford units, the electric choke system is supplied current to open the choke plate when underhood temperatures are between 80° and 110° F. For service information refer to the "Emission Control System" chapter.

Some 1977-78 2150 units are equipped with an altitude compensation aneroid to improve high altitude emission control and driveability. Intake air entering the bypass valve is metered into the air flow above the throttle plates, leaning the mixture for high altitude operation. Air flow is controlled by a valve activated by an aneroid attached to the rear of the carburetor main body. Also, these units are equipped with a choke in the bypass air intake, linked to the main choke.

The throttle plate, accelerating pump, power (enrichment) valve and fuel bowl are in the throttle body. The choke housing is attached to the throttle body.

The two bodies each contain a main and booster venturi, main fuel discharge, accelerating pump discharge, idle fuel discharge, and a throttle plate. On some units, an antistall dashpot is attached to the carburetor when the vehicle is equipped with an automatic transmission.

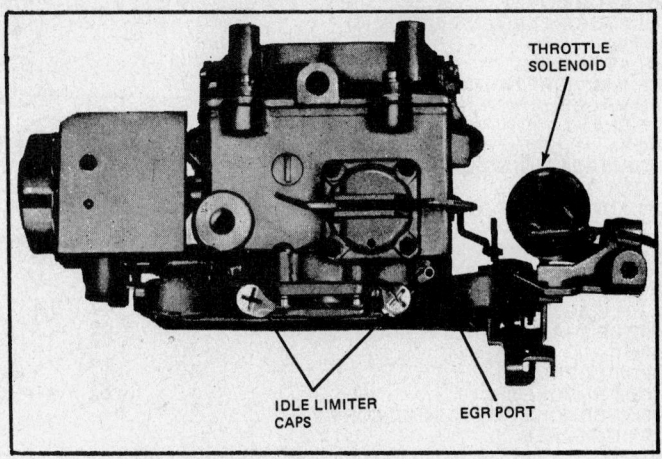

Fig. 2   Typical Motorcraft 2100 carburetor. 1974

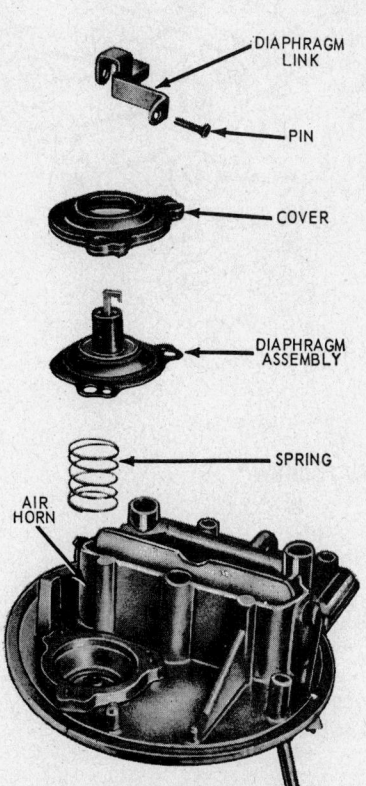

Fig. 4   Motorcraft 2100 choke diaphragm assembly

Float Level Adjustment

Fig. 5—This is a preliminary adjustment; the final adjustment must be made after the carburetor is mounted on the engine.

With air horn removed, float raised and fuel inlet needle seated, measure distance between top surface of throttle body and top surface of float. Take measurement near center of float at a point ⅛" from free end of float.

If a cardboard float gauge is used, place the gauge in the corner of the enlarged end section of the fuel bowl as shown. The gauge should touch the float near the end but not on the end radius.

Depress the float tab to seat the fuel inlet needle. The float height is measured from the gasket surface of the throttle body with gasket removed. If the float height is not as listed in the *Ford Specifications Chart*, bend tab on float as required to achieve the desired setting.

Fuel Level Adjustment

Fig. 6—With vehicle on a level surface, operate engine until normal temperature is reached, then stop engine and check fuel level as follows:
1. Remove carburetor air cleaner.

2. Remove air horn retaining screws and carburetor identification tag.
3. Temporarily leave air horn and gasket in position on throttle body and start engine.
4. Allow engine to idle for several minutes, then rotate air horn and remove air horn gasket to gain access to float or floats.
5. While engine is idling, use a standard depth gauge to measure vertical distance from top machined surface of throttle body to level of fuel in bowl. The measurement must be made at least ¼" away from any vertical surface to assure an accurate reading.
6. If the fuel level is not as listed in the **Specifications Chart,** stop the engine to avoid any fire hazard due to fuel spray when float setting is disturbed.
7. To adjust fuel level, bend float tab (contacting fuel inlet needle) upward in relation to original position to raise the fuel level, and downward to lower it.
8. Each time an adjustment is made to the float tab to alter the fuel level, the engine must be started and permitted to idle for at least three minutes to stabilize the fuel level. Check fuel level after each adjustment until the specified level is achieved.

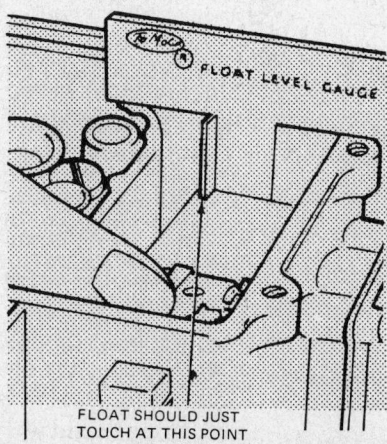

Fig. 5   Float level adjustment.

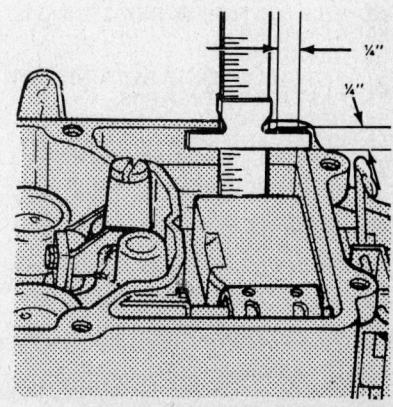

Fig. 6   Fuel level adjustment.

1. MODULATOR COVER
2. MODULATOR RETAINING SCREW (3)
3. PIVOT PIN
4. MODULATOR ARM
5. CHOKE VALVE RETAINING SCREW (2)
6. CHOKE VALVE
7. CHOKE SHAFT
8. AIR HORN
9. AIR HORN RETAINING SCREW (4)
10. AIR HORN GASKET
11. FLOAT AND LEVER ASSEMBLY
12. FLOAT SHAFT RETAINER
13. FLOAT SHAFT
14. NEEDLE RETAINING CLIP
15. CURB IDLE ADJUSTING SCREW
16. CURB IDLE ADJUSTING SCREW SPRING
17. THROTTLE SHAFT AND LEVER ASSEMBLY
18. DASHPOT
19. DASHPOT LOCKNUT
20. DASHPOT BRACKET
21. DASHPOT BRACKET RETAINING SCREW
22. ADJUSTING SCREW
23. CARRIAGE
24. ELECTRIC SOLENOID
25. MOUNTING BRACKET
26. THROTTLE VALVE RETAINING SCREW (4)
27. THROTTLE VALVE (2)
28. NEEDLE AND SEAT ASSEMBLY
29. NEEDLE SEAT GASKET
30. MAIN JET (2)
31. MAIN BODY
32. ELASTOMER VALVE
33. PUMP RETURN SPRING
34. PUMP DIAPHRAGM
35. PUMP LEVER PIN
36. PUMP COVER
37. PUMP ROD
38. PUMP ROD RETAINER
39. PUMP LEVER
40. PUMP COVER RETAINING SCREW (4)
41. FUEL INLET FITTING
42. POWER VALVE GASKET
43. POWER VALVE
44. POWER VALVE COVER GASKET
45. POWER VALVE COVER
46. POWER VALVE COVER
    RETAINING SCREW (4)
47. IDLE LIMITER CAP (2)
48. IDLE MIXTURE SCREW (2)

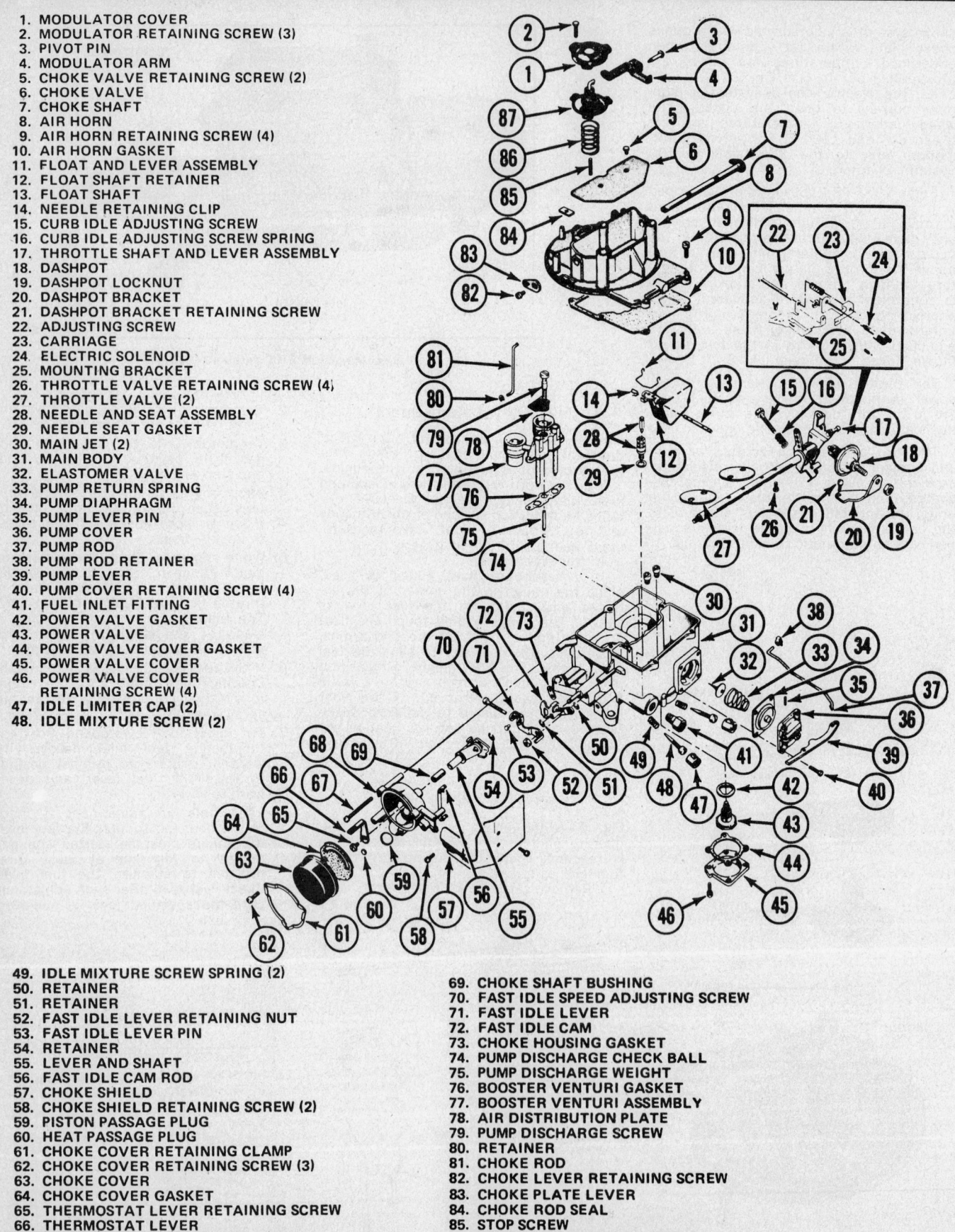

49. IDLE MIXTURE SCREW SPRING (2)
50. RETAINER
51. RETAINER
52. FAST IDLE LEVER RETAINING NUT
53. FAST IDLE LEVER PIN
54. RETAINER
55. LEVER AND SHAFT
56. FAST IDLE CAM ROD
57. CHOKE SHIELD
58. CHOKE SHIELD RETAINING SCREW (2)
59. PISTON PASSAGE PLUG
60. HEAT PASSAGE PLUG
61. CHOKE COVER RETAINING CLAMP
62. CHOKE COVER RETAINING SCREW (3)
63. CHOKE COVER
64. CHOKE COVER GASKET
65. THERMOSTAT LEVER RETAINING SCREW
66. THERMOSTAT LEVER
67. CHOKE HOUSING RETAINING SCREW (3)
68. CHOKE HOUSING

69. CHOKE SHAFT BUSHING
70. FAST IDLE SPEED ADJUSTING SCREW
71. FAST IDLE LEVER
72. FAST IDLE CAM
73. CHOKE HOUSING GASKET
74. PUMP DISCHARGE CHECK BALL
75. PUMP DISCHARGE WEIGHT
76. BOOSTER VENTURI GASKET
77. BOOSTER VENTURI ASSEMBLY
78. AIR DISTRIBUTION PLATE
79. PUMP DISCHARGE SCREW
80. RETAINER
81. CHOKE ROD
82. CHOKE LEVER RETAINING SCREW
83. CHOKE PLATE LEVER
84. CHOKE ROD SEAL
85. STOP SCREW
86. MODULATOR RETURN SPRING
87. MODULATOR DIAPHRAGM ASSEMBLY

Fig. 3   Exploded view of Model 2100 carburetor (Typical)

1. COMPENSATOR CHOKE SHAFT
2. RETAINER
3. COMPENSATOR CHOKE VALVE
4. CHOKE VALVE SCREW
5. COMPENSATOR CHOKE ROD
6. CHOKE VALVE
7. CHOKE SHAFT
8. AIR HORN
9. AIR HORN RETAINING SCREW (4)
10. AIR HORN GASKET
11. FLOAT SHAFT RETAINER
12. FLOAT AND LEVER ASSEMBLY
13. FLOAT SHAFT
14. NEEDLE RETAINING CLIP
15. CURB IDLE ADJUSTING SCREW
16. CURB IDLE ADJUSTING SCREW SPRING
17. THROTTLE SHAFT AND LEVER ASSEMBLY
18. DASHPOT
19. DASHPOT LOCKNUT
20. DASHPOT BRACKET
21. DASHPOT BRACKET RETAINING SCREW
22. ADJUSTING SCREW
23. CARRIAGE
24. ELECTRIC SOLENOID
25. MOUNTING BRACKET
26. THROTTLE VALVE RETAINING SCREW (4)
27. THROTTLE VALVE
28. NEEDLE AND SEAT ASSEMBLY
29. NEEDLE SEAT GASKET
30. MAIN JET (2)
31. MAIN BODY
32. ELASTOMER VALVE
33. PUMP RETURN SPRING
34. PUMP DIAPHRAGM
35. PUMP LEVER PIN
36. PUMP COVER
37. PUMP ROD
38. PUMP ROD RETAINER
39. PUMP LEVER
40. PUMP COVER RETAINING SCREW (4)
41. FUEL INLET FITTING
42. POWER VALVE GASKET
43. POWER VALVE
44. POWER VALVE COVER GASKET
45. POWER VALVE COVER
46. POWER VALVE COVER RETAINING SCREW (4)
47. IDLE LIMITER CAP (2)
48. IDLE MIXTURE SCREW (2)
49. IDLE MIXTURE SCREW SPRING (2)
50. RETAINER
51. RETAINER
52. FAST IDLE LEVER RETAINING NUT
53. FAST IDLE LEVER PIN
54. RETAINER
55. THERMOSTATIC CHOKE SHAFT
56. FAST IDLE CAM ROD
57. CHOKE SHIELD
58. CHOKE SHIELD RETAINING SCREW (2)
59. PISTON PASSAGE PLUG
60. HEAT PASSAGE PLUG
61. CHOKE COVER RETAINING CLAMP
62. CHOKE COVER RETAINING SCREW (3)
63. CHOKE COVER
64. CHOKE COVER GASKET
65. THERMOSTAT LEVER RETAINING SCREW
66. THERMOSTAT LEVER
67. CHOKE HOUSING RETAINING SCREW (3)
68. CHOKE HOUSING
69. CHOKE SHAFT BUSHING
70. FAST IDLE CAM LEVER ADJUSTING SCREW
71. CHOKE DIAPHRAGM

72. HOSE
73. LINK
74. SCREW
75. FAST IDLE SPEED ADJUSTING SCREW
76. FAST IDLE LEVER
77. FAST IDLE CAM
78. CHOKE HOUSING GASKET
79. PUMP DISCHARGE CHECK BALL
80. PUMP DISCHARGE WEIGHT
81. BOOSTER VENTURI GASKET
82. BOOSTER VENTURI ASSEMBLY
83. AIR DISTRIBUTION PLATE
84. PUMP DISCHARGE SCREW
85. RETAINER
86. CHOKE ROD
87. GASKET
88. COMPENSATION CHAMBER
89. GASKET
90. SCREW
91. ANEROID
92. SCREW
93. CHOKE LEVER RETAINING SCREW
94. CHOKE PLATE LEVER
95. CHOKE ROD SEAL

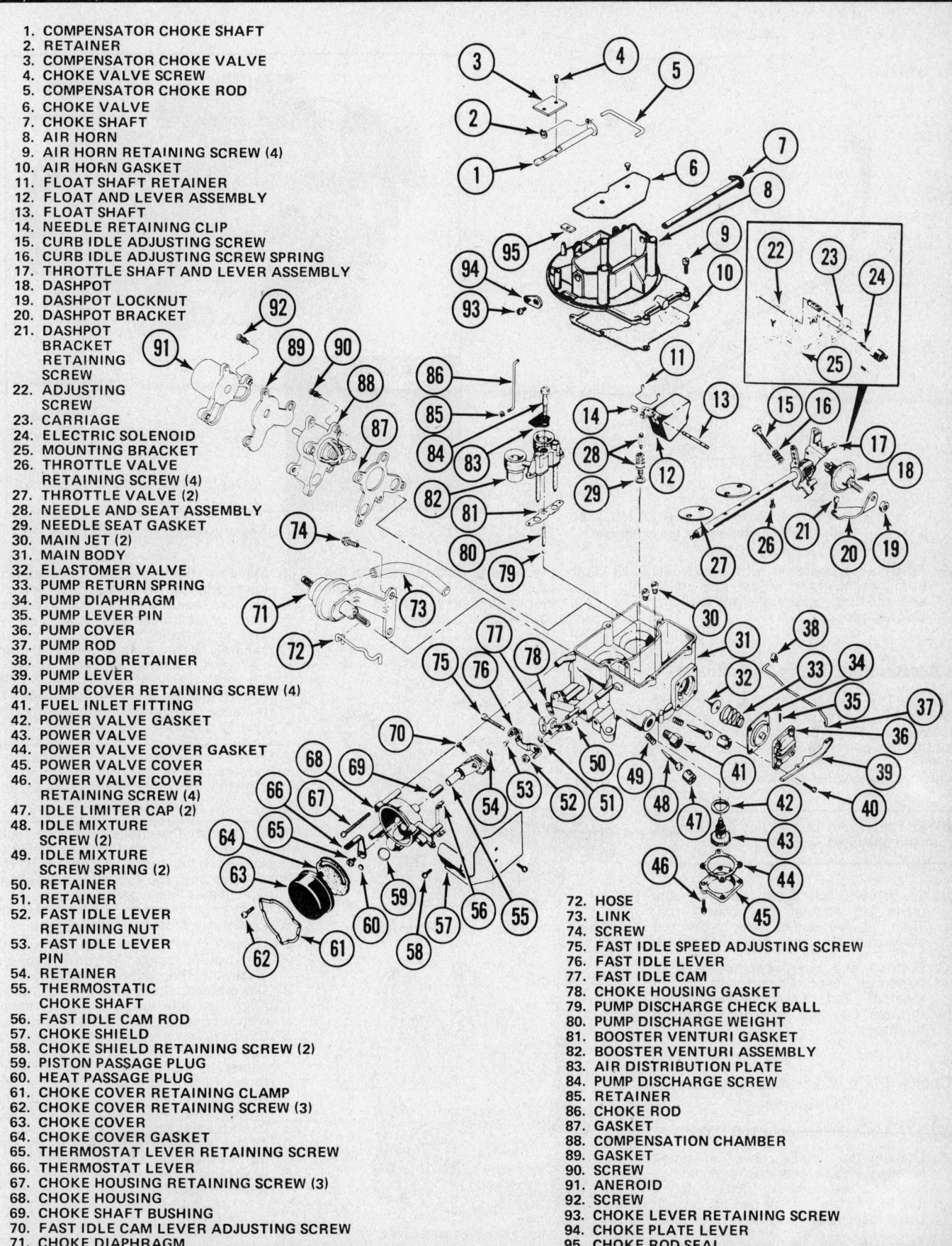

Fig. 3A   Exploded view of Model 2150 carburetor (Typical)

2–337

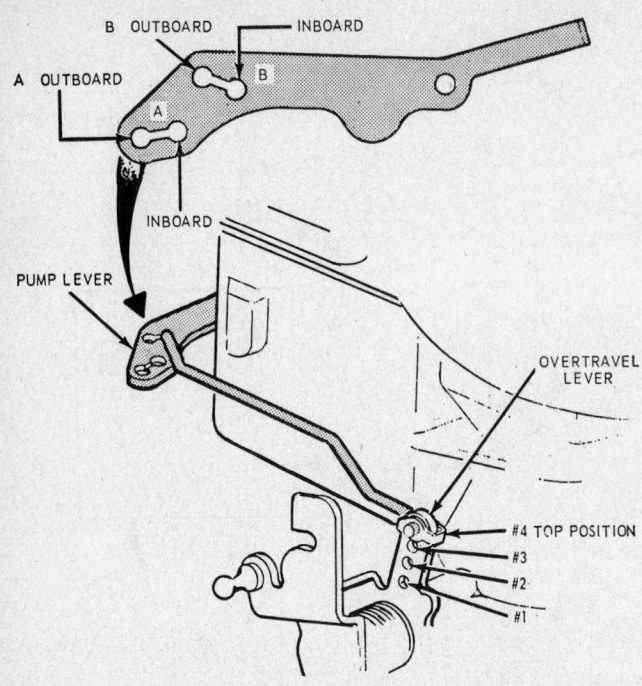

Fig. 7   Pump stroke adjusting points, 2100, 2150, with 4 holes in accelerating pump linkage

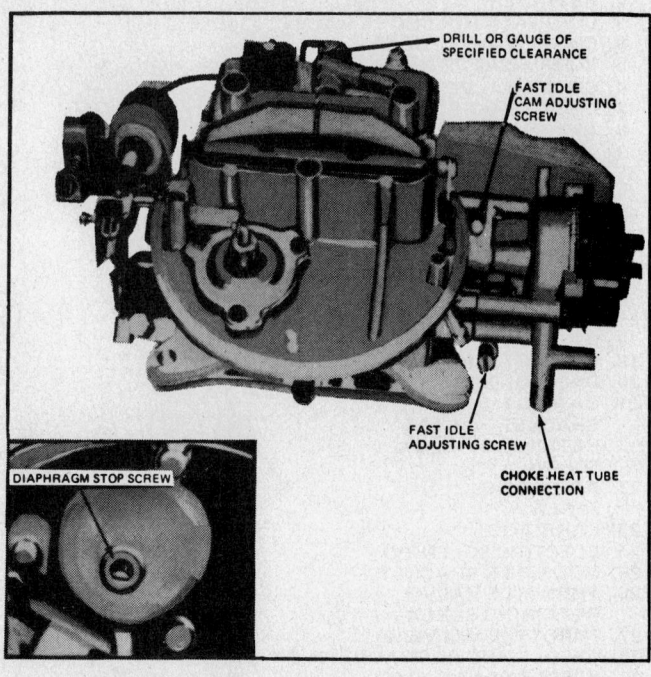

Fig. 8   Choke plate pulldown clearance 2100. 1974 Ford

9. Assemble carburetor with a new air horn gasket. Then adjust idle speed and mixture, and anti-stall dashpot, if so equipped.

Accelerating Pump Adjustment

Fig. 7—The primary throttle shaft lever (overtravel lever) has 4 holes and the accelerating pump link has 2 or 4 holes to control the pump stroke for various atmospheric temperatures, operating conditions and specific engine applications.

NOTE: The stroke should not be changed from the specified setting.

1. To release rod from retainer clip, press tab end of clip toward rod. Then, at the same time, press rod away from clip until it is disengaged.

2. Position clip over specified hole in overtravel lever. Press ends of clip together and insert operating rod through clip and lever. Release clip to engage rod.

Choke Plate Clearance (Pulldown) Adjustment

1974-77 American Motors 2100 Units

1. Loosen the choke cover retaining screws. Rotate the choke cover 1/4 turn counterclockwise (rich) from index and tighten the retaining screws. Disconnect the choke heat inlet tube.

2. Align the fast idle speed adjusting screw with the second step of the fast idle cam, Fig. 9.

3. Start the engine without moving the accelerator linkage. Turn the fast idle cam lever adjusting screw out counterclockwise 3 full turns.

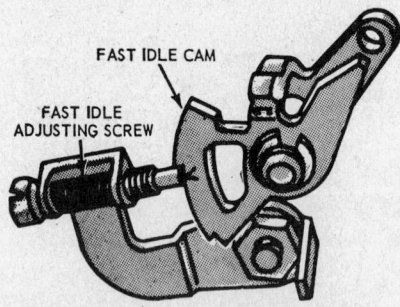

FAST IDLE CAM

FAST IDLE ADJUSTING SCREW

CONVENTIONAL ONE - PIECE FAST IDLE LEVER

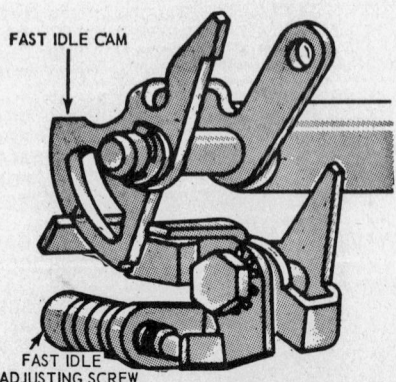

FAST IDLE CAM

FAST IDLE ADJUSTING SCREW

TWO - PIECE FAST IDLE LEVER

Fig. 9   Motorcraft fast idle adjustment 2100, 2150

4. Measure the clearance between the lower edge of the choke valve and the air horn wall. Refer to *2100 Specifications Chart* for the correct setting. Adjust by grasping the modulator arm securely with a pair of pliers at point "A" and twisting the arm at point "B" with a second pair of pliers. Twist toward the front of the carburetor to increase clearance and toward the rear to decrease clearance, Fig. 10.

CAUTION: Use extreme care while twisting the modulator arm to avoid damaging the nylon piston rod of the modulator assembly.

NOTE: Connect the choke heat tube. Turn the fast idle cam lever adjusting screw in (clockwise) 3 full turns. Do not reset the choke cover until the fast idle cam linkage adjustment has been performed.

1978 American Motors 2100 Units

1. Loosen choke cover retaining screws and rotate cover 1/4 turn counterclockwise, then tighten one screw.

2. Disconnect choke heat inlet tube. Align fast idle speed adjusting screw with second step of fast idle cam.

3. Start engine without moving accelerator linkage. Turn fast idle cam lever adjusting screw counterclockwise three turns. Measure clearance between upper edge of choke valve and air horn wall, Fig. 10A. Refer to 2100, 2150 Specifications Chart.

4. Adjust by turning set screw on bottom of modulator.

5. Stop engine and connect choke heat tube. Adjust fast idle cam clearance.

1974 Ford Units

Since the choke plate pulldown is set in production by means of an air-fuel meter, no specific clearance is indicated for pull-

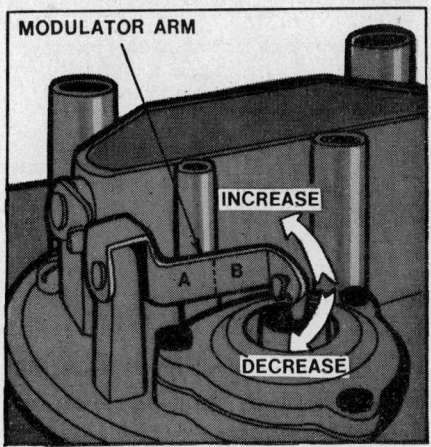

Fig. 10 Choke plate pulldown clearance 2100. 1974-77 American Motors

down adjustment. If the vehicle shows indication of leanness during cold starting, decrease the clearance between the choke plate and the air horn wall by 0.020 inch. If the engine shows signs of an overrich condition during cold starting, increase the pulldown clearance by 0.020 inch. If additional adjustment is required always make the adjustments in steps of 0.020 inch. If the original pulldown adjustment is lost, set the clearance between the choke plate and the air horn to 0.160 inch. Then adjust as required in steps of 0.020 inch, Fig. 8.

1975-78 Ford Units & 1977-78 American Motors 2150 Units

1. Set throttle on fast idle cam top step,

Fig. 9, then loosen choke thermostatic housing retaining screws and set housing 90° in rich direction.
2. Activate pulldown motor by manually forcing pulldown control diaphragm link in direction of applied vacuum or by applying vacuum to external vacuum tube.
3. Check clearance between lower edge of choke plate and center of carburetor air horn wall nearest fuel bowl Fig. 11. Refer to 2150 Specifications Chart. If clearance is not as specified, reset by adjusting diaphragm stop on end of choke pull-down diaphragm.

CAUTION: Do not attempt to turn the diaphragm adjusting screw without first loosening the Loctite which has been applied to the threads of the screw. The Loctite can be softened by heating the area around the screw with an electric soldering gun or by applying Loctite to the screw. When the Loctite has softened enough, the screw can be turned without causing any damage.

Fast Idle Cam Clearance

1974 Ford Units

1. Loosen the choke thermostatic spring housing retainer screws and set the housing 90 degrees in the rich direction.
2. Position the fast idle speed screw at the kickdown step of the fast idle cam. The kickdown step is identified on most units by a V stamped on the cam, Fig. 9. When a two-piece fast idle lever is used, a tang on the top lever will align with the V mark on the cam, Fig. 9.
3. Be sure the cam is at the kickdown

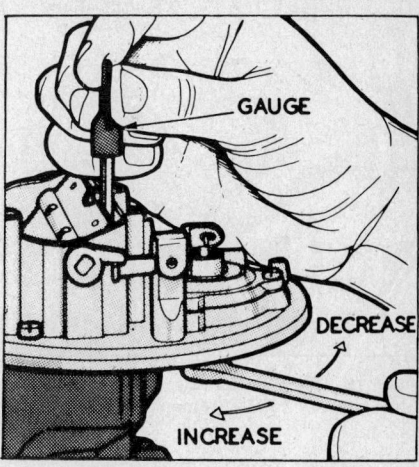

Fig. 10A Choke plate pulldown clearance adjust. 1978 American Motors 2100 units

position while checking or adjusting the fast idle cam clearance. Check clearance between the lower edge of the choke plate and the air horn wall. Refer to 2100, 2150 Specifications Chart. Adjust clearance by turning the fast idle cam clearance adjusting screw clockwise to increase and counterclockwise to decrease the clearance.
4. Set the choke thermostatic spring housing to specifications, Fig. 12. Adjust the anti-stall dashpot, idle speed and fuel mixture.

1974-78 American Motors Units

1. Push downward on fast idle cam lever until fast idle speed adjusting screw contacts the second step of cam and is against the high step shoulder.
2. Measure clearance between lower edge of choke valve and air horn wall. Refer to the 2100, 2150 Specifications Chart.
3. Adjust by turning fast idle cam lever screw, Fig. 13.
4. Set choke cover housing to specifications.

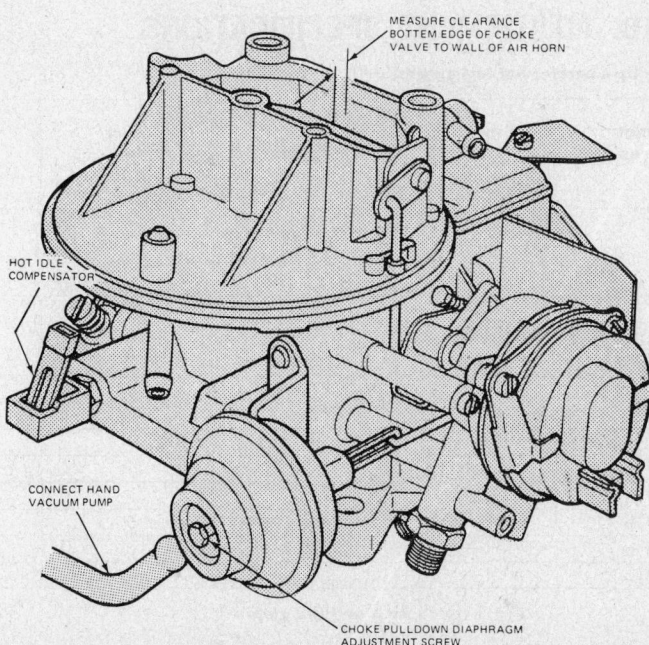

Fig. 11 Choke plate pulldown adjustment, 2150. 1975-78 Ford

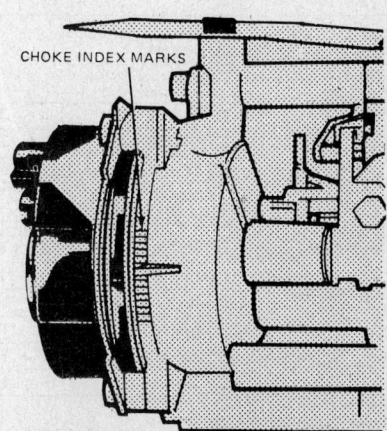

Fig. 12 Automatic choke adjustment. 2100, 2150

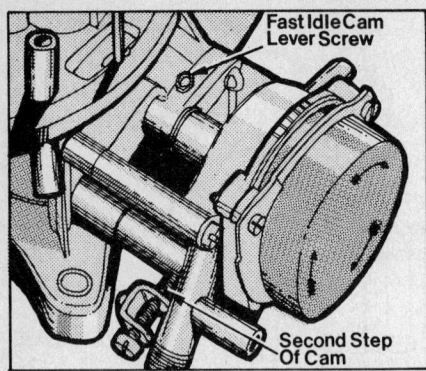

Fig. 13 Fast idle cam clearance adjustment 2100. 1974-78 American Motors

Fig. 14 Choke unloader adjustment 1974-78 American Motors

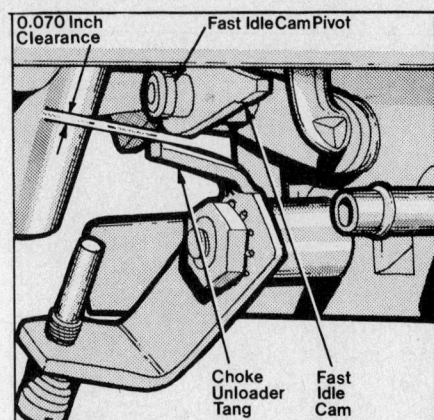

Fig. 15 Choke unloader to fast idle cam clearance. 1974-78 American Motors

Choke Unloader

1974-78 American Motors Units

1. Hold throttle fully open and apply pressure on choke valve toward the closed position.
2. Measure clearance between lower edge of choke valve and air horn wall. Refer to the 2100, 2150 Specifications Chart.
3. Adjust by bending the unloader tang contacting fast idle cam, Fig. 14. Bending the tang toward the cam increases the clearance and bending the tang away from the cam decreases the clearance.

NOTE: Do not bend unloader tang downward from a horizontal plane.

4. After making adjustment, open the

Fig. 16 Anti-stall dashpot adjustment. 2100

throttle until the unloader tang is directly below the fast idle cam pivot. A clearance of .070 inch must be obtained between the unloader tang and the edge of the fast idle cam, Fig. 15.

Automatic Choke Valve Tension

Turn thermostatic spring cover against spring tension until index mark on cover is aligned with mark specified in the *Ford Specifications Chart* on choke housing, Fig. 12.

Anti-Stall Dashpot Adjustment

Fig. 16—With engine idle speed and mixture properly adjusted and with engine at normal operating temperature, loosen dashpot lock nut. Hold throttle in closed position and depress plunger with screwdriver as shown. Check clearance between throttle lever and plunger tip. If clearance is not as listed in the *Ford Specifications Chart*, turn dashpot in its bracket as required to obtain the desired clearance. Tighten lock nut.

MODEL 2700 VV CARB. ADJUSTMENT SPECIFICATIONS

See Tune Up Chart for hot idle speeds.

Year	Carb Model (Code 9510)	Float Level (Dry)	Float Drop	Internal Vent	Venturi Valve Limiter	Fast Idle Cam	Choke Setting
FORD AND MERCURY							
1977	D7ZE-AC	$1\frac{3}{64}$	$1\frac{15}{32}$	.010	$\frac{61}{64}$	①	Index
	D7ZE-BD	$1\frac{3}{64}$	$1\frac{15}{32}$	.010	$\frac{13}{32}$	②	Index
	D7ZE-GD, GE	$1\frac{3}{64}$	$1\frac{15}{32}$	.010	$\frac{61}{64}$	①	Index
	D7ZE-GE	$1\frac{3}{64}$	$1\frac{15}{32}$	.010	$\frac{61}{64}$	①	Index
	77TF-MA, NA	$1\frac{3}{64}$	$1\frac{15}{32}$	.010	$\frac{61}{64}$	①	Index
1978	D8BE-EB	$1\frac{3}{64}$	$1\frac{15}{32}$	.010	$\frac{3}{4}$	①	Index
	D84E-DB	$1\frac{3}{64}$	$1\frac{15}{32}$	.010	$\frac{61}{64}$	①	Index
1979	D84E-KA	$1\frac{3}{64}$	$1\frac{15}{32}$	—	$\frac{61}{64}$	①	1 Rich
	D9AE-ACA	$1\frac{3}{64}$	$1\frac{15}{32}$	—	$\frac{3}{4}$	①	1 Rich
	D9ME-AA	$1\frac{3}{64}$	$1\frac{15}{32}$	—	$\frac{3}{4}$	①	1 Rich
	D9ZE-LB	$1\frac{3}{64}$	$1\frac{15}{32}$	—	$\frac{13}{32}$	③	1 Rich

①—1 Notch rich on third step.

②—Bobcat and Pinto, 4 Notches rich on second step. Except Bobcat and Pinto, 1 notch rich on third step.

③—1 Notch Rich on third step.

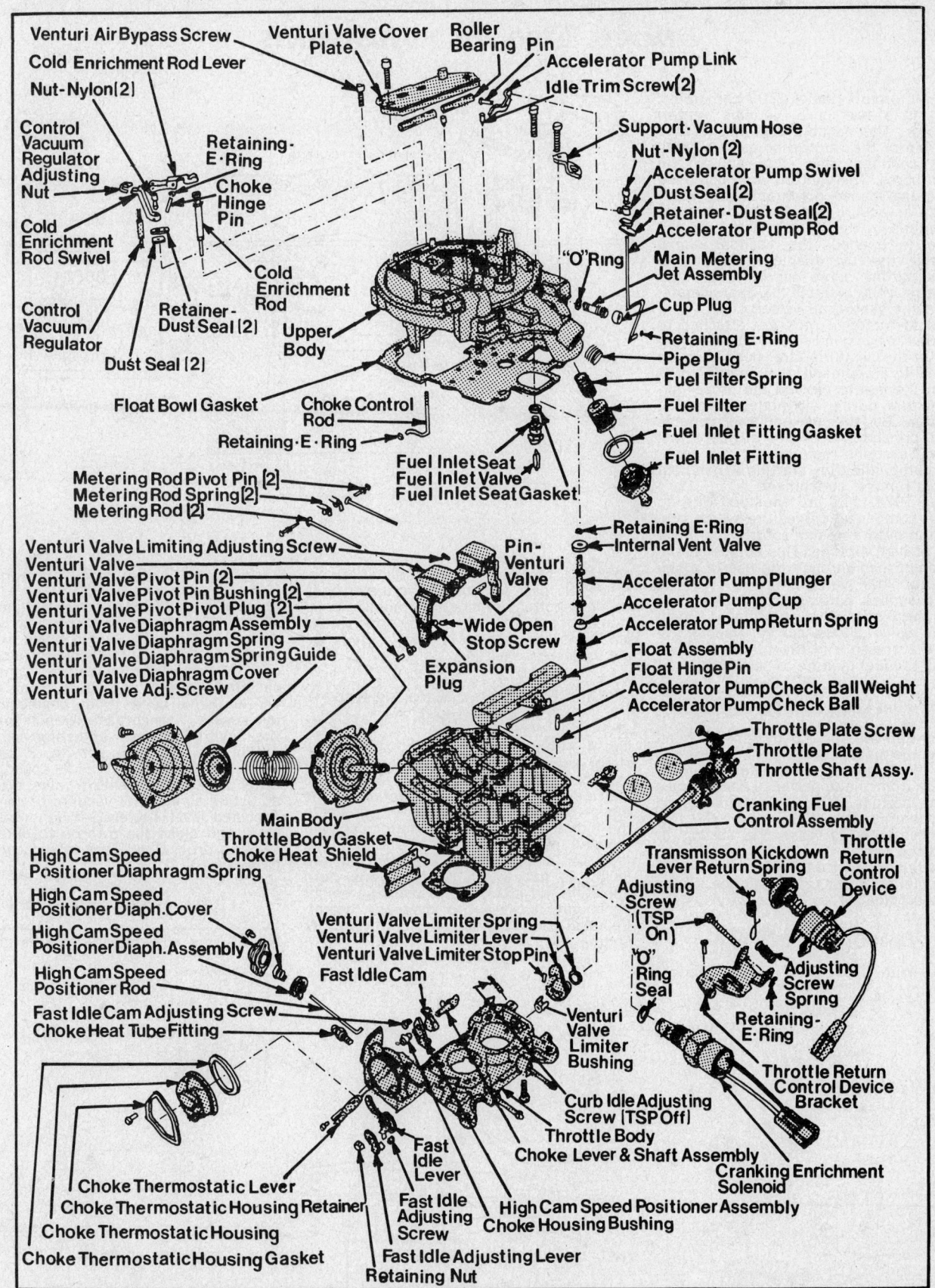

Fig. 1   Motorcraft model 2700 variable venturi carburetor, disassembled

MODEL 2700 VV ADJUSTMENTS

The Motorcraft model 2700 carburetor, Fig. 1, is a two bore, variable venturi carburetor. The variable venturis, located at the top of the throttle bores, are small oblong castings that slide across the throttle bores. The venturis are positioned by a spring loaded diaphram valve regulated by a vacuum signal obtained below the venturis in the throttle bores. As the throttle is opened, the vacuum signal increases, thereby, opening the venturis and permitting more air to enter the carburetor while maintaining approximately the same venturi air velocity.

Tapered metering rods are attached to the venturi valves and fit into the metering jets. As the venturis are positioned in response to air demand, the metering rods slide in the jets to provide the proper air-fuel mixture during all modes of engine operation. By the use of the variable venturi principle, the only auxiliary fuel metering systems required are the accelerator pump, idle trim, starting enrichment and cold running enrichment.

Some 1978 units are equipped with an altitude compensation feature which provides improved emission control and driveability at high altitude. This compensation is accomplished through the use of a bellows and pintle valve unit, Fig. 1A. The bellows senses barometric pressure and opens the pintle valve accordingly. Opening the valve allows control vacuum to lower the pressure in the fuel bowl area, causing the fuel mixture to be leaner.

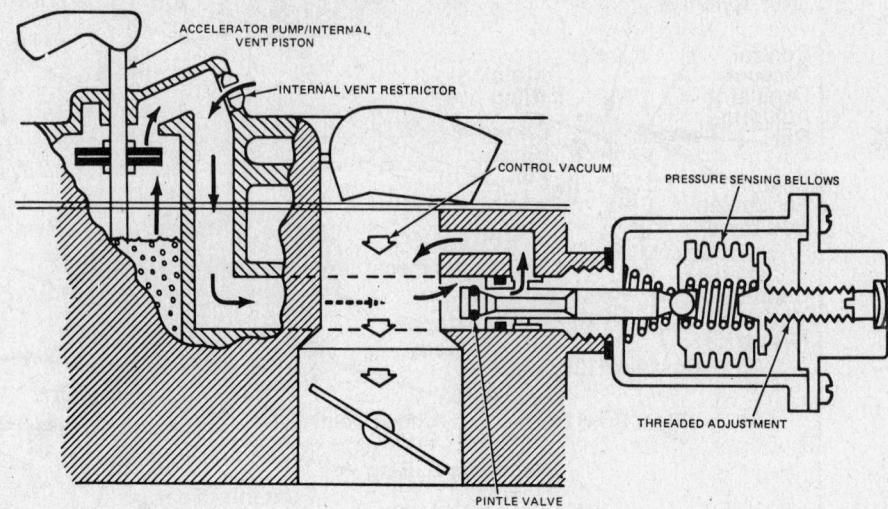

Fig. 1A   Altitude compensator. 1978 units

Fuel Level Adjustment

Fig. 2—Remove upper body assembly and replace the upper body gasket. With the upper body inverted, measure vertical distance from the upper body cast surface and the bottom of float. To adjust, bend float operating lever away from the fuel inlet needle to decrease the setting or toward the needle to increase the setting. After adjustment, the float pontoon must be parallel with the gasket surface. Check and adjust float drop, if necessary.

Float Drop Adjustment

Fig. 3—With upper body held in upright position, measure verticle distance between the cast surface of the upper body and the bottom of float. To adjust, bend stop tab on float lever away from hinge pin to increase setting or toward the hinge pin to decrease setting.

Cold Enrichment Metering Rod Adjustment

Fig. 4—Remove choke cap and install stator cap, tool T77L-9848-A as a weight to seat the cold enrichment rod. Install dial indicator with plunger contacting the top of the cold enrichment rod and zero the indicator. Remove the stator cap and reinstall at the index position. The dial indicator should read .125 inch. If rod height is not within specifications, turn adjusting nut clockwise to increase height or counterclockwise to decrease height. Reinstall choke cap and position at proper setting.

Control Vacuum Adjustment

Fig. 5—Install tachmeter to engine, then start engine at set idle speed to specifications. With a $5/32$ inch allen wrench, rotate venturi valve diaphram clockwise until the valve firmly closes. Connect a vacuum gauge to the vacuum tap on the venturi valve cover. With engine at curb idle, use a $1/8$ inch allen wrench to rotate the venturi bypass adjusting screw to obtain the specified setting. It may be necessary to readjust the idle speed at this time. Rotate the venturi valve diaphram adjusting screw until vacuum drops to the specified level, however, it is necessary to open and close the throttle to obtain the vacuum drop. Check and adjust curb idle, if necessary.

Internal Vent Adjustment

NOTE: This adjustment must be checked

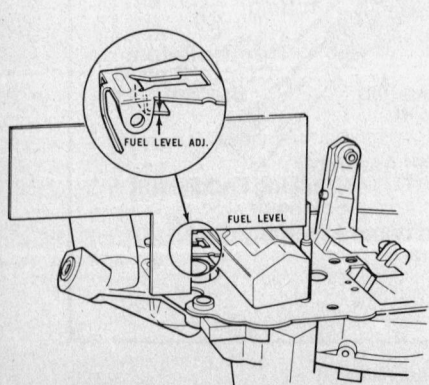

Fig. 2   Fuel level adjustment

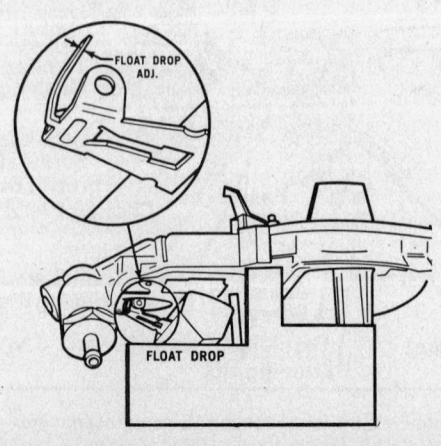

Fig. 3   Float drop adjustment

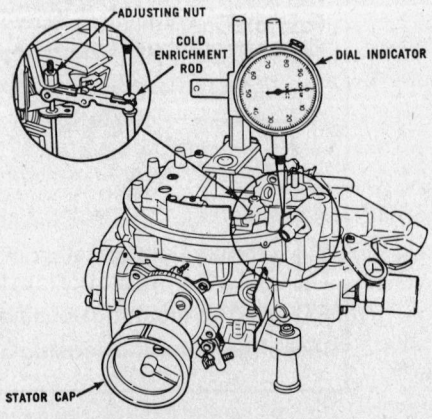

Fig. 4   Cold enrichment metering rod adjustment

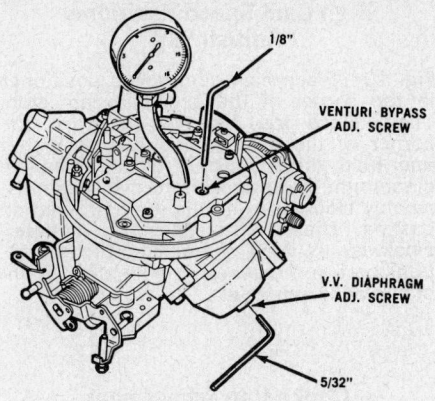

Fig. 5 Control vacuum adjustment

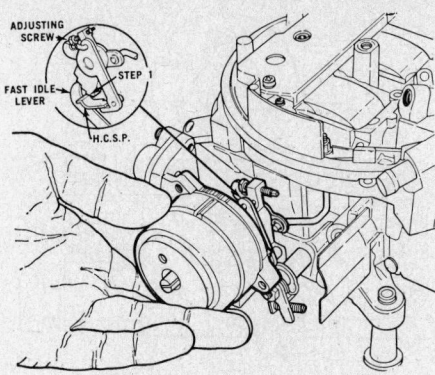

Fig. 7 Fast idle cam adjustment

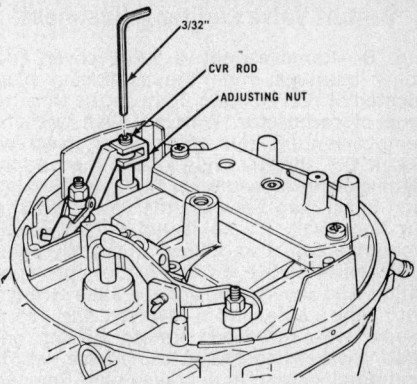

Fig. 9 Control vacuum regulator (CVR) adjustment, 1977 units

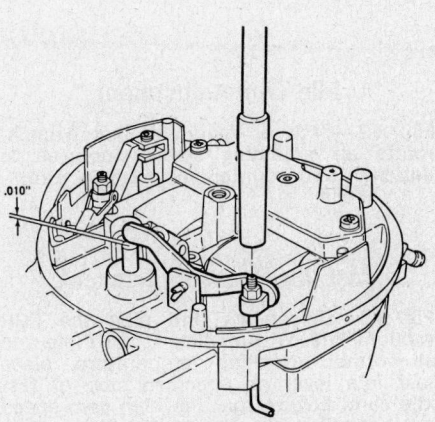

Fig. 6 Internal vent adjustment

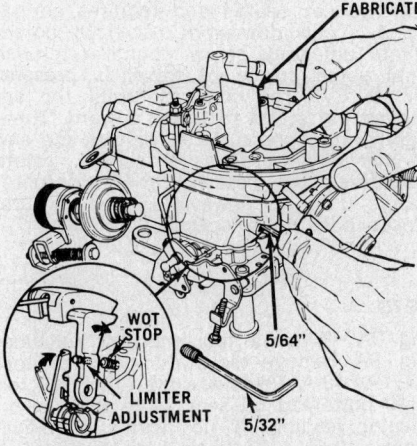

Fig. 8 Venturi valve limiter adjustment

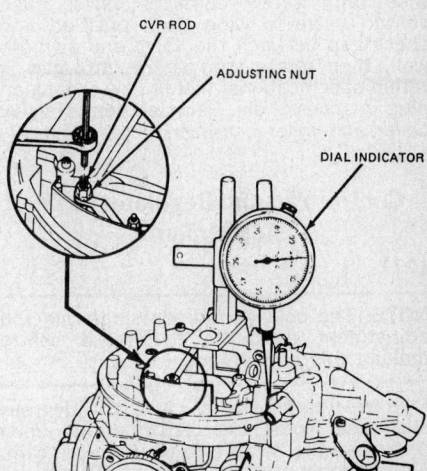

Fig. 9A Control vacuum regulator (CVR) adjustment. 1978 units

and adjusted, if necessary, whenever the curb idle is adjusted.

Fig. 6—With curb idle adjusted to specifications, place a .010 inch feeler gauge between the accelerator pump stem and the pump operating link. Rotate the nylon adjusting nut until a slight drag on the feeler gauge is obtained when removed.

Fast Idle Cam Adjustment

Fig. 7—Remove choke cap and place the fast idle lever in the corner of the specified step of the fast idle cam with the high cam speed positioner retracted. If adjust-

ment is performed on the bench, hold throttle closed with a rubber band to maintain cam position. Install stator cap, tool T77L-9848-A, and rotate clockwise until lever contacts adjusting screw. Rotate adjusting screw until index mark on stator cap aligns with the specified notch on the choke casting. Remove stator cap and reinstall choke cap.

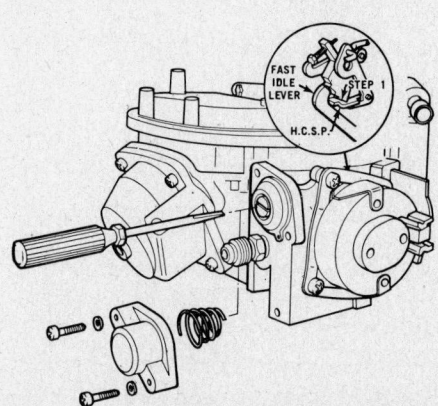

Fig. 10 High cam speed positioner adjustment

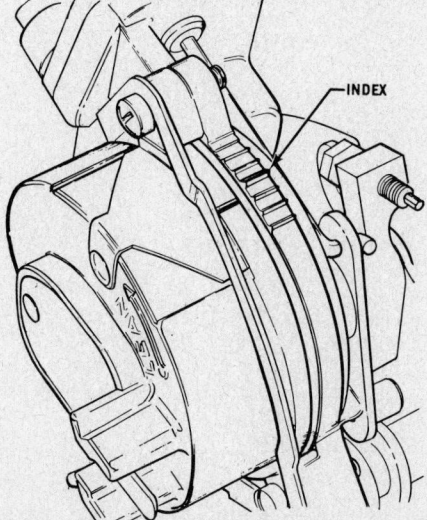

Fig. 11 Choke cap adjustment

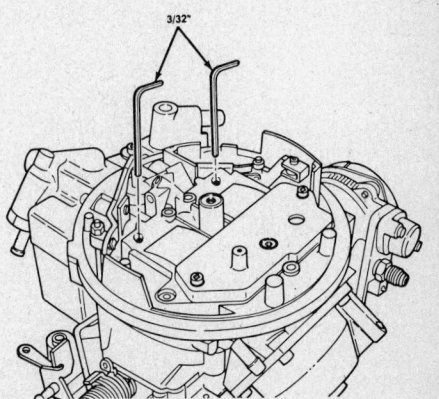

Fig. 12 Idle trim adjustment

Venturi Valve Limiter Adjustment

Fig. 8—Remove venturi valve cover and roller bearings, then the expansion plug located at rear of main body on the throttle side of carburetor. With an allen wrench, remove venturi valve wide open stop screw. Block the throttle wide open, then apply light closing pressure on the venturi valve and check gap between the valve and the air horn wall. If gap is not within specifications, adjust as follows: manually open the venturi valve to the wide open position and insert appropriate allen wrench into the hole from which the stop screw was removed. Rotate limiter adjusting screw clockwise to increase gap or counterclockwise to decrease gap. Remove allen wrench, apply light closing pressure to valve and recheck gap. If gap is within specifications, reinstall venturi valve wide open stop screw and rotate screw clockwise until screw contacts valve. Push venturi valve to wide open position and check gap between the valve and air horn wall, then rotate stop screw until gap is within specifications. Install new expansion plug in access hole. Reinstall venturi valve cover and roller bearings.

Control Vacuum Regulator (CVR) Adjustment

1977

NOTE: The cold enrichment metering rod adjustment must be performed before making this adjustment.

Fig. 9—Rotate choke cap 180 degrees clockwise from index position and open and close the throttle to position the cam. Lightly apply pressure on the CVR rod and, if any downward travel is present, the

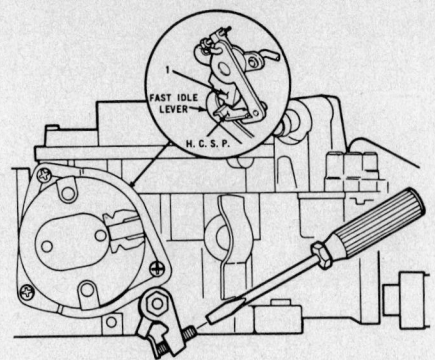

Fig. 13   Fast idle speed adjustment

valve is not seated and requires adjustment. If no downward travel is noted, rotate adjusting screw counter-clockwise until some downward travel is present. Rotate CVR rod clockwise until the adjusting nut starts to travel upward. Then, lightly apply pressure on the CVR rod and if any downward travel occurs, rotate adjusting screw clockwise in 1/4 turn increments until no downward travel occurs. Reset choke cap to specified setting.

1978

Fig. 9A—With the dial indicator installed, Fig. 9A, remove the stator cap with tool T77L-9848-A. Press downward on CVR rod until bottomed on seat. Note the dial indicator reading. If not within specifications, place a 3/8 inch box end wrench over CVR adjusting nut and, using a 3/32 inch allen wrench, turn CVR rod to adjust the travel.

High Cam Speed Positioner Adjustment

Fig. 10—Place high cam speed positioner in the corner of the specified cam step. Then, place the fast idle lever in the corner of the high cam speed positioner and hold throttle firmly closed. Remove diaphragm cover and rotate diaphragm assembly clockwise until lightly bottomed on casting, then rotate assembly counter-clockwise 1/2 to 1 1/2 turns, until the vacuum port and diaphragm hole align. Reinstall diaphragm cover.

Choke Cap Adjustment

Fig. 11—With choke cap installed, rotate choke cap clockwise until notch on cap is aligned with specified notch on housing.

Idle Trim Adjustment

Fig. 12—With a 3/32 inch allen wrench, rotate air adjusting screw clockwise to enrichen and counter-clockwise to lean.

Fast Idle Speed Adjustment

Fig. 13—Disconnect and plug the EGR vacuum line. With engine at curb idle and at normal operating temperature, place fast idle lever on specified step of fast idle cam. Ensure that the high cam speed positioner lever is disengaged, then rotate fast idle adjusting screw clockwise to increase speed or counter-clockwise to decrease speed.

MODEL 4300-4V ADJUSTMENT SPECIFICATIONS

See Tune Up Chart in car chapters for hot idle speeds.

Year	Carb. Model (Code 9510) ①	Idle Mixture Turns Open	Float Level (Dry)	Pump Setting (Hole No.)	Choke Plate Clearance (Pulldown)	Fast Idle Cam Linkage Setting	Fast Idle Speed (Hot Engine)	Auxiliary Inlet Valve Setting	Dechoke Clearance	Dashpot Setting	Choke Setting

AMERICAN MOTORS

Year	Carb. Model	Idle Mix	Float Level	Pump	Choke Plate Clr	Fast Idle Cam	Fast Idle Speed	Aux Inlet	Dechoke	Dashpot	Choke Setting
1974	4TA4	②	13/16	Center	.170	.160	1600	.050	.325	9/64	2 Rich
	4TA4 Police	②	25/32	Center	.170	.160	1600	.030	Preset	9/64	2 Rich
	4TM4	②	13/16	Center	.170	.160	1600	.050	.325	9/64	2 Rich

①—Tag attached to bowl cover.
②—Air/fuel ratio or idle CO% rating is found in Tune Up Specification tables in car chapters.

FORD AND MERCURY

Year	Carb. Model	Idle Mix	Float Level	Pump	Choke Plate Clr	Fast Idle Cam	Fast Idle Speed	Aux Inlet	Dechoke	Dashpot	Choke Setting
1974	D4AE-AA	②	3/4	#1	.230	.200	—	1/16	—	—	Index
	D4AE-NA	②	3/4	#1	.220	.200	—	1/16	—	—	Index
	D4OE-AA	②	13/16	#1	.180	.180	—	1/32	—	—	Index
	D4OE-BA	②	13/16	#1	.170	.170	—	1/32	—	—	Index
	D4TE-ATA	②	13/16	#1	.220	.180	—	1/16	—	—	Index
	D4VE-AB	②	3/4	#1	.220	.200	—	1/16	—	—	Index

①—Tag attached to bowl cover.　②—Air/fuel ratio or idle CO% rating is found in Tune Up Specification tables in car chapters.

MODEL 4300-4V ADJUSTMENTS

The model 4300, Figs. 1 thru 4, is a four barrel, three piece, separately cast design consisting of air horn, main body and mounting flange. A cast-in center fuel inlet has provision for a supplementary fuel inlet system. The fuel bowl is vented by an internal balance vent and a mechanical atmospheric vent operates during idle. An idle air by-pass system is designed to provide a consistent idle and a hot idle compensator is used to help stability.

The main (primary) fuel system has booster-type venturi cast integral with the air horn, and the main venturi are cast integral with the main body. The secondary throttle plates are mechanically operated from the primary linkage. On models 4300 and 4300-A, the air valve plates are located above the main venturis, Figs. 1 and 2, an integral hydraulic dashpot dampens sudden movement of the air valve plates to help prevent plate flutter and erratic engine operation. On model 4300-D the air valve plates are lo-

cated above the secondary bore. Secondary fuel supply is controlled by metering rods which are attached to the air valve plates, Fig. 4.

The automatic choke system consists of a standard bimetal thermostat. On Ford units, an electric choke system is incorporated which opens choke within 1-1½ minutes when underhood temperatures are above approximately 55° to 60°. On American Motors units, an electric choke system is also incorporated which opens choke when underhood temperatures are above approximately 95°. For service information refer to the "Emission Control System" chapter.

A single fuel bowl supplies both the primary and secondary fuel systems. Pontoon-type floats are used to help stabilize fuel level during cornering and hill-climbing. The accelerator pump is of the piston type. It is located in the fuel bowl for more positive displacement and a safeguard against external leaks.

Float Setting
Fig. 5
1. Adjust gauge to specified height.
2. Insert gauge into air horn outboard holes as shown.
3. Check clearance and alignment of float pontoons to gauge. Both pontoons should just touch gauge for proper setting. Align pontoons if necessary by slightly twisting pontoons.
4. If it is necessary to adjust float clearance, bend primary needle tab downward to raise float and upward to lower float.

NOTE: To raise float, insert open end of bending tool to *right* side of float lever tab and between needle and float hinge. Raise float lever off needle and bend tab downward.
To lower float, insert open end of bending tool to *left* side of float lever tab, between needle and float hinge. Support float lever and bend tab upward.

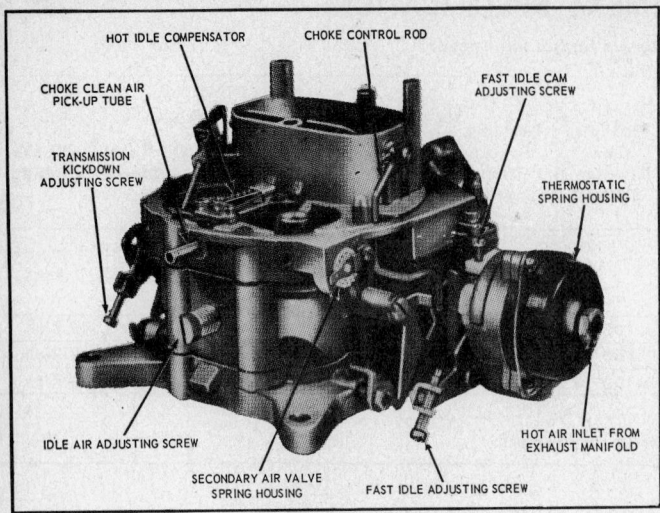

Fig. 1 Right rear view of 4300-4V carburetor

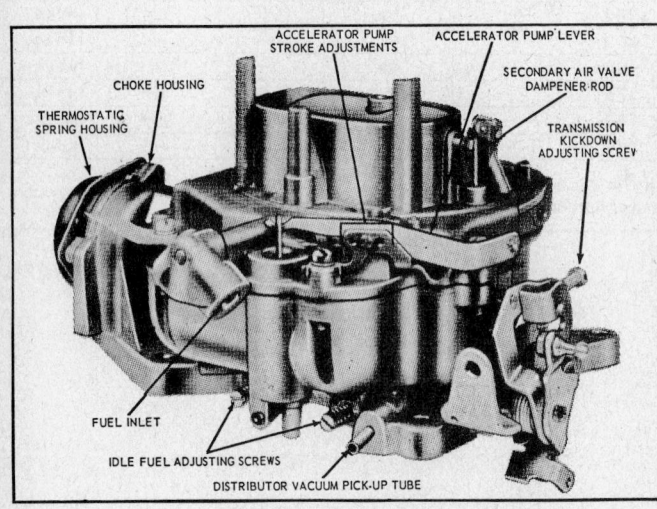

Fig. 2 Left front view of Model 4300-4V carburetor

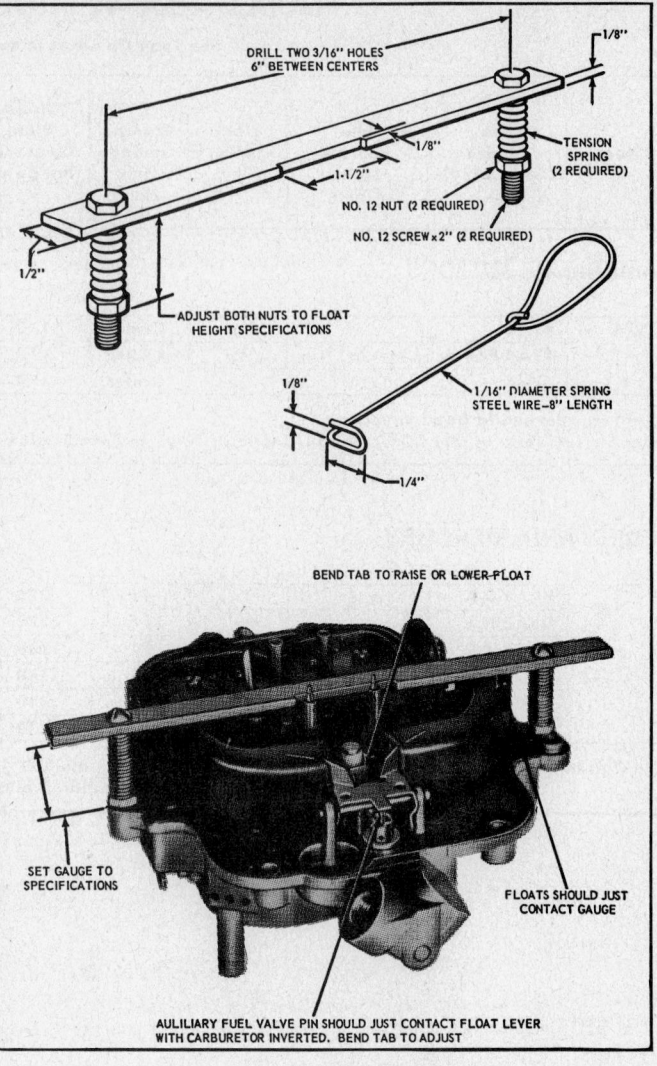

Fig. 5 Float setting

Auxiliary Valve Setting

1. Turn the air horn assembly upright allowing the float to hang freely.
2. Push up on the float until the primary fuel inlet needle lightly contacts its seat.
3. While holding the float in this position, measure the clearance between the float level auxiliary tab and the auxiliary inlet valve plunger.
4. Adjust by bending the tab. Refer to *4300 Specifications Chart.*

NOTE: To measure this clearance on a police fleet carburetor with a semi-articulating float, the float assembly must be positioned so that the bottom of both pontoons are same distance from gasket surface of air horn when primary fuel inlet is seated.

Fast Idle Speed Adjustment
Figs. 1 & 2

The fast idle adjusting screw contacts one edge of the fast idle cam. Each position on the fast idle cam permits a slower idle rpm as engine temperature rises and choking is reduced.

NOTE: Make certain the curb idle speed and mixture are adjusted to specification before attempting to set the fast idle speed.

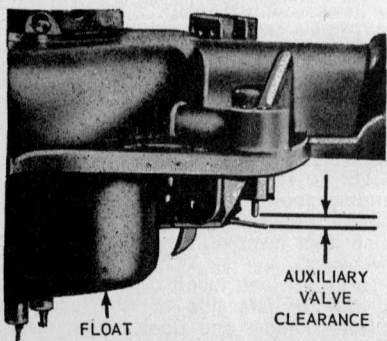

Fig. 6 Auxiliary valve setting.

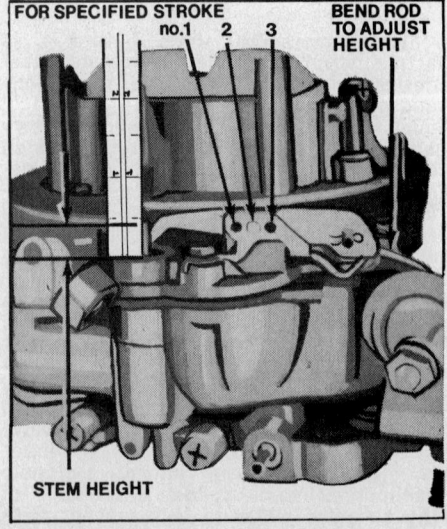

Fig. 7 Accelerator pump stroke adjustment

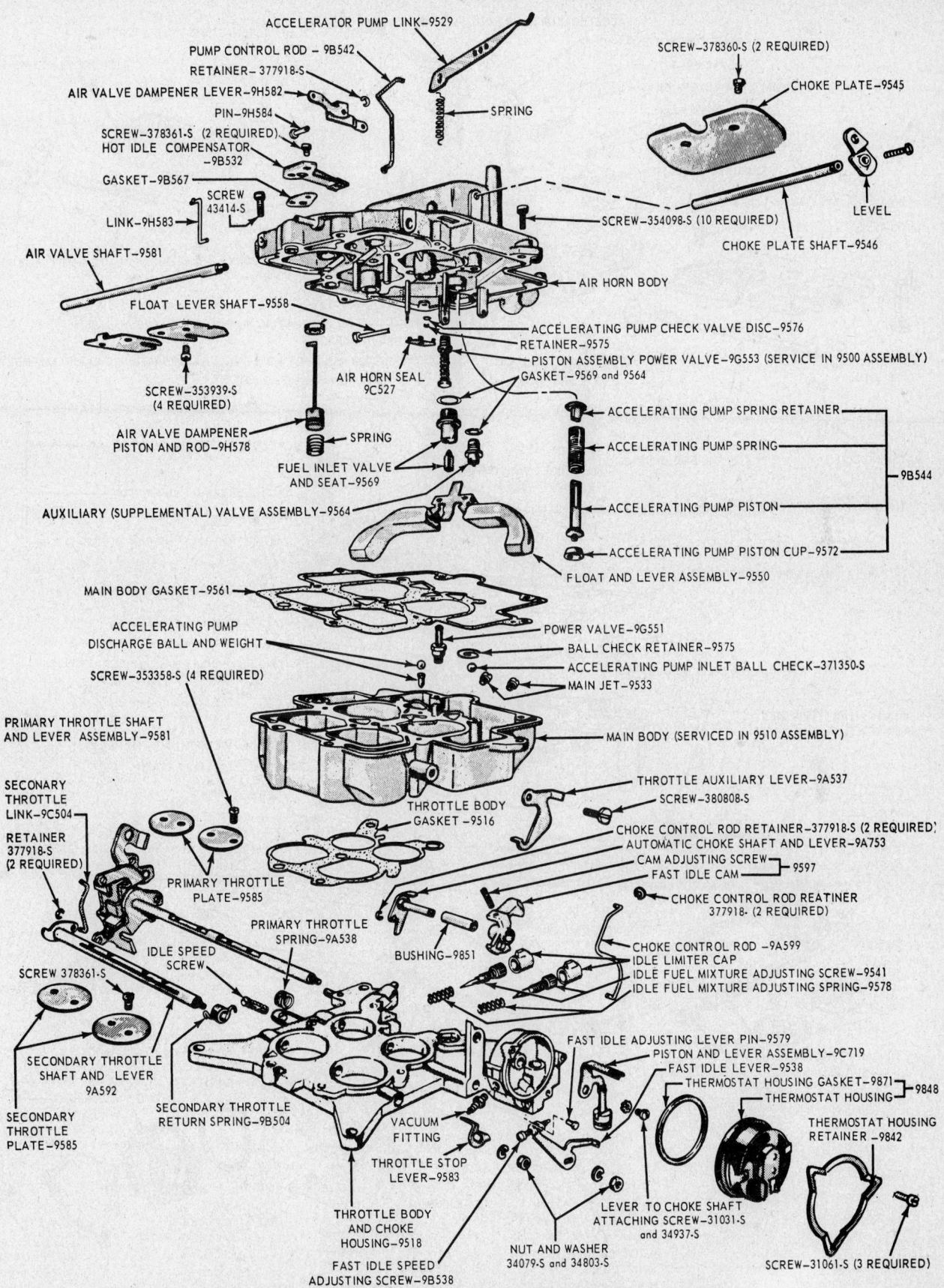

Fig. 3 Exploded view of a typical Motorcraft 4300A four-barrel carburetor.

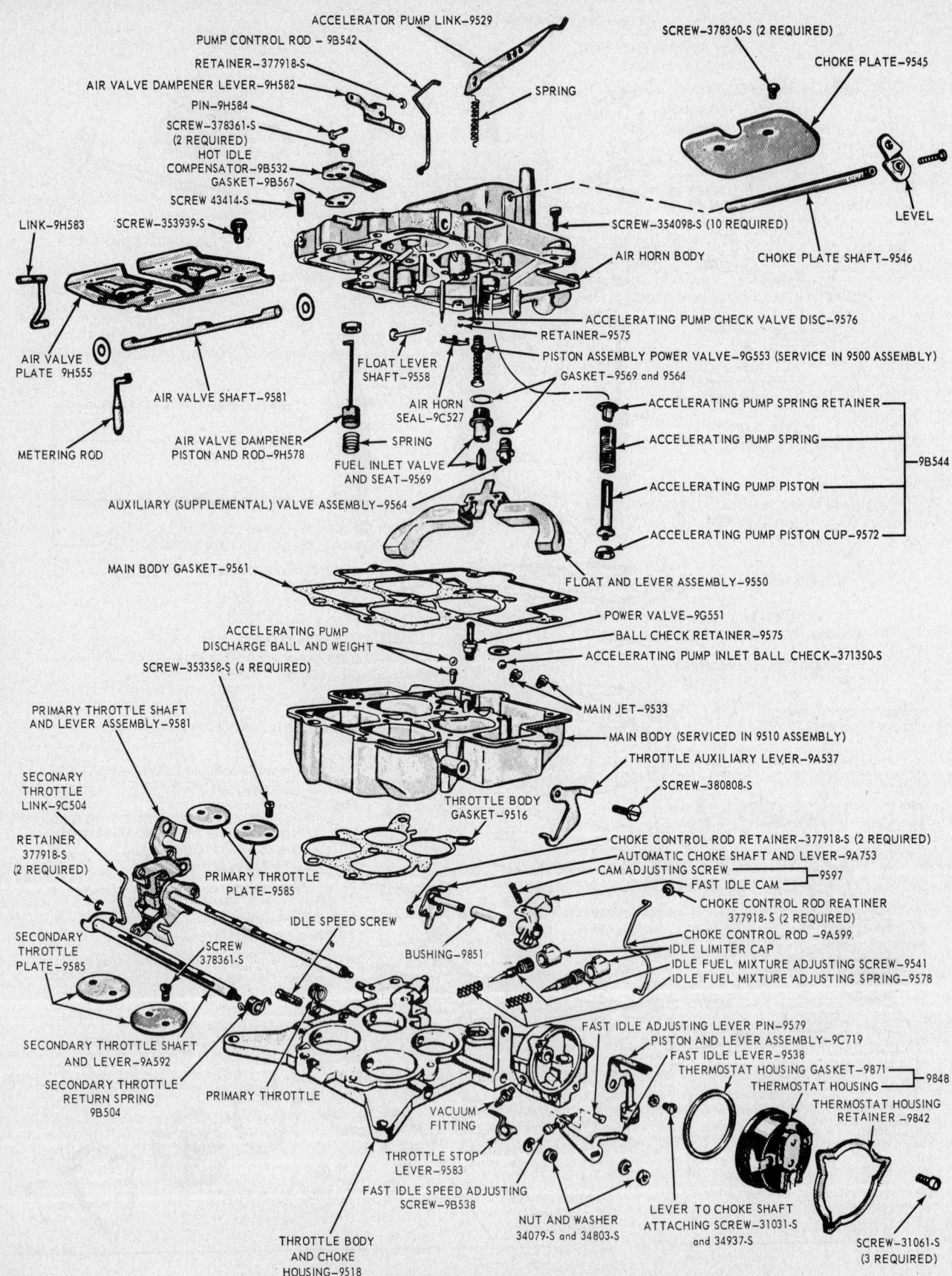

ACCELERATOR PUMP LINK—9529
PUMP CONTROL ROD — 9B542
RETAINER—377918-S
AIR VALVE DAMPENER LEVER—9H582
PIN—9H584
SCREW—378361-S (2 REQUIRED)
HOT IDLE COMPENSATOR—9B532
GASKET—9B567
SCREW 43414-S
LINK—9H583
SCREW—353939-S
AIR VALVE PLATE 9H555
AIR VALVE SHAFT—9581
METERING ROD
AIR VALVE DAMPENER PISTON AND ROD—9H578
FLOAT LEVER SHAFT—9558
AIR HORN SEAL—9C527
SPRING
FUEL INLET VALVE AND SEAT—9569
AUXILIARY (SUPPLEMENTAL) VALVE ASSEMBLY—9564
SCREW—378360-S (2 REQUIRED)
CHOKE PLATE—9545
LEVEL
SCREW—354098-S (10 REQUIRED)
AIR HORN BODY
CHOKE PLATE SHAFT—9546
ACCELERATING PUMP CHECK VALVE DISC—9576
RETAINER—9575
PISTON ASSEMBLY POWER VALVE—9G553 (SERVICE IN 9500 ASSEMBLY)
GASKET—9569 and 9564
ACCELERATING PUMP SPRING RETAINER
ACCELERATING PUMP SPRING
ACCELERATING PUMP PISTON
ACCELERATING PUMP PISTON CUP—9572
9B544
FLOAT AND LEVER ASSEMBLY—9550
MAIN BODY GASKET—9561
ACCELERATING PUMP DISCHARGE BALL AND WEIGHT
SCREW—353358-S (4 REQUIRED)
POWER VALVE—9G551
BALL CHECK RETAINER—9575
ACCELERATING PUMP INLET BALL CHECK—371350-S
PRIMARY THROTTLE SHAFT AND LEVER ASSEMBLY—9581
MAIN JET—9533
MAIN BODY (SERVICED IN 9510 ASSEMBLY)
THROTTLE AUXILIARY LEVER—9A537
SCREW—380808-S
SECONARY THROTTLE LINK—9C504
RETAINER 377918-S (2 REQUIRED)
PRIMARY THROTTLE PLATE—9585
SECONDARY THROTTLE PLATE—9585
SCREW 378361-S
SECONDARY THROTTLE SHAFT AND LEVER—9A592
SECONDARY THROTTLE RETURN SPRING 9B504
IDLE SPEED SCREW
BUSHING—9851
PRIMARY THROTTLE
THROTTLE BODY GASKET—9516
CHOKE CONTROL ROD RETAINER—377918-S (2 REQUIRED)
AUTOMATIC CHOKE SHAFT AND LEVER—9A753
CAM ADJUSTING SCREW
FAST IDLE CAM
9597
CHOKE CONTROL ROD REATINER 377918-S (2 REQUIRED)
CHOKE CONTROL ROD —9A599
IDLE LIMITER CAP
IDLE FUEL MIXTURE ADJUSTING SCREW—9541
IDLE FUEL MIXTURE ADJUSTING SPRING—9578
FAST IDLE ADJUSTING LEVER PIN—9579
PISTON AND LEVER ASSEMBLY—9C719
FAST IDLE LEVER—9538
THERMOSTAT HOUSING GASKET—9871
THERMOSTAT HOUSING
9848
THERMOSTAT HOUSING RETAINER —9842
VACUUM FITTING
THROTTLE STOP LEVER—9583
FAST IDLE SPEED ADJUSTING SCREW—9B538
NUT AND WASHER 34079-S and 34803-S
LEVER TO CHOKE SHAFT ATTACHING SCREW—31031-S and 34937-S
THROTTLE BODY AND CHOKE HOUSING—9518
SCREW—31061-S (3 REQUIRED)

Fig. 4   Exploded view of typical Motorcraft 4300-4V carburetor

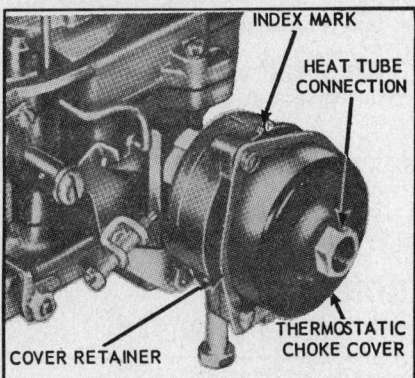

Fig. 8 Automatic choke setting (Typical)

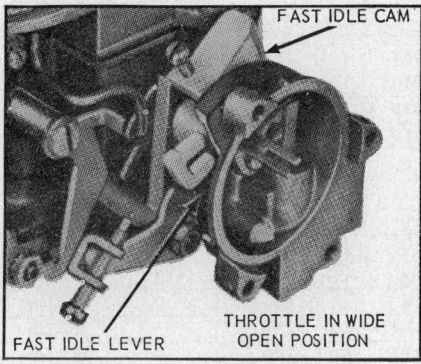

Fig. 9 Dechoke clearance setting

1. With the engine operating temperature normalized (hot), air cleaner removed and the tachometer attached, manually rotate the fast idle cam until the fast idle adjusting screw rests on the center step of the cam.
2. Adjust by turning the fast idle adjusting screw inward or outward as required. Refer to *4300 Specifications Chart*.

Accelerator Pump Stroke Adjustment
Fig. 7

The accelerator pump stroke has been calibrated to inject a pre-determined quantity of fuel into the air stream and help keep the exhaust emission level of the engine within the specified limits. The additional holes provided for pump stroke adjustment are for adjusting the stroke for specific engine applications.

NOTE: The stroke should not be changed from the specified setting.

If the pump stroke has been changed from the specified setting refer to the following instructions to correct the stroke to specification. Before adjusting the accelerator pump stroke, measure the height of the pump piston. Adjust by bending the pump control rod to correct the piston stem height. Refer to *4300 Specifications Chart*.

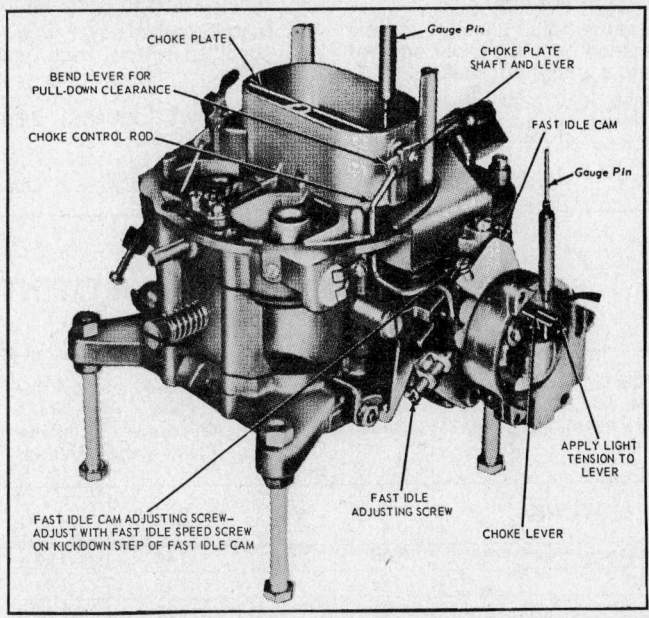

Fig. 10 Choke plate pulldown and fast idle cam adjustment

Automatic Choke Setting
Fig. 8

1. If carburetor is installed on engine, loosen choke heat tube nut.
2. Loosen choke cover retaining screws.
3. Rotate choke cover clockwise to reduce choking action or counterclockwise to increase choking action.
4. Tighten choke cover screws and choke heat tube nut.

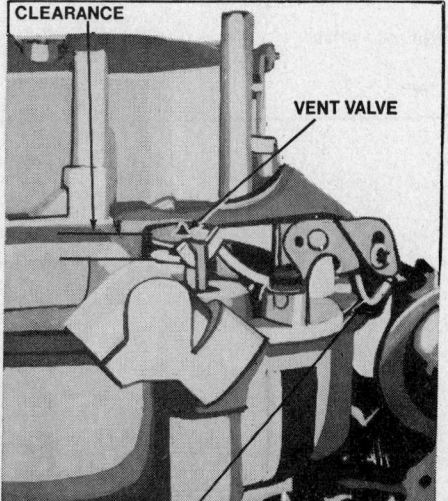

Fig. 11 Fuel bowl vent valve adjustment

Dechoke Clearance
Fig. 9

1. Open and hold throttle plate to wide open position.
2. Rotate choke plate toward closed position until pawl on fast idle speed lever contacts fast idle cam.
3. Check clearance between lower edge of choke plate and air horn wall.
4. Adjust clearance to specifications by bending pawl on fast idle speed lever forward to increase (backward to decrease) clearance.

Choke Plate Pulldown and Fast Idle Cam
Fig. 10

1. Remove choke cover.
2. Bend a .036" wire gauge at a 90° angle, approximately 1/8" from the end.
3. Insert bent edge of gauge between piston slot and upper edge of right hand slot in choke housing.
4. Rotate automatic choke lever counterclockwise until gauge is snug in piston slot. Exert light pressure on choke lever to hold gauge in place.
5. Using a gauge pin, check pulldown clearance between lower edge of choke plate and air horn wall.
6. Adjust pulldown clearance to specifications by bending adjusting arm on choke shaft lever. Bend downward to increase (upward to decrease) clearance.
7. Remove gauge and install choke cover loosely so it can rotate. Be sure thermostatic spring end is engaged in choke lever slot.
8. Rotate choke cover to 90° rich.
9. Position fast idle adjusting screw end to kickdown step on fast idle cam

FORD MOTORCRAFT CARBURETORS

and hold in this position.

10. Using a gauge pin, check fast idle cam clearance between lower edge of choke plate and air horn wall.

11. Adjust fast idle cam clearance to specifications by turning adjusting screw clockwise to increase (coun-terclockwise to decrease) clearance.

12. Install choke cover and rotate it to specified setting, then tighten cover.

Fuel Bowl External Vent Valve
Fig. 11

1. Set throttle plates in closed position.

2. Check clearance between vent valve and valve seat.

3. If clearance is not .070 inch, bend end of vent valve lever downward to decrease and upward to increase.

MODEL 4350-4V ADJUSTMENT SPECIFICATIONS

Year	Carb. Model (Code 9510)	Idle Mixture Turns Open	Float Level (Dry)	Pump Setting (Hole No.)	Choke Plate Clearance (Pulldown)	Fast Idle Cam Linkage Setting	Fast Idle Speed (Hot Engine)	Auxiliary Inlet Valve Setting	Dechoke Clearance	Metering Rod Setting	Choke Setting
AMERICAN MOTORS											
1975	5TA4	①	.900	②	.140	.160	1600③	.050	.325	.120	2 Rich
	5TA4D	①	29/32	—	.135	.135	1600③	.050	.325	—	2 Rich
	5TA4PD	①	15/16	—	.135	.135	1600③	.030	.325	—	2 Rich
1976	6TA4	①	29/32	—	.140	.135	1600③	.050	.325	—	2 Rich
FORD											
1975	D5AE-CA	①	31/32	#1	④	.160	1350	1/32	.300	.120	2 Rich
	D5AE-DA	①	31/32	#1	④	.160	1350	1/32	.300	.120	2 Rich
	D5VE-AD	①	15/16	#1	④	.160	1350	1/16	.300	⑤	2 Rich
	D5VE-BA	①	15/16	#1	④	.160	1350	1/16	.300	⑤	2 Rich
1976	D6AE-BA	①	1.00	#2	.140	.140	1350	.030	.300	—	2 Rich
	D6AE-BB	①	1.00	#2	.140	.140	1350	.030	.300	—	2 Rich
	D6AE-CA	①	1.00	#2	⑥	.140	1350	.030	.300	—	2 Rich
	D6AE-DA	①	.960	#2	⑦	.160	1350	.030	.300	—	2 Rich
	D6AE-EA	①	1.00	#2	.140	.140	1350	.030	.300	—	2 Rich
	D6AE-EB	①	1.00	#2	.140	.140	1350	.030	.300	—	2 Rich
	D6AE-FA	①	1.00	#2	⑥	.140	1350	.030	.300	—	2 Rich
	D6FE-TA	①	1.00	#2	.160	.160	1350	.030	.300	—	2 Rich
1977	D7VE-SA	①	1.00	#1	⑥	.140	—	.030	.300	—	Index
1978	D8VE-FA	①	1.00	#1	.160	.170	—	.030	.300	—	Index
	D8VE-GA	①	1.00	#1	.160	.170	—	.030	.300	—	Index

①—Air/fuel ratio or idle CO% rating is found in Tune Up Specification tables in car chapters.
②—In lower hole of throttle shaft lever assembly.
③—On second step of fast idle cam with TCS solenoid and EGR disconnected.
④—Initial setting; .160". Delayed setting; .190".
⑤—Check setting before disassembly and reset to original setting.
⑥—Initial setting; .140". Delayed setting; .190".
⑦—Initial setting; .160". Delayed setting; .210".

MODEL 4350-4V ADJUSTMENTS

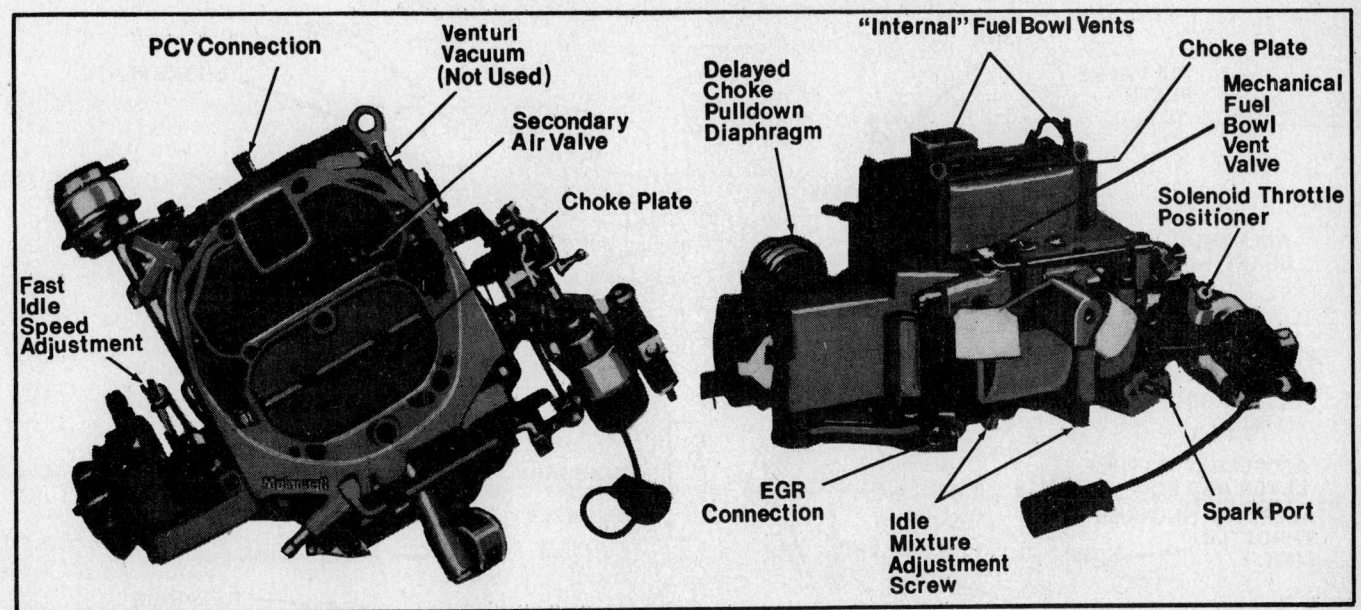

Fig. 1 Motorcraft 4350 4V carburetor assembly

The model 4350, Figs. 1, 2 and 2A, is a four barrel, three piece, separately cast design consisting of an upper body, main body and throttle body. The fuel bowl is vented by a mechanical fuel bowl vent valve to the carbon canister which opens when the engine is off and closes when the engine is running.

The upper main body consists of the choke plate, boost venturi assembly, secondary air valve, acceleration pump plunger, mechanical fuel vent valve and fuel inlet and float system.

The main body consists of the fuel bowl, primary fuel metering system vacuum piston and rods.

The throttle body consists of the primary and secondary throttle plates. The primary throttle is actuated by the accelerator linkage and the secondary throttle is actuated by a linkage from the primary throttle lever. A lockout tang coupled to the automatic choke linkage, prevents operation until choke is fully off. The secondary throttle shaft is split and loosely coupled in the center to permit tighter

secondary plate seating.

Primary fuel metering is accomplished by tapered metering rods that are raised or lowered according to engine vacuum and are limited by a mechanical system and throttle plate opening.

Fuel inlet is controlled by twin floats on either side of the carburetor. The piston type accelerator pump is suspended into the pump well by a linkage and operating rod which are part of upper body.

The choke system consists of a bimetallic thermostatic choke system which operates when underhood temperatures are below 60°F and an electric assist choke system which operates when underhood temperatures are above 60°F. On Ford models, this carburetor is equipped with a vacuum operated delayed choke system, Fig. 6, which operates in addition to the usual pulldown system. On American Motors models, a thermostatic bypass valve, which is integral with the choke heat tube, helps prevent premature choke valve opening. For service information on the choke system, refer to the "Emission Control System" chapter.

Some 1977-78 carburetors are equipped with high altitude compensation to provide improved high altitude emission control and driveability. Air passing the bypass intake is metered into the air flow below the primary, thus providing the leaner air fuel mixture required at high altitudes. Air flow is controlled by a valve controlled by an aneroid attached to the rear of the carburetor. To provide improved cold engine starts at high altitudes, the bypass is equipped with a choke plate connected to the main choke system.

Accelerator Pump Adjustment

The piston-to-shaft pin position which is

the only adjustment, is pre-set to deliver the correct amount of fuel for the engine on which it is installed and should not be changed from the specified setting. Do not attempt to adjust the accelerator pump stroke by turning the vacuum limiter level adjusting nut. This adjustment is pre-set and changing it could affect driveability.

1. Remove air horn assembly, then disconnect accelerator pump from operating lever by depressing spring and sliding arm out of pump shaft slot.
2. Disassemble spring and nylon keeper retaining adjustment pin. Refer to 4350 specifications chart. If pin is not in specified hole, remove it, reposition shaft in specified hole and reinstall pin, Fig. 3.
3. Slide nylon retainer over pin and position spring on shaft, then compress spring on shaft and install pump on arm.

Fig. 3 Accelerator pump stroke adjustment

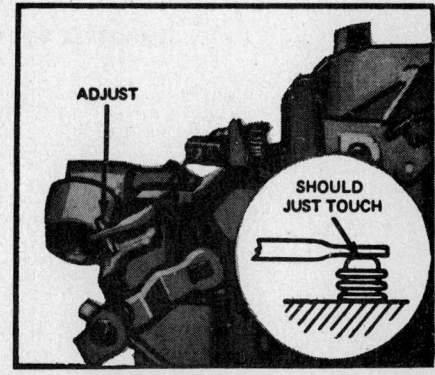

Fig. 4 Mechanical fuel vent valve adjustment

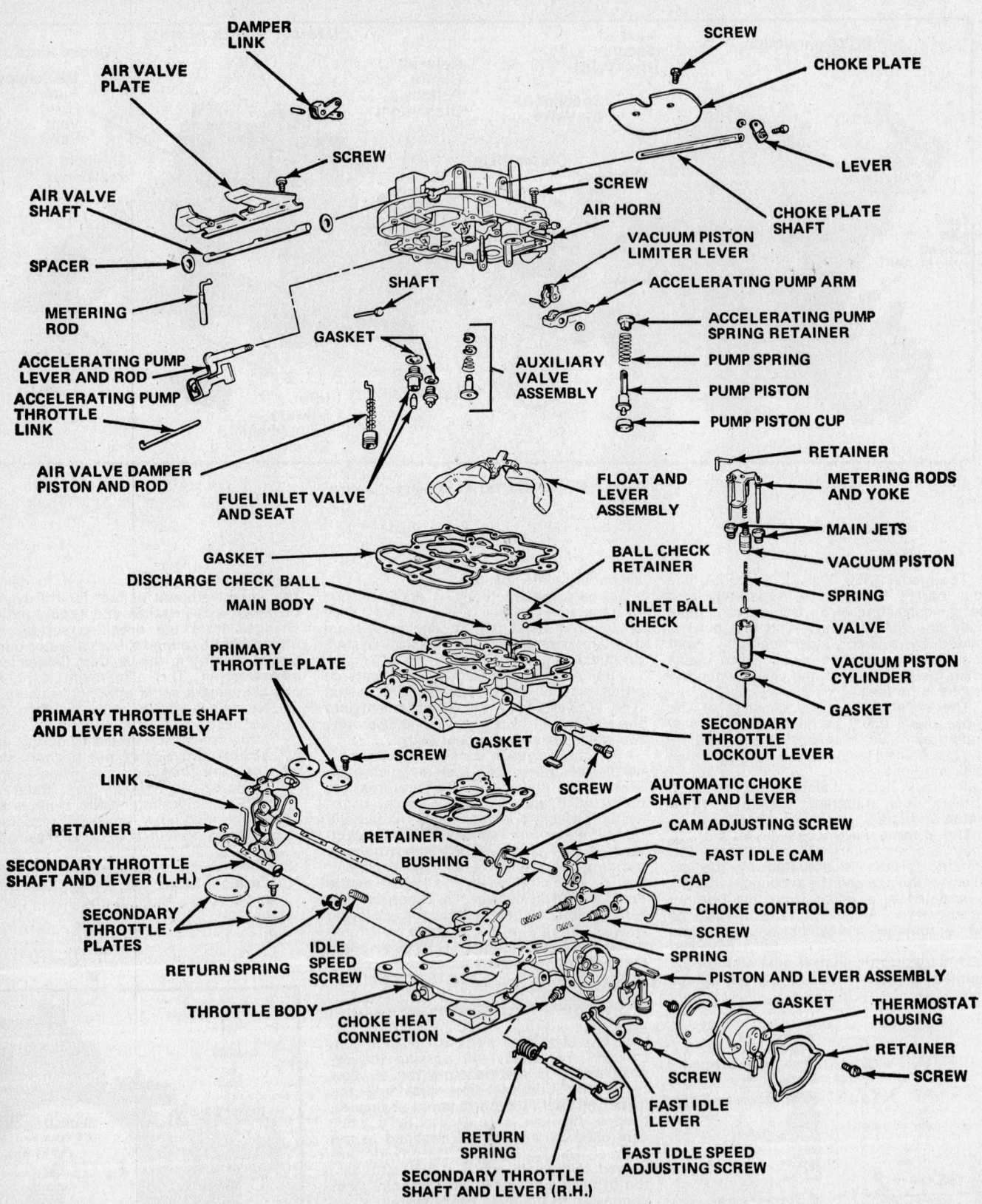

Fig. 2   Exploded view of 4350 4V carburetor without altitude compensation

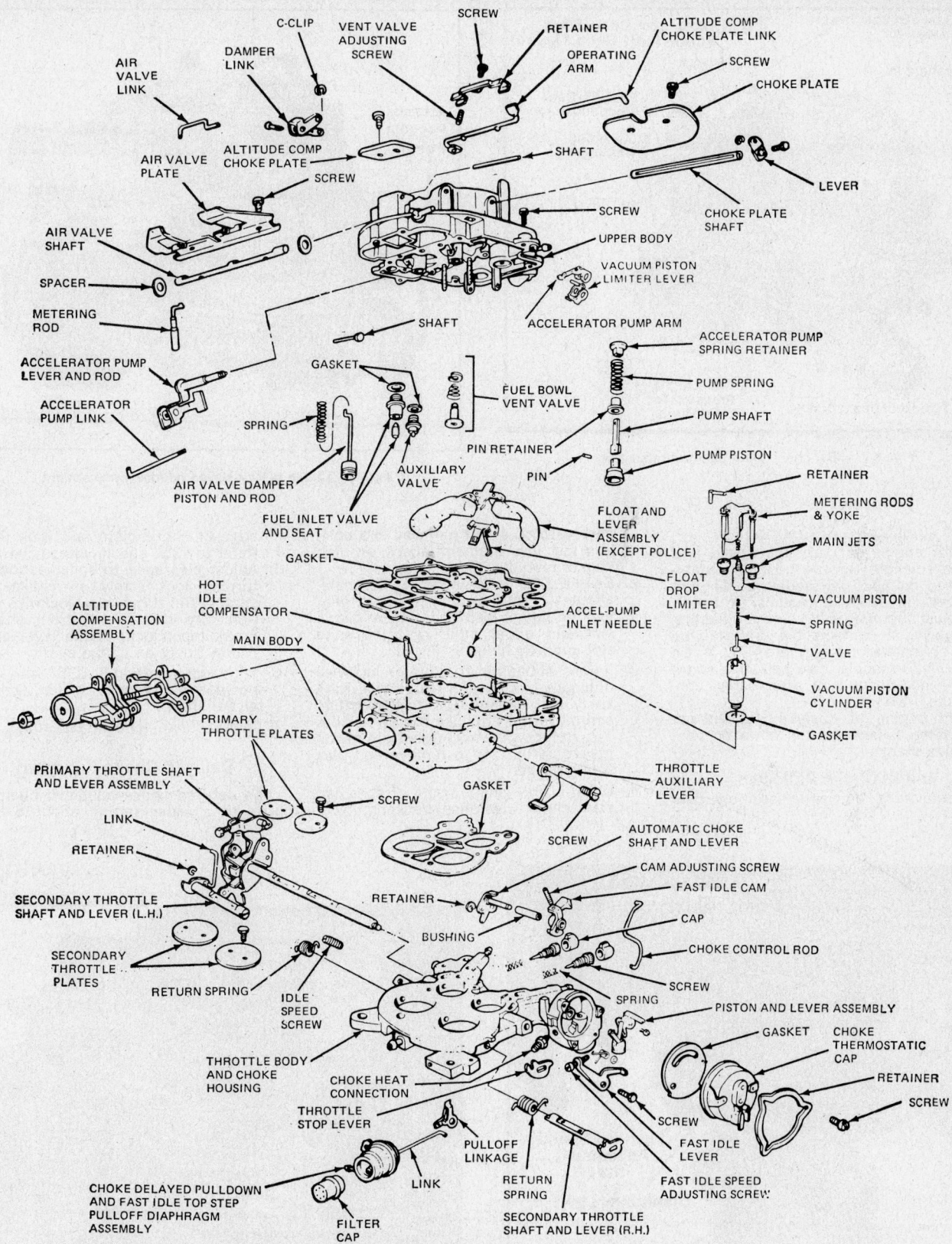

Fig. 2A Exploded view of 4350 4V carburetor with high altitude compensation.

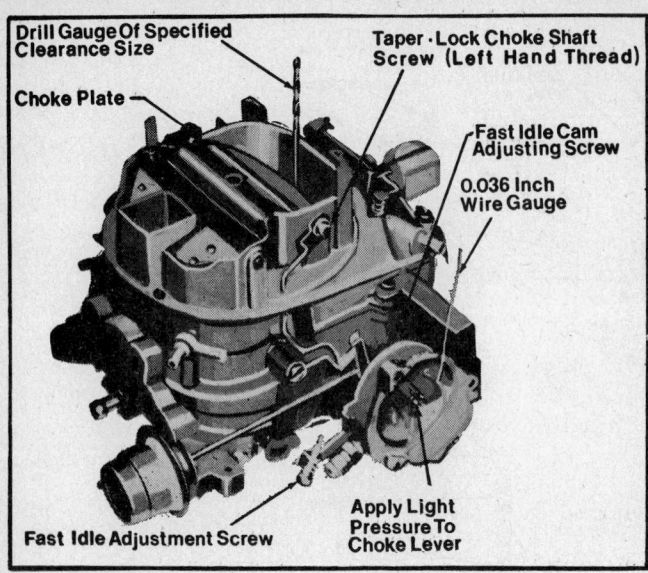

Fig. 5   Initial choke plate pulldown adjustment

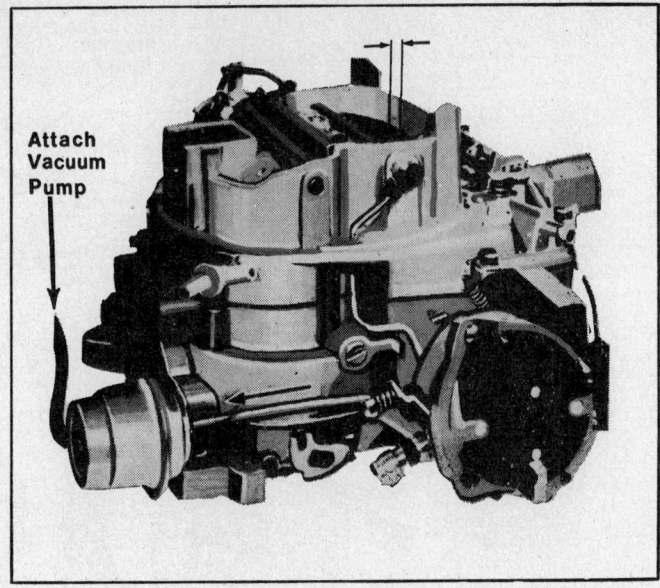

Fig. 6   Choke plate delayed pulldown adjustment

Vent Valve Adjustment

1. With engine at curb idle speed and the solenoid throttle positioner energized on 1975-76 models or de-energized on 1977-78 models (if used), adjust the vent valve so the adjusting screw just contacts the drive tab on the accelerator pump lever, Fig. 4. On 1977-78 models, turn adjusting screw one additional turn after screw contacts drive tab.
2. With engine off, observe that vent operating linkage pushes down on vent valve stem.

Initial Choke Pulldown

1. Remove choke housing assembly, then

open throttle about half-way and position fast idle adjusting screw on high step of fast idle cam.
2. Bend a .036″ wire gauge at 90° angle, about ⅛″ from end, then insert bent end of gauge between choke piston slot and upper edge of right hand slot in choke housing, Fig. 5.
3. Rotate choke lever counterclockwise until gauge is snug in piston slot, then apply light force to lever to hold gauge and move top of choke rod away from carburetor while moving bottom of rod toward carburetor to remove end play from linkage.
4. Using a drill gauge or pin of specified size, check clearance between lower

edge of choke plate and wall, Fig. 5. Refer to 4350 specifications chart.
5. Adjust clearance to specifications, by turning lock screw on choke plate shaft 3 full turns in a clockwise direction. Pry choke lever from shaft to break taper lock. Choke lever should rotate freely on choke shaft.
6. With drill gauge and .036″ wire gauge positioned as above, tighten, screw on choke shaft.
7. Install choke housing assembly.

Delayed Choke Pulldown

The delayed choke pulldown opens the choke to a wider setting about 6 to 18

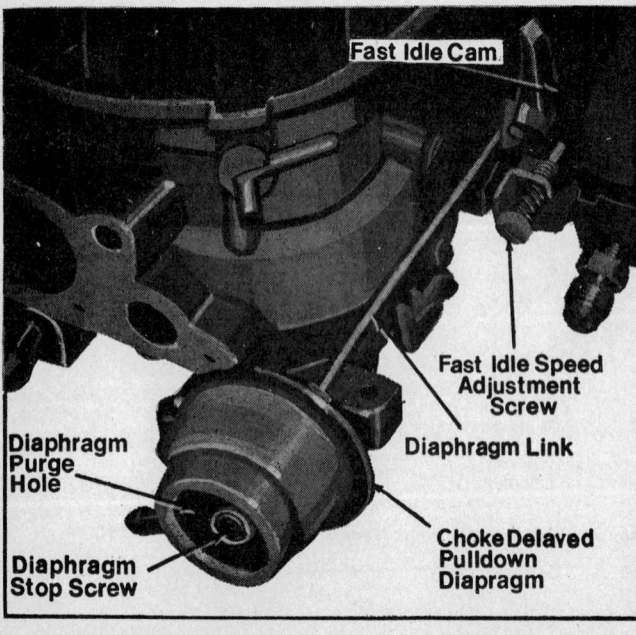

Fig. 7   Choke plate delayed pulldown stop screw adjustment

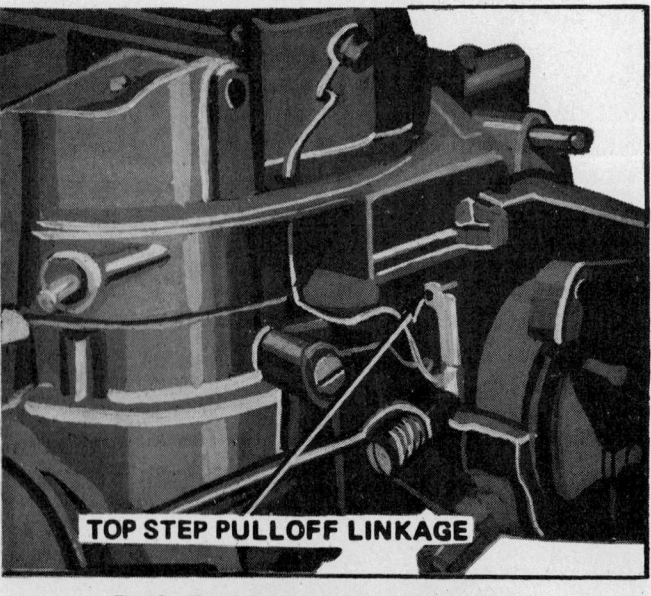

Fig. 8   Fast idle top step pulloff adjustment

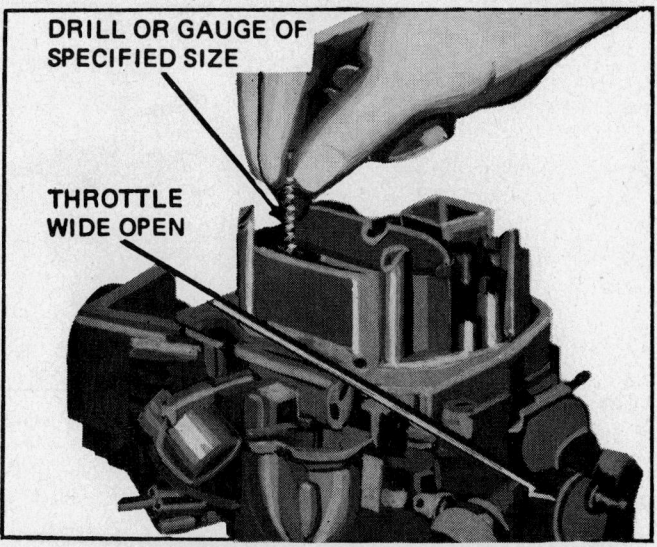

DRILL OR GAUGE OF SPECIFIED SIZE

THROTTLE WIDE OPEN

Fig. 9   Dechoke clearance adjustment

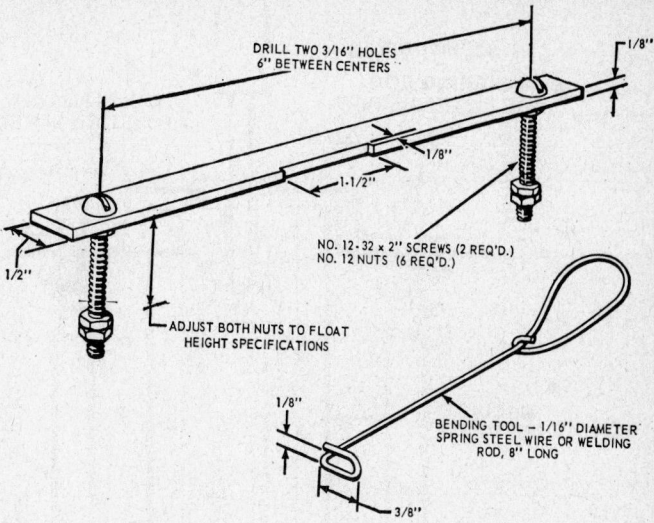

DRILL TWO 3/16" HOLES 6" BETWEEN CENTERS

1/8"

1/8"

1-1/2"

1/2"

NO. 12-32 x 2" SCREWS (2 REQ'D.)
NO. 12 NUTS (6 REQ'D.)

ADJUST BOTH NUTS TO FLOAT HEIGHT SPECIFICATIONS

1/8"

BENDING TOOL – 1/16" DIAMETER SPRING STEEL WIRE OR WELDING ROD, 8" LONG

3/8"

Fig. 10   Float setting gauge and bending tool

seconds after the engine is started.

1. With throttle set on fast idle cam, note position of index marks on choke housing, then loosen retaining screws and rotate cap 90° in closing (rich) direction.
2. Connect a vacuum source of 14-18 inches Hg. to vacuum supply port of delayed choke pulldown diaphragm and check clearance between lower edge of choke plate and wall, Fig. 6. Refer to 4350 specifications chart.
3. Adjust clearance to specifications by turning stop screw on delayed choke pulldown diaphragm, Fig. 7.

Fast Idle Top Step Pulloff

1. Operate delayed pulldown diaphragm manually or by applying 14 to 18 inches Hg.
2. Position fast idle speed screw on top step fast idle cam with choke plate

closed. If necessary, rotate choke housing cap to close choke plate.
3. Observe that fast idle speed adjusting screw drops to second step of cam as delayed choke pulldown diaphragm is operated, Fig. 8.

Dechoke (Unloader) Clearance

1. Hold throttle plate fully open and apply pressure on choke valve toward close position.
2. Measure clearance between lower edge of choke valve and air horn wall. Fig. 9. Refer to 4350 Specifications Chart.
3. Adjust clearance to specifications by bending unloader tang which contacts fast idle cam forward to increase or rearward to decrease clearance.

NOTE: Do not bend tang downward from a horizontal plane. After adjustment, make

certain that there is at least .070 inch clearance between unloader tang and choke housing with throttle fully open.

Float Setting

To simplify float setting, refer to Fig. 10 for construction of an adjustable float gauge and float tab bending tool.

1. Adjust gauge to specified height and insert gauge into air horn, Fig. 11.
2. Check clearance and alignment of floats to gauge. Refer to 4350 Specifications Chart. Both floats should just touch gauge. If necessary, align floats by twisting floats slightly.
3. To raise float setting, insert open end of bending tool to right side of float lever tab between needle and float hinge. Raise float lever off needle and bend tab downward.
4. To lower float setting, insert open end

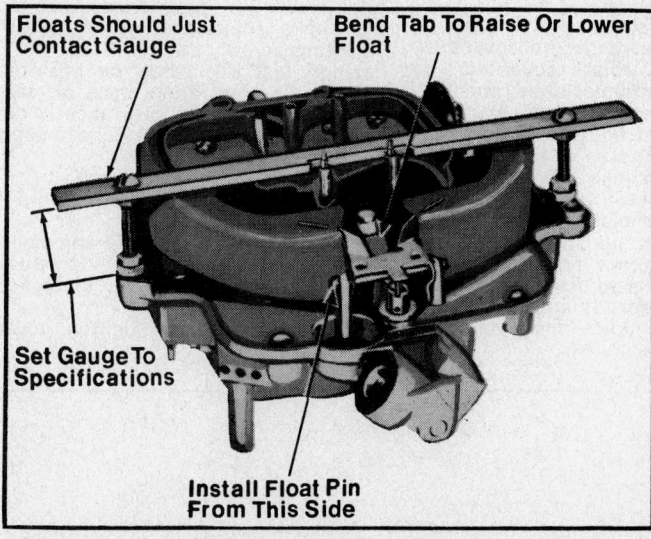

Floats Should Just Contact Gauge

Bend Tab To Raise Or Lower Float

Set Gauge To Specifications

Install Float Pin From This Side

Fig. 11   Float setting

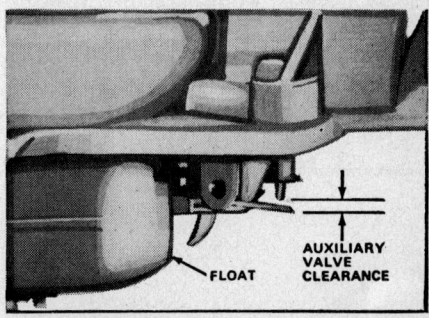

AUXILIARY VALVE CLEARANCE

FLOAT

Fig. 12   Auxiliary inlet valve adjustment

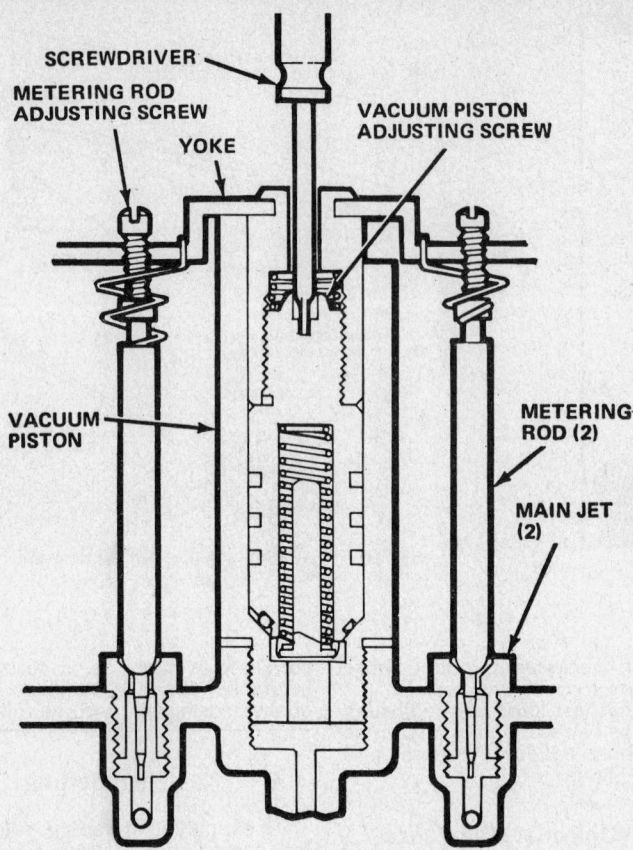

Fig. 13 Metering rod adjustment

SCREWDRIVER
METERING ROD ADJUSTING SCREW
YOKE
VACUUM PISTON ADJUSTING SCREW
VACUUM PISTON
METERING ROD (2)
MAIN JET (2)

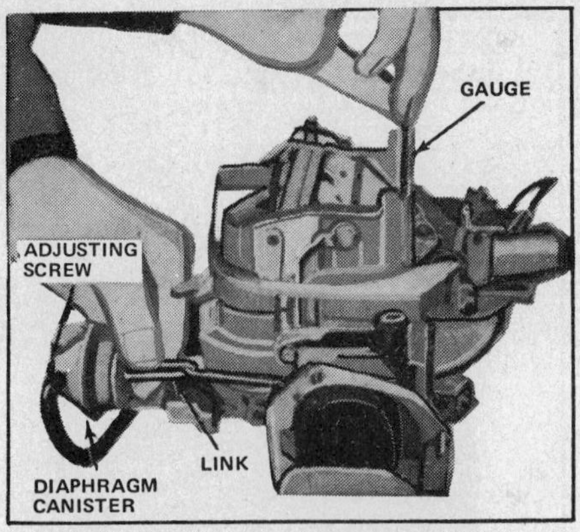

Fig. 14 Initial choke valve clearance adjustment. 1975 American Motors units with vacuum diaphragm

GAUGE
ADJUSTING SCREW
LINK
DIAPHRAGM CANISTER

of bending tool to left side of float lever tab between needle and float hinge. Support float lever and bend tap upward.

5. If above gauge is not available, invert upper body and measure distance from top of float to gasket surface of upper body. Adjust alignment and height of floats with bending tool as described previously.

Auxiliary Valve Setting

Check auxiliary valve clearance as shown in Fig. 12. If necessary to adjust clearance, use bending tool, Fig. 10.

Vacuum Piston & Metering Rods Adjustment

1. Remove air horn assembly, then depress metering rod hanger and turn vacuum piston adjusting screw and metering rod adjusting screws until metering rod hanger is fully seated against vacuum cylinder top face, Fig. 13.

2. Hold metering rod hanger in full downward position and turn each metering rod adjusting screw clockwise until the metering rod hanger starts to rise. Metering rods are now properly positioned in relation to vacuum piston.

3. Turn vacuum piston adjusting screw clockwise until specified clearance between metering rod hanger and vacuum cylinder top face is obtained.

Fast Idle Cam

1. Loosen choke cover screws and rotate cover to align index marks on cover and housing. Then, rotate cover an additional 90° counterclockwise and tighten attaching screws.

2. Place fast idle speed adjusting screw on kickdown (center) step of fast idle cam. Fully close choke plate and check clearance between air horn and lower edge of choke plate. Adjust by turning fast idle cam adjusting screw, ensuring adjusting screw remains on kickdown step during adjustment.

3. Loosen choke cove screws and rotate cover to specified index mark and tighten cover screws.

American Motors Units With Vacuum Diaphragm

Initial Choke Valve Clearance

1. Loosen choke cover screws, open throttle and rotate choke cover until choke valve closes. Then, tighten one cover screw to hold cover in place.
2. Close throttle. The fast idle screw should be on top step of cam.
3. Bottom choke diaphragm on setscrew, however, do not press on links, Fig. 14.
4. Measure clearance between air horn and lower edge of choke valve, Fig. 14. Adjust by turning adjusting screw at rear of diaphragm housing.
5. Adjust fast idle cam linkage.
6. Loosen choke cover screw and set choke cover to specifications.

Choke Plate Indexing

1. Loosen choke lever attaching screw and pry lever from choke shaft to permit choke valve rotation.

NOTE: The choke lever attaching screw has a left hand thread.

2. Loosen choke cover screws and rotate cover 90° counterclockwise so the choke shaft lever contacts cam adjusting screw.
3. Position fast idle screw on top step of fast idle cam. Then, back off cam adjusting screw until clearance is obtained between screw and choke shaft lever.
4. Turn cam adjusting screw until it contacts choke shaft lever, then turn 6-7 additional turns.
5. Manually close choke plate and tighten choke shaft lever attaching screw.
6. Adjust initial choke valve clearance and fast idle cam linkage.
7. Set choke cover and tighten cover screws.

MODEL 5200 ADJUSTMENT SPECIFICATIONS

See Tune Up Chart in car chapters for hot idle speeds.

Year	Carb. Model (9510) ①	Idle Mixture Turns Open	Float Level	Pump Setting (Hole)	Choke Pulldown	Dechoke Clearance	Fast Idle Speed	Fast Idle Cam Clearance	Dashpot Setting	Choke Setting
1974	D42E-AA	②	.460	#2	.280	.255	—	.1575	—	Index
	D42E-AC	②	.460	#2	.280	.255	—	.158	—	Index
	D42E-BA	②	.460	#2	.280	.255	—	.1575	—	1 Rich
	D42E-CB	②	.460	#2	.280	.255	—	.1575	—	Index
	D42E-CD	②	.460	#2	.280	.255	—	.158	—	Index
	D42E-DB	②	.460	#2	.280	.255	—	.1575	—	1 Rich
	D42F-EA	②	.460	#2	.236	.255	—	.1575	—	Index
	D42F-EB	②	.460	#2	.236	.255	—	.158	—	Index
	D42F-FA	②	.460	#2	.236	.255	—	.1575	—	Index
	D42F-GA	②	.460	#2	.236	.255	—	.1575	—	Index
	D42E-KA	②	.460	#2	.280	.255	—	.158	—	1 Rich
	D4ZE-AA	②	.430	#2	.195	.256	—	.195	—	1 Rich
	D4ZE-BA	②	.430	#2	.195	.256	—	.195	—	1 Rich
	D4ZE-BC	②	.435	#2	.195	.255	—	.195	—	1 Rich
	D4ZE-CA	②	.430	#2	.195	.256	—	.195	—	1 Rich
	D4ZE-DA	②	.430	#2	.195	.256	—	.195	—	1 Rich
	D4ZE-DC	②	.435	#2	.195	.255	—	.195	—	1 Rich
1975	D52E-AA	②	.460	#2	.197	.256	1800	.098	—	1 Lean
	D52E-BA	②	.460	#2	.197	.256	1800	.098	—	1 Lean
	D52E-CA	②	.460	#2	.197	.256	1800	.098	—	1 Lean
	D52E-DB	②	.460	#2	.197	.256	1800	.098	—	1 Lean
	D5ZE-EA	②	.460	#2	.197	.256	1800	.098	—	1 Lean
	D5ZE-FA	②	.460	#2	.197	.256	1800	.098	—	1 Lean
	D5ZE-GA	②	.460	#2	.197	.256	1800	.098	—	1 Lean
	D5ZE-HB	②	.460	#2	.197	.256	1800	.098	—	1 Lean
1976	D6EE-AA	②	.460	#2	.276	.256	1500	.158	—	1 Lean
	D6EE-BA	②	.460	#2	.236	.256	2000	.118	—	1 Lean
	D6EE-CA	②	.460	#2	.276	.256	1500	.158	—	1 Lean
	D6EE-DA	②	.460	#2	.236	.256	1800	.118	—	1 Lean
	D6EE-EA	②	.460	#2	.197	.256	2000	.079	—	Index
	D6EE-FA	②	.460	#2	.236	.256	1500	.118	—	1 Lean
	D6EE-JA	②	.460	#2	.276	.256	1500	.197	—	1 Lean
	D6EE-LA	②	.460	#2	.276	.256	1500	.158	—	Index
	D6ZE-EA	②	.460	#2	.276	.256	1500	.158	—	1 Lean
	D6ZE-FA	②	.460	#2	.236	.256	2000	.118	—	1 Lean
	D6ZE-GA	②	.460	#2	.276	.256	1500	.158	—	1 Lean
	D6ZE-HA	②	.460	#2	.236	.256	1800	.118	—	1 Lean
	D6ZE-LA	②	.460	#2	.236	.256	1500	.118	—	Index
	D6ZE-RA	②	.460	#2	.276	.256	1500	.197	—	1 Lean
1977	D7EE-BGA	②	29/64	#2	.24	.24	—	.12	—	Index
	D7EE-BHA	②	29/64	#2	.24	.24	—	.12	—	Index
	D7EE-BLA	②	29/64	#2	.24	.24	—	.12	—	1 Rich
	D7EE-BMA	②	29/64	#2	.24	.24	—	.12	—	1 Rich
1978	D8BE-FA	②	29/64	#2	.24	.24	—	.12	—	2 Rich
	D8BE-HA	②	29/64	#2	.24	.24	—	.12	—	1 Rich
	D8EE-CA	②	29/64	#2	.24	.24	—	.12	—	1 Rich
	D8EE-DA	②	29/64	#2	.24	.24	—	.12	—	2 Rich
	D8EE-JA	②	29/64	#2	.24	.24	—	.12	—	2 Rich
	D8EE-KA	②	29/64	#2	.24	.24	—	.12	—	1 Rich
	D8ZE-RA	②	29/64	#2	.24	.24	—	.12	—	1 Rich
	D8ZE-SA	②	29/64	#2	.24	.24	—	.12	—	1 Rich
1979	D9BE-AAA	②	.460	#2	.24	.24	—	.12	—	2 Rich
	D9BE-ABA	②	.460	#2	.24	.24	—	.12	—	2 Rich
	D9EE-AMA	②	.460	#2	.24	.24	—	.12	—	2 Rich
	D9EE-ANA	②	.460	#2	.24	.24	—	.12	—	1 Rich
	D9EE-ASA	②	.460	#2	.24	.24	—	.12	—	1 Rich
	D9EE-AYA	②	.460	#2	.24	.24	—	.12	—	1 Rich
	D9ZE-ND	②	.460	#3	.24	.24	—	.12	—	2 Rich

①—Tag attached to carburetor
②—Air/fuel ratio or idle CO% rating is found in Tune Up Specification tables in car chapters.

MODEL 5200 ADJUSTMENTS

This carburetor is a two stage, two venturi carburetor, Figs. 1 and 2. The primary stage or venturi is smaller than the secondary venturi. The secondary is operated by mechanical linkage.

The primary stage includes a curb idle system, accelerator pump system, idle transfer system, main metering system and power enrichment system.

The secondary stage includes a transfer system, main metering system, and power system. Both the primary and secondary systems draw fuel from a common fuel bowl.

The automatic choke on 1974-76 models is equipped with a housing for coolant flow and an electric heater assist. On 1977-78 models, the automatic choke is equipped with only the electric heater assist.

Some 1977 units are equipped with an altitude compensation feature which is controlled by the driver. This is a two piece manual system that utilizes the carburetor supplemental metering system when the dash panel control is placed in the "Sea Level" position and the normal fuel metering system when the control is in the "Altitude" position.

1978 units are equipped with a vacuum operated, solenoid assisted fuel bowl vent which is called a "Switching Bowl Vent". With the engine "Off", a spring holds the external vent open, closing the internal vent passage. In this position, the fuel bowl vapors pass to the evaporative emission canister. When the engine is started, manifold vacuum acting on the diaphragm overcomes the spring pressure and pulls the external vent to the seated position, uncovering the internal vent passage. A holding solenoid, connected to the ignition circuit, holds the vent closed to prevent the vent opening under low vacuum conditions. The vent will close only when the ignition is turned "Off".

Dry Float Setting

Fig. 3—With the bowl cover held in an inverted position and the float tang resting lightly on the spring loaded fuel inlet needle, measure the clearance between the edge of the float and the bowl cover. Adjust clearance by bending the float tang up or down as required, Fig. 4.

NOTE: Do not scratch or damage the tang. Adjust both floats equally.

Dechoke Clearance

Fig. 5—Hold throttle lever in wide open position and take slack out of choke linkage by applying finger pressure to top edge of choke plate. Measure clearance between lower edge of choke plate and air horn wall. Adjust by bending tab on fast idle lever where it touches the fast idle cam.

Choke Plate Vacuum Pull-Down

Fig. 6—Remove the three screws and ring retaining choke spring cover and pull the water cover and/or choke spring cover from carburetor. On 1974-77 units, place fast idle cam on high step. On 1978 units, place fast idle cam on second step. Push the diaphragm stem back against its stop. Place gauge rod or drill between the lower edge of the choke plate and the air horn wall. Remove the slack from the choke linkage by applying finger pressure to the top edge of the choke plate. Adjust the choke plate-to-air horn clearance by removing the plug from the diaphragm and turning the adjusting screw in or out as required.

Fast Idle Cam Clearance

Fig. 7—Insert specified drill or gauge between the lower edge of the choke plate and the air horn wall. With the fast idle screw held on the second step of the fast idle cam, measure the clearance between the tang of the choke lever and the arm on the fast idle cam. Adjust clearance by bending choke lever tang up or down as required. Refer to 5200 Specifications Chart.

Secondary Throttle Stop Screw Adjustment

Fig. 8—Back off the secondary throttle stop screw until the secondary throttle plate seats in its bore. Turn the screw in until it touches the tab on the secondary throttle lever. On all units except when used on 2800 cc engines, turn the screw inward an additional 1/4 turn. On units used on 2800 cc engines, turn screw inward an additional 3/4 turn.

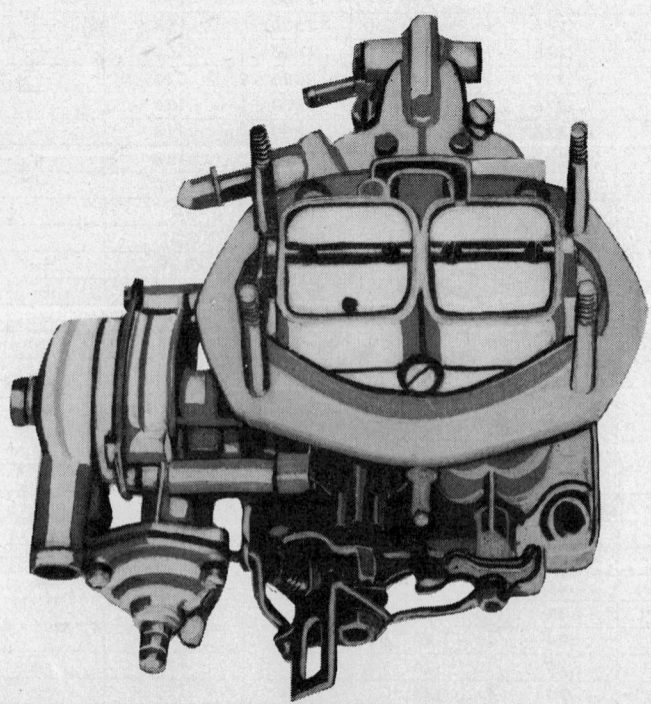

Fig. 1   Model 5200-2V carburetor

Fig. 4   Float adjusting point

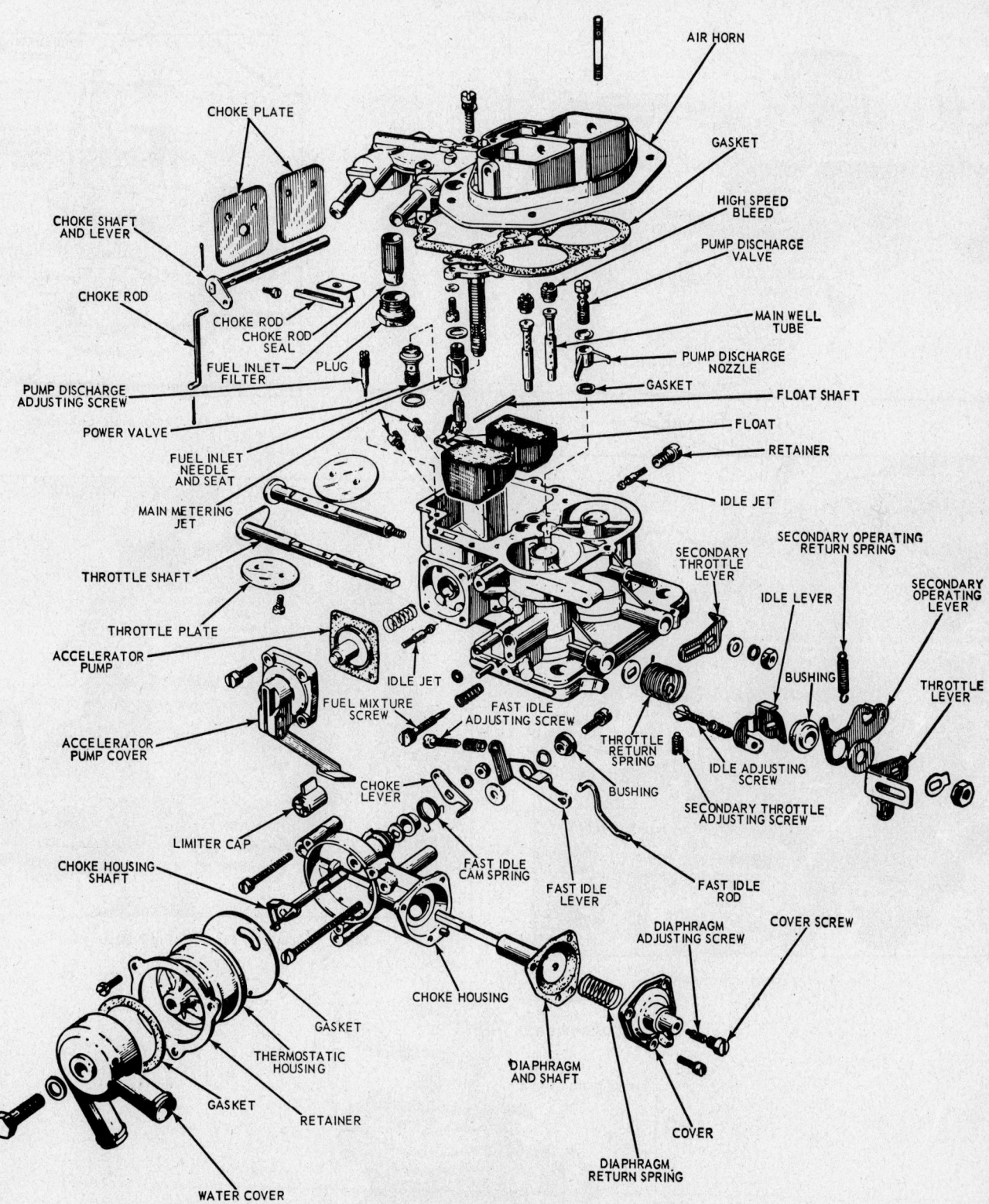

CHOKE PLATE

AIR HORN

GASKET

HIGH SPEED BLEED

PUMP DISCHARGE VALVE

CHOKE SHAFT AND LEVER

CHOKE ROD

CHOKE ROD
CHOKE ROD SEAL

FUEL INLET FILTER

PLUG

PUMP DISCHARGE ADJUSTING SCREW

POWER VALVE

FUEL INLET NEEDLE AND SEAT

MAIN METERING JET

THROTTLE SHAFT

THROTTLE PLATE

ACCELERATOR PUMP

ACCELERATOR PUMP COVER

LIMITER CAP

CHOKE HOUSING SHAFT

MAIN WELL TUBE

PUMP DISCHARGE NOZZLE

GASKET

FLOAT SHAFT

FLOAT

RETAINER

IDLE JET

SECONDARY OPERATING RETURN SPRING

SECONDARY THROTTLE LEVER

IDLE LEVER

SECONDARY OPERATING LEVER

BUSHING

THROTTLE LEVER

IDLE JET

FUEL MIXTURE SCREW

FAST IDLE ADJUSTING SCREW

THROTTLE RETURN SPRING

IDLE ADJUSTING SCREW

SECONDARY THROTTLE ADJUSTING SCREW

BUSHING

CHOKE LEVER

FAST IDLE CAM SPRING

FAST IDLE LEVER

FAST IDLE ROD

DIAPHRAGM ADJUSTING SCREW

COVER SCREW

CHOKE HOUSING

GASKET

THERMOSTATIC HOUSING

GASKET

RETAINER

DIAPHRAGM AND SHAFT

COVER

DIAPHRAGM RETURN SPRING

WATER COVER

**Fig. 2   Exploded view of model 5200 carburetor. All bolts and screws are Metric thread.
Early production Metric heads; later production U.S. heads**

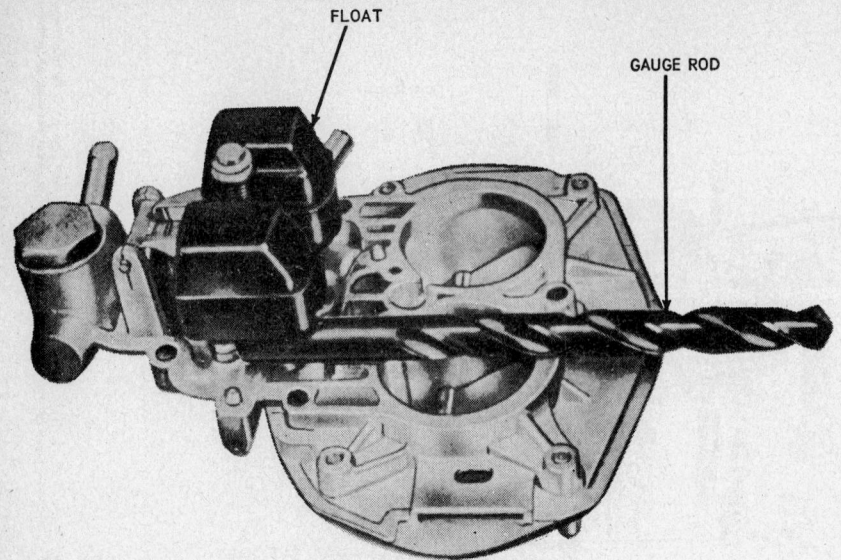

FLOAT

GAUGE ROD

Fig. 3   Dry float setting

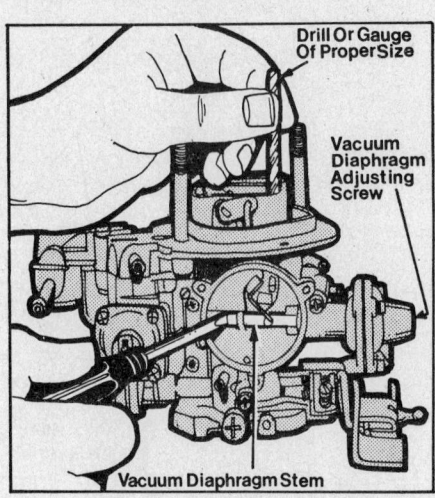

Drill Or Gauge Of Proper Size

Vacuum Diaphragm Adjusting Screw

Vacuum Diaphragm Stem

Fig. 6   Choke plate pull-down

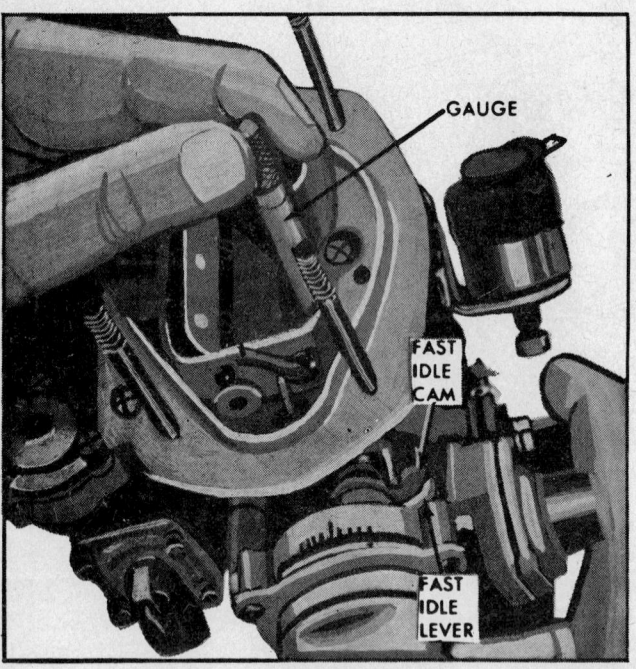

GAUGE

FAST IDLE CAM

FAST IDLE LEVER

Fig. 5   De-choke adjustment

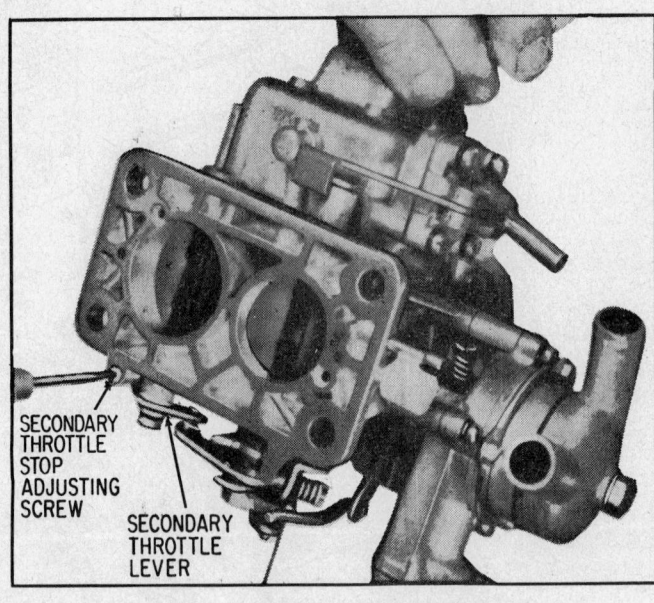

SECONDARY THROTTLE STOP ADJUSTING SCREW

SECONDARY THROTTLE LEVER

Fig. 8   Secondary throttle stop adjustment

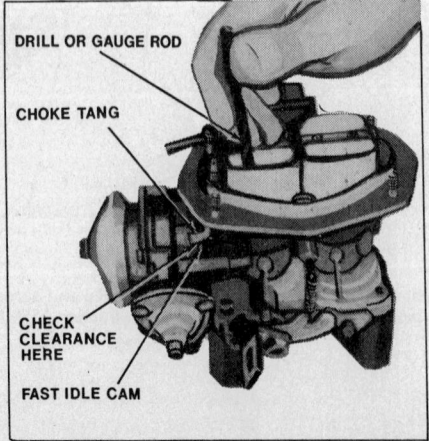

DRILL OR GAUGE ROD

CHOKE TANG

CHECK CLEARANCE HERE

FAST IDLE CAM

Fig. 7   Fast idle cam clearance

MODEL 2GC, 2GE, 2GV CARBURETOR ADJUSTMENT SPECIFICATIONS

See Tune Up Chart in car chapters for hot idle speeds.

Year	Carb. Production No.	Float Level	Float Drop	Pump Rod	Idle Vent	Intermediate Choke Rod	Vacuum Break Throttle Lever Side	Vacuum Break Choke Side	Choke Setting	Choke Rod	Choke Unloader
1974	7043060	21/32	1 9/32	1 11/32	—	.120	—	.160	1 Lean	.085	.180
	7043062, 063	21/32	1 9/32	1 5/16	—	.120	—	.170	1 Lean	.085	.180
	7043070	23/32	1 9/32	1 11/32	—	.120	—	.160	1 Lean	.085	.180
	7043071	23/32	1 9/32	1 5/16	—	.120	—	.200	1 Lean	.085	.180
	7043072	23/32	1 9/32	1 5/16	—	.120	—	.170	1 Lean	.085	.180
	7043119, 134	1 9/32	1 9/32	1 7/16	—	—	—	.130	—	.245	.325
	7044063	21/32	1 9/32	1 5/16	—	.120	—	.160	1 Lean	.085	.180
	7044065, 066	21/32	1 9/32	1 11/32	—	.120	—	.180	1 Lean	.085	.180
	7044067	21/32	1 9/32	1 11/32	—	.120	—	.180	1 Lean	.085	.180
	7044111, 113	1 9/32	1 9/32	1 1/2	—	—	—	.140	—	.200	.250
	7044112, 114	1 9/32	1 9/32	1 9/16	—	—	—	.130	—	.245	.325
	7044115, 117	1 9/32	1 9/32	1 21/32	—	—	—	.140	—	.200	.250
	7044116, 118	1 9/32	1 9/32	1 9/16	—	—	—	.130	—	.245	.325
	7044120	1 9/32	1 9/32	1 21/32	—	—	—	.130	—	.200	.250
	7044121, 123	1 9/32	1 9/32	1 21/32	—	—	—	.140	—	.200	.250
	7044124	1 9/32	1 9/32	1 9/16	—	—	—	.130	—	.200	.325
	7044125, 126	1 9/32	1 9/32	1 21/32	—	—	—	.140	—	.200	.250
	7044127, 129	1 9/32	1 9/32	1 21/32	—	—	—	.140	—	.200	.250
	7044141	15/32	1 9/32	1 15/32	—	—	.160	.120	—	.080	.180
	7044142, 144	15/32	1 9/32	1 15/32	—	—	.140	.120	—	.080	.180
	7044442, 444	15/32	1 9/32	1 15/32	—	—	.150	.120	—	.080	.180
1975	7045101	17/32	1 7/32	1 5/8	—	.120	—	.130	3 Rich	.400	.330
	7045102	17/32	1 7/32	1 5/8	—	.120	—	.130	Index	.400	.330
	7045105	9/16	1 7/32	1 5/8	—	.120	—	.130	3 Rich	.400	.330
	7045106	9/16	1 7/32	1 5/8	—	.120	—	.130	Index	.400	.330
	7045111	11/16	1 1/4	1 5/8	—	.120	—	.130	Index	.400	.330
	7045112, 114	11/16	1 1/4	1 5/8	—	.120	—	.130	Index	.400	.350
	7045115	11/16	1 1/4	1 5/8	—	.120	—	.130	Index	.400	.350
	7045123, 124	11/16	1 1/4	1 5/8	—	.120	—	.130	Index	.400	.350
	7045140, 143	15/32	1 9/32	1 19/32	①	.120	.140	.120	1 Rich	.080	.180
	7045145	7/16	1 9/32	1 19/32	—	.120	.180	.120	1 Lean	.080	.140
	7045147	7/16	1 9/32	1 19/32	—	.120	.120	.120	1 Lean	.080	.140
	7045148, 149	7/16	1 9/32	1 19/32	—	.120	.120	.120	1 Rich	.080	.140
	7045160, 161	9/16	1 7/32	1 11/32	①	.120	.145	.265	1 Rich	.085	.180
	7045162	9/16	1 7/32	1 9/32	①	.120	.145	.260	1 Rich	.085	.180
	7045163	9/16	1 7/32	1 11/32	①	.120	.145	.265	1 Rich	.085	.180
	7045167	9/16	1 7/32	1 5/16	①	.120	.145	.310	1 Rich	.085	.180
	7045171	9/16	1 7/32	1 9/32	①	.120	.145	.260	1 Rich	.085	.180
	7045173	9/16	1 7/32	1 11/32	①	.120	.145	.265	1 Rich	.085	.180
	7045401	21/32	1 7/32	1 19/32	—	.120	—	.130	Index	.380	.350
	7045402	21/32	1 7/32	1 19/32	—	.120	—	.130	Index	.375	.350
	7045405, 406	21/32	Float	1 19/32	—	.120	—	.130	Index	.380	.350
	7045441	7/16	1 9/32	1 19/32	—	.120	.130	.110	1 Rich	.080	.180
	7045447, 448	7/16	1 9/32	1 19/32	—	.120	.120	.120	1 Lean	.080	.140
	7045449	7/16	1 9/32	1 19/32	—	.120	.120	.120	1 Lean	.080	.140
1976	17056101, 102	17/32	1 9/32	1 21/32	—	.120	—	.130	Index	.260	.325
	17056103	17/32	1 9/32	1 21/32	—	.120	—	.130	Index	.260	.325
	17056104, 105	17/32	1 9/32	1 21/32	—	.120	—	.140	Index	.260	.325
	17056108, 109	9/16	1 5/32	1 21/32	—	.120	—	.140	Index	.260	.325
	17056110, 112	9/16	1 5/32	1 21/32	—	.120	—	.140	Index	.260	.325
	17056111, 113	9/16	1 5/32	1 11/16	—	.120	—	.130	Index	.260	.325
	17056114	11/16	1 7/32	1 11/16	—	.120	—	.130	1 Rich	.260	.325
	17056121, 122	11/16	1 9/32	1 21/32	—	.120	—	.130	Index	.260	.325
	17056132	11/16	1 9/32	1 21/32	—	.120	—	.130	Index	.260	.325

Continued

MODEL 2GC, 2GE, 2GV CARBURETOR ADJUSTMENT SPECIFICATIONS—Continued

See Tune Up Chart in car chapters for hot idle speeds.

Year	Carb. Production No.	Float Level	Float Drop	Pump Rod	Idle Vent	Intermediate Choke Rod	Vacuum Break Throttle Lever Side	Vacuum Break Choke Side	Choke Setting	Choke Rod	Choke Unloader
1976	17056140, 143	15/32	15/32	1 9/16	①	.120	.140	.100	1 Rich	.080	.180
	17056141	15/32	15/32	1 5/8	①	.120	.200	.030	1 Rich	.080	.180
	17056144	15/32	15/32	1 5/8	①	.120	.180	.030	1 Rich	.080	.180
	17056145	7/16	15/32	1 19/32	—	.120	.110	.100	1 Rich	.080	.140
	17056146, 148	7/16	15/32	1 19/32	—	.120	.120	.100	1 Rich	.080	.140
	17056149	7/16	15/32	1 19/32	—	.120	.120	.100	1 Rich	.080	.140
	17056160, 161	9/16	1 9/32	1 11/32	①	.120	.165	.285	1 Rich	.085	.180
	17056162, 164	9/16	1 9/32	1 11/32	①	.120	.165	.285	1 Rich	.085	.180
	17056163	9/16	1 9/32	1 11/32	①	.120	.145	.285	1 Rich	.085	.180
	17056402	17/32	1 9/32	1 21/32	—	.120	—	.130	1 Rich	.260	.325
	17056404, 405	17/32	1 9/32	1 21/32	—	.120	—	.140	Index	.260	.325
	17056408	9/16	15/32	1 21/32	—	.120	—	.140	Index	.260	.325
	17056410, 412	9/16	1 9/32	1 11/16	—	.120	—	.140	Index	.260	.325
	17056430	9/16	15/32	1 21/32	—	.120	—	.140	Index	.260	.325
	17056432	9/16	1 9/32	1 21/32	—	.120	—	.140	Index	.260	.325
	17056446, 447	7/16	15/32	1 19/32	—	.120	.130	.110	1 Rich	.080	.140
	17056448, 449	7/16	15/32	1 19/32	—	.120	.130	.110	1 Rich	.080	.140
1977	17057104, 105	7/16	1 9/32	1 21/32	—	.120	—	②	Index	.260	.325
	17057107, 109	7/16	1 9/32	1 17/32	—	.120	—	②	Index	.260	.325
	17057108, 110	19/32	1 9/32	1 21/32	—	.120	—	②	Index	.260	.325
	17057111, 113	19/32	1 9/32	1 17/32	—	.120	—	②	Index	.260	.325
	17057112	19/32	1 9/32	1 21/32	—	.120	—	②	Index	.260	.325
	17057114	19/32	1 9/32	1 17/32	—	.120	—	②	Index	.260	.325
	17057121, 123	19/32	1 9/32	1 17/32	—	.120	—	②	Index	.260	.325
	17057140	15/32	15/32	1 9/32	—	.120	.140	.100	1 Rich	.080	.180
	17057141, 145	7/16	15/32	1 1/2	—	.120	.110	.040	1 Rich	.080	.140
	17057143, 144	7/16	15/32	1 17/32	—	.120	.130	.100	1 Rich	.080	.140
	17057146, 148	7/16	15/32	1 17/32	—	.120	.100	.040	3 Rich	.080	.140
	17057147	7/16	15/32	1 1/2	—	.120	.110	.040	1 Rich	.080	.140
	17057149	7/16	15/32	1 9/16	—	.120	.110	.040	1 Lean	.080	.140
	17057180, 182	7/16	15/32	1 17/32	—	.120	.110	.060	1 Rich	.080	.140
	17057188, 190	19/32	1 9/32	1 21/32	—	.120	—	②	Index	.260	.325
	17057192, 194	19/32	1 9/32	1 21/32	—	.120	—	②	Index	.260	.325
	17057404	1/2	1 9/32	1 21/32	—	.120	—	③	1/2 Lean	.260	.325
	17057405	1/2	1 9/32	1 5/8	—	.120	—	③	1/2 Lean	.260	.325
	17057408, 410	21/32	1 9/32	1 5/8	—	.120	—	③	1 Lean	.260	.325

Continued

MODEL 2GC, 2GE, 2GV CARBURETOR ADJUSTMENT SPECIFICATIONS—Continued

See Tune Up Chart in car chapters for hot idle speeds.

Year	Carb. Production No.	Float Level	Float Drop	Pump Rod	Idle Vent	Intermediate Choke Rod	Vacuum Break Throttle Lever Side	Vacuum Break Choke Side	Choke Setting	Choke Rod	Choke Unloader
1977	17057412	21/32	1 9/32	1 5/8	—	.120	—	③	1 Lean	.260	.325
	17057414	21/32	1 9/32	1 21/32	—	.120	—	③	1 Lean	.260	.325
	17057445	7/16	1 5/32	1 1/2	—	.120	.140	.110	1 Lean	.080	.140
	17057446, 447	7/16	1 5/32	1 1/2	—	.120	.130	.110	1 Rich	.080	.140
	17057448	7/16	1 5/32	1 1/2	—	.120	.130	.110	1 Rich	.080	.140
1978	17058102, 103	15/32	1 9/32	1 17/32	—	.120	—	④	Index	.260	.325
	17058104, 105	15/32	1 9/32	1 21/32	—	.120	—	②	Index	.260	.325
	17058107, 109	15/32	1 9/32	1 17/32	—	.120	—	②	Index	.260	.325
	17058108, 110	19/32	1 9/32	1 21/32	—	.120	—	④	Index	.260	.325
	17058111	15/32	1 9/32	1 17/32	—	.120	—	②	Index	.260	.325
	17058112, 114	19/32	1 9/32	1 21/32	—	.120	—	④	Index	.260	.325
	17058113	19/32	1 9/32	1 17/32	—	.120	—	②	Index	.260	.325
	17058121, 123	19/32	1 9/32	1 17/32	—	.120	—	②	Index	.260	.325
	17058126, 128	19/32	1 9/32	1 17/32	—	.120	—	.130	Index	.260	.325
	17058140	7/16	1 5/32	1 19/32	—	.120	.110	.070	1 Rich	.080	.140
	17058141	7/16	1 5/32	1 19/32	①	.120	.140	.100	1 Rich	.080	.140
	17058143	7/16	1 5/32	1 9/16	①	.120	.110	.080	1 Rich	.080	.140
	17058144	7/16	1 5/32	1 5/8	①	.120	.110	.060	1 Rich	.080	.140
	17058145	7/16	1 5/32	1 19/32	①	.120	.110	.060	1 Rich	.080	.140
	17058147	7/16	1 5/32	1 19/32	①	.120	.140	.100	1 Rich	.080	.140
	17058148, 149	7/16	1 5/32	1 19/32	①	.120	.110	.080	1 Rich	.080	.140
	17058182, 183	7/16	1 5/32	1 19/32	①	.120	.110	.080	1 Rich	.080	.140
	17058185	7/16	1 5/32	1 19/32	①	.120	.110	.050	1 Rich	.080	.140
	17058187, 189	7/16	1 5/32	1 19/32	①	.120	.110	.080	1 Rich	.080	.140
	17058188	7/16	1 5/32	1 19/32	①	.120	.120	.050	1 Rich	.080	.140
	17058404, 405	1/2	1 9/32	1 21/32	—	.120	—	③	1/2 Lean	.260	.325
	17058408, 410	21/32	1 9/32	1 21/32	—	.120	—	③	1/2 Lean	.260	.325
	17058412, 414	21/32	1 9/32	1 21/32	—	.120	—	③	1/2 Lean	.260	.325
	17058444	7/16	1 5/32	1 19/32	①	.120	.140	.100	1 Rich	.080	.140
	17058446	7/16	1 5/32	1 19/32	①	.120	.130	.110	1 Rich	.080	.140
	17058447	7/16	1 5/32	1 19/32	①	.120	.150	.110	1 Rich	.080	.140
	17058448	7/16	1 5/32	1 19/32	①	.120	.140	.110	1 Rich	.080	.140

①—With idle speed properly adjusted, the vent valve should be just closed at idle.
②—.130 inch before first scheduled tune-up; .160 inch after first scheduled tune-up.
③—.140 inch before first scheduled tune-up; .160 inch after first scheduled tune-up.
④—.130 inch before first scheduled tune-up; .150 inch after first scheduled tune-up.

MODEL 2GC, 2GE, 2GV ADJUSTMENTS

Models 2GC, 2GE and 2GV use an automatic choke, Figs. 1 and 2.

There are two different types of automatic choke systems used on these units; 1) The carburetor mounted thermostatic coil, Fig. 3 and, 2) the well type, Fig. 4.

Float Level Adjustment

Figs. 5 & 6—Adjust float level as directed for the type of float shown in the specification listed in the *Rochester Specifications Chart*.

Float Drop Adjustment

Figs. 7 & 8—Adjust float drop as directed for the type of float shown in the specification listed in the *Rochester Specifications Chart*.

Pump Rod Adjustment

Fig. 9—Back out idle stop screw and completely close throttle valves in bore. Place proper size gauge listed in the *Rochester Specifications Chart* on top of air horn ring. Bend pump rod at lower angle to obtain specified dimension to top of pump rod.

Idle Vent Adjustment

Fig. 10—Open throttle until vent valve just closes. Place proper size gauge on top of air horn ring. Dimension to top of pump rod should be as specified in the *Rochester Specifications Chart*. Adjust by bending tang on pump lever.

Bowl Vent Adjustment

Fig. 11—Set idle speed to specifications, then with idle screw on second step of fast idle cam, vent valve should just be closed. To adjust, turn vent valve screw.

Intermediate Choke Rod Adjustment

2GC & 2GE Models, Fig. 12—Remove thermostat cover and coil assembly, then with fast idle screw on high step of cam and choke valve closed, the edge of choke lever must align with edge of .120″ plug gauge as shown. To adjust, bend choke rod at point shown.

Vacuum Break Adjustment

Figs. 13 & 14—Place fast idle screw on high step of cam, then using an outside vacuum source, seat vacuum diaphragm. On purge type vacuum diaphragms, cover bleed hole so that diaphragm will not bleed down. Hold choke towards closed position, then with vacuum diaphragm seated and rod in end of slot in plunger, check clearance between upper edge of choke valve and air horn wall. Refer to *Rochester Specifications Chart*. To adjust, bend vacuum break rod at point shown.

Automatic Choke Setting

Carburetor Mounted Choke, Fig. 15—Place idle screw on high step of fast idle cam, then loosen three retaining screws and rotate choke cover against coil tension until index mark is in line with specified point on choke housing (see *Rochester Specifications Chart*).

Choke Rod Adjustment

Fig. 16—It is important to position both slow idle and fast idle screws as follows

Fig. 1   Rochester Model 2GV two-barrel carburetor (typical)

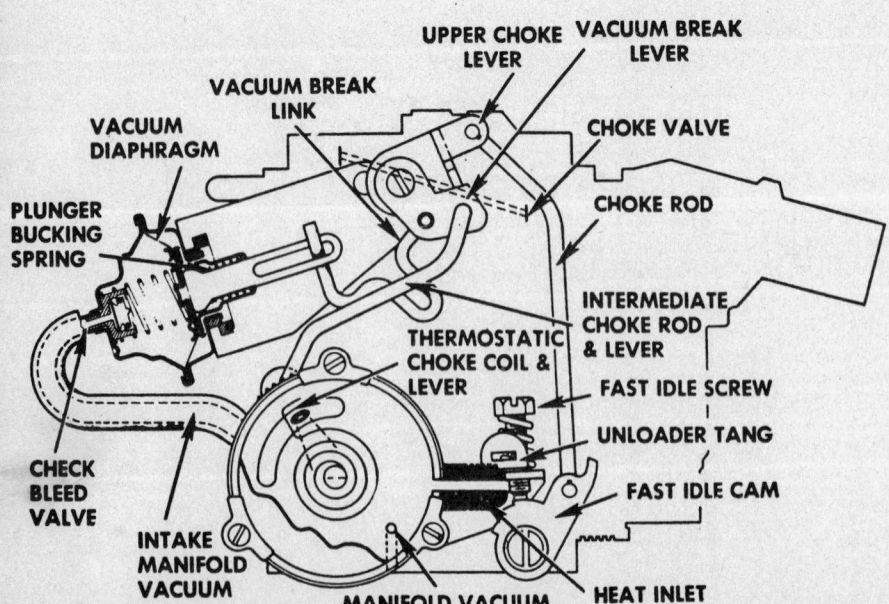

Fig. 3   Carburetor mounted automatic choke

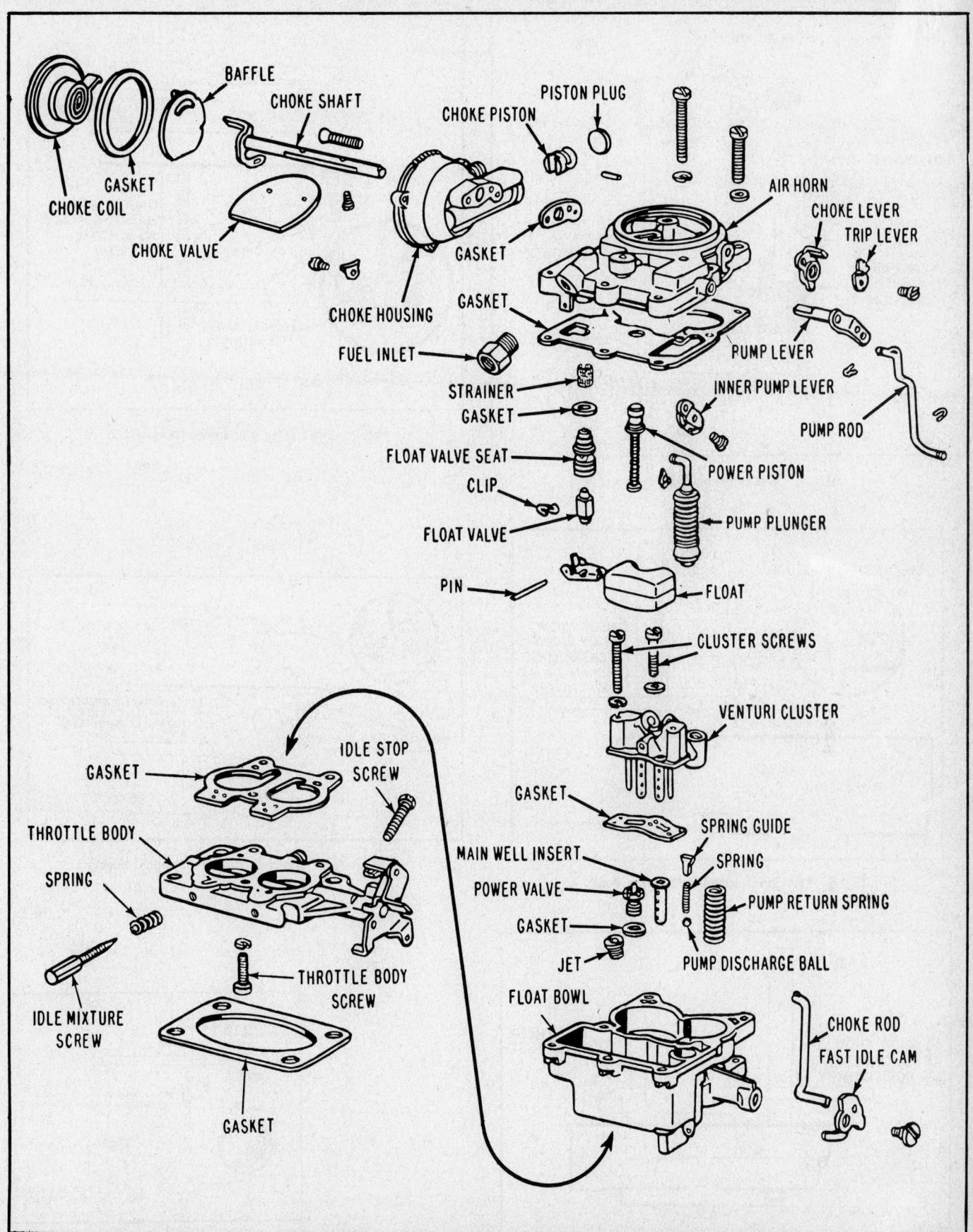

Fig. 2   Exploded view of typical Rochester two-barrel carburetor

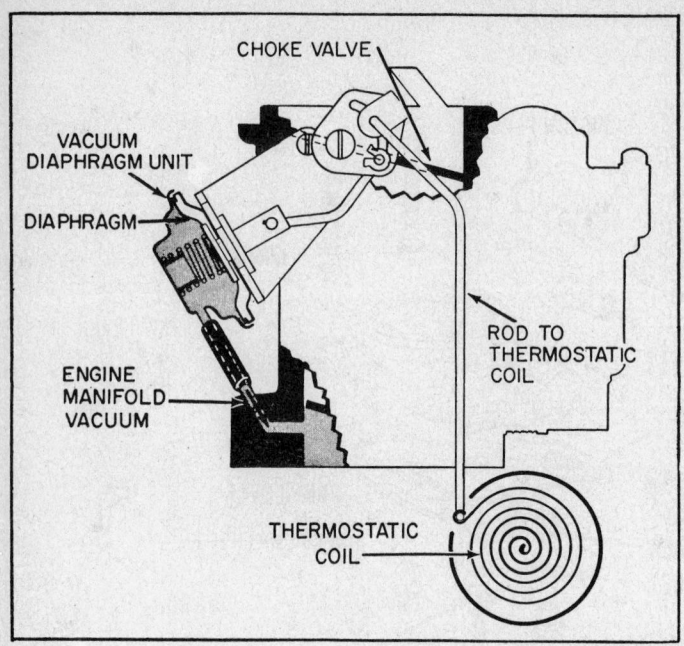

Fig. 4   Well-type choke. 2GV models

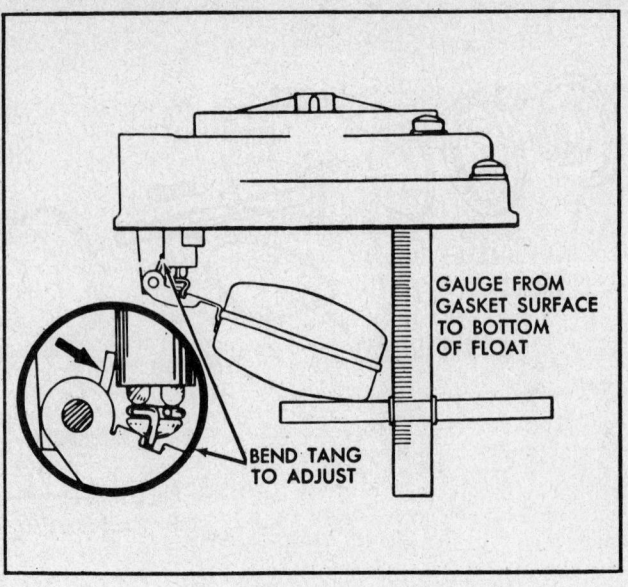

Fig. 7   Float drop adjustment (brass float)

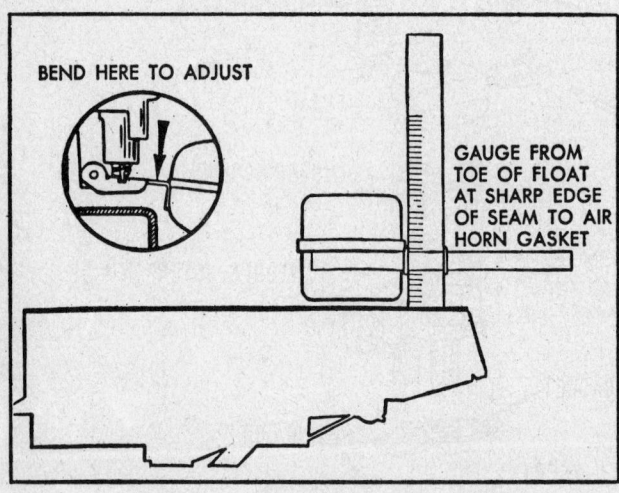

Fig. 5   Float level adjustment (brass float)

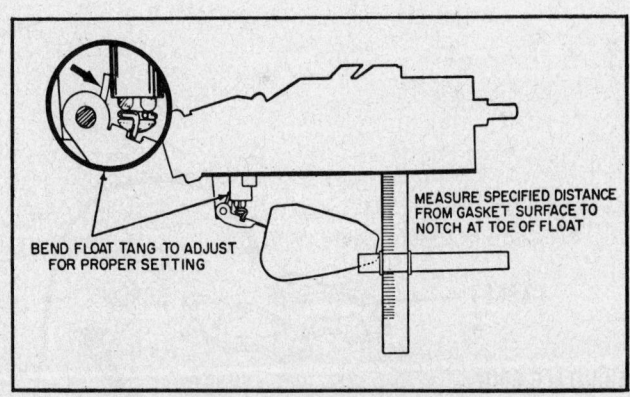

Fig. 8   Float drop adjustment (nitrophyl float)

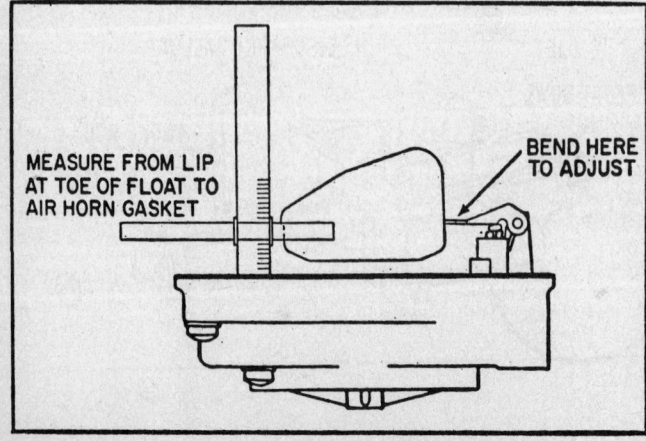

Fig. 6   Float level adjustment (nitrophyl float)

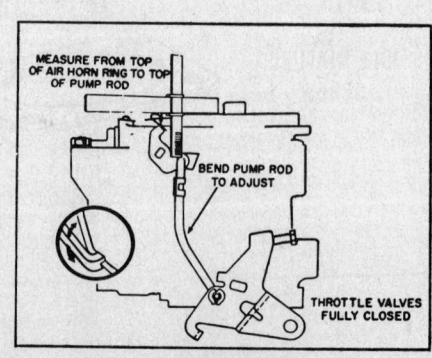

Fig. 9   Pump rod adjustment

before making choke rod adjustment.

1. On models using a single idle stop screw, turn stop screw in until it just contacts bottom step of fast idle cam. Then turn screw in one full turn farther.

2. On models using both a slow idle and a fast idle screw, turn slow idle stop screw in until it just contacts stop. Then turn this screw in one full turn from this point. Next turn the fast idle screw in until it touches bottom step of fast idle cam.

3. On all models, place idle screw on second step of fast idle cam against shoulder of high step. While holding screw in this position, check clearance between upper edge of choke valve and air horn wall as shown. Adjust to specified dimension by bending tang on choke lever and collar assembly (see *Rochester Specifications Chart*).

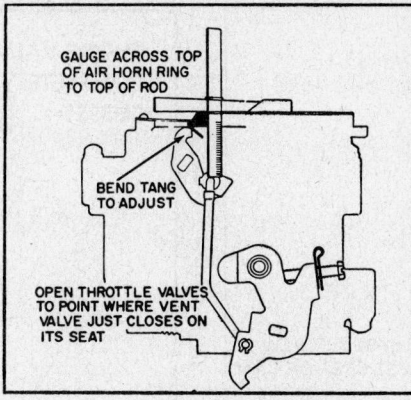

Fig. 10 Idle vent adjustment for 2GC, 2GV carburetors

Choke Unloader Adjustment

Fig. 17—With throttle valves held wide open, the choke valve should be open just enough to admit the specified gauge between upper edge of choke valve and air horn wall (see *Rochester Specifications Chart*). To adjust, bend tang on throttle lever.

Thermostatic Coil Rod Adjustment

1974 Buick, Fig. 18—Disconnect upper end of thermostatic coil rod from choke. Hold choke valve completely closed and pull upward on coil rod to end of its travel. Rod should just fit into notch in lever as shown. To adjust, bend rod at point shown.

1974 Chevrolet, Fig. 19—Disconnect upper end of coil rod from choke lever. Hold choke valve completely open and push downward on coil rod to end of its travel. On 1974 Chevrolet, rod should fit in bottom of slot in lever. To adjust, bend lever with screwdriver in slot as shown.

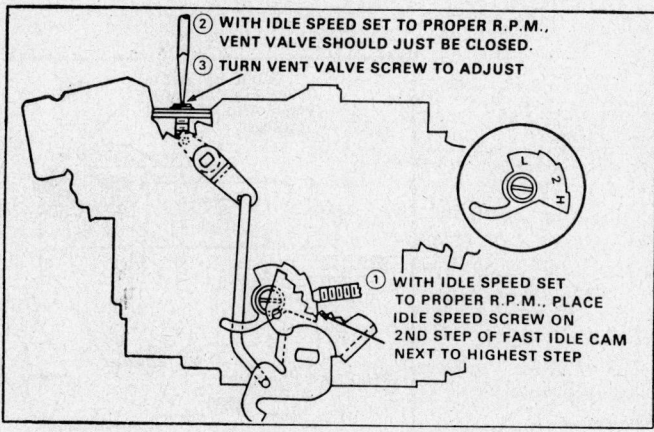

Fig. 11 Bowl vent adjustment

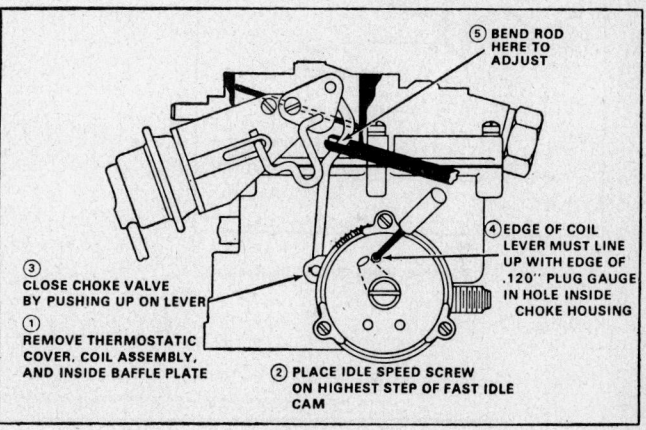

Fig. 12 Intermediate choke rod adjustment

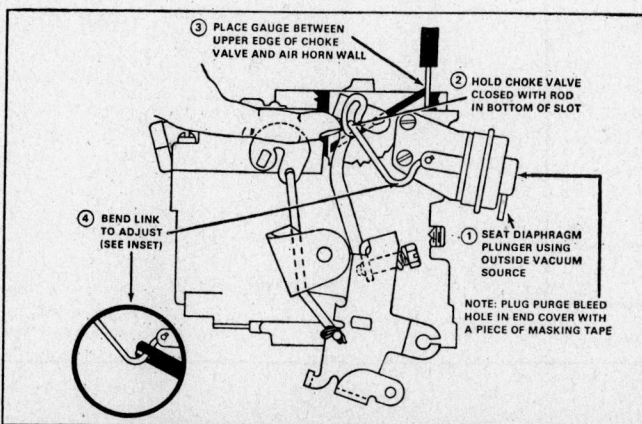

Fig. 13 Primary (throttle lever side) vacuum break adjustment

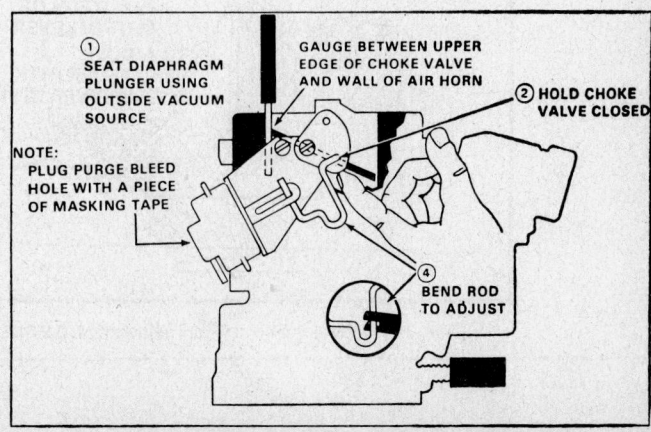

Fig. 14 Auxiliary (choke side) vacuum break adjustment

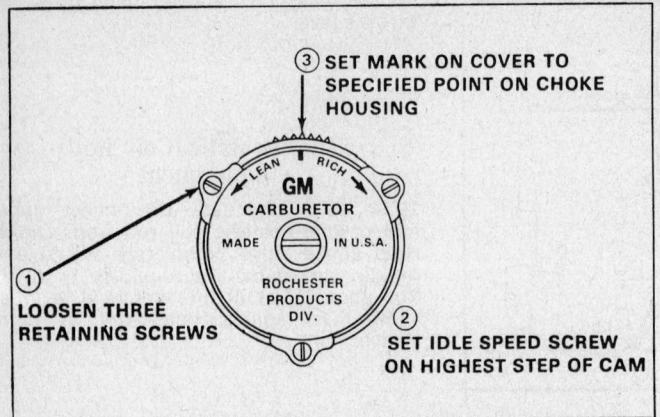

Fig. 15   Automatic choke adjustment for 2GC, 2GE carburetors

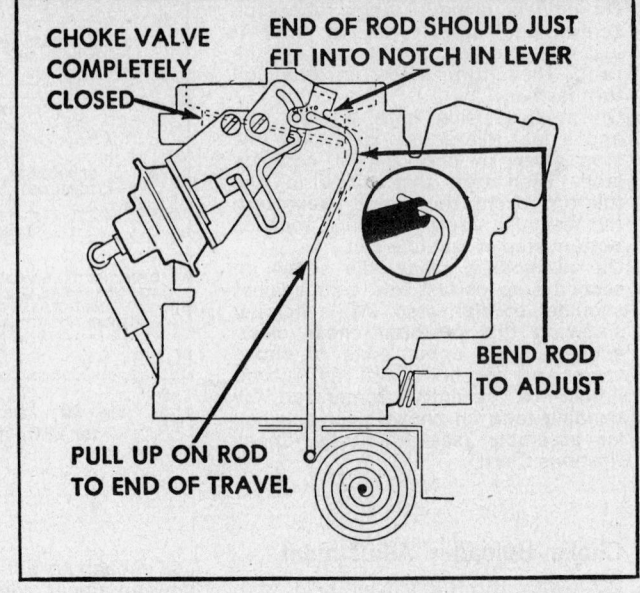

Fig. 18   Thermostatic coil rod adjustment. 1974 Buick

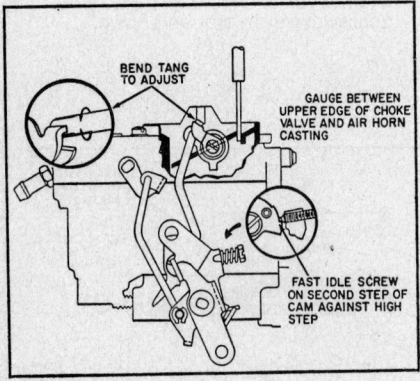

Fig. 16   Choke rod adjustment

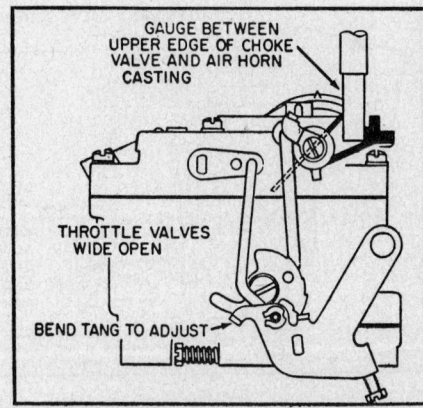

Fig. 17   Choke unloader adjustment for 2GC, 2GE, 2GV carburetors

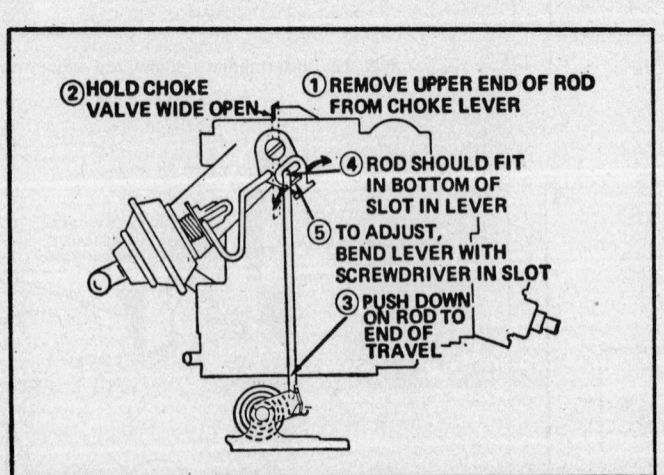

Fig. 19   Thermostatic coil rod adjustment. 1974 Chevrolet

QUADRAJET 4MC & 4MV ADJUSTMENT SPECIFICATIONS

See Tune Up Chart in car chapters for hot idle speeds.

Year	Carb. Model	Float Level	Pump Rod Hole	Pump Rod Adj.	Fast Idle (Bench)	Choke Rod	Vacuum Break	Air Valve Dash-pot	Choke Setting	Choke Unloader	Air Valve Lockout	Secondary Metering Rods	Air-Valve Valve Spring Wind-Up
BUICK													
1974	7044240	13/32	Inner	1/4	2	.130	.215②	.030	—	.325	.015	53/64	7/16
	7044241	13/32	Inner	1/4	2	.130	.215②	.030	—	.325	.015	53/64	7/16
	7044242	13/32	Inner	1/4	2	.130	.200④	.030	—	.325	.015	53/64	7/16
	7044244	15/32	Outer	3/8	2	.130	.170①	.030	—	.325	.015	53/64	11/16
	7044246	15/32	Outer	3/8	2	.130	.170①	.030	—	.325	.015	53/64	11/16
	7044540	13/32	Inner	1/4	2	.130	.215②	.030	—	.325	.015	53/64	7/16
	7044544	15/32	Outer	3/8	2	.130	.170①	.030	—	.325	.015	53/64	11/16
	7044546	15/32	Outer	3/8	2	.130	.170①	.030	—	.325	.015	53/64	11/16

①—Secondary adjustment .150″.   ②—Secondary adjustment .160″.   ③—Secondary adjustment .195″.   ④—Secondary adjustment .180″.

Year	Carb. Model	Float Level	Pump Rod Hole	Pump Rod Adj.	Fast Idle (Bench)	Choke Rod	Vacuum Break	Air Valve Dash-pot	Choke Setting	Choke Unloader	Air Valve Lockout	Secondary Metering Rods	Air-Valve Valve Spring Wind-Up
CADILLAC													
1974	7044230	1/4	Inner	1/4	1½ Turns	.110	.185	.025	—	.300	.030	.840	3/8
	7044232	3/8	Inner	1/4	1½ Turns	.110	.200	.025	—	.300	.030	.840	1/2
	7044233	9/32	Outer	11/32	1½ Turns	.110	.185	.025	—	.300	.030	.840	3/8
	7044234	1/4	Outer	11/32	1½ Turns	.090	.200	.025	—	.300	.030	.840	5/16
	7044235	3/8	Outer	11/32	1½ Turns	.090	.200	.025	—	.300	.030	.840	3/8
	7044530	1/4	Inner	1/4	1½ Turns	.110	.185	.025	—	.300	.030	.840	3/8
	7044532	3/8	Inner	1/4	1½ Turns	.110	.200	.025	—	.300	.030	.840	1/2
CHECKER MOTORS													
1974	7044502	1/4	Inner	—	—	.430	.230	—	—	.450	—	—	7/8
1976–77	7045583	11/32	Inner	.275	—	.430	.230	.015	—	.450	—	—	7/8
CHEVROLET ENGINES													
1974	7044201	3/8	Inner	13/32	2 Turns	.430	.250	.015	—	.450	—	—	7/16
	7044202	1/4	Inner	13/32	2 Turns	.430	.230	.015	—	.450	—	—	7/8
	7044203	1/4	Inner	13/32	2 Turns	.430	.230	.015	—	.450	—	—	7/8
	7044206	1/4	Inner	13/32	2 Turns	.430	.230	.015	—	.450	—	—	7/8
	7044207	1/4	Inner	13/32	2 Turns	.430	.230	.015	—	.450	—	—	7/8
	7044208	1/4	Inner	13/32	2 Turns	.430	.230	.015	—	.450	—	—	1 Turn
	7044209	1/4	Inner	13/32	2 Turns	.430	.230	.015	—	.450	—	—	1 Turn
	7044210	1/4	Inner	13/32	2 Turns	.430	.230	.015	—	.450	—	—	1 Turn
	7044211	1/4	Inner	13/32	2 Turns	.430	.230	.015	—	.450	—	—	1 Turn
	7044221	3/8	Inner	13/32	2 Turns	.430	.250	.015	—	.450	—	—	7/16
	7044223	3/8	Inner	13/32	2 Turns	.430	.220	.015	—	.450	—	—	7/16
	7044225	3/8	Inner	13/32	2 Turns	.430	.220	.015	—	.450	—	—	7/16
	7044226	1/4	Inner	13/32	2 Turns	.430	.230	.015	—	.450	—	—	3/4
	7044500	3/8	Inner	13/32	2 Fast	.430	.250	.015	—	.450	—	—	7/16
	7044502	1/4	Inner	13/32	2 Turns	.430	.230	.015	—	.450	—	—	7/8
	7044503	1/4	Inner	13/32	2 Turns	.430	.230	.015	—	.450	—	—	7/8
	7044505	3/8	Inner	—	2 Turns	.430	.250	.015	—	.450	—	—	7/16
	7044506	1/4	Inner	13/32	2 Turns	.430	.230	.015	—	.450	—	—	7/8
	7044507	1/4	Inner	13/32	2 Turns	.430	.230	.015	—	.450	—	—	7/8
	7044508	3/8	Inner	13/32	2 Turns	.430	.250	.015	—	.450	—	—	7/16
	7044509	1/4	Inner	13/32	2 Turns	.430	.230	.015	—	.450	—	—	7/8
	7044526	1/4	Inner	13/32	2 Turns	.430	.230	.015	—	.450	—	—	3/4

Continued

GM DELCO/ROCHESTER CARBURETORS

QUADRAJET 4MC & 4MV ADJUSTMENT SPECIFICATIONS—Continued

See Tune Up Chart in car chapters for hot idle speeds.

Year	Carb. Model	Float Level	Pump Rod Hole	Pump Rod Adj.	Fast Idle (Bench)	Choke Rod	Vacuum Break	Air Valve Dash-pot	Choke Setting	Choke Unloader	Air Valve Lockout	Secondary Metering Rods	Air-Valve Valve Spring Wind-Up
OLDSMOBILE													
1974	7043250	¼	Inner	—	2 Turns	.230	.200	.030	Index	.300	.035	—	½
	7043251	¼	Inner	—	2 Turns	.230	.200	.030	Index	.300	.035	—	¾
	7043252	¼	Inner	—	2 Turns	.230	.200	.030	1 Rich	.300	.035	—	¾
	7043255	¼	Inner	—	2 Turns	.230	.200	.030	Index	.300	.035	—	½
	7043256	¼	Inner	—	2 Turns	.230	.200	.030	Index	.300	.035	—	½
	7043257	¼	Inner	—	2 Turns	.230	.200	.030	Index	.300	.035	—	½
	7043259	¼	Inner	⅜	—	.230	.200	.030	Index	.300	.035	.070	—
	7044152	—	—	—	—	—	.200	—	—	—	—	—	—
	7044557	¼	Inner	⅜	2 Turns	.230	.200	.030	1 Rich	.300	.035	.070	¾
	7044558	¼	Inner	⅜	2 Turns	.230	.200	.030	Index	.300	.035	.070	¾
	7044559	¼	Inner	⅜	2 Turns	.230	.275	.030	Index	.275	.035	.070	¾
PONTIAC													
1974	7043263	¹³⁄₃₂	Inner	.410	—	.205	.290	.025	Index	.310	.015	—	⅝
	7044262	¹³⁄₃₂	Inner	.410	2 Turns	.200	.260	.025	Index	.300	.010	—	⅜
	7044266	¹³⁄₃₂	Inner	.410	2 Turns	.200	.260	.025	Index	.300	.010	—	½
	7044267	¹³⁄₃₂	Inner	.410	—	.205	.260	.025	—	.310	.015	—	⅜
	7044268	¹³⁄₃₂	Inner	.410	2 Turns	.200	.260	.025	—	.300	.010	—	½
	7044269	¹³⁄₃₂	Inner	.410	2 Turns	.200	.290	.025	—	.300	.010	—	½
	7044270	¹³⁄₃₂	Inner	.410	2 Turns	.200	.290	.025	—	.300	.010	—	¾
	7044272	¹³⁄₃₂	Outer	.315	2 Turns	.200	.290	.025	—	.300	.010	—	⅜
	7044273	¹³⁄₃₂	Inner	.410	2 Turns	.200	.290	.025	—	.300	.010	—	¾
	7044274	¹³⁄₃₂	Outer	.315	2 Turns	.200	.290	.025	—	.300	.010	—	⁹⁄₁₆
	7044560	¹³⁄₃₂	Inner	.410	2 Turns	.200	.260	.025	—	.300	.010	—	⅜
	7044568	¹³⁄₃₂	Inner	.410	2 Turns	.200	.260	.025	—	.300	.010	—	½

QUADRAJET 4MV, 4MC ADJUSTMENTS

The Quadrajet unit, Figs. 1, 2, has two stages in operation. The primary (fuel inlet) side has small bores with a triple venturi equipped with plain tube nozzles. The triple venturi feature, plus the smaller primary bores, give a more stable and finer fuel control in the idle and economy ranges of operation. Fuel metering in the primary side is accomplished with tapered metering rods positioned by a manifold vacuum responsive piston.

The secondary side has two very large bores which have greatly increased air capacity to meet all engine demands. The air valve principle is used in the secondary side for metering control and supplements fuel flow from the primary bores.

Using the air valve principle, fuel is metered in direct proportion to the air passing through the secondary bores.

The fuel reservoir is centrally located to avoid problems of fuel slosh causing engine turn cut-out and delayed fuel flow to the carburetor bores. The float system uses a single float pontoon for ease of service. The float needle valve is pressure balanced to overcome problems encountered with high fuel pump pressures and to permit use of a small float to control fuel "shut-off" through the large fuel inlet needle seat. It has a synthetic tip which gives added insurance against flooding problems casued by dirt.

The primary side of the carburetor has six systems of operation: float, idle, main metering, power, pump and choke. The secondary side has one metering system which supplements the primary main metering system and receives fuel from a common float chamber.

Model 4MV Choke System

Fig. 3—The choke system consists of a choke valve located in the primary air horn bore, a vacuum diaphragm unit, fast idle cam, connecting linkage, air valve lockout lever and a thermostatic coil. Some applications may use a split choke pick-up spring or a vacuum break modulating spring. The thermostatic coil is located in the engine manifold and is connected to the intermediate choke shaft and lever assembly. Choke operation is controlled by a combination of engine intake manifold vacuum, the offset choke valve, temperature and throttle position.

Model 4MC Choke System

Fig. 4—The choke consists of a choke valve located in the primary air horn bore, a choke housing and vacuum diaphragm assembly, fast idle cam, connecting linkage, air valve lockout lever, and thermostatic coil. Choke operation is controlled by a combination of intake manifold vacuum, the offset choke valve, temperature, and throttle position.

Air Valve Operation

Fig. 5—When the engine reaches a point where the primary bores cannot meet engine air and fuel demands, the primary throttle lever, through connecting linkage to the secondary throttle shaft lever, begins to open the secondary throttle valves. As air flow through the secondary bores creates a low pressure (vacuum) beneath the air valve, atmospheric pressure on top of the air valve forces the air valve open against spring tension. This allows the required air for increased engine speed to flow past the air valve.

Air Valve Dashpot Operation

Fig. 6—The secondary air valve has an attached piston assembly which acts as a damper to prevent oscillation of the valve due to engine pulsations. The damper piston operates in a well that is filled with fuel from the float bowl. The motion of the piston is retarded by fuel which must by-pass the piston when it moves up in the fuel well. The piston is attached loosely to a plunger rod. The rod has a rubber seal which retains the damper piston to the plunger rod and also acts as a valve. The purpose of the valve is to seat on the piston when the air valve opens and the piston rod moves upward. This closes off the area through the center of the piston and slows down the air valve opening to prevent secondary discharge nozzle lag.

ADJUSTMENTS
Float Level Adjustment

Fig. 7—With adjustable T-scale, measure from top of float bowl gasket surface

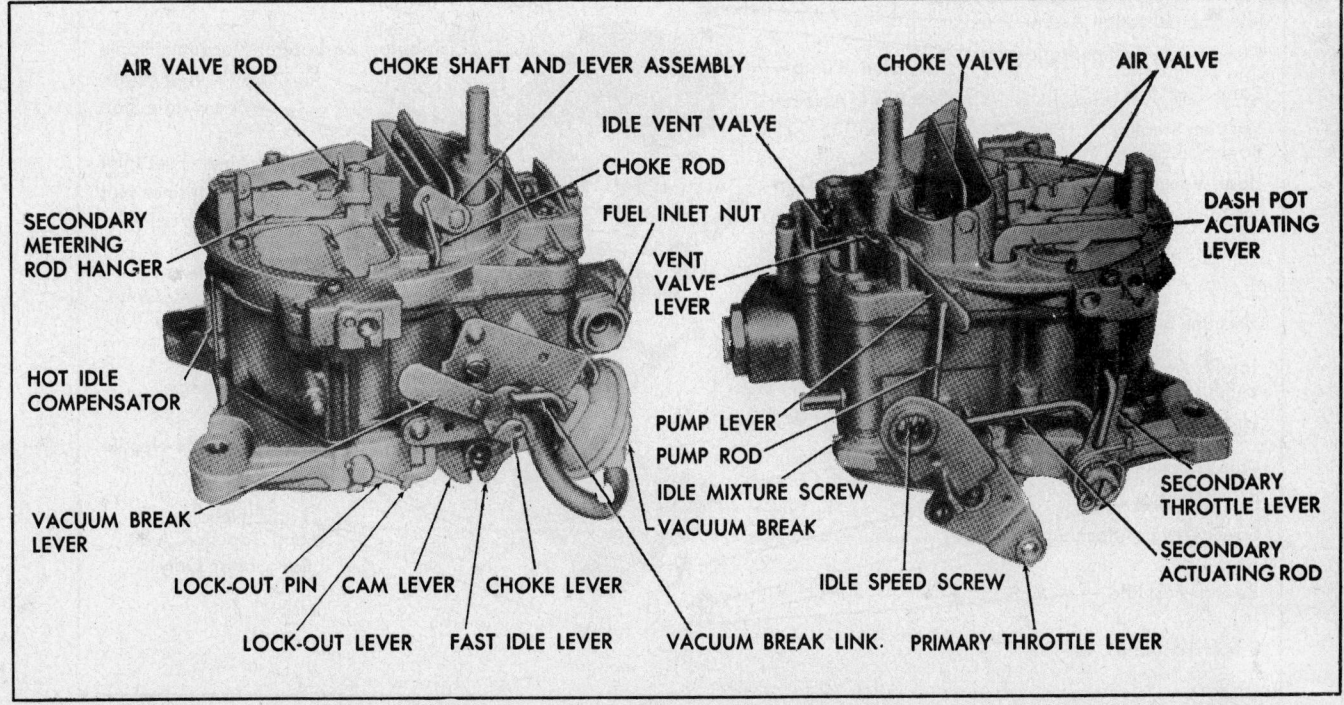

Fig. 1   Quadrajet Model 4MV carburetor

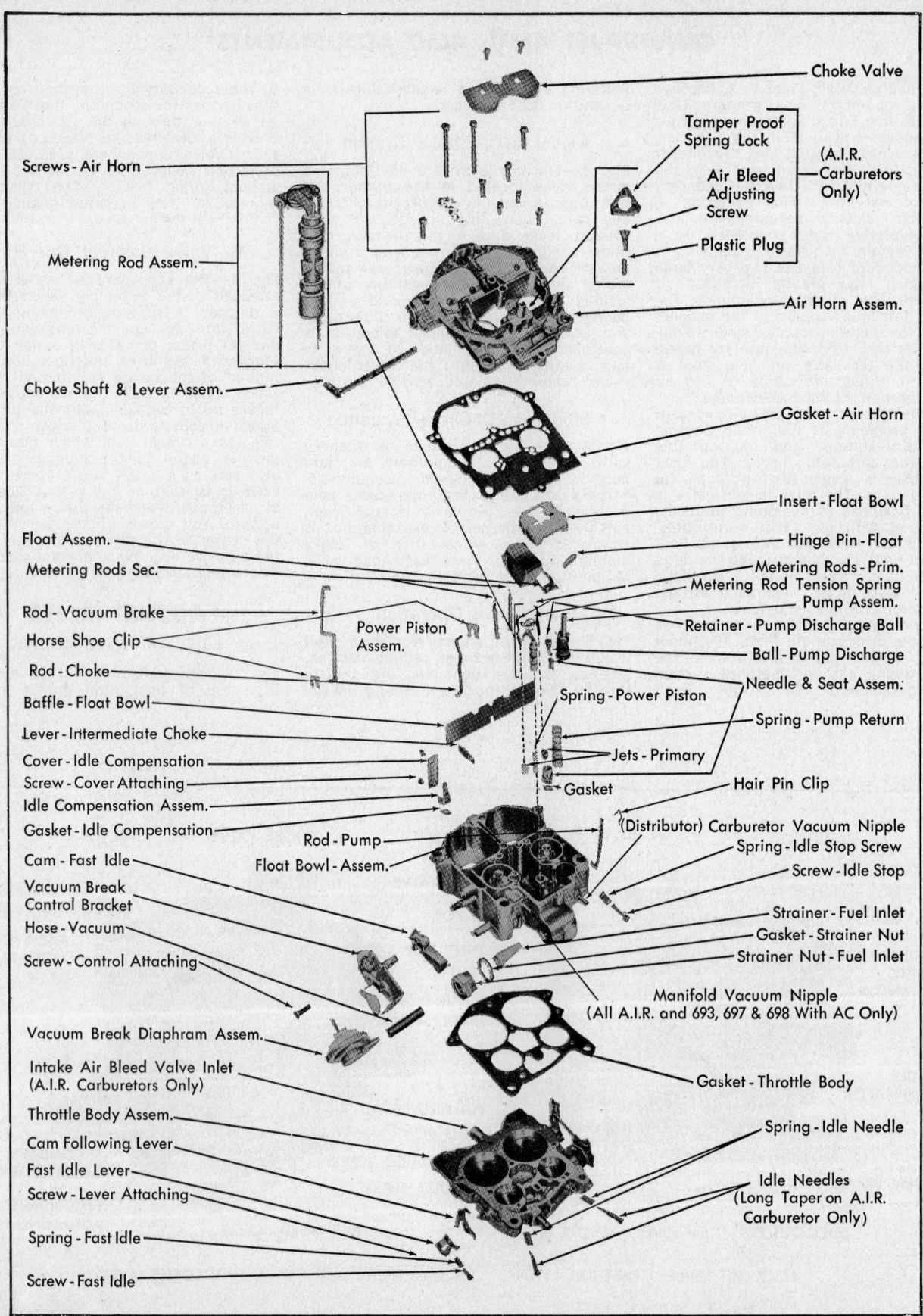

Fig. 2 4MV Quadrajet carburetor. Typical

Choke Valve

Tamper Proof Spring Lock

Air Bleed Adjusting Screw

Plastic Plug

(A.I.R. Carburetors Only)

Screws - Air Horn

Metering Rod Assem.

Air Horn Assem.

Choke Shaft & Lever Assem.

Gasket - Air Horn

Insert - Float Bowl

Hinge Pin - Float

Float Assem.

Metering Rods Sec.

Metering Rods - Prim.

Metering Rod Tension Spring

Rod - Vacuum Brake

Power Piston Assem.

Pump Assem.

Horse Shoe Clip

Retainer - Pump Discharge Ball

Rod - Choke

Ball - Pump Discharge

Baffle - Float Bowl

Needle & Seat Assem.

Spring - Power Piston

Lever - Intermediate Choke

Spring - Pump Return

Cover - Idle Compensation

Jets - Primary

Screw - Cover Attaching

Gasket

Idle Compensation Assem.

Hair Pin Clip

Gasket - Idle Compensation

(Distributor) Carburetor Vacuum Nipple

Cam - Fast Idle

Rod - Pump

Spring - Idle Stop Screw

Float Bowl - Assem.

Screw - Idle Stop

Vacuum Break Control Bracket

Strainer - Fuel Inlet

Hose - Vacuum

Gasket - Strainer Nut

Screw - Control Attaching

Strainer Nut - Fuel Inlet

Manifold Vacuum Nipple (All A.I.R. and 693, 697 & 698 With AC Only)

Vacuum Break Diaphram Assem.

Gasket - Throttle Body

Intake Air Bleed Valve Inlet (A.I.R. Carburetors Only)

Throttle Body Assem.

Spring - Idle Needle

Cam Following Lever

Fast Idle Lever

Screw - Lever Attaching

Idle Needles (Long Taper on A.I.R. Carburetor Only)

Spring - Fast Idle

Screw - Fast Idle

(gasket removed) to top of float at toe (locate gauging point 1/16″ back from toe). Adjust as directed in the illustration to the dimension listed in the *Rochester Specifications Chart*. Make sure retaining pin is held firmly in place and tang of float is seated on float needle.

Pump Rod Adjustment

Fig. 8—With throttle valves completely closed and pump rod in specified hole in pump lever, measure from top of choke valve wall (next to vent stack) to top of pump stem. Dimension should be as listed in the *Rochester Specifications Chart*. To adjust, bend pump lever as required.

Idle Vent Adjustment

Fig. 9—After pump rod adjustment has been made, open primary throttle valve to a point where the idle vent just closes. With T-scale, measure distance from top of choke valve wall (next to vent stack) to top of pump plunger stem. If dimension is not as specified in the *Rochester Specifications Chart*, bend wire tang on pump lever.

Fast Idle Adjustment

Fig. 10—With primary throttle valves completely closed, and the cam follower over the high step of the fast idle cam, adjust fast idle screw after screw makes contact with lever. Refer to *4MC and 4MV Specifications Chart*.

Choke Coil Lever Adjustment

4MC, Fig. 11

With thermostatic coil assembly removed from choke housing, push up on coil tang to close choke valve. Insert a .120 inch gauge into hole in choke housing. The choke coil lever should contact the gauge. If not, bend choke rod to adjust.

Choke Rod Adjustment

Fig. 12—With the fast idle adjustment made, and cam follower on second step of fast idle cam and against the high step, rotate choke valve toward closed position by pushing down on vacuum break lever (Model 4MV) or thermostatic coil tang (Model 4MC). Dimension between lower edge of choke valve (at choke lever end) should be as specified in the *Rochester Specifications Chart*. Adjust by bending choke rod on 4MV models or bending fast idle cam tang on 4MC models.

Vacuum Break Adjustment

4MC, Fig. 13

With cam follower on highest step of fast idle cam, seat the diaphragm using an external vacuum source. Rotate choke coil lever counter-clockwise until tang on outside lever contacts vacuum break rod. Dimension between lower end of choke valve and air horn wall should be as specified in *4MC and 4MV Specifications Chart*. To adjust, bend lower end of vacuum break rod.

4MV, All Exc. 1974 Chevrolet & Cadillac
Fig. 14—Using an external vacuum source, seat vacuum break diaphragm.

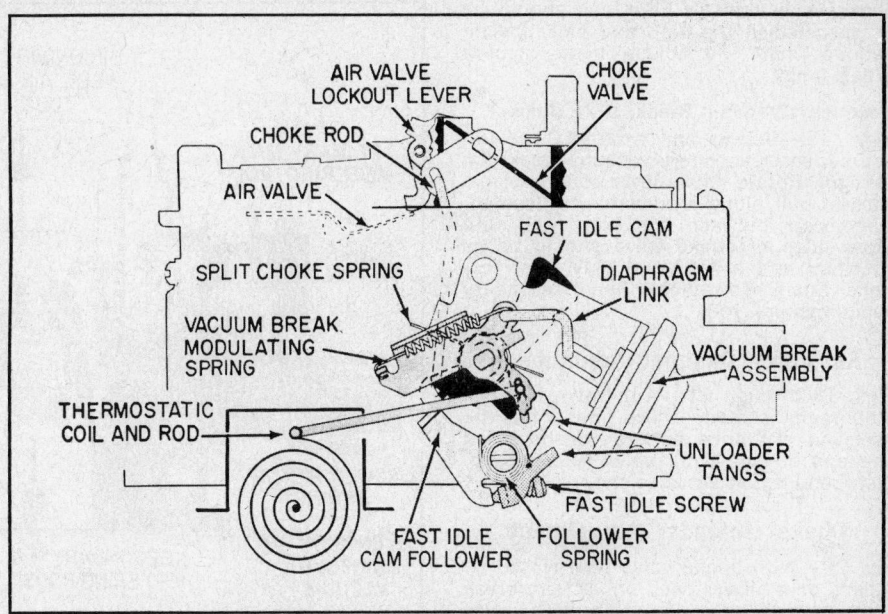

Fig. 3   Rochester Model 4MV choke system

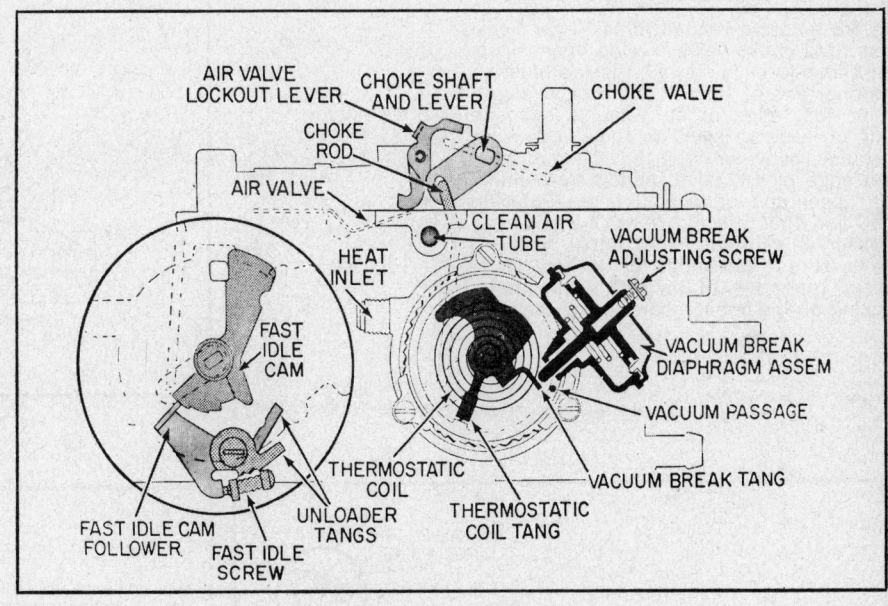

Fig. 4   Rochester Model 4MC choke system

Push upward on vacuum break lever until tang contacts rod. Dimension between lower end of choke valve and air horn wall should be as specified in the *4MC and 4MV Specifications Chart*. To adjust, bend vacuum break tang.

4MV, 1974 Chevrolet
Fig. 16—Using an external vacuum source, seat vacuum break diaphragm. Open primary throttle valves so fast idle cam follower clears fast idle cam steps. Rotate choke coil lever counterclockwise until rod end contacts end of slot in lev-

er. Dimension between lower edge of choke valve and air horn wall should be as specified in the *4MC and 4MV Specifications Chart*. To adjust, bend vacuum link.

4MV, 1974 Caddilac
Fig. 17—Using an external vacuum source, seat vacuum break diaphragm. Rotate vacuum break lever counter-clockwise until tang contacts rod and the choke vacuum diaphragm plunger spring is compressed. Dimension between lower edge of

choke valve and air horn wall should be as specified in the 4MC and 4MV Specifications Chart. To adjust, bend vacuum break tang.

Secondary Vacuum Break, 1974 Buick

Fig. 18—Using an external vacuum source, seat secondary vacuum break diaphragm. Rotate choke lever counter-clockwise to pull plunger outward until seated. Dimension between air horn wall and lower edge of choke valve should be as specified in the 4MC and 4MV Specifications Chart. To adjust, bend secondary vacuum break rod.

Air Valve Dashpot Adjustment

Figs. 19 through 21—With vacuum break diaphragm seated, there must be the specified clearance between dashpot rod and end of slot in air valve lever. To adjust, bend rod at air valve end.

Choke Unloader Adjustment

Fig. 22—With choke valve held closed by means of a rubber band on vacuum break lever, open throttle valves fully. With valves in this position, dimension between lower edge of choke valve and air horn wall should be as specified. To adjust, bend tang on fast idle lever.

Air Valve Lockout Adjustment

Fig. 23—Rotate vacuum break lever clockwise until choke valve is wide open. If upper choke lever is slotted, the rod must be in upper end of slot. Open air valve slightly so that edge of air valve is opposite tang on lockout lever, as shown. Measure distance between tang on lockout lever and edge of air valve. Adjust by bending the upper end of lockout lever. Refer to *4MC and 4MV Specifications Chart.*

After adjustment, close choke valve to make sure lower edge of lockout lever clears top edge of air valve for proper locking during choke operation. If the lock-

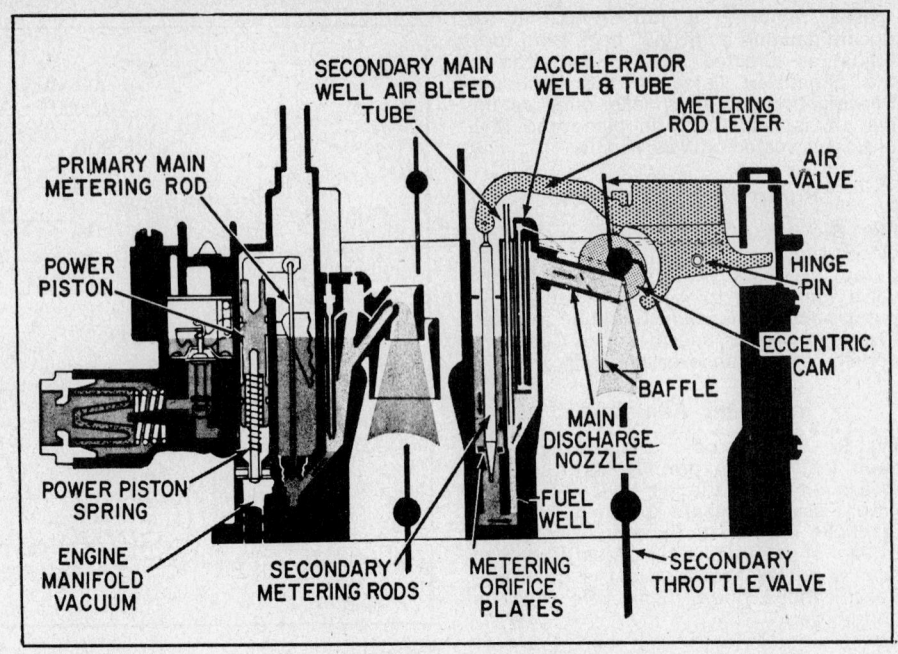

Fig. 5   Diagram of Quadrajet power system

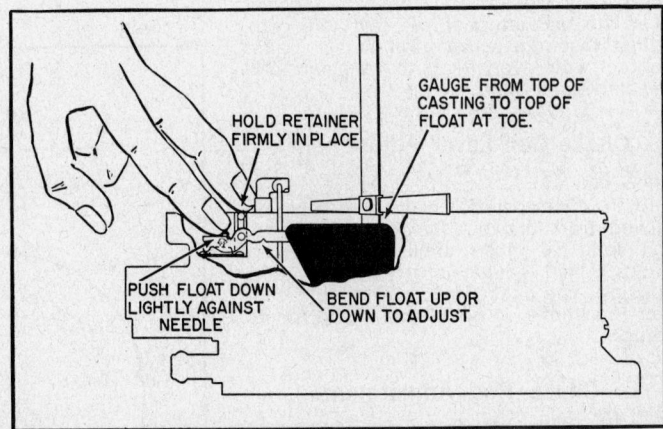

Fig. 7   Quadrajet float level adjustment

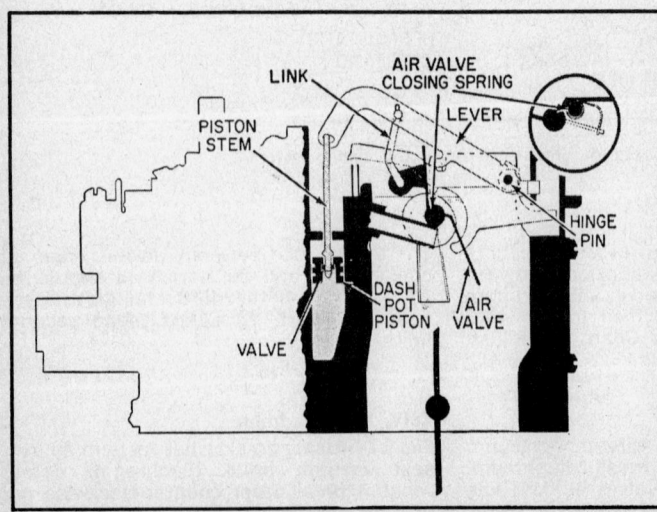

Fig. 6   Quadrajet air valve dashpot

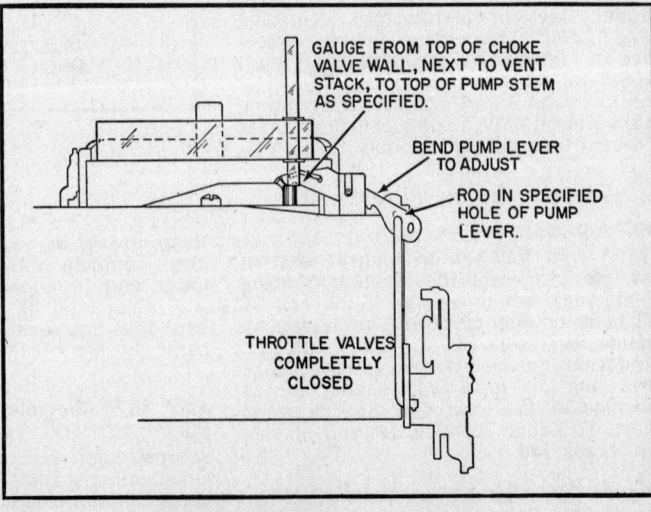

Fig. 8   Quadrajet pump rod adjustment

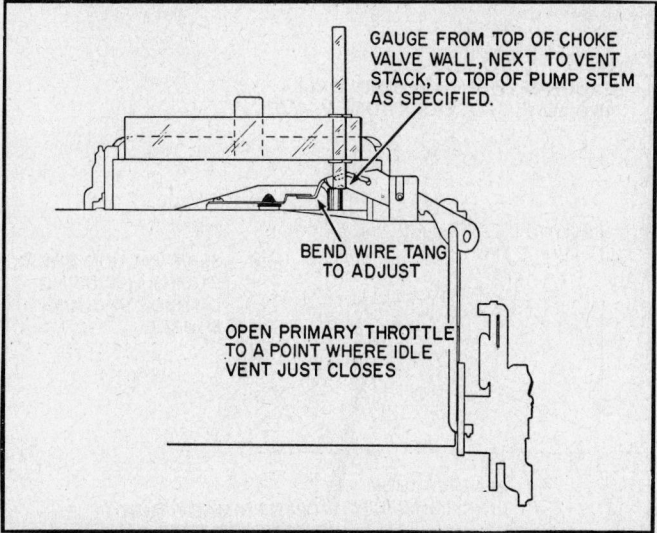

GAUGE FROM TOP OF CHOKE VALVE WALL, NEXT TO VENT STACK, TO TOP OF PUMP STEM AS SPECIFIED.

BEND WIRE TANG TO ADJUST

OPEN PRIMARY THROTTLE TO A POINT WHERE IDLE VENT JUST CLOSES

Fig. 9   Quadrajet idle vent adjustment

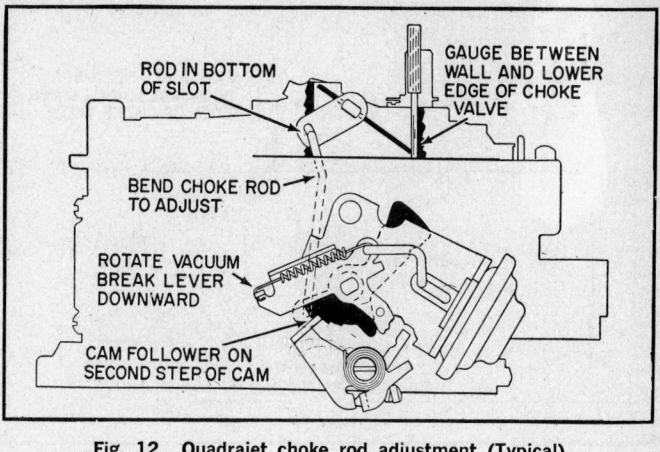

ROD IN BOTTOM OF SLOT

GAUGE BETWEEN WALL AND LOWER EDGE OF CHOKE VALVE

BEND CHOKE ROD TO ADJUST

ROTATE VACUUM BREAK LEVER DOWNWARD

CAM FOLLOWER ON SECOND STEP OF CAM

Fig. 12   Quadrajet choke rod adjustment (Typical)

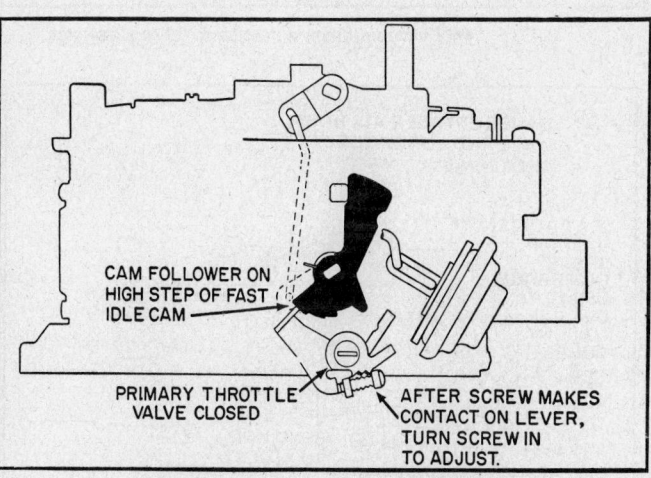

CAM FOLLOWER ON HIGH STEP OF FAST IDLE CAM

PRIMARY THROTTLE VALVE CLOSED

AFTER SCREW MAKES CONTACT ON LEVER, TURN SCREW IN TO ADJUST.

Fig. 10   Quadrajet fast idle adjustment

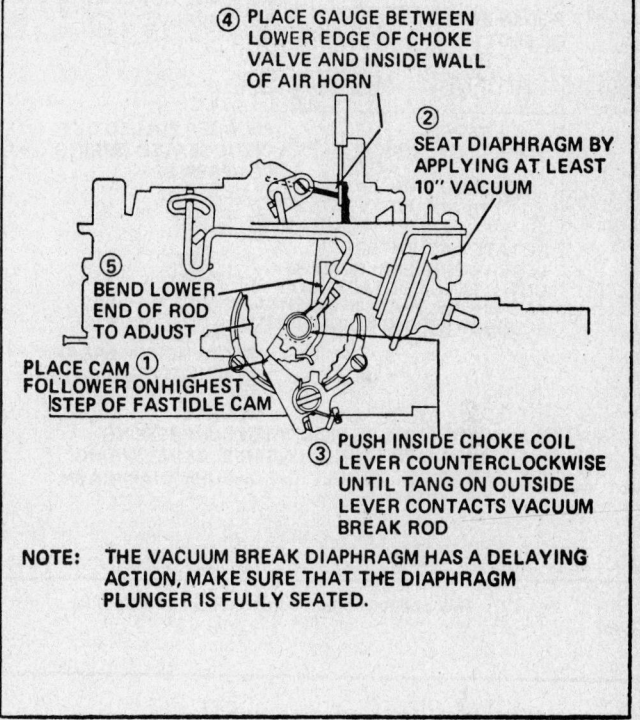

④ PLACE GAUGE BETWEEN LOWER EDGE OF CHOKE VALVE AND INSIDE WALL OF AIR HORN

② SEAT DIAPHRAGM BY APPLYING AT LEAST 10" VACUUM

⑤ BEND LOWER END OF ROD TO ADJUST

① PLACE CAM FOLLOWER ON HIGHEST STEP OF FASTIDLE CAM

③ PUSH INSIDE CHOKE COIL LEVER COUNTERCLOCKWISE UNTIL TANG ON OUTSIDE LEVER CONTACTS VACUUM BREAK ROD

NOTE: THE VACUUM BREAK DIAPHRAGM HAS A DELAYING ACTION, MAKE SURE THAT THE DIAPHRAGM PLUNGER IS FULLY SEATED.

Fig. 13   4MC vacuum break adjustment

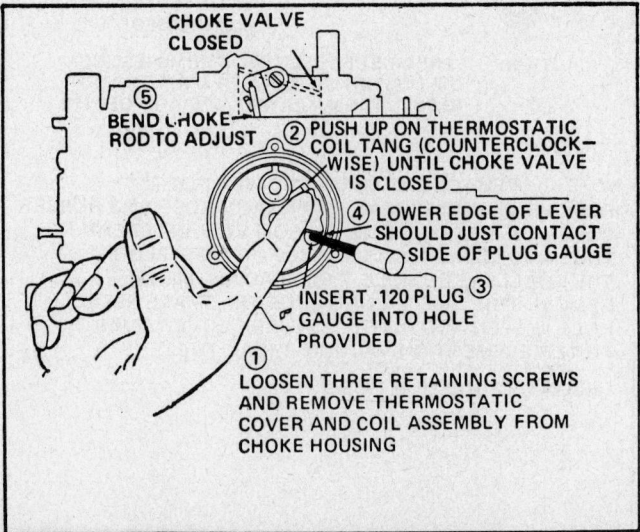

CHOKE VALVE CLOSED

⑤ BEND CHOKE ROD TO ADJUST

② PUSH UP ON THERMOSTATIC COIL TANG (COUNTERCLOCK-WISE) UNTIL CHOKE VALVE IS CLOSED

④ LOWER EDGE OF LEVER SHOULD JUST CONTACT SIDE OF PLUG GAUGE

③ INSERT .120 PLUG GAUGE INTO HOLE PROVIDED

① LOOSEN THREE RETAINING SCREWS AND REMOVE THERMOSTATIC COVER AND COIL ASSEMBLY FROM CHOKE HOUSING

Fig. 11   4MC choke coil lever adjustment

out lever does not swing over top edge of air valve make sure air valve is properly seated. File the top edge of valve for clearance.

Secondary Throttle Valve Lockout Adjustment

Lockout–Pin Clearance Fig. 24

With choke valve and both primary and secondary throttle valves fully closed, the lockout lever should not contact lockout pin. Clearance must not exceed .015". Bend lockout pin to adjust.

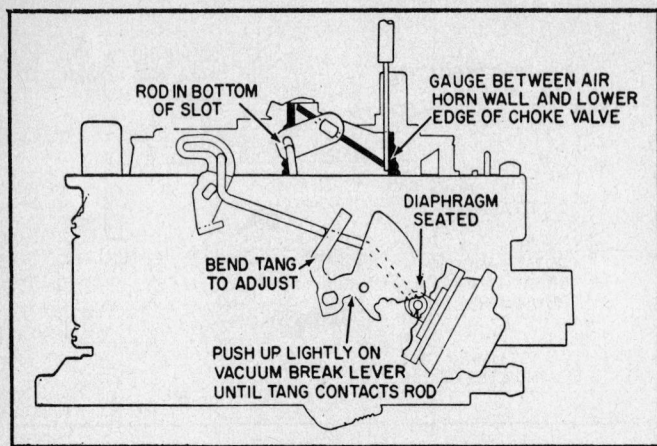

Fig. 14   4MV vacuum break adjustment, Exc. 1974 Chevrolet & Cadillac

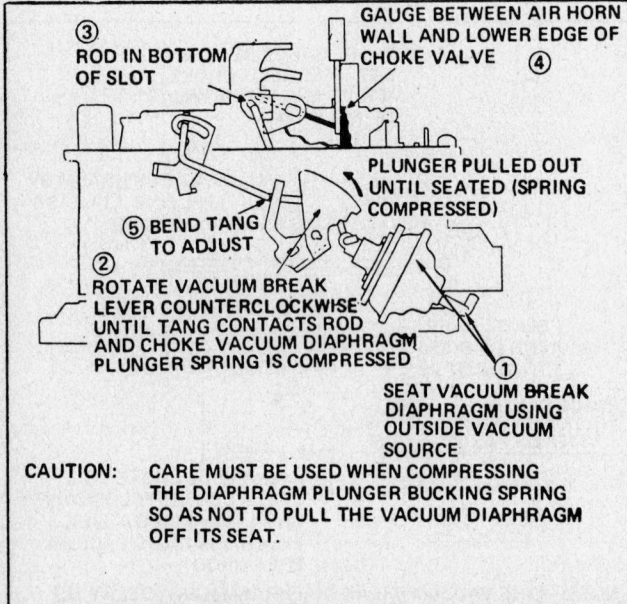

Fig. 17   4MV vacuum break adjustment. 1974 Cadillac

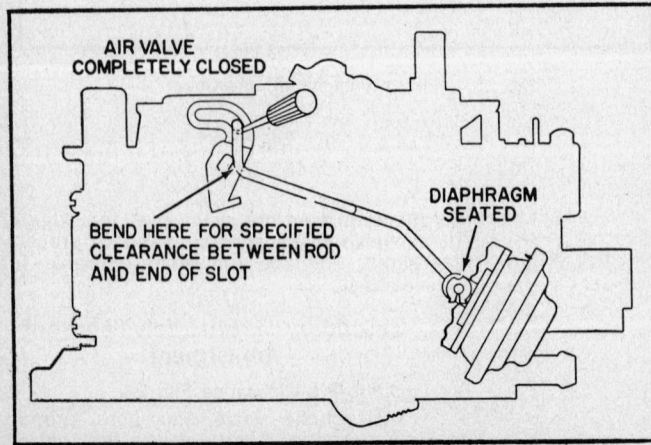

Fig. 19   Quadrajet air valve dashpot adjustment. All exc. 1974 Chevrolet & Cadillac

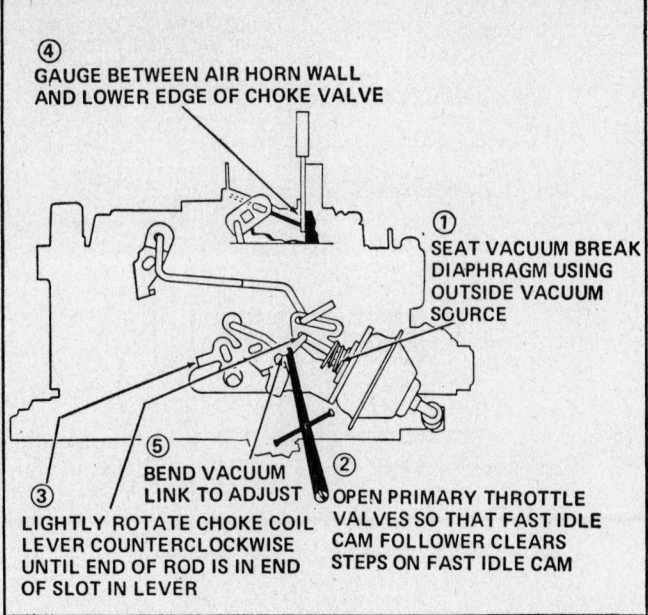

Fig. 16   4MV vacuum break adjustment. 1974 Chevrolet

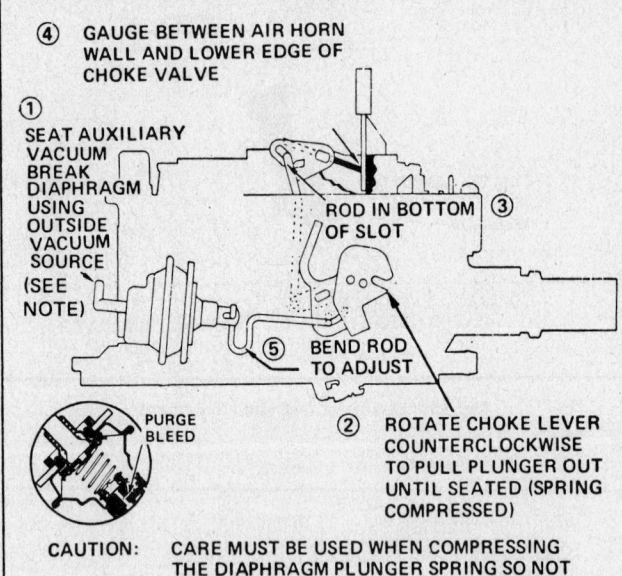

NOTE: IF PURGE FILTER IS USED (SEE INSET), REMOVE VACUUM BREAK DIAPHRAGM HOSE AND RUBBER COVER ON FILTER ELEMENT FROM VACUUM BREAK TUBE AND, USING A SMALL PIECE OF TAPE, PLUG THE SMALL BLEED HOLE. AFTER ADJUSTMENT, REMOVE THE TAPE MAKING SURE THE SMALL BLEED HOLE IS OPEN AND INSTALL RUBBER COVER OVER FILTER ELEMENT ON VACUUM BREAK TUBE.

RECONNECT VACUUM HOSE.

Fig. 18   4MV secondary vacuum break adjustment. 1974 Buick

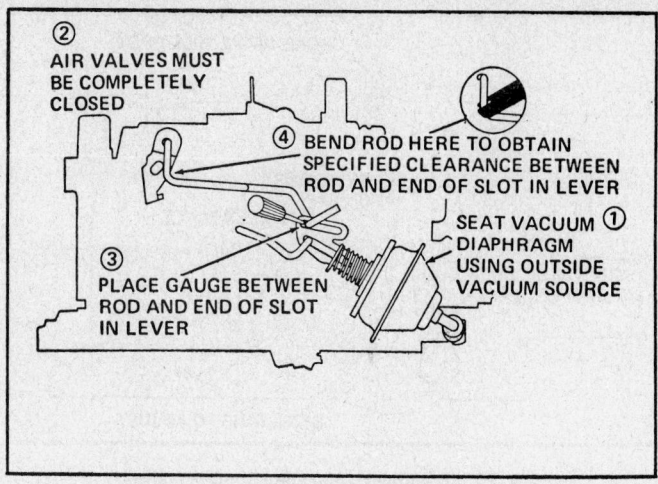

Fig. 20 Quadrajet air valve dashpot adjustment. 1974 Chevrolet

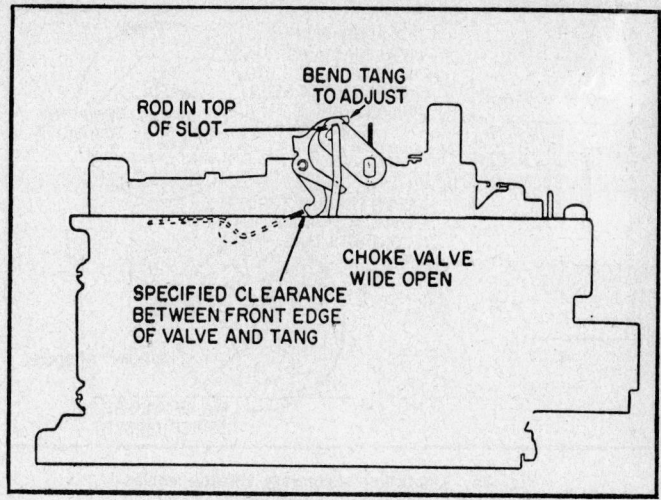

Fig. 23 Quadrajet air valve lockout adjustment

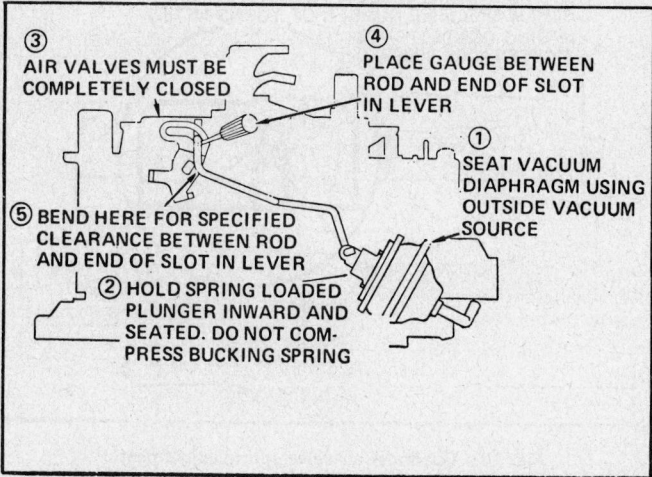

Fig. 21 Quadrajet air valve dashpot adjustment. 1974 Cadillac

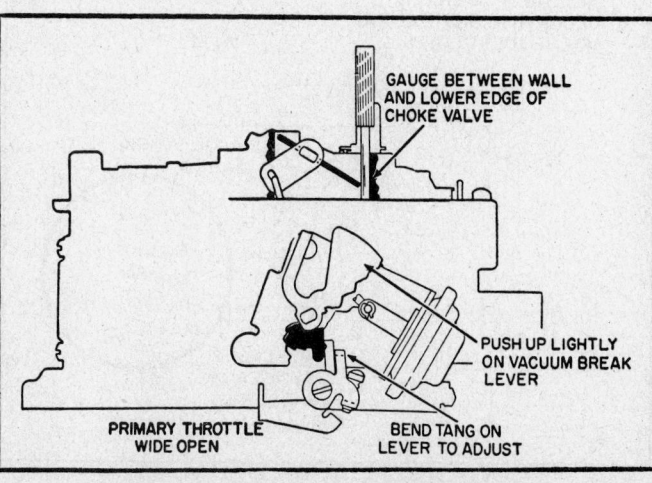

Fig. 22 Quadrajet unloader adjustment (Typical)

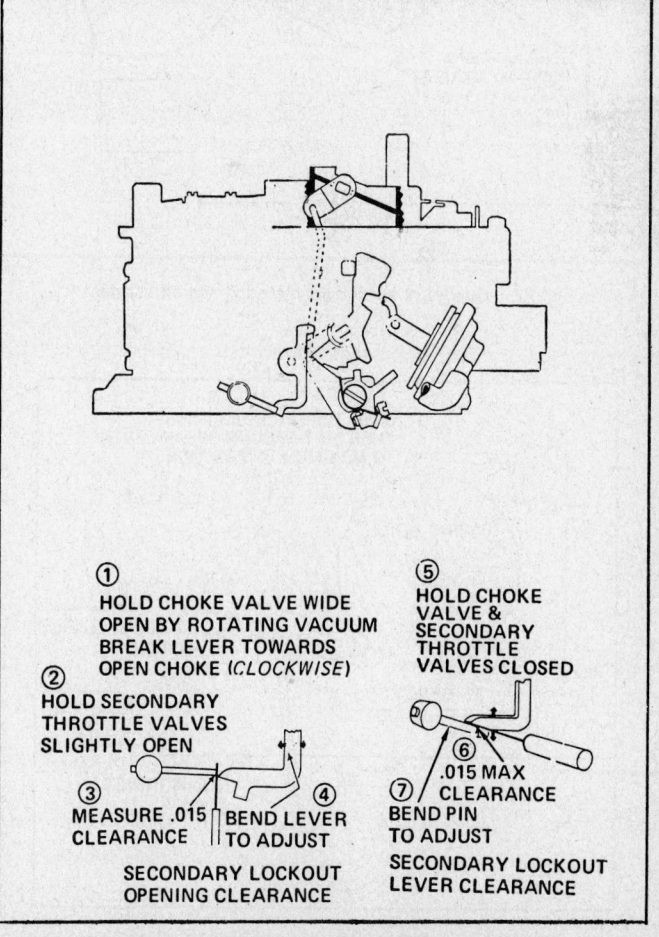

Fig. 24 Quadrajet secondary lockout adjustment

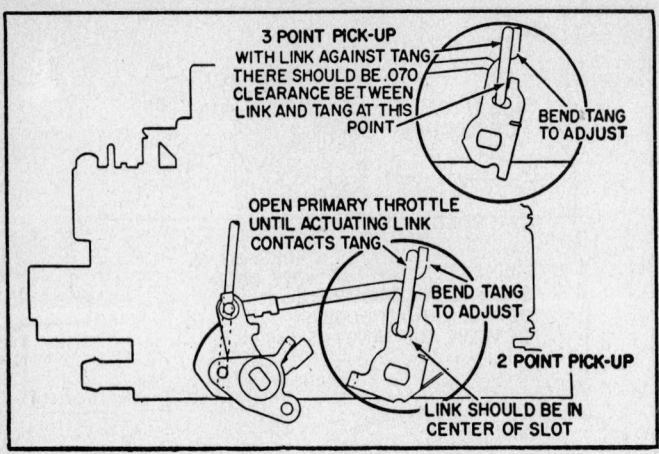

Fig. 25 Quadrajet secondary throttle valves opening adjustment

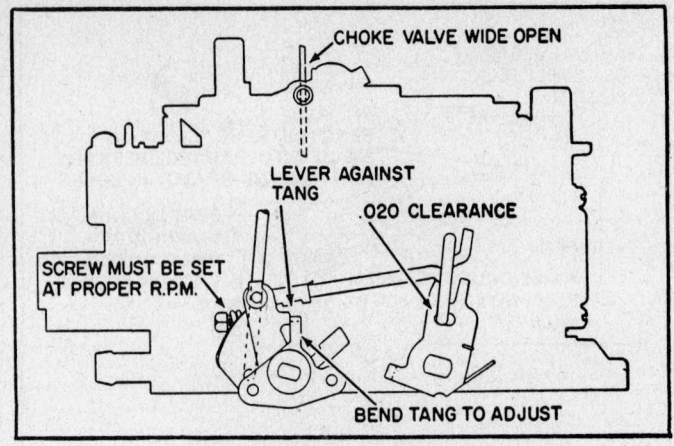

Fig. 26 Quadrajet secondary throttle valves closing adjustment

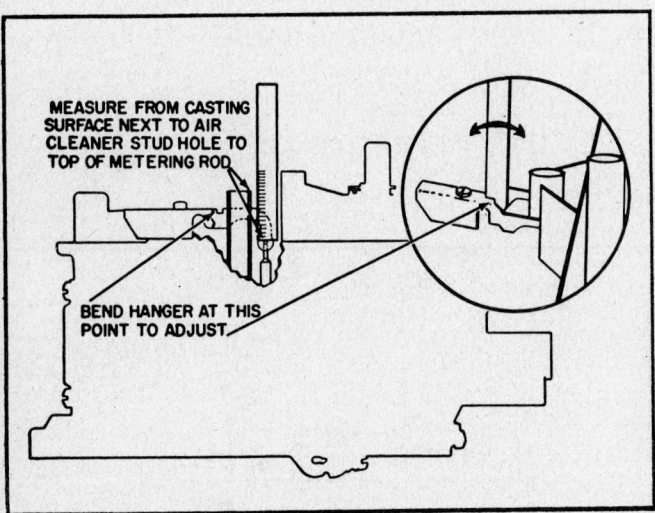

Fig. 27 Quadrajet secondary metering rod adjustment

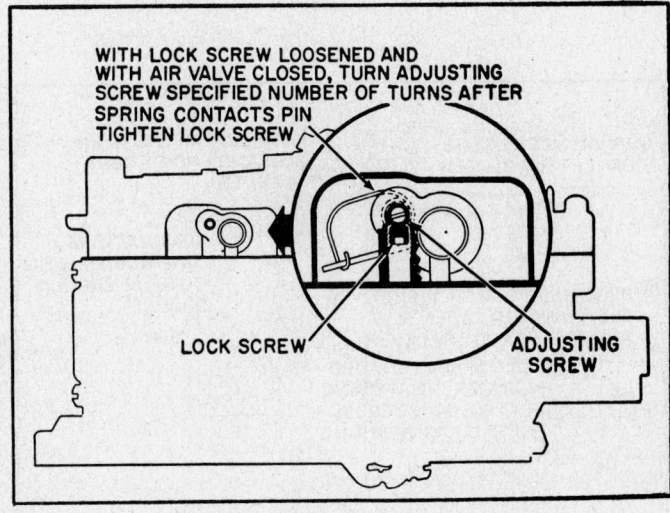

Fig. 28 Quadrajet air valve spring adjustment

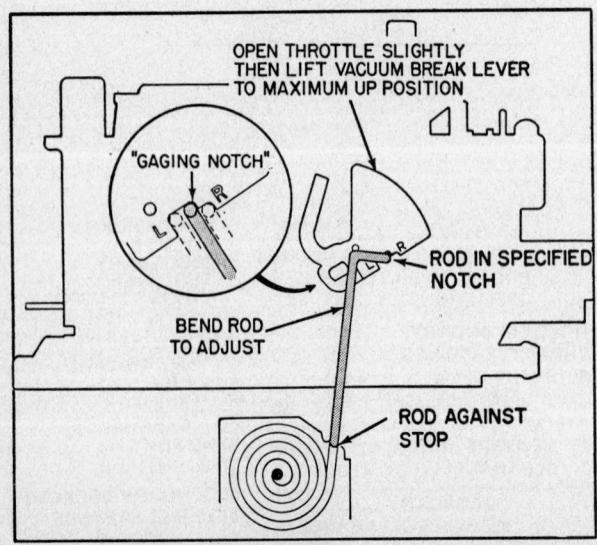

Fig. 29 4MV Choke coil adjustment. Typical

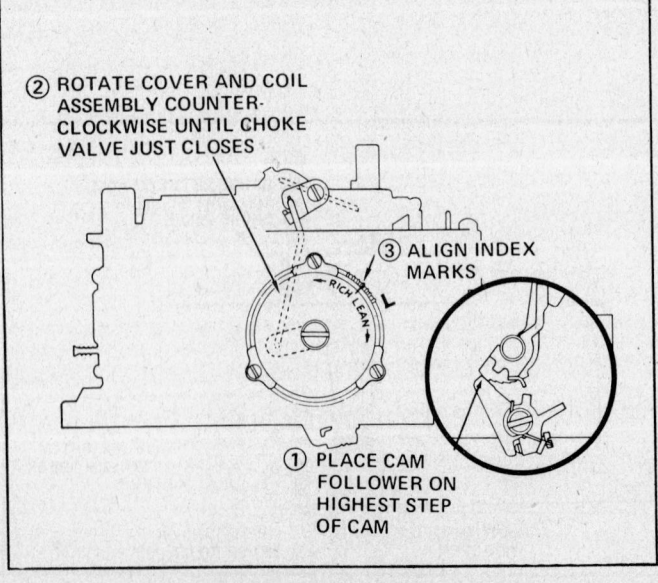

Fig. 30 4MC choke coil adjustment

Opening Clearance, Fig. 24

Hold choke valve wide open by rotating vacuum break lever toward open choke clockwise. With secondary throttle valves held partially open measure the clearance between lockout pin and toe of lockout lever.

Secondary Throttle Valves, Adjust

Throttle Opening, Fig. 25

With a two-point pickup, open primary throttle valves until actuating link contacts tang on secondary lever. With valves in this position, bottom of link should be in center slot of secondary lever.

With a three-point pickup, there should be .070" clearance between link and tang as indicated. If necessary to adjust, bend tang on secondary lever.

Throttle Closing, Fig. 26

Set curb idle screw to recommended rpm (listed in *Tune-Up Specifications* table in car chapters), making sure cam follower is not resting on fast idle cam. The 4MV should have .020" and 4MC .070" clearance between actuating link

and front of slot in secondary lever when tang of actuating lever on primary shaft is against pin. If necessary to adjust, bend tang on primary actuating lever.

Secondary Metering Rod Adjustment

Fig. 27

Measure from top of metering rod to top of air horn casting next to air cleaner stud hole. Dimension should be as specified. To adjust, bend metering rod hanger at point shown. *Make sure both rods are adjusted to the same dimension.*

Air Valve Spring Adjustment

Fig. 28

To adjust the air valve spring wind-up, loosen Allen head lockscrew and turn adjusting screw counterclockwise to remove all spring tension. With air valve closed, turn adjusting screw clockwise the specified number of turns after the torsion spring contacts pin on shaft. Hold adjusting screw in this position and tighten lock screw.

Choke Coil Rod Adjustment

1974 Buick, Cadillac & Chevrolet, Fig. 29

1. Remove choke coil assmebly to disengage choke rod from vacuum break lever.
2. Reinstall coil assembly but do not install rod into lever.
3. With choke valve completely closed, fast idle cam in cold start position, and vacuum break lever in maximum upward position, pull choke rod upward to end of travel. Upper end of rod should be positioned in gauging notch, Fig. 29. Bend choke rod to adjust and reassemble coil assembly, rod and lever.

1974 Oldsmobile & Pontiac, Fig. 30

Place the fast idle cam follower on the highest step of the fast idle cam. Rotate choke cover and coil assembly counterclockwise until the choke valve just closes and the index point on cover aligns with the center index point on the choke housing.

QUADRAJET M4M SERIES ADJUSTMENT SPECIFICATIONS

See Tune Up Chart in car chapters for hot idle speeds.

Year	Carb. Production No.	Float Level	Pump Rod Hole	Pump Rod Adj.	Bowl Vent	Fast Idle (Bench)	Choke Coil Lever	Choke Rod	Vacuum Break Front	Vacuum Break Rear	Air-Valve Dash-pot	Choke Setting	Choke Unloader	Air-Valve Valve Spring Wind-Up
1975	7045183	15/32	Inner	9/32	.075	3	.120	.135	.190	.140	.030	2 Rich	.230	1/2
	7045184, 185	15/32	Inner	9/32	.075	3	.120	.135	.190	.140	.030	2 Rich	.230	3/4
	7045200, 220	17/32	Inner	9/32	—	3	.120	.060	.200	①	.015	Index	.270	9/16
	7045202, 206	15/32	Inner	9/32	—	3	.120	.300	.180	.170	.015	Index	.325	7/8
	7045203, 207	15/32	Inner	9/32	—	3	.120	.300	.180	.170	.015	2 Lean	.325	7/8
	7045210, 222	15/32	Inner	9/32	—	3	.120	.300	.180	.170	.015	Index	.325	7/8
	7045211, 223	15/32	Inner	9/32	—	3	.120	.300	.180	.170	.015	2 Lean	.325	7/8
	7045218	5/16	Inner	9/32	—	3	.120	.325	.180	.170	.015	Index	.325	3/4
	7045219	5/16	Inner	9/32	—	3	.120	.325	.180	.170	.015	2 Lean	.325	3/4
	7045224	15/32	Inner	9/32	—	3	.120	.325	.200	.170	.015	Index	.325	3/4
	7045228	15/32	Inner	9/32	—	3	.120	.325	.180	.170	.015	Index	.325	3/4
	7045230	15/32	Outer	3/8	.075	3	.120	.080	.160	.130	.030	2 Rich	.215	7/16
	7045240	15/32	Inner	3/8	—	3	.120	.095	.135	.120	.015	1 Rich	.235	7/16
	7045244, 246	3/8	Outer	3/8	—	2	.120	.095	.130	.115	.015	1 Rich	.235	3/4
	7045250	15/32	Inner	9/32	.075	3	.120	.135	.190	.140	.030	2 Rich	.230	1/2
	7045251	15/32	Inner	9/32	.075	3	.120	.135	.190	.140	.030	2 Rich	.230	3/4
	7045260, 262	1/2	Inner	9/32	—	3	.120	.130	.150	.260	.030	Index	.230	1/2
	7045261, 263	17/32	Inner	9/32	—	3	.120	.130	.150	.260	.030	Index	.230	1/2
	7045264, 274	17/32	Inner	9/32	—	3	.120	.130	.150	.260	.030	Index	.230	1/2
	7045266	1/2	Inner	9/32	—	3	.120	.130	.160	.260	.030	Index	.230	1/2
	7045268	17/32	Inner	9/32	—	3	.120	.130	.150	.260	.030	Index	.230	7/16
	7045269	17/32	Inner	9/32	—	3	.120	.130	.160	.265	.030	Index	.230	7/16
	7045294	15/32	Inner	9/32	—	3	.120	.300	.180	.170	.015	Index	.330	7/8
	7045483	15/32	Inner	9/32	.075	3	.120	.135	.190	.140	.030	2 Rich	.230	1/2
	7045484	15/32	Inner	9/32	.075	3	.120	.135	.190	.140	.030	2 Rich	.230	3/4
	7045485	15/32	Inner	9/32	.075	3	.120	.135	.200	.140	.030	2 Rich	.230	3/4
	7045502, 503	15/32	Inner	9/32	—	3	.120	.300	.190	.170	.015	2 Rich	.325	7/8
	7045504	15/32	Inner	9/32	—	3	.120	.300	.180	.170	.015	2 Rich	.325	7/8
	7045506, 507	15/32	Inner	9/32	—	3	.120	.300	.190	.170	.015	2 Rich	.325	7/8
	7045512, 517	17/32	Inner	9/32	—	2	.120	.060	.180	①	.015	Index	.270	9/16
	7045530	15/32	Outer	3/8	.075	2 1/4	.120	.080	.180	.180	.030	1 Rich	.215	1/2
	7045541, 548	15/32	Outer	3/8	—	2	.120	.095	.135	.120	.015	1 Rich	.235	7/16
	7045544	3/8	Outer	3/8	—	2	.120	.095	.145	.130	.015	1 Rich	.235	3/4
	7045546	5/16	Outer	15/32	—	3	.120	.095	.145	.130	.015	1 Rich	.240	3/4

Continued

QUADRAJET M4M SERIES ADJUSTMENT SPECIFICATIONS—Continued

See Tune Up Chart in car chapters for hot idle speeds.

Year	Carb. Production No.	Float Level	Pump Rod Hole	Pump Rod Adj.	Bowl Vent	Fast Idle (Bench)	Choke Coil Lever	Choke Rod	Vacuum Break Front	Vacuum Break Rear	Air-Valve Dash-pot	Choke Setting	Choke Unloader	Air-Valve Valve Spring Wind-Up
	7045550	15/32	Inner	9/32	.075	3	.120	.135	.190	.140	.030	2 Rich	.230	1/2
	7045551	15/32	Inner	9/32	.075	3	.120	.135	.190	.140	.030	1 Rich	.230	3/4
	7045562, 564	17/32	Inner	9/32	—	3	.120	.130	.150	.260	.030	Index	.230	1/2
	7045566	17/32	Inner	9/32	—	3	.120	.130	.160	.260	.030	Index	.230	1/2
	7045568	17/32	Inner	9/32	—	3	.120	.130	.150	.260	.030	Index	.230	7/16
1976	17056200	13/32	Inner	9/32	—	3	.120	.195	.235	.235	.015	Index	.230	7/8
	17056202, 206	13/32	Inner	9/32	—	3	.120	.325	.185	—	.015	2 Lean	.230	7/8
	17056203, 207	13/32	Inner	9/32	—	3	.120	.325	.185	—	.015	3 Lean	.325	7/8
	17056210, 226	13/32	Inner	9/32	—	3	.120	.325	.185	—	.015	2 Lean	.325	1
	17056211	13/32	Inner	9/32	—	3	.120	.325	.170	—	.015	2 Lean	.325	1
	17056228	13/32	Inner	9/32	—	3	.120	.325	.185	—	.015	2 Lean	.325	7/8
	17056230, 232	13/32	Outer	3/8	—	2	.120	.080	.170	.140	.030	2 Rich	.230	3/8
	17056240	15/32	Inner	9/32	—	2	.120	.095	.140	.125	.015	1 Rich	.250	7/16
	17056244, 246	5/16	Outer	3/8	—	2	.120	.095	.130	.120	.015	1 Rich	.250	3/4
	17056250, 253	13/32	Inner	9/32	—	3	.120	.130	.190	.140	.030	2 Rich	.230	1/2
	17056251, 252	13/32	Inner	9/32	—	3	.120	.130	.190	.140	.030	2 Rich	.230	3/4
	17056255, 256	13/32	Inner	9/32	—	3	.120	.130	.190	.140	.030	2 Rich	.230	3/4
	17056257	13/32	Inner	9/32	—	3	.120	.130	.190	.140	.030	2 Rich	.230	3/4
	17056258, 259	13/32	Inner	9/32	—	3	.120	.130	.190	.140	.030	2 Rich	.230	1/2
	17056261, 263	17/32	Outer	3/8	—	3	.120	.125	.170	.250	.030	1 Rich	.230	5/8
	17056262, 264	17/32	Outer	3/8	—	3	.120	.125	.160	.250	.030	1 Rich	.230	1/2
	17056266, 274	17/32	Outer	3/8	—	3	.120	.130	.160	.250	.030	1 Rich	.230	1/2
	17056502, 503	13/32	Inner	9/32	—	3	.120	.325	.185	—	.015	2 Lean	.325	7/8
	17056506, 507	13/32	Inner	9/32	—	3	.120	.325	.185	—	.015	2 Lean	.325	7/8
	17056528	13/32	Inner	9/32	—	3	.120	.325	.185	—	.015	2 Lean	.325	7/8
	17056530	13/32	Inner	9/32	—	2	.120	.080	.170	.170	.030	2 Rich	.230	3/8
	17056540	15/32	Outer	3/8	—	2	.120	.095	.135	.125	.015	1 Rich	.250	7/16
	17056544, 546	5/16	Outer	3/8	—	2	.120	.095	.130	.130	.015	Index	.250	3/4
	17056550, 553	13/32	Inner	9/32	—	3	.120	.130	.190	.140	.030	2 Rich	.230	1/2
	17056551, 556	13/32	Inner	9/32	—	3	.120	.130	.190	.140	.030	1 Rich	.230	3/4
	17056552	13/32	Inner	9/32	—	3	.120	.130	.200	.140	.030	2 Rich	.230	3/4
	17056562, 566	17/32	Outer	3/8	—	3	.120	.125	.170	.250	.030	1 Rich	.230	1/2
	17056564	17/32	Outer	3/8	—	3	.120	.130	.150	.250	.030	1 Rich	.230	1/2
	17056568	17/32	Outer	3/8	—	3	.120	.125	.160	.250	.030	1 Rich	.230	1/2
1977	17057202, 204	15/32	Inner	9/32	—	3	.120	.325	②	—	.015	2 Lean	.280	7/8
	17057203	15/32	Inner	9/32	—	3	.120	.325	②	—	.015	3 Lean	.280	7/8
	17057210	15/32	Inner	9/32	—	3	.120	.325	③	—	.015	2 Lean	.280	1
	17057211	15/32	Inner	9/32	—	3	.120	.325	③	—	.015	3 Lean	.280	1
	17057226	15/32	Inner	9/32	—	3	.120	.325	.180	—	.015	2 Lean	.285	1
	17057228	13/32	Inner	9/32	—	3	.120	.325	③	—	.015	2 Lean	.280	1
	17057230	13/32	Inner	3/8	—	2	.120	.080	.140	.120	.030	2 Rich	.230	1/2
	17057231	17/32	Inner	3/8	—	2	.120	.080	.140	.140	.030	2 Rich	.230	3/4
	17057232	13/32	Outer	3/8	—	2	.120	.080	.140	.120	.030	2 Rich	.230	1/2
	17057233	13/32	Inner	3/8	—	2	.120	.080	.140	.140	.030	2 Rich	.230	3/4
	17057234	13/32	Inner	9/32	—	2	.120	.080	.140	.120	.030	2 Rich	.230	3/4
	17057235	17/32	Inner	9/32	—	2	.120	.080	.140	.120	.030	2 Rich	.230	3/4
	17057236	13/32	Inner	9/32	—	2	.120	.080	.140	.140	.030	2 Rich	.230	3/4
	17057241, 242	5/16	Outer	3/8	—	2	.120	.095	.120	.105	.015	1 Rich	.240	3/4
	17057248	5/16	Outer	3/8	—	3	.120	.095	.130	.110	.015	Index	.240	3/4
	17057250, 252	13/32	Inner	9/32	—	3	.120	.100	.135	.180	.030	2 Rich	.220	1/2
	17057253, 255	13/32	Inner	9/32	—	3	.120	.100	.135	.180	.030	2 Rich	.220	1/2
	17057256	13/32	Inner	9/32	—	3	.120	.100	.135	.180	.030	2 Rich	.220	1/2
	17057257, 258	15/32	Inner	9/32	—	3	.120	.100	.135	.225	.030	3 Rich	.220	1/2
	17057262, 266	17/32	Outer	3/8	—	3	.120	.130	.150	.240	.030	1 Rich	.220	1/2
	17057263	17/32	Outer	3/8	—	3	.120	.130	.165	.240	.030	1 Rich	.220	5/8
	17057274	17/32	Outer	3/8	—	3	.120	.130	.150	.240	.030	1 Rich	.220	1/2
	17057502, 504	15/32	Inner	9/32	—	3	.120	.325	④	—	.015	2 Lean	.280	7/8

Continued

QUADRAJET M4M SERIES ADJUSTMENT SPECIFICATIONS—Continued

See Tune Up Chart in car chapters for hot idle speeds.

Year	Carb. Production No.	Float Level	Pump Rod Hole	Pump Rod Adj.	Bowl Vent	Fast Idle (Bench)	Choke Coil Lever	Choke Rod	Vacuum Break Front	Vacuum Break Rear	Air-Valve Dash-pot	Choke Setting	Choke Unloader	Air-Valve Valve Spring Wind-Up
	17057510, 528	15/32	Inner	9/32	—	3	.120	.325	.180	—	.015	2 Lean	.280	1
	17057530, 533	13/32	Outer	7/16	—	2	.120	.080	.150	.150	.030	2 Rich	.230	½
	17057550, 553	13/32	Inner	9/32	—	3	.120	.100	.135	.225	.030	2 Rich	.220	½
	17057552	15/32	Inner	9/32	—	3	.120	.100	.135	.225	.030	3 Rich	.220	½
	17057582, 584	15/32	Outer	3/8	—	3	.120	.325	③	—	.015	2 Lean	.280	7/8
1978	17058202, 204	15/32	Inner	9/32	—	3	.120	46°	⑤	—	.015	2 Lean	42°	7/8
	17058203	15/32	Inner	9/32	—	3	.120	46°	⑤	—	.015	3 Lean	42°	7/8
	17058210, 228	15/32	Inner	9/32	—	3	.120	46°	⑥	—	.015	2 Lean	42°	1
	17058211	15/32	Inner	9/32	—	3	.120	46°	⑥	—	.015	3 Lean	42°	1
	17058230	13/32	Inner	9/32	—	3	.120	16°	25°	39°	.030	2 Rich	35°	½
	17058232	13/32	Inner	9/32	—	2	.120	16°	26°	28°	.030	2 Rich	35°	¾
	17058233	13/32	Inner	9/32	—	2	.120	16°	26°	28°	.030	2 Rich	35°	½
	17058240	7/32	Inner	9/32	—	3	.120	14½°	21°	23°	.015	Index	38°	¾
	17058241	5/16	Outer	3/8	—	3	.120	18°	21½°	19°	.015	1 Rich	38°	¾
	17058246	7/32	Outer	3/8	—	3	.120	14½°	23°	23°	.015	Index	38°	¾
	17058250, 253	13/32	Inner	9/32	—	3	.120	18°	23°	30½°	.030	2 Rich	35°	½
	17058254	15/32	Inner	9/32	—	3	.120	19°	24°	—	.030	3 Rich	35°	½
	17058257, 258	13/32	Inner	9/32	—	3	.120	19°	24°	36½°	.030	2 Rich	35°	½
	17058259	13/32	Inner	9/32	—	3	.120	19°	24°	30½°	.030	2 Rich	35°	½
	17058263	17/32	Outer	3/8	—	3	.120	23°	28°	40°	.030	Index	35°	5/8
	17058264, 278	17/32	Outer	3/8	—	3	.120	23½°	26°	40°	.030	1 Rich	35°	½
	17058266, 274	17/32	Outer	3/8	—	3	.120	23½°	26°	40°	.030	Index	35°	½
	17058272	15/32	Outer	3/8	—	3	.120	14½°	24°	32°	.030	2 Rich	36°	5/8
	17058276	17/32	Outer	3/8	—	3	.120	23½°	26°	40°	.030	Index	35°	½
	17058282, 284	15/32	Inner	9/32	—	3	.120	46°	27°	—	.015	Index	42°	7/8
	17058502, 504	15/32	Inner	9/32	—	3	.120	46°	⑦	—	.015	2 Lean	42°	7/8
	17058530, 531	13/32	Inner	9/32	—	2	.120	16°	26°	28°	.030	2 Rich	35°	½
	17058532, 533	13/32	Inner	9/32	—	2	.120	16°	26°	28°	.030	2 Rich	35°	½
	17058540	7/32	Inner	9/32	—	3	.120	14½°	21°	23°	.015	Index	38°	¾
	17058550, 553	13/32	Inner	9/32	—	3	.120	19°	24°	36½°	.030	2 Rich	35°	½
	17058555	13/32	Inner	9/32	—	3	.120	19°	24°	36½°	.030	2 Rich	35°	½
	17058559	15/32	Inner	9/32	—	3	.120	19°	24°	—	.030	3 Rich	36½°	½
	17058582, 584	15/32	Inner	9/32	—	3	.120	46°	⑥	—	.015	2 Lean	42°	7/8

①—Wide open.
②—.160 inch before first scheduled tune-up; .245 inch after first scheduled tune-up.
③—.180 inch before first scheduled tune-up; .275 inch after first scheduled tune-up.
④—.165 inch before first scheduled tune-up; .260 inch after first scheduled tune-up.
⑤—27° before first scheduled tune-up; 30° after first scheduled tune-up.
⑥—30° before first scheduled tune-up; 33° after first scheduled tune-up.
⑦—28° before first scheduled tune-up; 31° after first scheduled tune-up.

QUADRAJET M4M SERIES ADJUSTMENTS

The M4M Series (M4MC, M4MCA and M4MEA) Quadrajet carburetor, Fig. 1 is similar to the Quadrajet 4MC unit previously described in this chapter. However, some modifications have been made to the basic Quadrajet design.

An Adjustable Part Throttle (A.P.T.) feature incorporates an adjustable metering rod assembly operating in a fixed jet. On some models, a barometric pressure-sensitive aneroid (Bellows) is an integral part of the A.P.T. metering rod assembly. This provides a close tolerance control of fuel flow to the main metering system, thereby controlling air/fuel ratios during part throttle operation.

Some units use a multiple stage power enrichment system with two power pistons. One piston is an auxiliary power piston with a single metering rod operating in a fixed jet. The primary power piston with two metering rods operates in replaceable metering jets. This system provides sensitive control of the air/fuel ratio during light engine power requirements while providing richer mixtures during moderate to heavy engine loads.

All units use a bowl mounted choke housing with a thermostatic coil assembly. Also, a dual vacuum break system is used to improve cold engine warm-up and drive-away performance. Cadillac units use a three stage electric choke with a ceramic resistor for precise timing of the choke valve opening to improve engine warm-up performance. Refer of the "Emission Control System" chapter.

ADJUSTMENTS

Float Level Adjustment

Fig. 2—With an adjustable T-scale, measure distance from top of float bowl gasket surface, with gasket removed, to top of float at a point 3/16 inch back from toe. Dimension should be as specified in the M4M Series Specification Chart. To adjust, bend float arm.

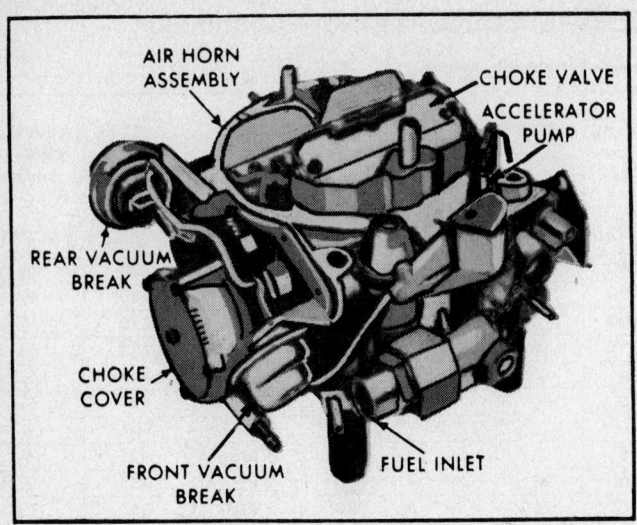

Fig. 1 Quadrajet M4M series carburetor (Typical)

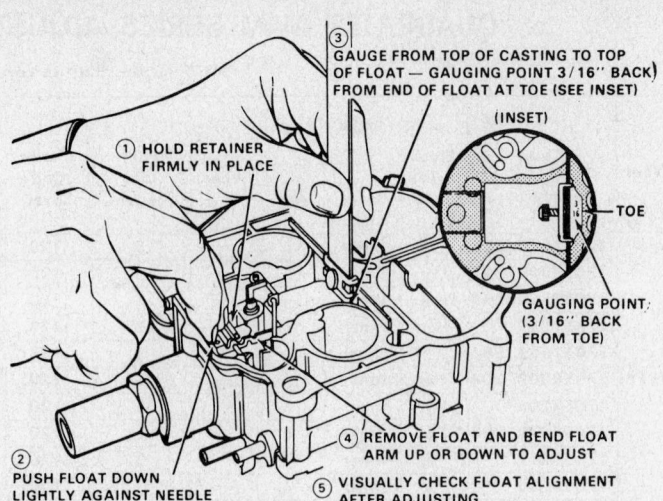

Fig. 2 Quadrajet M4M series float level adjustment

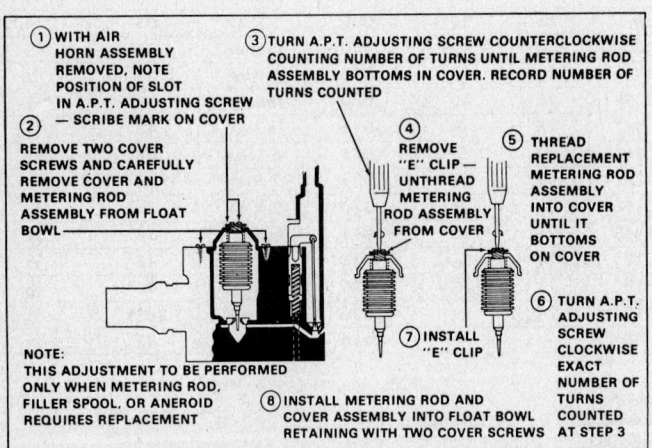

Fig. 3 Quadrajet M4M series A.P.T. metering rod adjustment

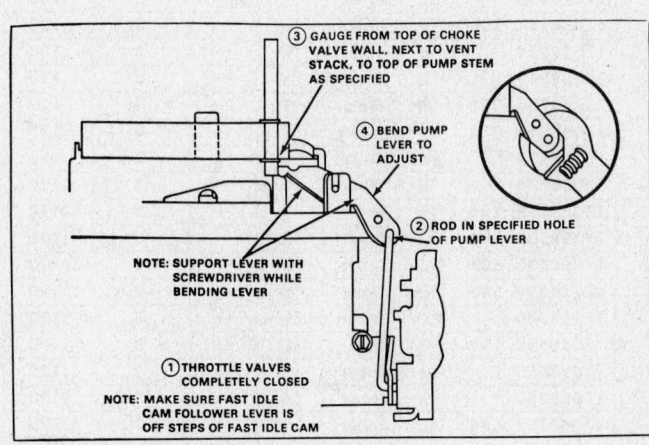

Fig. 4 Quadrajet M4M series pump rod adjustment. 1975-76

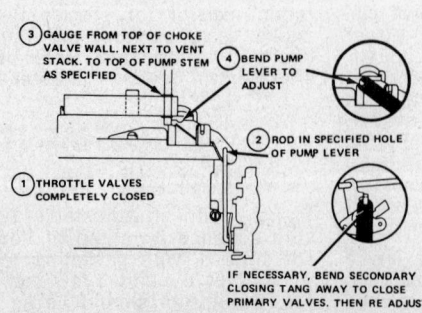

Fig. 4A Quadrajet M4M series pump rod adjustment . 1977-78

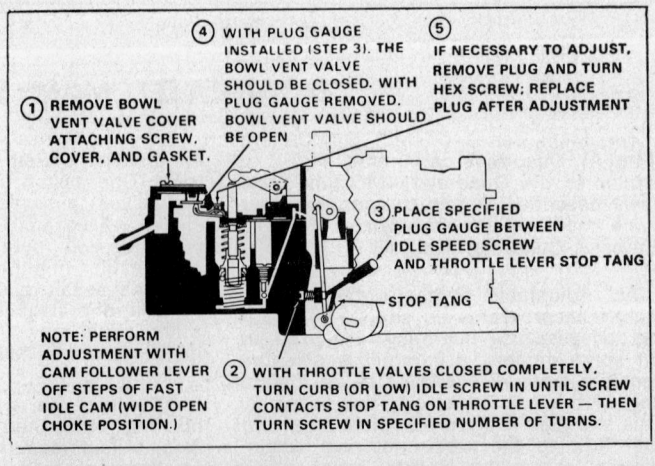

Fig. 5 Quadrajet M4M series bowl vent adjustment

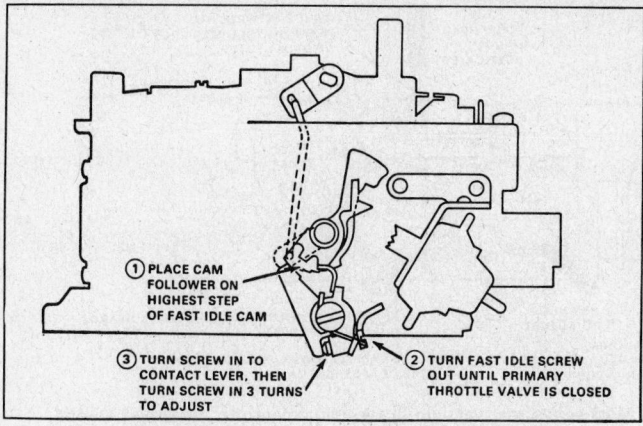

Fig. 6 Quadrajet M4M series fast idle adjustment (Bench)

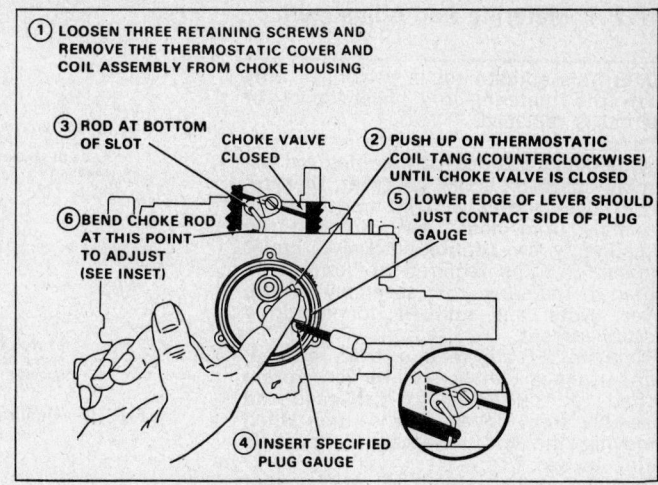

Fig. 7 Quadrajet M4M series choke coil lever adjustment

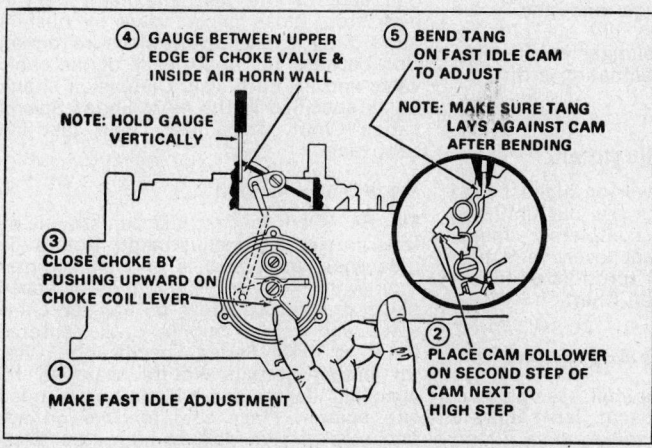

Fig. 8 Quadrajet M4M series choke rod adjustment. Plug gauge method

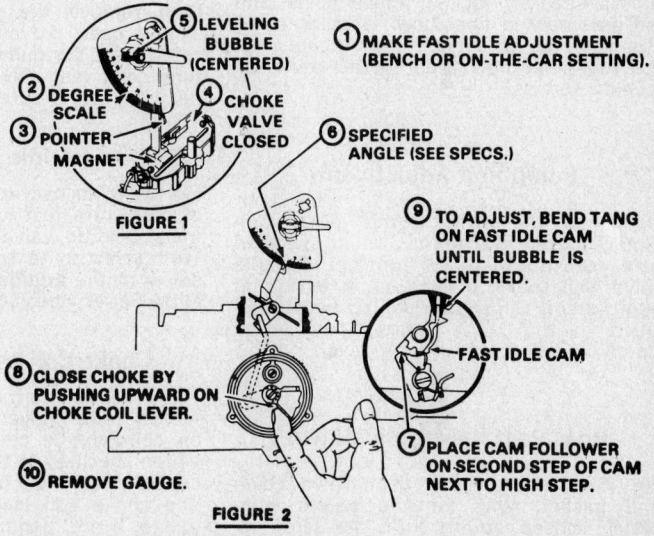

Fig. 8A Quadrajet M4M series choke rod adjustment. Angle gauge method

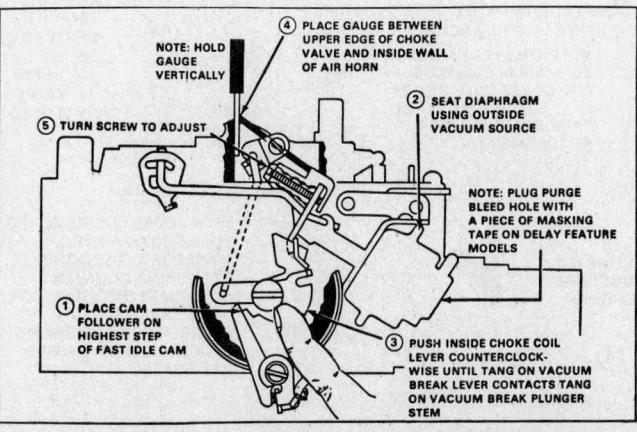

Fig. 9 Quadrajet M4M series front vacuum break adjustment. Plug gauge method

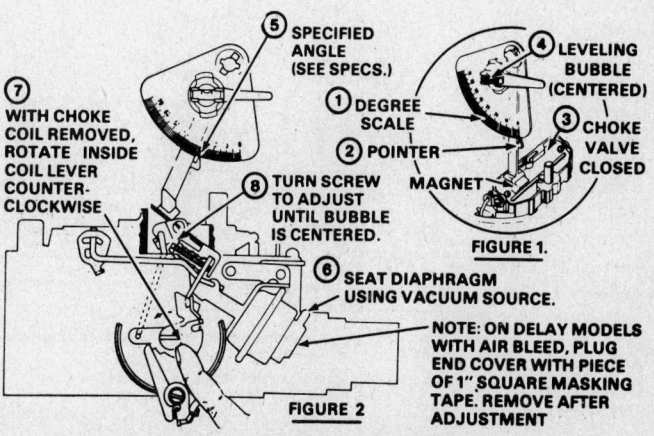

Fig. 9A Quadrajet M4M series front vacuum break adjustment. Angle gauge method

A.P.T. Metering Rod Adjustment

NOTE: This adjustment is performed only when the metering rod, filler spool or aneroid is replaced.

Fig. 3—Mark position of metering rod assembly adjusting screw on cover, then remove cover screws and lift metering rod assembly from float bowl. Rotating the adjusting screw counter-clockwise, count number of turns required to bottom the threaded metering rod assembly in the cover. Note this number for metering rod adjustment.

Remove "E" clip retainer from rod end, then using a small screwdriver, rotate slotted rod clockwise to disengage rod assembly from cover. Use caution when removing the rod assembly since it is spring loaded.

Install tension spring on replacement rod assembly, then thread the assembly into the cover until bottomed. Rotate the adjusting screw clockwise exactly the same number of turns from adjusting screw alignment mark noted previously. Install "E" clip in rod assembly groove, ensuring clip is securely locked. Place cover and rod assembly in float bowl, aligning cover assembly tab with float bowl tab nearest the fuel inlet nut, then install cover attaching screws.

Pump Rod Adjustment

Figs. 4 & 4A—With throttle valves completely closed and pump rod in specified hole, measure distance from top of choke valve wall (next to vent stack) to top of pump stem. Dimension should be as specified in the M4M Series Specification Chart. To adjust, bend pump lever.

Bowl Vent Valve Adjustment

Fig. 5—Remove bowl vent valve cover and gasket. With throttle valves completely closed, rotate curb idle screw inward until it contacts throttle lever stop tang, then an additional 1½ turns. Insert the gauge specified in the M4M Series Specification Chart between curb idle screw and throttle lever stop tang. The bowl vent valve should now be closed, then remove the gauge and the valve should open. To adjust, pry out plug located next to pump plunger shaft, then turn bowl vent valve, actuating arm allen head adjusting screw.

Fast Idle Adjustment

Fig. 6—With cam follower on highest step of cam, turn fast idle screw out until primary throttle valve is completely closed. Turn screw in to contact lever, then turn screw in the additional turns listed in the M4M Series Specification Chart.

Choke Coil Lever Adjustment

Fig. 7—With thermostic coil assembly removed from choke housing, push upward on coil tang to close choke valve. Insert gauge specified in the M4M Series Specification Chart into hole in choke housing. The choke coil lever should contact the gauge. If not, bend choke rod to adjust.

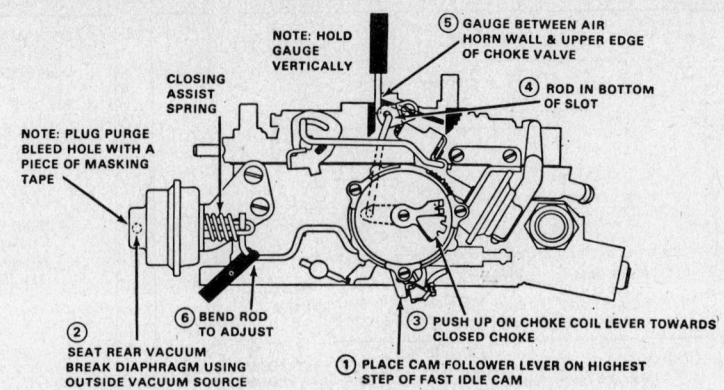

Fig. 10 Quadrajet M4M series rear vacuum break adjustment exc. Chevrolet V8-454. Plug gauge method

Choke Rod Adjustment

Plug Gauge Method

Fig. 8—With the fast idle adjustment performed, and the cam follower on the second step of the fast idle cam, next to high step, close choke valve by pushing upward on choke lever. Measure dimension between the upper edge of the choke valve and air horn wall. Dimension should be as specified in the M4M Series Specification Chart. To adjust, bend fast idle cam tang.

Angle Gauge Method

Fig. 8A—Perform fast idle adjustment before making this adjustment. Rotate degree scale until zero is opposite pointer, then with choke valve completely closed, place magnet squarely on top of choke valve and rotate bubble until centered. Refer to M4M Series Specification Chart for proper setting. Rotate scale so the specified degree for adjustment is opposite pointer. Place cam follower on second step of cam next to high step. Close choke by pushing upward on choke coil lever. To adjust, bend tang on fast idle cam until bubble is centered. Remove gauge.

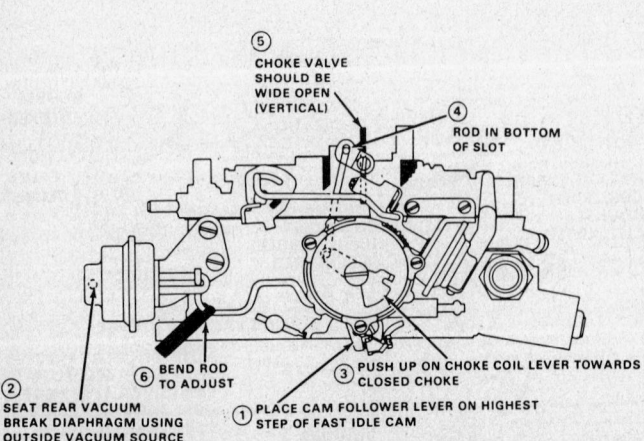

Fig. 10A Quadrajet M4M series rear vacuum break adjustment Chevrolet V8-454. Plug gauge method

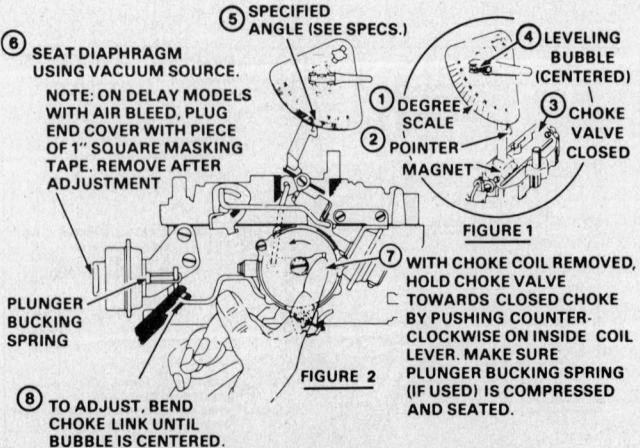

Fig. 10B Quadrajet M4M series rear vacuum break adjustment. Angle gauge method

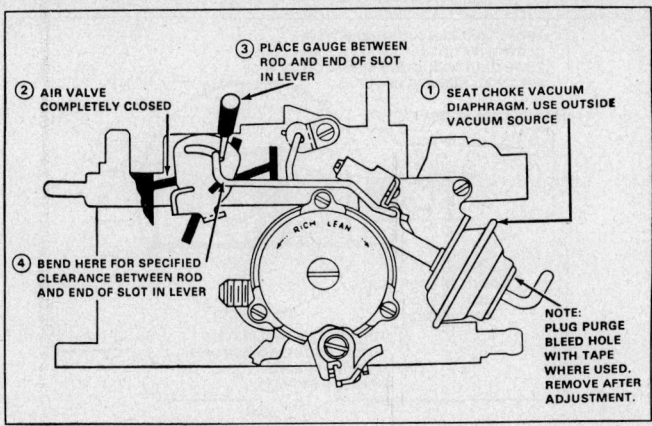

② AIR VALVE COMPLETELY CLOSED

③ PLACE GAUGE BETWEEN ROD AND END OF SLOT IN LEVER

① SEAT CHOKE VACUUM DIAPHRAGM. USE OUTSIDE VACUUM SOURCE

④ BEND HERE FOR SPECIFIED CLEARANCE BETWEEN ROD AND END OF SLOT IN LEVER

RICH LEAN

NOTE: PLUG PURGE BLEED HOLE WITH TAPE WHERE USED. REMOVE AFTER ADJUSTMENT.

Fig. 11 Quadrajet M4M series air-valve dashpot adjustment

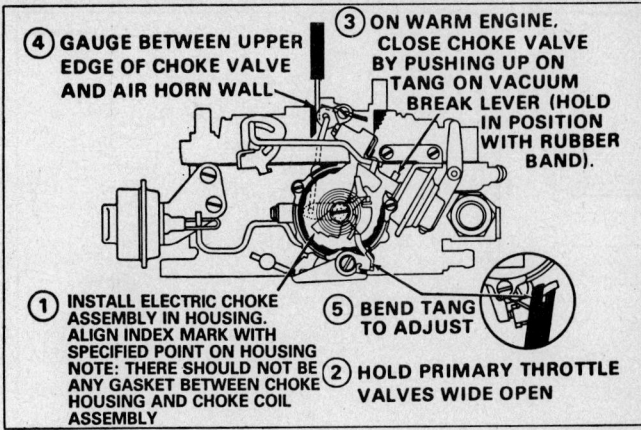

④ GAUGE BETWEEN UPPER EDGE OF CHOKE VALVE AND AIR HORN WALL

③ ON WARM ENGINE, CLOSE CHOKE VALVE BY PUSHING UP ON TANG ON VACUUM BREAK LEVER (HOLD IN POSITION WITH RUBBER BAND).

① INSTALL ELECTRIC CHOKE ASSEMBLY IN HOUSING. ALIGN INDEX MARK WITH SPECIFIED POINT ON HOUSING NOTE: THERE SHOULD NOT BE ANY GASKET BETWEEN CHOKE HOUSING AND CHOKE COIL ASSEMBLY

⑤ BEND TANG TO ADJUST

② HOLD PRIMARY THROTTLE VALVES WIDE OPEN

Fig. 13 Quadrajet M4M series choke unloader adjustment. Plug gauge method

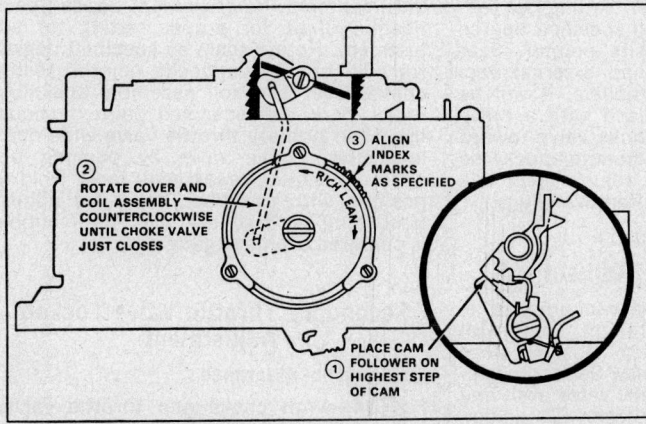

② ROTATE COVER AND COIL ASSEMBLY COUNTERCLOCKWISE UNTIL CHOKE VALVE JUST CLOSES

③ ALIGN INDEX MARKS AS SPECIFIED

RICH LEAN

PLACE CAM FOLLOWER ON HIGHEST STEP OF CAM

Fig. 12 Quadrajet M4M series automatic choke coil adjustment

⑦ HOLD PRIMARY THROTTLE VALVES WIDE OPEN.

⑤ SPECIFIED ANGLE (SEE SPECS.)

④ LEVELING BUBBLE (CENTERED)

① DEGREE SCALE

② POINTER MAGNET

③ CHOKE VALVE CLOSED

FIGURE 1

FIGURE 2

⑨ BEND TANG TO ADJUST UNTIL BUBBLE IS CENTERED.

⑥ INSTALL CHOKE THERMOSTATIC COVER AND COIL ASSEMBLY IN HOUSING. ALIGN INDEX MARK WITH SPECIFIED POINT ON HOUSING.

⑧ ON WARM ENGINE, CLOSE CHOKE VALVE BY PUSHING UP ON TANG ON VACUUM BREAK LEVER (HOLD IN POSITION WITH RUBBER BAND).

Fig. 13A Quadrajet M4M series choke unloader adjustment. Angle gauge method

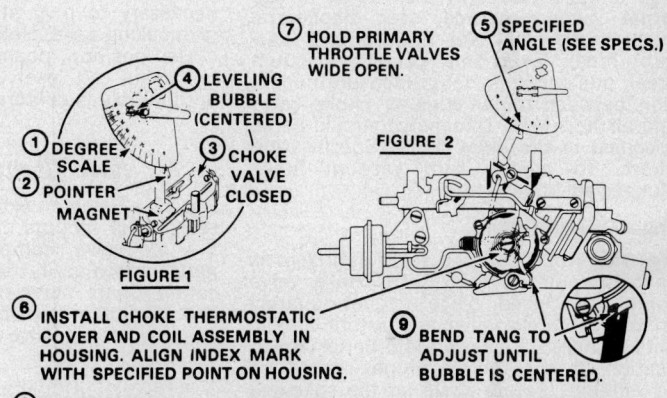

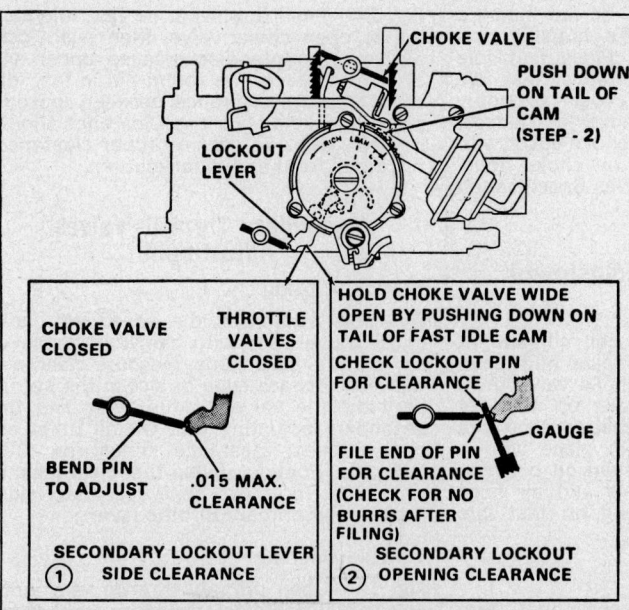

CHOKE VALVE

PUSH DOWN ON TAIL OF CAM (STEP - 2)

LOCKOUT LEVER

RICH LEAN

CHOKE VALVE CLOSED

THROTTLE VALVES CLOSED

BEND PIN TO ADJUST

.015 MAX. CLEARANCE

① SECONDARY LOCKOUT LEVER SIDE CLEARANCE

HOLD CHOKE VALVE WIDE OPEN BY PUSHING DOWN ON TAIL OF FAST IDLE CAM CHECK LOCKOUT PIN FOR CLEARANCE

FILE END OF PIN FOR CLEARANCE (CHECK FOR NO BURRS AFTER FILING)

GAUGE

② SECONDARY LOCKOUT OPENING CLEARANCE

Fig. 14 Quadrajet M4M series secondary throttle valve lockout adjustment

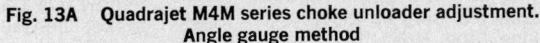
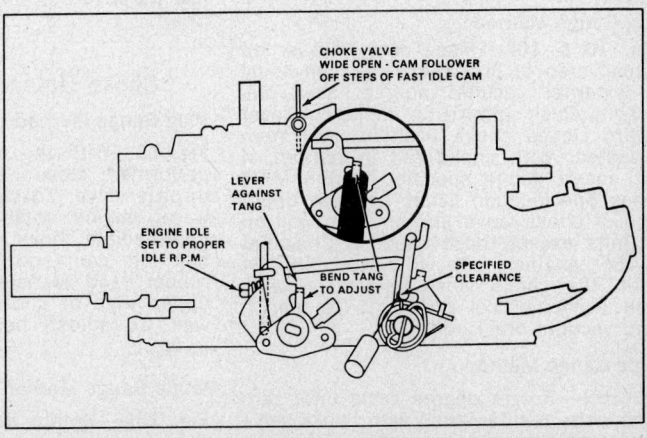

CHOKE VALVE WIDE OPEN - CAM FOLLOWER OFF STEPS OF FAST IDLE CAM

LEVER AGAINST TANG

ENGINE IDLE SET TO PROPER IDLE R.P.M.

BEND TANG TO ADJUST

SPECIFIED CLEARANCE

Fig. 15 Quadrajet M4M series secondary throttle valve closing adjustment

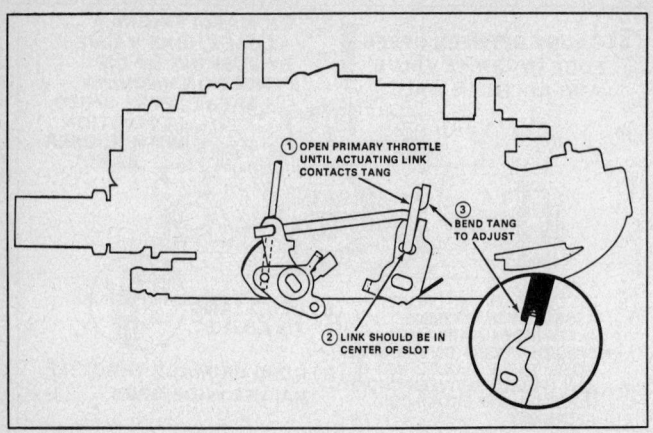

Fig. 16 Quadrajet M4M series secondary throttle valve opening adjustment

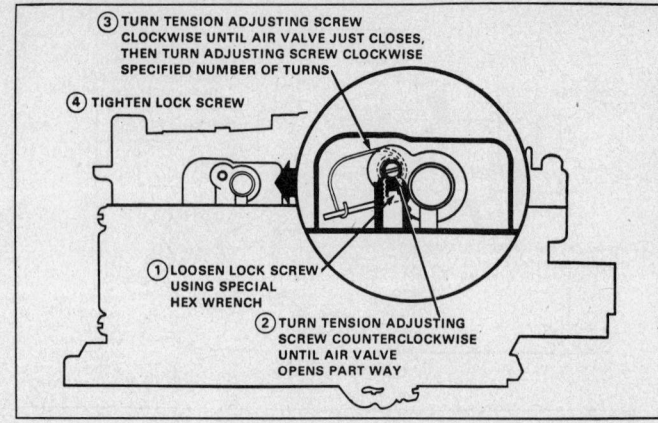

Fig. 17 Quadrajet M4M series air-valve spring wind-up adjustment

Front Vacuum Break Adjustment

Plug Gauge Method

Fig. 9—Place cam follower on highest step of fast idle cam, then using an external vacuum source, seat diaphragm. Push choke coil lever upward until vacuum break lever tang contacts vacuum break plunger stem tang. Measure dimension between upper edge of choke valve and air horn wall. Dimension should be as specified in the M4M Series Specification Chart. To adjust, turn vacuum break plunger adjusting screw.

Angle Gauge Method

Fig. 9A—Rotate degree scale until zero is opposite pointer, then with choke valve completely closed, place magnet squarely on top of choke valve and rotate bubble until centered. Refer to M4M Series Specification Chart to obtain proper setting for adjustment. Rotate scale so the specified degree for adjustment is opposite pointer. Seat choke diaphragm using an external vacuum source. On some models, it will be necessary to plug air bleed with a piece of masking tape. Hold choke valve toward closed position, pushing counter-clockwise on inside coil lever. To adjust, rotate screw until bubble is centered. Remove gauge.

Rear Vacuum Break Adjustment

Plug Gauge Method

Figs. 10 & 10A—Place cam follower on highest step of fast idle cam, then using an external vacuum source, seat diaphragm. Push upward on choke coil lever toward closed choke position until stem is seated. With choke rod in bottom of slot, insert gauge specified in the M4M Series Specification Chart between upper edge of choke valve and air horn wall on all units except those used on Chevrolet V8-454 engines. On Chevrolet V8-454 units, the choke valve should be wide open (fully vertical position). To adjust, bend vacuum break rod.

Angle Gauge Method

Fig. 10B—Rotate degree scale until zero is opposite pointer, then with choke valve completely closed, place magnet squarely on top of choke valve and rotate bubble until centered. Refer to M4M Series Speci-

fication Chart for proper setting for adjustment. Rotate scale so specified degree for adjustment is opposite pointer. Seat choke diaphragm using an external vacuum source. On some models, it will be necessary to plug air bleed with a piece of masking tape. Hold choke valve toward closed position, pushing counter-clockwise on inside coil lever. To adjust, bend link until bubble is centered. Remove gauge.

Air Valve Dashpot Adjustment

Fig. 11—Using an external vacuum source, seat choke vacuum diaphragm. Then, with the air valve completely closed, place gauge specified in the M4M Series Specification Chart between air valve rod and end of slot in air valve lever. To adjust, bend rod at air valve end.

Choke Coil Adjustment

Fig. 12—Install choke coil and cover assembly. On Cadillac units, do not install a gasket between the choke housing and electric choke assembly. Place fast idle cam follower on highest step of fast idle cam. Rotate coil and cover assembly counter-clockwise until choke just closes, then align index mark on choke cover with the specified index mark on choke housing. Refer to the M4M Series Specification Chart.

Choke Unloader Adjustment

Plug Gauge Method

Fig. 13—With the choke coil adjustment performed, close choke, valve and open throttle valve. To close choke valve on a warm engine, push upward on tang of intermediate choke lever that contacts the fast idle cam and hold in place with a rubber band. Measure dimension between upper edge of choke valve and air horn wall. To adjust, bend tang on fast idle lever.

Angle Gauge Method

Fig. 13A—Rotate degree scale until zero is opposite pointer, then with choke valve completely closed, place magnet squarely on top of choke valve and rotate bubble

until centered. Refer to M4M Series Specification Chart for proper setting for adjustment. Rotate scale so specified degree for adjustment is opposite pointer. Install choke cover and coil assembly and align index mark with specified point on housing. Hold primary throttle valve wide open and close choke valve by pushing upward on vacuum break lever tang. Hold in position with a rubber band. To adjust, bend tang on fast idle lever until bubble is centered. Remove gauge.

Secondary Throttle Valve Lockout Adjustment

Lockout-Pin Clearance

Fig. 14—With choke and throttle valves fully closed, measure clearance between lockout-pin and lockout lever. Maximum clearance should not exceed .015 inch. To adjust, bend lockout-pin.

Opening Clearance

Fig. 14—Push downward on fast idle cam tail to open choke valve, then push lockout lever counter-clockwise so upper end of lever contacts the round pin in fast idle cam. Measure clearance between lockout-pin and lockout lever toe. Clearance should be .015 inch. To obtain proper clearance, file metal from end of lockout-pin.

Secondary Throttle Valves Adjustment

Throttle Closing

Fig. 15—With curb idle speed set, hold choke valve open with cam follower lever off fast idle cam steps. Measure clearance between forward edge of slot in the secondary throttle valve pick-up lever and the secondary actuating rod. On all units except Pontiac, clearance should be .020 inch. On Pontiac units, the clearance is .025 inch. To adjust, bend secondary closing tang on primary throttle lever.

Throttle Opening

Fig. 16—Open primary throttle lever until link lightly contacts secondary lever tang. The bottom end of the link should be in the center of the slot in secondary lever. To adjust, bend tang on secondary lever.

Air Valve Spring Wind-Up Adjustment

Fig. 17—Remove front vacuum break diaphragm unit and air valve dashpot rod. Loosen lock screw and rotate spring adjusting screw counter-clockwise until air valve is partially open. Hold air valve closed, then rotate adjusting screw clockwise specified number of turns after the spring contacts pin. Refer to the M4M Series Specification Chart. Tighten lock screw and install air valve dashpot rod and the front vacuum break diaphragm unit.

DUAL-JET 2MC, M2MC, M2ME 200, 210 ADJUSTMENT SPECIFICATIONS

See Tune Up Chart in car chapters for hot idle speeds.

Year	Carb. Production No.	Float Level	Pump Rod Hole	Pump Rod Adj.	Choke Coil Lever	Choke Rod	Vacuum Break Rich	Vacuum Break Lean	Vacuum Break Front	Vacuum Break Rear	Choke Un-loader	Choke Setting
1975	7045156	3/16	Inner	9/32	.120	.105	.110	.175	—	—	.210	1 Rich
	7045297	3/16	Inner	3/16	.120	.105	.110	.210	—	—	.210	1 Rich
	7045298	3/16	Inner	9/32	.120	.105	.110	.175	—	—	.210	1 Rich
	7045354	3/16	Outer	9/32	.120	.105	.110	.210	—	—	.210	Index
	7045356, 598	3/16	Inner	3/16	.120	.105	.110	.210	—	—	.210	Index
	7045358	3/16	Outer	5/16	.120	.105	.110	.210	—	—	.210	Index
1976	17056152, 154	1/8	Inner	9/32	.120	.105	.110	.175	—	—	.210	1 Rich
	17056156, 158	1/8	Inner	9/32	.120	.105	.110	.175	—	—	.210	1 Rich
	17056157	1/8	Outer	3/16	.120	.105	.110	.175	—	—	.210	1 Rich
	17056452	1/8	Outer	3/16	.120	.105	.110	.175	—	—	.210	1 Rich
	17056454	1/8	Outer	3/16	.120	.105	.110	.210	—	—	.210	1 Rich
	17056455	1/8	Inner	9/32	.120	.120	.130	.210	—	—	.210	1 Rich
	17056456, 458	1/8	Outer	3/16	.120	.105	.110	.210	—	—	.210	1 Rich
	17056457	1/8	Outer	3/16	.120	.105	.110	.210	—	—	.210	Index
	17056459	1/8	Outer	3/16	.120	.105	.110	.210	—	—	.210	Index
1977	17057150, 151	1/8	Outer	11/32	.120	.085	.090	.160	—	—	.190	2 Rich
	17057156, 158	1/8	Outer	11/32	.120	.085	.090	.160	—	—	.190	1 Rich
	17057157	1/8	Outer	3/8	.120	.090	.100	.190	—	—	.190	1 Rich
	17057172, 176	11/32	Inner	1/4	.120	.075	—	—	①	②	.240	2 Rich
	17057173, 177	11/32	Outer	5/16	.120	.075	—	—	③	②	.240	2 Rich
1978	17058130, 131	1/4	Inner	1/4	.120	46°	—	—	24°	—	46°	Index
	17058132, 133	1/4	Inner	1/4	.120	46°	—	—	24°	—	46°	Index
	17058150, 152	3/8	Inner	1/4	.120	14°	—	—	35°	25°	35°	2 Rich
	17058151, 156	3/8	Outer	11/32	.120	14°	—	—	38°	25°	35°	2 Rich
	17058154, 155	3/8	Outer	11/32	.120	14°	—	—	27°	40°	35°	2 Rich
	17058158	3/8	Outer	11/32	.120	14°	—	—	38°	25°	35°	2 Rich
	17058160	11/32	Inner	1/4	.120	22.5°	—	—	25°	32°	33°	2 Rich
	17058192	5/16	Inner	9/32	.120	14.5°	—	—	21°	19°	50°	2 Rich
	17058450	3/8	Outer	11/32	.120	14°	—	—	27°	45°	35°	2 Rich
	17058496	1/4	Outer	3/8	.120	15°	—	—	24°	34°	38°	1 Rich
1979	17059134, 135	15/32	Inner	1/4	.120	38°	—	—	27°	—	38°	1 Lean
	17059136, 137	15/32	Inner	1/4	.120	38°	—	—	27°	—	38°	1 Lean
	17059150, 152	3/8	Inner	1/4	.120	14°	—	—	32°	23°	35°	2 Rich
	17059151	3/8	Outer	11/32	.120	14°	—	—	38°	25°	35°	2 Rich
	17059154	3/8	Outer	11/32	.120	14°	—	—	27°	40°	35°	2 Rich
	17059160	11/32	Inner	1/4	.120	20°	—	—	23°	33°	32°	2 Rich
	17059180, 190	11/32	Inner	1/4	.120	24.5°	—	—	19°	17°	38°	2 Rich
	17059184	11/32	Inner	1/4	.120	24.5°	—	—	19°	17°	35°	2 Rich
	17059191	11/32	Inner	9/32	.120	24.5°	—	—	19°	17°	38°	2 Rich
	17059193	13/32	Inner	1/4	.120	24.5°	—	—	19°	17°	35°	2 Rich
	17059194	11/32	Inner	1/4	.120	24.5°	—	—	19°	17°	35°	2 Rich
	17059196	11/32	Inner	1/4	.120	24.5°	—	—	23°	21°	42°	1 Rich
	17059430, 432	9/32	Inner	9/32	.120	38°	—	—	29°	—	38°	1 Lean
	17059434, 436	13/32	Inner	9/32	.120	38°	—	—	28°	—	38°	2 Lean
	17059450	3/8	Outer	11/32	.120	14°	—	—	27°	45°	35°	2 Rich
	17059491	11/32	Inner	9/32	.120	24.5°	—	—	23°	21°	42°	1 Rich
	17059492	11/32	Inner	9/32	.120	24.5°	—	—	19°	19°	42°	2 Rich
	17059496	5/16	Inner	3/8	.120	24.5°	—	—	21°	30°	38°	2 Rich
	17059498	11/32	Inner	9/32	.120	24.5°	—	—	23°	21°	42°	2 Rich

①—With angle gauge, 24°; with plug gauge, .135 inch.
②—Before first scheduled tune up—with angle gauge, 36°; with plug gauge, .225 inch.
    After first scheduled tune up—with angle gauge, 38°; with plug gauge, .240 inch.
③—With angle gauge, 28°; with plug gauge, .165 inch.

DUAL-JET 2MC, M2MC, M2ME 200, 210 ADJUSTMENTS

The Dual Jet carburetor, Figs. 1 and 2, is a two barrel, single stage unit, incorporating the design features of the primary side of the Quadrajet (four barrel) carburetor. The triple venturi stack up, plus the smaller 1⅜ inch bores results in good fuel metering control during all phases of operation.

The main metering system has a separate main well for each main nozzle for good fuel flow through the venturi.

An adjustable part throttle screw is used in the float bowl to aid in controlling fuel mixtures for good emission control. This screw is factory preset and should not be adjusted in service. However, if it becomes necessary to replace the float bowl, the new service float bowl will include the adjustable part throttle screw which has been preset.

Float Level Adjustment

Fig. 3—With adjustable T-scale, measure from top of float bowl gasket surface (gasket removed) to top of float at toe (locate gauging point ³⁄₁₆″ back from toe).

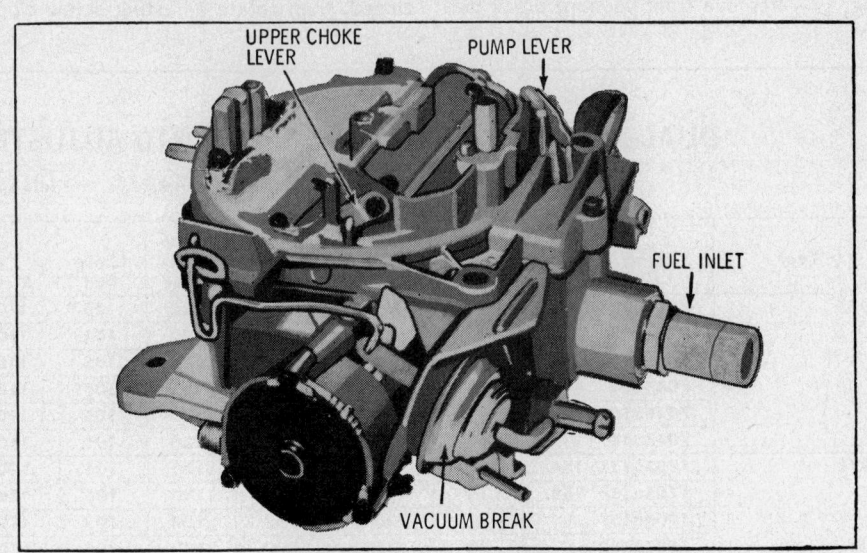

Fig. 1   Rochester Dual-Jet 2MC & M2MC 200 carburetor (typical)

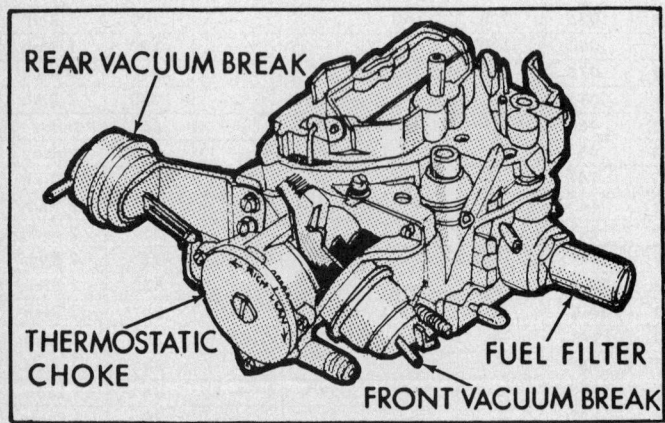

Fig. 2   Rochester Dual-Jet M2MC 210 carburetor

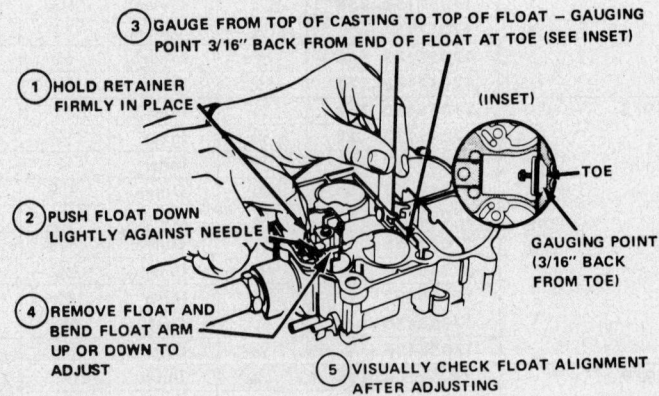

Fig. 3   Float level adjustment

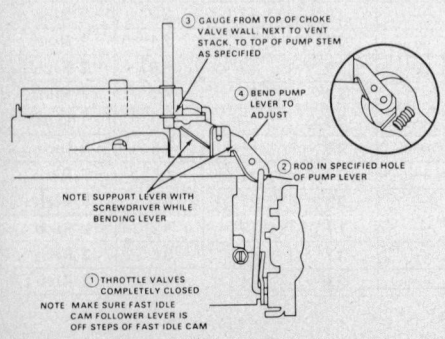

Fig. 4   Pump rod adjustment. 1975-76

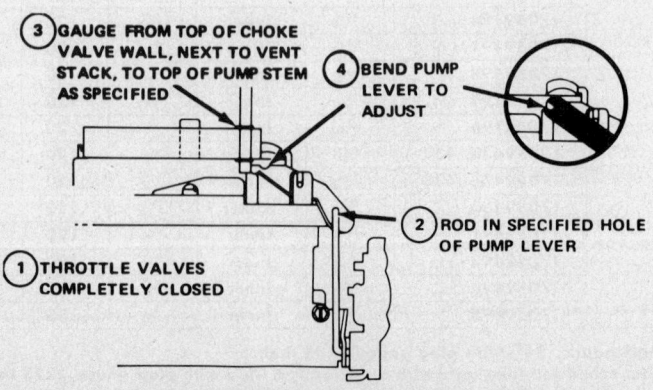

Fig. 5   Pump rod adjustment. 1977-78

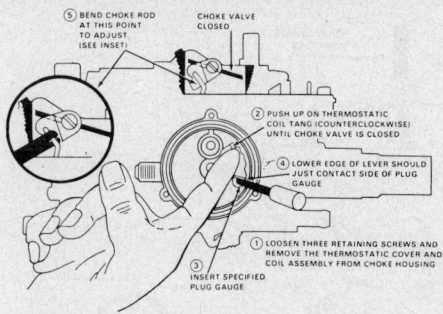

Fig. 6   Choke coil lever adjustment

edge of choke valve and air horn wall should be as specified in the 2MC Specifications Chart. Adjust by bending tang on intermediate choke lever.

Angle Gauge Method

Fig. 7A—Rotate degree scale until the zero is opposite pointer, then with choke valve completely closed, place magnet squarely on top of choke valve and rotate bubble until centered. Refer to the Specification Chart for proper setting for adjustment. Rotate scale so specified degree setting for adjustment is opposite pointer. Place cam follower on second step of cam, next to high step. Close choke by pushing upward on choke coil lever. To adjust, bend tang on fast idle lever until the bubble is centered.

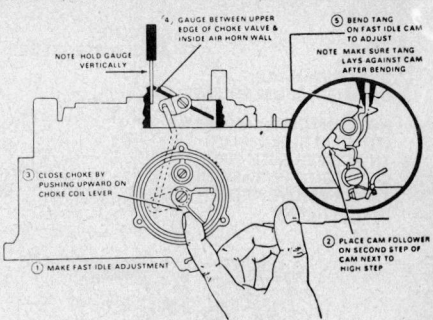

Fig. 7   Choke rod adjustment. Plug Gauge Method

Adjust as directed in the illustration to the dimension listed in the *2MC Specifications Chart*. Make sure retaining pin is held firmly in place and tang of float is seated on float needle.

Pump Rod Adjustment

Figs. 4 & 5—With throttle valves completely closed and pump rod in specified hole in pump lever, measure from top of choke valve wall (next to vent stack) to top of pump stem. Dimension should be as listed in the *2MC Specifications Chart*. To adjust, bend pump lever as required.

Choke Coil Lever Adjustment

Fig. 6—With thermostatic coil assembly removed, push upward on coil tang until choke valve closes. Insert gauge specified in the 2MC Specifications Chart into choke housing hole. The lower edge of choke coil lever should just contact gauge. To adjust, bend choke rod as required.

Choke Rod Adjustment

Plug Gauge Method

Fig. 7—With fast idle adjustment made, and cam follower on second step of fast idle cam and against the high step, push upward on choke coil lever until choke valve closes. Dimension between upper

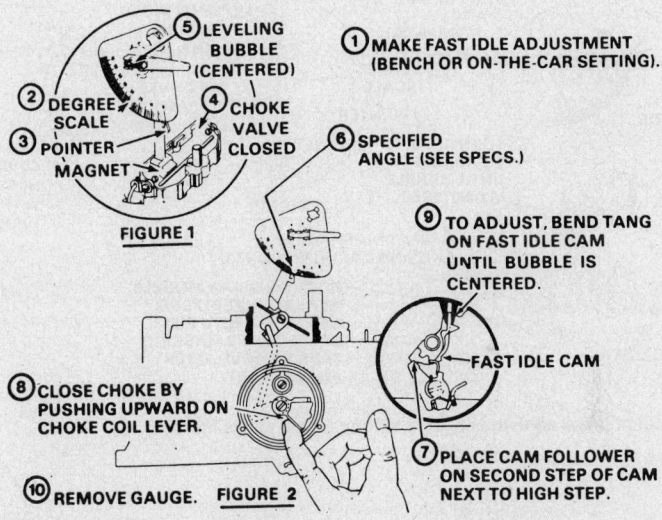

Fig. 7A   Choke rod adjustment. Angle gauge method

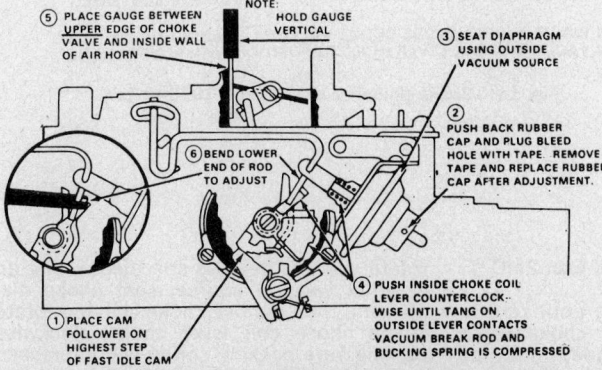

Fig. 8   Vacuum break adjustment, rich setting. 2MC units

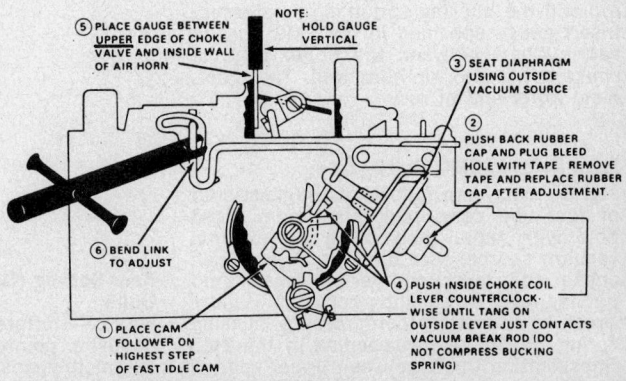

Fig. 9   Vacuum break adjustment, lean setting. 2MC units

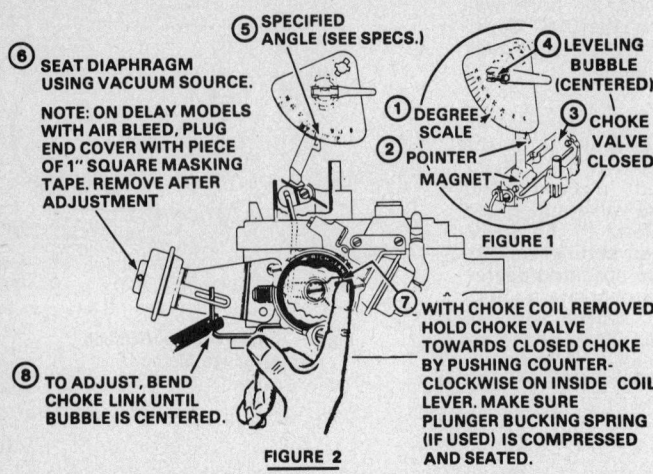

Fig. 10   Vacuum break adjustment, rear setting (angle gauge method)

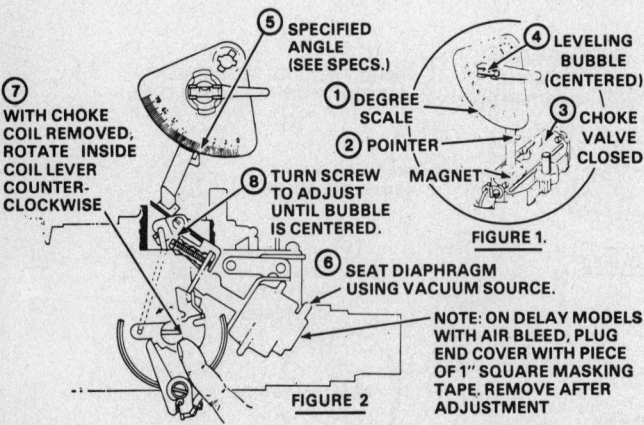

Fig. 11   Vacuum break adjustment, front setting (angle gauge method)

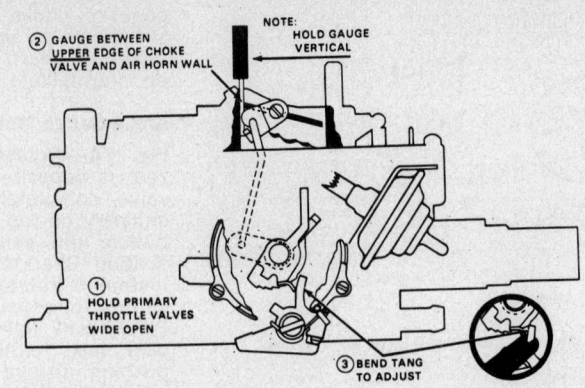

Fig. 12   Choke unloader adjustment. 1975-76 units

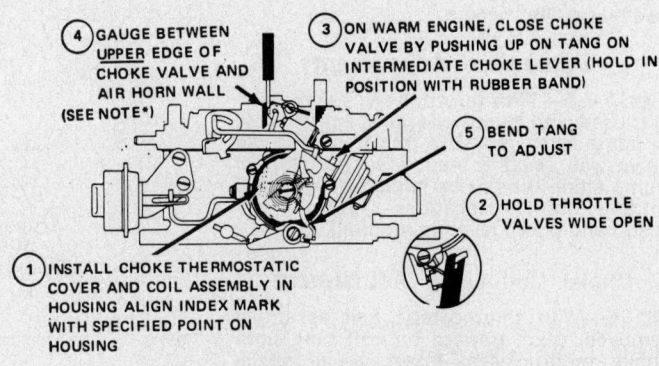

Fig. 13   Choke unloader adjustment. 1977 units

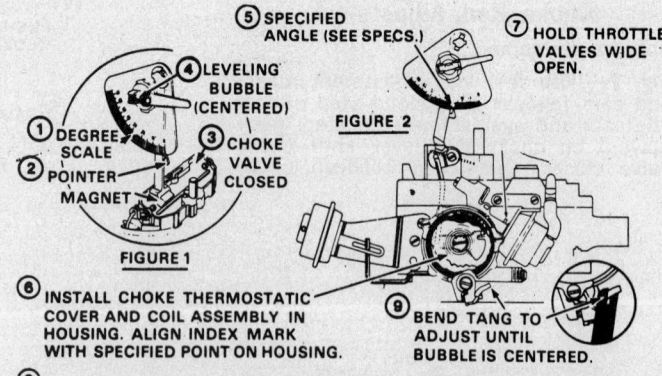

Fig. 14   Choke unloader adjustment. 1978 units

Vacuum Break Adjustment

Rich Setting, 2MC Units

Fig. 8—With cam follower on highest step of fast idle cam, plug diaphragm bleed hole with tape, then using an external vacuum source, seat the diaphragm. Push choke coil lever counter-clockwise until outside lever tang contacts vacuum break rod and the bucking spring is compressed. Insert gauge specified in the 2MC Specification Chart between the upper edge of choke valve and air horn wall. To adjust, bend lower end of rod.

Lean Setting, 2MC Units

Fig. 9—With cam follower on highest step of fast idle cam, plug diaphragm bleed hole with tape, then using an external vacuum source, seat the diaphragm. Push choke coil lever counter-clockwise until outside lever tang lightly contacts vacuum break rod without compressing bucking spring. Insert gauge specified in the 2MC Specification Chart between upper edge of choke valve and air horn wall. To adjust, bend upper end of rod.

Rear Setting (Gauge Method), Exc. 2MC Units

Fig. 10—Rotate degree scale until zero is opposite pointer, then with choke valve completely closed, place magnet on top of choke valve and rotate bubble until it is centered. Refer to Specification Chart and rotate scale to degrees specified. Using an external vacuum source, seat choke diaphragm, then remove choke coil and rotate inside choke coil lever counterclockwise making sure bucking spring is compressed and seated. To make final adjustment, bend link until bubble is centered.

Front Setting (Gauge Method), Exc. 2MC Units

Fig. 11—Rotate degree scale until zero is opposite pointer, then with choke valve completely closed, place gauge on top of choke valve and rotate bubble until it is centered. Refer to Specifications Chart and rotate gauge to degrees specified. Using an external vacuum source, seat choke vacuum diaphragm, then remove choke coil and rotate inside coil lever counterclockwise. To make final adjustment, turn screw in or out until bubble is centered.

Choke Unloader Adjustment

1975-76 Units

Fig. 12—With primary throttle valves held wide open, insert specified gauge between upper edge of choke valve and air horn wall. To adjust, bend fast idle lever tang.

1977 Units

Fig. 13—Install choke cover and coil assembly and align index mark with specified point on housing. Hold throttle valves

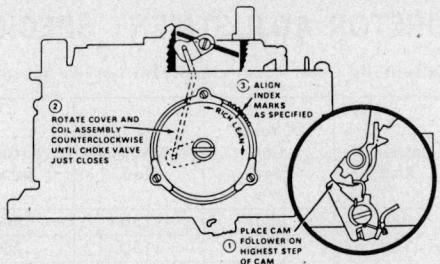

Fig. 15   Choke coil adjustment

wide open. On a warm engine, close choke valve by pushing upward on tang on intermediate choke lever and hold in position with a rubber band. Insert specified gauge between upper edge of choke valve and air horn wall. To adjust, bend fast idle lever tang.

1978 Units, Angle Gauge Method

Fig. 14—Rotate degree scale until the

zero is opposite pointer, then with choke valve completely closed, place magnet squarely on top of choke valve and rotate bubble until centered. Refer to the Specification Chart for proper setting for adjustment. Rotate scale until specified degree for adjustment is opposite pointer. Install choke cover and coil assembly and align index mark with specified point on housing. Hold throttle valves wide open. On a warm engine close choke valve by pushing upward on tang on vacuum break lever and hold in position with a rubber band. To adjust, bend fast idle lever tang until the bubble is centered.

Choke Coil Adjustment

Fig. 15—Place the fast idle cam follower on the highest step of the fast idle cam. Rotate choke cover and coil assembly counter-clockwise until the choke valve just closes and the index point on cover aligns with the specified index point on the choke housing.

MONOJET 1ME CARBURETOR ADJUSTMENT SPECIFICATIONS

See Tune Up Chart in car chapter for hot idle speeds.

Year	Carb. Part No. ①	Float Level	Metering Rod	Choke Coil Lever	Choke Rod	Vacuum Break	Unloader	Choke Setting	Fast Idle R.P.M.
1976	17056030	5/32	.072	—	.065	.070	.165	3 Rich	2200
	17056031	5/32	.072	—	.065	.070	.165	3 Rich	2000
	17056032	5/32	.073	—	.045	.070	.200	3 Rich	2200
	17056033	5/32	.073	—	.045	.070	.200	3 Rich	2000
	17056034	5/32	.073	—	.045	.070	.200	3 Rich	2200
	17056035	5/32	.073	—	.045	.070	.200	3 Rich	2000
	17056036	5/32	.072	—	.065	.070	.165	3 Rich	2200
	17056037	5/32	.072	—	.065	.070	.165	3 Rich	2000
	17056330	5/32	.072	—	.065	.070	.165	3 Rich	2200
	17056331	5/32	.072	—	.065	.070	.165	3 Rich	2000
	17056332	5/32	.073	—	.045	.070	.200	3 Rich	2200
	17056333	5/32	.073	—	.045	.070	.200	3 Rich	2000
	17056334	5/32	.073	—	.045	.070	.200	3 Rich	2200
	17056335	5/32	.073	—	.045	.120	.200	3 Rich	2000
1977	17057013	3/8	.080	.120	.100	.125	.325	1 Rich	2000
	17057014	3/8	.090	.120	.100	.125	.325	2 Rich	2000
	17057015	3/8	.080	.120	.100	.125	.325	1 Rich	2000
	17057016	3/8	.080	.120	.105	.105	.325	1 Lean	2000
	17057018	3/8	.080	.120	.085	.120	.325	2 Rich	2000
	17057020	3/8	.090	.120	.100	.125	.325	2 Rich	2000
	17057030	5/32	.080	.120	.050	.080	.200	2 Rich	2400
	17057031	5/32	.080	.120	.050	.080	.200	2 Rich	2300
	17057032	5/32	.080	.120	.050	.080	.200	2 Rich	2400
	17057034	5/32	.080	.120	.050	.080	.200	2 Rich	2400
	17057035	5/32	.080	.120	.050	.080	.200	2 Rich	2300
	17057042	5/32	.080	.120	.050	.075	.200	1 Rich	2400
	17057044	5/32	.080	.120	.050	.075	.200	1 Rich	2400
	17057045	5/32	.080	.120	.050	.075	.200	1 Rich	—
	17057310	3/8	.100	.120	—	—	—	Index	②
	17057312	3/8	.100	.120	—	—	—	Index	②
	17057314	3/8	.080	.120	.100	.110	.225	Index	1800
	17057318	3/8	.080	.120	.100	.110	.225	Index	1800
	17057332	5/32	.080	.120	.050	.075	.200	2 Rich	2400
	17057334	5/32	.080	.120	.050	.075	.200	2 Rich	2400
	17057335	5/32	.080	.120	.050	.075	.200	2 Rich	—

MONOJET 1ME CARBURETOR ADJUSTMENT SPECIFICATIONS—Continued

See Tune Up Chart in car chapter for hot idle speeds.

Year	Carb. Part No. ①	Float Level	Metering Rod	Choke Coil Lever	Choke Rod	Vacuum Break	Unloader	Choke Setting	Fast Idle R.P.M.
1978	17058013	⅜	.080	.120	.180	.200	.500	Index	2000
	17058014	⁵⁄₁₆	.100	.120	.180	.200	.500	Index	2100
	17058020	⁵⁄₁₆	.100	.120	.180	.200	.500	Index	2100
	17058031	⁵⁄₃₂	.080	.120	.105	.150	.500	2 Rich	2400
	17058032	⁵⁄₃₂	.080	.120	.080	.130	.500	3 Rich	2400
	17058033	⁵⁄₃₂	.080	.120	.080	.130	.500	2 Rich	2400
	17058034	⁵⁄₃₂	.080	.120	.080	.130	.500	3 Rich	2400
	17058035	⁵⁄₃₂	.080	.120	.080	.130	.500	3 Rich	2300
	17058036	⁵⁄₃₂	.080	.120	.080	.130	.500	3 Rich	2400
	17058037	⁵⁄₃₂	.080	.120	.080	.130	.500	2 Rich	2400
	17058038	⁵⁄₃₂	.080	.120	.080	.130	.500	3 Rich	2400
	17058042	⁵⁄₃₂	.080	.120	.080	③	.500	2 Rich	2400
	17058044	⁵⁄₃₂	.080	.120	.080	③	.500	2 Rich	2400
	17058045	⁵⁄₃₂	.080	.120	.080	③	.500	2 Rich	2300
	17058314	⅜	.100	.120	.190	.245	.400	Index	2000
	17058332	⁵⁄₃₂	.080	.120	.080	③	.500	2 Rich	2400
	17058334	⁵⁄₃₂	.080	.120	.080	③	.500	2 Rich	2400
	17058335	⁵⁄₃₂	.080	.120	.080	③	.500	2 Rich	2300
	17058339	⁵⁄₃₂	.080	.120	.080	③	.500	2 Rich	2400
1979	17059013	—	—	—	—	—	—	—	—
	17059014	—	—	—	—	—	—	—	—
	17059020	—	—	—	—	—	—	—	—
	17059314	—	—	—	—	—	—	—	—

①—On tag attached to carburetor.   ②—Exc. Calif. 2000 R.P.M. (N); Calif. 1800 R.P.M. (N).   ③—Below 30,000 miles, .130 inch; above 30,000 miles, .160 inch.

MONOJET 1ME ADJUSTMENTS

This Monojet carburetor is a single bore, downdraft carburetor incorporating a triple venturi in conjunction with a plain tube nozzle. The main metering system fuel flow is controlled by a main well air bleed and a variable orifice jet. Power enrichment is provided through a mechanically operated metering rod, connected by linkage to the throttle shaft. A fuel pull-over enrichment is used to supplement main metering mixtures at higher engine RPM.

An automatic choke system using an electrically heated choke coil is incorporated into this carburetor. The vacuum diaphragm unit, mounted externally on the air horn, is connected to the thermostatic coil lever through a connecting link. The electric choke coil is contained in a housing mounted on a bracket attached to the float bowl.

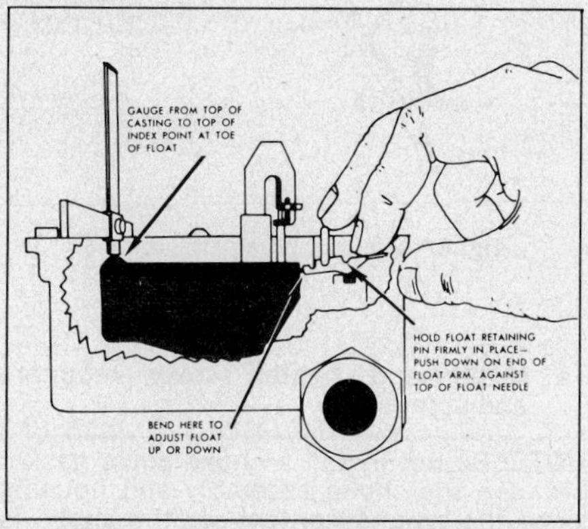

Fig. 1   Float level adjustment

Float Level Adjustment

Fig. 1

1. Hold float retaining pin firmly in place and float arm against top of float needle by pushing downward on float arm at point between needle seat and hinge pin as shown.
2. With adjustable T-scale, measure distance from top of float at toe to float bowl gasket surface (gasket removed). Measurement should be made at a point $1/16''$ in from end of flat surface at float toe (not on radius).
3. Bend float pontoon up or down at float arm junction to adjust.

Metering Rod Adjustment

Fig. 2

1. Remove metering rod by holding throttle valve wide open. Push downward on metering rod against spring tension, then slide metering rod out of slot in holder and remove from main metering jet.
2. To check adjustment, back out slow idle screw and rotate fast idle cam so that fast idle cam follower is not contacting steps on cam.
3. With throttle valve completely closed, apply pressure to top of power piston and hold piston down against its stop.
4. While holding downward pressure on power piston, swing metering rod holder over flat surface of bowl casting next to carburetor bore.
5. Use specified size drill and insert between bowl casting sealing bead and lower surface of metering rod holder. Drill should have a slide fit between both surfaces as shown.
6. To adjust, carefully bend metering rod holder up or down at point shown.
7. After adjustment, install metering rod.

Choke Coil Lever Adjustment

Fig. 3

1. With fast idle adjusting screw on fast idle cam high step, close choke valve.
2. Insert a .120 inch gauge pin through hole in lever and into casting. If holes do not align, bend link to adjust.

Fast Idle Adjustment

Fig. 4

1. Set normal engine idle speed.
2. Place fast idle cam follower tang on highest step of cam.
3. To adjust, insert screwdriver in slot provided in fast idle cam follower tang and bend inwards (towards cam) or outward to obtain specified dimension.

Choke Rod Adjustment

Fig. 5

1. With fast idle adjustment made, place fast idle cam follower on second step of fast idle cam and hold firmly against the rise to the high step.
2. Rotate choke towards direction of closed choke by applying force to choke coil lever.
3. Bend choke rod at point shown to give specified opening between upper edge of choke valve (at center of valve) and inside air horn wall.

Vacuum Break Adjustment

Fig. 6

1. With fast idle screw on fast idle cam high step, seat diaphragm using an outside vacuum source. Cover purge hole with a piece of tape.
2. Close choke valve to compress plunger bucking spring and seat plunger stem.
3. Place specified gauge between upper edge of choke valve and air horn wall. Bend link to adjust.

Unloader Adjustment

Fig. 7

1. With throttle valve wide open, hold choke valve closed with specified gauge between upper edge of choke valve and air horn wall.
2. If distance is not within specifications, bend unloader tang to adjust.

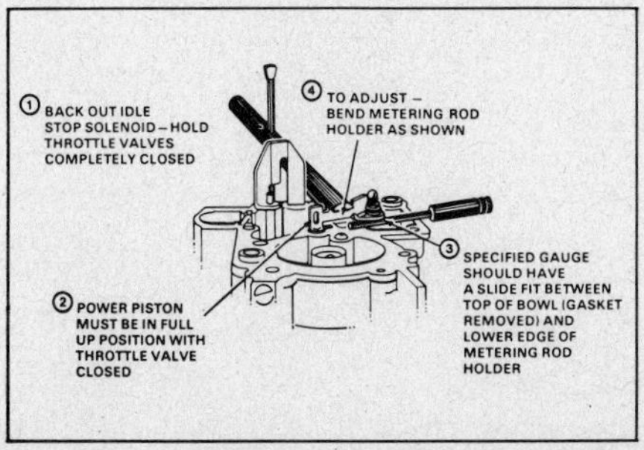

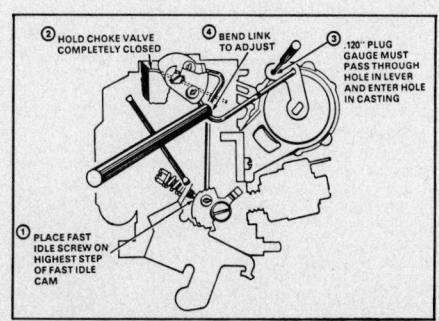

Fig. 2   Metering rod adjustment

Fig. 3   Choke coil lever adjustment

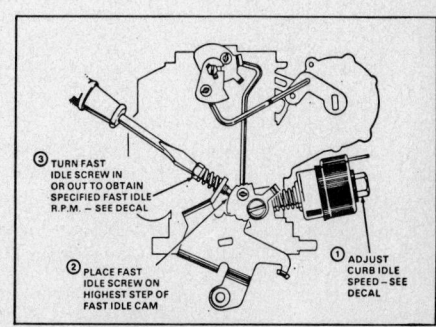

Fig. 4   Fast idle adjustment

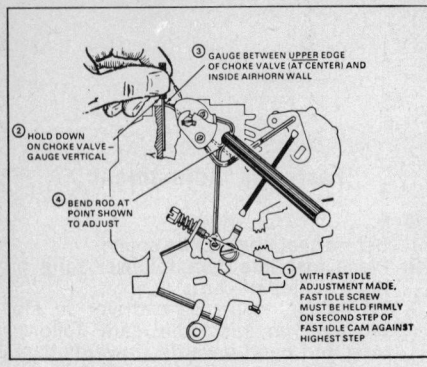

Fig. 5   Choke rod adjustment

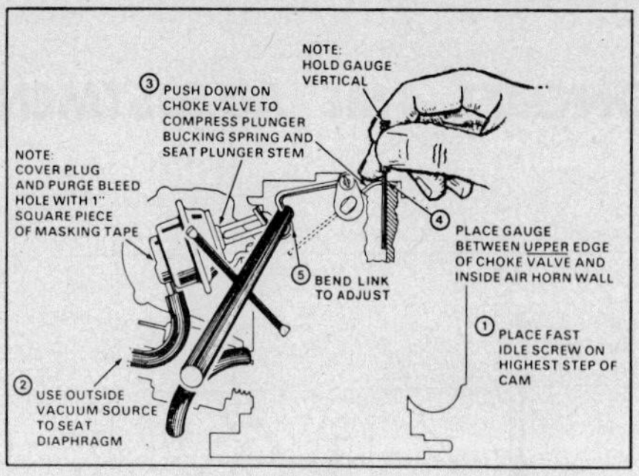

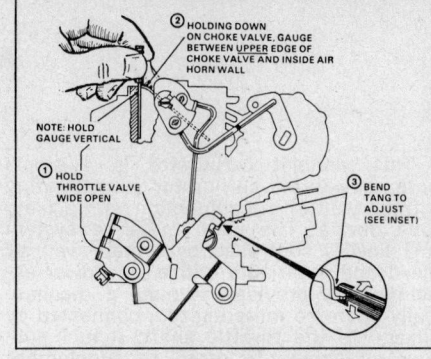

Fig. 6   Vacuum break adjustment

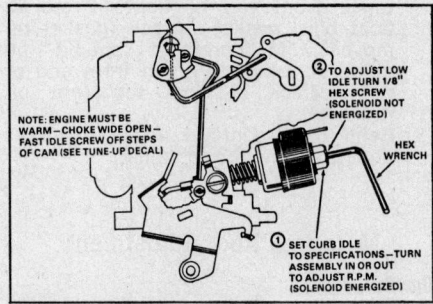

Fig. 7   Unloader adjustment

Choke Coil Adjustment

Fig. 8

1. Install electric choke assembly into housing, ensuring coil tang contacts lower side of coil lever pick-up arm.
2. Place fast cam follower on high step of cam.
3. Rotate cover and coil assembly counter-clockwise until choke valve just closes, then align cover index point with the specified mark on housing.

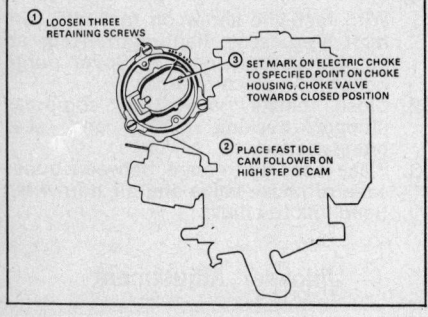

Fig. 8   Choke coil adjustment

4. Install and tighten cover retainers and screws.

NOTE: Do not install a choke cover gasket between the choke assembly and housing since the ground contact for the choke is provided by a metal plate at the rear of the choke assembly.

Low Idle & Curb Idle Speeds Adjustment

NOTE: On all models except vehicles equipped with automatic transmission and air conditioning, the idle solenoid wire will be color-coded tan. On vehicles equipped with automatic transmission and air conditioning, the solenoid wire is color-coded green with a double white stripe. The tan wire will be left disconnected.

Fig. 9

1. The engine should be at normal operating temperature with the air cleaner on, choke open and air conditioning off. Apply parking brake and chock wheels.
2. Disconnect and plug PCV hose at vapor canister and the vacuum advance hose from distributor.
3. On all models except equipped with automatic transmission and air conditioning, rotate solenoid body to adjust curb idle speed. Then, dis-

connect solenoid electrical connector. With automatic transmission in Drive or manual transmission in Neutral, turn 1/8 inch hex screw in end of solenoid to adjust low idle speed. Connect solenoid electrical connector.
4. On models equipped with automatic transmission and air conditioning, turn solenoid hex screw inward until fully bottomed. Rotate solenoid body to obtain 950 RPM. Then, rotate hex screw to obtain curb idle RPM.
5. On all models, unplug and connect PCV vapor canister hose and vacuum advance hose.

Fig. 9   Low & curb idle speeds adjustment

MONOJET MV ADJUSTMENT SPECIFICATIONS

See Tune Up Chart in car chapters for hot idle speeds.

Year	Carb. Part No. ①	Initial Idle Mix Screw Turns Open ②	Float Level	Metering Rod	Choke Rod	Vacuum Break	Auxiliary Vacuum Break	Unloader	Fast Idle R.P.M.
1974	7044014	②	11/32	.080	.230	.275	—	.500	1800
	7044017	②	11/32	.080	.275	.350	—	.500	1800
	7044023, 033	②	1/8	—	.080	.130	—	.375	2000
	7044024, 034	②	1/8	—	.080	.130	—	.375	2200
	7044314	②	11/32	.080	.245	.300	—	.500	1800
	7044323, 333	②	1/8	—	.080	.130	—	.375	2000
	7044324, 334	②	1/8	—	.080	.130	—	.375	2200
	7044336, 339	②	1/8	—	.245	.300	—	.500	1800
	7044337	②	1/8	—	.080	.130	—	.375	2000
	7044340	②	1/8	—	.080	.130	—	.375	2200
1975	7045012	②	11/32	.080	.160	.200	.215	.215	1700
	7045013	②	11/32	.080	.275	.350	.312	.275	1800
	7045018	②	1/8	.080	.230	.275	.312	.275	—
	7045024, 028	②	1/8	—	.080	.100	.450	.215	2400
	7045025, 027	②	1/8	—	.080	.100	.450	.215	2000
	7045029	②	1/8	—	.080	.100	.450	.215	2000
	7045038	②	11/32	.084	.080	.100	.312	.215	—
	7045314	②	11/32	.080	.230	.275	.312	.275	1700
1976	17056012, 014	②	11/32	.080	.090	.110	.215	.265	2200
	17056013, 015	②	11/32	.080	.090	.110	.215	.265	2100
	17056016	②	11/32	.080	.115	.140	—	.265	2200
	17056018	②	11/32	.080	.090	.110	.215	.265	2100
	17056022, 027	②	1/8	—	.045	.060	.450	.215	1500
	17056023, 026	②	1/8	—	.045	.060	.450	.215	2200
	17056313	②	11/32	.030	.105	.180	.320	.265	1700
	17056314	②	11/32	.030	.135	.150	.275	.265	1700

①—On tag attached to carburetor.
②—Air/fuel ratio or idle CO% rating is found in Tune Up Specification tables in car chapters.

MONOJET MV ADJUSTMENTS

The Monojet carburetor is a single-bore downdraft unit with a triple venturi coupled with a refined metering system which results in a unit having superior fuel mixture control and performance.

A plain tube nozzle is used in conjuction with the multiple venturi. Fuel flow through the main metering system is controlled by a mechanically and vacuum operated variable orifice jet. This consists of a specially tapered rod which operates in the fixed orifice main metering jet and is connected directly by linkage to the main throttle shaft. A vacuum-operated enrichment system is used in conjunction with the main metering system to provide good performance during moderate to heavy accelerations.

A separate and adjustable idle system is used in conjunction with the main metering system to meet fuel mixture requirements during engine idle and low speed operation. The off-idle discharge port is of a vertical slot design which gives good transition between curb idle and main metering system operation.

The idle system incorporates a hot idle compensator on some models where necessary to maintain a smooth engine idle during periods of extreme hot engine operation.

The main metering system has an adjustable flow feature which enables production to control the fuel mixture more accurately then attained heretofore.

The Monojet carburetor is designed to use an automatic choke system. The conventional choke valve is located in the air horn bore. The vacuum diaphragm unit is an integral part of the air horn. The automatic choke coil is manifold mounted and connects to the choke valve shaft by connecting linkage.

The choke system has a feature to give added enrichment during cold start. This feature greatly reduces starting time and yet allows the use of low torque thermostatic coils for increased economy.

The carburetor has internally balanced venting through a vent hole in the air horn. An external idle vent valve is used on some models where necessary for improved hot engine idle and starting.

Float Level Adjustment

Fig. 2

1. Hold float retaining pin firmly in place and float arm against top of float needle by pushing downward on float arm at point between needle seat and hinge pin as shown.
2. With adjustable T-scale, measure distance from top of float at toe to float bowl gasket surface (gasket removed). Measurement should be made at a point 1/16" in from end of flat surface at float toe (not on radius).
3. Bend float pontoon up or down at float arm junction to adjust.

Metering Rod Adjustment

Fig. 3

1. Remove metering rod by holding

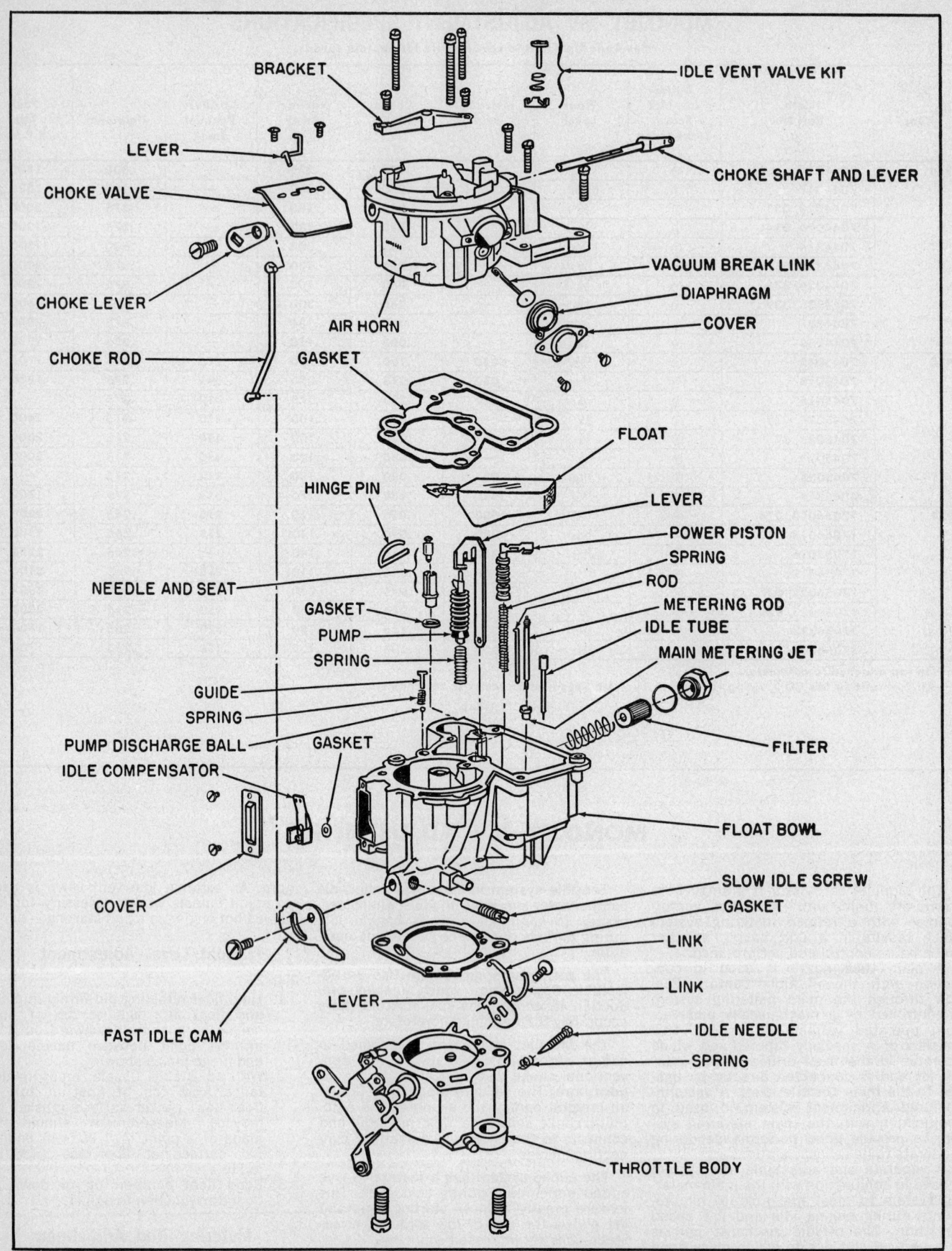

Fig. 1 Monojet Model MV carburetor.

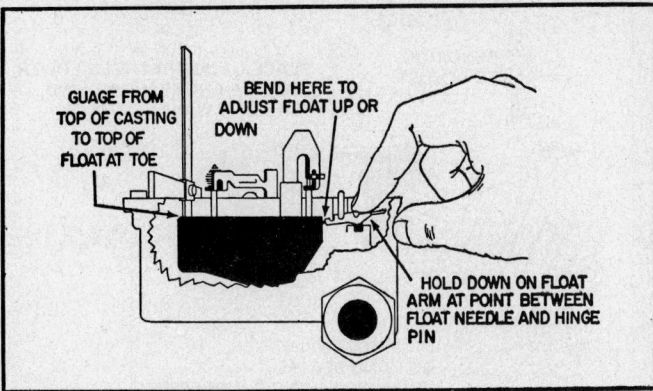

Fig. 2   Monojet float level adjustment

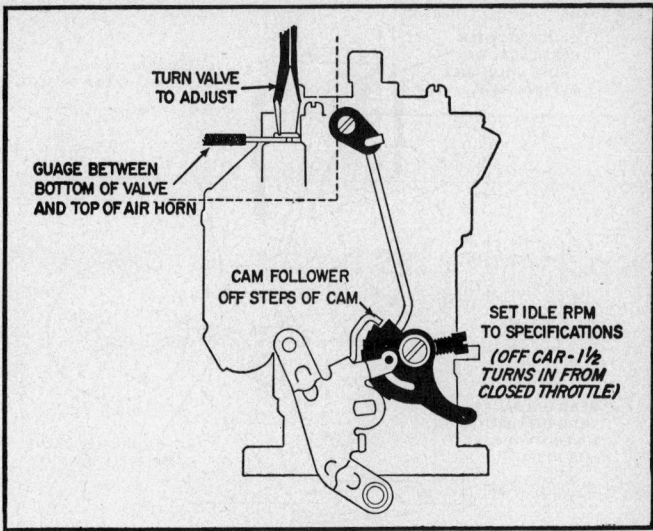

Fig. 4   Monojet idle vent adjustment

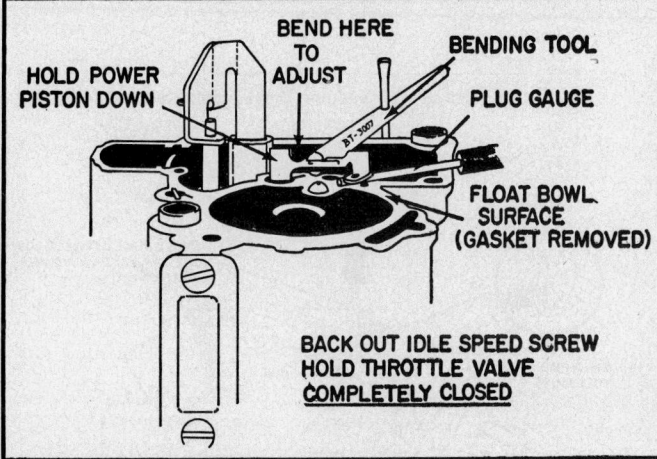

Fig. 3   Monojet metering rod adjustment

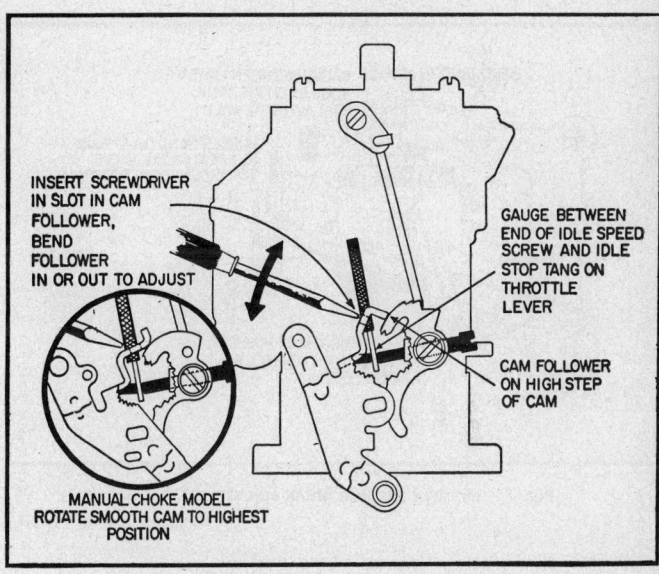

Fig. 5   Monojet fast idle adjustment (off car)—1974

throttle valve wide open. Push downward on metering rod against spring tension, then slide metering rod out of slot in holder and remove from main metering jet.

2. To check adjustment, back out slow idle screw and rotate fast idle cam so that fast idle cam follower is not contacting steps on cam.

3. With throttle valve completely closed, apply pressure to top of power piston and hold piston down against its stop.

4. While holding downward pressure on power piston, swing metering rod holder over flat surface of bowl casting next to carburetor bore.

5. Use specified size drill and insert between bowl casting sealing bead and lower surface of metering rod holder. Drill should have a slide fit between both surfaces as shown.

6. To adjust, carefully bend metering rod holder up or down at point shown.

7. After adjustment, install metering rod.

Idle Vent Adjustment
Fig. 4

1. Set engine idle rpm to specification

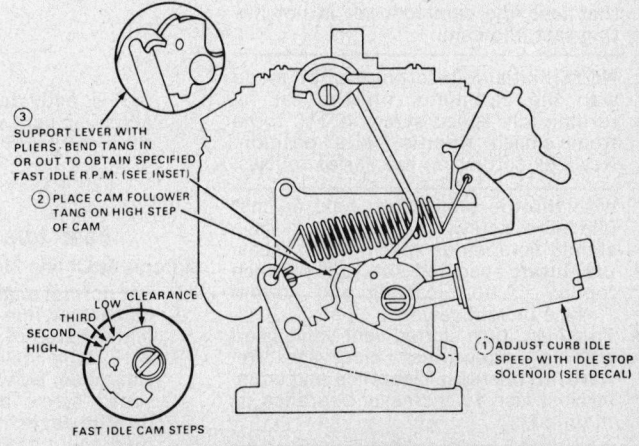

Fig. 5A   Monojet fast idle adjustment (off car). 1975-76

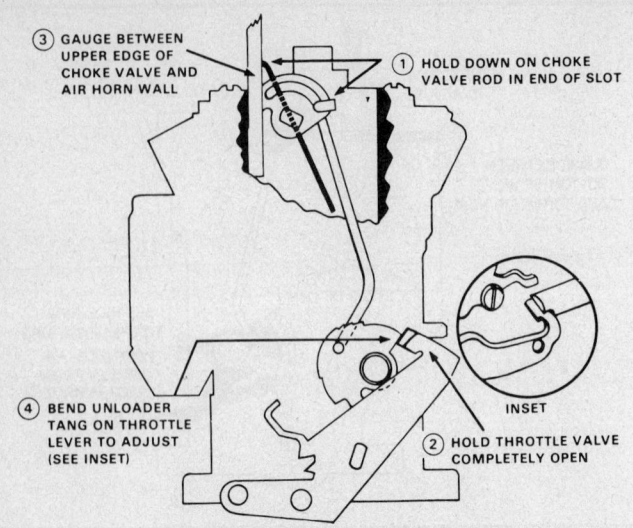

Fig. 6 Monojet choke rod adjustment

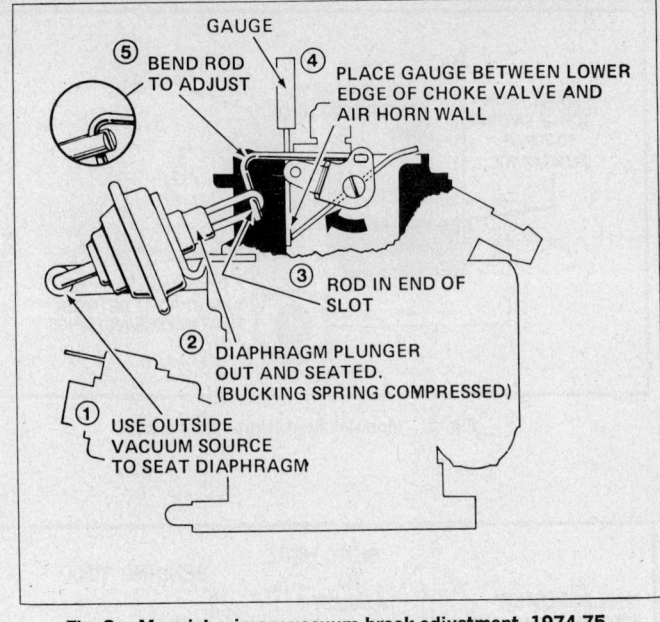

Fig. 8 Monojet primary vacuum break adjustment. 1974-75
4-140

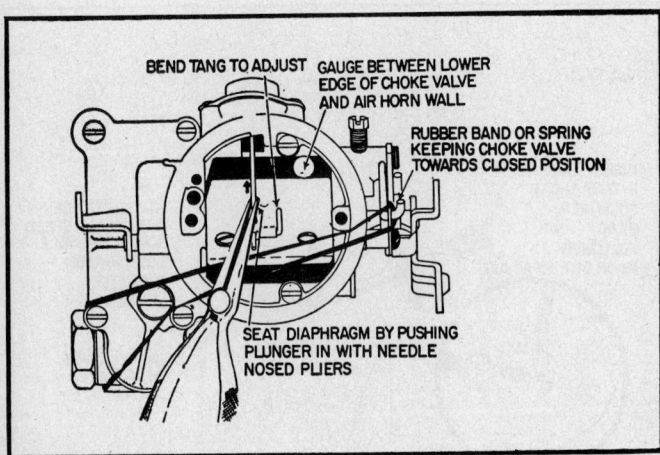

Fig. 7 Monojet vacuum break adjustment. 4-140

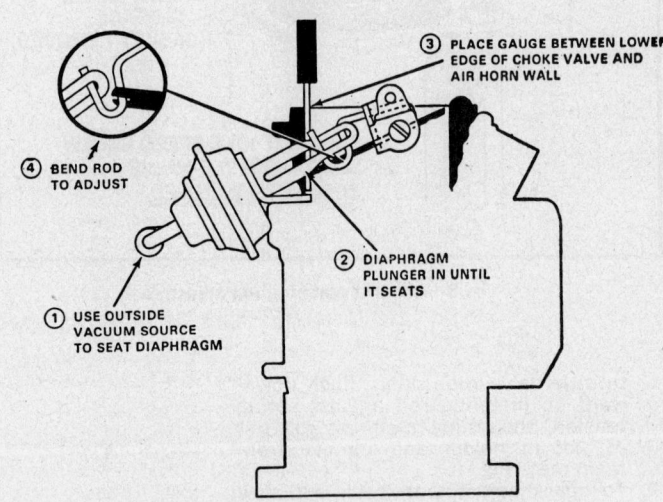

Fig. 9 Monojet primary vacuum break adjustment. 1974-75
All exc. 4-140

and hold choke valve wide open so that fast idle cam follower is not hitting fast idle cam.

NOTE: Initial idle setting can be made with the carburetor off the car by turning idle speed screw in 1½ turns from closed throttle valve position. Recheck setting on the car as follows:

2. With throttle stop screw held against idle stop screw, the idle vent valve should be open as specified. To measure, insert specified size drill between top of air horn casting and bottom surface of vent valve.
3. To adjust, turn slotted vent valve head with a screwdriver clockwise (inward) to decrease clearance and counterclockwise to increase clearance as required.

NOTE: On models provided with the idle stop solenoid, make sure solen-oid is activated when checking and adjusting vent valve.

Fast Idle Adjustment
Automatic Choke Models, Fig. 5
1. Set normal engine idle speed.
2. Place fast idle cam follower tang on highest step of cam.
3. With tang held against cam, check clearance between end of slow idle speed screw and idle stop tang on throttle lever. It should be as specified.
4. To adjust, insert screwdriver in slot provided in fast idle cam follower tang and bend inwards (towards cam) or outward to obtain specified dimension.

Choke Rod Adjustment
Automatic Choke Models, Fig. 6
1. With fast idle adjustment made, place fast idle cam follower on second step of fast idle cam and hold firmly against the rise to the high step.
2. Rotate choke towards direction of closed choke by applying force to choke coil lever.
3. Bend choke rod at point shown to give specified opening between upper

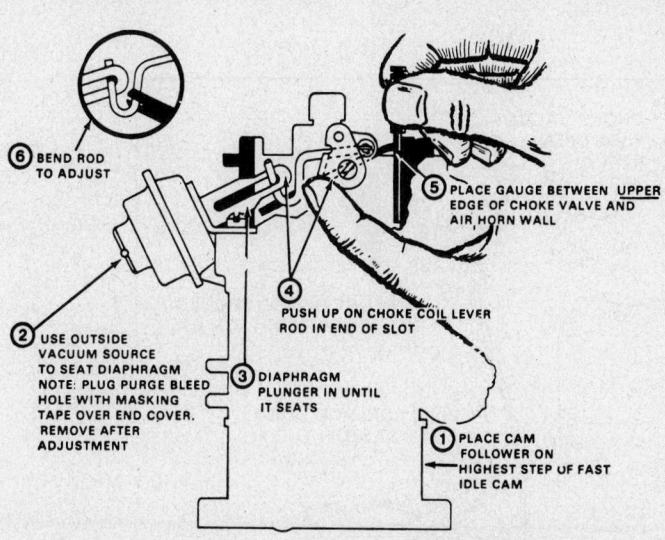

Fig. 10 Monojet primary vacuum break adjustment. 1976

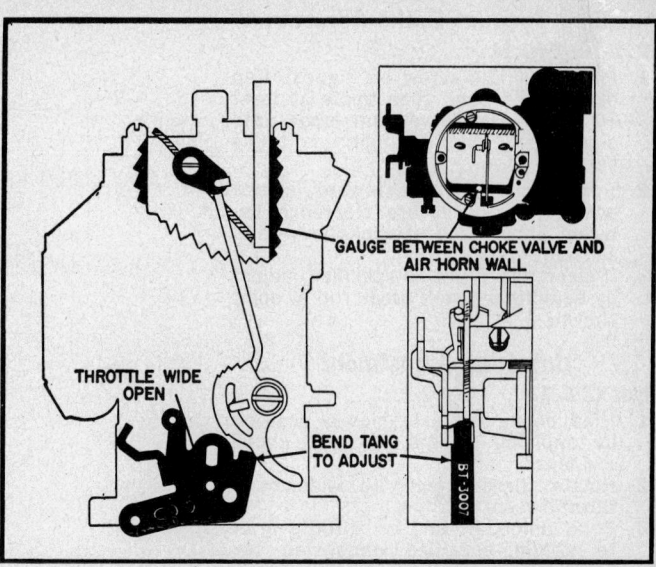

Fig. 12 Monojet unloader adjustment. 1974

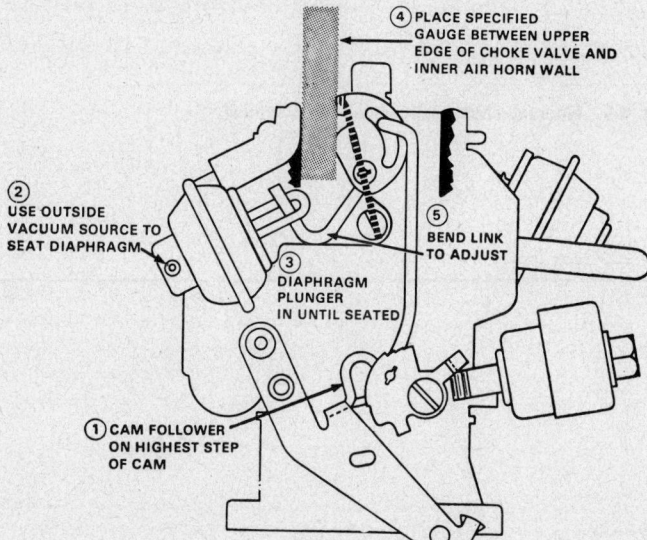

Fig. 11 Monojet auxiliary vacuum break adjustment. 1975-76

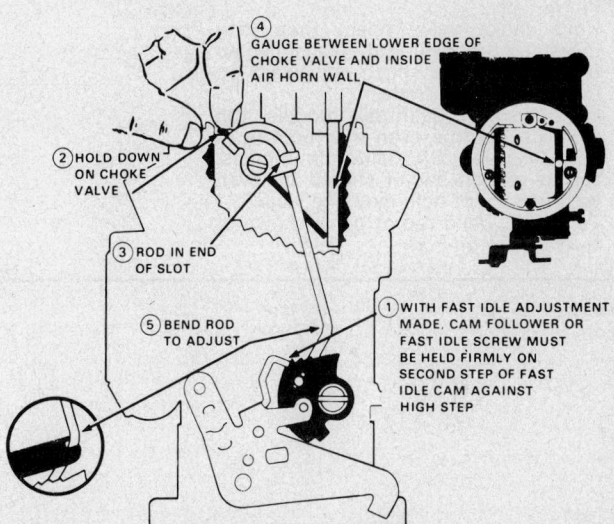

Fig. 13 Monojet unloader adjustment. 1975-76

edge of choke valve (at center of valve) and inside air horn wall.

Primary Vacuum Break Adjustment

4-140, Fig. 7

1. Open throttle valve so that cam follower on throttle lever will clear highest step on fast idle cam.
2. Rotate choke valve to closed position. If thermostatic coil is warm, hold choke valve closed with rubber band or spring attached between choke shaft lever and stationary part of carburetor.
3. Grasp vacuum break plunger rod with needle nose pliers and push straight inward until diaphragm seats.
4. With specified drill size, measure clearance between lower edge of

choke valve and inside air horn wall at center of valve as shown.
5. Bend end of vacuum break lever at point shown to adjust.

1974-75, Figs. 8 & 9

1. Apply outside vacuum to vacuum break diaphragm until plunger is fully seated.
2. With diaphragm in seated position, push choke valve to the closed choke position. Vacuum break rod should be at end of slot in the diaphragm plunger and spring loaded plunger fully compressed.
3. Measure clearance between lower edge of choke valve and inside air horn wall.
4. If clearance is not as specified, adjust

by bending vacuum break rod at point shown.

1976, Fig. 10

1. On all except 4-140 units, place cam follower on highest step of fast idle cam. Also, cover purge bleed hole with tape on vacuum break end cover.
2. On all units, with an outside vacuum source, apply vacuum to fully seat vacuum break plunger.
3. Push upward on choke coil lever.
4. Insert specified gauge between upper edge of choke valve and air horn wall.
5. If clearance is not within specifications, bend vacuum break rod to adjust.

Auxiliary Vacuum Brake Adjustment

1975-76, Fig. 11

1. Place fast idle screw on highest step of fast idle cam, then apply at least 10 inches Hg. to vacuum break until diaphragm and plunger is fully seated.
2. Rotate choke valve toward closed position and measure clearance between upper edge of choke valve and air horn wall.
3. If clearance is not as specified, adjust by bending vacuum break rod at point shown.

Unloader Adjustment

Figs. 12 & 13

1. Hold choke valve in closed position by applying a light force to choke coil lever.
2. Rotate throttle lever to wide open throttle valve position.
3. Bend unloader tang on throttle lever to obtain specified dimension between lower edge on 1974 or upper edge on 1975-76 of choke valve (at center) and air horn wall.

4-140, Fig. 14

1. Hold choke valve open, then with thermostatic coil rod disconnected from choke lever, push downward on rod to end of its travel.
2. On all except California models, top of rod should be even with bottom of hole in lever. On California models, top of pin on swivel should be even with bottom of hole in choke lever.
3. To adjust, bend rod at point shown or turn swivel on rod.

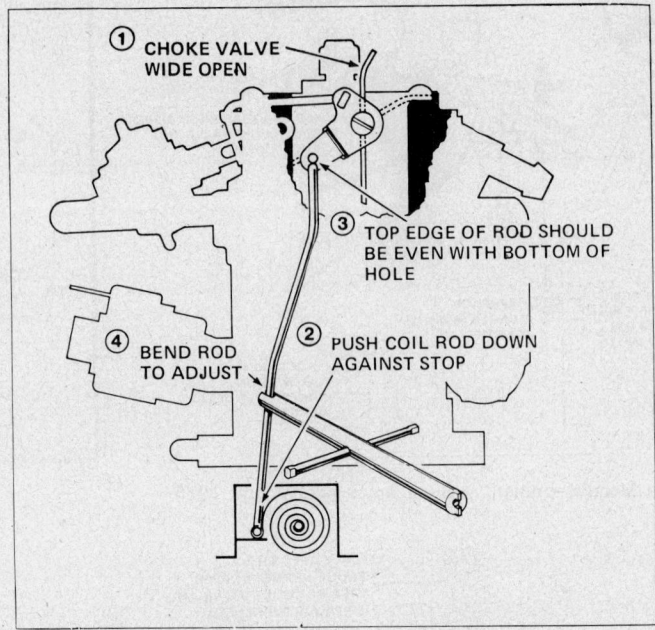

① CHOKE VALVE WIDE OPEN

③ TOP EDGE OF ROD SHOULD BE EVEN WITH BOTTOM OF HOLE

④ BEND ROD TO ADJUST

② PUSH COIL ROD DOWN AGAINST STOP

Fig. 14   Monojet choke coil adjustment. Typical

Holley Carburetor Section

1000 & 2000 SERIES CARB. ADJUSTMENT SPECIFICATIONS
See Tune Up Chart in car chapter for hot idle speeds.

Year	Carb. Part No.①	Carb. Model	Idle Mixture Turns Open	Float Level (Dry)	Fuel Level (Wet)	Pump Setting	Bowl Vent Clearance	Fast Idle Bench	Fast Idle On Car	Choke Unloader Clearance	Vacuum Kick Drill Size	Cam Position Drill Size	Choke Setting
CHRYSLER ENGINES													
1974	R-6721A	1945	②	3/64	—	11/16	—	.080	1600	.250	.140	.080	Fixed
	R-6722A	1945	②	3/64	—	13/16	—	.080	1800	.250	.090	.080	Fixed
	R-6723A	1945	②	3/64	—	11/16	—	.080	1600	.250	.140	.080	Fixed
	R-6724A	1945	②	3/64	—	3/4	—	.080	1800	.250	.080	.080	Fixed
	R-6725A⑥	1945	②	3/64	—	11/16	—	.080	1600	.250	.140	.080	Fixed
	R-6726A⑥	1945	②	3/64	—	3/4	—	.080	1800	.250	.090	.080	Fixed
	R-6731A	2245	②	.180	—	.255⑧	.015	.110	1800	.170	.150	.110	Fixed
	R-6737A	2245	②	.180	—	.255⑧	.015	.110	1600	.170	.150	.110	Fixed
1975	R-7017A	1945	②	3/64	—	2 7/32	—	.080	1600	.250	.130	.080	Fixed
	R-7018A	1945	②	3/64	—	2 21/64	—	.080	1700	.250	.090	.080	Fixed
	R-7019A	1945	②	3/64	—	2 7/32	—	.080	1600	.250	.130	.080	Fixed
	R-7020A	1945	②	3/64	—	2 21/64	—	.080	1700	.250	.090	.080	Fixed
	R-7027A	2245	②	3/16	—	1/4	.015	.110	1600	.170	.150	.110	Fixed
	R-7226A	2245	②	3/16	—	1/4	.015	.110	1600	.170	.150	.110	Fixed
	R-7329A	1945	②	3/64	—	2 7/32	—	.080	1700	.250	.130	.080	Fixed
1976	R-7356A	1945	②	⑦	—	2 7/32	1/16	.080	1600	.250	.110	.080	Fixed
	R-7357A	1945	②	⑦	—	2 21/32	1/16	.080	1700	.250	.100	.080	Fixed
	R-7360A	1945	②	⑦	—	2 7/32	—	.080	1600	.250	.110	.080	Fixed
	R-7361A	1945	②	3/64	—	2 21/32	—	.080	1700	.250	.100	.080	Fixed
	R-7364A	2245	②	3/16	—	1 7/64⑧	.025	.110	1600	.170	.150	.110	Fixed
	R-7366A	2245	②	3/16	—	1 7/64⑧	.025	.110	1600	.170	.150	.110	Fixed
	R-7661A	2245	②	3/16	—	1 7/64⑧	.025	.110	1600	.170	.150	.110	Fixed
1977	R-7632A	1945	②	⑦	—	2 7/32③	1/16	.080	1400	.250	.110	.080	Fixed
	R-7633A	1945	②	⑦	—	2 21/64④	1/16	.080	1700	.250	.110	.080	Fixed
	R-7635A	1945	②	⑦	—	2 21/64④	—	.080	1700	.250	.110	.080	Fixed
	R-7671A	2245	②	3/16	—	5/16⑧	.025	.110	1700	.170	.110	.110	Fixed
	R-7744A	1945	②	⑦	—	2 21/64④	1/16	.080	1700	.250	.130	.080	Fixed
	R-7745A	1945	②	⑦	—	2 7/32	1/16	.080	1600	.250	.150	.080	Fixed
	R-7746A	1945	②	⑦	—	2 21/64	1/16	.080	1700	.250	.110	.080	Fixed
	R-7764A	1945	②	⑦	—	2 7/32	1/16	.080	1700	.250	.110	.080	Fixed
	R-7765A	1945	②	⑦	—	2 21/64	1/16	.080	1700	.250	.110	.080	Fixed
1978	R-7988A	1945	②	⑦	—	2 7/32	1/16	.080	1400	.250	.110	.080	Fixed
	R-7989A	1945	②	⑦	—	2 21/64	1/16	.080	1600	.250	.110	.080	Fixed
	R-7990A	2280	②	5/16	—	⑨	.030	.070	1600	.310	.150	.070	Fixed
	R-7991A	2245	②	3/16	—	1 7/64⑧	.025	.110	1600	.170	.110	.110	Fixed
	R-8008A	1945	②	⑦	—	2 21/64	1/16	.080	1700	.250	.110	.080	Fixed
	R-8010A	1945	②	⑦	—	2 21/64	1/16	.080	1500	.250	.130	.080	Fixed
1979	R-8448A	2280	②	9/32	—	⑨	.030	.070	1600	.310	.150	.070	Fixed
	R-8450A	2245	②	3/16	—	1 7/64⑧	.025	.110	1600	.170	.110	.110	Fixed
	R-8452A	1945	②	⑦	—	1 5/8③	1/16	.080	1600	.250	.110	.080	Fixed
	R-8523A	1945	②	⑦	—	1 45/64⑧	1/16	.080	1400	.250	.110	.080	Fixed
	R-8680A	1945	②	⑦	—	1 5/8③	1/16	.080	1500	.250	.110	.080	Fixed

①—Located on tag attached to carburetor or on casting.
②—Air/fuel ratio or idle CO% rating is found in Tune Up chart in car chapters.
③—Slot #2
④—Slot #3

⑤—Unloader automatically set when fast idle cam is adjusted.
⑥—With California Emission package.
⑦—Flush with top of bowl cover gasket with bowl inverted.
⑧—Slot #1
⑨—Flush with top of bowl vent casting.

HOLLEY CARBURETORS

FORD & MERCURY ENGINES

Year	Carb. No.	Carb. Model	Float Level	Accel. Pump	Fast Idle Cam	Choke Pulldown	Dechoke	Choke Setting
1978	D8BE-AAA	1946	—	—	—	—	—	—
	D8BE-AB	1946	—	—	—	—	—	—
	D8BE-AGA	1946	—	—	—	—	—	—
	D8BE-AHA	1946	—	—	—	—	—	—
	D8BE-RA	1946	—	—	—	—	—	—
	D8BE-UC	1946	—	—	—	—	—	—
1979	D9BE-AEA	1946	—	—	—	—	—	—
	D9BE-KA	1946	—	—	—	—	—	—
	D9BE-LA	1946	—	—	—	—	—	—
	D9BE-MA	1946	—	—	—	—	—	—

1000 & 2000 SERIES CARBURETOR ADJUSTMENTS

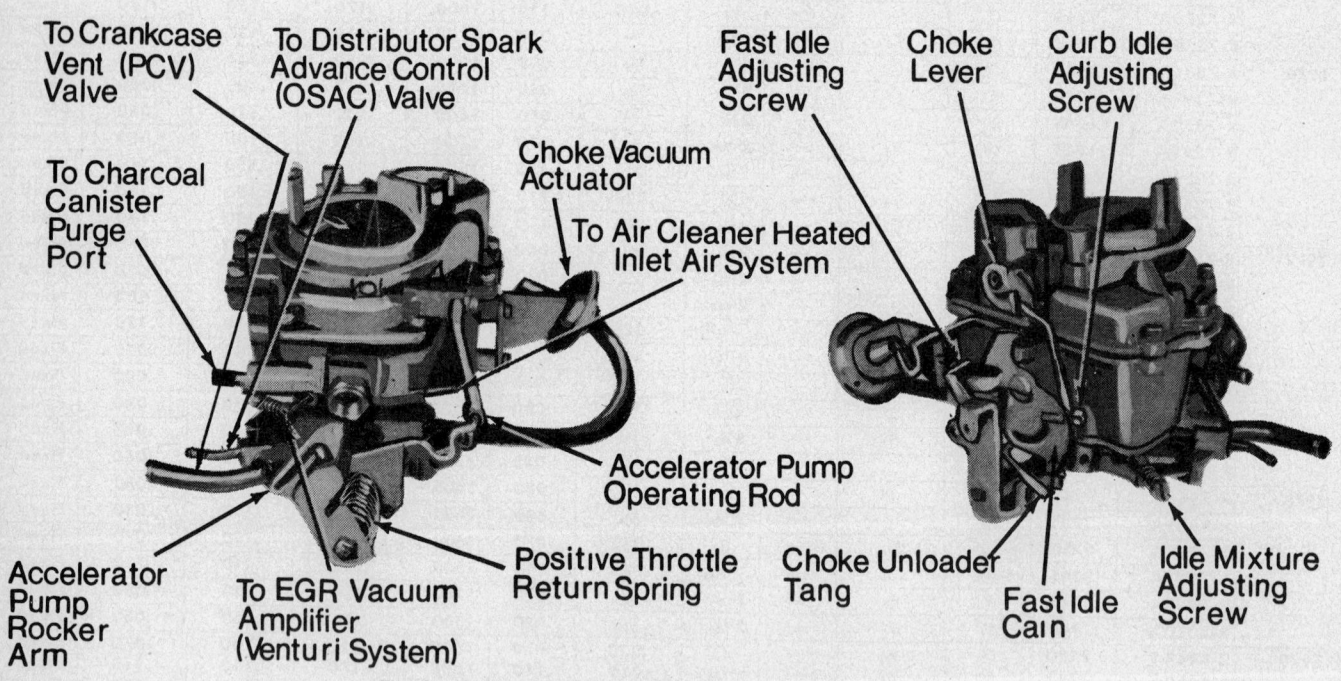

To Crankcase Vent (PCV) Valve

To Distributor Spark Advance Control (OSAC) Valve

To Charcoal Canister Purge Port

Choke Vacuum Actuator

To Air Cleaner Heated Inlet Air System

Fast Idle Adjusting Screw

Choke Lever

Curb Idle Adjusting Screw

Accelerator Pump Operating Rod

Accelerator Pump Rocker Arm

To EGR Vacuum Amplifier (Venturi System)

Positive Throttle Return Spring

Choke Unloader Tang

Fast Idle Cam

Idle Mixture Adjusting Screw

Fig. 1 Holley model 1945 single barrel carburetor. (Typical)

MODEL 1945

This single barrel carburetor, Fig. 1, utilizes dual cellular plastic floats to control the fuel level, thus permitting high angularity operation during the most severe operating conditions. Also, the float construction eliminates the possibility of a malfunction due to a punctured float.

On 1974-78 Chrysler units, an electric choke system is incorporated to open the choke at approximately 60 degrees F.

The accelerator pump is of the piston type and is operated by a rod and a link connected to the throttle lever.

The power enrichment system on all units, consists of a power valve installed near the center of the carburetor body and a vacuum piston located in the bowl cover. On 1974 California and all 1975 units, in addition to the vacuum operated enrichment system, a spring loaded mechanical modulator rod opens the power valve at 80 degrees of throttle opening regardless of engine vacuum.

On 1976-78 units, a spring-loaded modulated power valve is used. A vacuum passage in the throttle body transmits manifold vacuum to the vacuum piston chamber in the bowl cover. Under light throttle and load conditions, vacuum acting on the vacuum piston is sufficient to overcome the spring tension. When the throttle valve is opened to 55 degrees, vacuum acting on the vacuum piston is bled to the atmosphere and manifold vacuum is closed off. The throttle shaft is provided with a small hole which aligns with a port in the base of the carburetor when the throttle valve is opened to 55 degrees. This vents the vacuum piston chamber to the atmosphere, allowing the spring tension to open the power valve.

On 1975 vehicles with automatic transmissions, an idle enrichment system is used to reduce cold engine stalling by the use of an additional metering system which enrichens the mixture in the off idle position. This system is controlled by a vacuum diaphragm mounted near the top of the carburetor.

Dry Float Setting

Fig. 2—Hold float fulcrum retaining pin in position and invert carburetor bowl. Place a straight edge across surface of bowl, contracting float toes. Remove straight edge and measure distance float dropped from surface of fuel bowl. Refer to Holley

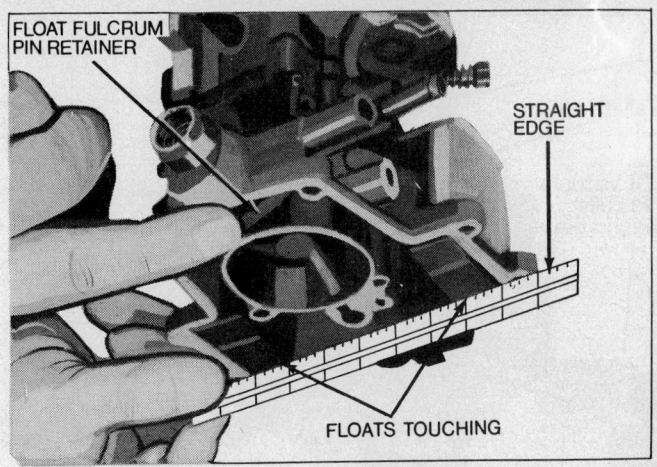

Fig. 2   Measuring float level. 1945 carburetor

Specifications Chart. Adjust by bending float tang to obtain proper dimension.

Bowl Vent Valve Adjustment

1976-78 Fig. 3—With throttle at curb idle, measure distance between the cover support surface and the flat on the plastic bowl vent lever. The distance should be 1/16 inch. If not within specifications, turn bowl vent lever adjusting screw to obtain specified distance.

Fast Idle Cam Position Adjustment

Fig. 4—With fast idle speed adjusting screw contacting second highest step on fast idle cam, move choke valve toward closed position with light pressure on choke shaft lever. Insert specified gauge between top of choke valve and wall of air horn. Refer to *Holley Specifications Chart*. An adjustment will be necessary if a slight

drag is not obtained as drill shank is being removed. Adjust by bending fast idle link at lower angle, until correct valve opening has been obtained.

Choke Vacuum Kick Adjustment

NOTE: Test can be made on or off vehicle.

Fig. 5—If adjustment is to be made with engine running, back off fast idle speed screw until choke can be closed to the kick position with engine at curb idle. (Note number of screw turns required so that fast idle can be returned to original adjustment). If an auxiliary vacuum source is to be used, open throttle valve (engine not running) and move choke to closed position. Release throttle first, then release choke.

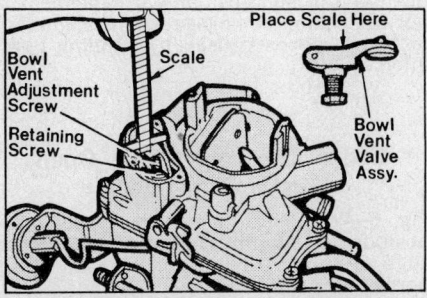

Fig. 3   Bowl vent valve adjustment.
1976-78 1945 carburetor

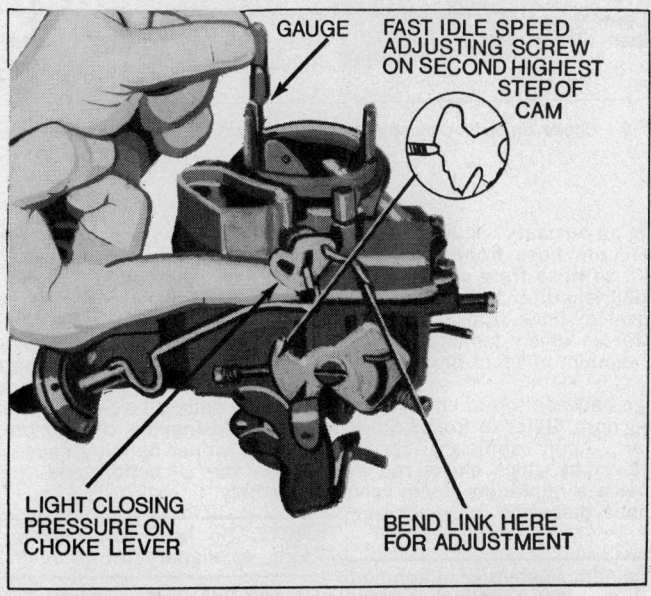

Fig. 4   Fast idle cam position adjustment. 1945 carburetor

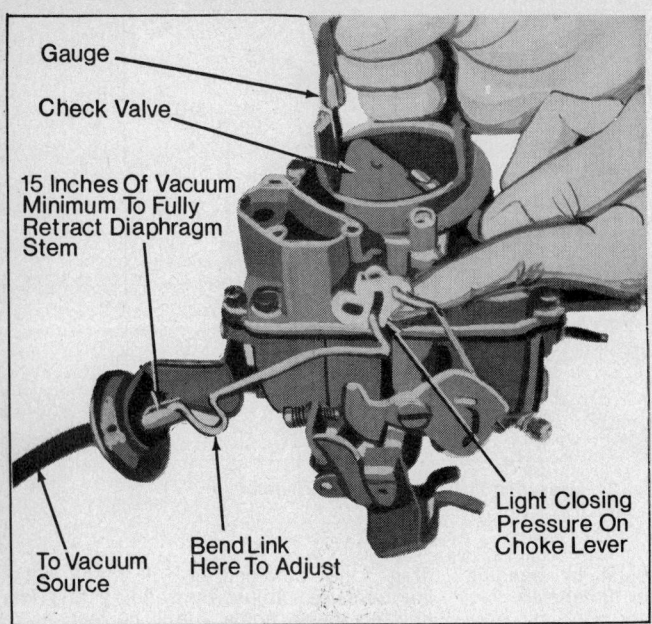

Fig. 5 Choke vacuum kick adjustment. 1945 carburetor

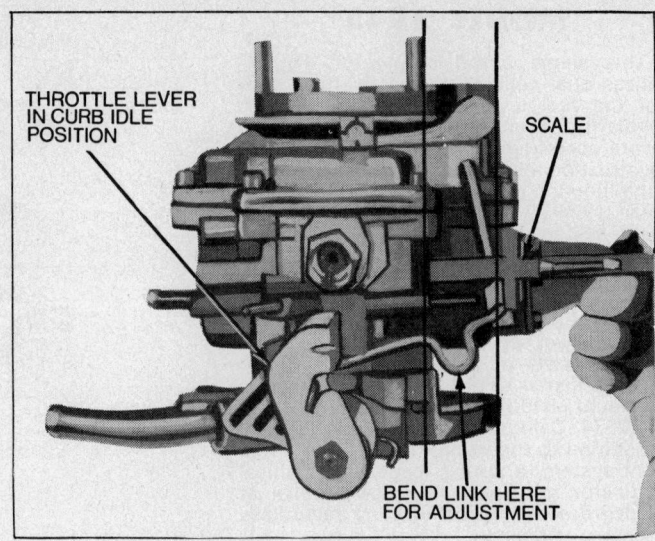

Fig. 7 Accelerator pump adjustment 1974. 1945 carburetor

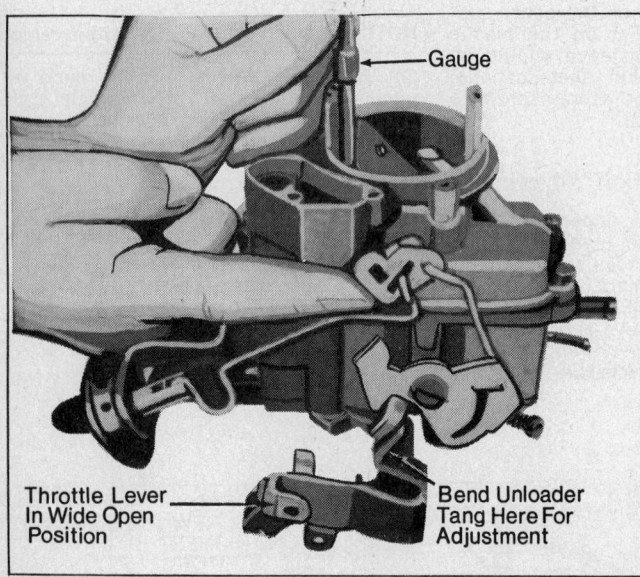

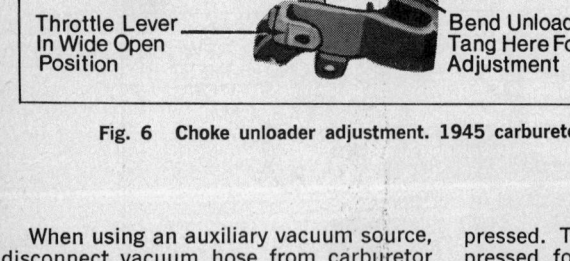

Fig. 6 Choke unloader adjustment. 1945 carburetor

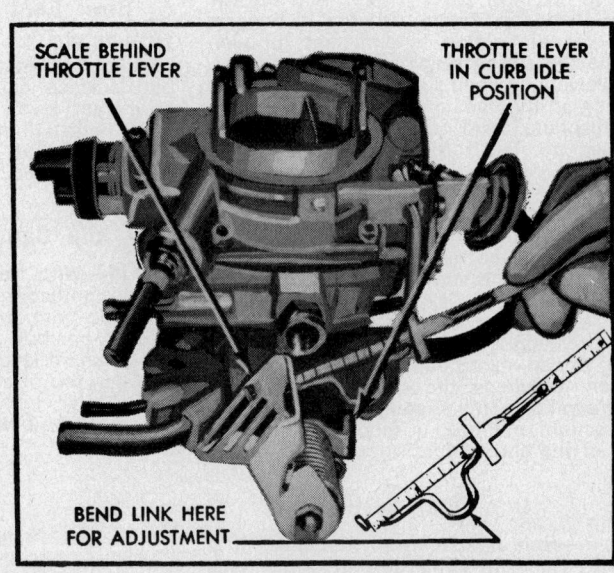

Fig. 8 Accelerator pump adjustment, 1975-78. 1945 carburetor

When using an auxiliary vacuum source, disconnect vacuum hose from carburetor and connect it to hose from vacuum supply with a small length of tube to act as a fitting. Removal of hose from diaphragm may require forces which damage the system. Apply a vacuum of 15 or more inches of mercury.

Insert gauge between top of choke valve and wall of air horn. Refer to *Holley Specifications Chart.* Apply sufficient closing pressure on lever to which choke rod attaches to provide a minimum choke valve opening without distortion of diaphragm link.

NOTE: The cylindrical stem of diaphragm extends as the internal spring is compressed. This spring must be fully compressed for proper measurement of vacuum kick adjustment.

Adjustment is necessary if slight drag is not obtained when removing the gauge. Shorten or lengthen diaphragm link to obtain correct choke valve opening. Length changes should be made by carefully opening or closing the U-bend provided in the link. Improper bending causes contact between the U-section and the diaphragm assembly.

NOTE: Do not apply twisting or bending force to diaphragm.

After completion of adjustment, reinstall

vacuum hose on correct carburetor fitting. Return fast idle screw to its original location if disturbed. Make following check. With no vacuum applied to diaphragm, the choke valve should move freely between open and closed positions. If movement is not free, examine linkage for misalignment or interferences caused by bending operation.

Choke Unloader (Wide Open Kick) Adjustment

Fig. 6—With throttle valves in wide open position, insert drill gauge between upper edge of choke valve and inner wall of air horn. Refer to *Holley Specifications Chart.* With a finger lightly pressing against shaft lever, a slight drag should be felt as drill is being withdrawn. Adjust by bending unloader tang on throttle lever until correct opening has been obtained.

Accelerator Pump Setting

Figs. 7 & 8—With throttle at curb idle position, on 1974 units, measure distance from vacuum passage casting to outer edge of hole in pump operating rod and on 1975-78 units, measure length of pump operating link. Refer to Holley Specifications Chart. Adjust by bending link between throttle lever and pump operating rod.

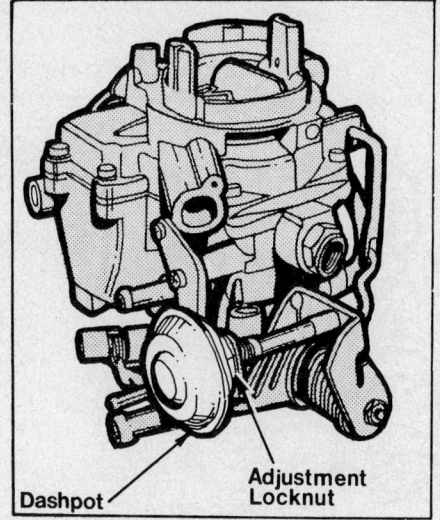

Fig. 9 Dashpot adjustment. 1945 carburetor

Dashpot Setting

Fig. 9—With curb idle speed and mixture properly set, install a tachometer on engine. Start engine and position throttle lever so actuating tab on lever contacts the dashpot stem, however, not depressing the stem. Permit the engine speed to stabilize. Engine speed should be 2300 RPM on 1974-76 models or 2500 RPM on 1977-78 models. To adjust, loosen locknut and turn the dashpot to obtain proper engine RPM.

MODEL 1946

This carburetor, Figs. 1 and 2, uses seven basic systems to provide the correct air/fuel mixture under various operating conditions. The systems are as follows: fuel inlet system, idle system, main metering system, power enrichment system, accelerator pump system, external fuel bowl vent system and automatic choke system. The carburetor is divided into three main assemblies which are the air horn assembly, the main body assembly and the throttle body assembly.

The air horn assembly contains the fuel bowl vent, enrichment valve piston and the accelerator pump piston, cup, spring and operating lever. Also contained in the air horn is the choke plate, shaft, lever, housing and choke cap. The idle air bleed and the high speed bleed restrictors are also found in the air horn assembly.

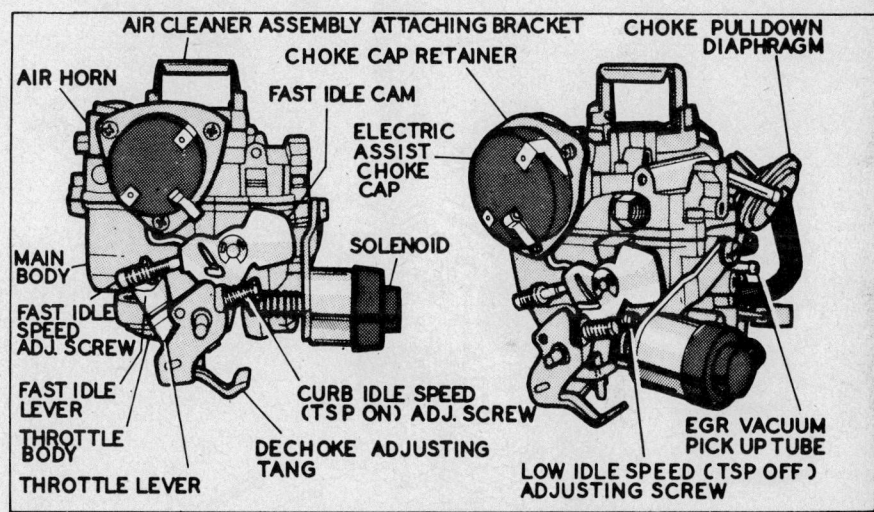

Fig. 1 Holley model 1946 one barrel carburetor

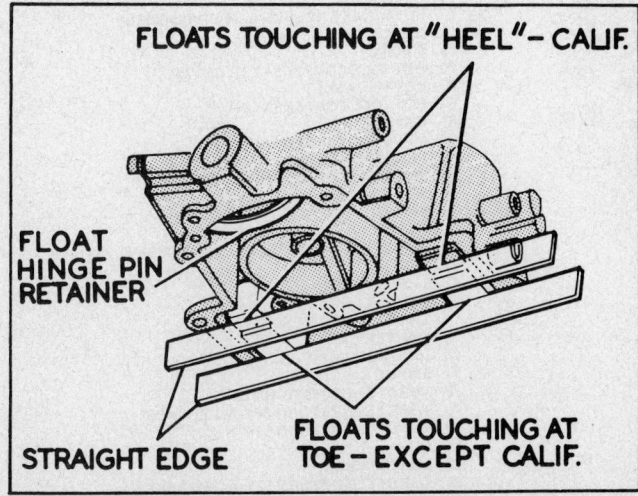

Fig. 3 Float adjustment. 1946 carburetor

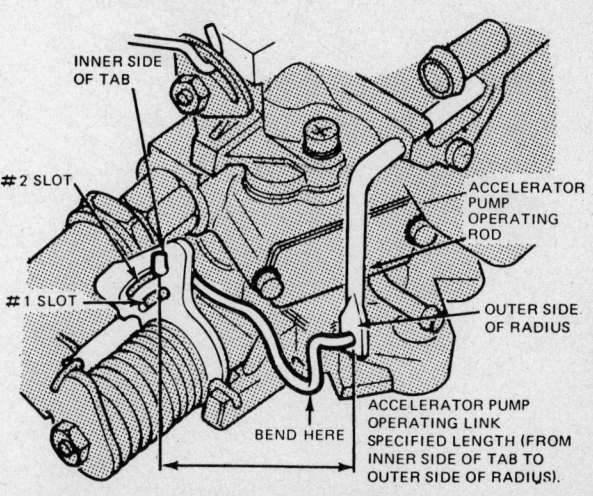

Fig. 4 Accelerator pump adjustment. 1946 carburetor

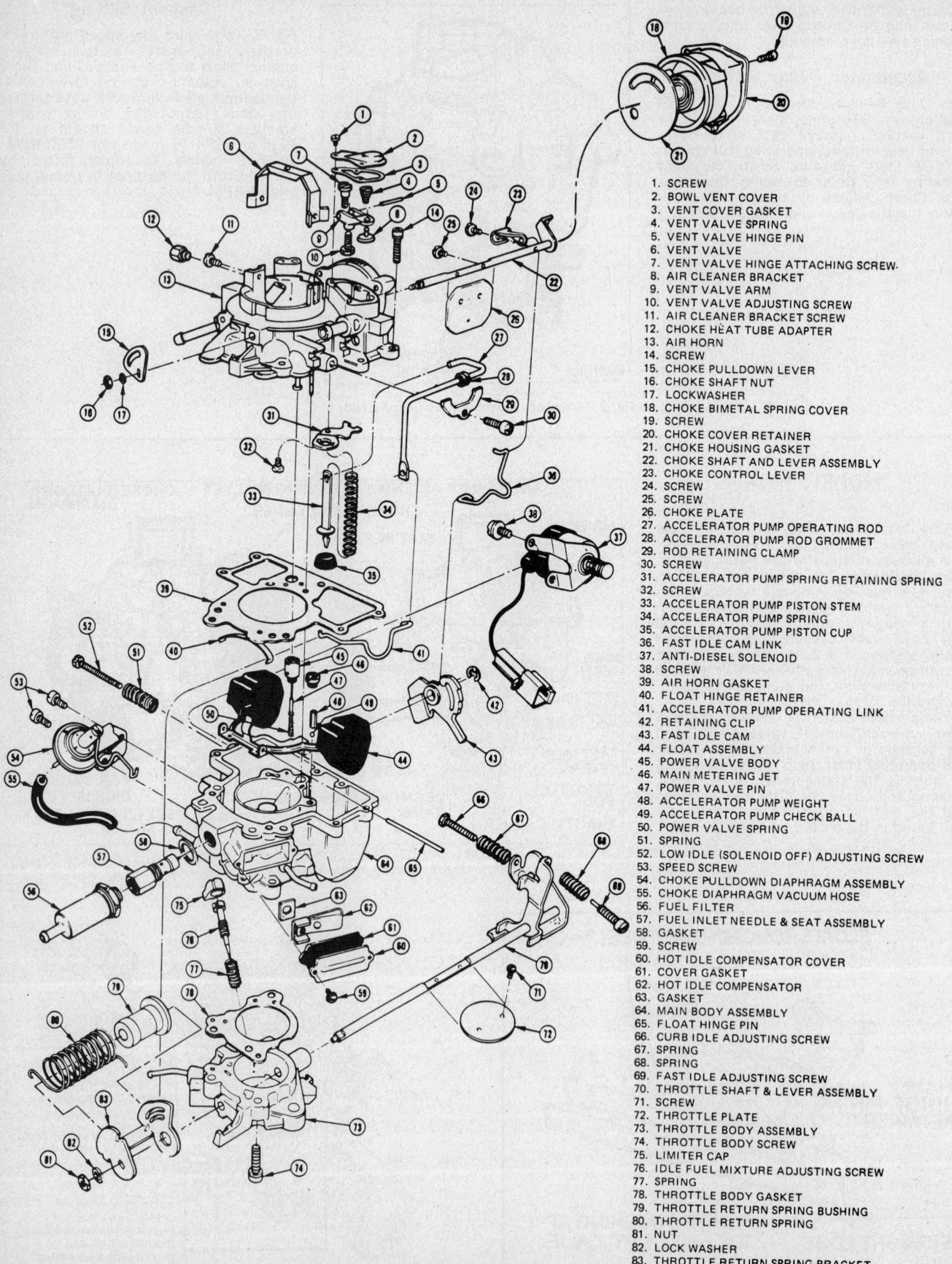

1. SCREW
2. BOWL VENT COVER
3. VENT COVER GASKET
4. VENT VALVE SPRING
5. VENT VALVE HINGE PIN
6. VENT VALVE
7. VENT VALVE HINGE ATTACHING SCREW
8. AIR CLEANER BRACKET
9. VENT VALVE ARM
10. VENT VALVE ADJUSTING SCREW
11. AIR CLEANER BRACKET SCREW
12. CHOKE HEAT TUBE ADAPTER
13. AIR HORN
14. SCREW
15. CHOKE PULLDOWN LEVER
16. CHOKE SHAFT NUT
17. LOCKWASHER
18. CHOKE BIMETAL SPRING COVER
19. SCREW
20. CHOKE COVER RETAINER
21. CHOKE HOUSING GASKET
22. CHOKE SHAFT AND LEVER ASSEMBLY
23. CHOKE CONTROL LEVER
24. SCREW
25. SCREW
26. CHOKE PLATE
27. ACCELERATOR PUMP OPERATING ROD
28. ACCELERATOR PUMP ROD GROMMET
29. ROD RETAINING CLAMP
30. SCREW
31. ACCELERATOR PUMP SPRING RETAINING SPRING
32. SCREW
33. ACCELERATOR PUMP PISTON STEM
34. ACCELERATOR PUMP SPRING
35. ACCELERATOR PUMP PISTON CUP
36. FAST IDLE CAM LINK
37. ANTI-DIESEL SOLENOID
38. SCREW
39. AIR HORN GASKET
40. FLOAT HINGE RETAINER
41. ACCELERATOR PUMP OPERATING LINK
42. RETAINING CLIP
43. FAST IDLE CAM
44. FLOAT ASSEMBLY
45. POWER VALVE BODY
46. MAIN METERING JET
47. POWER VALVE PIN
48. ACCELERATOR PUMP WEIGHT
49. ACCELERATOR PUMP CHECK BALL
50. POWER VALVE SPRING
51. SPRING
52. LOW IDLE (SOLENOID OFF) ADJUSTING SCREW
53. SPEED SCREW
54. CHOKE PULLDOWN DIAPHRAGM ASSEMBLY
55. CHOKE DIAPHRAGM VACUUM HOSE
56. FUEL FILTER
57. FUEL INLET NEEDLE & SEAT ASSEMBLY
58. GASKET
59. SCREW
60. HOT IDLE COMPENSATOR COVER
61. COVER GASKET
62. HOT IDLE COMPENSATOR
63. GASKET
64. MAIN BODY ASSEMBLY
65. FLOAT HINGE PIN
66. CURB IDLE ADJUSTING SCREW
67. SPRING
68. SPRING
69. FAST IDLE ADJUSTING SCREW
70. THROTTLE SHAFT & LEVER ASSEMBLY
71. SCREW
72. THROTTLE PLATE
73. THROTTLE BODY ASSEMBLY
74. THROTTLE BODY SCREW
75. LIMITER CAP
76. IDLE FUEL MIXTURE ADJUSTING SCREW
77. SPRING
78. THROTTLE BODY GASKET
79. THROTTLE RETURN SPRING BUSHING
80. THROTTLE RETURN SPRING
81. NUT
82. LOCK WASHER
83. THROTTLE RETURN SPRING BRACKET

Fig. 2   Holley model 1946 carburetor, disassembled

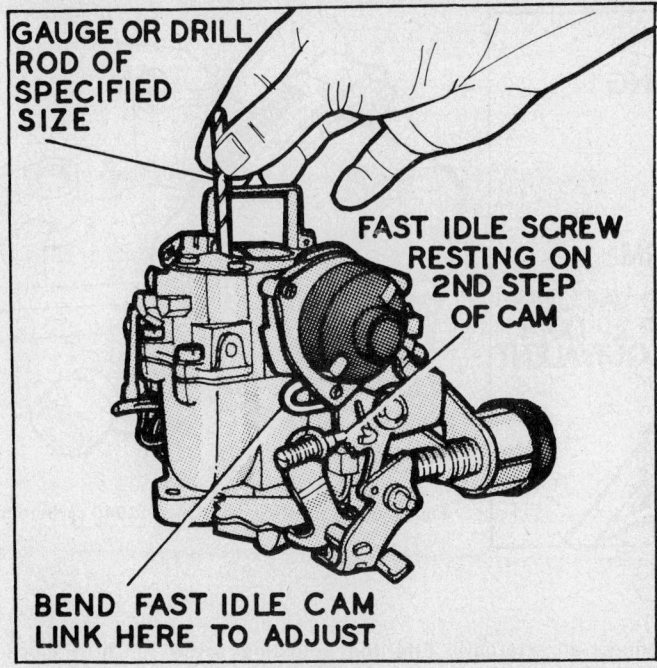

Fig. 5 Fast idle cam position adjustment. 1946 carburetor

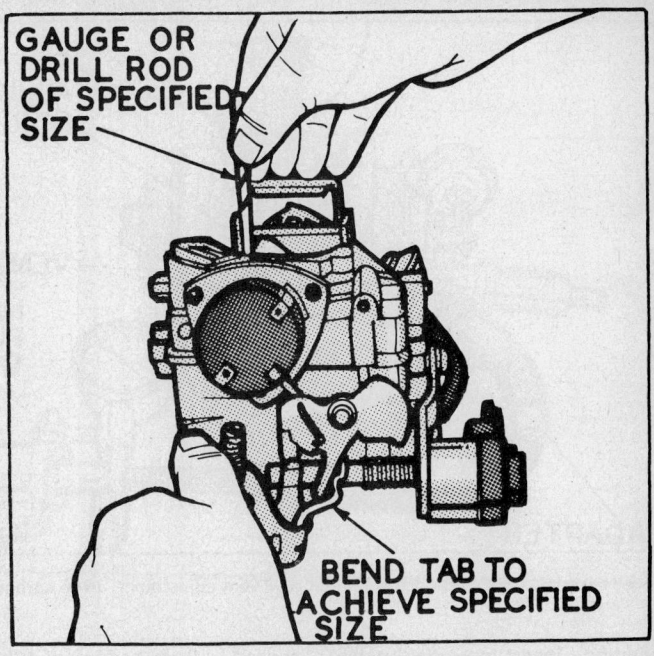

Fig. 7 Dechoke adjustment. 1946 carburetor

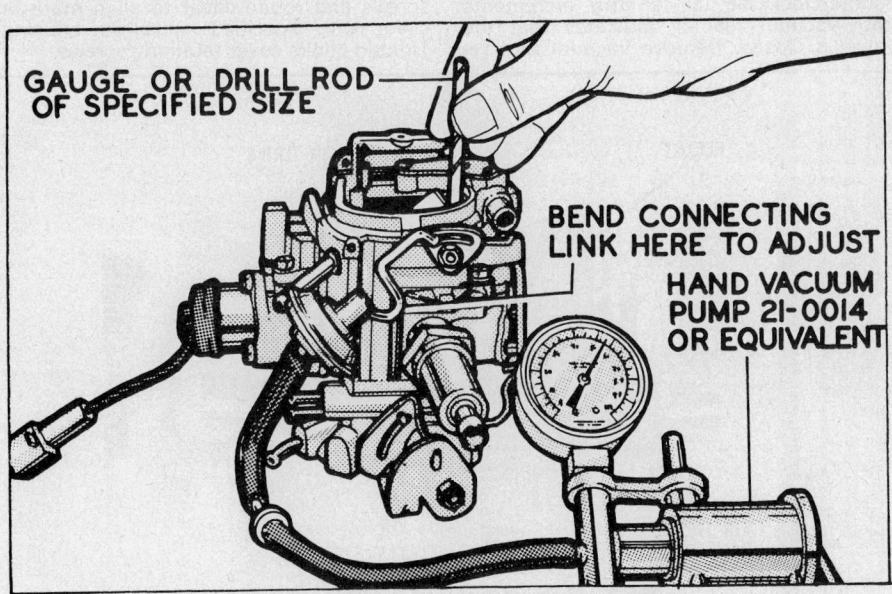

Fig. 6 Choke pulldown adjustment. 1946 carburetor

The main body assembly contains the fuel inlet system including the needle and seat assembly, the float, float hinge pin and retainer. The centrally located venturi contains two venturi vacuum boosters and the main discharge passage. The accelerator pump well, passages, check ball and weight, main metering jet, enrichment valve, idle tube and hot idle compensator are also located in the main body assembly. The venturi vacuum pick-up tube, manifold vacuum and EGR port vacuum pick-up tubes are incorporated in the main body assembly.

The throttle body assembly regulates air flow through the carburetor and provides the mounting flange for the carburetor. The throttle plate, shaft lever and return spring assemblies regulate air flow. Also located in the throttle body assembly are the spark vacuum port, EGR vacuum port, idle transfer slot, curb idle discharge port and the idle mixture adjusting screw.

Float Level Adjustment

Fig. 3—With air horn removed, place a finger over float hinge pin retainer and invert main body. Do not lose accelerator pump check ball and weight. Using a straight edge, check position of floats. The floats should touch the straight edge at points shown in illustration. To adjust, bend float tang.

Accelerator Pump Adjustment

Fig. 4—With the accelerator pump operating link in the specified slot, measure the length of the rod from inner side of tab to outer side of radius. To adjust, bend rod at U-joint.

Fast Idle Cam Position Adjustment

Fig. 5—With fast idle adjusting screw contacting second highest step of fast idle cam, move choke plate toward closed position. Insert specified gauge between upper edge of choke valve and air horn wall. To adjust, bend fast idle cam link.

Choke Pulldown Adjustment

Fig. 6—Loosen choke cover screw, rotate housing 90 degrees in the rich direction and tighten screws. Using an external vacuum source, apply sufficient vacuum to retract vacuum diaphragm. Push on small metal plate in the bottom of the linkage slot to ensure that the diaphragm is fully retracted. Insert specified gauge between upper edge of choke valve and air horn wall. To adjust, bend diaphragm link at U-bend.

Dechoke Adjustment

Fig. 7—With throttle held in wide open

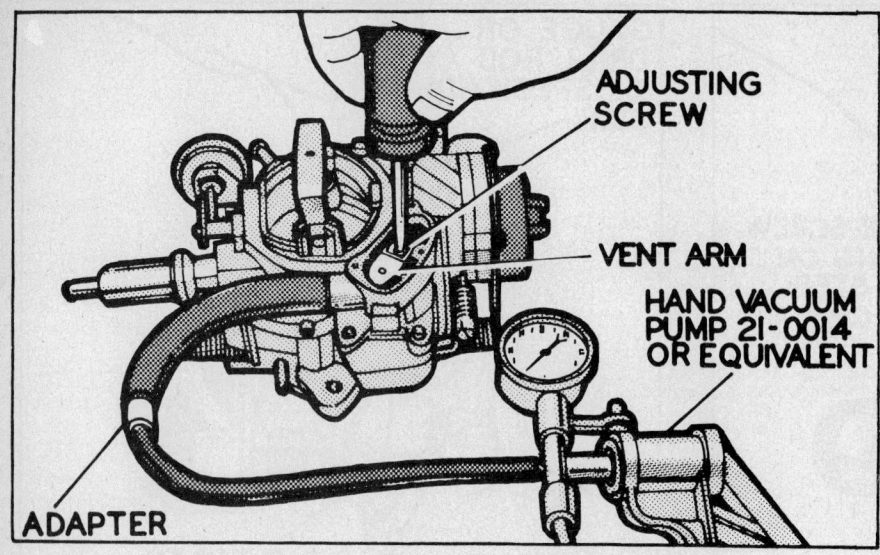

Fig. 8   External fuel bowl vent adjustment. 1946 carburetor

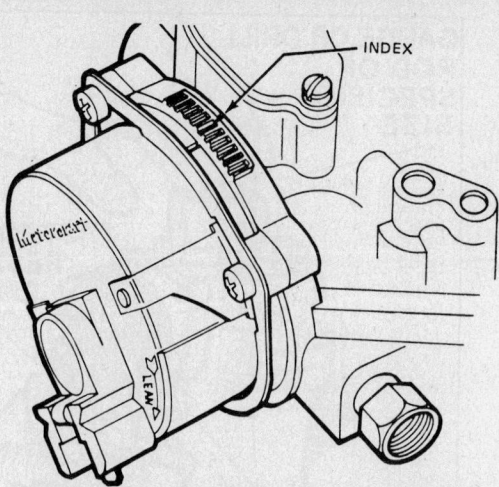

Fig. 9   Choke setting adjustment. 1946 carburetor

position, insert specified gauge between upper edge of choke valve and air horn wall. With light pressure against choke shaft lever, a slight drag should be felt when removing the gauge. To adjust, bend unloader tang on throttle lever.

External Fuel Bowl Vent Adjustment

Fig. 8—Disconnect canister vent hose from bowl vent tube. Connect an external vacuum source to bowl vent tube. Remove bowl vent cover, gasket and spring. Rotate vent adjusting screw clockwise until the adjusting screw protrudes $\frac{1}{8}$ inch or less above vent arm. Apply vacuum to vent tube and slowly turn the adjusting screw counterclockwise in $\frac{1}{8}$ turn increments until vacuum reading indicates that the valve is closed. Remove vacuum and ro-tate the adjusting screw $\frac{1}{2}$ turn clockwise. Install bowl vent spring, gasket and cover. Connect canister vent hose.

Choke Setting Adjustment

Fig. 9—Loosen choke cover retaining screws and rotate cover to align mark on cover with specified mark on housing. Tighten choke cover retaining screws.

MODEL 2245

This carburetor, Fig. 1, is a two-barrel unit but can be considered as two carburetors built side by side into one unit, utilizing the same fuel and air inlets. Each throat of the carburetor has its own throttle valve and main metering systems and are supplemented by the float, accelerating, idle and power systems. An electric choke system is incorporated to open choke at approximately 60° to 63°. For service information refer to the "Emission Control System" chapter.

On 1975-78 vehicles with automatic transmissions, an idle enrichment system is used to reduce cold engine stalling by the use of an additional metering system which enrichens the mixture in the off idle position. This system is controlled by a vacuum diaphragm mounted near the top of the carburetor.

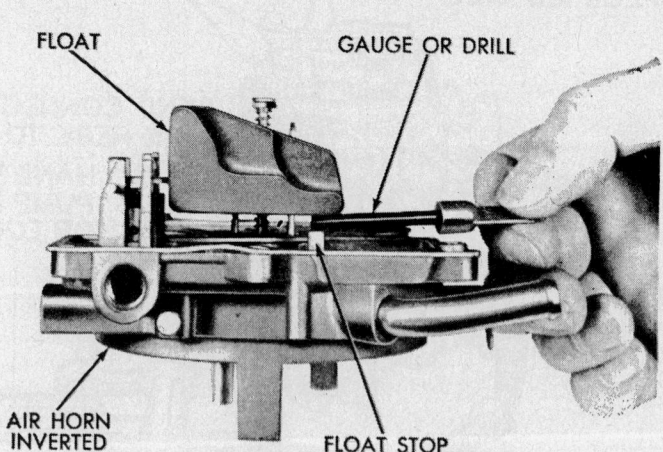

Fig. 2   Checking float level on 2245 carburetor

Float Adjustment

Invert air horn so that weight of float only is forcing needle against seat. Measure the clearance between top of float and float stop, Fig. 2. Be sure drill gauge is perfectly level when measuring. Refer to *Holley Specifications Chart*. Adjust by bending float lip toward or away from needle, using a narrow blade screwdriver, Fig. 3, until correct clearance of setting has been obtained.

Float Drop Adjustment

Check float drop, by holding air horn in an upright position. The bottom edge of float should be parallel to underside sur-face of air horn, Fig. 4. Adjust by bending tang on float arm until parallel surfaces have been obtained.

Fast Idle Cam Position Adjustment

Fig. 5—With fast idle speed adjusting screw contacting second highest step on fast idle cam, move choke valve toward closed position with light pressure on choke shaft lever. Insert specified gauge between top of choke valve and wall of air horn. Refer to *Holley Specifications Chart*. An adjustment will be necessary if a slight drag is not obtained as drill shank is be-ing removed. Adjust by bending fast idle link at angle, until correct valve opening has been obtained.

Choke Vacuum Kick Adjustment

NOTE: Test can be made on or off vehicle.

Fig. 6—If adjustment is to be made with engine running, back off fast idle speed screw until choke can be closed to the kick position with engine at curb idle. (Note number of screw turns required so that fast idle can be returned to original adjustment). If an auxiliary vacuum source is to be used, open throttle valve (engine

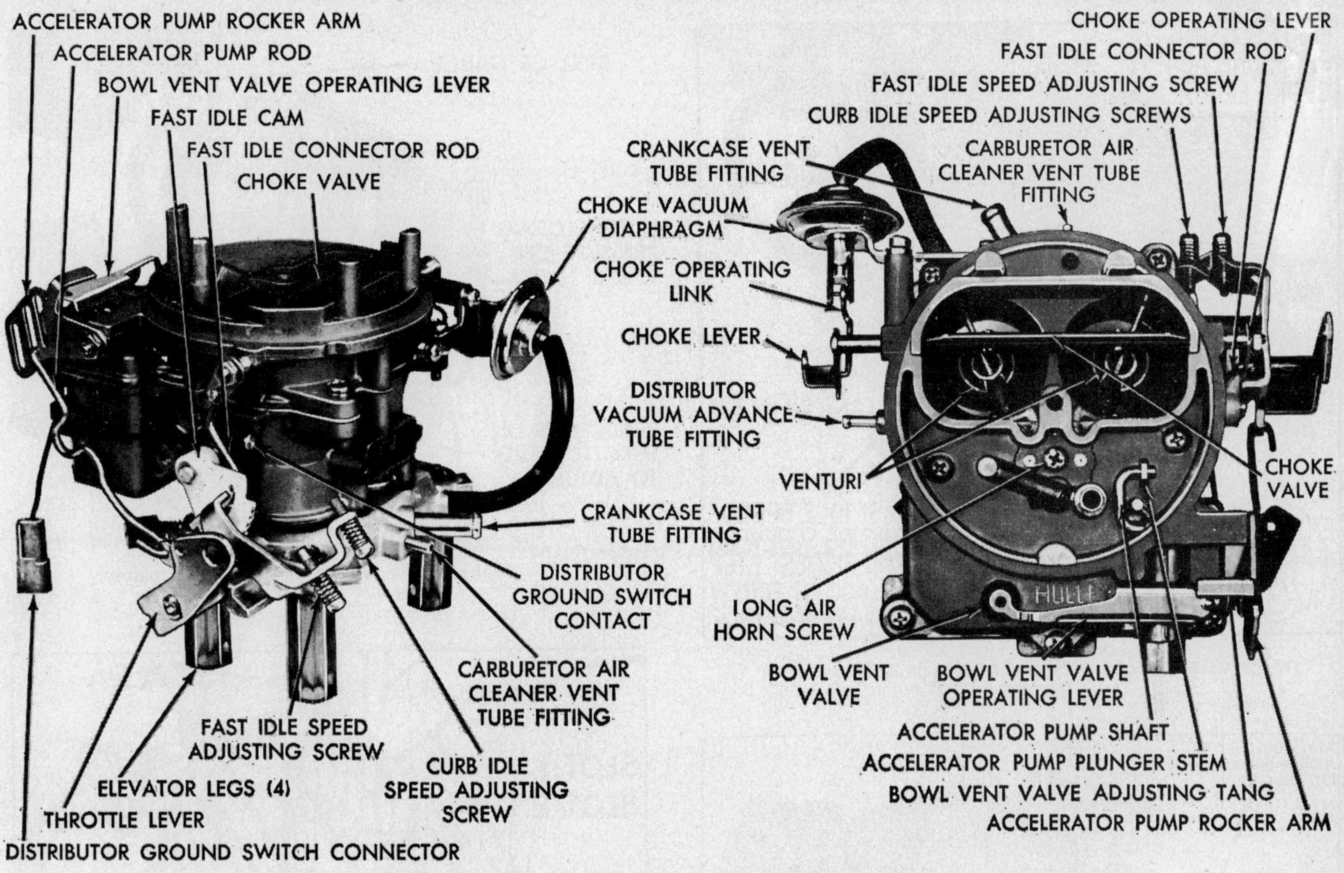

ACCELERATOR PUMP ROCKER ARM
ACCELERATOR PUMP ROD
BOWL VENT VALVE OPERATING LEVER
FAST IDLE CAM
FAST IDLE CONNECTOR ROD
CHOKE VALVE

CHOKE OPERATING LEVER
FAST IDLE CONNECTOR ROD
FAST IDLE SPEED ADJUSTING SCREW
CURB IDLE SPEED ADJUSTING SCREWS

CRANKCASE VENT TUBE FITTING
CARBURETOR AIR CLEANER VENT TUBE FITTING
CHOKE VACUUM DIAPHRAGM
CHOKE OPERATING LINK
CHOKE LEVER
DISTRIBUTOR VACUUM ADVANCE TUBE FITTING
VENTURI
CRANKCASE VENT TUBE FITTING
CHOKE VALVE
LONG AIR HORN SCREW
DISTRIBUTOR GROUND SWITCH CONTACT
BOWL VENT VALVE
BOWL VENT VALVE OPERATING LEVER
CARBURETOR AIR CLEANER VENT TUBE FITTING
ACCELERATOR PUMP SHAFT
FAST IDLE SPEED ADJUSTING SCREW
ACCELERATOR PUMP PLUNGER STEM
ELEVATOR LEGS (4)
CURB IDLE SPEED ADJUSTING SCREW
BOWL VENT VALVE ADJUSTING TANG
THROTTLE LEVER
ACCELERATOR PUMP ROCKER ARM
DISTRIBUTOR GROUND SWITCH CONNECTOR

Fig. 1   Holley model 2245 two-barrel carburetor (Typical)

not running) and move choke to closed position. Release throttle first, then release choke.

When using an auxiliary vacuum source, disconnect vacuum hose from carburetor and connect it to hose from vacuum supply with a small length of tube to act as a fitting. Removal of hose from diaphragm may require forces which damage the system. On 2245 units, apply 15 or more inches of vacuum to diaphragm.

Insert gauge between top of choke valve and wall of air horn. Refer to *Holley Specifications Chart.* Apply sufficient closing pressure on lever to which choke rod at-

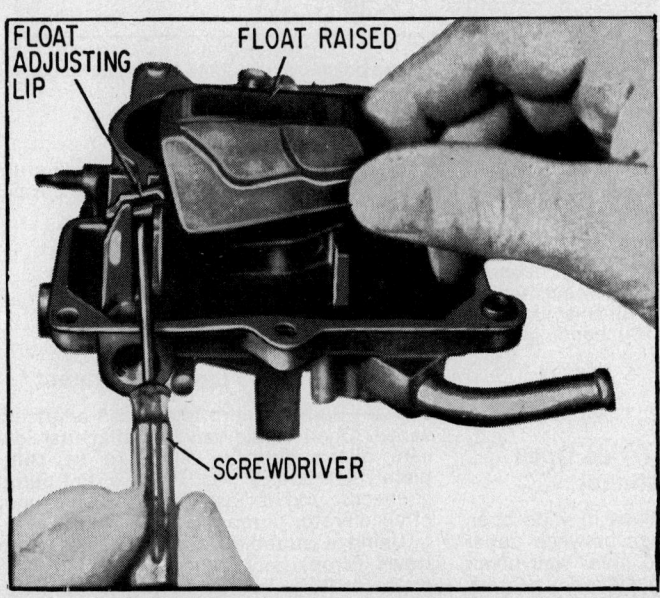

FLOAT ADJUSTING LIP
FLOAT RAISED
SCREWDRIVER

Fig. 3   Adjusting float on 2245 carburetor

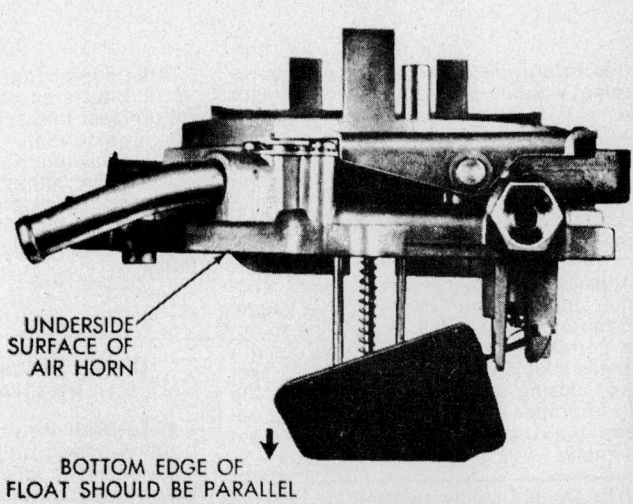

UNDERSIDE SURFACE OF AIR HORN

BOTTOM EDGE OF FLOAT SHOULD BE PARALLEL

Fig. 4   Checking float drop on 2245 carburetor

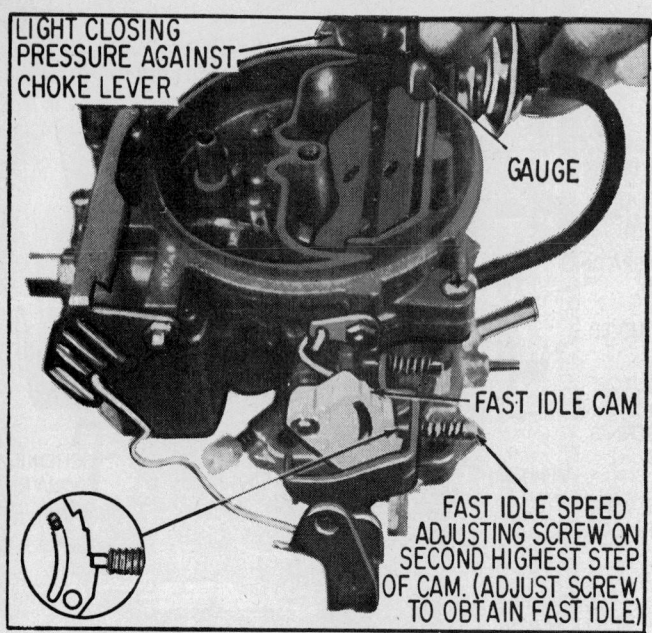

Fig. 5   Fast idle cam position adjustment on 2245 carburetor

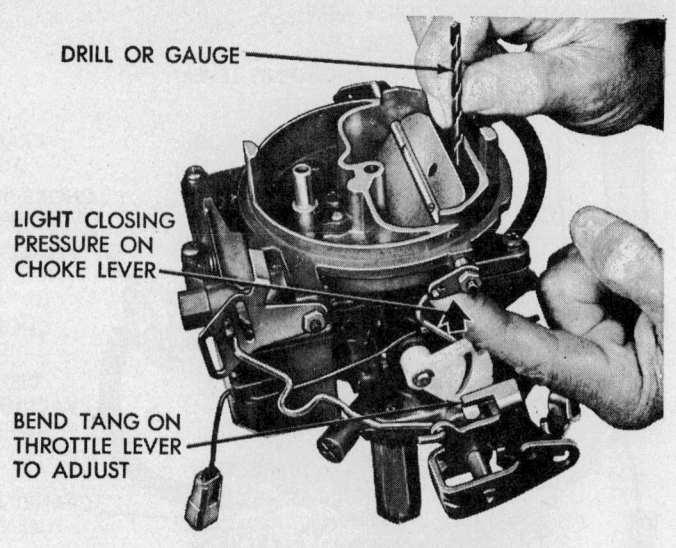

Fig. 7   Choke unloader adjustment on 2245 carburetor

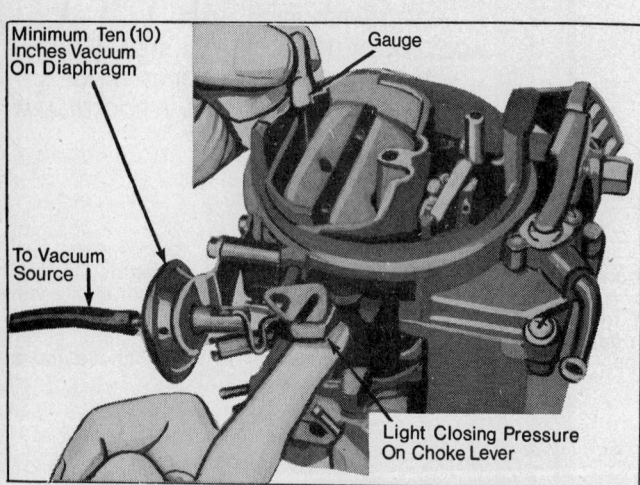

Fig. 6   Vacuum kick adjustment on 2245 carburetor

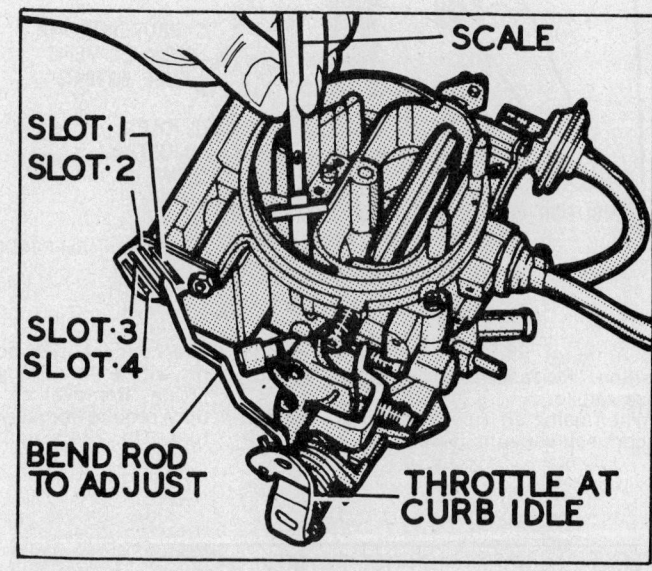

Fig. 8   Accelerator pump adjustment on 2245 carburetor

taches to provide a minimum choke valve opening without distortion of diaphragm link.

NOTE: The cylindrical stem of diaphragm extends as the internal spring is compressed. This spring must be fully compressed for proper measurement of vacuum kick adjustment.

Adjustment is necessary if slight drag is not obtained when removing the gauge. Shorten or lengthen diaphragm link to obtain correct choke valve opening. Length changes should be made by carefully opening or closing the U-bend provided in the link. Improper bending causes contact between the U-section and the diaphragm assembly.

NOTE: Do not apply twisting or bending force to diaphragm.

After completion of adjustment, reinstall vacuum hose on correct carburetor fitting. Return fast idle screw to its original location if disturbed. Make following check. With no vacuum applied to diaphragm, the choke valve should move freely between open and closed positions. If movement is not free, examine linkage for misalignment or interferences caused by bending operation.

Choke Unloader (Wide Open Kick) Adjustment

Fig. 7—With throttle valves in wide open position, insert drill gauge between upper edge of choke valve and inner wall of air horn. Refer to *Holley Specifications Chart*. With a finger lightly pressing against shaft lever, a slight drag should be felt as drill

is being withdrawn. Adjust by bending unloader tang on throttle lever until correct opening has been obtained.

Accelerator Pump Adjustment

Fig. 8—Back off curb idle speed adjusting screw. Open choke valve so that fast idle cam allows throttle valves to be completely seated in bores. Be sure that pump connector rod is installed in correct slot of accelerator pump rocker arm.

Using a suitable scale, measure pump travel (drop) between curb idle and wide open throttle. To adjust, bend pump operating rod until proper setting is obtained.

Bowl Vent Valve Clearance Adjustment

Fig. 9—With the throttle valves at curb idle, it should be possible to insert the specified gauge between the bowl vent valve plunger stem and operating rod. Refer to *Holley Specifications Chart.* Adjust by bending the tang on pump lever to change arc of contact with throttle lever, until correct clearance has been obtained.

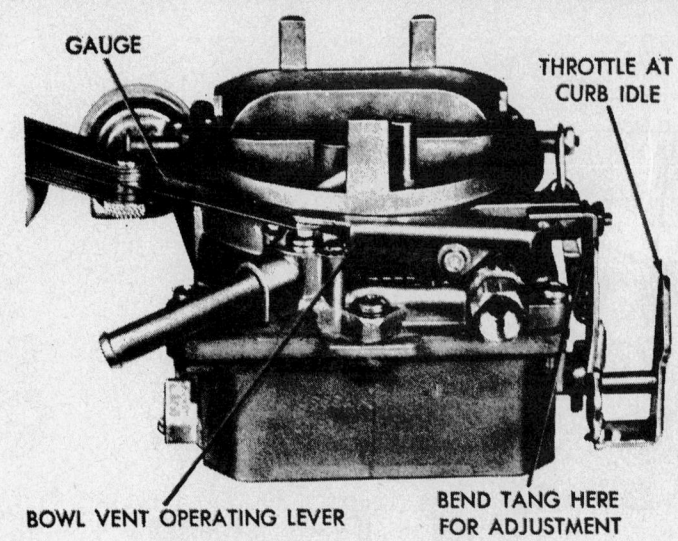

Fig. 9   Bowl vent adjustment on 2245 carburetor

MODEL 2280

This carburetor, Fig. 1, uses four basic metering systems. The basic idle system provides the proper air/fuel mixture for idle and low speed operations. The accelerator pump system provides additional fuel during acceleration. The main metering system provides the proper air/fuel mixture during normal cruising conditions. The power enrichment system, combining a mechanical and vacuum operated power valve, provides a richer mixture when higher engine power is required.

In addition to the four basic systems, there is a fuel inlet system which supplies fuel to the four basic systems and

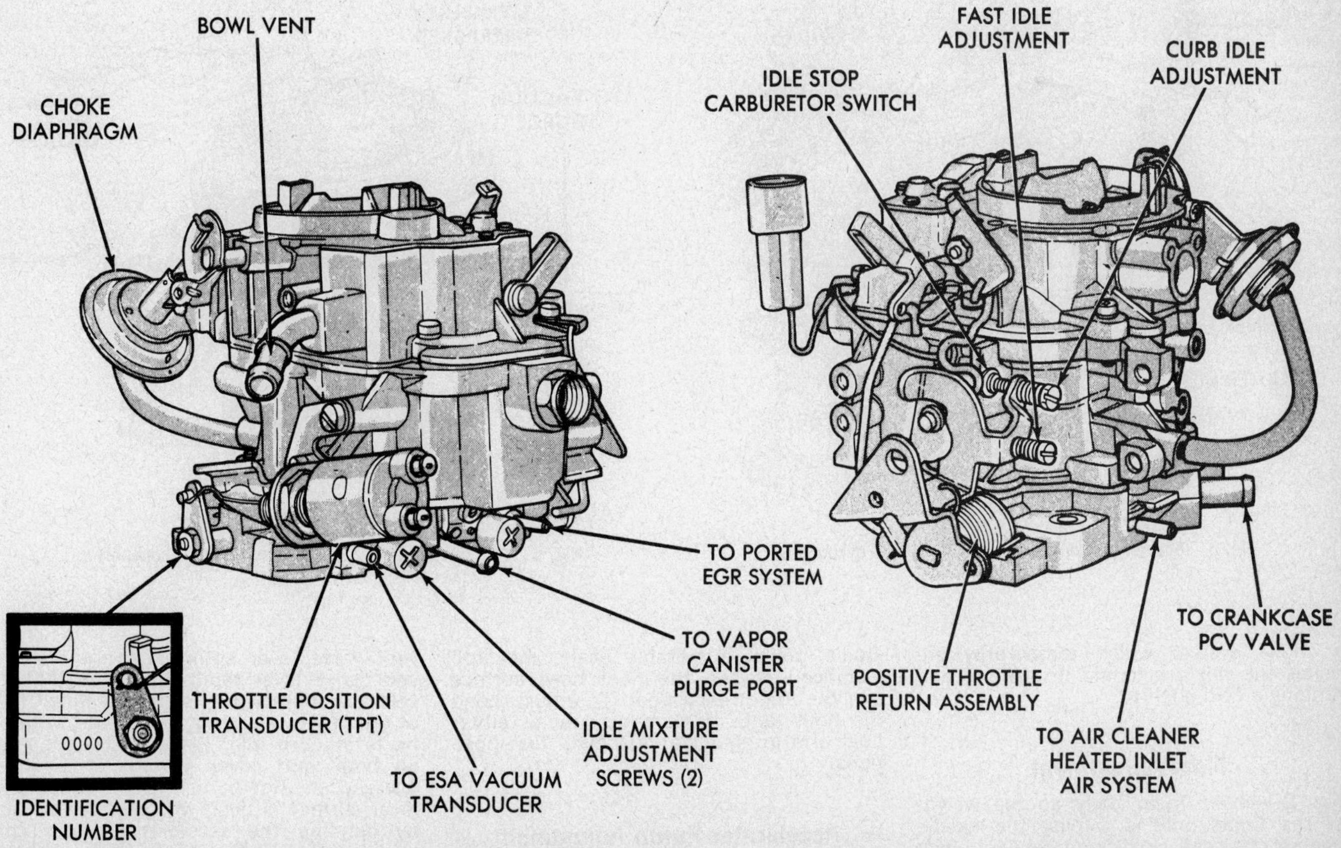

Fig. 1   Holley model 2280 two barrel carburetor

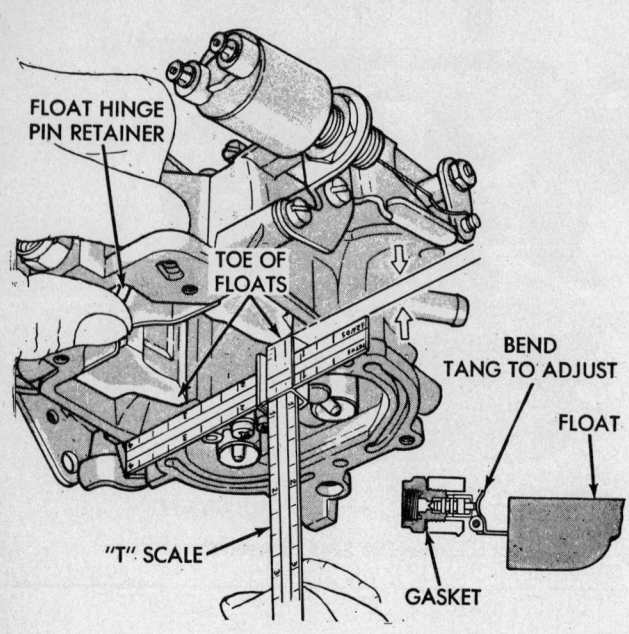

Fig. 2 Float adjustment. 2280 carburetor

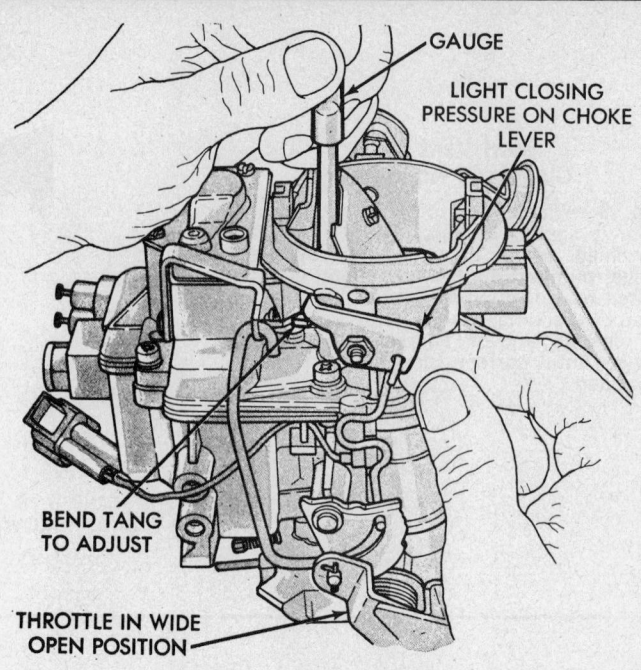

Fig. 4 Choke unloader adjustment. 2280 carburetor

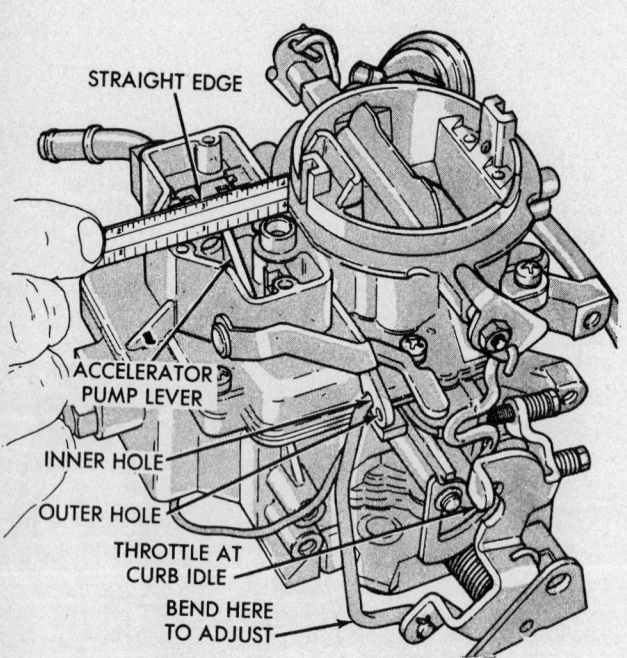

Fig. 3 Accelerator pump adjustment. 2280 carburetor

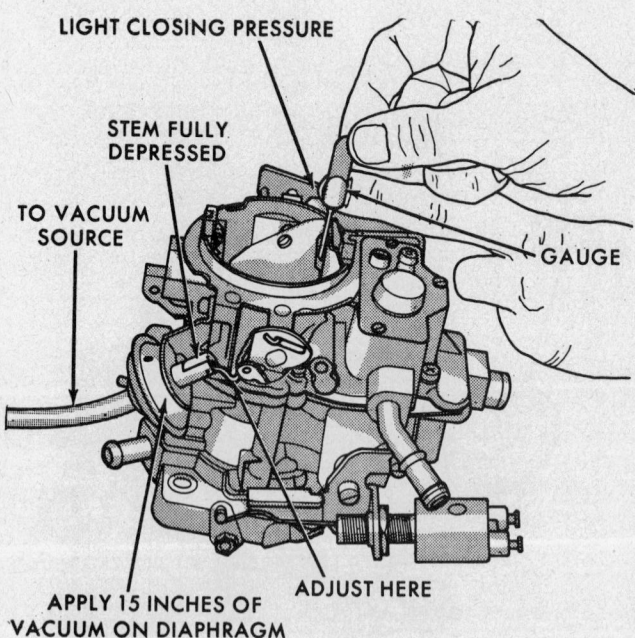

Fig. 5 Choke vacuum kick adjustment. 2280 carburetor

a choke system which temporarily enriches the mixture to aid in starting and running a cold engine.

Float Adjustment

Fig. 2—Invert main body so the weight of the floats only is forcing the needle against the seat. Hold finger against hinge pin retainer to fully seat in the float hinge cradle. Using a suitable scale, measure distance between the float bowl surface and the toe of each float. To adjust, bend the float tang. If necessary, bend either float arm to equalize individual float positions.

Accelerator Pump Adjustment

Fig. 3—Remove bowl vent cover plate and vent valve lever spring. Do not dislodge vent valve lever retainer. Ensure that accelerator pump rod is in the inner hole of the pump operating lever and the throttle is at curb idle. Place a straight edge on bowl vent cover surface of air horn over accelerator pump lever. Adjust until lever surface is flush with air horn surface by bending the accelerator pump connector rod. Install vent valve lever spring and bowl vent cover plate.

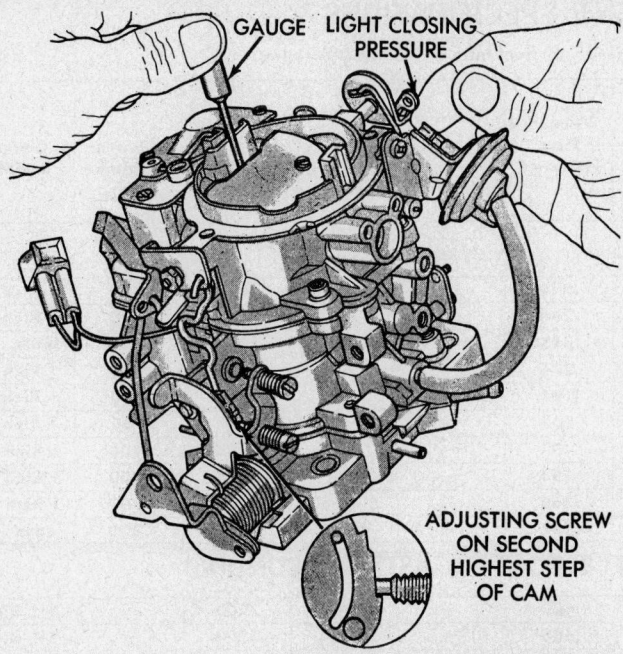

Fig. 6 Fast idle cam position adjustment. 2280 carburetor

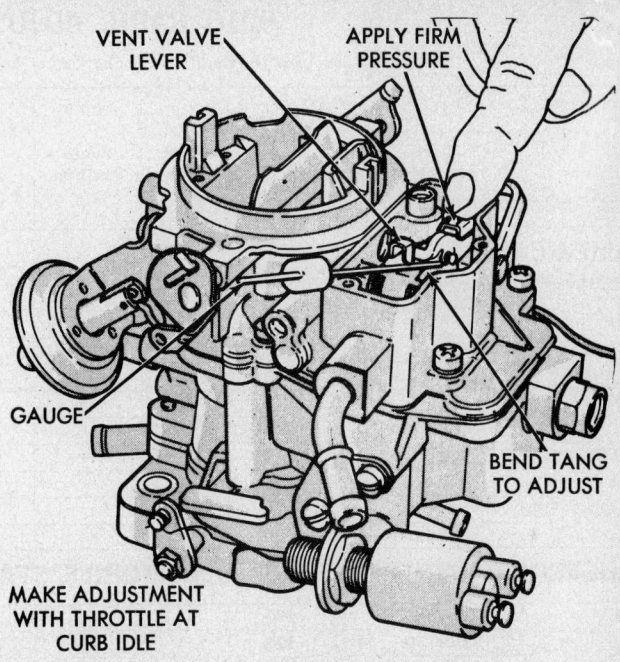

Fig. 7 Bowl vent valve adjustment. 2280 carburetor

NOTE: If this adjustment is changed, the bowl vent and mechanical power valve adjustments must be reset.

Choke Unloader Adjustment

Fig. 4—Hold throttle valves in wide open position. Lightly press finger against control lever to move choke valve toward closed position. Insert specified gauge between top of choke valve and air horn wall. To adjust, bend tang on accelerator pump lever.

Choke Vacuum Kick Adjustment

Fig. 5—Open throttle, close choke, then close throttle to trap fast idle cam at closed choke position. Apply approximately 15 inches of vacuum to diaphragm with an external vacuum source. Apply closing pressure on choke lever to completely compress spring in diaphragm stem without distorting linkage. The cylindrical stem of the diaphragm extends to a stop as the spring compresses. Insert specified gauge between top of choke valve and air horn wall. Adjust by bending diaphragm link at U-bend. Check for free movement between the open and adjusted positions.

Fast Idle Cam Position Adjustment

Fig. 6—With fast idle speed adjusting screw contacting second highest step of fast idle cam, move choke valve toward closed position with light pressure on choke shaft lever. Insert specified gauge between top of choke valve and air horn

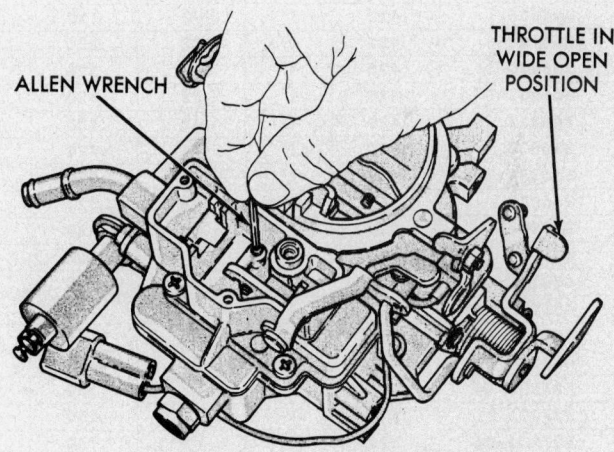

Fig. 8 Mechanical power valve adjustment. 2280 carburetor

wall. To adjust, bend U-bend in fast idle connector link to obtain proper setting.

Bowl Vent Valve Adjustment

Fig. 7—Remove bowl vent cover plate and vent valve lever spring. Do not dislodge vent valve lever retainer. With throttle at curb idle, press downward on vent valve lever where spring seats. Measure distance between contact surfaces of vent valve tang and vent valve lever. Adjust by bending end of vent valve lever. Install vent valve lever spring and bowl vent cover plate.

Mechanical Power Valve Adjustment

Fig. 8—Remove bowl vent cover plate, vent valve lever spring and retainer, then the vent valve lever and pivot pin. Hold throttle in wide open position. Insert a 5/64 inch allen wrench in mechanical power valve adjustment screw. Push screw downward and release to determine if clearance exists. Turn screw clockwise until zero clearance is obtained. Adjust by turning screw one turn counter-clockwise. Install vent valve lever, pivot pin and retainer, then the vent valve lever spring and bowl vent cover plate.

5210 CARB. ADJUSTMENT SPECIFICATIONS

See Tune Up Chart in car chapter for hot idle speeds, air/fuel ratio and idle CO% rating.

Year	Carb. Part No.	Float Level (Dry)	Float Drop	Pump Position	Fast Idle Cam Index	Vacuum Plate Pulldown	Vacuum Break Primary	Vacuum Break Secondary	Fast Idle Setting	Unloader Setting	Choke Setting
AMERICAN MOTORS											
1977	7711	.420	—	—	.140	.246	—	—	1600	.300	1 Rich
	7712	.420	—	—	.140	.246	—	—	1600	.300	1 Rich
	7799	.420	—	—	.135	.215	—	—	1600	.300	Index
	7846	.420	—	—	.101	.204	—	—	1600	.300	1 Rich
1978	8163	.420	—	—	.193	.191	—	—	1800	.300	1 Rich
	8164	.420	—	—	.204	.202	—	—	1800	.300	1 Rich
1979	7846	.420	—	—	.193	.191	—	—	1800	.300	1 Rich
	8548	.420	—	—	.204	.191	—	—	1800	.300	1 Rich
	8549	.420	—	—	.191	.266	—	—	1800	.300	1 Rich
	8675	.420	—	—	.173	.177	—	—	1800	.300	Index
CHEVROLET MONZA & VEGA, OLDSMOBILE STARFIRE & PONTIAC ASTRE & SUNBIRD											
1974	338168	.420	1″	#2	.140	.400	—	—	2200	—	3½ Rich
	338170	.420	1″	#2	.140	.400	—	—	2200	—	3½ Rich
	338179	.420	1″	#3	.140	.300	—	—	2000	—	2½ Rich
	338181	.420	1″	#3	.140	.300	—	—	2000	—	2½ Rich
1975	348659	.420	1″	—	—	.325	—	—	1600	—	3 Rich
	348660	.420	1″	#2	.110	.300	—	—	1600	—	4 Rich
	348661	.420	1″	—	—	.275	—	—	1600	—	3 Rich
	348662	.420	1″	#2	.110	.275	—	—	1600	—	4 Rich
	348663	.420	1″	—	—	.325	—	—	1600	—	3 Rich
	348664	.420	1″	#2	.110	.300	—	—	1600	—	4 Rich
	348665	.420	1″	—	—	.275	—	—	1600	—	3 Rich
	348666	.420	1″	#2	.110	.275	—	—	1600	—	4 Rich
1976	366829	.420	1″	#3	.320	.313	—	—	2200	.375	2 Rich
	366830	.420	1″	#2	.320	.288	—	—	2200	.375	3 Rich
	366831	.420	1″	#3	.320	.313	—	—	2200	.375	2 Rich
	366832	.420	1″	#2	.320	.288	—	—	2200	.375	3 Rich
	366833	.420	1″	#3	.320	.268	—	—	2200	.375	2 Rich
	366834	.420	1″	#2	.320	.268	—	—	2200	.375	3 Rich
	366840	.420	1″	#2	.320	.268	—	—	2200	.375	3 Rich
	366841	.420	1″	#3	.320	.268	—	—	2200	.375	2 Rich
1977	458102, 04	.420	1″	①	.120	—	.250	—	2500	.350	3 Rich
	458103, 05	.420	1″	①	.120	—	.250	—	2500	.350	3 Rich
	458106, 08	.420	1″	#1	.120	—	.275	—	2500	.400	3 Rich
	458107, 09	.420	1″	#2	.160	—	.275	.400	2500	.350	3 Rich
	458110, 12	.420	1″	#1	.160	—	.325	.400	2500	.350	3 Rich
	527200, 02	.520	1″	#2	.150	—	.300	—	2400	.400	4 Rich
	527201, 03	.520	1″	#2	.150	—	.325	—	2400	.400	4 Rich
	527204, 06	.520	1″	#2	.150	—	.325	—	2400	.400	2 Rich
1978	10001047	.520	1″	—	.150	—	.325	.400	2200	.350	1 Rich
	10001048	.520	1″	—	.150	—	.300	.400	2500	.350	2 Rich
	10001049	.520	1″	—	.150	—	.325	.400	2200	.350	1 Rich
	10001050	.520	1″	—	.150	—	.300	.400	2500	.350	2 Rich
	10001052	.520	1″	—	.150	—	.325	.400	2500	.350	2 Rich
	10001054	.520	1″	—	.150	—	.325	.400	2500	.350	2 Rich
	10004048	.520	1″	—	.150	—	.300	—	2400	.350	2 Rich
	10004049	.520	1″	—	.150	—	.300	—	2400	.350	2 Rich

①—Manual trans., #2; auto. trans., #1.

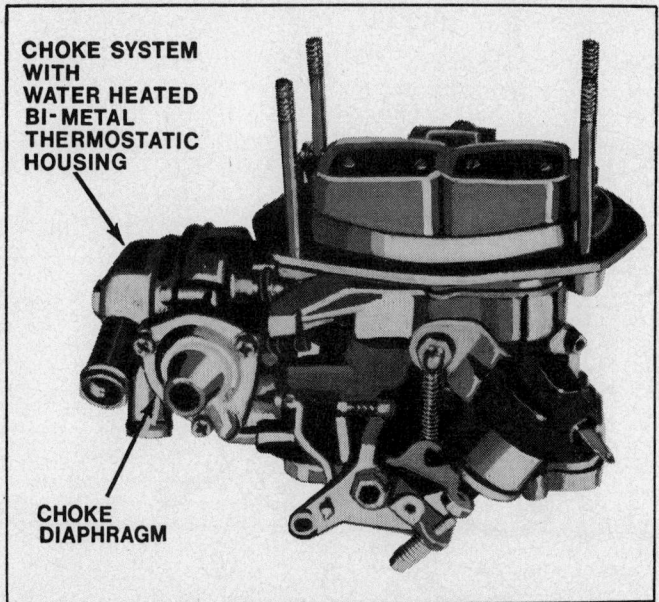

Fig. 1 Holley 5210 2 barrel carburetor

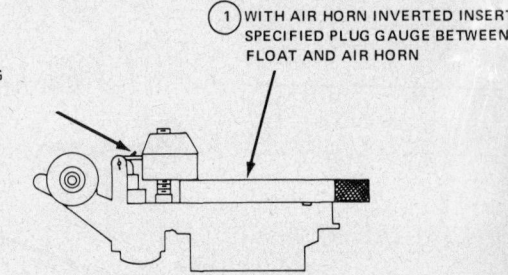

Fig. 3 Checking float level on 5210 carburetor

MODEL 5210

The Holley 5210 two-barrel carburetor, Figs. 1 and 2, has a number of unique features. An automatic choke system activated by a water heated bi-metal thermostatic coil and a primary venturi smaller in size than the secondary venturi.

An Exhaust Gas Recirculation (EGR) system is used on all applications with the EGR valve located in the intake manifold.

Carburetors used on 1977-78 vehicles use a primary and secondary vacuum break. The secondary vacuum break is used on some vehicles.

Float Adjustment

Fig. 3—With the air horn inverted and the float tang resting lightly on the spring loaded fuel inlet needle, measure the clearance between the bowl cover and the end of each float. Refer to *Holley 5210 Specifications Chart*. Adjust by bending the float tang as required.

Fast Idle Cam Index Adjustment

Fig. 4—Place the fast idle screw on the second step of the fast idle cam and against the shoulder of the first step. Place a drill or gauge on the down stream side of the choke plate. Refer to *5210 Specifications Chart*. Adjust by bending the choke lever tang.

NOTE: The dechoke is automatically set when the fast idle cam index is adjusted.

Vacuum Plate Pulldown Adjustment

Fig. 5—Remove the three hex headed screws and ring retaining the choke bi-metal cover. Do not remove the choke water housing screw if adjusting on the car. Pull the choke water housing and bi-metal cover assembly out of the way. With a screwdriver or suitable tool, push the diaphragm stem back against the stop. Place drill or gauge on the down stream side of the primary choke plate. Take all the slack out of the linkage. Refer to *5210 Specifications Chart*. Adjust by turning adjusting screw in or out with an 5/32 inch Allen wrench.

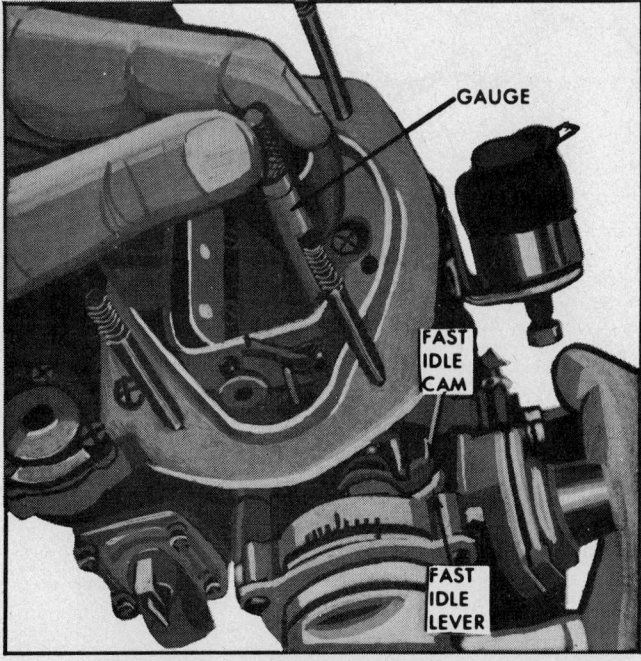

Fig. 4 Fast idle cam index adjustment 5210 Holley carburetor

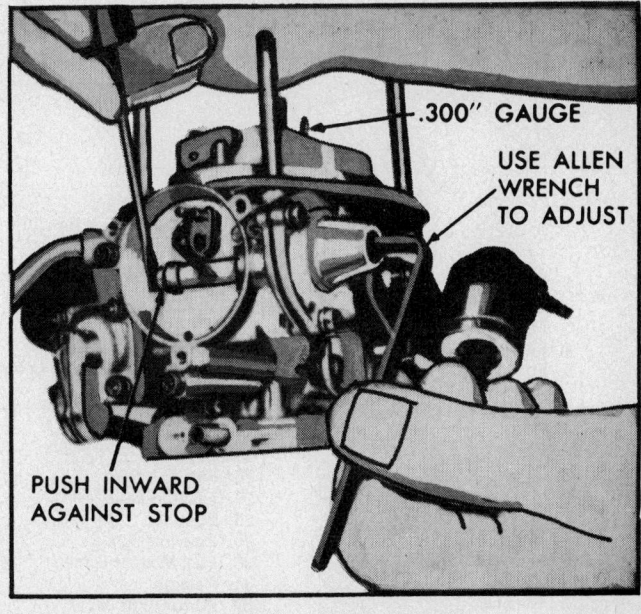

Fig. 5 Vacuum pull down adjustment 5210 Holley carburetor

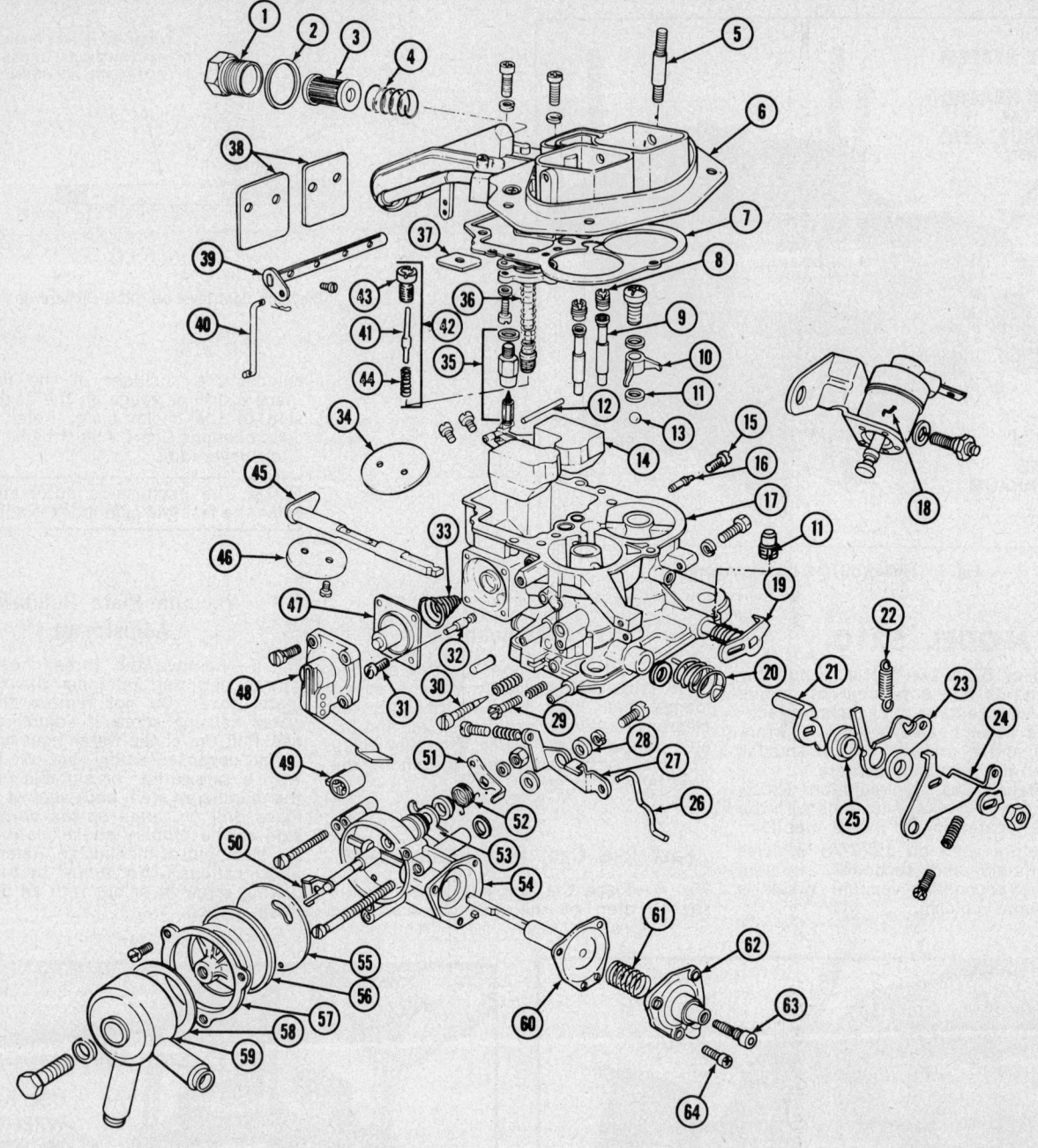

Fig. 2 Exploded view of a typical Holley 5210 carburetor

1. Fuel Inlet Nut
2. Gasket
3. Filter
4. Spring
5. Studs, Air Cleaner Attachment
6. Air Horn
7. Gasket
8. High Speed Bleed
9. Main Well Tube
10. Pump Discharge Nozzle
11. Gasket
12. Float Shaft
13. Discharge Check Ball
14. Float
15. Retainer
16. Secondary Idle Jet
17. Carburetor Body Assembly

18. Idle Stop Solenoid
19. Secondary Throttle Lever
20. Throttle Return Spring
21. Idle Lever
22. Secondary Operating Lever Return Spring
23. Secondary Operating Lever
24. Throttle Lever
25. Bushing
26. Fast Idle Rod
27. Fast Idle Lever
28. Bushing
29. Low Idle Screw
30. Fuel Mixture Screw
31. Retainer
32. Primary Idle Jet
33. Return Spring

34. Secondary Throttle Plate
35. Fuel Inlet Needle and Seat Assembly
36. Power Valve Economizer Assembly
37. Choke Rod Seal
38. Choke Plates
39. Choke Shaft and Lever
40. Choke Rod
41. Power Valve
42. Power Valve Assembly
43. Seat
44. Spring
45. Primary Throttle Shaft and Lever Assembly
46. Primary Throttle Plate
47. Accelerator Pump

48. Accelerator Pump Cover
49. Mixture Screw Limiter Cap
50. Choke Housing Shaft
51. Choke Lever
52. Fast Idle Cam Spring
53. Fast Idle Cam
54. Choke Housing
55. Gasket
56. Thermostatic Housing
57. Retainer
58. Gasket
59. Water Cover
60. Diaphragm and Shaft
61. Return Spring
62. Choke Diaphragm Cover
63. Hex Head Screw
64. Cover Screw

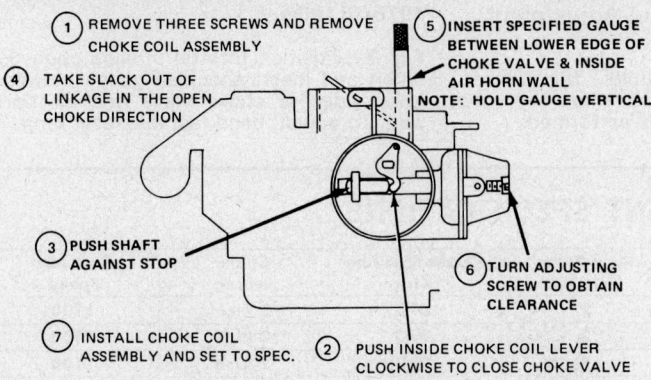

Fig. 5A Primary vacuum break adjustment 5210 Holley carburetor

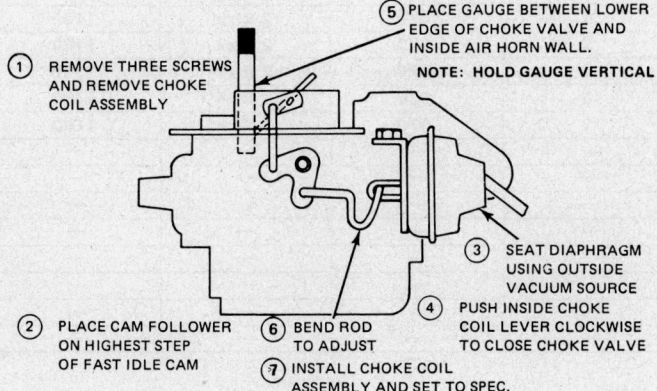

Fig. 5B Secondary vacuum break adjustment 5210 Holley carburetor

Vacuum Break

Primary

Fig. 5A—Remove choke coil assembly, then push inside choke coil lever clockwise to close choke valve and push shaft against stop to remove slack from linkage in open choke direction. Refer to 5210 Specifications Chart and insert specified gauge between lower edge of choke valve and inside air horn wall. Adjust by turning screw to obtain clearance.

Secondary

Fig. 5B—Remove choke coil assembly and place cam follower on highest step of fast idle cam. Using an outside vacuum source, seat diaphragm, then push inside choke coil lever clockwise to close choke valve. Refer to 5210 Specifications Chart and insert specified gauge between lower edge of choke valve and inside air horn wall. To adjust, bend rod.

Secondary Throttle Plate Adjustment

Fig. 6—Back out the secondary throttle stop screw, until the secondary throttle plate seats in the carburetor bore. Turn screw in until it makes contact with tab on the secondary throttle lever, then turn screw in an additional 1/4 turn.

Fast Idle Adjustment

Fig. 7—With engine at operating tempera-

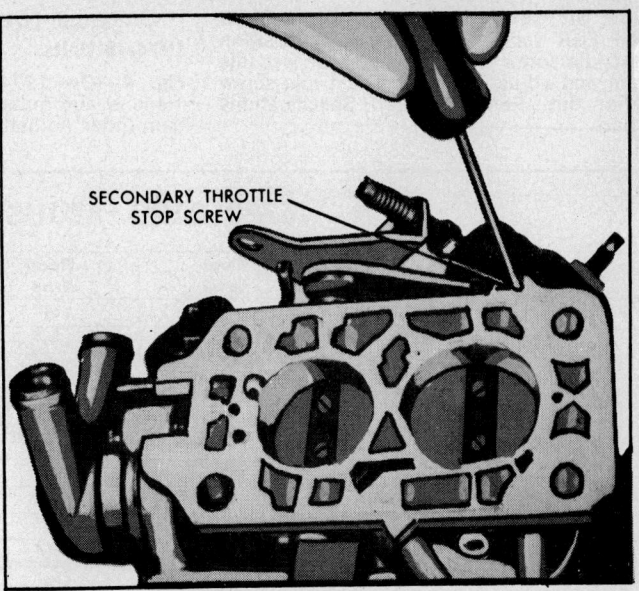

Fig. 6 Secondary throttle plate adjustment

Fig. 7 Fast idle adjustment 5210 Holley carburetor

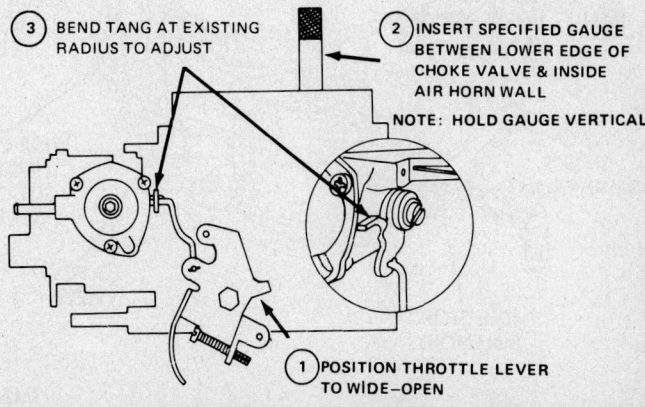

Fig. 8 Unloader adjustment. 1976-78 units

ture, air cleaner off, choke off, A/C off and EGR valve free to operate, position fast idle screw on second step of fast idle cam and adjust by turning fast idle screw in or out. Refer to 5210 Specifications Chart.

Unloader (Dechoke) Adjustment
1974-75 Units

Fig. 4—On 1974-75 units, this adjustment is automatically set when Fast Idle Cam Index Adjustment is performed.

1976-78 Units

Fig. 8—Position throttle in wide open position and insert specified gauge between lower edge of choke valve and air horn wall. To adjust, bend fast idle lever tang.

5220 CARB. ADJUSTMENT SPECIFICATIONS

Year	Model No.	Float Level	Float Drop	Acc. Pump Hole No.	Choke Vacuum Kick	Choke Setting	Fast Idle Speed
1978	R-8376A	.480	1⅞"	2	.070	2 Rich	1100
	R-8384A	.480	1⅞"	2	.070	2 Rich	1100
	R-8385A	.480	1⅞"	2	.070	2 Rich	1100
	R-8386A	.480	1⅞"	2	.070	2 Rich	1100
	R-8387A	.480	1⅞"	2	.070	2 Rich	1100
	R-8504A	.480	1⅞"	2	.070	2 Rich	1100
	R-8505A	.480	1⅞"	2	.070	2 Rich	1100
	R-8506A	.480	1⅞"	2	.070	2 Rich	1100
	R-8507A	.480	1⅞"	2	.070	2 Rich	1100
	R-8630A	.480	1⅞"	2	.070	2 Rich	1100
	R-8631A	.480	1⅞"	2	.070	2 Rich	1100
	R-8632A	.480	1⅞"	2	.070	2 Rich	1100
1979	R-8451A	—	—	—	—	—	—
	R-8524A	—	—	—	—	—	—
	R-8525A	—	—	—	—	—	—
	R-8526A	—	—	—	—	—	—
	R-8527A	—	—	—	—	—	—
	R-8528A	—	—	—	—	—	—
	R-8529A	—	—	—	—	—	—
	R-8530A	—	—	—	—	—	—

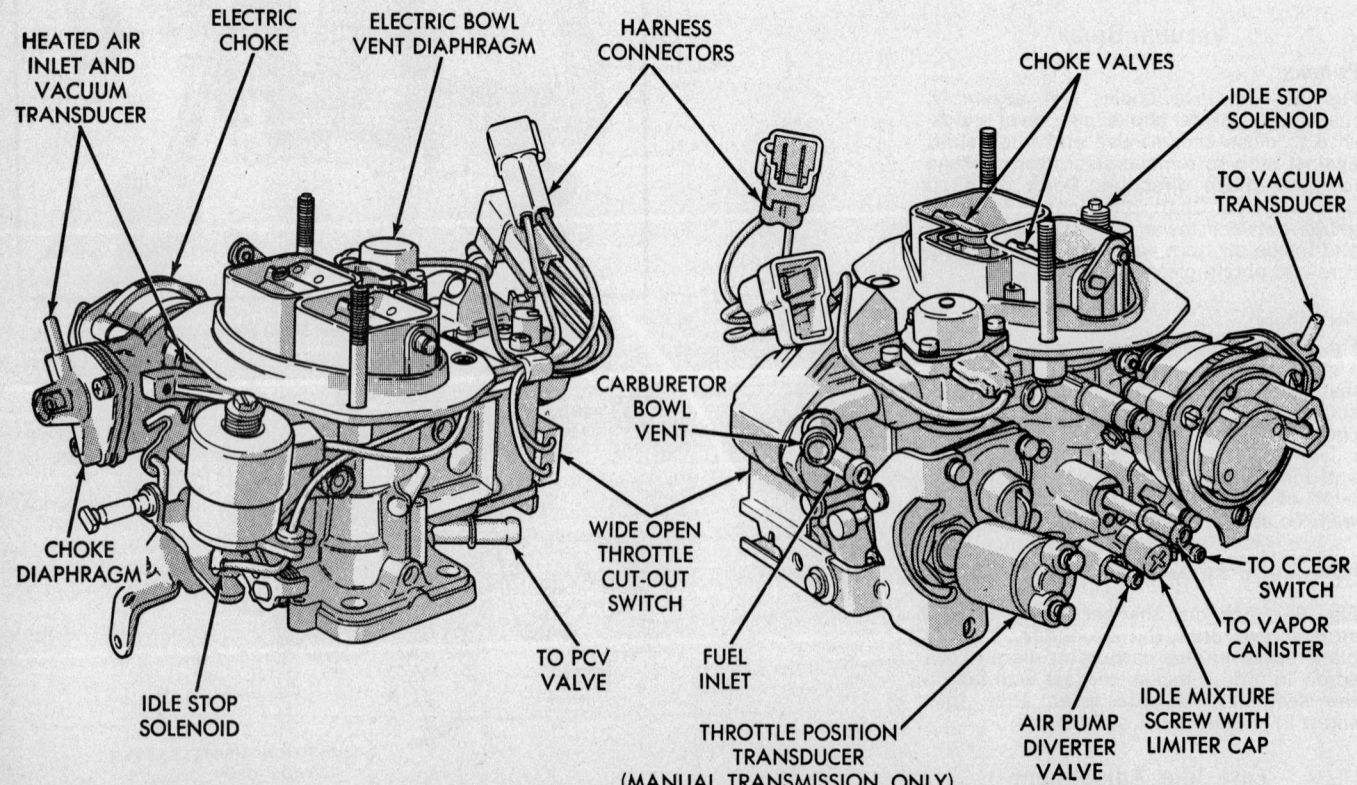

Fig. 1   Holley model 5220 carburetor. Vehicles equipped with air conditioning

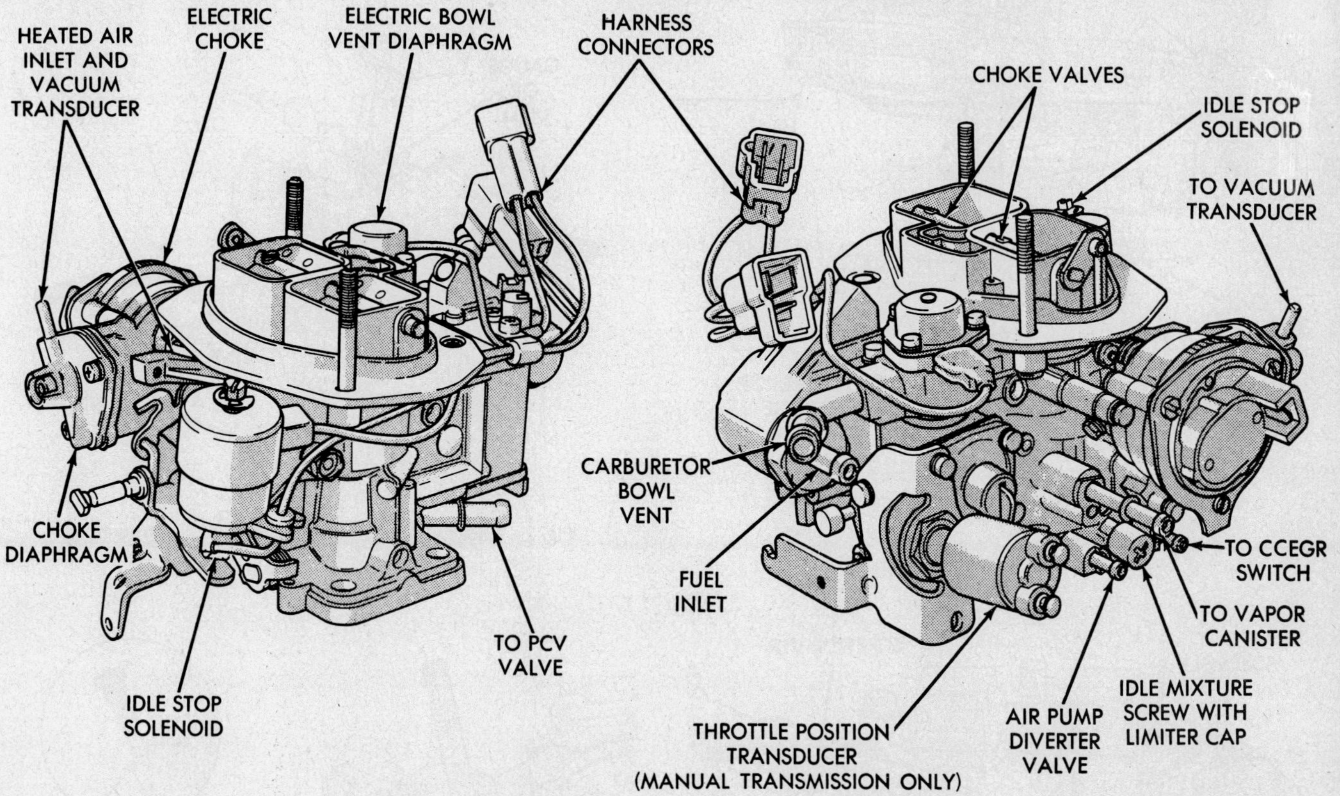

HEATED AIR INLET AND VACUUM TRANSDUCER

ELECTRIC CHOKE

ELECTRIC BOWL VENT DIAPHRAGM

HARNESS CONNECTORS

CHOKE VALVES

IDLE STOP SOLENOID

TO VACUUM TRANSDUCER

CHOKE DIAPHRAGM

IDLE STOP SOLENOID

TO PCV VALVE

CARBURETOR BOWL VENT

FUEL INLET

THROTTLE POSITION TRANSDUCER (MANUAL TRANSMISSION ONLY)

AIR PUMP DIVERTER VALVE

IDLE MIXTURE SCREW WITH LIMITER CAP

TO CCEGR SWITCH

TO VAPOR CANISTER

Fig. 2   Holley model 5220 carburetor. Vehicles less air conditioning

MODEL 5220

The Holley model 5220, Figs. 1 and 2, is a staged dual venturi carburetor. The primary bore or venturi is smaller than the secondary bore. The secondary stage is mechanically operated by linkage connect the primary and secondary throttle levers. The primary stage includes a curb idle and transfer system, diaphragm type accelerator pump system, main metering system and power enrichment system. The secondary stage includes a main metering system and power system. Both the primary and secondary venturi draw fuel from a common fuel bowl. The electric automatic choke has a bimetal two stage heating element. The carburetor also has an electronic solenoid and a vacuum operated bowl vent.

Float Level Adjustment

Figs. 3 & 4—Invert air horn and insert specified gauge between float and air horn. To adjust, use a small screwdriver to bend tang.

Float Drop Adjustment

Figs. 5 & 6—Using a suitable depth gauge, measure float drop. To adjust, use

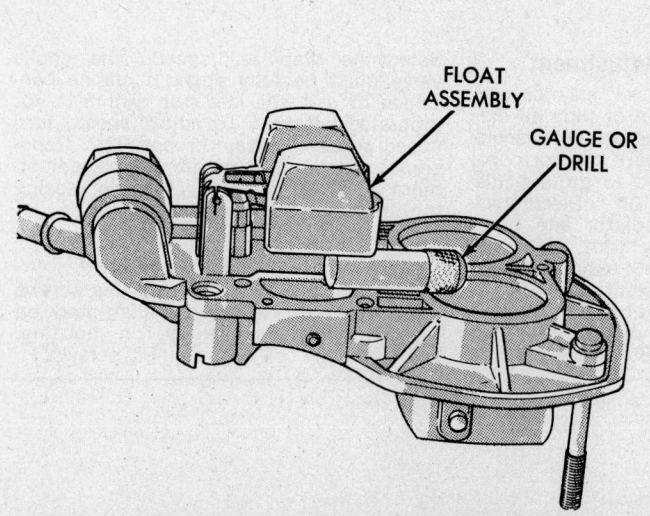

FLOAT ASSEMBLY

GAUGE OR DRILL

Fig. 3   Measuring float level. 5220 carburetor

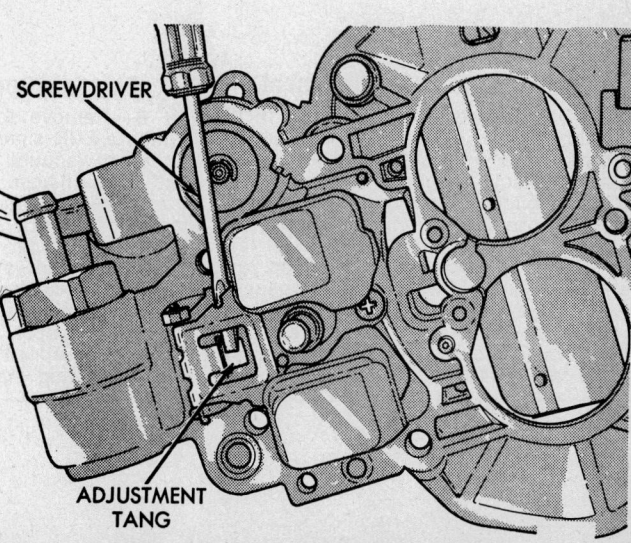

SCREWDRIVER

ADJUSTMENT TANG

Fig. 4   Adjusting float level. 5220 carburetor

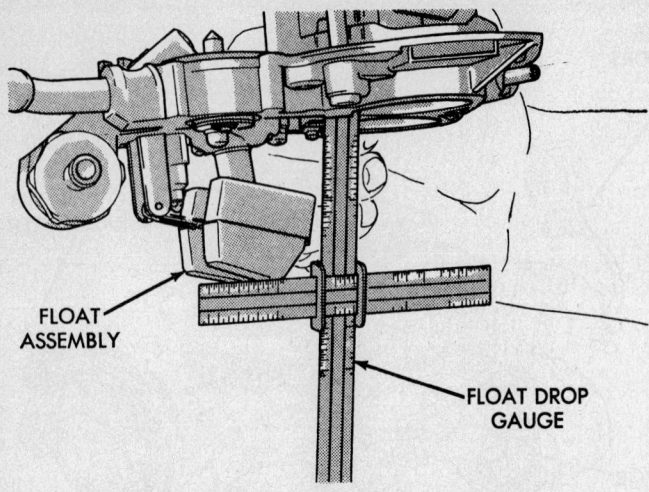

FLOAT ASSEMBLY

FLOAT DROP GAUGE

Fig. 5   Measuring float drop. 5220 carburetor

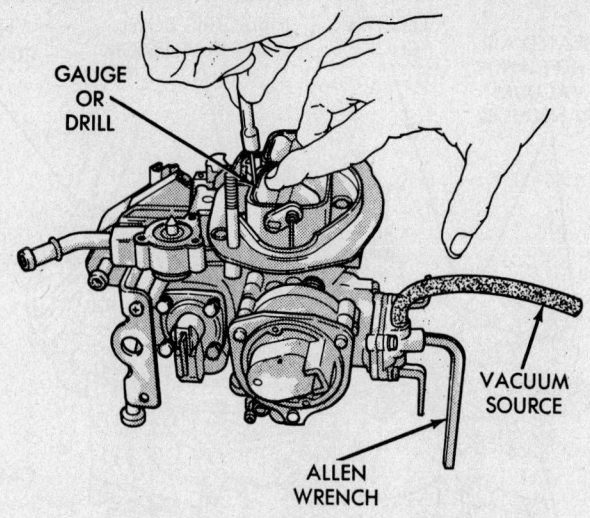

GAUGE OR DRILL

VACUUM SOURCE

ALLEN WRENCH

Fig. 7   Choke vacuum kick adjustment. 5220 carburetor

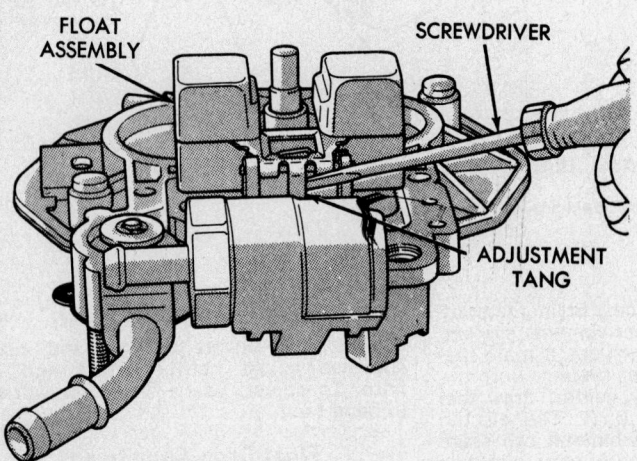

FLOAT ASSEMBLY

SCREWDRIVER

ADJUSTMENT TANG

Fig. 6   Adjusting float drop. 5220 carburetor

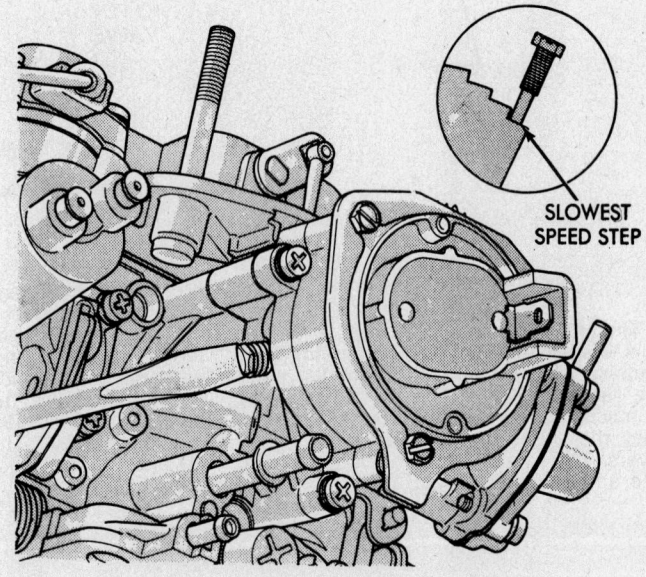

SLOWEST SPEED STEP

Fig. 8   Fast idle speed adjustment. 5220 carburetor

a small screwdriver to bend tang.

Choke Vacuum Kick Adjustment

Fig. 7—Open throttle, close choke, then close throttle to trap fast idle system in closed choke position. Using an external vacuum source, apply 15 inches of vacuum to choke diaphragm. Apply closing pressure to position choke at smallest opening without distorting linkage. An internal spring will compress to a stop inside choke system. Insert specified gauge between upper edge of choke valve and air horn wall at primary throttle end of carburetor. To adjust, rotate allen head screw in center of diaphragm housing.

Fast Idle Speed Adjustment

Fig. 8—Remove top of air cleaner and eliminate EGR signal. Cap or plug all disconnected vacuum fittings. Do not disconnect vacuum hose to spark control computer. Use a jumper wire to ground idle stop switch. Turn A/C "Off". Disconnect engine cooling fan at radiator and complete the circuit at plug with a jumper wire to energize fan. Apply parking brake, place transmission in Neutral with engine "Off", open throttle slightly and place lowest speed step of fast idle cam under adjusting screw. Start engine and determine stabilized speed. The choke valve must be fully open. If engine continues to rise, the idle stop switch is not grounded properly. To adjust speed, turn speed screw to obtain proper RPM. Reposition screw on cam after each adjustment to provide proper throttle closing torque and screw position.

Choke Setting Adjustment

Loosen choke coil cap retaining screws and rotate cap assembly to align mark on cap with specified mark on housing. Tighten choke coil cap retaining screws.

MODEL 6500

The Model 6500 carburetor, Fig. 1, is used with the Feedback Electronic Engine Control System. This carburetor is basically the same as the Motorcraft Model 5200 as described elsewhere in this chapter. The Model 6500 is equipped with an externally variable auxiliary fuel metering system in place of the enrichment valve used on the Motorcraft Model 5200. The auxiliary system consists of a metering valve assembly, metering valve operating piston and a diaphragm.

The feedback metering valve supplements fuel entering the main well through the conventional metering jet and channel. The amount of fuel entering the main well through the metering valve depends on the position of the tapered metering rod in the orifice. The position of the metering rod depends on the metering rod operating piston assembly.

Control vacuum from the vacuum regulator solenoid is transmitted to the cavity above the metering rod diaphragm. When no vacuum is present, the valve spring causes the valve to move to the lowest (richest) position and maximum fuel can pass through the orifice. As vacuum is applied to the diaphragm, spring pressure is overcome and the metering rod rises, reducing the orifice area and less fuel passes through the orifice. The metering valve is calibrated so the maximum vacuum signal supplied by the vacuum regulator solenoid raises the rod to the highest (leanest) position.

Adjustments

All adjustments for the Model 6500 are the same as the Motorcraft Model 5200 as described elsewhere in this chapter, however, the choke plate vacuum pulldown adjustment is different.

Choke Plate Vacuum Pulldown Adjustment

1. Remove choke cap, bi-metal heater assembly and plastic shield.
2. Place fast idle speed adjusting screw on top step of fast idle cam.
3. Using a suitable screwdriver, push diaphragm stem back against stop and place specified gauge between lower edge of choke valve and air horn wall, Fig. 3.
4. Remove slack from choke linkage by attaching a rubber band to choke operating lever, Fig. 3.
5. To adjust, rotate vacuum diaphragm adjusting screw as required to obtain proper setting, Fig. 4.

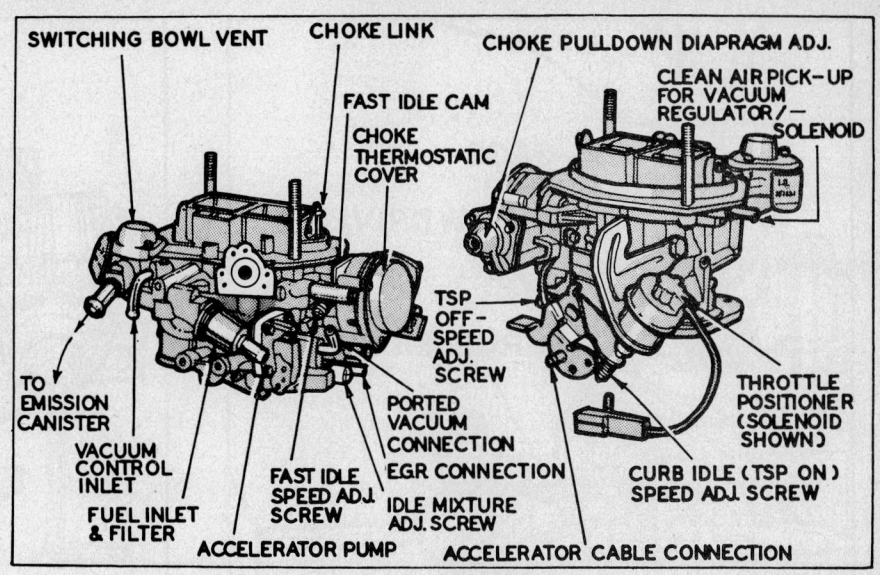

Fig. 1   Model 6500 carburetor

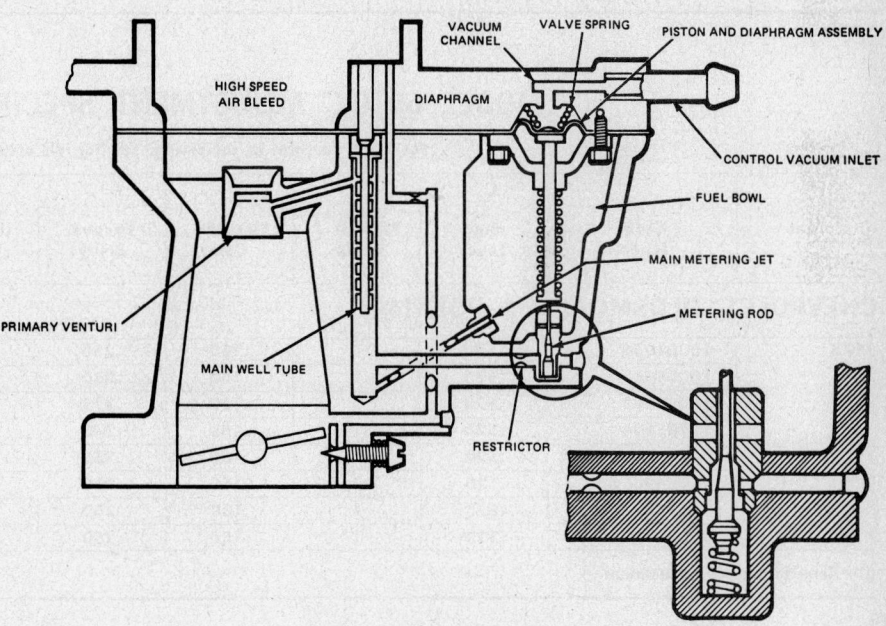

Fig. 2   Fuel metering system

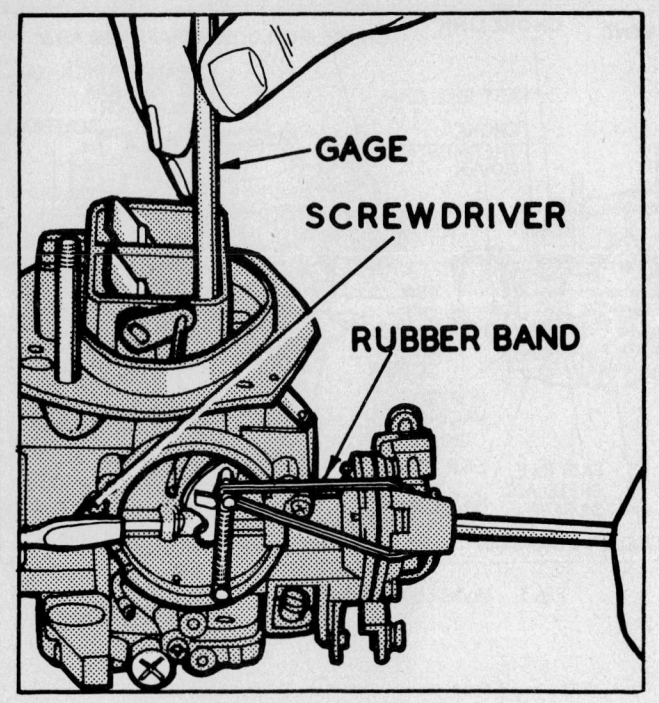

Fig. 3   Measuring choke plate vacuum pulldown

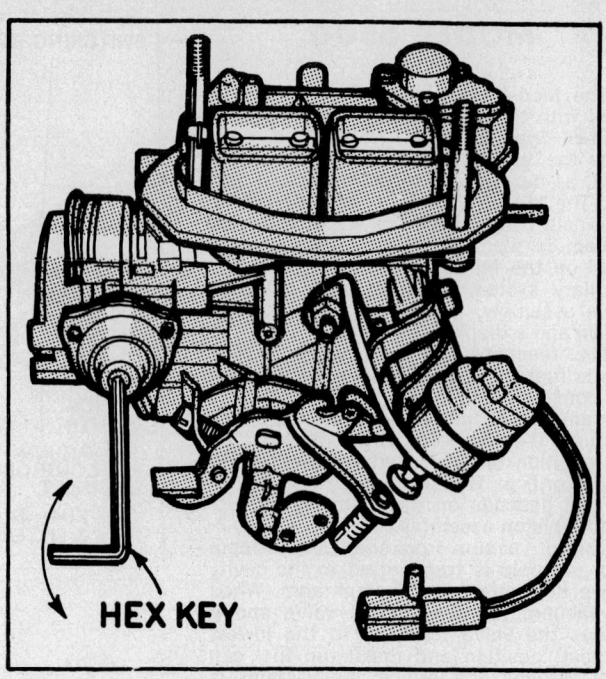

Fig. 4   Adjusting choke plate vacuum pulldown

MODEL 6510-C ADJUSTMENT SPECIFICATIONS

See Tune-Up chart in car chapter for hot idle speed.

Year	Carb. Model	Float Level	Float Drop	Fast Idle Cam	Vacuum Break	Unloader	Choke Coil	Secondary Throttle Stop Screw	Fast Idle Speed
CHEVROLET, OLDSMOBILE & PONTIAC									
1978	10001056	.520	1	.150	.250	.350	1 Rich	①	2400
	10001058	.520	1	.150	.250	.350	1 Rich	①	2400
	10005603	.520	1	.150	.275	.350	2 Rich	①	2000
	10005604	.520	1	.150	.275	.350	2 Rich	①	2000
1979	1000489	.520	1	.150	.250	.350	2 Rich	①	2200
	1000490	.520	1	.150	.250	.350	2 Rich	①	2200
	1000491	.520	1	.150	.250	.350	2 Rich	①	2200
	1000492	.520	1	.150	.250	.350	2 Rich	①	2200

①—Refer to text for adjustment.

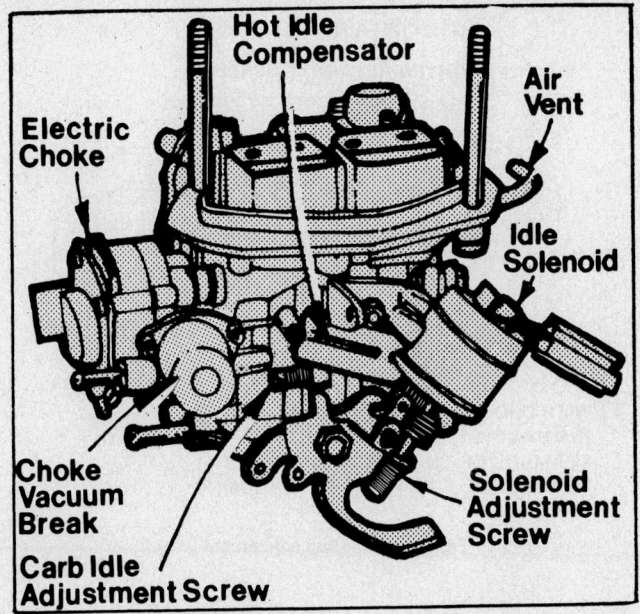

Fig. 1   Holley model 6510-C carburetor

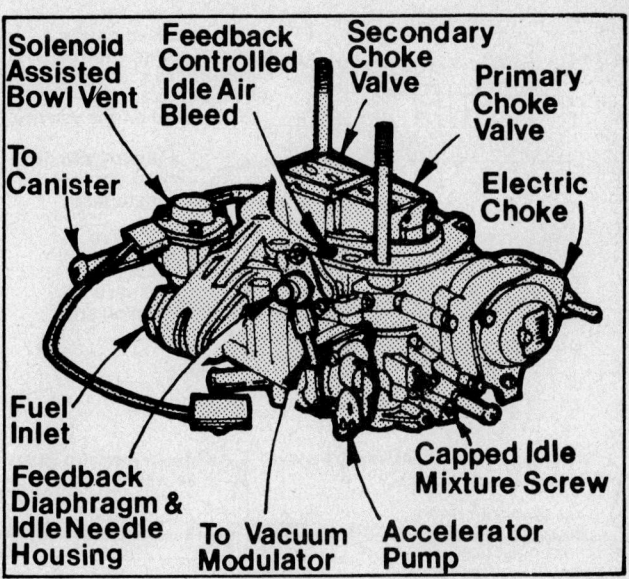

Fig. 2   Holley model 6510-C carburetor

MODEL 6510-C

Description

The Holley Model 6510-C carburetor, Figs. 1 and 2, is a controlled air-fuel ratio carburetor of a staged two barrel design with the primary bore smaller in size than the secondary bore. The secondary throttle is mechanically operated through interconnected linkage. This carburetor is used with the Electronic Fuel Control (EFC) system described elsewhere in this manual.

This carburetor utilizes four basic fuel metering systems: idle system, feedback controlled main metering system, acceleration system and power enrichment system.

The idle system is a separate factory adjusted system which provides a proper air-fuel mixture for both idle and low speed operation. The main metering system provides the correct air-fuel mixture for all normal and cruising speeds and aids in power enrichment. Fuel for acceleration is provided by the mechanically operated acceleration system. The power enrichment system consists of the accelerator pump discharge nozzle pullover and a secondary stage airflow regulated pullover system. These systems are used in conjunction with the main metering systems to provide adequate performance during periods of moderate to heavy acceleration.

Located in the primary bore are one or two vacuum ports for distributor vacuum spark advance, EGR vacuum and vapor canister purge depending upon emission control system usage.

A solenoid assisted vacuum operated bowl vent is used to vent the fuel vapors to the canister and not into the engine when the engine is operating. The vent is used in conjunction with existing internal venting through the air horn.

A hot idle compensator is used to maintain smooth engine idle during periods of excessive high temperature operation by allowing additional air to enter the primary throttle bore.

An electrically heated automatic choke system is used to provide correct air-fuel mixtures for cold start and warm-up operation. The automatic choke system is equipped with a vacuum break controlled by an external vacuum supply and a vacuum delay valve to prevent prolonged fast idle.

ADJUSTMENTS

Float Level Adjustment

Fig. 3—With air horn inverted, insert specified gauge between float and air horn. Bend tang to adjust.

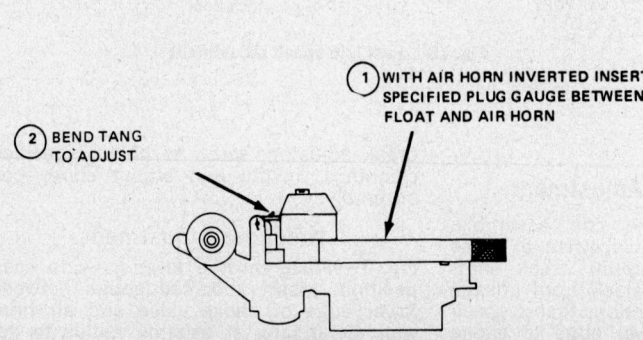

Fig. 3   Float level adjustment

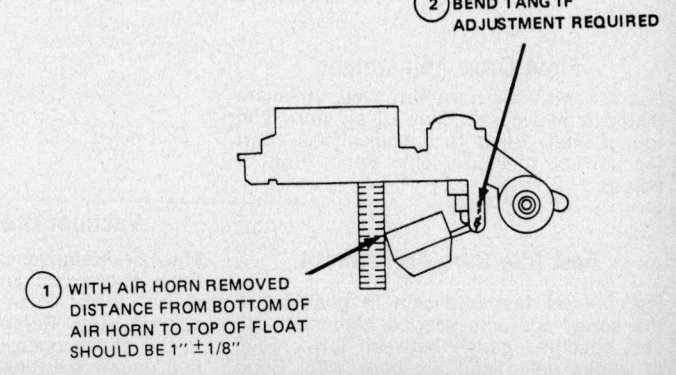

Fig. 4   Float drop adjustment

HOLLEY CARBURETORS

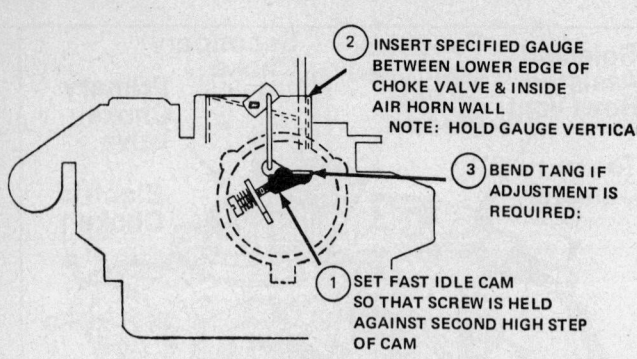

Fig. 5 Fast idle cam adjustment

② INSERT SPECIFIED GAUGE BETWEEN LOWER EDGE OF CHOKE VALVE & INSIDE AIR HORN WALL
NOTE: HOLD GAUGE VERTICAL

③ BEND TANG IF ADJUSTMENT IS REQUIRED:

① SET FAST IDLE CAM SO THAT SCREW IS HELD AGAINST SECOND HIGH STEP OF CAM

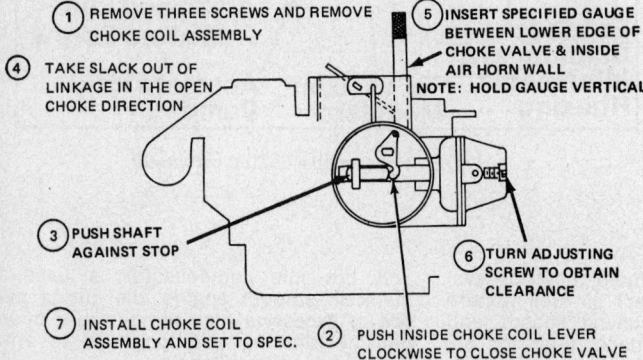

Fig. 6 Vacuum break adjustment

① REMOVE THREE SCREWS AND REMOVE CHOKE COIL ASSEMBLY

④ TAKE SLACK OUT OF LINKAGE IN THE OPEN CHOKE DIRECTION

③ PUSH SHAFT AGAINST STOP

⑦ INSTALL CHOKE COIL ASSEMBLY AND SET TO SPEC.

⑤ INSERT SPECIFIED GAUGE BETWEEN LOWER EDGE OF CHOKE VALVE & INSIDE AIR HORN WALL
NOTE: HOLD GAUGE VERTICAL

⑥ TURN ADJUSTING SCREW TO OBTAIN CLEARANCE

② PUSH INSIDE CHOKE COIL LEVER CLOCKWISE TO CLOSE CHOKE VALVE

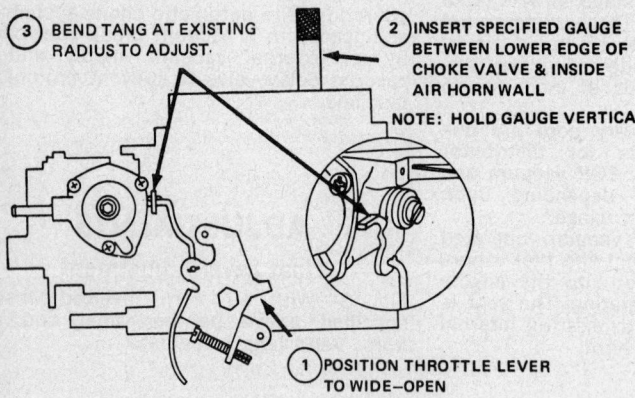

Fig. 7 Unloader adjustment

③ BEND TANG AT EXISTING RADIUS TO ADJUST

② INSERT SPECIFIED GAUGE BETWEEN LOWER EDGE OF CHOKE VALVE & INSIDE AIR HORN WALL
NOTE: HOLD GAUGE VERTICAL

① POSITION THROTTLE LEVER TO WIDE-OPEN

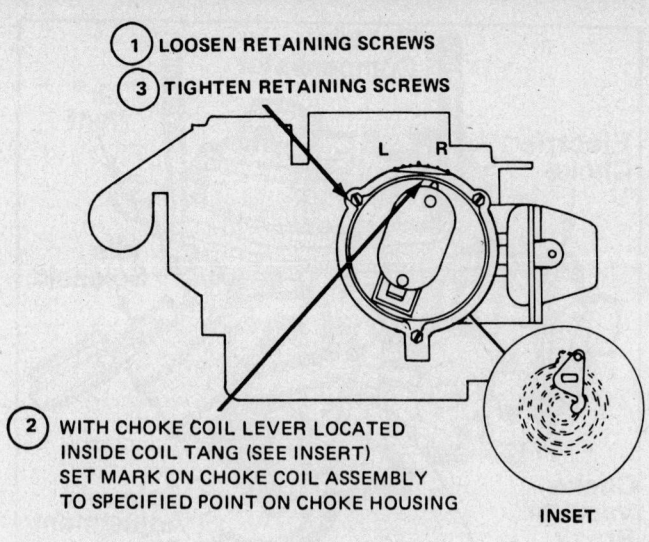

Fig. 8 Choke coil adjustment

① LOOSEN RETAINING SCREWS

③ TIGHTEN RETAINING SCREWS

② WITH CHOKE COIL LEVER LOCATED INSIDE COIL TANG (SEE INSERT) SET MARK ON CHOKE COIL ASSEMBLY TO SPECIFIED POINT ON CHOKE HOUSING

INSET

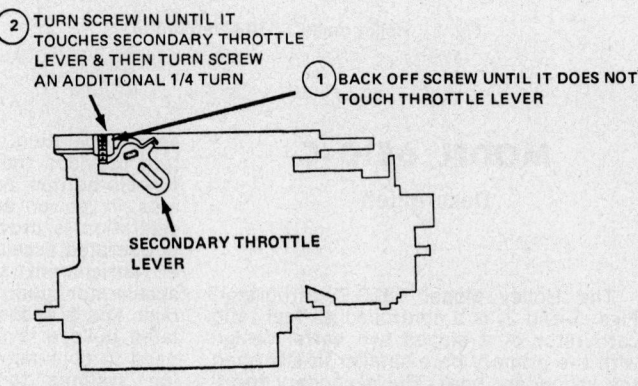

Fig. 9 Secondary throttle stop screw adjustment

② TURN SCREW IN UNTIL IT TOUCHES SECONDARY THROTTLE LEVER & THEN TURN SCREW AN ADDITIONAL 1/4 TURN

① BACK OFF SCREW UNTIL IT DOES NOT TOUCH THROTTLE LEVER

SECONDARY THROTTLE LEVER

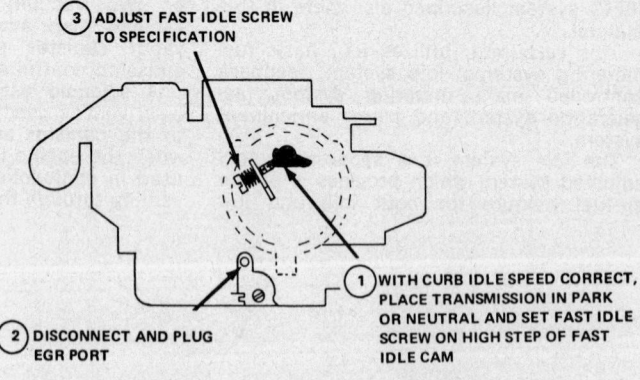

Fig. 10 Fast idle speed adjustment

③ ADJUST FAST IDLE SCREW TO SPECIFICATION

① WITH CURB IDLE SPEED CORRECT, PLACE TRANSMISSION IN PARK OR NEUTRAL AND SET FAST IDLE SCREW ON HIGH STEP OF FAST IDLE CAM

② DISCONNECT AND PLUG EGR PORT

Float Drop Adjustment

Fig. 4—With air horn removed, measure distance between bottom of air horn and top of float. Refer to specifications chart for correct measurement. Bend tang to adjust.

Fast Idle Cam Adjustment

Fig. 5—Set fast idle cam in position so the screw contacts second high step. Insert specified gauge between lower edge of choke valve and air horn wall. Bend tang to adjust.

Vacuum Break Adjustment

Fig. 6—Remove choke coil assembly. Push choke coil lever clockwise to close choke valve. Push vacuum break shaft against stop. Remove slack from linkage in the choke open direction. Insert specified gauge between lower edge of choke valve and air horn wall. Rotate vacuum break adjusting screw to obtain specified clearance. Install and adjust choke coil assembly.

Unloader Adjustment

Fig. 7—Place throttle lever in wide open position. Insert specified gauge between lower edge of choke valve and air horn wall. Bend tang at existing radius to adjust.

Choke Coil Adjustment

Fig. 8—Loosen choke coil cover retaining screws with choke coil lever located inside tang, rotate cover to align mark on cover with specified mark on choke coil housing. Tighten choke coil cover retaining screws.

Secondary Throttle Stop Screw Adjustment

Fig. 9—Back off secondary throttle stop screw until clear of throttle lever. Rotate screw inward until the screw contacts secondary throttle lever, then an additional ¼ turn.

Fast Idle Speed Adjustment

Fig. 10—With curb idle speed adjusted, place transmission in neutral or park and place fast idle screw on high step of cam. Disconnect and plug EGR port. Rotate fast idle adjusting screw to obtain specified fast idle speed.

TUNE UP SERVICE

CONTENTS

Tune up service has become increasingly important to the modern automotive engine with its vastly improved power and performance. Improved fuel and electrical systems and especially the exhaust emission controls with their inherently critical settings, engines have become more sensitive to usage and operating conditions, which have a decided effect on power and performance. It is important, therefore, that this service be performed on the engine every spring and fall or more often if conditions warrant.

In addition to the servicing of spark plugs, ignition points and condenser, a proper tune up includes a number of tests to check the condition of the engine and its related systems and uncover sources of future problems.

TUNE UP PROCEDURE

Since a quality tune up is dependent upon the proper operation of a number of systems, we have listed here in a logical sequence, the steps to be followed.

1. Diagnosis. This to consist of a compression test, cylinder balance test, oscilloscope check, manifold vacuum test, charging circuit and cranking voltage test.
2. Service spark plugs.
3. Service ignition system, secondary wiring, distributor and coil.
4. Check and service battery and charging system.
5. Service manifold heat valve, if used.
6. Service carburetor, linkage, fuel and air filters.
7. Check operation of various emission control devices.

Once these mechanical checks have been performed the tune up can be finalized. The final steps are:

1. Setting the dwell.
2. Setting slow idle, idle fuel mixture, choke and ignition timing.
3. Adjusting the fast idle.
4. Checking ignition output and secondary resistance.
5. Road test.

DIAGNOSIS & TESTING

Before a satisfactory tune up can be performed, the existing condition of the engine and its related systems must be determined. A tune up should not be attempted if tests indicate internal engine problems such as burnt valves, worn rings, blown head gasket, etc., until such conditions have been corrected.

Oscilloscope Test

Although oscilloscopes differ in many ways, they all display a light or "trace" on a screen which measures the voltage present at a given point and time. As the ignition system operates, its voltage creates a pattern on the screen. This pattern, when read in accordance with the manufacturer's instructions for the particular unit, indicates the condition of the entire ignition system.

Compression Test

An engine cannot be tuned to develop maximum power and smooth performance unless the proper compression is obtained in each cylinder.

CAUTION: When cranking the engine for a compression test or any other reason, the coil high tension cable should be removed from the distributor cap and grounded to the engine block or the distributor primary grounded with jumper wire.

1. Remove any foreign matter from around spark plugs by blowing out plug area with compressed air. Then remove plugs.
2. Remove air cleaner and block throttle and choke in wide open position.
3. Insert compression gauge firmly in spark plug opening and crank engine through at least four compression strokes to obtain highest possible reading.
4. Test and record compression of each cylinder. Compression should read within the limits given in the *Tune Up Charts* in the car chapters. Refer to chart, Fig. 1, for minimum compression pressures as indicated by percentages.
5. If one or more cylinders read low, inject about a tablespoon of engine oil on top of pistons in the low reading cylinders. Crank engine several times and recheck compression.
6. If compression is now higher, it indicates worn piston rings. If compression does not improve, valves are sticking or seating poorly. If two adjacent cylinders show low compression and injecting oil does not improve the condition, the cause

MAXIMUM PSI	MINIMUM PSI		MAXIMUM PSI	MINIMUM PSI		MAXIMUM PSI	MINIMUM PSI	
	75%	80%		75%	80%		75%	80%
134	101	107	174	131	139	214	160	171
136	102	109	176	132	141	216	162	173
138	104	110	178	133	142	218	163	174
140	105	112	180	135	144	220	165	176
142	107	114	182	136	146	222	166	178
144	108	115	184	138	147	224	168	179
146	110	117	186	140	149	226	169	181
148	111	118	188	141	150	228	171	182
150	113	120	190	142	152	230	172	184
152	114	122	192	144	154	232	174	186
154	115	123	194	145	155	234	175	187
156	117	125	196	147	157	236	177	189
158	118	126	198	148	158	238	178	190
160	120	128	200	150	160	240	180	192
162	121	130	202	151	162	242	181	194
164	123	131	204	153	163	244	183	195
166	124	133	206	154	165	246	184	197
168	126	134	208	156	166	248	186	198
170	127	136	210	157	168	250	187	200
172	129	138	212	158	170			

Fig. 1   Compression pressure limit chart

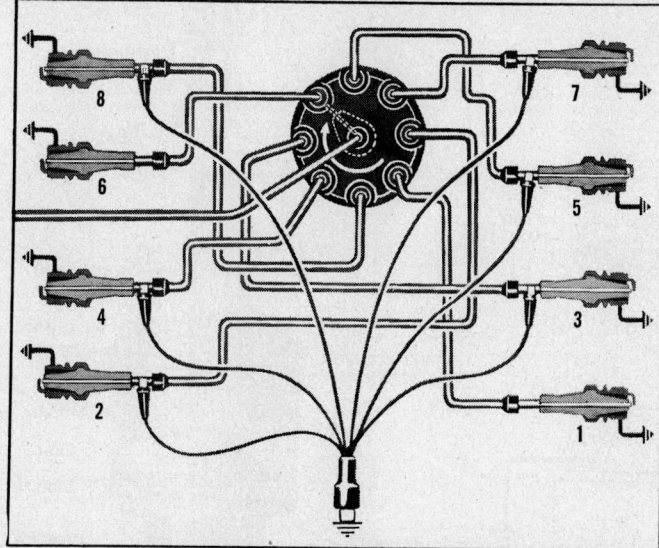

Fig. 1A Cylinder balance test connections. The firing order in this example is 1-8-4-3-6-5-7-2. Therefore, the cylinders to be tested together are 1-6, 8-5, 4-7, 3-2, using the grounding leads as shown

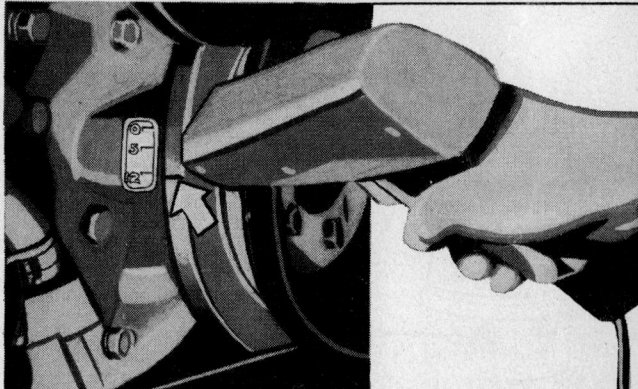

Fig. 2   Checking ignition timing with timing light

may be a head gasket leak between cylinders.

Cylinder Balance

CAUTION: When performing engine diagnosis on 1975-78 vehicles equipped with catalytic converters, a "Cylinder Balance Test", Fig. 1A, is *not* to be performed as damage to the catalytic converter will result. The alternate method of shorting out one cylinder at a time and noting the rpm drop of each individual cylinder can be used, but test should be performed as rapidly as possible.

It is sometimes difficult to locate a weak cylinder especially in an eight cylinder engine. A compression test, for example, will not locate a leaky intake manifold, a valve not opening properly due to a worn camshaft, or a defective spark plug.

With the cylinder balance test, the power output of one cylinder may be checked against another, using a set of grounding leads, Fig. 1A. When the power of each cylinder is not equal, the engine will lose power and run roughly. The cylinder balance test is as follows:
1. Connect a tachometer and vacuum gauge.
2. Start engine and run it at a fast idle.
3. Ground large clip of grounding leads and connect individual leads to all spark plugs *except the pair being tested,* Fig. 1A.
4. Divide the firing order in half and write down the first half over the second half. The cylinders to be tested together appear one over the other.

Firing Order   Pairs Tested
1-8-4-3-6-5-7-2 . . .1-6, 8-5, 4-7, 3-2
1-2-7-8-4-5-6-3 . . .1-4, 2-5, 7-6, 8-3

1-5-4-8-6-3-7-2 . . .1-6, 5-3, 4-7, 8-2
1-5-4-2-6-3-7-8 . . .1-6, 5-3, 4-7, 2-8
1-8-7-3-6-5-4-2 . . .1-6, 8-5, 7-4, 3-2
1-3-7-2-6-5-4-8 . . .1-6, 3-5, 7-4, 2-8
1-5-6-3-4-2-7-8 . . .1-4, 5-2, 6-7, 3-8
1-6-5-4-3-2 . . . . .1-4, 6-3, 5-2
1-5-3-6-2-4 . . . . .1-6, 5-2, 3-4
1-4-5-2-3-6 . . . . .1-2, 4-3, 5-6
1-3-4-2 . . . . .1-4, 3-2
1-4-3-2 . . . . .1-3, 4-2

5. Operate engine on each pair of cylinders in turn and note engine rpm and manifold vacuum for each pair. A variation of more than one inch of vacuum or 40 rpm between pairs of cylinders being tested indicates that the cylinders are off balance.
6. To isolate one weak cylinder, short out one bank of cylinders at a time. The bank giving the lower readings will include the weak cylinder.

Manifold Vacuum Test

NOTE: On some high performance engines, the camshaft provides such a great degree of valve overlap that vacuum at idle speed will be too low for an accurate test. For this reason, a vacuum test made on such units is of little value.

Manifold vacuum is affected by carburetor adjustment, valve timing, ignition timing, valve condition, cylinder compression, condition of positive crankcase ventilation system and leakage of manifold, carburetor, carburetor spacer or cylinder head gaskets.

Because abnormal gauge readings may indicate that more than one of the above factors are at fault, use care in analyzing an abnormal reading. For example, if the vacuum is low, the correction of one item may increase the vacuum enough to

indicate that the trouble has been corrected. It is important, therefore, that each cause of an abnormal reading be investigated and further tests conducted, where necessary, to arrive at the correct diagnosis of the trouble. To check manifold vacuum, proceed as follows:
1. Bring engine to operating temperature.
2. Connect an accurate vacuum gauge to the intake manifold.
3. Operate engine at recommended idle speed.
4. Check vacuum reading on gauge.

Test Conclusions

NORMAL READING: 18 inches or more. Allowance should be made for the effect of altitude on gauge reading.

LOW & STEADY: Loss of power in all cylinders possibly caused by late ignition or valve timing, or loss of compression.

VERY LOW: Intake manifold, carburetor spacer or head gasket leak.

NEEDLE FLUCTUATES STEADILY AS SPEED INCREASES: Partial or complete loss of power in one or more cylinders caused by a leaky head or manifold gasket, burnt valve, weak valve spring or a defect in the ignition system.

GRADUAL DROP IN READING AT IDLE SPEED: Excessive back pressure in exhaust system.

INTERMITTENT FLUCTUATION: Defect in ignition system or sticking valve.

SLOW FLUCTUATION OR DRIFTING OF NEEDLE: Improper idle mixture, carburetor, carburetor spacer, intake manifold gasket leak or restricted crankcase ventilation system.

Cranking Voltage Test

The condition of the starting circuit can be checked by connecting a voltmeter across the battery posts, grounding the coil so the engine will not fire and cranking the engine. If, during cranking, the voltage reading drops below 9.6 volts, there is high resistance in the circuit.

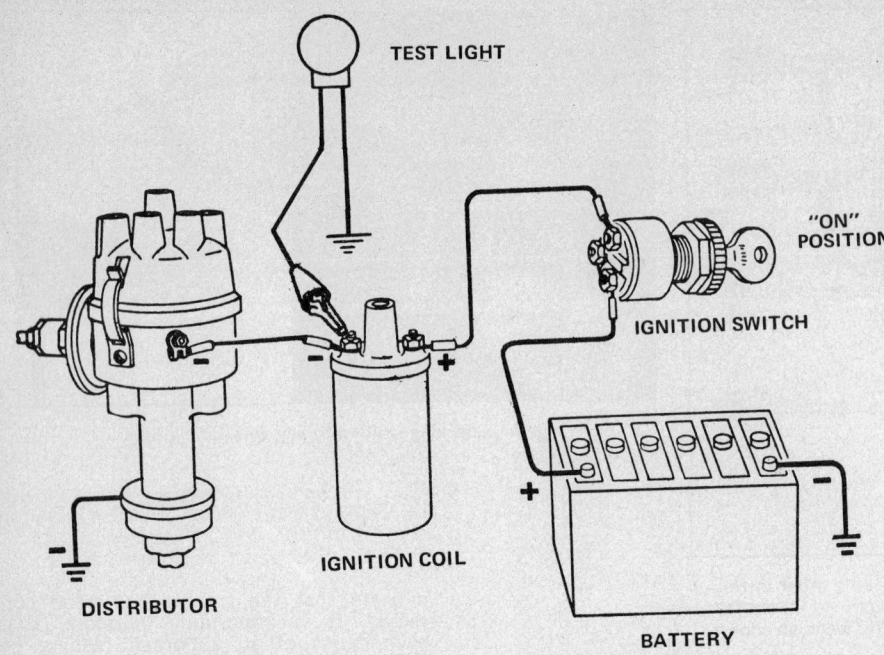

Fig. 3 Jumper light circuit for static ignition timing

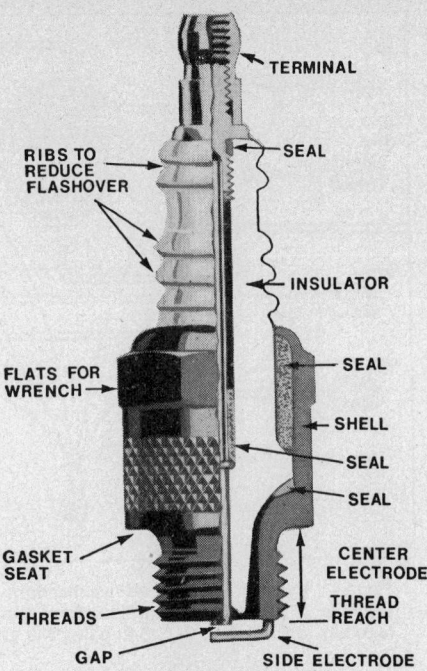

Fig. 4 Spark plug details

Charging Circuit Test

The performance of the charging circuit should be checked during any tune-up. See specific unit section of this manual for test procedures.

Ignition Timing

NOTE: When checking and setting ignition timing, ensure idle speed is set lower than the speed at which centrifugal advance begins unless otherwise specified. Refer to the Distributor Specifications Chart found in the car chapters.

The use of a timing light, Fig. 2, is recommended for checking and setting ignition timing. This setting is critical especially on units equipped with emission control systems.

NOTE: The use of an inductive type timing light is recommended when checking and setting ignition timing on electronic ignition systems.

Some engines have a provision for monolithic method of ignition timing utilizing a timing receptacle designed to accept an electronic probe. The receptacle is usually mounted at the front of the engine and the electronic probe is connected to electronic equipment which reads out the engine timing. These engines can also be timed using a timing light.

NOTE: The timing light should be connected to the proper spark plug lead by the use of an adapter. The boots around the connections should not be pierced to connect the light as this can cause spark arcing and misfiring.

Lacking a timing light, the timing can be set with the engine stopped by using a jumper light. Be sure to use a light bulb that corresponds with the vehicle voltage, Fig. 3.

1. Rotate engine until No. 1 cylinder is positioned at the specified timing mark.
2. Connect jumper light between distributor ignition terminal and ground.
3. Turn on ignition switch.
4. Loosen distributor and turn it in the direction of normal rotation until the points just close (light out). Then slowly turn the distributor in the opposite direction just to the exact point that the light goes on. Tighten distributor in this position.

Combustion Efficiency Test

This test checks the carburetor air/fuel mixture by measuring the amount of various chemicals present in the engine exhaust under different conditions. By following the manufacturer's instructions for the specific unit, the carburetor idle, intermediate, high speed and accelerator pump circuits can be checked for proper operation.

This test is especially important when working on engines equipped with exhaust emission controls because of the more critical mixture adjustments on such units.

SERVICE

Spark Plugs

1. Examine firing ends of plugs for evidence of oil fouling gas fouling, burned or overheated condition. *Oil fouling is usually identified by wet, sludgy deposits caused by excessive oil consumption. Gas fouling is identified by dry, black, fluffy deposits caused by incomplete combustion. Burned or overheated spark plugs are identified by white, burned or blistered insulator nose and badly burned electrodes. Improper fuel, insufficient cooling or improper ignition timing normally are the cause. Normal conditions are usually identified by white powdery deposits or rusty-brown to grayish-tan powdery deposits.*
2. Clean plugs with a suitable sand blast cleaner following the manufacturers instructions.
3. Remove carbon and other deposits from threads with a stiff wire brush.

NOTE: Do not use brush to clean electrodes as small pieces of wire can stick inside plug and later cause misfiring.

4. Dress electrodes with a small file to secure flat, parallel surfaces on both center and side electrodes, Fig. 4.
5. Use a round wire gauge to check the gap, Fig. 5, and adjust by bending the side (never center) electrode to the proper specifications as shown in the *Tune Up Charts* in the car chapters.
6. If gaskets are used, place new ones on plugs and torque plugs to specification.

IMPORTANT

Improper installation of spark plugs is one of the greatest single causes of unsatisfactory spark plug performance. Improper installation is the result of one or more of the following practices: 1) Installation of plugs with insufficient torque to fully seat the gasket; 2) excessive torque which changes gap settings; 3) installation of plugs on dirty gasket seal; 4) installation of plugs to corroded spark plug hole threads.

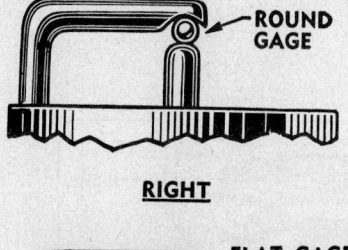

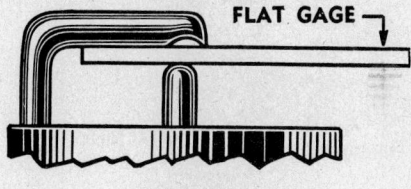

Fig. 5 Correct and incorrect spark plug gauges

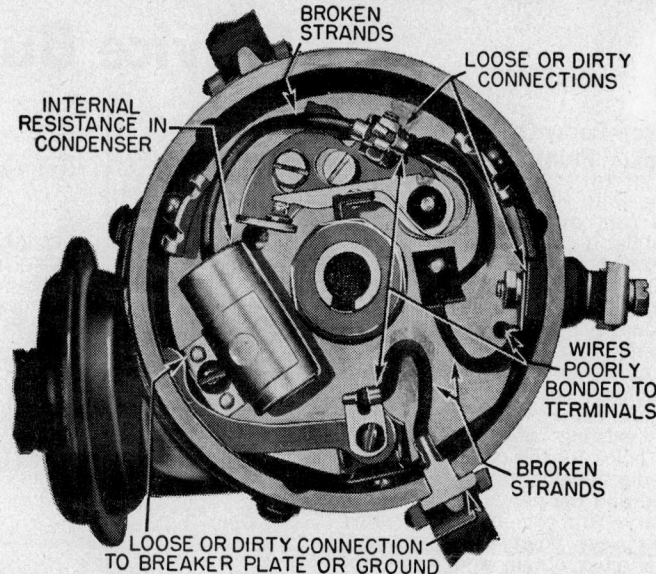

Fig. 6 What to look for when checking for high resistance in the primary circuit of the distributor. In addition to the points indicated, look for external circuit high resistance at ignition switch terminals, ammeter terminals, coil terminals and broken or poorly insulated wires in this circuit

Failure to install plugs properly will cause them to operate at excessively high temperatures and result in reduced operating life under mild operation or complete destruction under severe operation where the intense heat cannot be dissipated rapidly enough.

Always remove carbon deposits in hole threads before installing plugs. When corrosion is present in threads, normal torque is not sufficient to compress the plug gasket (if used) and early failure from overheating will result.

Always use a new gasket (if required) and wipe seats in head clean. The gasket must be fully compressed on clean seats to complete heat transfer and provide a gas tight seal in the cylinder. For this reason as well as the necessity of maintaining correct plug gap, the use of correct torque is extremely important during installation.

Ignition System

1. Check to be sure all connections are clean and tight. Repair or replace any wires that are frayed, loose or damaged, Fig. 6. Replace brittle or damaged spark plug wires.
2. Remove distributor cap, clean and inspect for cracks, carbon tracks and burned or corroded terminals. Replace cap if necessary.
3. Clean rotor and inspect for damage or deterioration. Replace rotor if necessary.
4. Check distributor centrifugal advance mechanism (if used) by turning distributor rotor in direction of running rotation as far as possible, then release rotor to see if springs return it to its retarded position. If rotor does not return readily, the distributor must be disassembled and cause of trouble corrected.
5. Check to see that the vacuum spark control operates freely by turning the movable breaker plate (if used) or distributor housing in a direction opposite to that of running rotation to see if the spring returns it to the

retarded position. Any stiffness in the operation of the spark control will affect ignition timing. Correct any interference or binding condition noted.
6. Examine distributor points and clean or replace if necessary. Points with an overall gray color and only slight roughness or pitting need not be replaced.
7. Dirty points should be cleaned with a clean point file. Use only a few strokes of the file. The file should not be used on other metals and should not be allowed to become dirty or greasy. *Never use emery cloth or sandpaper to clean points since particles will embed and cause arcing and rapid burning of points.* Do not attempt to remove all roughness nor dress the point surfaces down smooth. Merely remove scale or dirt.
8. Replace points that are badly burned or pitted. Where burned or badly pitted points are encountered, the ignition system and engine should be checked to determine the cause of the trouble so it can be eliminated. Unless the condition causing point burning is corrected, new points will provide no better service than the old points. See *distributor* chapter for an analysis of point burning or pitting, and for proper installation of points & condenser.

Battery & Cables

Inspect for signs of corrosion on battery, cables and surrounding area, loose or broken carriers, cracked or bulged cases, dirt and acid, electrolyte leakage and low electrolyte level. Fill cells to proper level with distilled water or water passed through a "demineralizer."

The top of the battery should be clean and the battery hold-down bolts properly tightened.

For best results when cleaning batteries, wash first with a dilute ammonia or soda solution to neutralize any acid present and then flush off with clean water. Care must be taken to keep vent plugs tight so that the neutralizing solution does not enter the battery.

To insure good contact, the battery cables should be tight on the battery posts. Oil battery terminal felt washer. If the battery posts or cables terminals are corroded, the cables should be cleaned separately with a soda solution and a wire brush.

If the battery has remained undercharged, check for a loose generator belt, defective generator, high resistance in charging circuit, oxidized voltage regulator contact points, or a low voltage setting.

If the battery has been using too much water, the voltage regulator setting is too high.

Fuel System

All fuel filters and the air cleaner element should be serviced during a tune up, including the sintered bronze "stone" used in some units.

Since carburetion is dependent in several ways on both compression and ignition, it should always be checked last when tuning an engine. Refer to the Carburetor Chapter for pertinent data on specific units.

Service Bulletins

Delco-Remy One-Piece Breaker Points (Uni-Set)

Beginning with 1972 some General Motors V-8 cars may be equipped with the new Uni-Set breaker points (one piece points and condenser, Fig. 7. Due to the limited availability of the Uni-Set for service, you should be aware of the alternatives to circumvent this problem.

1. A conversion kit is available (Part No. 1876065) which contains a breaker plate, contact set, radio shields, condenser and wick.
2. If the existing breaker plate has tapped holes for the condenser clamp and radio shields, it need not be changed and the conversion kit is not necessary. You can install the previous two piece points and condenser but you must obtain and install the radio shields.

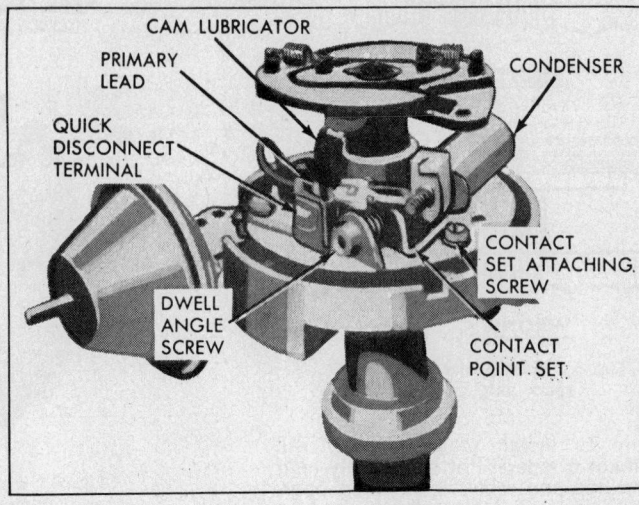

Fig. 7 Delco-Remy one-piece breaker points & condenser (Uni-Set)

Chevrolet Monza 2 + 2 Spark Plug Replacement

When replacing spark plugs on a V8-262 engine equipped with air conditioning and power steering, it is not necessary to release the engine mounts. The following procedure should be used: Have available a 1", 1½" and a 3" extension which are customarily used in spark plug servicing. Also needed are a ⅝" spark plug socket and a flex handle. Obtain a 5" to 6" length of windshield wiper hose which should be attached to the No. 3 spark plug end to facilitate installation, Fig. 8.

Insert a ¼" × 1½" stud or rod into the windshield wiper hose to achieve some rigidity in the windshield wiper hose structure as shown in Fig. 1. Then insert a ¼" × 1" bolt into other end of hose to allow for easier rotation. Now proceed to install No. 3 spark plug. Once the spark plug is started in the threads of the cylinder head, you may then remove the hose and proceed to tighten the spark plug with the appropriate tools. All other spark plugs can be replaced in the conventional manner using an applicable extension.

General Motors V6-231 Distributor Cap

All 1975-76 General Motors V6-231 engines use the basic design High Energy Ignition (H.E.I.) distributor, however, only six towers of the distributor cap are utilized. Under no circumstances can a V8 distributor cap, Fig. 9, be used on a V6 distributor since the terminals are specifically designed and manufactured for V6 applications, Fig. 10.

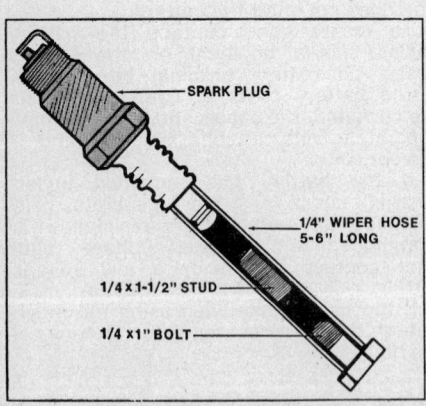

Fig. 8 Monza 2 + 2 spark plug replacement tool

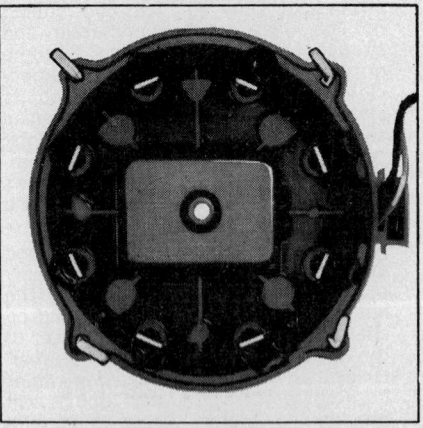

Fig. 9 General Motors V8 High Energy Ignition (H.E.I.) distributor cap terminals

Fig. 10 General Motors V6 High Energy Ignition (H.E.I.) distributor cap terminals

Ignition Coils & Resistors

IGNITION COILS

If poor ignition performance is obtained and the coil is suspected, it may be tested on the car or it may be removed for the test.

Ignition coils are often condemned when the trouble is actually in the ignition switch. A completely defective ignition switch will produce an open primary circuit, giving the same indications as if the coil were completely dead. A partly defective ignition switch will cause a weak spark.

By cutting the ignition switch out of the circuit, it can easily be determined whether the coil is defective or the fault lies in the ignition switch.

In the absence of any testing equipment a simple check of an ignition coil can be made as follows: Turn on ignition switch with breaker points closed. Remove the high tension cable from the center socket of the distributor cap and hold it 1/4" to 3/8" away from a clean spot on the engine. If the coil and other units connected to it are in good condition a spark should jump from the wire to the engine as the points are opened. If not, use a jumper wire from the distributor terminal to the engine; if the primary is in good condition a spark will occur.

All ignition coils with metal containers can be tested for grounded windings by placing one test clip on a clean part of the metal container and touching the other clip to the primary and high tension terminals. If the lamp lights or tiny sparks appear at the points of contact, the windings are grounded and the coil should be replaced.

Coil Polarity

Most coils are marked positive and negative at the primary terminals. When installing or connecting a coil be sure to make the connections as shown in Fig. 1. A reversal of this polarity may affect the performance of the engine (or the radio).

If the coil is not marked as to its polarity, it can be checked by holding any high tension wire about 1/4" away from its spark plug terminal with the engine

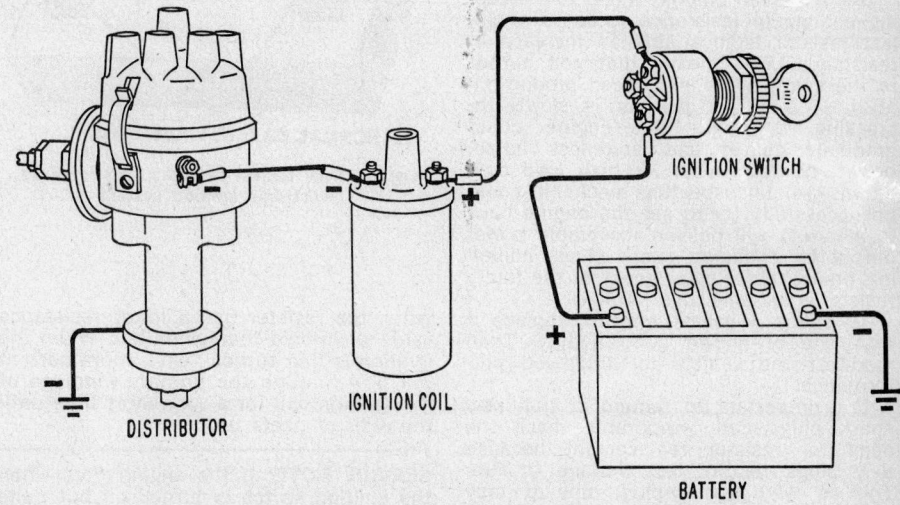

Fig. 1 Wiring connections for coil with negative grounded system

running. Insert the point of a wooden lead pencil between the spark plug and the wire, Fig. 2. If the spark flares and has a slight orange tinge on the spark plug side of the pencil, polarity is correct. If the spark flares on the cable side, coil connections should be reversed.

IGNITION RESISTORS

The purpose of the resistor is to prolong the service life of the distributor breaker points.

Block Type Ballast Resistors

Its basic purpose is to allow full battery voltage to the ignition coil during engine starting, and to reduce battery voltage to the coil when the engine is running. The higher voltage during starts means easier starts. But sustained high voltage to the breaker points can cause point failure. The reduced voltage during engine operation increases breaker point life.

These resistors are normally very dependable. But if one fails, it can be one of the most difficult of all ignition malfunctions to diagnose. An open resistor means that no current reaches the

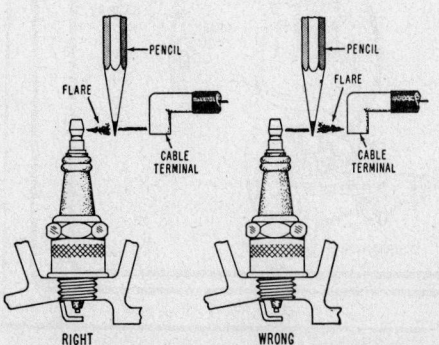

Fig. 2 Checking coil polarity

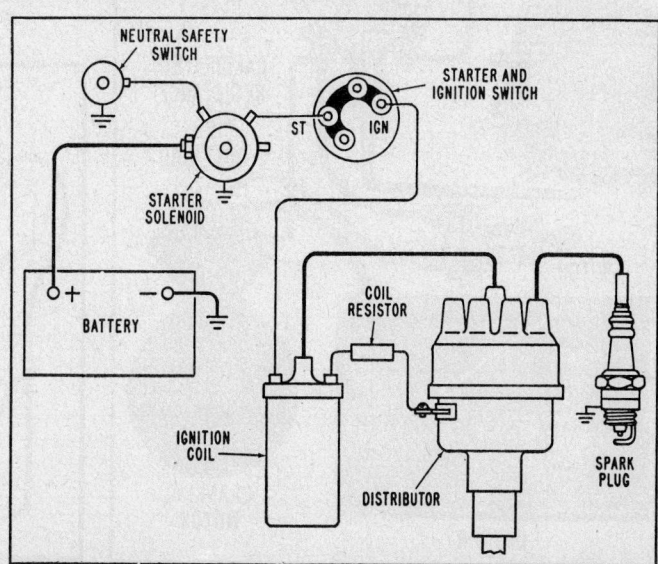

Fig. 3 Chrysler ignition circuit diagram with a temperature sensitive block-type resistor

coil and the engine cannot operate. It is possible for the resistance wire to warp or bend enough to touch the side of the case. When this happens, the engine may continue to run but the overall performance will be poor.

Resistors can change value. Any creeping change in resistance value of a ballast resistor is invariably an increase in resistance. This means that coil output to the spark plugs is reduced proportionately. If a ballast resistor is slowly increasing in value the engine could gradually deliver less and less horsepower, particularly under high load conditions. An unsuspecting mechanic could unsuccessfully try to get the engine back to where it will deliver acceptable power output by changing spark plugs, adjusting timing, etc. Replacement of the faulty resistor is the only cure in this case.

To check a ballast resistor, replace it with one of known good quality. Then road-test the vehicle for improved performance.

It is important to remember that new spark plugs can temporarily mask the need for resistor replacement because new plugs require less voltage to fire. This is why a new-plug tune-up may prove satisfactory for a time. But if the ballast resistor is faulty, eventually the engine will misfire under load.

On Chrysler Corp. standard ignition sys-

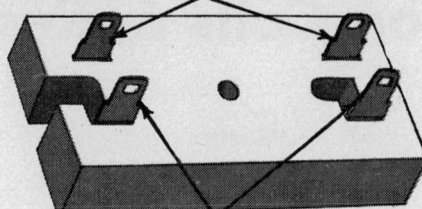

AUXILIARY BALLAST RESISTOR

NORMAL BALLAST RESISTOR

Fig. 4 Dual ballast resistor, Chrysler Corp. electronic ignition system

tems, the resistor has a lower resistance value when cold than when hot. When the ignition is first turned "On", more current will flow through the primary windings of the ignition coil for a very short time until the resistor heats up.

SERVICE NOTE: If the engine fires when the ignition switch is turned on but quits when the switch is released to its running position, it indicates that the resistor is defective and must be replaced.

A dual ballast resistor, Fig. 4, is used on Chrysler Corp. vehicles equipped with electronic ignition. The normal side of the resistor is a compensating resistance in the primary circuit. At low engine speeds, current is maintained for a longer period of time in this side of the resistor, causing the unit to heat up, in turn increasing resistance. This increased resistance reduces the primary circuit voltage, protecting the ignition coil from high voltage at low engine speeds.

As engine speed increases, the period of time in which current is maintained in the normal side of the resistor is shorter, causing the unit to cool, in turn decreasing resistance. This decreased resistance permits the primary circuit voltage to increase for high speed operation.

During engine start, the normal side of the ballast resistor is by-passed, allowing full battery voltage to be applied to the primary circuit.

The auxiliary side of the ballast resistor limits voltage to the control unit, thereby protecting the unit.

Wire Type Resistors

The special resistance wires used with 12-volt systems are five to six feet long and contained in the regular wiring harness. The wire is made of stainless steel or special alloy, plastic-coated and covered with a glass braid. There is a relatively small temperature rise and the resistance wire is switched out of the circuit for starting and back in again for running.

On Delco-Remy systems Fig. 5, the resistor is by-passed by means of a "finger" inside the solenoid switch housing which is attached to the additional switch terminal.

On Ford systems, Fig. 6, the resistor is by-passed through a terminal on the starter relay which is connected directly

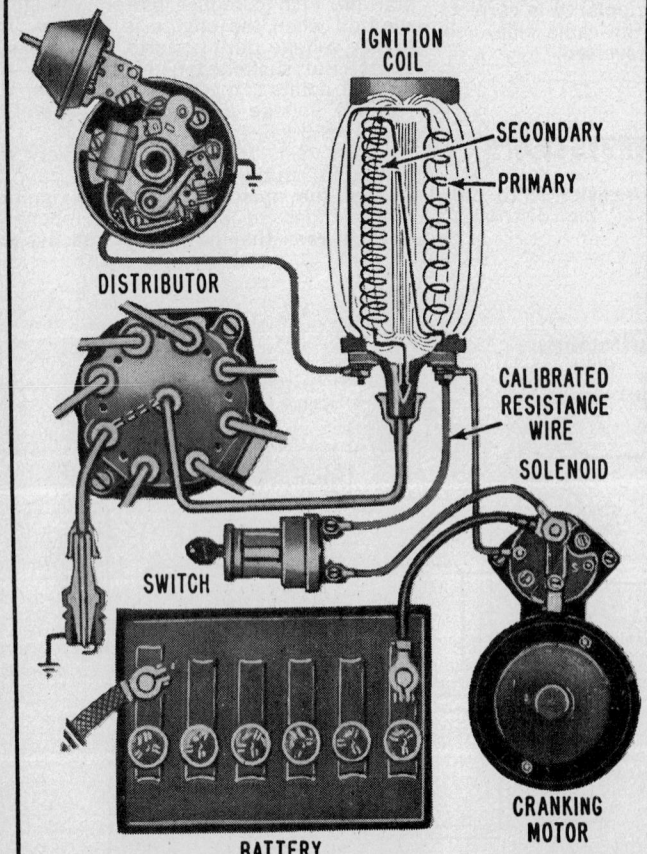

Fig. 5 Delco-Remy ignition circuit diagram with a resistance wire connected to a two-terminal ignition switch

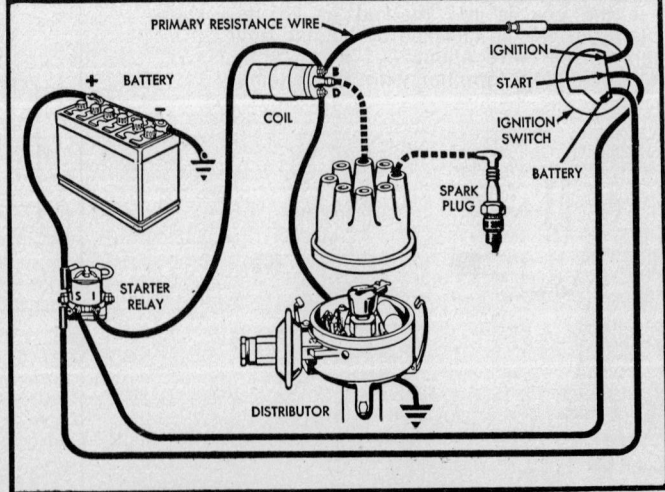

Fig. 6 Ford ignition circuit diagram with a resistance wire connected to a three-terminal ignition switch

to the positive terminal of the coil.

SERVICE NOTE: If the engine fires when the ignition switch is turned on but quits when the switch is released to the "run" position, it indicates that the resistance wire has lost its continuity or there is a bad connection at the resistor terminals. If the wire is defective, it must be replaced.

IMPORTANT: Do not attempt to operate the engine for an extended length of time with the resistor shorted out by means of a jumper wire as the breaker points will burn.

IGNITION COIL & RESISTOR SPECIFICATIONS

Year	Model	Coil Draw, Amps.		Coil Resistance, Ohms		Ignition Resistor Ohms @ 75°F.
		Engine Stopped	Engine Idling	Primary @ 75°F.	Secondary @ 75°F.	
AMERICAN MOTORS—All Models						
1974	6 Cyl.	3.5	1.6	1.40–1.65	3000–20000	1.80
	V8	3.5	1.6	1.77–2.05	3000–20000	1.35
1975	B.I.D.①	—	—	1.0–2.0	8000–12000	—
1976	B.I.D.①	—	—	1.0–2.0	9000–15000	—
1977	B.I.D.①	—	—	1.25–1.40	9000–15000	—
1978	Breakerless	—	—	1.13–1.23	7700–9300	1.35

①—Breakerless Inductive Discharge.

Year	Model	Coil Draw, Amps.		Coil Resistance, Ohms		Ignition Resistor Ohms @ 75°F.
		Engine Stopped	Engine Idling	Primary @ 75°F.	Secondary @ 75°F.	
BUICK—All Models						
1974	6 Cyl.	4.0	3.9	1.4–1.65	3000–20000	1.75–1.85
1974	V8	3.8	2.3	1.77–2.05	3000–20000	1.25–1.45
1975–78	H.E.I.①	0.25	1.0	0–1.0	6000–30000	—

①—High Energy Ignition.

Year	Model	Coil Draw, Amps.		Coil Resistance, Ohms		Ignition Resistor Ohms @ 75°F.
		Engine Stopped	Engine Idling	Primary @ 75°F.	Secondary @ 75°F.	
CADILLAC						
1974	Exc. Below	2.4	1.25	1.77–2.01	3000–20000	1.30–1.35
1974–78	H.E.I.①	—	—	0–1.0	6000–30000	—

①—High Energy Ignition.

Year	Model	Coil Draw, Amps.		Coil Resistance, Ohms		Ignition Resistor Ohms @ 75°F.
		Engine Stopped	Engine Idling	Primary @ 75°F.	Secondary @ 75°F.	
CHECKER MOTORS						
1974	6 Cyl.	4.0	1.8	1.41–1.65	3000–20000	1.80
	V8	4.0	1.8	1.77–2.05	3000–20000	1.35
1975–78	H.E.I.①	—	—	0–1.0	6000–30000	—

①—High Energy Ignition.

Year	Model	Coil Draw, Amps.		Coil Resistance, Ohms		Ignition Resistor Ohms @ 75°F.
		Engine Stopped	Engine Idling	Primary @ 75°F.	Secondary @ 75°F.	
CHEVROLET—(ALL) MODELS						
1974	4 & 6 Cyl.	4.0	1.8	1.41–1.65	3000–20000	1.80
	V8 Std. Ign.	4.0	1.8	1.77–2.05	3000–20000	1.35
1974–78	H.E.I.①	—	—	0–1.0	6000–30000	—

①—High Energy Ignition.
②—4-85 & 97, 0.25: 4-140 & 6-250, 4.0.
③—4-85 & 97, 1.5: 4-140 & 6-250, 1.8.

Continued

IGNITION COIL & RESISTOR SPECIFICATIONS—Continued

Year	Model	Coil Draw, Amps.		Coil Resistance, Ohms		Ignition Resistor Ohms @ 75°F.
		Engine Stopped	Engine Idling	Primary @ 75°F.	Secondary @ 75°F.	

CHRYSLER, DODGE, PLYMOUTH, IMPERIAL—All Models

Year	Model	Engine Stopped	Engine Idling	Primary @ 75°F.	Secondary @ 75°F.	Ignition Resistor Ohms @ 75°F.
1974	①	—	—	1.60–1.79	9400–11700	.50– .60③
	②	—	—	1.41–1.55	8000–10200	.50– .60③
1975–77	①	—	—	1.60–1.79	9400–11700	.50– .60③
	②	—	—	1.41–1.62	8000–11200	.50– .60③
1978	①	—	—	1.60–1.79	9400–11700	.50– .60③
	4 Cyl. ②	—	—	1.41–1.62	8000–11200	.50– .60③
	6 & V8②	—	—	1.34–1.55	9000–12200	.50– .60③

①Prestolite coils.　②Essex coils.
③Auxiliary (control unit side) 4.75—5.75 ohms.

FORD, MERCURY, LINCOLN, THUNDERBIRD—All Models

Year	Model	Engine Stopped	Engine Idling	Primary @ 75°F.	Secondary @ 75°F.	Ignition Resistor Ohms @ 75°F.
1974	Std. Ign.	4.5	2.5	1.40–1.54	7600–8800	1.30–1.40
1974–77	Breakerless	—	—	1.0–2.0	7000–13000	1.30–1.40
1978	DuraSpark I	—	—	.71–.77	7350–8250	—
	DuraSpark II	—	—	1.13–1.23	7700–9300	1.05–1.15

OLDSMOBILE—All Models

Year	Model	Engine Stopped	Engine Idling	Primary @ 75°F.	Secondary @ 75°F.	Ignition Resistor Ohms @ 75°F.
1974	Toronado	4.0	2.2	1.77–2.05	6500–20000	1.35
	6 Cyl.	4.0	1.8	1.40–1.65	3000–20000	1.80
	V8	4.0	2.0	1.77–2.05	6500–20000	1.35
1974–78	H.E.I.①	—	—	0–1.0	6000–30000	—

①—High Energy Ignition.

PONTIAC—All Models

Year	Model	Engine Stopped	Engine Idling	Primary @ 75°F.	Secondary @ 75°F.	Ignition Resistor Ohms @ 75°F.
1974	Six	...	...	1.4–1.65	3000–20000	...
	V8	...	...	1.8–2.2	3000–20000	...
	Unitized	...	...	0–.5	6000–9000	...
1975–78	H.E.I.③	①	②	0–1.0	6000–30000	—

①—4 cyl. 4.0　　②—4 cyl. 1.8　　③—High Energy Ignition.

Standard Ignition Distributors

CONTENTS

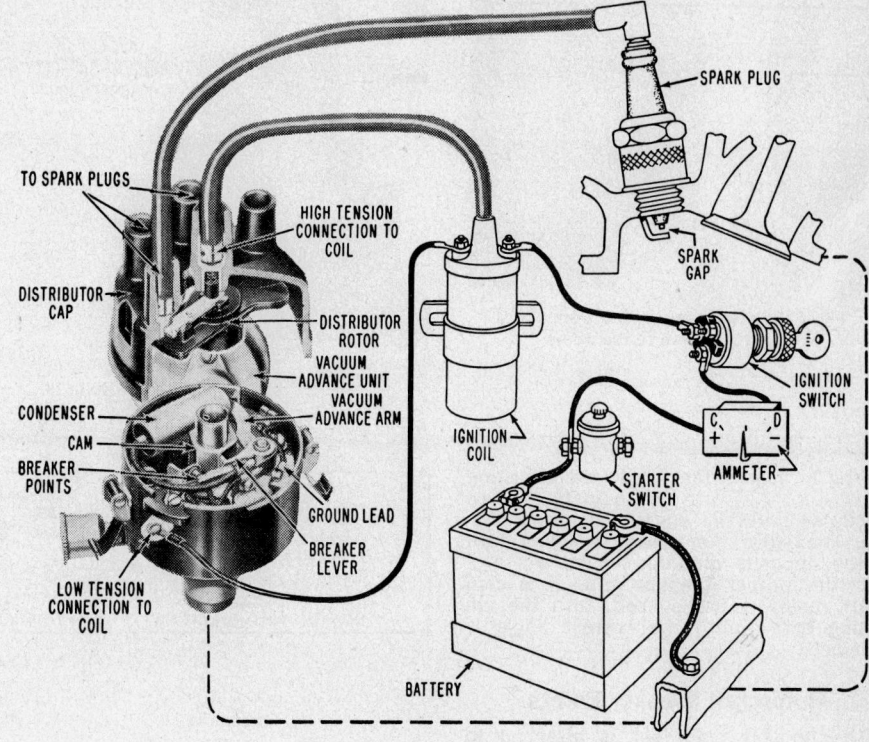

Fig. 1   Typical ignition system

BREAKER CONTACT POINTS

Contact Analysis

The normal color of points should be a light gray. If the contact surfaces are black it is usually caused by oil vapor or grease from the cam. If they are blue, the cause is usually excessive heating due to improper alignment, high resistance or open condenser circuit.

If the contacts develop a crater or depression on one point and a high spot of metal on the other, the cause is an electrolytic action transferring metal from one contact to the other, Fig. 2, due to an unbalanced ignition system, which can sometimes be improved by a slight change in condenser capacity. If the mound is on the positive point, Fig. 3, install a condenser of greater capacity; if on the negative point, Fig. 4, use a condenser of lesser capacity.

One of the most common causes of point failure is the presence of oil or grease on the contact surfaces, usually from over-lubrication of the wick at the top of the cam or too much grease on the rubbing block of the breaker arm.

Breaker Point Gap

If points are set too close, arcing and burning will occur, causing hard starting and poor low speed performance. If points are set too wide, the cam angle or dwell will be too small to allow saturation of the coil at high engine speeds, resulting in weak spark.

Contact point opening has a direct bearing on cam angle or dwell which is the number of degrees that the breaker cam rotates from the time the points close until they open again, Fig. 5. The cam angle or dwell increases as point opening is decreased and vice versa. If point gap is set with a feeler gauge, the cam angle or dwell should be checked either with a portable dwell meter or by installing the distributor in a distributor tester.

Breaker Arm Spring Tension

Breaker arm spring tension is important. If the tension is too great the arm will bounce, causing an interruption of the current in the coil and misfiring. If the spring tension is too little, the rubbing block will not follow the cam, causing a variation in cam dwell. The spring

tension should always be set at the high limit as given in the *Distributor Specifications* chart in the car chapter, as it will be reduced as the rubbing block wears.

Hook a spring scale on the breaker arm and pull in a straight line as shown in Fig. 6. Take a reading as the points start to separate under the slow and steady pull of the scale. If the tension is not within specifications, loosen the screw that holds the end of the point spring and slide the end of the spring in or out as necessary. Tighten the screw and recheck the spring tension.

Breaker Point Alignment

Check alignment of points with points closed, Fig. 7. Align new points where necessary but do not attempt to align used points. Instead, replace used points where serious misalignment is observed. After aligning points, adjust point gap.

Adjusting Breaker Gap

Specifications for breaker gap, *as measured with a feeler gauge*, are listed in the *Tune Up Specifications* in the car chapters. However, if at all possible, this should be set on a distributor tester, with a dial indicator, Fig. 8, or by hooking up a portable dwell meter with the distributor cap and rotor removed and,

while cranking the engine, setting the dwell.

NOTE: When setting the dwell with the engine cranking, be sure to ground the coil secondary lead and do not operate the starter for sustained periods at a time.

This eliminates the possibility of an incorrect gap because of rough points, Fig. 9.

The advantage of a distributor testing machine is that it not only measures cam angle or dwell but it also uncovers irregularities between cam lobes, point bounce, alignment of rubbing block with cam, alignment of contacts and breaker arm spring tension.

Delco-Remy Internal Adjustment Breaker Points

A slot is provided in the contact point assembly which allows easy dwell angle or breaker point adjustment, Fig. 10.

Delco-Remy External Adjustment Breaker Points

With engine running at idle speed, the breaker gap is adjusted by first raising the window provided in the cap and in-

Fig. 2 Showing how metal from one contact transfers to the other

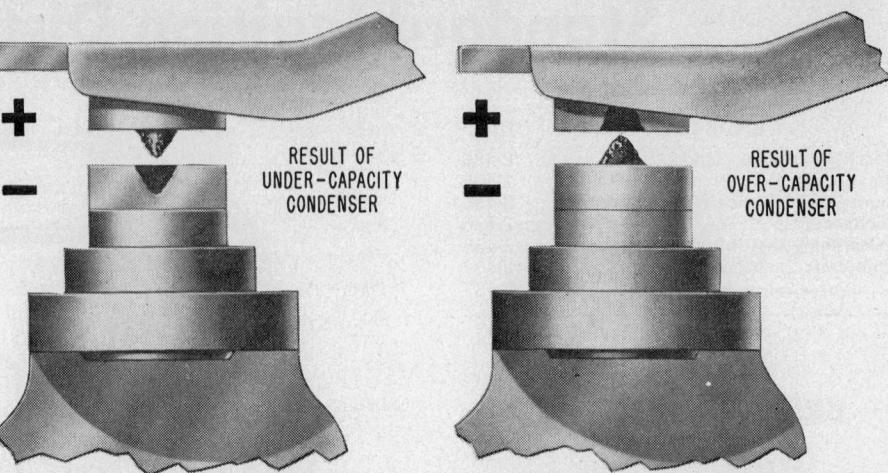

RESULT OF UNDER-CAPACITY CONDENSER

RESULT OF OVER-CAPACITY CONDENSER

Fig. 3 Mound on positive point

Fig. 4 Mound on negative point

serting a "hex" wrench into the adjusting screw, Fig. 11. Turn the adjusting screw clockwise until the engine begins to misfire. Then give the wrench one-half turn in the opposite direction which will provide the proper breaker gap. If a cam angle meter is to be used, turn the adjusting screw until the correct angle is obtained.

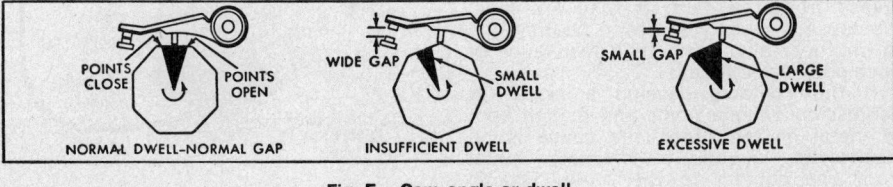

POINTS CLOSE   POINTS OPEN

NORMAL DWELL-NORMAL GAP

WIDE GAP   SMALL DWELL

INSUFFICIENT DWELL

SMALL GAP   LARGE DWELL

EXCESSIVE DWELL

Fig. 5 Cam angle or dwell

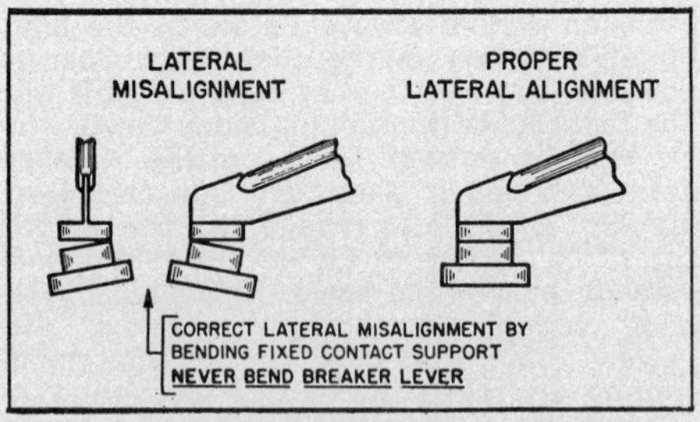

Motorcraft Breaker Points

The breaker point set is attached to the movable breaker plate. A slot in the stationary point bracket allows for easy breaker point adjustment, Fig. 12.

CONDENSER

A condenser should not be condemned because the points are burned or oxidized. Oil vapor, or grease from the cam, or high resistance may be the cause of such a condition.

Condensers should be tested with a good condenser tester for leakage, break-down, capacity, and resistance in series in the condenser circuit. Manufacturers of condenser testers furnish complete instructions as to their use.

CENTRIFUGAL ADVANCE

When engine speed increases, the spark must be introduced in the cylinder earlier in the cycle in order that the fuel charge can be ignited and will have time to burn and deliver its power to the piston. To provide this spark advance based on engine speed, the centrifugal advance mechanism is used.

This mechanism, Fig. 13, consists of

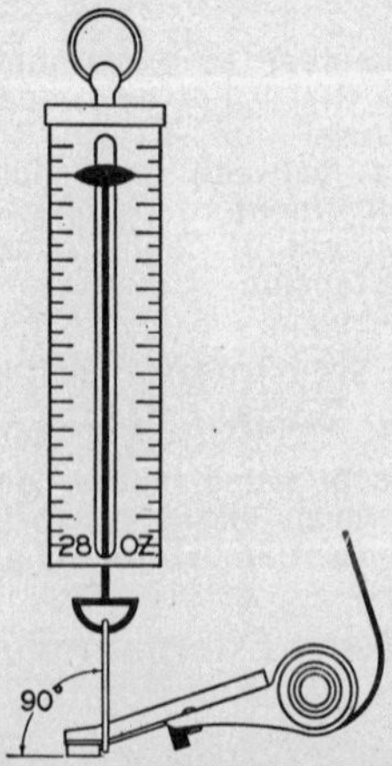

LATERAL MISALIGNMENT

PROPER LATERAL ALIGNMENT

CORRECT LATERAL MISALIGNMENT BY BENDING FIXED CONTACT SUPPORT NEVER BEND BREAKER LEVER

Fig. 7 Breaker point alignment

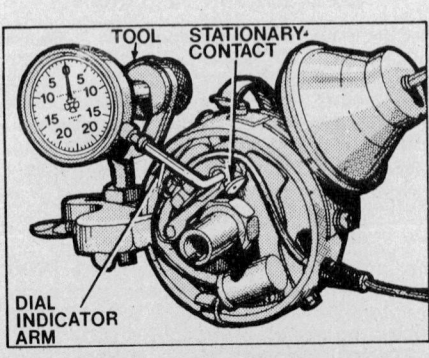

TOOL   STATIONARY CONTACT

DIAL INDICATOR ARM

Fig. 8 Dial indicator for measuring breaker gap

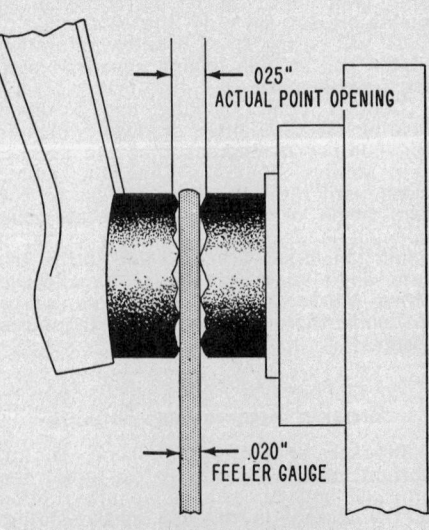

.025" ACTUAL POINT OPENING

.020" FEELER GAUGE

Fig. 9 Why flat feeler gauge will not provide accurate point spacing if points are rough

Fig. 6 Measuring breaker spring tension

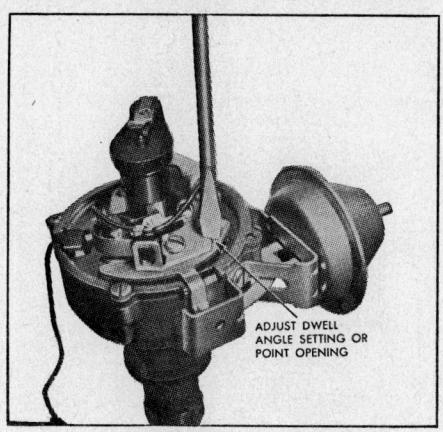

Fig. 10 Breaker point setting. Delco-Remy internally adjusted points

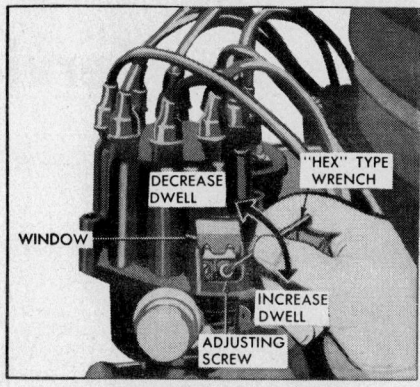

Fig. 11 Adjust breaker point gap through window in distributor cap

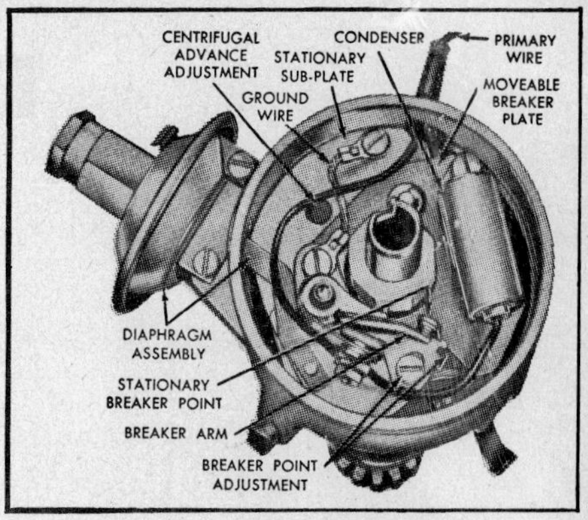

Fig. 12 Breaker plate installation. Motorcraft dual advance distributor (Typical)

VACUUM ADVANCE

Conventional Type

The vacuum advance unit consists of a spring loaded diaphragm, which is connected through linkage to the distributor breaker plate. The spring loaded side of the diaphragm is connected through a vacuum line to the carburetor or intake manifold. As vacuum increases, the diaphragm is drawn toward the source of vacuum, the diaphragm linkage is pulled with it and the breaker plate, attached to the linkage, is turned to advance the timing.

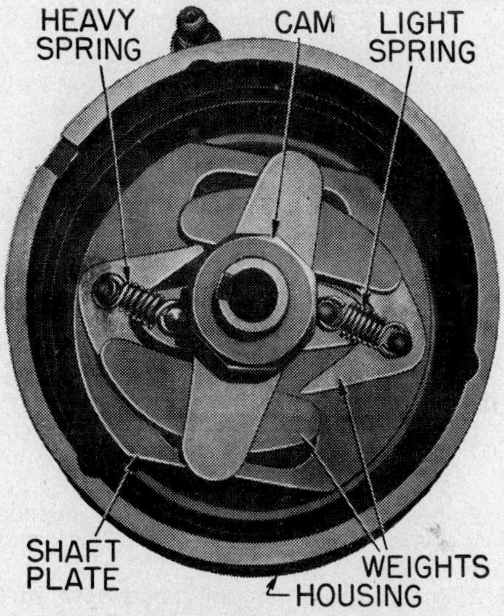

centrifugal advance weights which throw out against spring tension as the engine speed increases. This movement imparts, through a toggle arrangement, rotational motion to the breaker cam or plate, depending on the model, causing it to rotate a number of degrees with respect to the distributor drive shaft. This causes the points to be opened and closed earlier in the cycle so the spark is delivered to the cylinder earlier.

In servicing the distributor, all weights should be removed from the hinge pins, cleaned and checked for excessive wear, either in the weights or pins, or the plate which is slotted for the movement of the pins on top of the governor weights. Replacement should be made if there is any appreciable wear in the slots, as any wear at this point would change the characteristic of the spark advance.

If these parts are in good condition, the hinge pins should be lubricated before being reassembled, by greasing the hinge pins and filling the pockets in the governor weights with grease. Do not use vaseline for this purpose as its melting point is comparatively low.

When installing new centrifugal advance assemblies, it is important that the spacer washers between the housing and shaft be installed correctly. If incorrectly installed, the advance assembly will be too high, causing it to rub against the bottom of the breaker plate.

On some distributors, both springs are alike, while on others there is one heavy and one light spring, as in Fig. 13.

Fig. 13 Top view of Delco-Remy distributor with breaker plate removed to show centrifugal advance mechanism

Exhaust Emission Control Types

Chrysler

Some Chrysler engines have a solenoid incorporated in the distributor vacuum advance mechanism to retard the ignition timing when the throttle is closed. At closed throttle, electrical contacts on the carburetor throttle stop, with idle adjusting screw in the closed position, cause the distributor solenoid to energize. This retards the ignition timing to provide reduced exhaust emissions under hot idle conditions. Cold or part throttle starting is not penalized because the distributor solenoid is not energized unless the hot idle adjusting screw is against the throttle stop contact. Timing must be set at closed throttle to give accurate setting.

Ford Dual-Diaphragm

This unit consists of two independent diaphragms. The outer diaphragm uses carburetor vacuum to advance timing. The inner diaphragm uses intake manifold vacuum to provide additional retard during closed throttle operation.

Ford Single Diaphragm

This unit operates in the same manner as conventional units.

General Motors CCS

In this system, the advance is the ported type, that is the vacuum take-off is located above the throttle plate(s) so that during periods of closed throttle operation there is little or no vacuum reaching the advance unit and timing is retarded. As soon as the throttle is cracked, vacuum reaches the advance unit and timing is advanced.

NOTE: Some models of the Chevrolet V8-307 engine use the conventional type advance unit.

Distributor Service

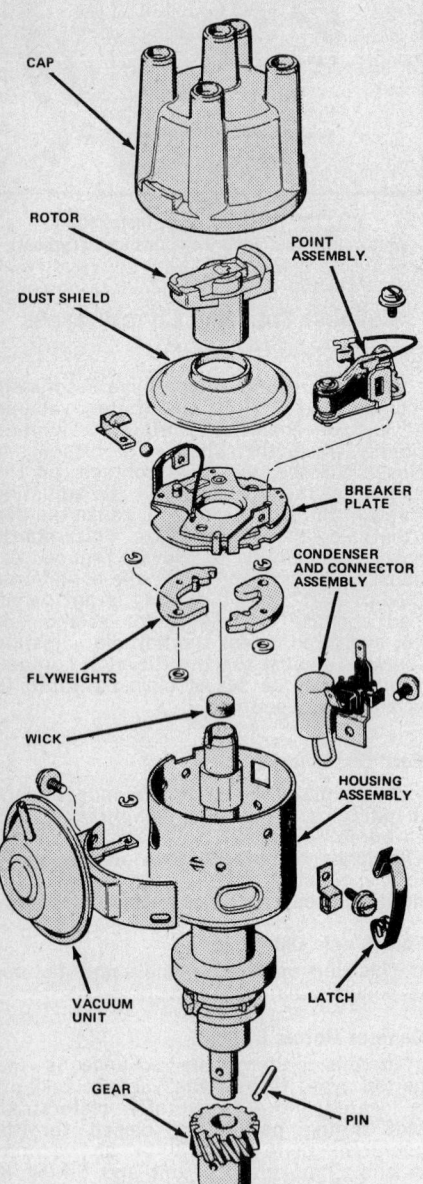

Fig. 1 Exploded view of Bosch distributor. American Motors 4-121 engine

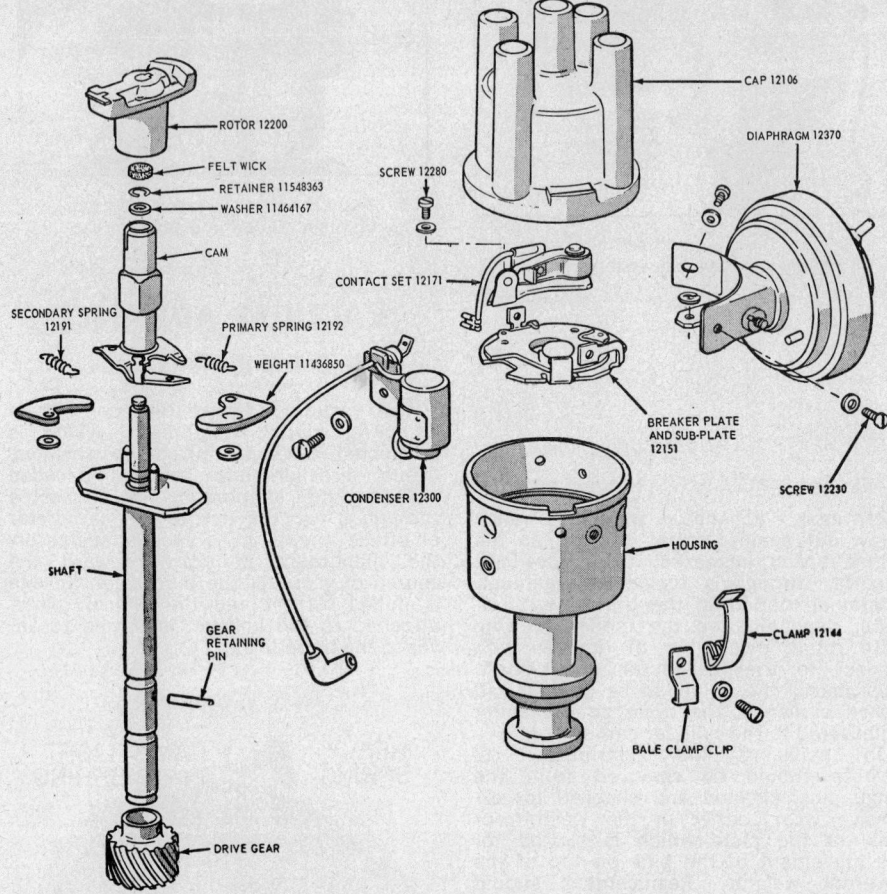

Fig. 2 Exploded view of Bosch distributor. Ford 2000cc engine

BOSCH DISTRIBUTOR SERVICE

NOTE: Replacement parts for servicing the distributor shaft, drive gear, bushing and cam are not available. In addition, the advance weights, advance springs and breaker plate are not serviceable since the breaker plate is permanently staked into the housing.

If distributor has been disassembled, refer to Figs. 1 and 2 at reassembly.

1. Lubricate pivot pins and install advance weights. Lubricate shaft and install cam assembly.
2. Install advance springs and advance plate, securing plate with clip and screws.
3. Insert grommet and condenser wire through hole in housing and install condenser and contact points.
4. Install vacuum advance unit. Hook vacuum advance rod over pin in advance plate and install snap ring.

DELCO-REMY DISTRIBUTOR SERVICE

External Adjustment Type

If the distributor has been disassembled, refer to Fig. 3 for guidance when reassembling.

1. Fill housing lubricating cavity with proper lubricant and install new plastic seal and felt washer.
2. Install vacuum advance unit, breaker plate and spring retainer on upper bushing.
3. Slide weight cam over mainshaft and install weights and springs.
4. Insert mainshaft assembly into housing, indexing assembly with drive gear and washers.
5. On Chevrolet Corvette units, install tachometer drive gear.
6. On all units, slide gear shims and drive gear over mainshaft and install retaining pin. Ensure shaft rotates freely.
7. Install breaker points and condenser.

Internal Adjustment Type

If the distributor has been disassembled, refer to Fig. 4 when reassembling. Fig. 5 shows the details of the breaker plate and attaching parts.

1. Replace cam assembly to shaft. Lubricate top end of shaft with light

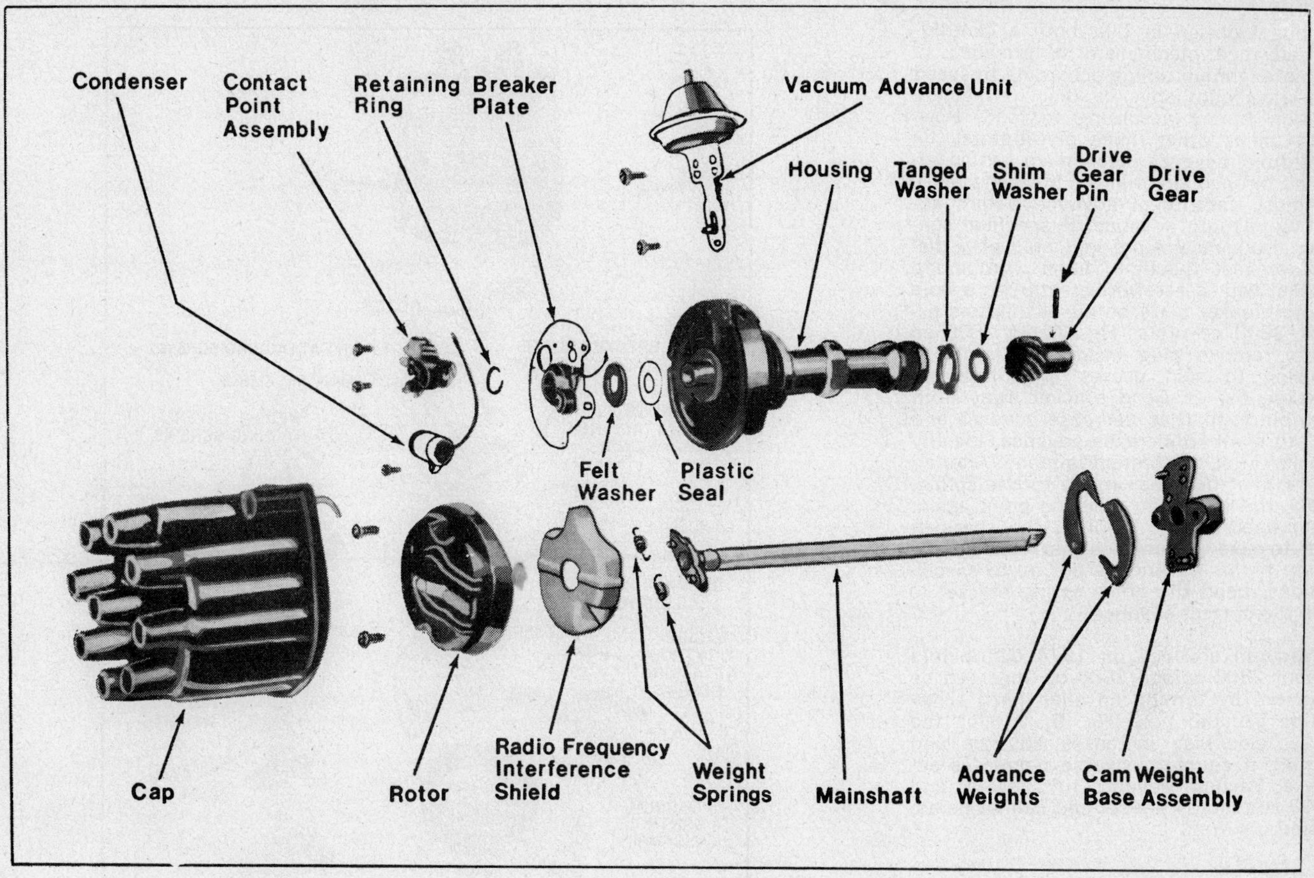

Condenser · Contact Point Assembly · Retaining Ring · Breaker Plate · Vacuum Advance Unit · Housing · Tanged Washer · Shim Washer · Drive Gear Pin · Drive Gear · Felt Washer · Plastic Seal · Cap · Rotor · Radio Frequency Interference Shield · Weight Springs · Mainshaft · Advance Weights · Cam Weight Base Assembly

Fig. 3 Delco-Remy external adjustment distributor

engine oil prior to replacing.
2. Install weights on their pivot pins. Install springs, weight cover and stop plate.
3. Lubricate shaft and install in housing.

4. Install thrust washers and driven gear to shaft and secure with roll pins. On Vega distributors, install damper cup on shaft and install pin. Check to see that shaft turns freely. Install driven gear with mark on hub in line with rotor segment.
5. Install breaker plate.
6. Attach condenser and breaker point set in proper location with appropriate attaching screws, Fig. 5. Connect primary and condenser leads to breaker point set quick disconnect terminal. *Contact point set pilot must engage matching hole in breaker plate.*
7. Attach vacuum control assembly to distributor housing, using upper mounting holes.
8. Adjust breaker arm spring tension and breaker gap.
9. Install rotor.

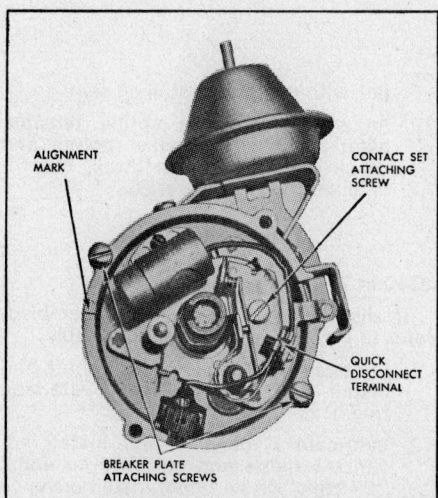

ALIGNMENT MARK · CONTACT SET ATTACHING SCREW · QUICK DISCONNECT TERMINAL · BREAKER PLATE ATTACHING SCREWS

Fig. 5 Breaker plate installation. Delco-Remy internal adjustment distributor

FORD MOTORCRAFT DISTRIBUTOR SERVICE

Dual Advance Distributor

This distributor, Fig. 6, is similar to con-

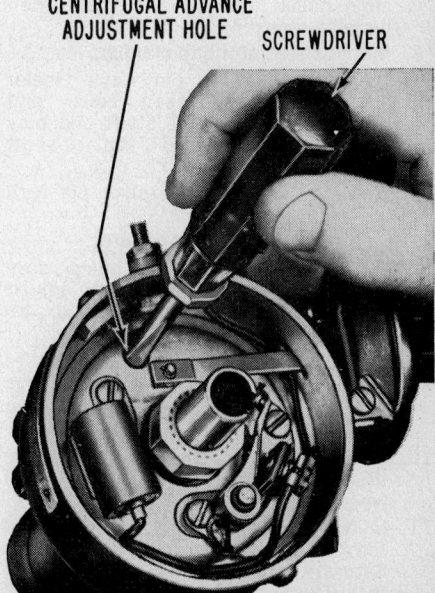

CENTRIFUGAL ADVANCE ADJUSTMENT HOLE · SCREWDRIVER

Fig. 7 Centrifugal advance adjustment all exc. 2800 cc units

TUNE UP SERVICE

ventional design in that both a centrifugal advance mechanism is provided to regulate ignition timing according to speed and a vacuum advance unit to regulate ignition timing according to load. However, unlike other make distributors, the centrifugal advance mechanism can be adjusted through a slot in the breaker plate.

Adjust centrifugal advance before adjusting vacuum advance. If specified centrifugal advance is not indicated on a distributor test machine, bend one spring bracket with a screwdriver through a hole in the breaker plate on all distributors except 2800 cc units, Fig. 7. On 2800 cc units, remove plug inside of distributor housing to gain access to adjustment bracket, Fig. 8. Bend bracket away from distributor shaft to decrease advance and toward shaft to increase advance. Identify bracket after adjustment is made. After an adjustment has been made to one spring, check the minimum advance point again. Then operate distributor at the specified rpm to give an advance just below maximum. If this advance is not up to specifications, bend the other spring bracket to give the correct advance.

Vacuum advance on 1974 distributors except 2300 cc and 2800 cc units can be adjusted by turning an allen head screw inside vacuum unit, Fig. 9. Turning the screw clockwise increases advance and turning it counterclockwise decreases advance. Vacuum advance on 2300 cc and 2800 cc units is pre-set and cannot be adjusted.

Distributor Service

Six & V8 Units

If the distributor has been disassembled, refer to Fig. 6 for guidance upon reassembly.

1. Oil shaft and slide it into distributor body.
2. Place collar in position on shaft and align holes in collar and shaft, then install a new pin.
3. Install distributor cap clamps.
4. Check shaft end play with feeler gauge placed between collar and base of distributor. If shaft end play is not within .024-.035", replace shaft and gear.
5. Fill grooves in weight pivot pin with ball bearing grease.
6. Position weights in distributor.
7. Install weight springs, being sure proper weight, spring and adjustment bracket are assembled together.
8. Install upper thrust washer.
9. Fill grooves in upper portion of distributor shaft with ball bearing grease.
10. Install cam assembly, being sure that slots in cam engage pins in weights.
11. Install cam retainer. Apply a light film of cam lubricant to cam lobes. Saturate wick with 10W engine oil. Install wick in cam.
12. Position stationary sub plate in distributor. Install one end of ground wire under plate retaining screw

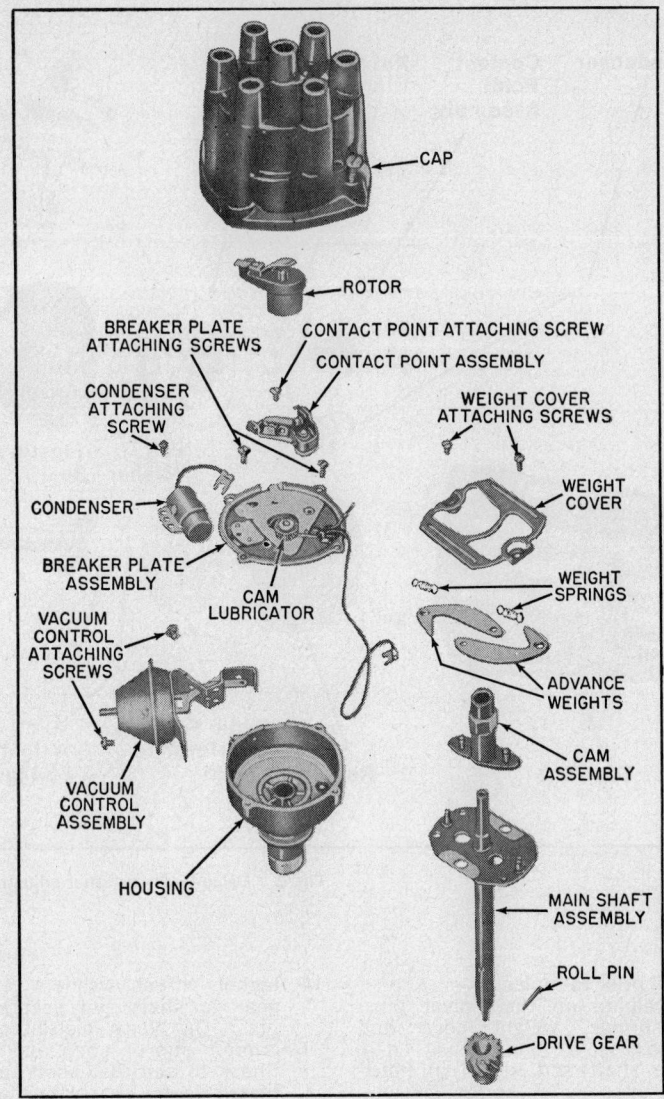

Fig. 4 Exploded view of typical Delco-Remy internal adjustment distributor

closest to diaphragm mounting flange.
13. Position movable breaker plate in distributor. Install spring washer on pivot pin. Place flat washer on spring washer. Be sure protruding edges of spring washer are facing upward. Install retainer.
14. Install new breaker point assembly. Install ground wire on breaker point attaching screw furthest from point adjustment slot.
15. Install condenser.
16. Working from inside to outside of distributor housing, pass primary wire through opening in distributor. Pull wire through opening until locating stop is flush with inside of distributor.
17. Connect condenser wire and primary wire to breaker points.
18. Position diaphragm and hook its link over pin on breaker plate. Install diaphragm attaching screws. Secure

link with retainer. Install oil seal.
19. Adjust breaker arm spring tension, align and adjust breaker points and check and adjust cam dwell, centrifugal and vacuum advance.

2300 cc & 2800 cc Units

If distributor has been disassembled, refer to Figs. 10 and 11 at reassembly.

1. Lubricate top of distributor shaft and install cam assembly, then retaining ring and felt wick.
2. Lubricate pivot pins and install advance weights and on 2800 cc units, "C" clips. On all units, install advance springs.
3. Place breaker plate into housing, ensuring mounting holes align. It may be necessary to lightly tap breaker

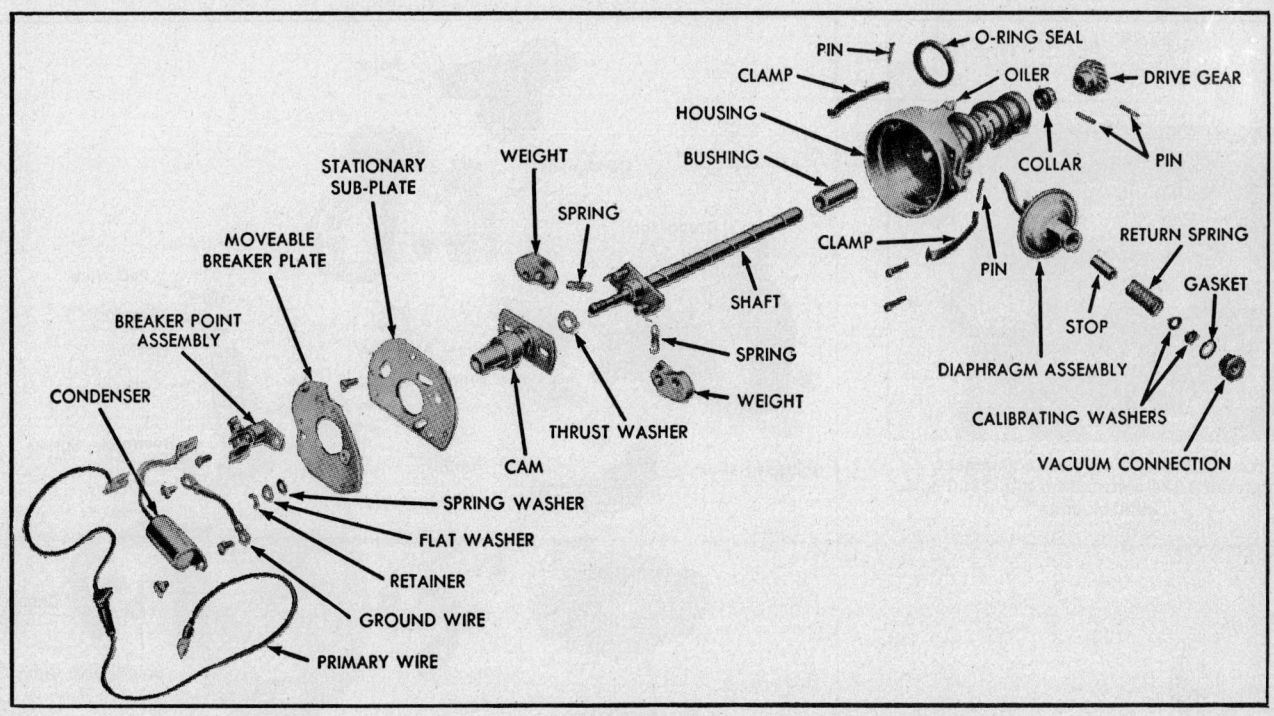

Fig. 6   Exploded view of Motorcraft V-8 dual-advance distributor. (Typical)

Fig. 8   Centrifugal advance adjustment. 2800 cc distributor

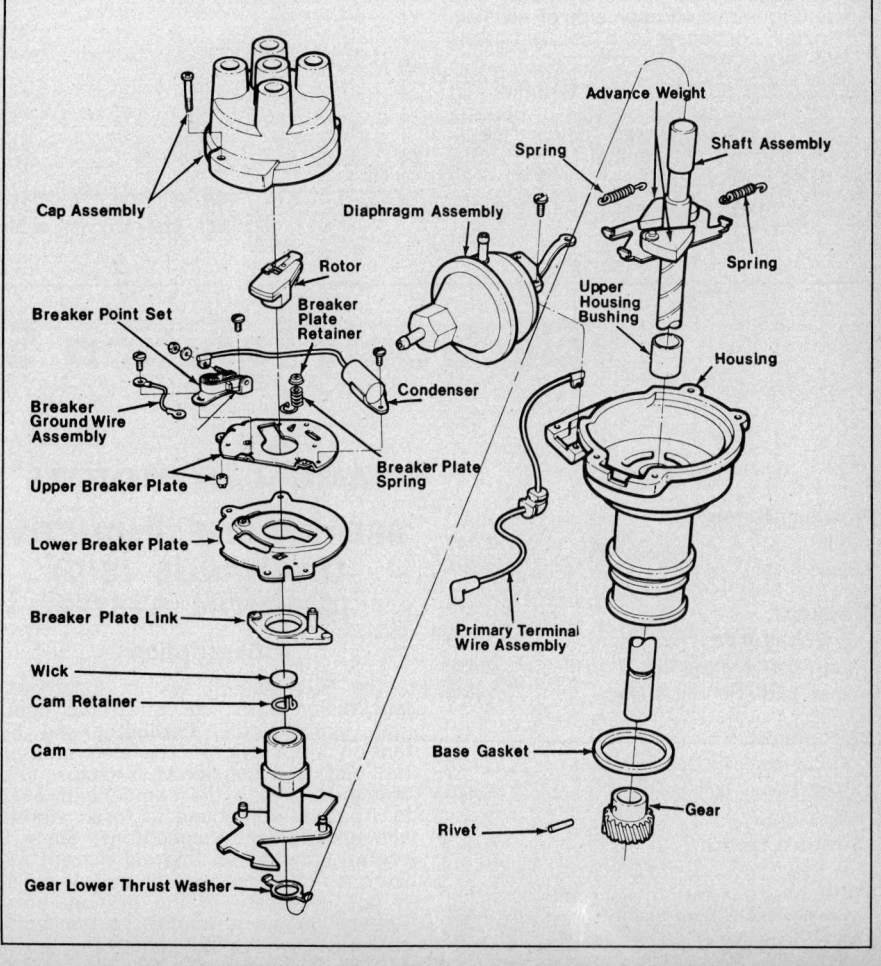

Fig. 10   Exploded view of Motorcraft 2300 cc dual advance distributor

2–441

Fig. 9 Vacuum advance adjustment.
Motorcraft 1974 distributors exc. 2300 cc &
2800 cc units

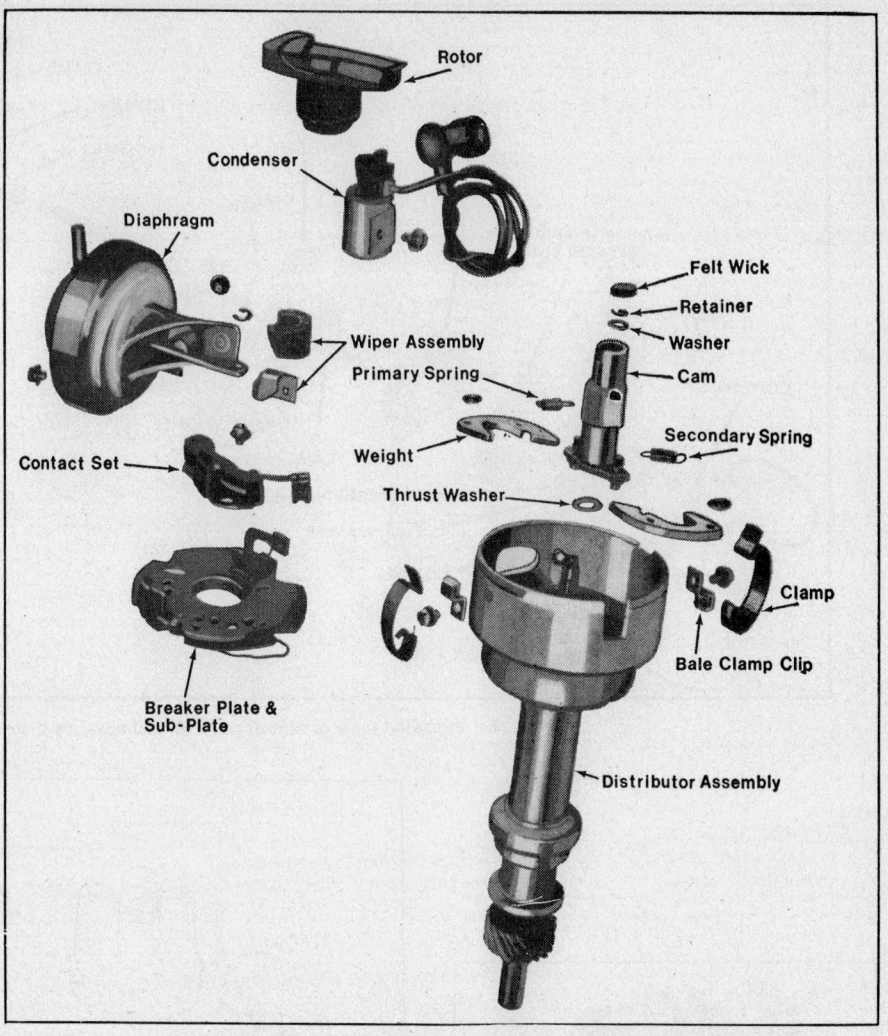

Fig. 11 Exploded view of Motorcraft 2800 cc dual advance distributor

plate to seat plate on swedged perches in housing.

4. Install vacuum advance unit, breaker points and cam wiper.

5. On 2300 cc units, route primary wire and grommet through side of housing. Install condenser and connect leads to terminal.

6. On 2800 cc units, place terminal and grommet into slot on side of housing and install condenser. Connect breaker point lead to terminal.

7. On all units, install rotor.

Electronic Ignition Systems

AMERICAN MOTORS

BREAKERLESS INDUCTIVE DISCHARGE (BID) IGNITION SYSTEM

Description

The BID ignition system incorporates four major units; an electronic control unit, ignition coil, distributor and high tension wires, Fig. 1. The electronic control unit is a solid-state, moisture resistant module with the components sealed in a potting compound to resist vibration and environmental conditions. Since the control unit has an internal current regulator, a resistance wire or ballast resistor is not necessary in the primary circuit. Battery voltage is applied to the ignition coil positive terminal when the ignition switch is in the "On" or "Start" position, therefore, an ignition system bypass is not required in this system. The primary coil circuit is electronically regulated by this unit.

The ignition coil is of standard construction and requires no special service. The function of the ignition coil in the BID ignition system is the same as for conventional ignition systems.

The distributor is conventional except the contact points, condenser and cam are replaced by a sensor and trigger wheel, and since no wearing occurs between the trigger wheel and sensor, dwell angle remains constant and requires no adjustment. The sensor is a small coil of fine wire and receives an alternating current signal from the electronic control unit. The sensor develops an electromagnetic field used to detect the presence of metal which are the leading edges of the trigger wheel teeth.

Operation

When the ignition switch is placed in the "Start" or "Run" position, the control unit is activated. An oscillator within the control unit excites the sensor coil, in turn developing the electromagnetic field. When a leading edge of a trigger wheel tooth enters the electromagnetic field, the tooth reduces the sensor oscillation strength to a predetermined level, in turn activating the demodulator circuit. The demodulator circuit controls a power transistor located in series with the coil primary circuit. The power transistor switches the coil primary circuit off, thereby inducing a high voltage in the coil secondary winding. The high voltage is then delivered to the spark plugs through the distributor rotor, cap and high tension wires.

System Quick Test, Fig. 2

The BID system may be tested quickly on the vehicle using No. 57 bulb and a jumper wire. Refer to Fig. 2 for procedure.

Comprehensive testing may be performed as outlined under "Troubleshooting".

Troubleshooting, Fig. 2A

1. Disconnect Electronic Control Unit (ECU) ground wire and the 4-wire connector. Using a small wire brush and solvent, clean the terminals. Leave connectors disconnected.
2. Disconnect battery cables, then momentarily move ignition switch to START and allow it to move to ON.
3. Measure resistance of entire ignition feed circuit by connecting an ohmmeter to battery positive B1 and F3 terminal in the 4-wire connector.
4. If resistance is less than 1 ohm, tighten main harness connector attaching screw to fully seat connector. If resistance is 1 ohm or more, isolate trouble area by connecting the ohmmeter and measuring the resistance of each portion of the ignition feed circuit between the following terminals: B1 and B2, B2 and A1, A1 and H1, F3 and C1, C1 and H2, H1 and H2, AV and DV. Clean, tighten or reposition connectors as needed.
5. Inspect coil primary connections for looseness and proper assembly. Wire terminals must be between channel washer and nut, channel washer tabs must be facing up. Reposition and tighten as needed.
6. Connect an ohmmeter between F3 and F4 terminals to measure coil primary circuit resistance. If resistance is 1-2 ohms, proceed to step 7. If resistance is less than 1 ohm, replace coil and proceed to step 8. If resistance is more than 2 ohms, isolate trouble and insure that the resistance between the following terminals is as follows: C1 and C2, 1-2 ohms; F3 and C1, 0 ohms; F4 and C2, 0 ohms. Replace coil or repair trouble area and proceed to step 7. If coil was replaced, proceed to step 8.
7. Measure coil secondary resistance by removing coil secondary wire from coil and connecting ohmmeter between C1 and C3.

NOTE: Set ohmmeter to the 1,000

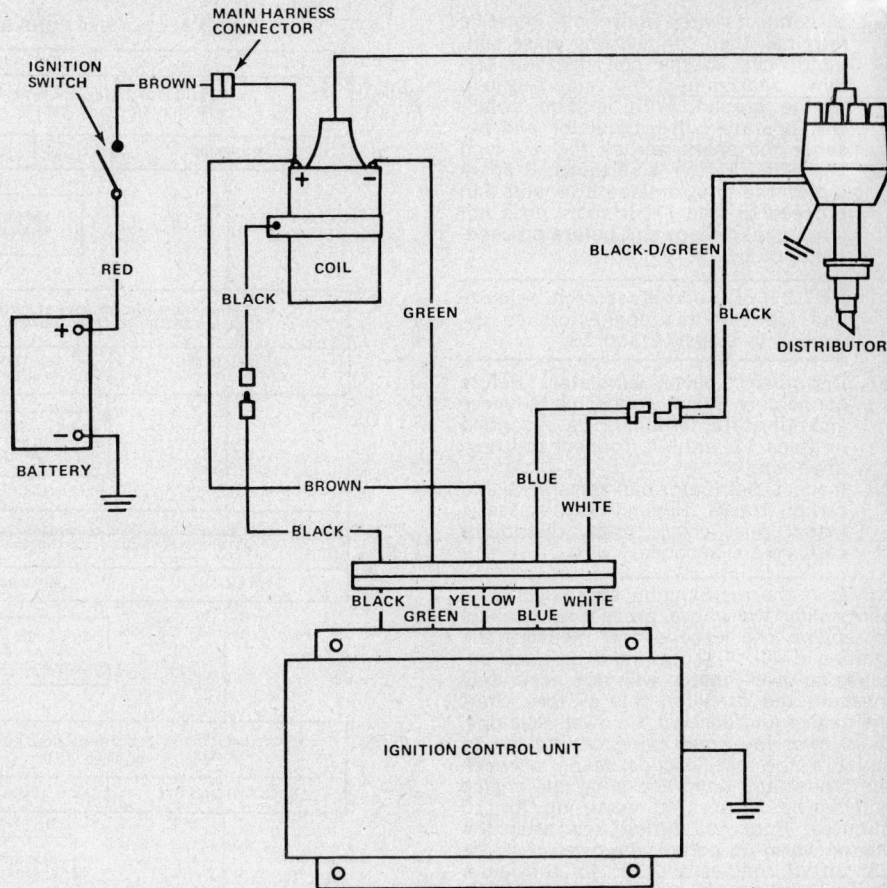

Fig. 1   BID ignition system wiring

ohm scale before testing secondary resistance.

If resistance is 9,000-15,000 ohms, reconnect coil secondary wire and proceed to step 8. If resistance is less than 9,000 ohms or more than 15,000 ohms, replace coil and reconnect coil secondary wire and proceed to Step 8.

8. Remove distributor cap, rotor and dust cover and check for 1.6-2.4 ohms resistance between F1 and F2 terminals.

NOTE: Pull and flex sensor wires, firmly squeeze molded sensor grommet at distributor, and apply firm side to side pressure on sensor post while checking resistance.

If resistance is as specified and steady, proceed to step 10. If resistance is too high or low, or if needle fluctuates or wavers, proceed to step 9.

9. Disconnect 2-wire connector and check for 1.6-2.4 ohms resistance between S1 and S2 terminals.

NOTE: Pull and flex sensor wires, firmly squeeze molded sensor wire grommet at distributor, and apply firm side to side pressure on sensor post.

If resistance is as specified and steady, proceed to step 10. If resistance is too high to too low, or if needle fluctuates or wavers, replace sensor and proceed to step 10.

10. Using a small wire brush and solvent, clean terminals S1, S2, S3 and S4.
11. Measure resistance of ECU ground circuit by connecting an ohmmeter between terminal G2 and battery negative cable G4. Resistance should be 0 ohms. Clean and tighten connections as needed.
12. Using pliers, squeeze terminals E1, E2, E3, E4 and G1 until terminals have a distinct oval shape, thereby assuring a tight fit when terminals are connected.
13. Using petroleum jelly, coat the male terminals in the 4-wire connector and ground connectors and around the outer edge of the terminal end of the ECU 4-wire connector.
14. Connect the 4-wire and ground connectors.
15. Connect Pulse Simulator J-25331 to the S3 and S4 terminals and reconnect battery cables. Remove coil secondary wire from distributor and place end of wire ½ inch from ground, then with ignition switch ON, operate simulator and observe for spark across the ½ inch gap. If spark jumps gap, proceed to step 17. If spark does not jump gap, proceed to step 16.

16. Disconnect wire from coil negative terminal, then connect one pulse simulator clip to the coil negative terminal and connect the remaining clip to the ground. With ignition switch ON, operate pulse simulator and observe for spark across the ½ inch gap when button is released. If spark jumps the gap, replace ECU unit and proceed to step 17. If spark does not jump gap, replace coil before proceeding to step 17.

NOTE: If ECU unit is replaced, squeeze and lubricate the connectors as described in steps 12 and 13.

17. Disconnect pulse simulator. Before connecting 2-wire connector, squeeze and lubricate terminals as described in steps 12 and 13. Connect coil negative wire.

18. Inspect distributor cap for cracks and carbon tracks. Replace as necessary. Install dust cover, rotor, distributor cap and coil secondary wire.

NOTE: If the malfunction still exists after performing the above procedure, connect an engine oscilloscope and measure the ignition dwell. A scope must be used because a dwell meter will not accurately measure the dwell on this system. Start the engine and observe the dwell readings, then lower the hood being careful not to squeeze the oscilloscope leads between the fender and hood and allow the engine and wiring harness to warm up for 10 minutes. Prior to, during and after the engine warm up period, the dwell must be 23° on V8 engines and 32° for 6 cylinder engines and the dwell must not vary more than 3° at any time. If the dwell readings are as specified at all times, the malfunction may be caused by the fuel system. If the fuel system checks out OK and the malfunction still exists, replace the ECU unit and recheck the dwell. If the dwell readings are still not as specified above, replace the ignition wiring harness and recheck the dwell as above. If the dwell is below specifications, disconnect the 4-wire connector and measure the sensor circuit resistance and integrity as described in step 8. If sensor circuit resistance and integrity are within specifications, replace ECU unit. If sensor circuit resistance is too high or too low, or if needle fluctuates, replace the sensor. Be sure to squeeze and lubricate the terminals as described in steps 12 and 13.

Component Replacement

1. Place distributor in a suitable holding fixture and remove cap, rotor and dust shield, Fig. 7.
2. Using a small gear puller, remove trigger wheel. Ensure puller jaws are gripping trigger wheel inner shoulder to prevent trigger wheel damage. Also, use a thick flat washer or nut as a spacer and do not press against small center shaft.
3. Loosen sensor locking screw approximately three turns, lift sensor lead grommet from distributor bowl and pull sensor leads from slot around sensor spring pivot pin. Release sensor spring, ensure spring clears sensor leads and slide sensor from bracket.

NOTE: The sensor locking screw uti-

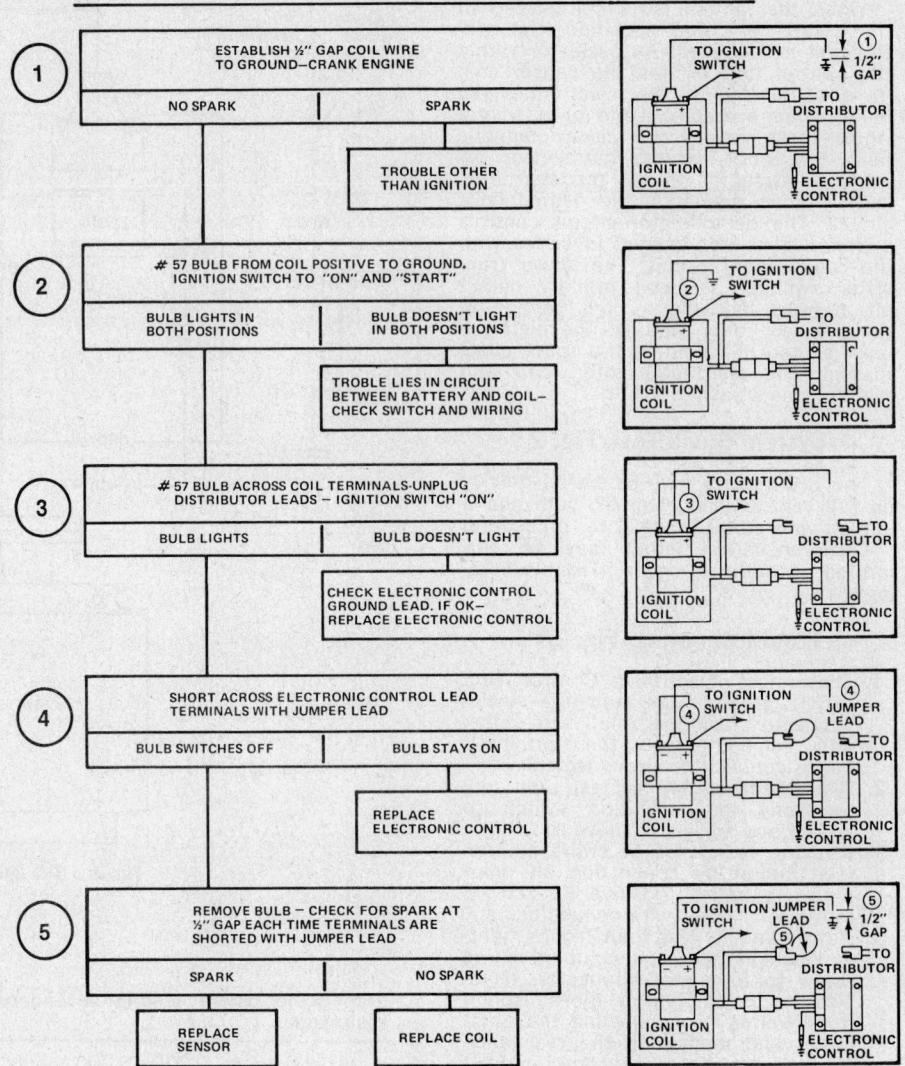

CHECK ALL CONNECTIONS BEFORE BEGINNING TEST

Fig. 2   American Motors BID system quick test

lizes a tamper proof head design and requires tool J-25097 for removal. However, if special tool is not available, use a small needlenose plier to remove screw. The service (replacement) sensor has a standard slotted head screw.

4. If vacuum control unit is to be replaced, remove retaining screw and vacuum unit.
5. Install new vacuum control unit and assemble sensor, sensor guide, flat washer and retaining screw.

NOTE: Install retaining screw far enough to hold assembly together and ensure it does not protrude past bottom of sensor.

6. If vacuum control has been replaced and original sensor is being used, replace special head screw with standard slotted head screw.

7. Install sensor assembly on vacuum chamber bracket, ensuring tip of sensor located properly in summing bar. Place sensor spring on sensor and route sensor leads around spring pivot pin, Fig. 4. Install sensor lead grommet and position leads away from trigger wheel.
8. Install sensor positioning gauge over yoke, ensure positioning is against flat of shaft, and move sensor sideways until gauge can be positioned. Snug retaining screw and check sensor position by removing and installing gauge, Fig. 5. When gauge can be removed and replaced without sensor side movement, sensor is positioned properly. Tighten retaining screw and check sensor position.
9. Place trigger wheel on yoke and check if sensor core is positioned approximately in center of trigger wheel legs. Bend a .050 inch gauge wire to dimension specified in Fig. 6, and place between trigger wheel

legs and sensor base. Press trigger wheel onto yoke until legs contact gauge wire.

10. Apply 3 to 5 drops of light engine oil to felt wick in top of yoke, then install dust shield, rotor and cap.

AMERICAN MOTORS SOLID STATE IGNITION SYSTEM

This ignition system, Fig. 7 is used on 1978 vehicles except those equipped with the four cylinder engine. The solid state ignition system consists of the ignition switch, electronic ignition control unit, ignition coil, primary resistance wire and bypass, distributor and spark plugs.

The electronic ignition control unit is a solid state, moisture resistant module. The component parts are sealed in a potting material to resist vibration and environmental conditions. The control unit is incorporated with reverse polarity protection and transient voltage protection.

The distributor incorporates a sensor and trigger wheel. Current flowing through the ignition coil creates a magnetic field in the primary windings. When the circuit is opened, the magnetic field collapses and induces a high voltage in the coil secondary windings. This circuit is electronically controlled by the electronic ignition control unit. The distributor sensor and trigger wheel provide the signal to operate the control unit. The trigger wheel is mounted on the distributor shaft and has one tooth for each cylinder. The sensor, a coil of fine wire mounted to a permanent magnet, develops an electromagnetic force that is sensitive to the presence of ferrous metal. The sensor detects the trigger wheel teeth as the teeth pass the sensor. When a trigger wheel tooth approaches the pole piece of the sensor, it reduces the reluctance of the magnetic field, increasing field strength. Field strength decreases as the tooth moves away from the pole piece. This increase and decrease of field strength generates an alternating current which is interpreted by the electronic ignition control unit. The control unit then opens and closes the ignition coil primary circuit.

Since there are no contacting surfaces and no wear occurs, dwell angle requires no adjustment. The dwell angle is electronically controlled by the electronic ignition control unit. When the coil circuit is switched open, an electronic timer in the control unit keeps the circuit open only long enough for the spark to discharge. Then, it automatically closes the ignition coil primary circuit.

Trouble Shooting

Secondary Circuit Test

1. Disconnect coil wire from distributor cap and, using insulated pliers, hold wire approximately ½ inch from a good engine ground.
2. Crank engine and observe wire for spark. If no spark occurs, proceed to Step 5. If spark occurs, proceed to Step 3.
3. Reconnect coil wire to distributor cap. Remove wire from one spark plug.

CAUTION: Do not remove wires from spark plugs on cylinders 3 or 5 on

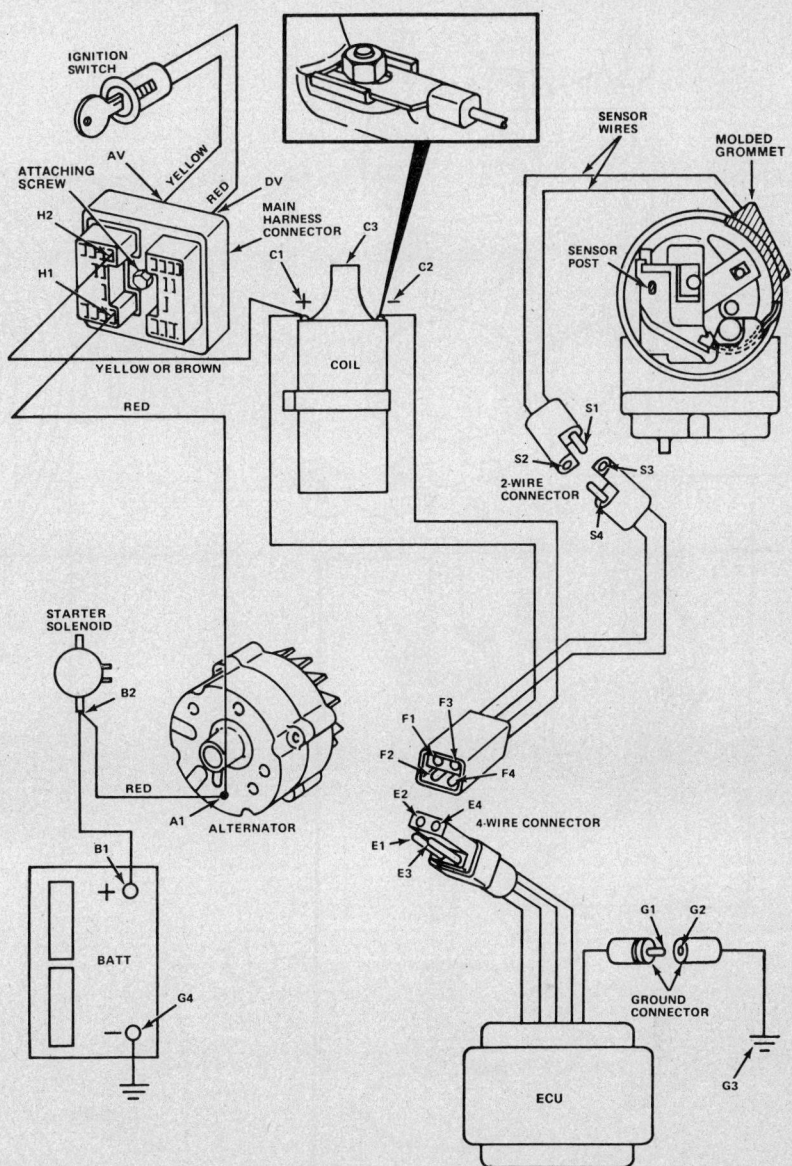

Fig. 2A   BID ignition system checkpoints

six cylinder engines or cylinders 3 or 4 on V8 engines when performing this test since the sensor may be damaged.

4. Using insulated pliers, hold wire approximately ½ inch from a good engine ground. Crank engine and observe wire for spark. If spark occurs, check for fuel system problems or incorrect ignition timing. If no spark occurs, check for defective distributor cap, rotor or spark plug wires.
5. If no spark occurs at coil wire, measure coil wire resistance. If resistance is greater than 10,000 ohms, replace wire.
6. If malfunction still exists, proceed to the following tests or diagnosis procedures.

Intermittent Failure Diagnosis

Since intermittent failure may be caused by loose or corroded terminals, defective components, poor ground connections or defective wiring, it is neces-

sary to check all wiring connections in the ignition system. Also, refer to Fig. 8 for further diagnosis.

Ignition Coil Primary Circuit Test

1. Turn ignition switch "On" and connect a voltmeter between ignition coil positive terminal and the ground. If voltage is 5.5-6.5 volts, proceed to Step 2. If battery voltage is noted, proceed to Step 4. If voltage is below 5.5 volts, disconnect condenser lead. If voltage is now 5.5-6.5 volts, replace condenser. If voltage is still not within specifications, proceed to Step 6.
2. Turn ignition switch to "Start" and measure voltage at coil positive terminal while cranking engine. If battery voltage is present while cranking engine, the ignition coil primary circuit is satisfactory. If voltage present is less than battery voltage, proceed to Step 3.
3. Check for shorted or open circuit in wire attached to starter "I" terminal.

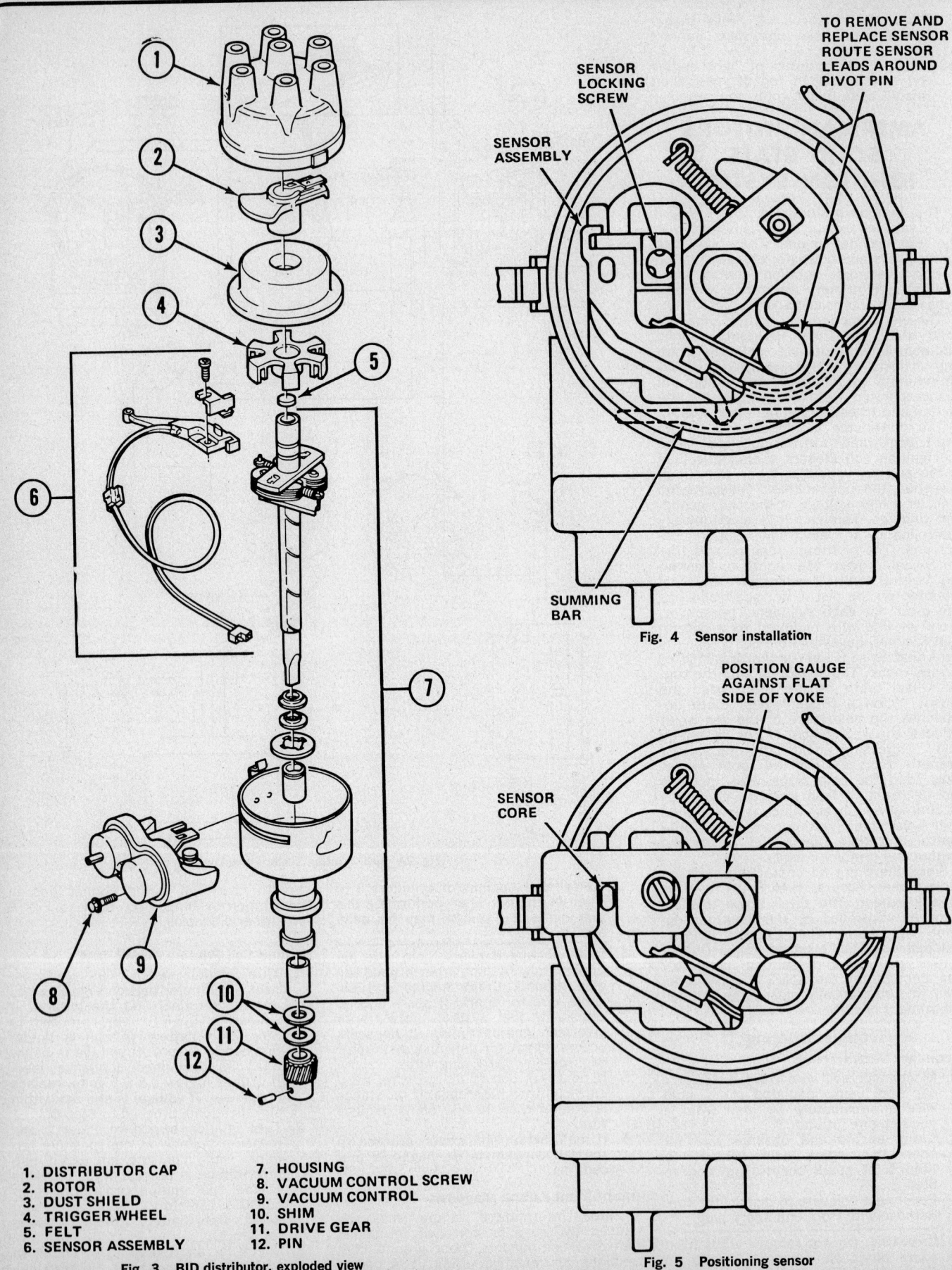

1. DISTRIBUTOR CAP
2. ROTOR
3. DUST SHIELD
4. TRIGGER WHEEL
5. FELT
6. SENSOR ASSEMBLY
7. HOUSING
8. VACUUM CONTROL SCREW
9. VACUUM CONTROL
10. SHIM
11. DRIVE GEAR
12. PIN

Fig. 3   BID distributor, exploded view

SENSOR LOCKING SCREW

SENSOR ASSEMBLY

TO REMOVE AND REPLACE SENSOR ROUTE SENSOR LEADS AROUND PIVOT PIN

SUMMING BAR

Fig. 4   Sensor installation

POSITION GAUGE AGAINST FLAT SIDE OF YOKE

SENSOR CORE

Fig. 5   Positioning sensor

Check for defective starter solenoid. Repair as necessary.

4. Place ignition switch in "On" position, disconnect wire from starter solenoid "I" terminal and measure voltage at ignition coil positive terminal. If voltage drops to 5.5-6.5 volts, replace starter solenoid. If voltage remains constant at battery voltage, connect a jumper wire between ignition coil negative terminal and the ground. If voltage drops to 5.5-6.5 volts, proceed to Step 5. If not, repair defective resistance wire and repeat Step 2.

5. Check continuity between ignition coil negative terminal and terminal "D4", Fig. 7. Also, check continuity between terminal "D1" and the ground. If continuity is present, replace electronic ignition control unit. If continuity is not present, locate and repair open circuit.

6. Turn ignition switch "Off" and measure resistance between ignition coil positive terminal and the dash connector "AV", Fig. 7. If resistance is greater than 1.40 ohms, repair or replace resistance wire. If resistance is 1.30-1.40 ohms, proceed to Step 7.

7. With ignition "Off", measure resistance between dash connector "AV" and ignition switch terminal "I1", Fig. 7. If resistance is less than .1 ohm, replace ignition switch or repair switch feed wire. If resistance is greater than .1 ohm, check and repair terminal connections at dash connector or defective wiring.

Coil Test

1. Inspect ignition coil for oil leaks, exterior damage and carbon tracks. If satisfactory, proceed to Step 2. If not, replace ignition coil.

2. Disconnect ignition coil connector and connect ohmmeter between coil terminals. If resistance is 1.13-1.23 ohms at 75° F. or 1.5 ohms at 200° F., proceed to Step 3. If not, replace ignition coil.

3. Connect ohmmeter between ignition coil center tower and the plus or minus terminal. Resistance should be 7700-9300 ohms. If not replace ignition coil.

Sensor & Control Unit Test

1. Disconnect the four wire connector at the control unit, Fig. 7. Disconnect coil wire from center tower of distributor and hold wire approximately ½ inch from a good engine ground with insulated pliers, then turn ignition "On". If spark is observed at coil wire, proceed to next step. If not, proceed to Step 5.

2. Measure resistance between terminals "D2" and "D3" of the harness connector, Fig. 7. If resistance is 400-800 ohms, proceed to Step 6. If not, proceed to next step.

3. Disconnect and connect the three wire connector at distributor and measure resistance between terminals "D2" and "D3" of the harness connector, Fig. 7. If resistance is now between 400-800 ohms, proceed to Step 6. If not, disconnect three wire connector at distributor and proceed to next step.

4. Measure resistance between terminals "B2" and "B3" of the distributor con-

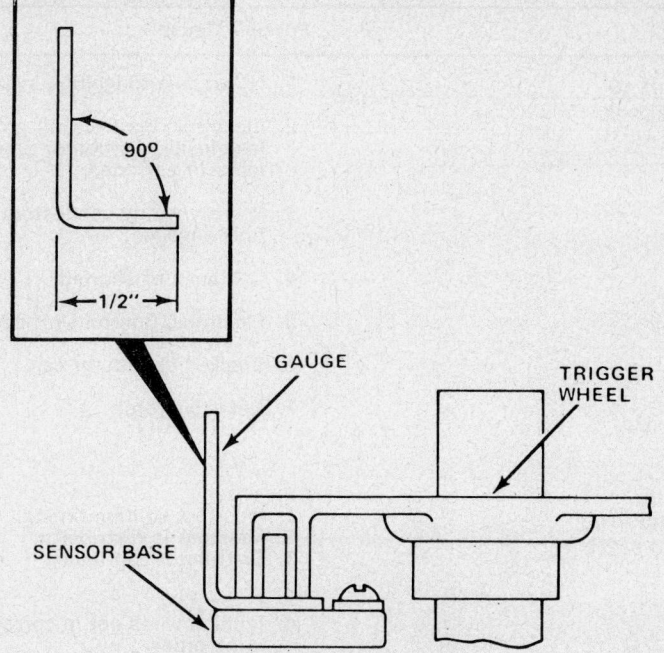

Fig. 6   Trigger wheel installation

nector, Fig. 7. If resistance is not 400-800 ohms, replace sensor. If resistance is 400-800 ohms, repair or replace harness between three wire and four wire connector.

5. Connect an ohmmeter between terminal "D1" of the harness connector, Fig. 7, and the battery negative terminal. If reading is below .002 ohm, repeat Step 2. If not, check for an improper ground. Check ground cable resistance, distributor to engine block resistance and distributor ground screw to terminal "D1" resistance, Fig. 7.

6. Using a voltmeter connected between terminals "D2" and "D3" of the harness connector, Fig. 7, observe reading while cranking engine. If voltmeter reading fluctuates, it indicates proper sensor and trigger wheel operation. If not, the trigger wheel is defective or the distributor is not rotating.

Ignition Feed To Control Unit Test

NOTE: Perform the "Ignition Coil Primary Circuit Test" before performing this test.

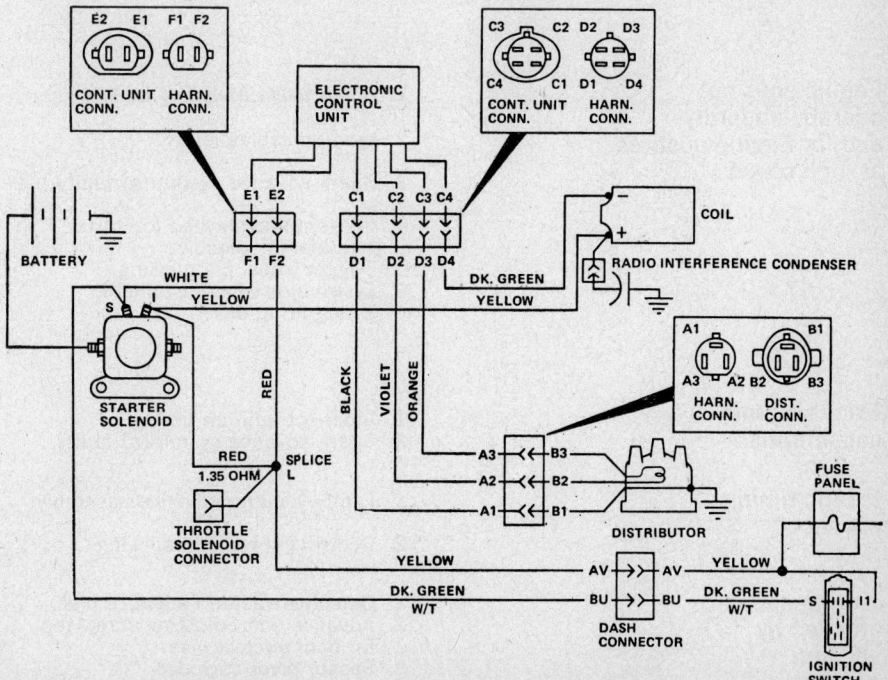

Fig. 7   American Motors solid state ignition system schematic

TUNE UP SERVICE

Condition	Possible Cause	Correction
Engine fails to start (no spark at plugs)	1. No voltage to ignition system.	1. Check battery, ignition switch and wiring. Repair as required.
	2. Electronic Control Unit ground lead inside distributor open, loose or corroded.	2. Clean, tighten or repair as required.
	3. Primary wiring connectors not fully engaged.	3. Clean and fully engage connectors.
	4. Coil open or shorted.	4. Test coil. Replace if faulty.
	5. Electronic Control Unit defective.	5. Replace Electronic Control Unit.
	6. Cracked distributor cap.	6. Replace cap.
	7. Defective rotor.	7. Replace rotor.
Engine backfires but fails to start	1. Incorrect ignition timing.	1. Check timing. Adjust as required.
	2. Moisture in distributor.	2. Dry cap and rotor.
	3. Distributor cap faulty.	3. Check cap for loose terminals, cracks and dirt. Clean or replace as required.
	4. Ignition wires not in correct firing order.	4. Install in correct order.
Engine runs only with key in start position	1. Open in resistance wire or excessive resistance.	1. Repair resistance wire.
Engine continues to run with key off	1. Defective starter solenoid.	1. Replace solenoid.
	2. Shorted diode in alternator indicator lamp circuit.	2. Replace diode.
Engine does not operate smoothly and/or Engine misfires at high speed	1. Spark plugs fouled or faulty.	1. Clean and gap plugs. Replace as required.
	2. Ignition cables faulty.	2. Check cables. Replace as required.
	3. Spark advance system(s) faulty.	3. Check operation. Repair as required.
	4. "I" terminal shorted to starter terminal in solenoid.	4. Replace solenoid.
	5. Trigger wheel pin missing.	5. Install pin.
	6. Distributor wires installed in wrong firing order.	6. Install wires correctly.
Excessive fuel consumption	1. Incorrect ignition timing.	1. Check timing. Adjust as required.
	2. Spark advance system(s) faulty.	2. Check operation. Repair as required.
Erratic timing advance	1. Faulty vacuum advance assembly.	1. Check operation. Replace if required.
	2. Centrifugal weights sticking.	2. Remove dirt, corrosion.
Timing not affected by vacuum	1. Defective vacuum advance unit.	1. Replace vacuum advance unit.
	2. Advance unit adjusting screw too far counterclockwise.	2. Turn screw clockwise to bring advance curve within specifications.
	3. Sensor pivot corroded.	3. Clean pivot.

Fig. 8   American Motors solid state ignition system service diagnosis chart

1. Disconnect two wire connector from control unit and connect a voltmeter between terminal "F2" and the ground, Fig. 7. Turn ignition "On". If voltmeter reading is within .2 volts of battery voltage, replace control unit and proceed to Step 3. If voltmeter reading is not within .2 volt of battery voltage, proceed to next step.
2. Locate and repair cause of voltage reduction as noted in Step 1. Check for a corroded dash connector or defective ignition switch. Then, check for spark at coil wire. Spark should be present at coil wire. If not, replace control unit.
3. Connect the two wire connector at control unit and disconnect the four wire connector from control unit. Connect an ammeter between terminal "C1" and the ground, Fig. 7. If ammeter reading is 1± .1 amp., the system is satisfactory. If ammeter reading is higher or lower, replace module.

Current Flow Test

1. Remove connector from coil.
2. Depress plastic barb and remove positive wire from connector. Remove negative wire in same manner.
3. Connect an ammeter between coil positive terminal and the disconnected positive wire.
4. Connect a jumper wire between coil negative terminal and the engine ground.
5. Turn ignition "On" and note ammeter reading. Reading should be approximately 7 amps. and not exceeding 7.6 amps. If reading exceeds 7.6 amps., replace ignition coil.
6. Remove jumper wire from coil negative terminal and connect the coil green wire to negative terminal. Ammeter reading should be approximately 4 amps. If reading is less than 3.5 amps., check for poor connections at the three wire and four wire connectors or a poor ground at distributor ground screw. If reading is greater than 5 amps., the control unit is defective, requiring replacement.
7. Start and run engine. Ammeter reading should be 2-2.4 amps. If not, replace control unit.

Distributor Service

Trigger Wheel & Sensor, Replace

1. Remove distributor cap and rotor, Fig. 9.
2. Remove trigger wheel with a suitable gear puller. Use a flat washer to prevent gear puller from contacting inner shaft. The trigger wheel may also be removed by using two screwdrivers to pry trigger wheel upward. Remove pin.
3. On six cylinder distributors, remove sensor retainers and washers from pivot pin on base plate.
4. On V8 distributors, remove sensor snap ring from shaft, then the retainer from vacuum unit to sensor drive pin and position vacuum unit lever aside.
5. On all distributors, remove ground screw from harness tab.
6. Remove sensor assembly from distributor housing.
7. Reverse procedure to assemble.

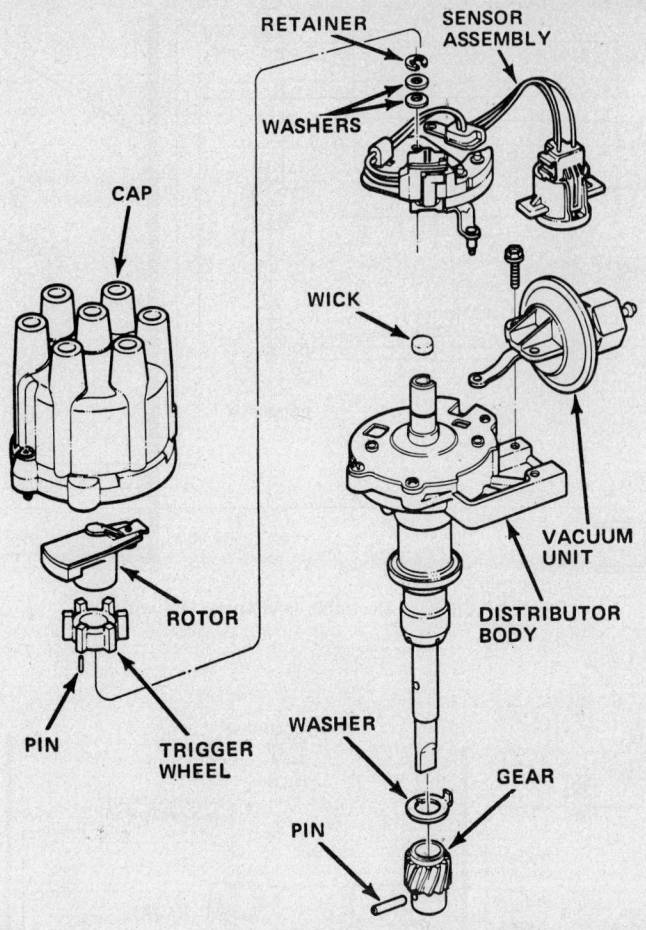

Fig. 9   American Motors distributor used with solid state ignition system (Typical)

Vacuum Unit, Replace

1. Disconnect vacuum hose.
2. On six cylinder distributors, remove vacuum unit attaching screws and the vacuum unit, Fig. 9. It is necessary to tilt the vacuum unit to disengage the link from the sensor pin and also loosen the base plate screws for clearance.
3. On V8 distributors, remove distributor cap and the retainer from the sensor pin. Remove vacuum unit attaching screws and the vacuum unit, Fig. 9.
4. Reverse procedure to install. If a new vacuum unit is installed, it must be calibrated as follows:
   a. Insert an appropriate size allen wrench into vacuum hose tube of original vacuum unit. Rotate allen wrench clockwise and note the number of turns required to bottom the adjusting screw.
   b. Insert allen wrench into vacuum hose tube of replacement vacuum unit. Turn the allen wrench clockwise until the adjusting screw is bottomed, then rotate allen wrench counterclockwise the number of turns noted in the previous step.

CHRYSLER CORP. EXC. LEAN BURN SYSTEMS

This system, Fig. 1, is composed of a magnetic distributor, an electronic control unit, a wiring harness, a production coil and a dual ballast resistor.

The distributor is essentially the same as the conventional type except the contacts have been replaced by a pickup coil and the cam by a reluctor. With a conventional contact type system, the voltage necessary to fire the spark plugs is developed by interrupting the current flowing through the primary of the ignition coil by opening a set of contacts. With the Electronic System, the voltage is produced the same way except that the current is interrupted by a transistor in the electronic control unit. This happens each time the control unit receives a "timing" pulse from the distributor magnetic pickup.

Since the magnetic pickup, reluctor and the control unit, which replace the contact points and cam, do not normally change or wear out with service, engine timing and dwell do not require periodic adjusting. This minimizes regular ignition maintenance of cleaning and replacing the spark plugs.

TROUBLE SHOOTING

Engine Will Not Start—Fuel System OK

1. Wiring harness electrical terminals

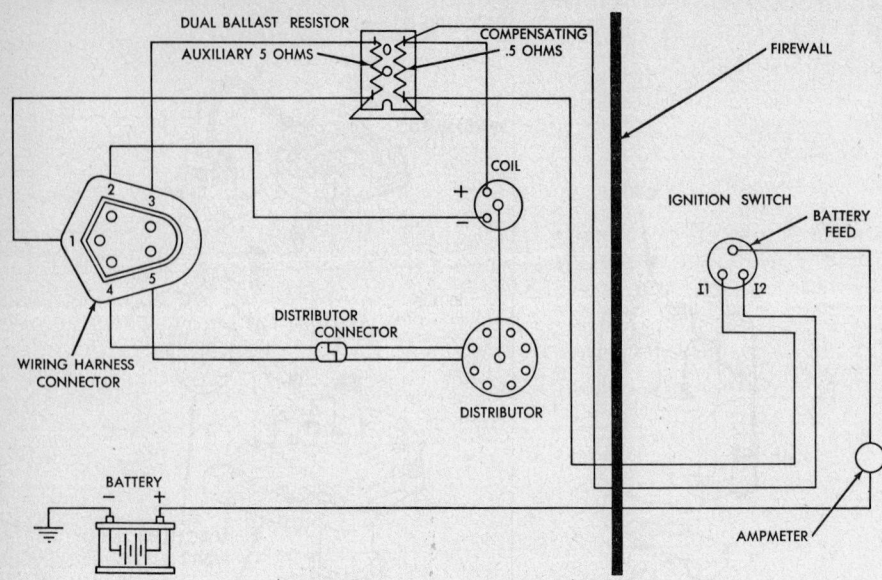

Fig. 1   Chrysler electronic ignition system wiring

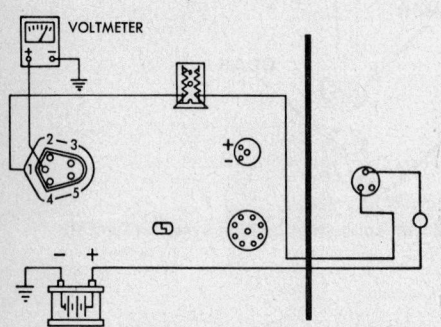

Fig. 2   Harness wiring test, No. 1 cavity

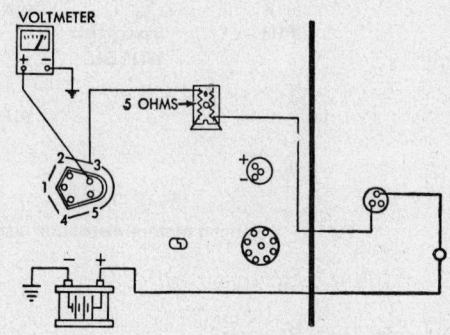

Fig. 4   Harness wiring test, No. 3 cavity

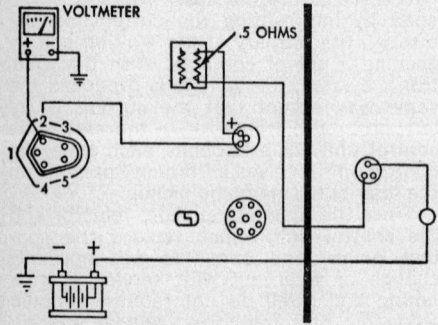

Fig. 3   Harness wiring test, No. 2 cavity

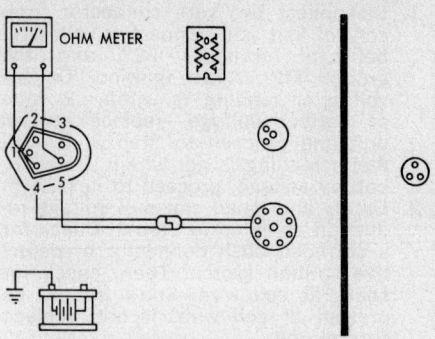

Fig. 5   Pick-up coil test, cavity Nos. 4 & 5

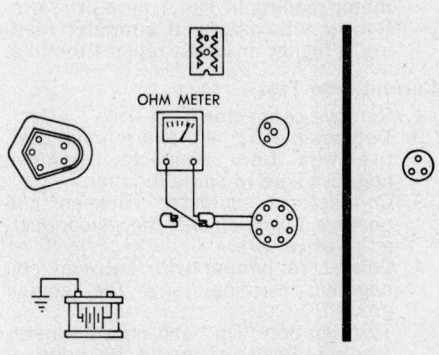

Fig. 6   Pick-up coil test, distributor lead connector

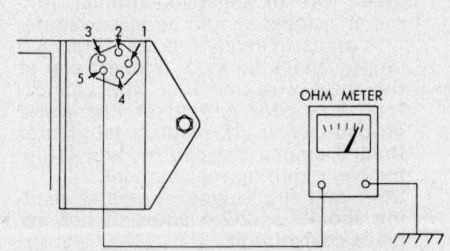

Fig. 7   Control unit ground circuit test

Engine Surges Severely—Not Lean Carburetor

1. Wiring.
2. Faulty pickup leads.
3. Ignition coil.

Engine Misses—Carburetion Good

1. Spark plugs.
2. Secondary cables.
3. Ignition coil.
4. Wiring.
5. Control unit.

SYSTEM TESTING

NOTE: To completely test components and circuits of the electronic ignition system, special testers should be used. However, in event the testers are not available, the following procedures may be utilized. A voltmeter with a 20,000 volt/ohm rating and an ohmmeter using a 1.5 volt battery for power should be used for testing. Be-

fore performing any electrical tests, ensure all wiring is properly connected.

Harness Wiring Test

1. Check battery voltage and note reading.
2. Disconnect harness connector from control unit.

CAUTION: Before disconnecting or connecting harness connector, ensure ignition switch is in the "Off" position.

3. Turn ignition switch to "On" position.
4. Connect the voltmeter between harness connector cavity No. 1 and the ground. Voltage reading should be within 1 volt of battery voltage earlier noted. If not, check circuit between cavity No. 1 and the battery, Fig. 2.

covered with grease.
2. Dual ballast.
3. Faulty ignition coil.
4. Faulty pickup or improper pickup air gap.
5. Faulty wiring.
6. Faulty control unit.

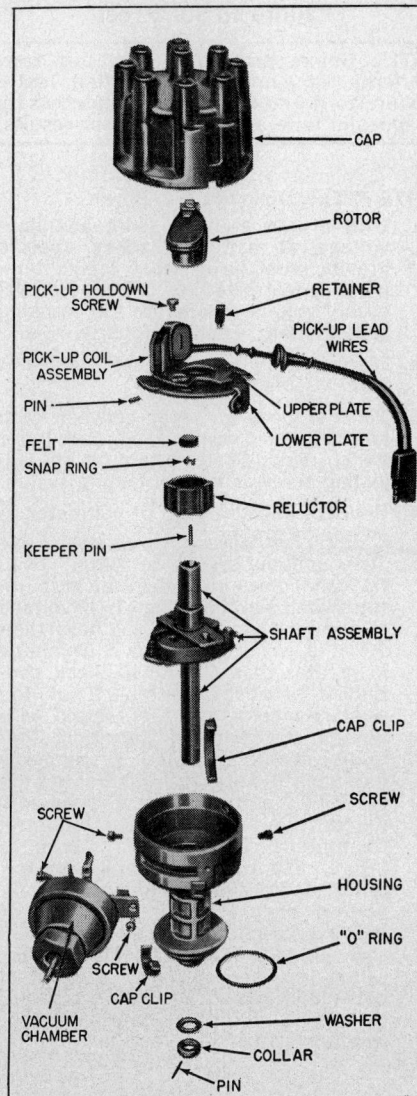

Fig. 8 Exploded view of typical Chrysler electronic distributor

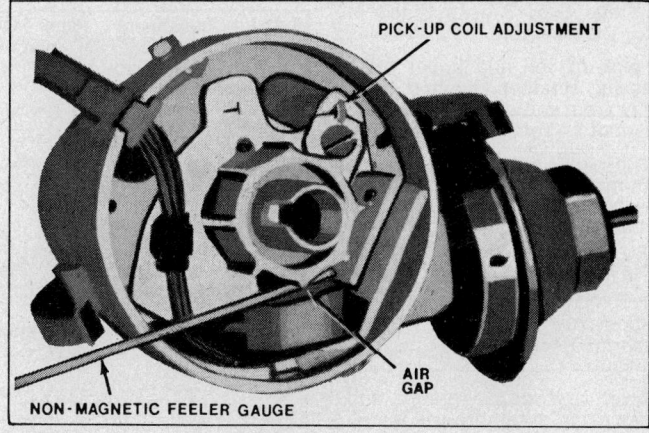

Fig. 9 Air gap adjustment

5. Test harness connector cavities numbers 2 and 3 in same manner. If voltage is not within specifications, check circuits between cavities numbers 2 and 3 and the battery, Figs. 3 and 4.

6. Turn ignition switch to "Off" position.

Distributor Pick-up Coil Test

1. Connect an ohmmeter between harness connector cavities numbers 4 and 5, Fig. 5. Resistance reading should be 150 to 900 ohms.

2. If reading is not as specified in above step, disconnect distributor dual lead connector and connect ohmmeter between the two leads on distributor side of connector, Fig. 6. If resistance is not between 150 and 900 ohms, replace pick-up coil.

3. Connect one ohmmeter lead to a good ground and the other lead to either

connector of the distributor. If ohm meter shows a reading, the pickup coil must be replaced.

Control Unit Ground Circuit Test

Connect an ohmmeter between control unit connector pin No. 5 and the ground, Fig. 7. If ohmmeter indicates infinite resistance, tighten bolts securing control unit to firewall and recheck resistance. If reading is still infinite, replace control unit.

Distributor Shaft & Bushing Wear Test

1. Remove distributor from vehicle and clamp distributor in a vise. Use extreme caution not to damage distributor.

2. Attach a dial indicator to housing so plunger rests against reluctor sleeve.

3. Place a wire loop around reluctor sleeve and hook a spring scale on the other end of the loop. Apply a one pound pull in line with indicator plunger and read movement on indicator. Movement must not exceed .006 inch. If movement exceeds limit, replace either housing or shaft to bring movement back within tolerance.

DISTRIBUTOR SERVICE
Distributor Disassemble

1. Remove rotor and vacuum advance unit, Fig. 8.

2. Remove reluctor. If reluctor cannot be pulled off easily, use two screwdrivers with a $7/16$ inch blade to pry up from bottom of reluctor. Use extreme caution not to damage teeth on reluctor.

3. Remove two screws from lower plate and lift out lower and upper plates and pick-up coil as an assembly.

4. On six cylinder distributors, remove drive gear retaining pin and slide gear

from shaft. Support gear so that gear teeth will not be damaged when pin is driven from shaft. On V8 distributors, remove shaft retaining pin and slide retainer from shaft.

5. Remove lower thrust washer by cleaning burrs from around pin hole.

6. Push up on shaft and remove through top of housing.

Distributor Assemble

1. Lubricate and test operation of governor weights. Inspect weight springs for distortion and bearing surfaces and pins for damage.

2. Lubricate upper thrust washer and install onto shaft. Install shaft into housing.

3. On six cylinder distributors, if drive gear is damaged, replace gear as outlined in the Standard Distributor section in this chapter. On V8 distributors, install shaft retainer and pin.

4. Install lower and upper plates and pick-up coil as an assembly.

5. Connect vacuum advance unit arm to pick-up plate and install vacuum unit mounting screws.

6. Place reluctor keeper pin into position on reluctor sleeve and slide reluctor downward on sleeve and press into place firmly. On V-8 distributors, the reluctor is installed with the two arrows on top.

NOTE: Distributors on V-8 engines may rotate either clockwise or counter-clockwise. The arrow at the keeper pin must point in the direction of distributor rotation. If not, remove reluctor and turn it 180 degrees and reinstall it. When removing reluctor, use care not to lose keeper pin.

7. Place 1 drop of light engine oil on felt pad on top of reluctor and install rotor.

Pick-up Replacement & Air Gap Adjustment

1. With distributor removed from vehicle,

perform Steps 1 to 3 as outlined in Distributor Disassemble.

2. Remove pick-up coil and upper plate by depressing retainer clip and moving it away from mounting stud. Pick-up coil cannot be removed from upper plate.

3. Lightly lubricate upper plate pivot pin and lower plate support pins with distributor lubricant. Install upper plate pivot pin through smallest hole in lower plate and install retainer clip.

NOTE: The upper plate must ride on the support pins on the lower plate.

4. Install lower and upper plates and pick-up coil as an assembly and install distributor into vehicle.

5. To set air gap, align one reluctor tooth with pick-up pole and install a non-magnetic feeler gauge——.008 inch on 1974-76 units or .006 inch on 1977-78 units, between reluctor tooth and pick-up pole, Fig. 9. Rotate pick-up coil until contact is made between reluctor tooth, feeler gauge and pick-up pole. Tighten pick-up coil hold down screw and remove feeler gauge. The feeler gauge should be removed without force. If not, readjust gap.

6. Perform a secondary gap check with a feeler gauge——.010 inch on 1974-76 units or .008 inch on 1977-78 units. Do not force feeler gauge between reluctor tooth and pick-up pole since it is possible to do so. Apply vacuum to vacuum control unit. Pick-up should not contact reluctor tooth. Readjust air gap if contact occurs.

NOTE: If pick-up contacts reluctor teeth on one side of shaft only, the distributor shaft most likely is bent and shaft replacement is required.

CHRYSLER ELECTRONIC LEAN BURN EXC. HORIZON & OMNI

Ignition System Starting Test

1. Remove the coil wire from distributor cap and hold end of wire about ¼ in. from a good engine ground. Crank engine and observe spark at coil wire.

2. The spark at the coil wire must be constant and bright blue in color. If so, continue to crank engine and slowly move coil wire away from ground. If arcing occurs at the coil tower, replace coil. If spark is weak or not constant or there is no spark, proceed to the "Failure To Start Test."

3. If spark is satisfactory and no arcing occurs at coil tower, the ignition system is producing the necessary high secondary voltage. However, this voltage is transmitted to the spark plugs by checking the distributor rotor, cap, spark plug wires, and spark plugs. If satisfactory, the ignition system is not faulty. It will be necessary to check the fuel system and engine mechanical components.

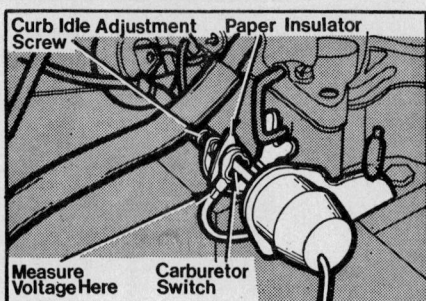

Fig. 1   Power & vacuum transducer tests

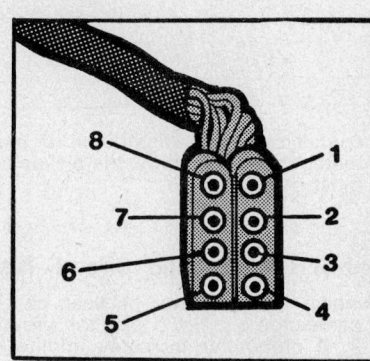

Fig. 2   Dual connector. 1976-77 Exc. Diplomat & LeBaron

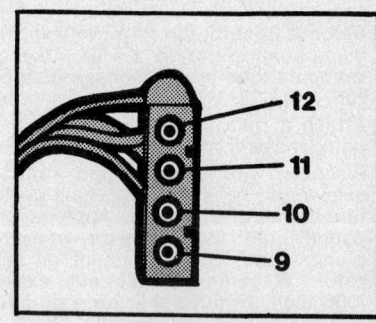

Fig. 3   Single connector. 1976-77 Exc. Diplomat & LeBaron

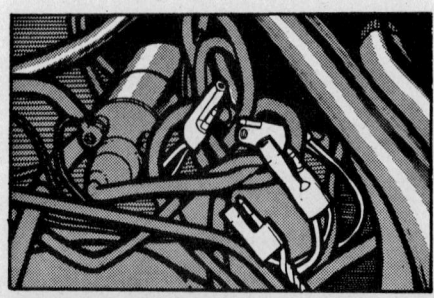

Fig. 4   Distributor leads. 1976-77 Exc. Diplomat & LeBaron

Failure To Start Test

NOTE: Before proceeding with this test, perform "Ignition System Starting Test". Failure to do so may lead to unnecessary diagnostic time and incorrect test results.

1976-77 Exc. Diplomat & LeBaron

1. With a voltmeter, measure and note voltage at battery. Battery specific gravity must be at least 1.220, temperature corrected, to deliver the necessary voltage to operate the cranking and ignition systems properly.

2. Disconnect wiring harness connector from "Coolant Switch."

3. Place a piece of paper between curb idle adjusting screw and carburetor switch, Fig. 1, or ensure curb idle adjusting screw is not contacting switch.

4. Connect negative lead of voltmeter to an engine ground.

5. Turn ignition switch to "Run" position and measure voltage at carburetor switch terminal, Fig. 1. If voltage is greater than 5 volts but less than 10 volts, proceed to Step 7. If voltage is greater than 10 volts, check continuity between terminal 2 of the dual connector and the ground with ignition switch in "Off" position. Continuity should be noted. If voltage is less than 5 volts, turn ignition switch to "OFF" and disconnect dual connector from bottom of "Spark Control Computer". Turn ignition switch to "Run" and measure voltage at terminal 4 of dual connector, Fig. 2. Voltage should be within 1 volt of battery voltage. If voltage is satisfactory, proceed to Step 6. If not, check wiring between terminal 4 of dual connector, Fig. 2, and ignition switch for opens, shorts or improper connections.

6. Turn ignition switch to "OFF" and disconnect single connector from bottom of "Spark Control Computer." Check continuity between terminal 11 of single connector, Fig. 3, and carburetor switch terminal. There should be continuity between these two points. If not, check wiring for opens, shorts or improper connections. If continuity is noted, check continuity between terminal 2 of dual connector, Fig. 2, and the ground. If continuity is noted, replace "Spark Control Computer". If not, check wiring for opens or improper connections and only proceed to Step 7 if engine still fails to start.

7. Turn ignition switch to "Run" and with positive lead of voltmeter, measure voltage at terminals 7 and 8 of disconnected leads from computer, Fig. 2. Voltage should be within 1 volt

PICK UP AIR GAP SPECIFICATIONS CHART

1976-77 Exc. Diplomat & LeBaron

	Set	Check
Start Pick Up	.008"	.010"
Run Pick Up	.012"	.014"

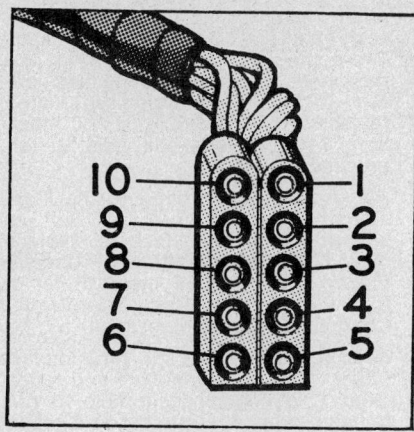

Fig. 5 Dual Connector. 1977 Diplomat & LeBaron; 1978 All

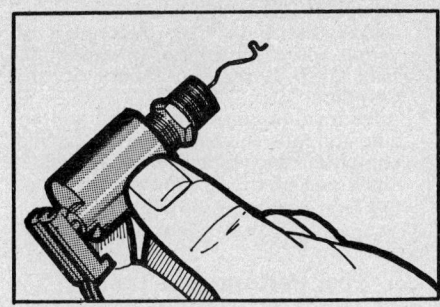

Fig. 7 Throttle transducer

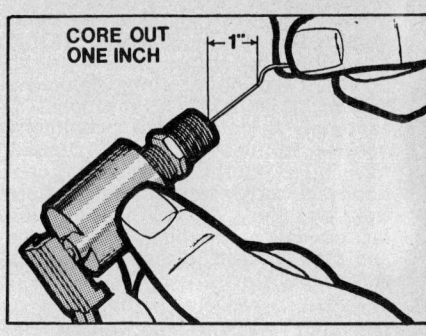

Fig. 8 Checking with test transducer

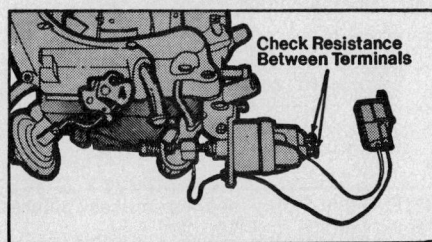

Fig. 6 Transducer terminal resistance & idle stop solenoid checks

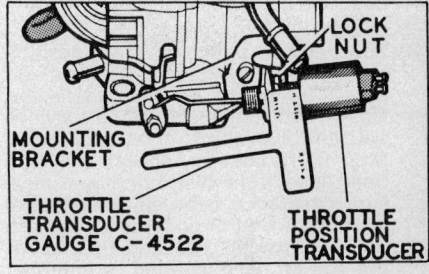

Fig. 9 Throttle position transducer adjustment. 1978

Pick-up Air Gap Specification Chart for air gap dimensions.

11. Install distributor cap, reconnect all wiring and start engine. If engine still fails to start, replace "Spark Control Computer".

12. After installing new computer and engine still fails to start, reinstall original one and repeat test procedure, since one of the test procedures may not have been performed correctly.

1977 Diplomat & LeBaron; 1978 All

1. With a voltmeter, measure and note battery voltage. Battery specific gravity must be at least 1.220, temperature corrected, to deliver the necessary voltage to operate the cranking and ignition systems properly.

2. Disconnect wiring harness connector from coolant switch.

3. Place a piece of paper between curb idle adjusting screw and carburetor switch, Fig. 1, or ensure curb idle adjusting screw is not contacting carburetor switch.

4. Connect negative lead of voltmeter to an engine ground.

5. Turn ignition switch to "Run" position and measure voltage at carburetor switch, Fig. 1. If voltage is greater than 5 volts but less than 10 volts, proceed to Step 7. If voltage is greater than 10 volts, turn ignition switch to "Off" position and disconnect dual connector from bottom of "Spark

of battery voltage. If so, proceed to Step 8. If not, proceed as follows:
Terminal 7—Check wiring and connections between connector and ignition switch. Also, check 5 ohm side of ballast resistor.
Terminal 8—Check wiring and connections between connector and ignition switch. Also, check primary windings of coil and 1/2 ohm side of ballast resistor.

8. Turn ignition switch to "OFF" position and measure resistance between terminals 5 and 6 of dual connector Fig. 2. Resistance should be between 150 and 900 ohms. If resistance is satisfactory, proceed to Step 9. If not, disconnect "Start Pick Up" coil leads from distributor and measure resistance at distributor leads, Fig. 4. If resistance is between 150 and 900 ohms, there is an open, shorted, or improper connection between distributor connector and terminals 5 and 6 of dual connector, Fig. 2. If resistance is not within specifications, the "Start Pick Up" coil is faulty.

9. Connect one lead of ohmmeter to engine ground and with other lead, check for continuity at each terminal of distributor leads, Fig. 4. There should be no continuity. Reconnect distributor leads and proceed to Step 10. If there is continuity, replace "Start Pick Up" coil.

10. Remove distributor cap and check and adjust air gap of "Start Pick Up" coil outlined under "Pick-up Replacement & Air Gap Adjustment", Chrysler Electronic Ignition System. Refer to the

Control Computer", Fig. 5, then check continuity between terminal 10 and the ground. If voltage is less than 5 volts, disconnect dual connector from "Spark Control Computer" with ignition switch in "Off" position. Then, turn ignition switch to "Run" position and measure voltage at terminal 2 of the dual connector, Fig. 5. Voltage should be within one volt of battery voltage. If voltage is satisfactory, proceed to Step 6. If not, check wiring between terminal 2, Fig. 5, and the ignition switch for opens, shorts or improper connections.

6. With ignition switch in "Off" position, check continuity between terminal 7

1976 CHRYSLER LEAN BURN SPECIFICATION CHART

Advance Schedules For Testing	Amount of Additional Advance[1]
Start Timer Advance Schedule	5° to 9°
Throttle Advance Schedule	
a) Test Transducer Core Out 1 inch	7° to 12° @ 75°F 4° to 7° @ 104°F
b) Test Transducer Core Moved Quickly In and Out	7° to 12° for approximately 1 second
Vacuum Transducer Advance Schedule	2° to 5° @ 16" minimum vacuum as soon as carb switch is isolated with paper 32° to 35° @ 16" minimum vacuum after 6 to 9 minutes

[1]—Additional advance does not include basic timing signal advance.

of dual connector, Fig. 5, and the carburetor switch terminal. There should be continuity between these two points. If not, check wiring for opens, shorts or improper connections. If continuity is noted, check continuity between terminal 10 of dual connector, Fig. 5, and the ground. If continuity is noted, replace "Spark Control Computer". If not, check wiring for opens or improper connections and only proceed to Step 7 if engine still fails to start.

7. Turn ignition switch to "Run" position and measure the voltage between terminal 1, Fig. 5, and the ground. Voltage should be within one volt of battery voltage. If so, proceed to Step 8. If not, proceed as follows: Terminal 1—Check wiring and connections between dual connector and ignition switch.

8. Turn ignition switch to "Off" position and measure resistance between terminals 5 and 9 of dual connector, Fig. 5. Resistance should be between 150 and 900 ohms. If so, proceed to Step 9. If not, disconnect "Pick-Up Coil" lead from distributor and measure resistance between terminals at distributor side of connector. If resistance is between 150 and 900 ohms, there is an open, shorted or improper connection between the distributor connector and terminals 5 and 9 of the dual connector. If resistance is still not within specifications, the "Pick-Up Coil" is faulty.

9. Check for continuity between each connector on distributor side of distributor connector and the engine ground. There should be no continuity. Reconnect distributor connector and proceed to Step 10. If continuity is present, replace "Pick-Up Coil".

10. Remove distributor cap and air gap of "Pick-Up Coil". Refer to "Pick-Up Replacement & Air Gap Adjustment",

Chrysler Electronic Ignition System. Adjust air gap if necessary.

11. Install distributor cap, reconnect all wiring and start engine. If engine still fails to start, replace "Spark Control Computer".

12. After installing new computer and engine still fails to start, reinstall original computer and repeat test procedure since one of the test procedures may not have been performed correctly.

Poor Performance Tests

Run Pick-Up Function Test, 1976-77 Exc. Diplomat & LeBaron

1. Start and run engine for about 1½ minutes. Then, disconnect "Start Pick Up" lead from distributor. If engine continues to run, reconnect "Start Pick Up" lead and proceed to "Start Timer Advance Schedule Test." If engine stopped proceed to Step 2.

2. Reconnect "Start Pick Up" lead at distributor, turn ignition switch to "OFF" and disconnect dual connector from bottom of "Spark Control Computer." Measure resistance between terminals 3 and 5 of dual connector, Fig. 2. Resistance should be between 150 and 900 ohms. If so, proceed to Step 3. If not, disconnect "Run Pick Up" coil leads from distributor and measure resistance at distributor leads. If resistance is now between 150 and 900 ohms, check for open, shorted or improper connections of the wiring between distributor connector and terminals 3 and 5 of dual connector, Fig. 2. If resistance is not within specifications, the "Run Pick Up" coil is faulty. Replace "Run Pick Up" coil and repeat Step 1. If engine still fails to run, proceed to Step 3.

3. Disconnect "Run Pick Up" coil from distributor. Connect one lead of ohmmeter to an engine ground and, with

other lead, check for continuity at each terminal of distributor leads. There should be no continuity. If not, reconnect distributor leads and proceed to Step 4. If continuity is noted, replace "Run Pick Up" coil and repeat Step 1. If engines still fails to run, proceed to Step 4.

4. Remove distributor cap and check and adjust air gap of "Run Pick Up" coil as outlined under "Pick-up Replacement & Air Gap Adjustment", Chrysler Electronic Ignition System. Refer to the Pick-up Air Gap Specification Chart for air gap dimensions.

5. If engine still fails to run, replace "Spark Control Computer" and repeat Step 1. If engine again fails to run, reinstall original computer and repeat complete test since one of the test procedures may not have been performed correctly.

Start Timer Advance Schedule Test

1. Connect an adjustable timing light to engine so total timing advance at crankshaft can be checked.

2. Start engine, snap throttle open and close and immediately place gear selector in drive.

NOTE: Fully apply service brakes before placing vehicle in drive.

Observe timing mark on crankshaft damper immediately after vehicle is in drive and adjust timing light so basic timing signal is observed at timing plate. The meter on the timing light should indicate amount of advance as indicated under specifications. Continue to observe timing for one minute on 1976 models or 90 seconds on 1977-78 models while adjusting timing light to maintain basic timing signal.

1977 CHRYSLER LEAN BURN SPECIFICATION CHART

Spark Control Computer	4091072① (4094022)②	4091073① (4094008)②	4091074① (4094023)②	4091195① (4106056)②
Start Timer Advance Schedule	5°–9°	5°–9°	5°–9°	8°
Delay Time In Seconds	90	90	90	90
Throttle Advance Schedule	10°③			
a) Test Transducer Core Out 1 inch	6°–10° @ 75°F 3°–6° @ 105°F	8°–12°	3°–5° @ 75°F 2°–3° @ 105°F	8°–12°
b) Test Transducer Core Moved Quickly In and Out	10°	10°	5°	—
Vacuum Advance Schedule				
a) Operating Vacuum Range	0 to 16 Inches Hg	0 to 16 Inches Hg	0 to 12 Inches Hg	0 to 14 Inches Hg
b) Advance Off Idle (Carb. Switch Isolated With Paper)	3°–5°	6°–8°	None	13°–15°
c) Accumulation Time in Minutes	7–9	7–9	7–9	8
d) Advance After Accumulation Time	34°	34°	28°	32°–36°
Speed Advance				
Ground Carb. Switch and Disconnect Throttle Transducer Before Checking	3°–5° @ 2000 rpm	1°–3° @ 2000 rpm	7°–9° @ 1200 rpm	1°–3° @ 2000 rpm 3°–7° @ 4000 rpm

Continued

1977 CHRYSLER LEAN BURN SPECIFICATION CHART—Continued

Spark Control Computer	4091421①	4091440①	4091468①	4091476①
	(4094021)②	(4094022)②	(4057923)②	(4094026)②
Start Timer Advance Schedule	5°–9°	5°–9°	8°	5°–9°
Delay Time In Seconds	90	90	90	90
Throttle Advance Schedule				
a) Test Transducer Core Out 1 inch	7°–9° @ 75°F 5°–7° @ 105°F	8°–12°	8°–12°	7°–9° @ 75°F 5°–7° @ 105°F
b) Test Transducer Core Moved Quickly In and Out	8°	10°	—	8°
Vacuum Advance Schedule				
a) Operating Vacuum Range	0 to 12 Inches Hg	0 to 16 Inches Hg	0 to 14 Inches Hg	0 to 12 Inches Hg
b) Advance Off Idle (Carb. Switch Isolated With Paper)	None	3°–5°	None	None
c) Accumulation Time in Minutes	7–9	7–9	8	7–9
d) Advance After Accumulation Time	30°	34°	32°–36°	28°
Speed Advance				
Ground Carb. Switch and Disconnect Throttle Transducer Before Checking	5°–7° @ 2000 rpm	2°–4° @ 2000 rpm	1°–3° @ 2000 rpm 3°–7° @ 4000 rpm	0°–2° @ 2000 rpm

Spark Control Computer	4091477①	4091946①	4091447①	4091448①
	(4094023)②	(4106057)②	(4106055)②	(4106056)②
Start Timer Advance Schedule	5°–9°	8°	8°	8°
Delay Time In Seconds	90	90	90	90
Throttle Advance Schedule				
a) Test Transducer Core Out 1 inch	4°–6°	3°–5°	3°–5°	3°–5°
b) Test Transducer Core Moved Quickly In and Out	5°	—	—	—
Vacuum Advance Schedule				
a) Operating Vacuum Range	0 to 12 Inches Hg	0 to 14 Inches Hg	0 to 14 Inches Hg	0 to 14 Inches Hg
b) Advance Off Idle (Carb. Switch Isolated With Paper)	None	4°–8°	None	10°–14°
c) Accumulation Time in Minutes	7–9	8	8	8
d) Advance After Accumulation Time	28°	26°–30°	32°–36°	26°–30°
Speed Advance				
Ground Carb. Switch and Disconnect Throttle Transducer Before Checking	7°–11° @ 2000 rpm	0°–3° @ 2000 rpm 1°–5° @ 4000 rpm	0°–3° @ 2000 rpm 1°–5° @ 4000 rpm	0°–3° @ 2000 rpm 1°–5° @ 4000 rpm

①—Production part number.
②—Remanufactured part number.
③—If equipped with remanufactured spark control computer, disregard temperature specifications since there is no air temperature sensor.

TUNE UP SERVICE

1978 CHRYSLER LEAN BURN SPECIFICATION CHART

Spark Control Computer	4091730①	4091731①	4091732①	4091786①
	(4106061)②	(4106067)②	(4106068)②	(4106069)②
Start Timer Advance Schedule	8°	8°	8°	8°
Delay Time In Seconds	60	60	60	60
Throttle Advance Schedule				
Test Transducer Core	7°–9° @ 100°F	4°–6° @ 100°F	5°–7° @ 100°F	5°–7° @ 100°F
Out 1 Inch	3°–6° @ 140°F	2°–4° @ 140°F	2°–5° @ 140°F	2°–4° @ 140°F
Vacuum Advance Schedule				
a) Operating Vacuum Range	0 to 12 Inches Hg	0 to 14 Inches Hg	0 to 14 Inches Hg	0 to 15.5 Inches Hg
b) Advance Off Idle (Carb. Switch Isolated With Paper)	None	7°–11°	None	5°–9°
c) Accumulation Time In Minutes	8	8	8	7
d) Advance After Accumulation Time	28°–32°	23°–27°	26°–30°	18°–22°
Speed Advance				
Ground Carb. Switch and Disconnect Throttle Transducer Before Checking	4°–8° @ 2000 rpm	4°–8° @ 2000 rpm	0°–3° @ 2000 rpm	0°–1° @ 2000 rpm
	8°–12° @ 4000 rpm	10°–14° @ 4000 rpm	2°–6° @ 4000 rpm	0°–2° @ 4000 rpm

Spark Control Computer	4091787①	4091788①	4091791①	4091923①
	(4106070)②	(4106071)②	(4106073)②	
Start Timer Advance Schedule	8°	8°	8°	8°
Delay Time In Seconds	60	60	60	60
Throttle Advance Schedule				
Test Transducer Core	5°–7° @ 100°F	7°–9° @ 100°F	4°–6° @ 100°F	5°–7° @ 100°F
Out 1 Inch	2°–4° @ 140°F	4°–6° @ 140°F	1°–4° @ 140°F	2°–5° @ 140°F
Vacuum Advance Schedule				
a) Operating Vacuum Range	0 to 14 Inches Hg	0 to 14 Inches Hg	0 to 12 Inches Hg	0 to 14 Inches Hg
b) Advance Off Idle (Carb. Switch Isolated With Paper)	None	7°–11°	None	8°–12°
c) Accumulation Time In Minutes	8	8	8	8
d) Advance After Accumulation Time	23°–27°	20°–24°	20°–24°	24°–28°
Speed Advance				
Ground Carb. Switch and Disconnect Throttle Transducer Before Checking	2°–5° @ 2000 rpm	1°–5° @ 2000 rpm	7°–11° @ 2000 rpm	1°–4° @ 2000 rpm
	7°–11° @ 4000 rpm	4°–8° @ 4000 rpm	8°–12° @ 4000 rpm	6°–10° @ 4000 rpm

1978 CHRYSLER LEAN BURN SPECIFICATION CHART—Continued

Spark Control Computer	4091924①	4091954①	4091955①	4111012①
	(4106075)②	(4106076)②	(4106077)②	(4106079)②
Start Timer Advance Schedule	8°	8°	8°	8°
Delay Time In Seconds	60	60	60	60
Throttle Advance Schedule				
Test Transducer Core	9°–11° @ 100°F	5°–7° @ 100°F	7°–9° @ 100°F	
Out 1 Inch	5°–8° @ 140°F	2°–5° @ 140°F	4°–6° @ 140°F	0°
Vacuum Advance Schedule				
a) Operating Vacuum Range	0 to 14 Inches Hg	0 to 15.5 Inches Hg	0 to 14 Inches Hg	0 to 15.5 Inches Hg
b) Advance Off Idle (Carb. Switch Isolated With Paper)	None	None	7°–11°	None
c) Accumulation Time In Minutes	8	8	7	8
d) Advance After Accumulation Time	21°–25°	18°–22°	20°–24°	18°–22°
Speed Advance				
Ground Carb. Switch and Disconnect Throttle Transducer Before Checking	10°–15° @ 2000 rpm	0°–1° @ 2000 rpm	1°–5° @ 2000 rpm	4°–8° @ 2000 rpm
	16°–21° @ 4000 rpm	0°–2° @ 4000 rpm	4°–8° @ 4000 rpm	6°–10° @ 4000 rpm

Spark Control Computer	4111013①	4111014①	4111015①	4111159①
	(4106080)②	(4106081)②	(4106082)②	(4106085)②
Start Timer Advance Schedule	8°	8°	8°	8°
Delay Time In Seconds	60	60	60	60
Throttle Advance Schedule				
Test Transducer Core	9°–11° @ 100°F	5°–7° @ 100°F	5°–7° @ 100°F	5°–7° @ 100°F
Out 1 Inch	5°–8° @ 140°F	2°–5° @ 140°F	2°–5° @ 140°F	2°–5° @ 140°F
Vacuum Advance Schedule				
a) Operating Vacuum Range	0 to 14 Inches Hg	0 to 12 Inches Hg	0 to 12 Inches Hg	0 to 15.5 Inches Hg
b) Advance Off Idle (Carb. Switch Isolated With Paper)	None	2°–6°	2°–6°	None
c) Accumulation Time In Minutes	8	8	8	8
d) Advance After Accumulation Time	21°–25°	18°–22°	18°–22°	18°–22°
Speed Advance				
Ground Carb. Switch and Disconnect Throttle Transducer Before Checking	10°–14° @ 2000 rpm	8°–12° @ 2000 rpm	8°–12° @ 2000 rpm	0–1° @ 2000 rpm
	16°–21° @ 4000 rpm	12°–16° @ 4000 rpm	12°–16° @ 4000 rpm	0–2° @ 4000 rpm

TUNE UP SERVICE

1978 CHRYSLER LEAN BURN SPECIFICATION CHART—Continued

Spark Control Computer	4111169①	4111170①	4111172①	4111217①
	(4106086)②	(4106087)②	(4106088)②	(4106089)②
Start Timer Advance Schedule	None	None	None	8°
Delay Time In Seconds	None	None	None	60
Throttle Advance Schedule				
Test Transducer Core	5°–7° @ 100°F	5°–7° @ 100°F	5°–7° @ 100°F	
Out 1 Inch	2°–5° @ 140°F	2°–5° @ 140°F	2°–7° @ 140°F	0°
Vacuum Advance Schedule				
a) Operating Vacuum Range	0 to 10 Inches Hg	0 to 10 Inches Hg	0 to 10 Inches Hg	4–14 Inches Hg
b) Advance Off Idle (Carb. Switch Isolated With Paper)	5°–9°	5°–9°	5°–9°	6°–10°
c) Accumulation Time In Minutes	8	8	8	7
d) Advance After Accumulation Time	16°–20°	16°–20°	16°–20°	18°–22°
Speed Advance				
Ground Carb. Switch and Disconnect Throttle Transducer Before Checking	1°–5° @ 2000 rpm	1°–5° @ 2000 rpm	1°–5° @ 2000 rpm	8°–12° @ 2000 rpm
	4°–8° @ 4000 rpm	4°–8° @ 4000 rpm	4°–8° @ 4000 rpm	12°–16° @ 4000 rpm

Spark Control Computer	4111218①	4111222①	4111253①	4111278①
Start Timer Advance Schedule	8°	8°	8°	8°
Delay Time In Seconds	60	60	60	60
Throttle Advance Schedule				
Test Transducer Core			5°–7° @ 100°F	7°–9° @ 100°F
Out 1 Inch	0°	0°	2°–5° @ 140°F	4°–6° @ 140°F
Vacuum Advance Schedule				
a) Operating Vacuum Range	4–14 Inches Hg	4–14 Inches Hg	0–10 Inches Hg	0–12 Inches Hg
b) Advance Off Idle (Carb. Switch Isolated With Paper)	2°–6°	2°–6°	None	None
c) Accumulation Time In Minutes	8	8	8	8
d) Advance After Accumulation Time	18°–22°	18°–22°	23°–27°	26°–30°
Speed Advance				
Ground Carb. Switch and Disconnect Throttle Transducer Before Checking	8°–12° @ 2000 rpm	8°–12° @ 2000 rpm	6°–11° @ 2000 rpm	0°–3° @ 2000 rpm
	12°–16° @ 4000 rpm	12°–16° @ 4000 rpm	11°–16° @ 4000 rpm	2°–6° @ 4000 rpm

reduce to the basic timing signal after approximately one minute. If timing did not increase and/or did not return to basic, replace "Spark Control Computer." If checked satisfactory, proceed to "Throttle Advance Schedule Test."

NOTE: Do not remove timing light since it is needed for further testing.

Speed Advance Schedule Test, 1977-78

NOTE: Before performing this test, ensure the basic timing signal and hot curb idle are within specifications. Disconnect wiring harness connector from throttle position transducer.

Start and run engine for two minutes. Increase engine speed to specified test level and adjust timing light so that basic timing is observed at timing indicator. The additional advance observed on the timing light meter should be as specified. Refer to the Chrysler Lean Burn Specification Charts. If advance is not within specifications, replace "Spark Control Computer" and repeat test.

Throttle Advance Schedule Test, 1976-77 Exc. Diplomat & LeBaron

NOTE: Before proceeding with test, ensure "Throttle Position Transducer" is adjusted properly.

1. Place ignition switch in the "OFF" position and disconnect single connector from bottom of "Spark Control Computer."

2. Measure resistance between terminals 9 and 10 of single connector, Fig. 3. Resistance should be between 50 and 90 ohms. If so, reconnect single connector and proceed to Step 3. If not, remove connector from "Throttle Position Transducer" and measure resistance at transducer terminals, Fig. 5. If resistance is between 50 and 90 ohms, there is an open, short, or improper connection of wiring between terminals 9 and 10 of single connector, Fig. 3, and the terminals connecting to the transducer. If resistance is not within specifications, replace "Throttle Position Transducer" and proceed to Step 3.

3. Reconnect all wiring and turn ignition switch to the "Run" position but do not start engine. Connect negative lead of a voltmeter to an engine ground. With positive lead of voltmeter, touch one terminal of "Throttle Position Transducer", Fig. 6, while fully opening throttle of carburetor and closing. Observe voltmeter reading. Repeat procedure with other terminal of transducer. Either of the terminals should show approximately a 2 volt change on voltmeter when throttle is opened and closed. If 2 volt change is noted, proceed to Step 4. If not, do not replace transducer since the "Spark Control Computer" can cause transducer to function improperly. It will be necessary to proceed to Step 4 to check malfunction.

1978 CHRYSLER LEAN BURN SPECIFICATION CHART—Continued

Spark Control Computer	4111283①	4145237①
Start Timer Advance Schedule	8°	8°
Delay Time In Seconds	60	60
Throttle Advance Schedule		
Test Transducer Core	7°–9° @ 100°F.	9°–11° @ 100°F.
Out 1 Inch	4°–6° @ 140°F.	5°–8° @ 140°F.
Vacuum Advance Schedule		
a) Operating Vacuum Range	0–12 Inches Hg	0–14 Inches Hg
b) Advance Off Idle (Carb. Switch Isolated With Paper	None	None
c) Accumulation Time In Minutes	8	8
d) Advance After Accumulation Time	26°–30°	26°–30°
Speed Advance		
Ground Carb. Switch and Disconnect Throttle Transducer	0–3° @ 2000 rpm	10°–14° @ 2000 rpm
Before Checking	2°–6° @ 4000 rpm	16°–21° @ 4000 rpm

①—Production part number.
②—Remanufactured part number.

4. Position throttle linkage on fast idle cam, ground carburetor switch with a jumper wire, disconnect wiring harness connector from "Throttle Position Transducer", and connect harness connector to a known good transducer of the same type suitable for testing.

5. Move core of test transducer inward to fully bottom out, start engine, wait 90 seconds, then move core outward about 1 inch, Fig. 8.

6. Adjust timing light so basic timing signal is observed at timing plate. The meter on the timing light should indicate additional amount of advance as listed under specifications. If advance is within specifications, move core back into transducer and timing should return to basic setting. If timing advanced and returned, proceed to Step 7. If timing did not advance and/or did not return, replace "Spark Control Computer." Also, after replacing computer, recheck "Throttle Position Transducer" as described in Step 3, to ensure transducer is satisfactory. If not, replace transducer.

7. Return timing light meter to zero and move core of test transducer inward and outward about 1 inch, Fig. 8, 5 or 6 times very quickly and observe timing marks. There should be additional advance as listed under specifications for about one second and then return to basic setting. If not, replace "Spark Control Computer". Also, if "Throttle Position Transducer" failed in Step 3, replace transducer since "Spark Control Computer" is not causing it to check unsatisfactory.

8. Remove test transducer and reconnect all wiring.

Throttle Advance Schedule Test, 1977 Diplomat & LeBaron; 1978 All

NOTE: Before performing this test, ensure "Throttle Position Transducer" is adjusted properly.

1. With ignition switch in "Off" position, disconnect dual connector from "Spark Control Computer".

2. Measure resistance between terminals 8 and 9 of dual connector. Resistance should be between 50 and 90 ohms. If resistance is within specifications, reconnect connector and proceed to Step 3. If not, disconnect connector from "Throttle Position Transducer" and measure resistance between transducer terminals. If resistance is between 50 and 90 ohms, there is an open, short or improper connection between terminals 8 and 9 of dual connector and the "Throttle Position Transducer". If resistance is not within specifications, replace "Throttle Position Transducer".

3. Position throttle linkage on fast idle cam, ground carburetor switch with a jumper wire, disconnect "Throttle Position Transducer" connector and connect connector to a known good transducer of the same type suitable for testing.

4. Move core of test transducer inward to fully bottom out, start engine, wait 90 seconds and move core outward approximately one inch.

5. Adjust timing light so basic timing signal is observed at timing plate. The timing light meter should indicate additional amount of advance as indicated in the Chrysler Lean Burn Specification Charts. If within specifications, move core back into transducer and timing should return to basic setting. If timing did not advance and/or did not return to basic setting, replace "Spark Control Computer". Retest "Throttle Position Transducer" after replacing "Spark Control Computer".

Poor Fuel Economy & Unusually High Idle Speed Tests

Coolant Switch Test

1. Connect one lead of ohmmeter to an engine ground.
2. Connect other lead of ohmmeter to terminal of coolant switch having the black wire with tracer connected.

For Engine Cold

1. Continuity should be present at terminal. If not, replace coolant switch.

NOTE: Disregard terminal of coolant switch having the orange wire connected since the wire has no function in the system.

For Engine Above 150° F.

1. Terminal reading should show no continuity. If continuity is noted, replace coolant switch.

NOTE: Disregard terminal of coolant switch having orange wire connected since the wire has no function in the system.

Vacuum Advance Schedule Test, 1976-77 Exc. Diplomat & LeBaron

1. Connect and adjust timing light to engine so total timing advance at crankshaft can be checked.
2. On 1976 models, disconnect wiring harness connector from coolant switch. Check "Idle Stop Solenoid" by turning ignition key to "Run" position, but do not start engine. Disconnect solenoid lead wire, push plunger inward until bottomed out, and while holding throttle linkage open, reconnect solenoid lead wire, Fig. 5. The solenoid plunger should extend and remain extended. Release throttle linkage and plunger should hold throttle linkage open. If not, replace "Idle Stop Solenoid". Start and run engine to reach operating temperature.
3. Ensure the transmission is in neutral and the parking brake is applied.
4. Place a piece of paper between carburetor switch and curb idle adjustment screw, Fig. 1. If curb idle adjustment screw is not contacting carburetor switch, ensure fast idle cam is not in fast idle position or is binding, linkage is not binding, or throttle stop screw is not over adjusted. Adjust timing light so basic timing signal can be observed at timing plate. The meter on the timing light should indicate additional amount of advance as listed under the specifications. If advance is not within specifications, replace

"Spark Control Computer". If advance is within specifications, run engine for approximately 6 to 9 minutes and ensure a minimum of 16 inches of vacuum is available at the transducer.
5. After 6 to 9 minutes, adjust timing light so basic timing signal can be observed at timing plate. The timing light meter should indicate additional amount of advance as listed under specifications. If advance is not within specifications, replace spark control computer. If advance is within specifications, proceed to next step.
6. Remove paper installed between carburetor switch and curb idle adjustment screw. The timing should return to the basic setting. If timing does not return to basic setting, ensure the curb idle adjustment screw is contacting carburetor switch. Then, turn engine off and check wire between Terminal 11 of single connector, Fig. 3, at bottom of computer for opens, shorts and improper connections. If wiring is satisfactory, repeat test. If timing will not return to basic setting, replace "Spark Control Computer".

Vacuum Advance Schedule Test, 1977 Diplomat & LeBaron; 1978 All

1. Connect and adjust timing light so that total timing advance at crankshaft can be checked.
2. Start engine, place transmission in neutral and apply parking brake.
3. With engine at normal operating temperature, place a piece of paper between carburetor switch and curb idle adjusting screw, Fig. 1. If curb idle adjusting screw is not contacting carburetor switch, ensure that fast idle cam is not on or is not binding, linkage is not binding or throttle stop screw is not over adjusted. Adjust timing light so basic timing is observed at timing plate. Run engine for nine minutes and ensure there is a minimum of 16 inches of vacuum at the transducer. The timing light meter should indicate the additional amount of advance as listed in the Chrysler Lean Burn Specification Chart. If advance is not within specifications, replace "Spark Control Computer."
4. Remove piece of paper between carburetor switch and curb idle adjusting screw. Timing should return to basic setting. If timing does not return to basic setting, ensure that curb idle adjusting screw is not contacting carburetor switch. Then, turn engine "Off" and check wire between terminal 7 of the dual connector and carburetor switch terminal for opens, shorts or improper connections. If check is satisfactory and if timing still will not return to basic setting, replace "Spark Control Computer".

THROTTLE POSITION TRANSDUCER ADJUSTMENT

1976-77

This adjustment can only be performed when the "Air Temperature Sensor", located inside the computer, is below 135° F. If necessary to adjust the transducer

when the engine is at operating temperature, it is necessary to cool the "Air Temperature Sensor".

NOTE: The "Air Temperature Sensor" may be cooled with a suitable cooling agent to rapidly lower the temperature of the sensor. To cool the sensor, remove the air cleaner top, insert the spray nozzle of the cooling agent into the computer and direct the spray over the sensor for approximately 15 seconds or until it is frosted.

If adjustment procedure takes longer than 3 or 4 minutes, turn engine off and re-cool "Air Temperature Sensor".

1. Start engine and wait at least 1½ minutes before proceeding with procedure.
2. Connect a jumper wire between carburetor switch terminal and the ground.
3. Disconnect electrical connector from transducer.
4. Check and adjust timing at crankshaft, if necessary.
5. Reconnect transducer electrical connector and recheck timing at crankshaft.
6. If timing is greater than specified, loosen transducer locknut and rotate transducer clockwise until timing returns to specified limits. Then, turn transducer an additional ½ turn clockwise and tighten locknut. If timing is at the specified limits, loosen transducer locknut and rotate transducer counter-clockwise until timing just starts to advance from specified limit. At that point, turn transducer an additional ½ turn and tighten locknut.

DISTRIBUTOR SERVICE

Distributor service procedures are the same as outlined under the "Distributor Service" procedures for the Chrysler System Except Lean Burn. Note that the pick-up coil replacement is the same for both distributors, however, the specifications are different. Refer to the "Pick-Up Air Gap" Specifications Chart for the air gap dimension on the Electronic Lean Burn System.

1978

1. Disconnect connector from transducer.
2. Loosen locknut.
3. Place special tool C-4522 between outer portion of transducer and transducer mounting bracket, Fig. 9.
4. Adjust transducer by rotating transducer until a clearance fit is obtained.
5. Tighten locknut and reconnect connector.

HORIZON & OMNI ELECTRONIC LEAN BURN SYSTEM

Ignition System Starting Test

1. Remove coil wire from distributor cap

1978 HORIZON & OMNI LEAN BURN SPECIFICATION CHART

Spark Control Computer	5206467①	5206501①	5206516①	5206525①
	(4106062)②	(4106063)②	—	(4106065)②
Start Timer Advance Schedule	8°	8°	8°	8°
Delay Time In Seconds	60	60	60	60
Throttle Advance Schedule	—	—	—	—
Test Transducer Core			4°–6° @ 100°F	4°–6° @ 100°F
Out 1 Inch	0°	0°	4°–6° @ 140°F	4°–6° @ 140°F
Vacuum Advance Schedule	—	—	—	—
a) Operating Vacuum Range	0 to 14 Inches Hg	0 to 14 Inches Hg	0 to 14 Inches Hg	0 to 14 Inches Hg
b) Advance Off Idle (Carb. Switch Isolated With Paper)	None	6°–10°	2°–6°	2°–6°
c) Accumulation Time In Minutes	8	7	8	8
d) Advance After Accumulation Time	18°–22°	18°–22°	18°–22°	18°–22°
Speed Advance	—	—	—	—
Ground Carb. Switch and Disconnect Throttle Transducer Before Checking	6°–10° @ 2000 rpm	6°–10° @ 2000 rpm	6°–10° @ 2000 rpm	5°–9° @ 2000 rpm
	18°–22° @ 6000 rpm	18°–22° @ 6000 rpm	18°–22° @ 6000 rpm	13°–17° @ 6000 rpm

Spark Control Computer	5206526①	5206666①
	(4106066)②	(4106112)②
Start Timer Advance Schedule	8°	8°
Delay Time In Seconds	60	60
Throttle Advance Schedule	—	—
Test Transducer Core		4°–6° @ 100°F
Out 1 Inch	0°	4°–6° @ 140°F
Vacuum Advance Schedule	—	—
a) Operating Vacuum Range	0 to 14 Inches Hg	0 to 14 Inches Hg
b) Advance Off Idle (Carb. Switch Isolated With Paper)	2°–6°	6°–10°
c) Accumulation Time In Minutes	8	7
d) Advance After Accumulation Time	18°–22°	18°–22°
Speed Advance	—	—
Ground Carb. Switch and Disconnect Throttle Transducer Before Checking	6°–10° @ 2000 rpm	5°–9° @ 2000 rpm
	18°–22° @ 6000 rpm	13°–17° @ 6000 rpm

①—Production part number.
②—Remanufactured part number.

and hold end of wire approximately 1/4 inch from a good engine ground. Crank engine and observe spark at coil wire.

2. The spark at the coil wire must be constant and bright blue in color. If so, continue to crank engine and slowly move coil wire away from the ground. If arcing occurs at the coil tower, replace coil. If spark is weak, not constant or there is no spark, proceed to the "Failure To Start Test".

3. If spark is satisfactory and no arcing occurs at the coil tower, the ignition system is producing the necessary high secondary voltage. However, this voltage is transmitted to the spark plugs by the distributor rotor, cap, spark plug wires and spark plugs and must also be checked. If satisfactory, the ignition system is not at fault. It will be necessary to check the fuel system and engine mechanical components.

Failure To Start Test

NOTE: Before performing this test, perform the "Ignition System Starting Test". Failure to do so may lead to unnecessary diagnostic time and incorrect test results.

1. With a voltmeter, measure and note battery voltage. Battery specific gravity must be at least 1.220, temperature corrected, to deliver the necessary voltage to operate the cranking and ignition systems properly.
2. Disconnect wire from ignition coil negative terminal.
3. Remove coil wire from distributor cap.
4. With ignition switch in "On" position and using a jumper wire, momentarily ground the ignition coil negative terminal while holding the coil wire 1/4 inch from a good engine ground. A spark should be obtained.
5. If no spark was obtained in Step 4, measure voltage at ignition coil positive terminal. Voltage should be at least 9 volts. If specified voltage is noted, the ignition coil is defective, requiring replacement. If specified voltage is not noted, check ballast resistor, wiring and connections. If engine still does not start, proceed to Step 6.

6. If spark was obtained in Step 4, turn ignition switch to "Off" position, reconnect ignition coil negative terminal wire and disconnect the distributor 3-wire harness, Fig. 1.

7. Turn ignition switch to "On" position and measure voltage between pin "B" on harness connector and the engine ground, Fig. 1. Voltage obtained should be battery voltage. If battery voltage is obtained, proceed to Step 11. If not, proceed to Step 8.

8. Turn ignition switch to "Off" position and disconnect the 10-wire harness connector from "Spark Control Computer", Fig. 2.

NOTE: Do not remove grease from harness connector or connector cavity since the grease is used to prevent moisture from corroding the terminals. There must be at least 1/4 inch of grease on the bottom of the computer connector cavity. If not, apply a liberal amount of Mopar Multi-purpose grease, part number 2932524, or equivalent over end of connector plug before reinstallation.

9. Check continuity between pin "B" of the distributor connector, Fig. 1, and terminal 3 of the "Spark Control Computer" connector, Fig. 2. If continuity is not noted, repair wire. If continuity exists, proceed to Step 10.

10. Turn ignition switch to "On" position and measure voltage between terminals 2 and 10 of the "Spark Control Computer" connector. Battery voltage should be obtained. If not, check wiring and connections. If battery voltage is obtained, the "Spark Control Computer" is defective, requiring replacement.

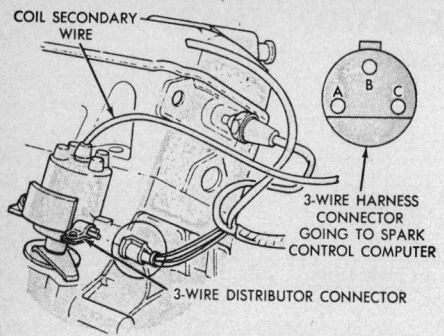

Fig. 1   Distributor 3-wire harness connector

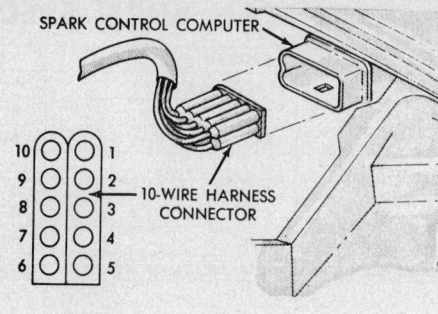

Fig. 2   Spark control computer 10-wire connector

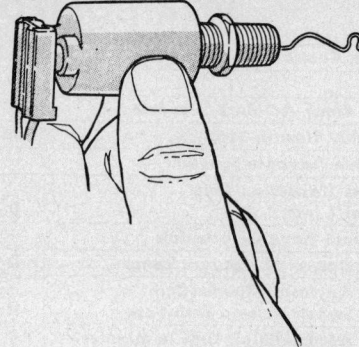

Fig. 3   Throttle position transducer

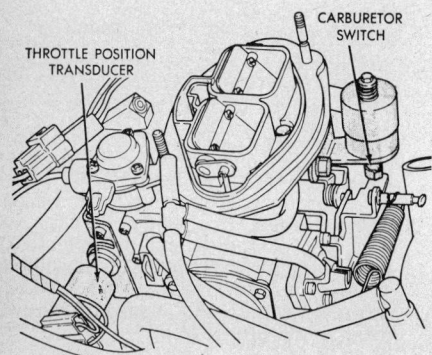

Fig. 4   Carburetor switch & throttle position transducer

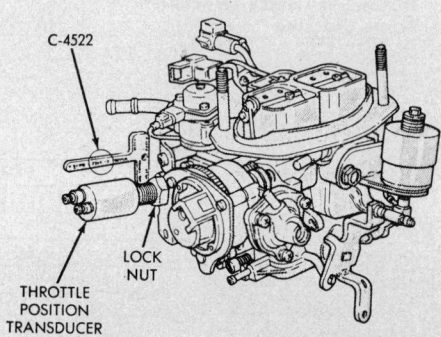

Fig. 5   Throttle position transducer adjustment

11. Connect "Spark Control Computer" 10-wire harness connector, turn ignition switch to "On" position and hold coil wire 1/4 inch from a good ground. Using a jumper wire, momentarily connect pins "A" and "C" of the distributor connector, Fig. 1. A spark should be obtained. If not, proceed to Step 12. If a spark is obtained, the Hall Effect Pick-up assembly is defective, requiring replacement.

12. Turn ignition to "Off" position and disconnect "Spark Control Computer" 10-wire harness connector, Fig. 2.

13. Check continuity between pin "C" of the 3-wire distributor connector, Fig. 1, and terminal 9 of the "Spark Control Computer" connector, Fig. 2. Also check continuity between pin "A" of distributor connector, Fig. 1, and terminal 5 of the "Spark Control Computer" connector, Fig. 2. If continuity exists, the "Spark Control Computer" is defective, requiring replacement. If no continuity exists, repair wiring and repeat Step 11.

Poor Performance Tests

Carburetor Switch Test

1. With ignition switch in "Off" position, disconnect 10-wire harness connector from "Spark Control Computer."

2. With throttle completely closed, check continuity between terminal 7 and the engine ground, Fig. 2. Continuity should exist. If not, check wiring and carburetor switch.

3. With throttle opened, check continuity between terminal 7 and the engine ground, Fig. 2. Continuity should not exist.

Coolant Switch Test

1. With ignition switch in "Off" position, disconnect wire from coolant switch.

2. Check continuity between coolant switch terminal and the engine ground. The ohmmeter readings should be as follows: Engine cold, below 150°—Continuity should exist. If not, replace coolant switch. Engine hot, above 150°—No continuity should exist. If continuity exists, replace coolant switch.

Start Advance Timing Test

1. Connect an adjustable timing light to engine so total timing advance can be checked.

2. Connect a jumper wire between carburetor switch and the engine ground.

3. Start engine and adjust timing light to align specified timing marks. The timing light meter should indicate the amount of advance listed in the Horizon & Omni Lean Burn Specification Chart. Continue to observe timing for 90 seconds while adjusting timing light to maintain basic timing signal. If timing did not increase and/or did not return to basic setting, replace "Spark Control Computer".

Speed Advance Test

1. Disconnect connector from "Throttle Position Transducer", manual transmission model.

2. Start and run engine for two minutes. Increase engine speed to specified test level and adjust timing light so basic timing setting can be observed at timing indicator. The timing light meter should indicate additional advance as listed in the Horizon and Omni Lean Burn Specification Chart. If not, replace "Spark Control Computer" and repeat test.

Throttle Advance Test, Manual Trans.

NOTE: Before performing this test, ensure the "Throttle Position Transducer" is properly adjusted.

1. With ignition switch in "Off" position, disconnect 10-wire harness connector from "Spark Control Computer", Fig. 2.

2. Measure resistance between terminals 8 and 9 of connector, Fig. 2. Resistance should be 50 to 90 ohms. If resistance is within specifications, connect connector and proceed to Step 3. If resistance is not within specifications, disconnect connector from "Throttle Position Transducer" and measure resistance between transducer terminals. If resistance is between 50 and 90 ohms, there is an open, short or improper connection between terminals 8 and 9 of "Spark Control Computer" connector and the "Throttle Position Transducer" connector. If resistance is not within specifications, replace "Throttle Position Transducer".

3. Place throttle linkage on fast idle cam, ground carburetor switch with a jumper wire, disconnect connector from "Throttle Position Transducer" and connect connector to a known good transducer of the same type suitable for testing.

4. Move core of test transducer inward until fully bottomed, Fig. 3.

5. Start engine, wait 90 seconds and move transducer core outward approximately one inch, Fig. 3.

6. Adjust timing light so timing marks are aligned. The timing light meter should indicate additional amount of advance as listed in the Horizon and Omni Lean Burn Specification Chart. If within specifications, move transducer core inward and timing should return to basic setting. If timing does not advance and/or did not return to basic setting, replace "Spark Con-

trol Computer''. After computer replacement, repeat test.

Vacuum Advance Test

1. Connect and adjust timing light to engine so total timing advance can be checked.
2. Start and run engine to obtain normal operating temperature with transmission in neutral and parking brake applied.
3. Place a piece of paper between carburetor switch and throttle lever, Fig. 4. If curb idle adjusting screw is not contacting carburetor switch, ensure fast idle cam is not on or binding, or throttle stop screw is not over adjusted. Adjust timing light so basic timing signal can be observed. Run engine for 9 minutes and ensure that a minimum of 16 inches of vacuum is present at transducer. The timing light meter should indicate additional amount of advance as listed in the Horizon and Omni Lean Burn Specification Chart. If not, replace ''Spark Control Computer''.

Throttle Position Transducer Adjustment

1. Disconnect connector from transducer.
2. Loosen lock nut.
3. Place special tool C-4522 between outer portion of transducer and transducer mounting bracket, Fig. 5.
4. Adjust transducer until a clearance fit is obtained.
5. Tighten lock nut and reconnect connector.

Distributor Service

Disassembly

1. Remove rotor from shaft, Fig. 6.
2. Remove screw holding pick-up lead.
3. Remove Hall Effect Pick-up Assembly lock springs and the pick-up assembly.
4. Remove two screws securing shield to distributor and the shield.
5. Mark position of drive gear on distributor shaft.
6. Remove roll pin with a suitable punch.
7. Remove drive gear, then the distributor shaft from housing.
8. Remove nylon spacer from shaft.

Assembly

1. Lightly lubricate housing bushings with engine oil.
2. Install shaft into housing, ensuring nylon spacer is resting on housing bushing.
3. Install drive gear onto distributor shaft in original position, aligning mating marks.
4. Drive in roll pin.
5. Install shield onto housing.
6. Place Hall Effect Pick-up Assembly into housing and secure with lock springs.
7. Secure Hall Effect Pick-up Assembly lead.
8. Install rotor onto shaft.

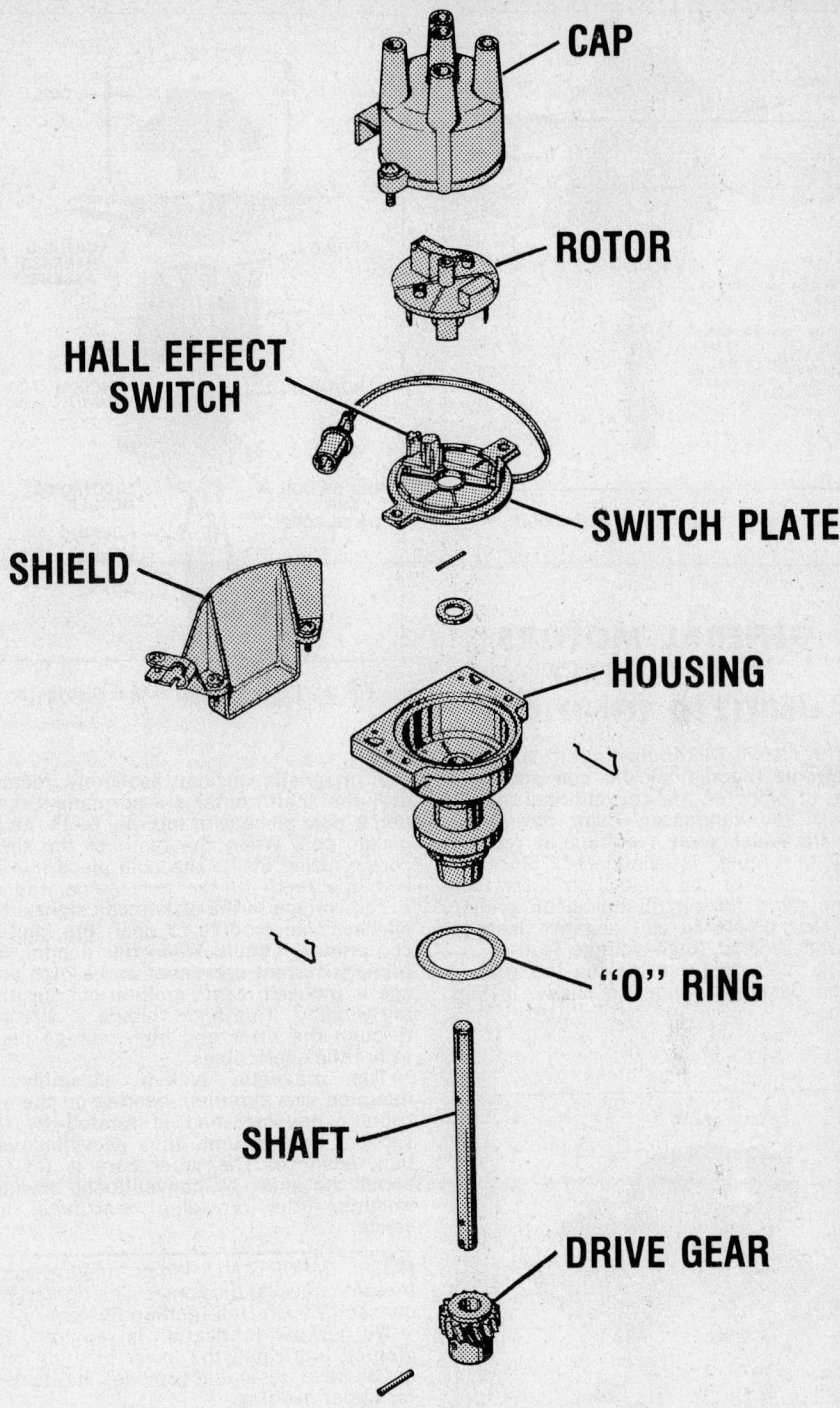

Fig. 6   Hall Effect electronic ignition distributor

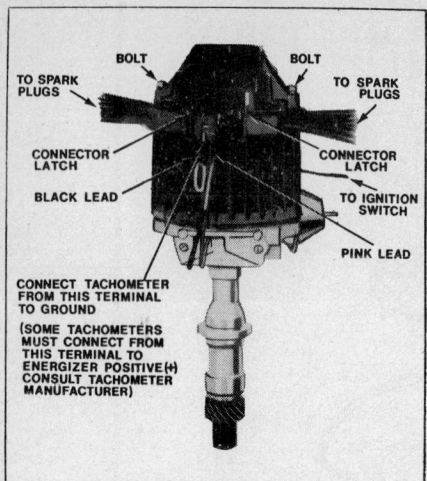

Fig. 1 Typical Unit Distributor

GENERAL MOTORS DELCO-REMY UNITIZED IGNITION

The "Unit Distributor" utilizes an all-electronic module, pickup coil and timer core in place of the conventional ignition points and condenser. Point pitting and rubbing block wear resulting in retarded ignition timing, is eliminated. Since the coil is part of the Unit Distributor there is no need for distributor-to-coil primary (breaker points to coil negative lead) or secondary lead (high voltage lead).

The main features making the Unit Ignition System unique are shown in Figs. 1 and 2.

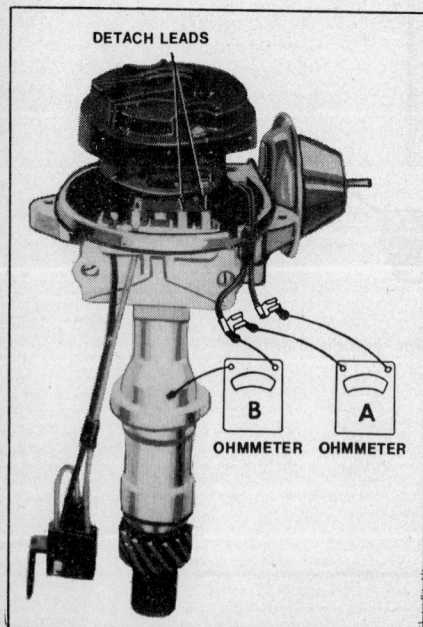

Fig. 4 Pickup coil test. Unit Distributor

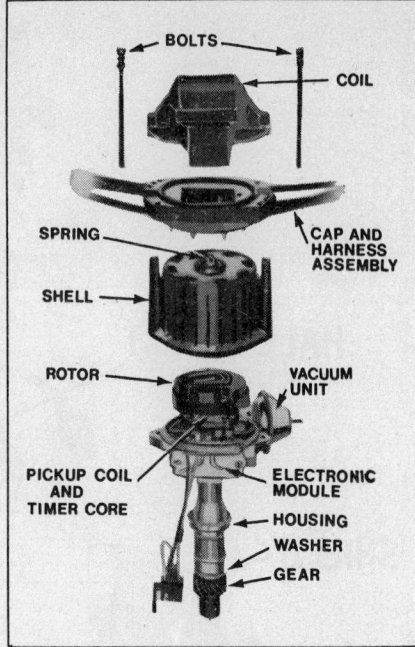

Fig. 2 Exploded view of Unit Distributor

A magnetic pickup assembly located over the shaft contains a permanent magnet, a pole piece with internal teeth, and a pickup coil. When the teeth of the timer core rotating inside the pole piece line up with the teeth of the pole piece, the induced voltage in the pickup coil signals the all-electronic module to open the ignition coil primary circuit. When this occurs, the primary current decreases and a high voltage is induced in the ignition coil secondary winding. This high voltage is directed through the rotor and high voltage leads to fire the spark plugs.

The magnetic pickup assembly is mounted over the main bearing on the distributor housing, and is rotated by the vacuum control unit, thus providing vacuum advance. The timer core is rotated about the shaft by conventional advance weights, thus providing centrifugal advance.

NOTE: IMPORTANT: When making compression checks, disconnect ignition switch connector from Unit Ignition System.

No periodic lubrication is required. Engine oil lubricates the lower bushing, and an oil-filled reservoir provides lubrication for upper bushing.

Trouble Diagnosis

Insure that the black and pink leads are connected, Fig. 1. Tighten both bolts, Fig. 1. Loose bolts may cause poor performance and radio interference.

NOTE: Before performing extensive diagnostic operations determine if fuel system is operating properly.

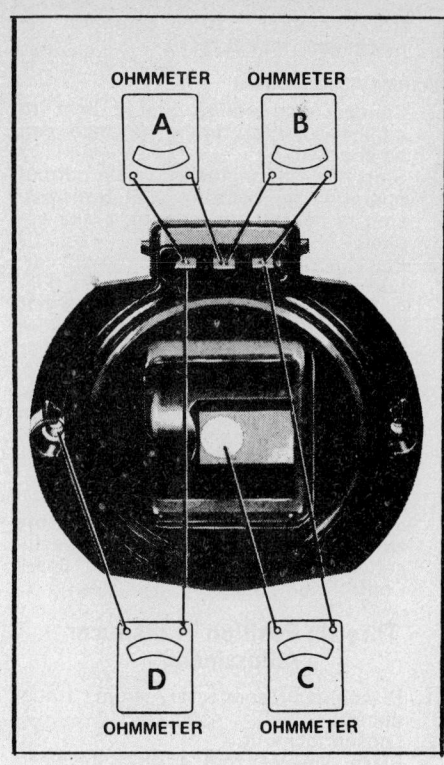

Fig. 3 Ignition Coil test. Unit Distributor

On Vehicle

Engine Will Not Start

1. Disconnected or loose ignition switch connector, Fig. 1.
   a. Connect voltmeter from ignition switch connector to ground.
   b. Turn on ignition switch.
   c. If reading is zero, circuit is open between connector and ignition switch.
   d. If reading is Energizer voltage, hold one spark lead with insulated pliers about 1/4" from dry area of engine

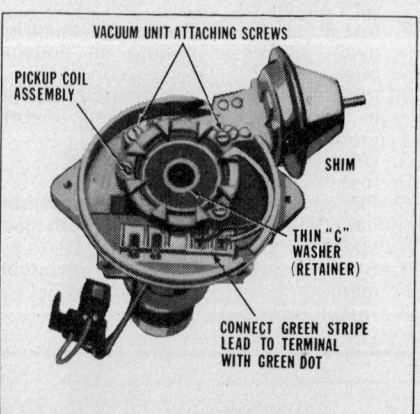

Fig. 5 Unit Distributor with shaft assembly removed

block while cranking engine. If a strong spark is present, ignition would appear to be trouble free. If no spark, follow "On Test Bench" procedure.

Engine Will Start, But Will Not Run. Rough Engine Operation, Miss or Surge

1. Spark plug lead arc-over, voltage leaking to ground or faulty spark plugs.
   a. If no defects are found, follow "On Test Bench" procedure.

On Test Bench

NOTE: Unit disassembled, Fig. 2.

Engine Will Not Start. Engine Will Start, But Will Not Run. Rough Engine Operation, Miss or Surge.

1. Inspect coil, eight inserts, shell and rotor for arc-over or leakage.
   a. Connect ohmmeter, Fig. 3.
   b. Tests "A" and "B" should have practically a zero result. If infinite on either reading, replace coil.
   c. Test "C" should result in 6000-9000 ohms. If outside range, replace coil.
   d. Test "D" should result in infinity. If not, replace coil.
   e. Connect vacuum source to vacuum unit.
   f. Connect ohmmeter, Fig. 4 and observe ohmmeter throughout vacuum range.

g. If test "A" reads less than 650 ohms, or more than 850 ohms at any time, replace pickup coil.
h. If test "B" does not read infinity at any time, replace pickup coil.
2. If no defects have been found, replace electronic module.

Pickup Coil Or Vacuum Unit Replacement, Fig. 5

1. Remove unit from engine.
2. Drive retaining pin out through gear.
3. Remove rotor and shaft assembly from housing.
4. Remove shim and "C" washer.
5. Remove pickup coil or vacuum unit.

MISAR ELECTRONIC SPARK TIMING (E.S.T.) SYSTEM

1977 Toronado

This system uses the basic H.E.I. distributor. However, the pick-up coil, pole piece and advance mechanisms have been deleted and the rotor has been redesigned, Fig. 1. This new system incorporates a crankshaft sensor, engine coolant temperature sensor and a controller unit.

The engine coolant temperature sensor resistance changes with changes in coolant temperature.

The electronic controller unit is mounted under the glove compartment and receives signals from the crankshaft sensor (crankshaft position and speed), engine coolant temperature sensor, engine vacuum and atmospheric pressure. The controller unit selects the most efficient advance as determined by the input signals and sends a signal to the distributor module to fire the spark plugs.

The electrical harness which connects these units together and to the vehicle harness, contains two vacuum hoses which are both connected to the controller unit. The white hose is connected to engine vacuum, while the black one is vented to atmospheric pressure outside of the vehicle.

The crankshaft sensor is mounted at the front of the engine with a disc located between the harmonic balancer and pulley.

A "Check Ignition" light, located in the instrument panel will go on under the following conditions:

1. Ignition switch is in start position. This mode provides a bulb check.
2. If system voltage is low and there is a heavy electrical load such as operation of power windows or other electrical accessories. Under this condition, the "check ignition" light will go off when the electrical load is removed, providing system voltage returns to normal. The alternator warning light may also go on under these conditions.
3. When checking reference timing and controller circuit is grounded.
4. If controller fails to advance spark timing.

1978 Toronado

This system is similar to the system used on the 1977 Toronado, except that the crankshaft sensor and pulse generator disc have been eliminated. The functions of the crankshaft sensor and pulse generator disc are performed by the pickup coil and timer core which are located in the distributor, Fig. 2. The electronic circuitry has also been redesigned, Fig. 3. The rotor mounting plate, Fig. 2, is constructed of brass, which is a non-magnetic metal. The reason for this is so that the brass mounting plate will prevent the signal produced by the pickup coil from being affected by magnetic attraction.

With these modifications, the ignition timing can be set by turning the distributor, however the reference timing connector must be grounded with a jumper wire.

1977 Toronado System Service & Diagnosis

Adjusting Distributor Position

1. Disconnect ignition feed wire and re-

Fig. 1   Redesigned rotor used on E.S.T. system. 1977 Toronado

NOTE EMPTY CAVITIES

move distributor cap.
2. Crank engine until rotor points toward rear of engine and number one piston is almost on TDC (0 degrees on timing indicator).
3. Using a socket on crankshaft bolt, turn crankshaft to 0 degrees.
4. White mark on rotor should be aligned with white mark on distributor housing, Fig. 4. If not, loosen distributor clamp bolt and turn distributor to align.

NOTE: This is the final distributor position.

5. Tighten distributor clamp bolt.

Adjusting Reference Timing

NOTE: Timing should be checked with a magnetic probe timing meter.

1. With distributor position correctly adjusted, connect the open reference timing connector (taped to harness), Fig. 5, to ground using a jumper wire.
2. With transmission in PARK, drive wheels blocked and parking brake applied, start engine and run at low idle. Timing should be at 20 degrees.

NOTE: Engine speed will not affect timing. Also, the "check timing" light shoud be on.

3. If timing is incorrect, stop engine, then loosen timing adjuster clamp bolts and rotate timing adjuster bolt, Fig. 6, clockwise to advance timing, or counterclockwise to retard timing. One complete turn equals about one degree.

NOTE: Do not rotate distributor in an attempt to adjust ignition timing.

4. Recheck timing. If correct, stop engine, then tighten adjuster bolt clamp bolts and disconnect jumper wire.

Crankshaft Sensor, Replace & Align

1. Turn ignition OFF and mark sensor position on mounting surfaces so that sensor can be installed in original position.
2. Disconnect sensor harness connector, then remove crankshaft sensor timing adjuster clamp bots and sensor.
3. Install crankshaft sensor in original position and leave adjuster clamp bolts slightly loose until after checking reference timing.
4. Check clearance between disc and crankshaft sensor, Fig. 7. To adjust, loosen clearance adjustment bolts, Fig. 6.
5. Reconnect harness connector.
6. Check reference timing.

System Diagnosis

Engine Will Not Start (Engine Cranks Normally, Battery Fully Charged)

1. Check EST fuse in fuse panel. If fuse is blown, proceed to step 2. If fuse is not blown, proceed to step 3.
2. Disconnect 3-wire connector near controller unit, then replace fuse and turn ignition ON. If fuse does not blow, locate and repair short in red wire from connector on controller unit to crankshaft sensor. If fuse blows again, locate and repair short circuit in pink wire with double-black stripes from 3-wire connector through instrument panel harness to fuse panel.
3. Check for spark at the spark plugs. If there is no spark, proceed to step 4. If there is spark, check distributor position and reference timing. If correct, trouble is not in ignition. Check fuel system and spark plugs.

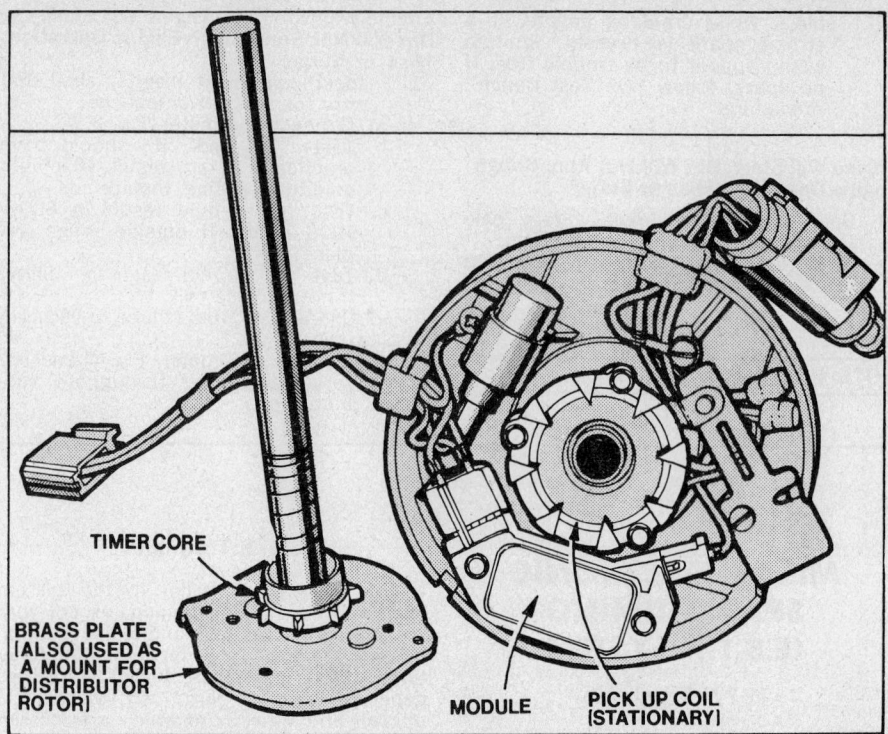

TIMER CORE

BRASS PLATE [ALSO USED AS A MOUNT FOR DISTRIBUTOR ROTOR]

MODULE **PICK UP COIL [STATIONARY]**

Fig. 2 Electronic Spark Timing (E.S.T.) distributor. 1978 Toronado

4. Inspect crankshaft sensor, disc and harness for damage. Check sensor alignment and clearance at disc. Check black ground wire and screw in distributor. If connection is good, turn ignition key to RUN position and check voltage as follows:

a. Ignition wire (black with pink stripe) at connector on distributor. If voltage is less than 12 volts, check wire from distributor to ignition switch for loose connections or open circuit. Also check ignition switch.
b. Terminal J (pink and red) wires in connector at controller unit. If voltage is less than 12 volts, check pink wire for loose connection or open circuit from connector at con-

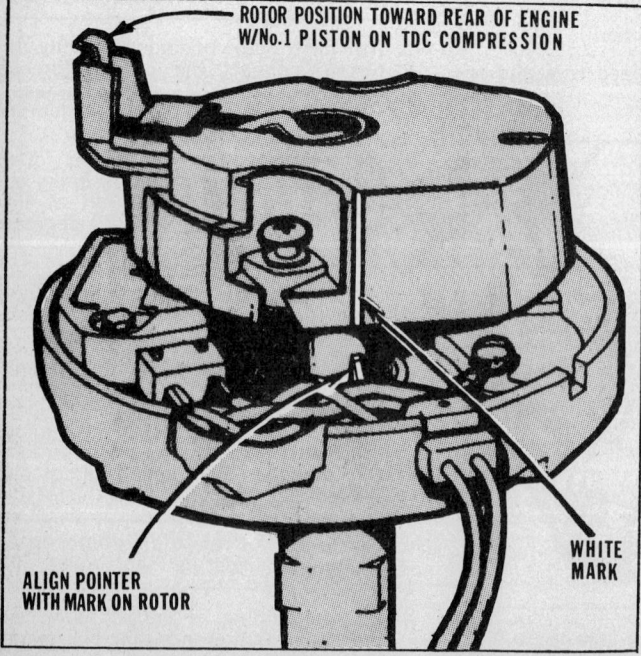

ROTOR POSITION TOWARD REAR OF ENGINE W/No.1 PISTON ON TDC COMPRESSION

ALIGN POINTER WITH MARK ON ROTOR

WHITE MARK

Fig. 4 Rotor and distributor alignment mark. 1977 Toronado

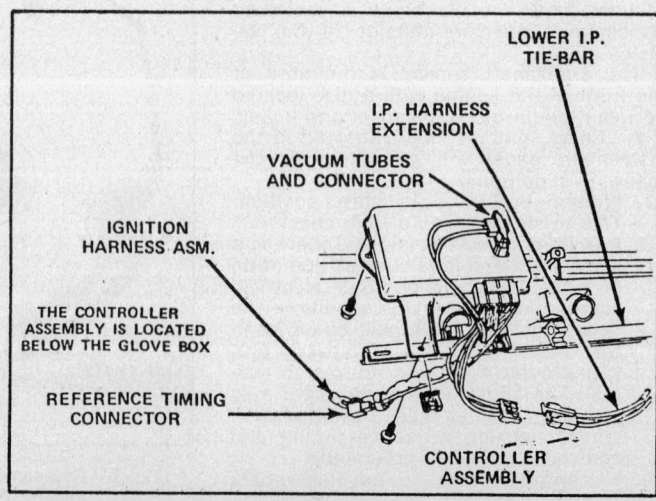

LOWER I.P. TIE-BAR

I.P. HARNESS EXTENSION

VACUUM TUBES AND CONNECTOR

IGNITION HARNESS ASM.

THE CONTROLLER ASSEMBLY IS LOCATED BELOW THE GLOVE BOX

REFERENCE TIMING CONNECTOR

CONTROLLER ASSEMBLY

Fig. 5 Reference timing connector. 1977 Toronado

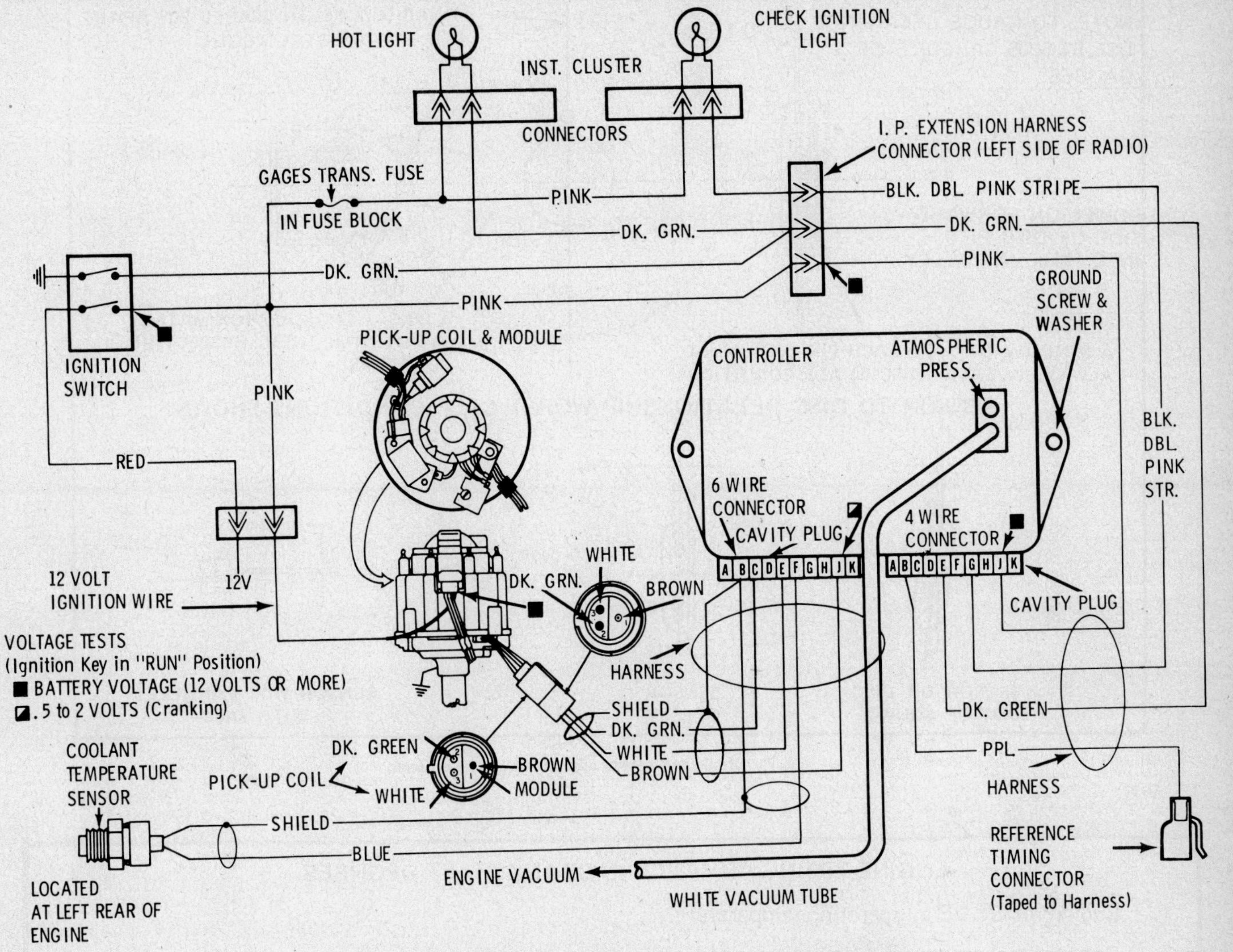

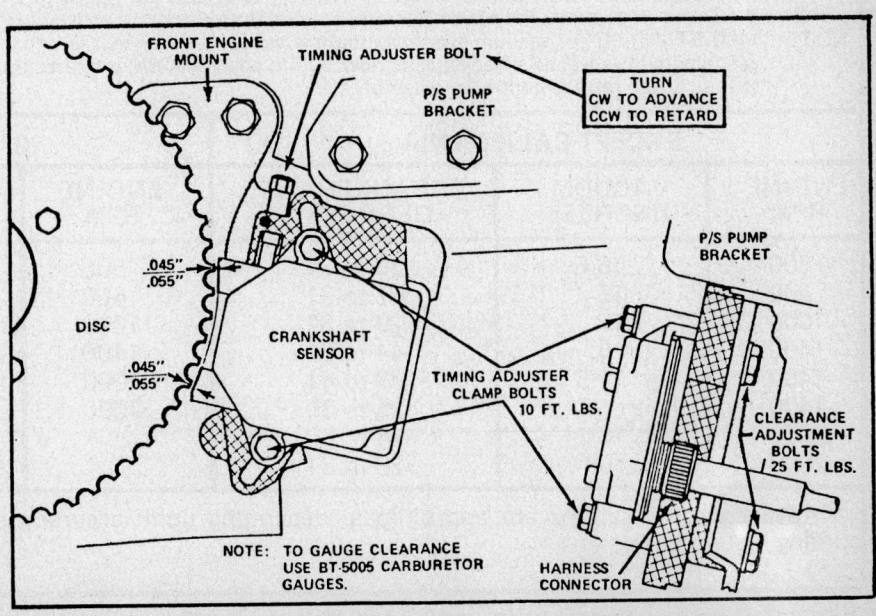

HOT LIGHT

CHECK IGNITION LIGHT

INST. CLUSTER
CONNECTORS

I. P. EXTENSION HARNESS
CONNECTOR (LEFT SIDE OF RADIO)

GAGES TRANS. FUSE
IN FUSE BLOCK

PINK

BLK. DBL. PINK STRIPE

DK. GRN.

DK. GRN.

DK. GRN.

PINK

PINK

IGNITION
SWITCH

PINK

PICK-UP COIL & MODULE

CONTROLLER

GROUND
SCREW &
WASHER

ATMOSPHERIC
PRESS.

RED

6 WIRE
CONNECTOR
CAVITY PLUG

4 WIRE
CONNECTOR

BLK.
DBL.
PINK
STR.

12 VOLT
IGNITION WIRE

12V

A B C D E F G H J K

A B C D E F G H J K

CAVITY PLUG

DK. GRN.

WHITE

BROWN

VOLTAGE TESTS
(Ignition Key in "RUN" Position)
■ BATTERY VOLTAGE (12 VOLTS OR MORE)
◧ .5 to 2 VOLTS (Cranking)

HARNESS

SHIELD
DK. GRN.
WHITE
BROWN

DK. GREEN

COOLANT
TEMPERATURE
SENSOR

DK. GREEN

PICK-UP COIL

WHITE

BROWN
MODULE

PPL

HARNESS

SHIELD

BLUE

ENGINE VACUUM

REFERENCE
TIMING
CONNECTOR
(Taped to Harness)

LOCATED
AT LEFT REAR OF
ENGINE

WHITE VACUUM TUBE

Fig. 3   Electronic Spark Timing (E.S.T.) wiring circuit. 1978 Toronado

troller unit to 3-wire connector near
controller, then the pink wire with
double-black stripes through instrument panel harness to fuse
panel.

c. Tan wire in 2-wire connector near
distributor. Do not disconnect wire.
Voltage should be .5-2 volts while
cranking the engine. If voltage is
not as specified, proceed to step 5.
If voltage is as specified, check
distributor, coil, and module. Replace defective parts.

5. Check voltage at terminal C (tan wire)
in connector at controller unit. Voltage should be .5-2 volts. If voltage is
not as specified, proceed to step 6.
If voltage is as specified, check tan
wire from controller to 2-wire connector near distributor for loose connection or open circuit. Replace or repair
as necessary.

6. Check voltage at terminal D (light
blue wire) in connector at controller
unit while cranking engine. Record

FRONT ENGINE
MOUNT

TIMING ADJUSTER BOLT

P/S PUMP
BRACKET

TURN
CW TO ADVANCE
CCW TO RETARD

.045"
.055"

DISC

CRANKSHAFT
SENSOR

P/S PUMP
BRACKET

.045"
.055"

TIMING ADJUSTER
CLAMP BOLTS
10 FT. LBS.

CLEARANCE
ADJUSTMENT
BOLTS
25 FT. LBS.

NOTE: TO GAUGE CLEARANCE
USE BT-5005 CARBURETOR
GAUGES

HARNESS
CONNECTOR

Fig. 6   Crankshaft sensor to disc clearance. 1977 Toronado

2-467

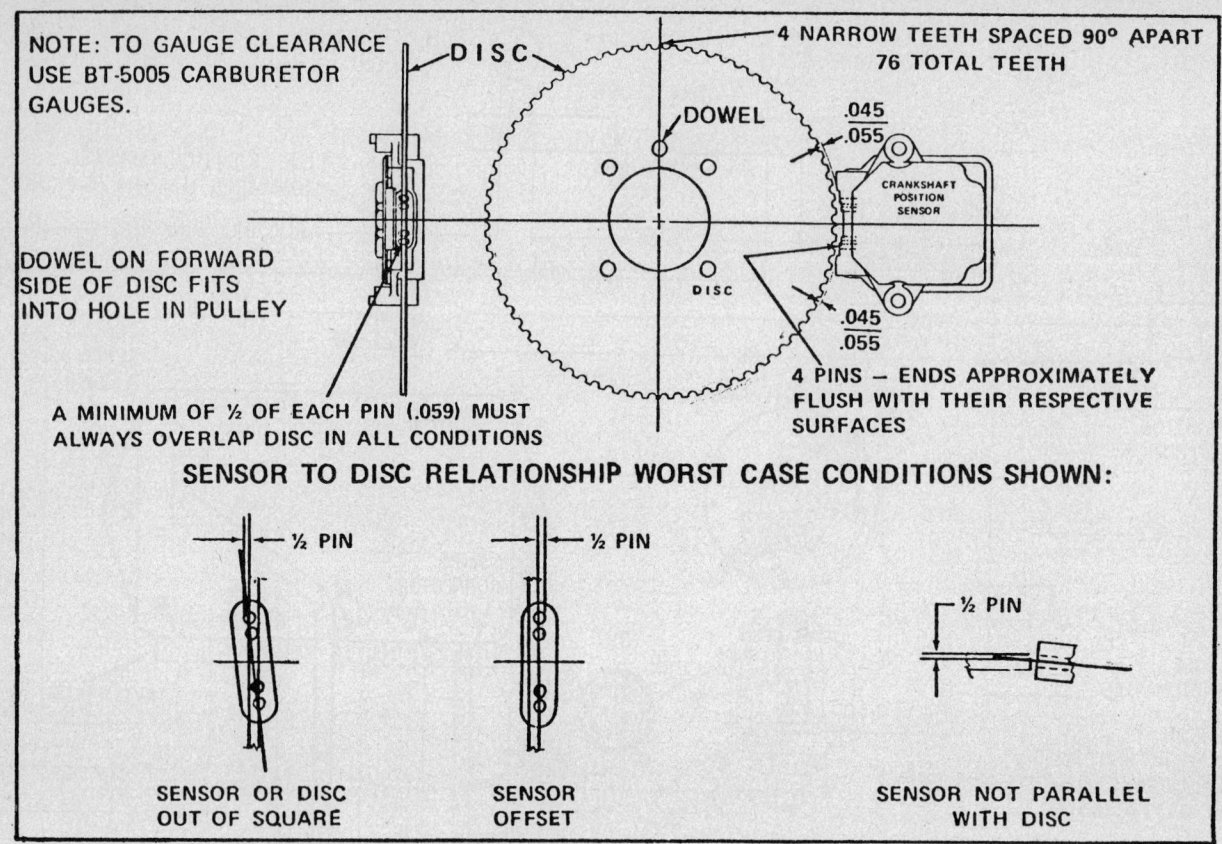

NOTE: TO GAUGE CLEARANCE USE BT-5005 CARBURETOR GAUGES.

DISC

4 NARROW TEETH SPACED 90° APART
76 TOTAL TEETH

DOWEL

.045
.055

CRANKSHAFT POSITION SENSOR

DOWEL ON FORWARD SIDE OF DISC FITS INTO HOLE IN PULLEY

DISC

.045
.055

A MINIMUM OF ½ OF EACH PIN (.059) MUST ALWAYS OVERLAP DISC IN ALL CONDITIONS

4 PINS — ENDS APPROXIMATELY FLUSH WITH THEIR RESPECTIVE SURFACES

SENSOR TO DISC RELATIONSHIP WORST CASE CONDITIONS SHOWN:

½ PIN

½ PIN

½ PIN

SENSOR OR DISC OUT OF SQUARE

SENSOR OFFSET

SENSOR NOT PARALLEL WITH DISC

Fig. 7   Crankshaft sensor alignment. 1977 Toronado

ENGINE TIMING ADVANCE IN CRANKSHAFT DEGREES

1. Engine **MUST BE** at operating temperature.

2. Connect tachometer and timing meter.

3. Disconnect controller assembly vacuum tube (white) from manifold vacuum "T". Plug "T" and connect vacuum pump and gauge to white tube. Use pump to get vacuum readings shown.

NOTE: 1400 RPM at 15" of vacuum gives maximum advance. If advance is less than specification, slowly increase vacuum to get maximum advance. If advance is now within specification, instruments/gauges used are inaccurate. If not within specification, replace controller assembly.

EXCEPT CALIFORNIA			CALIFORNIA		
ENGINE RPM	VACUUM (INCHES)	*CRANKSHAFT DEGREES	ENGINE RPM	VACUUM (INCHES)	*CRANKSHAFT DEGREES
600	16.5	29 to 34	600	13.5	17 to 20
600	15	27 to 31	600	12	17 to 20
1000	12	29 to 37	1000	12	19 to 22
1400	15	44 to 61	1400	15	44 to 61
1400	10.5	37 to 41	2000	18	31 to 49
1400	6	25 to 35	2000	0	31 to 34
2000	18	44 to 53			
2000	0	28 to 31			

＊Advance specifications are approximate depending upon accuracy of tachometer, vacuum gauge and timing meter.

Fig. 9   Engine timing advance specifications. 1977 Toronado

reading, then check voltage again with crankshaft sensor disconnected and placed aside so as not to damage it. If voltages are the same, proceed to step 7. If voltages are not the same, replace controller unit.

7. Turn ignition key to RUN position and check voltage at crankshaft sensor harness connector, Fig. 8. If voltages are as specified, proceed to step 8. If voltages are not as specified, replace harness.

8. Turn ignition key to RUN position and check voltage at both 8-10 volt terminals. If voltage is not 8-10 volts at both terminals, proceed to step 9. If voltage is as specified, replace crankshaft sensor.

9. Turn ignition key to RUN position and check voltage at controller unit. Voltage at terminals D (light blue) and E (purple) should be 8-10 volts. If voltage is as specified, replace harness. If voltage is not as specified, replace controller unit.

Engine Detonates (Recommended Octane Rating Fuel Used)

1. Check white vacuum hose from intake manifold to controller unit for kinks, obstructions, leakage or heat damage.

   NOTE: A partially obstructed hose would prevent fast drop of vacuum on acceleration.

   If hose is in good condition and not leaking, disconnect coolant temperature sensor and check resistance. At engine operating temperature, the resistance should be 500 to 2,000 ohms. At 70° F., the resistance should be 25,000 to 55,000 ohms. If resistance is as specified, proceed to step 2. If resistance is not as specified or if there is an open circuit in the sensor, replace sensor.

2. With ignition off, disconnect controller unit connector and connect a jumper wire between terminals B (black wire) and F (white wire) in connector. Connect an ohmmeter to the 2 terminals in coolant temperature harness connector.

3. If ohmmeter reading is less than 1 ohm, check crankshaft sensor alignment and disc for damage, Fig. 5. Check reference timing. If no damage is found and sensor alignment and reference timing are correct, replace controller unit.

4. If ohmmeter reading is more than 1 ohm or indicates an open circuit, check for open circuit in black and white wires. Repair or replace harness as necessary.

Engine Starts Then Stops When Key Is Turned to "RUN" Position

1. Turn ignition key to RUN, then disconnect crankshaft sensor connector and check voltages as shown in Fig. 8.

2. If voltage reading at 12 volt terminal or shield terminal are not as specified, repair or replace harness.

3. If voltage reading at either 8-10 volt terminal are not as specified, check voltage at controller unit connector from ground to terminal D (light blue) and E (purple). Reading should be

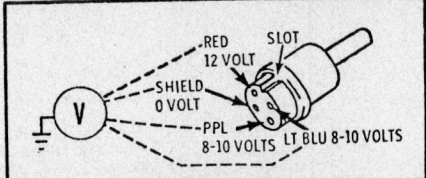

Fig. 8   Crankshaft sensor connector test connections

8-10 volts at both terminals. If both readings are as specified, replace harness. If readings are not as specified, replace controller unit.

4. If all voltage readings are as specified in Fig. 8, reconnect crankshaft sensor connector and connect jumper wire to reference timing connector (purple wire) near controller and connect jumper wire to ground.

5. Start engine and run at idle. Check voltage at controller unit connector terminal E (purple). Voltage reading should be 3-5 volts. If voltage is as specified, replace controller unit. If voltage is not as specified, check disc alignment, Fig. 7. If alignment is correct, replace crankshaft sensor.

Hard Starting, Rough Idle, Poor Performance (Battery Fully Charged)

1. Check fuel system, choke, spark plugs and cables.

2. Make sure harness connections to distributor, coolant temperature sensor and controller unit are good.

3. Inspect crankshaft sensor for alignment. Make sure clearance between sensor and disc is .045-.055 inches, Fig. 7. Also make sure harness and connector are in good condition.

4. Check all vacuum hoses for kinks, obstructions, leakage or heat damage. Repair or replace as necessary.

5. Check distributor cap and rotor for signs of arcing. Check ground wire and screw in distributor. Check module with tester J-24624.

6. Check distributor position and reference timing.

7. With engine idling, transmission in PARK and parking brakes applied, connect voltmeter to ground and touch other probe to ignition wire (black with pink stripe) in connector on distributor. If voltage is less than 12 volts, check for loose connection between distributor connector and ignition switch.

8. Connect voltmeter to ground and J terminal (pink and red wires) in controller unit. If less than 12 volts, check for loose connection through instrument panel harness connector to fuse panel.

9. If problem has not been located, proceed as follows:

10. Turn ignition key to RUN position, then disconnect crankshaft sensor connector and check voltage at 12 volt terminal and at shield terminal, Fig. 8. If voltages are as specified, proceed to step 11. If voltages are not as specified, repair or replace harness.

11. Turn ignition key to RUN position and check voltage at both 8-10 volt terminals. If voltages are as specified, proceed to step 12. If voltages are not

as specified, with crankshaft sensor disconnected, check for 8-10 volts at both terminals D (light blue) and E (purple) of controller unit. If voltages are as specified, replace harness, if not, replace controller unit.

12. Reconnect crankshaft sensor connector, then with key in RUN position and engine stopped, check reference voltage at controller unit connector terminal D (light blue). Record voltage, then check voltage again with engine at idle speed. If voltage readings are different, proceed to step 13. If voltage readings are the same, replace crankshaft sensor.

13. With engine idling, check for 3-5 volts at controller unit connector terminal E (purple). If voltage is as specified, proceed to step 14. If voltage is not as specified, replace crankshaft sensor.

14. With engine idling, check for 1-4 volts at tan wire in 2-wire connector near distributor. If voltage is as specified, proceed to step 15. If voltage is not as specified, replace controller unit assembly.

15. Check engine advance. Refer to chart in Fig. 9. If advance is not as specified, proceed to step 16. If advance is as specified, problem is not in ignition. Recheck steps 1, 3, 4, 5, and 6.

16. Disconnect coolant temperature sensor and check resistance of sensor at sensor terminals. At engine operating temperature, resistance should be 500 to 2,000 ohms. At 70° F., resistance should be 25,000 to 55,000 ohms. If resistance is as specified, proceed to step 17. If resistance is not as specified, replace coolant sensor.

17. With ignition OFF, disconnect controller unit connector and connect a jumper wire between terminals B (black wire) and F (white wire) in connector. Connect an ohmmeter to the 2 terminals in temperature sensor harness connector. If ohmmeter reads less than 1 ohm resistance, replace controller unit. If ohmmeter reads more than 1 ohm or indicates an open circuit, check for open circuit in black and white wires and repair or replace harness as necessary.

Hot Light ON (Ignition Key In "RUN" Position)

1. Check usual causes of "Hot Light On" condition. Correct as required.

2. Disconnect 2-wire connector at coolant temperature sensor and turn ignition to RUN position. If hot light remains on, proceed to step 3. If hot light goes off, replace coolant temperature sensor.

3. Turn ignition switch OFF, then disconnect 3-wire connector near controller unit and turn ignition switch to RUN. If hot light goes off, proceed to step 4. If hot light remains on, locate and repair short in dark green wire circuit from 3-wire connector to instrument cluster and to ignition switch.

4. Disconnect controller unit connector and connect an ohmmeter to the 2 terminals in coolant temperature sensor connector. Ohmmeter should indicate an open circuit. Connect ohmmeter to ground and connector termi-

nals. White wire terminal should indicate an open circuit. If all readings are as specified, replace controller unit. If all readings are not as specified, black and white wires are shorted together. Repair or replace harness as required.

"Check Ignition" Light "On" (Engine Running, Battery Fully Charged)

1. Check reference timing wire (purple) connector at controller unit, Fig. 3. The connector should be disconnected and not grounded.
2. With engine running, transmission in PARK and parking brakes applied, check voltage at controller unit terminal J (pink and red wires). If voltage is less than 11 volts, proceed to step 3. If voltage is above 11 volts, turn ignition key to RUN position (engine off) and disconnect 3-wire connector near controller unit. If light goes out, replace controller unit. If light remains on, circuit between H terminal and light is grounded. Repair or replace harness as required.
3. With all accessories turned off and engine running at fast idle, connect a voltmeter to battery. If voltmeter reading is more than 12 volts, proceed to step 4. If voltmeter reading is less than 12 volts, check fan belt tension and charging system.
4. Check for loose connection from terminal J in controller unit through instrument panel harness connectors to fuse panel. Repair as required.

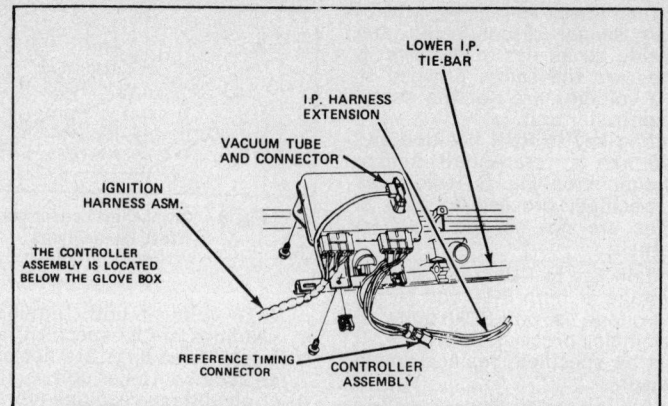

Fig. 10 Electronic Spark Timing (E.S.T.) reference timing connector 1978 Toronado

1978 Toronado System Service

Adjusting Reference Timing

1. Connect reference timing connector (taped to harness), Fig. 10, to ground using a suitable jumper wire.
2. Connect timing light or magnetic probe timing meter and start engine.

NOTE: The "Check Ignition" should be on if reference timing connector is properly connected.

3. Check timing. If timing is not to specifications, loosen distributor clamp bolt and turn distributor as necessary, then tighten clamp bolt.
4. Disconnect jumper wire from reference timing connector. The "Check Ignition" light should go out.

System Diagnosis

Refer to Fig. 11 for engine timing advance specifications, and to Figs. 12 thru 15 for system diagnosis.

NOTE: Make sure controller case is grounded at all times while performing diagnosis.

---

1. Engine **MUST BE** at operating temperature and timing set to specification.

2. Connect tachometer and timing meter. Do not ground reference timing connector.

3. Disconnect controller assembly vacuum tube (white) from manifold vacuum "T". Plug "T" and connect vacuum pump and gage to white tube. Use pump such as BT-7517 to get vacuum readings shown.

NOTE: 1400 RPM at 15" of vacuum gives maximum advance. If advance is less than specification, slowly increase vacuum to get maximum advance. If advance is now within specification, instruments/gages used are inaccurate. If not within specification, replace controller.

EXCEPT CALIFORNIA CARS			CALIFORNIA CARS		
ENGINE RPM	VACUUM (INCHES)	*CRANKSHAFT DEGREES	ENGINE RPM	VACUUM (INCHES)	*CRANKSHAFT DEGREES
600	16.5	29 to 34	600	13.5	15 to 22
600	15	27 to 31	600	12	15 to 22
1000	12	32 to 35	1000	12	17 to 25
1400	15	49 to 62	1400	15	39 to 65
1400	10.5	38 to 40	2000	18	24 to 33
1400	6	27 to 35	2000	0	23 to 32
2000	18	44 to 47			
2000	0	29 to 31			

* Advance specifications are approximate depending upon accuracy of tachometer, vacuum gage and timing meter.

Fig. 11 Electronic Spark Timing (E.S.T.) engine timing advance specifications. 1978

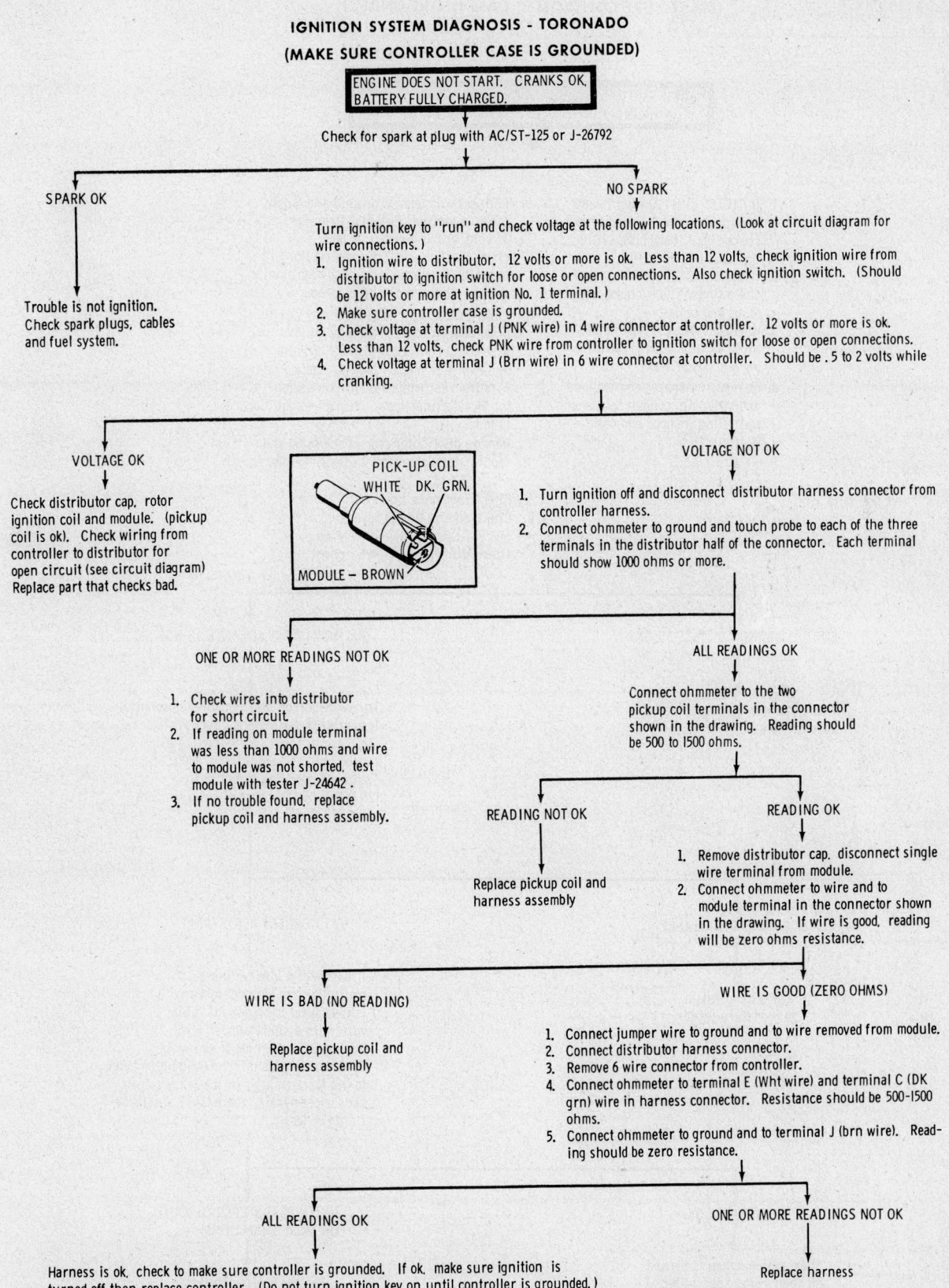

IGNITION SYSTEM DIAGNOSIS - TORONADO
(MAKE SURE CONTROLLER CASE IS GROUNDED)

ENGINE DOES NOT START. CRANKS OK,
BATTERY FULLY CHARGED.

Check for spark at plug with AC/ST-125 or J-26792

SPARK OK

Trouble is not ignition.
Check spark plugs, cables
and fuel system.

NO SPARK

Turn ignition key to "run" and check voltage at the following locations. (Look at circuit diagram for wire connections.)
1. Ignition wire to distributor. 12 volts or more is ok. Less than 12 volts, check ignition wire from distributor to ignition switch for loose or open connections. Also check ignition switch. (Should be 12 volts or more at ignition No. 1 terminal.)
2. Make sure controller case is grounded.
3. Check voltage at terminal J (PNK wire) in 4 wire connector at controller. 12 volts or more is ok. Less than 12 volts, check PNK wire from controller to ignition switch for loose or open connections.
4. Check voltage at terminal J (Brn wire) in 6 wire connector at controller. Should be .5 to 2 volts while cranking.

VOLTAGE OK

Check distributor cap, rotor
ignition coil and module. (pickup
coil is ok). Check wiring from
controller to distributor for
open circuit (see circuit diagram)
Replace part that checks bad.

PICK-UP COIL
WHITE DK. GRN.

MODULE – BROWN

VOLTAGE NOT OK

1. Turn ignition off and disconnect distributor harness connector from controller harness.
2. Connect ohmmeter to ground and touch probe to each of the three terminals in the distributor half of the connector. Each terminal should show 1000 ohms or more.

ONE OR MORE READINGS NOT OK

1. Check wires into distributor for short circuit.
2. If reading on module terminal was less than 1000 ohms and wire to module was not shorted, test module with tester J-24642.
3. If no trouble found, replace pickup coil and harness assembly.

ALL READINGS OK

Connect ohmmeter to the two
pickup coil terminals in the connector
shown in the drawing. Reading should
be 500 to 1500 ohms.

READING NOT OK

Replace pickup coil and
harness assembly

READING OK

1. Remove distributor cap, disconnect single wire terminal from module.
2. Connect ohmmeter to wire and to module terminal in the connector shown in the drawing. If wire is good, reading will be zero ohms resistance.

WIRE IS BAD (NO READING)

Replace pickup coil and
harness assembly

WIRE IS GOOD (ZERO OHMS)

1. Connect jumper wire to ground and to wire removed from module.
2. Connect distributor harness connector.
3. Remove 6 wire connector from controller.
4. Connect ohmmeter to terminal E (Wht wire) and terminal C (DK grn) wire in harness connector. Resistance should be 500-1500 ohms.
5. Connect ohmmeter to ground and to terminal J (brn wire). Reading should be zero resistance.

ALL READINGS OK

Harness is ok, check to make sure controller is grounded. If ok, make sure ignition is
turned off then replace controller. (Do not turn ignition key on until controller is grounded.)

ONE OR MORE READINGS NOT OK

Replace harness

Fig. 12   Electronic Spark Timing (E.S.T.) system diagnosis chart (part 1 of 4). 1978 Toronado

IGNITION SYSTEM DIAGNOSIS - TORONADO CONTINUED
(MAKE SURE CONTROLLER CASE IS GROUNDED)

HARD STARTING, ROUGH ENGINE, POOR PERFORMANCE
(Battery fully charged - 12 Volts or more)

---

1. If CHECK IGNITION light is on (engine running), use diagnosis chart CHECK IGNITION LIGHT ON - ENGINE RUNNING.
2. If CHECK IGNITION light is off, check fuel system, choke, spark plugs and cables.
3. Check all vacuum hoses and white vacuum tube to controller for pinches or leaks.
4. Make sure harness connections to distributor, coolant sensor and controller are good and controller is grounded.
5. Connect voltmeter to ground and touch probe to ignition wire at distributor 12 volts or more is ok. If less, check ignition wire from distributor to ignition switch. Also check ignition switch. Refer to circuit diagram.
6. Connect voltmeter to ground and touch probe to terminal J (PNK wire) in 4 wire connector at controller. Should be 12 volts or more. If less, check PNK wire from controller to ignition switch for loose connections. Also check ignition switch.
7. Remove distributor cap, check rotor and cap for signs of arcing. Check module with J-24642.
8. Check reference timing.
9. Check engine timing advance. See ENGINE TIMING ADVANCE IN CRANKSHAFT DEGREES chart.

ENGINE TIMING ADVANCE IS OK

Problem is not ignition. Recheck steps 2, 3 and 5.

ENGINE TIMING ADVANCE IS NOT OK

Turn ignition off and disconnect coolant temperature sensor and check resistance of sensor at sensor terminals. Resistance should be about 500 to 2,000 ohms. Engine at operating temperature. (25,000 to 55,000 ohms at room temperature.) 70°F. (21°C).

INCORRECT RESISTANCE

Replace coolant temperature sensor.

CORRECT RESISTANCE

1. Disconnect 6 wire connector at controller and connect terminal B (shield wire) to terminal F (blue wire) with a short jumper wire pushed into wire side of connector.
2. Check resistance by connecting ohmmeter to the two terminals in the temperature sensor connector. Resistance should be 1 ohm or less.

RESISTANCE OK

Make sure ignition is turned off then replace controller. (Do not turn ignition key on until controller is grounded.

METER READS OPEN CIRCUIT OR MORE THAN 1 OHM

Replace 6 wire connector harness.

Fig. 13 Electronic Spark Timing (E.S.T.) system diagnosis chart (part 2 of 4). 1978 Toronado

IGNITION SYSTEM DIAGNOSIS - TORONADO CONTINUED
(MAKE SURE CONTROLLER CASE IS GROUNDED)

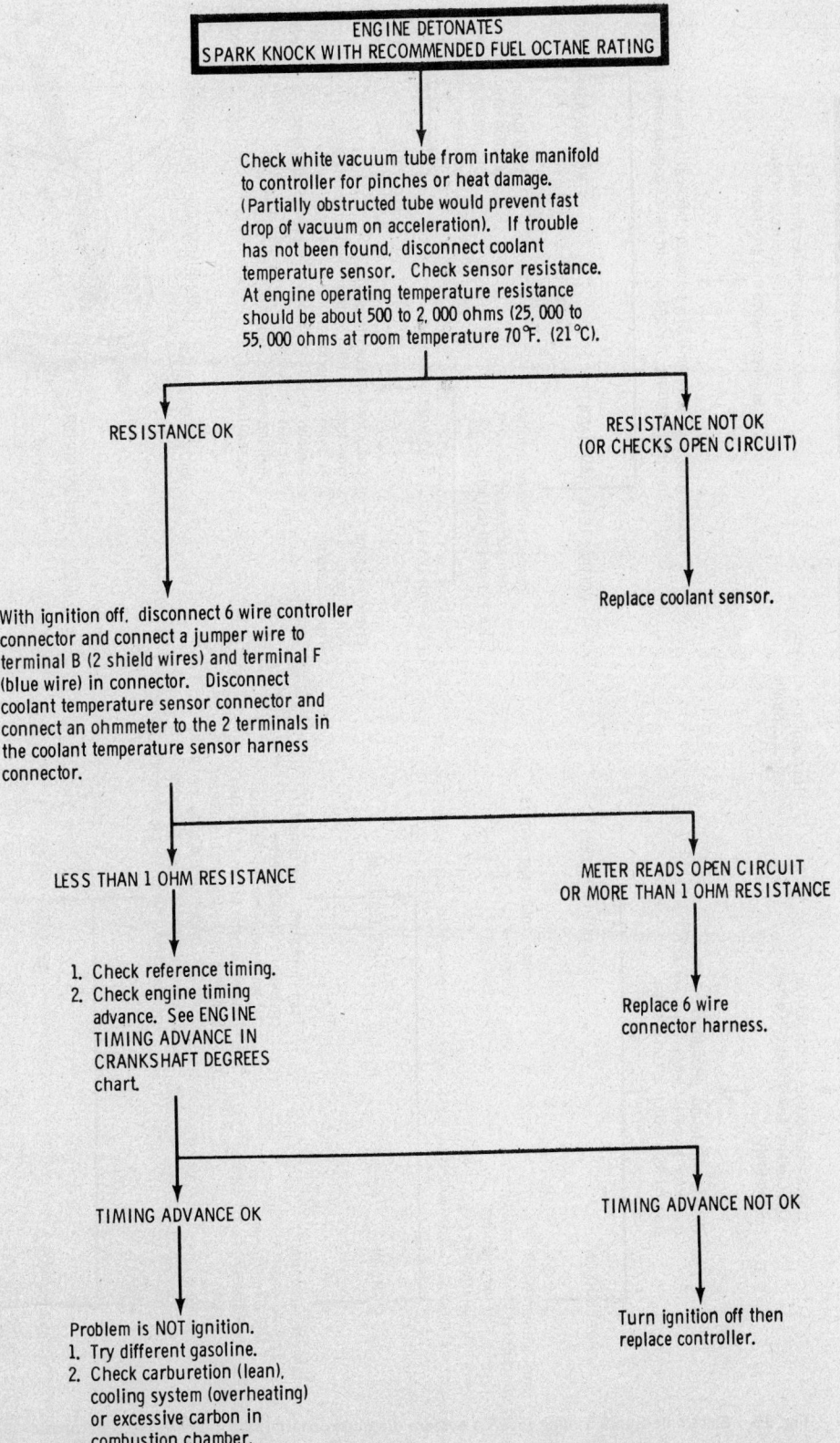

ENGINE DETONATES
SPARK KNOCK WITH RECOMMENDED FUEL OCTANE RATING

Check white vacuum tube from intake manifold to controller for pinches or heat damage. (Partially obstructed tube would prevent fast drop of vacuum on acceleration). If trouble has not been found, disconnect coolant temperature sensor. Check sensor resistance. At engine operating temperature resistance should be about 500 to 2,000 ohms (25,000 to 55,000 ohms at room temperature 70°F. (21°C).

RESISTANCE OK

RESISTANCE NOT OK
(OR CHECKS OPEN CIRCUIT)

Replace coolant sensor.

With ignition off, disconnect 6 wire controller connector and connect a jumper wire to terminal B (2 shield wires) and terminal F (blue wire) in connector. Disconnect coolant temperature sensor connector and connect an ohmmeter to the 2 terminals in the coolant temperature sensor harness connector.

LESS THAN 1 OHM RESISTANCE

METER READS OPEN CIRCUIT
OR MORE THAN 1 OHM RESISTANCE

1. Check reference timing.
2. Check engine timing advance. See ENGINE TIMING ADVANCE IN CRANKSHAFT DEGREES chart.

Replace 6 wire connector harness.

TIMING ADVANCE OK

TIMING ADVANCE NOT OK

Problem is NOT ignition.
1. Try different gasoline.
2. Check carburetion (lean), cooling system (overheating) or excessive carbon in combustion chamber.

Turn ignition off then replace controller.

Fig. 14   Electronic Spark Timing (E.S.T.) system diagnosis chart (part 3 of 4). 1978 Toronado

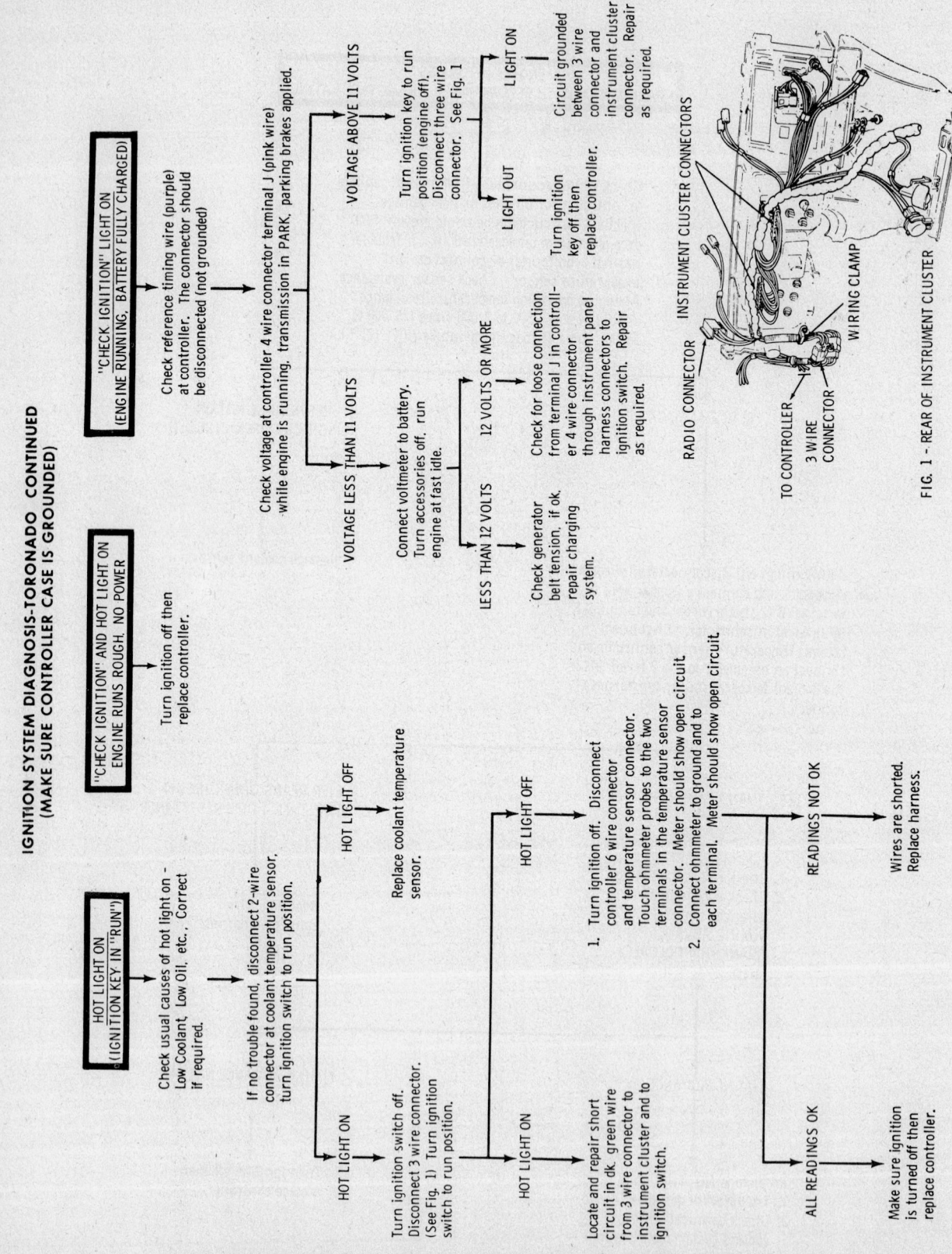

IGNITION SYSTEM DIAGNOSIS-TORONADO CONTINUED
(MAKE SURE CONTROLLER CASE IS GROUNDED)

"CHECK IGNITION" LIGHT ON (ENGINE RUNNING, BATTERY FULLY CHARGED)

Check reference timing wire (purple) at controller. The connector should be disconnected (not grounded)

→ Check voltage at controller 4 wire connector terminal J (pink wire) while engine is running. transmission in PARK, parking brakes applied.

VOLTAGE ABOVE 11 VOLTS

→ Turn ignition key to run position (engine off). Disconnect three wire connector. See Fig. 1

LIGHT ON

Circuit grounded between 3 wire connector and instrument cluster connector. Repair as required.

LIGHT OUT

Turn ignition key off then replace controller.

VOLTAGE LESS THAN 11 VOLTS

→ Connect voltmeter to battery. Turn accessories off. run engine at fast idle.

12 VOLTS OR MORE

Check for loose connection from terminal J in controller 4 wire connector through instrument panel harness connectors to ignition switch. Repair as required.

LESS THAN 12 VOLTS

Check generator belt tension. if ok. repair charging system.

"CHECK IGNITION" AND HOT LIGHT ON ENGINE RUNS ROUGH, NO POWER

Turn ignition off then replace controller.

HOT LIGHT ON (IGNITION KEY IN "RUN")

Check usual causes of hot light on - Low Coolant, Low Oil, etc., etc., Correct if required.

If no trouble found, disconnect 2-wire connector at coolant temperature sensor, turn ignition switch to run position.

HOT LIGHT OFF

Replace coolant temperature sensor.

HOT LIGHT ON

Turn ignition switch off. Disconnect 3 wire connector. (See Fig. 1) Turn ignition switch to run position.

HOT LIGHT OFF

1. Turn ignition off. Disconnect controller 6 wire connector and temperature sensor connector. Touch ohmmeter probes to the two terminals in the temperature sensor connector. Meter should show open circuit.
2. Connect ohmmeter to ground and to each terminal. Meter should show open circuit.

READINGS NOT OK

Wires are shorted. Replace harness.

ALL READINGS OK

Make sure ignition is turned off then replace controller.

HOT LIGHT ON

Locate and repair short circuit in dk. green wire from 3 wire connector to instrument cluster and to ignition switch.

RADIO CONNECTOR

INSTRUMENT CLUSTER CONNECTORS

WIRING CLAMP

TO CONTROLLER

3 WIRE CONNECTOR

FIG. 1 - REAR OF INSTRUMENT CLUSTER

Fig. 15   Electronic Spark Timing (E.S.T.) system diagnosis chart (part 4 of 4). 1978 Toronado

ELECTRONIC SPARK SELECTION (ESS) SYSTEM

1978 Seville

The Electronic Spark Selection (ESS) System is standard on all 1978 Seville models. This system is able to advance or retard the entire spark curve under certain operating conditions. This improves fuel economy at cruising speeds, reduces exhaust emissions and improves hot engine restarting.

Spark advance is retarded from normal engine timing during cranking, Fig. 1. Spark retard improved hot restarting by lessening the demand on the starting system since the spark is delivered to the cylinder when the piston is closer to top dead center. Ignition and the associated start of combustion pressure build-up in the cylinder occur closer to the point where the piston starts the downward motion at the beginning of the power stroke. This reduces demand on the starting system since the starter is not required to crank the engine a longer period of time against a high combustion pressure during engine starting.

Spark advance is also retarded from normal engine timing when coolant temperature is below approximately 130° F. (54° C.) on California vehicles only. This shortens the catalytic converter warm-up time thereby reducing exhaust gas hydrocarbon emissions. The catalytic converter is brought up to operating temperature faster since higher exhaust gas temperature is obtained when the spark is retarded.

There is no modification to normal ignition timing during normal city operation when outside of the cruise mode at normal operating temperature. Cruise conditions are identified by high manifold vacuums and high engine speeds. Normal spark advance occurs any time below the cruise mode and/or manifold vacuum points. California vehicles have retarded spark when the engine is cold as described previously. All other vehicles have normal spark advance at this time.

Spark timing is advanced over normal engine timing during cruise conditions to improve fuel economy, Fig. 1. Ignition occurs earlier in the compression stroke giving the fuel-air mixture more time to burn which increases efficiency and improves fuel economy.

This system includes an electronic decoder and a H.E.I. distributor which has been modified for the ESS system. The

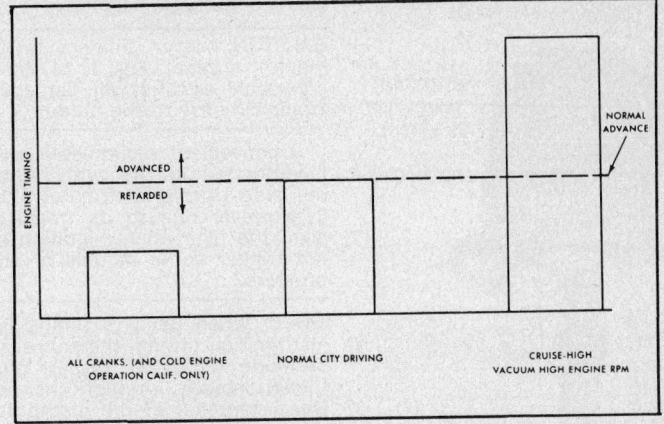

Fig. 1   Electronic Spark Selection (ESS) system operating modes

pick-up coil signal is sent to the electronic decoder to provide engine speed and ignition timing information. This signal is from the speed of the timer core and the relationship to the pole piece. The ESS system distributor has a five pin module in place of the 4 pin module used in conventional H.E.I. units. The electronic decoder output signal is sent to this new additional pin on the module. At this point, the decoder signal either delays or does not delay the shutting-off current in the primary winding in the ignition coil.

The spark is retarded from normal engine timing when current shut-off in the primary winding is delayed. Ignition then takes place at a later time when the piston is closer to top dead center.

Maximum delay of the primary winding current shut-off occurs when the engine is cranking and cold engine operation on California vehicles only. This is also the point of maximum spark retard from normal ignition timing. During normal city operation, the delay is less which results in normal advance during the normal city operation mode. Spark timing advanced over normal ignition timing occurs when there is no delay in shutting-off the primary current.

Existing components are utilized to provide input to the electronic decoder to further identify engine operating conditions which influence timing for any operating mode.

Engine coolant temperature is sensed indirectly at the EGR on/off solenoid. This solenoid valve is controlled by the electronic fuel injection system electronic control unit (ECU). Engine coolant temperature is an input to the ECU on all EFI equipped vehicles. On California vehicles, the ESS circuit to the EGR solenoid activates before the solenoid. On all except California vehicles, the ESS circuit to the EGR solenoid is activated after the solenoid.

The EFI ECU sends a signal to the EGR solenoid when the engine is cold through the solenoid windings to ground and closing the valve and shutting off EGR. There is approximately 12 volts across the solenoid when the engine is cold. On California vehicles, there is approximately 12 volts at the decoder when the engine is cold. On all except California vehicles, there is a ground potential at the decoder on cold engines. The decoder recognizes the difference in voltage and processes it as an input to retard the spark from normal ignition timing on California vehicles. Spark is not retarded on cold engine on all except California vehicles.

When the engine warms up, the ECU signal to the EGR solenoid is terminated to open the EGR valve. There is now a ground potential on warm engine on all vehicles, just like there was on all vehicles except California models. Therefore, the spark is not retarded from normal spark timing.

Diagnosis

Diagnosis of the Electronic Spark Selection (ESS) system must be accomplished through the use of a special tester, tool No. J-24642.

HIGH ENERGY IGNITION SYSTEM (H.E.I.)

The H.E.I. system utilizes an all-electronic module, pickup coil and timer core in place of the conventional ignition points and condenser (the condenser is used for noise suppression only). Point pitting and rubbing block wear resulting in retarded ignition timing, are eliminated.

NOTE: H.E.I. components are not interchangeable with "Unit Distributor" Components.

Since the coil is part of the H.E.I. distributor there is no need for distributor-to-coil primary (breaker points to coil negative lead) or secondary lead (high voltage lead).

NOTE: On late 1975 and all 1976-78 coils, the primary and secondary windings have been separated and a secondary coil ground lead is incorporated into the assembly.

The main features of H.E.I. system differentiating this system from the "Unit Ignition" system are shown in Figs. 1, 2 and 3.

The magnetic pickup consists of a rotating timer core attached to the distributor shaft, a stationary pole piece, permanent magnet and pickup coil.

When the distributor shaft rotates, the teeth of the timer core line up and pass the teeth of the pole piece inducing voltage in the pickup coil which signals the all-electronic module to open the ignition coil primary circuit. Maximum inductance occurs at the moment the timer core teeth are lined up with the teeth on the pole piece. At the instant the timer core teeth start to pass the pole teeth, the primary current decreases and a high voltage is

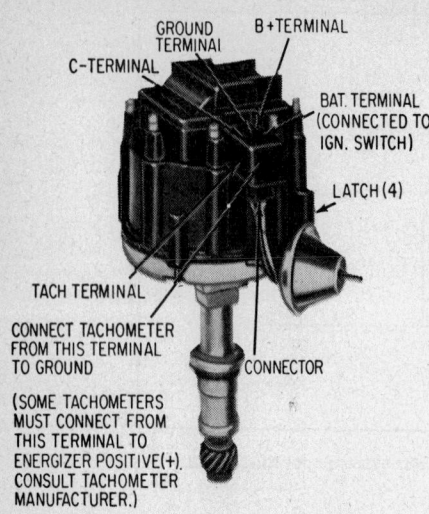

Fig. 1 H.E.I. distributor external components. V6 & V8 engines

viding centrifugal advance.

CAUTION: Never connect to ground the "tach" terminal, Fig. 1, of the distributor connector as this will damage the electronic circuitry of the module.

A convenient tachometer connection is incorporated in the wiring connector on the side of the distributor, Figs. 1 and 3. However due to its transistorized design, the high energy ignition system will not trigger some models of engine tachometers.

NOTE: When using a timing light to adjust ignition timing, the connection should be made at the No. 1 spark plug. Forcing foreign objects through the boot at the No. 1 terminal of the distributor cap will damage the boot and could cause engine misfiring.

The spark plug boot has been designed to form a tight seal around the spark plug and should be twisted ½ turn before removal.

System Diagnosis

With the wiring connector properly attached to connector at side of distributor cap and all the spark plug leads properly connected at plugs and at distributor terminals. Proceed as follows:

Engine Will Not Start
1. Connect voltmeter between "BAT" terminal lead on distributor connector and ground and turn on ignition switch.
2. If voltage is zero, there is an open circuit between the distributor and

induced in the ignition coil secondary winding and is directed through the rotor and high voltage leads to fire the spark plugs.

NOTE: Since this is a full 12 volt system it does not require a resistance wire.

The vacuum diaphragm is connected by linkage to the pole piece. When the diaphragm moves against spring pressure it rotates the pole piece allowing the poles to advance relative to the timer core. The timer core is rotated about the shaft by conventional advance weights, thus providing centrifugal advance.

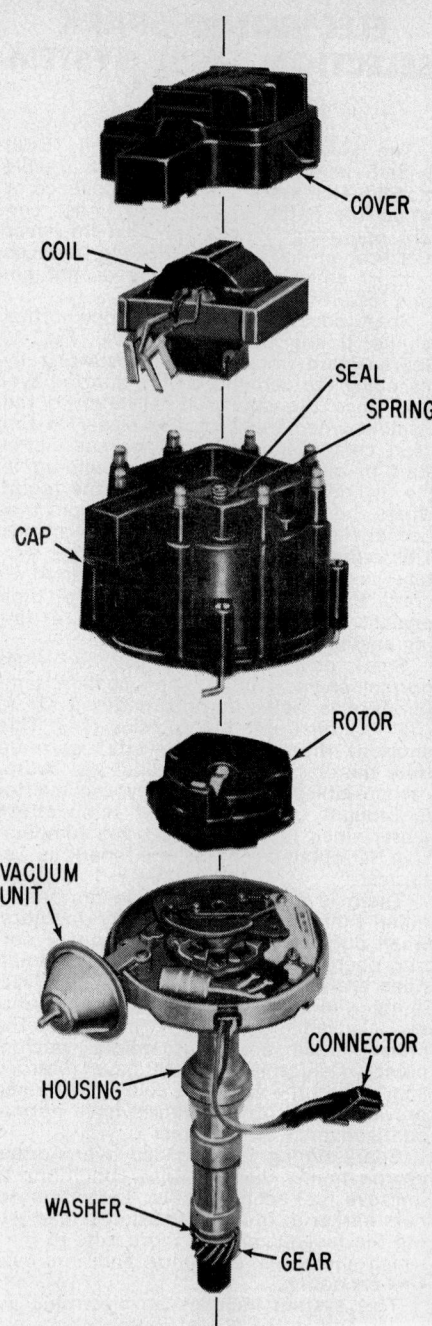

Fig. 2 H.E.I. distributor internal components. V6 & V8 engines

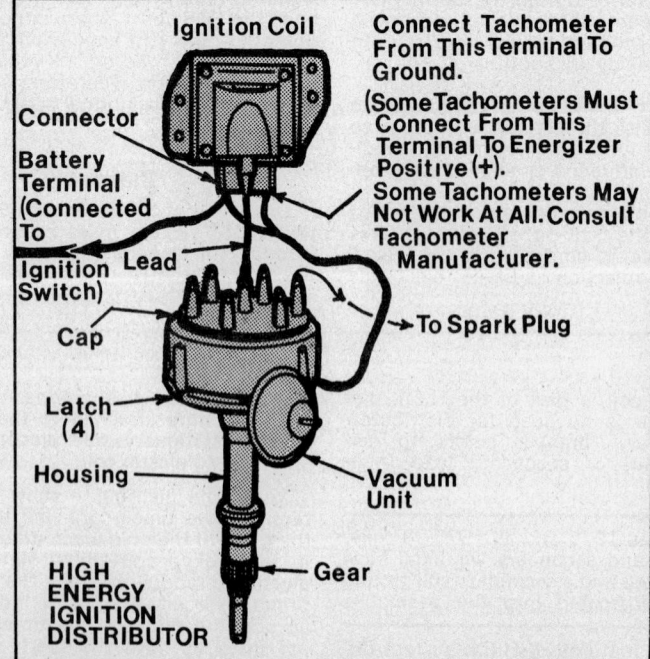

Fig. 3 H.E.I. distributor components. Inline 4 & 6 cyl. engines

the bulkhead connector; or between the bulkhead connector and the ignition switch; or between the ignition switch and the starter solenoid. Repair as required.
3. If reading is battery voltage, hold one spark plug lead with insulated pliers approximately ¼ inch away from a dry area of engine block and crank engine. If a spark is visible, the distributor has been eliminated as source of trouble. Check spark plugs and fuel system.
4. If there is no visible spark, perform

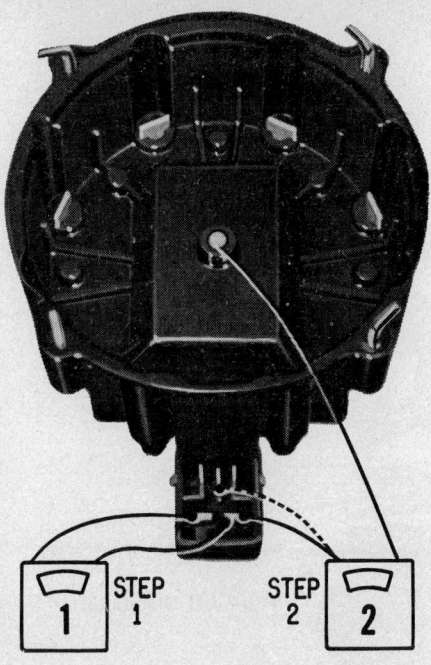

Fig. 4   H.E.I. distributor ignition coil ohmmeter test. V6 & V8 engines

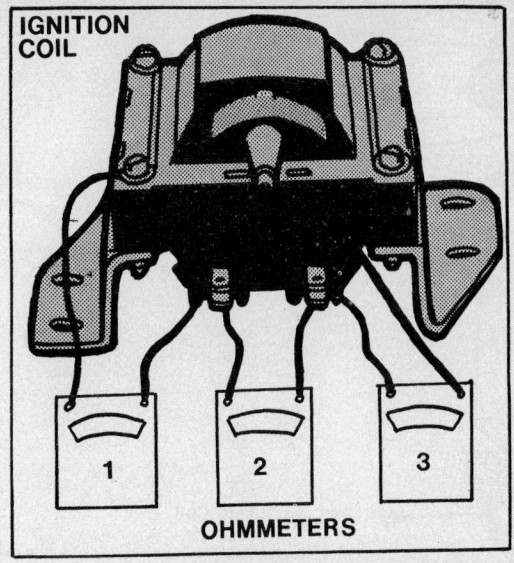

Fig. 5   H.E.I. distributor ignition coil ohmmeter test. Inline 4 & 6 cyl. engines

the "Component Checkout" and proceed as described further on.

Engine Starts But Runs Rough

1. Check for proper fuel delivery to carburetor.
2. Check all vacuum hoses for leakage.
3. Visually inspect and listen for sparks jumping to ground.
4. Check ignition timing.
5. Check centrifugal advance mechanism for proper operation.
6. Remove spark plugs and check for unusual defects, such as very wide gap, abnormal fouling, cracked insulators (inside and out), etc.
7. If no defects are found, perform the "Component Checkout" procedure as described below.

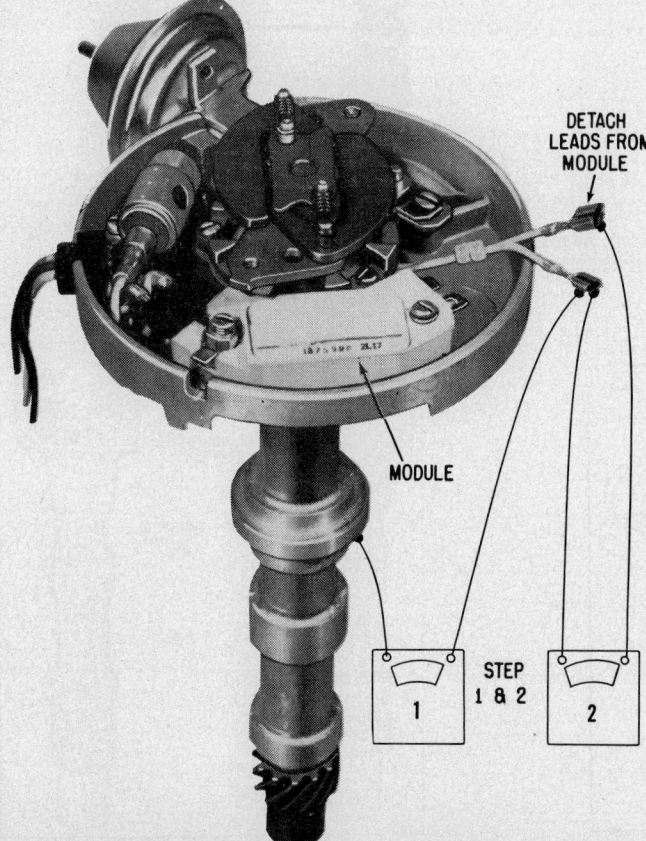

Fig. 6   Distributor pickup coil ohmmeter test

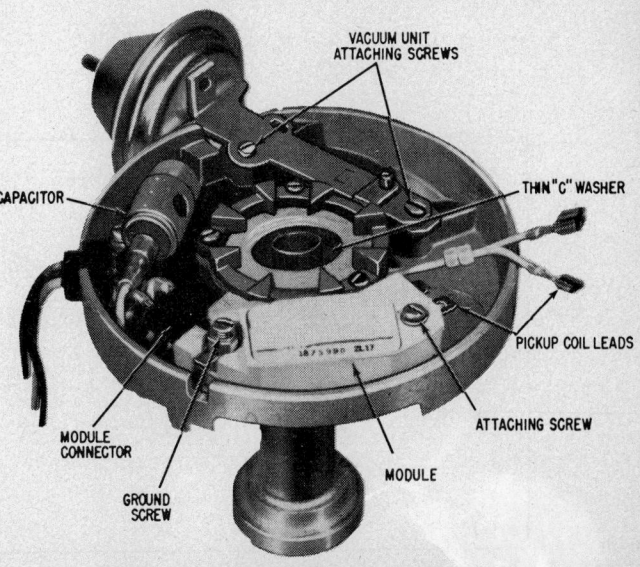

Fig. 7   H.E.I. distributor component replacement

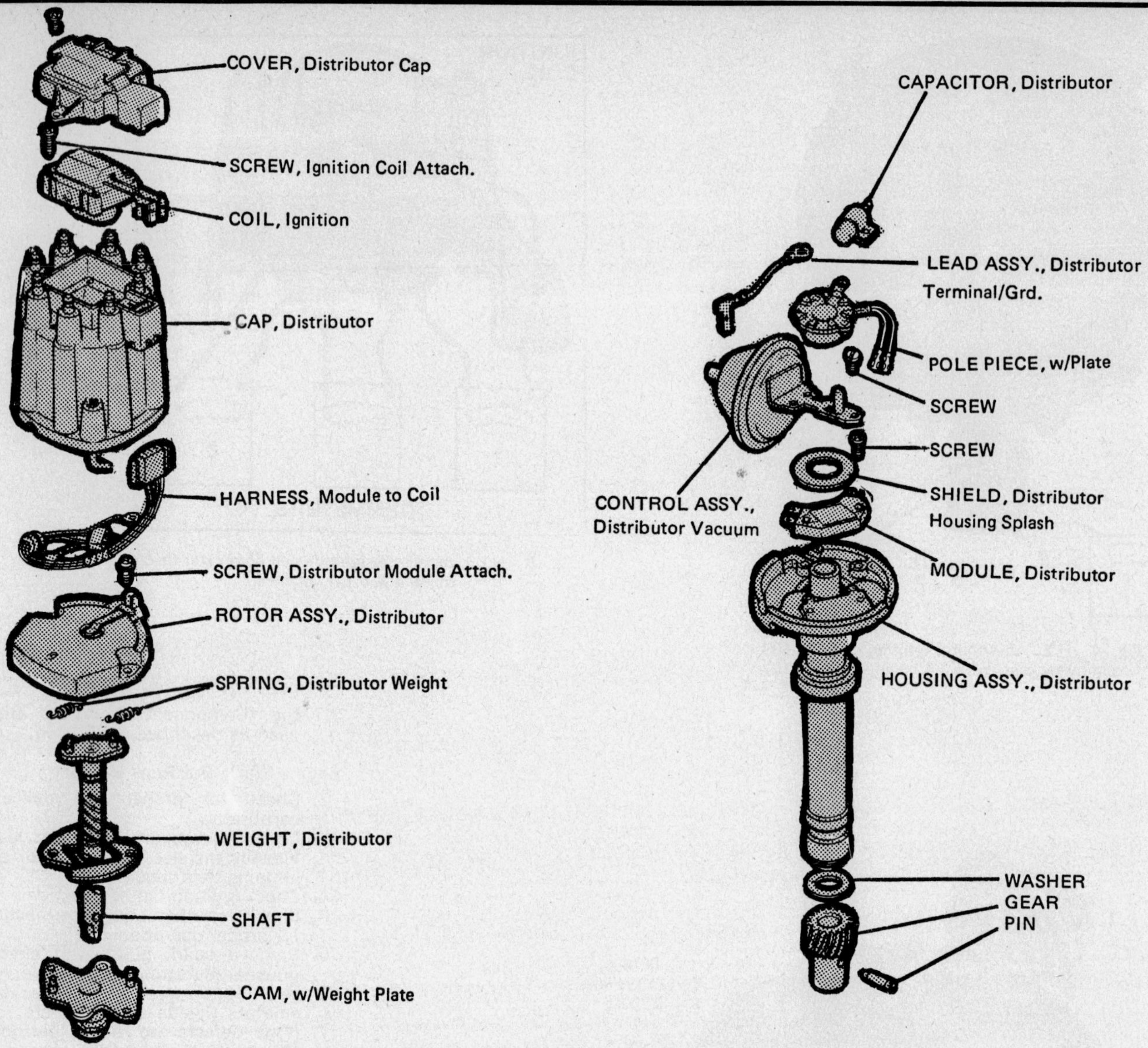

COVER, Distributor Cap
SCREW, Ignition Coil Attach.
COIL, Ignition
CAP, Distributor
HARNESS, Module to Coil
SCREW, Distributor Module Attach.
ROTOR ASSY., Distributor
SPRING, Distributor Weight
WEIGHT, Distributor
SHAFT
CAM, w/Weight Plate
CAPACITOR, Distributor
LEAD ASSY., Distributor
Terminal/Grd.
POLE PIECE, w/Plate
SCREW
SCREW
CONTROL ASSY.,
Distributor Vacuum
SHIELD, Distributor
Housing Splash
MODULE, Distributor
HOUSING ASSY., Distributor
WASHER
GEAR
PIN

Fig. 8 Exploded view of H.E.I. distributor (Typical). All except Cadillac with fuel injection

BATTERY TERMINAL
BATTERY TERMINAL
MUST BE INSERTED ON
THIS SIDE OF CONNECTOR

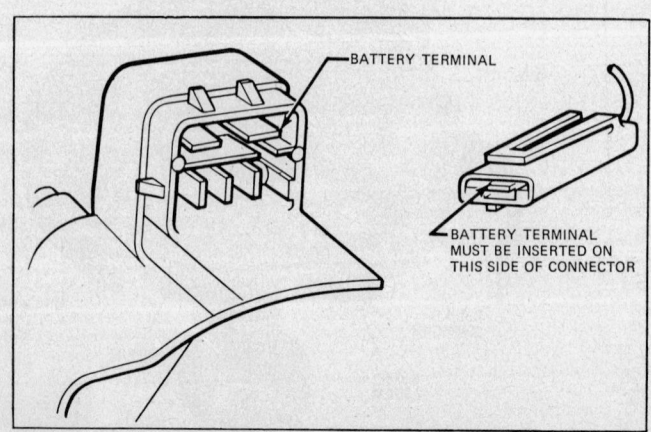

Fig. 9 H.E.I. distributor cap connector

ROUNDED
CASTING
FACE
POINTED
CASTING
FACE
DIMPLE

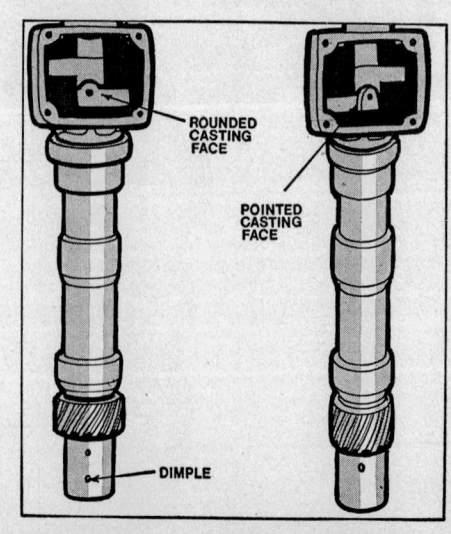

Fig. 11 Speed sensor location

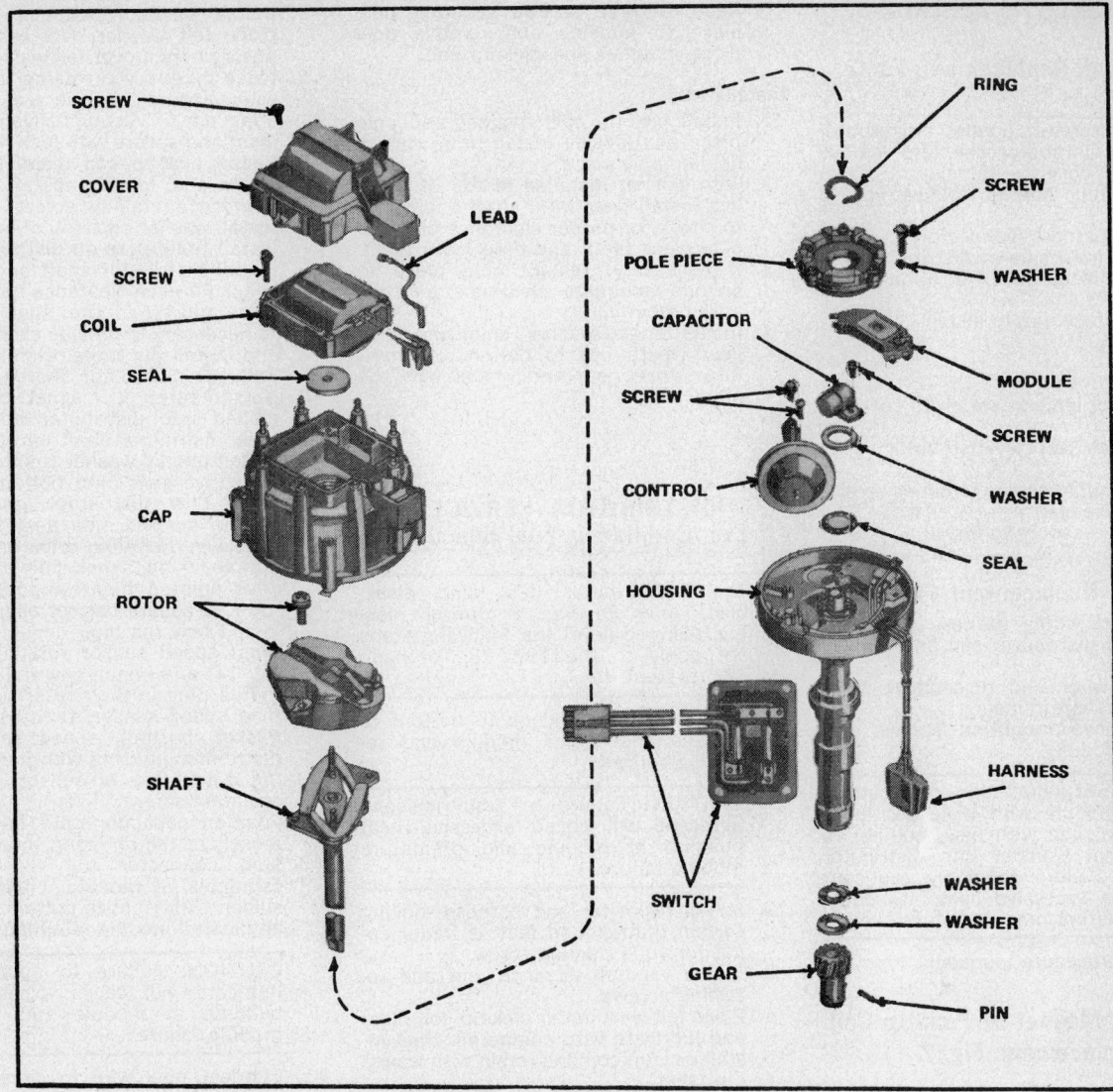

Fig. 10 Exploded view of H.E.I. distributor. Cadillac with fuel injection

Component Checkout

1. Remove cap and coil assembly.
2. Inspect cap, coil and rotor for spark arc-over.
3. On V6 and V8 engines:
   a. Connect ohmmeter, Fig. 4, step 1. If ohmmeter reading is other than zero or very near to zero, the ignition coil must be replaced.
   b. If no ohmmeter reading was observed in step 1, reconnect ohmmeter both ways, Fig. 4, step 2. If both ohmmeter readings are infinite on high scale, replace ignition coil.
4. On inline 4 and 6 cylinder engines:
   a. Connect ohmmeter, Fig. 5, step 1. If reading is not infinite, replace coil.
   b. Connect ohmmeter, Fig. 5, step 2. If reading is not zero or near zero, replace coil.
   c. Connect ohmmeter, Fig. 5, step 3. If reading is infinite, replace coil.
5. Connect an external vacuum source

to the vacuum advance unit. Replace vacuum unit if inoperative.
6. If vacuum unit is operating properly, connect ohmmeter, Fig. 6, step 1. If ohmmeter reading on middle scale is not infinite at all times, pick-up coil must be replaced.
7. With ohmmeter connected, Fig. 6, step 2, reading should be within 500 to 1500 ohms.

NOTE: Tester J-24624 is required to test the module. If this tester is not available, and malfunction still exists after performing the above checks, replace module.

SERVICE NOTE:

Some 1974-75 G. M. vehicles equipped with High Energy Ignition Systems (H. E. I.) may encounter a no-start condition or engine miss. These conditions may be caused by the battery ignition wire installed in such a way that the connector in distributor cap is bent and jammed on wrong side of blade in ignition

wire connector, Fig. 9. To correct this condition, proceed as folows:

1. Pry latch on black ignition wire connector and remove it from distributor, then unlock tang on blade and remove connector from blade.
2. Straighten blade, if bent. Bend tang on blade outboard to insure a positive lock when blade is reinstalled.
3. Slide connector over blade aligning tang with groove in connector until it bottoms, then pull lightly on wire to insure a positive lock.
4. Inspect blade in distributor cap connector. If bent, straighten and center.
5. Reinstall ignition wire connector by pushing straight up until latch is locked. The blade on distributor connector should be toward lock tab on ignition wire connector. When correctly installed, the connector should move freely while in the locked position.
6. Start engine and move connector. If engine does not start or misses, recheck above procedure.

TUNE UP SERVICE

COMPONENTS REPLACE

Ignition Coil Replacement, Fig. 2

V6 & V8 Engines
1. Remove screws holding distributor cover to distributor cap and remove distributor cover.
2. Remove four screws holding coil to cap.
3. Remove harness connector and battery wire from side of distributor cap.
4. Push coil leads out of position in cap and remove coil.
5. Reverse procedure to install.

Inline 4 & 6 Cyl. Engines
1. Disconnect ignition switch to coil lead from coil.
2. Disconnect coil to distributor leads from coil.
3. Remove coil to engine retaining screws and remove coil.
4. Reverse procedure to install.

Module Replacement, Fig. 7

1. Disconnect wiring harness connector at side of distributor cap and remove distributor.
2. Remove rotor and disconnect wires from module terminals.
3. Remove two mounting screws and remove module.

CAUTION: At installation, coat bottom of new module with dielectric lubricant (furnished with new module) to aid in heat transfer into distributor housing. Failure to apply lubricant will cause excessive heat at module and premature module failure.

4. Reverse procedure to install.

Pole Piece, Magnet or Pick-Up Coil Replacement, Fig. 7

Removal
1. With distributor removed, disconnect wires at module terminals.
2. Remove roll pin from drive gear by driving out with 1/8 inch diameter drift punch.
3. Remove gear, shim and the tanged washer from distributor shaft. Remove any burrs that may have been caused by removal of pin.
4. Remove distributor shaft from housing.
5. Remove washer from upper end of distributor housing.

NOTE: Bushings in the housing are not serviceable.

6. Remove three screws securing pole piece to housing and remove pole piece, magnet and pick-up coil.

Installation
1. Install pick-up coil, magnet and pole piece and loosely install three screws holding pole piece.
2. With washer installed at top of housing, install distributor shaft and rotate to check for proper clearance between pole piece teeth and timer core teeth.
3. If necessary, realign pole piece to provide adequate clearance and secure properly.
4. Install tanged washer, shim and drive gear (teeth up) to bottom of shaft. Align drive gear and install new roll pin.

DISTRIBUTOR SERVICE
Exc. Cadillac w/Fuel Injection

NOTE: If distributor has been disassembled, refer to Fig. 8 during reassembly. Also, some of the following steps do not apply to the 1977-78 Toronado (MISAR) system.

1. Liberally apply silicone to bottom of module and install module and retaining screws.

CAUTION: Failure to apply silicone lubricant will cause excessive heat build-up at module and premature module failure.

2. Install capacitor and harness making certain that ground lead is under capacitor and retaining screw.
3. Install vacuum advance unit and retaining screws.
4. Place felt wick under pick-up coil plate and lubricate with engine oil, then install pick-up coil and retain with waved C-washer.
5. Install distributor shaft into housing, then install drive gear onto shaft and install new roll pin.
6. On V8 engine distributors, install arc seal, coil and coil cover.

Cadillac w/Fuel Injection

NOTE: Close adherence to the following procedure is important, as several components may be installed in more than one way and could affect engine performance. Refer to Fig. 10 during assembly.

1. Install vacuum advance unit, then place felt washer over reservoir and position shim over felt washer.
2. Place pick-up coil retainer on housing with vacuum advance arm over actuating pin of vacuum advance mechanism and secure with lock ring.
3. Install pick-up coil magnet and pole piece and loosely install the three pole piece retaining screws.
4. Install washer onto top of housing and install timer core on distributor shaft.
5. Install distributor shaft and rotate to check for even clearance between pole piece and timer core. Align pole piece as necessary to provide even clearance and install the three retaining screws.
6. Pull out distributor shaft until speed sensor rotating magnet can be installed into distributor housing and push distributor shaft into position.
7. Install tanged washer (teeth up), shim and drive gear onto bottom of shaft. Note that distributor gear has a dimple on one side next to roll pin hole, Fig. 11. Align drive gear so that dimple is on same side of shaft as rotor pointer, then temporarily install rotor to assure correct alignment and install new roll pin.
8. Align speed sensor rotating magnet, Fig. 11, and install new roll pin.
9. Install plug in distributor housing behind speed sensor, then using a new gasket, position speed sensor onto distributor housing with harness coming out of top of sensor and install retaining screws.
10. Position capacitor onto housing and loosely install retaining screw, then install connector to "B" and "C" terminals of module. Liberally apply silicone lubricant to bottom of module and install module retaining screws.

CAUTION: Failure to apply silicone lubricant will cause excessive heat build-up at module and premature module failure.

11. Connect pink wire to capacitor stud and tighten screw, then connect white wire from pick-up coil to "W" terminal of module and connect white with green stripe wire from pick-up coil to "G" terminal of module.
12. Install advance cam over pins on shaft with stamped numbers facing down and install retaining rings.
13. Install advance weights with letters or numbers facing down and install springs with large loop in-board and offset up. Check weights for proper operation.
14. Install rotor and retaining screws.

NOTE: Assure that notch on side of rotor engages properly.

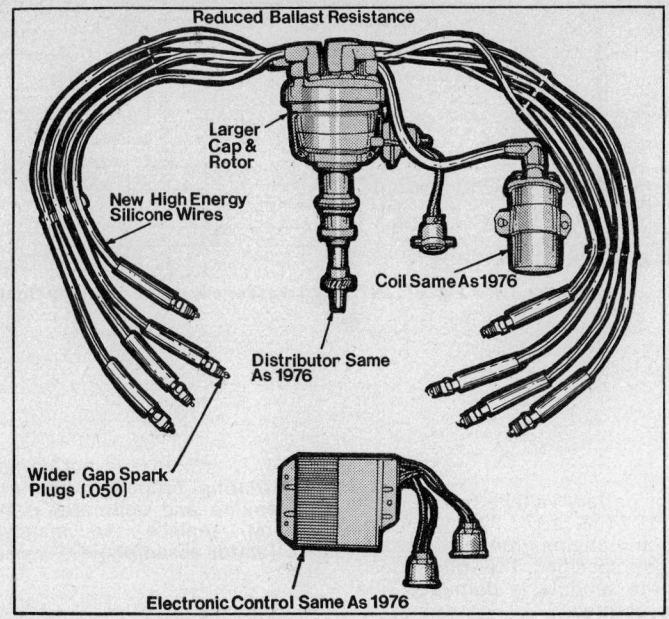

Fig. 1 Ford DuraSpark ignition system. 1977-78 exc. California 6-250 & V8 engines

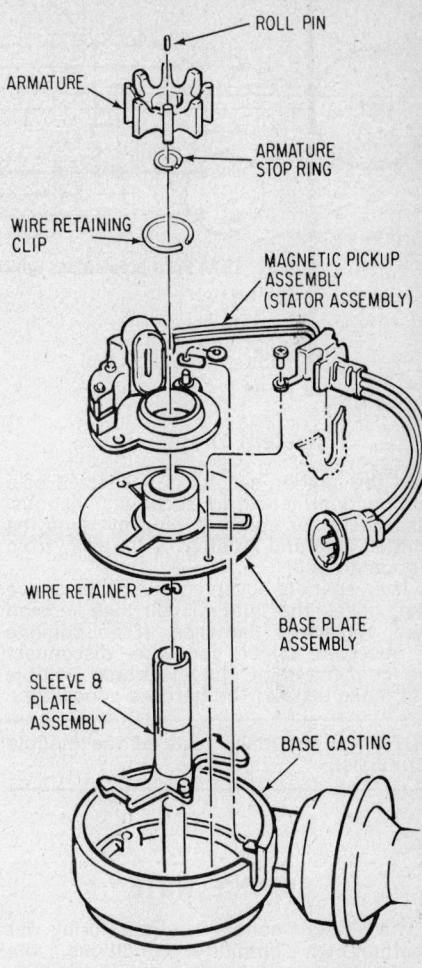

Fig. 4 Ford breakerless (B/L) distributor

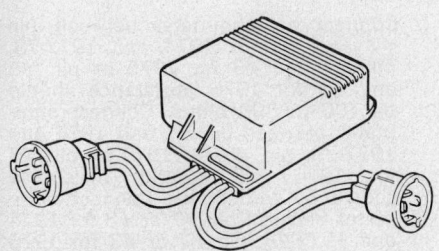

Fig. 2 Ford electronic module. B/L system

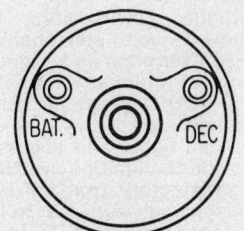

Fig. 3 Ford electronic ignition coil identification. B/L system

FORD SYSTEM

1974-76 Breakerless (B/L) & 1977-78 Dura Spark Solid State Ignition Systems

The B/L and Dura Spark ignition systems do not use points and are controlled by an electronic module. The Dura Spark system uses higher spark plug voltages during the starting and running modes, permitting the use of wider spark plug gaps required to ignite the leaner air/fuel mixtures.

Two versions of the Dura Spark system are used. The Dura Spark I system is used on California vehicles except 2300 cc and 2800 cc and the Dura Spark II system is used on all other applications. The Dura Spark I incorporates a new module ignition coil, distributor cap and adaptor, rotor and ignition wires. The module has a built-in current regulator which reduces overheating of the coil and module during operation. The ignition coil has revised primary and secondary windings necessary to supply the higher spark plug voltages. The Dura Spark II system, Fig. 1, uses a new distributor cap and adaptor, rotor and ignition wires. The higher spark plug

voltage in this system is obtained by reducing the value of the ballast resistor in the primary side of the ignition system.

The electronic module, Figs. 1 and 2, is the brain of this system and is well protected from outside elements such as heat and shock. The heat sink containing all the electronic devices is sealed in a mixture of epoxy and sand. This module can not be disassembled and must be replaced if malfunctioning.

New oil filled ignition coils are used, therefore conventional ignition coils are not to be used with these systems. The proper B/L coil is easily identified as it is all blue and terminals are labeled differently from conventional ignition coils "BAT" (battery) and "DEC" (Distributor Electronic Control), Fig. 3.

The ignition switch energizes the module through the white wire while engine is cranking and through the red wire when engine is running.

The distributor shaft and armature rotation, Fig. 4, causes the armature poles to pass by the core of the magnetic pick-up assembly. In turn cutting the magnetic field and signaling the electronic module, Figs. 5 thru 9, through the orange and purple wires to break the primary ignition

current, thus inducing secondary voltage in the coil to fire the spark plugs. The coil is then energized again by the primary circuit and ready for the next spark cycle. This primary circuit is controlled by a timing circuit in the module.

The ignition system is protected against electrical current produced during normal vehicle operation and against reverse polarity or high voltage accidentally applied if vehicle is jump started.

Total diagnosis of the system requires only a volt-ohmmeter tester.

CAUTION: The ignition system will be damaged if other than volt-ohm test procedures are used to check alternator output. This alternator test procedure is outlined in the "Ford Motorcraft Alternator" section, under "Voltmeter Test."

Do not use the volt-amp test procedure or any other test that utilizes a knife switch on the battery terminal.

Since the interval between the time that the module activates the primary ignition circuit and the time the distributor signal turns it off varies with engine speed. Consequently, a dwell measurement is insignificant.

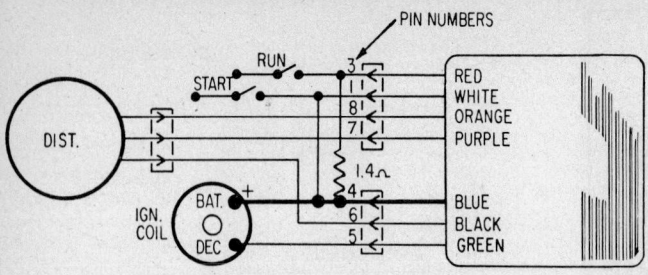

Fig. 5 1974 Ford breakerless ignition primary circuit

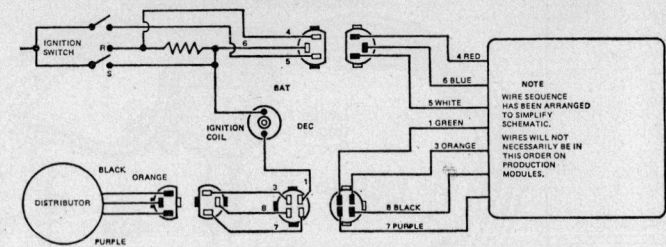

Fig. 6 1975 Ford breakerless ignition primary circuit

System Diagnosis

If the ignition system is suspected of a malfunction inspect for loose connections. Also check for spark at plug by removing ignition wire and holding 1/4 in. away from a good ground.

If no spark is observed during the above test, check the ignition coil high tension wire, replace if damaged. If no damage is observed at the coil wire, disconnect the connectors at the electronic module and make tests at the harness connectors.

NOTE: Do not make tests at the module terminals.

SERVICE NOTE

If a no start condition exists during wet weather/high humidity conditions, the cause may be high voltage leakage to ground at the coil to distributor wire boots due to excessive moisture and contamination (such as salt). To correct this condition proceed as follows:

1. Clean all moisture and dirt accumulation from exposed surfaces on the distributor cap and coil tower without removing wires from the cap or coil tower. If there is evidence of wire damage replace as necessary. Attempt to start the engine.
2. If the engine still does not start, remove the distributor to coil high tension wire and clean the coil tower, the center tower of the distributor cap and the distributor to coil wire. Apply Dow 4X or GE G-624 Silicone grease to the outer surfaces of the coil tower and the center tower of the cap and re-install the coil wire insuring that both ends are fully seated.
3. If condition persists, replace the coil to distributor high tension wire to provide new sealing qualities at the boot seals.

Voltage Tests At Harness Connectors, Figs. 10 thru 13

NOTE: If all the following tests comply with specifications replace the module.

Key On

1. Check for battery voltage between pin #3 for 1974 & 1977-78 or #4 for 1975-76 and engine ground. If voltage is less than specified, the voltage feed wire to the module is damaged and must be repaired.
2. Check for battery voltage between pin #5 for 1974 & 1977-78 or #1 for 1975-76 and engine ground. If voltage is less than specified proceed as follows:
   a. Without disconnecting the coil, connect voltmeter between coil "BAT" terminal and engine ground.
   b. Connect a jumper wire between the coil "DEC" terminal and engine ground.
   c. With all lights and accessories off, turn on the ignition switch.
   d. A satisfactory primary circuit will register between 4.9 to 7.9 volts for Breakerless & Dura Spark II systems, or 11 to 14 volts for Dura Spark I systems.
   e. If voltmeter readings are less than specified in previous step, check for worn primary circuit insulation, broken wire strands or loose-corroded terminals.
   f. On Breakerless and Dura Spark II systems, if voltage reading registered on voltmeter is greater than 7.9 volts, check and replace if necessary the resistance wire.

Cranking Engine

1. Check for 8 to 12 volts between pin #1 for 1974 & 1977-78 or pin #5 for 1975-76 and engine ground. On 1974-75, if voltage is not within specifications, the voltage feed wire to the module is damaged. On 1976-78, if reading is not more than 6 volts, the ignition by-pass circuit is open or grounded from either the starter solenoid or the ignition switch to pin #5 or primary connections at coil.
2. Check for 1/2 volt oscillation (using the 2.5 volt scale) between pin #7 and #8 for 1974 and 1977-78 pin #7 and #3 for 1975 or pin #3 and #8 for 1976. If the voltmeter does not register this oscillation, visually inspect distributor components. Make sure that the toothed armature is not damaged, is tight on sleeve and secured properly with the alignment pin, Fig.

4. If armature is not damaged and is rotating properly when cranking the engine and voltmeter is not oscillating, replace the magnetic pickup (stator assembly).

Resistance Test At Harness Connectors, Figs. 7 & 8

Key Off

1. Connect an ohmmeter between pin #7 and #8 for 1974 and 1977-78, pin #7 and #3 for 1975 or pin #8 and #3 for 1976, resistance should be 400 to 800 ohms. Connect ohmmeter between pin #6 and 1974 and 1977-78, pin #8 for 1975 or pin #7 for 1976 and ground, resistance should be zero ohms. Connect ohmmeter between pin #7 or #8 for 1974 and 1977-78, pin #7 or #3 for 1975 or pin #8 or #3 for 1976 and ground, resistance should be more than 70,000 ohms. If any of the above checks do not comply with specifications, the magnetic pick-up assembly (stator assembly) is not functioning and must be replaced.
2. Check secondary coil resistance between pin #3 for 1974 and 1977-78 or pin #4 for 1975-76 and coil tower. Also check primary coil resistance between pin #5 for 1974 and 1977-78 or pin #1 for 1975-76 and pin #4 for 1974, pin #6 for 1975 or coil "Bat" terminal for 1976. If secondary coil resistance is not within 7,000 to 13,000 ohms, or primary coil resistance is not within 1 to 2 ohms for Breakerless and Dura Spark II, or .5 to 1.5 for Dura Spark I, diagnose coil separately from rest of system. Follow procedures for testing standard ignition coils as outlined in the "TUNE UP SERVICE" chapter under "Ignition Coils & Resistors."
3. Check for a resistance of more than 4.0 ohms between pin #5 for 1974 or pin #1 for 1975-76 and engine ground. If resistance is less than specified, locate the short to ground either at the coil "DEC" terminal or in the green wire, Fig. 5.
4. If a resistance of 1.0 to 2.0 ohms is not obtained between pins #3 for 1974 and 1977-78 or pin #6 for 1975 and #4, replace the primary resistance wire.

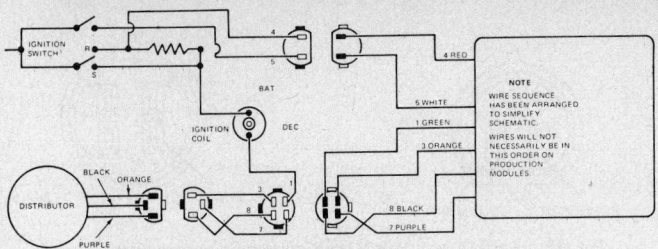

Fig. 7   1976 Ford breakerless ignition primary circuit

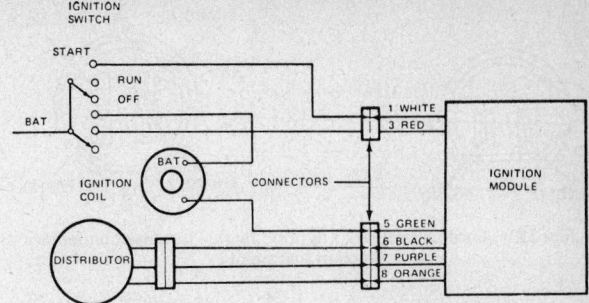

Fig. 8   Ford Dura Spark I ignition primary circuit

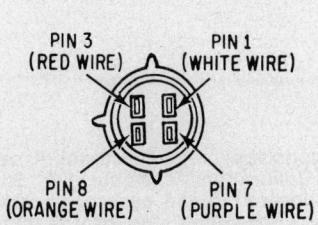

PIN 3
(RED WIRE)   PIN 1
(WHITE WIRE)

PIN 8
(ORANGE WIRE)   PIN 7
(PURPLE WIRE)

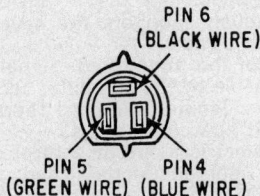

PIN 6
(BLACK WIRE)

PIN 5   PIN 4
(GREEN WIRE)   (BLUE WIRE)

Fig. 10   1974 Ford breakerless ignition female harness connectors system test points

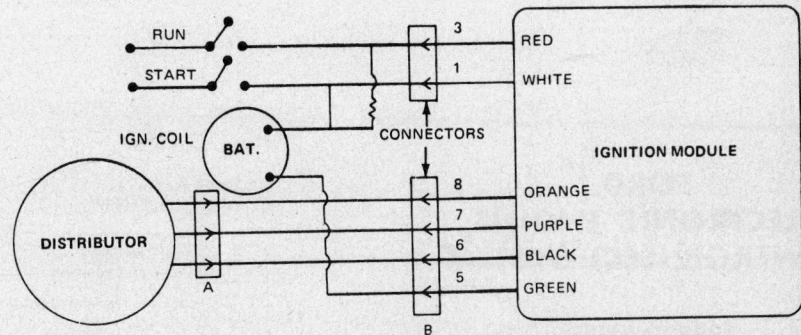

Fig. 9   Ford Dura Spark II ignition primary circuit

COMPONENT REPLACEMENT

Magnetic Pickup Assembly

Removal

1. Remove distributor cap and rotor, then disconnect distributor wiring harness plug, Fig. 4.
2. Using two screw drivers, pry armature from advance plate sleeve and remove roll pin.
3. Remove snap ring securing pickup assembly to base plate. On 4 and 6 cylinder models, remove washer and wave washer.
4. On all models, remove snap ring securing vacuum advance link to pickup assembly.
5. Remove pickup assembly ground screw and lift assembly from distributor.
6. Disconnect vacuum advance link from pickup assembly post.

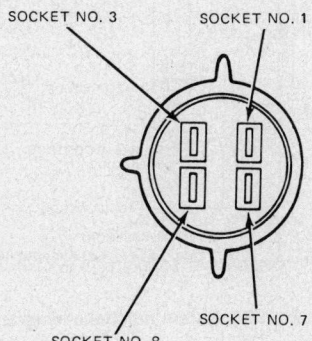

SOCKET NO. 3   SOCKET NO. 1

SOCKET NO. 8   SOCKET NO. 7

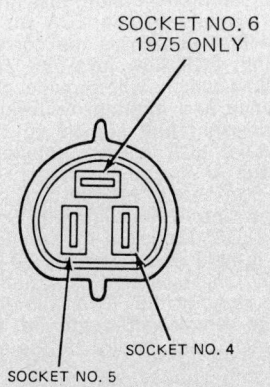

SOCKET NO. 6
1975 ONLY

SOCKET NO. 5   SOCKET NO. 4

Fig. 11   1975-76 Ford breakerless ignition female harness connectors (system test points)

Installation

1. Position pickup assembly over base plate and slide wiring harness into slot on side of distributor housing, Fig. 4.
2. On 4 and 6 cylinder models, install washers. On all models, install snap ring securing pickup assembly to base plate.
3. Position vacuum advance link on pickup assembly post and install snap ring.
4. Insert ground screw through wiring harness tab and install on base plate.
5. Install armature on advance plate sleeve, ensure roll pin is engaged in slot.
6. Install distributor rotor and cap, then connect distributor wiring harness plug to vehicle wiring harness.

Vacuum Advance Unit, Replace

1. Remove distributor cap and rotor.
2. Disconnect vacuum lines, then remove snap ring that secures vacuum advance link to pickup assembly.
3. Remove vacuum advance attaching screws, then tilt unit downward to disconnect link.
4. Carefully remove unit from distributor.
5. Reverse procedure to install.

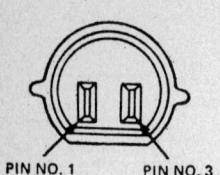

PIN NO. 5   PIN NO. 8

PIN NO. 1   PIN NO. 3

PIN NO. 7   PIN NO. 6

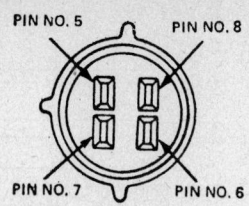

Fig. 12 Ford Dura Spark I ignition female harness connectors (system test points)

PIN NO. 8   PIN NO. 5

PIN NO. 1   PIN NO. 3

PIN NO. 7   PIN NO. 6

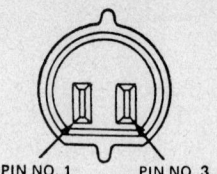
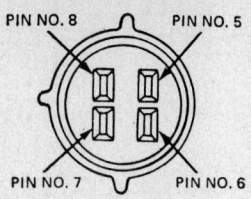

Fig. 13 Ford Dura Spark II ignition female harness connectors (system test points)

Fixed Base Plate, Replace

1. Remove distributor cap and rotor.
2. Remove vacuum advance unit and magnetic pickup assembly.
3. Remove attaching screws and lift base plate from distributor.
4. Reverse procedure to install.

FORD ELECTRONIC ENGINE CONTROL (EEC) SYSTEM

1978 Versailles

This system, Figs. 1 and 2 uses an integrated electronic engine control system designed to more precisely control ignition timing, EGR flow rate and Thermactor System air flow. The system consists of an Electronic Control Assembly (ECA), seven sensors, a Dura-Spark II ignition module and coil, a special distributor and an air pressure operated EGR system.

The seven sensors monitor the following ambient conditions and engine functions:
a. Manifold Absolute Pressure
b. Barometric Pressure
c. Engine Coolant Temperature
d. Inlet Air Temperature
e. Crankshaft Position
f. Throttle Position
g. EGR Valve Position

The sensors monitor these various engine and ambient conditions and send electrical signals to the ECA for evaluation. The ECA computes the correct ignition timing, EGR flow rate and Thermactor air flow which will provide the best performance and minimal emissions, and sends corresponding signals to the ignition module, EGR control solenoids and Thermactor air control solenoid.

If the ECA should malfunction, the system goes into the Limited Operation Strategy (LOS) Mode. In this mode, spark advance is held at a constant 10 degrees BTDC, and the EGR and Thermactor systems are deactivated. This allows operation of the vehicle, although with reduced performance, until repairs can be made.

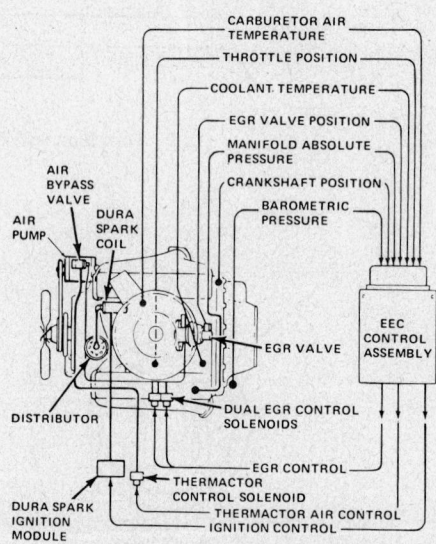

1978 302-VV Versailles
EEC FUNCTIONAL DIAGRAM

CARBURETOR AIR TEMPERATURE
THROTTLE POSITION
COOLANT TEMPERATURE
EGR VALVE POSITION
MANIFOLD ABSOLUTE PRESSURE
CRANKSHAFT POSITION
BAROMETRIC PRESSURE
AIR BYPASS VALVE
AIR PUMP
DURA SPARK COIL
EEC CONTROL ASSEMBLY
EGR VALVE
DISTRIBUTOR
DUAL EGR CONTROL SOLENOIDS
EGR CONTROL
THERMACTOR CONTROL SOLENOID
DURA SPARK IGNITION MODULE
THERMACTOR AIR CONTROL
IGNITION CONTROL

Fig. 2 EEC system functional diagram

puter consisting of a Processor Assembly and a Calibration Assembly, Fig. 3. This unit is located in the passenger compartment on the right side of the steering column.

The Processor Assembly is housed in an aluminum case and performs the following functions:
a. Continuously monitors the seven sensor input signals.
b. Converts the monitored signal to a form usable by the computer section.
c. Performs ignition timing, Thermactor and EGR flow calculations.
d. Sends electrical output control signals to the ignition module and control solenoids to adjust timing, Thermactor and EGR flow rates.
e. Provides a continuous reference voltage of about 9 volts to the sensors.

The Calibration Assembly is attached to the top of the Processor Assembly and contains the "memory" and programming for the processor assembly. The Calibration Assembly performs the following functions:
a. Provides calibration information for the particular vehicle, for use by the processor assembly.
b. Stores calculations for the processor assembly.
c. Recalls information from its memory when required.

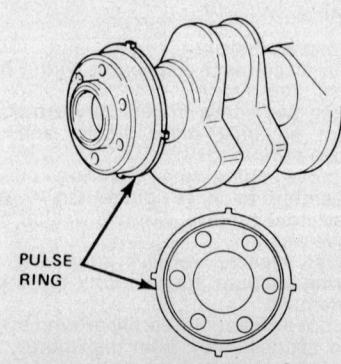

CALIBRATION ASSEMBLY
MOTORCRAFT
MOTORCRAFT No. 7318-9
PROCESSOR ASSEMBLY

Fig. 3 Electronic control assembly

System Components
Electronic Control Assembly (ECA)

The ECA is a solid-state, micro-com-

PULSE RING

Fig. 4 EEC crankshaft pulse ring

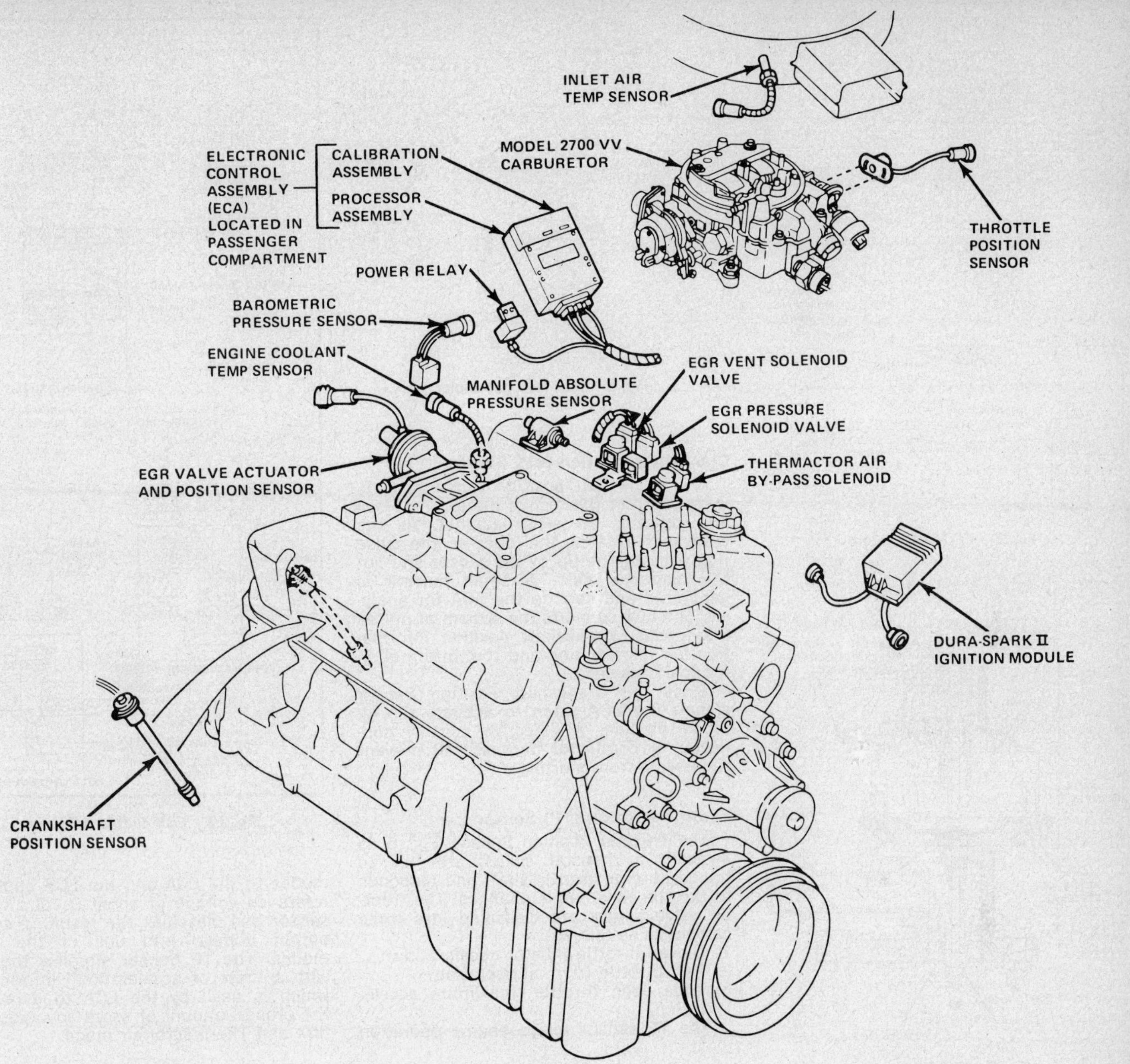

INLET AIR TEMP SENSOR

ELECTRONIC CONTROL ASSEMBLY (ECA) LOCATED IN PASSENGER COMPARTMENT

CALIBRATION ASSEMBLY

PROCESSOR ASSEMBLY

MODEL 2700 VV CARBURETOR

THROTTLE POSITION SENSOR

POWER RELAY

BAROMETRIC PRESSURE SENSOR

ENGINE COOLANT TEMP SENSOR

MANIFOLD ABSOLUTE PRESSURE SENSOR

EGR VENT SOLENOID VALVE

EGR PRESSURE SOLENOID VALVE

EGR VALVE ACTUATOR AND POSITION SENSOR

THERMACTOR AIR BY-PASS SOLENOID

DURA-SPARK II IGNITION MODULE

CRANKSHAFT POSITION SENSOR

Fig. 1   Electronic Engine Control (EEC) system

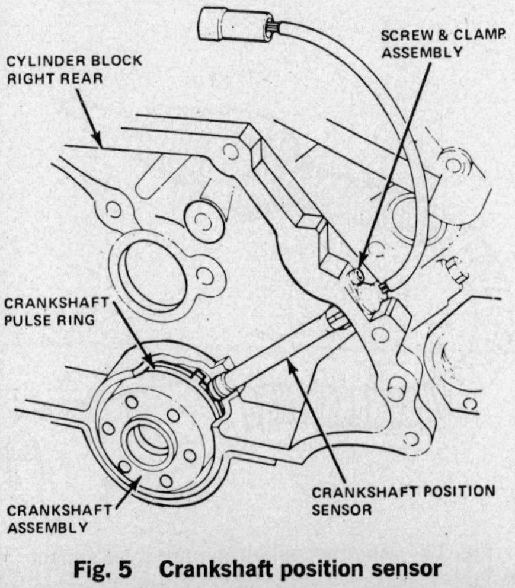

CYLINDER BLOCK RIGHT REAR

SCREW & CLAMP ASSEMBLY

CRANKSHAFT PULSE RING

CRANKSHAFT POSITION SENSOR

CRANKSHAFT ASSEMBLY

Fig. 5   Crankshaft position sensor

Power Relay

This relay is attached to the lower right hand side of the ECA mounting bracket and supplies battery voltage to the EEC system. It also protects the ECA from damage due to reversed polarity.

EEC Crankshaft

The rear of the crankshaft is fitted with a four-lobe "pulse ring," Fig. 4, to provide the EEC system with an accurate "reference timing" (indication when pistons reach top dead center).

The pulse ring is a ¼ inch thick powdered metal ring placed on the crankshaft during manufacture. It has four equally spaced lobes which indicate when the pistons are at TDC. Since four cylinders fire during each crankshaft revolution, only four lobes are required.

NOTE: The pulse ring is actually positioned 10 degrees before top dead center to establish the engine reference timing at 10 degrees.

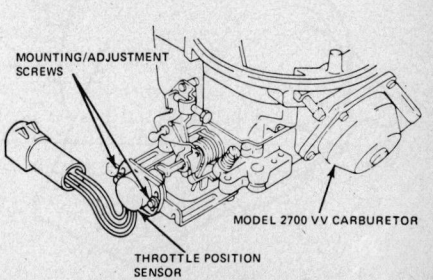

MOUNTING/ADJUSTMENT SCREWS

THROTTLE POSITION SENSOR

MODEL 2700 VV CARBURETOR

Fig. 6   Throttle position sensor

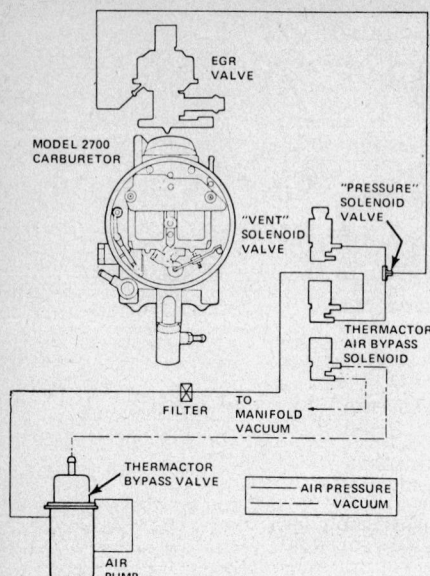

Fig. 7   EEC-EGR system

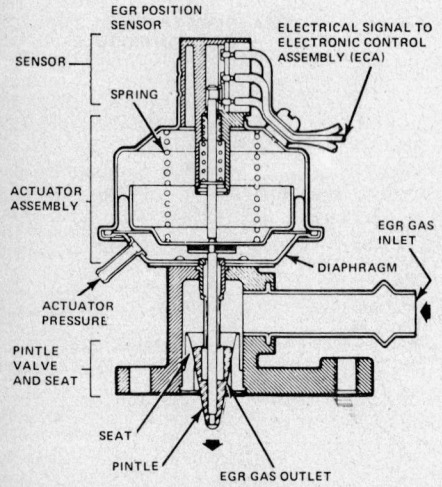

Fig. 8   EEC-EGR valve

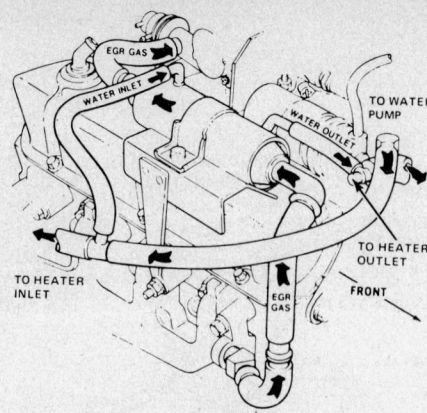

Fig. 9   EEC-EGR gas cooler

Crankshaft Position (CP) Sensor

The crankshaft position sensor, Fig. 5, is mounted at the rear of the engine block and contains an electromagnet. As the crankshaft rotates, the lobes on the pulse ring pass by the tip of the sensor and cut the magnetic field. A small current is generated and sent to the ECA for analysis. The ECA converts the stream of pulses into precise crankshaft position information for spark timing and rpm information for spark advance.

Since the Crankshaft Position Sensor signals the ECA when to activate the ignition module, a defective sensor, connector or connector harness will prevent the engine from starting.

Throttle Position (TP) Sensor

The Throttle Position Sensor, Fig. 6, is basically a rheostat switch attached to the carburetor throttle shaft and responds to throttle valve angle changes. The throttle valve angles are classified into three categories as follows:

1. Closed throttle (idle or deceleration)
2. Part throttle (normal operation)
3. Wide open throttle (maximum acceleration)

The TP sensor relays engine operation modes to the ECA and the ECA applies a reference voltage of about 9 volts to the sensor and classifies the resulting sensor output voltage into one of the three modes. The TP Sensor supplies the ECA with a "rate of acceleration" information which is used by the ECA to determine the proper amount of spark advance, EGR flow and Thermactor air mode.

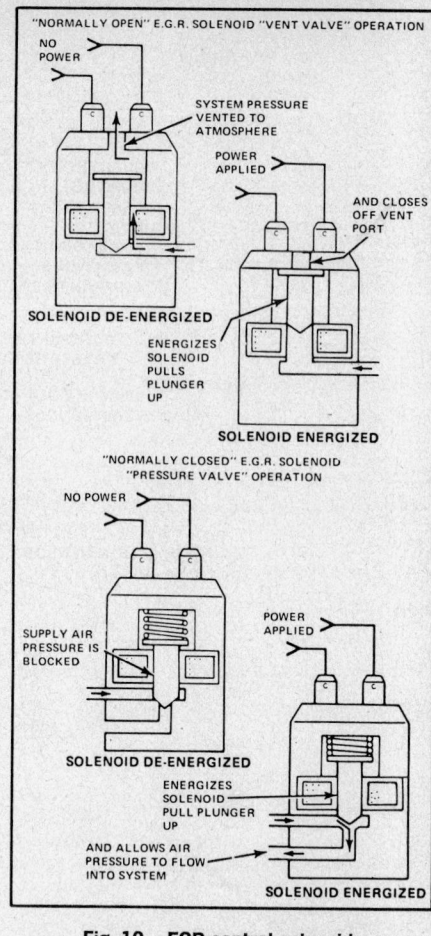

Fig. 10   EGR control solenoids

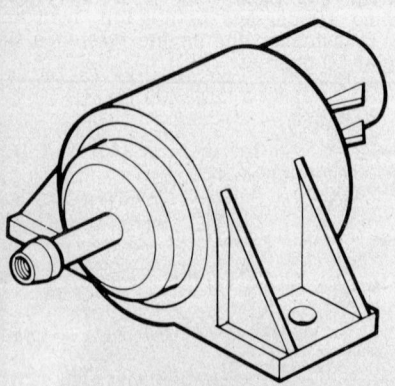

Fig. 11   Manifold absolute pressure (MAP) sensor

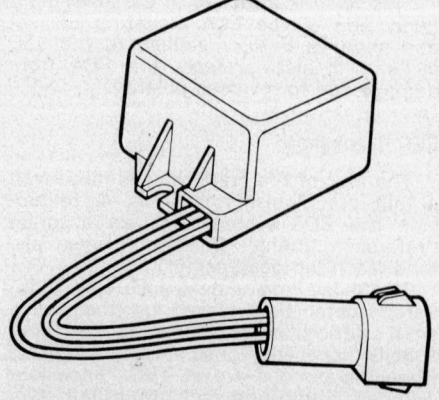

Fig. 12   Barometric pressure (BP) sensor

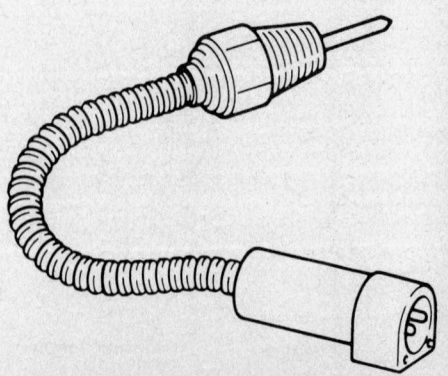

Fig. 13   Engine coolant temperature sensor

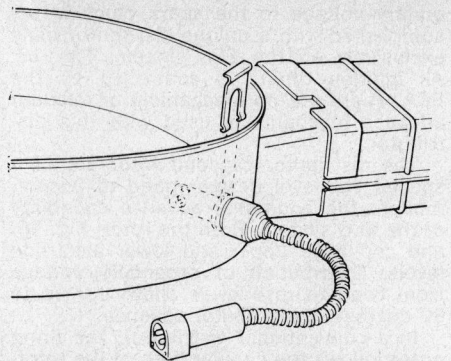

Fig. 14 Inlet air temperature (IAT) sensor

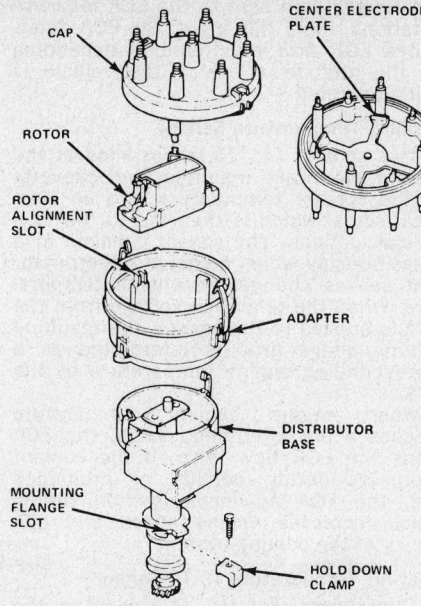

Fig. 15 EEC distributor exploded view

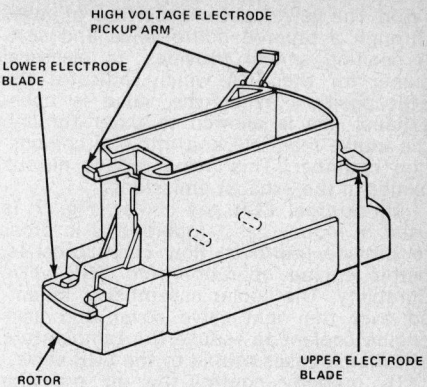

Fig. 16 EEC distributor rotor

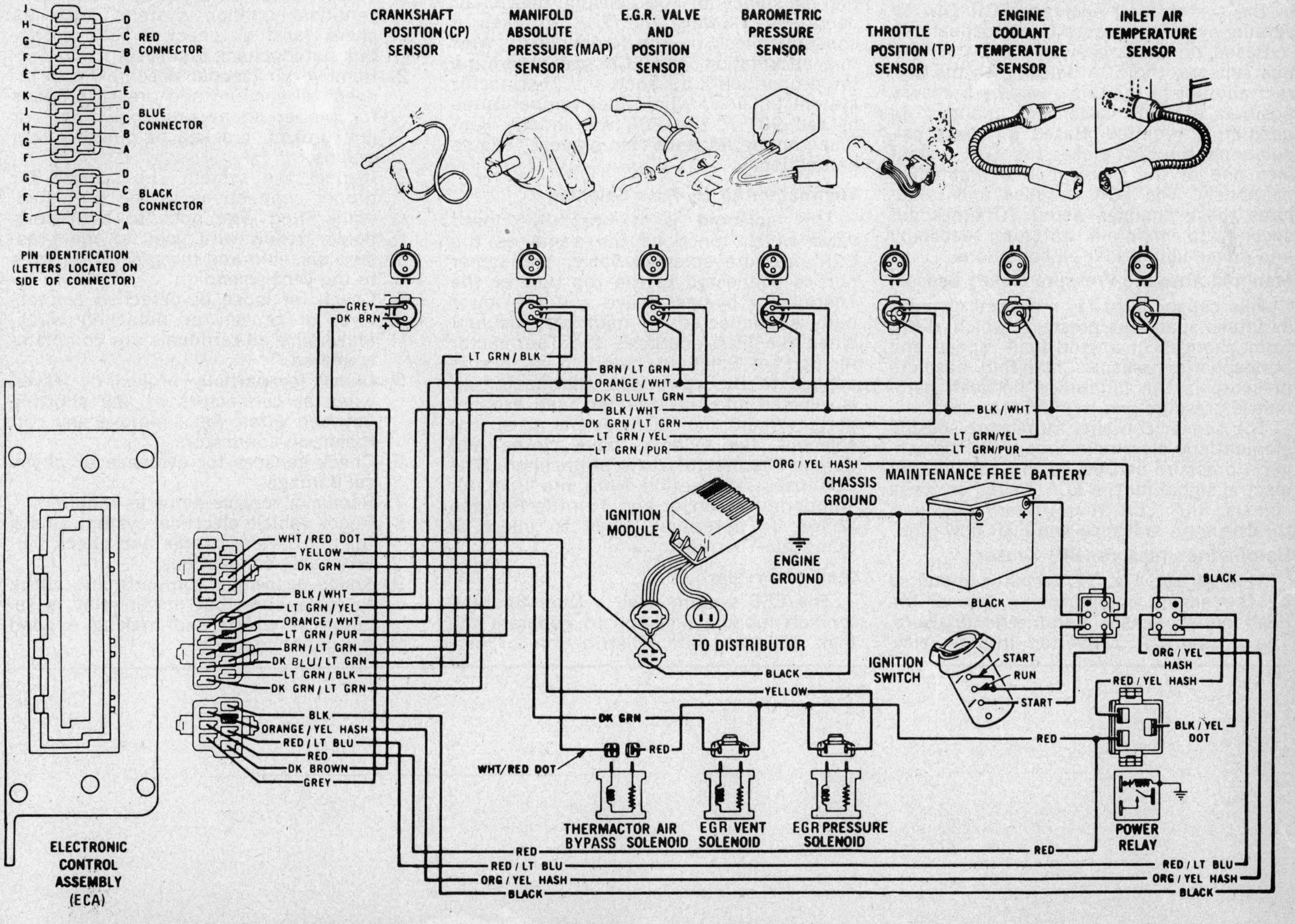

Exhaust Gas Recirculation (EGR)

The EGR system, Fig. 7, used on these vehicles consists of the EGR valve and sensor assembly, dual control solenoids and EGR cooler assembly. Indirectly related components consist of the Thermactor system and ECA.

The EGR gas flow is controlled by the

ECA which uses air pressure from the Thermactor system by-pass valve to operate the EGR valve. This is the opposite of conventional systems which use manifold vacuum for the same purpose.

The EGR valve, Fig. 8, is attached to a spacer which mounts under the carbu-

Fig. 17 EEC wiring schematic

retor. The valve controls the flow of gases through a tapered pintle valve and seat. A position sensor provides an electrical signal for the ECA which indicates the EGR position. When the valve is open, exhaust gas is allowed to enter through the intake manifold and into the combustion chamber. This helps reduce nitrous oxides in the exhaust emissions.

An external EGR gas cooler, Fig. 9, is used to reduce gas temperatures in order to provide improved flow characteristics, better engine operation and EGR valve durability. The cooler assembly is mounted over the right valve cover and uses engine coolant to reduce the temperature of exhaust gases routed to the EGR valve.

To properly control the air pressure used to operate the EGR valve and to also allow for application, hold and release of the air pressure, requires the use of a vent valve solenoid and a pressure valve solenoid, Fig. 10. The vent valve which is normally open has the outlet port normally connected to the inlet port when the solenoid is not operated. The pressure valve solenoid, which is normally closed, has the outlet port normally blocked when the solenoid is not operated.

The EGR valve is operated by air pressure supplied by the Thermactor by-pass valve. The pressure and vent solenoid valves work together and are controlled by the ECA to increase EGR flow by applying air pressure to the EGR valve, maintaining EGR flow by trapping air pressure in the system and decrease EGR flow by venting system pressure to atmosphere.

Based on data received from the various sensors, the ECA determines the correct amount of EGR flow required, checks position of EGR valve and changes its position if required. Based on these calculations, the ECA places the EGR system into one of the three modes mentioned previously. The ECA samples and calculates these changes about 10 times per second, to maintain optimum economy and driveability under all conditions.

Manifold Absolute Pressure (MAP) Sensor

This sensor, Fig. 11, monitors changes in intake manifold pressure which result from changes in engine load, speed and atmospheric pressure. Manifold absolute pressure is the difference between barometric pressure and manifold vacuum.

The sensor contains a pressure-sensing element and electronic circuitry which converts pressure sensed by the unit into an electric signal for the ECA. Based on these signals, the ECA then determines part throttle spark advance and EGR flow rate.

Barometric Pressure (BP) Sensor

This sensor, Fig. 12, which is mounted on the engine compartment side of the dash panel, senses barometric pressure. The pressure is converted into an electrical signal and sent to the ECA for computations. From this input, the ECA determines EGR flow requirements depending on the altitude at which the vehicle is being operated.

Coolant Temperature Sensor

This sensor, Fig. 13, is installed at the rear of the intake manifold, and converts engine coolant temperature into an electrical signal which is then fed to the ECA for calculations. The sensor consists of a brass housing which contains a thermistor that senses changes in engine temperature. When the reference voltage from the ECA is applied to the sensor, the resulting return voltage drop is interpreted as a corresponding engine temperature by the ECA.

When engine coolant temperature reaches a pre-determined value, the ECA stops the EGR flow. Also, if the coolant overheats during periods of prolonged idle, the ECA advances ignition timing which increases engine speed and efficiency of the cooling system.

Inlet Air Temperature (IAT) Sensor

This sensor, Fig. 14, is similar to the Coolant Temperature Sensor except for the addition of a protective shield near the tip.

This sensor is mounted in the air cleaner body near the duct and valve assembly and is sensitive to changes in inlet air temperature. As the temperature rises, the resistance of the sensing thermister decreases allowing the ECA to keep a constant check on the temperature. With this information, the ECA can determine the proper spark advance and Thermactor system air flow. When inlet temperatures exceed 90° F, the ECA will modify ignition timing advance to prevent engine detonation.

Thermactor Air By-Pass Solenoid

This solenoid is a normally closed valve which functions the same as the EGR pressure solenoid valve. The upper port is connected to the top port of the Thermactor by-pass valve and the lower port is connected to manifold vacuum. When the ECA energizes the Thermactor Air By-Pass Solenoid, manifold vacuum is applied to the valve and Thermactor air is injected into the cylinder head exhaust ports. When the ECA de-energizes the solenoid, the by-pass valve closes and dumps Thermactor air to atmosphere. The ECA uses information from the Inlet Air Temperature Sensor and Throttle Position Sensor to determine when to inject or dump the Thermactor air.

Ignition System

The EEC system uses a Dura Spark II ignition module and coil to generate the high voltage spark. Distribution of secondary voltage to the spark plugs is accomplished with a unique distributor used exclusively on the EEC system, Fig. 15. All ignition timing is controlled by the ECA. There are no mechanical or vacuum advance mechanisms used with this distributor.

The distributor cap and rotor are of a special two-level design made to accommodate the additional advance capability of the EEC system. Both the rotor, Fig. 16, and cap have upper and lower electrode levels. Distribution of secondary voltage from two separate levels allows for up to 30 degrees of distributor advance.

In a conventional distributor, the firing order follows the circular path of the rotor. In the EEC distributor, upper and lower level electrodes fire alternately in a pattern that jumps from one side of the cap to the other. Therefore, the engine firing order cannot be determined off the top of the distributor cap. The numbers molded in the cap are spark plug wire to cylinder identification numbers only.

System Diagnosis

Thoroughly checking out the EEC system components requires highly specialized diagnostic equipment. However, the following basic procedures can be followed which may correct the malfunction. Refer to Fig. 17 for a wiring schematic of this system.

1. Perform the usual checks that would be performed on a vehicle with a conventional ignition system, such as check for fuel, check if fuel is contaminated, check fuel system.
2. Remove air cleaner assembly and inspect all vacuum and pressure hoses for proper connection to fittings, or any broken, cracked or pinched conditions.
3. Inspect the system sub-harness for proper connections to the EGR solenoids. Red wire goes to both solenoids, yellow wire goes to the pressure solenoid and the green wire goes to the vent solenoid.
4. Check for loose or detached connectors, or broken or detached wires. Make sure all terminals are completely seated.
5. Check for partially broken or frayed wires at connectors or any shorting between wires. Also, remove any corrosion on connectors.
6. Check sensors for evidence of physical damage.
7. Repair or replace items as required.
8. Check vehicle electrical system. Check for full battery charge and check battery cable connections.
9. Inside passenger compartment, check to make sure that power relay is securely mounted and making a good ground connection.